presented to

_____

BY _____

_____

_____

ON THE OCCASION OF _____

_____

_____

DATE _____

THE GRASS WITHERS AND THE FLOWERS FALL,
BUT THE WORD OF OUR GOD STANDS FOREVER.

marriage

_____

AND _____

WERE UNITED IN MARRIAGE ON

_____

AT _____

BY _____

WITNESSED BY

MAID OF HONOR_____

BEST MAN _____

ATTENDANTS _____

_____

_____

_____

GENESIS 2:24

◆

FOR THIS REASON A MAN WILL LEAVE HIS FATHER
AND MOTHER AND BE UNITED TO HIS WIFE, AND
THEY WILL BECOME ONE FLESH.

births

NAME _____ DATE _____

BIRTHPLACE _____

NAME _____ DATE _____

BIRTHPLACE _____

NAME _____ DATE _____

BIRTHPLACE _____

NAME _____ DATE _____

BIRTHPLACE _____

NAME _____ DATE _____

BIRTHPLACE _____

◆ PSALM 127:3

SONS ARE A HERITAGE FROM THE LORD,
CHILDREN A REWARD FROM HIM.

baptisms

WAS BAPTIZED ON _____

AT _____

BY _____

WAS BAPTIZED ON _____

AT _____

BY _____

WAS BAPTIZED ON _____

AT _____

BY _____

WAS BAPTIZED ON _____

AT _____

BY _____

EPHESIANS 4:5

◆

ONE LORD, ONE FAITH, ONE BAPTISM.

deaths

NAME	DATE
NAME	DATE
NAME	DATE
NAME	DATE
NAME	DATE
NAME	DATE
NAME	DATE

◆ 1 CORINTHIANS 6:14

BY HIS POWER GOD RAISED
THE LORD FROM THE DEAD,
AND HE WILL RAISE US ALSO.

husband

THE FAMILY

NAME BIRTHPLACE DATES

BROTHERS AND SISTERS

PARENTS

FATHER   **MOTHER**

NAME   NAME

BIRTHPLACE DATES BIRTHPLACE DATES

GRANDPARENTS

PATERNAL   **MATERNAL**

GRANDFATHER   GRANDFATHER

BIRTHPLACE DATES BIRTHPLACE DATES

GRANDMOTHER   GRANDMOTHER

BIRTHPLACE DATES BIRTHPLACE DATES

GREAT-GRANDPARENTS

PATERNAL   **MATERNAL**

GRANDFATHER'S FATHER GRANDFATHER'S FATHER

BIRTHPLACE DATES BIRTHPLACE DATES

GRANDFATHER'S MOTHER GRANDFATHER'S MOTHER

BIRTHPLACE DATES BIRTHPLACE DATES

GRANDMOTHER'S FATHER GRANDMOTHER'S FATHER

BIRTHPLACE DATES BIRTHPLACE DATES

GRANDMOTHER'S MOTHER GRANDMOTHER'S MOTHER

BIRTHPLACE DATES BIRTHPLACE DATES

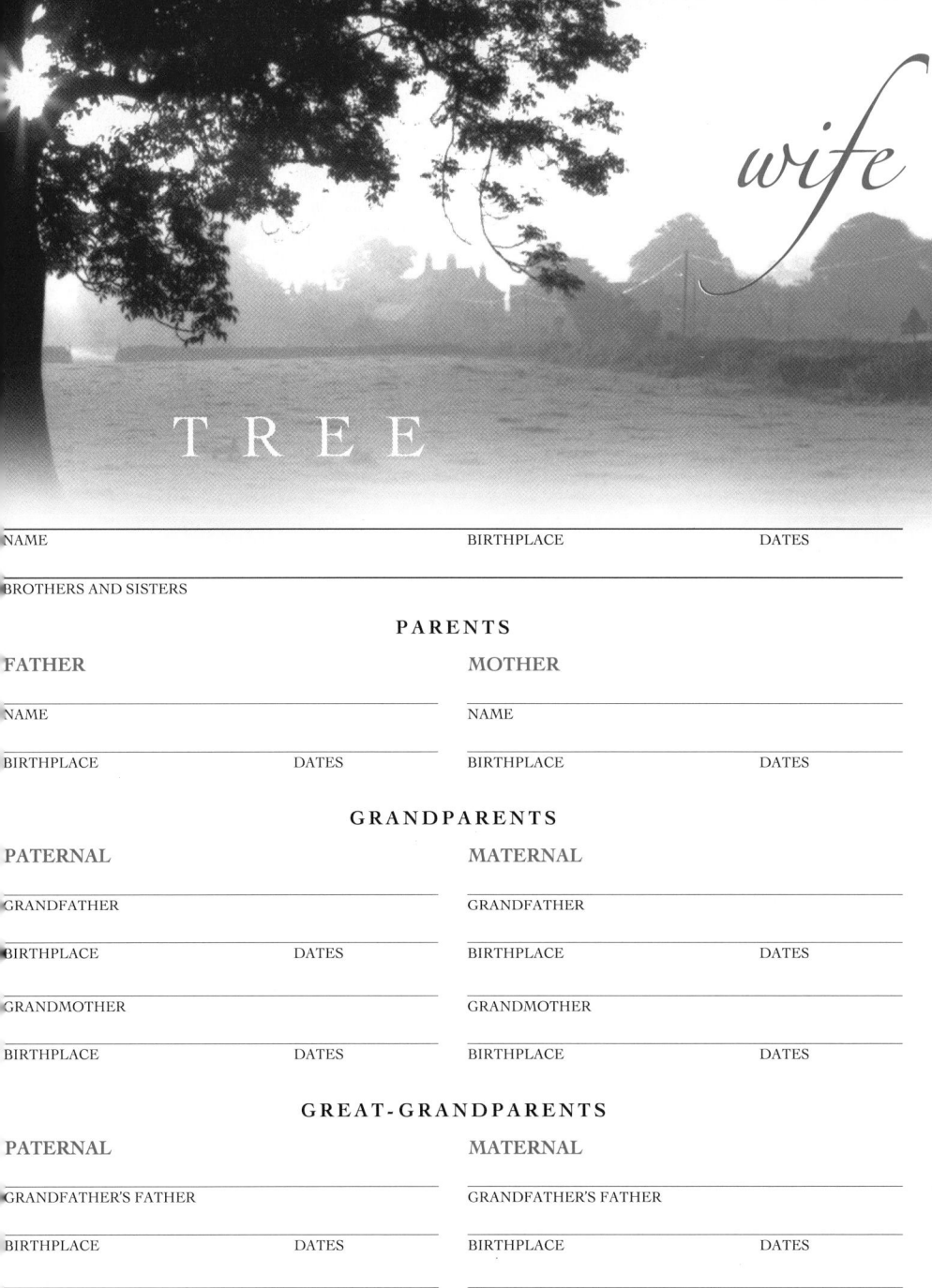

wife

TREE

NAME	BIRTHPLACE	DATES

BROTHERS AND SISTERS

PARENTS

FATHER	MOTHER
NAME	NAME

BIRTHPLACE	DATES	BIRTHPLACE	DATES

GRANDPARENTS

PATERNAL	MATERNAL
GRANDFATHER	GRANDFATHER

BIRTHPLACE	DATES	BIRTHPLACE	DATES

GRANDMOTHER	GRANDMOTHER

BIRTHPLACE	DATES	BIRTHPLACE	DATES

GREAT-GRANDPARENTS

PATERNAL	MATERNAL
GRANDFATHER'S FATHER	GRANDFATHER'S FATHER

BIRTHPLACE	DATES	BIRTHPLACE	DATES

GRANDFATHER'S MOTHER	GRANDFATHER'S MOTHER

BIRTHPLACE	DATES	BIRTHPLACE	DATES

GRANDMOTHER'S FATHER	GRANDMOTHER'S FATHER

BIRTHPLACE	DATES	BIRTHPLACE	DATES

GRANDMOTHER'S MOTHER	GRANDMOTHER'S MOTHER

BIRTHPLACE	DATES	BIRTHPLACE	DATES

special memories

EVENT

PLACE   DATE

EVENT

PLACE   DATE

EVENT

PLACE   DATE

EVENT

PLACE   DATE

◆ PSALM 118:29

GIVE THANKS TO THE LORD, FOR HE IS GOOD;
HIS LOVE ENDURES FOREVER.

APPLICATION® Study Bible

NIV | NEW INTERNATIONAL VERSION

Tyndale House Publishers, Inc.
Wheaton, Illinois

and

Zondervan Publishing House
Grand Rapids, Michigan

Copublished by:
Tyndale House Publishers, Inc.   Zondervan
Wheaton, Illinois 60189, USA   Grand Rapids, Michigan 49506, USA

Library of Congress Cataloging-in-Publication Data

Bible. English. New International. 1997.
  Life application study Bible : New International Version.
    p. cm.
  Includes indexes.
    ISBN 0-8423-4892-1 (hardcover : alk. paper). — ISBN 0-8423-4893-X
(hardcover indexed : alk. paper).
    I. Tyndale House Publishers. II. Title.
BS195.N37 1997
220.5′20814—dc21   97-2367

ISBN 0-8423-4892-1 Hardcover
ISBN 0-8423-4893-X Hardcover Indexed
ISBN 1-4143-0713-6 Hardcover Anniversary Edition

Printed in the United States of America

09 08 07 06 05
22 21 20 19 18 17 16

CONTENTS

THE NIV
CROSS-REFERENCE
SYSTEM

The New International Version has one of the most accurate and best-organized cross-reference systems available. The system used in this Bible contains more than 23,500 references.

The cross-references link words or phrases in the NIV text with counterpart Biblical references listed in a side column on every page. The raised letters containing these cross-references are set in a light italic typeface to distinguish them from the NIV text note letters, which use a bold typeface.

The lists of references are in Biblical order with one exception: If reference is made to a verse within the same chapter, that verse (indicated by "ver") is listed first.

In the Old Testament, some references are marked with an asterisk (*), which means that the Old Testament verse or phrase is quoted in the New Testament (see, for example, Genesis 1:3). The corresponding information is provided in the New Testament by the NIV text note (see 2 Corinthians 4:6).

Following is a list of abbreviations used in the cross-references:

ABBREVIATIONS FOR THE BOOKS OF THE BIBLE

Genesis . . . . Ge	Isaiah . . . . Isa	Romans . . . . Ro
Exodus. . . . . Ex	Jeremiah. . . . . Jer	1 Corinthians. 1Co
Leviticus . . . . Lev	Lamentations . . . . La	2 Corinthians. 2Co
Numbers . . . . Nu	Ezekiel. . . . . Eze	Galatians. . . . . Gal
Deuteronomy. . . . . Dt	Daniel . . . . Da	Ephesians . . . . Eph
Joshua. . . . . Jos	Hosea . . . . Hos	Philippians . . . . Php
Judges. . . . . Jdg	Joel. . . . . Joel	Colossians . . . . Col
Ruth . . . . Ru	Amos . . . . Am	1 Thessalonians. 1Th
1 Samuel. 1Sa	Obadiah . . . . Ob	2 Thessalonians. 2Th
2 Samuel. 2Sa	Jonah . . . . Jnh	1 Timothy 1Ti
1 Kings 1Ki	Micah . . . . Mic	2 Timothy 2Ti
2 Kings 2Ki	Nahum . . . . Na	Titus. . . . . Tit
1 Chronicles 1Ch	Habakkuk . . . . Hab	Philemon. . . . . Phm
2 Chronicles 2Ch	Zephaniah . . . . Zep	Hebrews . . . . Heb
Ezra . . . . Ezr	Haggai. . . . . Hag	James . . . . Jas
Nehemiah . . . . Ne	Zechariah . . . . Zec	1 Peter 1Pe
Esther . . . . Est	Malachi. . . . . Mal	2 Peter 2Pe
Job . . . . Job	Matthew. . . . . Mt	1 John. 1Jn
Psalms . . . . Ps	Mark. . . . . Mk	2 John. 2Jn
Proverbs . . . . Pr	Luke. . . . . Lk	3 John. 3Jn
Ecclesiastes. . . . . Ecc	John . . . . Jn	Jude. . . . . Jude
Song of Songs. . . . . SS	Acts . . . . Ac	Revelation . . . . Rev

THE NEW INTERNATIONAL VERSION is a completely new translation of the Holy Bible made by over a hundred scholars working directly from the best available Hebrew, Aramaic and Greek texts. It had its beginning in 1965 when, after several years of exploratory study by committees from the Christian Reformed Church and the National Association of Evangelicals, a group of scholars met at Palos Heights, Illinois, and concurred in the need for a new translation of the Bible in contemporary English. This group, though not made up of official church representatives, was transdenominational. Its conclusion was endorsed by a large number of leaders from many denominations who met in Chicago in 1966.

Responsibility for the new version was delegated by the Palos Heights group to a self-governing body of fifteen, the Committee on Bible Translation, composed for the most part of Biblical scholars from colleges, universities, and seminaries. In l967 the New York Bible Society (now the International Bible Society) generously undertook the financial sponsorship of the project—a sponsorship that made it possible to enlist the help of many distinguished scholars. The fact that participants from the United States, Great Britain, Canada, Australia, and New Zealand worked together gave the project its international scope. That they were from many denominations—including Anglican, Assemblies of God, Baptist, Brethren, Christian Reformed, Church of Christ, Evangelical Free, Lutheran, Mennonite, Methodist, Nazarene, Presbyterian, Wesleyan, and other churches—helped to safeguard the translation from sectarian bias.

How it was made helps to give the New International Version its distinctiveness. The translation of each book was assigned to a team of scholars. Next, one of the Intermediate Editorial Committees revised the initial translation, with constant reference to the Hebrew, Aramaic, or Greek. Their work then went to one of the General Editorial Committees, which checked it in detail and made another thorough revision. This revision in turn was carefully reviewed by the Committee on Bible Translation, which made further changes and then released the final version for publication. In this way the entire Bible underwent three revisions, during each of which the translation was examined for its faithfulness to the original languages and for its English style.

All this involved many thousands of hours of research and discussion regarding the meaning of the texts and the precise way of putting them into English. It may well be that no other translation has been made by a more thorough process of review and revision from committee to committee than this one.

From the beginning of the project, the Committee on Bible Translation held to certain goals for the New International Version: that it would be an accurate translation and one that would have clarity and literary quality and so prove suitable for public and private reading, teaching, preaching, memorizing, and liturgical use. The Committee also sought to preserve some measure of continuity with the long tradition of translating the Scriptures into English.

In working toward these goals, the translators were united in their commitment to the authority and infallibility of the Bible as God's Word in written form. They believe that it contains the divine answer to the deepest needs of humanity, that it sheds unique light on our path in a dark world, and that it sets forth the way to our eternal well-being.

The first concern of the translators has been the accuracy of the translation and its fidelity to the thought of the Biblical writers. They have weighed the significance of the lexical and grammatical details of the Hebrew, Aramaic and Greek texts. At the same time, they have striven for more than a word-for-word translation. Because thought patterns and syntax differ from language to language, faithful communication of the meaning of the writers of the Bible demands frequent modifications in sentence structure and constant regard for the contextual meanings of words.

A sensitive feeling for style does not always accompany scholarship. Accordingly the Committee on Bible Translation submitted the developing version to a number of stylistic consultants. Two of them read every book of both Old and New Testaments twice—once before and once after the last major revision—and made invaluable suggestions. Samples of the translation were tested for clarity and ease of reading by various kinds of people—young and old, highly educated and less well educated, ministers and laymen.

Concern for clear and natural English—that the New International Version should be idiomatic but not idiosyncratic, contemporary but not dated—motivated the translators and consultants. At the same time, they tried to reflect the differing styles of the Biblical writers. In view of the international use of English, the translators sought to avoid obvious Americanisms on the one hand and obvious Anglicisms on the other. A British edition reflects the comparatively few differences of significant idiom and of spelling.

As for the traditional pronouns "thou," "thee," and "thine" in reference to the Deity, the translators judged that to use these archaisms (along with the old verb forms such as "doest," "wouldest," and "hadst") would violate accuracy in translation. Neither Hebrew, Aramaic nor Greek uses special pronouns for the persons of the Godhead. A present-day translation is not enhanced by forms that in the time of the King James Version were used in everyday speech, whether referring to God or man.

For the Old Testament the standard Hebrew text, the Masoretic Text as published in the latest editions of *Biblia Hebraica,* was used throughout. The Dead Sea Scrolls contain material bearing on an earlier stage of the Hebrew text. They were consulted, as were the Samaritan Pentateuch and the ancient scribal traditions relating to textual changes. Sometimes a variant Hebrew reading in the margin of the Masoretic Text was followed instead of the text itself. Such instances, being variants within the Masoretic tradition, are not specified by footnotes. In rare cases, words in the consonantal text were divided differently from the way they appear in the Masoretic Text. Footnotes indicate this. The translators also consulted the more important early versions—the Septuagint; Aquila, Symmachus and Theodotion: the Vulgate; the Syriac Peshitta; the Targums; and for the Psalms the *Juxta Hebraica* of Jerome. Readings from these versions were occasionally followed where the Masoretic Text seemed doubtful and where accepted principles of textual criticism showed that one or more of these textual witnesses appeared to provide the correct reading. Such instances are footnoted. Sometimes vowel letters and vowel signs did not, in the judgment of the translators, represent the correct vowels for the original consonantal text. Accordingly some words were read with a different set of vowels. These instances are usually not indicated by footnotes.

The Greek text used in translating the New Testament was an eclectic one. No other piece of ancient literature has such an abundance of manuscript witnesses as does the New Testament. Where existing manuscripts differ, the translators made their choice of readings according to accepted principles of New Testament textual criticism. Footnotes call attention to places where there was uncertainty about what the original text was. The best current printed texts of the Greek New Testament were used.

There is a sense in which the work of translation is never wholly finished. This applies to all great literature and uniquely so to the Bible. In 1973 the New Testament in the New International Version was published. Since then, suggestions for corrections and revision have been received from various sources. The Committee on Bible Translation carefully considered the suggestions and adopted a number of them. These were incorporated in the first printing of the entire Bible in 1978. Additional revisions were made by the Committee on Bible Translation in 1983 and appear in printings after that date.

As in other ancient documents, the precise meaning of the Biblical texts is sometimes uncertain. This is more often the case with the Hebrew and Aramaic texts than with the

Greek text. Although archaeological and linguistic discoveries in this century aid in understanding difficult passages, some uncertainties remain. The more significant of these have been called to the reader's attention in the footnotes.

In regard to the divine name *YHWH,* commonly referred to as the *Tetragrammaton,* the translators adopted the device used in most English versions of rendering that name as "Lord," in capital letters to distinguish it from *Adonai,* another Hebrew word rendered "Lord," for which small letters are used. Wherever the two names stand together in the Old Testament as a compound name of God, they are rendered "Sovereign Lord."

Because for most readers today the phrases "the Lord of hosts" and "God of hosts" have little meaning, this version renders them "the Lord Almighty" and "God Almighty." These renderings convey the sense of the Hebrew, namely, "he who is sovereign over all the 'hosts' (powers) in heaven and on earth, especially over the 'hosts' (armies) of Israel." For readers unacquainted with Hebrew this does not make clear the distinction between *Sabaoth* ("hosts" or "Almighty") and *Shaddai* (which can be translated "Almighty"), but the latter occurs infrequently and is always footnoted. When *Adonai YHWH* and *Sabaoth* occur together, they are rendered "the Lord, the Lord Almighty."

As for other proper nouns, the familiar spellings of the King James Version are generally retained. Names traditionally spelled with "ch," except where it is final, are usually spelled in this translation with "k" or "c," since the Biblical languages do not have the sound that "ch" frequently indicates in English—for example in *chant.* For well-known names such as Zechariah, however, the traditional spelling has been retained. Variation in the spelling of names in the original languages has usually not been indicated. Where a person or place has two or more different names in the Hebrew, Aramaic or Greek texts, the more familiar one has generally been used, with footnotes where needed.

To achieve clarity the translators sometimes supplied words not in the original texts but required by the context. If there was uncertainty about such material, it is enclosed in brackets. Also for the sake of clarity or style, nouns, including some proper nouns, are sometimes substituted for pronouns, and vice versa. And though the Hebrew writers often shifted back and forth, between first, second and third personal pronouns without change of antecedent, this translation often makes them uniform, in accordance with English style and without the use of footnotes.

Poetical passages are printed as poetry, that is, with indentation of lines and with separate stanzas. These are generally designed to reflect the structure of Hebrew poetry. This poetry is normally characterized by parallelism in balanced lines. Most of the poetry in the Bible is in the Old Testament, and scholars differ regarding the scansion of Hebrew lines. The translators determined the stanza divisions for the most part by analysis of the subject matter. The stanzas therefore serve as poetic paragraphs.

As an aid to the reader, italicized sectional headings are inserted in most of the books. They are not to be regarded as part of the NIV text, are not for oral reading, and are not intended to dictate the interpretation of the sections they head.

The footnotes in this version are of several kinds, most of which need no explanation. Those giving alternative translations begin with "Or" and generally introduce the alternative with the last word preceding it in the text, except when it is a single-word alternative; in poetry quoted in a footnote a slant mark indicates a line division. Footnotes introduced by "Or" do not have uniform significance. In some cases two possible translations were considered to have about equal validity. In other cases, though the translators were convinced that the translation in the text was correct, they judged that another interpretation was possible and of sufficient importance to be represented in a footnote.

In the New Testament, footnotes that refer to uncertainty regarding the original text are introduced by "Some manuscripts" or similar expressions. In the Old Testament, evidence for the reading chosen is given first and evidence for the alternative is added after a semicolon (for example: Septuagint; Hebrew *father*). In such notes the term "Hebrew" refers to the Masoretic Text.

It should be noted that minerals, flora and fauna, architectural details, articles of clothing and jewelry, musical instruments and other articles cannot always be identified with precision. Also, measures of capacity in the Biblical period are particularly uncertain (see the table of weights and measures following the text).

Like all translations of the Bible, made as they are by imperfect man, this one undoubtedly falls short of its goals. Yet we are grateful to God for the extent to which he has enabled us to realize these goals and for the strength he has given us and our colleagues to complete our task. We offer this version of the Bible to him in whose name and for whose glory it has been made. We pray that it will lead many into a better understanding of the Holy Scriptures and a fuller knowledge of Jesus Christ the incarnate Word, of whom the Scriptures so faithfully testify.

The Committee on Bible Translation

June 1978
(Revised August 1983)

Names of the translators and editors may be secured
from the International Bible Society,
translation sponsors of the New International Version,
1820 Jet Stream Drive, Colorado Springs, Colorado, 80921-3696 U.S.A.

Senior Editorial Team
Dr. Bruce B. Barton
Ronald A. Beers
Dr. James C. Galvin
LaVonne Neff
Linda Chaffee Taylor
David R. Veerman

General Editor
Ronald A. Beers

Tyndale House Bible Editors
Dr. Philip W. Comfort
Robert Brown
Mark Norton
Leanne Roberts

Book Introductions
David R. Veerman

Book Outlines, Blueprints, Harmony
Dr. James C. Galvin

Megathemes
Dr. Bruce B. Barton

Map Development & Computer Operation
Linda Chaffee Taylor

Charts & Diagrams
Neil S. Wilson
Ronald A. Beers
David R. Veerman
Pamela York

Personality Profiles
Neil S. Wilson

Design & Development Team
Dr. Bruce B. Barton
Ronald A. Beers
Dr. James C. Galvin
David R. Veerman

Zondervan Development Team
Phil Herich
Michael A. Vander Klipp

Tyndale House Graphic Design
Timothy R. Botts
Dean Renninger

A Chronology of Bible Events and World Events
Dr. David Maas

Theological Reviewers
Dr. Kenneth S. Kantzer

General Theological Reviewer
Dean Emeritus and
Distinguished Professor of
Bible and Systematic Theology
Trinity Evangelical Divinity
School

Dr. V. Gilbert Beers
Former Editor of
Christianity Today magazine

Dr. Barry Beitzel
Associate Academic Dean
and Professor of Old Testament
and Semitic Languages
Trinity Evangelical Divinity
School

Dr. Edwin A. Blum
Associate Professor of
Historical Theology
Dallas Theological Seminary

Dr. Geoffrey W. Bromiley
Professor
Fuller Theological Seminary

Dr. George K. Brushaber
President
Bethel College & Seminary

Dr. L. Russ Bush
Associate Professor
Philosophy & Religion
Southwestern Baptist
Theological Seminary

C. Donald Cole
Pastor, Moody Radio Network

Mrs. Naomi E. Cole
Speaker & Seminar Leader

Dr. Walter A. Elwell
Dean
Wheaton College Graduate
School

Dr. Gerald F. Hawthorne
Professor of Greek
Wheaton College

Dr. Howard G. Hendricks
Professor-at-Large
Chairman
Center for Christian Leadership
Dallas Theological Seminary

Dr. Grant R. Osborne
Professor of New Testament
Trinity Evangelical Divinity
School

A special thanks to the nationwide staff of Youth for Christ/USA for their suggestions and field testing, and to the following additional contributing writers: V. Gilbert Beers, Neil Wilson, John Crosby, Joan Young, Jack Crabtree, Philip Craven, Bob Black, Bur Shilling, Arthur Deyo, Annie Lafrentz, Danny Sartin, William Hanawalt, William Bonikowsky, Brian Rathbun, Pamela Barden, Thomas Stobie, Robert Arnold, Greg Monaco, Larry Dunn, Lynn Ziegenfuss, Mitzie Barton, Mari-Jean Hamilton, Larry Kreider, Gary Dausey, William Roland, Kathy Howell, Philip Steffeck, James Coleman, Marty Grasley, O'Ann Steere, Julia Amstutz.

A special thanks also to the following people whose personal counsel, encouragement, and determination helped make this product a reality:

Dr. Kenneth N. Taylor
Translator of *The Living Bible*
Chairman of the Board
Tyndale House Publishers, Inc.

Mark D. Taylor
President
Tyndale House Publishers, Inc.

Dr. Wendell C. Hawley
Editor in Chief
Tyndale House Publishers, Inc.

Virginia Muir
Assistant Editor in Chief
Tyndale House Publishers, Inc.

Richard R. Wynn
Former President,
Youth for Christ/USA

Dr. Jay L. Kesler
Former President,
Taylor University

Jim and Patti Moffett
Household of God Ministry

A CHRONOLOGY OF BIBLE EVENTS AND WORLD EVENTS

THE TIMELINE on the following pages of the introduction gives you a visual overview of events in Bible times as compared to other famous world events. (The timelines in the individual Bible books are different—focusing on the events occurring in the books themselves.) This timeline gives the scope of Bible history from Creation to the resurrection of Christ and the beginnings of the church, along with key events that were occurring in other parts of the world.

| Creation *undated* | Noah builds the ark *undated* | | | Abraham born **2166** | Abraham enters Canaan **2091** |

2500 B.C. Egyptians discover papyrus and ink for writing and build the first libraries; iron objects manufactured in the ancient Near East

2400 Egyptians import gold from other parts of Africa

2331 Semitic chieftain, Sargon, conquers Sumer to become first "world conqueror"

2300 Horses domesticated in Egypt; chickens domesticated in Babylon; bows & arrows used in wars

2100 Glass made by the Mesopotamians; ziggurats (like the tower of Babel) built in Mesopotamia; earliest discovered drug, ethyl alcohol, used to alleviate pain

WHY THE
LIFE APPLICATION STUDY BIBLE
IS UNIQUE

Have you ever opened your Bible and asked the following:

- What does this passage really mean?
- How does it apply to my life?
- Why does some of the Bible seem irrelevant?
- What do these ancient cultures have to do with today?
- I love God; why can't I understand what he is saying to me through his Word?
- What's going on in the lives of these Bible people?

Many Christians do not read the Bible regularly. Why? Because in the pressures of daily living they cannot find a connection between the timeless principles of Scripture and the ever-present problems of day-by-day living.

God urges us to apply his Word (Isaiah 42:23; 1 Corinthians 10:11; 2 Thessalonians 3:4), but too often we stop at accumulating Bible knowledge. This is why the *Life Application Study Bible* was developed—to show how to put into practice what we have learned.

Isaac
born
2066

Jacob
& Esau
born
2006

Jacob
flees to
Haran
1929

Joseph
born
1915

Joseph
sold into
slavery
1898

Joseph
rules Egypt
1885

Joseph
dies
1805

Moses
born
1526

2000
Native Americans
immigrate to
North America
from northern Asia;
stock-breeding
and irrigation
used in China;
Stonehenge,
England, a center
for religious worship
is erected; bellows
used in India,
allowing for higher
furnace temperatures

1900
Egyptians use
irrigation systems
to control
Nile floods;
spoked wheel
invented in the
ancient Near East;
horses used
to pull vehicles

1750
Babylonian
mathematicians
already
understand
cube and
square root;
Hammurapi
of Babylon
provides
first of all
legal codes

1700
Egyptian
papyrus
document
describes
medical and
surgical
procedures

1500
Sundials
used in Egypt;
Mexican
Sun-Pyramid
built

Applying God's Word is a vital part of one's relationship with God; it is the evidence that we are obeying him. The difficulty in applying the Bible is not with the Bible itself, but with the reader's inability to bridge the gap between the past and present, the conceptual and practical. When we don't or can't do this, spiritual dryness, shallowness, and indifference are the results.

The words of Scripture itself cry out to us, "Do not merely listen to the word, and so deceive yourselves. Do what it says" (James 1:22). The *Life Application Study Bible* does just that. Developed by an interdenominational team of pastors, scholars, family counselors, and a national organization dedicated to promoting God's Word and spreading the gospel, the *Life Application Study Bible* took many years to complete, and all the work was reviewed by several renowned theologians under the directorship of Dr. Kenneth Kantzer.

The *Life Application Study Bible* does what a good resource Bible should—it helps you understand the context of a passage, gives important background and historical information, explains difficult words and phrases, and helps you see the interrelationships within Scripture. But it does much more. The *Life Application Study Bible* goes deeper into God's Word, helping you discover the timeless truth being communicated, see the relevance for your life, and make a personal application. While some study Bibles attempt application, over 75% of this Bible is application-oriented. The notes answer the questions, "So what?" and "What does this passage mean to me, my family, my friends, my job, my neighborhood, my church, my country?"

Imagine reading a familiar passage of Scripture and gaining fresh insight, as if it were the first time you had ever read it. How much richer your life would be if you left each Bible reading with a new perspective and a small change for the better. A small change every day adds up to a changed life—and that is the very purpose of Scripture.

The Exodus from Egypt **1446**

Ten Commandments given **1445**

Hebrews enter Canaan **1406**

Judges begin to rule Israel **1375**

Deborah becomes Israel's judge **1209**

Gideon becomes Israel's judge **1162**

Samuel born **1105**

Samson becomes Israel's judge **1075**

Saul becomes Israel's first king **1050**

David becomes Israel's king **1010**

1400 *First period of Chinese literature; intricate clock used in Egypt*

1380 *Palace of Knossos on island of Crete destroyed by earthquake*

1358 *Egyptian King Tutankhamen dies and is buried inside an immense treasure-laden tomb*

1250 *Silk fabrics manufactured in China*

1200 *Labor strike in Thebes; first Chinese dictionary*

1183 *Destruction of Troy during Trojan War*

WHAT IS APPLICATION?

The best way to define application is to first determine what it is *not*. Application is *not* just accumulating knowledge. This helps us discover and understand facts and concepts, but it stops there. History is filled with philosophers who knew what the Bible said, but failed to apply it to their lives, keeping them from believing and changing. Many think that understanding is the end goal of Bible study, but it is really only the beginning.

Application is *not* just illustration. Illustration only tells us how someone else handled a similar situation. While we may empathize with that person, we still have little direction for our personal situation.

Application is *not* just making a passage "relevant." Making the Bible relevant only helps us to see that the same lessons that were true in Bible times are true today; it does not show us how to apply them to the problems and pressures of our individual lives.

What, then, is application? Application begins by knowing and understanding God's Word and its timeless truths. *But you cannot stop there*. If you do, God's Word may not change your life, and it may become dull, difficult, tedious, and tiring. A good application focuses the truth of God's Word, shows the reader what to do about what is being read,

Solomon becomes Israel's king **970**

Temple in Jerusalem completed **959**

Kingdom of Israel divides **930**

Elijah prophesies in Israel **875**

Ahab becomes Israel's king **874**

Elisha prophesies in Israel **848**

Joash becomes Judah's king **835**

Jonah becomes a prophet **793**

1000
City of Peking built; Greek mythology fully developed; California Indians build wood-reed houses; Chinese mathematics utilizes root multiplication, geometry, proportions, and theory of motion; glazing of bricks and tiles begins in Near East

950
Gold vessels and jewelry popular in northern Europe

900
Celts invade Britain; Assyrians invent inflatable skins for soldiers to cross rivers

850
Evidence of highly developed metal and stone sculptures in Africa

814
Founding of Carthage, a Phoenician trading post

800
Development of caste system in India; Babylonian and Chinese astronomers understand planetary movements; spoked wheels used in Europe; Homer writes Iliad and Odyssey; ice skating a popular sport in northern Europe

776
First known date of Olympic games

and motivates the reader to respond to what God is teaching. All three are essential to application.

Application is putting into practice what we already know (see Mark 4:24 and Hebrews 5:14) and answering the question, "So what?" by confronting us with the right questions and motivating us to take action (see 1 John 2:5, 6 and James 2:17). Application is deeply personal—unique for each individual. It is making a relevant truth a personal truth, and involves developing a strategy and action plan to live your life in harmony with the Bible. It is the Biblical "how to" of life.

You may ask, "How can your application notes be relevant to my life?" Each application note has three parts: (1) an *explanation* that ties the note directly to the Scripture passage and sets up the truth that is being taught, (2) the *bridge* that explains the timeless truth and makes it relevant for today, (3) the *application* that shows you how to take the timeless truth and apply it to your personal situation. No note, by itself, can apply Scripture directly to your life. It can only teach, direct, lead, guide, inspire, recommend, and urge. It can give you the resources and direction you need to apply the Bible; but only *you* can take these resources and put them into practice.

A good note, therefore, should not only give you knowledge and understanding, but point you to application. Before you buy any kind of resource Bible, you should evaluate the notes and ask the following questions: (1) Does the note contain enough information to help me understand the point of the Scripture passage? (2) Does the note assume I know too much? (3) Does the note avoid denominational bias? (4) Do the notes touch most of life's experiences? (5) Does the note help me *apply* God's Word?

FEATURES OF THE LIFE APPLICATION STUDY BIBLE

NOTES

In addition to providing the reader with many application notes, the *Life Application Study Bible* offers several explanatory notes, which are notes that help the reader understand culture, history, context, difficult-to-understand passages, background, places, theological concepts, and the relationship of various passages in Scripture to other passages. Maps, charts, and diagrams are also found on the same page as the passages to which they relate. For an example of an application note, see Mark 15:47. For an example of an explanatory note, see Mark 11:1, 2. The abbreviation *ff* appears in some notes to indicate that the comments apply not only to the verse referenced but to the following passage as well.

BOOK INTRODUCTIONS

The Book Introductions are divided into several easy-to-find parts:

Timeline. This puts the Bible book into its historical setting. It lists the key events of each book and the date when they occurred. The alternative dates in parenthesis are based on a later dating of the Exodus.

King Nebuchadnezzar of Babylon dies **562**

Babylon overthrown by Cyrus of Persia **539**

First Jewish exiles return to Jerusalem **538**

New temple completed in Jerusalem **515**

Esther becomes queen of Persia **479**

563 Gautama Buddha, the founder of Buddhism, born in India

560 Aesop writes his fables

550 King Cyrus the Great conquers the Medes and founds the Persian empire; lock & key, water level, and carpenter's square invented

551 Confucius, famous Chinese scholar, born

540 Horseback postal service in Persian empire

534 Tragedy emerges as a form of Greek drama

525 Polo a sport among Persians

520 Public libraries open in Athens, Greece

509 Rome becomes a republic

500 Glass first imported into China from Near East; Indian surgeon Susrata performs cataract operation; origin of Halloween, a Celtic festival

490 First time Greek men choose short haircuts

Vital Statistics. This is a list of straight facts about the book—those pieces of information you need to know at a glance.

Overview. This is a summary of the book with general lessons and application that can be learned from the book as a whole.

Blueprint. This is the outline of the book. It is printed in easy-to-understand language and is designed for easy memorization. To the right of each main heading is a key lesson that is taught in that particular section.

Megathemes. This section gives the main themes of the Bible book, explains their significance, and then tells why they are still important for us today.

Map. This shows the key places found in that book and retells the story of the book from a geographical point of view.

OUTLINE
The *Life Application Study Bible* has a new, custom-made outline that was designed specifically from an application point of view. Several unique features should be noted:

1. To avoid confusion and to aid memory work, each book outline has only three levels for headings. Main outline heads are marked with a capital letter. Subheads are marked by a number. Minor explanatory heads have no letter or number.

2. Each main outline head marked by a letter also has a brief paragraph below it summarizing the Bible text and offering a general application.

3. Parallel passages are listed where they apply in the Gospels.

Ezra
returns to
Jerusalem
458

Nehemiah
builds
Jerusalem
wall
445

Malachi
becomes
a prophet
430

Aramaic
begins
to replace
Hebrew
as Jewish
language
390

460
Birth of
Democritus,
who introduced
an atomic theory
by arguing that
all bodies are
made of indivisible
and unchangeable
atoms

457
Golden Age
in Athens,
Greece
begins

448
The
Parthenon
built on
top of
Athens'
Acropolis

438
Greek sculptor
Phidias makes
a 60-foot-high
statue of Zeus—
one of the
seven wonders
of the ancient
world

430
Romans
agree to
concept of
a dictator
in times
of military
emergency

399
Socrates
condemned
to death by
Athenian jury

384
Aristotle
born

370
Plato writes
his most
famous book,
The Republic

469
Socrates,
philosopher
of the ancient
world, born

HARMONY OF THE GOSPELS

A harmony of the Gospels was developed specifically for this Bible. It is the first harmony that has ever been incorporated into the Bible text. Through a unique and simple numbering system (found both in the harmony feature and parenthesized in the subheads throughout the Gospels), you can read any Gospel account and see just where you are in relation to other events in the life of Christ. The harmony feature is located after the Gospel of John and explained in detail there.

PROFILE NOTES

Another unique feature of this Bible is the profiles of many Bible people, including their strengths and weaknesses, greatest accomplishments and mistakes, and key lessons from their lives. The profiles of these people are found in the Bible books where their stories occur.

MAPS

The *Life Application Study Bible* has numerous maps, building a thorough and comprehensive Bible atlas right into each Bible book. There are two kinds of maps: (1) A book introduction map, telling the story of that Bible book. (2) Thumbnail maps in the notes, plotting most geographic movements in the Bible.

CHARTS AND DIAGRAMS

Hundreds of charts and diagrams are included to help the reader better visualize difficult concepts or relationships. Most charts not only present the needed information but show the significance of the information as well.

Temple of Jerusalem plundered by Antiochus IV
169

Judas Maccabeus begins a revolt against Antiochus IV
165

312
Romans build first paved road, the "Appian Way," from Rome to Capua

330
Alexander the Great defeats the Persian empire

241
Romans conquer Sicily and add their first non-Italian territory to the Roman empire

255
Hebrew Old Testament translated into Greek and called the Septuagint

215
Great Wall of China built

139
Jews and astrologers banished from Rome

102
First Chinese ships reach east coast of India; ball bearings used in Danish cart wheels

100
Julius Caesar, first emperor of Rome, born

55
Romans conquer England and make it part of Roman empire until A.D. 442

51
Cleopatra becomes last independent Egyptian ruler of the ancient world

CROSS-REFERENCES

A carefully organized cross-reference system in the margins of the Bible text helps the reader find related passages quickly. See page ix for more information on the NIV Cross-Reference system.

TEXTUAL NOTES AND SECTIONAL HEADINGS

Directly related to the New International Version text, the textual notes examine such things as alternate translations, meaning of Hebrew and Greek terms, Old Testament quotations, and variant readings in ancient Biblical manuscripts. The NIV text also contains sectional headings in order to help you more easily understand the subject and content of each section. NOTE: The standard New International Version sectional headings have been altered for this particular edition, particularly in the Gospels where they have been eliminated in favor of the "Harmony of the Gospels" feature. The headings throughout the Gospels also include a parenthesized number, relating each passage to the "Harmony of the Gospels" feature.

A CHRISTIAN WORKER'S RESOURCE

The Christian Worker's Resource is a special supplement written just for you in mind. It includes five articles that you will find useful in your ministry: (1) "How to Become a Christian" includes the basic steps of becoming a believer, along with Bible verses you can use to guide someone to faith. (2) "How to Follow up with a New Believer" gives you fourteen discussion points to walk through with a new believer over the course of several weeks. These will help him or her to understand the basics of the Christian faith. (3) "Mining the Treasures of the *Life Application Study Bible*" gives you a taste of the

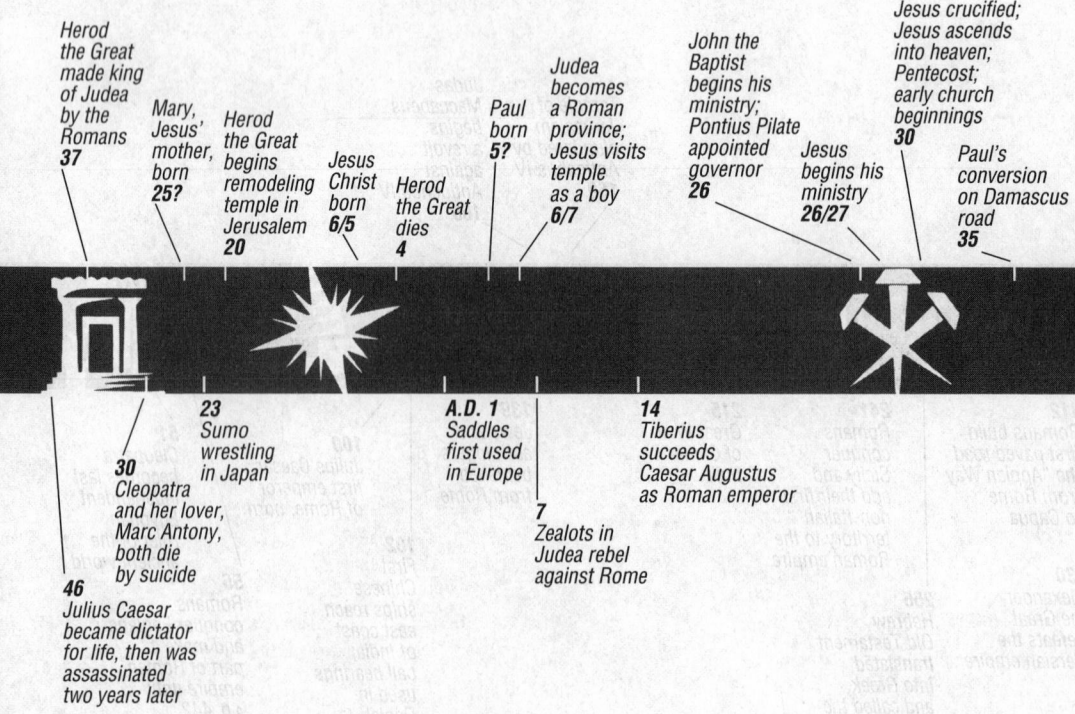

Herod
the Great
made king
of Judea
by the
Romans
37

Mary,
Jesus'
mother,
born
25?

Herod
the Great
begins
remodeling
temple in
Jerusalem
20

Jesus
Christ
born
6/5

Herod
the Great
dies
4

Paul
born
5?

Judea
becomes
a Roman
province;
Jesus visits
temple
as a boy
6/7

John the
Baptist
begins his
ministry;
Pontius Pilate
appointed
governor
26

Jesus
begins his
ministry
26/27

Jesus crucified;
Jesus ascends
into heaven;
Pentecost;
early church
beginnings
30

Paul's
conversion
on Damascus
road
35

30
Cleopatra
and her lover,
Marc Antony,
both die
by suicide

46
Julius Caesar
became dictator
for life, then was
assassinated
two years later

23
Sumo
wrestling
in Japan

A.D. 1
Saddles
first used
in Europe

7
Zealots in
Judea rebel
against Rome

14
Tiberius
succeeds
Caesar Augustus
as Roman emperor

depth of the study notes by offering often-asked questions in twenty-five categories (that you probably have been asked from time to time) and sends you to life application notes that help to answer those questions. (4) "So You've Been Asked to Speak" walks you through the process of preparing a talk or Bible study using the many features of the *Life Application Study Bible*. (5) Finally, "Taking the Step to Application" teaches you how to make application a natural part of your personal study, as well as a part of Bible studies you lead or talks you give.

MASTER INDEX
This book contains a complete index to all the notes, charts, maps, and personality profiles. With its emphasis on application, it is helpful for group Bible study, sermon preparation, teaching, or personal study.

DICTIONARY/CONCORDANCE
A concise concordance identifies terms of special interest and lists the important occurrences in context. Each word is followed by a brief definition.

Paul writes Romans; Paul imprisoned in Caesarea **57**

Paul writes "prison letters" **60**

Paul released from prison **62**

960 Jews commit mass suicide at Masada while under Roman attack **73**

Herod Agrippa appointed king of Judea **0**

Paul begins first missionary journey **46**

Paul's voyage to Rome **59**

Paul martyred **67?**

Romans destroy Jerusalem **70**

Apostle John writes Revelation **95**

43 London founded; first definite reference to diamonds

50 Romans begin using soap

54 Emperor Claudius poisoned by order of his wife; Nero becomes emperor

64 Fire burns much of Rome. Nero blames Christians for setting it

66 Painting on canvas

74 China opens silk trade with the west

79 Mount Vesuvius in Italy erupts, killing 30,000 people and burying cities of Pompeii and Herculaneum

68 Romans destroy a Jewish religious commune at Qumran. Before the Qumran community was captured, they hid their library of Bible manuscripts in a cave by the Dead Sea (discovered in 1948)

75 Rome begins construction of famous Colosseum

old TESTAMENT

GENESIS

VITAL STATISTICS

PURPOSE:
To record God's creation of the world and his desire to have a people set apart to worship him

AUTHOR:
Moses

ORIGINAL AUDIENCE:
The people of Israel

DATE WRITTEN:
1450–1410 B.C.

WHERE WRITTEN:
In the wilderness during Israel's wanderings, somewhere in the Sinai peninsula

SETTING:
The region presently known as the Middle East

KEY VERSES:
"So God created man in his own image, in the image of God he created him; male and female he created them" (1:27). "'I will make you into a great nation and I will bless you; I will make your name great, and you will be a blessing. I will bless those who bless you, and whoever curses you I will curse; and all peoples on earth will be blessed through you'" (12:2, 3).

KEY PEOPLE:
Adam, Eve, Noah, Abraham, Sarah, Isaac, Rebekah, Jacob, Joseph

BEGIN . . . start . . . commence . . . open. . . . There's something refreshing and optimistic about these words, whether they refer to the dawn of a new day, the birth of a child, the prelude of a symphony, or the first miles of a family vacation. Free of problems and full of promise, beginnings stir hope and imaginative visions of the future. *Genesis* means "beginnings" or "origin," and it unfolds the record of the beginning of the world, of human history, of family, of civilization, of salvation. It is the story of God's purpose and plan for his creation. As the book of beginnings, Genesis sets the stage for the entire Bible. It reveals the person and nature of God (Creator, Sustainer, Judge, Redeemer); the value and dignity of human beings (made in God's image, saved by grace, used by God in the world); the tragedy and consequences of sin (the fall, separation from God, judgment); and the promise and assurance of salvation (covenant, forgiveness, promised Messiah).

God. That's where Genesis begins. All at once we see him creating the world in a majestic display of power and purpose, culminating with a man and woman made like himself (1:26, 27). But before long, sin entered the world, and Satan was unmasked. Bathed in innocence, creation was shattered by the fall (the willful disobedience of Adam and Eve). Fellowship with God was broken, and evil began weaving its destructive web. In rapid succession, we read how Adam and Eve were expelled from the beautiful garden, their first son turned murderer, and evil bred evil until God finally destroyed everyone on earth except a small family led by Noah, the only godly person left.

As we come to Abraham on the plains of Canaan, we discover the beginning of God's covenant people and the broad strokes of his salvation plan: Salvation comes by faith, Abraham's descendants will be God's people, and the Savior of the world will come through this chosen nation. The stories of Isaac, Jacob, and Joseph that follow are more than interesting biographies. They emphasize the promises of God and the proof that he is faithful. The people we meet in Genesis are simple, ordinary people, yet through them, God did great things. These are vivid pictures of how God can and does use all kinds of people to accomplish his good purposes—even people like you.

Read Genesis and be encouraged. There is hope! No matter how dark the world situation seems, God has a plan. No matter how insignificant or useless you feel, God loves you and wants to use you in his plan. No matter how sinful and separated from God you are, his salvation is available. Read Genesis . . . and hope!

THE BLUEPRINT

A. THE STORY OF CREATION (1:1—2:3)

God created the sky, seas, and land. He created the plants, animals, fish, and birds. But he created human beings in his own image. At times, others may treat us disrespectfully. But we can be certain of our dignity and worth because we have been created in the image of God.

Jacob & Esau born 2006 (1840)	Jacob flees to Haran 1929 (1764)	Joseph born 1915 (1750)	Joseph sold into slavery 1898 (1733)	Joseph rules Egypt 1885 (1720)	Joseph dies 1805 (1640)

B. THE STORY OF ADAM (2:4—5:32)
 1. Adam and Eve
 2. Cain and Abel
 3. Adam's descendants

When Adam and Eve were created by God, they were without sin. But they became sinful when they disobeyed God and ate some fruit from the tree. Through Adam and Eve we learn about the destructive power of sin and its bitter consequences.

C. THE STORY OF NOAH (6:1—11:32)
 1. The flood
 2. Repopulating the earth
 3. The tower of Babel

Noah was spared from the destruction of the flood because he obeyed God and built the ark. Just as God protected Noah and his family, he still protects those who are faithful to him today.

D. THE STORY OF ABRAHAM (12:1—25:18)
 1. God promises a nation to Abram
 2. Abram and Lot
 3. God promises a son to Abram
 4. Sodom and Gomorrah
 5. Birth and near sacrifice of Isaac
 6. Isaac and Rebekah
 7. Abraham dies

Abraham was asked to leave his country, wander in Canaan, wait years for a son, and then sacrifice him as a burnt offering. Through these periods of sharp testing, Abraham remained faithful to God. His example teaches us what it means to live a life of faith.

E. THE STORY OF ISAAC (25:19—28:9)
 1. Jacob and Esau
 2. Isaac and Abimelech
 3. Jacob gets Isaac's blessing

Isaac did not demand his own way. He did not resist when he was about to be sacrificed, and he gladly accepted a wife chosen for him by others. Like Isaac, we must learn to put God's will ahead of our own.

F. THE STORY OF JACOB (28:10—36:43)
 1. Jacob starts a family
 2. Jacob returns home

Jacob did not give up easily. He faithfully served Laban for over 14 years. Later, he wrestled with God. Although Jacob made many mistakes, his hard work teaches us about living a life of service for our Lord.

G. THE STORY OF JOSEPH (37:1—50:26)
 1. Joseph is sold into slavery
 2. Judah and Tamar
 3. Joseph is thrown into prison
 4. Joseph is placed in charge of Egypt
 5. Joseph and his brothers meet in Egypt
 6. Jacob's family moves to Egypt
 7. Jacob and Joseph die in Egypt

Joseph was sold into slavery by his brothers and unjustly thrown into prison by his master. Through the life of Joseph, we learn that suffering, no matter how unfair, can develop strong character in us.

MEGATHEMES

THEME	EXPLANATION	IMPORTANCE
Beginnings	Genesis explains the beginning of many important realities: the universe, the earth, people, sin, and God's plan of salvation.	Genesis teaches us that the earth is well made and good. People are special to God and unique. God creates and sustains all life.
Disobedience	People are always facing great choices. Disobedience occurs when people choose not to follow God's plan of living.	Genesis explains why people are evil: They choose to do wrong. Even great Bible heroes failed God and disobeyed.
Sin	Sin ruins people's lives. It happens when we disobey God.	Living God's way makes life productive and fulfilling.
Promises	God makes promises to help and protect people. This kind of promise is called a "covenant."	God kept his promises then, and he keeps them now. He promises to love us, accept us, forgive us.
Obedience	The opposite of sin is obedience. Obeying God restores our relationship to him.	The only way to enjoy the benefits of God's promises is to obey him.
Prosperity	Prosperity is deeper than mere material wealth. True prosperity and fulfillment come as a result of obeying God.	When people obey God, they find peace with him, with others, and with themselves.
Israel	God started the nation of Israel in order to have a dedicated people who would (1) keep his ways alive in the world, (2) proclaim to the world what he is really like, and (3) prepare the world for the birth of Christ.	God is looking for people today to follow him. We are to proclaim God's truth and love to all nations, not just our own. We must be faithful to carry out the mission God has given us.

KEY PLACES IN GENESIS

Modern names and boundaries are shown in gray.

of Canaan. Along the way, they settled in the village of Haran for a while (11:31).

5 Shechem God urged Abram to leave Haran and go to a place where he would become the father of a great nation (12:1, 2). So Abram, Lot, and Sarai traveled to the land of Canaan and settled near a city called Shechem (12:6).

6 Hebron Abraham moved on to Hebron where he put down his deepest roots (13:18). Abraham, Isaac, and Jacob all lived and were buried here.

God created the universe and the earth. Then he made man and woman, giving them a home in a beautiful garden. Unfortunately, Adam and Eve disobeyed God and were banished from the garden (3:23).

1 Mountains of Ararat Adam and Eve's sin brought sin into the human race. Years later, sin had run rampant and God decided to destroy the earth with a great flood. But Noah, his family, and two of each animal were safe in the ark. When the floods receded, the ark rested on the mountains of Ararat (8:4).

2 Babel People never learn. Again sin abounded, and the pride of the people led them to build a huge tower as a monument to their own greatness—obviously they had no thought of God. As punishment, God scattered the people by giving them different languages (11:8, 9).

3 Ur of the Chaldeans Abram, a descendant of Shem and father of the Hebrew nation, was born in this great city (11:28).

4 Haran Terah, Abram, Lot, and Sarai left Ur and, following the fertile crescent of the Euphrates River, headed toward the land

7 Beersheba The well at Beersheba was a source of conflict between Abraham and King Abimelech and later became a sign of the oath that they swore there (21:31). Years later, as Isaac was moving from place to place, God appeared to him here and passed on to him the covenant he had made with his father, Abraham (26:23–25).

8 Bethel After deceiving his brother, Jacob left Beersheba and fled to Haran. Along the way, God revealed himself to Jacob in a dream and passed on to him the covenant he had made with Abraham and Isaac (28:10–22). Jacob lived in Haran, worked for Laban, and married Leah and Rachel (29:15–30). After a tense meeting with his brother, Esau, Jacob returned to Bethel (35:1).

9 Egypt Jacob had 12 sons, including Joseph, Jacob's favorite. Joseph's 10 older brothers grew jealous, until one day the brothers sold him to Midianite merchants going to Egypt. Eventually, Joseph rose from Egyptian slave to Pharaoh's "right-hand man," saving Egypt from famine. His entire family moved from Canaan to Egypt and settled there (46:3–7).

A. THE STORY OF CREATION (1:1—2:3)

We sometimes wonder how our world came to be. But here we find the answer. God created the earth and everything in it, and made humans like himself. Although we may not understand the complexity of just how he did it, it is clear that God did create all life. This shows not only God's authority over humanity, but his deep love for all people.

The Beginning

1 In the beginning *a* God created the heavens and the earth. *b* 2 Now the earth was *a* formless and empty, darkness was over the surface of the deep, and the Spirit of God was hovering over the waters.

a 2 Or possibly *became*

1:1
a Jn 1:1-2
b Isa 42:5; 44:24; 45:12, 18

1:1 The simple statement that God created the heavens and the earth is one of the most challenging concepts confronting the modern mind. The vast galaxy we live in is spinning at the incredible speed of 490,000 miles an hour. But even at this breakneck

speed, our galaxy still needs 200 million years to make one rotation. And there are over one billion other galaxies just like ours in the universe.

Some scientists say that the number of stars in creation is

1:3
*c*Ps 33:6, 9
*d*2Co 4:6*

1:5
*e*Ps 74:16

1:6
*f*Jer 10:12

1:7
*g*Ps 148:4

1:9
*h*Ps 104:6-9;
Jer 5:22; 2Pe 3:5

3 And God said,*c* "Let there be light," and there was light. *d* 4 God saw that the light was good, and he separated the light from the darkness. 5 God called the light "day," and the darkness he called "night."*e* And there was evening, and there was morning—the first day.

6 And God said, "Let there be an expanse *f* between the waters to separate water from water." 7 So God made the expanse and separated the water under the expanse from the water above it.*g* And it was so. 8 God called the expanse "sky." And there was evening, and there was morning—the second day.

9 And God said, "Let the water under the sky be gathered to one place,*h* and let dry ground appear." And it was so. 10 God called the dry ground "land," and the gathered waters he called "seas." And God saw that it was good.

11 Then God said, "Let the land produce vegetation: seed-bearing plants and trees on the land that bear fruit with seed in it, according to their various kinds."

BEGINNINGS
Origin of the universe

The Bible does not discuss the subject of evolution. Rather, its worldview assumes God created the world. The biblical view of creation is not in conflict with science; rather, it is in conflict with any worldview that starts without a creator.

Equally committed and sincere Christians have struggled with the subject of beginnings and come to **differing conclusions.** This, of course, is to be expected because the evidence is very old and, due to the ravages of the ages, quite fragmented. Students of the Bible and of science should avoid polarizations and black/white thinking. Students of the Bible must be careful not to make the Bible say what it doesn't say, and students of science must not make science say what it doesn't say.

The most important aspect of the continuing discussion is not the process of creation, but the origin of creation. **The world is not a product of blind chance and probability; God created it.** The Bible not only tells us that the world was created by God; more importantly, it tells us who this God is. It reveals God's personality, his character, and his plan for his creation. It also reveals **God's deepest desire: to relate to and fellowship with the people he created.** God took the ultimate step toward fellowship with us through his historic visit to this planet in the person of his Son, Jesus Christ. We can know in a very personal way this God who created the universe.

The heavens and the earth are here. We are here. God created all that we see and experience. The book of Genesis begins, "God created the heavens and the earth."

---

equal to all the grains of all the sands on all the beaches of the world. Yet this complex sea of spinning stars functions with remarkable order and efficiency. To say that the universe "just happened" or "evolved" requires more faith than to believe that God is behind these amazing statistics. God truly did create a wonderful universe.

God did not *need* to create the universe; he *chose* to create it. Why? God is love, and love is best expressed toward something or someone else—so God created the world and people as an expression of his love. We should avoid reducing God's creation to merely scientific terms. Remember that God created the universe because he loves us.

1:1ff The creation story teaches us much about God and ourselves. First, we learn about God: (1) he is creative; (2) as the Creator he is distinct from his creation; (3) he is eternal and in control of the world. We also learn about ourselves: (1) since God chose to create us, we are valuable in his eyes; (2) we are more important than the animals. (See 1:28 for more on our role in the created order.)

1:1ff Just how did God create the earth? This is still a subject of great debate. Some say that with a sudden explosion, the universe appeared. Others say that God started the process, and the universe evolved over billions of years. Almost every ancient religion has its own story to explain how the earth came to be. And almost every scientist has an opinion on the origin of the universe. But only the Bible shows one supreme God creating the earth out of his great love and giving all people a special place in it. We will never know all the answers to how God created the earth, but the Bible tells us that God did create it. That fact alone gives worth and dignity to all people.

1:2 Who created God? To ask that question is to assume there was another creator before God. At some time, however, we are

forced to stop asking that question and realize that there had to be something that has always existed. God is that infinite Being who has always been and who was created by no one. This is difficult to understand because finite minds cannot comprehend the infinite. For example, we can try to think of the highest number, but we can't do it. Likewise, we must not limit the infinite God by our finite understanding.

1:2 The statement "the earth was formless and empty" provides the setting for the creation narrative that follows. During the second and third days of creation, God gave *form* to the universe; during the next three days, God *filled* the earth with living beings. The "darkness . . . over the surface of the deep" was dispelled on the first day, when God created light.

1:2 The image of the Spirit of God hovering over the waters is similar to a mother bird caring for and protecting its young (see Deuteronomy 32:11, 12; Isaiah 31:5). God's Spirit was actively involved in the creation of the world (see Job 33:4; Psalm 104:30). God's care and protection are still active.

1:3—2:7 How long did it take God to create the world? There are two basic views about the days of creation: (1) each day was a literal 24-hour period; (2) each day represents an indefinite period of time (even millions of years).

The Bible does not say how long these time periods were. The real question, however, is not how long God took, but how he did it. God created the earth in an orderly fashion (he did not make plants before light), and he created men and women as unique beings capable of communication with him. No other part of creation can claim that remarkable privilege. It is not important how long it took God to create the world, whether a few days or a few billion years, but that he created it just the way he wanted it.

1:6 The "expanse between the waters" was a separation between the sea and the mists of the skies.

And it was so. [12]The land produced vegetation: plants bearing seed according to their kinds and trees bearing fruit with seed in it according to their kinds. And God saw that it was good. [13]And there was evening, and there was morning—the third day.

[14] And God said, "Let there be lights[i] in the expanse of the sky to separate the day from the night, and let them serve as signs to mark seasons[j] and days and years, [15]and let them be lights in the expanse of the sky to give light on the earth." And it was so. [16]God made two great lights—the greater light to govern[k] the day and the lesser light to govern[l] the night. He also made the stars. [m] [17]God set them in the expanse of the sky to give light on the earth, [18]to govern the day and the night, and to separate light from darkness. And God saw that it was good. [19]And there was evening, and there was morning—the fourth day.

[20] And God said, "Let the water teem with living creatures, and let birds fly above the earth across the expanse of the sky." [21]So God created the great creatures of the sea and every living and moving thing with which the water teems, according to their kinds, and every winged bird according to its kind. And God saw that it was good. [22]God blessed them and said, "Be fruitful and increase in number and fill the water in the seas, and let the birds increase on the earth." [23]And there was evening, and there was morning—the fifth day.

[24] And God said, "Let the land produce living creatures according to their kinds: livestock, creatures that move along the ground, and wild animals, each according to its kind." And it was so. [25]God made the wild animals according to their kinds, the livestock according to their kinds, and all the creatures that move along the ground according to their kinds. And God saw that it was good.

[26]Then God said, "Let us make man in our image, in our likeness, and let them rule over the fish of the sea and the birds of the air, over the livestock, over all the earth,[a] and over all the creatures that move along the ground."

[27] So God created man in his own image,
　　in the image of God he created him;
　　male and female[n] he created them.

[a]*26 Hebrew; Syriac all the wild animals*

1:14
[i]Ps 74:16
[j]Ps 104:19

1:16
[k]Ps 136:8
[l]Ps 136:9
[m]Ps 8:3; Isa 40:26

1:27
[n]Ge 5:2; Mt 19:4*;
Mk 10:6*

		DAYS OF CREATION
First Day	Light (so there was light and darkness)	
Second Day	Sky and water (waters separated)	
Third Day	Land and seas (waters gathered); vegetation	
Fourth Day	Sun, moon, and stars (to govern the day and the night and to mark seasons, days and years)	
Fifth Day	Fish and birds (to fill the waters and the sky)	
Sixth Day	Animals (to fill the earth) Man and woman (to care for the earth and to commune with God)	
Seventh Day	God rested and declared all he had made to be very good	

1:25 God saw that his work was good. People sometimes feel guilty for having a good time or for feeling good about an accomplishment. This need not be so. Just as God felt good about his work, we can be pleased with ours. However, we should not feel good about our work if God would not be pleased with it. What are you doing that pleases both you and God?

1:26 Why does God use the plural form, "Let *us* make man in *our* image"? One view says this is a reference to the Trinity—God the Father, Jesus Christ his Son, and the Holy Spirit—all of whom are God. Another view is that the plural wording is used to denote majesty. Kings traditionally use the plural form in speaking of themselves. From Job 33:4 and Psalm 104:30, we do know that God's Spirit was present in the creation. From Colossians 1:16 we know that Christ, God's Son, was at work in the creation.

1:26 In what ways are we made in God's image? God obviously did not create us exactly like himself because God has no physical body. Instead, we are reflections of God's glory. Some feel that

our reason, creativity, speech, or self-determination is the image of God. More likely, it is our entire self that reflects the image of God. We will never be totally like God because he is our supreme Creator. But we do have the ability to reflect his character in our love, patience, forgiveness, kindness, and faithfulness.

Knowing that we are made in God's image and thus share many of his characteristics provides a solid basis for self-worth. Human worth is not based on possessions, achievements, physical attractiveness, or public acclaim. Instead it is based on being made in God's image. Because we bear God's image, we can feel positive about ourselves. Criticizing or downgrading ourselves is criticizing what God has made and the abilities he has given us. Knowing that you are a person of worth helps you love God, know him personally, and make a valuable contribution to those around you.

1:27 God made both man and woman in his image. Neither man nor woman is made more in the image of God than the other.

1:28
*o*Ge 9:1, 7;
Lev 26:9

1:29
*p*Ps 104:14

1:30
*q*Ps 145:15

1:31
*r*Ps 104:24

2:2
*s*Ex 20:11; Heb 4:4*

2:5
*t*Ge 1:11

²⁸God blessed them and said to them, "Be fruitful and increase in number; fill the earth *o* and subdue it. Rule over the fish of the sea and the birds of the air and over every living creature that moves on the ground."

²⁹Then God said, "I give you every seed-bearing plant on the face of the whole earth and every tree that has fruit with seed in it. They will be yours for food. *p* ³⁰And to all the beasts of the earth and all the birds of the air and all the creatures that move on the ground—everything that has the breath of life in it—I give every green plant for food. *q* " And it was so.

³¹God saw all that he had made, *r* and it was very good. And there was evening, and there was morning—the sixth day.

2 Thus the heavens and the earth were completed in all their vast array.

²By the seventh day God had finished the work he had been doing; so on the seventh day he rested *a* from all his work. *s* ³And God blessed the seventh day and made it holy, because on it he rested from all the work of creating that he had done.

B. THE STORY OF ADAM (2:4—5:32)

Learning about our ancestors often helps us understand ourselves. Adam and Eve, our first ancestors, were the highlight of God's creation—the very reason God made the world. But they didn't always live the way God intended. Through their mistakes, we can learn important lessons about the way God wants us to live. Adam and Eve teach us much about the nature of sin and its consequences.

1. Adam and Eve

⁴This is the account of the heavens and the earth when they were created.

When the LORD God made the earth and the heavens— ⁵and no shrub of the field had yet appeared on the earth *b* and no plant of the field had yet sprung up, *t* for the LORD God had not sent rain on the earth *b* and there was no man to work the ground, ⁶but streams *c* came

*a*2 Or *ceased*; also in verse 3   *b*5 Or *land*; also in verse 6   *c*6 Or *mist*

WHAT THE BIBLE SAYS ABOUT MARRIAGE	
Genesis 2:18–24 . . .	Marriage is God's idea
Genesis 24:58–60 . .	Commitment is essential to a successful marriage
Genesis 29:10, 11 . .	Romance is important
Jeremiah 7:34	Marriage holds times of great joy
Malachi 2:14, 15	Marriage creates the best environment for raising children
Matthew 5:32	Unfaithfulness breaks the bond of trust, the foundation of all relationships
Matthew 19:6	Marriage is permanent
Romans 7:2, 3	Ideally, only death should dissolve marriage
Ephesians 5:21–33 . .	Marriage is based on the principled practice of love, not on feelings
Ephesians 5:23, 32 . .	Marriage is a living symbol of Christ and the church
Hebrews 13:4	Marriage is good and honorable

From the beginning the Bible places both man and woman at the pinnacle of God's creation. Neither sex is exalted, and neither is depreciated.

1:28 To "rule over" something is to have absolute authority and control over it. God has ultimate rule over the earth, and he exercises his authority with loving care. When God delegated some of his authority to the human race, he expected us to take responsibility for the environment and the other creatures that share our planet. We must not be careless and wasteful as we fulfill this charge. God was careful how he made this earth. We must not be careless about how we take care of it.

1:31 God saw that all he had created was very good. You are part of God's creation, and he is pleased with how he made you. If at times you feel worthless or of little value, remember that God made you for a good reason. You are valuable to him.

2:2, 3 We live in an action-oriented world! There always seems to be something to do and no time to rest. Yet God demonstrated that rest is appropriate and right. If God himself rested from his work, we should not be surprised that we also need rest. Jesus demonstrated this principle when he and his disciples left in a boat to get away from the crowds (see Mark 6:31, 32). Our times of rest refresh us for times of service.

2:3 That God *blessed* the seventh day means that he set it apart for holy use. The Ten Commandments emphasize this distinction by commanding the observance of the Sabbath (Exodus 20:1–17).

up from the earth and watered the whole surface of the ground— 7 the LORD God formed the man a from the dust u of the ground and breathed into his nostrils the breath of life, and the man became a living being. v

8 Now the LORD God had planted a garden in the east, in Eden; and there he put the man he had formed. 9 And the LORD God made all kinds of trees grow out of the ground—trees that were pleasing to the eye and good for food. In the middle of the garden were the tree of life w and the tree of the knowledge of good and evil.

10 A river watering the garden flowed from Eden; from there it was separated into four headwaters. 11 The name of the first is the Pishon; it winds through the entire land of Havilah, where there is gold. 12 (The gold of that land is good; aromatic resin b and onyx are also there.) 13 The name of the second river is the Gihon; it winds through the entire land of Cush. c 14 The name of the third river is the Tigris; x it runs along the east side of Asshur. And the fourth river is the Euphrates.

15 The LORD God took the man and put him in the Garden of Eden to work it and take care of it. 16 And the LORD God commanded the man, "You are free to eat from any tree in the garden; 17 but you must not eat from the tree of the knowledge of good and evil, for when you eat of it you will surely die." y

18 The LORD God said, "It is not good for the man to be alone. I will make a helper suitable for him."

19 Now the LORD God had formed out of the ground all the beasts of the field and all the birds of the air. He brought them to the man to see what he would name them; and whatever the man called each living creature, that was its name. 20 So the man gave names to all the livestock, the birds of the air and all the beasts of the field.

But for Adam d no suitable helper was found. 21 So the LORD God caused the man to fall into a deep sleep; and while he was sleeping, he took one of the man's ribs e and closed up the place with flesh. 22 Then the LORD God made a woman from the rib f he had taken out of the man, and he brought her to the man.

23 The man said,

"This is now bone of my bones
　and flesh of my flesh; z
she shall be called 'woman, g'
　for she was taken out of man."

a 7 The Hebrew for man (adam) sounds like and may be related to the Hebrew for ground (adamah); it is also the name Adam (see Gen. 2:20).　b 12 Or good; pearls　c 13 Possibly southeast Mesopotamia　d 20 Or the man　e 21 Or took part of the man's side　f 22 Or part　g 23 The Hebrew for woman sounds like the Hebrew for man.

2:7 uGe 3:19
v1Co 15:45*

2:9 wGe 3:22, 24; Rev 2:7; 22:2, 14, 19

2:14 xDa 10:4

2:17 yRo 5:12; 6:23

2:23 zEph 5:28-30

2:7 "From the dust of the ground" implies that there is nothing fancy about the chemical elements making up our bodies. The body is a lifeless shell until God brings it to life with his "breath of life." When God removes his life-giving breath, our bodies once again return to dust. Our lives and worth, therefore, come from God's Spirit. Many boast of their achievements and abilities as though they were the originator of their own strengths. Others feel worthless because their abilities do not stand out. In reality, our worth comes not from our achievements but from the God of the universe, who chooses to give us the mysterious and miraculous gift of life. Value life, as he does.

2:9 The name of the tree of the knowledge of good and evil implies that evil had already occurred, if not in the garden, then at the time of Satan's fall.

2:9, 16, 17 Were the tree of life and the tree of the knowledge of good and evil real trees? Two views are often expressed:

(1) The trees were real, but symbolic. Eternal life with God was pictured as eating from the tree of life.

(2) The trees were real, possessing special properties. By eating the fruit from the tree of life, Adam and Eve could have had eternal life, enjoying a permanent relationship as God's children.

In either case, Adam and Eve's sin separated them from the tree of life and thus kept them from obtaining eternal life. Interestingly, the tree of life again appears in a description in Revelation 22 of people enjoying eternal life with God.

2:15-17 God gave Adam responsibility for the garden and told him not to eat from the tree of the knowledge of good and evil.

Rather than physically preventing him from eating, God gave Adam a choice, and thus the possibility of choosing wrongly. God still gives us choices, and we, too, often choose wrongly. These wrong choices may cause us pain, but they can help us learn and grow and make better choices in the future. Living with the consequences of our choices teaches us to think and choose more carefully.

2:16, 17 Why would God place a tree in the garden and then forbid Adam to eat from it? God wanted Adam to obey, but God gave Adam the freedom to choose. Without choice, Adam would have been like a prisoner, and his obedience would have been hollow. The two trees provided an exercise in choice, with rewards for choosing to obey and sad consequences for choosing to disobey. When you are faced with the choice, always choose to obey God.

2:18-24 God's creative work was not complete until he made woman. He could have made her from the dust of the ground, as he made man. God chose, however, to make her from the man's flesh and bone. In so doing, he illustrated for us that in marriage man and woman symbolically become one flesh. This is a mystical union of the couple's hearts and lives. Throughout the Bible, God treats this special partnership seriously. If you are married or planning to be married, are you willing to keep the commitment that makes the two of you one? The goal in marriage should be more than friendship; it should be oneness.

2:21-23 God forms and equips men and women for various tasks, but all these tasks lead to the same goal—honoring God. Man gives life to woman; woman gives life to the world. Each role

2:24
a Mt 19:5*; 1Co 6:16*;
Eph 5:31*

24 For this reason a man will leave his father and mother and be united to his wife, and they will become one flesh. *a*

2:25
b Ge 3:7, 10-11

25 The man and his wife were both naked, *b* and they felt no shame.

ADAM

We can hardly imagine what it must have been like to be the first and only person on earth. It's one thing for us to be lonely; it was another for Adam, who had never known another human being. He missed much that makes us who we are—he had no childhood, no parents, no family or friends. He had to learn to be human on his own. Fortunately, God didn't let him struggle too long before presenting him with an ideal companion and mate, Eve. Theirs was a complete, innocent, and open oneness, without a hint of shame.

One of Adam's first conversations with his delightful new companion must have been about the rules of the garden. Before God made Eve he had already given Adam complete freedom in the garden, with the responsibility to tend and care for it. But one tree was off limits, the tree of the knowledge of good and evil. Adam would have told Eve all about this. She knew, when Satan approached her, that the tree's fruit was not to be eaten. However, she decided to eat the forbidden fruit. Then she offered some to Adam. At that moment, the fate of creation was on the line. Sadly, Adam didn't pause to consider the consequences. He went ahead and ate.

In that moment of small rebellion something large, beautiful, and free was shattered . . . God's perfect creation. Man was separated from God by his desire to act on his own. The effect on a plate glass window is the same whether a pebble or a boulder is hurled at it—the thousands of fragments can never be regathered.

In the case of man's sin, however, God already had a plan in motion to overcome the effects of the rebellion. The entire Bible is the story of how that plan unfolds, ultimately leading to God's own visit to earth through his Son, Jesus. His sinless life and death made it possible for God to offer forgiveness to all who want it. Our small and large acts of rebellion prove that we are descendants of Adam. Only by asking forgiveness of Jesus Christ can we become children of God.

Strengths and accomplishments:	• The first zoologist—one who names animals • The first landscape architect, placed in the garden to care for it • Father of the human race • The first person made in the image of God, and the first human to share an intimate personal relationship with God
Weaknesses and mistakes:	• Avoided responsibility and blamed others; chose to hide rather than to confront; made excuses rather than admitting the truth • Greatest mistake: teamed up with Eve to bring sin into the world
Lessons from his life:	• As Adam's descendants, we all reflect to some degree the image of God • God wants people who, though free to do wrong, choose instead to love him • We should not blame others for our faults • We cannot hide from God
Vital statistics:	• Where: Garden of Eden • Occupation: Caretaker, gardener, farmer • Relatives: Wife: Eve. Sons: Cain, Abel, Seth. Numerous other children. The only man who never had an earthly mother or father.
Key verses:	"The man said, 'The woman you put here with me—she gave me some fruit from the tree, and I ate it'" (Genesis 3:12). "For as in Adam all die, so in Christ all will be made alive" (1 Corinthians 15:22).

Adam's story is told in Genesis 1:26—5:5. He is also mentioned in 1 Chronicles 1:1; Job 31:33; Luke 3:38; Romans 5:14; 1 Corinthians 15:22, 45; 1 Timothy 2:13, 14.

carries exclusive privileges; there is no room for thinking that one sex is superior to the other.

2:24 God gave marriage as a gift to Adam and Eve. They were created perfect for each other. Marriage was not just for convenience, nor was it brought about by any culture. It was instituted by God and has three basic aspects: (1) the man leaves his parents and, in a public act, promises himself to his wife; (2) the man and woman are joined together by taking responsibility for each other's welfare and by loving the mate above all others; (3) the two become one flesh in the intimacy and commitment of sexual union that is reserved for marriage. Strong marriages include all three of these aspects.

2:25 Have you ever noticed how a little child can run naked through a room full of strangers without embarrassment? He

is not aware of his nakedness, just as Adam and Eve were not embarrassed in their innocence. But after Adam and Eve sinned, shame and awkwardness followed, creating barriers between themselves and God. We often experience these same barriers in marriage. Ideally a husband and wife have no barriers, feeling no embarrassment in exposing themselves to each other or to God. But, like Adam and Eve (3:7), we put on fig leaves (barriers) because we have areas we don't want our spouse, or God, to know about. Then we hide, just as Adam and Eve hid from God. In marriage, lack of spiritual, emotional, and intellectual intimacy usually precedes a breakdown of physical intimacy. In the same way, when we fail to expose our secret thoughts to God, we break our lines of communication with him.

The Fall of Man

3 Now the serpent[c] was more crafty than any of the wild animals the LORD God had made. He said to the woman, "Did God really say, 'You must not eat from any tree in the garden'?"

²The woman said to the serpent, "We may eat fruit from the trees in the garden, ³but God did say, 'You must not eat fruit from the tree that is in the middle of the garden, and you must not touch it, or you will die.'"

⁴"You will not surely die," the serpent said to the woman. ⁵"For God knows that when you eat of it your eyes will be opened, and you will be like God, knowing good and evil."

⁶When the woman saw that the fruit of the tree was good for food and pleasing to the eye, and also desirable for gaining wisdom, she took some and ate it. She also gave some to her husband, who was with her, and he ate it.[d] ⁷Then the eyes of both of them were opened, and they realized they were naked; so they sewed fig leaves together and made coverings for themselves.

⁸Then the man and his wife heard the sound of the LORD God as he was walking in the garden in the cool of the day, and they hid[e] from the LORD God among the trees of the garden. ⁹But the LORD God called to the man, "Where are you?"

3:1
c 2Co 11:3;
Rev 12:9; 20:2

3:6
d 1Ti 2:14

3:8
e Job 31:33

3:1 Disguised as a crafty serpent, Satan came to tempt Eve. At one time, Satan had been a glorious angel. But in pride, he rebelled against God and was cast out of heaven. As a created being, Satan has definite limitations. Although he is trying to tempt everyone away from God, he will not be the final victor. In 3:14, 15, God promises that Satan will be crushed by one of the woman's offspring, the Messiah.

3:1–6 Why does Satan tempt us? Temptation is Satan's invitation to give in to his kind of life and give up on God's kind of life. Satan tempted Eve and succeeded in getting her to sin. Ever since then, he's been busy getting people to sin. He even tempted Jesus (Matthew 4:11). But Jesus did not sin!

How could Eve have resisted temptation? By following the same guidelines we can follow. First, we must realize that *being tempted* is not a sin. We have not sinned until we *give in* to the temptation. Then, to resist temptation, we must (1) pray for strength to resist, (2) run, sometimes literally, and (3) say no when confronted with what we know is wrong. James 1:12 tells of the blessings and rewards for those who don't give in when tempted.

3:1–6 The serpent, Satan, tempted Eve by getting her to doubt God's goodness. He implied that God was strict, stingy, and selfish for not wanting Eve to share his knowledge of good and evil. Satan made Eve forget all that God had given her and, instead, focus on what God had forbidden. We fall into trouble, too, when we dwell on what God forbids rather than on the countless blessings and promises he has given us. The next time you are feeling sorry for yourself and what you don't have, consider all you *do* have and thank God. Then your doubts won't lead you into sin.

3:5 Adam and Eve got what they wanted: an intimate knowledge of both good and evil. But they got it by doing evil, and the results were disastrous. Sometimes we have the illusion that freedom is doing anything we want. But God says that true freedom comes from obedience and knowing what *not* to do. The restrictions he gives us are for our good, helping us avoid evil. We have the freedom to walk in front of a speeding car, but we don't need to be hit to realize it would be foolish to do so. Don't listen to Satan's temptations. You don't have to do evil to gain more experience and learn more about life.

3:5 Satan used a sincere motive to tempt Eve—"you will be like God." It wasn't wrong of Eve to want to be like God. To become more like God is humanity's highest goal. It is what we are supposed to do. But Satan misled Eve concerning the right way to accomplish this goal. He told her that she could become more like God by defying God's authority, by taking God's place and deciding for herself what was best for her life. In effect, he told her to become her own god.

But to become like God is not the same as trying to become God. Rather, it is to reflect his characteristics and to recognize his authority over your life. Like Eve, we often have a worthy goal but

try to achieve it in the wrong way. We act like a political candidate who pays off an election judge to be "voted" into office. When he does this, serving the people is no longer his highest goal.

Self-exaltation leads to rebellion against God. As soon as we begin to leave God out of our plans, we are placing ourselves above him. This is exactly what Satan wants us to do.

3:6 Satan tried to make Eve think that sin is good, pleasant, and desirable. A knowledge of both good and evil seemed harmless to her. People usually choose wrong things because they have become convinced that those things are good, at least for themselves. Our sins do not always appear ugly to us, and the pleasant sins are the hardest to avoid. So prepare yourself for the attractive temptations that may come your way. We cannot always prevent temptation, but there is always a way of escape (1 Corinthians 10:13). Use God's Word and God's people to help you stand against it.

3:6, 7 Notice what Eve did: She looked, she took, she ate, and she gave. The battle is often lost at the first look. Temptation often begins by simply seeing something you want. Are you struggling with temptation because you have not learned that looking is the first step toward sin? You would win over temptation more often if you followed Paul's advice to run from those things that produce evil thoughts (2 Timothy 2:22).

3:6, 7 One of the realities of sin is that its effects spread. After Eve sinned, she involved Adam in her wrongdoing. When we do something wrong, often we try to relieve our guilt by involving someone else. Like toxic waste spilled in a river, sin swiftly spreads. Recognize and confess your sin to God before you are tempted to pollute those around you.

3:7, 8 After sinning, Adam and Eve felt guilt and embarrassment over their nakedness. Their guilty feelings made them try to hide from God. A guilty conscience is a warning signal God placed inside you that goes off when you've done wrong. The worst step you could take is to eliminate the guilty feelings without eliminating the cause. That would be like using a pain killer but not treating the disease. Be glad those guilty feelings are there. They make you aware of your sin so you can ask God's forgiveness and then correct your wrongdoing.

3:8 The thought of two humans covered with fig leaves trying to hide from the all-seeing, all-knowing God is humorous. How could they be so silly as to think they could actually hide? Yet we do the same, acting as though God doesn't know what we're doing. Have the courage to share all you do and think with him. And don't try to hide—it can't be done. Honesty will strengthen your relationship with God.

3:8, 9 These verses show God's desire to have fellowship with us. They also show why we are afraid to have fellowship with him. Adam and Eve hid from God when they heard him approaching.

¹⁰He answered, "I heard you in the garden, and I was afraid because I was naked; so I hid."

¹¹And he said, "Who told you that you were naked? Have you eaten from the tree that I commanded you not to eat from?"

¹²The man said, "The woman you put here with me—she gave me some fruit from the tree, and I ate it."

¹³Then the LORD God said to the woman, "What is this you have done?"

The woman said, "The serpent deceived me, and I ate."

¹⁴So the LORD God said to the serpent, "Because you have done this,

"Cursed are you above all the livestock
    and all the wild animals!
You will crawl on your belly
    and you will eat dust
    all the days of your life.
¹⁵ And I will put enmity
    between you and the woman,
    and between your offspringᵃᶠ and hers;
he will crushᵇ your head,ᵍ
    and you will strike his heel."

¹⁶To the woman he said,

"I will greatly increase your pains in childbearing;
    with pain you will give birth to children.
Your desire will be for your husband,
    and he will rule over you."

¹⁷To Adam he said, "Because you listened to your wife and ate from the tree about which I commanded you, 'You must not eat of it,'

3:15
ᶠ 1 Jn 3:8
ᵍ Ro 16:20

ᵃ *15* Or *seed*   ᵇ *15* Or *strike*

SATAN'S PLAN AGAINST US	Doubt	Makes you question God's Word and his goodness
	Discouragement. . . .	Makes you look at your problems rather than at God
	Diversion	Makes the wrong things seem attractive so that you will want them more than the right things
	Defeat	Makes you feel like a failure so that you don't even try
	Delay	Makes you put off doing something so that it never gets done

God wanted to be with them, but because of their sin they were afraid to show themselves. Sin had broken their close relationship with God, just as it has broken ours. But Jesus Christ, God's Son, opens the way for us to renew our fellowship with him. God longs to be with us. He actively offers us his unconditional love. Our natural response is fear because we feel we can't live up to his standards. But understanding that he loves us, regardless of our faults, can help remove that dread.

3:11–13 Adam and Eve failed to heed God's warning recorded in 2:16, 17. They did not understand the reasons for his command, so they chose to act in another way that looked better to them. All of God's commands are for our own good, but we may not always understand the reasons behind them. People who trust God will obey because God asks them to, whether or not they understand why God commands it.

3:11–13 When God asked Adam about his sin, Adam blamed Eve. Then Eve blamed the serpent. How easy it is to excuse our sins by blaming someone else or circumstances. But God knows the truth, and he holds each of us responsible for what we do (see 3:14–19). Admit your wrong attitudes and actions and apologize to God. Don't try to get away with sin by blaming someone else.

3:14ff Adam and Eve chose their course of action (disobedience), and then God chose his. As a holy God, he could respond only in a way consistent with his perfect moral nature. He could not allow sin to go unchecked; he had to punish it. If the consequences of Adam and Eve's sin seem extreme, remember that their sin set in

motion the world's tendency toward disobeying God. That is why we sin today: Every human being ever born, with the exception of Jesus, has inherited the sinful nature of Adam and Eve (Romans 5:12–21). Adam and Eve's punishment reflects how seriously God views sin of any kind.

3:14–19 Adam and Eve learned by painful experience that because God is holy and hates sin, he must punish sinners. The rest of the book of Genesis recounts painful stories of lives ruined as a result of the fall. Disobedience is sin, and it breaks our fellowship with God. But, fortunately, when we disobey, God is willing to forgive us and to restore our relationship with him.

3:15 Satan is our enemy. He will do anything he can to get us to follow his evil, deadly path. The phrase "you will strike his heel" refers to Satan's repeated attempts to defeat Christ during his life on earth. "He will crush your head" foreshadows Satan's defeat when Christ rose from the dead. A strike on the heel is not deadly, but a blow to the head is. Already God was revealing his plan to defeat Satan and offer salvation to the world through his Son, Jesus Christ.

3:17–19 Adam and Eve's disobedience and fall from God's gracious presence affected all creation, including the environment. Years ago people thought nothing of polluting streams with chemical wastes and garbage. This seemed so insignificant, so small. Now we know that just two or three parts per million of certain chemicals can damage human health. Sin in our lives is similar to pollution in streams. Even small amounts are deadly.

> "Cursed[h] is the ground because of you;
> through painful toil you will eat of it
> all the days of your life.[i]
>
> [18] It will produce thorns and thistles for you,
> and you will eat the plants of the field.
> [19] By the sweat of your brow
> you will eat your food
> until you return to the ground,
> since from it you were taken;
> for dust you are
> and to dust you will return."[j]

[20]Adam[a] named his wife Eve,[b] because she would become the mother of all the living. [21]The LORD God made garments of skin for Adam and his wife and clothed them. [22]And the LORD God said, "The man has now become like one of us, knowing good and evil. He must not be allowed to reach out his hand and take also from the tree of life[k] and eat, and live forever." [23]So the LORD God banished him from the Garden of Eden to work the ground from which he had been taken. [24]After he drove the man out, he placed on the east side[c] of the Garden of Eden cherubim and a flaming sword flashing back and forth to guard the way to the tree of life.

2. Cain and Abel

4 Adam[a] lay with his wife Eve, and she became pregnant and gave birth to Cain.[d] She said, "With the help of the LORD I have brought forth[e] a man." [2]Later she gave birth to his brother Abel.

Now Abel kept flocks, and Cain worked the soil. [3]In the course of time Cain brought some of the fruits of the soil as an offering to the LORD. [4]But Abel brought fat portions from some of the firstborn of his flock. The LORD looked with favor on Abel and his offering,[l] [5]but on Cain and his offering he did not look with favor. So Cain was very angry, and his face was downcast.

[6]Then the LORD said to Cain, "Why are you angry? Why is your face downcast? [7]If you do what is right, will you not be accepted? But if you do not do what is right, sin is crouching at your door; it desires to have you, but you must master it."

[a]20,1 Or *The man*   [b]20 *Eve* probably means *living.*   [c]24 Or *placed in front*   [d]1 *Cain* sounds like the Hebrew for *brought forth* or *acquired.*   [e]1 Or *have acquired*

3:17
[h]Ro 8:20-22
[i]Ecc 2:23

3:19
[j]Ge 2:7; Ps 90:3;
Ecc 12:7

3:22
[k]Rev 22:14

4:4
[l]Heb 11:4

3:22–24 Life in the Garden of Eden was like living in heaven. Everything was perfect, and if Adam and Eve had obeyed God, they could have lived there forever. But after disobeying, Adam and Eve no longer deserved paradise, and God told them to leave. If they had continued to live in the garden and had eaten from the tree of life, they would have lived forever. But eternal life in a state of sin would mean forever trying to hide from God. Like Adam and Eve, all of us have sinned and are separated from fellowship with God. We do not have to stay separated, however. God is preparing a new earth as an eternal paradise for his people (see Revelation 22).

3:24 The cherubim were mighty angels of the Lord.

3:24 This is how Adam and Eve broke their relationship with God: (1) they became convinced their way was better than God's; (2) they became self-conscious and hid; (3) they tried to excuse and defend themselves. To build a relationship with God we must reverse those steps: (1) we must drop our excuses and self-defenses; (2) we must stop trying to hide from God; (3) we must become convinced that God's way is better than our way.

4:1 The phrase *lay with* is literally *he knew* and means he "had sexual intercourse with." Sexual union means oneness and total knowledge of the other person. Sexual intercourse is the most intimate of acts, sealing a social, physical, and spiritual relationship. That is why God has reserved it for marriage alone.

4:2 No longer was everything provided for Adam and Eve as it was in the Garden of Eden, where their daily tasks were refreshing and delightful. Now they had to struggle against the elements in order to provide food, clothing, and shelter for themselves and

their family. Cain became a farmer, while Abel was a shepherd. In parts of the Middle East today, these ancient occupations are still practiced much as they were in Cain and Abel's time.

4:3–5 The Bible does not say why God rejected Cain's sacrifice. Perhaps Cain's attitude was improper, or perhaps his offering was not up to God's standards. Proverbs 21:27 says, "The sacrifice of the wicked is detestable—how much more so when brought with evil intent!" God evaluates both our motives and the quality of what we offer him. When we give to God and others, we should have a joyful heart because of what we are able to give. We should not worry about how much we are giving up, for all things are God's in the first place. Instead, we should joyfully give to God our best in time, money, possessions, and talents.

4:6, 7 How do you react when someone suggests you have done something wrong? Do you move to correct the mistake or deny that you need to correct it? After Cain's sacrifice was rejected, God gave him the chance to right his wrong and try again. God even encouraged him to do this! But Cain refused, and the rest of his life is a startling example of what happens to those who refuse to admit their mistakes. The next time someone suggests you are wrong, take an honest look at yourself and choose God's way instead of Cain's.

4:7 For Cain to master the sin lurking at the entrance to his desires, he would have to give up his jealous anger so that sin would not find a foothold in his life. Sin is still crouching at our doors today. Like Cain, we will be victims of sin if we do not master it. But we cannot master sin in our own strength. Instead, we must turn to God to receive faith for ourselves and faith and strength from other believers. The Holy Spirit will help us master

4:8
m Mt 23:35;
1Jn 3:12

⁸ Now Cain said to his brother Abel, "Let's go out to the field."ᵃ And while they were in the field, Cain attacked his brother Abel and killed him. *m*

⁹ Then the LORD said to Cain, "Where is your brother Abel?"

"I don't know," he replied. "Am I my brother's keeper?"

¹⁰ The LORD said, "What have you done? Listen! Your brother's blood cries out to me from the ground. ¹¹ Now you are under a curse and driven from the ground, which opened its mouth to receive your brother's blood from your hand. ¹² When you work the ground, it will no longer yield its crops for you. You will be a restless wanderer on the earth."

¹³ Cain said to the LORD, "My punishment is more than I can bear. ¹⁴ Today you are driving

ᵃ8 Samaritan Pentateuch, Septuagint, Vulgate and Syriac; Masoretic Text does not have *"Let's go out to the field."*

We know very little about Eve, the first woman in the world, yet she is the mother of us all. She was the final piece in the intricate and amazing puzzle of God's creation. Adam now had another human being with whom to fellowship—someone with an equal share in God's image. Here was someone alike enough for companionship, yet different enough for relationship. Together they were greater than either could have been alone.

Eve was approached by Satan in the Garden of Eden, where she and Adam lived. He questioned her contentment. How could she be happy when she was not allowed to eat from one of the fruit trees? Satan helped Eve shift her focus from all that God had done and given to the one thing he had withheld. And Eve was willing to accept Satan's viewpoint without checking with God.

Sound familiar? How often is our attention drawn from the much which is ours to the little that isn't? We get that "I've got to have it" feeling. Eve was typical of us all, and we consistently show we are her descendants by repeating her mistakes. Our desires, like Eve's, can be quite easily manipulated. They are not the best basis for actions. We need to keep God in our decision-making process always. His Word, the Bible, is our guidebook in decision-making.

Strengths and accomplishments:	• First wife and mother • First female. As such she shared a special relationship with God, had co-responsibility with Adam over creation, and displayed certain characteristics of God
Weaknesses and mistakes:	• Allowed her contentment to be undermined by Satan • Acted impulsively without talking either to God or to her mate • Not only sinned, but shared her sin with Adam • When confronted, blamed others
Lessons from her life:	• The female shares in the image of God • The necessary ingredients for a strong marriage are commitment to each other, companionship with each other, complete oneness, absence of shame (2:24, 25) • The basic human tendency to sin goes back to the beginning of the human race
Vital statistics:	• Where: Garden of Eden • Occupation: Wife, helper, companion, co-manager of Eden • Relatives: Husband: Adam. Sons: Cain, Abel, Seth. Numerous other children.
Key verse:	"The LORD God said, 'It is not good for the man to be alone. I will make a helper suitable for him'" (Genesis 2:18).

Eve's story is told in Genesis 2:19—4:26. Her death is not mentioned in Scripture.

---

sin. This will be a lifelong battle that will not be over until we are face to face with Christ.

4:8–10 This is the first murder—taking a life by shedding human blood. Blood represents life (Leviticus 17:10–14). If blood is removed from a living creature, it will die. Because God created life, only God should take life away.

4:8–10 Adam and Eve's disobedience brought sin into the human race. They may have thought their sin—eating a piece of fruit—wasn't very bad, but notice how quickly their sinful nature developed in their children. Simple disobedience quickly degenerated into outright murder. Adam and Eve acted only against God, but Cain acted against both God and man. A small sin has a way of growing out of control. Let God help you with your "little" sins before they turn into tragedies.

4:11–15 Cain was severely punished for this murder. God

judges all sins and punishes appropriately, not out of vengeance, but because he desires to correct us and restore our fellowship with him. When you're corrected, don't resent it. Instead, renew your fellowship with God.

4:14 We have heard about only four people so far—Adam, Eve, Cain, and Abel. Two questions arise: Why was Cain worried about being killed by others, and where did he get his wife (see 4:17)?

Adam and Eve had numerous children; they had been told to "fill the earth" (1:28). Cain's guilt and fear over killing his brother were heavy, and he probably feared repercussions from his family. If he was capable of killing, so were they. The wife Cain chose may have been one of his sisters or a niece. The human race was still genetically pure, and there was no fear of side effects from marrying relatives.

me from the land, and I will be hidden from your presence;[n] I will be a restless wanderer on the earth, and whoever finds me will kill me."[o]

[15]But the LORD said to him, "Not so[a]; if anyone kills Cain[p], he will suffer vengeance seven times over." Then the LORD put a mark on Cain so that no one who found him would kill him. [16]So Cain went out from the LORD's presence and lived in the land of Nod,[b] east of Eden.

[17]Cain lay with his wife, and she became pregnant and gave birth to Enoch. Cain was then building a city, and he named it after his son Enoch. [18]To Enoch was born Irad, and Irad was the father of Mehujael, and Mehujael was the father of Methushael, and Methushael was the father of Lamech.

[19]Lamech married two women, one named Adah and the other Zillah. [20]Adah gave birth to Jabal; he was the father of those who live in tents and raise livestock. [21]His brother's name was Jubal; he was the father of all who play the harp and flute. [22]Zillah also had a son, Tubal-Cain, who forged all kinds of tools out of[c] bronze and iron. Tubal-Cain's sister was Naamah.

[23]Lamech said to his wives,

> "Adah and Zillah, listen to me;
>   wives of Lamech, hear my words.
> I have killed[d] a man for wounding me,
>   a young man for injuring me.
> [24] If Cain is avenged seven times,[q]
>   then Lamech seventy-seven times."

[25]Adam lay with his wife again, and she gave birth to a son and named him Seth,[e] [r] saying, "God has granted me another child in place of Abel, since Cain killed him." [26]Seth also had a son, and he named him Enosh.

At that time men began to call on[f] the name of the LORD. [s]

3. Adam's descendants
From Adam to Noah

5 This is the written account of Adam's line.

When God created man, he made him in the likeness of God. [t] [2]He created them male and female[u] and blessed them. And when they were created, he called them "man.[g] "

[3]When Adam had lived 130 years, he had a son in his own likeness, in his own image; and he named him Seth. [4]After Seth was born, Adam lived 800 years and had other sons and daughters. [5]Altogether, Adam lived 930 years, and then he died. [v]

4:14
[n]Ps 51:11
[o]Nu 35:19, 21, 27, 33
4:15
[p]Eze 9:4, 6

4:24
[q]ver 15

4:25
[r]Ge 5:3
4:26
[s]Ge 12:8;
1Ki 18:24;
Joel 2:32; Zep 3:9;
1Co 1:2

5:1
[t]Ge 1:27; Eph 4:24;
Col 3:10
5:2
[u]Ge 1:27

5:5
[v]Ge 3:19

---

a *15* Septuagint, Vulgate and Syriac; Hebrew *Very well*   b *16* Nod means *wandering* (see verses 12 and 14).
c *22* Or *who instructed all who work in*   d *23* Or *I will kill*   e *25 Seth* probably means *granted*.   f *26* Or *to proclaim*
g *2* Hebrew *adam*

4:15 The expression, "will suffer vengeance seven times over" means that the person's punishment would be complete, thorough, and much worse than that received by Cain for his sin.

4:19–26 Unfortunately, when left to themselves, people tend to get worse instead of better. This short summary of Lamech's family shows us the variety of talent and ability God gives humans. It also presents the continuous development of sin as time passes. Another killing occurred, presumably in self-defense. Violence is on the rise. Two distinct groups are appearing: (1) those who show indifference to sin and evil, and (2) those who call on the name of the Lord (the descendants of Seth, 4:26). Seth would take Abel's place as leader of a line of God's faithful people.

5:1ff The Bible contains several lists of ancestors, called *genealogies*. Two basic views concerning these lists include: (1) they are complete, recording the entire history of a family, tribe, or nation; or (2) they are not intended to be exhaustive and may

include only famous people or the heads of families. "Became the father of" could refer not just to a son, but also to a more distant descendant.

Why are genealogies included in the Bible? The Hebrews passed on their beliefs through oral tradition. For many years in many places, writing was primitive or nonexistent. Stories were told to children who passed them on to their children. Genealogies gave a skeletal outline that helped people remember the stories. For centuries these genealogies were added to and passed down from family to family. Even more important than preserving family tradition, genealogies were included to confirm the Bible's promise that the coming Messiah, Jesus Christ, would be born into the line of Abraham.

Genealogies point out that people are important to God as individuals. Therefore God refers to people by name, mentioning their life span and descendants. The next time you feel overwhelmed in a vast crowd, remember that the focus of God's attention and love is on the individual—and on you!

5:3–5 All human beings are related, going back to Adam and Eve. Mankind is a family that shares one flesh and blood. Remember this when prejudice enters your mind or hatred invades your feelings. Each person is a valuable and unique creation of God.

6 When Seth had lived 105 years, he became the father a of Enosh. 7 And after he became the father of Enosh, Seth lived 807 years and had other sons and daughters. 8 Altogether, Seth lived 912 years, and then he died.

9 When Enosh had lived 90 years, he became the father of Kenan. 10 And after he became the father of Kenan, Enosh lived 815 years and had other sons and daughters. 11 Altogether, Enosh lived 905 years, and then he died.

12 When Kenan had lived 70 years, he became the father of Mahalalel. 13 And after he became the father of Mahalalel, Kenan lived 840 years and had other sons and daughters. 14 Altogether, Kenan lived 910 years, and then he died.

15 When Mahalalel had lived 65 years, he became the father of Jared. 16 And after he became the father of Jared, Mahalalel lived 830 years and had other sons and daughters. 17 Altogether, Mahalalel lived 895 years, and then he died.

18 When Jared had lived 162 years, he became the father of Enoch. 19 And after he became the father of Enoch, Jared lived 800 years and had other sons and daughters. 20 Altogether, Jared lived 962 years, and then he died.

5:22
w ver 24; Ge 6:9; Mic 6:8

5:24
x 2Ki 2:1, 11; Heb 11:5

21 When Enoch had lived 65 years, he became the father of Methuselah. 22 And after he became the father of Methuselah, Enoch walked with God *w* 300 years and had other sons and daughters. 23 Altogether, Enoch lived 365 years. 24 Enoch walked with God; then he was no more, because God took him away. *x*

25 When Methuselah had lived 187 years, he became the father of Lamech. 26 And after he became the father of Lamech, Methuselah lived 782 years and had other sons and daughters. 27 Altogether, Methuselah lived 969 years, and then he died.

5:29
y Ge 3:17

28 When Lamech had lived 182 years, he had a son. 29 He named him Noah b and said, "He will comfort us in the labor and painful toil of our hands caused by the ground the LORD has cursed. *y*" 30 After Noah was born, Lamech lived 595 years and had other sons and daughters. 31 Altogether, Lamech lived 777 years, and then he died.

32 After Noah was 500 years old, he became the father of Shem, Ham and Japheth.

a *6 Father* may mean *ancestor*; also in verses 7-26.   b *29 Noah* sounds like the Hebrew for *comfort*.

Abel was the second child born into the world, but the first one to obey God. All we know about this man is that his parents were Adam and Eve, he was a shepherd, he presented pleasing sacrifices to God, and his short life was ended at the hands of his jealous older brother, Cain.

The Bible doesn't tell us why God liked Abel's gift and disliked Cain's, but both Cain and Abel knew what God expected. Only Abel obeyed. Throughout history, Abel is remembered for his obedience and faith (Hebrews 11:4), and he is called "righteous" (Matthew 23:35).

The Bible is filled with God's general guidelines and expectations for our lives. It is also filled with more specific directions. Like Abel, we must obey regardless of the cost and trust God to make things right.

ABEL

Strengths and accomplishments:	• First member of the Hall of Faith in Hebrews 11 • First shepherd • First martyr for truth (Matthew 23:35)
Lessons from his life:	• God hears those who come to him • God recognizes the innocent person and sooner or later punishes the guilty
Vital statistics:	• Where: Just outside of Eden • Occupation: Shepherd • Relatives: Parents: Adam and Eve. Brother: Cain.
Key verse:	"By faith Abel offered God a better sacrifice than Cain did. By faith he was commended as a righteous man, when God spoke well of his offerings. And by faith he still speaks, even though he is dead" (Hebrews 11:4).

Abel's story is told in Genesis 4:1–8. He is also mentioned in Matthew 23:35; Luke 11:51; Hebrews 11:4 and 12:24.

5:25–27 How did these people live so long? Some believe that the ages listed here were lengths of family dynasties rather than ages of individual men. Those who think these were actual ages offer three explanations: (1) the human race was more genetically pure in this early time period with less disease to shorten life spans; (2) no rain had yet fallen on the earth, and the expanse of water "above" (1:7) kept out harmful cosmic rays and shielded people from environmental factors that hasten aging; (3) God gave people longer lives so they would have time to "fill the earth" (1:28).

C. THE STORY OF NOAH (6:1—11:32)

Earth was no longer the perfect paradise that God had intended. It is frightening to see how quickly all of humanity forgot about God. Incredibly, in all the world, only one man and his family still worshiped God. That man was Noah. Because of his faithfulness and obedience, God saved him and his family from a vast flood that destroyed every other human being on earth. This section shows us how God hates sin and judges those who enjoy it.

1. The flood

6 When men began to increase in number on the earth and daughters were born to them, ² the sons of God saw that the daughters of men were beautiful, and they married any of them they chose. ³ Then the Lord said, "My Spirit will not contend with ᵃ man forever, for he is mortal ᵇ; his days will be a hundred and twenty years."

⁴ The Nephilim were on the earth in those days—and also afterward—when the sons of God went to the daughters of men and had children by them. They were the heroes of old, men of renown.

⁵ The Lord saw how great man's wickedness on the earth had become, and that every inclination of the thoughts of his heart was only evil all the time. ᶻ ⁶ The Lord was grieved ᵃ that he had made man on the earth, and his heart was filled with pain. ⁷ So the Lord said, "I will wipe mankind, whom I have created, from the face of the earth—men and animals, and creatures that move along the ground, and birds of the air—for I am grieved that I have made them." ⁸ But Noah found favor in the eyes of the Lord. ᵇ

⁹ This is the account of Noah.

Noah was a righteous man, blameless among the people of his time, ᶜ and he walked with God. ᵈ ¹⁰ Noah had three sons: Shem, Ham and Japheth.

¹¹ Now the earth was corrupt in God's sight and was full of violence. ¹² God saw how corrupt the earth had become, for all the people on earth had corrupted their ways. ᵉ ¹³ So God said to Noah, "I am going to put an end to all people, for the earth is filled with violence because of them. I am surely going to destroy both them and the earth. ¹⁴ So make yourself an ark of cypress ᶜ wood; make rooms in it and coat it with pitch ᶠ inside and out. ¹⁵ This is how you are to build it: The ark is to be 450 feet long, 75 feet wide and 45 feet high. ᵈ ¹⁶ Make a roof for it and finish ᵉ the ark to within 18 inches ᶠ of the top. Put a door in the side of the ark and make lower, middle and upper decks. ¹⁷ I am going to bring floodwaters on the earth to destroy all life under the heavens, every creature that has the breath of life in it. Everything

6:5
ᶻGe 8:21
6:6
ᵃIsa 63:10

6:8
ᵇGe 19:19;
Ex 33:12, 13, 17;
Lk 1:30; Ac 7:46

6:9
ᶜHeb 11:7; 2Pe 2:5
ᵈGe 5:22

6:12
ᵉPs 14:1-3

6:14
ᶠEx 2:3

ᵃ3 Or *My spirit will not remain in*   ᵇ3 Or *corrupt*   ᶜ14 The meaning of the Hebrew for this word is uncertain.
ᵈ15 Hebrew *300 cubits long, 50 cubits wide and 30 cubits high* (about 140 meters long, 23 meters wide and 13.5 meters high)   ᵉ16 Or *Make an opening for light by finishing*   ᶠ16 Hebrew *a cubit* (about 0.5 meter)

6:1–4 Some people have thought that the "sons of God" were fallen angels. But the "sons of God" were probably not angels, because angels do not marry or reproduce (Matthew 22:30; Mark 12:25). Some scholars believe this phrase refers to the descendants of Seth who intermarried with Cain's evil descendants ("the daughters of men"). This would have weakened the good influence of the faithful and increased moral depravity in the world, resulting in an explosion of evil. *Nephilim* refers to a powerful race of giants.

6:3 "His days will be a hundred and twenty years" means that God was allowing the people of Noah's day 120 years to change their sinful ways. God shows us his great patience with us as well. He is giving us time to quit living our way and begin living his way, the way he shows us in his Word. While 120 years seems like a long time, eventually the time ran out and the floodwaters swept across the earth. Your time also may be running out. Turn to God to forgive your sins. You can't see the stopwatch of God's patience, and there is no bargaining for additional time.

6:4 The Nephilim were giants, people probably nine or ten feet tall. These may have been the same people mentioned in Numbers 13:33. Goliath, who was nine feet tall, appears in 1 Samuel 17. The Nephilim used their physical advantage to oppress the people around them.

6:6, 7 Does this mean that God regretted creating humanity? Was he admitting he made a mistake? No, God does not change his mind (1 Samuel 15:29). Instead, he was expressing sorrow for what the people had done to themselves, as a parent might express sorrow over a rebellious child. God was sorry that the people chose sin and death instead of a relationship with him.

6:6–8 The people's sin grieved God. Our sins break God's heart as much as sin did in Noah's day. Noah, however, pleased God, although he was far from perfect. We can follow Noah's example and find "favor in the eyes of the Lord" in spite of the sin that surrounds us.

6:9 Saying that Noah was *righteous* and *blameless* does not mean that he never sinned (the Bible records one of his sins in 9:20ff). Rather it means that Noah wholeheartedly loved and obeyed God. For a lifetime he walked step by step in faith as a living example to his generation. Like Noah, we live in a world filled with evil. Are we influencing others or being influenced by them?

6:14 *Pitch* was a tarlike substance used to make the ark watertight.

6:15 The boat Noah built was no canoe! Picture yourself building a boat the length of one and a half football fields and as high as a four-story building. The ark was exactly six times longer than it was wide—the same ratio used by modern shipbuilders. This huge boat was probably built miles from any body of water by only a few faithful men who believed God's promises and obeyed his commands.

on earth will perish. ¹⁸But I will establish my covenant with you, and you will enter the ark—you and your sons and your wife and your sons' wives with you. ¹⁹You are to bring into the ark two of all living creatures, male and female, to keep them alive with you. ²⁰Two*g* of every kind of bird, of every kind of animal and of every kind of creature that moves along the ground will come to you to be kept alive. ²¹You are to take every kind of food that is to be eaten and store it away as food for you and for them."

²²Noah did everything just as God commanded him. *h*

6:20
g Ge 7:15

6:22
h Ge 7:5, 9, 16

7:1
i Ge 6:9

7:2
j Lev 10:10; 11:1-47

7 The Lord then said to Noah, "Go into the ark, you and your whole family, because I have found you righteous*i* in this generation. ²Take with you seven*a* of every kind of clean*j* animal, a male and its mate, and two of every kind of unclean animal, a male and its mate, ³and also seven of every kind of bird, male and female, to keep their various kinds alive throughout the earth. ⁴Seven days from now I will send rain on the earth for forty days and forty nights, and I will wipe from the face of the earth every living creature I have made."

a 2 Or seven pairs; also in verse 3

CAIN

In spite of parents' efforts and worries, conflicts between children in a family seem inevitable. Sibling relationships allow both competition and cooperation. In most cases, the mixture of loving and fighting eventually creates a strong bond between brothers and sisters. It isn't unusual, though, to hear parents say, "They fight so much I hope they don't kill each other before they grow up." In Cain's case, the troubling potential became a tragedy. And while we don't know many details of this first child's life, his story can still teach us.

Cain got angry. Furious. Both he and his brother Abel had made sacrifices to God, and his had been rejected. Cain's reaction gives us a clue that his attitude was probably wrong from the start. Cain had a choice to make. He could correct his attitude about his sacrifice to God, or he could take out his anger on his brother. His decision is a clear reminder of how often we are aware of opposite choices, yet choose the wrong just as Cain did. We may not be choosing to murder, but we are still intentionally choosing what we shouldn't.

The feelings motivating our behavior can't always be changed by simple thought-power. But here we can begin to experience God's willingness to help. Asking for his help to do what is right can prevent us from setting into motion actions that we will later regret.

Strengths and accomplishments:	• First human child • First to follow in father's profession, farming
Weaknesses and mistakes:	• When disappointed, reacted in anger • Took the negative option even when a positive possibility was offered • Was the first murderer
Lessons from his life:	• Anger is not necessarily a sin, but actions motivated by anger can be sinful. Anger should be the energy behind good action, not evil action • What we offer to God must be from the heart—the best we are and have • The consequences of sin may last a lifetime
Vital statistics:	• Where: Near Eden, which was probably located in present-day Iraq or Iran • Occupation: Farmer, then wanderer • Relatives: Parents: Adam and Eve. Brothers: Abel, Seth, and others not mentioned by name.
Key verse:	"If you do what is right, will you not be accepted? But if you do not do what is right, sin is crouching at your door; it desires to have you, but you must master it" (Genesis 4:7).

Cain's story is told in Genesis 4:1–17. He is also mentioned in Hebrews 11:4; 1 John 3:12; Jude 11.

6:18 A *covenant* is a promise. This is a familiar theme in Scripture—God making covenants with his people. How reassuring it is to know God's covenant is established with us. He is still our salvation and we are kept safe through our relationship with him. For more on the covenant see 9:8–17; 12:1–3; and 15:17–20.

6:22 Noah got right to work when God told him to build the ark. Other people must have been warned about the coming disaster (1 Peter 3:20), but apparently they did not expect it to happen. Today things haven't changed much. Each day thousands of people are warned of God's inevitable judgment, yet most of them don't

really believe it will happen. Don't expect people to welcome or accept your message of God's coming judgment on sin. Those who don't believe in God will deny his judgment and try to get you to deny God as well. But remember God's promise to Noah to keep him safe. This can inspire you to trust God for deliverance in the judgment that is sure to come.

7:1ff Pairs of every animal joined Noah in the ark; seven pairs were taken of those animals used for sacrifice—the "clean" animals. Scholars have estimated that almost 45,000 animals could have fit into the ark.

⁵And Noah did all that the LORD commanded him.

⁶Noah was six hundred years old when the floodwaters came on the earth. ⁷And Noah and his sons and his wife and his sons' wives entered the ark to escape the waters of the flood. ⁸Pairs of clean and unclean animals, of birds and of all creatures that move along the ground, ⁹male and female, came to Noah and entered the ark, as God had commanded Noah. ¹⁰And after the seven days the floodwaters came on the earth.

¹¹In the six hundredth year of Noah's life, on the seventeenth day of the second month—on that day all the springs of the great deep[k] burst forth, and the floodgates of the heavens[l] were opened. ¹²And rain fell on the earth forty days and forty nights.

¹³On that very day Noah and his sons, Shem, Ham and Japheth, together with his wife and the wives of his three sons, entered the ark. ¹⁴They had with them every wild animal according to its kind, all livestock according to their kinds, every creature that moves along the ground according to its kind and every bird according to its kind, everything with wings. ¹⁵Pairs of all creatures that have the breath of life in them came to Noah and entered the ark. ¹⁶The animals going in were male and female of every living thing, as God had commanded Noah. Then the LORD shut him in.

¹⁷For forty days the flood kept coming on the earth, and as the waters increased they lifted the ark high above the earth. ¹⁸The waters rose and increased greatly on the earth, and the ark floated on the surface of the water. ¹⁹They rose greatly on the earth, and all the high mountains under the entire heavens were covered. ²⁰The waters rose and covered the mountains to a depth of more than twenty feet.[a,b] ²¹Every living thing that moved on the earth perished—birds, livestock, wild animals, all the creatures that swarm over the earth, and all mankind.[m] ²²Everything on dry land that had the breath of life in its nostrils died. ²³Every living thing on the face of the earth was wiped out; men and animals and the creatures that move along the ground and the birds of the air were wiped from the earth.[n] Only Noah was left, and those with him in the ark.

²⁴The waters flooded the earth for a hundred and fifty days.

8 But God remembered Noah and all the wild animals and the livestock that were with him in the ark, and he sent a wind over the earth, and the waters receded. ²Now the springs of the deep and the floodgates of the heavens had been closed, and the rain had stopped falling from the sky. ³The water receded steadily from the earth. At the end of the hundred and fifty days the water had gone down, ⁴and on the seventeenth day of the seventh month the ark came to rest on the mountains of Ararat. ⁵The waters continued to recede until the tenth month, and on the first day of the tenth month the tops of the mountains became visible.

⁶After forty days Noah opened the window he had made in the ark ⁷and sent out a raven, and it kept flying back and forth until the water had dried up from the earth. ⁸Then he sent out a dove to see if the water had receded from the surface of the ground. ⁹But the dove could find no place to set its feet because there was water over all the surface of the earth; so it returned to Noah in the ark. He reached out his hand and took the dove and brought it back to himself in the ark. ¹⁰He waited seven more days and again sent out the dove from

a 20 Hebrew *fifteen cubits* (about 6.9 meters)   b 20 Or *rose more than twenty feet, and the mountains were covered*

7:11
k Eze 26:19
l Ge 8:2

7:21
m Ge 6:7, 13

7:23
n Mt 24:39;
Lk 17:27; 2Pe 2:5

MOUNTAINS OF ARARAT
Caspian Sea
Mediterranean Sea
N
•Jerusalem
Tigris River
Euphrates River
Nile River
Red Sea
Persian Gulf
0   100 Mi.
0 100 Km.

MOUNTAINS OF ARARAT The ark touched land in the mountains of Ararat, located in present-day Turkey. There it rested for almost eight months before Noah, his family, and the animals stepped onto dry land.

7:16 Many have wondered how this animal kingdom roundup happened. Did Noah and his sons spend years collecting all the animals? In reality the creation, along with Noah, was doing just as God had commanded. There seemed to be no problem gathering the animals—God took care of the details of that job while Noah was doing his part by building the ark. Often we do just the opposite of Noah. We worry about details over which we have no control, while neglecting specific areas (such as attitudes, relationships, responsibilities) that *are* under our control. Like Noah, concentrate on what God has given you to do, and leave the rest to God.

7:17–24 Was the flood a local event, or did it cover the entire earth? A universal flood was certainly possible. Enough water exists in the oceans to cover all dry land (the earth began that way; see 1:9, 10). Afterward, God promised never again to destroy the earth with a flood. Thus this flood must have either covered the entire earth or destroyed all the inhabitants of the earth. Remember, God's reason for sending the flood was to destroy all the earth's wickedness. It would have taken a major flood to accomplish this.

the ark. [11]When the dove returned to him in the evening, there in its beak was a freshly plucked olive leaf! Then Noah knew that the water had receded from the earth. [12]He waited seven more days and sent the dove out again, but this time it did not return to him.

[13]By the first day of the first month of Noah's six hundred and first year, the water had dried up from the earth. Noah then removed the covering from the ark and saw that the surface of the ground was dry. [14]By the twenty-seventh day of the second month the earth was completely dry.

[15]Then God said to Noah, [16]"Come out of the ark, you and your wife and your sons and their wives. [17]Bring out every kind of living creature that is with you—the birds, the animals, and all the creatures that move along the ground—so they can multiply on the earth and be fruitful and increase in number upon it." [o]

[18]So Noah came out, together with his sons and his wife and his sons' wives. [19]All the animals and all the creatures that move along the ground and all the birds—everything that moves on the earth—came out of the ark, one kind after another.

[20]Then Noah built an altar to the LORD [p] and, taking some of all the clean animals and clean birds, he sacrificed burnt offerings [q] on it. [21]The LORD smelled the pleasing aroma [r] and said in his heart: "Never again will I curse the ground [s] because of man, even though [a] every inclination of his heart is evil from childhood. And never again will I destroy all living creatures, [t] as I have done.

8:17
[o]Ge 1:22

8:20
[p]Ge 12:7-8
[q]Ge 22:2, 13;
Ex 10:25

8:21
[r]Lev 1:9, 13;
2Co 2:15
[s]Ge 3:17
[t]Ge 9:11, 15;
Isa 54:9

[a]21 Or man, for

The story of Noah's life involves not one, but two great and tragic floods. The world in Noah's day was flooded with evil. The number of those who remembered the God of creation, perfection, and love had dwindled to one. Of God's people, only Noah was left. God's response to the severe situation was a 120-year-long last chance, during which he had Noah build a graphic illustration of the message of his life. Nothing like a huge boat on dry land to make a point! For Noah, obedience meant a long-term commitment to a project.

Many of us have trouble sticking to any project, whether or not it is directed by God. It is interesting that the length of Noah's obedience was greater than the lifespan of people today. The only comparable long-term project is our very lives. But perhaps this is one great challenge Noah's life gives us—to live, in acceptance of God's grace, an entire lifetime of obedience and gratitude.

NOAH

Strengths and accomplishments:	• Only follower of God left in his generation • Second father of the human race • Man of patience, consistency, and obedience • First major shipbuilder
Weakness and mistake:	• Got drunk and embarrassed himself in front of his sons
Lessons from his life:	• God is faithful to those who obey him • God does not always protect us from trouble, but cares for us in spite of trouble • Obedience is a long-term commitment • We may be faithful, but our sinful nature always travels with us
Vital statistics:	• Where: We're not told how far from the Garden of Eden people had settled • Occupation: Farmer, shipbuilder, preacher • Relatives: Grandfather: Methuselah. Father: Lamech. Sons: Ham, Shem, and Japheth.
Key verse:	"Noah did everything just as God commanded him" (Genesis 6:22).

Noah's story is told in Genesis 5:29—10:32. He is also mentioned in 1 Chronicles 1:3, 4; Isaiah 54:9; Ezekiel 14:14, 20; Matthew 24:37, 38; Luke 3:36; 17:26, 27; Hebrews 11:7; 1 Peter 3:20; 2 Peter 2:5.

8:6–16 Occasionally Noah would send a bird out to test the earth and see if it was dry. But Noah didn't get out of the ark until God told him to. He was waiting for God's timing. God knew that even though the water was gone, the earth was not dry enough for Noah and his family to venture out. What patience Noah showed, especially after spending an entire year inside his boat! We, like Noah, must trust God to give us patience during those difficult times when we must wait.

8:21, 22 Countless times throughout the Bible we see God showing his love and patience toward men and women in order to save them. Although he realizes that their hearts are evil, he continues to try to reach them. When we sin or fall away from God, we surely deserve to be destroyed by his judgment. But God has promised never again to destroy everything on earth until the judgment day when Christ returns to destroy evil forever. Now every change of season is a reminder of his promise.

22 "As long as the earth endures,
    seedtime and harvest,
    cold and heat,
    summer and winter,
    day and night
    will never cease."

2. Repopulating the earth
God's Covenant With Noah

9 Then God blessed Noah and his sons, saying to them, "Be fruitful and increase in number and fill the earth. *u* 2 The fear and dread of you will fall upon all the beasts of the earth and all the birds of the air, upon every creature that moves along the ground, and upon all the fish of the sea; they are given into your hands. 3 Everything that lives and moves will be food for you. *v* Just as I gave you the green plants, I now give you everything.

4 "But you must not eat meat that has its lifeblood still in it. *w* 5 And for your lifeblood I will surely demand an accounting. I will demand an accounting from every animal. *x* And from each man, too, I will demand an accounting for the life of his fellow man. *y*

6 "Whoever sheds the blood of man,
    by man shall his blood be shed; *z*
for in the image of God *a*
    has God made man.

7 As for you, be fruitful and increase in number; multiply on the earth and increase upon it." *b*

8 Then God said to Noah and to his sons with him: 9 "I now establish my covenant with you *c* and with your descendants after you 10 and with every living creature that was with you—the birds, the livestock and all the wild animals, all those that came out of the ark with you—every living creature on earth. 11 I establish my covenant with you: Never again will all life be cut off by the waters of a flood; never again will there be a flood to destroy the earth."

12 And God said, "This is the sign of the covenant *d* I am making between me and you and every living creature with you, a covenant for all generations to come: 13 I have set my rainbow in the clouds, and it will be the sign of the covenant between me and the earth. 14 Whenever I bring clouds over the earth and the rainbow appears in the clouds, 15 I will remember my covenant *e* between me and you and all living creatures of every kind. Never again will the waters become a flood to destroy all life. 16 Whenever the rainbow appears in the clouds, I will see it and remember the everlasting covenant *f* between God and all living creatures of every kind on the earth."

17 So God said to Noah, "This is the sign of the covenant *g* I have established between me and all life on the earth."

The Sons of Noah

18 The sons of Noah who came out of the ark were Shem, Ham and Japheth. (Ham was the father of Canaan.) 19 These were the three sons of Noah, and from them came the people who were scattered over the earth.

20 Noah, a man of the soil, proceeded *a* to plant a vineyard. 21 When he drank some of its wine, he became drunk and lay uncovered inside his tent. 22 Ham, the father of Canaan, saw his father's nakedness and told his two brothers outside. 23 But Shem and Japheth took a garment and laid it across their shoulders; then they walked in backward and covered their

a 20 Or soil, was the first

9:1
u Ge 1:22

9:3
v Ge 1:29

9:4
w Lev 3:17;
17:10-14; Dt 12:16,
23-25; 1Sa 14:33

9:5
x Ex 21:28-32
y Ge 4:10

9:6
z Ex 21:12, 14;
Lev 24:17; Mt 26:52
a Ge 1:26

9:7
b Ge 1:22

9:9
c Ge 6:18

9:12
d Ge 17:11

9:15
e Lev 26:42, 45

9:16
f Ge 17:7, 13, 19

9:17
g ver 12; Ge 17:11

9:5 To "demand an accounting" means that God will require each person to account for his or her actions. We cannot harm or kill another human being without answering to God. A penalty must be paid. Justice will be served.

9:5, 6 Here God explains why murder is so wrong: To kill a person is to kill one made in God's image. Because all human beings are made in God's image, all people possess the qualities that distinguish them from animals: morality, reason, creativity, and self-worth. When we interact with others, we are interacting with beings made by God, beings to whom God offers eternal life. God wants us to recognize his image in all people.

9:8–17 Noah stepped out of the ark onto an earth devoid of human life. But God gave him a reassuring promise. This covenant had three parts: (1) never again will a flood do such destruction; (2) as long as the earth remains, the seasons will always come as expected; (3) a rainbow will be visible when it rains as a sign to all that God will keep his promises. The earth's order and seasons are still preserved, and rainbows still remind us of God's faithfulness to his Word.

9:20–27 Noah, the great hero of faith, got drunk—a poor example of godliness to his sons. Perhaps this story is included to show us that even godly people can sin and that their bad influence affects father's nakedness. Their faces were turned the other way so that they would not see their father's nakedness.

24 When Noah awoke from his wine and found out what his youngest son had done to him, 25 he said,

> "Cursed be Canaan!*h*
> The lowest of slaves
> will he be to his brothers.*i*"

26 He also said,

> "Blessed be the LORD, the God of Shem!
> May Canaan be the slave of Shem.*a*
> 27 May God extend the territory of Japheth*b*;
> may Japheth live in the tents of Shem,
> and may Canaan be his*c* slave."

28 After the flood Noah lived 350 years. 29 Altogether, Noah lived 950 years, and then he died.

The Table of Nations

10 This is the account of Shem, Ham and Japheth, Noah's sons, who themselves had sons after the flood.

The Japhethites

2 The sons*d* of Japheth:
Gomer, Magog, Madai, Javan, Tubal, Meshech and Tiras.
3 The sons of Gomer:
Ashkenaz, Riphath and Togarmah.*j*
4 The sons of Javan:
Elishah, Tarshish,*k* the Kittim and the Rodanim.*e* 5 (From these the maritime peoples spread out into their territories by their clans within their nations, each with its own language.)

The Hamites

6 The sons of Ham:
Cush, Mizraim,*f* Put and Canaan.*l*
7 The sons of Cush:
Seba, Havilah, Sabtah, Raamah and Sabteca.
The sons of Raamah:
Sheba and Dedan.

8 Cush was the father*g* of Nimrod, who grew to be a mighty warrior on the earth. 9 He was a mighty hunter before the LORD; that is why it is said, "Like Nimrod, a mighty hunter before

a26 Or be his slave *b27 Japheth sounds like the Hebrew for extend.* *c27 Or their* *d2 Sons may mean descendants or successors or nations; also in verses 3, 4, 6, 7, 20-23, 29 and 31.* *e4 Some manuscripts of the Masoretic Text and Samaritan Pentateuch (see also Septuagint and 1 Chron. 1:7); most manuscripts of the Masoretic Text Dodanim* *f6 That is, Egypt; also in verse 13* *g8 Father may mean ancestor or predecessor or founder; also in verses 13, 15, 24 and 26.*

9:25
h ver 18
i Ge 25:23

10:3
j Eze 38:6
10:4
k Jnh 1:3

10:6
l ver 15; Ge 9:18

BIBLE NATIONS DESCENDED FROM NOAH'S SONS	Shem	Ham	Japheth	
	Shem	Ham	Japheth	Shem's descendants were called Semites.
	Hebrews	Canaanites	Greeks	Abraham, David, and Jesus descended
	Chaldeans	Egyptians	Thracians	from Shem. Ham's descendants settled
	Assyrians	Philistines	Scythians	in Canaan, Egypt, and the rest of Africa.
	Persians	Hittites		Japheth's descendants settled for the most
	Syrians	Amorites		part in Europe and Asia Minor.

their families. Although the wicked people had all been killed, the possibility of evil still existed in the hearts of Noah and his family. Ham's mocking attitude revealed a severe lack of respect for his father and for God.

9:25 This verse has been wrongly used to support racial prejudice and even slavery. Noah's curse, however, wasn't directed toward any particular race, but rather at the Canaanite nation—a nation God knew would become wicked. The curse

was fulfilled when the Israelites entered the promised land and drove the Canaanites out (see the book of Joshua).

10:8, 9 Who was Nimrod? Not much is known about him except that he was a mighty hunter. But people with great gifts can become proud, and that is probably what happened to Nimrod. Some consider him the founder of the great, godless Babylonian empire.

the LORD." [10] The first centers of his kingdom were Babylon,[m] Erech, Akkad and Calneh, in[a] Shinar.[b] [11] From that land he went to Assyria,[n] where he built Nineveh, Rehoboth Ir,[c] Calah [12] and Resen, which is between Nineveh and Calah; that is the great city.

10:10
[m]Ge 11:9
10:11
[n]Mic 5:6

[13] Mizraim was the father of
the Ludites, Anamites, Lehabites, Naphtuhites, [14]Pathrusites, Casluhites (from whom the Philistines came) and Caphtorites.
[15] Canaan[o] was the father of
Sidon his firstborn,[d] and of the Hittites, [16]Jebusites, Amorites, Girgashites, [17]Hivites, Arkites, Sinites, [18]Arvadites, Zemarites and Hamathites.

10:15
[o]ver 6; Ge 9:18

Later the Canaanite clans scattered [19]and the borders of Canaan[p] reached from Sidon toward Gerar as far as Gaza, and then toward Sodom, Gomorrah, Admah and Zeboiim, as far as Lasha.
[20] These are the sons of Ham by their clans and languages, in their territories and nations.

10:19
[p]Ge 13:12; 17:8

The Semites

[21]Sons were also born to Shem, whose older brother was[e] Japheth; Shem was the ancestor of all the sons of Eber. [q]

10:21
[q]ver 24; Nu 24:24

[22] The sons of Shem:
Elam, Asshur, Arphaxad, Lud and Aram.
[23] The sons of Aram:
Uz,[r] Hul, Gether and Meshech.[f]
[24] Arphaxad was the father of[g] Shelah,
and Shelah the father of Eber. [s]
[25] Two sons were born to Eber:
One was named Peleg,[h] because in his time the earth was divided; his brother was named Joktan.
[26] Joktan was the father of
Almodad, Sheleph, Hazarmaveth, Jerah, [27]Hadoram, Uzal, Diklah, [28]Obal, Abimael, Sheba, [29]Ophir, Havilah and Jobab. All these were sons of Joktan.

10:23
[r]Job 1:1
10:24
[s]ver 21

[30] The region where they lived stretched from Mesha toward Sephar, in the eastern hill country.
[31] These are the sons of Shem by their clans and languages, in their territories and nations.

[32] These are the clans of Noah's sons,[t] according to their lines of descent, within their nations. From these the nations spread out over the earth [u] after the flood.

10:32
[t]ver 1
[u]Ge 9:19

3. The tower of Babel

11 Now the whole world had one language and a common speech. [2]As men moved eastward,[i] they found a plain in Shinar[b] and settled there.
[3]They said to each other, "Come, let's make bricks and bake them thoroughly." They used brick instead of stone, and tar for mortar. [4]Then they said, "Come, let us build ourselves a city, with a tower that reaches to the heavens,[v] so that we may make a name for ourselves and not be scattered over the face of the whole earth."

11:4
[v]Dt 1:28

[5]But the LORD came down [w] to see the city and the tower that the men were building. [6]The LORD said, "If as one people speaking the same language they have begun to do this, then nothing they plan to do will be impossible for them. [7]Come, let us[x] go down and confuse their language so they will not understand each other."[y]

11:5
[w]ver 7; Ge 18:21
11:7
[x]Ge 1:26
[y]Ge 42:23

[a]*10* Or *Erech and Akkad—all of them in*   [b]*10, 2* That is, Babylonia   [c]*11* Or *Nineveh with its city squares*   [d]*15* Or *of the Sidonians, the foremost*   [e]*21* Or *Shem, the older brother of*   [f]*23* See Septuagint and 1 Chron. 1:17; Hebrew *Mash*   [g]*24* Hebrew; Septuagint *father of Cainan, and Cainan was the father of*   [h]*25 Peleg* means *division.*   [i]*2* Or *from the east*; or *in the east*

11:3 The brick used to build this tower was man-made and not as hard as stone.

11:3, 4 The tower of Babel was most likely a ziggurat, a common structure in Babylonia at this time. Most often built as temples, ziggurats looked like pyramids with steps or ramps leading up the sides. Ziggurats stood as high as 300 feet and were often just as wide; thus they were the focal point of the city. The

people in this story built their tower as a monument to their own greatness, something for the whole world to see.

11:4 The tower of Babel was a great human achievement, a wonder of the world. But it was a monument to the people themselves rather than to God. We may build monuments to ourselves (expensive clothes, big house, fancy car, important job) to call attention to our achievements. These may not be

11:8
z Lk 1:51

8 So the LORD scattered them from there over all the earth,z and they stopped building the city. 9 That is why it was called Babel a—because there the LORD confused the language of the whole world. From there the LORD scattered them over the face of the whole earth.

From Shem to Abram

10 This is the account of Shem.

Two years after the flood, when Shem was 100 years old, he became the father b of Arphaxad. 11 And after he became the father of Arphaxad, Shem lived 500 years and had other sons and daughters.

12 When Arphaxad had lived 35 years, he became the father of Shelah. 13 And after he became the father of Shelah, Arphaxad lived 403 years and had other sons and daughters. c

14 When Shelah had lived 30 years, he became the father of Eber. 15 And after he became the father of Eber, Shelah lived 403 years and had other sons and daughters.

16 When Eber had lived 34 years, he became the father of Peleg. 17 And after he became the father of Peleg, Eber lived 430 years and had other sons and daughters.

18 When Peleg had lived 30 years, he became the father of Reu. 19 And after he became the father of Reu, Peleg lived 209 years and had other sons and daughters.

20 When Reu had lived 32 years, he became the father of Serug. 21 And after he became the father of Serug, Reu lived 207 years and had other sons and daughters.

22 When Serug had lived 30 years, he became the father of Nahor. 23 And after he became the father of Nahor, Serug lived 200 years and had other sons and daughters.

24 When Nahor had lived 29 years, he became the father of Terah. 25 And after he became the father of Terah, Nahor lived 119 years and had other sons and daughters.

11:26
a Jos 24:2

26 After Terah had lived 70 years, he became the father of Abram, Nahor a and Haran.

11:27
b ver 31; Ge 12:4

27 This is the account of Terah.

Terah became the father of Abram, Nahor and Haran. And Haran became the father of Lot. b 28 While his father Terah was still alive, Haran died in Ur of the Chaldeans, in the land

11:29
c Ge 17:15

of his birth. 29 Abram and Nahor both married. The name of Abram's wife was Sarai, c and the name of Nahor's wife was Milcah; she was the daughter of Haran, the father of both Mil-

11:30
d Ge 16:1

cah and Iscah. 30 Now Sarai was barren; she had no children. d

11:31
e Ge 15:7; Ne 9:7; Ac 7:4

31 Terah took his son Abram, his grandson Lot son of Haran, and his daughter-in-law Sarai, the wife of his son Abram, and together they set out from Ur of the Chaldeans e to go to Canaan. But when they came to Haran, they settled there.

32 Terah lived 205 years, and he died in Haran.

a 9 That is, Babylon; *Babel* sounds like the Hebrew for *confused.*   b 10 *Father* may mean *ancestor*; also in verses 11-25.   c 12,13 Hebrew; Septuagint (see also Luke 3:35, 36 and note at Gen. 10:24) *35 years, he became the father of Cainan.* 13 *And after he became the father of Cainan, Arphaxad lived 430 years and had other sons and daughters, and then he died. When Cainan had lived 130 years, he became the father of Shelah. And after he became the father of Shelah, Cainan lived 330 years and had other sons and daughters*

---

wrong in themselves, but when we use them to give us identity and self-worth, they take God's place in our lives. We are free to develop in many areas, but we are not free to think we have replaced God. What "towers" have you built in your life?

11:10–27 Here and in 10:22–31 appears a list of Shem's descendants, who were blessed (9:26). Because of that blessing from Shem's line came Abram and the entire Jewish nation, which would eventually conquer the land of Canaan in the days of Joshua.

11:26–28 Abram grew up in Ur of the Chaldeans, an important city in the ancient world. Archaeologists have discovered evidence of a flourishing civilization there in Abram's day. The city carried on an extensive trade with its neighbors and had a vast library. Growing up in Ur, Abram was probably well educated.

11:31 Terah left Ur to go to Canaan but settled in Haran instead. Why did he stop halfway? It may have been his health, the climate, or even fear. But this did not change Abram's calling ("the LORD had said to Abram," 12:1). He had respect for his father's leadership, but when Terah died Abram moved on to Canaan. God's will may come in stages. Just as the time in Haran was a transition period for Abram, so God may give us transition periods and times of waiting to help us depend on him and trust his timing. If we

patiently do his will during the transition times, we will be better prepared to serve him as we should when he calls us.

THE TOWER OF BABEL   The plain between the Tigris and Euphrates Rivers offered a perfect location for the city and tower "that reaches to the heavens."

D. THE STORY OF ABRAHAM (12:1—25:18)

Despite God's swift judgment of sin, most people ignored him and continued to sin. But a handful of people really tried to follow him. One of these was Abraham. God appeared to Abraham one day and promised to make his descendants into a great nation. Abram's part of the agreement was to obey God. Through sharp testing and an incident that almost destroyed his family, Abraham remained faithful to God. Throughout this section we discover how to live a life of faith.

1. God promises a nation to Abram
The Call of Abram

12 The LORD had said to Abram, "Leave your country, your people and your father's household and go to the land I will show you.*f*

12:1
f Ac 7:3*; Heb 11:8

² "I will make you into a great nation *g*
and I will bless you;
I will make your name great,
and you will be a blessing.

12:2
g Ge 17:2, 4; 18:18

³ I will bless those who bless you,
and whoever curses you I will curse;*h*
and all peoples on earth
will be blessed through you.*i*"

12:3
h Ge 27:29; Nu 24:9
i Ge 22:18; 26:4;
Ac 3:25; Gal 3:8*

⁴ So Abram left, as the LORD had told him; and Lot went with him. Abram was seventy-five years old when he set out from Haran. ⁵ He took his wife Sarai, his nephew Lot, all the possessions they had accumulated and the people*j* they had acquired in Haran, and they set out for the land of Canaan, and they arrived there.

12:5
j Ge 14:14

⁶ Abram traveled through the land as far as the site of the great tree of Moreh at Shechem. At that time the Canaanites were in the land. ⁷ The LORD appeared to Abram*k* and said, "To your offspring*a* I will give this land."*l* So he built an altar there to the LORD, who had appeared to him.

12:7
k Ge 17:1
l Ge 13:15, 17;
Ps 105:9-11

⁸ From there he went on toward the hills east of Bethel*m* and pitched his tent, with Bethel on the west and Ai on the east. There he built an altar to the LORD and called on the name of the LORD. ⁹ Then Abram set out and continued toward the Negev.

12:8
m Ge 13:3

a 7 Or *seed*

12:1-3 When God called him, Abram moved out in faith from Ur to Haran and finally to Canaan. God then established a covenant with Abram, telling him that he would found a great nation. Not only would this nation be blessed, God said, but the other nations of the earth would be blessed through Abram's descendants. Israel, the nation that would come from Abram, was to follow God and influence those with whom it came in contact. Through Abram's family tree, Jesus Christ was born to save humanity.

ABRAM'S JOURNEY TO CANAAN Abram, Sarai, and Lot traveled from Ur of the Chaldeans to Canaan by way of Haran. Though indirect, this route followed the rivers rather than attempting to cross the vast desert.

Through Christ, people can have a personal relationship with God and be blessed beyond measure.

12:2 God promised to bless Abram and make him great, but God had one condition. Abram had to do what God wanted him to do. This meant leaving his home and friends and traveling to a new land where God promised to build a great nation from Abram's family. Abram obeyed, walking away from his home for God's promise of even greater blessings in the future. God may be trying to lead you to a place of greater service and usefulness for him. Don't let the comfort and security of your present position make you miss God's plan for you.

12:5 God planned to develop a nation of people he would call his own. He called Abram from the godless, self-centered city of Ur to a fertile region called Canaan, where a God-centered, moral nation could be established. Though small in dimension, the land of Canaan was the focal point for most of the history of Israel as well as for the rise of Christianity. This small land given to one man, Abram, has had a tremendous impact on world history.

12:7 Abram built an altar to the Lord. Altars were used in many religions, but for God's people, altars were more than places of sacrifice. For them, altars symbolized communion with God and commemorated notable encounters with him. Built of rough stones and earth, altars often remained in place for years as continual reminders of God's protection and promises.

Abram regularly built altars to God for two reasons: (1) for prayer and worship, and (2) as reminders of God's promise to bless him. Abram couldn't survive spiritually without regularly renewing his love and loyalty to God. Building altars helped Abram remember that God was at the center of his life. Regular worship helps us remember what God desires and motivates us to obey him.

Abram in Egypt

¹⁰Now there was a famine in the land, and Abram went down to Egypt to live there for a while because the famine was severe. ¹¹As he was about to enter Egypt, he said to his wife Sarai, "I know what a beautiful woman you are. ¹²When the Egyptians see you, they will say, 'This is his wife.' Then they will kill me but will let you live. ¹³Say you are my sister, so that I will be treated well for your sake and my life will be spared because of you."

¹⁴When Abram came to Egypt, the Egyptians saw that she was a very beautiful woman. ¹⁵And when Pharaoh's officials saw her, they praised her to Pharaoh, and she was taken into his palace. ¹⁶He treated Abram well for her sake, and Abram acquired sheep and cattle, male and female donkeys, menservants and maidservants, and camels.

12:17
*n*1Ch 16:21

¹⁷But the LORD inflicted serious diseases on Pharaoh and his household *n* because of Abram's wife Sarai. ¹⁸So Pharaoh summoned Abram. "What have you done to me?" he said. "Why didn't you tell me she was your wife? ¹⁹Why did you say, 'She is my sister,' so that I took her to be my wife? Now then, here is your wife. Take her and go!" ²⁰Then Pharaoh gave orders about Abram to his men, and they sent him on his way, with his wife and everything he had.

2. Abram and Lot
Abram and Lot Separate

13 So Abram went up from Egypt to the Negev, with his wife and everything he had, and Lot went with him. ²Abram had become very wealthy in livestock and in silver and gold.

13:4
*o*Ge 12:7

³From the Negev he went from place to place until he came to Bethel, to the place between Bethel and Ai where his tent had been earlier ⁴and where he had first built an altar. *o* There Abram called on the name of the LORD.

13:7
*p*Ge 26:20, 21

⁵Now Lot, who was moving about with Abram, also had flocks and herds and tents. ⁶But the land could not support them while they stayed together, for their possessions were so great that they were not able to stay together. ⁷And quarreling *p* arose between Abram's herdsmen and the herdsmen of Lot. The Canaanites and Perizzites were also living in the land at that time.

12:10 When famine struck, Abram went to Egypt where there was food. Why would God allow a famine in the land where he had just called Abram? This was a test of Abram's faith, and Abram passed. He didn't question God's leading when facing this difficulty. Many believers find that when they determine to follow God, they immediately encounter great obstacles. The next time you face such a test, don't try to second-guess what God is doing. Use the intelligence God gave you, as Abram did when he temporarily moved to Egypt, and wait for new opportunities.

12:11–13 Abram, acting out of fear, asked Sarai to tell a half-truth by saying she was his sister. She *was* his half sister, but she was also his wife (see 20:12).

Abram's intent was to deceive the Egyptians. He feared that if they knew the truth, they would kill him to get Sarai. She would have been a desirable addition to Pharaoh's harem because of her wealth, beauty, and potential for political alliance. As Sarai's brother, Abram would have been given a place of honor. As her husband, however, his life would be in danger because Sarai could not enter Pharaoh's harem unless Abram was dead. So Abram lost faith in God's protection, even after all God had promised him, and told a half-truth. This shows how lying compounds the effects of sin. When he lied, Abram's problems multiplied.

13:1, 2 In Abram's day, sheep and cattle owners could acquire great wealth. Abram's wealth not only included silver and gold, but also livestock. These animals were a valuable commodity used for food, clothing, tent material, and sacrifices. They were often traded for other goods and services. Abram was able to watch his wealth grow and multiply daily.

13:5–9 Facing a potential conflict with his nephew Lot, Abram took the initiative in settling the dispute. He gave Lot first choice, even though Abram, being older, had the right to choose first. Abram also showed a willingness to risk being cheated. Abram's example shows us how to respond to difficult family situations: (1) take the initiative in resolving conflicts; (2) let others have first

choice, even if that means not getting what we want; (3) put family peace above personal desires.

13:7, 8 Surrounded by hostile neighbors, the herdsmen of Abram and Lot should have pulled together. Instead, they let petty jealousy tear them apart. Similar situations exist today. Christians often bicker while Satan is at work all around them.

Rivalries, arguments, and disagreements among believers can be destructive in three ways. (1) They damage goodwill, trust, and peace—the foundations of good human relations. (2) They hamper progress toward important goals. (3) They make us self-centered rather than love-centered. Jesus understood how destructive arguments among brothers could be.

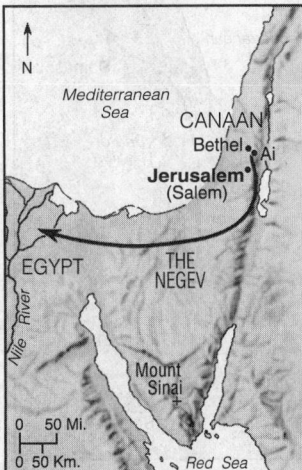

ABRAM'S JOURNEY TO EGYPT
A famine could cause the loss of a shepherd's wealth. So Abram traveled through the Negev to Egypt, where there was plenty of food and good land for his flocks.

8 So Abram said to Lot, "Let's not have any quarreling between you and me, or between your herdsmen and mine, for we are brothers. 9 Is not the whole land before you? Let's part company. If you go to the left, I'll go to the right; if you go to the right, I'll go to the left."

10 Lot looked up and saw that the whole plain of the Jordan was well watered, like the garden of the LORD, q like the land of Egypt, toward Zoar. r (This was before the LORD destroyed Sodom and Gomorrah.) s 11 So Lot chose for himself the whole plain of the Jordan and set out toward the east. The two men parted company: 12 Abram lived in the land of Canaan, while Lot lived among the cities of the plain and pitched his tents near Sodom. 13 Now the men of Sodom were wicked and were sinning greatly against the LORD. t

14 The LORD said to Abram after Lot had parted from him, "Lift up your eyes from where you are and look north and south, east and west. 15 All the land that you see I will give to you and your offspring a forever. u 16 I will make your offspring like the dust of the earth, so that if anyone could count the dust, then your offspring could be counted. 17 Go, walk through the length and breadth of the land, v for I am giving it to you."

18 So Abram moved his tents and went to live near the great trees of Mamre w at Hebron, where he built an altar to the LORD.

13:10
q Ge 2:8-10
r Ge 19:22, 30
s Ge 19:17-29

13:13
t Ge 18:20; 2Pe 2:8

13:15
u Ge 12:7; Gal 3:16*

13:17
v Nu 13:17-25

13:18
w Ge 14:13, 24

Abram Rescues Lot

14 At this time Amraphel king of Shinar, b Arioch king of Ellasar, Kedorlaomer king of Elam and Tidal king of Goiim 2 went to war against Bera king of Sodom, Birsha king of Gomorrah, Shinab king of Admah, Shemeber king of Zeboiim, and the king of Bela (that is, Zoar). 3 All these latter kings joined forces in the Valley of Siddim (the Salt Sea c x). 4 For twelve years they had been subject to Kedorlaomer, but in the thirteenth year they rebelled.

5 In the fourteenth year, Kedorlaomer and the kings allied with him went out and defeated the Rephaites in Ashteroth Karnaim, the Zuzites in Ham, the Emites in Shaveh Kiriathaim 6 and the Horites y in the hill country of Seir, as far as El Paran near the desert. 7 Then they turned back and went to En Mishpat (that is, Kadesh), and they conquered the whole territory of the Amalekites, as well as the Amorites who were living in Hazazon Tamar.

8 Then the king of Sodom, the king of Gomorrah, the king of Admah, the king of Zeboiim and the king of Bela (that is, Zoar) marched out and drew up their battle lines in the Valley of Siddim 9 against Kedorlaomer king of Elam, Tidal king of Goiim, Amraphel king of Shinar and Arioch king of Ellasar—four kings against five. 10 Now the Valley of Siddim was full of tar pits, and when the kings of Sodom and Gomorrah fled, some of the men fell into them and

14:3
x Nu 34:3, 12; Jos 3:16

14:6
y Dt 2:12, 22

a 15 Or seed; also in verse 16   b 1 That is, Babylonia; also in verse 9   c 3 That is, the Dead Sea

---

In his final prayer before being betrayed and arrested, Jesus asked God that his followers be "one" (John 17:21).

13:10, 11 Lot's character is revealed by his choices. He took the best share of the land even though it meant living near

LOT'S RESCUE
Having conquered Sodom, Kedorlaomer left for his home country, taking many captives with him. Abram learned what had happened and chased Kedorlaomer past Dan and beyond Damascus. There he defeated the king and rescued the captives, among them Lot.

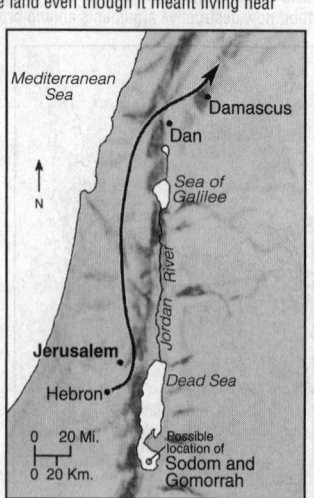

Sodom, a city known for its sin. He was greedy, wanting the best for himself, without thinking about his uncle Abram's needs or what was fair.

Life presents a series of choices. We too can choose the best while ignoring the needs and feelings of others. But this kind of choice, as Lot's life shows, leads to problems. When we stop making choices in God's direction, our only option is to make choices in the wrong direction.

13:12 Good pasture and available water seemed like a wise choice to Lot at first. But he failed to recognize that wicked Sodom could provide temptations strong enough to destroy his family. Have you chosen to live or work in a "Sodom"? Even though you may be strong enough to resist the temptations, other members of your family may not be. While God commands us to reach people in the "Sodom" near us, we must be careful not to become like the very people we are trying to reach.

14:4–16 Who was Kedorlaomer, and why was he important? In Abram's time, most cities had their own kings. Wars and rivalries among kings were common. A conquered city paid tribute to the victorious king. Nothing is known about Kedorlaomer except what we read in the Bible, but apparently he was quite powerful. Five cities including Sodom had paid tribute to him for 12 years. The five cities formed an alliance and rebelled by withholding tribute. Kedorlaomer reacted swiftly and reconquered them all. When he defeated Sodom, he captured Lot, his family, and his possessions. Abram, with only 318 men, chased Kedorlaomer's army and attacked him near Damascus. With God's help, he defeated them and recovered Lot, his family, and their possessions.

the rest fled to the hills. ¹¹The four kings seized all the goods of Sodom and Gomorrah and all their food; then they went away. ¹²They also carried off Abram's nephew Lot and his possessions, since he was living in Sodom.

14:13
z ver 24; Ge 13:18

14:14
a Ge 15:3

¹³One who had escaped came and reported this to Abram the Hebrew. Now Abram was living near the great trees of Mamre *z* the Amorite, a brother *a* of Eshcol and Aner, all of whom were allied with Abram. ¹⁴When Abram heard that his relative had been taken captive, he called out the 318 trained men born in his household *a* and went in pursuit as far as Dan. ¹⁵During the night Abram divided his men to attack them and he routed them, pursuing them as far as Hobah, north of Damascus. ¹⁶He recovered all the goods and brought back his relative Lot and his possessions, together with the women and the other people.

14:17
b 2Sa 18:18

¹⁷After Abram returned from defeating Kedorlaomer and the kings allied with him, the king of Sodom came out to meet him in the Valley of Shaveh (that is, the King's Valley). *b*

a 13 Or *a relative;* or *an ally*

LOT

Some people simply drift through life. Their choices, when they can muster the will to choose, tend to follow the course of least resistance. Lot, Abram's nephew, was such a person.

While still young, Lot lost his father. Although this must have been hard on him, he was not left without strong role models in his grandfather Terah and his uncle Abram, who raised him. Still, Lot did not develop their sense of purpose. Throughout his life he was so caught up in the present moment that he seemed incapable of seeing the consequences of his actions. It is hard to imagine what his life would have been like without Abram's careful attention and God's intervention.

By the time Lot drifted out of the picture, his life had taken an ugly turn. He had so blended into the sinful culture of his day that he did not want to leave it. Then his daughters committed incest with him. His drifting finally took him in a very specific direction—destruction.

Lot, however, is called "righteous" in the New Testament (2 Peter 2:7, 8). Ruth, a descendant of Moab, was an ancestor of Jesus, even though Moab was born as a result of Lot's incestuous relationship with one of his daughters. Lot's story gives hope to us that God forgives and often brings about positive circumstances from evil.

What is the direction of your life? Are you headed toward God or away from him? If you're a drifter, the choice for God may seem difficult, but it is the one choice that puts all other choices in a different light.

Strengths and accomplishments:	• He was a successful businessman • Peter calls him a righteous man (2 Peter 2:7, 8)
Weaknesses and mistakes:	• When faced with decisions, he tended to put off deciding, then chose the easiest course of action • When given a choice, his first reaction was to think of himself
Lesson from his life:	• God wants us to do more than drift through life; he wants us to be an influence for him
Vital statistics:	• Where: Lived first in Ur of the Chaldeans, then moved to Canaan with Abram. Eventually he moved to the wicked city of Sodom • Occupation: Wealthy sheep and cattle rancher; also a city official • Relatives: Father: Haran. Adopted by Abram when his father died. The name of his wife, who turned into a pillar of salt, is not mentioned.
Key verse:	"When he hesitated, the men grasped his hand and the hands of his wife and of his two daughters and led them safely out of the city, for the LORD was merciful to them" (Genesis 19:16).

Lot's story is told in Genesis 11—14; 19. He is also mentioned in Deuteronomy 2:9; Luke 17:28–32; 2 Peter 2:7, 8.

14:12 Lot's greedy desire for the best of everything led him into sinful surroundings. His burning desire for possessions and success cost him his freedom and enjoyment. As a captive to Kedorlaomer, he faced torture, slavery, or death. In much the same way, we can be enticed into doing things or going places we shouldn't. The prosperity we long for is captivating; it can both entice us and enslave us if our motives are not in line with God's desires.

14:14–16 These incidents portray two of Abram's characteristics: (1) He had courage that came from God. Facing a powerful foe, he attacked. (2) He was prepared. He had taken time to train his men

for a potential conflict. We never know when we will be called upon to complete difficult tasks. Like Abram, we should prepare for those times and take courage from God when they come.

14:14–16 When Abram learned that Lot was a prisoner, he immediately tried to rescue his nephew. It would have been easier and safer not to become involved. But with Lot in serious trouble, Abram acted at once. Sometimes we must get involved in a messy or painful situation in order to help others. We should be willing to act immediately when others need our help.

18Then Melchizedek[c] king of Salem[a][d] brought out bread and wine. He was priest of God Most High, 19and he blessed Abram, saying,

> "Blessed be Abram by God Most High,
>   Creator[b] of heaven and earth.[e]
> 20 And blessed be[c] God Most High,[f]
>   who delivered your enemies into your hand."

Then Abram gave him a tenth of everything.[g]

21The king of Sodom said to Abram, "Give me the people and keep the goods for yourself."

22But Abram said to the king of Sodom, "I have raised my hand to the Lord, God Most High, Creator of heaven and earth, and have taken an oath 23that I will accept nothing belonging to you, not even a thread or the thong of a sandal, so that you will never be able to say, 'I made Abram rich.' 24I will accept nothing but what my men have eaten and the share that belongs to the men who went with me—to Aner, Eshcol and Mamre. Let them have their share."

3. God promises a son to Abram
God's Covenant With Abram

15 After this, the word of the Lord came to Abram in a vision:

> "Do not be afraid,[h] Abram.
>   I am your shield,[d][i]
>   your very great reward.[e]"

2But Abram said, "O Sovereign Lord, what can you give me since I remain childless and the one who will inherit[f] my estate is Eliezer of Damascus?" 3And Abram said, "You have given me no children; so a servant in my household will be my heir."

4Then the word of the Lord came to him: "This man will not be your heir, but a son coming from your own body will be your heir." 5He took him outside and said, "Look up at the heavens and count the stars—if indeed you can count them." Then he said to him, "So shall your offspring be."[j]

6Abram believed the Lord, and he credited it to him as righteousness.[k]

7He also said to him, "I am the Lord, who brought you out of Ur of the Chaldeans to give you this land to take possession of it."

---

a 18 That is, Jerusalem   **b** 19 Or *Possessor*; also in verse 22   **c** 20 Or *And praise be to*   **d** 1 Or *sovereign*   **e** 1 Or *shield; / your reward will be very great*   **f** 2 The meaning of the Hebrew for this phrase is uncertain.

14:18 *Ps 110:4; Heb 5:6*   *Heb 7:2*
14:19 *ver 22*
14:20 *Ge 24:27*   *Heb 7:4*
15:1 *Ge 21:17; 26:24; Isa 41:10, 13-14*   *Dt 33:29*
15:5 *Ro 4:18*; Heb 11:12*
15:6 *Ro 4:3*, 20-24*; Gal 3:6*; Jas 2:23**

14:18 Who was Melchizedek? He was obviously a God-fearing man, for his name means "king of righteousness," and king of Salem means "king of peace." He was a "priest of God Most High" (Hebrews 7:1, 2). He recognized God as Creator of heaven and earth. What else is known about him? Four main theories have been suggested. (1) Melchizedek was a respected king of that region. Abram was simply showing him the respect he deserved. (2) The name Melchizedek may have been a standing title for all the kings of Salem. (3) Melchizedek was a type of Christ (Hebrews 7:3). A type is an Old Testament event or teaching that is so closely related to what Christ did that it illustrates a lesson about Christ. (4) Melchizedek was the appearance on earth of the preincarnate Christ in a temporary bodily form.

14:20 Abram gave one-tenth of the booty to Melchizedek. Even in some pagan religions, it was traditional to give a tenth of one's earnings to the gods. Abram followed accepted tradition; however, he refused to take any booty from the king of Sodom. Even though this huge amount would significantly increase what he could have given to God, he chose to reject it for more important reasons—he didn't want the ungodly king of Sodom to say, "I have made Abram rich." Instead, Abram wanted him to say, "God has made Abram rich." In this case, accepting the gifts would have focused everyone's attention on Abram or the king of Sodom rather than on God, the giver of victory. When people look at us, they need to see what God has accomplished in our lives.

15:1 Why would Abram be afraid? Perhaps he feared revenge from the kings he had just defeated (14:15). God gave him two good reasons for courage: (1) he promised to defend Abram ("I am your shield"), and (2) he promised to be Abram's "very great reward." When you fear what lies ahead, remember that God will stay with you through difficult times and that he has promised you great blessings.

15:2, 3 Eliezer was Abram's most trusted servant, acting as household administrator ("chief servant," see Genesis 24). According to custom, if Abram were to die without a son, his eldest servant would become his heir. Although Abram loved his servant, he wanted a son to carry on the family line.

15:5 Abram wasn't promised wealth or fame; he already had that. Instead God promised descendants like the stars in the sky or the grains of sand on the seashore (22:17), too numerous to count. To appreciate the vast number of stars scattered through the sky, you need to be, like Abram, away from any distractions. Or pick up a handful of sand and try to count the grains—it can't be done! Just when Abram was despairing of ever having an heir, God promised descendants too numerous to imagine. God's blessings are beyond our imaginations!

15:6 Although Abram had been demonstrating his faith through his actions, it was his belief in the Lord, not his actions, that made Abram right with God (Romans 4:1–5). We too can have a right relationship with God by trusting him. Our outward actions—church attendance, prayer, good deeds—will not by themselves make us right with God. A right relationship is based on faith—the heartfelt inner confidence that God is who he says he is and does what he says he will do. Right actions will follow naturally as by-products.

8 But Abram said, "O Sovereign LORD, how can I know that I will gain possession of it?" 9 So the LORD said to him, "Bring me a heifer, a goat and a ram, each three years old, along with a dove and a young pigeon."

10 Abram brought all these to him, cut them in two and arranged the halves opposite each other; the birds, however, he did not cut in half. 11 Then birds of prey came down on the carcasses, but Abram drove them away.

12 As the sun was setting, Abram fell into a deep sleep,[l] and a thick and dreadful darkness came over him. 13 Then the LORD said to him, "Know for certain that your descendants will be strangers in a country not their own, and they will be enslaved and mistreated four hundred years.[m] 14 But I will punish the nation they serve as slaves, and afterward they will come out[n] with great possessions.[o] 15 You, however, will go to your fathers in peace and be buried at a good old age.[p] 16 In the fourth generation your descendants will come back here, for the sin of the Amorites has not yet reached its full measure."

15:12
[l] Ge 2:21

15:13
[m] Ex 12:40; Ac 7:6, 17

15:14
[n] Ac 7:7*
[o] Ex 12:32-38

15:15
[p] Ge 25:8

MELCHIZEDEK

Do you like a good mystery? History is full of them! They usually involve people. One of the most mysterious people in the Bible is the King of Peace, Melchizedek. He appeared one day in the life of Abraham (then Abram) and was never heard from again. What happened that day, however, was to be remembered throughout history and eventually became a subject of a New Testament letter (Hebrews).

This meeting between Abram and Melchizedek was most unusual. Although the two men were strangers and foreigners to each other, they shared a most important characteristic: both worshiped and served the one God who made heaven and earth. This was a great moment of triumph for Abram. He had just defeated an army and regained the freedom of a large group of captives. If there was any doubt in his mind about whose victory it was, Melchizedek set the record straight by reminding Abram, "Blessed be God Most High, who delivered your enemies into your hand" (Genesis 14:20). Abram recognized that this man worshiped the same God he did.

Melchizedek was one of a small group of God-honoring people throughout the Old Testament who came in contact with the Jews (Israelites) but were not Jews themselves. This indicates that the requirement to be a follower of God is not genetic, but is based on faithfully obeying his teachings and recognizing his greatness.

Do you let God speak to you through other people? In evaluating others, do you consider God's impact on their lives? Are you aware of the similarities between yourself and others who worship God, even if their form of worship is quite different from yours? Do you know the God of the Bible well enough to know if you truly worship him? Allow Melchizedek, Abraham, David, and Jesus, along with many other persons in the Bible, to show you this great God, Creator of heaven and earth. He wants you to know how much he loves you; he wants you to know him personally.

Strengths and accomplishments:	• The first priest/king of Scripture—a leader with a heart tuned to God • Good at encouraging others to serve God wholeheartedly • A man whose character reflected his love for God • A person in the Old Testament who reminds us of Jesus and who some believe really was Jesus
Lesson from his life:	• Live for God and you're likely to be at the right place at the right time. Examine your heart: to whom or what is your greatest loyalty? If you can honestly answer *God*, you are living for him.
Vital statistics:	• Where: Ruled in Salem, site of the future Jerusalem • Occupation: King of Salem and priest of God Most High
Key verses:	"This Melchizedek was king of Salem and priest of God Most High. He met Abraham returning from the defeat of the kings and blessed him, . . . Just think how great he was: Even the patriarch Abraham gave him a tenth of the plunder!" (Hebrews 7:1, 4).

Melchizedek's story is told in Genesis 14:17–20. He is also mentioned in Psalm 110:4; Hebrews 5—7.

15:8 Abram was looking for confirmation and assurance that he was doing God's will. We also want assurance when we ask for guidance. But we can know for sure that what we are doing is right if we do what the Bible says. Abram didn't have the Bible—but we do.

15:13, 14 The book of Exodus tells the story of the enslavement and miraculous deliverance of Abram's descendants.

15:16 The Amorites were one of the nations living in Canaan,

the land God promised Abram. God knew the people would grow more wicked and would someday need to be punished. Part of that punishment would involve taking away their land and giving it to Abram's descendants. God in his mercy was giving the Amorites plenty of time to repent, but he already knew they would not. At the right time, they would have to be punished. Everything God does is true to his character. He is merciful, knows all, and acts justly—and his timing is perfect.

[17]When the sun had set and darkness had fallen, a smoking firepot with a blazing torch appeared and passed between the pieces. [18]On that day the LORD made a covenant with Abram and said, "To your descendants I give this land, from the river[a] of Egypt to the great river, the Euphrates— [19]the land of the Kenites, Kenizzites, Kadmonites, [20]Hittites, Perizzites, Rephaites, [21]Amorites, Canaanites, Girgashites and Jebusites."

Hagar and Ishmael

16 Now Sarai, Abram's wife, had borne him no children. But she had an Egyptian maidservant named Hagar; [2]so she said to Abram, "The LORD has kept me from having children. Go, sleep with my maidservant; perhaps I can build a family through her."[q]

Abram agreed to what Sarai said. [3]So after Abram had been living in Canaan[r] ten years, Sarai his wife took her Egyptian maidservant Hagar and gave her to her husband to be his wife. [4]He slept with Hagar, and she conceived.

When she knew she was pregnant, she began to despise her mistress. [5]Then Sarai said to Abram, "You are responsible for the wrong I am suffering. I put my servant in your arms, and now that she knows she is pregnant, she despises me. May the LORD judge between you and me."[s]

[6]"Your servant is in your hands," Abram said. "Do with her whatever you think best." Then Sarai mistreated Hagar; so she fled from her.

[7]The angel of the LORD found Hagar near a spring in the desert; it was the spring that is beside the road to Shur. [8]And he said, "Hagar, servant of Sarai, where have you come from, and where are you going?"

"I'm running away from my mistress Sarai," she answered.

[9]Then the angel of the LORD told her, "Go back to your mistress and submit to her." [10]The angel added, "I will so increase your descendants that they will be too numerous to count."

[11]The angel of the LORD also said to her:

> "You are now with child
> and you will have a son.
> You shall name him Ishmael,[b]
> for the LORD has heard of your misery.
> [12] He will be a wild donkey of a man;
> his hand will be against everyone
> and everyone's hand against him,
> and he will live in hostility
> toward[c] all his brothers.[t]"

[a]18 Or Wadi   [b]11 Ishmael means God hears.   [c]12 Or live to the east / of

16:2
qGe 30:3-4, 9-10

16:3
rGe 12:5

16:5
sGe 31:53

16:12
tGe 25:18

15:17 Why did God send this strange vision to Abram? God's covenant with Abram was serious business. It represented an incredible promise from God and a huge responsibility for Abram. To confirm this promise, God gave Abram a sign—the smoking firepot and a blazing torch. The fire and smoke suggest God's holiness, his zeal for righteousness, and his judgment on all the nations. God took the initiative, gave the confirmation, and followed through on his promises. God's passing through the pieces was a visible assurance to Abram that the covenant God had made was real.

16:1–3 Sarai gave Hagar to Abram as a substitute wife, a common practice of that time. A married woman who could not have children was shamed by her peers and was often required to give a female servant to her husband in order to produce heirs. The children born to the servant woman were considered the children of the wife. Abram was acting in line with the custom of the day, but his action showed a lack of faith that God would fulfill his promise.

16:3 Sarai took matters into her own hands by giving Hagar to Abram. Like Abram she had trouble believing God's promise that was apparently directed specifically toward Abram and Sarai. Out of this lack of faith came a series of problems. This invariably happens when we take over for God, trying to make his promise come true through efforts that are not in line with his specific directions. In this case, time was the greatest test of Abram and Sarai's willingness to let God work in their lives. Sometimes we too must simply wait. When we ask God for something and have to wait, we can be tempted to take matters into our own hands and interfere with God's plans.

16:5 Although Sarai arranged for Hagar to have a child by Abram, she later blamed Abram for the results. It is often easier to strike out in frustration and accuse someone else than to admit an error and ask forgiveness. (Adam and Eve did the same thing in 3:12, 13.)

16:6 Sarai took out her anger against Abram and separately against Hagar, and her treatment was harsh enough to cause Hagar to run away. Anger, especially when it arises from our own shortcomings, can be dangerous.

16:8 Hagar was running away from her mistress and her problem. The angel of the Lord gave her this advice: (1) to return

¹³She gave this name to the LORD who spoke to her: "You are the God who sees me," for she said, "I have now seen ª the One who sees me." ¹⁴That is why the well was called Beer Lahai Roi ᵇ; it is still there, between Kadesh and Bered.

¹⁵So Hagar bore Abram a son, and Abram gave the name Ishmael to the son she had borne. ¹⁶Abram was eighty-six years old when Hagar bore him Ishmael.

ª 13 Or seen the back of   ᵇ 14 Beer Lahai Roi means well of the Living One who sees me.

ISHMAEL

Have you ever wondered if you were born into the wrong family? We don't know much about how Ishmael viewed life, but that question must have haunted him at times. His life, his name, and his position were bound up in a conflict between two jealous women. Sarah (Sarai), impatient with God's timetable, had taken matters into her own hands, deciding to have a child through another woman. Hagar, servant that she was, submitted to being used this way. But her pregnancy gave birth to strong feelings of superiority toward Sarah. Into this tense atmosphere, Ishmael was born.

For 13 years Abraham thought Ishmael's birth had fulfilled God's promise. He was surprised to hear God say that the promised child would be Abraham and Sarah's very own. Sarah's pregnancy and Isaac's birth must have had a devastating impact on Ishmael. Until then he had been treated as a son and heir, but this late arrival made his future uncertain. During Isaac's weaning celebration, Sarah caught Ishmael teasing his half brother. As a result, Hagar and Ishmael were permanently expelled from Abraham's family.

Much of what happened throughout his life cannot be blamed on Ishmael. He was caught in a process much bigger than himself. However, his own actions showed that he had chosen to become part of the problem and not part of the solution. He chose to live under his circumstances rather than above them.

The choice he made is one we must all make. There are circumstances over which we have no control (heredity, for instance), but there are others that we can control (decisions we make). At the heart of the matter is the sin-oriented nature we all inherited. It can be partly controlled, although not overcome, by human effort. In the context of history, Ishmael's life represents the mess we make when we don't try to change the things we could change. The God of the Bible has offered a solution. His answer is not control, but a changed life. To have a changed life, turn to God, trust him to forgive your sinful past, and begin to change your attitude toward him and others.

Strengths and accomplishments:	• One of the first to experience the physical sign of God's covenant, circumcision • Known for his ability as an archer and hunter • Fathered 12 sons who became leaders of warrior tribes
Weakness and mistake:	• Failed to recognize the place of his half brother, Isaac, and mocked him
Lesson from his life:	• God's plans incorporate people's mistakes
Vital statistics:	• Where: Canaan and Egypt • Occupation: Hunter, archer, warrior • Relatives: Parents: Hagar and Abraham. Half brother: Isaac.
Key verses:	"God heard the boy crying, and the angel of God called to Hagar from heaven and said to her, 'What is the matter, Hagar? Do not be afraid; God has heard the boy crying as he lies there. Lift the boy up and take him by the hand, for I will make him into a great nation'" (Genesis 21:17, 18).

Ishmael's story is told in Genesis 16—17; 25:12–18; 28:8, 9; 36:1–3. He is also mentioned in 1 Chronicles 1:28–31; Romans 9:7–9; Galatians 4:21–31.

and face Sarai, the cause of her problem, and (2) to submit to her. Hagar needed to work on her attitude toward Sarai, no matter how justified it may have been. Running away from problems rarely solves them. It is wise to return to our problems, face them squarely, accept God's promise of help, correct our attitudes, and act as we should.

16:13 We have watched three people make serious mistakes: (1) Sarai, who took matters into her own hands and gave her maidservant to Abram; (2) Abram, who went along with the plan but, when circumstances began to go wrong, refused to help solve the problem; and (3) Hagar, who ran away from the problem. In spite of this messy situation, God demonstrated his ability to work in all things for good (Romans 8:28). Sarai and Abram still received the son they so desperately wanted, and God solved Hagar's problem despite Abram's refusal to get involved. No problem is too complicated for God if you are willing to let him help you.

The Covenant of Circumcision

17 When Abram was ninety-nine years old, the LORD appeared to him and said, "I am God Almighty^a;^u walk before me and be blameless.^v 2 I will confirm my covenant between me and you and will greatly increase your numbers."

3 Abram fell facedown, and God said to him, 4 "As for me, this is my covenant with you: You will be the father of many nations. 5 No longer will you be called Abram^b; your name will be Abraham,^{c w} or I have made you a father of many nations. ^x 6 I will make you very fruitful;^y I will make nations of you, and kings will come from you. 7 I will establish my covenant as an everlasting covenant between me and you and your descendants after you for the generations to come, to be your God and the God of your descendants after you.^z 8 The whole land of Canaan, where you are now an alien, I will give as an everlasting possession to you and your descendants after you;^a and I will be their God."

9 Then God said to Abraham, "As for you, you must keep my covenant, you and your descendants after you for the generations to come. 10 This is my covenant with you and your descendants after you, the covenant you are to keep: Every male among you shall be circumcised.^b 11 You are to undergo circumcision, and it will be the sign of the covenant^c between me and you. 12 For the generations to come every male among you who is eight days old must be circumcised,^d including those born in your household or bought with money from a foreigner—those who are not your offspring. 13 Whether born in your household or bought with your money, they must be circumcised. My covenant in your flesh is to be an everlasting covenant. 14 Any uncircumcised male, who has not been circumcised in the flesh, will be cut off from his people; he has broken my covenant."

15 God also said to Abraham, "As for Sarai your wife, you are no longer to call her Sarai; her name will be Sarah. 16 I will bless her and will surely give you a son by her. I will bless her so that she will be the mother of nations; kings of peoples will come from her."

17 Abraham fell facedown; he laughed^e and said to himself, "Will a son be born to a man a hundred years old? Will Sarah bear a child at the age of ninety?" 18 And Abraham said to God, "If only Ishmael might live under your blessing!"

19 Then God said, "Yes, but your wife Sarah will bear you a son,^f and you will call him Isaac.^d I will establish my covenant with him as an everlasting covenant for his descendants after him. 20 And as for Ishmael, I have heard you: I will surely bless him; I will make him fruitful and will greatly increase his numbers.^g He will be the father of twelve rulers,^h and I will make him into a great nation. ⁱ 21 But my covenant I will establish with Isaac, whom Sarah will bear to you by this time next year." 22 When he had finished speaking with Abraham, God went up from him.

17:1 ^uGe 28:3 ^vDt 18:13
17:5 ^wver 15; Ne 9:7 ^xRo 4:17*
17:6 ^yGe 35:11
17:7 ^zRo 9:8; Gal 3:16
17:8 ^aGe 12:7
17:10 ^bver 23; Ac 7:8
17:11 ^cRo 4:11
17:12 ^dLev 12:3
17:17 ^eGe 18:12; 21:6
17:19 ^fGe 18:14; 21:2
17:20 ^gGe 16:10 ^hGe 25:12-16 ⁱGe 21:18

^a1 Hebrew *El-Shaddai* ^b5 *Abram* means *exalted father.* ^c5 *Abraham* means *father of many.* ^d19 *Isaac* means *he laughs.*

17:1 The Lord told Abram, "I am God Almighty; walk before me and be blameless." God has the same message for us today. We are to obey the Lord in every respect because he is God—that is reason enough. If you don't think the benefits of obedience are worth it, consider who God is—the only one with the power and ability to meet your every need.

17:2–8 Why did God repeat his covenant to Abram? Twice before, he had mentioned this agreement (Genesis 12 and 15). Here, however, God was bringing it into focus and preparing to carry it out. He revealed to Abram several specific parts of his covenant: (1) God would give Abram many descendants; (2) many nations would descend from him; (3) God would maintain his covenant with Abram's descendants; (4) God would give Abram's descendants the land of Canaan.

17:5 In the Bible, people's names were very important—a name described a person's character or experience. Therefore, shortly before the promised son was conceived, God changed Abram's name (which meant "exalted father") to Abraham (which meant "father of many"). From this point on, the Bible calls him Abraham.

17:5–14 God was making a covenant, or contract, between himself and Abraham. The terms were simple: Abraham would obey God and circumcise all the males in his household; God's part was to give Abraham heirs, property, power, and wealth. Most contracts are even trades: We give something and, in turn, receive something of equal value. But when we become part of

God's covenant family, the blessings we receive far outweigh what we must give up.

17:9, 10 Why did God require circumcision? (1) As a sign of obedience to him in all matters. (2) As a sign of belonging to his covenant people. Once circumcised, the man would be identified as one of God's chosen people (eventually the Jews) forever. (3) As a symbol of "cutting off" the old life of sin, purifying one's heart, and dedicating oneself to God. (4) Possibly as a health measure.

Circumcision more than any other practice separated God's people from their pagan neighbors. In Abraham's day, this was essential to develop the pure worship of the one true God.

17:17–27 How could Abraham doubt God? It seemed incredible that he and Sarah in their advanced years could have a child. Abraham, the man God considered righteous because of his faith, had trouble believing God's promise to him. Despite his doubts, however, Abraham followed God's commands (17:22–27). Even people of great faith may have doubts. When God seems to want the impossible and you begin to doubt his leading, be like Abraham. Focus on God's commitment to fulfill his promises to you, and then continue to obey.

17:20 God did not forget Ishmael. Although he was not to be Abraham's heir, he would also be the father of a great nation. Regardless of your circumstances, God has not forgotten you. Obey him and trust in his plan.

23On that very day Abraham took his son Ishmael and all those born in his household or bought with his money, every male in his household, and circumcised them, as God told him. 24Abraham was ninety-nine years old when he was circumcised, 25and his son Ishmael was thirteen; 26Abraham and his son Ishmael were both circumcised on that same day. 27And every male in Abraham's household, including those born in his household or bought from a foreigner, was circumcised with him.

4. Sodom and Gomorrah
The Three Visitors

18:1
*j*Ge 13:18; 14:13
18:2
*k*ver 16, 22;
Heb 13:2

18 The LORD appeared to Abraham near the great trees of Mamre*j* while he was sitting at the entrance to his tent in the heat of the day. 2Abraham looked up and saw three men*k* standing nearby. When he saw them, he hurried from the entrance of his tent to meet them and bowed low to the ground.

3He said, "If I have found favor in your eyes, my lord,*a* do not pass your servant by. 4Let a

a3 Or *O Lord*

We all know that there are consequences to any action we take. What we do can set into motion a series of events that may continue long after we're gone. Unfortunately, when we are making a decision most of us think only of the immediate consequences. These are often misleading because they are short-lived.

Abraham had a choice to make. His decision was between setting out with his family and belongings for parts unknown or staying right where he was. He had to decide between the security of what he already had and the uncertainty of traveling under God's direction. All he had to go on was God's promise to guide and bless him. Abraham could hardly have been expected to visualize how much of the future was resting on his decision of whether to go or stay, but his obedience affected the history of the world. His decision to follow God set into motion the development of the nation that God would eventually use as his own when he visited earth himself. When Jesus Christ came to earth, God's promise was fulfilled; through Abraham the entire world was blessed.

You probably don't know the long-term effects of most decisions you make. But shouldn't the fact that there will be long-term results cause you to think carefully and seek God's guidance as you make choices and take action today?

Strengths and accomplishments:	• His faith pleased God • Became the founder of the Jewish nation • Was respected by others and was courageous in defending his family at any cost • Was not only a caring father to his own family, but practiced hospitality to others • Was a successful and wealthy rancher • Usually avoided conflicts, but when they were unavoidable, he allowed his opponent to set the rules for settling the dispute
Weakness and mistake:	• Under direct pressure, he distorted the truth
Lessons from his life:	• God desires dependence, trust, and faith in him—not faith in our ability to please him • God's plan from the beginning has been to make himself known to all people
Vital statistics:	• Where: Born in Ur of the Chaldeans; spent most of his life in the land of Canaan • Occupation: Wealthy livestock owner • Relatives: Brothers: Nahor and Haran. Father: Terah. Wife: Sarah. Nephew: Lot. Sons: Ishmael and Isaac. • Contemporaries: Abimelech, Melchizedek
Key verse:	"Abram believed the LORD, and he credited it to him as righteousness" (Genesis 15:6).

Abraham's story is told in Genesis 11—25. He is also mentioned in Exodus 2:24; Acts 7:2–8; Romans 4; Galatians 3; Hebrews 2; 6; 7; 11.

18:2–5 Abraham was eager to show hospitality to these three visitors, as was Lot (19:2). In Abraham's day, a person's reputation was largely connected to his hospitality—the sharing of home and food. Even strangers were to be treated as highly honored guests. Meeting another's need for food or shelter was and still is one of the most immediate and practical ways to obey God. It is also a time-honored relationship builder. Hebrews 13:2 suggests that we, like Abraham, might actually entertain angels. This thought should be on our minds the next time we have the opportunity to meet a stranger's needs.

little water be brought, and then you may all wash your feet *j* and rest under this tree. 5Let me get you something to eat, so you can be refreshed and then go on your way—now that you have come to your servant."

"Very well," they answered, "do as you say."

6So Abraham hurried into the tent to Sarah. "Quick," he said, "get three seahs *a* of fine flour and knead it and bake some bread."

7Then he ran to the herd and selected a choice, tender calf and gave it to a servant, who hurried to prepare it. 8He then brought some curds and milk and the calf that had been prepared, and set these before them. While they ate, he stood near them under a tree.

9"Where is your wife Sarah?" they asked him.

"There, in the tent," he said.

10Then the LORD *b* said, "I will surely return to you about this time next year, and Sarah your wife will have a son." *m*

Now Sarah was listening at the entrance to the tent, which was behind him. 11Abraham and Sarah were already old and well advanced in years, *n* and Sarah was past the age of childbearing. *o* 12So Sarah laughed *p* to herself as she thought, "After I am worn out and my master *c q* is old, will I now have this pleasure?"

13Then the LORD said to Abraham, "Why did Sarah laugh and say, 'Will I really have a child, now that I am old?' 14Is anything too hard for the LORD? *r* I will return to you at the appointed time next year and Sarah will have a son."

15Sarah was afraid, so she lied and said, "I did not laugh."

But he said, "Yes, you did laugh."

Abraham Pleads for Sodom

16When the men got up to leave, they looked down toward Sodom, and Abraham walked along with them to see them on their way. 17Then the LORD said, "Shall I hide from Abraham what I am about to do? 18Abraham will surely become a great and powerful nation, *s* and all nations on earth will be blessed through him. 19For I have chosen him, so that he will direct his children *t* and his household after him to keep the way of the LORD by doing what is right and just, so that the LORD will bring about for Abraham what he has promised him."

20Then the LORD said, "The outcry against Sodom and Gomorrah is so great and their sin so grievous 21that I will go down and see if what they have done is as bad as the outcry that has reached me. If not, I will know."

22The men turned away and went toward Sodom, but Abraham remained standing before the LORD. *d* 23Then Abraham approached him and said: "Will you sweep away the righteous with the wicked? *u* 24What if there are fifty righteous people in the city? Will you really sweep it away and not spare *e* the place for the sake of the fifty righteous people in it? *v* 25Far be it from you to do such a thing—to kill the righteous with the wicked, treating the righteous and the wicked alike. Far be it from you! Will not the Judge *f* of all the earth do right?" *w*

a6 That is, probably about 20 quarts (about 22 liters)   *b10* Hebrew *Then he*   *c12* Or *husband*   *d22* Masoretic Text; an ancient Hebrew scribal tradition *but the LORD remained standing before Abraham*   *e24* Or *forgive*; also in verse 26   *f25* Or *Ruler*

18:4
*j*Ge 19:2; 43:24

18:10
*m*Ro 9:9*

18:11
*n*Ge 17:17
*o*Ro 4:19

18:12
*p*Ge 17:17; 21:6
*q*1Pe 3:6

18:14
*r*Jer 32:17, 27;
Lk 1:37

18:18
*s*Gal 3:8*

18:19
*t*Dt 4:9-10; 6:7

18:23
*u*Nu 16:22

18:24
*v*Jer 5:1

18:25
*w*Job 8:3, 20;
Isa 3:10-11

18:14 "Is anything too hard for the LORD?" The obvious answer is, "Of course not!" This question reveals much about God. Make it a habit to insert your specific needs into the question. "Is this day in my life too hard for the Lord?" "Is this habit I'm trying to break too hard for him?" "Is the communication problem I'm having too hard for him?" Asking the question this way reminds you that God is personally involved in your life and nudges you to ask for his power to help you.

18:15 Sarah lied because she was afraid of being discovered. Fear is the most common motive for lying. We are afraid that our inner thoughts and emotions will be exposed or our wrongdoings discovered. But lying causes greater complications than telling the truth and brings even more problems. You will be far better off telling the truth right from the start.

18:20–33 Did Abraham change God's mind? Of course not. The more likely answer is that God changed Abraham's mind. Abraham knew that God is just and that he punishes sin, but he may have wondered about God's mercy. Abraham seemed to be probing God's mind to see how merciful he really was. He left his conversation with God convinced that God was both kind and fair.

Our prayers won't change God's mind, but they may change ours just as Abraham's prayer changed his. Prayer helps us better understand the mind of God.

18:20–33 Why did God let Abraham question his justice and intercede for a wicked city? Abraham knew that God must punish sin, but he also knew from experience that God is merciful to sinners. God knew there were not ten righteous people in the city, but he was merciful enough to allow Abraham to intercede. He was also merciful enough to help Lot, Abraham's nephew, get out of Sodom before it was destroyed. God does not take pleasure in destroying the wicked, but he must punish sin. He is both just and merciful. We should be thankful that God's mercy extends to us.

18:21 God gave the men of Sodom a fair test. He was not ignorant of the city's wicked practices, but in his fairness and patience he gave the people of Sodom one last chance to repent. God is still waiting, giving people the opportunity to turn to him (2 Peter 3:9). Those who are wise will turn to him before his patience wears out.

18:25 Was God being unfair to the people of Sodom? Did he really plan to destroy the righteous with the wicked? On the contrary, God's fairness stood out. (1) He agreed to spare the

26 The LORD said, "If I find fifty righteous people in the city of Sodom, I will spare the whole place for their sake."

18:27
×Ge 2:7; 3:19

27 Then Abraham spoke up again: "Now that I have been so bold as to speak to the Lord, though I am nothing but dust and ashes,× 28 what if the number of the righteous is five less than fifty? Will you destroy the whole city because of five people?"

"If I find forty-five there," he said, "I will not destroy it."

29 Once again he spoke to him, "What if only forty are found there?"

He said, "For the sake of forty, I will not do it."

30 Then he said, "May the Lord not be angry, but let me speak. What if only thirty can be found there?"

He answered, "I will not do it if I find thirty there."

31 Abraham said, "Now that I have been so bold as to speak to the Lord, what if only twenty can be found there?"

He said, "For the sake of twenty, I will not destroy it."

32 Then he said, "May the Lord not be angry, but let me speak just once more. What if only ten can be found there?"

SARAH

There probably isn't anything harder to do than wait, whether we are expecting something good, something bad, or an unknown.

One way we often cope with a long wait (or even a short one) is to begin helping God get his plan into action. Sarah tried this approach. She was too old to expect to have a child of her own, so she thought God must have something else in mind. From Sarah's limited point of view this could only be to give Abraham a son through another woman—a common practice in her day. The plan seemed harmless enough. Abraham would sleep with Sarah's maidservant, who would then give birth to a child. Sarah would take the child as her own. The plan worked beautifully—at first. But as you read about the events that followed, you will be struck by how often Sarah must have regretted the day she decided to push God's timetable ahead.

Another way we cope with a long wait is to gradually conclude that what we're waiting for is never going to happen. Sarah waited 90 years for a baby! When God told her she would finally have one of her own, she laughed, not so much from a lack of faith in what God could do, but from doubt about what he could do *through her*. When confronted about her laughter, she lied—as she had seen her husband do from time to time. She probably didn't want her true feelings to be known.

What parts of your life seem to be on hold right now? Do you understand that this may be part of God's plan for you? The Bible has more than enough clear direction to keep us busy while we're waiting for some particular part of life to move ahead.

Strengths and accomplishments:	• Was intensely loyal to her own child • Became the mother of a nation and an ancestor of Jesus • Was a woman of faith, the first woman listed in the Hall of Faith in Hebrews 11
Weaknesses and mistakes:	• Had trouble believing God's promises to her • Attempted to work problems out on her own, without consulting God • Tried to cover her faults by blaming others
Lessons from her life:	• God responds to faith even in the midst of failure • God is not bound by what usually happens; he can stretch the limits and cause unheard-of events to occur
Vital statistics:	• Where: Married Abram in Ur of the Chaldeans, then moved with him to Canaan • Occupation: Wife, mother, household manager • Relatives: Father: Terah. Husband: Abraham. Half brothers: Nahor and Haran. Nephew: Lot. Son: Isaac.
Key verse:	"By faith Abraham, even though he was past age—and Sarah herself was barren—was enabled to become a father because he considered him faithful who had made the promise" (Hebrews 11:11).

Sarah's story is told in Genesis 11—25. She is also mentioned in Isaiah 51:2; Romans 4:19; 9:9; Hebrews 11:11; 1 Peter 3:6.

---

entire city if only ten righteous people lived there. (2) He showed great mercy toward Lot, apparently the only man in the city who had any kind of relationship with him (and even that was questionable). (3) He showed great patience toward Lot, almost forc-ing him to leave Sodom before it was destroyed. Remember God's patience when you are tempted to think he is unfair. Even the most godly people deserve his justice. We should be glad God doesn't direct his justice toward us as he did toward Sodom.

He answered, "For the sake of ten, I will not destroy it."

33 When the LORD had finished speaking with Abraham, he left, and Abraham returned home.

Sodom and Gomorrah Destroyed

19 The two angels arrived at Sodom in the evening, and Lot was sitting in the gateway of the city. When he saw them, he got up to meet them and bowed down with his face to the ground. 2 "My lords," he said, "please turn aside to your servant's house. You can wash your feet and spend the night and then go on your way early in the morning."

"No," they answered, "we will spend the night in the square."

3 But he insisted so strongly that they did go with him and entered his house. He prepared a meal for them, baking bread without yeast, and they ate.ʸ 4 Before they had gone to bed, all the men from every part of the city of Sodom—both young and old—surrounded the house. 5 They called to Lot, "Where are the men who came to you tonight? Bring them out to us so that we can have sex with them."ᶻ

6 Lot went outside to meet them and shut the door behind him 7 and said, "No, my friends. Don't do this wicked thing. 8 Look, I have two daughters who have never slept with a man. Let me bring them out to you, and you can do what you like with them. But don't do anything to these men, for they have come under the protection of my roof."

9 "Get out of our way," they replied. And they said, "This fellow came here as an alien, and now he wants to play the judge!ᵃ We'll treat you worse than them." They kept bringing pressure on Lot and moved forward to break down the door.

10 But the men inside reached out and pulled Lot back into the house and shut the door. 11 Then they struck the men who were at the door of the house, young and old, with blindness so that they could not find the door.

12 The two men said to Lot, "Do you have anyone else here—sons-in-law, sons or daughters, or anyone else in the city who belongs to you?ᵇ Get them out of here, 13 because we are going to destroy this place. The outcry to the LORD against its people is so great that he has sent us to destroy it."ᶜ

14 So Lot went out and spoke to his sons-in-law, who were pledged to marryᵃ his daughters. He said, "Hurry and get out of this place, because the LORD is about to destroy the city! ᵈ" But his sons-in-law thought he was joking.

15 With the coming of dawn, the angels urged Lot, saying, "Hurry! Take your wife and your two daughters who are here, or you will be swept away when the city is punished."

16 When he hesitated, the men grasped his hand and the hands of his wife and of his two

ᵃ14 Or *were married to*

19:3
ʸGe 18:6

19:5
ᶻJdg 19:22;
Ro 1:24-27

19:9
ᵃEx 2:14

19:12
ᵇGe 7:1

19:13
ᶜ1Ch 21:15

19:14
ᵈNu 16:21

18:33 God showed Abraham that asking for anything is allowed, with the understanding that God's answers come from God's perspective. They are not always in harmony with our expectations, for only he knows the whole story. Are you missing God's answer to a prayer because you haven't considered any possible answers other than the one you expect?

19:1 The gateway of the city was the meeting place for city officials and other men to discuss current events and transact business. It was a place of authority and status where a person could see and be seen. Evidently Lot held an important position in the government or associated with those who did because the angels found him at the city gate. Perhaps Lot's status in Sodom was one reason he was so reluctant to leave (19:16, 18–22).

19:8 How could any father give his daughters to be ravished by a mob of perverts, just to protect two strangers? Possibly Lot was scheming to save both the girls and the visitors, hoping the girls' fiancés would rescue them or that the homosexual men would be disinterested in the girls and simply go away. Although it was the custom of the day to protect guests at any cost, this terrible suggestion reveals how deeply sin had been absorbed into Lot's life. He had become hardened to evil acts in an evil city. Whatever Lot's motives were, we see here an illustration of Sodom's terrible wickedness—a wickedness so great that God had to destroy the entire city.

19:13 God promised to spare Sodom if only ten righteous people lived there (18:32). Obviously not even ten could be found,

because the angels arrived to destroy the city. Archaeological evidence points to an advanced civilization in this area during Abraham's day. Most researchers also confirm some kind of sudden and devastating destruction. It is now widely thought that the buried city lies beneath the waters of the southern end of the Dead Sea. The story of Sodom reveals that the people of Lot's day had to deal with the same kinds of repulsive sins the world faces today. We should follow Abraham's example of trusting God. His selfless faith contrasts with the self-gratifying people of Sodom.

19:14 Lot had lived so long and so contented among ungodly people that he was no longer a believable witness for God. He had allowed his environment to shape him, rather than he shaping his environment. Do those who know you see you as a witness for God, or are you just one of the crowd, blending in unnoticed? Lot had compromised to the point that he was almost useless to God. When he finally made a stand, nobody listened. Have you too become useless to God because you are too much like your environment? To make a difference, you must first decide to be different in your faith and your conduct.

19:16 Lot hesitated, so the angel grasped his hand and rushed him to safety. Lot did not want to abandon the wealth, position, and comfort he enjoyed in Sodom. It is easy to criticize Lot for being hypnotized by Sodom when the choice seems so clear to us. To be wiser than Lot, we must see that our hesitation to obey stems from the false attractions of our culture's pleasures.

19:16–29 Notice how God's mercy toward Abraham extended to

19:17
e ver 26

daughters and led them safely out of the city, for the Lᴏʀᴅ was merciful to them. [17] As soon as they had brought them out, one of them said, "Flee for your lives! Don't look back, *e* and don't stop anywhere in the plain! Flee to the mountains or you will be swept away!"

[18] But Lot said to them, "No, my lords, *a* please! [19] Your *b* servant has found favor in your *b* eyes, and you *b* have shown great kindness to me in sparing my life. But I can't flee to the mountains; this disaster will overtake me, and I'll die. [20] Look, here is a town near enough to run to, and it is small. Let me flee to it—it is very small, isn't it? Then my life will be spared."

[21] He said to him, "Very well, I will grant this request too; I will not overthrow the town you speak of. [22] But flee there quickly, because I cannot do anything until you reach it." (That is why the town was called Zoar. *c*)

19:24
f Dt 29:23; Isa 1:9; 13:19
g Lk 17:29

[23] By the time Lot reached Zoar, the sun had risen over the land. [24] Then the Lᴏʀᴅ rained down burning sulfur on Sodom and Gomorrah *f*—from the Lᴏʀᴅ out of the heavens. *g* [25] Thus he overthrew those cities and the entire plain, including all those living in the cities—and also the vegetation in the land. [26] But Lot's wife looked back, *h* and she became a pillar of salt. *i*

19:26
h ver 17
i Lk 17:32

[27] Early the next morning Abraham got up and returned to the place where he had stood before the Lᴏʀᴅ. *j* [28] He looked down toward Sodom and Gomorrah, toward all the land of the plain, and he saw dense smoke rising from the land, like smoke from a furnace. *k*

19:27
j Ge 18:22

19:28
k Rev 18:9

[29] So when God destroyed the cities of the plain, he remembered Abraham, and he brought Lot out of the catastrophe that overthrew the cities where Lot had lived.

Lot and His Daughters

[30] Lot and his two daughters left Zoar and settled in the mountains, for he was afraid to stay in Zoar. He and his two daughters lived in a cave. [31] One day the older daughter said to the younger, "Our father is old, and there is no man around here to lie with us, as is the custom all over the earth. [32] Let's get our father to drink wine and then lie with him and preserve our family line through our father."

[33] That night they got their father to drink wine, and the older daughter went in and lay with him. He was not aware of it when she lay down or when she got up.

[34] The next day the older daughter said to the younger, "Last night I lay with my father. Let's get him to drink wine again tonight, and you go in and lie with him so we can preserve our family line through our father." [35] So they got their father to drink wine that night also, and the younger daughter went and lay with him. Again he was not aware of it when she lay down or when she got up.

19:37
l Dt 2:9

19:38
m Dt 2:19

[36] So both of Lot's daughters became pregnant by their father. [37] The older daughter had a son, and she named him Moab *d*; he is the father of the Moabites *l* of today. [38] The younger daughter also had a son, and she named him Ben-Ammi *e*; he is the father of the Ammonites *m* of today.

a 18 Or *No, Lord*; or *No, my lord*   *b 19* The Hebrew is singular.   *c 22 Zoar* means *small*.   *d 37 Moab* sounds like the Hebrew for *from father*.   *e 38 Ben-Ammi* means *son of my people*.

Lot and his family. Because Abraham pleaded for Lot, God was merciful and saved Lot from the fiery destruction of Sodom. A righteous person can often affect others for good. James says that the prayers of a righteous person are powerful (see James 5:16). All Christians should follow Abraham's example and pray for others to be saved.

19:24 In the story of Sodom and Gomorrah, we see two facets of God's character: his great patience (agreeing to spare a wicked city for ten good people) and his fierce anger (destroying both cities). As we grow spiritually, we should find ourselves developing a deeper respect for God because of his anger toward sin, and also a deeper love for God because of his patience when we sin.

19:26 Lot's wife turned back to look at the smoldering city of Sodom. Clinging to the past, she was unwilling to turn completely away. Are you looking back longingly at sin while trying to move forward with God? You can't make progress with God as long as you are holding on to pieces of your old life. Jesus said it this way in Matthew 6:24: "No one can serve two masters."

19:30–38 In this pitiful sequel to the story of the destruction of Sodom, we see two women compelled to preserve their family line. They were driven not by lust, but by desperation—they feared they would never marry. Lot's tendency to compromise

and refusal to act reached its peak. He should have found right partners for his daughters long before this; Abraham's family wasn't far away. Now the two daughters stooped to incest, showing their acceptance of the morals of Sodom. We are most likely to sin when we are desperate for what we feel we must have.

19:30–38 Why doesn't the Bible openly condemn these sisters for what they did? In many cases, the Bible does not judge people for their actions. It simply reports the events. However, incest is clearly condemned in other parts of Scripture (Leviticus 18:6–18; 20:11, 12, 17, 19–21; Deuteronomy 22:30; 27:20–23; Ezekiel 22:11; 1 Corinthians 5:1). Perhaps the consequence of their action—Moab and Ammon became enemies of Israel—was God's way of judging their sin.

19:37, 38 Moab and Ben-Ammi were the products of incest. They became the fathers of two of Israel's greatest enemies, the Moabites and the Ammonites. These nations settled east of the Jordan River, and Israel never conquered them. Because of the family connection, Moses was forbidden to attack them (Deuteronomy 2:9). Ruth, great-grandmother of David and an ancestor of Jesus, was from Moab.

Abraham and Abimelech

20 Now Abraham moved on from thereⁿ into the region of the Negev and lived between Kadesh and Shur. For a while he stayed in Gerar, ² and there Abraham said of his wife Sarah, "She is my sister. ^o" Then Abimelech king of Gerar sent for Sarah and took her.

³ But God came to Abimelech in a dream one night and said to him, "You are as good as dead because of the woman you have taken; she is a married woman."

⁴ Now Abimelech had not gone near her, so he said, "Lord, will you destroy an innocent nation? ⁵ Did he not say to me, 'She is my sister,' and didn't she also say, 'He is my brother'? I have done this with a clear conscience and clean hands."

⁶ Then God said to him in the dream, "Yes, I know you did this with a clear conscience, and so I have kept you from sinning against me. That is why I did not let you touch her. ⁷ Now return the man's wife, for he is a prophet, and he will pray for you^p and you will live. But if you do not return her, you may be sure that you and all yours will die."

⁸ Early the next morning Abimelech summoned all his officials, and when he told them all that had happened, they were very much afraid. ⁹ Then Abimelech called Abraham in and said, "What have you done to us? How have I wronged you that you have brought such great guilt upon me and my kingdom? You have done things to me that should not be done." ¹⁰ And Abimelech asked Abraham, "What was your reason for doing this?"

¹¹ Abraham replied, "I said to myself, 'There is surely no fear of God ^q in this place, and they will kill me because of my wife.'^r ¹² Besides, she really is my sister, the daughter of my father though not of my mother; and she became my wife. ¹³ And when God had me wander from my father's household, I said to her, 'This is how you can show your love to me: Everywhere we go, say of me, "He is my brother."'"

¹⁴ Then Abimelech brought sheep and cattle and male and female slaves and gave them to Abraham,^s and he returned Sarah his wife to him. ¹⁵ And Abimelech said, "My land is before you; live wherever you like."^t

¹⁶ To Sarah he said, "I am giving your brother a thousand shekels^a of silver. This is to cover the offense against you before all who are with you; you are completely vindicated."

¹⁷ Then Abraham prayed to God, and God healed Abimelech, his wife and his slave girls so they could have children again, ¹⁸ for the LORD had closed up every womb in Abimelech's household because of Abraham's wife Sarah. ^u

5. Birth and near sacrifice of Isaac
The Birth of Isaac

21 Now the LORD was gracious to Sarah as he had said, and the LORD did for Sarah what he had promised. ² Sarah became pregnant and bore a son to Abraham in his old age,^v at the very time God had promised him. ³ Abraham gave the name Isaac^{b w} to the son Sarah bore him. ⁴ When his son Isaac was eight days old, Abraham circumcised him,^x as God commanded him. ⁵ Abraham was a hundred years old when his son Isaac was born to him.

^a *16* That is, about 25 pounds (about 11.5 kilograms)   ^b *3 Isaac* means *he laughs.*

20:1
ⁿ Ge 18:1
20:2
^o ver 12; Ge 12:13; 26:7

20:7
^p ver 17; 1Sa 7:5; Job 42:8

20:11
^q Ps 36:1
^r Ge 12:12; 26:7

20:14
^s Ge 12:16
20:15
^t Ge 13:9

20:18
^u Ge 12:17

21:2
^v Gal 4:22; Heb 11:11
21:3
^w Ge 17:19
21:4
^x Ge 17:10, 12; Ac 7:8

20:2 Abraham had used this same trick before to protect himself (12:11–13). Although Abraham is one of our heroes of faith, he did not learn his lesson well enough the first time. In fact, by giving in to the temptation again, he risked turning a sinful act into a sinful pattern of lying whenever he suspected his life was in danger.

No matter how much we love God, certain temptations are especially difficult to resist. These are the vulnerable spots in our spiritual armor. As we struggle with these weaknesses, we can be encouraged to know that God is watching out for us just as he did for Abraham.

20:6 Abimelech had unknowingly taken a married woman to be his wife and was about to commit adultery. But God somehow prevented him from touching Sarah and held him back from sinning. What mercy on God's part! How many times has God done the same for us, holding us back from sin in ways we can't even detect? We have no way of knowing—we just know from this story that he can. God works just as often in ways we can't see as in ways we can.

20:11–13 Because Abraham mistakenly assumed that Abimelech was a wicked man, he made a quick decision to tell a half-truth. Abraham thought it would be more effective to deceive Abimelech

than to trust God to work in the king's life. Don't assume that God will not work in a situation that has potential problems. You may not completely understand the situation, and God may intervene when you least expect it.

20:17, 18 Why did God punish Abimelech when he had no idea Sarah was married? (1) Even though Abimelech's intentions were good, as long as Sarah was living in his harem he was in danger of sinning. A person who eats a poisonous toadstool, thinking it's a harmless mushroom, no doubt has perfectly good intentions—but will still suffer. Sin is a poison that damages us and those around us, whatever our intentions. (2) The punishment, closing up "every womb in Abimelech's household," lasted only as long as Abimelech was in danger of sleeping with Sarah. It was meant to change the situation, not to harm Abimelech. (3) The punishment clearly showed that Abraham was in league with almighty God. This incident may have made Abimelech respect and fear Abraham's God.

21:1–7 Who could believe that Abraham would have a son at 100 years of age—and live to raise him to adulthood? But doing the impossible is everyday business for God. Our big problems won't seem so impossible if we let God handle them.

21:6
y Ge 17:17

⁶Sarah said, "God has brought me laughter,ʸ and everyone who hears about this will laugh with me." ⁷And she added, "Who would have said to Abraham that Sarah would nurse children? Yet I have borne him a son in his old age."

Hagar and Ishmael Sent Away

⁸The child grew and was weaned, and on the day Isaac was weaned Abraham held a great feast. ⁹But Sarah saw that the son whom Hagar the Egyptian had borne to Abraham was mocking, ¹⁰and she said to Abraham, "Get rid of that slave woman and her son, for that slave woman's son will never share in the inheritance with my son Isaac."ᶻ

21:10
z Gal 4:30*

¹¹The matter distressed Abraham greatly because it concerned his son.ᵃ ¹²But God said to him, "Do not be so distressed about the boy and your maidservant. Listen to whatever Sarah

21:11
a Ge 17:18

ISAAC

A name carries great authority. It sets you apart. It triggers memories. The sound of it calls you to attention anywhere.

Many Bible names accomplished even more. They were often descriptions of important facts about one's past and hopes for the future. The choice of the name *Isaac*, "he laughs," for Abraham and Sarah's son must have created a variety of feelings in them each time it was spoken. At times it must have recalled their shocked laughter at God's announcement that they would be parents in their old age. At other times, it must have brought back the joyful feelings of receiving their long-awaited answer to prayer for a child. Most importantly, it was a testimony to God's power in making his promise a reality.

In a family of forceful initiators, Isaac was the quiet, "mind-my-own-business" type unless he was specifically called on to take action. He was the protected only child from the time Sarah got rid of Ishmael until Abraham arranged his marriage to Rebekah.

In his own family, Isaac had the patriarchal position, but Rebekah had the power. Rather than stand his ground, Isaac found it easier to compromise or lie to avoid confrontations.

In spite of these shortcomings, Isaac was part of God's plan. The model his father gave him included a great gift of faith in the one true God. God's promise to create a great nation through which he would bless the world was passed on by Isaac to his twin sons.

It is usually not hard to identify with Isaac in his weaknesses. But consider for a moment that God works through people in spite of their shortcomings and, often, through them. As you pray, put into words your desire to be available to God. You will discover that his willingness to use you is even greater than your desire to be used.

Strengths and accomplishments:	• He was the miracle child born to Sarah and Abraham when Sarah was 90 years old and Abraham was 100 • He was the first descendant in fulfillment of God's promise to Abraham • He seems to have been a caring and consistent husband, at least until his sons were born • He demonstrated great patience
Weaknesses and mistakes:	• Under pressure he tended to lie • In conflict he sought to avoid confrontation • He played favorites between his sons and alienated his wife
Lessons from his life:	• Patience often brings rewards • Both God's plans and his promises are larger than people • God keeps his promises! He remains faithful though we are often faithless • Playing favorites is sure to bring family conflict
Vital statistics:	• Where: The area called the Negev, in the southern part of Palestine, between Kadesh and Shur (Genesis 20:1) • Occupation: Wealthy livestock owner • Relatives: Parents: Abraham and Sarah. Half brother: Ishmael. Wife: Rebekah. Sons: Jacob and Esau.
Key verse:	"Then God said, 'Yes, but your wife Sarah will bear you a son, and you will call him Isaac. I will establish my covenant with him as an everlasting covenant for his descendants after him'" (Genesis 17:19).

Isaac's story is told in Genesis 17:15—35:29. He is also mentioned in Romans 9:7, 8; Hebrews 11:17–20; James 2:21–24.

21:7 After repeated promises, a visit by two angels, and the appearance of the Lord himself, Sarah finally cried out with surprise and joy at the birth of her son. Because of her doubt, worry, and fear, she had forfeited the peace she could have felt in God's wonderful promise to her. The way to bring peace to a troubled heart is to focus on God's promises. Trust him to do what he says.

tells you, because it is through Isaac that your offspring[a] will be reckoned.[b] [13]I will make the son of the maidservant into a nation also, because he is your offspring."

[14]Early the next morning Abraham took some food and a skin of water and gave them to Hagar. He set them on her shoulders and then sent her off with the boy. She went on her way and wandered in the desert of Beersheba.

[15]When the water in the skin was gone, she put the boy under one of the bushes. [16]Then she went off and sat down nearby, about a bowshot away, for she thought, "I cannot watch the boy die." And as she sat there nearby, she[b] began to sob.

[17]God heard the boy crying,[c] and the angel of God called to Hagar from heaven and said to her, "What is the matter, Hagar? Do not be afraid; God has heard the boy crying as he lies there. [18]Lift the boy up and take him by the hand, for I will make him into a great nation."

[19]Then God opened her eyes and she saw a well of water. So she went and filled the skin with water and gave the boy a drink.

[20]God was with the boy[d] as he grew up. He lived in the desert and became an archer. [21]While he was living in the Desert of Paran, his mother got a wife for him[e] from Egypt.

The Treaty at Beersheba

[22]At that time Abimelech and Phicol the commander of his forces said to Abraham, "God is with you in everything you do. [23]Now swear to me here before God that you will not deal falsely with me or my children or my descendants. Show to me and the country where you are living as an alien the same kindness I have shown to you."

[24]Abraham said, "I swear it."

[25]Then Abraham complained to Abimelech about a well of water that Abimelech's servants had seized.[f] [26]But Abimelech said, "I don't know who has done this. You did not tell me, and I heard about it only today."

[27]So Abraham brought sheep and cattle and gave them to Abimelech, and the two men made a treaty.[g] [28]Abraham set apart seven ewe lambs from the flock, [29]and Abimelech asked Abraham, "What is the meaning of these seven ewe lambs you have set apart by themselves?"

[30]He replied, "Accept these seven lambs from my hand as a witness[h] that I dug this well." [31]So that place was called Beersheba,[c] because the two men swore an oath there.

[32]After the treaty had been made at Beersheba, Abimelech and Phicol the commander of his forces returned to the land of the Philistines. [33]Abraham planted a tamarisk tree in Beersheba, and there he called upon the name of the LORD, the Eternal God. [34]And Abraham stayed in the land of the Philistines for a long time.

Abraham Tested

22 Some time later God tested[i] Abraham. He said to him, "Abraham!" "Here I am," he replied.

a *12* Or *seed*   b *16* Hebrew; Septuagint *the child*   c *31* *Beersheba* can mean *well of seven* or *well of the oath.*

21:12
b Ro 9:7*;
Heb 11:18*

21:17
c Ex 3:7

21:20
d Ge 28:15

21:21
e Ge 24:4, 38

21:25
f Ge 26:15, 18,
20-22

21:27
g Ge 26:28, 31

21:30
h Ge 31:44, 47,
48, 50, 52

22:1
i Dt 8:2, 16;
Heb 11:17;
Jas 1:12-13

21:18 What happened to Ishmael, and who are his descendants? Ishmael became ruler of a large tribe or nation. The Ishmaelites were nomads living in the Desert of Sinai and Paran, south of Israel. One of Ishmael's daughters married Esau, Ishmael's nephew (28:9). The Bible pictures the Ishmaelites as hostile to Israel and to God (Psalm 83:6).

21:31 Beersheba, the southernmost city of Israel, lay on the edge of a vast desert that stretched as far as Egypt to the southwest and Mount Sinai to the south. The area described as being from Dan in the north to Beersheba in the south was often used to describe the traditional boundaries of the promised land (2 Samuel 17:11). Beersheba's southern location and the presence of several wells in the area may explain why Abraham settled there. Beersheba was also the home of Isaac, Abraham's son.

22:1 God tested Abraham, not to trip him and watch him fall, but to deepen his capacity to obey God and thus to develop his character. Just as fire refines ore to extract precious metals, God refines us through difficult circumstances. When we are tested we can complain, or we can try to see how God is stretching us to develop our character.

ABRAHAM'S TRIP TO MOUNT MORIAH
Abraham and Isaac traveled the 50 or 60 miles from Beersheba to Mount Moriah in about three days. This was a very difficult time for Abraham, who was on his way to sacrifice his beloved son, Isaac.

22:2
j Jn 3:16

²Then God said, "Take your son *j*, your only son, Isaac, whom you love, and go to the region of Moriah. Sacrifice him there as a burnt offering on one of the mountains I will tell you about."

³Early the next morning Abraham got up and saddled his donkey. He took with him two of his servants and his son Isaac. When he had cut enough wood for the burnt offering, he set out for the place God had told him about. ⁴On the third day Abraham looked up and saw the place in the distance. ⁵He said to his servants, "Stay here with the donkey while I and the boy go over there. We will worship and then we will come back to you."

22:6
k Jn 19:17

⁶Abraham took the wood for the burnt offering and placed it on his son Isaac, *k* and he himself carried the fire and the knife. As the two of them went on together, ⁷Isaac spoke up and said to his father Abraham, "Father?"

"Yes, my son?" Abraham replied.

"The fire and wood are here," Isaac said, "but where is the lamb for the burnt offering?"

Escape of some kind is usually the most tempting solution to our problems. In fact, it can become a habit. Hagar was a person who used that approach. When the going got tough, she usually got going—in the other direction.

However, it is worthwhile to note that the biggest challenges Hagar faced were brought on by *other* people's choices. Sarah chose her to bear Abraham's child, and Hagar probably had little to say in the matter.

It isn't hard to understand how Hagar's pregnancy caused her to look down on Sarah. But that brought on hard feelings, and Sarah consequently punished Hagar. This motivated her first escape. When she returned to the family and gave birth to Ishmael, Sarah's continued barrenness must have contributed to bitterness on both sides.

When Isaac was finally born, Sarah looked for any excuse to have Hagar and Ishmael sent away. She found it when she caught Ishmael teasing Isaac. In the desert, out of water and facing the death of her son, Hagar once again tried to escape. She walked away so she wouldn't have to watch her son die. Once again, God graciously intervened.

Have you noticed how patiently God operates to make our escape attempts fail? Have you begun to learn that escape is only a temporary solution? God's continual desire is for us to face our problems with his help. We experience his help most clearly in and through conflicts and difficulties, not away from them. Are there problems in your life for which you've been using the "Hagar solution"? Choose one of those problems, ask for God's help, and begin to face it today.

Strength and accomplishment:	• Mother of Abraham's first child, Ishmael, who became founder of the Arab nations
Weaknesses and mistakes:	• When faced with problems, she tended to run away • Her pregnancy brought out strong feelings of pride and arrogance
Lessons from her life:	• God is faithful to his plan and promises, even when humans complicate the process • God shows himself as one who knows us and wants to be known by us • The New Testament uses Hagar as a symbol of those who would pursue favor with God by their own efforts, rather than by trusting in his mercy and forgiveness
Vital statistics:	• Where: Canaan and Egypt • Occupation: Servant, mother • Relatives: Son: Ishmael
Key verse:	"Then the angel of the LORD told her, 'Go back to your mistress and submit to her'" (Genesis 16:9).

Hagar's story is told in Genesis 16—21. She is also mentioned in Galatians 4:24, 25.

22:3 That morning Abraham began one of the greatest acts of obedience in recorded history. He traveled 50 miles to Mount Moriah near the site of Jerusalem. Over the years he had learned many tough lessons about the importance of obeying God. This time his obedience was prompt and complete. Obeying God is often a struggle because it may mean giving up something we truly want. We should not expect our obedience to God to be easy or to come naturally.

22:6 We don't know how Abraham carried the fire. Perhaps he carried a live coal or a flint to start a fire.

22:7, 8 Why did God ask Abraham to perform human sacrifice? Pagan nations practiced human sacrifice, but God condemned this as a terrible sin (Leviticus 20:1–5). God did not want Isaac to die, but he wanted Abraham to sacrifice Isaac in his heart so it would be clear that Abraham loved God more than he loved his promised and long-awaited son. God was testing Abraham. The purpose of testing is to strengthen our character and deepen our commitment to God and his perfect timing. Through this difficult experience, Abraham strengthened his commitment to obey God. He also learned about God's ability to provide.

[8]Abraham answered, "God himself will provide the lamb for the burnt offering, my son." And the two of them went on together.

[9]When they reached the place God had told him about, Abraham built an altar there and arranged the wood on it. He bound his son Isaac and laid him on the altar, on top of the wood. [10]Then he reached out his hand and took the knife to slay his son. [11]But the angel of the LORD called out to him from heaven, "Abraham! Abraham!"

"Here I am," he replied.

[12]"Do not lay a hand on the boy," he said. "Do not do anything to him. Now I know that you fear God, because you have not withheld from me your son, your only son.["]

[13]Abraham looked up and there in a thicket he saw a ram[a] caught by its horns. He went over and took the ram and sacrificed it as a burnt offering instead of his son.[m] [14]So Abraham called that place The LORD Will Provide. And to this day it is said, "On the mountain of the LORD it will be provided."

[15]The angel of the LORD called to Abraham from heaven a second time [16]and said, "I swear by myself,[n] declares the LORD, that because you have done this and have not withheld your son, your only son, [17]I will surely bless you and make your descendants[o] as numerous as the stars in the sky[p] and as the sand on the seashore.[q] Your descendants will take possession of the cities of their enemies,[r] [18]and through your offspring[b] all nations on earth will be blessed,[s] because you have obeyed me."

[19]Then Abraham returned to his servants, and they set off together for Beersheba. And Abraham stayed in Beersheba.

Nahor's Sons

[20]Some time later Abraham was told, "Milcah is also a mother; she has borne sons to your brother Nahor: [21]Uz the firstborn, Buz his brother, Kemuel (the father of Aram), [22]Kesed, Hazo, Pildash, Jidlaph and Bethuel." [23]Bethuel became the father of Rebekah.[t] Milcah bore these eight sons to Abraham's brother Nahor. [24]His concubine, whose name was Reumah, also had sons: Tebah, Gaham, Tahash and Maacah.

The Death of Sarah

23 Sarah lived to be a hundred and twenty-seven years old. [2]She died at Kiriath Arba[u] (that is, Hebron) in the land of Canaan, and Abraham went to mourn for Sarah and to weep over her.

[3]Then Abraham rose from beside his dead wife and spoke to the Hittites.[c] He said, [4]"I am an alien and a stranger[v] among you. Sell me some property for a burial site here so I can bury my dead."

---

[a] 13 Many manuscripts of the Masoretic Text, Samaritan Pentateuch, Septuagint and Syriac; most manuscripts of the Masoretic Text *a ram behind ⌊him⌋*   [b] 18 Or *seed*   [c] 3 Or *the sons of Heth*; also in verses 5, 7, 10, 16, 18 and 20

Side references

22:12 *l* ver 2; Jn 3:16

22:13 *m* Ro 8:32

22:16 *n* Heb 6:13

22:17 *o* Heb 6:14*; *p* Ge 15:5; *q* Ge 26:24; *r* Ge 24:60

22:18 *s* Ac 3:25*; Gal 3:8*

22:23 *t* Ge 24:15

23:2 *u* Jos 14:15

23:4 *v* Ps 105:12; Heb 11:9, 13

CAVE OF MACHPELAH

Sarah died in Hebron. Abraham bought the cave of Machpelah, near Hebron, as her burial place. Abraham was also buried there, as were his son and grandson, Isaac and Jacob.

Mediterranean Sea
Sea of Galilee
Jordan River
Jerusalem (Salem)
Hebron
Cave of Machpelah
Dead Sea
0   20 Mi.
0   20 Km.
N

22:12 It is difficult to let go of what we deeply love. What could be more proper than to love your only child? Yet when we do give to God what he asks, he returns to us far more than we could dream. The spiritual benefits of his blessings far outweigh our sacrifices. Have you withheld your love, your children, or your time from him? Trust him to provide (22:8).

22:13 Notice the parallel between the ram offered on the altar as a substitute for Isaac and Christ offered on the cross as a substitute for us. Whereas God stopped Abraham from sacrificing his son, God did not spare his own Son, Jesus, from dying on the cross. If Jesus had lived, the rest of humankind would have died. God sent his only Son to die for us so that we could be spared from the eternal death we deserve and instead receive eternal life (John 3:16).

22:15–18 Abraham received abundant blessings because he obeyed God. God promised to give Abraham's descendants the ability to conquer their enemies. In addition, God promised Abraham children and grandchildren who would in turn bless the whole earth. People's lives would be changed as a result of knowing of the faith of Abraham and his descendants. We often think of blessings as gifts that we will enjoy. But when God blesses us, his blessings may also overflow to others—today and into eternity.

23:1–4 In Abraham's day, death and burial were steeped in ritual and traditions. Failing to honor a dead person demonstrated the

23:6
ʷGe 14:14-16;
24:35

5 The Hittites replied to Abraham, 6 "Sir, listen to us. You are a mighty prince ʷ among us. Bury your dead in the choicest of our tombs. None of us will refuse you his tomb for burying your dead."

7 Then Abraham rose and bowed down before the people of the land, the Hittites. 8 He said to them, "If you are willing to let me bury my dead, then listen to me and intercede with Ephron son of Zohar on my behalf 9 so he will sell me the cave of Machpelah, which belongs to him and is at the end of his field. Ask him to sell it to me for the full price as a burial site among you."

23:10
ˣRu 4:4

10 Ephron the Hittite was sitting among his people and he replied to Abraham in the hearing of all the Hittites who had come to the gate ˣ of his city. 11 "No, my lord," he said. "Listen to me; I give ᵃ you the field, and I give ᵃ you the cave that is in it. I give ᵃ it to you in the presence of my people. Bury your dead."

12 Again Abraham bowed down before the people of the land 13 and he said to Ephron in their hearing, "Listen to me, if you will. I will pay the price of the field. Accept it from me so I can bury my dead there."

14 Ephron answered Abraham, 15 "Listen to me, my lord; the land is worth four hundred shekels ᵇ of silver, but what is that between me and you? Bury your dead."

23:16
ʸJer 32:9

16 Abraham agreed to Ephron's terms and weighed out for him the price he had named in the hearing of the Hittites: four hundred shekels of silver, ʸ according to the weight current among the merchants.

23:17
ᶻGe 25:9; 49:30-32;
50:13

17 So Ephron's field in Machpelah near Mamre ᶻ—both the field and the cave in it, and all the trees within the borders of the field—was deeded 18 to Abraham as his property in the presence of all the Hittites who had come to the gate of the city. 19 Afterward Abraham buried his wife Sarah in the cave in the field of Machpelah near Mamre (which is at Hebron) in the land of Canaan. 20 So the field and the cave in it were deeded to Abraham by the Hittites as a burial site.

6. Isaac and Rebekah

24:1
ᵃver 35

24:3
ᵇGe 14:19

24:4
ᶜGe 12:1

24 Abraham was now old and well advanced in years, and the LORD had blessed him in every way. ᵃ 2 He said to the chief ᶜ servant in his household, the one in charge of all that he had, "Put your hand under my thigh. 3 I want you to swear by the LORD, the God of heaven and the God of earth, ᵇ that you will not get a wife for my son from the daughters of the Canaanites, among whom I am living, 4 but will go to my country and my own relatives ᶜ and get a wife for my son Isaac."

5 The servant asked him, "What if the woman is unwilling to come back with me to this land? Shall I then take your son back to the country you came from?"

ᵃ11 Or *sell*   ᵇ15 That is, about 10 pounds (about 4.5 kilograms)   ᶜ2 Or *oldest*

---

greatest possible lack of respect. An improper burial was the equivalent of a curse. Mourning was an essential part of the death ritual. Friends and relatives would cry loudly for the whole neighborhood to hear. Because there were no funeral homes or undertakers, these same friends and relatives would help prepare the body for burial, which usually would take place on the same day because of the warm climate.

23:4–6 Abraham was in a foreign land looking for a place to bury his wife. Strangers offered to help him because he was "a mighty prince," and they respected him. Although Abraham had not put down roots in the area, his reputation was above reproach. Those who invest their time and money in serving God often earn a pleasant return on their investment—a good reputation and the respect of others.

23:10–15 The polite interchange between Abraham and Ephron was typical of bargaining at that time. Ephron graciously offered to give his land to Abraham at no charge; Abraham insisted on paying for it; Ephron politely mentioned the price but said, in effect, that it wasn't important; Abraham paid the 400 shekels of silver. Both men knew what was going on as they went through the bargaining process. If Abraham had accepted the land as a gift when it was offered, he would have insulted Ephron, who then would have rescinded his offer. Many Middle Eastern shopkeepers still follow this bargaining ritual with their customers.

23:16 Four hundred shekels of silver was a high price for the piece of property Abraham bought. The Hittites weren't thrilled about foreigners buying their property, so Abraham had little bargaining leverage.

Ephron asked an outrageous price. The custom of the day was to ask double the fair market value of the land, fully expecting the buyer to offer half the stated price. Abraham, however, did not bargain. He simply paid the initial price. He was not trying to take anything he didn't deserve. Even though God had promised the land to Abraham, he did not just take it away from Ephron.

24:2, 9 In Abraham's culture, putting a hand under the thigh was how an agreement was sealed or a covenant ratified. To accomplish the same purpose, we shake hands, swear oaths, or sign documents in the presence of a notary public.

24:4 Abraham wanted Isaac to marry within the family. This was a common and acceptable practice at this time that had the added advantage of avoiding intermarriage with pagan neighbors. A son's wife was usually chosen by the parents. It was common for a woman to be married in her early teens although Rebekah was probably older.

⁶"Make sure that you do not take my son back there," Abraham said. ⁷"The LORD, the God
of heaven, who brought me out of my father's household and my native land and who spoke
to me and promised me on oath, saying, 'To your offspringᵃ ᵈ I will give this land'ᵉ—he will
send his angel before youᶠ so that you can get a wife for my son from there. ⁸If the woman is
unwilling to come back with you, then you will be released from this oath of mine. Only do
not take my son back there." ⁹So the servant put his hand under the thigh of his master
Abraham and swore an oath to him concerning this matter.

¹⁰Then the servant took ten of his master's camels and left, taking with him all kinds of
good things from his master. He set out for Aram Naharaimᵇ and made his way to the town
of Nahor. ¹¹He had the camels kneel down near the well outside the town; it was toward
evening, the time the women go out to draw water.ᵍ

¹²Then he prayed, "O LORD, God of my master Abraham,ʰ give me success today, and
show kindness to my master Abraham. ¹³See, I am standing beside this spring, and the
daughters of the townspeople are coming out to draw water. ¹⁴May it be that when I say to a
girl, 'Please let down your jar that I may have a drink,' and she says, 'Drink, and I'll water your
camels too'—let her be the one you have chosen for your servant Isaac. By this I will know
that you have shown kindness to my master."

¹⁵Before he had finished praying, Rebekahⁱ came out with her jar on her shoulder. She
was the daughter of Bethuel son of Milcah, who was the wife of Abraham's brother Nahor.
¹⁶The girl was very beautiful,ʲ a virgin; no man had ever lain with her. She went down to the
spring, filled her jar and came up again.

¹⁷The servant hurried to meet her and said, "Please give me a little water from your jar."

¹⁸"Drink, my lord," she said, and quickly lowered the jar to her hands and gave him a drink.

¹⁹After she had given him a drink, she said, "I'll draw water for your camels too, until they
have finished drinking." ²⁰So she quickly emptied her jar into the trough, ran back to the
well to draw more water, and drew enough for all his camels. ²¹Without saying a word, the
man watched her closely to learn whether or not the LORD had made his journey successful.

²²When the camels had finished drinking, the man took out a gold nose ring weighing a
bekaᶜ and two gold bracelets weighing ten shekels.ᵈ ²³Then he asked, "Whose daughter
are you? Please tell me, is there room in your father's house for us to spend the night?"

²⁴She answered him, "I am the daughter of Bethuel, the son that Milcah bore to Nahor."
²⁵And she added, "We have plenty of straw and fodder, as well as room for you to spend the
night."

²⁶Then the man bowed down and worshiped the LORD,ᵏ ²⁷saying, "Praise be to the LORD,
the God of my master Abraham, who has not abandoned his kindness and faithfulness to my
master. As for me, the LORD has led me on the journey to the house of my master's relatives."

24:7
ᵈGal 3:16*
ᵉGe 12:7; 13:15
ᶠEx 23:20, 23

24:11
ᵍver 13; 1Sa 9:11

24:12
ʰver 27, 42, 48;
Ge 26:24; Ex 3:6,
15, 16

24:15
ⁱGe 22:23

24:16
ʲGe 26:7

24:26
ᵏver 48, 52

ᵃ*7* Or *seed*   ᵇ*10* That is, Northwest Mesopotamia   ᶜ*22* That is, about 1/5 ounce (about 5.5 grams)   ᵈ*22* That is,
about 4 ounces (about 110 grams)

24:6 Abraham wanted Isaac to stay in Canaan, but he didn't
want him to marry one of the local girls. This contrasts to the
way Hagar selected a wife for Ishmael in 21:21. To have Isaac
stay and marry, or send him back to marry a relative would have
been easier. But Abraham wanted to obey God in the *who* as well
as in the *where.* Make your obedience full and complete.

24:11 The well, the chief source of water for an entire village,
was usually located outside town along the main road. Many
people had to walk a mile or more for their water. They could use
only what they could carry home. Farmers and shepherds would
come from nearby fields to draw water for their animals. The well
was a good place to meet new friends or to chat with old ones.
Rebekah would have visited the well twice daily to draw water
for her family.

24:12 Abraham's servant asked God for guidance in this very
important task. Obviously Eliezer (see 15:2) had learned much
about faith and about God from his master. What are your family
members, friends, and associates learning about God from watching you? Be like Abraham, setting an example of dependent faith.
And be like Eliezer, asking God for guidance before any venture.

24:14 Was it right for Abraham's servant to ask God for such a
specific sign? The sign he requested was only slightly out of the
ordinary. The hospitality of the day required women at the well to

offer water to weary travelers, but not to their animals. Eliezer
was simply asking God to show him a woman with an attitude
of service—someone who would go beyond the expected. An
offer to water his camels would indicate that kind of attitude.
Eliezer did not ask for a woman with looks or wealth. He knew
the importance of finding a woman with the right heart, and he
asked God to help him with this task.

24:15, 16 Rebekah had physical beauty, but the servant was
looking for a sign of inner beauty. Appearance is important to us,
and we spend time and money improving it. But how much effort
do we put into developing our inner beauty? Patience, kindness,
and joy are the beauty treatments that help us become truly
lovely—on the inside.

24:18–21 Rebekah's servant spirit was clearly demonstrated as
she willingly and quickly drew water for Eliezer and his camels.
The pots used for carrying water were large and heavy. A thirsty
camel drinks a lot of water—up to 25 gallons after a week's
travel. Seeing Rebekah go to work, Eliezer knew this was a
woman with a heart for doing far more than the bare minimum.
Do you have a servant spirit? When asked to help or when you
see a need, go beyond the minimum.

24:26, 27 As soon as Abraham's servant knew that God had
answered his prayer, he thanked God for his goodness and

24:29
l ver 4; Ge 29:5, 12, 13

24:31
m Ge 26:29

24:32
n Ge 43:24; Jdg 19:21

24:35
o ver 1

24:36
p Ge 21:2, 10
q Ge 25:5

24:37
r ver 3

24:39
s ver 5

24:40
t ver 7

24:41
u ver 8

24:42
v ver 12

24:43
w ver 13

24:45
x 1Sa 1:13
y ver 15

24:48
z ver 26

28 The girl ran and told her mother's household about these things. 29 Now Rebekah had a brother named Laban,*l* and he hurried out to the man at the spring. 30 As soon as he had seen the nose ring, and the bracelets on his sister's arms, and had heard Rebekah tell what the man said to her, he went out to the man and found him standing by the camels near the spring. 31 "Come, you who are blessed by the LORD,"*m* he said. "Why are you standing out here? I have prepared the house and a place for the camels."

32 So the man went to the house, and the camels were unloaded. Straw and fodder were brought for the camels, and water for him and his men to wash their feet.*n* 33 Then food was set before him, but he said, "I will not eat until I have told you what I have to say."

"Then tell us," Laban said.

34 So he said, "I am Abraham's servant. 35 The LORD has blessed my master abundantly,*o* and he has become wealthy. He has given him sheep and cattle, silver and gold, menservants and maidservants, and camels and donkeys. 36 My master's wife Sarah has borne him a son in her*a* old age,*p* and he has given him everything he owns.*q* 37 And my master made me swear an oath, and said, 'You must not get a wife for my son from the daughters of the Canaanites, in whose land I live,*r* 38 but go to my father's family and to my own clan, and get a wife for my son.'

39 "Then I asked my master, 'What if the woman will not come back with me?'*s*

40 "He replied, 'The LORD, before whom I have walked, will send his angel with you*t* and make your journey a success, so that you can get a wife for my son from my own clan and from my father's family. 41 Then, when you go to my clan, you will be released from my oath even if they refuse to give her to you—you will be released from my oath.'*u*

42 "When I came to the spring today, I said, 'O LORD, God of my master Abraham, if you will, please grant success*v* to the journey on which I have come. 43 See, I am standing beside this spring;*w* if a maiden comes out to draw water and I say to her, "Please let me drink a little water from your jar," 44 and if she says to me, "Drink, and I'll draw water for your camels too," let her be the one the LORD has chosen for my master's son.'

45 "Before I finished praying in my heart,*x* Rebekah came out, with her jar on her shoulder.*y* She went down to the spring and drew water, and I said to her, 'Please give me a drink.'

46 "She quickly lowered her jar from her shoulder and said, 'Drink, and I'll water your camels too.' So I drank, and she watered the camels also.

47 "I asked her, 'Whose daughter are you?'

"She said, 'The daughter of Bethuel son of Nahor, whom Milcah bore to him.'

"Then I put the ring in her nose and the bracelets on her arms, 48 and I bowed down and worshiped the LORD.*z* I praised the LORD, the God of my master Abraham, who had led me on the right road to get the granddaughter of my master's brother for his son. 49 Now if you

a 36 Or *his*

ELEIZER: PROFILE OF A TRUE SERVANT

Have you ever approached a responsiblity with this kind of single-mindedness and careful planning, while ultimately depending on God?

---

guidance. God will also use and lead us if we are available like Eliezer. Our first response should be praise and thanksgiving that God would choose to work in and through us.

24:42, 48 When Eliezer told his story to Laban, he spoke openly of God and his goodness. Often we do the opposite, afraid that we will be misunderstood, rejected, or seen as too religious. Instead, we should share openly what God is doing for us.

will show kindness and faithfulness[a] to my master, tell me; and if not, tell me, so I may know which way to turn."

[50] Laban and Bethuel answered, "This is from the LORD;[b] we can say nothing to you one way or the other.[c] [51] Here is Rebekah; take her and go, and let her become the wife of your master's son, as the LORD has directed."

[52] When Abraham's servant heard what they said, he bowed down to the ground before the LORD.[d] [53] Then the servant brought out gold and silver jewelry and articles of clothing and gave them to Rebekah; he also gave costly gifts to her brother and to her mother. [54] Then he and the men who were with him ate and drank and spent the night there.

When they got up the next morning, he said, "Send me on my way[e] to my master."

[55] But her brother and her mother replied, "Let the girl remain with us ten days or so; then you[a] may go."

[56] But he said to them, "Do not detain me, now that the LORD has granted success to my journey. Send me on my way so I may go to my master."

[57] Then they said, "Let's call the girl and ask her about it." [58] So they called Rebekah and asked her, "Will you go with this man?"

"I will go," she said.

[59] So they sent their sister Rebekah on her way, along with her nurse[f] and Abraham's servant and his men. [60] And they blessed Rebekah and said to her,

> "Our sister, may you increase
>   to thousands upon thousands;[g]
> may your offspring possess
>   the gates of their enemies."[h]

[61] Then Rebekah and her maids got ready and mounted their camels and went back with the man. So the servant took Rebekah and left.

[62] Now Isaac had come from Beer Lahai Roi,[i] for he was living in the Negev. [63] He went out to the field one evening to meditate,[b][j] and as he looked up, he saw camels approaching. [64] Rebekah also looked up and saw Isaac. She got down from her camel [65] and asked the servant, "Who is that man in the field coming to meet us?"

"He is my master," the servant answered. So she took her veil and covered herself.

[66] Then the servant told Isaac all he had done. [67] Isaac brought her into the tent of his mother Sarah, and he married Rebekah. So she became his wife, and he loved her; and Isaac was comforted after his mother's death.

7. Abraham dies
The Death of Abraham

25 Abraham took[c] another wife, whose name was Keturah. [2] She bore him Zimran, Jokshan, Medan, Midian, Ishbak and Shuah. [3] Jokshan was the father of Sheba and Dedan; the descendants of Dedan were the Asshurites, the Letushites and the Leummites. [4] The sons of Midian were Ephah, Epher, Hanoch, Abida and Eldaah. All these were descendants of Keturah.

[5] Abraham left everything he owned to Isaac.[k] [6] But while he was still living, he gave gifts to the sons of his concubines and sent them away from his son Isaac to the land of the east.

[7] Altogether, Abraham lived a hundred and seventy-five years. [8] Then Abraham breathed his last and died at a good old age,[l] an old man and full of years; and he was gathered to his people.[m] [9] His sons Isaac and Ishmael buried him in the cave of Machpelah near Mamre, in the field of Ephron son of Zohar the Hittite, [10] the field Abraham had bought from the Hittites.[d][n] There Abraham was buried with his wife Sarah. [11] After Abraham's death, God blessed his son Isaac, who then lived near Beer Lahai Roi.

[a]55 Or she   [b]63 The meaning of the Hebrew for this word is uncertain.   [c]1 Or had taken   [d]10 Or the sons of Heth

Cross references

24:49 [a]Ge 47:29; Jos 2:14
24:50 [b]Ps 118:23 [c]Ge 31:7, 24, 29, 42
24:52 [d]ver 26
24:54 [e]ver 56, 59
24:59 [f]Ge 35:8
24:60 [g]Ge 17:16 [h]Ge 22:17
24:62 [i]Ge 16:14; 25:11
24:63 [j]Ps 1:2; 77:12; 119:15, 27, 48, 97, 148; 143:5
25:5 [k]Ge 24:36
25:8 [l]Ge 15:15 [m]Ge 35:29; 49:29, 33
25:10 [n]Ge 23:16

24:60 "May your offspring possess the gates of their enemies" means "May you overcome all your enemies."

24:64, 65 When Rebekah learned that the man coming to greet them was Isaac, her husband-to-be, she followed two oriental customs. She dismounted from her camel to show respect, and she placed a veil over her face as a bride.

25:1–6 Abraham took another wife, Keturah, after Sarah died. Although the sons and grandson of Abraham and Keturah received many gifts from Abraham, all his property and authority went to Isaac, his principle heir.

Ishmael's Sons

25:12
*o*Ge 16:15

¹²This is the account of Abraham's son Ishmael, whom Sarah's maidservant, Hagar the Egyptian, bore to Abraham. *o*

¹³These are the names of the sons of Ishmael, listed in the order of their birth: Nebaioth the firstborn of Ishmael, Kedar, Adbeel, Mibsam, ¹⁴Mishma, Dumah, Massa, ¹⁵Hadad, Tema,

25:16
*p*Ge 17:20
25:17
*q*ver 8
25:18
*r*Ge 16:12

Jetur, Naphish and Kedemah. ¹⁶These were the sons of Ishmael, and these are the names of the twelve tribal rulers *p* according to their settlements and camps. ¹⁷Altogether, Ishmael lived a hundred and thirty-seven years. He breathed his last and died, and he was gathered to his people. *q* ¹⁸His descendants settled in the area from Havilah to Shur, near the border of Egypt, as you go toward Asshur. And they lived in hostility toward *a* all their brothers. *r*

E. THE STORY OF ISAAC (25:19—28:9)

Isaac inherited everything from his father, including God's promise to make his descendants into a great nation. As a boy, Isaac did not resist as his father prepared to sacrifice him, and as a man, he gladly accepted the wife that others chose for him. Through Isaac, we learn how to let God guide our lives and place his will ahead of our own.

1. Jacob and Esau

¹⁹This is the account of Abraham's son Isaac.

25:20
*s*Ge 24:29

Abraham became the father of Isaac, ²⁰and Isaac was forty years old when he married Rebekah daughter of Bethuel the Aramean from Paddan Aram *b* and sister of Laban *s* the Aramean.

a 18 Or *lived to the east of*   *b* 20 That is, Northwest Mesopotamia

Some people are initiators. They help get the ball rolling. Rebekah would easily stand out in this group. Her life was characterized by initiative. When she saw a need she took action, even though the action was not always right.

It was Rebekah's initiative that first caught the attention of Eliezer, the servant Abraham sent to find a wife for Isaac. It was common courtesy to give a drink to a stranger, but it took added character to also fetch water for ten thirsty camels. Later, after hearing the details of Eliezer's mission, Rebekah was immediately willing to be Isaac's bride.

Several later events help us see how initiative can be misdirected. Rebekah was aware that God's plan would be channeled through Jacob, not Esau (Genesis 25:23). So not only did Jacob become her favorite; she actually planned ways to ensure that he would over-shadow his older twin. Meanwhile, Isaac preferred Esau. This created a conflict between the couple. She felt justified in deceiving her husband when the time came to bless the sons, and her ingenious plan was carried out to perfection.

Most of the time we try to justify the things we choose to do. Often we attempt to add God's approval to our actions. While it is true that our actions will not spoil God's plan, it is also true that we are responsible for what we do and must always be cautious about our motives. When thinking about a course of action, are you simply seeking God's stamp of approval on something you've already decided to do? Or are you willing to set the plan aside if the principles and commands of God's Word are against the action? Initiative and action are admirable and right when they are controlled by God's wisdom.

Strengths and accomplishments:	• When confronted with a need, she took immediate action • She was accomplishment oriented
Weaknesses and mistakes:	• Her initiative was not always balanced by wisdom • She favored one of her sons • She deceived her husband
Lessons from her life:	• Our actions must be guided by God's Word • God makes use even of our mistakes in his plan • Parental favoritism hurts a family
Vital statistics:	• Where: Haran, Canaan • Occupation: Wife, mother, household manager • Relatives: Grandparents: Nahor and Milcah. Father: Bethuel. Husband: Isaac. Brother: Laban. Twin sons: Esau and Jacob.
Key verses:	"Isaac brought her into the tent of his mother Sarah, and he married Rebekah. So she became his wife, and he loved her; and Isaac was comforted after his mother's death" (Genesis 24:67). "Isaac, who had a taste for wild game, loved Esau, but Rebekah loved Jacob" (Genesis 25:28).

Rebekah's story is told in Genesis 24—49. She is also mentioned in Romans 9:10.

[21]Isaac prayed to the LORD on behalf of his wife, because she was barren. The LORD answered his prayer, and his wife Rebekah became pregnant. [22]The babies jostled each other within her, and she said, "Why is this happening to me?" So she went to inquire of the LORD. [23]The LORD said to her,

> "Two nations are in your womb,
> and two peoples from within you will be separated;
> one people will be stronger than the other,
> and the older will serve the younger.[t]"

[24]When the time came for her to give birth, there were twin boys in her womb. [25]The first to come out was red, and his whole body was like a hairy garment;[u] so they named him Esau.[a] [26]After this, his brother came out, with his hand grasping Esau's heel;[v] so he was named Jacob.[b][w] Isaac was sixty years old when Rebekah gave birth to them.

[27]The boys grew up, and Esau became a skillful hunter, a man of the open country, while Jacob was a quiet man, staying among the tents. [28]Isaac, who had a taste for wild game, loved Esau, but Rebekah loved Jacob.

[29]Once when Jacob was cooking some stew, Esau came in from the open country, famished. [30]He said to Jacob, "Quick, let me have some of that red stew! I'm famished!" (That is why he was also called Edom.[c])

[31]Jacob replied, "First sell me your birthright."

[32]"Look, I am about to die," Esau said. "What good is the birthright to me?"

[33]But Jacob said, "Swear to me first." So he swore an oath to him, selling his birthright[x] to Jacob.

[34]Then Jacob gave Esau some bread and some lentil stew. He ate and drank, and then got up and left.

So Esau despised his birthright.

2. Isaac and Abimelech

26 Now there was a famine in the land[y]—besides the earlier famine of Abraham's time—and Isaac went to Abimelech king of the Philistines in Gerar. [z] [2]The LORD appeared[a] to Isaac and said, "Do not go down to Egypt; live in the land where I tell you to live.[b] [3]Stay in

[a]*25 Esau* may mean *hairy*; he was also called Edom, which means *red*.   [b]*26 Jacob* means *he grasps the heel* (figuratively, *he deceives*).   [c]*30 Edom* means *red*.

25:23
[t]Ge 27:29, 40; Mal 1:3; Ro 9:11-12*

25:25
[u]Ge 27:11

25:26
[v]Hos 12:3
[w]Ge 27:36

25:33
[x]Heb 12:16

26:1
[y]Ge 12:10
[z]Ge 20:1

26:2
[a]Ge 12:7
[b]Ge 12:1

25:21 As Isaac pleaded with God for children, so the Bible encourages us to ask and even plead for our most personal and important requests. God wants to grant our requests, but he wants us to ask him. Even then, as Isaac learned, God may decide to withhold his answer for a while in order to (1) deepen our insight into what we really need, (2) broaden our appreciation for his answers, or (3) allow us to mature so we can use his gifts more wisely.

ISAAC'S MOVE TO GERAR

Isaac had settled near Beer Lahai Roi ("the well of the Living One who sees me"), where his sons, Jacob and Esau, were born. A famine drove him to Gerar. But when he became wealthy, his jealous neighbors asked him to leave. From Gerar he moved to Beersheba.

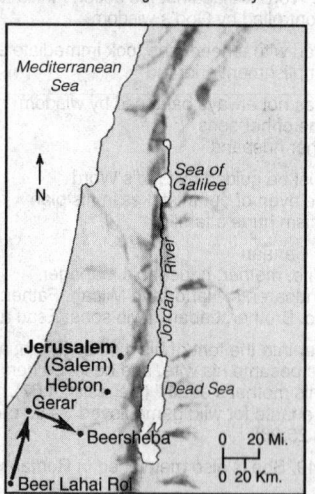

Mediterranean Sea
N
Sea of Galilee
Jordan River
Jerusalem (Salem)
Hebron
Gerar
Dead Sea
Beersheba
Beer Lahai Roi
0   20 Mi.
0   20 Km.

25:31 A birthright was a special honor given to the firstborn son. It included a double portion of the family inheritance along with the honor of one day becoming the family's leader. The oldest son could sell his birthright or give it away if he chose, but in so doing, he would lose both material goods and his leadership position. By trading his birthright, Esau showed complete disregard for the spiritual blessings that would have come his way if he had kept it. In effect, Esau "despised" his birthright (25:34).

25:32, 33 Esau traded the lasting benefits of his birthright for the immediate pleasure of food. He acted on impulse, satisfying his immediate desires without pausing to consider the long-range consequences of what he was about to do. We can fall into the same trap. When we see something we want, our first impulse is to get it. At first we feel intensely satisfied and sometimes even powerful because we have obtained what we set out to get. But immediate pleasure often loses sight of the future. We can avoid making Esau's mistake by comparing the short-term satisfaction with its long-range consequences before we act.

Esau exaggerated his hunger. "I am about to die," he said. This thought made his choice much easier because if he was starving, what good was an inheritance anyway? The pressure of the moment distorted his perspective and made his decision seem urgent. We often experience similar pressures. For example, when we feel sexual pressure, a marriage vow may seem unimportant. We might feel such great pressure in one area that nothing else seems to matter and we lose our perspective. Getting through that short, pressure-filled moment is often the most difficult part of overcoming a temptation.

26:1 The Philistines would become some of Israel's fiercest enemies. The Philistines were one group of a number of migrat-

26:3
*c*Ge 12:2; 22:16-18
*d*Ge 12:7; 13:15

26:4
*e*Ge 15:5; 22:17

26:7
*f*Ge 12:13; 20:2, 12

this land for a while, and I will be with you and will bless you. *c* For to you and your descendants I will give all these lands *d* and will confirm the oath I swore to your father Abraham. 4 I will make your descendants as numerous as the stars in the sky *e* and will give them all these lands, and through your offspring *a* all nations on earth will be blessed, 5 because Abraham obeyed me and kept my requirements, my commands, my decrees and my laws." 6 So Isaac stayed in Gerar.

7 When the men of that place asked him about his wife, he said, "She is my sister, *f*" because he was afraid to say, "She is my wife." He thought, "The men of this place might kill me on account of Rebekah, because she is beautiful."

8 When Isaac had been there a long time, Abimelech king of the Philistines looked down from a window and saw Isaac caressing his wife Rebekah. 9 So Abimelech summoned Isaac and said, "She is really your wife! Why did you say, 'She is my sister'?"

Isaac answered him, "Because I thought I might lose my life on account of her."

*a*4 Or *seed*

ESAU

Common sense isn't all that common. In fact, the common thread in many decisions is that they don't make sense. Esau's life was filled with choices he must have regretted bitterly. He appears to have been a person who found it hard to consider consequences, reacting to the need of the moment without realizing what he was giving up to meet that need. Trading his birthright for a bowl of stew was the clearest example of this weakness. He also chose wives in direct opposition to his parents' wishes. He learned the hard way.

What are you willing to trade for the things you want? Do you find yourself, at times, willing to negotiate *anything* for what you feel you need *now*? Do your family, spouse, integrity, body, or soul get included in these deals? Do you sometimes feel that the important parts of life escaped while you were grabbing for something else?

If so, your initial response, like Esau's, may be deep anger. In itself that isn't wrong, as long as you direct the energy of that anger toward a solution and not toward yourself or others as the cause of the problem. Your greatest need is to find a focal point other than "what I need now." The only worthy focal point is God. A relationship with him will not only give an ultimate purpose to your life; it will also be a daily guideline for living. Meet him in the pages of the Bible.

Strengths and accomplishments:	• Ancestor of the Edomites • Known for his archery skill • Able to forgive after explosive anger
Weaknesses and mistakes:	• When faced with important decisions, tended to choose according to the immediate need rather than the long-range effect • Angered his parents by poor marriage choices
Lessons from his life:	• God allows certain events in our lives to accomplish his overall purposes, but we are still responsible for our actions • Consequences are important to consider • It is possible to have great anger and yet not sin
Vital statistics:	• Where: Canaan • Occupation: Skillful hunter • Relatives: Parents: Isaac and Rebekah. Brother: Jacob. Wives: Judith, Basemath, and Mahalath.
Key verses:	"Make every effort to live in peace with all men and to be holy; without holiness no one will see the Lord. See to it that no one misses the grace of God and that no bitter root grows up to cause trouble and defile many. See that no one is sexually immoral, or is godless like Esau, who for a single meal sold his inheritance rights as the oldest son. Afterward, as you know, when he wanted to inherit this blessing, he was rejected. He could bring about no change of mind, though he sought the blessing with tears" (Hebrews 12:14–17).

Esau's story is told in Genesis 25—36. He is also mentioned in Malachi 1:2, 3; Romans 9:13; Hebrews 12:16, 17.

---

ing sea peoples from the Aegean Sea who had settled in Palestine. They arrived by way of Crete and Cyprus and were used as mercenaries by Canaanite rulers. These people, living along the southwest coast, were few but ferocious in battle. Although friendly to Isaac, this small group was the forerunner of the nation that would plague Israel during the time of Joshua, the judges, and David. This King Abimelech was not the same Abimelech that Abraham encountered (chapter 22). *Abimelech* may have been a dynastic name of the Philistine rulers.

26:7–11 Isaac was afraid that the men in Gerar would kill him to get his beautiful wife, Rebekah. So he lied, claiming that Rebekah was his sister. Where did he learn that trick? He may have known about the actions of his father, Abraham (see 12:10–14 and 20:1–4). Parents help shape the world's future by the way they shape their children's values. The first step toward helping children live rightly is for the parents to live rightly. Your actions are often copied by those closest to you. What kind of example are you setting for your children?

10 Then Abimelech said, "What is this you have done to us? *g* One of the men might well have slept with your wife, and you would have brought guilt upon us."

11 So Abimelech gave orders to all the people: "Anyone who molests this man or his wife shall surely be put to death."

12 Isaac planted crops in that land and the same year reaped a hundredfold, because the LORD blessed him. *h* 13 The man became rich, and his wealth continued to grow until he became very wealthy. 14 He had so many flocks and herds and servants that the Philistines envied him. 15 So all the wells *i* that his father's servants had dug in the time of his father Abraham, the Philistines stopped up, filling them with earth.

16 Then Abimelech said to Isaac, "Move away from us; you have become too powerful for us."

17 So Isaac moved away from there and encamped in the Valley of Gerar and settled there. 18 Isaac reopened the wells that had been dug in the time of his father Abraham, which the Philistines had stopped up after Abraham died, and he gave them the same names his father had given them.

19 Isaac's servants dug in the valley and discovered a well of fresh water there. 20 But the herdsmen of Gerar quarreled with Isaac's herdsmen and said, "The water is ours!" So he named the well Esek, *a* because they disputed with him. 21 Then they dug another well, but they quarreled over that one also; so he named it Sitnah. *b* 22 He moved on from there and dug another well, and no one quarreled over it. He named it Rehoboth, *c* saying, "Now the LORD has given us room and we will flourish *j* in the land."

23 From there he went up to Beersheba. 24 That night the LORD appeared to him and said, "I am the God of your father Abraham. *k* Do not be afraid, for I am with you; I will bless you and will increase the number of your descendants for the sake of my servant Abraham." *l*

25 Isaac built an altar *m* there and called on the name of the LORD. There he pitched his tent, and there his servants dug a well.

26 Meanwhile, Abimelech had come to him from Gerar, with Ahuzzath his personal adviser and Phicol the commander of his forces. *n* 27 Isaac asked them, "Why have you come to me, since you were hostile to me and sent me away?"

28 They answered, "We saw clearly that the LORD was with you; *o* so we said, 'There ought to be a sworn agreement between us'—between us and you. Let us make a treaty with you 29 that you will do us no harm, just as we did not molest you but always treated you well and sent you away in peace. And now you are blessed by the LORD."

30 Isaac then made a feast for them, and they ate and drank. 31 Early the next morning the men swore an oath *p* to each other. Then Isaac sent them on their way, and they left him in peace.

32 That day Isaac's servants came and told him about the well they had dug. They said, "We've found water!" 33 He called it Shibah, *d* and to this day the name of the town has been Beersheba. *e*

34 When Esau was forty years old, he married Judith daughter of Beeri the Hittite, and also Basemath daughter of Elon the Hittite. *q* 35 They were a source of grief to Isaac and Rebekah. *r*

a *20 Esek* means *dispute.*   b *21 Sitnah* means *opposition.*   c *22 Rehoboth* means *room.*   d *33 Shibah* can mean *oath* or *seven.*   e *33 Beersheba* can mean *well of the oath* or *well of seven.*

26:10
g Ge 20:9

26:12
h ver 3

26:15
i Ge 21:30

26:22
j Ge 17:6

26:24
k Ge 24:12
l Ge 17:7

26:25
m Ge 12:7, 8; 13:4, 18; Ps 116:17

26:26
n Ge 21:22

26:28
o Ge 21:22

26:31
p Ge 21:31

26:34
q Ge 36:2

26:35
r Ge 27:46

26:12-16 God kept his promise to bless Isaac. The neighboring Philistines grew jealous because everything Isaac did seemed to go right. So they filled his wells with dirt and tried to get rid of him. Jealousy is a dividing force strong enough to tear apart the mightiest of nations or the closest of friends. It forces you to separate yourself from what you were longing for in the first place. When you find yourself becoming jealous of others, try thanking God for their good fortune. Before striking out in anger, consider what you could lose—a friend, a job, a spouse?

26:17, 18 The desolate Gerar area was located on the edge of a desert. Water was as precious as gold. A person who dug a well was staking a claim to the land. Some wells had locks to keep thieves from stealing the water. To "stop" or plug up someone's well was an act of war; it was one of the most serious crimes in the land. Isaac had every right to fight back when the Philistines ruined his wells, yet he chose to keep the peace. In the end, the Philistines respected him for his patience.

26:17-22 Three times Isaac and his men dug new wells. When the first two disputes arose, Isaac moved on. Finally room was available for everyone. Rather than start a huge conflict, Isaac compromised for the sake of peace. Would you be willing to forsake an important position or valuable possession to keep peace? Ask God for the wisdom to know when to withdraw and when to stand and fight.

26:26-31 With his enemies wanting to make a peace treaty, Isaac was quick to respond, turning the occasion into a celebration. We should be just as receptive to those who want to make peace with us. When God's influence in our lives attracts people—even enemies—we must take the opportunity to reach out to them with God's love.

26:34, 35 Esau married pagan women, and this upset his parents greatly. Most parents can be a storehouse of good advice, because they have a lifetime of insight into their children's character. You may not agree with everything your parents say, but at least talk with them and listen carefully. This will help avoid the hard feelings Esau experienced.

3. Jacob gets Isaac's blessing

27 When Isaac was old and his eyes were so weak that he could no longer see, he called for Esau his older son and said to him, "My son."

"Here I am," he answered.

27:3
s Ge 25:27

²Isaac said, "I am now an old man and don't know the day of my death. ³Now then, get your weapons—your quiver and bow—and go out to the open country s to hunt some wild game for me. ⁴Prepare me the kind of tasty food I like and bring it to me to eat, so that I may give you my blessing before I die."

JACOB

Abraham, Isaac, and Jacob are among the most significant people in the Old Testament. It is important to realize that this significance is not based upon their personal characters, but upon the character of God. They were all men who earned the grudging respect and even fear of their peers; they were wealthy and powerful, and yet each was capable of lying, deceit, and selfishness. They were not the perfect heroes we might have expected; instead, they were just like us, trying to please God, but often falling short.

Jacob was the third link in God's plan to start a nation from Abraham. The success of that plan was more often in spite of than because of Jacob's life. Before Jacob was born, God promised that his plan would be worked out through Jacob and not his twin brother, Esau. Although Jacob's methods were not always respectable, his skill, determination, and patience have to be admired. As we follow him from birth to death, we are able to see God's work.

Jacob's life had four stages, each marked by a personal encounter with God. In the first stage, Jacob lived up to his name, which means "he grasps the heel" (figuratively, "he deceives"). He grabbed Esau's heel at birth, and by the time he fled from home, he had also grabbed his brother's birthright and blessing. During his flight, God first appeared to him. Not only did God confirm to Jacob his blessing, but he awakened in Jacob a personal knowledge of himself. In the second stage, Jacob experienced life from the other side, being manipulated and deceived by Laban. But there is a curious change: the Jacob of stage one would simply have left Laban, whereas the Jacob of stage two, after deciding to leave, waited six years for God's permission. In the third stage, Jacob was in a new role as grabber. This time, by the Jordan River, he grabbed on to God and wouldn't let go. He realized his dependence on the God who had continued to bless him. His relationship to God became essential to his life, and his name was changed to Israel, "he struggles with God." Jacob's last stage of life was to be grabbed—God achieved a firm hold on him. In responding to Joseph's invitation to come to Egypt, Jacob was clearly unwilling to make a move without God's approval.

Can you think of times when God has made himself known to you? Do you allow yourself to meet him as you study his Word? What difference have these experiences made in your life? Are you more like the young Jacob, forcing God to track you down in the desert of your own plans and mistakes? Or are you more like the Jacob who placed his desires and plans before God for his approval before taking any action?

Strengths and accomplishments:	• Father of the 12 tribes of Israel • Third in the Abrahamic line of God's plan • Determined, willing to work long and hard for what he wanted • Good businessman
Weaknesses and mistakes:	• When faced with conflict, relied on his own resources rather than going to God for help • Tended to accumulate wealth for its own sake
Lessons from his life:	• Security does not lie in the accumulation of goods • All human intentions and actions—for good or evil—are woven by God into his ongoing plan
Vital statistics:	• Where: Canaan • Occupation: Shepherd, livestock owner • Relatives: Parents: Isaac and Rebekah. Brother: Esau. Father-in-law: Laban. Wives: Rachel and Leah. Twelve sons and one daughter are mentioned in the Bible.
Key verse:	"I am with you and will watch over you wherever you go, and I will bring you back to this land. I will not leave you until I have done what I have promised you" (Genesis 28:15).

Jacob's story is told in Genesis 25—50. He is also mentioned in Hosea 12:2–5; Matthew 1:2; 22:32; Acts 3:13; 7:46; Romans 9:11–13; 11:26; Hebrews 11:9, 20, 21.

⁵Now Rebekah was listening as Isaac spoke to his son Esau. When Esau left for the open country to hunt game and bring it back, ⁶Rebekah said to her son Jacob, "Look, I overheard your father say to your brother Esau, ⁷'Bring me some game and prepare me some tasty food to eat, so that I may give you my blessing in the presence of the LORD before I die.' ⁸Now, my son, listen carefully and do what I tell you: ᵗ ⁹Go out to the flock and bring me two choice young goats, so I can prepare some tasty food for your father, just the way he likes it. ¹⁰Then take it to your father to eat, so that he may give you his blessing before he dies."

¹¹Jacob said to Rebekah his mother, "But my brother Esau is a hairy man,ᵘ and I'm a man with smooth skin. ¹²What if my father touches me?ᵛ I would appear to be tricking him and would bring down a curse on myself rather than a blessing."

¹³His mother said to him, "My son, let the curse fall on me. Just do what I say; go and get them for me."

¹⁴So he went and got them and brought them to his mother, and she prepared some tasty food, just the way his father liked it. ¹⁵Then Rebekah took the best clothes ᵂ of Esau her older son, which she had in the house, and put them on her younger son Jacob. ¹⁶She also covered his hands and the smooth part of his neck with the goatskins. ¹⁷Then she handed to her son Jacob the tasty food and the bread she had made.

¹⁸He went to his father and said, "My father."

"Yes, my son," he answered. "Who is it?"

¹⁹Jacob said to his father, "I am Esau your firstborn. I have done as you told me. Please sit up and eat some of my game so that you may give me your blessing."ˣ

²⁰Isaac asked his son, "How did you find it so quickly, my son?"

"The LORD your God gave me success," he replied.

²¹Then Isaac said to Jacob, "Come near so I can touch you,ʸ my son, to know whether you really are my son Esau or not."

²²Jacob went close to his father Isaac, who touched him and said, "The voice is the voice of Jacob, but the hands are the hands of Esau." ²³He did not recognize him, for his hands were hairy like those of his brother Esau; ᶻ so he blessed him. ²⁴"Are you really my son Esau?" he asked.

"I am," he replied.

²⁵Then he said, "My son, bring me some of your game to eat, so that I may give you my blessing."ᵃ

Jacob brought it to him and he ate; and he brought some wine and he drank. ²⁶Then his father Isaac said to him, "Come here, my son, and kiss me."

²⁷So he went to him and kissed him ᵇ. When Isaac caught the smell of his clothes,ᶜ he blessed him and said,

> "Ah, the smell of my son
>   is like the smell of a field
>   that the LORD has blessed.
> ²⁸ May God give you of heaven's dewᵈ
>   and of earth's richness—
>   an abundance of grain and new wine.ᵉ

27:8
ᵗver 13, 43

27:11
ᵘGe 25:25

27:12
ᵛver 22

27:15
ᵂver 27

27:19
ˣver 4

27:21
ʸver 12

27:23
ᶻver 16

27:25
ᵃver 4

27:27
ᵇHeb 11:20
ᶜSS 4:11

27:28
ᵈDt 33:13
ᵉDt 33:28

27:5-10 When Rebekah learned that Isaac was preparing to bless Esau, she quickly devised a plan to trick him into blessing Jacob instead. Although God had already told her that Jacob would become the family leader (25:23–26), Rebekah took matters into her own hands. She resorted to doing something wrong to try to bring about what God had already said would happen. For Rebekah, the end justified the means. No matter how good we think our goals are, we should not attempt to achieve them by doing what is wrong. Would God approve of the methods you are using to accomplish your goals?

27:11, 12 How we react to a moral dilemma often exposes our real motives. Frequently we are more worried about getting caught than about doing what is right. Jacob did not seem concerned about the deceitfulness of his mother's plan; instead he was afraid of getting in trouble while carrying it out. If you are worried about getting caught, you are probably in a position that is less than honest. Let your fear of getting caught be a warning to do right. Jacob paid a huge price for carrying out this dishonest plan.

27:11-13 Jacob hesitated when he heard Rebekah's deceitful plan. Although he questioned it for the wrong reason (fear of getting caught), he protested and thus gave him one last chance to reconsider. But Rebekah had become so wrapped up in her plan that she no longer saw clearly what she was doing. Sin had trapped her and was degrading her character. Correcting yourself in the middle of doing wrong may bring hurt and disappointment, but it also will bring freedom from sin's control.

27:24 Although Jacob got the blessing he wanted, deceiving his father cost him dearly. These are some of the consequences of that deceit: (1) he never saw his mother again; (2) his brother wanted to kill him; (3) he was deceived by his uncle, Laban; (4) his family became torn by strife; (5) Esau became the founder of an enemy nation; (6) he was exiled from his family for years. Ironically, Jacob would have received the birthright and blessing anyway (25:23). Imagine how different his life would have been had he and his mother waited for God to work his way, in his time!

27:29
f Isa 49:7, 23
g Ge 9:25; 25:23
h Ge 12:3

²⁹ May nations serve you
　　and peoples bow down to you.*f*
Be lord over your brothers,
　　and may the sons of your mother bow down to you.*g*
May those who curse you be cursed
　　and those who bless you be blessed.*h*"

27:31
i ver 4

³⁰After Isaac finished blessing him and Jacob had scarcely left his father's presence, his brother Esau came in from hunting. ³¹He too prepared some tasty food and brought it to his father. Then he said to him, "My father, sit up and eat some of my game, so that you may give me your blessing."*i*

³²His father Isaac asked him, "Who are you?"

"I am your son," he answered, "your firstborn, Esau."

27:33
j Ge 28:3, 4;
Ro 11:29

³³Isaac trembled violently and said, "Who was it, then, that hunted game and brought it to me? I ate it just before you came and I blessed him—and indeed he will be blessed!*j*"

27:34
k Heb 12:17

³⁴When Esau heard his father's words, he burst out with a loud and bitter cry*k* and said to his father, "Bless me—me too, my father!"

³⁵But he said, "Your brother came deceitfully and took your blessing."

27:36
l Ge 25:26
m Ge 25:33

³⁶Esau said, "Isn't he rightly named Jacob*a* ?*l* He has deceived me these two times: He took my birthright,*m* and now he's taken my blessing!" Then he asked, "Haven't you reserved any blessing for me?"

27:37
n ver 28

³⁷Isaac answered Esau, "I have made him lord over you and have made all his relatives his servants, and I have sustained him with grain and new wine. *n* So what can I possibly do for you, my son?"

27:38
o Heb 12:17

³⁸Esau said to his father, "Do you have only one blessing, my father? Bless me too, my father!" Then Esau wept aloud. *o*

27:39
p ver 28

³⁹His father Isaac answered him,

"Your dwelling will be
　　away from the earth's richness,
　　away from the dew*p* of heaven above.

27:40
q Ge 25:23
r 2Ki 8:20-22

⁴⁰ You will live by the sword
　　and you will serve your brother.*q*
But when you grow restless,
　　you will throw his yoke
　　from off your neck.*r*"

Jacob Flees to Laban

⁴¹Esau held a grudge against Jacob because of the blessing his father had given him. He said to himself, "The days of mourning for my father are near; then I will kill my brother Jacob."

⁴²When Rebekah was told what her older son Esau had said, she sent for her younger son Jacob and said to him, "Your brother Esau is consoling himself with the thought of killing

27:43
s Ge 11:31

you. ⁴³Now then, my son, do what I say: Flee at once to my brother Laban in Haran. *s* ⁴⁴Stay with him for a while until your brother's fury subsides. ⁴⁵When your brother is no longer angry with you and forgets what you did to him, I'll send word for you to come back from there. Why should I lose both of you in one day?"

a 36 Jacob means *he grasps the heel* (figuratively, *he deceives*).

27:33 In ancient times, a person's word was binding (much like a written contract today), especially when it was a formal oath. This is why Isaac's blessing was irrevocable.

27:33-37 Before the father died, he performed a ceremony of blessing, in which he officially handed over the birthright to the rightful heir. Although the firstborn son was entitled to the birthright, it was not actually his until the blessing was pronounced. Before the blessing was given, the father could take the birthright away from the oldest son and give it to a more deserving son. But after the blessing was given, the birthright could no longer be taken away. This is why fathers usually waited until late in life to pronounce the blessing. Although Jacob had been given the birthright by his older brother years before, he still needed his father's blessing to make it binding.

27:41 Esau was so angry at Jacob that he failed to see his own wrong in giving away the birthright in the first place. Jealous anger blinds us from seeing the benefits we have and makes us dwell on what we don't have.

27:41 When Esau lost the valuable family blessing, his future suddenly changed. Reacting in anger, he decided to kill Jacob. When you lose something of great value, or if others conspire against you and succeed, anger is the first and most natural reaction. But you can control your feelings by (1) recognizing your reaction for what it is, (2) praying for strength, and (3) asking God for help to see the opportunities that even your bad situation may provide.

46 Then Rebekah said to Isaac, "I'm disgusted with living because of these Hittite women. If Jacob takes a wife from among the women of this land, from Hittite women like these, my life will not be worth living." *t*

28 So Isaac called for Jacob and blessed*a* him and commanded him: "Do not marry a Canaanite woman. *u* 2 Go at once to Paddan Aram,*b* to the house of your mother's father Bethuel. Take a wife for yourself there, from among the daughters of Laban, your mother's brother. 3 May God Almighty*c v* bless you and make you fruitful*w* and increase your numbers until you become a community of peoples. 4 May he give you and your descendants the blessing given to Abraham,*x* so that you may take possession of the land where you now live as an alien,*y* the land God gave to Abraham." 5 Then Isaac sent Jacob on his way, and he went to Paddan Aram, to Laban son of Bethuel the Aramean, the brother of Rebekah, who was the mother of Jacob and Esau.

6 Now Esau learned that Isaac had blessed Jacob and had sent him to Paddan Aram to take a wife from there, and that when he blessed him he commanded him, "Do not marry a Canaanite woman," 7 and that Jacob had obeyed his father and mother and had gone to Paddan Aram. 8 Esau then realized how displeasing the Canaanite women were to his father Isaac;*z* 9 so he went to Ishmael and married Mahalath, the sister of Nebaioth and daughter of Ishmael son of Abraham, in addition to the wives he already had.

F. THE STORY OF JACOB (28:10—36:43)
Jacob did everything, both right and wrong, with great zeal. He deceived his own brother, Esau, and his father Isaac. He wrestled with an angel and worked fourteen years to marry the woman he loved. Through Jacob we learn how a strong leader can also be a servant. We also see how wrong actions will always come back to haunt us.

1. Jacob starts a family
Jacob's Dream at Bethel

10 Jacob left Beersheba and set out for Haran. 11 When he reached a certain place, he stopped for the night because the sun had set. Taking one of the stones there, he put it under his head and lay down to sleep. 12 He had a dream in which he saw a stairway*d* resting on the earth, with its top reaching to heaven, and the angels of God were ascending and descending on it. *a* 13 There above it*e* stood the Lord, and he said: "I am the Lord, the God of your father Abraham and the God of Isaac. *b* I will give you and your descendants the land*c* on which you are lying. 14 Your descendants will be like the dust of the earth, and you*d* will spread out to the west and to the east, to the north and to the south. All peoples on earth will be blessed through you and your offspring. *e* 15 I am with you and will watch over you wherever you go, and I will bring you back to this land. I will not leave you until I have done what I have promised you."

16 When Jacob awoke from his sleep, he thought, "Surely the Lord is in this place, and I was not aware of it." 17 He was afraid and said, "How awesome is this place! *f* This is none other than the house of God; this is the gate of heaven."

a 1 Or *greeted*   *b 2* That is, Northwest Mesopotamia; also in verses 5, 6 and 7   *c 3* Hebrew *El-Shaddai*
d 12 Or *ladder*   *e 13* Or *There beside him*

27:46
t Ge 26:35

28:1
u Ge 24:3

28:3
v Ge 17:1
w Ge 17:6

28:4
x Ge 12:2, 3
y Ge 17:8

28:8
z Ge 26:35

28:12
a Jn 1:51

28:13
b Ge 26:24
c Ge 13:15

28:14
d Ge 26:4
e Ge 12:3; 18:18;
22:18; Gal 3:8

28:17
f Ex 3:5; Jos 5:15

28:9 Ishmael was Isaac's half brother, the son of Abraham and Hagar, Sarah's maidservant (16:1–4, 15). After marrying two foreign girls (26:34), Esau hoped his marriage into Ishmael's family would please his parents, Isaac and Rebekah.

28:10–15 God's covenant promise to Abraham and Isaac was offered to Jacob as well. But it was not enough to be Abraham's grandson; Jacob had to establish his own personal relationship with God. God has no grandchildren; each person must have a personal relationship with him. It is not enough to hear wonderful stories about Christians in your family. You need to become part of the story yourself (see Galatians 3:6, 7).

JACOB'S TRIP TO HARAN
After deceiving Esau, Jacob ran for his life, traveling more than 400 miles to Haran, where an uncle, Laban, lived. In Haran, Jacob married and started a family.

28:19
g Jdg 1:23, 26
28:20
h Ge 31:13
i ver 15
28:21
j Jdg 11:31
k Dt 26:17
28:22
l Ge 35:7, 14
m Ge 14:20;
Lev 27:30

[18]Early the next morning Jacob took the stone he had placed under his head and set it up as a pillar and poured oil on top of it. [19]He called that place Bethel,*a* though the city used to be called Luz.*g*

[20]Then Jacob made a vow,*h* saying, "If God will be with me and will watch over me*i* on this journey I am taking and will give me food to eat and clothes to wear [21]so that I return safely*j* to my father's house, then the LORD*b* will be my God*k* [22]and*c* this stone that I have set up as a pillar will be God's house,*l* and of all that you give me I will give you a tenth.*m*"

Jacob Arrives in Paddan Aram

29 Then Jacob continued on his journey and came to the land of the eastern peoples. [2]There he saw a well in the field, with three flocks of sheep lying near it because the flocks were watered from that well. The stone over the mouth of the well was large. [3]When all the flocks were gathered there, the shepherds would roll the stone away from the well's mouth and water the sheep. Then they would return the stone to its place over the mouth of the well.

[4]Jacob asked the shepherds, "My brothers, where are you from?"

"We're from Haran," they replied.

[5]He said to them, "Do you know Laban, Nahor's grandson?"

"Yes, we know him," they answered.

[6]Then Jacob asked them, "Is he well?"

"Yes, he is," they said, "and here comes his daughter Rachel with the sheep."

[7]"Look," he said, "the sun is still high; it is not time for the flocks to be gathered. Water the sheep and take them back to pasture."

[8]"We can't," they replied, "until all the flocks are gathered and the stone has been rolled away from the mouth of the well. Then we will water the sheep."

[9]While he was still talking with them, Rachel came with her father's sheep, for she was a shepherdess. [10]When Jacob saw Rachel daughter of Laban, his mother's brother, and Laban's sheep, he went over and rolled the stone away from the mouth of the well and

29:12
n Ge 24:28

watered his uncle's sheep. [11]Then Jacob kissed Rachel and began to weep aloud. [12]He had told Rachel that he was a relative of her father and a son of Rebekah. So she ran and told her father.*n*

29:13
o Ge 24:29
29:14
p Jdg 9:2

[13]As soon as Laban*o* heard the news about Jacob, his sister's son, he hurried to meet him. He embraced him and kissed him and brought him to his home, and there Jacob told him all these things. [14]Then Laban said to him, "You are my own flesh and blood."*p*

Jacob Marries Leah and Rachel

After Jacob had stayed with him for a whole month, [15]Laban said to him, "Just because you are a relative of mine, should you work for me for nothing? Tell me what your wages should be."

[16]Now Laban had two daughters; the name of the older was Leah, and the name of the younger was Rachel. [17]Leah had weak*d* eyes, but Rachel was lovely in form, and beautiful. [18]Jacob was in love with Rachel and said, "I'll work for you seven years in return for your younger daughter Rachel."

[19]Laban said, "It's better that I give her to you than to some other man. Stay here with

a 19 Bethel means *house of God.* *b 20,21* Or *Since God . . . father's house, the* LORD *c 21,22* Or *house, and the* LORD *will be my God,* *22then* *d 17* Or *delicate*

28:19 Bethel was about ten miles north of Jerusalem and 60 miles north of Beersheba, where Jacob left his family. This was where Abraham made one of his first sacrifices to God when he entered the land. At first, Bethel became an important center for worship; later, it was a center of idol worship. The prophet Hosea condemned its evil practices.

28:20–22 Was Jacob trying to bargain with God? It is possible that he, in his ignorance of how to worship and serve God, treated God like a servant who would perform a service for a tip. More likely, Jacob was not bargaining, but pledging his future to God. He may have been saying, in effect, "Because you have blessed me, I will follow you." Whether Jacob was bargaining or pledging, God blessed him. But God also had some difficult lessons for Jacob to learn.

29:18–27 It was the custom of the day for a man to present a dowry, or substantial gift, to the family of his future wife. This was to compensate the family for the loss of the girl. Jacob's dowry was not a material possession, for he had none to offer. Instead he agreed to work seven years for Laban. But there was another custom of the land that Laban did not tell Jacob. The older daughter had to be married first. By giving Jacob Leah and not Rachel, Laban tricked him into promising another seven years of hard work.

me." 20 So Jacob served seven years to get Rachel, but they seemed like only a few days to him because of his love for her.

21 Then Jacob said to Laban, "Give me my wife. My time is completed, and I want to lie with her. q"

22 So Laban brought together all the people of the place and gave a feast. r 23 But when evening came, he took his daughter Leah and gave her to Jacob, and Jacob lay with her. 24 And Laban gave his servant girl Zilpah to his daughter as her maidservant.

25 When morning came, there was Leah! So Jacob said to Laban, "What is this you have done to me? s I served you for Rachel, didn't I? Why have you deceived me? t"

26 Laban replied, "It is not our custom here to give the younger daughter in marriage before the older one. 27 Finish this daughter's bridal week; then we will give you the younger one also, in return for another seven years of work."

28 And Jacob did so. He finished the week with Leah, and then Laban gave him his daughter Rachel to be his wife. 29 Laban gave his servant girl Bilhah to his daughter Rachel as her maidservant. 30 Jacob lay with Rachel also, and he loved Rachel more than Leah. And he worked for Laban another seven years. u

Jacob's Children

31 When the LORD saw that Leah was not loved, v he opened her womb, w but Rachel was barren. 32 Leah became pregnant and gave birth to a son. She named him Reuben, a for she said, "It is because the LORD has seen my misery. x Surely my husband will love me now."

33 She conceived again, and when she gave birth to a son she said, "Because the LORD heard that I am not loved, he gave me this one too." So she named him Simeon. b

34 Again she conceived, and when she gave birth to a son she said, "Now at last my husband will become attached to me, because I have borne him three sons." So he was named Levi. c y

35 She conceived again, and when she gave birth to a son she said, "This time I will praise the LORD." So she named him Judah. d z Then she stopped having children.

30 When Rachel saw that she was not bearing Jacob any children, a she became jealous of her sister. So she said to Jacob, "Give me children, or I'll die!"

2 Jacob became angry with her and said, "Am I in the place of God, who has kept you from having children?" b

3 Then she said, "Here is Bilhah, my maidservant. Sleep with her so that she can bear children for me and that through her I too can build a family." c

4 So she gave him her servant Bilhah as a wife. Jacob slept with her, d 5 and she became pregnant and bore him a son. 6 Then Rachel said, "God has vindicated me; he has listened to my plea and given me a son." Because of this she named him Dan. e

a 32 Reuben sounds like the Hebrew for he has seen my misery; the name means see, a son.   b 33 Simeon probably means one who hears.   c 34 Levi sounds like and may be derived from the Hebrew for attached.   d 35 Judah sounds like and may be derived from the Hebrew for praise.   e 6 Dan here means he has vindicated.

29:21
q Jdg 15:1

29:22
r Jdg 14:10;
Jn 2:1-2

29:25
s Ge 12:18
t Ge 27:36

29:30
u Ge 31:41

29:31
v Dt 21:15-17
w Ge 11:30; 30:1;
Ps 127:3

29:32
x Ge 16:11; 31:42

29:34
y Ge 49:5-7

29:35
z Ge 49:8; Mt 1:2-3

30:1
a Ge 29:31;
1Sa 1:5-6

30:2
b Ge 16:2; 29:31

30:3
c Ge 16:2

30:4
d Ge 16:3-4

29:20–28 People often wonder if working a long time for something they desire is worth it. Jacob worked seven years to marry Rachel. After being tricked, he agreed to work seven more years for her (although he did get to marry Rachel shortly after he married Leah)! The most important goals and desires are worth working and waiting for. Movies and television have created the illusion that people have to wait only about an hour to solve their problems or get what they want. Don't be trapped into thinking the same is true in real life. Patience is hardest when we need it the most, but it is the key to achieving our goals.

29:23–25 Jacob was enraged when he learned that Laban had tricked him. The deceiver of Esau was now deceived himself. How natural it is for us to become upset at an injustice done to us while closing our eyes to the injustices we do to others. Sin has a way of coming back to haunt us.

29:28–30 Although Jacob was tricked by Laban, he kept his part of the bargain. There was more at stake than just Jacob's hurt. There was Rachel to think about, as well as God's plan for his life. When we are tricked by others, keeping our part of the bargain may still be wise. Nursing our wounds or plotting revenge makes us unable to see from God's perspective.

29:32 Today parents usually give their children names that sound good or have sentimental appeal. But the Old Testament portrays a more dynamic use of names. Parents often chose names that reflected the situation at the time of the birth. They sometimes hoped their children would fulfill the meaning of the names given them. Later the parents could look back and see if their grown children had lived up to their names. Sometimes a person's name was changed because his or her character and name did not match. This happened to Jacob ("he grasps the heel," figuratively, "he deceives"), whose name was changed to Israel ("he struggles with God"). Jacob's character had changed to the point that he was no longer seen as a deceiver, but as a God-honoring man.

30:3 Each of the three great patriarchs (Abraham, Isaac, and Jacob) had wives who had difficulty conceiving children. It is interesting to note how each man reacted to his wife's predicament. Abraham had relations with Sarah's maidservant in order to have his own child, thus introducing bitterness and jealousy into his family. Isaac, by contrast, prayed to God when his wife was barren. God eventually answered his prayers, and Rebekah had twin sons. Jacob, however, followed his grandfather's example and had children by his wives' maidservants, leading to sad and sometimes bitter consequences.

30:4–13 Rachel and Leah were locked in a cruel contest. In their

7 Rachel's servant Bilhah conceived again and bore Jacob a second son. 8 Then Rachel said, "I have had a great struggle with my sister, and I have won." So she named him Naphtali. a

30:9
e ver 4

9 When Leah saw that she had stopped having children, she took her maidservant Zilpah and gave her to Jacob as a wife. e 10 Leah's servant Zilpah bore Jacob a son. 11 Then Leah said, "What good fortune!" b So she named him Gad. c

30:13
f Lk 1:48

12 Leah's servant Zilpah bore Jacob a second son. 13 Then Leah said, "How happy I am! The women will call me happy." f So she named him Asher. d

14 During wheat harvest, Reuben went out into the fields and found some mandrake plants, which he brought to his mother Leah. Rachel said to Leah, "Please give me some of your son's mandrakes."

15 But she said to her, "Wasn't it enough that you took away my husband? Will you take my son's mandrakes too?"

"Very well," Rachel said, "he can sleep with you tonight in return for your son's mandrakes."

16 So when Jacob came in from the fields that evening, Leah went out to meet him. "You

a 8 *Naphtali* means *my struggle.*   b 11 Or *"A troop is coming!"*   c 11 *Gad* can mean *good fortune* or *a troop.*
d 13 *Asher* means *happy.*

RACHEL

History seems to repeat itself here. Twice a town well at Haran was the site of significant events in one family's story. It was here that Rebekah met Eliezer, Abraham's servant, who had come to find a wife for Isaac. Some 40 years later, Rebekah's son Jacob returned the favor by serving his cousin Rachel and her sheep from the same well. The relationship that developed between them not only reminds us that romance is not a modern invention, but also teaches us a few lessons about patience and love.

Jacob's love for Rachel was both patient and practical. Jacob had the patience to wait seven years for her, but he kept busy in the meantime. His commitment to Rachel kindled a strong loyalty within her. In fact, her loyalty to Jacob got out of hand and became self-destructive. She was frustrated by her barrenness and desperate to compete with her sister for Jacob's affection. She was trying to gain from Jacob what he had already given: devoted love.

Rachel's attempts to earn the unearnable are a picture of a much greater error we can make. Like her, we find ourselves trying somehow to earn love—God's love. But apart from his Word, we end up with one of two false ideas. Either we think we've been good enough to deserve his love or we recognize we aren't able to earn his love and assume that it cannot be ours. If the Bible makes no other point, it shouts this one: God loves us! His love had no beginning and is incredibly patient. All we need to do is respond, not try to earn what is freely offered. God has said in many ways, "I love you. I have demonstrated that love to you by all I've done for you. I have even sacrificed my Son, Jesus, to pay the price for what is unacceptable about you—your sin. Now, live because of my love. Respond to me; love me with your whole being; give yourself to me in thanksgiving, not as payment." Live life fully, in the freedom of knowing you are loved.

Strengths and accomplishments:	• She showed great loyalty to her family • She mothered Joseph and Benjamin after being barren for many years
Weaknesses and mistakes:	• Her envy and competitiveness marred her relationship with her sister, Leah • She was capable of dishonesty when she took her loyalty too far • She failed to recognize that Jacob's devotion was not dependent on her ability to have children
Lessons from her life:	• Loyalty must be controlled by what is true and right • Love is accepted, not earned
Vital statistics:	• Where: Haran • Occupation: Shepherdess, housewife • Relatives: Father: Laban. Aunt: Rebekah. Sister: Leah. Husband: Jacob. Sons: Joseph and Benjamin.
Key verse:	"So Jacob served seven years to get Rachel, but they seemed like only a few days to him because of his love for her" (Genesis 29:20).

Rachel's story is told in Genesis 29:1—35:20. She is also mentioned in Ruth 4:11.

---

race to have more children, they both gave their maidservants to Jacob as concubines. Jacob would have been wise to refuse, even though this was an accepted custom of the day. The fact that a custom is socially acceptable does not mean it is wise or right.

You will be spared much heartbreak if you look at the potential consequences, to you or others, of your actions. Are you doing anything now that might cause future problems?

must sleep with me," she said. "I have hired you with my son's mandrakes." So he slept with her that night.

[17] God listened to Leah, and she became pregnant and bore Jacob a fifth son. [18] Then Leah said, "God has rewarded me for giving my maidservant to my husband." So she named him Issachar.[a]

[19] Leah conceived again and bore Jacob a sixth son. [20] Then Leah said, "God has presented me with a precious gift. This time my husband will treat me with honor, because I have borne him six sons." So she named him Zebulun.[b]

[21] Some time later she gave birth to a daughter and named her Dinah.

[22] Then God remembered Rachel;[g] he listened to her and opened her womb.[h] [23] She became pregnant and gave birth to a son and said, "God has taken away my disgrace."[i] [24] She named him Joseph,[c] and said, "May the LORD add to me another son."[j]

Jacob's Flocks Increase

[25] After Rachel gave birth to Joseph, Jacob said to Laban, "Send me on my way[k] so I can go back to my own homeland. [26] Give me my wives and children, for whom I have served you,[l] and I will be on my way. You know how much work I've done for you."

[27] But Laban said to him, "If I have found favor in your eyes, please stay. I have learned by divination that[d] the LORD has blessed me because of you."[m] [28] He added, "Name your wages,[n] and I will pay them."

[29] Jacob said to him, "You know how I have worked for you and how your livestock has fared under my care. [30] The little you had before I came has increased greatly, and the LORD has blessed you wherever I have been. But now, when may I do something for my own household?"

[31] "What shall I give you?" he asked.

"Don't give me anything," Jacob replied. "But if you will do this one thing for me, I will go on tending your flocks and watching over them: [32] Let me go through all your flocks today and remove from them every speckled or spotted sheep, every dark-colored lamb and every spotted or speckled goat.[o] They will be my wages. [33] And my honesty will testify for me in the future, whenever you check on the wages you have paid me. Any goat in my possession that is not speckled or spotted, or any lamb that is not dark-colored, will be considered stolen."

[34] "Agreed," said Laban. "Let it be as you have said." [35] That same day he removed all the male goats that were streaked or spotted, and all the speckled or spotted female goats (all that had white on them) and all the dark-colored lambs, and he placed them in the care of his sons. [36] Then he put a three-day journey between himself and Jacob, while Jacob continued to tend the rest of Laban's flocks.

[37] Jacob, however, took fresh-cut branches from poplar, almond and plane trees and made white stripes on them by peeling the bark and exposing the white inner wood of the branches. [38] Then he placed the peeled branches in all the watering troughs, so that they would be directly in front of the flocks when they came to drink. When the flocks were in heat and came to drink, [39] they mated in front of the branches. And they bore young that were streaked or speckled or spotted. [40] Jacob set apart the young of the flock by themselves, but made the rest face the streaked and dark-colored animals that belonged to Laban. Thus he made separate flocks for himself and did not put them with Laban's animals. [41] Whenever the stronger females were in heat, Jacob would place the branches in the troughs in front of the animals so they would mate near the branches, [42] but if the animals were weak, he would not place them there. So the weak animals went to Laban and the strong ones to Jacob. [43] In this way the man grew exceedingly prosperous and came to own large flocks, and maidservants and menservants, and camels and donkeys.[p]

---

[a] 18 Issachar sounds like the Hebrew for reward.   [b] 20 Zebulun probably means honor.   [c] 24 Joseph means may he add.   [d] 27 Or possibly have become rich and

30:22
[g] 1Sa 1:19-20
[h] Ge 29:31

30:23
[i] Isa 4:1; Lk 1:25

30:24
[j] Ge 35:17

30:25
[k] Ge 24:54

30:26
[l] Ge 29:20, 30; Hos 12:12

30:27
[m] Ge 26:24; 39:3, 5

30:28
[n] Ge 29:15

30:32
[o] Ge 31:8, 12

30:43
[p] Ge 12:16; 13:2; 24:35; 26:13-14

30:22-24 Eventually God answered Rachel's prayers and gave her a child of her own. In the meantime, however, she had given her maidservant to Jacob. Trusting God when nothing seems to happen is difficult. But it is harder still to live with the consequences of taking matters into our own hands. Resist the temptation to think God has forgotten you. Have patience and courage to wait for God to act.

30:37-43 It is unclear what this method was or how it worked. Some say that there was a belief among herdsmen that vivid impressions at mating time influenced the offspring. Most likely, the selective breeding and God's promise of provision were the main reasons that Jacob's flocks increased.

31:41
k Ge 29:30
l ver 7

31:42
m ver 53
n Ge 29:32

31:44
o Ge 21:27; 26:28
p Jos 24:27

31:45
q Ge 28:18

31:49
r Jdg 11:29;
1Sa 7:5-6

31:50
s Jer 29:23; 42:5

31:53
t Ge 16:5

I worked for you fourteen years for your two daughters *k* and six years for your flocks, and you changed my wages ten times. *l* 42 If the God of my father, the God of Abraham and the Fear of Isaac, *m* had not been with me, you would surely have sent me away empty-handed. But God has seen my hardship and the toil of my hands, *n* and last night he rebuked you."

43 Laban answered Jacob, "The women are my daughters, the children are my children, and the flocks are my flocks. All you see is mine. Yet what can I do today about these daughters of mine, or about the children they have borne? 44 Come now, let's make a covenant, *o* you and I, and let it serve as a witness between us." *p*

45 So Jacob took a stone and set it up as a pillar. *q* 46 He said to his relatives, "Gather some stones." So they took stones and piled them in a heap, and they ate there by the heap. 47 Laban called it Jegar Sahadutha, *a* and Jacob called it Galeed. *b*

48 Laban said, "This heap is a witness between you and me today." That is why it was called Galeed. 49 It was also called Mizpah, *c r* because he said, "May the LORD keep watch between you and me when we are away from each other. 50 If you mistreat my daughters or if you take any wives besides my daughters, even though no one is with us, remember that God is a witness *s* between you and me."

51 Laban also said to Jacob, "Here is this heap, and here is this pillar I have set up between you and me. 52 This heap is a witness, and this pillar is a witness, that I will not go past this heap to your side to harm you and that you will not go past this heap and pillar to my side to harm me. 53 May the God of Abraham and the God of Nahor, the God of their father, judge between us." *t*

a 47 The Aramaic Jegar Sahadutha means witness heap.   *b 47 The Hebrew Galeed means witness heap.*
c 49 Mizpah means watchtower.

We're all selfish, but some of us have a real corner on the weakness. Laban's whole life was stamped by self-centeredness. His chief goal was to look out for himself. The way he treated others was controlled by that goal. He made profitable arrangements for his sister Rebekah's marriage to Isaac and used his daughters' lives as bargaining chips. Jacob eventually out-maneuvered Laban, but the older man was unwilling to admit defeat. His hold on Jacob was broken, but he still tried to maintain some kind of control by getting Jacob to promise to be gone for good. He realized that Jacob and Jacob's God were more than he could handle.

On the surface, we may find it difficult to identify with Laban. But his selfishness is one point we have in common. Like him, we often have a strong tendency to control people and events to our benefit. Our "good" reasons for treating others the way we do may simply be a thin cover on our self-centered motives. We may not even recognize our own selfishness. One way to discover it is to examine our willingness to admit we're wrong. Laban could not bring himself to do this. If you ever amaze yourself by what you say and do to avoid facing up to wrong actions, you are getting a glimpse of your selfishness in action. Recognizing selfishness is painful, but it is the first step on the road back to God.

Strengths and accomplishments:	• Controlled two generations of marriages in the Abrahamic family (Rebekah, Rachel, Leah) • Quick-witted
Weaknesses and mistakes:	• Manipulated others for his own benefit • Unwilling to admit wrongdoing • Benefited financially by using Jacob, but never fully benefited spiritually by knowing and worshiping Jacob's God
Lessons from his life:	• Those who set out to use people will eventually find themselves used • God's plan cannot be blocked
Vital statistics:	• Where: Haran • Occupation: Wealthy sheep breeder • Relatives: Father: Bethuel. Sister: Rebekah. Brother-in-law: Isaac. Daughters: Rachel and Leah. Son-in-law: Jacob.
Key verse:	"If the God of my father, the God of Abraham and the Fear of Isaac, had not been with me, you would surely have sent me away empty-handed. But God has seen my hardship and the toil of my hands, and last night he rebuked you" (Genesis 31:42).

Laban's story is told in Genesis 24:1—31:55.

---

and advancement, (3) enhances your reputation, (4) builds others' confidence in you, (5) gives you more experience and knowledge, and (6) develops your spiritual maturity.

31:49 To be binding, an agreement had to be witnessed by a third party. In this case, Jacob and Laban used God as their witness that they would keep their word.

So Jacob took an oath in the name of the Fear of his father Isaac.*u* 54 He offered a sacrifice there in the hill country and invited his relatives to a meal. After they had eaten, they spent the night there.

55 Early the next morning Laban kissed his grandchildren and his daughters and blessed them. Then he left and returned home.

Jacob Prepares to Meet Esau

32 Jacob also went on his way, and the angels of God met him. 2 When Jacob saw them, he said, "This is the camp of God!" So he named that place Mahanaim.*a*

3 Jacob sent messengers ahead of him to his brother Esau in the land of Seir, the country of Edom.*v* 4 He instructed them: "This is what you are to say to my master Esau: 'Your servant Jacob says, I have been staying with Laban and have remained there till now. 5 I have cattle and donkeys, sheep and goats, menservants and maidservants.*w* Now I am sending this message to my lord, that I may find favor in your eyes.*x*'"

6 When the messengers returned to Jacob, they said, "We went to your brother Esau, and now he is coming to meet you, and four hundred men are with him."*y*

7 In great fear and distress Jacob divided the people who were with him into two groups,*b* and the flocks and herds and camels as well. 8 He thought, "If Esau comes and attacks one group,*c* the group*c* that is left may escape."

9 Then Jacob prayed, "O God of my father Abraham, God of my father Isaac, O LORD, who said to me, 'Go back to your country and your relatives, and I will make you prosper,'*z* 10 I am unworthy of all the kindness and faithfulness*a* you have shown your servant. I had only my staff when I crossed this Jordan, but now I have become two groups. 11 Save me, I pray, from the hand of my brother Esau, for I am afraid he will come and attack me, and also the mothers with their children.*b* 12 But you have said, 'I will surely make you prosper and will make your descendants like the sand of the sea, which cannot be counted.*c*'"

13 He spent the night there, and from what he had with him he selected a gift*d* for his brother Esau: 14 two hundred female goats and twenty male goats, two hundred ewes and twenty rams, 15 thirty female camels with their young, forty cows and ten bulls, and twenty female donkeys and ten male donkeys. 16 He put them in the care of his servants, each herd by itself, and said to his servants, "Go ahead of me, and keep some space between the herds."

17 He instructed the one in the lead: "When my brother Esau meets you and asks, 'To whom do you belong, and where are you going, and who owns all these animals in front of you?' 18 then you are to say, 'They belong to your servant Jacob. They are a gift sent to my lord Esau, and he is coming behind us.'"

19 He also instructed the second, the third and all the others who followed the herds: "You are to say the same thing to Esau when you meet him. 20 And be sure to say, 'Your servant Jacob is coming behind us.'" For he thought, "I will pacify him with these gifts I am sending on ahead; later, when I see him, perhaps he will receive me." 21 So Jacob's gifts went on ahead of him, but he himself spent the night in the camp.

Jacob Wrestles With God

22 That night Jacob got up and took his two wives, his two maidservants and his eleven sons and crossed the ford of the Jabbok.*e* 23 After he had sent them across the stream, he sent over all his possessions. 24 So Jacob was left alone, and a man wrestled with him till daybreak. 25 When the man saw that he could not overpower him, he touched the socket of Jacob's hip so that his hip was wrenched as he wrestled with the man. 26 Then the man said, "Let me go, for it is daybreak."

a 2 Mahanaim means *two camps.*   *b 7* Or *camps;* also in verse 10   *c 8* Or *camp*

31:53
u ver 42

32:3
v Ge 25:30; 36:8, 9

32:5
w Ge 12:16; 30:43
x Ge 33:8, 10, 15

32:6
y Ge 33:1

32:9
z Ge 31:13

32:10
a Ge 24:27

32:11
b Ge 27:41

32:12
c Ge 28:13-15;
Hos 1:10

32:13
d Ge 43:11, 15, 25,
26; Pr 18:16

32:22
e Dt 2:37; 3:16

32:1 Why did angels of God meet Jacob? In Bible times, angels often intervened in human situations. Although angels usually would appear in human form, these angels must have looked different, for Jacob recognized them at once. The reason these angels met Jacob is unclear; but because of their visit, Jacob knew God was with him.

32:3 The last time Jacob had seen Esau, his older brother had been ready to kill him for stealing the family blessing (25:29— 27:42). Esau was so angry he had vowed to kill Jacob as soon

as their father, Isaac, died (27:41). Fearing their reunion, Jacob sent a messenger ahead with gifts. He hoped to buy Esau's favor.

32:9–12 How would you feel knowing you were about to meet the person you had cheated out of his most precious possession? Jacob had taken Esau's birthright (25:33) and his blessings (27:27–40). Now he was about to meet this brother for the first time in 20 years, and he was frantic with fear. He collected his thoughts, however, and decided to pray. When we face a difficult conflict, we can run about frantically or we can pause to pray. Which approach will be more effective?

32:26
f Hos 12:4

But Jacob replied, "I will not let you go unless you bless me." *f*

27 The man asked him, "What is your name?"

"Jacob," he answered.

32:28
g Ge 17:5; 35:10

28 Then the man said, "Your name will no longer be Jacob, but Israel,*a g* because you have struggled with God and with men and have overcome."

29 Jacob said, "Please tell me your name."

But he replied, "Why do you ask my name?" Then he blessed him there.

32:30
h Ge 16:13;
Ex 24:11; Jdg 6:22

30 So Jacob called the place Peniel,*b* saying, "It is because I saw God face to face,*h* and yet my life was spared."

a 28 Israel means *he struggles with God.*   *b 30 Peniel* means *face of God.*

LEAH

Leah lived in a blunt and painful world. She observed it with sad eyes. Women in her day were considered property. Daughters were traded by their fathers in business deals. Leah's father Laban gave her to a man who did not love her. Perhaps it would be more fair to say that Jacob didn't love her as much as he loved her younger sister Rachel. But God loved her.

Leah apparently could not see very well, but her sister looked great! In fact, Jacob agreed to work seven years for Rachel's hand in marriage. Jacob kept his end of the contract, but Laban deceived his future son-in-law. He substituted Leah for Rachel under the wedding veil. By the time Jacob knew a switch had been made, he was already married. Laban excused his deception by citing a local custom that a younger daughter could not marry ahead of an older one. After a brief confrontation, Laban agreed to give Rachel to Jacob in exchange for another seven years of work. And although Leah was not his first choice, Jacob accepted her as his wife.

Leah revealed how she felt toward Jacob in the name she gave their first son, Reuben. The name expressed her desire to be noticed by her husband. Because Leah and Rachel competed for Jacob's attention, there was constant friction in the family. They measured their worth against each other by their ability to bear children. Leah was winning the fertility contest handily when Rachel died bearing her second child, Benjamin. Leah's victory carried little satisfaction. The Scriptures mention no more children born to Jacob. Ironically, the greatest honor Jacob finally gave Leah was to bury her with his parents and grandparents in the cave at Machpelah (Genesis 49:31).

When we fail to live at peace with the important people in our lives, we leave behind a tragic story. Although God loved Leah, we are not told of her response to him. Her inability to appreciate God's love also made her unable to love others. When we struggle to love others, we can be helped by reflecting on the fact that God loves us. If God's love doesn't free us, we need to think again!

Strengths and accomplishments:	• Bore Jacob six sons and one daughter • Collaborated with Jacob and Rachel to outwit Laban's ruthless manipulation • She is honored as one of the mothers of Israel (Ruth 4:11)
Weaknesses and mistakes:	• Envied her sister Rachel over Jacob's love • Competed with Rachel for Jacob's attention and respect
Lessons from her life:	• Even wrong motives can't entirely cover the truth—Leah gave God specific credit in the birth of five of her sons • Opportunities for joy can be missed through wrong motives toward others • God has a way of using unexpected people to accomplish his purposes and plans
Vital statistics:	• Where: Paddan Aram • Occupation: Wife and mother • Relatives: Father: Laban. Husband: Jacob. Daughter: Dinah. Sons: Reuben, Simeon, Levi, Judah, Issachar, and Zebulun.
Key verse:	"Then Leah said, 'God has presented me with a precious gift. This time my husband will treat me with honor, because I have borne him six sons.' So she named him Zebulun" (Genesis 30:20).

Leah's story is told in Genesis 29—35. She is also mentioned in Genesis 46:15, 18, 31 and Ruth 4:11.

32:26 Jacob continued this wrestling match all night just to be blessed. He was persistent. God encourages persistence in all areas of our lives, including the spiritual. Where in your spiritual life do you need more persistence? Strong character develops as you struggle through tough conditions.

32:27–29 God gave many Bible people new names (Abraham, Sarah, Peter). Their new names were symbols of how God had changed their lives. Here we see how Jacob's character had changed. Jacob, the ambitious deceiver, became Israel, the one who struggles with God and overcomes.

[31] The sun rose above him as he passed Peniel,[a] and he was limping because of his hip. [32] Therefore to this day the Israelites do not eat the tendon attached to the socket of the hip, because the socket of Jacob's hip was touched near the tendon.

Jacob Meets Esau

33 Jacob looked up and there was Esau, coming with his four hundred men;[i] so he divided the children among Leah, Rachel and the two maidservants. [2] He put the maidservants and their children in front, Leah and her children next, and Rachel and Joseph in the rear. [3] He himself went on ahead and bowed down to the ground[j] seven times as he approached his brother.

[4] But Esau ran to meet Jacob and embraced him; he threw his arms around his neck and kissed him. And they wept.[k] [5] Then Esau looked up and saw the women and children. "Who are these with you?" he asked.

Jacob answered, "They are the children God has graciously given your servant.[l]"

[6] Then the maidservants and their children approached and bowed down. [7] Next, Leah and her children came and bowed down. Last of all came Joseph and Rachel, and they too bowed down.

[8] Esau asked, "What do you mean by all these droves I met?"[m]

"To find favor in your eyes, my lord," he said.

[9] But Esau said, "I already have plenty, my brother. Keep what you have for yourself."

[10] "No, please!" said Jacob. "If I have found favor in your eyes, accept this gift from me. For to see your face is like seeing the face of God, now that you have received me favorably. [11] Please accept the present[n] that was brought to you, for God has been gracious to me and I have all I need." And because Jacob insisted, Esau accepted it.

[12] Then Esau said, "Let us be on our way; I'll accompany you."

[13] But Jacob said to him, "My lord knows that the children are tender and that I must care for the ewes and cows that are nursing their young. If they are driven hard just one day, all the animals will die. [14] So let my lord go on ahead of his servant, while I move along slowly at the pace of the droves before me and that of the children, until I come to my lord in Seir.[o]"

[15] Esau said, "Then let me leave some of my men with you."

"But why do that?" Jacob asked. "Just let me find favor in the eyes of my lord."

[a] *31* Hebrew *Penuel*, a variant of *Peniel*

33:1
i Ge 32:6

33:3
j Ge 42:6

33:4
k Ge 45:14-15

33:5
l Ge 48:9; Ps 127:3; Isa 8:18

33:8
m Ge 32:14-16

33:11
n 1Sa 25:27

33:14
o Ge 32:3

33:1–11 Jacob must have been amazed to see Esau's change of heart when the two brothers met again (33:10). Esau was no longer bitter over losing his birthright and blessing (27:36–41); instead, he was content with what he had. Life can bring us some bad situations. We can feel cheated, as Esau did, but we don't have to remain bitter. We can remove bitterness from our lives by honestly expressing our feelings to God, forgiving those who have wronged us, and being content with what we have.

JACOB'S JOURNEY TO SHECHEM After a joyful reunion with his brother, Esau (who journeyed from Edom), Jacob set up camp in Succoth. Later he moved on to Shechem where his daughter, Dinah, was raped and two of his sons took revenge on the city.

33:3 Bowing to the ground seven times was the sign of respect given to a king. Jacob was taking every precaution as he met Esau, hoping to dispel any thoughts of revenge.

33:4 Esau greeted his brother, Jacob, with a great hug. Imagine how difficult this must have been for a man who once actually plotted his brother's death (27:41). But time away from each other allowed the bitter wounds to heal. With the passing of time, each brother was able to see that their relationship was more important than their real estate.

33:11 Why did Jacob send gifts ahead for Esau? In Bible times, gifts were given for several reasons. (1) This may have been a bribe. Gifts are still given to win someone over or buy his or her support. Esau may first have refused Jacob's gifts (33:9) because he didn't want or need a bribe. He had already forgiven Jacob, and he had ample wealth of his own. (2) This may have been an expression of affection. (3) It may have been the customary way of greeting someone before an important meeting. Such gifts were often related to a person's occupation. This explains why Jacob sent Esau—who was a herdsman—sheep, goats, and cattle.

33:14-17 Why did Jacob imply that he was going to Seir but then stop at Succoth? We don't know the answer, but perhaps Jacob decided to stop there as they journeyed because Succoth is a beautiful site on the eastern side of the Jordan River. Whatever the reason, Jacob and Esau parted in peace. Then they lived fairly close to each other until after their father's death (36:6–8).

33:17
p Jdg 8:5, 6,
8, 14-16

33:18
q Jos 24:1; Jdg 9:1

33:19
r Jos 24:32
s Jn 4:5

34:1
t Ge 30:21

34:6
u Jdg 14:2-5

¹⁶So that day Esau started on his way back to Seir. ¹⁷Jacob, however, went to Succoth,*p* where he built a place for himself and made shelters for his livestock. That is why the place is called Succoth.*a*

¹⁸After Jacob came from Paddan Aram,*b* he arrived safely at the*c* city of Shechem*q* in Canaan and camped within sight of the city. ¹⁹For a hundred pieces of silver,*d* he bought from the sons of Hamor, the father of Shechem,*r* the plot of ground*s* where he pitched his tent. ²⁰There he set up an altar and called it El Elohe Israel.*e*

Dinah and the Shechemites

34 Now Dinah,*t* the daughter Leah had borne to Jacob, went out to visit the women of the land. ²When Shechem son of Hamor the Hivite, the ruler of that area, saw her, he took her and violated her. ³His heart was drawn to Dinah daughter of Jacob, and he loved the girl and spoke tenderly to her. ⁴And Shechem said to his father Hamor, "Get me this girl as my wife."

⁵When Jacob heard that his daughter Dinah had been defiled, his sons were in the fields with his livestock; so he kept quiet about it until they came home.

⁶Then Shechem's father Hamor went out to talk with Jacob.*u* ⁷Now Jacob's sons had come in from the fields as soon as they heard what had happened. They were filled with

a 17 Succoth means *shelters.* *b 18* That is, Northwest Mesopotamia *c 18* Or *arrived at Shalem, a* *d 19* Hebrew *hundred kesitahs;* a kesitah was a unit of money of unknown weight and value. *e 20 El Elohe Israel* can mean *God, the God of Israel* or *mighty is the God of Israel.*

As far as we know, Dinah was Jacob's only daughter. She lived among ten older and two younger brothers. She grew up in a family rocked by struggle between two sisters married to the same man. Dinah's mother, Leah, knew that Jacob loved her sister and rival Rachel. We don't know how the bitterness and jealousy between these women affected the only girl-child in the family. By the time Dinah was a teenager, her family was living in Shechem, a town north of Bethel and Jerusalem in the promised land.

Apparently no one really paid much attention to Dinah until she went out for a walk in town one day. She was noticed and raped by Shechem, the son of the ruler of the city. Violated and shamed, Dinah found herself in the center of a family crisis. Shechem asked his father to arrange a marriage with Dinah. But in Jacob's and his sons' eyes, Dinah had been damaged and their family had been insulted. Jacob failed to provide any fatherly leadership in this situation and his sons took matters into their own hands. The results were treacherous and bloody.

In all of this, the victim was overlooked. Dinah was neither comforted nor consulted. Instead, she was treated with almost as much disrespect by her family as she was by Shechem. By handing her over to Shechem, they used Dinah as bait in a trap that led to the murder of all the men in the village. Dinah's brothers profited from the massacre of Shechem. Jacob was angry at his sons for their actions, but did nothing. Meanwhile, Dinah slipped back into oblivion. Her story reminds us of the tragedies that occur when family members are careless with each other. Someone ends up paying a high price.

You probably know someone who can identify closely with Dinah. Perhaps you have experienced that same anonymity as a victim who was unnoticed or forgotten. Remember several glimmers of hope: Even when everyone else forgets, God doesn't; when no one seems to notice, God sees; when no one seems to care, God cares; when you feel all alone, you aren't. And one of the first lessons God will teach you as you depend on him is that there are others who also care and are willing to help. Begin to speak to God today in prayer about your past.

Strengths and accomplishments:	• Jacob's only daughter
Lessons from her life:	• Thoughtless avengers often hurt the original victims a second time • Family members can be trampled in the rush for family honor
Vital statistics:	• Where: Paddan Aram • Relatives: Parents: Jacob and Leah. Twelve brothers. Aunt: Rachel. Grandparents: Isaac and Rebekah, Laban. Uncle: Esau.
Key verse:	"Some time later she gave birth to a daughter and named her Dinah" (Genesis 30:21).

Dinah's story is told in Genesis 34. Her birth is mentioned in Genesis 30:21; she is last mentioned in Genesis 46:15.

34:1–4 Shechem may have been a victim of "love at first sight," but his actions were impulsive and evil. Not only did he sin against Dinah; he sinned against the entire family (34:6, 7). The consequences of his deed were severe both for his family and

for Jacob's (34:25–31). Even Shechem's declared love for Dinah could not excuse the evil he did by raping her. Don't allow sexual passion to boil over into evil actions. Passion must be controlled.

grief and fury, because Shechem had done a disgraceful thing in ª Israel ᵛ by lying with
Jacob's daughter—a thing that should not be done.

⁸But Hamor said to them, "My son Shechem has his heart set on your daughter. Please
give her to him as his wife. ⁹Intermarry with us; give us your daughters and take our daughters for yourselves. ¹⁰You can settle among us;ʷ the land is open to you.ˣ Live in it, tradeᵇ in
it,ʸ and acquire property in it."

¹¹Then Shechem said to Dinah's father and brothers, "Let me find favor in your eyes, and
I will give you whatever you ask. ¹²Make the price for the brideᶻ and the gift I am to bring as
great as you like, and I'll pay whatever you ask me. Only give me the girl as my wife."

¹³Because their sister Dinah had been defiled, Jacob's sons replied deceitfully as they
spoke to Shechem and his father Hamor. ¹⁴They said to them, "We can't do such a thing; we
can't give our sister to a man who is not circumcised. ª That would be a disgrace to us. ¹⁵We
will give our consent to you on one condition only: that you become like us by circumcising
all your males.ᵇ ¹⁶Then we will give you our daughters and take your daughters for ourselves.
We'll settle among you and become one people with you. ¹⁷But if you will not agree to be circumcised, we'll take our sisterᶜ and go."

¹⁸Their proposal seemed good to Hamor and his son Shechem. ¹⁹The young man, who
was the most honored of all his father's household, lost no time in doing what they said, because he was delighted with Jacob's daughter. ²⁰So Hamor and his son Shechem went to the
gate of their city to speak to their fellow townsmen. ²¹"These men are friendly toward us,"
they said. "Let them live in our land and trade in it; the land has plenty of room for them. We
can marry their daughters and they can marry ours. ²²But the men will consent to live with
us as one people only on the condition that our males be circumcised, as they themselves
are. ²³Won't their livestock, their property and all their other animals become ours? So let
us give our consent to them, and they will settle among us."

²⁴All the men who went out of the city gate agreed with Hamor and his son Shechem, and
every male in the city was circumcised.

²⁵Three days later, while all of them were still in pain, two of Jacob's sons, Simeon and
Levi, Dinah's brothers, took their swordsᶜ and attacked the unsuspecting city, killing every
male. ᵈ ²⁶They put Hamor and his son Shechem to the sword and took Dinah from Shechem's house and left. ²⁷The sons of Jacob came upon the dead bodies and looted the city
whereᵈ their sister had been defiled. ²⁸They seized their flocks and herds and donkeys and
everything else of theirs in the city and out in the fields. ²⁹They carried off all their wealth
and all their women and children, taking as plunder everything in the houses.

³⁰Then Jacob said to Simeon and Levi, "You have brought trouble on me by making me a
stench to the Canaanites and Perizzites, the people living in this land. We are few in number, and if they join forces against me and attack me, I and my household will be destroyed."

³¹But they replied, "Should he have treated our sister like a prostitute?"

Jacob Returns to Bethel

35 Then God said to Jacob, "Go up to Bethelᵉ and settle there, and build an altar there to
God, who appeared to you when you were fleeing from your brother Esau."ᶠ

²So Jacob said to his householdᵍ and to all who were with him, "Get rid of the foreign godsʰ
you have with you, and purify yourselves and change your clothes.ⁱ ³Then come, let us go up to
Bethel, where I will build an altar to God, who answered me in the day of my distressʲ and who
has been with me wherever I have gone." ⁴So they gave Jacob all the foreign gods they had and
the rings in their ears, and Jacob buried them under the oak at Shechem. ⁵Then they set out,
and the terror of God fell upon the towns all around them so that no one pursued them.

ª7 Or *against*   ᵇ10 Or *move about freely*; also in verse 21   ᶜ17 Hebrew *daughter*   ᵈ27 Or *because*

34:7
ᵛDt 22:21;
Jdg 20:6; 2Sa 13:12

34:10
ʷGe 47:6, 27
ˣGe 13:9; 20:15
ʸGe 42:34

34:12
ᶻEx 22:16;
Dt 22:29; 1Sa 18:25

34:14
ªGe 17:14

34:15
ᵇEx 12:48

34:25
ᶜGe 49:5
ᵈGe 49:7

35:1
ᵉGe 28:19
ᶠGe 27:43

35:2
ᵍGe 18:19;
Jos 24:15
ʰGe 31:19
ⁱEx 19:10, 14

35:3
ʲGe 32:7

34:25–31 Why did Simeon and Levi take such harsh action
against the city of Shechem? Jacob's family saw themselves
as set apart from others. God wanted them to remain separate
from their pagan neighbors. But the brothers wrongly thought
that being set apart also meant being better. This arrogant
attitude led to the terrible slaughter of innocent people.

34:27–29 When Shechem raped Dinah, the consequences were
far greater than he could have imagined. Dinah's brothers were outraged and took revenge. Pain, deceit, and murder followed. Sexual
sin is devastating because its consequences are so far reaching.

34:30, 31 In seeking revenge against Shechem, Simeon and Levi
lied, stole, and murdered. Their desire for justice was right, but
their ways of achieving it were wrong. Because of their sin, their
father cursed them with his dying breath (49:5–7). Generations
later, their descendants lost the part of the promised land allotted
to them. When tempted to return evil for evil, leave revenge to God
and spare yourself the dreadful consequences of sin.

35:2 Why did the people have these idols ("foreign gods")? Idols
were sometimes seen more as good luck charms than as gods.
Some Israelites, even though they worshiped God, had idols in

35:6
k Ge 28:19
35:8
l Ge 24:59
35:9
m Ge 32:29
35:10
n Ge 17:5
35:11
o Ge 17:1
p Ge 28:3
q Ge 17:6
35:12
r Ge 13:15; 28:13
35:13
s Ge 17:22
35:14
t Ge 28:18
35:15
u Ge 28:19

⁶Jacob and all the people with him came to Luz *k* (that is, Bethel) in the land of Canaan. ⁷There he built an altar, and he called the place El Bethel,*a* because it was there that God revealed himself to him when he was fleeing from his brother.

⁸Now Deborah, Rebekah's nurse,*l* died and was buried under the oak below Bethel. So it was named Allon Bacuth.*b*

⁹After Jacob returned from Paddan Aram,*c* God appeared to him again and blessed him.*m* ¹⁰God said to him, "Your name is Jacob,*d* but you will no longer be called Jacob; your name will be Israel.*e*"*n* So he named him Israel.

¹¹And God said to him, "I am God Almighty*f*;*o* be fruitful and increase in number. A nation*p* and a community of nations will come from you, and kings will come from your body.*q* ¹²The land I gave to Abraham and Isaac I also give to you, and I will give this land to your descendants after you.*r*" ¹³Then God went up from him*s* at the place where he had talked with him.

¹⁴Jacob set up a stone pillar at the place where God had talked with him, and he poured out a drink offering on it; he also poured oil on it.*t* ¹⁵Jacob called the place where God had talked with him Bethel.*g u*

The Deaths of Rachel and Isaac

¹⁶Then they moved on from Bethel. While they were still some distance from Ephrath, Rachel began to give birth and had great difficulty. ¹⁷And as she was having great difficulty in childbirth, the midwife said to her, "Don't be afraid, for you have another son."*v* ¹⁸As she breathed her last—for she was dying—she named her son Ben-Oni.*h* But his father named him Benjamin.*i*

35:17
v Ge 30:24

¹⁹So Rachel died and was buried on the way to Ephrath (that is, Bethlehem). ²⁰Over her tomb Jacob set up a pillar, and to this day that pillar marks Rachel's tomb.*w*

35:20
w 1Sa 10:2

²¹Israel moved on again and pitched his tent beyond Migdal Eder. ²²While Israel was living in that region, Reuben went in and slept with his father's concubine*x* Bilhah, and Israel heard of it.

35:22
x Ge 49:4; 1Ch 5:1

a 7 El Bethel means *God of Bethel.*   *b 8 Allon Bacuth* means *oak of weeping.*   *c 9* That is, Northwest Mesopotamia; also in verse 26   *d 10 Jacob* means *he grasps the heel* (figuratively, *he deceives*).   *e 10 Israel* means *he struggles with God.*   *f 11* Hebrew *El-Shaddai*   *g 15 Bethel* means *house of God.*   *h 18 Ben-Oni* means *son of my trouble.* *i 18 Benjamin* means *son of my right hand.*

---

their homes, just as some Christians today own good luck trinkets. Jacob believed that idols should have no place in his household. He wanted nothing to divert his family's spiritual focus.

Jacob ordered his household to get rid of their gods. Unless we remove idols from our lives, they can ruin our faith. What idols do we have? An idol is anything we put before God. Idols don't have to be physical objects; they can be thoughts or desires. Like Jacob, we should get rid of anything that could stand between us and God.

35:4 Why did the people give Jacob their earrings? Jewelry in itself was not evil, but in Jacob's day earrings were often worn as good luck charms to ward off evil. The people in his family had to cleanse themselves of all pagan influences, including reminders of foreign gods.

35:10 God reminded Jacob of his new name, Israel, which meant "he struggles with God." Although Jacob's life was littered with difficulties and trials, his new name was a tribute to his desire to stay close to God despite life's disappointments.

Many people believe that Christianity should offer a problem-free life. Consequently, as life gets tough, they draw back disappointed. Instead, they should determine to prevail with God through life's storm. Problems and difficulties are painful but inevitable; you might as well see them as opportunities for growth. You can't prevail with God unless you have troubles to prevail over.

35:13, 14 This oil used to anoint the pillar was olive oil of the finest grade of purity. It was expensive, so using it showed the high value placed on the anointed object. Jacob was showing the greatest respect for the place where he had met with God.

35:22 Reuben's sin was costly, although not right away. As the oldest son, he stood to receive a double portion of the family inheritance and a place of leadership among his people. Reuben may have thought he had gotten away with his sin. No more is

mentioned of it until Jacob, on his deathbed, assembled his family for the final blessing. Suddenly Jacob took away Reuben's double portion and gave it to someone else. The reason? "You went up onto your father's bed, onto my couch and defiled it" (49:4).

Sin's consequences can plague us long after the sin is committed. When we do something wrong, we may think we can escape unnoticed, only to discover later that the sin has been quietly breeding serious consequences.

JACOB'S JOURNEY BACK TO HEBRON
After Jacob's sons Simeon and Levi destroyed Shechem, God told Jacob to move to Bethel, where God reminded him that his name had been changed to Israel. He then traveled to Hebron, but along the way, his dear wife Rachel died near Ephrath (Bethlehem).

Jacob had twelve sons:

23 The sons of Leah:

Reuben the firstborn of Jacob,

Simeon, Levi, Judah, Issachar and Zebulun.

24 The sons of Rachel:

Joseph y and Benjamin. z

25 The sons of Rachel's maidservant Bilhah:

Dan and Naphtali.

26 The sons of Leah's maidservant Zilpah:

Gad and Asher.

These were the sons of Jacob, who were born to him in Paddan Aram.

35:24
y Ge 30:24
z ver 18

27 Jacob came home to his father Isaac in Mamre, a near Kiriath Arba (that is, Hebron), where Abraham and Isaac had stayed. 28 Isaac lived a hundred and eighty years. 29 Then he breathed his last and died and was gathered to his people, b old and full of years. c And his sons Esau and Jacob buried him. d

35:27
a Ge 13:18
35:29
b Ge 25:8
c Ge 15:15
d Ge 25:9

Esau's Descendants

36 This is the account of Esau (that is, Edom). e

36:1
e Ge 25:30

2 Esau took his wives from the women of Canaan: f Adah daughter of Elon the Hittite, g and Oholibamah daughter of Anah and granddaughter of Zibeon the Hivite— 3 also Basemath daughter of Ishmael and sister of Nebaioth.

36:2
f Ge 28:8-9
g Ge 26:34

4 Adah bore Eliphaz to Esau, Basemath bore Reuel, h 5 and Oholibamah bore Jeush, Jalam and Korah. These were the sons of Esau, who were born to him in Canaan.

36:4
h 1Ch 1:35

6 Esau took his wives and sons and daughters and all the members of his household, as well as his livestock and all his other animals and all the goods he had acquired in Canaan, i and moved to a land some distance from his brother Jacob. 7 Their possessions were too great for them to remain together; the land where they were staying could not support them both because of their livestock. j 8 So Esau k (that is, Edom) settled in the hill country of Seir. l

36:6
i Ge 12:5
36:7
j Ge 13:6
36:8
k Dt 2:4
l Ge 32:3

9 This is the account of Esau the father of the Edomites in the hill country of Seir.

10 These are the names of Esau's sons:

Eliphaz, the son of Esau's wife Adah, and Reuel, the son of Esau's wife Basemath.

11 The sons of Eliphaz:

Teman, Omar, Zepho, Gatam and Kenaz.

12 Esau's son Eliphaz also had a concubine named Timna, who bore him Amalek. m These were grandsons of Esau's wife Adah. n

36:12
m Ex 17:8, 16;
Nu 24:20; 1Sa 15:2
n ver 16

13 The sons of Reuel:

Nahath, Zerah, Shammah and Mizzah. These were grandsons of Esau's wife Basemath.

14 The sons of Esau's wife Oholibamah daughter of Anah and granddaughter of Zibeon, whom she bore to Esau:

Jeush, Jalam and Korah.

15 These were the chiefs o among Esau's descendants:

The sons of Eliphaz the firstborn of Esau:

Chiefs Teman, Omar, Zepho, Kenaz, 16 Korah, a Gatam and Amalek. These were the chiefs descended from Eliphaz in Edom; they were grandsons of Adah.

36:15
o Ex 15:15

17 The sons of Esau's son Reuel: p

Chiefs Nahath, Zerah, Shammah and Mizzah. These were the chiefs descended from Reuel in Edom; they were grandsons of Esau's wife Basemath.

36:17
p 1Ch 1:37

a 16 Masoretic Text; Samaritan Pentateuch (see also Gen. 36:11 and 1 Chron. 1:36) does not have *Korah.*

36:9 The Edomites were descendants of Esau who lived south and east of the Dead Sea. The country featured rugged mountains and desolate desert. Several major roads led through Edom because it was rich in natural resources. During the exodus, God told Israel to leave the Edomites alone (Deuteronomy 2:4, 5) because they were "brothers." But Edom refused to let them enter the land, and later they became bitter enemies of King David. The nations of Edom and Israel shared the same ancestor, Isaac, and the same border. Israel looked down on the Edomites because they had intermarried with the Canaanites.

36:15ff The title "chief" is equivalent to "head of the clan."

¹⁸ The sons of Esau's wife Oholibamah:

Chiefs Jeush, Jalam and Korah. These were the chiefs descended from Esau's wife Oholibamah daughter of Anah.

¹⁹These were the sons of Esau (that is, Edom), and these were their chiefs.

36:20
*q*Ge 14:6;
Dt 2:12, 22

²⁰These were the sons of Seir the Horite,*q* who were living in the region:

Lotan, Shobal, Zibeon, Anah, ²¹Dishon, Ezer and Dishan. These sons of Seir in Edom were Horite chiefs.

²² The sons of Lotan:

Hori and Homam.*a* Timna was Lotan's sister.

²³ The sons of Shobal:

Alvan, Manahath, Ebal, Shepho and Onam.

²⁴ The sons of Zibeon:

Aiah and Anah. This is the Anah who discovered the hot springs*b* in the desert while he was grazing the donkeys of his father Zibeon.

²⁵ The children of Anah:

Dishon and Oholibamah daughter of Anah.

²⁶ The sons of Dishon*c*:

Hemdan, Eshban, Ithran and Keran.

²⁷ The sons of Ezer:

Bilhan, Zaavan and Akan.

²⁸ The sons of Dishan:

Uz and Aran.

²⁹ These were the Horite chiefs:

Lotan, Shobal, Zibeon, Anah, ³⁰Dishon, Ezer and Dishan. These were the Horite chiefs, according to their divisions, in the land of Seir.

The Rulers of Edom

36:31
*r*1Ch 1:43

³¹These were the kings who reigned in Edom before any Israelite king*r* reigned*d*:

³² Bela son of Beor became king of Edom. His city was named Dinhabah.

³³ When Bela died, Jobab son of Zerah from Bozrah succeeded him as king.

³⁴ When Jobab died, Husham from the land of the Temanites succeeded him as king.

36:35
*s*Ge 19:37;
Ru 1:1, 6

³⁵ When Husham died, Hadad son of Bedad, who defeated Midian in the country of Moab,*s* succeeded him as king. His city was named Avith.

³⁶ When Hadad died, Samlah from Masrekah succeeded him as king.

³⁷ When Samlah died, Shaul from Rehoboth on the river*e* succeeded him as king.

³⁸ When Shaul died, Baal-Hanan son of Acbor succeeded him as king.

³⁹ When Baal-Hanan son of Acbor died, Hadad*f* succeeded him as king. His city was named Pau, and his wife's name was Mehetabel daughter of Matred, the daughter of Me-Zahab.

⁴⁰These were the chiefs descended from Esau, by name, according to their clans and regions:

Timna, Alvah, Jetheth, ⁴¹Oholibamah, Elah, Pinon, ⁴²Kenaz, Teman, Mibzar, ⁴³Magdiel and Iram. These were the chiefs of Edom, according to their settlements in the land they occupied.

This was Esau the father of the Edomites.

G. THE STORY OF JOSEPH (37:1—50:26)

Joseph, one of Jacob's 12 sons, was obviously the favorite. Hated by his brothers for this, Joseph was sold to slave traders only to emerge as ruler of all Egypt. Through Joseph, we learn how suffering, no matter how unfair, develops strong character and deep wisdom.

1. Joseph is sold into slavery
Joseph's Dreams

37:1
*t*Ge 17:8

37 Jacob lived in the land where his father had stayed,*t* the land of Canaan.

²This is the account of Jacob.

---

a22 Hebrew *Hemam*, a variant of *Homam* (see 1 Chron. 1:39)   *b24* Vulgate; Syriac *discovered water;* the meaning of the Hebrew for this word is uncertain.   *c26* Hebrew *Dishan*, a variant of *Dishon*   *d31* Or *before an Israelite king reigned over them*   *e37* Possibly the Euphrates   *f39* Many manuscripts of the Masoretic Text, Samaritan Pentateuch and Syriac (see also 1 Chron. 1:50); most manuscripts of the Masoretic Text *Hadar*

Joseph, a young man of seventeen, was tending the flocks[u] with his brothers, the sons of Bilhah and the sons of Zilpah, his father's wives, and he brought their father a bad report[v] about them.

3Now Israel loved Joseph more than any of his other sons, because he had been born to him in his old age;[w] and he made a richly ornamented[a] robe for him. 4When his brothers saw that their father loved him more than any of them, they hated him[x] and could not speak a kind word to him.

5Joseph had a dream, and when he told it to his brothers, they hated him all the more. 6He said to them, "Listen to this dream I had: 7We were binding sheaves of grain out in the field when suddenly my sheaf rose and stood upright, while your sheaves gathered around mine and bowed down to it."[y]

8His brothers said to him, "Do you intend to reign over us? Will you actually rule us?"[z] And they hated him all the more because of his dream and what he had said.

9Then he had another dream, and he told it to his brothers. "Listen," he said, "I had another dream, and this time the sun and moon and eleven stars were bowing down to me."

10When he told his father as well as his brothers, his father rebuked him and said, "What is this dream you had? Will your mother and I and your brothers actually come and bow down to the ground before you?"[a] 11His brothers were jealous of him,[b] but his father kept the matter in mind.[c]

Joseph Sold by His Brothers

12Now his brothers had gone to graze their father's flocks near Shechem, 13and Israel said to Joseph, "As you know, your brothers are grazing the flocks near Shechem. Come, I am going to send you to them."

"Very well," he replied.

14So he said to him, "Go and see if all is well with your brothers and with the flocks, and bring word back to me." Then he sent him off from the Valley of Hebron.

When Joseph arrived at Shechem, 15a man found him wandering around in the fields and asked him, "What are you looking for?"

16He replied, "I'm looking for my brothers. Can you tell me where they are grazing their flocks?"

17"They have moved on from here," the man answered. "I heard them say, 'Let's go to Dothan.'[d]"

So Joseph went after his brothers and found them near Dothan. 18But they saw him in the distance, and before he reached them, they plotted to kill him.[e]

19"Here comes that dreamer!" they said to each other. 20"Come now, let's kill him and throw him into one of these cisterns and say that a ferocious animal devoured him. Then we'll see what comes of his dreams."[f]

a3 The meaning of the Hebrew for *richly ornamented* is uncertain; also in verses 23 and 32.

37:2 [u]Ps 78:71 [v]1Sa 2:24
37:3 [w]Ge 44:20
37:4 [x]Ge 27:41
37:7 [y]Ge 42:6, 9; 43:26, 28; 44:14; 50:18
37:8 [z]Ge 49:26
37:10 [a]Ge 27:29
37:11 [b]Ac 7:9 [c]Lk 2:19, 51
37:17 [d]2Ki 6:13
37:18 [e]Mk 14:1
37:20 [f]Ge 50:20

JOSEPH GOES TO MEET HIS BROTHERS
Jacob asked Joseph to go find his brothers, who were grazing their flocks near Shechem. When Joseph arrived, he learned that his brothers had gone on to Dothan, which lay along a major trade route to Egypt. There the jealous brothers sold Joseph as a slave to a group of Midianite merchants on their way to Egypt.

37:3 In Joseph's day, everyone had a robe or cloak. Robes were used for warmth, to bundle up belongings for a trip, to wrap babies, to sit on, or even to serve as security for a loan. Most robes were knee length, short sleeved, and plain. In contrast, Joseph's robe was probably of the kind worn by royalty—long sleeved, ankle length, and colorful. The robe became a symbol of Jacob's favoritism toward Joseph, and it aggravated the already strained relations between Joseph and his brothers. Favoritism in families may be unavoidable, but its divisive effects should be minimized. Parents may not be able to change their feelings toward a favorite child, but they can change their actions toward the others.

37:6–11 Joseph's brothers were already angry over the possibility of being ruled by their little brother. Joseph then fueled the fire with his immature attitude and boastful manner. No one enjoys a braggart. Joseph learned this the hard way. His angry brothers sold him into slavery to get rid of him. After several years of hardship, Joseph learned an important lesson: Because our talents and knowledge come from God, it is more appropriate to thank him for them than to brag about them. Later, Joseph gave God the credit (41:16).

37:19, 20 Could jealousy ever make you feel like killing someone? Before saying, "Of course not," look at what happened in

37:21
g Ge 42:22

²¹When Reuben heard this, he tried to rescue him from their hands. "Let's not take his life," he said. g ²²"Don't shed any blood. Throw him into this cistern here in the desert, but don't lay a hand on him." Reuben said this to rescue him from them and take him back to his father.

²³So when Joseph came to his brothers, they stripped him of his robe—the richly ornamented robe he was wearing— ²⁴and they took him and threw him into the cistern. Now the cistern was empty; there was no water in it.

37:25
h ver 28

²⁵As they sat down to eat their meal, they looked up and saw a caravan of Ishmaelites coming from Gilead. Their camels were loaded with spices, balm and myrrh, and they were on their way to take them down to Egypt. h

37:26
i ver 20; Ge 4:10

37:27
j Ge 42:21

²⁶Judah said to his brothers, "What will we gain if we kill our brother and cover up his blood? i ²⁷Come, let's sell him to the Ishmaelites and not lay our hands on him; after all, he is our brother, j our own flesh and blood." His brothers agreed.

37:28
k Jdg 6:1-3
l Ge 45:4-5;
Ps 105:17; Ac 7:9

²⁸So when the Midianite k merchants came by, his brothers pulled Joseph up out of the cistern and sold him for twenty shekels ᵃ of silver to the Ishmaelites, who took him to Egypt. l

ᵃ28 That is, about 8 ounces (about 0.2 kilogram)

As a youngster, Joseph was overconfident. His natural self-assurance, increased by being Jacob's favorite son and by knowing of God's designs on his life, was unbearable to his ten older brothers, who eventually conspired against him. But this self-assurance, molded by pain and combined with a personal knowledge of God, allowed him to survive and prosper where most would have failed. He added quiet wisdom to his confidence and won the hearts of everyone he met—Potiphar, the warden, other prisoners, the pharaoh, and after many years, even those ten brothers.

Perhaps you can identify with one or more of these hardships Joseph experienced: he was betrayed and deserted by his family; he was exposed to sexual temptation, and punished for doing the right thing; he endured a long imprisonment and was forgotten by those he helped. As you read his story, note what Joseph did in each case. His positive response transformed each setback into a step forward. He didn't spend much time asking "Why?" His approach was "What shall I do now?" Those who met Joseph were aware that wherever he went and whatever he did, God was with him. When you're facing a setback, the beginning of a Joseph-like attitude is to acknowledge that God is with you. There is nothing like his presence to shed new light on a dark situation.

Strengths and accomplishments:	• Rose in power from slave to ruler of Egypt • Was known for his personal integrity • Was a man of spiritual sensitivity • Prepared a nation to survive a famine
Weakness and mistake:	• His youthful pride caused friction with his brothers
Lessons from his life:	• What matters is not so much the events or circumstances of life, but our response to them • With God's help, any situation can be used for good, even when others intend it for evil
Vital statistics:	• Where: Canaan, Egypt • Occupation: Shepherd, slave, convict, ruler • Relatives: Parents: Jacob and Rachel. Eleven brothers and one sister named in the Bible. Wife: Asenath. Sons: Manasseh and Ephraim.
Key verse:	"So Pharaoh asked them, 'Can we find anyone like this man, one in whom is the spirit of God?'" (Genesis 41:38).

Joseph's story is told in Genesis 30—50. He is also mentioned in Hebrews 11:22.

---

this story. Ten men were willing to kill their younger brother over a robe and a few reported dreams. Their deep jealousy had grown into ugly rage, completely blinding them to what was right. Jealousy can be difficult to recognize because our reasons for it seem to make sense. But left unchecked, jealousy grows quickly and leads to serious sins. The longer you cultivate jealous feelings, the harder it is to uproot them. The time to deal with jealousy is when you notice yourself keeping score of others' recognition, awards, and achievements.

37:26, 27 The brothers were worried about bearing the guilt of Joseph's death. Judah suggested an option that was not right but would leave them innocent of murder. Sometimes we jump at a solution because it is the lesser of two evils but still is not the right action to take. When someone proposes a seemingly workable solution, first ask, "Is it right?"

29When Reuben returned to the cistern and saw that Joseph was not there, he tore his clothes. m 30He went back to his brothers and said, "The boy isn't there! Where can I turn now?"n

31Then they got Joseph's robe, o slaughtered a goat and dipped the robe in the blood. 32They took the ornamented robe back to their father and said, "We found this. Examine it to see whether it is your son's robe."

33He recognized it and said, "It is my son's robe! Some ferocious animalp has devoured him. Joseph has surely been torn to pieces."

34Then Jacob tore his clothes, put on sackcloth and mourned for his son many days. 35All his sons and daughters came to comfort him, but he refused to be comforted. "No," he said, "in mourning will I go down to the gravea q to my son." So his father wept for him.

36Meanwhile, the Midianitesb sold Joseph in Egypt to Potiphar, one of Pharaoh's officials, the captain of the guard. r

2. Judah and Tamar

38 At that time, Judah left his brothers and went down to stay with a man of Adullam named Hirah. 2There Judah met the daughter of a Canaanite man named Shua.s He married her and lay with her; 3she became pregnant and gave birth to a son, who was named Er. t 4She conceived again and gave birth to a son and named him Onan. 5She gave birth to still another son and named him Shelah. It was at Kezib that she gave birth to him.

6Judah got a wife for Er, his firstborn, and her name was Tamar. 7But Er, Judah's firstborn, was wicked in the Lord's sight; so the Lord put him to death. u

8Then Judah said to Onan, "Lie with your brother's wife and fulfill your duty to her as a brother-in-law to produce offspring for your brother."v 9But Onan knew that the offspring would not be his; so whenever he lay with his brother's wife, he spilled his semen on the ground to keep from producing offspring for his brother. 10What he did was wicked in the Lord's sight; so he put him to death also. w

11Judah then said to his daughter-in-law Tamar, "Live as a widow in your father's house until my son Shelah grows up."x For he thought, "He may die too, just like his brothers." So Tamar went to live in her father's house.

a35 Hebrew Sheol b36 Samaritan Pentateuch, Septuagint, Vulgate and Syriac (see also verse 28); Masoretic Text Medanites

37:29	mJob 1:20
37:30	nver 22; Ge 42:13, 36
37:31	over 3, 23
37:33	pver 20
37:35	qGe 42:38; 44:22, 29, 31
37:36	rGe 39:1
38:2	s1Ch 2:3
38:3	tver 6; Ge 46:12
38:7	u1Ch 2:3
38:8	vDt 25:5-6; Mt 22:24-28
38:10	wGe 46:12
38:11	xRu 1:13

TAMAR	Canaanite	Genesis 38:1–30	**WOMEN IN JESUS' FAMILY TREE**
RAHAB	Canaanite	Joshua 6:22–25	
RUTH	Moabite	Ruth 4:13–22	
BATHSHEBA	Israelite	2 Samuel 12:24, 25	

37:28 Although Joseph's brothers didn't kill him outright, they wouldn't expect him to survive for long as a slave. They were quite willing to let cruel slave traders do their dirty work for them. Joseph faced a 30-day journey through the desert, probably chained and on foot. He would be treated like baggage, and once in Egypt, would be sold as a piece of merchandise. His brothers thought they would never see him again. But God was in control of Joseph's life and had other plans.

37:29, 30 Reuben returned to the cistern to find Joseph, but his little brother was gone. His first response, in effect, was "What is going to happen to me?" rather than "What is going to happen to Joseph?" In a tough situation, are you usually concerned first about yourself? Consider the person most affected by the problem, and you will be more likely to find a solution for it.

37:31–35 To cover their evil action, Jacob's sons deceived their father into thinking Joseph was dead. Jacob himself had deceived others many times (including his own father; 27:35). Even though he didn't know it at this point, Jacob was learning by hard experience the painfulness and destructive consequences of deceit.

37:34 Tearing one's clothes and wearing sackcloth (rough cloth like burlap) were signs of mourning, much like wearing black today.

37:36 Imagine the culture shock Joseph experienced upon arriving in Egypt. Joseph had lived as a nomad, traveling the countryside with his family, caring for sheep. Suddenly he was thrust into the world's most advanced civilization with great pyramids, beautiful homes, sophisticated people, and a new language. While Joseph saw Egypt's skill and intelligence at their best, he also saw the Egyptians' spiritual blindness. They worshiped countless gods related to every aspect of life.

38:1ff This chapter vividly contrasts the immoral character of Judah with the moral character of Joseph. Judah's lack of integrity resulted in family strife and deception. Chapter 39 shows how Joseph's integrity and wise choices reflect his godly character. His faithfulness was rewarded with blessings greater than he could imagine, both for himself and for his family.

38:8–10 This law about marrying a widow in the family is explained in Deuteronomy 25:5–10. Its purpose was to ensure that a childless widow would have a son who would receive her late husband's inheritance and who, in turn, would care for her. Because Judah's son (Tamar's husband) had no children, there was no family line through which the inheritance and the blessing of the covenant could continue. God killed Onan because he refused to fulfill his obligation to his brother and to Tamar.

Now Joseph was well-built and handsome, 7 and after a while his master's wife took notice of Joseph and said, "Come to bed with me!"

39:8
l Pr 6:23-24

39:9
m Ge 20:6; 42:18;
2Sa 12:13

8 But he refused. *l* "With me in charge," he told her, "my master does not concern himself with anything in the house; everything he owns he has entrusted to my care. 9 No one is greater in this house than I am. My master has withheld nothing from me except you, because you are his wife. How then could I do such a wicked thing and sin against God?" *m* 10 And though she spoke to Joseph day after day, he refused to go to bed with her or even be with her.

POTIPHAR AND HIS WIFE

Potiphar, the captain of Pharaoh's royal guard, had a large household and a wife with too much time on her hands. One day he purchased Joseph from some Ishmaelite slave traders and put him to work in his home. This was the best decision Potiphar ever made. Joseph was not only talented; God was also with him. Because of Joseph, Potiphar began to prosper greatly.

While Potiphar was benefiting from Joseph's good work ethic, Potiphar's wife was noticing Joseph's good looks. She tried to seduce her young Hebrew servant, but Joseph continually resisted her advances. Denied the thrill of chasing and capturing her prey, of feeling a few moments of illicit pleasure, Potiphar's wife became angry and hurt. One day, after she had been scorned again, she accused Joseph of attempted rape. Consumed with selfish feelings, she wanted to punish Joseph.

Potiphar had Joseph thrown into prison. We don't know if he realized what was going on in his house, but he sided with his wife. Because he listened to a faithless woman, Potiphar jailed an innocent man and got rid of the best overseer in all of Egypt. Had Potiphar been more observant, he would have seen that Joseph was not merely an administrative windfall, he was also a young man of integrity. Perhaps he did see Joseph's character but didn't have enough himself to face the truth. In any case, Potiphar and his wife deserved each other.

We need to be careful that we are not guilty of over-emphasizing talent and under-emphasizing character. Both qualities are important, but character matters far more in the long run. Selfishness, faithlessness, and deceit have no place in a person who wants to develop character. Potiphar and his wife show us that anyone can be a judge of talent, but it takes insight and courage to be a judge of character.

Strengths and accomplishments:	• Potiphar reached a high rank in Pharaoh's court • Enjoyed the temporary blessing of having Joseph, God's servant, as their slave
Weaknesses and mistakes:	• Neither recognized the amazing person who lived in their house • Both failed in judging character—Potiphar toward his wife and Joseph, his wife toward Joseph • Falsely accused and imprisoned Joseph, their faithful servant
Lessons from their life:	• A lasting marriage requires faithfulness and hard work • God can accomplish his purposes through other's mistakes and sins • God blesses many people who clearly don't deserve his grace and help • One person with character stands out among those who possess little of it
Vital statistics:	• Where: Egypt • Occupation: Palace official and wife
Key verse:	"From the time he put him in charge of his household and of all that he owned, the LORD blessed the household of the Egyptian because of Joseph. The blessing of the LORD was on everything Potiphar had, both in the house and in the field" (Genesis 39:5).

The story of Potiphar and his wife is told in Genesis 37:36 and Genesis 39.

surrounded themselves with alabaster vases, paintings, beautiful rugs, and hand-carved chairs. Dinner was served on golden tableware, and the rooms were lighted with gold lampstands. Servants, like Joseph, worked on the first floor, while the family occupied the upper stories.

39:9 Potiphar's wife failed to seduce Joseph, who resisted this temptation by saying it would be a sin against God. Joseph didn't say, "I'd be hurting you," or "I'd be sinning against Potiphar," or "I'd be sinning against myself." Under pressure, such excuses

are easily rationalized away. Remember that sexual sin is not just between two consenting adults. It is an act of disobedience against God.

39:10-15 Joseph avoided Potiphar's wife as much as possible. He refused her advances and finally *ran* from her. Sometimes merely trying to avoid temptations is not enough. We must turn and run from them, especially when the temptations seem very strong, as is often the case in sexual temptations.

[11]One day he went into the house to attend to his duties, and none of the household servants was inside. [12]She caught him by his cloak[n] and said, "Come to bed with me!" But he left his cloak in her hand and ran out of the house.

[13]When she saw that he had left his cloak in her hand and had run out of the house, [14]she called her household servants. "Look," she said to them, "this Hebrew has been brought to us to make sport of us! He came in here to sleep with me, but I screamed.[o] [15]When he heard me scream for help, he left his cloak beside me and ran out of the house."

[16]She kept his cloak beside her until his master came home. [17]Then she told him this story:[p] "That Hebrew slave you brought us came to me to make sport of me. [18]But as soon as I screamed for help, he left his cloak beside me and ran out of the house."

[19]When his master heard the story his wife told him, saying, "This is how your slave treated me," he burned with anger.[q] [20]Joseph's master took him and put him in prison,[r] the place where the king's prisoners were confined.

But while Joseph was there in the prison, [21]the LORD was with him; he showed him kindness and granted him favor in the eyes of the prison warden.[s] [22]So the warden put Joseph in charge of all those held in the prison, and he was made responsible for all that was done there. [23]The warden paid no attention to anything under Joseph's care, because the LORD was with Joseph and gave him success in whatever he did.[t]

The Cupbearer and the Baker

40 Some time later, the cupbearer and the baker of the king of Egypt offended their master, the king of Egypt. [2]Pharaoh was angry with his two officials, the chief cupbearer and the chief baker, [3]and put them in custody in the house of the captain of the guard,[u] in the same prison where Joseph was confined. [4]The captain of the guard assigned them to Joseph, and he attended them.

After they had been in custody for some time, [5]each of the two men—the cupbearer and the baker of the king of Egypt, who were being held in prison—had a dream the same night, and each dream had a meaning of its own.

[6]When Joseph came to them the next morning, he saw that they were dejected. [7]So he asked Pharaoh's officials who were in custody with him in his master's house, "Why are your faces so sad today?"

[8]"We both had dreams," they answered, "but there is no one to interpret them."[v]

Then Joseph said to them, "Do not interpretations belong to God?[w] Tell me your dreams."

[9]So the chief cupbearer told Joseph his dream. He said to him, "In my dream I saw a vine in front of me, [10]and on the vine were three branches. As soon as it budded, it blossomed, and its clusters ripened into grapes. [11]Pharaoh's cup was in my hand, and I took the grapes, squeezed them into Pharaoh's cup and put the cup in his hand."

[12]"This is what it means,[x]" Joseph said to him. "The three branches are three days. [13]Within three days Pharaoh will lift up your head and restore you to your position, and you will put Pharaoh's cup in his hand, just as you used to do when you were his cupbearer. [14]But when all goes well with you, remember me and show me kindness;[y] mention me to Pharaoh and get me out of this prison. [15]For I was forcibly carried off from the land of the Hebrews, and even here I have done nothing to deserve being put in a dungeon."

[16]When the chief baker saw that Joseph had given a favorable interpretation, he said to Joseph, "I too had a dream: On my head were three baskets of bread.[a] [17]In the top basket

[a] 16 Or three wicker baskets

39:12
[n] Pr 7:13
39:14
[o] Dt 22:24, 27

39:17
[p] Ex 23:1, 7

39:19
[q] Pr 6:34
39:20
[r] Ps 105:18
39:21
[s] Ex 3:21

39:23
[t] ver 3

40:3
[u] Ge 39:20

40:8
[v] Ge 41:8, 15
[w] Ge 41:16;
Da 2:22, 28, 47

40:12
[x] Da 2:36; 4:19

40:14
[y] Jos 2:12

39:20 Prisons were grim places with vile conditions. They were used to house forced laborers or, like Joseph, the accused who were awaiting trial. Prisoners were guilty until proven innocent, and there was no right to a speedy trial. Many prisoners never made it to court because trials were held at the whim of the ruler. Joseph was in prison two years until he appeared before Pharaoh, and then he was called out to interpret a dream, not to stand trial.

39:21-23 As a prisoner and slave, Joseph could have seen his situation as hopeless. Instead, he did his best with each small task given him. His diligence and positive attitude were soon noticed by the warden, who promoted him to prison administrator. Are you facing a seemingly hopeless predicament? At work, at home, or at school, follow Joseph's example by taking each

small task and doing your best. Remember how God turned Joseph's situation around. He will see your efforts and can reverse even overwhelming odds.

40:1-3 The cupbearer and the baker were two of the most trusted men in Pharaoh's kingdom. The baker was in charge of making the pharaoh's food, and the cupbearer tasted all of Pharaoh's food and drink before giving it to him, in case any of it was contaminated or poisoned. These trusted men must have been suspected of a serious wrong, perhaps of conspiring against Pharaoh. Later the cupbearer was released and the baker executed.

40:8 When the subject of dreams came up, Joseph focused everyone's attention on God. Rather than using the situation to make himself look good, he turned it into a powerful witness for the Lord.

were all kinds of baked goods for Pharaoh, but the birds were eating them out of the basket on my head."

40:18
z ver 12

40:19
a ver 13

18"This is what it means," Joseph said. "The three baskets are three days. *z* 19Within three days Pharaoh will lift off your head *a* and hang you on a tree. *a* And the birds will eat away your flesh."

20Now the third day was Pharaoh's birthday, and he gave a feast for all his officials. He lifted up the heads of the chief cupbearer and the chief baker in the presence of his officials: 21He restored the chief cupbearer to his position, so that he once again put the cup into Pharaoh's hand, *b* 22but he hanged *b* the chief baker, *c* just as Joseph had said to them in his interpretation. *d*

40:21
b ver 13

40:22
c ver 19
d Ps 105:19

23The chief cupbearer, however, did not remember Joseph; he forgot him.

4. Joseph is placed in charge of Egypt
Pharaoh's Dreams

41 When two full years had passed, Pharaoh had a dream: He was standing by the Nile, 2when out of the river there came up seven cows, sleek and fat, and they grazed among the reeds. 3After them, seven other cows, ugly and gaunt, came up out of the Nile and stood beside those on the riverbank. 4And the cows that were ugly and gaunt ate up the seven sleek, fat cows. Then Pharaoh woke up.

5He fell asleep again and had a second dream: Seven heads of grain, healthy and good, were growing on a single stalk. 6After them, seven other heads of grain sprouted—thin and scorched by the east wind. 7The thin heads of grain swallowed up the seven healthy, full heads. Then Pharaoh woke up; it had been a dream.

41:8
e Da 2:1, 3; 4:5, 19
f Ex 7:11, 22;
Da 2:2, 27; 4:7

8In the morning his mind was troubled, *e* so he sent for all the magicians *f* and wise men of Egypt. Pharaoh told them his dreams, but no one could interpret them for him.

41:10
g Ge 40:2

41:11
h Ge 40:5

41:12
i Ge 40:12

41:13
j Ge 40:22

9Then the chief cupbearer said to Pharaoh, "Today I am reminded of my shortcomings. 10Pharaoh was once angry with his servants, *g* and he imprisoned me and the chief baker in the house of the captain of the guard. 11Each of us had a dream the same night, and each dream had a meaning of its own. *h* 12Now a young Hebrew was there with us, a servant of the captain of the guard. We told him our dreams, and he interpreted them for us, giving each man the interpretation of his dream. *i* 13And things turned out exactly as he interpreted them to us: I was restored to my position, and the other man was hanged. *b* *j*"

41:14
k Ps 105:20;
Da 2:25

14So Pharaoh sent for Joseph, and he was quickly brought from the dungeon. *k* When he had shaved and changed his clothes, he came before Pharaoh.

41:15
l Da 5:16

15Pharaoh said to Joseph, "I had a dream, and no one can interpret it. But I have heard it said of you that when you hear a dream you can interpret it." *l*

41:16
m Ge 40:8; Da 2:30;
Ac 3:12; 2Co 3:5

16"I cannot do it," Joseph replied to Pharaoh, "but God will give Pharaoh the answer he desires." *m*

17Then Pharaoh said to Joseph, "In my dream I was standing on the bank of the Nile, 18when out of the river there came up seven cows, fat and sleek, and they grazed among the reeds. 19After them, seven other cows came up—scrawny and very ugly and lean. I had never seen such ugly cows in all the land of Egypt. 20The lean, ugly cows ate up the seven fat cows that came up first. 21But even after they ate them, no one could tell that they had done so; they looked just as ugly as before. Then I woke up.

a 19 Or *and impale you on a pole*   *b 22,13* Or *impaled*

One secret of effective witnessing is to recognize opportunities to relate God to the other person's experience. When the opportunity arises, we must have the courage to speak, as Joseph did.

40:23 When Pharaoh's cupbearer was freed from prison, he forgot about Joseph. Two full years passed before Joseph had another opportunity to be freed (41:1). Yet Joseph's faith was deep, and he would be ready when the next chance came. When we feel passed by, overlooked, or forgotten, we shouldn't be surprised that people are often ungrateful. In similar situations, we should trust God as Joseph did. More opportunities may be waiting.

41:8 Magicians and wise men were common in the palaces of ancient rulers. Their job description included studying sacred arts and sciences, reading the stars, interpreting dreams, predicting the future, and performing magic. These men had power (see Exodus 7:11, 12), but their power was satanic. They were unable

to interpret Pharaoh's dream, but God had revealed it to Joseph in prison.

41:14 Our most important opportunities may come when we least expect them. Joseph was brought hastily from the dungeon and pushed before Pharaoh. Did he have time to prepare? Yes and no. He had no warning that he would be suddenly pulled from prison and questioned by the king. Yet Joseph was ready for almost any thing because of his right relationship with God. It was not Joseph's knowledge of dreams that helped him interpret their meaning. It was his knowledge of God. Be ready for opportunities by staying close to God. Then, when he calls you to a task, you'll be ready.

41:16 Joseph made sure that he gave the credit to God. We should be careful to do the same. To take the honor for ourselves is a form of stealing God's honor. Don't be silent when you know you should be giving glory and credit to God.

²²"In my dreams I also saw seven heads of grain, full and good, growing on a single stalk. ²³After them, seven other heads sprouted—withered and thin and scorched by the east wind. ²⁴The thin heads of grain swallowed up the seven good heads. I told this to the magicians, but none could explain it to me."

²⁵Then Joseph said to Pharaoh, "The dreams of Pharaoh are one and the same. God has revealed to Pharaoh what he is about to do.[n] ²⁶The seven good cows are seven years, and the seven good heads of grain are seven years; it is one and the same dream. ²⁷The seven lean, ugly cows that came up afterward are seven years, and so are the seven worthless heads of grain scorched by the east wind: They are seven years of famine.[o]

²⁸"It is just as I said to Pharaoh: God has shown Pharaoh what he is about to do. ²⁹Seven years of great abundance[p] are coming throughout the land of Egypt, ³⁰but seven years of famine[q] will follow them. Then all the abundance in Egypt will be forgotten, and the famine will ravage the land. ³¹The abundance in the land will not be remembered, because the famine that follows it will be so severe. ³²The reason the dream was given to Pharaoh in two forms is that the matter has been firmly decided by God, and God will do it soon.

³³"And now let Pharaoh look for a discerning and wise man and put him in charge of the land of Egypt. ³⁴Let Pharaoh appoint commissioners over the land to take a fifth of the harvest of Egypt during the seven years of abundance. ³⁵They should collect all the food of these good years that are coming and store up the grain under the authority of Pharaoh, to be kept in the cities for food.[r] ³⁶This food should be held in reserve for the country, to be used during the seven years of famine that will come upon Egypt, so that the country may not be ruined by the famine."

³⁷The plan seemed good to Pharaoh and to all his officials. ³⁸So Pharaoh asked them, "Can we find anyone like this man, in whom is the spirit of God[a]?"[s]

³⁹Then Pharaoh said to Joseph, "Since God has made all this known to you, there is no one so discerning and wise as you. ⁴⁰You shall be in charge of my palace, and all my people are to submit to your orders.[t] Only with respect to the throne will I be greater than you."

Joseph in Charge of Egypt

⁴¹So Pharaoh said to Joseph, "I hereby put you in charge of the whole land of Egypt."[u] ⁴²Then Pharaoh took his signet ring[v] from his finger and put it on Joseph's finger. He dressed him in robes of fine linen and put a gold chain around his neck.[w] ⁴³He had him ride in a chariot as his second-in-command,[b] and men shouted before him, "Make way[c]!" Thus he put him in charge of the whole land of Egypt.

⁴⁴Then Pharaoh said to Joseph, "I am Pharaoh, but without your word no one will lift hand or foot in all Egypt." ⁴⁵Pharaoh gave Joseph the name Zaphenath-Paneah and gave him Asenath daughter of Potiphera, priest of On,[d] to be his wife. And Joseph went throughout the land of Egypt.

⁴⁶Joseph was thirty years old when he entered the service of Pharaoh king of Egypt. And Joseph went out from Pharaoh's presence and traveled throughout Egypt. ⁴⁷During the seven years of abundance the land produced plentifully. ⁴⁸Joseph collected all the food produced in those seven years of abundance in Egypt and stored it in the cities. In each city he put the food grown in the fields surrounding it. ⁴⁹Joseph stored up huge quantities of grain, like the sand of the sea; it was so much that he stopped keeping records because it was beyond measure.

**Cross references (margin):**

41:25 ⁿDa 2:45

41:27 °2Ki 8:1

41:29 ᵖver 47

41:30 �q ver 54; Ge 47:13

41:35 ʳver 48

41:38 ˢNu 27:18; Job 32:8; Da 4:8-9, 18; 5:11, 14

41:40 ᵗPs 105:21-22; Ac 7:10

41:41 ᵘGe 42:6

41:42 ᵛEst 3:10
ʷDa 5:7, 16, 29

ᵃ38 Or *of the gods*   ᵇ43 Or *in the chariot of his second-in-command;* or *in his second chariot*   ᶜ43 Or *Bow down*
ᵈ45 That is, Heliopolis; also in verse 50

41:28-36 After interpreting Pharaoh's dream, Joseph gave the king a survival plan for the next 14 years. The only way to prevent starvation was through careful planning; without a famine plan Egypt would have turned from prosperity to ruin. Many find detailed planning boring and unnecessary. But planning is a responsibility, not an option. Joseph was able to save a nation by translating God's plan for Egypt into practical actions (implementation).

41:38 Pharaoh recognized that Joseph was a man "in whom is the spirit of God." You probably won't get to interpret dreams for a king, but those who know you should be able to see God in you, through your kind words, merciful acts, and wise advice. Do your relatives, neighbors, and coworkers see you as a person in whom the Spirit of God lives?

41:39, 40 Joseph rose quickly to the top, from prison walls to Pharaoh's palace. His training for this important position involved being first a slave and then a prisoner. In each situation he learned the importance of serving God and others. Whatever your situation, no matter how undesirable, consider it part of your training program for serving God.

41:45 Pharaoh may have been trying to make Joseph more acceptable by giving him an Egyptian name and wife. He probably wanted to (1) play down the fact that Joseph was a nomadic shepherd, an occupation disliked by the Egyptians, (2) make Joseph's name easier for Egyptians to pronounce and remember, and (3) show how highly he was honored by giving him the daughter of a prominent Egyptian official.

41:46 Joseph was 30 years old when he became second-in-

41:52
ˣGe 17:6; 49:22

41:54
ʸver 30; Ps 105:11;
Ac 7:11

⁵⁰Before the years of famine came, two sons were born to Joseph by Asenath daughter of Potiphera, priest of On. ⁵¹Joseph named his firstborn Manassehᵃ and said, "It is because God has made me forget all my trouble and all my father's household." ⁵²The second son he named Ephraimᵇ and said, "It is because God has made me fruitfulˣ in the land of my suffering."

⁵³The seven years of abundance in Egypt came to an end, ⁵⁴and the seven years of famine began,ʸ just as Joseph had said. There was famine in all the other lands, but in the whole land of Egypt there was food. ⁵⁵When all Egypt began to feel the famine, the people cried to Pharaoh for food. Then Pharaoh told all the Egyptians, "Go to Joseph and do what he tells you."

⁵⁶When the famine had spread over the whole country, Joseph opened the storehouses and sold grain to the Egyptians, for the famine was severe throughout Egypt. ⁵⁷And all the countries came to Egypt to buy grain from Joseph, because the famine was severe in all the world.

5. Joseph and his brothers meet in Egypt
Joseph's Brothers Go to Egypt

42:1
ᶻAc 7:12

42:2
ᵃGe 43:8

42:4
ᵇver 38

42:5
ᶜAc 7:11

42:6
ᵈGe 41:41
ᵉGe 37:7-10

42:9
ᶠGe 37:7

42:13
ᵍGe 37:30, 33;
44:20

42:15
ʰ1Sa 17:55

42 When Jacob learned that there was grain in Egypt,ᶻ he said to his sons, "Why do you just keep looking at each other?" ²He continued, "I have heard that there is grain in Egypt. Go down there and buy some for us, so that we may live and not die."ᵃ

³Then ten of Joseph's brothers went down to buy grain from Egypt. ⁴But Jacob did not send Benjamin, Joseph's brother, with the others, because he was afraid that harm might come to him.ᵇ ⁵So Israel's sons were among those who went to buy grain, for the famine was in the land of Canaan also.ᶜ

⁶Now Joseph was the governor of the land,ᵈ the one who sold grain to all its people. So when Joseph's brothers arrived, they bowed down to him with their faces to the ground.ᵉ ⁷As soon as Joseph saw his brothers, he recognized them, but he pretended to be a stranger and spoke harshly to them. "Where do you come from?" he asked.

"From the land of Canaan," they replied, "to buy food."

⁸Although Joseph recognized his brothers, they did not recognize him. ⁹Then he remembered his dreamsᶠ about them and said to them, "You are spies! You have come to see where our land is unprotected."

¹⁰"No, my lord," they answered. "Your servants have come to buy food. ¹¹We are all the sons of one man. Your servants are honest men, not spies."

¹²"No!" he said to them. "You have come to see where our land is unprotected."

¹³But they replied, "Your servants were twelve brothers, the sons of one man, who lives in the land of Canaan. The youngest is now with our father, and one is no more."ᵍ

¹⁴Joseph said to them, "It is just as I told you: You are spies! ¹⁵And this is how you will be tested: As surely as Pharaoh lives,ʰ you will not leave this place unless your youngest brother comes here. ¹⁶Send one of your number to get your brother; the rest of you will be kept in prison, so that your words may be tested to see if you are telling the truth. If you are not, then as surely as Pharaoh lives, you are spies!" ¹⁷And he put them all in custody for three days.

ᵃ51 *Manasseh* sounds like and may be derived from the Hebrew for *forget*.   ᵇ52 *Ephraim* sounds like the Hebrew for *twice fruitful.*

---

command in Egypt. At age 17, he had been sold into slavery by his brothers. Thus he had spent 13 years as an Egyptian slave and in prison.

41:54 Famine was a catastrophe because ancient peoples relied almost exclusively on their own crops for food. Almost perfect conditions were needed to produce good crops because there were no chemical fertilizers or pesticides. Any variances in rainfall or insect activity could cause crop failure and great hunger. Lack of storage, refrigeration, or transportation turned a moderate famine into a desperate situation. The famine Joseph prepared for was especially severe because seven years of famine came one right after the other. Without God's intervention, the Egyptian nation would have crumbled.

42:1, 2 Why was grain so valuable in those days? As a food source it was universal and used in nearly everything eaten. It could be dried and stored much longer than any vegetables, milk products, or meat. It was so important that it was even used as money.

42:4 Jacob was especially fond of Benjamin because he was Joseph's only full brother and—as far as Jacob knew—the only

surviving son of his beloved wife, Rachel. Benjamin was Jacob's youngest son and a child of his old age.

42:7 Joseph could have revealed his identity to his brothers at once. But Joseph's last memory of them may well have been staring in horror at their faces as slave traders carried him away. Were his brothers still evil and treacherous, or had they changed over the years? Joseph decided to put them through a few tests to find out.

42:8, 9 Joseph remembered his dreams about his brothers bowing down to him (37:6–9). Those dreams were coming true! As a young boy, Joseph had been boastful about his dreams. As a man, he no longer flaunted his superior status. He did not feel the need to say "I told you so." It was not yet time to reveal his identity, so he kept quiet. Sometimes it is best to remain quiet, even when we would like to have the last word.

42:15 Joseph was testing his brothers to make sure they had not been as cruel to Benjamin as they had been to him. Benjamin was his only full brother, and he wanted to see him face to face.

[18]On the third day, Joseph said to them, "Do this and you will live, for I fear God: [i] [19]If you are honest men, let one of your brothers stay here in prison, while the rest of you go and take grain back for your starving households. [20]But you must bring your youngest brother to me, [j] so that your words may be verified and that you may not die." This they proceeded to do.

[21]They said to one another, "Surely we are being punished because of our brother. We saw how distressed he was when he pleaded with us for his life, but we would not listen; that's why this distress [k] has come upon us."

[22]Reuben replied, "Didn't I tell you not to sin against the boy? [l] But you wouldn't listen! Now we must give an accounting [m] for his blood." [23]They did not realize that Joseph could understand them, since he was using an interpreter.

[24]He turned away from them and began to weep, but then turned back and spoke to them again. He had Simeon taken from them and bound before their eyes.

[25]Joseph gave orders to fill their bags with grain, to put each man's silver back in his sack, and to give them provisions for their journey. [n] After this was done for them, [26]they loaded their grain on their donkeys and left.

[27]At the place where they stopped for the night one of them opened his sack to get feed for his donkey, and he saw his silver in the mouth of his sack. [28]"My silver has been returned," he said to his brothers. "Here it is in my sack."

Their hearts sank and they turned to each other trembling and said, "What is this that God has done to us?"

[29]When they came to their father Jacob in the land of Canaan, they told him all that had happened to them. They said, [30]"The man who is lord over the land spoke harshly to us [o] and treated us as though we were spying on the land. [31]But we said to him, 'We are honest men; we are not spies. [32]We were twelve brothers, sons of one father. One is no more, and the youngest is now with our father in Canaan.'

[33]"Then the man who is lord over the land said to us, 'This is how I will know whether you are honest men: Leave one of your brothers here with me, and take food for your starving households and go. [34]But bring your youngest brother to me so I will know that you are not spies but honest men. Then I will give your brother back to you, and you can trade [a] in the land.' [p]'"

[35]As they were emptying their sacks, there in each man's sack was his pouch of silver! When they and their father saw the money pouches, they were frightened. [36]Their father Jacob said to them, "You have deprived me of my children. Joseph is no more and Simeon is no more, and now you want to take Benjamin. [q] Everything is against me!"

[37]Then Reuben said to his father, "You may put both of my sons to death if I do not bring him back to you. Entrust him to my care, and I will bring him back."

[38]But Jacob said, "My son will not go down there with you; his brother is dead [r] and he is the only one left. If harm comes to him on the journey you are taking, you will bring my gray head down to the grave [b] [s] in sorrow."

The Second Journey to Egypt

43 Now the famine was still severe in the land. [t] [2]So when they had eaten all the grain they had brought from Egypt, their father said to them, "Go back and buy us a little more food."

[3]But Judah said to him, "The man warned us solemnly, 'You will not see my face again unless your brother is with you.' [u] [4]If you will send our brother along with us, we will go down and buy food for you. [5]But if you will not send him, we will not go down, because the man said to us, 'You will not see my face again unless your brother is with you.'"

[6]Israel asked, "Why did you bring this trouble on me by telling the man you had another brother?"

[7]They replied, "The man questioned us closely about ourselves and our family. 'Is your father still living?' he asked us. 'Do you have another brother?' [v] We simply answered his questions. How were we to know he would say, 'Bring your brother down here'?"

[a]34 Or *move about freely*   [b]38 Hebrew *Sheol*

42:18 [i]Lev 25:43

42:20 [j]ver 15, 34; Ge 43:5

42:21 [k]Hos 5:15

42:22 [l]Ge 37:21-22   [m]Ge 9:5

42:25 [n]Ro 12:17, 20-21

42:30 [o]ver 7

42:34 [p]Ge 34:10

42:36 [q]Ge 43:14

42:38 [r]Ge 37:33   [s]Ge 37:35

43:1 [t]Ge 12:10; 41:56-57

43:3 [u]Ge 42:15; 44:23

43:7 [v]Ge 42:13

42:22 Reuben couldn't resist saying "I told you so." To "give an accounting for his blood" means that they thought they were being punished by God for what they had done to Joseph. Apparently the intervening years had not lessened their guilt. Selling Joseph into slavery amounted to death in their minds, for they surely never expected to see him again.

43:1 Jacob and his sons had no relief from the famine. They could not see God's overall plan of sending them to Egypt to

43:9
w Ge 42:37; 44:32;
Phm 1:18-19

43:11
x Ge 32:20;
Pr 18:16
y Ge 37:25; Jer 8:22

43:12
z Ge 42:25

43:16
a Ge 44:1, 4, 12

43:21
b ver 15;
Ge 42:27, 35

43:24
c ver 16
d Ge 18:4; 24:32

43:26
e Ge 37:7, 10

43:28
f Ge 37:7

43:29
g Ge 42:13

43:30
h Ge 42:24; 45:2,
14, 15; 46:29

8 Then Judah said to Israel his father, "Send the boy along with me and we will go at once, so that we and you and our children may live and not die. 9 I myself will guarantee his safety; you can hold me personally responsible for him. If I do not bring him back to you and set him here before you, I will bear the blame before you all my life. *w* 10 As it is, if we had not delayed, we could have gone and returned twice."

11 Then their father Israel said to them, "If it must be, then do this: Put some of the best products of the land in your bags and take them down to the man as a gift *x* —a little balm *y* and a little honey, some spices and myrrh, some pistachio nuts and almonds. 12 Take double the amount of silver with you, for you must return the silver that was put back into the mouths of your sacks. *z* Perhaps it was a mistake. 13 Take your brother also and go back to the man at once. 14 And may God Almighty *a* grant you mercy before the man so that he will let your other brother and Benjamin come back with you. As for me, if I am bereaved, I am bereaved."

15 So the men took the gifts and double the amount of silver, and Benjamin also. They hurried down to Egypt and presented themselves to Joseph. 16 When Joseph saw Benjamin with them, he said to the steward of his house, *a* "Take these men to my house, slaughter an animal and prepare dinner; they are to eat with me at noon."

17 The man did as Joseph told him and took the men to Joseph's house. 18 Now the men were frightened when they were taken to his house. They thought, "We were brought here because of the silver that was put back into our sacks the first time. He wants to attack us and overpower us and seize us as slaves and take our donkeys."

19 So they went up to Joseph's steward and spoke to him at the entrance to the house. 20 "Please, sir," they said, "we came down here the first time to buy food. 21 But at the place where we stopped for the night we opened our sacks and each of us found his silver—the exact weight—in the mouth of his sack. So we have brought it back with us. *b* 22 We have also brought additional silver with us to buy food. We don't know who put our silver in our sacks."

23 "It's all right," he said. "Don't be afraid. Your God, the God of your father, has given you treasure in your sacks; I received your silver." Then he brought Simeon out to them.

24 The steward took the men into Joseph's house, *c* gave them water to wash their feet *d* and provided fodder for their donkeys. 25 They prepared their gifts for Joseph's arrival at noon, because they had heard that they were to eat there.

26 When Joseph came home, they presented to him the gifts they had brought into the house, and they bowed down before him to the ground. *e* 27 He asked them how they were, and then he said, "How is your aged father you told me about? Is he still living?"

28 They replied, "Your servant our father is still alive and well." And they bowed low to pay him honor. *f*

29 As he looked about and saw his brother Benjamin, his own mother's son, he asked, "Is this your youngest brother, the one you told me about?" *g* And he said, "God be gracious to you, my son." 30 Deeply moved at the sight of his brother, Joseph hurried out and looked for a place to weep. He went into his private room and wept *h* there.

31 After he had washed his face, he came out and, controlling himself, said, "Serve the food."

a 14 Hebrew *El-Shaddai*

---

be reunited with Joseph and fed from Egypt's storehouses. If you are praying for relief from suffering or pressure and God is not bringing it as quickly as you would like, remember that God may be leading you to special treasures.

43:9 Judah accepted full responsibility for Benjamin's safety. He did not know what that might mean for him, but he was determined to do his duty. In the end, Judah's stirring words caused Joseph to break down with emotion and reveal himself to his brothers (44:18-34). Accepting responsibilities is difficult, but it builds character and confidence, earns others' respect, and motivates us to complete our work. When you have been given an assignment to complete or a responsibility to fulfill, commit yourself to seeing it through.

43:11 These gifts of balm, honey, spices, myrrh, pistachio nuts, and almonds were highly valuable specialty items not common in Egypt. Because of the famine, they were even more rare.

43:12 Joseph's brothers arrived home from Egypt only to find in their grain sacks the money they had used to pay for the grain (42:35). Some months later, when it was time to return to Egypt for more food, Jacob instructed them to take extra money so they could pay for the previous purchase as well as for additional grain. Jacob did not try to get away with anything. He was a man of integrity who paid for what he bought, whether he had to or not. We should follow his example and guard our integrity. A reputation for honesty is worth far more than the money we might save by compromising it.

43:23 How did the money get into the sacks? Most likely, Joseph instructed his steward to replace the money and then explain it with this response. Note that the steward credited their God, not some Egyptian deity.

³²They served him by himself, the brothers by themselves, and the Egyptians who ate with him by themselves, because Egyptians could not eat with Hebrews, for that is detestable to Egyptians. *i* ³³The men had been seated before him in the order of their ages, from the firstborn to the youngest; and they looked at each other in astonishment. ³⁴When portions were served to them from Joseph's table, Benjamin's portion was five times as much as anyone else's. *j* So they feasted and drank freely with him.

43:32
i Ge 46:34

43:34
j Ge 37:3; 45:22

A Silver Cup in a Sack

44 Now Joseph gave these instructions to the steward of his house: "Fill the men's sacks with as much food as they can carry, and put each man's silver in the mouth of his sack. ²Then put my cup, the silver one, in the mouth of the youngest one's sack, along with the silver for his grain." And he did as Joseph said.

³As morning dawned, the men were sent on their way with their donkeys. ⁴They had not gone far from the city when Joseph said to his steward, "Go after those men at once, and when you catch up with them, say to them, 'Why have you repaid good with evil? ⁵Isn't this the cup my master drinks from and also uses for divination? This is a wicked thing you have done.'"

⁶When he caught up with them, he repeated these words to them. ⁷But they said to him, "Why does my lord say such things? Far be it from your servants to do anything like that! ⁸We even brought back to you from the land of Canaan the silver we found inside the mouths of our sacks. *k* So why would we steal silver or gold from your master's house? ⁹If any of your servants is found to have it, he will die; *l* and the rest of us will become my lord's slaves."

44:8
k Ge 42:25; 43:21

44:9
l Ge 31:32

¹⁰"Very well, then," he said, "let it be as you say. Whoever is found to have it will become my slave; the rest of you will be free from blame."

¹¹Each of them quickly lowered his sack to the ground and opened it. ¹²Then the steward proceeded to search, beginning with the oldest and ending with the youngest. And the cup was found in Benjamin's sack. ¹³At this, they tore their clothes. *m* Then they all loaded their donkeys and returned to the city.

44:13
m Ge 37:29; Nu 14:6

¹⁴Joseph was still in the house when Judah and his brothers came in, and they threw themselves to the ground before him. *n* ¹⁵Joseph said to them, "What is this you have done? Don't you know that a man like me can find things out by divination? *o*"

44:14
n Ge 37:7, 10

44:15
o ver 5

¹⁶"What can we say to my lord?" Judah replied. "What can we say? How can we prove our innocence? God has uncovered your servants' guilt. We are now my lord's slaves *p*—we ourselves and the one who was found to have the cup."

44:16
p ver 9

¹⁷But Joseph said, "Far be it from me to do such a thing! Only the man who was found to have the cup will become my slave. The rest of you, go back to your father in peace."

¹⁸Then Judah went up to him and said: "Please, my lord, let your servant speak a word to my lord. Do not be angry *q* with your servant, though you are equal to Pharaoh himself. ¹⁹My lord asked his servants, 'Do you have a father or a brother?' ²⁰And we answered, 'We have an aged father, and there is a young son born to him in his old age. *r* His brother is dead, *s* and he is the only one of his mother's sons left, and his father loves him.' *t*

44:18
q Ge 18:30;
Ex 32:22

44:20
r Ge 37:3
s Ge 37:33
t Ge 42:13

43:32 Why did Joseph eat by himself? He was following the laws of the Egyptians' caste system. Egyptians considered themselves highly intelligent and sophisticated. They looked upon shepherds and nomads as uncultured and even vulgar. As a Hebrew, Joseph could not eat with Egyptians even though he outranked them. As foreigners and shepherds, his brothers were lower in rank than any Egyptian citizens, so they had to eat separately too.

44:2 Joseph's silver cup was a symbol of his authority. It was thought to have supernatural powers, and to steal it would be a serious crime. Such goblets were used for predicting the future. A person poured water into the cup and interpreted the reflections, ripples, and bubbles. Joseph wouldn't have needed his cup, since God told him everything he needed to know about the future.

44:13 Tearing clothes was an expression of deep sorrow, a customary manner of showing grief. The brothers were terrified that Benjamin might be harmed.

44:15 Did Joseph really practice divination? Probably not—he would have no desire or need to because of his relationship with

God. This statement was probably part of the test to emphasize how important the cup was.

44:16–34 When Judah was younger, he had showed no regard for his brother Joseph or his father, Jacob. First he had convinced his brothers to sell Joseph as a slave (37:27); then he had joined his brothers in lying to his father about Joseph's fate (37:32). But what a change had taken place in Judah! The man who had sold one favored little brother into slavery now offered to become a slave himself to save another favored little brother. He was so concerned for his father and younger brother that he was willing to die for them. When you are ready to give up hope on yourself or someone else, remember that God can work a complete change in even the most selfish personality.

44:18–34 Judah finally could take no more and stepped forward to plead his case. This was risky because Joseph could have had him killed. But Judah courageously defended himself and his brothers and pled for mercy. And he offered to put himself in Benjamin's place. At times we should be silent, but at times we

44:21
*u*Ge 42:15

44:23
*v*Ge 43:5

44:27
*w*Ge 46:19
44:28
*x*Ge 37:33
44:29
*y*Ge 42:38
44:30
*z*1Sa 18:1

44:32
*a*Ge 43:9

45:3
*b*Ac 7:13

45:4
*c*Ge 37:28
45:5
*d*ver 7-8; Ge 50:20;
Ps 105:17

45:8
*e*Jdg 17:10
*f*Ge 41:41

45:10
*g*Ge 47:1

45:13
*h*Ac 7:14

21"Then you said to your servants, 'Bring him down to me so I can see him for myself.' *u* 22And we said to my lord, 'The boy cannot leave his father; if he leaves him, his father will die.' 23But you told your servants, 'Unless your youngest brother comes down with you, you will not see my face again.' *v* 24When we went back to your servant my father, we told him what my lord had said.

25"Then our father said, 'Go back and buy a little more food.' 26But we said, 'We cannot go down. Only if our youngest brother is with us will we go. We cannot see the man's face unless our youngest brother is with us.'

27"Your servant my father said to us, 'You know that my wife bore me two sons. *w* 28One of them went away from me, and I said, "He has surely been torn to pieces."*x* And I have not seen him since. 29If you take this one from me too and harm comes to him, you will bring my gray head down to the grave*a* in misery.'*y*

30"So now, if the boy is not with us when I go back to your servant my father and if my father, whose life is closely bound up with the boy's life,*z* 31sees that the boy isn't there, he will die. Your servants will bring the gray head of our father down to the grave in sorrow. 32Your servant guaranteed the boy's safety to my father. I said, 'If I do not bring him back to you, I will bear the blame before you, my father, all my life!'*a*

33"Now then, please let your servant remain here as my lord's slave in place of the boy, and let the boy return with his brothers. 34How can I go back to my father if the boy is not with me? No! Do not let me see the misery that would come upon my father."

Joseph Makes Himself Known

45 Then Joseph could no longer control himself before all his attendants, and he cried out, "Have everyone leave my presence!" So there was no one with Joseph when he made himself known to his brothers. 2And he wept so loudly that the Egyptians heard him, and Pharaoh's household heard about it.

3Joseph said to his brothers, "I am Joseph! Is my father still living?"*b* But his brothers were not able to answer him, because they were terrified at his presence.

4Then Joseph said to his brothers, "Come close to me." When they had done so, he said, "I am your brother Joseph, the one you sold into Egypt!*c* 5And now, do not be distressed and do not be angry with yourselves for selling me here, because it was to save lives that God sent me ahead of you. *d* 6For two years now there has been famine in the land, and for the next five years there will not be plowing and reaping. 7But God sent me ahead of you to preserve for you a remnant on earth and to save your lives by a great deliverance.*b*

8"So then, it was not you who sent me here, but God. He made me father*e* to Pharaoh, lord of his entire household and ruler of all Egypt.*f* 9Now hurry back to my father and say to him, 'This is what your son Joseph says: God has made me lord of all Egypt. Come down to me; don't delay. 10You shall live in the region of Goshen*g* and be near me—you, your children and grandchildren, your flocks and herds, and all you have. 11I will provide for you there, because five years of famine are still to come. Otherwise you and your household and all who belong to you will become destitute.'

12"You can see for yourselves, and so can my brother Benjamin, that it is really I who am speaking to you. 13Tell my father about all the honor accorded me in Egypt and about everything you have seen. And bring my father down here quickly.*h*"

a29 Hebrew *Sheol*; also in verse 31   *b7* Or *save you as a great band of survivors*

should speak up, even if there could be serious repercussions. When faced with a situation that needs a strong voice and courageous action, remember Judah, and speak up.

44:32, 33 Judah had promised Jacob that he would guarantee young Benjamin's safety (43:9). Now Judah had a chance to keep that promise. Becoming a slave was a terrible fate, but Judah was determined to keep his word to his father. He showed great courage in carrying out his promise. Accepting a responsibility means carrying it out with determination and courage, regardless of the personal sacrifice.

44:33 Joseph wanted to see if his brothers' attitudes had changed for the better, so he tested the way they treated each other. Judah, the brother who had stepped forward with the plan to sell Joseph (37:27), now stepped forward to take Benjamin's punishment so that Benjamin could return to their father. This courageous act

convinced Joseph that his brothers had dramatically changed for the better.

45:4–8 Although Joseph's brothers had wanted to get rid of him, God used even their evil actions to fulfill his ultimate plan. He sent Joseph ahead to preserve their lives, save Egypt, and prepare the way for the beginning of the nation of Israel. God is sovereign. His plans are not dictated by human actions. When others intend evil toward you, remember that they are only God's tools. As Joseph said to his brothers, "You intended to harm me, but God intended it for good to accomplish what is now being done, the saving of many lives" (50:20).

¹⁴Then he threw his arms around his brother Benjamin and wept, and Benjamin embraced him, weeping. ¹⁵And he kissed all his brothers and wept over them. Afterward his brothers talked with him.

¹⁶When the news reached Pharaoh's palace that Joseph's brothers had come, Pharaoh and all his officials were pleased. ¹⁷Pharaoh said to Joseph, "Tell your brothers, 'Do this: Load your animals and return to the land of Canaan, ¹⁸and bring your father and your families back to me. I will give you the best of the land of Egypt/ and you can enjoy the fat of the land.'

¹⁹"You are also directed to tell them, 'Do this: Take some carts/ from Egypt for your children and your wives, and get your father and come. ²⁰Never mind about your belongings, because the best of all Egypt will be yours.'"

²¹So the sons of Israel did this. Joseph gave them carts, as Pharaoh had commanded, and he also gave them provisions for their journey. ²²To each of them he gave new clothing, but to Benjamin he gave three hundred shekels ᵃ of silver and five sets of clothes. ²³And this is what he sent to his father: ten donkeys loaded with the best things of Egypt, and ten female donkeys loaded with grain and bread and other provisions for his journey. ²⁴Then he sent his brothers away, and as they were leaving he said to them, "Don't quarrel on the way!"

²⁵So they went up out of Egypt and came to their father Jacob in the land of Canaan. ²⁶They told him, "Joseph is still alive! In fact, he is ruler of all Egypt." Jacob was stunned; he did not believe them. ²⁷But when they told him everything Joseph had said to them, and when he saw the carts ᵏ Joseph had sent to carry him back, the spirit of their father Jacob revived. ²⁸And Israel said, "I'm convinced! My son Joseph is still alive. I will go and see him before I die."

6. Jacob's family moves to Egypt
Jacob Goes to Egypt

46 So Israel set out with all that was his, and when he reached Beersheba, he offered sacrifices to the God of his father Isaac.

²And God spoke to Israel in a vision at night/ and said, "Jacob! Jacob!"

"Here I am," he replied.

³"I am God, the God of your father,"ᵐ he said. "Do not be afraid to go down to Egypt, for I will make you into a great nationⁿ there. ⁴I will go down to Egypt with you, and I will surely bring you back again. ᵒ And Joseph's own hand will close your eyes.ᵖ"

ᵃ*22 That is, about 7 1/2 pounds (about 3.5 kilograms)*

45:18
ⁱGe 27:28; 46:34;
47:6, 11, 27

45:19
ʲGe 46:5

45:27
ᵏver 19

46:2
ˡGe 15:1;
Job 33:14-15

46:3
ᵐGe 28:13
ⁿGe 12:2

46:4
ᵒGe 28:15; 48:21;
Ex 3:8
ᵖGe 50:1, 24

45:17–20 Joseph had been rejected, kidnapped, enslaved, and imprisoned. Although his brothers had been unfaithful to him, he graciously forgave them and shared his prosperity. Joseph demonstrated how God forgives us and showers us with goodness even though we have sinned against him. The same forgiveness and blessings are ours if we ask for them.

JACOB MOVES TO EGYPT
After hearing the joyful news that Joseph was alive, Jacob packed up and moved his family to Egypt. Stopping first in Beersheba, Jacob offered sacrifices and received assurance from God that Egypt was where he should go. Jacob and his family settled in the region of Goshen, in the northeastern part of Egypt.

45:26, 27 Jacob needed some evidence before he could believe the incredible news that Joseph was alive. Similarly, Thomas refused to believe that Jesus had risen from the dead until he could see and touch him (John 20:25). It is hard to change what you believe without all the facts—or sometimes even with the facts. Good news can be difficult to believe. Don't ever give up hope that God has a wonderful future in store for you.

46:3, 4 The Israelites did become a great nation, and Jacob's descendants eventually returned to Canaan. The book of Exodus recounts the story of Israel's slavery in Egypt for 400 years (fulfilling God's words to Abraham in 15:13–16), and the book of Joshua gives an exciting account of the Israelites entering and conquering Canaan, the promised land.

46:3, 4 God told Jacob to leave his home and travel to a strange and faraway land. But God reassured him by promising to go with him and take care of him. When new situations or surroundings frighten you, recognize that experiencing fear is normal. To be paralyzed by fear, however, is an indication that you question God's ability to take care of you.

46:4 Jacob never returned to Canaan. This was a promise to his descendants that they would return. "Joseph's own hand will close your eyes" refers to Joseph attending to Jacob as he faced death. It was God's promise to Jacob that he would never know the pain of being lonely again.

46:6
qDt 26:5; Jos 24:4;
Ps 105:23; Isa 52:4;
Ac 7:15

5 Then Jacob left Beersheba, and Israel's sons took their father Jacob and their children and their wives in the carts that Pharaoh had sent to transport him. 6 They also took with them their livestock and the possessions they had acquired in Canaan, and Jacob and all his offspring went to Egypt.q 7 He took with him to Egypt his sons and grandsons and his daughters and granddaughters—all his offspring.

8 These are the names of the sons of Israel (Jacob and his descendants) who went to Egypt:

Reuben the firstborn of Jacob.
9 The sons of Reuben:
Hanoch, Pallu, Hezron and Carmi.

46:10
rEx 6:15

10 The sons of Simeon:
Jemuel,r Jamin, Ohad, Jakin, Zohar and Shaul the son of a Canaanite woman.
11 The sons of Levi:
Gershon, Kohath and Merari.

46:12
s1Ch 2:5

12 The sons of Judah:
Er, Onan, Shelah, Perez and Zerah (but Er and Onan had died in the land of Canaan).
The sons of Perez:s
Hezron and Hamul.
13 The sons of Issachar:
Tola, Puah,a Jashubb and Shimron.

a 13 Samaritan Pentateuch and Syriac (see also 1 Chron. 7:1); Masoretic Text *Puvah*   b 13 Samaritan Pentateuch and some Septuagint manuscripts (see also Num. 26:24 and 1 Chron. 7:1); Masoretic Text *Iob*

JUDAH

People who are leaders stand out. They don't necessarily look or act a certain way until the need for their action is apparent. Among their skills are outspokenness, decisiveness, action, and control. These skills can be used for great good or great evil. Jacob's fourth son, Judah, was a natural leader. The events of his life provided many opportunities to exercise those skills. Unfortunately Judah's decisions were often shaped more by the pressures of the moment than by a conscious desire to cooperate with God's plan. But when he did recognize his mistakes, he was willing to admit them. His experience with Tamar and the final confrontation with Joseph are both examples of Judah's willingness to bear the blame when confronted. It was one of the qualities he passed on to his descendant David.

Whether or not we have Judah's natural leadership qualities, we share with him a tendency to be blind toward our own sin. Too often, however, we don't share his willingness to admit mistakes. From Judah we can learn that it is not wise to wait until our errors force us to admit to wrongdoing. It is far better to admit our mistakes openly, to shoulder the blame, and to seek forgiveness.

Strengths and accomplishments:	• Was a natural leader—outspoken and decisive • Thought clearly and took action in high-pressure situations • Was willing to stand by his word and put himself on the line when necessary • Was the fourth son of 12, through whom God would eventually bring David and Jesus, the Messiah
Weaknesses and mistakes:	• Suggested to his brothers they sell Joseph into slavery • Failed to keep his promise to his daughter-in-law, Tamar
Lessons from his life:	• God is in control, far beyond the immediate situation • Procrastination often makes matters worse • Judah's offer to substitute his life for Benjamin's is a picture of what his descendant Jesus would do for all people
Vital statistics:	• Where: Canaan and Egypt • Occupation: Shepherd • Relatives: Parents: Jacob and Leah. Wife: The daughter of Shua (1 Chronicles 2:3). Daughter-in-law: Tamar. Eleven brothers, at least one sister, and at least five sons.
Key verses:	"Judah, your brothers will praise you; your hand will be on the neck of your enemies; your father's sons will bow down to you. You are a lion's cub, O Judah; you return from the prey, my son. Like a lion he crouches and lies down, like a lioness—who dares to rouse him? The scepter will not depart from Judah, nor the ruler's staff from between his feet, until he comes to whom it belongs and the obedience of the nations is his" (Genesis 49:8–10).

Judah's story is told in Genesis 29:35—50:26. He is also mentioned in 1 Chronicles 2—4.

14 The sons of Zebulun:

Sered, Elon and Jahleel.

15These were the sons Leah bore to Jacob in Paddan Aram,ª besides his daughter Dinah. These sons and daughters of his were thirty-three in all.

16 The sons of Gad:

Zephon,b t Haggi, Shuni, Ezbon, Eri, Arodi and Areli.

46:16
t Nu 26:15

17 The sons of Asher: u

Imnah, Ishvah, Ishvi and Beriah.

Their sister was Serah.

The sons of Beriah:

Heber and Malkiel.

46:17
u Ge 30:13;
1Ch 7:30-31

18These were the children born to Jacob by Zilpah, whom Laban had given to his daughter Leah—sixteen in all.

19 The sons of Jacob's wife Rachel:

Joseph and Benjamin. 20In Egypt, Manasseh v and Ephraim were born to Joseph by Asenath daughter of Potiphera, priest of On. c

46:20
v Ge 41:51

21 The sons of Benjamin: w

Bela, Beker, Ashbel, Gera, Naaman, Ehi, Rosh, Muppim, Huppim and Ard.

46:21
w 1Ch 7:6-12

22These were the sons of Rachel who were born to Jacob—fourteen in all.

23 The son of Dan:

Hushim.

24 The sons of Naphtali:

Jahziel, Guni, Jezer and Shillem.

25These were the sons born to Jacob by Bilhah,ˣ whom Laban had given to his daughter Rachelʸ—seven in all.

46:25
x Ge 30:8
y Ge 29:29

26All those who went to Egypt with Jacob—those who were his direct descendants, not counting his sons' wives—numbered sixty-six persons. z 27With the two sons d who had been born to Joseph in Egypt, the members of Jacob's family, which went to Egypt, were seventye in all. a

46:26
z Ex 1:5; Dt 10:22
46:27
a Ac 7:14

28Now Jacob sent Judah ahead of him to Joseph to get directions to Goshen. When they arrived in the region of Goshen, 29Joseph had his chariot made ready and went to Goshen to meet his father Israel. As soon as Joseph appeared before him, he threw his arms around his fatherf and wept for a long time. b

46:29
b Ge 45:14-15

30Israel said to Joseph, "Now I am ready to die, since I have seen for myself that you are still alive."

31Then Joseph said to his brothers and to his father's household, "I will go up and speak to Pharaoh and will say to him, 'My brothers and my father's household, who were living in the land of Canaan, have come to me. c 32The men are shepherds; they tend livestock, and they have brought along their flocks and herds and everything they own.' 33When Pharaoh calls you in and asks, 'What is your occupation?' d 34you should answer, 'Your servants have tended livestock from our boyhood on, just as our fathers did.' Then you will be allowed to settle in the region of Goshen, for all shepherds are detestable to the Egyptians. e"

46:31
c Ge 47:1
46:33
d Ge 47:3
46:34
e Ge 43:32; Ex 8:26

47 Joseph went and told Pharaoh, "My father and brothers, with their flocks and herds and everything they own, have come from the land of Canaan and are now in Goshen." f 2He chose five of his brothers and presented them before Pharaoh.

3Pharaoh asked the brothers, "What is your occupation?" g

"Your servants are shepherds," they replied to Pharaoh, "just as our fathers were." 4They also said to him, "We have come to live here awhile,h because the famine is severe in Canaani and your servants' flocks have no pasture. So now, please let your servants settle in Goshen."j

47:1
f Ge 46:31
47:3
g Ge 46:33
47:4
h Ge 15:13; Dt 26:5
i Ge 43:1
j Ge 46:34

a 15 That is, Northwest Mesopotamia   b 16 Samaritan Pentateuch and Septuagint (see also Num. 26:15); Masoretic Text *Ziphion*   c 20 That is, Heliopolis   d 27 Hebrew; Septuagint *the nine children*   e 27 Hebrew (see also Exodus 1:5 and footnote); Septuagint (see also Acts 7:14) *seventy-five*   f 29 Hebrew *around him*

46:31–34 Jacob moved his whole family to Egypt, but they wanted to live apart from the Egyptians. To ensure this, Joseph told them to let Pharaoh know they were shepherds. Although Pharaoh may have been sympathetic to shepherds (for he was probably descended from the nomadic Hyksos line), the Egyptian culture would not willingly accept shepherds among them. The strategy worked, and Jacob's family was able to benefit from Pharaoh's generosity as well as from the Egyptians' prejudice.

47:1–6 Joseph's faithfulness affected his entire family. When he was in the pit and in prison, Joseph must have wondered about his

5 Pharaoh said to Joseph, "Your father and your brothers have come to you, 6 and the land of Egypt is before you; settle your father and your brothers in the best part of the land. Let them live in Goshen. And if you know of any among them with special ability, put them in charge of my own livestock."

7 Then Joseph brought his father Jacob in and presented him before Pharaoh. After Jacob blessed a Pharaoh, 8 Pharaoh asked him, "How old are you?"

47:9
k Ge 25:7
l Ge 35:28

9 And Jacob said to Pharaoh, "The years of my pilgrimage are a hundred and thirty. *k* My years have been few and difficult, and they do not equal the years of the pilgrimage of my fathers." *l* 10 Then Jacob blessed b Pharaoh *m* and went out from his presence.

47:10
m ver 7

47:11
n Ex 1:11; 12:37

11 So Joseph settled his father and his brothers in Egypt and gave them property in the best part of the land, the district of Rameses, *n* as Pharaoh directed. 12 Joseph also provided his father and his brothers and all his father's household with food, according to the number of their children.

Joseph and the Famine

47:13
o Ge 41:30; Ac 7:11

47:14
p Ge 41:56

13 There was no food, however, in the whole region because the famine was severe; both Egypt and Canaan wasted away because of the famine. *o* 14 Joseph collected all the money that was to be found in Egypt and Canaan in payment for the grain they were buying, and he brought it to Pharaoh's palace. *p* 15 When the money of the people of Egypt and Canaan was gone, all Egypt came to Joseph and said, "Give us food. Why should we die before your eyes? Our money is used up."

16 "Then bring your livestock," said Joseph. "I will sell you food in exchange for your livestock, since your money is gone." 17 So they brought their livestock to Joseph, and he gave them food in exchange for their horses, their sheep and goats, their cattle and donkeys. And he brought them through that year with food in exchange for all their livestock.

18 When that year was over, they came to him the following year and said, "We cannot hide from our lord the fact that since our money is gone and our livestock belongs to you, there is nothing left for our lord except our bodies and our land. 19 Why should we perish before your eyes—we and our land as well? Buy us and our land in exchange for food, and we with our land will be in bondage to Pharaoh. Give us seed so that we may live and not die, and that the land may not become desolate."

47:22
q Dt 14:28-29;
Ezr 7:24

20 So Joseph bought all the land in Egypt for Pharaoh. The Egyptians, one and all, sold their fields, because the famine was too severe for them. The land became Pharaoh's, 21 and Joseph reduced the people to servitude, c from one end of Egypt to the other. 22 However, he did not buy the land of the priests, because they received a regular allotment from Pharaoh and had food enough from the allotment q Pharaoh gave them. That is why they did not sell their land.

23 Joseph said to the people, "Now that I have bought you and your land today for Pharaoh, here is seed for you so you can plant the ground. 24 But when the crop comes in, give a fifth of it to Pharaoh. The other four-fifths you may keep as seed for the fields and as food for yourselves and your households and your children."

25 "You have saved our lives," they said. "May we find favor in the eyes of our lord; we will be in bondage to Pharaoh."

47:26
r ver 22

26 So Joseph established it as a law concerning land in Egypt—still in force today—that a fifth of the produce belongs to Pharaoh. It was only the land of the priests that did not become Pharaoh's. *r*

27 Now the Israelites settled in Egypt in the region of Goshen. They acquired property there and were fruitful and increased greatly in number.

7. Jacob and Joseph die in Egypt

47:29
s Dt 31:14

28 Jacob lived in Egypt seventeen years, and the years of his life were a hundred and forty-seven. 29 When the time drew near for Israel to die, s he called for his son Joseph and said to

a 7 Or *greeted*   b 10 Or *said farewell to*   c 21 Samaritan Pentateuch and Septuagint (see also Vulgate); Masoretic Text *and he moved the people into the cities*

---

future. Instead of despairing, he faithfully obeyed God and did what was right. Here we see one of the exciting results. We may not always see the effects of our faith, but we can be sure that God will honor faithfulness.

47:29-31 Putting a hand under the thigh was a sign of making a promise, much like shaking hands today. Jacob had Joseph prom-

ise to bury him in his homeland. Few things were written in this culture, so a person's word carried as much force as a written contract does today. People today seem to find it easy to say, "I didn't mean that." God's people, however, are to speak the truth and live the truth. Let your words be as binding as a written contract.

him, "If I have found favor in your eyes, put your hand under my thigh *t* and promise that you will show me kindness and faithfulness. Do not bury me in Egypt, ³⁰ but when I rest with my fathers, carry me out of Egypt and bury me where they are buried." *u*

"I will do as you say," he said.

³¹ "Swear to me," he said. Then Joseph swore to him, and Israel worshiped as he leaned on the top of his staff. *a*

Manasseh and Ephraim

48 Some time later Joseph was told, "Your father is ill." So he took his two sons Manasseh and Ephraim along with him. ² When Jacob was told, "Your son Joseph has come to you," Israel rallied his strength and sat up on the bed.

³ Jacob said to Joseph, "God Almighty *b* appeared to me at Luz *v* in the land of Canaan, and there he blessed me *w* ⁴ and said to me, 'I am going to make you fruitful and will increase your numbers. I will make you a community of peoples, and I will give this land as an everlasting possession to your descendants after you.'

⁵ "Now then, your two sons born to you in Egypt *x* before I came to you here will be reckoned as mine; Ephraim and Manasseh will be mine, *y* just as Reuben and Simeon are mine. ⁶ Any children born to you after them will be yours; in the territory they inherit they will be reckoned under the names of their brothers. ⁷ As I was returning from Paddan, *c* to my sorrow Rachel died in the land of Canaan while we were still on the way, a little distance from Ephrath. So I buried her there beside the road to Ephrath" (that is, Bethlehem). *z*

⁸ When Israel saw the sons of Joseph, he asked, "Who are these?"

⁹ "They are the sons God has given me here," *a* Joseph said to his father.

Then Israel said, "Bring them to me so I may bless them."

¹⁰ Now Israel's eyes were failing because of old age, and he could hardly see. *b* So Joseph brought his sons close to him, and his father kissed them *c* and embraced them.

¹¹ Israel said to Joseph, "I never expected to see your face again, and now God has allowed me to see your children too."

¹² Then Joseph removed them from Israel's knees and bowed down with his face to the ground. ¹³ And Joseph took both of them, Ephraim on his right toward Israel's left hand and Manasseh on his left toward Israel's right hand, and brought them close to him. ¹⁴ But Israel reached out his right hand and put it on Ephraim's head, though he was the younger, and crossing his arms, he put his left hand on Manasseh's head, even though Manasseh was the firstborn.

¹⁵ Then he blessed *d* Joseph and said,

"May the God before whom my fathers
    Abraham and Isaac walked,
the God who has been my shepherd
    all my life to this day,
¹⁶ the Angel who has delivered me from all harm
    —may he bless these boys. *e*
May they be called by my name
    and the names of my fathers Abraham and Isaac,
and may they increase greatly
    upon the earth."

47:29
t Ge 24:2

47:30
u Ge 49:29-32;
50:5, 13

48:3
v Ge 28:19
w Ge 28:13; 35:9-12

48:5
x Ge 41:50-52;
46:20
y Jos 14:4

48:7
z Ge 35:19

48:9
a Ge 33:5

48:10
b Ge 27:1
c Ge 27:27

48:15
d Ge 17:1

48:16
e Heb 11:21

a 31 Or *Israel bowed down at the head of his bed*   *b* 3 Hebrew *El-Shaddai*   *c* 7 That is, Northwest Mesopotamia

---

48:8–20 Jacob gave Ephraim, instead of his older brother Manasseh, the greater blessing. When Joseph objected, Jacob refused to listen because God had told him that Ephraim would become greater. God often works in unexpected ways. When he chooses people to fulfill his plans, he always goes deeper than appearance, tradition, or position. He sometimes surprises us by choosing the less obvious person, at least by human reasoning. God can use you to carry out his plans, even if you don't think you have all the qualifications.

48:11 When Joseph became a slave, Jacob thought he was dead and wept in despair (37:30). But eventually God's plan allowed Jacob to regain not only his son, but his grandchildren as well. Circumstances are never so bad that they are beyond

God's help. Jacob regained his son. Job got a new family (Job 42:10–17). Mary regained her brother Lazarus (John 11:1–44). We need never despair because we belong to a loving God. We don't yet know what good he may bring out of a seemingly hopeless situation.

48:15 Jacob spoke of God as his shepherd throughout his life. In his old age, he could clearly see his dependence upon God. This marks a total attitude change from that of his scheming and dishonest youth. To develop an attitude like Jacob's, let God shepherd you as you trust in his provision and care. When people chase after what they want with no thought of God, they are willing to do anything, even what is wrong, in order to get it. It is far better to trust God and realize that all good things come from his hand.

48:17
f ver 14

[17]When Joseph saw his father placing his right hand on Ephraim's head *f* he was displeased; so he took hold of his father's hand to move it from Ephraim's head to Manasseh's head. [18]Joseph said to him, "No, my father, this one is the firstborn; put your right hand on his head."

48:19
g Ge 25:23

[19]But his father refused and said, "I know, my son, I know. He too will become a people, and he too will become great. Nevertheless, his younger brother will be greater than he,*g* and his descendants will become a group of nations." [20]He blessed them that day and said,

> "In your*a* name will Israel pronounce this blessing:
> 'May God make you like Ephraim and Manasseh.'"

48:21
h Ge 26:3; 46:4
i Ge 28:13; 50:24

48:22
j Jos 24:32; Jn 4:5

So he put Ephraim ahead of Manasseh.

[21]Then Israel said to Joseph, "I am about to die, but God will be with you*b* *h* and take you*b* back to the land of your*b* fathers. *i* [22]And to you, as one who is over your brothers, I give the ridge of land*c* *j* I took from the Amorites with my sword and my bow."

Jacob Blesses His Sons

49:1
k Nu 24:14

49

Then Jacob called for his sons and said: "Gather around so I can tell you what will happen to you in days to come.*k*

> [2] "Assemble and listen, sons of Jacob;
> listen to your father Israel.

49:3
l Ge 29:32
m Dt 21:17

> [3] "Reuben, you are my firstborn,*l*
> my might, the first sign of my strength,*m*
> excelling in honor, excelling in power.

49:4
n Ge 35:22;
Dt 27:20

> [4] Turbulent as the waters, you will no longer excel,
> for you went up onto your father's bed,
> onto my couch and defiled it.*n*

a20 The Hebrew is singular.   *b21* The Hebrew is plural.   *c22* Or *And to you I give one portion more than to your brothers—the portion*

PARALLELS BETWEEN JOSEPH AND JESUS
Genesis
37—50

Joseph	Parallels	Jesus
37:3	Their fathers loved them dearly	Matthew 3:17
37:2	Shepherds of their fathers' sheep	John 10:11, 27
37:13, 14	Sent by father to brothers	Hebrews 2:11
37:4	Hated by brothers	John 7:5
37:20	Others plotted to harm them	John 11:53
39:7	Tempted	Matthew 4:1
37:25	Taken to Egypt	Matthew 2:14, 15
37:23	Robes taken from them	John 19:23
37:28	Sold for the price of a slave	Matthew 26:15
39:20	Bound in chains	Matthew 27:2
39:16–18	Falsely accused	Matthew 26:59, 60
40:2, 3	Placed with two other prisoners, one who was saved and the other lost	Luke 23:32
41:46	Both 30 years old at the beginning of public recognition	Luke 3:23
41:41	Exalted after suffering	Philippians 2:9–11
45:1–15	Forgave those who wronged them	Luke 23:34
45:7	Saved their nation	Matthew 1:21
50:20	What people did to hurt them God turned to good	1 Corinthians 2:7, 8

48:20–22 Jacob was giving these young boys land occupied by the Philistines and Canaanites. His gift became reality when the tribes of Ephraim and Manasseh occupied the east and west sides of the Jordan River (Joshua 16).

49:3–28 Jacob blessed each of his sons and then made a prediction about each one's future. The way the men had lived played an important part in Jacob's blessing and prophecy. Our past also affects our present and future. By sunrise tomorrow, our actions of today will have become part of the past. Yet they will already have begun to shape the future. What actions can you choose or avoid that will positively shape your future?

49:4 The oldest son was supposed to receive a double inheritance, but Reuben lost his special honor. Unruly and untrustworthy, especially in his younger days, he had gone so far as to sleep with one of his father's concubines. Jacob could not give the birthright blessing to such a dishonorable son.

5 "Simeon and Levi are brothers—
    their swords[a] are weapons of violence.
6 Let me not enter their council,
    let me not join their assembly,[o]
for they have killed men in their anger[p]
    and hamstrung oxen as they pleased.
7 Cursed be their anger, so fierce,
    and their fury, so cruel!
I will scatter them in Jacob
    and disperse them in Israel.[q]

8 "Judah,[b] your brothers will praise you;
    your hand will be on the neck of your enemies;
    your father's sons will bow down to you.[r]
9 You are a lion's[s] cub, O Judah;
    you return from the prey, my son.
Like a lion he crouches and lies down,
    like a lioness—who dares to rouse him?
10 The scepter will not depart from Judah,[t]
    nor the ruler's staff from between his feet,
until he comes to whom it belongs[c]
    and the obedience of the nations is his.[u]
11 He will tether his donkey to a vine,
    his colt to the choicest branch;
he will wash his garments in wine,
    his robes in the blood of grapes.
12 His eyes will be darker than wine,
    his teeth whiter than milk.[d]

13 "Zebulun[v] will live by the seashore
    and become a haven for ships;
    his border will extend toward Sidon.

14 "Issachar is a rawboned[e] donkey
    lying down between two saddlebags.[f]
15 When he sees how good is his resting place
    and how pleasant is his land,
he will bend his shoulder to the burden
    and submit to forced labor.

16 "Dan[g] will provide justice for his people
    as one of the tribes of Israel.
17 Dan[x] will be a serpent by the roadside,
    a viper along the path,
that bites the horse's heels
    so that its rider tumbles backward.

18 "I look for your deliverance, O LORD.

19 "Gad[h][y] will be attacked by a band of raiders,
    but he will attack them at their heels.

49:6
o Pr 1:15; Eph 5:11
p Ge 34:26

49:7
q Jos 19:1, 9

49:8
r 1Ch 5:2

49:9
s Nu 24:9

49:10
t Nu 24:17, 19;
Ps 60:7
u Ps 2:9; Isa 42:1, 4

49:13
v Dt 33:18-19

49:16
w Dt 33:22

49:17
x Jdg 18:27

49:19
y Dt 33:20

a 5 The meaning of the Hebrew for this word is uncertain.   b 8 Judah sounds like and may be derived from the Hebrew for praise.   c 10 Or until Shiloh comes; or until he comes to whom tribute belongs   d 12 Or will be dull from wine, / his teeth white from milk   e 14 Or strong   f 14 Or campfires   g 16 Dan here means he provides justice.   h 19 Gad can mean attack and band of raiders.

49:8-12 Judah had sold Joseph into slavery and tried to defraud his daughter-in-law. So why did Jacob grant him this blessing? God had chosen Judah to be the ancestor of Israel's line of kings (that is the meaning of "the scepter will not depart from Judah"). This may have been due to Judah's dramatic change of character (44:33, 34). Judah's line would produce the promised Messiah, Jesus.

49:10 "Until he comes to whom it belongs" may also be trans-

lated, "until Shiloh comes." What is Shiloh? The meaning of this difficult passage is disputed. Shiloh may be another name for the Messiah, because its literal meaning is "sent." Shiloh might also refer to the Tent of Meeting set up at the city of Shiloh (Joshua 18:1).

49:18 In the middle of his prophecy to Dan, Jacob exclaimed, "I look for your deliverance, O LORD." He was emphasizing to Dan that he would be a strong leader only if he trusted in God,

49:20
z Dt 33:24

20 "Asher's *z* food will be rich;
   he will provide delicacies fit for a king.

49:21
a Dt 33:23

21 "Naphtali *a* is a doe set free
   that bears beautiful fawns.*a*

49:22
b Dt 33:13-17

22 "Joseph *b* is a fruitful vine,
   a fruitful vine near a spring,
   whose branches climb over a wall.*b*

23 With bitterness archers attacked him;
   they shot at him with hostility.

49:24
c Ps 18:34
d Ps 132:2, 5;
Isa 1:24; 41:10
e Isa 28:16

24 But his bow remained steady,
   his strong arms*c* stayed*c* limber,
   because of the hand of the Mighty One of Jacob,*d*
   because of the Shepherd, the Rock of Israel,*e*

49:25
f Ge 28:13
g Ge 27:28

25 because of your father's God,*f* who helps you,
   because of the Almighty,*d* who blesses you
   with blessings of the heavens above,
   blessings of the deep that lies below,*g*
   blessings of the breast and womb.

49:26
h Dt 33:15-16

26 Your father's blessings are greater
   than the blessings of the ancient mountains,
   than*e* the bounty of the age-old hills.
   Let all these rest on the head of Joseph,
   on the brow of the prince among*f* his brothers.*h*

27 "Benjamin is a ravenous wolf;
   in the morning he devours the prey,
   in the evening he divides the plunder."

28 All these are the twelve tribes of Israel, and this is what their father said to them when he blessed them, giving each the blessing appropriate to him.

*a*21 Or free; / he utters beautiful words   *b*22 Or Joseph is a wild colt, / a wild colt near a spring, / a wild donkey on a terraced hill   *c*23,24 Or archers will attack... will shoot... will remain... will stay   *d*25 Hebrew *Shaddai*   *e*26 Or of my progenitors, / as great as   *f*26 Or The one separated from

JACOB'S SONS AND THEIR NOTABLE DESCENDANTS		
Jacob's 12 sons were the ancestors of the 12 tribes of Israel. The entire nation of Israel came from these men.	REUBEN	none
	SIMEON	none
	LEVI	Aaron, Moses, Eli, John the Baptist
	JUDAH	David, Jesus
	DAN	Samson
	NAPHTALI	Barak, Elijah (?)
	GAD	Jephthah (?)
	ASHER	none
	ISSACHAR	none
	ZEBULUN	none
	JOSEPH	Joshua, Gideon, Samuel
	BENJAMIN	Saul, Esther, Paul

not in his natural strength or ability. Those who are strong, attractive, or talented often find it easier to trust in themselves than in God who gave them their gifts. Remember to thank God for what you are and have so your trust does not become misplaced.

49:22 Joseph would have some heroic descendants. Among them were Joshua, who would lead the Israelites into the promised land (Joshua 1:10, 11); Deborah, Gideon, and Jephthah, judges of Israel (Judges 4:4; 6:11, 12; 11:11); and Samuel, a great prophet (1 Samuel 3:19).

49:23, 24 These verses celebrate the times God rescued Joseph

when his enemies attacked him. So often we struggle by ourselves, forgetting that God is able to help us fight our battles, whether they are against people with weapons or against spiritual forces. Joseph was able to draw closer to God as adversity mounted. To trust God to rescue you shows great faith. Can you trust him when injury or persecution is directed at you? Such spiritual battles require teamwork between courageous, faithful people and a mighty God.

The Death of Jacob

29 Then he gave them these instructions: "I am about to be gathered to my people.[i] Bury me with my fathers in the cave in the field of Ephron the Hittite, 30 the cave in the field of Machpelah, near Mamre in Canaan, which Abraham bought as a burial place from Ephron the Hittite, along with the field. 31 There Abraham[j] and his wife Sarah[k] were buried, there Isaac and his wife Rebekah[l] were buried, and there I buried Leah. 32 The field and the cave in it were bought from the Hittites.[a] "

33 When Jacob had finished giving instructions to his sons, he drew his feet up into the bed, breathed his last and was gathered to his people.[m]

50 Joseph threw himself upon his father and wept over him and kissed him.[n] 2 Then Joseph directed the physicians in his service to embalm his father Israel. So the physicians embalmed him,[o] 3 taking a full forty days, for that was the time required for embalming. And the Egyptians mourned for him seventy days.

4 When the days of mourning had passed, Joseph said to Pharaoh's court, "If I have found favor in your eyes, speak to Pharaoh for me. Tell him, 5 'My father made me swear an oath and said, "I am about to die; bury me in the tomb I dug for myself[p] in the land of Canaan."[q] Now let me go up and bury my father; then I will return.'"

6 Pharaoh said, "Go up and bury your father, as he made you swear to do."

7 So Joseph went up to bury his father. All Pharaoh's officials accompanied him—the dignitaries of his court and all the dignitaries of Egypt— 8 besides all the members of Joseph's household and his brothers and those belonging to his father's household. Only their children and their flocks and herds were left in Goshen. 9 Chariots and horsemen[b] also went up with him. It was a very large company.

10 When they reached the threshing floor of Atad, near the Jordan, they lamented loudly and bitterly;[r] and there Joseph observed a seven-day period[s] of mourning for his father. 11 When the Canaanites who lived there saw the mourning at the threshing floor of Atad, they said, "The Egyptians are holding a solemn ceremony of mourning." That is why that place near the Jordan is called Abel Mizraim.[c]

12 So Jacob's sons did as he had commanded them: 13 They carried him to the land of Canaan and buried him in the cave in the field of Machpelah, near Mamre, which Abraham had bought as a burial place from Ephron the Hittite, along with the field.[t] 14 After burying his father, Joseph returned to Egypt, together with his brothers and all the others who had gone with him to bury his father.

Joseph Reassures His Brothers

15 When Joseph's brothers saw that their father was dead, they said, "What if Joseph holds a grudge against us and pays us back for all the wrongs we did to him?"[u] 16 So they sent word to Joseph, saying, "Your father left these instructions before he died: 17 'This is what you are to say to Joseph: I ask you to forgive your brothers the sins and the wrongs they committed in treating you so badly.' Now please forgive the sins of the servants of the God of your father." When their message came to him, Joseph wept.

---

[a] 32 Or the sons of Heth   [b] 9 Or charioteers   [c] 11 Abel Mizraim means mourning of the Egyptians.

49:29
[i] Ge 25:8

49:31
[j] Ge 25:9
[k] Ge 23:19
[l] Ge 35:29

49:33
[m] ver 29; Ge 25:8; Ac 7:15

50:1
[n] Ge 46:4

50:2
[o] ver 26; 2Ch 16:14

50:5
[p] Isa 22:16
[q] Ge 47:31

50:10
[r] Ac 8:2
[s] 1Sa 31:13; Job 2:13

50:13
[t] Ge 23:20; Ac 7:16

50:15
[u] Ge 37:28

50:1–11 When Jacob died at the age of 147, Joseph wept and mourned for months. When someone close to us dies, we need a long period of time to work through our grief. Crying and sharing our feelings with others helps us recover and go on with life. Allow yourself and others the freedom to grieve over the loss of a loved one, and give yourself time enough to complete your grieving process.

50:2, 3 Embalming was typical for Egyptians but unusual for nomadic shepherds. Believing that the dead went to the next world in their physical bodies, the Egyptians embalmed bodies to preserve them so they could function in the world to come. Jacob's family allowed him to be embalmed as a sign of courtesy and respect to the Egyptians.

50:5 Joseph had proven trustworthy as Pharaoh's adviser. Because of his good record, Pharaoh had little doubt that he would return to Egypt as promised after burying his father

in Canaan. Privileges and freedom often result when we have demonstrated our trustworthiness. Since trust must be built gradually over time, take every opportunity to prove your reliability even in minor matters.

50:12, 13 Abraham had purchased the cave in the field of Machpelah as a burial place for his wife, Sarah (23:1–9). It was to be a burial place for his entire family. Jacob was Abraham's grandson, and Jacob's sons returned to Canaan to bury him in this cave along with Abraham and Isaac. Their desire to be buried in this cave expressed their faith in God's promise to give their descendants the land of Canaan.

50:15–21 Now that Jacob (or Israel) was dead, the brothers feared revenge from Joseph. Could he really have forgiven them for selling him into slavery? But to their surprise, Joseph not only forgave them but reassured them, offering to care for them and their families. Joseph's forgiveness was complete. He

50:18
v Ge 37:7

50:19
w Ro 12:19;
Heb 10:30

50:20
x Ro 8:28
y Ge 45:5

50:21
z Ge 45:11

50:24
a Ge 12:7; 26:3;
28:13; 35:12

[18]His brothers then came and threw themselves down before him. v "We are your slaves," they said.

[19]But Joseph said to them, "Don't be afraid. Am I in the place of God? w [20]You intended to harm me, but God intended it for good x to accomplish what is now being done, the saving of many lives. y [21]So then, don't be afraid. I will provide for you and your children. z" And he reassured them and spoke kindly to them.

The Death of Joseph

[22]Joseph stayed in Egypt, along with all his father's family. He lived a hundred and ten years [23]and saw the third generation of Ephraim's children. Also the children of Makir son of Manasseh were placed at birth on Joseph's knees. a

[24]Then Joseph said to his brothers, "I am about to die. But God will surely come to your aid and take you up out of this land to the land he promised on oath to Abraham, Isaac and Jacob." a [25]And Joseph made the sons of Israel swear an oath and said, "God will surely come to your aid, and then you must carry my bones up from this place."

[26]So Joseph died at the age of a hundred and ten. And after they embalmed him, he was placed in a coffin in Egypt.

a 23 That is, were counted as his

---

demonstrated how God graciously accepts us even though we don't deserve it. Because God forgives us even when we have ignored or rejected him, we should graciously forgive others.

50:20 God brought good from the brothers' evil deed, Potiphar's wife's false accusation, the cupbearer's neglect, and seven years of famine. The experiences in Joseph's life taught him that God brings good from evil for those who trust him. Do you trust God enough to wait patiently for him to bring good out of bad situations? You can trust him because, as Joseph learned, God can overrule people's evil intentions to bring about his intended results.

50:24 Joseph was ready to die. He had no doubts that God would keep his promise and one day bring the Israelites back to their homeland. What a tremendous example! The secret of that kind of faith is a lifetime of trusting God. Your faith is like a muscle—it grows with exercise, gaining strength over time. After a lifetime of exercising trust, your faith can be as strong as Joseph's. Then at your death, you can be confident that God

will fulfill all his promises to you and to all those faithful to him who may live after you.

50:24 This verse sets the stage for what would begin to happen in Exodus and come to completion in Joshua. God was going to make Jacob's family into a great nation, lead them out of Egypt, and bring them into the land he had promised them. The nation would rely heavily on this promise, and Joseph emphasized his belief that God would do what he had promised.

50:26 The book of Genesis gives us rich descriptions of the lives of many great men and women who walked with God. They sometimes succeeded and often failed. Yet we learn much by reading the biographies of these people. Where did they get their motivation and courage? They got it by realizing God was with them despite their inadequacies. Knowing this should encourage us to be faithful to God, to rely on him for guidance, and to utilize the potential he has given us.

EXODUS

Joseph
dies
1805 B.C.
(1640 B.C.)

VITAL STATISTICS

PURPOSE:
To record the events of Israel's deliverance from Egypt and development as a nation

AUTHOR:
Moses

ORIGINAL AUDIENCE:
The people of Israel

DATE WRITTEN:
1450–1410 B.C., approximately the same as Genesis

WHERE WRITTEN:
In the desert during Israel's wanderings, somewhere in the Sinai peninsula

SETTING:
Egypt. God's people, once highly favored in the land, are now slaves. God is about to set them free.

KEY VERSES:
"The LORD said, 'I have indeed seen the misery of my people in Egypt. I have heard the crying out because of their slave drivers, and I am concerned about their suffering. . . . So now, go. I am sending you to Pharaoh to bring my people the Israelites out of Egypt'" (3:7, 10).

KEY PEOPLE:
Moses, Miriam, Pharaoh, Pharaoh's daughter, Jethro, Aaron, Joshua, Bezalel

KEY PLACES:
Egypt, Goshen, Nile River, Midian, Red Sea, Sinai peninsula, Mount Sinai

SPECIAL FEATURES:
Exodus relates more miracles than any other Old Testament book and is noted for containing the Ten Commandments.

GET UP . . . leave . . . take off—these words sound good to those trapped or enslaved. Some resist their marching orders, however, preferring present surroundings to a new, unknown environment. It's not easy to trade the comfortable security of the known for an uncertain future. But what if God gives the order to move? Will we follow his lead? Exodus describes a series of God's calls and the responses of his people.

Four hundred years had passed since Joseph moved his family to Egypt. These descendants of Abraham had now grown to over two million strong. To Egypt's new pharaoh, the Hebrews were foreigners, and their numbers were frightening. Pharaoh decided to make them slaves so they wouldn't upset his balance of power. As it turned out, that was his biggest mistake, for God then came to the rescue of his people.

Through a series of strange events, a Hebrew boy named Moses became a prince in Pharaoh's palace and then an outcast in a desert land. God visited Moses in the mysterious flames of a burning bush, and, after some discussion, Moses agreed to return to Egypt to lead God's people out of slavery. Pharaoh was confronted, and through a cycle of plagues and promises made and broken, Israel was torn from his grasp.

Mobilizing this mass of humanity was no easy task, but they marched out of Egypt, through the Red Sea, and into the desert behind Moses and the pillars of cloud and fire. Despite continual evidence of God's love and power, the people complained and began to yearn for their days in Egypt. God provided for their physical and spiritual needs with food and a place to worship, but he also judged their disobedience and unbelief. Then in the dramatic Sinai meeting with Moses, God gave his laws for right living.

God led Moses and the nation of Israel, and he wants to lead us as well. Is he preparing you, like Moses, for a specific task? He will be with you; obey and follow. Is he delivering you from an enemy or a temptation? Trust him, and do what he says. Have you heard his clear moral directions? Read, study, and obey his Word. Is he calling you to true worship? Discover God's presence in your life, in your home, and in the body of assembled believers. Exodus is the exciting story of God's guidance. Read with the determination to follow God wherever he leads.

THE BLUEPRINT

A. ISRAEL IN EGYPT (1:1—12:30)
    1. Slavery in Egypt
    2. God chooses Moses
    3. God sends Moses to Pharaoh
    4. Plagues strike Egypt
    5. The Passover

When the Israelites were enslaved in Egypt, God heard their cries and rescued them. We can be confident that God still hears the cries of his people. Just as he delivered the Israelites from their captors, he delivers us from sin, death, and evil.

B. ISRAEL IN THE DESERT
    (12:31—18:27)
    1. The exodus
    2. Crossing the sea
    3. Complaining in the desert

After crossing the Red Sea, the Israelites became quarrelsome and discontent. Like the Israelites, we find it easy to complain and be dissatisfied. Christians still have struggles, but we should never allow difficulties and unpleasant circumstances to turn us away from trusting God.

C. ISRAEL AT SINAI (19:1—40:38)
    1. Giving the law
    2. Tabernacle instructions
    3. Breaking the law
    4. Tabernacle construction

God revealed his law to the Israelites at Sinai. Through the law, they learned more about what God is like and how he expected his people to live. The law is still instructional for us, for it exposes our sin and shows us God's standard for living.

MEGATHEMES

THEME	EXPLANATION	IMPORTANCE
Slavery	During the Israelites' 400-year stay in the land of Egypt, they became enslaved to the Egyptians. Pharaoh, the king of Egypt, oppressed them cruelly. They prayed to God for deliverance from this situation.	Like the Israelites, we need both human and divine leadership to escape from the slavery of sin. After their escape, the memory of slavery helped the Israelites learn to treat others generously. We need to stand against those who oppress others.
Rescue/ Redemption	God rescued Israel through the leader Moses and through mighty miracles. The Passover celebration was an annual reminder of their escape from slavery.	God delivers us from the slavery of sin. Jesus Christ celebrated the Passover with his disciples at the Last Supper and then went on to rescue us from sin by dying in our place.
Guidance	God guided Israel out of Egypt by using the plagues, Moses' heroic courage, the miracle of the Red Sea, and the Ten Commandments. God is a trustworthy guide.	Although God is all-powerful and can do miracles, he normally leads us by wise leadership and team effort. His Word gives us the wisdom to make daily decisions and govern our lives.
Ten Commandments	God's law system had three parts. The Ten Commandments were the first part, containing the absolutes of spiritual and moral life. The civil law was the second part, giving the people rules to manage their lives. The ceremonial law was the third part, showing them patterns for building the tabernacle and for regular worship.	God was teaching Israel the importance of choice and responsibility. When they obeyed the conditions of the law, he blessed them; if they forgot or disobeyed, he punished them or allowed calamities to come. Many great countries of the world base their laws on the moral system set up in the book of Exodus. God's moral law is valid today.
The Nation	God founded the nation of Israel to be the source of truth and salvation to all the world. His relationship to his people was loving yet firm. The Israelites had no army, schools, governors, mayors, or police when they left Egypt. God had to instruct them in their constitutional laws and daily practices. He showed them how to worship and how to have national holidays.	Israel's newly formed nation had all the behavioral characteristics of Christians today. We are often disorganized, sometimes rebellious, and sometimes victorious. God's Person and Word are still our only guides. If our churches reflect his leadership, they will be effective in serving him.

LEBANON

↑ N

Mediterranean Sea

SYRIA

Sea of Galilee

Samaria•

Jerusalem•

ISRAEL

Dead Sea

JORDAN

• Baal Zephon
Rameses
•Pithom

GOSHEN

• Marah

DESERT OF SIN

Elim•

EGYPT

•Rephidim

MIDIAN

Mount Sinai

Nile River

SAUDI ARABIA

0   50 Mi.

0   50 Mi.

Red Sea

Modern names and boundaries are shown in gray.

God commissioned him for the job of leading the Hebrew people out of Egypt (2:15—4:31).

5 Baal Zephon Slavery was not to last because God planned to deliver his people. After choosing Moses and Aaron to be his spokesmen to Pharaoh, God worked a series of dramatic miracles in the land of Egypt to convince Pharaoh to let the Hebrews go (5:1—12:33). When finally freed, the entire nation set out with the riches of Egypt (12:34–36). One of their first stops was at Baal Zephon (14:2), where Pharaoh, who had changed his mind, chased the Hebrews and trapped them against the sea. But God parted the waters and led the people through the sea on dry land. When Pharaoh's army tried to pursue, the waters collapsed around them, and they were drowned (14:5–31).

6 Marah Moses now led the people southward. The long trek across the desert brought hot tempers and parched throats for this mass of people. At Marah, the water they found was bitter, but God sweetened it (15:22–25).

7 Elim As they continued their journey, the Hebrews (now called Israelites) came to Elim, an oasis with 12 springs (15:27).

8 Desert of Sin Leaving Elim, the people headed into the Desert of Sin. Here the people became hungry, so God provided them with manna that came from heaven and covered the ground each morning (16:1, 13–15). The people ate this manna until they entered the promised land.

9 Rephidim Moses led the people

1 Goshen This area was given to Jacob and his family when they moved to Egypt (Genesis 47:5, 6). It became the Hebrews' homeland for 400 years and remained separate from the main Egyptian centers, for Egyptian culture looked down upon shepherds and nomads. As the years passed, Jacob's family grew into a large nation (1:7).

2, 3 Pithom and Rameses During the Israelites' stay in the land of Egypt, a pharaoh came to the throne who had no respect for these descendants of Joseph and feared their large numbers. He forced them into slavery in order to oppress and subdue them. Out of their slave labor, the supply cities of Pithom and Rameses were built (1:11).

4 Midian Moses, an Egyptian prince who was born a Hebrew, killed an Egyptian and fled for his life to Midian. Here he became a shepherd and married a woman named Zipporah. While he was here,

to Rephidim where they found no water. But God miraculously provided water from a rock (17:1, 5, 6). Here the Israelites encountered their first test in battle: The Amalekites attacked and were defeated (17:9–13). Moses' father-in-law, Jethro, then arrived on the scene with some sound advice on delegating responsibilities (18).

10 Mount Sinai God had previously appeared to Moses on this mountain and commissioned him to lead Israel (3:1–10). Now Moses returned with the people God had asked him to lead. For almost a year the people camped at the foot of Mount Sinai. During this time God gave them his Ten Commandments as well as other laws for right living. He also provided the blueprint for building the tabernacle (19—40). God was forging a holy nation, prepared to live for and serve him alone.

A. ISRAEL IN EGYPT (1:1—12:30)

Joseph brought his family to Egypt and protected them there. But after Joseph's death, as they multiplied into a nation, they were forced into slavery. God then prepared Moses to free his people from slavery and lead them out of Egypt. To help Moses, God unleashed ten plagues upon the land. After the tenth plague, Pharaoh let the people go. On the night before the great exodus, God's new nation celebrated the Passover. Just as God delivered Israel from Egypt, he delivers us from sin, death, and evil.

1. Slavery in Egypt

The Israelites Oppressed

1:1
a Ge 46:8

1:5
b Ge 46:26

1:6
c Ge 50:26

1:7
d Ge 46:3; Ac 7:17

1:9
e Ps 105:24-25

1:11
f Ex 3:7
g Ge 15:13
h Ge 47:11

1:14
i Ex 2:23; Nu 20:15

1 These are the names of the sons of Israel *a* who went to Egypt with Jacob, each with his family: 2 Reuben, Simeon, Levi and Judah; 3 Issachar, Zebulun and Benjamin; 4 Dan and Naphtali; Gad and Asher. 5 The descendants of Jacob numbered seventy *a* in all; *b* Joseph was already in Egypt.

6 Now Joseph and all his brothers and all that generation died, *c* 7 but the Israelites were fruitful and multiplied greatly and became exceedingly numerous, *d* so that the land was filled with them.

8 Then a new king, who did not know about Joseph, came to power in Egypt. 9 "Look," he said to his people, "the Israelites have become much too numerous *e* for us. 10 Come, we must deal shrewdly with them or they will become even more numerous and, if war breaks out, will join our enemies, fight against us and leave the country."

11 So they put slave masters *f* over them to oppress them with forced labor, *g* and they built Pithom and Rameses *h* as store cities for Pharaoh. 12 But the more they were oppressed, the more they multiplied and spread; so the Egyptians came to dread the Israelites 13 and worked them ruthlessly. 14 They made their lives bitter with hard labor in brick and mortar and with all kinds of work in the fields; in all their hard labor the Egyptians used them ruthlessly. *i*

15 The king of Egypt said to the Hebrew midwives, whose names were Shiphrah and Puah, 16 "When you help the Hebrew women in childbirth and observe them on the delivery stool,

a 5 Masoretic Text (see also Gen. 46:27); Dead Sea Scrolls and Septuagint (see also Acts 7:14 and note at Gen. 46:27) *seventy-five*

1:1 The children of Israel (or Israelites) were the descendants of Jacob, whose name was changed to Israel after he wrestled with the angel (see Genesis 32:24–30). Jacob's family had moved to Egypt at the invitation of Joseph, one of Jacob's sons who had become a great ruler under Pharaoh. Jacob's family grew into a large nation. But, as foreigners and newcomers, their lives were quite different from the Egyptians. The Hebrews worshiped one God; the Egyptians worshiped many gods. The Hebrews were wanderers; the Egyptians had a deeply rooted culture. The Hebrews were shepherds; the Egyptians were builders. The Hebrews were also physically separated from the rest of the Egyptians: They lived in Goshen, north of the great Egyptian cultural centers.

1:9, 10 Pharaoh was afraid the Israelites were becoming so numerous that they would organize and threaten his kingdom, so he made them slaves and oppressed them to kill their spirit and stop their growth. Slavery was an ancient practice used by almost all nations to employ conquered people and other captives. Most likely, the great pyramids of Egypt were built with slave labor. Although Israel was not a conquered nation, the people were foreigners and thus lacked the rights of native Egyptians.

1:11 There were levels of slavery in Egypt. Some slaves worked long hours in mud pits while others were skilled carpenters, jewelers, and craftsmen. Regardless of their skill or level, all slaves were watched closely by brutal slave masters, supervisors whose assignment was to keep the slaves working as fast as possible. They were specialists at making a slave's life miserable.

1:11 Ancient records indicate that these cities were built in 1290 B.C., which is why some scholars believe the exodus occurred early in the 13th century. Looking at other evidence, however, other scholars believe the Hebrews left Egypt in

1446 B.C. How could they build two cities 150 years after they left? These scholars suggest that Rameses II, the pharaoh in 1290 B.C., did not build the cities of Pithom and Rameses. Instead, he renamed two cities that actually had been built 150 years previously. It was a common practice for an Egyptian ruler to make improvements on a city and then take credit for building it, thus wiping out all records of previous founders. Also see the second note on 13:17, 18.

1:12 The Egyptians tried to wear down the Hebrew people by forcing them into slavery and mistreating them. Instead, the Hebrews multiplied and grew stronger. When we are burdened or mistreated, we may feel defeated. But our burdens can make us stronger and develop qualities in us that will prepare us for the future. We cannot be overcomers without troubles to overcome. Be true to God in the hard times because even the worst situations can make us better people.

1:15–17 Shiphrah and Puah may have been supervisors over the midwives, or else these two were given special mention. Hebrew midwives helped women give birth and cared for the baby until the mother was stronger. When Pharaoh ordered the midwives to kill the Hebrew baby boys, he was asking the wrong group of people. Midwives were committed to helping babies be born, not to killing them. These women showed great courage and love for God by risking their lives to disobey Pharaoh's command. Note: A delivery stool was the stool upon which a woman crouched when delivering her baby.

if it is a boy, kill him; but if it is a girl, let her live." [17]The midwives, however, feared[j] God and did not do what the king of Egypt had told them to do; they let the boys live. [18]Then the king of Egypt summoned the midwives and asked them, "Why have you done this? Why have you let the boys live?"

[19]The midwives answered Pharaoh, "Hebrew women are not like Egyptian women; they are vigorous and give birth before the midwives arrive."

[20]So God was kind to the midwives and the people increased and became even more numerous. [21]And because the midwives feared God, he gave them families[k] of their own.

[22]Then Pharaoh gave this order to all his people: "Every boy that is born[a] you must throw into the Nile, but let every girl live."[l]

1:17
[j]ver 21; Pr 16:6

1:21
[k]1Sa 2:35

1:22
[l]Ac 7:19

2. God chooses Moses
The Birth of Moses

2 Now a man of the house of Levi married a Levite woman,[m] [2]and she became pregnant and gave birth to a son. When she saw that he was a fine child, she hid him for three months. [n] [3]But when she could hide him no longer, she got a papyrus basket for him and coated it with tar and pitch. Then she placed the child in it and put it among the reeds along the bank of the Nile. [4]His sister[o] stood at a distance to see what would happen to him.

[5]Then Pharaoh's daughter went down to the Nile to bathe, and her attendants were walking along the river bank. She saw the basket among the reeds and sent her slave girl to get it. [6]She opened it and saw the baby. He was crying, and she felt sorry for him. "This is one of the Hebrew babies," she said.

[7]Then his sister asked Pharaoh's daughter, "Shall I go and get one of the Hebrew women to nurse the baby for you?"

[8]"Yes, go," she answered. And the girl went and got the baby's mother. [9]Pharaoh's daughter said to her, "Take this baby and nurse him for me, and I will pay you." So the woman took the baby and nursed him. [10]When the child grew older, she took him to Pharaoh's daughter and he became her son. She named him Moses,[b] saying, "I drew him out of the water."

2:1
[m]Ex 6:20

2:2
[n]Ac 7:20;
Heb 11:23

2:4
[o]Ex 15:20;
Nu 26:59

[a]22 Masoretic Text; Samaritan Pentateuch, Septuagint and Targums *born to the Hebrews*   [b]10 Moses sounds like the Hebrew for *draw out.*

1:17–21 Against Pharaoh's orders, the midwives spared the Hebrew babies. Their faith in God gave them the courage to take a stand for what they knew was right. In this situation, disobeying the authority was proper. God does not expect us to obey those in authority when they ask us to disobey him or his Word. The Bible is filled with examples of those who were willing to sacrifice their very lives in order to obey God or save others. Esther and Mordecai (Esther 3:2; 4:13–16) and Shadrach, Meshach, and Abednego (Daniel 3:16–18) are some of the people who took a bold stand for what was right. Whole nations can be caught up in immorality (racial hatred, slavery, prison cruelty); thus following the majority or the authority is not always right. Whenever we are ordered to disobey God's Word, we must "obey God rather than men" (Acts 5:29).

1:19–21 Did God bless the Hebrew midwives for lying to Pharaoh? God blessed them not because they lied, but because they saved the lives of innocent children. This doesn't mean that a lie was necessarily the best way to answer Pharaoh. The midwives were blessed, however, for not violating the higher law of God that forbids the senseless slaughter of innocent lives.

2:1, 2 Although a name is not mentioned yet, the baby in this story was Moses. Moses' mother and father were named Jochebed and Amram. His brother was Aaron and his sister, Miriam.

2:3 This tiny boat made of papyrus reeds was fashioned by a woman who knew what she was doing. Egyptian river boats were made with these same reeds and waterproofed with tar. The reeds, which grew as tall as sixteen feet, could be gathered in swampy areas along the Nile. Thus a small basket hidden among the reeds would be well insulated from the weather and difficult to see.

2:3ff Moses' mother knew how wrong it would be to destroy

her child. But there was little she could do to change Pharaoh's new law. Her only alternative was to hide the child and later place him in a tiny papyrus basket on the river. God used her courageous act to place her son, the Hebrew of his choice, in the house of Pharaoh. Do you sometimes feel surrounded by evil and frustrated by how little you can do about it? When faced with evil, look for ways to act against it. Then trust God to use your effort, however small it seems, in his war against evil.

2:5 Who was Pharaoh's daughter? There are two popular explanations. (1) Some think that Hatshepsut was the woman who pulled Moses from the river. Her husband was Pharaoh Thutmose II. (This would match the earlier exodus date.) Apparently Hatshepsut could not have children, so Thutmose had a son by another woman, and this son became heir to the throne. Hatshepsut would have considered Moses a gift from the gods because now she had her own son who would be the legal heir to the throne. (2) Some think the princess who rescued baby Moses was the daughter of Rameses II, an especially cruel Pharaoh who would have made life miserable for the Hebrew slaves. (This would match the later exodus date.)

2:7, 8 Miriam, the baby's sister, saw that Pharaoh's daughter had discovered Moses. Quickly she took the initiative to suggest a nurse (her mother) who might care for the baby. The Bible doesn't say if Miriam was afraid to approach the Egyptian princess, or if the princess was suspicious of the Hebrew girl. But Miriam did approach her, and the princess bought the services of Miriam and her mother. Their family was reunited. Special opportunities may come our way unexpectedly. Don't let the fear of what might happen cause you to miss an opportunity. Be alert for the opportunities God gives you, and take full advantage of them.

2:9 Moses' mother was reunited with her baby! God used her courageous act of saving and hiding her baby to begin his plan

Moses Flees to Midian

2:11
p Ac 7:23;
Heb 11:24-26

2:13
q Ac 7:26

2:14
r Ac 7:27*

2:16
s Ex 3:1
t Ge 24:11

2:17
u Ge 29:10

2:18
v Nu 10:29

2:21
w Ex 18:2

2:23
x Ex 3:7,9; Dt 26:7;
Jas 5:4

2:24
y Ps 105:10,42

2:25
z Ex 3:7; 4:31

¹¹One day, after Moses had grown up, he went out to where his own people *p* were and watched them at their hard labor. He saw an Egyptian beating a Hebrew, one of his own people. ¹²Glancing this way and that and seeing no one, he killed the Egyptian and hid him in the sand. ¹³The next day he went out and saw two Hebrews fighting. He asked the one in the wrong, "Why are you hitting your fellow Hebrew?" *q*

¹⁴The man said, "Who made you ruler and judge over us? *r* Are you thinking of killing me as you killed the Egyptian?" Then Moses was afraid and thought, "What I did must have become known."

¹⁵When Pharaoh heard of this, he tried to kill Moses, but Moses fled from Pharaoh and went to live in Midian, where he sat down by a well. ¹⁶Now a priest of Midian *s* had seven daughters, and they came to draw water *t* and fill the troughs to water their father's flock. ¹⁷Some shepherds came along and drove them away, but Moses got up and came to their rescue and watered their flock. *u*

¹⁸When the girls returned to Reuel *v* their father, he asked them, "Why have you returned so early today?"

¹⁹They answered, "An Egyptian rescued us from the shepherds. He even drew water for us and watered the flock."

²⁰"And where is he?" he asked his daughters. "Why did you leave him? Invite him to have something to eat."

²¹Moses agreed to stay with the man, who gave his daughter Zipporah *w* to Moses in marriage. ²²Zipporah gave birth to a son, and Moses named him Gershom,ᵃ saying, "I have become an alien in a foreign land."

²³During that long period, the king of Egypt died. The Israelites groaned in their slavery and cried out, and their cry *x* for help because of their slavery went up to God. ²⁴God heard their groaning and he remembered his covenant *y* with Abraham, with Isaac and with Jacob. ²⁵So God looked on the Israelites and was concerned *z* about them.

ᵃ22 *Gershom* sounds like the Hebrew for *an alien there.*

---

to rescue his people from Egypt. God doesn't need much from us to accomplish his plan for our lives. Focusing on our human predicament may paralyze us because the situation may appear humanly impossible. But concentrating on God and his power will help us see the way out. Right now you may feel unable to see through your troubles. Focus instead on God, and trust him for the way out. That is all he needs to begin his work in you.

2:12–14 Moses tried to make sure no one was watching before he killed the Egyptian. But as it turned out, someone did see, and Moses had to flee the country. Sometimes we mistakenly think we can get away with doing wrong if no one sees or catches us. Sooner or later, however, doing wrong will catch up with us as it did with Moses. Even if we are not caught in this life, we will still have to face God and his evaluation of our actions.

2:15 To escape punishment for killing the Egyptian, Moses ran away to Midian. He became a stranger in a strange land, separated from his home and family. It took many years after this incident for Moses to be ready to serve God. But he trusted God instead of fearing the king (Hebrews 11:27). We may feel abandoned or isolated because of something we have done. But though we feel afraid and separated, we should not give up. Moses didn't. He trusted God to deliver him, no matter how dark his past or bleak his future.

2:17 How did Moses handle these shepherds so easily? As an Egyptian prince, Moses would have been well trained in the Egyptian military, the most advanced army in the world. Even a large group of shepherds would have been no match for the sophisticated fighting techniques of this trained warrior.

2:18 Reuel is also called Jethro in 3:1.

2:23–25 God's rescue doesn't always come the moment we want it. God had promised to bring the Hebrew slaves

out of Egypt (Genesis 15:16; 46:3, 4). The people had waited a long time for that promise to be kept, but God rescued them when he knew the right time had come. God knows the best time to act. When you feel that God has forgotten you in your troubles, remember that God has a time schedule we can't see.

MOSES FLEES TO MIDIAN
After murdering an Egyptian, Moses escaped into Midian. There he married Zipporah and became a shepherd.

Moses and the Burning Bush

3 Now Moses was tending the flock of Jethro his father-in-law, the priest of Midian, and he led the flock to the far side of the desert and came to Horeb, the mountain of God. [2] There the angel of the Lord appeared to him in flames of fire from within a bush.[a] Moses saw that though the bush was on fire it did not burn up. [3] So Moses thought, "I will go over and see this strange sight—why the bush does not burn up."

[4] When the Lord saw that he had gone over to look, God called to him from within the bush, "Moses! Moses!"

And Moses said, "Here I am."

[5] "Do not come any closer," God said. "Take off your sandals, for the place where you are standing is holy ground." [6] Then he said, "I am the God of your father, the God of Abraham, the God of Isaac and the God of Jacob."[b] At this, Moses hid his face, because he was afraid to look at God.

[7] The Lord said, "I have indeed seen the misery of my people in Egypt. I have heard them crying out because of their slave drivers, and I am concerned[c] about their suffering. [8] So I have come down to rescue them from the hand of the Egyptians and to bring them up out of that land into a good and spacious land, a land flowing with milk and honey[d]—the home of the Canaanites, Hittites, Amorites, Perizzites, Hivites and Jebusites. [9] And now the cry of the Israelites has reached me, and I have seen the way the Egyptians are oppressing them. [10] So now, go. I am sending you to Pharaoh to bring my people the Israelites out of Egypt."[e]

[11] But Moses said to God, "Who am I, that I should go to Pharaoh and bring the Israelites out of Egypt?"

[12] And God said, "I will be with you. And this will be the sign to you that it is I who have sent you: When you have brought the people out of Egypt, you[a] will worship God on this mountain."

[13] Moses said to God, "Suppose I go to the Israelites and say to them, 'The God of your fathers has sent me to you,' and they ask me, 'What is his name?' Then what shall I tell them?"

[14] God said to Moses, "I am who I am.[b] This is what you are to say to the Israelites: 'I am[f] has sent me to you.'"

[a] 12 The Hebrew is plural.   [b] 14 Or *I will be what I will be*

3:2 [a] Dt 33:16; Ac 7:30

3:6 [b] Mt 22:32*; Ac 7:32*

3:7 [c] Ex 2:25

3:8 [d] ver 17

3:10 [e] Mic 6:4

3:14 [f] Ex 6:2-3; Jn 8:58; Heb 13:8

3:1 What a contrast between Moses' life as an Egyptian prince and his life as a Midianite shepherd! As a prince he had everything done for him; he was the famous son of an Egyptian princess. As a shepherd he had to do everything for himself; he was holding the very job he had been taught to despise (Genesis 43:32; 46:32–34), and he lived as an unknown foreigner. What a humbling experience this must have been for Moses! But God was preparing him for leadership. Living the life of a shepherd and nomad, Moses learned about the ways of the people he would be leading and also about life in the desert. Moses couldn't appreciate this lesson, but God was getting him ready to free Israel from Pharaoh's grasp.

3:1 Mount Horeb is another name for Mount Sinai, where God would give the people his revealed law, known today as the Ten Commandments (3:12; 19:1—20:21).

3:2 God spoke to Moses from an unexpected source: a burning bush. When Moses saw it, he went to investigate. God may use unexpected sources when communicating to us too, whether people, thoughts, or experiences. Be willing to investigate, and be open to God's surprises.

3:2–4 Moses saw a burning bush and spoke with God. Many people in the Bible experienced God in visible (not necessarily human) form. Abraham saw the smoking firepot and blazing torch (Genesis 15:17); Jacob wrestled with a man (Genesis 32:24–29). When the slaves were freed from Egypt, God led them by pillars of cloud and fire (13:17–22). God made such appearances to encourage his new nation, to guide them, and to prove the reliability of his verbal message.

3:5, 6 At God's command, Moses removed his sandals and covered his face. Taking off his shoes was an act of reverence, conveying his own unworthiness before God. God is our friend, but he is also our sovereign Lord. To approach him frivolously shows a lack of respect and sincerity. When you

come to God in worship, do you approach him casually, or do you come as though you were an invited guest before a king? If necessary, adjust your attitude so it is suitable for approaching a holy God.

3:8 "The home of the Canaanites" is the land of Israel and Jordan today. *Canaanites* was a term for all the various tribes living in that land.

3:10ff Moses made excuses because he felt inadequate for the job God asked him to do. It was natural for him to feel that way. He *was* inadequate all by himself. But God wasn't asking Moses to work alone. He offered other resources to help (God himself, Aaron, and the ability to do miracles). God often calls us to tasks that seem too difficult, but he doesn't ask us to do them alone. God offers us his resources, just as he did to Moses. We should not hide behind our inadequacies, as Moses did, but look beyond ourselves to the great resources available. Then we can allow God to use our unique contributions.

3:13–15 The Egyptians had many gods by many different names. Moses wanted to know God's name so the Hebrew people would know exactly who had sent him to them. God called himself, *I am*, a name describing his eternal power and unchangeable character. In a world where values, morals, and laws change constantly, we can find stability and security in our unchanging God. The God who appeared to Moses is the same God who can live in us today. Hebrews 13:8 says God is the same "yesterday and today and forever." Because God's nature is stable and trustworthy, we are free to follow and enjoy him rather than spend our time trying to figure him out.

3:14, 15 *Yahweh* is derived from the Hebrew word for "I am." God reminded Moses of his covenant promises to Abraham (Genesis 12:1–3; 15; 17), Isaac (Genesis 26:2–5), and Jacob (Genesis 28:13–15), and used the name *I am* to show his

3:15
g Ps 135:13

¹⁵God also said to Moses, "Say to the Israelites, 'The Lord,ᵃ the God of your fathers—the God of Abraham, the God of Isaac and the God of Jacob—has sent me to you.' This is my name*g* forever, the name by which I am to be remembered from generation to generation.

¹⁶"Go, assemble the elders of Israel and say to them, 'The Lord, the God of your fathers—the God of Abraham, Isaac and Jacob—appeared to me and said: I have watched over you and have seen what has been done to you in Egypt. ¹⁷And I have promised to bring you up

3:17
h Ge 15:16

out of your misery in Egypt *h* into the land of the Canaanites, Hittites, Amorites, Perizzites, Hivites and Jebusites—a land flowing with milk and honey.'

3:18
i Ex 4:1,8,31
j Ex 5:1,3

¹⁸"The elders of Israel will listen *i* to you. Then you and the elders are to go to the king of Egypt and say to him, 'The Lord, the God of the Hebrews, has met with us. Let us take a three-day journey into the desert to offer sacrifices*j* to the Lord our God.' ¹⁹But I know that the king of Egypt will not let you go unless a mighty hand compels him. ²⁰So I will stretch out

3:20
k Ex 6:1,6; 9:15
l Dt 6:22; Ne 9:10
m Ex 12:31-33

my hand*k* and strike the Egyptians with all the wonders*l* that I will perform among them. After that, he will let you go. *m*

3:22
n Ex 11:2

²¹"And I will make the Egyptians favorably disposed toward this people, so that when you leave you will not go empty-handed. ²²Every woman is to ask her neighbor and any woman living in her house for articles of silver and gold *n* and for clothing, which you will put on your sons and daughters. And so you will plunder the Egyptians."

Signs for Moses

4 Moses answered, "What if they do not believe me or listen to me and say, 'The Lord did not appear to you'?"

4:2
o ver 17,20

²Then the Lord said to him, "What is that in your hand?"

"A staff," *o* he replied.

³The Lord said, "Throw it on the ground."

Moses threw it on the ground and it became a snake, and he ran from it. ⁴Then the Lord said to him, "Reach out your hand and take it by the tail." So Moses reached out and took hold of the snake and it turned back into a staff in his hand. ⁵"This," said the Lord, "is so that they may believe that the Lord, the God of their fathers—the God of Abraham, the God of Isaac and the God of Jacob—has appeared to you."

4:6
p Nu 12:10;
2Ki 5:1,27

⁶Then the Lord said, "Put your hand inside your cloak." So Moses put his hand into his cloak, and when he took it out, it was leprous,ᵇ like snow.*p*

⁷"Now put it back into your cloak," he said. So Moses put his hand back into his cloak, and when he took it out, it was restored, like the rest of his flesh.

ᵃ15 The Hebrew for Lord sounds like and may be derived from the Hebrew for *I am* in verse 14.　ᵇ6 The Hebrew word was used for various diseases affecting the skin—not necessarily leprosy.

---

unchanging nature. What God promised to the great patriarchs hundreds of years earlier he would fulfill through Moses. His wisdom spans the ages, and his promises give meaning and direction to our lives.

3:16, 17 God told Moses to tell the people what he saw and heard at the burning bush. Our God is a God who acts and speaks. One of the most convincing ways to tell others about him is to describe what he has done and how he has spoken to his people. If you are trying to explain God to others, talk about what he has done for you, for people you know, or for people whose stories are told in the Bible.

3:17 "A land flowing with milk and honey" is a poetic word picture expressing the beauty and productivity of the promised land.

3:18–20 The leaders of Israel would accept God's message, and the leaders of Egypt would reject it. God knew what both reactions would be before they happened. This is more than good psychology—God knows the future. Any believer can trust his or her future to God because God already knows what is going to happen.

3:22 The jewels and clothing were not merely borrowed—they were asked for and easily received. The Egyptians were so glad to see the Israelites go that they sent them out with gifts. These items were used later in building the tabernacle (35:5, 22). The promise of being able to plunder the Egyptians seemed impossible to Moses at this time.

4:1 Moses' reluctance and fear were caused by overanticipation. He was worried about how the people might respond to him. We often build up events in our minds and then panic over what might go wrong. God does not ask us to go where he has not provided the means to help. Go where he leads, trusting him to supply courage, confidence, and resources at the right moment.

4:2–4 A shepherd's staff was commonly a three- to six-foot wooden rod with a curved hook at the top. The shepherd used it for walking, guiding his sheep, killing snakes, and many other tasks. Still, it was just a stick. But God used the simple shepherd's staff Moses carried as a sign to teach him an important lesson. God sometimes takes joy in using ordinary things for extraordinary purposes. What are the ordinary things in your life—your voice, a pen, a hammer, a broom, a musical instrument? While it is easy to assume God can use only special skills, you must not hinder his use of the everyday contributions you can make. Little did Moses imagine the power his simple staff would wield when it became the staff of God.

4:6, 7 Leprosy was one of the most feared diseases of this time. There was no cure, and a great deal of suffering preceded eventual death. Through this experience, Moses learned that God could cause or cure any kind of problem. He saw that God indeed had all power and was commissioning him to exercise that power to lead the Hebrews out of Egypt.

⁸Then the LORD said, "If they do not believe you or pay attention to the first miraculous sign, they may believe the second. ⁹But if they do not believe these two signs or listen to you, take some water from the Nile and pour it on the dry ground. The water you take from the river will become blood*q* on the ground."

¹⁰Moses said to the LORD, "O Lord, I have never been eloquent, neither in the past nor since you have spoken to your servant. I am slow of speech and tongue."

¹¹The LORD said to him, "Who gave man his mouth? Who makes him deaf or mute? Who gives him sight or makes him blind?*r* Is it not I, the LORD? ¹²Now go; I will help you speak and will teach you what to say."*s*

¹³But Moses said, "O Lord, please send someone else to do it."

¹⁴Then the LORD's anger burned against Moses and he said, "What about your brother, Aaron the Levite? I know he can speak well. He is already on his way to meet*t* you, and his heart will be glad when he sees you. ¹⁵You shall speak to him and put words in his mouth;*u* I will help both of you speak and will teach you what to do. ¹⁶He will speak to the people for you, and it will be as if he were your mouth and as if you were God to him. ¹⁷But take this staff*v* in your hand so you can perform miraculous signs with it."

Moses Returns to Egypt

¹⁸Then Moses went back to Jethro his father-in-law and said to him, "Let me go back to my own people in Egypt to see if any of them are still alive."

Jethro said, "Go, and I wish you well."

¹⁹Now the LORD had said to Moses in Midian, "Go back to Egypt, for all the men who wanted to kill*w* you are dead.*x*" ²⁰So Moses took his wife and sons, put them on a donkey and started back to Egypt. And he took the staff of God in his hand.

²¹The LORD said to Moses, "When you return to Egypt, see that you perform before Pharaoh all the wonders I have given you the power to do. But I will harden his heart*y* so that he will not let the people go. ²²Then say to Pharaoh, 'This is what the LORD says: Israel is my firstborn son,*z* ²³and I told you, "Let my son go, so he may worship me." But you refused to let him go; so I will kill your firstborn son.'"*a*

²⁴At a lodging place on the way, the LORD met ⌊Moses⌋*a* and was about to kill*b* him. ²⁵But Zipporah took a flint knife, cut off her son's foreskin*c* and touched ⌊Moses'⌋ feet with it.*b* "Surely you are a bridegroom of blood to me," she said. ²⁶So the LORD let him alone. (At that time she said "bridegroom of blood," referring to circumcision.)

²⁷The LORD said to Aaron, "Go into the desert to meet Moses." So he met Moses at the mountain*d* of God and kissed him. ²⁸Then Moses told Aaron everything the LORD had sent him to say, and also about all the miraculous signs he had commanded him to perform.

*a*24 Or ⌊Moses' son⌋; Hebrew *him*   *b*25 Or *and drew near* ⌊Moses'⌋ *feet*

4:9
*q*Ex 7:17-21

4:11
*r*Ps 94:9

4:12
*s*Isa 50:4; Jer 1:9; Mt 10:19-20; Mk 13:11; Lk 12:12

4:14
*t*ver 27

4:15
*u*Nu 23:5,12,16

4:17
*v*ver 2

4:19
*w*Ex 2:15
*x*Ex 2:23

4:21
*y*Ex 7:3,13; 9:12,35; Dt 2:30; Jn 12:40

4:22
*z*Jer 31:9; Hos 11:1; Ro 9:4

4:23
*a*Ex 12:12,29

4:24
*b*Nu 22:22

4:25
*c*Jos 5:2,3

4:27
*d*Ex 3:1

4:10–13 Moses pleaded with God to let him out of his mission. After all, he was not a good speaker and would probably embarrass both himself and God. But God looked at Moses' problem quite differently. All Moses needed was some help, and who better than God could help him say and do the right things. God made his mouth and would give him the words to say. It is easy for us to focus on our weaknesses, but if God asks us to do something, then he will help us get the job done. If the job involves some of our weak areas, then we can trust that he will provide words, strength, courage, and ability where needed.

4:14 God finally agreed to let Aaron speak for Moses. Moses' feelings of inadequacy were so strong that he could not trust even God's ability to help him. Moses had to deal with his deep sense of inadequacy many times. When we face difficult or frightening situations, we must be willing to let God help us.

4:16 The phrase, "as if you were God to him," means that Moses would tell Aaron what to say as God was telling him.

4:17–20 Moses clung tightly to the shepherd's staff as he left for Egypt to face the greatest challenge of his life. The staff was his assurance of God's presence and power. When feeling uncertain, some people need something to stabilize and reassure them. For assurance when facing great trials, God has given promises from his Word and examples from great heroes of faith. Any Christian may cling tightly to these. As we grow in faith, we will outgrow

our need for physical or temporary assurances and be able to trust God's Word alone.

4:24–26 God was about to kill Moses because Moses had not circumcised his son. Why hadn't Moses done this? Remember that Moses had spent half his life in Pharaoh's palace and half his life in the Midianite desert. He might not have been too familiar with God's laws, especially since all the requirements of God's covenant with Israel (Genesis 17) had not been actively carried out for over 400 years. In addition, Moses' wife, due to her Midianite background, may have opposed circumcision. But Moses could not effectively serve as deliverer of God's people until he had fulfilled the conditions of God's covenant, and one of those conditions was circumcision. Before they could go any farther, Moses and his family had to follow God's commands completely. Under Old Testament law, failing to circumcise your son was to remove yourself and your family from God's blessings. Moses learned that disobeying God was even more dangerous than tangling with an Egyptian pharaoh.

4:25, 26 Why did Zipporah perform the circumcision? It may have been Zipporah who, as a Midianite unfamiliar with the circumcision requirement, had persuaded Moses not to circumcise their son. If she prevented the action, now she would have to perform it. It is also possible that Moses became ill as a result of permitting disobedience, and so Zipporah had to perform the circumcision herself to save both her husband and son. This

4:29
e Ex 3:16

4:31
f Ex 3:18

5:2
g Job 21:15
h Ex 3:19

5:4
i Ex 1:11

²⁹ Moses and Aaron brought together all the elders *e* of the Israelites, ³⁰ and Aaron told them everything the Lord had said to Moses. He also performed the signs before the people, ³¹ and they believed. *f* And when they heard that the Lord was concerned about them and had seen their misery, they bowed down and worshiped.

3. God sends Moses to Pharaoh
Bricks Without Straw

5 Afterward Moses and Aaron went to Pharaoh and said, "This is what the Lord, the God of Israel, says: 'Let my people go, so that they may hold a festival to me in the desert.'"

² Pharaoh said, "Who is the Lord,*g* that I should obey him and let Israel go? I do not know the Lord and I will not let Israel go." *h*

³ Then they said, "The God of the Hebrews has met with us. Now let us take a three-day journey into the desert to offer sacrifices to the Lord our God, or he may strike us with plagues or with the sword."

⁴ But the king of Egypt said, "Moses and Aaron, why are you taking the people away from their labor? *i* Get back to your work!" ⁵ Then Pharaoh said, "Look, the people of the land are now numerous, and you are stopping them from working."

⁶ That same day Pharaoh gave this order to the slave drivers and foremen in charge of the people: ⁷ "You are no longer to supply the people with straw for making bricks; let them go and gather their own straw. ⁸ But require them to make the same number of bricks as before; don't reduce the quota. They are lazy; that is why they are crying out, 'Let us go and sacrifice to our God.' ⁹ Make the work harder for the men so that they keep working and pay no attention to lies."

¹⁰ Then the slave drivers and the foremen went out and said to the people, "This is what Pharaoh says: 'I will not give you any more straw. ¹¹ Go and get your own straw wherever you can find it, but your work will not be reduced at all.'" ¹² So the people scattered all over Egypt to gather stubble to use for straw. ¹³ The slave drivers kept pressing them, saying, "Complete the work required of you for each day, just as when you had straw." ¹⁴ The Israelite foremen appointed by Pharaoh's slave drivers were beaten and were asked, "Why didn't you meet your quota of bricks yesterday or today, as before?"

¹⁵ Then the Israelite foremen went and appealed to Pharaoh: "Why have you treated your servants this way? ¹⁶ Your servants are given no straw, yet we are told, 'Make bricks!' Your servants are being beaten, but the fault is with your own people."

---

would not have made her happy—hence, her unflattering comment to Moses.

5:1, 2 Pharaoh was familiar with many gods (Egypt was filled with them), but he had never heard of the God of Israel. Pharaoh assumed that the God of the Hebrew slaves couldn't be very powerful. At first, Pharaoh was not at all worried about Moses' message, for he had not yet seen any evidence of the Lord's power.

5:3 Pharaoh would not listen to Moses and Aaron because he did not know or respect God. People who do not know God may not listen to his word or his messengers. Like Moses and Aaron, we need to persist. When others reject you or your faith, don't be surprised or discouraged. Continue to tell them about God, trusting him to open minds and soften stubborn hearts.

5:4–9 Moses and Aaron took their message to Pharaoh just as God directed. The unhappy result was harder work and more oppression for the Hebrews. Sometimes hardship comes as a result of obeying God. Are you following God but still suffering— or suffering even worse than before? If your life is miserable, don't assume you have fallen out of God's favor. You may be suffering for doing good in an evil world.

5:7, 8 Mixing straw with mud made bricks stronger and more durable. Pharaoh had supplied the slaves with straw, but now he made them find their own straw and keep up their production quota as well.

5:15–21 The foremen were caught in the middle. First they tried to get the people to produce the same amount, then they complained to Pharaoh, finally they turned on Moses. Perhaps you have felt caught in the middle at work, or in relationships in your

family or church. Complaining or turning on the leadership does not solve the problem. In the case of these supervisors, God had a larger purpose in mind, just as he might in your situation. So rather than turning on the leadership when you feel pressured by both sides, turn to God to see what else he might be doing in this situation.

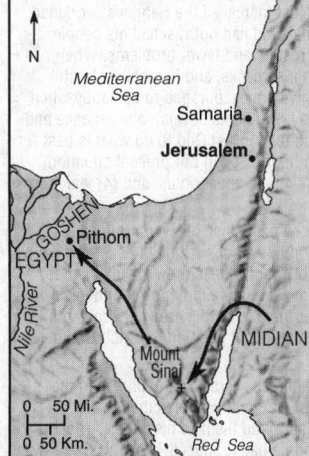

MOSES RETURNS TO EGYPT
God appeared to Moses in a mysterious burning bush on Mount Sinai (also called Mount Horeb). Later Aaron met Moses at the mountain, and together they returned to Egypt, a 200-mile trip.

[17]Pharaoh said, "Lazy, that's what you are—lazy! That is why you keep saying, 'Let us go and sacrifice to the LORD.' [18]Now get to work. You will not be given any straw, yet you must produce your full quota of bricks."

[19]The Israelite foremen realized they were in trouble when they were told, "You are not to reduce the number of bricks required of you for each day." [20]When they left Pharaoh, they found Moses and Aaron waiting to meet them, [21]and they said, "May the LORD look upon you and judge you! You have made us a stench to Pharaoh and his officials and have put a sword in their hand to kill us."

God Promises Deliverance

[22]Moses returned to the LORD and said, "O Lord, why have you brought trouble upon this people? Is this why you sent me? [23]Ever since I went to Pharaoh to speak in your name, he has brought trouble upon this people, and you have not rescued your people at all."

6 Then the LORD said to Moses, "Now you will see what I will do to Pharaoh: Because of my mighty hand[j] he will let them go;[k] because of my mighty hand he will drive them out of his country."[l]

[2]God also said to Moses, "I am the LORD. [3]I appeared to Abraham, to Isaac and to Jacob as God Almighty,[a] [m] but by my name[n] the LORD[b] [o] I did not make myself known to them.[c] [4]I also established my covenant[p] with them to give them the land of Canaan, where they lived as aliens.[q] [5]Moreover, I have heard the groaning[r] of the Israelites, whom the Egyptians are enslaving, and I have remembered my covenant.

[6]"Therefore, say to the Israelites: 'I am the LORD, and I will bring you out from under the yoke of the Egyptians. I will free you from being slaves to them, and I will redeem[s] you with an outstretched arm and with mighty acts of judgment. [7]I will take you as my own people, and I will be your God.[t] Then you will know that I am the LORD your God, who brought you out from under the yoke of the Egyptians. [8]And I will bring you to the land[u] I swore with uplifted hand to give to Abraham, to Isaac and to Jacob. I will give it to you as a possession. I am the LORD.'"

[9]Moses reported this to the Israelites, but they did not listen to him because of their discouragement and cruel bondage.

[10]Then the LORD said to Moses, [11]"Go, tell Pharaoh king of Egypt to let the Israelites go out of his country."

[12]But Moses said to the LORD, "If the Israelites will not listen to me, why would Pharaoh listen to me, since I speak with faltering lips[d]?"

Family Record of Moses and Aaron

[13]Now the LORD spoke to Moses and Aaron about the Israelites and Pharaoh king of Egypt, and he commanded them to bring the Israelites out of Egypt.

a 3 Hebrew El-Shaddai   **b** 3 See note at Exodus 3:15.   **c** 3 Or Almighty, and by my name the LORD did I not let myself be known to them?   **d** 12 Hebrew I am uncircumcised of lips; also in verse 30

6:1
[j] Ex 3:19
[k] Ex 3:20
[l] Ex 12:31,33,39
6:3
[m] Ge 17:1
[n] Ps 83:18; Isa 52:6
[o] Ex 3:14
6:4
[p] Ge 15:18
[q] Ge 28:4,13
6:5
[r] Ex 2:23
6:6
[s] Dt 7:8; 1Ch 17:21
6:7
[t] Dt 4:20; 2Sa 7:24
6:8
[u] Ge 15:18

5:22, 23 Pharaoh had just increased the Hebrews' workload, and Moses protested that God had not rescued his people. Moses expected faster results and fewer problems. When God is at work, suffering, setbacks, and hardship may still occur. In James 1:2–4, we are encouraged to be happy when difficulties come our way. Problems develop our patience and character by teaching us to (1) trust God to do what is best for us, (2) look for ways to honor God in our present situation, (3) remember that God will not abandon us, and (4) watch for God's plan for us.

6:6 Small problems need only small answers. But when we face great problems, God has an opportunity to exercise his great power. As the Hebrews' troubles grew steadily worse, God planned to intervene with his mighty power and perform great miracles to deliver them. How big are your problems? Big problems put you in a perfect position to watch God give big answers.

6:6–8 God's promises in these verses were fulfilled to the letter when the Hebrews left Egypt. He freed them from slavery, became their God, and accepted them as his people. Then he led them toward the land he had promised. When the Hebrews were rescued from slavery, they portrayed the drama of salvation for all of us. When God redeems us from sin he delivers us, accepts us, and becomes our God. Then he leads us to a new life as we follow him.

6:9–12 When Moses gave God's message to the people, they were too discouraged to listen. The Hebrews didn't want to hear any more about God and his promises because the last time they listened to Moses, all they got was more work and greater suffering. Sometimes a clear message from God is followed by a period when no change in the situation is apparent. During that time, seeming setbacks may turn people away from wanting to hear more about God. If you are a leader, don't give up. Keep bringing people God's message as Moses did. By focusing on God who must be obeyed rather than on the results to be achieved, good leaders see beyond temporary setbacks and reversals.

6:10–12 Think how hard it must have been for Moses to bring God's message to Pharaoh when his own people had trouble believing it. Eventually the Hebrews believed that God had sent Moses, but for a time he must have felt very alone. Moses obeyed God, however, and what a difference it made! When the chances for success appear slim, remember that anyone can obey God when the task is easy and everyone is behind it. Only those with persistent faith can obey when the task seems impossible.

14These were the heads of their families a:

The sons of Reuben the firstborn son of Israel were Hanoch and Pallu, Hezron and Carmi. These were the clans of Reuben.

15The sons of Simeon were Jemuel, Jamin, Ohad, Jakin, Zohar and Shaul the son of a Canaanite woman. These were the clans of Simeon.

16These were the names of the sons of Levi according to their records: Gershon, *v* Kohath and Merari. *w* Levi lived 137 years.

17The sons of Gershon, by clans, were Libni and Shimei. *x*

18The sons of Kohath were Amram, Izhar, Hebron and Uzziel. *y* Kohath lived 133 years.

19The sons of Merari were Mahli and Mushi. *z*

These were the clans of Levi according to their records.

20Amram married his father's sister Jochebed, who bore him Aaron and Moses. *a* Amram lived 137 years.

21The sons of Izhar *b* were Korah, Nepheg and Zicri.

22The sons of Uzziel were Mishael, Elzaphan *c* and Sithri.

23Aaron married Elisheba, daughter of Amminadab and sister of Nahshon, and she bore him Nadab and Abihu, Eleazar and Ithamar.

24The sons of Korah were Assir, Elkanah and Abiasaph. These were the Korahite clans.

25Eleazar son of Aaron married one of the daughters of Putiel, and she bore him Phinehas. *d*

These were the heads of the Levite families, clan by clan.

26It was this same Aaron and Moses to whom the LORD said, "Bring the Israelites out of Egypt by their divisions." 27They were the ones who spoke to Pharaoh king of Egypt about bringing the Israelites out of Egypt. It was the same Moses and Aaron.

Aaron to Speak for Moses

28Now when the LORD spoke to Moses in Egypt, 29he said to him, "I am the LORD. Tell Pharaoh king of Egypt everything I tell you."

30But Moses said to the LORD, "Since I speak with faltering lips, why would Pharaoh listen to me?"

7 Then the LORD said to Moses, "See, I have made you like God *e* to Pharaoh, and your brother Aaron will be your prophet. 2You are to say everything I command you, and your brother Aaron is to tell Pharaoh to let the Israelites go out of his country. 3But I will harden Pharaoh's heart, *f* and though I multiply my miraculous signs and wonders in Egypt, 4he will not listen *g* to you. Then I will lay my hand on Egypt and with mighty acts of judgment I will bring out my divisions, my people the Israelites. 5And the Egyptians will know that I am the LORD when I stretch out my hand *h* against Egypt and bring the Israelites out of it."

6Moses and Aaron did just as the LORD commanded *i* them. 7Moses was eighty years old *j* and Aaron eighty-three when they spoke to Pharaoh.

Aaron's Staff Becomes a Snake

8The LORD said to Moses and Aaron, 9"When Pharaoh says to you, 'Perform a miracle, *k*' then say to Aaron, 'Take your staff and throw it down before Pharaoh,' and it will become a snake." *l*

10So Moses and Aaron went to Pharaoh and did just as the LORD commanded. Aaron threw his staff down in front of Pharaoh and his officials, and it became a snake. 11Pharaoh

a 14 The Hebrew for *families* here and in verse 25 refers to units larger than clans.

6:16 *v*Ge 46:11 *w*Nu 3:17

6:17 *x*1Ch 6:17

6:18 *y*1Ch 6:2,18

6:19 *z*1Ch 6:19

6:20 *a*Ex 2:1-2

6:21 *b*1Ch 6:38

6:22 *c*Lev 10:4

6:25 *d*Nu 25:7,11; Jos 24:33

7:1 *e*Ex 4:16

7:3 *f*Ex 4:21

7:4 *g*Ex 11:9

7:5 *h*Ex 3:20

7:6 *i*ver 2

7:7 *j*Dt 34:7; Ac 7:23,30

7:9 *k*Isa 7:11 *l*Ex 4:2-5

6:14-25 This genealogy or family tree was placed here to identify more firmly Moses and Aaron. Genealogies were used to establish credentials and authority as well as outlining the history of a family.

6:26 To bring the Israelites out of Egypt by their divisions means that they would be brought out in tribes, clans, or family groups.

7:1 God made Moses "like God to Pharaoh"—in other words, a powerful person who deserved to be listened to. Pharaoh himself was considered a god, so he recognized Moses as one of his peers. His refusal to give in to Moses shows, however, that he did not feel inferior to Moses.

7:11 How were these sorcerers and magicians able to duplicate Moses' miracles? Some of their feats involved trickery or illusion, and some may have used satanic power since worshiping gods of the underworld was part of their religion. Ironically, whenever the sorcerers duplicated one of Moses' plagues, it only made matters worse. If the magicians had been as powerful as God, they would have reversed the plagues, not added to them.

then summoned wise men and sorcerers, and the Egyptian magicians *m* also did the same things by their secret arts: *n* ¹²Each one threw down his staff and it became a snake. But Aaron's staff swallowed up their staffs. ¹³Yet Pharaoh's heart became hard and he would not listen to them, just as the LORD had said.

7:11
m Ge 41:8
n ver 22; Ex 8:7,18

4. Plagues strike Egypt
The Plague of Blood

¹⁴Then the LORD said to Moses, "Pharaoh's heart is unyielding; he refuses to let the people go. ¹⁵Go to Pharaoh in the morning as he goes out to the water. Wait on the bank of the Nile to meet him, and take in your hand the staff that was changed into a snake. ¹⁶Then say to him, 'The LORD, the God of the Hebrews, has sent me to say to you: Let my people go, so that they may worship *o* me in the desert. But until now you have not listened. ¹⁷This is what the LORD says: By this you will know that I am the LORD: With the staff that is in my hand I will strike the water of the Nile, and it will be changed into blood.*p* ¹⁸The fish in the Nile will die, and the river will stink; the Egyptians will not be able to drink its water.'" *q*

7:16
o Ex 3:18

7:17
p Ex 4:9; Rev 16:4

7:18
q ver 21,24

¹⁹The LORD said to Moses, "Tell Aaron, 'Take your staff and stretch out your hand*r* over the waters of Egypt—over the streams and canals, over the ponds and all the reservoirs'—and they will turn to blood. Blood will be everywhere in Egypt, even in the wooden buckets and stone jars."

7:19
r Ex 14:21

²⁰Moses and Aaron did just as the LORD had commanded. He raised his staff in the presence of Pharaoh and his officials and struck the water of the Nile, and all the water was changed into blood.*s* ²¹The fish in the Nile died, and the river smelled so bad that the Egyptians could not drink its water. Blood was everywhere in Egypt.

7:20
s Ps 78:44; 105:29

²²But the Egyptian magicians did the same things by their secret arts,*t* and Pharaoh's heart became hard; he would not listen to Moses and Aaron, just as the LORD had said. ²³Instead, he turned and went into his palace, and did not take even this to heart. ²⁴And all the Egyptians dug along the Nile to get drinking water, because they could not drink the water of the river.

7:22
t ver 11

The Plague of Frogs

8 ²⁵Seven days passed after the LORD struck the Nile. ¹Then the LORD said to Moses, "Go to Pharaoh and say to him, 'This is what the LORD says: Let my people go, so that they may worship me. ²If you refuse to let them go, I will plague your whole country with frogs. ³The Nile will teem with frogs. They will come up into your palace and your bedroom and onto your bed, into the houses of your officials and on your people, and into your ovens and kneading troughs. ⁴The frogs will go up on you and your people and all your officials.'"

⁵Then the LORD said to Moses, "Tell Aaron, 'Stretch out your hand with your staff *u* over the streams and canals and ponds, and make frogs come up on the land of Egypt.'"

8:5
u Ex 7:19

⁶So Aaron stretched out his hand over the waters of Egypt, and the frogs*v* came up and covered the land. ⁷But the magicians did the same things by their secret arts; *w* they also made frogs come up on the land of Egypt.

8:6
v Ps 78:45; 105:30

8:7
w Ex 7:11

⁸Pharaoh summoned Moses and Aaron and said, "Pray*x* to the LORD to take the frogs away from me and my people, and I will let your people go to offer sacrifices to the LORD."

8:8
x Ex 9:28; 10:17

7:12 God performed a miracle by turning Aaron's staff into a snake, and Pharaoh's magicians did the same through trickery or sorcery. Although miracles can help us believe, it is dangerous to rely on them alone. Satan can imitate some parts of God's work and lead people astray. Pharaoh focused on the miracle rather than the message. We can avoid this error by letting the Word of God be the basis of our faith. No miracle from God would endorse any message that is contrary to the teachings of his Word.

7:17 God dramatically turned the waters of the Nile into blood to show Pharaoh who he was. Do you sometimes wish for miraculous signs so you can be sure about God? God has given you the miracle of eternal life through your faith in him, something Pharaoh never obtained. This is a quiet miracle and, though less evident right now, just as extraordinary as water turned to blood. The desire for spectacular signs may cause us to ignore the more subtle miracles God is working every day.

7:20 Egypt was a large country, but most of the population lived along the banks of the Nile River. This 3,000-mile waterway was truly a river of life for the Egyptians. It made life possible in a land that was mostly desert by providing water for drinking, farming, bathing, and fishing. Egyptian society was a ribbon of civilization lining the banks of this life source, rarely reaching very far into the surrounding desert. Without the Nile's water, Egypt could not have existed. Imagine Pharaoh's dismay when Moses turned this sacred river to blood!

8:3ff Moses predicted that every house in Egypt would be infested with frogs. The poor of Egypt lived in small, mud-brick houses of one or two rooms with palm-trunk roofs. The homes of the rich, however, were often two or three stories high, surrounded by landscaped gardens and enclosed by a high wall. Servants lived and worked on the first floor while the family occupied the upper floors. Thus if the frogs got into the royal bedrooms, they had infiltrated even the upper floors. No place in Egypt would be safe from them.

⁹Moses said to Pharaoh, "I leave to you the honor of setting the time for me to pray for you and your officials and your people that you and your houses may be rid of the frogs, except for those that remain in the Nile."

8:10
ʸ Ex 9:14; Dt 33:26;
Isa 46:9; Jer 10:6

¹⁰"Tomorrow," Pharaoh said.

Moses replied, "It will be as you say, so that you may know there is no one like the Lᴏʀᴅ our God. ʸ ¹¹The frogs will leave you and your houses, your officials and your people; they will remain only in the Nile."

¹²After Moses and Aaron left Pharaoh, Moses cried out to the Lᴏʀᴅ about the frogs he had brought on Pharaoh. ¹³And the Lᴏʀᴅ did what Moses asked. The frogs died in the houses, in the courtyards and in the fields. ¹⁴They were piled into heaps, and the land reeked of them. ¹⁵But when Pharaoh saw that there was relief, he hardened his heart and would not listen to Moses and Aaron, just as the Lᴏʀᴅ had said.

The Plague of Gnats

8:17
ᶻ Ps 105:31

¹⁶Then the Lᴏʀᴅ said to Moses, "Tell Aaron, 'Stretch out your staff and strike the dust of the ground,' and throughout the land of Egypt the dust will become gnats." ¹⁷They did this, and when Aaron stretched out his hand with the staff and struck the dust of the ground, gnats ᶻ came upon men and animals. All the dust throughout the land of Egypt became gnats. ¹⁸But when the magicians tried to produce gnats by their secret arts,ᵃ they could not. And the gnats were on men and animals.

8:18
ᵃ Ex 7:11

¹⁹The magicians said to Pharaoh, "This is the finger of God." But Pharaoh's heart was hard and he would not listen, just as the Lᴏʀᴅ had said.

The Plague of Flies

8:20
ᵇ Ex 7:15

²⁰Then the Lᴏʀᴅ said to Moses, "Get up early in the morningᵇ and confront Pharaoh as he goes to the water and say to him, 'This is what the Lᴏʀᴅ says: Let my people go, so that they may worship me. ²¹If you do not let my people go, I will send swarms of flies on you and your officials, on your people and into your houses. The houses of the Egyptians will be full of flies, and even the ground where they are.

8:22
ᶜ Ex 9:4,6,26;
10:23; 11:7

²²"'But on that day I will deal differently with the land of Goshen, where my people live;ᶜ no swarms of flies will be there, so that you will know that I, the Lᴏʀᴅ, am in this land. ²³I will make a distinction ᵃ between my people and your people. This miraculous sign will occur tomorrow.'"

8:24
ᵈ Ps 78:45; 105:31

²⁴And the Lᴏʀᴅ did this. Dense swarms of flies poured into Pharaoh's palace and into the houses of his officials, and throughout Egypt the land was ruined by the flies. ᵈ

²⁵Then Pharaoh summoned Moses and Aaron and said, "Go, sacrifice to your God here in the land."

²⁶But Moses said, "That would not be right. The sacrifices we offer the Lᴏʀᴅ our God would be detestable to the Egyptians. And if we offer sacrifices that are detestable in their eyes, will they not stone us? ²⁷We must take a three-day journey into the desert to offer sacrifices ᵉ to the Lᴏʀᴅ our God, as he commands us."

8:27
ᵉ Ex 3:18

²⁸Pharaoh said, "I will let you go to offer sacrifices to the Lᴏʀᴅ your God in the desert, but you must not go very far. Now prayᶠ for me."

8:28
ᶠ ver 8

8:29
ᵍ ver 15

²⁹Moses answered, "As soon as I leave you, I will pray to the Lᴏʀᴅ, and tomorrow the flies will leave Pharaoh and his officials and his people. Only be sure that Pharaoh does not act deceitfullyᵍ again by not letting the people go to offer sacrifices to the Lᴏʀᴅ."

ᵃ23 Septuagint and Vulgate; Hebrew *will put a deliverance*

8:15 After repeated warnings, Pharaoh still refused to obey God. He hardened his heart every time there was a break in the plagues. His stubborn disobedience brought suffering upon himself and his entire country. While persistence is good, stubbornness is usually self-centered. Stubbornness toward God amounts to rebellion against him. Rebellion will not only bring you grief, but it also may affect those who stand with you.

8:19 Some people think, "If only I could see a miracle, I could believe in God." God gave Pharaoh just such an opportunity. When gnats infested Egypt, even the magicians agreed that this was God's work ("the finger of God")—but still Pharaoh refused to believe. He was stubborn, and stubbornness can blind a person to the truth. When you rid yourself of stubbornness, you may be surprised by abundant evidence of God's work in your life.

8:25–29 Pharaoh wanted a compromise. He would allow the Hebrews to sacrifice, but only if they would do it nearby. God's requirement, however, was firm: The Hebrews had to leave Egypt. Sometimes people urge believers to compromise and give only partial obedience to God's commands. But commitment and obedience to God cannot be negotiated. When it comes to obeying God, half measures won't do.

8:26 The Israelites would be sacrificing animals that the Egyptians regarded as sacred, and this would be offensive to them. Moses was concerned about a violent reaction to sacrificing these animals near the Egyptians.

30 Then Moses left Pharaoh and prayed to the LORD, 31 and the LORD did what Moses asked: The flies left Pharaoh and his officials and his people; not a fly remained. 32 But this time also Pharaoh hardened his heart *h* and would not let the people go.

8:32
h Ex 4:21

The Plague on Livestock

9 Then the LORD said to Moses, "Go to Pharaoh and say to him, 'This is what the LORD, the God of the Hebrews, says: "Let my people go, so that they may worship *i* me." 2 If you refuse to let them go and continue to hold them back, 3 the hand of the LORD will bring a terrible plague on your livestock in the field—on your horses and donkeys and camels and on your cattle and sheep and goats. 4 But the LORD will make a distinction between the livestock of Israel and that of Egypt, *j* so that no animal belonging to the Israelites will die.'"

9:1
i Ex 8:1

9:4
j Ex 8:22

5 The LORD set a time and said, "Tomorrow the LORD will do this in the land." 6 And the next day the LORD did it: All the livestock of the Egyptians died, but not one animal belonging to the Israelites died. 7 Pharaoh sent men to investigate and found that not even one of the animals of the Israelites had died. Yet his heart was unyielding and he would not let the people go. *k*

9:7
k Ex 7:14; 8:32

The Plague of Boils

8 Then the LORD said to Moses and Aaron, "Take handfuls of soot from a furnace and have Moses toss it into the air in the presence of Pharaoh. 9 It will become fine dust over the whole land of Egypt, and festering boils *l* will break out on men and animals throughout the land."

9:9
l Rev 16:2

10 So they took soot from a furnace and stood before Pharaoh. Moses tossed it into the air, and festering boils broke out on men and animals. 11 The magicians could not stand before Moses because of the boils that were on them and on all the Egyptians. 12 But the LORD hardened Pharaoh's heart *m* and he would not listen to Moses and Aaron, just as the LORD had said to Moses.

9:12
m Ex 4:21

The Plague of Hail

13 Then the LORD said to Moses, "Get up early in the morning, confront Pharaoh and say to him, 'This is what the LORD, the God of the Hebrews, says: Let my people go, so that they may worship me, 14 or this time I will send the full force of my plagues against you and against your officials and your people, so you may know *n* that there is no one like me in all the earth. 15 For by now I could have stretched out my hand and struck you and your people with a plague that would have wiped you off the earth. 16 But I have raised you up [a] for this very purpose, that I might show you my power *o* and that my name might be proclaimed in all the earth. 17 You still set yourself against my people and will not let them go. 18 Therefore, at this time tomorrow I will send the worst hailstorm that has ever fallen on Egypt, from the day it was founded till now. 19 Give an order now to bring your livestock and everything you have in the field to a place of shelter, because the hail will fall on every man and animal that has not been brought in and is still out in the field, and they will die.'"

9:14
n Ex 8:10

9:16
o Ro 9:17*

20 Those officials of Pharaoh who feared the word of the LORD hurried to bring their slaves and their livestock inside. 21 But those who ignored the word of the LORD left their slaves and livestock in the field.

22 Then the LORD said to Moses, "Stretch out your hand toward the sky so that hail will fall all over Egypt—on men and animals and on everything growing in the fields of Egypt." 23 When Moses stretched out his staff toward the sky, the LORD sent thunder *p* and hail, *q* and lightning flashed down to the ground. So the LORD rained hail on the land of Egypt; 24 hail fell and lightning flashed back and forth. It was the worst storm in all the land of Egypt since it had become a nation. 25 Throughout Egypt hail struck everything in the fields—both men

9:23
p Ps 18:13
q Jos 10:11;
Ps 78:47;
Eze 38:22;
Rev 8:7; 16:21

a 16 Or *have spared you*

9:1 This was the fifth time God sent Moses back to Pharaoh with the demand, "Let my people go!" By this time, Moses may have been tired and discouraged, but he continued to obey. Is there a difficult conflict you must face again and again? Don't give up when you know what the right thing is to do. As Moses discovered, persistence is rewarded.

9:12 God gave Pharaoh many opportunities to heed Moses' warnings. But finally God seemed to say, "All right, Pharaoh, have it your way," and Pharaoh's heart became permanently

hardened. Did God intentionally harden Pharaoh's heart and overrule his free will? No, he simply confirmed that Pharaoh freely chose a life of resisting God. Similarly, after a lifetime of resisting God, you may find it impossible to turn to him. Don't wait until just the *right* time before turning to God. Do it now while you still have the chance. If you continually ignore God's voice, eventually you will be unable to hear it at all.

9:20, 21 If all the Egyptian livestock were killed in the earlier plague (9:6), how could the slaves of Pharaoh bring their live-

9:25
r Ps 105:32-33

9:26
s ver 4
t Ex 8:22; 10:23;
11:7

9:27
u Ex 10:16
v 2Ch 12:6; La 1:18

9:28
w Ex 8:8

9:29
x 1Ki 8:22,38;
Ps 143:6
y Ps 24:1

9:35
z Ex 4:21

and animals; it beat down everything growing in the fields and stripped every tree. r 26 The only place it did not hail was the land of Goshen, s where the Israelites were. t

27 Then Pharaoh summoned Moses and Aaron. "This time I have sinned," u he said to them. "The LORD is in the right, v and I and my people are in the wrong. 28 Pray to the LORD, for we have had enough thunder and hail. I will let you go; w you don't have to stay any longer."

29 Moses replied, "When I have gone out of the city, I will spread out my hands x in prayer to the LORD. The thunder will stop and there will be no more hail, so you may know that the earth y is the LORD's. 30 But I know that you and your officials still do not fear the LORD God." 31 (The flax and barley were destroyed, since the barley had headed and the flax was in bloom. 32 The wheat and spelt, however, were not destroyed, because they ripen later.)

33 Then Moses left Pharaoh and went out of the city. He spread out his hands toward the LORD; the thunder and hail stopped, and the rain no longer poured down on the land. 34 When Pharaoh saw that the rain and hail and thunder had stopped, he sinned again: He and his officials hardened their hearts. 35 So Pharaoh's heart z was hard and he would not let the Israelites go, just as the LORD had said through Moses.

THE PLAGUES ON EGYPT	Reference	Plague	What Happened	Result
	7:14–24	Blood	Fish die, the river smells, the people are without water	Pharaoh's magicians duplicate the miracle by "secrets arts," and Pharaoh is unmoved
	8:1–15	Frogs	Frogs come up from the water and completely cover the land	Again Pharaoh's magicians duplicate the miracle by sorcery, and Pharaoh is unmoved
	8:16–19	Gnats	All the dust of Egypt becomes a massive swarm of gnats	Magicians are unable to duplicate this; they say it is the "finger of God," but Pharaoh's heart remains hard
	8:20–32	Flies	Swarms of flies cover the land	Pharaoh promises to let the Hebrews go but then hardens his heart and refuses
	9:1–7	Livestock	All the Egyptian livestock die—but none of Israel's is even sick	Pharaoh still refuses to let the people go
	9:8–12	Boils	Horrible boils break out on everyone in Egypt	Magicians cannot respond because they are struck down with boils as well—Pharaoh refuses to listen
	9:13–35	Hail	Hailstorms kill all the slaves and animals left out or unprotected and strip or destroy almost every plant	Pharaoh admits his sin but then changes his mind and refuses to let Israel go
	10:1–20	Locusts	Locusts cover Egypt and eat everything left after the hail	Everyone advises Pharaoh to let the Hebrews go, but God hardens Pharaoh's heart and he refuses
	10:21–29	Darkness	Total darkness covers Egypt for three days so no one can even move—except the Hebrews, who have light as usual	Pharaoh again promises to let Israel go but again changes his mind
	11:1—12:33	Death of Firstborn	The firstborn of all the people and cattle of Egypt die—but Israel is spared	Pharaoh and the Egyptians urge Israel to leave quickly; after they are gone, Pharaoh again changes his mind and chases after them

stock in from the fields? The answer is probably that the earlier plague killed all the animals in the fields (9:3), but not those in the shelters.

9:27-34 After promising to let the Hebrews go, Pharaoh immediately broke his promise and brought even more trouble upon the land. His actions reveal that his repentance was not real. We do damage to ourselves and to others if we pretend to change but don't mean it.

The Plague of Locusts

10 Then the LORD said to Moses, "Go to Pharaoh, for I have hardened his heart *a* and the hearts of his officials so that I may perform these miraculous signs of mine among them [2] that you may tell your children *b* and grandchildren how I dealt harshly with the Egyptians and how I performed my signs among them, and that you may know that I am the LORD."

10:1
a Ex 4:21

10:2
b Dt 4:9; Ps 44:1

[3] So Moses and Aaron went to Pharaoh and said to him, "This is what the LORD, the God of the Hebrews, says: 'How long will you refuse to humble *c* yourself before me? Let my people go, so that they may worship me. [4] If you refuse to let them go, I will bring locusts into your country tomorrow. [5] They will cover the face of the ground so that it cannot be seen. They will devour what little you have left *d* after the hail, including every tree that is growing in your fields. [6] They will fill your houses and those of all your officials and all the Egyptians—something neither your fathers nor your forefathers have ever seen from the day they settled in this land till now.'" Then Moses turned and left Pharaoh.

10:3
c Jas 4:10

10:5
d Joel 1:4

[7] Pharaoh's officials said to him, "How long will this man be a snare *e* to us? Let the people go, so that they may worship the LORD their God. Do you not yet realize that Egypt is ruined?" *f* [8] Then Moses and Aaron were brought back to Pharaoh. "Go, worship the LORD your God," he said. "But just who will be going?"

10:7
e Ex 23:33;
Jos 23:13

10:7
f Ex 8:19

[9] Moses answered, "We will go with our young and old, with our sons and daughters, and with our flocks and herds, because we are to celebrate a festival to the LORD."

[10] Pharaoh said, "The LORD be with you—if I let you go, along with your women and children! Clearly you are bent on evil. *a* [11] No! Have only the men go; and worship the LORD, since that's what you have been asking for." Then Moses and Aaron were driven out of Pharaoh's presence.

[12] And the LORD said to Moses, "Stretch out your hand *g* over Egypt so that locusts will swarm over the land and devour everything growing in the fields, everything left by the hail."

10:12
g Ex 7:19

[13] So Moses stretched out his staff over Egypt, and the LORD made an east wind blow across the land all that day and all that night. By morning the wind had brought the locusts; [14] they invaded all Egypt and settled down in every area of the country in great numbers. Never before had there been such a plague of locusts, *h* nor will there ever be again. [15] They covered all the ground until it was black. They devoured *i* all that was left after the hail—everything growing in the fields and the fruit on the trees. Nothing green remained on tree or plant in all the land of Egypt.

10:14
h Joel 2:1-11,25

10:15
i Ps 105:34-35

[16] Pharaoh quickly summoned Moses and Aaron and said, "I have sinned *j* against the LORD your God and against you. [17] Now forgive my sin once more and pray to the LORD your God to take this deadly plague away from me."

10:16
j Ex 9:27

[18] Moses then left Pharaoh and prayed to the LORD. [19] And the LORD changed the wind to a very strong west wind, which caught up the locusts and carried them into the Red Sea. *b* Not a locust was left anywhere in Egypt. [20] But the LORD hardened Pharaoh's heart, *k* and he would not let the Israelites go.

10:20
k Ex 4:21

The Plague of Darkness

[21] Then the LORD said to Moses, "Stretch out your hand toward the sky so that darkness will spread over Egypt—darkness that can be felt." [22] So Moses stretched out his hand toward the sky, and total darkness *l* covered all Egypt for three days. [23] No one could see anyone else or leave his place for three days. Yet all the Israelites had light in the places where they lived.

10:22
l Ps 105:28

a 10 Or *Be careful, trouble is in store for you!*   *b* 19 Hebrew *Yam Suph*; that is, Sea of Reeds

---

10:2 God told Moses that his miraculous experiences with Pharaoh should be retold to his descendants. What stories Moses had to tell! Living out one of the greatest dramas in Biblical history, he witnessed events few people would ever see. It is important to tell our children about God's work in our past and to help them see what he is doing right now. What are the turning points in your life where God intervened? What is God doing for you now? Your stories will form the foundations of your children's belief in God.

10:22 As each gloomy plague descended upon the land, the Egyptian people realized how powerless their own gods were

to stop it. Hapi, the god of the Nile River, could not prevent the waters from turning to blood (7:20). Hathor, the crafty cow-goddess, was helpless as Egyptian livestock died in droves (9:6). Amon-Re, the sun-god and chief of the Egyptian gods, could not stop an eerie darkness from covering the land for three full days (10:21, 22). The Egyptian gods were (1) not personal, centering around images like the sun or the river; (2) numerous; (3) not exclusive (any and all could be worshiped). By contrast, the God of the Hebrews was (1) a living personal Being, (2) the only true God, and (3) the only God who should be worshiped. God was proving to both the Hebrews and the Egyptians that he alone is the living and all-powerful God.

10:24
m ver 8-10

24 Then Pharaoh summoned Moses and said, "Go, worship the LORD. Even your women and children *m* may go with you; only leave your flocks and herds behind."

25 But Moses said, "You must allow us to have sacrifices and burnt offerings to present to the LORD our God. 26 Our livestock too must go with us; not a hoof is to be left behind. We have to use some of them in worshiping the LORD our God, and until we get there we will not know what we are to use to worship the LORD."

27 But the LORD hardened Pharaoh's heart, and he was not willing to let them go. 28 Pharaoh said to Moses, "Get out of my sight! Make sure you do not appear before me again! The day you see my face you will die."

10:29
n Heb 11:27

29 "Just as you say," Moses replied, "I will never appear *n* before you again."

The Plague on the Firstborn

11 Now the LORD had said to Moses, "I will bring one more plague on Pharaoh and on Egypt. After that, he will let you go from here, and when he does, he will drive you out

11:2
o Ex 3:21,22

completely. 2 Tell the people that men and women alike are to ask their neighbors for articles of silver and gold." *o* 3 (The LORD made the Egyptians favorably disposed toward the people, and Moses himself was highly regarded in Egypt by Pharaoh's officials and by the people.)

11:4
p Ex 12:29

4 So Moses said, "This is what the LORD says: 'About midnight *p* I will go throughout Egypt. 5 Every firstborn son in Egypt will die, from the firstborn son of Pharaoh, who sits on the throne, to the firstborn son of the slave girl, who is at her hand mill, and all the firstborn of

11:6
q Ex 12:30

the cattle as well. 6 There will be loud wailing *q* throughout Egypt—worse than there has ever been or ever will be again. 7 But among the Israelites not a dog will bark at any man or animal.'

11:7
r Ex 8:22

Then you will know that the LORD makes a distinction *r* between Egypt and Israel. 8 All these

11:8
s Ex 12:31-33

officials of yours will come to me, bowing down before me and saying, 'Go, *s* you and all the people who follow you!' After that I will leave." Then Moses, hot with anger, left Pharaoh.

11:9
t Ex 7:4

9 The LORD had said to Moses, "Pharaoh will refuse to listen *t* to you—so that my wonders may be multiplied in Egypt." 10 Moses and Aaron performed all these wonders before Pha-

11:10
u Ex 4:21

raoh, but the LORD hardened Pharaoh's heart, *u* and he would not let the Israelites go out of his country.

5. The Passover

12:2
v Ex 13:4; Dt 16:1

12 The LORD said to Moses and Aaron in Egypt, 2 "This month is to be for you the first month, *v* the first month of your year. 3 Tell the whole community of Israel that on the tenth day of this month each man is to take a lamb*a* for his family, one for each household. 4 If

a3 The Hebrew word can mean *lamb* or *kid*; also in verse 4.

10:27, 28 Why was Pharaoh so reluctant to let the people go? The Hebrews were Egypt's free labor—the builders of their great cities. As Egypt's leader, Pharaoh would not easily let such a great resource go.

11:7 Moses told Pharaoh that God made a distinction between Egypt and Israel. At this time the distinction was very clear in God's mind: He knew the Hebrews would become his chosen people. The distinction was taking shape in Moses' mind also. But the Hebrews still saw the distinction only in terms of slave and free. Later, when they were in the desert, God would teach them the laws, principles, and values that would make them distinct as his people. Remember that God sees us in terms of what we will become and not just what we are right now.

11:9, 10 You may wonder how Pharaoh could be so foolish as to see God's miraculous power and still not listen to Moses. But Pharaoh had his mind made up long before the plagues began. He couldn't believe that someone was greater than he. This stubborn unbelief led to a heart so hard that even a major catastrophe couldn't soften him. Finally, it took the greatest of all calamities, the loss of his son, to force him to recognize God's authority. But even then he wanted God to leave, not to rule his country. We must not wait for great calamities to drive us to God, but must open our hearts and minds to his direction now.

11:10 Did God really harden Pharaoh's heart and force him to do wrong? Before the ten plagues began, Moses and Aaron announced what God would do if Pharaoh didn't let the people go. But their message only made Pharaoh stubborn—he was

hardening his own heart. In so doing, he defied both God and his messengers. Through the first six plagues, Pharaoh's heart grew even more stubborn. After the sixth plague, God passed judgment. Sooner or later, evil people will be punished for their sins. When it became evident that Pharaoh wouldn't change, God confirmed Pharaoh's prideful decision and set the painful consequences of his actions in motion. God didn't force Pharaoh to reject him; rather, he gave him every opportunity to change his mind. In Ezekiel 33:11, God says, "I take no pleasure in the death of the wicked."

12:1–3 Certain holidays were instituted by God himself. Passover was a holiday designed to celebrate Israel's deliverance from Egypt and to remind the people of what God had done. Holidays can be important today, too, as annual reminders of what God has done for us. Develop traditions in your family to highlight the religious significance of certain holidays. These serve as reminders to the older people and learning experiences for the younger ones.

12:3ff For the Israelites to be spared from the plague of death, a lamb with no defects had to be killed and its blood placed on the doorframes of each home. What was the significance of the lamb? In killing the lamb, the Israelites shed innocent blood. The lamb was a sacrifice, a substitute for the person who would have died in the plague. From this point on, the Hebrew people would clearly understand that for them to be spared from death, an innocent life had to be sacrificed in their place.

any household is too small for a whole lamb, they must share one with their nearest neighbor, having taken into account the number of people there are. You are to determine the amount of lamb needed in accordance with what each person will eat. 5The animals you choose must be year-old males without defect,*w* and you may take them from the sheep or the goats. 6Take care of them until the fourteenth day of the month,*x* when all the people of the community of Israel must slaughter them at twilight.*y* 7Then they are to take some of the blood and put it on the sides and tops of the doorframes of the houses where they eat the lambs. 8That same night*z* they are to eat the meat roasted*a* over the fire, along with bitter herbs, and bread made without yeast. 9Do not eat the meat raw or cooked in water, but roast it over the fire—head, legs and inner parts. 10Do not leave any of it till morning;*b* if some is left till morning, you must burn it. 11This is how you are to eat it: with your cloak tucked into your belt, your sandals on your feet and your staff in your hand. Eat it in haste;*c* it is the LORD's Passover.

12"On that same night I will pass through*d* Egypt and strike down every firstborn—both men and animals—and I will bring judgment on all the gods*e* of Egypt. I am the LORD. 13The blood will be a sign for you on the houses where you are; and when I see the blood, I will pass over you. No destructive plague will touch you when I strike Egypt.

14"This is a day you are to commemorate;*f* for the generations to come you shall celebrate it as a festival to the LORD—a lasting ordinance.*g* 15For seven days you are to eat bread made without yeast.*h* On the first day remove the yeast from your houses, for whoever eats anything with yeast in it from the first day through the seventh must be cut off*i* from Israel. 16On the first day hold a sacred assembly, and another one on the seventh day. Do no work at all on these days, except to prepare food for everyone to eat—that is all you may do.

17"Celebrate the Feast of Unleavened Bread, because it was on this very day that I brought your divisions out of Egypt.*j* Celebrate this day as a lasting ordinance for the generations to come. 18In the first month*k* you are to eat bread made without yeast, from the evening of the fourteenth day until the evening of the twenty-first day. 19For seven days no yeast is to be found in your houses. And whoever eats anything with yeast in it must be cut off from the community of Israel, whether he is an alien or native-born. 20Eat nothing made with yeast. Wherever you live, you must eat unleavened bread."

21Then Moses summoned all the elders of Israel and said to them, "Go at once and select the animals for your families and slaughter the Passover lamb. 22Take a bunch of hyssop, dip it into the blood in the basin and put some of the blood*l* on the top and on both sides of the doorframe. Not one of you shall go out the door of his house until morning. 23When the LORD goes through the land to strike down the Egyptians, he will see the blood on the top and sides of the doorframe and will pass over*m* that doorway, and he will not permit the destroyer to enter your houses and strike you down.

24"Obey these instructions as a lasting ordinance for you and your descendants. 25When you enter the land that the LORD will give you as he promised, observe this ceremony. 26And when your children ask you, 'What does this ceremony mean to you?' 27then tell them, 'It is the Passover*n* sacrifice to the LORD, who passed over the houses of the Israelites in Egypt and spared our homes when he struck down the Egyptians.'" Then the people bowed down and worshiped. 28The Israelites did just what the LORD commanded Moses and Aaron.

12:5
*w*Lev 22:18-21

12:6
*x*Lev 23:5;
Nu 9:1-3,5,11
*y*Dt 16:4,6

12:8
*z*Ex 34:25
*a*Dt 16:7

12:10
*b*Ex 34:25

12:11
*c*Dt 16:3

12:12
*d*Ex 11:4
*e*Nu 33:4

12:14
*f*Ex 13:9
*g*Ex 13:5,10

12:15
*h*Ex 23:15;
Lev 23:6; Dt 16:3
*i*Nu 9:13

12:17
*j*Ex 13:3

12:18
*k*ver 2; Lev 23:5-8

12:22
*l*ver 7

12:23
*m*ver 13

12:27
*n*ver 11

12:6-11 The Feast of the Passover was to be an annual holiday in honor of the night when the Lord "passed over" the homes of the Israelites. The Hebrews followed God's instructions by placing the blood of a lamb on the doorframes of their homes. That night the firstborn son of every family who did not have blood on the doorframes was killed. The lamb had to be killed in order to get the blood that would protect them. (This foreshadowed the death of Christ, the Lamb of God, who gave his blood for the sins of all people.) Inside their homes, the Israelites ate a meal of roast lamb, bitter herbs, and bread made without yeast. Unleavened bread could be made quickly because the dough did not have to rise. Thus they could leave at any time. Bitter herbs signified the bitterness of slavery.

12:11 Eating the Passover feast while dressed for travel was a sign of the Hebrews' faith. Although they were not yet free, they were to prepare themselves, for God had said he would lead them out of Egypt. Their preparation was an act of faith. Preparing ourselves for the fulfillment of God's promises, however unlikely they may seem, demonstrates our faith.

12:17, 23 Passover and the Feast of Unleavened Bread became an annual remembrance of how God delivered the Hebrews from Egypt. Each year the people would pause to remember the day when the destroyer (God's angel of death) passed over their homes. They gave thanks to God for saving them from death and bringing them out of a land of slavery and sin. Believers today have experienced a day of deliverance as well—the day we were delivered from spiritual death and slavery to sin. The Lord's Supper is our Passover remembrance of our new life and freedom from sin. The next time struggles and trials come, remember how God has delivered you in the past and focus on his promise of new life with him.

12:29
o Ex 11:4
p Ex 4:23
12:30
q Ex 11:6

²⁹At midnight o the LORD struck down all the firstborn p in Egypt, from the firstborn of Pharaoh, who sat on the throne, to the firstborn of the prisoner, who was in the dungeon, and the firstborn of all the livestock as well. ³⁰Pharaoh and all his officials and all the Egyptians got up during the night, and there was loud wailing q in Egypt, for there was not a house without someone dead.

B. ISRAEL IN THE DESERT (12:31—18:27)

As Egypt buried its dead, the Hebrew slaves left the country, a free people at last. Pharaoh made one last attempt to bring them back, but the people escaped when God miraculously parted the waters of the Red Sea. But on the other side, the people soon became dissatisfied and complained bitterly to Moses and Aaron about their trek through the desert. Through these experiences of the Hebrews, we learn that the Christian life is not always trouble-free. We still have struggles and often complain bitterly to God about conditions in our lives.

1. The exodus

³¹During the night Pharaoh summoned Moses and Aaron and said, "Up! Leave my people, you and the Israelites! Go, worship the LORD as you have requested. ³²Take your flocks and herds, as you have said, and go. And also bless me."

³³The Egyptians urged the people to hurry and leave the country. "For otherwise," they

THE HEBREW CALENDAR	Month	Today's Calendar	Bible Reference	Israel's Holidays
A Hebrew month began in the middle of a month on our calendar today. Crops are planted in November and December and harvested in March and April.	1 Nisan (Abib)	March–April	Exodus 13:4; 23:15; 34:18; Deuteronomy 16:1	Passover (Leviticus 23:5) Unleavened Bread (Leviticus 23:6) Firstfruits (Leviticus 23:10)
	2 Iyyar (Ziv)	April–May	1 Kings 6:1, 37	Second Passover (Numbers 9:10, 11)
	3 Sivan	May–June	Esther 8:9	Pentecost (Weeks) (Leviticus 23:16)
	4 Tammuz	June–July		
	5 Ab	July–August		
	6 Elul	August–September	Nehemiah 6:15	
	7 Tishri (Ethanaim)	September–October	1 Kings 8:2	Trumpets (Numbers 29:1; Leviticus 23:24) Day of Atonement (Leviticus 23:27) Tabernacles (Booths) (Leviticus 23:34)
	8 Marcheshvan (Bul)	October–November	1 Kings 6:38	
	9 Kislev	November–December	Nehemiah 1:1	Dedication (Hanukkah) (John 10:22)
	10 Tebeth	December–January	Esther 2:16	
	11 Shebat	January–February	Zechariah 1:7	
	12 Adar	February–March	Esther 3:7	Purim (Esther 9:24–32)

12:29, 30 Every firstborn child of the Egyptians died, but the Israelite children were spared because the blood of the lamb had been placed on their doorframes. So begins the story of redemption, the central theme of the Bible.

Redemption means "to buy back" or "to save from captivity by paying a ransom." One way to buy back a slave was to offer an equivalent or superior slave in exchange. That is the way God chose to buy us back—he offered his Son in exchange for us.

In Old Testament times, God accepted symbolic offerings. Jesus had not yet been sacrificed, so God accepted the life of an animal in place of the life of the sinner. When Jesus came, he substituted his perfect life for our sinful lives, taking the penalty for sin that we deserve. Thus he redeemed us from the power of sin and restored us to God. Jesus' sacrifice made animal sacrifice no longer necessary.

We must recognize that if we want to be freed from the deadly consequences of our sins, a tremendous price must be paid. But we don't have to pay it. Jesus Christ, our substitute, has already redeemed us by his death on the cross. Our part is to trust him and accept his gift of eternal life. Our sins have been paid for, and the way has been cleared for us to begin a relationship with God (Titus 2:14; Hebrews 9:13–15, 23–26).

said, "we will all die!" 34 So the people took their dough before the yeast was added, and carried it on their shoulders in kneading troughs wrapped in clothing. 35 The Israelites did as Moses instructed and asked the Egyptians for articles of silver and gold *r* and for clothing. 36 The LORD had made the Egyptians favorably disposed toward the people, and they gave them what they asked for; so they plundered *s* the Egyptians.

37 The Israelites journeyed from Rameses to Succoth. *t* There were about six hundred thousand men *u* on foot, besides women and children. 38 Many other people went up with them, as well as large droves of livestock, both flocks and herds. 39 With the dough they had brought from Egypt, they baked cakes of unleavened bread. The dough was without yeast because they had been driven out of Egypt and did not have time to prepare food for themselves.

40 Now the length of time the Israelite people lived in Egypt *a* was 430 years. *v* 41 At the end of the 430 years, to the very day, all the LORD's divisions left Egypt. 42 Because the LORD kept vigil that night to bring them out of Egypt, on this night all the Israelites are to keep vigil to honor the LORD for the generations to come. *w*

Passover Restrictions

43 The LORD said to Moses and Aaron, "These are the regulations for the Passover:
"No foreigner is to eat of it. 44 Any slave you have bought may eat of it after you have circumcised *x* him, 45 but a temporary resident and a hired worker may not eat of it.

46 "It must be eaten inside one house; take none of the meat outside the house. Do not break any of the bones. *y* 47 The whole community of Israel must celebrate it.

48 "An alien living among you who wants to celebrate the LORD's Passover must have all the males in his household circumcised; then he may take part like one born in the land. *z* No uncircumcised male may eat of it. 49 The same law applies to the native-born and to the alien *a* living among you."

50 All the Israelites did just what the LORD had commanded Moses and Aaron. 51 And on that very day the LORD brought the Israelites out of Egypt by their divisions.

Consecration of the Firstborn

13 The LORD said to Moses, 2 "Consecrate to me every firstborn male. *b* The first offspring of every womb among the Israelites belongs to me, whether man or animal."

3 Then Moses said to the people, "Commemorate this day, the day you came out of Egypt, out of the land of slavery, because the LORD brought you out of it with a mighty hand. Eat nothing containing yeast. 4 Today, in the month of Abib, you are leaving. 5 When the LORD brings you into the land of the Canaanites, Hittites, Amorites, Hivites and Jebusites *c*—the land he swore to your forefathers to give you, a land flowing with milk and honey—you are to observe this ceremony *d* in this month: 6 For seven days eat bread made without yeast and on the seventh day hold a festival *e* to the LORD. 7 Eat unleavened bread during those seven days; nothing with yeast in it is to be seen among you, nor shall any yeast be seen anywhere within your borders. 8 On that day tell your son, 'I do this because of what the LORD did for me when I came out of Egypt.' 9 This observance will be for you like a sign on your hand and a reminder on your forehead *f* that the law of the LORD is to be on your lips. For the LORD brought you out of Egypt with his mighty hand. 10 You must keep this ordinance at the appointed time year after year.

a 40 Masoretic Text; Samaritan Pentateuch and Septuagint *Egypt and Canaan*

12:35
r Ex 3:22
12:36
s Ex 3:22

12:37
t Nu 33:3-5
u Nu 11:13,21

12:40
v Ge 15:13; Ac 7:6;
Gal 3:17
12:42
w Dt 16:1,6

12:44
x Ge 17:12-13

12:46
y Nu 9:12; Jn 19:36*
12:48
z Nu 9:14
12:49
a Nu 15:15-16,29

13:2
b ver 12,13,15;
Ex 22:29; Lk 2:23*

13:5
c Ex 3:8
d Ex 12:25-26

13:6
e Ex 12:15-20

13:9
f Dt 6:8

12:34 A kneading trough was a large bowl made of wood, bronze, or pottery and used for kneading dough. Bread was made by mixing water and flour in the trough with a small piece of leavened dough saved from the previous day's batch. Bread was the primary food in the Hebrews' diet, and thus it was vital to bring the trough along. It could be easily carried on the shoulder.

12:37, 38 The total number of people leaving Egypt is estimated to have been about two million. The "many other people" may have been Egyptians and others who were drawn to the Hebrews by God's mighty works and who decided to leave Egypt with them.

13:2 *Consecrate* means to sacrifice or to consider something as belonging to God. This dedication practice described in 13:11–16 was to remind the people of their deliverance through God.

13:4 "In the month of Abib" corresponds to late March and early April on our calendar.

13:6–9 The Feast of Unleavened Bread marked the Hebrews as a unique people—as though they were branded on their hands and foreheads. What do you do that marks you as a follower of God? The way you raise your children, demonstrate love for others, show concern for the poor, and live in devotion to God—these actions will leave visible marks for all to see. While national groups are marked by customs and traditions, Christians are marked by loving one another (John 13:34, 35).

13:12
g Lk 2:23*

13:13
h Ex 34:20
i Nu 18:15

13:16
j ver 9

13:17
k Ex 14:11;
Nu 14:1-4; Dt 17:16

13:19
l Jos 24:32
m Ge 50:24-25

13:20
n Nu 33:6

13:21
o Ex 14:19,24;
Ps 78:14; 1Co 10:1

[11]"After the LORD brings you into the land of the Canaanites and gives it to you, as he promised on oath to you and your forefathers, [12]you are to give over to the LORD the first offspring of every womb. All the firstborn males of your livestock belong to the LORD. *g* [13]Redeem with a lamb every firstborn donkey, but if you do not redeem it, break its neck. *h* Redeem every firstborn among your sons. *i*

[14]"In days to come, when your son asks you, 'What does this mean?' say to him, 'With a mighty hand the LORD brought us out of Egypt, out of the land of slavery. [15]When Pharaoh stubbornly refused to let us go, the LORD killed every firstborn in Egypt, both man and animal. This is why I sacrifice to the LORD the first male offspring of every womb and redeem each of my firstborn sons.' [16]And it will be like a sign on your hand and a symbol on your forehead *j* that the LORD brought us out of Egypt with his mighty hand."

2. Crossing the sea

[17]When Pharaoh let the people go, God did not lead them on the road through the Philistine country, though that was shorter. For God said, "If they face war, they might change their minds and return to Egypt." *k* [18]So God led the people around by the desert road toward the Red Sea. *a* The Israelites went up out of Egypt armed for battle.

[19]Moses took the bones of Joseph *l* with him because Joseph had made the sons of Israel swear an oath. He had said, "God will surely come to your aid, and then you must carry my bones up with you from this place." *b m*

[20]After leaving Succoth they camped at Etham on the edge of the desert. *n* [21]By day the LORD went ahead of them in a pillar of cloud *o* to guide them on their way and by night in a pillar of fire to give them light, so that they could travel by day or night. [22]Neither the pillar of cloud by day nor the pillar of fire by night left its place in front of the people.

a 18 Hebrew *Yam Suph;* that is, Sea of Reeds   *b 19* See Gen. 50:25.

13:12–14 What did it mean to "redeem every firstborn among your sons"? During the night the Israelites escaped from Egypt, God spared the oldest son of every house marked with blood on the doorframes. Because God saved the lives of the firstborn, he had a rightful claim to them. But God commanded the Israelites to buy their sons back from him. This ritual served three main purposes: (1) it was a reminder to the people of how God had spared their sons from death and freed them all from slavery; (2) it showed God's high respect for human life in contrast to the pagan gods who, their worshipers believed, demanded human sacrifice; (3) it looked forward to the day when Jesus Christ would buy us back by paying the price for our sin once and for all.

13:17, 18 God doesn't always work in the way that seems best to us. Instead of guiding the Israelites along the direct route from Egypt to the promised land, he took them by a longer route to avoid fighting with the Philistines. If God does not lead you along the shortest path to your goal, don't complain or resist. Follow him willingly and trust him to lead you safely around unseen obstacles. He can see the end of your journey from the beginning, and he knows the safest and best route.

13:17, 18 When did the Hebrews leave Egypt? There are two theories. The *early* theory says the exodus occurred around 1446–1445 B.C. The *late* theory suggests the exodus happened between 1300 and 1200 B.C. Those who hold to the earlier date point to 1 Kings 6:1, where the Bible clearly states that Solomon began building the temple 480 years after the Hebrews left Egypt. Since almost all scholars agree that Solomon began building the temple in 966, this puts the exodus in the year 1446. But those who hold to the later date suggest that the 480 years cannot be taken literally. They point to Exodus 1:11, which says that the Hebrews built the store cities of Pithom and Rameses, named after Pharaoh Rameses II, who reigned around 1290 B.C. Regardless of which date is correct, the fact is that God led the Hebrews out of Egypt, just as he had promised. This showed his great power and his great love for his people.

13:21, 22 God gave the Hebrews a pillar of cloud and a pillar of fire so they would know day and night that God was with them on their journey to the promised land. What has God given us so

that we can have the same assurance? The Bible—something the Israelites did not have. He also has given us the Holy Spirit to remind us of what the Bible says and to guide us each day (John 14:26). Look to God's Word for reassurance of his presence. As the Hebrews looked to the pillars of cloud and fire, we can look to God's Word day and night to know he is with us, helping us on our journey.

13:21, 22 The pillars of fire and cloud were examples of *theophany*—God appearing in a physical form. In this form, God lighted Israel's path, protected them from their enemies, provided reassurance, controlled their movements, and inspired the burning zeal that Israel should have for their God.

THE EXODUS
The Israelites left Succoth and camped first at Etham before going toward Baal Zephon to camp by the sea (14:2). God miraculously brought them across the sea, into the Desert of Shur (15:22). After stopping at the oasis of Elim, the people moved into the Desert of Sin (16:1).

14 Then the LORD said to Moses, 2 "Tell the Israelites to turn back and encamp near Pi Hahiroth, between Migdol *p* and the sea. They are to encamp by the sea, directly opposite Baal Zephon. 3 Pharaoh will think, 'The Israelites are wandering around the land in confusion, hemmed in by the desert.' 4 And I will harden Pharaoh's heart, *q* and he will pursue them. But I will gain glory *r* for myself through Pharaoh and all his army, and the Egyptians will know that I am the LORD." So the Israelites did this.

5 When the king of Egypt was told that the people had fled, Pharaoh and his officials changed their minds about them and said, "What have we done? We have let the Israelites go and have lost their services!" 6 So he had his chariot made ready and took his army with him. 7 He took six hundred of the best chariots, along with all the other chariots of Egypt, with officers over all of them. 8 The LORD hardened the heart *s* of Pharaoh king of Egypt, so that he pursued the Israelites, who were marching out boldly. *t* 9 The Egyptians—all Pharaoh's horses and chariots, horsemen *a* and troops—pursued the Israelites and overtook *u* them as they camped by the sea near Pi Hahiroth, opposite Baal Zephon.

10 As Pharaoh approached, the Israelites looked up, and there were the Egyptians, marching after them. They were terrified and cried *v* out to the LORD. 11 They said to Moses, "Was it because there were no graves in Egypt that you brought us to the desert to die? What have you done to us by bringing us out of Egypt? 12 Didn't we say to you in Egypt, 'Leave us alone; let us serve the Egyptians'? It would have been better for us to serve the Egyptians than to die in the desert!"

13 Moses answered the people, "Do not be afraid. Stand firm and you will see *w* the deliverance the LORD will bring you today. The Egyptians you see today you will never see *x* again. 14 The LORD will fight *y* for you; you need only to be still." *z*

15 Then the LORD said to Moses, "Why are you crying out to me? Tell the Israelites to move on. 16 Raise your staff and stretch out your hand over the sea to divide the water so that the Israelites can go through the sea on dry ground. 17 I will harden the hearts of the Egyptians so that they will go in after them. *a* And I will gain glory through Pharaoh and all his army, through his chariots and his horsemen. 18 The Egyptians will know that I am the LORD when I gain glory through Pharaoh, his chariots and his horsemen."

19 Then the angel of God, who had been traveling in front of Israel's army, withdrew and went behind them. The pillar of cloud *b* also moved from in front and stood behind them, 20 coming between the armies of Egypt and Israel. Throughout the night the cloud brought darkness to the one side and light to the other side; so neither went near the other all night long.

21 Then Moses stretched out his hand over the sea, and all that night the LORD drove the sea back with a strong east wind and turned it into dry land. The waters were divided, *c* 22 and the Israelites went through the sea on dry ground, *d* with a wall of water on their right and on their left.

a 9 Or charioteers; also in verses 17, 18, 23, 26 and 28

14:2
p Nu 33:7

14:4
q Ex 4:21
r Ro 9:17,22-23

14:8
s ver 4
t Nu 33:3

14:9
u Ex 15:9

14:10
v Ne 9:9

14:13
w 2Ch 20:17;
Isa 41:10,13-14
x ver 30

14:14
y Ex 15:3; Dt 1:30;
2Ch 20:29
z Ps 46:10;
Isa 30:15

14:17
a ver 4

14:19
b Ex 13:21

14:21
c Isa 63:12

14:22
d Heb 11:29

14:6–9 Six hundred Egyptian war chariots were bearing down on the helpless Israelites, who were trapped between the mountains and the sea. The war chariots each carried two people—one to drive and one to fight. These chariots were made of a wood or leather cab placed over two wheels, and they were pulled by horses. These were the armored tanks of Bible times. But even their power was no match for God, who destroyed both the chariots and their soldiers.

14:10, 11 Trapped against the sea, the Israelites faced the Egyptian army sweeping in for the kill. The Israelites thought they were doomed. After watching God's powerful hand deliver them from Egypt, their only response was fear, whining, and despair. Where was their trust in God? Israel had to learn from repeated experience that God was able to provide for them. God has preserved these examples in the Bible so that we can learn to trust him the first time. By focusing on God's faithfulness in the past we can face crises with confidence rather than with fear and complaining.

14:11, 12 This is the first instance of grumbling and complaining by the Israelites. Grumbling would become a major problem for the people on this journey. Their lack of faith in God is startling. Yet how often do we find ourselves doing the same thing—complaining over inconveniences or discomforts? The Israelites

were about to learn some tough lessons. Had they trusted God, they would have been spared much grief.

14:13, 14 The people were hostile and despairing, but Moses encouraged them to watch the wonderful way God would rescue them. Moses had a positive attitude! When it looked as if they were trapped, Moses called upon God to intervene. We may not be chased by an army, but we may still feel trapped. Instead of giving in to despair, we should adopt Moses' attitude to "stand firm and . . . see the deliverance the LORD will bring."

14:15 The Lord told Moses to stop praying and get moving! Prayer must have a vital place in our lives, but there is also a place for action. Sometimes we know what to do, but we pray for more guidance as an excuse to postpone doing it. If we know what we should do, then it is time to get moving.

14:21 There was no apparent way of escape, but the Lord opened up a dry path through the sea. Sometimes we find ourselves caught in a problem and see no way out. Don't panic; God can open up a way.

14:21, 22 Some scholars believe the Israelites did not cross the main body of the Red Sea but one of the shallow lakes or marshes north of it that dry up at certain times of the year, or perhaps a smaller branch of the Red Sea where the water would have been

23 The Egyptians pursued them, and all Pharaoh's horses and chariots and horsemen followed them into the sea. 24 During the last watch of the night the LORD looked down from the pillar of fire and cloud at the Egyptian army and threw it into confusion. 25 He made the wheels of their chariots come off a so that they had difficulty driving. And the Egyptians said, "Let's get away from the Israelites! The LORD is fighting for them against Egypt."

26 Then the LORD said to Moses, "Stretch out your hand over the sea so that the waters may flow back over the Egyptians and their chariots and horsemen." 27 Moses stretched out his

a 25 Or *He jammed the wheels of their chariots* (see Samaritan Pentateuch, Septuagint and Syriac)

MOSES

Some people can't stay out of trouble. When conflict breaks out, they always manage to be nearby. Reaction is their favorite action. This was Moses. He seemed drawn to what needed to be righted. Throughout his life, he was at his finest and his worst responding to the conflicts around him. Even the burning bush experience was an illustration of his character. Having spotted the fire and seen that the bush did not burn, he had to investigate. Whether jumping into a fight to defend a Hebrew slave or trying to referee a struggle between two kinsmen, when Moses saw conflict, he reacted.

Over the years, however, an amazing thing happened to Moses' character. He didn't stop reacting, but rather learned to react correctly. The kaleidoscopic action of each day of leading two million people in the desert was more than enough challenge for Moses' reacting ability. Much of the time he served as a buffer between God and the people. At one moment he had to respond to God's anger at the people's stubbornness and forgetfulness. At another moment he had to react to the people's bickering and complaining. At still another moment he had to react to their unjustified attacks on his character.

Leadership often involves reaction. If we want to react with instincts consistent with God's will, we must develop habits of obedience to God. Consistent obedience to God is best developed in times of less stress. Then when stress comes, our natural reaction will be to obey God.

In our age of lowering moral standards, we find it almost impossible to believe that God would punish Moses for the one time he disobeyed outright. What we fail to see, however, is that God did not reject Moses; Moses simply disqualified himself to enter the promised land. Personal greatness does not make a person immune to error or its consequences.

In Moses we see an outstanding personality shaped by God. But we must not misunderstand what God did. He did not change who or what Moses was; he did not give Moses new abilities and strengths. Instead, he took Moses' characteristics and molded them until they were suited to his purposes. Does knowing this make a difference in your understanding of God's purpose in your life? He is trying to take what he created in the first place and use it for its intended purposes. The next time you talk with God, don't ask, "What should I change into?" but "How should I use my own abilities and strengths to do your will?"

Strengths and accomplishments:	• Egyptian education; desert training • Greatest Jewish leader; set the exodus in motion • Prophet and lawgiver; recorder of the Ten Commandments • Author of the Pentateuch
Weaknesses and mistakes:	• Failed to enter the promised land because of disobedience to God • Did not always recognize and use the talents of others
Lessons from his life:	• God prepares, then uses. His timetable is life-sized • God does his greatest work through frail people
Vital statistics:	• Where: Egypt, Midian, Desert of Sinai • Occupations: Prince, shepherd, leader of the Israelites • Relatives: Sister: Miriam. Brother: Aaron. Wife: Zipporah. Sons: Gershom and Eliezer.
Key verses:	"By faith Moses, when he had grown up, refused to be known as the son of Pharaoh's daughter. He chose to be mistreated along with the people of God rather than to enjoy the pleasures of sin for a short time" (Hebrews 11:24, 25).

Moses' story is told in the books of Exodus through Deuteronomy. He is also mentioned in Acts 7:20–44; Hebrews 11:23–29.

shallow enough to wade across. But the Bible clearly states that the Lord "drove the sea back with a strong east wind and turned it into dry land" (14:21; see also Joshua 3:15, 16; and 2 Kings 2:13, 14). Also, the water was deep enough to cover the chariots (14:28). The God who created the earth and water performed a mighty miracle at exactly the right time to demonstrate his great power and love for his people.

14:27, 28 No evidence of this great exodus has been discovered in Egyptian historical records. This was because it was a common practice for Egyptian pharaohs not to record their defeats. They even went so far as to take existing records and delete the names of traitors and political adversaries. Pharaoh would have been especially anxious not to record that his great army was destroyed chasing a band of runaway slaves. Since either the Egyptians failed to record the exodus or the record has not yet been found, it is impossible to place a precise date on the event.

hand over the sea, and at daybreak the sea went back to its place. The Egyptians were fleeing toward[a] it, and the LORD swept them into the sea.[e] 28 The water flowed back and covered the chariots and horsemen—the entire army of Pharaoh that had followed the Israelites into the sea. Not one of them survived.

29 But the Israelites went through the sea on dry ground, with a wall of water on their right and on their left. 30 That day the LORD saved[f] Israel from the hands of the Egyptians, and Israel saw the Egyptians lying dead on the shore. 31 And when the Israelites saw the great power the LORD displayed against the Egyptians, the people feared the LORD and put their trust[g] in him and in Moses his servant.

14:27
e Ex 15:1,21;
Ps 106:11

14:30
f Ps 106:8,10,21

14:31
g Jn 2:11

The Song of Moses and Miriam

15 Then Moses and the Israelites sang this song to the LORD:

"I will sing[h] to the LORD,
    for he is highly exalted.
The horse and its rider
    he has hurled into the sea.
2 The LORD is my strength and my song;
    he has become my salvation.
He is my God, and I will praise him,
    my father's God, and I will exalt[i] him.
3 The LORD is a warrior;[j]
    the LORD is his name.
4 Pharaoh's chariots and his army[k]
    he has hurled into the sea.
The best of Pharaoh's officers
    are drowned in the Red Sea.[b]
5 The deep waters have covered them;
    they sank to the depths like a stone.[l]

6 "Your right hand,[m] O LORD,
    was majestic in power.
Your right hand, O LORD,
    shattered the enemy.
7 In the greatness of your majesty
    you threw down those who opposed you.
You unleashed your burning anger;
    it consumed them like stubble.
8 By the blast of your nostrils[n]
    the waters piled up.[o]
The surging waters stood firm like a wall;
    the deep waters congealed in the heart of the sea.

9 "The enemy boasted,
    'I will pursue,[p] I will overtake them.
I will divide the spoils;
    I will gorge myself on them.
I will draw my sword
    and my hand will destroy them.'
10 But you blew with your breath,
    and the sea covered them.
They sank like lead
    in the mighty waters.[q]

15:1
h Ps 106:12

15:2
i Ex 3:6,15-16

15:3
j Rev 19:11

15:4
k Ex 14:6-7

15:5
l Ne 9:11

15:6
m Ps 118:15

15:8
n Ex 14:21
o Ps 78:13

15:9
p Ex 14:5-9

15:10
q Ex 14:27-28

a 27 Or from   b 4 Hebrew Yam Suph; that is, Sea of Reeds; also in verse 22

15:1ff Music played an important part in Israel's worship and celebration. Singing was an expression of love and thanks, and it was a creative way to pass down oral traditions. Some say this song of Moses is the oldest recorded song in the world. It was a festive epic poem celebrating God's victory, lifting the hearts and voices of the people outward and upward. After having been delivered from great danger, they sang with joy! Psalms and hymns can be great ways to express relief, praise, and thanks when you have been through trouble.

15:8 The phrase, "the deep waters congealed in the heart of the sea" means that the waters became like hard walls for them to walk between.

15:11
r Ex 8:10
s Isa 6:3
t Ps 8:1

11 "Who among the gods is like you,r O Lᴏʀᴅ?
> Who is like you—
>   majestic in holiness,s
>   awesome in glory,t
>   working wonders?
12 You stretched out your right hand
> and the earth swallowed them.

15:13
u Ne 9:12
v Ps 78:54

13 "In your unfailing love you will lead u
> the people you have redeemed.
> In your strength you will guide them
>   to your holy dwelling.v

15:14
w Dt 2:25

14 The nations will hear and tremble;w
> anguish will grip the people of Philistia.

15:15
x Nu 22:3
y Jos 5:1

15 The chiefs of Edom will be terrified,
> the leaders of Moab will be seized with trembling,x
> the peoplea of Canaan will melty away;

15:16
z Ps 74:2

16 terror and dread will fall upon them.
> By the power of your arm
>   they will be as still as a stone—
> until your people pass by, O Lᴏʀᴅ,
> until the people you boughtb z pass by.

15:17
a Ps 44:2
b Ps 78:54,68

17 You will bring them in and planta them
> on the mountainb of your inheritance—
> the place, O Lᴏʀᴅ, you made for your dwelling,
> the sanctuary, O Lord, your hands established.
18 The Lᴏʀᴅ will reign
> for ever and ever."

15:19
c Ex 14:28

15:20
d Nu 26:59
e 1Sa 18:6;
Ps 150:4

19When Pharaoh's horses, chariots and horsemenc went into the sea,c the Lᴏʀᴅ brought the waters of the sea back over them, but the Israelites walked through the sea on dry ground. 20Then Miriamd the prophetess, Aaron's sister, took a tambourine in her hand, and all the women followed her, with tambourines and dancing. e 21Miriam sang to them:

a 15 Or rulers   b 16 Or created   c 19 Or charioteers

FAMOUS SONGS IN THE BIBLE

Where	Purpose of Song
Exodus 15:1–21	Moses' song of deliverance and praise after God led Israel out of Egypt and saved them by parting the Red Sea; Miriam joined in the singing, too
Numbers 21:17	Israel's song of praise to God for giving them water in the desert
Deuteronomy 32:1–43	Moses' song of Israel's history with thanksgiving and praise as the Hebrews were about to enter the promised land
Judges 5:2–31	Deborah and Barak's song of praise thanking God for Israel's victory over King Jabin's army at Mount Tabor
2 Samuel 22:2–51	David's song of thanks and praise to God for rescuing him from Saul and his other enemies
Song of Songs	Solomon's song of love celebrating the union of husband and wife
Isaiah 26:1	Isaiah's prophetic song about how the redeemed will sing in the new Jerusalem
Ezra 3:11	Israel's song of praise at the completion of the temple's foundation
Luke 1:46–55	Mary's song of praise to God for the conception of Jesus
Luke 1:68–79	Zechariah's song of praise for the birth of his son
Acts 16:25	Paul and Silas sang hymns in prison
Revelation 5:9, 10	The "new song" of the 24 elders acclaiming Christ as worthy to break the seven seals of God's scroll
Revelation 14:3	The song of the 144,000 redeemed from the earth
Revelation 15:3, 4	The song of all the redeemed in praise of the Lamb who redeemed them

---

15:20 Miriam was called a prophetess not only because she received revelations from God (Numbers 12:1, 2; Micah 6:4) but also for her musical skill. Prophecy and music were often closely related in the Bible (1 Samuel 10:5; 1 Chronicles 25:1).

> "Sing to the LORD,
>   for he is highly exalted.
> The horse and its rider
>   he has hurled into the sea."

3. Complaining in the desert
The Waters of Marah and Elim

22 Then Moses led Israel from the Red Sea and they went into the Desert of Shur. For three days they traveled in the desert without finding water. 23 When they came to Marah, they could not drink its water because it was bitter. (That is why the place is called Marah. a f) 24 So the people grumbled against Moses, saying, "What are we to drink?"

25 Then Moses cried out to the LORD, and the LORD showed him a piece of wood. He threw it into the water, and the water became sweet.

There the LORD made a decree and a law for them, and there he tested them. 26 He said, "If you listen carefully to the voice of the LORD your God and do what is right in his eyes, if you pay attention to his commands and keep all his decrees,g I will not bring on you any of the diseasesh I brought on the Egyptians, for I am the LORD, who heals you."

27 Then they came to Elim, where there were twelve springs and seventy palm trees, and they campedi there near the water.

Manna and Quail

16 The whole Israelite community set out from Elim and came to the Desert of Sin,j which is between Elim and Sinai, on the fifteenth day of the second month after they had come out of Egypt. 2 In the desert the whole community grumbledk against Moses and Aaron. 3 The Israelites said to them, "If only we had died by the LORD's hand in Egypt! There we sat around pots of meat and ate all the foodl we wanted, but you have brought us out into this desert to starve this entire assembly to death."

4 Then the LORD said to Moses, "I will rain down bread from heavenm for you. The people are to go out each day and gather enough for that day. In this way I will test them and see whether they will follow my instructions. 5 On the sixth day they are to prepare what they bring in, and that is to be twicen as much as they gather on the other days."

6 So Moses and Aaron said to all the Israelites, "In the evening you will know that it was the LORD who brought you out of Egypt, 7 and in the morning you will see the glory of the LORD, because he has heard your grumbling against him. Who are we, that you should grumble against us?"o 8 Moses also said, "You will know that it was the LORD when he gives you meat to eat in the evening and all the bread you want in the morning, because he has heard your grumbling against him. Who are we? You are not grumbling against us, but against the LORD."

9 Then Moses told Aaron, "Say to the entire Israelite community, 'Come before the LORD, for he has heard your grumbling.'"

a 23 *Marah* means *bitter.*

15:23
f Nu 33:8

15:26
g Dt 7:12
h Dt 28:27,58-60

15:27
i Nu 33:9

16:1
j Nu 33:11,12

16:2
k 1Co 10:10

16:3
l Nu 11:4,34

16:4
m Dt 8:3; Jn 6:31*

16:5
n ver 22

16:7
o Nu 16:11

15:23, 27 The waters of Marah are contrasted with the springs of Elim. Marah stood for the unbelieving, grumbling attitude of the people who would not trust God. Elim stands for God's bountiful provision. How easy it is to grumble and complain too quickly, only to be embarrassed by God's help! We must be patient for God's kindness and help. Don't let a negative attitude erode your trust in God.

15:26 God promised that if the people obeyed him they would not suffer from the diseases that plagued the Egyptians. Little did they know that many of the moral laws he later gave them were designed to keep them free from sickness. For example, following God's law against prostitution would keep them free of venereal disease. God's laws for us are often designed to keep us from harm. Men and women are complex beings. Our physical, emotional, and spiritual lives are intertwined. Modern medicine is now acknowledging what these laws assumed. If we want God to care for us, we need to submit to his directions for living.

16:1 The Desert of Sin was a vast and hostile environment of sand and stone. Its barren surroundings provided the perfect place for God to test and shape the character of his people.

16:2 It happened again. As the Israelites encountered danger, shortages, and inconvenience, they complained bitterly and longed to be back in Egypt. But as always, God provided for their needs. Difficult circumstances often lead to stress, and complaining is a natural response. The Israelites didn't really want to be back in Egypt; they just wanted life to get a little easier. In the pressure of the moment, they could not focus on the cause of their stress (in this case, lack of trust in God); they could only think about the quickest way of escape. When pressure comes your way, resist the temptation to make a quick escape. Instead, focus on God's power and wisdom to help you deal with the cause of your stress.

16:4, 5 God promised to meet the Hebrews' need for food in the desert, but he decided to test their obedience. God wanted to see if they would obey his detailed instructions. We can learn to trust him as our Lord only by following. We can learn to obey by taking small steps of obedience.

16:10
ᵖver 7

¹⁰While Aaron was speaking to the whole Israelite community, they looked toward the desert, and there was the gloryᵖ of the LORD appearing in the cloud.

¹¹The LORD said to Moses, ¹²"I have heard the grumbling of the Israelites. Tell them, 'At twilight you will eat meat, and in the morning you will be filled with bread. Then you will know that I am the LORD your God.'"

16:13
�q Nu 11:31;
Ps 78:27-28;
105:40

16:14
ʳ Nu 11:7-9

¹³That evening quail�q came and covered the camp, and in the morning there was a layer of dew around the camp. ¹⁴When the dew was gone, thin flakes like frostʳ on the ground appeared on the desert floor. ¹⁵When the Israelites saw it, they said to each other, "What is it?" For they did not know what it was.

Moses said to them, "It is the bread the LORD has given you to eat. ¹⁶This is what the LORD has commanded: 'Each one is to gather as much as he needs. Take an omerª for each person you have in your tent.'"

16:18
ˢ 2Co 8:15*

¹⁷The Israelites did as they were told; some gathered much, some little. ¹⁸And when they measured it by the omer, he who gathered much did not have too much, and he who gathered little did not have too little.ˢ Each one gathered as much as he needed.

16:19
ᵗ Ex 12:10

¹⁹Then Moses said to them, "No one is to keep any of it until morning."ᵗ

²⁰However, some of them paid no attention to Moses; they kept part of it until morning, but it was full of maggots and began to smell. So Moses was angry with them.

²¹Each morning everyone gathered as much as he needed, and when the sun grew hot, it melted away. ²²On the sixth day, they gathered twice as much—two omersᵇ for each person—and the leaders of the community came and reported this to Moses. ²³He said to them,

16:23
ᵘ Ge 2:3; Ex 20:8;
23:12

"This is what the LORD commanded: 'Tomorrow is to be a day of rest, a holy Sabbathᵘ to the LORD. So bake what you want to bake and boil what you want to boil. Save whatever is left and keep it until morning.'"

²⁴So they saved it until morning, as Moses commanded, and it did not stink or get maggots in it. ²⁵"Eat it today," Moses said, "because today is a Sabbath to the LORD. You will not find any of it on the ground today. ²⁶Six days you are to gather it, but on the seventh day, the Sabbath, there will not be any."

16:28
ᵛ Ps 78:10

²⁷Nevertheless, some of the people went out on the seventh day to gather it, but they found none. ²⁸Then the LORD said to Moses, "How long will youᶜ refuse to keep my commandsᵛ and my instructions? ²⁹Bear in mind that the LORD has given you the Sabbath; that is why on the sixth day he gives you bread for two days. Everyone is to stay where he is on the seventh day; no one is to go out." ³⁰So the people rested on the seventh day.

16:31
ʷ Nu 11:7-9

³¹The people of Israel called the bread manna.ᵈ ʷ It was white like coriander seed and tasted like wafers made with honey. ³²Moses said, "This is what the LORD has commanded: 'Take an omer of manna and keep it for the generations to come, so they can see the bread I gave you to eat in the desert when I brought you out of Egypt.'"

16:33
ˣ Heb 9:4

³³So Moses said to Aaron, "Take a jar and put an omer of mannaˣ in it. Then place it before the LORD to be kept for the generations to come."

16:34
ʸ Ex 25:16,21,22

16:35
ᶻ Jos 5:12

³⁴As the LORD commanded Moses, Aaron put the manna in front of the Testimony,ʸ that it might be kept. ³⁵The Israelites ate manna forty years, until they came to a land that was settled; they ate manna until they reached the border of Canaan.ᶻ

³⁶(An omer is one tenth of an ephah.)

ª *16* That is, probably about 2 quarts (about 2 liters); also in verses 18, 32, 33 and 36   ᵇ *22* That is, probably about 4 quarts (about 4.5 liters)   ᶜ *28* The Hebrew is plural.   ᵈ *31 Manna* means *What is it?* (see verse 15).

16:14–16 Manna (16:31) appeared on the ground each day as thin flakes like frost. The people gathered it, ground it like grain, and made it into honey-tasting pancakes. For the Israelites the manna was a gift—it came every day and was just what they needed. It satisfied their temporary physical need. In John 6:48–51 Jesus compares himself to manna. Christ is our daily bread who satisfies our eternal, spiritual need.

16:23 The Israelites were not to work on the Sabbath—not even to cook food. Why? God knew that the busy routine of daily living could distract people from worshiping him. It is so easy to let work, family responsibilities, and recreation crowd our schedules so tightly that we don't take time to worship. Carefully guard your time with God.

16:32 The Hebrews put some manna in a special jar as a reminder of the way God provided for them in the desert. Symbols

have always been an important part of Christian worship also. We use special objects as symbols to remind us of God's work. Such symbols can be valuable aids to our worship as long as we are careful to keep them from becoming objects of worship.

16:36 "An omer is one tenth of an ephah"—this is about two quarts or one tenth of a bushel.

Water From the Rock

17 The whole Israelite community set out from the Desert of Sin, [a] traveling from place to place as the LORD commanded. They camped at Rephidim, but there was no water for the people to drink. [2] So they quarreled with Moses and said, "Give us water [b] to drink."

Moses replied, "Why do you quarrel with me? Why do you put the LORD to the test?" [c]

[3] But the people were thirsty for water there, and they grumbled [d] against Moses. They said, "Why did you bring us up out of Egypt to make us and our children and livestock die of thirst?"

[4] Then Moses cried out to the LORD, "What am I to do with these people? They are almost ready to stone [e] me."

[5] The LORD answered Moses, "Walk on ahead of the people. Take with you some of the elders of Israel and take in your hand the staff with which you struck the Nile, and go. [6] I will stand there before you by the rock at Horeb. Strike the rock, and water [f] will come out of it for the people to drink." So Moses did this in the sight of the elders of Israel. [7] And he called the place Massah [a] and Meribah [b] because the Israelites quarreled and because they tested the LORD saying, "Is the LORD among us or not?"

The Amalekites Defeated

[8] The Amalekites [g] came and attacked the Israelites at Rephidim. [9] Moses said to Joshua, "Choose some of our men and go out to fight the Amalekites. Tomorrow I will stand on top of the hill with the staff of God in my hands."

[10] So Joshua fought the Amalekites as Moses had ordered, and Moses, Aaron and Hur went to the top of the hill. [11] As long as Moses held up his hands, the Israelites were winning, but whenever he lowered his hands, the Amalekites were winning. [12] When Moses' hands grew tired, they took a stone and put it under him and he sat on it. Aaron and Hur held his hands up—one on one side, one on the other—so that his hands remained steady till sunset. [13] So Joshua overcame the Amalekite army with the sword.

[14] Then the LORD said to Moses, "Write [h] this on a scroll as something to be remembered and make sure that Joshua hears it, because I will completely blot out the memory of Amalek from under heaven."

[15] Moses built an altar and called it The LORD is my Banner. [16] He said, "For hands were lifted up to the throne of the LORD. The [c] LORD will be at war against the Amalekites from generation to generation."

17:1
[a]Ex 16:1

17:2
[b]Nu 20:2
[c]Dt 6:16;
Ps 78:18,41;
1Co 10:9

17:3
[d]Ex 15:24; 16:2-3

17:4
[e]Nu 14:10

17:6
[f]Nu 20:11;
1Co 10:4

17:8
[g]Dt 25:17-19

17:14
[h]Ex 34:27

[a] 7 *Massah* means *testing.* [b] 7 *Meribah* means *quarreling.* [c] 16 Or *"Because a hand was against the throne of the LORD, the*

17:2 Again the people complained about their problem instead of praying. Some problems can be solved by careful thought or by rearranging our priorities. Some can be solved by discussion

JOURNEY TO MOUNT SINAI
God miraculously supplied food and water in the desert for the Israelites. In the Desert of Sin, he provided manna (16). At Rephidim, he provided water from a rock (17:1–7). Finally God brought them to the foot of Mount Sinai, where he gave them his holy laws.

and good counsel, but some problems can be solved only by prayer. We should make a determined effort to pray when we feel like complaining, because complaining only raises our level of stress. Prayer quiets our thoughts and emotions and prepares us to listen.

17:8 The Amalekites were descendants of Amalek, a grandson of Esau. They were a fierce nomadic tribe that lived in the desert region of the Dead Sea. They made part of their livelihood by conducting frequent raids on other settlements and carrying off plundered goods. They killed for pleasure. One of the greatest insults in Israelite culture was to call someone "a friend of Amalek." When the Israelites entered the region, the Amalekites saw this as a perfect opportunity for both pleasure and profit. But this hostile tribe was moving in on the wrong group—a people led by God. For the Israelite slaves to defeat such a war-like nation was more than enough proof that God was with them as he had promised to be.

17:9 Here we meet Joshua for the first time. Later he would become the great leader who would bring God's people into the promised land. As a general of the Israelite army, he was gaining valuable experience for the greater battles ahead.

17:10–13 Aaron and Hur stood by Moses' side and held up his arms to ensure victory against Amalek. We need to "lift up the hands" of our spiritual leaders as well. Shouldering some responsibility, lending a word of encouragement, or offering a prayer are ways of refreshing spiritual leaders in their work.

Jethro Visits Moses

18:1
*Ex 2:16; 3:1

18 Now Jethro, the priest of Midian *i* and father-in-law of Moses, heard of everything God had done for Moses and for his people Israel, and how the LORD had brought Israel out of Egypt.

18:2
*Ex 4:25

18:3
k Ac 7:29
l Ex 2:22

² After Moses had sent away his wife Zipporah, *j* his father-in-law Jethro received her ³ and her two sons. *k* One son was named Gershom, *a* for Moses said, "I have become an alien in a foreign land"; *l* ⁴ and the other was named Eliezer, *b* for he said, "My father's God was my helper; he saved me from the sword of Pharaoh."

18:5
m Ex 3:1

⁵ Jethro, Moses' father-in-law, together with Moses' sons and wife, came to him in the desert, where he was camped near the mountain *m* of God. ⁶ Jethro had sent word to him, "I, your father-in-law Jethro, am coming to you with your wife and her two sons."

18:7
n Ge 43:28

⁷ So Moses went out to meet his father-in-law and bowed down *n* and kissed him. They greeted each other and then went into the tent. ⁸ Moses told his father-in-law about everything the LORD had done to Pharaoh and the Egyptians for Israel's sake and about all the hardships they had met along the way and how the LORD had saved them.

18:10
o Ps 68:19-20

⁹ Jethro was delighted to hear about all the good things the LORD had done for Israel in rescuing them from the hand of the Egyptians. ¹⁰ He said, "Praise be to the LORD, *o* who rescued you from the hand of the Egyptians and of Pharaoh, and who rescued the people from

---

a 3 Gershom sounds like the Hebrew for *an alien there.*   *b 4 Eliezer* means *my God is helper.*

JETHRO

People such as Jethro and Melchizedek—not Israelites, but nevertheless worshipers of the true God—play an important role in the Old Testament. They remind us of God's commitment to the world. God chose one nation through which to work, but his love and concern are for all nations!

Jethro's religious background prepared him for, rather than prevented him from, responding in faith to God. When he saw and heard what God had done for the Israelites, he worshiped God wholeheartedly. We can guess that for 40 years as Moses' father-in-law, Jethro had been watching God at work, molding a leader. Moses' and Jethro's relationship must have been close, for Moses readily accepted his father-in-law's advice. Each benefited from knowing the other. Jethro met God through Moses, and Moses received hospitality, his wife, and wisdom from Jethro.

The greatest gift one person can give another is an introduction to God. But that gift is hindered if the believer's attitude is, "I have the greatest gift to pass on to you, while you have nothing to give me in return." Real friends give to and receive from each other. The importance of introducing a friend to God does not make the friend's gifts to us insignificant. Rather, the believer is doubly blessed—first by receiving the gifts the friend wishes to give; then by growing in knowledge of the Lord. For we discover that in introducing another person to God, we increase our own awareness of God. As we give God away, he gives himself even more to us.

Is all you know about God a miscellaneous collection of trivia, or do you have a living relationship with him? Only with a vital relationship can you pass on to others the excitement of allowing God to guide your life. Have you reached the point of saying, with Jethro, "I know that the LORD is greater than all other gods" (Exodus 18:11)?

Strengths and accomplishments:	• As father-in-law to Moses, he came to recognize the one true God • He was a practical troubleshooter and organizer
Lessons from his life:	• Supervision and administration are team efforts • God's plan includes all nations
Vital statistics:	• Where: The land of Midian and the Desert of Sinai • Occupations: Shepherd, priest • Relatives: Daughter: Zipporah. Son-in-law: Moses. Son: Hobab.
Key verse:	"Jethro was delighted to hear about all the good things the LORD had done for Israel in rescuing them from the hand of the Egyptians" (Exodus 18:9).

Jethro's story is told in Exodus 2:15—3:1; 18:1–27. He is also mentioned in Judges 1:16.

18:7 Jethro entered Moses' tent where the two talked. Tents were the homes of shepherds. In shape and design, they resembled the tents of today, but they were very large and made of a thick cloth woven from goat or camel hair. This fabric breathed in warm weather and contracted in stormy weather to offer protection from the winter winds and rains. The floor was often covered with animal-skin rugs, while curtains divided the inside space into rooms.

18:8–11 Moses told his father-in-law all that God had done, convincing him that the Lord was greater than any other god. Our relatives are often the hardest people to tell about God. Yet we should look for opportunities to tell them what God is doing in our lives because we can have an important influence on them.

the hand of the Egyptians. [11]Now I know that the LORD is greater than all other gods, for he did this to those who had treated Israel arrogantly."[p] [12]Then Jethro, Moses' father-in-law, brought a burnt offering and other sacrifices to God, and Aaron came with all the elders of Israel to eat bread with Moses' father-in-law in the presence of God.

[13]The next day Moses took his seat to serve as judge for the people, and they stood around him from morning till evening. [14]When his father-in-law saw all that Moses was doing for the people, he said, "What is this you are doing for the people? Why do you alone sit as judge, while all these people stand around you from morning till evening?"

[15]Moses answered him, "Because the people come to me to seek God's will.[q] [16]Whenever they have a dispute, it is brought to me, and I decide between the parties and inform them of God's decrees and laws."

[17]Moses' father-in-law replied, "What you are doing is not good. [18]You and these people who come to you will only wear yourselves out. The work is too heavy for you; you cannot handle it alone.[r] [19]Listen now to me and I will give you some advice, and may God be with you. You must be the people's representative before God and bring their disputes[s] to him. [20]Teach them the decrees and laws,[t] and show them the way to live[u] and the duties they are to perform.[v] [21]But select capable men[w] from all the people—men who fear God, trustworthy men who hate dishonest gain[x]—and appoint them as officials[y] over thousands, hundreds, fifties and tens. [22]Have them serve as judges for the people at all times, but have them bring every difficult case[z] to you; the simple cases they can decide themselves. That will make your load lighter, because they will share[a] it with you. [23]If you do this and God so commands, you will be able to stand the strain, and all these people will go home satisfied."

[24]Moses listened to his father-in-law and did everything he said. [25]He chose capable men from all Israel and made them leaders of the people, officials over thousands, hundreds, fifties and tens.[b] [26]They served as judges for the people at all times. The difficult cases they brought to Moses, but the simple ones they decided themselves.[c]

[27]Then Moses sent his father-in-law on his way, and Jethro returned to his own country.[d]

C. ISRAEL AT SINAI (19:1—40:38)

After escaping through the Red Sea, the Hebrews traveled through the desert and arrived at Sinai, God's holy mountain. There they received the Ten Commandments, as well as instructions for building a tabernacle as a center of worship. Through Israel's experiences at Mount Sinai, we learn about the importance of obedience in our relationship with God. His laws help expose sin, and they give standards for righteous living.

1. Giving the law
At Mount Sinai

19 In the third month after the Israelites left Egypt—on the very day—they came to the Desert of Sinai. [2]After they set out from Rephidim,[e] they entered the Desert of Sinai, and Israel camped there in the desert in front of the mountain.

[3]Then Moses went up to God, and the LORD called[f] to him from the mountain and said, "This is what you are to say to the house of Jacob and what you are to tell the people of Israel: [4]'You yourselves have seen what I did to Egypt,[g] and how I carried you on eagles' wings and

18:11
[p]Lk 1:51

18:15
[q]Nu 9:6,8;
Dt 17:8-13

18:18
[r]Nu 11:11,14,17
18:19
[s]Nu 27:5
18:20
[t]Dt 5:1
[u]Ps 143:8
[v]Dt 1:18
18:21
[w]Ac 6:3
[x]Dt 16:19
[y]Dt 1:13,15;
2Ch 19:5-10
18:22
[z]Dt 1:17-18
[a]Nu 11:17

18:25
[b]Dt 1:13-15
18:26
[c]ver 22
18:27
[d]Nu 10:29-30

19:2
[e]Ex 17:1

19:3
[f]Ac 7:38
19:4
[g]Dt 29:2

18:12 This reunion turned into a large celebration. The Israelites frequently shared a sacrificial meal among themselves. A burnt offering was sacrificed to God, and then the meal taken from the sacrifice was dedicated to God and eaten ceremonially as a fellowship dinner.

18:13-26 Moses was spending so much time and energy hearing the Hebrews' complaints that he could not get to other important work. Jethro suggested that Moses delegate most of this work to others and focus his efforts on jobs only he could do. People in positions of responsibility sometimes feel they are the only ones who can do necessary tasks; but others are capable of handling part of the load. Delegation relieved Moses' stress and improved the quality of the government. It helped prepare them for the system of government set up in Canaan. Proper delegation can multiply your effectiveness while giving others a chance to grow.

18:16 Moses not only decided these cases, he also taught the people God's laws. Whenever we help others settle disputes or resolve conflicts, we should also look for opportunities to teach about God.

19:2, 3 Mount Sinai (also called Mount Horeb) is one of the most sacred locations in Israel's history. Located in the south-central Sinai peninsula, this mountain is where Moses met God in a burning bush, God made his covenant with Israel, and Elijah heard God in the gentle whisper. Here God gave his people the laws and guidelines for right living. They learned the potential blessings of obedience (34:4–28) and the tragic consequences of disobedience (34:32).

19:4-6 God had a reason for rescuing the Israelites from slavery. Now he was ready to tell them what it was: Israel was to become a kingdom of priests and a holy nation where anyone could approach God freely. It didn't take long, however, for the people to corrupt God's plan. God then established Aaron's descendants from the tribe of Levi as priests, representing what the entire nation should have been (Leviticus 8; 9). But with the coming of Jesus Christ, God has once again extended his plan to all believers. We are to become holy, a "royal priesthood" (1 Peter 2:9). The death and resurrection of Christ has allowed each of us to approach God freely.

19:5
h Dt 5:2
i Dt 10:14
19:6
j 1Pe 2:5
k Dt 7:6

19:8
l Ex 24:3,7

19:9
m ver 16;
Ex 24:15-16

19:10
n Lev 11:44

19:13
o Heb 12:20*

19:16
p Heb 12:18-19;
Rev 4:1

19:18
q Ps 104:32
r Ps 68:8

19:19
s Ne 9:13
t Ps 81:7

19:21
u Ex 3:5; 1Sa 6:19

19:22
v Lev 10:3

19:23
w ver 12

brought you to myself. [5]Now if you obey me fully and keep my covenant,h then out of all nations you will be my treasured possession. Although the whole earth i is mine, [6]youa will be for me a kingdom of priestsj and a holy nation.'k These are the words you are to speak to the Israelites."

[7]So Moses went back and summoned the elders of the people and set before them all the words the LORD had commanded him to speak. [8]The people all responded together, "We will do everything the LORD has said."l So Moses brought their answer back to the LORD.

[9]The LORD said to Moses, "I am going to come to you in a dense cloud,m so that the people will hear me speaking with you and will always put their trust in you." Then Moses told the LORD what the people had said.

[10]And the LORD said to Moses, "Go to the people and consecraten them today and tomorrow. Have them wash their clothes [11]and be ready by the third day, because on that day the LORD will come down on Mount Sinai in the sight of all the people. [12]Put limits for the people around the mountain and tell them, 'Be careful that you do not go up the mountain or touch the foot of it. Whoever touches the mountain shall surely be put to death. [13]He shall surely be stonedo or shot with arrows; not a hand is to be laid on him. Whether man or animal, he shall not be permitted to live.' Only when the ram's horn sounds a long blast may they go up to the mountain."

[14]After Moses had gone down the mountain to the people, he consecrated them, and they washed their clothes. [15]Then he said to the people, "Prepare yourselves for the third day. Abstain from sexual relations."

[16]On the morning of the third day there was thunder and lightning, with a thick cloud over the mountain, and a very loud trumpet blast.p Everyone in the camp trembled. [17]Then Moses led the people out of the camp to meet with God, and they stood at the foot of the mountain. [18]Mount Sinai was covered with smoke,q because the LORD descended on it in fire. The smoke billowed up from it like smoke from a furnace, the whole mountain b trembled r violently, [19]and the sound of the trumpet grew louder and louder. Then Moses spoke and the voices of God answered t him.c

[20]The LORD descended to the top of Mount Sinai and called Moses to the top of the mountain. So Moses went up [21]and the LORD said to him, "Go down and warn the people so they do not force their way through to seeu the LORD and many of them perish. [22]Even the priests, who approach v the LORD, must consecrate themselves, or the LORD will break out against them."

[23]Moses said to the LORD, "The people cannot come up Mount Sinai, because you yourself warned us, 'Put limits w around the mountain and set it apart as holy.'"

[24]The LORD replied, "Go down and bring Aaron up with you. But the priests and the people must not force their way through to come up to the LORD, or he will break out against them."

[25]So Moses went down to the people and told them.

a 5,6 Or possession, for the whole earth is mine. 6 You   b 18 Most Hebrew manuscripts; a few Hebrew manuscripts and Septuagint all the people   c 19 Or and God answered him with thunder

---

19:5 Why did God choose Israel as his nation? God knew that no nation on earth was good enough to deserve to be called his people, his "treasured possession." He chose Israel, not because of anything they had done, but in his love and mercy he chose Israel in spite of the wrong the nation had done and would do. Why did he want to have a special nation on earth? To represent his way of life, to teach his Word, and to be an agent of salvation to the world. "All nations on earth" would be blessed through Abraham's descendants (Genesis 18:18). Gentiles and kings would come to the Lord through Israel, predicted Isaiah (Isaiah 60:3). Through the nation of Israel, the Messiah, God's chosen Son, would be born. God chose one nation and put it through a rigorous training program, so that one day it could be a channel for his blessings to the whole world.

19:5–8 In Genesis 15 and 17, God made a covenant with Abraham, promising to make his descendants into a great nation. Now that promise was being realized as God restated his agreement with the Israelite nation, the descendants of Abraham. God promised to bless and care for them. The people promised to obey him. The covenant was thus sealed. But the good intentions of the people quickly wore off. Have you made a commitment to God? How are you holding up your end of the bargain?

19:9–11 Moses was told to consecrate the people. This meant getting them physically and spiritually ready to meet God. The people were to set themselves apart from sin and even ordinary daily routine in order to dedicate themselves to God. The act of washing and preparing served to get their minds and hearts ready. When we meet God for worship, we should set aside the cares and preoccupations of everyday life. Use your time of physical preparation to get your mind ready to meet God.

19:22 By stating that he "will break out against them," the Lord was saying that he would destroy anyone who was not fully consecrated and ready to meet him.

19:23 Because God's glory and power were so strong, and because God is completely holy, the people could not come to him. God did this to show that he was not like the idols of Egypt that could be seen and touched. Now, however, we are invited to approach God because of what Christ has done for us (Hebrews 12:18–24). Jesus is superior to Moses because Jesus opens the way for us to come to God with great joy.

The Ten Commandments

20 And God spoke all these words:

2 "I am the LORD your God, who brought you out of Egypt, out of the land of slavery.

3 "You shall have no other gods before[a] me. *x*

4 "You shall not make for yourself an idol in the form of anything in heaven above or on the earth beneath or in the waters below. 5 You shall not bow down to them or worship them; for I, the LORD your God, am a jealous God, *y* punishing the children for the sin of the fathers to the third and fourth generation *z* of those who hate me, 6 but showing love to a thousand *a* ¦ generations ¦ of those who love me and keep my commandments.

7 "You shall not misuse the name of the LORD your God, for the LORD will not hold anyone guiltless who misuses his name. *b*

8 "Remember the Sabbath *c* day by keeping it holy. 9 Six days you shall labor and do all your work, *d* 10 but the seventh day is a Sabbath to the LORD your God. On it you shall not do any work, neither you, nor your son or daughter, nor your manservant or maidservant, nor your animals, nor the alien within your gates. 11 For in six days the LORD made the heavens and the earth, the sea, and all that is in them, but he rested *e* on the seventh day. Therefore the LORD blessed the Sabbath day and made it holy.

12 "Honor your father and your mother, *f* so that you may live long in the land the LORD your God is giving you.

13 "You shall not murder. *g*

14 "You shall not commit adultery.

15 "You shall not steal. *h*

16 "You shall not give false testimony against your neighbor. *i*

17 "You shall not covet *j* your neighbor's house. You shall not covet your neighbor's wife, or his manservant or maidservant, his ox or donkey, or anything that belongs to your neighbor."

a 3 Or besides

20:3
x Jer 35:15

20:5
y Dt 4:24
z Jer 32:18

20:6
a Dt 7:9

20:7
b Lev 19:12

20:8
c Ex 31:13-16

20:9
d Lk 13:14

20:11
e Ge 2:2

20:12
f Mt 15:4*; Eph 6:2

20:13
g Ro 13:9*

20:15
h Mt 19:18*

20:16
i Ex 23:1,7

20:17
j Ro 7:7*; 13:9*; Eph 5:3

20:1ff Why were the Ten Commandments necessary for God's new nation? At the foot of Mount Sinai, God showed his people the true function and beauty of his laws. The commandments were designed to lead Israel to a life of practical holiness. In them, people could see the nature of God and his plan for how they should live. The commands and guidelines were intended to direct the community to meet the needs of each individual in a loving and responsible manner. By Jesus' time, however, most people looked at the law the wrong way. They saw it as a means to prosperity in both this world and the next. And they thought that to obey every law was the way to earn God's protection from foreign invasion and natural disaster. Lawkeeping became an end in itself, not the means to fulfill God's ultimate law of love.

20:1–6 The Israelites had just come from Egypt, a land of many idols and many gods. Because each god represented a different aspect of life, it was common to worship many gods in order to get the maximum number of blessings. When God told his people to worship and believe in him, that wasn't so hard for them—he was just one more god to add to the list. But when he said, "You shall have no other gods before me," that was difficult for the people to accept. But if they didn't learn that the God who led them out of Egypt was the only true God, they could not be his people— no matter how faithfully they kept the other nine commandments. Thus, God made this his first commandment. Today we can allow many things to become gods to us. Money, fame, work, or pleasure can become gods when we concentrate too much on them for personal identity, meaning, and security. No one sets out with the intention of worshiping these things. But by the amount of time we devote to them, they can grow into gods that ultimately control our thoughts and energies. Letting God hold the central place in our lives keeps these things from turning into gods.

20:7 God's name is special because it carries his personal identity. Using it frivolously or in a curse is so common today that we

may fail to realize how serious it is. The way we use God's name conveys how we really feel about him. We should respect his name and use it appropriately, speaking it in praise or worship rather than in curse or jest. We should not take lightly the abuse or dishonor of his name.

20:8–11 The Sabbath was a day set aside for rest and worship. God commanded a Sabbath because human beings need to spend unhurried time in worship and rest each week. A God who is concerned enough to provide a day each week for us to rest is indeed wonderful. To observe a regular time of rest and worship in our fast-paced world demonstrates how important God is to us, and it gives us the extra benefit of refreshing our spirits. Don't neglect God's provision.

20:12 This is the first commandment with a promise attached. To live in peace for generations in the promised land, the Israelites would need to respect authority and build strong families. But what does it mean to "honor" parents? Partly, it means speaking well of them and politely to them. It also means acting in a way that shows them courtesy and respect (but not to obey them if this means disobedience to God). It means following their teaching and example of putting God first. Parents have a special place in God's sight. Even those who find it difficult to get along with their parents are still commanded to honor them.

20:16 Giving false testimony means lying in court. God knew that Israel could not survive unless its system of justice was incorruptible. We should be honest in our private dealings as well as in our public statements. In either situation, we "give false testimony" by leaving something out of a story, telling a half-truth, twisting the facts, or inventing a falsehood. God warns us against deception. Even though deception is a way of life for many people, God's people must not give in to it!

20:17 To covet is to wish to have the possessions of others. It goes beyond simply admiring someone else's possessions or

20:18
[k] Ex 19:16-19;
Heb 12:18-19

20:19
[l] Dt 5:5,23-27

20:20
[m] Pr 16:6

[18] When the people saw the thunder and lightning and heard the trumpet [k] and saw the mountain in smoke, they trembled with fear. They stayed at a distance [19] and said to Moses, "Speak to us yourself and we will listen. But do not have God speak to us or we will die." [l]

[20] Moses said to the people, "Do not be afraid. God has come to test you, so that the fear of God will be with you to keep you from sinning." [m]

[21] The people remained at a distance, while Moses approached the thick darkness where God was.

Idols and Altars

[22] Then the LORD said to Moses, "Tell the Israelites this: 'You have seen for yourselves that I have spoken to you from heaven: [23] Do not make any gods to be alongside me; do not make for yourselves gods of silver or gods of gold.

20:24
[n] Ge 12:2

[24] "'Make an altar of earth for me and sacrifice on it your burnt offerings and fellowship offerings,[a] your sheep and goats and your cattle. Wherever I cause my name to be honored, I will come to you and bless [n] you. [25] If you make an altar of stones for me, do not build it with dressed stones, for you will defile it if you use a tool on it. [26] And do not go up to my altar on steps, lest your nakedness be exposed on it.'

[a] 24 Traditionally *peace offerings*

THE TEN COMMAND-MENTS AND THE WORDS OF JESUS

The Ten Commandments said . . .	Jesus said . . .
Exodus 20:3 "You shall have no other gods before me."	Matthew 4:10 "Worship the Lord your God and serve him only."
Exodus 20:4 "You shall not make for yourself an idol."	Luke 16:13 "No servant can serve two masters."
Exodus 20:7 "You shall not misuse the name of the LORD your God."	Matthew 5:34 "Do not swear at all: either by heaven, for it is God's throne. . . ."
Exodus 20:8 "Remember the Sabbath day by keeping it holy."	Mark 2:27, 28 "The Sabbath was made for man, not man for the Sabbath. So the Son of Man is Lord even of the Sabbath."
Exodus 20:12 "Honor your father and your mother."	Matthew 10:37 "Anyone who loves his father or mother more than me is not worthy of me."
Exodus 20:13 "You shall not murder."	Matthew 5:22 "Anyone who is angry with his brother will be subject to judgment."
Exodus 20:14 "You shall not commit adultery."	Matthew 5:28 "Anyone who looks at a woman lustfully has already committed adultery with her in his heart."
Exodus 20:15 "You shall not steal."	Matthew 5:40 "If someone wants to sue you and take your tunic, let him have your cloak as well."
Exodus 20:16 "You shall not give false testimony."	Matthew 12:36 "Men will have to give account on the day of judgment for every careless word they have spoken."
Exodus 20:17 "You shall not covet."	Luke 12:15 "Be on your guard against all kinds of greed."

---

thinking, "I'd like to have one of those." Coveting includes envy—resenting the fact that others have what you don't. God knows, however, that possessions never make anyone happy for long. Since only God can supply all our needs, true contentment is found only in him. When you begin to covet, try to determine if a more basic need is leading you to envy. For example, you may covet someone's success, not because you want to take it away from him, but because you would like to feel as appreciated by others as he is. If this is the case, pray that God will help you deal with your resentment and meet your basic needs.

20:18 Sometimes God speaks to his people with a majestic display of power; at other times he speaks quietly. Why the difference? God speaks in the way that best accomplishes his purposes. At Sinai, the awesome display of light and sound was necessary to show Israel God's great power and authority. Only then would they listen to Moses and Aaron.

20:20 Throughout the Bible we find this phrase, "Do not be

afraid." God wasn't trying to scare the people. He was showing his mighty power so the Israelites would know he was the true God and would therefore obey him. If they would do this, he would make his power available to them. God wants us to follow him out of love rather than fear. To overcome fear, we must think more about his love. 1 John 4:18 says, "Perfect love drives out fear."

20:24–26 Why were specific directions given for building altars? God's people had no Bible and few religious traditions to learn from. God had to start from scratch and teach them how to worship him. God gave specific instructions about building altars because he wanted to control the way sacrifices were offered. To prevent idolatry from creeping into worship, God did not allow the altar stones to be cut or shaped into any form. Nor did God let the people build an altar just anywhere. This was designed to prevent them from starting their own religions or making changes in the way God wanted things done. God is not against creativity, but he is against us creating our own religion.

21

"These are the laws *o* you are to set before them:

21:1
o Dt 4:14

Hebrew Servants

2 "If you buy a Hebrew servant, he is to serve you for six years. But in the seventh year, he shall go free, without paying anything. 3 If he comes alone, he is to go free alone; but if he has a wife when he comes, she is to go with him. 4 If his master gives him a wife and she bears him sons or daughters, the woman and her children shall belong to her master, and only the man shall go free.

5 "But if the servant declares, 'I love my master and my wife and children and do not want to go free,' *p* 6 then his master must take him before the judges. *a* He shall take him to the door or the doorpost and pierce his ear with an awl. Then he will be his servant for life. *q*

21:5
p Dt 15:16
21:6
q Ne 5:5

7 "If a man sells his daughter as a servant, she is not to go free as menservants do. 8 If she does not please the master who has selected her for himself, *b* he must let her be redeemed. He has no right to sell her to foreigners, because he has broken faith with her. 9 If he selects her for his son, he must grant her the rights of a daughter. 10 If he marries another woman, he must not deprive the first one of her food, clothing and marital rights. *r* 11 If he does not provide her with these three things, she is to go free, without any payment of money.

21:10
r 1Co 7:3-5

Personal Injuries

12 "Anyone who strikes a man and kills him shall surely be put to death. *s* 13 However, if he does not do it intentionally, but God lets it happen, he is to flee to a place *t* I will designate. 14 But if a man schemes and kills another man deliberately, take him away from my altar and put him to death. *u*

15 "Anyone who attacks *c* his father or his mother must be put to death.

16 "Anyone who kidnaps another and either sells him or still has him when he is caught must be put to death. *v*

17 "Anyone who curses his father or mother must be put to death. *w*

21:12
s Ge 9:6
21:13
t Nu 35:10-34;
Dt 19:2-13
21:14
u Dt 19:11-12;
1Ki 2:28-34
21:16
v Dt 24:7
21:17
w Mk 7:10*

18 "If men quarrel and one hits the other with a stone or with his fist *d* and he does not die but is confined to bed, 19 the one who struck the blow will not be held responsible if the other gets up and walks around outside with his staff; however, he must pay the injured man for the loss of his time and see that he is completely healed.

20 "If a man beats his male or female slave with a rod and the slave dies as a direct result, he must be punished, 21 but he is not to be punished if the slave gets up after a day or two, since the slave is his property.

22 "If men who are fighting hit a pregnant woman and she gives birth prematurely *e* but there is no serious injury, the offender must be fined whatever the woman's husband demands and the court allows. 23 But if there is serious injury, you are to take life for life, 24 eye for eye, tooth for tooth, *x* hand for hand, foot for foot, 25 burn for burn, wound for wound, bruise for bruise.

21:24
x Mt 5:38*

26 "If a man hits a manservant or maidservant in the eye and destroys it, he must let the servant go free to compensate for the eye. 27 And if he knocks out the tooth of a manservant or maidservant, he must let the servant go free to compensate for the tooth.

28 "If a bull gores a man or a woman to death, the bull must be stoned to death, *y* and its meat must not be eaten. But the owner of the bull will not be held responsible. 29 If, however, the bull has had the habit of goring and the owner has been warned but has not kept it penned up and it kills a man or woman, the bull must be stoned and the owner also must be put to death. 30 However, if payment is demanded of him, he may redeem his life by paying whatever is demanded. 31 This law also applies if the bull gores a son or daughter. 32 If the

21:28
y Ge 9:5

a 6 Or before God   *b* 8 Or master so that he does not choose her   *c* 15 Or kills   *d* 18 Or with a tool   *e* 22 Or she has a miscarriage

---

21:1ff These laws were given because everything we do has consequences. It is vital to think before acting, to consider the effects of our choices. Think of your plans for today and consider what their long-range results will be. As we deal with others, we should keep the principles of these laws in mind. We should act responsibly and justly with all people—friends and enemies alike.

21:2 The Hebrews, though freed from slavery, had slaves (or servants) themselves. A person could become a slave because of poverty, debt, or even crime. But Hebrew slaves were treated as humans, not property, and were allowed to work their way to freedom. The Bible acknowledges the existence of slavery but never encourages it.

21:24, 25 The "eye for eye" rule was instituted as a guide for judges, not as a rule for personal relationships or to justify revenge. This rule made the punishment fit the crime, thereby preventing the cruel and barbaric punishments that characterized many ancient countries. Jesus used this principle to teach us not to retaliate (Matthew 5:38–48). Judges, parents, teachers, and others who work bull gores a male or female slave, the owner must pay thirty shekels[a] [z] of silver to the master of the slave, and the bull must be stoned.

21:32
[z] Zec 11:12-13;
Mt 26:15

[33] "If a man uncovers a pit or digs one and fails to cover it and an ox or a donkey falls into it, [34] the owner of the pit must pay for the loss; he must pay its owner, and the dead animal will be his.

[35] "If a man's bull injures the bull of another and it dies, they are to sell the live one and divide both the money and the dead animal equally. [36] However, if it was known that the bull had the habit of goring, yet the owner did not keep it penned up, the owner must pay, animal for animal, and the dead animal will be his.

Protection of Property

22 "If a man steals an ox or a sheep and slaughters it or sells it, he must pay back[a] five head of cattle for the ox and four sheep for the sheep.

22:1
[a] 2Sa 12:6

[2] "If a thief is caught breaking in[b] and is struck so that he dies, the defender is not guilty of bloodshed; [3] but if it happens[b] after sunrise, he is guilty of bloodshed.

22:2
[b] Mt 24:43

"A thief must certainly make restitution, but if he has nothing, he must be sold[c] to pay for his theft.

22:3
[c] Ex 21:2

[4] "If the stolen animal is found alive in his possession—whether ox or donkey or sheep—he must pay back double.

[5] "If a man grazes his livestock in a field or vineyard and lets them stray and they graze in another man's field, he must make restitution from the best of his own field or vineyard.

[6] "If a fire breaks out and spreads into thornbushes so that it burns shocks of grain or standing grain or the whole field, the one who started the fire must make restitution.

[7] "If a man gives his neighbor silver or goods for safekeeping and they are stolen from the neighbor's house, the thief, if he is caught, must pay back double. [8] But if the thief is not found, the owner of the house must appear before the judges[c] to determine whether he has laid his hands on the other man's property. [9] In all cases of illegal possession of an ox, a donkey, a sheep, a garment, or any other lost property about which somebody says, 'This is mine,' both parties are to bring their cases before the judges.[d] The one whom the judges declare[d] guilty must pay back double to his neighbor.

22:9
[d] Dt 25:1

[10] "If a man gives a donkey, an ox, a sheep or any other animal to his neighbor for safekeeping and it dies or is injured or is taken away while no one is looking, [11] the issue between them will be settled by the taking of an oath[e] before the LORD that the neighbor did not lay hands on the other person's property. The owner is to accept this, and no restitution is required. [12] But if the animal was stolen from the neighbor, he must make restitution to the owner. [13] If it was torn to pieces by a wild animal, he shall bring in the remains as evidence and he will not be required to pay for the torn animal.[f]

22:11
[e] Heb 6:16

22:13
[f] Ge 31:39

[14] "If a man borrows an animal from his neighbor and it is injured or dies while the owner is not present, he must make restitution. [15] But if the owner is with the animal, the borrower will not have to pay. If the animal was hired, the money paid for the hire covers the loss.

Social Responsibility

[16] "If a man seduces a virgin[g] who is not pledged to be married and sleeps with her, he must pay the bride-price, and she shall be his wife. [17] If her father absolutely refuses to give her to him, he must still pay the bride-price for virgins.

22:16
[g] Dt 22:28

[18] "Do not allow a sorceress to live.

[a] *32 That is, about 12 ounces (about 0.3 kilogram)*   [b] *3 Or if he strikes him*   [c] *8 Or before God; also in verse 9*
[d] *9 Or whom God declares*

---

with people must make wise decisions in order for discipline to be effective. A punishment too harsh is unfair, and one too lenient is powerless to teach. Ask God for wisdom before you judge.

22:1ff These are not a collection of picky laws but are case studies of God's principles in action. God was taking potential situations and showing how his laws would work in the Israelites' everyday lives. These case studies had several objectives: (1) to protect the nation, (2) to organize the nation, and (3) to focus the nation's attention on God. The laws listed here do not cover every possible situation but give practical examples that make it easier to decide what God wants.

22:3ff Throughout chapter 22 we find examples of the principle

of restitution—making wrongs right. For example, if a man stole an animal, he had to repay double the beast's market value. If you have done someone wrong, perhaps you should go beyond what is expected to make things right. This will (1) help ease any pain you've caused, (2) help the other person be more forgiving, and (3) make you more likely to think before you do it again.

22:18 Why did God's laws speak so strongly against sorcery (Leviticus 19:31; 20:6, 27; Deuteronomy 18:10–12)? Sorcery was punishable by death because it was a crime against God himself. To invoke evil powers violated the first commandment to "have no other gods." Sorcery was rebellion against God and his authority. In essence, it was teaming up with Satan instead of with God.

19"Anyone who has sexual relations with an animal [h] must be put to death.

20"Whoever sacrifices to any god other than the LORD must be destroyed. [a] [i]

21"Do not mistreat an alien or oppress him, for you were aliens [j] in Egypt.

22"Do not take advantage of a widow or an orphan. 23 If you do and they cry out [k] to me, I will certainly hear their cry. [l] 24 My anger will be aroused, and I will kill you with the sword; your wives will become widows and your children fatherless. [m]

25"If you lend money to one of my people among you who is needy, do not be like a moneylender; charge him no interest. [b] 26 If you take your neighbor's cloak as a pledge, return it to him by sunset, 27 because his cloak is the only covering he has for his body. What else will he sleep in? When he cries out to me, I will hear, for I am compassionate.

28"Do not blaspheme God [c] or curse the ruler of your people. [n]

29"Do not hold back offerings [o] from your granaries or your vats. [d]

"You must give me the firstborn of your sons. [p] 30 Do the same with your cattle and your sheep. [q] Let them stay with their mothers for seven days, but give them to me on the eighth day. [r]

31"You are to be my holy people. [s] So do not eat the meat of an animal torn by wild beasts; throw it to the dogs.

Laws of Justice and Mercy

23 "Do not spread false reports. Do not help a wicked man by being a malicious witness. 2"Do not follow the crowd in doing wrong. When you give testimony in a lawsuit, do not pervert justice by siding with the crowd, 3 and do not show favoritism to a poor man in his lawsuit.

4"If you come across your enemy's ox or donkey wandering off, be sure to take it back to him. 5 If you see the donkey [t] of someone who hates you fallen down under its load, do not leave it there; be sure you help him with it.

6"Do not deny justice to your poor people in their lawsuits. 7 Have nothing to do with a false charge [u] and do not put an innocent or honest person to death, for I will not acquit the guilty.

8"Do not accept a bribe, [v] for a bribe blinds those who see and twists the words of the righteous.

9"Do not oppress an alien; [w] you yourselves know how it feels to be aliens, because you were aliens in Egypt.

Sabbath Laws

10"For six years you are to sow your fields and harvest the crops, 11 but during the seventh year let the land lie unplowed and unused. Then the poor among your people may get food from it, and the wild animals may eat what they leave. Do the same with your vineyard and your olive grove.

[a] 20 The Hebrew term refers to the irrevocable giving over of things or persons to the LORD, often by totally destroying them.   [b] 25 Or *excessive interest*   [c] 28 Or *Do not revile the judges*   [d] 29 The meaning of the Hebrew for this phrase is uncertain.

22:19
[h] Lev 18:23
22:20
[i] Dt 17:2-5
22:21
[j] Dt 10:19
22:23
[k] Lk 18:7
[l] Ps 18:6
22:24
[m] Ps 69:24; 109:9
22:28
[n] Ac 23:5*
22:29
[o] Ex 23:15,16,19
[p] Ex 13:2
22:30
[q] Ex 13:12; Dt 15:19
[r] Lev 22:27
22:31
[s] Lev 19:2

23:5
[t] Dt 22:4
23:7
[u] Eph 4:25
23:8
[v] Dt 10:17

23:9
[w] Ex 22:21

22:21 God warned the Israelites not to treat aliens unfairly because they themselves were once strangers in Egypt. It is not easy coming into a new environment where you feel alone and out of place. Are there strangers in your corner of the world? Refugees? New arrivals at school? Immigrants from another country? Be sensitive to their struggles, and express God's love by your kindness and generosity.

22:22–27 The Hebrew law code is noted for its fairness and social responsibility toward the poor. God insisted that the poor and powerless be well treated and given the chance to restore their fortunes. We should reflect God's concern for the poor by giving and by helping those less fortunate than ourselves.

22:26 Why did the law insist on returning a person's cloak by evening? The cloak was one of an Israelite's most valuable possessions. Making clothing was difficult and time-consuming. As a result, cloaks were expensive, and most people owned only one. The cloak was used as a blanket, a sack to carry things in, a place to sit, a pledge for a debt, and, of course, clothing.

22:29 The Israelites were to be prompt in giving God their offerings and not hold anything back. The first of the harvest was to be dedicated to him. Since God doesn't send payment overdue

notices, it is easy to take care of other financial responsibilities while letting our gifts to God slide. Giving to God first out of what he has allowed you to have demonstrates that he has first priority in your life.

23:1 Making up or spreading false reports was strictly forbidden by God. Gossip, slander, and false witnessing would undermine families, strain neighborhood cooperation, and make chaos of the justice system. Destructive gossip still causes problems. Even if you do not initiate a lie, you become responsible if you pass it along. Don't circulate rumors; squelch them.

23:2, 3 Justice is often perverted in favor of the rich. Here the people are warned against twisting justice in favor of the poor. Justice should be impartial, treating rich and poor alike. Giving special privileges to either rich or poor only makes justice for everyone more unlikely. Withstand the pressure of the crowd to sway your decision about a person. Let the fairness God shows to each of us guide your judgment.

23:4, 5 The thought of being kind to enemies was new and startling in a world where revenge was the common form of justice. God not only introduced this idea to the Israelites, he made it law! If a man found a lost animal owned by his enemy, he was to return

¹²"Six days do your work, but on the seventh day do not work, so that your ox and your donkey may rest and the slave born in your household, and the alien as well, may be refreshed.

¹³"Be careful to do everything I have said to you. Do not invoke the names of other gods; do not let them be heard on your lips.

The Three Annual Festivals

¹⁴"Three times[x] a year you are to celebrate a festival to me.

¹⁵"Celebrate the Feast of Unleavened Bread;[y] for seven days eat bread made without yeast, as I commanded you. Do this at the appointed time in the month of Abib, for in that month you came out of Egypt.

"No one is to appear before me empty-handed.[z]

¹⁶"Celebrate the Feast of Harvest with the firstfruits[a] of the crops you sow in your field.

"Celebrate the Feast of Ingathering at the end of the year, when you gather in your crops from the field.

¹⁷"Three times[b] a year all the men are to appear before the Sovereign LORD.

¹⁸"Do not offer the blood of a sacrifice to me along with anything containing yeast.

"The fat of my festival offerings must not be kept until morning.

¹⁹"Bring the best of the firstfruits of your soil to the house of the LORD your God.

"Do not cook a young goat in its mother's milk.[c]

God's Angel to Prepare the Way

²⁰"See, I am sending an angel ahead of you to guard you along the way and to bring you to the place I have prepared. ²¹Pay attention to him and listen to what he says. Do not rebel against him; he will not forgive your rebellion,[d] since my Name is in him. ²²If you listen carefully to what he says and do all that I say, I will be an enemy to your enemies and will oppose those who oppose you. ²³My angel will go ahead of you and bring you into the land of the Amorites, Hittites, Perizzites, Canaanites, Hivites and Jebusites,[e] and I will wipe them out. ²⁴Do not bow down before their gods or worship[f] them or follow their practices.[g] You must demolish them and break their sacred stones to pieces. ²⁵Worship the LORD your God,[h] and his blessing[i] will be on your food and water. I will take away sickness[j] from among you, ²⁶and none will miscarry or be barren[k] in your land. I will give you a full life span.

²⁷"I will send my terror ahead of you and throw into confusion[l] every nation you encounter. I will make all your enemies turn their backs and run. ²⁸I will send the hornet[m] ahead of you to drive the Hivites, Canaanites and Hittites out of your way. ²⁹But I will not drive them out in a single year, because the land would become desolate and the wild animals[n] too numerous for you. ³⁰Little by little I will drive them out before you, until you have increased enough to take possession of the land.

³¹"I will establish your borders from the Red Sea[a] to the Sea of the Philistines,[b] and from the desert to the River.[c][o] I will hand over to you the people who live in the land and you will drive them out[p] before you. ³²Do not make a covenant with them or with their gods. ³³Do not let them live in your land, or they will cause you to sin against me, because the worship of their gods will certainly be a snare to you."

[a]*31 Hebrew Yam Suph; that is, Sea of Reeds*   [b]*31 That is, the Mediterranean*   [c]*31 That is, the Euphrates*

23:14
[x]Ex 34:23,24

23:15
[y]Ex 12:17
[z]Ex 34:20

23:16
[a]Ex 34:22

23:17
[b]Dt 16:16

23:19
[c]Dt 14:21

23:21
[d]Ps 78:8,40,56

23:23
[e]Jos 24:8,11

23:24
[f]Ex 20:5
[g]Dt 12:30-31

23:25
[h]Dt 6:13; Mt 4:10
[i]Dt 28:1-14
[j]Ex 15:26

23:26
[k]Dt 7:14

23:27
[l]Dt 7:23

23:28
[m]Jos 24:12

23:29
[n]Dt 7:22

23:31
[o]Ge 15:18
[p]Jos 21:44

---

it at once, even if his enemy might use it to harm him. Jesus clearly taught in Luke 10:30–37 to reach out to all people in need, even our enemies. Following the laws of right living is hard enough with friends. When we apply God's laws of fairness and kindness to our enemies, we show how different we are from the world.

23:20, 21 Who was this angel that went with the Israelites? Most likely the angel was a manifestation of God. God is not present in all the angels in this way. Angels are God's created messengers (Hebrews 1:14). God chose to make himself known in this special way for a special purpose. God was in the angel in the same way he was present in the pillars of cloud and fire (13:21, 22). "My Name is in him" means the essential nature and power of God were made known in this angel.

23:24, 25 If you're in the furnace, it's easy to catch on fire. God warned the Israelites about their neighbors whose beliefs and actions could turn them away from him. We also live among neighbors whose values may be completely different from ours.

We are called to maintain a lifestyle that shows our faith. This can be a struggle, especially if our Christian lifestyle differs from the norm. Our lives should demonstrate that obeying God takes precedence over conforming to our neighbors' way of life. God's Word, not society, dictates how we should live.

23:29 Not all of God's solutions are instantaneous. Nor does delay justify inaction. In this case, God's cause would require constant cooperation, persistence, and effort by the Israelites. Success would come step by step.

23:32, 33 God continually warned the people to avoid false religions and false gods. In Egypt they had been surrounded by idols and sorcerers, but leaving that land did not mean they were free from pagan religious influences. The land of Canaan was just as infested with idol worship. God knew his people needed extra strength, so he continually emphasized guarding against the influence of pagan religions.

The Covenant Confirmed

24 Then he said to Moses, "Come up to the Lord, you and Aaron, Nadab and Abihu, and seventy of the elders *q* of Israel. You are to worship at a distance, ²but Moses alone is to approach the Lord; the others must not come near. And the people may not come up with him."

³When Moses went and told the people all the Lord's words and laws, they responded with one voice, "Everything the Lord has said we will do." *r* ⁴Moses then wrote *s* down everything the Lord had said.

He got up early the next morning and built an altar at the foot of the mountain and set up twelve stone pillars representing the twelve tribes of Israel. ⁵Then he sent young Israelite men, and they offered burnt offerings and sacrificed young bulls as fellowship offerings *a* to the Lord. ⁶Moses took half of the blood *t* and put it in bowls, and the other half he sprinkled on the altar. ⁷Then he took the Book of the Covenant and read it to the people. They responded, "We will do everything the Lord has said; we will obey."

⁸Moses then took the blood, sprinkled it on the people and said, "This is the blood of the covenant that the Lord has made with you in accordance with all these words."

⁹Moses and Aaron, Nadab and Abihu, and the seventy elders of Israel went up ¹⁰and saw the God of Israel. Under his feet was something like a pavement made of sapphire, *b u* clear as the sky *v* itself. ¹¹But God did not raise his hand against these leaders of the Israelites; they saw *w* God, and they ate and drank.

¹²The Lord said to Moses, "Come up to me on the mountain and stay here, and I will give you the tablets of stone, *x* with the law and commands I have written for their instruction."

¹³Then Moses set out with Joshua his aide, and Moses went up on the mountain of God. ¹⁴He said to the elders, "Wait here for us until we come back to you. Aaron and Hur are with you, and anyone involved in a dispute can go to them."

¹⁵When Moses went up on the mountain, the cloud *y* covered it, ¹⁶and the glory of the Lord settled on Mount Sinai. For six days the cloud covered the mountain, and on the seventh day the Lord called to Moses from within the cloud. ¹⁷To the Israelites the glory of the Lord looked like a consuming fire *z* on top of the mountain. ¹⁸Then Moses entered the cloud as he went on up the mountain. And he stayed on the mountain forty *a* days and forty nights.

2. Tabernacle instructions
Offerings for the Tabernacle

25 The Lord said to Moses, ²"Tell the Israelites to bring me an offering. You are to receive the offering for me from each man whose heart prompts *b* him to give. ³These are the offerings you are to receive from them: gold, silver and bronze; ⁴blue, purple and scarlet yarn and fine linen; goat hair; ⁵ram skins dyed red and hides of sea cows *c*; acacia wood; ⁶olive oil *c* for the light; spices for the anointing oil and for the fragrant incense; ⁷and onyx stones and other gems to be mounted on the ephod *d* and breastpiece. *e*

⁸"Then have them make a sanctuary *f* for me, and I will dwell *g* among them. ⁹Make this tabernacle and all its furnishings exactly like the pattern *h* I will show you.

*a*5 Traditionally *peace offerings*   *b*10 Or *lapis lazuli*   *c*5 That is, dugongs

24:1
*q*Nu 11:16

24:3
*r*Ex 19:8
24:4
*s*Dt 31:9

24:6
*t*Heb 9:18

24:10
*u*Eze 1:26
*v*Rev 4:3
24:11
*w*Ge 32:30
24:12
*x*Ex 32:15-16

24:15
*y*Ex 19:9
24:17
*z*Heb 12:18,29
24:18
*a*Dt 9:9

25:2
*b*Ex 35:21;
2Co 8:11-12; 9:7
25:6
*c*Ex 27:20;
30:22-32
25:7
*d*Ex 28:4,6-14
*e*Ex 28:15-30
25:8
*f*Ex 36:1-5
*g*Ex 29:45;
Rev 21:3
25:9
*h*ver 40

24:6–8 To understand this unusual covenant ratification ceremony, we need to understand the Bible's view of sin and forgiveness. God is the sovereign judge of the universe. He is also absolutely holy. As the holy judge of all, he condemns sin and judges it worthy of death. In the Old Testament God accepted the death of an animal as a substitute for the sinner. The animal's shed blood was proof that one life had been given for another. So on the one hand, blood symbolized the death of the animal, but it also symbolized the life that was spared as a result. Of course the death of the animal that brought forgiveness in the Old Testament was only a temporary provision, looking forward to the death of Jesus Christ (Hebrews 9:9—10:24).

In this ceremony described here, Moses sprinkled half the blood from the sacrificed animals on the altar to show that the sinner could once again approach God because something had died in his place. He sprinkled the other half of the blood on the people to show that the penalty for their sin had been paid and

they could be reunited with God. Through this symbolic act God's promises to Israel were reaffirmed and lessons were taught to us about the future sacrificial death (or atonement) of Jesus Christ.

25:1ff Chapters 25 through 31 record God's directions for building the tabernacle. Chapters 35 through 39 tell how these instructions were carried out. But what can all these ancient, complicated construction details show us today? First, the high quality of the precious materials making up the tabernacle shows God's greatness and transcendence. Second, the curtain surrounding the Most Holy Place shows God's moral perfection as symbolized by his separation from the common and unclean. Third, the portable nature of the tabernacle shows God's desire to be with his people as they traveled. Fourth, the tabernacle, its furnishings, and the service performed there provide a picture of the atonement that would one day come through Jesus Christ.

The Ark

10"Have them make a chest of acacia wood—two and a half cubits long, a cubit and a half wide, and a cubit and a half high.ᵃ ¹¹Overlay it with pure gold, both inside and out, and make a gold molding around it. ¹²Cast four gold rings for it and fasten them to its four feet, with two rings on one side and two rings on the other. ¹³Then make poles of acacia wood and overlay them with gold. ¹⁴Insert the poles into the rings on the sides of the chest to carry it. ¹⁵The poles are to remain in the rings of this ark; they are not to be removed. ¹⁶Then put in the ark the Testimony,ⁱ which I will give you.

17"Make an atonement coverᵇ of pure gold—two and a half cubits long and a cubit and a half wide. ᶜ ¹⁸And make two cherubim out of hammered gold at the ends of the cover. ¹⁹Make one cherub on one end and the second cherub on the other; make the cherubim of one piece with the cover, at the two ends. ²⁰The cherubim are to have their wings spread upward, overshadowingʲ the cover with them. The cherubim are to face each other, looking toward the cover. ²¹Place the cover on top of the arkᵏ and put in the ark the Testimony,ˡ which I will give you. ²²There, above the cover between the two cherubim ᵐ that are over the ark of the Testimony, I will meetⁿ with you and give you all my commands for the Israelites.

The Table

23"Make a table of acacia wood—two cubits long, a cubit wide and a cubit and a half high.ᵈ ²⁴Overlay it with pure gold and make a gold molding around it. ²⁵Also make around it a rim a handbreadthᵉ wide and put a gold molding on the rim. ²⁶Make four gold rings for the table and fasten them to the four corners, where the four legs are. ²⁷The rings are to be close to the rim to hold the poles used in carrying the table. ²⁸Make the poles of acacia wood, overlay them with gold and carry the table with them. ²⁹And make its plates and dishes of pure gold, as well as its pitchers and bowls for the pouring out of offerings.ᵒ ³⁰Put the bread of the Presenceᵖ on this table to be before me at all times.

The Lampstand

31"Make a lampstand of pure gold and hammer it out, base and shaft; its flowerlike cups, buds and blossoms shall be of one piece with it. ³²Six branches are to extend from the sides of the lampstand—three on one side and three on the other. ³³Three cups shaped like almond flowers with buds and blossoms are to be on one branch, three on the

25:16
ⁱDt 31:26; Heb 9:4

25:20
ʲ1Ki 8:7; Heb 9:5
25:21
ᵏEx 26:34
ˡver 16
25:22
ᵐNu 7:89; Ps 80:1
ⁿEx 29:42-43

25:29
ᵒNu 4:7
25:30
ᵖLev 24:5-9

---

a 10 That is, about 3 3/4 feet (about 1.1 meters) long and 2 1/4 feet (about 0.7 meter) wide and high   b 17 Traditionally a mercy seat   c 17 That is, about 3 3/4 feet (about 1.1 meters) long and 2 1/4 feet (about 0.7 meter) wide   d 23 That is, about 3 feet (about 0.9 meter) long and 1 1/2 feet (about 0.5 meter) wide and 2 1/4 feet (about 0.7 meter) high   e 25 That is, about 3 inches (about 8 centimeters)

THEOPHANIES IN THE SCRIPTURE
Appearances of God

At the foot of Mount Sinai, God appeared to the people of Israel in a physical form. This is called a *theophany.* Here are some of the other times God appeared to Bible people.

Verse	Theophany
Genesis 16:7	The angel of the Lord appeared to Sarah's maidservant, Hagar, announcing the birth of Abraham's son Ishmael
Genesis 18:1–11	The Lord appeared to Abraham, foretelling Isaac's birth
Genesis 22:11, 12	The angel of the Lord stopped Abraham from sacrificing Isaac
Exodus 3:2	The angel of the Lord appeared to Moses in flames in a bush
Exodus 14:19	The angel of God appeared to Israel in pillars of cloud and fire to guide them through the desert
Exodus 33:11	The Lord spoke to Moses face to face
Daniel 3:25	One "like a son of the gods" appeared as the fourth man with Shadrach, Meshach, and Abednego in the fiery furnace

("Angel of the Lord" is a reverential way to refer to God.)

25:10 Much of the tabernacle and its furniture was made of acacia wood. Acacia trees flourished in barren regions and were fairly common in Old Testament times. The wood was brownish-orange and very hard, making it an excellent material for furniture. Acacia wood is still used in furniture-making today. A cubit is about 1 1/2 feet or .43 meter.

25:17 The cover of the ark of the Testimony was called the atonement cover. This is where, between the two golden cherubim (mighty angels), the presence of God would dwell in a cloud above their outstretched wings. The atonement cover was where the highest and most perfect act of atonement would be made when the high priest would enter the Most Holy Place on the Day of Atonement to atone for the sins of all the people (30:10).

next branch, and the same for all six branches extending from the lampstand. [34]And on the lampstand there are to be four cups shaped like almond flowers with buds and blossoms. [35]One bud shall be under the first pair of branches extending from the lampstand, a second bud under the second pair, and a third bud under the third pair—six branches in all. [36]The buds and branches shall all be of one piece with the lampstand, hammered out of pure gold.

[37]"Then make its seven lamps and set them up on it so that they light the space in front of it. [38]Its wick trimmers and trays are to be of pure gold. [39]A talent[a] of pure gold is to be used for the lampstand and all these accessories. [40]See that you make them according to the pattern[q] shown you on the mountain.

The Tabernacle

26 "Make the tabernacle with ten curtains of finely twisted linen and blue, purple and scarlet yarn, with cherubim worked into them by a skilled craftsman. [2]All the curtains are to be the same size—twenty-eight cubits long and four cubits wide.[b] [3]Join five of the curtains together, and do the same with the other five. [4]Make loops of blue material along the edge of the end curtain in one set, and do the same with the end curtain in the other set. [5]Make fifty loops on one curtain and fifty loops on the end curtain of the other set, with the loops opposite each other. [6]Then make fifty gold clasps and use them to fasten the curtains together so that the tabernacle is a unit.

[7]"Make curtains of goat hair for the tent over the tabernacle—eleven altogether. [8]All eleven curtains are to be the same size—thirty cubits long and four cubits wide.[c] [9]Join five of the curtains together into one set and the other six into another set. Fold the sixth curtain double at the front of the tent. [10]Make fifty loops along the edge of the end curtain in one set and also along the edge of the end curtain in the other set. [11]Then make fifty bronze clasps and put them in the loops to fasten the tent together as a unit. [12]As for the additional length of the tent curtains, the half curtain that is left over is to hang down at the rear of the tabernacle. [13]The tent curtains will be a cubit[d] longer on both sides; what is left will hang over the sides of the tabernacle so as to cover it. [14]Make for the tent a covering of ram skins dyed red, and over that a covering of hides of sea cows.[e] [r]

[15]"Make upright frames of acacia wood for the tabernacle. [16]Each frame is to be ten cubits long and a cubit and a half wide,[f] [17]with two projections set parallel to each other. Make all the frames of the tabernacle in this way. [18]Make twenty frames for the south side of the tabernacle [19]and make forty silver bases to go under them—two bases for each frame, one under each projection. [20]For the other side, the north side of the tabernacle, make twenty frames [21]and forty silver bases—two under each frame. [22]Make six frames for the far end, that is, the west end of the tabernacle, [23]and make two frames for the corners at the far end. [24]At these two corners they must be double from the bottom all the way to the top, and fitted into a single ring; both shall be like that. [25]So there will be eight frames and sixteen silver bases—two under each frame.

[26]"Also make crossbars of acacia wood: five for the frames on one side of the tabernacle, [27]five for those on the other side, and five for the frames on the west, at the far end of the tabernacle. [28]The center crossbar is to extend from end to end at the middle of the frames. [29]Overlay the frames with gold and make gold rings to hold the crossbars. Also overlay the crossbars with gold.

[30]"Set up the tabernacle according to the plan[s] shown you on the mountain.

[31]"Make a curtain[t] of blue, purple and scarlet yarn and finely twisted linen, with cherubim[u] worked into it by a skilled craftsman. [32]Hang it with gold hooks on four posts of acacia wood overlaid with gold and standing on four silver bases. [33]Hang the curtain from the clasps and place the ark of the Testimony behind the curtain.[v] The curtain will separate the Holy Place from the Most Holy Place.[w] [34]Put the atonement cover[x] on the ark of the Testimony in the Most Holy Place. [35]Place the table outside the curtain on the north side of the tabernacle and put the lampstand[y] opposite it on the south side.

[a]39 That is, about 75 pounds (about 34 kilograms)   [b]2 That is, about 42 feet (about 12.5 meters) long and 6 feet (about 1.8 meters) wide   [c]8 That is, about 45 feet (about 13.5 meters) long and 6 feet (about 1.8 meters) wide   [d]13 That is, about 1 1/2 feet (about 0.5 meter)   [e]14 That is, dugongs   [f]16 That is, about 15 feet (about 4.5 meters) long and 2 1/4 feet (about 0.7 meter) wide

25:40
[q]Ex 26:30; Ac 7:44; Heb 8:5*

26:14
[r]Ex 36:19

26:30
[s]Ex 25:9,40; Ac 7:44; Heb 8:5
26:31
[t]Mt 27:51; Heb 9:3
[u]Ex 36:35
26:33
[v]Ex 40:3,21
[w]Heb 9:2-3
26:34
[x]Ex 25:21; 40:20
26:35
[y]Ex 40:22,24

26:31-33 This curtain separated the two sacred rooms in the tabernacle—the Holy Place and the Most Holy Place.

The priest entered the Holy Place each day to commune with God and to tend to the altar of incense, the lampstand, and

³⁶"For the entrance to the tent make a curtain of blue, purple and scarlet yarn and finely twisted linen—the work of an embroiderer. ³⁷Make gold hooks for this curtain and five posts of acacia wood overlaid with gold. And cast five bronze bases for them.

The Altar of Burnt Offering

27 "Build an altar of acacia wood, three cubits[a] high; it is to be square, five cubits long and five cubits wide.[b] ²Make a horn at each of the four corners, so that the horns and the altar are of one piece, and overlay the altar with bronze. ³Make all its utensils of bronze—its pots to remove the ashes, and its shovels, sprinkling bowls, meat forks and firepans. ⁴Make a grating for it, a bronze network, and make a bronze ring at each of the four corners of the network. ⁵Put it under the ledge of the altar so that it is halfway up the altar. ⁶Make poles of acacia wood for the altar and overlay them with bronze. ⁷The poles are to be inserted into the rings so they will be on two sides of the altar when it is carried. ⁸Make the altar hollow, out of boards. It is to be made just as you were shown ᶻ on the mountain.

27:8
ᶻ Ex 25:9,40

The Courtyard

⁹"Make a courtyard for the tabernacle. The south side shall be a hundred cubits[c] long and is to have curtains of finely twisted linen, ¹⁰with twenty posts and twenty bronze bases and with silver hooks and bands on the posts. ¹¹The north side shall also be a hundred cubits long and is to have curtains, with twenty posts and twenty bronze bases and with silver hooks and bands on the posts.

¹²"The west end of the courtyard shall be fifty cubits[d] wide and have curtains, with ten posts and ten bases. ¹³On the east end, toward the sunrise, the courtyard shall also be fifty cubits wide. ¹⁴Curtains fifteen cubits[e] long are to be on one side of the entrance, with three posts and three bases, ¹⁵and curtains fifteen cubits long are to be on the other side, with three posts and three bases.

¹⁶"For the entrance to the courtyard, provide a curtain twenty cubits[f] long, of blue, purple and scarlet yarn and finely twisted linen—the work of an embroiderer—with four posts and four bases. ¹⁷All the posts around the courtyard are to have silver bands and hooks, and bronze bases. ¹⁸The courtyard shall be a hundred cubits long and fifty cubits wide,[g] with curtains of finely twisted linen five cubits[h] high, and with bronze bases. ¹⁹All the other articles used in the service of the tabernacle, whatever their function, including all the tent pegs for it and those for the courtyard, are to be of bronze.

Oil for the Lampstand

²⁰"Command the Israelites to bring you clear oil of pressed olives for the light so that the lamps may be kept burning. ²¹In the Tent of Meeting,ᵃ outside the curtain that is in front of the Testimony,ᵇ Aaron and his sons are to keep the lamps burning before the LORD from evening till morning. This is to be a lasting ordinanceᶜ among the Israelites for the generations to come.

27:21
ᵃ Ex 28:43
ᵇ Ex 26:31,33
ᶜ Lev 3:17; 16:34

ᵃ*1* That is, about 4 1/2 feet (about 1.3 meters)   ᵇ*1* That is, about 7 1/2 feet (about 2.3 meters) long and wide   ᶜ*9* That is, about 150 feet (about 46 meters); also in verse 11   ᵈ*12* That is, about 75 feet (about 23 meters); also in verse 13   ᵉ*14* That is, about 22 1/2 feet (about 6.9 meters); also in verse 15   ᶠ*16* That is, about 30 feet (about 9 meters)   ᵍ*18* That is, about 150 feet (about 46 meters) long and 75 feet (about 23 meters) wide   ʰ*18* That is, about 7 1/2 feet (about 2.3 meters)

---

the table with the bread of the Presence. The Most Holy Place was where God himself dwelt, his presence resting on the atonement cover, which covered the ark of the Testimony. Only the high priest could enter the Most Holy Place. Even he could do so only once a year (on the Day of Atonement) to make atonement for the sins of the nation as a whole. When Jesus Christ died on the cross, the curtain in the temple (which had replaced the tabernacle) tore from top to bottom (Mark 15:38), symbolizing our free access to God because of Jesus' death. No longer did people have to approach God through priests and sacrifices.

27:1 The altar of burnt offering was the first thing the Israelites saw as they entered the tabernacle courtyard. Here sacrifices were constantly made. Its vivid presence constantly reminded the people that they could only come to God by means of the sacrifice. It was the only way their sins could be forgiven and

taken away. In Hebrews 10:1–18, Jesus Christ is portrayed as the ultimate sacrifice. This teaches that we are not to seek any other means to having a personal relationship with God. No counseling theory, Eastern mysticism, or modern ideas of spirituality can remove our sin. Jesus is our only High Priest today. Put all your confidence in him.

The Priestly Garments

28 "Have Aaron*d* your brother brought to you from among the Israelites, along with his sons Nadab and Abihu, Eleazar and Ithamar, so they may serve me as priests.*e* ²Make sacred garments*f* for your brother Aaron, to give him dignity and honor. ³Tell all the skilled men*g* to whom I have given wisdom*h* in such matters that they are to make garments for Aaron, for his consecration, so he may serve me as priest. ⁴These are the garments they are to make: a breastpiece,*i* an ephod, a robe,*j* a woven tunic,*k* a turban and a sash. They are to make these sacred garments for your brother Aaron and his sons, so they may serve me as priests. ⁵Have them use gold, and blue, purple and scarlet yarn, and fine linen.

28:1
*d*Heb 5:4
*e*Nu 18:1-7;
Heb 5:1
28:2
*f*Ex 29:5,29; 31:10
28:3
*g*Ex 31:6
*h*Ex 31:3
28:4
*i*ver 15-30
*j*ver 31-35
*k*ver 39

The Ephod

⁶"Make the ephod of gold, and of blue, purple and scarlet yarn, and of finely twisted linen—the work of a skilled craftsman. ⁷It is to have two shoulder pieces attached to two of its corners, so it can be fastened. ⁸Its skillfully woven waistband is to be like it—of one piece with the ephod and made with gold, and with blue, purple and scarlet yarn, and with finely twisted linen.

⁹"Take two onyx stones and engrave on them the names of the sons of Israel ¹⁰in the order of their birth—six names on one stone and the remaining six on the other. ¹¹Engrave the names of the sons of Israel on the two stones the way a gem cutter engraves a seal. Then mount the stones in gold filigree settings ¹²and fasten them on the shoulder pieces of the ephod as memorial stones for the sons of Israel. Aaron is to bear the names on his shoulders as a memorial before the Lord. ¹³Make gold filigree settings ¹⁴and two braided chains of pure gold, like a rope, and attach the chains to the settings.

The Breastpiece

¹⁵"Fashion a breastpiece for making decisions—the work of a skilled craftsman. Make it like the ephod: of gold, and of blue, purple and scarlet yarn, and of finely twisted linen. ¹⁶It is to be square—a span*a* long and a span wide—and folded double. ¹⁷Then mount four rows of precious stones on it. In the first row there shall be a ruby, a topaz and a beryl; ¹⁸in the second row a turquoise, a sapphire*b* and an emerald; ¹⁹in the third row a jacinth, an agate and an amethyst; ²⁰in the fourth row a chrysolite, an onyx and a jasper.*c* Mount them in gold filigree settings. ²¹There are to be twelve stones, one for each of the names of the sons of Israel, each engraved like a seal with the name of one of the twelve tribes.

²²"For the breastpiece make braided chains of pure gold, like a rope. ²³Make two gold rings for it and fasten them to two corners of the breastpiece. ²⁴Fasten the two gold chains to the rings at the corners of the breastpiece, ²⁵and the other ends of the chains to the two settings, attaching them to the shoulder pieces of the ephod at the front. ²⁶Make two gold rings and attach them to the other two corners of the breastpiece on the inside edge next to the ephod. ²⁷Make two more gold rings and attach them to the bottom of the shoulder pieces on the front of the ephod, close to the seam just above the waistband of the ephod. ²⁸The rings of the breastpiece are to be tied to the rings of the ephod with blue cord, connecting it to the waistband, so that the breastpiece will not swing out from the ephod.

a 16 That is, about 9 inches (about 22 centimeters)   *b 18* Or *lapis lazuli*   *c 20* The precise identification of some of these precious stones is uncertain.

28:1ff God was teaching his people how to worship him. To do so, he needed ministers to oversee the operations of the tabernacle and to help the people maintain their relationship with God. These men were called priests and Levites, and they could only be members of the tribe of Levi. Chapters 28 and 29 give some details about priests. Not only was a priest from the tribe of Levi, but he also was a descendant of Aaron, Israel's first high priest. Priests had more responsibilities than Levites. As high priest, Aaron was in charge of all the priests and Levites. The priests performed the daily sacrifices, maintained the tabernacle, and counseled the people on how to follow God. They were the people's representatives before God and thus were required to live worthy of their office. Jesus is now our high priest (Hebrews 8). Daily sacrifices are no longer required because he sacrificed himself on the cross for our sins. Today ministers no longer sacrifice animals. Instead they lead us in prayer and teach us about both the benefits and the commandments that characterize our new life as Christians.

28:3 The tailors who made Aaron's garments were given wisdom by God in order to do their task. All of us have special skills. God wants to fill us with his Spirit so we will use those skills for his glory. Think about your special talents and abilities and the ways you could use them for God's work in the world. As you focus on helping and giving to others, God will show you the best ways to do it and give you wisdom to accomplish the task.

28:6–13 The ephod was a kind of apron elaborately embroidered with two pieces, back and front, joined at the shoulder with a band at the waist. On each shoulder strap was a stone with six of the 12 tribes of Israel engraved on it. The priest symbolically carried the burden of the whole nation on his shoulders as he represented them before God.

29"Whenever Aaron enters the Holy Place, he will bear the names of the sons of Israel over his heart on the breastpiece of decision as a continuing memorial before the LORD. 30Also put the Urim and the Thummim *l* in the breastpiece, so they may be over Aaron's heart whenever he enters the presence of the LORD. Thus Aaron will always bear the means of making decisions for the Israelites over his heart before the LORD.

Other Priestly Garments

31"Make the robe of the ephod entirely of blue cloth, 32with an opening for the head in its center. There shall be a woven edge like a collar *a* around this opening, so that it will not tear. 33Make pomegranates of blue, purple and scarlet yarn around the hem of the robe, with gold bells between them. 34The gold bells and the pomegranates are to alternate around the hem of the robe. 35Aaron must wear it when he ministers. The sound of the bells will be heard when he enters the Holy Place before the LORD and when he comes out, so that he will not die.

36"Make a plate of pure gold and engrave on it as on a seal: HOLY TO THE LORD. *m* 37Fasten a blue cord to it to attach it to the turban; it is to be on the front of the turban. 38It will be on Aaron's forehead, and he will bear the guilt *n* involved in the sacred gifts the Israelites consecrate, whatever their gifts may be. It will be on Aaron's forehead continually so that they will be acceptable to the LORD.

39"Weave the tunic of fine linen and make the turban of fine linen. The sash is to be the work of an embroiderer. 40Make tunics, sashes and headbands for Aaron's sons, *o* to give them dignity and honor. 41After you put these clothes on your brother Aaron and his sons, anoint and ordain them. Consecrate them so they may serve me as priests. *p*

42"Make linen undergarments *q* as a covering for the body, reaching from the waist to the thigh. 43Aaron and his sons must wear them whenever they enter the Tent of Meeting *r* or approach the altar to minister in the Holy Place, so that they will not incur guilt and die. *s*

"This is to be a lasting ordinance for Aaron and his descendants.

Consecration of the Priests

29 "This is what you are to do to consecrate them, so they may serve me as priests: Take a young bull and two rams without defect. 2And from fine wheat flour, without yeast, make bread, and cakes mixed with oil, and wafers spread with oil. *t* 3Put them in a basket and present them in it—along with the bull and the two rams. 4Then bring Aaron and his sons to the entrance to the Tent of Meeting and wash them with water. *u* 5Take the garments and dress Aaron with the tunic, the robe of the ephod, the ephod itself and the breastpiece. Fasten the ephod on him by its skillfully woven waistband. *v* 6Put the turban on his head and attach the sacred diadem *w* to the turban. 7Take the anointing oil *x* and anoint him by pouring it on his head. 8Bring his sons and dress them in tunics 9and put headbands on them. Then tie sashes on Aaron and his sons. *b y* The priesthood is theirs by a lasting ordinance. *z* In this way you shall ordain Aaron and his sons.

10"Bring the bull to the front of the Tent of Meeting, and Aaron and his sons shall lay their hands on its head. 11Slaughter it in the LORD's presence at the entrance to the Tent of Meeting. 12Take some of the bull's blood and put it on the horns *a* of the altar with your finger, and pour out the rest of it at the base of the altar. 13Then take all the fat *b* around the inner parts, the covering of the liver, and both kidneys with the fat on them, and burn them on the altar. 14But burn the bull's flesh and its hide and its offal outside the camp. *c* It is a sin offering.

a 32 The meaning of the Hebrew for this word is uncertain.   *b 9* Hebrew; Septuagint *on them*

28:30
l Lev 8:8; Nu 27:21

28:36
m Zec 14:20

28:38
n Lev 10:17;
Nu 18:1

28:40
o ver 4

28:41
p Ex 29:7-9; 30:30;
Lev 8:1-36

28:42
q Lev 6:10;
Eze 44:18

28:43
r Ex 27:21
s Ex 20:26

29:2
t Lev 6:19-23

29:4
u Ex 40:12

29:5
v Ex 28:8

29:6
w Lev 8:9

29:7
x Ex 30:25,30,31;
Lev 8:12; 21:10

29:9
y Ex 28:40
z Nu 18:7

29:12
a Ex 27:2

29:13
b Lev 3:3,5,9

29:14
c Lev 4:11-12,21;
Heb 13:11

28:30 The Urim and the Thummim were used by the priest to make decisions. These names mean "Curses" and "Perfections" and refer to the nature of God whose will they revealed. They were kept in a pouch and taken out or shaken out to get either a yes or no decision.

29:1ff Why did God set up the priesthood? God had originally intended that his chosen people be a "kingdom of priests" with both the nation as a whole and each individual dealing directly with God. But the people's sin prevented this from happening because a sinful person is not worthy to approach a perfect God. God then appointed priests from the tribe of Levi and set up the system of sacrifices to help the people approach him. He promised to forgive the people's sins if they would offer certain sacrifices administered by the priests on behalf of the people. Through these priests and their work, God wished to prepare all people for the coming of Jesus Christ, who would once again offer a direct relationship with God for anyone who would come to him. But until Christ came, the priests were the people's representatives before God. Through this Old Testament system, we can better understand the significance of what Christ did for us (see Hebrews 10:1–14).

29:10–41 Why were there such detailed rituals in connection with these sacrifices? Partly, it was for quality control. A centralized, standardized form of worship prevented problems of belief which could arise from individuals creating their own worship. Also, it differentiated the Hebrews from the pagan Canaanites they would meet in the promised land. By closely following God's instructions, the Hebrews could not possibly join the Canaanites in their immoral religious practices. Finally, it showed Israel that God was serious about his relationship with them.

15"Take one of the rams, and Aaron and his sons shall lay their hands on its head. 16Slaughter it and take the blood and sprinkle it against the altar on all sides. 17Cut the ram into pieces and wash the inner parts and the legs, putting them with the head and the other pieces. 18Then burn the entire ram on the altar. It is a burnt offering to the LORD, a pleasing aroma,*d* an offering made to the LORD by fire.

29:18
*d*Ge 8:21

19"Take the other ram, and Aaron and his sons shall lay their hands on its head. 20Slaughter it, take some of its blood and put it on the lobes of the right ears of Aaron and his sons, on the thumbs of their right hands, and on the big toes of their right feet. Then sprinkle blood against the altar on all sides. 21And take some of the blood *e* on the altar and some of the anointing oil*f* and sprinkle it on Aaron and his garments and on his sons and their garments. Then he and his sons and their garments will be consecrated.*g*

29:21
*e*Heb 9:22
*f*Ex 30:25,31
*g*ver 1

22"Take from this ram the fat, the fat tail, the fat around the inner parts, the covering of the liver, both kidneys with the fat on them, and the right thigh. (This is the ram for the ordination.) 23From the basket of bread made without yeast, which is before the LORD, take a loaf, and a cake made with oil, and a wafer. 24Put all these in the hands of Aaron and his sons and wave them before the LORD as a wave offering.*h* 25Then take them from their hands and burn them on the altar along with the burnt offering for a pleasing aroma to the LORD, an offering made to the LORD by fire. 26After you take the breast of the ram for Aaron's ordination, wave it before the LORD as a wave offering, and it will be your share.

29:24
*h*Lev 7:30

27"Consecrate those parts of the ordination ram that belong to Aaron and his sons:*i* the breast that was waved and the thigh that was presented. 28This is always to be the regular share from the Israelites for Aaron and his sons. It is the contribution the Israelites are to make to the LORD from their fellowship offerings.*a*

29:27
*i*Lev 7:31,34

29"Aaron's sacred garments will belong to his descendants so that they can be anointed and ordained in them.*j* 30The son who succeeds him as priest and comes to the Tent of Meeting to minister in the Holy Place is to wear them seven days.

29:29
*j*Nu 20:26,28

31"Take the ram for the ordination and cook the meat in a sacred place. 32At the entrance to the Tent of Meeting, Aaron and his sons are to eat the meat of the ram and the bread that is in the basket. 33They are to eat these offerings by which atonement was made for their ordination and consecration. But no one else may eat*k* them, because they are sacred. 34And if any of the meat of the ordination ram or any bread is left over till morning, burn it up. It must not be eaten, because it is sacred.

29:33
*k*Lev 10:14;
22:10,13

35"Do for Aaron and his sons everything I have commanded you, taking seven days to ordain them. 36Sacrifice a bull each day*l* as a sin offering to make atonement. Purify the altar by making atonement for it, and anoint it to consecrate it. 37For seven days make atonement for the altar and consecrate it. Then the altar will be most holy, and whatever touches it will be holy.*m*

29:36
*l*Heb 10:11
29:37
*m*Ex 40:10

38"This is what you are to offer on the altar regularly each day:*n* two lambs a year old. 39Offer one in the morning and the other at twilight. 40With the first lamb offer a tenth of an ephah*b* of fine flour mixed with a quarter of a hin*c* of oil from pressed olives, and a quarter of a hin of wine as a drink offering. 41Sacrifice the other lamb at twilight with the same grain offering and its drink offering as in the morning—a pleasing aroma, an offering made to the LORD by fire.

29:38
*n*Nu 28:3-8

42"For the generations to come *o* this burnt offering is to be made regularly at the entrance to the Tent of Meeting before the LORD. There I will meet you and speak to you;*p* 43there also I will meet with the Israelites, and the place will be consecrated by my glory.*q*

29:42
*o*Ex 30:8
*p*Ex 25:22
29:43
*q*1Ki 8:11

44"So I will consecrate the Tent of Meeting and the altar and will consecrate Aaron and his sons to serve me as priests. 45Then I will dwell*r* among the Israelites and be their God.*s* 46They will know that I am the LORD their God, who brought them out of Egypt so that I might dwell among them. I am the LORD their God.*t*

29:45
*r*Ex 25:8; Lev 26:12
*s*2Co 6:16;
Rev 21:3
29:46
*t*Ex 20:2

a28 Traditionally *peace offerings*   *b40* That is, probably about 2 quarts (about 2 liters)   *c40* That is, probably about 1 quart (about 1 liter)

29:37 Notice the overwhelming emphasis on the holiness of God. The priests, the clothes, the tabernacle, and the sacrifice had to be clean and consecrated, prepared to meet God. In contrast, today we tend to take God for granted, rushing into worship and treating him with almost casual disregard. But we worship the almighty Creator and Sustainer of the universe. Remember that profound truth when you pray or worship, and come before him with reverence and repentance.

29:45, 46 God's action in bringing the Israelites out of Egypt showed his great desire to be with them and protect them. Throughout the Bible, God shows that he is not an absentee landlord. He wants to live among us, even in our hearts. Don't exclude God from your life. Allow him to be your God as you

The Altar of Incense

30 "Make an altar of acacia wood for burning incense. [2]It is to be square, a cubit long and a cubit wide, and two cubits high[a]—its horns of one piece with it. [3]Overlay the top and all the sides and the horns with pure gold, and make a gold molding around it. [4]Make two gold rings for the altar below the molding—two on opposite sides—to hold the poles used to carry it. [5]Make the poles of acacia wood and overlay them with gold. [6]Put the altar in front of the curtain that is before the ark of the Testimony—before the atonement cover[u] that is over the Testimony—where I will meet with you.

[7]"Aaron must burn fragrant incense on the altar every morning when he tends the lamps. [8]He must burn incense again when he lights the lamps at twilight so incense will burn regularly before the LORD for the generations to come. [9]Do not offer on this altar any other incense[v] or any burnt offering or grain offering, and do not pour a drink offering on it. [10]Once a year Aaron shall make atonement[w] on its horns. This annual atonement must be made with the blood of the atoning sin offering for the generations to come. It is most holy to the LORD."

Atonement Money

[11]Then the LORD said to Moses, [12]"When you take a census[x] of the Israelites to count them, each one must pay the LORD a ransom[y] for his life at the time he is counted. Then no plague will come on them when you number them. [13]Each one who crosses over to those already counted is to give a half shekel,[b] according to the sanctuary shekel,[z] which weighs twenty gerahs. This half shekel is an offering to the LORD. [14]All who cross over, those twenty years old or more, are to give an offering to the LORD. [15]The rich are not to give more than a half shekel and the poor are not to give less when you make the offering to the LORD to atone for your lives. [16]Receive the atonement money from the Israelites and use it for the service of the Tent of Meeting. It will be a memorial for the Israelites before the LORD, making atonement for your lives."

Basin for Washing

[17]Then the LORD said to Moses, [18]"Make a bronze basin,[a] with its bronze stand, for washing. Place it between the Tent of Meeting and the altar, and put water in it. [19]Aaron and his sons are to wash their hands and feet[b] with water from it. [20]Whenever they enter the Tent of Meeting, they shall wash with water so that they will not die. Also, when they approach the altar to minister by presenting an offering made to the LORD by fire, [21]they shall wash their hands and feet so that they will not die. This is to be a lasting ordinance[c] for Aaron and his descendants for the generations to come."

Anointing Oil

[22]Then the LORD said to Moses, [23]"Take the following fine spices: 500 shekels[c] of liquid myrrh, half as much (that is, 250 shekels) of fragrant cinnamon, 250 shekels of fragrant cane, [24]500 shekels of cassia—all according to the sanctuary shekel—and a hin[d] of olive oil. [25]Make these into a sacred anointing oil, a fragrant blend, the work of a perfumer. [d] It will be the sacred anointing oil. [26]Then use it to anoint[e] the Tent of Meeting, the ark of the Testimony, [27]the table and all its articles, the lampstand and its accessories, the altar of incense, [28]the altar of burnt offering and all its utensils, and the basin with its stand. [29]You shall consecrate them so they will be most holy, and whatever touches them will be holy.

30:6
u Ex 25:22

30:9
v Lev 10:1

30:10
w Lev 16:18-19,30

30:12
x Nu 1:2,49
y Nu 31:50

30:13
z Mt 17:24

30:18
a Ex 38:8; 40:7,30

30:19
b Ex 40:31-32

30:21
c Ex 27:21; 28:43

30:25
d Ex 37:29

30:26
e Lev 8:10

a 2 That is, about 1 1/2 feet (about 0.5 meter) long and wide and about 3 feet (about 0.9 meter) high   *b 13* That is, about 1/5 ounce (about 6 grams); also in verse 15   *c 23* That is, about 12 1/2 pounds (about 6 kilograms)   *d 24* That is, probably about 4 quarts (about 4 liters)

---

obey his Word and communicate with him in prayer. Let him be your resident landlord.

30:10 This once-a-year ceremony was called the Day of Atonement. On this day a sacrifice was made for the sins of the entire Israelite nation. This was the only day the high priest could enter the Most Holy Place, the innermost room of the tabernacle. Here he asked God to forgive the people. The Day of Atonement served as a reminder that the daily, weekly, and monthly sacrifices could cover sins only temporarily. It pointed toward Jesus Christ, the perfect atonement, who could remove sins forever.

30:11–16 The atonement money was like a census tax. It

continued the principle that all the people belonged to God and therefore needed to be redeemed by a sacrifice. Whenever a census took place, everyone, both rich and poor, was required to pay a ransom. God does not discriminate between people (see Acts 10:34; Galatians 3:28). All of us need mercy and forgiveness because of our sinful thoughts and actions. There is no way the rich person can buy off God, and no way the poor can avoid paying. God's demand is that all of us come humbly before him to be forgiven and brought into his family.

30"Anoint Aaron and his sons and consecrate ᶠ them so they may serve me as priests. 31Say to the Israelites, 'This is to be my sacred anointing oil for the generations to come. 32Do not pour it on men's bodies and do not make any oil with the same formula. It is sacred, and you are to consider it sacred. 33Whoever makes perfume like it and whoever puts it on anyone other than a priest must be cut off ᵍ from his people.'"

30:30
ᶠLev 8:2,12,30

30:33
ᵍver 38

Incense

34Then the LORD said to Moses, "Take fragrant spices—gum resin, onycha and galbanum—and pure frankincense, all in equal amounts, 35and make a fragrant blend of incense, the work of a perfumer. It is to be salted and pure and sacred. 36Grind some of it to powder and place it in front of the Testimony in the Tent of Meeting, where I will meet with you. It shall be most holy to you. 37Do not make any incense with this formula for yourselves; consider it holy to the LORD. 38Whoever makes any like it to enjoy its fragrance must be cut off from his people."

Bezalel and Oholiab

31 Then the LORD said to Moses, 2"See, I have chosen Bezalelʰ son of Uri, the son of Hur, of the tribe of Judah, 3and I have filled him with the Spirit of God, with skill, ability and knowledge in all kinds of crafts— 4to make artistic designs for work in gold, silver and bronze, 5to cut and set stones, to work in wood, and to engage in all kinds of craftsmanship. 6Moreover, I have appointed Oholiab son of Ahisamach, of the tribe of Dan, to help him. Also I have given skill to all the craftsmen to make everything I have commanded you: 7the Tent of Meeting, ⁱ the ark of the Testimonyʲ with the atonement cover ᵏ on it, and all the other furnishings of the tent— 8the tableˡ and its articles, the pure gold lampstandᵐ and all its accessories, the altar of incense, 9the altar of burnt offering and all its utensils, the basin with its stand— 10and also the woven garments, both the sacred garments for Aaron the priest and the garments for his sons when they serve as priests, 11and the anointing oilⁿ and fragrant incense for the Holy Place. They are to make them just as I commanded you."

31:2
ʰEx 36:1,2

31:7
ⁱEx 36:8-38
ʲEx 37:1-5
ᵏEx 37:6

31:8
ˡEx 37:10-16
ᵐEx 37:17-24

31:11
ⁿEx 30:22-32

The Sabbath

12Then the LORD said to Moses, 13"Say to the Israelites, 'You must observe my Sabbaths. This will be a signᵒ between me and you for the generations to come, so you may know that I am the LORD, who makes you holy. ᵃ

14"'Observe the Sabbath, because it is holy to you. Anyone who desecrates it must be put to death;ᵖ whoever does any work on that day must be cut off from his people. 15For six days, work�q is to be done, but the seventh day is a Sabbath of rest, holy to the LORD. Whoever does any work on the Sabbath day must be put to death. 16The Israelites are to observe the Sabbath, celebrating it for the generations to come as a lasting covenant. 17It will be a signʳ between me and the Israelites forever, for in six days the LORD made the heavens and the earth, and on the seventh day he abstained from work and rested. ˢ'"

18When the LORD finished speaking to Moses on Mount Sinai, he gave him the two tablets of the Testimony, the tablets of stone inscribed by the finger of God. ᵗ

31:13
ᵒEze 20:12,20

31:14
ᵖNu 15:32-36

31:15
qEx 20:8-11

31:17
ʳver 13
ˢGe 2:2-3

31:18
ᵗEx 32:15-16

ᵃ 13 Or *who sanctifies you*; or *who sets you apart as holy*

30:34–38 The Israelites often burned incense, but this holy incense could be burned only in the tabernacle. Here God gave the recipe for this special incense. The sweet-smelling incense was burned in shallow dishes called censers and was used to show honor and reverence to God. It was like prayer lifting up to God. It was also a vital part of the sacred ceremony on the Day of Atonement, when the high priest carried his smoking censer into the Most Holy Place. This incense, like the sacred anointing oil, was so holy that the people were strictly forbidden to copy it for personal use.

31:1–11 God regards all the skills of his people, not merely those with theological or ministerial abilities. Our tendency is to regard only those who are up front and in leadership roles. God gave Bezalel and Oholiab Spirit-filled abilities in artistic craftsmanship. Take notice of all the abilities God gives his people. Don't diminish your skills if they are not like Moses' and Aaron's.

31:12–17 The Sabbath had two purposes: It was a time *to rest* and a time *to remember* what God had done. We need rest. Without time out from the bustle, life loses its meaning. In our day, as in Moses' day, taking time out is not easy. But God reminds us that without Sabbaths we will forget the purpose for all of our activity and lose the balance crucial to a faithful life. Make sure your Sabbath provides a time of both refreshment and remembrance of God.

31:18 The two tablets of the Testimony contained the Ten Commandments. These were not the only code of laws in the ancient world. Other law codes had come into existence when cities or nations decided that there must be standards of judgment, ways to correct specific wrongs. But God's laws for Israel were unique in that: (1) they alleviated the harsh judgments typical of the day; (2) they were egalitarian—the poor and the powerful received the same punishment; (3) they did not separate religious and social law. All law rested on God's authority.

3. Breaking the law

The Golden Calf

32 When the people saw that Moses was so long in coming down from the mountain, they gathered around Aaron and said, "Come, make us gods[a] who will go before us. As for this fellow Moses who brought us up out of Egypt, we don't know what has happened to him."

2Aaron answered them, "Take off the gold earrings that your wives, your sons and your daughters are wearing, and bring them to me." 3So all the people took off their earrings and brought them to Aaron. 4He took what they handed him and made it into an idol cast in the shape of a calf,[u] fashioning it with a tool. Then they said, "These are your gods,[b] O Israel, who brought you up out of Egypt."

5When Aaron saw this, he built an altar in front of the calf and announced, "Tomorrow there will be a festival to the LORD." 6So the next day the people rose early and sacrificed burnt offerings and presented fellowship offerings.[c] Afterward they sat down to eat and drink and got up to indulge in revelry.[v]

7Then the LORD said to Moses, "Go down, because your people, whom you brought up out of Egypt, have become corrupt.[w] 8They have been quick to turn away from what I commanded them and have made themselves an idol[x] cast in the shape of a calf. They have bowed down to it and sacrificed to it and have said, 'These are your gods, O Israel, who brought you up out of Egypt.'[y]

9"I have seen these people," the LORD said to Moses, "and they are a stiff-necked[z] people. 10Now leave me alone so that my anger may burn against them and that I may destroy them. Then I will make you into a great nation."[a]

11But Moses sought the favor[b] of the LORD his God. "O LORD," he said, "why should your anger burn against your people, whom you brought out of Egypt with great power and a mighty hand? 12Why should the Egyptians say, 'It was with evil intent that he brought them out, to kill them in the mountains and to wipe them off the face of the earth'?[c] Turn from your fierce anger; relent and do not bring disaster on your people. 13Remember your servants Abraham, Isaac and Israel, to whom you swore by your own self:[d] 'I will make your descendants as numerous as the stars in the sky and I will give your descendants all this land[e] I promised them, and it will be their inheritance forever.'" 14Then the LORD relented[f] and did not bring on his people the disaster he had threatened.

15Moses turned and went down the mountain with the two tablets of the Testimony in his hands.[g] They were inscribed on both sides, front and back. 16The tablets were the work of God; the writing was the writing of God, engraved on the tablets.

a1 Or *a god*; also in verses 23 and 31   b4 Or *This is your god*; also in verse 8   c6 Traditionally *peace offerings*

32:4
uDt 9:16; Ac 7:41

32:6
v1Co 10:7*

32:7
wGe 6:11-12; Dt 9:12

32:8
xEx 20:4
y1Ki 12:28

32:9
zEx 33:3,5; 34:9; Isa 48:4; Ac 7:51

32:10
aNu 14:12; Dt 9:14

32:11
bDt 9:18

32:12
cNu 14:13-16

32:13
dGe 22:16; Heb 6:13
eGe 12:7

32:14
fPs 106:45

32:15
gDt 9:15

32:1–10 Idols again! Even though Israel had seen the invisible God in action, they still wanted the familiar gods they could see and shape into whatever image they desired. How much like them we are! Our great temptation is still to shape God to our liking, to make him convenient to obey or ignore. God responds in great anger when his mercy is trampled on. The gods we create blind us to the love our loving God wants to shower on us. God cannot work in us when we elevate anyone or anything above him. What false gods in your life are preventing the true God from living in you?

32:4, 5 Two popular Egyptian gods, Hapi (Apis) and Hathor, were thought of as a bull and a heifer. The Canaanites around them worshiped Baal, thought of as a bull. Baal was their sacred symbol of power and fertility and was closely connected to immoral sexual practices. No doubt the Israelites, fresh from Egypt, found it quite natural to make a golden calf to represent the God that had just delivered them from their oppressors. They were weary of a god without a face. But in doing so, they were ignoring the command he had just given them: "You shall not make for yourself an idol in the form of anything in heaven above or on the earth beneath or in the waters below" (20:4). They may even have thought they were worshiping God. Their apparent sincerity was no substitute for obedience or excuse for disobedience.

Even if we do not make idols, we are often guilty of trying to make God in our image, molding him to fit our expectations, desires, and circumstances. When we do this, we end up worshiping ourselves rather than the God who created us—and self-worship, today as in the Israelites' time, leads to all kinds of immorality. What is your favorite image of God? Is it Biblical? Is it adequate? Do you need to destroy it in order to worship the immeasurably powerful God who delivered you from bondage to sin?

32:9-14 God was ready to destroy the whole nation because of their sin. But Moses pleaded for mercy, and God spared them. This is one of the countless examples in the Bible of God's mercy. Although we deserve his anger, he is willing to forgive and restore us to himself. We can receive God's forgiveness from sin by asking him. Like Moses, we can pray that he will forgive others and use us to bring them the message of his mercy.

32:14 How could God relent? God did not change his mind in the same way that a parent decides not to discipline a child. Instead, God changed his behavior to remain consistent with his nature. When God first wanted to destroy the people, he was acting consistently with his justice. When Moses interceded for the people, God relented in order to act consistently with his mercy. God had often told the people that if they changed their ways, he would not condemn them. They changed, and God forgave them as he had promised.

[17] When Joshua heard the noise of the people shouting, he said to Moses, "There is the sound of war in the camp."

[18] Moses replied:

> "It is not the sound of victory,
>   it is not the sound of defeat;
>   it is the sound of singing that I hear."

[19] When Moses approached the camp and saw the calf *h* and the dancing, his anger burned and he threw the tablets out of his hands, breaking them to pieces *i* at the foot of the mountain. [20] And he took the calf they had made and burned it in the fire; then he ground it to powder, scattered it on the water *j* and made the Israelites drink it.

[21] He said to Aaron, "What did these people do to you, that you led them into such great sin?"

[22] "Do not be angry, my lord," Aaron answered. "You know how prone these people are to evil. *k* [23] They said to me, 'Make us gods who will go before us. As for this fellow Moses who brought us up out of Egypt, we don't know what has happened to him.' [24] So I told them, 'Whoever has any gold jewelry, take it off.' Then they gave me the gold, and I threw it into the fire, and out came this calf!"

[25] Moses saw that the people were running wild and that Aaron had let them get out of control and so become a laughingstock to their enemies. [26] So he stood at the entrance to the camp and said, "Whoever is for the LORD, come to me." And all the Levites rallied to him.

[27] Then he said to them, "This is what the LORD, the God of Israel, says: 'Each man strap a sword to his side. Go back and forth through the camp from one end to the other, each killing his brother and friend and neighbor.'" [28] The Levites did as Moses commanded, and that day about three thousand of the people died. [29] Then Moses said, "You have been set apart to the LORD today, for you were against your own sons and brothers, and he has blessed you this day."

[30] The next day Moses said to the people, "You have committed a great sin. *l* But now I will go up to the LORD; perhaps I can make atonement for your sin."

[31] So Moses went back to the LORD and said, "Oh, what a great sin these people have committed! They have made themselves gods of gold. *m* [32] But now, please forgive their sin—but if not, then blot me out of the book *n* you have written."

[33] The LORD replied to Moses, "Whoever has sinned against me I will blot out of my book. [34] Now go, lead the people to the place I spoke of, and my angel will go before you. However, when the time comes for me to punish, I will punish them for their sin."

[35] And the LORD struck the people with a plague because of what they did with the calf Aaron had made.

33

Then the LORD said to Moses, "Leave this place, you and the people you brought up out of Egypt, and go up to the land I promised on oath to Abraham, Isaac and Jacob, saying, 'I will give it to your descendants.' *o* [2] I will send an angel before you and drive out the Canaanites, Amorites, Hittites, Perizzites, Hivites and Jebusites. [3] Go up to the land flowing with milk and honey. *p* But I will not go with you, because you are a stiff-necked people and I might destroy you on the way."

[4] When the people heard these distressing words, they began to mourn *q* and no one put on any ornaments. [5] For the LORD had said to Moses, "Tell the Israelites, 'You are a stiff-necked people. If I were to go with you even for a moment, I might destroy you. Now take off your ornaments and I will decide what to do with you.'" [6] So the Israelites stripped off their ornaments at Mount Horeb.

Cross-references
32:19 *h* Dt 9:16; *i* Dt 9:17
32:20 *j* Dt 9:21
32:22 *k* Dt 9:24
32:30 *l* 1Sa 12:20
32:31 *m* Ex 20:23
32:32 *n* Ps 69:28; Da 12:1; Rev 3:5; 21:27
33:1 *o* Ge 12:7
33:3 *p* Ex 3:8
33:4 *q* Nu 14:39

32:19, 20 Overwhelmed by the actual sight of the blatant idolatry and revelry, Moses broke the tablets containing the commandments which had already been broken in the hearts and actions of the people. There is a place for righteous anger. However angry Moses might have been, God was angrier still— he wanted to kill all the people. Anger at sin is a sign of spiritual vitality. Don't squelch this kind of anger. But when you are justifiably angry at sin, be careful not to do anything that you will regret later.

32:21–24 Aaron's decision nearly cost him his life. His absurd excuse shows the spiritual decline in his leadership and in the people. Those who function as spokespersons and assistants need to be doubly sure their theology and morality are in tune with God so they will not be influenced by pressure from people. For more information on Aaron, see his Profile on the next page.

33:5, 6 This was not a permanent ban on all jewelry. It was a temporary sign of repentance and mourning. In 35:22 we read that the people still had jewelry.

The Tent of Meeting

33:9
r Ps 99:7

⁷Now Moses used to take a tent and pitch it outside the camp some distance away, calling it the "tent of meeting." Anyone inquiring of the Lᴏʀᴅ would go to the tent of meeting outside the camp. ⁸And whenever Moses went out to the tent, all the people rose and stood at the entrances to their tents, watching Moses until he entered the tent. ⁹As Moses went into the tent, the pillar of cloud would come down and stay at the entrance, while the Lᴏʀᴅ spoke *r* with Moses. ¹⁰Whenever the people saw the pillar of cloud standing at the entrance to the tent, they all stood and worshiped, each at the entrance to his tent. ¹¹The Lᴏʀᴅ would speak to Moses face to face, *s* as a man speaks with his friend. Then Moses would return to the camp, but his young aide Joshua son of Nun did not leave the tent.

33:11
s Nu 12:8; Dt 34:10

Moses and the Glory of the Lᴏʀᴅ

33:12
t ver 17

33:13
u Ps 25:4
v Dt 9:26,29

33:14
w Isa 63:9

¹²Moses said to the Lᴏʀᴅ, "You have been telling me, 'Lead these people,' but you have not let me know whom you will send with me. You have said, 'I know you by name *t* and you have found favor with me.' ¹³If you are pleased with me, teach me your ways *u* so I may know you and continue to find favor with you. Remember that this nation is your people." *v*
¹⁴The Lᴏʀᴅ replied, "My Presence *w* will go with you, and I will give you rest."

Effective teamwork happens when each team member uses his or her special skills. Ideally, each member's strengths will contribute something important to the team effort. In this way, members make up for one another's weaknesses. Aaron made a good team with Moses. He provided Moses with one skill Moses lacked—effective public speaking. But while Aaron was necessary to Moses, he needed Moses as well. Without a guide, Aaron had little direction of his own. There was never any doubt as to who God's chosen and trained leader was. The pliability that made Aaron a good follower made him a weak leader. His major failures were caused by his inability to stand alone. His yielding to public pressure and making an idol was a good example of this weakness.

Most of us have more of the follower than the leader in us. We may even be good followers, following a good leader. But no leader is perfect, and no human deserves our complete allegiance. Only God deserves our complete loyalty and obedience. We need to be effective team members in using the skills and abilities God has given us. But if the team or the leader goes against God's Word, we must be willing to stand alone.

Strengths and accomplishments:	• First high priest of God in Israel • Effective communicator; Moses' mouthpiece
Weaknesses and mistakes:	• Pliable personality; gave in to people's demands for a golden calf • Joined with Moses in disobeying God's orders about the water-giving rock • Joined sister Miriam in complaining against Moses
Lessons from his life:	• God gives individuals special abilities, which he weaves together for his use • The very skills that make a good team player sometimes also make a poor leader
Vital statistics:	• Where: Egypt, Desert of Sinai • Occupations: Priest; Moses' second in command • Relatives: Brother: Moses. Sister: Miriam. Sons: Nadab, Abihu, Eleazar, and Ithamar.
Key verses:	"Then the Lᴏʀᴅ's anger burned against Moses and he said, 'What about your brother, Aaron the Levite? I know he can speak well. He is already on his way to meet you, and his heart will be glad when he sees you. . . . He will speak to the people for you, and it will be as if he were your mouth and as if you were God to him'" (Exodus 4:14, 16).

Aaron's story is told in Exodus 1:1—Deuteronomy 10:6. He is also mentioned in Hebrews 7:11.

33:11 God and Moses talked face to face in the Tent of Meeting, just as friends do. Why did Moses find such favor with God? It certainly was not because he was perfect, gifted, or powerful. Rather, it was because God chose Moses, and Moses in turn relied wholeheartedly on God's wisdom and direction. Friendship with God was a true privilege for Moses, out of reach for the other Hebrews. But it is not out of reach for us today. Jesus called his disciples—and, by extension, all of his followers—his friends

(John 15:15). He has called you to be his friend. Will you accept his invitation to openly communicate with him? He desires this kind of relationship with you.

33:11 Joshua, Moses' aide, did not leave the tent, probably because he was guarding it. No doubt there were curious people who would have dared to go inside.

¹⁵Then Moses said to him, "If your Presence does not go with us, do not send us up from here. ¹⁶How will anyone know that you are pleased with me and with your people unless you go with us? What else will distinguish me and your people from all the other people on the face of the earth?"

¹⁷And the LORD said to Moses, "I will do the very thing you have asked, because I am pleased with you and I know you by name."

¹⁸Then Moses said, "Now show me your glory."

¹⁹And the LORD said, "I will cause all my goodness to pass in front of you, and I will proclaim my name, the LORD, in your presence. I will have mercy on whom I will have mercy, and I will have compassion on whom I will have compassion.ˣ ²⁰But," he said, "you cannot see my face, for no one may see me and live."

33:19
ˣRo 9:15*

²¹Then the LORD said, "There is a place near me where you may stand on a rock. ²²When my glory passes by, I will put you in a cleft in the rock and cover you with my hand until I have passed by. ²³Then I will remove my hand and you will see my back; but my face must not be seen."

The New Stone Tablets

34 The LORD said to Moses, "Chisel out two stone tablets like the first ones, and I will write on them the words that were on the first tablets, which you broke.ʸ ²Be ready in the morning, and then come up on Mount Sinai.ᶻ Present yourself to me there on top of the mountain. ³No one is to come with you or be seen anywhere on the mountain;ᵃ not even the flocks and herds may graze in front of the mountain."

34:1
ʸEx 32:19
34:2
ᶻEx 19:11
34:3
ᵃEx 19:12-13,21

⁴So Moses chiseled out two stone tablets like the first ones and went up Mount Sinai early in the morning, as the LORD had commanded him; and he carried the two stone tablets in his hands. ⁵Then the LORD came down in the cloud and stood there with him and proclaimed his name, the LORD. ⁶And he passed in front of Moses, proclaiming, "The LORD, the LORD, the compassionate and gracious God, slow to anger, abounding in loveᵇ and faithfulness, ⁷maintaining love to thousands,ᶜ and forgiving wickedness, rebellion and sin.ᵈ Yet he does not leave the guilty unpunished; he punishes the children and their children for the sin of the fathers to the third and fourth generation."

34:6
ᵇNe 9:17
34:7
ᶜEx 20:6
ᵈPs 103:3

⁸Moses bowed to the ground at once and worshiped. ⁹"O Lord, if I have found favor in your eyes," he said, "then let the Lord go with us. Although this is a stiff-necked people, forgive our wickedness and our sin, and take us as your inheritance."

¹⁰Then the LORD said: "I am making a covenantᵉ with you. Before all your people I will do wonders never before done in any nation in all the world.ᶠ The people you live among will see how awesome is the work that I, the LORD, will do for you. ¹¹Obey what I command you today. I will drive out before you the Amorites, Canaanites, Hittites, Perizzites, Hivites and Jebusites.ᵍ ¹²Be careful not to make a treaty with those who live in the land where you are

34:10
ᵉDt 5:2-3
ᶠDt 4:32
34:11
ᵍEx 33:2

33:18–23 Moses wanted to see God's glory. He wanted assurance of God's presence with him, Aaron, and Joshua, and also he desired to know that presence experientially. Because we are finite and morally imperfect, we cannot exist and see God as he is. To see God from behind means we can only see where God has passed by. We can only know him by what he does and how he acts. We cannot comprehend God as he really is apart from Jesus Christ (John 14:9). Jesus promised to show himself to those who believe (John 14:21).

34:6, 7 Moses had asked to see God's glory (33:18), and this was God's response. What is God's glory? It is his character, his nature, his way of relating to his creatures. Notice that God did not give Moses a vision of his power and majesty, but rather of his love. God's glory is revealed in his mercy, grace, compassion, faithfulness, forgiveness, and justice. God's love and mercy are truly wonderful, and we benefit from them. We can respond and give glory to God when our characters resemble his.

34:6, 7 Many people think the God of the Old Testament is a God of wrath, only to be feared. These words from God revealed to Moses the very heart or essence of God's nature (33:19).

What do we learn from these assurances to Moses? God is compassionate, gracious, loving, faithful, and forgiving. Don't accept anyone's argument that the God of the Old Testament is merely vengeful. Instead, remember that God is "slow to anger," and his love cannot be diminished.

34:7 Why would sins affect children and grandchildren? This is no arbitrary punishment. Children still suffer for the sins of their parents. Consider child abuse or alcoholism, for example. While these sins are obvious, sins like selfishness and greed can be passed along as well. The dire consequences of sin are not limited to the individual family member. Be careful not to treat sin casually, but repent and turn from it. The sin may cause you little pain now, but it could sting in a most tender area of your life later—your children and grandchildren.

34:12–14 God told the Israelites not to join in religious rites with the sinful people around them, but to give their absolute loyalty and exclusive devotion to him. Pagan worship simply cannot be mixed with the worship of the holy God. As Jesus pointed out, "No servant can serve two masters. . . . You cannot serve both God and Money" (Luke 16:13). Love of money is the god of this age, and many Christians attempt to make a treaty with this enslaving god. Are you trying to worship two gods at once? Where is your first allegiance?

34:12
h Ex 23:32-33
34:13
i 2Ki 18:4
34:14
j Ex 20:3
34:15
k Nu 25:2
34:16
l Dt 7:3
34:18
m Ex 12:15
34:19
n Ex 13:2
34:20
o Ex 13:13,15
34:21
p Ex 20:9
34:22
q Ex 23:16
34:23
r Ex 23:14
34:26
s Ex 23:19
34:28
t Ex 24:18
u ver 1; Ex 31:18
v Dt 4:13; 10:4
34:29
w Ex 32:15
x Mt 17:2;
2Co 3:7,13
34:33
y 2Co 3:13
35:1
z Ex 34:32
35:3
a Ex 16:23

going, or they will be a snare h among you. 13Break down their altars, smash their sacred stones and cut down their Asherah poles. a i 14Do not worship any other god, j for the LORD, whose name is Jealous, is a jealous God.

15"Be careful not to make a treaty with those who live in the land; for when they prostitute themselves to their gods and sacrifice to them, they will invite you and you will eat their sacrifices. k 16And when you choose some of their daughters as wives l for your sons and those daughters prostitute themselves to their gods, they will lead your sons to do the same.

17"Do not make cast idols.

18"Celebrate the Feast of Unleavened Bread. For seven days eat bread made without yeast, m as I commanded you. Do this at the appointed time in the month of Abib, for in that month you came out of Egypt.

19"The first offspring n of every womb belongs to me, including all the firstborn males of your livestock, whether from herd or flock. 20Redeem the firstborn donkey with a lamb, but if you do not redeem it, break its neck. o Redeem all your firstborn sons.

"No one is to appear before me empty-handed.

21"Six days you shall labor, but on the seventh day you shall rest; p even during the plowing season and harvest you must rest.

22"Celebrate the Feast of Weeks with the firstfruits of the wheat harvest, and the Feast of Ingathering q at the turn of the year. b 23Three times r a year all your men are to appear before the Sovereign LORD, the God of Israel. 24I will drive out nations before you and enlarge your territory, and no one will covet your land when you go up three times each year to appear before the LORD your God.

25"Do not offer the blood of a sacrifice to me along with anything containing yeast, and do not let any of the sacrifice from the Passover Feast remain until morning.

26"Bring the best of the firstfruits of your soil to the house of the LORD your God.

"Do not cook a young goat in its mother's milk." s

27Then the LORD said to Moses, "Write down these words, for in accordance with these words I have made a covenant with you and with Israel." 28Moses was there with the LORD forty days and forty nights t without eating bread or drinking water. And he wrote on the tablets u the words of the covenant—the Ten Commandments. v

The Radiant Face of Moses

29When Moses came down from Mount Sinai with the two tablets of the Testimony in his hands, w he was not aware that his face was radiant x because he had spoken with the LORD. 30When Aaron and all the Israelites saw Moses, his face was radiant, and they were afraid to come near him. 31But Moses called to them; so Aaron and all the leaders of the community came back to him, and he spoke to them. 32Afterward all the Israelites came near him, and he gave them all the commands the LORD had given him on Mount Sinai.

33When Moses finished speaking to them, he put a veil y over his face. 34But whenever he entered the LORD's presence to speak with him, he removed the veil until he came out. And when he came out and told the Israelites what he had been commanded, 35they saw that his face was radiant. Then Moses would put the veil back over his face until he went in to speak with the LORD.

4. Tabernacle construction
Sabbath Regulations

35 Moses assembled the whole Israelite community and said to them, "These are the things the LORD has commanded z you to do: 2For six days, work is to be done, but the seventh day shall be your holy day, a Sabbath of rest to the LORD. Whoever does any work on it must be put to death. 3Do not light a fire in any of your dwellings on the Sabbath day. a"

a 13 That is, symbols of the goddess Asherah   b 22 That is, in the fall

---

34:13 Asherah poles were wooden poles that stood by Baal's altar (see Judges 6:25). Asherah was the goddess who was the consort (wife) of Baal. She represented good luck in agriculture and fertility.

34:18 The month of Abib corresponds to the end of March and the beginning of April.

34:28-35 Moses' face was radiant after he spent time with God. The people could clearly see God's presence in him. How often do you spend time alone with God? Although your face may not light up a room, time spent in prayer, reading the Bible, and meditating should have such an effect on your life that people will know you have been with God.

Materials for the Tabernacle

⁴Moses said to the whole Israelite community, "This is what the Lᴏʀᴅ has commanded: ⁵From what you have, take an offering for the Lᴏʀᴅ. Everyone who is willing is to bring to the Lᴏʀᴅ an offering of gold, silver and bronze; ⁶blue, purple and scarlet yarn and fine linen; goat hair; ⁷ram skins dyed red and hides of sea cows ᵃ; acacia wood; ⁸olive oil for the light; spices for the anointing oil and for the fragrant incense; ⁹and onyx stones and other gems to be mounted on the ephod and breastpiece.

¹⁰"All who are skilled among you are to come and make everything the Lᴏʀᴅ has commanded:ᵇ ¹¹the tabernacleᶜ with its tent and its covering, clasps, frames, crossbars, posts and bases; ¹²the ark with its poles and the atonement cover and the curtain that shields it; ¹³the tableᵈ with its poles and all its articles and the bread of the Presence; ¹⁴the lampstand that is for light with its accessories, lamps and oil for the light; ¹⁵the altarᵉ of incense with its poles, the anointing oil and the fragrant incense; the curtain for the doorway at the entrance to the tabernacle; ¹⁶the altar of burnt offering with its bronze grating, its poles and all its utensils; the bronze basin with its stand; ¹⁷the curtains of the courtyard with its posts and bases, and the curtain for the entrance to the courtyard; ¹⁸the tent pegs for the tabernacle and for the courtyard, and their ropes; ¹⁹the woven garments worn for ministering in the sanctuary— both the sacred garments ᶠ for Aaron the priest and the garments for his sons when they serve as priests."

²⁰Then the whole Israelite community withdrew from Moses' presence, ²¹and everyone who was willing and whose heart moved him came and brought an offering to the Lᴏʀᴅ for the work on the Tent of Meeting, for all its service, and for the sacred garments. ²²All who were willing, men and women alike, came and brought gold jewelry of all kinds: brooches, earrings, rings and ornaments. They all presented their gold as a wave offering to the Lᴏʀᴅ. ²³Everyone who had blue, purple or scarlet yarn or fine linen, or goat hair, ram skins dyed red or hides of sea cows brought them. ²⁴Those presenting an offering of silver or bronze brought it as an offering to the Lᴏʀᴅ, and everyone who had acacia wood for any part of the work brought it. ²⁵Every skilled woman spun with her hands and brought what she had spun—blue, purple or scarlet yarn or fine linen. ²⁶And all the women who were willing and had the skill spun the goat hair. ²⁷The leaders brought onyx stones and other gems to be mounted on the ephod and breastpiece. ²⁸They also brought spices and olive oil for the light and for the anointing oil and for the fragrant incense. ²⁹All the Israelite men and women who were willingᵍ brought to the Lᴏʀᴅ freewill offeringsʰ for all the work the Lᴏʀᴅ through Moses had commanded them to do.

Bezalel and Oholiab

³⁰Then Moses said to the Israelites, "See, the Lᴏʀᴅ has chosen Bezalel son of Uri, the son of Hur, of the tribe of Judah, ³¹and he has filled him with the Spirit of God, with skill, ability and knowledge in all kinds of craftsⁱ— ³²to make artistic designs for work in gold, silver and bronze, ³³to cut and set stones, to work in wood and to engage in all kinds of artistic craftsmanship. ³⁴And he has given both him and Oholiabʲ son of Ahisamach, of the tribe of Dan,

ᵃ7 That is, dugongs; also in verse 23

35:10
ᵇEx 31:6

35:11
ᶜEx 26:1-37

35:13
ᵈEx 25:23-30

35:15
ᵉEx 30:1-6

35:19
ᶠEx 28:2; 31:10

35:29
ᵍver 21; 1Ch 29:9
ʰver 4-9; Ex 25:1-7;
36:3; 2Ki 12:4

35:31
ⁱver 35; 2Ch 2:7,14

35:34
ʲEx 31:6

35:5–21 God did not require these special offerings, but he appealed to people with generous hearts. Only those who were willing to give were invited to participate. God loves cheerful givers (2 Corinthians 9:7). Our giving should be from love and generosity, not from a guilty conscience. Review what God has done for you. Has he blessed you with enough to meet your daily needs? Thank him, and then cheerfully give so others' needs can be met. Learn the joy of giving wholeheartedly to God.

35:10–19 Moses asked people with various abilities to help with the tabernacle. Every one of God's people has been given special abilities. We are responsible to develop these abilities—even the ones not considered religious—and to use them for God's glory. We can become skilled through study, by watching others, and through practice. Work on your skills or abilities that could help your church or community.

35:20–24 Where did the Israelites, who were once Egyptian slaves, get all this gold and jewelry? When the Hebrews left Egypt, they took with them items they requested from the Egyptians. The

Egyptians had been so glad for them to go that they readily gave these valuables to the Hebrews (3:22; 12:35, 36). This included gold, silver, jewels, linen, skins, and other valuables.

35:21 Those whose hearts were stirred gave cheerfully to the Tent of Meeting (also called the tabernacle). With great enthusiasm they gave because they knew how important their giving was to the completion of God's house. Moses had carefully explained the need and the plans for the tabernacle, and so many people responded generously. For God to stir our hearts, we must be informed. If your church has a stewardship campaign, get involved and learn all you can. Find out about evangelistic missions and ministries to the poor. God will use this knowledge to stir your heart.

35:26 Those who spun cloth made a beautiful contribution to the tabernacle. Good workers take pride in the quality and beauty of their work. God is concerned with the quality and beauty of what you do. Whether you are a corporate executive or a drugstore cashier, your work should reflect the creative abilities God has given you.

35:34
k 2Ch 2:14

35:35
l ver 31; Ex 31:3,6

36:1
m Ex 28:3
n Ex 25:8

36:2
o Ex 31:2
p Ex 31:6
q Ex 25:2; 35:21,26;
1Ch 29:5

36:3
r Ex 35:29

36:5
s 2Ch 24:14; 31:10;
2Co 8:2-3

36:7
t 1Ki 7:47

the ability to teach k others. [35] He has filled them with skill to do all kinds of work l as craftsmen, designers, embroiderers in blue, purple and scarlet yarn and fine linen, and weavers—

36

all of them master craftsmen and designers. [1] So Bezalel, Oholiab and every skilled person m to whom the LORD has given skill and ability to know how to carry out all the work of constructing the sanctuary n are to do the work just as the LORD has commanded."

[2] Then Moses summoned Bezalel o and Oholiab p and every skilled person to whom the LORD had given ability and who was willing q to come and do the work. [3] They received from Moses all the offerings r the Israelites had brought to carry out the work of constructing the sanctuary. And the people continued to bring freewill offerings morning after morning. [4] So all the skilled craftsmen who were doing all the work on the sanctuary left their work [5] and said to Moses, "The people are bringing more than enough s for doing the work the LORD commanded to be done."

[6] Then Moses gave an order and they sent this word throughout the camp: "No man or woman is to make anything else as an offering for the sanctuary." And so the people were restrained from bringing more, [7] because what they already had was more t than enough to do all the work.

The Tabernacle

[8] All the skilled men among the workmen made the tabernacle with ten curtains of finely twisted linen and blue, purple and scarlet yarn, with cherubim worked into them by a skilled craftsman. [9] All the curtains were the same size—twenty-eight cubits long and four cubits wide. a [10] They joined five of the curtains together and did the same with the other five. [11] Then they made loops of blue material along the edge of the end curtain in one set, and

a 9 That is, about 42 feet (about 12.5 meters) long and 6 feet (about 1.8 meters) wide

KEY TABERNACLE PIECES	Name	Function and Significance
	Ark of the Covenant	• A golden rectangular box that contained the Ten Commandments • Symbolized God's covenant with Israel's people • Located in the Most Holy Place
	Atonement Cover	• The lid to the ark of the covenant • Symbolized the presence of God among his people
	Curtain	• The curtain that divided the two sacred rooms of the tabernacle—the Holy Place and the Most Holy Place • Symbolized how the people were separated from God because of sin
	Table	• A wooden table located in the Holy Place of the tabernacle. The bread of the Presence and various utensils were kept on this table
	Bread of the Presence	• Twelve loaves of baked bread, one for each tribe of Israel • Symbolized the spiritual nourishment God offers his people
	Lampstands and Lamps	• A golden lampstand located in the Holy Place, which held seven burning oil lamps • The lampstand lit the Holy Place for the priests
	Altar of Incense	• An altar in the Holy Place in front of the curtain • Used for burning God's special incense and symbolic of acceptable prayer
	Anointing Oil	• A special oil used to anoint the priests and all the pieces in the tabernacle • A sign of being set apart for God
	Altar of Burnt Offering	• The bronze altar outside the tabernacle used for the sacrifices • Symbolized how sacrifice restored one's relationship with God
	Basin	• A large basin outside the tabernacle used by the priests to cleanse themselves before performing their duties • Symbolized the need for spiritual cleansing

36:8, 9 Making cloth (spinning and weaving) took a great deal of time in Moses' day. To own more than two or three changes of clothes was a sign of wealth. The effort involved in making enough cloth for the tabernacle was staggering. The tabernacle would never have been built without tremendous community involvement. Today, churches and neighborhoods often require this same kind of pulling together. Without it, many essential services wouldn't get done.

36:35 Cherubim are mighty angels.

the same was done with the end curtain in the other set. [12]They also made fifty loops on one curtain and fifty loops on the end curtain of the other set, with the loops opposite each other. [13]Then they made fifty gold clasps and used them to fasten the two sets of curtains together so that the tabernacle was a unit. [u]

[14]They made curtains of goat hair for the tent over the tabernacle—eleven altogether. [15]All eleven curtains were the same size—thirty cubits long and four cubits wide. [a] [16]They joined five of the curtains into one set and the other six into another set. [17]Then they made fifty loops along the edge of the end curtain in one set and also along the edge of the end curtain in the other set. [18]They made fifty bronze clasps to fasten the tent together as a unit. [v] [19]Then they made for the tent a covering of ram skins dyed red, and over that a covering of hides of sea cows. [b]

[20]They made upright frames of acacia wood for the tabernacle. [21]Each frame was ten cubits long and a cubit and a half wide, [c] [22]with two projections set parallel to each other. They made all the frames of the tabernacle in this way. [23]They made twenty frames for the south side of the tabernacle [24]and made forty silver bases to go under them—two bases for each frame, one under each projection. [25]For the other side, the north side of the tabernacle, they made twenty frames [26]and forty silver bases—two under each frame. [27]They made six frames for the far end, that is, the west end of the tabernacle, [28]and two frames were made for the corners of the tabernacle at the far end. [29]At these two corners the frames were double from the bottom all the way to the top and fitted into a single ring; both were made alike. [30]So there were eight frames and sixteen silver bases—two under each frame.

[31]They also made crossbars of acacia wood: five for the frames on one side of the tabernacle, [32]five for those on the other side, and five for the frames on the west, at the far end of the tabernacle. [33]They made the center crossbar so that it extended from end to end at the middle of the frames. [34]They overlaid the frames with gold and made gold rings to hold the crossbars. They also overlaid the crossbars with gold.

[35]They made the curtain [w] of blue, purple and scarlet yarn and finely twisted linen, with cherubim worked into it by a skilled craftsman. [36]They made four posts of acacia wood for it and overlaid them with gold. They made gold hooks for them and cast their four silver bases. [37]For the entrance to the tent they made a curtain of blue, purple and scarlet yarn and finely twisted linen—the work of an embroiderer; [x] [38]and they made five posts with hooks for them. They overlaid the tops of the posts and their bands with gold and made their five bases of bronze.

The Ark

37 Bezalel [y] made the ark [z] of acacia wood—two and a half cubits long, a cubit and a half wide, and a cubit and a half high. [d] [2]He overlaid it with pure gold, [a] both inside and out, and made a gold molding around it. [3]He cast four gold rings for it and fastened them to its four feet, with two rings on one side and two rings on the other. [4]Then he made poles of acacia wood and overlaid them with gold. [5]And he inserted the poles into the rings on the sides of the ark to carry it.

[6]He made the atonement cover [b] of pure gold—two and a half cubits long and a cubit and a half wide. [e] [7]Then he made two cherubim [c] out of hammered gold at the ends of the cover. [8]He made one cherub on one end and the second cherub on the other; at the two ends he made them of one piece with the cover. [9]The cherubim had their wings spread upward, overshadowing [d] the cover with them. The cherubim faced each other, looking toward the cover. [e]

The Table

[10]They [f] made the table [f] of acacia wood—two cubits long, a cubit wide, and a cubit and a half high. [g] [11]Then they overlaid it with pure gold [g] and made a gold molding around it. [12]They also made around it a rim a handbreadth [h] wide and put a gold molding on the rim.

36:13
[u] ver 18

36:18
[v] ver 13

36:35
[w] Ex 39:38;
Mt 27:51; Lk 23:45;
Heb 9:3
36:37
[x] Ex 27:16

37:1
[y] Ex 31:2
[z] Ex 30:6; 39:35;
Dt 10:3
37:2
[a] ver 11,26

37:6
[b] Ex 26:34; 31:7;
Heb 9:5
37:7
[c] Eze 41:18
37:9
[d] Heb 9:5
[e] Dt 10:3

37:10
[f] Heb 9:2
37:11
[g] ver 2

---

[a] 15 That is, about 45 feet (about 13.5 meters) long and 6 feet (about 1.8 meters) wide   [b] 19 That is, dugongs
[c] 21 That is, about 15 feet (about 4.5 meters) long and 2 1/4 feet (about 0.7 meter) wide   [d] 1 That is, about 3 3/4 feet
(about 1.1 meters) long and 2 1/4 feet (about 0.7 meter) wide and high   [e] 6 That is, about 3 3/4 feet (about 1.1 meters)
long and 2 1/4 feet (about 0.7 meter) wide   [f] 10 Or He; also in verses 11-29   [g] 10 That is, about 3 feet (about 0.9
meter) long, 1 1/2 feet (about 0.5 meter) wide, and 2 1/4 feet (about 0.7 meter) high   [h] 12 That is, about 3 inches
(about 8 centimeters)

37:1 The ark (also called the ark of the Testimony or ark of the covenant) was built to hold the Ten Commandments. It symbolized God's covenant with his people. Two gold angels called cherubim were placed on its top. The ark was Israel's most sacred object and was kept in the Most Holy Place in the tabernacle. Only once each year, the high priest entered the Most Holy Place to sprinkle blood on the top of the ark (called the atonement cover) to atone for the sins of the entire nation.

¹³They cast four gold rings for the table and fastened them to the four corners, where the four legs were. ¹⁴The rings^h were put close to the rim to hold the poles used in carrying the table. ¹⁵The poles for carrying the table were made of acacia wood and were overlaid with gold. ¹⁶And they made from pure gold the articles for the table—its plates and dishes and bowls and its pitchers for the pouring out of drink offerings.

37:14
*h*ver 27

The Lampstand

¹⁷They made the lampstandⁱ of pure gold and hammered it out, base and shaft; its flower-like cups, buds and blossoms were of one piece with it. ¹⁸Six branches extended from the sides of the lampstand—three on one side and three on the other. ¹⁹Three cups shaped like almond flowers with buds and blossoms were on one branch, three on the next branch and the same for all six branches extending from the lampstand. ²⁰And on the lampstand were four cups shaped like almond flowers with buds and blossoms. ²¹One bud was under the first pair of branches extending from the lampstand, a second bud under the second pair, and a third bud under the third pair—six branches in all. ²²The buds and the branches were all of one piece with the lampstand, hammered out of pure gold.^j

²³They made its seven lamps,^k as well as its wick trimmers and trays, of pure gold. ²⁴They made the lampstand and all its accessories from one talent^a of pure gold.

37:17
*i*Heb 9:2; Rev 1:12

37:22
*j*ver 17; Nu 8:4
37:23
*k*Ex 40:4,25

The Altar of Incense

²⁵They made the altar of incense^l out of acacia wood. It was square, a cubit long and a cubit wide, and two cubits high^b—its horns^m of one piece with it. ²⁶They overlaid the top and all the sides and the horns with pure gold, and made a gold molding around it. ²⁷They made two gold rings below the molding—two on opposite sides—to hold the poles used to carry it. ²⁸They made the poles of acacia wood and overlaid them with gold. ⁿ

²⁹They also made the sacred anointing oil^o and the pure, fragrant incense^p—the work of a perfumer.

37:25
*l*Ex 30:34-36;
Lk 1:11; Heb 9:4;
Rev 8:3
*m*Ex 27:2; Rev 9:13
37:28
*n*Ex 25:13
37:29
*o*Ex 31:11
*p*Ex 30:1,25

The Altar of Burnt Offering

38 They^c built the altar of burnt offering of acacia wood, three cubits^d high; it was square, five cubits long and five cubits wide.^e ²They made a horn at each of the four corners, so that the horns and the altar were of one piece, and they overlaid the altar with bronze. ³They made all its utensils of bronze—its pots, shovels, sprinkling bowls, meat forks and firepans. ⁴They made a grating for the altar, a bronze network, to be under its ledge, halfway up the altar. ⁵They cast bronze rings to hold the poles for the four corners of the bronze grating. ⁶They made the poles of acacia wood and overlaid them with bronze. ⁷They inserted the poles into the rings so they would be on the sides of the altar for carrying it. They made it hollow, out of boards.

Basin for Washing

⁸They made the bronze basin^q and its bronze stand from the mirrors of the women^r who served at the entrance to the Tent of Meeting.

38:8
*q*Ex 30:18
*r*Dt 23:17; 1Sa 2:22

The Courtyard

⁹Next they made the courtyard. The south side was a hundred cubits^f long and had curtains of finely twisted linen, ¹⁰with twenty posts and twenty bronze bases, and with silver hooks and bands on the posts. ¹¹The north side was also a hundred cubits long and had twenty posts and twenty bronze bases, with silver hooks and bands on the posts.

¹²The west end was fifty cubits^g wide and had curtains, with ten posts and ten bases, with silver hooks and bands on the posts. ¹³The east end, toward the sunrise, was also fifty cubits wide. ¹⁴Curtains fifteen cubits^h long were on one side of the entrance, with three posts and three bases, ¹⁵and curtains fifteen cubits long were on the other side of the entrance to the courtyard, with three posts and three bases. ¹⁶All the curtains around the courtyard were of finely twisted linen. ¹⁷The bases for the posts were bronze. The hooks and bands on the posts were silver, and their tops were overlaid with silver; so all the posts of the courtyard had silver bands.

¹⁸The curtain for the entrance to the courtyard was of blue, purple and scarlet yarn and

*a*24 That is, about 75 pounds (about 34 kilograms)   *b*25 That is, about 1 1/2 feet (about 0.5 meter) long and wide, and about 3 feet (about 0.9 meter) high   *c*1 Or *He*; also in verses 2-9   *d*1 That is, about 4 1/2 feet (about 1.3 meters)   *e*1 That is, about 7 1/2 feet (about 2.3 meters) long and wide   *f* That is, about 150 feet (about 46 meters)   *g*12 That is, about 75 feet (about 23 meters)   *h*14 That is, about 22 1/2 feet (about 6.9 meters) finely twisted linen—the work of an embroiderer. It was twenty cubits[a] long and, like the curtains of the courtyard, five cubits[b] high, [19]with four posts and four bronze bases. Their hooks and bands were silver, and their tops were overlaid with silver. [20]All the tent pegs of the tabernacle and of the surrounding courtyard were bronze.

The Materials Used

[21]These are the amounts of the materials used for the tabernacle, the tabernacle of the Testimony,[s] which were recorded at Moses' command by the Levites under the direction of Ithamar[t] son of Aaron, the priest. [22](Bezalel[u] son of Uri, the son of Hur, of the tribe of Judah, made everything the LORD commanded Moses; [23]with him was Oholiab son of Ahisamach, of the tribe of Dan—a craftsman and designer, and an embroiderer in blue, purple and scarlet yarn and fine linen.) [24]The total amount of the gold from the wave offering used for all the work on the sanctuary was 29 talents and 730 shekels,[c] according to the sanctuary shekel.[v]

[25]The silver obtained from those of the community who were counted in the census[w] was 100 talents and 1,775 shekels,[d] according to the sanctuary shekel— [26]one beka per person,[x] that is, half a shekel,[e] according to the sanctuary shekel,[y] from everyone who had crossed over to those counted, twenty years old or more,[z] a total of 603,550 men.[a] [27]The 100 talents[f] of silver were used to cast the bases[b] for the sanctuary and for the curtain— 100 bases from the 100 talents, one talent for each base. [28]They used the 1,775 shekels[h] to make the hooks for the posts, to overlay the tops of the posts, and to make their bands.

[29]The bronze from the wave offering was 70 talents and 2,400 shekels.[i] [30]They used it to make the bases for the entrance to the Tent of Meeting, the bronze altar with its bronze grating and all its utensils, [31]the bases for the surrounding courtyard and those for its entrance and all the tent pegs for the tabernacle and those for the surrounding courtyard.

The Priestly Garments

39 From the blue, purple and scarlet yarn[c] they made woven garments for ministering in the sanctuary.[d] They also made sacred garments[e] for Aaron, as the LORD commanded Moses.

The Ephod

[2]They[j] made the ephod of gold, and of blue, purple and scarlet yarn, and of finely twisted linen. [3]They hammered out thin sheets of gold and cut strands to be worked into the blue, purple and scarlet yarn and fine linen—the work of a skilled craftsman. [4]They made shoulder pieces for the ephod, which were attached to two of its corners, so it could be fastened. [5]Its skillfully woven waistband was like it—of one piece with the ephod and made with gold, and with blue, purple and scarlet yarn, and with finely twisted linen, as the LORD commanded Moses.

[6]They mounted the onyx stones in gold filigree settings and engraved them like a seal with the names of the sons of Israel. [7]Then they fastened them on the shoulder pieces of the ephod as memorial[f] stones for the sons of Israel, as the LORD commanded Moses.

The Breastpiece

[8]They fashioned the breastpiece[g]—the work of a skilled craftsman. They made it like the ephod: of gold, and of blue, purple and scarlet yarn, and of finely twisted linen. [9]It was square—a span[k] long and a span wide—and folded double. [10]Then they mounted four rows of precious stones on it. In the first row there was a ruby, a topaz and a beryl; [11]in the second row a turquoise, a sapphire[l] and an emerald; [12]in the third row a jacinth, an agate and an

38:21
[s]Nu 1:50,53; 9:15; 10:11; 17:7; 2Ch 24:6; Ac 7:44; Rev 15:5
[t]Nu 4:28,33
38:22
[u]Ex 31:2
38:24
[v]Ex 30:13
38:25
[w]Ex 30:12
38:26
[x]Ex 30:12
[y]Ex 30:13
[z]Ex 30:14
[a]Ex 12:37; Nu 1:46
38:27
[b]Ex 26:19

39:1
[c]Ex 35:23
[d]Ex 35:19
[e]ver 41; Ex 28:2

39:7
[f]Lev 24:7; Jos 4:7

39:8
[g]Lev 8:8

[a]18 That is, about 30 feet (about 9 meters)   [b]18 That is, about 7 1/2 feet (about 2.3 meters)   [c]24 The weight of the gold was a little over one ton (about 1 metric ton).   [d]25 The weight of the silver was a little over 3 3/4 tons (about 3.4 metric tons).   [e]26 That is, about 1/5 ounce (about 5.5 grams)   [f]27 That is, about 3 3/4 tons (about 3.4 metric tons)   [h]28 That is, about 45 pounds (about 20 kilograms)   [i]29 The weight of the bronze was about 2 1/2 tons (about 2.4 metric tons).   [j]2 Or He; also in verses 7, 8 and 22   [k]9 That is, about 9 inches (about 22 centimeters)   [l]11 Or lapis lazuli

38:21 In building the tabernacle, Moses laid out the steps, but Ithamar supervised the project. We all have different talents and abilities. God didn't ask Moses to build the tabernacle but to motivate the experts to do it. Look for the areas where God has gifted you and then seek opportunities to allow God to use your gifts.

39:1–21 The priests wore a uniform to the tabernacle each day. Some of the pieces of their uniform were not only beautiful but also significant. Two parts of the high priest's uniform were the ephod and breastpiece. The ephod looked like a vest and was worn over the outer clothing. The breastpiece was fitted to the ephod (and sometimes was called the ephod). The breastpiece was made of colored linens about nine inches square. On its

39:14
h Rev 21:12

amethyst; [13]in the fourth row a chrysolite, an onyx and a jasper.[a] They were mounted in gold filigree settings. [14]There were twelve stones, one for each of the names of the sons of Israel, each engraved like a seal with the name of one of the twelve tribes. [h]

[15]For the breastpiece they made braided chains of pure gold, like a rope. [16]They made two gold filigree settings and two gold rings, and fastened the rings to two of the corners of the breastpiece. [17]They fastened the two gold chains to the rings at the corners of the breastpiece, [18]and the other ends of the chains to the two settings, attaching them to the shoulder pieces of the ephod at the front. [19]They made two gold rings and attached them to the other two corners of the breastpiece on the inside edge next to the ephod. [20]Then they made two more gold rings and attached them to the bottom of the shoulder pieces on the front of the ephod, close to the seam just above the waistband of the ephod. [21]They tied the rings of the breastpiece to the rings of the ephod with blue cord, connecting it to the waistband so that the breastpiece would not swing out from the ephod—as the LORD commanded Moses.

Other Priestly Garments

[22]They made the robe of the ephod entirely of blue cloth—the work of a weaver— [23]with an opening in the center of the robe like the opening of a collar,[b] and a band around this opening, so that it would not tear. [24]They made pomegranates of blue, purple and scarlet yarn and finely twisted linen around the hem of the robe. [25]And they made bells of pure gold and attached them around the hem between the pomegranates. [26]The bells and pomegranates alternated around the hem of the robe to be worn for ministering, as the LORD commanded Moses.

[27]For Aaron and his sons, they made tunics of fine linen—the work of a weaver— [28]and the turban of fine linen, the linen headbands and the undergarments of finely twisted linen. [29]The sash was of finely twisted linen and blue, purple and scarlet yarn—the work of an embroiderer—as the LORD commanded Moses.

[30]They made the plate, the sacred diadem, out of pure gold and engraved on it, like an inscription on a seal: HOLY TO THE LORD. [31]Then they fastened a blue cord to it to attach it to the turban, as the LORD commanded Moses.

Moses Inspects the Tabernacle

39:32
i ver 42-43; Ex 25:9

[32]So all the work on the tabernacle, the Tent of Meeting, was completed. The Israelites did everything just as the LORD commanded Moses. [i] [33]Then they brought the tabernacle to Moses: the tent and all its furnishings, its clasps, frames, crossbars, posts and bases; [34]the covering of ram skins dyed red, the covering of hides of sea cows[c] and the shielding curtain; [35]the ark of the Testimony with its poles and the atonement cover; [36]the table with all its articles and the bread of the Presence; [37]the pure gold lampstand with its row of lamps and all its accessories, and the oil for the light; [38]the gold altar, the anointing oil, the fragrant incense, and the curtain for the entrance to the tent; [39]the bronze altar with its bronze grating, its poles and all its utensils; the basin with its stand; [40]the curtains of the courtyard with its posts and bases, and the curtain for the entrance to the courtyard; the ropes and tent pegs for the courtyard; all the furnishings for the tabernacle, the Tent of Meeting; [41]and the woven garments worn for ministering in the sanctuary, both the sacred garments for Aaron the priest and the garments for his sons when serving as priests.

[42]The Israelites had done all the work just as the LORD had commanded Moses.

---

a 13 The precise identification of some of these precious stones is uncertain.   *b 23* The meaning of the Hebrew for this word is uncertain.   *c 34* That is, dugongs

---

front were attached 12 precious stones, each inscribed with the name of a tribe of Israel. This symbolized how the high priest represented all the people before God. The breastpiece also contained pockets that held two stones or plates called the Urim and Thummim. The high priest could determine God's will for the nation by consulting the Urim and Thummim. (See the note on 28:30.)

39:32 The tabernacle was finally complete to the last detail. God was keenly interested in every minute part. The Creator of the universe was concerned about even the little things. Matthew 10:30 says that God knows the number of hairs on our heads. This shows that God is greatly interested in you. Don't be afraid

to talk with him about any of your concerns—no matter how small or unimportant they might seem.

39:42 Moses had learned his management lesson well. He gave important responsibilities to others and then trusted them to do the job. Great leaders, like Moses, give plans and direction while letting others participate on the team. If you are a leader, trust your assistants with key responsibilities.

43 Moses inspected the work and saw that they had done it just as the LORD had commanded. So Moses blessedⁱ them.

Setting Up the Tabernacle

40 Then the LORD said to Moses: 2"Set up the tabernacle, the Tent of Meeting,ᵏ on the first day of the first month.ˡ 3Place the arkᵐ of the Testimony in it and shield the ark with the curtain. 4Bring in the table and set out what belongs on it.ⁿ Then bring in the lampstand and set up its lamps. 5Place the gold altar of incense in front of the ark of the Testimony and put the curtain at the entrance to the tabernacle.

6"Place the altar of burnt offering in front of the entrance to the tabernacle, the Tent of Meeting; 7place the basinᵒ between the Tent of Meeting and the altar and put water in it. 8Set up the courtyard around it and put the curtain at the entrance to the courtyard.

9"Take the anointing oil and anointᵖ the tabernacle and everything in it; consecrate it and all its furnishings, and it will be holy. 10Then anoint the altar of burnt offering and all its utensils; consecrate�q the altar, and it will be most holy. 11Anoint the basin and its stand and consecrate them.

12"Bring Aaron and his sons to the entrance to the Tent of Meeting and wash them with water.ʳ 13Then dress Aaron in the sacred garments,ˢ anoint him and consecrateᵗ him so he may serve me as priest. 14Bring his sons and dress them in tunics. 15Anoint them just as you anointed their father, so they may serve me as priests. Their anointing will be to a priesthood that will continue for all generations to come.ᵘ" 16Moses did everything just as the LORD commanded him.

17So the tabernacle ᵛ was set up on the first day of the first month ʷ in the second year. 18When Moses set up the tabernacle, he put the bases in place, erected the frames, inserted the crossbars and set up the posts. 19Then he spread the tent over the tabernacle and put the covering over the tent, as the LORD commanded him.

20He took the Testimonyˣ and placed it in the ark, attached the poles to the ark and put the atonement cover over it. 21Then he brought the ark into the tabernacle and hung the shielding curtainʸ and shielded the ark of the Testimony, as the LORD commanded him.

22Moses placed the tableᶻ in the Tent of Meeting on the north side of the tabernacle outside the curtain 23and set out the bread on it before the LORD, as the LORD commanded him.

24He placed the lampstandᵃ in the Tent of Meeting opposite the table on the south side of the tabernacle 25and set up the lampsᵇ before the LORD, as the LORD commanded him.

26Moses placed the gold altar ᶜ in the Tent of Meeting in front of the curtain 27and burned fragrant incense on it, as the LORD commanded him. 28Then he put up the curtain at the entrance to the tabernacle.

29He set the altar of burnt offering near the entrance to the tabernacle, the Tent of Meeting, and offered on it burnt offerings and grain offerings,ᵈ as the LORD commanded him.

30He placed the basin between the Tent of Meeting and the altar and put water in it for washing, 31and Moses and Aaron and his sons used it to wash their hands and feet. 32They washed whenever they entered the Tent of Meeting or approached the altar, as the LORD commanded Moses.

33Then Moses set up the courtyard around the tabernacle and altar and put up the curtain at the entrance to the courtyard. And so Moses finished the work.

39:43
ⁱLev 9:22,23;
Nu 6:23-27;
2Sa 6:18;
1Ki 8:14,55;
2Ch 30:27

40:2
ᵏNu 1:1
ˡver 17; Ex 12:2

40:3
ᵐEx 26:33

40:4
ⁿEx 25:30

40:7
ᵒEx 30:18

40:9
ᵖEx 30:26

40:10
qEx 29:36

40:12
ʳLev 8:1-13

40:13
ˢEx 28:41
ᵗLev 8:12

40:15
ᵘEx 29:9; Nu 25:13

40:17
ᵛNu 7:1
ʷver 2

40:20
ˣEx 16:34; 25:16;
Heb 9:4

40:21
ʸEx 26:33

40:22
ᶻEx 26:35

40:24
ᵃEx 26:35

40:25
ᵇEx 25:37

40:26
ᶜver 5; Ex 30:6

40:29
ᵈver 6

39:43 Moses inspected the finished work, saw that it was done the way God wanted, and then blessed the people. A good leader follows up on assigned tasks and gives rewards for good work. In whatever responsible position you find yourself, follow up to make sure that tasks are completed as intended, and show your appreciation to the people who have helped.

40:1ff Moses was careful to obey God's instructions in the smallest detail. Notice that he didn't make a reasonable facsimile of God's description, but an exact copy. We should follow

Moses' example and be fastidious about our obedience. If God has told you to do something, do it, do it right, and do it completely.

40:16 God told Moses how to build the tabernacle, and Moses delegated jobs in order to do it. God allows people to participate with him in carrying out his will. Your task is not just to sit and watch God work, but to give your best effort when work needs to be done.

40:17-33 The physical care of the tabernacle required a long list of tasks, and each was important to the work of God's house. This principle is important to remember today when God's house is the church. There are many seemingly unimportant tasks that must be done to keep your church building maintained. Washing dishes, painting walls, or shoveling snow may not seem very spiritual. But they are vital to the ministry of the church and have an important role in our worship of God.

The Glory of the LORD

40:34
e Nu 9:15-23

34 Then the cloud *e* covered the Tent of Meeting, and the glory of the LORD filled the tabernacle. 35 Moses could not enter the Tent of Meeting because the cloud had settled upon it, and the glory of the LORD filled the tabernacle.

40:36
f Nu 9:17-23;
Ne 9:19

40:38
g Ex 13:21; Nu 9:15

36 In all the travels of the Israelites, whenever the cloud lifted from above the tabernacle, they would set out; *f* 37 but if the cloud did not lift, they did not set out—until the day it lifted. 38 So the cloud *g* of the LORD was over the tabernacle by day, and fire was in the cloud by night, in the sight of all the house of Israel during all their travels.

40:34 The tabernacle was God's home on earth. He filled it with his glory—the overpowering sense of his presence. Almost 500 years later, Solomon built the temple, which replaced the tabernacle as the central place of worship. God also filled the temple with his glory (2 Chronicles 5:13, 14). But when Israel turned from God, his glory and presence departed from the temple and it was destroyed by invading armies (2 Kings 25). The temple was rebuilt in 516 B.C. God's glory returned in even greater splendor nearly five centuries later when Jesus Christ, God's Son, entered it and taught. When Jesus was crucified, God's glory again left the temple. However, God no longer needed a physical building after Jesus rose from the dead. God's temple now is his church, the body of believers.

40:38 The Israelites were once Egyptian slaves making bricks without straw. Here they were following the pillar of cloud and the pillar of fire, carrying the tabernacle they had built for God. Exodus begins in gloom and ends in glory. This parallels our progress through the Christian life. We begin as slaves to sin, are redeemed by God, and end our pilgrimage living with God forever. The lessons the Israelites learned along the way we also need to learn.

LEVITICUS

Joseph
dies
1805 B.C.
(1640 B.C.)

VITAL STATISTICS

PURPOSE:
A handbook for the priests and
Levites outlining their duties
in worship, and a guidebook
of holy living for the Hebrews

AUTHOR:
Moses

ORIGINAL AUDIENCE:
The people of Israel

DATE WRITTEN:
1445–1444 B.C.

WHERE WRITTEN:
In the desert during Israel's
wanderings, somewhere in the
Sinai peninsula

SETTING:
At the foot of Mount Sinai. God
is teaching the Israelites how
to live as holy people.

KEY VERSE:
"Be holy because I, the LORD your
God, am holy" (19:2).

KEY PEOPLE:
Moses, Aaron, Nadab, Abihu,
Eleazar, Ithamar

KEY PLACE:
Mount Sinai

SPECIAL FEATURE:
Holiness is mentioned more times
(152) than in any other book of
the Bible.

"GOD seems so far away . . . if only I could see or hear him." Have you ever felt this way—struggling with loneliness, burdened by despair, riddled with sin, overwhelmed by problems? Made in God's image, we were created to have a close relationship with him; thus, when fellowship is broken, we are incomplete and need restoration. Communion with the living God is the essence of worship. It is vital, touching the very core of our lives. Perhaps this is why a whole book of the Bible is dedicated to worship. After Israel's dramatic exit from Egypt, the nation was camped at the foot of Mount Sinai for two years to listen to God (Exodus 19 to Numbers 10). It was a time of resting, teaching, building, and meeting with him face to face. Redemption in Exodus is the foundation for cleansing, worship, and service in Leviticus.

The overwhelming message of Leviticus is the holiness of God—"Be holy because I, the LORD your God, am holy" (19:2). But how can unholy people approach a holy God? The answer—first sin must be dealt with. Thus the opening chapters of Leviticus give detailed instructions for offering sacrifices, which were the active symbols of repentance and obedience. Whether bulls, grain, goats, or sheep, the sacrificial offerings had to be perfect, with no defects or bruises—pictures of the ultimate sacrifice to come, Jesus, the Lamb of God. Jesus has come and opened the way to God by giving up his life as the final sacrifice in our place. True worship and oneness with God begin as we confess our sin and accept Christ as the only one who can redeem us from sin and help us approach God.

In Leviticus, sacrifices, priests, and the sacred Day of Atonement opened the way for the Israelites to come to God. God's people were also to worship him with their lives. Thus we read of purity laws (chapters 11—15) and rules for daily living, concerning family responsibilities, sexual conduct, relationships, worldliness (chapters 18—20), and vows (chapter 27). These instructions involve one's holy walk with God, and the patterns of spiritual living still apply today. Worship, therefore, has a horizontal aspect—that is, God is honored by our lives as we relate to others.

The final emphasis in Leviticus is celebration. The book gives instructions for the feasts. These were special, regular, and corporate occasions for remembering what God had done, giving thanks to him, and rededicating lives to his service (chapter 23). Our Christian traditions and holidays are different, but they are necessary ingredients of worship. We, too, need special days of worship and celebration with our spiritual brothers and sisters to remember God's goodness in our lives.

As you read Leviticus, rededicate yourself to holiness, worshiping God in private confession, public service, and group celebration.

1:4
*e*Ex 29:10,15;
Lev 3:2
*f*2Ch 29:23-24

1:5
*g*Heb 12:24

1:9
*h*Ge 8:21; Eph 5:2

1:10
*i*ver 3

1:14
*j*Lev 5:7

1:16
*k*Lev 6:10

1:17
*l*Ge 15:10

He must present it at the entrance to the Tent of Meeting so that it*a* will be acceptable to the LORD. [4] He is to lay his hand on the head*e* of the burnt offering, and it will be accepted on his behalf to make atonement*f* for him. [5] He is to slaughter the young bull before the LORD, and then Aaron's sons the priests shall bring the blood and sprinkle it against the altar on all sides*g* at the entrance to the Tent of Meeting. [6] He is to skin the burnt offering and cut it into pieces. [7] The sons of Aaron the priest are to put fire on the altar and arrange wood on the fire. [8] Then Aaron's sons the priests shall arrange the pieces, including the head and the fat, on the burning wood that is on the altar. [9] He is to wash the inner parts and the legs with water, and the priest is to burn all of it on the altar. It is a burnt offering, an offering made by fire, an aroma pleasing to the LORD. *h*

[10] "If the offering is a burnt offering from the flock, from either the sheep or the goats,*i* he is to offer a male without defect. [11] He is to slaughter it at the north side of the altar before the LORD, and Aaron's sons the priests shall sprinkle its blood against the altar on all sides. [12] He is to cut it into pieces, and the priest shall arrange them, including the head and the fat, on the burning wood that is on the altar. [13] He is to wash the inner parts and the legs with water, and the priest is to bring all of it and burn it on the altar. It is a burnt offering, an offering made by fire, an aroma pleasing to the LORD.

[14] "If the offering to the LORD is a burnt offering of birds, he is to offer a dove or a young pigeon.*j* [15] The priest shall bring it to the altar, wring off the head and burn it on the altar; its blood shall be drained out on the side of the altar. [16] He is to remove the crop with its contents*b* and throw it to the east side of the altar, where the ashes*k* are. [17] He shall tear it open by the wings, not severing it completely,*l* and then the priest shall burn it on the wood that is on the fire on the altar. It is a burnt offering, an offering made by fire, an aroma pleasing to the LORD.

a3 Or *he*   *b16* Or *crop and the feathers*; the meaning of the Hebrew for this word is uncertain.

THE OFFERINGS	Offering	Purpose	Significance	Christ, the Perfect Offering
Listed here are the five key offerings the Israelites made to God. They made these offerings in order to have their sins forgiven and to restore their fellowship with God. The death of Jesus Christ made these sacrifices unnecessary. Because of his death, our sins were completely forgiven, and fellowship with God has been restored.	Burnt Offering (Lev. 1—voluntary)	To make payment for sins in general	Showed a person's devotion to God	Christ's death was the perfect offering
	Grain Offering (Lev. 2—voluntary)	To show honor and respect to God in worship	Acknowledged that all we have belongs to God	Christ was the perfect man, who gave all of himself to God and others
	Fellowship Offering (Lev. 3—voluntary)	To express gratitude to God	Symbolized peace and fellowship with God	Christ is the only way to fellowship with God
	Sin Offering (Lev. 4—required)	To make payment for unintentional sins of uncleanness, neglect, or thoughtlessness	Restored the sinner to fellowship with God; showed seriousness of sin	Christ's death restores our fellowship with God
	Guilt Offering (Lev. 5—required)	To make payment for sins against God and others. A sacrifice was made to God, and the injured person was repaid or compensated	Provided compensation for injured parties	Christ's death takes away the deadly consequences of sin

---

of the people's commitment to God. (4) By their nature, sacrifices required the use of all the senses in worship, encouraging a whole-person response to God. Some sacrifices were voluntary while others were required. The sacrificial system taught a combination of requirement before God, but also presented opportunities for heartfelt voluntary response to God.

1:3–13 Why are there such detailed regulations for each offering? God had a purpose in giving these commands. Starting from scratch, he was teaching his people a whole new way of life, cleansing them from the many pagan practices they had learned in Egypt, and restoring true worship of himself. The strict details kept Israel from slipping back into their old lifestyle. In addition, each law paints a graphic picture of the seriousness of sin and of God's great mercy in forgiving sinners.

1:4ff Israel was not the only nation to sacrifice animals. Many other religions did it as well to try to please their gods. Some cultures even included human sacrifice, which was strictly forbidden by God. However, the meaning of Israel's animal sacrifices was clearly different from that of their pagan neighbors. Israelites sacrificed animals, not just to appease God's wrath, but as a substitute for the punishment they deserved for their sins. A sacrifice showed faith in God and commitment to his laws. Most important, this system foreshadowed the day when the Lamb of God (Jesus Christ) would die and conquer sin once and for all.

1:13 The "aroma pleasing to the LORD" is a way of saying that God accepted the sacrifice because of the people's attitude.

The Grain Offering

2 "'When someone brings a grain offering^m to the LORD, his offering is to be of fine flour. He is to pour oil on it, put incense on it ^2 and take it to Aaron's sons the priests. The priest shall take a handful of the fine flour and oil, together with all the incense, and burn this as a memorial portion ^n on the altar, an offering made by fire, an aroma pleasing to the LORD. ^3 The rest of the grain offering belongs to Aaron and his sons; ^o it is a most holy part of the offerings made to the LORD by fire.

^4 "'If you bring a grain offering baked in an oven, it is to consist of fine flour: cakes made without yeast and mixed with oil, or ^a wafers made without yeast and spread with oil. ^5 If your grain offering is prepared on a griddle, it is to be made of fine flour mixed with oil, and without yeast. ^6 Crumble it and pour oil on it; it is a grain offering. ^7 If your grain offering is cooked in a pan, it is to be made of fine flour and oil. ^8 Bring the grain offering made of these things to the LORD; present it to the priest, who shall take it to the altar. ^9 He shall take out the memorial portion ^p from the grain offering and burn it on the altar as an offering made by fire, an aroma pleasing to the LORD. ^10 The rest of the grain offering belongs to Aaron and his sons; ^q it is a most holy part of the offerings made to the LORD by fire.

^11 "'Every grain offering you bring to the LORD must be made without yeast, ^r for you are not to burn any yeast or honey in an offering made to the LORD by fire. ^12 You may bring them to the LORD as an offering of the firstfruits, ^s but they are not to be offered on the altar as a pleasing aroma. ^13 Season all your grain offerings with salt. Do not leave the salt of the covenant ^t of your God out of your grain offerings; add salt to all your offerings.

^14 "'If you bring a grain offering of firstfruits ^u to the LORD, offer crushed heads of new grain roasted in the fire. ^15 Put oil and incense on it; it is a grain offering. ^16 The priest shall burn the memorial portion ^v of the crushed grain and the oil, together with all the incense, as an offering made by fire to the LORD.

The Fellowship Offering

3 "'If someone's offering is a fellowship offering, ^b ^w and he offers an animal from the herd, whether male or female, he is to present before the LORD an animal without defect. ^x ^2 He is to lay his hand on the head of his offering and slaughter it ^y at the entrance to the Tent of Meeting. Then Aaron's sons the priests shall sprinkle the blood against the altar on all sides. ^3 From the fellowship offering he is to bring a sacrifice made to the LORD by fire: all the fat that covers the inner parts or is connected to them, ^4 both kidneys with the fat on them near the loins, and the covering of the liver, which he will remove with the kidneys. ^5 Then Aaron's sons are to burn it on the altar on top of the burnt offering ^z that is on the burning wood, as an offering made by fire, an aroma pleasing to the LORD.

^a 4 Or *and*   ^b 1 Traditionally *peace offering*; also in verses 3, 6 and 9

**Margin references:**

2:1 ^m Lev 6:14-18
2:2 ^n ver 9,16; Lev 5:12; 6:15; Ac 10:4
2:3 ^o Lev 10:12,13
2:9 ^p ver 2
2:10 ^q ver 3
2:11 ^r Lev 6:16
2:12 ^s Lev 23:10
2:13 ^t Nu 18:19
2:14 ^u Lev 23:10
2:16 ^v ver 2
3:1 ^w Lev 7:11-34 ^x Lev 22:21
3:2 ^y Lev 1:5
3:5 ^z Ex 29:13,38-42

2:1ff The grain offering accompanied all burnt offerings and was a gift of thanks to God. It reminded the people that their food came from God and that therefore they owed their lives to him. Three kinds of grain offerings are listed: (1) fine flour with oil and incense, (2) baked cakes or wafers of fine flour and oil, and (3) roasted kernels of grain (corn) with oil and incense. The absence of yeast symbolized the absence of sin, and the oil symbolized God's presence. Part of the grain offering was burned on the altar as a gift to God, and the rest was eaten by the priests. The offerings helped support them in their work.

2:11 Why was no yeast allowed in the grain offerings? Yeast is a bacterial fungus or mold and is, therefore, an appropriate symbol for sin. It grows in bread dough just as sin grows in a life. A little yeast will affect the whole loaf, just as a little sin can ruin a whole life. Jesus expanded this analogy by warning about the "yeast of the Pharisees and Sadducees" (Matthew 16:6; Mark 8:15). How do you visualize the effects of sin in your life? What do you do to eliminate sin from your attitudes and actions?

2:13 The offerings were seasoned with salt as a reminder of the people's covenant (contract) with God. Salt is a good symbol of God's activity in a person's life, because it penetrates, preserves, and aids in healing. God wants to be active in your life. Let him become part of you, penetrating every aspect of your life, preserv-

ing you from the evil all around, and healing you of your sins and shortcomings.

2:13 In ancient Middle Eastern lands, an agreement was sealed with a gift of salt to show the strength and permanence of the contract. Salt also points to the effects of a truthful agreement—it changes behavior. In Matthew 5:13 believers are called "the salt of the earth." Let the salt you use each day remind you that you are now one of God's covenant people who actively helps preserve and purify the world.

2:14, 15 Crushed heads of new grain mixed with oil and baked was typical food for the average person. This offering was a token presentation of a person's daily food. In this way, people acknowledged God as provider of their food. Even a poor person could fulfill this offering. God was pleased by the motivation and the dedication of the persons making it.

3:1ff A person gave a fellowship (or peace) offering as an expression of gratitude and a means of maintaining fellowship between himself and God. The animal's sacrificed life emphasized the value of gratitude and maintaining harmony with God. Neither peace with God nor thanks to God was to be considered a cheap or unimportant gift. Because it symbolized peace with God, part of the offering could be eaten by the person presenting it.

3:2 The altar was inside the walls of the tabernacle gate but outside the Tent of Meeting.

3:6
ᵃver 1

6 "'If he offers an animal from the flock as a fellowship offering ᵃ to the LORD, he is to offer a male or female without defect. 7 If he offers a lamb, he is to present it before the LORD. 8 He is to lay his hand on the head of his offering and slaughter it in front of the Tent of Meeting. Then Aaron's sons shall sprinkle its blood against the altar on all sides. 9 From the fellowship offering he is to bring a sacrifice made to the LORD by fire: its fat, the entire fat tail cut off close to the backbone, all the fat that covers the inner parts or is connected to them, 10 both kidneys with the fat on them near the loins, and the covering of the liver,

3:11
ᵇLev 21:6,17

which he will remove with the kidneys. 11 The priest shall burn them on the altar as food,ᵇ an offering made to the LORD by fire.

12 "'If his offering is a goat, he is to present it before the LORD. 13 He is to lay his hand on its head and slaughter it in front of the Tent of Meeting. Then Aaron's sons shall sprinkle its blood against the altar on all sides. 14 From what he offers he is to make this offering to the LORD by fire: all the fat that covers the inner parts or is connected to them, 15 both kidneys with the fat on them near the loins, and the covering of the liver, which he will remove with the kidneys. 16 The priest shall burn them on the altar as food, an offering made by fire, a pleasing aroma. All the fat is the LORD's.

3:17
ᶜLev 7:25-26;
17:10-16

17 "'This is a lasting ordinance for the generations to come, wherever you live: You must not eat any fat or any blood.ᶜ'"

The Sin Offering

4:2
ᵈLev 5:15-18;
Heb 9:7

4 The LORD said to Moses, 2 "Say to the Israelites: 'When anyone sins unintentionallyᵈ and does what is forbidden in any of the LORD's commands—

4:4
ᵉLev 1:3

3 "'If the anointed priest sins, bringing guilt on the people, he must bring to the LORD a young bull without defect as a sin offering for the sin he has committed. 4 He is to present the bull at the entrance to the Tent of Meeting before the LORD.ᵉ He is to lay his hand on its head and slaughter it before the LORD. 5 Then the anointed priest shall take some of the bull's blood and carry it into the Tent of Meeting. 6 He is to dip his finger into the blood and sprinkle some of it seven times before the LORD, in front of the curtain of the sanctuary.

4:7
ᶠLev 8:15
ᵍLev 5:9; 9:9; 16:18

7 The priest shall then put some of the blood on the horns of the altar of fragrant incense that is before the LORD in the Tent of Meeting. The rest of the bull's blood he shall pour out at the base of the altarᶠ of burnt offeringᵍ at the entrance to the Tent of Meeting. 8 He shall

4:8
ʰLev 3:3-5

remove all the fatʰ from the bull of the sin offering—the fat that covers the inner parts or is connected to them, 9 both kidneys with the fat on them near the loins, and the covering of the liver, which he will remove with the kidneys— 10 just as the fat is removed from the oxᵃ

4:11
ⁱNu 19:5
4:12
ʲHeb 13:11
ᵏLev 6:11

sacrificed as a fellowship offering.ᵇ Then the priest shall burn them on the altar of burnt offering. 11 But the hide of the bull and all its flesh, as well as the head and legs, the inner parts and offalⁱ— 12 that is, all the rest of the bull—he must take outside the campʲ to a place ceremonially clean,ᵏ where the ashes are thrown, and burn it in a wood fire on the ash heap.

4:13
ˡver 2; Lev 5:2-4,17;
Nu 15:24-26

13 "'If the whole Israelite community sins unintentionallyˡ and does what is forbidden in any of the LORD's commands, even though the community is unaware of the matter, they are guilty. 14 When they become aware of the sin they committed, the assembly must bring a

4:14
ᵐver 3
ⁿver 23,28

young bullᵐ as a sin offeringⁿ and present it before the Tent of Meeting. 15 The elders of the community are to lay their hands on the bull's headᵒ before the LORD, and the bull shall be

4:15
ᵒLev 1:4; 8:14,22;
Nu 8:10

slaughtered before the LORD. 16 Then the anointed priest is to take some of the bull's blood into the Tent of Meeting. 17 He shall dip his finger into the blood and sprinkle it before the

4:17
ᵖver 6

LORDᵖ seven times in front of the curtain. 18 He is to put some of the blood on the horns of the altar that is before the LORD in the Tent of Meeting. The rest of the blood he shall pour out at the base of the altar of burnt offering at the entrance to the Tent of Meeting. 19 He

ᵃ 10 The Hebrew word can include both male and female. ᵇ 10 Traditionally *peace offering*; also in verses 26, 31 and 35

4:1ff Have you ever done something wrong without realizing it until later? Although your sin was unintentional, it was still sin. God's commands served to make the Israelites aware of their sins (even the unintentional ones) so they could be forgiven for them, and to keep the people from repeating those sins. Leviticus 4 and 5 mention some of these unintentional sins and the way the Israelites could be forgiven for them. As you read more of God's laws, keep in mind that they were meant to teach and guide the people. Let them help you become more aware of sin in your life.

4:3 The sin offering was for those who: (1) committed a sin without realizing it or (2) committed a sin out of weakness or negligence as opposed to outright rebellion against God. Both individuals and groups could be guilty of unintentional sin. Different animals were sacrificed for the different kinds of sin. The death of Jesus Christ was the final sin offering in the Bible (Hebrews 9:25–28 tells why).

shall remove all the fat from it and burn it on the altar, [20]and do with this bull just as he did with the bull for the sin offering. In this way the priest will make atonement for them, and they will be forgiven. [q] [21]Then he shall take the bull outside the camp and burn it as he burned the first bull. This is the sin offering for the community.

[22]"'When a leader sins unintentionally[r] and does what is forbidden in any of the commands of the LORD his God, he is guilty. [23]When he is made aware of the sin he committed, he must bring as his offering a male goat without defect. [24]He is to lay his hand on the goat's head and slaughter it at the place where the burnt offering is slaughtered before the LORD. It is a sin offering. [25]Then the priest shall take some of the blood of the sin offering with his finger and put it on the horns of the altar of burnt offering and pour out the rest of the blood at the base of the altar. [s] [26]He shall burn all the fat on the altar as he burned the fat of the fellowship offering. In this way the priest will make atonement for the man's sin, and he will be forgiven.

[27]"'If a member of the community sins unintentionally[t] and does what is forbidden in any of the LORD's commands, he is guilty. [28]When he is made aware of the sin he committed, he must bring as his offering for the sin he committed a female goat without defect. [29]He is to lay his hand on the head[u] of the sin offering[v] and slaughter it at the place of the burnt offering. [30]Then the priest is to take some of the blood with his finger and put it on the horns of the altar of burnt offering and pour out the rest of the blood at the base of the altar. [31]He shall remove all the fat, just as the fat is removed from the fellowship offering, and the priest shall burn it on the altar as an aroma pleasing to the LORD. [w] In this way the priest will make atonement for him, and he will be forgiven.

[32]"'If he brings a lamb as his sin offering, he is to bring a female without defect. [33]He is to lay his hand on its head and slaughter it for a sin offering at the place where the burnt offering is slaughtered. [34]Then the priest shall take some of the blood of the sin offering with his finger and put it on the horns of the altar of burnt offering and pour out the rest of the blood at the base of the altar. [35]He shall remove all the fat, just as the fat is removed from the lamb of the fellowship offering, and the priest shall burn it on the altar[x] on top of the offerings made to the LORD by fire. In this way the priest will make atonement for him for the sin he has committed, and he will be forgiven.

5 "If a person sins because he does not speak up when he hears a public charge to testify[y] regarding something he has seen or learned about, he will be held responsible.

[2]"'Or if a person touches anything ceremonially unclean—whether the carcasses of unclean wild animals or of unclean livestock or of unclean creatures that move along the ground[z]—even though he is unaware of it, he has become unclean and is guilty.

[3]"'Or if he touches human uncleanness[a]—anything that would make him unclean—even though he is unaware of it, when he learns of it he will be guilty.

[4]"'Or if a person thoughtlessly takes an oath to do anything, whether good or evil—in any matter one might carelessly swear about—even though he is unaware of it, in any case when he learns of it he will be guilty.

[5]"'When anyone is guilty in any of these ways, he must confess[b] in what way he has sinned [6]and, as a penalty for the sin he has committed, he must bring to the LORD a female lamb or goat from the flock as a sin offering; and the priest shall make atonement for him for his sin.

[7]"'If he cannot afford[c] a lamb, he is to bring two doves or two young pigeons to the LORD as a penalty for his sin—one for a sin offering and the other for a burnt offering. [8]He is to

4:20
[q]Nu 15:25

4:22
[r]ver 2

4:25
[s]ver 7,18,30,34;
Lev 9:9

4:27
[t]ver 2; Nu 15:27

4:29
[u]ver 4,24
[v]Lev 1:4

4:31
[w]Ge 8:21

4:35
[x]ver 26,31

5:1
[y]Pr 29:24

5:2
[z]Lev 11:11,24-40

5:3
[a]Nu 19:11-16

5:5
[b]Lev 16:21; 26:40;
Nu 5:7

5:7
[c]Lev 12:8

5:4 Have you ever sworn to do or not do something and then realized how foolish your promise was? God's people are called to keep their word, even if they make promises that are tough to keep. Jesus was warning against swearing (in the sense of making vows or oaths) when he said, "Simply let your 'Yes' be 'Yes,' and your 'No,' 'No'; anything beyond this comes from the evil one" (Matthew 5:37). Our word should be enough. If we feel we have to strengthen it with an oath, something is wrong with our sincerity. The only promises we ought not to keep are prom-

ises that lead to sin. A wise and self-controlled person avoids making rash promises.

5:5 The entire system of sacrifices could not help a sinner unless he brought his offering with an attitude of repentance and a willingness to confess sin. Today, because of Christ's death on the cross, we do not have to sacrifice animals. But it is still vital to confess sin, because genuine confession shows realization of sin, awareness of God's holiness, humility before God, and willingness to turn from this sin (Psalm 51:16, 17). Even Jesus' death will be of little value to us if we do not repent and follow him. It is like a vaccine for a dangerous disease—it won't help unless it enters the bloodstream.

bring them to the priest, who shall first offer the one for the sin offering. He is to wring its head from its neck, not severing it completely, [9]and is to sprinkle some of the blood of the sin offering against the side of the altar; the rest of the blood must be drained out at the base of the altar. [d] It is a sin offering. [10]The priest shall then offer the other as a burnt offering in the prescribed way[e] and make atonement for him for the sin he has committed, and he will be forgiven.

[11]"'If, however, he cannot afford two doves or two young pigeons, he is to bring as an offering for his sin a tenth of an ephah[a] of fine flour for a sin offering. He must not put oil or incense on it, because it is a sin offering. [12]He is to bring it to the priest, who shall take a handful of it as a memorial portion and burn it on the altar on top of the offerings made to the LORD by fire. It is a sin offering. [13]In this way the priest will make atonement for him for any of these sins he has committed, and he will be forgiven. The rest of the offering will belong to the priest,[f] as in the case of the grain offering.'"

The Guilt Offering

[14]The LORD said to Moses: [15]"When a person commits a violation and sins unintentionally in regard to any of the LORD's holy things, he is to bring to the LORD as a penalty a ram from the flock, one without defect and of the proper value in silver, according to the sanctuary shekel.[b] It is a guilt offering. [16]He must make restitution[g] for what he has failed to do in regard to the holy things, add a fifth of the value[h] to that and give it all to the priest, who will make atonement for him with the ram as a guilt offering, and he will be forgiven.

[17]"If a person sins and does what is forbidden in any of the LORD's commands, even though he does not know it,[i] he is guilty and will be held responsible. [18]He is to bring to the priest as a guilt offering a ram from the flock, one without defect and of the proper value. In this way the priest will make atonement for him for the wrong he has committed unintentionally, and he will be forgiven.[j] [19]It is a guilt offering; he has been guilty of[c] wrongdoing against the LORD."

6 The LORD said to Moses: [2]"If anyone sins and is unfaithful to the LORD by deceiving his neighbor about something entrusted to him or left in his care[k] or stolen, or if he cheats him, [3]or if he finds lost property and lies about it,[l] or if he swears falsely, or if he commits any such sin that people may do— [4]when he thus sins and becomes guilty, he must return what he has stolen or taken by extortion, or what was entrusted to him, or the lost property he found, [5]or whatever it was he swore falsely about. He must make restitution[m] in full, add a fifth of the value to it and give it all to the owner on the day he presents his guilt offering.[n] [6]And as a penalty he must bring to the priest, that is, to the LORD, his guilt offering,[o] a ram from the flock, one without defect and of the proper value. [7]In this way the priest will make atonement for him before the LORD, and he will be forgiven for any of these things he did that made him guilty."

The Burnt Offering

[8]The LORD said to Moses: [9]"Give Aaron and his sons this command: 'These are the regulations for the burnt offering: The burnt offering is to remain on the altar hearth throughout the night, till morning, and the fire must be kept burning on the altar. [10]The priest shall then put on his linen clothes, with linen undergarments next to his body,[p] and shall remove the ashes of the burnt offering that the fire has consumed on the altar and place them beside the altar. [11]Then he is to take off these clothes and put on others, and carry the ashes outside

---

5:9 [d]Lev 4:7,18

5:10 [e]Lev 1:14-17

5:13 [f]Lev 2:3

5:16 [g]Lev 6:4 [h]Lev 22:14; Nu 5:7

5:17 [i]Lev 4:2

5:18 [j]ver 15

6:2 [k]Ex 22:7

6:3 [l]Dt 22:1-3

6:5 [m]Nu 5:7 [n]Lev 5:15

6:6 [o]Lev 5:15

6:10 [p]Ex 28:39-42,43

---

[a]11 That is, probably about 2 quarts (about 2 liters)   [b]15 That is, about 2/5 ounce (about 11.5 grams)   [c]19 Or *has made full expiation for his*

5:14–19 The guilt offering was a way of taking care of sin committed unintentionally. It was for those who sinned in some way against "holy things"—the tabernacle or the priesthood—as well as for those who unintentionally sinned against someone. In either case, a ram with no defects had to be sacrificed, plus those harmed by the sin had to be compensated for their loss, plus a 20 percent penalty. Even though Christ's death has made guilt offerings unnecessary for us today, we still need to make things right with those we hurt.

6:1–7 Here we discover that stealing involves more than just taking from someone. Finding something and not returning it or failing to return something borrowed are other forms of stealing. These are sins against God and not just your neighbor, a stranger, or a large business. If you have gotten something deceitfully, then confess your sin to God, apologize to the owner, and return the stolen items—with interest.

the camp to a place that is ceremonially clean. [12]The fire on the altar must be kept burning; it must not go out. Every morning the priest is to add firewood and arrange the burnt offering on the fire and burn the fat of the fellowship offerings[a] on it. [13]The fire must be kept burning on the altar continuously; it must not go out.

The Grain Offering

[14]"'These are the regulations for the grain offering: Aaron's sons are to bring it before the LORD, in front of the altar. [15]The priest is to take a handful of fine flour and oil, together with all the incense on the grain offering, and burn the memorial portion on the altar as an aroma pleasing to the LORD. [16]Aaron and his sons[q] shall eat the rest of it, but it is to be eaten without yeast[r] in a holy place; they are to eat it in the courtyard of the Tent of Meeting. [17]It must not be baked with yeast; I have given it as their share of the offerings made to me by fire. Like the sin offering and the guilt offering, it is most holy. [18]Any male descendant of Aaron may eat it.[s] It is his regular share of the offerings made to the LORD by fire for the generations to come. Whatever touches them will become holy.[b]'"

[19]The LORD also said to Moses, [20]"This is the offering Aaron and his sons are to bring to the LORD on the day he[c] is anointed: a tenth of an ephah[d] of fine flour as a regular grain offering,[t] half of it in the morning and half in the evening. [21]Prepare it with oil on a griddle;[u] bring it well-mixed and present the grain offering broken[e] in pieces as an aroma pleasing to the LORD. [22]The son who is to succeed him as anointed priest shall prepare it. It is the LORD's regular share and is to be burned completely. [23]Every grain offering of a priest shall be burned completely; it must not be eaten."

The Sin Offering

[24]The LORD said to Moses, [25]"Say to Aaron and his sons: 'These are the regulations for the sin offering: The sin offering is to be slaughtered before the LORD in the place[v] the burnt offering is slaughtered; it is most holy. [26]The priest who offers it shall eat it; it is to be eaten in a holy place,[w] in the courtyard of the Tent of Meeting. [27]Whatever touches any of the flesh will become holy, and if any of the blood is spattered on a garment, you must wash it in a holy place. [28]The clay pot[x] the meat is cooked in must be broken; but if it is cooked in a bronze pot, the pot is to be scoured and rinsed with water. [29]Any male in a priest's family may eat it;[y] it is most holy. [30]But any sin offering whose blood is brought into the Tent of Meeting to make atonement in the Holy Place must not be eaten; it must be burned.

The Guilt Offering

7 "'These are the regulations for the guilt offering,[z] which is most holy: [2]The guilt offering is to be slaughtered in the place where the burnt offering is slaughtered, and its blood is to be sprinkled against the altar on all sides. [3]All its fat shall be offered: the fat tail and the fat that covers the inner parts, [4]both kidneys with the fat on them near the loins, and the covering of the liver, which is to be removed with the kidneys. [5]The priest shall burn them on the altar as an offering made to the LORD by fire. It is a guilt offering. [6]Any male in a priest's family may eat it,[a] but it must be eaten in a holy place; it is most holy.[b]

[7]"'The same law applies to both the sin offering and the guilt offering: They belong to the priest[c] who makes atonement with them. [8]The priest who offers a burnt offering for anyone may keep its hide for himself. [9]Every grain offering baked in an oven or cooked in a pan or on a griddle[d] belongs to the priest who offers it, [10]and every grain offering, whether mixed with oil or dry, belongs equally to all the sons of Aaron.

The Fellowship Offering

[11]"'These are the regulations for the fellowship offering[f] a person may present to the LORD: [12]"'If he offers it as an expression of thankfulness, then along with this thank offering he

6:16
q Lev 2:3
r Lev 2:11

6:18
s ver 29; Nu 18:9-10

6:20
t Ex 29:2
6:21
u Lev 2:5

6:25
v Lev 1:5,11

6:26
w ver 16

6:28
x Lev 11:33; 15:12
6:29
y ver 18

7:1
z Lev 5:14–6:7

7:6
a Lev 6:18
b Lev 2:3
7:7
c Lev 6:17,26
7:9
d Lev 2:5

a 12 Traditionally *peace offerings*   b 18 Or *Whoever touches them must be holy*; similarly in verse 27   c 20 Or *each*
d 20 That is, probably about 2 quarts (about 2 liters)   e 21 The meaning of the Hebrew for this word is uncertain.
f 11 Traditionally *peace offering*; also in verses 13-37

6:12, 13 While the previous offerings and sacrifices were ones that the people did, the section from 6:8—7:38 deals with general and continual priestly duties. The burnt offering was presented in the morning and evening for the whole nation (see Exodus 29:38–43). The holy fire on the altar had to keep burning because God had started it. This represented God's continual presence in the sacrificial system. It showed the people that only by God's gracious favor could their sacrifices be acceptable. God's fire is present in each believer's life today. He lights the fire when the Holy Spirit comes to live in us, and he tends it so that we will grow in grace as we walk with him. When we are aware that God lives in us, we have confidence to come to him for forgiveness and restoration. We can carry out our work with strength and enthusiasm.

7:11-18 The fellowship offering was divided into three kinds

7:12
e Lev 2:4

7:13
f Am 4:5

7:15
g Lev 22:30

7:16
h Lev 19:5-8

7:18
i Lev 19:7

7:20
j Lev 22:3-7

7:23
k Lev 3:17; 17:13-14

7:26
l Ge 9:4

7:27
m Lev 17:10-24;
Ac 15:20,29

7:30
n Nu 6:20

7:31
o ver 34

7:34
p Ex 29:27;
Nu 18:18-19

is to offer cakes of bread made without yeast and mixed with oil, wafers *e* made without yeast and spread with oil, and cakes of fine flour well-kneaded and mixed with oil. ¹³Along with his fellowship offering of thanksgiving he is to present an offering with cakes of bread made with yeast. *f* ¹⁴He is to bring one of each kind as an offering, a contribution to the LORD; it belongs to the priest who sprinkles the blood of the fellowship offerings. ¹⁵The meat of his fellowship offering of thanksgiving must be eaten on the day it is offered; he must leave none of it till morning. *g*

¹⁶"If, however, his offering is the result of a vow or is a freewill offering, the sacrifice shall be eaten on the day he offers it, but anything left over may be eaten on the next day. *h* ¹⁷Any meat of the sacrifice left over till the third day must be burned up. ¹⁸If any meat of the fellowship offering is eaten on the third day, it will not be accepted. *i* It will not be credited to the one who offered it, for it is impure; the person who eats any of it will be held responsible.

¹⁹"Meat that touches anything ceremonially unclean must not be eaten; it must be burned up. As for other meat, anyone ceremonially clean may eat it. ²⁰But if anyone who is unclean eats any meat of the fellowship offering belonging to the LORD, that person must be cut off from his people. *j* ²¹If anyone touches something unclean—whether human uncleanness or an unclean animal or any unclean, detestable thing—and then eats any of the meat of the fellowship offering belonging to the LORD, that person must be cut off from his people.'"

Eating Fat and Blood Forbidden

²²The LORD said to Moses, ²³"Say to the Israelites: 'Do not eat any of the fat of cattle, sheep or goats. *k* ²⁴The fat of an animal found dead or torn by wild animals may be used for any other purpose, but you must not eat it. ²⁵Anyone who eats the fat of an animal from which an offering by fire may be*a* made to the LORD must be cut off from his people. ²⁶And wherever you live, you must not eat the blood *l* of any bird or animal. ²⁷If anyone eats blood, *m* that person must be cut off from his people.'"

The Priests' Share

²⁸The LORD said to Moses, ²⁹"Say to the Israelites: 'Anyone who brings a fellowship offering to the LORD is to bring part of it as his sacrifice to the LORD. ³⁰With his own hands he is to bring the offering made to the LORD by fire; he is to bring the fat, together with the breast, and wave the breast before the LORD as a wave offering. *n* ³¹The priest shall burn the fat on the altar, but the breast belongs to Aaron and his sons. *o* ³²You are to give the right thigh of your fellowship offerings to the priest as a contribution. ³³The son of Aaron who offers the blood and the fat of the fellowship offering shall have the right thigh as his share. ³⁴From the fellowship offerings of the Israelites, I have taken the breast that is waved and the thigh that is presented and have given them to Aaron the priest and his sons *p* as their regular share from the Israelites.'"

³⁵This is the portion of the offerings made to the LORD by fire that were allotted to Aaron and his sons on the day they were presented to serve the LORD as priests. ³⁶On the day they were anointed, the LORD commanded that the Israelites give this to them as their regular share for the generations to come.

a 25 Or *fire is*

---

according to purpose: thanksgiving offering, vow offering, and freewill offering. A thanksgiving offering was appropriate whenever one wished to show thanks to God, as when recovering from a serious illness, or surviving a dangerous calamity (Psalm 107). A vow offering was given in fulfillment of a vow (2 Samuel 15:7, 8). The freewill offering, however, needed no special occasion or reason.

7:22–27 The fat portions were regarded as the best portions; therefore, it was appropriate to dedicate them only to God. Because blood was the river of life, and life was God's gift and his alone, blood had to be returned to God and not used by people.

7:28–30 God told the people of Israel to bring their fellowship offerings personally, with their own hands. They were to take time and effort to express thanks to God. You are the best person to express your thankfulness to God and to others. Do you leave it to others to express thanks to someone who

has been helpful? Do you rely on the one leading in prayer to thank God for you? Take time to communicate your personal gratitude both to God and to others who have helped and blessed you.

7:31–36 The offering that was waved before the altar was called the wave offering. The part of the offering the priests waved was theirs to keep. The waving motion toward and away from the altar symbolized the offering of the sacrifice to God and his returning it to the priests. These offerings helped to care for the priests, who cared for God's house. The New Testament teaches that ministers should be paid by the people they serve (1 Corinthians 9:10). We should give generously to those who minister to us.

37 These, then, are the regulations for the burnt offering, the grain offering, the sin offering, the guilt offering, the ordination offering and the fellowship offering, 38 which the LORD gave Moses on Mount Sinai on the day he commanded the Israelites to bring their offerings to the LORD, *q* in the Desert of Sinai.

2. Instructions for the priests
The Ordination of Aaron and His Sons

8 The LORD said to Moses, 2 "Bring Aaron and his sons, their garments, the anointing oil, *r* the bull for the sin offering, the two rams and the basket containing bread made without yeast, *s* 3 and gather the entire assembly *t* at the entrance to the Tent of Meeting." 4 Moses did as the LORD commanded him, and the assembly gathered at the entrance to the Tent of Meeting.

5 Moses said to the assembly, "This is what the LORD has commanded to be done." 6 Then Moses brought Aaron and his sons forward and washed them with water. *u* 7 He put the tunic on Aaron, tied the sash around him, clothed him with the robe and put the ephod on him. He also tied the ephod to him by its skillfully woven waistband; so it was fastened on him. 8 He placed the breastpiece on him and put the Urim and Thummim *v* in the breastpiece. 9 Then he placed the turban on Aaron's head and set the gold plate, the sacred diadem, *w* on the front of it, as the LORD commanded Moses.

10 Then Moses took the anointing oil *x* and anointed the tabernacle and everything in it, and so consecrated them. 11 He sprinkled some of the oil on the altar seven times, anointing the altar and all its utensils and the basin with its stand, to consecrate them. 12 He poured some of the anointing oil on Aaron's head and anointed him to consecrate him. *y* 13 Then he brought Aaron's sons forward, put tunics on them, tied sashes around them and put headbands on them, as the LORD commanded Moses.

14 He then presented the bull *z* for the sin offering, *a* and Aaron and his sons laid their hands on its head. 15 Moses slaughtered the bull and took some of the blood, and with his finger he put it on all the horns of the altar *b* to purify the altar. *c* He poured out the rest of the blood at the base of the altar. So he consecrated it to make atonement for it. *d* 16 Moses also took all the fat around the inner parts, the covering of the liver, and both kidneys and their fat, and burned it on the altar. 17 But the bull with its hide and its flesh and its offal *e* he burned up outside the camp, *f* as the LORD commanded Moses.

7:38
q Lev 1:2

8:2
r Ex 30:23-25,30
s Ex 29:2-3

8:3
t Nu 8:9

8:6
u Ex 29:4

8:8
v Ex 28:30

8:9
w Ex 28:36

8:10
x ver 2

8:12
y Ex 30:30

8:14
z Lev 4:3
a Ps 66:15; Eze 43:19

8:15
b Lev 4:7
c Heb 9:22
d Eze 43:20

8:17
e Lev 4:11
f Lev 4:12

7:37 The ordination offering refers to the offering given at the ceremony when priests were inducted into office (8:22).

7:38 God gave his people many rituals and instructions to follow. All the rituals in Leviticus were meant to teach the people valuable lessons. But over time, the people became indifferent to the meanings of these rituals and they began to lose touch with God. When your church appears to be conducting dry, meaningless rituals, instead of criticizing or becoming discouraged, try rediscovering the original meaning and purpose behind each. Your worship will be revitalized.

8:1ff Why did Aaron and his sons need to be cleansed and set apart? Although all the men from the tribe of Levi were dedicated for service to God, only Aaron's descendants could be priests. They alone had the honor and responsibility of performing the sacrifices. These priests had to cleanse and dedicate themselves before they could help the people do the same.

The ceremony described in Leviticus 8 and 9 was their ordination ceremony. Aaron and his sons were washed with water (8:6), clothed with special garments (8:7–9), and anointed with oil (8:12). They placed their hands on a young bull as it was killed (8:14), and on two rams as they were killed (8:18, 19, 22). This showed that holiness came from God alone, not from the priestly role. Similarly, we are not spiritually cleansed because we have a religious position, reputation, or title. Spiritual cleansing comes only from God. No matter how high our position or how long we have held it, we must depend on God for spiritual vitality.

8:2, 3 Why were priests needed in Israel? In Exodus 19:6, the Israelites were instructed to be a kingdom of priests; ideally they would all be holy and relate to God. But from the time of Adam's fall, sin has separated humans and God, and people have needed

mediators to help them find forgiveness. At first, the patriarchs—heads of households like Abraham and Job—were priests of the house or clan and made sacrifices for the family. When the Israelites left Egypt, the descendants of Aaron, from the tribe of Levi, were chosen to serve as priests for the nation. The priests stood in the gap between God and people. They were the full-time spiritual leaders and overseers of offerings. The priestly system was a concession to people's inability, because of sin, to confront and relate to God individually and corporately. In Christ, this imperfect system was transformed. Jesus Christ himself is our High Priest. Now all believers can approach God through him.

8:8 What were the Urim and Thummim? Little is known about them, but they were probably precious stones or flat objects that God used to give guidance to his people. The high priest kept them in a pouch attached to his breastpiece. Some scholars think the Urim may have been the *no* answer and the Thummim the *yes* answer. After a time of prayer for guidance, the priest would shake one of the stones out of the pouch, and God would cause the proper one to fall out. Another view is that the Urim and Thummim were small flat objects, each with a *yes* side and a *no* side. The priest spilled both from his pouch. If both landed on the *yes* sides, God's answer was positive. Two *no* sides were negative. A *yes* and a *no* meant no reply. God had a specific purpose for using this method of guidance—he was teaching a nation the principles of following him. Our situation is not the same, however, so we must not invent ways like this for God to guide us.

8:12 What was the significance of anointing Aaron as high priest? The high priest had special duties that no other priest had. He alone could enter the Most Holy Place in the tabernacle on the

18He then presented the ram for the burnt offering, and Aaron and his sons laid their hands on its head. 19Then Moses slaughtered the ram and sprinkled the blood against the altar on all sides. 20He cut the ram into pieces and burned the head, the pieces and the fat. 21He washed the inner parts and the legs with water and burned the whole ram on the altar as a burnt offering, a pleasing aroma, an offering made to the Lord by fire, as the Lord commanded Moses.

22He then presented the other ram, the ram for the ordination, and Aaron and his sons laid their hands on its head. 23Moses slaughtered the ram and took some of its blood and put it on the lobe of Aaron's right ear, on the thumb of his right hand and on the big toe of his right foot. 24Moses also brought Aaron's sons forward and put some of the blood on the lobes of their right ears, on the thumbs of their right hands and on the big toes of their right feet. Then he sprinkled blood against the altar on all sides. 25He took the fat, the fat tail, all the fat around the inner parts, the covering of the liver, both kidneys and their fat and the right thigh. 26Then from the basket of bread made without yeast, which was before the Lord, he took a cake of bread, and one made with oil, and a wafer; he put these on the fat portions and on the right thigh. 27He put all these in the hands of Aaron and his sons and waved them before the Lord as a wave offering. 28Then Moses took them from their hands and burned them on the altar on top of the burnt offering as an ordination offering, a pleasing aroma, an offering made to the Lord by fire. 29He also took the breast—Moses' share of the ordination ram—and waved it before the Lord as a wave offering, as the Lord commanded Moses.

30Then Moses took some of the anointing oil and some of the blood from the altar and sprinkled them on Aaron and his garments and on his sons and their garments. So he consecrated Aaron and his garments and his sons and their garments.

31Moses then said to Aaron and his sons, "Cook the meat at the entrance to the Tent of Meeting and eat it there with the bread from the basket of ordination offerings, as I commanded, saying,a 'Aaron and his sons are to eat it.' 32Then burn up the rest of the meat and the bread. 33Do not leave the entrance to the Tent of Meeting for seven days, until the days of your ordination are completed, for your ordination will last seven days. 34What has been done today was commanded by the Lordg to make atonement for you. 35You must stay at the entrance to the Tent of Meeting day and night for seven days and do what the Lord requires,h so you will not die; for that is what I have been commanded." 36So Aaron and his sons did everything the Lord commanded through Moses.

The Priests Begin Their Ministry

9 On the eighth dayi Moses summoned Aaron and his sons and the elders of Israel. 2He said to Aaron, "Take a bull calf for your sin offering and a ram for your burnt offering, both without defect, and present them before the Lord. 3Then say to the Israelites: 'Take a male goat for a sin offering, a calf and a lamb—both a year old and without defect—for a burnt offering, 4and an oxb and a ram for a fellowship offeringc to sacrifice before the Lord, together with a grain offering mixed with oil. For today the Lord will appear to you.j'"

5They took the things Moses commanded to the front of the Tent of Meeting, and the entire assembly came near and stood before the Lord. 6Then Moses said, "This is what the Lord has commanded you to do, so that the glory of the Lordk may appear to you."

7Moses said to Aaron, "Come to the altar and sacrifice your sin offering and your burnt offering and make atonement for yourself and the people; sacrifice the offering that is for the people and make atonement for them, as the Lord has commanded.l"

8So Aaron came to the altar and slaughtered the calf as a sin offeringm for himself. 9His sons brought the blood to him, and he dipped his finger into the blood and put it on the horns of the altar; the rest of the blood he poured out at the base of the altar. 10On the altar he burned the fat, the kidneys and the covering of the liver from the sin offering, as the Lord commanded Moses; 11the flesh and the hiden he burned up outside the camp.o

8:34
g Heb 7:16

8:35
h Nu 3:7; Dt 11:1; 1Ki 2:3

9:1
i Eze 43:27

9:4
j Ex 29:43

9:6
k ver 23

9:7
l Heb 5:1,3; 7:27

9:8
m Lev 4:1-12

9:11
n Lev 4:11
o Lev 8:17

a31 Or *I was commanded:*   b4 The Hebrew word can include both male and female; also in verses 18 and 19.
c4 Traditionally *peace offering*; also in verses 18 and 22

annual Day of Atonement to atone for the sins of the nation. Therefore he was in charge of all the other priests. The high priest was a picture of Jesus Christ, who is our High Priest (Hebrews 7:26–28).
8:36 Aaron and his sons did "everything the Lord commanded." Considering the many detailed lists of Leviticus, that was a remarkable feat. They knew what God wanted, how he wanted it

done, and with what attitude it was to be carried out. This can serve as a model for how carefully we ought to obey God. God wants us to be thoroughly holy people, not a rough approximation of the way his followers should be.

¹²Then he slaughtered the burnt offering. His sons handed him the blood, and he sprinkled it against the altar on all sides. ¹³They handed him the burnt offering piece by piece, including the head, and he burned them on the altar. ¹⁴He washed the inner parts and the legs and burned them on top of the burnt offering on the altar.

¹⁵Aaron then brought the offering that was for the people. He took the goat for the people's sin offering and slaughtered it and offered it for a sin offering as he did with the first one.

¹⁶He brought the burnt offering and offered it in the prescribed way.ᵖ ¹⁷He also brought the grain offering, took a handful of it and burned it on the altar in addition to the morning's burnt offering.�q

¹⁸He slaughtered the ox and the ram as the fellowship offering for the people.ʳ His sons handed him the blood, and he sprinkled it against the altar on all sides. ¹⁹But the fat portions of the ox and the ram—the fat tail, the layer of fat, the kidneys and the covering of the liver—²⁰these they laid on the breasts, and then Aaron burned the fat on the altar. ²¹Aaron waved the breasts and the right thigh before the LORD as a wave offering,ˢ as Moses commanded.

²²Then Aaron lifted his hands toward the people and blessed them. ᵗ And having sacrificed the sin offering, the burnt offering and the fellowship offering, he stepped down.

²³Moses and Aaron then went into the Tent of Meeting. When they came out, they blessed the people; and the glory of the LORDᵘ appeared to all the people. ²⁴Fireᵛ came out from the presence of the LORD and consumed the burnt offering and the fat portions on the altar. And when all the people saw it, they shouted for joy and fell facedown. ʷ

The Death of Nadab and Abihu

10 Aaron's sons Nadab and Abihuˣ took their censers, put fire in themʸ and added incense; and they offered unauthorized fire before the LORD, contrary to his command. ²So fire came out from the presence of the LORD and consumed them, and they died before the LORD. ³Moses then said to Aaron, "This is what the LORD spoke of when he said:

> "'Among those who approach meᶻ
> I will show myself holy;ᵃ
> in the sight of all the people
> I will be honored.'"

Aaron remained silent.

⁴Moses summoned Mishael and Elzaphan,ᵇ sons of Aaron's uncle Uzziel, and said to them, "Come here; carry your cousins outside the camp, away from the front of the sanctuary." ⁵So they came and carried them, still in their tunics, outside the camp, as Moses ordered.

⁶Then Moses said to Aaron and his sons Eleazar and Ithamar, "Do not let your hair become unkempt,ᵃ ᶜ and do not tear your clothes, or you will die and the LORD will be angry with the whole community. ᵈ But your relatives, all the house of Israel, may mourn for those the LORD has destroyed by fire. ⁷Do not leave the entrance to the Tent of Meeting or you will die, because the LORD's anointing oilᵉ is on you." So they did as Moses said.

ᵃ6 Or *Do not uncover your heads*

9:16
ᵖLev 1:1-13
9:17
qLev 2:1-2
9:18
ʳLev 3:1-11
9:21
ˢLev 7:30-34
9:22
ᵗNu 6:23; Dt 21:5;
Lk 24:50
9:23
ᵘver 6
9:24
ᵛJdg 6:21; 2Ch 7:1
ʷ1Ki 18:39

10:1
ˣNu 3:2-4
ʸLev 16:12

10:3
ᶻEx 19:22
ᵃEx 30:29;
Lev 21:6; Eze 28:22

10:4
ᵇEx 6:22

10:6
ᶜLev 21:10
ᵈNu 16:22; Jos 7:1

10:7
ᵉLev 21:12

9:22, 23 In 9:6 Moses said to the people, "This is what the LORD has commanded you to do, so that the glory of the LORD may appear to you." Moses, Aaron, and the people then got to work and followed God's instructions. Soon after, the glory of the Lord appeared. Often we look for God's glorious acts without concern for following his instructions. Do you serve God in the daily routines of life, or do you wait for him to do a mighty act? If you depend on his glorious acts, you may find yourself sidestepping your everyday duty to obey.

9:24 As a display of his mighty power, God sent fire from the sky to consume Aaron's offering. The people fell to the ground in awe. Some people wonder if God really exists because they don't see his activity in the world. But God is at work in today's world just as he was in Moses' world. Where a large body of believers is active for him, God tends not to display his power in the form of mighty physical acts. Instead he works to change the world through the work of these believers. When you realize that, you will begin to see acts of love and faith that are just as supernatural.

10:1 What was the unauthorized fire that Nadab and Abihu

offered before the Lord? The fire on the altar of burnt offering was never to go out (6:12, 13), implying that it was holy. It is possible that Nadab and Abihu brought coals of fire to the altar from another source, making the sacrifice unholy. It has also been suggested that the two priests gave an offering at an unprescribed time. Whatever explanation is correct, the point is that Nadab and Abihu abused their office as priests in a flagrant act of disrespect to God, who had just reviewed with them precisely how they were to conduct worship. As leaders, they had special responsibility to obey God. In their position, they could easily lead many people astray. If God has commissioned you to lead or teach others, never take that role for granted or abuse it. Stay faithful to God and follow his instructions.

10:2 Aaron's sons were careless about following the laws for sacrifices. In response, God destroyed them with a blast of fire. Performing the sacrifices was an act of obedience. Doing them correctly showed respect for God. It is easy for us to grow careless about obeying God, to live our way instead of God's. But if one way were just as good as another, God would not have commanded us to live his way. He always has good reasons for

10:9
ʰEze 44:21;
Lk 1:15; 1Ti 3:3;
Tit 1:7

⁸Then the LORD said to Aaron, ⁹"You and your sons are not to drink wine or other fermented drink ʰ whenever you go into the Tent of Meeting, or you will die. This is a lasting ordinance for the generations to come. ¹⁰You must distinguish between the holy and the common, between the unclean and the clean, ¹¹and you must teach the Israelites all the decrees the LORD has given them through Moses."

10:12
ᵍLev 6:14-18

¹²Moses said to Aaron and his remaining sons, Eleazar and Ithamar, "Take the grain offering left over from the offerings made to the LORD by fire and eat it prepared without yeast beside the altar,ᵍ for it is most holy. ¹³Eat it in a holy place, because it is your share and your sons' share of the offerings made to the LORD by fire; for so I have been commanded. ¹⁴But you and your sons and your daughters may eat the breast that was waved and the thigh that was presented. Eat them in a ceremonially clean place; they have been given to you and your children as your share of the Israelites' fellowship offerings. ᵃ ¹⁵The thigh ʰ that was

10:15
ʰLev 7:34

presented and the breast that was waved must be brought with the fat portions of the offerings made by fire, to be waved before the LORD as a wave offering. This will be the regular share for you and your children, as the LORD has commanded."

ᵃ 14 Traditionally *peace offerings*

NADAB/ABIHU

Some brothers, like Cain and Abel or Jacob and Esau, get each other in trouble. Nadab and Abihu got in trouble together.

Although little is known of their early years, the Bible gives us an abundance of information about the environment in which they grew up. Born in Egypt, they were eyewitnesses of God's mighty acts of the exodus. They saw their father, Aaron, their uncle, Moses, and their aunt, Miriam, in action many times. They had firsthand knowledge of God's holiness as few men have ever had, and for a while at least, they followed God wholeheartedly (Leviticus 8:36). But at a crucial moment they chose to treat with indifference the clear instructions from God. The consequence of their sin was fiery, instant, and shocking to all.

We are in danger of making the same mistake as these brothers when we treat lightly the justice and holiness of God. We must draw near to God while realizing that there is a proper fear of God. Don't forget that the opportunity to know God personally is based on his gracious invitation to an always unworthy people, not a gift to be taken for granted. Do your thoughts about God include a humble recognition of his great holiness?

Strengths and accomplishments:	• Oldest sons of Aaron • Primary candidates to become high priest after their father • Involved with the original consecration of the tabernacle • Commended for doing "everything the LORD commanded" (Leviticus 8:36)
Weakness and mistake:	• Treated lightly God's direct commands
Lesson from their lives:	• Sin has deadly consequences
Vital statistics:	• Where: The Sinai peninsula • Occupation: Priests-in-training • Relatives: Father: Aaron. Uncle and Aunt: Moses and Miriam. Brothers: Eleazar and Ithamar.
Key verses:	"Aaron's sons Nadab and Abihu took their censers, put fire in them and added incense; and they offered unauthorized fire before the LORD, contrary to his command. So fire came out from the presence of the LORD and consumed them, and they died before the LORD" (Leviticus 10:1, 2).

The story of Nadab and Abihu is told in Leviticus 8—10. They are also mentioned in Exodus 24:1, 9; 28:1; Numbers 3:2–4; 26:60, 61.

---

his commands, and we always place ourselves in danger when we consciously or carelessly disobey them.

10:8–11 The priests were not to drink wine or other alcoholic beverages before going into the tabernacle. If their senses were dulled by alcohol, they might repeat Nadab and Abihu's sin and bring something unholy into the worship ceremony. In addition, drinking would disqualify them to teach the people God's requirements of self-discipline. Drunkenness was associated with pagan practices and the Jewish priests were supposed to be distinctively different.

10:10, 11 This passage (along with 19:1, 2) shows the focus of Leviticus. The Ten Commandments recorded in Exodus 20 were God's fundamental laws. Leviticus explained and supplemented those laws with many other guidelines and principles that helped the Israelites put them into practice. The purpose of God's laws was to teach people how to distinguish right from wrong, the sacred from the common, the clean from the unclean. The nation who lived by God's laws would obviously be set apart, dedicated to his service.

[16]When Moses inquired about the goat of the sin offering[i] and found that it had been burned up, he was angry with Eleazar and Ithamar, Aaron's remaining sons, and asked, [17]"Why didn't you eat the sin offering[j] in the sanctuary area? It is most holy; it was given to you to take away the guilt of the community by making atonement for them before the LORD. [18]Since its blood was not taken into the Holy Place,[k] you should have eaten the goat in the sanctuary area, as I commanded."

[19]Aaron replied to Moses, "Today they sacrificed their sin offering and their burnt offering[l] before the LORD, but such things as this have happened to me. Would the LORD have been pleased if I had eaten the sin offering today?" [20]When Moses heard this, he was satisfied.

3. Instructions for the people
Clean and Unclean Food

11 The LORD said to Moses and Aaron, [2]"Say to the Israelites: 'Of all the animals that live on land, these are the ones you may eat: [3]You may eat any animal that has a split hoof completely divided and that chews the cud.

[4]"'There are some that only chew the cud or only have a split hoof, but you must not eat them. The camel, though it chews the cud, does not have a split hoof; it is ceremonially unclean for you. [5]The coney,[a] though it chews the cud, does not have a split hoof; it is unclean for you. [6]The rabbit, though it chews the cud, does not have a split hoof; it is unclean for you. [7]And the pig,[m] though it has a split hoof completely divided, does not chew the cud; it is unclean for you. [8]You must not eat their meat or touch their carcasses; they are unclean for you.[n]

[9]"'Of all the creatures living in the water of the seas and the streams, you may eat any that have fins and scales. [10]But all creatures in the seas or streams that do not have fins and scales—whether among all the swarming things or among all the other living creatures in the water—you are to detest. [11]And since you are to detest them, you must not eat their meat and you must detest their carcasses. [12]Anything living in the water that does not have fins and scales is to be detestable to you.

[13]"'These are the birds you are to detest and not eat because they are detestable: the eagle, the vulture, the black vulture, [14]the red kite, any kind of black kite, [15]any kind of raven, [16]the horned owl, the screech owl, the gull, any kind of hawk, [17]the little owl, the cormorant, the great owl, [18]the white owl, the desert owl, the osprey, [19]the stork, any kind of heron, the hoopoe and the bat.[b]

[20]"'All flying insects that walk on all fours are to be detestable to you. [21]There are, however, some winged creatures that walk on all fours that you may eat: those that have jointed legs for hopping on the ground. [22]Of these you may eat any kind of locust,[o] katydid, cricket or grasshopper. [23]But all other winged creatures that have four legs you are to detest.

[24]"'You will make yourselves unclean by these; whoever touches their carcasses will be unclean till evening. [25]Whoever picks up one of their carcasses must wash his clothes, and he will be unclean till evening.

[26]"'Every animal that has a split hoof not completely divided or that does not chew the cud is unclean for you; whoever touches ⌊the carcass of⌋ any of them will be unclean. [27]Of

a 5 That is, the hyrax or rock badger   b 19 The precise identification of some of the birds, insects and animals in this chapter is uncertain.

10:16–20 The priest who offered the sin offering was supposed to eat a portion of the animal and then burn the rest (6:24–30). Moses was angry because Eleazar and Ithamar burned the sin offering, but did not eat any of it. Aaron explained to Moses that his two sons did not feel it appropriate to eat the sacrifice after their two brothers, Nadab and Abihu, had just been killed for sacrificing wrongly. Moses then understood that Eleazar and Ithamar were not trying to disobey God. They were simply afraid and upset over what had just happened to their brothers.

11:8 God had strictly forbidden eating the meat of certain "unclean" animals; to make sure, he forbade even touching them. He wanted the people to be totally separated from those things he had forbidden. So often we flirt with temptation, rationalizing that at least we are technically keeping the commandment not to commit the sin. But God wants us to separate ourselves completely from all sin and tempting situations. Perhaps this passage has made you aware of areas of your life where you have "technical" innocence

but in which you have actually been involved in sin. It's time to cross back over the line and stay there.

11:25 In order to worship, people need to be prepared. Some acts of disobedience, some natural acts (such as childbirth, menstruation, or sex), or some accidents (such as touching a dead or diseased body) would make people ceremonially unclean and thus forbidden to participate in worship. This did not imply that they had sinned or were rejected by God, but it insured that all worship was done decently and in order. This chapter describes many of the intentional or accidental occurrences that would disqualify people from worship until they were "cleansed" or straightened out. Similarly, we need to be [prepared] for worship. We cannot live any way we want during the week and then rush into God's presence on Sunday. We should prepare ourselves through repentance, correction of errors where possible, and thoughtful anticipation of what it will mean to be in God's presence with other believers.

10:16
[i]Lev 9:3
10:17
[j]Lev 6:24-30
10:18
[k]Lev 6:26,30
10:19
[l]Lev 9:12

11:7
[m]Isa 65:4
11:8
[n]Heb 9:10

11:22
[o]Mt 3:4; Mk 1:6

24 "When someone has a burn on his skin and a reddish-white or white spot appears in the raw flesh of the burn, 25 the priest is to examine the spot, and if the hair in it has turned white, and it appears to be more than skin deep, it is an infectious disease that has broken out in the burn. The priest shall pronounce him unclean; it is an infectious skin disease. 26 But if the priest examines it and there is no white hair in the spot and if it is not more than skin deep and has faded, then the priest is to put him in isolation for seven days. 27 On the seventh day the priest is to examine him,[i] and if it is spreading in the skin, the priest shall pronounce him unclean; it is an infectious skin disease. 28 If, however, the spot is unchanged and has not spread in the skin but has faded, it is a swelling from the burn, and the priest shall pronounce him clean; it is only a scar from the burn.

29 "If a man or woman has a sore on the head or on the chin, 30 the priest is to examine the sore, and if it appears to be more than skin deep and the hair in it is yellow and thin, the priest shall pronounce that person unclean; it is an itch, an infectious disease of the head or chin. 31 But if, when the priest examines this kind of sore, it does not seem to be more than skin deep and there is no black hair in it, then the priest is to put the infected person in isolation for seven days. 32 On the seventh day the priest is to examine the sore, and if the itch has not spread and there is no yellow hair in it and it does not appear to be more than skin deep, 33 he must be shaved except for the diseased area, and the priest is to keep him in isolation another seven days. 34 On the seventh day the priest is to examine the itch, and if it has not spread in the skin and appears to be no more than skin deep, the priest shall pronounce him clean. He must wash his clothes, and he will be clean. 35 But if the itch does spread in the skin after he is pronounced clean, 36 the priest is to examine him, and if the itch has spread in the skin, the priest does not need to look for yellow hair; the person is unclean.[j] 37 If, however, in his judgment it is unchanged and black hair has grown in it, the itch is healed. He is clean, and the priest shall pronounce him clean.

38 "When a man or woman has white spots on the skin, 39 the priest is to examine them, and if the spots are dull white, it is a harmless rash that has broken out on the skin; that person is clean.

40 "When a man has lost his hair and is bald,[k] he is clean. 41 If he has lost his hair from the front of his scalp and has a bald forehead, he is clean. 42 But if he has a reddish-white sore on his bald head or forehead, it is an infectious disease breaking out on his head or forehead. 43 The priest is to examine him, and if the swollen sore on his head or forehead is reddish-white like an infectious skin disease, 44 the man is diseased and is unclean. The priest shall pronounce him unclean because of the sore on his head.

45 "The person with such an infectious disease must wear torn clothes, let his hair be unkempt,[a] cover the lower part of his face[l] and cry out, 'Unclean! Unclean!'[m] 46 As long as he has the infection he remains unclean. He must live alone; he must live outside the camp.[n]

Regulations About Mildew

47 "If any clothing is contaminated with mildew—any woolen or linen clothing, 48 any woven or knitted material of linen or wool, any leather or anything made of leather— 49 and if the contamination in the clothing, or leather, or woven or knitted material, or any leather article, is greenish or reddish, it is a spreading mildew and must be shown to the priest. 50 The priest is to examine the mildew[o] and isolate the affected article for seven days. 51 On the seventh day he is to examine it, and if the mildew has spread in the clothing, or the woven or knitted material, or the leather, whatever its use, it is a destructive mildew; the article is unclean.[p] 52 He must burn up the clothing, or the woven or knitted material of wool or linen, or any leather article that has the contamination in it, because the mildew is destructive; the article must be burned up.

53 "But if, when the priest examines it, the mildew has not spread in the clothing, or the woven or knitted material, or the leather article, 54 he shall order that the contaminated article be washed. Then he is to isolate it for another seven days. 55 After the affected article has been washed, the priest is to examine it, and if the mildew has not changed its appearance, even though it has not spread, it is unclean. Burn it with fire, whether the mildew has affected

a 45 Or *clothes, uncover his head*

13:27
[i] ver 5

13:36
[j] ver 30

13:40
[k] 2Ki 2:23; Isa 15:2; Eze 29:18; Am 8:10

13:45
[l] Eze 24:17,22; Mic 3:7
[m] La 4:15

13:46
[n] Nu 5:1-4; 12:14; 2Ki 7:3; 15:5; Lk 17:12

13:50
[o] Eze 44:23

13:51
[p] Lev 14:44

13:45, 46 A person with an infectious skin disease had to perform this strange ritual to protect others from coming too near. Because the disease described in Leviticus was highly contagious, it was important that people stay away from those who had it.

one side or the other. ⁵⁶If, when the priest examines it, the mildew has faded after the article has been washed, he is to tear the contaminated part out of the clothing, or the leather, or the woven or knitted material. ⁵⁷But if it reappears in the clothing, or in the woven or knitted material, or in the leather article, it is spreading, and whatever has the mildew must be burned with fire. ⁵⁸The clothing, or the woven or knitted material, or any leather article that has been washed and is rid of the mildew, must be washed again, and it will be clean."

⁵⁹These are the regulations concerning contamination by mildew in woolen or linen clothing, woven or knitted material, or any leather article, for pronouncing them clean or unclean.

Cleansing From Infectious Skin Diseases

14 The LORD said to Moses, ²"These are the regulations for the diseased person at the time of his ceremonial cleansing, when he is brought to the priest: �q ³The priest is to go outside the camp and examine him. If the person has been healed of his infectious skin disease,ᵃ ⁴the priest shall order that two live clean birds and some cedar wood, scarlet yarn and hyssop be brought for the one to be cleansed. ʳ ⁵Then the priest shall order that one of the birds be killed over fresh water in a clay pot. ⁶He is then to take the live bird and dip it, together with the cedar wood, the scarlet yarn and the hyssop, into the blood of the bird that was killed over the fresh water. ⁷Seven times he shall sprinkleˢ the one to be cleansed of the infectious disease and pronounce him clean. Then he is to release the live bird in the open fields.

⁸"The person to be cleansed must wash his clothes,ᵗ shave off all his hair and bathe with water; then he will be ceremonially clean. After this he may come into the camp, but he must stay outside his tent for seven days. ⁹On the seventh day he must shave off all his hair; he must shave his head, his beard, his eyebrows and the rest of his hair. He must wash his clothes and bathe himself with water, and he will be clean.

¹⁰"On the eighth day he must bring two male lambs and one ewe lamb a year old, each without defect, along with three-tenths of an ephahᵇ of fine flour mixed with oil for a grain offering, and one logᶜ of oil. ¹¹The priest who pronounces him clean shall present both the one to be cleansed and his offerings before the LORD at the entrance to the Tent of Meeting.

¹²"Then the priest is to take one of the male lambs and offer it as a guilt offering,ᵘ along with the log of oil; he shall wave them before the LORD as a wave offering. ᵛ ¹³He is to slaughter the lamb in the holy placeʷ where the sin offering and the burnt offering are slaughtered. Like the sin offering, the guilt offering belongs to the priest;ˣ it is most holy. ¹⁴The priest is to take some of the blood of the guilt offering and put it on the lobe of the right ear of the one to be cleansed, on the thumb of his right hand and on the big toe of his right foot.ʸ ¹⁵The priest shall then take some of the log of oil, pour it in the palm of his own left hand, ¹⁶dip his right forefinger into the oil in his palm, and with his finger sprinkle some of it before the LORD seven times. ¹⁷The priest is to put some of the oil remaining in his palm on the lobe of the right ear of the one to be cleansed, on the thumb of his right hand and on the big toe of his right foot, on top of the blood of the guilt offering. ¹⁸The rest of the oil in his palm the priest shall put on the head of the one to be cleansed and make atonement for him before the LORD.

¹⁹"Then the priest is to sacrifice the sin offering and make atonement for the one to be cleansed from his uncleanness. After that, the priest shall slaughter the burnt offering ²⁰and offer it on the altar, together with the grain offering, and make atonement for him, and he will be clean.

²¹"If, however, he is poorᶻ and cannot afford these, he must take one male lamb as a guilt offering to be waved to make atonement for him, together with a tenth of an ephahᵈ of fine flour mixed with oil for a grain offering, a log of oil, ²²and two doves or two young pigeons, which he can afford, one for a sin offering and the other for a burnt offering.

²³"On the eighth day he must bring them for his cleansing to the priest at the entrance to the Tent of Meeting, before the LORD. ᵃ ²⁴The priest is to take the lamb for the guilt offering, together with the log of oil,ᵇ and wave them before the LORD as a wave offering. ᶜ ²⁵He shall slaughter the lamb for the guilt offering and take some of its blood and put it on the lobe of the right ear of the one to be cleansed, on the thumb of his right hand and on the big toe of his right foot. ᵈ ²⁶The priest is to pour some of the oil into the palm of his own left hand, ²⁷and with his right forefinger sprinkle some of the oil from his palm seven times before the LORD. ²⁸Some of the oil in his palm he is to put on the same places he put the blood of the guilt offering—on the lobe of the right ear of the one to be cleansed, on the thumb of his right

14:2
�q Mt 8:2-4;
Mk 1:40-44;
Lk 5:12-14; 17:14
14:4
ʳ Nu 19:6

14:7
ˢ 2Ki 5:10,14
14:8
ᵗ Lev 11:25; 13:6

14:12
ᵘ Lev 5:18; 6:6-7
ᵛ Ex 29:24
14:13
ʷ Ex 29:11
ˣ Lev 6:24-30; 7:7
14:14
ʸ Ex 29:20; Lev 8:23

14:21
ᶻ Lev 5:7; 12:8

14:23
ᵃ ver 10,11
14:24
ᵇ ver 10
ᶜ ver 12
14:25
ᵈ ver 14

ᵃ3 Traditionally *leprosy*; the Hebrew word was used for various diseases affecting the skin—not necessarily leprosy; also elsewhere in this chapter.　ᵇ10 That is, probably about 6 quarts (about 6.5 liters)　ᶜ10 That is, probably about 2/3 pint (about 0.3 liter); also in verses 12, 15, 21 and 24　ᵈ21 That is, probably about 2 quarts (about 2 liters) hand and on the big toe of his right foot. ²⁹The rest of the oil in his palm the priest shall put on the head of the one to be cleansed, to make atonement for him before the LORD. ³⁰Then he shall sacrifice the doves or the young pigeons, which the person can afford, ³¹one*a* as a sin offering and the other as a burnt offering, *e* together with the grain offering. In this way the priest will make atonement before the LORD on behalf of the one to be cleansed."

³²These are the regulations for anyone who has an infectious skin disease and who cannot afford the regular offerings for his cleansing.

Cleansing From Mildew

³³The LORD said to Moses and Aaron, ³⁴"When you enter the land of Canaan, which I am giving you as your possession, *f* and I put a spreading mildew in a house in that land, ³⁵the owner of the house must go and tell the priest, 'I have seen something that looks like mildew in my house.' ³⁶The priest is to order the house to be emptied before he goes in to examine the mildew, so that nothing in the house will be pronounced unclean. After this the priest is to go in and inspect the house. ³⁷He is to examine the mildew on the walls, and if it has greenish or reddish depressions that appear to be deeper than the surface of the wall, ³⁸the priest shall go out the doorway of the house and close it up for seven days. ³⁹On the seventh day the priest shall return to inspect the house. If the mildew has spread on the walls, ⁴⁰he is to order that the contaminated stones be torn out and thrown into an unclean place outside the town. ⁴¹He must have all the inside walls of the house scraped and the material that is scraped off dumped into an unclean place outside the town. ⁴²Then they are to take other stones to replace these and take new clay and plaster the house.

⁴³"If the mildew reappears in the house after the stones have been torn out and the house scraped and plastered, ⁴⁴the priest is to go and examine it and, if the mildew has spread in the house, it is a destructive mildew; the house is unclean. *g* ⁴⁵It must be torn down—its stones, timbers and all the plaster—and taken out of the town to an unclean place.

⁴⁶"Anyone who goes into the house while it is closed up will be unclean till evening. ⁴⁷Anyone who sleeps or eats in the house must wash his clothes.

⁴⁸"But if the priest comes to examine it and the mildew has not spread after the house has been plastered, he shall pronounce the house clean, because the mildew is gone. ⁴⁹To purify the house he is to take two birds and some cedar wood, scarlet yarn and hyssop. *h* ⁵⁰He shall kill one of the birds over fresh water in a clay pot. ⁵¹Then he is to take the cedar wood, the hyssop,*i* the scarlet yarn and the live bird, dip them into the blood of the dead bird and the fresh water, and sprinkle the house seven times. ⁵²He shall purify the house with the bird's blood, the fresh water, the live bird, the cedar wood, the hyssop and the scarlet yarn. ⁵³Then he is to release the live bird in the open fields outside the town. In this way he will make atonement for the house, and it will be clean.*j*"

⁵⁴These are the regulations for any infectious skin disease,*k* for an itch, ⁵⁵for mildew*l* in clothing or in a house, ⁵⁶and for a swelling, a rash or a bright spot,*m* ⁵⁷to determine when something is clean or unclean.

These are the regulations for infectious skin diseases and mildew.

a31 Septuagint and Syriac; Hebrew *³¹such as the person can afford, one*

**Marginal references:**
14:31 *e* Lev 5:7
14:34 *f* Ge 17:8; Nu 32:22; Dt 7:1; 32:49
14:44 *g* Lev 13:51
14:49 *h* ver 4
14:51 *i* Ps 51:7
14:53 *j* ver 20
14:54 *k* Lev 13:2,30
14:55 *l* Lev 13:47-52
14:56 *m* Lev 13:2

14:34, 35 This mildew was dry rot or mineral crystals affecting stone walls. These specific cleansing procedures designated for mildewed clothing and buildings were fully required by the law (vv. 44–57). Why was mildew so dangerous? This fungus could spread rapidly and promote disease. It was therefore important to check its spread as soon as possible. In extreme cases, if the fungus had done enough damage, the clothing was burned or the house destroyed.

14:54-57 God told the Israelites how to diagnose infectious skin diseases and mildew so they could avoid them or treat them. These laws were given for the people's health and protection. They helped the Israelites avoid diseases that were serious threats in that time and place. Although they wouldn't have understood the medical reasons for some of these laws, their obedience to them made them healthier. Many of God's laws must have seemed strange to the Israelites. His laws, however, helped them avoid not only physical contamination, but also moral and spiritual infection.

The Word of God still provides a pattern for physically, spiri-

tually, and morally healthy living. We may not always understand the wisdom of God's laws, but if we obey them, we will thrive. Does this mean we are to follow the Old Testament health and dietary restrictions? In general, the basic principles of health and cleanliness are still healthful practices, but it would be legalistic, if not wrong, to adhere to each specific restriction today. Some of these regulations were intended to mark the Israelites as different from the wicked people around them. Others were given to prevent God's people from becoming involved in pagan religious practices, one of the most serious problems of the day. Still others related to quarantines in a culture where exact medical diagnosis was impossible. Today, for example, physicians can diagnose the different forms of leprosy, and they know which ones are contagious. Treatment methods have greatly improved, and quarantine for leprosy is rarely necessary.

Discharges Causing Uncleanness

15 The LORD said to Moses and Aaron, [2]"Speak to the Israelites and say to them: 'When any man has a bodily discharge,[n] the discharge is unclean. [3]Whether it continues flowing from his body or is blocked, it will make him unclean. This is how his discharge will bring about uncleanness:

[4]"'Any bed the man with a discharge lies on will be unclean, and anything he sits on will be unclean. [5]Anyone who touches his bed must wash his clothes[o] and bathe with water, and he will be unclean till evening. [6]Whoever sits on anything that the man with a discharge sat on must wash his clothes and bathe with water, and he will be unclean till evening.

[7]"'Whoever touches the man who has a discharge must wash his clothes and bathe with water, and he will be unclean till evening.

[8]"'If the man with the discharge spits on someone who is clean, that person must wash his clothes and bathe with water, and he will be unclean till evening.

[9]"'Everything the man sits on when riding will be unclean, [10]and whoever touches any of the things that were under him will be unclean till evening; whoever picks up those things must wash his clothes and bathe with water, and he will be unclean till evening.

[11]"'Anyone the man with a discharge touches without rinsing his hands with water must wash his clothes and bathe with water, and he will be unclean till evening.

[12]"'A clay pot[p] that the man touches must be broken, and any wooden article[q] is to be rinsed with water.

[13]"'When a man is cleansed from his discharge, he is to count off seven days[r] for his ceremonial cleansing; he must wash his clothes and bathe himself with fresh water, and he will be clean. [14]On the eighth day he must take two doves or two young pigeons[s] and come before the LORD to the entrance to the Tent of Meeting and give them to the priest. [15]The priest is to sacrifice them, the one for a sin offering[t] and the other for a burnt offering.[u] In this way he will make atonement before the LORD for the man because of his discharge.[v]

[16]"'When a man has an emission of semen,[w] he must bathe his whole body with water, and he will be unclean till evening. [17]Any clothing or leather that has semen on it must be washed with water, and it will be unclean till evening. [18]When a man lies with a woman and there is an emission of semen,[x] both must bathe with water, and they will be unclean till evening.

[19]"'When a woman has her regular flow of blood, the impurity of her monthly period[y] will last seven days, and anyone who touches her will be unclean till evening.

[20]"'Anything she lies on during her period will be unclean, and anything she sits on will be unclean. [21]Whoever touches her bed must wash his clothes and bathe with water, and he will be unclean till evening. [22]Whoever touches anything she sits on must wash his clothes and bathe with water, and he will be unclean till evening. [23]Whether it is the bed or anything she was sitting on, when anyone touches it, he will be unclean till evening.

[24]"'If a man lies with her and her monthly flow[z] touches him, he will be unclean for seven days; any bed he lies on will be unclean.

[25]"'When a woman has a discharge of blood for many days at a time other than her monthly period[a] or has a discharge that continues beyond her period, she will be unclean as long as she has the discharge, just as in the days of her period. [26]Any bed she lies on while her discharge continues will be unclean, as is her bed during her monthly period, and anything she sits on will be unclean, as during her period. [27]Whoever touches them will be unclean; he must wash his clothes and bathe with water, and he will be unclean till evening.

[28]"'When she is cleansed from her discharge, she must count off seven days, and after that she will be ceremonially clean. [29]On the eighth day she must take two doves or two young pigeons and bring them to the priest at the entrance to the Tent of Meeting. [30]The priest is to sacrifice one for a sin offering and the other for a burnt offering. In this way he will make atonement for her before the LORD for the uncleanness of her discharge.

[31]"'You must keep the Israelites separate from things that make them unclean, so they will not die in their uncleanness for defiling my dwelling place,[a] [b] which is among them.'"

[a] 31 Or *my tabernacle*

15:2
[n]Lev 22:4; Nu 5:2; 2Sa 3:29; Mt 9:20

15:5
[o]Lev 11:25

15:12
[p]Lev 6:28
[q]Lev 11:32

15:13
[r]Lev 8:33

15:14
[s]Lev 14:22

15:15
[t]Lev 5:7
[u]Lev 14:31
[v]Lev 14:18,19

15:16
[w]Lev 22:4; Dt 23:10

15:18
[x]1Sa 21:4

15:19
[y]Lev 12:2

15:24
[z]Lev 20:18

15:25
[a]Mt 9:20; Mk 5:25; Lk 8:43

15:31
[b]Nu 19:13,20; Eze 5:11; 23:38

15:18 The verses in this section are not implying that sex is dirty or disgusting. God created sex for (1) the enjoyment of married couples, (2) the continuation of the race, and (3) the preservation of the covenant. Everything must be seen and done with a view toward God's love and ultimate authority. Sex is not separate from spirituality and God's care. God is concerned about our sexual habits. He designed us, including our sexuality, as wonderfully complex and unified creations. We tend to separate our physical and spiritual lives, but there is an inseparable intertwining. God must be Lord over our whole selves—including our private lives.

15:32
c ver 2

15:33
d ver 19,24,25

32 These are the regulations for a man with a discharge, for anyone made unclean by an emission of semen,*c* 33 for a woman in her monthly period, for a man or a woman with a discharge, and for a man who lies with a woman who is ceremonially unclean. *d*

4. Instructions for the altar
The Day of Atonement

16:1
e Lev 10:1

16:2
f Ex 30:10; Heb 9:7
g Ex 25:22

16 The LORD spoke to Moses after the death of the two sons of Aaron who died when they approached the LORD. *e* 2 The LORD said to Moses: "Tell your brother Aaron not to come whenever he chooses *f* into the Most Holy Place behind the curtain in front of the atonement cover on the ark, or else he will die, because I appear *g* in the cloud over the atonement cover.

16:4
h Ex 28:39
i Ex 28:42

16:5
j Lev 4:13-21
k 2Ch 29:23

3 "This is how Aaron is to enter the sanctuary area: with a young bull for a sin offering and a ram for a burnt offering. 4 He is to put on the sacred linen tunic, with linen undergarments next to his body; he is to tie the linen sash around him and put on the linen turban. *h* These are sacred garments; *i* so he must bathe himself with water before he puts them on. 5 From the Israelite community *j* he is to take two male goats *k* for a sin offering and a ram for a burnt offering.

16:6
l Lev 9:7; Heb 5:3;
7:27; 9:7,12

6 "Aaron is to offer the bull for his own sin offering to make atonement for himself and his household. *l* 7 Then he is to take the two goats and present them before the LORD at the entrance to the Tent of Meeting. 8 He is to cast lots for the two goats—one lot for the LORD and the other for the scapegoat.*a* 9 Aaron shall bring the goat whose lot falls to the LORD and sacrifice it for a sin offering. 10 But the goat chosen by lot as the scapegoat shall be presented alive before the LORD to be used for making atonement by sending it into the desert as a scapegoat.

16:12
m Lev 10:1
n Ex 30:34-38

16:14
o Heb 9:7,13,25
p Lev 4:6

11 "Aaron shall bring the bull for his own sin offering to make atonement for himself and his household, and he is to slaughter the bull for his own sin offering. 12 He is to take a censer full of burning coals *m* from the altar before the LORD and two handfuls of finely ground fragrant incense *n* and take them behind the curtain. 13 He is to put the incense on the fire before the LORD, and the smoke of the incense will conceal the atonement cover above the Testimony, so that he will not die. 14 He is to take some of the bull's blood *o* and with his finger sprinkle it on the front of the atonement cover; then he shall sprinkle some of it with his finger seven times before the atonement cover.*p*

16:15
q Heb 9:7,12

15 "He shall then slaughter the goat for the sin offering for the people *q* and take its blood behind the curtain and do with it as he did with the bull's blood: He shall sprinkle it on the

a 8 That is, the goat of removal; Hebrew *azazel*; also in verses 10 and 26

In what ways do you acknowledge your relationship with God in your sexuality?

15:32, 33 God is concerned about health. He upholds the dignity of the person, the dignity of the body, and the dignity of the sexual experience. His commands call the people to avoid unhealthy practices and promote healthy ones with practical instructions. Washing was a God-directed means to maintain physical health; acts of purification or cleansing were God-directed means to preserve spiritual dignity. Millennia before the rise of the AIDS epidemic, God's directions already preserved people from known and unknown dangers. This shows God's high regard for sex and sexuality. In our day, sex has been degraded by shocking media exposure. It has become public domain, not private celebration. We are called to have a high regard for sex, both in good health and in purity. Our deepest form of gratitude to God for the gift of sex is expressed in how we use the gift.

16:1ff The Day of Atonement was the greatest day of the year for Israel. The Hebrew word for *atone* means "to cover." Old Testament sacrifices could not actually remove sins, only cover them. On this day, the people confessed their sins as a nation, and the high priest went into the Most Holy Place to make atonement for them. Sacrifices were made and blood was shed so that the people's sins could be "covered" until Christ's sacrifice on the cross would give people the opportunity to have their sin removed forever.

16:1–25 Aaron had to spend hours preparing himself to meet God. But we can approach God anytime (Hebrews 4:16). What a privilege! We are offered easier access to God than the high priests of Old Testament times! Still, we must never forget that God is holy nor let this privilege cause us to approach God carelessly. The way to God has been opened to us by Christ. But easy access to God does not eliminate our need to prepare our hearts as we draw near in prayer.

16:5–28 This event with the two goats occurred on the Day of Atonement. The two goats represented the two ways God was dealing with the Israelites' sin: (1) he was forgiving their sin through the first goat, which was sacrificed, and (2) he was removing their guilt through the second goat, the scapegoat that was sent into the desert. The same ritual had to be repeated every year. Jesus Christ's death replaced this system once and for all. We can have our sins forgiven and guilt removed by placing our trust in Christ (Hebrews 10:1–18).

16:12 A censer was a dish or shallow bowl that hung by a chain or was carried with tongs. Inside the censer were placed incense (a combination of sweet-smelling spices) and burning coals from the altar. On the Day of Atonement, the high priest entered the Most Holy Place carrying a smoking censer. The smoke shielded him from the ark of the covenant and the presence of God—otherwise he would die. Incense may also have had a very practical purpose. The sweet smell drew the people's attention to the morning and evening sacrifices and helped cover the sometimes foul smell.

atonement cover and in front of it. [16]In this way he will make atonement[r] for the Most Holy Place because of the uncleanness and rebellion of the Israelites, whatever their sins have been. He is to do the same for the Tent of Meeting, which is among them in the midst of their uncleanness. [17]No one is to be in the Tent of Meeting from the time Aaron goes in to make atonement in the Most Holy Place until he comes out, having made atonement for himself, his household and the whole community of Israel.

[18]"Then he shall come out to the altar that is before the LORD and make atonement for it. He shall take some of the bull's blood and some of the goat's blood and put it on all the horns of the altar. [19]He shall sprinkle some of the blood on it with his finger seven times to cleanse it and to consecrate it from the uncleanness of the Israelites.

[20]"When Aaron has finished making atonement for the Most Holy Place, the Tent of Meeting and the altar, he shall bring forward the live goat. [21]He is to lay both hands on the head of the live goat and confess over it all the wickedness and rebellion of the Israelites—all their sins—and put them on the goat's head. He shall send the goat away into the desert in the care of a man appointed for the task. [22]The goat will carry on itself all their sins to a solitary place; and the man shall release it in the desert.

[23]"Then Aaron is to go into the Tent of Meeting and take off the linen garments he put on before he entered the Most Holy Place, and he is to leave them there.[s] [24]He shall bathe himself with water in a holy place and put on his regular garments.[t] Then he shall come out and sacrifice the burnt offering for himself and the burnt offering for the people, to make atonement for himself and for the people. [25]He shall also burn the fat of the sin offering on the altar.

[26]"The man who releases the goat as a scapegoat must wash his clothes and bathe himself with water; afterward he may come into the camp. [27]The bull and the goat for the sin offerings, whose blood was brought into the Most Holy Place to make atonement, must be taken outside the camp;[u] their hides, flesh and offal are to be burned up. [28]The man who burns them must wash his clothes and bathe himself with water; afterward he may come into the camp.

[29]"This is to be a lasting ordinance for you: On the tenth day of the seventh month you must deny yourselves[a][v] and not do any work—whether native-born or an alien living among you— [30]because on this day atonement will be made for you, to cleanse you. Then, before the LORD, you will be clean from all your sins. [31]It is a sabbath of rest, and you must deny yourselves; it is a lasting ordinance. [32]The priest who is anointed and ordained to succeed his father as high priest is to make atonement. He is to put on the sacred linen garments[w] [33]and make atonement for the Most Holy Place, for the Tent of Meeting and the altar, and for the priests and all the people of the community.

[34]"This is to be a lasting ordinance for you: Atonement is to be made once a year[x] for all the sins of the Israelites."

And it was done, as the LORD commanded Moses.

Eating Blood Forbidden

17 The LORD said to Moses, [2]"Speak to Aaron and his sons and to all the Israelites and say to them: 'This is what the LORD has commanded: [3]Any Israelite who sacrifices an ox,[b] a lamb or a goat in the camp or outside of it [4]instead of bringing it to the entrance to the Tent of Meeting to present it as an offering to the LORD in front of the tabernacle of the LORD[y]—that man shall be considered guilty of bloodshed; he has shed blood and must be cut off from his people. [5]This is so the Israelites will bring to the LORD the sacrifices they are now making in the open fields. They must bring them to the priest, that is, to the LORD, at the entrance to the Tent of Meeting and sacrifice them as fellowship offerings.[c] [6]The priest is to sprinkle the blood against the altar of the LORD at the entrance to the Tent of Meeting and

16:16
[r] Ex 29:36

16:23
[s] Eze 42:14; 44:19
16:24
[t] ver 3-5

16:27
[u] Heb 13:11

16:29
[v] Lev 23:27,32;
Nu 29:7; Isa 58:3

16:32
[w] ver 4

16:34
[x] Heb 9:7,25

17:4
[y] Dt 12:5-21

---

[a]29 Or *must fast*; also in verse 31   [b]3 The Hebrew word can include both male and female.   [c]5 Traditionally *peace offerings*

17:1ff Chapters 17—26 are sometimes called the "holiness code" because they focus on what it means to live a holy life. The central verse is 19:2, "Be holy because I, the LORD your God, am holy."

17:3–9 Why were the Israelites prohibited from sacrificing outside the tabernacle area? God had established specific times and places for sacrifices, and each occasion was permeated with

symbolism. If people sacrificed on their own, they might easily add to or subtract from God's laws to fit their own lifestyles. Many pagan religions allowed every individual priest to set his own rules; God's command helped the Israelites resist the temptation to follow the pagan pattern. When the Israelites slipped into idolatry, it was because "everyone did as he saw fit" (Judges 17:6).

17:6
zNu 18:17
17:7
a2Ch 11:15
bEx 32:8; 34:15;
Dt 32:17;
1Co 10:20

17:10
cDt 12:16,23
17:11
dHeb 9:22

17:13
eDt 12:16
17:14
fver 11

17:15
gEx 22:31

burn the fat as an aroma pleasing to the LORD. z 7 They must no longer offer any of their sacrifices to the goat idolsa a to whom they prostitute themselves. b This is to be a lasting ordinance for them and for the generations to come.'

8 "Say to them: 'Any Israelite or any alien living among them who offers a burnt offering or sacrifice 9 and does not bring it to the entrance to the Tent of Meeting to sacrifice it to the LORD—that man must be cut off from his people.

10 "'Any Israelite or any alien living among them who eats any blood—I will set my face against that person who eats blood c and will cut him off from his people. 11 For the life of a creature is in the blood, and I have given it to you to make atonement for yourselves on the altar; it is the blood that makes atonement for one's life. d 12 Therefore I say to the Israelites, "None of you may eat blood, nor may an alien living among you eat blood."

13 "'Any Israelite or any alien living among you who hunts any animal or bird that may be eaten must drain out the blood and cover it with earth, e 14 because the life of every creature is its blood. That is why I have said to the Israelites, "You must not eat the blood of any creature, because the life of every creature is its blood; anyone who eats it must be cut off." f

15 "'Anyone, whether native-born or alien, who eats anything found dead or torn by wild animals g must wash his clothes and bathe with water, and he will be ceremonially unclean till evening; then he will be clean. 16 But if he does not wash his clothes and bathe himself, he will be held responsible.'"

B. LIVING A HOLY LIFE (18:1—27:34)

After the sacrificial system for forgiving sins was in place, the people were instructed on how to live as forgiven people. Applying these standards to our lives helps us grow in obedience and live a life pleasing to God.

a 7 Or demons

OLD/NEW SYSTEMS OF SACRIFICE	Old System of Sacrifice	New System of Sacrifice
	Was temporary (Hebrews 8:13)	Is permanent (Hebrews 7:21)
	Aaron first high priest (Leviticus 16:32)	Jesus only High Priest (Hebrews 4:14)
	From tribe of Levi (Hebrews 7:5)	From tribe of Judah (Hebrews 7:14)
	Ministered on earth (Hebrews 8:4)	Ministers in heaven (Hebrews 8:1, 2)
	Used blood of animals (Leviticus 16:15)	Uses blood of Christ (Hebrews 10:4–12)
	Required many sacrifices (Hebrews 10:1–3)	Requires one sacrifice (Hebrews 9:28)
	Needed perfect animals (Leviticus 22:19)	Needs a perfect life (Hebrews 5:9)
	Required careful approach to tabernacle (Leviticus 16:2)	Encourages confident approach to throne (Hebrews 4:16)
	Looked forward to new system (Hebrews 10:1)	Sets aside old system (Hebrews 10:9)

17:7 The goat idols (also called demons) were objects of worship and sacrifice in ancient times, particularly in Egypt from which they had recently escaped. God did not want the people to make this kind of sacrifice in the desert or in the promised land where they were heading.

17:11–14 How does blood make atonement for sin? When offered with the right attitude, the sacrifice and the blood shed from it made forgiveness of sin possible. On the one hand, blood represented the sinner's life, infected by his sin and headed for death. On the other hand, the blood represented the innocent life of the animal that was sacrificed in place of the guilty person making the offering. The death of the animal (of which the blood was proof) fulfilled the penalty of death. God therefore granted forgiveness to the sinner. It is God who forgives based on the faith of the person doing the sacrificing.

17:14 Why was eating or drinking blood prohibited? The prohibition against eating blood can be traced all the way back to Noah (Genesis 9:4). God prohibited eating or drinking blood for several reasons. (1) To discourage pagan practices. Israel was to be separate and distinct from the foreign nations around them.

Eating blood was a common pagan practice. It was often done in hopes of gaining the characteristics of the slain animal (strength, speed, etc.). God's people were to rely on him, not on ingested blood, for their strength. (2) To preserve the symbolism of the sacrifice. Blood symbolized the life of the animal that was sacrificed in the sinner's place. To drink it would change the symbolism of the sacrificial penalty and destroy the evidence of the sacrifice. (3) To protect the people from infection because many deadly diseases are transmitted through the blood. The Jews took this prohibition seriously, and that is why Jesus' hearers were so upset when Jesus told them to drink his blood (John 6:53–56). However, Jesus, as God himself and the last sacrifice ever needed for sins, was asking believers to identify with him completely. He wants us to take his life into us, and he wants to participate in our lives as well.

1. Standards for the people
Unlawful Sexual Relations

18 The LORD said to Moses, 2"Speak to the Israelites and say to them: 'I am the LORD your God. *h* 3You must not do as they do in Egypt, where you used to live, and you must not do as they do in the land of Canaan, where I am bringing you. Do not follow their practices. 4You must obey my laws and be careful to follow my decrees. I am the LORD your God. 5Keep my decrees and laws, for the man who obeys them will live by them.*i* I am the LORD.

6"'No one is to approach any close relative to have sexual relations. I am the LORD.

7"'Do not dishonor your father*j* by having sexual relations with your mother. She is your mother; do not have relations with her.

8"'Do not have sexual relations with your father's wife; that would dishonor your father.

9"'Do not have sexual relations with your sister, *k* either your father's daughter or your mother's daughter, whether she was born in the same home or elsewhere.

10"'Do not have sexual relations with your son's daughter or your daughter's daughter; that would dishonor you.

11"'Do not have sexual relations with the daughter of your father's wife, born to your father; she is your sister.

12"'Do not have sexual relations with your father's sister;*l* she is your father's close relative.

13"'Do not have sexual relations with your mother's sister, because she is your mother's close relative.

14"'Do not dishonor your father's brother by approaching his wife to have sexual relations; she is your aunt. *m*

15"'Do not have sexual relations with your daughter-in-law. She is your son's wife; do not have relations with her.

16"'Do not have sexual relations with your brother's wife; that would dishonor your brother.

17"'Do not have sexual relations with both a woman and her daughter. *n* Do not have sexual relations with either her son's daughter or her daughter's daughter; they are her close relatives. That is wickedness.

18"'Do not take your wife's sister as a rival wife and have sexual relations with her while your wife is living.

19"'Do not approach a woman to have sexual relations during the uncleanness of her monthly period. *o*

20"'Do not have sexual relations with your neighbor's wife*p* and defile yourself with her.

21"'Do not give any of your children to be sacrificed*a* to Molech,*q* for you must not profane the name of your God. *r* I am the LORD.

22"'Do not lie with a man as one lies with a woman;*s* that is detestable.

23"'Do not have sexual relations with an animal and defile yourself with it. A woman must not present herself to an animal to have sexual relations with it; that is a perversion. *t*

24"'Do not defile yourselves in any of these ways, because this is how the nations that I am going to drive out before you became defiled. 25Even the land was defiled; so I punished it for its sin, and the land vomited out its inhabitants. 26But you must keep my decrees and my laws. The native-born and the aliens living among you must not do any of these detestable things, 27for all these things were done by the people who lived in the land before you, and the land became defiled. 28And if you defile the land, it will vomit you out as it vomited out the nations that were before you.

*a*21 Or *to be passed through* ⌊*the fire*⌋

18:2
h Ex 6:7

18:5
i Eze 20:11;
Ro 10:5*; Gal 3:12*

18:7
j Lev 20:11

18:9
k Lev 20:17

18:12
l Lev 20:19

18:14
m Lev 20:20

18:17
n Lev 20:14

18:19
o Lev 15:24; 20:18

18:20
p Ex 20:14;
Lev 20:10;
Mt 5:27,28;
1Co 6:9; Heb 13:4

18:21
q Lev 20:2-5
r Lev 19:12

18:22
s Lev 20:13

18:23
t Ex 22:19

18:3 The Israelites moved from one idol-infested country (Egypt) to another (Canaan). They also had contact with other cultures (Moab). As God helped them form a new culture, he warned them to leave all aspects of their pagan background and surroundings behind. He also warned them how easy it would be to slip into the pagan culture of Canaan, where they were going. Canaan's society and religions appealed to worldly desires, especially sexual immorality and drunkenness. The Israelites were to keep themselves pure and set apart for God. God did not want his people absorbed into the surrounding culture and environment. Society may pressure us to conform to its way of life and thought, but yielding to that pressure will (1) create confusion as to which side we should

be on and (2) eliminate our effectiveness in serving God. Follow God by obeying his Word, and don't let the culture around you mold your thoughts and actions.

18:6-18 Marrying relatives was prohibited by God for physical, social, and moral reasons. Children born to near relatives may experience serious health problems. Without these specific laws, sexual promiscuity would have been more likely, first in families, then outside. Improper sexual relations destroy family life.

18:6-27 Several abominations, or wicked actions, are listed here: (1) having sexual relations with close relatives, (2) committing adultery, (3) offering children as sacrifices, (4) having homosexual relations, and (5) having sexual relations with animals.

18:30
u Dt 11:1

29"'Everyone who does any of these detestable things—such persons must be cut off from their people. 30 Keep my requirements *u* and do not follow any of the detestable customs that were practiced before you came and do not defile yourselves with them. I am the LORD your God.'"

Various Laws

19 The LORD said to Moses, 2 "Speak to the entire assembly of Israel and say to them: 'Be holy because I, the LORD your God, am holy.

19:3
v Ex 20:12

3 "'Each of you must respect his mother and father, *v* and you must observe my Sabbaths. I am the LORD your God.

19:4
w Ex 20:4,23

4 "'Do not turn to idols or make gods of cast metal for yourselves. *w* I am the LORD your God.

5 "'When you sacrifice a fellowship offering *a* to the LORD, sacrifice it in such a way that it will be accepted on your behalf. 6 It shall be eaten on the day you sacrifice it or on the next day; anything left over until the third day must be burned up. 7 If any of it is eaten on the third day, it is impure and will not be accepted. 8 Whoever eats it will be held responsible because he has desecrated what is holy to the LORD; that person must be cut off from his people.

19:9
x Dt 24:19-22

9 "'When you reap the harvest of your land, do not reap to the very edges of your field or gather the gleanings of your harvest. *x* 10 Do not go over your vineyard a second time or pick up the grapes that have fallen. Leave them for the poor and the alien. I am the LORD your God.

19:11
y Ex 20:15
z Eph 4:25

11 "'Do not steal. *y*

"'Do not lie. *z*

"'Do not deceive one another.

19:12
a Ex 20:7; Mt 5:33

12 "'Do not swear falsely by my name *a* and so profane the name of your God. I am the LORD.

13 "'Do not defraud your neighbor or rob him.

"'Do not hold back the wages of a hired man overnight.

19:14
b Dt 27:18

14 "'Do not curse the deaf or put a stumbling block in front of the blind, *b* but fear your God. I am the LORD.

15 "'Do not pervert justice; do not show partiality to the poor or favoritism to the great, but judge your neighbor fairly.

16 "'Do not go about spreading slander among your people.

"'Do not do anything that endangers your neighbor's life. I am the LORD.

19:17
c 1Jn 2:9; 3:15
d Mt 18:15; Lk 17:3

17 "'Do not hate your brother in your heart. *c* Rebuke your neighbor frankly *d* so you will not share in his guilt.

19:18
e Ro 12:19
f Ps 103:9
g Mt 5:43*; 19:16*;
22:39*; Ro 13:9*

18 "'Do not seek revenge *e* or bear a grudge *f* against one of your people, but love your neighbor as yourself. *g* I am the LORD.

19 "'Keep my decrees.

"'Do not mate different kinds of animals.

19:19
h Dt 22:9
i Dt 22:11

"'Do not plant your field with two kinds of seed. *h*

"'Do not wear clothing woven of two kinds of material. *i*

20 "'If a man sleeps with a woman who is a slave girl promised to another man but who has not been ransomed or given her freedom, there must be due punishment. Yet they are not to be put to death, because she had not been freed. 21 The man, however, must bring a ram to the entrance to the Tent of Meeting for a guilt offering to the LORD. 22 With the ram of the

a 5 Traditionally *peace offering*

These practices were common in pagan religions and cultures, and it is easy to see why God dealt harshly with those who began to follow them. Such practices lead to disease, deformity, and death. They disrupt family life and society and reveal a low regard for the value of oneself and of others. Society today takes some of these practices lightly, even trying to make them acceptable. But they are still sins in God's eyes. If you consider them acceptable, you are not judging by God's standards.

19:9, 10 This law was a protection for the poor and the alien (foreigner) and a reminder that God owned the land; the people were only caretakers. Laws such as this showed God's generosity and liberality. As people of God, the Israelites were to reflect his nature and characteristics in their attitudes and actions. Ruth and Naomi were two people who benefited from this merciful law (Ruth 2:2).

19:9, 10 God instructed the Hebrews to provide for those in need. He required that the people leave the edges of their fields unharvested, providing food for travelers and the poor. It is easy to ignore the poor or forget about those who have less than we do. But God desires generosity. In what ways can you leave the "edges of your field" for those in need?

19:10–35 "Do not . . ." Some people think the Bible is nothing but a book of don'ts. But Jesus neatly summarized all these rules when he said to love God with all your heart, and your neighbor as yourself. He called these the greatest commandments (or rules) of all (Matthew 22:34–40). By carrying out Jesus' simple commands, we find ourselves following all of God's other laws as well.

guilt offering the priest is to make atonement for him before the LORD for the sin he has committed, and his sin will be forgiven.

23 "'When you enter the land and plant any kind of fruit tree, regard its fruit as forbidden.a For three years you are to consider it forbiddena; it must not be eaten. 24 In the fourth year all its fruit will be holy, an offering of praise to the LORD. 25 But in the fifth year you may eat its fruit. In this way your harvest will be increased. I am the LORD your God.

26 "'Do not eat any meat with the blood still in it.j

"'Do not practice divination or sorcery.k

27 "'Do not cut the hair at the sides of your head or clip off the edges of your beard. l

28 "'Do not cut your bodies for the dead or put tattoo marks on yourselves. I am the LORD.

29 "'Do not degrade your daughter by making her a prostitute,m or the land will turn to prostitution and be filled with wickedness.

30 "'Observe my Sabbaths and have reverence for my sanctuary. I am the LORD. n

31 "'Do not turn to mediums or seek out spiritists, for you will be defiled by them. I am the LORD your God.

32 "'Rise in the presence of the aged, show respect for the elderly and revere your God. I am the LORD.

33 "'When an alien lives with you in your land, do not mistreat him. 34 The alien living with you must be treated as one of your native-born. Love him as yourself, for you were aliens in Egypt. I am the LORD your God.

35 "'Do not use dishonest standards when measuring length, weight or quantity. 36 Use honest scales and honest weights, an honest ephahb and an honest hin.c I am the LORD your God, who brought you out of Egypt.

37 "'Keep all my decrees and all my laws and follow them. I am the LORD.'"

Punishments for Sin

20 The LORD said to Moses, 2 "Say to the Israelites: 'Any Israelite or any alien living in Israel who givesd any of his children to Molech must be put to death. The people of the community are to stone him. 3 I will set my face against that man and I will cut him off from his people; for by giving his children to Molech, he has defiled my sanctuary and profaned my holy name.o 4 If the people of the community close their eyes when that man gives one of his children to Molech and they fail to put him to death, 5 I will set my face against that man and his family and will cut off from their people both him and all who follow him in prostituting themselves to Molech.

6 "'I will set my face against the person who turns to mediums and spiritists to prostitute himself by following them, and I will cut him off from his people.p

7 "'Consecrate yourselves and be holy, because I am the LORD your God. 8 Keep my decrees and follow them. I am the LORD, who makes you holy.e q

9 "'If anyone curses his father or mother,r he must be put to death.s He has cursed his father or his mother, and his blood will be on his own head.

a23 Hebrew uncircumcised   b36 An ephah was a dry measure.   c36 A hin was a liquid measure.   d2 Or sacrifices; also in verses 3 and 4   e8 Or who sanctifies you; or who sets you apart as holy

19:26
j Lev 17:10
k Dt 18:10

19:27
l Lev 21:5

19:29
m Dt 23:18

19:30
n Lev 26:2

20:3
o Lev 18:21

20:6
p Lev 19:31

20:8
q Ex 31:13

20:9
r Dt 27:16
s Ex 21:17

19:32 People often find it easy to dismiss the opinions of the elderly and avoid taking time to visit with them. But the fact that God commanded the Israelites to honor the elderly shows how seriously we should take the responsibility of respecting those older than we. Their wisdom gained from experience can save us from many pitfalls. How do you show respect and honor to your elders?

19:33, 34 How do you feel when you encounter foreigners (aliens), especially those who don't speak your language? Are you impatient? Do you think or act as if they should go back where they came from? Are you tempted to take advantage of them? God says to treat foreigners as you'd treat fellow countrymen, to love them as you love yourself. In reality, we are all foreigners in this world, because it is only our temporary home. View strangers, newcomers, and foreigners as opportunities to demonstrate God's love.

20:1–3 Sacrificing children to the gods was a common practice in ancient religions. The Ammonites, Israel's neighbors, made child sacrifice to Molech (their national god) a vital part of their religion. They saw this as the greatest gift they could offer to ward

off evil or appease angry gods. God made it clear that this practice was detestable and strictly forbidden. In Old Testament times as well as New, his character made human sacrifice unthinkable. (1) Unlike the pagan gods, he is a God of love, who does not need to be appeased (Exodus 34:6). (2) He is a God of life, who prohibits murder and encourages practices that lead to health and happiness (Deuteronomy 30:15, 16). (3) He is God of the helpless, who shows special concern for children (Psalm 72:4). (4) He is a God of unselfishness who, instead of demanding human sacrifices, sacrificed himself for us (Isaiah 53:4, 5).

20:6 Everyone is interested in what the future holds, and we often look to others for guidance. But God warned about looking to the occult for advice. Mediums and spiritists were outlawed because God was not the source of their information. At best, occult practitioners are fakes whose predictions cannot be trusted. At worst, they are in contact with evil spirits and are thus extremely dangerous. We don't need to look to the occult for information about the future. God has given us the Bible so that we may obtain all the information we need—and the Bible's teaching is trustworthy.

¹⁰"'If a man commits adultery with another man's wife—with the wife of his neighbor—both the adulterer and the adulteress must be put to death.

¹¹"'If a man sleeps with his father's wife, he has dishonored his father. Both the man and the woman must be put to death; their blood will be on their own heads.

¹²"'If a man sleeps with his daughter-in-law, both of them must be put to death. What they have done is a perversion; their blood will be on their own heads.

20:13
*t*Lev 18:22

¹³"'If a man lies with a man as one lies with a woman, both of them have done what is detestable. *t* They must be put to death; their blood will be on their own heads.

20:14
*u*Dt 27:23

¹⁴"'If a man marries both a woman and her mother, it is wicked. Both he and they must be burned in the fire, so that no wickedness will be among you. *u*

20:15
*v*Lev 18:23

¹⁵"'If a man has sexual relations with an animal, *v* he must be put to death, and you must kill the animal.

¹⁶"'If a woman approaches an animal to have sexual relations with it, kill both the woman and the animal. They must be put to death; their blood will be on their own heads.

20:17
*w*Lev 18:9

¹⁷"'If a man marries his sister *w*, the daughter of either his father or his mother, and they have sexual relations, it is a disgrace. They must be cut off before the eyes of their people. He has dishonored his sister and will be held responsible.

¹⁸"'If a man lies with a woman during her monthly period and has sexual relations with her, he has exposed the source of her flow, and she has also uncovered it. Both of them must be cut off from their people.

20:19
*x*Lev 18:12-13

¹⁹"'Do not have sexual relations with the sister of either your mother or your father, *x* for that would dishonor a close relative; both of you would be held responsible.

20:20
*y*Lev 18:14

²⁰"'If a man sleeps with his aunt, *y* he has dishonored his uncle. They will be held responsible; they will die childless.

20:21
*z*Lev 18:16

²¹"'If a man marries his brother's wife, *z* it is an act of impurity; he has dishonored his brother. They will be childless.

20:22
*a*Lev 18:25-28

20:23
*b*Lev 18:3

20:24
*c*Ex 33:16

²²"'Keep all my decrees and laws and follow them, so that the land *a* where I am bringing you to live may not vomit you out. ²³You must not live according to the customs of the nations *b* I am going to drive out before you. Because they did all these things, I abhorred them. ²⁴But I said to you, "You will possess their land; I will give it to you as an inheritance, a land flowing with milk and honey." I am the LORD your God, who has set you apart from the nations. *c*

20:25
*d*Lev 11:1-47;
Dt 14:3-21

²⁵"'You must therefore make a distinction between clean and unclean animals and between unclean and clean birds. *d* Do not defile yourselves by any animal or bird or anything that moves along the ground—those which I have set apart as unclean for you. ²⁶You are to be holy to me *a* because I, the LORD, am holy, and I have set you apart from the nations to be my own.

20:27
*e*Lev 19:31

²⁷"'A man or woman who is a medium or spiritist among you must be put to death. *e* You are to stone them; their blood will be on their own heads.'"

2. Rules for priests

21 The LORD said to Moses, "Speak to the priests, the sons of Aaron, and say to them: 'A priest must not make himself ceremonially unclean for any of his people who die, ²except for a close relative, such as his mother or father, his son or daughter, his brother,

a26 Or be my holy ones

20:10–21 This list of commands against sexual sins includes extremely harsh punishments. Why? God had no tolerance for such acts for the following reasons: (1) they shatter the mutual commitment of married partners; (2) they destroy the sanctity of the family; (3) they twist people's mental well-being; and (4) they spread disease. Sexual sin has always been widely available, but the glorification of sex between people who are not married to each other often hides deep tragedy and hurt behind the scenes. When society portrays sexual sins as attractive, it is easy to forget the dark side. God had good reasons for prohibiting sexual sins: He loves us and wants the very best for us.

20:10–21 The detestable acts listed here were very common in the pagan nations of Canaan; their religions were rampant with sex goddesses, temple prostitution, and other gross sins. The Canaanites' immoral religious practices reflected a decadent culture that tended to corrupt whoever came in contact with it. By contrast, God was building a nation to make a positive influence on the

world. He did not want the Israelites to adopt the Canaanites' practices and slide into debauchery. So he prepared the people for what they would face in the promised land by commanding them to steer clear of sexual sins. God still expects those who worship him to maintain sexual purity in their lives.

20:22, 23 God gave many rules to his people—but not without reason. He did not withhold good from them; he only prohibited those acts that would bring them to ruin. All of us understand God's physical laws of nature. For example, jumping off a ten-story building means death because of the law of gravity. But some of us don't understand how God's spiritual laws work. God forbids us to do certain things because he wants to keep us from self-destruction. Next time you are drawn to a forbidden physical or emotional pleasure, remind yourself that its consequences might be suffering and separation from the God who is trying to help you.

21:1, 2 To become ceremonially unclean for "any of his people who die" means touching a dead body.

³or an unmarried sister who is dependent on him since she has no husband—for her he may make himself unclean. ⁴He must not make himself unclean for people related to him by marriage,ᵃ and so defile himself.

⁵"'Priests must not shave their heads or shave off the edges of their beardsᶠ or cut their bodies.ᵍ ⁶They must be holy to their God and must not profane the name of their God.ʰ Because they present the offerings made to the LORD by fire,ⁱ the food of their God, they are to be holy.

⁷"'They must not marry women defiled by prostitution or divorced from their husbands,ʲ because priests are holy to their God. ⁸Regard them as holy,ᵏ because they offer up the food of your God. Consider them holy, because I the LORD am holy—I who make you holy.ᵇ

⁹"'If a priest's daughter defiles herself by becoming a prostitute, she disgraces her father; she must be burned in the fire.ˡ

¹⁰"'The high priest, the one among his brothers who has had the anointing oil poured on his head and who has been ordained to wear the priestly garments, must not let his hair become unkemptᶜ or tear his clothes.ᵐ ¹¹He must not enter a place where there is a dead body. He must not make himself unclean,ⁿ even for his father or mother, ¹²nor leave the sanctuary of his God or desecrate it, because he has been dedicated by the anointing oilᵒ of his God. I am the LORD.

¹³"'The woman he marries must be a virgin. ¹⁴He must not marry a widow, a divorced woman, or a woman defiled by prostitution, but only a virgin from his own people, ¹⁵so he will not defile his offspring among his people. I am the LORD, who makes him holy.ᵈ'"

¹⁶The LORD said to Moses, ¹⁷"Say to Aaron: 'For the generations to come none of your descendants who has a defect may come near to offer the food of his God. ¹⁸No man who has any defectᵖ may come near: no man who is blind or lame, disfigured or deformed; ¹⁹no man with a crippled foot or hand, ²⁰or who is hunchbacked or dwarfed, or who has any eye defect, or who has festering or running sores or damaged testicles.�q ²¹No descendant of Aaron the priest who has any defect is to come near to present the offerings made to the LORD by fire. He has a defect; he must not come near to offer the food of his God. ²²He may eat the most holy food of his God, as well as the holy food; ²³yet because of his defect, he must not go near the curtain or approach the altar, and so desecrate my sanctuary. I am the LORD, who makes them holy.ᵉ'"

²⁴So Moses told this to Aaron and his sons and to all the Israelites.

22 The LORD said to Moses, ²"Tell Aaron and his sons to treat with respect the sacred offerings the Israelites consecrate to me, so they will not profane my holy name. I am the LORD.

³"Say to them: 'For the generations to come, if any of your descendants is ceremonially unclean and yet comes near the sacred offerings that the Israelites consecrate to the LORD, that person must be cut off from my presence.ʳ I am the LORD.

⁴"'If a descendant of Aaron has an infectious skin diseaseᶠ or a bodily discharge,ˢ he may not eat the sacred offerings until he is cleansed. He will also be unclean if he touches something defiled by a corpse or by anyone who has an emission of semen, ⁵or if he touches any crawling thingᵗ that makes him unclean, or any person who makes him unclean, whatever the uncleanness may be. ⁶The one who touches any such thing will be unclean till evening. He must not eat any of the sacred offerings unless he has bathed himself with water. ⁷When the sun goes down, he will be clean, and after that he may eat the sacred offerings, for they are his food.ᵘ ⁸He must not eat anything found dead or torn by wild animals,ᵛ and so become unclean through it. I am the LORD.

21:5
ᶠEze 44:20
ᵍLev 19:28
21:6
ʰLev 18:21
ⁱLev 3:11
21:7
ʲver 13,14
21:8
ᵏver 6
21:9
ˡGe 38:24
21:10
ᵐLev 10:6
21:11
ⁿLev 19:28
21:12
ᵒLev 10:7

21:18
ᵖLev 22:19-25
21:20
qDt 23:1

22:3
ʳLev 7:20,21

22:4
ˢLev 14:1-32
22:5
ᵗLev 11:24-28,43

22:7
ᵘNu 18:11

22:8
ᵛEx 22:31;
Lev 17:15

ᵃ4 Or *unclean as a leader among his people*   ᵇ8 Or *who sanctify you;* or *who set you apart as holy*   ᶜ10 Or *not uncover his head*   ᵈ15 Or *who sanctifies him;* or *who sets him apart as holy*   ᵉ23 Or *who sanctifies them;* or *who sets them apart as holy*   ᶠ4 Traditionally *leprosy;* the Hebrew word was used for various diseases affecting the skin—not necessarily leprosy.

21:16–23 Was God unfairly discriminating against handicapped people when he said they were unqualified to offer sacrifices? Just as God demanded that no imperfect animals be used for sacrifice, he required that no handicapped priests offer sacrifices. This was not meant as an insult; rather, it had to do with the fact that the priest must match as closely as possible the perfect God he served. Of course, such perfection was not fully realized until Jesus Christ came. Because they were Levites, the handicapped priests were protected and supported with food from the sacrifices. They were not abandoned; they still had opportunity to perform many essential services within the tabernacle.

22:1–9 Why were there so many specific guidelines for the priests? The Israelites would have been quite familiar with priests from Egypt. Egyptian priests were mainly interested in politics. They viewed religion as a way to gain power. Thus the Israelites would have been suspicious of the establishment of a new priestly order. But God wanted his priests to serve him and the people. Their duties were religious—to help people draw near to God and worship him. They could not use their position to gain power because they were not allowed to own land or take money from anyone. All these guidelines reassured the people and helped the priests accomplish their purpose.

22:9
w ver 16; Ex 28:43

9 "'The priests are to keep my requirements so that they do not become guilty and die *w* for treating them with contempt. I am the LORD, who makes them holy. *a*

10 "'No one outside a priest's family may eat the sacred offering, nor may the guest of a priest or his hired worker eat it. 11But if a priest buys a slave with money, or if a slave is born in his household, that slave may eat his food. 12If a priest's daughter marries anyone other than a priest, she may not eat any of the sacred contributions. 13But if a priest's daughter becomes a widow or is divorced, yet has no children, and she returns to live in her father's house as in her youth, she may eat of her father's food. No unauthorized person, however, may eat any of it.

22:14
x Lev 5:15
22:16
y ver 9

14 "'If anyone eats a sacred offering by mistake, he must make restitution to the priest for the offering and add a fifth of the value *x* to it. 15The priests must not desecrate the sacred offerings the Israelites present to the LORD 16by allowing them to eat the sacred offerings and so bring upon them guilt requiring payment. *y* I am the LORD, who makes them holy.'"

Unacceptable Sacrifices

17The LORD said to Moses, 18"Speak to Aaron and his sons and to all the Israelites and say to them: 'If any of you—either an Israelite or an alien living in Israel—presents a gift for a burnt offering to the LORD, either to fulfill a vow or as a freewill offering, 19you must present a male without defect from the cattle, sheep or goats in order that it may be accepted on

22:20
z Dt 15:21;
Heb 9:14; 1Pe 1:19
22:21
a Lev 3:6

your behalf. 20Do not bring anything with a defect, *z* because it will not be accepted on your behalf. 21When anyone brings from the herd or flock a fellowship offering*b a* to the LORD to fulfill a special vow or as a freewill offering, it must be without defect or blemish to be acceptable. 22Do not offer to the LORD the blind, the injured or the maimed, or anything with warts or festering or running sores. Do not place any of these on the altar as an offering made to the LORD by fire. 23You may, however, present as a freewill offering an ox *c* or a sheep that is deformed or stunted, but it will not be accepted in fulfillment of a vow. 24You must not offer to the LORD an animal whose testicles are bruised, crushed, torn or cut. You must not do this in your own land, 25and you must not accept such animals from the hand of

22:25
b Lev 21:6

a foreigner and offer them as the food of your God. *b* They will not be accepted on your behalf, because they are deformed and have defects.'"

22:27
c Ex 22:30
22:28
d Dt 22:6,7
22:29
e Lev 7:12

26The LORD said to Moses, 27"When a calf, a lamb or a goat is born, it is to remain with its mother for seven days. *c* From the eighth day on, it will be acceptable as an offering made to the LORD by fire. 28Do not slaughter a cow or a sheep and its young on the same day. *d*

29"When you sacrifice a thank offering*e* to the LORD, sacrifice it in such a way that it will be accepted on your behalf. 30It must be eaten that same day; leave none of it till morning. I am the LORD.

22:31
f Dt 4:2,40
22:32
g Lev 18:21

31"Keep *f* my commands and follow them. I am the LORD. 32Do not profane my holy name. *g* I must be acknowledged as holy by the Israelites. I am the LORD, who makes*d* you holy*e* 33and who brought you out of Egypt to be your God. I am the LORD."

3. Seasons and feasts

23:2
h ver 4,37,44;
Nu 29:39
23:3
i Ex 20:9

23 The LORD said to Moses, 2"Speak to the Israelites and say to them: 'These are my appointed feasts,*h* the appointed feasts of the LORD, which you are to proclaim as sacred assemblies.

The Sabbath

23:3
i Ex 20:10;
31:13-17;
Lev 19:3; Dt 5:13;
Heb 4:9,10

3"'There are six days when you may work,*i* but the seventh day is a Sabbath of rest,*j* a day of sacred assembly. You are not to do any work; wherever you live, it is a Sabbath to the LORD.

a9 Or *who sanctifies them;* or *who sets them apart as holy;* also in verse 16   *b21* Traditionally *peace offering*
c23 The Hebrew word can include both male and female.   *d32* Or *made   e32* Or *who sanctifies you;* or *who sets you apart as holy*

22:19–25 Animals with defects were not acceptable as sacrifices because they did not represent God's holy nature. Furthermore, the animal had to be without blemish in order to foreshadow the perfect, sinless life of Jesus Christ. When we give our best time, talent, and treasure to God rather than what is tarnished or common, we demonstrate the true meaning of worship and testify to God's supreme worth. What kind of quality can people see in your service and giving?

23:1ff Feasts played a major role in Israel's culture. Israel's feasts were different from those of any other nation because, being

ordained by God, they were times of celebrating with him, not times of moral depravity. God wanted to set aside special days for the people to come together for rest, refreshment, and remembering with thanksgiving all he had done for them.

23:1–4 God established several national holidays each year for celebration, fellowship, and worship. Much can be learned about people by observing the holidays they celebrate and the way they celebrate them. Take note of your holiday traditions. What do they say about your values? In what ways do your celebrations and holidays reflect your relationship with God?

The Passover and Unleavened Bread

4" 'These are the LORD's appointed feasts, the sacred assemblies you are to proclaim at their appointed times: 5 The LORD's Passover begins at twilight on the fourteenth day of the first month.ᵏ 6 On the fifteenth day of that month the LORD's Feast of Unleavened Bread begins; for seven days you must eat bread made without yeast. 7 On the first day hold a sacred assembly and do no regular work. 8 For seven days present an offering made to the LORD by fire. And on the seventh day hold a sacred assembly and do no regular work.'"

Firstfruits

9 The LORD said to Moses, 10 "Speak to the Israelites and say to them: 'When you enter the land I am going to give you and you reap its harvest, bring to the priest a sheaf of the first grain you harvest. 11 He is to wave the sheaf before the LORD so it will be accepted on your behalf; the priest is to wave it on the day after the Sabbath. 12 On the day you wave the sheaf, you must sacrifice as a burnt offering to the LORD a lamb a year old without defect, 13 together with its grain offeringˡ of two-tenths of an ephahᵃ of fine flour mixed with oil—an offering made to the LORD by fire, a pleasing aroma—and its drink offering of a quarter of a hinᵇ of wine. 14 You must not eat any bread, or roasted or new grain, until the very day you bring this offering to your God. This is to be a lasting ordinance for the generations to come, wherever you live.

Feast of Weeks

15" 'From the day after the Sabbath, the day you brought the sheaf of the wave offering, count off seven full weeks. 16 Count off fifty days up to the day after the seventh Sabbath,ᵐ and then present an offering of new grain to the LORD. 17 From wherever you live, bring two loaves made of two-tenths of an ephah of fine flour, baked with yeast, as a wave offering of firstfruitsⁿ to the LORD. 18 Present with this bread seven male lambs, each a year old and without defect, one young bull and two rams. They will be a burnt offering to the LORD, together with their grain offerings and drink offerings—an offering made by fire, an aroma pleasing to the LORD. 19 Then sacrifice one male goat for a sin offering and two lambs, each a year old, for a fellowship offering.ᶜ 20 The priest is to wave the two lambs before the LORD as a wave offering, together with the bread of the firstfruits. They are a sacred offering to the LORD for the priest. 21 On that same day you are to proclaim a sacred assemblyᵒ and do no regular work.ᵖ This is to be a lasting ordinance for the generations to come, wherever you live.

22" 'When you reap the harvest�q of your land, do not reap to the very edges of your field or gather the gleanings of your harvest. Leave them for the poor and the alien. I am the LORD your God.'"

Feast of Trumpets

23 The LORD said to Moses, 24 "Say to the Israelites: 'On the first day of the seventh month you are to have a day of rest, a sacred assembly commemorated with trumpet blasts.ʳ 25 Do no regular work, but present an offering made to the LORD by fire.'"

Day of Atonement

26 The LORD said to Moses, 27 "The tenth day of this seventh monthˢ is the Day of Atonement. Hold a sacred assemblyᵗ and deny yourselves,ᵈ and present an offering made to the LORD by fire. 28 Do no work on that day, because it is the Day of Atonement, when atonement is made for you before the LORD your God. 29 Anyone who does not deny himself on that day must be cut off from his people.ᵘ 30 I will destroy from among his peopleᵛ anyone who does

ᵃ*13* That is, probably about 4 quarts (about 4.5 liters); also in verse 17　　ᵇ*13* That is, probably about 1 quart (about 1 liter)　　ᶜ*19* Traditionally *peace offering*　　ᵈ*27* Or *and fast;* also in verses 29 and 32

23:5
ᵏEx 12:18-19

23:13
ˡLev 2:14-16

23:16
ᵐNu 28:26; Ac 2:1
23:17
ⁿEx 34:22; Lev 2:12

23:21
ᵒver 2
ᵖver 3
23:22
qLev 19:9

23:24
ʳLev 25:9; Nu 29:1

23:27
ˢLev 16:29
ᵗNu 29:7
23:29
ᵘGe 17:14
23:30
ᵛLev 20:3

23:6 The Feast of Unleavened Bread reminded Israel of their escape from Egypt. For seven days they ate unleavened bread, just as they had eaten it back then (Exodus 12:14, 15). The symbolism of this bread made without yeast was important to the Israelites. First, because the bread was unique, it illustrated Israel's uniqueness as a nation. Second, because yeast was a symbol of sin, the yeast-less bread represented Israel's moral purity. Third, the baking method reminded them to obey quickly. Their ancestors left the yeast out of their dough so they could leave Egypt quickly without waiting for the dough to rise.

23:9–14 The Feast of Firstfruits required that the first crops harvested be offered to God. The Israelites could not eat the food from their harvest until they had made this offering. Today God still expects us to set aside his portion first, not last. Giving leftovers to God is no way to express thanks. What do the "firstfruits" represent in your life?

23:15–22 The Feast of Weeks was a festival praising God for a bountiful harvest.

23:23, 24 Most of the trumpets used were rams' horns, although some of the more special trumpets were made of beaten silver.

any work on that day. ³¹You shall do no work at all. This is to be a lasting ordinance for the generations to come, wherever you live. ³²It is a sabbath of rest for you, and you must deny yourselves. From the evening of the ninth day of the month until the following evening you are to observe your sabbath."

Feast of Tabernacles

23:34
ʷEx 23:16;
Dt 16:13; Jn 7:2

³³The LORD said to Moses, ³⁴"Say to the Israelites: 'On the fifteenth day of the seventh month the LORD's Feast of Tabernaclesʷ begins, and it lasts for seven days. ³⁵The first day is a sacred assembly; do no regular work. ³⁶For seven days present offerings made to the LORD by fire, and on the eighth day hold a sacred assembly and present an offering made to the LORD by fire. It is the closing assembly; do no regular work.

³⁷("These are the LORD's appointed feasts, which you are to proclaim as sacred assemblies for bringing offerings made to the LORD by fire—the burnt offerings and grain offerings, sacrifices and drink offerings required for each day. ³⁸These offerings are in addition to those for the LORD's Sabbaths andᵃ in addition to your gifts and whatever you have vowed and all the freewill offerings you give to the LORD.)

23:39
ˣEx 23:16
23:40
ʸNe 8:14-17

³⁹"'So beginning with the fifteenth day of the seventh month, after you have gathered the crops of the land, celebrate the festival to the LORD for seven days;ˣ the first day is a day of rest, and the eighth day also is a day of rest. ⁴⁰On the first day you are to take choice fruit from the trees, and palm fronds, leafy branches and poplars,ʸ and rejoice before the LORD your God for seven days. ⁴¹Celebrate this as a festival to the LORD for seven days each year. This is to be a lasting ordinance for the generations to come; celebrate it in the seventh month. ⁴²Live in booths for seven days: All native-born Israelites are to live in booths ⁴³so your descendants will know that I had the Israelites live in booths when I brought them out of Egypt. I am the LORD your God.'"

⁴⁴So Moses announced to the Israelites the appointed feasts of the LORD.

ᵃ*38* Or *These feasts are in addition to the* LORD's *Sabbaths, and these offerings are*

THE FEASTS
Besides enjoying one Sabbath day of rest each week, the Israelites also enjoyed 19 days when national holidays were celebrated.

Festival	What It Celebrated	Its Importance
Passover One day (Leviticus 23:5)	When God spared the lives of Israel's firstborn children in Egypt and freed the Hebrews from slavery	Reminded the people of God's deliverance
Unleavened Bread Seven days (Leviticus 23:6–8)	The exodus from Egypt	Reminded the people they were leaving the old life behind and entering a new way of living
Firstfruits One day (Leviticus 23:9–14)	The first crops of the barley harvest	Reminded the people how God provided for them
Pentecost (Weeks) One day (Leviticus 23:15–22)	The end of the barley harvest and beginning of the wheat harvest	Showed joy and thanksgiving over the bountiful harvest
Trumpets One day (Leviticus 23:23–25)	The beginning of the seventh month (civil new year)	Expressed joy and thanksgiving to God
Day of Atonement One day (Leviticus 23:26–32)	The removal of sin from the people and the nation	Restored fellowship with God
Shelters Seven days (Leviticus 23:33–43)	God's protection and guidance in the desert	Renewed Israel's commitment to God and trust in his guidance and protection

---

Trumpets were blown to announce the beginning of each month as well as the start of festivals.

23:33-43 The Feast of Tabernacles was a special celebration involving the whole family (see 23:34; Exodus 23:16; Deuteronomy 16:13). Like Passover, this feast taught family members of all ages about God's nature and what he had done for them and was a time of renewed commitment to God. Our families also need rituals of celebration to renew our faith and to pass it on to our children. In addition to Christmas and Easter, we should select other special days to commemorate God's goodness.

23:44 Worship involves both celebration and confession. But in Israel's national holidays, the balance seems heavily tipped in favor of celebration—five joyous occasions to two solemn ones. The God of the Bible encourages joy! God does not intend for religion to be only meditation and introspection. He also wants us to celebrate. Serious reflection and immediate confession of sin is essential, of course. But this should be balanced by celebrating who God is and what he has done for his people. What special occasions on your calendar would you describe as times for joy? Which would be times for confession? How are you doing with the five-to-two balance?

Oil and Bread Set Before the LORD

24 The LORD said to Moses, [2]"Command the Israelites to bring you clear oil of pressed olives for the light so that the lamps may be kept burning continually. [3]Outside the curtain of the Testimony in the Tent of Meeting, Aaron is to tend the lamps before the LORD from evening till morning, continually. This is to be a lasting ordinance for the generations to come. [4]The lamps on the pure gold lampstand before the LORD must be tended continually.

[5]"Take fine flour and bake twelve loaves of bread, [z] using two-tenths of an ephah [a] for each loaf. [6]Set them in two rows, six in each row, on the table of pure gold [a] before the LORD. [7]Along each row put some pure incense as a memorial portion to represent the bread and to be an offering made to the LORD by fire. [8]This bread is to be set out before the LORD regularly, [b] Sabbath after Sabbath, on behalf of the Israelites, as a lasting covenant. [9]It belongs to Aaron and his sons, [c] who are to eat it in a holy place, because it is a most holy part of their regular share of the offerings made to the LORD by fire."

A Blasphemer Stoned

[10]Now the son of an Israelite mother and an Egyptian father went out among the Israelites, and a fight broke out in the camp between him and an Israelite. [11]The son of the Israelite woman blasphemed the Name with a curse; so they brought him to Moses. (His mother's name was Shelomith, the daughter of Dibri the Danite.) [12]They put him in custody until the will of the LORD should be made clear to them. [d]

[13]Then the LORD said to Moses: [14]"Take the blasphemer outside the camp. All those who heard him are to lay their hands on his head, and the entire assembly is to stone him. [e] [15]Say to the Israelites: 'If anyone curses his God, he will be held responsible; [16]anyone who blasphemes the name of the LORD must be put to death. [f] The entire assembly must stone him. Whether an alien or native-born, when he blasphemes the Name, he must be put to death.

[17]"'If anyone takes the life of a human being, he must be put to death. [g] [18]Anyone who takes the life of someone's animal must make restitution [h]—life for life. [19]If anyone injures his neighbor, whatever he has done must be done to him: [20]fracture for fracture, eye for eye, tooth for tooth. [i] As he has injured the other, so he is to be injured. [21]Whoever kills an animal must make restitution, but whoever kills a man must be put to death. [j] [22]You are to have the same law for the alien [k] and the native-born. [l] I am the LORD your God.'"

[23]Then Moses spoke to the Israelites, and they took the blasphemer outside the camp and stoned him. The Israelites did as the LORD commanded Moses.

The Sabbath Year

25 The LORD said to Moses on Mount Sinai, [2]"Speak to the Israelites and say to them: 'When you enter the land I am going to give you, the land itself must observe a sabbath to the LORD. [3]For six years sow your fields, and for six years prune your vineyards and gather their crops. [4]But in the seventh year the land is to have a sabbath of rest, a sabbath to the LORD. Do not sow your fields or prune your vineyards. [5]Do not reap what grows of itself or harvest the grapes of your untended vines. The land is to have a year of rest. [6]Whatever the land yields during the sabbath year will be food for you—for yourself, your manservant and maidservant, and the hired worker and temporary resident who live among you, [7]as well as for your livestock and the wild animals in your land. Whatever the land produces may be eaten.

The Year of Jubilee

[8]"'Count off seven sabbaths of years—seven times seven years—so that the seven sabbaths of years amount to a period of forty-nine years. [9]Then have the trumpet [m] sounded

a5 That is, probably about 4 quarts (about 4.5 liters)

24:5
z Ex 25:30
24:6
a Ex 25:23-30
24:8
b Nu 4:7; 2Ch 2:4
24:9
c Lev 8:31; Mt 12:4;
Mk 2:26; Lk 6:4

24:12
d Ex 18:16;
Nu 15:34
24:14
e Dt 13:9; 17:5,7
24:16
f 1Ki 21:10,13

24:17
g Ex 21:12;
Nu 35:30-31
24:18
h ver 21
24:20
i Mt 5:38*
24:21
j ver 17
24:22
k Ex 12:49
l Nu 15:16

25:9
m Lev 23:24

24:13 This punishment for blasphemy (cursing God) seems extreme by modern standards. But it shows how seriously God expects us to take our relationship with him. Often we use his name in swearing, or we act as though he doesn't exist. We should be careful how we speak and act, treating God with reverence. Eventually, he will have the last word.

24:17–22 This was a code for judges, not an endorsement of personal vengeance. In effect, it was saying that the punishment should fit the crime, but it should not go beyond.

25:1–7 The sabbath year provided one year in seven for the fields to lay fallow (unplowed). This was good management of natural resources and reminded the people of God's control and provision for them.

25:8–17 The Year of Jubilee was meant to be celebrated every 50 years. It included canceling all debts, freeing all slaves, and returning to its original owners all land that had been sold. There is no indication in the Bible that the Year of Jubilee was ever carried out. If Israel had followed this practice faithfully, they would have been a society without permanent poverty.

everywhere on the tenth day of the seventh month; on the Day of Atonement sound the

25:10
n Jer 34:8,15,17

trumpet throughout your land. [10]Consecrate the fiftieth year and proclaim liberty[n] through-out the land to all its inhabitants. It shall be a jubilee for you; each one of you is to return to his family property and each to his own clan. [11]The fiftieth year shall be a jubilee for you; do not sow and do not reap what grows of itself or harvest the untended vines. [12]For it is a jubilee and is to be holy for you; eat only what is taken directly from the fields.

25:13
o ver 10

[13]"'In this Year of Jubilee [o] everyone is to return to his own property.

25:15
p Lev 27:18,23

[14]"'If you sell land to one of your countrymen or buy any from him, do not take advantage of each other. [15]You are to buy from your countryman on the basis of the number of years[p] since the Jubilee. And he is to sell to you on the basis of the number of years left for harvest-ing crops. [16]When the years are many, you are to increase the price, and when the years are few, you are to decrease the price, because what he is really selling you is the number of

25:17
q Lev 19:14
r Lev 19:32

crops. [17]Do not take advantage of each other, but fear your God. [q] I am the LORD your God.[r]

[18]"'Follow my decrees and be careful to obey my laws, and you will live safely in the land.[s]

25:18
s Lev 26:4,5;
Dt 12:10

[19]Then the land will yield its fruit, and you will eat your fill and live there in safety. [20]You may ask, "What will we eat in the seventh year[t] if we do not plant or harvest our crops?" [21]I

25:20
t ver 4

will send you such a blessing in the sixth year that the land will yield enough for three years.

25:22
u Lev 26:10

[22]While you plant during the eighth year, you will eat from the old crop and will continue to eat from it until the harvest of the ninth year comes in. [u]

25:23
v Ex 19:5
w Ge 23:4;
Ps 39:12;
Heb 11:13

[23]"'The land must not be sold permanently, because the land is mine [v] and you are but aliens [w] and my tenants. [24]Throughout the country that you hold as a possession, you must provide for the redemption of the land.

25:25
x Ru 2:20
y Ru 4:4

[25]"'If one of your countrymen becomes poor and sells some of his property, his nearest relative[x] is to come and redeem[y] what his countryman has sold. [26]If, however, a man has no one to redeem it for him but he himself prospers and acquires sufficient means to redeem it, [27]he is to determine the value for the years since he sold it and refund the balance to the man to whom he sold it; he can then go back to his own property. [28]But if he does not ac-quire the means to repay him, what he sold will remain in the possession of the buyer until the Year of Jubilee. It will be returned in the Jubilee, and he can then go back to his property.

[29]"'If a man sells a house in a walled city, he retains the right of redemption a full year af-ter its sale. During that time he may redeem it. [30]If it is not redeemed before a full year has passed, the house in the walled city shall belong permanently to the buyer and his descen-dants. It is not to be returned in the Jubilee. [31]But houses in villages without walls around them are to be considered as open country. They can be redeemed, and they are to be re-turned in the Jubilee.

25:32
z Nu 35:1-8

[32]"'The Levites always have the right to redeem their houses in the Levitical towns, [z] which they possess. [33]So the property of the Levites is redeemable—that is, a house sold in any town they hold—and is to be returned in the Jubilee, because the houses in the towns of the Levites are their property among the Israelites. [34]But the pastureland belonging to their towns must not be sold; it is their permanent possession.

25:35
a Dt 15:8

[35]"'If one of your countrymen becomes poor and is unable to support himself among you, help him [a] as you would an alien or a temporary resident, so he can continue to live

25:36
b Ex 22:25;
Dt 23:19-20

among you. [36]Do not take interest [b] of any kind[a] from him, but fear your God, so that your countryman may continue to live among you. [37]You must not lend him money at interest or sell him food at a profit. [38]I am the LORD your God, who brought you out of Egypt to give you the land of Canaan and to be your God.

a 36 Or *take excessive interest*; similarly in verse 37

25:23 The people would one day possess land in Canaan, but in God's plan, only God's ownership was absolute. He wanted his people to avoid greed and materialism. If you have the attitude that you are taking care of the Lord's property, you will make what you have more available to others. This is difficult to do if you have an attitude of ownership. Think of yourself as a manager of all that is under your care, not as an owner.

25:35ff The Bible places great emphasis on assisting the poor and helpless, especially orphans, widows, and the handicapped. In Israelite society, no paid work was available to women; thus, a widow and her children had no livelihood. Neither was there work available for the seriously handicapped in this nation of farmers and shepherds. The poor were to be helped without

charging any interest. Individual and family responsibility for the poor was crucial since there was no government aid.

25:35–37 God said that neglecting the poor was a sin. Perma-nent poverty was not allowed in Israel. Financially secure families were responsible to help and house those in need. Many times we do nothing, not because we lack compassion, but because we are overwhelmed by the size of the problem and don't know where to begin. God doesn't expect you to eliminate poverty, nor does he expect you to neglect your family while providing for others. He does, however, expect that when you see an individual in need, you will reach out with whatever help you can offer, including hospitality.

³⁹"'If one of your countrymen becomes poor among you and sells himself to you, do not make him work as a slave. ^c ⁴⁰He is to be treated as a hired worker or a temporary resident among you; he is to work for you until the Year of Jubilee. ⁴¹Then he and his children are to be released, and he will go back to his own clan and to the property ^d of his forefathers. ⁴²Because the Israelites are my servants, whom I brought out of Egypt, they must not be sold as slaves. ⁴³Do not rule over them ruthlessly, ^e but fear your God.

⁴⁴"'Your male and female slaves are to come from the nations around you; from them you may buy slaves. ⁴⁵You may also buy some of the temporary residents living among you and members of their clans born in your country, and they will become your property. ⁴⁶You can will them to your children as inherited property and can make them slaves for life, but you must not rule over your fellow Israelites ruthlessly.

⁴⁷"'If an alien or a temporary resident among you becomes rich and one of your countrymen becomes poor and sells himself to the alien living among you or to a member of the alien's clan, ⁴⁸he retains the right of redemption after he has sold himself. One of his relatives may redeem him: ⁴⁹An uncle or a cousin or any blood relative in his clan may redeem him. Or if he prospers, he may redeem himself. ⁵⁰He and his buyer are to count the time from the year he sold himself up to the Year of Jubilee. The price for his release is to be based on the rate paid to a hired man ^f for that number of years. ⁵¹If many years remain, he must pay for his redemption a larger share of the price paid for him. ⁵²If only a few years remain until the Year of Jubilee, he is to compute that and pay for his redemption accordingly. ⁵³He is to be treated as a man hired from year to year; you must see to it that his owner does not rule over him ruthlessly.

⁵⁴"'Even if he is not redeemed in any of these ways, he and his children are to be released in the Year of Jubilee, ⁵⁵for the Israelites belong to me as servants. They are my servants, whom I brought out of Egypt. I am the LORD your God.

4. Receiving God's blessing
Reward for Obedience

26 ¹"'Do not make idols^g or set up an image or a sacred stone for yourselves, and do not place a carved stone in your land to bow down before it. I am the LORD your God.

²"'Observe my Sabbaths and have reverence for my sanctuary. ^h I am the LORD.

³"'If you follow my decrees and are careful to obeyⁱ my commands, ⁴I will send you rain in its season, and the ground will yield its crops and the trees of the field their fruit. ⁵Your threshing will continue until grape harvest and the grape harvest will continue until planting, and you will eat all the food you want^j and live in safety in your land. ^k

⁶"'I will grant peace in the land,^l and you will lie down and no one will make you afraid. I will remove savage beasts^m from the land, and the sword will not pass through your country. ⁷You will pursue your enemies, and they will fall by the sword before you. ⁸Five of you will chase a hundred, and a hundred of you will chase ten thousand, and your enemies will fall by the sword before you. ⁿ

⁹"'I will look on you with favor and make you fruitful and increase your numbers,^o and I will keep my covenant with you. ¹⁰You will still be eating last year's harvest when you will have to move it out to make room for the new.^p ¹¹I will put my dwelling place^a ^q among you, and I will not abhor you. ¹²I will walk among you and be your God, and you will be my people.^r ¹³I am the LORD your God, who brought you out of Egypt so that you would no longer be slaves to the Egyptians; I broke the bars of your yoke and enabled you to walk with heads held high.

^a 11 Or *my tabernacle*

25:39
^cEx 21:2; Dt 15:12; 1Ki 9:22
25:41
^dver 28

25:43
^eEx 1:13

25:50
^fJob 7:1

26:1
^gEx 20:4; Dt 5:8

26:2
^hLev 19:30
26:3
ⁱDt 28:1,9
26:5
^jAm 9:13
^kLev 25:18
26:6
^lPs 29:11; 147:14
^mver 22
26:8
ⁿDt 32:30
26:9
^oGe 17:6
26:10
^pLev 25:22
26:11
^qEx 25:8
26:12
^r2Co 6:16*

25:44 Why did God allow the Israelites to purchase slaves? Under Hebrew laws, slaves were treated differently from slaves in other nations. They were seen as human beings with dignity, and not as animals. Hebrew slaves, for example, took part in the religious festivals and rested on the Sabbath. Nowhere does the Bible condone slavery, but it recognizes its existence. God's laws offered many guidelines for treating slaves properly.

26:1ff This chapter presents the two paths of obedience and disobedience that God set before the people (see also Deuteronomy 28). The people of the Old Testament were warned over and over against worshiping idols. We wonder how they could deceive themselves with these objects of wood and stone. Yet

God could well give us the same warning, for we are prone to put idols before him. Idolatry is making anything more important than God, and our lives are full of that temptation. Money, looks, success, reputation, security—these are today's idols. As you look at these false gods that promise everything you want but nothing you need, does idolatry seem so far removed from your experience?

26:13 Imagine the joy of a slave set free. God took the children of Israel out of bitter slavery and gave them freedom and dignity. We too are set free when we accept Christ's payment that redeems us from sin's slavery. We no longer need to be bogged down in shame over our past sins; we can walk with

Punishment for Disobedience

26:14
s Dt 28:15-68;
Mal 2:2

26:16
t Dt 28:22,35
u 1Sa 2:33

26:17
v Ps 106:41
w ver 36,37; Ps 53:5

26:19
x Isa 25:11

26:20
y Ps 127:1

26:23
z Jer 2:30

26:26
a Mic 6:14

26:29
b Dt 28:53

26:30
c 2Ch 34:3; Eze 6:3
d Eze 6:6

26:31
e Ps 74:3-7

26:32
f Jer 9:11

26:33
g Dt 4:27; Eze 12:15

26:34
h 2Ch 36:21

26:36
i Eze 21:7

¹⁴"'But if you will not listen to me and carry out all these commands,ˢ ¹⁵and if you reject my decrees and abhor my laws and fail to carry out all my commands and so violate my covenant, ¹⁶then I will do this to you: I will bring upon you sudden terror, wasting diseases and fever ᵗ that will destroy your sight and drain away your life. ᵘ You will plant seed in vain, because your enemies will eat it. ¹⁷I will set my face against you so that you will be defeated by your enemies; those who hate you will rule over you,ᵛ and you will flee even when no one is pursuing you. ʷ

¹⁸"'If after all this you will not listen to me, I will punish you for your sins seven times over. ¹⁹I will break down your stubborn pride ˣ and make the sky above you like iron and the ground beneath you like bronze. ²⁰Your strength will be spent in vain,ʸ because your soil will not yield its crops, nor will the trees of the land yield their fruit.

²¹"'If you remain hostile toward me and refuse to listen to me, I will multiply your afflictions seven times over, as your sins deserve. ²²I will send wild animals against you, and they will rob you of your children, destroy your cattle and make you so few in number that your roads will be deserted.

²³"'If in spite of these things you do not accept my correctionᶻ but continue to be hostile toward me, ²⁴I myself will be hostile toward you and will afflict you for your sins seven times over. ²⁵And I will bring the sword upon you to avenge the breaking of the covenant. When you withdraw into your cities, I will send a plague among you, and you will be given into enemy hands. ²⁶When I cut off your supply of bread,ᵃ ten women will be able to bake your bread in one oven, and they will dole out the bread by weight. You will eat, but you will not be satisfied.

²⁷"'If in spite of this you still do not listen to me but continue to be hostile toward me, ²⁸then in my anger I will be hostile toward you, and I myself will punish you for your sins seven times over. ²⁹You will eat the flesh of your sons and the flesh of your daughters.ᵇ ³⁰I will destroy your high places,ᶜ cut down your incense altars ᵈ and pile your dead bodies on the lifeless forms of your idols, and I will abhor you. ³¹I will turn your cities into ruins and lay waste your sanctuaries,ᵉ and I will take no delight in the pleasing aroma of your offerings. ³²I will lay waste the land,ᶠ so that your enemies who live there will be appalled. ³³I will scatter you among the nationsᵍ and will draw out my sword and pursue you. Your land will be laid waste, and your cities will lie in ruins. ³⁴Then the land will enjoy its sabbath years all the time that it lies desolate and you are in the country of your enemies;ʰ then the land will rest and enjoy its sabbaths. ³⁵All the time that it lies desolate, the land will have the rest it did not have during the sabbaths you lived in it.

³⁶"'As for those of you who are left, I will make their hearts so fearful in the lands of their enemies that the sound of a windblown leaf will put them to flight.ⁱ They will run as though fleeing from the sword, and they will fall, even though no one is pursuing them. ³⁷They will stumble over one another as though fleeing from the sword, even though no one is pursuing them. So you will not be able to stand before your enemies. ³⁸You will perish among the nations; the land of your enemies will devour you. ³⁹Those of you who are left will waste away in the lands of their enemies because of their sins; also because of their fathers' sins they will waste away.

---

dignity because God has forgiven us and forgotten them. But just as the Israelites were still in danger of returning to a slave mentality, we need to beware of the temptation to return to our former sinful patterns.

26:18 If the Israelites obeyed, there would be peace in the land. If they disobeyed, disaster would follow. God used sin's consequences to draw them to repentance, not to get back at them. Today, sin's consequences are not always so apparent. When calamity strikes us we may not know the reason. It may be (1) the result of our own disobedience, (2) the result of someone else's sin, (3) the result of natural disaster. Because we don't know, we should search our hearts and be sure we are at peace with God. His Spirit, like a great searchlight, will reveal those areas we need to deal with. Because calamity is not always the result of wrongdoing, we must guard against assigning or accepting blame for every tragedy we encounter. Misplaced guilt is one of Satan's favorite weapons against believers.

26:33-35 In 2 Kings 17 and 25 the warning pronounced in these verses came true. The people persistently disobeyed, and eventually they were conquered and carried off to the lands of Assyria and Babylonia. The nation was held in captivity for 70 years, making up for all of the years that the Israelites did not observe the law of the sabbath year (2 Chronicles 36:21).

[40] " 'But if they will confess their sins and the sins of their fathers [i]—their treachery against me and their hostility toward me, [41]which made me hostile toward them so that I sent them into the land of their enemies—then when their uncircumcised hearts are humbled and they pay for their sin, [42]I will remember my covenant with Jacob and my covenant with Isaac and my covenant with Abraham, and I will remember the land. [43]For the land will be deserted by them and will enjoy its sabbaths while it lies desolate without them. They will pay for their sins because they rejected my laws and abhorred my decrees. [44]Yet in spite of this, when they are in the land of their enemies, I will not reject them or abhor[k] them so as to destroy them completely,[l] breaking my covenant with them. I am the LORD their God. [45]But for their sake I will remember the covenant with their ancestors whom I brought out of Egypt[m] in the sight of the nations to be their God. I am the LORD.' "

[46]These are the decrees, the laws and the regulations that the LORD established on Mount Sinai between himself and the Israelites through Moses. [n]

Redeeming What Is the LORD's

27 The LORD said to Moses, [2]"Speak to the Israelites and say to them: 'If anyone makes a special vow to dedicate persons to the LORD by giving equivalent values, [3]set the value of a male between the ages of twenty and sixty at fifty shekels[a] of silver, according to the sanctuary shekel[b];[o] [4]and if it is a female, set her value at thirty shekels.[c] [5]If it is a person between the ages of five and twenty, set the value of a male at twenty shekels[d] and of a female at ten shekels.[e] [6]If it is a person between one month and five years, set the value of a male at five shekels[f][p] of silver and that of a female at three shekels[g] of silver. [7]If it is a person sixty years old or more, set the value of a male at fifteen shekels[h] and of a female at ten shekels. [8]If anyone making the vow is too poor to pay the specified amount, he is to present the person to the priest, who will set the value for him according to what the man making the vow can afford.

[9]" 'If what he vowed is an animal that is acceptable as an offering to the LORD, such an animal given to the LORD becomes holy. [10]He must not exchange it or substitute a good one for a bad one, or a bad one for a good one; if he should substitute one animal for another, both it and the substitute become holy. [11]If what he vowed is a ceremonially unclean animal—one that is not acceptable as an offering to the LORD—the animal must be presented to the priest, [12]who will judge its quality as good or bad. Whatever value the priest then sets, that is what it will be. [13]If the owner wishes to redeem the animal, he must add a fifth to its value.

[14]" 'If a man dedicates his house as something holy to the LORD, the priest will judge its quality as good or bad. Whatever value the priest then sets, so it will remain. [15]If the man who dedicates his house redeems it, [q] he must add a fifth to its value, and the house will again become his.

---

[a]*3* That is, about 1 1/4 pounds (about 0.6 kilogram); also in verse 16　　[b]*3* That is, about 2/5 ounce (about 11.5 grams); also in verse 25　　[c]*4* That is, about 12 ounces (about 0.3 kilogram)　　[d]*5* That is, about 8 ounces (about 0.2 kilogram)　　[e]*5* That is, about 4 ounces (about 110 grams); also in verse 7　　[f]*6* That is, about 2 ounces (about 55 grams)　　[g]*6* That is, about 1 1/4 ounces (about 35 grams)　　[h]*7* That is, about 6 ounces (about 170 grams)

### Cross references (margin)

26:40 [i] 1Jn 1:9

26:44 [k] Ro 11:2　[l] Dt 4:31

26:45 [m] Ex 6:8

26:46 [n] Lev 7:38; 27:34

27:3 [o] Ex 30:13

27:6 [p] Nu 18:16

27:15 [q] ver 13,20

26:40-45 These verses show what God meant when he said he is slow to anger (Exodus 34:6). Even if the Israelites chose to disobey and were scattered among their enemies, God would still give them the opportunity to repent and return to him. His purpose was not to destroy them, but to help them grow. Our day-to-day experiences and hardships are sometimes overwhelming; unless we can see that God's purpose is to bring about continual growth in us, we may despair. The hope we need is well expressed in Jeremiah 29:11, 12: "'For I know the plans I have for you,' declares the LORD, 'plans to prosper you and not to harm you, plans to give you hope and a future. Then you will call upon me and come and pray to me, and I will listen to you.'" To retain hope while we suffer shows we understand God's merciful ways of relating to his people.

27:1ff The Israelites were required to give or dedicate certain things to the Lord and to his service: the firstfruits of their harvests, firstborn animals, their firstborn sons, a tithe of their increase. Many wished to go beyond this and dedicate themselves or another family member, additional animals, a house, or a field to God. In these cases, it was possible to donate money instead of the actual person, animal, or property. Some people made rash or unrealistic vows. To urge them to think about it first, a 20 percent penalty was put on those items purchased back by money. This chapter explains how valuations were to be made and what to do if a donor later wished to buy back what had been donated to God.

27:9, 10 God taught the Israelites that when they made a vow to him, they must not go back on their promise even if it turned out to cost more than expected. (This applied to animals; humans could be redeemed or purchased back.) God takes our promises seriously. If you vow to give 10 percent of your income and suddenly some unexpected bills come along, your faithful stewardship will be costly. God, however, expects you to fulfill your vow even if it is difficult to do so.

27:14-25 Real estate could be given as a voluntary offering in much the same way that today people give property through a will or donate the proceeds from the sale of property to the church or Christian organizations.

27:18
r Lev 25:15

27:21
s Lev 25:10
t Nu 18:14;
Eze 44:29

27:24
u Lev 25:28

27:25
v Ex 30:13

27:26
w Ex 13:2,12

27:27
x ver 11

27:28
y Jos 6:17-19

27:30
z Ge 28:22; Mal 3:8

27:33
a ver 10

27:34
b Lev 26:46

16"'If a man dedicates to the Lord part of his family land, its value is to be set according to the amount of seed required for it—fifty shekels of silver to a homer^a of barley seed. 17If he dedicates his field during the Year of Jubilee, the value that has been set remains. 18But if he dedicates his field after the Jubilee, the priest will determine the value according to the number of years that remain^r until the next Year of Jubilee, and its set value will be reduced. 19If the man who dedicates the field wishes to redeem it, he must add a fifth to its value, and the field will again become his. 20If, however, he does not redeem the field, or if he has sold it to someone else, it can never be redeemed. 21When the field is released in the Jubilee,^s it will become holy, like a field devoted to the Lord; ^t it will become the property of the priests.^b

22"'If a man dedicates to the Lord a field he has bought, which is not part of his family land, 23the priest will determine its value up to the Year of Jubilee, and the man must pay its value on that day as something holy to the Lord. 24In the Year of Jubilee the field will revert to the person from whom he bought it,^u the one whose land it was. 25Every value is to be set according to the sanctuary shekel,^v twenty gerahs to the shekel.

26"'No one, however, may dedicate the firstborn of an animal, since the firstborn already belongs to the Lord;^w whether an ox^c or a sheep, it is the Lord's. 27If it is one of the unclean animals,^x he may buy it back at its set value, adding a fifth of the value to it. If he does not redeem it, it is to be sold at its set value.

28"'But nothing that a man owns and devotes^{d y} to the Lord—whether man or animal or family land—may be sold or redeemed; everything so devoted is most holy to the Lord.

29"'No person devoted to destruction^e may be ransomed; he must be put to death.

30"'A tithe^z of everything from the land, whether grain from the soil or fruit from the trees, belongs to the Lord; it is holy to the Lord. 31If a man redeems any of his tithe, he must add a fifth of the value to it. 32The entire tithe of the herd and flock—every tenth animal that passes under the shepherd's rod—will be holy to the Lord. 33He must not pick out the good from the bad or make any substitution.^a If he does make a substitution, both the animal and its substitute become holy and cannot be redeemed.'"

34These are the commands the Lord gave Moses on Mount Sinai for the Israelites.^b

^a16 That is, probably about 6 bushels (about 220 liters)   ^b21 Or *priest*   ^c26 The Hebrew word can include both male and female.   ^d28 The Hebrew term refers to the irrevocable giving over of things or persons to the Lord.   ^e29 The Hebrew term refers to the irrevocable giving over of things or persons to the Lord, often by totally destroying them.

27:29 Things devoted to destruction applies to personal property or persons placed under God's ban, such as captured plunder from idol-worshipers or idols themselves. These were to be destroyed and could not be redeemed.

27:33 Many of the principles regarding sacrifices and tithes were intended to encourage inward attitudes as well as outward actions. If a person gives grudgingly, he shows that he has a stingy heart. God wants us to be cheerful givers (2 Corinthians 9:7) who give with gratitude to him.

27:34 The book of Leviticus is filled with the commands God gave his people at the foot of Mount Sinai. From these commands

we can learn much about God's nature and character. At first glance, Leviticus seems irrelevant to our high-tech world. But digging a little deeper, we realize that the book still speaks to us today—God has not changed, and his principles are for all times. As people and society change, we need constantly to search for ways to apply the principles of God's law to our present circumstances. God was the same in Leviticus as he is today and will be forever (Hebrews 13:8).

NUMBERS

VITAL STATISTICS

PURPOSE:
To tell the story of how Israel prepared to enter the promised land, how they sinned and were punished, and how they prepared to try again

AUTHOR:
Moses

ORIGINAL AUDIENCE:
The people of Israel

DATE WRITTEN:
1450–1410 B.C.

WHERE WRITTEN:
In the desert during Israel's wanderings, somewhere in the Sinai peninsula

SETTING:
The vast desert of the Sinai region, as well as lands just south and east of Canaan

KEY VERSES:
"Not one of the men who saw my glory and the miraculous signs I performed in Egypt and in the desert but who disobeyed me and tested me ten times—not one of them will ever see the land I promised on oath to their forefathers. No one who has treated me with contempt will ever see it" (14:22, 23).

KEY PEOPLE:
Moses, Aaron, Miriam, Joshua, Caleb, Eleazar, Korah, Balaam

KEY PLACES:
Mount Sinai, promised land (Canaan), Kadesh, Mount Hor, plains of Moab

EVERY parent knows the shrill whine of a young child—a slow, high-pitched complaint that grates on the eardrums and aggravates the soul. The tone of voice is difficult to bear, but the real irritation is the underlying cause—discontentment and disobedience. As the "children" of Israel journeyed from the foot of Mount Sinai to the land of Canaan, they grumbled, whined, and complained at every turn. They focused on their present discomforts. Faith had fled, and they added an extra 40 years to their trip.

Numbers, which records the tragic story of Israel's unbelief, should serve as a dramatic lesson for all of God's people. God loves us and wants the very best for us. He can and should be trusted. Numbers also gives a clear portrayal of God's patience. Again and again he withholds judgment and preserves the nation. But his patience must not be taken for granted. His judgment will come. We must obey.

As Numbers begins, the nation of Israel was camped at the foot of Mount Sinai. The people had received God's laws and were preparing to move. A census was taken to determine the number of men fit for military service. Next, the people were set apart for God. God was making the people, both spiritually and physically, ready to receive their inheritance.

But then the complaining began. First, the people complained about the food. Next, it was over Moses' authority. God punished some people but spared the nation because of Moses' prayers. The nation then arrived at Kadesh, and spies were sent into Canaan to assess its strength. Ten returned with fearful stories of giants. Only Caleb and Joshua encouraged the nation to "go up and take possession of the land" (13:30). The minority report fell on deaf ears full of the ominous message of the majority. Because of their unbelief, God declared that the present generation would not live to see the promised land. Thus the "wanderings" began. These desert wanderings featured a continuous pattern of grumbling, defiance, discipline, and death. How much better it would have been to have trusted God and entered his land! Then the terrible waiting began—waiting for the old generation to die off and waiting to see if the new generation could faithfully obey God.

Numbers ends as it begins, with preparation. This new generation of Israelites was numbered and sanctified. After defeating numerous armies, they settled on the east side of the Jordan River. Then they faced their greatest test: to cross the river and possess the beautiful land God had promised to them.

The lesson is clear. God's people must trust him, moving ahead by *faith* if they are to claim his promised land.

THE BLUEPRINT

A. PREPARING FOR THE JOURNEY
(1:1—10:10)
   1. The first census of the nation
   2. The role of the Levites
   3. The purity of the camp
   4. Receiving guidance for the journey

As part of their preparations, the Lord gave strict guidelines to the Israelites regarding purity in the camp. He wanted them to have a lifestyle distinct from the nations around them. He wanted them to be a holy people. Similarly, we should concern ourselves with purity in the church.

B. FIRST APPROACH TO THE PROMISED LAND (10:11—14:45)
   1. The people complain
   2. Miriam and Aaron oppose Moses
   3. The spies incite rebellion

The Israelites were prevented from entering the promised land because of their unbelief. Throughout history, God's people have continued to struggle with lack of faith. We must prevent unbelief from gaining a foothold in our lives, for it will keep us from enjoying the blessings that God has promised.

C. WANDERING IN THE DESERT
(15:1—21:35)
   1. Additional regulations
   2. Many leaders rebel against Moses
   3. Duties of priests and Levites
   4. The new generation

When the people complained against God and criticized Moses, they were severely punished. Over 14,000 people died as a result of rebellion against Moses. As a result of Korah's rebellion, Korah, Dathan, and Abiram and their households died, along with 250 false priests. Dissatisfaction and discontent, if allowed to remain in our lives, can easily lead to disaster. We should refrain from complaining and criticizing our leaders.

D. SECOND APPROACH TO THE PROMISED LAND (22:1—36:13)
   1. The story of Balaam
   2. The second census of the nation
   3. Instructions concerning offerings
   4. Vengeance on the Midianites
   5. The Transjordan tribes
   6. Camped on the plains of Moab

The Moabites and Midianites could not get Balaam to curse Israel, but they did get him to give advice on how to draw the Israelites to idol worship. Balaam knew what was right, but he gave in to the temptation of material rewards and sinned. Knowing what is right alone is never enough. We must also do what is right.

MEGATHEMES

THEME	EXPLANATION	IMPORTANCE
Census	Moses counted the Israelites twice. The first census organized the people into marching units to better defend themselves. The second prepared them to conquer the country east of the Jordan River.	People have to be organized, trained, and led to be effective in great movements. It is always wise to count the cost before setting out on some great undertaking. When we are aware of the obstacles before us, we can more easily avoid them. In God's work, we must remove barriers in our relationships with others so that our effectiveness is not diminished.
Rebellion	At Kadesh, 12 spies were sent out into the land of Canaan to report on the fortifications of the enemies. When the spies returned, 10 said that they should give up and go back to Egypt. As a result, the people refused to enter the land. Faced with a choice, Israel rebelled against God. Rebellion did not start with an uprising, but with griping and murmuring against Moses and God.	Rebellion against God is always a serious matter. It is not something to take lightly, for God's punishment for sin is often very severe. Our rebellion does not usually begin with all-out warfare, but in subtle ways—with griping and criticizing. Make sure your negative comments are not the product of a rebellious spirit.
Wandering	Because they rebelled, the Israelites wandered 40 years in the desert. This shows how severely God can punish sin. Forty years was enough time for all those who held on to Egypt's customs and values to die off. It gave time to train up a new generation in the ways of God.	God judges sin harshly because he is holy. The wanderings in the desert demonstrate how serious God considers flagrant disobedience of his commands. Purging our lives of sin is vital to God's purpose.
Canaan	Canaan is the promised land. It was the land God had promised to Abraham, Isaac, and Jacob—the land of the covenant. Canaan was to be the dwelling place of God's people, those set apart for true spiritual worship.	Although God's punishment for sin is often severe, he offers reconciliation and hope— his love is truly amazing. Just as God's love and law led Israel to the promised land, God desires to give purpose and destiny to our lives.

KEY PLACES IN NUMBERS

Modern names and boundaries are shown in gray.

from each tribe was sent to spy out the new land. After 40 days they returned, and all but Joshua and Caleb were too afraid to enter. Because of their lack of faith, the Israelites were made to wander in the desert for 40 years (12:16—19:22).

3 Kadesh With the years of wandering nearing an end, the Israelites set their sights once again on the promised land. Kadesh was the oasis where they spent most of their desert years. Miriam died here. And it was here that Moses angrily struck the rock, which kept him from entering the promised land (20).

4 Arad When the king there heard that Israel was on the move, he attacked, but he was soundly defeated. Moses then led the people southward and eastward around the Dead Sea (21:1–3).

5 Edom The Israelites wanted to travel through Edom, but the king of Edom refused them passage (20:14–22). So they traveled around Edom and became very discouraged. The people complained, and God sent venomous snakes to punish them. Only by looking at a bronze snake on a pole could those bitten be healed (21:4–9).

6 Ammon Next, King Sihon of the Amorites refused Israel passage. When he attacked, Israel defeated his army and conquered the territory as far as the border of Ammon (21:21–32).

7 Bashan Moses sent spies to Bashan. King Og attacked, but he was also defeated (21:33–35).

8 Plains of Moab The people camped on the plains of Moab, east of the

1 Mount Sinai Numbers begins at Mount Sinai in the Desert of Sinai with Moses taking a census of the men eligible for battle. As the battle preparations began, the people also prepared for the spiritual warfare they would face. The promised land was full of wicked people who would try to entice the Israelites to sin. God, therefore, taught Moses and the Israelites how to live rightly (1:1—12:15).

2 Desert of Paran After a full year at Mount Sinai, the Israelites broke camp and began their march toward the promised land by moving into the Desert of Paran. From there, one leader

Jordan River across from Jericho. They were on the verge of entering the promised land (22:1).

9 Moab King Balak of Moab, terrified of the Israelites, called upon Balaam, a famous sorcerer, to curse Israel from the mountains above where the Israelites camped. But the Lord caused Balaam to bless them instead (22:2—24:25).

10 Gilead The tribes of Reuben and Gad decided to settle in the fertile country of Gilead east of the Jordan River because it was a good land for their sheep. But first they promised to help the other tribes conquer the land west of the Jordan River (32).

A. PREPARING FOR THE JOURNEY (1:1—10:10)

At Mount Sinai, the Israelites received specific directions for their lifestyle in the new land God would give to them. A census was taken and the second Passover was celebrated, marking one year of freedom from slavery in Egypt. The people were now prepared to continue their journey to the promised land. Just as the Lord prepared the Israelites, he prepares us for our journey through life.

1. The first census of the nation

1:1
a Ex 40:2

1:2
b Ex 30:11-16;
Nu 26:2

1:3
c Ex 30:14

1:4
d ver 16
e Dt 1:15

1:5
f Rev 7:5

1:7
g Ru 4:20;
1Ch 2:10; Lk 3:32

1 The LORD spoke to Moses in the Tent of Meeting *a* in the Desert of Sinai on the first day of the second month of the second year after the Israelites came out of Egypt. He said: ²"Take a census *b* of the whole Israelite community by their clans and families, listing every man by name, one by one. ³You and Aaron are to number by their divisions all the men in Israel twenty years old or more *c* who are able to serve in the army. ⁴One man from each tribe, each the head of his family, *d* is to help you. *e* ⁵These are the names of the men who are to assist you:

      from Reuben, *f* Elizur son of Shedeur;
  ⁶from Simeon, Shelumiel son of Zurishaddai;
  ⁷from Judah, Nahshon son of Amminadab; *g*
  ⁸from Issachar, Nethanel son of Zuar;
  ⁹from Zebulun, Eliab son of Helon;
  ¹⁰from the sons of Joseph:
    from Ephraim, Elishama son of Ammihud;
    from Manasseh, Gamaliel son of Pedahzur;
  ¹¹from Benjamin, Abidan son of Gideoni;
  ¹²from Dan, Ahiezer son of Ammishaddai;
  ¹³from Asher, Pagiel son of Ocran;

1:14
h Nu 2:14

  ¹⁴from Gad, Eliasaph son of Deuel; *h*
  ¹⁵from Naphtali, Ahira son of Enan."

1:16
i Ex 18:25
j ver 4; Nu 7:2

1:18
k Ezr 2:59

¹⁶These were the men appointed from the community, the leaders *i* of their ancestral tribes. They were the heads of the clans of Israel. *j*

¹⁷Moses and Aaron took these men whose names had been given, ¹⁸and they called the whole community together on the first day of the second month. The people indicated their ancestry *k* by their clans and families, and the men twenty years old or more were listed by name, one by one, ¹⁹as the LORD commanded Moses. And so he counted them in the Desert of Sinai:

1:20
l Nu 26:5-11

²⁰From the descendants of Reuben *l* the firstborn son of Israel:
    All the men twenty years old or more who were able to serve in the army were listed by name, one by one, according to the records of their clans and families. ²¹The number from the tribe of Reuben was 46,500.

1:1 As the book of Numbers opens, the Israelites had been camped near Mount Sinai for more than a year. There they had received all the laws and regulations recorded in the book of Leviticus. They had been transformed into a new nation and equipped for their task. At this time, they were ready to move out and receive their land. In preparation, Moses and Aaron were told to number all the men who were able to serve in the army. This book is named for this census, or numbering, of the people.

1:1 The Tent of Meeting was the smaller structure inside the larger tabernacle. The Tent of Meeting contained the sanctuary (or Holy Place) in one part, and the Most Holy Place with the ark in another part. These two parts were separated by a curtain. God revealed himself to Moses in the Most Holy Place. Sometimes the Tent of Meeting refers to the whole tabernacle (see 2:2).

   Exodus 33:7 mentions the "tent of meeting" as the place where Moses met with God before the tabernacle was constructed. Many believe that the tent of meeting in Exodus served the same function as the one described here.

1:2–15 Taking a census was long and tedious, but it was an important task. The fighting men had to be counted to determine Israel's military strength before entering the promised land. In addition, the tribes had to be organized to determine the amount of land each would need, as well as to provide genealogical records. Without such a census, the task of conquering and organizing the promised land would have been more difficult. Whenever we are at a crossroads, it is important to take inventory of our resources. We will serve more effectively if, before plunging in, we set aside time to take a "census" of all we have— possessions, relationships, spiritual condition, time, goals.

1:20–46 If there were 603,550 men, not counting the Levites or women and children, the total population must have numbered more than two million Israelites. How could such a large population grow from Jacob's family of 70 who moved down to Egypt? The book of Exodus tells us that the Israelites who descended from Jacob's family "multiplied greatly" (Exodus 1:7). Because they remained in Egypt more than 400 years, they had plenty of time to grow into a large group of people. After leaving Egypt, they were able to survive in the desert because God miraculously provided the food and water they needed. The leaders of Moab were terrified because of the large number of Israelites (22:3).

22 From the descendants of Simeon: *m*

All the men twenty years old or more who were able to serve in the army were counted and listed by name, one by one, according to the records of their clans and families. 23 The number from the tribe of Simeon was 59,300.

1:22
m Nu 26:12-14

24 From the descendants of Gad: *n*

All the men twenty years old or more who were able to serve in the army were listed by name, according to the records of their clans and families. 25 The number from the tribe of Gad was 45,650.

1:24
n Nu 26:15-18

26 From the descendants of Judah: *o*

All the men twenty years old or more who were able to serve in the army were listed by name, according to the records of their clans and families. 27 The number from the tribe of Judah was 74,600.

1:26
o Nu 26:19-22

28 From the descendants of Issachar: *p*

All the men twenty years old or more who were able to serve in the army were listed by name, according to the records of their clans and families. 29 The number from the tribe of Issachar was 54,400.

1:28
p Nu 26:23-25

30 From the descendants of Zebulun: *q*

All the men twenty years old or more who were able to serve in the army were listed by name, according to the records of their clans and families. 31 The number from the tribe of Zebulun was 57,400.

1:30
q Nu 26:26-27

32 From the sons of Joseph:

From the descendants of Ephraim: *r*

All the men twenty years old or more who were able to serve in the army were listed by name, according to the records of their clans and families. 33 The number from the tribe of Ephraim was 40,500.

1:32
r Nu 26:35-37

34 From the descendants of Manasseh: *s*

All the men twenty years old or more who were able to serve in the army were listed by name, according to the records of their clans and families. 35 The number from the tribe of Manasseh was 32,200.

1:34
s Nu 26:28-34

36 From the descendants of Benjamin: *t*

All the men twenty years old or more who were able to serve in the army were listed by name, according to the records of their clans and families. 37 The number from the tribe of Benjamin was 35,400.

1:36
t Nu 26:38-41

38 From the descendants of Dan: *u*

All the men twenty years old or more who were able to serve in the army were listed by name, according to the records of their clans and families. 39 The number from the tribe of Dan was 62,700.

1:38
u Nu 26:42-43

40 From the descendants of Asher: *v*

All the men twenty years old or more who were able to serve in the army were listed by name, according to the records of their clans and families. 41 The number from the tribe of Asher was 41,500.

1:40
v Nu 26:44-47

42 From the descendants of Naphtali: *w*

All the men twenty years old or more who were able to serve in the army were listed by name, according to the records of their clans and families. 43 The number from the tribe of Naphtali was 53,400.

1:42
w Nu 26:48-50

44 These were the men counted by Moses and Aaron and the twelve leaders of Israel, each one representing his family. 45 All the Israelites twenty years old or more who were able to serve in Israel's army were counted according to their families. 46 The total number was 603,550. *x*

1:46
x Ex 12:37; 38:26;
Nu 2:32; 26:51

47 The families of the tribe of Levi, *y* however, were not counted along with the others. 48 The LORD had said to Moses: 49 "You must not count the tribe of Levi or include them in the census of the other Israelites. 50 Instead, appoint the Levites to be in charge of the tabernacle of the Testimony—over all its furnishings and everything belonging to it. They are to carry the tabernacle and all its furnishings; they are to take care of it and encamp around it.

1:47
y Nu 2:33; 26:57

1:52
zNu 2:2

⁵¹Whenever the tabernacle is to move, the Levites are to take it down, and whenever the tabernacle is to be set up, the Levites shall do it. Anyone else who goes near it shall be put to death. ⁵²The Israelites are to set up their tents by divisions, each man in his own camp under his own standard.ᶻ ⁵³The Levites, however, are to set up their tents around the tabernacle of the Testimony so that wrath will not fall on the Israelite community. The Levites are to be responsible for the care of the tabernacle of the Testimony."

⁵⁴The Israelites did all this just as the LORD commanded Moses.

The Arrangement of the Tribal Camps

2:2
aNu 1:52

2 The LORD said to Moses and Aaron: ²"The Israelites are to camp around the Tent of Meeting some distance from it, each man under his standardᵃ with the banners of his family."

2:3
bNu 10:14

³On the east, toward the sunrise, the divisions of the camp of Judah are to encamp under their standard. The leader of the people of Judah is Nahshon son of Amminadab.ᵇ ⁴His division numbers 74,600.

⁵The tribe of Issachar will camp next to them. The leader of the people of Issachar is Nethanel son of Zuar. ⁶His division numbers 54,400.

⁷The tribe of Zebulun will be next. The leader of the people of Zebulun is Eliab son of Helon. ⁸His division numbers 57,400.

2:9
cNu 10:14

⁹All the men assigned to the camp of Judah, according to their divisions, number 186,400. They will set out first.ᶜ

¹⁰On the south will be the divisions of the camp of Reuben under their standard. The leader of the people of Reuben is Elizur son of Shedeur. ¹¹His division numbers 46,500.

¹²The tribe of Simeon will camp next to them. The leader of the people of Simeon is Shelumiel son of Zurishaddai. ¹³His division numbers 59,300.

¹⁴The tribe of Gad will be next. The leader of the people of Gad is Eliasaph son of Deuel.ᵃ ¹⁵His division numbers 45,650.

2:16
dNu 10:18

¹⁶All the men assigned to the camp of Reuben,ᵈ according to their divisions, number 151,450. They will set out second.

¹⁷Then the Tent of Meeting and the camp of the Levites will set out in the middle of the camps. They will set out in the same order as they encamp, each in his own place under his standard.

a14 Many manuscripts of the Masoretic Text, Samaritan Pentateuch and Vulgate (see also Num. 1:14); most manuscripts of the Masoretic Text *Reuel*

ARRANGEMENT OF TRIBES AROUND THE TABERNACLE WHILE IN THE DESERT

		DAN		
	ASHER		NAPHTALI	
BENJAMIN		Merari (Son of Levi)		ISSACHAR
EPHRAIM	Gershon (Son of Levi)	TABERNACLE	Moses Aaron Sons of Aaron	JUDAH
MANASSEH		Kohath (Son of Levi)		ZEBULUN
	GAD		SIMEON	
		REUBEN		

2:2 The nation of Israel was organized according to tribes for several reasons. (1) It was an effective way to manage and govern a large group. (2) It made dividing the promised land easier. (3) It was part of their culture and heritage (people were not known by a last name, but by their family, clan, and tribe). (4) It made it easier to keep detailed genealogies, and genealogies were the only way to prove membership in God's chosen nation. (5) It made travel much more efficient. The people followed the tribe's standard (a kind of flag) and thus stayed together and kept from getting lost.

¹⁸On the west will be the divisions of the camp of Ephraim under their standard. The leader of the people of Ephraim is Elishama son of Ammihud. ¹⁹His division numbers 40,500.

²⁰The tribe of Manasseh will be next to them. The leader of the people of Manasseh is Gamaliel son of Pedahzur.ᵉ ²¹His division numbers 32,200.

²²The tribe of Benjamin will be next. The leader of the people of Benjamin is Abidan son of Gideoni. ²³His division numbers 35,400.

²⁴All the men assigned to the camp of Ephraim,ᶠ according to their divisions, number 108,100. They will set out third.

²⁵On the north will be the divisions of the camp of Dan, under their standard. The leader of the people of Dan is Ahiezer son of Ammishaddai. ²⁶His division numbers 62,700.

²⁷The tribe of Asher will camp next to them. The leader of the people of Asher is Pagiel son of Ocran.ᵍ ²⁸His division numbers 41,500.

²⁹The tribe of Naphtali will be next. The leader of the people of Naphtali is Ahira son of Enan. ³⁰His division numbers 53,400.

³¹All the men assigned to the camp of Dan number 157,600. They will set out last,ʰ under their standards.

³²These are the Israelites, counted according to their families. All those in the camps, by their divisions, number 603,550.ⁱ ³³The Levites, however, were not countedʲ along with the other Israelites, as the LORD commanded Moses.

³⁴So the Israelites did everything the LORD commanded Moses; that is the way they encamped under their standards, and that is the way they set out, each with his clan and family.

2. The role of the Levites
The Levites

3 This is the account of the family of Aaron and Moses at the time the LORD talked with Moses on Mount Sinai.

²The names of the sons of Aaron were Nadab the firstborn and Abihu, Eleazar and Ithamar.ᵏ ³Those were the names of Aaron's sons, the anointed priests, who were ordained to serve as priests. ⁴Nadab and Abihu, however, fell dead before the LORDˡ when they made an offering with unauthorized fire before him in the Desert of Sinai.ᵐ They had no sons; so only Eleazar and Ithamar served as priests during the lifetime of their father Aaron.

⁵The LORD said to Moses, ⁶"Bring the tribe of Levi and present them to Aaron the priest to assist him.ⁿ ⁷They are to perform duties for him and for the whole community at the Tent of Meeting by doing the work of the tabernacle. ⁸They are to take care of all the furnishings of the Tent of Meeting, fulfilling the obligations of the Israelites by doing the work of the tabernacle. ⁹Give the Levites to Aaron and his sons;ᵒ they are the Israelites who are to be given wholly to him.ᵃ ¹⁰Appoint Aaron and his sons to serve as priests;ᵖ anyone else who approaches the sanctuary must be put to death."�q

2:20
ᵉNu 1:10

2:24
ᶠNu 10:22

2:27
ᵍNu 1:13

2:31
ʰNu 10:25

2:32
ⁱEx 38:26; Nu 1:46
2:33
ʲNu 1:47

3:2
ᵏEx 6:23

3:4
ˡLev 10:2
ᵐLev 10:1

3:6
ⁿNu 8:6-22; 18:1-7

3:9
ᵒNu 8:19; 18:6

3:10
ᵖEx 29:9
qNu 1:51

ᵃ9 Most manuscripts of the Masoretic Text; some manuscripts of the Masoretic Text, Samaritan Pentateuch and Septuagint (see also Num. 8:16) *to me*

2:34 This must have been one of the biggest campsites the world has ever seen! It would have taken about 12 square miles to set up tents for just the 600,000 fighting men—not to mention the women and children. Moses must have had a difficult time managing such a group. In the early stages of the journey and at Mount Sinai, the people were generally obedient to both God and Moses. But when the people left Mount Sinai and traveled across the rugged desert, they began to complain, grumble, and disobey. Soon problems erupted, and Moses could no longer effectively manage the Israelites. The books of Exodus, Leviticus, and Numbers present a striking contrast between how much we can accomplish when we obey God and how little we can accomplish when we don't.

3:4 See Leviticus 10:1, 2 for the story of Nadab and Abihu.

3:5–13 At the time of the first Passover (Exodus 13:2), God instructed every Israelite family to dedicate its firstborn son to him (see 3:40–51 and 8:16). They were set apart to assist

Moses and Aaron in ministering to the people. This was only a temporary measure, however. Here God chose all the men from the tribe of Levi to replace the firstborn sons from every Israelite tribe. These men, called Levites, were set apart to care for the tabernacle and minister to the people. All the priests had to belong to the tribe of Levi, but not all Levites were priests. The Levites were to be 25 years old before entering service. They probably received five years of on-the-job training before being admitted to full service at age 30.

3:10 Aaron and his descendants were appointed to the priesthood. There is a tremendous contrast between the priesthood of Aaron in the Old Testament and the priesthood of Christ in the New Testament. Aaron and his descendants were the only ones who could carry out the duties of the priests and approach God's dwelling place. Now that Christ is our High Priest—our intermediary with God—anyone who follows him is also called a priest (1 Peter 2:5, 9). Now all Christians may come into God's presence

3:12
r ver 41; Nu 8:16,18
3:13
s Ex 13:12

3:15
t ver 39

3:17
u Ex 6:16
3:18
v Ex 6:17

3:25
w Ex 26:36; Nu 4:25

3:27
x 1Ch 26:23

3:31
y Ex 25:10-22
z Ex 25:31

3:36
a Nu 4:32

3:38
b Nu 18:5
c ver 10

3:39
d Nu 26:62

3:41
e ver 12

¹¹The LORD also said to Moses, ¹²"I have taken the Levites from among the Israelites in place of the first male offspring *r* of every Israelite woman. The Levites are mine, ¹³for all the firstborn are mine. *s* When I struck down all the firstborn in Egypt, I set apart for myself every firstborn in Israel, whether man or animal. They are to be mine. I am the LORD."

¹⁴The LORD said to Moses in the Desert of Sinai, ¹⁵"Count *t* the Levites by their families and clans. Count every male a month old or more." ¹⁶So Moses counted them, as he was commanded by the word of the LORD.

¹⁷ These were the names of the sons of Levi:

Gershon, Kohath and Merari. *u*

¹⁸ These were the names of the Gershonite clans:

Libni and Shimei. *v*

¹⁹ The Kohathite clans:

Amram, Izhar, Hebron and Uzziel.

²⁰ The Merarite clans:

Mahli and Mushi.

These were the Levite clans, according to their families.

²¹To Gershon belonged the clans of the Libnites and Shimeites; these were the Gershonite clans. ²²The number of all the males a month old or more who were counted was 7,500. ²³The Gershonite clans were to camp on the west, behind the tabernacle. ²⁴The leader of the families of the Gershonites was Eliasaph son of Lael. ²⁵At the Tent of Meeting the Gershonites were responsible for the care of the tabernacle and tent, its coverings, the curtain at the entrance *w* to the Tent of Meeting, ²⁶the curtains of the courtyard, the curtain at the entrance to the courtyard surrounding the tabernacle and altar, and the ropes—and everything related to their use.

²⁷To Kohath belonged the clans of the Amramites, Izharites, Hebronites and Uzzielites; *x* these were the Kohathite clans. ²⁸The number of all the males a month old or more was 8,600. *a* The Kohathites were responsible for the care of the sanctuary. ²⁹The Kohathite clans were to camp on the south side of the tabernacle. ³⁰The leader of the families of the Kohathite clans was Elizaphan son of Uzziel. ³¹They were responsible for the care of the ark, *y* the table, the lampstand, *z* the altars, the articles of the sanctuary used in ministering, the curtain, and everything related to their use. ³²The chief leader of the Levites was Eleazar son of Aaron, the priest. He was appointed over those who were responsible for the care of the sanctuary.

³³To Merari belonged the clans of the Mahlites and the Mushites; these were the Merarite clans. ³⁴The number of all the males a month old or more who were counted was 6,200. ³⁵The leader of the families of the Merarite clans was Zuriel son of Abihail; they were to camp on the north side of the tabernacle. ³⁶The Merarites were appointed *a* to take care of the frames of the tabernacle, its crossbars, posts, bases, all its equipment, and everything related to their use, ³⁷as well as the posts of the surrounding courtyard with their bases, tent pegs and ropes.

³⁸Moses and Aaron and his sons were to camp to the east of the tabernacle, toward the sunrise, in front of the Tent of Meeting. They were responsible for the care of the sanctuary *b* on behalf of the Israelites. Anyone else who approached the sanctuary was to be put to death. *c*

³⁹The total number of Levites counted at the LORD's command by Moses and Aaron according to their clans, including every male a month old or more, was 22,000. *d*

⁴⁰The LORD said to Moses, "Count all the firstborn Israelite males who are a month old or more and make a list of their names. ⁴¹Take the Levites for me in place of all the firstborn of the Israelites, *e* and the livestock of the Levites in place of all the firstborn of the livestock of the Israelites. I am the LORD."

a 28 Hebrew; some Septuagint manuscripts *8,300*

without fear because God's own Son encourages his followers to do so. We can put guilt behind us and experience forgiveness when we have a special relationship with God based on what Christ has done for us.

42 So Moses counted all the firstborn of the Israelites, as the LORD commanded him. 43 The total number of firstborn males a month old or more, listed by name, was 22,273.[f]

44 The LORD also said to Moses, 45 "Take the Levites in place of all the firstborn of Israel, and the livestock of the Levites in place of their livestock. The Levites are to be mine. I am the LORD. 46 To redeem[g] the 273 firstborn Israelites who exceed the number of the Levites, 47 collect five shekels[a] [h] for each one, according to the sanctuary shekel,[i] which weighs twenty gerahs.[j] 48 Give the money for the redemption of the additional Israelites to Aaron and his sons."

49 So Moses collected the redemption money from those who exceeded the number redeemed by the Levites. 50 From the firstborn of the Israelites he collected silver weighing 1,365 shekels,[b] [k] according to the sanctuary shekel. 51 Moses gave the redemption money to Aaron and his sons, as he was commanded by the word of the LORD.

The Kohathites

4 The LORD said to Moses and Aaron: 2 "Take a census of the Kohathite branch of the Levites by their clans and families. 3 Count all the men from thirty to fifty years of age[l] who come to serve in the work in the Tent of Meeting.

4 "This is the work of the Kohathites in the Tent of Meeting: the care of the most holy things. 5 When the camp is to move, Aaron and his sons are to go in and take down the shielding curtain and cover the ark of the Testimony with it. 6 Then they are to cover this with hides of sea cows,[c] spread a cloth of solid blue over that and put the poles in place.

7 "Over the table of the Presence[m] they are to spread a blue cloth and put on it the plates, dishes and bowls, and the jars for drink offerings; the bread that is continually there[n] is to remain on it. 8 Over these they are to spread a scarlet cloth, cover that with hides of sea cows and put its poles in place.

9 "They are to take a blue cloth and cover the lampstand that is for light, together with its lamps, its wick trimmers and trays,[o] and all its jars for the oil used to supply it. 10 Then they are to wrap it and all its accessories in a covering of hides of sea cows and put it on a carrying frame.

11 "Over the gold altar[p] they are to spread a blue cloth and cover that with hides of sea cows and put its poles in place.

12 "They are to take all the articles used for ministering in the sanctuary, wrap them in a blue cloth, cover that with hides of sea cows and put them on a carrying frame.

13 "They are to remove the ashes from the bronze altar[q] and spread a purple cloth over it. 14 Then they are to place on it all the utensils used for ministering at the altar, including the firepans, meat forks, shovels and sprinkling bowls. Over it they are to spread a covering of hides of sea cows and put its poles in place.

15 "After Aaron and his sons have finished covering the holy furnishings and all the holy articles, and when the camp is ready to move, the Kohathites are to come to do the carrying.[r] But they must not touch the holy things or they will die.[s] The Kohathites are to carry those things that are in the Tent of Meeting.

16 "Eleazar son of Aaron, the priest, is to have charge of the oil for the light,[t] the fragrant incense, the regular grain offering[u] and the anointing oil. He is to be in charge of the entire tabernacle and everything in it, including its holy furnishings and articles."

17 The LORD said to Moses and Aaron, 18 "See that the Kohathite tribal clans are not cut off from the Levites. 19 So that they may live and not die when they come near the most holy things,[v] do this for them: Aaron and his sons are to go into the sanctuary and assign to each man his work and what he is to carry. 20 But the Kohathites must not go in to look[w] at the holy things, even for a moment, or they will die."

The Gershonites

21 The LORD said to Moses, 22 "Take a census also of the Gershonites by their families and clans. 23 Count all the men from thirty to fifty years of age[x] who come to serve in the work at the Tent of Meeting.

3:43 [f]ver 39
3:46 [g]Ex 13:13; Nu 18:15
3:47 [h]Lev 27:6 [i]Ex 30:13 [j]Lev 27:25
3:50 [k]ver 46-48
4:3 [l]ver 23; Nu 8:25; 1Ch 23:3,24,27
4:7 [m]Lev 24:6 [n]Ex 25:30
4:9 [o]Ex 25:31,37,38
4:11 [p]Ex 30:1
4:13 [q]Ex 27:1-8
4:15 [r]Nu 7:9 [s]2Sa 6:6,7
4:16 [t]Ex 25:6 [u]Ex 29:41
4:19 [v]ver 15
4:20 [w]Ex 19:21
4:23 [x]ver 3

[a]47 That is, about 2 ounces (about 55 grams)   [b]50 That is, about 35 pounds (about 15.5 kilograms)   [c]6 That is, dugongs; also in verses 8, 10, 11, 12, 14 and 25

4:2ff The Kohathites, Gershonites (4:21), and Merarites (4:29) were families of Levites who were assigned special tasks in Israel's worship. For the jobs described in this chapter, a Levite had to be between 30 and 50 years old. They were expected to carry out their duties as described here in every detail. In fact, failure to do so would mean death (4:20). This contrasted greatly from the religious practices of the Egyptians who could purchase amulets and potions. Their idols could be handled. The God of the

4:25
y Nu 3:25

24 "This is the service of the Gershonite clans as they work and carry burdens: 25 They are to carry the curtains of the tabernacle, the Tent of Meeting, y its covering and the outer covering of hides of sea cows, the curtains for the entrance to the Tent of Meeting, 26 the curtains of the courtyard surrounding the tabernacle and altar, the curtain for the entrance, the ropes and all the equipment used in its service. The Gershonites are to do all that needs to be done with these things. 27 All their service, whether carrying or doing other work, is to be done under the direction of Aaron and his sons. You shall assign to them as their responsibility all they are to carry. 28 This is the service of the Gershonite clans at the Tent of Meeting. Their duties are to be under the direction of Ithamar son of Aaron, the priest.

The Merarites

4:31
z Nu 3:36

29 "Count the Merarites by their clans and families. 30 Count all the men from thirty to fifty years of age who come to serve in the work at the Tent of Meeting. 31 This is their duty as they perform service at the Tent of Meeting: to carry the frames of the tabernacle, its crossbars, posts and bases, z 32 as well as the posts of the surrounding courtyard with their bases, tent pegs, ropes, all their equipment and everything related to their use. Assign to each man the specific things he is to carry. 33 This is the service of the Merarite clans as they work at the Tent of Meeting under the direction of Ithamar son of Aaron, the priest."

The Numbering of the Levite Clans

4:34
a ver 2

4:37
b Nu 3:27

34 Moses, Aaron and the leaders of the community counted the Kohathites a by their clans and families. 35 All the men from thirty to fifty years of age who came to serve in the work in the Tent of Meeting, 36 counted by clans, were 2,750. 37 This was the total of all those in the Kohathite clans b who served in the Tent of Meeting. Moses and Aaron counted them according to the LORD's command through Moses.

4:38
c Ge 46:11

38 The Gershonites c were counted by their clans and families. 39 All the men from thirty to fifty years of age who came to serve in the work at the Tent of Meeting, 40 counted by their clans and families, were 2,630. 41 This was the total of those in the Gershonite clans who served at the Tent of Meeting. Moses and Aaron counted them according to the LORD's command.

4:45
d ver 29

42 The Merarites were counted by their clans and families. 43 All the men from thirty to fifty years of age who came to serve in the work at the Tent of Meeting, 44 counted by their clans, were 3,200. 45 This was the total of those in the Merarite clans. d Moses and Aaron counted them according to the LORD's command through Moses.

4:47
e ver 3

46 So Moses, Aaron and the leaders of Israel counted all the Levites by their clans and families. 47 All the men from thirty to fifty years of age e who came to do the work of serving and carrying the Tent of Meeting 48 numbered 8,580. 49 At the LORD's command through Moses, each was assigned his work and told what to carry.

Thus they were counted, as the LORD commanded Moses.

3. The purity of the camp

5:2
f Lev 13:46
g Lev 15:2
h Lev 13:3;
Nu 9:6-10

5:3
i Lev 26:12;
2Co 6:16

5 The LORD said to Moses, 2 "Command the Israelites to send away from the camp anyone who has an infectious skin disease a f or a discharge g of any kind, or who is ceremonially unclean h because of a dead body. 3 Send away male and female alike; send them outside the camp so they will not defile their camp, where I dwell among them. i" 4 The Israelites did this; they sent them outside the camp. They did just as the LORD had instructed Moses.

Restitution for Wrongs

5:6
j Lev 6:2

5:7
k Lev 5:5; 26:40;
Jos 7:19; Lk 19:8
l Lev 6:5

5 The LORD said to Moses, 6 "Say to the Israelites: 'When a man or woman wrongs another in any way b and so is unfaithful j to the LORD, that person is guilty 7 and must confess k the

a 2 Traditionally *leprosy* ; the Hebrew word was used for various diseases affecting the skin—not necessarily leprosy.
b 6 Or *woman commits any wrong common to mankind*

Hebrews was not to be handled or reduced to common elements. He is greater than anything in his creation. Worshiping our holy God must not be taken lightly.

4:27, 28 The Gershonites could receive directions from any of Aaron's sons, but they were directly responsible to Ithamar only. The lines of authority and accountability were clearly communicated to all. As you function with others in service to God, make sure the lines of authority between you and those you work with are clearly understood. Good communication builds good relationships.

5:5–8 God included restitution, a unique concept for that day, as part of his law for Israel. When someone was robbed, the guilty person was required to restore the loss to the victim and pay an additional interest penalty. When we have wronged others, we ought to do more than apologize. We should look for ways to set matters right and, if possible, leave the victim even better off than when we harmed him or her. When we have been wronged, we should still seek restoration rather than striking out in revenge.

sin he has committed. He must make full restitution *l* for his wrong, add one fifth to it and give it all to the person he has wronged. [8] But if that person has no close relative to whom restitution can be made for the wrong, the restitution belongs to the LORD and must be given to the priest, along with the ram with which atonement is made for him. *m* [9] All the sacred contributions the Israelites bring to a priest will belong to him. *n* [10] Each man's sacred gifts are his own, but what he gives to the priest will belong to the priest. *o* '"

The Test for an Unfaithful Wife

[11] Then the LORD said to Moses, [12] "Speak to the Israelites and say to them: 'If a man's wife goes astray and is unfaithful to him [13] by sleeping with another man, *p* and this is hidden from her husband and her impurity is undetected (since there is no witness against her and she has not been caught in the act), [14] and if feelings of jealousy come over her husband and he suspects his wife and she is impure—or if he is jealous and suspects her even though she is not impure— [15] then he is to take his wife to the priest. He must also take an offering of a tenth of an ephah[a] of barley flour on her behalf. He must not pour oil on it or put incense on it, because it is a grain offering for jealousy, a reminder *q* offering to draw attention to guilt.

[16] "'The priest shall bring her and have her stand before the LORD. [17] Then he shall take some holy water in a clay jar and put some dust from the tabernacle floor into the water. [18] After the priest has had the woman stand before the LORD, he shall loosen her hair *r* and place in her hands the reminder offering, the grain offering for jealousy, while he himself holds the bitter water that brings a curse. [19] Then the priest shall put the woman under oath and say to her, "If no other man has slept with you and you have not gone astray and become impure while married to your husband, may this bitter water that brings a curse not harm you. [20] But if you have gone astray while married to your husband and you have defiled yourself by sleeping with a man other than your husband"— [21] here the priest is to put the woman under this curse of the oath *s* —"may the LORD cause your people to curse and denounce you when he causes your thigh to waste away and your abdomen to swell. *b* [22] May this water *t* that brings a curse enter your body so that your abdomen swells and your thigh wastes away. *c* "

"'Then the woman is to say, "Amen. So be it. *u* "

[23] "'The priest is to write these curses on a scroll and then wash them off into the bitter water. [24] He shall have the woman drink the bitter water that brings a curse, and this water will enter her and cause bitter suffering. [25] The priest is to take from her hands the grain offering for jealousy, wave it before the LORD *v* and bring it to the altar. [26] The priest is then to take a handful of the grain offering as a memorial offering and burn it on the altar; after that, he is to have the woman drink the water. [27] If she has defiled herself and been unfaithful to her husband, then when she is made to drink the water that brings a curse, it will go into her and cause bitter suffering; her abdomen will swell and her thigh waste away, *d* and she will become accursed *w* among her people. [28] If, however, the woman has not defiled herself and is free from impurity, she will be cleared of guilt and will be able to have children.

[29] "'This, then, is the law of jealousy when a woman goes astray *x* and defiles herself while married to her husband, [30] or when feelings of jealousy come over a man because he suspects his wife. The priest is to have her stand before the LORD and is to apply this entire law to her. [31] The husband will be innocent of any wrongdoing, but the woman will bear the consequences of her sin.'"

The Nazirite

6 The LORD said to Moses, [2] "Speak to the Israelites and say to them: 'If a man or woman wants to make a special vow *y*, a vow of separation to the LORD as a Nazirite, *z* [3] he must abstain from wine *a* and other fermented drink and must not drink vinegar made from wine or from other fermented drink. He must not drink grape juice or eat grapes or raisins. [4] As

a 15 That is, probably about 2 quarts (about 2 liters)   b 21 Or *causes you to have a miscarrying womb and barrenness*
c 22 Or *body and cause you to be barren and have a miscarrying womb*   d 27 Or *suffering; she will have barrenness and a miscarrying womb*

**Cross references (margin):**
5:8 *m* Lev 6:6,7
5:9 *n* Lev 6:17
5:10 *o* Lev 10:13
5:13 *p* Lev 18:20
5:15 *q* Eze 29:16
5:18 *r* 1Co 11:6
5:21 *s* Jos 6:26; 1Sa 14:24; Ne 10:29
5:22 *t* Ps 109:18 *u* Dt 27:15
5:25 *v* Lev 8:27
5:27 *w* Jer 29:18; 42:18
5:29 *x* ver 19
6:2 *y* Ac 21:23 *z* Jdg 13:5; 16:17; Am 2:11,12
6:3 *a* Lk 1:15

5:11–31 This test for adultery served to remove a jealous husband's suspicion. Trust between husband and wife had to be completely eroded for a man to bring his wife to the priest for this type of test. Today priests and pastors help restore marriages by counseling couples who have lost faith in each other. Men and women should strengthen the bond of trust in marriage. Flirtatious and intimate communication with someone you're not married to can build suspicion and weaken trust. Guard your heart and guard your marriage in order to maintain trust and strengthen your bond with your spouse.

6:1, 2 In Moses' day, a personal vow was as binding as a written contract. It was one thing to say you would do something, but it was considered much more serious when you made a solemn vow to do it. God instituted the Nazirite vow long as he is a Nazirite, he must not eat anything that comes from the grapevine, not even the seeds or skins.

6:5
b 1Sa 1:11

5 "'During the entire period of his vow of separation no razor may be used on his head.b He must be holy until the period of his separation to the Lord is over; he must let the hair of his head grow long. 6 Throughout the period of his separation to the Lord he must not go near a dead body. c 7 Even if his own father or mother or brother or sister dies, he must not make himself ceremonially unclean d on account of them, because the symbol of his separation to God is on his head. 8 Throughout the period of his separation he is consecrated to the Lord.

6:6
c Nu 19:11-22
6:7
d Nu 9:6

9 "'If someone dies suddenly in his presence, thus defiling the hair he has dedicated, he must shave his head on the day of his cleansing—the seventh day. 10 Then on the eighth day he must bring two doves or two young pigeons e to the priest at the entrance to the Tent of Meeting. 11 The priest is to offer one as a sin offering and the other as a burnt offering to make atonement for him because he sinned by being in the presence of the dead body. That same day he is to consecrate his head. 12 He must dedicate himself to the Lord for the period of his separation and must bring a year-old male lamb as a guilt offering. The previous days do not count, because he became defiled during his separation.

6:10
e Lev 5:7; 14:22

13 "'Now this is the law for the Nazirite when the period of his separation is over.f He is to be brought to the entrance to the Tent of Meeting. 14 There he is to present his offerings to the Lord: a year-old male lamb without defect for a burnt offering, a year-old ewe lamb without defect for a sin offering,g a ram without defect for a fellowship offering,a 15 together with their grain offerings and drink offerings, and a basket of bread made without yeast—cakes made of fine flour mixed with oil, and wafers spread with oil.h

6:13
f Ac 21:26
6:14
g Lev 14:10
6:15
h Ex 29:2

16 "'The priest is to present them before the Lord and make the sin offering and the burnt offering. 17 He is to present the basket of unleavened bread and is to sacrifice the ram as a fellowship offering to the Lord, together with its grain offering and drink offering.

18 "'Then at the entrance to the Tent of Meeting, the Nazirite must shave off the hair that he dedicated.i He is to take the hair and put it in the fire that is under the sacrifice of the fellowship offering.

6:18
i ver 9; Ac 21:24

19 "'After the Nazirite has shaved off the hair of his dedication, the priest is to place in his hands a boiled shoulder of the ram, and a cake and a wafer from the basket, both made without yeast. 20 The priest shall then wave them before the Lord as a wave offering; they are holy and belong to the priest, together with the breast that was waved and the thigh that was presented. After that, the Nazirite may drink wine.

21 "'This is the law of the Nazirite who vows his offering to the Lord in accordance with his separation, in addition to whatever else he can afford. He must fulfill the vow he has made, according to the law of the Nazirite.'"

The Priestly Blessing

6:23
j 1Ch 23:13

22 The Lord said to Moses, 23 "Tell Aaron and his sons, 'This is how you are to blessj the Israelites. Say to them:

6:24
k Dt 28:3-6

24 "'"The Lord bless youk
       and keep you;

6:25
l Ps 80:3; 119:135
m Ge 43:29;
Ps 25:16; 86:16

25 the Lord make his face shine upon youl
       and be gracious to you;m

6:26
n Ps 4:6; 44:3

26 the Lord turn his facen toward you
       and give you peace."'

6:27
o Dt 28:10;
2Ch 7:14

27 "So they will put my nameo on the Israelites, and I will bless them."

a 14 Traditionally peace offering; also in verses 17 and 18

---

for people who wanted to devote some time exclusively to serving him. This vow could be taken for as little as 30 days or as long as a lifetime. It was voluntary, with one exception—parents could take the vow for their young children, making them Nazirites for life. The vow included three distinct restrictions: (1) he must abstain from wine and fermented drink; (2) his hair could not be cut, and his beard could not be shaved; (3) touching a dead body was prohibited. The purpose of the Nazirite vow was to raise up a group of leaders devoted completely to God. Samson, Samuel, and John the Baptist were probably Nazirites for life.

6:24–26 A blessing was one way of asking for God's divine favor to rest upon others. The ancient blessing in these verses helps us understand what a blessing was supposed to do. Its five parts conveyed hope that God would (1) bless and keep them (favor and protect); (2) make his face shine upon them (be pleased); (3) be gracious (merciful and compassionate); (4) turn his face toward them (give his approval); (5) give peace. When you ask God to bless others or yourself, you are asking him to do these five things. The blessing you offer will not only help the one receiving it, it will also demonstrate love, encourage others, and provide a model of caring to others.

Offerings at the Dedication of the Tabernacle

7 When Moses finished setting up the tabernacle,[p] he anointed it and consecrated it and all its furnishings. He also anointed and consecrated the altar and all its utensils. ²Then the leaders of Israel,[q] the heads of families who were the tribal leaders in charge of those who were counted, made offerings. ³They brought as their gifts before the LORD six covered carts and twelve oxen—an ox from each leader and a cart from every two. These they presented before the tabernacle.

⁴The LORD said to Moses, ⁵"Accept these from them, that they may be used in the work at the Tent of Meeting. Give them to the Levites as each man's work requires."

⁶So Moses took the carts and oxen and gave them to the Levites. ⁷He gave two carts and four oxen to the Gershonites,[r] as their work required, ⁸and he gave four carts and eight oxen to the Merarites,[s] as their work required. They were all under the direction of Ithamar son of Aaron, the priest. ⁹But Moses did not give any to the Kohathites, because they were to carry on their shoulders[t] the holy things, for which they were responsible.

¹⁰When the altar was anointed, the leaders brought their offerings for its dedication[u] and presented them before the altar. ¹¹For the LORD had said to Moses, "Each day one leader is to bring his offering for the dedication of the altar."

¹²The one who brought his offering on the first day was Nahshon son of Amminadab of the tribe of Judah.

¹³His offering was one silver plate weighing a hundred and thirty shekels,[a] and one silver sprinkling bowl weighing seventy shekels,[b] both according to the sanctuary shekel, each filled with fine flour mixed with oil as a grain offering; ¹⁴one gold dish weighing ten shekels,[c] filled with incense; ¹⁵one young bull, one ram and one male lamb a year old, for a burnt offering; ¹⁶one male goat for a sin offering;[v] ¹⁷and two oxen, five rams, five male goats and five male lambs a year old, to be sacrificed as a fellowship offering.[d][w] This was the offering of Nahshon son of Amminadab.

¹⁸On the second day Nethanel son of Zuar,[x] the leader of Issachar, brought his offering. ¹⁹The offering he brought was one silver plate weighing a hundred and thirty shekels, and one silver sprinkling bowl weighing seventy shekels, both according to the sanctuary shekel, each filled with fine flour mixed with oil as a grain offering; ²⁰one gold dish weighing ten shekels, filled with incense; ²¹one young bull, one ram and one male lamb a year old, for a burnt offering; ²²one male goat for a sin offering; ²³and two oxen, five rams, five male goats and five male lambs a year old, to be sacrificed as a fellowship offering. This was the offering of Nethanel son of Zuar.

²⁴On the third day, Eliab son of Helon,[y] the leader of the people of Zebulun, brought his offering. ²⁵His offering was one silver plate weighing a hundred and thirty shekels, and one silver sprinkling bowl weighing seventy shekels, both according to the sanctuary shekel, each filled with fine flour mixed with oil as a grain offering; ²⁶one gold dish weighing ten shekels, filled with incense; ²⁷one young bull, one ram and one male lamb a year old, for a burnt offering; ²⁸one male goat for a sin offering; ²⁹and two oxen, five rams, five male goats and five male lambs a year old, to be sacrificed as a fellowship offering. This was the offering of Eliab son of Helon.

³⁰On the fourth day Elizur son of Shedeur,[z] the leader of the people of Reuben, brought his offering. ³¹His offering was one silver plate weighing a hundred and thirty shekels, and one silver sprinkling bowl weighing seventy shekels, both according to the sanctuary shekel, each filled with fine flour mixed with oil as a grain offering; ³²one gold dish weighing ten shekels, filled with incense; ³³one young bull, one ram and one male lamb a year old, for a burnt offering; ³⁴one male goat for a sin offering; ³⁵and two oxen, five rams, five male goats and five male lambs a year old, to be sacrificed as a fellowship offering. This was the offering of Elizur son of Shedeur.

7:1 [p] Ex 40:17
7:2 [q] Nu 1:5-16
7:7 [r] Nu 4:24-26,28
7:8 [s] Nu 4:31-33
7:9 [t] Nu 4:15
7:10 [u] 2Ch 7:9
7:16 [v] Lev 4:3,23
7:17 [w] Lev 3:1
7:18 [x] Nu 1:8
7:24 [y] Nu 1:9
7:30 [z] Nu 1:5

a 13 That is, about 3 1/4 pounds (about 1.5 kilograms); also elsewhere in this chapter   b 13 That is, about 1 3/4 pounds (about 0.8 kilogram); also elsewhere in this chapter   c 14 That is, about 4 ounces (about 110 grams); also elsewhere in this chapter   d 17 Traditionally peace offering; also elsewhere in this chapter

7:1ff After the tabernacle was set up, anointed, and consecrated, the leaders of the 12 tribes brought gifts and offerings for its use and maintenance. All of the people participated—it was everyone's tabernacle.

7:36
a Nu 1:6

36 On the fifth day Shelumiel son of Zurishaddai, *a* the leader of the people of Simeon, brought his offering.

37 His offering was one silver plate weighing a hundred and thirty shekels, and one silver sprinkling bowl weighing seventy shekels, both according to the sanctuary shekel, each filled with fine flour mixed with oil as a grain offering; 38 one gold dish weighing ten shekels, filled with incense; 39 one young bull, one ram and one male lamb a year old, for a burnt offering; 40 one male goat for a sin offering; 41 and two oxen, five rams, five male goats and five male lambs a year old, to be sacrificed as a fellowship offering. This was the offering of Shelumiel son of Zurishaddai.

7:42
b Nu 1:14

42 On the sixth day Eliasaph son of Deuel, *b* the leader of the people of Gad, brought his offering.

43 His offering was one silver plate weighing a hundred and thirty shekels, and one silver sprinkling bowl weighing seventy shekels, both according to the sanctuary shekel, each filled with fine flour mixed with oil as a grain offering; 44 one gold dish weighing ten shekels, filled with incense; 45 one young bull, one ram and one male lamb a year old, for a burnt offering; 46 one male goat for a sin offering; 47 and two oxen, five rams, five male goats and five male lambs a year old, to be sacrificed as a fellowship offering. This was the offering of Eliasaph son of Deuel.

7:48
c Nu 1:10

48 On the seventh day Elishama son of Ammihud, *c* the leader of the people of Ephraim, brought his offering.

49 His offering was one silver plate weighing a hundred and thirty shekels, and one silver sprinkling bowl weighing seventy shekels, both according to the sanctuary shekel, each filled with fine flour mixed with oil as a grain offering; 50 one gold dish weighing ten shekels, filled with incense; 51 one young bull, one ram and one male lamb a year old, for a burnt offering; 52 one male goat for a sin offering; 53 and two oxen, five rams, five male goats and five male lambs a year old, to be sacrificed as a fellowship offering. This was the offering of Elishama son of Ammihud.

7:54
d Nu 1:10; 2:20

54 On the eighth day Gamaliel son of Pedahzur, *d* the leader of the people of Manasseh, brought his offering.

55 His offering was one silver plate weighing a hundred and thirty shekels, and one silver sprinkling bowl weighing seventy shekels, both according to the sanctuary shekel, each filled with fine flour mixed with oil as a grain offering; 56 one gold dish weighing ten shekels, filled with incense; 57 one young bull, one ram and one male lamb a year old, for a burnt offering; 58 one male goat for a sin offering; 59 and two oxen, five rams, five male goats and five male lambs a year old, to be sacrificed as a fellowship offering. This was the offering of Gamaliel son of Pedahzur.

7:60
e Nu 1:11

60 On the ninth day Abidan son of Gideoni, *e* the leader of the people of Benjamin, brought his offering.

61 His offering was one silver plate weighing a hundred and thirty shekels, and one silver sprinkling bowl weighing seventy shekels, both according to the sanctuary shekel, each filled with fine flour mixed with oil as a grain offering; 62 one gold dish weighing ten shekels, filled with incense; 63 one young bull, one ram and one male lamb a year old, for a burnt offering; 64 one male goat for a sin offering; 65 and two oxen, five rams, five male goats and five male lambs a year old, to be sacrificed as a fellowship offering. This was the offering of Abidan son of Gideoni.

7:66
f Nu 1:12; 2:25

66 On the tenth day Ahiezer son of Ammishaddai, *f* the leader of the people of Dan, brought his offering.

67 His offering was one silver plate weighing a hundred and thirty shekels, and one silver sprinkling bowl weighing seventy shekels, both according to the sanctuary shekel, each filled with fine flour mixed with oil as a grain offering; 68 one gold dish weighing ten shekels, filled with incense; 69 one young bull, one ram and one male lamb a year old, for a burnt offering; 70 one male goat for a sin offering; 71 and two oxen, five rams, five male goats and five male lambs a year old, to be sacrificed as a fellowship offering. This was the offering of Ahiezer son of Ammishaddai.

7:72
g Nu 1:13

72 On the eleventh day Pagiel son of Ocran, *g* the leader of the people of Asher, brought his offering.

73 His offering was one silver plate weighing a hundred and thirty shekels, and one silver sprinkling bowl weighing seventy shekels, both according to the sanctuary shekel, each filled with fine flour mixed with oil as a grain offering; 74 one gold dish weighing ten shekels, filled with incense; 75 one young bull, one ram and one male lamb a year old, for a burnt offering; 76 one male goat for a sin offering; 77 and two oxen, five rams, five male goats and five male lambs a year old, to be sacrificed as a fellowship offering. This was the offering of Pagiel son of Ocran.

78 On the twelfth day Ahira son of Enan, *h* the leader of the people of Naphtali, brought his offering.

7:78
h Nu 1:15; 2:29

79 His offering was one silver plate weighing a hundred and thirty shekels, and one silver sprinkling bowl weighing seventy shekels, both according to the sanctuary shekel, each filled with fine flour mixed with oil as a grain offering; 80 one gold dish weighing ten shekels, filled with incense; 81 one young bull, one ram and one male lamb a year old, for a burnt offering; 82 one male goat for a sin offering; 83 and two oxen, five rams, five male goats and five male lambs a year old, to be sacrificed as a fellowship offering. This was the offering of Ahira son of Enan.

84 These were the offerings of the Israelite leaders for the dedication of the altar when it was anointed: *i* twelve silver plates, twelve silver sprinkling bowls and twelve gold dishes. 85 Each silver plate weighed a hundred and thirty shekels, and each sprinkling bowl seventy shekels. Altogether, the silver dishes weighed two thousand four hundred shekels,*a* according to the sanctuary shekel. 86 The twelve gold dishes filled with incense weighed ten shekels each, according to the sanctuary shekel. Altogether, the gold dishes weighed a hundred and twenty shekels. *b* 87 The total number of animals for the burnt offering came to twelve young bulls, twelve rams and twelve male lambs a year old, together with their grain offering. Twelve male goats were used for the sin offering. 88 The total number of animals for the sacrifice of the fellowship offering came to twenty-four oxen, sixty rams, sixty male goats and sixty male lambs a year old. These were the offerings for the dedication of the altar after it was anointed.*j*

7:84
i ver 1,10

7:88
j ver 1,10

89 When Moses entered the Tent of Meeting to speak with the LORD,*k* he heard the voice speaking to him from between the two cherubim above the atonement cover *l* on the ark of the Testimony. And he spoke with him.

7:89
k Ex 25:21,22
l Ps 80:1; 99:1

Setting Up the Lamps

8 The LORD said to Moses, 2 "Speak to Aaron and say to him, 'When you set up the seven lamps, they are to light the area in front of the lampstand.*m*'"

8:2
m Ex 25:37

3 Aaron did so; he set up the lamps so that they faced forward on the lampstand, just as the LORD commanded Moses. 4 This is how the lampstand was made: It was made of hammered gold *n*—from its base to its blossoms. The lampstand was made exactly like the pattern the LORD had shown Moses.

8:4
n Ex 25:18,36

The Setting Apart of the Levites

5 The LORD said to Moses: 6 "Take the Levites from among the other Israelites and make them ceremonially clean. *o* 7 To purify them, do this: Sprinkle the water of cleansing*p* on them; then have them shave their whole bodies*q* and wash their clothes, and so purify themselves. 8 Have them take a young bull with its grain offering of fine flour mixed with oil;*r* then you are to take a second young bull for a sin offering. 9 Bring the Levites to the front of the Tent of Meeting *s* and assemble the whole Israelite community. *t* 10 You are to bring the Levites before the LORD, and the Israelites are to lay their hands on them. 11 Aaron is to present the Levites before the LORD as a wave offering from the Israelites, so that they may be ready to do the work of the LORD.

8:6
o Isa 52:11
8:7
p Nu 19:9,17
q Lev 14:9
8:8
r Lev 2:1
8:9
s Ex 40:12
t Lev 8:3

*a*85 That is, about 60 pounds (about 28 kilograms)   *b*86 That is, about 3 pounds (about 1.4 kilograms)

7:89 Imagine hearing the very voice of God! Moses must have trembled at the sound. Yet we have God's words recorded for us in the Bible, and we should have no less reverence and awe for them. God sometimes spoke directly to his people to tell them the proper way to live. The Bible records these conversations to give us insights into God's character. How tragic when we take these very words of God lightly. Like Moses, we have the privilege of talking to God, but God answers us differently—through his written Word and the guidance of his Holy Spirit. To receive this guidance, we need to seek to know God as Moses did.

8:1–4 The lamps provided light for the priests as they carried out their duties. The light was also an expression of God's presence. Jesus said, "I am the light of the world" (John 8:12). The golden lampstand is still one of the major symbols of the Jewish faith.

8:12
u Ex 29:10

¹²"After the Levites lay their hands on the heads of the bulls,*u* use the one for a sin offering to the LORD and the other for a burnt offering, to make atonement for the Levites. ¹³Have the Levites stand in front of Aaron and his sons and then present them as a wave offering to the LORD. ¹⁴In this way you are to set the Levites apart from the other Israelites, and the Levites will be mine. *v*

8:14
v Nu 3:12

8:15
w Ex 29:24

8:16
x Nu 3:12

8:17
y Ex 13:2

¹⁵"After you have purified the Levites and presented them as a wave offering,*w* they are to come to do their work at the Tent of Meeting. ¹⁶They are the Israelites who are to be given wholly to me. I have taken them as my own in place of the firstborn, the first male offspring*x* from every Israelite woman. ¹⁷Every firstborn male in Israel, whether man or animal, is mine. When I struck down all the firstborn in Egypt, I set them apart for myself.*y* ¹⁸And I have taken the Levites in place of all the firstborn sons in Israel. ¹⁹Of all the Israelites, I have given the Levites as gifts to Aaron and his sons*z* to do the work at the Tent of Meeting on behalf of the Israelites*a* and to make atonement for them*b* so that no plague will strike the Israelites when they go near the sanctuary."

8:19
z Nu 3:9
a Nu 1:53
b Nu 16:46

8:21
c ver 7

²⁰Moses, Aaron and the whole Israelite community did with the Levites just as the LORD commanded Moses. ²¹The Levites purified themselves and washed their clothes.*c* Then Aaron presented them as a wave offering before the LORD and made atonement for them to purify them. ²²After that, the Levites came to do their work at the Tent of Meeting under the supervision of Aaron and his sons. They did with the Levites just as the LORD commanded Moses.

8:24
d 1Ch 23:3

²³The LORD said to Moses, ²⁴"This applies to the Levites: Men twenty-five years old or more*d* shall come to take part in the work at the Tent of Meeting, ²⁵but at the age of fifty, they must retire from their regular service and work no longer. ²⁶They may assist their brothers in performing their duties at the Tent of Meeting, but they themselves must not do the work. This, then, is how you are to assign the responsibilities of the Levites."

The Passover

9:1
e Nu 1:1

9 The LORD spoke to Moses in the Desert of Sinai in the first month of the second year after they came out of Egypt.*e* He said, ²"Have the Israelites celebrate the Passover at the appointed time. ³Celebrate it at the appointed time, at twilight on the fourteenth day of this month, in accordance with all its rules and regulations."

9:5
f Ex 12:1-13;
Jos 5:10

⁴So Moses told the Israelites to celebrate the Passover, ⁵and they did so in the Desert of Sinai at twilight on the fourteenth day of the first month.*f* The Israelites did everything just as the LORD commanded Moses.

9:6
g Ex 18:15; Nu 27:2

⁶But some of them could not celebrate the Passover on that day because they were ceremonially unclean on account of a dead body. So they came to Moses and Aaron*g* that same day ⁷and said to Moses, "We have become unclean because of a dead body, but why should we be kept from presenting the LORD's offering with the other Israelites at the appointed time?"

⁸Moses answered them, "Wait until I find out what the LORD commands concerning you."

9:11
h Ex 12:8

9:12
i Ex 12:46;
Jn 19:36*

9:13
j Ge 17:14; Ex 12:15

⁹Then the LORD said to Moses, ¹⁰"Tell the Israelites: 'When any of you or your descendants are unclean because of a dead body or are away on a journey, they may still celebrate the LORD's Passover. ¹¹They are to celebrate it on the fourteenth day of the second month at twilight. They are to eat the lamb, together with unleavened bread and bitter herbs.*h* ¹²They must not leave any of it till morning or break any of its bones.*i* When they celebrate the Passover, they must follow all the regulations. ¹³But if a man who is ceremonially clean and not on a journey fails to celebrate the Passover, that person must be cut off from his people*j* because

---

8:25, 26 Why were the Levites supposed to retire at age 50? The reasons were probably more practical than theological. (1) Moving the tabernacle and its furniture through the desert required strength. The younger men were more suited for the work of lifting the heavy articles. (2) The Levites over 50 did not stop working altogether. They were allowed to assist with various light duties in the tabernacle. This helped the younger men assume more responsibilities, and it allowed the older men to be in a position to advise and counsel them.

9:2 This is the second Passover. The first was instituted in Egypt and recorded in Exodus 12. Passover and the Feast of Unleavened Bread were eight-day religious observances (Leviticus 23:5, 6) commemorating the Israelites' escape from slavery in Egypt by God's power.

9:6–12 Several men came to Moses because of the predica-

ment they faced: They were "unclean" because of contact with a dead body (or entering the home of a person who had died), and this prevented them from participating in the Passover meal. Notice that God did not adjust the requirements of the Passover. The standards of holiness were maintained, and the men were not allowed to participate. But God did make an exception and allowed the men to celebrate the Passover at a later date. This upheld the sacred requirements while allowing the men to participate in the feast—a duty for all Israelite men. Sometimes we face predicaments where the most obvious solution might cause us to compromise God's standards. Like Moses, we should use wisdom and prayer to reach a workable solution.

he did not present the LORD's offering at the appointed time. That man will bear the consequences of his sin.

14"'An alien *k* living among you who wants to celebrate the LORD's Passover must do so in accordance with its rules and regulations. You must have the same regulations for the alien and the native-born.'"

9:14
k Ex 12:48,49

4. Receiving guidance for the journey
The Cloud Above the Tabernacle

15On the day the tabernacle, the Tent of the Testimony, was set up, the cloud *l* covered it. From evening till morning the cloud above the tabernacle looked like fire. *m* 16That is how it continued to be; the cloud covered it, and at night it looked like fire. 17Whenever the cloud lifted from above the Tent, the Israelites set out; wherever the cloud settled, the Israelites encamped. *n* 18At the LORD's command the Israelites set out, and at his command they encamped. As long as the cloud stayed over the tabernacle, they remained in camp. 19When the cloud remained over the tabernacle a long time, the Israelites obeyed the LORD's order and did not set out. 20Sometimes the cloud was over the tabernacle only a few days; at the LORD's command they would encamp, and then at his command they would set out. 21Sometimes the cloud stayed only from evening till morning, and when it lifted in the morning, they set out. Whether by day or by night, whenever the cloud lifted, they set out. 22Whether the cloud stayed over the tabernacle for two days or a month or a year, the Israelites would remain in camp and not set out; but when it lifted, they would set out. 23At the LORD's command they encamped, and at the LORD's command they set out. They obeyed the LORD's order, in accordance with his command through Moses.

9:15
l Ex 40:34
m Ex 13:21

9:17
n Ex 40:36-38;
Nu 10:11,12;
1Co 10:1

The Silver Trumpets

10 The LORD said to Moses: 2"Make two trumpets of hammered silver, and use them for calling the community together and for having the camps set out. 3When both are sounded, the whole community is to assemble before you at the entrance to the Tent of Meeting. 4If only one is sounded, the leaders *o*—the heads of the clans of Israel—are to assemble before you. 5When a trumpet blast is sounded, the tribes camping on the east are to set out. *p* 6At the sounding of a second blast, the camps on the south are to set out. *q* The blast will be the signal for setting out. 7To gather the assembly, blow the trumpets, *r* but not with the same signal.

8"The sons of Aaron, the priests, are to blow the trumpets. This is to be a lasting ordinance for you and the generations to come. *s* 9When you go into battle in your own land against an enemy who is oppressing you, *t* sound a blast on the trumpets. Then you will be remembered by the LORD your God and rescued from your enemies. *u* 10Also at your times of rejoicing—your appointed feasts and New Moon festivals—you are to sound the trumpets *v* over your burnt offerings and fellowship offerings, *a* and they will be a memorial for you before your God. I am the LORD your God."

10:4
o Ex 18:21

10:5
p ver 14

10:6
q ver 18

10:7
r Joel 2:1

10:8
s Nu 31:6

10:9
t Jdg 2:18
u Ps 106:4

10:10
v Lev 23:24

a 10 Traditionally *peace offerings*

9:14 God said regarding foreigners and the Passover, "You must have the same regulations for the alien and the native-born." This principle designed for foreigners doesn't mean we mandate our religion to our neighbors, but in our homes we should live out our convictions. When we have guests in our homes, whether visitors or family, we may be tempted to change or water down our Christian practices. If family devotions, attending church, and mealtime prayers are your practices, don't change these when you have guests. Holidays such as Christmas and Easter should not be reduced to nothing more than society's expressions. Further, you should maintain your family standards even when guests visit—for example, unmarried couples who are guests should not be allowed to sleep together. Maintain your Christian standards and principles. You never know what influence you may have on the guests in your home.

9:15–22 A pillar of cloud by day and a pillar of fire by night guided and protected the Israelites as they traveled across the desert. Some have said this pillar may have been a burning bowl of pitch whose smoke was visible during the day and whose fire

could be seen at night. However, a bowl of pitch would not have lifted itself up and moved ahead of the people, and the Bible is clear that the cloud and fire moved in accordance with the will of God. The cloud and the fire were not merely natural phenomena; they were the vehicle of God's presence and the visible evidence of his moving and directing his people.

9:23 The Israelites traveled and camped as God guided. When you follow God's guidance, you know you are where God wants you, whether you're moving or staying in one place. You are physically somewhere right now. Instead of praying, "God, what do you want me to do next?" ask, "God, what do you want me to do while I'm right here?" Direction from God is not just for your next big move. He has a purpose in placing you where you are right now. Begin to understand God's purpose for your life by discovering what he wants you to do now!

10:1–10 The two silver trumpets were used to coordinate the tribes as they moved through the desert. To keep so many people in tight formations required clear communication and control. Trumpet blasts also reminded Israel of God's protection over them.

B. FIRST APPROACH TO THE PROMISED LAND (10:11—14:45)

As the Israelites approached the promised land, Moses sent leaders to spy out the land and its people. But the spies returned with a discouraging report. Only Joshua and Caleb wanted to proceed, but the Israelites had already made up their minds and began to complain. As punishment for their lack of faith, God condemned them to wander in the desert for 40 years. Our obedience must be complete and timely.

1. The people complain

The Israelites Leave Sinai

10:11
w Nu 9:17

¹¹On the twentieth day of the second month of the second year, the cloud lifted *w* from above the tabernacle of the Testimony. ¹²Then the Israelites set out from the Desert of Sinai and traveled from place to place until the cloud came to rest in the Desert of Paran. ¹³They set out, this first time, at the LORD's command through Moses.

10:14
x Nu 2:3-9

¹⁴The divisions of the camp of Judah went first, under their standard. *x* Nahshon son of Amminadab was in command. ¹⁵Nethanel son of Zuar was over the division of the tribe of Issachar, ¹⁶and Eliab son of Helon was over the division of the tribe of Zebulun. ¹⁷Then the tabernacle was taken down, and the Gershonites and Merarites, who carried it, set out. *y*

10:17
y Nu 4:21-32

10:18
z Nu 2:10-16

¹⁸The divisions of the camp of Reuben went next, under their standard. *z* Elizur son of Shedeur was in command. ¹⁹Shelumiel son of Zurishaddai was over the division of the tribe of Simeon, ²⁰and Eliasaph son of Deuel was over the division of the tribe of Gad. ²¹Then the Kohathites set out, carrying the holy things. *a* The tabernacle was to be set up before they arrived.

10:21
a Nu 4:20

10:22
b Nu 2:24

²²The divisions of the camp of Ephraim *b* went next, under their standard. Elishama son of Ammihud was in command. ²³Gamaliel son of Pedahzur was over the division of the tribe of Manasseh, ²⁴and Abidan son of Gideoni was over the division of the tribe of Benjamin.

10:25
c Nu 2:31; Jos 6:9

²⁵Finally, as the rear guard *c* for all the units, the divisions of the camp of Dan set out, under their standard. Ahiezer son of Ammishaddai was in command. ²⁶Pagiel son of Ocran was over the division of the tribe of Asher, ²⁷and Ahira son of Enan was over the division of the tribe of Naphtali. ²⁸This was the order of march for the Israelite divisions as they set out.

10:29
d Ex 2:18
e Ge 12:7

²⁹Now Moses said to Hobab son of Reuel *d* the Midianite, Moses' father-in-law, "We are setting out for the place about which the LORD said, 'I will give it to you.' *e* Come with us and we will treat you well, for the LORD has promised good things to Israel."

³⁰He answered, "No, I will not go; I am going back to my own land and my own people."

10:31
f Job 29:15

³¹But Moses said, "Please do not leave us. You know where we should camp in the desert, and you can be our eyes. *f* ³²If you come with us, we will share with you whatever good things the LORD gives us."

10:33
g Dt 1:33

³³So they set out *g* from the mountain of the LORD and traveled for three days. The ark of the covenant of the LORD went before them during those three days to find them a place to rest. ³⁴The cloud of the LORD was over them by day when they set out from the camp. *h*

10:34
h Nu 9:15-23

³⁵Whenever the ark set out, Moses said,

ISRAEL'S DEPARTURE FROM SINAI

It has been two years since Israel left Egypt. Having received God's travel instructions through Moses, Israel set out from Mount Sinai into the Desert of Paran on their way toward the promised land.

0   50 Mi.

0   50 Km.

N

Mediterranean Sea

CANAAN

Jerusalem •

EGYPT

Nile River

DESERT OF PARAN

Mount Sinai

• Hazeroth

Red Sea

10:21 Those who travel, move, or face new challenges know what it is to be uprooted. Life is full of changes, and few things remain stable. The Israelites were constantly moving through the desert. They were able to handle change only because God's presence in the tabernacle was always with them. The portable tabernacle signified God and his people moving together. For us, stability does not mean lack of change, but moving with God in every circumstance.

10:29–32 By complimenting Hobab's desert skills, Moses let him know he was needed. People cannot know you appreciate them if you do not tell them they are important to you. Complimenting those who deserve it builds lasting relationships and helps people know they are valued. Think about those who have helped you this month. What can you do to let them know how much you need and appreciate them?

"Rise up, O Lord!
May your enemies be scattered;[i]
may your foes flee before you."

10:35
[i] Ps 68:1

36 Whenever it came to rest, he said,

"Return, O Lord,
to the countless thousands of Israel."

Fire From the LORD

11 Now the people complained about their hardships in the hearing of the Lord, and when he heard them his anger was aroused. Then fire from the Lord burned among them[j] and consumed some of the outskirts of the camp. 2 When the people cried out to Moses, he prayed to the Lord[k] and the fire died down. 3 So that place was called Taberah,[a] because fire from the Lord had burned among them.

11:1
[j] Lev 10:2

11:2
[k] Nu 21:7

Quail From the LORD

4 The rabble with them began to crave other food,[l] and again the Israelites started wailing[m] and said, "If only we had meat to eat! 5 We remember the fish we ate in Egypt at no cost—also the cucumbers, melons, leeks, onions and garlic.[n] 6 But now we have lost our appetite; we never see anything but this manna!"

7 The manna was like coriander seed[o] and looked like resin. 8 The people went around gathering it, and then ground it in a handmill or crushed it in a mortar. They cooked it in a pot or made it into cakes. And it tasted like something made with olive oil. 9 When the dew[p] settled on the camp at night, the manna also came down.

11:4
[l] Ex 12:38
[m] Ps 78:18

11:5
[n] Ex 16:3

11:7
[o] Ex 16:31

11:9
[p] Ex 16:13

10 Moses heard the people of every family wailing, each at the entrance to his tent. The Lord became exceedingly angry, and Moses was troubled. 11 He asked the Lord, "Why have you brought this trouble on your servant? What have I done to displease you that you put the burden of all these people on me? 12 Did I conceive all these people? Did I give them birth? Why do you tell me to carry them in my arms, as a nurse carries an infant,[q] to the land you promised on oath to their forefathers?[r] 13 Where can I get meat for all these people? They keep wailing to me, 'Give us meat to eat!' 14 I cannot carry all these people by myself; the burden is too heavy for me.[s] 15 If this is how you are going to treat me, put me to death right now—if I have found favor in your eyes—and do not let me face my own ruin."

11:12
[q] Isa 49:23
[r] Ex 13:5

11:14
[s] Ex 18:18

16 The Lord said to Moses: "Bring me seventy of Israel's elders who are known to you as leaders and officials among the people. Have them come to the Tent of Meeting, that they may stand there with you. 17 I will come down and speak with you there, and I will take of the Spirit that is on you and put the Spirit on them.[t] They will help you carry the burden of the people so that you will not have to carry it alone.[u]

11:17
[t] ver 25,29;
1Sa 10:6
[u] Ex 18:18

18 "Tell the people: 'Consecrate yourselves[v] in preparation for tomorrow, when you will eat meat. The Lord heard you when you wailed, "If only we had meat to eat! We were better off in Egypt!"[w] Now the Lord will give you meat, and you will eat it. 19 You will not eat it for just one day, or two days, or five, ten or twenty days, 20 but for a whole month—until it comes out of your nostrils and you loathe it[x]—because you have rejected the Lord, who is among you, and have wailed before him, saying, "Why did we ever leave Egypt?"'"

11:18
[v] Ex 19:10
[w] Ac 7:39

11:20
[x] Ps 78:29

[a] 3 *Taberah* means *burning*.

11:1, 6–15 The Israelites complained, and then Moses complained. But God responded positively to Moses and negatively to the rest of the people. Why? The people complained *to one another*, and nothing was accomplished. Moses took his complaint *to God*, who could solve any problem. Many of us are good at complaining to each other. We need to learn to take our problems to the One who can do something about them.

11:4 The *rabble* refers to a mixed crowd of Egyptians and others who had followed Israel out of Egypt (Exodus 12:38).

11:4–6 Dissatisfaction comes when our attention shifts from what we have to what we don't have. The people of Israel didn't seem to notice what God was doing for them—setting them free, making them a nation, giving them a new land—because they were so wrapped up in what God wasn't doing for them. They could think of nothing but the delicious Egyptian food they had

left behind. Somehow they forgot that the brutal whip of Egyptian slavery was the cost of eating that food. Before we judge the Israelites too harshly, it's helpful to think about what occupies our attention most of the time. Are we grateful for what God has given us, or are we always thinking about what we would like to have? We should not allow our unfulfilled desires to cause us to forget God's gifts of life, food, health, work, and friends.

11:4–9 Every morning the Israelites drew back their tent doors and witnessed a miracle. Covering the ground was white, fluffy manna—food from heaven. But soon that wasn't enough. Feeling it was their right to have more, they forgot what they already had. They didn't ask God to fill their need; instead they demanded meat, and they stopped trusting God to care for them. "If only we had meat to eat!" they complained to Moses as they reminisced about the good food they had in Egypt. God gave them what they

²¹But Moses said, "Here I am among six hundred thousand men on foot, and you say, 'I will give them meat to eat for a whole month!' ²²Would they have enough if flocks and herds were slaughtered for them? Would they have enough if all the fish in the sea were caught for them?"

11:23
ʸIsa 50:2; 59:1

²³The LORD answered Moses, "Is the LORD's arm too short?ʸ You will now see whether or not what I say will come true for you."

11:25
ᶻNu 12:5
ᵃver 17

²⁴So Moses went out and told the people what the LORD had said. He brought together seventy of their elders and had them stand around the Tent. ²⁵Then the LORD came down in the cloudᶻ and spoke with him,ᵃ and he took of the Spirit that was on him and put the Spirit on the seventy elders. When the Spirit rested on them, they prophesied, but they did not do so again.ᵃ

²⁶However, two men, whose names were Eldad and Medad, had remained in the camp. They were listed among the elders, but did not go out to the Tent. Yet the Spirit also rested on them, and they prophesied in the camp. ²⁷A young man ran and told Moses, "Eldad and Medad are prophesying in the camp."

11:28
ᵇMk 9:38-40

²⁸Joshua son of Nun, who had been Moses' aide since youth, spoke up and said, "Moses, my lord, stop them!"ᵇ

ᵃ25 Or prophesied and continued to do so

ISRAEL'S COMPLAINING		Complaint	Sin	Result
	11:1	About their hardships	Complained about their problems instead of praying to God about them	Thousands of people were destroyed when God sent a plague of fire to punish them
	11:4	About the lack of meat	Lusted after things they didn't have	God sent quail; but as the people began to eat, God struck them with a plague that killed many
	14:1–4	About being stuck in the desert, facing the giants of the promised land, and wishing to return to Egypt	Openly rebelled against God's leaders and failed to trust in his promises	All who complained were not allowed to enter the promised land, being doomed to wander in the desert until they died
	16:3	About Moses' and Aaron's authority and leadership	Were greedy for more power and authority	The families, friends, and possessions of Korah, Dathan, and Abiram were swallowed up by the earth. Fire then burned up the 250 other men who rebelled
	16:41	That Moses and Aaron caused the deaths of Korah and his conspirators	Blamed others for their own troubles	God began to destroy Israel with a plague. Moses and Aaron made atonement for the people, but 14,700 of them were killed
	20:2, 3	About the lack of water	Refused to believe that God would provide as he had promised	Moses sinned along with the people. For this he was barred from entering the promised land
	21:5	That God and Moses brought them into the desert	Failed to recognize that their problems were brought on by their own disobedience	God sent venomous snakes that killed many people and seriously injured many others

---

asked for, but they paid dearly for it when a plague struck the camp (see 11:18–20, 31–34). When you ask God for something, he may grant your request. But if you approach him with a sinful attitude, getting what you want may prove costly.

11:21, 22 Moses had witnessed God's power in spectacular miracles, yet at this time he questioned God's ability to feed the wandering Israelites. If Moses doubted God's power, how much easier it is for us to do the same. But completely depending upon God is essential, regardless of our level of spiritual maturity. When we begin to rely on our own understanding, we are in danger of ignoring God's assessment of the situation. By remembering his past works and his present power, we can be sure that we are not cutting off his potential help.

11:23 How strong is God? It is easy to trust God when we see his mighty acts (the Israelites saw many), but after a while, in the routine of daily life, his strength may appear to diminish. God doesn't change, but our view of him often does. The monotony of day-by-day living lulls us into forgetting how powerful God can be. As Moses learned, God's strength is always available.

11:26–29 This incident is similar to a story told in Mark 9:38–41. The disciples wanted Jesus to forbid others to drive out demons because they were not part of the disciples' group. But this type of narrow attitude was condemned by both Moses and Jesus. Beware of putting limits on God—he can work through whomever he chooses.

²⁹But Moses replied, "Are you jealous for my sake? I wish that all the LORD's people were prophets^c and that the LORD would put his Spirit on them!" ³⁰Then Moses and the elders of Israel returned to the camp.

³¹Now a wind went out from the LORD and drove quail^d in from the sea. It brought them^a down all around the camp to about three feet^b above the ground, as far as a day's walk in any direction. ³²All that day and night and all the next day the people went out and gathered quail. No one gathered less than ten homers. ^c Then they spread them out all around the camp. ³³But while the meat was still between their teeth ^e and before it could be consumed, the anger of the LORD burned against the people, and he struck them with a severe plague.^f ³⁴Therefore the place was named Kibroth Hattaavah,^d because there they buried the people who had craved other food.

³⁵From Kibroth Hattaavah the people traveled to Hazeroth^g and stayed there.

2. Miriam and Aaron oppose Moses

12 Miriam and Aaron began to talk against Moses because of his Cushite wife,^h for he had married a Cushite. ²"Has the LORD spoken only through Moses?" they asked. "Hasn't he also spoken through us?" And the LORD heard this.

³(Now Moses was a very humble man, more humble than anyone else on the face of the earth.)

⁴At once the LORD said to Moses, Aaron and Miriam, "Come out to the Tent of Meeting, all three of you." So the three of them came out. ⁵Then the LORD came down in a pillar of cloud;ⁱ he stood at the entrance to the Tent and summoned Aaron and Miriam. When both of them stepped forward, ⁶he said, "Listen to my words:

> "When a prophet of the LORD is among you,
> I reveal myself to him in visions,^j
> I speak to him in dreams.^k
> ⁷ But this is not true of my servant Moses;^l
> he is faithful in all my house.^m
> ⁸ With him I speak face to face,
> clearly and not in riddles;ⁿ
> he sees the form of the LORD.^o
> Why then were you not afraid
> to speak against my servant Moses?"

⁹The anger of the LORD burned against them, and he left them.

¹⁰When the cloud lifted from above the Tent, there stood Miriam—leprous,^e like snow.^p Aaron turned toward her and saw that she had leprosy;^q ¹¹and he said to Moses, "Please, my lord, do not hold against us the sin we have so foolishly committed.^r ¹²Do not let her be like a stillborn infant coming from its mother's womb with its flesh half eaten away."

^a*31* Or *They flew*   ^b*31* Hebrew *two cubits* (about 1 meter)   ^c*32* That is, probably about 60 bushels (about 2.2 kiloliters)   ^d*34 Kibroth Hattaavah* means *graves of craving.*   ^e*10* The Hebrew word was used for various diseases affecting the skin—not necessarily leprosy.

### Cross references (margin)

11:29 ^c1Co 14:5

11:31 ^dEx 16:13; Ps 78:26-28

11:33 ^ePs 78:30 ^fPs 106:15

11:35 ^gNu 33:17

12:1 ^hEx 2:21

12:5 ⁱNu 11:25

12:6 ^jGe 15:1; 46:2 ^kGe 31:10; 1Ki 3:5; Heb 1:1

12:7 ^lPs 105:26 ^mHeb 3:2,5

12:8 ⁿDt 34:10 ^oPs 17:15

12:10 ^pDt 24:9 ^q2Ki 5:1,27

12:11 ^r2Sa 19:19; 24:10

11:29 Moses was looking forward to the day when all God's people would experience the pouring out of God's Spirit. The prophet Joel recorded God's promise to pour out his Spirit on all believers (Joel 2:28, 29), and this was fulfilled at Pentecost (Acts 2:16–21). Believers today can be sure that they have the Holy Spirit when they become Christians (Romans 8:9). We also can pray to live by the Holy Spirit's power (Galatians 5:16–26). If you wish to have the Holy Spirit's power, pray for him to fill your life with his presence and strengthen you to follow Christ.

11:34 Craving or lusting is more than inappropriate sexual desire. It can be an unnatural or greedy desire for anything (sports, knowledge, possessions, influence over others). In this circumstance, God punished the Israelites for craving good food! Their desire was not wrong; the sin was in allowing that desire to turn into greed. They felt it was their right to have fine food, and they could think of nothing else. When you become preoccupied with something until it affects your perspective on everything else, you have moved from desire to lust.

12:1 Moses didn't have a Jewish wife because he lived with the Egyptians the first 40 years of his life, and he was in the desert the next 40 years. The woman is probably not Zipporah, his first wife, who was a Midianite (see Exodus 2:21). A Cushite was an Ethiopian. There is no explanation given for why Miriam objected to this woman.

12:1 People often argue over minor disagreements, leaving the real issue untouched. Such was the case when Miriam and Aaron came to Moses with a complaint. They represented the priests and the prophets, the two most powerful groups next to Moses. The real issue was their growing jealousy of Moses' position and influence. Since they could not find fault with the way Moses was leading the people, they chose to criticize his wife. Rather than face the problem squarely by dealing with their envy and pride, they chose to create a diversion from the real issue. When you are in a disagreement, stop and ask yourself if you are arguing over the real issue or if you have introduced a smoke screen by attacking someone's character. If you are unjustly criticized, remember that your critics may be afraid to face the real problem. Don't take this type of criticism personally. Ask God to help you identify the real issue and deal with it.

12:11 Aaron asked that the sin he and Miriam committed not be

12:14
s Lev 13:46;
Nu 5:2-3

¹³So Moses cried out to the LORD, "O God, please heal her!"

¹⁴The LORD replied to Moses, "If her father had spit in her face, would she not have been in disgrace for seven days? Confine her outside the camp*s* for seven days; after that she can be brought back." ¹⁵So Miriam was confined outside the camp for seven days, and the people did not move on till she was brought back.

¹⁶After that, the people left Hazeroth and encamped in the Desert of Paran.

3. The spies incite rebellion
Exploring Canaan

13:2
t Dt 1:22

13 The LORD said to Moses, ²"Send some men to explore*t* the land of Canaan, which I am giving to the Israelites. From each ancestral tribe send one of its leaders."

³So at the LORD's command Moses sent them out from the Desert of Paran. All of them were leaders of the Israelites. ⁴These are their names:

from the tribe of Reuben, Shammua son of Zaccur;
⁵ from the tribe of Simeon, Shaphat son of Hori;

Ask older brothers or sisters what their greatest trial in life is and they will often answer, "My younger brother (or sister)!" This is especially true when the younger sibling is more successful than the older. The bonds of family loyalty can be strained to the breaking point.

When we first meet Miriam she is involved in one of history's most unusual babysitting jobs. She is watching her infant brother float on the Nile River in a waterproof cradle. Miriam's quick thinking allowed Moses to be raised by his own mother. Her protective superiority, reinforced by that event, must have been hard to give up as she watched her little brother rise to greatness.

Eventually Moses' choice of a wife gave Miriam an opportunity to criticize. It was natural for her insecurity to break out over this issue. With Moses married, Miriam was clearly no longer the most important woman in his life. The real issue, however, was not the kind of woman Moses had married. It was the fact that he was now the most important man in Israel. "Has the Lord spoken only through Moses? . . . Hasn't he also spoken through us?" No mention is made of Moses' response, but God had a quick answer for Miriam and Aaron. Without denying their role in his plan, God clearly pointed out his special relationship with Moses. Miriam was stricken with leprosy, a deadly disease, as punishment for her insubordination. But Moses, true to his character, intervened for his sister so that God healed Miriam of her leprosy.

Before criticizing someone else, we need to pause long enough to discover our own motives. Failing to do this can bring disastrous results. What is often labeled "constructive criticism" may actually be destructive jealousy, since the easiest way to raise our own status is to bring someone else down. Are you willing to question your motives before you offer criticism? Does the critical finger you point need to be pointed first toward yourself?

Strengths and accomplishments:	• Quick thinker under pressure • Able leader • Songwriter • Prophetess
Weaknesses and mistakes:	• Was jealous of Moses' authority • Openly criticized Moses' leadership
Lesson from her life:	• The motives behind criticism are often more important to deal with than the criticism itself
Vital statistics:	• Where: Egypt, Sinai peninsula • Relatives: Brothers: Aaron and Moses
Key verses:	"Then Miriam the prophetess, Aaron's sister, took a tambourine in her hand, and all the women followed her, with tambourines and dancing. Miriam sang to them: 'Sing to the Lord, for he is highly exalted. The horse and its rider he has hurled into the sea'" (Exodus 15:20, 21).

Miriam's story is told in Exodus 2; 15; and Numbers 12; 20. She is also mentioned in Deuteronomy 24:9; 1 Chronicles 6:3; Micah 6:4.

---

held against them. It is easy to look back at our mistakes and recognize their foolishness. It is much harder to recognize foolish plans while we are carrying them out because somehow then they seem appropriate. To get rid of foolish ideas before they turn into foolish actions requires eliminating our wrong thoughts and motives. Failing to do this caused Miriam and Aaron much grief.

12:14 Spitting in someone's face was considered the ultimate insult and a sign of shame imposed on wrongdoers. The religious leaders spat in Jesus' face to insult him (Matthew 26:67). God punished Miriam for her smug attitude toward not only Moses' authority, but also God's. He struck her with leprosy, then ordered her out of the camp for a week. This punishment was actually quite lenient. A week was the length of time she would have been excluded if her father had spat in her face. How much more she deserved for wronging God! Once again, God was merciful while retaining an effective discipline.

6 from the tribe of Judah, Caleb son of Jephunneh;
7 from the tribe of Issachar, Igal son of Joseph;
8 from the tribe of Ephraim, Hoshea son of Nun;
9 from the tribe of Benjamin, Palti son of Raphu;
10 from the tribe of Zebulun, Gaddiel son of Sodi;
11 from the tribe of Manasseh (a tribe of Joseph), Gaddi son of Susi;
12 from the tribe of Dan, Ammiel son of Gemalli;
13 from the tribe of Asher, Sethur son of Michael;
14 from the tribe of Naphtali, Nahbi son of Vophsi;
15 from the tribe of Gad, Geuel son of Maki.

16These are the names of the men Moses sent to explore the land. (Moses gave Hoshea son of Nun the name Joshua.)

17When Moses sent them to explore Canaan, he said, "Go up through the Negev and on into the hill country. 18See what the land is like and whether the people who live there are strong or weak, few or many. 19What kind of land do they live in? Is it good or bad? What kind of towns do they live in? Are they unwalled or fortified? 20How is the soil? Is it fertile or poor? Are there trees on it or not? Do your best to bring back some of the fruit of the land.*u*" (It was the season for the first ripe grapes.)

13:20
*u*Dt 1:25

21So they went up and explored the land from the Desert of Zin as far as Rehob, toward Lebo*a* Hamath. 22They went up through the Negev and came to Hebron, where Ahiman, Sheshai and Talmai,*v* the descendants of Anak, lived. (Hebron had been built seven years before Zoan in Egypt.)*w* 23When they reached the Valley of Eshcol,*b* they cut off a branch bearing a single cluster of grapes. Two of them carried it on a pole between them, along with some pomegranates and figs. 24That place was called the Valley of Eshcol because of the cluster of grapes the Israelites cut off there. 25At the end of forty days they returned from exploring the land.

13:22
*v*Jos 15:14
*w*Ps 78:12,43

Report on the Exploration

26They came back to Moses and Aaron and the whole Israelite community at Kadesh in the Desert of Paran. There they reported to them and to the whole assembly and showed

*a*21 Or *toward the entrance to*   *b*23 *Eshcol* means *cluster*; also in verse 24.

13:17–20 Moses decided what information was needed before the people could enter the promised land, and he took careful steps to get that information. When you are making decisions or assuming new responsibilities, remember these two important steps. Ask yourself what you need to know about the opportunity, and then obtain that knowledge. Common sense is a valuable aid in accomplishing God's purposes. See Proverbs 12:15 and 15:22.

13:25–29 God told the Israelites that the promised land was rich and fertile. Not only that, he promised that this bountiful land would be theirs. When the spies reported back to Moses, they gave plenty of good reasons for entering the land, but they couldn't stop focusing on their fear. Talk of giants (descendants of Anak) and fortified cities made it easy to forget about God's promise to help. When facing a tough decision, don't let the negatives cause you to lose sight of the positives. Weigh both sides carefully. Don't let potential difficulties blind you to God's power to help and his promise to guide.

13:26 Although Kadesh was only a desert oasis, it was a crossroads in Israel's history. When the spies returned to Kadesh from scouting the new land, the people had to decide either to enter the land or to retreat. They chose to retreat and were condemned to wander 40 years in the desert. It was also at Kadesh that Moses disobeyed God (20:7–12). For this, he too was denied entrance into the promised land. Aaron and Miriam died there, for they could not enter the new land either. Kadesh was near Canaan's southern borders, but because of the Israelites' lack of faith, they needed more than a lifetime to go from Kadesh to the promised land.

ROUTE OF THE SPIES The spies traveled from Kadesh at the southernmost edge of the Desert of Zin to Rehob at the northernmost edge and back, a round trip of about 500 miles.

13:27
x Ex 3:8
y Dt 1:25

13:28
z Dt 1:28

them the fruit of the land. 27 They gave Moses this account: "We went into the land to which you sent us, and it does flow with milk and honey! *x* Here is its fruit. *y* 28 But the people who live there are powerful, and the cities are fortified and very large. *z* We even saw descendants of Anak there. 29 The Amalekites live in the Negev; the Hittites, Jebusites and Amorites live in the hill country; and the Canaanites live near the sea and along the Jordan."

30 Then Caleb silenced the people before Moses and said, "We should go up and take possession of the land, for we can certainly do it."

13:31
a Dt 1:28; 9:1;
Jos 14:8

13:32
b Nu 14:36,37

31 But the men who had gone up with him said, "We can't attack those people; they are stronger than we are." *a* 32 And they spread among the Israelites a bad report *b* about the land they had explored. They said, "The land we explored devours those living in it. All the people we saw there are of great size. 33 We saw the Nephilim there (the descendants of Anak come from the Nephilim). We seemed like grasshoppers in our own eyes, and we looked the same to them."

The People Rebel

14 That night all the people of the community raised their voices and wept aloud. 2 All the Israelites grumbled against Moses and Aaron, and the whole assembly said to them, "If only we had died in Egypt! Or in this desert! 3 Why is the LORD bringing us to this land only to let us fall by the sword? Our wives and children will be taken as plunder. Wouldn't it be better for us to go back to Egypt?" 4 And they said to each other, "We should choose a leader and go back to Egypt."

14:5
c Nu 16:4,22,45

14:7
d Nu 13:27

14:8
e Dt 10:15
f Nu 13:27

14:9
g Dt 9:7,23,24
h Dt 1:21; 7:18; 20:1

14:10
i Ex 17:4
j Lev 9:23

5 Then Moses and Aaron fell facedown *c* in front of the whole Israelite assembly gathered there. 6 Joshua son of Nun and Caleb son of Jephunneh, who were among those who had explored the land, tore their clothes 7 and said to the entire Israelite assembly, "The land we passed through and explored is exceedingly good. *d* 8 If the LORD is pleased with us, *e* he will lead us into that land, a land flowing with milk and honey, *f* and will give it to us. 9 Only do not rebel *g* against the LORD. And do not be afraid of the people of the land, *h* because we will swallow them up. Their protection is gone, but the LORD is with us. Do not be afraid of them."

10 But the whole assembly talked about stoning *i* them. Then the glory of the LORD *j* appeared at the Tent of Meeting to all the Israelites. 11 The LORD said to Moses, "How long will these people treat me with contempt? How long will they refuse to believe in me, in spite of

---

13:27 The promised land, also called the land of Canaan, was indeed bountiful, as the 12 spies discovered. The Bible often calls it the land flowing with milk and honey. Although the land was relatively small—150 miles long and 60 miles wide—its lush hillsides were covered with fig, date, and nut trees. It was the land God had promised to Abraham, Isaac, and Jacob.

13:28 The "descendants of Anak" were a race of abnormally large people. The family of Goliath may have been descended from these people (see 2 Samuel 21:16–22).

13:28, 29 The fortified cities the spies talked about were surrounded by high walls as much as 20 feet thick and 25 feet tall. Guards were often stationed on top, where there was a commanding view of the countryside. Some of the inhabitants, said the spies, were formidable men—from seven to nine feet tall—so that the Israelites felt like grasshoppers next to them (13:33). The fortified cities and the giants struck fear into the hearts of most of the spies.

13:30–32 Imagine standing before a crowd and loudly voicing an unpopular opinion! Caleb was willing to take the unpopular stand to do as God had commanded. To be effective when you go against the crowd, you must: (1) have the facts (Caleb had seen the land himself); (2) have the right attitude (Caleb trusted God's promise to give Israel the land); (3) state clearly what you believe (Caleb said, "We can certainly do it").

13:33 The Nephilim were giants who lived on the earth before the flood (Genesis 6:4).

13:33—14:4 The negative opinion of ten men caused a great rebellion among the people. Because it is human nature to accept opinion as fact, we must be especially careful when voicing our negative opinions. What we say may heavily influence the actions of those who trust us to give sound advice.

14:1–4 When the chorus of despair went up, everyone joined in. Their greatest fears were being realized. Losing their perspective, the people were caught up in the emotion of the moment, forgetting what they knew about God's character. What if the people had spent as much energy moving forward as they did moving back? They could have enjoyed their land—instead they never even entered it. When a cry of despair goes up around you, consider the larger perspective before you join in. You have better ways to use your energy than to complain.

14:5–9 With great miracles, God had led the Israelites out of slavery, through the desolate desert, and up to the very edge of the promised land. He had protected them, fed them, and fulfilled every promise. Yet when encouraged to take that last step of faith and enter the land, the people refused. After witnessing so many miracles, why did they stop trusting God? Why did they refuse to enter the promised land when that had been their goal since leaving Egypt? They were afraid. Often we do the same thing. We trust God to handle the smaller issues but doubt his ability to take care of the big problems, the tough decisions, the frightening situations. Don't stop trusting God just as you are ready to reach your goal. He brought you this far and won't let you down now. We can continue trusting God by remembering all he has done for us.

14:6 Tearing clothing was a customary way of showing deep sorrow, mourning, or despair. Joshua and Caleb were greatly distressed by the people's refusal to enter the land.

14:6–10 Two wise men, Joshua and Caleb, encouraged the people to act on God's promise and move ahead into the land. The people rejected their advice and even talked of killing them. Don't be too quick to reject advice you don't like. Evaluate it carefully, comparing it to the teaching in God's Word. The advice may be God's message.

all the miraculous signs I have performed among them? [12]I will strike them down with a plague and destroy them, but I will make you into a nation[k] greater and stronger than they."

[13]Moses said to the LORD, "Then the Egyptians will hear about it! By your power you brought these people up from among them.[l] [14]And they will tell the inhabitants of this land about it. They have already heard[m] that you, O LORD, are with these people and that you, O LORD, have been seen face to face, that your cloud stays over them, and that you go before them in a pillar of cloud by day and a pillar of fire by night.[n] [15]If you put these people to death all at one time, the nations who have heard this report about you will say, [16]'The LORD was not able to bring these people into the land he promised them on oath; so he slaughtered them in the desert.'

[17]"Now may the Lord's strength be displayed, just as you have declared: [18]'The LORD is slow to anger, abounding in love and forgiving sin and rebellion.[o] Yet he does not leave the guilty unpunished; he punishes the children for the sin of the fathers to the third and fourth generation.'[p] [19]In accordance with your great love, forgive[q] the sin of these people, just as you have pardoned them from the time they left Egypt until now."

[20]The LORD replied, "I have forgiven them, as you asked. [21]Nevertheless, as surely as I live and as surely as the glory of the LORD fills the whole earth,[r] [22]not one of the men who saw my glory and the miraculous signs I performed in Egypt and in the desert but who disobeyed me and tested me ten times— [23]not one of them will ever see the land I promised on oath to their forefathers. No one who has treated me with contempt will ever see it. [24]But because my servant Caleb has a different spirit and follows me wholeheartedly,[s] I will bring him into the land he went to, and his descendants will inherit it.[t] [25]Since the Amalekites and Canaanites are living in the valleys, turn back tomorrow and set out toward the desert along the route to the Red Sea.[a]"

[26]The LORD said to Moses and Aaron: [27]"How long will this wicked community grumble against me? I have heard the complaints of these grumbling Israelites. [28]So tell them, 'As surely as I live,[u] declares the LORD, I will do to you the very things I heard you say: [29]In this desert your bodies will fall—every one of you twenty years old or more[v] who was counted in the census and who has grumbled against me. [30]Not one of you will enter the land I swore with uplifted hand to make your home, except Caleb son of Jephunneh and Joshua son of Nun. [31]As for your children that you said would be taken as plunder, I will bring them in to enjoy the land you have rejected. [32]But you—your bodies will fall[w] in this desert. [33]Your children will be shepherds here for forty years, suffering for your unfaithfulness, until the last of your bodies lies in the desert. [34]For forty years—one year for each of the forty days you explored the land[x]—you will suffer for your sins and know what it is like to have me against you.' [35]I, the LORD, have spoken, and I will surely do these things[y] to this whole wicked community, which has banded together against me. They will meet their end in this desert; here they will die."

[a]25 Hebrew Yam Suph; that is, Sea of Reeds

14:12
[k]Ex 32:10
14:13
[l]Ex 32:11-14;
Ps 106:23
14:14
[m]Ex 15:14
[n]Ex 13:21

14:18
[o]Ex 34:6
[p]Ex 20:5
14:19
[q]Ex 34:9

14:21
[r]Ps 72:19

14:24
[s]Jos 14:8,14
[t]Nu 32:12

14:28
[u]ver 21
14:29
[v]Nu 1:45

14:32
[w]1Co 10:5

14:34
[x]Nu 13:25

14:35
[y]Nu 23:19

14:17-20 Moses pleaded with God, asking him to forgive his people. His plea reveals several characteristics of God: (1) God is immensely patient; (2) God's love is one promise we can always count on; (3) God forgives again and again; and (4) God is merciful, listening to and answering our requests. God has not changed since Moses' day. Like Moses, we can rely on God's love, patience, forgiveness, and mercy.

14:20-23 The people of Israel had a clearer view of God than any people before them, for they had both his laws and his physical presence. Their refusal to follow God after witnessing his miraculous deeds and listening to his words made the judgment against them more severe. Increased opportunity brings increased responsibility. As Jesus said: "From everyone who has been given much, much will be demanded" (Luke 12:48). How much greater is our responsibility to obey and serve God—we have the whole Bible, and we know God's Son, Jesus Christ.

14:22 God wasn't exaggerating when he said that the Israelites had already failed ten times to trust and obey him. Here is a list of their ten failures: (1) lacking trust at the crossing of the Red Sea (Exodus 14:11, 12); (2) complaining over bitter water at Marah (Exodus 15:24); (3) complaining in the Desert of Sin (Exodus 16:3); (4) collecting more than the daily quota of manna (Exodus 16:20); (5) collecting manna on the Sabbath (Exodus 16:27-29);

(6) complaining over lack of water at Rephidim (Exodus 17:2, 3); (7) engaging in idolatry with a golden calf (Exodus 32:7-10); (8) complaining at Taberah (Numbers 11:1, 2); (9) more complaining over the lack of delicious food (Numbers 11:4); (10) failing to trust God and enter the promised land (Numbers 14:1-4).

14:24 The fulfillment of this verse is recorded in Joshua 14:6-15 when Caleb received his inheritance in the promised land. Caleb followed God with all his heart and was rewarded for his obedience. Are you wholehearted in your commitment to obey God?

14:34 God's judgment came in the form the people feared most. The people were afraid of dying in the desert, so God punished them by making them wander in the desert until they died. Now they wished they had the problem of facing the giants and the fortified cities of the promised land. Failing to trust God often brings even greater problems than those we originally faced. When we run from God, we inevitably run into problems.

14:35 Was this judgment—wandering 40 years in the desert— too harsh? Not compared to the instant death that God first threatened (14:12). Instead, God allowed the people to live. God had brought his people to the edge of the promised land, just as he said he would. He was ready to give them the rich land, but the people didn't want it (14:1, 2). By this time, God had put up with a lot. At least ten times the people had refused to trust and obey

14:36
z Nu 13:32

36 So the men Moses had sent to explore the land, who returned and made the whole community grumble against him by spreading a bad report *z* about it— 37 these men responsible for spreading the bad report about the land were struck down and died of a plague before the LORD. 38 Of the men who went to explore the land, only Joshua son of Nun and Caleb son of Jephunneh survived.

14:39
a Ex 33:4

14:40
b Dt 1:41

14:41
c 2Ch 24:20

14:42
d Dt 1:42

39 When Moses reported this to all the Israelites, they mourned *a* bitterly. 40 Early the next morning they went up toward the high hill country. "We have sinned *b*," they said. "We will go up to the place the LORD promised."

41 But Moses said, "Why are you disobeying the LORD's command? This will not succeed! *c* 42 Do not go up, because the LORD is not with you. You will be defeated by your enemies, *d* 43 for the Amalekites and Canaanites will face you there. Because you have turned away from the LORD, he will not be with you and you will fall by the sword."

14:44
e Dt 1:43

14:45
f Nu 21:3; Dt 1:44

44 Nevertheless, in their presumption they went up *e* toward the high hill country, though neither Moses nor the ark of the LORD's covenant moved from the camp. 45 Then the Amalekites and Canaanites who lived in that hill country came down and attacked them and beat them down all the way to Hormah. *f*

C. WANDERING IN THE DESERTS (15:1—21:35)

After their disobedience and unsuccessful attempt to enter the promised land, the Israelites were condemned to wander 40 years in the desert. Even in the midst of this punishment, the people continued to rebel, and thus God continued to punish them. But the hearts of the people remained hard and rebellious. Hard hearts toward God may bring similar calamity to us.

CALEB

The voice of the minority is not often given a hearing. Nevertheless, truth cannot be measured by numbers. On the contrary, it often stands against majority opinion. Truth remains unchanged because it is guaranteed by the character of God. God is truth; what he says is the last word. At times, a person must even stand alone on the side of truth.

Caleb was not so much a man of great faith as a man of faith in a great God! His boldness rested on his understanding of God, not on his confidence in Israel's abilities to conquer the land. He could not agree with the majority, for that would be to disagree with God.

We, on the other hand, often base our decisions on what everyone else is doing. Few of us are first-order cowards like the ten spies. We are more like the people of Israel, getting our cowardice secondhand. Our search for right and wrong usually starts with questions such as "What do the experts say?" or "What do my friends say?" The question we most often avoid is "What does God say?" The principles we learn as we study the Bible provide a dependable road map for life. They draw us into a personal relationship with the God whose Word is the Bible. The God who gave Caleb his boldness is the same God who offers us the gift of eternal life through his Son, Jesus. That's truth worth believing!

Strengths and accomplishments:	• One of the spies sent by Moses to survey the land of Canaan • One of the only two adults who left Egypt and entered the promised land • Voiced the minority opinion in favor of conquering the land • Expressed faith in God's promises, in spite of apparent obstacles
Lessons from his life:	• Majority opinion is not an accurate measurement of right and wrong • Boldness based on God's faithfulness is appropriate • For courage and faith to be effective, they must combine words and actions
Vital statistics:	• Where: From Egypt to the Sinai peninsula to the promised land, specifically Hebron • Occupations: Spy, soldier, shepherd
Key verse:	"But because my servant Caleb has a different spirit and follows me wholeheartedly, I will bring him into the land he went to, and his descendants will inherit it" (Numbers 14:24).

Caleb's story is told in Numbers 13; 14 and Joshua 14; 15. He is also mentioned in Judges 1 and 1 Chronicles 4:15.

him (14:22). The whole nation (except for Joshua, Caleb, Moses, and Aaron) showed contempt for and distrust of God. But God's punishment was not permanent. In 40 years, a new generation would have a chance to enter Canaan (Joshua 1—3).

14:40-44 When the Israelites realized their foolish mistake, they were suddenly ready to return to God. But God didn't confuse

their admission of guilt with true repentance because he knew their hearts. Sure enough, they soon went their own way again. Sometimes right actions or good intentions come too late. We must not only do what is right, but also do it at the right time. God wants complete and instant obedience.

1. Additional regulations
Supplementary Offerings

15 The LORD said to Moses, ²"Speak to the Israelites and say to them: 'After you enter the land I am giving you as a home ³and you present to the LORD offerings made by fire, from the herd or the flock,ᵍ as an aroma pleasing to the LORD—whether burnt offerings or sacrifices, for special vows or freewill offerings or festival offeringsʰ— ⁴then the one who brings his offering shall present to the LORD a grain offeringⁱ of a tenth of an ephahᵃ of fine flour mixed with a quarter of a hinᵇ of oil. ⁵With each lamb for the burnt offering or the sacrifice, prepare a quarter of a hin of wine as a drink offering.

⁶"'With a ram prepare a grain offeringⁱ of two-tenths of an ephahᶜ of fine flour mixed with a third of a hinᵈ of oil, ⁷and a third of a hin of wine as a drink offering. Offer it as an aroma pleasing to the LORD.

⁸"'When you prepare a young bull as a burnt offering or sacrifice, for a special vow or a fellowship offeringᵉ to the LORD, ⁹bring with the bull a grain offering of three-tenths of an ephahᶠ of fine flour mixed with half a hinᵍ of oil. ¹⁰Also bring half a hin of wine as a drink offering. It will be an offering made by fire, an aroma pleasing to the LORD. ¹¹Each bull or ram, each lamb or young goat, is to be prepared in this manner. ¹²Do this for each one, for as many as you prepare.

¹³"'Everyone who is native-born must do these things in this way when he brings an offering made by fire as an aroma pleasing to the LORD. ¹⁴For the generations to come, whenever an alien or anyone else living among you presents an offering made by fire as an aroma pleasing to the LORD, he must do exactly as you do. ¹⁵The community is to have the same rules for you and for the alien living among you; this is a lasting ordinance for the generations to come.ᵏ You and the alien shall be the same before the LORD: ¹⁶The same laws and regulations will apply both to you and to the alien living among you.'"

¹⁷The LORD said to Moses, ¹⁸"Speak to the Israelites and say to them: 'When you enter the land to which I am taking you ¹⁹and you eat the food of the land,ˡ present a portion as an offering to the LORD. ²⁰Present a cake from the first of your ground meal and present it as an offering from the threshing floor.ᵐ ²¹Throughout the generations to come you are to give this offering to the LORD from the first of your ground meal.

Offerings for Unintentional Sins

²²"'Now if you unintentionally fail to keep any of these commands the LORD gave Mosesⁿ— ²³any of the LORD's commands to you through him, from the day the LORD gave them and continuing through the generations to come— ²⁴and if this is done unintentionally without the community being aware of it, then the whole community is to offer a young bull for a burnt offeringᵒ as an aroma pleasing to the LORD, along with its prescribed grain offering and drink offering, and a male goat for a sin offering. ²⁵The priest is to make atonement for the whole Israelite community, and they will be forgiven,ᵖ for it was not intentional and they have brought to the LORD for their wrong an offering made by fire and a sin offering. ²⁶The whole Israelite community and the aliens living among them will be forgiven, because all the people were involved in the unintentional wrong.

²⁷"'But if just one person sins unintentionally,�q he must bring a year-old female goat for a sin offering. ²⁸The priest is to make atonement before the LORD for the one who erred by sinning unintentionally, and when atonement has been made for him, he will be forgiven.ʳ ²⁹One and the same law applies to everyone who sins unintentionally, whether he is a native-born Israelite or an alien.

³⁰"'But anyone who sins defiantly,ˢ whether native-born or alien, blasphemes the LORD, and that person must be cut off from his people. ³¹Because he has despised the LORD's word and broken his commands,ᵗ that person must surely be cut off; his guilt remains on him.ᵘ'"

15:3 ᵍLev 1:2 ʰLev 23:1-44
15:4 ⁱLev 6:14
15:6 ʲNu 28:12
15:15 ᵏver 29; Nu 9:14
15:19 ˡJos 5:11,12
15:20 ᵐLev 2:14
15:22 ⁿLev 4:2
15:24 ᵒLev 4:14
15:25 ᵖLev 4:20
15:27 qLev 4:27
15:28 ʳLev 4:35
15:30 ˢDt 17:13; Ps 19:13
15:31 ᵗ2Sa 12:9; Pr 13:13 ᵘLev 5:1; Eze 18:20

ᵃ*4* That is, probably about 2 quarts (about 2 liters)   ᵇ*4* That is, probably about 1 quart (about 1 liter); also in verse 5   ᶜ*6* That is, probably about 4 quarts (about 4.5 liters)   ᵈ*6* That is, probably about 1 1/4 quarts (about 1.2 liters); also in verse 7   ᵉ*8* Traditionally *peace offering*   ᶠ*9* That is, probably about 6 quarts (about 6.5 liters)   ᵍ*9* That is, probably about 2 quarts (about 2 liters); also in verse 10

15:3 "An aroma pleasing to the LORD" means that God would be pleased with their sacrifices.

15:30, 31 God was willing to forgive those who made unintentional errors if they realized their mistakes quickly and corrected them. However, those who defiantly and deliberately sinned received a harsher judgment. Intentional sin grows out of an improper attitude toward God. A child who knowingly disobeys his parents challenges their authority and dares them to respond. Both the act and the attitude have to be dealt with.

16:42
ʷver 19

⁴²But when the assembly gathered in opposition ʷ to Moses and Aaron and turned toward the Tent of Meeting, suddenly the cloud covered it and the glory of the Lᴏʀᴅ appeared. ⁴³Then Moses and Aaron went to the front of the Tent of Meeting, ⁴⁴and the Lᴏʀᴅ said to Moses, ⁴⁵"Get away from this assembly so I can put an end to them at once." And they fell facedown.

16:46
ˣNu 25:13
ʸNu 8:19
16:47
ᶻNu 25:6-8
16:48
ᵃPs 106:30
16:49
ᵇver 32

⁴⁶Then Moses said to Aaron, "Take your censer and put incense in it, along with fire from the altar, and hurry to the assembly to make atonement ˣ for them. Wrath has come out from the Lᴏʀᴅ; the plague ʸ has started." ⁴⁷So Aaron did as Moses said, and ran into the midst of the assembly. The plague had already started among the people, ᶻ but Aaron offered the incense and made atonement for them. ⁴⁸He stood between the living and the dead, and the plague stopped. ᵃ ⁴⁹But 14,700 people died from the plague, in addition to those who had died because of Korah. ᵇ ⁵⁰Then Aaron returned to Moses at the entrance to the Tent of Meeting, for the plague had stopped.

The Budding of Aaron's Staff

17 The Lᴏʀᴅ said to Moses, ²"Speak to the Israelites and get twelve staffs from them, one from the leader of each of their ancestral tribes. Write the name of each man on his staff. ³On the staff of Levi write Aaron's name, for there must be one staff for the head of

---

KORAH

Some notorious historical figures might have remained anonymous if they hadn't tried to grab on to more than they could hold. But by refusing to be content with what they had, and by trying to get more than they deserved, they ended up with nothing. Korah, one of the Israelite leaders, was such a person.

Korah was a Levite who assisted in the daily functions of the tabernacle. Shortly after Israel's great rebellion against God (Numbers 13; 14), Korah instigated his own mini-rebellion. He recruited a grievance committee and confronted Moses and Aaron. Their list of complaints boils down to three statements: (1) you are no better than anyone else; (2) everyone in Israel has been chosen of the Lord; (3) we don't need to obey you. It is amazing to see how Korah twisted the first two statements—both true—to reach the wrong conclusion.

Moses would have agreed that he was no better than anyone else. He would also have agreed that all Israelites were God's chosen people. But Korah's application of these truths was wrong. Not all Israelites were chosen to lead. Korah's hidden claim was this: "I have as much right to lead as Moses does." His error cost him not only his job—a position of service that he enjoyed—but also his life.

Korah's story gives us numerous warnings: (1) Don't let desire for what someone else has make you discontented with what you already have. (2) Don't try to raise your own self-esteem by attacking someone else's. (3) Don't use part of God's Word to support what you want, rather than allowing its entirety to shape your wants. (4) Don't expect to find satisfaction in power and position; God may want to work through you in the position you are now in.

Strengths and accomplishments:	• Popular leader; influential figure during the exodus • Mentioned among the chief men of Israel (Exodus 6) • One of the first Levites appointed for special service in the tabernacle
Weaknesses and mistakes:	• Failed to recognize the significant position God had placed him in • Forgot that his fight was against someone greater than Moses • Allowed greed to blind his common sense
Lessons from his life:	• There is sometimes a fine line between goals and greed • If we are discontented with what we have, we may lose it without gaining anything better
Vital statistics:	• Where: Egypt, Sinai peninsula • Occupation: Levite (tabernacle assistant)
Key verses:	"Moses also said to Korah, 'Now listen, you Levites! Isn't it enough for you that the God of Israel has separated you from the rest of the Israelite community and brought you near himself to do the work at the Lᴏʀᴅ's tabernacle and to stand before the community and minister to them? He has brought you and all your fellow Levites near himself, but now you are trying to get the priesthood too'" (Numbers 16:8–10).

Korah's story is told in Numbers 16:1–40. He is also mentioned in Numbers 26:9; Jude 11.

---

often dissatisfied, skeptical, complaining, or bitter—beware! These attitudes lead to rebellion and separation from God. Any

choice to side against God is a step in the direction of letting go of him completely and making your own way through life.

each ancestral tribe. 4 Place them in the Tent of Meeting in front of the Testimony, where I meet with you. c 5 The staff belonging to the man I choose d will sprout, and I will rid myself of this constant grumbling against you by the Israelites."

17:4
cEx 25:22
17:5
dNu 16:5

6 So Moses spoke to the Israelites, and their leaders gave him twelve staffs, one for the leader of each of their ancestral tribes, and Aaron's staff was among them. 7 Moses placed the staffs before the LORD in the Tent of the Testimony.

8 The next day Moses entered the Tent of the Testimony and saw that Aaron's staff, which represented the house of Levi, had not only sprouted but had budded, blossomed and produced almonds. 9 Then Moses brought out all the staffs from the LORD's presence to all the Israelites. They looked at them, and each man took his own staff.

10 The LORD said to Moses, "Put back Aaron's staff in front of the Testimony, to be kept as a sign to the rebellious. This will put an end to their grumbling against me, so that they will not die." 11 Moses did just as the LORD commanded him.

12 The Israelites said to Moses, "We will die! We are lost, we are all lost! 13 Anyone who even comes near the tabernacle of the LORD will die. e Are we all going to die?"

17:13
eNu 1:51

3. Duties of priests and Levites

18 The LORD said to Aaron, "You, your sons and your father's family are to bear the responsibility for offenses against the sanctuary, f and you and your sons alone are to bear the responsibility for offenses against the priesthood. 2 Bring your fellow Levites from your ancestral tribe to join you and assist you when you and your sons minister g before the Tent of the Testimony. 3 They are to be responsible to you and are to perform all the duties of the Tent, but they must not go near the furnishings of the sanctuary or the altar, or both they and you will die. h 4 They are to join you and be responsible for the care of the Tent of Meeting—all the work at the Tent—and no one else may come near where you are.

18:1
fEx 28:38
18:2
gNu 3:10
18:3
hNu 4:15

5 "You are to be responsible for the care of the sanctuary and the altar, so that wrath will not fall on the Israelites again. 6 I myself have selected your fellow Levites from among the Israelites as a gift to you, i dedicated to the LORD to do the work at the Tent of Meeting. 7 But only you and your sons may serve as priests in connection with everything at the altar and inside the curtain. j I am giving you the service of the priesthood as a gift. Anyone else who comes near the sanctuary must be put to death."

18:6
iNu 3:9
18:7
jHeb 9:3,6

Offerings for Priests and Levites

8 Then the LORD said to Aaron, "I myself have put you in charge of the offerings presented to me; all the holy offerings the Israelites give me I give to you and your sons as your portion and regular share. k 9 You are to have the part of the most holy offerings that is kept from the fire. From all the gifts they bring me as most holy offerings, whether grain or sin l or guilt offerings, that part belongs to you and your sons. 10 Eat it as something most holy; every male shall eat it. m You must regard it as holy.

18:8
kLev 6:16;
7:6,31-34,36
18:9
lLev 6:25
18:10
mLev 6:16

11 "This also is yours: whatever is set aside from the gifts of all the wave offerings n of the Israelites. I give this to you and your sons and daughters as your regular share. Everyone in your household who is ceremonially clean o may eat it.

18:11
nEx 29:26
oLev 22:1-16

12 "I give you all the finest olive oil and all the finest new wine and grain they give the LORD as the firstfruits of their harvest. p 13 All the land's firstfruits that they bring to the LORD will be yours. Everyone in your household who is ceremonially clean may eat it.

18:12
pEx 23:19;
Ne 10:35

14 "Everything in Israel that is devoted a to the LORD is yours. 15 The first offspring of every womb, both man and animal, that is offered to the LORD is yours. q But you must redeem every firstborn son and every firstborn male of unclean animals. r 16 When they are a month old, you must redeem them at the redemption price set at five shekels b s of silver, according to the sanctuary shekel, which weighs twenty gerahs.

18:15
qEx 13:2
rEx 13:13
18:16
sLev 27:6

a 14 The Hebrew term refers to the irrevocable giving over of things or persons to the LORD.   b 16 That is, about 2 ounces (about 55 grams)

17:5, 10 After witnessing spectacular miracles, seeing the Egyptians punished by the plagues, and experiencing the actual presence of God, the Israelites still complained and rebelled. We wonder how they could be so blind and ignorant, and yet we often repeat this same pattern. We have centuries of evidence, the Bible in many translations, and the convincing results of archaeological and historical studies. But people today continue to disobey God and go their own way. Like the Israelites, we are more concerned about our physical condition than our spiritual condition. We can escape this pattern only by paying attention to all the signs of God's presence that we have been given. Has God guided and protected you? Has he answered your prayers? Do you know people who have experienced remarkable blessings and healings? Do you know Bible stories about the way God has led his people? Focus your thoughts on what God has done, and rebellion will become unthinkable.

18:17
*t*Lev 3:2

18:19
*u*2Ch 13:5

18:20
*v*Dt 10:9; 18:1-2;
Jos 13:33;
Eze 44:28

18:21
*w*Lev 27:30-33

18:22
*x*Nu 1:51

18:26
*y*Ne 10:38

18:32
*z*Lev 22:15
*a*Lev 19:8

19:2
*b*Dt 21:3

19:3
*c*Nu 3:4
*d*Lev 4:12,21

19:5
*e*Ex 29:14

19:6
*f*Lev 14:4

19:9
*g*Heb 9:13
*h*ver 13

19:11
*i*Lev 21:1; Nu 5:2
*j*Nu 31:19

19:12
*k*ver 19; Nu 31:19

17"But you must not redeem the firstborn of an ox, a sheep or a goat; they are holy. Sprinkle their blood *t* on the altar and burn their fat as an offering made by fire, an aroma pleasing to the LORD. 18Their meat is to be yours, just as the breast of the wave offering and the right thigh are yours. 19Whatever is set aside from the holy offerings the Israelites present to the LORD I give to you and your sons and daughters as your regular share. It is an everlasting covenant of salt *u* before the LORD for both you and your offspring."

20The LORD said to Aaron, "You will have no inheritance in their land, nor will you have any share among them; I am your share and your inheritance *v* among the Israelites.

21"I give to the Levites all the tithes in Israel as their inheritance *w* in return for the work they do while serving at the Tent of Meeting. 22From now on the Israelites must not go near the Tent of Meeting, or they will bear the consequences of their sin and will die. *x* 23It is the Levites who are to do the work at the Tent of Meeting and bear the responsibility for offenses against it. This is a lasting ordinance for the generations to come. They will receive no inheritance among the Israelites. 24Instead, I give to the Levites as their inheritance the tithes that the Israelites present as an offering to the LORD. That is why I said concerning them: 'They will have no inheritance among the Israelites.'"

25The LORD said to Moses, 26"Speak to the Levites and say to them: 'When you receive from the Israelites the tithe I give you as your inheritance, you must present a tenth of that tithe as the LORD's offering. *y* 27Your offering will be reckoned to you as grain from the threshing floor or juice from the winepress. 28In this way you also will present an offering to the LORD from all the tithes you receive from the Israelites. From these tithes you must give the LORD's portion to Aaron the priest. 29You must present as the LORD's portion the best and holiest part of everything given to you.'

30"Say to the Levites: 'When you present the best part, it will be reckoned to you as the product of the threshing floor or the winepress. 31You and your households may eat the rest of it anywhere, for it is your wages for your work at the Tent of Meeting. 32By presenting the best part *z* of it you will not be guilty in this matter; then you will not defile the holy offerings *a* of the Israelites, and you will not die.'"

The Water of Cleansing

19 The LORD said to Moses and Aaron: 2"This is a requirement of the law that the LORD has commanded: Tell the Israelites to bring you a red heifer without defect or blemish and that has never been under a yoke. *b* 3Give it to Eleazar *c* the priest; it is to be taken outside the camp *d* and slaughtered in his presence. 4Then Eleazar the priest is to take some of its blood on his finger and sprinkle it seven times toward the front of the Tent of Meeting. 5While he watches, the heifer is to be burned—its hide, flesh, blood and offal. *e* 6The priest is to take some cedar wood, hyssop and scarlet wool *f* and throw them onto the burning heifer. 7After that, the priest must wash his clothes and bathe himself with water. He may then come into the camp, but he will be ceremonially unclean till evening. 8The man who burns it must also wash his clothes and bathe with water, and he too will be unclean till evening.

9"A man who is clean shall gather up the ashes of the heifer *g* and put them in a ceremonially clean place outside the camp. They shall be kept by the Israelite community for use in the water of cleansing; *h* it is for purification from sin. 10The man who gathers up the ashes of the heifer must also wash his clothes, and he too will be unclean till evening. This will be a lasting ordinance both for the Israelites and for the aliens living among them.

11"Whoever touches the dead body *i* of anyone will be unclean for seven days. *j* 12He must purify himself with the water on the third day and on the seventh day; *k* then he will be clean. But if he does not purify himself on the third and seventh days, he will not be clean.

18:25, 26 Even the Levites, who were ministers, had to tithe to support the Lord's work. No one was exempt from returning to God a portion of what was received. Though the Levites owned no land and operated no great enterprises, they were to treat their income the same as everyone else did by giving a portion to care for the needs of the other Levites and of the tabernacle. The tithing principle is still relevant. God expects all his followers to supply the material needs of those who devote themselves to meeting the spiritual needs of the community of faith. Ask God to direct you about what you should give and to help you give generously.

19:9, 10 What is the significance of the red heifer's ashes? When a person touched a dead body, he was considered unclean (i.e., unable to approach God in worship). This ritual purified the unclean person so that once again he could offer sacrifices and worship God. Death was the strongest of defilements because it was the final result of sin. Thus a special sacrifice—a red heifer—was required. It had to be offered by someone who was not unclean. When it had been burned on the altar, its ashes were used to purify water for ceremonial cleansing—not so much physically as symbolically. The unclean person then washed himself, and often his clothes and belongings, with this purified water as an act of becoming clean again.

13Whoever touches the dead body of anyone and fails to purify himself defiles the LORD's tabernacle.*l* That person must be cut off from Israel.*m* Because the water of cleansing has not been sprinkled on him, he is unclean; his uncleanness remains on him.

14"This is the law that applies when a person dies in a tent: Anyone who enters the tent and anyone who is in it will be unclean for seven days, 15and every open container without a lid fastened on it will be unclean.

16"Anyone out in the open who touches someone who has been killed with a sword or someone who has died a natural death, or anyone who touches a human bone or a grave, will be unclean for seven days.

17"For the unclean person, put some ashes*n* from the burned purification offering into a jar and pour fresh water over them. 18Then a man who is ceremonially clean is to take some hyssop, dip it in the water and sprinkle the tent and all the furnishings and the people who were there. He must also sprinkle anyone who has touched a human bone or a grave or someone who has been killed or someone who has died a natural death. 19The man who is clean is to sprinkle the unclean person on the third and seventh days, and on the seventh day he is to purify him.*o* The person being cleansed must wash his clothes and bathe with water, and that evening he will be clean. 20But if a person who is unclean does not purify himself, he must be cut off from the community, because he has defiled the sanctuary of the LORD. The water of cleansing has not been sprinkled on him, and he is unclean. 21This is a lasting ordinance for them.

"The man who sprinkles the water of cleansing must also wash his clothes, and anyone who touches the water of cleansing will be unclean till evening. 22Anything that an unclean person touches becomes unclean, and anyone who touches it becomes unclean till evening."

4. The new generation
Water From the Rock

20 In the first month the whole Israelite community arrived at the Desert of Zin, and they stayed at Kadesh.*p* There Miriam died and was buried.

2 Now there was no water for the community,*q* and the people gathered in opposition to Moses and Aaron. 3They quarreled*r* with Moses and said, "If only we had died when our brothers fell dead before the LORD!*s* 4Why did you bring the LORD's community into this desert, that we and our livestock should die here?*t* 5Why did you bring us up out of Egypt to this terrible place? It has no grain or figs, grapevines or pomegranates. And there is no water to drink!"

6Moses and Aaron went from the assembly to the entrance to the Tent of Meeting and fell facedown,*u* and the glory of the LORD appeared to them. 7The LORD said to Moses, 8"Take the staff, and you and your brother Aaron gather the assembly together. Speak to that rock before their eyes and it will pour out its water.*v* You will bring water out of the rock for the community so they and their livestock can drink."

19:13
*l*Lev 15:31
*m*Lev 7:20; 22:3

19:17
*n*ver 9

19:19
*o*Eze 36:25; Heb 10:22

20:1
*p*Nu 33:36

20:2
*q*Ex 17:1

20:3
*r*Ex 17:2
*s*Nu 14:2; 16:31-35

20:4
*t*Ex 14:11; 17:3; Nu 14:3; 16:13

20:6
*u*Nu 14:5

20:8
*v*Ex 17:6; Isa 43:20

20:1 It had been 37 years since Israel's first spy mission into the promised land (Numbers 13; 14) and 40 years since the exodus from Egypt. The Bible is virtually silent about those 37 years of aimless wandering. The generation of those who had lived in Egypt had almost died off, and the new generation would soon be ready to enter the land. Moses, Aaron, Joshua, and Caleb were among the few who remained from those who had left Egypt. Once again they camped at Kadesh, the site of the first spy mission that had ended in disaster. Moses hoped the people were ready for a fresh start.

20:3-5 After 37 years in the desert, the Israelites forgot that their wanderings were a result of their parents' and their own sin. They could not accept the fact that they brought their problems upon themselves, so they blamed Moses for their condition. Often our troubles result from our own disobedience or lack of faith. We cannot blame God for our sins. Until we face this reality, we will have little peace and no spiritual growth.

EVENTS AT KADESH
After wandering in the desert for 40 years, Israel arrived at Kadesh, where Miriam died. There was not enough water, and the people complained bitterly. Moses struck a rock, and it gave enough water for everyone. The king of Edom refused Israel passage through his land, forcing them to travel around his country.

20:9
wNu 17:10

20:10
xPs 106:32,33

20:11
yEx 17:6; 1Co 10:4

20:12
zNu 27:14
aDt 1:37

20:13
bEx 17:7

20:16
cEx 2:23
dEx 14:19

9So Moses took the staff from the LORD's presence,w just as he commanded him. 10He and Aaron gathered the assembly together in front of the rock and Moses said to them, "Listen, you rebels, must we bring you water out of this rock?"x 11Then Moses raised his arm and struck the rock twice with his staff. Watery gushed out, and the community and their livestock drank.

12But the LORD said to Moses and Aaron, "Because you did not trust in me enough to honor me as holyz in the sight of the Israelites, you will not bring this community into the land I give them."a

13These were the waters of Meribah,a b where the Israelites quarreled with the LORD and where he showed himself holy among them.

Edom Denies Israel Passage

14Moses sent messengers from Kadesh to the king of Edom, saying:

"This is what your brother Israel says: You know about all the hardships that have come upon us. 15Our forefathers went down into Egypt, and we lived there many years. The Egyptians mistreated us and our fathers, 16but when we cried out to the LORD, he heard our cryc and sent an angel d and brought us out of Egypt.

a 13 Meribah means *quarreling.*

ELEAZAR

An understudy must know the lead role completely and be willing to step into it at a moment's notice. Eleazar was an excellent understudy, well trained for his eventual leading role. However, his moments in the spotlight were painful. On one occasion, he watched his two older brothers burn to death for failing to take God's holiness seriously. Later, as his father was dying, he was made high priest, surely one of the most responsible—and therefore potentially most stressful—positions in Israel.

An understudy benefits from having both the script and a human model of the role. Ever since childhood, Eleazar had been able to observe Moses and Aaron. Now he could learn from watching Joshua. In addition, he had God's laws to guide him as he worked as priest and adviser to Joshua.

Strengths and accomplishments:	• Succeeded his father, Aaron, as high priest • Completed his father's work by helping lead the people into the promised land • Teamed up with Joshua • Acted as God's spokesman to the people
Lessons from his life:	• Concentrating on our present challenges and responsibilities is the best way to prepare for what God has planned for our future • God's desire is consistent obedience throughout our lives
Vital statistics:	• Where: Desert of Sinai, promised land • Occupations: Priest and high priest • Relatives: Father: Aaron. Brothers: Nadab, Abihu, and Ithamar. Aunt and uncle: Miriam and Moses. • Contemporaries: Joshua, Caleb
Key verses:	"At Mount Hor, near the border of Edom, the LORD said to Moses and Aaron, . . . 'Get Aaron and his son Eleazar and take them up Mount Hor. Remove Aaron's garments and put them on his son Eleazar'" (Numbers 20:23–26).

Eleazar is mentioned in Exodus 6:23; Leviticus 10:16–20; Numbers 3:1–4; 4:16; 16:36–40; 20:25–29; 26:1–3, 63; 27:2, 15–23; 32:2; 34:17; Deuteronomy 10:6; Joshua 14:1; 17:4; 24:33.

20:12 The Lord had told Moses to speak to the rock; however, Moses struck it, not once, but twice. God did the miracle; yet Moses was taking credit for it when he said, "we bring you water out of this rock." For this he was forbidden to enter the promised land. Was God's punishment of Moses too harsh? After all, the people had nagged him, slandered him, and rebelled against both him and God. Now they were at it again (20:5). But Moses was the leader and model for the entire nation. Because of this great responsibility to the people, he could not be let off lightly. By striking the rock, Moses disobeyed God's direct command and dishonored God in the presence of his people.

20:14 Two brothers became the ancestors of two nations. The Edomites descended from Esau; the Israelites from Jacob. Thus the Edomites were "brothers" to the Israelites. Israel sent a brotherly message to Edom requesting passage through their land on the main road, a well-traveled trade route. Israel promised to stay on the road, thus harmlessly bypassing Edom's fields, vineyards, and wells. Edom refused, however, because they did not trust Israel's word. They were afraid that this great horde of people would either attack them or devour their crops (Deuteronomy 2:4, 5). Because brothers should not fight, God told the Israelites to turn back and travel by a different route to the promised land.

"Now we are here at Kadesh, a town on the edge of your territory. [17]Please let us pass through your country. We will not go through any field or vineyard, or drink water from any well. We will travel along the king's highway and not turn to the right or to the left until we have passed through your territory. [e]"

[18]But Edom answered:

"You may not pass through here; if you try, we will march out and attack you with the sword."

[19]The Israelites replied:

"We will go along the main road, and if we or our livestock drink any of your water, we will pay for it. [f] We only want to pass through on foot—nothing else."

[20]Again they answered:

"You may not pass through."

Then Edom came out against them with a large and powerful army. [21]Since Edom refused to let them go through their territory, Israel turned away from them. [g]

The Death of Aaron

[22]The whole Israelite community set out from Kadesh and came to Mount Hor. [23]At Mount Hor, near the border of Edom, the LORD said to Moses and Aaron, [24]"Aaron will be gathered to his people. [h] He will not enter the land I give the Israelites, because both of you rebelled against my command at the waters of Meribah. [25]Get Aaron and his son Eleazar and take them up Mount Hor. [26]Remove Aaron's garments and put them on his son Eleazar, for Aaron will be gathered to his people; he will die there."

[27]Moses did as the LORD commanded: They went up Mount Hor in the sight of the whole community. [28]Moses removed Aaron's garments and put them on his son Eleazar. [i] And Aaron died there[j] on top of the mountain. Then Moses and Eleazar came down from the mountain, [29]and when the whole community learned that Aaron had died, the entire house of Israel mourned for him[k] thirty days.

Arad Destroyed

21 When the Canaanite king of Arad,[l] who lived in the Negev, heard that Israel was coming along the road to Atharim, he attacked the Israelites and captured some of them. [2]Then Israel made this vow to the LORD: "If you will deliver these people into our hands, we will totally destroy[a] their cities." [3]The LORD listened to Israel's plea and gave the Canaanites over to them. They completely destroyed them and their towns; so the place was named Hormah. [b]

The Bronze Snake

[4]They traveled from Mount Hor[m] along the route to the Red Sea,[c] to go around Edom. But the people grew impatient on the way; [5]they spoke against God[n] and against Moses, and said, "Why have you brought us up out of Egypt to die in the desert? There is no bread! There is no water! And we detest this miserable food!"

[6]Then the LORD sent venomous snakes[o] among them; they bit the people and many

20:17
[e] Nu 21:22

20:19
[f] Dt 2:6,28

20:21
[g] Dt 2:8; Jdg 11:18

20:24
[h] Ge 25:8

20:28
[i] Ex 29:29
[j] Nu 33:38; Dt 10:6

20:29
[k] Dt 34:8

21:1
[l] Nu 33:40

21:4
[m] Nu 20:22

21:5
[n] Ps 78:19

21:6
[o] Dt 8:15

---

a2 The Hebrew term refers to the irrevocable giving over of things or persons to the LORD, often by totally destroying them; also in verse 3.   b3 *Hormah* means *destruction.*   c4 Hebrew *Yam Suph;* that is, Sea of Reeds

---

20:17 The king's highway was an old caravan route. Long before this time it was used as a major public road.

20:21 Moses tried to negotiate and reason with the Edomite king. When nothing worked, he was left with two choices—force a conflict or avoid it. Moses knew there would be enough barriers in the days and months ahead. There was no point in adding another one unnecessarily. Sometimes conflict is unavoidable. Sometimes, however, it isn't worth the consequences. Open warfare may seem heroic, courageous, and even righteous, but it is not always the best choice. At times, we should follow Moses' example and find another way to solve our problems, even if it is harder for us to do.

20:28 Aaron died just before entering the promised land, probably as punishment for his sin of rebellion (Exodus 32; Numbers

12:1–9). This was the first time that a new high priest was appointed. The priestly clothing was removed from Aaron and placed on his son Eleazar, following the commands recorded in the book of Leviticus.

21:5 In Psalm 78, we learn the sources of Israel's complaining: (1) their spirits were not faithful to God (78:8); (2) they refused to obey God's law (78:10); (3) they forgot the miracles God had done for them (78:11). Our complaining often has its roots in one of these thoughtless actions and attitudes. If we can deal with the cause of our complaining, it will not take hold and grow in our lives.

21:6 God used venomous snakes to punish the people for their unbelief and complaining. The Desert of Sinai has a variety of snakes. Some hide in the sand and attack without warning. Both

21:6
p 1Co 10:9

21:7
q Ps 78:34
r Ac 8:24

21:9
s 2Ki 18:4
t Jn 3:14-15

21:11
u Nu 33:44

21:12
v Dt 2:13,14

21:15
w Dt 2:9,18

21:17
x Ex 15:1

Israelites died.*p* 7 The people came to Moses *q* and said, "We sinned when we spoke against the Lord and against you. Pray that the Lord *r* will take the snakes away from us." So Moses prayed for the people.

8 The Lord said to Moses, "Make a snake and put it up on a pole; anyone who is bitten can look at it and live." 9 So Moses made a bronze snake *s* and put it up on a pole. Then when anyone was bitten by a snake and looked at the bronze snake, he lived. *t*

The Journey to Moab

10 The Israelites moved on and camped at Oboth. 11 Then they set out from Oboth and camped in Iye Abarim, in the desert that faces Moab *u* toward the sunrise. 12 From there they moved on and camped in the Zered Valley. *v* 13 They set out from there and camped alongside the Arnon, which is in the desert extending into Amorite territory. The Arnon is the border of Moab, between Moab and the Amorites. 14 That is why the Book of the Wars of the Lord says:

> "... Waheb in Suphah *a* and the ravines,
>   the Arnon 15 and *b* the slopes of the ravines
> that lead to the site of Ar *w*
>   and lie along the border of Moab."

16 From there they continued on to Beer, the well where the Lord said to Moses, "Gather the people together and I will give them water."

17 Then Israel sang this song: *x*

> "Spring up, O well!
>   Sing about it,
> 18 about the well that the princes dug,
>   that the nobles of the people sank—
> the nobles with scepters and staffs."

a 14 The meaning of the Hebrew for this phrase is uncertain.   *b 14,15* Or *"I have been given from Suphah and the ravines / of the Arnon 15to*

---

the Israelites and the Egyptians had a great fear of snakes. A bite by a poisonous snake often meant a slow death with intense suffering.

21:8, 9 When the bronze snake was hung on the pole, the Israelites didn't know the fuller meaning Jesus Christ would bring to this event (see John 3:14, 15). Jesus explained that just as the Israelites were healed of their sickness by looking at the snake on the pole, all believers today can be saved from the sickness of sin by looking to Jesus' death on the cross. It was not the snake that healed the people, but their belief that God could heal them. This belief was demonstrated by their obedience to God's instructions. In the same way, we should continue to look to Christ (see Hebrews 12:2).

21:14 There is no other existing record of the Book of the Wars of the Lord. Most likely, it was a collection of victory songs or poems.

EVENTS IN THE DESERT   Israel next met resistance from the king of Arad but soundly defeated him. The next stop was Mount Hor (where Aaron had died); then they traveled south and east around Edom. After camping at Oboth, they moved toward the Arnon River and onto the plains of Moab near Mount Pisgah.

Then they went from the desert to Mattanah, [19]from Mattanah to Nahaliel, from Nahaliel to Bamoth, [20]and from Bamoth to the valley in Moab where the top of Pisgah overlooks the wasteland.

Defeat of Sihon and Og

[21]Israel sent messengers to say to Sihon king of the Amorites:

[22]"Let us pass through your country. We will not turn aside into any field or vineyard, or drink water from any well. We will travel along the king's highway until we have passed through your territory.y"

[23]But Sihon would not let Israel pass through his territory. He mustered his entire army and marched out into the desert against Israel. When he reached Jahaz,z he fought with Israel. [24]Israel, however, put him to the sworda and took over his land from the Arnon to the Jabbok, but only as far as the Ammonites, because their border was fortified. [25]Israel captured all the cities of the Amorites and occupied them, including Heshbon and all its surrounding settlements. [26]Heshbon was the city of Sihon king of the Amorites, who had fought against the former king of Moab and had taken from him all his land as far as the Arnon.

[27]That is why the poets say:

"Come to Heshbon and let it be rebuilt;
   let Sihon's city be restored.

[28] "Fire went out from Heshbon,
      a blaze from the city of Sihon.b
   It consumed Ar of Moab,
      the citizens of Arnon's heights.c
[29] Woe to you, O Moab!
      You are destroyed, O people of Chemosh!d
   He has given up his sons as fugitives
      and his daughters as captives
   to Sihon king of the Amorites.

[30] "But we have overthrown them;
      Heshbon is destroyed all the way to Dibon.e
   We have demolished them as far as Nophah,
      which extends to Medeba."

[31]So Israel settled in the land of the Amorites. [32]After Moses had sent spies to Jazer,f the Israelites captured its surrounding settlements and drove out the Amorites who were there. [33]Then they turned and went up along the road toward Bashan, and Og king of Bashan and his whole army marched out to meet them in battle at Edrei.g

21:22
yNu 20:17

21:23
zDt 2:32
21:24
aDt 2:33;
Ps 135:10-11

21:28
bJer 48:45
cIsa 15:2

21:29
dJdg 11:24;
1Ki 11:7,33;
2Ki 23:13

21:30
eNu 32:3;
Jer 48:18,22

21:32
fNu 32:1,3,35;
Jer 48:32
21:33
gDt 3:1,10;
Jos 13:12,31

21:27–30 Chemosh, the national god of Moab, was worshiped as a god of war. This false god, however, was no help to this nation when it fought against Israel. Israel's God was stronger than any of Canaan's war gods.

BATTLES WITH SIHON AND OG
King Sihon refused passage to the Israelites through his land, and he attacked Israel at Jahaz. Israel defeated him, occupying the land between the Arnon and Jabbok Rivers, including the capital city, Heshbon. As they moved north, they defeated King Og of Bashan at Edrei.

21:34
h Dt 3:2

34 The LORD said to Moses, "Do not be afraid of him, for I have handed him over to you, with his whole army and his land. Do to him what you did to Sihon king of the Amorites, who reigned in Heshbon. *h*"

35 So they struck him down, together with his sons and his whole army, leaving them no survivors. And they took possession of his land.

D. SECOND APPROACH TO THE PROMISED LAND (22:1—36:13)
Now the old generation has died and a new generation stands poised at the border, ready to enter the promised land. Neighboring nations, however, cause Israel to begin worshiping other gods. Without Moses' quick action, the nation may never have entered Canaan. We must never let down our guard in resisting sin.

1. The story of Balaam
Balak Summons Balaam

22:1
i Nu 33:48

22:3
j Ex 15:15

22 Then the Israelites traveled to the plains of Moab and camped along the Jordan across from Jericho.*a i*

2 Now Balak son of Zippor saw all that Israel had done to the Amorites, 3 and Moab was terrified because there were so many people. Indeed, Moab was filled with dread *j* because of the Israelites.

4 The Moabites said to the elders of Midian, "This horde is going to lick up everything around us, as an ox licks up the grass of the field."

22:5
k Dt 23:4

So Balak son of Zippor, who was king of Moab at that time, 5 sent messengers to summon Balaam son of Beor, *k* who was at Pethor, near the River, *b* in his native land. Balak said:

22:6
l Nu 23:7,11,13

"A people has come out of Egypt; they cover the face of the land and have settled next to me. 6 Now come and put a curse *l* on these people, because they are too powerful for me. Perhaps then I will be able to defeat them and drive them out of the country. For I know that those you bless are blessed, and those you curse are cursed."

7 The elders of Moab and Midian left, taking with them the fee for divination. When they came to Balaam, they told him what Balak had said.

22:8
m ver 19

8 "Spend the night here," Balaam said to them, "and I will bring you back the answer the LORD gives me. *m*" So the Moabite princes stayed with him.

9 God came to Balaam and asked, "Who are these men with you?"

10 Balaam said to God, "Balak son of Zippor, king of Moab, sent me this message: 11 'A people that has come out of Egypt covers the face of the land. Now come and put a curse on them for me. Perhaps then I will be able to fight them and drive them away.'"

12 But God said to Balaam, "Do not go with them. You must not put a curse on those people, because they are blessed."

a 1 Hebrew *Jordan of Jericho*; possibly an ancient name for the Jordan River   *b* 5 That is, the Euphrates

---

THE SNAKE IN THE DESERT	Israelites	Christians
Compare the texts for yourself: Numbers 21:7–9 and John 3:14, 15.	Bitten by snakes .... Bitten by sin	
	Little initial pain, then intense suffering .... Little initial pain, then intense suffering	
	Physical death from snakes' poison .... Spiritual death from sin's poison	
	Bronze snake lifted up in the desert .... Christ lifted up on the cross	
	Looking to the snake spared one's life .... Looking to Christ saves from eternal death	

21:34 God assured Moses that Israel's enemy was conquered even before the battle began! God wants to give us victory over our enemies (which are usually problems related to sin rather than armed soldiers). But first we must believe that he can help us. Second, we must trust him to help us. Third, we must take the steps he shows us.

22:4–6 Balaam was a sorcerer, one called upon to place curses on others. Belief in curses and blessings was common in Old Testament times. Sorcerers were thought to have power with the gods. Thus the king of Moab wanted Balaam to use his powers with the God of Israel to place a curse on Israel—hoping that, by magic, God would turn against his people. Neither Balaam nor Balak had any idea whom they were dealing with!

22:9 Why would God speak through a sorcerer like Balaam? God wanted to give a message to the Moabites, and they had already chosen to employ Balaam. So Balaam was available for God to use, much as he used the wicked pharaoh to accomplish his will in Egypt (Exodus 10:1). Balaam entered into his prophetic role seriously, but his heart was mixed. He had some knowledge of God, but not enough to forsake his magic and turn wholeheartedly to God. Although this story leads us to believe he turned completely to God, later passages in the Bible show that Balaam couldn't resist the tempting pull of money and idolatry (31:16; 2 Peter 2:15; Jude 11).

[13]The next morning Balaam got up and said to Balak's princes, "Go back to your own country, for the LORD has refused to let me go with you."

[14]So the Moabite princes returned to Balak and said, "Balaam refused to come with us."

[15]Then Balak sent other princes, more numerous and more distinguished than the first. [16]They came to Balaam and said:

"This is what Balak son of Zippor says: Do not let anything keep you from coming to me, [17]because I will reward you handsomely and do whatever you say. Come and put a curse[n] on these people for me."

22:17
[n] ver 6

[18]But Balaam answered them, "Even if Balak gave me his palace filled with silver and gold, I could not do anything great or small to go beyond the command of the LORD my God.[o] [19]Now stay here tonight as the others did, and I will find out what else the LORD will tell me."

22:18
[o] ver 38; Nu 24:13; 1Ki 22:14; 2Ch 18:13

[20]That night God came to Balaam and said, "Since these men have come to summon you, go with them, but do only what I tell you."[p]

22:20
[p] ver 35,38; Nu 23:5,12,16,26; 24:13

Balaam's Donkey

[21]Balaam got up in the morning, saddled his donkey and went with the princes of Moab. [22]But God was very angry when he went, and the angel of the LORD[q] stood in the road to oppose him. Balaam was riding on his donkey, and his two servants were with him. [23]When the donkey saw the angel of the LORD standing in the road with a drawn sword in his hand, she turned off the road into a field. Balaam beat her to get her back on the road.

22:22
[q] Ex 23:20

[24]Then the angel of the LORD stood in a narrow path between two vineyards, with walls on both sides. [25]When the donkey saw the angel of the LORD, she pressed close to the wall, crushing Balaam's foot against it. So he beat her again.

[26]Then the angel of the LORD moved on ahead and stood in a narrow place where there was no room to turn, either to the right or to the left. [27]When the donkey saw the angel of the LORD, she lay down under Balaam, and he was angry[r] and beat her with his staff. [28]Then the LORD opened the donkey's mouth,[s] and she said to Balaam, "What have I done to you to make you beat me these three times?"

22:27
[r] Jas 1:19
22:28
[s] 2Pe 2:16

[29]Balaam answered the donkey, "You have made a fool of me! If I had a sword in my hand, I would kill you right now.[t]"

22:29
[t] Pr 12:10; Mt 15:19

[30]The donkey said to Balaam, "Am I not your own donkey, which you have always ridden, to this day? Have I been in the habit of doing this to you?"

"No," he said.

[31]Then the LORD opened Balaam's eyes,[u] and he saw the angel of the LORD standing in the road with his sword drawn. So he bowed low and fell facedown.

22:31
[u] Ge 21:19

[32]The angel of the LORD asked him, "Why have you beaten your donkey these three times? I have come here to oppose you because your path is a reckless one before me.[a]

[a] 32 The meaning of the Hebrew for this clause is uncertain.

22:20–23 God let Balaam go with Balak's messengers, but he was angry about Balaam's greedy attitude. Balaam claimed that he would not go against God just for money, but his resolve was beginning to slip. His greed for the wealth offered by the king blinded him so that he could not see how God was trying to stop him. Though we may know what God wants us to do, we can become blinded by the desire for money, possessions, or prestige. We can avoid Balaam's mistake by looking past the allure of fame or fortune to the long-range benefits of following God.

22:27 Donkeys were all-purpose vehicles used for transportation, carrying loads, grinding grain, and plowing fields. They were usually highly dependable, which explains why Balaam became so angry when his donkey refused to move.

22:29 The donkey saved Balaam's life but made him look foolish in the process, so Balaam lashed out at the donkey. We sometimes strike out at blameless people who get in our way because we are embarrassed or our pride is hurt. Lashing out at others can be a sign that something is wrong with us. Don't allow your own hurt pride to lead you to hurt others.

Mediterranean Sea

↑ N

Sea of Galilee

CANAAN

Jordan River

Jerusalem

Mount Peor
Mount Pisgah
Bamoth Baal

Dead Sea   Arnon

0   20 Mi.
0   20 Km.

MOAB

THE STORY OF BALAAM

At King Balak's request, Balaam traveled nearly 400 miles to curse Israel. Balak took Balaam to Bamoth Baal ("the high places of Baal"), then to Mount Pisgah, and finally to Mount Peor. Each place looked over the plains of Moab, where the Israelites were camped. But to the king's dismay, Balaam blessed, not cursed, Israel.

22:34
vNu 14:40;
1Sa 15:24,30;
2Sa 12:13

22:36
wNu 21:13

22:38
xNu 23:5,16,26

22:41
yNu 21:28
zNu 23:13

23:2
aver 14,30

23:3
bver 15

³³The donkey saw me and turned away from me these three times. If she had not turned away, I would certainly have killed you by now, but I would have spared her."

³⁴Balaam said to the angel of the LORD, "I have sinned. ᵛ I did not realize you were standing in the road to oppose me. Now if you are displeased, I will go back."

³⁵The angel of the LORD said to Balaam, "Go with the men, but speak only what I tell you." So Balaam went with the princes of Balak.

³⁶When Balak heard that Balaam was coming, he went out to meet him at the Moabite town on the Arnon ʷ border, at the edge of his territory. ³⁷Balak said to Balaam, "Did I not send you an urgent summons? Why didn't you come to me? Am I really not able to reward you?"

³⁸"Well, I have come to you now," Balaam replied. "But can I say just anything? I must speak only what God puts in my mouth." ˣ

³⁹Then Balaam went with Balak to Kiriath Huzoth. ⁴⁰Balak sacrificed cattle and sheep, and gave some to Balaam and the princes who were with him. ⁴¹The next morning Balak took Balaam up to Bamoth Baal, ʸ and from there he saw part of the people. ᶻ

Balaam's First Oracle

23 Balaam said, "Build me seven altars here, and prepare seven bulls and seven rams for me." ²Balak did as Balaam said, and the two of them offered a bull and a ram on each altar. ᵃ

³Then Balaam said to Balak, "Stay here beside your offering while I go aside. Perhaps the LORD will come to meet with me. ᵇ Whatever he reveals to me I will tell you." Then he went off to a barren height.

BALAAM

Balaam was one of those noteworthy Old Testament characters who, though not one of God's chosen people, was willing to acknowledge that Yahweh (the Lord) was indeed a powerful God. But he did not believe in the Lord as the only true God. His story exposes the deception of maintaining an outward facade of spirituality over a corrupt inward life. Balaam was a man ready to obey God's command as long as he could profit from doing so. This mixture of motives—obedience and profit—eventually led to Balaam's death. Although he realized the awesome power of Israel's God, his heart was occupied with the wealth he could gain in Moab. There he returned to die when the armies of Israel invaded.

Eventually, each of us lives through the same process. Who and what we are will somehow come to the surface, destroying any masks we may have put on to cover up our real selves. Efforts spent on keeping up appearances would be much better spent on finding the answer to sin in our lives. We can avoid Balaam's mistake by facing ourselves and realizing that God is willing to accept us, forgive us, and literally make us over from within. Don't miss this great discovery that eluded Balaam.

Strengths and accomplishments:	• Widely known for his effective curses and blessings • Obeyed God and blessed Israel, in spite of Balak's bribe
Weaknesses and mistakes:	• Encouraged the Israelites to worship idols (Numbers 31:16) • Returned to Moab and was killed in war
Lessons from his life:	• Motives are just as important as actions • Your treasure is where your heart is
Vital statistics:	• Where: Lived near the Euphrates River, traveled to Moab • Occupations: Sorcerer, prophet • Relative: Father: Beor • Contemporaries: Balak (king of Moab), Moses, Aaron
Key verses:	"They have left the straight way and wandered off to follow the way of Balaam son of Beor, who loved the wages of wickedness. But he was rebuked for his wrongdoing by a donkey—a beast without speech—who spoke with a man's voice and restrained the prophet's madness" (2 Peter 2:15, 16).

Balaam's story is told in Numbers 22:1—24:25. He is also mentioned in Numbers 31:7, 8, 16; Deuteronomy 23:4, 5; Joshua 24:9, 10; Nehemiah 13:2; Micah 6:5; 2 Peter 2:15, 16; Jude 11; Revelation 2:14.

22:41 Bamoth Baal means the high places of Baal near Heshbon and Dibon. It was the first stopping point on the way to the high plains of Moab. From this vantage point, they could see the entire Israelite camp.

23:1–3 The number seven was sacred among many of the nations and religions at this time. A "barren height" means a place at a higher elevation on the mountain, without foliage.

⁴God met with him,ᶜ and Balaam said, "I have prepared seven altars, and on each altar I have offered a bull and a ram."

⁵The LORD put a message in Balaam's mouth ᵈ and said, "Go back to Balak and give him this message."

⁶So he went back to him and found him standing beside his offering, with all the princes of Moab. ⁷Then Balaam uttered his oracle: ᵉ

"Balak brought me from Aram,
    the king of Moab from the eastern mountains.
'Come,' he said, 'curse Jacob for me;
    come, denounce Israel.'ᶠ
⁸ How can I curse
    those whom God has not cursed?
How can I denounce
    those whom the LORD has not denounced?
⁹ From the rocky peaks I see them,
    from the heights I view them.
I see a people who live apart
    and do not consider themselves one of the nations.ᵍ
¹⁰ Who can count the dust of Jacobʰ
    or number the fourth part of Israel?
Let me die the death of the righteous,
    and may my end be like theirs!"

¹¹Balak said to Balaam, "What have you done to me? I brought you to curse my enemies, but you have done nothing but bless them!"

¹²He answered, "Must I not speak what the LORD puts in my mouth?"ⁱ

Balaam's Second Oracle

¹³Then Balak said to him, "Come with me to another place where you can see them; you will see only a part but not all of them. And from there, curse them for me." ¹⁴So he took him to the field of Zophim on the top of Pisgah, and there he built seven altars and offered a bull and a ram on each altar.

¹⁵Balaam said to Balak, "Stay here beside your offering while I meet with him over there."

¹⁶The LORD met with Balaam and put a message in his mouth and said, "Go back to Balak and give him this message."

¹⁷So he went to him and found him standing beside his offering, with the princes of Moab. Balak asked him, "What did the LORD say?"

¹⁸Then he uttered his oracle:

"Arise, Balak, and listen;
    hear me, son of Zippor.
¹⁹ God is not a man, that he should lie,
    nor a son of man, that he should change his mind.ʲ
Does he speak and then not act?
    Does he promise and not fulfill?
²⁰ I have received a command to bless;
    he has blessed,ᵏ and I cannot change it.

²¹ "No misfortune is seen in Jacob,ˡ
    no misery observed in Israel.ᵃ
The LORD their God is with them;
    the shout of the Kingᵐ is among them.
²² God brought them out of Egypt;ⁿ
    they have the strength of a wild ox.

ᵃ21 Or He has not looked on Jacob's offenses / or on the wrongs found in Israel.

23:4
ᶜver 16

23:5
ᵈDt 18:18; Jer 1:9

23:7
ᵉver 18; Nu 24:3,21
ᶠNu 22:6

23:9
ᵍDt 32:8; 33:28

23:10
ʰGe 13:16

23:12
ⁱNu 22:20,38

23:19
ʲ1Sa 15:29;
Mal 3:6; Jas 1:17

23:20
ᵏGe 22:17;
Nu 22:12

23:21
ˡPs 32:2,5; Ro 4:7-8
ᵐPs 89:15-18

23:22
ⁿNu 24:8

23:27 Balak took Balaam to several places to try to entice him to curse the Israelites. He thought a change of scenery might help change Balaam's mind. But changing locations won't change God's will. We must learn to face the source of our problems. Moving to escape problems only makes solving them more difficult. Problems rooted in us are not solved by a change of scenery. A change in location or job may only distract us from the need for us to change our heart.

Moab Seduces Israel

25:1
h Jos 2:1
i 1Co 10:8; Rev 2:14
j Nu 31:16

25:2
k Ex 20:5

25:3
l Ps 106:28

25:4
m Dt 4:3
n Dt 13:17

25 While Israel was staying in Shittim,h the men began to indulge in sexual immorality i with Moabite women,j 2 who invited them to the sacrifices to their gods.k The people ate and bowed down before these gods. 3 So Israel joined in worshiping the Baal of Peor. l And the LORD's anger burned against them.

4 The LORD said to Moses, "Take all the leaders of these people, kill them and expose them in broad daylight before the LORD,m so that the LORD's fierce anger n may turn away from Israel."

5 So Moses said to Israel's judges, "Each of you must put to death those of your men who have joined in worshiping the Baal of Peor."

6 Then an Israelite man brought to his family a Midianite woman right before the eyes of Moses and the whole assembly of Israel while they were weeping at the entrance to the Tent of Meeting. 7 When Phinehas son of Eleazar, the son of Aaron, the priest, saw this, he left the assembly, took a spear in his hand 8 and followed the Israelite into the tent. He drove the spear through both of them—through the Israelite and into the woman's body. Then the plague against the Israelites was stopped;o 9 but those who died in the plague p numbered 24,000.

25:8
o Ps 106:30

25:9
p 1Co 10:8

25:11
q Ps 106:30
r Ex 20:5

25:12
s Isa 54:10;
Mal 2:4,5

10 The LORD said to Moses, 11 "Phinehas son of Eleazar, the son of Aaron, the priest, has turned my anger away from the Israelites;q for he was as zealous as I am for my honor r among them, so that in my zeal I did not put an end to them. 12 Therefore tell him I am making my covenant of peace s with him. 13 He and his descendants will have a covenant of a lasting priesthood, because he was zealous for the honor of his God and made atonement for the Israelites."

25:15
t Nu 31:8

25:17
u Nu 31:1-3

14 The name of the Israelite who was killed with the Midianite woman was Zimri son of Salu, the leader of a Simeonite family. 15 And the name of the Midianite woman who was put to death was Cozbi daughter of Zur, a tribal chief of a Midianite family. t

16 The LORD said to Moses, 17 "Treat the Midianites u as enemies and kill them, 18 because they treated you as enemies when they deceived you in the affair of Peor and their sister Cozbi, the daughter of a Midianite leader, the woman who was killed when the plague came as a result of Peor."

2. The second census of the nation

26:2
v Ex 30:11-16

26:3
w Nu 33:48
x Nu 22:1

26 After the plague the LORD said to Moses and Eleazar son of Aaron, the priest, 2 "Take a census v of the whole Israelite community by families—all those twenty years old or more who are able to serve in the army of Israel." 3 So on the plains of Moab w by the Jordan across from Jericho,a x Moses and Eleazar the priest spoke with them and said, 4 "Take a census of the men twenty years old or more, as the LORD commanded Moses."

a 3 Hebrew *Jordan of Jericho*; possibly an ancient name for the Jordan River; also in verse 63

25:1 This verse shows the great challenge Israel had to face. The most dangerous problem for Moses and Joshua was not Jericho's hostile army, but the ever-present temptation to compromise with the pagan Canaanite religions and cultures.

25:1, 2 The Bible doesn't say how the Israelite men got involved in sexual immorality. We do know that sacred prostitution was a common practice among Canaanite religions. At first, they didn't think about worshiping idols; they were just interested in sex. Before long they started attending local feasts and family celebrations that involved idol worship. Soon they were in over their heads, absorbed into the practices of the pagan culture. Their desire for fun and pleasure caused them to loosen their spiritual commitment. Have you relaxed your standards in order to justify your desires?

25:1–3 This combination of sexual sin and idolatry, it turns out, was Balaam's idea (see 31:16; Revelation 2:14), the same Balaam who had just blessed Israel and who appeared to be on their side. It is easy to see how the Israelites were misled, for Balaam seemed to say and do all the right things—at least for a while (22—24). Not until Balaam had inflicted great damage on them did the Israelites realize that he was greedy, used sorcery, and was deeply involved in pagan religious practices. We must be careful to weigh both the words and the deeds of those who claim to offer spiritual help.

25:3 Baal was the most popular god in Canaan, the land Israel

was about to enter. Represented by a bull, symbol of strength and fertility, he was the god of the rains and harvest. The Israelites were continually attracted to Baal worship, in which prostitution played a large part, throughout their years in Canaan. Because Baal was so popular, his name was often used as a generic title for all the local gods.

25:6 The phrase "brought to his family" meant that she was brought into his tent for sex. Zimri (25:14) so disregarded the law of God that he brought the woman right into the camp.

25:10, 11 It is clear from Phinehas's story that some anger is proper and justified. Phinehas was angry because of his zeal for the Lord. But how can we know when our anger is appropriate and when it should be restrained? Ask these questions when you become angry: (1) Why am I angry? (2) Whose rights are being violated (mine or another's)? (3) Is the truth (a principle of God) being violated? If only your rights are at stake, it may be wiser to keep angry feelings under control. But if the truth is at stake, anger is often justified, although violence and retaliation are usually the wrong way to express it (Phinehas's case was unique). If we are becoming more and more like God, we should be angered by sin.

25:12, 13 Phinehas's act made atonement for the nation of Israel; in effect, what he did averted God's judgment. Because of this, his descendants would become the high priests of Israel. They continued so throughout the history of the tabernacle and the temple.

These were the Israelites who came out of Egypt:

5 The descendants of Reuben, the firstborn son of Israel, were:
    through Hanoch, the Hanochite clan;
    through Pallu, the Palluite clan;
 6 through Hezron, the Hezronite clan;
    through Carmi, the Carmite clan.
7 These were the clans of Reuben; those numbered were 43,730.

8 The son of Pallu was Eliab, 9 and the sons of Eliab were Nemuel, Dathan and Abiram. The same Dathan and Abiram were the community officials who rebelled against Moses and Aaron and were among Korah's followers when they rebelled against the LORD. *y* 10 The earth opened its mouth and swallowed them along with Korah, whose followers died when the fire devoured the 250 men. And they served as a warning sign. *z* 11 The line of Korah, however, did not die out.

12 The descendants of Simeon by their clans were:
    through Nemuel, the Nemuelite clan;
    through Jamin, *a* the Jaminite clan;
    through Jakin, the Jakinite clan;
13 through Zerah, *b* the Zerahite clan;
    through Shaul, the Shaulite clan.
14 These were the clans of Simeon; there were 22,200 men.

15 The descendants of Gad by their clans were:
    through Zephon, *c* the Zephonite clan;
    through Haggi, the Haggite clan;
    through Shuni, the Shunite clan;
16 through Ozni, the Oznite clan;
    through Eri, the Erite clan;
17 through Arodi, *a* the Arodite clan;
    through Areli, the Arelite clan.
18 These were the clans of Gad; *d* those numbered were 40,500.

19 Er and Onan were sons of Judah, but they died *e* in Canaan.
20 The descendants of Judah by their clans were:
    through Shelah, *f* the Shelanite clan;
    through Perez, the Perezite clan;
    through Zerah, the Zerahite clan.
21 The descendants of Perez were:
    through Hezron, the Hezronite clan;
    through Hamul, the Hamulite clan.
22 These were the clans of Judah; *g* those numbered were 76,500.

23 The descendants of Issachar by their clans were:
    through Tola, *h* the Tolaite clan;
    through Puah, the Puite *b* clan;
24 through Jashub, the Jashubite clan;
    through Shimron, the Shimronite clan.
25 These were the clans of Issachar; *i* those numbered were 64,300.

26 The descendants of Zebulun by their clans were:
    through Sered, the Seredite clan;
    through Elon, the Elonite clan;
    through Jahleel, the Jahleelite clan.
27 These were the clans of Zebulun; those numbered were 60,500.

28 The descendants of Joseph by their clans through Manasseh and Ephraim were:

29 The descendants of Manasseh:
    through Makir, *j* the Makirite clan (Makir was the father of Gilead);
    through Gilead, the Gileadite clan.

26:9
y Nu 16:2

26:10
z Nu 16:35,38

26:12
a 1Ch 4:24

26:13
b Ge 46:10

26:15
c Ge 46:16

26:18
d Nu 1:25

26:19
e Ge 38:2-10; 46:12

26:20
f 1Ch 2:3

26:22
g Nu 1:27

26:23
h Ge 46:13

26:25
i Nu 1:29

26:29
j Jos 17:1

---

a 17 Samaritan Pentateuch and Syriac (see also Gen. 46:16); Masoretic Text *Arod* *b 23* Samaritan Pentateuch, Septuagint, Vulgate and Syriac (see also 1 Chron. 7:1); Masoretic Text *through Puvah, the Punite*

26:30
k Jos 17:2; Jdg 6:11

26:33
l Nu 27:1

26:37
m Nu 1:33

26:38
n Ge 46:21

26:41
o Nu 1:37

26:42
p Ge 46:23

26:47
q Nu 1:41

26:53
r Jos 11:23; 14:1
26:54
s Nu 33:54
26:55
t Nu 34:14

30 These were the descendants of Gilead:
    through Iezer,k the Iezerite clan;
    through Helek, the Helekite clan;
31 through Asriel, the Asrielite clan;
    through Shechem, the Shechemite clan;
32 through Shemida, the Shemidaite clan;
    through Hepher, the Hepherite clan.
33 (Zelophehad l son of Hepher had no sons; he had only daughters, whose names were
    Mahlah, Noah, Hoglah, Milcah and Tirzah.)
34 These were the clans of Manasseh; those numbered were 52,700.

35 These were the descendants of Ephraim by their clans:
    through Shuthelah, the Shuthelahite clan;
    through Beker, the Bekerite clan;
    through Tahan, the Tahanite clan.
36 These were the descendants of Shuthelah:
    through Eran, the Eranite clan.
37 These were the clans of Ephraim;m those numbered were 32,500.

These were the descendants of Joseph by their clans.

38 The descendants of Benjamin n by their clans were:
    through Bela, the Belaite clan;
    through Ashbel, the Ashbelite clan;
    through Ahiram, the Ahiramite clan;
39 through Shupham,a the Shuphamite clan;
    through Hupham, the Huphamite clan.
40 The descendants of Bela through Ard and Naaman were:
    through Ard,b the Ardite clan;
    through Naaman, the Naamite clan.
41 These were the clans of Benjamin;o those numbered were 45,600.

42 These were the descendants of Dan by their clans:
    through Shuham,p the Shuhamite clan.
These were the clans of Dan: 43 All of them were Shuhamite clans; and those numbered were 64,400.

44 The descendants of Asher by their clans were:
    through Imnah, the Imnite clan;
    through Ishvi, the Ishvite clan;
    through Beriah, the Beriite clan;
45 and through the descendants of Beriah:
    through Heber, the Heberite clan;
    through Malkiel, the Malkielite clan.
46 (Asher had a daughter named Serah.)
47 These were the clans of Asher;q those numbered were 53,400.

48 The descendants of Naphtali by their clans were:
    through Jahzeel, the Jahzeelite clan;
    through Guni, the Gunite clan;
49 through Jezer, the Jezerite clan;
    through Shillem, the Shillemite clan.
50 These were the clans of Naphtali; those numbered were 45,400.

51 The total number of the men of Israel was 601,730.

52 The LORD said to Moses, 53 "The land is to be allotted to them as an inheritance based on the number of names.r 54 To a larger group give a larger inheritance, and to a smaller group a smaller one; each is to receive its inheritance according to the numbers of those listed. 55 Be sure that the land is distributed by lot.t What each group inherits will be according to the

a 39 A few manuscripts of the Masoretic Text, Samaritan Pentateuch, Vulgate and Syriac (see also Septuagint); most manuscripts of the Masoretic Text *Shephupham*   b 40 Samaritan Pentateuch and Vulgate (see also Septuagint); Masoretic Text does not have *through Ard.*

names for its ancestral tribe. 56 Each inheritance is to be distributed by lot among the larger and smaller groups."

57 These were the Levites u who were counted by their clans:
through Gershon, the Gershonite clan;
through Kohath, the Kohathite clan;
through Merari, the Merarite clan.
58 These also were Levite clans:
the Libnite clan,
the Hebronite clan,
the Mahlite clan,
the Mushite clan,
the Korahite clan.
(Kohath was the forefather of Amram; 59 the name of Amram's wife was Jochebed, a descendant of Levi, who was born to the Levites a in Egypt. To Amram she bore Aaron, Moses v and their sister Miriam. 60 Aaron was the father of Nadab and Abihu, Eleazar and Ithamar. w 61 But Nadab and Abihu x died when they made an offering before the LORD with unauthorized fire.) y

62 All the male Levites a month old or more numbered 23,000. They were not counted z along with the other Israelites because they received no inheritance a among them.

63 These are the ones counted by Moses and Eleazar the priest when they counted the Israelites on the plains of Moab by the Jordan across from Jericho. 64 Not one of them was among those counted b by Moses and Aaron the priest when they counted the Israelites in the Desert of Sinai. 65 For the LORD had told those Israelites they would surely die in the desert, c and not one of them was left except Caleb son of Jephunneh and Joshua son of Nun.

Zelophehad's Daughters

27 The daughters of Zelophehad d son of Hepher, the son of Gilead, the son of Makir, e the son of Manasseh, belonged to the clans of Manasseh son of Joseph. The names of the daughters were Mahlah, Noah, Hoglah, Milcah and Tirzah. They approached 2 the entrance to the Tent of Meeting and stood before Moses, Eleazar the priest, the leaders and the whole assembly, and said, 3 "Our father died in the desert. f He was not among Korah's followers, who banded together against the LORD, g but he died for his own sin and left no sons. 4 Why should our father's name disappear from his clan because he had no son? Give us property among our father's relatives."

5 So Moses brought their case before the LORD h 6 and the LORD said to him, 7 "What Zelophehad's daughters are saying is right. You must certainly give them property as an inheritance among their father's relatives and turn their father's inheritance over to them.

8 "Say to the Israelites, 'If a man dies and leaves no son, turn his inheritance over to his daughter. 9 If he has no daughter, give his inheritance to his brothers. 10 If he has no brothers, give his inheritance to his father's brothers. 11 If his father had no brothers, give his inheritance to the nearest relative in his clan, that he may possess it. This is to be a legal requirement i for the Israelites, as the LORD commanded Moses.'"

Joshua to Succeed Moses

12 Then the LORD said to Moses, "Go up this mountain in the Abarim range j and see the land k I have given the Israelites. 13 After you have seen it, you too will be gathered to your people, l as your brother Aaron was, 14 for when the community rebelled at the waters in the Desert of Zin, both of you disobeyed my command to honor me as holy m before their eyes." (These were the waters of Meribah n Kadesh, in the Desert of Zin.)

a 59 Or Jochebed, a daughter of Levi, who was born to Levi

Cross references:
26:57 u Ge 46:11
26:59 v Ex 6:20
26:60 w Nu 3:2
26:61 x Lev 10:1-2; y Nu 3:4
26:62 z Nu 1:47; a Nu 18:23
26:64 b Dt 2:14-15; Heb 3:17
26:65 c Nu 14:28; 1Co 10:5
27:1 d Nu 26:33; e Nu 36:1
27:3 f Nu 26:65; g Nu 16:2
27:5 h Nu 9:8
27:11 i Nu 35:29
27:12 j Nu 33:47; Jer 22:20; k Dt 32:48-52
27:13 l Nu 31:2
27:14 m Nu 20:12; n Dt 32:51; Ps 106:32

26:64 A new census for a new generation. Thirty-eight years had elapsed since the first great census recorded in Numbers (see 1:1—2:33). During that time, every Israelite man and woman over 20 years of age—except Caleb, Joshua, and Moses—had died, and yet God's laws and the spiritual character of the nation were still intact. Numbers records some dramatic miracles. This is a quiet but powerful miracle often overlooked: A whole nation moved from one land to another, lost its entire adult population, yet managed to maintain its spiritual direction. Sometimes it may feel like God isn't working dramatic miracles in our lives. But God often works in quiet ways to bring about his long-range purposes.

27:3 "Died for his own sin" means that he died a natural death. His death fell under the judgment of the entire nation for believing the faithless spies.

27:3, 4 Up to this point, the Hebrew law gave sons alone the right to inherit. The daughters of Zelophehad, having no brothers,

27:16
*o*Nu 16:22

27:17
*p*Dt 31:2; Mt 9:36;
Mk 6:34

27:18
*q*Nu 11:25-29
*r*Dt 34:9

27:19
*s*Dt 31:7

27:20
*t*Jos 1:16,17

27:21
*u*Ex 28:30

[15] Moses said to the Lord, [16] "May the Lord, the God of the spirits of all mankind, *o* appoint a man over this community [17] to go out and come in before them, one who will lead them out and bring them in, so the Lord's people will not be like sheep without a shepherd." *p*

[18] So the Lord said to Moses, "Take Joshua son of Nun, a man in whom is the spirit, *a q* and lay your hand on him. *r* [19] Have him stand before Eleazar the priest and the entire assembly and commission him in their presence. *s* [20] Give him some of your authority so the whole Israelite community will obey him. *t* [21] He is to stand before Eleazar the priest, who will obtain decisions for him by inquiring of the Urim *u* before the Lord. At his command he and the entire community of the Israelites will go out, and at his command they will come in."

[22] Moses did as the Lord commanded him. He took Joshua and had him stand before Eleazar the priest and the whole assembly. [23] Then he laid his hands on him and commissioned him, as the Lord instructed through Moses.

3. Instructions concerning offerings
Daily Offerings

28:2
*v*Lev 3:11

28:3
*w*Ex 29:38

28:5
*x*Lev 2:1

28:7
*y*Ex 29:41

28 The Lord said to Moses, [2] "Give this command to the Israelites and say to them: 'See that you present to me at the appointed time the food *v* for my offerings made by fire, as an aroma pleasing to me.' [3] Say to them: 'This is the offering made by fire that you are to present to the Lord: two lambs a year old without defect, as a regular burnt offering each day. *w* [4] Prepare one lamb in the morning and the other at twilight, [5] together with a grain offering of a tenth of an ephah *b* of fine flour mixed with a quarter of a hin *c* of oil *x* from pressed olives. [6] This is the regular burnt offering instituted at Mount Sinai as a pleasing aroma, an offering made to the Lord by fire. [7] The accompanying drink offering *y* is to be a quarter of a hin of fermented drink with each lamb. Pour out the drink offering to the Lord at the sanctuary. [8] Prepare the second lamb at twilight, along with the same kind of grain offering and drink offering that you prepare in the morning. This is an offering made by fire, an aroma pleasing to the Lord.

Sabbath Offerings

[9] "'On the Sabbath day, make an offering of two lambs a year old without defect, together with its drink offering and a grain offering of two-tenths of an ephah *d* of fine flour mixed with oil. [10] This is the burnt offering for every Sabbath, in addition to the regular burnt offering *z* and its drink offering.

28:10
*z*ver 3

Monthly Offerings

28:11
*a*Nu 10:10

28:12
*b*Nu 15:6
*c*Nu 15:9

[11] "'On the first of every month, *a* present to the Lord a burnt offering of two young bulls, one ram and seven male lambs a year old, all without defect. [12] With each bull there is to be a grain offering *b* of three-tenths of an ephah *e c* of fine flour mixed with oil; with the ram, a grain offering of two-tenths of an ephah of fine flour mixed with oil; [13] and with each lamb, a grain offering of a tenth of an ephah of fine flour mixed with oil. This is for a burnt offering,

a 18 Or *Spirit*   *b 5* That is, probably about 2 quarts (about 2 liters); also in verses 13, 21 and 29   *c 5* That is, probably about 1 quart (about 1 liter); also in verses 7 and 14   *d 9* That is, probably about 4 quarts (about 4.5 liters); also in verses 12, 20 and 28   *e 12* That is, probably about 6 quarts (about 6.5 liters); also in verses 20 and 28

---

came to Moses to ask for their father's possessions. God told Moses that if a man died without sons, his inheritance would go to his daughters (27:8). But the daughters could keep it only if they married within their own tribe, probably so the territorial lines would remain intact (36:5–12).

27:15–17 Moses asked God to appoint a leader who was capable of directing both external and internal affairs—one who could lead them in battle, but who would also care for their needs. The Lord responded by appointing Joshua. Many people want to be known as leaders. Some are very capable of reaching their goals, while others care deeply for the people in their charge. The best leaders are both goal-oriented and people-oriented.

27:15–21 Moses did not want to leave his work without making sure a new leader was ready to replace him. First he asked God to help him find a replacement. Then, when Joshua was selected, Moses gave him a variety of tasks to ease the transition into his new position. Moses also clearly told the people that Joshua had the authority and the ability to lead the nation. His display of

confidence in Joshua was good for both Joshua and the people. To minimize leadership gaps, anyone in a leadership position should train others to carry on the duties should he or she suddenly or eventually have to leave. While you have the opportunity, follow Moses' pattern: pray, select, develop, and commission.

28:1, 2 Offerings had to be brought regularly and presented according to prescribed rituals under the priests' supervision. Following these rituals took time, and this gave the people the opportunity to prepare their hearts for worship. Unless our hearts are ready, worship is meaningless. By contrast, God is delighted, and we get more from it, when our hearts are prepared to come before him in a spirit of thankfulness.

28:9, 10 Why were extra offerings made on the Sabbath day? The Sabbath was a special day of rest and worship commemorating both creation (Exodus 20:8–11) and the deliverance from Egypt (Deuteronomy 5:12–15). Because of the significance of this special day, it was only natural to offer extra sacrifices on it.

a pleasing aroma, an offering made to the LORD by fire. [14]With each bull there is to be a drink offering of half a hin[a] of wine; with the ram, a third of a hin[b]; and with each lamb, a quarter of a hin. This is the monthly burnt offering to be made at each new moon during the year. [15]Besides the regular burnt offering [d] with its drink offering, one male goat is to be presented to the LORD as a sin offering.

28:15
[d]ver 3,23,24

The Passover

[16]"'On the fourteenth day of the first month the LORD's Passover [e] is to be held. [17]On the fifteenth day of this month there is to be a festival; for seven days eat bread made without yeast. [f] [18]On the first day hold a sacred assembly and do no regular work. [g] [19]Present to the LORD an offering made by fire, a burnt offering of two young bulls, one ram and seven male lambs a year old, all without defect. [20]With each bull prepare a grain offering of three-tenths of an ephah of fine flour mixed with oil; with the ram, two-tenths; [21]and with each of the seven lambs, one-tenth. [22]Include one male goat as a sin offering to make atonement for you. [23]Prepare these in addition to the regular morning burnt offering. [24]In this way prepare the food for the offering made by fire every day for seven days as an aroma pleasing to the LORD; it is to be prepared in addition to the regular burnt offering and its drink offering. [25]On the seventh day hold a sacred assembly and do no regular work.

28:16
[e]Ex 12:6,18;
Lev 23:5; Dt 16:1
28:17
[f]Lev 23:6
28:18
[g]Ex 12:16

Feast of Weeks

[26]"'On the day of firstfruits,[h] when you present to the LORD an offering of new grain during the Feast of Weeks,[i] hold a sacred assembly and do no regular work.[j] [27]Present a burnt offering of two young bulls, one ram and seven male lambs a year old as an aroma pleasing to the LORD. [28]With each bull there is to be a grain offering of three-tenths of an ephah of fine flour mixed with oil; with the ram, two-tenths; [29]and with each of the seven lambs, one-tenth. [30]Include one male goat to make atonement for you. [31]Prepare these together with their drink offerings, in addition to the regular burnt offering [k] and its grain offering. Be sure the animals are without defect.

28:26
[h]Ex 34:22
[i]Ex 23:16
[j]Dt 16:10

28:31
[k]ver 3,19

Feast of Trumpets

29 "'On the first day of the seventh month hold a sacred assembly and do no regular work. [l] It is a day for you to sound the trumpets. [2]As an aroma pleasing to the LORD, prepare a burnt offering of one young bull, one ram and seven male lambs a year old, all without defect. [3]With the bull prepare a grain offering of three-tenths of an ephah[c] of fine flour mixed with oil; with the ram, two-tenths [d]; [4]and with each of the seven lambs, one-tenth. [e] [5]Include one male goat as a sin offering to make atonement for you. [6]These are in addition to the monthly[m] and daily burnt offerings[n] with their grain offerings and drink offerings as specified. They are offerings made to the LORD by fire—a pleasing aroma.

29:1
[l]Lev 23:24

29:6
[m]Nu 28:11
[n]Nu 28:3

Day of Atonement

[7]"'On the tenth day of this seventh month hold a sacred assembly. You must deny yourselves[f] and do no work. [o] [8]Present as an aroma pleasing to the LORD a burnt offering of one young bull, one ram and seven male lambs a year old, all without defect. [9]With the bull prepare a grain offering of three-tenths of an ephah of fine flour mixed with oil; with the ram, two-tenths; [10]and with each of the seven lambs, one-tenth. [11]Include one male goat as a sin offering, in addition to the sin offering for atonement and the regular burnt offering[p] with its grain offering, and their drink offerings.

29:7
[o]Ex 31:15;
Lev 16:29;
23:26-32

29:11
[p]Lev 16:3; Nu 28:3

[a]14 That is, probably about 2 quarts (about 2 liters)   [b]14 That is, probably about 1 1/4 quarts (about 1.2 liters)
[c]3 That is, probably about 6 quarts (about 6.5 liters); also in verses 9 and 14   [d]3 That is, probably about 4 quarts
(about 4.5 liters); also in verses 9 and 14   [e]4 That is, probably about 2 quarts (about 2 liters); also in verses 10 and 15
[f]7 Or must fast

29:1ff God placed many holidays on Israel's calendar. The Feast of Trumpets was one of three great holidays celebrated in the seventh month (the Feast of Tabernacles and Day of Atonement were the other two). These holidays provided a time to refresh the mind and body and to renew one's commitment to God. If you feel tired or far from God, try taking a "spiritual holiday." Separate yourself from your daily routine and concentrate on renewing your commitment to God.

29:1, 2 The Feast of Trumpets demonstrated three important principles that we should follow in our worship today: (1) The

people gathered together to celebrate and worship. There is an extra benefit to be gained from worshiping with other believers. (2) The normal daily routine was suspended, and no hard work was done. It takes time to worship, and setting aside the time allows us to adjust our attitudes before and reflect afterwards. (3) The people sacrificed animals as burnt offerings to God. We show our commitment to God when we give something of value to him. God desires wholehearted worship. Our gift of money presented generously to God's work also demonstrates our thanks to him. The best gift, of course, is ourselves.

Feast of Tabernacles

12"'On the fifteenth day of the seventh month, hold a sacred assembly and do no regular work. Celebrate a festival to the LORD for seven days. 13Present an offering made by fire as an aroma pleasing to the LORD, a burnt offering of thirteen young bulls, two rams and fourteen male lambs a year old, all without defect. 14With each of the thirteen bulls prepare a grain offering of three-tenths of an ephah of fine flour mixed with oil; with each of the two rams, two-tenths; 15and with each of the fourteen lambs, one-tenth. 16Include one male goat as a sin offering, in addition to the regular burnt offering with its grain offering and drink offering.

17"'On the second day q prepare twelve young bulls, two rams and fourteen male lambs a year old, all without defect. 18With the bulls, rams and lambs, prepare their grain offerings r and drink offerings according to the number specified. s 19Include one male goat as a sin offering, in addition to the regular burnt offering with its grain offering, and their drink offerings.

20"'On the third day prepare eleven bulls, two rams and fourteen male lambs a year old, all without defect. 21With the bulls, rams and lambs, prepare their grain offerings and drink offerings according to the number specified. 22Include one male goat as a sin offering, in addition to the regular burnt offering with its grain offering and drink offering.

23"'On the fourth day prepare ten bulls, two rams and fourteen male lambs a year old, all without defect. 24With the bulls, rams and lambs, prepare their grain offerings and drink offerings according to the number specified. 25Include one male goat as a sin offering, in addition to the regular burnt offering with its grain offering and drink offering.

26"'On the fifth day prepare nine bulls, two rams and fourteen male lambs a year old, all without defect. 27With the bulls, rams and lambs, prepare their grain offerings and drink offerings according to the number specified. 28Include one male goat as a sin offering, in addition to the regular burnt offering with its grain offering and drink offering.

29"'On the sixth day prepare eight bulls, two rams and fourteen male lambs a year old, all without defect. 30With the bulls, rams and lambs, prepare their grain offerings and drink offerings according to the number specified. 31Include one male goat as a sin offering, in addition to the regular burnt offering with its grain offering and drink offering.

32"'On the seventh day prepare seven bulls, two rams and fourteen male lambs a year old, all without defect. 33With the bulls, rams and lambs, prepare their grain offerings and drink offerings according to the number specified. 34Include one male goat as a sin offering, in addition to the regular burnt offering with its grain offering and drink offering.

35"'On the eighth day hold an assembly t and do no regular work. 36Present an offering made by fire as an aroma pleasing to the LORD, a burnt offering of one bull, one ram and seven male lambs a year old, all without defect. 37With the bull, the ram and the lambs, prepare their grain offerings and drink offerings according to the number specified. 38Include one male goat as a sin offering, in addition to the regular burnt offering with its grain offering and drink offering.

39"'In addition to what you vow and your freewill offerings, prepare these for the LORD at your appointed feasts: u your burnt offerings, v grain offerings, drink offerings and fellowship offerings. a'"

40Moses told the Israelites all that the LORD commanded him.

Vows

30 Moses said to the heads of the tribes of Israel: w "This is what the LORD commands: 2When a man makes a vow to the LORD or takes an oath to obligate himself by a pledge, he must not break his word but must do everything he said. x

3"When a young woman still living in her father's house makes a vow to the LORD or

a39 Traditionally *peace offerings*

29:17
q Lev 23:36
29:18
r ver 9
s Nu 15:4-12

29:35
t Lev 23:36

29:39
u Lev 23:2
v 1Ch 23:31;
2Ch 31:3

30:1
w Nu 1:4
30:2
x Dt 23:21-23;
Ps 50:14

30:1, 2 Moses reminded the people that their promises to God and others must be kept. In ancient times, people did not sign written contracts. A person's word was as binding as a signature. To make a vow even more binding, an offering was given along with it. No one was forced by law to make a vow; but once made, vows had to be fulfilled. Breaking a vow meant a broken trust and a broken relationship. Trust is still the basis of our relationships with God and others. A broken promise today is just as harmful as it was in Moses' day.

30:3–8 Under Israelite law, parents could overrule their children's vows. This helped young people avoid the consequences of making foolish promises or costly commitments. From this law comes an important principle for both parents and children. Young people still living at home should seek their parents' help when they make decisions. A parent's experience could save a child from a serious mistake. Parents, however, should exercise their authority with caution and grace. They should let children learn from their mistakes while protecting them from disaster.

obligates herself by a pledge [4] and her father hears about her vow or pledge but says nothing to her, then all her vows and every pledge by which she obligated herself will stand. [5] But if her father forbids her when he hears about it, none of her vows or the pledges by which she obligated herself will stand; the LORD will release her because her father has forbidden her.

[6] "If she marries after she makes a vow or after her lips utter a rash promise by which she obligates herself [7] and her husband hears about it but says nothing to her, then her vows or the pledges by which she obligated herself will stand. [8] But if her husband forbids her when he hears about it, he nullifies the vow that obligates her or the rash promise by which she obligates herself, and the LORD will release her.

[9] "Any vow or obligation taken by a widow or divorced woman will be binding on her.

[10] "If a woman living with her husband makes a vow or obligates herself by a pledge under oath [11] and her husband hears about it but says nothing to her and does not forbid her, then all her vows or the pledges by which she obligated herself will stand. [12] But if her husband nullifies them when he hears about them, then none of the vows or pledges that came from her lips will stand. *y* Her husband has nullified them, and the LORD will release her. [13] Her husband may confirm or nullify any vow she makes or any sworn pledge to deny herself. [14] But if her husband says nothing to her about it from day to day, then he confirms all her vows or the pledges binding on her. He confirms them by saying nothing to her when he hears about them. [15] If, however, he nullifies them some time after he hears about them, then he is responsible for her guilt."

[16] These are the regulations the LORD gave Moses concerning relationships between a man and his wife, and between a father and his young daughter still living in his house.

4. Vengeance on the Midianites

31 The LORD said to Moses, [2] "Take vengeance on the Midianites for the Israelites. After that, you will be gathered to your people. *z*"

[3] So Moses said to the people, "Arm some of your men to go to war against the Midianites and to carry out the LORD's vengeance on them. [4] Send into battle a thousand men from each of the tribes of Israel." [5] So twelve thousand men armed for battle, a thousand from each tribe, were supplied from the clans of Israel. [6] Moses sent them into battle, a thousand from each tribe, along with Phinehas son of Eleazar, the priest, who took with him articles from the sanctuary and the trumpets *a* for signaling.

[7] They fought against Midian, as the LORD commanded Moses, and killed every man. *b* [8] Among their victims were Evi, Rekem, Zur, Hur and Reba *c*—the five kings of Midian. They also killed Balaam son of Beor with the sword. *d* [9] The Israelites captured the Midianite women and children and took all the Midianite herds, flocks and goods as plunder. [10] They burned all the towns where the Midianites had settled, as well as all their camps. [11] They took all the plunder and spoils, including the people and animals, *e* [12] and brought the captives, spoils and plunder to Moses and Eleazar the priest and the Israelite assembly at their camp on the plains of Moab, by the Jordan across from Jericho. *a*

[13] Moses, Eleazar the priest and all the leaders of the community went to meet them outside the camp. [14] Moses was angry with the officers of the army—the commanders of thousands and commanders of hundreds—who returned from the battle.

[15] "Have you allowed all the women to live?" he asked them. [16] "They were the ones who followed Balaam's advice *f* and were the means of turning the Israelites away from the LORD

a 12 Hebrew *Jordan of Jericho*; possibly an ancient name for the Jordan River

30:12
y Eph 5:22

31:2
z Nu 20:26; 27:13

31:6
a Nu 10:9

31:7
b Dt 20:13;
Jdg 21:11;
1Ki 11:15,16
31:8
c Jos 13:21
d Jos 13:22
31:11
e Dt 20:14

31:16
f 2Pe 2:15

31:1ff The Midianites were a nomadic people who descended from Abraham and his second wife, Keturah. The land of Midian lay far to the south of Canaan, but large bands of Midianites roamed many miles from their homeland, searching for grazing areas for their flocks. Such a group was near the promised land when the Israelites arrived. When Moses fled from Egypt (Exodus 2), he took refuge in the land of Midian. His wife and father-in-law were Midianites. Despite this alliance, the Israelites and Midianites were always bitter enemies.

31:14–16 Because Midianites were responsible for enticing Israel into Baal worship, God commanded Israel to destroy them (25:16–18). But Israel took the women as captives, rather than killing

them, probably because of the tempting enticements of the Midianites' sinful lifestyle. When we discover sin in our lives, we must deal with it completely. When the Israelites later entered the promised land, it was their indifferent attitude to sin that eventually ruined them. Moses dealt with the sin promptly and completely. When God points out sin, move quickly to remove it from your life.

31:16 Balaam's story (22:1—24:25), taken alone, would lead us to believe that Balaam was an honest and God-fearing man. But here is the first of much Biblical evidence that Balaam was not the good man he might appear to be. For more on Balaam, see the notes on 22:9 and 25:1–3, and Balaam's Profile in chapter 22, p. 231.

31:16
gNu 25:1-9

31:17
hDt 7:2; 20:16-18;
Jdg 21:11

31:19
iNu 19:12

31:23
j1Co 3:13
kNu 19:9,17

31:24
lLev 11:25

in what happened at Peor,g so that a plague struck the LORD's people. 17Now kill all the boys. And kill every woman who has slept with a man,h 18but save for yourselves every girl who has never slept with a man.

19"All of you who have killed anyone or touched anyone who was killed must stay outside the camp seven days. On the third and seventh days you must purify yourselvesi and your captives. 20Purify every garment as well as everything made of leather, goat hair or wood."

21Then Eleazar the priest said to the soldiers who had gone into battle, "This is the requirement of the law that the LORD gave Moses: 22Gold, silver, bronze, iron, tin, lead 23and anything else that can withstand fire must be put through the fire,j and then it will be clean. But it must also be purified with the water of cleansing.k And whatever cannot withstand fire must be put through that water. 24On the seventh day wash your clothes and you will be clean.l Then you may come into the camp."

Dividing the Spoils

25The LORD said to Moses, 26"You and Eleazar the priest and the family heads of the community are to count all the people and animals that were captured. 27Dividem the spoils between the soldiers who took part in the battle and the rest of the community. 28From the soldiers who fought in the battle, set apart as tribute for the LORDn one out of every five hundred, whether persons, cattle, donkeys, sheep or goats. 29Take this tribute from their half share and give it to Eleazar the priest as the LORD's part. 30From the Israelites' half, select one out of every fifty, whether persons, cattle, donkeys, sheep, goats or other animals. Give them to the Levites, who are responsible for the care of the LORD's tabernacle.o" 31So Moses and Eleazar the priest did as the LORD commanded Moses.

31:27
mJos 22:8

31:28
nNu 18:21

31:30
oNu 3:7; 18:3

32The plunder remaining from the spoils that the soldiers took was 675,000 sheep, 3372,000 cattle, 3461,000 donkeys 35and 32,000 women who had never slept with a man.

36The half share of those who fought in the battle was:

337,500 sheep, 37of which the tribute for the LORDp was 675;
38 36,000 cattle, of which the tribute for the LORD was 72;
39 30,500 donkeys, of which the tribute for the LORD was 61;
40 16,000 people, of which the tribute for the LORD was 32.

31:37
pver 38-41

41Moses gave the tribute to Eleazar the priest as the LORD's part,q as the LORD commanded Moses.

42The half belonging to the Israelites, which Moses set apart from that of the fighting men— 43the community's half—was 337,500 sheep, 44 36,000 cattle, 45 30,500 donkeys 46and 16,000 people. 47From the Israelites' half, Moses selected one out of every fifty persons and animals, as the LORD commanded him, and gave them to the Levites, who were responsible for the care of the LORD's tabernacle.

31:41
qNu 18:8

48Then the officers who were over the units of the army—the commanders of thousands and commanders of hundreds—went to Moses 49and said to him, "Your servants have counted the soldiers under our command, and not one is missing. 50So we have brought as an offering to the LORD the gold articles each of us acquired—armlets, bracelets, signet rings, earrings and necklaces—to make atonement for ourselvesr before the LORD."

31:50
rEx 30:16

51Moses and Eleazar the priest accepted from them the gold—all the crafted articles. 52All the gold from the commanders of thousands and commanders of hundreds that Moses and Eleazar presented as a gift to the LORD weighed 16,750 shekels.a 53Each soldier had taken plunders for himself. 54Moses and Eleazar the priest accepted the gold from the commanders of thousands and commanders of hundreds and brought it into the Tent of Meeting as a memorial for the Israelites before the LORD.

31:53
sDt 20:14

a52 That is, about 420 pounds (about 190 kilograms)

31:25-30 Moses told the Israelites to give a portion of the war spoils to God. Another portion was to go to the people who remained behind. Similarly, the money we earn is not ours alone. Everything we possess comes directly or indirectly from God and ultimately belongs to him. We should return a portion to him (a "tribute") and also share a portion with those in need.

31:48-50 After carefully accounting for all their men, the officers discovered that not one soldier had been lost in battle. At once they thanked God. After going through tough times, we should be quick to thank God for delivering us and protecting us from severe loss.

5. The Transjordan tribes

32 The Reubenites and Gadites, who had very large herds and flocks, saw that the lands of Jazer[t] and Gilead were suitable for livestock.[u] 2So they came to Moses and Eleazar the priest and to the leaders of the community, and said, 3"Ataroth, Dibon, Jazer, Nimrah,[v] Heshbon, Elealeh, Sebam, Nebo and Beon[w]— 4the land the LORD subdued[x] before the people of Israel—are suitable for livestock, and your servants have livestock. 5If we have found favor in your eyes," they said, "let this land be given to your servants as our possession. Do not make us cross the Jordan."

6Moses said to the Gadites and Reubenites, "Shall your countrymen go to war while you sit here? 7Why do you discourage the Israelites from going over into the land the LORD has given them?[y] 8This is what your fathers did when I sent them from Kadesh Barnea to look over the land.[z] 9After they went up to the Valley of Eshcol[a] and viewed the land, they discouraged the Israelites from entering the land the LORD had given them. 10The LORD's anger was aroused that day and he swore this oath: 11'Because they have not followed me wholeheartedly, not one of the men twenty years old or more who came up out of Egypt will see the land I promised on oath to Abraham, Isaac and Jacob[b]— 12not one except Caleb son of Jephunneh the Kenizzite and Joshua son of Nun, for they followed the LORD wholeheartedly.'[c] 13The LORD's anger burned against Israel and he made them wander in the desert forty years, until the whole generation of those who had done evil in his sight was gone.[d]

14"And here you are, a brood of sinners, standing in the place of your fathers and making the LORD even more angry with Israel. 15If you turn away from following him, he will again leave all this people in the desert, and you will be the cause of their destruction.[e]"

16Then they came up to him and said, "We would like to build pens here for our livestock and cities for our women and children. 17But we are ready to arm ourselves and go ahead of the Israelites[f] until we have brought them to their place. Meanwhile our women and children will live in fortified cities, for protection from the inhabitants of the land. 18We will not return to our homes until every Israelite has received his inheritance.[g] 19We will not receive any inheritance with them on the other side of the Jordan, because our inheritance has come to us on the east side of the Jordan."[h]

20Then Moses said to them, "If you will do this—if you will arm yourselves before the LORD for battle,[i] 21and if all of you will go armed over the Jordan before the LORD until he has driven his enemies out before him— 22then when the land is subdued before the LORD, you may return and be free from your obligation to the LORD and to Israel. And this land will be your possession before the LORD.[j]

*Cross-references (right margin):*
32:1 [t]Nu 21:32 [u]Ex 12:38
32:3 [v]ver 36 [w]ver 38
32:4 [x]Nu 21:34
32:7 [y]Nu 13:27–14:4
32:8 [z]Nu 13:3,26; Dt 1:19-25
32:9 [a]Dt 1:24
32:11 [b]Nu 14:28-30
32:12 [c]Nu 14:24,30; Dt 1:36
32:13 [d]Nu 14:28-35; 26:64,65
32:15 [e]Dt 30:17-18; 2Ch 7:20
32:17 [f]Jos 4:12,13
32:18 [g]Jos 22:1-4
32:19 [h]Jos 12:1
32:20 [i]Dt 3:18
32:22 [j]Dt 3:18-20

32:1ff Three tribes (Reuben, Gad, and the half-tribe of Manasseh) wanted to live east of the Jordan River (sometimes referred to as the Transjordan area) on land they had already conquered.

PREPARING TO ENTER THE PROMISED LAND
The Israelites had been camped in the plains of Moab, across from Jericho. From this position, they were ready to enter the promised land.

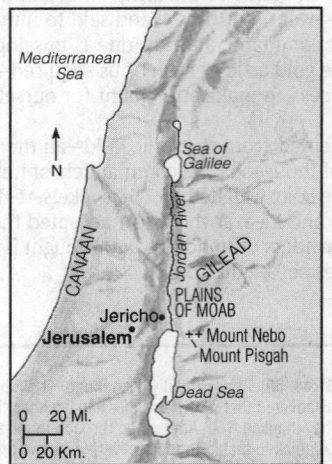

Mediterranean Sea

N

Sea of Galilee

Jordan River

CANAAN

GILEAD

PLAINS OF MOAB

Jericho
Jerusalem

Mount Nebo
Mount Pisgah

Dead Sea

0 20 Mi.
0 20 Km.

Moses immediately assumed they had selfish motives and were trying to avoid helping the others fight for the land across the river. But Moses jumped to the wrong conclusion. In dealing with people, we must find out all the facts before making up our minds. We shouldn't automatically assume that their motives are wrong, even if their plans sound suspicious.

32:16 A simple pen for livestock had four roughly built stone walls, high enough to keep wild animals out. Sometimes the top of the wall was lined with thorns to further discourage predators and thieves. The pen's single entrance made it easier for a shepherd to guard his flock. Often several shepherds used a single pen and took turns guarding the entrance. Mingling the animals was no problem since each flock responded readily to its own shepherd's voice. The three tribes who chose to remain east of the Jordan River wanted to build pens to protect their flocks and cities to protect their families before the men crossed the river to help the rest of the tribes conquer the promised land.

32:16–19 The land on the east side of the Jordan had been conquered. The hard work was done by all of the tribes together. But the tribes of Reuben and Gad and the half-tribe of Manasseh did not stop after their land was cleared. They promised to keep working with the others until everyone's land was conquered. After others have helped you, do you make excuses to escape helping them? Finish the whole job, even those parts that may not benefit you directly.

32:23
k Ge 4:7

32:24
l ver 1,16

23 "But if you fail to do this, you will be sinning against the Lord; and you may be sure that your sin will find you out. k 24 Build cities for your women and children, and pens for your flocks, l but do what you have promised."

32:26
m Jos 1:14

25 The Gadites and Reubenites said to Moses, "We your servants will do as our lord commands. 26 Our children and wives, our flocks and herds will remain here in the cities of Gilead. m 27 But your servants, every man armed for battle, will cross over to fight before the Lord, just as our lord says."

32:28
n Jos 1:13

28 Then Moses gave orders about them n to Eleazar the priest and Joshua son of Nun and to the family heads of the Israelite tribes. 29 He said to them, "If the Gadites and Reubenites, every man armed for battle, cross over the Jordan with you before the Lord, then when the land is subdued before you, give them the land of Gilead as their possession. 30 But if they do not cross over with you armed, they must accept their possession with you in Canaan."

31 The Gadites and Reubenites answered, "Your servants will do what the Lord has said. 32 We will cross over before the Lord into Canaan armed, but the property we inherit will be on this side of the Jordan."

32:33
o Nu 21:24;
Jos 12:6

33 Then Moses gave to the Gadites, the Reubenites and the half-tribe of Manasseh son of Joseph the kingdom of Sihon king of the Amorites and the kingdom of Og king of Bashan— the whole land with its cities and the territory around them. o

32:34
p Dt 2:36

32:36
q ver 3

34 The Gadites built up Dibon, Ataroth, Aroer, p 35 Atroth Shophan, Jazer, Jogbehah, 36 Beth Nimrah q and Beth Haran as fortified cities, and built pens for their flocks. 37 And the Reubenites rebuilt Heshbon, Elealeh and Kiriathaim, 38 as well as Nebo and Baal Meon (these names were changed) and Sibmah. They gave names to the cities they rebuilt.

32:39
r Ge 50:23

32:41
s Dt 3:14; Jdg 10:4

32:42
t 2Sa 18:18;
Ps 49:11

39 The descendants of Makir r son of Manasseh went to Gilead, captured it and drove out the Amorites who were there. 40 So Moses gave Gilead to the Makirites, the descendants of Manasseh, and they settled there. 41 Jair, a descendant of Manasseh, captured their settlements and called them Havvoth Jair. a s 42 And Nobah captured Kenath and its surrounding settlements and called it Nobah after himself. t

6. Camped on the plains of Moab
Stages in Israel's Journey

33 Here are the stages in the journey of the Israelites when they came out of Egypt by divisions under the leadership of Moses and Aaron. 2 At the Lord's command Moses recorded the stages in their journey. This is their journey by stages:

33:3
u Ex 14:8

33:4
v Ex 12:12

3 The Israelites set out from Rameses on the fifteenth day of the first month, the day after the Passover. They marched out boldly u in full view of all the Egyptians, 4 who were burying all their firstborn, whom the Lord had struck down among them; for the Lord had brought judgment on their gods. v

5 The Israelites left Rameses and camped at Succoth.

33:6
w Ex 13:20

6 They left Succoth and camped at Etham, on the edge of the desert. w

33:7
x Ex 14:2

7 They left Etham, turned back to Pi Hahiroth, to the east of Baal Zephon, and camped near Migdol. x

33:8
y Ex 14:22

8 They left Pi Hahiroth b and passed through the sea y into the desert, and when they had traveled for three days in the Desert of Etham, they camped at Marah.

33:9
z Ex 15:27

9 They left Marah and went to Elim, where there were twelve springs and seventy palm trees, and they camped z there.

10 They left Elim and camped by the Red Sea. c

33:11
a Ex 16:1

11 They left the Red Sea and camped in the Desert of Sin. a

12 They left the Desert of Sin and camped at Dophkah.

13 They left Dophkah and camped at Alush.

a 41 Or *them the settlements of Jair*　　b 8 Many manuscripts of the Masoretic Text, Samaritan Pentateuch and Vulgate; most manuscripts of the Masoretic Text *left from before Hahiroth*　　c 10 Hebrew *Yam Suph*; that is, Sea of Reeds; also in verse 11

33:1ff Look at the map in the introduction to the book of Numbers to see the travels of the Israelites.

33:2 Moses recorded the Israelites' journeys as God instructed him, providing a record of their spiritual as well as geographic progress. Have you made spiritual progress lately? Recording your thoughts about God and lessons you have learned over a period of time can be a valuable aid to spiritual growth. A record

of your spiritual pilgrimage will let you check up on your progress and avoid repeating past mistakes.

33:4 God "brought judgment on their gods" by sending the plagues. See the note on Exodus 10:22 for a further explanation.

¹⁴They left Alush and camped at Rephidim, where there was no water for the people to drink.

¹⁵They left Rephidim ᵇ and camped in the Desert of Sinai. ᶜ

¹⁶They left the Desert of Sinai and camped at Kibroth Hattaavah. ᵈ

¹⁷They left Kibroth Hattaavah and camped at Hazeroth. ᵉ

¹⁸They left Hazeroth and camped at Rithmah.

¹⁹They left Rithmah and camped at Rimmon Perez.

²⁰They left Rimmon Perez and camped at Libnah.

²¹They left Libnah and camped at Rissah.

²²They left Rissah and camped at Kehelathah.

²³They left Kehelathah and camped at Mount Shepher.

²⁴They left Mount Shepher and camped at Haradah.

²⁵They left Haradah and camped at Makheloth.

²⁶They left Makheloth and camped at Tahath.

²⁷They left Tahath and camped at Terah.

²⁸They left Terah and camped at Mithcah.

²⁹They left Mithcah and camped at Hashmonah.

³⁰They left Hashmonah and camped at Moseroth. ᶠ

³¹They left Moseroth and camped at Bene Jaakan.

³²They left Bene Jaakan and camped at Hor Haggidgad.

³³They left Hor Haggidgad and camped at Jotbathah.

³⁴They left Jotbathah and camped at Abronah.

³⁵They left Abronah and camped at Ezion Geber. ᵍ

³⁶They left Ezion Geber and camped at Kadesh, in the Desert of Zin. ʰ

³⁷They left Kadesh and camped at Mount Hor, ⁱ on the border of Edom. ³⁸At the LORD's command Aaron the priest went up Mount Hor, where he died ʲ on the first day of the fifth month of the fortieth year after the Israelites came out of Egypt. ᵏ ³⁹Aaron was a hundred and twenty-three years old when he died on Mount Hor.

⁴⁰The Canaanite king of Arad, ˡ who lived in the Negev of Canaan, heard that the Israelites were coming.

⁴¹They left Mount Hor and camped at Zalmonah.

⁴²They left Zalmonah and camped at Punon.

⁴³They left Punon and camped at Oboth. ᵐ

⁴⁴They left Oboth and camped at Iye Abarim, on the border of Moab.

⁴⁵They left Iyim ᵃ and camped at Dibon Gad.

⁴⁶They left Dibon Gad and camped at Almon Diblathaim.

⁴⁷They left Almon Diblathaim and camped in the mountains of Abarim, near Nebo.

⁴⁸They left the mountains of Abarim and camped on the plains of Moab by the Jordan across from Jericho. ᵇ ⁿ ⁴⁹There on the plains of Moab they camped along the Jordan from Beth Jeshimoth to Abel Shittim. ᵒ

⁵⁰On the plains of Moab by the Jordan across from Jericho the LORD said to Moses, ⁵¹"Speak to the Israelites and say to them: 'When you cross the Jordan into Canaan, ⁵²drive out all the inhabitants of the land before you. Destroy all their carved images and their cast idols, and demolish all their high places. ᵖ ⁵³Take possession of the land and settle in it, for I have given you the land to possess. ⁵⁴Distribute the land by lot, according to your clans. �q To a larger group give a larger inheritance, and to a smaller group a smaller one. Whatever falls to them by lot will be theirs. Distribute it according to your ancestral tribes.

ᵃ45 That is, Iye Abarim   ᵇ48 Hebrew *Jordan of Jericho*; possibly an ancient name for the Jordan River; also in verse 50

33:15
ᵇEx 17:1
ᶜEx 19:1

33:16
ᵈNu 11:34

33:17
ᵉNu 11:35

33:30
ᶠDt 10:6

33:35
ᵍDt 2:8

33:36
ʰNu 20:1

33:37
ⁱNu 20:22

33:38
ʲDt 10:6
ᵏNu 20:25-28

33:40
ˡNu 21:1

33:43
ᵐNu 21:10

33:48
ⁿNu 22:1

33:49
ᵒNu 25:1

33:52
ᵖEx 23:24; Dt 7:2,5

33:54
qNu 26:54

33:50-53 God told Moses that before the Israelites settled in the promised land they should drive out the wicked inhabitants and destroy their idols. In Colossians 3, Paul encourages us to live as Christians in the same manner: throwing away our old way of living and moving ahead into our new life of obedience to God and faith in Jesus Christ. Like the Israelites moving into the promised land, we can destroy the wickedness in our lives or we can settle down and live with it. To move in and possess the new life, we must drive out the sinful thoughts and practices to make room for the new.

33:50-56 Why were the Israelites told to destroy the people living in Canaan? God had several compelling reasons for giving this command: (1) God was stamping out the wickedness of an extremely sinful nation. The Canaanites brought on their own punishment. Idol worship expressed their deepest evil desires. It ultimately led to the worship of Satan and the total rejection of God. (2) God was using Moses and Israel to judge Canaan for its sins in fulfillment of the prophecy in Genesis 9:25. (3) God wanted to remove all trace of pagan beliefs and practices from the land. He did not want his people to mix or compromise with

33:55
ʳJos 23:13

55"'But if you do not drive out the inhabitants of the land, those you allow to remain will become barbs in your eyes and thorns ʳ in your sides. They will give you trouble in the land where you will live. 56And then I will do to you what I plan to do to them.'"

Boundaries of Canaan

34:2
ˢGe 17:8; Dt 1:7-8;
Ps 78:54-55

34 The Lᴏʀᴅ said to Moses, 2"Command the Israelites and say to them: 'When you enter Canaan, the land that will be allotted to you as an inheritance ˢ will have these boundaries:

34:3
ᵗJos 15:1-3

34:4
ᵘNu 32:8

34:5
ᵛJos 15:4

3"'Your southern side will include some of the Desert of Zin ᵗ along the border of Edom. On the east, your southern boundary will start from the end of the Salt Sea.ᵃ 4cross south of Scorpionᵇ Pass, continue on to Zin and go south of Kadesh Barnea. ᵘ Then it will go to Hazar Addar and over to Azmon, 5where it will turn, join the Wadi of Egyptᵛ and end at the Sea.ᶜ

6"'Your western boundary will be the coast of the Great Sea. This will be your boundary on the west.

34:7
ʷEze 47:15-17

7"'For your northern boundary,ʷ run a line from the Great Sea to Mount Hor 8and from Mount Hor to Leboᵈ Hamath. Then the boundary will go to Zedad, 9continue to Ziphron and end at Hazar Enan. This will be your boundary on the north.

34:11
ˣ2Ki 23:33
ʸDt 3:17

10"'For your eastern boundary, run a line from Hazar Enan to Shepham. 11The boundary will go down from Shepham to Riblahˣ on the east side of Ain and continue along the slopes east of the Sea of Kinnereth.ᵉ ʸ 12Then the boundary will go down along the Jordan and end at the Salt Sea.

"'This will be your land, with its boundaries on every side.'"

34:13
ᶻJos 14:1-5

34:14
ᵃNu 32:33

13Moses commanded the Israelites: "Assign this land by lot as an inheritance. ᶻ The Lᴏʀᴅ has ordered that it be given to the nine and a half tribes, 14because the families of the tribe of Reuben, the tribe of Gad and the half-tribe of Manasseh have received their inheritance.ᵃ 15These two and a half tribes have received their inheritance on the east side of the Jordan of Jericho,ᶠ toward the sunrise."

34:17
ᵇJos 14:1

34:18
ᶜNu 1:4,16

16The Lᴏʀᴅ said to Moses, 17"These are the names of the men who are to assign the land for you as an inheritance: Eleazar the priest and Joshua ᵇ son of Nun. 18And appoint one leader from each tribe to helpᶜ assign the land. 19These are their names:

Caleb son of Jephunneh,
    from the tribe of Judah;

ᵃ*3* That is, the Dead Sea; also in verse 12   ᵇ*4* Hebrew *Akrabbim*   ᶜ*5* That is, the Mediterranean; also in verses 6 and 7   ᵈ*8* Or *to the entrance to*   ᵉ*11* That is, Galilee   ᶠ*15 Jordan of Jericho* was possibly an ancient name for the Jordan River.

---

idolatry in any way. The Israelites did not fully understand God's reasons, and they did not carry out his command. This eventually led them to compromise and corruption. In all areas of life, we should obey God's Word without question because we know he is just, even if we cannot fully understand his overall purposes.

33:55 If you don't do the job right the first time, it often becomes much more difficult to accomplish. God warned that if the Israelites did not drive the wicked inhabitants out of the promised land, later these people would become a source of great irritation. That is exactly what happened. Just as the Israelites were hesitant to clear out all the wicked people, we are sometimes hesitant to clear out all the sin in our lives, either because we are afraid of it (as the Israelites feared the giants), or because it seems harmless and attractive (as sexual sin seemed). But Hebrews 12:1, 2 tells us to throw off "the sin that so easily entangles" us. We all have "idols" we don't want to let go of (a bad habit, an unhealthy relationship, a certain lifestyle). If we allow these idols to dominate us, they will cause serious problems later.

34:1ff The land was given by God as an inheritance; no tribe was to claim its own land. The boundaries declared by God are larger than the area actually occupied by the Hebrews. The boundaries correspond more to the land conquered by David and to the ideal territory portrayed by Ezekiel (Ezekiel 47; 48). The size of the land portrays God's generosity. He always gives us more than we could ask or think.

34:16–29 In God's plan for settling the land, he (1) explained what to do, (2) communicated this clearly to Moses, and

(3) assigned specific people to oversee the apportionment of the land. No plan is complete until each job is assigned and everyone understands his or her responsibilities. When you have a job to do, determine what must be done, give clear instructions, and put people in charge of each part.

THE BORDERS OF THE PROMISED LAND
The borders of the promised land stretched from the Deserts of Zin and Kadesh in the south to Lebo Hamath and Riblah in the north, and from the Mediterranean seacoast (the Great Sea) on the west to the Jordan River on the east. The land of Gilead was also included.

20 Shemuel son of Ammihud,
    from the tribe of Simeon;
21 Elidad son of Kislon,
    from the tribe of Benjamin;
22 Bukki son of Jogli,
    the leader from the tribe of Dan;
23 Hanniel son of Ephod,
    the leader from the tribe of Manasseh son of Joseph;
24 Kemuel son of Shiphtan,
    the leader from the tribe of Ephraim son of Joseph;
25 Elizaphan son of Parnach,
    the leader from the tribe of Zebulun;
26 Paltiel son of Azzan,
    the leader from the tribe of Issachar;
27 Ahihud son of Shelomi,
    the leader from the tribe of Asher;
28 Pedahel son of Ammihud,
    the leader from the tribe of Naphtali."

29 These are the men the LORD commanded to assign the inheritance to the Israelites in the land of Canaan.

Towns for the Levites

35 On the plains of Moab by the Jordan across from Jericho,[a] the LORD said to Moses, 2 "Command the Israelites to give the Levites towns to live in[d] from the inheritance the Israelites will possess. And give them pasturelands around the towns. 3 Then they will have towns to live in and pasturelands for their cattle, flocks and all their other livestock.

4 "The pasturelands around the towns that you give the Levites will extend out fifteen hundred feet[b] from the town wall. 5 Outside the town, measure three thousand feet[c] on the east side, three thousand on the south side, three thousand on the west and three thousand on the north, with the town in the center. They will have this area as pastureland for the towns.

Cities of Refuge

6 "Six of the towns you give the Levites will be cities of refuge, to which a person who has killed someone may flee. [e] In addition, give them forty-two other towns. 7 In all you must give the Levites forty-eight towns, together with their pasturelands. 8 The towns you give the Levites from the land the Israelites possess are to be given in proportion to the inheritance of each tribe: Take many towns from a tribe that has many, but few from one that has few."[f]

35:2
[d]Lev 25:32-34

35:6
[e]Jos 20:7-9;
21:3,13

35:8
[f]Nu 26:54

a 1 Hebrew *Jordan of Jericho*; possibly an ancient name for the Jordan River   b 4 Hebrew *a thousand cubits* (about 450 meters)   c 5 Hebrew *two thousand cubits* (about 900 meters)

35:2, 3 The Levites were ministers. They were supported by the tithes of the people who gave them homes, flocks, and pasturelands. Likewise, we are responsible to provide for the needs of our ministers and missionaries so they can be free to do their God-ordained work.

35:6 Of the 48 cities given to the Levites, six were cities of refuge. These six cities were probably put under the Levites' supervision because they would be the most impartial judges. Such cities were needed because the ancient customs of justice called for revenge in the event of the death of a relative or loved one (2 Samuel 14:7). The Levites would hold a preliminary hearing outside the gates while the accused person was kept in the city until the time of his trial. If the killing was judged accidental, the person would stay in the city until the death of the high priest. At that time, he would be allowed to go free, and he could start a new life without worrying about avengers. If it was not accidental, the person would be delivered to the slain person's avengers. This system of justice shows how God's law and his mercy go hand in hand.

CITIES OF REFUGE
Six of the Levites' cities were designated as cities of refuge. They were spaced throughout the land and protected those who had accidentally committed a crime or who were awaiting trial.

35:11
g Ex 21:13

35:12
h Jos 20:3

35:16
i Ex 21:12;
Lev 24:17

9Then the LORD said to Moses: 10"Speak to the Israelites and say to them: 'When you cross the Jordan into Canaan, 11select some towns to be your cities of refuge, to which a person who has killed someone accidentally*g* may flee. 12They will be places of refuge from the avenger,*h* so that a person accused of murder may not die before he stands trial before the assembly. 13These six towns you give will be your cities of refuge. 14Give three on this side of the Jordan and three in Canaan as cities of refuge. 15These six towns will be a place of refuge for Israelites, aliens and any other people living among them, so that anyone who has killed another accidentally can flee there.

16"'If a man strikes someone with an iron object so that he dies, he is a murderer; the murderer shall be put to death.*i* 17Or if anyone has a stone in his hand that could kill, and he strikes someone so that he dies, he is a murderer; the murderer shall be put to death. 18Or if anyone has a wooden object in his hand that could kill, and he hits someone so that he dies, he is a murderer; the murderer shall be put to death. 19The avenger of blood shall put the murderer to death; when he meets him, he shall put him to death. 20If anyone with malice

PRIESTS IN ISRAEL'S HISTORY	Priest	Importance	Reference
Numbers 35:25–28 mentions the death of a high priest. Each new high priest had to come from the lineage of Aaron. Listed here are the ones whose stories are told elsewhere in the Bible.	Aaron	Moses' brother and first priest	Exodus 28:1–3
	Eleazar	Watched two of his brothers die in a fire from God because they did not follow God's instructions. He obeyed God and became chief leader of the tabernacle.	Leviticus 10 Numbers 3:32
	Phinehas	Executed a young Israelite idol worshiper and his Midianite mistress to end a plague. He was then promised that his priestly line would never end.	Numbers 25:1–15
	Ahitub	A priest during King Saul's reign	1 Samuel 14:3
	Zadok	A faithful high priest under King David. He and Nathan anointed Solomon as the next king.	2 Samuel 8:17 1 Kings 1:38, 39
	Ahimaaz	Carried the message of Absalom's death to King David but was apparently afraid to tell about it.	2 Samuel 18:19-29
	Azariah	High priest under King Solomon	1 Kings 4:2
	Azariah	High priest under Uzziah. He rebuked the king for burning incense himself.	2 Chronicles 26:17–21
		When Hezekiah became king, he reopened the temple. Azariah again served as high priest.	2 Chronicles 26:17–21
	Amariah	King Jehoshaphat appointed him to judge religious disputes.	2 Chronicles 19:11
	Hilkiah	Found the Book of the Law during Josiah's reign	2 Kings 22:3–13 2 Chronicles 34:14–21
	Azariah	Probably one of the first to return to Israel from Babylon	1 Chronicles 9:10, 11
	Seraiah	The father of Ezra	Ezra 7:1-5

35:11–28 If anyone died because of violence, murder was assumed, but the murder suspect was not automatically assumed guilty. The cities of refuge assured the accused that justice would be served. But if he or she left the city, then he or she would be assumed guilty and able to be killed by the avenging party. The people were to be intolerant of the sin, yet impartial to the accused so that he or she could have a fair trial. The cities of refuge represented God's concern for justice in a culture that did not always protect the innocent. It is unjust both to overlook wrongdoing and to jump to conclusions about guilt. When someone is accused of wrongdoing, stand up for justice, protect those not yet proven guilty, and listen carefully to all sides of the story.

aforethought shoves another or throws something at him intentionally[j] so that he dies [21]or
if in hostility he hits him with his fist so that he dies, that person shall be put to death; he is a
murderer. The avenger of blood shall put the murderer to death when he meets him.

[22]"'But if without hostility someone suddenly shoves another or throws something at
him unintentionally [23]or, without seeing him, drops a stone on him that could kill him, and
he dies, then since he was not his enemy and he did not intend to harm him, [24]the assembly[k] must judge between him and the avenger of blood according to these regulations.
[25]The assembly must protect the one accused of murder from the avenger of blood and
send him back to the city of refuge to which he fled. He must stay there until the death of
the high priest, who was anointed with the holy oil.[l]

[26]"'But if the accused ever goes outside the limits of the city of refuge to which he has
fled [27]and the avenger of blood finds him outside the city, the avenger of blood may kill
the accused without being guilty of murder. [28]The accused must stay in his city of refuge
until the death of the high priest; only after the death of the high priest may he return to
his own property.

[29]"'These are to be legal requirements for you throughout the generations to come,
wherever you live.

[30]"'Anyone who kills a person is to be put to death as a murderer only on the testimony of
witnesses. But no one is to be put to death on the testimony of only one witness.[m]

[31]"'Do not accept a ransom for the life of a murderer, who deserves to die. He must surely
be put to death.

[32]"'Do not accept a ransom for anyone who has fled to a city of refuge and so allow him to
go back and live on his own land before the death of the high priest.

[33]"'Do not pollute the land where you are. Bloodshed pollutes the land,[n] and atonement
cannot be made for the land on which blood has been shed, except by the blood of the one
who shed it. [34]Do not defile the land[o] where you live and where I dwell, for I, the LORD, dwell
among the Israelites.'"

Inheritance of Zelophehad's Daughters

36 The family heads of the clan of Gilead[p] son of Makir, the son of Manasseh, who
were from the clans of the descendants of Joseph, came and spoke before Moses
and the leaders, the heads of the Israelite families. [2]They said, "When the LORD commanded my lord to give the land as an inheritance to the Israelites by lot, he ordered you to
give the inheritance of our brother Zelophehad[q] to his daughters. [3]Now suppose they
marry men from other Israelite tribes; then their inheritance will be taken from our
ancestral inheritance and added to that of the tribe they marry into. And so part of the inheritance allotted to us will be taken away. [4]When the Year of Jubilee[r] for the Israelites
comes, their inheritance will be added to that of the tribe into which they marry, and their
property will be taken from the tribal inheritance of our forefathers."

[5]Then at the LORD's command Moses gave this order to the Israelites: "What the tribe
of the descendants of Joseph is saying is right. [6]This is what the LORD commands for Zelophehad's daughters: They may marry anyone they please as long as they marry within the
tribal clan of their father. [7]No inheritance[s] in Israel is to pass from tribe to tribe, for every
Israelite shall keep the tribal land inherited from his forefathers. [8]Every daughter who inherits land in any Israelite tribe must marry someone in her father's tribal clan,[t] so that
every Israelite will possess the inheritance of his fathers. [9]No inheritance may pass from
tribe to tribe, for each Israelite tribe is to keep the land it inherits."

35:20
[j]Ex 21:14

35:24
[k]ver 12

35:25
[l]Ex 29:7

35:30
[m]Dt 17:6; 19:15;
Mt 18:16; 2Co 13:1

35:33
[n]Ge 9:6; Ps 106:38

35:34
[o]Lev 18:24,25

36:1
[p]Nu 26:29

36:2
[q]Nu 26:33; 27:1,7

36:4
[r]Lev 25:10

36:7
[s]1Ki 21:3

36:8
[t]1Ch 23:22

36:1–9 Zelophehad had five daughters but no sons. After
he died, his daughters appealed to Moses. Because the inheritance normally passed only through the male line, the family
line of Zelophehad would have disappeared. God told Moses
that if a man died without sons, then the inheritance would
go to his daughters (27:8). But the question of marriage arose.
If the daughters were to marry outside of their tribe, the land
would belong to another tribe at the Year of Jubilee. So Moses
commanded that in such cases the women should marry men
in their own clan and tribe so that each tribe would retain its
original inheritance. Later, when the tribes received their land
under Joshua, the daughters of Zelophehad received their
inheritance as God had instructed (Joshua 17:3–6).

We don't have to look far to find those who want to be
considered "special cases" and "exceptions to the rule,"
but wise leaders will sort out those who have legitimate
concerns and make sure that justice is done in these special
situations.

36:11
u Nu 27:1

10So Zelophehad's daughters did as the LORD commanded Moses. ¹¹Zelophehad's daughters—Mahlah, Tirzah, Hoglah, Milcah and Noah *u*—married their cousins on their father's side. ¹²They married within the clans of the descendants of Manasseh son of Joseph, and their inheritance remained in their father's clan and tribe.

¹³These are the commands and regulations the LORD gave through Moses to the Israelites on the plains of Moab by the Jordan across from Jericho. *a*

a 13 Hebrew *Jordan of Jericho*; possibly an ancient name for the Jordan River

EIGHT WORDS FOR LAW	Word	Meaning	Examples	Significance
Hebrew law served as the personal and national guide for living under God's authority. It directed the moral, spiritual, and social life. Its purpose was to produce better understanding of God and greater commitment to him.	Torah	Direction, Guidance, Instruction	Exodus 24:12; Isaiah 13:3	Need for law in general; a command from a higher person to a lower
	Mitswah	Commandment, Command	Genesis 26:5; Exodus 15:26; 20:2–17	God's specific instruction to be obeyed rather than a general law; used of the Ten Commandments
	Mishpat	Judgment, Ordinance	Genesis 18:19; Deuteronomy 16:18; 17:9	Refers to the civil, social, and sanitation laws
	Eduth	Admonition, Testimony	Exodus 25:22	Refers to God's law as he deals with his people
	Huqqim	Statutes, Oracles	Leviticus 18:4; Deuteronomy 4:1	Dealt with the royal pronouncements; mainly connected to worship and feasts
	Piqqudim	Orders, Precepts	Psalms 19:8; 103:18	Used often in the psalms to describe God's orders and assignments
	Dabar	Word	Exodus 34:28; Deuteronomy 4:13	Used to indicate divine oracles or revelations of God
	Dath	Royal Edict, Public Law	Ezekiel 7:26; Daniel 6:8, 12	Refers to the divine law or Jewish religious traditions in general

36:13 The book of Numbers covers 39 years and closes with the Israelites poised near the banks of the Jordan River with the promised land in sight. The wanderings in the desert have come to an end, and the people are preparing for their next big move—the conquest of the land. The apostle Paul says that the events described in Numbers are examples that warn us and help us avoid the Israelites' mistakes (1 Corinthians 10:1–12). From their experiences we learn that unbelief is disastrous. We also learn not to long for the sinful pleasures of the past, to avoid complaining, and to stay away from all forms of sexual sin. We must not weaken our biblical beliefs by compromising them with our culture's values. If we choose to let God lead our lives, we should not ignore his message in the book of Numbers.

DEUTERONOMY

DESERT WANDERINGS

VITAL STATISTICS

PURPOSE:
To remind the people of what God had done and encourage them to rededicate their lives to him

AUTHOR:
Moses (except for the final summary, which was probably written by Joshua after Moses' death)

ORIGINAL AUDIENCE:
Israel (the new generation entering the promised land)

DATE WRITTEN:
About 1407/6 B.C.

SETTING:
The east side of the Jordan River, in view of Canaan

KEY VERSE:
"Know therefore that the LORD your God is God; he is the faithful God, keeping his covenant of love to a thousand generations of those who love him and keep his commands" (7:9).

KEY PEOPLE:
Moses, Joshua

KEY PLACE:
The Arabah in Moab

CLASS reunions, photo albums, familiar songs, and old neighborhoods—like longtime friends they awaken our memories and stir our emotions. The past is a kaleidoscope of promises, failures, victories, and embarrassments. Sometimes we want to forget memories that are too painful. As the years pass, however, remembrances of unpleasant events usually fade into our subconscious. But there is a time to remember: Mistakes should not be repeated; commitments made must be fulfilled; and the memory of special events can encourage us and move us to action.

The book of Deuteronomy is written in the form of a treaty between a king and his vassal state typical of the second millenium B.C. It calls Israel to remember who God is and what he has done. Lacking faith, the old generation had wandered for 40 years and had died in the desert. They left Egypt behind, but never knew the promised land. Then on the east bank of the Jordan River, Moses prepared the sons and daughters of that faithless generation to possess the land. After a brief history lesson emphasizing God's great acts on behalf of his people, Moses reviewed the law. Then he restated the covenant—God's contract with his people.

The lessons are clear. Because of what God has done, Israel should have hope and follow him; because of what he expects, they should listen and obey; because of who he is, they should love him completely. Learning these lessons will prepare them to possess the promised land.

As you hear the message of Deuteronomy, remember how God has expressed his kindness in your life, and then commit yourself anew to trust, love, and obey him.

THE BLUEPRINT

A. **WHAT GOD HAS DONE FOR US: MOSES' FIRST ADDRESS (1:1—4:43)**

Moses reviewed the mighty acts of God for the nation of Israel. Remembering God's special involvement in our lives gives us hope and encouragement for the future.

B. **PRINCIPLES FOR GODLY LIVING: MOSES' SECOND ADDRESS (4:44—28:68)**
   1. The Ten Commandments
   2. Love the Lord your God
   3. Laws for proper worship
   4. Laws for ruling the nation
   5. Laws for human relationships
   6. Consequences of obedience and disobedience

Obeying God's laws brought blessings to the Israelites and disobeying brought misfortune. This was part of the written agreement God made with his people. Although we are not part of this covenant, the principle holds true: Obedience and disobedience carry inevitable consequences in this life and the next.

C. **A CALL FOR COMMITMENT TO GOD: MOSES' THIRD ADDRESS (29:1—30:20)**

Moses called the people to commitment. God still calls us to be committed to love him with all our heart, soul, mind, and strength.

D. **THE CHANGE IN LEADERSHIP: MOSES' LAST DAYS (31:1—34:12)**

Although Moses made some serious mistakes, he had lived uprightly and carried out God's commands. Moses died with integrity. We too may make some serious mistakes, but that should not stop us from living with integrity and godly commitment.

MEGATHEMES

THEME	EXPLANATION	IMPORTANCE
History	Moses reviewed the mighty acts of God whereby he liberated Israel from slavery in Egypt. He recounted how God had helped them and how the people had disobeyed.	By reviewing God's promises and mighty acts in history, we can learn about his character. We come to know God more intimately through understanding how he has acted in the past. We can also avoid mistakes in our own lives through learning from Israel's past failures.
Laws	God reviewed his laws for the people. The legal contract between God and his people had to be renewed by the new generation about to enter the promised land.	Commitment to God and his truth cannot be taken for granted. Each generation and each person must respond afresh to God's call for obedience.
Love	God's faithful and patient love is portrayed more often than his punishment. God shows his love by being faithful to his people and his promises. In response, God desires love from the heart, not merely a legalistic keeping of his law.	God's love forms the foundation for our trust in him. We trust him because he loves us. Because God loves us, we should maintain justice and respect.
Choices	God reminded his people that in order to ratify his covenant, they must choose the path of obedience. A personal decision to obey would bring benefits to their lives; rebellion would bring severe calamity.	Our choices make a difference. Choosing to follow God benefits us and improves our relationships with others. Choosing to abandon God's ways brings harm to ourselves and others.
Teaching	God commanded the Israelites to teach their children his ways. They were to use ritual, instruction, and memorization to make sure their children understood God's principles and passed them on to the next generation.	Quality teaching for our children must be a priority. It is important to pass on God's truth to future generations in our traditions. But God desires that his truth be in our hearts and minds and not merely in our traditions.

A. WHAT GOD HAS DONE FOR US: MOSES' FIRST ADDRESS (1:1—4:43)

God has led his people out of Egypt and through the great desert for 40 years. Now they stand ready to enter the promised land. But before the Israelites go into the land, Moses has some important advice to give them. He delivers his advice in three parts. In the first part, Moses reviews the history of God's previous care for the people of Israel. Through God's actions in the past, we can learn about the God we serve today.

The Command to Leave Horeb

1 These are the words Moses spoke to all Israel in the desert east of the Jordan—that is, in the Arabah—opposite Suph, between Paran and Tophel, Laban, Hazeroth and Dizahab. ²(It takes eleven days to go from Horeb to Kadesh Barnea ᵃ by the Mount Seir road.) ³In the fortieth year, ᵇ on the first day of the eleventh month, Moses proclaimed to the Israelites all that the Lord had commanded him concerning them. ⁴This was after he had defeated Sihon king of the Amorites, who reigned in Heshbon, and at Edrei had defeated Og ᶜ king of Bashan, who reigned in Ashtaroth.

1:2
ᵃNu 13:26; Dt 9:23

1:3
ᵇNu 33:38

1:4
ᶜNu 21:33-35

1:1, 2 The Israelites spent 40 years on a journey that should have lasted 11 days. It wasn't distance that stood between them and the promised land. It was the condition of their hearts. God's purpose went deeper than simply transporting a huge group of people to a new land. He was preparing them to live in obedience to him once they arrived. What good was the promised land if the Israelites were just as wicked as the nations already living there? The journey was a painful but necessary part of their preparation. Through it God taught the Israelites who he was: the living God, the Leader of their nation. He also taught them who they were: people who were fallen, sinful, prone to rebellion and doubt. He gave his rebellious people the law to help them understand how to relate to God and to other people. Your spiritual pilgrimage may be lengthy, and you may face pain, discouragement, and difficulties. But remember that God isn't just trying to keep you alive. He wants to prepare you to live for service and devotion to him.

1:1–5 The 40 years of desert wandering come to an end in this book. The events of Deuteronomy cover only a week or two of the 11th month of the 40th year (1:3). The 12th and last month was spent in mourning for Moses (34:8). Then the Israelites entered the promised land the first month of the 41st year after the exodus (Joshua 4:19).

⁵East of the Jordan in the territory of Moab, Moses began to expound this law, saying:

⁶The LORD our God said to us *d* at Horeb, "You have stayed long enough at this mountain. ⁷Break camp and advance into the hill country of the Amorites; go to all the neighboring peoples in the Arabah, in the mountains, in the western foothills, in the Negev and along the coast, to the land of the Canaanites and to Lebanon, *e* as far as the great river, the Euphrates. ⁸See, I have given you this land. Go in and take possession of the land that the LORD swore *f* he would give to your fathers—to Abraham, Isaac and Jacob—and to their descendants after them."

The Appointment of Leaders

⁹At that time I said to you, "You are too heavy a burden for me to carry alone. *g* ¹⁰The LORD your God has increased your numbers so that today you are as many *h* as the stars in the sky. *i* ¹¹May the LORD, the God of your fathers, increase you a thousand times and bless you as he has promised! *j* ¹²But how can I bear your problems and your burdens and your disputes all by myself? ¹³Choose some wise, understanding and respected men from each of your tribes, and I will set them over you."

¹⁴You answered me, "What you propose to do is good."

¹⁵So I took *k* the leading men of your tribes, wise and respected men, and appointed them to have authority over you—as commanders of thousands, of hundreds, of fifties and of tens and as tribal officials. ¹⁶And I charged your judges at that time: Hear the disputes between your brothers and judge fairly, *l* whether the case is between brother Israelites or between one of them and an alien. ¹⁷Do not show partiality *m* in judging; hear both small and great alike. Do not be afraid of any man, for judgment belongs to God. Bring me any case too hard for you, and I will hear it. *n* ¹⁸And at that time I told you everything you were to do.

Spies Sent Out

¹⁹Then, as the LORD our God commanded us, we set out from Horeb and went toward the hill country of the Amorites through all that vast and dreadful desert *o* that you have seen, and so we reached Kadesh Barnea. ²⁰Then I said to you, "You have reached the hill country of the Amorites, which the LORD our God is giving us. ²¹See, the LORD your God has given you the land. Go up and take possession of it as the LORD, the God of your fathers, told you. Do not be afraid; *p* do not be discouraged."

1:6 *d* Nu 10:13
1:7 *e* Dt 11:24
1:8 *f* Ge 12:7; 26:4; 28:13
1:9 *g* Ex 18:18
1:10 *h* Ge 15:5 *i* Dt 10:22; 28:62
1:11 *j* Ex 32:13
1:15 *k* Ex 18:25
1:16 *l* Dt 16:18
1:17 *m* Jas 2:1 *n* Ex 18:26
1:19 *o* Dt 8:15
1:21 *p* Jos 1:6,9,18

1:6, 7 Notice that Moses' summary of Israel's 40-year journey begins at Mount Horeb (Sinai), not in Egypt. Why did Moses leave out the first part of the exodus? Moses was not giving an itinerary—he was summarizing the nation's development. In Moses' mind the nation of Israel began at the base of Mount

EVENTS IN DEUTERONOMY
The book of Deuteronomy opens with Israel camped east of the Jordan River in the Arabah in the land of Moab. Just before the people crossed the river into the promised land, Moses delivered an inspirational speech indicating how they were to live.

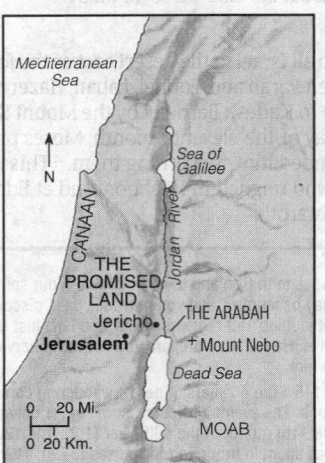

Sinai, not in Egypt, for it was at Mount Sinai that God gave his covenant to the people (Exodus 19; 20). Along with this covenant came knowledge and responsibility. After the people chose to follow God, they had to know *how* to follow him. Therefore, God gave them a comprehensive set of laws and guidelines that stated how he wanted them to live (these are found in the books of Exodus, Leviticus, and Numbers). The people could no longer say they didn't know the difference between right and wrong. Now that the people had promised to follow God and knew how to follow him, they had a responsibility to do it. When God tells you to break camp and move out to face a challenge he gives you, will you be ready to obey?

1:9–13 It was a tremendous burden for Moses to lead the nation by himself. He could not accomplish the task single-handedly. As nations, organizations, and churches grow, they become increasingly complex. Conflicting needs and quarrels arise. No longer can one leader make all the decisions. Like Moses, you may have a natural tendency to try to do all the work alone. You may be afraid or embarrassed to ask for help. Moses made a wise decision to share the leadership with others. Rather than trying to handle larger responsibilities alone, look for ways of sharing the load so that others may exercise their God-given gifts and abilities.

1:13–18 Moses identified some of the inner qualities of good leaders: (1) wisdom, (2) understanding, and (3) respect. These characteristics differ markedly from the ones that often help elect leaders today: good looks, wealth, popularity, willingness to do anything to get to the top. The qualities Moses identified should be evident in us as we lead, and we should look for them in those we elect to positions of leadership.

22 Then all of you came to me and said, "Let us send men ahead to spy out the land for us and bring back a report about the route we are to take and the towns we will come to."

23 The idea seemed good to me; so I selected twelve of you, one man from each tribe.

1:24
q Nu 13:21-25

24 They left and went up into the hill country, and came to the Valley of Eshcol *q* and explored it. 25 Taking with them some of the fruit of the land, they brought it down to us and reported, "It is a good land that the LORD our God is giving us."

Rebellion Against the LORD

1:26
r Nu 14:1-4

1:27
s Dt 9:28

1:28
t Nu 13:33; Dt 9:1-3

1:30
u Ex 14:14

26 But you were unwilling to go up; *r* you rebelled against the command of the LORD your God. 27 You grumbled *s* in your tents and said, "The LORD hates us; so he brought us out of Egypt to deliver us into the hands of the Amorites to destroy us. 28 Where can we go? Our brothers have made us lose heart. They say, 'The people are stronger and taller than we are; the cities are large, with walls up to the sky. We even saw the Anakites *t* there.'"

29 Then I said to you, "Do not be terrified; do not be afraid of them. 30 The LORD your God, who is going before you, will fight *u* for you, as he did for you in Egypt, before your very eyes,

1:31
v Dt 32:10-12;
Ac 13:18

1:32
w Ps 106:24

1:33
x Ex 13:21

1:34
y Nu 14:23,28-30

31 and in the desert. There you saw how the LORD your God carried *v* you, as a father carries his son, all the way you went until you reached this place."

32 In spite of this, you did not trust *w* in the LORD your God, 33 who went ahead of you on your journey, in fire by night and in a cloud by day, *x* to search out places for you to camp and to show you the way you should go.

34 When the LORD heard what you said, he was angry and solemnly swore: *y* 35 "Not a man of this evil generation shall see the good land I swore to give your forefathers, 36 except Caleb son of Jephunneh. He will see it, and I will give him and his descendants the land he set his feet on, because he followed the LORD wholeheartedly."

1:37
z Dt 3:26
a Nu 20:12

1:38
b Nu 14:30

1:39
c Nu 14:3

1:40
d Nu 14:25

37 Because of you the LORD became angry *z* with me also and said, "You shall not enter *a* it, either. 38 But your assistant, Joshua *b* son of Nun, will enter it. Encourage him, because he will lead Israel to inherit it. 39 And the little ones that you said would be taken captive, *c* your children who do not yet know good from bad—they will enter the land. I will give it to them and they will take possession of it. 40 But as for you, turn around and set out toward the desert along the route to the Red Sea. *a d*"

41 Then you replied, "We have sinned against the LORD. We will go up and fight, as the LORD our God commanded us." So every one of you put on his weapons, thinking it easy to go up into the hill country.

1:42
e Nu 14:41-43

42 But the LORD said to me, "Tell them, 'Do not go up and fight, because I will not be with you. You will be defeated by your enemies.'" *e*

43 So I told you, but you would not listen. You rebelled against the LORD's command and in your arrogance you marched up into the hill country. 44 The Amorites who lived in those hills came out against you; they chased you like a swarm of bees *f* and beat you down from Seir all the way to Hormah. 45 You came back and wept before the LORD, but he paid no attention to your weeping and turned a deaf ear to you. 46 And so you stayed in Kadesh *g* many days—all the time you spent there.

1:44
f Ps 118:12

1:46
g Nu 20:1

a 40 Hebrew *Yam Suph;* that is, Sea of Reeds

1:22 The spies had been sent into the land to determine not *whether* they should enter, but *where* they should enter. Upon returning, however, most of the spies had concluded that the land was not worth the obstacles. God would give the Israelites the power to conquer the land, but they were afraid of the risk and decided not to enter. God gives us the power to overcome our obstacles, but just as the Israelites were filled with fear and skepticism, we often let difficulties control our lives. When we follow God regardless of the difficulties, we demonstrate courageous, overcoming faith.

1:23–40 Moses retold the story of the spy mission into the promised land (Numbers 13; 14). When the spies returned with reports of giants (Anakites) and walled cities, the people were afraid to move ahead and began to complain about their predicament. But the minority report of Joshua and Caleb pointed out that the land was fertile, the enemy was vulnerable, and God was on their side. We become fearful and immobile when we focus on the negative aspects of a situation. How much better it is to focus on the positive—God's direction and promises.

When confronted with an important decision and you know what you should do, move out in faith. Focus on the positives while trusting God to overcome the negatives. Problems don't have to rob you of the victory.

1:28 Canaan was a land with giants and imposing fortresses. The "Anakites" may have been seven to nine feet tall. Many of the land's fortified cities had walls as high as 30 feet. The Israelites' fear was understandable, but not justified, for the all-powerful God had already promised them victory.

Wanderings in the Desert

2 Then we turned back and set out toward the desert along the route to the Red Sea,[a] as the LORD had directed me. For a long time we made our way around the hill country of Seir.

[2] Then the LORD said to me, [3] "You have made your way around this hill country long enough; now turn north. [4] Give the people these orders:[h] 'You are about to pass through the territory of your brothers the descendants of Esau, who live in Seir. They will be afraid of you, but be very careful. [5] Do not provoke them to war, for I will not give you any of their land, not even enough to put your foot on. I have given Esau the hill country of Seir as his own.[i] [6] You are to pay them in silver for the food you eat and the water you drink.'"

[7] The LORD your God has blessed you in all the work of your hands. He has watched[j] over your journey through this vast desert. These forty years the LORD your God has been with you, and you have not lacked anything.

[8] So we went on past our brothers the descendants of Esau, who live in Seir. We turned from the Arabah road, which comes up from Elath and Ezion Geber, and traveled along the desert road of Moab.

[9] Then the LORD said to me, "Do not harass the Moabites or provoke them to war, for I will not give you any part of their land. I have given Ar to the descendants of Lot[k] as a possession."

[10] (The Emites[l] used to live there—a people strong and numerous, and as tall as the Anakites. [11] Like the Anakites, they too were considered Rephaites, but the Moabites called them Emites. [12] Horites used to live in Seir, but the descendants of Esau drove them out. They destroyed the Horites from before them and settled in their place, just as Israel did[m] in the land the LORD gave them as their possession.)

[13] And the LORD said, "Now get up and cross the Zered Valley." So we crossed the valley.

[14] Thirty-eight years passed from the time we left Kadesh Barnea until we crossed the Zered Valley. By then, that entire generation[n] of fighting men had perished from the camp, as the LORD had sworn to them.[o] [15] The LORD's hand was against them until he had completely eliminated them from the camp.

[16] Now when the last of these fighting men among the people had died, [17] the LORD said to me, [18] "Today you are to pass by the region of Moab at Ar. [19] When you come to the Ammonites,[p] do not harass them or provoke them to war, for I will not give you possession of any land belonging to the Ammonites. I have given it as a possession to the descendants of Lot."

[20] (That too was considered a land of the Rephaites, who used to live there; but the Ammonites called them Zamzummites. [21] They were a people strong and numerous, and as tall as the Anakites. The LORD destroyed them from before the Ammonites, who drove them out and settled in their place. [22] The LORD had done the same for the descendants of Esau, who lived in Seir,[q] when he destroyed the Horites from before them. They drove them out and have lived in their place to this day. [23] And as for the Avvites[r] who lived in villages as far as Gaza, the Caphtorites[s] coming out from Caphtor[b] [t] destroyed them and settled in their place.)

Defeat of Sihon King of Heshbon

[24] "Set out now and cross the Arnon Gorge.[u] See, I have given into your hand Sihon the Amorite, king of Heshbon, and his country. Begin to take possession of it and engage him in battle. [25] This very day I will begin to put the terror and fear of you on all the nations under heaven. They will hear reports of you and will tremble[v] and be in anguish because of you."

[a] *1* Hebrew *Yam Suph*; that is, Sea of Reeds   [b] *23* That is, Crete

2:4 [h] Nu 20:14-21
2:5 [i] Jos 24:4
2:7 [j] Dt 8:2-4
2:9 [k] Ge 19:36-38
2:10 [l] Ge 14:5
2:12 [m] ver 22
2:14 [n] Nu 14:29-35 [o] Dt 1:34-35
2:19 [p] Ge 19:38
2:22 [q] Ge 36:8
2:23 [r] Jos 13:3 [s] Ge 10:14 [t] Am 9:7
2:24 [u] Jdg 11:13,18
2:25 [v] Ex 15:14-16

2:4–6 When the Israelites passed through Seir, God advised them to be careful. The Israelites were known as warriors, and the children of Esau—the Edomites—would be understandably nervous as the great crowd passed through their land. God warned the Israelites not to start a fight, to respect the Edomites' territory, and to pay for whatever they used. God wanted the Israelites to deal justly with these neighbors. We must also act justly in dealing with others. Recognize the rights of others, even your opponents. By behaving wisely and justly you may be able to establish or restore a relationship.

2:11 Both Moab and Ammon had removed a tall Anakim-like people usually known as the Rephaites, but called Emites by the Moabites and Zamzummites by the Ammonites (2:20). If our enemies seem overwhelming, we must remember that God can deliver us as he did the Israelites.

2:14, 15 Israel did not have to spend 40 years on the way to the promised land. God sentenced them to desert wanderings because they rejected his love, rebelled against his authority, ignored his commands for right living, and willfully broke their end of the agreement made in Exodus 19:8 and 24:3–8. In short, they disobeyed God. We often make life's journey more difficult than necessary by disobedience. Accept God's love, read and follow his commands in the Bible, and make a promise to stick with God whatever your situation. You will find that your life will be less complicated and more rewarding.

2:25 God told Moses he would make the enemy nations terrified of Israel. By worldly standards, Israel's army was not intimidating, but Israel had God on its side. Moses no longer had to worry about his enemies because his enemies were worried about him. God often goes before us in our daily battles, preparing the way

2:27
w Nu 21:21-22
2:28
x Nu 20:19

2:30
y Nu 21:23

2:32
z Nu 21:23

2:34
a Dt 3:6; 7:2

2:36
b Dt 3:12; 4:48

2:37
c Nu 21:24

26 From the desert of Kedemoth I sent messengers to Sihon king of Heshbon offering peace and saying, 27 "Let us pass through your country. We will stay on the main road; we will not turn aside to the right or to the left. *w* 28 Sell us food to eat and water to drink for their price in silver. Only let us pass through on foot *x*— 29 as the descendants of Esau, who live in Seir, and the Moabites, who live in Ar, did for us—until we cross the Jordan into the land the LORD our God is giving us." 30 But Sihon king of Heshbon refused to let us pass through. For the LORD your God had made his spirit stubborn *y* and his heart obstinate in order to give him into your hands, as he has now done.

31 The LORD said to me, "See, I have begun to deliver Sihon and his country over to you. Now begin to conquer and possess his land."

32 When Sihon and all his army came out to meet us in battle *z* at Jahaz, 33 the LORD our God delivered him over to us and we struck him down, together with his sons and his whole army. 34 At that time we took all his towns and completely destroyed *a a* them—men, women and children. We left no survivors. 35 But the livestock and the plunder from the towns we had captured we carried off for ourselves. 36 From Aroer *b* on the rim of the Arnon Gorge, and from the town in the gorge, even as far as Gilead, not one town was too strong for us. The LORD our God gave us all of them. 37 But in accordance with the command of the LORD our God, you did not encroach on any of the land of the Ammonites, *c* neither the land along the course of the Jabbok nor that around the towns in the hills.

Defeat of Og King of Bashan

3:1
d Nu 21:33

3 Next we turned and went up along the road toward Bashan, and Og king of Bashan with his whole army marched out to meet us in battle at Edrei. *d* 2 The LORD said to me, "Do not be afraid of him, for I have handed him over to you with his whole army and his land. Do to him what you did to Sihon king of the Amorites, who reigned in Heshbon."

3:4
e 1Ki 4:13

3 So the LORD our God also gave into our hands Og king of Bashan and all his army. We struck them down, leaving no survivors. 4 At that time we took all his cities. There was not one of the sixty cities that we did not take from them—the whole region of Argob, Og's kingdom in Bashan. *e* 5 All these cities were fortified with high walls and with gates and bars, and there were also a great many unwalled villages. 6 We completely destroyed *a* them, as we had done with Sihon king of Heshbon, destroying *a f* every city—men, women and children. 7 But all the livestock and the plunder from their cities we carried off for ourselves.

3:6
f Dt 2:24,34

8 So at that time we took from these two kings of the Amorites the territory east of the Jordan, from the Arnon Gorge as far as Mount Hermon. 9 (Hermon is called Sirion *g* by the Sidonians; the Amorites call it Senir.) 10 We took all the towns on the plateau, and all Gilead, and all Bashan as far as Salecah and Edrei, towns of Og's kingdom in Bashan. 11 (Only Og king of Bashan was left of the remnant of the Rephaites. *h* His bed *b* was made of iron and was more than thirteen feet long and six feet wide. *c* It is still in Rabbah *i* of the Ammonites.)

3:9
g Ps 29:6
3:11
h Ge 14:5
i 2Sa 12:26;
Jer 49:2

Division of the Land

3:12
j Nu 32:32-38;
Dt 2:36

12 Of the land that we took over at that time, I gave the Reubenites and the Gadites the territory north of Aroer *j* by the Arnon Gorge, including half the hill country of Gilead, together with its towns. 13 The rest of Gilead and also all of Bashan, the kingdom of Og, I gave to the half-tribe of Manasseh. (The whole region of Argob in Bashan used to be known as a land of the Rephaites. 14 Jair, *k* a descendant of Manasseh, took the whole region of Argob as far as the border of the Geshurites and the Maacathites; it was named after him, so that to this day Bashan is called Havvoth Jair. *d*) 15 And I gave Gilead to Makir. *l* 16 But to the Reubenites and the Gadites I gave the territory extending from Gilead down to the Arnon Gorge (the middle of the gorge being the border) and out to the Jabbok River, which is the border of the Ammonites. 17 Its western border was the Jordan in the Arabah, from Kinnereth *m* to the Sea of the Arabah (the Salt Sea *e*), below the slopes of Pisgah.

3:14
k Nu 32:41

3:15
l Nu 32:39-40

3:17
m Nu 34:11

a 34,6 The Hebrew term refers to the irrevocable giving over of things or persons to the LORD, often by totally destroying them.   *b 11* Or *sarcophagus*   *c 11* Hebrew *nine cubits long and four cubits wide* (about 4 meters long and 1.8 meters wide)   *d 14* Or *called the settlements of Jair*   *e 17* That is, the Dead Sea

---

and overcoming barriers. We need to follow him wholeheartedly and be alert to his leading.

3:1-3 The Israelites faced a big problem—the well-trained army of Og, king of Bashan. The Israelites hardly stood a chance. But they won because God fought for them. God can help his people

regardless of the problems they face. No matter how insurmountable the obstacles may seem, remember that God is sovereign, and he will keep his promises.

[18]I commanded you at that time: "The LORD your God has given you this land to take pos- | **3:18**
session of it. But all your able-bodied men, armed for battle, must cross over ahead of your | [n]Nu 32:17
brother Israelites. [n] [19]However, your wives, your children and your livestock (I know you
have much livestock) may stay in the towns I have given you, [20]until the LORD gives rest to
your brothers as he has to you, and they too have taken over the land that the LORD your God
is giving them, across the Jordan. After that, each of you may go back to the possession I
have given you."

Moses Forbidden to Cross the Jordan

[21]At that time I commanded Joshua: "You have seen with your own eyes all that the LORD
your God has done to these two kings. The LORD will do the same to all the kingdoms over
there where you are going. [22]Do not be afraid [o] of them; the LORD your God himself will | **3:22**
fight for you." | [o]Dt 1:29

[23]At that time I pleaded with the LORD: [24]"O Sovereign LORD, you have begun to show to | **3:24**
your servant your greatness and your strong hand. For what god [p] is there in heaven or on | [p]Ex 15:11; Ps 86:8
earth who can do the deeds and mighty works you do? [25]Let me go over and see the good | **3:25**
land [q] beyond the Jordan—that fine hill country and Lebanon." | [q]Dt 4:22

[26]But because of you the LORD was angry [r] with me and would not listen to me. "That is | **3:26**
enough," the LORD said. "Do not speak to me anymore about this matter. [27]Go up to the top | [r]Dt 1:37
of Pisgah and look west and north and south and east. Look at the land with your own eyes, | **3:27**
since you are not going to cross this Jordan. [s] [28]But commission [t] Joshua, and encourage and | [s]Nu 27:12
strengthen him, for he will lead this people across and will cause them to inherit the land | **3:28**
that you will see." [29]So we stayed in the valley near Beth Peor. [u] | [t]Nu 27:18-23
| **3:29**
| [u]Dt 34:6

Obedience Commanded

4 Hear now, O Israel, the decrees and laws I am about to teach you. Follow them so that | **4:1**
you may live [v] and may go in and take possession of the land that the LORD, the God of | [v]Dt 30:15-20
your fathers, is giving you. [2]Do not add [w] to what I command you and do not subtract from it, | **4:2**
but keep the commands of the LORD your God that I give you. | [w]Dt 12:32; Jos 1:7

[3]You saw with your own eyes what the LORD did at Baal Peor. The LORD your God destroyed from among you everyone who followed the Baal of Peor, [4]but all of you who held
fast to the LORD your God are still alive today.

[5]See, I have taught you decrees and laws as the LORD my God commanded me, so that you
may follow them in the land you are entering to take possession of it. [6]Observe them carefully, for this will show your wisdom and understanding to the nations, who will hear about
all these decrees and say, "Surely this great nation is a wise and understanding people."
[7]What other nation is so great [x] as to have their gods near [y] them the way the LORD our God is | **4:7**
near us whenever we pray to him? [8]And what other nation is so great as to have such righ- | [x]2Sa 7:23
teous decrees and laws as this body of laws I am setting before you today? | [y]Isa 55:6

3:21, 22 What encouraging news for Joshua, who was to lead his men against the persistent forces of evil in the promised land! Since God promised to help him win every battle, he had nothing to fear. Our battles may not be against godless armies, but they are just as real as Joshua's. Whether we are resisting temptation or battling fear, God has promised to fight with and for us as we place our hope and confidence in him.

3:26–28 God had made it clear that Moses would not enter the promised land (Numbers 20:12). So God told Moses to commission Joshua as the new leader and encourage him in this new role. This is a good example to churches and organizations who must eventually replace their leaders. Good leaders prepare their people to function without them by discovering those with leadership potential, providing the training they need, and looking for ways to encourage them.

4:2 What is meant by adding to or subtracting from God's commands? These laws were the word of God, and they were complete. How could any human being, with limited wisdom and knowledge, edit God's perfect laws? To add to the laws would make them a burden; to subtract from the laws would make them incomplete. Thus the laws were to remain unchanged. To presume to make changes in God's law is to assume a position of authority over God who gave the laws (Matthew 5:17–19;

15:3–9; Revelation 22:18, 19). The religious leaders at the time of Christ did exactly this; they elevated their own laws to the same level as God's. Jesus rebuked them for this (Matthew 23:1–4).

4:8 Do the laws God gave to the Israelites still apply to Christians today? God's laws are designed to guide all people toward lifestyles that are healthy, upright, and devoted to God. Their purpose was to point out sin (or potential sin) and show the proper way to deal with that sin. The Ten Commandments, the heart of God's law, are just as applicable today as they were 3,000 years ago because they proclaim a lifestyle endorsed by God. They are the perfect expression of who God is and how he wants people to live.

But God gave other laws besides the Ten Commandments. Are these just as important? God never issued a law that didn't have a purpose. However, many of the laws we read in the Pentateuch were directed specifically to people of that time and culture. Although a specific law may not apply to us, the timeless truth or principle behind the law does.

For example, Christians do not practice animal sacrifice in worship. However, the principles behind the sacrifices—forgiveness for sin and thankfulness to God—still apply. The sacrifices pointed to the ultimate sacrifice made for us by Jesus Christ. The New Testament says that with the death and resurrection of Jesus Christ the Old Testament laws were fulfilled. This means that

4:9
z Pr 4:23
a Eph 6:4

4:11
b Ex 19:18

4:13
c Ex 34:28

4:16
d Ex 20:4-5; Dt 5:8

4:19
e Dt 17:3

4:20
f 1Ki 8:51; Jer 11:4

4:21
g Dt 1:37

4:22
h Dt 3:25

4:23
i ver 9,16

4:24
j Ex 24:17; Dt 9:3; Heb 12:29

4:25
k 2Ki 17:2,17

4:26
l Dt 30:18-19

4:28
m Dt 28:36,64
n Ps 115:4-8

4:29
o 2Ch 15:4; Isa 55:6

9 Only be careful,[z] and watch yourselves closely so that you do not forget the things your eyes have seen or let them slip from your heart as long as you live. Teach[a] them to your children and to their children after them. 10 Remember the day you stood before the LORD your God at Horeb, when he said to me, "Assemble the people before me to hear my words so that they may learn to revere me as long as they live in the land and may teach them to their children." 11 You came near and stood at the foot of the mountain while it blazed with fire[b] to the very heavens, with black clouds and deep darkness. 12 Then the LORD spoke to you out of the fire. You heard the sound of words but saw no form; there was only a voice. 13 He declared to you his covenant, the Ten Commandments,[c] which he commanded you to follow and then wrote them on two stone tablets. 14 And the LORD directed me at that time to teach you the decrees and laws you are to follow in the land that you are crossing the Jordan to possess.

Idolatry Forbidden

15 You saw no form of any kind the day the LORD spoke to you at Horeb out of the fire. Therefore watch yourselves very carefully, 16 so that you do not become corrupt and make for yourselves an idol,[d] an image of any shape, whether formed like a man or a woman, 17 or like any animal on earth or any bird that flies in the air, 18 or like any creature that moves along the ground or any fish in the waters below. 19 And when you look up to the sky and see the sun,[e] the moon and the stars—all the heavenly array—do not be enticed into bowing down to them and worshiping things the LORD your God has apportioned to all the nations under heaven. 20 But as for you, the LORD took you and brought you out of the iron-smelting furnace,[f] out of Egypt, to be the people of his inheritance, as you now are.

21 The LORD was angry with me[g] because of you, and he solemnly swore that I would not cross the Jordan and enter the good land the LORD your God is giving you as your inheritance. 22 I will die in this land; I will not cross the Jordan; but you are about to cross over and take possession of that good land.[h] 23 Be careful not to forget the covenant[i] of the LORD your God that he made with you; do not make for yourselves an idol in the form of anything the LORD your God has forbidden. 24 For the LORD your God is a consuming fire,[j] a jealous God.

25 After you have had children and grandchildren and have lived in the land a long time— if you then become corrupt and make any kind of idol, doing evil[k] in the eyes of the LORD your God and provoking him to anger, 26 I call heaven and earth as witnesses against you[l] this day that you will quickly perish from the land that you are crossing the Jordan to possess. You will not live there long but will certainly be destroyed. 27 The LORD will scatter you among the peoples, and only a few of you will survive among the nations to which the LORD will drive you. 28 There you will worship man-made gods[m] of wood and stone, which cannot see or hear or eat or smell.[n] 29 But if from there you seek[o] the LORD your God, you will find

---

while the Old Testament laws help us recognize our sins and correct our wrongdoings, it is Jesus Christ who takes our sins away. Jesus is now our primary example to follow because he alone perfectly obeyed the law and modeled its true intent.

4:9 Moses wanted to make sure that the people did not forget all they had seen God do, so he urged parents to teach their children about God's great miracles. This helped parents remember God's faithfulness and provided the means for passing on from one generation to the next the stories recounting God's great acts. It is easy to forget the wonderful ways God has worked in the lives of his people. But you can remember God's great acts of faithfulness by telling your children, friends, or associates what you have seen him do.

4:19 God was not excusing the other nations for their idol worship. He was simply saying that while judgment might be delayed for those other nations, it would be swift and complete for Israel because Israel knew God's laws. We must remember that idol worship was not just keeping statues around the house—harmless lumps of clay, wood, or iron. It was the commitment to the other evil qualities, beliefs, and practices the idol represented (such as murder, prostitution, cruelty in war, self-centeredness). When the strengths and attributes of powerful humans or animals are revered or the cycles of nature are honored without reference to God who created them, this is idolatry. Because God had so clearly revealed himself in Israel's history, the Israelites had no excuse for worshiping any person or power but the one true God.

4:24 God is a consuming fire. Because he is morally perfect, he hates sin and cannot accept those who practice it. Moses' sin kept him from entering the promised land, and no sacrifice could remove that judgment. Sin kept us from entering God's presence, but Jesus Christ paid the penalty for our sin and removed God's judgment forever by his death. Trusting in Jesus Christ will save you from God's anger and will allow you to begin a personal relationship with him.

4:24 Jealousy is a demand for someone else's exclusive affection or loyalty. Some jealousy is bad. It is destructive for a person to get upset when his or her spouse talks to someone of the opposite sex. But other jealousy is good. It is right for a man to demand that his wife treat him, and only him, as her husband. Usually we use the word *jealousy* only for the bad reaction. But God's kind of jealousy is appropriate and good. He is defending his word and guarding his high honor. He makes a strong, exclusive demand on us: We must treat only the Lord—and no one else in all the universe—as God.

4:29 Do you want to know God? God promised the Israelites that they would find him when they searched with all their hearts and souls. God is knowable and wants to be known—but we have to want to know him. Acts of service and worship must be accompanied by sincere devotion of the heart. As Hebrews 11:6 says, "Anyone who comes to him must believe that he exists and that he rewards those who earnestly seek him." God will reward those who pursue a relationship with him.

him if you look for him with all your heart and with all your soul. *p* 30 When you are in distress and all these things have happened to you, then in later days *q* you will return to the LORD your God and obey him. 31 For the LORD your God is a merciful *r* God; he will not abandon or destroy you or forget the covenant with your forefathers, which he confirmed to them by oath.

4:29
p Dt 30:1-3,10
4:30
q Hos 3:5
4:31
r 2Ch 30:9;
Ps 116:5

The LORD Is God

32 Ask now about the former days, long before your time, from the day God created man on the earth; ask from one end of the heavens to the other. Has anything so great as this ever happened, or has anything like it ever been heard of? 33 Has any other people heard the voice of God *a* speaking out of fire, as you have, and lived? *s* 34 Has any god ever tried to take for himself one nation out of another nation, by testings, by miraculous signs and wonders, *t* by war, by a mighty hand and an outstretched arm, or by great and awesome deeds, like all the things the LORD your God did for you in Egypt before your very eyes?

4:33
s Dt 5:24-26
4:34
t Dt 7:19

35 You were shown these things so that you might know that the LORD is God; besides him there is no other. *u* 36 From heaven he made you hear his voice *v* to discipline you. On earth he showed you his great fire, and you heard his words from out of the fire. 37 Because he loved *w* your forefathers and chose their descendants after them, he brought you out of Egypt by his Presence and his great strength, 38 to drive out before you nations greater and stronger than you and to bring you into their land to give it to you for your inheritance, as it is today.

4:35
u Dt 32:39; 1Sa 2:2;
Isa 45:5,18
4:36
v Ex 19:9,19
4:37
w Dt 10:15

39 Acknowledge and take to heart this day that the LORD is God in heaven above and on the earth below. There is no other. *x* 40 Keep *y* his decrees and commands, which I am giving you today, so that it may go well with you and your children after you and that you may live long in the land the LORD your God gives you for all time.

4:39
x Jos 2:11
4:40
y Lev 22:31

Cities of Refuge

41 Then Moses set aside three cities east of the Jordan, 42 to which anyone who had killed a person could flee if he had unintentionally killed his neighbor without malice aforethought. He could flee into one of these cities and save his life. 43 The cities were these: Bezer in the desert plateau, for the Reubenites; Ramoth in Gilead, for the Gadites; and Golan in Bashan, for the Manassites.

B. PRINCIPLES FOR GODLY LIVING: MOSES' SECOND ADDRESS (4:44—28:68)

After reviewing the history of Israel's journey, Moses recounts the Ten Commandments and the other laws given to the Israelites at Mount Sinai. He urges them to obey the law and reminds them of the consequences of disobeying God's laws. The Ten Commandments and all of God's laws point out to us where we fall short and show us how we should act as God's people.

Introduction to the Law

44 This is the law Moses set before the Israelites. 45 These are the stipulations, decrees and laws Moses gave them when they came out of Egypt 46 and were in the valley near Beth Peor east of the Jordan, in the land of Sihon *z* king of the Amorites, who reigned in Heshbon and was defeated by Moses and the Israelites as they came out of Egypt. 47 They took possession of his land and the land of Og king of Bashan, the two Amorite kings east of the Jordan. 48 This land extended from Aroer *a* on the rim of the Arnon Gorge to Mount Siyon *b* (that is, Hermon), 49 and included all the Arabah east of the Jordan, as far as the Sea of the Arabah, *c* below the slopes of Pisgah.

4:46
z Nu 21:26; Dt 3:29
4:48
a Dt 2:36

a 33 Or *of a god*   *b* 48 Hebrew; Syriac (see also Deut. 3:9) *Sirion*   *c* 49 That is, the Dead Sea

---

4:32 How tempted we are to look everywhere else but to God for our guidance and leadership! We trust medical doctors, financial advisers, and news commentators, but do we trust God? Get God's advice first (4:39, 40), and recognize his authority over every dimension of life.

4:40 Was Israel guaranteed prosperity for obeying God's laws? Yes—but we have to look carefully at what that means. God's laws were designed to make his chosen nation devout, healthy, just, and merciful. When the people followed those laws, they prospered. This does not mean, however, that no sickness, no sadness, and no misunderstandings existed among them. Rather, it means that as a nation they prospered and that individuals' problems were handled as fairly as possible. Today God's promise of prosperity—his constant presence, comfort, and the resources to live as we should—extends to all believers. We will face trials; Jesus told us that. But we will avoid the misery that directly results from intentional sin, and we will know that a great treasure awaits us in heaven.

1. The Ten Commandments

5 Moses summoned all Israel and said:
Hear, O Israel, the decrees and laws I declare in your hearing today. Learn them and be sure to follow them. ²The LORD our God made a covenant*b* with us at Horeb. ³It was not with our fathers that the LORD made this covenant, but with us, with all of us who are alive here today. ⁴The LORD spoke*c* to you face to face out of the fire on the mountain. ⁵(At that time I stood between the LORD and you to declare to you the word of the LORD, because you were afraid*d* of the fire and did not go up the mountain.) And he said:

⁶ "I am the LORD your God, who brought you out of Egypt, out of the land of slavery.
⁷ "You shall have no other gods before*a* me.
⁸ "You shall not make for yourself an idol in the form of anything in heaven above or on the earth beneath or in the waters below. ⁹You shall not bow down to them or worship them; for I, the LORD your God, am a jealous God, punishing the children for the sin of the fathers to the third and fourth generation of those who hate me,*e* ¹⁰but showing love to a thousand ⌞generations⌟ of those who love me and keep my commandments.*f*
¹¹ "You shall not misuse the name of the LORD your God, for the LORD will not hold anyone guiltless who misuses his name. *g*
¹² "Observe the Sabbath day by keeping it holy, as the LORD your God has commanded you. ¹³Six days you shall labor and do all your work, ¹⁴but the seventh day*h* is a Sabbath to the LORD your God. On it you shall not do any work, neither you, nor your son or daughter, nor your manservant or maidservant, nor your ox, your donkey or any of your animals, nor the alien within your gates, so that your manservant and maidservant may rest, as you do. ¹⁵Remember that you were slaves in Egypt and that the LORD your God brought you out of there with a mighty hand and an outstretched arm. Therefore the LORD your God has commanded you to observe the Sabbath day.
¹⁶ "Honor your father and your mother,*i* as the LORD your God has commanded you, so that you may live long and that it may go well with you in the land the LORD your God is giving you.
¹⁷ "You shall not murder.*j*
¹⁸ "You shall not commit adultery. *k*

a 7 Or *besides*

Margin references:
5:2 *b* Ex 19:5
5:4 *c* Dt 4:12,33,36
5:5 *d* Ex 20:18,21
5:9 *e* Ex 34:7
5:10 *f* Jer 32:18
5:11 *g* Lev 19:12
5:14 *h* Ge 2:2
5:16 *i* Eph 6:2-3*
5:17 *j* Mt 5:21-22*
5:18 *k* Mt 5:27-30; Lk 18:20*

5:1 The people had entered into a covenant with God, and Moses commanded them to hear, learn, and obey his statutes. Christians also have entered into a covenant with God through Jesus Christ and should be responsive to what God expects. Moses' threefold command to the Israelites provides excellent advice for all God's followers. *Hearing* is absorbing and accepting information about God. *Learning* is understanding its meaning and implications. *Following* is putting into action all we have learned and understood. All three parts are essential to a growing relationship with God.

5:7 A *god* is whatever people use as a driving force in their lives. Some people literally worship other gods by joining cults or strange religions. In a more subtle way, many of us worship other gods by building our lives around something other than the one true God. If your greatest desire is for popularity, power, or money, you are devoting yourself to something other than God. To put God first, (1) recognize what is taking his place in your life; (2) renounce this substitute god as unworthy of your devotion; (3) ask God for forgiveness; (4) restructure your priorities so that love for God is the motive for everything you do; (5) examine yourself daily to be sure you are giving God first place.

5:8, 9 How would you feel if someone took a picture of you, framed it, stared at it a lot, showed it to others, but completely ignored the real you? God does not want to be treated this way either. He wants a genuine relationship with us, not mere ritual. He wants us to know him. God knows that if we put anything other than him at the center of our lives, we will not reach our potential and become all that he wants us to be.

5:11 We are familar with the sin to be avoided in this commandment, that we should not misuse the name of the Lord by saying it in an empty or worthless way. But there is also a good work that is commanded: to use God's name to praise him and ascribe to him glory. This is the opposite of misusing his name. While you might be able to keep yourself from swearing, how have you done at finding time to praise God and honor his name?

5:16 Obeying our parents is our main task when we are young, but honoring them should continue even beyond their death. One way to honor parents is to provide for them in times of financial need or when they are ill and unable to care for themselves. Perhaps the best way to honor them is to pass on their Christ-honoring values to our children. Honoring involves all that sons and daughters do with their lives—the way they work and talk, the values they hold, and the morals they practice. What are you doing to show respect to your parents? Are you living in a way that brings honor to them?

5:17 "But I don't murder people," you may say. Good. That fulfills the letter of the law. But Jesus explained that hateful anger breaks this commandment (Matthew 5:21, 22). Have you ever been so angry with someone who mistreated you that for a moment you wished that person were dead? Have you ever fantasized that you could get rid of someone? Jesus' teaching concerning this law demonstrates that we are capable of murder in our hearts. Even if we are legally innocent, we are all morally guilty of murder and need to ask God's forgiveness. We need to commit ourselves to the opposite of hatred and anger—love and reconciliation.

19 "You shall not steal.

20 "You shall not give false testimony against your neighbor.

21 "You shall not covet your neighbor's wife. You shall not set your desire on your neighbor's house or land, his manservant or maidservant, his ox or donkey, or anything that belongs to your neighbor."[l]

5:21 [l] Ro 7:7*

22 These are the commandments the LORD proclaimed in a loud voice to your whole assembly there on the mountain from out of the fire, the cloud and the deep darkness; and he added nothing more. Then he wrote them on two stone tablets[m] and gave them to me.

5:22 [m] Ex 31:18; Dt 4:13

23 When you heard the voice out of the darkness, while the mountain was ablaze with fire, all the leading men of your tribes and your elders came to me. 24 And you said, "The LORD our God has shown us his glory and his majesty, and we have heard his voice from the fire. Today we have seen that a man can live even if God speaks with him. 25 But now, why should we die? This great fire will consume us, and we will die if we hear the voice of the LORD our God any longer.[n] 26 For what mortal man has ever heard the voice of the living God speaking out of fire, as we have, and survived?[o] 27 Go near and listen to all that the LORD our God says. Then tell us whatever the LORD our God tells you. We will listen and obey."

5:25 [n] Dt 18:16

5:26 [o] Dt 4:33

28 The LORD heard you when you spoke to me and the LORD said to me, "I have heard what this people said to you. Everything they said was good.[p] 29 Oh, that their hearts would be inclined to fear me[q] and keep all my commands[r] always, so that it might go well with them and their children forever!

5:28 [p] Dt 18:17

5:29 [q] Ps 81:8,13 [r] Isa 48:18

30 "Go, tell them to return to their tents. 31 But you stay here with me so that I may give you all the commands, decrees and laws you are to teach them to follow in the land I am giving them to possess."

32 So be careful to do what the LORD your God has commanded you; do not turn aside to the right or to the left.[s] 33 Walk in all the way that the LORD your God has commanded you, so that you may live and prosper and prolong your days[t] in the land that you will possess.

5:32 [s] Dt 17:11,20; 28:14; Jos 1:7

5:33 [t] Dt 4:40

2. Love the LORD your God

6 These are the commands, decrees and laws the LORD your God directed me to teach you to observe in the land that you are crossing the Jordan to possess, 2 so that you, your children and their children after them may fear[u] the LORD your God as long as you live by keeping all his decrees and commands that I give you, and so that you may enjoy long life. 3 Hear, O Israel, and be careful to obey so that it may go well with you and that you may increase greatly in a land flowing with milk and honey,[v] just as the LORD, the God of your fathers, promised you.

6:2 [u] Dt 10:12-13

6:3 [v] Ex 3:8

4 Hear, O Israel: The LORD our God, the LORD is one.[a][w] 5 Love[x] the LORD your God with all your heart and with all your soul and with all your strength. 6 These commandments that I

6:4 [w] 1Co 8:4

6:5 [x] Mt 22:37*

[a]4 Or *The LORD our God is one LORD*; or *The LORD is our God, the LORD is one*; or *The LORD is our God, the LORD alone*

5:21 To covet means to ardently desire another person's prosperity. We are not to set our desires on anything that belongs to someone else. Not only can such cravings make us miserable, they can also lead us to other sins such as adultery and stealing. Envying others is a useless exercise because God is able to provide everything we really need, even if he does not always give us everything we want. To stop coveting, we need to practice being content with what we have. The apostle Paul emphasizes the significance of contentment in Philippians 4:11. It's a matter of perspective. Instead of thinking about what we don't have, we should thank God for what he has given and strive to be content. After all, our most important possession is free and available to everyone—eternal life through Christ.

5:29 God told Moses that he wanted the people to incline their hearts to fear him—to *want* to respect and obey him. There is a difference between doing something because it is required and doing something because we want to. God is not interested in forced religious exercises and rule-keeping. He wants our hearts and lives completely dedicated to him. If we love him, obedience will follow.

6:3 For a nation that had wandered 40 years in a parched desert, a land flowing with milk and honey sounded like paradise. It brought to mind rich crops, rushing streams, gentle rains, and lush fields filled with livestock. The Israelites could have had all

that 40 years earlier. Numbers 13 and 14 explain how the people missed their chance. Now Moses was determined to help the people avoid the same mistake by whetting their appetite for the beautiful land and then clearly explaining the conditions for entering the land.

6:4 Monotheism—belief in only one God—was a distinctive feature of Hebrew religion. Many ancient religions believed in many gods. But the God of Abraham, Isaac, and Jacob is the God of the whole earth, the only true God. This was an important insight for the nation of Israel because they were about to enter a land filled with people who believed in many gods. Both then and today, there are people who prefer to place their trust in many different values, belief systems, and "gods." But the day is coming when God will be recognized as the only one. He will be the king over the whole earth (Zechariah 14:9).

6:4–9 This passage provides the central theme of Deuteronomy. It sets a pattern that helps us relate the Word of God to our daily lives. We are to love God, think constantly about his commandments, teach his commandments to our children, and live each day by the guidelines in his Word. God emphasized the importance of parents teaching the Bible to their children. The church and Christian schools cannot be used to escape from this responsibility. The Bible provides so many opportunities for object lessons and practical teaching that it would be a shame to study it only one

6:6
y Dt 11:18

6:7
z Eph 6:4

6:9
a Dt 11:20

6:10
b Jos 24:13

6:11
c Dt 8:10

6:13
d Mt 4:10*

6:15
e Dt 4:24

6:16
f Mt 4:7*

6:17
g Ps 119:4

6:20
h Ex 13:14

give you today are to be upon your hearts. y 7Impress them on your children. Talk about them when you sit at home and when you walk along the road, when you lie down and when you get up. z 8Tie them as symbols on your hands and bind them on your foreheads. 9Write them on the doorframes of your houses and on your gates. a

10When the LORD your God brings you into the land he swore to your fathers, to Abraham, Isaac and Jacob, to give you—a land with large, flourishing cities you did not build, b 11houses filled with all kinds of good things you did not provide, wells you did not dig, and vineyards and olive groves you did not plant—then when you eat and are satisfied, c 12be careful that you do not forget the LORD, who brought you out of Egypt, out of the land of slavery.

13Fear the LORD your God, serve him only d and take your oaths in his name. 14Do not follow other gods, the gods of the peoples around you; 15for the LORD your God e, who is among you, is a jealous God and his anger will burn against you, and he will destroy you from the face of the land. 16Do not test the LORD your God f as you did at Massah. 17Be sure to keep the commands of the LORD your God and the stipulations and decrees he has given you. g 18Do what is right and good in the LORD's sight, so that it may go well with you and you may go in and take over the good land that the LORD promised on oath to your forefathers, 19thrusting out all your enemies before you, as the LORD said.

20In the future, when your son asks you, h "What is the meaning of the stipulations, decrees and laws the LORD our God has commanded you?" 21tell him: "We were slaves of Pharaoh in Egypt, but the LORD brought us out of Egypt with a mighty hand. 22Before our eyes the LORD sent miraculous signs and wonders—great and terrible—upon Egypt and Pharaoh and his whole household. 23But he brought us out from there to bring us in and give us the land that he promised on oath to our forefathers. 24The LORD commanded us to obey all

---

BROKEN COMMANDMENTS

The Ten Commandments were God's standard for right living (5:6–21). To obey them was to obey God. Yet throughout the Old Testament, we can see how each commandment was broken. As you read the stories, notice the tragic consequences that occurred as a result of violating God's law.

Ten Commandments	Notable Violations
"You shall have no other gods before me."	Solomon (1 Kings 11)
"You shall not make for yourself an idol. . . . You shall not bow down to them or worship them. . . ."	The golden calf-idol incident (Exodus 32); generations after Joshua (Judges 2:10–14; 2 Kings 21:1–15; Jeremiah 1:16)
"You shall not misuse the name of the LORD your God. . . ."	Zedekiah (Ezekiel 17:15–21)
"Observe the Sabbath day by keeping it holy."	Judah (2 Chronicles 36:21)
"Honor your father and your mother."	Eli's sons—Hophni and Phinehas (1 Samuel 2:12, 23–25)
"You shall not murder."	Hazael (2 Kings 8:15)
"You shall not commit adultery."	David (2 Samuel 11:2–5)
"You shall not steal."	Ahab (1 Kings 21:1–19)
"You shall not give false testimony against your neighbor."	Saul (1 Samuel 15:13–25)
"You shall not covet your neighbor's wife. You shall not set your desire on your neighbor's house or land . . . or anything that belongs to your neighbor."	Achan (Joshua 7:19–26)

---

day a week. Eternal truths are most effectively learned in the loving environment of a God-fearing home.

6:5 Jesus said that loving God with all of ourselves is the first and greatest commandment (Matthew 22:37–39). This command, combined with the command to love your neighbor (Leviticus 19:18), encompasses all the other Old Testament laws.

6:7 The Hebrews were extremely successful at making religion an integral part of life. The reason for their success was that religious education was life-oriented, not information-oriented. They used the context of daily life to teach about God. The key to teaching your children to love God is stated simply and clearly in these verses. If you want your children to follow God, you must make God a part of your everyday experiences. You must teach your children diligently to see God in all aspects of life, not just those that are church related.

6:10–13 Moses warned the people not to forget God when they entered the promised land and became prosperous. Prosperity,

more than poverty, can dull our spiritual vision because it tends to make us self-sufficient and eager to acquire still more of everything—except God. The same thing can happen in our church. Once we become successful in terms of numbers, programs, and buildings, we can easily become self-sufficient and less sensitive to our need for God. This leads us to concentrate on self-preservation rather than thankfulness and service to God.

6:24 Does the phrase "so that we might always prosper" mean that we can expect only prosperity and no suffering when we obey God? What is promised here is a right relationship with God for all those who love him with all their heart. It speaks of a good relationship with God and the ultimate benefit of knowing him. It is not blanket protection against poverty, adversity, or suffering. We can have this right relationship with God by obeying his command to love him with all that we are.

these decrees and to fear the LORD our God, *i* so that we might always prosper and be kept alive, as is the case today. 25And if we are careful to obey all this law before the LORD our God, as he has commanded us, that will be our righteousness."

6:24
i Jer 32:39

Driving Out the Nations

7 When the LORD your God brings you into the land you are entering to possess and drives out before you many nations *j*—the Hittites, Girgashites, Amorites, Canaanites, Perizzites, Hivites and Jebusites, seven nations larger and stronger than you— 2and when the LORD your God has delivered them over to you and you have defeated them, then you must destroy them totally.ª Make no treatyᵏ with them, and show them no mercy. 3Do not intermarry with them. *l* Do not give your daughters to their sons or take their daughters for your sons, 4for they will turn your sons away from following me to serve other gods, and the LORD's anger will burn against you and will quickly destroy you. 5This is what you are to do to them: Break down their altars, smash their sacred stones, cut down their Asherah polesᵇ and burn their idols in the fire. *m* 6For you are a people holy *n* to the LORD your God. The LORD your God has chosen o you out of all the peoples on the face of the earth to be his people, his treasured possession.

7:1
j Dt 31:3

7:2
ᵏ Ex 23:32

7:3
l Ex 34:15-16

7:5
m Ex 23:24

7:6
n Ex 19:5-6
o Dt 14:2

7The LORD did not set his affection on you and choose you because you were more numerous than other peoples, for you were the fewest of all peoples.*p* 8But it was because the LORD loved you and kept the oath he swore to your forefathers that he brought you out with a mighty hand and redeemed you from the land of slavery,q from the power of Pharaoh king of Egypt. 9Know therefore that the LORD your God is God; he is the faithful God,*r* keeping his covenant of love *s* to a thousand generations of those who love him and keep his commands. 10But

7:7
p Dt 10:22

7:8
q Ex 13:14

7:9
r 1Co 1:9
s Ne 1:5

> those who hate him he will repay to their face by destruction;
> he will not be slow to repay to their face those who hate him.

11Therefore, take care to follow the commands, decrees and laws I give you today.

12If you pay attention to these laws and are careful to follow them, then the LORD your God will keep his covenant of love with you, as he swore to your forefathers. *t* 13He will love you and bless you and increase your numbers. He will bless the fruit of your womb, the crops of your land—your grain, new wine and oil—the calves of your herds and the lambs of your flocks in the land that he swore to your forefathers to give you. 14You will be blessed more than any other people; none of your men or women will be childless, nor any of your livestock without young. *u* 15The LORD will keep you free from every disease. *v* He will not inflict on you the horrible diseases you knew in Egypt, but he will inflict them on all who hate you. 16You must destroy all the peoples the LORD your God gives over to you. Do not look on them with pity *w* and do not serve their gods, for that will be a snare to you.

7:12
t Dt 28:1-14

7:14
u Ex 23:26

7:15
v Ex 15:26

7:16
w ver 2

17You may say to yourselves, "These nations are stronger than we are. How can we drive them out?" 18But do not be afraid of them; remember well what the LORD your God did to Pharaoh and to all Egypt. *x* 19You saw with your own eyes the great trials, the miraculous signs and wonders, the mighty hand and outstretched arm, with which the LORD your God brought you out. The LORD your God will do the same to all the peoples you now fear. *y* 20Moreover, the LORD your God will send the hornetᶻ among them until even the survivors

7:18
x Ps 105:5

7:19
y Dt 4:34

7:20
ᶻ Jos 24:12

ª2 The Hebrew term refers to the irrevocable giving over of things or persons to the LORD, often by totally destroying them; also in verse 26.   ᵇ5 That is, symbols of the goddess Asherah; here and elsewhere in Deuteronomy

---

7:2 God told the Israelites to completely destroy their enemies. How can a God of love and mercy wipe out everyone, even children? Although God is loving and merciful, he is also just. These enemy nations were as much a part of God's creation as Israel was, and God does not allow evil to continue unchecked. God had punished Israel by keeping out of the promised land all those who had disobeyed. The command to destroy these nations was both a judgment (9:4–6) and a safety measure. On one hand, the people living in the land were being judged for their sin, and Israel was God's instrument of judgment—just as God would one day use other nations to judge Israel for its sin (2 Chronicles 36:17; Isaiah 10:12). On the other hand, God's command was designed to protect the nation of Israel from being ruined by the idolatry

and immorality of its enemies. To think that God is too "nice" to judge sin would be to underestimate him.

7:5 Asherah was a Canaanite mother goddess of the sea, associated with Baal. Baal was the most worshiped god of the Canaanites. Most often cast in the form of a bull, he symbolized strength and fertility and was considered the god of agriculture. Asherah was Baal's female consort. She was worshiped by means of wooden pillars (here called "poles").

7:6–8 How did Israel deserve to be chosen above all of the other nations at that time? It was not a matter of Israel's merit, but of God keeping his promise to their ancestors. Just as God chose the nation of Israel, he has chosen all believers today to be a part of his treasured possession. Similarly, it is not because of our merit that we have come to faith in Christ. Instead God chose us out of his goodness and grace.

7:22
a Ex 23:28-30

who hide from you have perished. ²¹Do not be terrified by them, for the LORD your God, who is among you, is a great and awesome God. ²²The LORD your God will drive out those nations before you, little by little. *a* You will not be allowed to eliminate them all at once, or the wild animals will multiply around you. ²³But the LORD your God will deliver them over to you, throwing them into great confusion until they are destroyed. ²⁴He will give their kings into your hand, and you will wipe out their names from under heaven. No one will be able to stand up against you; you will destroy them. ²⁵The images of their gods you are to burn *b* in the fire. Do not covet the silver and gold on them, and do not take it for yourselves, or you will be ensnared *c* by it, for it is detestable to the LORD your God. ²⁶Do not bring a detestable thing into your house or you, like it, will be set apart for destruction. Utterly abhor and detest it, for it is set apart for destruction.

7:25
b 1Ch 14:12
c Jdg 8:27

Do Not Forget the LORD

8:1
d Dt 4:1

8 Be careful to follow every command I am giving you today, so that you may live *d* and increase and may enter and possess the land that the LORD promised on oath to your forefathers. ²Remember how the LORD your God led you all the way in the desert these forty years, to humble you and to test you in order to know what was in your heart, whether or not you would keep his commands. ³He humbled you, causing you to hunger and then feeding you with manna, which neither you nor your fathers had known, to teach you that man does not live on bread alone but on every word that comes from the mouth of the LORD. *e* ⁴Your

8:3
e Mt 4:4*; Lk 4:4*

DANGER IN PLENTY
"When you eat and are satisfied, be careful that you do not forget the LORD" (Deuteronomy 6:11, 12). It is often most difficult to follow God when life is easy—we can fall prey to temptation and fall away from God. Here are some notable examples of this truth.

Person	Reference	Comment
ADAM	Genesis 3	Adam lived in a perfect world and had a perfect relationship with God. His needs were met; he had everything. But he fell to Satan's deception.
NOAH	Genesis 9	Noah and his family had survived the flood, and the whole world was theirs. They were prosperous, and life was easy. Noah shamed himself by becoming drunk and cursed his son Ham.
THE NATION OF ISRAEL	Judges 2	God had given Israel the promised land—rest at last with no more wandering. But as soon as brave and faithful Joshua died, they fell into the idolatrous practices of the Canaanites.
DAVID	2 Samuel 11	David ruled well, and Israel was a dominant nation politically, economically, and militarily. In the midst of prosperity and success, he committed adultery with Bathsheba and had her husband, Uriah, murdered.
SOLOMON	1 Kings 11	Solomon truly had it all: power, wealth, fame, and wisdom. But his very abundance was the source of his downfall. He loved his pagan, idolatrous wives so much that he allowed himself and Israel to copy their detestable religious rites.

7:21-24 Moses told the Israelites that God would destroy Israel's enemies, but not all at once. God had the power to destroy those nations instantly, but he chose to do it in stages, "little by little." In the same way and with the same power, God could miraculously and instantaneously change your life. Usually, however, he chooses to help you gradually, teaching you one lesson at a time. Rather than expecting instant spiritual maturity and solutions to all your problems, slow down and work one step at a time, trusting God to make up the difference between where you should be and where you are now. You'll soon look back and see that a miraculous transformation has occurred.

7:25, 26 Moses warned Israel against becoming ensnared by the idols of the defeated nations by coveting the silver or gold on them. We may think it's all right to be close to sin as long as we don't participate. "After all," we say, "I won't do anything wrong!" But being close can hurt us as we become attracted and finally give in. Avoid the snare of sin by first reigning in your desires. Then stay as far away from sin as you can.

8:3 Jesus quoted this verse when the devil tempted him to turn stones into bread (Matthew 4:4). Many people think that life is based on satisfying their appetites. If they can earn enough

money to dress, eat, and play in high style, they think they are living "the good life." But such things do not satisfy our deepest longings. In the end they leave us empty and dissatisfied. Real life, according to Moses, comes from total commitment to God and living by every word that comes from him. How can we live by his word? (1) Recognize our need for it. (2) Agree that God alone can truly satisfy us. (3) Pray for God's presence, wisdom, and direction as we read. (4) Savor the relationship you have with him through Christ. (5) Practice what he teaches you.

8:4 It's usually easy for us to take God's protection for granted. We seldom take notice or thank God when our car doesn't break down, our clothes don't rip, or our tools don't break. The people of Israel also failed to take notice, it seems, for they didn't even notice that in 40 years of wandering in the desert, their clothes didn't wear out and their feet didn't swell. Thus, they did not remember to give thanks to God for these blessings. What has been working well for you? What has been giving you good service? What has been lasting for a long time without breaking down or apart? Remember to thank God for these quiet blessings.

clothes did not wear out and your feet did not swell during these forty years.[f] 5 Know then in your heart that as a man disciplines his son, so the LORD your God disciplines you.[g]

6 Observe the commands of the LORD your God, walking in his ways and revering him. 7 For the LORD your God is bringing you into a good land—a land with streams and pools of water, with springs flowing in the valleys and hills;[h] 8 a land with wheat and barley, vines and fig trees, pomegranates, olive oil and honey; 9 a land where bread will not be scarce and you will lack nothing; a land where the rocks are iron and you can dig copper out of the hills.

10 When you have eaten and are satisfied,[i] praise the LORD your God for the good land he has given you. 11 Be careful that you do not forget the LORD your God, failing to observe his commands, his laws and his decrees that I am giving you this day. 12 Otherwise, when you eat and are satisfied, when you build fine houses and settle down, 13 and when your herds and flocks grow large and your silver and gold increase and all you have is multiplied, 14 then your heart will become proud and you will forget the LORD your God, who brought you out of Egypt, out of the land of slavery. 15 He led you through the vast and dreadful desert, that thirsty and waterless land, with its venomous snakes[j] and scorpions. He brought you water out of hard rock.[k] 16 He gave you manna to eat in the desert, something your fathers had never known,[l] to humble and to test you so that in the end it might go well with you. 17 You may say to yourself, "My power and the strength of my hands have produced this wealth for me." 18 But remember the LORD your God, for it is he who gives you the ability to produce wealth,[m] and so confirms his covenant, which he swore to your forefathers, as it is today.

19 If you ever forget the LORD your God and follow other gods and worship and bow down to them, I testify against you today that you will surely be destroyed.[n] 20 Like the nations the LORD destroyed before you, so you will be destroyed for not obeying the LORD your God.

Not Because of Israel's Righteousness

9 Hear, O Israel. You are now about to cross the Jordan to go in and dispossess nations greater and stronger than you, with large cities that have walls up to the sky. 2 The people are strong and tall—Anakites! You know about them and have heard it said: "Who can stand up against the Anakites?"[o] 3 But be assured today that the LORD your God is the one who goes across ahead of you[p] like a devouring fire.[q] He will destroy them; he will subdue them before you. And you will drive them out and annihilate them quickly,[r] as the LORD has promised you.

4 After the LORD your God has driven them out before you, do not say to yourself,[s] "The LORD has brought me here to take possession of this land because of my righteousness." No, it is on account of the wickedness of these nations[t] that the LORD is going to drive them out before you. 5 It is not because of your righteousness or your integrity that you are going in to take possession of their land; but on account of the wickedness of these nations, the LORD your God will drive them out before you, to accomplish what he swore[u] to your fathers, to Abraham, Isaac and Jacob. 6 Understand, then, that it is not because of your righteousness that the LORD your God is giving you this good land to possess, for you are a stiff-necked people.[v]

The Golden Calf

7 Remember this and never forget how you provoked the LORD your God to anger in the desert. From the day you left Egypt until you arrived here, you have been rebellious against the LORD. 8 At Horeb you aroused the LORD's wrath so that he was angry enough to destroy you. 9 When I went up on the mountain to receive the tablets of stone, the tablets of the covenant that the LORD had made with you, I stayed on the mountain forty days and forty nights; I ate no bread and drank no water.[w] 10 The LORD gave me two stone tablets inscribed by the finger of God. On them were all the commandments the LORD proclaimed to you on the mountain out of the fire, on the day of the assembly.

8:4
[f] Dt 29:5

8:5
[g] Pr 3:11-12; Heb 12:5-11

8:7
[h] Dt 11:9-12

8:10
[i] Dt 6:10-12

8:15
[j] Nu 21:6
[k] Nu 20:11

8:16
[l] Ex 16:15

8:18
[m] Pr 10:22; Hos 2:8

8:19
[n] Dt 4:26; 30:18

9:2
[o] Nu 13:22,28,32-33

9:3
[p] Dt 31:3
[q] Dt 4:24
[r] Dt 7:23-24

9:4
[s] Dt 8:17
[t] Lev 18:21,24-30

9:5
[u] Ge 12:7

9:6
[v] ver 13

9:9
[w] Ex 24:12,15,18

8:10 This verse is traditionally cited as the reason we say grace before or after meals. Its purpose, however, was to warn the Israelites not to forget God when their needs and wants were satisfied. Let your table prayers serve as a constant reminder of the Lord's goodness to you and your duty to those who are less fortunate.

8:11–20 In times of plenty, we often take credit for our prosperity and become proud that our own hard work and cleverness have made us rich. It is easy to get so busy collecting and managing wealth that we push God right out of our lives. But it is God who gives us everything we have, and it is God who asks us to manage it for him.

9:2, 3 The Anakites were enormous people, some seven to nine feet tall. Goliath, probably a descendant of this race, was over nine feet tall (1 Samuel 17:4–7). Unfortunately, these great men used their stature as a means of intimidation rather than for noble causes. Their appearance alone frightened the Israelite spies (Numbers 13:28), and their bad reputation may have been the deciding factor that kept the Israelites out of the land 40 years earlier (Numbers 13; 14). Moses used all his persuasive power to convince his people that God could handle these bullies. He used the illustration of God as a devouring fire, for not even a giant could stand up to that.

9:12
ˣEx 32:7-8

9:13
ʸEx 32:9

9:14
ᶻEx 32:10

9:15
ᵃEx 32:15

9:18
ᵇEx 34:28

9:21
ᶜEx 32:20

9:22
ᵈNu 11:3
ᵉEx 17:7
ᶠNu 11:34

9:24
ᵍDt 31:27

9:25
ʰver 18

9:26
ⁱEx 32:11

9:29
ʲDt 4:20

¹¹At the end of the forty days and forty nights, the Lᴏʀᴅ gave me the two stone tablets, the tablets of the covenant. ¹²Then the Lᴏʀᴅ told me, "Go down from here at once, because your people whom you brought out of Egypt have become corrupt. ˣ They have turned away quickly from what I commanded them and have made a cast idol for themselves."

¹³And the Lᴏʀᴅ said to me, "I have seen this people ʸ, and they are a stiff-necked people indeed! ¹⁴Let me alone, ᶻ so that I may destroy them and blot out their name from under heaven. And I will make you into a nation stronger and more numerous than they."

¹⁵So I turned and went down from the mountain while it was ablaze with fire. And the two tablets of the covenant were in my hands. ᵃ ¹⁶When I looked, I saw that you had sinned against the Lᴏʀᴅ your God; you had made for yourselves an idol cast in the shape of a calf. You had turned aside quickly from the way that the Lᴏʀᴅ had commanded you. ¹⁷So I took the two tablets and threw them out of my hands, breaking them to pieces before your eyes.

¹⁸Then once again I fell ᵇ prostrate before the Lᴏʀᴅ for forty days and forty nights; I ate no bread and drank no water, because of all the sin you had committed, doing what was evil in the Lᴏʀᴅ's sight and so provoking him to anger. ¹⁹I feared the anger and wrath of the Lᴏʀᴅ, for he was angry enough with you to destroy you. But again the Lᴏʀᴅ listened to me. ²⁰And the Lᴏʀᴅ was angry enough with Aaron to destroy him, but at that time I prayed for Aaron too. ²¹Also I took that sinful thing of yours, the calf you had made, and burned it in the fire. Then I crushed it and ground it to powder as fine as dust and threw the dust into a stream that flowed down the mountain. ᶜ

²²You also made the Lᴏʀᴅ angry at Taberah, ᵈ at Massah ᵉ and at Kibroth Hattaavah. ᶠ

²³And when the Lᴏʀᴅ sent you out from Kadesh Barnea, he said, "Go up and take possession of the land I have given you." But you rebelled against the command of the Lᴏʀᴅ your God. You did not trust him or obey him. ²⁴You have been rebellious against the Lᴏʀᴅ ever since I have known you. ᵍ

²⁵I lay prostrate before the Lᴏʀᴅ those forty days and forty nights because the Lᴏʀᴅ had said he would destroy you. ʰ ²⁶I prayed to the Lᴏʀᴅ and said, "O Sovereign Lᴏʀᴅ, do not destroy your people, your own inheritance that you redeemed by your great power and brought out of Egypt with a mighty hand. ⁱ ²⁷Remember your servants Abraham, Isaac and Jacob. Overlook the stubbornness of this people, their wickedness and their sin. ²⁸Otherwise, the country from which you brought us will say, 'Because the Lᴏʀᴅ was not able to take them into the land he had promised them, and because he hated them, he brought them out to put them to death in the desert.' ²⁹But they are your people, your inheritance ʲ that you brought out by your great power and your outstretched arm."

ᵃ15 Or *And I had the two tablets of the covenant with me, one in each hand*

OBEDIENCE
Deuteronomy 8:1 tells us to obey God's commandments. We do this by obeying God with . . .

OUR HEART	By loving him more than any relationship, activity, achievement, or possession
OUR WILL	By committing ourselves completely to him
OUR MIND	By seeking to know him and his Word, so his principles and values form the foundation of all we think and do
OUR BODY	By recognizing that our strengths, talents, and sexuality are given to us by God to be used for pleasure and fulfillment according to his rules, not ours
OUR FINANCES . . .	By deciding that all of the resources we have ultimately come from God, and that we are to be managers of them and not owners
OUR FUTURE	By deciding to make service to God and man the main purpose of our life's work

---

9:18 From the record of this event in Exodus 32, it seems as though Moses acted immediately, grinding the golden calf into powder, and forcing the people to drink water mixed with it. But evidently, Moses had first spent 40 days and nights interceding for the people.

9:23 Moses was reminding the people of the nation's unbelief 40 years earlier, when they had been afraid to enter Canaan. The Israelites had not believed God would be able to help them in spite of all he had already done. They refused to follow because they looked only to their own limited resources instead of to God. Unbelief is the root of many sins and problems. When you feel lost, it may be because you're looking everywhere but to God for your help and guidance. (See Psalms 81:6–12; 95:8; 106:13–20; Hebrews 3.)

Tablets Like the First Ones

10 At that time the LORD said to me, "Chisel out two stone tablets[k] like the first ones and come up to me on the mountain. Also make a wooden chest.[a] ²I will write on the tablets the words that were on the first tablets, which you broke. Then you are to put them in the chest."[l]

³So I made the ark out of acacia wood and chiseled[m] out two stone tablets like the first ones, and I went up on the mountain with the two tablets in my hands. ⁴The LORD wrote on these tablets what he had written before, the Ten Commandments he had proclaimed[n] to you on the mountain, out of the fire, on the day of the assembly. And the LORD gave them to me. ⁵Then I came back down the mountain and put the tablets in the ark[o] I had made, as the LORD commanded me, and they are there now.

⁶(The Israelites traveled from the wells of the Jaakanites to Moserah.[p] There Aaron died and was buried, and Eleazar his son succeeded him as priest. ⁷From there they traveled to Gudgodah and on to Jotbathah, a land with streams of water. [q] ⁸At that time the LORD set apart the tribe of Levi[r] to carry the ark of the covenant of the LORD, to stand before the LORD to minister[s] and to pronounce blessings[t] in his name, as they still do today. ⁹That is why the Levites have no share or inheritance among their brothers; the LORD is their inheritance, as the LORD your God told them.)

¹⁰Now I had stayed on the mountain forty days and nights, as I did the first time, and the LORD listened to me at this time also. It was not his will to destroy you. ¹¹"Go," the LORD said to me, "and lead the people on their way, so that they may enter and possess the land that I swore to their fathers to give them."

Fear the LORD

¹²And now, O Israel, what does the LORD your God ask of you[u] but to fear the LORD your God, to walk in all his ways, to love him, to serve the LORD your God with all your heart[v] and with all your soul, ¹³and to observe the LORD's commands and decrees that I am giving you today for your own good?

¹⁴To the LORD your God belong the heavens, even the highest heavens,[w] the earth and everything in it. ¹⁵Yet the LORD set his affection on your forefathers and loved[x] them, and he chose you, their descendants, above all the nations, as it is today. ¹⁶Circumcise[y] your hearts, therefore, and do not be stiff-necked[z] any longer. ¹⁷For the LORD your God is God of gods and Lord of lords, the great God, mighty and awesome, who shows no partiality[a] and accepts no bribes. ¹⁸He defends the cause of the fatherless and the widow,[b] and loves the alien, giving him food and clothing. ¹⁹And you are to love those who are aliens, for you yourselves were aliens in Egypt. [c] ²⁰Fear the LORD your God and serve him. Hold fast[d] to him and take your oaths in his name. [e] ²¹He is your praise; he is your God, who performed for you those great and awesome wonders you saw with your own eyes. ²²Your forefathers who went down into Egypt were seventy in all,[f] and now the LORD your God has made you as numerous as the stars in the sky.

ᵃ 1 That is, an ark

10:1
ᵏEx 25:10; 34:1-2
10:2
ˡEx 25:16,21
10:3
ᵐEx 34:4
10:4
ⁿEx 20:1
10:5
ᵒEx 40:20
10:6
ᵖNu 33:30-31,38
10:7
�q Nu 33:32-34
10:8
ʳNu 3:6
ˢDt 18:5
ᵗDt 21:5
10:12
ᵘMic 6:8
ᵛDt 6:5
10:14
ʷ1Ki 8:27
10:15
ˣDt 4:37
10:16
ʸJer 4:4
ᶻDt 9:6
10:17
ᵃAc 10:34
10:18
ᵇPs 68:5
10:19
ᶜLev 19:34
10:20
ᵈDt 11:22
ᵉPs 63:11
10:22
ᶠGe 46:26-27

10:5 The tablets of the law were still in the ark about 500 years later when Solomon put it in his newly built temple (1 Kings 8:9). The ark last appears in the Israelite's history during the reign of Josiah, about 300 years after Solomon (2 Chronicles 35:3).

10:12, 13 Often we ask, "What does God expect of me?" Here Moses gives a summary that is simple in form and easy to remember. Here are the essentials: (1) Fear God (have respect for him). (2) Walk in all his ways (follow him). (3) Love him. (4) Serve him with all your heart and soul. (5) Observe his commands. How often we complicate faith with man-made rules, regulations, and requirements. Are you frustrated and burned out from trying hard to please God? Concentrate on his real requirements and find peace. Respect, follow, love, serve, and obey.

10:16–19 God required all male Israelites to be circumcised, but he wanted them to go beyond performing the surgery to

understanding its meaning. They needed to submit to God inside, in their hearts, as well as outside, in their bodies. Then they could begin to imitate God's love and justice in their relationships with others. If our hearts are right with God, then our relationships with other people can be made right too. When your heart has been cleansed and you have been reconciled to God, you will begin to see a difference in the way you treat others.

10:17 In saying that the Lord is God of gods and Lord of lords, Moses was distinguishing the true God from all the local gods worshiped throughout the land. Then Moses went a step further, calling God "mighty and awesome." He has such awesome power and justice that people cannot stand before him without his mercy. Fortunately, his mercy toward his people is unlimited. When we begin to grasp the extent of God's mercy toward us, we see what true love is and how deeply God loves us. Although our sins deserve severe judgment, God has chosen to show love and mercy to all who seek him.

10:20 "Take your oaths in his name" means that God alone should have their allegiance.

Love and Obey the LORD

11:1
g Dt 10:12

11 Love *g* the LORD your God and keep his requirements, his decrees, his laws and his commands always. ²Remember today that your children were not the ones who saw and experienced the discipline of the LORD your God: his majesty, his mighty hand, his outstretched arm; ³the signs he performed and the things he did in the heart of Egypt, both to Pharaoh king of Egypt and to his whole country; ⁴what he did to the Egyptian army, to its horses and chariots, how he overwhelmed them with the waters of the Red Sea ᵃ as they were pursuing you, and how the LORD brought lasting ruin on them. ⁵It was not your children who saw what he did for you in the desert until you arrived at this place, ⁶and what he did *h* to Dathan and Abiram, sons of Eliab the Reubenite, when the earth opened its mouth right in the middle of all Israel and swallowed them up with their households, their tents and every living thing that belonged to them. ⁷But it was your own eyes that saw all these great things the LORD has done.

11:6
h Nu 16:1-35

⁸Observe therefore all the commands I am giving you today, so that you may have the strength to go in and take over the land that you are crossing the Jordan to possess, *i* ⁹and so that you may live long *j* in the land that the LORD swore to your forefathers to give to them and their descendants, a land flowing with milk and honey. *k* ¹⁰The land you are entering to take over is not like the land of Egypt, from which you have come, where you planted your seed and irrigated it by foot as in a vegetable garden. ¹¹But the land you are crossing the Jordan to take possession of is a land of mountains and valleys that drinks rain from heaven. *l* ¹²It is a land the LORD your God cares for; the eyes of the LORD your God are continually on it from the beginning of the year to its end.

11:8
i Jos 1:7

11:9
j Dt 4:40
k Ex 3:8

11:11
l Dt 8:7

¹³So if you faithfully obey the commands I am giving you today—to love the LORD your God and to serve him with all your heart and with all your soul— ¹⁴then I will send rain *m* on your land in its season, both autumn and spring rains, *n* so that you may gather in your grain, new wine and oil. ¹⁵I will provide grass in the fields for your cattle, and you will eat and be satisfied.

11:14
m Dt 28:12
n Joel 2:23

¹⁶Be careful, or you will be enticed to turn away and worship other gods and bow down to them. ¹⁷Then the LORD's anger will burn against you, and he will shut *o* the heavens so that it will not rain and the ground will yield no produce, and you will soon perish *p* from the good land the LORD is giving you. ¹⁸Fix these words of mine in your hearts and minds; tie them as symbols on your hands and bind them on your foreheads. *q* ¹⁹Teach them to your children, *r* talking about them when you sit at home and when you walk along the road, when you lie down and when you get up. *s* ²⁰Write them on the doorframes of your houses and on your gates, *t* ²¹so that your days and the days of your children may be many in the land that the LORD swore to give your forefathers, as many as the days that the heavens are above the earth.

11:17
o 1Ki 8:35
p Dt 4:26

11:18
q Dt 6:6-8

11:19
r Dt 6:7
s Dt 4:9-10

11:20
t Dt 6:9

11:22
u Dt 6:17

²²If you carefully observe *u* all these commands I am giving you to follow—to love the LORD your God, to walk in all his ways and to hold fast to him— ²³then the LORD will drive out all these nations before you, and you will dispossess nations larger and stronger than you. *v* ²⁴Every place where you set your foot will be yours: *w* Your territory will extend from the desert to Lebanon, and from the Euphrates River to the western sea. ᵇ ²⁵No man will be able to stand against you. The LORD your God, as he promised you, will put the terror and fear of you on the whole land, wherever you go. *x*

11:23
v Dt 9:1

11:24
w Ge 15:18;
Ex 23:31; Jos 1:3

11:25
x Dt 7:24

11:26
y Dt 30:1,15,19

²⁶See, I am setting before you today a blessing and a curse *y*— ²⁷the blessing *z* if you obey

11:27
z Dt 28:1-14

ᵃ4 Hebrew *Yam Suph*; that is, Sea of Reeds   ᵇ24 That is, the Mediterranean

---

11:7 Israel had strong reasons to believe in God and obey his commands. They had witnessed a parade of mighty miracles that demonstrated God's love and care for them. Incredibly, they still had trouble remaining faithful. Because few of us have seen such dramatic miracles, it may seem even more difficult for us to obey God and remain faithful. But we have the Bible, the written record of God's acts throughout history. Reading God's Word gives us a panoramic view of both the miracles Israel saw and others they didn't see. The lessons from the past, the instructions for the present, and the glimpses into the future give us many opportunities to strengthen our faith in God.

11:26 What is God's curse? It is not a magician's spell. To understand it, we must remember the conditions of the covenant between God and Israel. Both parties had agreed to the terms.

The blessings would benefit Israel if they kept their part of the covenant: They would receive the land, live there forever, have fruitful crops, and expel their enemies. The curse would fall on Israel only if they broke their agreement; then they would forfeit God's blessing and would be in danger of crop failure, invasion, and expulsion from their land. Joshua later reviewed these blessings and curses with the entire nation (Joshua 8:34).

11:26 It is amazing that God set before the Israelites a choice between a blessing and a curse. It is even more amazing that most of them, through their disobedience, chose the curse. We have the same fundamental choice today. We can live for ourselves or live in service to God. To choose our own way is to travel on a dead-end road, but to choose God's way is to receive eternal life (John 5:24).

the commands of the LORD your God that I am giving you today; 28 the curse if you disobey[a] the commands of the LORD your God and turn from the way that I command you today by following other gods, which you have not known. 29 When the LORD your God has brought you into the land you are entering to possess, you are to proclaim on Mount Gerizim the blessings, and on Mount Ebal the curses. [b] 30 As you know, these mountains are across the Jordan, west of the road,[a] toward the setting sun, near the great trees of Moreh,[c] in the territory of those Canaanites living in the Arabah in the vicinity of Gilgal. 31 You are about to cross the Jordan to enter and take possession of the land the LORD your God is giving you. When you have taken it over and are living there, 32 be sure that you obey all the decrees and laws I am setting before you today.

11:28
[a] Dt 28:15

11:29
[b] Dt 27:12-13;
Jos 8:33

11:30
[c] Ge 12:6

3. Laws for proper worship
The One Place of Worship

12 These are the decrees and laws you must be careful to follow in the land that the LORD, the God of your fathers, has given you to possess—as long as you live in the land. [d] 2 Destroy completely all the places on the high mountains and on the hills and under every spreading tree where the nations you are dispossessing worship their gods. 3 Break down their altars, smash their sacred stones and burn their Asherah poles in the fire; cut down the idols of their gods and wipe out their names from those places.

12:1
[d] Dt 4:9-10

4 You must not worship the LORD your God in their way. 5 But you are to seek the place the LORD your God will choose from among all your tribes to put his Name there for his dwelling. To that place you must go; 6 there bring your burnt offerings and sacrifices, your tithes and special gifts, what you have vowed to give and your freewill offerings, and the firstborn of your herds and flocks. 7 There, in the presence of the LORD your God, you and your families shall eat and shall rejoice [e] in everything you have put your hand to, because the LORD your God has blessed you.

12:7
[e] ver 12,18;
Dt 14:26

8 You are not to do as we do here today, everyone as he sees fit, 9 since you have not yet reached the resting place and the inheritance the LORD your God is giving you. 10 But you will cross the Jordan and settle in the land the LORD your God is giving you as an inheritance, and he will give you rest from all your enemies around you so that you will live in safety. 11 Then to the place the LORD your God will choose as a dwelling for his Name [f]—there you are to bring everything I command you: your burnt offerings and sacrifices, your tithes and special gifts, and all the choice possessions you have vowed to the LORD. 12 And there rejoice [g] before the LORD your God, you, your sons and daughters, your menservants and maidservants, and the Levites from your towns, who have no allotment or inheritance [h] of their own. 13 Be careful not to sacrifice your burnt offerings anywhere you please. 14 Offer them only at the place the LORD will choose in one of your tribes, and there observe everything I command you.

12:11
[f] ver 5

12:12
[g] ver 7
[h] Dt 10:9

15 Nevertheless, you may slaughter your animals in any of your towns and eat as much of the meat as you want, as if it were gazelle or deer,[i] according to the blessing the LORD your God gives you. Both the ceremonially unclean and the clean may eat it. 16 But you must not

12:15
[i] Dt 14:5

12:16
[j] Lev 17:10-12

[a] 30 Or *Jordan, westward*

12:2, 3 When taking over a nation, the Israelites were supposed to destroy every pagan altar and idol in the land. God knew it would be easy for them to change their beliefs if they started using those altars, so nothing was to remain that might tempt them to worship idols. We too should ruthlessly find and remove any centers of false worship in our lives. These may be activities, attitudes, possessions, relationships, places, or habits—anything that tempts us to turn our hearts from God and do wrong. We should never flatter ourselves by thinking we're too strong to be tempted. Israel learned that lesson the hard way.

12:12, 18 The Hebrews placed great emphasis on family worship. Whether offering a sacrifice or attending a great feast, the family was often together. This gave the children a healthy attitude toward worship, and it put extra meaning into it for the adults. Watching a family member confess his or her sin was just as important as celebrating a great holiday together. Although there are appropriate times to separate people by ages, some of the most meaningful worship can be experienced only when shared by old and young.

12:13, 14 While the pagans offered sacrifices to their gods, they offered them in many places. In contrast, the Israelites were only to offer sacrifices in the prescribed manner and in the prescribed places. This restriction was meant to ensure purity of worship for the nation of Israel. Later, they would neglect this injunction and offer sacrifices at the high places where pagan deities were worshiped. (See, for example, 2 Kings 23 where Josiah destroyed the other altars.) We should take steps to safeguard the purity of worship in our congregations. If we all individualized and customized worship to suit our own preferences, we would lose the benefit of worshiping as a body of believers.

12:16 Eating blood was forbidden for several reasons: (1) it was an integral part of the pagan practices of the land the Israelites were about to enter; (2) it represented life, which is sacred to God; (3) it reminded the people that life and strength come from God, not from drinking or eating blood; (4) it was a symbol of the sacrifice that had to be made for sin. (For more on why eating blood was prohibited, see the note on Leviticus 17:14.)

eat the blood;^j pour it out on the ground like water. ¹⁷You must not eat in your own towns the tithe of your grain and new wine and oil, or the firstborn of your herds and flocks, or whatever you have vowed to give, or your freewill offerings or special gifts. ¹⁸Instead, you are to eat them in the presence of the LORD your God at the place the LORD your God will choose—you, your sons and daughters, your menservants and maidservants, and the Levites from your towns—and you are to rejoice ^k before the LORD your God in everything you put your hand to. ¹⁹Be careful not to neglect the Levites^l as long as you live in your land.

²⁰When the LORD your God has enlarged your territory as he promised ^m you, and you crave meat and say, "I would like some meat," then you may eat as much of it as you want. ²¹If the place where the LORD your God chooses to put his Name is too far away from you, you may slaughter animals from the herds and flocks the LORD has given you, as I have commanded you, and in your own towns you may eat as much of them as you want. ²²Eat them as you would gazelle or deer. ⁿ Both the ceremonially unclean and the clean may eat. ²³But be sure you do not eat the blood, ^o because the blood is the life, and you must not eat the life with the meat. ²⁴You must not eat the blood; pour it out on the ground like water. ²⁵Do not eat it, so that it may go well^p with you and your children after you, because you will be doing what is right in the eyes of the LORD.

²⁶But take your consecrated things and whatever you have vowed to give, and go to the place the LORD will choose. ²⁷Present your burnt offerings ^q on the altar of the LORD your God, both the meat and the blood. The blood of your sacrifices must be poured beside the altar of the LORD your God, but you may eat the meat. ²⁸Be careful to obey all these regulations I am giving you, so that it may always go well with you and your children after you, because you will be doing what is good and right in the eyes of the LORD your God.

²⁹The LORD your God will cut off before you the nations you are about to invade and dispossess. But when you have driven them out and settled in their land, ³⁰and after they have been destroyed before you, be careful not to be ensnared by inquiring about their gods, saying, "How do these nations serve their gods? We will do the same." ³¹You must not worship the LORD your God in their way, because in worshiping their gods, they do all kinds of detestable things the LORD hates. They even burn their sons ^r and daughters in the fire as sacrifices to their gods.

³²See that you do all I command you; do not add ^s to it or take away from it.

Worshiping Other Gods

13 If a prophet,^t or one who foretells by dreams, appears among you and announces to you a miraculous sign or wonder, ²and if the sign or wonder of which he has spoken takes place, and he says, "Let us follow other gods" (gods you have not known) "and let us worship them," ³you must not listen to the words of that prophet or dreamer. The LORD your God is testing ^u you to find out whether you love him with all your heart and with all your soul. ⁴It is the LORD your God you must follow, ^v and him you must revere. Keep his commands and obey him; serve him and hold fast to him. ⁵That prophet or dreamer must be put to death, because he preached rebellion against the LORD your God, who brought you out of Egypt and redeemed you from the land of slavery; he has tried to turn you from the way the LORD your God commanded you to follow. You must purge the evil from among you.

12:18
^kver 7,12

12:19
^lDt 14:27

12:20
^mGe 15:18;
Dt 11:24

12:22
ⁿver 15

12:23
^over 16;
Lev 17:11,14

12:25
^pDt 4:40

12:27
^qLev 1:5,9,13

12:31
^rDt 18:10

12:32
^sDt 4:2

13:1
^tMt 24:24

13:3
^uDt 8:2,16

13:4
^v2Ki 23:3

12:30, 31 God did not want the Israelites even to ask about the pagan religions surrounding them. Idolatry completely permeated the land of Canaan. It was too easy to get drawn into the subtle temptations of seemingly harmless practices. Sometimes curiosity can cause us to stumble. Knowledge of evil is harmful if the evil becomes too tempting to resist. To resist curiosity about harmful practices shows discretion and obedience.

13:1–3 Attractive leaders are not always led by God. Moses warned the Israelites against false prophets who encouraged worship of other gods. New ideas from inspiring people may sound good, but we must judge them by whether or not they are consistent with God's Word. When people claim to speak for God today, check them in these areas: Are they telling the truth? Is their focus on God? Are their words consistent with what you already know to be true? Some people speak the truth while directing you toward God, but others speak persuasively

while directing you toward themselves. It is even possible to say the right words but still lead people in the wrong direction. God is not against new ideas, but he is for discernment. When you hear a new, attractive idea, examine it carefully before getting too excited. False prophets are still around today. The wise person will carefully test ideas against the truth of God's Word.

13:2–11 The Israelites were warned not to listen to false prophets or to anyone else who tried to get them to worship other gods—even if this person was a close friend or family member. The temptation to abandon God's commands often sneaks up on us. It may come not with a loud shout but in a whispering doubt. And whispers can be very persuasive, especially if they come from loved ones. But love for relatives should not take precedence over devotion to God. We can overcome whispered temptations by pouring out our hearts to God in prayer and by diligently studying his Word.

⁶If your very own brother, or your son or daughter, or the wife you love, or your closest friend secretly entices ʷ you, saying, "Let us go and worship other gods" (gods that neither you nor your fathers have known, ⁷gods of the peoples around you, whether near or far, from one end of the land to the other), ⁸do not yield to him or listen to him. Show him no pity. Do not spare him or shield him. ⁹You must certainly put him to death. ˣ Your hand must be the first in putting him to death, and then the hands of all the people. ¹⁰Stone him to death, because he tried to turn you away from the LORD your God, who brought you out of Egypt, out of the land of slavery. ¹¹Then all Israel will hear and be afraid,ʸ and no one among you will do such an evil thing again.

¹²If you hear it said about one of the towns the LORD your God is giving you to live in ¹³that wicked men ᶻ have arisen among you and have led the people of their town astray, saying, "Let us go and worship other gods" (gods you have not known), ¹⁴then you must inquire, probe and investigate it thoroughly. And if it is true and it has been proved that this detestable thing has been done among you, ¹⁵you must certainly put to the sword all who live in that town. Destroy it completely,ᵃ both its people and its livestock. ¹⁶Gather all the plunder of the town into the middle of the public square and completely burn the town and all its plunder as a whole burnt offering to the LORD your God. It is to remain a ruinᵃ forever, never to be rebuilt. ¹⁷None of those condemned thingsᵃ shall be found in your hands, so that the LORD will turn from his fierce anger;ᵇ he will show you mercy, have compassion on you, and increase your numbers, as he promised on oath to your forefathers, ¹⁸because you obey the LORD your God, keeping all his commands that I am giving you today and doing what is right in his eyes.

Clean and Unclean Food

14 You are the childrenᶜ of the LORD your God. Do not cut yourselves or shave the front of your heads for the dead, ²for you are a people holy to the LORD your God. Out of all the peoples on the face of the earth, the LORD has chosen you to be his treasured possession.ᵈ

³Do not eat any detestable thing. ᵉ ⁴These are the animals you may eat:ᶠ the ox, the sheep, the goat, ⁵the deer, the gazelle, the roe deer, the wild goat, the ibex, the antelope and the mountain sheep. ᵇ ⁶You may eat any animal that has a split hoof divided in two and that chews the cud. ⁷However, of those that chew the cud or that have a split hoof completely divided you may not eat the camel, the rabbit or the coney.ᶜ Although they chew the cud, they do not have a split hoof; they are ceremonially unclean for you. ⁸The pig is also unclean; although it has a split hoof, it does not chew the cud. You are not to eat their meat or touch their carcasses.ᵍ

⁹Of all the creatures living in the water, you may eat any that has fins and scales. ¹⁰But anything that does not have fins and scales you may not eat; for you it is unclean.

¹¹You may eat any clean bird. ¹²But these you may not eat: the eagle, the vulture, the black vulture, ¹³the red kite, the black kite, any kind of falcon, ¹⁴any kind of raven, ¹⁵the horned owl, the screech owl, the gull, any kind of hawk, ¹⁶the little owl, the great owl, the white owl, ¹⁷the desert owl, the osprey, the cormorant, ¹⁸the stork, any kind of heron, the hoopoe and the bat.

ᵃ 15, 17 The Hebrew term refers to the irrevocable giving over of things or persons to the LORD, often by totally destroying them.   ᵇ 5 The precise identification of some of the birds and animals in this chapter is uncertain.
ᶜ 7 That is, the hyrax or rock badger

13:6
ʷDt 17:2-7

13:9
ˣDt 17:5,7

13:11
ʸDt 19:20

13:13
ᶻver 2,6

13:16
ᵃJos 8:28

13:17
ᵇNu 25:4

14:1
ᶜLev 21:5; Ro 8:14
14:2
ᵈDt 7:6

14:3
ᵉEze 4:14
14:4
ᶠLev 11:2-45

14:8
ᵍLev 11:26-27

13:12–16 A city that completely rejected God was to be destroyed so as not to lead the rest of the nation astray. But Israel was not to take action against a city until the rumor about its rejecting God was proven true. This guideline saved many lives when the leaders of Israel wrongly accused three tribes of falling away from their faith (Joshua 22). If we hear of friends who have wandered from the Lord or of entire congregations that have fallen away, we should check the facts and find the truth before doing or saying anything that could prove harmful. There are times, of course, when God wants us to take action—to rebuke a wayward friend, to discipline a child, to reject false teaching—but first we must be sure we have all the facts straight.

14:1 The actions described here refer to a cult of the dead. Many other religions today have some kind of worship of or service to the dead. But Christianity and Judaism are very different from other religions because they focus on serving God in this life.

Don't let concern or worry over the dead distract you from the tasks that God has for you while you are still alive.

14:3–21 Why was Israel forbidden to eat certain foods? There are several reasons: (1) Predatory animals ate the blood of other animals, and scavengers ate dead animals. Because the people could not eat blood or animals they found dead, they could not eat animals that did these things either. (2) Some forbidden animals had bad associations in the Israelite culture, as bats, snakes, and spiders do for some people today. Some may have been used in pagan religious practices (Isaiah 66:17). To the Israelites, the unclean animals represented sin or unhealthy habits. (3) Perhaps some restrictions were given to Israel just to remind them continually that they were a different and separate people committed to God. Although we no longer must follow these laws about food (Acts 10:9–16), we can still learn from them the lesson that holiness is to be carried into all parts of life. We can't

¹⁹All flying insects that swarm are unclean to you; do not eat them. ²⁰But any winged creature that is clean you may eat.

²¹Do not eat anything you find already dead. ^h You may give it to an alien living in any of your towns, and he may eat it, or you may sell it to a foreigner. But you are a people holy to the LORD your God.

Do not cook a young goat in its mother's milk. ⁱ

14:21
^hLev 17:15
ⁱEx 34:26

Tithes

²²Be sure to set aside a tenth^j of all that your fields produce each year. ²³Eat the tithe of your grain, new wine and oil, and the firstborn of your herds and flocks in the presence of the LORD your God at the place he will choose as a dwelling for his Name, ^k so that you may learn to revere the LORD your God always. ²⁴But if that place is too distant and you have been blessed by the LORD your God and cannot carry your tithe (because the place where the LORD will choose to put his Name is so far away), ²⁵then exchange your tithe for silver, and take the silver with you and go to the place the LORD your God will choose. ²⁶Use the silver to buy whatever you like: cattle, sheep, wine or other fermented drink, or anything you wish. Then you and your household shall eat there in the presence of the LORD your God and rejoice. ^l ²⁷And do not neglect the Levites living in your towns, for they have no allotment or inheritance of their own. ^m

²⁸At the end of every three years, bring all the tithes of that year's produce and store it in your towns, ⁿ ²⁹so that the Levites (who have no allotment or inheritance of their own) and the aliens, ^o the fatherless and the widows who live in your towns may come and eat and be satisfied, and so that the LORD your God may bless^p you in all the work of your hands.

14:22
^jLev 27:30
14:23
^kDt 12:5

14:26
^lDt 12:7-8

14:27
^mNu 18:20

14:28
ⁿDt 26:12
14:29
^oDt 26:12
^pDt 15:10

The Year for Canceling Debts

15 At the end of every seven years you must cancel debts. ^q ²This is how it is to be done: Every creditor shall cancel the loan he has made to his fellow Israelite. He shall not require payment from his fellow Israelite or brother, because the LORD's time for canceling debts has been proclaimed. ³You may require payment from a foreigner, ^r but you must cancel any debt your brother owes you. ⁴However, there should be no poor among you, for in the land the LORD your God is giving you to possess as your inheritance, he will richly bless you, ⁵if only you fully obey the LORD your God and are careful to follow all these commands I am giving you today. ⁶For the LORD your God will bless you as he has promised, and you will lend to many nations but will borrow from none. You will rule over many nations but none will rule over you. ^s

⁷If there is a poor man among your brothers in any of the towns of the land that the LORD your God is giving you, do not be hardhearted or tightfisted ^t toward your poor brother. ⁸Rather be openhanded ^u and freely lend him whatever he needs. ⁹Be careful not to harbor this wicked thought: "The seventh year, the year for canceling debts, is near," so that you do

15:1
^qDt 31:10

15:3
^rDt 23:20

15:6
^sDt 28:12-13,44

15:7
^t1Jn 3:17
15:8
^uMt 5:42

---

restrict holiness only to the spiritual side; we must be holy in the everyday practical part of life as well. Health practices, finances, use of leisure—all provide opportunities to put holy living into daily living.

14:21 This prohibition against cooking a young goat in its mother's milk may reflect a Canaanite fertility rite. Or it may just mean that the Israelites were not to take what was intended to promote life and use it to kill or destroy life. This commandment is also given in Exodus 23:19.

14:22, 23 The Bible makes the purpose of tithing very clear—to teach us to fear the Lord and to put him first in our lives. We are to give God the first and best of what we earn. For example, what we do first with our money shows what we value most. Giving the first part of our paycheck to God immediately focuses our attention on him. It also reminds us that all we have belongs to him. A habit of regular tithing can keep God at the top of our priority list and give us a proper perspective on everything else we have.

14:28, 29 The Bible supports an organized system of caring for the poor. God told his people to use their tithe every third year for those who were helpless, hungry, or poor. These regulations were designed to prevent the country from sinking under crushing poverty and oppression. It was everyone's responsibility to

care for those less fortunate. Families were to help other family members, and towns were to help members of their community. National laws protected the rights of the poor, but helping the poor was also an active part of religious life. God counts on believers to provide for the needy, and we should use what God has given us to aid those less fortunate. Look beyond your regular giving and think of ways to help the needy. This will help you show your regard for God as Creator of all people, share God's goodness with others, and draw them to him. It is a practical and essential way to make faith work in everyday life.

15:7–11 God told the Israelites to help the poor among them when they arrived in the promised land. This was an important part of possessing the land. Many people conclude that people are poor through some fault of their own. This kind of reasoning makes it easy to close their hearts and hands to the needy. But we are not to invent reasons for ignoring the poor. We are to respond to their needs no matter who or what was responsible for their condition. Who are the poor in your community? How could your church help them? If your church does not have a program to identify the poor and assist in fulfilling their needs, why not help start one? What can you do to help someone in need?

not show ill will toward your needy brother and give him nothing. He may then appeal to the LORD against you, and you will be found guilty of sin. *v* 10 Give generously to him and do so without a grudging heart; *w* then because of this the LORD your God will bless you in all your work and in everything you put your hand to. 11 There will always be poor people in the land. Therefore I command you to be openhanded toward your brothers and toward the poor and needy in your land. *x*

Freeing Servants

12 If a fellow Hebrew, a man or a woman, sells himself to you and serves you six years, in the seventh year you must let him go free. *y* 13 And when you release him, do not send him away empty-handed. 14 Supply him liberally from your flock, your threshing floor and your winepress. Give to him as the LORD your God has blessed you. 15 Remember that you were slaves in Egypt and the LORD your God redeemed you. That is why I give you this command today.

16 But if your servant says to you, "I do not want to leave you," because he loves you and your family and is well off with you, 17 then take an awl and push it through his ear lobe into the door, and he will become your servant for life. Do the same for your maidservant.

18 Do not consider it a hardship to set your servant free, because his service to you these six years has been worth twice as much as that of a hired hand. And the LORD your God will bless you in everything you do.

The Firstborn Animals

19 Set apart for the LORD your God every firstborn male *z* of your herds and flocks. Do not put the firstborn of your oxen to work, and do not shear the firstborn of your sheep. 20 Each year you and your family are to eat them in the presence of the LORD your God at the place he will choose. *a* 21 If an animal has a defect, is lame or blind, or has any serious flaw, you must not sacrifice it to the LORD your God. *b* 22 You are to eat it in your own towns. Both the ceremonially unclean and the clean may eat it, as if it were gazelle or deer. *c* 23 But you must not eat the blood; pour it out on the ground like water. *d*

Passover

16 Observe the month of Abib *e* and celebrate the Passover of the LORD your God, because in the month of Abib he brought you out of Egypt by night. 2 Sacrifice as the Passover to the LORD your God an animal from your flock or herd at the place the LORD will choose as a dwelling for his Name. 3 Do not eat it with bread made with yeast, but for seven days eat unleavened bread, the bread of affliction, because you left Egypt in haste *f* —so that all the days of your life you may remember the time of your departure from Egypt. 4 Let no yeast be found in your possession in all your land for seven days. Do not let any of the meat you sacrifice on the evening of the first day remain until morning.

5 You must not sacrifice the Passover in any town the LORD your God gives you 6 except in the place he will choose as a dwelling for his Name. There you must sacrifice the Passover in the evening, when the sun goes down, on the anniversary *a* of your departure from Egypt. 7 Roast *g* it and eat it at the place the LORD your God will choose. Then in the morning return to your tents. 8 For six days eat unleavened bread and on the seventh day hold an assembly *h* to the LORD your God and do no work.

Feast of Weeks

9 Count off seven weeks *i* from the time you begin to put the sickle to the standing grain. *j* 10 Then celebrate the Feast of Weeks to the LORD your God by giving a freewill offering in proportion to the blessings the LORD your God has given you. 11 And rejoice *k* before the LORD your God at the place he will choose as a dwelling for his Name—you, your sons and daughters, your menservants and maidservants, the Levites *l* in your towns, and the aliens, the fatherless and the widows living among you. 12 Remember that you were slaves in Egypt, *m* and follow carefully these decrees.

a 6 Or *down, at the time of day*

Cross-references
15:9 *v* Dt 24:15
15:10 *w* 2Co 9:5
15:11 *x* Mt 26:11; Mk 14:7; Jn 12:8
15:12 *y* Ex 21:2; Lev 25:39
15:19 *z* Ex 13:2
15:20 *a* Dt 12:5-7,17,18
15:21 *b* Lev 22:19-25
15:22 *c* Dt 12:15,22
15:23 *d* Dt 12:16
16:1 *e* Ex 12:2
16:3 *f* Ex 12:11,15,19
16:7 *g* Ex 12:8
16:8 *h* Ex 12:16
16:9 *i* Ex 34:22; Lev 23:15 *j* Ex 23:16
16:11 *k* Dt 12:7 *l* Dt 12:12
16:12 *m* Dt 15:15

15:12-15 The Israelites were to release their servants after six years, sending them away with enough food so that they would be amply supplied until their needs could be met by some other means. This humanitarian act recognized that God created each person with dignity and worth. It also reminded the Israelites that they, too, had once been slaves in Egypt, and that their present freedom was a gift from God. We do not have servants such as these today, but God's instructions still apply to us: We must still be sure to treat our employees with respect and economic fairness.

Feast of Tabernacles

16:13
n Lev 23:34

[13]Celebrate the Feast of Tabernacles for seven days after you have gathered the produce of your threshing floor *n* and your winepress. [14]Be joyful at your Feast—you, your sons and daughters, your menservants and maidservants, and the Levites, the aliens, the fatherless and the widows who live in your towns. [15]For seven days celebrate the Feast to the LORD your God at the place the LORD will choose. For the LORD your God will bless you in all your harvest and in all the work of your hands, and your joy will be complete.

16:16
o Ex 23:14,16
p Ex 34:20

[16]Three times a year all your men must appear before the LORD your God at the place he will choose: at the Feast of Unleavened Bread, the Feast of Weeks and the Feast of Tabernacles. *o* No man should appear before the LORD empty-handed: *p* [17]Each of you must bring a gift in proportion to the way the LORD your God has blessed you.

4. Laws for ruling the nation
Judges

16:19
q Ex 23:2,8
r Dt 1:17

[18]Appoint judges and officials for each of your tribes in every town the LORD your God is giving you, and they shall judge the people fairly. [19]Do not pervert justice *q* or show partiality. *r* Do not accept a bribe, for a bribe blinds the eyes of the wise and twists the words of the righteous. [20]Follow justice and justice alone, so that you may live and possess the land the LORD your God is giving you.

Worshiping Other Gods

[21]Do not set up any wooden Asherah pole *a* beside the altar you build to the LORD your God, [22]and do not erect a sacred stone, for these the LORD your God hates.

17:1
s Dt 15:21

17 Do not sacrifice to the LORD your God an ox or a sheep that has any defect or flaw in it, for that would be detestable to him. *s*

17:2
t Dt 13:6-11

[2]If a man or woman living among you in one of the towns the LORD gives you is found doing evil in the eyes of the LORD your God in violation of his covenant, *t* [3]and contrary to my command has worshiped other gods, bowing down to them or to the sun or the moon or the stars of the sky, [4]and this has been brought to your attention, then you must investigate it thoroughly. If it is true and it has been proved that this detestable thing has been done in Israel, [5]take the man or woman who has done this evil deed to your city gate and stone that person to death. [6]On the testimony of two or three witnesses a man shall be put to death, but no one shall be put to death on the testimony of only one witness. *u* [7]The hands of the witnesses must be the first in putting him to death, and then the hands of all the people. You must purge the evil *v* from among you.

17:6
u Nu 35:30;
Dt 19:15; Mt 18:16

17:7
v Dt 13:5,9

Law Courts

17:8
w Dt 12:5

[8]If cases come before your courts that are too difficult for you to judge—whether bloodshed, lawsuits or assaults—take them to the place the LORD your God will choose. *w* [9]Go to

a 21 Or *Do not plant any tree dedicated to Asherah*

16:16, 17 Three times a year every male was to make a journey to the sanctuary in the city that would be designated as Israel's religious capital. At these festivals, each participant was encouraged to give what he could in proportion to what God had given him. God does not expect us to give more than we can, but we will be blessed when we give cheerfully. For some, 10 percent may be a burden. For most of us, that would be far too little. Look at what you have and then give in proportion to what you have been given.

16:18–20 These verses anticipated a great problem the Israelites would face when they arrived in the promised land. Although they had Joshua as their national leader, they failed to complete the task and choose other spiritual leaders who would lead the tribes, districts, and cities with justice and God's wisdom. Because they did not appoint wise judges and faithful administrators, rebellion and injustice plagued their communities. It is a serious responsibility to appoint or elect wise and just officials. In your sphere of influence—home, church, school, job—are you ensuring that justice and godliness prevail? Failing to choose leaders who uphold justice can lead to much trouble, as Israel would discover.

17:1 The fact that this command was included probably indicates that some Israelites were sacrificing imperfect or deformed animals to God. Then, as now, it is difficult and expensive to offer God our best (i.e., the first part of what we earn). It is always tempting to shortchange God because we think we won't get caught. But our giving shows our real priorities. When we give God the leftovers, it is obvious that he is not at the center of our lives. Give God the honor of having first claim on your money, time, and talents.

17:6, 7 A person was not put to death on the testimony of only one witness. On the witness of two or three, a person could be condemned and then sentenced to death by stoning. The condemned person was taken outside the city gates, and the witnesses were the first to throw heavy stones down on him or her. Bystanders would then pelt the dying person with stones. This system would "purge the evil" by putting the idolater to death. At the same time, it protected the rights of accused persons two ways. First, by requiring several witnesses, it prevented any angry individual from giving "false testimony." Second, by requiring the accusers to throw the first stones, it made them think twice about accusing unjustly. They were responsible to finish what they had started.

the priests, who are Levites, and to the judge who is in office at that time. Inquire of them and they will give you the verdict. ˣ ¹⁰You must act according to the decisions they give you at the place the LORD will choose. Be careful to do everything they direct you to do. ¹¹Act according to the law they teach you and the decisions they give you. Do not turn aside from what they tell you, to the right or to the left. ¹²The man who shows contempt for the judge or for the priest who stands ministering there to the LORD your God must be put to death. You must purge the evil from Israel. ¹³All the people will hear and be afraid, and will not be contemptuous again.

17:9
ˣDt 19:17

The King

¹⁴When you enter the land the LORD your God is giving you and have taken possession of it and settled in it, and you say, "Let us set a king over us like all the nations around us," ʸ ¹⁵be sure to appoint over you the king the LORD your God chooses. He must be from among your own brothers. ᶻ Do not place a foreigner over you, one who is not a brother Israelite. ¹⁶The king, moreover, must not acquire great numbers of horses for himself ᵃ or make the people return to Egypt to get more of them, ᵇ for the LORD has told you, "You are not to go back that way again." ¹⁷He must not take many wives, ᶜ or his heart will be led astray. He must not accumulate large amounts of silver and gold.

17:14
ʸ1Sa 8:5,19-20
17:15
ᶻJer 30:21
17:16
ᵃ1Ki 4:26; 10:26
ᵇ1Ki 10:28;
Eze 17:15
17:17
ᶜ1Ki 11:3

¹⁸When he takes the throne of his kingdom, he is to write for himself on a scroll a copy of this law, taken from that of the priests, who are Levites. ¹⁹It is to be with him, and he is to read it all the days of his life so that he may learn to revere the LORD his God and follow carefully all the words of this law and these decrees ²⁰and not consider himself better than his brothers and turn from the law to the right or to the left. ᵈ Then he and his descendants will reign a long time over his kingdom in Israel.

17:20
ᵈDt 5:32

Offerings for Priests and Levites

18 The priests, who are Levites—indeed the whole tribe of Levi—are to have no allotment or inheritance with Israel. They shall live on the offerings made to the LORD by fire, for that is their inheritance. ᵉ ²They shall have no inheritance among their brothers; the LORD is their inheritance, as he promised them.

18:1
ᵉDt 10:9; 1Co 9:13

³This is the share due the priests from the people who sacrifice a bull or a sheep: the shoulder, the jowls and the inner parts. ᶠ ⁴You are to give them the firstfruits of your grain, new wine and oil, and the first wool from the shearing of your sheep, ᵍ ⁵for the LORD your God has chosen them and their descendants out of all your tribes to stand and minister ʰ in the LORD's name always.

18:3
ᶠLev 7:28-34
18:4
ᵍNu 18:12
18:5
ʰDt 10:8

⁶If a Levite moves from one of your towns anywhere in Israel where he is living, and comes in all earnestness to the place the LORD will choose, ⁷he may minister in the name of the LORD his God like all his fellow Levites who serve there in the presence of the LORD. ⁸He is to share equally in their benefits, even though he has received money from the sale of family possessions. ⁱ

18:8
ⁱNe 12:44,47

17:14-20 God was not encouraging Israel to appoint a king to rule their nation. He was actually against the idea because he was their King, and the people were to obey and follow him. But God knew that the people would one day demand a king for selfish reasons—they would want to be like the nations around them (1 Samuel 8). If they insisted on having a king, he wanted to make sure they chose the right person. That is why he included these instructions both for the people's benefit as they chose their king and for the king himself as he sought to lead the nation according to God's laws.

17:16, 17 Israel's kings did not heed this warning, and their behavior led to their downfall. Solomon had everything going for him, but when he became rich, built up a large army, and married many wives, his heart turned from God (1 Kings 11). Out of Solomon's sin came Israel's disobedience, division, and captivity.

17:18-20 The king was to be a man of God's Word. He was to (1) make for himself a copy of the law, (2) keep it with him all the time, (3) read from it every day, and (4) obey it completely. Through this process he would learn respect for God, keep himself from feeling more important than others, and avoid neglecting God in times of prosperity. We can't know what God wants except through his Word, and his Word won't affect our lives unless we read and think about it regularly. With the abundant availability of the Bible today, it is not difficult to gain access to the source of the King's wisdom. What is more of a challenge is following its directives.

18:1-8 The priests and Levites served much the same function as our ministers today. Their duties included (1) teaching the people about God, (2) setting an example of godly living, (3) caring for the sanctuary and its workers, and (4) distributing the offerings. Because priests and Levites could not own property or pursue outside business interests, God made special arrangements so that people would not take advantage of them. Often churches take advantage of the men and women God has brought to lead them. For example, ministers may not be paid in accordance with their skills or the time they put in. Or pastors may be expected to attend every evening meeting, even if this continual absence is harmful to their families. As you look at your own church in light of God's Word, what ways do you see to honor the leaders God has given you?

Detestable Practices

18:10
l Dt 12:31

9 When you enter the land the LORD your God is giving you, do not learn to imitate the detestable ways of the nations there. 10 Let no one be found among you who sacrifices his son or daughter in a the fire, who practices divination *j* or sorcery, interprets omens, engages in witchcraft, 11 or casts spells, or who is a medium or spiritist or who consults the dead. 12 Anyone who does these things is detestable to the LORD, and because of these detestable practices the LORD your God will drive out those nations before you. 13 You must be blameless before the LORD your God.

The Prophet

18:15
k Ac 3:22*

18:16
l Ex 20:19

18:18
m Isa 51:16
n Jn 4:25-26

18:19
o Ac 3:23*

14 The nations you will dispossess listen to those who practice sorcery or divination. But as for you, the LORD your God has not permitted you to do so. 15 The LORD your God will raise up for you a prophet like me from among your own brothers. *k* You must listen to him. 16 For this is what you asked of the LORD your God at Horeb on the day of the assembly when you said, "Let us not hear the voice of the LORD our God nor see this great fire anymore, or we will die." *l*

17 The LORD said to me: "What they say is good. 18 I will raise up for them a prophet like you from among their brothers; I will put my words *m* in his mouth, and he will tell them everything I command him. *n* 19 If anyone does not listen to my words that the prophet speaks in my name, I myself will call him to account. *o* 20 But a prophet who presumes to speak in my name anything I have not commanded him to say, or a prophet who speaks in the name of other gods, must be put to death."

18:22
p Jer 28:9
q ver 20

21 You may say to yourselves, "How can we know when a message has not been spoken by the LORD?" 22 If what a prophet proclaims in the name of the LORD does not take place or come true, that is a message the LORD has not spoken. *p* That prophet has spoken presumptuously. *q* Do not be afraid of him.

Cities of Refuge

19

When the LORD your God has destroyed the nations whose land he is giving you, and when you have driven them out and settled in their towns and houses, 2 then set aside for yourselves three cities centrally located in the land the LORD your God is giving you to possess. 3 Build roads to them and divide into three parts the land the LORD your God is giving you as an inheritance, so that anyone who kills a man may flee there.

4 This is the rule concerning the man who kills another and flees there to save his life— one who kills his neighbor unintentionally, without malice aforethought. 5 For instance, a man may go into the forest with his neighbor to cut wood, and as he swings his ax to fell a tree, the head may fly off and hit his neighbor and kill him. That man may flee to one of

---

a 10 Or *who makes his son or daughter pass through*

18:10 Child sacrifice and occult practices were strictly forbidden by God. These practices were common among pagan religions. Israel's own neighbors actually sacrificed their children to the god Molech (Leviticus 20:2–5). Other neighboring religions used supernatural means, such as contacting the spirit world, to foretell the future and gain guidance. Because of these wicked practices, God would drive out the pagan nations (18:12). The Israelites were to replace their evil practices with the worship of the one true God.

18:10–13 The Israelites were naturally curious about the occult practices of the Canaanite religions. But Satan is behind the occult, and God flatly forbade Israel to have anything to do with it. Today people are still fascinated by horoscopes, fortune-telling, witchcraft, and bizarre cults. Often their interest comes from a desire to know and control the future. But Satan is no less dangerous today than he was in Moses' time. In the Bible, God tells us all we need to know about what is going to happen. The information Satan offers is likely to be distorted or completely false. With the trustworthy guidance of the Holy Spirit through the Bible and the church, we don't need to turn to occult sources for faulty information.

18:15 Who is this prophet? Stephen used this verse to support his claim that Jesus Christ is God's Son, the Messiah (Acts 7:37).

The coming of Jesus Christ to earth was not an afterthought, but part of God's original plan.

18:21, 22 As in the days of ancient Israel, some people today claim to have messages from God. God still speaks to his people, but we must be cautious before saying that someone is God's spokesman. How can we tell when people are speaking for the Lord? (1) We can see whether or not their prophecies come true—the ancient test for judging prophets. (2) We can check their words against the Bible. God never contradicts himself, so if someone says something contrary to the Bible, we can know that this is not God's word. (See 13:1–11.)

19:2–7 Every society must deal with the problem of murder. But how should society treat those who have innocently or accidentally killed someone? God had an answer for the Israelites. Since revenge was common and swift in Moses' day, God had the Israelites set apart several "cities of refuge." Anyone who claimed to have accidentally killed someone could flee to one of these cities until he could have a fair trial. If he was found innocent of intentional murder, he could remain in that city and be safe from those seeking revenge. This is a beautiful example of how God blended his justice and mercy toward his people. (For more information on cities of refuge, see the note on Numbers 35:6.)

these cities and save his life. 6 Otherwise, the avenger of blood might pursue him in a rage, overtake him if the distance is too great, and kill him even though he is not deserving of death, since he did it to his neighbor without malice aforethought. 7 This is why I command you to set aside for yourselves three cities.

8 If the LORD your God enlarges your territory, as he promised on oath to your forefathers, and gives you the whole land he promised them, 9 because you carefully follow all these laws I command you today—to love the LORD your God and to walk always in his ways*r*—then you are to set aside three more cities. 10 Do this so that innocent blood will not be shed in your land, which the LORD your God is giving you as your inheritance, and so that you will not be guilty of bloodshed.

11 But if a man hates his neighbor and lies in wait for him, assaults and kills him, and then flees to one of these cities, 12 the elders of his town shall send for him, bring him back from the city, and hand him over to the avenger of blood to die. 13 Show him no pity. You must purge from Israel the guilt of shedding innocent blood, so that it may go well with you.

14 Do not move your neighbor's boundary stone set up by your predecessors in the inheritance you receive in the land the LORD your God is giving you to possess. *s*

Witnesses

15 One witness is not enough to convict a man accused of any crime or offense he may have committed. A matter must be established by the testimony of two or three witnesses.*t*

16 If a malicious witness*u* takes the stand to accuse a man of a crime, 17 the two men involved in the dispute must stand in the presence of the LORD before the priests and the judges*v* who are in office at the time. 18 The judges must make a thorough investigation, and if the witness proves to be a liar, giving false testimony against his brother, 19 then do to him as he intended to do to his brother. *w* You must purge the evil from among you. 20 The rest of the people will hear of this and be afraid, and never again will such an evil thing be done among you. 21 Show no pity: *x* life for life, eye for eye, tooth for tooth, hand for hand, foot for foot. *y*

Going to War

20 When you go to war against your enemies and see horses and chariots and an army greater than yours, do not be afraid *z* of them, because the LORD your God, who brought you up out of Egypt, will be with you. 2 When you are about to go into battle, the priest shall come forward and address the army. 3 He shall say: "Hear, O Israel, today you are going into battle against your enemies. Do not be fainthearted or afraid; do not be terrified or give way to panic before them. 4 For the LORD your God is the one who goes with you to fight*a* for you against your enemies to give you victory."

5 The officers shall say to the army: "Has anyone built a new house and not dedicated it? Let him go home, or he may die in battle and someone else may dedicate it. 6 Has anyone planted a vineyard and not begun to enjoy it? Let him go home, or he may die in battle and someone else enjoy it. 7 Has anyone become pledged to a woman and not married her? Let him go home, or he may die in battle and someone else marry her. *b*" 8 Then the officers shall add, "Is any man afraid or fainthearted? Let him go home so that his brothers will not become disheartened too."*c* 9 When the officers have finished speaking to the army, they shall appoint commanders over it.

10 When you march up to attack a city, make its people an offer of peace. 11 If they accept and open their gates, all the people in it shall be subject to forced labor and shall work for you. 12 If they refuse to make peace and they engage you in battle, lay siege to that city. 13 When the LORD your God delivers it into your hand, put to the sword all the men in it. *d* 14 As for the women, the children, the livestock *e* and everything else in the city, you may take

19:9
r Jos 20:7-8

19:14
s Dt 27:17

19:15
t Nu 35:30; Dt 17:6; Mt 18:16*; 2Co 13:1*

19:16
u Ps 27:12

19:17
v Dt 17:9

19:19
w Pr 19:5,9

19:21
x ver 13
y Ex 21:24; Lev 24:20; Mt 5:38*

20:1
z Dt 31:6,8

20:4
a Dt 1:30

20:7
b Dt 24:5

20:8
c Jdg 7:3

20:13
d Nu 31:7

20:14
e Jos 8:2

19:12 The "avenger of blood" was the nearest male relative to the person killed. He acted as the family protector (see Numbers 35:19).

19:21 This principle was for the judges to use, not a plan for personal vengeance. This attitude toward punishment may seem primitive, but it was actually a breakthrough for justice and fairness in ancient times when most nations used arbitrary methods to punish criminals. This guideline reflects a concern for even-handedness and justice—ensuring that those who violated the law were not punished more severely than their particular crime

deserved. In the same spirit of justice, a false witness was to receive the same punishment the accused person would have suffered. The principle of making the punishment fit the crime should still be observed today.

20:1 Just like the Israelites, we sometimes face overwhelming opposition. Whether at school, at work, or even at home, we can feel outnumbered and helpless. God bolstered the Israelites' confidence by reminding them that he was always with them and that he had already saved them from the potential danger. We too can feel secure when we consider that God is able to overcome even the most difficult odds.

these as plunder for yourselves. And you may use the plunder the Lord your God gives you from your enemies. [15]This is how you are to treat all the cities that are at a distance from you and do not belong to the nations nearby.

20:16
f Dt 7:2; Jos 11:14

[16]However, in the cities of the nations the Lord your God is giving you as an inheritance, do not leave alive anything that breathes.*f* [17]Completely destroy*a* them—the Hittites, Amorites, Canaanites, Perizzites, Hivites and Jebusites—as the Lord your God has commanded

20:18
g Ex 23:33

you. [18]Otherwise, they will teach you to follow all the detestable things they do in worshiping their gods, and you will sin*g* against the Lord your God.

[19]When you lay siege to a city for a long time, fighting against it to capture it, do not destroy its trees by putting an ax to them, because you can eat their fruit. Do not cut them down. Are the trees of the field people, that you should besiege them?*b* [20]However, you may cut down trees that you know are not fruit trees and use them to build siege works until the city at war with you falls.

5. Laws for human relationships
Atonement for an Unsolved Murder

21 If a man is found slain, lying in a field in the land the Lord your God is giving you to possess, and it is not known who killed him, [2]your elders and judges shall go out and measure the distance from the body to the neighboring towns. [3]Then the elders of the town nearest the body shall take a heifer that has never been worked and has never worn a yoke

21:5
h Dt 17:8-11

[4]and lead her down to a valley that has not been plowed or planted and where there is a flowing stream. There in the valley they are to break the heifer's neck. [5]The priests, the sons of Levi, shall step forward, for the Lord your God has chosen them to minister and to pronounce blessings in the name of the Lord and to decide all cases of dispute and assault.*h*

21:6
i Mt 27:24

[6]Then all the elders of the town nearest the body shall wash their hands*i* over the heifer whose neck was broken in the valley, [7]and they shall declare: "Our hands did not shed this blood, nor did our eyes see it done. [8]Accept this atonement for your people Israel, whom you have redeemed, O Lord, and do not hold your people guilty of the blood of an innocent

21:9
j Dt 19:13

man." And the bloodshed will be atoned for. [9]So you will purge*j* from yourselves the guilt of shedding innocent blood, since you have done what is right in the eyes of the Lord.

Marrying a Captive Woman

[10]When you go to war against your enemies and the Lord your God delivers them into your hands and you take captives, [11]if you notice among the captives a beautiful woman and are attracted to her, you may take her as your wife. [12]Bring her into your home and have her

21:12
k Lev 14:9
21:13
l Ps 45:10

shave her head,*k* trim her nails [13]and put aside the clothes she was wearing when captured. After she has lived in your house and mourned her father and mother for a full month,*l* then you may go to her and be her husband and she shall be your wife. [14]If you are not pleased with her, let her go wherever she wishes. You must not sell her or treat her as a slave, since you have dishonored her.

The Right of the Firstborn

21:15
m Ge 29:33
21:16
n 1Ch 26:10

[15]If a man has two wives, and he loves one but not the other, and both bear him sons but the firstborn is the son of the wife he does not love,*m* [16]when he wills his property to his sons, he must not give the rights of the firstborn to the son of the wife he loves in preference to his actual firstborn, the son of the wife he does not love.*n* [17]He must acknowledge the son

---

a 17 The Hebrew term refers to the irrevocable giving over of things or persons to the Lord, often by totally destroying them.   *b 19* Or *down to use in the siege, for the fruit trees are for the benefit of man.*

20:13–18 "Put to the sword" means to kill. How could a merciful and just God order the destruction of entire population centers? He did this to protect his people from idol worship, which was certain to bring ruin to Israel (20:18). In fact, because Israel did not completely destroy these evil people as God commanded, Israel was constantly oppressed by them and experienced greater bloodshed and destruction than if they had followed God's instructions in the first place. (See 7:2–6.)

20:20 Archaeologists have uncovered the remnants of many well-fortified cities in Canaan. Some had tall walls (up to 30 feet high), ramparts, moats, and towers. Accustomed to fighting on the open plains, the Israelites were going to have to learn new battle strategies to conquer these massive fortresses.

21:1–9 When a crime was committed and the criminal got away, the whole community was held responsible. In much the same way, if a city has a dangerous intersection and someone is killed there, the community may be held responsible for both damages and repairs. God was pointing to the need for the whole community to feel a keen sense of responsibility for what was going on around them and to move to correct any situations that were potentially harmful—physically, socially, or morally.

of his unloved wife as the firstborn by giving him a double share of all he has. That son is the first sign of his father's strength. *o* The right of the firstborn belongs to him.

21:17
o Ge 49:3

A Rebellious Son

¹⁸If a man has a stubborn and rebellious son who does not obey his father and mother and will not listen to them when they discipline him, ¹⁹his father and mother shall take hold of him and bring him to the elders at the gate of his town. ²⁰They shall say to the elders, "This son of ours is stubborn and rebellious. He will not obey us. He is a profligate and a drunkard." ²¹Then all the men of his town shall stone him to death. You must purge the evil from among you. All Israel will hear of it and be afraid. *p*

21:21
p Dt 13:11

Various Laws

²²If a man guilty of a capital offense is put to death and his body is hung on a tree, ²³you must not leave his body on the tree overnight. *q* Be sure to bury him that same day, because anyone who is hung on a tree is under God's curse. *r* You must not desecrate the land the LORD your God is giving you as an inheritance.

21:23
q Jos 8:29; 10:27; Jn 19:31
r Gal 3:13*

22 If you see your brother's ox or sheep straying, do not ignore it but be sure to take it back to him. *s* ²If the brother does not live near you or if you do not know who he is, take it home with you and keep it until he comes looking for it. Then give it back to him. ³Do the same if you find your brother's donkey or his cloak or anything he loses. Do not ignore it.

22:1
s Ex 23:4-5

⁴If you see your brother's donkey or his ox fallen on the road, do not ignore it. Help him get it to its feet.

⁵A woman must not wear men's clothing, nor a man wear women's clothing, for the LORD your God detests anyone who does this.

⁶If you come across a bird's nest beside the road, either in a tree or on the ground, and the mother is sitting on the young or on the eggs, do not take the mother with the young. *t* ⁷You may take the young, but be sure to let the mother go, so that it may go well with you and you may have a long life. *u*

22:6
t Lev 22:28
22:7
u Dt 4:40

⁸When you build a new house, make a parapet around your roof so that you may not bring the guilt of bloodshed on your house if someone falls from the roof.

⁹Do not plant two kinds of seed in your vineyard; *v* if you do, not only the crops you plant but also the fruit of the vineyard will be defiled. *a*

22:9
v Lev 19:19

¹⁰Do not plow with an ox and a donkey yoked together.

22:11
w Lev 19:19

¹¹Do not wear clothes of wool and linen woven together. *w*

¹²Make tassels on the four corners of the cloak you wear. *x*

22:12
x Nu 15:37-41

Marriage Violations

¹³If a man takes a wife and, after lying with her, dislikes her ¹⁴and slanders her and gives her a bad name, saying, "I married this woman, but when I approached her, I did not find

a 9 Or be forfeited to the sanctuary

21:18–21 Disobedient and rebellious children were to be brought before the elders of the city and stoned to death. There is no Biblical or archaeological evidence that this punishment was ever carried out, but the point was that disobedience and rebellion were not to be tolerated in the home or allowed to continue unchecked. These principles must never be used to justify or overlook abuse or harsh treatment of children. While firm guidance may be needed with strong consequences for disobedience, the Bible does not condone physical, verbal, or emotional abuse of children.

22:1–4 The Hebrews were to care for and return lost animals or possessions to their rightful owners. The way of the world, by contrast, is "Finders keepers, losers weepers." To go beyond the finders-keepers rule by protecting and returning the property of others keeps us from being envious and greedy.

22:5 This verse commands men and women not to reverse their sexual roles. It is not a statement about clothing styles. Today role rejections are common—there are men who want to become women and women who want to become men. It's not the clothing style that offends God, but using the style to act out a different sex role. God had a purpose in making us uniquely male and female.

22:8–11 These are practical laws, helpful for establishing good habits for everyday living. Verse 8: Since people used their flat

roofs as porches, a guardrail (parapet) was a wise safety precaution. Verse 9: If you plant two different crops side by side, one of them will not survive, since the stronger, taller one will block the sunlight and take most of the vital nutrients from the soil. Verse 10: A donkey and an ox, due to differences in strength and size, cannot pull a plow evenly. Verse 11: Two different kinds of thread wear unevenly and wash differently. Combining them reduces the life of the garment. Don't think of God's laws as arbitrary restrictions. Look for the reasons behind the laws. They are not made just to teach or restrict, but also to protect and help us.

22:13–30 Why did God include all these laws about sexual sins? Instructions about sexual behavior would have been vital for three million people on a 40-year camping trip. But they would be equally important when they entered the promised land and settled down as a nation. Paul, in Colossians 3:5–8, recognizes the importance of strong rules about sex for believers because sexual sins have the power to disrupt and destroy the church. Sins involving sex are not innocent dabblings in forbidden pleasures, as is so often portrayed, but powerful destroyers of relationships. They confuse and tear down the climate of respect, trust, and credibility so essential for solid marriages and secure children.

proof of her virginity," 15then the girl's father and mother shall bring proof that she was a virgin to the town elders at the gate. 16The girl's father will say to the elders, "I gave my daughter in marriage to this man, but he dislikes her. 17Now he has slandered her and said, 'I did not find your daughter to be a virgin.' But here is the proof of my daughter's virginity." Then her parents shall display the cloth before the elders of the town, 18and the elders shall take the man and punish him. 19They shall fine him a hundred shekels of silver *a* and give them to the girl's father, because this man has given an Israelite virgin a bad name. She shall continue to be his wife; he must not divorce her as long as he lives.

20If, however, the charge is true and no proof of the girl's virginity can be found, 21she shall be brought to the door of her father's house and there the men of her town shall stone her to death. She has done a disgraceful thing *y* in Israel by being promiscuous while still in her father's house. You must purge the evil from among you.

22If a man is found sleeping with another man's wife, both the man who slept with her and the woman must die. *z* You must purge the evil from Israel.

23If a man happens to meet in a town a virgin pledged to be married and he sleeps with her, 24you shall take both of them to the gate of that town and stone them to death—the girl because she was in a town and did not scream for help, and the man because he violated another man's wife. You must purge the evil from among you.

25But if out in the country a man happens to meet a girl pledged to be married and rapes her, only the man who has done this shall die. 26Do nothing to the girl; she has committed no sin deserving death. This case is like that of someone who attacks and murders his neighbor, 27for the man found the girl out in the country, and though the betrothed girl screamed, there was no one to rescue her.

28If a man happens to meet a virgin who is not pledged to be married and rapes her and they are discovered, *a* 29he shall pay the girl's father fifty shekels of silver. *b* He must marry the girl, for he has violated her. He can never divorce her as long as he lives.

30A man is not to marry his father's wife; he must not dishonor his father's bed. *b*

Exclusion From the Assembly

23 No one who has been emasculated by crushing or cutting may enter the assembly of the LORD.

2No one born of a forbidden marriage *c* nor any of his descendants may enter the assembly of the LORD, even down to the tenth generation.

3No Ammonite or Moabite or any of his descendants may enter the assembly of the LORD, even down to the tenth generation. *c* 4For they did not come to meet you with bread and water on your way when you came out of Egypt, and they hired Balaam *d* son of Beor from Pethor in Aram Naharaim *d* to pronounce a curse on you. 5However, the LORD your God would not listen to Balaam but turned the curse into a blessing for you, because the LORD your God loves you. 6Do not seek a treaty of friendship with them as long as you live. *e*

7Do not abhor an Edomite, for he is your brother. *f* Do not abhor an Egyptian, because you lived as an alien in his country. 8The third generation of children born to them may enter the assembly of the LORD.

Uncleanness in the Camp

9When you are encamped against your enemies, keep away from everything impure. 10If one of your men is unclean because of a nocturnal emission, he is to go outside the camp and stay there. *g* 11But as evening approaches he is to wash himself, and at sunset he may return to the camp.

12Designate a place outside the camp where you can go to relieve yourself. 13As part of your equipment have something to dig with, and when you relieve yourself, dig a hole and cover up your excrement. 14For the LORD your God moves *h* about in your camp to protect you and to deliver your enemies to you. Your camp must be holy, so that he will not see among you anything indecent and turn away from you.

Miscellaneous Laws

15If a slave has taken refuge with you, do not hand him over to his master. *i* 16Let him live among you wherever he likes and in whatever town he chooses. Do not oppress him.

22:21
y Ge 34:7; Dt 13:5

22:22
z Lev 20:10; Jn 8:5

22:28
a Ex 22:16
22:30
b Lev 18:8;
Dt 27:20; 1Co 5:1

23:3
c Ne 13:2
23:4
d Nu 22:5-6
23:6
e Ezr 9:12

23:7
f Ge 25:26

23:10
g Lev 15:16

23:14
h Lev 26:12

23:15
i 1Sa 30:15

a 19 That is, about 2 1/2 pounds (about 1 kilogram)   b 29 That is, about 1 1/4 pounds (about 0.6 kilogram)   c 2 Or one of illegitimate birth   d 4 That is, Northwest Mesopotamia

¹⁷No Israelite man or woman is to become a shrine prostitute. ¹⁸You must not bring the earnings of a female prostitute or of a male prostitute[a] into the house of the LORD your God to pay any vow, because the LORD your God detests them both.

¹⁹Do not charge your brother interest, whether on money or food or anything else that may earn interest.[j] ²⁰You may charge a foreigner interest, but not a brother Israelite, so that the LORD your God may bless you in everything you put your hand to in the land you are entering to possess.

²¹If you make a vow to the LORD your God, do not be slow to pay it, for the LORD your God will certainly demand it of you and you will be guilty of sin.[k] ²²But if you refrain from making a vow, you will not be guilty. ²³Whatever your lips utter you must be sure to do, because you made your vow freely to the LORD your God with your own mouth.

²⁴If you enter your neighbor's vineyard, you may eat all the grapes you want, but do not put any in your basket. ²⁵If you enter your neighbor's grainfield, you may pick kernels with your hands, but you must not put a sickle to his standing grain.[l]

24 If a man marries a woman who becomes displeasing to him because he finds something indecent about her, and he writes her a certificate of divorce,[m] gives it to her and sends her from his house, ²and if after she leaves his house she becomes the wife of another man, ³and her second husband dislikes her and writes her a certificate of divorce, gives it to her and sends her from his house, or if he dies, ⁴then her first husband, who divorced her, is not allowed to marry her again after she has been defiled. That would be detestable in the eyes of the LORD. Do not bring sin upon the land the LORD[n] your God is giving you as an inheritance.

⁵If a man has recently married, he must not be sent to war or have any other duty laid on him. For one year he is to be free to stay at home and bring happiness to the wife he has married.[o]

⁶Do not take a pair of millstones—not even the upper one—as security for a debt, because that would be taking a man's livelihood as security.

⁷If a man is caught kidnapping one of his brother Israelites and treats him as a slave or sells him, the kidnapper must die.[p] You must purge the evil from among you.

⁸In cases of leprous[b] diseases be very careful to do exactly as the priests, who are Levites, instruct you. You must follow carefully what I have commanded them.[q] ⁹Remember what the LORD your God did to Miriam along the way after you came out of Egypt.[r]

¹⁰When you make a loan of any kind to your neighbor, do not go into his house to get what he is offering as a pledge. ¹¹Stay outside and let the man to whom you are making the loan bring the pledge out to you. ¹²If the man is poor, do not go to sleep with his pledge in your possession. ¹³Return his cloak to him by sunset[s] so that he may sleep in it. Then he will thank you, and it will be regarded as a righteous act in the sight of the LORD your God.

23:19
[j] Ex 22:25;
Lev 25:35-37

23:21
[k] Nu 30:1-2

23:25
[l] Mt 12:1; Mk 2:23;
Lk 6:1

24:1
[m] Mt 5:31*; 19:7-9;
Mk 10:4-5

24:4
[n] Jer 3:1

24:5
[o] Dt 20:7

24:7
[p] Ex 21:16

24:8
[q] Lev 13:1-46
24:9
[r] Nu 12:10

24:13
[s] Ex 22:26

---

a *18* Hebrew *of a dog*   **b** *8* The Hebrew word was used for various diseases affecting the skin—not necessarily leprosy.

23:17, 18 Prostitution was not overlooked in God's law—it was strictly forbidden. To forbid this practice may seem obvious to us, but it may not have been so obvious to the Israelites. Almost every other religion known to them included prostitution as an integral part of its worship services. Prostitution makes a mockery of God's original idea for sex, treating sex as an isolated physical act rather than an act of commitment to another. Outside of marriage, sex destroys relationships. Within marriage, if approached with the right attitude, it can be a relationship builder. God frequently had to warn the people against the practice of extramarital sex. Today we still need to hear his warnings; young people need to be reminded about premarital sex, and adults need to be reminded about sexual fidelity.

23:24, 25 This commandment guarded against selfishly holding on to one's possessions. It also insured that no one had to go hungry. It was not, however, an excuse for taking advantage of one's neighbor. The Pharisees did not interpret this appropriately when they accused Jesus and the disciples of harvesting on the Sabbath (Matthew 12:1, 2).

24:1–4 Some think this passage supports divorce, but that is not the case. It simply recognizes a practice that already existed in Israel. All four verses must be read to understand the point of the passage; it certainly is not suggesting that a man divorce his wife

on a whim. Divorce was a permanent and final act for the couple. Once divorced and remarried to others, they could never be remarried to each other (24:4). This restriction was to prevent casual remarriage after a frivolous separation. The intention was to make people think twice before divorcing.

24:5 Recently married couples were to remain together their first year. This was to avoid placing an excessive burden upon a new, unproven relationship and to give it a chance to mature and strengthen before confronting it with numerous responsibilities. A gardener starts a tiny seedling in a small pot and allows it to take root before planting it in the field. Let your marriage grow strong by protecting your relationship from too many outside pressures and distractions—especially in the beginning. And don't expect or demand so much from newlyweds that they have inadequate time or energy to establish their marriage.

24:10–22 Throughout the Old Testament God told his people to treat the poor with justice. The powerless and poverty-stricken are often looked upon by some people as incompetent or lazy when, in fact, those facing that situation may be victims of oppression and circumstance. God says we must do all we can to help those who are needy. His justice did not permit the Israelites to insist on profits or quick payment from those who were less fortunate. Instead, his laws gave the poor every opportunity to better their situation,

24:15
t Lev 19:13
u Jas 5:4

24:16
v Jer 31:29-30;
Eze 18:20

24:19
w Lev 19:9; 23:22

25:1
x Dt 19:17

25:3
y 2Co 11:24

25:4
z 1Ti 5:18*

25:5
a Mt 22:24;
Lk 20:28

25:6
b Ru 4:5,10

25:7
c Ru 4:1-2,5-6

25:9
d Ru 4:7-8,11

25:13
e Lev 19:35-37

25:16
f Pr 11:1

¹⁴Do not take advantage of a hired man who is poor and needy, whether he is a brother Israelite or an alien living in one of your towns. ¹⁵Pay him his wages each day before sunset, because he is poor and is counting on it. *t* Otherwise he may cry to the LORD against you, and you will be guilty of sin. *u*

¹⁶Fathers shall not be put to death for their children, nor children put to death for their fathers; each is to die for his own sin. *v*

¹⁷Do not deprive the alien or the fatherless of justice, or take the cloak of the widow as a pledge. ¹⁸Remember that you were slaves in Egypt and the LORD your God redeemed you from there. That is why I command you to do this.

¹⁹When you are harvesting in your field and you overlook a sheaf, do not go back to get it. *w* Leave it for the alien, the fatherless and the widow, so that the LORD your God may bless you in all the work of your hands. ²⁰When you beat the olives from your trees, do not go over the branches a second time. Leave what remains for the alien, the fatherless and the widow. ²¹When you harvest the grapes in your vineyard, do not go over the vines again. Leave what remains for the alien, the fatherless and the widow. ²²Remember that you were slaves in Egypt. That is why I command you to do this.

25 When men have a dispute, they are to take it to court and the judges will decide the case, *x* acquitting the innocent and condemning the guilty. ²If the guilty man deserves to be beaten, the judge shall make him lie down and have him flogged in his presence with the number of lashes his crime deserves, ³but he must not give him more than forty lashes. *y* If he is flogged more than that, your brother will be degraded in your eyes.

⁴Do not muzzle an ox while it is treading out the grain. *z*

⁵If brothers are living together and one of them dies without a son, his widow must not marry outside the family. Her husband's brother shall take her and marry her and fulfill the duty of a brother-in-law to her. *a* ⁶The first son she bears shall carry on the name of the dead brother so that his name will not be blotted out from Israel. *b*

⁷However, if a man does not want to marry his brother's wife, she shall go to the elders at the town gate and say, "My husband's brother refuses to carry on his brother's name in Israel. He will not fulfill the duty of a brother-in-law to me." *c* ⁸Then the elders of his town shall summon him and talk to him. If he persists in saying, "I do not want to marry her," ⁹his brother's widow shall go up to him in the presence of the elders, take off one of his sandals, *d* spit in his face and say, "This is what is done to the man who will not build up his brother's family line." ¹⁰That man's line shall be known in Israel as The Family of the Unsandaled.

¹¹If two men are fighting and the wife of one of them comes to rescue her husband from his assailant, and she reaches out and seizes him by his private parts, ¹²you shall cut off her hand. Show her no pity.

¹³Do not have two differing weights in your bag—one heavy, one light. *e* ¹⁴Do not have two differing measures in your house—one large, one small. ¹⁵You must have accurate and honest weights and measures, so that you may live long in the land the LORD your God is giving you. ¹⁶For the LORD your God detests anyone who does these things, anyone who deals dishonestly. *f*

---

while providing humane options for those who couldn't. None of us is completely isolated from the poor; many of us face needs at one time or another. God wants us to treat each other fairly and do our part to help meet one another's needs.

24:19–21 God's people were instructed to leave some of their harvest in the fields so travelers and the poor could gather it. This second gathering, called gleaning, was a way for them to provide food for themselves. Years later, Ruth obtained food for herself and Naomi by gleaning behind the reapers in Boaz's field, picking up the leftovers (Ruth 2:2). Because this law was being obeyed years after it was written, Ruth, a woman in Christ's lineage, was able to find food.

25:1–3 At first glance these verses appear irrelevant today. But a closer look reveals some important principles about discipline. Are you responsible for the discipline of a child, a student, or an employee? Three important points will help you carry out your responsibility: (1) let the punishment follow quickly after the offense; (2) let the degree of punishment reflect the seriousness of the offense; and (3) don't overdo the punishment. Discipline that is swift, just, and restrained makes its point while preserving the dignity of the offender.

25:4 What is the point of this Old Testament regulation? Oxen were often used to tread out the grain on a threshing floor. The animal was attached by poles to a large millstone. As it walked around the millstone, its hooves trampled the grain, separating the kernels from the chaff. At the same time, the millstone ground the grain into flour. To muzzle the ox would prevent it from eating while it was working. Paul used this illustration in the New Testament to argue that people productive in Christian work should not be denied its benefits—they should receive financial support (2 Corinthians 9:10; 1 Timothy 5:17, 18). The fact that a person is in Christian ministry doesn't mean he or she should be unfairly paid. There is also a broader application: Don't be stingy with those who work for you.

25:5–10 This law describes a "levirate" marriage, the marriage of a widow to the brother of her dead husband. The purpose of such a marriage was to carry on the dead man's name and inheritance. Family ties were an important aspect of Israelite culture. The best way to be remembered was through your line of descendants. If a widow married someone outside the family, her first husband's line would come to an end. Tamar fought for this right in Genesis 38.

[17] Remember what the Amalekites[g] did to you along the way when you came out of Egypt. [18] When you were weary and worn out, they met you on your journey and cut off all who were lagging behind; they had no fear of God. [19] When the LORD your God gives you rest from all the enemies around you in the land he is giving you to possess as an inheritance, you shall blot out the memory of Amalek[h] from under heaven. Do not forget!

Firstfruits and Tithes

26 When you have entered the land the LORD your God is giving you as an inheritance and have taken possession of it and settled in it, [2] take some of the firstfruits[i] of all that you produce from the soil of the land the LORD your God is giving you and put them in a basket. Then go to the place the LORD your God will choose as a dwelling for his Name [3] and say to the priest in office at the time, "I declare today to the LORD your God that I have come to the land the LORD swore to our forefathers to give us." [4] The priest shall take the basket from your hands and set it down in front of the altar of the LORD your God. [5] Then you shall declare before the LORD your God: "My father was a wandering Aramean, and he went down into Egypt with a few people[j] and lived there and became a great nation, powerful and numerous. [6] But the Egyptians mistreated us and made us suffer,[k] putting us to hard labor. [7] Then we cried out to the LORD, the God of our fathers, and the LORD heard our voice[l] and saw our misery, toil and oppression. [8] So the LORD brought us out of Egypt with a mighty hand and an outstretched arm, with great terror and with miraculous signs and wonders.[m] [9] He brought us to this place and gave us this land, a land flowing with milk and honey;[n] [10] and now I bring the firstfruits of the soil that you, O LORD, have given me." Place the basket before the LORD your God and bow down before him. [11] And you and the Levites[o] and the aliens among you shall rejoice in all the good things the LORD your God has given to you and your household.

[12] When you have finished setting aside a tenth of all your produce in the third year, the year of the tithe,[p] you shall give it to the Levite, the alien, the fatherless and the widow, so that they may eat in your towns and be satisfied. [13] Then say to the LORD your God: "I have removed from my house the sacred portion and have given it to the Levite, the alien, the fatherless and the widow, according to all you commanded. I have not turned aside from your commands nor have I forgotten any of them. [q] [14] I have not eaten any of the sacred portion while I was in mourning, nor have I removed any of it while I was unclean, nor have I offered any of it to the dead. I have obeyed the LORD my God; I have done everything you commanded me. [15] Look down from heaven, your holy dwelling place, and bless your people Israel and the land you have given us as you promised on oath to our forefathers, a land flowing with milk and honey."

Follow the LORD's Commands

[16] The LORD your God commands you this day to follow these decrees and laws; carefully observe them with all your heart and with all your soul. [17] You have declared this day that the LORD is your God and that you will walk in his ways, that you will keep his decrees, commands and laws, and that you will obey him. [18] And the LORD has declared this day that you are his people, his treasured possession[r] as he promised, and that you are to keep all his commands. [19] He has declared that he will set you in praise, fame and honor high above all the nations[s] he has made and that you will be a people holy[t] to the LORD your God, as he promised.

6. Consequences of obedience and disobedience
The Altar on Mount Ebal

27 Moses and the elders of Israel commanded the people: "Keep all these commands that I give you today. [2] When you have crossed the Jordan into the land the LORD your God is giving you, set up some large stones and coat them with plaster.[u] [3] Write on them all

25:17
[g] Ex 17:8

25:19
[h] 1Sa 15:2-3

26:2
[i] Ex 23:16,19; Nu 18:13

26:5
[j] Ge 43:1-2; 46:27; Dt 10:22

26:6
[k] Ex 1:11,14

26:7
[l] Ex 2:23-25

26:8
[m] Dt 4:34

26:9
[n] Ex 3:8

26:11
[o] Dt 12:7

26:12
[p] Dt 14:28-29

26:13
[q] Ps 119:141, 153,176

26:18
[r] Dt 7:6

26:19
[s] Dt 28:1,13,44
[t] Dt 7:6

27:2
[u] Jos 8:31

26:5–10 This recitation of God's dealings with his people helped the people remember what God had done for them. What is the history of your relationship with God? Can you put into clear and concise words what God has done for you? Find a friend with whom you can share your spiritual journey. Telling your stories to each other will help you clearly understand your personal spiritual history, as well as encouraging and inspiring you both. Note: *Wandering* can mean lost or dying. Also, Arameans were the people of northern Syria and among the ancestors of Abraham. This is also used as a reference to Jacob, who spent many years there (Genesis 29—31) and got his two wives in Aram.

26:12 This law is repeated from 14:28–29. The people were to give their tithe to the needy every third year. This amounts to one-third of their giving on a three-year cycle. Though we are not under this law today, the New Testament reminds us not to forget the poor. Consider giving one-third of your annual contribution to overseas ministries, or to relief for the poor, orphans, and widows.

the words of this law when you have crossed over to enter the land the LORD your God is giving you, a land flowing with milk and honey, just as the LORD, the God of your fathers, promised you. 4And when you have crossed the Jordan, set up these stones on Mount Ebal, as I command you today, and coat them with plaster. 5Build there an altar v to the LORD your God, an altar of stones. Do not use any iron tool w upon them. 6Build the altar of the LORD your God with fieldstones and offer burnt offerings on it to the LORD your God. 7Sacrifice fellowship offeringsa there, eating them and rejoicing in the presence of the LORD your God. 8And you shall write very clearly all the words of this law on these stones you have set up."

27:5
v Jos 8:31
w Ex 20:25

Curses From Mount Ebal

9Then Moses and the priests, who are Levites, said to all Israel, "Be silent, O Israel, and listen! You have now become the people of the LORD your God. 10Obey the LORD your God and follow his commands and decrees that I give you today."

11On the same day Moses commanded the people:

12When you have crossed the Jordan, these tribes shall stand on Mount Gerizim to bless the people: Simeon, Levi, Judah, Issachar, Joseph and Benjamin. x 13And these tribes shall stand on Mount Ebal to pronounce curses: Reuben, Gad, Asher, Zebulun, Dan and Naphtali.

27:12
x Jos 8:35

14The Levites shall recite to all the people of Israel in a loud voice:

15"Cursed is the man who carves an image or casts an idol y—a thing detestable to the LORD, the work of the craftsman's hands—and sets it up in secret."

Then all the people shall say, "Amen!"

27:15
y Ex 20:4; 34:17

16"Cursed is the man who dishonors his father or his mother." z

Then all the people shall say, "Amen!"

27:16
z Ex 21:17

17"Cursed is the man who moves his neighbor's boundary stone."

Then all the people shall say, "Amen!"

18"Cursed is the man who leads the blind astray on the road." a

Then all the people shall say, "Amen!"

27:18
a Lev 19:14

19"Cursed is the man who withholds justice from the alien, b the fatherless or the widow." c

Then all the people shall say, "Amen!"

27:19
b Dt 24:19
c Dt 10:18

20"Cursed is the man who sleeps with his father's wife, for he dishonors his father's bed." d

Then all the people shall say, "Amen!"

27:20
d Lev 18:7; Dt 22:30

21"Cursed is the man who has sexual relations with any animal." e

Then all the people shall say, "Amen!"

27:21
e Lev 18:23

22"Cursed is the man who sleeps with his sister, the daughter of his father or the daughter of his mother." f

Then all the people shall say, "Amen!"

27:22
f Lev 18:9

23"Cursed is the man who sleeps with his mother-in-law."

Then all the people shall say, "Amen!"

24"Cursed is the man who kills g his neighbor secretly."

Then all the people shall say, "Amen!"

27:24
g Lev 24:17;
Nu 35:31

a 7 Traditionally *peace offerings*

27:5, 6 The Lord had specified an altar made of uncut stones (fieldstones) so that the people would not begin worshiping the altars as idols. To use a chisel on a stone of the altar would be to profane it (Exodus 20:24–26). Additionally, because the Israelites did not have the capacity to work with iron at this time, using iron tools might mean using the cooperation and expertise of other nations.

27:9, 10 Moses was reviewing the law with the new generation of people. When we decide to believe in God, we must also decide to follow his ways. What we do shows what we really believe. Can people tell that you are a member of God's family?

27:15–26 These curses were a series of oaths, spoken by the priests and affirmed by the people, by which the people promised to stay away from wrong actions. By saying *Amen*, "So be it," the people took responsibility for their actions. Sometimes looking at a list of curses like this gives us the idea that God has a bad

temper and is out to crush anyone who steps out of line. But we need to see these restrictions not as threats, but as loving warnings about the plain facts of life. Just as we warn children to stay away from hot stoves and busy streets, God warns us to stay away from dangerous actions. The natural law of his universe makes it clear that wrongdoing toward others or God has tragic consequences. God is merciful enough to tell us this truth plainly. Motivated by love and not anger, his strong words help us avoid the serious consequences that result from neglecting God or wronging others. But God does not leave us with only curses or consequences. Immediately following these curses, we discover the great blessings (positive consequences) that come from living for God (28:1–14). These give us extra incentive to obey God's laws. While all these blessings may not come in our lifetime on earth, those who obey God will experience the fullness of his blessing when he establishes the new heaven and the new earth.

25 "Cursed is the man who accepts a bribe to kill an innocent person." *h*

        Then all the people shall say, "Amen!"

26 "Cursed is the man who does not uphold the words of this law by carrying them out." *i*

        Then all the people shall say, "Amen!"

27:25 h Ex 23:7-8

27:26 i Gal 3:10*

Blessings for Obedience

28 If you fully obey the LORD your God and carefully follow all his commands I give you today, the LORD your God will set you high above all the nations on earth. *j* 2 All these blessings will come upon you and accompany you if you obey the LORD your God:

3 You will be blessed in the city and blessed in the country. *k*

4 The fruit of your womb will be blessed, and the crops of your land and the young of your livestock—the calves of your herds and the lambs of your flocks.

5 Your basket and your kneading trough will be blessed.

6 You will be blessed when you come in and blessed when you go out. *l*

28:1 j Dt 26:19

28:3 k Ge 39:5

28:6 l Ps 121:8

7 The LORD will grant that the enemies who rise up against you will be defeated before you. They will come at you from one direction but flee from you in seven.

8 The LORD will send a blessing on your barns and on everything you put your hand to. The LORD your God will bless you in the land he is giving you.

9 The LORD will establish you as his holy people, *m* as he promised you on oath, if you keep the commands of the LORD your God and walk in his ways. 10 Then all the peoples on earth will see that you are called by the name *n* of the LORD, and they will fear you. 11 The LORD will grant you abundant prosperity—in the fruit of your womb, the young of your livestock and the crops of your ground—in the land he swore to your forefathers to give you.

12 The LORD will open the heavens, the storehouse of his bounty, to send rain *o* on your land in season and to bless all the work of your hands. You will lend to many nations but will borrow from none. 13 The LORD will make you the head, not the tail. If you pay attention to the commands of the LORD your God that I give you this day and carefully follow them, you will always be at the top, never at the bottom. 14 Do not turn aside from any of the commands I give you today, to the right or to the left, *p* following other gods and serving them.

28:9 m Ex 19:6

28:10 n 2Ch 7:14

28:12 o Lev 26:4

28:14 p Dt 5:32

Curses for Disobedience

15 However, if you do not obey *q* the LORD your God and do not carefully follow all his commands and decrees I am giving you today, all these curses will come upon you and overtake you: *r*

16 You will be cursed in the city and cursed in the country.

17 Your basket and your kneading trough will be cursed.

18 The fruit of your womb will be cursed, and the crops of your land, and the calves of your herds and the lambs of your flocks.

19 You will be cursed when you come in and cursed when you go out.

28:15 q Lev 26:14 r Jos 23:15

20 The LORD will send on you curses, *s* confusion and rebuke *t* in everything you put your hand to, until you are destroyed and come to sudden ruin because of the evil you have done in forsaking him. *a* 21 The LORD will plague you with diseases until he has destroyed you from the land you are entering to possess. *u* 22 The LORD will strike you with wasting disease, with fever and inflammation, with scorching heat and drought, *v* with blight and mildew, which will plague you until you perish. *w* 23 The sky over your head will be bronze, the ground beneath you iron. 24 The LORD will turn the rain of your country into dust and powder; it will come down from the skies until you are destroyed.

25 The LORD will cause you to be defeated before your enemies. You will come at them from one direction but flee from them in seven, and you will become a thing of horror to all the kingdoms on earth. *x* 26 Your carcasses will be food for all the birds of the air and the beasts of the earth, and there will be no one to frighten them away. *y* 27 The LORD will afflict you with the boils of Egypt and with tumors, festering sores and the itch, from which you

28:20 s Mal 2:2 t Isa 51:20

28:21 u Lev 26:25

28:22 v Lev 26:16 w Am 4:9

28:25 x Jer 15:4

28:26 y Jer 7:33; 16:4

a 20 Hebrew me

28:23, 24 This curse is referring to a drought.

cannot be cured. 28 The LORD will afflict you with madness, blindness and confusion of mind. 29 At midday you will grope about like a blind man in the dark. You will be unsuccessful in everything you do; day after day you will be oppressed and robbed, with no one to rescue you.

30 You will be pledged to be married to a woman, but another will take her and ravish her. z You will build a house, but you will not live in it. a You will plant a vineyard, but you will not even begin to enjoy its fruit. 31 Your ox will be slaughtered before your eyes, but you will eat none of it. Your donkey will be forcibly taken from you and will not be returned. Your sheep will be given to your enemies, and no one will rescue them. 32 Your sons and daughters will be given to another nation, and you will wear out your eyes watching for them day after day, powerless to lift a hand. 33 A people that you do not know will eat what your land and labor produce, and you will have nothing but cruel oppression all your days. b 34 The sights you see will drive you mad. 35 The LORD will afflict your knees and legs with painful boils that cannot be cured, spreading from the soles of your feet to the top of your head.

36 The LORD will drive you and the king c you set over you to a nation unknown to you or your fathers. d There you will worship other gods, gods of wood and stone. e 37 You will become a thing of horror and an object of scorn and ridicule to all the nations where the LORD will drive you. f

38 You will sow much seed in the field but you will harvest little, g because locusts will devour h it. 39 You will plant vineyards and cultivate them but you will not drink the wine or gather the grapes, because worms will eat them. 40 You will have olive trees throughout your country but you will not use the oil, because the olives will drop off. 41 You will have sons and daughters but you will not keep them, because they will go into captivity. 42 Swarms of locusts will take over all your trees and the crops of your land.

43 The alien who lives among you will rise above you higher and higher, but you will sink lower and lower. i 44 He will lend to you, but you will not lend to him. j He will be the head, but you will be the tail.

45 All these curses will come upon you. They will pursue you and overtake you until you are destroyed, because you did not obey the LORD your God and observe the commands and decrees he gave you. 46 They will be a sign and a wonder to you and your descendants forever. k 47 Because you did not serve the LORD your God joyfully and gladly in the time of prosperity, 48 therefore in hunger and thirst, in nakedness and dire poverty, you will serve the enemies the LORD sends against you. He will put an iron yoke l on your neck until he has destroyed you.

49 The LORD will bring a nation against you from far away, from the ends of the earth, m like an eagle n swooping down, a nation whose language you will not understand, 50 a fierce-looking nation without respect for the old or pity for the young. 51 They will devour the young of your livestock and the crops of your land until you are destroyed. They will leave you no grain, new wine or oil, nor any calves of your herds or lambs of your flocks until you are ruined. 52 They will lay siege to all the cities throughout your land until the high fortified walls in which you trust fall down. They will besiege all the cities throughout the land the LORD your God is giving you. o

53 Because of the suffering that your enemy will inflict on you during the siege, you will eat the fruit of the womb, the flesh of the sons and daughters the LORD your God has given you. p 54 Even the most gentle and sensitive man among you will have no compassion on his own brother or the wife he loves or his surviving children, 55 and he will not give to one of them any of the flesh of his children that he is eating. It will be all he has left because of the suffering your enemy will inflict on you during the siege of all your cities. 56 The most gentle and sensitive woman among you—so sensitive and gentle that she would not venture to touch the ground with the sole of her foot—will begrudge the husband she loves and her own son or daughter 57 the afterbirth from her womb and the children she bears. For she intends to eat them secretly during the siege and in the distress that your enemy will inflict on you in your cities.

28:30
z Jer 8:10
a Am 5:11

28:33
b Jer 5:15-17

28:36
c 2Ki 17:4,6;
24:12,14
d Jer 16:13
e Dt 4:28

28:37
f Jer 24:9

28:38
g Mic 6:15;
Hag 1:6,9
h Joel 1:4

28:43
i ver 13

28:44
j ver 12

28:46
k Isa 8:18

28:48
l Jer 28:13-14

28:49
m Jer 5:15
n Hos 8:1

28:52
o Zep 1:14-16,17

28:53
p Lev 26:29;
Jer 19:9; La 2:20

28:34 One of the curses for those who rejected God was that they would go mad from seeing all the tragedy around them. Do you ever feel that you will go mad if you hear about one more rape, kidnapping, murder, or war? Much of the world's evil is a result of people's failure to acknowledge and serve God. When you hear bad news, don't groan helplessly as do unbelievers who

have no hope for the future. Remind yourself that in spite of it all, God has ultimate control and will one day come back to make everything right.

28:36 This happened when Assyria and Babylonia took the Israelites captive to their lands (2 Kings 17:23; 25:11).

58 If you do not carefully follow all the words of this law, which are written in this book, and do not revere this glorious and awesome name—the LORD your God— 59 the LORD will send fearful plagues on you and your descendants, harsh and prolonged disasters, and severe and lingering illnesses. 60 He will bring upon you all the diseases of Egypt that you dreaded, and they will cling to you. 61 The LORD will also bring on you every kind of sickness and disaster not recorded in this Book of the Law, until you are destroyed. 62 You who were as numerous as the stars in the sky q will be left but few in number, because you did not obey the LORD your God. 63 Just as it pleased the LORD to make you prosper and increase in number, so it will please him to ruin and destroy you. You will be uprooted from the land you are entering to possess.

64 Then the LORD will scatter r you among all nations, from one end of the earth to the other. There you will worship other gods—gods of wood and stone, which neither you nor your fathers have known. 65 Among those nations you will find no repose, no resting place for the sole of your foot. There the LORD will give you an anxious mind, eyes weary with longing, and a despairing heart. s 66 You will live in constant suspense, filled with dread both night and day, never sure of your life. 67 In the morning you will say, "If only it were evening!" and in the evening, "If only it were morning!"—because of the terror that will fill your hearts and the sights that your eyes will see. 68 The LORD will send you back in ships to Egypt on a journey I said you should never make again. There you will offer yourselves for sale to your enemies as male and female slaves, but no one will buy you.

28:62
q Dt 4:27; 10:22

28:64
r Dt 4:27

28:65
s Lev 26:16,36

C. A CALL FOR COMMITMENT TO GOD: MOSES' THIRD ADDRESS (29:1—30:20)

After reviewing God's laws, Moses calls for commitment, urging the people to honor the contract they had previously made with God. Knowing God's Word is not enough; we must obey it.

Renewal of the Covenant

29 These are the terms of the covenant the LORD commanded Moses to make with the Israelites in Moab, in addition to the covenant he had made with them at Horeb. t 2 Moses summoned all the Israelites and said to them:

Your eyes have seen all that the LORD did in Egypt to Pharaoh, to all his officials and to all his land. 3 With your own eyes you saw those great trials, those miraculous signs and great wonders. 4 But to this day the LORD has not given you a mind that understands or eyes that see or ears that hear. u 5 During the forty years that I led you through the desert, your clothes did not wear out, nor did the sandals on your feet. v 6 You ate no bread and drank no wine or other fermented drink. I did this so that you might know that I am the LORD your God. w

7 When you reached this place, Sihon king of Heshbon and Og king of Bashan came out to fight against us, but we defeated them. x 8 We took their land and gave it as an inheritance to the Reubenites, the Gadites and the half-tribe of Manasseh. y

9 Carefully follow z the terms of this covenant, so that you may prosper in everything you do. 10 All of you are standing today in the presence of the LORD your God—your leaders and chief men, your elders and officials, and all the other men of Israel, 11 together with your children and your wives, and the aliens living in your camps who chop your wood and carry your water. a 12 You are standing here in order to enter into a covenant with the LORD your God, a covenant the LORD is making with you this day and sealing with an oath, 13 to confirm

29:1
t Dt 5:2-3

29:4
u Isa 6:10;
Ac 28:26-27;
Ro 11:8*

29:5
v Dt 8:4

29:6
w Dt 8:3

29:7
x Nu 21:21-24,33-35

29:8
y Nu 32:33;
Dt 3:12-13

29:9
z Dt 4:6; Jos 1:7

29:11
a Jos 9:21,23,27

28:64 This severe warning tragically came true when Israel was defeated and carried away into captivity by Assyria (722 B.C.), and Judah to Babylonia (586 B.C.). Later, in A.D. 70, Roman oppression forced many Jews to flee their homeland. Thus the people were dispersed throughout the various nations.

29:1ff At Mount Sinai, 40 years earlier, God and Israel had made a covenant (Exodus 19; 20). Although there were many parts to the covenant (read the books of Exodus, Leviticus, and Numbers), its purpose can be summed up in two sentences: God promised to bless the Israelites by making them the nation through whom the rest of the world could know God. In return, the Israelites promised to love and obey God in order to receive physical and spiritual blessings. Here Moses reviewed this covenant. God was still keeping his part of the bargain (and he always would), but the Israelites were already neglecting their

part. Moses restated the covenant to warn the people that if they did not keep their part of the agreement, they would experience severe discipline.

29:5 Just as the people of Israel did not notice God's care for them along their journey, we sometimes do not notice all of the ways that God takes care of us—that all of our daily needs have been supplied and we have been well fed and well clothed. Worse yet, we mistakenly take the credit ourselves for being good providers instead of recognizing God's hand in the process.

29:9 What is the best way to prosper in life? For the Israelites, their first step was to keep their part of the covenant. They were to love God with all of their heart, soul, and strength (6:4, 5). We, too, are to seek first the kingdom of God and his righteousness (Matthew 6:33); then true success in life will follow as a blessing from the hand of God.

29:13
b Ge 17:7; Ex 6:7

you this day as his people, that he may be your God *b* as he promised you and as he swore to your fathers, Abraham, Isaac and Jacob. ¹⁴I am making this covenant, with its oath, not only with you ¹⁵who are standing here with us today in the presence of the LORD our God but also with those who are not here today.

¹⁶You yourselves know how we lived in Egypt and how we passed through the countries on the way here. ¹⁷You saw among them their detestable images and idols of wood and stone, of silver and gold.

29:18
c Heb 12:15

¹⁸Make sure there is no man or woman, clan or tribe among you today whose heart turns away from the LORD our God to go and worship the gods of those nations; make sure there is no root among you that produces such bitter poison. *c*

¹⁹When such a person hears the words of this oath, he invokes a blessing on himself and therefore thinks, "I will be safe, even though I persist in going my own way." This will bring di-

29:20
d Ps 74:1; 79:5
e Dt 9:14

saster on the watered land as well as the dry. *a* ²⁰The LORD will never be willing to forgive him; his wrath and zeal will burn *d* against that man. All the curses written in this book will fall upon him, and the LORD will blot *e* out his name from under heaven. ²¹The LORD will single him out from all the tribes of Israel for disaster, according to all the curses of the covenant written in this Book of the Law.

29:22
f Jer 19:8

²²Your children who follow you in later generations and foreigners who come from distant lands will see the calamities that have fallen on the land and the diseases with which the LORD has afflicted it. *f* ²³The whole land will be a burning waste of salt and sulfur—nothing planted,

29:23
g Zep 2:9
29:24
h Jer 22:8-9

nothing sprouting, no vegetation growing on it. It will be like the destruction of Sodom and Gomorrah, *g* Admah and Zeboiim, which the LORD overthrew in fierce anger. ²⁴All the nations will ask: "Why has the LORD done this to this land? *h* Why this fierce, burning anger?"

²⁵And the answer will be: "It is because this people abandoned the covenant of the LORD, the God of their fathers, the covenant he made with them when he brought them out of Egypt. ²⁶They went off and worshiped other gods and bowed down to them, gods they did not know, gods he had not given them. ²⁷Therefore the LORD's anger burned against this land, so that he brought on it all the curses written in this book. ²⁸In furious anger and in great wrath the LORD

29:28
i 1Ki 14:15;
2Ch 7:20

uprooted *i* them from their land and thrust them into another land, as it is now."

²⁹The secret things belong to the LORD our God, but the things revealed belong to us and to our children forever, that we may follow all the words of this law.

Prosperity After Turning to the LORD

30:1
j Dt 11:26
k 1Ki 8:47
30:2
l Dt 4:30
30:3
m Ps 126:4
n Jer 32:37;
Eze 34:13
o Jer 29:14
30:4
p Ne 1:8-9; Isa 43:6
30:6
q Jer 32:39

30 When all these blessings and curses *j* I have set before you come upon you and you take them to heart wherever the LORD your God disperses you among the nations, *k* ²and when you and your children return *l* to the LORD your God and obey him with all your heart and with all your soul according to everything I command you today, ³then the LORD your God will restore your fortunes *b* *m* and have compassion on you and gather *n* you again from all the nations where he scattered you. *o* ⁴Even if you have been banished to the most distant land under the heavens, from there the LORD your God will gather you and bring you back. *p* ⁵He will bring you to the land that belonged to your fathers, and you will take possession of it. He will make you more prosperous and numerous than your fathers. ⁶The LORD your God will circumcise your hearts and the hearts of your descendants, *q* so that you may love him with all your heart and with all your soul, and live. ⁷The LORD your God will put all

a 19 Or *way, in order to add drunkenness to thirst."*   *b 3* Or *will bring you back from captivity*

29:18 Moses cautioned that the day the Hebrews chose to turn from God, a root would be planted that would produce bitter poison (see Hebrews 12:15). When we decide to do what we know is wrong, we plant an evil seed that begins to grow out of control, eventually yielding a crop of sorrow and pain. But we can prevent those seeds of sin from taking root. If you have done something wrong, confess it to God and others immediately. If the seed never finds fertile soil, its bitter fruit will never ripen.

29:29 There are some secrets God has chosen not to reveal to us, possibly for the following reasons: (1) our finite minds cannot fully understand the infinite aspects of God's nature and the universe (Ecclesiastes 3:11); (2) some things are unnecessary for us to know until we are more mature; (3) God is infinite and all-knowing, and we do not have the capacity to know everything he does. This verse shows that although God has not told us everything there is to know about obeying him, he has told us enough.

Thus disobedience comes from an act of the will, not a lack of knowledge. Through God's Word we know enough about him to be saved by faith and to serve him. We must not use the limitation of our knowledge as an excuse to reject his claim on our life.

30:1–6 Moses told the Hebrews that when they were ready to return to God, he would be ready to receive them. God's mercy is unbelievable. It goes far beyond what we can imagine. Even if the Jews deliberately walked away from him and ruined their lives, God would still take them back. God would give them inward spiritual renewal (circumcise their hearts). God wants to forgive us and bring us back to himself too. Some people will not learn this until their world has crashed in around them. Then the sorrow and pain seem to open their eyes to what God has been saying all along. Are you separated from God by sin? No matter how far you have wandered, God promises a fresh beginning if only you will turn to him.

these curses on your enemies who hate and persecute you. 8 You will again obey the LORD and follow all his commands I am giving you today. 9 Then the LORD your God will make you most prosperous in all the work of your hands and in the fruit of your womb, the young of your livestock and the crops of your land.*r* The LORD will again delight in you and make you prosperous, just as he is delighted in your fathers, 10 if you obey the LORD your God and keep his commands and decrees that are written in this Book of the Law and turn to the LORD your God with all your heart and with all your soul.

30:9
r Jer 32:41

The Offer of Life or Death

11 Now what I am commanding you today is not too difficult for you or beyond your reach. 12 It is not up in heaven, so that you have to ask, "Who will ascend into heaven to get it and proclaim it to us so we may obey it?"*s* 13 Nor is it beyond the sea, so that you have to ask, "Who will cross the sea to get it and proclaim it to us so we may obey it?" 14 No, the word is very near you; it is in your mouth and in your heart so you may obey it.

30:12
s Ro 10:6*

15 See, I set before you today life and prosperity, death and destruction.*t* 16 For I command you today to love the LORD your God, to walk in his ways, and to keep his commands, decrees and laws; then you will live and increase, and the LORD your God will bless you in the land you are entering to possess.

30:15
t Dt 11:26

17 But if your heart turns away and you are not obedient, and if you are drawn away to bow down to other gods and worship them, 18 I declare to you this day that you will certainly be destroyed.*u* You will not live long in the land you are crossing the Jordan to enter and possess.

30:18
u Dt 8:19

19 This day I call heaven and earth as witnesses against you*v* that I have set before you life and death, blessings and curses. Now choose life, so that you and your children may live 20 and that you may love the LORD your God, listen to his voice, and hold fast to him. For the LORD is your life, and he will give you many years in the land he swore to give to your fathers, Abraham, Isaac and Jacob.

30:19
v Dt 4:26

D. THE CHALLENGE IN LEADERSHIP: MOSES' LAST DAYS (31:1—34:12)
Realizing that he is about to die, Moses commissions Joshua, records the laws in a permanent form, and teaches a special song to the Israelites. Thus Moses prepared the people for his departure. Similarly, we should not allow others to become dependent upon us for their spiritual growth, but help them to become dependent upon God.

Joshua to Succeed Moses

31 Then Moses went out and spoke these words to all Israel: 2 "I am now a hundred and twenty years old*w* and I am no longer able to lead you. The LORD has said to me, 'You shall not cross the Jordan.'*x* 3 The LORD your God himself will cross over ahead of you.*y* He will destroy these nations before you, and you will take possession of their land. Joshua also will cross over ahead of you, as the LORD said. 4 And the LORD will do to them what he did to Sihon and Og, the kings of the Amorites, whom he destroyed along with their land. 5 The LORD will deliver*z* them to you, and you must do to them all that I have commanded you. 6 Be strong and courageous.*a* Do not be afraid or terrified because of them, for the LORD your God goes with you;*b* he will never leave you nor forsake*c* you."

31:2
w Dt 34:7
x Dt 3:23,26

31:3
y Dt 9:3

31:5
z Dt 7:2

31:6
a Jos 10:25
b Dt 1:29; 20:4
c Heb 13:5*

7 Then Moses summoned Joshua and said*d* to him in the presence of all Israel, "Be strong and courageous, for you must go with this people into the land that the LORD swore to their forefathers to give them, and you must divide it among them as their inheritance. 8 The LORD himself goes before you and will be with you; he will never leave you nor forsake you. Do not be afraid; do not be discouraged."

31:7
d Dt 1:38; 3:28

The Reading of the Law

9 So Moses wrote down this law and gave it to the priests, the sons of Levi, who carried*e* the ark of the covenant of the LORD, and to all the elders of Israel. 10 Then Moses commanded

31:9
e ver 25; Nu 4:15

30:11–14 God has called us to keep his commands, while reminding us that his laws are not hidden from us or beyond our reach. Have you ever said you would obey God if you knew what he wanted? Have you ever complained that obedience is too difficult for a mere human? These are unacceptable excuses. God's laws are written in the Bible and are clearly evident in the world around us. Obeying them is reasonable, sensible, and beneficial. The most difficult part of obeying God's laws is simply deciding to start now. Paul refers to this passage in Romans 10:5–8.

30:19, 20 Moses challenged Israel to choose life, to obey God, and therefore continue to experience his blessings. God doesn't force his will on anyone. He lets us decide whether to follow him or reject him. This decision, however, is a life-or-death matter. God wants us to realize this, for he would like us all to choose life. Daily, in each new situation, we must affirm and reinforce this commitment.

31:10–13 The laws were to be read to the whole assembly so that everyone, including the children, could hear them. Every

31:10
f Dt 15:1
g Lev 23:34

31:11
h Dt 16:16
i Jos 8:34-35

31:12
j Dt 4:10

them: "At the end of every seven years, in the year for canceling debts,*f* during the Feast of Tabernacles,*g* [11]when all Israel comes to appear*h* before the LORD your God at the place he will choose, you shall read this law*i* before them in their hearing. [12]Assemble the people—men, women and children, and the aliens living in your towns—so they can listen and learn*j* to fear the LORD your God and follow carefully all the words of this law. [13]Their children, who do not know this law, must hear it and learn to fear the LORD your God as long as you live in the land you are crossing the Jordan to possess."

Israel's Rebellion Predicted

[14]The LORD said to Moses, "Now the day of your death is near. Call Joshua and present yourselves at the Tent of Meeting, where I will commission him." So Moses and Joshua came and presented themselves at the Tent of Meeting.

31:15
k Ex 33:9

31:16
l Jdg 2:12
m Jdg 10:6,13

31:17
n Jdg 6:13
o Nu 14:42

[15]Then the LORD appeared at the Tent in a pillar of cloud, and the cloud stood over the entrance to the Tent.*k* [16]And the LORD said to Moses: "You are going to rest with your fathers, and these people will soon prostitute*l* themselves to the foreign gods of the land they are entering. They will forsake*m* me and break the covenant I made with them. [17]On that day I will become angry with them and forsake*n* them; I will hide my face from them, and they will be destroyed. Many disasters and difficulties will come upon them, and on that day they will ask, 'Have not these disasters come upon us because our God is not with us?'*o* [18]And I will certainly hide my face on that day because of all their wickedness in turning to other gods.

31:20
p Dt 32:15-17

[19]"Now write down for yourselves this song and teach it to the Israelites and have them sing it, so that it may be a witness for me against them. [20]When I have brought them into the land flowing with milk and honey, the land I promised on oath to their forefathers, and when they eat their fill and thrive, they will turn to other gods*p* and worship them, rejecting me and breaking my covenant. [21]And when many disasters and difficulties come upon them, this song will testify against them, because it will not be forgotten by their descendants. I know what they are disposed to do, even before I bring them into the land I promised them on oath." [22]So Moses wrote down this song that day and taught it to the Israelites.

31:23
q ver 7
r Jos 1:6

[23]The LORD gave this command*q* to Joshua son of Nun: "Be strong and courageous,*r* for you will bring the Israelites into the land I promised them on oath, and I myself will be with you."

[24]After Moses finished writing in a book the words of this law from beginning to end, [25]he gave this command to the Levites who carried the ark of the covenant of the LORD: [26]"Take this Book of the Law and place it beside the ark of the covenant of the LORD your God. There it will remain as a witness against you. [27]For I know how rebellious and stiff-necked*s* you are. If you have been rebellious against the LORD while I am still alive and with you, how much more will you rebel after I die! [28]Assemble before me all the elders of your tribes and all your officials, so that I can speak these words in their hearing and call heaven and earth to testify against them.*t* [29]For I know that after my death you are sure to become utterly corrupt and to turn from the way I have commanded you. In days to come, disaster will fall upon you because you will do evil in the sight of the LORD and provoke him to anger by what your hands have made."

31:27
s Dt 9:6,24

31:28
t Dt 4:26; 32:1

---

seven years the entire nation would gather together and listen as a priest read the law to them. There were no books, Bibles, or newsstands to spread God's word, so the people had to rely on word of mouth and an accurate memory. Memorization was an important part of worship because if everyone knew the law, ignorance would be no excuse for breaking it. To fulfill God's purpose and will in our lives, we need the content and substance of his Word in our hearts and minds. For the Hebrews, this process began in childhood. Teaching our children and new believers should be one of our top priorities. Our finest teachers, best resources, and most careful thought should be directed toward showing young believers how to follow God in all life's situations.

31:23 Joshua had been appointed to take over the leadership of Israel and guide the people into the promised land (Moses could not enter the land due to his disobedience—Numbers 20:12). Joshua, first mentioned in Exodus 17:9, had been Moses' assistant for many years (Joshua 1:1). One of his key qualifications was his faith. As one of the 12 spies to first enter Canaan, only he and Caleb believed that God could help Israel conquer the

land (Numbers 13:1—14:30). Moses told Joshua to be strong and courageous twice in this chapter (31:7, 23). Indeed, this was a frightening task with three million people to care for, settle disputes for, and lead into battle. Finding courage would be Joshua's greatest test. He was strong and courageous because he knew God was with him and because he had faith that God would do all he had promised Israel.

31:27-29 Moses knew that the Israelites, in spite of all they had seen of God's work, were rebellious at heart. They deserved God's punishment, although they often received his mercy instead. We too are stubborn and rebellious by nature. Throughout our lives we struggle with sin. Repentance once a month or once a week is not enough. We must constantly turn from our sins to God and let him, in his mercy, save us.

The Song of Moses

30And Moses recited the words of this song from beginning to end in the hearing of the whole assembly of Israel:

32 Listen, O heavens,u and I will speak;
    hear, O earth, the words of my mouth.
2 Let my teaching fall like rain
    and my words descend like dew,v
like showers on new grass,
    like abundant rain on tender plants.

3 I will proclaim the name of the LORD. w
    Oh, praise the greatness of our God!
4 He is the Rock, his works are perfect,x
    and all his ways are just.
A faithful God who does no wrong,
    upright and just is he.

5 They have acted corruptly toward him;
    to their shame they are no longer his children,
    but a warped and crooked generation.a y
6 Is this the way you repayz the LORD,
    O foolish and unwise people?
Is he not your Father,a your Creator,b
    who made you and formed you?

7 Remember the days of old;
    consider the generations long past.
Ask your father and he will tell you,
    your elders, and they will explain to you.
8 When the Most High gave the nations their inheritance,
    when he divided all mankind,b
he set up boundaries for the peoples
    according to the number of the sons of Israel.c
9 For the LORD's portionc is his people,
    Jacob his allotted inheritance.

10 In a desert land he found him,
    in a barren and howling waste.
He shielded him and cared for him;
    he guarded him as the apple of his eye,d
11 like an eagle that stirs up its nest
    and hovers over its young,e
that spreads its wings to catch them
    and carries them on its pinions.
12 The LORD alone led him;
    no foreign god was with him.

13 He made him ride on the heightsf of the land
    and fed him with the fruit of the fields.
He nourished him with honey from the rock,
    and with oil from the flinty crag,
14 with curds and milk from herd and flock
    and with fattened lambs and goats,

32:1
uIsa 1:2

32:2
vIsa 55:11

32:3
wEx 33:19

32:4
x2Sa 22:31

32:5
yDt 31:29

32:6
zPs 116:12
aIsa 63:16

32:8
bGe 11:8; Ac 17:26

32:9
cJer 10:16

32:10
dPs 17:8; Zec 2:8

32:11
eEx 19:4

32:13
fIsa 58:14

a5 Or *Corrupt are they and not his children, / a generation warped and twisted to their shame*   b6 Or *Father, who bought you*   c8 Masoretic Text; Dead Sea Scrolls (see also Septuagint) *sons of God*

32:1ff Moses was not only a great prophet but also a song leader. After three sermons, he changed the form of his message to singing. Sometimes reciting something in a different form makes it easier to remember. This song gives a brief history of Israel. It reminds the people of their mistakes, warns them to avoid repetition of those mistakes, and offers the hope that comes only in trusting God.

32:10 The Israelites had no excuse for abandoning God. He had shielded them like a kindly shepherd. He had guarded them like a

32:14
g Ps 81:16

with choice rams of Bashan
    and the finest kernels of wheat.*g*
You drank the foaming blood of the grape.

32:15
h Dt 31:20
i Isa 1:4,28

15 Jeshurun*a* grew fat*h* and kicked;
    filled with food, he became heavy and sleek.
He abandoned*i* the God who made him
    and rejected the Rock his Savior.

32:16
j 1Co 10:22

16 They made him jealous*j* with their foreign gods
    and angered him with their detestable idols.

32:17
k Dt 28:64

17 They sacrificed to demons, which are not God—
    gods they had not known,*k*
    gods that recently appeared,
    gods your fathers did not fear.
18 You deserted the Rock, who fathered you;
    you forgot the God who gave you birth.

32:19
l Ps 106:40

19 The LORD saw this and rejected them
    because he was angered by his sons and daughters.*l*

32:20
m Dt 31:17,29

20 "I will hide my face*m* from them," he said,
    "and see what their end will be;
for they are a perverse generation,
    children who are unfaithful.

32:21
n Ro 10:19*

21 They made me jealous by what is no god
    and angered me with their worthless idols.
I will make them envious by those who are not a people;
    I will make them angry by a nation that has no understanding.*n*

32:22
o La 4:11

22 For a fire has been kindled by my wrath,
    one that burns to the realm of death*b* below.*o*
It will devour the earth and its harvests
    and set afire the foundations of the mountains.

32:23
p Dt 29:21

23 "I will heap calamities*p* upon them
    and spend my arrows against them.

32:24
q Dt 28:22
r Lev 26:22

24 I will send wasting famine against them,
    consuming pestilence*q* and deadly plague;
I will send against them the fangs of wild beasts,*r*
    the venom of vipers that glide in the dust.

32:25
s Eze 7:15
t 2Ch 36:17

25 In the street the sword will make them childless;
    in their homes terror will reign.*s*
Young men and young women will perish,
    infants and gray-haired men.*t*

32:26
u Dt 4:27

26 I said I would scatter*u* them
    and blot out their memory from mankind,

a 15 Jeshurun means *the upright one*, that is, Israel.   *b* 22 Hebrew *to Sheol*

VARIETY IN WORSHIP
Israel's worship used all of the senses. They reinforced the meaning of the ceremony. Every sense can be used to worship God.

SIGHT	The beauty and symbolism of the tabernacle; every color and hue had a meaning	
HEARING	The use of music; there were instructions for the use of a variety of instruments, and the Bible records many songs	
TOUCH	The head of the animal to be sacrificied was touched, symbolizing the fact that it was taking their place	
SMELL	The sacrifices were burned, emitting a familiar aroma	
TASTE	The feasts were celebrations and memorials—much of the food was symbolic	

---

person protects the pupil (apple) of his eye. He had been the encircling protector, like a mother eagle who protects her young.

The Lord alone had led them. And he alone leads us. Let us remember to trust in him.

²⁷ but I dreaded the taunt of the enemy,
    lest the adversary misunderstand
and say, 'Our hand has triumphed;
    the LORD has not done all this.'"

²⁸ They are a nation without sense,
    there is no discernment in them.
²⁹ If only they were wise and would understand this
    and discern what their end will be!
³⁰ How could one man chase a thousand,
    or two put ten thousand to flight,ᵛ
unless their Rock had sold them,
    unless the LORD had given them up?ʷ
³¹ For their rock is not like our Rock,
    as even our enemies concede.
³² Their vine comes from the vine of Sodom
    and from the fields of Gomorrah.
Their grapes are filled with poison,
    and their clusters with bitterness.
³³ Their wine is the venom of serpents,
    the deadly poison of cobras.ˣ

³⁴ "Have I not kept this in reserve
    and sealed it in my vaults?
³⁵ It is mine to avenge; I will repay.ʸ
    In due time their foot will slip;
their day of disaster is near
    and their doom rushes upon them."

³⁶ The LORD will judge his people
    and have compassion on his servantsᶻ
when he sees their strength is gone
    and no one is left, slave or free.
³⁷ He will say: "Now where are their gods,
    the rock they took refuge in,ᵃ
³⁸ the gods who ate the fat of their sacrifices
    and drank the wine of their drink offerings?
Let them rise up to help you!
    Let them give you shelter!

³⁹ "See now that I myself am He!ᵇ
    There is no god besides me.ᶜ
I put to death and I bring to life,
    I have wounded and I will heal,
    and no one can deliver out of my hand.ᵈ
⁴⁰ I lift my hand to heaven and declare:
    As surely as I live forever,
⁴¹ when I sharpen my flashing swordᵉ
    and my hand grasps it in judgment,
I will take vengeance on my adversaries
    and repay those who hate me.ᶠ
⁴² I will make my arrows drunk with blood,
    while my sword devours flesh:ᵍ
the blood of the slain and the captives,
    the heads of the enemy leaders."

⁴³ Rejoice,ʰ O nations, with his people,ᵃ·ᵇ
    for he will avenge the blood of his servants;
he will take vengeance on his enemies
    and make atonement for his land and people.ⁱ

ᵃ43 Or *Make his people rejoice, O nations* ᵇ43 Masoretic Text; Dead Sea Scrolls (see also Septuagint) *people, /
and let all the angels worship him /*

32:30
ᵛLev 26:8
ʷPs 44:12

32:33
ˣPs 58:4

32:35
ʸRo 12:19*;
Heb 10:30*

32:36
ᶻPs 135:14;
Joel 2:14

32:37
ᵃJdg 10:14;
Jer 2:28

32:39
ᵇIsa 41:4
ᶜIsa 45:5
ᵈPs 50:22

32:41
ᵉIsa 66:16
ᶠJer 50:29

32:42
ᵍJer 46:10,14

32:43
ʰRo 15:10*
ⁱPs 85:1; Rev 19:2

44 Moses came with Joshua[a] son of Nun and spoke all the words of this song in the hearing of the people. 45 When Moses finished reciting all these words to all Israel, 46 he said to them, "Take to heart all the words I have solemnly declared to you this day,[j] so that you may command your children to obey carefully all the words of this law. 47 They are not just idle words for you—they are your life. By them you will live long in the land you are crossing the Jordan to possess."

Moses to Die on Mount Nebo

48 On that same day the LORD told Moses, 49 "Go up into the Abarim[k] Range to Mount Nebo in Moab, across from Jericho, and view Canaan, the land I am giving the Israelites as their own possession. 50 There on the mountain that you have climbed you will die and be gathered to your people, just as your brother Aaron died on Mount Hor and was gathered to his people. 51 This is because both of you broke faith with me in the presence of the Israelites at the waters of Meribah Kadesh in the Desert of Zin[l] and because you did not uphold my holiness among the Israelites. 52 Therefore, you will see the land only from a distance;[m] you will not enter the land I am giving to the people of Israel."

Moses Blesses the Tribes

33 This is the blessing that Moses the man of God pronounced on the Israelites before his death. 2 He said:

> "The LORD came from Sinai
>   and dawned over them from Seir;
>   he shone forth from Mount Paran.[n]
> He came with[b] myriads of holy ones[o]
>   from the south, from his mountain slopes.[c]
> 3 Surely it is you who love the people;
>   all the holy ones are in your hand.
> At your feet they all bow down,[p]
>   and from you receive instruction,
> 4 the law that Moses gave us,
>   the possession of the assembly of Jacob.[q]
> 5 He was king over Jeshurun[d]
>   when the leaders of the people assembled,
>   along with the tribes of Israel.
>
> 6 "Let Reuben live and not die,
>   nor[e] his men be few."

7 And this he said about Judah:[r]

> "Hear, O LORD, the cry of Judah;
>   bring him to his people.
> With his own hands he defends his cause.
>   Oh, be his help against his foes!"

8 About Levi he said:

> "Your Thummim and Urim[s] belong
>   to the man you favored.
> You tested him at Massah;
>   you contended with him at the waters of Meribah.[t]
> 9 He said of his father and mother,[u]
>   'I have no regard for them.'

**Cross references (left margin):**

32:46 [j] Eze 40:4

32:49 [k] Nu 27:12

32:51 [l] Nu 20:11-13

32:52 [m] Dt 34:1-3

33:2 [n] Hab 3:3 [o] Da 7:10; Rev 5:11

33:3 [p] Lk 10:39

33:4 [q] Ps 119:111

33:7 [r] Ge 49:10

33:8 [s] Ex 28:30 [t] Ex 17:7

33:9 [u] Ex 32:26-29

---

[a] 44 Hebrew *Hoshea*, a variant of *Joshua*   [b] 2 Or *from*   [c] 2 The meaning of the Hebrew for this phrase is uncertain.   [d] 5 *Jeshurun* means *the upright one*, that is, Israel; also in verse 26.   [e] 6 Or *but let*

32:46, 47 Moses urged the people to think about God's word and teach it to their children. The Bible can sit on your bookshelf and gather dust, or you can make it a vital part of your life by regularly setting aside time to study it. When you discover the wisdom of God's message, you will want to apply it to your life and pass it on to your family and others. The Bible is not merely good reading—it's real help for real life.

33:6–25 Note the difference in blessings God gave each tribe.

To one he gave the best land, to another strength, to another safety. Too often we see someone with a particular blessing and think that God must love that person more than others. Think rather that God draws out in all people their unique talents. All these gifts are needed to complete his plan. Don't be envious of the gifts others have. Instead, look for the gifts God has given you, and resolve to do the tasks he has uniquely qualified you to do.

He did not recognize his brothers
or acknowledge his own children,
but he watched over your word
and guarded your covenant.

10 He teaches your precepts to Jacob
and your law to Israel.
He offers incense before you
and whole burnt offerings on your altar. *v*

11 Bless all his skills, O LORD,
and be pleased with the work of his hands.
Smite the loins of those who rise up against him;
strike his foes till they rise no more."

12About Benjamin he said:

"Let the beloved of the LORD rest secure in him,
for he shields him all day long,
and the one the LORD loves rests between his shoulders."

13About Joseph *w* he said:

"May the LORD bless his land
with the precious dew from heaven above
and with the deep waters that lie below;*x*

14 with the best the sun brings forth
and the finest the moon can yield;

15 with the choicest gifts of the ancient mountains
and the fruitfulness of the everlasting hills;

16 with the best gifts of the earth and its fullness
and the favor of him who dwelt in the burning bush.*y*
Let all these rest on the head of Joseph,
on the brow of the prince among*a* his brothers.

17 In majesty he is like a firstborn bull;
his horns are the horns of a wild ox. *z*
With them he will gore*a* the nations,
even those at the ends of the earth.
Such are the ten thousands of Ephraim;
such are the thousands of Manasseh."

18About Zebulun *b* he said:

"Rejoice, Zebulun, in your going out,
and you, Issachar, in your tents.

19 They will summon peoples to the mountain*c*
and there offer sacrifices of righteousness;*d*
they will feast on the abundance of the seas,
on the treasures hidden in the sand."

20About Gad he said:

"Blessed is he who enlarges Gad's domain!
Gad lives there like a lion,
tearing at arm or head.

21 He chose the best land for himself;
the leader's portion was kept for him.
When the heads of the people assembled,
he carried out the LORD's righteous will,*e*
and his judgments concerning Israel."

---

a 16 Or *of the one separated from*

33:10
v Ps 51:19

33:13
w Ge 49:25
x Ge 27:28

33:16
y Ex 3:2

33:17
z Nu 23:22
a Ps 44:5

33:18
b Ge 49:13-15

33:19
c Isa 2:3
d Ps 4:5

33:21
e Jos 4:12

33:20, 21 The people of the tribe of Gad received the best of the new land because they obeyed God by punishing Israel's wicked enemies. Punishment is unpleasant for both the giver and the receiver, but it is a necessary part of growth. If you are in a position that sometimes requires you to correct others, don't hold back from fulfilling your task.

33:22
f Ge 49:16

22 About Dan *f* he said:

"Dan is a lion's cub,
   springing out of Bashan."

23 About Naphtali he said:

"Naphtali is abounding with the favor of the LORD
   and is full of his blessing;
   he will inherit southward to the lake."

33:24
g Ge 49:21
h Ge 49:20;
Job 29:6

24 About Asher *g* he said:

"Most blessed of sons is Asher;
   let him be favored by his brothers,
   and let him bathe his feet in oil. *h*
25 The bolts of your gates will be iron and bronze,
   and your strength will equal your days.

33:26
i Ex 15:11

26 "There is no one like the God of Jeshurun, *i*
   who rides on the heavens to help you
   and on the clouds in his majesty.

33:27
j Ps 90:1
k Jos 24:18

27 The eternal God is your refuge, *j*
   and underneath are the everlasting arms.
He will drive out your enemy before you, *k*
   saying, 'Destroy him!'

33:28
l Ge 27:28

28 So Israel will live in safety alone;
   Jacob's spring is secure
in a land of grain and new wine,
   where the heavens drop dew. *l*

33:29
m Ps 144:15
n Ps 115:9-11

29 Blessed are you, O Israel! *m*
   Who is like you,
   a people saved by the LORD?
He is your shield and helper *n*
   and your glorious sword.
Your enemies will cower before you,
   and you will trample down their high places. *a*"

The Death of Moses

34:1
o Dt 32:49
p Dt 32:52

34 Then Moses climbed Mount Nebo from the plains of Moab to the top of Pisgah, across from Jericho. *o* There the LORD showed *p* him the whole land—from Gilead to Dan, 2 all of Naphtali, the territory of Ephraim and Manasseh, all the land of Judah as far as

a 29 Or *will tread upon their bodies*

THE DEATH OF MOSES

Just before Moses died, he climbed Mount Nebo. Although he could not enter the promised land, God showed him its beauty from Mount Nebo's peak.

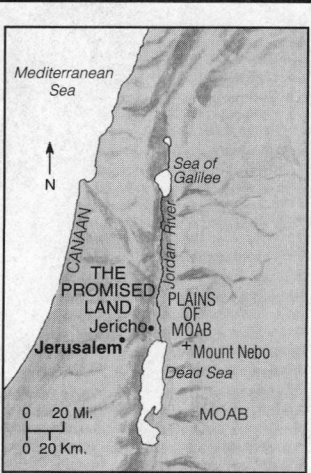

Mediterranean Sea

N

Sea of Galilee

CANAAN

Jordan River

THE PROMISED LAND

PLAINS OF MOAB

Jericho•

Jerusalem•

+ Mount Nebo

Dead Sea

MOAB

0   20 Mi.

0   20 Km.

Understand that realistic discipline is important to character development. Always strive to be both just and merciful, keeping in mind the best interests of the person who must receive the punishment.

33:24 Bathing feet in oil was a sign of prosperity.

33:27 Moses' song declares that God is our refuge, our only true security. How often we entrust our lives to other things—perhaps money, career, a noble cause, or a lifelong dream. But our only true refuge is the eternal God, who always holds out his arms to catch us when the shaky supports that we trust collapse and we fall. No storm can destroy us when we take refuge in him. Those without God, however, must forever be cautious. One mistake may wipe them out. Living for God in this world may look like risky business. But it is the godless who are on shaky ground. Because God is our refuge, we can dare to be bold.

the western sea,[a] [q] [3]the Negev and the whole region from the Valley of Jericho, the City of Palms,[r] as far as Zoar. [4]Then the LORD said to him, "This is the land I promised on oath to Abraham, Isaac and Jacob when I said, 'I will give it[s] to your descendants.' I have let you see it with your eyes, but you will not cross over into it."

[5]And Moses the servant of the LORD died[t] there in Moab, as the LORD had said. [6]He buried him[b] in Moab, in the valley opposite Beth Peor, but to this day no one knows where his grave is.[u] [7]Moses was a hundred and twenty years old[v] when he died, yet his eyes were not weak[w] nor his strength gone. [8]The Israelites grieved for Moses in the plains of Moab thirty days, until the time of weeping and mourning was over.

[9]Now Joshua son of Nun was filled with the spirit[c] of wisdom[x] because Moses had laid his hands on him.[y] So the Israelites listened to him and did what the LORD had commanded Moses.

[10]Since then, no prophet has risen in Israel like Moses,[z] whom the LORD knew face to face,[a] [11]who did all those miraculous signs and wonders the LORD sent him to do in Egypt—to Pharaoh and to all his officials and to his whole land. [12]For no one has ever shown the mighty power or performed the awesome deeds that Moses did in the sight of all Israel.

[a]2 That is, the Mediterranean   [b]6 Or *He was buried*   [c]9 Or *Spirit*

34:2
[q]Dt 11:24

34:3
[r]2Ch 28:15

34:4
[s]Ge 12:7

34:5
[t]Dt 32:50; Jos 1:1-2

34:6
[u]Jude 1:9

34:7
[v]Dt 31:2
[w]Ge 27:1

34:9
[x]Isa 11:2
[y]Nu 27:18,23

34:10
[z]Dt 18:15,18
[a]Ex 33:11;
Nu 12:6,8; Dt 5:4

34:4, 10 Moses was the only person who ever spoke with God face to face (Exodus 33:11; Numbers 12:8). He was called Israel's greatest prophet. Yet even this great man was not allowed to enter the promised land because he disobeyed God (Numbers 20:12). No matter how good we are, or how much we've done for God, we sometimes disobey him. The result of our disobedience is that we will be disciplined. God disciplined Moses severely, but still called him his friend. When you experience the sting of God's discipline, respond as Moses did. Don't turn away in anger, embarrassment, or resentment. Instead, turn toward God with love, openness, and a desire to do better.

34:10-12 Moses, the man who did not want to be sent to Egypt because he was "slow of speech" (Exodus 4:10), delivered the three addresses to Israel that make up the book of Deuteronomy. God gave him the power to develop from a stuttering shepherd into a national leader and powerful orator. His courage, humility, and wisdom molded the Hebrew slaves into a nation. But Moses was one person who did not let success go to his head. In the end, God was still Moses' best friend. His love, respect, and awe for God had grown daily throughout his life. Moses knew that it was not any greatness in himself that made him successful; it was the greatness of the all-powerful God in whom he trusted. There were many great and powerful prophets during the time of the kings. But it would be more than a thousand years before one greater than Moses would appear—Jesus.

KEY PLACES IN JOSHUA

Mediterranean Sea
LEBANON
N
SYRIA
Hazor
Sea of Galilee
ISRAEL
Jordan River
Mount Ebal +
Shechem
Mount Gerizim +
Shiloh
Ai
Gibeon
Gilgal
Jericho
Shittim
VALLEY OF AIJALON
Jerusalem
JORDAN
Dead Sea

0   20 Mi.

0   20 Km.

The broken lines (– · – ·) indicate modern boundaries.

4 Jericho The walled city of Jericho seemed a formidable enemy. But when Joshua followed God's plans, the great walls were no obstacle. The city was conquered with only the obedient marching of the people (6:1–27).

5 Ai Victory could not continue without obedience to God. That is why the disobedience of one man, Achan, brought defeat to the entire nation in the first battle against Ai. But once the sin was recognized and punished, God told Joshua to take heart and try Ai once again. This time the city was taken (7:1—8:29).

6 The Mountains of Ebal and Gerizim After the defeat of Ai, Joshua built an altar at Mount Ebal. Then the people divided themselves, half at the foot of Mount Ebal, half at the foot of Mount Gerizim. The priests stood between the mountains holding the ark of the covenant as Joshua read God's law to all the people (8:30–35).

7 Gibeon It was just after the Israelites reaffirmed their covenant with God that their leaders made a major mistake in judgment: They were tricked into making a peace treaty with the city of Gibeon. The Gibeonites pretended that they had traveled a long distance and asked the Israelites for a treaty. The leaders made the agreement without consulting God. The trick was soon discovered, but because the treaty had been made, Israel could not go back on its word. As a result, the Gibeonites saved their own lives, but they were forced to become Israel's slaves (9:1–27).

8 Valley of Aijalon The king of Jerusalem was very angry at Gibeon for making a peace treaty with the Israelites. He gathered armies from four other cities to attack the city. Gibeon summoned Joshua for help. Joshua took immediate action. Leaving Gilgal, he attacked the coalition by surprise. As the battle waged on and moved into the Valley of Aijalon, Joshua prayed for the sun to stand still until the enemy could be destroyed (10:1–43).

1 Shittim The story of Joshua begins with the Israelites camping at Shittim. The Israelites under Joshua were ready to enter and conquer Canaan. But before the nation moved out, Joshua received instructions from God (1:1–18).

2 Jordan River The entire nation prepared to cross this river, which was swollen from spring rains. After the spies returned from Jericho with a positive report, Joshua prepared the priests and people for a miracle. As the priests carried the ark into the Jordan River, the water stopped flowing, and the entire nation crossed on dry ground into the promised land (2:1—4:24).

3 Gilgal After crossing the Jordan River, the Israelites camped at Gilgal, where they renewed their commitment to God and celebrated the Passover, the feast commemorating their deliverance from Egypt (see Exodus). As Joshua made plans for the attack on Jericho, an angel appeared to him (5:1–15).

9 Hazor Up north in Hazor, King Jabin mobilized the kings of the surrounding cities to unite and crush Israel. But God gave Joshua and Israel victory (11:1–23).

10 Shiloh After the armies of Canaan were conquered, Israel gathered at Shiloh to set up the tabernacle. This movable building had been the nation's center of worship during their years of wandering. The seven tribes who had not received their land were given their allotments (18:1—19:51).

11 Shechem Before Joshua died he called the entire nation together at Shechem to remind them that it was God who had given them their land and that only with God's help could they keep it. The people vowed to follow God. As long as Joshua was alive, the land was at rest from war and trouble (24:1–33).

JOSHUA

Exodus from Egypt 1446 B.C. (1280 B.C.)	Israelites enter Canaan 1406 (1240)	Judges begin to rule 1375 (1220)	THE DAYS OF

CONQUEST OF CANAAN

VITAL STATISTICS

PURPOSE:
To give the history of Israel's conquest of the promised land

AUTHOR:
Joshua, except for the ending, which may have been written by the high priest, Phinehas, an eyewitness to the events recounted there

ORIGINAL AUDIENCE:
The people of Israel

SETTING:
Canaan, also called the promised land, which occupied the same general geographical territory of modern-day Israel

KEY VERSE:
"Go through the camp and tell the people, 'Get your supplies ready. Three days from now you will cross the Jordan here to go in and take possession of the land the LORD your God is giving you for your own.'" (1:11).

KEY PEOPLE:
Joshua, Rahab, Achan, Phinehas, Eleazar

KEY PLACES:
Jericho, Ai, Mount Ebal, Mount Gerizim, Gibeon, Gilgal, Shiloh, Shechem

SPECIAL FEATURE:
Out of over a million people, Joshua and Caleb were the only two who left Egypt and entered the promised land.

REMEMBER the childhood game "follow the leader"? The idea was to mimic the antics of the person in front of you in the line of boys and girls winding through the neighborhood. Being a follower was all right, but being leader was the most fun, creating imaginative routes and tasks for everyone else to copy.

In real life, great leaders are rare. Often, men and women are elected or appointed to leadership positions but then falter or fail to act. Others abuse their power to satisfy their egos, crushing their subjects and squandering resources. But without faithful, ethical, and effective leaders, people wander.

For 40 years, Israel had journeyed a circuitous route through the desert, but *not* because they were following their leader. Quite the opposite was true—with failing faith, they had refused to obey God and to conquer Canaan. So they wandered. Finally, the new generation was ready to cross the Jordan and possess the land. Having distinguished himself as a man of faith and courage (he and Caleb had given the minority scout report recorded in Numbers 13:30—14:9), Joshua was chosen to be Moses' successor. This book records Joshua's leadership of the people of God as they finished their march and conquered the promised land.

Joshua was a brilliant military leader and a strong spiritual influence. But the key to his success was his submission to God. When God spoke, Joshua listened and obeyed. Joshua's obedience served as a model. As a result, Israel remained faithful to God throughout Joshua's lifetime.

The book of Joshua is divided into two main parts. The first narrates the events surrounding the conquest of Canaan. After crossing the Jordan River on dry ground, the Israelites camped near the mighty city of Jericho. God commanded the people to conquer Jericho by marching around the city 13 times, blowing trumpets, and shouting. Because they followed God's unique battle strategy, they won (chapter 6). After the destruction of Jericho, they set out against the small town of Ai. Their first attack was driven back because one of the Israelites (Achan) had sinned (chapter 7). After the men of Israel stoned Achan and his family—purging the community of its sin—the Israelites succeeded in capturing Ai (chapter 8). In their next battle against the Amorites, God even provided extended daylight to aid them in their victory (chapter 10). Finally, after defeating other assorted Canaanites led by Jabin and his allies (chapter 11), they possessed most of the land.

Part two of the book of Joshua records the assignment and settlement of the captured territory (chapters 13—22). The book concludes with Joshua's farewell address and his death (chapters 23—24).

Joshua was committed to obeying God, and this book is about obedience. Whether conquering enemies or settling the land, God's people were required to do it God's way. In his final message to the people, Joshua underscored the importance of obeying God. "So be very careful to love the LORD your God" (23:11), and "choose for yourselves this day whom you will serve. . . . But as for me and my household, we will serve the LORD" (24:15). Read Joshua and make a fresh commitment to obey God today. Decide to follow your Lord wherever he leads and whatever it costs.

*United
kingdom
under
Saul
1050
(1045)*

*David
becomes
king
1010*

THE BLUEPRINT

A. ENTERING THE PROMISED LAND
(1:1—5:12)
1. Joshua leads the nation
2. Crossing the Jordan

Joshua demonstrated his faith in God as he took up the challenge to lead the nation. The Israelites reaffirmed their commitment to God by obediently setting out across the Jordan River to possess the land. As we live the Christian life, we need to cross over from the old life to the new, put off our selfish desires, and press on to possess all God has planned for us. Like Joshua and Israel, we need courageous faith to live the new life.

B. CONQUERING THE PROMISED LAND
(5:13—12:24)
1. Joshua attacks the center of the land
2. Joshua attacks the southern kings
3. Joshua attacks the northern kings
4. Summary of conquests

Joshua and his army moved from city to city, cleansing the land of its wickedness by destroying every trace of idol worship. Conflict with evil is inevitable, and we should be as merciless as Israel in destroying sin in our lives.

C. DIVIDING THE PROMISED LAND
(13:1—24:33)
1. The tribes receive their land
2. Special cities are set aside
3. Eastern tribes return home
4. Joshua's farewell to Israel

Joshua urged the Israelites to continue to follow the Lord and worship him alone. The people had seen God deliver them from many enemies and miraculously provide for all their needs, but they were prone to wander from the Lord. Even though we may have experienced God at work in our lives, we, too, must continually renew our commitment to obey him above all other authority and to worship him alone.

MEGATHEMES

THEME	EXPLANATION	IMPORTANCE
Success	God gave success to the Israelites when they obeyed his master plan, not when they followed their own desires. Victory came when they trusted in him rather than in their military power, money, muscle, or mental capacity.	God's work done in God's way will bring his success. The standard for success, however, is not to be set by the society around us but by God's Word. We must adjust our minds to God's way of thinking in order to see his standard for success.
Faith	The Israelites demonstrated their faith by trusting God daily to save and guide them. By noticing how God fulfilled his promises in the past, they developed strong confidence that he would be faithful in the future.	Our strength to do God's work comes from trusting him. His promises reassure us of his love and that he will be there to guide us in the decisions and struggles we face. Faith begins with believing he can be trusted.
Guidance	God gave instructions to Israel for every aspect of their lives. His law guided their daily living, and his specific marching orders gave them victory in battle.	Guidance from God for daily living can be found in his Word. By staying in touch with God, we will have the needed wisdom to meet the great challenges of life.
Leadership	Joshua was an example of an excellent leader. He was confident in God's strength, courageous in the face of opposition, and willing to seek God's advice.	To be a strong leader like Joshua, we must be ready to listen and to move quickly when God instructs us. Once we have his instructions, we must be diligent in carrying them out. Strong leaders are led by God.
Conquest	God commanded his people to conquer the Canaanites and take all their land. Completing this mission would have fulfilled God's promise to Abraham and brought judgment on the evil people living there. Unfortunately, Israel never finished the job.	The Israelites were faithful in accomplishing their mission at first, but their commitment faltered. To love God means more than being enthusiastic about him. We must complete all the work he gives us and apply his instructions to every corner of our lives.

A. ENTERING THE PROMISED LAND (1:1—5:12)

After wandering for 40 years in the desert, a new generation is ready to enter Canaan. But first God prepares both Joshua and the nation by teaching them the importance of courageous and consistent faith. The nation then miraculously crosses the Jordan River to begin the long-awaited conquest of the promised land. Like Joshua, we, too, need faith to begin and continue living the Christian life.

1. Joshua leads the nation

The LORD Commands Joshua

1 After the death of Moses the servant of the LORD,[a] the LORD said to Joshua son of Nun, Moses' aide: 2"Moses my servant is dead. Now then, you and all these people, get ready to cross the Jordan River[b] into the land I am about to give to them—to the Israelites. 3I will give you every place where you set your foot,[c] as I promised Moses. 4Your territory will extend from the desert to Lebanon, and from the great river, the Euphrates[d]—all the Hittite country—to the Great Sea[a] on the west. 5No one will be able to stand up against you[e] all the days of your life. As I was with Moses, so I will be with you; I will never leave you nor forsake[f] you.

6"Be strong and courageous, because you will lead these people to inherit the land I swore to their forefathers[g] to give them. 7Be strong and very courageous. Be careful to obey all the law my servant Moses gave you; do not turn from it to the right or to the left,[h] that you may be successful wherever you go. 8Do not let this Book of the Law depart from your mouth; meditate on it day and night, so that you may be careful to do everything written in it. Then you will be prosperous and successful.[i] 9Have I not commanded you? Be strong and courageous. Do not be terrified; do not be discouraged, for the LORD your God will be with you wherever you go."[j]

10So Joshua ordered the officers of the people: 11"Go through the camp and tell the people, 'Get your supplies ready. Three days from now you will cross the Jordan here to go in and take possession of the land the LORD your God is giving you for your own.'"

12But to the Reubenites, the Gadites and the half-tribe of Manasseh,[k] Joshua said, 13"Remember the command that Moses the servant of the LORD gave you: 'The LORD your God is

a4 That is, the Mediterranean

1:1 [a]Dt 34:5
1:2 [b]ver 11
1:3 [c]Dt 11:24
1:4 [d]Ge 15:18
1:5 [e]Dt 7:24 [f]Dt 31:6-8
1:6 [g]Dt 31:23
1:7 [h]Dt 5:32
1:8 [i]Ps 1:1-3
1:9 [j]Dt 31:7-8; Jer 1:8
1:12 [k]Nu 32:20-22

1:1 As the book of Joshua opens, the Israelites are camped along the east bank of the Jordan River at the very edge of the promised land and they are completing the mourning period for Moses, who has just died (Deuteronomy 34:7, 8). Thirty-nine years earlier (after spending a year at Mount Sinai receiving God's law), the Israelites had an opportunity to enter the promised land, but they failed to trust God to give them victory. As a result, God did not allow them to enter the land, but made them wander in the desert until the disobedient generation had all died.

During their desert wanderings, the Israelites obeyed God's laws. They also taught the new generation to obey God's laws so that they might enter the promised land (also called Canaan). As the children grew, they were often reminded that faith and obedience to God brought victory, while unbelief and disobedience brought tragedy. When the last of the older generation had died and the new generation had become adults, the Israelites prepared to make their long-awaited claim on the promised land.

1:1-5 Joshua succeeded Moses as Israel's leader. What qualifications did he have to become the leader of a nation? (1) God appointed him (Numbers 27:18–23). (2) He was one of only two living eyewitnesses to the Egyptian plagues and the exodus from Egypt. (3) He was Moses' personal aide for 40 years. (4) Of the 12 spies, only he and Caleb showed complete confidence that God would help them conquer the land.

1:2 Because Joshua had assisted Moses for many years, he was well prepared to take over the leadership of the nation. Changes in leadership are common in many organizations. At such times, a smooth transition is essential for the establishment of the new administration. This doesn't happen unless new leaders are trained. If you are currently in a leadership position, begin preparing someone to take your place. Then, when you leave or are promoted, operations can continue to run efficiently. If you want

to be a leader, learn from others so that you will be prepared when the opportunity comes.

1:5 Joshua's new job consisted of leading more than two million people into a strange new land and conquering it. What a challenge—even for a man of Joshua's caliber! Every new job is a challenge. Without God it can be frightening. With God it can be a great adventure. Just as God was with Joshua, he is with us as we face our new challenges. We may not conquer nations, but every day we face tough situations, difficult people, and temptations. God promises, however, that he will never abandon us or fail to help us. By asking God to direct us we can conquer many of life's challenges.

1:6–8 Many people think that prosperity and success come from having power, influential personal contacts, and a relentless desire to get ahead. But the strategy for gaining prosperity that God taught Joshua goes against such criteria. He said that to succeed Joshua must (1) be strong and courageous because the task ahead would not be easy, (2) obey God's law, and (3) constantly read and study the Book of the Law—God's Word. To be successful, follow God's words to Joshua. You may not succeed by the world's standards, but you will be a success in God's eyes—and his approval is most important.

1:12–15 During the previous year, the tribes of Reuben and Gad and the half-tribe of Manasseh had asked Moses if they could settle just east of the promised land. The area was excellent pastureland for their large flocks. Moses agreed to give them the land on one condition—that they help their fellow tribes enter and conquer the promised land. Only after the land was conquered could they return to their homes. Now it was time for these three tribes to live up to their agreement.

1:13 God was giving the people rest. This was wonderful news to these people who had been on the move for their entire lives. The people who had no land would be given a land of their own, and they would be able to settle and to "rest."

1:13
l Dt 3:18-20
1:15
m Jos 22:1-4

giving you rest *l* and has granted you this land.' [14] Your wives, your children and your livestock may stay in the land that Moses gave you east of the Jordan, but all your fighting men, fully armed, must cross over ahead of your brothers. You are to help your brothers [15] until the LORD gives them rest, as he has done for you, and until they too have taken possession of the land that the LORD your God is giving them. After that, you may go back and occupy your own land, which Moses the servant of the LORD gave you east of the Jordan toward the sunrise." *m*

[16] Then they answered Joshua, "Whatever you have commanded us we will do, and wherever you send us we will go. [17] Just as we fully obeyed Moses, so we will obey you. Only may the LORD your God be with you as he was with Moses. [18] Whoever rebels against your word and does not obey your words, whatever you may command them, will be put to death. Only be strong and courageous!"

Rahab and the Spies

2:1
n Jas 2:25
o Nu 25:1
p Heb 11:31

2 Then Joshua son of Nun secretly sent two spies *n* from Shittim. *o* "Go, look over the land," he said, "especially Jericho." So they went and entered the house of a prostitute *a* named Rahab *p* and stayed there.

[2] The king of Jericho was told, "Look! Some of the Israelites have come here tonight to spy out the land." [3] So the king of Jericho sent this message to Rahab: "Bring out the men who came to you and entered your house, because they have come to spy out the whole land."

a 1 Or possibly *an innkeeper*

TAKE THE LAND God's Plan for the Promised Land		
Genesis 12:1–3	God promised to bless Abraham and make his descendants into a great nation	
Genesis 15:16	God would choose the right time for Israel to enter Canaan, because the nations living there then would be wicked and ripe for judgment (their sin would reach full measure)	
Genesis 17:7, 8	God promised to give all the land of Canaan to Abraham's descendants	
Exodus 33:1–3	God promised to help the Israelites drive out all the evil nations from Canaan	
Deuteronomy 4:5–8	The Israelites were to be an example of right living to the whole world; this would not work if they intermingled with the wicked Canaanites	
Deuteronomy 7:1–5	The Israelites were to utterly wipe out the Canaanites because of their wickedness and because of Israel's call to purity	
Deuteronomy 12:2	The Israelites were to completely destroy the Canaanite altars so nothing would tempt them away from worshiping God alone	

God told Joshua to lead the Israelites into the promised land (also called Canaan) and conquer it. This was not an act of imperialism or aggression but an act of judgment. Here are some of the earlier passages in the Bible where God promised to give this land to the Israelites and the reasons for doing so.

1:16 If everyone had tried to conquer the promised land his own way, chaos would have resulted. In order to complete the enormous task of conquering the land, everyone had to agree to the leader's plan and be willing to support and obey him. If we are going to complete the tasks God has given us, we must fully agree to his plan, pledge ourselves to obey it, and put his principles into action. Agreeing to God's plan means both knowing what the plan is (as found in the Bible) and carrying it out daily.

1:18 When God commissioned Joshua, he was told three times to be strong and courageous (see 1:6, 7, 9). Here, Joshua was given the same kind of encouragement from the people. Apparently, he took God's message to heart, and found the strength and courage he needed in his relationship with God. The next time you are afraid to do what you know is right, remember that strength and courage are readily available from God.

2:1 Why did Joshua send the spies secretly? As far as he knew, he would be attacking a heavily fortified city using conventional warfare tactics. He needed strategic information about the city for the upcoming battle. But he also knew that this might draw criticism from the other leaders. After all, the last time spies were

sent, the report they brought back caused disastrous problems (see Numbers 13:1—14:4). While he did not want to move ahead without information, he also did not want to cause the people to stumble and question his wisdom and ability to lead the nation.

2:1 Why would the spies stop at the house of Rahab, a prostitute? (1) It was a good place to gather information and have no questions asked in return. (2) Rahab's house was in an ideal location for a quick escape because it was built into the city wall (2:15). (3) God directed the spies to Rahab's house because he knew her heart was open to him and that she would be instrumental in the Israelite victory over Jericho. God often uses people with simple faith to accomplish his great purposes, no matter what kind of past they have had or how insignificant they seem to be. Rahab didn't allow her past to keep her from the new role God had for her.

4But the woman had taken the two men and hidden them.q She said, "Yes, the men came to me, but I did not know where they had come from. 5At dusk, when it was time to close the city gate, the men left. I don't know which way they went. Go after them quickly. You may catch up with them." 6(But she had taken them up to the roof and hidden them under the stalks of flaxr she had laid out on the roof.) 7So the men set out in pursuit of the spies on the road that leads to the fords of the Jordan, and as soon as the pursuers had gone out, the gate was shut.

8Before the spies lay down for the night, she went up on the roof 9and said to them, "I know that the LORD has given this land to you and that a great fears of you has fallen on us, so that all who live in this country are melting in fear because of you. 10We have heard how the LORD dried upt the water of the Red Seaa for you when you came out of Egypt, and what you did to Sihon and Og,u the two kings of the Amorites east of the Jordan, whom you completely destroyed.b 11When we heard of it, our hearts melted and everyone's courage failed because of you,v for the LORD your God is God in heaven above and on the earth w below. 12Now then, please swear to me by the LORD that you will show kindness to my family, because I have shown kindness to you. Give me a sure signx 13that you will spare the lives of my father and mother, my brothers and sisters, and all who belong to them, and that you will save us from death."

14"Our lives for your lives!" the men assured her. "If you don't tell what we are doing, we will treat you kindly and faithfullyy when the LORD gives us the land."

15So she let them down by a rope through the window, for the house she lived in was part of the city wall. 16Now she had said to them, "Go to the hills so the pursuers will not find you. Hide yourselves there three days until they return, and then go on your way."

17The men said to her, "This oathz you made us swear will not be binding on us 18unless, when we enter the land, you have tied this scarlet cord in the window through which you let us down, and unless you have brought your father and mother, your brothers and all your familya into your house. 19If anyone goes outside your house into the street, his blood will be on his own head; we will not be responsible. As for anyone who is in the house with you, his blood will be on our headb if a hand is laid on him. 20But if you tell what we are doing, we will be released from the oath you made us swear."

a 10 Hebrew Yam Suph; that is, Sea of Reeds   b 10 The Hebrew term refers to the irrevocable giving over of things or persons to the LORD, often by totally destroying them.

Ref	Cross-reference
2:4	q 2Sa 17:19-20
2:6	r Jas 2:25
2:9	s Ex 23:27; Dt 2:25
2:10	t Ex 14:21; u Nu 21:21,24,34-35
2:11	v Ex 15:14; Jos 5:1; w Dt 4:39
2:12	x ver 18
2:14	y Jdg 1:24
2:17	z Ge 24:8
2:18	a ver 12
2:19	b Mt 27:25

2:4, 5 Was Rahab justified in lying to save the lives of the spies? Although the Bible does not speak negatively about her lie, it is clear that lying is sin. In Hebrews 11:31, however, Rahab is commended for her faith in God. Her lie is not mentioned. Several explanations have been offered: (1) God forgave Rahab's lie because of her faith; (2) Rahab was simply deceiving the enemy, a normal and acceptable practice in wartime; (3) because Rahab was not a Jew, she could not be held responsible for keeping the moral standards set forth in God's law; (4) Rahab broke a lesser principle—telling the truth—to uphold a higher principle—protecting God's people.

There may have been another way to save the lives of the Israelite spies. But under the pressure of the moment, Rahab had to make a choice. Most of us will face dilemmas at one time or another. We may feel that there is no perfect solution to our problem. Fortunately, God does not demand that our judgment be perfect in all situations. He simply asks us to put our trust in him and to do the best we know how. Rahab did that and was commended for her faith.

2:6 Flax was harvested in the fields and piled high on the rooftops to dry. It was then made into yarn, which was used to make linen cloth. Flax grows to a height of three or four feet. Stacked on the roof, it made an excellent hiding place for the spies.

2:8–13 Many would assume that Rahab—a pagan, a Canaanite, and a prostitute—would never be interested in God. Yet Rahab was willing to risk everything she had for a God she barely knew. We must not gauge a person's interest in God by his or her background, lifestyle, or appearance. We should let nothing get in the way of our telling people the Good News.

2:11 Rahab recognized something that many of the Israelites did not—the God of heaven is not an ordinary god! He is all-powerful. The people of Jericho were afraid because they had heard the news of God's extraordinary power in defeating the armies across the Jordan River. Today we can worship this same powerful, miracle-working God. He is powerful enough to destroy mighty, wicked armies, as he did in Jericho. He is also powerful enough to save us from certain death, as he did with Rahab.

2:15 In Joshua's day it was common to build houses on city walls. Many cities had two walls about 12 to 15 feet apart. Houses were built on wooden logs laid across the tops of the two walls. Rahab may have lived in such a house with a window that looked out over the outside wall.

SPY MISSION TO JERICHO
Two spies left the Israelite camp at Shittim, crossed the Jordan River, and slipped into Jericho. The city was built around an oasis in the midst of a hot and desolate valley 840 feet below sea level. Jericho was the first major city the Israelites set out to conquer.

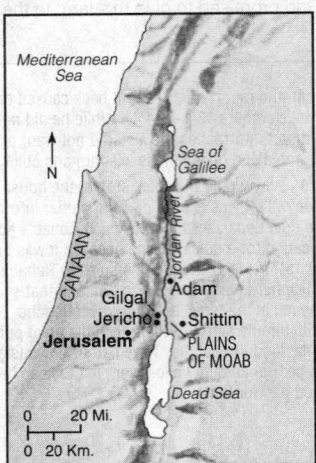

Mediterranean Sea
N
Sea of Galilee
CANAAN
Jordan River
Adam
Gilgal
Jericho
Shittim
Jerusalem
PLAINS OF MOAB
Dead Sea
0   20 Mi.
0   20 Km.

²¹"Agreed," she replied. "Let it be as you say." So she sent them away and they departed. And she tied the scarlet cord in the window.

²²When they left, they went into the hills and stayed there three days, until the pursuers had searched all along the road and returned without finding them. ²³Then the two men started back. They went down out of the hills, forded the river and came to Joshua son of Nun and told him everything that had happened to them. ²⁴They said to Joshua, "The LORD has surely given the whole land into our hands; all the people are melting in fear because of us."

2. Crossing the Jordan

3:1
c Jos 2:1

3:2
d Jos 1:11

3:3
e Dt 31:9

3 Early in the morning Joshua and all the Israelites set out from Shittim *c* and went to the Jordan, where they camped before crossing over. ²After three days the officers went throughout the camp,*d* ³giving orders to the people: "When you see the ark of the covenant of the LORD your God, and the priests,*e* who are Levites, carrying it, you are to move out from your positions and follow it. ⁴Then you will know which way to go, since you have never

JOSHUA

One of the greatest challenges facing leaders is to replace themselves, training others to become leaders. Many outstanding accomplishments have been started by someone with great ability whose life or career ended before the vision became reality. The fulfillment of that dream then became the responsibility of that person's successor. Death is the ultimate deadline for leadership. One of the best tests of our leadership is our willingness and ability to train another for our position.

Moses made an excellent decision when he chose Joshua as his assistant. That choice was later confirmed by God himself when he instructed Moses to commission Joshua as his successor (Numbers 27:15–23). Joshua had played a key role in the exodus from Egypt. Introduced as the field general of Israel's army, he was the only person allowed to accompany Moses partway up the mountain when Moses received the law. Joshua and Caleb were the only 2 among the 12 scouts to bring back an encouraging report after being sent into the promised land the first time. Other references show him to have been Moses' constant shadow. His basic training was living with Moses—experiencing firsthand what it meant to lead God's people. This was modeling at its best!

Who is your Moses? Who is your Joshua? You are part of the chain of God's ongoing work in the world. You are modeling yourself after others, and others are patterning their lives after you. How important is God to those you want to be like? Do those who are watching you see God reflected in every area of your life? Ask God to lead you to a trustworthy Moses. Ask him to make you a good Joshua.

Strengths and accomplishments:	• Moses' assistant and successor • One of only two adults who experienced Egyptian slavery and lived to enter the promised land • Led the Israelites into their God-given homeland • Brilliant military strategist • Faithful to ask God's direction in the challenges he faced
Lessons from his life:	• Effective leadership is often the product of good preparation and encouragement • The persons after whom we pattern ourselves will have a definite effect on us • A person committed to God provides the best model for us
Vital statistics:	• Where: Egypt, the wilderness of Sinai, Canaan (the promised land) • Occupations: Special assistant to Moses, warrior, leader • Relative: Father: Nun • Contemporaries: Moses, Caleb, Miriam, Aaron
Key verses:	"Moses did as the LORD commanded him. He took Joshua and had him stand before Eleazar the priest and the whole assembly. Then he laid his hands on him and commissioned him, as the LORD had instructed through Moses" (Numbers 27:22, 23).

Joshua is also mentioned in Exodus 17:9–14; 24:13; 32:17; 33:11; Numbers 11:28; 13—14; 26:65; 27:18–23; 32:11, 12, 28; 34:17; Deuteronomy 1:38; 3:21, 28; 31:3, 7, 14, 23; 34:9; the book of Joshua; Judges 2:6–9; and 1 Kings 16:34.

3:2–4 The ark of the covenant was Israel's most sacred treasure. It was a symbol of God's presence and power. The ark was a golden rectangular box with two cherubim (angels) facing each other on the lid. Inside the ark were the tablets of the Ten Commandments Moses received from God, a jar of manna (the bread God miraculously sent from heaven during the desert wanderings), and Aaron's staff (the symbol of the high priest's authority). According to God's law, only the Levites could carry the ark. The ark was constructed at the same time as the tabernacle (Exodus 37:1–9) and placed in the sanctuary's most sacred room.

been this way before. But keep a distance of about a thousand yards[a] between you and the ark; do not go near it."

5 Joshua told the people, "Consecrate yourselves,[f] for tomorrow the LORD will do amazing things among you."

6 Joshua said to the priests, "Take up the ark of the covenant and pass on ahead of the people." So they took it up and went ahead of them.

7 And the LORD said to Joshua, "Today I will begin to exalt you in the eyes of all Israel, so they may know that I am with you as I was with Moses.[g] 8 Tell the priests who carry the ark of the covenant: 'When you reach the edge of the Jordan's waters, go and stand in the river.'"

9 Joshua said to the Israelites, "Come here and listen to the words of the LORD your God. 10 This is how you will know that the living God[h] is among you and that he will certainly drive out before you the Canaanites, Hittites, Hivites, Perizzites, Girgashites, Amorites and Jebusites.[i] 11 See, the ark of the covenant of the Lord of all the earth[j] will go into the Jordan ahead of you. 12 Now then, choose twelve men[k] from the tribes of Israel, one from each tribe. 13 And as soon as the priests who carry the ark of the LORD—the Lord of all the earth—set foot in the Jordan, its waters flowing downstream will be cut off and stand up in a heap."

14 So when the people broke camp to cross the Jordan, the priests carrying the ark of the covenant went ahead[l] of them. 15 Now the Jordan is at flood stage[m] all during harvest. Yet as soon as the priests who carried the ark reached the Jordan and their feet touched the water's edge, 16 the water from upstream stopped flowing.[n] It piled up in a heap a great distance away, at a town called Adam in the vicinity of Zarethan, while the water flowing down to the Sea of the Arabah (the Salt Sea[b]) was completely cut off. So the people crossed over opposite Jericho. 17 The priests who carried the ark of the covenant of the LORD stood firm on dry ground in the middle of the Jordan, while all Israel passed by until the whole nation had completed the crossing on dry ground.[o]

a 4 Hebrew *about two thousand cubits* (about 900 meters)   b 16 That is, the Dead Sea

3:5 f Ex 19:10,14; Jos 7:13

3:7 g Jos 1:5

3:10 h Dt 5:26 i Dt 7:1

3:11 j Zec 6:5

3:12 k Jos 4:2,4

3:14 l Ac 7:44-45

3:15 m Jos 4:18; 1Ch 12:15

3:16 n Ps 66:6

3:17 o Ex 14:22,29

3:5 Before entering the promised land, the Israelites were to perform a consecration (purification) ceremony. This was often done before making a sacrifice or, as in this case, before witnessing a great act of God. God's law stated that a person could become unclean for many reasons—eating certain foods (Leviticus 11), giving birth (Leviticus 12), dealing with disease (Leviticus 13, 14), touching a dead person (Numbers 19:11–22). God used these various outward signs of uncleanness to illustrate a person's inward uncleanness that comes as a result of sin. The consecration ceremony pictured the importance of approaching God with a pure heart. Like the Israelites, we need God's forgiveness before we approach him.

3:9 Just before crossing over into the promised land, Joshua gathered the people to hear the words of the Lord. Their excitement was high. No doubt they wanted to rush on, but Joshua made them stop and listen. We live in a fast-paced age where everyone rushes just to keep up. It is easy to get caught up in our tasks, becoming too busy for what God says is most important—listening to his words. Before making your schedule, take time to focus on what God wants from all your activities. Knowing what God has said before you rush into your day can help you avoid foolish mistakes.

3:10 Why would God help the Israelites drive out these nations from their native land? God had punished Israel first for its disobedience. He then turned to the rest of the nations. Genesis 15:16 implies that the people of Canaan were wicked and deserved to be punished for their terrible sins. Israel was to be a vehicle for this punishment. More important was the fact that Israel, as a holy nation, could not live among such evil

and idolatrous people. To do so would be to invite sin into their lives. The only way to prevent Israel from being infected by evil religions was to drive out those who practiced them. Israel, however, failed to drive everyone out as God had told them to do. It wasn't long before Israel—the nation God chose to be his holy people—began following the evil practices of the Canaanites.

3:13, 14 The Israelites were eager to enter the promised land, conquer nations, and live peacefully. But first they had to cross the flood-level waters of the Jordan River. God gave them specific instructions: in order to cross, the priests had to step into the water. What if these priests had been afraid to take that first step? Often God provides no solution to our problems until we trust him and move ahead with what we know we should do. What are the rivers, or obstacles, in your life? In obedience to God, take that first step.

3:13–17 God had parted the waters of the Red Sea to let the people out of Egypt (Exodus 14), and here he parted the Jordan River to let them enter Canaan. These miracles showed Israel that God keeps his promises. God's presence among his people and his faithfulness to them made the entire journey from Egypt to the promised land possible. He was with them at the end of their wanderings just as he was with them in the beginning.

3:15, 16 The Israelites crossed the Jordan River in the spring, when it was overflowing its banks. God chose the time when the river was at its highest to demonstrate his power—parting the waters so that the entire nation could cross on dry ground. Some say that God used a natural occurrence (such as a landslide) to stop the waters of the Jordan; others say he did it by a direct act. In either case, God showed his great power by working a miracle of timing and location to allow his people to cross the river on dry ground. This testimony of God's supernatural power served to build the Israelites' hope in God and to give them a great reputation with their enemies, who greatly outnumbered them.

4:1
P Dt 27:2

4:2
q Jos 3:12

4:3
r ver 20
s ver 19

4:6
t Ex 12:26; 13:14

4:7
u Jos 3:13

4:8
v ver 20

4:14
w Jos 3:7

4:20
x ver 3,8

4:22
y Jos 3:17

4:23
z Ex 14:21

4:24
a 1Ki 8:42-43;
Ps 106:8

4:24
b Ex 15:16;
1Ch 29:12;
Ps 89:13
c Ex 14:31

4 When the whole nation had finished crossing the Jordan, *p* the LORD said to Joshua, 2 "Choose twelve men *q* from among the people, one from each tribe, 3 and tell them to take up twelve stones *r* from the middle of the Jordan from right where the priests stood and to carry them over with you and put them down at the place where you stay tonight. *s*"

4 So Joshua called together the twelve men he had appointed from the Israelites, one from each tribe, 5 and said to them, "Go over before the ark of the LORD your God into the middle of the Jordan. Each of you is to take up a stone on his shoulder, according to the number of the tribes of the Israelites, 6 to serve as a sign among you. In the future, when your children ask you, 'What do these stones mean?' *t* 7 tell them that the flow of the Jordan was cut off *u* before the ark of the covenant of the LORD. When it crossed the Jordan, the waters of the Jordan were cut off. These stones are to be a memorial to the people of Israel forever."

8 So the Israelites did as Joshua commanded them. They took twelve stones from the middle of the Jordan, according to the number of the tribes of the Israelites, as the LORD had told Joshua; *v* and they carried them over with them to their camp, where they put them down. 9 Joshua set up the twelve stones that had been *a* in the middle of the Jordan at the spot where the priests who carried the ark of the covenant had stood. And they are there to this day.

10 Now the priests who carried the ark remained standing in the middle of the Jordan until everything the LORD had commanded Joshua was done by the people, just as Moses had directed Joshua. The people hurried over, 11 and as soon as all of them had crossed, the ark of the LORD and the priests came to the other side while the people watched. 12 The men of Reuben, Gad and the half-tribe of Manasseh crossed over, armed, in front of the Israelites, as Moses had directed them. 13 About forty thousand armed for battle crossed over before the LORD to the plains of Jericho for war.

14 That day the LORD exalted *w* Joshua in the sight of all Israel; and they revered him all the days of his life, just as they had revered Moses.

15 Then the LORD said to Joshua, 16 "Command the priests carrying the ark of the Testimony to come up out of the Jordan."

17 So Joshua commanded the priests, "Come up out of the Jordan."

18 And the priests came up out of the river carrying the ark of the covenant of the LORD. No sooner had they set their feet on the dry ground than the waters of the Jordan returned to their place and ran at flood stage as before.

19 On the tenth day of the first month the people went up from the Jordan and camped at Gilgal on the eastern border of Jericho. 20 And Joshua set up at Gilgal the twelve stones *x* they had taken out of the Jordan. 21 He said to the Israelites, "In the future when your descendants ask their fathers, 'What do these stones mean?' 22 tell them, 'Israel crossed the Jordan on dry ground.' *y* 23 For the LORD your God dried up the Jordan before you until you had crossed over. The LORD your God did to the Jordan just what he had done to the Red Sea *b* when he dried it up before us until we had crossed over. *z* 24 He did this so that all the peoples of the earth might know *a* that the hand of the LORD is powerful *b* and so that you might always fear the LORD your God. *c*"

a 9 Or *Joshua also set up twelve stones*   *b 23* Hebrew *Yam Suph*; that is, Sea of Reeds

---

4:1ff After the people safely crossed the river, what would be next? Conquering the land? Not yet. First, God directed them to build a memorial from 12 stones drawn from the river by 12 men, one from each tribe. This may seem like an insignificant step in their mission of conquering the land, but God did not want his people to plunge into their task unprepared. They were to focus on him and remember who was guiding them. As you are busy doing your God-given tasks, set aside quiet moments, times to build your own memorial to God's power. Too much activity may shift your focus away from God.

4:14 The Israelites revered Joshua for his role in leading them across the Jordan River. He, like Moses, would receive Israel's praises generation after generation. Although Israel was not a world power at that time, Joshua's reputation for handling his responsibilities God's way brought him greater glory than if he had been a hero in a "superpower" nation. Doing right is more important than doing well.

4:21–24 The memorial of 12 stones was to be a constant reminder of the day the Israelites crossed the Jordan River on dry ground. Their children would see the stones, hear the story, and learn about God. Do you have traditions—special dates or special places—to help your children learn about God's work in your life? Do you take time to tell them what God has done for you—forgiving and saving you, answering your prayers, supplying your needs? Retelling your story will help keep memories of God's faithfulness alive in your family.

Circumcision at Gilgal

5 Now when all the Amorite kings west of the Jordan and all the Canaanite kings along the coast *d* heard how the LORD had dried up the Jordan before the Israelites until we had crossed over, their hearts melted *e* and they no longer had the courage to face the Israelites. ²At that time the LORD said to Joshua, "Make flint knives *f* and circumcise the Israelites again." ³So Joshua made flint knives and circumcised the Israelites at Gibeath Haaraloth. *a*

⁴Now this is why he did so: All those who came out of Egypt—all the men of military age—died in the desert on the way after leaving Egypt. *g* ⁵All the people that came out had been circumcised, but all the people born in the desert during the journey from Egypt had not. ⁶The Israelites had moved about in the desert forty years *h* until all the men who were of military age when they left Egypt had died, since they had not obeyed the LORD. For the LORD had sworn to them that they would not see the land that he had solemnly promised their fathers to give us, *i* a land flowing with milk and honey. ⁷So he raised up their sons in their place, and these were the ones Joshua circumcised. They were still uncircumcised because they had not been circumcised on the way. ⁸And after the whole nation had been circumcised, they remained where they were in camp until they were healed.

⁹Then the LORD said to Joshua, "Today I have rolled away the reproach of Egypt from you." So the place has been called Gilgal *b* to this day.

¹⁰On the evening of the fourteenth day of the month, while camped at Gilgal on the plains of Jericho, the Israelites celebrated the Passover. ¹¹The day after the Passover, that very day, they ate some of the produce of the land: unleavened bread and roasted grain. ¹²The manna stopped the day after *c* they ate this food from the land; there was no longer any manna for the Israelites, but that year they ate of the produce of Canaan. *j*

5:1 *d*Nu 13:29
*e*Jos 2:9-11

5:2 *f*Ex 4:25

5:4 *g*Dt 2:14

5:6 *h*Dt 2:7
*i*Nu 14:23,29-35;
Dt 2:14

5:12 *j*Ex 16:35

B. CONQUERING THE PROMISED LAND (5:13—12:24)

After crossing the Jordan River, the Israelites begin to conquer Canaan. Jericho is the first to fall. Then Israel suffers its first defeat because of one man's disobedience. After the people remove the sin from their community, they strike again—this time with success. Soon great kings attack from the north and south, but they are defeated because God is with Israel. Evil could not be tolerated in the promised land, nor can it be tolerated in our lives. We, like Israel, must ruthlessly remove sin from our lives before it takes control of us.

*a*3 Gibeath Haaraloth means *hill of foreskins.* *b*9 Gilgal sounds like the Hebrew for *roll.* *c*12 Or *the day*

5:1 The Amorites and Canaanites were the two major groups living in Canaan at the time of Israel's invasion. The Canaanites worshiped a variety of gods, but Baal was their favorite. Canaanite culture was materialistic, and their religion, sensual. The Israelites continually turned to Baal after entering Canaan. The Amorite gods also infected Israel's worship and turned people away from worshiping the true God. Worshiping these false gods eventually brought about Israel's downfall.

5:1 The Israelites spent 39 years in the desert unnecessarily because they were terrified of the Canaanites. They underestimated God's ability. The Israelites' first attempt to enter the promised land had failed (Numbers 13; 14). Here Israel saw that the Canaanites were terrified of their army. The Canaanites had heard about Israel's great victories through God (2:9–11), and they hoped that the Jordan River would slow Israel down or discourage them from entering Canaan. But news that the Israelites had crossed the Jordan on dry land caused any courage the Canaanites still had to melt away.

Don't underestimate God. If we are faithful to God, he will cause great opposition to disappear. God can change the attitudes of those who oppose him.

5:2, 3 The rite of circumcision marked Israel's position as God's covenant people. When God made the original covenant with Abraham, he required that each male be circumcised as a sign of cutting off the old life and beginning a new life with God (Genesis 17:13). Other cultures at that time used circumcision as a sign of entry into adulthood, but only Israel used it as a sign of following God.

5:8, 9 Located about two miles northeast of Jericho, Gilgal was Israel's base camp and their temporary center of government and worship during their invasion of Canaan. Here the people renewed their commitment to God and covenant with him before attempting to conquer the new land. At Gilgal the angelic commander of the Lord's army appeared to Joshua with further instructions for battle and encouragement for the conquest (5:13–15). After the conquest, Gilgal continued to be an important place in Israel. It was here that Israel's first king, Saul, was crowned (1 Samuel 11:14, 15).

5:10 This joyous Passover was the first to be celebrated in the promised land and only the third celebrated by Israel since the exodus from Egypt. The last time was at the foot of Mount Sinai, 39 years earlier. This celebration reminded Israel of God's mighty miracles that brought them out of Egypt. There they had to eat in fear and haste; here they ate in celebration of God's blessings and promises. (See Exodus 12 for a description of the night the angel "passed over" the Israelites' homes.)

5:11, 12 God supplied manna to the hungry Israelites during their 40 years in the desert (Exodus 16:14–31). In the bountiful promised land they no longer needed this daily food supply because the land was ready for planting and harvesting. God had miraculously provided food for the Israelites while they were in the desert; here he provided food from the land itself. Prayer is not an alternative to preparation, and faith is not a substitute for hard work. God can and does provide miraculously for his people as needed, but he also expects them to use their God-given talents and resources to provide for themselves. If your prayers have gone unanswered, perhaps what you need is within your reach. Pray instead for the wisdom to see it and the energy and motivation to do it.

1. Joshua attacks the center of the land
The Fall of Jericho

5:13
k Ge 18:2; 32:24

[13] Now when Joshua was near Jericho, he looked up and saw a man *k* standing in front of him with a drawn sword in his hand. Joshua went up to him and asked, "Are you for us or for our enemies?"

5:14
l Ge 17:3

[14] "Neither," he replied, "but as commander of the army of the LORD I have now come." Then Joshua fell facedown *l* to the ground in reverence, and asked him, "What message does my Lord[a] have for his servant?"

5:15
m Ex 3:5

[15] The commander of the LORD's army replied, "Take off your sandals, for the place where you are standing is holy." *m* And Joshua did so.

**6 ** Now Jericho was tightly shut up because of the Israelites. No one went out and no one came in.

6:2
n Dt 7:24

[2] Then the LORD said to Joshua, "See, I have delivered *n* Jericho into your hands, along with

a 14 Or lord

RAHAB

Rahab was a prostitute in the city of Jericho. As a prostitute, she lived on the edge of society, one stop short of rejection. Her house, built right into the city wall, provided both lodging and favors to travelers. It was a natural place for the Israelite spies to stay, as they would be mistaken for Rahab's customers.

Stories about the Israelites had been circulating for some time, but now it was evident that the Israelites were about to invade. Living on the wall, Rahab felt especially vulnerable. Yet while she shared the general mood of fear with the rest of Jericho's population, she alone turned to the Lord for her salvation. Her faith gave her the courage to hide the spies and lie to the authorities. Rahab knew her position was dangerous; she could have been killed if she had been caught harboring the Israelites. Rahab took the risk, however, because she sensed that the Israelites relied on a God worth trusting. And God rewarded Rahab by promising safety for her and her family.

God works through people—like Rahab—whom we are inclined to reject. God remembers her because of her faith, not her profession. If at times you feel like a failure, remember that Rahab rose above her situation through her trust in God. You can do the same!

Strengths and accomplishments:	• Relative of Boaz, and thus an ancestor of David and Jesus • One of only two women listed in the Hall of Faith in Hebrews 11 • Resourceful, willing to help others at great cost to herself
Weakness and mistake:	• She was a prostitute
Lesson from her life:	• She did not let fear affect her faith in God's ability to deliver
Vital statistics:	• Where: Jericho • Occupations: Prostitute/innkeeper, later became a wife • Relatives: Ancestor of David and Jesus (Matthew 1:5) • Contemporary: Joshua
Key verse:	"By faith the prostitute Rahab, because she welcomed the spies, was not killed with those who were disobedient" (Hebrews 11:31).

Rahab's story is told in Joshua 2 and 6:22, 23. She is also mentioned in Matthew 1:5; Hebrews 11:31; and James 2:25.

5:14, 15 This was an angel of superior rank, the commander of the Lord's army. Some say he was an appearance of God in human form. As a sign of respect, Joshua took off his sandals. Although Joshua was Israel's leader, he was still subordinate to God, the absolute Leader. Awe and respect are the responses due to our holy God. How can we show respect for God? By our attitudes and actions. We should recognize God's power, authority, and deep love, and our actions must model our absolute reverence for God. Respect for God is just as important today as it was in Joshua's day, even though removing shoes is no longer our cultural way of showing it.

6:1 The city of Jericho, built thousands of years before Joshua was born, was one of the oldest cities in the world. In some places it had fortified walls up to 25 feet high and 20 feet thick. Soldiers standing guard on top of the walls could see for miles. Jericho was a symbol of military power and strength—the Canaanites considered it invincible.

Israel would attack this city first, and its destruction would put the fear of Israel into the heart of every person in Canaan. The Canaanites saw Israel's God as a nature god because he parted the Jordan and as a war god because he defeated Sihon and Og. But the Canaanites did not consider him a fortress god—one who could prevail against a walled city. The defeat of Jericho showed not only that Israel's God was superior to the Canaanite gods, but also that he was invincible.

6:2–5 God told Joshua that Jericho was already delivered into his hands—the enemy was already defeated! What confidence Joshua must have had as he went into battle! Christians also fight against a defeated enemy. Our enemy, Satan, has been defeated by Christ (Romans 8:37–39; Hebrews 2:14, 15; 1 John 3:8). Although we still fight battles every day and sin runs rampant in the world, we have the assurance that the war has already been won. We do not have to be paralyzed by the power of a defeated enemy; we can overcome him through Christ's power.

its king and its fighting men. ³March around the city once with all the armed men. Do this for six days. ⁴Have seven priests carry trumpets of rams' horns in front of the ark. On the seventh day, march around the city seven times, with the priests blowing the trumpets. ⁵When you hear them sound a long blast on the trumpets, have all the people give a loud shout; then the wall of the city will collapse and the people will go up, every man straight in."

⁶So Joshua son of Nun called the priests and said to them, "Take up the ark of the covenant of the LORD and have seven priests carry trumpets in front of it." ⁷And he ordered the people, "Advance! March around the city, with the armed guard going ahead of the ark of the LORD."

⁸When Joshua had spoken to the people, the seven priests carrying the seven trumpets before the LORD went forward, blowing their trumpets, and the ark of the LORD's covenant followed them. ⁹The armed guard marched ahead of the priests who blew the trumpets, and the rear guard followed the ark. All this time the trumpets were sounding. ¹⁰But Joshua had commanded the people, "Do not give a war cry, do not raise your voices, do not say a word until the day I tell you to shout. Then shout!" ¹¹So he had the ark of the LORD carried around the city, circling it once. Then the people returned to camp and spent the night there.

¹²Joshua got up early the next morning and the priests took up the ark of the LORD. ¹³The seven priests carrying the seven trumpets went forward, marching before the ark of the LORD and blowing the trumpets. The armed men went ahead of them and the rear guard followed the ark of the LORD, while the trumpets kept sounding. ¹⁴So on the second day they marched around the city once and returned to the camp. They did this for six days.

¹⁵On the seventh day, they got up at daybreak and marched around the city seven times in the same manner, except that on that day they circled the city seven times. ¹⁶The seventh time around, when the priests sounded the trumpet blast, Joshua commanded the people, "Shout! For the LORD has given you the city! ¹⁷The city and all that is in it are to be devoted[a] ᵒ to the LORD. Only Rahab the prostitute ᵇ and all who are with her in her house shall be spared, because she hidᵖ the spies we sent. ¹⁸But keep away from the devoted things,�q so that you will not bring about your own destruction by taking any of them. Otherwise you will make the camp of Israel liable to destruction and bring trouble on it. ¹⁹All the silver and gold and the articles of bronze and iron are sacred to the LORD and must go into his treasury."

²⁰When the trumpets sounded, the people shouted, and at the sound of the trumpet, when the people gave a loud shout, the wall collapsed; so every man charged straight in, and they took the city.ʳ ²¹They devoted the city to the LORD and destroyedˢ with the sword every living thing in it—men and women, young and old, cattle, sheep and donkeys.

²²Joshua said to the two men who had spied out the land, "Go into the prostitute's house and bring her out and all who belong to her, in accordance with your oath to her.ᵗ" ²³So the young men who had done the spying went in and brought out Rahab, her father and mother and brothers and all who belonged to her.ᵘ They brought out her entire family and put them in a place outside the camp of Israel.

²⁴Then they burned the whole city and everything in it, but they put the silver and gold and the articles of bronze and iron ᵛ into the treasury of the LORD's house. ²⁵But Joshua spared Rahab the prostitute, with her family and all who belonged to her, because she hid the men Joshua had sent as spies to Jerichoʷ—and she lives among the Israelites to this day.

6:17
ᵒ Lev 27:28
ᵖ Jos 2:4

6:18
q Jos 7:1

6:20
ʳ Heb 11:30

6:21
ˢ Dt 20:16

6:22
ᵗ Jos 2:14;
Heb 11:31

6:23
ᵘ Jos 2:13

6:24
ᵛ ver 19

6:25
ʷ Jos 2:6

ᵃ 17 The Hebrew term refers to the irrevocable giving over of things or persons to the LORD, often by totally destroying them; also in verses 18 and 21.   ᵇ 17 Or possibly *innkeeper*; also in verses 22 and 25

6:3–5 Why did God give Joshua all these complicated instructions for the battle? Several answers are possible: (1) God was making it undeniably clear that the battle would depend upon him, and not upon Israel's weapons and expertise. This is why priests carrying the ark, not soldiers, led the Israelites into battle. (2) God's method of taking the city accentuated the terror already felt in Jericho (2:9). (3) This strange military maneuver was a test of the Israelites' faith and their willingness to follow God completely. The blowing of the trumpets had a special significance. They had been instructed to blow the same trumpets used in the religious festivals in their battles to remind them that their victory would come from the Lord, not their own military might (Numbers 10:9).

6:21 Why did God demand that the Israelites destroy almost everyone and everything in Jericho? He was carrying out severe judgment against the wickedness of the Canaanites. This judgment,

or *ban*, usually required that everything be destroyed (Deuteronomy 12:2, 3; 13:12–18). Because of their evil practices and intense idolatry, the Canaanites were a stronghold of rebellion against God. This threat to the right kind of living that God required had to be removed. If not, it would affect all Israel like a cancerous growth (as it did in the sad story told in the book of Judges). A few people and some items in Jericho were not destroyed, but this was a special case. Rahab and her household were saved because she had faith in God and because she helped the Israelite spies. The silver and gold and articles of bronze and iron were kept, not to enrich the people, but to beautify the tabernacle and its services.

God's purpose in all this was to keep the people's faith and religion uncontaminated. He did not want the plunder to remind Israel of Canaanite practices.

God also wants us to be pure. He wants us to clean up our

6:26
×1Ki 16:34

26At that time Joshua pronounced this solemn oath: "Cursed before the Lord is the man who undertakes to rebuild this city, Jericho:

"At the cost of his firstborn son
    will he lay its foundations;
at the cost of his youngest
    will he set up its gates."×

6:27
y Jos 1:5
z Jos 9:1

27So the Lord was with Joshua,y and his fame spread z throughout the land.

Achan's Sin

7:1
a Jos 6:18

7 But the Israelites acted unfaithfully in regard to the devoted things a; a Achan son of Carmi, the son of Zimri,b the son of Zerah, of the tribe of Judah, took some of them. So the Lord's anger burned against Israel.

2Now Joshua sent men from Jericho to Ai, which is near Beth Aven to the east of Bethel, and told them, "Go up and spy out the region." So the men went up and spied out Ai.

3When they returned to Joshua, they said, "Not all the people will have to go up against Ai. Send two or three thousand men to take it and do not weary all the people, for only a few

7:4
b Lev 26:17;
Dt 28:25

men are there." 4So about three thousand men went up; but they were routed by the men of Ai,b 5who killed about thirty-six of them. They chased the Israelites from the city gate as far as the stone quarriesc and struck them down on the slopes. At this the hearts of the people melted and became like water.

7:6
c Job 2:12;
Rev 18:19

6Then Joshua tore his clothes and fell facedown to the ground before the ark of the Lord, remaining there till evening. The elders of Israel did the same, and sprinkled dust c on their heads. 7And Joshua said, "Ah, Sovereign Lord, why did you ever bring this people across the Jordan to deliver us into the hands of the Amorites to destroy us? If only we had been content to stay on the other side of the Jordan! 8O Lord, what can I say, now that Israel has been

7:9
d Ex 32:12

routed by its enemies? 9The Canaanites and the other people of the country will hear about this and they will surround us and wipe out our name from the earth. d What then will you do for your own great name?"

a 1 The Hebrew term refers to the irrevocable giving over of things or persons to the Lord, often by totally destroying them; also in verses 11, 12, 13 and 15.   b 1 See Septuagint and 1 Chron. 2:6; Hebrew *Zabdi*; also in verses 17 and 18.   c 5 Or *as far as Shebarim*

---

behavior when we begin a new life with him. We must not let the desire for personal gain distract us from our spiritual purpose. We must also reject any objects that are reminders of a life of rebellion against God. (For more information on how Israel handled its plunder, see the note on Numbers 31:25–30.)

6:26 This curse was fulfilled in 1 Kings 16:34 when a man, Hiel, rebuilt Jericho and consequently lost his oldest and youngest sons. It is very possible that Hiel sacrificed his sons and placed them in the foundation and gate masonry to ward off evil.

7:1 "The devoted things" refers to all the clothing, cattle, and other plunder that God said Israel should destroy when they conquered Jericho (see 6:17–19). It was not that they found a good use for something that was going to be thrown out anyway. This was a serious offense because it was in direct defiance to an explicit command of God (see Deuteronomy 20:16–18).

7:1ff Notice the results of Achan's sin: (1) many men died (7:5); (2) Israel's army melted in fear (7:5); (3) Joshua questioned God (7:7–9); (4) God threatened to withdraw his presence from the people (7:12); (5) Achan and his family had to be destroyed (7:24–26).

When Israel eliminated the sin from their community, these were the results: (1) God's encouragement (8:1); (2) God's presence in battle (8:1); (3) God's guidance and promise of victory (8:2); (4) God's permission to keep the plunder and livestock from the battle for themselves (8:2). Throughout Israel's history, blessings came when the people got rid of their sin. You will also experience blessings when you turn from your sin and follow God's plan wholeheartedly.

7:6 Joshua and the elders tore their clothing and sprinkled dust on their heads as signs of deep mourning before God. They were confused by their defeat at the small city of Ai after the spectacu-

lar Jericho victory, so they went before God in deep humility and sorrow to receive his instructions. When our lives fall apart, we also should turn to God for direction and help. Like Joshua and the elders, we should humble ourselves so that we will be able to hear God's words.

7:7 When Joshua first went against Ai (7:3), he did not consult God but relied on the strength of his army to defeat the small city. Only after Israel was defeated did they turn to God and ask what happened.

Too often we rely on our own skills and strength, especially when the task before us seems easy. We go to God only when the obstacles seem too great. However, only God knows what lies ahead. Consulting him, even when we are on a winning streak, may save us from grave mistakes or misjudgments. God may want us to learn lessons, remove pride, or consult others before he will work through us.

7:7–9 Imagine praying this way to God. This is not a formal church prayer; it is the prayer of a man who is afraid and confused by what is happening around him. Joshua poured out his real thoughts to God. Hiding your needs from God is ignoring the only one who can really help. God welcomes your honest prayers and wants you to express your true feelings to him. Any believer can become more honest in prayer by remembering that God is all-knowing and all-powerful and that his love is everlasting.

¹⁰The Lord said to Joshua, "Stand up! What are you doing down on your face? ¹¹Israel has sinned; they have violated my covenant, ᵉ which I commanded them to keep. They have taken some of the devoted things; they have stolen, they have lied, they have put them with their own possessions. ¹²That is why the Israelites cannot stand against their enemies; they turn their backs and run because they have been made liable to destruction. I will not be with you anymore unless you destroy whatever among you is devoted to destruction.

¹³"Go, consecrate the people. Tell them, 'Consecrate yourselves ᶠ in preparation for tomorrow; for this is what the Lord, the God of Israel, says: That which is devoted is among you, O Israel. You cannot stand against your enemies until you remove it.

¹⁴"'In the morning, present yourselves tribe by tribe. The tribe that the Lord takesᵍ shall come forward clan by clan; the clan that the Lord takes shall come forward family by family; and the family that the Lord takes shall come forward man by man. ¹⁵He who is caught with the devoted things shall be destroyed by fire, along with all that belongs to him. ʰ He has violated the covenantⁱ of the Lord and has done a disgraceful thing in Israel!'"ʲ

¹⁶Early the next morning Joshua had Israel come forward by tribes, and Judah was taken. ¹⁷The clans of Judah came forward, and he took the Zerahites. He had the clan of the Zerahites come forward by families, and Zimri was taken. ¹⁸Joshua had his family come forward man by man, and Achan son of Carmi, the son of Zimri, the son of Zerah, of the tribe of Judah, was taken.

¹⁹Then Joshua said to Achan, "My son, give gloryᵏ to the Lord,ᵃ the God of Israel, and give him the praise. ᵇ Tellˡ me what you have done; do not hide it from me."

²⁰Achan replied, "It is true! I have sinned against the Lord, the God of Israel. This is what I have done: ²¹When I saw in the plunder a beautiful robe from Babylonia, ᶜ two hundred shekels ᵈ of silver and a wedge of gold weighing fifty shekels, ᵉ I coveted them and took them. They are hidden in the ground inside my tent, with the silver underneath."

²²So Joshua sent messengers, and they ran to the tent, and there it was, hidden in his tent, with the silver underneath. ²³They took the things from the tent, brought them to Joshua and all the Israelites and spread them out before the Lord.

²⁴Then Joshua, together with all Israel, took Achan son of Zerah, the silver, the robe, the gold wedge, his sons and daughters, his cattle, donkeys and sheep, his tent and all that he had, to the Valley of Achor.ᵐ ²⁵Joshua said, "Why have you brought this troubleⁿ on us? The Lord will bring trouble on you today."

Then all Israel stoned him,ᵒ and after they had stoned the rest, they burned them. ²⁶Over Achan they heaped up a large pile of rocks, which remains to this day. Then the Lord turned from his fierce anger. Therefore that place has been called the Valley of Achorᶠ ever since.

7:11
ᵉJos 6:17-19

7:13
ᶠJos 3:5; 6:18

7:14
ᵍPr 16:33

7:15
ʰ1Sa 14:39
ⁱver 11
ʲGe 34:7

7:19
ᵏJer 13:16; Jn 9:24*
ˡ1Sa 14:43

7:24
ᵐJos 15:7

7:25
ⁿJos 6:18
ᵒDt 17:5

ᵃ*19* A solemn charge to tell the truth   ᵇ*19* Or *and confess to him*   ᶜ*21* Hebrew *Shinar*   ᵈ*21* That is, about 5 pounds (about 2.3 kilograms)   ᵉ*21* That is, about 1 1/4 pounds (about 0.6 kilogram)   ᶠ*26* *Achor* means *trouble*.

7:10–12 Why did Achan's sin bring judgment on the entire nation? Although it was one man's failure, God saw it as national disobedience to a national law. God needed the entire nation to be committed to the job they had agreed to do—conquer the land. Thus, when one person failed, everyone failed. If Achan's sin went unpunished, unlimited looting could break out. The nation as a whole had to take responsibility for preventing this undisciplined disobedience.

Achan's sin was not merely his keeping some of the plunder (God allowed it in some cases), but his disobeying God's explicit command to destroy everything connected with Jericho. Achan's sin was indifference to the evil and idolatry of the city, not just a desire for money and clothes. God would not protect Israel's army again until the sin was removed and the army returned to obeying him without reservation. God is not content with our doing what is right some of the time. He wants us to do what is right all the time. We are under his orders to eliminate any thoughts, practices, or possessions that hinder our devotion to him.

7:13 "Consecrate yourselves" meant that the Israelites were to undergo purification rites like those mentioned in 3:5 when they were preparing to cross the Jordan River. Such rites prepared the people to approach God and constantly reminded them of their sinfulness and his holiness.

7:24, 25 Achan underestimated God and didn't take his commands seriously (6:18). Taking a robe, along with some silver and gold, may have seemed a small thing to Achan, but the effects of his sin were felt by the entire nation, especially his family. Like Achan, our actions affect more people than just ourselves. Beware of the temptation to rationalize your sins by saying they are too small or too personal to hurt anyone but you.

7:24–26 Why did Achan's entire family pay for his sin? The biblical record does not tell us if they were accomplices to his crime, but in the ancient world, the family was treated as a whole. Achan, as the head of his family, was like a tribal chief. If he prospered, the family prospered with him. If he suffered, so did they. Many Israelites had already died in battle because of Achan's sin. Now he was to be completely cut off from Israel.

Achan's entire family was to be stoned along with him so that no trace of the sin would remain in Israel. In our permissive and individualistic culture we have a hard time understanding such a decree, but in ancient cultures this punishment was common. The punishment fit the crime: Achan had disobeyed God's command to destroy everything in Jericho; thus everything that belonged to Achan had to be destroyed. Sin has drastic consequences, so we should take drastic measures to avoid it.

Ai Destroyed

8:1
pDt 31:6
qDt 1:21; Jos 1:9
rJos 6:2
8:2
sver 27; Dt 20:14

8 Then the LORD said to Joshua, "Do not be afraid;p do not be discouraged. q Take the whole army with you, and go up and attack Ai. For I have delivered r into your hands the king of Ai, his people, his city and his land. 2You shall do to Ai and its king as you did to Jericho and its king, except that you may carry off their plunder and livestock for yourselves. s Set an ambush behind the city."

3So Joshua and the whole army moved out to attack Ai. He chose thirty thousand of his best fighting men and sent them out at night 4with these orders: "Listen carefully. You are to set an ambush behind the city. Don't go very far from it. All of you be on the alert. 5I and all those with me will advance on the city, and when the men come out against us, as they did before, we will flee from them. 6They will pursue us until we have lured them away from the city, for they will say, 'They are running away from us as they did before.' So when we flee from them, 7you are to rise up from ambush and take the city. The LORD your God will give it into your hand. 8When you have taken the city, set it on fire. Do what the LORD has commanded. See to it; you have my orders."

9Then Joshua sent them off, and they went to the place of ambush and lay in wait between Bethel and Ai, to the west of Ai—but Joshua spent that night with the people.

8:10
tGe 22:3

10Early the next morning t Joshua mustered his men, and he and the leaders of Israel marched before them to Ai. 11The entire force that was with him marched up and approached the city and arrived in front of it. They set up camp north of Ai, with the valley between them and the city. 12Joshua had taken about five thousand men and set them in ambush between Bethel and Ai, to the west of the city. 13They had the soldiers take up their positions—all those in the camp to the north of the city and the ambush to the west of it. That night Joshua went into the valley.

8:14
uJdg 20:34
8:15
vJdg 20:36
wJos 15:61; 16:1;
18:12
8:16
xJdg 20:31
8:18
yEx 17:9-12

14When the king of Ai saw this, he and all the men of the city hurried out early in the morning to meet Israel in battle at a certain place overlooking the Arabah. But he did not know u that an ambush had been set against him behind the city. 15Joshua and all Israel let themselves be driven back v before them, and they fled toward the desert. w 16All the men of Ai were called to pursue them, and they pursued Joshua and were lured away x from the city. 17Not a man remained in Ai or Bethel who did not go after Israel. They left the city open and went in pursuit of Israel.

18Then the LORD said to Joshua, "Hold out toward Ai the javelin that is in your hand,y for

---

8:1 After Israel had been cleansed from Achan's sin, Joshua prepared to attack Ai again—this time to win. Joshua had learned some lessons that we can follow: (1) confess your sins when God reveals them to you (7:19–21); (2) when you fail, refocus on God, deal with the problem, and move on (7:22–25; 8:1). God wants the cycle of sin, repentance, and forgiveness to strengthen us, not weaken us. The lessons we learn from our failures should make us better able to handle the same situation the second time around. Because God is eager to give us cleansing, forgiveness, and strength, the only way to lose is to give up. We can tell what kind of people we are by what we do on the second and third attempts.

8:2 Why did God allow the Israelites to keep the plunder and livestock this time? Israel's laws for handling the spoils of war covered two situations. (1) Cities like Jericho which were under God's *ban* (judgment for idolatry) could not be looted (see Deuteronomy 20:16–18). God's people were to be kept holy and separate from every influence of idolatry. (2) The distribution of plunder from cities not under the ban was a normal part of warfare. It provided the army and the nation with the necessary food, flocks, and weapons needed to sustain itself in wartime. Ai was not under the ban. The conquering army needed the food and equipment. Because soldiers were not paid, the loot was part of their incentive and reward for going to war.

8:3 The conquest of Ai was very important to the Israelites. Only 11 miles away from Jericho, Ai was a key stronghold for the Caananites and a buffer fortress for Bethel (8:12). If the Caananite kings got wind of an Israelite defeat at Ai, they could unite in a coordinated attack. They did not know that God had restored his power and protection to Joshua's troops. We must

depend on God with absolute obedience to be sure of the victory he has promised.

8:18, 19 The Lord gave Joshua the city. Yesterday's defeat became today's victory. Once sin is dealt with, forgiveness and victory lie ahead. With God's direction we need not stay discouraged or burdened with guilt. No matter how difficult a setback sin may bring, we must renew our efforts to carry out God's will.

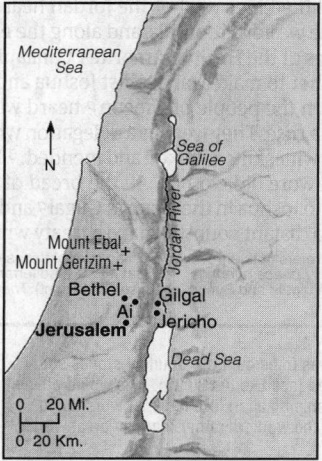

THE BATTLE FOR AI
During the night, Joshua sent one detachment of soldiers to the west of Ai to lie in wait. The next morning he led a second group north of Ai. When the army of Ai attacked, the Israelites to the north pretended to scatter, only to turn on the enemy as the men lying in ambush moved in and burned the city.

into your hand I will deliver the city." So Joshua held out his javelin *z* toward Ai. ¹⁹As soon as he did this, the men in the ambush rose quickly from their position and rushed forward. They entered the city and captured it and quickly set it on fire. *a*

²⁰The men of Ai looked back and saw the smoke of the city rising against the sky, but they had no chance to escape in any direction, for the Israelites who had been fleeing toward the desert had turned back against their pursuers. ²¹For when Joshua and all Israel saw that the ambush had taken the city and that smoke was going up from the city, they turned around and attacked the men of Ai. ²²The men of the ambush also came out of the city against them, so that they were caught in the middle, with Israelites on both sides. Israel cut them down, leaving them neither survivors nor fugitives. *b* ²³But they took the king of Ai alive and brought him to Joshua.

²⁴When Israel had finished killing all the men of Ai in the fields and in the desert where they had chased them, and when every one of them had been put to the sword, all the Israelites returned to Ai and killed those who were in it. ²⁵Twelve thousand men and women fell that day—all the people of Ai. *c* ²⁶For Joshua did not draw back the hand that held out his javelin until he had destroyed *a* all who lived in Ai. *d* ²⁷But Israel did carry off for themselves the livestock and plunder of this city, as the LORD had instructed Joshua. *e*

²⁸So Joshua burned Ai and made it a permanent heap of ruins, *f* a desolate place to this day. ²⁹He hung the king of Ai on a tree and left him there until evening. At sunset, *g* Joshua ordered them to take his body from the tree and throw it down at the entrance of the city gate. And they raised a large pile of rocks over it, which remains to this day.

The Covenant Renewed at Mount Ebal

³⁰Then Joshua built on Mount Ebal an altar to the LORD, the God of Israel, ³¹as Moses the servant of the LORD had commanded the Israelites. He built it according to what is written in the Book of the Law of Moses—an altar of uncut stones, on which no iron tool *h* had been used. On it they offered to the LORD burnt offerings and sacrificed fellowship offerings. *b* *i* ³²There, in the presence of the Israelites, Joshua copied on stones the law of Moses, which he had written. *j* ³³All Israel, aliens and citizens alike, with their elders, officials and judges, were standing on both sides of the ark of the covenant of the LORD, facing those who carried it—the priests, who were Levites. *k* Half of the people stood in front of Mount Gerizim and half of them in front of Mount Ebal, *l* as Moses the servant of the LORD had formerly commanded when he gave instructions to bless the people of Israel.

³⁴Afterward, Joshua read all the words of the law—the blessings and the curses—just as it is written in the Book of the Law. *m* ³⁵There was not a word of all that Moses had commanded that Joshua did not read to the whole assembly of Israel, including the women and children, and the aliens who lived among them. *n*

2. Joshua attacks the southern kings

The Gibeonite Deception

9 Now when all the kings west of the Jordan heard about these things—those in the hill country, in the western foothills, and along the entire coast of the Great Sea *c* *o* as far as Lebanon (the kings of the Hittites, Amorites, Canaanites, Perizzites, Hivites and Jebusites)— ²they came together to make war against Joshua and Israel.

³However, when the people of Gibeon *p* heard what Joshua had done to Jericho and Ai, ⁴they resorted to a ruse: They went as a delegation whose donkeys were loaded *d* with worn-out sacks and old wineskins, cracked and mended. ⁵The men put worn and patched sandals on their feet and wore old clothes. All the bread of their food supply was dry and moldy. ⁶Then they went to Joshua in the camp at Gilgal *q* and said to him and the men of Israel, "We have come from a distant country; make a treaty with us."

a 26 The Hebrew term refers to the irrevocable giving over of things or persons to the LORD, often by totally destroying them.   *b 31* Traditionally *peace offerings*   *c 1* That is, the Mediterranean   *d 4* Most Hebrew manuscripts; some Hebrew manuscripts, Vulgate and Syriac (see also Septuagint) *They prepared provisions and loaded their donkeys*

**Side references:**

8:18 *z* ver 26
8:19 *a* ver 8
8:22 *b* Dt 7:2
8:25 *c* Dt 20:16-18
8:26 *d* Ex 17:12
8:27 *e* ver 2
8:28 *f* Dt 13:16
8:29 *g* Dt 21:23
8:31 *h* Ex 20:25; *i* Dt 27:6-7
8:32 *j* Dt 27:8
8:33 *k* Dt 31:12; *l* Dt 11:29; 27:11-14
8:34 *m* Dt 31:11
8:35 *n* Dt 31:12
9:1 *o* Nu 34:6
9:3 *p* Jos 10:2
9:6 *q* Jos 5:10

8:30, 31 The altar was to be built out of uncut stones so it would not be profaned (see Exodus 20:25). This would prevent the people from worshiping altars like idols, or worshiping the craftsmanship of the workers rather than the great works of God.

8:32 It was most likely the Ten Commandments (recorded in Exodus 20) that Joshua copied on stones. These were the heart of all God's laws, and are still to be followed today.

9:1–6 As the news about their victory became widespread, the Israelites experienced opposition in two forms: direct (kings in the area began to unite against them); and indirect (the Gibeonites resorted to deception). We can expect similar

9:7
r Jos 11:19
s Ex 23:32

7 The men of Israel said to the Hivites, r "But perhaps you live near us. How then can we make a treaty s with you?"

8 "We are your servants," they said to Joshua.

But Joshua asked, "Who are you and where do you come from?"

9:9
t Dt 20:15
u ver 24; Jos 2:9
9:10
v Nu 21:24,35

9 They answered: "Your servants have come from a very distant country t because of the fame of the Lord your God. For we have heard reports u of him: all that he did in Egypt, 10 and all that he did to the two kings of the Amorites east of the Jordan—Sihon king of Heshbon, and Og king of Bashan, who reigned in Ashtaroth. v 11 And our elders and all those living in our country said to us, 'Take provisions for your journey; go and meet them and say to them, "We are your servants; make a treaty with us."' 12 This bread of ours was warm when we packed it at home on the day we left to come to you. But now see how dry and moldy it is. 13 And these wineskins that we filled were new, but see how cracked they are. And our clothes and sandals are worn out by the very long journey."

9:14
w Nu 27:21

14 The men of Israel sampled their provisions but did not inquire w of the Lord. 15 Then Joshua made a treaty of peace with them to let them live, and the leaders of the assembly ratified it by oath.

9:17
x Jos 18:25
9:18
y Ps 15:4

16 Three days after they made the treaty with the Gibeonites, the Israelites heard that they were neighbors, living near them. 17 So the Israelites set out and on the third day came to their cities: Gibeon, Kephirah, Beeroth x and Kiriath Jearim. 18 But the Israelites did not attack them, because the leaders of the assembly had sworn an oath y to them by the Lord, the God of Israel.

The whole assembly grumbled against the leaders, 19 but all the leaders answered, "We have given them our oath by the Lord, the God of Israel, and we cannot touch them now.

9:21
z ver 15
a Dt 29:11

20 This is what we will do to them: We will let them live, so that wrath will not fall on us for breaking the oath we swore to them." 21 They continued, "Let them live, z but let them be woodcutters and water carriers a for the entire community." So the leaders' promise to them was kept.

9:22
b ver 16
9:23
c Ge 9:25

22 Then Joshua summoned the Gibeonites and said, "Why did you deceive us by saying, 'We live a long way from you,' while actually you live near b us? 23 You are now under a curse: c You will never cease to serve as woodcutters and water carriers for the house of my God."

24 They answered Joshua, "Your servants were clearly told how the Lord your God had commanded his servant Moses to give you the whole land and to wipe out all its inhabitants from before you. So we feared for our lives because of you, and that is why we did this. 25 We are now in your hands. d Do to us whatever seems good and right to you."

9:25
d Ge 16:6
9:27
e Dt 12:5

26 So Joshua saved them from the Israelites, and they did not kill them. 27 That day he made the Gibeonites woodcutters and water carriers for the community and for the altar of the Lord at the place the Lord would choose. e And that is what they are to this day.

The Sun Stands Still

10:1
f Jos 8:1
g Dt 20:16; Jos 8:22
h Jos 9:15

10 Now Adoni-Zedek king of Jerusalem heard that Joshua had taken Ai f and totally destroyed a g it, doing to Ai and its king as he had done to Jericho and its king, and that the people of Gibeon had made a treaty of peace h with Israel and were living near them. 2 He and his people were very much alarmed at this, because Gibeon was an important city, like one of the royal cities; it was larger than Ai, and all its men were good fighters. 3 So Adoni-Zedek king

a 1 The Hebrew term refers to the irrevocable giving over of things or persons to the Lord, often by totally destroying them; also in verses 28, 35, 37, 39 and 40.

---

opposition as we obey God's commands. To guard against these pressures, we must rely on God and communicate daily with him. He will give us strength to endure the direct and indirect pressures and wisdom to see through deception.

9:14–17 When the leaders sampled these men's provisions, they saw that the bread was dry and moldy, the wineskins were cracked, and the clothes and sandals worn out. But they did not see through the deception. After the promise had been made and the treaty ratified, the facts came out—Israel's leaders had been deceived. God had specifically instructed Israel to make no treaties with the inhabitants of Canaan (Exodus 23:32; 34:12; Numbers 33:55; Deuteronomy 7:2; 20:17, 18). As a strategist, Joshua knew enough to talk to God before leading his troops into battle. But the peace treaty seemed innocent enough, so Joshua

and the leaders made this decision on their own. By failing to seek God's guidance and rushing ahead with their own plans, they had to deal with angry people and an awkward alliance. Once again, they had forgotten to go to God; yet how often we do the same. A new situation arises, and we forget to seek God's wisdom and guidance. When we learn the lessons of the past and apply them to today, we save ourselves a lot of trouble.

9:19, 20 Joshua and his advisers had made a mistake. But because they had given an oath to protect the Gibeonites, they would keep their word. The oath was not nullified by the Gibeonites' trickery. God had commanded that oaths be kept (Leviticus 5:4; 27:1, 28), and breaking an oath was serious. This encourages us not to take our promises lightly.

of Jerusalem appealed to Hoham king of Hebron,[i] Piram king of Jarmuth, Japhia king of Lachish[j] and Debir king of Eglon. [4]"Come up and help me attack Gibeon," he said, "because it has made peace[k] with Joshua and the Israelites."

[5]Then the five kings of the Amorites[l]—the kings of Jerusalem, Hebron, Jarmuth, Lachish and Eglon—joined forces. They moved up with all their troops and took up positions against Gibeon and attacked it.

[6]The Gibeonites then sent word to Joshua in the camp at Gilgal: "Do not abandon your servants. Come up to us quickly and save us! Help us, because all the Amorite kings from the hill country have joined forces against us."

[7]So Joshua marched up from Gilgal with his entire army,[m] including all the best fighting men. [8]The LORD said to Joshua, "Do not be afraid[n] of them; I have given them into your hand. Not one of them will be able to withstand you."

[9]After an all-night march from Gilgal, Joshua took them by surprise. [10]The LORD threw them into confusion before Israel,[o] who defeated them in a great victory at Gibeon. Israel pursued them along the road going up to Beth Horon and cut them down all the way to Azekah and Makkedah. [11]As they fled before Israel on the road down from Beth Horon to Azekah, the LORD hurled large hailstones[p] down on them from the sky, and more of them died from the hailstones than were killed by the swords of the Israelites.

[12]On the day the LORD gave the Amorites over to Israel, Joshua said to the LORD in the presence of Israel:

> "O sun, stand still over Gibeon,
>   O moon, over the Valley of Aijalon."
> [13] So the sun stood still,[q]
>   and the moon stopped,
>   till the nation avenged itself on[a] its enemies,

as it is written in the Book of Jashar.[r]

The sun stopped in the middle of the sky and delayed going down about a full day. [14]There has never been a day like it before or since, a day when the LORD listened to a man. Surely the LORD was fighting[s] for Israel!

[15]Then Joshua returned with all Israel to the camp at Gilgal.[t]

Five Amorite Kings Killed

[16]Now the five kings had fled and hidden in the cave at Makkedah. [17]When Joshua was told that the five kings had been found hiding in the cave at Makkedah, [18]he said, "Roll large

a 13 Or *nation triumphed over*

### Cross references (margin)

10:3
[i] Ge 13:18
[j] Isa 36:2; 37:8;
Jer 34:7

10:4
[k] Jos 9:15

10:5
[l] Nu 13:29

10:7
[m] Jos 8:1

10:8
[n] Jos 1:9

10:10
[o] Dt 7:23

10:11
[p] Ps 18:12

10:13
[q] Hab 3:11
[r] 2Sa 1:18

10:14
[s] ver 42

10:15
[t] ver 43

10:5–8 This alliance of enemy kings from the south actually helped Joshua and his army. Because the enemies had united to attack Gibeon, Joshua didn't have to spend the time and resources required to wage separate campaigns against each fortified city represented in the coalition. Joshua confidently confronted this coalition of armies and defeated them in a single battle because he trusted God to give Israel the victory.

10:6, 7 Joshua's response shows his integrity. After having been deceived by the Gibeonites, Joshua and the leaders could have been slow about their attempt to rescue them. Instead, they immediately responded to their call for help. How willing would you be to help someone who had deceived you, even though you had forgiven him or her? We should take our word just as seriously as Joshua did.

10:12–14 How did the sun stand still? Of course, in relation to the earth the sun always stands still—it is the earth that travels around the sun. But the terminology used in Joshua should not cause us to doubt the miracle. After all, we are not confused when someone tells us the sun rises or sets. The point is that the day was prolonged, not that God used a particular method to prolong it.

Two explanations have been given for how this event occurred: (1) A slowing of the earth's normal rotation gave Joshua more time, as the original Hebrew language seems to indicate. (2) Some unusual refraction of the sun's rays gave additional hours of light. Regardless of God's chosen method, the Bible is clear that the day was prolonged by a miracle, and that God's intervention turned the tide of battle for his people.

10:13 The Book of Jashar (also mentioned in 2 Samuel 1:18) was probably a collection of historical events put to music. Many parts of the Bible contain quotations from previous books, songs,

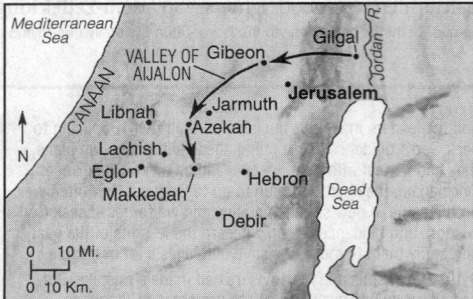

THE BATTLE FOR GIBEON Five Amorite kings conspired to destroy Gibeon. Israel came to the aid of the Gibeonites. The Israelites attacked the enemy armies outside of Gibeon and chased them through the Valley of Aijalon as far as Makkedah and Azekah.

rocks up to the mouth of the cave, and post some men there to guard it. 19But don't stop! Pursue your enemies, attack them from the rear and don't let them reach their cities, for the LORD your God has given them into your hand."

10:20
uDt 20:16

20So Joshua and the Israelites destroyed them completely u—almost to a man—but the few who were left reached their fortified cities. 21The whole army then returned safely to Joshua in the camp at Makkedah, and no one uttered a word against the Israelites.

22Joshua said, "Open the mouth of the cave and bring those five kings out to me." 23So they brought the five kings out of the cave—the kings of Jerusalem, Hebron, Jarmuth, Lachish and Eglon. 24When they had brought these kings to Joshua, he summoned all the men of Israel and said to the army commanders who had come with him, "Come here and put your feet v on the necks of these kings." So they came forward and placed their feet on their necks.

10:24
vMal 4:3

25Joshua said to them, "Do not be afraid; do not be discouraged. Be strong and courageous. This is what the LORD will do to all the enemies you are going to fight." 26Then Joshua struck and killed the kings and hung them on five trees, and they were left hanging on the trees until evening.

10:27
wDt 21:23

27At sunset w Joshua gave the order and they took them down from the trees and threw them into the cave where they had been hiding. At the mouth of the cave they placed large rocks, which are there to this day.

10:28
xDt 20:16
yJos 6:21

28That day Joshua took Makkedah. He put the city and its king to the sword and totally destroyed everyone in it. He left no survivors. x And he did to the king of Makkedah as he had done to the king of Jericho. y

Southern Cities Conquered

29Then Joshua and all Israel with him moved on from Makkedah to Libnah and attacked it. 30The LORD also gave that city and its king into Israel's hand. The city and everyone in it Joshua put to the sword. He left no survivors there. And he did to its king as he had done to the king of Jericho.

31Then Joshua and all Israel with him moved on from Libnah to Lachish; he took up positions against it and attacked it. 32The LORD handed Lachish over to Israel, and Joshua took it on the second day. The city and everyone in it he put to the sword, just as he had done to Libnah. 33Meanwhile, Horam king of Gezer had come up to help Lachish, but Joshua defeated him and his army—until no survivors were left.

34Then Joshua and all Israel with him moved on from Lachish to Eglon; they took up positions against it and attacked it. 35They captured it that same day and put it to the sword and totally destroyed everyone in it, just as they had done to Lachish.

10:36
zJos 14:13; 15:13;
Jdg 1:10

36Then Joshua and all Israel with him went up from Eglon to Hebron z and attacked it. 37They took the city and put it to the sword, together with its king, its villages and everyone in it. They left no survivors. Just as at Eglon, they totally destroyed it and everyone in it.

10:38
aJos 15:15;
Jdg 1:11

38Then Joshua and all Israel with him turned around and attacked Debir. a 39They took the city, its king and its villages, and put them to the sword. Everyone in it they totally destroyed. They left no survivors. They did to Debir and its king as they had done to Libnah and its king and to Hebron.

40So Joshua subdued the whole region, including the hill country, the Negev, the western

---

poems, or other spoken and written materials. Because God guided the writer of this book to select this material, his message comes with divine authority.

10:24 Placing a foot on the neck of a captive was a common military practice in the ancient Near East. It symbolized the victor's domination of his captives. These proud kings had boasted of their power. Now all Israel could see that God was superior to any earthly army.

10:25 With God's help, Israel won the battle against five Amorite armies. Such a triumph was part of God's daily business as he worked with his people for victory. Joshua told his men never to be afraid because God would give them similar victories over all their enemies. God has often protected us and won victories for us. The same God who empowered Joshua and who has led us in the past will help us with our present and future needs. Reminding ourselves of his help in the past will give us hope for the struggles that lie ahead.

10:32 Notice that in every Israelite victory, the text gives the credit to the Lord. All of Israel's victories came from God. When we are successful, we may be tempted to take all the credit and glory as though we succeeded by ourselves, in our own strength. In reality, *God* gives us the victories; and he alone delivers us from our enemies. We should give him the credit and praise him for his goodness.

10:40–43 God had commanded Joshua to take the leadership in ridding the land of sin so God's people could occupy it. Joshua did his part thoroughly—leading the united army to weaken the inhabitants. When God orders us to stop sinning, we must not pause to debate, consider the options, negotiate a compromise, or rationalize. Instead, like Joshua, our response must be swift and complete. We must be ruthless in avoiding relationships and activities that can lead us into sin.

foothills and the mountain slopes, together with all their kings.[b] He left no survivors. He totally destroyed all who breathed, just as the LORD, the God of Israel, had commanded. [c] 41 Joshua subdued them from Kadesh Barnea to Gaza and from the whole region of Goshen[d] to Gibeon. 42 All these kings and their lands Joshua conquered in one campaign, because the LORD, the God of Israel, fought[e] for Israel.

43 Then Joshua returned with all Israel to the camp at Gilgal.

3. Joshua attacks the northern kings

11 When Jabin king of Hazor heard of this, he sent word to Jobab king of Madon, to the kings of Shimron and Acshaph, 2 and to the northern kings who were in the mountains, in the Arabah[f] south of Kinnereth, in the western foothills and in Naphoth Dor[a] on the west; 3 to the Canaanites in the east and west; to the Amorites, Hittites, Perizzites and Jebusites in the hill country; and to the Hivites below Hermon in the region of Mizpah. 4 They came out with all their troops and a large number of horses and chariots—a huge army, as numerous as the sand on the seashore.[g] 5 All these kings joined forces and made camp together at the Waters of Merom, to fight against Israel.

6 The LORD said to Joshua, "Do not be afraid of them, because by this time tomorrow I will hand all of them over[h] to Israel, slain. You are to hamstring[i] their horses and burn their chariots."

7 So Joshua and his whole army came against them suddenly at the Waters of Merom and attacked them, 8 and the LORD gave them into the hand of Israel. They defeated them and pursued them all the way to Greater Sidon, to Misrephoth Maim,[j] and to the Valley of Mizpah on the east, until no survivors were left. 9 Joshua did to them as the LORD had directed: He hamstrung their horses and burned their chariots.

10 At that time Joshua turned back and captured Hazor and put its king to the sword. (Hazor had been the head of all these kingdoms.) 11 Everyone in it they put to the sword. They totally destroyed[b] them, not sparing anything that breathed, [k] and he burned up Hazor itself.

12 Joshua took all these royal cities and their kings and put them to the sword. He totally destroyed them, as Moses the servant of the LORD had commanded. [l] 13 Yet Israel did not burn any of the cities built on their mounds—except Hazor, which Joshua burned. 14 The Israelites carried off for themselves all the plunder and livestock of these cities, but all the people they put to the sword until they completely destroyed them, not sparing anyone that breathed. 15 As the LORD commanded his servant Moses, so Moses commanded Joshua, and Joshua did it; he left nothing undone of all that the LORD commanded Moses.[m]

a 2 Or *in the heights of Dor*   b 11 The Hebrew term refers to the irrevocable giving over of things or persons to the LORD, often by totally destroying them; also in verses 12, 20 and 21.

10:40
b Dt 7:24
c Dt 20:16-17
10:41
d Jos 11:16
10:42
e ver 14

11:2
f Jos 12:3

11:4
g Jdg 7:12

11:6
h Jos 10:8
i 2Sa 8:4

11:8
j Jos 13:6

11:11
k Dt 20:16-17

11:12
l Nu 33:50-52;
Dt 7:2

11:15
m Ex 34:11; Jos 1:7

THE BATTLE FOR HAZOR
Kings from the north joined together to battle the Israelites who controlled the southern half of Canaan. They gathered at the Waters of Merom, but Joshua attacked them by surprise— the enemies' chariots were useless in the dense forests. Hazor, the largest Canaanite center in Galilee, was destroyed.

11:1–5 Two kings of Hazor were named Jabin. The other, apparently a weak ruler, is mentioned in Judges 4:2, 3. The Jabin of this story was quite powerful because he was able to build an alliance with dozens of kings. By all appearances, Jabin had a clear advantage over Joshua and his outnumbered forces. But those who honor God can be victorious regardless of the odds.

11:10–13 Victorious invaders usually kept captured cities intact, moving into them and making them centers of commerce and defense. For example, Moses predicted in Deuteronomy 6:10–12 that Israel would occupy cities they themselves had not built. Joshua, however, burned Hazor. As a former capital of the land, Hazor symbolized the wicked culture that Israel had come to destroy. In addition, its capture and destruction broke the backbone of the federation and weakened the will of the people to resist.

11:15 Joshua carefully obeyed all the instructions given by God. This theme of obedience is repeated frequently in the book of Joshua, partly because obedience is one aspect of life that each individual believer can control. We can't always control our understanding because we may not have all the facts. We can't control what other people do or how they treat us. However, we can control our choice to obey God. Whatever new challenges we may face, the Bible contains relevant instructions that we can choose to ignore or choose to follow.

4. Summary of conquests

¹⁶So Joshua took this entire land: the hill country, all the Negev, the whole region of Goshen, the western foothills, [n] the Arabah and the mountains of Israel with their foothills, ¹⁷from Mount Halak, which rises toward Seir, to Baal Gad in the Valley of Lebanon [o] below Mount Hermon. He captured all their kings and struck them down, putting them to death. [p] ¹⁸Joshua waged war against all these kings for a long time. ¹⁹Except for the Hivites living in Gibeon, [q] not one city made a treaty of peace with the Israelites, who took them all in battle. ²⁰For it was the LORD himself who hardened their hearts to wage war against Israel, so that he might destroy them totally, exterminating them without mercy, as the LORD had commanded Moses.

²¹At that time Joshua went and destroyed the Anakites [r] from the hill country: from Hebron, Debir and Anab, from all the hill country of Judah, and from all the hill country of Israel. Joshua totally destroyed them and their towns. ²²No Anakites were left in Israelite territory; only in Gaza, Gath [s] and Ashdod did any survive. ²³So Joshua took the entire land, [t] just as the LORD had directed Moses, and he gave it as an inheritance to Israel according to their tribal divisions.

Then the land had rest from war.

List of Defeated Kings

12 These are the kings of the land whom the Israelites had defeated and whose territory they took over east of the Jordan, from the Arnon Gorge to Mount Hermon, [u] including all the eastern side of the Arabah:

²Sihon king of the Amorites,
who reigned in Heshbon. He ruled from Aroer on the rim of the Arnon Gorge—from the middle of the gorge—to the Jabbok River, which is the border of the Ammonites. This included half of Gilead. ³He also ruled over the eastern Arabah from the Sea of Kinnereth [a] [v] to the Sea of the Arabah (the Salt Sea [b]), to Beth Jeshimoth, [w] and then southward below the slopes of Pisgah.

⁴And the territory of Og king of Bashan,
one of the last of the Rephaites, who reigned in Ashtaroth [x] and Edrei. ⁵He ruled over Mount Hermon, Salecah, [y] all of Bashan to the border of the people of Geshur and Maacah, and half of Gilead to the border of Sihon king of Heshbon.

⁶Moses, the servant of the LORD, and the Israelites conquered them. And Moses the servant of the LORD gave their land to the Reubenites, the Gadites and the half-tribe of Manasseh to be their possession. [z]

⁷These are the kings of the land that Joshua and the Israelites conquered on the west side of the Jordan, from Baal Gad in the Valley of Lebanon [a] to Mount Halak, which rises toward Seir (their lands Joshua gave as an inheritance to the tribes of Israel according to their tribal divisions— ⁸the hill country, the western foothills, the Arabah, the mountain slopes, the desert and the Negev [b]—the lands of the Hittites, Amorites, Canaanites, Perizzites, Hivites and Jebusites):

⁹ the king of Jericho [c]	one
the king of Ai [d] (near Bethel)	one

[a] *3 That is, Galilee*   [b] *3 That is, the Dead Sea*

Side notes (left margin references):
11:16 [n] Jos 10:41
11:17 [o] Jos 12:7 [p] Dt 7:24
11:19 [q] Jos 9:3
11:21 [r] Nu 13:22,33
11:22 [s] 1Sa 17:4
11:23 [t] Jos 21:43-45
12:1 [u] Dt 3:8
12:3 [v] Jos 11:2 [w] Jos 13:20
12:4 [x] Dt 1:4
12:5 [y] Dt 3:10
12:6 [z] Nu 32:29,33
12:7 [a] Jos 11:17
12:8 [b] Jos 11:16
12:9 [c] Jos 6:2 [d] Jos 8:29

11:15 Joshua followed every detail of God's commands to Moses. It is usually difficult to complete someone else's project, but Joshua stepped into Moses' job, building upon what Moses had started, and brought it to completion. A new person starting a new job usually brings a new style and personality to that job. But the church or any other organization cannot work effectively if every change of personnel means starting from scratch. True servants will step in and continue or complete good work that others have begun.

11:18 The conquest of much of the land of Canaan seems to have happened quickly (we can read about it in one sitting), but it actually took seven years. We often expect quick changes in our lives and quick victories over sin. Our journey with God is a lifelong process, however, and the changes and victories may take time. It is easy to grow impatient with God and feel like

giving up hope because things are moving too slowly. When we are close to a situation, it is difficult to see progress. But when we look back we can see that God never stopped working.

11:21, 22 The Anakites were the tribes of giants the Israelite spies described when they gave their negative report on the promised land (Numbers 13; 14). This time the people did not let their fear of the giants prevent them from engaging in battle and claiming the land God had promised.

12:1ff Chapter 12 is a summary of the first half of the book of Joshua. It lists the kings and nations conquered by Joshua to both the east and the west of the Jordan River. As long as the people trusted and obeyed God, one evil nation after another fell in defeat.

10 the king of Jerusalem	one
the king of Hebron	one
11 the king of Jarmuth	one
the king of Lachish	one
12 the king of Eglon	one
the king of Gezer[e]	one
13 the king of Debir	one
the king of Geder	one
14 the king of Hormah	one
the king of Arad	one
15 the king of Libnah	one
the king of Adullam	one
16 the king of Makkedah	one
the king of Bethel	one
17 the king of Tappuah	one
the king of Hepher[f]	one

12:12
[e] Jos 10:33

12:17
[f] 1Ki 4:10

THE CONQUERED LAND

Joshua displayed brilliant military strategy in the way he went about conquering the land of Canaan. He first captured the well-fortified Jericho to gain a foothold in Canaan and to demonstrate the awesome might of the God of Israel. Then he gained the hill country around Bethel and Gibeon. From there he subdued towns in the lowlands. Then his army conquered important cities in the north, such as Hazor. In all, Israel conquered land both east (12:1–6) and west (12:7–24) of the Jordan River; from Mount Hermon in the north to beyond the Negev to Mount Halak in the south. Thirty-one kings and their cities had been defeated. The Israelites had overpowered the Hittites, the Amorites, the Canaanites, the Perizzites, the Hivites, and the Jebusites. Other peoples living in Canaan were yet to be conquered.

The broken lines (—·—·) indicate modern boundaries.

¹⁸ the king of Aphek	one
the king of Lasharon	one
¹⁹ the king of Madon	one
the king of Hazor	one
²⁰ the king of Shimron Meron	one
the king of Acshaph	one
²¹ the king of Taanach	one
the king of Megiddo	one
²² the king of Kedesh*g*	one
the king of Jokneam in Carmel	one
²³ the king of Dor (in Naphoth Dor*a*)	one
the king of Goyim in Gilgal	one
²⁴ the king of Tirzah	one

12:22
g Jos 19:37

thirty-one kings in all.

C. DIVIDING THE PROMISED LAND (13:1—24:33)

After seven years of battle, Israel gained control of the land, which was then divided and allotted to the tribes. Joshua dismisses the army, for it was now each tribe's responsibility to clear
out the remaining enemies from their own areas. Joshua continues to encourage the people
to remain faithful to God so they can remain in the land. The promised land was Israel's
earthly inheritance. But Israel also had a spiritual inheritance in which we can share when we
live a life of faithfulness to God.

1. The tribes receive their land

Land Still to Be Taken

13:1
h Jos 14:10

13 When Joshua was old and well advanced in years,*h* the LORD said to him, "You are very
old, and there are still very large areas of land to be taken over.

13:3
i Jdg 3:3

² "This is the land that remains: all the regions of the Philistines and Geshurites: ³ from the Shihor River on the east of Egypt to the territory of Ekron on the north, all of it counted as Canaanite (the territory of the five Philistine rulers*i* in Gaza, Ashdod,

a 23 Or *in the heights of Dor*

13—19 The following chapters describe how the promised land was to be divided among the 12 tribes. First, the tribe of Levi was not to have any land because they were to spend all their energies serving the people, not their own interests (13:14; 21). Second, the tribes of Reuben and Gad and the half-tribe of Manasseh had already received land east of the Jordan River, which had been given to them by Moses (Numbers 32). Third, the tribes of Judah and Joseph (Ephraim and the other half-tribe of Manasseh) had received land that their ancestor Jacob had promised them 450 years earlier (Genesis 48:22; Joshua 15—17). The rest of the tribes divided up the remaining land by casting lots (chapter 18).

Through Jacob's original blessing of his sons (Genesis 49) and Moses' blessing of the 12 tribes (Deuteronomy 33), the type of land each tribe would receive was already known. The two blessings were prophetic, for although Joshua cast lots to determine the land to be given to each of the remaining tribes, the allotments came out just as Jacob and Moses had predicted.

13:1 Joshua was getting old—he was between 85 and 100 years of age at this time. God, however, still had work for him to do. Our culture often glorifies the young and strong and sets aside those who are older. Yet older people are filled with the wisdom that comes with experience. They are very capable of serving if given the chance and should be encouraged to do so. Believers are never allowed to retire from God's service. Those past retirement age should not assume that age disqualifies or excuses them from serving God.

13:7 Much of the land was unconquered at this point, but God's plan was to go ahead and include it in the divisions among the tribes. God's desire was that it would eventually be conquered by the Israelites. God knows the future, and as he leads you he already knows about the victories that lie ahead. But just as the Israelites still had to go to battle and fight, we must still face the trials and fight the battles of our unconquered land.

What are our unconquered lands? They may be overseas missionary territories, new languages in which to translate the Bible, new missionary areas in our neighborhoods, interest groups or institutions that need redemptive work, unchallenged public problems or ethical issues, unconfessed sin in our lives, or underdeveloped talents and resources. What territory has God given you to conquer? This territory is your "promised land." Our inheritance will be a new heaven and a new earth (Revelation 21:1) if we fulfill the mission God has given us to do.

**THE LAND
YET TO BE
CONQUERED**
Canaan was now controlled by the Israelites, although much land and several cities still needed to be conquered. Joshua told the people to include both conquered and unconquered lands in the territorial allotments (13:7). He was certain the people would complete the conquest as God had commanded.

Ashkelon, Gath and Ekron—that of the Avvites);[j] [4]from the south, all the land of the Canaanites, from Arah of the Sidonians as far as Aphek, the region of the Amorites,[k] [5]the area of the Gebalites[a];[l] and all Lebanon to the east, from Baal Gad below Mount Hermon to Lebo[b] Hamath.

[6]"As for all the inhabitants of the mountain regions from Lebanon to Misrephoth Maim,[m] that is, all the Sidonians, I myself will drive them out before the Israelites. Be sure to allocate this land to Israel for an inheritance, as I have instructed you, [7]and divide it as an inheritance among the nine tribes and half of the tribe of Manasseh."

Division of the Land East of the Jordan

[8]The other half of Manasseh,[c] the Reubenites and the Gadites had received the inheritance that Moses had given them east of the Jordan, as he, the servant of the LORD, had assigned[n] it to them.

[9]It extended from Aroer[o] on the rim of the Arnon Gorge, and from the town in the middle of the gorge, and included the whole plateau of Medeba as far as Dibon, [10]and all the towns of Sihon king of the Amorites, who ruled in Heshbon, out to the border of the Ammonites.[p] [11]It also included Gilead, the territory of the people of Geshur and Maacah, all of Mount Hermon and all Bashan as far as Salecah— [12]that is, the whole kingdom of Og in Bashan,[q] who had reigned in Ashtaroth[r] and Edrei and had survived as one of the last of the Rephaites. Moses had defeated them and taken over their land. [13]But the Israelites did not drive out the people of Geshur and Maacah, so they continue to live among the Israelites to this day.

[14]But to the tribe of Levi he gave no inheritance, since the offerings made by fire to the LORD, the God of Israel, are their inheritance, as he promised them.[s]

[15]This is what Moses had given to the tribe of Reuben, clan by clan:

[16]The territory from Aroer[t] on the rim of the Arnon Gorge, and from the town in the middle of the gorge, and the whole plateau past Medeba [17]to Heshbon and all its towns on the plateau, including Dibon, Bamoth Baal, Beth Baal Meon, [18]Jahaz,[u] Kedemoth, Mephaath, [19]Kiriathaim,[v] Sibmah, Zereth Shahar on the hill in the valley, [20]Beth Peor, the slopes of Pisgah, and Beth Jeshimoth— [21]all the towns on the plateau and the entire realm of Sihon king of the Amorites, who ruled at Heshbon. Moses had defeated him and the Midianite chiefs, Evi, Rekem, Zur, Hur and Reba[w]—princes allied with Sihon— who lived in that country. [22]In addition to those slain in battle, the Israelites had put to the sword Balaam son of Beor, who practiced divination. [23]The boundary of the Reubenites was the bank of the Jordan. These towns and their villages were the inheritance of the Reubenites, clan by clan.

a5 That is, the area of Byblos   b5 Or *to the entrance to*   c8 Hebrew *With it* (that is, with the other half of Manasseh)

**Cross references (right margin):**
13:3   *j* Dt 2:23
13:4   *k* Am 2:10
13:5   *l* 1Ki 5:18
13:6   *m* Jos 11:8
13:8   *n* Jos 12:6
13:9   *o* ver 16
13:10   *p* Nu 21:24
13:12   *q* Dt 3:11   *r* Jos 12:4
13:14   *s* Dt 18:1-2
13:16   *t* ver 9; Jos 12:2
13:18   *u* Nu 21:23
13:19   *v* Nu 32:37
13:21   *w* Nu 31:8

THE TRIBES EAST OF THE JORDAN
Joshua assigned territory to the tribes of Reuben, Gad, and the half-tribe of Manasseh on the east side of the Jordan where they had chosen to remain because of the wonderful livestock country (Numbers 32:1–5).

13:13 One reason the Israelites encountered so many problems as they settled the land was that they failed to conquer *fully* the land and drive out all its inhabitants. The cancer-like presence of the remaining pagan peoples of Canaan caused unending difficulties for the Israelites, as the book of Judges records. Just as they failed to remove completely the sin from the land, believers today often fail to remove completely the sin from their lives—also with disastrous results. As a self-test, reread the Ten Commandments in Exodus 20:1–17. Ask yourself, Am I tolerating sinful practices or thoughts? Have I accepted half-measures as good enough? Do I condemn the faults of others but condone my own?

13:15–23 Because of Joseph's godly character (Genesis 49:22–26), the tribes descended from him—Ephraim and Manasseh— were given the richest, most fertile land in all of Canaan. Judah, who offered himself in exchange for his brother Benjamin's safety (Genesis 44:18–34), received the largest portion of land, which eventually became the southern kingdom and the seat of David's dynasty. Reuben, who slept with one of his father's wives (Genesis 49:4), was given desert land, the region described here. The blessings Jacob gave to his sons according to their character seem also to be reflected in the characteristics of the land each tribe later received.

24 This is what Moses had given to the tribe of Gad, clan by clan:

25 The territory of Jazer,ˣ all the towns of Gilead and half the Ammonite country as far as Aroer, near Rabbah; 26 and from Heshbon to Ramath Mizpah and Betonim, and from Mahanaim to the territory of Debir; 27 and in the valley, Beth Haram, Beth Nimrah, Succoth and Zaphon with the rest of the realm of Sihon king of Heshbon (the east side of the Jordan, the territory up to the end of the Sea of Kinnereth ᵃ ʸ). 28 These towns and their villages were the inheritance of the Gadites, clan by clan.

29 This is what Moses had given to the half-tribe of Manasseh, that is, to half the family of the descendants of Manasseh, clan by clan:

30 The territory extending from Mahanaim and including all of Bashan, the entire realm of Og king of Bashan—all the settlements of Jair ᶻ in Bashan, sixty towns, 31 half of Gilead, and Ashtaroth and Edrei (the royal cities of Og in Bashan). This was for the descendants of Makir son of Manasseh—for half of the sons of Makir, clan by clan.

32 This is the inheritance Moses had given when he was in the plains of Moab across the Jordan east of Jericho. 33 But to the tribe of Levi, Moses had given no inheritance; the LORD, the God of Israel, is their inheritance,ᵃ as he promised them. ᵇ

Division of the Land West of the Jordan

14 Now these are the areas the Israelites received as an inheritance in the land of Canaan, which Eleazar the priest, Joshua son of Nun and the heads of the tribal clans of Israel allotted to them.ᶜ 2 Their inheritances were assigned by lot ᵈ to the nine-and-a-half tribes, as the LORD had commanded through Moses. 3 Moses had granted the two-and-a-half tribes their inheritance east of the Jordan ᵉ but had not granted the Levites an inheritance among the rest,ᶠ 4 for the sons of Joseph had become two tribes—Manasseh and Ephraim. ᵍ The Levites received no share of the land but only towns to live in, with pasturelands for their flocks and herds. 5 So the Israelites divided the land, just as the LORD had commanded Moses.

Hebron Given to Caleb

6 Now the men of Judah approached Joshua at Gilgal, and Caleb son of Jephunneh ʰ the Kenizzite said to him, "You know what the LORD said to Moses the man of God at Kadesh Barnea ᶦ about you and me. 7 I was forty years old when Moses the servant of the LORD sent me from Kadesh Barnea to explore the land. And I brought him back a report according to my convictions,ʲ 8 but my brothers who went up with me made the hearts of the people melt with fear. I, however, followed the LORD my God wholeheartedly. ᵏ 9 So on that day Moses swore to me, 'The land on which your feet have walked will be your inheritance and that of your children ᶦ forever, because you have followed the LORD my God wholeheartedly.'ᵇ

10 "Now then, just as the LORD promised, he has kept me alive for forty-five years since the time he said this to Moses, while Israel moved about in the desert. So here I am today, eighty-five years old! 11 I am still as strong ᵐ today as the day Moses sent me out; I'm just as

ᵃ27 That is, Galilee   ᵇ9 Deut. 1:36

13:25
ˣNu 21:32
13:27
ʸNu 34:11

13:30
ᶻNu 32:41

13:33
ᵃNu 18:20
ᵇver 14

14:1
ᶜNu 34:17-18
14:2
ᵈNu 26:55
14:3
ᵉNu 32:33
ᶠJos 13:14
14:4
ᵍGe 48:5

14:6
ʰNu 14:30
ᶦNu 13:26
14:7
ʲNu 13:30; 14:6-9
14:8
ᵏNu 14:24
14:9
ᶦDt 1:36

14:11
ᵐDt 34:7

13:29 The tribe of Manasseh was divided into two half-tribes. This occurred when many people from the tribe wanted to settle east of the Jordan River in an area that was especially suited for their flocks (Numbers 32:33). The rest of the tribe preferred to settle west of the Jordan River in the land of Canaan.

13:33 The tribe of Levi was dedicated to serving God. The Levites needed more time and mobility than a landowner could possibly have. Giving them land would mean saddling them with responsibilities and loyalties that would hinder their service to God. Instead, God arranged for the other tribes to meet the Levites' needs through donations. (See Numbers 35:2–4 for how the Levites were to receive cities within each tribal territory.)

14:5 The land was divided exactly as God had instructed Moses years before. Joshua did not change a word. He followed God's commands precisely. Often we believe that *almost* is close enough, and this idea can carry over into our spiritual lives. For example, we may follow God's Word as long as we agree with it, but ignore it when the demands seem harsh. But God is looking for people who follow instructions thoroughly.

14:6–12 Caleb was faithful from the start. As one of the original spies sent into the promised land (Numbers 13:30–33), he saw great cities and giants, yet he knew God would help the people conquer the land. Because of Caleb's faith, God promised him a personal inheritance of land (Numbers 14:24; Deuteronomy 1:34–36). Here, 45 years later, the land was given to him. Caleb's faith was still unwavering. Although his inherited land still had giants, Caleb knew the Lord would help him conquer them. Like Caleb, we must be faithful to God, not only at the start of our walk with him, but through our entire lives. We must never allow ourselves to rest on our past accomplishments or reputations.

14:6–12 When Joshua gave Caleb his inheritance, it fulfilled a promise God had made to Caleb 45 years earlier. We expect such integrity and reliability from God, but do we expect the same from his followers? How about you? Is your word this reliable? Would you honor a 45-year-old promise? God would—and does. Even today he is honoring promises he made *thousands* of years ago. In fact, some of his greatest promises are yet to be fulfilled. This gives us much to look forward to. Let your faith grow as you realize that God keeps his word.

vigorous to go out to battle now as I was then. [12]Now give me this hill country that the LORD promised me that day. You yourself heard then that the Anakites[n] were there and their cities were large and fortified, but, the LORD helping me, I will drive them out just as he said."

[13]Then Joshua blessed[o] Caleb son of Jephunneh and gave him Hebron as his inheritance. [14]So Hebron has belonged to Caleb son of Jephunneh the Kenizzite ever since, because he followed the LORD, the God of Israel, wholeheartedly. [15](Hebron used to be called Kiriath Arba after Arba, who was the greatest man among the Anakites.)

Then the land had rest[p] from war.

Allotment for Judah

15 The allotment for the tribe of Judah, clan by clan, extended down to the territory of Edom,[q] to the Desert of Zin in the extreme south.

[2]Their southern boundary started from the bay at the southern end of the Salt Sea,[a] [3]crossed south of Scorpion[b] Pass,[r] continued on to Zin and went over to the south of Kadesh Barnea. Then it ran past Hezron up to Addar and curved around to Karka. [4]It then passed along to Azmon[s] and joined the Wadi of Egypt, ending at the sea. This is their[c] southern boundary.

[5]The eastern boundary is the Salt Sea as far as the mouth of the Jordan.

The northern boundary started from the bay of the sea at the mouth of the Jordan, [6]went up to Beth Hoglah and continued north of Beth Arabah to the Stone of Bohan[t] son of Reuben. [7]The boundary then went up to Debir from the Valley of Achor[u] and turned north to Gilgal, which faces the Pass of Adummim south of the gorge. It continued along to the waters of En Shemesh and came out at En Rogel. [8]Then it ran up the Valley of Ben Hinnom along the southern slope of the Jebusite[v] city (that is, Jerusalem). From there it climbed to the top of the hill west of the Hinnom Valley at the northern end of the Valley of Rephaim. [9]From the hilltop the boundary headed toward the spring of the waters of Nephtoah,[w] came out at the towns of Mount Ephron and went down toward Baalah[x] (that is, Kiriath Jearim). [10]Then it curved westward from Baalah to Mount Seir, ran along the northern slope of Mount Jearim (that is, Kesalon), continued down to Beth Shemesh and crossed to Timnah.[y] [11]It went to the northern slope of Ekron, turned toward Shikkeron, passed along to Mount Baalah and reached Jabneel. The boundary ended at the sea.

[12]The western boundary is the coastline of the Great Sea.[d][z]
These are the boundaries around the people of Judah by their clans.

[13]In accordance with the LORD's command to him, Joshua gave to Caleb son of Jephunneh a portion in Judah—Kiriath Arba, that is, Hebron. (Arba was the forefather of Anak.)[a] [14]From Hebron Caleb drove out the three Anakites—Sheshai, Ahiman and Talmai[b]—descendants of Anak. [15]From there he marched against the people living in Debir (formerly called Kiriath Sepher). [16]And Caleb said, "I will give my daughter Acsah[c] in marriage to the man who attacks and captures Kiriath Sepher." [17]Othniel[d] son of Kenaz, Caleb's brother, took it; so Caleb gave his daughter Acsah to him in marriage.

[18]One day when she came to Othniel, she urged him[e] to ask her father for a field. When she got off her donkey, Caleb asked her, "What can I do for you?"

[19]She replied, "Do me a special favor. Since you have given me land in the Negev, give me also springs of water." So Caleb gave her the upper and lower springs.

[20]This is the inheritance of the tribe of Judah, clan by clan:

[21]The southernmost towns of the tribe of Judah in the Negev toward the boundary of Edom were:

Kabzeel, Eder,[e] Jagur, [22]Kinah, Dimonah, Adadah, [23]Kedesh, Hazor, Ithnan, [24]Ziph,

---

14:12 [n]Nu 13:33

14:13 [o]Jos 22:6,7

14:15 [p]Jos 11:23

15:1 [q]Nu 34:3

15:3 [r]Nu 34:4

15:4 [s]Nu 34:5

15:6 [t]Jos 18:17

15:7 [u]Jos 7:24

15:8 [v]ver 63

15:9 [w]Jos 18:15
[x]1Ch 13:6

15:10 [y]Ge 38:12

15:12 [z]Nu 34:6

15:13 [a]Jos 14:13-15

15:14 [b]Nu 13:22

15:16 [c]Jdg 1:12

15:17 [d]Jdg 3:9,11

15:21 [e]Ge 35:21

---

[a]2 That is, the Dead Sea; also in verse 5 [b]3 Hebrew *Akrabbim* [c]4 Hebrew *your* [d]12 That is, the Mediterranean; also in verse 47 [e]18 Hebrew and some Septuagint manuscripts; other Septuagint manuscripts (see also note at Judges 1:14) *Othniel, he urged her*

14:15 The Anakites were a race of giants who inhabited parts of the land before Joshua's conquest.

15:4 Notice that these boundaries and descriptions of the promised land are very specific. God was telling Israel exactly what to do, and he was giving them just what they needed. They had no excuse for disobedience.

15:16–19 Othniel became Israel's first judge after Joshua's death (Judges 1:13; 3:9–11). He played an important role in reforming Israel by chasing away an oppressive enemy army and bringing peace back to the land. Thus Caleb's legacy of faithfulness continued to the next generation.

15:19 Acsah asked Caleb for springs of water because her land

Telem, Bealoth, 25 Hazor Hadattah, Kerioth Hezron (that is, Hazor), 26 Amam, Shema, Moladah, 27 Hazar Gaddah, Heshmon, Beth Pelet, 28 Hazar Shual, Beersheba, Biziothiah, 29 Baalah, Iim, Ezem, 30 Eltolad, Kesil, Hormah, 31 Ziklag, f Madmannah, Sansannah, 32 Lebaoth, Shilhim, Ain and Rimmon—a total of twenty-nine towns and their villages.

15:31
f 1Sa 27:6

33 In the western foothills:

15:33
g Jdg 13:25; 16:31

Eshtaol, g Zorah, Ashnah, 34 Zanoah, En Gannim, Tappuah, Enam, 35 Jarmuth, Adullam, h Socoh, Azekah, 36 Shaaraim, Adithaim and Gederah (or Gederothaim) a —fourteen towns and their villages.

15:35
h 1Sa 22:1

37 Zenan, Hadashah, Migdal Gad, 38 Dilean, Mizpah, Joktheel, i 39 Lachish, j Bozkath, Eglon, 40 Cabbon, Lahmas, Kitlish, 41 Gederoth, Beth Dagon, Naamah and Makkedah—sixteen towns and their villages.

15:38
i 2Ki 14:7

15:39
j Jos 10:3; 2Ki 14:19

42 Libnah, Ether, Ashan, 43 Iphtah, Ashnah, Nezib, 44 Keilah, Aczib and Mareshah—nine towns and their villages.

45 Ekron, with its surrounding settlements and villages; 46 west of Ekron, all that were in the vicinity of Ashdod, together with their villages; 47 Ashdod, its surrounding settlements and villages; and Gaza, its settlements and villages, as far as the Wadi of Egypt k and the coastline of the Great Sea. l

15:47
k ver 4
l Nu 34:6

48 In the hill country:

Shamir, Jattir, Socoh, 49 Dannah, Kiriath Sannah (that is, Debir), 50 Anab, Eshtemoh, Anim, 51 Goshen, m Holon and Giloh—eleven towns and their villages.

15:51
m Jos 10:41; 11:16

52 Arab, Dumah, Eshan, 53 Janim, Beth Tappuah, Aphekah, 54 Humtah, Kiriath Arba (that is, Hebron) and Zior—nine towns and their villages.

55 Maon, Carmel, Ziph, Juttah, 56 Jezreel, Jokdeam, Zanoah, 57 Kain, Gibeah and Timnah—ten towns and their villages.

58 Halhul, Beth Zur, Gedor, 59 Maarath, Beth Anoth and Eltekon—six towns and their villages.

60 Kiriath Baal (that is, Kiriath Jearim n) and Rabbah—two towns and their villages.

15:60
n Jos 18:14

61 In the desert:

Beth Arabah, Middin, Secacah, 62 Nibshan, the City of Salt and En Gedi—six towns and their villages.

63 Judah could not o dislodge the Jebusites p, who were living in Jerusalem; to this day the Jebusites live there with the people of Judah.

15:63
o Jdg 1:21
p 2Sa 5:6

Allotment for Ephraim and Manasseh

16:2
q Jos 18:13

16 The allotment for Joseph began at the Jordan of Jericho, b east of the waters of Jericho, and went up from there through the desert into the hill country of Bethel. 2 It went on from Bethel (that is, Luz q), c crossed over to the territory of the Arkites in Ataroth, 3 descended westward to the territory of the Japhletites as far as the region of Lower Beth Horon and on to Gezer, ending at the sea.

4 So Manasseh and Ephraim, the descendants of Joseph, received their inheritance.

5 This was the territory of Ephraim, clan by clan:

16:5
r Jos 18:13

The boundary of their inheritance went from Ataroth Addar r in the east to Upper Beth Horon 6 and continued to the sea. From Micmethath s on the north it curved eastward to Taanath Shiloh, passing by it to Janoah on the east. 7 Then it went down from Janoah to Ataroth and Naarah, touched Jericho and came out at the Jordan. 8 From Tappuah the border went west to the Kanah Ravine t and ended at the sea. This was the inheritance of the tribe of the Ephraimites, clan by clan. 9 It also included all the towns and their villages that were set aside for the Ephraimites within the inheritance of the Manassites.

16:6
s Jos 17:7

16:8
t Jos 17:9

10 They did not dislodge the Canaanites living in Gezer; to this day the Canaanites live among the people of Ephraim but are required to do forced labor. u

16:10
u Jos 17:13;
Jdg 1:28-29;
1Ki 9:16

a 36 Or Gederah and Gederothaim   b 1 Jordan of Jericho was possibly an ancient name for the Jordan River.
c 2 Septuagint; Hebrew Bethel to Luz

---

was in the south and was very arid. Caleb probably granted her request as a wedding present (see 15:17).

16:1ff Although Joseph was one of Jacob's 12 sons, he did not have a tribe named after him. This was because Joseph, as the oldest son of Jacob's wife Rachel, received a double portion of

the inheritance. Joseph's double portion was divided between his two sons, Ephraim and Manasseh, whom Jacob considered as his own (Genesis 48:5). The largest territory and the greatest influence in the northern half of Israel belonged to their tribes.

17 This was the allotment for the tribe of Manasseh as Joseph's firstborn,ᵛ that is, for Makir, Manasseh's firstborn. Makir was the ancestor of the Gileadites, who had received Gilead and Bashan because the Makirites were great soldiers. ²So this allotment was for the rest of the people of Manasseh—the clans of Abiezer,ʷ Helek, Asriel, Shechem, Hepher and Shemida. These are the other male descendants of Manasseh son of Joseph by their clans.

³Now Zelophehad son of Hepher,ˣ the son of Gilead, the son of Makir, the son of Manasseh, had no sons but only daughters,ʸ whose names were Mahlah, Noah, Hoglah, Milcah and Tirzah. ⁴They went to Eleazar the priest, Joshua son of Nun, and the leaders and said, "The Lᴏʀᴅ commanded Moses to give us an inheritance among our brothers." So Joshua gave them an inheritance along with the brothers of their father, according to the Lᴏʀᴅ's command.ᶻ ⁵Manasseh's share consisted of ten tracts of land besides Gilead and Bashan east of the Jordan, ⁶because the daughters of the tribe of Manasseh received an inheritance among the sons. The land of Gilead belonged to the rest of the descendants of Manasseh.

⁷The territory of Manasseh extended from Asher to Micmethathᵃ east of Shechem. The boundary ran southward from there to include the people living at En Tappuah. ⁸(Manasseh had the land of Tappuah, but Tappuahᵇ itself, on the boundary of Manasseh, belonged to the Ephraimites.) ⁹Then the boundary continued south to the Kanah Ravine.ᶜ There were towns belonging to Ephraim lying among the towns of Manasseh, but the boundary of Manasseh was the northern side of the ravine and ended at the sea. ¹⁰On the south the land belonged to Ephraim, on the north to Manasseh. The territory of Manasseh reached the sea and bordered Asher on the north and Issachar on the east.

¹¹Within Issachar and Asher, Manasseh also had Beth Shan,ᵈ Ibleam and the people of Dor, Endor, Taanach and Megiddo, together with their surrounding settlements (the third in the list is Naphothᵃ).

¹²Yet the Manassites were not ableᵉ to occupy these towns, for the Canaanites were determined to live in that region. ¹³However, when the Israelites grew stronger, they subjected the Canaanites to forced labor but did not drive them out completely.ᶠ

¹⁴The people of Joseph said to Joshua, "Why have you given us only one allotment and one portion for an inheritance? We are a numerous people and the Lᴏʀᴅ has blessed us abundantly."ᵍ

¹⁵"If you are so numerous," Joshua answered, "and if the hill country of Ephraim is too small for you, go up into the forest and clear land for yourselves there in the land of the Perizzites and Rephaites."

¹⁶The people of Joseph replied, "The hill country is not enough for us, and all the Canaanites who live in the plain have iron chariots,ʰ both those in Beth Shan and its settlements and those in the Valley of Jezreel."

¹⁷But Joshua said to the house of Joseph—to Ephraim and Manasseh—"You are numerous and very powerful. You will have not only one allotment ¹⁸but the forested hill country as well. Clear it, and its farthest limits will be yours; though the Canaanites have iron chariots and though they are strong, you can drive them out."

Division of the Rest of the Land

18 The whole assembly of the Israelites gathered at Shilohⁱ and set up the Tent of Meeting there. The country was brought under their control, ²but there were still seven Israelite tribes who had not yet received their inheritance.

ᵃ11 That is, Naphoth Dor

17:1
ᵛGe 41:51
17:2
ʷNu 26:30
17:3
ˣNu 27:1
ʸNu 26:33
17:4
ᶻNu 27:5-7
17:7
ᵃJos 16:6
17:8
ᵇJos 16:8
17:9
ᶜJos 16:8
17:11
ᵈ1Ch 7:29
17:12
ᵉJdg 1:27
17:13
ᶠJos 16:10
17:14
ᵍNu 26:28-37
17:16
ʰJdg 1:19; 4:3,13
18:1
ⁱJos 19:51; Jer 7:12

16:10 Occasionally this short phrase appears: "They did not dislodge" the people of the land (see also 15:63; 17:12). This was contrary to God's explicit desire and command (13:1–6). The failure to remove completely the pagan people and their gods from the land would cause many problems for the nation. The book of Judges records many of these struggles.

17:3, 4 Although women did not traditionally inherit property in Israelite society, Moses put justice ahead of tradition and gave these five women the land they deserved (see Numbers 27:1–11). In fact, God told Moses to add a law that would help other women in similar circumstances to inherit property as well. Joshua was now carrying out this law. It is easy to refuse to honor a reasonable request because "we have never done it that way before." But, like Moses and Joshua, we should look carefully at the purpose of the law and the merits of each case before deciding.

17:14, 15 Notice the two contrasting attitudes toward settling the promised land: Caleb took what God gave him and moved ahead to fulfill God's plan for him (14:12). He was confident that God would help him drive out the wicked inhabitants and that he would soon fully occupy his land (15:14, 15). In contrast, the two tribes of Joseph were given rich land and lots of it, but they were afraid to drive out the inhabitants and take full possession of it. Instead they begged for more land. But Joshua asked them to prove their sincerity first by clearing the unclaimed forest areas. They agreed, but they failed to carry through (Judges 1:27).

18:1, 2 With most of the conquest behind them, Israel moved its religious center from Gilgal (see the note on 5:8, 9) to Shiloh. This was probably the first permanent location for the tabernacle. Its central location in the land made it easier for the people to attend the special worship services and yearly feasts.

³So Joshua said to the Israelites: "How long will you wait before you begin to take possession of the land that the LORD, the God of your fathers, has given you? ⁴Appoint three men from each tribe. I will send them out to make a survey of the land and to write a description of it, according to the inheritance of each. Then they will return to me. ⁵You are to divide the land into seven parts. Judah is to remain in its territory on the south *ʲ* and the house of Joseph in its territory on the north. *ᵏ* ⁶After you have written descriptions of the seven parts of the land, bring them here to me and I will cast lots for you in the presence of the LORD our God. ⁷The Levites, however, do not get a portion among you, because the priestly service of the LORD is their inheritance. *ˡ* And Gad, Reuben and the half-tribe of Manasseh have already received their inheritance on the east side of the Jordan. Moses the servant of the LORD gave it to them."

⁸As the men started on their way to map out the land, Joshua instructed them, "Go and make a survey of the land and write a description of it. Then return to me, and I will cast lots for you here at Shiloh in the presence of the LORD." ⁹So the men left and went through the land. They wrote its description on a scroll, town by town, in seven parts, and returned to Joshua in the camp at Shiloh. ¹⁰Joshua then cast lots for them in Shiloh in the presence of the LORD, and there he distributed the land to the Israelites according to their tribal divisions. *ᵐ*

Allotment for Benjamin

¹¹The lot came up for the tribe of Benjamin, clan by clan. Their allotted territory lay between the tribes of Judah and Joseph:

¹²On the north side their boundary began at the Jordan, passed the northern slope of Jericho and headed west into the hill country, coming out at the desert *ⁿ* of Beth Aven. ¹³From there it crossed to the south slope of Luz *ᵒ* (that is, Bethel *ᵖ*) and went down to Ataroth Addar *ᵍ* on the hill south of Lower Beth Horon.

¹⁴From the hill facing Beth Horon on the south the boundary turned south along the western side and came out at Kiriath Baal (that is, Kiriath Jearim), a town of the people of Judah. This was the western side.

¹⁵The southern side began at the outskirts of Kiriath Jearim on the west, and the boundary came out at the spring of the waters of Nephtoah. *ʳ* ¹⁶The boundary went down

18:5
ʲ Jos 15:1
ᵏ Jos 16:1-4

18:7
ˡ Jos 13:33

18:10
ᵐ Jos 19:51

18:12
ⁿ Jos 16:1

18:13
ᵒ Ge 28:19
ᵖ Jdg 1:23
ᵍ Jos 16:5

18:15
ʳ Jos 15:9

The family of Samuel, a great priest and prophet, later would often travel to Shiloh, and Samuel would be taken there when a small boy (1 Samuel 1:3, 22). The tabernacle would remain in Shiloh through the period of the judges (about 300 years). Apparently the city was destroyed by the Philistines when the ark of the covenant was captured (1 Samuel 4; 5). Shiloh never lived up to its reputation as Israel's religious center, for later references in the Bible point to the wickedness and idolatry in the city (Psalm 78:56–60; Jeremiah 7:12–15).

18:2ff Seven of the tribes had not yet been assigned their land. They gathered at Shiloh, where Joshua cast lots to determine which areas would be given to them. Using the sacred lottery, God would make the choice, not Joshua or any other human leader.

By this time, the Canaanites were, in most places, so weakened that they were no longer a threat. Instead of fulfilling God's command to destroy the remaining Canaanites, however, these seven tribes would often take the path of least resistance. As nomadic people, they may have been reluctant to settle down, preferring to depend economically on the people they were supposed to eliminate. Others may have feared the high cost of continued warfare. Trading for goods was easier and more profitable than destroying the suppliers and having to provide for themselves.

18:3–6 Joshua asked why some of the tribes were putting off the job of possessing the land. Often we delay doing jobs that seem large, difficult, boring, or disagreeable. But to continue putting them off shows lack of discipline, poor stewardship of time, and, in some cases, disobedience to God. Jobs we don't enjoy require concentration, teamwork, twice as much time, lots of encouragement, and accountability. Remember this when you are tempted to procrastinate.

18:8 Making decisions by casting lots was a common practice among the Hebrews. Little is known about the actual method used in Joshua's day. A type of dice may have been used. Another possibility is that two urns were used: one containing tribal names; the other, the divisions of the land. Drawing one name from each urn matched a tribe to a region. The Urim and Thummim (explained in

the note on Leviticus 8:8) may also have been used. No matter how it was done, the process removed human choice from the decision-making process and allowed God to match tribes and lands as he saw fit.

18:11 The tribe of Benjamin was given a narrow strip of land that served as a buffer zone between Judah and Ephraim, the two tribes that would later dominate the land.

18:16 The Valley of Ben Hinnom became associated with the worship of Molech (the Ammonite god) in Jeremiah's time. These terrible rites involved the sacrifice of children. Later the valley was used for burning garbage and the corpses of criminals and animals. Thus the name became a synonym for hell.

THE TRIBES WEST OF THE JORDAN Judah, Ephraim, and the other half-tribe of Manasseh were the first tribes to receive land west of the Jordan because of their past acts of faith. The remaining seven tribes— Benjamin, Zebulun, Issachar, Asher, Naphtali, Simeon, and Dan—were slow to conquer and possess the land allotted to them.

to the foot of the hill facing the Valley of Ben Hinnom, north of the Valley of Rephaim. It continued down the Hinnom Valley[s] along the southern slope of the Jebusite city and so to En Rogel.[t] [17]It then curved north, went to En Shemesh, continued to Geliloth, which faces the Pass of Adummim, and ran down to the Stone of Bohan[u] son of Reuben. [18]It continued to the northern slope of Beth Arabah[a][v] and on down into the Arabah. [19]It then went to the northern slope of Beth Hoglah and came out at the northern bay of the Salt Sea,[b] at the mouth of the Jordan in the south. This was the southern boundary.

[20]The Jordan formed the boundary on the eastern side.

These were the boundaries that marked out the inheritance of the clans of Benjamin on all sides.

[21]The tribe of Benjamin, clan by clan, had the following cities:

Jericho, Beth Hoglah, Emek Keziz, [22]Beth Arabah, Zemaraim, Bethel, [23]Avvim, Parah, Ophrah, [24]Kephar Ammoni, Ophni and Geba[w]—twelve towns and their villages.

[25]Gibeon, Ramah, Beeroth, [26]Mizpah, Kephirah, Mozah, [27]Rekem, Irpeel, Taralah, [28]Zelah,[x] Haeleph, the Jebusite city[y] (that is, Jerusalem), Gibeah and Kiriath—fourteen towns and their villages.

This was the inheritance of Benjamin for its clans.

Allotment for Simeon

19 The second lot came out for the tribe of Simeon, clan by clan. Their inheritance lay within the territory of Judah.[z] [2]It included:

Beersheba (or Sheba),[c] Moladah, [3]Hazar Shual, Balah, Ezem, [4]Eltolad, Bethul, Hormah, [5]Ziklag, Beth Marcaboth, Hazar Susah, [6]Beth Lebaoth and Sharuhen—thirteen towns and their villages;

[7]Ain, Rimmon, Ether and Ashan—four towns and their villages— [8]and all the villages around these towns as far as Baalath Beer (Ramah in the Negev).

This was the inheritance of the tribe of the Simeonites, clan by clan. [9]The inheritance of the Simeonites was taken from the share of Judah, because Judah's portion was more than they needed. So the Simeonites received their inheritance within the territory of Judah.

Allotment for Zebulun

[10]The third lot came up for Zebulun, clan by clan:

The boundary of their inheritance went as far as Sarid. [11]Going west it ran to Maralah, touched Dabbesheth, and extended to the ravine near Jokneam.[a] [12]It turned east from Sarid toward the sunrise to the territory of Kisloth Tabor and went on to Daberath and up to Japhia. [13]Then it continued eastward to Gath Hepher and Eth Kazin; it came out at Rimmon and turned toward Neah. [14]There the boundary went around on the north to Hannathon and ended at the Valley of Iphtah El. [15]Included were Kattath, Nahalal, Shimron, Idalah and Bethlehem. There were twelve towns and their villages.

[16]These towns and their villages were the inheritance of Zebulun, clan by clan.

Allotment for Issachar

[17]The fourth lot came out for Issachar, clan by clan. [18]Their territory included:

Jezreel, Kesulloth, Shunem, [b] [19]Hapharaim, Shion, Anaharath, [20]Rabbith, Kishion, Ebez, [21]Remeth, En Gannim, En Haddah and Beth Pazzez. [22]The boundary touched Tabor,[c] Shahazumah and Beth Shemesh, and ended at the Jordan. There were sixteen towns and their villages.

[23]These towns and their villages were the inheritance of the tribe of Issachar, clan by clan.

Allotment for Asher

[24]The fifth lot came out for the tribe of Asher, clan by clan. [25]Their territory included:

Helkath, Hali, Beten, Acshaph, [26]Allammelech, Amad and Mishal. On the west the boundary touched Carmel and Shihor Libnath. [27]It then turned east toward Beth Dagon, touched Zebulun and the Valley of Iphtah El, and went north to Beth Emek and Neiel, passing Cabul[d] on the left. [28]It went to Abdon,[d] Rehob,[e] Hammon and Kanah, as far as Greater Sidon.[f] [29]The boundary then turned back toward Ramah and went to the fortified city of Tyre, turned toward Hosah and came out at the sea in the region of Aczib,[g] [30]Ummah, Aphek and Rehob. There were twenty-two towns and their villages.

[31]These towns and their villages were the inheritance of the tribe of Asher, clan by clan.

a 18 Septuagint; Hebrew slope facing the Arabah   b 19 That is, the Dead Sea   c 2 Or Beersheba, Sheba; 1 Chron. 4:28 does not have Sheba.   d 28 Some Hebrew manuscripts (see also Joshua 21:30); most Hebrew manuscripts Ebron

18:16
s Jos 15:8;
2Ki 23:10
t Jos 15:7
18:17
u Jos 15:6
18:18
v Jos 15:6

18:24
w Isa 10:29
18:28
x 2Sa 21:14
y Jos 15:8

19:1
z ver 9

19:11
a Jos 12:22

19:18
b 1Sa 28:4; 2Ki 4:8

19:22
c Jdg 4:6,12;
Ps 89:12

19:27
d 1Ki 9:13
19:28
e Jdg 1:31
f Ge 10:19; Jos 11:8
19:29
g Jdg 1:31

Allotment for Naphtali

32 The sixth lot came out for Naphtali, clan by clan:

33 Their boundary went from Heleph and the large tree in Zaanannim, passing Adami Nekeb and Jabneel to Lakkum and ending at the Jordan. 34 The boundary ran west through Aznoth Tabor and came out at Hukkok. It touched Zebulun on the south, Asher on the west and the Jordan[a] on the east. 35 The fortified cities were Ziddim, Zer, Hammath, Rakkath, Kinnereth, 36 Adamah, Ramah, Hazor, 37 Kedesh, Edrei, En Hazor, 38 Iron, Migdal El, Horem, Beth Anath and Beth Shemesh. There were nineteen towns and their villages.

19:39
h Dt 33:23

39 These towns and their villages were the inheritance of the tribe of Naphtali, clan by clan.[h]

Allotment for Dan

40 The seventh lot came out for the tribe of Dan, clan by clan. 41 The territory of their inheritance included:

19:42
i Jdg 1:35

Zorah, Eshtaol, Ir Shemesh, 42 Shaalabbin, Aijalon,[i] Ithlah, 43 Elon, Timnah, Ekron, 44 Eltekeh, Gibbethon, Baalath, 45 Jehud, Bene Berak, Gath Rimmon, 46 Me Jarkon and Rakkon, with the area facing Joppa.

19:47
j Jdg 18:1
k Jdg 18:27,29

47 (But the Danites had difficulty taking possession of their territory,[j] so they went up and attacked Leshem, took it, put it to the sword and occupied it. They settled in Leshem and named it Dan after their forefather.)[k]

48 These towns and their villages were the inheritance of the tribe of Dan, clan by clan.

Allotment for Joshua

19:50
l Jos 24:30

49 When they had finished dividing the land into its allotted portions, the Israelites gave Joshua son of Nun an inheritance among them, 50 as the LORD had commanded. They gave him the town he asked for—Timnath Serah[b][l] in the hill country of Ephraim. And he built up the town and settled there.

19:51
m Jos 14:1; 18:10

51 These are the territories that Eleazar the priest, Joshua son of Nun and the heads of the tribal clans of Israel assigned by lot at Shiloh in the presence of the LORD at the entrance to the Tent of Meeting. And so they finished dividing the land. *m*

2. Special cities are set aside
Cities of Refuge

20

Then the LORD said to Joshua: 2 "Tell the Israelites to designate the cities of refuge, as I instructed you through Moses, 3 so that anyone who kills a person accidentally and unintentionally may flee there and find protection from the avenger of blood.

20:4
n Ru 4:1

4 "When he flees to one of these cities, he is to stand in the entrance of the city gate[n] and state his case before the elders of that city. Then they are to admit him into their city and give him a place to live with them. 5 If the avenger of blood pursues him, they must not surrender the one accused, because he killed his neighbor unintentionally and without malice aforethought. 6 He is to stay in that city until he has stood trial before the assembly[o] and until the death of the high priest who is serving at that time. Then he may go back to his own home in the town from which he fled."

20:6
o Nu 35:12
20:7
p Jos 21:32;
1Ch 6:76
q Jos 21:11
r Lk 1:39

7 So they set apart Kedesh[p] in Galilee in the hill country of Naphtali, Shechem in the hill country of Ephraim, and Kiriath Arba (that is, Hebron[q]) in the hill country of Judah.[r] 8 On

---

a 34 Septuagint; Hebrew *west, and Judah, the Jordan,*   **b** 50 Also known as *Timnath Heres* (see Judges 2:9)

19:47, 48 The tribe of Dan found that some of their land was difficult to conquer, so they chose to migrate to Leshem where they knew victory would be easier. Anyone can trust God when the going is easy. It is when everything looks impossible that our faith and courage are put to the test. Have faith that God is great enough to tackle your most difficult situations.

19:49 There were several good reasons for establishing these well-set boundaries instead of turning the promised land into a single undivided nation. (1) The boundaries gave each tribe ownership of an area, promoting loyalty and unity that would strengthen each tribe. (2) The boundaries delineated areas of responsibility and privilege, which would help each tribe develop and mature. (3) The boundaries reduced conflicts that might have broken out if everyone had wanted to live in the choicest areas. (4) The bound-

aries fulfilled the promised inheritance to each tribe that began to be given as early as the days of Jacob (Genesis 48:21, 22).

20:6 A new nation in a new land needed a new government. Many years earlier God had told Moses how this government should function. One of the tasks God wanted the Israelites to do when they entered the promised land was to designate certain cities as "cities of refuge." These were to be scattered throughout the land. Their purpose was to prevent injustice, especially in cases of revenge. For example, if someone accidentally killed another person, he could flee to a city of refuge where he was safe until he could have a fair trial. The Levites were in charge of these cities. They were to ensure that God's principles of justice and fairness were kept. (For more on cities of refuge, see the notes on Numbers 35:6; 35:11–28.)

the east side of the Jordan of Jericho[a] they designated Bezer[s] in the desert on the plateau in the tribe of Reuben, Ramoth in Gilead in the tribe of Gad, and Golan in Bashan in the tribe of Manasseh. [9]Any of the Israelites or any alien living among them who killed someone accidentally could flee to these designated cities and not be killed by the avenger of blood prior to standing trial before the assembly.[t]

20:8
s Jos 21:36

20:9
t Ex 21:13; Nu 35:15

Towns for the Levites

21 Now the family heads of the Levites approached Eleazar the priest, Joshua son of Nun, and the heads of the other tribal families of Israel[u] [2]at Shiloh in Canaan and said to them, "The LORD commanded through Moses that you give us towns to live in, with pasturelands for our livestock."[v] [3]So, as the LORD had commanded, the Israelites gave the Levites the following towns and pasturelands out of their own inheritance:

[4]The first lot came out for the Kohathites, clan by clan. The Levites who were descendants of Aaron the priest were allotted thirteen towns from the tribes of Judah, Simeon and Benjamin. [w] [5]The rest of Kohath's descendants were allotted ten towns from the clans of the tribes of Ephraim, Dan and half of Manasseh.

[6]The descendants of Gershon were allotted thirteen towns from the clans of the tribes of Issachar, Asher, Naphtali and the half-tribe of Manasseh in Bashan.

[7]The descendants of Merari, clan by clan, received twelve towns from the tribes of Reuben, Gad and Zebulun.

[8]So the Israelites allotted to the Levites these towns and their pasturelands, as the LORD had commanded through Moses.

[9]From the tribes of Judah and Simeon they allotted the following towns by name [10](these towns were assigned to the descendants of Aaron who were from the Kohathite clans of the Levites, because the first lot fell to them):

[11]They gave them Kiriath Arba (that is, Hebron[x]), with its surrounding pastureland, in the hill country of Judah. (Arba was the forefather of Anak.) [12]But the fields and villages around the city they had given to Caleb son of Jephunneh as his possession.

[13]So to the descendants of Aaron the priest they gave Hebron (a city of refuge for one accused of murder), Libnah,[y] [14]Jattir, Eshtemoa, [15]Holon, Debir, [16]Ain, Juttah[z] and Beth Shemesh,[a] together with their pasturelands—nine towns from these two tribes.

[17]And from the tribe of Benjamin they gave them Gibeon, Geba,[b] [18]Anathoth and Almon, together with their pasturelands—four towns.

[19]All the towns for the priests, the descendants of Aaron, were thirteen, together with their pasturelands.

[20]The rest of the Kohathite clans of the Levites were allotted towns from the tribe of Ephraim:

21:1
u Jos 14:1

21:2
v Nu 35:2-3

21:4
w ver 19

21:11
x Jos 15:13; 1Ch 6:55

21:13
y Jos 15:42; 1Ch 6:57

21:16
z Jos 15:55
a Jos 15:10

21:17
b Jos 18:24

---

a 8 Jordan of Jericho was possibly an ancient name for the Jordan River.

21:2 The Levites were to minister on behalf of all the people, so they were given cities scattered throughout the land. Although Jerusalem was far away from the homes of many Israelites, almost no one lived more than a day's journey from a Levitical city.

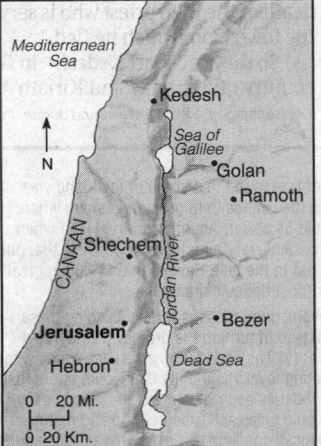

THE CITIES OF REFUGE

A city of refuge was just that— refuge for someone who committed an unintentional murder that would evoke revenge from the victim's friends and relatives. The six cities of refuge were spaced throughout the land so that a person was never too far from one.

21:21
c Jos 20:7

²¹In the hill country of Ephraim they were given Shechem *c* (a city of refuge for one accused of murder) and Gezer, ²²Kibzaim and Beth Horon, together with their pasturelands—four towns.

²³Also from the tribe of Dan they received Eltekeh, Gibbethon, ²⁴Aijalon and Gath Rimmon, together with their pasturelands—four towns.

²⁵From half the tribe of Manasseh they received Taanach and Gath Rimmon, together with their pasturelands—two towns.

²⁶All these ten towns and their pasturelands were given to the rest of the Kohathite clans.

21:27
d Jos 12:5
e Nu 35:6

²⁷The Levite clans of the Gershonites were given:
from the half-tribe of Manasseh,
Golan in Bashan *d* (a city of refuge for one accused of murder *e*) and Be Eshtarah, together with their pasturelands—two towns;
²⁸from the tribe of Issachar,
Kishion, Daberath, ²⁹Jarmuth and En Gannim, together with their pasturelands—four towns;
³⁰from the tribe of Asher,
Mishal, Abdon, ³¹Helkath and Rehob, together with their pasturelands—four towns;

21:32
f Jos 20:7

³²from the tribe of Naphtali,
Kedesh in Galilee (a city of refuge for one accused of murder *f*), Hammoth Dor and Kartan, together with their pasturelands—three towns.
³³All the towns of the Gershonite clans were thirteen, together with their pasturelands.

21:34
g 1Ch 6:77

³⁴The Merarite clans (the rest of the Levites) were given:
from the tribe of Zebulun, *g*
Jokneam, Kartah, ³⁵Dimnah and Nahalal, together with their pasturelands—four towns;
³⁶from the tribe of Reuben,

21:36
h Jos 20:8

Bezer, *h* Jahaz, ³⁷Kedemoth and Mephaath, together with their pasturelands—four towns;
³⁸from the tribe of Gad,

21:38
i Dt 4:43

Ramoth *i* in Gilead (a city of refuge for one accused of murder), Mahanaim, ³⁹Heshbon and Jazer, together with their pasturelands—four towns in all.
⁴⁰All the towns allotted to the Merarite clans, who were the rest of the Levites, were twelve.

21:41
j Nu 35:7

⁴¹The towns of the Levites in the territory held by the Israelites were forty-eight in all, together with their pasturelands. *j* ⁴²Each of these towns had pasturelands surrounding it; this was true for all these towns.

21:43
k Dt 11:31

21:44
l Jos 1:13
m Dt 7:24

21:45
n Jos 23:14; Ne 9:8

⁴³So the LORD gave Israel all the land he had sworn to give their forefathers, and they took possession *k* of it and settled there. ⁴⁴The LORD gave them rest *l* on every side, just as he had sworn to their forefathers. Not one of their enemies withstood them; the LORD handed all their enemies over to them. *m* ⁴⁵Not one of all the LORD's good promises *n* to the house of Israel failed; every one was fulfilled.

3. Eastern tribes return home

22 Then Joshua summoned the Reubenites, the Gadites and the half-tribe of Manasseh ²and said to them, "You have done all that Moses the servant of the LORD commanded, and you have obeyed me in everything I commanded. ³For a long time now—to this very day—you have not deserted your brothers but have carried out the mission the LORD

22:4
o Dt 3:20
p Nu 32:18

your God gave you. ⁴Now that the LORD your God has given your brothers rest as he promised, return to your homes *o* in the land that Moses the servant of the LORD gave you on the other side of the Jordan. *p* ⁵But be very careful to keep the commandment and the law that Moses

22:5
q Dt 5:29
r Dt 6:6,17

the servant of the LORD gave you: to love the LORD your God, to walk in all his ways, to obey his commands, *q* to hold fast to him and to serve him with all your heart and all your soul. *r*"

21:43–45 God proved faithful in fulfilling every promise he had given to Israel. Fulfillment of some promises took several years, but "every one was fulfilled." God's promises will be fulfilled according to his timetable, not ours, but we know that his word is sure. The more we learn of those promises God has fulfilled and continues to fulfill, the easier it is to hope for those yet to come. Sometimes we become impatient, wanting God to act in a certain way *now*. Instead, we should faithfully do what we know he wants us to do and trust him for the future.

22:2–4 Before the conquest had begun, these tribes were given land on the east side of the Jordan River. But before they could settle down, they had to first promise to help the other tribes conquer the land on the west side (Numbers 32:20–22). They had patiently and diligently carried out their promised duties. Joshua commended them for doing just that. At last they were permitted to return to their families and build their cities. Follow-through is vital in God's work. Beware of the temptation to quit early and leave God's work undone.

6 Then Joshua blessed s them and sent them away, and they went to their homes. 7 (To the half-tribe of Manasseh Moses had given land in Bashan, t and to the other half of the tribe Joshua gave land on the west side u of the Jordan with their brothers.) When Joshua sent them home, he blessed them, 8 saying, "Return to your homes with your great wealth—with large herds of livestock, with silver, gold, bronze and iron, and a great quantity of clothing—and divide v with your brothers the plunder w from your enemies."

9 So the Reubenites, the Gadites and the half-tribe of Manasseh left the Israelites at Shiloh in Canaan to return to Gilead, x their own land, which they had acquired in accordance with the command of the LORD through Moses.

10 When they came to Geliloth near the Jordan in the land of Canaan, the Reubenites, the Gadites and the half-tribe of Manasseh built an imposing altar there by the Jordan. 11 And when the Israelites heard that they had built the altar on the border of Canaan at Geliloth near the Jordan on the Israelite side, 12 the whole assembly of Israel gathered at Shiloh y to go to war against them.

13 So the Israelites sent Phinehas z son of Eleazar, the priest, to the land of Gilead—to Reuben, Gad and the half-tribe of Manasseh. 14 With him they sent ten of the chief men, one for each of the tribes of Israel, each the head of a family division among the Israelite clans. a

15 When they went to Gilead—to Reuben, Gad and the half-tribe of Manasseh—they said to them: 16 "The whole assembly of the LORD says: 'How could you break faith with the God of Israel like this? How could you turn away from the LORD and build yourselves an altar in rebellion b against him now? 17 Was not the sin of Peor c enough for us? Up to this very day we have not cleansed ourselves from that sin, even though a plague fell on the community of the LORD! 18 And are you now turning away from the LORD?

"'If you rebel against the LORD today, tomorrow he will be angry with the whole community of Israel. 19 If the land you possess is defiled, come over to the LORD's land, where the LORD's tabernacle stands, and share the land with us. But do not rebel against the LORD or against us by building an altar for yourselves, other than the altar of the LORD our God. 20 When Achan son of Zerah acted unfaithfully regarding the devoted things, a d did not wrath come upon the whole community of Israel? He was not the only one who died for his sin.'" e

21 Then Reuben, Gad and the half-tribe of Manasseh replied to the heads of the clans of Israel: 22 "The Mighty One, God, the LORD! The Mighty One, God, f the LORD! He knows! g And let Israel know! If this has been in rebellion or disobedience to the LORD, do not spare us this day. 23 If we have built our own altar to turn away from the LORD and to offer burnt offerings and grain offerings, or to sacrifice fellowship offerings b on it, may the LORD himself call us to account. h

24 "No! We did it for fear that some day your descendants might say to ours, 'What do you have to do with the LORD, the God of Israel? 25 The LORD has made the Jordan a boundary between us and you—you Reubenites and Gadites! You have no share in the LORD.' So your descendants might cause ours to stop fearing the LORD.

26 "That is why we said, 'Let us get ready and build an altar—but not for burnt offerings or sacrifices.' 27 On the contrary, it is to be a witness i between us and you and the generations that follow, that we will worship the LORD at his sanctuary with our burnt offerings, sacrifices and fellowship offerings. j Then in the future your descendants will not be able to say to ours, 'You have no share in the LORD.'

28 "And we said, 'If they ever say this to us, or to our descendants, we will answer: Look at

22:6
s Ex 39:43
22:7
t Nu 32:33
u Jos 17:2,5
22:8
v Nu 31:27
w 1Sa 30:16
22:9
x Nu 32:26,29

22:12
y Jos 18:1

22:13
z Nu 25:7
22:14
a Nu 1:4

22:16
b Dt 12:13-14

22:17
c Nu 25:1-9

22:20
d Jos 7:1
e Jos 7:5

22:22
f Dt 10:17
g 1Ki 8:39
22:23
h Dt 18:19;
1Sa 20:16

22:27
i Jos 24:27
j Dt 12:6

a 20 The Hebrew term refers to the irrevocable giving over of things or persons to the LORD, often by totally destroying them.   b 23 Traditionally peace offerings; also in verse 27

22:5 Here Joshua briefly restated the central message Moses gave the people in Deuteronomy: Obedience should be based on love for God. Although the Israelites had completed their military responsibility, Joshua reminded them of their spiritual responsibility. Sometimes we think so much about what we are to do that we neglect thinking about who we are to be. If we know we are God's children, we will love him and joyfully serve him. We must not let daily service take away from our love for God.

22:11–34 When the tribes of Reuben and Gad and the half-tribe of Manasseh built an altar at the Jordan River, the rest of Israel feared that these tribes were starting their own religion and rebelling against God. But before beginning an all-out war, Phinehas led a delegation to learn the truth, following the principle taught

in Deuteronomy 13:12–19. He was prepared to negotiate rather than fight if a battle was not necessary. When he learned that the altar was for a memorial rather than for pagan sacrifice, war was averted and unity restored.

As nations and as individuals, we would benefit from a similar approach to resolving conflicts. Assuming the worst about the intentions of others only brings trouble. Israel averted the threat of civil war by asking before assaulting. Beware of reacting before you hear the whole story.

22:17 For the story of how Israel turned away from God and began to worship Baal at Peor, see Numbers 25:1–18.

22:20 For the story of Achan, a man who allowed greed to get the best of him, see chapter 7.

the replica of the Lord's altar, which our fathers built, not for burnt offerings and sacrifices, but as a witness between us and you.'

22:29
k Dt 12:13-14

²⁹"Far be it from us to rebel against the Lord and turn away from him today by building an altar for burnt offerings, grain offerings and sacrifices, other than the altar of the Lord our God that stands before his tabernacle. *k*"

22:31
l Lev 26:11-12;
2Ch 15:2

³⁰When Phinehas the priest and the leaders of the community—the heads of the clans of the Israelites—heard what Reuben, Gad and Manasseh had to say, they were pleased. ³¹And Phinehas son of Eleazar, the priest, said to Reuben, Gad and Manasseh, "Today we know that the Lord is with us,*l* because you have not acted unfaithfully toward the Lord in this matter. Now you have rescued the Israelites from the Lord's hand."

22:33
m 1Ch 29:20

³²Then Phinehas son of Eleazar, the priest, and the leaders returned to Canaan from their meeting with the Reubenites and Gadites in Gilead and reported to the Israelites. ³³They were glad to hear the report and praised God. *m* And they talked no more about going to war against them to devastate the country where the Reubenites and the Gadites lived.

³⁴And the Reubenites and the Gadites gave the altar this name: A Witness Between Us that the Lord is God.

4. Joshua's farewell to the leaders

23:1
n Jos 21:44
o Jos 13:1
23:2
p Jos 24:1

23 After a long time had passed and the Lord had given Israel rest *n* from all their enemies around them, Joshua, by then old and well advanced in years,*o* ²summoned all Israel—their elders, leaders, judges and officials*p*—and said to them: "I am old and well advanced in years. ³You yourselves have seen everything the Lord your God has done to all these nations for your sake; it was the Lord your God who fought for you. ⁴Remember how I have allotted as an inheritance for your tribes all the land of the nations that remain—the nations I conquered—between the Jordan and the Great Sea*a* in the west. ⁵The Lord your God himself will drive them out of your way. He will push them out before you, and you will take possession of their land, as the Lord your God promised you.

23:6
q Jos 1:7
23:7
r Ex 23:13
23:8
s Dt 10:20
23:9
t Dt 11:23
23:10
u Lev 26:8
v Dt 3:22
23:12
w Dt 7:3

⁶"Be very strong; be careful to obey all that is written in the Book of the Law of Moses, without turning aside to the right or to the left. *q* ⁷Do not associate with these nations that remain among you; do not invoke the names of their gods or swear*r* by them. You must not serve them or bow down to them. ⁸But you are to hold fast to the Lord *s* your God, as you have until now.

⁹"The Lord has driven out before you great and powerful nations;*t* to this day no one has been able to withstand you. ¹⁰One of you routs a thousand, *u* because the Lord your God fights for you,*v* just as he promised. ¹¹So be very careful to love the Lord your God.

¹²"But if you turn away and ally yourselves with the survivors of these nations that remain among you and if you intermarry with them *w* and associate with them, ¹³then you may be sure that the Lord your God will no longer drive out these nations before you. Instead, they will become snares and traps for you, whips on your backs and thorns in your eyes, until you perish from this good land, which the Lord your God has given you.

23:14
x 1Ki 2:2
23:15
y Dt 28:15

¹⁴"Now I am about to go the way of all the earth. *x* You know with all your heart and soul that not one of all the good promises the Lord your God gave you has failed. Every promise has been fulfilled; not one has failed. ¹⁵But just as every good promise of the Lord your God has come true, so the Lord will bring on you all the evil he has threatened, until he has destroyed you from this good land he has given you.*y* ¹⁶If you violate the covenant of the Lord your God,

*a*4 That is, the Mediterranean

22:26–28 The tribes were concerned that, without some visible sign of unity between the people on the two sides of the Jordan, future generations might see conflict between them. The altar, patterned after the altar of the Lord, was to remind these people that they all worshiped the same God. Often we need to be reminded of the faith of our fathers. What actions demonstrate to your children your reliance on God and remind them of what he has done? Take the time to establish family traditions that will help your children remember.

23:6–13 Joshua knew the nation's weak spots. Before dying, he called the people together and gave commands to help them where they were most likely to slip: (1) follow all that is written in the Book of the Law of Moses without turning aside; (2) don't associate with the pagan nations or worship their gods; (3) don't intermarry

with the pagan nations. These temptations were right in their backyard. Our associations and relationships can be temptations to us as well. It's wise to identify our weak spots *before* we break down. Then we can develop strategies to overcome these temptations instead of being overcome by them.

23:8 Joshua was dying and so he called all the leaders of the nation together to give them his final words of encouragement and instruction. His whole message can be summarized in this verse, "Hold fast to the Lord your God." Joshua had been a living example of those words, and he wanted that to be his legacy. For what do you want to be remembered, and what do you want to pass on to your children and associates? You can leave them nothing better than the admonition to hold on to God and to the memory of a person who did.

which he commanded you, and go and serve other gods and bow down to them, the LORD's anger will burn against you, and you will quickly perish from the good land he has given you."

The Covenant Renewed at Shechem

24 Then Joshua assembled all the tribes of Israel at Shechem. He summoned the elders, leaders, judges and officials of Israel,ᶻ and they presented themselves before God.

²Joshua said to all the people, "This is what the LORD, the God of Israel, says: 'Long ago your forefathers, including Terah the father of Abraham and Nahor, lived beyond the Riverᵃ and worshiped other gods.ᵃ ³But I took your father Abraham from the land beyond the River and led him throughout Canaanᵇ and gave him many descendants. I gave him Isaac, ⁴and to Isaac I gave Jacob and Esau.ᶜ I assigned the hill country of Seirᵈ to Esau, but Jacob and his sons went down to Egypt.ᵉ

⁵"Then I sent Moses and Aaron,ᶠ and I afflicted the Egyptians by what I did there, and I brought you out. ⁶When I brought your fathers out of Egypt, you came to the sea, and the Egyptians pursued them with chariots and horsemenᵇ as far as the Red Sea.ᶜ ⁷But they cried to the LORD for help, and he put darkness between you and the Egyptians; he brought the sea over them and covered them. You saw with your own eyes what I did to the Egyptians. Then you lived in the desert for a long time.

⁸"'I brought you to the land of the Amorites who lived east of the Jordan. They fought against you, but I gave them into your hands. I destroyed them from before you, and you took possession of their land.ᵍ ⁹When Balak son of Zippor,ʰ the king of Moab, prepared to fight against Israel, he sent for Balaam son of Beor to put a curse on you. ¹⁰But I would not listen to Balaam, so he blessed you again and again, and I delivered you out of his hand.

¹¹"Then you crossed the Jordanⁱ and came to Jericho.ʲ The citizens of Jericho fought against you, as did also the Amorites, Perizzites, Canaanites, Hittites, Girgashites, Hivites and Jebusites, but I gave them into your hands. ¹²I sent the hornetᵏ ahead of you, which drove them out before you—also the two Amorite kings. You did not do it with your own sword and bow. ¹³So I gave you a land on which you did not toil and cities you did not build; and you live in them and eat from vineyards and olive groves that you did not plant.'ˡ

¹⁴"Now fear the LORD and serve him with all faithfulness.ᵐ Throw away the gods your forefathers worshiped beyond the River and in Egypt, and serve the LORD. ¹⁵But if serving the LORD seems undesirable to you, then choose for yourselves this day whom you will serve, whether the gods your forefathers served beyond the River, or the gods of the Amorites, in whose land you are living. But as for me and my household, we will serve the LORD."

¹⁶Then the people answered, "Far be it from us to forsake the LORD to serve other gods! ¹⁷It was the LORD our God himself who brought us and our fathers up out of Egypt, from that

ᵃ2 That is, the Euphrates; also in verses 3, 14 and 15 ᵇ6 Or charioteers ᶜ6 Hebrew Yam Suph; that is, Sea of Reeds

24:1 ᶻJos 23:2
24:2 ᵃGe 11:32
24:3 ᵇGe 12:1
24:4 ᶜGe 25:26 ᵈDt 2:5 ᵉGe 46:5-6
24:5 ᶠEx 3:10
24:8 ᵍNu 21:31
24:9 ʰNu 22:2
24:11 ⁱJos 3:16-17 ʲJos 6:1
24:12 ᵏEx 23:28; Ps 44:3,6-7
24:13 ˡDt 6:10-11
24:14 ᵐDt 10:12; 18:13; 1Sa 12:24; 2Co 1:12

23:12–16 This chilling prediction about the consequences of intermarriage with the Canaanite nations eventually became a reality. Numerous stories in the book of Judges show what Israel had to suffer because of failure to follow God wholeheartedly. God was supremely loving and patient with Israel, just as he is today. But we must not confuse his patience with us as approval of or indifference to our sin. Beware of demanding your own way because eventually you may get it—along with all its painful consequences.

JOSHUA'S FINAL SPEECH
Joshua called all the Israelites to Shechem to hear his final words. He challenged the people to make a conscious choice to always serve God. Soon afterward, Joshua died and was buried in his hometown of Timnath Serah.

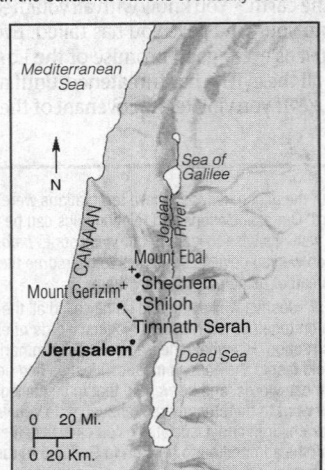

24:15 The people had to decide whether they would obey the Lord, who had proven his trustworthiness, or obey the local gods, which were only man-made idols. It's easy to slip into a quiet rebellion—going about life in your own way. But the time comes when you have to choose who or what will control you. The choice is yours. Will it be God, your own limited personality, or another imperfect substitute? Once you have chosen to be controlled by God's Spirit, reaffirm your choice every day.

24:15 In taking a definite stand for the Lord, Joshua again displayed his spiritual leadership. Regardless of what others decided, Joshua had made a commitment to God, and he was willing to set the example of living by that decision. The way we live shows others the strength of our commitment to serving God.

24:16-18, 21 All the people boldly claimed that they would never forsake the Lord. But they did not keep that promise. Very soon God would charge them with breaking their contract with him (Judges 2:2, 3). Talk is cheap. It is easy to say we will land of slavery, and performed those great signs before our eyes. He protected us on our entire journey and among all the nations through which we traveled. ¹⁸And the LORD drove out before us all the nations, including the Amorites, who lived in the land. We too will serve the LORD, because he is our God."

24:19
ⁿEx 20:5
ᵒEx 23:21

¹⁹Joshua said to the people, "You are not able to serve the LORD. He is a holy God; he is a jealous God. ⁿ He will not forgive your rebellion ᵒ and your sins. ²⁰If you forsake the LORD ᵖ and serve foreign gods, he will turn and bring disaster on you and make an end of you,�q after he has been good to you."

24:20
ᵖ1Ch 28:9,20
qJos 23:15

²¹But the people said to Joshua, "No! We will serve the LORD."

24:22
ʳPs 119:30,173

²²Then Joshua said, "You are witnesses against yourselves that you have chosenʳ to serve the LORD."

"Yes, we are witnesses," they replied.

²³"Now then," said Joshua, "throw away the foreign gods that are among you and yield your hearts to the LORD, the God of Israel."

24:24
ˢEx 19:8

²⁴And the people said to Joshua, "We will serve the LORD our God and obey him."ˢ

24:25
ᵗEx 24:8

²⁵On that day Joshua made a covenantᵗ for the people, and there at Shechem he drew up for them decrees and laws. ²⁶And Joshua recorded these things in the Book of the Law of God. ᵘ Then he took a large stone and set it up there under the oak near the holy place of the LORD.

24:26
ᵘDt 31:24

24:27
ᵛJos 22:27

²⁷"See!" he said to all the people. "This stone will be a witnessᵛ against us. It has heard all the words the LORD has said to us. It will be a witness against you if you are untrue to your God."

Buried in the Promised Land

²⁸Then Joshua sent the people away, each to his own inheritance.

24:30
ʷJos 19:50

²⁹After these things, Joshua son of Nun, the servant of the LORD, died at the age of a hundred and ten. ³⁰And they buried him in the land of his inheritance, at Timnath Serahᵃ ʷ in the hill country of Ephraim, north of Mount Gaash.

24:31
ˣJdg 2:7

³¹Israel served the LORD throughout the lifetime of Joshua and of the eldersˣ who outlived him and who had experienced everything the LORD had done for Israel.

24:32
ʸGe 50:25;
Ex 13:19
ᶻGe 33:19

³²And Joseph's bones, which the Israelites had brought up from Egypt,ʸ were buried at Shechem in the tract of landᶻ that Jacob bought for a hundred pieces of silverᵇ from the sons of Hamor, the father of Shechem. This became the inheritance of Joseph's descendants.

24:33
ᵃJos 22:13

³³And Eleazar son of Aaronᵃ died and was buried at Gibeah, which had been allotted to his son Phinehas in the hill country of Ephraim.

ᵃ30 Also known as *Timnath Heres* (see Judges 2:9)   ᵇ32 Hebrew *hundred kesitahs*; a kesitah was a unit of money of unknown weight and value.

---

follow God, but it is much more important to live like it. Yet the nation followed God through Joshua's lifetime, a great tribute to Joshua's faith in God and powerful leadership.

24:23 Joshua told the Israelites to throw away their foreign gods, or idols. To follow God requires destroying whatever gets in the way of worshiping him. We have our own form of idols—greed, wrong priorities, jealousies, prejudices—that get in the way of worshiping God. God is not satisfied if we merely hide these idols. We must completely remove them from our lives.

24:24–26 The covenant between Israel and God was that the people would worship and obey the Lord alone. Their purpose was to become a holy nation that would influence the rest of the world for God. The conquest of Canaan was a means to achieve this purpose, but Israel became preoccupied with the land and lost sight of the Lord God.

The same can happen in our lives. We can spend so much time on the means that we forget the end—to glorify God. Churches may make this mistake as well. For example, the congregation may pour all of its energies into a new facility, only to become self-satisfied or fearful of letting certain groups use it. If this happens, they have focused on the building and lost sight of its purpose—to bring others to God.

24:29–31 The book of Joshua opens with a new leader being handed a seemingly impossible task—to lead the nation in taking over the land of Canaan. By following God closely, Joshua led the people through military victories and faithful spiritual obedience. In 24:16 we read that the people were sure they would never forsake the Lord. The response of the whole nation during these many years is a tribute both to Joshua's leadership and to the God he faithfully served.

24:33 Joshua and Eleazar died, but not before laying before the people the fundamentals of what it means to have faith in God. We are to fear and serve the Lord alone (24:14). This is based on a choice: to obey him instead of following other gods (24:15). We are incapable, however, of properly worshiping him because of our rebellion and sins (24:19). By choosing God as Lord we enter into a covenant with him (24:25) whereby he promises not only to forgive and love us, but also to enable us by his Spirit to do his work here on earth. This covenant requires us to renounce the principles and practices of the culture around us that are hostile to God's plan (24:23). This is not to be done alone, but by binding ourselves together with others who have faith in God. (See Deuteronomy 30:15–20 for a similar message from Moses.)

JUDGES

VITAL STATISTICS

PURPOSE:
To show that God's judgment against sin is certain, and his forgiveness of sin and restoration to relationship are just as certain for those who repent

AUTHOR:
Possibly Samuel

ORIGINAL AUDIENCE:
The people of Israel

SETTING:
The land of Canaan, later called Israel. God had helped the Israelites conquer Canaan, which had been inhabited by a host of wicked nations. But they were in danger of losing this promised land because they compromised their convictions and disobeyed God.

KEY VERSE:
"In those days Israel had no king; everyone did as he saw fit" (17:6).

KEY PEOPLE:
Othniel, Ehud, Deborah, Gideon, Abimelech, Jephthah, Samson, Delilah

SPECIAL FEATURE:
Records Israel's first civil war

REAL heroes are hard to find these days. Modern research and the media have made the foibles and weaknesses of our leaders very apparent; we search in vain for men and women to emulate. The music, movie, and sports industries produce a steady stream of "stars" who shoot to the top and then quickly fade from view.

Judges is a book about heroes—12 men and women who delivered Israel from its oppressors. These judges were not perfect; in fact, they included an assassin, a sexually promiscuous man, and a person who broke all the laws of hospitality. But they were submissive to God, and God used them.

Judges is also a book about sin and its consequences. Like a minor cut or abrasion that becomes infected when left untreated, sin grows and soon poisons the whole body. The book of Joshua ends with the nation taking a stand for God, ready to experience all the blessings of the promised land. After settling in Canaan, however, the Israelites lost their spiritual commitment and motivation. When Joshua and the elders died, the nation experienced a leadership vacuum, leaving them without a strong central government. Instead of enjoying freedom and prosperity in the promised land, Israel entered the dark ages of her history.

Simply stated, the reason for this rapid decline was sin—individual and corporate. The first step away from God was incomplete obedience (1:11—2:5); the Israelites refused to eliminate the enemy completely from the land. This led to intermarriage and idolatry (2:6—3:7) and everyone doing "as he saw fit" (17:6). Before long the Israelites became captives. Out of their desperation they begged God to rescue them. In faithfulness to his promise and out of his loving-kindness, God would raise up a judge to deliver his people, and for a time there would be peace. Then complacency and disobedience would set in, and the cycle would begin again.

The book of Judges spans a period of over 325 years, recording six successive periods of oppression and deliverance, and the careers of 12 deliverers. Their captors included the Mesopotamians, Moabites, Philistines, Canaanites, Midianites, and Ammonites. God used a variety of deliverers—from Othniel to Samson—to lead his people to freedom and true worship. God's deliverance through the judges is a powerful demonstration of his love and mercy toward his people.

As you read the book of Judges, take a good look at these heroes from Jewish history. Note their dependence on God and obedience to his commands. Observe Israel's repeated downward spiral into sin, refusing to learn from history and living only for the moment. But most of all, stand in awe of God's mercy as he delivers his people over and over again.

| Gideon 1162–1122 (1146–1106) | Samuel born 1105 (1083) | Samson 1075–1055 (1083–1063) | Saul anointed king 1050 (1045) | David becomes king 1010 |

THE BLUEPRINT

A. THE MILITARY FAILURE OF ISRAEL (1:1—3:6)
1. Incomplete conquest of the land
2. Disobedience and defeat

The tribes had compromised God's command to drive out the inhabitants of the land. Incomplete removal of evil often means disaster in the end. We must beware of compromising with wickedness.

B. THE RESCUE OF ISRAEL BY THE JUDGES (3:7—16:31)
1. First period: Othniel
2. Second period: Ehud and Shamgar
3. Third period: Deborah and Barak
4. Fourth period: Gideon, Tola, and Jair
5. Fifth period: Jephthah, Ibzan, Elon, and Abdon
6. Sixth period: Samson

Repeatedly we see the nation of Israel sinning against God and God allowing suffering to come upon the land and the people. Sin always has its consequences. Where there is sin we can expect suffering to follow. Rather than living in an endless cycle of abandoning God and then crying out to him for rescue, we should seek to live a consistent life of faithfulness.

C. THE MORAL FAILURE OF ISRAEL (17:1—21:25)
1. Idolatry in the tribe of Dan
2. War against the tribe of Benjamin

Despite the efforts of Israel's judges, the people still would not turn wholeheartedly to God. They all did whatever they thought was best for themselves. The result was the spiritual, moral, and political decline of the nation. Our lives will also fall into decline and decay unless we live by the guidelines God has given us.

MEGATHEMES

THEME	EXPLANATION	IMPORTANCE
Decline/ Compromise	Whenever a judge died, the people faced decline and failure because they compromised their high spiritual purpose in many ways. They abandoned their mission to drive all the people out of the land, and they adopted the customs of the people living around them.	Society has many rewards to offer those who compromise their faith: wealth, acceptance, recognition, power, and influence. When God gives us a mission, it must not be polluted by a desire for approval from society. We must keep our eyes on Christ, who is our Judge and Deliverer.
Decay/Apostasy	Israel's moral downfall had its roots in the fierce independence that each tribe cherished. It led to everyone doing whatever seemed right in his own eyes. There was no unity in government or in worship. Law and order broke down. Finally, idol worship and man-made religion led to the complete abandoning of faith in God.	We can expect decay when we value anything more highly than God. If we value our own independence more than dedication to God, we have placed an idol in our hearts. Soon our lives become temples to that god. We must constantly regard God's first claim on our lives and all our desires.
Defeat/ Oppression	God used evil oppressors to punish the Israelites for their sin, to bring them to the point of repentance, and to test their allegiance to him.	Rebellion against God leads to disaster. God may use defeat to bring wandering hearts back to him. When all else is stripped away, we recognize the importance of serving only him.
Repentance	Decline, decay, and defeat caused the people to cry out to God for help. They vowed to turn from idolatry and to turn to God for mercy and deliverance. When they repented, God delivered them.	Idolatry gains a foothold in our hearts when we make anything more important than God. We must identify modern idols in our hearts, renounce them, and turn to God for his love and mercy.
Deliverance/ Heroes	Because Israel repented, God raised up heroes to deliver his people from their path of sin and the oppression it brought. He used many kinds of people to accomplish this purpose by filling them with his Holy Spirit.	God's Holy Spirit is available to all people. Anyone who is dedicated to God can be used for his service. Real heroes recognize the futility of human effort without God's guidance and power.

KEY PLACES IN JUDGES

The broken lines (— · — ·) indicate modern boundaries.

1 Bokim The book of Judges opens with the Israelites continuing their conquest of the promised land. Their failure to obey God and destroy all the evil inhabitants soon came back to haunt them in two ways: (1) The enemies reorganized and counterattacked, and (2) Israel turned away from God, adopting the evil and idolatrous practices of the inhabitants of the land. The angel of the Lord appeared at Bokim to inform the Israelites that their sin and disobedience had broken their agreement with God and would result in punishment through oppression (1:1—3:11).

2 Jericho The nation of Moab was one of the first to oppress Israel. Moab's King Eglon conquered much of Israel—including the city of Jericho ("the City of Palms")— and forced the people to pay unreasonable taxes. The messenger chosen to deliver this tax money to King Eglon was named Ehud. But he had more than money to deliver, for he drew his hidden sword and killed the Moabite king. Ehud then escaped, only to return with an army

that chased out the Moabites and freed Israel from its oppressors (3:12–31).

3 Hazor After Ehud's death, King Jabin of Hazor conquered Israel and oppressed the people for 20 years. Then Deborah became Israel's leader. She summoned Barak to fight Commander Sisera, the leader of King Jabin's army. Together Deborah and Barak led their army into battle against Jabin's forces in the land between Mount Tabor and the Kishon River and conquered them (4:1—5:31).

4 Hill of Moreh After 40 years of peace, the Midianites began to harass the Israelites by destroying their flocks and crops. When the Israelites finally cried out to God, he chose Gideon, a poor and humble farmer, to be their deliverer. After struggling with doubt and feelings of inferiority, Gideon took courage and knocked down his town's altar to Baal, causing a great uproar among the citizens. Filled with the Spirit of God, he attacked the vast army of Midian, which was camped near the hill of Moreh. With just a handful of men he sent the enemy running away in confusion (6:1—7:25).

5 Shechem Even great leaders make mistakes. Gideon's relations with a concubine in Shechem resulted in the birth of a son named Abimelech. Abimelech turned out to be treacherous and power hungry—stirring up the people to proclaim him king. To carry out his plan, he went so far as to kill 69 of his 70 half brothers. Eventually some men of Shechem rebelled against Abimelech, but he gathered together an army and defeated them. His lust for power led him to ransack two other cities, but he was killed by a woman who dropped a millstone onto his head (8:28—9:57).

6 Land of Ammon Again Israel turned completely from God; so God turned from them. But when the Ammonites mobilized their army to attack, Israel threw away her idols and called upon God once again. Jephthah, a prostitute's son who had been run out of Israel, was asked to return and lead Israel's forces against the enemy. After defeating the Ammonites, Jephthah became involved in a war with the tribe of Ephraim over a misunderstanding (10:1—12:15).

7 Timnah Israel's next judge, Samson, was a miracle child promised by God to a barren couple. He was the one who would begin to free Israel from their next and most powerful oppressor, the Philistines. According to God's command, Samson was to be a Nazirite—one who took a vow to be set apart for special service to God. One of the stipulations of the vow was that Samson's hair could never be cut. But when Samson grew up, he did not always take his special responsibility to God seriously. He even fell in love with a Philistine girl in Timnah and asked to marry her. Before the wedding, Samson held a party for some men in the city, using a riddle to place a bet with them. The men, however, forced Samson's fiancée into giving the answer. Furious at being tricked, Samson paid his bet with the lives of 30 Philistines who lived in the nearby city of Ashkelon (13:1—14:20).

8 Valley of Sorek   Samson killed thousands of Philistines with his incredible strength. The nation's leaders looked for a way to stop him. They got their chance when another Philistine woman stole Samson's heart. Her name was Delilah, and she lived in the Valley of Sorek. In exchange for a great sum of money, Delilah deceived Samson into confiding in her the secret of his strength. One night while he slept, Delilah had his hair cut off. As a result, Samson fell helplessly into the hands of the enemy (15:1—16:20).

9 Gaza   Samson was blinded and led captive to a prison in Gaza. There his hair began to grow again. After a while, the Philistines held a great festival to celebrate Samson's imprisonment and to humiliate him before the crowds. When he was brought out as the entertainment, he literally brought down the house when he pushed on the main pillars of the banquet hall and killed the thousands trapped inside. The prophecy that he would begin to free Israel from the Philistines had come true (16:21—31).

10 Hill Country of Ephraim   In the hill country of Ephraim lived a man named Micah. Micah hired his own priest to perform priestly duties in the shrine that housed his collection of idols. He thought he was pleasing God with all his religiosity! Like many of the Israelites, Micah assumed that his own opinions of what was right would agree with God's (17:1–13).

11 Dan   The tribe of Dan migrated north in order to find new territory. They sent spies ahead of them to scout out the land. One night the spies stopped at Micah's home. Looking for some assurance of victory, the spies stole Micah's idols and priest. Rejoining the tribe, they came upon the city of Laish and slaughtered the unarmed and innocent citizens, renaming the conquered city Dan. Micah's idols were then set up in the city and became the focal point of the tribe's worship for many years (18:1–31).

12 Gibeah   The extent to which many people had fallen away from God became clear in Gibeah, a village in the territory of Benjamin. A man and his concubine were traveling north toward the hill country of Ephraim. They stopped for the night in Gibeah, thinking they would be safe. But some perverts in the city gathered around the home where they were staying and demanded that the man come out to have sexual relations with them. Instead, the man and his host pushed the concubine out the door. She was raped and abused all night. When the man found her lifeless body the next morning, he cut it into 12 pieces and sent the parts to each tribe of Israel. This tragic event demonstrated that the nation had sunk to its lowest spiritual level (19:1–30).

13 Mizpah   The leaders of Israel came to Mizpah to decide how to punish the wicked men from the city of Gibeah. When the city leaders refused to turn the criminals over, the whole nation of Israel took vengeance upon both Gibeah and the tribe of Benjamin where the city was located. When the battle ended, the entire tribe had been destroyed except for a handful of men who took refuge in the hills. Israel had become morally depraved. The stage was now set for the much-needed spiritual renewal that would come under the prophet Samuel (20:1—21:25).

A. THE MILITARY FAILURE OF ISRAEL (1:1—3:6)

By faithfully obeying the Lord, Joshua led the Israelites to military victory. After his death, however, the tribes failed to clear the inhabitants from the land, so the Lord withdrew his promise to help drive the people out and bless the Israelites in battle. The new generation abandoned God and worshiped idols. This part of Judges shows what can happen when we neglect to teach our children to follow the Lord.

1. Incomplete conquest of the land
Israel Fights the Remaining Canaanites

1:1
*a*Nu 27:21

1:2
*b*Ge 49:8

1 After the death of Joshua, the Israelites asked the Lord, "Who will be the first *a* to go up and fight for us against the Canaanites?"
²The Lord answered, "Judah *b* is to go; I have given the land into their hands."

1:1   The people of Israel had finally entered and taken control of the land promised to their ancestors (Genesis 12:7; Exodus 3:16, 17). The book of Judges continues the story of this conquest that began in the book of Joshua. Through God's strength, the Israelites had conquered many enemies and overcome many difficulties, but their work was not yet finished. They had effectively met many political and military challenges, but facing spiritual challenges was more difficult. The unholy but attractive lifestyle of the Canaanites proved more dangerous than their military might. The Israelites gave in to the pressure and compromised their faith. If we attempt to meet life's challenges with human effort alone, we will find the pressures and temptations around us too great to resist.

1:1   Soon after Joshua died, Israel began to lose its firm grip on the land. Although Joshua was a great commander, the people missed his spiritual leadership even more than his military skill, for he had kept the people focused on God and his purposes. Joshua had been the obvious successor to Moses, but there was no obvious successor to Joshua. During this crisis of leadership, Israel had to learn that no matter how powerful and wise the current leader was, their real leader was God. We often focus our hope and confidence on some influential leader, failing to realize that in reality it is God who is in command. Acknowledge God as your commander in chief, and avoid the temptation of relying too heavily on human leaders, regardless of their spiritual wisdom.

1:1   The Canaanites were all the people who lived in Canaan (the promised land). They lived in city-states where each city had its own government, army, and laws. One reason Canaan was so difficult to conquer was that each city had to be defeated individually. There was no single king who could surrender the entire country into the hands of the Israelites.

Canaan's greatest threat to Israel was not its army, but its religion. Canaanite religion idealized evil traits: cruelty in war, sexual immorality, selfish greed, and materialism. It was a "me first, anything goes" society. Obviously, the religions of Israel and Canaan could not coexist.

1:2   The book of Joshua tells of a swift and thorough conquest of enemy armies and cities, while the book of Judges seems to suggest a more lengthy and gradual conquest. When the Israelites first entered the promised land (Joshua 1—12), they united as one army to crush the inhabitants until they were too weak to retaliate. Then, after the land was divided among the 12 tribes (Joshua 13—24), each tribe was responsible for driving out the remaining enemy from its own territory. The book of Judges tells of their failure to do this.

Some tribes were more successful than others. Under Joshua, they all began strong, but soon most were sidetracked by fear, weariness, lack of discipline, or pursuit of their own interests. As a result, their faith began to fade away, and "everyone did as he saw fit" (17:6). In order for our faith to survive, it must be practiced day by day. It must penetrate every aspect of our lives. Beware of starting out strong and then getting sidetracked from your real purpose—loving God and living for him.

3 Then the men of Judah said to the Simeonites their brothers, "Come up with us into the territory allotted to us, to fight against the Canaanites. We in turn will go with you into yours." So the Simeonites *c* went with them.

4 When Judah attacked, the LORD gave the Canaanites and Perizzites *d* into their hands and they struck down ten thousand men at Bezek. 5 It was there that they found Adoni-Bezek and fought against him, putting to rout the Canaanites and Perizzites. 6 Adoni-Bezek fled, but they chased him and caught him, and cut off his thumbs and big toes.

7 Then Adoni-Bezek said, "Seventy kings with their thumbs and big toes cut off have picked up scraps under my table. Now God has paid me back *e* for what I did to them." They brought him to Jerusalem, and he died there.

8 The men of Judah attacked Jerusalem *f* also and took it. They put the city to the sword and set it on fire.

9 After that, the men of Judah went down to fight against the Canaanites living in the hill country, the Negev and the western foothills. 10 They advanced against the Canaanites living in Hebron (formerly called Kiriath Arba) and defeated Sheshai, Ahiman and Talmai. *g*

11 From there they advanced against the people living in Debir (formerly called Kiriath Sepher). 12 And Caleb said, "I will give my daughter Acsah in marriage to the man who attacks and captures Kiriath Sepher." 13 Othniel son of Kenaz, Caleb's younger brother, took it; so Caleb gave his daughter Acsah to him in marriage.

14 One day when she came to Othniel, she urged him *a* to ask her father for a field. When she got off her donkey, Caleb asked her, "What can I do for you?"

15 She replied, "Do me a special favor. Since you have given me land in the Negev, give me also springs of water." Then Caleb gave her the upper and lower springs.

16 The descendants of Moses' father-in-law, *h* the Kenite, *i* went up from the City of Palms *b j* with the men of Judah to live among the people of the Desert of Judah in the Negev near Arad. *k*

17 Then the men of Judah went with the Simeonites their brothers and attacked the Canaanites living in Zephath, and they totally destroyed *c* the city. Therefore it was called Hormah. *d* / 18 The men of Judah also took *e* Gaza, Ashkelon and Ekron—each city with its territory.

19 The LORD was with the men of Judah. They took possession of the hill country, but they were unable to drive the people from the plains, because they had iron chariots. *m* 20 As

1:3 *c* ver 17
1:4 *d* Ge 13:7
1:7 *e* Lev 24:19
1:8 *f* ver 21; Jos 15:63
1:10 *g* Jos 15:14
1:16 *h* Nu 10:29 *i* Jdg 4:11 *j* Dt 34:3 *k* Nu 21:1
1:17 *l* Nu 21:3
1:19 *m* Jos 17:16

a 14 Hebrew; Septuagint and Vulgate *Othniel, he urged her*   *b 16* That is, Jericho   *c 17* The Hebrew term refers to the irrevocable giving over of things or persons to the LORD, often by totally destroying them.   *d 17 Hormah* means *destruction.*   *e 18* Hebrew; Septuagint *Judah did not take*

1:6 The maiming of Adoni-Bezek was one example in a long string of actions that demonstrated Israel's tendency to disobey God's instructions by only giving partial obedience. Enemy kings were supposed to be executed, not humiliated. This defeated king recognized God's righteous punishment more clearly than God's

people acknowledged God's commands. When we understand what God tells us to do, we run great danger if we don't carry out both the letter and the spirit of his words.

1:8 Although the Israelites conquered Jerusalem, they did not occupy the city until the days of David (2 Samuel 5:6–10).

1:12–15 This same event is recorded in Joshua 15:16–19. Caleb was one of the original spies who scouted out the promised land (Numbers 13—14) and, with Joshua, encouraged the people to conquer it. For his faithfulness, he was given the land of his choice.

JUDAH FIGHTS FOR ITS LAND

The tribe of Judah wasted no time beginning their conquest of the territory allotted to them. With help from the tribe of Simeon, Jerusalem was conquered, as were the Canaanites in the Negev and along the coast. Hebron and Debir fell to Judah, and later Gaza, Ashkelon, and Ekron.

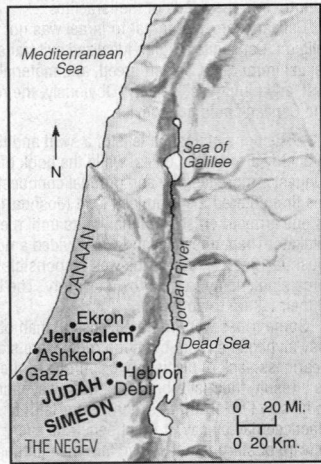

1:17 Why did God order the Israelites to drive the Canaanites from their land? Although the command seems cruel, the Israelites were under God's order to execute judgment on those wicked people. The other nations were to be judged for their sin as God had judged Israel by forcing them to wander for 40 years before they were allowed to enter the promised land. Over 700 years earlier, God had told Abraham that when the Israelites entered the promised land, the gross evil of the native people would be ready for judgment (Genesis 15:16). But God wasn't playing favorites with the Israelites because eventually they too would be severely punished for becoming as evil as the people they were ordered to drive out (2 Kings 17; 25; Jeremiah 6:18; 19; Ezekiel 8). God is not partial; all people are eligible for God's gracious forgiveness as well as for his firm justice.

1:19 Canaanite chariots pulled by horses were among the most sophisticated weapons of the day. Israelite foot soldiers were absolutely powerless when a speeding iron chariot bore down upon them. This is why Israel preferred to fight in the hills where chariots couldn't venture.

1:20
n Jos 14:9; 15:13-14

1:21
o Jos 15:63

1:23
p Ge 28:19

1:24
q Jos 2:12,14

1:25
r Jos 6:25

1:27
s Jos 17:11

1:29
t Jos 16:10

Moses had promised, Hebron n was given to Caleb, who drove from it the three sons of Anak. 21 The Benjamites, however, failed o to dislodge the Jebusites, who were living in Jerusalem; to this day the Jebusites live there with the Benjamites.

22 Now the house of Joseph attacked Bethel, and the LORD was with them. 23 When they sent men to spy out Bethel (formerly called Luz), p 24 the spies saw a man coming out of the city and they said to him, "Show us how to get into the city and we will see that you are treated well. q" 25 So he showed them, and they put the city to the sword but spared r the man and his whole family. 26 He then went to the land of the Hittites, where he built a city and called it Luz, which is its name to this day.

27 But Manasseh did not drive out the people of Beth Shan or Taanach or Dor or Ibleam s or Megiddo and their surrounding settlements, for the Canaanites were determined to live in that land. 28 When Israel became strong, they pressed the Canaanites into forced labor but never drove them out completely. 29 Nor did Ephraim drive out the Canaanites living in Gezer, but the Canaanites continued to live there among them. t 30 Neither did Zebulun drive out the Canaanites living in Kitron or Nahalol, who remained among them; but they did subject them to forced labor. 31 Nor did Asher drive out those living in Acco or Sidon or Ahlab or Aczib or Helbah or Aphek or Rehob, 32 and because of this the people of Asher lived among the Canaanite inhabitants of the land. 33 Neither did Naphtali drive out those living in Beth Shemesh or Beth Anath; but the Naphtalites too lived among the Canaanite inhabitants of the land, and those living in Beth Shemesh and Beth Anath became forced laborers for them. 34 The Amorites confined the Danites to the hill country, not allowing them to come down into the plain. 35 And the Amorites were determined also to hold out in Mount Heres, Aijalon and Shaalbim, but when the power of the house of

THE JUDGES OF ISRAEL	Judge	Years of Judging	Memorable Act(s)	Reference
	OTHNIEL	40	He captured a powerful Canaanite city	Judges 3:7–11
	EHUD	80	He killed Eglon and defeated the Moabites	Judges 3:12-30
	SHAMGAR	unrecorded	He killed 600 Philistines with an oxgoad	Judges 3:31
	DEBORAH (w/Barak)	40	She defeated Sisera and the Canaanites and later sang a victory song with Barak	Judges 4; 5
	GIDEON	40	He destroyed his family idols, used a fleece to determine God's will, raised an army of 10,000, and defeated 135,000 Midianites with 300 soldiers	Judges 6—8
	TOLA	23	He judged Israel for 23 years	Judges 10:1, 2
	JAIR	22	He had 30 sons	Judges 10:3–5
	JEPHTHAH	6	He made a rash vow, defeated the Ammonites, and later battled jealous Ephraim	Judges 10:6—12:7
	IBZAN	7	He had 30 sons and 30 daughters	Judges 12:8–10
	ELON	10	Unrecorded	Judges 12:11, 12
	ABDON	8	He had 40 sons and 30 grandsons, each of whom had his own donkey	Judges 12:13–15
	SAMSON	20	He was a Nazirite, killed a lion with his bare hands, burned the Philistine wheat fields, killed 1,000 Philistines with a donkey's jawbone, tore off an iron gate, was betrayed by Delilah, and destroyed thousands of Philistines in one last mighty act	Judges 13—16

1:21ff Tribe after tribe failed to drive the evil Canaanites from their land. Why didn't they follow through and completely obey God's commands? (1) They had been fighting for a long time and were tired. Although the goal was in sight, they lacked the discipline and energy to reach it. (2) They were afraid the enemy was too strong—the iron chariots seemed invincible. (3) After Joshua's death, power and authority were decentralized to the tribal leaders, and the tribes were no longer unified in purpose. (4) Spiritual decay had infected them from within. They thought

they could handle the temptation and be more prosperous by doing business with the Canaanites.

We, too, often choose to tolerate sin rather than drive it from our lives. We may know what to do but just don't follow through. This results in a gradual deterioration of our relationship with God. In our battles, we may grow tired and want rest, but we need more than a break from our work. We need to know that God loves us and has given us a purpose for life. Victory comes from living according to his purpose, willing to fully obey him.

Joseph increased, they too were pressed into forced labor. ³⁶ The boundary of the Amorites was from Scorpion ᵃ Pass ᵘ to Sela and beyond.

1:36
ᵘ Jos 15:3

The Angel of the LORD at Bokim

2 The angel of the LORD went up from Gilgal to Bokim ᵛ and said, "I brought you up out of
Egypt ʷ and led you into the land that I swore to give to your forefathers. ˣ I said, 'I will
never break my covenant with you, ² and you shall not make a covenant with the people of
this land, but you shall break down their altars.' Yet you have disobeyed me. Why have you
done this? ³ Now therefore I tell you that I will not drive them out before you; ʸ they will be
⌊thorns⌋ in your sides and their gods will be a snare ᶻ to you."

2:1
ᵛ ver 5
ʷ Ex 20:2
ˣ Ge 17:8

2:3
ʸ Jos 23:13
ᶻ Ps 106:36

⁴ When the angel of the LORD had spoken these things to all the Israelites, the people wept
aloud, ⁵ and they called that place Bokim. ᵇ There they offered sacrifices to the LORD.

2. Disobedience and defeat

⁶ After Joshua had dismissed the Israelites, they went to take possession of the land, each to
his own inheritance. ⁷ The people served the LORD throughout the lifetime of Joshua and of the
elders who outlived him and who had seen all the great things the LORD had done for Israel.

⁸ Joshua son of Nun, the servant of the LORD, died at the age of a hundred and ten. ⁹ And they
buried him in the land of his inheritance, at Timnath Heres ᶜ ᵃ in the hill country of Ephraim,
north of Mount Gaash.

2:9
ᵃ Jos 19:50

¹⁰ After that whole generation had been gathered to their fathers, another generation
grew up, who knew neither the LORD nor what he had done for Israel. ᵇ ¹¹ Then the Israelites
did evil in the eyes of the LORD and served the Baals. ᶜ ¹² They forsook the LORD, the God of
their fathers, who had brought them out of Egypt. They followed and worshiped various gods
of the peoples around them. ᵈ They provoked the LORD to anger ¹³ because they forsook him
and served Baal and the Ashtoreths. ¹⁴ In his anger against Israel the LORD handed them over ᵉ
to raiders who plundered them. He sold them to their enemies all around, whom they were
no longer able to resist. ᶠ ¹⁵ Whenever Israel went out to fight, the hand of the LORD was
against them to defeat them, just as he had sworn to them. They were in great distress.

2:10
ᵇ Ex 5:2; 1Sa 2:12
2:11
ᶜ Jdg 3:7
2:12
ᵈ Dt 31:16
2:14
ᵉ Ps 106:41
ᶠ Dt 28:25

ᵃ*36* Hebrew *Akrabbim*   ᵇ*5* Bokim means *weepers.*   ᶜ*9* Also known as *Timnath Serah* (see Joshua 19:50 and 24:30)

2:1–3 This event marks a significant change in Israel's relationship with God. At Mount Sinai, God made a sacred and binding
agreement with the Israelites called a covenant (Exodus 19:5–8).
God's part was to make Israel a special nation (see the note on
Genesis 12:1–3), to protect them, and to give them unique blessings for following him. Israel's part was to love God and obey his
laws. But because they rejected and disobeyed God, the agreement
to protect them was no longer in effect. But God wasn't going to
abandon his people. They would receive wonderful blessings if
they asked God to forgive them and sincerely followed him again.

Although God's agreement to help Israel conquer the land was
no longer in effect, his promise to make Israel a nation through
whom the whole world would be blessed (fulfilled in the Messiah's
coming) remained valid. God still wanted the Israelites to be a holy
people (just as he wants us to be holy), and he often used oppression to bring them back to him, just as he warned he would (Leviticus 26; Deuteronomy 28). The book of Judges records a number
of instances where God allowed his people to be oppressed so that
they would repent of their sins and return to him.

Too often people want God to fulfill his promises while excusing themselves from their responsibilities. Before you claim God's
promises, ask, "Have I done my part?"

2:4 The people of Israel knew they had sinned, and they wept
loudly, responding with deep sorrow. Because we have a tendency
to sin, only repentance is the true measure of spiritual sensitivity.
Repentance means not only confessing sins and asking God to
forgive us, but also abandoning our sinful ways. But we cannot
do this sincerely unless we are truly sorry for our sinful actions.
Tears alone are not enough. When we are aware that we have done
wrong, we should admit it plainly to God rather than try to cover
it up or hope we can get away with it.

2:7–9 The account of Joshua's death is found here and at the end
of the book of Joshua (24:29). Either this account is a summary of
what happened earlier, or the account in the book of Joshua omit-

ted the events in the first chapter of Judges. (For more on Joshua,
see his Profile in Joshua 2, p. 305.)

2:10ff One generation died, and the next did not follow God.
Judges 2:10—3:7 is a brief preview of the cycle of sin, judgment,
and repentance that Israel experienced again and again. Each
generation failed to teach the next generation to love and follow
God. Yet this was at the very center of God's law (Deuteronomy
6:4–9). It is tempting to leave the job of teaching the Christian faith
to the church or Christian school. Yet God says that the responsibility for this task belongs primarily to the family. Because children
learn so much by our example, the home offers the most effective
place to pass on the faith to the next generation.

2:11–15 Baal was the god of the storm and rains; therefore, he
was thought to control vegetation and agriculture. Ashtoreth was
the mother goddess of love, war, and fertility (she was also called
Astarte or Ishtar). Temple prostitution and child sacrifice were a
part of the worship of these Canaanite idols. This generation of
Israelites abandoned the faith of their parents and began worshiping the gods of their neighbors. Many things can tempt us to
abandon what we know is right. The desire to be accepted by our
neighbors can lead us into behavior that is unacceptable to God.
Don't be lulled into compromise or pressured into disobedience.

2:12–15 God often saved his harshest criticism and punishment
for those who worshiped idols. Why were idols so bad in God's
sight? To worship an idol violated the first two of the Ten Commandments (Exodus 20:3–6). The Canaanites had gods for almost
every season, activity, or place. To them, the Lord was just another
god to add to their collection of gods. Israel, by contrast, was to
worship only the Lord. They could not possibly believe that God
was the one true God and at the same time bow to an idol. Idol
worshipers could not see their god as their creator because they
created it. These idols represent sensual, carnal, and immoral
aspects of human nature. God's nature is spiritual and moral.

2:16
g Ps 106:43

2:17
h ver 7

2:19
i Jdg 3:12

2:20
j ver 14; Jos 23:16

2:22
k Jdg 3:1,14

3:1
l Jdg 2:21-22

¹⁶Then the LORD raised up judges,ª who saved *g* them out of the hands of these raiders. ¹⁷Yet they would not listen to their judges but prostituted themselves to other gods and worshiped them. Unlike their fathers, they quickly turned from the way in which their fathers had walked, the way of obedience to the LORD's commands. *h* ¹⁸Whenever the LORD raised up a judge for them, he was with the judge and saved them out of the hands of their enemies as long as the judge lived; for the LORD had compassion on them as they groaned under those who oppressed and afflicted them. ¹⁹But when the judge died, the people returned to ways even more corrupt *i* than those of their fathers, following other gods and serving and worshiping them. They refused to give up their evil practices and stubborn ways.

²⁰Therefore the LORD was very angry *j* with Israel and said, "Because this nation has violated the covenant that I laid down for their forefathers and has not listened to me, ²¹I will no longer drive out before them any of the nations Joshua left when he died. ²²I will use them to test *k* Israel and see whether they will keep the way of the LORD and walk in it as their forefathers did." ²³The LORD had allowed those nations to remain; he did not drive them out at once by giving them into the hands of Joshua.

3 These are the nations the LORD left to test *l* all those Israelites who had not experienced any of the wars in Canaan ²(he did this only to teach warfare to the descendants of the

ª *16* Or *leaders*; similarly in verses 17-19

WHY DID ISRAEL WANT TO WORSHIP IDOLS?

Worshiping God	*Worshiping Idols*
Long-range benefits	Short-range benefits
Gratification postponed	Self-gratification immediate
Morality required	Sensuality approved
High ethical standards demanded	Low ethical standards tolerated
Neighbors' sins disapproved	Neighbors' sins approved
Unseen God worshiped	Visible idols worshiped
Unselfishness expected	Selfishness condoned
Business relations hindered	Business relations improved
Strict religious practices maintained	Religious practices loosely regulated
Changed life demanded	Changed life not demanded
Ethical stand expected	Compromise and cooperation practiced
Concern for others taught	No concern for others expected

The temptation to follow false gods because of short-term benefits, good feelings, easy "rules," or convenience was always present. *But the benefits were deceptive because the gods were false.* We worship God because he is the one and only true God.

Adding the worship of idols to the worship of God could not be tolerated.

2:15, 16 Despite Israel's disobedience, God showed his great mercy by raising up judges to save the people from their oppressors. Mercy has been defined as "not giving a person what he or she deserves." This is exactly what God did for Israel and what he does for us. Our disobedience demands judgment! But God shows mercy toward us by providing an escape from sin's penalty through Jesus Christ, who alone saves us from sin. When we pray for forgiveness, we are asking for what we do not deserve. Yet when we take this step and trust in Christ's saving work on our behalf, we can experience God's forgiveness.

2:16–19 Throughout this period of history Israel went through seven cycles of (1) rebelling against God, (2) being overrun by enemy nations, (3) being delivered by a God-fearing judge, (4) remaining loyal to God under that judge, and (5) again forgetting God when the judge died. We tend to follow the same cycle—remaining loyal to God as long as we are near those who are devoted to him. But when we are on our own, the pressure to be drawn away from God increases. Determine to be faithful to God despite the difficult situations you encounter. Recognize the importance of maintaining contact with other believers.

2:17 Why would the people of Israel turn so quickly from their faith in God? Simply put, the Canaanite religion appeared more attractive to the sensual nature and offered more short-range benefits (sexual permissiveness and increased fertility in childbearing and farming). One of its most attractive features was that people could remain selfish and yet fulfill their religious requirements. They could do almost anything they wished and still be obeying at least one of the many Canaanite gods. Male and female prostitution were not only allowed, but encouraged as forms of worship.

Faith in the one true God, however, does not offer short-range benefits that appeal to our sinful human nature. The essence of sin is selfishness; the essence of God's way of life is selflessness. We must seek Christ's help to live God's way.

3:1–4 We learn from chapter 1 that these enemy nations were still in the land because the Israelites had failed to obey God and drive them out. Now God would allow the enemies to remain in order to "test" the Israelites; that is, to give them an opportunity to exercise faith and obedience. By now the younger generation that had not fought in the great battles of conquest was coming of age. It was their job to complete the conquest of the land. There were many obstacles yet to be overcome in their new homeland. How they would handle these obstacles would be a test of their faith.

Perhaps God has left obstacles in your life—hostile people, difficult situations, baffling problems—to allow you to develop faith and obedience.

Israelites who had not had previous battle experience). ³the five^m rulers of the Philistines, all the Canaanites, the Sidonians, and the Hivites living in the Lebanon mountains from Mount Baal Hermon to Lebo^a Hamath. ⁴They were left to test the Israelites to see whether they would obey the LORD's commands, which he had given their forefathers through Moses.

⁵The Israelites lived ^n among the Canaanites, Hittites, Amorites, Perizzites, Hivites and Jebusites. ⁶They took their daughters in marriage and gave their own daughters to their sons, and served their gods. ^o

B. THE RESCUE OF ISRAEL BY THE JUDGES (3:7—16:31)
The Israelites began a series of cycles of sinning, worshiping idols, being punished, crying out for help, being rescued by a judge sent from God, obeying God for a while, then falling back into idolatry. They were conquered by Syria, Moab, Canaan, Midian, Ammon, and Philistia. They even faced the threat of civil war. Just as God sent help to the people when they cried out to him, he will deliver us when we call on him.

1. First period: Othniel
Othniel

⁷The Israelites did evil in the eyes of the LORD; they forgot the LORD^p their God and served the Baals and the Asherahs. ^q ⁸The anger of the LORD burned against Israel so that he sold them into the hands of Cushan-Rishathaim king of Aram Naharaim,^b to whom the Israelites were subject for eight years. ⁹But when they cried out ^r to the LORD, he raised up for them a deliverer, Othniel ^s son of Kenaz, Caleb's younger brother, who saved them. ¹⁰The Spirit of the LORD came upon him,^t so that he became Israel's judge^c and went to war. The LORD gave Cushan-Rishathaim king of Aram into the hands of Othniel, who overpowered him. ¹¹So the land had peace for forty years, until Othniel son of Kenaz died.

2. Second period: Ehud and Shamgar
Ehud

¹²Once again the Israelites did evil in the eyes of the LORD,^u and because they did this evil the LORD gave Eglon king of Moab power over Israel. ¹³Getting the Ammonites and Amalekites to join him, Eglon came and attacked Israel, and they took possession of the City of Palms.^d^v ¹⁴The Israelites were subject to Eglon king of Moab for eighteen years.
¹⁵Again the Israelites cried out to the LORD, and he gave them a deliverer—Ehud, a left-

3:3
^mJos 13:3

3:5
^nPs 106:35
3:6
^oEx 34:16; Dt 7:3-4

3:7
^pDt 4:9
^qJdg 2:11,13
3:9
^rver 15
^sJdg 1:13
3:10
^tNu 11:25,29;
Jdg 6:34

3:12
^uJdg 2:11,14

3:13
^vJdg 1:16

^a3 Or *to the entrance to*   ^b8 That is, Northwest Mesopotamia   ^c10 Or *leader*   ^d13 That is, Jericho

---

3:5–7 The Israelites discovered that relationships affect faith. The men and women of the surrounding nations were attractive to the Israelites. Soon they intermarried, and the Israelites accepted their pagan gods. This was clearly prohibited by God (Exodus 34:15–17; Deuteronomy 7:1–4). By accepting these gods into their homes, the Israelites gradually began to accept the immoral practices associated with them. Most Israelites didn't start out determined to be idolaters; they just added the idols to the worship of God. But before long they found themselves absorbed in pagan worship.

A similar danger faces us. We want to befriend those who don't know God, but through those friendships we can become entangled in unhealthy practices. Friendships with unbelievers are important, but we must accept people without compromising or adopting their patterns of behavior.

3:7 Baal was the most worshiped god of the Canaanites. Most often cast in the form of a bull, he symbolized strength and fertility and was considered the god of agriculture. Asherah was Baal's female consort, mother goddess of the sea who was worshiped by means of wooden pillars that substituted for sacred trees. In times of famine, the Canaanites believed Baal was angry with them and was withholding rain as punishment. Archaeologists have uncovered many Baal idols in Israel. It is difficult to imagine the people of Israel trading worship of the Lord for worship of idols of wood, stone, and iron, but we do the same when we forsake worshiping God for other activities, hobbies, or priorities. Our idols are not made of wood or stone, but they are every bit as sinful.

3:9 Othniel was Israel's first judge. In 1:13 we read that he volunteered to lead an attack against a fortified city. Here he

was to lead the nation back to God. Othniel had a rich spiritual heritage—his uncle was Caleb, a man with unwavering faith in God (Numbers 13:30; 14:24). Othniel's leadership brought the people back to God and freed them from the oppression of the king of Aram, Naharaim. But after Othniel's death, it didn't take the Israelites long to fall back into their neighbors' comfortable but sinful ways.

3:10 This phrase, "The Spirit of the LORD came upon him," was also spoken of the judges Gideon, Jephthah, and Samson, among others. It expresses a temporary and spontaneous increase of physical, spiritual, or mental strength. This was an extraordinary and supernatural occurrence to prepare a person for a special task. The Holy Spirit is available to all believers today, but he will come upon believers in an extraordinary way for special tasks. We should ask the Holy Spirit's help as we face our daily problems as well as life's major challenges.

3:12, 13 The Moabites, Ammonites, and Amalekites were nomadic tribes that lived near each other east and southeast of Canaan. These tribes were notorious raiders, possessing great military skill. This was the first time nations outside Canaan attacked the Israelites in their own land.

3:15 Ehud is called a *deliverer*. In the broadest sense, all the judges can be looked upon as foreshadowing the perfect Deliverer, Jesus Christ. While Ehud delivered Israel from its enemies, Jesus delivers us from sin, our greatest enemy.

3:15–30 This unusual story demonstrates how God can use us just the way he made us. Being left-handed in Ehud's day was considered an exceptional ability. Many Benjaminites were left-handed (see 20:16), making them highly specialized troops, able handed man, the son of Gera the Benjamite. The Israelites sent him with tribute to Eglon king of Moab. ¹⁶Now Ehud had made a double-edged sword about a foot and a half ᵃ long, which he strapped to his right thigh under his clothing. ¹⁷He presented the tribute to Eglon king of Moab, who was a very fat man. ¹⁸After Ehud had presented the tribute, he sent on their way the men who had carried it. ¹⁹At the idols ᵇ near Gilgal he himself turned back and said, "I have a secret message for you, O king."

The king said, "Quiet!" And all his attendants left him.

²⁰Ehud then approached him while he was sitting alone in the upper room of his summer palace ᶜ and said, "I have a message from God for you." As the king rose from his seat, ²¹Ehud reached with his left hand, drew the sword from his right thigh and plunged it into the king's belly. ²²Even the handle sank in after the blade, which came out his back. Ehud did not pull the sword out, and the fat closed in over it. ²³Then Ehud went out to the porch ᵈ; he shut the doors of the upper room behind him and locked them.

²⁴After he had gone, the servants came and found the doors of the upper room locked. They said, "He must be relieving himself ʷ in the inner room of the house." ²⁵They waited to the point of embarrassment, but when he did not open the doors of the room, they took a key and unlocked them. There they saw their lord fallen to the floor, dead.

²⁶While they waited, Ehud got away. He passed by the idols and escaped to Seirah. ²⁷When he arrived there, he blew a trumpet ˣ in the hill country of Ephraim, and the Israelites went down with him from the hills, with him leading them.

²⁸"Follow me," he ordered, "for the LORD has given Moab, your enemy, into your hands. ʸ" So they followed him down and, taking possession of the fords of the Jordan ᶻ that led to

3:24
ʷ1Sa 24:3

3:27
ˣJdg 6:34

3:28
ʸJdg 7:9,15
ᶻJdg 7:24; 12:5

ᵃ16 Hebrew *a cubit* (about 0.5 meter)   ᵇ19 Or *the stone quarries*; also in verse 26   ᶜ20 The meaning of the Hebrew for this phrase is uncertain.   ᵈ23 The meaning of the Hebrew for this word is uncertain.

EHUD

At first glance, Ehud's career as a judge in Israel may not seem relevant to us. He clearly lived in another time. He took radical and violent action to free his people. His murder of Eglon shocks us. His war on Moab was swift and deadly. His life is difficult to relate to. But our commitment to God's Word challenges us not to ignore this leader. As we read about his life, some questions come to mind: (1) When was the last time God showed me something wrong in my life and I took immediate and painful action to correct the error? (2) When was the last time I asked God to show me how he could use something unique about me (as he used Ehud's left-handedness)? (3) When was the last time I made a plan to obey God in some specific area of my life and then followed through on that plan? (4) When was the last time my life was an example to others of obedience to God?

The enemies we face are as real as Ehud's, but they are most often within ourselves. The battles we fight are not against other people but against the power of sin. We need God's help in doing battle against sin. We also need to remember that he has already won the war. He has defeated sin at the cross of his Son, Jesus. His help is the cause of each success, and his forgiveness is sufficient for each failure.

Strengths and accomplishments:	• Second judge of Israel • A man of direct action, a frontline leader • Used a perceived weakness (left-handedness) to do a great work for God • Led the revolt against Moabite domination and gave Israel 80 years of peace
Lessons from his life:	• Some conditions call for radical action • God responds to the cry of repentance • God is ready to use our unique qualities to accomplish his work
Vital statistics:	• Where: Born during the last years of the desert wanderings or during Israel's early years in the promised land • Occupation: Messenger, judge • Relative: Father: Gera • Contemporary: Eglon of Moab
Key verse:	"Again the Israelites cried out to the LORD, and he gave them a deliverer—Ehud, a left-handed man, the son of Gera the Benjamite" (Judges 3:15).

His story is told in Judges 3:12–30.

---

to use a sling or bow with tactics designed to repel right-handed warriors. Eglon's bodyguard never checked Israel's messengers for left-handed weapons. But God used Ehud's overlooked ability to give Israel victory. Let God use you the way you are to accomplish his work.

Moab, they allowed no one to cross over. ²⁹At that time they struck down about ten thousand Moabites, all vigorous and strong; not a man escaped. ³⁰That day Moab was made subject to Israel, and the land had peace for eighty years.

Shamgar

³¹After Ehud came Shamgar son of Anath,ᵃ who struck down six hundred Philistines with an oxgoad. He too saved Israel.

3:31
ᵃJdg 5:6

3. Third period: Deborah and Barak
Deborah

4 After Ehud died, the Israelites once again did evilᵇ in the eyes of the Lord. ²So the Lord sold them into the hands of Jabin, a king of Canaan, who reigned in Hazor.ᶜ The commander of his army was Sisera,ᵈ who lived in Harosheth Haggoyim. ³Because he had nine hundred iron chariotsᵉ and had cruelly oppressed the Israelites for twenty years, they cried to the Lord for help.

⁴Deborah, a prophetess, the wife of Lappidoth, was leadingᵃ Israel at that time. ⁵She held court under the Palm of Deborah between Ramah and Bethel in the hill country of Ephraim, and the Israelites came to her to have their disputes decided. ⁶She sent for Barak son of Abinoamᶠ from Kedesh in Naphtali and said to him, "The Lord, the God of Israel, commands you: 'Go, take with you ten thousand men of Naphtali and Zebulun and lead the way to Mount Tabor. ⁷I will lure Sisera, the commander of Jabin's army, with his chariots and his troops to the Kishon Riverᵍ and give him into your hands.'"

⁸Barak said to her, "If you go with me, I will go; but if you don't go with me, I won't go."

ᵃ4 Traditionally judging

4:1
ᵇJdg 2:19

4:2
ᶜJos 11:1
ᵈver 13,16; Ps 83:9

4:3
ᵉJdg 1:19

4:6
ᶠHeb 11:32

4:7
ᵍPs 83:9

3:31 To kill 600 Philistines with an oxgoad was quite a feat. An oxgoad was a long stick with a small flat piece of iron on one side and a sharp point on the other. The sharp side was used to drive the oxen during the times of plowing, and the flat end was used to clean the mud off the plow. Eight-foot-long ancient oxgoads have been found. In times of crisis they could easily have been used as spears, as in Shamgar's case. Oxgoads are still used in the Middle East to drive oxen.

4:1 Israel sinned "in the eyes of the Lord." Our sins harm both ourselves and others, but all sin is ultimately against God because it disregards his commands and his authority over us. When confessing his sin David prayed, "Against you, you only, have I sinned and done what is evil in your sight" (Psalm 51:4). Recognizing the seriousness of sin is the first step toward removing it from our lives.

4:2, 3 Nothing more is known about Jabin. Joshua had defeated a king by that name years earlier and burned the city of Hazor to

the ground (Joshua 11:1–11). Either the city was rebuilt by this time, or Jabin was hoping to rebuild it.

This is the only time during the period of the judges when the Israelites' enemies came from within their land. The Israelites had failed to drive out all the Canaanites. These Canaanites had regrouped and were attempting to restore their lost power. If the Israelites had obeyed God in the first place and had driven the Canaanites from the land, this incident would not have happened.

4:2, 3 Chariots were the tanks of the ancient world. Made of iron or wood, they were pulled by one or two horses and were the most feared and powerful weapons of the day. Some chariots even had razor-sharp knives extending from the wheels designed to mutilate helpless foot soldiers. The Canaanite army had 900 iron chariots. Israel was not powerful enough to defeat such an invincible army. Therefore, Jabin and Sisera had no trouble oppressing the people—until a faithful woman named Deborah called upon God.

4:3 After 20 years of unbearable circumstances, the Israelites finally cried to the Lord for help. But God should be the first place we turn when we are facing struggles or dilemmas. The Israelites chose to go their own way and got into a mess. We often do the same. Trying to control our own lives without God's help leads to struggle and confusion. By contrast, when we stay in daily contact with the Lord, we are less likely to create painful circumstances for ourselves. This is a lesson the Israelites never fully learned. When struggles come our way, God wants us to come to him first, seeking his strength and guidance.

4:4ff The Bible records several women who held national leadership positions, and Deborah was an exceptional woman. Obviously she was the best person for the job, and God chose her to lead Israel. God can choose anyone to lead his people, young or old, man or woman. Don't let your prejudices get in the way of those God may have chosen to lead you.

4:6–8 Was Barak cowardly or just in need of support? We don't know Barak's character, but we see the character of a great leader in Deborah, who took charge as God directed. Deborah told Barak that God would be with him in battle, but that was not enough for Barak. He wanted Deborah to go with him. Barak's request shows that at heart he trusted human strength more than God's promise. A person of real faith steps out at God's command, even if he or she must do so alone.

EHUD FREES ISRAEL FROM MOAB
When King Eglon of Moab conquered part of Israel, he set up his throne in the city of Jericho. Ehud was chosen to take Israel's tribute there. After delivering Israel's tribute, Ehud killed King Eglon and escaped into the hill country of Ephraim. From there he gathered together an army to cut off any Moabites trying to escape across the Jordan River.

4:10
h Jdg 5:15,18

4:11
i Jdg 1:16

4:14
j Dt 9:3; 2Sa 5:24

4:15
k Jos 10:10

4:16
l Ps 83:9

4:19
m Jdg 5:25

4:21
n Jdg 5:26

⁹"Very well," Deborah said, "I will go with you. But because of the way you are going about this,ᵃ the honor will not be yours, for the Lᴏʀᴅ will hand Sisera over to a woman." So Deborah went with Barak to Kedesh, ¹⁰where he summoned ʰ Zebulun and Naphtali. Ten thousand men followed him, and Deborah also went with him.

¹¹Now Heber the Kenite had left the other Kenites, ⁱ the descendants of Hobab, Moses' brother-in-law,ᵇ and pitched his tent by the great tree in Zaanannim near Kedesh.

¹²When they told Sisera that Barak son of Abinoam had gone up to Mount Tabor, ¹³Sisera gathered together his nine hundred iron chariots and all the men with him, from Harosheth Haggoyim to the Kishon River.

¹⁴Then Deborah said to Barak, "Go! This is the day the Lᴏʀᴅ has given Sisera into your hands. Has not the Lᴏʀᴅ gone aheadʲ of you?" So Barak went down Mount Tabor, followed by ten thousand men. ¹⁵At Barak's advance, the Lᴏʀᴅ routedᵏ Sisera and all his chariots and army by the sword, and Sisera abandoned his chariot and fled on foot. ¹⁶But Barak pursued the chariots and army as far as Harosheth Haggoyim. All the troops of Sisera fell by the sword; not a man was left. ˡ

¹⁷Sisera, however, fled on foot to the tent of Jael, the wife of Heber the Kenite, because there were friendly relations between Jabin king of Hazor and the clan of Heber the Kenite.

¹⁸Jael went out to meet Sisera and said to him, "Come, my lord, come right in. Don't be afraid." So he entered her tent, and she put a covering over him.

¹⁹"I'm thirsty," he said. "Please give me some water." She opened a skin of milk, ᵐ gave him a drink, and covered him up.

²⁰"Stand in the doorway of the tent," he told her. "If someone comes by and asks you, 'Is anyone here?' say 'No.'"

²¹But Jael, Heber's wife, picked up a tent peg and a hammer and went quietly to him while he lay fast asleep, exhausted. She drove the peg through his temple into the ground, and he died. ⁿ

²²Barak came by in pursuit of Sisera, and Jael went out to meet him. "Come," she said, "I will show you the man you're looking for." So he went in with her, and there lay Sisera with the tent peg through his temple—dead.

²³On that day God subdued Jabin, the Canaanite king, before the Israelites. ²⁴And the hand of the Israelites grew stronger and stronger against Jabin, the Canaanite king, until they destroyed him.

ᵃ9 Or *But on the expedition you are undertaking*   ᵇ11 Or *father-in-law*

THE JUDGES' FUNCTIONS

Judges of Israel could be

saviors (deliverers) and redeemers (Gideon) . . . *or* mediators and administrators (Tola)

providers of rest and peace (Ehud and Jair) . . . . *or* rude, petty dictators (Jephthah)

famous and powerful (Samson) . . . . *or* hardworking yet unsung (Elon and Abdon)

leaders of the nation (Othniel and Deborah) . . . . *or* local heroes (Shamgar and Ibzan)

Regardless of an individual judge's leadership style, each one demonstrated that God's judgment follows apostasy, while repentance brings restoration.

4:9 How did Deborah command such respect? She was responsible for leading the people into battle, but more than that, she influenced them to live for God after the battle was over. Her personality drew people together and commanded the respect of even Barak, a military general. She was also a prophetess, whose main role was to encourage the people to obey God. Those who lead must not forget about the spiritual condition of those being led. A true leader is concerned for persons, not just success.

4:11 Heber was Jael's husband (4:17). He was from the Kenite tribe, descendants of Moses' father-in-law, and longtime allies of Israel. But for some reason, Heber decided to remain neutral in this war, maybe because Jabin's army appeared to have the military advantage. It was probably Heber who told Sisera that the Israelites were camped near Mount Tabor (4:12; see map). Although Heber threw in his lot with Jabin and his forces, his wife, Jael, did not (4:21).

4:18–21 Sisera couldn't have been more pleased when Jael offered him her tent as a hiding place. First, because Jael was the wife of Heber, a man friendly to Sisera's forces (see the note on 4:11), he thought she could be trusted. Second, because men were never allowed to enter a woman's tent, no one would think to look for Sisera there.

Even though her husband, Heber, apparently sided with Sisera's forces, Jael certainly did not. Because women of that day were in charge of pitching the tents, Jael had no problem driving the tent peg into Sisera's head while he slept. Deborah's prediction was thus fulfilled: the honor of conquering Sisera went to a brave and resourceful woman (4:9).

The Song of Deborah

5 On that day Deborah and Barak son of Abinoam sang this song:[o]

2 "When the princes in Israel take the lead,
  when the people willingly offer themselves—
    praise the LORD!

3 "Hear this, you kings! Listen, you rulers!
  I will sing to[a] the LORD, I will sing;
  I will make music to[b] the LORD, the God of Israel.[p]

4 "O LORD, when you went out from Seir,[q]
  when you marched from the land of Edom,
    the earth shook, the heavens poured,
    the clouds poured down water.[r]

5 The mountains quaked[s] before the LORD, the One of Sinai,
  before the LORD, the God of Israel.

6 "In the days of Shamgar son of Anath,[t]
  in the days of Jael,[u] the roads were abandoned;
    travelers took to winding paths.

7 Village life[c] in Israel ceased,
  ceased until I,[d] Deborah, arose,
    arose a mother in Israel.

8 When they chose new gods,[v]
  war came to the city gates,
and not a shield or spear was seen
    among forty thousand in Israel.

9 My heart is with Israel's princes,
  with the willing volunteers among the people.
    Praise the LORD!

10 "You who ride on white donkeys,[w]
  sitting on your saddle blankets,
  and you who walk along the road,
    consider 11 the voice of the singers[e] at the watering places.
    They recite the righteous acts[x] of the LORD,
    the righteous acts of his warriors[f] in Israel.

"Then the people of the LORD
  went down to the city gates.

	5:1 [o]Ex 15:1
	5:3 [p]Ps 27:6
	5:4 [q]Dt 33:2 [r]Ps 68:8
	5:5 [s]Ps 68:8; 97:5
	5:6 [t]Jdg 3:31 [u]Jdg 4:17
	5:8 [v]Dt 32:17
	5:10 [w]Jdg 10:4; 12:14
	5:11 [x]1Sa 12:7; Mic 6:5

a3 Or of   b3 Or / with song I will praise   c7 Or Warriors   d7 Or you   e11 Or archers; the meaning of the Hebrew for this word is uncertain.   f11 Or villagers

KING JABIN IS DEFEATED
Deborah traveled from her home between Ramah and Bethel to march with Barak and the Israelite army against Hazor. Sisera, commander of Hazor's army, assembled his men at Harosheth Haggoyim. In spite of Sisera's 900 chariots and expertly trained army, Israel was victorious.

Mediterranean Sea
N
Hazor
Sea of Galilee
Harosheth Haggoyim
Kishon R.
Kedesh
Mount Tabor
Jordan R.
Bethel
Ramah
Jerusalem
Dead Sea
0   20 Mi.
0   20 Km.   ✦ Battle site

5:1ff Music and singing were a cherished part of Israel's culture. Chapter 5 is a song, possibly composed and sung by Deborah and Barak. It sets to music the story of Israel's great victory recounted in chapter 4. This victory song was accompanied by joyous celebration. It proclaimed God's greatness by giving him credit for the victory. It was an excellent way to preserve and retell this wonderful story from generation to generation. (Other songs in the Bible are listed in the chart in Exodus 15.)

5:1ff In victory, Barak and Deborah sang praises to God. Songs of praise focus our attention on God, give us an outlet for spiritual celebration, and remind us of God's faithfulness and character. Whether you are experiencing a great victory or a major dilemma, singing praises to God can have a positive effect on your attitude.

5:8 War was the inevitable result when Israel chose to follow false gods. Although God had given Israel clear directions, the people failed to put his words into practice. Without God at the center of their national life, pressure from the outside soon became greater than power from within, and they were an easy prey for their enemies. If you are letting a desire for recognition, craving for power, or love of money rule your life, you may find yourself besieged by enemies—stress, anxiety, illness, fatigue.

5:12
y Ps 57:8
z Ps 68:18

12 'Wake up,y wake up, Deborah!
Wake up, wake up, break out in song!
Arise, O Barak!
Take captive your captives,z O son of Abinoam.'

13 "Then the men who were left
came down to the nobles;
the people of the LORD
came to me with the mighty.

14 Some came from Ephraim, whose roots were in Amalek;
Benjamin was with the people who followed you.
From Makir captains came down,
from Zebulun those who bear a commander's staff.

5:15
a Jdg 4:10

15 The princes of Issachar were with Deborah;a
yes, Issachar was with Barak,
rushing after him into the valley.
In the districts of Reuben
there was much searching of heart.

16 Why did you stay among the campfiresa
to hear the whistling for the flocks?
In the districts of Reuben
there was much searching of heart.

a 16 Or *saddlebags*

DEBORAH

Wise leaders are rare. They accomplish great amounts of work without direct involvement because they know how to work through other people. They are able to see the big picture that often escapes those directly involved, so they make good mediators, advisers, and planners. Deborah fit this description perfectly. She had all these leadership skills, and she had a remarkable relationship with God. The insight and confidence God gave this woman placed her in a unique position in the Old Testament. Deborah is among the outstanding women of history.

Her story shows that she was not power hungry. She wanted to serve God. Whenever praise came her way, she gave God the credit. She didn't deny or resist her position in the culture as a woman and wife, but she never allowed herself to be hindered by it either. Her story shows that God can accomplish great things through people who are willing to be led by him.

Deborah's life challenges us in several ways. She reminds us of the need to be available both to God and to others. She encourages us to spend our efforts on what we can do rather than on worrying about what we can't do. Deborah challenges us to be wise leaders. She demonstrates what a person can accomplish when God is in control.

Strengths and accomplishments:	• Fourth and only female judge of Israel • Special abilities as a mediator, adviser, and counselor • When called on to lead, was able to plan, direct, and delegate • Known for her prophetic power • A writer of songs
Lessons from her life:	• God chooses leaders by his standards, not ours • Wise leaders choose good helpers
Vital statistics:	• Where: Canaan • Occupations: Prophetess and judge • Relative: Husband: Lappidoth • Contemporaries: Barak, Jael, Jabin of Hazor, Sisera
Key verse:	"Deborah, a prophetess, the wife of Lappidoth, was leading Israel at that time" (Judges 4:4).

Her story is told in Judges 4; 5.

Keep God at the center of your life, and you will have the power you need to fight these destroyers.

5:15-17 Four tribes—Reuben, Gilead (either Gad or Manasseh), Dan, and Asher—were accused of not lending a helping hand in the battle. No reasons are given for their refusal to help their fellow Israelites, but they may be the same ones that stopped them from driving out the Canaanites in the first place: (1) lack of reliance on God for help, (2) lack of effort, (3) fear of the enemy, and (4) fear of antagonizing those with whom they did business and thus from whom they prospered. This disobedience showed both a lack of commitment to God's plan and a weak faith in God's power.

17 Gilead stayed beyond the Jordan.
 And Dan, why did he linger by the ships?
 Asher remained on the coast[b]
 and stayed in his coves.
18 The people of Zebulun risked their very lives;
 so did Naphtali on the heights of the field.[c]

19 "Kings came, they fought;
 the kings of Canaan fought
 at Taanach by the waters of Megiddo,[d]
 but they carried off no silver, no plunder.
20 From the heavens[e] the stars fought,
 from their courses they fought against Sisera.
21 The river Kishon[f] swept them away,
 the age-old river, the river Kishon.
 March on, my soul; be strong!
22 Then thundered the horses' hoofs—
 galloping, galloping go his mighty steeds.
23 'Curse Meroz,' said the angel of the LORD.
 'Curse its people bitterly,
 because they did not come to help the LORD,
 to help the LORD against the mighty.'

24 "Most blessed of women be Jael,[g]
 the wife of Heber the Kenite,
 most blessed of tent-dwelling women.
25 He asked for water, and she gave him milk;[h]
 in a bowl fit for nobles she brought him curdled milk.
26 Her hand reached for the tent peg,
 her right hand for the workman's hammer.
 She struck Sisera, she crushed his head,
 she shattered and pierced his temple.
27 At her feet he sank,
 he fell; there he lay.
 At her feet he sank, he fell;
 where he sank, there he fell—dead.

28 "Through the window peered Sisera's mother;
 behind the lattice she cried out,
 'Why is his chariot so long in coming?
 Why is the clatter of his chariots delayed?'
29 The wisest of her ladies answer her;
 indeed, she keeps saying to herself,
30 'Are they not finding and dividing the spoils:[i]
 a girl or two for each man,
 colorful garments as plunder for Sisera,
 colorful garments embroidered,
 highly embroidered garments for my neck—
 all this as plunder?'

31 "So may all your enemies perish, O LORD!
 But may they who love you be like the sun[j]
 when it rises in its strength."

Then the land had peace forty years.

4. Fourth period: Gideon, Tola, and Jair
Gideon

6 Again the Israelites did evil in the eyes of the LORD,[k] and for seven years he gave them into the hands of the Midianites. 2 Because the power of Midian was so oppressive,[l] the Israelites prepared shelters for themselves in mountain clefts, caves and strongholds. [m]

5:17
[b] Jos 19:29

5:18
[c] Jdg 4:6,10

5:19
[d] Jdg 1:27

5:20
[e] Jos 10:11

5:21
[f] Jdg 4:7

5:24
[g] Jdg 4:17

5:25
[h] Jdg 4:19

5:30
[i] Ex 15:9

5:31
[j] Ps 19:4

6:1
[k] Jdg 2:11

6:2
[l] 1Sa 13:6
[m] Heb 11:38

6:4
ⁿLev 26:16;
Dt 28:30,51
6:5
ᵒJdg 7:12

³Whenever the Israelites planted their crops, the Midianites, Amalekites and other eastern peoples invaded the country. ⁴They camped on the land and ruined the cropsⁿ all the way to Gaza and did not spare a living thing for Israel, neither sheep nor cattle nor donkeys. ⁵They came up with their livestock and their tents like swarms of locusts. ᵒ It was impossible to count the men and their camels; they invaded the land to ravage it. ⁶Midian so impoverished the Israelites that they cried out to the LORD for help.

6:8
ᵖJdg 2:1
6:9
ᑫPs 44:2
6:10
ʳJer 10:2

⁷When the Israelites cried to the LORD because of Midian, ⁸he sent them a prophet, who said, "This is what the LORD, the God of Israel, says: I brought you up out of Egypt,ᵖ out of the land of slavery. ⁹I snatched you from the power of Egypt and from the hand of all your oppressors. I drove them from before you and gave you their land. ᑫ ¹⁰I said to you, 'I am the LORD your God; do not worship the gods of the Amorites,ʳ in whose land you live.' But you have not listened to me."

6:11
ˢJos 17:2
ᵗHeb 11:32
6:12
ᵘJos 1:5

¹¹The angel of the LORD came and sat down under the oak in Ophrah that belonged to Joash the Abiezrite,ˢ where his son Gideonᵗ was threshing wheat in a winepress to keep it from the Midianites. ¹²When the angel of the LORD appeared to Gideon, he said, "The LORD is with you,ᵘ mighty warrior."

6:13
ᵛPs 44:1

¹³"But sir," Gideon replied, "if the LORD is with us, why has all this happened to us? Where are all his wonders that our fathers toldᵛ us about when they said, 'Did not the LORD bring us up out of Egypt?' But now the LORD has abandoned us and put us into the hand of Midian."

6:14
ʷHeb 11:34

¹⁴The LORD turned to him and said, "Go in the strength you haveʷ and save Israel out of Midian's hand. Am I not sending you?"

6:15
ˣ1Sa 9:21

¹⁵"But Lord,ᵃ" Gideon asked, "how can I save Israel? My clan is the weakest in Manasseh, and I am the least in my family.ˣ"

6:16
ʸEx 3:12; Jos 1:5

¹⁶The LORD answered, "I will be with you,ʸ and you will strike down all the Midianites together."

6:17
ᶻver 36-37

¹⁷Gideon replied, "If now I have found favor in your eyes, give me a signᶻ that it is really you talking to me. ¹⁸Please do not go away until I come back and bring my offering and set it before you."

And the LORD said, "I will wait until you return."

6:19
ᵃGe 18:7-8

¹⁹Gideon went in, prepared a young goat, and from an ephahᵇ of flour he made bread without yeast. Putting the meat in a basket and its broth in a pot, he brought them out and offered them to him under the oak. ᵃ

ᵃ*15* Or *sir*　ᵇ*19* That is, probably about 3/5 bushel (about 22 liters)

6:2 The Midianites were desert people descended from Abraham's second wife, Keturah (Genesis 25:1, 2). From this relationship came a nation that was always in conflict with Israel. Years earlier the Israelites, while still wandering in the desert, battled the Midianites and almost totally destroyed them (Numbers 31:1–20). Because of their failure to completely destroy them, however, the tribe repopulated. Here they were once again oppressing Israel.

6:6 Again the Israelites hit rock bottom before turning back to God. How much suffering they could have avoided if they had trusted him! Turning to God shouldn't be a last resort; we should look to him for help each day. This isn't to say life will always be easy. There will be struggles, but God will give us the strength to live through them. Don't wait until you're at the end of your rope. Call on God first in every situation.

6:11 The Old Testament records several appearances of the angel of the Lord: Genesis 16:7; 22:11; 31:11; Exodus 3:2; 14:19; Judges 2:1; 13:3; Zechariah 3:1–6. It is not known whether the same angel appeared in each case. The angel mentioned here appears to be separate from God in one place (6:12) and yet the same as God in another place (6:14). This has led some to believe that the angel was a special appearance of Jesus Christ prior to his mission on earth as recorded in the New Testament. It is also possible that as a special messenger from God, the angel had authority to speak for God. In either case, God sent a special messenger to deliver an important message to Gideon.

6:11 Threshing was the process of separating the grains of wheat from the useless outer shell called chaff. This was normally done in a large area, often on a hill, where the wind could blow away the lighter chaff when the farmer tossed the beaten wheat

into the air. If Gideon had done this, however, he would have been an easy target for the bands of raiders who were overrunning the land. Therefore, he was forced to thresh his wheat in a winepress, a pit that was probably hidden from view and that would not be suspected as a place to find a farmer's crops.

6:13 Gideon questioned God about the problems he and his nation faced and about God's apparent lack of help. What he didn't acknowledge was the fact that the people had brought calamity upon themselves when they decided to disobey and neglect God. How easy it is to overlook personal accountability and blame our problems on God and others. Unfortunately this does not solve our problems. It brings us no closer to God, and it escorts us to the very edge of rebellion and backsliding.

When problems come, the first place to look is within. Our immediate response should be confession to God of sins that may have created our problems.

6:14–16 "I will be with you," God told Gideon, and God promised to give him the strength he needed to overcome the opposition. In spite of this clear promise for strength, Gideon made excuses. Seeing only his limitations and weaknesses, he failed to see how God could work through him.

Like Gideon, we are called to serve God in specific ways. Although God promises us the tools and strength we need, we often make excuses. But reminding God of our limitations only implies that he does not know all about us or that he has made a mistake in evaluating our character. Don't spend time making excuses. Instead spend it doing what God wants.

20The angel of God said to him, "Take the meat and the unleavened bread, place them on this rock,*b* and pour out the broth." And Gideon did so. 21With the tip of the staff that was in his hand, the angel of the LORD touched the meat and the unleavened bread. *c* Fire flared from the rock, consuming the meat and the bread. And the angel of the LORD disappeared. 22When Gideon realized *d* that it was the angel of the LORD, he exclaimed, "Ah, Sovereign LORD! I have seen the angel of the LORD face to face!"*e*

23But the LORD said to him, "Peace! Do not be afraid. You are not going to die."

24So Gideon built an altar to the LORD there and called it The LORD is Peace. To this day it stands in Ophrah of the Abiezrites.

25That same night the LORD said to him, "Take the second bull from your father's herd, the one seven years old. *a* Tear down your father's altar to Baal and cut down the Asherah pole*b f* beside it. 26Then build a proper kind of*c* altar to the LORD your God on the top of this height. Using the wood of the Asherah pole that you cut down, offer the second *d* bull as a burnt offering."

27So Gideon took ten of his servants and did as the LORD told him. But because he was afraid of his family and the men of the town, he did it at night rather than in the daytime.

28In the morning when the men of the town got up, there was Baal's altar, demolished, with the Asherah pole beside it cut down and the second bull sacrificed on the newly built altar!

29They asked each other, "Who did this?"

When they carefully investigated, they were told, "Gideon son of Joash did it."

30The men of the town demanded of Joash, "Bring out your son. He must die, because he has broken down Baal's altar and cut down the Asherah pole beside it."

31But Joash replied to the hostile crowd around him, "Are you going to plead Baal's cause? Are you trying to save him? Whoever fights for him shall be put to death by morning! If Baal really is a god, he can defend himself when someone breaks down his altar." 32So that day they called Gideon "Jerub-Baal,*e g*" saying, "Let Baal contend with him," because he broke down Baal's altar.

33Now all the Midianites, Amalekites and other eastern peoples joined forces and crossed over the Jordan and camped in the Valley of Jezreel. *h* 34Then the Spirit of the LORD came upon*i* Gideon, and he blew a trumpet,*j* summoning the Abiezrites to follow him. 35He sent messengers throughout Manasseh, calling them to arms, and also into Asher, Zebulun and Naphtali, so that they too went up to meet them.

36Gideon said to God, "If you will save Israel by my hand as you have promised— 37look, I will place a wool fleece on the threshing floor. If there is dew only on the fleece and all the ground is dry, then I will know*k* that you will save Israel by my hand, as you said." 38And that is what happened. Gideon rose early the next day; he squeezed the fleece and wrung out the dew—a bowlful of water.

6:20
b Jdg 13:19
6:21
c Lev 9:24
6:22
d Jdg 13:16,21
e Jdg 13:22
6:25
f Ex 34:13
6:32
g Jdg 7:1;
1Sa 12:11
6:33
h Jos 17:16
6:34
i Jdg 3:10
j Jdg 3:27
6:37
k Ge 24:14

a25 Or Take a full-grown, mature bull from your father's herd   b25 That is, a symbol of the goddess Asherah; here and elsewhere in Judges   c26 Or build with layers of stone an   d26 Or full-grown; also in verse 28   e32 Jerub-Baal means let Baal contend.

6:22, 23 Why was Gideon afraid of seeing an angel? The Israelites believed that no one could see God and live (see God's words to Moses in Exodus 33:20). Evidently Gideon thought this also applied to angels.

6:25–30 After God called Gideon to be Israel's deliverer, he immediately asked him to tear down the altar of the pagan god, Baal—an act that would test Gideon's faith and commitment. Canaanite religion was very political, so an attack on a god was often seen as an attack on the local government supporting that god. If caught, Gideon would face serious social problems and probable physical attack. (For more on Baal and Asherah, see the notes on 2:11–15 and 3:7.)

Gideon took a great risk by following God's higher law, which specifically forbids idol worship (Exodus 20:1–5). After learning what Gideon had done, the townspeople wanted to kill him. Many of those people were fellow Israelites. This shows how immoral God's people had become. God said in Deuteronomy 13:6–11 that idolaters must be stoned to death, but these Israelites wanted to stone Gideon for tearing down an idol and worshiping God! When you begin to accomplish something for God, you may be criticized by the very people who should support you.

6:33 The armies of Midian and Amalek camped in the Valley of Jezreel, the agricultural center for the area. Whoever controlled the valley's rich and fertile land controlled the people who lived in and around it. Because of the valley's vast resources, many major trade routes converged at the pass which led into it. This made it the site of many great battles. Gideon's men attacked the enemy armies from the hills, and the only escape route was through the pass toward the Jordan River. That is why Gideon urged some of his troops to take control of the river's crossing points (7:24).

6:37–39 Was Gideon testing God, or was he simply asking God for more encouragement? In either case, though his motive was right (to obey God and defeat the enemy), his method was less than ideal. Gideon seems to have known that his requests might displease God (6:39), and yet he demanded two miracles (6:37, 39) even after witnessing the miraculous fire from the rock (6:21). It is true that to make good decisions, we need facts. Gideon had all the facts, but still he hesitated. He delayed obeying God because he wanted even more proof.

Demanding extra signs was an indication of unbelief. Fear often makes us wait for more confirmation when we should be taking action. Visible signs are unnecessary if they only confirm what we already know is true.

Today the greatest means of God's guidance is his Word, the

6:39
l Ge 18:32

39 Then Gideon said to God, "Do not be angry with me. Let me make just one more request. *l* Allow me one more test with the fleece. This time make the fleece dry and the ground covered with dew." 40 That night God did so. Only the fleece was dry; all the ground was covered with dew.

Gideon Defeats the Midianites

7:1
m Jdg 6:32

7:2
n Dt 8:17

7:3
o Dt 20:8

7:4
p 1Sa 14:6

7 Early in the morning, Jerub-Baal *m* (that is, Gideon) and all his men camped at the spring of Harod. The camp of Midian was north of them in the valley near the hill of Moreh. 2 The LORD said to Gideon, "You have too many men for me to deliver Midian into their hands. In order that Israel may not boast against me that her own strength *n* has saved her, 3 announce now to the people, 'Anyone who trembles with fear may turn back and leave Mount Gilead. *o* '" So twenty-two thousand men left, while ten thousand remained.

4 But the LORD said to Gideon, "There are still too many *p* men. Take them down to the water, and I will sift them for you there. If I say, 'This one shall go with you,' he shall go; but if I say, 'This one shall not go with you,' he shall not go."

5 So Gideon took the men down to the water. There the LORD told him, "Separate those who lap the water with their tongues like a dog from those who kneel down to drink." 6 Three hundred men lapped with their hands to their mouths. All the rest got down on their knees to drink.

7:7
q 1Sa 14:6

7 The LORD said to Gideon, "With the three hundred men that lapped I will save you and give the Midianites into your hands. Let all the other men go, each to his own place." *q* 8 So Gideon sent the rest of the Israelites to their tents but kept the three hundred, who took over the provisions and trumpets of the others.

GOD USES COMMON PEOPLE	Person	Known as	Task	Reference
God uses all sorts of people to do his work— like you and me!	JACOB	A deceiver	To "father" the Israelite nation	Genesis 27—28
	JOSEPH	A slave	To save his family	Genesis 39ff
	MOSES	Shepherd in exile (and murderer)	To lead Israel out of bondage, to the promised land	Exodus 3
	GIDEON	A farmer	To deliver Israel from Midian	Judges 6:11–14
	JEPHTHAH	Son of a prostitute	To deliver Israel from the Ammonites	Judges 11
	HANNAH	A homemaker	To be the mother of Samuel	1 Samuel 1
	DAVID	A shepherd boy and last-born of the family	To be Israel's greatest king	1 Samuel 16
	EZRA	A scribe	To lead the return to Judah and to write some of the Bible	Ezra; Nehemiah
	ESTHER	A slave girl	To save her people from massacre	Esther
	MARY	A peasant girl	To be the mother of Christ	Luke 1:27–38
	MATTHEW	A tax collector	To be an apostle and Gospel writer	Matthew 9:9
	LUKE	A Greek physician	To be a companion of Paul and a Gospel writer	Colossians 4:14
	PETER	A fisherman	To be an apostle, a leader of the early church, and a writer of two New Testament letters	Matthew 4:18–20

Bible. Unlike Gideon, we have God's complete, revealed Word. If you want to have more of God's guidance, don't ask for signs; study the Bible (2 Timothy 3:16, 17).

6:39 After seeing the miracle of the wet fleece, why did Gideon ask for another miracle? Perhaps he thought the results of the first test could have happened naturally. A thick fleece could retain moisture long after the sun had dried the surrounding ground. "Putting out fleeces" is a poor decision-making method. Those who do this put limitations on God. They ask him to fit their expectations. The results of such experiments are usually inconclusive and thus fail to make us any more confident about our choices. Don't let a "fleece" become a substitute for God's wisdom that comes through Bible study and prayer.

7:2 Self-sufficiency is a handicap when it causes us to believe we can do what needs to be done in our own strength. To prevent this attitude among Gideon's soldiers, God reduced their number from 32,000 to 300. With an army this vastly outnumbered, there could be no doubt that victory was from God. The men could not take the credit. Like Gideon, we must recognize the danger of fighting in our own strength. We can be confident of victory against life's challenges and temptations only if we put our confidence in God and not ourselves.

Now the camp of Midian lay below him in the valley. [9]During that night the Lord said to Gideon, "Get up, go down against the camp, because I am going to give it into your hands. [10]If you are afraid to attack, go down to the camp with your servant Purah [11]and listen to what they are saying. Afterward, you will be encouraged to attack the camp." So he and Purah his servant went down to the outposts of the camp. [12]The Midianites, the Amalekites and all the other eastern peoples had settled in the valley, thick as locusts. Their camels could no more be counted than the sand on the seashore.

[13]Gideon arrived just as a man was telling a friend his dream. "I had a dream," he was saying. "A round loaf of barley bread came tumbling into the Midianite camp. It struck the tent with such force that the tent overturned and collapsed."

[14]His friend responded, "This can be nothing other than the sword of Gideon son of Joash, the Israelite. God has given the Midianites and the whole camp into his hands."

[15]When Gideon heard the dream and its interpretation, he worshiped God. He returned to the camp of Israel and called out, "Get up! The Lord has given the Midianite camp into your hands." [16]Dividing the three hundred men into three companies, he placed trumpets and empty jars in the hands of all of them, with torches inside.

[17]"Watch me," he told them. "Follow my lead. When I get to the edge of the camp, do exactly as I do. [18]When I and all who are with me blow our trumpets, then from all around the camp blow yours and shout, 'For the Lord and for Gideon.'"

[19]Gideon and the hundred men with him reached the edge of the camp at the beginning of the middle watch, just after they had changed the guard. They blew their trumpets and broke the jars that were in their hands. [20]The three companies blew the trumpets and smashed the jars. Grasping the torches in their left hands and holding in their right hands the trumpets they were to blow, they shouted, "A sword for the Lord and for Gideon!" [21]While each man held his position around the camp, all the Midianites ran, crying out as they fled.

[22]When the three hundred trumpets sounded, the Lord caused the men throughout the camp to turn on each other with their swords. The army fled to Beth Shittah toward Zererah as far as the border of Abel Meholah near Tabbath. [23]Israelites from Naphtali, Asher and all Manasseh were called out, and they pursued the Midianites. [24]Gideon sent messengers throughout the hill country of Ephraim, saying, "Come down against the Midianites and seize the waters of the Jordan ahead of them as far as Beth Barah."

So all the men of Ephraim were called out and they took the waters of the Jordan as far as Beth Barah. [25]They also captured two of the Midianite leaders, Oreb and Zeeb. They killed Oreb at the rock of Oreb, and Zeeb at the winepress of Zeeb. They pursued the Midianites and brought the heads of Oreb and Zeeb to Gideon, who was by the Jordan.

7:9
r Jos 2:24

7:12
s Jdg 8:10
t Jdg 6:5
u Jos 11:4

7:21
v 2Ki 7:7

7:22
w 1Sa 14:20

7:23
x Jdg 6:35

7:24
y Jdg 3:28

7:25
z Jdg 8:3; Ps 83:11
a Isa 10:26
b Jdg 8:4

7:10, 11 Facing overwhelming odds, Gideon was afraid. God understood his fear, but he didn't excuse Gideon from his task. Instead he allowed Gideon to slip into the enemy camp and overhear a conversation that would give him courage (7:12–15). Are you facing a battle with internal or external foes that have defeated you in the past or appear invincible today? God can give you the strength you need for any situation. And don't be startled by the way he helps you. Like Gideon, you must listen to God and be ready to take the first step. Only after you begin to obey God will you find the courage to move ahead.

GIDEON'S BATTLE

In spite of Deborah and Barak's victory, the Canaanites still caused trouble in this fertile region. God appeared to Gideon at Ophrah and called him to defeat them. With only 300 fighting men, Gideon routed thousands of Midianites, chasing them to Zererah and Abel Meholah.

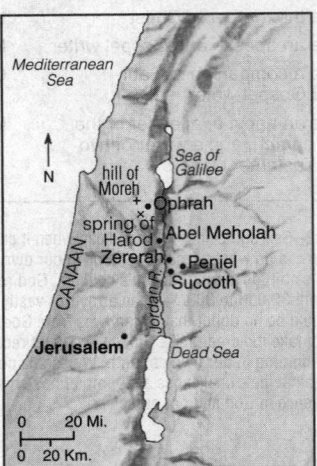

7:12 Midianites were camel-riding marauders composed of five families linked to Abraham through Midian, the son of Abraham's second wife, Keturah. They inhabited the desert regions from the Dead Sea to the Red Sea.

7:13 An enemy soldier dreamed of a loaf of barley bread tumbling into camp. Barley grain was only half the value of wheat, and the bread made from it was considered inferior. In the same way, Israel's tiny band of men was considered inferior to the vast forces of Midian and Amalek. But God would make the underdog Israelites seem invincible.

7:19 The night was divided equally into three watches. The beginning of the middle watch would have been around 10:00 p.m. Many in the camp would have still been awake.

7:21 Gideon's warriors simply watched as the army of Midian fell into panic, confusion, and disordered retreat. Not one man had to draw a sword to defeat the enemy. Gideon's small army could never have brought about such a victory in its own strength. God wanted to demonstrate to Israel that victory depends not on strength or numbers, but on obedience and commitment to him.

Zebah and Zalmunna

8:1
c Jdg 12:1

8 Now the Ephraimites asked Gideon, "Why have you treated us like this? Why didn't you call us when you went to fight Midian?" c And they criticized him sharply. 2 But he answered them, "What have I accomplished compared to you? Aren't the gleanings of Ephraim's grapes better than the full grape harvest of Abiezer? 3 God gave Oreb and

GIDEON

Most of us want to know God's plan for our lives, but we're not always sure how to find it. One common misunderstanding is the idea that God's guidance will come to us out of the blue, that it has nothing to do with what we're doing now. But if we're always looking around for God's next assignment, we run the risk of ruining whatever we're working on right now. Fortunately, the Bible points to a kind of guidance that does not put our current projects in jeopardy. In the Bible's descriptions of how God guided many people, we can see that often God's call came while people were completely immersed in the challenge of the moment. A good example of this kind of guidance is seen in Gideon's life.

Gideon had a limited vision, but he was committed to it. His challenge was to obtain food for his family even though hostile invaders were making the growing, gathering, and preparation of the food almost impossible. Gideon was resourceful. He put a winepress to double duty by turning it into a sunken threshing floor. It lacked ventilation to blow the chaff away, but at least it was hidden from the Midianites. Gideon was working in his threshing floor when God sent him a messenger with a challenge.

Gideon was surprised by what God told him to do. He did not want to jump into a task for which he was ill prepared. The angel had to overcome three objections before Gideon was convinced: (1) Gideon's feelings of responsibility for his family's welfare, (2) his doubts about the call itself, and (3) his feelings of inadequacy for the job. Once Gideon was convinced, however, he obeyed with zest, resourcefulness, and speed. He dedicated those personality traits to God, with whom he was now personally acquainted.

Gideon had his weak moments and failures, but he was still God's servant. If you can easily see yourself in Gideon's weakness, can you also see yourself in being willing to serve? Remember Gideon as a man who obeyed God by giving his attention to the task at hand. Then give your full attention to believing God will prepare you for tomorrow when it comes.

Strengths and accomplishments:	• Israel's fifth judge. A military strategist who was expert at surprise • A member of the Hall of Faith in Hebrews 11 • Defeated the Midianite army • Was offered a hereditary kingship by the men of Israel • Though slow to be convinced, acted on his convictions
Weaknesses and mistakes:	• Feared that his own limitations would prevent God from working • Collected Midianite gold and made a symbol that became an evil object of worship • Through a concubine, fathered a son who would bring great grief and tragedy to both Gideon's family and the nation of Israel • Failed to establish the nation in God's ways; after he died they all went back to idol worship
Lessons from his life:	• God calls in the middle of our present obedience. As we are faithful, he gives us more responsibility • God expands and uses the abilities he has already built into us • God uses us in spite of our limitations and failures • Even those who make great spiritual progress can easily fall into sin if they don't consistently follow God
Vital statistics:	• Where: Ophrah, Valley of Jezreel, spring of Harod • Occupations: Farmer, warrior, and judge • Relatives: Father: Joash. Son: Abimelech. • Contemporaries: Zebah, Zalmunna
Key verses:	"'But Lord,' Gideon asked, 'how can I save Israel? My clan is the weakest in Manasseh, and I am the least in my family.' The LORD answered, 'I will be with you, and you will strike down all the Midianites together'" (Judges 6:15, 16).

His story is told in Judges 6—8. He is also mentioned in Hebrews 11:32.

8:1–3 Ephraim's leaders felt left out because Gideon had not called them to join the battle, but had left them in place to "clean up" the escaping Midianites ("the gleanings"), and so they angrily confronted him. Gideon assured the leaders of Ephraim that their accomplishment was even greater than his own clan's (Abiezer). His diplomatic explanation pointed out that this rear guard had managed to capture the enemy's generals, thus cutting off the leaders from their army. Not every necessary job is a highly visible leadership role. Much of the necessary labor of any effective enterprise is considered by many to be dirty work. But such work is vital to getting any big task done. Engineers and millionaires may design and finance an elegant building, but it is the bricklayers who get the work done. Pride causes us to want recognition. Are you content to be God's bricklayer, or do you resent the work God has given you?

Zeeb,*d* the Midianite leaders, into your hands. What was I able to do compared to you?" At this, their resentment against him subsided. **8:3**
d Jdg 7:25

⁴Gideon and his three hundred men, exhausted yet keeping up the pursuit, came to the Jordan and crossed it. ⁵He said to the men of Succoth,*e* "Give my troops some bread; they are worn out, and I am still pursuing Zebah and Zalmunna, the kings of Midian." **8:5**
e Ge 33:17

⁶But the officials of Succoth said, "Do you already have the hands of Zebah and Zalmunna in your possession? Why should we give bread to your troops?"*f* **8:6**
f ver 15

⁷Then Gideon replied, "Just for that, when the LORD has given Zebah and Zalmunna*g* into my hand, I will tear your flesh with desert thorns and briers." **8:7**
g Jdg 7:15

⁸From there he went up to Peniel*a h* and made the same request of them, but they answered as the men of Succoth had. ⁹So he said to the men of Peniel, "When I return in triumph, I will tear down this tower." **8:8**
h Ge 32:30

¹⁰Now Zebah and Zalmunna were in Karkor with a force of about fifteen thousand men, all that were left of the armies of the eastern peoples; a hundred and twenty thousand swordsmen had fallen.*i* ¹¹Gideon went up by the route of the nomads east of Nobah and Jogbehah and fell upon the unsuspecting army. ¹²Zebah and Zalmunna, the two kings of Midian, fled, but he pursued them and captured them, routing their entire army. **8:10**
i Jdg 7:12

¹³Gideon son of Joash then returned from the battle by the Pass of Heres. ¹⁴He caught a young man of Succoth and questioned him, and the young man wrote down for him the names of the seventy-seven officials of Succoth, the elders of the town. ¹⁵Then Gideon came and said to the men of Succoth, "Here are Zebah and Zalmunna, about whom you taunted me by saying, 'Do you already have the hands of Zebah and Zalmunna in your possession? Why should we give bread to your exhausted men?'" ¹⁶He took the elders of the town and taught the men of Succoth a lesson by punishing them with desert thorns and briers. ¹⁷He also pulled down the tower of Peniel and killed the men of the town.*k* **8:15**
j ver 6

8:17
k ver 9

¹⁸Then he asked Zebah and Zalmunna, "What kind of men did you kill at Tabor?*l*" **8:18**
l Jdg 4:6

"Men like you," they answered, "each one with the bearing of a prince."

¹⁹Gideon replied, "Those were my brothers, the sons of my own mother. As surely as the LORD lives, if you had spared their lives, I would not kill you." ²⁰Turning to Jether, his oldest son, he said, "Kill them!" But Jether did not draw his sword, because he was only a boy and was afraid.

²¹Zebah and Zalmunna said, "Come, do it yourself. 'As is the man, so is his strength.'" So Gideon stepped forward and killed them, and took the ornaments*m* off their camels' necks. **8:21**
m ver 26; Ps 83:11

Gideon's Ephod

²²The Israelites said to Gideon, "Rule over us—you, your son and your grandson—because you have saved us out of the hand of Midian."

²³But Gideon told them, "I will not rule over you, nor will my son rule over you. The LORD will rule*n* over you." ²⁴And he said, "I do have one request, that each of you give me an earring from your share of the plunder." (It was the custom of the Ishmaelites*o* to wear gold earrings.) **8:23**
n 1Sa 8:7; 10:19; 12:12

8:24
o Ge 25:13

a 8 Hebrew *Penuel,* a variant of *Peniel;* also in verses 9 and 17

8:5, 9 The leaders of Succoth and Peniel refused to help Gideon, probably fearing Midian's revenge should he fail (Gideon's army was 300 men chasing 15,000). They should have realized that victory was certain because God was with Gideon. But they were so worried about saving themselves that they never thought about God's power to save.

Because of fear for ourselves, we may not recognize God's presence in other people and therefore miss God's victory. Then we must face the often bitter consequences of failing to join forces with those God has chosen to do his work. Because God will prevail with or without you, be quick to join others who are engaged in his work. Lend support with your time, money, talents, and prayer.

8:11 The Midianites were escaping into the desert area, where the tent-dwelling nomads lived. They didn't expect Gideon to follow them that far.

8:15–17 Gideon carried out the threat he had made in 8:7. It is difficult to determine whether this act of revenge was justified or whether he should have left the punishment up to God. Gideon was God's appointed leader, but the officials of Succoth and Peniel refused to help him in any way because they feared the enemy. They showed neither faith nor respect for God nor the man God had chosen to save them. We should help others because it is right, regardless of whether we will benefit personally.

8:20, 21 For a king to be killed by a boy was humiliating because it would look as though he was no match for a boy ("As is the man, so is his strength"). The two men wanted to avoid that disgrace, as well as the slower and more painful death which an inexperienced swordsman might inflict.

8:23 The people wanted to make Gideon their king, but Gideon stressed that the Lord was to rule over them. Despite his inconsistencies, Gideon never lost sight of the importance, for both a nation and an individual, of putting God first. Is God first in your life? If he is, he must affect every dimension of your life, not just what you do in church.

25 They answered, "We'll be glad to give them." So they spread out a garment, and each man threw a ring from his plunder onto it. 26 The weight of the gold rings he asked for came to seventeen hundred shekels,ᵃ not counting the ornaments, the pendants and the purple garments worn by the kings of Midian or the chains that were on their camels' necks. 27 Gideon made the gold into an ephod,ᵖ which he placed in Ophrah, his town. All Israel prostituted themselves by worshiping it there, and it became a snareᑫ to Gideon and his family.

Gideon's Death

28 Thus Midian was subdued before the Israelites and did not raise its head again. During Gideon's lifetime, the land enjoyed peace forty years.

29 Jerub-Baal son of Joash went back home to live. 30 He had seventy sonsʳ of his own, for he had many wives. 31 His concubine, who lived in Shechem, also bore him a son, whom he named Abimelech.ˢ 32 Gideon son of Joash died at a good old age and was buried in the tomb of his father Joash in Ophrah of the Abiezrites.

33 No sooner had Gideon died than the Israelites again prostituted themselves to the Baals.ᵗ They set up Baal-Berithᵘ as their godᵛ and 34 did not remember the Lᴏʀᴅ their God, who had rescued them from the hands of all their enemies on every side. 35 They also failed to show kindness to the family of Jerub-Baal (that is, Gideon) for all the good things he had done for them.

Abimelech

9 Abimelechʷ son of Jerub-Baal went to his mother's brothers in Shechem and said to them and to all his mother's clan, 2 "Ask all the citizens of Shechem, 'Which is better for you: to have all seventy of Jerub-Baal's sons rule over you, or just one man?' Remember, I am your flesh and blood.ˣ"

3 When the brothers repeated all this to the citizens of Shechem, they were inclined to

ᵃ26 That is, about 43 pounds (about 19.5 kilograms)

**Cross references (left margin):**
8:27
ᵖ Jdg 17:5
ᑫ Dt 7:16; Ps 106:39

8:30
ʳ Jdg 9:2,5,18,24

8:31
ˢ Jdg 9:1

8:33
ᵗ Jdg 2:11,13,19
ᵘ Jdg 9:4
ᵛ Jdg 9:27,46

9:1
ʷ Jdg 8:31

9:2
ˣ Ge 29:14

8:26, 27 Those who were very wealthy put ornaments on their camels as a way of displaying their riches. Women wore vast amounts of jewelry as well, often up to 15 pairs of earrings. Jewelry was also worn for good luck. After Gideon's rise to power, he seems to have become carried away with this accumulation of wealth. Eventually it led the Israelites to idolatry.

8:27 An ephod was a linen garment worn by priests over their chests. It was considered holy (Exodus 28:5–35; 39:2–24; Leviticus 8:7, 8). Gideon probably had good motives for making the ephod (a visible remembrance commemorating the victory). Unfortunately, the people began to worship the ephod as an idol. Sadly, many decisions that stem from good motives produce negative results. Perhaps no one stops to ask, "What might go wrong?" or "Is there a possibility of negative consequences?" In your plans and decisions, take time to anticipate how a good idea might lead to a potential problem.

8:31 This relationship between Gideon and a concubine produced a son who tore apart Gideon's family and caused tragedy for the nation. Gideon's story illustrates the fact that heroes in battle are not always heroes in daily life. Gideon led the nation but could not lead his family. No matter who you are, moral laxness will cause problems. Just because you have won a single battle with temptation does not mean you will automatically win the next one. We need to be constantly watchful against temptation. Sometimes Satan's strongest attacks come after a victory.

8:33 Baal-Berith means "Baal [lord] of the covenant." Worship of the idol may have combined elements of both the Israelite and Canaanite religions.

9:1–3 With Gideon dead, Abimelech wanted to take his father's place. (Jerub-Baal is another name for Gideon; see 6:32.) To set his plan in motion he went to the city of Shechem, his mother's hometown, to drum up support. Here he felt kinship with the residents. These relatives were Canaanites and would be glad to unite against Israel. Shechem was an important city, a crossroads for trade routes and a natural link between the coastal plain and the Jordan Valley. Whoever controlled Shechem would dominate the countryside.

9:2–5 Israel's king was to be the Lord and not a man. But Abimelech wanted to usurp the position reserved for God alone. In his selfish quest, he killed all but one of his 70 half brothers. People with selfish desires often seek to fulfill them in ruthless ways. Examine your ambitions to see if they are self-centered or God-centered. Be sure you always fulfill your desires in ways that God would approve.

ABIMELECH'S FALL
Gideon's illegitimate son killed 69 of his half brothers in Ophrah and returned to Shechem to be acclaimed king. But three years later, Shechem rebelled. From Arumah, Abimelech attacked Shechem, Beth Millo ("the tower at Shechem"), and Thebez, where he was killed.

Mediterranean Sea
Sea of Galilee
Ophrah
Thebez
Shechem
Mount Gerizim
Arumah
Jerusalem
Jordan River
Dead Sea
CANAAN
N
0   20 Mi.
0   20 Km.

follow Abimelech, for they said, "He is our brother." [4] They gave him seventy shekels[a] of silver from the temple of Baal-Berith,[y] and Abimelech used it to hire reckless adventurers, who became his followers. [5] He went to his father's home in Ophrah and on one stone murdered his seventy brothers, the sons of Jerub-Baal. But Jotham, the youngest son of Jerub-Baal, escaped by hiding.[z] [6] Then all the citizens of Shechem and Beth Millo gathered beside the great tree at the pillar in Shechem to crown Abimelech king.

[7] When Jotham was told about this, he climbed up on the top of Mount Gerizim[a] and shouted to them, "Listen to me, citizens of Shechem, so that God may listen to you. [8] One day the trees went out to anoint a king for themselves. They said to the olive tree, 'Be our king.'

[9] "But the olive tree answered, 'Should I give up my oil, by which both gods and men are honored, to hold sway over the trees?'

[10] "Next, the trees said to the fig tree, 'Come and be our king.'

[11] "But the fig tree replied, 'Should I give up my fruit, so good and sweet, to hold sway over the trees?'

[12] "Then the trees said to the vine, 'Come and be our king.'

[13] "But the vine answered, 'Should I give up my wine, which cheers both gods and men, to hold sway over the trees?'

[14] "Finally all the trees said to the thornbush, 'Come and be our king.'

[15] "The thornbush said to the trees, 'If you really want to anoint me king over you, come and take refuge in my shade;[b] but if not, then let fire come out of the thornbush and consume the cedars of Lebanon!'

[16] "Now if you have acted honorably and in good faith when you made Abimelech king, and if you have been fair to Jerub-Baal and his family, and if you have treated him as he deserves— [17] and to think that my father fought for you, risked his life to rescue you from the hand of Midian [18] (but today you have revolted against my father's family, murdered his seventy sons[c] on a single stone, and made Abimelech, the son of his slave girl, king over the citizens of Shechem because he is your brother)— [19] if then you have acted honorably and in good faith toward Jerub-Baal and his family today, may Abimelech be your joy, and may you be his, too! [20] But if you have not, let fire come out from Abimelech and consume you, citizens of Shechem and Beth Millo, and let fire come out from you, citizens of Shechem and Beth Millo, and consume Abimelech!"

[21] Then Jotham fled, escaping to Beer, and he lived there because he was afraid of his brother Abimelech.

[22] After Abimelech had governed Israel three years, [23] God sent an evil spirit[d] between Abimelech and the citizens of Shechem, who acted treacherously against Abimelech. [24] God did this in order that the crime against Jerub-Baal's seventy sons, the shedding[e] of their blood, might be avenged on their brother Abimelech and on the citizens of Shechem, who had helped him[f] murder his brothers. [25] In opposition to him these citizens of Shechem set men on the hilltops to ambush and rob everyone who passed by, and this was reported to Abimelech.

a4 That is, about 1 3/4 pounds (about 0.8 kilogram)

9:4 y Jdg 8:33
9:5 z 2Ki 11:2
9:7 a Dt 11:29; Jn 4:20
9:15 b Isa 30:2
9:18 c ver 5-6; Jdg 8:30
9:23 d 1Sa 16:14,23; 18:10
9:24 e Nu 35:33 f Dt 27:25

9:4 Politics played a major part in pagan religions such as the worship of Baal-Berith. Governments often went so far as to hire temple prostitutes to bring in additional money. In many cases a religious system was set up and supported by the government so the offerings could fund community projects. Religion became a profit-making business. In Israel's religion, this was strictly forbidden. God's system of religion was designed to come from an attitude of the heart, not from calculated plans and business opportunities. It was also designed to serve people and help those in need, not to oppress the needy. Is your faith genuine and sincere, or is it based on convenience, comfort, and availability?

9:6 Abimelech was declared ruler of Israel at Shechem, the site of other key Bible events. It was one of Abraham's first stops upon arriving in Canaan (Genesis 12:6, 7). When Jacob lived there, two of his sons killed all the men in Shechem because the prince's son raped their sister (Genesis 34). Joseph's bones were buried in Shechem (Joshua 24:32); Israel renewed its covenant with God there (Joshua 24); and the kingdom of Israel would split apart at this same city (1 Kings 12).

9:7-15 In Jotham's parable the trees represented Gideon's 70 sons, and the thornbush represented Abimelech. Jotham's point was this: a productive person would be too busy doing good to want to bother with power politics. A worthless person, on the other hand, would be glad to accept the honor—but he would destroy the people he ruled. Abimelech, like a thornbush, could offer Israel no real protection or security. Jotham's parable came true when Abimelech destroyed the city of Shechem (9:45), burned "the tower of Shechem" (the city of Beth Millo, 9:46-49), and was finally killed at Thebez (9:53, 54).

9:16 Jotham told the story about the trees in order to help the people set good priorities. He did not want them to appoint a leader of low character. As we serve in leadership positions, we should examine our motives. Do we just want praise, prestige, or power? In the parable, the good trees chose to be productive and to provide benefits to people. Make sure these are your priorities as you aspire to leadership.

9:22-24 Abimelech was the opposite of what God wanted in a judge, but it was three years before God moved against him,

9:27
g Jdg 8:33
9:28
h Ge 34:2,6

9:29
i 2Sa 15:4

9:33
j 1Sa 10:7

²⁶Now Gaal son of Ebed moved with his brothers into Shechem, and its citizens put their confidence in him. ²⁷After they had gone out into the fields and gathered the grapes and trodden them, they held a festival in the temple of their god. *g* While they were eating and drinking, they cursed Abimelech. ²⁸Then Gaal son of Ebed said, "Who is Abimelech, and who is Shechem, that we should be subject to him? Isn't he Jerub-Baal's son, and isn't Zebul his deputy? Serve the men of Hamor, *h* Shechem's father! Why should we serve Abimelech? ²⁹If only this people were under my command! *i* Then I would get rid of him. I would say to Abimelech, 'Call out your whole army!'" *a*

³⁰When Zebul the governor of the city heard what Gaal son of Ebed said, he was very angry. ³¹Under cover he sent messengers to Abimelech, saying, "Gaal son of Ebed and his brothers have come to Shechem and are stirring up the city against you. ³²Now then, during the night you and your men should come and lie in wait in the fields. ³³In the morning at sunrise, advance against the city. When Gaal and his men come out against you, do whatever your hand finds to do. *j*"

a 29 Septuagint; Hebrew him." Then he said to Abimelech, "Call out your whole army!"

ABIMELECH

People who desire power always outnumber those who are able to use power wisely once they have it. Perhaps this is because power has a way of taking over and controlling the person using it. This is especially true in cases of inherited but unmerited power. Abimelech's life shows us what happens when hunger for power corrupts judgment.

Abimelech's position in Gideon's family as the son of a concubine must have created great tension between him and Gideon's many other sons. One against 70: such odds can either crush a person or make him ruthless. It is obvious which direction Abimelech chose. Gideon's position as warrior and judge had placed Abimelech in an environment of power; Gideon's death provided an opportunity for this son to seize power. Once the process began, the disastrous results were inevitable. A person's thirst for power is not satisfied when he gets power—it only becomes more intense. Abimelech's life was consumed by that thirst. Eventually, he could not tolerate any threat to his power.

By this time, ownership had changed: Abimelech no longer had power—power had him. One lesson we can learn from his life is that our goals control our actions. The amount of control is related to the importance of the goal. Abimelech's most important goal was to have power. His lust for power led him to wipe out not only his brothers, but also whole cities that refused to submit to him. Nothing but death could stop his bloodthirsty drive to conquer. How ironic that he was fatally injured by a woman with a farm implement! The contrast between Abimelech and the great people of the Bible is great. He wanted to control the nation; they were willing to be controlled by God.

Strengths and accomplishments:	• The first self-declared king of Israel • Qualified tactical planner and organizer
Weaknesses and mistakes:	• Power hungry and ruthless • Overconfident • Took advantage of his father's position without imitating his father's character • Had 69 of his 70 half brothers killed
Vital statistics:	• Where: Shechem, Arumah, Thebez • Occupations: Self-acclaimed king, judge, political troublemaker • Relatives: Father: Gideon. Only surviving brother: Jotham.
Key verses:	"Thus God repaid the wickedness that Abimelech had done to his father by murdering his seventy brothers. God also made the men of Shechem pay for all their wickedness. The curse of Jotham son of Jerub-Baal came on them" (Judges 9:56, 57).

His story is told in Judges 8:31—9:57. He is also mentioned in 2 Samuel 11:21.

---

fulfilling Jotham's parable. Those three years must have seemed like forever to Jotham. Why wasn't Abimelech punished sooner for his evil ways?

We are not alone when we wonder why evil seems to prevail (Job 10:3; 21:1–18; Jeremiah 12:1; Habakkuk 1:2–4, 12–17). God promises to deal with sin, but in his time, not ours. Actually it is good news that God doesn't punish *us* immediately because we all have sinned and deserve God's punishment. God, in his mercy, often spares us from immediate punishment and allows us time to turn from our sins and turn to him in repentance. Trusting God

for justice means (1) we must first recognize our own sins and repent, and (2) we may face a difficult time of waiting for the wicked to be punished. But in God's time, all evil will be destroyed.

9:23 This evil spirit was not just an attitude of strife, it was a demon. It was not Satan himself, but one of the fallen angels under Satan's influence. God used this evil spirit to bring about judgment on Shechem. First Samuel 16:14 records how God judged Saul in a similar way.

34 So Abimelech and all his troops set out by night and took up concealed positions near Shechem in four companies. 35 Now Gaal son of Ebed had gone out and was standing at the entrance to the city gate just as Abimelech and his soldiers came out from their hiding place.

36 When Gaal saw them, he said to Zebul, "Look, people are coming down from the tops of the mountains!"

Zebul replied, "You mistake the shadows of the mountains for men."

37 But Gaal spoke up again: "Look, people are coming down from the center of the land, and a company is coming from the direction of the soothsayers' tree."

38 Then Zebul said to him, "Where is your big talk now, you who said, 'Who is Abimelech that we should be subject to him?' Aren't these the men you ridiculed? k Go out and fight them!"

39 So Gaal led out a the citizens of Shechem and fought Abimelech. 40 Abimelech chased him, and many fell wounded in the flight—all the way to the entrance to the gate. 41 Abimelech stayed in Arumah, and Zebul drove Gaal and his brothers out of Shechem.

42 The next day the people of Shechem went out to the fields, and this was reported to Abimelech. 43 So he took his men, divided them into three companies and set an ambush in the fields. When he saw the people coming out of the city, he rose to attack them. 44 Abimelech and the companies with him rushed forward to a position at the entrance to the city gate. Then two companies rushed upon those in the fields and struck them down. 45 All that day Abimelech pressed his attack against the city until he had captured it and killed its people. Then he destroyed the city l and scattered salt m over it.

46 On hearing this, the citizens in the tower of Shechem went into the stronghold of the temple n of El-Berith. 47 When Abimelech heard that they had assembled there, 48 he and all his men went up Mount Zalmon. o He took an ax and cut off some branches, which he lifted to his shoulders. He ordered the men with him, "Quick! Do what you have seen me do!" 49 So all the men cut branches and followed Abimelech. They piled them against the stronghold and set it on fire over the people inside. So all the people in the tower of Shechem, about a thousand men and women, also died.

50 Next Abimelech went to Thebez and besieged it and captured it. 51 Inside the city, however, was a strong tower, to which all the men and women—all the people of the city—fled. They locked themselves in and climbed up on the tower roof. 52 Abimelech went to the tower and stormed it. But as he approached the entrance to the tower to set it on fire, 53 a woman dropped an upper millstone on his head and cracked his skull. p

54 Hurriedly he called to his armor-bearer, "Draw your sword and kill me, q so that they can't say, 'A woman killed him.'" So his servant ran him through, and he died. 55 When the Israelites saw that Abimelech was dead, they went home.

56 Thus God repaid the wickedness that Abimelech had done to his father by murdering his seventy brothers. 57 God also made the men of Shechem pay for all their wickedness. r The curse of Jotham son of Jerub-Baal came on them.

Tola

10 After the time of Abimelech a man of Issachar, Tola son of Puah, the son of Dodo, rose to save s Israel. He lived in Shamir, in the hill country of Ephraim. 2 He led b Israel twenty-three years; then he died, and was buried in Shamir.

a 39 Or Gaal went out in the sight of   b 2 Traditionally judged; also in verse 3

9:38
k ver 28-29

9:45
l ver 20; 2Ki 3:25
m Dt 29:23

9:46
n Jdg 8:33
9:48
o Ps 68:14

9:53
p 2Sa 11:21

9:54
q 1Sa 31:4

9:57
r ver 20

10:1
s Jdg 2:16

9:45 To scatter salt over a conquered city was a ritual to symbolize the perpetual desolation of the city. It would not be rebuilt for 150 years.

9:53 In times of battle, women were sometimes asked to join the men at the city wall to drop heavy objects on the soldiers below. A millstone would have been an ideal object for this purpose. It was a round stone about 18 inches in diameter with a hole in the center. Millstones were used to grind grain into flour. The grain was placed between two millstones. The top millstone was turned, crushing the grain.

Abimelech's death was especially humiliating: he was killed by a woman, not by fighting; and he was killed by a farm implement instead of a weapon. Abimelech therefore asked his armor-bearer to stab him with his sword before he died from the blow of the millstone.

9:56, 57 Gideon, Abimelech's father, succeeded in military battles, but sometimes failed in his personal struggles. Gideon was not condemned for taking a concubine (8:31), but the family problems that resulted from this relationship are clearly stated.

In the end, Abimelech killed 69 of his 70 half brothers, tore apart a nation, and then was killed himself. From Gideon's life we learn that no matter how much good we do for God's kingdom, sin in our lives will still produce powerful, damaging consequences.

9:56, 57 Jotham's curse is found in 9:16–20.

10:1–5 In five verses we read about two men who judged Israel for a total of 45 years, yet all we know about them besides the length of their rules is that one had 30 sons who rode around on 30 donkeys. What are you doing for God that is worth noting? When your life is over, will people remember more than just what was in your bank account or the number of years you lived?

Jair

10:4
t Nu 32:41

³He was followed by Jair of Gilead, who led Israel twenty-two years. ⁴He had thirty sons, who rode thirty donkeys. They controlled thirty towns in Gilead, which to this day are called Havvoth Jair.ᵃ *t* ⁵When Jair died, he was buried in Kamon.

5. Fifth period: Jephthah, Ibzan, Elon, and Abdon
Jephthah

10:6
u Jdg 2:13
v Dt 32:15

10:7
w Dt 31:17

⁶Again the Israelites did evil in the eyes of the LORD. They served the Baals and the Ashtoreths,*u* and the gods of Aram, the gods of Sidon, the gods of Moab, the gods of the Ammonites and the gods of the Philistines. And because the Israelites forsook the LORD *v* and no longer served him, ⁷he became angry*w* with them. He sold them into the hands of the Philistines and the Ammonites, ⁸who that year shattered and crushed them. For eighteen years they oppressed all the Israelites on the east side of the Jordan in Gilead, the land of the Amorites. ⁹The Ammonites also crossed the Jordan to fight against Judah, Benjamin and the house of Ephraim; and Israel was in great distress. ¹⁰Then the Israelites cried out to the LORD, "We have sinned against you, forsaking our God and serving the Baals."*x*

10:10
x 1Sa 12:10

10:11
y Nu 21:21;
Jdg 3:13

10:12
z Ps 106:42

¹¹The LORD replied, "When the Egyptians, the Amorites, the Ammonites,*y* the Philistines, ¹²the Sidonians, the Amalekites and the Maonitesᵇ oppressed you*z* and you cried to me for help, did I not save you from their hands? ¹³But you have forsaken me and served other gods, so I will no longer save you. ¹⁴Go and cry out to the gods you have chosen. Let them save you when you are in trouble!"

10:15
a 1Sa 3:18

10:16
b Jos 24:23;
Jer 18:8

10:17
c Jdg 11:29

¹⁵But the Israelites said to the LORD, "We have sinned. Do with us whatever you think best,ᵃ but please rescue us now." ¹⁶Then they got rid of the foreign gods among them and served the LORD. *b* And he could bear Israel's misery no longer.

¹⁷When the Ammonites were called to arms and camped in Gilead, the Israelites assembled and camped at Mizpah. *c* ¹⁸The leaders of the people of Gilead said to each other, "Whoever will launch the attack against the Ammonites will be the head of all those living in Gilead."

11:1
d Heb 11:32

11:3
e 2Sa 10:6,8

11 Jephthah*d* the Gileadite was a mighty warrior. His father was Gilead; his mother was a prostitute. ²Gilead's wife also bore him sons, and when they were grown up, they drove Jephthah away. "You are not going to get any inheritance in our family," they said, "because you are the son of another woman." ³So Jephthah fled from his brothers and settled in the land of Tob,*e* where a group of adventurers gathered around him and followed him.

ᵃ4 Or *called the settlements of Jair*   ᵇ12 Hebrew; some Septuagint manuscripts *Midianites*

10:6 Baal and Ashtoreth are explained in the notes on 2:11–15 and 3:7. The gods of Aram and Sidon are very similar. The gods of Moab and Ammon were Chemosh and Molech. The Philistine gods were Dagon, Ashtoreth, Asherah, and Baal-Zebul.

10:9, 10 Once again the Israelites suffered for many years before they gave up their sinful ways and called out to God for help (see 4:1–3; 6:1–7). Notice that when the Israelites were at the end of their rope they did not look to their pagan gods for help, but to the only One who was really able to help.

Is God your last resort? So much unnecessary suffering takes place because we don't call on God until we've used up all other resources. Rather than waiting until the situation becomes desperate, turn to God first. He has the necessary resources to meet every kind of problem.

10:11–16 These verses show how difficult it can be to follow God over the long haul. The Israelites always seemed to forget God when all was well. But despite being rejected by his own people, God never failed to rescue them when they called out to him in repentance. God never fails to rescue us either. We act just like the Israelites when we put God outside our daily events instead of at the center of them. Just as a loving parent feels rejected when a child rebels, so God feels great rejection when we ignore or neglect him (1 Samuel 8:4–9; 10:17–19; John 12:44–50). We should strive to stay close to God rather than see how far we can go before judgment comes.

10:17, 18 The power of the Ammonite nation was at its peak during the period of the judges. The people were descendants

of Ammon, conceived when Lot's younger daughter slept with her drunk father (Genesis 19:30–38). The land of Ammon was located just east of the Jordan River across from Jerusalem. South of Ammon lay the land of Moab, the nation conceived when Lot's older daughter slept with her father. Moab and Ammon were usually allies. It was a formidable task to defeat these nations.

11:1, 2 Jephthah, an illegitimate son of Gilead, was chased out of the country by his half brothers. He suffered as a result of another's decision and not for any wrong he had done. Yet in spite of his brothers' rejection, God used him. If you are suffering from unfair rejection, don't blame others and become discouraged. Remember how God used Jephthah despite his unjust circumstances, and realize that he is able to use you even if you feel rejected by some.

11:3 Circumstances beyond his control forced Jephthah away from his people and into life as an outcast. Today, both believers and nonbelievers may drive away those who do not fit the norms dictated by our society, neighborhoods, or churches. Often, as in Jephthah's case, great potential is wasted because of prejudice—a refusal to look beyond ill-conceived stereotypes. Look around you to see if there are potential Jephthahs being kept out due to factors beyond their control. As a Christian you know that everyone can have a place in God's family. Can you do anything to help these people gain acceptance for their character and abilities?

⁴Some time later, when the Ammonites ᶠ made war on Israel, ⁵the elders of Gilead went to get Jephthah from the land of Tob. ⁶"Come," they said, "be our commander, so we can fight the Ammonites."

11:4
ᶠJdg 10:9

⁷Jephthah said to them, "Didn't you hate me and drive me from my father's house?ᵍ Why do you come to me now, when you're in trouble?"

11:7
ᵍGe 26:27

⁸The elders of Gilead said to him, "Nevertheless, we are turning to you now; come with us to fight the Ammonites, and you will be our head ʰ over all who live in Gilead."

11:8
ʰJdg 10:18

⁹Jephthah answered, "Suppose you take me back to fight the Ammonites and the LORD gives them to me—will I really be your head?"

¹⁰The elders of Gilead replied, "The LORD is our witness;ⁱ we will certainly do as you say."

11:10
ⁱJer 42:5

¹¹So Jephthah went with the elders of Gilead, and the people made him head and commander over them. And he repeated all his words before the LORD in Mizpah.ʲ

11:11
ʲJdg 10:17

¹²Then Jephthah sent messengers to the Ammonite king with the question: "What do you have against us that you have attacked our country?"

¹³The king of the Ammonites answered Jephthah's messengers, "When Israel came up out of Egypt, they took away my land from the Arnon to the Jabbok,ᵏ all the way to the Jordan. Now give it back peaceably."

11:13
ᵏNu 21:24

¹⁴Jephthah sent back messengers to the Ammonite king, ¹⁵saying:

"This is what Jephthah says: Israel did not take the land of Moab or the land of the Ammonites. ¹⁶But when they came up out of Egypt, Israel went through the desert to the Red Sea ᵃ and on to Kadesh. ˡ ¹⁷Then Israel sent messengers to the king of Edom, saying, 'Give us permission to go through your country,' but the king of Edom would not listen. They sent also to the king of Moab, and he refused. So Israel stayed at Kadesh.

11:16
ˡNu 20:1

¹⁸"Next they traveled through the desert, skirted the lands of Edom ᵐ and Moab, passed along the eastern side ⁿ of the country of Moab, and camped on the other side of the Arnon. They did not enter the territory of Moab, for the Arnon was its border.

11:18
ᵐNu 21:4
ⁿDt 2:8

¹⁹"Then Israel sent messengers to Sihon king of the Amorites, who ruled in Heshbon, and said to him, 'Let us pass through your country to our own place.' ᵒ ²⁰Sihon, however, did not trust Israel ᵇ to pass through his territory. He mustered all his men and encamped at Jahaz and fought with Israel.

11:19
ᵒNu 21:21-22;
Dt 2:26-27

²¹"Then the LORD, the God of Israel, gave Sihon and all his men into Israel's hands, and they defeated them. Israel took over all the land of the Amorites who lived in that country, ²²capturing all of it from the Arnon to the Jabbok and from the desert to the Jordan.ᵖ

11:22
ᵖDt 2:36

²³"Now since the LORD, the God of Israel, has driven the Amorites out before his people Israel, what right have you to take it over? ²⁴Will you not take what your god Chemosh ᑫ gives you? Likewise, whatever the LORD our God has given us, we will possess. ²⁵Are you better than Balak son of Zippor, ʳ king of Moab? Did he ever quarrel with Israel or fight with them?ˢ ²⁶For three hundred years Israel occupied ᵗ Heshbon, Aroer, the surrounding settlements and all the towns along the Arnon. Why didn't you retake them during that time? ²⁷I have not wronged you, but you are doing me wrong by waging war against me. Let the LORD, the Judge,ᶜ ᵘ decide ᵛ the dispute this day between the Israelites and the Ammonites."

11:24
ᑫNu 21:29; 1Ki 11:7

11:25
ʳNu 22:2
ˢJos 24:9

11:26
ᵗNu 21:25

11:27
ᵘGe 18:25
ᵛGe 16:5; 31:53;
1Sa 24:12,15

²⁸The king of Ammon, however, paid no attention to the message Jephthah sent him.

²⁹Then the Spirit ʷ of the LORD came upon Jephthah. He crossed Gilead and Manasseh,

11:29
ʷJdg 3:10

ᵃ *16* Hebrew *Yam Suph*; that is, Sea of Reeds ᵇ *20* Or *however, would not make an agreement for Israel*
ᶜ *27* Or *Ruler*

11:11 What does it mean that Jephthah repeated all his words before the Lord? Those making covenants in ancient times often made them at shrines so that they would be witnessed by deities. Often a written copy was also deposited at the shrine. This was much like a coronation ceremony for Jephthah.

11:14ff Jephthah sent messengers to the Ammonite king wanting to know why the Israelites in the land of Gilead were being attacked (11:12). The king replied that Israel had stolen this land and he wanted it back (11:13).

Jephthah sent another message to the king (11:14–27). In it he gave three arguments against the king's claim: (1) Gilead was never the king's land in the first place because Israel took

it from the Amorites, not the Ammonites (11:16–22); (2) Israel should possess land given by Israel's God, and Ammon should possess land given by Ammon's god; (3) no one had contested Israel's ownership of the land since its conquest 300 years earlier (11:25, 26).

To Jephthah's credit, he tried to solve the problem without bloodshed. But the king of Ammon ignored his message and prepared his troops for battle.

11:27 Over the years, Israel had many judges to lead them. But Jephthah recognized the Lord as the people's true Judge, the only One who could really lead them and help them conquer the invading enemies.

passed through Mizpah of Gilead, and from there he advanced against the Ammonites. [30] And Jephthah made a vow to the LORD: "If you give the Ammonites into my hands, [31] whatever comes out of the door of my house to meet me when I return in triumph from the Ammonites will be the LORD's, and I will sacrifice it as a burnt offering."

[32] Then Jephthah went over to fight the Ammonites, and the LORD gave them into his hands. [33] He devastated twenty towns from Aroer to the vicinity of Minnith, [x] as far as Abel Keramim. Thus Israel subdued Ammon.

[34] When Jephthah returned to his home in Mizpah, who should come out to meet him but his daughter, dancing to the sound of tambourines! [y] She was an only child. Except for her he had neither son nor daughter. [35] When he saw her, he tore his clothes and cried, "Oh! My daughter! You have made me miserable and wretched, because I have made a vow to the LORD that I cannot break. [z]"

[36] "My father," she replied, "you have given your word to the LORD. Do to me just as you promised, now that the LORD has avenged you of your enemies, the Ammonites. [37] But grant me this one request," she said. "Give me two months to roam the hills and weep with my friends, because I will never marry."

11:33
x Eze 27:17

11:34
y Jer 31:4

11:35
z Nu 30:2;
Ecc 5:2,4,5

RASH VOWS

Ecclesiastes 5:2 says: "Do not be quick with your mouth, do not be hasty in your heart to utter anything before God." Scripture records the vows of many men and women. Some of these vows proved to be rash and unwise, and others, though extreme, were kept to the letter by those who made them. Let us learn from the examples in God's Word not to make rash vows.

Person	Vow	Result	Reference
JACOB	To "choose" the true God and to give back a tenth to him if he kept him safe	God protected Jacob, who kept his vow to follow God	Genesis 28:20
JEPHTHAH	To offer to the Lord whoever came out to meet him after battle (it turned out to be his daughter)	He lost his daughter	Judges 11:30, 31
HANNAH	To give her son back to God if God would give her a son	When Samuel was born, she dedicated him to God	1 Samuel 1:9–11
SAUL	To kill anyone who ate before evening (Jonathan, his son, had not heard the command and broke it)	Saul would have killed Jonathan if soldiers had not intervened	1 Samuel 14:24–45
DAVID	To be kind to Jonathan's family	Mephibosheth, Jonathan's son, was treated royally by David	2 Samuel 9:7
ITTAI	To remain loyal to David	He became one of the great men in David's army	2 Samuel 15:21
MICAIAH	To say only what God told him to say	He was put in prison	1 Kings 22:14
JOB	That he was not rebelling against God	His fortunes were restored	Job 42:10
HEROD ANTIPAS	To give Herodias's daughter anything she requested	Herod was forced to order John the Baptist's death	Mark 6:22, 23
PAUL	To offer a sacrifice of thanksgiving in Jerusalem	He made the sacrifice despite the danger	Acts 18:18

11:30, 31 In God's law, a vow was a promise to God that should not be broken (Numbers 30:1, 2; Deuteronomy 23:21–23). It carried as much force as a written contract. Many people made vows in Biblical times. Some, like Jephthah's, were very foolish.

11:30, 31 When Jephthah made his vow, did he stop to consider that a person, not a sheep or goat, might come out to meet him? Scholars are divided over the issue. Those who say Jephthah was considering human sacrifice use the following arguments: (1) He was from an area where pagan religion and human sacrifice were common. In his eyes, it may not have seemed like a sin. (2) Jephthah may not have had a background in religious law. Perhaps he was ignorant of God's command against human sacrifice.

Those who say Jephthah could not have been thinking about human sacrifice point to other evidence: (1) As leader of the people, Jephthah must have been familiar with God's laws; human sacrifice was clearly forbidden (Leviticus 18:21; 20:1–5).

(2) No legitimate priest would have helped Jephthah carry out his vow if a person was to be the sacrifice.

Whatever Jephthah had in mind when he made the vow, did he or did he not sacrifice his daughter? Some think he did, because his vow was to make a burnt offering. Some think he did not, and they offer several reasons: (1) If the girl was to die, she would not have spent her last two months in the hills. (2) God would not have honored a vow based on a wicked practice. (3) Verse 39 says that she never married, not that she died, implying that she was set apart for service to God, not killed.

11:34, 35 Jephthah's rash vow brought him unspeakable grief. In the heat of emotion or personal turmoil it is easy to make foolish promises to God. These promises may sound very spiritual when we make them, but they may produce only guilt and frustration when we are forced to fulfill them. Making spiritual "deals" only brings disappointment. God does not want promises for the future, but obedience for today.

38"You may go," he said. And he let her go for two months. She and the girls went into the hills and wept because she would never marry. 39After the two months, she returned to her father and he did to her as he had vowed. And she was a virgin.

From this comes the Israelite custom 40that each year the young women of Israel go out for four days to commemorate the daughter of Jephthah the Gileadite.

Jephthah and Ephraim

12 The men of Ephraim called out their forces, crossed over to Zaphon and said to Jephthah, "Why did you go to fight the Ammonites without calling us to go with you? *a* We're going to burn down your house over your head."

2Jephthah answered, "I and my people were engaged in a great struggle with the Ammonites, and although I called, you didn't save me out of their hands. 3When I saw that you wouldn't help, I took my life in my hands *b* and crossed over to fight the Ammonites, and the LORD gave me the victory over them. Now why have you come up today to fight me?"

4Jephthah then called together the men of Gilead and fought against Ephraim. The Gileadites struck them down because the Ephraimites had said, "You Gileadites are renegades from Ephraim and Manasseh." 5The Gileadites captured the fords of the Jordan *c* leading to Ephraim, and whenever a survivor of Ephraim said, "Let me cross over," the men of Gilead asked him, "Are you an Ephraimite?" If he replied, "No," 6they said, "All right, say 'Shibboleth.'" If he said, "Sibboleth," because he could not pronounce the word correctly, they seized him and killed him at the fords of the Jordan. Forty-two thousand Ephraimites were killed at that time.

7Jephthah led *a* Israel six years. Then Jephthah the Gileadite died, and was buried in a town in Gilead.

Ibzan, Elon and Abdon

8After him, Ibzan of Bethlehem led Israel. 9He had thirty sons and thirty daughters. He gave his daughters away in marriage to those outside his clan, and for his sons he brought in thirty young women as wives from outside his clan. Ibzan led Israel seven years. 10Then Ibzan died, and was buried in Bethlehem.

11After him, Elon the Zebulunite led Israel ten years. 12Then Elon died, and was buried in Aijalon in the land of Zebulun.

13After him, Abdon son of Hillel, from Pirathon, led Israel. 14He had forty sons and thirty grandsons, who rode on seventy donkeys. *d* He led Israel eight years. 15Then Abdon son of Hillel died, and was buried at Pirathon in Ephraim, in the hill country of the Amalekites. *e*

a 7 Traditionally *judged*; also in verses 8-14

	12:1 *a* Jdg 8:1
	12:3 *b* 1Sa 19:5
	12:5 *c* Jdg 3:28
	12:14 *d* Jdg 5:10
	12:15 *e* Jdg 5:14

12:1ff Israel had just won a great battle, but instead of joy, there was pettiness and quarreling. The tribe of Ephraim was angry and jealous that they were not invited to join in the fighting (although Jephthah said he had invited them). The insults of the Ephraimites enraged Jephthah, who called out his troops and killed 42,000 men from Ephraim.

Jephthah usually spoke before he acted, but this time his revenge was swift. It cost Israel dearly, and it might have been avoided. Insulting others and being jealous are not right responses when we feel left out. But seeking revenge for an insult is just as wrong, and very costly.

12:4–7 The men of the tribe of Ephraim caused Jephthah trouble just as they had Gideon (8:1–3). Jephthah captured the fords of the Jordan, the boundary of Ephraim, and was able to defeat his countrymen as they crossed the river. He used a pronunciation test. *Shibboleth* is the word for stream. The Ephraimites pronounced "sh" as "s," so Jephthah's army could easily identify them.

12:8–15 There is little else known about these three judges or their importance. The large number of children and cattle are an indication of the wealth of these men.

Mediterranean Sea

N

Sea of Galilee

Zaphon • Jabbok R.
fords of the Jordan • Mizpah
EPHRAIM GILEAD
Jerusalem • AMMON
Dead Sea

CANAAN
Jordan River

0 20 Mi.
0 20 Km.

JEPHTHAH'S VICTORY
The Ephraimites mobilized an army because they were angry at not being included in the battle against Ammon. They planned to attack Jephthah at his home in Gilead. Jephthah captured the fords of the Jordan at the Jabbok River and killed the Ephraimites who tried to cross.

6. Sixth period: Samson

The Birth of Samson

13:1
f Jdg 2:11

13:2
g Jos 19:41

13:3
h ver 10
i Lk 1:13

13:4
j ver 14; Nu 6:2-4;
Lk 1:15

13:5
k Nu 6:5; 1Sa 1:11
l Nu 6:2,13
m 1Sa 7:13

13 Again the Israelites did evil in the eyes of the Lord, so the Lord delivered them into the hands of the Philistines *f* for forty years.

²A certain man of Zorah,*g* named Manoah, from the clan of the Danites, had a wife who was sterile and remained childless. ³The angel of the Lord appeared to her *h* and said, "You are sterile and childless, but you are going to conceive and have a son. *i* ⁴Now see to it that you drink no wine or other fermented drink and that you do not eat anything unclean,*j* ⁵because you will conceive and give birth to a son. No razor *k* may be used on his head, because the boy is to be a Nazirite,*l* set apart to God from birth, and he will begin *m* the deliverance of Israel from the hands of the Philistines."

It's hard not to admire people whose word can be depended on completely and whose actions are consistent with their words. For such people, talking is not avoiding action; it is the beginning of action. People like this can make excellent negotiators. They approach a conflict with the full intention of settling issues verbally, but they do not hesitate to use other means if verbal attempts fail. Jephthah was this kind of person.

In most of his conflicts, Jephthah's first move was to talk. In the war with the Ammonites, his strategy was negotiation. He clarified the issues so that everyone knew the cause of the conflict. His opponent's response determined his next action.

The fate of Jephthah's daughter is difficult to understand. We are not sure what Jephthah meant by his vow recorded in Judges 11:31. In any case, his vow was unnecessary. We do not know what actually happened to his daughter—whether she was burned as an offering or set apart as a virgin, thus denying Jephthah any hope of descendants since she was his only child. What we do know is that Jephthah was a person of his word, even when it was a word spoken in haste, and even when keeping his word caused him great pain.

How do you approach conflicts? There is a big difference between trying to settle a conflict through words and simply counterattacking someone verbally. How dependable are the statements you make? Do your children, friends, and fellow workers know you to be a person of your word? The measure of your trustworthiness is your willingness to take responsibility, even if you must pay a painful price because of something you said.

Strengths and accomplishments:	• Listed in the Hall of Faith in Hebrews 11 • Controlled by God's Spirit • Brilliant military strategist who negotiated before fighting
Weaknesses and mistakes:	• Was bitter over the treatment he received from his half brothers • Made a rash and foolish vow that was costly
Lesson from his life:	• A person's background does not prevent God from working powerfully in his or her life
Vital statistics:	• Where: Gilead • Occupations: Warrior, judge • Relative: Father: Gilead
Key verse:	"Then Jephthah went over to fight the Ammonites, and the Lord gave them into his hands" (Judges 11:32).

His story is told in Judges 11:1—12:7. He is also mentioned in 1 Samuel 12:11 and Hebrews 11:32.

13:1 The Philistines lived on the west side of Canaan, along the Mediterranean seacoast. From Samson's day until the time of David they were the major enemy force in the land and a constant threat to Israel. The Philistines were fierce warriors; they had the advantage over Israel in numbers, tactical expertise, and technology. They knew the secret of making weapons out of iron (1 Samuel 13:19–22). But none of that mattered when God was fighting for Israel.

13:1ff Once again the cycle of sin, judgment, and repentance began (3:8, 9, 14, 15; 4:1–4; 6:1–14; 10:6—11:11). The Israelites would not turn to God unless they had been stunned by suffering, oppression, and death. This suffering was not caused by God, but resulted from the fact that the people ignored God, their Judge and Ruler. What will it take for you to follow God? The warnings in God's Word are clear: if we continue to harden our hearts against God, we can expect the same fate as Israel.

13:5 Samson was to be a Nazirite—a person who took a vow to be set apart for God's service. Samson's parents made the vow for him. A Nazirite vow was sometimes temporary, but in Samson's case, it was for life. As a Nazirite, Samson could not cut his hair, touch a dead body, or drink anything containing alcohol.

Although Samson often used poor judgment and sinned terribly, he accomplished much when he determined to be set apart for God. In this way he was like the nation Israel. As long as the Israelites remained set apart for God, the nation thrived. But they fell into terrible sin when they ignored God.

13:5 Manoah's wife was told that her son would *begin* the deliverance of Israel from Philistine oppression. It wasn't until David's day that the Philistine opposition was completely crushed (2 Samuel 8:1). Samson's part in subduing the Philistines was just the beginning, but it was important nonetheless. It was the task God had given Samson to do. Be faithful in following God even if you don't see instant results, because you might be beginning an important job that others will finish.

JEPHTHAH

⁶Then the woman went to her husband and told him, "A man of God ⁿ came to me. He looked like an angel of God, very awesome. I didn't ask him where he came from, and he didn't tell me his name. ⁷But he said to me, 'You will conceive and give birth to a son. Now then, drink no wine or other fermented drink and do not eat anything unclean, because the boy will be a Nazirite of God from birth until the day of his death.'"

⁸Then Manoah prayed to the LORD: "O Lord, I beg you, let the man of God you sent to us come again to teach us how to bring up the boy who is to be born."

⁹God heard Manoah, and the angel of God came again to the woman while she was out in the field; but her husband Manoah was not with her. ¹⁰The woman hurried to tell her husband, "He's here! The man who appeared to me the other day!"

¹¹Manoah got up and followed his wife. When he came to the man, he said, "Are you the one who talked to my wife?"

"I am," he said.

¹²So Manoah asked him, "When your words are fulfilled, what is to be the rule for the boy's life and work?"

¹³The angel of the LORD answered, "Your wife must do all that I have told her. ¹⁴She must not eat anything that comes from the grapevine, nor drink any wine or other fermented drink nor eat anything unclean. ⁰ She must do everything I have commanded her."

¹⁵Manoah said to the angel of the LORD, "We would like you to stay until we prepare a young goat ᵖ for you."

¹⁶The angel of the LORD replied, "Even though you detain me, I will not eat any of your food. But if you prepare a burnt offering, offer it to the LORD." (Manoah did not realize that it was the angel of the LORD.)

¹⁷Then Manoah inquired of the angel of the LORD, "What is your name, so that we may honor you when your word comes true?"

¹⁸He replied, "Why do you ask my name? It is beyond understanding. ᵃ " ¹⁹Then Manoah took a young goat, together with the grain offering, and sacrificed it on a rock �q to the LORD. And the LORD did an amazing thing while Manoah and his wife watched: ²⁰As the flame ʳ blazed up from the altar toward heaven, the angel of the LORD ascended in the flame. Seeing this, Manoah and his wife fell with their faces to the ground. ²¹When the angel of the LORD did not show himself again to Manoah and his wife, Manoah realized that it was the angel of the LORD.

²²"We are doomed ˢ to die!" he said to his wife. "We have seen ᵗ God!"

²³But his wife answered, "If the LORD had meant to kill us, he would not have accepted a burnt offering and grain offering from our hands, nor shown us all these things or now told us this."

²⁴The woman gave birth to a boy and named him Samson. ᵘ He grew ᵛ and the LORD blessed him, ²⁵and the Spirit of the LORD began to stir ʷ him while he was in Mahaneh Dan, ˣ between Zorah and Eshtaol.

Samson's Marriage

14 Samson went down to Timnah and saw there a young Philistine woman. ²When he returned, he said to his father and mother, "I have seen a Philistine woman in Timnah; now get her for me as my wife." ʸ

ᵃ 18 Or *is wonderful*

13:6
ⁿver 8; 1Sa 2:27;
9:6

13:14
⁰ver 4

13:15
ᵖJdg 6:19

13:19
qJdg 6:20

13:20
ʳLev 9:24

13:22
ˢDt 5:26
ᵗJdg 6:22

13:24
ᵘHeb 11:32
ᵛ1Sa 3:19

13:25
ʷJdg 3:10
ˣJdg 18:12

14:2
ʸGe 21:21

13:18 Why did the angel keep his name a secret? In those days people believed that if they knew someone's name, they knew his character and how to control him. By not giving his name, the angel was not allowing himself to be controlled by Manoah. He was also saying that his name was a mystery beyond understanding and too wonderful to imagine. Manoah asked the angel for an answer that he wouldn't have understood. Sometimes we ask God questions and then receive no answer. This may not be because God is saying no. We may have asked for knowledge beyond our ability to understand or accept.

13:19 Manoah sacrificed a grain offering to the Lord. A grain offering was grain, oil, and flour shaped into a cake and burned on the altar along with the *burnt offering* (the young goat). The grain offering, described in Leviticus 2, was offered to God as a sign of honor, respect, and worship. It was an acknowledgment that because the Israelites' food came from God, they owed their lives to him. With the grain offering, Manoah showed his desire to serve God and demonstrated his respect.

13:25 Samson's tribe, Dan, continued to wander in their inherited land (18:1), which was yet unconquered (Joshua 19:47, 48). Samson must have grown up with his warlike tribe's yearnings for a permanent and settled territory. Thus his visits to the tribal army camp stirred his heart, and God's Spirit began preparing him for his role as judge and leader against the Philistines.

Perhaps there are things that stir your heart. These may indicate areas where God wants to use you. God uses a variety of means to develop and prepare us: hereditary traits, environmental influences, and personal experiences. As with Samson, this preparation often begins long before adulthood. Work at being sensitive to the Holy Spirit's leading and the tasks God has prepared for you. Your past may be more useful to you than you imagine.

14:3
z Ex 34:16

3 His father and mother replied, "Isn't there an acceptable woman among your relatives or among all our people? Must you go to the uncircumcised Philistines to get a wife? z"

14:4
a Jos 11:20
b Jdg 13:1

But Samson said to his father, "Get her for me. She's the right one for me." 4 (His parents did not know that this was from the LORD, who was seeking an occasion to confront the Philistines; a for at that time they were ruling over Israel.) b 5 Samson went down to Timnah together with his father and mother. As they approached the vineyards of Timnah, suddenly a young lion came roaring toward him. 6 The Spirit of the LORD came upon him in power c so that he tore the lion apart with his bare hands as he might have torn a young goat. But he told neither his father nor his mother what he had done. 7 Then he went down and talked with the woman, and he liked her.

14:6
c Jdg 3:10

SAMSON

It is sad to be remembered for what one might have been. Samson had tremendous potential. Not many people have started life with credentials like his. Born as a result of God's plan in the lives of Manoah and his wife, Samson was to do a great work for God—to "begin the deliverance of Israel from the hands of the Philistines." To help him accomplish God's plan, he was given enormous physical strength.

Because Samson wasted his strength on practical jokes and getting out of scrapes, and because he eventually gave it up altogether to satisfy the woman he loved, we tend to see him as a failure. We remember him as the judge in Israel who spent his last days grinding grain in an enemy prison, and we say, "What wasted potential!"

Yes, Samson wasted his life. He could have strengthened his nation. He could have returned his people to the worship of God. He could have wiped out the Philistines. But even though he did none of those things, Samson still accomplished the purpose announced by the angel who visited his parents before his birth. In his final act, Samson began to rescue Israel from the Philistines.

Interestingly, the New Testament does not mention Samson's failures or his heroic feats of strength. In Hebrews 11:33, he is simply listed with others "who through faith conquered kingdoms, administered justice, and gained what was promised," and in other ways were given superhuman aid. In the end, Samson recognized his dependence on God. When he died, God turned his failures and defeats into victory. Samson's story teaches us that it is never too late to start over. However badly we may have failed in the past, today is not too late for us to put our complete trust in God.

Strengths and accomplishments:	• Dedicated to God from birth as a Nazirite • Known for his feats of strength • Listed in the Hall of Faith in Hebrews 11 • Began to free Israel from Philistine oppression
Weaknesses and mistakes:	• Violated his vow and God's laws on many occasions • Was controlled by sensuality • Confided in the wrong people • Used his gifts and abilities unwisely
Lessons from his life:	• Great strength in one area of life does not make up for great weaknesses in other areas • God's presence does not overwhelm a person's will • God can use a person of faith in spite of his or her mistakes
Vital statistics:	• Where: Zorah, Timnah, Ashkelon, Gaza, Valley of Sorek • Occupation: Judge • Relative: Father: Manoah • Contemporaries: Delilah, Samuel (who might have been born while Samson was a judge)
Key verse:	"You will conceive and give birth to a son. No razor may be used on his head, because the boy is to be a Nazirite, set apart to God from birth, and he will begin the deliverance of Israel from the hands of the Philistines" (Judges 13:5).

His story is told in Judges 13—16. He is also mentioned in Hebrews 11:32.

14:3 Samson's parents objected to his marrying the Philistine woman for several reasons: (1) It was against God's law (Exodus 34:15–17; Deuteronomy 7:1–4). A stark example of what happened when the Israelites married pagans can be found in 3:5–7. (2) The Philistines were Israel's greatest enemies. Marriage to a hated Philistine would be a disgrace to Samson's family. But Samson's father gave in to Samson's demand and allowed the marriage, even though he had the right to refuse his son.

14:6 "The Spirit of the LORD came upon him in power" refers to the unusual physical strength given him by the Spirit of the Lord. Samson did not seem to be affected in any other ways than increased physical strength.

8Some time later, when he went back to marry her, he turned aside to look at the lion's carcass. In it was a swarm of bees and some honey, 9which he scooped out with his hands and ate as he went along. When he rejoined his parents, he gave them some, and they too ate it. But he did not tell them that he had taken the honey from the lion's carcass.

10Now his father went down to see the woman. And Samson made a feast there, as was customary for bridegrooms. 11When he appeared, he was given thirty companions.

12"Let me tell you a riddle,*d* " Samson said to them. "If you can give me the answer within the seven days of the feast,*e* I will give you thirty linen garments and thirty sets of clothes.*f* 13If you can't tell me the answer, you must give me thirty linen garments and thirty sets of clothes."

"Tell us your riddle," they said. "Let's hear it."

14He replied,

> "Out of the eater, something to eat;
>   out of the strong, something sweet."

For three days they could not give the answer.

15On the fourth*a* day, they said to Samson's wife, "Coax*g* your husband into explaining the riddle for us, or we will burn you and your father's household to death.*h* Did you invite us here to rob us?"

16Then Samson's wife threw herself on him, sobbing, "You hate me! You don't really love me.*i* You've given my people a riddle, but you haven't told me the answer."

"I haven't even explained it to my father or mother," he replied, "so why should I explain it to you?" 17She cried the whole seven days of the feast. So on the seventh day he finally told her, because she continued to press him. She in turn explained the riddle to her people.

18Before sunset on the seventh day the men of the town said to him,

> "What is sweeter than honey?
>   What is stronger than a lion?"

Samson said to them,

> "If you had not plowed with my heifer,
>   you would not have solved my riddle."

19Then the Spirit of the LORD came upon him in power.*j* He went down to Ashkelon, struck down thirty of their men, stripped them of their belongings and gave their clothes to those who had explained the riddle. Burning with anger, he went up to his father's house. 20And Samson's wife was given to the friend*k* who had attended him at his wedding.

Samson's Vengeance on the Philistines

15 Later on, at the time of wheat harvest, Samson took a young goat and went to visit his wife. He said, "I'm going to my wife's room." But her father would not let him go in.

a 15 Some Septuagint manuscripts and Syriac; Hebrew *seventh*

14:12
d Eze 17:2
e Ge 29:27
f Ge 45:22; 2Ki 5:5

14:15
g Jdg 16:5; Ecc 7:26
h Jdg 15:6

14:16
i Jdg 16:15

14:19
j Nu 11:25;
Jdg 3:10; 6:34;
13:25; 1Sa 11:6;
Isa 11:2

14:20
k Jdg 15:2,6;
Jn 3:29

14:18 "If you had not plowed with my heifer" means "If you had not manipulated my wife." If they hadn't threatened his wife, they wouldn't have learned the answer to his riddle.

14:19 Samson impulsively used the special gift God gave him for selfish purposes. Today, God distributes abilities and skills throughout the church (1 Corinthians 12:1ff). The apostle Paul states that these gifts are to be used "that the body of Christ may be built up;" that is, to build up the church (Ephesians 4:12). To use these abilities for selfish purposes is to rob the church and fellow believers of strength. As you use the gifts God has given you, be sure you are helping others, not just yourself.

15:1ff Samson's reply in 15:11 tells the story of this chapter: "I merely did to them what they did to me." Revenge is an uncontrollable monster. Each act of retaliation brings another. It is a boomerang that cannot be thrown without cost to the thrower. The revenge cycle can be halted only by forgiveness.

SAMSON'S VENTURES Samson grew up in Zorah and wanted to marry a Philistine girl from Timnah. Tricked at his own wedding feast, he went to Ashkelon and killed some Philistine men and stole their clothes to pay off a bet. Samson then let himself be captured and brought to Lehi, where he snapped his ropes and killed 1,000 people.

15:2
*l*Jdg 14:20

2 "I was so sure you thoroughly hated her," he said, "that I gave her to your friend. *l* Isn't her younger sister more attractive? Take her instead."

3 Samson said to them, "This time I have a right to get even with the Philistines; I will really harm them." 4 So he went out and caught three hundred foxes and tied them tail to tail in pairs. He then fastened a torch to every pair of tails, 5 lit the torches and let the foxes loose in the standing grain of the Philistines. He burned up the shocks and standing grain, together with the vineyards and olive groves.

15:6
*m*Jdg 14:15

6 When the Philistines asked, "Who did this?" they were told, "Samson, the Timnite's son-in-law, because his wife was given to his friend."

So the Philistines went up and burned her and her father to death. *m* 7 Samson said to them, "Since you've acted like this, I won't stop until I get my revenge on you." 8 He attacked them viciously and slaughtered many of them. Then he went down and stayed in a cave in the rock of Etam.

15:9
*n*ver 14,17,19

9 The Philistines went up and camped in Judah, spreading out near Lehi. *n* 10 The men of Judah asked, "Why have you come to fight us?"

"We have come to take Samson prisoner," they answered, "to do to him as he did to us."

15:11
*o*Jdg 14:4

11 Then three thousand men from Judah went down to the cave in the rock of Etam and said to Samson, "Don't you realize that the Philistines are rulers over us? *o* What have you done to us?"

He answered, "I merely did to them what they did to me."

12 They said to him, "We've come to tie you up and hand you over to the Philistines." Samson said, "Swear to me that you won't kill me yourselves."

15:14
*p*Jdg 14:19

13 "Agreed," they answered. "We will only tie you up and hand you over to them. We will not kill you." So they bound him with two new ropes and led him up from the rock. 14 As he approached Lehi, the Philistines came toward him shouting. The Spirit of the LORD came upon him in power. *p* The ropes on his arms became like charred flax, and the bindings dropped from his hands. 15 Finding a fresh jawbone of a donkey, he grabbed it and struck down a thousand men. *q*

15:15
*q*Lev 26:8;
Jos 23:10

16 Then Samson said,

> "With a donkey's jawbone
>   I have made donkeys of them. *a*
> With a donkey's jawbone
>   I have killed a thousand men."

17 When he finished speaking, he threw away the jawbone; and the place was called Ramath Lehi. *b*

15:18
*r*Jdg 16:28

18 Because he was very thirsty, he cried out to the LORD, *r* "You have given your servant this great victory. Must I now die of thirst and fall into the hands of the uncircumcised?" 19 Then God opened up the hollow place in Lehi, and water came out of it. When Samson drank, his strength returned and he revived. *s* So the spring was called En Hakkore, *c* and it is still there in Lehi.

15:19
*s*Ge 45:27;
Isa 40:29

15:20
*t*Jdg 13:1; 16:31

20 Samson led *d* Israel for twenty years *t* in the days of the Philistines.

Samson and Delilah

16 One day Samson went to Gaza, where he saw a prostitute. He went in to spend the night with her. 2 The people of Gaza were told, "Samson is here!" So they surrounded the place and lay in wait for him all night at the city gate. They made no move during the night, saying, "At dawn we'll kill him."

a 16 Or *made a heap or two*; the Hebrew for *donkey* sounds like the Hebrew for *heap.*   *b 17 Ramath Lehi* means *jawbone hill.*   *c 19 En Hakkore* means *caller's spring.*   *d 20* Traditionally *judged*

15:14–17 The Lord's strength came upon Samson, but he was proud and boasted only of his own strength. "With a donkey's jawbone I have killed a thousand men," he said, and later asked God to refresh him because of *his* accomplishments (15:16–18). Pride can cause us to take credit for work we've done only because of God's strength.

15:18 Samson was physically and emotionally exhausted. After a great personal victory, his attitude declined quickly into self-pity— "Must I now die of thirst?" Emotionally, we are most vulnerable after a great effort or when faced with real physical needs. Severe depression often follows great achievements, so don't be surprised if you feel drained after a personal victory.

During these times of vulnerability, avoid the temptation to think that God owes you for your efforts. It was *his* strength that gave you victory. Concentrate on keeping your attitudes, actions, and words focused on God instead of yourself.

15:20 Apparently Samson was appointed Israel's judge after this victory over the Philistines.

3 But Samson lay there only until the middle of the night. Then he got up and took hold of the doors of the city gate, together with the two posts, and tore them loose, bar and all. He lifted them to his shoulders and carried them to the top of the hill that faces Hebron.

4 Some time later, he fell in love with a woman in the Valley of Sorek whose name was Delilah. 5 The rulers of the Philistines ᵘ went to her and said, "See if you can lure ᵛ him into showing you the secret of his great strength and how we can overpower him so we may tie him up and subdue him. Each one of us will give you eleven hundred shekels ᵃ of silver."

16:5
ᵘ Jos 13:3
ᵛ Jdg 14:15

6 So Delilah said to Samson, "Tell me the secret of your great strength and how you can be tied up and subdued."

7 Samson answered her, "If anyone ties me with seven fresh thongs ᵇ that have not been dried, I'll become as weak as any other man."

8 Then the rulers of the Philistines brought her seven fresh thongs that had not been dried, and she tied him with them. 9 With men hidden in the room, she called to him, "Samson, the Philistines are upon you!" But he snapped the thongs as easily as a piece of string snaps when it comes close to a flame. So the secret of his strength was not discovered.

10 Then Delilah said to Samson, "You have made a fool of me; ʷ you lied to me. Come now, tell me how you can be tied."

16:10
ʷ ver 13

11 He said, "If anyone ties me securely with new ropes that have never been used, I'll become as weak as any other man."

12 So Delilah took new ropes and tied him with them. Then, with men hidden in the room, she called to him, "Samson, the Philistines are upon you!" But he snapped the ropes off his arms as if they were threads.

13 Delilah then said to Samson, "Until now, you have been making a fool of me and lying to me. Tell me how you can be tied."

He replied, "If you weave the seven braids of my head into the fabric ⌐on the loom⌐ and tighten it with the pin, I'll become as weak as any other man." So while he was sleeping, Delilah took the seven braids of his head, wove them into the fabric 14 and ᶜ tightened it with the pin.

Again she called to him, "Samson, the Philistines are upon you!" He awoke from his sleep and pulled up the pin and the loom, with the fabric.

15 Then she said to him, "How can you say, 'I love you,' ˣ when you won't confide in me? This is the third time you have made a fool of me and haven't told me the secret of your great strength." 16 With such nagging she prodded him day after day until he was tired to death.

16:15
ˣ Jdg 14:16

17 So he told her everything. ʸ "No razor has ever been used on my head," he said, "because I have been a Nazirite ᶻ set apart to God since birth. If my head were shaved, my strength would leave me, and I would become as weak as any other man."

16:17
ʸ Mic 7:5
ᶻ Nu 6:2,5; Jdg 13:5

ᵃ5 That is, about 28 pounds (about 13 kilograms)   ᵇ7 Or *bowstrings*; also in verses 8 and 9   ᶜ13,14 Some Septuagint manuscripts; Hebrew "⌐I can⌐ if you weave the seven braids of my head into the fabric [on the loom]." 14 So she

---

16:5 The Philistines were ruled by five rulers, not just one. Each ruler ruled from a different city—Ashdod, Ashkelon, Ekron, Gath, or Gaza. Each of these cities was an important center for trade and commerce. Given Delilah's character, it is little wonder that she betrayed Samson when these rich and powerful men paid her a personal visit.

16:15 Samson was deceived because he wanted to believe Delilah's lies. Although he could strangle a lion, he could not smother his burning lust and see Delilah for who she really was. How can you keep your desire for love and sexual pleasure from deceiving you? (1) You must decide what kind of a person you will love *before* passion takes over. Determine whether a person's character and faith in God are as desirable as his or her physical appearance. (2) Because most of the time you spend with your spouse will *not* involve sex, your companion's personality, temperament, and commitment to solve problems must be as gratifying as his or her kisses. (3) Be patient. Time and observation often reveal what is beneath the pleasant appearance and attentive touch.

16:16, 17 Delilah kept asking Samson for the secret of his strength until he finally grew tired of hearing her nagging and gave in. This was the second time that Samson allowed himself to be worn down by constant nagging (14:17). What a pitiful excuse for disobedience. Don't allow anyone—no matter how attractive, persuasive, or persistent—to talk you into doing wrong.

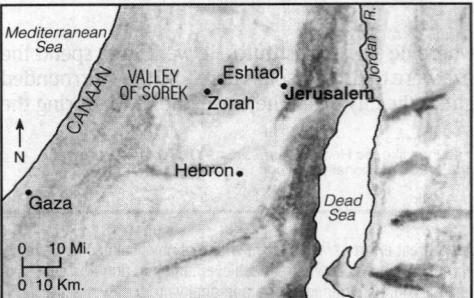

SAMSON AND DELILAH   Samson was seduced by a Philistine woman named Delilah who lived in the Valley of Sorek. She betrayed the secret of his strength to the Philistines, who captured him and led him away in chains to Gaza. There he died. His relatives buried him between Zorah and Eshtaol.

[18] When Delilah saw that he had told her everything, she sent word to the rulers of the Philistines, "Come back once more; he has told me everything." So the rulers of the Philistines returned with the silver in their hands. [19] Having put him to sleep on her lap, she called a man to shave off the seven braids of his hair, and so began to subdue him. [a] And his strength left him. [a]

[20] Then she called, "Samson, the Philistines are upon you!"

He awoke from his sleep and thought, "I'll go out as before and shake myself free." But he did not know that the LORD had left him. [b]

[21] Then the Philistines seized him, gouged out his eyes and took him down to Gaza. Binding him with bronze shackles, they set him to grinding in the prison. [22] But the hair on his head began to grow again after it had been shaved.

The Death of Samson

[23] Now the rulers of the Philistines assembled to offer a great sacrifice to Dagon [c] their god and to celebrate, saying, "Our god has delivered Samson, our enemy, into our hands."

16:19
a Pr 7:26-27

16:20
b Nu 14:42;
Jos 7:12;
1Sa 16:14; 18:12;
28:15

16:23
c 1Sa 5:2

[a] 19 Hebrew; some Septuagint manuscripts *and he began to weaken*

A person's greatest accomplishment may well be helping others accomplish great things. Likewise, a person's greatest failure may be preventing others from achieving greatness. Delilah played a minor role in Samson's life, but her effect was devastating, for she influenced him to betray his special calling from God. Motivated by greed, Delilah used her persistence to wear down Samson. His infatuation with her made Samson a vulnerable target. For all his physical strength, he was no match for her, and he paid a great price for giving in to her. Delilah is never mentioned again in the Bible. Her unfaithfulness to Samson brought ruin to him and to her people.

Are people helped by knowing you? Do they find that knowing you challenges them to be the best they can be? Even more important, does knowing you help their relationship with God? What do your demands for their time and attention tell them about your real care for them? Are you willing to be God's instrument in the lives of others?

DELILAH

Strength and accomplishment:	• Persistent when faced with obstacles
Weaknesses and mistakes:	• Valued money more than relationships • Betrayed the man who trusted her
Lesson from her life:	• We need to be careful to place our trust only in people who are trustworthy
Vital statistics:	• Where: Valley of Sorek • Contemporary: Samson
Key verses:	"With such nagging she prodded him day after day until he was tired to death. So he told her everything" (Judges 16:16, 17).

Her story is told in Judges 16.

16:19 Delilah was a deceitful woman with honey on her lips and poison in her heart. Cold and calculating, she toyed with Samson, pretending to love him while looking for personal gain. How could Samson be so foolish? Four times Delilah took advantage of him. If he didn't realize what was happening after the first or second experience, surely he should have understood the situation by the fourth time! We think Samson is foolish, but how many times do we allow ourselves to be deceived by flattery and give in to temptation and wrong beliefs? Avoid falling prey to deceit by asking God to help you distinguish between deception and truth.

16:21 Samson, the mighty warrior, became a slave. Rather than kill him, the Philistines preferred to humiliate him by gouging out his eyes and making him grind grain. Samson now had plenty of time to wonder if Delilah's charms were worth spending the rest of his life in humiliation.

Although God did not completely abandon Samson (16:28–30), he allowed Samson's decision to stand, and the consequences of his decision followed naturally. We may choose to be close to God or to go our own way, but there are consequences resulting from our choice. Samson didn't choose to be captured, but he chose to be with Delilah, and he could not escape the consequences of his decision.

16:21 Blinded and without strength, Samson was taken to Gaza where he would spend the rest of his short life. Gaza was one of the five capital cities of the Philistines. Known for its many wells, Gaza was a vital stop along a great caravan route that connected Egypt to the south with Aram to the north. The Philistines probably showed off their prize captive, Samson, to many dignitaries passing through.

Ironically, it was in Gaza that Samson had earlier demonstrated his great strength by uprooting the city gates (16:1–3). Now he was an example of weakness.

16:23, 24 Dagon was the chief god of the Philistines, the god of grain and harvest. Many temples were built to Dagon, and the worship there included human sacrifice. The temples were also the local entertainment centers. Just as people today crowd into theaters, Philistine townspeople crowded into the local temple. They sat on the flat temple roof and looked into the courtyard below. What they often saw was the torture and humiliation of prisoners.

Since the Philistines had control over the Israelites, they thought their god was stronger. But when the ark of God was placed before Dagon in a similar temple, the idol fell over and broke into pieces (1 Samuel 5:1–7). God's strength goes beyond numbers or physical might.

24 When the people saw him, they praised their god,*d* saying,

> "Our god has delivered our enemy
>   into our hands,*e*
> the one who laid waste our land
>   and multiplied our slain."

25 While they were in high spirits,*f* they shouted, "Bring out Samson to entertain us." So they called Samson out of the prison, and he performed for them.

When they stood him among the pillars, 26 Samson said to the servant who held his hand, "Put me where I can feel the pillars that support the temple, so that I may lean against them." 27 Now the temple was crowded with men and women; all the rulers of the Philistines were there, and on the roof were about three thousand men and women watching Samson perform. 28 Then Samson prayed to the LORD,*g* "O Sovereign LORD, remember me. O God, please strengthen me just once more, and let me with one blow get revenge*h* on the Philistines for my two eyes." 29 Then Samson reached toward the two central pillars on which the temple stood. Bracing himself against them, his right hand on the one and his left hand on the other, 30 Samson said, "Let me die with the Philistines!" Then he pushed with all his might, and down came the temple on the rulers and all the people in it. Thus he killed many more when he died than while he lived.

31 Then his brothers and his father's whole family went down to get him. They brought him back and buried him between Zorah and Eshtaol in the tomb of Manoah his father. He had led*a* Israel twenty years.*i*

C. THE MORAL FAILURE OF ISRAEL (17:1—21:25)

This section shows Israel falling into idolatry, moral decline, and petty fighting. Israel, the nation that was to set the example for spiritual living, had instead become morally depraved. When Israel did serve God, and that was seldom, it was often from selfish motives. Selfish obedience does not bring us far. Genuine obedience is motivated by a love and reverence for God himself.

1. Idolatry in the tribe of Dan
Micah's Idols

17 Now a man named Micah from the hill country of Ephraim 2 said to his mother, "The eleven hundred shekels*b* of silver that were taken from you and about which I heard you utter a curse—I have that silver with me; I took it."

Then his mother said, "The LORD bless you, my son!"

3 When he returned the eleven hundred shekels of silver to his mother, she said, "I solemnly consecrate my silver to the LORD for my son to make a carved image and a cast idol.*j* I will give it back to you."

4 So he returned the silver to his mother, and she took two hundred shekels*c* of silver and gave them to a silversmith, who made them into the image and the idol. And they were put in Micah's house.

5 Now this man Micah had a shrine, and he made an ephod*k* and some idols and installed one of his sons as his priest. 6 In those days Israel had no king;*l* everyone did as he saw fit.*m*

---

a31 Traditionally *judged*   *b2* That is, about 28 pounds (about 13 kilograms)   *c4* That is, about 5 pounds (about 2.3 kilograms)

Marginal references:
16:24 *d* Da 5:4; *e* 1Sa 31:9; 1Ch 10:9
16:25 *f* Jdg 9:27
16:28 *g* Jdg 15:18; *h* Jer 15:15
16:31 *i* Jdg 15:20
17:3 *j* Ex 20:4,23
17:5 *k* Jdg 8:27
17:6 *l* Jdg 18:1; 19:1; *m* Dt 12:8

16:28-30 In spite of Samson's past, God still answered his prayer and destroyed the pagan temple and worshipers. God still loved him. He was willing to hear Samson's prayer of confession and repentance and use him this final time. One of the effects of sin in our lives is to keep us from feeling like praying. But perfect moral behavior is not a condition for prayer. Don't let guilt feelings over sin keep you from your only means of restoration. No matter how long you have been away from God, he is ready to hear from you and restore you to a right relationship. Every situation can be salvaged if you are willing to turn again to him. If God could still work in Samson's situation, he can certainly make something worthwhile out of yours.

17:2 Micah and his mother seemed to be good and moral and may have sincerely desired to worship God, but they disobeyed God by following their own desires instead of doing what God wanted. The attitude that prevailed in Micah's day was this: "Every-

one did as he saw fit" (17:6). This is remarkably similar to today's prevailing attitudes. But God has given us standards. He has not left our conduct up to us and our opinions. We can avoid conforming to society's low standards by taking God's commands seriously and applying them to life. Independence and self-reliance are positive traits, but only within the framework of God's standards.

17:6 Today, as in Micah's day, everyone seems to put his or her own interests first. Time has not changed human nature. Most people still reject God's right way of living. The people in Micah's time replaced the true worship of God with a homemade version of worship. As a result, justice was soon replaced by revenge and chaos. Ignoring God's direction led to confusion and destruction. Anyone who has not submitted to God will end up doing whatever seems right at the time. This tendency is present in all of us. To know what is really right and to have the strength to do it, we need to draw closer to God and his Word.

17:7
n Jdg 19:1;
Ru 1:1-2; Mic 5:2;
Mt 2:1

17:10
o Jdg 18:19

18:1
p Jdg 17:6
q Jos 19:47

18:2
r Jdg 13:25
s Jdg 17:1

18:4
t Jdg 17:12

18:6
u 1Ki 22:6
18:7
v Jos 19:47
w ver 28

⁷A young Levite from Bethlehem in Judah,*n* who had been living within the clan of Judah, ⁸left that town in search of some other place to stay. On his way*a* he came to Micah's house in the hill country of Ephraim.

⁹Micah asked him, "Where are you from?"

"I'm a Levite from Bethlehem in Judah," he said, "and I'm looking for a place to stay."

¹⁰Then Micah said to him, "Live with me and be my father and priest,*o* and I'll give you ten shekels*b* of silver a year, your clothes and your food." ¹¹So the Levite agreed to live with him, and the young man was to him like one of his sons. ¹²Then Micah installed the Levite, and the young man became his priest and lived in his house. ¹³And Micah said, "Now I know that the LORD will be good to me, since this Levite has become my priest."

Danites Settle in Laish

18 In those days Israel had no king.*p*

And in those days the tribe of the Danites was seeking a place of their own where they might settle, because they had not yet come into an inheritance among the tribes of Israel.*q* ²So the Danites*r* sent five warriors from Zorah and Eshtaol to spy out the land and explore it. These men represented all their clans. They told them, "Go, explore the land."

The men entered the hill country of Ephraim and came to the house of Micah,*s* where they spent the night. ³When they were near Micah's house, they recognized the voice of the young Levite; so they turned in there and asked him, "Who brought you here? What are you doing in this place? Why are you here?"

⁴He told them what Micah had done for him, and said, "He has hired me and I am his priest.*t*"

⁵Then they said to him, "Please inquire of God to learn whether our journey will be successful."

⁶The priest answered them, "Go in peace.*u* Your journey has the LORD's approval."

⁷So the five men left and came to Laish,*v* where they saw that the people were living in safety, like the Sidonians, unsuspecting and secure. And since their land lacked nothing, they were prosperous.*c* Also, they lived a long way from the Sidonians*w* and had no relationship with anyone else.*d*

⁸When they returned to Zorah and Eshtaol, their brothers asked them, "How did you find things?"

a 8 Or *To carry on his profession*   *b 10* That is, about 4 ounces (about 110 grams)   *c 7* The meaning of the Hebrew for this clause is uncertain.   *d 7* Hebrew; some Septuagint manuscripts *with the Arameans*

17:7–12 Apparently the Israelites no longer supported the priests and Levites with their tithes because so many of the people no longer worshiped God. The young Levite in this story probably left his home in Bethlehem because the money he received from the people there was not enough to live on. But Israel's moral decay affected even the priests and Levites. This man accepted money (17:10, 11), idols (18:20), and position (17:12) in a way that was inconsistent with God's laws. While Micah revealed the religious downfall of individual Israelites, this priest illustrated the religious downfall of priests and Levites.

18:1 The Danites had been assigned enough land to meet their needs (Joshua 19:40–48). However, because they failed to trust God to help them conquer their territory, the Amorites forced them into the hill country and wouldn't let them settle in the plains (1:34). Rather than fight for their allotted territory, they preferred to look for new land in the north where resistance from the enemy wouldn't be so tough. It was while they were traveling north that some of their men passed Micah's home and stole some of his idols.

18:4–6 Priests and their assistants were all members of the tribe of Levi (Numbers 3:5–13). They were to serve the people, teach them how to worship God, and perform the rituals involved in the worship services both at the tabernacle in Shiloh and in the designated cities throughout the land. But this disobedient priest showed disrespect for God because (1) he performed his duties in a way that (2) He priestly duties were to be performed only in the tabernacle or a designated city. This requirement was intended to prevent God's laws from being changed. (2) He

carried idols with him (18:20). (3) He claimed to speak for God when God had not spoken through him (18:6).

18:11–26 Through this entire incident, no one desired to worship God; instead, they wanted to use God for selfish gain. Today some people go to church to feel better, be accepted,

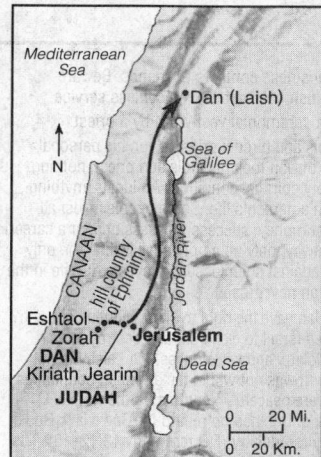

THE TRIBE OF DAN MOVES NORTH
Troops from the tribe of Dan traveled from Zorah and Eshtaol into the hill country of Ephraim, where they persuaded Micah's priest to come with them. They continued north to Laish, where they ruthlessly butchered its citizens. The city was renamed Dan, and the priest's idols became the focus of their worship.

⁹They answered, "Come on, let's attack them! We have seen that the land is very good. Aren't you going to do something? Don't hesitate to go there and take it over.ˣ ¹⁰When you get there, you will find an unsuspecting people and a spacious land that God has put into your hands, a land that lacks nothingʸ whatever."

¹¹Then six hundred menᶻ from the clan of the Danites, armed for battle, set out from Zorah and Eshtaol. ¹²On their way they set up camp near Kiriath Jearim in Judah. This is why the place west of Kiriath Jearim is called Mahaneh Danᵃ ᵃ to this day. ¹³From there they went on to the hill country of Ephraim and came to Micah's house.

¹⁴Then the five men who had spied out the land of Laish said to their brothers, "Do you know that one of these houses has an ephod, other household gods, a carved image and a cast idol? Now you know what to do." ¹⁵So they turned in there and went to the house of the young Levite at Micah's place and greeted him. ¹⁶The six hundred Danites,ᵇ armed for battle, stood at the entrance to the gate. ¹⁷The five men who had spied out the land went inside and took the carved image, the ephod, the other household gods and the cast idol while the priest and the six hundred armed men stood at the entrance to the gate.

¹⁸When these men went into Micah's house and took the carved image, the ephod, the other household gods and the cast idol, the priest said to them, "What are you doing?"

¹⁹They answered him, "Be quiet!ᶜ Don't say a word. Come with us, and be our father and priest. ᵈ Isn't it better that you serve a tribe and clan in Israel as priest rather than just one man's household?" ²⁰Then the priest was glad. He took the ephod, the other household gods and the carved image and went along with the people. ²¹Putting their little children, their livestock and their possessions in front of them, they turned away and left.

²²When they had gone some distance from Micah's house, the men who lived near Micah were called together and overtook the Danites. ²³As they shouted after them, the Danites turned and said to Micah, "What's the matter with you that you called out your men to fight?"

²⁴He replied, "You took the gods I made, and my priest, and went away. What else do I have? How can you ask, 'What's the matter with you?'"

²⁵The Danites answered, "Don't argue with us, or some hot-tempered men will attack you, and you and your family will lose your lives." ²⁶So the Danites went their way, and Micah, seeing that they were too strong for him, turned around and went back home.

²⁷Then they took what Micah had made, and his priest, and went on to Laish, against a peaceful and unsuspecting people. They attacked them with the sword and burned down their city. ᵉ ²⁸There was no one to rescue them because they lived a long way from Sidonᶠ and had no relationship with anyone else. The city was in a valley near Beth Rehob.ᵍ

The Danites rebuilt the city and settled there. ²⁹They named it Dan after their forefather Dan, who was born to Israel—though the city used to be called Laish. ʰ ³⁰There the Danites set up for themselves the idols, and Jonathan son of Gershom,ⁱ the son of Moses,ᵇ and his sons were priests for the tribe of Dan until the time of the captivity of the land. ³¹They continued to use the idols Micah had made, all the time the house of God was in Shiloh.ʲ

18:9 ˣNu 13:30; 1Ki 22:3
18:10 ʸDt 8:9
18:11 ᶻver 16,17
18:12 ᵃJdg 13:25
18:16 ᵇver 11
18:19 ᶜJob 21:5; 29:9; 40:4 ᵈJdg 17:10
18:27 ᵉJos 19:47
18:28 ᶠver 7 ᵍ2Sa 10:6
18:29 ʰJos 19:47
18:30 ⁱEx 2:22; Jdg 17:3,5
18:31 ʲJos 18:1

ᵃ 12 *Mahaneh Dan* means *Dan's camp.* ᵇ 30 An ancient Hebrew scribal tradition, some Septuagint manuscripts and Vulgate; Masoretic Text *Manasseh*

relieve guilt, and gain business contacts or friends. Beware of following God for selfish gain rather than selfless service.

18:14 An ephod was a ceremonial vest worn by a priest.

18:24 Micah made idols and hired a priest to run his personal religion. When the men of Dan took his idols and priest, nothing remained. What an empty spiritual condition! An idol is anything that takes God's place in a person's life. Some people invest all their energy in pursuit of money, success, possessions, or a career. If these idols are taken away, only an empty shell is left. The only way to protect yourself against such loss is to invest your life in the living God, whom you can never lose.

18:27 Did the tribe of Dan have the right to kill the citizens of Laish? No. God had commanded Israel to clean out and destroy certain cities because of their idolatry and wickedness, but Laish did not fall under that judgment. It was not within the assigned boundaries of Dan, and its people were peaceful in contrast to the warlike Canaanites. But the tribe of Dan had no regard for God's law. God's law said to destroy a city for idolatry (Deuteronomy 13:12–15). The Danites themselves were guilty of this sin. This story shows how far some of the tribes had wandered away from God.

18:27 Just because the Danites successfully defeated Laish doesn't mean their actions were right. Their idolatry showed that God was not guiding them. Today many justify their wrong actions by outward signs of success. They think that wealth, popularity, or lack of suffering is an indication of God's blessing. But many stories in the Bible indicate that evil and earthly success can go hand in hand (see, for example, 2 Kings 14:23–29). Success doesn't indicate God's approval. Don't allow personal success to become a measuring rod of whether or not you are pleasing God.

18:30, 31 The tribe of Dan had stolen Micah's idols, and now they set them up in Laish. Although the Danites were actually denying God by worshiping these images (Exodus 20:1–5), they probably assumed they were worshiping God through them (see the note on Exodus 32:4, 5). Worshiping images of God is *not* worshiping God, even if it resembles true worship in some ways. People repeat the same mistake today when they claim to be Christians without really believing in God's power or changing their conduct to conform to his expectations. Godliness cannot be merely a claim. It must be a reality in our motives and in our actions.

18:31 Shiloh was probably destroyed during the events reported

2. War against the tribe of Benjamin

A Levite and His Concubine

19:1
k Jdg 18:1

19 In those days Israel had no king.
Now a Levite who lived in a remote area in the hill country of Ephraim*k* took a concubine from Bethlehem in Judah. 2 But she was unfaithful to him. She left him and went back to her father's house in Bethlehem, Judah. After she had been there four months, 3 her husband went to her to persuade her to return. He had with him his servant and two donkeys. She took him into her father's house, and when her father saw him, he gladly welcomed him. 4 His father-in-law, the girl's father, prevailed upon him to stay; so he remained with him three days, eating and drinking, and sleeping there.

19:5
l ver 8; Ge 18:5

5 On the fourth day they got up early and he prepared to leave, but the girl's father said to his son-in-law, "Refresh yourself *l* with something to eat; then you can go." 6 So the two of them sat down to eat and drink together. Afterward the girl's father said, "Please stay tonight and enjoy yourself." 7 And when the man got up to go, his father-in-law persuaded him, so he stayed there that night. 8 On the morning of the fifth day, when he rose to go, the girl's father said, "Refresh yourself. Wait till afternoon!" So the two of them ate together.

9 Then when the man, with his concubine and his servant, got up to leave, his father-in-law, the girl's father, said, "Now look, it's almost evening. Spend the night here; the day is nearly over. Stay and enjoy yourself. Early tomorrow morning you can get up and be on your

19:10
m 1Ch 11:4-5

way home." 10 But, unwilling to stay another night, the man left and went toward Jebus *m* (that is, Jerusalem), with his two saddled donkeys and his concubine.

11 When they were near Jebus and the day was almost gone, the servant said to his master, "Come, let's stop at this city of the Jebusites and spend the night."

19:13
n Jos 18:25

12 His master replied, "No. We won't go into an alien city, whose people are not Israelites. We will go on to Gibeah." 13 He added, "Come, let's try to reach Gibeah or Ramah *n* and spend the night in one of those places." 14 So they went on, and the sun set as they neared Gibeah in Benjamin. 15 There they stopped to spend the night. They went and sat in the city square, but no one took them into his home for the night.

19:16
o Ps 104:23

16 That evening *o* an old man from the hill country of Ephraim, who was living in Gibeah (the men of the place were Benjamites), came in from his work in the fields. 17 When he looked and saw the traveler in the city square, the old man asked, "Where are you going? Where did you come from?"

19:18
p Jdg 18:31

18 He answered, "We are on our way from Bethlehem in Judah to a remote area in the hill country of Ephraim where I live. I have been to Bethlehem in Judah and now I am going to the house of the LORD. *p* No one has taken me into his house. 19 We have both straw and fodder for our donkeys and bread and wine for ourselves your servants—me, your maidservant, and the young man with us. We don't need anything."

20 "You are welcome at my house," the old man said. "Let me supply whatever you need.

19:21
q Ge 24:32-33

Only don't spend the night in the square." 21 So he took him into his house and fed his donkeys. After they had washed their feet, they had something to eat and drink. *q*

---

in 1 Samuel 4 and 5, not long after the time described here. Because Shiloh was the religious center for Israel, all adult males were required to travel there for certain religious feasts. The tribe of Dan, however, set up idols and priests in the new territory they conquered. The fact that they were over 80 miles away from Shiloh may have been their excuse for not fulfilling the law's requirements. This act was a further demonstration of their disregard for God.

18:31 The true worship of God should have been maintained through the Levitical priests scattered throughout the land and the influence of the tabernacle in Shiloh. This story shows how pagan influences and moral depravity had crept into every corner of Israelite culture. Although 300 years had passed since they entered the promised land, they still had not destroyed the idolatry and evil practices within it.

There may be a tendency in your life to allow "harmless" habits to have their own small corners, but they can become dominating forces. The values, attitudes, and practices you have adopted from the world's system can be exposed by applying the light of God's truth to them. Once you see them for what they are, you can begin to uproot them.

19:1—21:25 What is the significance of this tragic story? When the Israelites' faith in God disintegrated, their unity as a nation also disintegrated. They could have taken complete possession of the land if they had obeyed God and trusted him to keep his promises. But when they forgot him, they lost their purpose, and soon "everyone did as he saw fit" (21:25). When they stopped letting God lead them, they became no better than the evil people around them. When they made laws for their own benefit, they set standards far below God's. When you leave God out of your life you may be shocked at what you are capable of doing (19:30).

19:1 Having concubines was an accepted part of Israelite society although this is not what God intended (Genesis 2:24). A concubine had most of the duties but only some of the privileges of a wife. Although she was legally attached to one man, she and her children usually did not have the inheritance rights of the legal wife and legitimate children. Her primary purpose was giving the man sexual pleasure, bearing additional children, and contributing more help to the household or estate. Concubines were often foreign prisoners of war. But they could also be Israelites, as was probably the case in this story.

22 While they were enjoying themselves, some of the wicked men *r* of the city surrounded the house. Pounding on the door, they shouted to the old man who owned the house, "Bring out the man who came to your house so we can have sex with him. *s*"

23 The owner of the house went outside and said to them, "No, my friends, don't be so vile. Since this man is my guest, don't do this disgraceful thing. *t* 24 Look, here is my virgin daughter, *u* and his concubine. I will bring them out to you now, and you can use them and do to them whatever you wish. But to this man, don't do such a disgraceful thing."

25 But the men would not listen to him. So the man took his concubine and sent her outside to them, and they raped her and abused her throughout the night, and at dawn they let her go. 26 At daybreak the woman went back to the house where her master was staying, fell down at the door and lay there until daylight.

27 When her master got up in the morning and opened the door of the house and stepped out to continue on his way, there lay his concubine, fallen in the doorway of the house, with her hands on the threshold. 28 He said to her, "Get up; let's go." But there was no answer. Then the man put her on his donkey and set out for home.

29 When he reached home, he took a knife and cut up his concubine, limb by limb, into twelve parts and sent them into all the areas of Israel. *v* 30 Everyone who saw it said, "Such a thing has never been seen or done, not since the day the Israelites came up out of Egypt. Think about it! Consider it! Tell us what to do! *w*"

Israelites Fight the Benjamites

20 Then all the Israelites *x* from Dan to Beersheba and from the land of Gilead came out as one man and assembled *y* before the LORD in Mizpah. 2 The leaders of all the people of the tribes of Israel took their places in the assembly of the people of God, four hundred thousand soldiers *z* armed with swords. 3 (The Benjamites heard that the Israelites had gone up to Mizpah.) Then the Israelites said, "Tell us how this awful thing happened."

4 So the Levite, the husband of the murdered woman, said, "I and my concubine came to Gibeah in Benjamin to spend the night. *a* 5 During the night the men of Gibeah came after me and surrounded the house, intending to kill me. *b* They raped my concubine, and she died. *c* 6 I took my concubine, cut her into pieces and sent one piece to each region of Israel's inheritance, *d* because they committed this lewd and disgraceful act *e* in Israel. 7 Now, all you Israelites, speak up and give your verdict. *f*"

8 All the people rose as one man, saying, "None of us will go home. No, not one of us will return to his house. 9 But now this is what we'll do to Gibeah: We'll go up against it as the lot directs. 10 We'll take ten men out of every hundred from all the tribes of Israel, and a hundred from a thousand, and a thousand from ten thousand, to get provisions for the army. Then, when the army arrives at Gibeah *a* in Benjamin, it can give them what they deserve for all this vileness done in Israel." 11 So all the men of Israel got together and united as one man against the city.

a 10 One Hebrew manuscript; most Hebrew manuscripts *Geba,* a variant of *Gibeah*

19:22
r Dt 13:13
s Ge 19:4-5;
Ro 1:26-27

19:23
t Ge 34:7; Dt 22:21;
2Sa 13:12

19:24
u Ge 19:8

19:29
v 1Sa 11:7

19:30
w Jdg 20:7

20:1
x Jdg 21:5
y 1Sa 7:5

20:2
z Jdg 8:10

20:4
a Jdg 19:15

20:5
b Jdg 19:22
c Jdg 19:25-26

20:6
d Jdg 19:29
e Jos 7:15

20:7
f Jdg 19:30

19:24 Nowhere is the unwritten law of hospitality stronger than in the Middle East. Protecting a guest at any cost ranked at the top of a man's code of honor. But here the hospitality code turned to fanaticism. The rape and abuse of a daughter and companion was preferable to the *possibility* of a conflict between a guest and a neighbor. The two men were selfish (they didn't want to get hurt themselves); they lacked courage (they didn't want to face a conflict even when lives were at stake); and they disobeyed God's law (they allowed deliberate abuse and murder). What drastic consequences can result when social protocol carries more authority than moral convictions!

19:29, 30 Although this was a terrible way to spread the news, it effectively communicated the horror of the crime and called the people to action. Saul used a similar method in 1 Samuel 11:7. Ironically, the man who alerted Israel to the murder of his concubine was just as guilty for her death as the men who actually killed her.

19:30 The horrible crime described in this chapter wasn't Israel's worst offense. Even worse was the nation's failure to establish a government based upon God's moral principles, where the law of God was the law of the land. As a result, laws were usually not enforced and crime was ignored. Sexual perversion and lawlessness were a by-product of Israel's disobedience to God. The Israelites weren't willing to speak up until events had gone too far.

Whenever we get away from God and his Word, all sorts of evil can follow. Our drifting away from God may be slow and almost imperceptible, with the ultimate results affecting a future generation. We must continually call our nation back to God and work toward the establishment of God's moral and spiritual reign in the heart of every person.

20:1 Dan was the northernmost city in Israel, and Beersheba, the southernmost. The two were often mentioned together as a reference to the entire nation.

20:5 In reporting the events in Gibeah, the man conveniently left out the fact that he had handed over his concubine to satisfy the mob's demands. He wanted justice for the threats made against himself rather than placing any value on the life of the woman or holding himself partly responsible for her death. How easy it is to give only partial facts or twist events to remove our own culpability when we are seeking to shift blame to someone

¹²The tribes of Israel sent men throughout the tribe of Benjamin, saying, "What about this awful crime that was committed among you? ¹³Now surrender those wicked men^g of Gibeah so that we may put them to death and purge the evil from Israel."

20:13
^g Dt 13:13

But the Benjamites would not listen to their fellow Israelites. ¹⁴From their towns they came together at Gibeah to fight against the Israelites. ¹⁵At once the Benjamites mobilized twenty-six thousand swordsmen from their towns, in addition to seven hundred chosen men from those living in Gibeah. ¹⁶Among all these soldiers there were seven hundred chosen men who were left-handed,^h each of whom could sling a stone at a hair and not miss.

20:16
^h Jdg 3:15;
1Ch 12:2

¹⁷Israel, apart from Benjamin, mustered four hundred thousand swordsmen, all of them fighting men.

¹⁸The Israelites went up to Bethel^a and inquired of God.ⁱ They said, "Who of us shall go first to fight^j against the Benjamites?"

20:18
ⁱ ver 26-27;
Nu 27:21
^j ver 23,28

The LORD replied, "Judah shall go first."

¹⁹The next morning the Israelites got up and pitched camp near Gibeah. ²⁰The men of Israel went out to fight the Benjamites and took up battle positions against them at Gibeah. ²¹The Benjamites came out of Gibeah and cut down twenty-two thousand Israelites on the battlefield that day. ²²But the men of Israel encouraged one another and again took up their positions where they had stationed themselves the first day. ²³The Israelites went up and wept before the LORD until evening,^k and they inquired of the LORD. They said, "Shall we go up again to battle against the Benjamites, our brothers?"

20:23
^k Jos 7:6

The LORD answered, "Go up against them."

²⁴Then the Israelites drew near to Benjamin the second day. ²⁵This time, when the Benjamites came out from Gibeah to oppose them, they cut down another eighteen thousand Israelites, all of them armed with swords.

²⁶Then the Israelites, all the people, went up to Bethel, and there they sat weeping before the LORD. They fasted that day until evening and presented burnt offerings and fellowship offerings^b to the LORD. ²⁷And the Israelites inquired of the LORD. (In those days the ark of the covenant of God was there, ²⁸with Phinehas son of Eleazar, the son of Aaron, ministering before it.) They asked, "Shall we go up again to battle with Benjamin our brother, or not?"

The LORD responded, "Go, for tomorrow I will give them into your hands."

²⁹Then Israel set an ambush^l around Gibeah. ³⁰They went up against the Benjamites on the third day and took up positions against Gibeah as they had done before. ³¹The Benjamites came out to meet them and were drawn away^m from the city. They began to inflict casualties on the Israelites as before, so that about thirty men fell in the open field and on the roads—the one leading to Bethel and the other to Gibeah.

20:29
^l Jos 8:2,4
20:31
^m Jos 8:16

³²While the Benjamites were saying, "We are defeating them as before," the Israelites were saying, "Let's retreat and draw them away from the city to the roads."

³³All the men of Israel moved from their places and took up positions at Baal Tamar, and the Israelite ambush charged out of its place on the west^c of Gibeah.^d ³⁴Then ten thousand of Israel's finest men made a frontal attack on Gibeah. The fighting was so heavy that the Benjamites did not realizeⁿ how near disaster was. ³⁵The LORD defeated Benjamin before Israel, and on that day the Israelites struck down 25,100 Benjamites, all armed with swords. ³⁶Then the Benjamites saw that they were beaten.

20:34
ⁿ Jos 8:14

Now the men of Israel had given way before Benjamin, because they relied on the ambush they had set near Gibeah. ³⁷The men who had been in ambush made a sudden dash into Gibeah, spread out and put the whole city to the sword.^o ³⁸The men of Israel had arranged with

20:37
^o Jos 8:19

^a *18* Or *to the house of God*; also in verse 26   ^b *26* Traditionally *peace offerings*   ^c *33* Some Septuagint manuscripts and Vulgate; the meaning of the Hebrew for this word is uncertain.   ^d *33* Hebrew *Geba*, a variant of *Gibeah*

---

else. This incident reveals the depths of perversion and violence that develop when a culture abandon's God's ways.

20:13 Perhaps the Benjamite leaders had been given distorted facts about the serious crime in their territory, or perhaps they were too proud to admit that some of their people had stooped so low. In either case, they would not listen to the rest of Israel and hand over the accused criminals. They were more loyal to their own tribe than to God's law.

By covering for their kinsmen, the entire tribe of Benjamin sank to a level of immorality as low as the criminals'. Through this act, we get a glimpse of how thoroughly the nation's moral fabric had unraveled. The time period of the judges ends in a

bloody civil war that sets the stage for the spiritual renewal to come under Samuel (see 1 Samuel).

20:27, 28 This is the only place in Judges where the ark of the covenant is mentioned. This probably indicates how seldom the people consulted God.

Phinehas, the high priest, was also the high priest under Joshua (Joshua 22:13). The reference to Phinehas as high priest and the location of the tabernacle in Bethel instead of Shiloh probably indicate that the events of this story occurred during the early years of the judges.

the ambush that they should send up a great cloud of smoke from the city, [39] and then the men of Israel would turn in the battle.

The Benjamites had begun to inflict casualties on the men of Israel (about thirty), and they said, "We are defeating them as in the first battle."[p] [40] But when the column of smoke began to rise from the city, the Benjamites turned and saw the smoke of the whole city going up into the sky. [41] Then the men of Israel turned on them, and the men of Benjamin were terrified, because they realized that disaster had come upon them. [42] So they fled before the Israelites in the direction of the desert, but they could not escape the battle. And the men of Israel who came out of the towns cut them down there. [43] They surrounded the Benjamites, chased them and easily[a] overran them in the vicinity of Gibeah on the east. [44] Eighteen thousand Benjamites fell, all of them valiant fighters. [45] As they turned and fled toward the desert to the rock of Rimmon,[q] the Israelites cut down five thousand men along the roads. They kept pressing after the Benjamites as far as Gidom and struck down two thousand more.

[46] On that day twenty-five thousand Benjamite swordsmen fell, all of them valiant fighters. [47] But six hundred men turned and fled into the desert to the rock of Rimmon, where they stayed four months. [48] The men of Israel went back to Benjamin and put all the towns to the sword, including the animals and everything else they found. All the towns they came across they set on fire.

Wives for the Benjamites

21 The men of Israel had taken an oath at Mizpah: "Not one of us will give[r] his daughter in marriage to a Benjamite."

[2] The people went to Bethel,[b] where they sat before God until evening, raising their voices and weeping bitterly. [3] "O Lord, the God of Israel," they cried, "why has this happened to Israel? Why should one tribe be missing from Israel today?"

[4] Early the next day the people built an altar and presented burnt offerings and fellowship offerings.[c][s]

[5] Then the Israelites asked, "Who from all the tribes of Israel[t] has failed to assemble before the Lord?" For they had taken a solemn oath that anyone who failed to assemble before the Lord at Mizpah should certainly be put to death.

[6] Now the Israelites grieved for their brothers, the Benjamites. "Today one tribe is cut off from Israel," they said. [7] "How can we provide wives for those who are left, since we have taken an oath by the Lord not to give them any of our daughters in marriage?" [8] Then they asked, "Which one of the tribes of Israel failed to assemble before the Lord at Mizpah?" They discovered that no one from Jabesh Gilead[u] had come to the camp for the assembly. [9] For when they counted the people, they found that none of the people of Jabesh Gilead were there.

[10] So the assembly sent twelve thousand fighting men with instructions to go to Jabesh Gilead and put to the sword those living there, including the women and children. [11] "This is what you are to do," they said. "Kill every male and every woman who is not a virgin.[v]" [12] They found among the people living in Jabesh Gilead four hundred young women who had never slept with a man, and they took them to the camp at Shiloh in Canaan.

[13] Then the whole assembly sent an offer of peace to the Benjamites at the rock of Rimmon.[w] [14] So the Benjamites returned at that time and were given the women of Jabesh Gilead who had been spared. But there were not enough for all of them.

a43 The meaning of the Hebrew for this word is uncertain.   b2 Or to the house of God   c4 Traditionally peace offerings

Cross references

20:39 p ver 32

20:45 q Jos 15:32; Jdg 21:13

21:1 r ver 7,18

21:4 s Jdg 20:26; 2Sa 24:25

21:5 t Jdg 5:23

21:8 u 1Sa 11:1

21:11 v Nu 31:17-18

21:13 w Jdg 20:47

20:46-48 The effects of the horrible rape and murder should never have been felt outside the community where the crime happened. The local people should have brought the criminals to justice and corrected the laxness that originally permitted the crime. Instead, first the town and then the entire tribe defended this wickedness, even going to war over it.

To prevent unresolved problems from turning into major conflicts, firm action must be taken quickly, wisely, and forcefully *before* the situation gets out of hand.

20:48 The tribe of Benjamin eventually recovered from this slaughter. Saul, Israel's first king, was from this tribe (1 Samuel 9:21). So were Queen Esther (Esther 2:5-7) and the apostle Paul

(Romans 11:1). But the tribe was always known for being smaller than the rest (as in Psalm 68:27).

21:8-12 The Israelites moved from one mess to another. Because of a rash vow made in the heat of emotion (21:5), here they destroyed another town. Israel probably justified their action with the following arguments: (1) An oath could not be broken, and Israel had vowed that anyone who did not help them fight the Benjamites would be killed. (2) Because all the women from Benjamin had been killed, the few remaining men needed wives to prevent the tribe from disappearing. To spare the unmarried women from Jabesh Gilead seemed the right solution.

We do not know all the circumstances behind the brutal massacre at Jabesh Gilead, but it seems that the rest of Israel

¹⁵The people grieved for Benjamin, because the Lord had made a gap in the tribes of Israel. ¹⁶And the elders of the assembly said, "With the women of Benjamin destroyed, how shall we provide wives for the men who are left? ¹⁷The Benjamite survivors must have heirs," they said, "so that a tribe of Israel will not be wiped out. ¹⁸We can't give them our daughters as wives, since we Israelites have taken this oath: 'Cursed be anyone who gives a wife to a Benjamite.' ¹⁹But look, there is the annual festival of the Lord in Shiloh, to the north of Bethel, and east of the road that goes from Bethel to Shechem, and to the south of Lebonah."

21:21
×Ex 15:20;
Jdg 11:34

²⁰So they instructed the Benjamites, saying, "Go and hide in the vineyards ²¹and watch. When the girls of Shiloh come out to join in the dancing,× then rush from the vineyards and each of you seize a wife from the girls of Shiloh and go to the land of Benjamin. ²²When their fathers or brothers complain to us, we will say to them, 'Do us a kindness by helping them, because we did not get wives for them during the war, and you are innocent, since you did not give your daughters to them.'"

21:23
yJdg 20:48

²³So that is what the Benjamites did. While the girls were dancing, each man caught one and carried her off to be his wife. Then they returned to their inheritance and rebuilt the towns and settled in them.y

²⁴At that time the Israelites left that place and went home to their tribes and clans, each to his own inheritance.

21:25
zJdg 17:6; 18:1;
19:1

²⁵In those days Israel had no king; everyone did as he saw fit.z

---

followed Benjamin's pattern. They put tribal loyalties above God's commands, and they justified wrong actions to correct past mistakes.

21:25 During the time of the judges, the people of Israel experienced trouble because everyone became his own authority and acted on his own opinions of right and wrong. This produced horrendous results. Our world is similar. Individuals, groups, and societies have made themselves the final authorities without reference to God. When people selfishly satisfy their personal desires at all costs, everyone pays the price.

It is the ultimate heroic act to submit all our plans, desires, and motives to God. Men like Gideon, Jephthah, and Samson are known for their heroism in battle. But their personal lives were far from heroic.

To be truly heroic, we must go into battle each day in our home, job, church, and society to make God's kingdom a reality. Our weapons are the standards, morals, truths, and convictions we receive from God's Word. We will lose the battle if we gather the spoils of earthly treasures rather than seeking the treasures of heaven.

RUTH

WHEN someone says, "Let me tell you about my mother-in-law," we expect some kind of negative statement or humorous anecdote. That's because the mother-in-law caricature has been a standard centerpiece of ridicule or comedy. The book of Ruth, however, tells a different story. Ruth loved her mother-in-law, Naomi. Recently widowed, Ruth begged to stay with Naomi wherever she went, even though it would mean leaving her homeland, ending her plea with, "Your people will be my people and your God my God" (1:16). Naomi agreed, and Ruth traveled with her to Bethlehem.

Not much is said about Naomi except that she loved and cared for Ruth. Obviously, Naomi's life was a powerful witness to the reality of God. Ruth was drawn to her—and to the God she worshiped. In the succeeding months, God led this young Moabite widow to a man named Boaz, whom she eventually married. As a result, she became the great-grandmother of David and an ancestor in the line of the Messiah. What a profound impact Naomi's life made!

The book of Ruth is also the story of God's grace in the midst of difficult circumstances. Ruth's story occurred during the time of the judges—a period of disobedience, idolatry, and violence. Even in times of crisis and deepest despair, there are those who follow God and through whom God works. No matter how discouraging or antagonistic the world may seem, there are always people who follow God. He will use anyone who is open to him to achieve his purposes. Ruth was a Moabitess, and Boaz was a descendant of Rahab, a former prostitute from Jericho. Nevertheless, their offspring continued the family line through which the Messiah came into our world.

Read this book and be encouraged. God is at work in the world, and he wants to use you. God could use you, as he used Naomi, to bring family and friends to him.

THE BLUEPRINT

1. Ruth remains loyal to Naomi (1:1–22)
2. Ruth gleans in Boaz's field (2:1–23)
3. Ruth follows Naomi's plan (3:1–18)
4. Ruth and Boaz are married (4:1–22)

When we first meet Ruth, she is a destitute widow. We follow her as she joins God's people, gleans in the grainfields, and risks her honor at the threshing floor of Boaz. In the end, we see Ruth becoming the wife of Boaz. What a picture of how we come to faith in Christ. We begin with no hope and are rebellious aliens with no part in the kingdom of God. Then as we risk everything by putting our faith in Christ, God saves us, forgives us, rebuilds our lives, and gives us blessings that will last through eternity. Boaz's redeeming of Ruth is a picture of Christ redeeming us.

MEGATHEMES

THEME	EXPLANATION	IMPORTANCE
Faithfulness	Ruth's faithfulness to Naomi as a daughter-in-law and friend is a great example of love and loyalty. Ruth, Naomi, and Boaz are also faithful to God and his laws. Throughout the story we see God's faithfulness to his people.	Ruth's life was guided by faithfulness toward God and showed itself in loyalty toward the people she knew. To be loyal and loving in relationships, we must imitate God's faithfulness in our relationships with others.
Kindness	Ruth showed great kindness to Naomi. In turn, Boaz showed kindness to Ruth—a despised Moabite woman with no money. God showed his kindness to Ruth, Naomi, and Boaz by bringing them together for his purposes.	Just as Boaz showed his kindness by buying back land to guarantee Ruth and Naomi's inheritance, so Christ showed his kindness by dying for us to guarantee our eternal life. God's kindness should motivate us to love and honor him.

Integrity	Ruth showed high moral character by being loyal to Naomi, by her clean break from her former land and customs, and by her hard work in the fields. Boaz showed integrity in his moral standards, his honesty, and by following through on his commitments.	When we have experienced God's faithfulness and kindness, we should respond by showing integrity. Just as the values by which Ruth and Boaz lived were in sharp contrast to those of the culture portrayed in the book of Judges, so our lives should stand out from the world around us.
Protection	We see God's care and protection over the lives of Naomi and Ruth. His supreme control over circumstances brings them safety and security. He guides the minds and activities of people to fulfill his purposes.	No matter how devastating our present situation may be, our hope is in God. His resources are infinite. We must believe that he can work in the life of any person—whether that person is a king or a stranger in a foreign land. Trust his protection.
Prosperity/ Blessing	Ruth and Naomi came to Bethlehem as poor widows, but they soon became prosperous through Ruth's marriage to Boaz. Ruth became the great-grandmother of King David. Yet the greatest blessing was not the money, the marriage, or the child; it was the quality of love and respect between Ruth, Boaz, and Naomi.	We tend to think of blessings in terms of prosperity rather than the high-quality relationships God makes possible for us. No matter what our economic situation, we can love and respect the people God has brought into our lives. In so doing, we give and receive blessings. Love is the greatest blessing.

1. Ruth remains loyal to Naomi

Naomi and Ruth

1:1
a Jdg 2:16-18
b Jdg 3:30

1:2
c Ge 35:19

1 In the days when the judges ruled,*a a* there was a famine in the land, and a man from Bethlehem in Judah, together with his wife and two sons, went to live for a while in the country of Moab.*b* 2 The man's name was Elimelech, his wife's name Naomi, and the names of his two sons were Mahlon and Kilion. They were Ephrathites from Bethlehem,*c* Judah. And they went to Moab and lived there.

3 Now Elimelech, Naomi's husband, died, and she was left with her two sons. 4 They married Moabite women, one named Orpah and the other Ruth. After they had lived there about ten years, 5 both Mahlon and Kilion also died, and Naomi was left without her two sons and her husband.

1:6
d Ex 4:31
e Mt 6:11

6 When she heard in Moab that the LORD had come to the aid of his people*d* by providing food*e* for them, Naomi and her daughters-in-law prepared to return home from there. 7 With her two daughters-in-law she left the place where she had been living and set out on the road that would take them back to the land of Judah.

8 Then Naomi said to her two daughters-in-law, "Go back, each of you, to your mother's

a 1 Traditionally *judged*

1:1 The story of Ruth takes place sometime during the period of the rule of the judges. These were dark days for Israel, when "everyone did as he saw fit" (Judges 17:6; 21:25). But during those dark and evil times, there were still some who followed God. Naomi and Ruth are beautiful examples of loyalty, friendship, and commitment—to God and to each other.

1:1, 2 Moab was the land east of the Dead Sea. It was one of the nations that oppressed Israel during the period of the judges (Judges 3:12ff), so there was hostility between the two nations. The famine must have been quite severe in Israel for Elimelech to move his family here. They were called Ephrathites because Ephrath was an earlier name for Bethlehem. Even if Israel had already defeated Moab, there still would have been tensions between them.

1:4, 5 Friendly relations with the Moabites were discouraged (Deuteronomy 23:3–6) but probably not forbidden, since the Moabites lived outside the promised land. Marrying a Canaanite (and all those living within the borders of the promised land), however, was against God's law (Deuteronomy 7:1–4). Moabites were not allowed to worship at the tabernacle because they had not let the Israelites pass through their land during the exodus from Egypt.

As God's chosen nation, Israel should have set the standards of high moral living for the other nations. Ironically it was Ruth, a Moabitess, whom God used as an example of genuine spiritual character. This shows just how bleak life had become in Israel during those days.

1:8, 9 There was almost nothing worse than being a widow in the ancient world. Widows were taken advantage of or ignored. They were almost always poverty stricken. God's law, therefore, provided that the nearest relative of the dead husband should care for the widow; but Naomi had no relatives in Moab, and she did not know if any of her relatives were alive in Israel.

Even in her desperate situation, Naomi had a selfless attitude. Although she had decided to return to Israel, she encouraged Ruth and Orpah to stay in Moab and start their lives over, even though this would mean hardship for her. Like Naomi, we must consider the needs of others and not just our own. As Naomi discovered, when you act selflessly, others are encouraged to follow your example.

home. May the LORD show kindness ƒ to you, as you have shown to your dead and to me. ⁹May the LORD grant that each of you will find rest ⁹ in the home of another husband."

Then she kissed them and they wept aloud ¹⁰and said to her, "We will go back with you to your people."

¹¹But Naomi said, "Return home, my daughters. Why would you come with me? Am I going to have any more sons, who could become your husbands? ʰ ¹²Return home, my daughters; I am too old to have another husband. Even if I thought there was still hope for me—even if I had a husband tonight and then gave birth to sons— ¹³would you wait until they grew up? Would you remain unmarried for them? No, my daughters. It is more bitter for me than for you, because the LORD's hand has gone out against me! ⁱ"

¹⁴At this they wept again. Then Orpah kissed her mother-in-law good-by, but Ruth clung to her.

¹⁵"Look," said Naomi, "your sister-in-law is going back to her people and her gods. Go back with her."

¹⁶But Ruth replied, "Don't urge me to leave you ʲ or to turn back from you. Where you go I will go, and where you stay I will stay. Your people will be my people and your God my God. ¹⁷Where you die I will die, and there I will be buried. May the LORD deal with me, be it ever so severely, ᵏ if anything but death separates you and me." ¹⁸When Naomi realized that Ruth was determined to go with her, she stopped urging her. ˡ

¹⁹So the two women went on until they came to Bethlehem. When they arrived in Bethlehem, the whole town was stirred ᵐ because of them, and the women exclaimed, "Can this be Naomi?"

²⁰"Don't call me Naomi,ᵃ" she told them. "Call me Mara,ᵇ because the Almightyᶜ has made my life very bitter. ²¹I went away full, but the LORD has brought me back empty.ⁿ Why call me Naomi? The LORD has afflictedᵈ me; the Almighty has brought misfortune upon me."

²²So Naomi returned from Moab accompanied by Ruth the Moabitess, her daughter-in-law, arriving in Bethlehem as the barley harvest ᵒ was beginning.

ᵃ*20 Naomi means pleasant;* also in verse 21. ᵇ*20 Mara means bitter.* ᶜ*20 Hebrew Shaddai;* also in verse 21
ᵈ*21 Or has testified against*

1:8 ƒRu 2:20; 2Ti 1:16
1:9 ⁹Ru 3:1
1:11 ʰGe 38:11; Dt 25:5
1:13 ⁱJdg 2:15; Job 19:21; Ps 32:4
1:16 ʲ2Ki 2:2
1:17 ᵏ1Sa 3:17; 2Ki 6:31
1:18 ˡAc 21:14
1:19 ᵐMt 21:10
1:21 ⁿJob 1:21
1:22 ᵒEx 9:31

1:11 Naomi's comment here ("sons, who could become your husbands") refers to *levirate marriage,* the obligation of a dead man's brother to care for the widow (Deuteronomy 25:5–10). This law kept the widow from poverty and provided a way for the family name of the dead husband to continue.

Naomi, however, had no other sons for Ruth or Orpah to marry, so she encouraged them to remain in their homeland and remarry. Orpah agreed, which was her right. But Ruth was willing to give up the possibility of security and children in order to care for Naomi.

1:16 Ruth was a Moabitess, but that didn't stop her from worshiping the true God, nor did it stop God from accepting her

worship and blessing her greatly. The Jews were not the only people God loved. God chose the Jews to be the people through whom the rest of the world would come to know him. This was fulfilled when Jesus Christ was born as a Jew. Through him, the entire world can come to know God. Acts 10:35 says that "[God] accepts men from every nation who fear him and do what is right." God accepts all who worship him; he works through people regardless of their race, sex, or nationality. The book of Ruth is a perfect example of God's impartiality. Although Ruth belonged to a race often despised by Israel, she was blessed because of her faithfulness. She became a great-grandmother of King David and a direct ancestor of Jesus. No one should feel disqualified to serve God because of race, sex, or national background. And God can use every circumstance to build his kingdom.

1:20, 21 Naomi had experienced severe hardships. She had left Israel married and secure; she returned widowed and poor. Naomi changed her name to express the bitterness and pain she felt. Naomi was not rejecting God by openly expressing her pain. However, she seems to have lost sight of the tremendous resources she had in her relationship with Ruth and with God. When you face bitter times, God welcomes your honest prayers, but be careful not to overlook the love, strength, and resources that he provides in your present relationships. And don't allow bitterness and disappointment to blind you to your opportunities.

1:22 Bethlehem was about five miles southwest of Jerusalem. The town was surrounded by lush fields and olive groves. Its harvests were abundant.

Ruth and Naomi's return to Bethlehem was certainly part of God's plan because in this town David would be born (1 Samuel 16:1), and, as predicted by the prophet Micah (Micah 5:2), Jesus Christ would also be born there. This move, then, was more than merely convenient for Ruth and Naomi. It led to the fulfillment of Scripture.

1:22 Because Israel's climate is quite moderate, there are two harvests each year, in the spring and in the fall. The barley harvest

SETTING FOR THE STORY
Elimelech, Naomi, and their sons traveled from Bethlehem to Moab because of a famine. After her husband and sons died, Naomi returned to Bethlehem with her daughter-in-law Ruth.

2. Ruth gleans in Boaz's field
Ruth Meets Boaz

2:1
p Ru 3:2,12

2 Now Naomi had a relative*p* on her husband's side, from the clan of Elimelech, a man of standing, whose name was Boaz.

2:2
q Lev 19:9; Dt 24:19

²And Ruth the Moabitess said to Naomi, "Let me go to the fields and pick up the leftover grain *q* behind anyone in whose eyes I find favor."

Naomi said to her, "Go ahead, my daughter." ³So she went out and began to glean in the fields behind the harvesters. As it turned out, she found herself working in a field belonging to Boaz, who was from the clan of Elimelech.

2:4
r Lk 1:28; 2Th 3:16
s Ps 129:7-8

⁴Just then Boaz arrived from Bethlehem and greeted the harvesters, "The LORD be with you!*r*"

"The LORD bless you!*s*" they called back.

⁵Boaz asked the foreman of his harvesters, "Whose young woman is that?"

RUTH & NAOMI

The stories of several people in the Bible are woven together so closely that they are almost inseparable. We know more about their relationship than we know about them as individuals. And in an age that worships individualism, their stories become helpful models of good relationships. Naomi and Ruth are beautiful examples of this blending of lives. Their cultures, family backgrounds, and ages were very different. As mother-in-law and daughter-in-law, they probably had as many opportunities for tension as for tenderness. And yet they were bound to each other.

They shared deep sorrow, great affection for each other, and an overriding commitment to the God of Israel. And yet as much as they depended on each other, they also gave each other freedom in their commitment to one another. Naomi was willing to let Ruth return to her family. Ruth was willing to leave her homeland to go to Israel. Naomi even helped arrange Ruth's marriage to Boaz although it would change their relationship.

God was at the center of their intimate communication. Ruth came to know the God of Israel through Naomi. The older woman allowed Ruth to see, hear, and feel all the joy and anguish of her relationship to God. How often do you feel that your thoughts and questions about God should be left out of a close relationship? How often do you share your unedited thoughts about God with your spouse or friends? Sharing openly about our relationship with God can bring depth and intimacy to our relationships with others.

Strengths and accomplishments:	• A relationship where the greatest bond was faith in God • A relationship of strong mutual commitment • A relationship in which each person tried to do what was best for the other
Lesson from their lives:	• God's living presence in a relationship overcomes differences that might otherwise create division and disharmony
Vital statistics:	• Where: Moab, Bethlehem • Occupation: Wives, widows • Relatives: Elimelech, Mahlon, Kilion, Orpah, Boaz
Key verses:	"But Ruth replied, 'Don't urge me to leave you or to turn back from you. Where you go I will go, and where you stay I will stay. Your people will be my people and your God my God. Where you die I will die, and there I will be buried. May the LORD deal with me, be it ever so severely, if anything but death separates you and me'" (Ruth 1:16, 17).

Their story is told in the book of Ruth. Ruth is also mentioned in Matthew 1:5.

took place in the spring, and it was during this time of hope and plenty that Ruth and Naomi returned to Bethlehem. Bethlehem was a farming community, and because it was the time of the harvest, there was plenty of leftover grain in the fields. This grain could be collected, or *gleaned,* and then made into food. (See the note on 2:2 for more information on gleaning.)

2:1 A clan is a group of families with a common ancestor.

2:2 When the wheat and barley were ready to be harvested, reapers were hired to cut down the stalks and tie them into bundles. Israelite law demanded that the corners of the fields not be harvested. In addition, any grain that was dropped was to be left for poor people who picked it up (this was called *gleaning*) and used it for food (Leviticus 19:9; 23:22; Deuteronomy 24:19). The purpose of this law was to feed the poor and to prevent the

owners from hoarding. This law served as a type of welfare program in Israel. Because she was a widow with no means of providing for herself, Ruth went into the fields to glean the grain.

2:2, 3 Ruth made her home in a foreign land. Instead of depending on Naomi or waiting for good fortune to happen, she took the initiative. She went to work. She was not afraid of admitting her need or working hard to supply it. When Ruth went out to the fields, God provided for her. If you are waiting for God to provide, consider this: He may be waiting for you to take the first step to demonstrate just how important your need is.

6 The foreman replied, "She is the Moabitess*t* who came back from Moab with Naomi. 7 She said, 'Please let me glean and gather among the sheaves behind the harvesters.' She went into the field and has worked steadily from morning till now, except for a short rest in the shelter."

8 So Boaz said to Ruth, "My daughter, listen to me. Don't go and glean in another field and don't go away from here. Stay here with my servant girls. 9 Watch the field where the men are harvesting, and follow along after the girls. I have told the men not to touch you. And whenever you are thirsty, go and get a drink from the water jars the men have filled."

10 At this, she bowed down with her face to the ground. *u* She exclaimed, "Why have I found such favor in your eyes that you notice me—a foreigner?"

11 Boaz replied, "I've been told all about what you have done for your mother-in-law *v* since the death of your husband—how you left your father and mother and your homeland and came to live with a people you did not know before. *w* 12 May the LORD repay you for what you have done. May you be richly rewarded by the LORD, *x* the God of Israel, under whose wings *y* you have come to take refuge. *z*"

13 "May I continue to find favor in your eyes, my lord," she said. "You have given me comfort and have spoken kindly to your servant—though I do not have the standing of one of your servant girls."

14 At mealtime Boaz said to her, "Come over here. Have some bread and dip it in the wine vinegar."

When she sat down with the harvesters, he offered her some roasted grain. She ate all she wanted and had some left over. *a* 15 As she got up to glean, Boaz gave orders to his men, "Even if she gathers among the sheaves, don't embarrass her. 16 Rather, pull out some stalks for her from the bundles and leave them for her to pick up, and don't rebuke her."

17 So Ruth gleaned in the field until evening. Then she threshed the barley she had gathered, and it amounted to about an ephah. *a* 18 She carried it back to town, and her mother-in-law saw how much she had gathered. Ruth also brought out and gave her what she had left over *b* after she had eaten enough.

19 Her mother-in-law asked her, "Where did you glean today? Where did you work? Blessed be the man who took notice of you!"

Then Ruth told her mother-in-law about the one at whose place she had been working. "The name of the man I worked with today is Boaz," she said.

20 "The LORD bless him!" Naomi said to her daughter-in-law. "He has not stopped showing his kindness *c* to the living and the dead." She added, "That man is our close relative; he is one of our kinsman-redeemers. *d*"

21 Then Ruth the Moabitess said, "He even said to me, 'Stay with my workers until they finish harvesting all my grain.'"

22 Naomi said to Ruth her daughter-in-law, "It will be good for you, my daughter, to go with his girls, because in someone else's field you might be harmed."

23 So Ruth stayed close to the servant girls of Boaz to glean until the barley and wheat harvests *e* were finished. And she lived with her mother-in-law.

a 17 That is, probably about 3/5 bushel (about 22 liters)

2:6
t Ru 1:22

2:10
u 1Sa 25:23

2:11
v Ru 1:14
w Ru 1:16-17

2:12
x 1Sa 24:19
y Ps 17:8
z Ru 1:16

2:14
a ver 18

2:18
b ver 14

2:20
c Ru 3:10
d Ru 3:9,12

2:23
e Dt 16:9

2:7 Ruth's task, though menial, tiring, and perhaps degrading, was done faithfully. What is your attitude when the task you have been given is not up to your true potential? The task at hand may be all you can do, or it may be the work God wants you to do. Or, as in Ruth's case, it may be a test of your character that can open up new doors of opportunity.

2:10–12 Ruth's life exhibited admirable qualities: she was hardworking, loving, kind, faithful, and brave. These qualities gained for her a good reputation, but only because she displayed them *consistently* in all areas of her life. Wherever Ruth went or whatever she did, her character remained the same.

Your reputation is formed by the people who watch you at work, in town, at home, in church. A good reputation comes by *consistently* living out the qualities you believe in—no matter what group of people or surroundings you are in.

2:15, 16 The characters in the book of Ruth are classic examples of good people in action. Boaz went far beyond the intent of the gleaners' law in demonstrating his kindness and generosity. Not only did he let Ruth glean in his field, he also told his workers

to let some of the grain fall in her path. Out of his abundance, he provided for the needy. How often do you go beyond the accepted patterns of providing for those less fortunate? Do more than the minimum for others.

2:19, 20 Naomi had felt bitter (1:20, 21), but her faith in God was still alive, and she praised God for Boaz's kindness to Ruth. In her sorrows, she still trusted God and acknowledged his goodness. We may feel bitter about a situation, but we must never despair. Today is always a new opportunity for experiencing God's care. (For more on kinsman-redeemer, see the note on 3:1–9.)

2:20 Though Ruth may not have always recognized God's guidance, he had been with her every step of the way. She went to glean and "just happened" to end up in the field owned by Boaz who "just happened" to be a close relative. This was more than mere coincidence. As you go about your daily tasks, God is working in your life in ways you may not even notice. We must not close the door on what God can do. Events do not occur by luck or coincidence. We should have faith that God is directing our lives for his purpose.

3. Ruth follows Naomi's plan
Ruth and Boaz at the Threshing Floor

3 One day Naomi her mother-in-law said to her, "My daughter, should I not try to find a home[a] for you, where you will be well provided for? [2] Is not Boaz, with whose servant girls you have been, a kinsman of ours? Tonight he will be winnowing barley on the threshing floor. [3] Wash and perfume yourself,[f] and put on your best clothes. Then go down to the threshing floor, but don't let him know you are there until he has finished eating and drinking. [4] When

3:3
*f*2Sa 14:2

a 1 Hebrew *find rest* (see Ruth 1:9)

BOAZ

Heroes are easier to admire than to define. They are seldom conscious of their moments of heroism, and others may not recognize their acts as heroic. Heroes simply do the right thing at the right time, whether or not they realize the impact their action will have. Perhaps the one quality they share is a tendency to think of others before they think of themselves. Boaz was a hero.

In his dealings with other people, he was always sensitive to their needs. His words to his employees, relatives, and others were colored with kindness. He offered help openly, not grudgingly. When he discovered who Ruth was, he took several steps to help her because she had been faithful to his relative Naomi. When Naomi advised Ruth to request his protection, he was ready to marry her if the legal complications could be worked out.

Boaz not only did what was right; he also did it right away. Of course he could not foresee all that his actions would accomplish. He could not have known that the child he would have by Ruth would be an ancestor of both David and Jesus. He only met the challenge of taking the right action in the situation facing him.

We are faced with this challenge in our daily choices. Like Naomi's nearer relative, we are often more concerned with making the easy choice than with making the right one. Yet more often than not, the right choice is clear. Ask God to give you a special awareness in your choices today as well as renewed commitment to make the right ones.

Strengths and accomplishments:	• A man of his word • Sensitive to those in need, caring for his workers • A keen sense of responsibility, integrity • A successful and shrewd businessman
Lessons from his life:	• It can be heroic to do what must be done and to do it right • God often uses little decisions to carry out his big plan
Vital statistics:	• Where: Bethlehem • Occupation: Wealthy farmer • Relatives: Elimelech, Naomi, Ruth
Key verse:	"I have also acquired Ruth the Moabitess, Mahlon's widow, as my wife, in order to maintain the name of the dead with his property, so that his name will not disappear from among his family or from the town records. Today you are witnesses!" (Ruth 4:10).

His story is told in the book of Ruth. He is also mentioned in Matthew 1:5.

3:1-9 As widows, Ruth and Naomi could only look forward to difficult times. (See the note on 1:8, 9 for more on a widow's life.) But when Naomi heard the news about Boaz, her hope for the future was renewed (2:20). Typical of her character, she thought first of Ruth, encouraging her to see if Boaz would take the responsibility of being a "kinsman-redeemer" to her (2:20).

A kinsman-redeemer was a relative who volunteered to take responsibility for the extended family. When a woman's husband died, the law (Deuteronomy 25:5–10) provided that she could marry a brother of her dead husband. But Naomi had no more sons. In such a case, the nearest relative to the deceased husband could become a kinsman-redeemer and marry the widow. The nearest relative did not have to marry the widow. If he chose not to, the next nearest relative could take his place. If no one chose to help the widow, she would probably live in poverty the rest of her life because in Israelite culture the inheritance was passed on to the son or nearest male relative, not to the wife. To take the sting out of these inheritance rules, there were laws for gleaning and kinsman-redeemers.

We have a kinsman-redeemer in Jesus Christ, who, though he was God, came to earth as a man in order to save us. By his death on the cross, he has redeemed us from sin and hopeless-

ness and thereby purchased us to be his own possession (1 Peter 1:18, 19). This guarantees our eternal inheritance.

3:2 The threshing floor was the place where the grain was separated from the harvested wheat. The wheat stalks were crushed, either by hand or by oxen, and the valuable grain (inner kernels) separated from the worthless chaff (the outside shell). The floor was made from rock or soil and located outside the village, usually on an elevated site where the winds would blow away the lighter chaff when the crushed wheat was thrown into the air (or winnowed). Boaz spent the night beside the threshing floor for two reasons: (1) to prevent theft and (2) to wait for his turn to thresh grain. (Threshing was often done at night because daylight hours were spent harvesting.)

3:4 Naomi's advice seems strange, but she was not suggesting a seductive act. In reality, Naomi was telling Ruth to act in accordance with Israelite custom and law. It was common for a servant to lie at the feet of his master and even share a part of his covering. By observing this custom, Ruth would inform Boaz that he could be her kinsman-redeemer—that he could find someone to marry her or marry her himself. It was family business, nothing romantic. But the story later became beautifully romantic as Ruth and Boaz developed an unselfish love and deep respect for each other.

he lies down, note the place where he is lying. Then go and uncover his feet and lie down. He will tell you what to do."

5"I will do whatever you say," Ruth answered. 6So she went down to the threshing floor and did everything her mother-in-law told her to do.

7When Boaz had finished eating and drinking and was in good spirits,*g* he went over to lie down at the far end of the grain pile. Ruth approached quietly, uncovered his feet and lay down. 8In the middle of the night something startled the man, and he turned and discovered a woman lying at his feet.

9"Who are you?" he asked.

"I am your servant Ruth," she said. "Spread the corner of your garment over me, since you are a kinsman-redeemer. *h*"

10"The LORD bless you, my daughter," he replied. "This kindness is greater than that which you showed earlier: You have not run after the younger men, whether rich or poor. 11And now, my daughter, don't be afraid. I will do for you all you ask. All my fellow townsmen know that you are a woman of noble character.*i* 12Although it is true that I am near of kin, there is a kinsman-redeemer nearer than*j* I. 13Stay here for the night, and in the morning if he wants to redeem,*k* good; let him redeem. But if he is not willing, as surely as the LORD lives I will do it. Lie here until morning."

14So she lay at his feet until morning, but got up before anyone could be recognized; and he said, "Don't let it be known that a woman came to the threshing floor."*l*

15He also said, "Bring me the shawl you are wearing and hold it out." When she did so, he poured into it six measures of barley and put it on her. Then he*a* went back to town.

16When Ruth came to her mother-in-law, Naomi asked, "How did it go, my daughter?"

Then she told her everything Boaz had done for her 17and added, "He gave me these six measures of barley, saying, 'Don't go back to your mother-in-law empty-handed.'"

18Then Naomi said, "Wait, my daughter, until you find out what happens. For the man will not rest until the matter is settled today."

4. Ruth and Boaz are married
Boaz Marries Ruth

4 Meanwhile Boaz went up to the town gate and sat there. When the kinsman-redeemer he had mentioned*m* came along, Boaz said, "Come over here, my friend, and sit down." So he went over and sat down.

2Boaz took ten of the elders of the town and said, "Sit here," and they did so. 3Then he said to the kinsman-redeemer, "Naomi, who has come back from Moab, is selling the piece of land that belonged to our brother Elimelech. 4I thought I should bring the matter to your attention and suggest that you buy it in the presence of these seated here and in the presence of the elders of my people. If you will redeem it, do so. But if you*b* will not, tell me, so I will know. For no one has the right to do it except you,*n* and I am next in line."

a 15 Most Hebrew manuscripts; many Hebrew manuscripts, Vulgate and Syriac *she*   *b 4* Many Hebrew manuscripts, Septuagint, Vulgate and Syriac; most Hebrew manuscripts *he*

3:7 *g* Jdg 19:6,9,22; 2Sa 13:28

3:9 *h* Ru 2:20

3:11 *i* Pr 12:4

3:12 *j* Ru 4:1

3:13 *k* Dt 25:5; Mt 22:24

3:14 *l* Ro 14:16; 2Co 8:21

4:1 *m* Ru 3:12

4:4 *n* Lev 25:25; Jer 32:7-8

3:5 As a foreigner, Ruth may have thought that Naomi's advice was odd. But Ruth followed the advice because she knew Naomi was kind, trustworthy, and filled with moral integrity. Each of us knows a parent, older friend, or relative who is always looking out for our best interests. Be willing to listen to the advice of those older and wiser than you are. The experience and knowledge of such a person can be invaluable. Imagine what Ruth's life would have been like had she ignored her mother-in-law.

3:12 Ruth and Naomi must have assumed that Boaz was their closest relative. Boaz, too, must have already considered marrying Ruth because his answer to her shows he had been thinking about it. He couldn't have considered marrying Naomi because she was probably too old to bear any more children (1:11, 12). One man in the city was a nearer relative than Boaz, and this man had the first right to take Ruth as his wife. If he chose not to, then Boaz could marry Ruth (3:13).

3:18 Naomi implied that Boaz would follow through with his promise at once. He obviously had a reputation for keeping his word and would not rest until his task was completed. Such reliable people stand out in any age and culture. Do others regard

you as one who will do what you say? Keeping your word and following through on assignments should be high on anyone's priority list. Building a reputation for integrity, however, must be done one brick, one act, at a time.

4:1 Boaz knew he could find his relative at the town gate. This was the center of activity. No one could enter or leave the town without traveling through the gate. Merchants set up their temporary shops near the gate, which also served as "city hall." Here city officials gathered to transact business. Because there was so much activity, it was a good place to find witnesses (4:2) and an appropriate place for Boaz to make his transaction.

4:3 Boaz cleverly presented his case to the relative. First he brought in new information not yet mentioned in the story—Elimelech, Naomi's former husband, still had some property in the area that was now for sale. As the nearest relative, this man had the first right to buy the land, which he agreed to do (Leviticus 25:25). But then Boaz said that according to the law, if the relative bought the property he also had to marry the widow (probably because Mahlon, Ruth's former husband and Elimelech's son, had inherited the property). At this stipulation, the relative backed down. He did not

"I will redeem it," he said.

4:5
o Ge 38:8; Dt 25:5-6

[5] Then Boaz said, "On the day you buy the land from Naomi and from Ruth the Moabitess, you acquire [a] the dead man's widow, in order to maintain the name of the dead with his property." [o]

4:6
p Ru 3:13

[6] At this, the kinsman-redeemer said, "Then I cannot redeem[p] it because I might endanger my own estate. You redeem it yourself. I cannot do it."

4:7
q Dt 25:7-9

[7] (Now in earlier times in Israel, for the redemption and transfer of property to become final, one party took off his sandal and gave it to the other. This was the method of legalizing transactions in Israel.)[q]

[8] So the kinsman-redeemer said to Boaz, "Buy it yourself." And he removed his sandal.

4:10
r Dt 25:6

[9] Then Boaz announced to the elders and all the people, "Today you are witnesses that I have bought from Naomi all the property of Elimelech, Kilion and Mahlon. [10] I have also acquired Ruth the Moabitess, Mahlon's widow, as my wife, in order to maintain the name of the dead with his property, so that his name will not disappear from among his family or from the town records. [r] Today you are witnesses!"

4:11
s Ps 127:3

[11] Then the elders and all those at the gate said, "We are witnesses. May the LORD make the woman who is coming into your home like Rachel and Leah,[s] who together built up the house of Israel. May you have standing in Ephrathah and be famous in Bethlehem.

4:12
t ver 18; Ge 38:29

[12] Through the offspring the LORD gives you by this young woman, may your family be like that of Perez,[t] whom Tamar bore to Judah."

The Genealogy of David

4:13
u Ge 29:31; 33:5;
Ru 3:11

[13] So Boaz took Ruth and she became his wife. Then he went to her, and the LORD enabled her to conceive,[u] and she gave birth to a son. [14] The women [v] said to Naomi: "Praise be to the LORD, who this day has not left you without a kinsman-redeemer. May he become famous throughout Israel! [15] He will renew your life and sustain you in your old age. For your daughter-in-law, who loves you and who is better to you than seven sons,[w] has given him birth."

4:14
v Lk 1:58

4:15
w Ru 1:16-17;
2:11-12

[16] Then Naomi took the child, laid him in her lap and cared for him. [17] The women living there said, "Naomi has a son." And they named him Obed. He was the father of Jesse, the father of David.

4:18
x Mt 1:3-6

[18] This, then, is the family line of Perez[x]:

Perez was the father of Hezron,
[19] Hezron the father of Ram,
   Ram the father of Amminadab,
[20] Amminadab the father of Nahshon,
   Nahshon the father of Salmon,[b]
[21] Salmon the father of Boaz,
   Boaz the father of Obed,
[22] Obed the father of Jesse,
   and Jesse the father of David.

[a]*5* Hebrew; Vulgate and Syriac *Naomi, you acquire Ruth the Moabitess,*   [b]*20* A few Hebrew manuscripts, some Septuagint manuscripts and Vulgate (see also verse 21 and Septuagint of 1 Chron. 2:11); most Hebrew manuscripts *Salma*

---

want to complicate his inheritance. He may have feared that if he had a son through Ruth, some of his estate would transfer away from his family to the family of Elimelech. Whatever his reason, the way was now clear for Boaz to marry Ruth.

4:15 Ruth's love for her mother-in-law was known and recognized throughout the town. From the beginning of the book of Ruth to the end, her kindness toward others remained unchanged.

4:15 God brought great blessings out of Naomi's tragedy, even greater than "seven sons," or an abundance of heirs. Throughout her tough times, Naomi continued to trust God. And God, in his time, blessed her greatly. Even in our sorrow and calamity, God can bring great blessings. Be like Naomi, and don't turn your back on God when tragedy strikes. Instead of asking "How can God allow this to happen to me?" trust him. He will be with you in the hard times.

4:16, 17 To some, the book of Ruth may be just a nice story about a girl who was fortunate. But in reality, the events recorded in Ruth were part of God's preparations for the births of David and of Jesus, the promised Messiah. Just as Ruth was unaware of this larger purpose in her life, we will not know the full purpose and importance of our lives until we are able to look back from the perspective of eternity. We must make our choices with God's eternal values in mind. Taking moral short-cuts and living for short-range pleasures are not good ways to move ahead. Because of Ruth's faithful obedience, her life and legacy were significant even though she couldn't see all the results. Live in faithfulness to God, knowing that the significance of your life will extend beyond your lifetime. The rewards will outweigh any sacrifice you may have made.

1 SAMUEL

Judges		Samuel	Saul
begin		born	born
to rule		1105	1080
1375 B.C.		(1083)	
(1220 B.C.)			

VITAL STATISTICS

PURPOSE:
To record the life of Samuel, Israel's last judge; the reign and decline of Saul, the first king; and the choice and preparation of David, Israel's greatest king

AUTHOR:
Possibly Samuel, but also includes writings from the prophets Nathan and Gad (1 Chronicles 29:29)

ORIGINAL AUDIENCE:
The people of Israel

SETTING:
The book begins in the days of the judges and describes Israel's transition from a theocracy (led by God) to a monarchy (led by a king).

KEY VERSES:
"And the Lord told him: 'Listen to all that the people are saying to you; it is not you they have rejected, but they have rejected me as their king. . . . Now listen to them; but warn them solemnly and let them know what the king who will reign over them will do'" (8:7, 9).

KEY PEOPLE:
Eli, Hannah, Samuel, Saul, Jonathan, David

"RUNNERS, take your marks," the starter barks his signal, and the crowd turns quiet attention to the athletes walking toward the line. "Get set" . . . in position now, muscles tense, nervously anticipating the sound of the gun. It resounds! And the race begins. In any contest, the start is important, but the finish is even more crucial. Often a front-runner will lose strength and fade to the middle of the pack. And there is the tragedy of the brilliant beginner who sets the pace for a time, but does not even finish. He quits the race burned out, exhausted, or injured.

First Samuel is a book of great beginnings . . . and tragic endings. It begins with Eli as high priest during the time of the judges. As a religious leader, Eli certainly must have begun his life with a close relationship to God. In his communication with Hannah, and in his training of her son Samuel, he demonstrated a clear understanding of God's purposes and call (chapters 1; 3). But his life ended in ignominy as his sacrilegious sons were judged by God, and the sacred ark of the covenant fell into enemy hands (chapter 4). Eli's death marked the decline of the influence of the priesthood and the rise of the prophets in Israel.

Samuel was dedicated to God's service by his mother, Hannah. He became one of Israel's greatest prophets. He was a man of prayer who finished the work of the judges, began the school of the prophets, and anointed Israel's first kings. But even Samuel was not immune to finishing poorly. Like Eli's family, Samuel's sons turned away from God, taking bribes and perverting justice. The people rejected the leadership of the judges and priests and clamored for a king "as all the other nations have" (8:5).

Saul also started quickly. A striking figure, this handsome (9:2) and humble (9:21; 10:22) man was God's choice as Israel's first king (10:24). His early reign was marked by leadership (chapter 11) and bravery (14:46–48). But he disobeyed God (chapter 15), became jealous and paranoid (chapters 18—19), and finally had his kingship taken away from him by God (chapter 16). Saul's life continued steadily downward. Obsessed with killing David (chapters 19—30), he consulted a medium (chapter 28) and finally committed suicide (chapter 31).

Among the events of Saul's life stands another great beginner—David. A man who followed God (13:14; 16:7), David ministered to Saul (chapter 16), killed Goliath (chapter 17), and became a great warrior. But we'll have to wait until the book of 2 Samuel to see how David finished.

As you read 1 Samuel, note the transition from theocracy to monarchy; exult in the classic stories of David and Goliath, David and Jonathan, David and Abigail; and watch the rise of the influence of the prophets. But in the midst of reading all the history and adventure, determine to run your race as God's person from start to finish.

Samson becomes judge 1075 (1083)	Saul becomes king 1050 (1045)	David born 1040	David anointed; Goliath slain 1025	David becomes king over Judah 1010	David becomes king over all Israel 1003	Solomon becomes king 970	The kingdom is divided 930

THE BLUEPRINT

A. ELI AND SAMUEL
(1:1—7:17)
1. Samuel's birth and childhood
2. War with the Philistines

We see a vivid contrast between young Samuel and Eli's sons. Eli's sons were selfish, but Samuel was helpful. Eli's sons defrauded people, but Samuel grew in wisdom and gave the people messages from God. As an adult, Samuel became a prophet, priest, and judge over Israel. A person's actions reflect his character. This was true of Samuel and of Eli's sons. It is also true of us. Strive, like Samuel, to keep your heart pure before God.

B. SAMUEL AND SAUL
(8:1—15:35)
1. Saul becomes king of Israel
2. God rejects Saul for disobedience

Saul showed great promise. He was strong, tall, and modest. God's Spirit came upon him, and Samuel was his counselor. But Saul deliberately disobeyed God and became an evil king. We must not base our hopes or future on our potential. Instead, we must consistently obey God in all areas of life. God evaluates obedience, not potential.

C. SAUL AND DAVID
(16:1—31:13)
1. Samuel anoints David
2. David and Goliath
3. David and Jonathan become friends
4. Saul pursues David
5. Saul's defeat and death

David quickly killed Goliath but waited patiently for God to deal with Saul. Although David was anointed to be Israel's next king, he had to wait years to realize this promise. The difficult circumstances in life and the times of waiting often refine, teach, and prepare us for the future responsibilities God has for us.

MEGATHEMES

THEME	EXPLANATION	IMPORTANCE
King	Because Israel suffered from corrupt priests and judges, the people wanted a king. They wanted to be organized like the surrounding nations. Though it was against his original purpose, God chose a king for them.	Establishing a monarchy did not solve Israel's problems. What God desires is the genuine devotion of each person's mind and heart to him. No government or set of laws can substitute for the rule of God in your heart and life.
God's Control	Israel prospered as long as the people regarded God as their true king. When the leaders strayed from God's law, God intervened in their personal lives and overruled their actions. In this way, God maintained ultimate control over Israel's history.	God is always at work in this world, even when we can't see what he is doing. No matter what kinds of pressures we must endure or how many changes we must face, God is ultimately in control of our situation. Being confident of God's sovereignty, we can face the difficult situations in our lives with boldness.
Leadership	God guided his people using different forms of leadership: judges, priests, prophets, kings. Those whom he chose for these different offices, such as Eli, Samuel, Saul, and David, portrayed different styles of leadership. Yet the success of each leader depended on his devotion to God, not his position, leadership style, wisdom, age, or strength.	When Eli, Samuel, Saul, and David disobeyed God, they faced tragic consequences. Sin affected what they accomplished for God and how some of them raised their children. Being a real leader means letting God guide all aspects of your activities, values, and goals, including the way you raise your children.
Obedience	For God, "to obey is better than sacrifice" (15:22). God wanted his people to obey, serve, and follow him with a whole heart rather than to maintain a superficial commitment based on tradition or ceremonial systems.	Although we are free from the sacrificial system of the Jewish law, we may still rely on outward observances to substitute for inward commitment. God desires that all our work and worship be motivated by genuine, heartfelt devotion to him.
God's Faithfulness	God faithfully kept the promises he made to Israel. He responded to his people with tender mercy and swift justice. In showing mercy, he faithfully acted in the best interest of his people. In showing justice, he was faithful to his word and perfect moral nature.	Because God is faithful, he can be counted on to be merciful toward us. Yet God is also just, and he will not tolerate rebellion against him. His faithfulness and unselfish love should inspire us to dedicate ourselves to him completely. We must never take his mercy for granted.

LEBANON

N

SYRIA

Mediterranean
Sea

Sea of
Galilee

Mount
Gilboa

ISRAEL

Jordan River

CANAAN

Ebenezer

Shiloh

Mizpah

Gilgal

JORDAN

Kiriath Jearim. Ramah

Jerusalem

Gath

VALLEY
OF ELAH

Dead
Sea

DESERT
OF ZIPH

En Gedi

Ziklag

DESERT
OF MAON

0   20 Mi.

0   20 Km.

The broken lines (— ·— ·) indicate modern boundaries.

Ebenezer, and the ark was captured. However, the Philistines soon found out that the ark was not quite the great battle trophy they expected, for God sent plagues upon every Philistine city into which the ark was brought. Finally, the Philistines sent it back to Kiriath Jearim in Israel (4:1—7:1).

4 Mizpah The Israelites' defeat made them realize that God was no longer blessing them. Samuel called the people together at Mizpah and asked them to fast and pray in sorrow for their sins. The assembly at Mizpah was a tempting target for the confident Philistines who advanced for an attack. But God intervened and routed their mighty army. Meanwhile, Samuel was judging cases throughout Israel. But as Samuel grew old, the people came to him at Ramah (his home base) demanding a king in order to be like the other nations. At Mizpah, Saul was chosen by sacred appointment to be Israel's first king with the blessing, but not the approval, of God and Samuel (7:2—10:27).

5 Gilgal A battle with the Ammonites proved Saul's leadership abilities to the people of Israel. He protected the people of Jabesh Gilead and scattered the Ammonite army. Samuel and the people crowned Saul as king of Israel at Gilgal (11:1–15).

6 Valley of Elah Saul won many other battles, but over time he proved to be arrogant, sinful, and rebellious, so God finally rejected him as king. Unknown to Saul, a young shepherd and musician named David was anointed to be Israel's next king. But it would be many years before David sat upon the throne. Ironically, Saul hired David to play the harp in his palace. Saul grew to like David so much that he made him his personal armor-bearer. In one particular battle with the Philistines in the Valley of Elah, David killed Goliath, the Philistines' mightiest soldier. But this victory was the beginning of the end of Saul's love for David. The Israelites

1 Ramah Samuel was born in Ramah. Before his birth, Samuel's mother, Hannah, made a promise to God that she would dedicate her son to serve God alongside the priests in the tabernacle at Shiloh (1:1—2:11).

2 Shiloh The focal point of Israel's worship was at Shiloh, where the tabernacle and the ark of the covenant resided. Eli was the high priest, but his sons, Hophni and Phinehas, were evil men who took advantage of the people. Samuel, however, served God faithfully, and God blessed him as he grew (2:12—3:21).

3 Kiriath Jearim Israel was constantly at odds with the Philistines, and another battle was brewing. Hophni and Phinehas brought the ark of the covenant from Shiloh to the battlefield, believing that its mere presence would bring the Israelites victory. The Israelites were defeated by the Philistines at

praised David more than Saul, causing Saul to become so jealous that he plotted to kill David (12:1—22:23).

7 The Desert Even anointed kings are not exempt from troubles. David literally ran for his life from King Saul, hiding with his band of followers in the Desert of Ziph (where the men of Ziph constantly betrayed him), the Desert of Maon, and the Desert of En Gedi. Though he had opportunities to kill Saul, David refused to do so because Saul was God's anointed king (23:1—26:25).

8 Gath David moved his men and family to Gath, the Philistine city where King Achish lived. Saul then stopped chasing him. The Philistines seemed to welcome this famous fugitive from Israel (27:1–4).

9 Ziklag Desiring privacy in return for his pretended loyalty to King Achish, David asked for a city in which to house his men and family. Achish gave him Ziklag. From there David conducted raids against the cities of the Geshurites, Girzites, and Amalekites, making sure no one escaped to tell the tale (27:5–12). David later conquered the Amalekites after they raided Ziklag (30:1–31).

10 Mount Gilboa War with the Philistines broke out again in the north, near Mount Gilboa. Saul, who no longer relied on God, consulted a medium in a desperate attempt to contact

Samuel for help. In the meantime, David was sent back to Ziklag because the Philistine commanders did not trust his loyalty in battle against Israel. The Philistines slaughtered the Israelites on Mount Gilboa, killing King Saul and his three sons, including David's loyal friend Jonathan. Without God, Saul led a bitter and misguided life. The consequences of his sinful actions affected not only him but hurt his family and the entire nation as well (28:1—31:13).

A. ELI AND SAMUEL (1:1—7:17)

Israel has been ruled by judges for over 200 years. Eli and Samuel are the last of those judges. Samuel is born near the end of Eli's life. He grows up in the tabernacle as a priest-in-training under Eli and is well qualified to serve Israel as both a priest and a judge. Although the nation has fallen away from God, it is clear that God is preparing Samuel from the very beginning to lead the nation back to right living. God is always in control; he is able to bring his people back to him.

1. Samuel's birth and childhood
The Birth of Samuel

1:1
a 1Ch 6:27,34

1 There was a certain man from Ramathaim, a Zuphite*a* from the hill country of Ephraim, whose name was Elkanah*a* son of Jeroham, the son of Elihu, the son of Tohu, the son of Zuph, an Ephraimite. ²He had two wives; one was called Hannah and the other Peninnah. Peninnah had children, but Hannah had none.

1:3
b Dt 12:5-7
c Jos 18:1

³Year after year this man went up from his town to worship*b* and sacrifice to the Lord Almighty at Shiloh,*c* where Hophni and Phinehas, the two sons of Eli, were priests of the Lord.

1:4
d Dt 12:17-18

1:5
e Ge 16:1; 30:2

1:6
f Job 24:21

1:8
g Ru 4:15

⁴Whenever the day came for Elkanah to sacrifice,*d* he would give portions of the meat to his wife Peninnah and to all her sons and daughters. ⁵But to Hannah he gave a double portion because he loved her, and the Lord had closed her womb.*e* ⁶And because the Lord had closed her womb, her rival kept provoking her in order to irritate her.*f* ⁷This went on year after year. Whenever Hannah went up to the house of the Lord, her rival provoked her till she wept and would not eat. ⁸Elkanah her husband would say to her, "Hannah, why are you weeping? Why don't you eat? Why are you downhearted? Don't I mean more to you than ten sons?*g*"

a 1 Or *from Ramathaim Zuphim*

1:1 The book of 1 Samuel begins in the days when the judges still ruled Israel, possibly during the closing years of Samson's life. Samuel was Israel's last judge and the first priest and prophet to serve during the time of a king. He was the best example of what a good judge should be, governing the people by God's word and not by his own impulses. Samuel was the man who anointed Saul as Israel's first king.

1:2 Although many great Old Testament leaders (such as Abraham, Jacob, and David) had more than one wife, this was not God's original intention for marriage. Genesis 2:24 states that in marriage, two people become one flesh. Why then did polygamy exist among God's people? First, it was to produce more offspring to help in the man's work and to assure the continuation of the man's family line. Numerous children were a symbol of status and wealth. Second, in societies where many young men were killed in battle, polygamy became an accepted way of supporting women who otherwise would have remained unmarried and, very likely, destitute. Nevertheless, polygamy often caused serious family problems, as we see in this story of Hannah and Peninnah.

1:3 The tabernacle (Tent of Meeting) was located at Shiloh, the religious center of the nation (see Joshua 18:1). Three times a year all Israelite men were required to attend a religious feast held at the tabernacle: the Passover with the Feast of Unleavened Bread, the Feast of Weeks, and the Feast of Tabernacles (Deuteronomy 16:16). Elkanah made this pilgrimage regularly to fulfill God's commands. (See Exodus 23:14–17 for the regulations concerning the pilgrimage, and see the note on Exodus 40:34 for more on the tabernacle.)

1:6 Hannah had been unable to conceive children, and in Old Testament times, a childless woman was considered a failure. Her barrenness was a social embarrassment for her husband. Children were a very important part of the society's economic structure. They were a source of labor for the family, and it was their duty to care for their parents in their old age. If a wife could not bear children she was often obligated, by ancient Middle Eastern custom, to give one of her servant girls to her husband to bear children for her. Although Elkanah could have left Hannah (a husband was permitted to divorce a barren wife), he remained lovingly devoted to her despite social criticism and his rights under civil law.

1:7 Part of God's plan for Hannah involved postponing her years of childbearing. While Peninnah and Elkanah looked at Hannah's outward circumstances, God was moving ahead with his plan. Think of those in your world who are struggling with God's timing in answering their prayers and who need your love and help. By supporting those who are struggling, you may help them remain steadfast in their faith and confident in his timing to bring fulfillment to their lives.

1:8 Hannah knew her husband loved her, but even his encouragement could not comfort her. She could not keep from listening to Peninnah's jeers and letting Peninnah's words erode her self-confidence. Although we cannot keep others from unjustly criticizing us, we can choose how we will react to their hurtful words. Rather than dwelling upon our problems, we can enjoy the loving relationships God has given us. By so doing, we can exchange self-pity for hope.

⁹Once when they had finished eating and drinking in Shiloh, Hannah stood up. Now Eli the priest was sitting on a chair by the doorpost of the LORD's temple.ᵃ ʰ ¹⁰In bitterness of soul Hannah wept much and prayed to the LORD. ¹¹And she made a vow, saying, "O LORD Almighty, if you will only look upon your servant's misery and remember me, and not forget your servant but give her a son, then I will give him to the LORD for all the days of his life, and no razorⁱ will ever be used on his head."

¹²As she kept on praying to the LORD, Eli observed her mouth. ¹³Hannah was praying in her heart, and her lips were moving but her voice was not heard. Eli thought she was drunk ¹⁴and said to her, "How long will you keep on getting drunk? Get rid of your wine."

¹⁵"Not so, my lord," Hannah replied, "I am a woman who is deeply troubled. I have not been drinking wine or beer; I was pouringʲ out my soul to the LORD. ¹⁶Do not take your servant for a wicked woman; I have been praying here out of my great anguish and grief."

¹⁷Eli answered, "Go in peace,ᵏ and may the God of Israel grant you what you have asked of him.ˡ"

¹⁸She said, "May your servant find favor in your eyes.ᵐ" Then she went her way and ate something, and her face was no longer downcast.

¹⁹Early the next morning they arose and worshiped before the LORD and then went back to their home at Ramah. Elkanah lay with Hannah his wife, and the LORD rememberedⁿ her. ²⁰So in the course of time Hannah conceived and gave birth to a son. She named him Samuel,ᵇ saying, "Because I asked the LORD for him."

Hannah Dedicates Samuel

²¹When the man Elkanah went up with all his family to offer the annualᵒ sacrifice to the LORD and to fulfill his vow, ²²Hannah did not go. She said to her husband, "After the boy is weaned, I will take him and presentᵖ him before the LORD, and he will live there always."

²³"Do what seems best to you," Elkanah her husband told her. "Stay here until you have weaned him; only may the LORD make goodᵠ hisᶜ word." So the woman stayed at home and nursed her son until she had weaned him.

²⁴After he was weaned, she took the boy with her, young as he was, along with a three-year-old bull,ᵈ ʳ an ephahᵉ of flour and a skin of wine, and brought him to the house of the LORD at Shiloh. ²⁵When they had slaughtered the bull, they brought the boy to Eli, ²⁶and she

1:9 ʰ 1Sa 3:3
1:11 ⁱ Nu 6:1-21; Jdg 13:5
1:15 ʲ Ps 62:8
1:17 ᵏ Jdg 18:6; Mk 5:34 ˡ Ps 20:3-5
1:18 ᵐ Ru 2:13
1:19 ⁿ Ge 30:22
1:21 ᵒ ver 3
1:22 ᵖ Lk 2:22
1:23 ᵠ Nu 30:7
1:24 ʳ Dt 12:5; Jos 18:1

ᵃ*9* That is, tabernacle   ᵇ*20 Samuel* sounds like the Hebrew for *heard of God.*   ᶜ*23* Masoretic Text; Dead Sea Scrolls, Septuagint and Syriac *your*   ᵈ*24* Dead Sea Scrolls, Septuagint and Syriac; Masoretic Text *with three bulls*
ᵉ*24* That is, probably about 3/5 bushel (about 22 liters)

1:10 Hannah had good reason to feel discouraged and bitter. She was unable to bear children; she shared her husband with a woman who ridiculed her (1:7); her loving husband could not solve her problem (1:8); and even the high priest misunderstood her motives (1:14). But instead of retaliating or giving up hope, Hannah prayed. She brought her problem honestly before God.

THE JOURNEY TO SHILOH
Each year Elkanah and his family traveled from their home at Ramah to Shiloh, where they worshiped and sacrificed at God's tabernacle.

Each of us may face times of barrenness when nothing "comes to birth" in our work, service, or relationships. It is difficult to pray in faith when we feel so ineffective. But, as Hannah discovered, prayer opens the way for God to work (1:19, 20).

1:11 Be careful what you promise in prayer because God may take you up on it. Hannah so desperately wanted a child that she was willing to strike a bargain with God. God took her up on her promise, and to Hannah's credit, she did her part, even though it was painful (1:27, 28).

Although we are not in a position to barter with God, he may still choose to answer a prayer that has an attached promise. When you pray, ask yourself, "Will I follow through on any promises I make to God if he grants my request?" It is dishonest and dangerous to ignore a promise, especially to God. God keeps his promises, and he expects you to keep yours.

1:18 Earlier Hannah had been discouraged to the point of being physically sick and unable to eat. At this point, she returned home well and happy. The change in her attitude may be attributed to three factors: (1) she honestly prayed to God (1:11); (2) she received encouragement from Eli (1:17); (3) she resolved to leave the problem with God (1:18). This is the antidote for discouragement: tell God how you really feel and leave your problems with him. Then rely upon the support of good friends and counselors.

1:26–28 To do what she promised (1:11), Hannah gave up what she wanted most—her son—and presented him to Eli to serve in the house of the Lord. In dedicating her only son to God, Hannah was dedicating her entire life and future to God. Because Samuel's life was from God, Hannah was not really giving him up. Rather, she was returning him to God who had given Samuel to Hannah in said to him, "As surely as you live, my lord, I am the woman who stood here beside you praying to the LORD. 27 I prayed for this child, and the LORD has granted me what I asked of him. 28 So now I give him to the LORD. For his whole life he will be given over to the LORD." And he worshiped the LORD there.

Hannah's Prayer

2 Then Hannah prayed and said: *s*

2:1
s Lk 1:46-55
t Isa 12:2-3

> "My heart rejoices in the LORD;
>   in the LORD my horn *a* *t* is lifted high.

a 1 *Horn* here symbolizes strength; also in verse 10.

ELKANAH & PENINNAH

Husbands can be insensitive for many reasons, but often they simply suffer from ignorance. Elkanah had two wives, which doubled his opportunities to seem insensitive. One of the wives, Peninnah, was able to give Elkanah many children. The other wife, Hannah, owned Elkanah's heart but was unable to get pregnant. Peninnah, jealous that providing Elkanah with heirs didn't turn his affections toward her, treated Hannah with disdain. Yet Elkanah seemed oblivious to the turmoil around him.

Although the events leading up to the birth of Samuel primarily involved Hannah, both Elkanah and Peninnah played significant roles. Peninnah's competitiveness and derision drove Hannah to prayer; Elkanah's simple love allowed Hannah to entrust their child Samuel into God's care. Elkanah didn't realize how much a little attention toward Peninnah could have cooled the simmering emotions in his home. Nor did he understand that his love for Hannah didn't make up for the emptiness of her womb.

The glimpse God gives us of that tense household provides a helpful backdrop for God's purposes, which are not thwarted by human shortcomings. He worked within the strain and stress of those relationships to bring Samuel into the world—one of the most significant figures in the Old Testament. When our relational systems seem too snarled to be unraveled or salvaged, we need to remember that God not only displays his creativity by making things from scratch, but also by bringing order and beauty out of messes.

Strengths and accomplishments:	• Elkanah supported Hannah's decision to leave Samuel in Shiloh to be raised as a priest • Regular trips to Shiloh acknowledged God's importance to the entire family
Weaknesses and mistakes:	• Elkanah did not understand what would have helped each of his wives • Peninnah made things worse by taking out her disappointment and anger on Hannah
Lessons from their lives:	• Ignorance is not a good excuse for insensitivity • Jealousy is not a good excuse for bad behavior • God works in the middle of family messes
Vital statistics:	• Where: Ramathaim • Occupation: Unknown • Relatives: Elkanah and Peninnah had an unknown number of children together; Elkanah and Hannah bore two daughters and four sons, including Samuel • Contemporary: Eli the priest
Key verse:	"Elkanah her husband would say to her, 'Hannah, why are you weeping? Why don't you eat? Why are you downhearted? Don't I mean more to you than ten sons?'" (1 Samuel 1:8).

Their story is told in 1 Samuel 1—2.

---

the first place. These verses illustrate the kind of gifts we should give to God. Do your gifts cost you little (Sunday mornings, a comfortable tithe), or are they gifts of sacrifice? Are you presenting God with tokens, or are you presenting him with your entire life?

1:28 Samuel was probably three years old—the customary age for weaning—when his mother left him at the tabernacle. By saying, "I give him to the LORD," Hannah meant that she was dedicating Samuel to God for lifetime service. She did not, of course, forget her much-wanted son. She visited him regularly. And each year she brought him a robe just like Eli's (2:19). In later years, Samuel lived in Ramah (7:17), his parents' hometown (1:19, 20).

2:1–10 Hannah praised God for his answer to her prayer for a son. The theme of her poetic prayer is her confidence in God's sovereignty and her thankfulness for everything he had done. Mary, the mother of Jesus, modeled her own praise song, called the Magnificat, after Hannah's prayer (Luke 1:46–55). Like Hannah and Mary, we should be confident of God's ultimate control over the events in our lives, and we should be thankful for the ways God has blessed us. By praising God for all good gifts, we acknowledge his ultimate control over all the affairs of life.

My mouth boasts over my enemies,
    for I delight in your deliverance.

2 "There is no one holy[a] [u] like the LORD;
    there is no one besides you;
    there is no Rock like our God.

3 "Do not keep talking so proudly
    or let your mouth speak such arrogance,
for the LORD is a God who knows,
    and by him deeds[v] are weighed. [w]

4 "The bows of the warriors are broken,
    but those who stumbled are armed with strength.
5 Those who were full hire themselves out for food,
    but those who were hungry hunger no more.
She who was barren[x] has borne seven children,
    but she who has had many sons pines away.

6 "The LORD brings death and makes alive;[y]
    he brings down to the grave[b] and raises up.
7 The LORD sends poverty and wealth;
    he humbles and he exalts. [z]
8 He raises the poor from the dust
    and lifts the needy from the ash heap;
he seats them with princes
    and has them inherit a throne of honor. [a]

"For the foundations[b] of the earth are the LORD's;
    upon them he has set the world.
9 He will guard the feet[c] of his saints,
    but the wicked will be silenced in darkness.

"It is not by strength that one prevails;
10   those who oppose the LORD will be shattered. [d]
He will thunder[e] against them from heaven;
    the LORD will judge[f] the ends of the earth.

"He will give strength to his king
    and exalt the horn[g] of his anointed."

11 Then Elkanah went home to Ramah, but the boy ministered[h] before the LORD under Eli the priest.

a2 Or *no Holy One*   b6 Hebrew *Sheol*

2:2
[u] Ex 15:11

2:3
[v] 1Sa 16:7
[w] Pr 16:2

2:5
[x] Ps 113:9; Jer 15:9

2:6
[y] Dt 32:39

2:7
[z] Ps 75:7

2:8
[a] Job 36:7
[b] Job 38:4

2:9
[c] Ps 91:12

2:10
[d] Ps 2:9
[e] Ps 18:13
[f] Ps 96:13
[g] Ps 89:24

2:11
[h] 1Sa 3:1

2:2 Hannah praised God for being a Rock—firm, strong, and unchanging. In our fast-paced world, friends come and go, and circumstances change. It's difficult to find a solid foundation that will not change. Those who devote their lives to achievements, causes, or possessions have as their security that which is finite and changeable. The possessions that we work so hard to obtain will all pass away. But God is always present. Hope in him. He will never fail.

2:3 No doubt as Hannah said these words, she was thinking of Peninnah's arrogance and chiding. Hannah did not have to get even with Peninnah. She knew that God is all-knowing, and that he will judge all sin and pride. Hannah wisely left judgment up to God. Resist the temptation to take justice into your own

hands. God will weigh your deeds as well as those who have wronged you.

2:10 Because we live in a world where evil abounds and where war and terrorism always threaten, we may forget that God is in control. Hannah saw God as (1) solid as a rock (2:2), (2) the one who knows what we do (2:3), (3) sovereign over all the affairs of people (2:4–8), and (4) the supreme judge who administers perfect justice (2:10). Remembering God's sovereign control helps us put both world and personal events in perspective.

2:11 Samuel "ministered before the LORD under Eli the priest." In other words, Samuel was Eli's helper or assistant. In this role, Samuel's responsibilities would have included opening the tabernacle doors each morning (3:15), cleaning the furniture, and sweeping the floors. As he grew older, Samuel would have assisted Eli in offering sacrifices. The fact that he was wearing a linen ephod (a garment worn only by priests) shows that he was a priest-in-training (2:18). Because Samuel was Eli's helper, he was God's helper too. When you serve others—even in carrying out ordinary tasks—you are serving God. Because ultimately we serve God, every job has dignity.

Eli's Wicked Sons

2:12
Jer 2:8

¹²Eli's sons were wicked men; they had no regard *i* for the LORD. ¹³Now it was the practice of the priests with the people that whenever anyone offered a sacrifice and while the meat was being boiled, the servant of the priest would come with a three-pronged fork in his hand. ¹⁴He would plunge it into the pan or kettle or caldron or pot, and the priest would take for himself whatever the fork brought up. This is how they treated all the Israelites who came to Shiloh. ¹⁵But even before the fat was burned, the servant of the priest would come and say to the man who was sacrificing, "Give the priest some meat to roast; he won't accept boiled meat from you, but only raw."

¹⁶If the man said to him, "Let the fat be burned up first, and then take whatever you want," the servant would then answer, "No, hand it over now; if you don't, I'll take it by force."

Hannah's prayer shows us that all we have and receive is on loan from God. Hannah might have had many excuses for being a possessive mother. But when God answered her prayer, she followed through on her promise to dedicate Samuel to God's service.

She discovered that the greatest joy in having a child is to give that child fully and freely back to God. She entered motherhood prepared to do what all mothers must eventually do— let go of their children.

When children are born, they are completely dependent upon their parents for all their basic necessities. This causes some parents to forget that those same children will grow toward independence within the span of a few short years. Being sensitive to the different stages of that healthy process will greatly strengthen family relationships; resisting or denying that process will cause great pain. We must gradually let go of our children in order to allow them to become mature, interdependent adults.

HANNAH

Strengths and accomplishments:	• Mother of Samuel, Israel's greatest judge • Fervent in worship; effective in prayer • Willing to follow through on even a costly commitment
Weakness and mistake:	• Struggled with her sense of self-worth because she was unable to have children
Lessons from her life:	• God hears and answers prayer • Our children are gifts from God • God is concerned for the oppressed and afflicted
Vital statistics:	• Where: Ephraim • Occupation: Homemaker • Relatives: Husband: Elkanah. Son: Samuel. Later, three other sons and two daughters. • Contemporary: Eli, the priest
Key verses:	"And she said to him, 'As surely as you live, my lord, I am the woman who stood here beside you praying to the LORD. I prayed for this child, and the LORD has granted me what I asked of him. So now I give him to the LORD. For his whole life he will be given over to the LORD'" (1 Samuel 1:26–28).

Her story is told in 1 Samuel 1, 2.

2:12ff The law stipulated that the needs of all the Levites were to be met through the people's tithes (Numbers 18:20–24; Joshua 13:14, 33). Because Eli's sons were priests, they were to be taken care of this way. But Eli's sons took advantage of their position to satisfy their lust for power, possessions, and control. Their contempt and arrogance toward both people and worship undermined the integrity of the whole priesthood.

Eli knew that his sons were evil, but he did little to correct or stop them, even when the integrity of God's sanctuary was threatened. As the high priest, Eli should have responded by executing his sons (Numbers 15:22–31). No wonder he chose not to confront the situation. But by ignoring their selfish actions, Eli let his sons ruin their own lives and the lives of many others. There are times when serious problems must be confronted, even if the process and consequences could be painful.

2:13, 14 This fork was a utensil used in the tabernacle for offering sacrifices. Made of bronze (Exodus 27:3), it usually had three prongs to hook the meat that was to be offered on the altar. Eli's sons used the fork to take more meat from the pot than was due them.

2:13–17 What were Eli's sons doing wrong? They were taking parts of the sacrifices *before* they were offered to God on the altar. They were also eating meat before the fat was burned off. This was against God's laws (Leviticus 3:3–5). In effect, Eli's sons were treating God's offerings with contempt. Offerings were given to show honor and respect to God while seeking forgiveness for sins, but through their irreverence, Eli's sons were actually sinning while making the offerings. To add to their sins, they were also sleeping with the women who served there (2:22).

Like Eli's sons, some religious leaders look down on the faith of ordinary people and treat their offerings to God casually or even with contempt. God harshly judges those who lead his people astray or scorn what is devoted to him (Numbers 18:32).

¹⁷This sin of the young men was very great in the Lord's sight, for they^a were treating the Lord's offering with contempt.^j

2:17
/Mal 2:7-9

¹⁸But Samuel was ministering ^k before the Lord—a boy wearing a linen ephod. ¹⁹Each year his mother made him a little robe and took it to him when she went up with her husband to offer the annual^l sacrifice. ²⁰Eli would bless Elkanah and his wife, saying, "May the Lord give you children by this woman to take the place of the one she prayed^m for and gave to the Lord." Then they would go home. ²¹And the Lord was gracious to Hannah;ⁿ she conceived and gave birth to three sons and two daughters. Meanwhile, the boy Samuel grew^o up in the presence of the Lord.

2:18
kver 11
2:19
lSa 1:3
2:20
m1Sa 1:11,27-28
2:21
nGe 21:1
over 26

²²Now Eli, who was very old, heard about everything his sons were doing to all Israel and how they slept with the women^p who served at the entrance to the Tent of Meeting. ²³So he said to them, "Why do you do such things? I hear from all the people about these wicked deeds of yours. ²⁴No, my sons; it is not a good report that I hear spreading among the Lord's people. ²⁵If a man sins against another man, God^b may mediate for him; but if a man sins against the Lord, who will^q intercede for him?" His sons, however, did not listen to their father's rebuke, for it was the Lord's will to put them to death.

2:22
pEx 38:8

2:25
qNu 15:30;
Jos 11:20

²⁶And the boy Samuel continued to grow^r in stature and in favor with the Lord and with men.

2:26
rver 21; Lk 2:52

Prophecy Against the House of Eli

²⁷Now a man of God^s came to Eli and said to him, "This is what the Lord says: 'Did I not clearly reveal myself to your father's house when they were in Egypt under Pharaoh? ²⁸I chose^t your father out of all the tribes of Israel to be my priest, to go up to my altar, to burn incense, and to wear an ephod in my presence. I also gave your father's house all the offerings made with fire by the Israelites. ²⁹Why do you^c scorn my sacrifice and offering that I prescribed for my dwelling?^u Why do you honor your sons more than me by fattening yourselves on the choice parts of every offering made by my people Israel?'

2:27
sEx 4:14-16
2:28
tEx 28:1

2:29
uDt 12:5

³⁰"Therefore the Lord, the God of Israel, declares: 'I promised that your house and your father's house would minister before me forever. ^v' But now the Lord declares: 'Far be it from me! Those who honor me I will honor, but those who despise^w me will be disdained. ³¹The time is coming when I will cut short your strength and the strength of your father's house, so that there will not be an old man in your family line^x ³²and you will see distress in my dwelling. Although good will be done to Israel, in your family line there will never be an old man.^y ³³Every one of you that I do not cut off from my altar will be spared only to blind your eyes with tears and to grieve your heart, and all your descendants will die in the prime of life.

2:30
vEx 29:9
wMal 2:9
2:31
x1Sa 4:11-18;
22:16-20
2:32
yZec 8:4

^a17 Or men   ^b25 Or the judges   ^c29 The Hebrew is plural.

2:18 Samuel wore a linen ephod. *Ephods,* long sleeveless vests made of plain linen, were worn by all priests. The high priest's ephod carried special significance. It was embroidered with a variety of bright colors. Attached to it was the breastplate, a bib-like garment with gold embroidered shoulder straps. Twelve precious gemstones were attached to the breastplate, each stone representing one of the tribes of Israel. A pouch on the ephod held the Urim and the Thummim, two small objects used to determine God's will in certain national matters.

2:21 God honored the desires of faithful Hannah. We never hear about Peninnah or her children again, but Samuel was used mightily by God. God also gave Hannah five children in addition to Samuel. God often blesses us in ways we do not expect. Hannah never expected to have a child at her age, much less six children! Don't resent God's timing. His blessings might not be immediate, but they will come if we are faithful to do what he says in his Word.

2:23–25 Eli's sons knew better, but they continued to disobey God deliberately by cheating, seducing, and robbing the people. Therefore, God planned to kill them. Any sin is wrong, but sin carried out deliberately and deceitfully is the worst kind. When we sin out of ignorance, we deserve punishment. But when we sin intentionally, the consequences will be more severe. Don't ignore God's warnings about sin. Abandon sin before it becomes a way of life.

2:25 Does a loving God really will or want to put people to death? Consider the situation in the tabernacle. A person made an offering in order to have his sins forgiven, and Eli's sons stole the offering and made a sham of the person's repentant attitude. God, in his love for Israel, could not permit this situation to continue. He allowed Eli's sons to die as a result of their own boastful presumption. They took the ark into battle, thinking it would protect them. But God withdrew his protection, and the wicked sons of Eli were killed (4:10, 11).

2:29 Eli had a difficult time rearing his sons. He apparently did not take any strong disciplinary action with them when he became aware of their wrongdoing. But Eli was not just a father trying to handle his rebellious sons; he was the high priest ignoring the sins of priests under his jurisdiction. As a result, the Lord took the necessary disciplinary action that Eli would not.

Eli was guilty of honoring his sons above God by letting them continue in their sinful ways. Is there a situation in your life, family, or work that you allow to continue even though you know it is wrong? If so, you may become as guilty as those engaged in the wrong act.

2:31, 35, 36 For the fulfillment of this prediction see 1 Kings 2:26, 27. This is where Solomon removed Abiathar from his position, thus ending Eli's line. Then God raised up Zadok, a priest under David and then high priest under Solomon. Zadok's line was probably still in place as late as the days of Ezra.

2:34
z 1Sa 4:11
a 1Ki 13:3

2:35
b 2Sa 7:11,27;
1Ki 11:38

34"'And what happens to your two sons, Hophni and Phinehas, will be a sign to you—they will both die z on the same day. a 35 I will raise up for myself a faithful priest, who will do according to what is in my heart and mind. I will firmly establish his house, and he will minister before my anointed b one always. 36 Then everyone left in your family line will come and bow down before him for a piece of silver and a crust of bread and plead, "Appoint me to some priestly office so I can have food to eat."'"

The LORD Calls Samuel

3:1
c 1Sa 2:11
d Ps 74:9
e Am 8:11

3 The boy Samuel ministered c before the LORD under Eli. In those days the word of the LORD was rare; d there were not many visions. e

ELI

Eli was one Old Testament person with a very modern problem. The recognition and respect he earned in public did not extend to his handling of his private affairs. He may have been an excellent priest, but he was a poor parent. His sons brought him grief and ruin. He lacked two important qualities needed for effective parental discipline: firm resolve and corrective action.

Eli responded to situations rather than solving them. But even his responses tended to be weak. God pointed out his sons' errors, but Eli did little to correct them. The contrast between God's dealing with Eli and Eli's dealing with his sons is clear—God gave warning, spelled out the consequences of disobedience, and then acted. Eli only warned. Children need to learn that their parents' words and actions go together. Both love and discipline must be spoken as well as acted out.

But Eli had another problem. He was more concerned with the symbols of his religion than with the God they represented. For Eli, the ark of the covenant had become a relic to be protected rather than a reminder of the Protector. His faith shifted from the Creator to the created.

It may be easier to worship things we can see, whether buildings, people, or Scripture itself, but such tangible things have no power in themselves. This book you hold is either merely a respectable religious relic, or it is the sharp and effective Word of God. Your attitude toward it is largely shaped by your relationship to the God from whom it comes. A relic or antique has to be carefully stored away; God's Word has to be used and obeyed. Which attitude accurately describes your approach to the Word of God?

Strengths and accomplishments:	• Judged Israel for 40 years • Spoke with Hannah, the mother of Samuel, and assured her of God's blessing • Reared and trained Samuel, the greatest judge of Israel
Weaknesses and mistakes:	• Failed to discipline his sons or correct them when they sinned • Tended to react to situations rather than take decisive action • Saw the ark of the covenant as a relic to be cherished rather than as a symbol of God's presence with Israel
Lessons from his life:	• Parents need to discipline their children responsibly • Life is more than simply reacting; it demands action • Past victories cannot substitute for present trust
Vital statistics:	• Where: Shiloh • Occupations: High priest and judge of Israel • Relatives: Sons: Hophni and Phinehas • Contemporary: Samuel
Key verses:	"And the LORD said to Samuel: 'See, I am about to do something in Israel that will make the ears of everyone who hears of it tingle. At that time I will carry out against Eli everything I spoke against his family—from beginning to end. For I told him that I would judge his family forever because of the sin he knew about; his sons made themselves contemptible, and he failed to restrain them. Therefore, I swore to the house of Eli, "The guilt of Eli's house will never be atoned for by sacrifice or offering"'" (1 Samuel 3:11–14).

His story is told in 1 Samuel 1—4. He is also mentioned in 1 Kings 2:26, 27.

2:35 "My anointed one" refers to the king (see 2:10). God was saying that his faithful priest would serve his king forever.

3:1–5 Although God had spoken directly and audibly with Moses and Joshua, his word became rare during the three centuries of rule by judges. By Eli's time, no prophets were speaking God's messages to Israel. Why? Look at the attitude of Eli's sons. They either refused to listen to God or allowed greed to get in the way of any communication with him.

Listening and responding is vital in a relationship with God. Although God does not always use the sound of a human voice, he always speaks clearly through his Word. To receive his messages, we must be ready to listen and to act upon what he tells us. Like Samuel, be ready to say "Here I am" when God calls you to action.

2 One night Eli, whose eyes were becoming so weak that he could barely see, was lying down in his usual place. 3 The lamp of God had not yet gone out, and Samuel was lying down in the temple a of the Lord, where the ark of God was. 4 Then the Lord called Samuel.

Samuel answered, "Here I am." 5 And he ran to Eli and said, "Here I am; you called me." But Eli said, "I did not call; go back and lie down." So he went and lay down.

6 Again the Lord called, "Samuel!" And Samuel got up and went to Eli and said, "Here I am; you called me."

"My son," Eli said, "I did not call; go back and lie down."

7 Now Samuel did not yet know the Lord: The word of the Lord had not yet been revealed f to him.

8 The Lord called Samuel a third time, and Samuel got up and went to Eli and said, "Here I am; you called me."

Then Eli realized that the Lord was calling the boy. 9 So Eli told Samuel, "Go and lie down, and if he calls you, say, 'Speak, Lord, for your servant is listening.'" So Samuel went and lay down in his place.

10 The Lord came and stood there, calling as at the other times, "Samuel! Samuel!"

Then Samuel said, "Speak, for your servant is listening."

11 And the Lord said to Samuel: "See, I am about to do something in Israel that will make the ears of everyone who hears of it tingle. g 12 At that time I will carry out against Eli everything h I spoke against his family—from beginning to end. 13 For I told him that I would judge his family forever because of the sin he knew about; his sons made themselves contemptible, b and he failed to restrain i them. 14 Therefore, I swore to the house of Eli, 'The guilt of Eli's house will never be atoned j for by sacrifice or offering.'"

15 Samuel lay down until morning and then opened the doors of the house of the Lord. He was afraid to tell Eli the vision, 16 but Eli called him and said, "Samuel, my son."

Samuel answered, "Here I am."

17 "What was it he said to you?" Eli asked. "Do not hide it from me. May God deal with you, be it ever so severely, if you hide from me anything he told you." 18 So Samuel told him everything, hiding nothing from him. Then Eli said, "He is the Lord; let him do what is good in his eyes." k

19 The Lord was with l Samuel as he grew m up, and he let none n of his words fall to the ground. 20 And all Israel from Dan to Beersheba o recognized that Samuel was attested as a prophet of the Lord. 21 The Lord continued to appear at Shiloh, and there he revealed himself to Samuel through his word.

4

And Samuel's word came to all Israel.

2. War with the Philistines
The Philistines Capture the Ark

Now the Israelites went out to fight against the Philistines. The Israelites camped at Ebenezer, p and the Philistines at Aphek. 2 The Philistines deployed their forces to meet Israel,

---

a *3* That is, tabernacle   b *13* Masoretic Text; an ancient Hebrew scribal tradition and Septuagint *sons blasphemed God*

3:7
f Ac 19:12

3:11
g 2Ki 21:12
3:12
h 1Sa 2:27-36
3:13
i 1Sa 2:12,17, 22, 29-31
3:14
j 1Sa 2:25

3:18
k Isa 39:8

3:19
l Ge 39:2
m 1Sa 2:21
n 1Sa 9:6
3:20
o Jdg 20:1
4:1
p 1Sa 7:12

3:2, 3 The ark of God was kept in the Most Holy Place, the innermost room of the tabernacle where only the high priest could enter once a year. In front of the Most Holy Place was the Holy Place, a small room where the other sacred furniture of the tabernacle was kept (the altar of incense, the bread of the Presence, the lampstand). Just outside the Holy Place was a court with small rooms where the priests were to stay. Samuel probably slept here with the other priests, only a few yards away from the ark.

3:8, 9 One would naturally expect an audible message from God to be given to the priest Eli and not to the child Samuel. Eli was older and more experienced, and he held the proper position. But God's chain of command is based on faith, not on age or position. In finding faithful followers, God may use unexpected channels. Be prepared for the Lord to work at any place, at any time, and through anyone he chooses.

3:13 Eli had spent his entire life in service to God. His responsibility was to oversee all the worship in Israel. But in pursuing this great mission he neglected the responsibilities in his own home. Don't let your desire to do God's work cause you to neglect your family. If you do, your mission may degenerate into a quest for personal importance, and your family will suffer the consequences of your neglect.

3:14 *Atoned for* means "forgiven." God was saying that the sin of Eli's sons could not be covered by sacrifice and that they would be punished.

3:20 The phrase "from Dan to Beersheba" was often used to describe the boundaries of the promised land. Dan was one of the northernmost cities in the land, and Beersheba one of the cities farthest south. In this context, it was a way of emphasizing that *everyone* in Israel knew that Samuel was called to be a prophet.

4:1 The Philistines, descendants of Noah's son Ham, settled along the southeastern Mediterranean coast between Egypt and Gaza. They were originally one of the "Sea Peoples" who had migrated to the Middle East in ships from Greece and Crete. By Samuel's time, these warlike people were well established in five of Gaza's cities in southwest Canaan and were constantly pressing inland against the Israelites. Throughout this time, the Philistines were Israel's major enemy.

and as the battle spread, Israel was defeated by the Philistines, who killed about four thousand of them on the battlefield. ³When the soldiers returned to camp, the elders of Israel asked, "Why did the LORD bring defeat upon us today before the Philistines? Let us bring the ark of the LORD's covenant from Shiloh, so that itᵃ may go with us and save us from the hand of our enemies."

4:4
ᵠ2Sa 6:2

⁴So the people sent men to Shiloh, and they brought back the ark of the covenant of the LORD Almighty, who is enthroned between the cherubim. ᵠ And Eli's two sons, Hophni and Phinehas, were there with the ark of the covenant of God.

⁵When the ark of the LORD's covenant came into the camp, all Israel raised such a great shout that the ground shook. ⁶Hearing the uproar, the Philistines asked, "What's all this shouting in the Hebrew camp?"

ᵃ3 Or he

ISRAELITES VERSUS PHILISTINES	Location of the Battle	Winner	Comments	Reference
The Israelites and Philistines were archenemies and constantly fought. Here are some of their confrontations, found in 1 and 2 Samuel. When the Israelites trusted God for the victory, they always won.	Aphek to Ebenezer	Philistines	The ark was captured and Eli's sons killed	1 Samuel 4:1–11
	Mizpah	Israelites	After the ark was returned, the Philistines planned to attack again, but God confused them. Israel chased the Philistines back to Beth Car	1 Samuel 7:7–14
	Geba	Israelites under Jonathan	One detachment destroyed	1 Samuel 13:3, 4
	Gilgal	A standoff	The Israelites lost their nerve and hid	1 Samuel 13:6–17
	Micmash	Israelites	Jonathan and his armor-bearer said it didn't matter how many enemies there were. If God was with them, they would win. They began the battle, and the army completed it	1 Samuel 13:23—14:23
	Valley of Elah	Israelites	David and Goliath	1 Samuel 17:1–58
	?	Israelites	David killed 200 Philistines to earn a wife	1 Samuel 18:17–30
	Keilah	Israelites under David	David protected the threshing floors from Philistine looters	1 Samuel 23:1–5
	Aphek, Jezreel, to Mount Gilboa	Philistines	Saul and Jonathan killed	1 Samuel 29:1; 31:1–13
	Baal Perazim	Israelites	The Philistines tried to capture King David	2 Samuel 5:17–25
	Metheg Ammah (possibly near Gath)	Israelites	There was very little trouble with the Philistines after this defeat	2 Samuel 8:1
	?	Israelites	Abishai saved David from a Philistine giant	2 Samuel 21:15–17
	Gob	Israelites	Other giants were killed, including Goliath's brother (see NIV text note)	2 Samuel 21:18–22

4:3 The ark of the covenant contained the Ten Commandments given by God to Moses. The ark was supposed to be kept in the Most Holy Place, a sacred part of the tabernacle that only the high priest could enter once a year. Hophni and Phinehas desecrated the room by unlawfully entering it and removing the ark.

The Israelites rightly recognized the great holiness of the ark, but they thought that the ark itself—the wood and metal box—was their source of power. They began to use it as a good luck charm, expecting it to protect them from their enemies. A symbol of God does not guarantee his presence and power. Their attitude toward the ark came perilously close to idol worship. When the ark was captured by their enemies, they thought that Israel's glory was gone (4:19–22) and that God had deserted them (7:1, 2). God uses his power according to his own wisdom and will. He responds to the faith of those who seek him.

4:4 "The LORD Almighty, who is enthroned between the cheru-

bim" conveys that God's presence rested on the ark of the covenant between the two golden cherubim (or angels) attached to its lid. The people believed that the ark would bring victory when Hophni and Phinehas carried it into battle.

4:5–8 The Philistines were afraid because they remembered stories about God's intervention for Israel when they left Egypt. But Israel had turned away from God and was clinging to only a form of godliness, a symbol of former victories.

People (and churches) often try to live on the memories of God's blessings. The Israelites wrongly assumed that because God had given them victory in the past, he would do it again, even though they had strayed far from him. Today, as in Bible times, spiritual victories come through a continually renewed relationship with God. Don't live off the past. Keep your relationship with God new and fresh.

When they learned that the ark of the Lord had come into the camp, [7]the Philistines were afraid. "A god has come into the camp," they said. "We're in trouble! Nothing like this has happened before. [8]Woe to us! Who will deliver us from the hand of these mighty gods? They are the gods who struck the Egyptians with all kinds of plagues in the desert. [9]Be strong, Philistines! Be men, or you will be subject to the Hebrews, as they[r] have been to you. Be men, and fight!"

[10]So the Philistines fought, and the Israelites were defeated[s] and every man fled to his tent. The slaughter was very great; Israel lost thirty thousand foot soldiers. [11]The ark of God was captured, and Eli's two sons, Hophni and Phinehas, died.[t]

Death of Eli

[12]That same day a Benjamite ran from the battle line and went to Shiloh, his clothes torn and dust[u] on his head. [13]When he arrived, there was Eli[v] sitting on his chair by the side of the road, watching, because his heart feared for the ark of God. When the man entered the town and told what had happened, the whole town sent up a cry.

[14]Eli heard the outcry and asked, "What is the meaning of this uproar?"

The man hurried over to Eli, [15]who was ninety-eight years old and whose eyes[w] were set so that he could not see. [16]He told Eli, "I have just come from the battle line; I fled from it this very day."

Eli asked, "What happened, my son?"

[17]The man who brought the news replied, "Israel fled before the Philistines, and the army has suffered heavy losses. Also your two sons, Hophni and Phinehas, are dead, and the ark of God has been captured."

[18]When he mentioned the ark of God, Eli fell backward off his chair by the side of the gate. His neck was broken and he died, for he was an old man and heavy. He had led[a] Israel forty years.

[19]His daughter-in-law, the wife of Phinehas, was pregnant and near the time of delivery. When she heard the news that the ark of God had been captured and that her father-in-law and her husband were dead, she went into labor and gave birth, but was overcome by her labor pains. [20]As she was dying, the women attending her said, "Don't despair; you have given birth to a son." But she did not respond or pay any attention.

[21]She named the boy Ichabod,[b] saying, "The glory has departed from Israel"—because of the capture of the ark of God and the deaths of her father-in-law and her husband. [22]She said, "The glory has departed from Israel, for the ark of God has been captured."

a 18 Traditionally *judged*   b 21 *Ichabod* means *no glory*.

4:9
r Jdg 13:1;
1Co 16:13

4:10
s ver 2; Dt 28:25

4:11
t 1Sa 2:34;
Ps 78:61,64

4:12
u Jos 7:6; 2Sa 1:2;
Ne 9:1

4:13
v 1Sa 1:9

4:15
w 1Sa 3:2

THE ARK'S TRAVELS Eli's sons took the ark from Shiloh to the battlefield on the lower plains at Ebenezer and Aphek. The Philistines captured the ark and took it to Ashdod, Gath, and Ekron. Plagues forced the people to send the ark back to Israel, where it finally was taken by cattle-drawn carts to Beth Shemesh and on to the home of Eleazar in Kiriath Jearim.

4:11 This event fulfills the prophecy in 2:34 stating that Eli's sons, Hophni and Phinehas, would die "on the same day."

4:12 At this time, the city of Shiloh was Israel's religious center (Joshua 18:1; 1 Samuel 4:3). The tabernacle was permanently set up there. Because Israel did not have a civil capital—a seat of national government—Shiloh was the natural place for a messenger to deliver the sad news from the battle. Many scholars believe that it was during this battle that Shiloh was destroyed (Jeremiah 7:12; 26:2–6; also see the note on 7:1).

4:18 Eli was Israel's judge and high priest. His death marked the end of the dark period of the judges when most of the nation ignored God. Although Samuel was also a judge, his career saw the transition from Israel's rule by judges to the nation's monarchy. He began the great revival that Israel would experience for the next century. The Bible does not say who became the next high priest (Samuel was not eligible because he was not a direct descendant of Aaron), but Samuel acted as high priest at this time by offering the important sacrifices throughout Israel.

4:19–22 This incident illustrates the spiritual darkness and decline of Israel. This young boy, Ichabod, was supposed to succeed his father Phinehas in the priesthood, but his father had been killed because he was an evil man who desecrated the tabernacle. The terror of God's leaving his people overshadowed the joy of childbirth. When sin dominates our lives, even God-given joys and pleasures seem empty.

The Ark in Ashdod and Ekron

5:1
x 1Sa 4:1; 7:12

5:2
y Jdg 16:23

5:3
z Isa 19:1; 46:7

5:4
a Eze 6:6; Mic 1:7

5 After the Philistines had captured the ark of God, they took it from Ebenezer x to Ashdod. 2 Then they carried the ark into Dagon's temple and set it beside Dagon. y 3 When the people of Ashdod rose early the next day, there was Dagon, fallen z on his face on the ground before the ark of the LORD! They took Dagon and put him back in his place. 4 But the following morning when they rose, there was Dagon, fallen on his face on the ground before the ark of the LORD! His head and hands had been broken a off and were lying on the threshold; only his body remained. 5 That is why to this day neither the priests of Dagon nor any others who enter Dagon's temple at Ashdod step on the threshold.

5:6
b Ex 9:3
c Ps 78:66
d 1Sa 6:5

6 The LORD's hand b was heavy upon the people of Ashdod and its vicinity; he brought devastation c upon them and afflicted them with tumors. a d 7 When the men of Ashdod saw what was happening, they said, "The ark of the god of Israel must not stay here with us, because his hand is heavy upon us and upon Dagon our god." 8 So they called together all the rulers of the Philistines and asked them, "What shall we do with the ark of the god of Israel?"

They answered, "Have the ark of the god of Israel moved to Gath." So they moved the ark of the God of Israel.

5:9
e 1Sa 7:13

9 But after they had moved it, the LORD's hand was against that city, throwing it into a great panic. e He afflicted the people of the city, both young and old, with an outbreak of tumors. b 10 So they sent the ark of God to Ekron.

As the ark of God was entering Ekron, the people of Ekron cried out, "They have brought the ark of the god of Israel around to us to kill us and our people." 11 So they called together

5:11
f ver 6,8-9

all the rulers f of the Philistines and said, "Send the ark of the god of Israel away; let it go back to its own place, or it c will kill us and our people." For death had filled the city with panic; God's hand was very heavy upon it. 12 Those who did not die were afflicted with tumors, and the outcry of the city went up to heaven.

The Ark Returned to Israel

6:2
g Ge 41:8; Ex 7:11

6 When the ark of the LORD had been in Philistine territory seven months, 2 the Philistines called for the priests and the diviners g and said, "What shall we do with the ark of the LORD? Tell us how we should send it back to its place."

6:3
h Ex 23:15; Dt 16:16
i Lev 5:15

3 They answered, "If you return the ark of the god of Israel, do not send it away empty, h but by all means send a guilt offering i to him. Then you will be healed, and you will know why his hand has not been lifted from you."

6:4
j Jos 13:3; Jdg 3:3

4 The Philistines asked, "What guilt offering should we send to him?"

6:5
k 1Sa 5:6-11
l Jos 7:19; Isa 42:12

6:6
m Ex 12:31,33

They replied, "Five gold tumors and five gold rats, according to the number j of the Philistine rulers, because the same plague has struck both you and your rulers. 5 Make models of the tumors k and of the rats that are destroying the country, and pay honor l to Israel's god. Perhaps he will lift his hand from you and your gods and your land. 6 Why do you harden your hearts as the Egyptians and Pharaoh did? When he d treated them harshly, did they m not send the Israelites out so they could go on their way?

a 6 Hebrew; Septuagint and Vulgate *tumors. And rats appeared in their land, and death and destruction were throughout the city* b 9 Or *with tumors in the groin* (see Septuagint) c 11 Or *he* d 6 That is, God

5:1ff Dagon was the chief god of the Philistines, whom they believed sent rain and assured a bountiful harvest. But the Philistines, like most of their pagan neighbors, worshiped many gods. The more gods they could have on their side, the more secure they felt. That was why they wanted the ark, thinking that if it helped the Israelites, it could help them too. But when the people living nearby began to get sick and die, the Philistines realized that the ark was not a good omen. It was a source of greater power than they had ever seen—power they could not control.

5:6, 7 Although the Philistines had just witnessed a great victory by Israel's God over their god, Dagon, they didn't act upon that insight until they were afflicted with tumors (possibly bubonic plague). Similarly, today many people don't respond to biblical truth until they experience pain. Are you willing to listen to God for truth's sake, or do you turn to him only when you are hurting?

5:8 The Philistines were governed by five rulers, or lords. Each lord lived in a different city—Gath, Ekron, Ashdod, Ashkelon,

Gaza. The ark was taken to three of these capital cities, and each time it brought great trouble and chaos to the citizens.

6:3 What was this guilt offering supposed to accomplish? This was a normal reaction to trouble in the Canaanite religion. The Philistines thought their problems were the result of their gods being angry. They recognized their guilt in taking the ark and now were trying everything they could to placate Israel's God. The diviners (6:2) probably helped choose the gift they thought would placate Yahweh. But the offering consisted of images of tumors and rats, not the kind of guilt offering prescribed in God's laws (Leviticus 5:14—6:7; 7:1–10). How easy it is to design our own methods of acknowledging God rather than serving him in the way he requires.

7"Now then, get a new cart[n] ready, with two cows that have calved and have never been yoked.[o] Hitch the cows to the cart, but take their calves away and pen them up. 8Take the ark of the LORD and put it on the cart, and in a chest beside it put the gold objects you are sending back to him as a guilt offering. Send it on its way, 9but keep watching it. If it goes up to its own territory, toward Beth Shemesh,[p] then the LORD has brought this great disaster on us. But if it does not, then we will know that it was not his hand that struck us and that it happened to us by chance."

10So they did this. They took two such cows and hitched them to the cart and penned up their calves. 11They placed the ark of the LORD on the cart and along with it the chest containing the gold rats and the models of the tumors. 12Then the cows went straight up toward Beth Shemesh, keeping on the road and lowing all the way; they did not turn to the right or to the left. The rulers of the Philistines followed them as far as the border of Beth Shemesh.

13Now the people of Beth Shemesh were harvesting their wheat in the valley, and when they looked up and saw the ark, they rejoiced at the sight. 14The cart came to the field of Joshua of Beth Shemesh, and there it stopped beside a large rock. The people chopped up the wood of the cart and sacrificed the cows as a burnt offering[q] to the LORD. 15The Levites took down the ark of the LORD, together with the chest containing the gold objects, and placed them on the large rock. On that day the people of Beth Shemesh offered burnt offerings and made sacrifices to the LORD. 16The five rulers of the Philistines saw all this and then returned that same day to Ekron.

17These are the gold tumors the Philistines sent as a guilt offering to the LORD—one each[r] for Ashdod, Gaza, Ashkelon, Gath and Ekron. 18And the number of the gold rats was according to the number of Philistine towns belonging to the five rulers—the fortified towns with their country villages. The large rock, on which[a] they set the ark of the LORD, is a witness to this day in the field of Joshua of Beth Shemesh.

19But God struck down[s] some of the men of Beth Shemesh, putting seventy[b] of them to death because they had looked into the ark of the LORD. The people mourned because of the heavy blow the LORD had dealt them, 20and the men of Beth Shemesh asked, "Who can stand[t] in the presence of the LORD, this holy God? To whom will the ark go up from here?"

21Then they sent messengers to the people of Kiriath Jearim, saying, "The Philistines have returned the ark of the LORD. Come down and take it up to your place." 1So the men of

7 Kiriath Jearim came and took up the ark of the LORD. They took it to Abinadab's[u] house on the hill and consecrated Eleazar his son to guard the ark of the LORD.

Samuel Subdues the Philistines at Mizpah

2It was a long time, twenty years in all, that the ark remained at Kiriath Jearim, and all the people of Israel mourned and sought after the LORD. 3And Samuel said to the whole house

a 18 A few Hebrew manuscripts (see also Septuagint); most Hebrew manuscripts *villages as far as Greater Abel, where*   b 19 A few Hebrew manuscripts; most Hebrew manuscripts and Septuagint *50,070*

6:7
n 2Sa 6:3
o Nu 19:2

6:9
p ver 3; Jos 15:10

6:14
q 1Ki 19:21

6:17
r ver 4

6:19
s 2Sa 6:7

6:20
t 2Sa 6:9; Mal 3:2

7:1
u 2Sa 6:3

6:7–12 The Philistine priests and diviners devised a test to see if God was really the one who had caused all their recent troubles. Two cows who had just given birth were hitched to a cart and sent toward Israel's border carrying the ark of the covenant. For a cow to leave her nursing calf, she would have to go against all her motherly instincts. Only God, who has power over the natural order, could cause this to happen. God sent the cows to Israel, not to pass the Philistines' test, but to show them his mighty power.

6:9 The Philistines acknowledged the existence of the Hebrew God, but only as one of many deities whose favor they sought. Thinking of God in this way made it easy for them to ignore his demand that people worship him alone. Many people "worship" God this way. They see God as just one ingredient in a successful life. But God is far more than an ingredient—he is the source of life itself. Are you a "Philistine," seeing God's favor as only an ingredient of the good life?

6:19 Why were people killed for looking into the ark? The Israelites had made an idol of the ark. They had tried to harness God's power, to use it for their own purposes (victory in battle). But the Lord of the universe cannot be controlled by humans. To protect the Israelites from his power, he had warned them not even to look at the sacred sanctuary objects in the Most Holy Place or they would die (Numbers 4:20). Only Levites were

allowed to move the ark. Because of their disobedience, God carried out his promised judgment.

God could not allow the people to think they could use his power for their own ends. He could not permit them to disregard his warnings and come into his presence lightly. He did not want the cycle of disrespect, disobedience, and defeat to start all over again. God did not kill the men of Beth Shemesh to be cruel. He killed them because overlooking their presumptuous sin would encourage the whole nation of Israel to ignore him.

7:1 The ark was taken to Kiriath Jearim, a city near the battlefield, for safekeeping, and Eleazar was given the task of caring for it. Why wasn't it taken back to the tabernacle at Shiloh? Shiloh had probably been defeated and destroyed by the Philistines in an earlier battle (4:1–18; Jeremiah 26:2–6) because of the evil deeds of its priests (2:12–17). Apparently, the tabernacle and its furniture were saved because we read that the tabernacle was set up in Nob during Saul's reign (21:1–6) and in Gibeon during the reigns of David and Solomon (1 Chronicles 16:39; 21:29, 30; 2 Chronicles 1). Shiloh, however, is never again mentioned in the historical books of the Old Testament. Samuel's new home became Ramah (7:15–17; 8:4), his birthplace (further evidence of Shiloh's destruction).

7:2, 3 Israel mourned and sorrow gripped the nation for 20 years. The ark was put away like an unwanted box in an attic,

7:3
ᵛJos 24:14
ʷJdg 2:12-13
ˣJoel 2:12
ʸDt 6:13; Lk 4:8

of Israel, "If you are returning to the LORD with all your hearts, then rid ᵛ yourselves of the foreign gods and the Ashtoreths ʷ and commit ˣ yourselves to the LORD and serve him only, ʸ and he will deliver you out of the hand of the Philistines." ⁴So the Israelites put away their Baals and Ashtoreths, and served the LORD only.

⁵Then Samuel said, "Assemble all Israel at Mizpah and I will intercede with the LORD for

SAMUEL

We often wonder about the childhoods of great people. We have little information about the early years of most of the people mentioned in the Bible. One delightful exception is Samuel; he came as a result of God's answer to Hannah's fervent prayer for a child. (In fact, the name *Samuel* comes from the Hebrew expression, "heard of God.") God shaped Samuel from the start. Like Moses, Samuel was called to fill many different roles: judge, priest, prophet, counselor, and God's man at a turning point in the history of Israel. God worked through Samuel because Samuel was willing to be one thing: God's servant.

Samuel showed that those whom God finds faithful in small things will be trusted with greater things. He grew up assisting the high priest (Eli) in the tabernacle until God directed him to other responsibilities. God was able to use Samuel because he was genuinely dedicated to God.

Samuel moved ahead because he was listening to God's directions. Too often we ask God to control our lives without making us give up the goals for which we strive. We ask God to help us get where *we* want to go. The first step in correcting this tendency is to turn over both the control and destination of our lives to him. The second step is to do what we *already know* God requires of us. The third step is to listen for further direction from his Word—God's map for life.

Strengths and accomplishments:	• Used by God to assist Israel's transition from a loosely governed tribal people to a monarchy • Anointed the first two kings of Israel • Was the last and most effective of Israel's judges • Is listed in the Hall of Faith in Hebrews 11
Weakness and mistake:	• Was unable to lead his sons into a close relationship with God
Lessons from his life:	• The significance of what people accomplish is directly related to their relationship with God • The kind of person we are is more important than anything we might do
Vital statistics:	• Where: Ephraim • Occupations: Judge, prophet, priest • Relatives: Mother: Hannah. Father: Elkanah. Sons: Joel and Abijah. • Contemporaries: Eli, Saul, David
Key verses:	"The LORD was with Samuel as he grew up, and he let none of his words fall to the ground. And all Israel from Dan to Beersheba recognized that Samuel was attested as a prophet of the LORD" (1 Samuel 3:19, 20).

His story is told in 1 Samuel 1—28. He is also mentioned in Psalm 99:6; Jeremiah 15:1; Acts 3:24; 13:20; Hebrews 11:32.

and it seemed as if the Lord had abandoned his people. Samuel, now a grown man, roused them to action by saying that if they were truly sorry, they should do something about it. How easy it is for us to complain about our problems, even to God, while we refuse to act, change, and do what he requires. We don't even take the advice he has already given us. Do you ever feel as if God has abandoned you? Check to see if there is anything he has already told you to do. You may not receive new guidance from God until you have acted on his previous directions.

7:3 Samuel urged the Israelites to get rid of their foreign gods. Idols today are much more subtle than gods of wood and stone, but they are just as dangerous. Whatever holds first place in our lives or controls us is our god. Money, success, material goods, pride, or anything else can be an idol if it takes the place of God in our lives. The Lord alone is worthy of our service and worship, and we must let nothing rival him. If we have "foreign gods," we need to ask God to help us dethrone them, making the true God our first priority.

7:4 Baal was believed to be the son of El, chief deity of the Canaanites. Baal was regarded as the god of thunder and rain, thus he controlled vegetation and agriculture. Ashtoreth was a goddess of love and war (she was called Ishtar in Babylon and Astarte or Aphrodite in Greece). She represented fertility. The Canaanites believed that by the sexual union of Baal and Ashtoreth, the earth would be magically rejuvenated and made fertile.

7:5 Mizpah held special significance for the Israelite nation. It was there that the Israelites had gathered to mobilize against the tribe of Benjamin (Judges 20:1). Samuel was appointed to be leader (7:6), and Saul, Israel's first king, would be identified and presented to the people (10:17ff).

you." 6 When they had assembled at Mizpah, they drew water and poured it out before the LORD. On that day they fasted and there they confessed, "We have sinned against the LORD." And Samuel was leader a z of Israel at Mizpah.

7 When the Philistines heard that Israel had assembled at Mizpah, the rulers of the Philistines came up to attack them. And when the Israelites heard of it, they were afraid a because of the Philistines. 8 They said to Samuel, "Do not stop crying b out to the LORD our God for us, that he may rescue us from the hand of the Philistines." 9 Then Samuel c took a suckling lamb and offered it up as a whole burnt offering to the LORD. He cried out to the LORD on Israel's behalf, and the LORD answered him.

10 While Samuel was sacrificing the burnt offering, the Philistines drew near to engage Israel in battle. But that day the LORD thundered d with loud thunder against the Philistines and threw them into such a panic e that they were routed before the Israelites. 11 The men of Israel rushed out of Mizpah and pursued the Philistines, slaughtering them along the way to a point below Beth Car.

12 Then Samuel took a stone f and set it up between Mizpah and Shen. He named it Ebenezer, b saying, "Thus far has the LORD helped us." 13 So the Philistines were subdued g and did not invade Israelite territory again.

Throughout Samuel's lifetime, the hand of the LORD was against the Philistines. 14 The towns from Ekron to Gath that the Philistines had captured from Israel were restored to her, and Israel delivered the neighboring territory from the power of the Philistines. And there was peace between Israel and the Amorites.

15 Samuel continued as judge over Israel all the days of his life. 16 From year to year he went on a circuit from Bethel to Gilgal to Mizpah, judging Israel in all those places. 17 But he always went back to Ramah, where his home was, and there he also judged Israel. And he built an altar there to the LORD.

**Cross references (right margin):**
7:6 z Jdg 10:10; Ne 9:1
7:7 a 1Sa 17:11
7:8 b Isa 37:4
7:9 c Ps 99:6
7:10 d 1Sa 2:10; 2Sa 22:14-15 e Jos 10:10
7:12 f Jos 4:9
7:13 g Jdg 13:1,5; 1Sa 13:5

B. SAMUEL AND SAUL (8:1—15:35)

Samuel judges Israel well, saves them from the Philistines, and leads them back to God. But when he retires, the nation does not want another judge. Instead, they demand to be given a king in order to be like the nations around them. Although God is unhappy with their request, he tells Samuel to anoint Saul as Israel's first king. Saul is a skillful soldier who successfully leads the nation into many battles against their enemies. But in God's eyes Saul is a failure because he constantly disobeys and does things his own way. God eventually rejects Saul as king. Sometimes we want to go our own way rather than follow the ways of God. This will always end in ruin as it did for Saul.

1. Saul becomes king of Israel
Israel Asks for a King

8 When Samuel grew old, he appointed h his sons as judges for Israel. 2 The name of his firstborn was Joel and the name of his second was Abijah, and they served at Beersheba. 3 But his sons did not walk in his ways. They turned aside after dishonest gain and accepted bribes and perverted justice.

8:1 h Dt 16:18-19

a 6 Traditionally *judge*   b 12 Ebenezer means *stone of help.*

7:6 Pouring water on the ground "before the LORD" was a sign of repenting from sin, turning from idols, and determining to obey God alone.

7:6 Samuel became the last in the long line of Israel's judges (leaders), a line that began when Israel first conquered the promised land. For a list of these judges, see the chart in Judges 2, p. 341. A judge was both a political and a religious leader. God was Israel's true leader, while the judge was to be God's spokesman to the people and administrator of justice throughout the land. While some of Israel's judges relied more on their own judgment than on God's, Samuel's obedience and dedication to God made him one of the greatest judges in Israel's history. (For more on Samuel as a judge, see the note on 4:18.)

7:12 The Israelites had great difficulty with the Philistines, but God rescued them. In response, the people set up a large stone as a memorial of God's great help and deliverance. During tough times, we may need to remember the crucial turning points in our past to help us through the present. Memorials can help us remember God's past victories and gain confidence and strength for the present.

7:14 In Joshua's time, the Amorites were a powerful tribe scattered throughout the hill country on both sides of the Jordan with a heavy concentration occupying the east side of the Jordan River opposite the Dead Sea. In the context of this verse, however, *Amorites* is another general name for all the inhabitants of Canaan who were not Israelites.

8:1–3 As an old man, Samuel appointed his sons to be judges over Israel in his place. But they turned out to be corrupt, much like Eli's sons (2:12). We don't know why Samuel's sons went wrong, but we do know that Eli was held responsible for his own sons' corruption (2:29–34).

It is impossible to know if Samuel was a bad parent. His children were old enough to be on their own. We must be careful not to blame ourselves for the sins of our children. On the other hand, parenthood is an awesome responsibility, and nothing is more important than molding and shaping our children's lives.

If your grown children are not following God, realize that you can't control them any longer. Don't blame yourself for something that is no longer your responsibility. But if your children are still

8:4
i 1Sa 7:17

8:5
j Dt 17:14-20

8:7
k Ex 16:8;
1Sa 10:19

8:9
l ver 11-18

8:11
m 1Sa 14:52

8:14
n Eze 46:18
o 1Ki 21:7,15

8:18
p Mic 3:4

8:19
q Jer 44:16

[4] So all the elders of Israel gathered together and came to Samuel at Ramah. *i* [5] They said to him, "You are old, and your sons do not walk in your ways; now appoint a king *j* to lead *a* us, such as all the other nations have."

[6] But when they said, "Give us a king to lead us," this displeased Samuel; so he prayed to the LORD. [7] And the LORD told him: "Listen to all that the people are saying to you; it is not you they have rejected, but they have rejected me as their king. *k* [8] As they have done from the day I brought them up out of Egypt until this day, forsaking me and serving other gods, so they are doing to you. [9] Now listen to them; but warn them solemnly and let them know *l* what the king who will reign over them will do."

[10] Samuel told all the words of the LORD to the people who were asking him for a king. [11] He said, "This is what the king who will reign over you will do: He will take *m* your sons and make them serve with his chariots and horses, and they will run in front of his chariots. [12] Some he will assign to be commanders of thousands and commanders of fifties, and others to plow his ground and reap his harvest, and still others to make weapons of war and equipment for his chariots. [13] He will take your daughters to be perfumers and cooks and bakers. [14] He will take the best of your *n* fields and vineyards *o* and olive groves and give them to his attendants. [15] He will take a tenth of your grain and of your vintage and give it to his officials and attendants. [16] Your menservants and maidservants and the best of your cattle *b* and donkeys he will take for his own use. [17] He will take a tenth of your flocks, and you yourselves will become his slaves. [18] When that day comes, you will cry out for relief from the king you have chosen, and the LORD will not answer *p* you in that day."

[19] But the people refused *q* to listen to Samuel. "No!" they said. "We want a king over us.

a 5 Traditionally *judge*; also in verses 6 and 20   *b* 16 Septuagint; Hebrew *young men*

THE PROBLEMS WITH HAVING A KING

Problems (warned by Samuel)	Reference	Fulfillment
Drafting young men into the army	8:11, 12	14:52—"Whenever Saul saw a mighty or brave man, he took him into his service."
Having the young men "run in front of his [the king's] chariots"	8:11	2 Samuel 15:1—"Absalom provided himslef with a chariot and horses and with fifty men to run ahead of him."
Making slave laborers	8:12, 17	2 Chronicles 2:17, 18—Solomon assigned laborers to build the temple.
Taking the best of your fields and vineyards	8:14	1 Kings 21:5–16—Jezebel stole Naboth's vineyard.
Using your property for his personal gain	8:14–16	1 Kings 9:10–14—Solomon gave away 20 towns to Hiram of Tyre.
Demanding a tenth of your harvest and flocks	8:15, 17	1 Kings 12:1–16—Rehoboam was going to demand heavier taxation than Solomon.

---

in your care, know that what you do and teach can profoundly affect your children and lasts a lifetime.

8:4–9 Israel wanted a king for several reasons: (1) Samuel's sons were not fit to lead Israel. (2) The 12 tribes of Israel continually had problems working together because each tribe had its own leader and territory. It was hoped that a king would unite the tribes into one nation and one army. (3) The people wanted to be like the neighboring nations. This is exactly what God didn't want. Having a king would make it easy to forget that God was their real leader. It was not wrong for Israel to want a king; God had mentioned the possibility in Deuteronomy 17:14–20. Yet, in reality, the people were rejecting God as their leader. The Israelites wanted laws, an army, and a human monarch in the place of God. They wanted to run the nation through human strength, even though only God's strength could make them flourish in the hostile land of Canaan.

8:5, 6 The people clamored for a king, thinking that a new system of government would bring about a change in the nation. But because their basic problem was disobedience to God, their other problems would only continue under the new administration. What they needed was a unified faith, not a uniform rule.

Had the Israelites submitted to God's leadership, they would have thrived beyond their expectations (Deuteronomy 28:1). Our

obedience is weak if we ask God to lead our family or personal life but continue to live by the world's standards and values. Faith in God must touch all the practical areas of life.

8:19, 20 Samuel carefully explained all the negative consequences of having a king, but the Israelites refused to listen. When you have an important decision to make, weigh the positives and negatives carefully, considering everyone who might be affected by your choice. When you want something badly enough, it is difficult to see the potential problems. But don't discount the negatives. Unless you have a plan to handle each one, they will cause you great difficulty later.

8:19, 20 Israel was called to be a holy nation, separate from and unique among all others (Leviticus 20:26). The Israelites' motive in asking for a king was to be like the nations around them. This was in total opposition to God's original plan. It was not their desire for a king that was wrong, but their reasons for wanting a king.

Often we let others' values and actions dictate our attitudes and behavior. Have you ever made a wrong choice because you wanted to be like everyone else? Be careful that the values of your friends or "heroes" don't pull you away from what God says is right. When God's people want to be like unbelievers, they are heading for spiritual disaster.

²⁰Then we will be like all the other nations,ʳ with a king to lead us and to go out before us and fight our battles."

²¹When Samuel heard all that the people said, he repeated it before the LORD. ²²The LORD answered, "Listenˢ to them and give them a king."

Then Samuel said to the men of Israel, "Everyone go back to his town."

8:20
ʳ ver 5

8:22
ˢ ver 7

Samuel Anoints Saul

9 There was a Benjamite, a man of standing, whose name was Kishᵗ son of Abiel, the son of Zeror, the son of Becorath, the son of Aphiah of Benjamin. ²He had a son named Saul, an impressive young man without equal among the Israelites—a head tallerᵘ than any of the others.

9:1
ᵗ 1Sa 14:51; 1Ch 9:39

9:2
ᵘ 1Sa 10:23

³Now the donkeys belonging to Saul's father Kish were lost, and Kish said to his son Saul, "Take one of the servants with you and go and look for the donkeys." ⁴So he passed through the hill country of Ephraim and through the area around Shalisha,ᵛ but they did not find them. They went on into the district of Shaalim, but the donkeys were not there. Then he passed through the territory of Benjamin, but they did not find them.

9:4
ᵛ 2Ki 4:42

⁵When they reached the district of Zuph, Saul said to the servant who was with him, "Come, let's go back, or my father will stop thinking about the donkeys and start worrying about us."

⁶But the servant replied, "Look, in this town there is a man of God;ʷ he is highly respected, and everythingˣ he says comes true. Let's go there now. Perhaps he will tell us what way to take."

9:6
ʷ Dt 33:1
ˣ 1Sa 3:19

⁷Saul said to his servant, "If we go, what can we give the man? The food in our sacks is gone. We have no giftʸ to take to the man of God. What do we have?"

9:7
ʸ 1Ki 14:3; 2Ki 8:8

⁸The servant answered him again. "Look," he said, "I have a quarter of a shekelᵃ of silver. I will give it to the man of God so that he will tell us what way to take." ⁹(Formerly in Israel, if a man went to inquire of God, he would say, "Come, let us go to the seer," because the prophet of today used to be called a seer.)ᶻ

9:9
ᶻ 2Sa 24:11; 1Ch 26:28; Isa 30:10

¹⁰"Good," Saul said to his servant. "Come, let's go." So they set out for the town where the man of God was.

¹¹As they were going up the hill to the town, they met some girls coming out to draw water, and they asked them, "Is the seer here?"

¹²"He is," they answered. "He's ahead of you. Hurry now; he has just come to our town today, for the people have a sacrifice at the high place. ¹³As soon as you enter the town, you will find him before he goes up to the high place to eat. The people will not begin eating until he comes, because he must bless the sacrifice; afterward, those who are invited will eat. Go up now; you should find him about this time."

¹⁴They went up to the town, and as they were entering it, there was Samuel, coming toward them on his way up to the high place.

ᵃ8 That is, about 1/10 ounce (about 3 grams)

9:3 Saul was sent by his father on an important mission—to find their stray donkeys. Donkeys were all-purpose animals, the "pickup trucks" of Bible times. Used for transportation, hauling, and farming, they were considered necessities. Even the poorest family owned one. To own many donkeys was a sign of wealth, and to lose them was a disaster. Saul's father was wealthy, and his many donkeys were evidence of that wealth.

9:3ff Often we think that events just happen to us, but as we learn from this story about Saul, God may use common occurrences to lead us where he wants. It is important to evaluate all situations as potential "divine appointments" designed to shape our lives. Think of all the good and bad circumstances that have affected you lately. Can you see God's purpose in them? Perhaps he is building a certain quality in you or leading you to serve him in a new area.

9:6 The city where the servant said the prophet lived was probably Ramah, where Samuel moved after the Philistine battle near Shiloh (7:17). Saul's lack of knowledge about Samuel showed his ignorance of spiritual matters. Saul and Samuel even lived in the same territory, Benjamin.

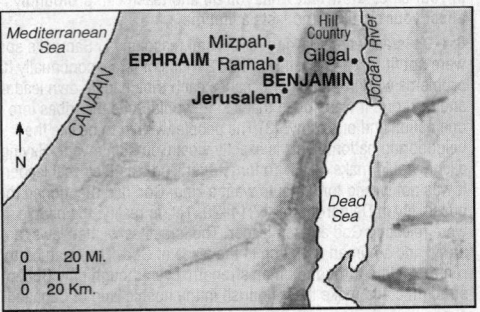

SAUL CHOSEN AS KING Saul and a servant searched for their lost donkeys in the hill country of Ephraim and the territory of Benjamin. They went to Ramah, looking for help from Samuel the prophet. While Saul was there, he found himself unexpectedly anointed by Samuel as Israel's first king. Samuel called Israel together at Mizpah to tell them God's choice for their king.

9:16
a 1Sa 10:1
b Ex 3:7-9

9:17
c 1Sa 16:12

9:20
d ver 3
e 1Sa 8:5; 12:13

9:21
f 1Sa 15:17
g Jdg 20:35,46

9:25
h Dt 22:8; Ac 10:9

¹⁵Now the day before Saul came, the LORD had revealed this to Samuel: ¹⁶"About this time tomorrow I will send you a man from the land of Benjamin. Anoint *a* him leader over my people Israel; he will deliver *b* my people from the hand of the Philistines. I have looked upon my people, for their cry has reached me."

¹⁷When Samuel caught sight of Saul, the LORD said to him, "This *c* is the man I spoke to you about; he will govern my people."

¹⁸Saul approached Samuel in the gateway and asked, "Would you please tell me where the seer's house is?"

¹⁹"I am the seer," Samuel replied. "Go up ahead of me to the high place, for today you are to eat with me, and in the morning I will let you go and will tell you all that is in your heart. ²⁰As for the donkeys *d* you lost three days ago, do not worry about them; they have been found. And to whom is all the desire *e* of Israel turned, if not to you and all your father's family?"

²¹Saul answered, "But am I not a Benjamite, from the smallest tribe *f* of Israel, and is not my clan the least of all the clans of the tribe of Benjamin? *g* Why do you say such a thing to me?"

²²Then Samuel brought Saul and his servant into the hall and seated them at the head of those who were invited—about thirty in number. ²³Samuel said to the cook, "Bring the piece of meat I gave you, the one I told you to lay aside."

²⁴So the cook took up the leg with what was on it and set it in front of Saul. Samuel said, "Here is what has been kept for you. Eat, because it was set aside for you for this occasion, from the time I said, 'I have invited guests.'" And Saul dined with Samuel that day.

²⁵After they came down from the high place to the town, Samuel talked with Saul on the roof *h* of his house. ²⁶They rose about daybreak and Samuel called to Saul on the roof, "Get ready, and I will send you on your way." When Saul got ready, he and Samuel went outside together. ²⁷As they were going down to the edge of the town, Samuel said to Saul, "Tell the servant to go on ahead of us"—and the servant did so—"but you stay here awhile, so that I may give you a message from God."

RELIGIOUS AND POLITICAL CENTERS OF ISRAEL
During the period of the judges, Israel may have had more than one capital. This may explain why the Scriptures overlap with reference to some cities.

Gilgal	Joshua 4:19; Judges 2:1; Hosea 4:15; Micah 6:5
Shiloh	Joshua 18:1–10; 19:51; Judges 18:31; 1 Samuel 1:3; Jeremiah 7:12–14
Shechem	Joshua 24:1
Ramah	1 Samuel 7:17; 8:4
Mizpah	Judges 11:11; 20:1; 1 Samuel 10:17
Bethel	Judges 20:18, 26; 1 Samuel 10:3
Gibeah (political center only)	1 Samuel 10:26
Gibeon (religious center only)	1 Kings 3:4; 2 Chronicles 1:2, 3
Jerusalem	1 Kings 8:1ff; Psalm 51:16–19

Samuel called the Israelites together at Mizpah, where he would anoint Saul as their first king. Up to this point, the political seat of the nation seems to have been the religious center of the nation as well. Above are the cities which probably served as both the religious and political centers of Israel since the days of Joshua. Saul may have been the first Israelite leader to separate the nation's religious center (probably Mizpah at this time) from its political center (Gibeah—1 Samuel 11:4; 26:1). Politically, the nation grew strong for a while. But when Saul and his officials stopped seeking God's will, internal jealousies and strife soon began to decay the nation from within. When David became king, he brought the ark of the covenant back to Jerusalem, his capital. King Solomon then completely united the religious and political centers at Jerusalem.

9:21 "Why do you say such a thing to me?" Saul's outburst reveals a problem he would face repeatedly—feeling inferior. Like a leaf tossed about by the wind, Saul vacillated between his feelings and his convictions. Everything he said and did was selfish because he was worried about himself. For example, Saul said his clan was "the least" in the smallest tribe in Israel, but 9:1 says his father was "a man of standing." (The tribe of Benjamin was the smallest because they were nearly wiped out as punishment for their immorality—see Judges 19—21.) Saul didn't want to face

the responsibility God had given him. Later, Saul kept some war plunder that he shouldn't have and then tried to blame his soldiers (15:21) while claiming that they had really taken it to sacrifice to God (15:15).

Although Saul had been called by God and had a mission in life, he struggled constantly with jealousy, insecurity, arrogance, impulsiveness, and deceit. He did not decide to be wholeheartedly committed to God. Because Saul would not let God's love give rest to his heart, he never became God's man.

10 Then Samuel took a flask[j] of oil and poured it on Saul's head and kissed him, saying, "Has not the LORD anointed you leader over his inheritance?[a] [2]When you leave me today, you will meet two men near Rachel's tomb,[j] at Zelzah on the border of Benjamin. They will say to you, 'The donkeys you set out to look for have been found. And now your father has stopped thinking about them and is worried about you. He is asking, "What shall I do about my son?"'

[3]"Then you will go on from there until you reach the great tree of Tabor. Three men going up to God at Bethel[k] will meet you there. One will be carrying three young goats, another three loaves of bread, and another a skin of wine. [4]They will greet you and offer you two loaves of bread, which you will accept from them.

[5]"After that you will go to Gibeah of God, where there is a Philistine outpost.[l] As you approach the town, you will meet a procession of prophets coming down from the high place with lyres, tambourines, flutes and harps[m] being played before them, and they will be prophesying. [6]The Spirit[n] of the LORD will come upon you in power, and you will prophesy with them; and you will be changed into a different person. [7]Once these signs are fulfilled, do whatever your hand finds to do, for God is with[o] you.

[8]"Go down ahead of me to Gilgal.[p] I will surely come down to you to sacrifice burnt offerings and fellowship offerings,[b] but you must wait seven days until I come to you and tell you what you are to do."

Saul Made King

[9]As Saul turned to leave Samuel, God changed Saul's heart, and all these signs were fulfilled that day. [10]When they arrived at Gibeah, a procession of prophets met him; the Spirit of God came upon him in power, and he joined in their prophesying.[q] [11]When all those who had formerly known him saw him prophesying with the prophets, they asked each other, "What is this[r] that has happened to the son of Kish? Is Saul also among the prophets?"

[12]A man who lived there answered, "And who is their father?" So it became a saying: "Is Saul also among the prophets?" [13]After Saul stopped prophesying, he went to the high place.

[14]Now Saul's uncle asked him and his servant, "Where have you been?"

"Looking for the donkeys," he said. "But when we saw they were not to be found, we went to Samuel."

[15]Saul's uncle said, "Tell me what Samuel said to you."

[16]Saul replied, "He assured us that the donkeys had been found." But he did not tell his uncle what Samuel had said about the kingship.

[17]Samuel summoned the people of Israel to the LORD at Mizpah[s] [18]and said to them, "This is what the LORD, the God of Israel, says: 'I brought Israel up out of Egypt, and I delivered you from the power of Egypt and all the kingdoms that oppressed[t] you.' [19]But you have now rejected your God, who saves you out of all your calamities and distresses. And you have said, 'No, set a king[u] over us.' So now present yourselves before the LORD by your tribes and clans."

---

[a]*1 Hebrew; Septuagint and Vulgate* over his people Israel? You will reign over the LORD's people and save them from the power of their enemies round about. And this will be a sign to you that the LORD has anointed you leader over his inheritance: *[b]8 Traditionally* peace offerings

**Marginal references:**

10:1 [j]2Ki 9:1,3,6
10:2 [j]Ge 35:20
10:3 [k]Ge 35:7-8
10:5 [l]1Sa 13:3; [m]2Ki 3:15
10:6 [n]Nu 11:25; 1Sa 19:23-24
10:7 [o]Jdg 6:12
10:8 [p]1Sa 11:14-15
10:10 [q]ver 5-6; 1Sa 19:20
10:11 [r]Mt 13:54; Jn 7:15
10:17 [s]1Sa 7:5
10:18 [t]Jdg 6:8-9
10:19 [u]1Sa 8:5-7

10:1 When an Israelite king took office he was not only crowned, he was anointed. The coronation was the political act of establishing the king as ruler; the anointing was the religious act of making the king God's representative to the people. A king was always anointed by a priest or prophet. The special anointing oil was a mixture of olive oil, myrrh, and other expensive spices. It was poured over the king's head to symbolize the presence and power of the Holy Spirit of God in his life. This anointing ceremony was to remind the king of his great responsibility to lead his people by God's wisdom and not his own.

10:6 How could Saul be so filled with the Spirit and yet later commit such evil acts? Throughout the Old Testament, God's Spirit "came upon" a person temporarily so that God could use him or her for great acts. This happened frequently to Israel's judges when they were called by God to rescue the nation (Judges 3:8–10). This was not always a permanent, abiding influence, but sometimes a temporary manifestation of the Holy Spirit. Yet, at times in the Old Testament, the Spirit even came upon unbelievers to enable them to do unusual tasks (Numbers 24; 2 Chronicles 36:22, 23). The Holy Spirit gave the person power to do what God

asked, but it did not always produce the other fruits of the Spirit, such as self-control. Saul, in his early years as king, was a different person (10:1–10) as a result of the Holy Spirit's work in him. But as Saul's power grew, so did his pride. After a while he refused to seek God; the Spirit left him (16:14); and his good attitude melted away.

10:10, 11 A prophet is someone who speaks God's words. While God told many prophets to predict certain events, what God wanted most was for them to instruct and inspire people to live in faithfulness to God. When Saul's friends heard inspired words coming from Saul they exclaimed, "Is Saul also among the prophets?" This was an expression of surprise at worldly Saul's becoming religious. It is equivalent to "What? Has he got religion?"

10:19 Israel's true king was God, but the nation demanded another. Imagine wanting a human being instead of God as guide and leader! Throughout history, men and women have rejected God, and they continue to do it today. Are you rejecting God by pushing him aside and acknowledging someone or something else as your "king" or top priority? Learn from these stories of Israel's kings, and don't push God aside.

²⁰When Samuel brought all the tribes of Israel near, the tribe of Benjamin was chosen. ²¹Then he brought forward the tribe of Benjamin, clan by clan, and Matri's clan was chosen. Finally Saul son of Kish was chosen. But when they looked for him, he was not to be found. ²²So they inquired further of the LORD, "Has the man come here yet?"

And the LORD said, "Yes, he has hidden himself among the baggage."

10:23
ᵛ1Sa 9:2

10:24
ʷ2Sa 21:6
ˣ1Ki 1:25,34,39

²³They ran and brought him out, and as he stood among the people he was a head taller ᵛ than any of the others. ²⁴Samuel said to all the people, "Do you see the man the LORD has chosen? ʷ There is no one like him among all the people."

Then the people shouted, "Long live ˣ the king!"

SAUL

First impressions can be deceiving, especially when the image created by a person's appearance is contradicted by his or her qualities and abilities. Saul presented the ideal visual image of a king, but the tendencies of his character often went contrary to God's commands for a king. Saul was God's chosen leader, but this did not mean he was capable of being king on his own.

During his reign, Saul had his greatest successes when he obeyed God. His greatest failures resulted from acting on his own. Saul had the raw materials to be a good leader—appearance, courage, and action. Even his weaknesses could have been used by God if Saul had recognized them and left them in God's hands. His own choices cut him off from God and eventually alienated him from his own people.

From Saul we learn that while our strengths and abilities make us useful, it is our weaknesses that make us usable. Our skills and talents make us tools, but our failures and shortcomings remind us that we need a Craftsman in control of our lives. Whatever we accomplish on our own is only a hint of what God could do through our lives. Does he control your life?

Strengths and accomplishments:	• First God-appointed king of Israel • Known for his personal courage and generosity • Stood tall, with a striking appearance
Weaknesses and mistakes:	• His leadership abilities did not match the expectations created by his appearance • Impulsive by nature, he tended to overstep his bounds • Jealous of David, he tried to kill him • He specifically disobeyed God on several occasions
Lessons from his life:	• God wants obedience from the heart, not mere acts of religious ritual • Obedience always involves sacrifice; but sacrifice is not always obedience • God wants to make use of our strengths and weaknesses • Weaknesses should help us remember our need for God's guidance and help
Vital statistics:	• Where: The land of Benjamin • Occupation: King of Israel • Relatives: Father: Kish. Wife: Ahinoam. Sons: Jonathan, Malki-Shua, Abinadab, Ish-Bosheth (and possibly Ishvi). Daughters: Merab and Michal.
Key verses:	"But Samuel replied: 'Does the LORD delight in burnt offerings and sacrifices as much as in obeying the voice of the LORD? To obey is better than sacrifice, and to heed is better than the fat of rams. For rebellion is like the sin of divination, and arrogance like the evil of idolatry. Because you have rejected the word of the LORD, he has rejected you as king'" (1 Samuel 15:22, 23).

His story is told in 1 Samuel 9—31. He is also mentioned in Acts 13:21.

10:20 The Israelites chose their first king by casting lots—perhaps by using the Urim and Thummim, two plates or flat stones carried by the high priest. The fact that Saul was chosen may seem like luck, but it was really the opposite. God had instructed the Israelites to make the Urim and Thummim for the specific purpose of consulting him in times such as this (Exodus 28:30; Numbers 27:12–21). By using the Urim and Thummim, the Israelites were taking the decision out of their own hands and turning it over to God.

Only the high priest could use the Urim and Thummim, which were designed to give only yes or no answers.

10:22 When the Israelites assembled to choose a king, Saul already knew he was the one (10:1). Instead of coming forward, however, he hid among the baggage. Often we hide from important responsibilities because we are afraid of failure, afraid of what others will think, or perhaps unsure about how to proceed. Prepare now to step up to your future responsibilities. Count on God's provision rather than your feelings of adequacy.

²⁵ Samuel explained to the people the regulations ʸ of the kingship. He wrote them down on a scroll and deposited it before the LORD. Then Samuel dismissed the people, each to his own home.

²⁶ Saul also went to his home in Gibeah, ᶻ accompanied by valiant men whose hearts God had touched. ²⁷ But some troublemakers said, "How can this fellow save us?" They despised him and brought him no gifts. But Saul kept silent.

Saul Rescues the City of Jabesh

11 Nahash ᵃ the Ammonite went up and besieged Jabesh Gilead. ᵇ And all the men of Jabesh said to him, "Make a treaty with us, and we will be subject to you."

² But Nahash the Ammonite replied, "I will make a treaty with you only on the condition that I gouge out the right eye of every one of you and so bring disgrace ᶜ on all Israel."

³ The elders of Jabesh said to him, "Give us seven days so we can send messengers throughout Israel; if no one comes to rescue us, we will surrender to you."

⁴ When the messengers came to Gibeah ᵈ of Saul and reported these terms to the people, they all wept aloud. ⁵ Just then Saul was returning from the fields, behind his oxen, and he asked, "What is wrong with the people? Why are they weeping?" Then they repeated to him what the men of Jabesh had said.

⁶ When Saul heard their words, the Spirit ᵉ of God came upon him in power, and he burned with anger. ⁷ He took a pair of oxen, cut them into pieces, and sent the pieces by messengers throughout Israel, ᶠ proclaiming, "This is what will be done to the oxen of anyone ᵍ who does not follow Saul and Samuel." Then the terror of the LORD fell on the people, and they turned out as one man. ⁸ When Saul mustered them at Bezek, ʰ the men of Israel numbered three hundred thousand and the men of Judah thirty thousand.

⁹ They told the messengers who had come, "Say to the men of Jabesh Gilead, 'By the time the sun is hot tomorrow, you will be delivered.'" When the messengers went and reported this to the men of Jabesh, they were elated. ¹⁰ They said to the Ammonites, "Tomorrow we will surrender ⁱ to you, and you can do to us whatever seems good to you."

10:25
ʸ1Sa 8:11-18

10:26
ᶻ1Sa 11:4

11:1
ᵃ1Sa 12:12
ᵇJdg 21:8

11:2
ᶜ1Sa 17:26

11:4
ᵈ1Sa 10:5,26

11:6
ᵉJdg 3:10

11:7
ᶠJdg 19:29
ᵍJdg 21:5

11:8
ʰJdg 1:4

11:10
ⁱver 3

10:25 The kings of Israel, unlike kings of other nations, had specific regulations outlined for them (Deuteronomy 17:14–20). Pagan kings were considered gods; they made their own laws and answered to no one. By contrast, Israel's king had to answer to a higher authority—the Lord of heaven and earth. The Israelites now had a king like everyone else, just as they wanted. But Samuel, in his charge to both the king and the people, wanted to make sure that the rule of Israel's king would be different from that of his pagan counterparts. "Deposited it before the LORD" means that Samuel put the book, as a witness to the agreement, in a special place at Mizpah.

SAUL DEFEATS THE AMMONITES
The Ammonites prepared to attack Jabesh Gilead. The people of Jabesh sent messengers to Saul in Gibeah asking for help. Saul mobilized an army at Bezek and then attacked the Ammonites. After the battle, the Israelites returned to Gilgal to crown Saul as king.

10:26, 27 Some men became Saul's constant companions, while others despised him. Criticism will always be directed toward those who lead because they are out in front. At this time, Saul took no notice of those who seemed to be against him, although later he would become consumed with jealousy (19:1–3; 26:17–21). As you lead, listen to constructive criticism, but don't spend valuable time and energy worrying about those who may oppose you. Instead, focus your attention on those who are ready and willing to help.

11:1ff At this time, Israel was very susceptible to invasion by marauding tribes such as these Ammonites from east of the Jordan River. Saul's leadership in battle against this warlike tribe helped unify the nation and proved that he was a worthy military ruler. Saul's kingship was solidified when he saved the nation from disgrace and spared the people who had criticized him.

11:3 Why would Nahash give the city of Jabesh Gilead seven days to find an army to help them? Because Israel was still disorganized, Nahash was betting that no one would come to the city's aid. He was hoping to take the city without a fight and avoid a battle. He also may not have been prepared to attack the city because a siege against its walls could last weeks or months.

11:6 Anger is a powerful emotion. Often it may drive people to hurt others with words or physical violence. But anger directed at sin and the mistreatment of others is not wrong. Saul was angered by the Ammonites' threat to humiliate and mistreat his fellow Israelites. The Holy Spirit used Saul's anger to bring justice and freedom. When injustice or sin makes you angry, ask God how you can channel that anger in constructive ways to help bring about a positive change.

11:8 Judah, one of the 12 tribes of Israel, is often mentioned separately from the other 11. There are several reasons for this. Judah was the largest tribe (Numbers 1:20–46), and it was the tribe from which most of Israel's kings would come (Genesis 49:8–12). Later, Judah would be one of the few tribes to return to God after a century of captivity under a hostile foreign power.

11:11
j Jdg 7:16

[11] The next day Saul separated his men into three divisions;[j] during the last watch of the night they broke into the camp of the Ammonites and slaughtered them until the heat of the day. Those who survived were scattered, so that no two of them were left together.

Saul Confirmed as King

11:12
k Lk 19:27

[12] The people then said to Samuel, "Who[k] was it that asked, 'Shall Saul reign over us?' Bring these men to us and we will put them to death."

11:13
l 2Sa 19:22
m 1Sa 19:5

[13] But Saul said, "No one shall be put to death today,[l] for this day the LORD has rescued[m] Israel."

11:14
n 1Sa 10:8

[14] Then Samuel said to the people, "Come, let us go to Gilgal[n] and there reaffirm the kingship." [15] So all the people went to Gilgal and confirmed Saul as king in the presence of the LORD. There they sacrificed fellowship offerings[a] before the LORD, and Saul and all the Israelites held a great celebration.

Samuel's Farewell Speech

12:2
o 1Sa 8:5

12:3
p 1Sa 24:6;
2Sa 1:14

12 Samuel said to all Israel, "I have listened to everything you said to me and have set a king over you. [2] Now you have a king as your leader.[o] As for me, I am old and gray, and my sons are here with you. I have been your leader from my youth until this day. [3] Here I stand. Testify against me in the presence of the LORD and his anointed.[p] Whose ox have I taken? Whose donkey have I taken? Whom have I cheated? Whom have I oppressed? From whose hand have I accepted a bribe to make me shut my eyes? If I have done any of these, I will make it right."

[4] "You have not cheated or oppressed us," they replied. "You have not taken anything from anyone's hand."

12:5
q Ac 23:9
r Ex 22:4

[5] Samuel said to them, "The LORD is witness against you, and also his anointed is witness this day, that you have not found anything[q] in my hand.[r]"

"He is witness," they said.

12:7
s Mic 6:1-5

[6] Then Samuel said to the people, "It is the LORD who appointed Moses and Aaron and brought your forefathers up out of Egypt. [7] Now then, stand here, because I am going to confront[s] you with evidence before the LORD as to all the righteous acts performed by the LORD for you and your fathers.

12:8
t Ex 2:23
u Ex 3:10

[8] "After Jacob entered Egypt, they cried[t] to the LORD for help, and the LORD sent[u] Moses and Aaron, who brought your forefathers out of Egypt and settled them in this place.

12:9
v Jdg 3:7
w Jdg 4:2
x Jdg 10:7
y Jdg 3:12

[9] "But they forgot[v] the LORD their God; so he sold them into the hand of Sisera,[w] the commander of the army of Hazor, and into the hands of the Philistines[x] and the king of Moab,[y] who fought against them. [10] They cried out to the LORD and said, 'We have sinned; we have forsaken the LORD and served the Baals and the Ashtoreths. But now deliver us from the hands of our enemies, and we will serve you.' [11] Then the LORD sent Jerub-Baal,[b][z] Barak,[c][a]

12:11
z Jdg 6:14,32
a Jdg 4:6
b Jdg 11:1

Jephthah[b] and Samuel,[d] and he delivered you from the hands of your enemies on every side, so that you lived securely.

---

a 15 Traditionally *peace offerings*   *b* 11 Also called *Gideon*   *c* 11 Some Septuagint manuscripts and Syriac; Hebrew *Bedan*   *d* 11 Hebrew; some Septuagint manuscripts and Syriac *Samson*

Judah would also be the tribe through which the Messiah would come (Micah 5:2).

11:14 Saul had been anointed by Samuel at Ramah (10:1); then Saul was publicly chosen at Mizpah (10:17–27); his defeat of the Ammonites confirmed his kingship in the people's minds; at this time, all the people confirm his rule.

11:15 The Israelites sacrificed fellowship offerings to God as they made Saul their first king. The instructions for giving these offerings are given in Leviticus 3. The fellowship offering was an expression of gratitude and thanksgiving to God, symbolizing the peace that comes to those who know him and who live in accordance with his commands. Although God did not want his people to have a human king, the people were demonstrating through their offerings that he was still their true King. Unfortunately, this attitude did not last, just as God had predicted (8:7–19).

12:1ff Samuel continued to serve the people as their priest, prophet, and judge, but Saul exercised more and more political and military control over the tribes (see 7:15).

12:1–3 In his farewell speech, Samuel asked the Israelites to point out any wrongs he had committed during his time as Israel's judge. By doing so, Samuel was reminding them that he could be trusted to tell the truth. He was also reminding them that having a king was their idea, not his. Samuel was setting the stage for the miraculous thunderstorm recorded in 12:16–19, so that the people could not blame him when God punished them for their selfish motives.

12:10 "The Baals and the Ashtoreths" were pagan gods. See the note on 7:4 for more information.

12:11 Jerub-Baal was the name given to Gideon when he demolished the altar of Baal (see Judges 6:32).

¹²"But when you saw that Nahash^c king of the Ammonites was moving against you, you said to me, 'No, we want a king to rule^d over us'—even though the LORD your God was your king. ¹³Now here is the king^e you have chosen, the one you asked for; see, the LORD has set a king over you. ¹⁴If you fear^f the LORD and serve and obey him and do not rebel against his commands, and if both you and the king who reigns over you follow the LORD your God—good! ¹⁵But if you do not obey the LORD, and if you rebel against^g his commands, his hand will be against you, as it was against your fathers.

¹⁶"Now then, stand still and see^h this great thing the LORD is about to do before your eyes! ¹⁷Is it not wheat harvest now? I will call upon the LORD to send thunder and rain.ⁱ And you will realize what an evil^j thing you did in the eyes of the LORD when you asked for a king."

¹⁸Then Samuel called upon the LORD, and that same day the LORD sent thunder and rain. So all the people stood in awe^k of the LORD and of Samuel.

¹⁹The people all said to Samuel, "Pray to the LORD your God for your servants so that we will not die, for we have added to all our other sins the evil of asking for a king."

²⁰"Do not be afraid," Samuel replied. "You have done all this evil; yet do not turn away from the LORD, but serve the LORD with all your heart. ²¹Do not turn away after useless^l idols.^m They can do you no good, nor can they rescue you, because they are useless. ²²For the sake of his great nameⁿ the LORD will not reject his people, because the LORD was pleased to make^o you his own. ²³As for me, far be it from me that I should sin against the LORD by failing to pray^p for you. And I will teach^q you the way that is good and right. ²⁴But be sure to fear^r the LORD and serve him faithfully with all your heart; consider what great^s things he has done for you. ²⁵Yet if you persist in doing evil, both you and your king will be swept^t away."

2. God rejects Saul for disobedience
Samuel Rebukes Saul

13 Saul was ˌthirtyˌ^a years old when he became king, and he reigned over Israel ˌforty-ˌ^b two years.

²Saul^c chose three thousand men from Israel; two thousand were with him at Micmash and in the hill country of Bethel, and a thousand were with Jonathan at Gibeah in Benjamin. The rest of the men he sent back to their homes.

³Jonathan attacked the Philistine outpost^u at Geba, and the Philistines heard about it. Then Saul had the trumpet blown throughout the land and said, "Let the Hebrews hear!" ⁴So all Israel heard the news: "Saul has attacked the Philistine outpost, and now Israel has become a stench to the Philistines." And the people were summoned to join Saul at Gilgal.

a *1 A few late manuscripts of the Septuagint; Hebrew does not have* thirty. **b** *1 See the round number in Acts 13:21; Hebrew does not have* forty-. **c** *1,2 Or* and when he had reigned over Israel two years, *2he*

12:12
c 1Sa 11:1
d 1Sa 8:6,19

12:13
e 1Sa 8:5;
Hos 13:11

12:14
f Jos 24:14

12:15
g Jos 24:20

12:16
h Ex 14:13

12:17
i Pr 26:1
j 1Sa 8:6-7

12:18
k Ex 14:31

12:21
l Hab 2:18
m Dt 11:16

12:22
n Jos 7:9
o Dt 7:7

12:23
p Col 1:9; 2Ti 1:3
q 1Ki 8:36

12:24
r Ecc 12:13
s Dt 10:21

12:25
t Jos 24:20

13:3
u 1Sa 10:5

12:12–15 God granted the nation's request for a king, but his commands and requirements remained the same. God was to be their true King, and both Saul and the people were to be subject to his laws. No person is ever exempt from God's laws. No human action is outside his jurisdiction. God is the true King of every area of life. We must recognize his kingship and pattern our relationships, worklife, and homelife according to his principles.

12:17 The wheat harvest came near the end of the dry season during the months of May and June. Because rain rarely fell during this period, a great thunderstorm was considered a miraculous event. It was not a beneficial miracle, however, because rain during the wheat harvest could damage the crops and cause them to rot quickly. This unusual occurrence showed God's displeasure with Israel's demand for a king.

12:22 Why did God make Israel "his people"? God did not choose them because they deserved it (Deuteronomy 7:7, 8), but in order that they might become his channel of blessing to all people through the Messiah (Genesis 12:1–3). Because God chose the people of Israel, he would never abandon them; but because they were his special nation, he would often punish them for their disobedience in order to bring them back to a right relationship with him.

12:23 Is failing to pray for others a sin? Samuel's words seem to indicate that it is. His actions illustrate two of God's people's responsibilities: (1) they should pray consistently for others (Ephesians 6:18), and (2) they should teach others the right way to God (2 Timothy 2:2). Samuel disagreed with the Israelites' demand for a king, but he assured them that he would continue to pray for them and teach them. We may disagree with others, but we shouldn't stop praying for them.

12:24 This is the second time in his farewell speech that Samuel reminded the people to take time to consider what great things God had done for them (see 12:7). Taking time for reflection allows us to focus our attention upon God's goodness and strengthens our faith. Sometimes we are so progress- and future-oriented that we fail to take time to recall all that God has already done. Remember what God has done for you so that you may move ahead with gratitude.

13:3, 4 Jonathan attacked and destroyed the Philistine outpost, but Saul took all the credit for it. Although this was normal in that culture, it didn't make his action right. Saul's growing pride started out small—taking credit for a battle that was won by his son. Left unchecked, his pride grew into an ugly obsession; thus it destroyed him, tore his family apart, and threatened the well-being of the nation. Taking credit for the accomplishments of others indicates that pride is controlling your life. When you notice pride taking a foothold, take immediate steps to put it in check by giving credit to those who deserve it.

13:6
ᵛJdg 6:2

⁵The Philistines assembled to fight Israel, with three thousandᵃ chariots, six thousand charioteers, and soldiers as numerous as the sand on the seashore. They went up and camped at Micmash, east of Beth Aven. ⁶When the men of Israel saw that their situation was critical and that their army was hard pressed, they hid in caves and thickets, among the rocks, and in pits and cisterns. ᵛ ⁷Some Hebrews even crossed the Jordan to the land of Gad and Gilead.

13:8
ʷ1Sa 10:8

Saul remained at Gilgal, and all the troops with him were quaking with fear. ⁸He waited sevenʷ days, the time set by Samuel; but Samuel did not come to Gilgal, and Saul's men began to scatter. ⁹So he said, "Bring me the burnt offering and the fellowship offerings.ᵇ" And Saul offered up the burnt offering. ¹⁰Just as he finished making the offering, Samuel arrived, and Saul went out to greet him.

¹¹"What have you done?" asked Samuel.

Saul replied, "When I saw that the men were scattering, and that you did not come at the set time, and that the Philistines were assembling at Micmash, ¹²I thought, 'Now the Philistines will come down against me at Gilgal, and I have not sought the LORD's favor.' So I felt compelled to offer the burnt offering."

13:13
ˣ2Ch 16:9
ʸ1Sa 15:23,24

¹³"You acted foolishly,ˣ" Samuel said. "You have not keptʸ the command the LORD your God gave you; if you had, he would have established your kingdom over Israel for all time. ¹⁴But now your kingdomᶻ will not endure; the LORD has sought out a man after his own heartᵃ and appointed him leader of his people, because you have not kept the LORD's command."

13:14
ᶻ1Sa 15:28
ᵃAc 13:22

13:15
ᵇ1Sa 14:2

¹⁵Then Samuel left Gilgalᶜ and went up to Gibeah ᵇ in Benjamin, and Saul counted the men who were with him. They numbered about six hundred.

ᵃ5 Some Septuagint manuscripts and Syriac; Hebrew *thirty thousand*   ᵇ9 Traditionally *peace offerings*
ᶜ15 Hebrew; Septuagint *Gilgal and went his way; the rest of the people went after Saul to meet the army, and they went out of Gilgal*

GLOOM AND DOOM
Samuel's messages to Israel

Reference	Message
3:11–14	Judgment will come to the house of Eli.
7:1–4	The nation must turn from idol worship.
8:10–22	Your kings will bring you nothing but trouble.
12:25	If you continue in sin, you will be destroyed by God.
13:13, 14	Saul's kingdom will not continue.
15:17–31	Saul, you have sinned before God.

It wasn't easy being a prophet. Most of the messages they had to give were very unpleasant to hear. They preached of repentance, judgment, impending destruction, sin, and, in general, how displeased God was over the behavior of his people. Prophets were not the most popular people in town (unless they were *false* prophets and said just what the people wanted to hear). But popularity was not the bottom line for true prophets of God—it was obedience to God and faithfully proclaiming his word. Samuel is a good example of a faithful prophet.

God has words for us to proclaim as well. And although his messages are loaded with "good news," there is also "bad news" to give. May we, like true prophets, faithfully deliver *all* God's words, regardless of their popularity or lack of it.

13:6 When we forget who is on our side or see only our own resources, we tend to panic at the sight of the opposition. The Israelites became terrified and hid when they saw the mighty Philistine army. They forgot that God was on their side and that he couldn't be defeated. As you face problems and temptations, focus your attention on God and his resources, trusting him to help you (Romans 8:31–37).

13:9 Rather than waiting for a priest, Saul offered the sacrifice himself. This was against God's laws (Deuteronomy 12:5–14) and against the specific instructions of Samuel (10:8). Under pressure from the approaching Philistines, he took matters into his own hands and disobeyed God. He was doing a good thing (offering a sacrifice to God before a crucial battle), but he did it in the wrong way. Like Saul, our true spiritual character is revealed under pressure. The methods we use to accomplish our goals are as important as the attainment of those goals.

13:11, 12 It is difficult to trust God when you feel your resources slipping away. When Saul felt that time was running out, he became impatient with God's timing. In thinking that the ritual was all he needed, he substituted the ritual for faith in God.

When faced with a difficult decision, don't allow impatience to drive you to disobey God. When you know what God wants, follow his plan regardless of the consequences. God often uses delays to test our obedience and patience.

13:12, 13 Saul had plenty of excuses for his disobedience. But Samuel zeroed in on the real issue: "You have not kept the command the LORD your God gave you." Like Saul, we often gloss over our mistakes and sins, trying to justify and spiritualize our actions because of our "special" circumstances. Our excuses, however, are nothing more than disobedience. God knows our true motives. He forgives, restores, and blesses only when we are honest about our sins. By trying to hide his sins behind excuses, Saul lost his kingship (13:14).

Israel Without Weapons

[16]Saul and his son Jonathan and the men with them were staying in Gibeah[a] in Benjamin, while the Philistines camped at Micmash. [17]Raiding parties went out from the Philistine camp in three detachments. One turned toward Ophrah[c] in the vicinity of Shual, [18]another toward Beth Horon,[d] and the third toward the borderland overlooking the Valley of Zeboim[e] facing the desert.

[19]Not a blacksmith[f] could be found in the whole land of Israel, because the Philistines had said, "Otherwise the Hebrews will make swords or spears!" [20]So all Israel went down to the Philistines to have their plowshares, mattocks, axes and sickles[b] sharpened. [21]The price was two thirds of a shekel[c] for sharpening plowshares and mattocks, and a third of a shekel[d] for sharpening forks and axes and for repointing goads.

[22]So on the day of the battle not a soldier with Saul and Jonathan had a sword or spear[g] in his hand; only Saul and his son Jonathan had them.

Jonathan Attacks the Philistines

[23]Now a detachment of Philistines had gone out to the pass at Micmash. **14** [1]One day Jonathan son of Saul said to the young man bearing his armor, "Come, let's go over to the Philistine outpost on the other side." But he did not tell his father.

[2]Saul was staying on the outskirts of Gibeah[h] under a pomegranate tree in Migron. With him were about six hundred men, [3]among whom was Ahijah, who was wearing an ephod. He was a son of Ichabod's[i] brother Ahitub[j] son of Phinehas, the son of Eli,[k] the LORD's priest in Shiloh. No one was aware that Jonathan had left.

[4]On each side of the pass[l] that Jonathan intended to cross to reach the Philistine outpost was a cliff; one was called Bozez, and the other Seneh. [5]One cliff stood to the north toward Micmash, the other to the south toward Geba.

[6]Jonathan said to his young armor-bearer, "Come, let's go over to the outpost of those uncircumcised[m] fellows. Perhaps the LORD will act in our behalf. Nothing can hinder the LORD from saving, whether by many[n] or by few."

[7]"Do all that you have in mind," his armor-bearer said. "Go ahead; I am with you heart and soul."

13:17
c Jos 18:23
13:18
d Jos 18:13-14
e Ne 11:34
13:19
f 2Ki 24:14

13:22
g Jdg 5:8

14:2
h 1Sa 13:15
14:3
i 1Sa 4:21
j 1Sa 22:11,20
k 1Sa 2:28
14:4
l 1Sa 13:23
14:6
m Jer 9:26
n Jdg 7:4

---

a *16 Two Hebrew manuscripts; most Hebrew manuscripts* Geba, *a variant of* Gibeah   b *20 Septuagint; Hebrew* plowshares   c *21 Hebrew* pim; *that is, about 1/4 ounce (about 8 grams)*   d *21 That is, about 1/8 ounce (about 4 grams)*

13:19-22 Israel was in no position to conquer anyone. The army had no iron weapons, and there were no facilities for turning their tools into weapons. In fact, if an Israelite wanted to sharpen his tools, he had to pay a Philistine blacksmith to do it because the Philistines had a carefully guarded monopoly on iron and blacksmithing. And they charged high prices for sharp-ening farm implements. The Philistines' tight control over the technology, along with their surprise raids, demoralized the Israelites and kept them in subjection.

Against such superiority, the Israelites were at a serious disadvantage. How could they hope to rout their oppressors? Only with God's help. God wanted to give Israel victory without swords, so they would realize their true source of strength.

14:1 Why would Jonathan go alone to attack the Philistines? Jonathan may have been weary of the long, hopeless standoff in the battle; he trusted God to give the victory and wanted to act on that trust. He also knew that the number of Philistines was no problem for God. Perhaps he didn't tell his father about his mission because he thought Saul would not let him go.

14:1ff In this chapter we read about the miserable job Saul did as leader: he had no communication with Jonathan (14:1, 17); he made a foolish curse (14:24); and he ignored the well-being of his own soldiers (14:31). Saul's poor leadership was not a result of personality traits but of decaying spiritual character. What we do is often a direct result of our spiritual condition. We cannot ignore the importance of spiritual character in effective leadership.

14:6 Jonathan and his armor-bearer weren't much of a force to attack the huge Philistine army. But while everyone else was afraid, they trusted God, knowing that the size of the enemy army would not restrict God's ability to help them. God honored the faith and brave action of these two men with a tremendous victory.

Have you ever felt surrounded by the "enemy" or faced overwhelming odds? God is never intimidated by the size of the enemy or the complexity of a problem. With him, there are always enough resources to resist the pressures and win the battle. If God has called you to action, then bravely commit what resources you have to God, and rely upon him to lead you to victory.

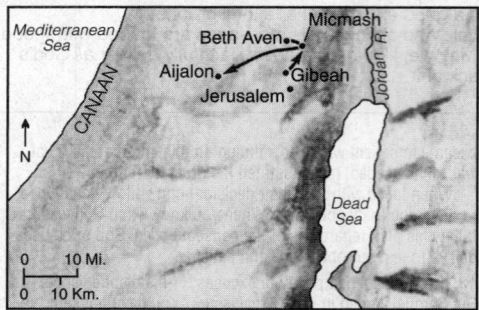

JONATHAN'S BRAVERY Jonathan, Saul's son, left the camp at Gibeah and crept to the Philistine camp at Micmash. With God's help, Jonathan and his armor-bearer surprised the Philistines, who panicked and began killing each other! Saul's army heard the commotion and chased the Philistines as far as Beth Aven and Aijalon.

14:10
o Ge 24:14

8 Jonathan said, "Come, then; we will cross over toward the men and let them see us. 9 If they say to us, 'Wait there until we come to you,' we will stay where we are and not go up to them. 10 But if they say, 'Come up to us,' we will climb up, because that will be our sign o that the LORD has given them into our hands."

14:12
p 2Sa 5:24

11 So both of them showed themselves to the Philistine outpost. "Look!" said the Philistines. "The Hebrews are crawling out of the holes they were hiding in." 12 The men of the outpost shouted to Jonathan and his armor-bearer, "Come up to us and we'll teach you a lesson."

So Jonathan said to his armor-bearer, "Climb up after me; the LORD has given them into the hand p of Israel."

13 Jonathan climbed up, using his hands and feet, with his armor-bearer right behind him. The Philistines fell before Jonathan, and his armor-bearer followed and killed behind him. 14 In that first attack Jonathan and his armor-bearer killed some twenty men in an area of about half an acre. a

Israel Routs the Philistines

14:15
q Ge 35:5; 2Ki 7:5-7
r 1Sa 13:17

15 Then panic q struck the whole army—those in the camp and field, and those in the outposts and raiding r parties—and the ground shook. It was a panic sent by God. b

16 Saul's lookouts at Gibeah in Benjamin saw the army melting away in all directions. 17 Then Saul said to the men who were with him, "Muster the forces and see who has left us." When they did, it was Jonathan and his armor-bearer who were not there.

18 Saul said to Ahijah, "Bring the ark of God." (At that time it was with the Israelites.) c

14:19
s Nu 27:21

19 While Saul was talking to the priest, the tumult in the Philistine camp increased more and more. So Saul said to the priest, s "Withdraw your hand."

14:20
t Jdg 7:22;
2Ch 20:23

20 Then Saul and all his men assembled and went to the battle. They found the Philistines in total confusion, striking t each other with their swords. 21 Those Hebrews who had previously been with the Philistines and had gone up with them to their camp went over to the Israelites who were with Saul and Jonathan. 22 When all the Israelites who had hidden u in the hill country of Ephraim heard that the Philistines were on the run, they joined the battle in hot pursuit. 23 So the LORD rescued v Israel that day, and the battle moved on beyond Beth Aven. w

14:22
u 1Sa 13:6

14:23
v Ex 14:30;
Ps 44:6-7
w 1Sa 13:5

Jonathan Eats Honey

14:24
x Jos 6:26

24 Now the men of Israel were in distress that day, because Saul had bound the people under an oath, x saying, "Cursed be any man who eats food before evening comes, before I have avenged myself on my enemies!" So none of the troops tasted food.

25 The entire army d entered the woods, and there was honey on the ground. 26 When they went into the woods, they saw the honey oozing out, yet no one put his hand to his mouth, because they feared the oath. 27 But Jonathan had not heard that his father had bound the people with the oath, so he reached out the end of the staff that was in his hand and dipped it into the honeycomb. He raised his hand to his mouth, and his eyes brightened. e 28 Then one of the soldiers told him, "Your father bound the army under a strict oath, saying, 'Cursed be any man who eats food today!' That is why the men are faint."

14:29
y 1Ki 18:18

29 Jonathan said, "My father has made trouble y for the country. See how my eyes brightened f when I tasted a little of this honey. 30 How much better it would have been if the men had eaten today some of the plunder they took from their enemies. Would not the slaughter of the Philistines have been even greater?"

---

a 14 Hebrew *half a yoke*; a "yoke" was the land plowed by a yoke of oxen in one day.   b 15 Or *a terrible panic*
c 18 Hebrew; Septuagint *"Bring the ephod." (At that time he wore the ephod before the Israelites.)*   d 25 Or *Now all the people of the land*   e 27 Or *his strength was renewed*   f 29 Or *my strength was renewed*

14:12 Jonathan did not have the authority to lead all the troops into battle, but he could start a small skirmish in one corner of the enemy camp. When he did, panic broke out among the Philistines, the Hebrews who had been drafted into the Philistine army revolted, and the men who were hiding in the hills regained their courage and returned to fight.

When you are facing a difficult situation that is beyond your control, ask yourself, "What steps can I take now to work toward a solution?" A few small steps may be just what is needed to begin the chain of events leading to eventual victory.

14:19 "Withdraw your hand" refers to the use of the Urim and Thummim. They were withdrawn from the linen ephod (vest) as a way to determine God's will (see the note on 10:20). Saul was

rushing the formalities of getting an answer from God so he could hurry and get into battle to take advantage of the confusion of the Philistines.

14:24 Saul made an oath without thinking through the implications. The results? (1) His men were too tired to fight; (2) they were so hungry they ate meat that still contained blood, which was against God's law (14:32); (3) Saul almost killed his own son (14:42–44).

Saul's impulsive oath sounded heroic, but it had disastrous side effects. If you are in the middle of a conflict, guard against impulsive statements that you may be forced to honor.

³¹That day, after the Israelites had struck down the Philistines from Micmash to Aijalon, they were exhausted. ³²They pounced on the plunder *z* and, taking sheep, cattle and calves, they butchered them on the ground and ate them, together with the blood. *a* ³³Then someone said to Saul, "Look, the men are sinning against the Lᴏʀᴅ by eating meat that has blood in it."

"You have broken faith," he said. "Roll a large stone over here at once." ³⁴Then he said, "Go out among the men and tell them, 'Each of you bring me your cattle and sheep, and slaughter them here and eat them. Do not sin against the Lᴏʀᴅ by eating meat with blood still in it.'"

So everyone brought his ox that night and slaughtered it there. ³⁵Then Saul built an altar *b* to the Lᴏʀᴅ; it was the first time he had done this.

³⁶Saul said, "Let us go down after the Philistines by night and plunder them till dawn, and let us not leave one of them alive."

"Do whatever seems best to you," they replied.

But the priest said, "Let us inquire of God here."

³⁷So Saul asked God, "Shall I go down after the Philistines? Will you give them into Israel's hand?" But God did not answer *c* him that day.

³⁸Saul therefore said, "Come here, all you who are leaders of the army, and let us find out what sin has been committed *d* today. ³⁹As surely as the Lᴏʀᴅ who rescues Israel lives, *e* even if it lies with my son Jonathan, he must die." But not one of the men said a word.

⁴⁰Saul then said to all the Israelites, "You stand over there; I and Jonathan my son will stand over here."

"Do what seems best to you," the men replied.

⁴¹Then Saul prayed to the Lᴏʀᴅ, the God of Israel, "Give *f* me the right answer."*a* And Jonathan and Saul were taken by lot, and the men were cleared. ⁴²Saul said, "Cast the lot between me and Jonathan my son." And Jonathan was taken.

⁴³Then Saul said to Jonathan, "Tell me what you have done." *g*

So Jonathan told him, "I merely tasted a little honey with the end of my staff. And now must I die?"

⁴⁴Saul said, "May God deal with me, be it ever so severely, *h* if you do not die, Jonathan."

⁴⁵But the men said to Saul, "Should Jonathan die—he who has brought about this great deliverance in Israel? Never! As surely as the Lᴏʀᴅ lives, not a hair *i* of his head will fall to the ground, for he did this today with God's help." So the men rescued *j* Jonathan, and he was not put to death.

⁴⁶Then Saul stopped pursuing the Philistines, and they withdrew to their own land.

⁴⁷After Saul had assumed rule over Israel, he fought against their enemies on every side:

a41 Hebrew; Septuagint *"Why have you not answered your servant today? If the fault is in me or my son Jonathan, respond with Urim, but if the men of Israel are at fault, respond with Thummim."*

**Cross references (right margin):**

14:32
z 1Sa 15:19
a Lev 17:10-14

14:35
b 1Sa 7:17

14:37
c 1Sa 28:6,15

14:38
d 1Sa 10:19

14:39
e 2Sa 12:5

14:41
f Ac 1:24

14:43
g Jos 7:19

14:44
h Ru 1:17

14:45
i 1Ki 1:52
j 2Sa 14:11

14:32-34 One of the oldest and strongest Hebrew food laws was the prohibition against eating meat containing the animal's blood (Leviticus 7:26, 27). This law began in Noah's day (Genesis 9:4) and was still observed by the early Christians (Acts 15:27–29). It was wrong to eat blood because blood represented life and life belonged to God. (For a further explanation, see Leviticus 17:10–14.)

14:35, 36 After being king for several years, Saul finally built his first altar to God, but only as a last resort. Throughout Saul's reign he consistently approached God only after he had tried everything else. This was in sharp contrast to the priest, who suggested that God be consulted *first*. How much better if Saul had gone to God first, building an altar as his first official act as king. God is too great to be an afterthought. When we turn to him first, we will never have to turn to him as a last resort.

14:39 This is the second of Saul's foolish curses. Saul made the first of his two oaths (14:24–26) because he was overly anxious to defeat the Philistines and wanted to give his soldiers an incentive to finish the battle quickly. In the Bible, God never asked people to make oaths or vows, but if they did, he expected them to keep them (Leviticus 5:4; Numbers 30).

Saul's curse was not something God would have condoned, but still it was an oath. And Jonathan, although he didn't know about Saul's oath, was nevertheless guilty of breaking it. Like Jephthah (Judges 11), Saul made an oath that risked the life of his own child. Fortunately, the people intervened and spared Jonathan's life.

14:39 Saul had issued a ridiculous command and had driven his men to sin, but still he wouldn't back down even if he had to kill his son. When we make ridiculous statements, it is difficult to admit we are wrong. Sticking to the story, just to save face, only compounds the problem. It takes more courage to admit a mistake than to hold resolutely to an error.

14:43 Jonathan's spiritual character was in striking contrast to Saul's. Jonathan admitted what he had done; he did not try to make excuses. Even though he was unaware of Saul's oath, Jonathan was willing to accept the consequences of his actions. When you do wrong, even unintentionally, respond like Jonathan, not like Saul.

14:44, 45 Saul made another foolish statement, this time because he was more concerned about saving face than being right. To spare Jonathan's life would require him to admit he had acted foolishly, an embarrassment for a king. Saul was really more interested in protecting his image than in enforcing his vow. Fortunately, the people came to Jonathan's rescue. Don't be like Saul. Admit your mistakes, and show that you are more interested in doing what is right than in looking good.

14:47 Why was Saul so successful right after he had disobeyed God and been told that his reign would end (13:13, 14)? Sometimes ungodly people win battles. Victory is neither guaranteed nor limited to the righteous. God provides according to his will. God

14:48
k 1Sa 15:2,7

Moab, the Ammonites, Edom, the kings[a] of Zobah, and the Philistines. Wherever he turned, he inflicted punishment on them.[b] 48 He fought valiantly and defeated the Amalekites,[k] delivering Israel from the hands of those who had plundered them.

Saul's Family

14:49
l 1Sa 31:2; 1Ch 8:33

49 Saul's sons were Jonathan, Ishvi and Malki-Shua.[l] The name of his older daughter was Merab, and that of the younger was Michal. 50 His wife's name was Ahinoam daughter of Ahimaaz. The name of the commander of Saul's army was Abner son of Ner, and Ner was Saul's uncle.

14:51
m 1Sa 9:1

51 Saul's father Kish[m] and Abner's father Ner were sons of Abiel.

52 All the days of Saul there was bitter war with the Philistines, and whenever Saul saw a mighty or brave man, he took him into his service.

The LORD Rejects Saul as King

15:1
n 1Sa 9:16

15:2
o Ex 17:8-14;
Nu 24:20;
Dt 25:17-19

15 Samuel said to Saul, "I am the one the LORD sent to anoint[n] you king over his people Israel; so listen now to the message from the LORD. 2 This is what the LORD Almighty says: 'I will punish the Amalekites[o] for what they did to Israel when they waylaid them as they came up from Egypt. 3 Now go, attack the Amalekites and totally destroy[c] everything that belongs to them. Do not spare them; put to death men and women, children and infants, cattle and sheep, camels and donkeys.'"

15:6
p Ex 18:10,19;
Nu 10:29-32;
Jdg 1:16; 4:1

4 So Saul summoned the men and mustered them at Telaim—two hundred thousand foot soldiers and ten thousand men from Judah. 5 Saul went to the city of Amalek and set an ambush in the ravine. 6 Then he said to the Kenites,[p] "Go away, leave the Amalekites so that I do not destroy you along with them; for you showed kindness to all the Israelites when they came up out of Egypt." So the Kenites moved away from the Amalekites.

15:7
q 1Sa 14:48
r Ge 16:7; 25:17-18

15:8
s 1Sa 30:1

15:9
t ver 3,15

7 Then Saul attacked the Amalekites[q] all the way from Havilah to Shur,[r] to the east of Egypt. 8 He took Agag king of the Amalekites alive,[s] and all his people he totally destroyed with the sword. 9 But Saul and the army spared[t] Agag and the best of the sheep and cattle, the fat calves[d] and lambs—everything that was good. These they were unwilling to destroy completely, but everything that was despised and weak they totally destroyed.

15:11
u Ge 6:6; 2Sa 24:16
v 1Ki 9:6-7

10 Then the word of the LORD came to Samuel: 11 "I am grieved[u] that I have made Saul king, because he has turned away from me and has not carried out my instructions."[v] Samuel was troubled, and he cried out to the LORD all that night.

15:12
w Jos 15:55

12 Early in the morning Samuel got up and went to meet Saul, but he was told, "Saul has gone to Carmel.[w] There he has set up a monument in his own honor and has turned and gone on down to Gilgal."

a 47 Masoretic Text; Dead Sea Scrolls and Septuagint *king*   *b* 47 Hebrew; Septuagint *he was victorious*   *c* 3 The Hebrew term refers to the irrevocable giving over of things or persons to the LORD, often by totally destroying them; also in verses 8, 9, 15, 18, 20 and 21.   *d* 9 Or *the grown bulls*; the meaning of the Hebrew for this phrase is uncertain.

---

might have given Saul success for the sake of the people, not for Saul. He may have left Saul on the throne for a while to utilize his military talents so that David, Israel's next king, could spend more time focusing on the nation's spiritual battles. Regardless of God's reasons for delaying Saul's demise, his reign ended exactly the way God had foretold. The timing of God's plans and promises are known only to him. Our task is to commit our ways to God and then trust him for the outcome.

15:2, 3 Why did God command such utter destruction? The Amalekites were a band of guerrilla terrorists. They lived by attacking other nations and carrying off their wealth and their families. They were the first to attack the Israelites as they entered the promised land, and they continued to raid Israelite camps at every opportunity. God knew that the Israelites could never live peacefully in the promised land as long as the Amalekites existed. He also knew that their corrupt, idolatrous religious practices threatened Israel's relationship with him. The only way to protect the Israelites' bodies and souls was to utterly destroy the people of this warlike nation and all their possessions, including their idols.

15:9 Saul and his men did not destroy all the plunder from the battle as God commanded (15:3). The law of devoting something—setting it aside—entirely for destruction was well known to the Israelites. Anything under God's ban was to be completely

destroyed (Deuteronomy 20:16–18). This was set up in order to prevent idolatry from taking hold in Israel because many of the valuables were idols. To break this law was punishable by death (Joshua 7). It showed disrespect and disregard for God because it directly violated his command.

When we gloss over sin in order to protect what we have or for material gain, we aren't being shrewd; we are disobeying God's law. Selective obedience is just another form of disobedience.

15:11 When God said he was grieved that he had made Saul king, was he saying he had made a mistake? God's comment was an expression of sorrow, not an admission of error (Genesis 6:5–7). An omniscient God cannot make a mistake (15:29); therefore, God did not change his mind. He did, however, change his attitude toward Saul when Saul changed. Saul's heart no longer belonged to God, but to his own interests.

15:12 Saul built a monument in honor of himself. What a contrast to Moses and Joshua, who gave all the credit to God.

13When Samuel reached him, Saul said, "The LORD bless you! I have carried out the LORD's instructions."

14But Samuel said, "What then is this bleating of sheep in my ears? What is this lowing of cattle that I hear?"

15Saul answered, "The soldiers brought them from the Amalekites; they spared the best of the sheep and cattle to sacrifice to the LORD your God, but we totally destroyed the rest."

16"Stop!" Samuel said to Saul. "Let me tell you what the LORD said to me last night."

"Tell me," Saul replied.

17Samuel said, "Although you were once small in your own eyes, did you not become the head of the tribes of Israel? The LORD anointed you king over Israel. 18And he sent you on a mission, saying, 'Go and completely destroy those wicked people, the Amalekites; make war on them until you have wiped them out.' 19Why did you not obey the LORD? Why did you pounce on the plunder and do evil in the eyes of the LORD?"

20"But I did obey the LORD," Saul said. "I went on the mission the LORD assigned me. I completely destroyed the Amalekites and brought back Agag their king. 21The soldiers took sheep and cattle from the plunder, the best of what was devoted to God, in order to sacrifice them to the LORD your God at Gilgal."

22But Samuel replied:

> "Does the LORD delight in burnt offerings and sacrifices
>> as much as in obeying the voice of the LORD?
> To obey is better than sacrifice,[x]
>> and to heed is better than the fat of rams.
> 23 For rebellion is like the sin of divination,
>> and arrogance like the evil of idolatry.
> Because you have rejected[y] the word of the LORD,
>> he has rejected you as king."

24Then Saul said to Samuel, "I have sinned. I violated the LORD's command and your instructions. I was afraid[z] of the people and so I gave in to them. 25Now I beg you, forgive my sin and come back with me, so that I may worship the LORD."

26But Samuel said to him, "I will not go back with you. You have rejected the word of the LORD, and the LORD has rejected you as king over Israel!"

27As Samuel turned to leave, Saul caught hold of the hem of his robe, and it tore.[a] 28Samuel said to him, "The LORD has torn[b] the kingdom of Israel from you today and has given it to one of your neighbors—to one better than you. 29He who is the Glory of Israel does not lie or change[c] his mind; for he is not a man, that he should change his mind."

30Saul replied, "I have sinned. But please honor[d] me before the elders of my people and before Israel; come back with me, so that I may worship the LORD your God." 31So Samuel went back with Saul, and Saul worshiped the LORD.

15:22
[x] Isa 1:11-15; Hos 6:6; Mic 6:6-8; Mk 12:33; Heb 10:6-9

15:23
[y] 1Sa 13:13

15:24
[z] Isa 51:12-13

15:27
[a] 1Ki 11:11,31

15:28
[b] 1Sa 28:17

15:29
[c] Nu 23:19; Eze 24:14

15:30
[d] Jn 12:43

15:13, 14 Saul thought he had won a great victory over the Amalekites, but God saw it as a great failure because Saul had disobeyed him and then lied to Samuel about the results of the battle. Saul may have thought his lie wouldn't be detected, or that what he did was not wrong. Saul was deceiving himself.

Dishonest people soon begin to believe the lies they construct around themselves. Then they lose the ability to tell the difference between truth and lies. By believing your own lies you deceive yourself, you will alienate yourself from God, and you will lose credibility in all your relationships. In the long run, honesty wins out.

15:22, 23 This is the first of numerous places in the Bible where the theme "to obey is better than sacrifice" is stated (Psalms 40:6–8; 51:16, 17; Proverbs 21:3; Isaiah 1:11–17; Jeremiah 7:21–23; Hosea 6:6; Micah 6:6–8; Matthew 12:7; Mark 12:33; Hebrews 10:8, 9). Was Samuel saying that sacrifice is unimportant? No, he was urging Saul to look at his reasons for making the sacrifice rather than at the sacrifice itself. A sacrifice was a ritual transaction between a person and God that physically demonstrated a relationship between them. But if the person's heart was not truly repentant or if he did not truly love

God, the sacrifice was a hollow ritual. Religious ceremonies or rituals are empty unless they are performed with an attitude of love and obedience. "Being religious" (going to church, serving on a committee, giving to charity) is not enough if we do not act out of devotion and obedience to God.

15:23 Rebellion and arrogance are serious sins. They involve far more than being independent and strong-minded. Scripture equates them with divination (witchcraft) and idolatry, sins worthy of death (Exodus 22:18; Leviticus 20:6; Deuteronomy 13:12–15; 18:10; Micah 5:10–14).

Saul became both rebellious and arrogant, so it is little wonder that God finally rejected him and took away his kingdom. Rebellion against God is perhaps the most serious sin of all because as long as a person rebels, he or she closes the door to forgiveness and restoration with God.

15:26 Saul's excuses had come to an end. It was the time of reckoning. God wasn't rejecting Saul as a person; the king could still seek forgiveness and restore his relationship with God, but it was too late to get his kingdom back. If you do not act responsibly with what God has entrusted to you, eventually you will run out of excuses. All of us must one day give an account for our actions (Romans 14:12; Revelation 22:12).

15:33
e Jdg 1:7

32 Then Samuel said, "Bring me Agag king of the Amalekites."

Agag came to him confidently,ª thinking, "Surely the bitterness of death is past." 33 But Samuel said,

"As your sword has made women childless,
    so will your mother be childless among women."*e*

15:34
f 1Sa 11:4

15:35
g 1Sa 19:24
h 1Sa 16:1

And Samuel put Agag to death before the LORD at Gilgal.

34 Then Samuel left for Ramah, but Saul went up to his home in Gibeah *f* of Saul. 35 Until the day Samuel *g* died, he did not go to see Saul again, though Samuel mourned *h* for him. And the LORD was grieved that he had made Saul king over Israel.

C. SAUL AND DAVID (16:1—31:13)

While Saul is still on the throne, Samuel anoints David as Israel's next king. Young David then bravely conquers Goliath, the Philistine champion, and establishes a lifelong friendship with Jonathan, Saul's son. When Saul realizes that David will become king one day, he grows very jealous and tries to kill David on several occasions. David escapes into Philistine territory until Saul is killed in battle. When treated unjustly, we should not take matters into our own hands. God, who is faithful and just, sees all that is happening and will judge all evil.

1. Samuel anoints David

16:1
i 1Sa 15:35
j 1Sa 15:23
k 2Ki 9:1
l Ps 78:70; Ac 13:22

16 The LORD said to Samuel, "How long will you mourn *i* for Saul, since I have rejected *j* him as king over Israel? Fill your horn with oil *k* and be on your way; I am sending you to Jesse of Bethlehem. I have chosen *l* one of his sons to be king."

2 But Samuel said, "How can I go? Saul will hear about it and kill me."

16:3
m Ex 4:15
n 1Sa 9:16

The LORD said, "Take a heifer with you and say, 'I have come to sacrifice to the LORD.' 3 Invite Jesse to the sacrifice, and I will show *m* you what to do. You are to anoint *n* for me the one I indicate."

16:4
o 1Ki 2:13; 2Ki 9:17

4 Samuel did what the LORD said. When he arrived at Bethlehem, the elders of the town trembled when they met him. They asked, "Do you come in peace? *o*"

16:5
p Ex 19:10,22

5 Samuel replied, "Yes, in peace; I have come to sacrifice to the LORD. Consecrate *p* yourselves and come to the sacrifice with me." Then he consecrated Jesse and his sons and invited them to the sacrifice.

16:6
q 1Sa 17:13

6 When they arrived, Samuel saw Eliab *q* and thought, "Surely the LORD's anointed stands here before the LORD."

16:7
r 1Ki 8:39

7 But the LORD said to Samuel, "Do not consider his appearance or his height, for I have rejected him. The LORD does not look at the things man looks at. Man looks at the outward appearance, but the LORD looks at the heart." *r*

16:8
s 1Sa 17:13

8 Then Jesse called Abinadab *s* and had him pass in front of Samuel. But Samuel said, "The LORD has not chosen this one either." 9 Jesse then had Shammah pass by, but Samuel said, "Nor has the LORD chosen this one." 10 Jesse had seven of his sons pass before Samuel, but Samuel said to him, "The LORD has not chosen these." 11 So he asked Jesse, "Are these all the sons you have?"

"There is still the youngest," Jesse answered, "but he is tending the sheep."

Samuel said, "Send for him; we will not sit down *b* until he arrives."

16:12
t 1Sa 9:17

12 So he *t* sent and had him brought in. He was ruddy, with a fine appearance and handsome features.

ª 32 Or *him trembling, yet*   *b* 11 Some Septuagint manuscripts; Hebrew *not gather around*

15:30 Saul was more concerned about what others would think of him than he was about the status of his relationship with God (15:24). He begged Samuel to go with him to worship as a public demonstration that Samuel still supported him. If Samuel had refused, the people probably would have lost all confidence in Saul.

16:5 Samuel "consecrated" Jesse and his sons to prepare them to come before God in worship or to offer a sacrifice. For more on this ceremony, see Genesis 35:2; Exodus 19:10, 14; and the note on Joshua 3:5.

16:7 Saul was tall and handsome; he was an impressive-looking man. Samuel may have been trying to find someone who looked like Saul to be Israel's next king, but God warned him against judging by appearance alone. When people judge by outward appearance, they may overlook quality individuals who lack the particular physical qualities society currently admires. Appearance doesn't reveal what people are really like or what their true value is.

Fortunately, God judges by faith and character, not appearances. And because only God can see on the inside, only he can accurately judge people. Most people spend hours each week maintaining their outward appearance; they should do even more to develop their inner character. While everyone can see your face, only you and God know what your heart really looks like. What steps are you taking to improve your heart's attitude?

Then the LORD said, "Rise and anoint him; he is the one."

[13]So Samuel took the horn of oil and anointed him in the presence of his brothers, and from that day on the Spirit of the LORD came upon David in power. [u] Samuel then went to Ramah.

16:13
[u]1Sa 10:1,6,9-10;
11:6

David in Saul's Service

[14]Now the Spirit of the LORD had departed [v] from Saul, and an evil[a] spirit [w] from the LORD tormented him.

[15]Saul's attendants said to him, "See, an evil spirit from God is tormenting you. [16]Let our lord command his servants here to search for someone who can play the harp. [x] He will play when the evil spirit from God comes upon you, and you will feel better."

16:14
[v]Jdg 16:20
[w]Jdg 9:23
16:16
[x]2Ki 3:15

[17]So Saul said to his attendants, "Find someone who plays well and bring him to me."

[18]One of the servants answered, "I have seen a son of Jesse of Bethlehem who knows how to play the harp. He is a brave man and a warrior. He speaks well and is a fine-looking man. And the LORD is with [y] him."

16:18
[y]1Sa 3:19;
17:32-37

[19]Then Saul sent messengers to Jesse and said, "Send me your son David, who is with the sheep." [20]So Jesse took a donkey loaded with bread, [z] a skin of wine and a young goat and sent them with his son David to Saul.

16:20
[z]1Sa 10:27

[21]David came to Saul and entered his service. [a] Saul liked him very much, and David became one of his armor-bearers. [22]Then Saul sent word to Jesse, saying, "Allow David to remain in my service, for I am pleased with him."

16:21
[a]Ge 41:46

[23]Whenever the spirit from God came upon Saul, David would take his harp and play. Then relief would come to Saul; he would feel better, and the evil spirit [b] would leave him.

16:23
[b]ver 14-16

2. David and Goliath

17 Now the Philistines gathered their forces for war and assembled at Socoh in Judah. They pitched camp at Ephes Dammim, between Socoh and Azekah. [2]Saul and the Israelites assembled and camped in the Valley of Elah and drew up their battle line to meet the Philistines. [3]The Philistines occupied one hill and the Israelites another, with the valley between them.

[4]A champion named Goliath, [c] who was from Gath, came out of the Philistine camp. He was over nine feet[b] tall. [5]He had a bronze helmet on his head and wore a coat of scale armor

17:4
[c]Jos 11:21-22;
2Sa 21:19

[a]*14* Or *injurious*; also in verses 15, 16 and 23   [b]*4* Hebrew *was six cubits and a span* (about 3 meters)

16:13 David was anointed king, but it was done in secret; he was not publicly anointed until much later (2 Samuel 2:4; 5:3). Saul was still legally the king, but God was preparing David for his future responsibilities. The anointing oil poured over David's head stood for holiness. It was used to set people or objects apart for God's service. Each king and high priest of Israel was anointed with oil. This commissioned him as God's representative to the nation. Although God rejected Saul's kingship by not allowing any of his descendants to sit on Israel's throne, Saul himself remained in his position until his death.

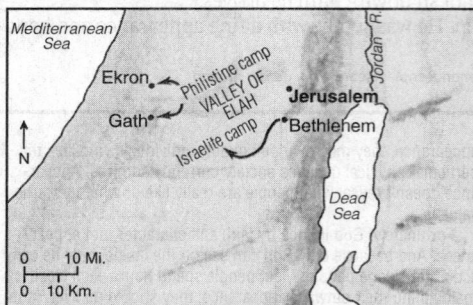

DAVID AND GOLIATH The armies of Israel and Philistia faced each other across the Valley of Elah. David arrived from Bethlehem and offered to fight the giant Goliath. After David defeated Goliath, the Israelite army chased the Philistines to Ekron and Gath (Goliath's hometown).

16:14 What was this evil spirit the Lord sent? Perhaps Saul was simply depressed. Or perhaps the Holy Spirit had left Saul, and God allowed an evil spirit (a demon) to torment him as judgment for his disobedience (this would demonstrate God's power over the spirit world—1 Kings 22:19–23). Either way, Saul was driven to insanity, which led him to attempt to murder David.

16:15, 16 Harps were popular musical instruments in Saul's day, and their music is still known for its soothing qualities. The simplest harps were merely two pieces of wood fastened at right angles to each other. The strings were stretched across the wood to give the harp a triangular shape. Simple strings could be made of twisted grasses, but better strings were made of dried animal intestine. Harps could have up to 40 strings and were louder than the smaller three- or four-stringed instruments called lyres. David, known for his shepherding skills and bravery, was also an accomplished harpist and musician who would eventually write many of the psalms found in the Bible.

16:19–21 When Saul asked David to be in his service, he obviously did not know that David had been secretly anointed king (16:12). Saul's invitation presented an excellent opportunity for the young man and future king to gain firsthand information about leading a nation ("David went back and forth from Saul" 17:15).

Sometimes our plans—even the ones we think God has approved—have to be put on hold indefinitely. Like David, we can use this waiting time profitably. We can choose to learn and grow in our present circumstances, whatever they may be.

17:4–7 When they had first approached the promised land, most of the Israelites had been afraid to enter because of the giants living there (Numbers 13:32, 33). King Og of Bashan needed a bed over 13 feet long (Deuteronomy 3:11). Now Goliath, over nine feet tall, taunted Israel's soldiers and appeared invincible to of bronze weighing five thousand shekels a; 6on his legs he wore bronze greaves, and a bronze javelin was slung on his back. 7His spear shaft was like a weaver's rod, and its iron point weighed six hundred shekels. b His shield bearer went ahead of him.

17:8
d1Sa 8:17

8Goliath stood and shouted to the ranks of Israel, "Why do you come out and line up for battle? Am I not a Philistine, and are you not the servants of Saul? Choose d a man and have him come down to me. 9If he is able to fight and kill me, we will become your subjects; but if I overcome him and kill him, you will become our subjects and serve us." 10Then the Philis-tine said, "This day I defy e the ranks of Israel! Give me a man and let us fight each other." 11On hearing the Philistine's words, Saul and all the Israelites were dismayed and terrified.

17:10
ever 26,45

17:12
f1Ch 2:13-15
gGe 35:19
h1Sa 16:11

12Now David was the son of an Ephrathite named Jesse, f who was from Bethlehem g in Ju-dah. Jesse had eight h sons, and in Saul's time he was old and well advanced in years. 13Jesse's three oldest sons had followed Saul to the war: The firstborn was Eliab; i the second, Abina-dab; and the third, Shammah. j 14David was the youngest. The three oldest followed Saul, 15but David went back and forth from Saul to tend his father's sheep k at Bethlehem.

17:13
i1Sa 16:6
j1Sa 16:9

17:15
k1Sa 16:19

16For forty days the Philistine came forward every morning and evening and took his stand.

a5 That is, about 125 pounds (about 57 kilograms)   b7 That is, about 15 pounds (about 7 kilograms)

GOLIATH

Goliath was a giant with an attitude. As champion of the Philistines, he immobilized an entire army of Israelites by challenging one of them to duel with him. He made them forget they had an absolute champion in the Lord their God. It took a bold shepherd boy named David to remind them all they were the armies of the living God.

Goliath was a problem to be faced on his terms but not with his weapons. Goliath's strengths were so obvious (size, armor, arrogance) that others missed his vulnerability. For Goliath had a glaring weakness that never occurred to him until David's stone struck him down. When David was given Goliath's kind of weapons, David quickly concluded he couldn't even function—much less fight—with those tools. Goliath's strengths would have been David's handicaps. Armor plating and heavy weapons were of little use to the shepherd boy. David went with the two weapons he knew he could rely on: his trust in God and his shepherd's sling. When others looked at Goliath, they saw an opponent too powerful to defeat; when David looked at Goliath, he saw a target too big to miss!

David had armor to match Goliath's, but it was invisible. He was spiritually equipped. Ephesians 6:10–18 describes in detail the resources that God places at our disposal. How unfortunate that we face our world each day on its terms and too often try to wield its weapons. God's weapons are not as obvious, but they never fail us! How much of your spiritual armor are you wearing today?

Strengths and accomplishments:	• Designated champion of the Philistine army • Held the entire army of Israel at bay by intimidation and derision • Recognized as a giant in his day
Weaknesses and mistakes:	• Defied the armies of the living God • Failed to take David seriously
Lessons from his life:	• Strengths often conceal weaknesses • God will not be mocked • God transforms strength into weakness and weakness into strength • God equips those who trust him with spiritual armor
Vital statistics:	• Where: Gath • Occupation: Soldier • Relatives: At least one brother • Contemporaries: Saul, Jonathan, David
Key verse:	"Who is this uncircumcised Philistine that he should defy the armies of the living God?" (1 Samuel 17:26b).

Goliath's story is told in 1 Samuel 17.

---

them. Saul, the tallest of the Israelites, may have been especially worried because he was obviously the best match for Goliath. In God's eyes, however, Goliath was no different than anyone else.

17:9 An army often avoided the high cost of battle by pitting its strongest warrior against the strongest warrior of the enemy. This avoided great bloodshed because the winner of the fight was considered the winner of the battle. Goliath had the definite advantage against David from a human standpoint. But Goliath didn't realize that in fighting David, he also had to fight God.

17:16 Why would this go on for 40 days without one side attack-ing the other? They were camped on opposite sides of a valley with steep walls. Whoever would rush down the valley and up the steep cliffs would be at a disadvantage at the beginning of the battle and probably suffer great casualties. Each side was waiting for the other to attack first.

¹⁷Now Jesse said to his son David, "Take this ephah ᵃ of roasted grain and these ten loaves of bread for your brothers and hurry to their camp. ¹⁸Take along these ten cheeses to the commander of their unit.ᵇ See how your brothers ⁱ are and bring back some assurance ᶜ from them. ¹⁹They are with Saul and all the men of Israel in the Valley of Elah, fighting against the Philistines."

²⁰Early in the morning David left the flock with a shepherd, loaded up and set out, as Jesse had directed. He reached the camp as the army was going out to its battle positions, shouting the war cry. ²¹Israel and the Philistines were drawing up their lines facing each other. ²²David left his things with the keeper of supplies, ran to the battle lines and greeted his brothers. ²³As he was talking with them, Goliath, the Philistine champion from Gath, stepped out from his lines and shouted his usual ᵐ defiance, and David heard it. ²⁴When the Israelites saw the man, they all ran from him in great fear.

²⁵Now the Israelites had been saying, "Do you see how this man keeps coming out? He comes out to defy Israel. The king will give great wealth to the man who kills him. He will also give him his daughter ⁿ in marriage and will exempt his father's family from taxes in Israel."

²⁶David asked the men standing near him, "What will be done for the man who kills this Philistine and removes this disgrace ᵒ from Israel? Who is this uncircumcised ᵖ Philistine that he should defy �q the armies of the living God?"

²⁷They repeated to him what they had been saying and told him, "This is what will be done for the man who kills him."

²⁸When Eliab, David's oldest brother, heard him speaking with the men, he burned with anger ʳ at him and asked, "Why have you come down here? And with whom did you leave those few sheep in the desert? I know how conceited you are and how wicked your heart is; you came down only to watch the battle."

²⁹"Now what have I done?" said David. "Can't I even speak?" ³⁰He then turned away to someone else and brought up the same matter, and the men answered him as before. ³¹What David said was overheard and reported to Saul, and Saul sent for him.

³²David said to Saul, "Let no one lose heart ˢ on account of this Philistine; your servant will go and fight him."

³³Saul replied, "You are not able to go out against this Philistine and fight him; you are only a boy, and he has been a fighting man from his youth."

³⁴But David said to Saul, "Your servant has been keeping his father's sheep. When a lion or a bear came and carried off a sheep from the flock, ³⁵I went after it, struck it and rescued the sheep from its mouth. When it turned on me, I seized it by its hair, struck it and killed it. ³⁶Your servant has killed both the lion and the bear; this uncircumcised Philistine will be like one of them, because he has defied the armies of the living God. ³⁷The LORD who delivered me from the paw of the lion ᵗ and the paw of the bear will deliver me from the hand of this Philistine."

Saul said to David, "Go, and the LORD be with ᵘ you."

³⁸Then Saul dressed David in his own tunic. He put a coat of armor on him and a bronze helmet on his head. ³⁹David fastened on his sword over the tunic and tried walking around, because he was not used to them.

"I cannot go in these," he said to Saul, "because I am not used to them." So he took them off. ⁴⁰Then he took his staff in his hand, chose five smooth stones from the stream, put them in the pouch of his shepherd's bag and, with his sling in his hand, approached the Philistine.

⁴¹Meanwhile, the Philistine, with his shield bearer in front of him, kept coming closer to David. ⁴²He looked David over and saw that he was only a boy, ruddy and handsome, ᵛ and he despised him. ⁴³He said to David, "Am I a dog, ʷ that you come at me with sticks?" And the Philistine cursed David by his gods. ⁴⁴"Come here," he said, "and I'll give your flesh to the birds of the air and the beasts of the field! ˣ"

ᵃ *17* That is, probably about 3/5 bushel (about 22 liters)   ᵇ *18* Hebrew *thousand*   ᶜ *18* Or *some token*; or *some pledge of spoils*

17:18
ⁱGe 37:14

17:23
ᵐver 8-10

17:25
ⁿJos 15:16

17:26
ᵒ1Sa 11:2
ᵖ1Sa 14:6
qver 10

17:28
ʳGe 37:4,8,11

17:32
ˢDt 20:3; 1Sa 16:18

17:37
ᵗ2Ti 4:17
ᵘ1Sa 20:13;
1Ch 22:11,16

17:42
ᵛ1Sa 16:12
17:43
ʷ1Sa 24:14;
2Sa 3:8
17:44
ˣ1Ki 20:10-11

17:26 What a difference perspective can make. Most of the onlookers saw only a giant. David, however, saw a mortal man defying almighty God. Goliath was a target too big to miss. He knew he would not be alone when he faced Goliath; God would fight with him. He looked at his situation from God's point of view. Who or what are the "giants" you are facing? Viewing impossible situations from God's point of view helps us put giant problems in perspective. Once we see clearly, we can fight more effectively.

17:28–32 Criticism couldn't stop David. While the rest of the army stood around, he knew the importance of taking action. With God to fight for him, there was no reason to wait. People may try to discourage you with negative comments or mockery, but continue to do what you know is right. By doing what is right, you will be pleasing God, whose opinion matters most.

17:45
y 2Ch 32:8;
Heb 11:32-34

17:46
z 1Ki 18:36;
2Ki 19:19

17:47
a Hos 1:7
b 2Ch 14:11

45 David said to the Philistine, "You come against me with sword and spear and javelin, but I come against you in the name y of the LORD Almighty, the God of the armies of Israel, whom you have defied. 46 This day the LORD will hand you over to me, and I'll strike you down and cut off your head. Today I will give the carcasses of the Philistine army to the birds of the air and the beasts of the earth, and the whole world will know that there is a God in Israel. z 47 All those gathered here will know that it is not by sword a or spear that the LORD saves; b for the battle is the LORD's, and he will give all of you into our hands."

48 As the Philistine moved closer to attack him, David ran quickly toward the battle line to meet him. 49 Reaching into his bag and taking out a stone, he slung it and struck the Philistine on the forehead. The stone sank into his forehead, and he fell facedown on the ground.

When we think of David, we think: shepherd, poet, giant-killer, king, ancestor of Jesus—in short, one of the greatest men in the Old Testament. But alongside that list stands another: betrayer, liar, adulterer, murderer. The first list gives qualities we all might like to have; the second, qualities that might be true of any one of us. The Bible makes no effort to hide David's failures. Yet he is remembered and respected for his heart for God. Knowing how much more we share in David's failures than in his greatness, we should be curious to find out what made God refer to David as "a man after my own heart" (Acts 13:22).

David, more than anything else, had an unchangeable belief in the faithful and forgiving nature of God. He was a man who lived with great zest. He sinned many times, but he was quick to confess his sins. His confessions were from the heart, and his repentance was genuine. David never took God's forgiveness lightly or his blessing for granted. In return, God never held back from David either his forgiveness or the consequences of his actions. David experienced the joy of forgiveness even when he had to suffer the consequences of his sins.

We tend to get these two reversed. Too often we would rather avoid the consequences than experience forgiveness. Another big difference between us and David is that while he sinned greatly, he did not sin repeatedly. He learned from his mistakes because he accepted the suffering they brought. Often we don't seem to learn from our mistakes or the consequences that result from those mistakes. What changes would it take for God to find this kind of obedience in you?

Strengths and accomplishments:	• Greatest king of Israel • Ancestor of Jesus Christ • Listed in the Hall of Faith in Hebrews 11 • A man described by God himself as a man after his own heart
Weaknesses and mistakes:	• Committed adultery with Bathsheba • Arranged the murder of Uriah, Bathsheba's husband • Directly disobeyed God in taking a census of the people • Did not deal decisively with the sins of his children
Lessons from his life:	• Willingness to honestly admit our mistakes is the first step in dealing with them • Forgiveness does not remove the consequences of sin • God greatly desires our complete trust and worship
Vital statistics:	• Where: Bethlehem, Jerusalem • Occupations: Shepherd, musician, poet, soldier, king • Relatives: Father: Jesse. Wives: included Michal, Ahinoam, Bathsheba, Abigail. Sons: included Absalom, Amnon, Solomon, Adonijah. Daughters: included Tamar. Seven brothers. • Contemporaries: Saul, Jonathan, Samuel, Nathan
Key verses:	"O Sovereign LORD, you are God! Your words are trustworthy, and you have promised these good things to your servant. Now be pleased to bless the house of your servant, that it may continue forever in your sight; for you, O Sovereign LORD, have spoken, and with your blessing the house of your servant will be blessed forever" (2 Samuel 7:28, 29).

His story is told in 1 Samuel 16—1 Kings 2. He is also mentioned in Amos 6:5; Matthew 1:1, 6; 22:43–45; Luke 1:32; Acts 13:22; Romans 1:3; Hebrews 11:32.

17:48–49 David was able to move faster than Goliath because David carried no heavy weapons or armor. David was an expert marksman with a sling, and as he advanced on Goliath, he stayed out of range of Goliath's huge weapons. What made David effective, however, was more than his ability with a sling; it was his courage and his faith in God. To fight like David we need David's

kind of fearlessness. David had grown strong in his confidence by trusting God when he had encountered wild animals while guarding his father's sheep (17:34–37). When you face towering problems, recall how God has helped you in the past. Take heart because God gives you strength. Use the skills God has already given you and move forward.

⁵⁰So David triumphed over the Philistine with a sling and a stone; without a sword in his hand he struck down the Philistine and killed him.

⁵¹David ran and stood over him. He took hold of the Philistine's sword and drew it from the scabbard. After he killed him, he cut off his head with the sword.

When the Philistines saw that their hero was dead, they turned and ran. ⁵²Then the men of Israel and Judah surged forward with a shout and pursued the Philistines to the entrance of Gath ᵃ and to the gates of Ekron. Their dead were strewn along the Shaaraim ᶜ road to Gath and Ekron. ⁵³When the Israelites returned from chasing the Philistines, they plundered their camp. ⁵⁴David took the Philistine's head and brought it to Jerusalem, and he put the Philistine's weapons in his own tent.

⁵⁵As Saul watched David ᵈ going out to meet the Philistine, he said to Abner, commander of the army, "Abner, whose son is that young man?"

Abner replied, "As surely as you live, O king, I don't know."

⁵⁶The king said, "Find out whose son this young man is."

⁵⁷As soon as David returned from killing the Philistine, Abner took him and brought him before Saul, with David still holding the Philistine's head.

⁵⁸"Whose son are you, young man?" Saul asked him.

David said, "I am the son of your servant Jesse of Bethlehem."

17:52
ᶜJos 15:36

17:55
ᵈ1Sa 16:21

3. David and Jonathan become friends
Saul's Jealousy of David

18 After David had finished talking with Saul, Jonathan became one in spirit with David, and he loved ᵉ him as himself. ᶠ ²From that day Saul kept David with him and did not let him return to his father's house. ³And Jonathan made a covenant with David because he loved him as himself. ⁴Jonathan took off the robe he was wearing and gave it to David, along with his tunic, and even his sword, his bow and his belt.

⁵Whatever Saul sent him to do, David did it so successfully ᵇ that Saul gave him a high rank in the army. This pleased all the people, and Saul's officers as well.

⁶When the men were returning home after David had killed the Philistine, the women came out from all the towns of Israel to meet King Saul with singing and dancing,ᵍ with joyful songs and with tambourines ʰ and lutes. ⁷As they danced, they sang:

18:1
ᵉ2Sa 1:26
ᶠGe 44:30

18:6
ᵍEx 15:20
ʰJdg 11:34

18:7
ⁱ1Sa 21:11

> "Saul has slain his thousands,
> and David his tensⁱ of thousands."

⁸Saul was very angry; this refrain galled him. "They have credited David with tens of thousands," he thought, "but me with only thousands. What more can he get but the kingdom?" ⁹And from that time on Saul kept a jealous eye on David.

¹⁰The next day an evilᶜ spiritʲ from God came forcefully upon Saul. He was prophesying in his house, while David was playing the harp, as he usuallyᵏ did. Saul had a spear in his hand ¹¹and he hurled it, saying to himself,ˡ "I'll pin David to the wall." But David eludedᵐ him twice.

18:10
ʲ1Sa 16:14
ᵏ1Sa 19:7

18:11
ˡ1Sa 20:7,33
ᵐ1Sa 19:10

ᵃ52 Some Septuagint manuscripts; Hebrew *a valley*   ᵇ5 Or *wisely*   ᶜ10 Or *injurious*

17:55–58 Although David had played his harp many times in front of Saul, Saul's question to Abner seems to show he didn't know David very well. Perhaps, since David was scheduled to marry Saul's daughter if he was successful (17:25), Saul wanted to know more about his family. Or possibly Saul's unstable mental condition (16:14) may have prevented him from recognizing David.

18:1–4 When David and Jonathan met, they became close friends at once. Their friendship is one of the deepest and closest recorded in the Bible: (1) they based their friendship on commitment to God, not just each other; (2) they let nothing come between them, not even career or family problems; (3) they drew closer together when their friendship was tested; (4) they remained friends to the end.

Jonathan, the prince of Israel, later realized that David, and not he, would be the next king (23:17). But that did not weaken his love for David. Jonathan would much rather lose the throne of Israel than lose his closest friend.

18:8 Saul's appreciation for David turned to jealousy as people began to applaud David's exploits. In a jealous rage, Saul attempted to murder David by hurling his spear at him (18:11, 12).

Jealousy may not seem to be a major sin, but in reality, it is one step short of murder. Jealousy starts as you resent a rival; it leads to your wishing he or she were removed; then it manifests itself in your seeking ways to harm that person in word or action. Beware of letting jealousy get a foothold in your life.

18:10 The note on 16:14 explains what this evil spirit might have been.

18:11, 12 Saul tried to kill David because he was jealous of David's popularity, yet David continued to protect and comfort Saul. Perhaps people have been jealous of you and have even attacked you in some way. They may be intimidated by your strengths, which make them conscious of their own shortcomings. It would be natural to strike back or to avoid them. A better response is to befriend them (Matthew 5:43, 44) and to ask God for the strength to continue to love them, as David kept on loving Saul.

18:13
n 2Sa 5:2

18:14
o Ge 39:3

18:16
p ver 5

18:17
q 1Sa 17:25
r 1Sa 25:28
s ver 25

18:18
t 1Sa 9:21;
2Sa 7:18

18:19
u 2Sa 21:8
v Jdg 7:22

18:20
w ver 28

18:25
x Ex 22:17;
1Sa 14:24

18:27
y 2Sa 3:14

[12]Saul was afraid of David, because the LORD was with David but had left Saul. [13]So he sent David away from him and gave him command over a thousand men, and David led the troops in their campaigns. *n* [14]In everything he did he had great success,*a* *o* because the LORD was with him. [15]When Saul saw how successful*b* he was, he was afraid of him. [16]But all Israel and Judah loved David, because he led them in their campaigns. *p*

[17]Saul said to David, "Here is my older daughter*q* Merab. I will give her to you in marriage; only serve me bravely and fight the battles*r* of the LORD." For Saul said to himself,*s* "I will not raise a hand against him. Let the Philistines do that!"

[18]But David said to Saul, "Who am I,*t* and what is my family or my father's clan in Israel, that I should become the king's son-in-law?" [19]So*c* when the time came for Merab,*u* Saul's daughter, to be given to David, she was given in marriage to Adriel of Meholah. *v*

[20]Now Saul's daughter Michal*w* was in love with David, and when they told Saul about it, he was pleased. [21]"I will give her to him," he thought, "so that she may be a snare to him and so that the hand of the Philistines may be against him." So Saul said to David, "Now you have a second opportunity to become my son-in-law."

[22]Then Saul ordered his attendants: "Speak to David privately and say, 'Look, the king is pleased with you, and his attendants all like you; now become his son-in-law.'"

[23]They repeated these words to David. But David said, "Do you think it is a small matter to become the king's son-in-law? I'm only a poor man and little known."

[24]When Saul's servants told him what David had said, [25]Saul replied, "Say to David, 'The king wants no other price*x* for the bride than a hundred Philistine foreskins, to take revenge on his enemies.'" Saul's plan was to have David fall by the hands of the Philistines.

[26]When the attendants told David these things, he was pleased to become the king's son-in-law. So before the allotted time elapsed, [27]David and his men went out and killed two hundred Philistines. He brought their foreskins and presented the full number to the king so that he might become the king's son-in-law. Then Saul gave him his daughter Michal*y* in marriage.

[28]When Saul realized that the LORD was with David and that his daughter Michal loved David, [29]Saul became still more afraid of him, and he remained his enemy the rest of his days.

[30]The Philistine commanders continued to go out to battle, and as often as they did, David met with more success*d* than the rest of Saul's officers, and his name became well known.

a 14 Or he was very wise   *b* 15 Or wise   *c* 19 Or However,   *d* 30 Or David acted more wisely

---

GOD USES SIMPLE OBJECTS	Object	Reference	Who Used It?	How Was It Used?
God often uses simple, ordinary objects to accomplish his tasks in the world.	A staff	Exodus 4:2–4	Moses	To work miracles before Pharaoh
	Trumpets	Joshua 6:3–5	Joshua	To flatten the walls of Jericho
	A fleece	Judges 6:36–40	Gideon	To confirm God's will
	Trumpets, jars, and torches	Judges 7:19–22	Gideon	To defeat the Midianites
It is important only that they be dedicated to him for his use.	Jawbone	Judges 15:15	Samson	To kill 1,000 Philistines
	Small stone	1 Samuel 17:40	David	To kill Goliath
	Oil	2 Kings 4:1–7	Elisha	To demonstrate God's power to provide
What do you have that God can use?	A river	2 Kings 5:9–14	Elisha	To heal a man of leprosy
Anything and everything is a possible "instrument" for him.	Linen belt	Jeremiah 13:1–11	Jeremiah	As an object lesson of God's wrath
	Pottery	Jeremiah 19:1–13	Jeremiah	As an object lesson of God's wrath
	Iron pan, water, and food	Ezekiel 4:1–17	Ezekiel	As an object lesson of judgment
	Five loaves and two fish	Mark 6:30–44	Jesus	To feed a crowd of over 5,000 people

---

18:15–18 While Saul's popularity made him proud and arrogant, David remained humble (18:23), even when the entire nation praised him. Although David succeeded in almost everything he tried and became famous throughout the land, he refused to use his popular support to his advantage against Saul. Don't allow popularity to twist your perception of your own importance. It's comparatively easy to be humble when you're not on center stage, but how will you react to praise and honor?

Saul Tries to Kill David

19 Saul told his son Jonathan and all the attendants to kill David. But Jonathan was very fond of David ²and warned him, "My father Saul is looking for a chance to kill you. Be on your guard tomorrow morning; go into hiding and stay there. ³I will go out and stand with my father in the field where you are. I'll speak to him about you and will tell you what I find out."

⁴Jonathan spoke well of David to Saul his father and said to him, "Let not the king do wrong*z* to his servant David; he has not wronged you, and what he has done has benefited you greatly. ⁵He took his life in his hands when he killed the Philistine. The LORD won a great victory*a* for all Israel, and you saw it and were glad. Why then would you do wrong to an innocent*b* man like David by killing him for no reason?"

⁶Saul listened to Jonathan and took this oath: "As surely as the LORD lives, David will not be put to death."

⁷So Jonathan called David and told him the whole conversation. He brought him to Saul, and David was with Saul as before.

⁸Once more war broke out, and David went out and fought the Philistines. He struck them with such force that they fled before him.

⁹But an evil*a* spirit*c* from the LORD came upon Saul as he was sitting in his house with his spear in his hand. While David was playing the harp, ¹⁰Saul tried to pin him to the wall with his spear, but David eluded him as Saul drove the spear into the wall. That night David made good his escape.

¹¹Saul sent men to David's house to watch it and to kill him in the morning. But Michal, David's wife, warned him, "If you don't run for your life tonight, tomorrow you'll be killed." ¹²So Michal let David down through a window, *d* and he fled and escaped. ¹³Then Michal took an idol*b* and laid it on the bed, covering it with a garment and putting some goats' hair at the head.

¹⁴When Saul sent the men to capture David, Michal said, "He is ill."

¹⁵Then Saul sent the men back to see David and told them, "Bring him up to me in his bed so that I may kill him." ¹⁶But when the men entered, there was the idol in the bed, and at the head was some goats' hair.

¹⁷Saul said to Michal, "Why did you deceive me like this and send my enemy away so that he escaped?"

Michal told him, "He said to me, 'Let me get away. Why should I kill you?'"

¹⁸When David had fled and made his escape, he went to Samuel at Ramah and told him all that Saul had done to him. Then he and Samuel went to Naioth and stayed there. ¹⁹Word came to Saul: "David is in Naioth at Ramah"; ²⁰so he sent men to capture him. But when they saw a group of prophets prophesying, with Samuel standing there as their leader, the Spirit of God came upon*e* Saul's men and they also prophesied. *f* ²¹Saul was told about it, and he sent more men, and they prophesied too. Saul sent men a third time, and they also prophesied. ²²Finally, he himself left for Ramah and went to the great cistern at Secu. And he asked, "Where are Samuel and David?"

"Over in Naioth at Ramah," they said.

²³So Saul went to Naioth at Ramah. But the Spirit of God came even upon him, and he walked along prophesying until he came to Naioth. ²⁴He stripped*g* off his robes and also prophesied in Samuel's presence. He lay that way all that day and night. This is why people say, "Is Saul also among the prophets?"

a9 Or *injurious*   *b13* Hebrew *teraphim*; also in verse 16

19:4
*z*Ge 42:22

19:5
*a*1Sa 11:13; 17:49-50
*b*1Sa 20:32

19:9
*c*1Sa 16:14; 18:10-11

19:12
*d*Jos 2:15; Ac 9:25

19:20
*e*Nu 11:25
*f*1Sa 10:5

19:24
*g*Isa 20:2

19:1, 2 Is it ever right to disobey your father, as Jonathan did here? It is clearly a principle of Scripture that when a father instructs a son to break God's laws, the son should obey God rather than man. This principle assumes that the son is old enough to be accountable and to see through any deception. A son's role is to be respectful, helpful, and obedient to his father (Ephesians 6:1–3), but not to follow commands or advice that violate God's laws.

19:20–24 This was the second time that Saul surprised everyone by joining a group of prophets and prophesying. This seems to be a group of people in Spirit-filled ecstasy. It was very powerful and contagious to anyone who found them. We do not know if they were speaking messages from God or merely joining in ecstatic expression. The first time this happened to Saul (chapter 10) was right after he was anointed king and did not want to accept the responsibility. This time Saul was consumed with jealousy over David's growing popularity, but the Spirit of God immobilized him so he was unable to harm David. Although Saul was receptive to the Spirit of God and was caught up in prophesying, his heart and mind were far from loving God and thinking God's thoughts.

David and Jonathan

20:1
h 1Sa 24:9

20 Then David fled from Naioth at Ramah and went to Jonathan and asked, "What have I done? What is my crime? How have I wronged*h* your father, that he is trying to take my life?"

2 "Never!" Jonathan replied. "You are not going to die! Look, my father doesn't do anything, great or small, without confiding in me. Why would he hide this from me? It's not so!"

3 But David took an oath and said, "Your father knows very well that I have found favor in your eyes, and he has said to himself, 'Jonathan must not know this or he will be grieved.' Yet as surely as the LORD lives and as you live, there is only a step between me and death."

4 Jonathan said to David, "Whatever you want me to do, I'll do for you."

20:5
i Nu 10:10; 28:11
j 1Sa 19:2

20:6
k 1Sa 17:58

20:7
l 1Sa 25:17

20:8
m 1Sa 18:3; 23:18
n 2Sa 14:32

5 So David said, "Look, tomorrow is the New Moon festival,*i* and I am supposed to dine with the king; but let me go and hide*j* in the field until the evening of the day after tomorrow. 6 If your father misses me at all, tell him, 'David earnestly asked my permission to hurry to Bethlehem,*k* his hometown, because an annual sacrifice is being made there for his whole clan.' 7 If he says, 'Very well,' then your servant is safe. But if he loses his temper,*l* you can be sure that he is determined to harm me. 8 As for you, show kindness to your servant, for you have brought him into a covenant*m* with you before the LORD. If I am guilty, then kill*n* me yourself! Why hand me over to your father?"

9 "Never!" Jonathan said. "If I had the least inkling that my father was determined to harm you, wouldn't I tell you?"

10 David asked, "Who will tell me if your father answers you harshly?"

11 "Come," Jonathan said, "let's go out into the field." So they went there together.

20:13
o Ru 1:17; 1Sa 3:17
p 1Sa 17:37

12 Then Jonathan said to David: "By the LORD, the God of Israel, I will surely sound out my father by this time the day after tomorrow! If he is favorably disposed toward you, will I not send you word and let you know? 13 But if my father is inclined to harm you, may the LORD deal with me, be it ever so severely,*o* if I do not let you know and send you away safely. May the LORD be with*p* you as he has been with my father. 14 But show me unfailing kindness like that of the LORD as long as I live, so that I may not be killed, 15 and do not ever cut off your kindness from my family*q*—not even when the LORD has cut off every one of David's enemies from the face of the earth."

20:15
q 2Sa 9:7

20:17
r 1Sa 18:3

16 So Jonathan made a covenant with the house of David, saying, "May the LORD call David's enemies to account." 17 And Jonathan had David reaffirm his oath*r* out of love for him, because he loved him as he loved himself.

20:18
s ver 5,25

20:19
t 1Sa 19:2

18 Then Jonathan said to David: "Tomorrow is the New Moon festival. You will be missed, because your seat will be empty.*s* 19 The day after tomorrow, toward evening, go to the place where you hid*t* when this trouble began, and wait by the stone Ezel. 20 I will shoot three arrows to the side of it, as though I were shooting at a target. 21 Then I will send a boy and say, 'Go, find the arrows.' If I say to him, 'Look, the arrows are on this side of you; bring them here,' then come, because, as surely as the LORD lives, you are safe; there is no danger. 22 But if I say to the boy, 'Look, the arrows are beyond you,' then you must go, because the LORD has sent you away. 23 And about the matter you and I discussed—remember, the LORD is witness*u* between you and me forever."

20:23
u ver 14-15;
Ge 31:50

24 So David hid in the field, and when the New Moon festival came, the king sat down to eat. 25 He sat in his customary place by the wall, opposite Jonathan,*a* and Abner sat next to Saul, but David's place was empty. 26 Saul said nothing that day, for he thought, "Something must have

a 25 Septuagint; Hebrew *wall. Jonathan arose*

20:5 At the beginning of each month, the Israelites gathered to celebrate the New Moon festival. While this was mainly a time to be enjoyed, it was also a way to dedicate the next month to God. Other nations had celebrations during the full moon and worshiped the moon itself. The Israelites, however, celebrated their festival at the time of the new moon, when the moon was not visible in the sky. This was an added precaution against false worship. Nothing in the creation is to be worshiped—only the Creator.

20:15 Jonathan asked David to keep a promise to treat his children kindly in the future. Years later David took great pains to fulfill this promise: he invited Jonathan's son Mephibosheth into his palace to live (2 Samuel 9).

20:26 Because the New Moon festival involved making a sacrifice to God (Numbers 28:11–15), those attending the feast had to be ceremonially clean according to God's laws (Exodus 19:10; Leviticus 15; Numbers 19:11–22; also see the note on Joshua 3:5). This cleansing involved washing the body and clothes before approaching God to offer a sacrifice. The outward cleansing was a symbol of the inward desire for a purified heart and right relationship with God. Today our hearts are purified by faith in God through the death of Jesus Christ on our behalf (Hebrews 10:10, 22) and by reading and heeding God's Word (John 17:17).

happened to David to make him ceremonially unclean—surely he is unclean. *v* ²⁷But the next day, the second day of the month, David's place was empty again. Then Saul said to his son Jonathan, "Why hasn't the son of Jesse come to the meal, either yesterday or today?"

²⁸Jonathan answered, "David earnestly asked me for permission *w* to go to Bethlehem. ²⁹He said, 'Let me go, because our family is observing a sacrifice in the town and my brother has ordered me to be there. If I have found favor in your eyes, let me get away to see my brothers.' That is why he has not come to the king's table."

³⁰Saul's anger flared up at Jonathan and he said to him, "You son of a perverse and rebellious woman! Don't I know that you have sided with the son of Jesse to your own shame and to the shame of the mother who bore you? ³¹As long as the son of Jesse lives on this earth, neither you nor your kingdom will be established. Now send and bring him to me, for he must die!"

³²"Why *x* should he be put to death? What has he done?" Jonathan asked his father. ³³But Saul hurled his spear at him to kill him. Then Jonathan knew that his father intended *y* to kill David.

³⁴Jonathan got up from the table in fierce anger; on that second day of the month he did not eat, because he was grieved at his father's shameful treatment of David.

³⁵In the morning Jonathan went out to the field for his meeting with David. He had a small boy with him, ³⁶and he said to the boy, "Run and find the arrows I shoot." As the boy ran, he shot an arrow beyond him. ³⁷When the boy came to the place where Jonathan's arrow had fallen, Jonathan called out after him, "Isn't the arrow beyond you?" ³⁸Then he shouted, "Hurry! Go quickly! Don't stop!" The boy picked up the arrow and returned to his master. ³⁹(The boy knew nothing of all this; only Jonathan and David knew.) ⁴⁰Then Jonathan gave his weapons to the boy and said, "Go, carry them back to town."

⁴¹After the boy had gone, David got up from the south side ˌof the stoneˌ and bowed down before Jonathan three times, with his face to the ground. Then they kissed each other and wept together—but David wept the most.

⁴²Jonathan said to David, "Go in peace, *z* for we have sworn friendship with each other in the name of the Lord, saying, 'The Lord is witness between you and me, and between your descendants and my descendants forever.'" Then David left, and Jonathan went back to the town.

4. Saul pursues David
David at Nob

21 David went to Nob, to Ahimelech the priest. Ahimelech trembled *a* when he met him, and asked, "Why are you alone? Why is no one with you?"

²David answered Ahimelech the priest, "The king charged me with a certain matter and said to me, 'No one is to know anything about your mission and your instructions.' As for my men, I have told them to meet me at a certain place. ³Now then, what do you have on hand? Give me five loaves of bread, or whatever you can find."

### Margin references:
20:26 *v* Lev 7:20-21; 15:5
20:28 *w* ver 6
20:32 *x* 1Sa 19:4; Mt 27:23
20:33 *y* ver 7; 1Sa 18:11,17
20:42 *z* 1Sa 1:17
21:1 *a* 1Sa 16:4

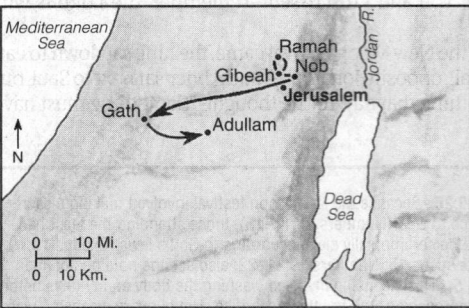

DAVID'S ESCAPE David learned of Saul's plans to kill him and fled to Samuel at Ramah. Returning to Gibeah to say good-bye to Jonathan, he then escaped to Nob, where he received food and a sword from the priest. He then fled to Gath in Philistine territory. When the Philistines became suspicious, he escaped to the cave of Adullam, where many men joined him.

20:31, 32 Saul was still trying to secure his throne for future generations even though he had already been told his dynasty would end with him (13:13, 14). Even worse, he was trying to do this by sinful human means, because he knew he would get no help from God. Jonathan could have made a move to become the next king by killing his rival, but he bypassed this opportunity because of his love for both God and David (23:16–18).

21:1ff This is the first time Ahimelech is mentioned. Either he was the Ahijah mentioned in 14:3, 18, or, more likely, he was Ahijah's successor. In either case, Ahimelech had to go against the law to give the consecrated bread to David because the bread was supposed to be given only to the priests (Leviticus 24:5–9). But Ahimelech put David's need and life ahead of religious ceremony and fed him the consecrated food. This upheld a higher law of love (Leviticus 19:18). Centuries later, Jesus would refer to this incident to show that God's laws should be applied with compassion. To do good and to save life is God's greater law (Matthew 12:1–8; Luke 6:1–5).

21:2 David lied to protect himself from Saul (21:10). Some excuse this lie because a war was going on, and it is the duty of a good soldier to deceive the enemy. But nowhere is David's lie

21:4
b Lev 24:8-9
c Mt 12:4

⁴But the priest answered David, "I don't have any ordinary bread *b* on hand; however, there is some consecrated *c* bread here—provided the men have kept themselves from women."

21:6
d Lev 24:8-9;
Mt 12:3-4

⁵David replied, "Indeed women have been kept from us, as usual whenever*a* I set out. The men's things *b* are holy even on missions that are not holy. How much more so today!" ⁶So the priest gave him the consecrated bread,*d* since there was no bread there except the bread of the Presence that had been removed from before the LORD and replaced by hot bread on the day it was taken away.

21:7
e 1Sa 22:9,22

⁷Now one of Saul's servants was there that day, detained before the LORD; he was Doeg*e* the Edomite, Saul's head shepherd.

⁸David asked Ahimelech, "Don't you have a spear or a sword here? I haven't brought my sword or any other weapon, because the king's business is urgent."

21:9
f 1Sa 17:51
g 1Sa 17:2

⁹The priest replied, "The sword *f* of Goliath the Philistine, whom you killed in the Valley of Elah,*g* is here; it is wrapped in a cloth behind the ephod. If you want it, take it; there is no sword here but that one."

David said, "There is none like it; give it to me."

a5 Or from us in the past few days since   *b5 Or bodies*

JONATHAN

Loyalty is one of life's most costly qualities; it is the most selfless part of love. To be loyal, you cannot live only for yourself. Loyal people not only stand by their commitments, they are willing to suffer for them. Jonathan is a shining example of loyalty. Sometimes he was forced to deal with conflicting loyalties: to his father, Saul, and to his friend David. His solution to that conflict teaches us both how to be loyal and what must guide loyalty. In Jonathan, truth always guided loyalty.

Jonathan realized that the source of truth was God, who demanded his ultimate loyalty. It was his relationship with God that gave Jonathan the ability to deal effectively with the complicated situations in his life. He was loyal to Saul because Saul was his father and the king. He was loyal to David because David was his friend. His loyalty to God guided him through the conflicting demands of his human relationships.

The conflicting demands of our relationships challenge us as well. If we attempt to settle these conflicts only at the human level, we will be constantly dealing with a sense of betrayal. But if we communicate to our friends that our ultimate loyalty is to God and his truth, many of our choices will be much clearer. The truth in his Word, the Bible, will bring light to our decisions. Do those closest to you know who has your greatest loyalty?

Strengths and accomplishments:	• Brave, loyal, and a natural leader • The closest friend David ever had • Did not put his personal well-being ahead of those he loved • Depended on God
Lessons from his life:	• Loyalty is one of the strongest parts of courage • An allegiance to God puts all other relationships in perspective • Great friendships are costly
Vital statistics:	• Occupation: Military leader • Relatives: Father: Saul. Mother: Ahinoam. Brothers: Malki-Shua, Abinadab, Ish-Bosheth (and possibly Ishvi). Sisters: Merab and Michal. Son: Mephibosheth.
Key verse:	"I grieve for you, Jonathan my brother; you were very dear to me. Your love for me was wonderful, more wonderful than that of women" (2 Samuel 1:26).

His story is told in 1 Samuel 13—31. He is also mentioned in 2 Samuel 9.

---

condoned. In fact, the opposite is true because his lie led to the death of 85 priests (22:9–19). David's small lie seemed harmless enough, but it led to tragedy. The Bible makes it very clear that lying is wrong (Leviticus 19:11). Lying, like every other sin, is serious in God's sight and may lead to all sorts of harmful consequences. Don't minimize or categorize sins. All sins must be avoided whether or not we can foresee their potential consequences.

21:5 The men's bodies were ceremonially clean because they had not had sexual intercourse during this journey. Therefore, the priest allowed them to eat the consecrated bread.

21:6 Once a week on the Sabbath, a priest entered the Holy Place in the tabernacle and placed 12 freshly baked loaves of bread on a small table. This bread, called the bread of the Presence, symbolized God's presence among his people as well as his loving care that met their physical needs. The bread that was replaced was to be eaten only by the priests on duty.

21:9 An ephod was a vest worn by the priest (see the second note on 2:18 for a more detailed explanation). David didn't know Goliath's sword was there probably because David was a young man when he killed the giant and he had spent much of his time at home.

David at Gath

¹⁰ That day David fled from Saul and went to Achish king of Gath. ¹¹ But the servants of Achish said to him, "Isn't this David, the king of the land? Isn't he the one they sing about in their dances:

> "'Saul has slain his thousands,
>   and David his tens of thousands'?"ʰ

¹² David took these words to heart and was very much afraid of Achish king of Gath. ¹³ So he pretended to be insaneⁱ in their presence; and while he was in their hands he acted like a madman, making marks on the doors of the gate and letting saliva run down his beard.

¹⁴ Achish said to his servants, "Look at the man! He is insane! Why bring him to me? ¹⁵ Am I so short of madmen that you have to bring this fellow here to carry on like this in front of me? Must this man come into my house?"

David at Adullam and Mizpah

22 David left Gath and escaped to the caveʲ of Adullam. When his brothers and his father's household heard about it, they went down to him there. ²All those who were in distress or in debt or discontented gatheredᵏ around him, and he became their leader. About four hundred men were with him.

³ From there David went to Mizpah in Moab and said to the king of Moab, "Would you let my father and mother come and stay with you until I learn what God will do for me?" ⁴ So he left them with the king of Moab, and they stayed with him as long as David was in the stronghold.

⁵ But the prophet Gadˡ said to David, "Do not stay in the stronghold. Go into the land of Judah." So David left and went to the forest of Hereth.

Saul Kills the Priests of Nob

⁶ Now Saul heard that David and his men had been discovered. And Saul, spear in hand, was seated under the tamarisk tree on the hill at Gibeah, with all his officials standing around him. ⁷ Saul said to them, "Listen, men of Benjamin! Will the son of Jesse give all of you fields and vineyards? Will he make all of you commandersᵐ of thousands and commanders of hundreds? ⁸ Is that why you have all conspired against me? No one tells me when my son makes a covenantⁿ with the son of Jesse. None of you is concerned about me or tells me that my son has incited my servant to lie in wait for me, as he does today."

⁹ But Doeg the Edomite, who was standing with Saul's officials, said, "I saw the son of Jesse come to Ahimelech son of Ahitub at Nob.ᵒ ¹⁰ Ahimelech inquired of the LORD for him; he also gave him provisionsᵖ and the sword of Goliath the Philistine."

¹¹ Then the king sent for the priest Ahimelech son of Ahitub and his father's whole family, who were the priests at Nob, and they all came to the king. ¹² Saul said, "Listen now, son of Ahitub."

21:11
ʰ 1Sa 18:7; 29:5

21:13
ⁱ Ps 34 Title

22:1
ʲ 2Sa 23:13

22:2
ᵏ 1Sa 25:13

22:5
ˡ 2Sa 24:11; 1Ch 21:9; 2Ch 29:25

22:7
ᵐ 1Sa 8:14

22:8
ⁿ 1Sa 18:3

22:9
ᵒ 1Sa 21:1

22:10
ᵖ 1Sa 21:6

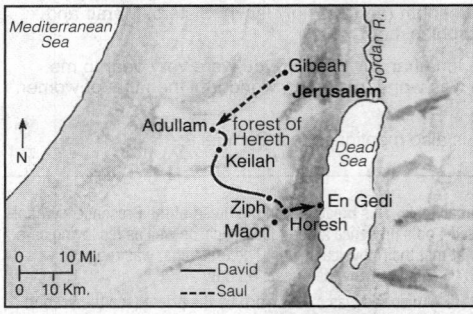

DAVID FLEES FROM SAUL David and his men attacked the Philistines at Keilah from the forest of Hereth. Saul came from Gibeah to attack David, but David escaped into the Desert of Ziph. At Horesh he met Jonathan, who encouraged him. Then he fled into the Desert of Maon and into the strongholds of En Gedi.

21:10–15 Gath was one of the five major Philistine cities. Why did the Philistines allow their archenemy, David, into their camp? The Philistines may have been initially happy to accept a defector who was a high military leader. Any enemy of Saul would have been a friend of theirs. They could not have known that David had been anointed Israel's next king (16:13). Soon, however, the Philistines became nervous about David's presence. After all, he had slain thousands of their people (18:7). David then protected himself by acting insane because it was the custom not to harm mentally unstable people.

22:2 Those in distress, in debt, or discontented joined David, who himself was an outlaw. These people were outcasts themselves and could only improve their lot by helping David become king. David's control over this band of men again shows his resourcefulness and ability to lead and motivate others. It is difficult enough to build an army out of good men, but it takes even greater leadership to build one out of the kind of men that followed David. This group eventually formed the core of his military leadership (2 Samuel 23:8ff).

22:7, 8 Apparently Saul's key officers were from the tribe of Benjamin, just as he was. David was from the neighboring tribe of Judah. Saul was appealing to tribal loyalty to maintain his hold on the throne.

"Yes, my lord," he answered.

¹³Saul said to him, "Why have you conspired against me, you and the son of Jesse, giving him bread and a sword and inquiring of God for him, so that he has rebelled against me and lies in wait for me, as he does today?"

¹⁴Ahimelech answered the king, "Who of all your servants is as loyal as David, the king's son-in-law, captain of your bodyguard and highly respected in your household? ¹⁵Was that day the first time I inquired of God for him? Of course not! Let not the king accuse your servant or any of his father's family, for your servant knows nothing at all about this whole affair."

¹⁶But the king said, "You will surely die, Ahimelech, you and your father's whole family."

22:17
ᵠEx 1:17

¹⁷Then the king ordered the guards at his side: "Turn and kill the priests of the LORD, because they too have sided with David. They knew he was fleeing, yet they did not tell me."

But the king's officials were not willingᵠ to raise a hand to strike the priests of the LORD.

22:18
ʳ1Sa 2:18,31

¹⁸The king then ordered Doeg, "You turn and strike down the priests." So Doeg the Edomite turned and struck them down. That day he killed eighty-five men who wore the linen ephod.ʳ ¹⁹He also put to the sword Nob, the town of the priests, with its men and women, its children and infants, and its cattle, donkeys and sheep.

22:20
ˢ1Sa 23:6,9
ᵗ1Sa 2:32
22:22
ᵘ1Sa 21:7
22:23
ᵛ1Ki 2:26

²⁰But Abiathar,ˢ a son of Ahimelech son of Ahitub, escaped and fled to join David.ᵗ ²¹He told David that Saul had killed the priests of the LORD. ²²Then David said to Abiathar: "That day, when Doegᵘ the Edomite was there, I knew he would be sure to tell Saul. I am responsible for the death of your father's whole family. ²³Stay with me; don't be afraid; the man who is seeking your lifeᵛ is seeking mine also. You will be safe with me."

David Saves Keilah

23:1
ʷJos 15:44
23:2
ˣver 4,12

23 When David was told, "Look, the Philistines are fighting against Keilahʷ and are looting the threshing floors," ²he inquiredˣ of the LORD, saying, "Shall I go and attack these Philistines?"

The LORD answered him, "Go, attack the Philistines and save Keilah."

³But David's men said to him, "Here in Judah we are afraid. How much more, then, if we go to Keilah against the Philistine forces!"

⁴Once again David inquired of the LORD, and the LORD answered him, "Go down to Keilah, for I am going to give the Philistines into your hand." ⁵So David and his men went to Keilah, fought the Philistines and carried off their livestock. He inflicted heavy losses on the Philistines and saved the people of Keilah.

23:6
ʸ1Sa 22:20

⁶(Now Abiatharʸ son of Ahimelech had brought the ephod down with him when he fled to David at Keilah.)

22:18 Why would Saul have his own priests killed? Saul suspected a conspiracy among Jonathan, David, and the priests. His suspicion came from Doeg's report of seeing David talking to Ahimelech, the high priest, and receiving food and a weapon from him (22:9, 10). Saul's action showed his mental and emotional instability and how far he had strayed from God.

By destroying everything in Nob, Saul was placing the city under the ban (declaring it to be utterly destroyed) described in Deuteronomy 13:12–17, which was supposed to be used only in cases of idolatry and rebellion against God. But it was Saul, not the priests, who had rebelled against God.

22:18, 19 Why did God allow 85 innocent priests and their families to be killed? Their deaths served to dramatize to the nation how a king could become an evil tyrant. Where were Saul's advisers? Where were the elders of Israel? Sometimes God allows evil to develop to teach us not to let evil systems flourish. Serving God is not a ticket to wealth, success, or health. God does not promise to protect good people from evil in this world, but he does promise that ultimately all evil will be abolished. Those who have remained faithful through their trials will experience great rewards in the age to come (Matthew 5:11, 12; Revelation 21:1–7; 22:1–21).

22:20 Abiathar escaped to David with an ephod (23:6), a priestly garment containing the Urim and Thummim, two objects David used to consult God. The ephod was probably the only symbol of the priesthood that survived Saul's raid and made it into David's camp (23:6). Saul destroyed Israel's

priesthood, but when David became king, he installed Abiathar as the new high priest. Abiathar remained in that position during David's entire reign.

23:1 Threshing floors were open, circular areas where the grain kernels were separated from their husks. (In order to separate the grain from the husk, farmers would toss their grain into the air. The wind would blow the husks away, leaving only the grain. This process is called *winnowing*.) By looting the threshing floors, the Philistines were robbing Keilah's citizens of all their food supplies. (For more on threshing, see the note on Ruth 3:2.)

23:2 Through the Urim and Thummim that Abiathar the priest brought (23:6), David sought the Lord's guidance *before* he took action. He listened to God's directions and then proceeded accordingly. Rather than trying to find God's will *after* the fact or having to ask God to undo the results of our hasty decisions, we should take time to discern God's will beforehand. We can hear him speak through the counsel of others, his Word, and the leading of his Spirit in our hearts, as well as through circumstances.

23:6 An ephod was a sleeveless linen vest worn by priests. The high priest's ephod was brightly colored and had a breastplate with 12 gemstones representing each tribe. The Urim and Thummim were kept in a pouch of the high priest's ephod. (See the note on 2:18 for a more detailed explanation of the ephod.)

Saul Pursues David

7 Saul was told that David had gone to Keilah, and he said, "God has handed him over to me, for David has imprisoned himself by entering a town with gates and bars." 8 And Saul called up all his forces for battle, to go down to Keilah to besiege David and his men.

9 When David learned that Saul was plotting against him, he said to Abiathar z the priest, "Bring the ephod." 10 David said, "O Lᴏʀᴅ, God of Israel, your servant has heard definitely that Saul plans to come to Keilah and destroy the town on account of me. 11 Will the citizens of Keilah surrender me to him? Will Saul come down, as your servant has heard? O Lᴏʀᴅ, God of Israel, tell your servant."

And the Lᴏʀᴅ said, "He will."

12 Again David asked, "Will the citizens of Keilah surrender me and my men to Saul?"

And the Lᴏʀᴅ said, "They will."

13 So David and his men, a about six hundred in number, left Keilah and kept moving from place to place. When Saul was told that David had escaped from Keilah, he did not go there.

14 David stayed in the desert strongholds and in the hills of the Desert of Ziph. Day after day Saul searched b for him, but God did not give David into his hands.

15 While David was at Horesh in the Desert of Ziph, he learned that Saul had come out to take his life. 16 And Saul's son Jonathan went to David at Horesh and helped him find strength in God. 17 "Don't be afraid," he said. "My father Saul will not lay a hand on you. You will be king c over Israel, and I will be second to you. Even my father Saul knows this." 18 The two of them made a covenant d before the Lᴏʀᴅ. Then Jonathan went home, but David remained at Horesh.

19 The Ziphites e went up to Saul at Gibeah and said, "Is not David hiding among us in the strongholds at Horesh, on the hill of Hakilah, south of Jeshimon? 20 Now, O king, come down whenever it pleases you to do so, and we will be responsible for handing him over to the king."

21 Saul replied, "The Lᴏʀᴅ bless you for your concern f for me. 22 Go and make further preparation. Find out where David usually goes and who has seen him there. They tell me he is very crafty. 23 Find out about all the hiding places he uses and come back to me with definite information. a Then I will go with you; if he is in the area, I will track him down among all the clans of Judah."

24 So they set out and went to Ziph ahead of Saul. Now David and his men were in the Desert of Maon, g in the Arabah south of Jeshimon. 25 Saul and his men began the search, and when David was told about it, he went down to the rock and stayed in the Desert of Maon. When Saul heard this, he went into the Desert of Maon in pursuit of David.

26 Saul h was going along one side of the mountain, and David and his men were on the other side, hurrying to get away from Saul. As Saul and his forces were closing in on David and his men to capture them, 27 a messenger came to Saul, saying, "Come quickly! The Philistines are raiding the land." 28 Then Saul broke off his pursuit of David and went to meet the Philistines. That is why they call this place Sela Hammahlekoth. b 29 And David went up from there and lived in the strongholds of En Gedi. i

David Spares Saul's Life

24 After Saul returned from pursuing the Philistines, he was told, "David is in the Desert of En Gedi. i" 2 So Saul took three thousand chosen men from all Israel and set out to look for David and his men near the Crags of the Wild Goats.

3 He came to the sheep pens along the way; a cave was there, and Saul went in to relieve k

a 23 Or *me at Nacon*   b 28 *Sela Hammahlekoth* means *rock of parting.*

23:9 z 1Sa 30:7

23:13 a 1Sa 22:2; 25:13

23:14 b Ps 54:3-4

23:17 c 1Sa 24:20

23:18 d 1Sa 18:3; 20:16,42; 2Sa 21:7

23:19 e 1Sa 26:1

23:21 f 1Sa 22:8

23:24 g Jos 15:55; 1Sa 25:2

23:26 h Ps 17:9

23:29 i 2Ch 20:2

24:1 j 1Sa 23:28-29

24:3 k Jdg 3:24

23:7 When Saul heard that David was trapped in a walled town (one with gates and bars), he thought God was putting David at his mercy. Saul wanted to kill David so badly that he would have interpreted any sign as God's approval to move ahead with his plan. Had Saul known God better, he would have known what God wanted and would not have misread the situation as God's approval for murder.

Not every opportunity is sent from God. We may want something so much that we assume any opportunity to obtain it is of divine origin. As we see from Saul's case, however, this may not be true. An opportunity to do something against God's will can never be from God because God does not tempt us. When opportunities come your way, double-check your motives. Make sure you are following God's desires, and not just your own.

23:16–18 This may have been the last time David and Jonathan were together. As true friends they were more than just companions who enjoyed each other's company. They encouraged each other's faith in God and trusted each other with their deepest thoughts and closest confidences. These are the marks of true friendship.

24:3 David and his 600 men found the Desert of En Gedi a good place to hide because of the many caves in the area. These caves himself. David and his men were far back in the cave. [4]The men said, "This is the day the LORD spoke of when he said a to you, 'I will give your enemy into your hands for you to deal with as you wish.'" Then David crept up unnoticed and cut off a corner of Saul's robe.

24:5
l 2Sa 24:10
24:6
m 1Sa 26:11

[5]Afterward, David was conscience-stricken *l* for having cut off a corner of his robe. [6]He said to his men, "The LORD forbid that I should do such a thing to my master, the LORD's anointed, *m* or lift my hand against him; for he is the anointed of the LORD." [7]With these words David rebuked his men and did not allow them to attack Saul. And Saul left the cave and went his way.

[8]Then David went out of the cave and called out to Saul, "My lord the king!" When Saul looked behind him, David bowed down and prostrated himself with his face to the ground. [9]He said to Saul, "Why do you listen when men say, 'David is bent on harming you'? [10]This day you have seen with your own eyes how the LORD delivered you into my hands in the cave. Some urged me to kill you, but I spared you; I said, 'I will not lift my hand against my master, because he is the LORD's anointed.'

24:11
n 1Sa 26:20

[11]See, my father, look at this piece of your robe in my hand! I cut off the corner of your robe but did not kill you. Now understand and recognize that I am not guilty of wrongdoing or rebellion. I have not wronged you, but you are hunting *n* me down to take my life. [12]May the LORD judge between you and me. And may the LORD

24:12
o Jdg 11:27
24:14
p 1Sa 17:43
24:15
q ver 12
r Ps 35:1,23
24:16
s 1Sa 26:17
24:17
t Ge 38:26
u Mt 5:44
24:18
v 1Sa 26:23

avenge *o* the wrongs you have done to me, but my hand will not touch you. [13]As the old saying goes, 'From evildoers come evil deeds,' so my hand will not touch you.

[14]"Against whom has the king of Israel come out? Whom are you pursuing? A dead dog? *p* A flea? [15]May the LORD be our judge *q* and decide between us. May he consider my cause and uphold *r* it; may he vindicate me by delivering me from your hand."

[16]When David finished saying this, Saul asked, "Is that your voice, *s* David my son?" And he wept aloud. [17]"You are more righteous than I," *t* he said. "You have treated me well, *u* but I have treated you badly. [18]You have just now told me of the good you did to me; the LORD delivered *v*

a 4 Or "Today the LORD is saying

LIFE OF DAVID VERSUS LIFE OF SAUL

Life of David	Life of Saul
David was God's kind of king (2 Samuel 7:8–16)	Saul was man's kind of king (1 Samuel 10:23, 24)
David was a man after God's heart (Acts 13:22)	Saul was a man after people's praise (1 Samuel 18:6–8)
David's kingship was eternal (through Jesus) (2 Samuel 7:29)	Saul's kingship was rejected (1 Samuel 15:23)
David was kind and benevolent (2 Samuel 9; 1 Chronicles 19:2)	Saul was cruel (1 Samuel 20:30–34; 22:11–19)
David was forgiving (1 Samuel 26)	Saul was unforgiving (1 Samuel 14:44; 18:9)
David repented (2 Samuel 12:13; 24:10)	When confronted, Saul lied (1 Samuel 15:10–31)
David was courageous (1 Samuel 17; 1 Chronicles 18)	Saul was fearful (1 Samuel 17:11; 18:12)
David was at peace with God (Psalms 4:8; 37:11)	Saul was separated from God (1 Samuel 16:14)

---

were used by local people for housing and as tombs. For David's men they were places of refuge. These caves can still be seen today. Some are large enough to hold thousands of people.

24:4 Scripture does not record that God made any such statement to David or his men. The men were probably offering their own interpretation of some previous event such as David's anointing (16:13) or Jonathan's prediction that David would become king (23:17). When David's men saw Saul entering their cave, they wrongly assumed that this was an indication from God that they should act.

24:5, 6 David had great respect for Saul, in spite of the fact that Saul was trying to kill him. Although Saul was sinning and rebelling against God, David still respected the position he held as God's anointed king. David knew he would one day be king, and he also knew it was not right to strike down the man God had

placed on the throne. If he assassinated Saul, he would be setting a precedent for his own opponents to remove him some day.

Romans 13:1–7 teaches that God has placed the government and its leaders in power. We may not know why, but, like David, we are to respect the positions and roles of those to whom God has given authority. There is one exception, however. Because God is our highest authority, we should not allow a leader to pressure us to violate God's law.

24:16–19 The means we use to accomplish a goal are just as important as the goal we are trying to accomplish. David's goal was to become king, so his men urged him to kill Saul when he had the chance. David's refusal was not an example of cowardice but of courage—the courage to stand against the group and do what he knew was right. Don't compromise your moral standards by giving in to group pressure or taking the easy way out.

me into your hands, but you did not kill me. 19When a man finds his enemy, does he let him get away unharmed? May the LORD reward you well for the way you treated me today. 20I know that you will surely be king and that the kingdom of Israel will be established in your hands. 21Now swear w to me by the LORD that you will not cut off my descendants or wipe out my name from my father's family."

22So David gave his oath to Saul. Then Saul returned home, but David and his men went up to the stronghold. x

David, Nabal and Abigail

25 Now Samuel died, y and all Israel assembled and mourned z for him; and they buried him at his home in Ramah.

Then David moved down into the Desert of Maon. a 2A certain man in Maon, a who had property there at Carmel, was very wealthy. He had a thousand goats and three thousand sheep, which he was shearing in Carmel. 3His name was Nabal and his wife's name was Abigail. She was an intelligent and beautiful woman, but her husband, a Calebite, was surly and mean in his dealings.

4While David was in the desert, he heard that Nabal was shearing sheep. 5So he sent ten young men and said to them, "Go up to Nabal at Carmel and greet him in my name. 6Say to him: 'Long life to you! Good health to you and your household! And good health to all that is yours! b

7"'Now I hear that it is sheep-shearing time. When your shepherds were with us, we did not mistreat c them, and the whole time they were at Carmel nothing of theirs was missing. 8Ask your own servants and they will tell you. Therefore be favorable toward my young men, since we come at a festive time. Please give your servants and your son David whatever d you can find for them.'"

9When David's men arrived, they gave Nabal this message in David's name. Then they waited.

10Nabal answered David's servants, "Who e is this David? Who is this son of Jesse? Many servants are breaking away from their masters these days. 11Why should I take my bread and water, and the meat I have slaughtered for my shearers, and give it to men coming from who knows where?"

12David's men turned around and went back. When they arrived, they reported every word. 13David said to his men, "Put on your swords!" So they put on their swords, and David put on his. About four hundred men went up with David, while two hundred stayed with the supplies. f

14One of the servants told Nabal's wife Abigail: "David sent messengers from the desert to give our master his greetings, but he hurled insults at them. 15Yet these men were very good to us. They did not mistreat g us, and the whole time we were out in the fields near them nothing was missing. 16Night and day they were a wall h around us all the time we were herding our sheep near them. 17Now think it over and see what you can do, because disaster is hanging over our master and his whole household. He is such a wicked man that no one can talk to him."

18Abigail lost no time. She took two hundred loaves of bread, two skins of wine, five dressed sheep, five seahs b of roasted grain, a hundred cakes of raisins and two hundred cakes of pressed figs, and loaded them on donkeys. 19Then she told her servants, "Go on ahead; i I'll follow you." But she did not tell her husband Nabal.

a *1 Some Septuagint manuscripts; Hebrew* Paran   b *18 That is, probably about a bushel (about 37 liters)*

24:21
w Ge 21:23;
2Sa 21:1-9

24:22
x 1Sa 23:29

25:1
y 1Sa 28:3
z Dt 34:8

25:2
a Jos 15:55

25:6
b 1Ch 12:18

25:7
c ver 15
25:8
d Ne 8:10

25:10
e Jdg 9:28

25:13
f 1Sa 30:24

25:15
g ver 7

25:16
h Ex 14:22

25:19
i Ge 32:20

24:21, 22 David kept his promise—he never took revenge on Saul's family or descendants. Most of Saul's sons were killed later, however, by the Philistines (31:2) and the Gibeonites (2 Samuel 21:1–14). David had promised to be kind to the descendants of Saul's son Jonathan (20:14, 15), and he kept this promise when he invited Mephibosheth to live in his palace (2 Samuel 9).

25:1 Saul was king, but Samuel had been the nation's spiritual leader. As a young boy and an older man, Samuel was always careful to listen to (3:10; 9:14–17) and obey (3:21; 10:1, 2) the

Lord. With Samuel gone, Israel would be without this spiritual leadership until David became king. (For more on Samuel, read his Profile in chapter 8, p. 403.)

25:2–11 Nabal rudely refused David's request to feed his 600 men. If we sympathize with Nabal, it is because customs are so different today. First, simple hospitality demanded that travelers—any number of them—be fed. Nabal was very rich and could have easily afforded to meet David's request. Second, David wasn't asking for a handout. He and his men had been protecting Nabal's work force, and part of Nabal's prosperity was due to David's vigilance. We should be generous with those who protect us and help us prosper, even if we are not obligated to do so by law or custom.

25:21
/Ps 109:5

25:22
k 1Sa 3:17; 20:13
/1Ki 14:10

25:26
m 2Sa 18:32

25:27
n Ge 33:11;
1Sa 30:26

25:28
o 2Sa 7:11,26
p 1Sa 18:17
q 1Sa 24:11

25:29
r Jer 10:18

25:32
s Ex 18:10

25:33
t ver 26

20As she came riding her donkey into a mountain ravine, there were David and his men descending toward her, and she met them. 21David had just said, "It's been useless—all my watching over this fellow's property in the desert so that nothing of his was missing. He has paid/ me back evil for good. 22May God deal with David,a be it ever so severely,k if by morning I leave alive one male/ of all who belong to him!"

23When Abigail saw David, she quickly got off her donkey and bowed down before David with her face to the ground. 24She fell at his feet and said: "My lord, let the blame be on me alone. Please let your servant speak to you; hear what your servant has to say. 25May my lord pay no attention to that wicked man Nabal. He is just like his name—his name is Fool, and folly goes with him. But as for me, your servant, I did not see the men my master sent.

26"Now since the LORD has kept you, my master, from bloodshed and from avenging yourself with your own hands, as surely as the LORD lives and as you live, may your enemies and all who intend to harm my master be like Nabal. m 27And let this gift, n which your servant has brought to my master, be given to the men who follow you. 28Please forgive your servant's offense, for the LORD will certainly make a lasting o dynasty for my master, because he fights the LORD's battles. p Let no wrongdoing q be found in you as long as you live. 29Even though someone is pursuing you to take your life, the life of my master will be bound securely in the bundle of the living by the LORD your God. But the lives of your enemies he will hurl r away as from the pocket of a sling. 30When the LORD has done for my master every good thing he promised concerning him and has appointed him leader over Israel, 31my master will not have on his conscience the staggering burden of needless bloodshed or of having avenged himself. And when the LORD has brought my master success, remember your servant."

32David said to Abigail, "Praises be to the LORD, the God of Israel, who has sent you today to meet me. 33May you be blessed for your good judgment and for keeping me from bloodshed t this day and from avenging myself with my own hands. 34Otherwise, as surely as the

a 22 Some Septuagint manuscripts; Hebrew with David's enemies

---

ABIGAIL

Some men don't deserve their wives. Abigail was probably the best woman Nabal could afford, and he got even more than he bargained for when he arranged to marry her. She was beautiful and more suited than he was to manage his wealth. But Nabal took this wife for granted.

In spite of his shortcomings, Nabal's household did what they could to keep him out of trouble. This loyalty must have been inspired by Abigail. Although her culture and her husband placed a low value on her, she made the most of her skills and opportunities. David was impressed with her abilities, and when Nabal died, he married her.

Abigail was an effective counselor to both of the men in her life, working hard to prevent them from making rash moves. By her swift action and skillful negotiation, she kept David from taking vengeance upon Nabal. She saw the big picture and left plenty of room for God to get involved.

Do you, like Abigail, look beyond the present crisis to the big picture? Do you use your skills to promote peace? Are you loyal without being blind? What challenge or responsibility do you face today that needs a person under God's control?

Strengths and accomplishments:	• Sensible and capable • A persuasive speaker, able to see beyond herself
Lessons from her life:	• Life's tough situations can bring out the best in people • One does not need a prestigious title to play a significant role
Vital statistics:	• Where: Carmel • Occupation: Homemaker • Relatives: First husband: Nabal. Second husband: David. Son: Kileab (Daniel). • Contemporaries: Saul, Michal, Ahinoam
Key verses:	"David said to Abigail, 'Praise be to the LORD, the God of Israel, who has sent you today to meet me. May you be blessed for your good judgment and for keeping me from bloodshed this day and from avenging myself with my own hands'" (1 Samuel 25:32, 33).

Her story is told in 1 Samuel 25—2 Samuel 2. She is also mentioned in 1 Chronicles 3:1.

25:24 David was in no mood to listen when he set out for Nabal's property (25:13, 22). Nevertheless, he stopped to hear what Abigail had to say. If he had ignored her, he would have been guilty of taking vengeance into his own hands. No matter how right we think we are, we must always be careful to stop and listen to others. The extra time and effort can save us pain and trouble in the long run.

LORD, the God of Israel, lives, who has kept me from harming you, if you had not come quickly to meet me, not one male belonging to Nabal would have been left alive by daybreak."

35 Then David accepted from her hand what she had brought him and said, "Go home in peace. I have heard your words and granted *u* your request."

36 When Abigail went to Nabal, he was in the house holding a banquet like that of a king. He was in high spirits and very drunk. So she told him nothing until daybreak. 37 Then in the morning, when Nabal was sober, his wife told him all these things, and his heart failed him and he became like a stone. 38 About ten days later, the LORD struck Nabal and he died.

39 When David heard that Nabal was dead, he said, "Praise be to the LORD, who has upheld my cause against Nabal for treating me with contempt. He has kept his servant from doing wrong and has brought Nabal's wrongdoing down on his own head."

Then David sent word to Abigail, asking her to become his wife. 40 His servants went to Carmel and said to Abigail, "David has sent us to you to take you to become his wife."

41 She bowed down with her face to the ground and said, "Here is your maidservant, ready to serve you and wash the feet of my master's servants." 42 Abigail quickly got on a donkey and, attended by her five maids, went with David's messengers and became his wife. 43 David had also married Ahinoam *v* of Jezreel, and they both were his wives. *w* 44 But Saul had given his daughter Michal, David's wife, to Paltiel *a x* son of Laish, who was from Gallim. *y*

David Again Spares Saul's Life

26 The Ziphites *z* went to Saul at Gibeah and said, "Is not David hiding on the hill of Hakilah, which faces Jeshimon?"

2 So Saul went down to the Desert of Ziph, with his three thousand chosen men of Israel, to search there for David. 3 Saul made his camp beside the road on the hill of Hakilah facing Jeshimon, but David stayed in the desert. When he saw that Saul had followed him there, 4 he sent out scouts and learned that Saul had definitely arrived. *b*

5 Then David set out and went to the place where Saul had camped. He saw where Saul and Abner *a* son of Ner, the commander of the army, had lain down. Saul was lying inside the camp, with the army encamped around him.

6 David then asked Ahimelech the Hittite and Abishai son of Zeruiah, *b* Joab's brother, "Who will go down into the camp with me to Saul?"

"I'll go with you," said Abishai.

7 So David and Abishai went to the army by night, and there was Saul, lying asleep inside the camp with his spear stuck in the ground near his head. Abner and the soldiers were lying around him.

8 Abishai said to David, "Today God has delivered your enemy into your hands. Now let me pin him to the ground with one thrust of my spear; I won't strike him twice."

a 44 Hebrew Palti, a variant of Paltiel *b 4 Or had come to Nacon*

25:35
u Ge 19:21;
1Sa 20:42;
2Ki 5:19

25:43
v Jos 15:56
w 1Sa 27:3

25:44
x 2Sa 3:15
y Isa 10:30

26:1
z 1Sa 23:19

26:5
a 1Sa 17:55

26:6
b 1Ch 2:16

25:36 Because Nabal was drunk, Abigail waited until morning to tell him what she had done. Abigail knew that Nabal, in his drunkenness, may not have understood her or may have reacted foolishly. When discussing difficult matters with people, especially family members, timing is everything. Ask God for wisdom to know the best time for confrontation and for bringing up touchy subjects.

25:44 The story of David and Michal does not end here. (See 2 Samuel 3:12–16 for the next episode.)

26:5–9 Abishai showed great courage when he volunteered to go into Saul's camp with David. In the heat of emotion, Abishai wanted to kill Saul, but David restrained him. Although Abishai was only trying to protect David, his leader, David could not hurt Saul because of his respect for Saul's authority and position as God's anointed king. Abishai may have disagreed with David, but he also respected the one in authority over him. Eventually he became the greatest warrior in David's army (2 Samuel 23:18, 19).

26:8ff The strongest moral decisions are the ones we make before temptation strikes. David was determined to follow God and this carried over into his decision not to murder God's anointed king, Saul, even when his men and the circumstances seemed to make it a feasible option. Who would you have been like in such a situation—David or David's men? To be like David and follow God, we must realize that we can't do wrong in order to execute justice. Even when our closest friends counsel us to do something that seems right, we must always put God's commands first.

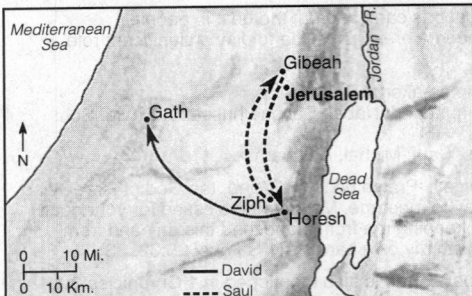

SAUL CHASES DAVID The men of Ziph again betrayed David to Saul, who was in his palace in Gibeah. Saul took 3,000 troops to the area around Horesh in order to find David. David could have killed Saul, but he refused. Saul, feeling foolish at David's kindness, returned to Gibeah, and David went to Gath.

26:9
c 2Sa 1:14

26:10
d 1Sa 25:38
e Dt 31:14
f 1Sa 31:6

26:12
g Ge 2:21; 15:12

26:17
h 1Sa 24:16

26:18
i 1Sa 24:9,11-14

26:19
j 2Sa 16:11

26:20
k 1Sa 24:14

26:21
l 1Sa 15:24
m 1Sa 24:17

⁹But David said to Abishai, "Don't destroy him! Who can lay a hand on the LORD's anointed *c* and be guiltless? ¹⁰As surely as the LORD lives," he said, "the LORD himself will strike *d* him; either his time *e* will come and he will die, *f* or he will go into battle and perish. ¹¹But the LORD forbid that I should lay a hand on the LORD's anointed. Now get the spear and water jug that are near his head, and let's go."

¹²So David took the spear and water jug near Saul's head, and they left. No one saw or knew about it, nor did anyone wake up. They were all sleeping, because the LORD had put them into a deep sleep. *g*

¹³Then David crossed over to the other side and stood on top of the hill some distance away; there was a wide space between them. ¹⁴He called out to the army and to Abner son of Ner, "Aren't you going to answer me, Abner?"

Abner replied, "Who are you who calls to the king?"

¹⁵David said, "You're a man, aren't you? And who is like you in Israel? Why didn't you guard your lord the king? Someone came to destroy your lord the king. ¹⁶What you have done is not good. As surely as the LORD lives, you and your men deserve to die, because you did not guard your master, the LORD's anointed. Look around you. Where are the king's spear and water jug that were near his head?"

¹⁷Saul recognized David's voice and said, "Is that your voice, *h* David my son?"

David replied, "Yes it is, my lord the king." ¹⁸And he added, "Why is my lord pursuing his servant? What have I done, and what wrong *i* am I guilty of? ¹⁹Now let my lord the king listen to his servant's words. If the LORD has incited you against me, then may he accept an offering. *j* If, however, men have done it, may they be cursed before the LORD! They have now driven me from my share in the LORD's inheritance and have said, 'Go, serve other gods.' ²⁰Now do not let my blood fall to the ground far from the presence of the LORD. The king of Israel has come out to look for a flea *k*—as one hunts a partridge in the mountains."

²¹Then Saul said, "I have sinned. *l* Come back, David my son. Because you considered my life precious *m* today, I will not try to harm you again. Surely I have acted like a fool and have erred greatly."

²²"Here is the king's spear," David answered. "Let one of your young men come over and get it. ²³The LORD rewards every man for his righteousness and faithfulness. The LORD delivered you into my hands today, but I would not lay a hand on the LORD's anointed. ²⁴As surely as I valued your life today, so may the LORD value my life and deliver me from all trouble."

²⁵Then Saul said to David, "May you be blessed, my son David; you will do great things and surely triumph."

So David went on his way, and Saul returned home.

5. Saul's defeat and death
David Among the Philistines

27 But David thought to himself, "One of these days I will be destroyed by the hand of Saul. The best thing I can do is to escape to the land of the Philistines. Then Saul will give up searching for me anywhere in Israel, and I will slip out of his hand."

26:9 Why did David refuse to kill Saul? God had placed Saul in power and had not yet removed him. David did not want to run ahead of God's timing. We are in similar situations when we have leaders in church or government who are unfaithful or incompetent. It may be easy for us to criticize or move against a leader oblivious to God's hidden purposes and timing. Determining not to do wrong, David left Saul's destiny in God's hands. While we should not ignore sin or sit back and allow evil leaders to carry on their wickedness, neither should we take actions that are against God's laws. We should work for righteousness while trusting God.

26:15, 16 David could have killed Saul and Abner, but he would have disobeyed God and set into motion possible cycles of vengeance and assassination. Instead, he took a spear and water jug, showing that he could have killed the king, but had not done it. And he made the point that he had great respect for both God and God's anointed king. When you need to make a point, look for creative, God-honoring ways to do so. It will have a more significant impact.

26:25 Saul had opportunities to kill David, but he never did. Why? First, every time David and Saul were face to face, David did something generous for Saul. The king did not want to respond to David's kindness with cruelty in front of all his men. Second, David had a large following in Israel. By killing him, Saul would risk his hold on the kingdom. Third, God had appointed David to become king of Israel and was protecting him.

27:1–3 For the second time, David sought refuge from Saul in Philistine territory (21:10–15). The once-great conqueror of Philistines now had permission to live under the protection of King Achish of Gath. Previously David had acted insane in front of this king. Evidently Achish had forgotten that incident or had overlooked it in light of David's current situation. Achish certainly would have known about the split between Saul and David and would have been glad to shelter this Israelite traitor. In return, Achish would have expected military support from David and his 600 warriors. David further strengthened his position with Achish by leading Achish to believe that he was conducting raids on Israel and by pretending loyalty to the Philistine ruler.

2 So David and the six hundred men[n] with him left and went[o] over to Achish son of Maoch king of Gath. 3 David and his men settled in Gath with Achish. Each man had his family with him, and David had his two wives:[p] Ahinoam of Jezreel and Abigail of Carmel, the widow of Nabal. 4 When Saul was told that David had fled to Gath, he no longer searched for him.

5 Then David said to Achish, "If I have found favor in your eyes, let a place be assigned to me in one of the country towns, that I may live there. Why should your servant live in the royal city with you?"

6 So on that day Achish gave him Ziklag,[q] and it has belonged to the kings of Judah ever since. 7 David lived in Philistine territory a year and four months.

8 Now David and his men went up and raided the Geshurites, the Girzites and the Amalekites.[r] (From ancient times these peoples had lived in the land extending to Shur and Egypt.) 9 Whenever David attacked an area, he did not leave a man or woman alive, but took sheep and cattle, donkeys and camels, and clothes. Then he returned to Achish.

10 When Achish asked, "Where did you go raiding today?" David would say, "Against the Negev of Judah" or "Against the Negev of Jerahmeel[s]" or "Against the Negev of the Kenites.[t]" 11 He did not leave a man or woman alive to be brought to Gath, for he thought, "They might inform on us and say, 'This is what David did.'" And such was his practice as long as he lived in Philistine territory. 12 Achish trusted David and said to himself, "He has become so odious to his people, the Israelites, that he will be my servant forever."

Saul and the Witch of Endor

28 In those days the Philistines gathered[u] their forces to fight against Israel. Achish said to David, "You must understand that you and your men will accompany me in the army."

2 David said, "Then you will see for yourself what your servant can do."

Achish replied, "Very well, I will make you my bodyguard for life."

3 Now Samuel was dead,[v] and all Israel had mourned for him and buried him in his own town of Ramah. Saul had expelled the mediums and spiritists[w] from the land.

4 The Philistines assembled and came and set up camp at Shunem,[x] while Saul gathered all the Israelites and set up camp at Gilboa.[y] 5 When Saul saw the Philistine army, he was afraid; terror filled his heart. 6 He inquired[z] of the Lord, but the Lord did not answer him by dreams or Urim[a] or prophets. 7 Saul then said to his attendants, "Find me a woman who is a medium, so I may go and inquire of her."

27:2
n 1Sa 25:13
o 1Sa 21:10

27:3
p 1Sa 25:43

27:6
q Jos 15:31; 19:5

27:8
r 1Sa 15:7-8

27:10
s 1Ch 2:9,25
t Jdg 1:16

28:1
u 1Sa 29:1

28:3
v 1Sa 25:1
w Lev 19:31;
Dt 18:10-11

28:4
x 2Ki 4:8
y 1Sa 31:1,3

28:6
z 1Ch 10:13-14;
Pr 1:28
a Ex 28:30

27:4 Saul finally stopped pursuing David. His army was not strong enough to invade Philistine territory just to seek one man. Besides, the immediate threat to Saul's throne was gone while David was out of the country.

27:5–7 Gath was one of five principal cities in Philistia, and Achish was one of five corulers. David may have wanted to move out of this important city to avoid potential skirmishes or attacks upon his family. He may also have wanted to escape the close scrutiny of the Philistine officials. Achish let David move to Ziklag, where he lived until Saul's death (2 Samuel 2:1).

27:8, 9 David probably conducted these guerrilla-style raids because these three tribes were known for their surprise attacks and cruel treatment of innocent people. These desert tribes were a danger not just to the Philistines, but especially to the Israelites, the people David would one day lead.

27:10–12 Was David wrong in falsely reporting his activities to Achish? No doubt David was lying, but he may have felt his strategy was justified in a time of war against a pagan enemy. David knew he would one day be Israel's king. The Philistines were still his enemies, but this was an excellent place to hide from Saul. When Achish asked David to go into battle against Israel, David agreed, once again pretending loyalty to the Philistines (28:1ff). Whether he would have actually fought Saul's army we can't know, but we can be sure that his ultimate loyalty was to God and not to Achish or Saul.

28:1, 2 Achish's request put David in a difficult position. To refuse to help Achish fight the Israelites would give away David's loyalty to Israel and endanger the lives of his soldiers and family. But to fight his own people would hurt the very people he loved

and would soon lead. David, however, never had to solve his dilemma because God protected him. The other Philistine leaders objected to his presence in battle; thus, he did not have to fight his countrymen.

28:3–8 Saul had banned all mediums and spiritists (those who consult with the spirits of the dead) from Israel, but in desperation he turned to one for counsel. Although he had removed the sin of witchcraft from the land, he did not remove it from his heart. We may make a great show of denouncing sin, but if our hearts do not change, the sins will return. Knowing what is right and condemning what is wrong do not take the place of *doing* what is right.

28:5, 6 The Urim, along with the Thummim, was used by the high priest to determine God's guidance in certain matters. (See the notes on 2:18 and 10:20 for further information on the use of the Urim and Thummim.)

28:5–7 Saul was overwhelmed at the sight of the Philistine army, and so he turned to the occult. Regard life's difficulties and obstacles as reminders to turn you in God's direction and make you depend upon him. As we see from Saul's story, turning to anything or anyone else leads only to disaster.

28:7, 8 God had strictly forbidden the Israelites to have anything to do with divination, sorcery, witchcraft, mediums, spiritists, or anyone who consults the dead (Deuteronomy 18:9–14). In fact, sorcerers were to be put to death (Exodus 22:18). Occult practices were carried on in the name of pagan gods, and people turned to the occult for answers that God would not give.

Practitioners of the occult have Satan and demons as the source of their information; God does not reveal his will to them.

"There is one in Endor," they said.

[8] So Saul disguised himself, putting on other clothes, and at night he and two men went to the woman. "Consult [b] a spirit for me," he said, "and bring up for me the one I name."

[9] But the woman said to him, "Surely you know what Saul has done. He has cut off [c] the mediums and spiritists from the land. Why have you set a trap for my life to bring about my death?"

[10] Saul swore to her by the LORD, "As surely as the LORD lives, you will not be punished for this."

[11] Then the woman asked, "Whom shall I bring up for you?"

"Bring up Samuel," he said.

[12] When the woman saw Samuel, she cried out at the top of her voice and said to Saul, "Why have you deceived me? You are Saul!"

[13] The king said to her, "Don't be afraid. What do you see?"

The woman said, "I see a spirit [a] coming up out of the ground."

[14] "What does he look like?" he asked.

"An old man wearing a robe [d] is coming up," she said.

Then Saul knew it was Samuel, and he bowed down and prostrated himself with his face to the ground.

[15] Samuel said to Saul, "Why have you disturbed me by bringing me up?"

"I am in great distress," Saul said. "The Philistines are fighting against me, and God has turned [e] away from me. He no longer answers me, either by prophets or by dreams. So I have called on you to tell me what to do."

[16] Samuel said, "Why do you consult me, now that the LORD has turned away from you and become your enemy? [17] The LORD has done what he predicted through me. The LORD has torn the kingdom out of your hands and given it to one of your neighbors—to David. [18] Because you did not obey the LORD or carry out his fierce wrath against the Amalekites, the LORD has done this to you today. [19] The LORD will hand over both Israel and you to the Philistines, and tomorrow you and your sons will be with me. The LORD will also hand over the army of Israel to the Philistines."

[20] Immediately Saul fell full length on the ground, filled with fear because of Samuel's words. His strength was gone, for he had eaten nothing all that day and night.

[21] When the woman came to Saul and saw that he was greatly shaken, she said, "Look, your maidservant has obeyed you. I took my life [f] in my hands and did what you told me to do. [22] Now please listen to your servant and let me give you some food so you may eat and have the strength to go on your way."

[23] He refused and said, "I will not eat."

But his men joined the woman in urging him, and he listened to them. He got up from the ground and sat on the couch.

[a] 13 Or *see spirits;* or *see gods*

28:8
[b] Dt 18:10-11; Isa 8:19
28:9
[c] ver 3
28:14
[d] 1Sa 15:27
28:15
[e] ver 6; 1Sa 18:12
28:21
[f] Jdg 12:3; 1Sa 19:5

THE BATTLE AT GILBOA
David pretended loyalty to Achish, but when war broke out with Israel, he was sent to Ziklag from Aphek. The Philistines defeated the Israelites at Mount Gilboa. David returned to Ziklag to find that the Amalekites had destroyed Ziklag. So David and his men pursued the Amalekite raiders and slaughtered them, recovering all that was taken.

Instead he speaks through his own channels: the Bible, his Son Jesus Christ, and the Holy Spirit.

28:12 Did Samuel really come back from the dead at the medium's call? The medium shrieked at the appearance of Samuel—she knew too well that the spirits she usually contacted were either contrived or satanic. Somehow Samuel's appearance revealed to her that she was dealing with a power far greater than she had known. She did not call up Samuel by trickery or by the power of Satan; God brought Samuel back to give Saul a prediction regarding his fate, a message Saul already knew. This in no way justifies efforts to contact the dead or communicate with persons or spirits from the past. God is against all such practices (Galatians 5:19-21).

28:15 God did not answer Saul's appeals because Saul had not followed God's previous directions. Sometimes people wonder why their prayers are not answered. But if they don't fulfill the responsibilities God has already given them, they should not be surprised when he does not give further guidance.

24 The woman had a fattened calf at the house, which she butchered at once. She took some flour, kneaded it and baked bread without yeast. 25 Then she set it before Saul and his men, and they ate. That same night they got up and left.

Achish Sends David Back to Ziklag

29 The Philistines gathered*g* all their forces at Aphek,*h* and Israel camped by the spring in Jezreel. 2 As the Philistine rulers marched with their units of hundreds and thousands, David and his men were marching at the rear *i* with Achish. 3 The commanders of the Philistines asked, "What about these Hebrews?"

Achish replied, "Is this not David, who was an officer of Saul king of Israel? He has already been with me for over a year,*j* and from the day he left Saul until now, I have found no fault in him."

4 But the Philistine commanders were angry with him and said, "Send the man back, that he may return to the place you assigned him. He must not go with us into battle, or he will turn *k* against us during the fighting. How better could he regain his master's favor than by taking the heads of our own men? 5 Isn't this the David they sang about in their dances:

> "'Saul has slain his thousands,
>   and David his tens of thousands'?"*l*

6 So Achish called David and said to him, "As surely as the Lord lives, you have been reliable, and I would be pleased to have you serve with me in the army. From the day you came to me until now, I have found no fault in you, but the rulers *m* don't approve of you. 7 Turn back and go in peace; do nothing to displease the Philistine rulers."

8 "But what have I done?" asked David. "What have you found against your servant from the day I came to you until now? Why can't I go and fight against the enemies of my lord the king?"

9 Achish answered, "I know that you have been as pleasing in my eyes as an angel *n* of God; nevertheless, the Philistine commanders *o* have said, 'He must not go up with us into battle.' 10 Now get up early, along with your master's servants who have come with you, and leave*p* in the morning as soon as it is light."

11 So David and his men got up early in the morning to go back to the land of the Philistines, and the Philistines went up to Jezreel.

David Destroys the Amalekites

30 David and his men reached Ziklag*q* on the third day. Now the Amalekites*r* had raided the Negev and Ziklag. They had attacked Ziklag and burned it, 2 and had taken captive the women and all who were in it, both young and old. They killed none of them, but carried them off as they went on their way.

3 When David and his men came to Ziklag, they found it destroyed by fire and their wives and sons and daughters taken captive. 4 So David and his men wept aloud until they had no strength left to weep. 5 David's two wives*s* had been captured—Ahinoam of Jezreel and Abigail, the widow of Nabal of Carmel. 6 David was greatly distressed because the men were talking of stoning*t* him; each one was bitter in spirit because of his sons and daughters. But David found strength in the Lord his God.

7 Then David said to Abiathar the priest, the son of Ahimelech, "Bring me the ephod. *u*" Abiathar brought it to him, 8 and David inquired *v* of the Lord, "Shall I pursue this raiding party? Will I overtake them?"

29:1 *g*1Sa 28:1
*h*1Sa 4:1
29:2 *i*1Sa 28:2
29:3 *j*1Sa 27:7; Da 6:5
29:4 *k*1Sa 14:21
29:5 *l*1Sa 18:7; 21:11
29:6 *m*ver 3
29:9 *n*2Sa 14:17,20; 19:27
*o*ver 4
29:10 *p*1Ch 12:19
30:1 *q*1Sa 29:4,11
*r*1Sa 15:7; 27:8
30:5 *s*1Sa 25:43
30:6 *t*Ex 17:4
30:7 *u*1Sa 23:9
30:8 *v*1Sa 23:2

29:4 The other Philistine commanders knew that David was the one who, as a young man, had killed their champion, Goliath (17:32–54), had killed hundreds of Philistine soldiers (18:27), and was the hero of Israelite victory songs (21:11). They were afraid that, in the heat of battle, David might turn against them. Although David was upset at this at first, God used the commanders' suspicion to keep him from having to fight against Saul and his countrymen.

30:6 Faced with the tragedy of losing their families, David's soldiers began to turn against him and even talked about killing him. Instead of planning a rescue, they looked for someone to blame. But David found his strength in God and began looking for a solution instead of a scapegoat. When facing problems, remember that it is useless to look for someone to blame or criticize. Instead, consider how you can help find a solution.

30:7 David couldn't go to the tabernacle to ask the Lord for guidance because it was in Saul's territory. Therefore he called for the ephod, the only tabernacle-related object he possessed. In the presence of the priest and this priestly garment, he asked God for direction. When David called for the ephod, he was really asking the priest to bring him the Urim and Thummim, which were kept in a pouch attached to the ephod. Only the high priest could carry and use the Urim and Thummim. (For more information on the ephod and its contents, see the note on Exodus 39:1–21.)

"Pursue them," he answered. "You will certainly overtake them and succeed in the rescue."

30:10
ʷver 9,21

⁹David and the six hundred men with him came to the Besor Ravine, where some stayed behind, ¹⁰for two hundred men were too exhausted ʷ to cross the ravine. But David and four hundred men continued the pursuit.

30:12
ˣJdg 15:19

¹¹They found an Egyptian in a field and brought him to David. They gave him water to drink and food to eat— ¹²part of a cake of pressed figs and two cakes of raisins. He ate and was revived, ˣ for he had not eaten any food or drunk any water for three days and three nights.

¹³David asked him, "To whom do you belong, and where do you come from?"

He said, "I am an Egyptian, the slave of an Amalekite. My master abandoned me when I became ill three days ago. ¹⁴We raided the Negev of the Kerethites ʸ and the territory belonging to Judah and the Negev of Caleb. ᶻ And we burned Ziklag."

30:14
ʸ2Sa 8:18;
Eze 25:16
ᶻJos 14:13

¹⁵David asked him, "Can you lead me down to this raiding party?"

He answered, "Swear to me before God that you will not kill me or hand me over to my master, and I will take you down to them."

¹⁶He led David down, and there they were, scattered over the countryside, eating, drinking and reveling because of the great amount of plunder they had taken from the land of the Philistines and from Judah. ¹⁷David fought them from dusk until the evening of the next day, and none of them got away, except four hundred young men who rode off on camels and fled. ᵃ ¹⁸David recovered everything the Amalekites had taken, including his two wives. ¹⁹Nothing was missing: young or old, boy or girl, plunder or anything else they had taken. David brought everything back. ²⁰He took all the flocks and herds, and his men drove them ahead of the other livestock, saying, "This is David's plunder."

30:17
ᵃ1Sa 15:3

²¹Then David came to the two hundred men who had been too exhausted ᵇ to follow him and who were left behind at the Besor Ravine. They came out to meet David and the people with him. As David and his men approached, he greeted them. ²²But all the evil men and troublemakers among David's followers said, "Because they did not go out with us, we will not share with them the plunder we recovered. However, each man may take his wife and children and go."

30:21
ᵇver 10

²³David replied, "No, my brothers, you must not do that with what the Lᴏʀᴅ has given us. He has protected us and handed over to us the forces that came against us. ²⁴Who will listen to what you say? The share of the man who stayed with the supplies is to be the same as that of him who went down to the battle. All will share alike. ᶜ" ²⁵David made this a statute and ordinance for Israel from that day to this.

30:24
ᶜNu 31:27;
Jos 22:8

30:27
ᵈJos 19:8
ᵉJos 15:48

²⁶When David arrived in Ziklag, he sent some of the plunder to the elders of Judah, who were his friends, saying, "Here is a present for you from the plunder of the Lᴏʀᴅ's enemies."

²⁷He sent it to those who were in Bethel, Ramoth ᵈ Negev and Jattir; ᵉ ²⁸to those in Aroer, ᶠ Siphmoth, Eshtemoa ²⁹and Racal; to those in the towns of the Jerahmeelites ᵍ and the Kenites; ³⁰to those in Hormah, ʰ Bor Ashan, Athach ³¹and Hebron; ⁱ and to those in all the other places where David and his men had roamed.

30:28
ᶠJos 13:16

30:29
ᵍ1Sa 27:10

30:30
ʰJdg 1:17

30:31
ⁱJos 14:13

Saul Takes His Life

31:1
ʲ1Sa 28:4;
1Ch 10:1-12

31

Now the Philistines fought against Israel; the Israelites fled before them, and many fell slain on Mount Gilboa. ʲ ²The Philistines pressed hard after Saul and his sons, and

---

30:11–15 The Amalekites cruelly left this slave to die, but God used him to lead David and his men to the Amalekite camp. David and his men treated the young man kindly, and he returned the kindness by leading them to the enemy. Treat those you meet with respect and dignity no matter how insignificant they may seem. You never know how God will use them to help you or haunt you, depending upon your response to them.

30:24, 25 David made a law that those who stayed with the supplies were to be treated equally with those who fought in battle. Today it takes several people to provide the support services needed for every soldier in battle. In the church and other organizations, we need to treat those who provide support services equally with those on the front lines. Without bookkeepers, secretaries, trainers, and administrators, those

with a public ministry would be unable to do their jobs. Are you on the front lines? Don't forget those who are backing you up. Are you in the support group? Realize that your position, although it may be less glamorous or exciting, is vital to the work of the entire group.

they killed his sons Jonathan, Abinadab and Malki-Shua. ³The fighting grew fierce around Saul, and when the archers overtook him, they wounded ᵏ him critically.

⁴Saul said to his armor-bearer, "Draw your sword and run me through,ˡ or these uncircumcised fellows will come and run me through and abuse me."

But his armor-bearer was terrified and would not do it; so Saul took his own sword and fell on it. ⁵When the armor-bearer saw that Saul was dead, he too fell on his sword and died with him. ⁶So Saul and his three sons and his armor-bearer and all his men died together that same day.

⁷When the Israelites along the valley and those across the Jordan saw that the Israelite army had fled and that Saul and his sons had died, they abandoned their towns and fled. And the Philistines came and occupied them.

⁸The next day, when the Philistines came to strip the dead, they found Saul and his three sons fallen on Mount Gilboa. ⁹They cut off his head and stripped off his armor, and they sent messengers throughout the land of the Philistines to proclaim the newsᵐ in the temple of their idols and among their people. ¹⁰They put his armor in the temple of the Ashtorethsⁿ and fastened his body to the wall of Beth Shan.ᵒ

¹¹When the people of Jabesh Gileadᵖ heard of what the Philistines had done to Saul, ¹²all their valiant men journeyed through the night to Beth Shan. They took down the bodies of Saul and his sons from the wall of Beth Shan and went to Jabesh, where they burned them. ¹³Then they took their bones �q and buried them under a tamarisk tree at Jabesh, and they fasted seven days.

31:3
ᵏ2Sa 1:6

31:4
ˡJdg 9:54

31:9
ᵐ2Sa 1:20

31:10
ⁿJdg 2:12-13
ᵒJos 17:11

31:11
ᵖ1Sa 11:1

31:13
q2Sa 21:12-14

31:3, 4 The Philistines had a well-earned reputation for torturing their captives. Saul no doubt knew about Samson's fate (Judges 16:18–31) and did not want to risk physical mutilation or other abuse. When his armor-bearer refused to kill him, he took his own life.

31:3, 4 Saul was tall, handsome, strong, rich, and powerful, but all of this was not enough to make him someone we should emulate. He was big physically, but he was small in God's eyes. He was handsome, but his sin made him ugly. He was strong, but his lack of faith made him weak. He was rich, but he was spiritually bankrupt. He could give orders to many, but he couldn't command their respect or allegiance. Saul looked good on the outside, but he was decaying on the inside. A right relationship with God and a strong character are much more valuable than a good-looking exterior.

31:3, 4 Saul's armor-bearer faced a moral dilemma—should he carry out a sinful order from a man he was supposed to obey? He knew he should obey his master, the king, but he also knew murder was wrong. He decided not to kill Saul.

There is a difference between following an order with which you don't agree and following one you know is wrong. It is never right or ethical to carry out a wrong act, no matter who gives the order or what the consequences for disobedience may be. What shapes your choice when you face a moral dilemma? Have the courage to follow God's law above human commands.

31:4 Saul faced death the same way he faced life. He took matters into his own hands without thinking of God or asking for his guidance. If our lives aren't the way we would like them to be now, we can't assume that change will come more easily later. When nearing death, we will respond to God the same

way we have been responding all along. Coming face to face with death only shows us what we are *really* like. How do you want to face death? Start facing life that way right now.

31:10 To put Saul's armor in the Philistine temple gave credit to a pagan goddess for victory over Saul. Ashtoreth was a goddess of fertility and sex. Beth Shan was a town on the eastern slopes of Mount Gilboa, overlooking the Jordan Valley.

31:13 Consider the difference between the last judge of Israel and its first king. Saul, the king, was characterized by inconsistency, disobedience, and self-will. He did not have a heart for God. Samuel, the judge, was characterized by consistency, obedience, and a deep desire for God's will. He had a genuine desire for God.

When God called Samuel, he said, "Speak, Lᴏʀᴅ, for your servant is listening" (3:9). But when God, through Samuel, called Saul, Saul replied, "Why do you say such a thing to me?" (9:21). Saul was dedicated to himself; Samuel was dedicated to God.

31:13 Saul's death was also the death of an ideal—Israel could no longer believe that having a king like the other nations would solve all their troubles. The real problem was not the form of government, but the sinful king. Saul tried to please God by spurts of religiosity, but real spirituality takes a lifetime of consistent obedience.

Heroic spiritual lives are built by stacking days of obedience one on top of the other. Like a brick, each obedient act is small in itself, but in time the acts will pile up, and a huge wall of strong character will be built—a great defense against temptation. We should strive for consistent obedience each day.

KEY PLACES IN 2 SAMUEL

N

Mediterranean
Sea

LEBANON

Abel Beth Maacah

ARAM

SYRIA

Sea of
Galilee

Helam

ISRAEL

CANAAN

Forest of
Ephraim

Mahanaim

Jordan River

Rabbah

AMMON
JORDAN

Jerusalem

PHILISTIA

Gath

Hebron

Dead
Sea

Ziklag

MOAB

EDOM

| 0 | 20 Mi. |
| 0 | 20 Km. |

The broken lines (— · —) indicate modern boundaries.

they did give David sanctuary when he was hiding from Saul (1 Samuel 27). But when Saul died and David became king, the Philistines planned to defeat him. In a battle near Jerusalem, David and his troops routed the Philistines (5:17–25), but they were not completely subdued until David conquered Metheg Ammah (possibly near Gath) (8:1).

4 Moab During the time of the judges, Moab controlled many cities in Israel and demanded heavy taxes (Judges 3:12–30). David conquered Moab and, in turn, levied tribute from them (8:2).

5 Edom Though the Edomites and the Israelites traced their ancestry back to the same man, Isaac (Genesis 25:19–23), they were long-standing enemies. David defeated Edom and forced them to pay tribute also (8:14).

6 Rabbah The Ammonites insulted David's delegation and turned a peace-making mission into angry warfare. The Ammonites called troops from Aram, but David defeated this alliance first at Helam, then at Rabbah, the capital city (10:1—12:31).

7 Mahanaim David had victory in the field, but problems at home. His son Absalom incited a rebellion

1 Hebron After Saul's death, David moved from the Philistine city of Ziklag to Hebron, where the tribe of Judah crowned him king. But the rest of Israel's tribes backed Saul's son Ish-Bosheth and crowned him king at Mahanaim. As a result, there was war between Judah and the rest of the tribes of Israel until Ish-Bosheth was assassinated. Then all of Israel pledged loyalty to David as their king (1:1—5:5).

2 Jerusalem One of David's first battles as king occurred at the fortress city of Jerusalem. David and his troops took the city by surprise, and it became his capital. It was here that David brought the ark of the covenant and made a special agreement with God (5:6—7:29).

3 Gath The Philistines were Israel's constant enemy, though

and crowned himself king at Hebron. David and his men fled to Mahanaim. Acting on bad advice, Absalom mobilized his army to fight David (13:1—17:29).

8 Forest of Ephraim The armies of Absalom and David fought in the forest of Ephraim. Absalom's hair got caught in a tree, and Joab, David's general, found and killed him. With Absalom's death the rebellion died, and David was welcomed back to Jerusalem (18:1—19:43).

9 Abel Beth Maacah A man named Sheba also incited a rebellion against David. He fled to Abel-beth-maacah, but Joab and a small troop besieged the city. The citizens of Abel Beth Maacah killed Sheba themselves (20:1–26). David's victories laid the foundation for the peaceful reign of his son Solomon.

2 SAMUEL

Judges
begin
to rule
1375 B.C.
(1220 B.C.)

Saul
becomes
king
1050
(1045)

VITAL STATISTICS

PURPOSES:
(1) to record the history of David's reign;
(2) to demonstrate effective leadership under God;
(3) to reveal that one person can make a difference;
(4) to show the personal qualities that please God;
(5) to depict David as an ideal leader of an imperfect kingdom, and to foreshadow Christ, who will be the ideal leader of a new and perfect kingdom (chapter 7)

AUTHOR:
Unknown. Some have suggested that Nathan's son Zabud may have been the author (1 Kings 4:5).
The book also includes the writings of Nathan and Gad (1 Chronicles 29:29).

ORIGINAL AUDIENCE:
The people of Israel

DATE WRITTEN:
930 B.C.; written soon after David's reign, 1010–970 B.C.

SETTING:
The land of Israel under David's rule

KEY VERSE:
"And David knew that the LORD had established him as king over Israel and had exalted his kingdom for the sake of his people Israel" (5:12).

KEY PEOPLE:
David, Joab, Bathsheba, Nathan, Absalom

SPECIAL FEATURES:
This book was named after the prophet who anointed David and guided him in living for God.

THE CHILD enters the room with long gown flowing, trailing well behind her high-heeled shoes. The wide-brimmed hat rests precariously atop her head, tilted to the right, and the long necklace swings like a pendulum as she walks. Following close is the "man." His fingertips peek out of the coat sleeves that are already pushed upward six inches. With feet shuffling in the double-sized boots, his unsteady steps belie his confident smile. Children at play, dressing up—they copy Mom and Dad, having watched them dress and walk. Models . . . everyone has them . . . people we emulate, people who are our ideals. Unconsciously, perhaps, we copy their actions and adopt their ideas.

Among all the godly role models mentioned in the Bible, probably no one stands out more than King David. Born halfway between Abraham and Jesus, he became God's leader for all of Israel and the ancestor of the Messiah. David was "a man after [God's] own heart" (1 Samuel 13:14). What are the personal qualities that David possessed that pleased God?

The book of 2 Samuel tells David's story. As you read, you will be filled with excitement as he is crowned king over Judah and then king over all of Israel (5:1–5), praising God as he brings the ark of the covenant back to the tabernacle (6:1–23) and exulting as he leads his armies to victory over all their enemies and completes the conquest of the promised land begun by Joshua (8—10). David accomplished much.

But David was human, and during dark times he stumbled and fell into sin. The record of lust, adultery, and murder is not easy to read (11—13) and reveals that even great people who try to follow God are susceptible to temptation and sin.

Godliness does not guarantee an easy and carefree life. David had family problems—his own son incited the entire nation to rebellion and crowned himself king (14:1—18:33). And greatness can cause pride, as we see in David's sinful act of taking a census in order to glory in the strength of his nation (24:1–25). But the story of this fallen hero does not end in tragedy. Through repentance, his fellowship and peace with God were restored, but he had to face the consequences of the sins he committed (12—20). These consequences stayed with him the rest of his life as a reminder of his sinful deeds and his need for God.

As you read 2 Samuel, look for David's godlike characteristics—his faithfulness, patience, courage, generosity, commitment, honesty—as well as other God-honoring characteristics, such as modesty and penitence. Valuable lessons can be learned from his sins and from his repentance. You, like David, can become a person after God's own heart.

Saul dies; David is king over Judah 1010	David becomes king over all Israel 1003	David and Bathsheba sin 997(?)	Solomon born 991	David's census 980(?)	David dies; Solomon made king 970	The kingdom is divided 930

THE BLUEPRINT

A. DAVID'S SUCCESSES
   (1:1—10:19)
   1. David becomes king over Judah
   2. David becomes king over Israel
   3. David conquers the surrounding nations

David took the fractured kingdom that Saul had left behind and built a strong, united power. Forty years later, David would turn this kingdom over to his son Solomon. David had a heart for God. He was a king who governed God's people by God's principles, and God blessed him greatly. We may not have David's earthly success, but following God is, ultimately, the most successful decision we can make.

B. DAVID'S STRUGGLES
   (11:1—24:25)
   1. David and Bathsheba
   2. Turmoil in David's family
   3. National rebellion against David
   4. The later years of David's rule

David sinned with Bathsheba and then tried to cover his sin by having her husband killed. Although he was forgiven for his sin, the consequences remained—he experienced trouble and distress, both with his family and with the nation. God is always ready to forgive, but we must live with the consequences of our actions. Covering up our sin will only multiply sin's painful consequences.

MEGATHEMES

THEME	EXPLANATION	IMPORTANCE
Kingdom Growth	Under David's leadership, Israel's kingdom grew rapidly. With the growth came many changes: from tribal independence to central-ized government, from the leadership of judges to a monarchy, from decentralized worship to worship at Jerusalem.	No matter how much growth or how many changes we experience, God provides for us if we love him and highly regard his principles. God's work done in God's way never lacks God's supply of wisdom and energy.
Personal Greatness	David's popularity and influence increased greatly. He realized that the Lord was behind his success because he wanted to pour out his kindness on Israel. David regarded God's interests as more important than his own.	God graciously pours out his favor on us because of what Christ has done. God does not regard personal greatness as something to be used selfishly, but as an instrument to carry out his work among his people. The greatness we should desire is to love others as God loves us.
Justice	King David showed justice, mercy, and fairness to Saul's family, enemies, rebels, allies, and close friends alike. His just rule was grounded in his faith in and knowledge of God. God's perfect moral nature is the standard for justice.	Although David was the most just of all Israel's kings, he was still imperfect. His use of justice offered hope for a heavenly, ideal kingdom. This hope will never be satisfied in our hearts until Christ, the Son of David, comes to rule in perfect justice forever.
Consequences of Sin	David abandoned his purpose as leader and king in time of war. His desire for prosperity and ease led him from triumph to trouble. Because David committed adultery with Bathsheba, he experienced consequences of his sin that destroyed both his family and the nation.	Temptation quite often comes when a person's life is aimless. We sometimes think that sinful pleasures and freedom from God's restraint will bring us a feeling of vitality; but sin creates a cycle of suffering that is not worth the fleeting pleasures it offers.
Feet of Clay	David not only sinned with Bathsheba, he murdered an innocent man. He neglected to discipline his sons when they got involved in rape and murder. This great hero showed a lack of character in some of his most impor-tant personal decisions. The man of iron had feet of clay.	Sin should never be considered as a mere weak-ness or flaw. Sin is fatal and must be eradicated from our lives. David's life teaches us to have compassion for all people, including those whose sinful nature leads them into sinful acts. It serves as a warning to us not to excuse sin in our own lives, even in times of success.

A. DAVID'S SUCCESSES (1:1—10:19)

After years of running from Saul, David was finally crowned king over the tribe of Judah. The rest of Israel, however, followed Ish-Bosheth, Saul's son. David did not attempt to take the tribes by force but placed the matter in God's hands. After a few years Ish-Bosheth was assassinated, and the rest of the tribes finally put their support behind David. David moved the capital to Jerusalem, defeated the surrounding nations, and even showed kindness to Saul's family. We may not understand why God seems to move slowly at times, but we must trust him and be faithful with what he has given us.

1. David becomes king over Judah
David Hears of Saul's Death

1 After the death of Saul, David returned from defeating *a* the Amalekites and stayed in Ziklag two days. ²On the third day a man arrived from Saul's camp, with his clothes torn and with dust on his head.*b* When he came to David, he fell to the ground to pay him honor.

³"Where have you come from?" David asked him.

He answered, "I have escaped from the Israelite camp."

⁴"What happened?" David asked. "Tell me."

He said, "The men fled from the battle. Many of them fell and died. And Saul and his son Jonathan are dead."

⁵Then David said to the young man who brought him the report, "How do you know that Saul and his son Jonathan are dead?"

⁶"I happened to be on Mount Gilboa,*c*" the young man said, "and there was Saul, leaning on his spear, with the chariots and riders almost upon him. ⁷When he turned around and saw me, he called out to me, and I said, 'What can I do?'

⁸"He asked me, 'Who are you?'

"'An Amalekite,*d*' I answered.

⁹"Then he said to me, 'Stand over me and kill me! I am in the throes of death, but I'm still alive.'

¹⁰"So I stood over him and killed him, because I knew that after he had fallen he could not survive. And I took the crown*e* that was on his head and the band on his arm and have brought them here to my lord."

¹¹Then David and all the men with him took hold of their clothes and tore them. ¹²They mourned and wept and fasted till evening for Saul and his son Jonathan, and for the army of the LORD and the house of Israel, because they had fallen by the sword.

¹³David said to the young man who brought him the report, "Where are you from?"

"I am the son of an alien, an Amalekite," he answered.

¹⁴David asked him, "Why were you not afraid to lift your hand to destroy the LORD's anointed?*f*"

1:1
a 1Sa 30:17

1:2
b 1Sa 4:12

1:6
c 1Sa 31:2-4

1:8
d 1Sa 15:2

1:10
e Jdg 9:54

1:14
f 1Sa 24:6; 26:9

1:1 David had great faith in God. He waited for God to fulfill his promises. The book of 1 Samuel tells of David's struggles as he waited to become king of Israel (Samuel had anointed David as king of Israel many years earlier). King Saul became jealous of David because the people were praising him for his accomplishments. Eventually, Saul's jealousy became so intense that he tried to kill David. As a result, David had to run and hide. For many years David hid from Saul in enemy territory and in the barren desert south and east of Jerusalem. David may have wondered when God's promise that he would be king would come true, but his struggles prepared him for the great responsibilities he would later face. The book of 2 Samuel tells how David was finally rewarded for his patience and consistent faith in God.

1:1 When Saul died, David and his men were still living in Ziklag, a Philistine city. Because Saul had driven him out of Israel, David had pretended to be loyal to Achish, a Philistine ruler (1 Samuel 27). There he was safe from Saul.

1:11, 12 "They mourned and wept and fasted till evening." David and his men were visibly shaken over Saul's death. Their actions showed their genuine sorrow over the loss of their king, their friend Jonathan, and the other soldiers of Israel who died that day. They were not ashamed to grieve. Today, some people consider expressing emotions to be a sign of weakness. Those who wish to appear strong try to hide their feelings. But expressing our grief can help us deal with our intense sorrow when a loved one dies.

1:13 The man identified himself as an Amalekite from Saul's camp (1:2). He may have been an Amalekite under Israelite jurisdiction, but more likely he was a battlefield scavenger. Obviously the man was lying both about his identity and about what happened on the battlefield. (Compare his story with the account in 1 Samuel 31:3, 4.) Because he had Saul's crown with him, something the Philistines wouldn't have left behind, we can infer that he found Saul dead on the battlefield before the Philistines arrived (1 Samuel 31:8).

A life of deceit leads to disaster. The man lied to gain some personal reward for killing David's rival, but he misread David's character. If David had rewarded him for murdering the king, David would have shared his guilt. Instead, David had the messenger killed. Lying can bring disaster upon the liar, even for something he or she has not done.

1:13 The Amalekites were a fierce nomadic tribe that frequently conducted surprise raids on Canaanite villages. They had been Israel's enemies since Moses' time. David had just destroyed an Amalekite band of raiders who had burned his city and kidnapped its women and children (1 Samuel 30:1–20). This man was probably unaware of David's recent confrontations with Amalekites, or he may not have come. Instead, he incurred David's wrath by

1:15
g 2Sa 4:12
h 2Sa 4:10

[15]Then David called one of his men and said, "Go, strike him down!"*g* So he struck him down, and he died.*h* [16]For David had said to him, "Your blood be on your own head. Your own mouth testified against you when you said, 'I killed the LORD's anointed.'"

David's Lament for Saul and Jonathan

1:18
i Jos 10:13

[17]David took up this lament concerning Saul and his son Jonathan, [18]and ordered that the men of Judah be taught this lament of the bow (it is written in the Book of Jashar):*i*

1:19
j ver 27

[19] "Your glory, O Israel, lies slain on your heights.
　　How the mighty have fallen!*j*

1:20
k Mic 1:10
l 1Sa 31:8
m Ex 15:20;
1Sa 18:6

[20] "Tell it not in Gath,*k*
　　proclaim it not in the streets of Ashkelon,
lest the daughters of the Philistines*l* be glad,
　　lest the daughters of the uncircumcised rejoice.*m*

1:21
n 1Sa 31:1
o Isa 21:5

[21] "O mountains of Gilboa,*n*
　　may you have neither dew nor rain,
　　nor fields that yield offerings ⌊of grain⌋.
For there the shield of the mighty was defiled,
　　the shield of Saul—no longer rubbed with oil.*o*

1:22
p Isa 34:3,7
q 1Sa 18:4

[22] From the blood*p* of the slain,
　　from the flesh of the mighty,
　　the bow*q* of Jonathan did not turn back,
　　the sword of Saul did not return unsatisfied.

1:23
r Jer 4:13
s Jdg 14:18

[23] "Saul and Jonathan—
　　in life they were loved and gracious,
　　and in death they were not parted.
They were swifter than eagles,*r*
　　they were stronger than lions.*s*

[24] "O daughters of Israel,
　　weep for Saul,
who clothed you in scarlet and finery,
　　who adorned your garments with ornaments of gold.

CHARACTERS IN THE DRAMA OF 2 SAMUEL It can be confusing to keep track of all the characters introduced in the first few chapters of 2 Samuel. Here is some help.	Character	Relation	Position	Whose Side?
	Joab	Son of Zeruiah, David's half sister	One of David's military leaders and, later, commander in chief	David's
	Abner	Saul's cousin	Saul's commander in chief	Saul and Ish-Bosheth's, but made overtures to David
	Abishai	Joab's brother	High officer in David's army—Commander of "the Three"	Joab and David's
	Asahel	Joab and Abishai's brother	High officer—one of David's 30 select warriors ("mighty men")	Joab and David's
	Ish-Bosheth	Saul's son	Saul and Abner's selection as king	Saul's

---

posing as an enemy of Israel and claiming to have killed God's chosen king.

1:15, 16 Why did David consider it a crime to kill the king, even though Saul was his enemy? David believed that God anointed Saul, and only God could remove him from office. If it became casual or commonplace to assassinate the king, the whole society would become chaotic. It was God's job, not David's, to judge Saul's sins (Leviticus 19:18). We must realize that God has placed rulers in authority over us, and we should respect their positions (Romans 13:1–5).

1:17, 18 David was a talented musician. He played the harp (1 Samuel 16:23), he brought music into the worship services

of the temple (1 Chronicles 25), and he wrote many of the psalms. Here we are told that he wrote a lament in memory of Saul and his son Jonathan, David's closest friend. Music played an important role in Israel's history. (For other famous songs in the Bible, see the chart in Exodus 15, p. 119.)

1:17–27 Saul had caused much trouble for David, but when he died, David composed a lament in memory of the king and his son. David had every reason to hate Saul, but he chose not to. Instead, he chose to look at the good Saul had done and to ignore the times when Saul had attacked him. It takes courage to lay aside hatred and hurt and to respect the positive side of another person, especially an enemy.

25 "How the mighty have fallen in battle!
  Jonathan lies slain on your heights.
26 I grieve for you, Jonathan my brother;
  you were very dear to me.
  Your love for me was wonderful,*t*
  more wonderful than that of women.

27 "How the mighty have fallen!
  The weapons of war have perished!"*u*

1:26
t 1Sa 18:1

1:27
u ver 19,25

David Anointed King Over Judah

2 In the course of time, David inquired*v* of the Lord. "Shall I go up to one of the towns of Judah?" he asked.

The Lord said, "Go up."

David asked, "Where shall I go?"

"To Hebron,"*w* the Lord answered.

2 So David went up there with his two wives, Ahinoam of Jezreel and Abigail, the widow of Nabal of Carmel. 3 David also took the men who were with him, each with his family, and they settled in Hebron and its towns. 4 Then the men of Judah came to Hebron and there they anointed*x* David king over the house of Judah.

When David was told that it was the men of Jabesh Gilead*y* who had buried Saul, 5 he sent messengers to the men of Jabesh Gilead to say to them, "The Lord bless*z* you for showing this kindness to Saul your master by burying him. 6 May the Lord now show you kindness and faithfulness, and I too will show you the same favor because you have done this. 7 Now then, be strong and brave, for Saul your master is dead, and the house of Judah has anointed me king over them."

2:1
v 1Sa 23:2,11-12
w Ge 13:18;
1Sa 30:31

2:4
x 2Sa 5:3-5
y 1Sa 31:11-13

2:5
z 1Sa 23:21

War Between the Houses of David and Saul

8 Meanwhile, Abner*a* son of Ner, the commander of Saul's army, had taken Ish-Bosheth son of Saul and brought him over to Mahanaim. 9 He made him king over Gilead, Ashuri*a* and Jezreel, and also over Ephraim, Benjamin and all Israel.

a 9 Or Asher

2:8
a 1Sa 14:50

1:26 By saying that Jonathan's love was "more wonderful than that of women," David was not implying that he had a sexual relationship with Jonathan. Homosexual acts were absolutely forbidden in Israel. Leviticus 18:22 calls homosexuality "detestable," and Leviticus 20:13 decrees the death penalty for those who practice homosexuality. David was simply restating the deep brotherhood and faithful friendship he had with Jonathan. (For more on their friendship, see the note on 1 Samuel 18:1–4.)

2:1 Although David knew he would become king (1 Samuel 16:13; 23:17; 24:20), and although the time seemed right now that Saul was dead, David still asked God if he should move back to Judah, the home territory of his tribe. Before moving ahead with what seems obvious, first bring the matter to God, who alone knows the best timing.

2:1 God told David to return to Hebron, where he would soon be crowned king of Judah. David made Hebron his capital because (1) it was the largest city in Judah at that time; (2) it was secure against attack; (3) it was located near the center of Judah's territory, an ideal location for a capital city; (4) many key trade routes converged at Hebron, making it difficult for supply lines to be cut off in wartime.

2:4 The men of Judah publicly anointed David as their king. David had been anointed king by Samuel years earlier (1 Samuel 16:13), but that ceremony had taken place in private. This one was like inaugurating a public official who has already been elected to office. The rest of Israel, however, didn't accept David's kingship for seven and a half years (2:10, 11).

2:4–7 David sent a message thanking the men of Jabesh Gilead who had risked their lives to bury Saul's body (1 Samuel 31:11–13). Saul had rescued Jabesh Gilead from certain defeat when Nahash the Ammonite had surrounded the city (1 Samuel 11), so these citizens showed their gratitude and kindness. In his message, he also suggested that they follow Judah's lead and acknowledge him as their king. Jabesh Gilead was to the north in the land of Gilead, and David was seeking to gain support among the 10 remaining tribes who had not yet recognized him as king.

JOAB VERSUS ABNER
David was crowned king of Judah in Hebron; Ish-Bosheth was crowned king of Israel in Mahanaim. The opposing armies of Judah and Israel met at Gibeon for battle— Judah under Joab, Israel under Abner.

Mediterranean Sea
N
Sea of Galilee
Jordan River
CANAAN
Mahanaim
Gibeon
Jerusalem
Bethlehem
Hebron
Dead Sea
0   20 Mi.
0   20 Km.
—— Judah's army
----- Israel's army

2:11
b 2Sa 5:5
2:12
c Jos 18:25
2:13
d 1Ch 2:16

¹⁰Ish-Bosheth son of Saul was forty years old when he became king over Israel, and he reigned two years. The house of Judah, however, followed David. ¹¹The length of time David was king in Hebron over the house of Judah was seven years and six months. *b*

¹²Abner son of Ner, together with the men of Ish-Bosheth son of Saul, left Mahanaim and went to Gibeon. *c* ¹³Joab *d* son of Zeruiah and David's men went out and met them at the pool of Gibeon. One group sat down on one side of the pool and one group on the other side. ¹⁴Then Abner said to Joab, "Let's have some of the young men get up and fight hand to hand in front of us."

"All right, let them do it," Joab said.

ABNER

The honest compliments of an opponent are often the best measure of someone's greatness. Although Abner and David frequently saw each other across battle lines, the Bible gives a glimpse of the respect they had for each other. As a young man, David had served under Abner. But later, Saul's campaign to kill David was carried out by Abner. After Saul's death, Abner temporarily upheld the power of the king's family. But the struggle between Abner and Saul's heir, Ish-Bosheth, brought about Abner's decision to support David's claim to the throne. It was during his efforts to unite the kingdom that Abner was murdered by Joab.

Several years earlier, in a battle between Ish-Bosheth's army under Abner and David's forces under Joab, Abner fled and was pursued by Joab's brother, Asahel. Abner told Asahel twice to stop following him. But the eager young soldier refused, so Abner killed him. Joab was determined to avenge his brother.

Abner realized Saul's family was doomed to defeat and that David would be the next king, so he decided to change sides. He hoped that in exchange for his delivering Saul's kingdom, David would make him commander in chief of his army. David's willingness to accept this proposal was probably another reason for Joab's action.

Abner lived by his wits and his will. To him, God was someone with whom he would cooperate if it suited his plans. Otherwise he did what seemed best for him at the time. We can identify with Abner's tendency to give God conditional cooperation. Obedience is easy when the instructions in God's Word fit in with our plans. But our allegiance to God is tested when his plans are contrary to ours. What action should you take today in obedience to God's Word?

Strengths and accomplishments:	• Commander in chief of Saul's army and a capable military leader • Held Israel together for several years under the weak king Ish-Bosheth • Recognized and accepted God's plan to make David king over all Israel and Judah
Weaknesses and mistakes:	• He had selfish motives in his effort to reunite Judah and Israel rather than godly conviction • He slept with one of the royal concubines after Saul's death
Lesson from his life:	• God requires more than conditional, halfhearted cooperation
Vital statistics:	• Where: Territory of Benjamin • Occupation: Commander of the armies under Saul and Ish-Bosheth • Relatives: Father: Ner. Cousin: Saul. Son: Jaasiel. • Contemporaries: David, Asahel, Joab, Abishai
Key verse:	"Then the king said to his men, 'Do you not realize that a prince and a great man has fallen in Israel this day?'" (2 Samuel 3:38).

Abner's story is told in 1 Samuel 14:50—2 Samuel 4:12. He is also mentioned in 1 Kings 2:5, 32; 1 Chronicles 26:28; 27:16—22.

2:10, 11 David ruled over Judah for seven and a half years, while Ish-Bosheth reigned in Israel for only two years. The five-year gap may be due to Ish-Bosheth's not assuming the throne immediately after Saul's death. Because of constant danger from the Philistines in the northern part of Israel, five years may have passed before Ish-Bosheth could begin his reign. During that time, Abner, commander of his army, probably played a principal role in driving out the Philistines and leading the northern confederacy. Regardless of when Ish-Bosheth began to rule, his control was weak and limited. The Philistines still dominated the area, and Ish-Bosheth was intimidated by Abner (3:11).

2:12ff With Israel divided, there was constant tension between north and south. David's true rival in the north, however, was not Ish-Bosheth but Abner. In this incident, Abner suggested a

"dagger match" between the champions of his army and the champions of David's army, led by Joab. The fact that this confrontation occurred at the pool of Gibeon (located in Saul's home territory of Benjamin) suggests that Joab's men were pushing northward, gaining more territory. Abner may have suggested this confrontation in hopes of stopping Joab's advance.

Twelve men from each side were supposed to fight each other, and the side with the most survivors would be declared the winner. The confrontation between David and Goliath (1 Samuel 17) was a similar battle strategy—a way to avoid terrible bloodshed from an all-out war. In this case, however, all 24 champions were killed before either side could claim victory. Nothing was accomplished, and the civil war continued.

15So they stood up and were counted off—twelve men for Benjamin and Ish-Bosheth son of Saul, and twelve for David. 16Then each man grabbed his opponent by the head and thrust his dagger into his opponent's side, and they fell down together. So that place in Gibeon was called Helkath Hazzurim.a

17The battle that day was very fierce, and Abner and the men of Israel were defeatede by David's men.

2:17
e 2Sa 3:1

18The three sons of Zeruiah were there: Joab, Abishai and Asahel.f Now Asahel was as fleet-footed as a wild gazelle.g 19He chased Abner, turning neither to the right nor to the left as he pursued him. 20Abner looked behind him and asked, "Is that you, Asahel?"

2:18
f 1Ch 2:16
g 1Ch 12:8

"It is," he answered.

21Then Abner said to him, "Turn aside to the right or to the left; take on one of the young men and strip him of his weapons." But Asahel would not stop chasing him.

22Again Abner warned Asahel, "Stop chasing me! Why should I strike you down? How could I look your brother Joab in the face?"h

2:22
h 2Sa 3:27

23But Asahel refused to give up the pursuit; so Abner thrust the butt of his spear into Asahel's stomach,i and the spear came out through his back. He fell there and died on the spot. And every man stopped when he came to the place where Asahel had fallen and died.

2:23
i 2Sa 3:27; 4:6

24But Joab and Abishai pursued Abner, and as the sun was setting, they came to the hill of Ammah, near Giah on the way to the wasteland of Gibeon. 25Then the men of Benjamin rallied behind Abner. They formed themselves into a group and took their stand on top of a hill.

26Abner called out to Joab, "Must the sword devour forever? Don't you realize that this will end in bitterness? How long before you order your men to stop pursuing their brothers?"

27Joab answered, "As surely as God lives, if you had not spoken, the men would have continued the pursuit of their brothers until morning.b"

28So Joab blew the trumpet, and all the men came to a halt; they no longer pursued Israel, nor did they fight anymore.

29All that night Abner and his men marched through the Arabah. They crossed the Jordan, continued through the whole Bithronc and came to Mahanaim.

30Then Joab returned from pursuing Abner and assembled all his men. Besides Asahel, nineteen of David's men were found missing. 31But David's men had killed three hundred and sixty Benjamites who were with Abner. 32They took Asahel and buried him in his father's tomb at Bethlehem. Then Joab and his men marched all night and arrived at Hebron by daybreak.

3 The war between the house of Saul and the house of David lasted a long time.j David grew stronger and stronger, while the house of Saul grew weaker and weaker.

3:1
j 1Ki 14:30

2 Sons were born to David in Hebron:

His firstborn was Amnon the son of Ahinoamk of Jezreel;

3:2
k 1Sa 25:43;
1Ch 3:1-3

3 his second, Kileab the son of Abigail the widow of Nabal of Carmel;

the third, Absalom the son of Maacah daughter of Talmai king of Geshur;l

3:3
l 1Sa 27:8;
2Sa 13:37

4 the fourth, Adonijahm the son of Haggith;

the fifth, Shephatiah the son of Abital;

3:4
m 1Ki 1:5,11

5 and the sixth, Ithream the son of David's wife Eglah.

These were born to David in Hebron.

a 16 Helkath Hazzurim means field of daggers or field of hostilities.   b 27 Or spoken this morning, the men would not have taken up the pursuit of their brothers; or spoken, the men would have given up the pursuit of their brothers by morning   c 29 Or morning; or ravine; the meaning of the Hebrew for this word is uncertain.

2:21–23 Abner repeatedly warned Asahel to turn back or risk losing his life, but Asahel refused to turn from his self-imposed duty. Persistence is a good trait if it is for a worthy cause. But if the goal is only personal honor or gain, persistence may be no more than stubbornness. Asahel's stubbornness not only cost his life, but it also spurred unfortunate disunity in David's army for years to come (3:26, 27; 1 Kings 2:28–35). Before you decide to pursue a goal, make sure it is worthy of your devotion.

2:28 This battle ended with a victory for Joab's troops (2:17), but war in the divided nation continued until David was finally crowned king over all Israel (5:1–5).

3:1 The events recorded in chapter 2 led to a long war between David's followers and the troops loyal to Abner and Ish-Bosheth. Civil war rocked the country at great cost to both sides. This war occurred because Israel and Judah had lost sight of God's vision

and purpose: to settle the land (Genesis 12:7), to drive out the Canaanites (Deuteronomy 7:1–4), and to obey God's laws (Deuteronomy 8:1). Instead of uniting to accomplish these goals, they fought each other. When you face conflict, step back from the hostilities and consider whether you and your enemy have common goals that are bigger than your differences. Appeal to those interests as you work for a settlement.

3:2–5 David suffered much heartache because of his many wives. Polygamy was a socially acceptable practice for kings at this time, although God specifically warned against it (Deuteronomy 17:14–17). Sadly, the numerous sons born to David's wives caused him great trouble. Rape (13:14), murder (13:28), rebellion (15:13), and greed (1 Kings 1:5, 6) all resulted from the jealous rivalries among the half brothers. Solomon, one of David's sons and his successor to the throne, also took many wives who eventually turned him away from God (1 Kings 11:3, 4).

Abner Goes Over to David

6 During the war between the house of Saul and the house of David, Abner had been strengthening his own position in the house of Saul. **7** Now Saul had had a concubine[n] named Rizpah[o] daughter of Aiah. And Ish-Bosheth said to Abner, "Why did you sleep with my father's concubine?"

8 Abner was very angry because of what Ish-Bosheth said and he answered, "Am I a dog's head[p]—on Judah's side? This very day I am loyal to the house of your father Saul and to his family and friends. I haven't handed you over to David. Yet now you accuse me of an offense involving this woman! **9** May God deal with Abner, be it ever so severely, if I do not do for David what the LORD promised[q] him on oath **10** and transfer the kingdom from the house of Saul and establish David's throne over Israel and Judah from Dan to Beersheba."[r] **11** Ish-Bosheth did not dare to say another word to Abner, because he was afraid of him.

12 Then Abner sent messengers on his behalf to say to David, "Whose land is it? Make an agreement with me, and I will help you bring all Israel over to you."

13 "Good," said David. "I will make an agreement with you. But I demand one thing of you: Do not come into my presence unless you bring Michal daughter of Saul when you come to see me."[s] **14** Then David sent messengers to Ish-Bosheth son of Saul, demanding, "Give me my wife Michal,[t] whom I betrothed to myself for the price of a hundred Philistine foreskins."

15 So Ish-Bosheth gave orders and had her taken away from her husband Paltiel[u] son of Laish. **16** Her husband, however, went with her, weeping behind her all the way to Bahurim.[v] Then Abner said to him, "Go back home!" So he went back.

17 Abner conferred with the elders of Israel and said, "For some time you have wanted to make David your king. **18** Now do it! For the LORD promised David, 'By my servant David I will rescue my people Israel from the hand of the Philistines[w] and from the hand of all their enemies.'"[x]

19 Abner also spoke to the Benjamites in person. Then he went to Hebron to tell David everything that Israel and the whole house of Benjamin[y] wanted to do. **20** When Abner, who had twenty men with him, came to David at Hebron, David prepared a feast for him and his men. **21** Then Abner said to David, "Let me go at once and assemble all Israel for my lord the king, so that they may make a compact[z] with you, and that you may rule over all that your heart desires."[a] So David sent Abner away, and he went in peace.

Joab Murders Abner

22 Just then David's men and Joab returned from a raid and brought with them a great deal of plunder. But Abner was no longer with David in Hebron, because David had sent him away, and he had gone in peace. **23** When Joab and all the soldiers with him arrived, he was told that Abner son of Ner had come to the king and that the king had sent him away and that he had gone in peace.

24 So Joab went to the king and said, "What have you done? Look, Abner came to you. Why did you let him go? Now he is gone! **25** You know Abner son of Ner; he came to deceive you and observe your movements and find out everything you are doing."

3:7
[n] 2Sa 16:21-22
[o] 2Sa 21:8-11

3:8
[p] 1Sa 24:14;
2Sa 9:8

3:9
[q] 1Sa 15:28;
1Ki 19:2

3:10
[r] Jdg 20:1

3:13
[s] 1Sa 18:20

3:14
[t] 1Sa 18:27

3:15
[u] 1Sa 25:44

3:16
[v] 2Sa 16:5; 19:16

3:18
[w] 1Sa 9:16
[x] 1Sa 15:28

3:19
[y] 1Ch 12:2,16,29

3:21
[z] ver 10,12
[a] 1Ki 11:37

3:6, 7 To sleep with any of the king's wives or concubines was to make a claim to the throne, and it was considered treason. Because Ish-Bosheth was a weak ruler, Abner was running the country; thus he may have felt justified in sleeping with Saul's concubine. Ish-Bosheth, however, saw that Abner's power was becoming too great.

3:7 Ish-Bosheth may have been right to speak out against Abner's behavior, but he didn't have the moral strength to maintain his authority (3:11). Lack of moral backbone became the root of Israel's troubles over the next four centuries. Only 4 of the next 40 kings of Israel were called "good." It takes courage and strength to stand firm in your convictions and to confront wrongdoing in the face of opposition. When you believe something is wrong, do not let yourself be talked out of your position. Firmly attack the wrong and uphold the right.

3:8 By saying, "Am I a dog's head?" Abner meant, "Am I a traitor for Judah?" He may have been refuting the accusation that he was trying to take over the throne, or he may have been angry that Ish-Bosheth scolded him after Abner had helped put

him on the throne in the first place. Prior to this conversation, Abner realized that he could not keep David from eventually taking over Israel. Because he was angry at Ish-Bosheth, Abner devised a plan to turn over the kingdom of Israel to David.

3:13, 14 Michal had been married to David. Saul had arranged the marriage as a reward for David's acts of bravery (1 Samuel 17:25; 18:24–27). Later, however, in one of his jealous fits, Saul took Michal away from David and forced her to marry Paltiel (1 Samuel 25:44). Now David wanted his wife back before he would begin to negotiate peace with the northern tribes. Perhaps David still loved her (but see 6:20–23 for the tension in their relationship). More likely, he thought that marriage to Saul's daughter would strengthen his claim to rule all Israel and demonstrate that he had no animosity toward Saul's house. Paltiel was the unfortunate victim caught in the web of Saul's jealousy.

3:19 Because Saul, Ish-Bosheth, and Abner were all from the tribe of Benjamin, the support of the elders of that tribe meant that Abner was serious about his offer. There was a strong possibility of overcoming tribal jealousies and uniting the kingdom.

26 Joab then left David and sent messengers after Abner, and they brought him back from the well of Sirah. But David did not know it. 27 Now when Abner returned to Hebron, Joab took him aside into the gateway, as though to speak with him privately. And there, to avenge the blood of his brother Asahel, Joab stabbed him in the stomach, and he died.b

28 Later, when David heard about this, he said, "I and my kingdom are forever innocent before the LORD concerning the blood of Abner son of Ner. 29 May his blood fall upon the head of Joab and upon all his father's house!c May Joab's house never be without someone who has a running sore or leprosya or who leans on a crutch or who falls by the sword or who lacks food."

30 (Joab and his brother Abishai murdered Abner because he had killed their brother Asahel in the battle at Gibeon.)

31 Then David said to Joab and all the people with him, "Tear your clothes and put on sackcloth and walk in mourningd in front of Abner." King David himself walked behind the bier. 32 They buried Abner in Hebron, and the king wepte aloud at Abner's tomb. All the people wept also.

33 The king sang this lament for Abner:

"Should Abner have died as the lawless die?
34   Your hands were not bound,
      your feet were not fettered.
   You fell as one falls before wicked men."

And all the people wept over him again.

35 Then they all came and urged David to eat something while it was still day; but David took an oath, saying, "May God deal with me, be it ever so severely,f if I taste breadg or anything else before the sun sets!"

36 All the people took note and were pleased; indeed, everything the king did pleased them. 37 So on that day all the people and all Israel knew that the king had no part in the murder of Abner son of Ner.

38 Then the king said to his men, "Do you not realize that a prince and a great man has fallen in Israel this day? 39 And today, though I am the anointed king, I am weak, and these sons of Zeruiah are too strong for me.h May the LORD repay the evildoer according to his evil deeds!"

Ish-Bosheth Murdered

4 When Ish-Bosheth son of Saul heard that Abneri had died in Hebron, he lost courage, and all Israel became alarmed. 2 Now Saul's son had two men who were leaders of raiding bands. One was named Baanah and the other Recab; they were sons of Rimmon the Beerothite from the tribe of Benjamin—Beerothj is considered part of Benjamin, 3 because the people of Beeroth fled to Gittaimk and have lived there as aliens to this day.

a29 The Hebrew word was used for various diseases affecting the skin—not necessarily leprosy.

3:27 b2Sa 2:22; 20:9-10; 1Ki 2:5
3:29 c1Ki 2:31-33
3:31 dGe 37:34
3:32 ePr 24:17
3:35 fRu 1:17 g2Sa 1:12; 12:17
3:39 h2Sa 19:5-7
4:1 i2Sa 3:27; Ezr 4:4
4:2 jJos 9:17; 18:25
4:3 kNe 11:33

3:26-29 Joab took revenge for the death of his brother instead of leaving justice to God. But that revenge backfired on him (1 Kings 2:31-34). God will repay those who deserve it (Romans 12:19). Refuse to rejoice when your enemies suffer, and don't try to get revenge. Seeking revenge will ruin your own peace of mind and increase the chances of further retaliation.

3:27 Abner killed Joab's brother Asahel in self-defense. Joab then killed Abner to avenge his brother's death and also to save his position of military leadership. People who killed in self-defense were supposed to be safe in cities of refuge (Numbers 35:22-25). Joab showed his disrespect for God's laws by killing Abner out of revenge in Hebron, a city of refuge (Joshua 20:7).

3:29 David was saying that Joab's descendants would be unclean, unhealthy, and in want. Why did David say such harsh words about Joab? David was upset over Abner's death for several reasons. (1) He was grieved over the loss of a skilled military officer. (2) He wanted to place the guilt of Abner's murder on Joab, not himself. (3) He was on the verge of becoming king over the entire nation, and utilizing Abner was the key to winning over the northern tribes. Abner's death could have revived the civil war. (4) Joab violated David's agreement to protect Abner. Joab's murderous act ruined David's plans, and David was especially angry that his own commander had committed the crime.

3:31 By walking behind the bier, or casket, David was leading the mourning.

3:31ff David ordered Joab to mourn, possibly because few people were aware that Joab had committed the crime and because David did not want any further trouble. If this is true, David was thinking more about strengthening his kingdom than about justice.

3:39 Joab and Abishai were the two sons of Zeruiah David mentioned. David had an especially hard time controlling Joab because, although he was intensely loyal, he was strong willed, preferring to do things his own way. In exchange for his loyalty, however, David was willing to give him the flexibility he craved.

Joab's murder of Abner is an example of his fierce independence. While David opposed the murder, he allowed it to remain unpunished because (1) to punish Joab could cause the troops to rebel; (2) Joab was David's nephew, and any harsh treatment could cause family problems; (3) Joab was from the tribe of Judah, and David didn't want rebellion from his own tribe; (4) to get rid of Joab would mean losing a skilled and competent commander who had been invaluable in strengthening his army.

4:1 Ish-Bosheth was a man who took his courage from another man (Abner) rather than from God. When Abner died, Ish-Bosheth was left with nothing. In crisis and under pressure, he collapsed in

4:4
*¹*2Sa 9:3,6;
1Ch 8:34; 9:40

⁴(Jonathan son of Saul had a son who was lame in both feet. He was five years old when the news about Saul and Jonathan came from Jezreel. His nurse picked him up and fled, but as she hurried to leave, he fell and became crippled. His name was Mephibosheth.)*ˡ*

4:6
*ᵐ*2Sa 2:23

⁵Now Recab and Baanah, the sons of Rimmon the Beerothite, set out for the house of Ish-Bosheth, and they arrived there in the heat of the day while he was taking his noonday rest. ⁶They went into the inner part of the house as if to get some wheat, and they stabbed*ᵐ* him in the stomach. Then Recab and his brother Baanah slipped away.

⁷They had gone into the house while he was lying on the bed in his bedroom. After they stabbed and killed him, they cut off his head. Taking it with them, they traveled all night by way of the Arabah. ⁸They brought the head of Ish-Bosheth to David at Hebron and said to the king, "Here is the head of Ish-Bosheth son of Saul, your enemy, who tried to take your life. This day the LORD has avenged my lord the king against Saul and his offspring."

4:9
*ⁿ*1Ki 1:29
4:10
*ᵒ*2Sa 1:2-16
4:11
*ᵖ*Ge 9:5

⁹David answered Recab and his brother Baanah, the sons of Rimmon the Beerothite, "As surely as the LORD lives, who has delivered*ⁿ* me out of all trouble, ¹⁰when a man told me, 'Saul is dead,' and thought he was bringing good news, I seized him and put him to death in Ziklag. *ᵒ* That was the reward I gave him for his news! ¹¹How much more—when wicked men have killed an innocent man in his own house and on his own bed—should I not now demand his blood*ᵖ* from your hand and rid the earth of you!"

4:12
*q*2Sa 1:15

¹²So David gave an order to his men, and they killed them. *q* They cut off their hands and feet and hung the bodies by the pool in Hebron. But they took the head of Ish-Bosheth and buried it in Abner's tomb at Hebron.

2. David becomes king over Israel

5:2
*ʳ*1Sa 18:5,13,16
*ˢ*1Sa 16:1

5 All the tribes of Israel came to David at Hebron and said, "We are your own flesh and blood. ²In the past, while Saul was king over us, you were the one who led Israel on their military campaigns. *ʳ* And the LORD said to you, 'You will shepherd *ˢ* my people Israel, and you will become their ruler.'"

5:3
*ᵗ*2Sa 3:21

³When all the elders of Israel had come to King David at Hebron, the king made a compact *ᵗ* with them at Hebron before the LORD, and they anointed David king over Israel.

5:4
*ᵘ*Lk 3:23
*ᵛ*1Ch 26:31
5:5
*ʷ*2Sa 2:11; 1Ch 3:4

⁴David was thirty years old *ᵘ* when he became king, and he reigned forty *ᵛ* years. ⁵In Hebron he reigned over Judah seven years and six months, *ʷ* and in Jerusalem he reigned over all Israel and Judah thirty-three years.

---

fear. Fear can paralyze us, but faith and trust in God can overcome fear (2 Timothy 1:6–8; Hebrews 13:6). If we trust in God, we will be free to respond boldly to the events around us.

4:4 The rest of Mephibosheth's story is told in chapters 9; 16:1–4; and 19:24–30.

4:11 David called Ish-Bosheth an "innocent man." As Saul's son, Ish-Bosheth had reason to think he was in line for the throne. He was not wicked for wanting to be king; rather, he was simply too weak to stand against injustice. Although David knew Ish-Bosheth was not the strong leader needed to unite Israel, he had no intention of killing him. God had promised the kingdom to David, and he knew that God would fulfill his promise.

When David learned of Ish-Bosheth's death, he was angry. He had never harmed Saul, and he thought the assassins' method was cowardly. David wanted to unite Israel, not drive a permanent wedge between him and Ish-Bosheth's supporters. To show that he had nothing to do with the extermination of Saul's royal line, he ordered the assassins killed and gave Ish-Bosheth a proper burial. All the tribes of Israel, recognizing in David the strong leader they needed, pledged their loyalty to him. No doubt the Philistine threat and David's military reputation (1 Samuel 18:7) also helped unify the people.

5:3–5 This was the third time David was anointed king. First he was privately anointed by Samuel (1 Samuel 16:13). Then he was made king over the tribe of Judah (2:4). Finally he was crowned king over all Israel. As an outlaw, life had looked bleak, but God's promise to make him king over all Israel was now being fulfilled. Although the kingdom would be divided again in less than 75 years, David's dynasty would reign over Judah, the southern kingdom, for over 400 years.

5:4, 5 David did not become king over all Israel until he was 37 years old, although he had been promised the kingdom many years earlier (1 Samuel 16:13). During those years, David had to wait patiently for the fulfillment of God's promise. If you feel pressured to achieve instant results and success, remember David's patience. Just as his time of waiting prepared him for his important task, a waiting period may help prepare you by strengthening your character.

DAVID DEFEATS THE PHILISTINES The Philistines camped in the Valley of Rephaim. David defeated them at Baal Perazim, but they remained in the valley. He attacked again and chased them from Gibeon to Gezer.

David Conquers Jerusalem

6The king and his men marched to Jerusalem *x* to attack the Jebusites, who lived there. The Jebusites said to David, "You will not get in here; even the blind and the lame can ward you off." They thought, "David cannot get in here." 7Nevertheless, David captured the fortress of Zion, the City of David. *y*

8On that day, David said, "Anyone who conquers the Jebusites will have to use the water shaft*a* to reach those 'lame and blind' who are David's enemies.*b*" That is why they say, "The 'blind and lame' will not enter the palace."

9David then took up residence in the fortress and called it the City of David. He built up the area around it, from the supporting terraces*c* inward. 10And he became more and more powerful,*z* because the LORD God Almighty was with him.

11Now Hiram*a* king of Tyre sent messengers to David, along with cedar logs and carpenters and stonemasons, and they built a palace for David. 12And David knew that the LORD had established him as king over Israel and had exalted his kingdom for the sake of his people Israel.

13After he left Hebron, David took more concubines and wives*b* in Jerusalem, and more sons and daughters were born to him. 14These are the names of the children born to him there: *c* Shammua, Shobab, Nathan, Solomon, 15Ibhar, Elishua, Nepheg, Japhia, 16Elishama, Eliada and Eliphelet.

David Defeats the Philistines

17When the Philistines heard that David had been anointed king over Israel, they went up in full force to search for him, but David heard about it and went down to the stronghold. *d* 18Now the Philistines had come and spread out in the Valley of Rephaim; *e* 19so David inquired*f* of the LORD, "Shall I go and attack the Philistines? Will you hand them over to me?"

The LORD answered him, "Go, for I will surely hand the Philistines over to you."

20So David went to Baal Perazim, and there he defeated them. He said, "As waters break out, the LORD has broken out against my enemies before me." So that place was called Baal Perazim. *d g* 21The Philistines abandoned their idols there, and David and his men carried them off.

22Once more the Philistines came up and spread out in the Valley of Rephaim; 23so David inquired of the LORD, and he answered, "Do not go straight up, but circle around behind them and attack them in front of the balsam trees. 24As soon as you hear the sound *h* of

5:6 *x*Jdg 1:8
5:7 *y*1Ki 2:10
5:10 *z*2Sa 3:1
5:11 *a*1Ki 5:1,18
5:13 *b*Dt 17:17
5:14 *c*1Ch 3:5
5:17 *d*2Sa 23:14; 1Ch 11:16
5:18 *e*Jos 15:8
5:19 *f*1Sa 23:2
5:20 *g*Isa 28:21
5:24 *h*2Ki 7:6

*a*8 Or *use scaling hooks*   *b*8 Or *are hated by David*   *c*9 Or *the Millo*   *d*20 *Baal Perazim* means *the lord who breaks out.*

5:6 The fortress city of Jerusalem was located on a high ridge near the center of the united Israelite kingdom. It was considered neutral territory because it stood on the border of the territory of the tribes of Benjamin and Judah and it was still occupied by the Jebusites, a Canaanite tribe that had never been expelled from the land (Judges 1:21). Because of its strategic advantages, David made Jerusalem his capital.

5:6, 7 The Jebusites had a clear military advantage, and they boasted of their security behind the impregnable walls of Jerusalem, also called Zion. But they soon discovered that their walls would not protect them. David caught them by surprise by entering the city through the water tunnel.

Only in God are we truly safe and secure. Anything else is false security. Whether you are surrounded by mighty walls of stone, a comfortable home, or a secure job, no one can predict what tomorrow may bring. Our relationship with God is the only security that cannot be taken away.

5:12 "David knew that the LORD had established him . . ." Although the pagan kingdoms based their greatness on conquest, power, armies, and wealth, David knew that his greatness came only from God. To be great means keeping a close relationship with God personally and nationally. To do this, David had to keep his ambition under control. Although he was famous, successful, and well liked, he gave God first place in his life and served the people according to God's purposes. Do you seek greatness from God or from people? In the drive for success, remember to keep your ambition under God's control.

5:17 "The stronghold" is the mountain stronghold in the Desert of Judah that David used when defending himself against Saul (see 23:14 and 1 Chronicles 12:8).

5:17 The Philistine oppression of Israel had begun in the days of Samson (Judges 13—16). The Philistines were still Israel's most powerful enemy although David was once considered a friend and ally (1 Samuel 27; 29). Because they occupied much of Israel's northern territory, they apparently did not bother David while he was king of Judah to the south. But when they learned that David was planning to unite all Israel, they tried to stop him.

5:19 How could David get such a clear message from God? He may have prayed and been urged to action by the Holy Spirit. He may have asked God through a prophet. Most likely, however, he went to the high priest, who consulted God through the Urim and Thummim that God had told the Israelites to use for just such a purpose. (For more on the Urim and Thummim, see the notes on Leviticus 8:8 and 1 Samuel 10:20.)

5:19–25 David fought his battles the way God instructed him. In each instance he (1) asked if he should fight or not, (2) followed instructions carefully, and (3) gave God the glory. We can err in our "battles" by ignoring these steps and instead: (1) do what we want without considering God's will, (2) do things our way and ignore advice in the Bible or from other wise people, and (3) take the glory ourselves or give it to someone else without acknowledging the help we received from God. All these responses are sinful.

5:24
j Jdg 4:14

marching in the tops of the balsam trees, move quickly, because that will mean the Lᴏʀᴅ has gone out in front *j* of you to strike the Philistine army." ²⁵ So David did as the Lᴏʀᴅ commanded him, and he struck down the Philistines all the way from Gibeon ᵃ to Gezer.

The Ark Brought to Jerusalem

6:2
j 1Sa 4:4
k Lev 24:16

6 David again brought together out of Israel chosen men, thirty thousand in all. ² He and all his men set out from Baalah of Judah ᵇ to bring up from there the ark *j* of God, which is called by the Name, ᶜ ᵏ the name of the Lᴏʀᴅ Almighty, who is enthroned between the cherubim that are on the ark. ³ They set the ark of God on a new cart *l* and brought it from the house of Abinadab, which was on the hill. Uzzah and Ahio, sons of Abinadab, were guiding the new cart ⁴ with the ark of God on it, ᵈ and Ahio was walking in front of it. ⁵ David and the whole house of Israel were celebrating with all their might before the Lᴏʀᴅ, with songs ᵉ and with harps, lyres, tambourines, sistrums and cymbals.

6:3
l 1Sa 6:7

⁶ When they came to the threshing floor of Nacon, Uzzah reached out and took hold of ᵐ the ark of God, because the oxen stumbled. ⁷ The Lᴏʀᴅ's anger burned against Uzzah because of his irreverent act; therefore God struck him down ⁿ and he died there beside the ark of God.

6:6
m Nu 4:15,19-20;
1Ch 13:9
6:7
n 1Sa 6:19

⁸ Then David was angry because the Lᴏʀᴅ's wrath had broken out against Uzzah, and to this day that place is called Perez Uzzah. *f*

ᵃ25 Septuagint (see also 1 Chron. 14:16); Hebrew *Geba*   ᵇ2 That is, Kiriath Jearim; Hebrew *Baale Judah*, a variant of *Baalah of Judah*   ᶜ2 Hebrew; Septuagint and Vulgate do not have the *Name*.   ᵈ3,4 Dead Sea Scrolls and some Septuagint manuscripts; Masoretic Text *cart* ⁴*and they brought it with the ark of God from the house of Abinadab, which was on the hill*   ᵉ5 See Dead Sea Scrolls, Septuagint and 1 Chronicles 13:8; Masoretic Text *celebrating before the Lᴏʀᴅ with all kinds of instruments made of pine.*   *f*8 Perez Uzzah means *outbreak against Uzzah.*

CRITICIZING GOD'S LEADERS It is dangerous to criticize God's leaders. Consider the consequences for these men and women.	*Person/Situation*	*Result*	*Reference*
	Miriam: Mocked Moses because he had a Cushite wife	Stricken with leprosy	Numbers 12
	Korah and followers: Led the people of Israel to rebel against Moses' leadership	Swallowed by the earth	Numbers 16
	Michal: Despised David because he danced before the Lord	Remained childless	2 Samuel 6
	Shimei: Cursed and threw stones at David	Executed at Solomon's order	2 Samuel 16 1 Kings 2
	Youths: Mocked Elisha and laughed at his baldness	Killed by bears	2 Kings 2
	Sanballat and Tobiah: Spread rumors and lies to stop the building of Jerusalem's walls	Frightened and humiliated	Nehemiah 2; 4; 6
	Hananiah: Contradicted Jeremiah's prophecies with false predictions	Died two months later	Jeremiah 28
	Bar-Jesus, a sorcerer: Lied about Paul in an attempt to turn the proconsul against him	Stricken with blindness	Acts 13

5:25 After David became king, his first order of business was to subdue his enemies—a task the nation had failed to complete when they first entered the land (Judges 2:1–4). David knew this had to be done in order to (1) protect the nation, (2) unify the kingdom, and (3) prepare for building the temple (which would unify religion under God and help abolish idolatrous influences).

6:3 The ark of God was Israel's national treasure and was ordinarily kept in the tabernacle. When the ark was returned to Israel after a brief Philistine captivity (1 Samuel 4:1—7:2), it was kept in Abinadab's home for 20 years. David saw how God blessed Abinadab, and he wanted to bring the ark to Jerusalem to ensure God's blessing on the entire nation. (See the notes on Exodus 37:1 and Joshua 3:2–4 for more information on the ark.)

6:6, 7 Uzzah was only trying to protect the ark, so was God's anger against Uzzah just? According to Numbers 4:5–15, the ark was to be moved only by the Levites, who were to carry it using the carrying poles—they were *never* to touch the ark itself. To touch it was a capital offense under Hebrew law (Numbers 4:15). God's action was directed against both David and Uzzah. David placed the ark on a cart, following the Philistines' example

(1 Samuel 6:7, 8) rather than God's commands. Uzzah, though sincere in his desire to protect the ark, had to face the consequences of the sin of touching it. Also, Uzzah may not have been a Levite. As David sought to bring Israel back into a relationship with God, God had to remind the nation dramatically that enthusiasm must be accompanied by obedience to his laws. The next time David tried to bring the ark to Jerusalem, he was careful to handle it correctly (1 Chronicles 15:1–15).

6:8–12 David was angry that a well-meaning man had been killed and that his plans for a joyous return of the ark had been spoiled (6:8). He undoubtedly knew that the fault was his own for transporting the ark carelessly. After cooling down, he had the ark put into temporary storage while he waited to see if the Lord would allow him to bring it to Jerusalem. This also gave David time to consider the right way to transport the ark. The fact that God blessed the home of Obed-Edom was a sign to David that he could try once again to move the ark to Jerusalem.

⁹David was afraid of the Lord that day and said, "How can the ark of the Lord ever come to me?" ¹⁰He was not willing to take the ark of the Lord to be with him in the City of David. Instead, he took it aside to the house of Obed-Edom the Gittite. ¹¹The ark of the Lord remained in the house of Obed-Edom the Gittite for three months, and the Lord blessed him and his entire household. ᵒ

¹²Now King David ᵖ was told, "The Lord has blessed the household of Obed-Edom and everything he has, because of the ark of God." So David went down and brought up the ark of God from the house of Obed-Edom to the City of David with rejoicing. ¹³When those who were carrying the ark of the Lord had taken six steps, he sacrificed �q a bull and a fattened calf. ¹⁴David, wearing a linen ephod,ʳ danced ˢ before the Lord with all his might, ¹⁵while he and the entire house of Israel brought up the ark of the Lord with shouts and the sound of trumpets.

¹⁶As the ark of the Lord was entering the City of David, Michal daughter of Saul watched from a window. And when she saw King David leaping and dancing before the Lord, she despised him in her heart.

¹⁷They brought the ark of the Lord and set it in its place inside the tent that David had pitched for it,ᵗ and David sacrificed burnt offeringsᵘ and fellowship offeringsᵃ before the Lord. ¹⁸After he had finished sacrificing the burnt offerings and fellowship offerings, he blessed the people in the name of the Lord Almighty. ¹⁹Then he gave a loaf of bread, a cake of dates and a cake of raisins to each person in the whole crowd of Israelites, both men and women. And all the people went to their homes.

²⁰When David returned home to bless his household, Michal daughter of Saul came out to meet him and said, "How the king of Israel has distinguished himself today, disrobingᵛ in the sight of the slave girls of his servants as any vulgar fellow would!"

²¹David said to Michal, "It was before the Lord, who chose me rather than your father or anyone from his house when he appointed ʷ me ruler over the Lord's people Israel—I will celebrate before the Lord. ²²I will become even more undignified than this, and I will be humiliated in my own eyes. But by these slave girls you spoke of, I will be held in honor."

²³And Michal daughter of Saul had no children to the day of her death.

God's Promise to David

7 After the king was settled in his palaceˣ and the Lord had given him rest from all his enemies around him, ²he said to Nathan the prophet, "Here I am, living in a palaceʸ of cedar, while the ark of God remains in a tent."ᶻ

³Nathan replied to the king, "Whatever you have in mind, go ahead and do it, for the Lord is with you."

⁴That night the word of the Lord came to Nathan, saying:

⁵"Go and tell my servant David, 'This is what the Lord says: Are youᵃ the one to build me a house to dwell in?ᵇ ⁶I have not dwelt in a house from the day I brought the Israelites up out of Egypt to this day. I have been moving from place to place with a tentᶜ as

ᵃ17 Traditionally *peace offerings*; also in verse 18

Cross references
6:11 ᵒGe 39:5
6:12 ᵖ1Ki 8:1; 1Ch 15:25
6:13 �q1Ki 8:5,62
6:14 ʳ1Sa 2:18 ˢEx 15:20
6:17 ᵗ1Ch 15:1 ᵘ1Ki 8:62-64
6:20 ᵛver 14,16
6:21 ʷ1Sa 13:14
7:1 ˣ1Ch 17:1
7:2 ʸ2Sa 5:11 ᶻEx 26:1
7:5 ᵃ1Ki 8:19 ᵇ1Ki 5:3-5
7:6 ᶜEx 40:18,34

6:14 David wore a linen ephod, the priest's apron, possibly because it was a religious celebration.

6:16ff Michal was David's first wife, but here she is called daughter of Saul, possibly to show how similar her attitude was to her father's. Her contempt for David probably did not start with David's grand entrance into the city. Perhaps she thought it was undignified to be so concerned with public worship at a time when it was so unimportant in the kingdom. Or maybe she thought it was not fitting for a king to display such emotion. She may have resented David's taking her from Paltiel (see the note on 3:13, 14). Whatever the reason, this contempt she felt toward her husband escalated into a difficult confrontation, and Michal ended up childless for life. Feelings of bitterness and resentment that go unchecked will destroy a relationship. Deal with your feelings before they escalate into open warfare.

6:17 Only a priest could place the sacrifices on the altar. Leviticus 1:2–13 indicates that anyone who was ceremonially clean could assist a priest in offering the sacrifice (see the notes on Joshua 3:5; 1 Samuel 20:26). So David probably offered these

sacrifices to God with the aid of a priest. Solomon did the same (1 Kings 8:62–65).

7:1ff This chapter records the covenant God made with David, promising to carry on David's line forever. This promise would be fully realized in the birth of Jesus Christ. Although the word *covenant* is not specifically stated in the Bible text here, it is used elsewhere to describe this occasion (23:5; Psalm 89:3, 4, 28, 34–37).

7:2 This is the first time Nathan the prophet is mentioned. God made certain that a prophet was living during the reign of each of the kings of Israel. The prophet's main tasks were to urge the people to follow God and to communicate God's laws and plans to the king. Most of the kings rejected the prophets God sent. But at least God had given them the opportunity to listen and obey. In earlier years, judges and priests had the role of prophets. Samuel served as judge, priest, and prophet, bridging the gap between the period of the judges and the monarchy.

7:5 In this message from Nathan, God is saying that he doesn't want David to build a "house" for him. Why didn't God want David to build the temple? God told David that his job was to unify and

7:6
d 1Ki 8:16

7:7
e Lev 26:11-12

7:8
f 1Sa 16:11

7:9
g 2Sa 5:10
h Ps 18:37-42

7:10
i Isa 5:1-7
j Ps 89:22-23

my dwelling. *d* 7 Wherever I have moved with all the Israelites, did I ever say to any of their rulers whom I commanded to shepherd my people Israel, "Why have you not built me a house of cedar?*e*"'

8 "Now then, tell my servant David, 'This is what the LORD Almighty says: I took you from the pasture and from following the flock *f* to be ruler over my people Israel. 9 I have been with you wherever you have gone, *g* and I have cut off all your enemies from before you. *h* Now I will make your name great, like the names of the greatest men of the earth. 10 And I will provide a place for my people Israel and will plant *i* them so that they can have a home of their own and no longer be disturbed. Wicked *j* people will not oppress them anymore, as they did at the beginning 11 and have done ever since the

MICHAL

Sometimes love is not enough—especially if that love is little more than the strong emotional attraction that grows between a hero and an admirer. To Michal, Saul's daughter, the courageous young David must have seemed like a dream come true. Her feelings about this hero gradually became obvious to others, and eventually, her father heard about her love for David. He saw this as an opportunity to get rid of his rival for the people's loyalty. He promised Michal's hand in marriage in exchange for David's success in the impossible task of killing 100 Philistines. But David was victorious, and so Saul lost a daughter and saw his rival become even more popular with the people.

Michal's love for David did not have time to be tested by the realities of marriage. Instead, she became involved in saving David's life. Her quick thinking helped him escape, but it cost her Saul's anger and her separation from David. Her father gave her to another man, Paltiel, but David eventually took her back.

Unlike her brother Jonathan, Michal did not have the kind of deep relationship with God that would have helped her through the difficulties in her life. Instead she became bitter. She could not share David's joyful worship of God, so she hated it. As a result, she never bore David any children.

Beyond feeling sorry for her, we need to see Michal as a person mirroring our own tendencies. How quickly and easily we become bitter with life's unexpected turns. But bitterness cannot remove or change the bad things that have happened. Often bitterness only makes a bad situation worse. On the other hand, a willingness to respond to God gives him the opportunity to bring good out of the difficult situations. That willingness has two parts: asking God for his guidance and looking for that guidance in his Word.

Strengths and accomplishments:	• Loved David and became his first wife • Saved David's life • Could think and act quickly when it was needed
Weaknesses and mistakes:	• Lied under pressure • Allowed herself to become bitter over her circumstances • In her unhappiness, she hated David for loving God
Lessons from her life:	• We are not as responsible for what happens to us as we are for how we respond to our circumstances • Disobedience to God almost always harms us as well as others
Vital statistics:	• Occupations: Daughter of one king, Saul, and wife of another, David • Relatives: Parents: Saul and Ahinoam. Brothers: Jonathan, Malki-Shua, Abinadab, Ish-Bosheth (and possibly Ishvi). Sister: Merab. Husbands: David and Paltiel.
Key verse:	"As the ark of the LORD was entering the City of David, Michal daughter of Saul watched from a window. And when she saw King David leaping and dancing before the LORD, she despised him in her heart" (2 Samuel 6:16).

Michal's story is told in 1 Samuel 14—2 Samuel 6. She is also mentioned in 1 Chronicles 15:29.

---

lead Israel and to destroy its enemies. This huge task would require David to shed a great deal of blood. In 1 Chronicles 28:3, we learn that God did not want his temple built by a warrior. Therefore, David made the plans and collected the materials so that his son Solomon could begin work on the temple as soon as he became king (1 Kings 5—7). David accepted his part in God's plan and did not try to go beyond it. Sometimes God says no to our plans. When he does, we should utilize the other opportunities he gives us.

7:8–16 David's request was good, but God said no. This does not mean that God rejected David. In fact, God was planning to do something even greater in David's life than allowing him the pres-

tige of building the temple. Although God turned down David's request, he promised to continue the house (or dynasty) of David forever. David's earthly dynasty ended four centuries later, but Jesus Christ, a direct descendant of David, was the ultimate fulfillment of this promise (Acts 2:22–36). Christ will reign for eternity—now in his spiritual kingdom and in heaven, and later, on earth, in the new Jerusalem (Luke 1:30–33; Revelation 21). Have you prayed with good intentions, only to have God say no? This is God's way of directing you to a greater purpose in your life. Accepting God's no requires as great a faith as carrying out his yes.

time I appointed leaders[a][k] over my people Israel. I will also give you rest from all your enemies.

"'The Lord declares to you that the Lord himself will establish[l] a house[m] for you: [12]When your days are over and you rest[n] with your fathers, I will raise up your offspring to succeed you, who will come from your own body, and I will establish his kingdom. [13]He is the one who will build a house for my Name, and I will establish the throne of his kingdom forever. [14]I will be his father, and he will be my son.[o] When he does wrong, I will punish him with the rod[p] of men, with floggings inflicted by men. [15]But my love will never be taken away from him, as I took it away from Saul, whom I removed from before you. [16]Your house and your kingdom will endure forever before me[b]; your throne will be established forever.'"

[17]Nathan reported to David all the words of this entire revelation.

David's Prayer

[18]Then King David went in and sat before the Lord, and he said:

"Who am I, O Sovereign Lord, and what is my family, that you have brought me this far? [19]And as if this were not enough in your sight, O Sovereign Lord, you have also spoken about the future of the house of your servant. Is this your usual way of dealing with man,[q] O Sovereign Lord?

[20]"What more can David say to you? For you know your servant, O Sovereign Lord. [21]For the sake of your word and according to your will, you have done this great thing and made it known to your servant.

[22]"How great you are,[r] O Sovereign Lord! There is no one like you, and there is no God but you, as we have heard with our own ears.[s] [23]And who is like your people Israel[t]—the one nation on earth that God went out to redeem as a people for himself, and to make a name for himself, and to perform great and awesome wonders by driving out nations and their gods from before your people, whom you redeemed[u] from Egypt?[c] [24]You have established your people Israel as your very own[v] forever, and you, O Lord, have become their God.[w]

[25]"And now, Lord God, keep forever the promise you have made concerning your servant and his house. Do as you promised, [26]so that your name will be great forever. Then men will say, 'The Lord Almighty is God over Israel!' And the house of your servant David will be established before you.

[27]"O Lord Almighty, God of Israel, you have revealed this to your servant, saying, 'I will build a house for you.' So your servant has found courage to offer you this prayer. [28]O Sovereign Lord, you are God! Your words are trustworthy,[x] and you have promised these good things to your servant. [29]Now be pleased to bless the house of your servant, that it may continue forever in your sight; for you, O Sovereign Lord, have spoken, and with your blessing[y] the house of your servant will be blessed forever."

3. David conquers the surrounding nations
David's Victories

8 In the course of time, David defeated the Philistines and subdued them, and he took Metheg Ammah from the control of the Philistines.

[2]David also defeated the Moabites.[z] He made them lie down on the ground and measured them off with a length of cord. Every two lengths of them were put to death, and the third length was allowed to live. So the Moabites became subject to David and brought tribute.

**Side references:**

7:11
[k] 1Sa 12:9-11
[l] 1Sa 25:28
[m] ver 27

7:12
[n] 1Ki 2:1

7:14
[o] Heb 1:5*
[p] Ps 89:30-33

7:19
[q] Isa 55:8-9

7:22
[r] Dt 3:24
[s] Ps 44:1

7:23
[t] Dt 4:32-38
[u] Dt 9:26

7:24
[v] Dt 26:18
[w] Ps 48:14

7:28
[x] Jn 17:17

7:29
[y] Nu 6:23-27

8:2
[z] Nu 24:17

---

[a] 11 Traditionally *judges*   [b] 16 Some Hebrew manuscripts and Septuagint; most Hebrew manuscripts *you*   [c] 23 See Septuagint and 1 Chron. 17:21; Hebrew *wonders for your land and before your people, whom you redeemed from Egypt, from the nations and their gods.*

7:18ff This section records David's prayer expressing his humble acceptance of God's promise to extend his dynasty forever. David realized that these blessings were given to him and his descendants in order that Israel might benefit from them. They would help fulfill God's greater purpose and prom-

ises that through the nation the whole world would be blessed (Genesis 12:1–3).

8:1–5 Part of God's covenant with David included the promise that the Israelites' enemies would be defeated and would no longer oppress them (7:10, 11). God fulfilled this promise by helping David defeat the opposing nations. Several enemies are

8:3
a 2Sa 10:16,19
8:4
b Jos 11:9

³Moreover, David fought Hadadezer *a* son of Rehob, king of Zobah, when he went to restore his control along the Euphrates River. ⁴David captured a thousand of his chariots, seven thousand charioteers *a* and twenty thousand foot soldiers. He hamstrung *b* all but a hundred of the chariot horses.

8:5
c 1Ki 11:24

⁵When the Arameans of Damascus *c* came to help Hadadezer king of Zobah, David struck down twenty-two thousand of them. ⁶He put garrisons in the Aramean kingdom of Damascus, and the Arameans became subject to him and brought tribute. The LORD gave David victory wherever he went.

8:7
d 1Ki 10:16

⁷David took the gold shields *d* that belonged to the officers of Hadadezer and brought them to Jerusalem. ⁸From Tebah *b* and Berothai, towns that belonged to Hadadezer, King David took a great quantity of bronze.

⁹When Tou *c* king of Hamath heard that David had defeated the entire army of Hadadezer, ¹⁰he sent his son Joram *d* to King David to greet him and congratulate him on his victory in battle over Hadadezer, who had been at war with Tou. Joram brought with him articles of silver and gold and bronze.

8:11
e 1Ki 7:51

¹¹King David dedicated *e* these articles to the LORD, as he had done with the silver and gold from all the nations he had subdued: ¹²Edom *e* and Moab, the Ammonites and the Philistines, and Amalek. He also dedicated the plunder taken from Hadadezer son of Rehob, king of Zobah.

8:13
f 2Ki 14:7

¹³And David became famous after he returned from striking down eighteen thousand Edomites *f* in the Valley of Salt. *f*

8:14
g Nu 24:17-18
h Ge 27:29,37-40

¹⁴He put garrisons throughout Edom, and all the Edomites *g* became subject to David. *h* The LORD gave David victory wherever he went.

a 4 Septuagint (see also Dead Sea Scrolls and 1 Chron. 18:4); Masoretic Text *captured seventeen hundred of his chariots*   *b* 8 See some Septuagint manuscripts (see also 1 Chron. 18:8); Hebrew *Betah*.   *c* 9 Hebrew *Toi*, a variant of *Tou*; also in verse 10   *d* 10 A variant of *Hadoram*   *e* 12 Some Hebrew manuscripts, Septuagint and Syriac (see also 1 Chron. 18:11); most Hebrew manuscripts *Aram*   *f* 13 A few Hebrew manuscripts, Septuagint and Syriac (see also 1 Chron. 18:12); most Hebrew manuscripts *Aram* (that is, Arameans)

COVENANTS	Name and Reference	God's Promise	Sign
A covenant is a legally binding obligation (promise). Throughout history God has made covenants with his people— he would keep his side if they would keep theirs. Here are seven covenants found in the Bible.	In Eden Genesis 3:15	Satan and mankind will be enemies.	Pain of childbirth
	Noah Genesis 9:8–17	God would never again destroy the earth with a flood.	Rainbow
	Abraham Genesis 15:12–21; 17:1–14	Abraham's descendants would become a great nation if they obeyed God. God would be their God forever.	Smoking firepot and blazing torch
	At Mount Sinai Exodus 19:5, 6	Israel would be God's special people, a holy nation. But they would have to keep their part of the covenant— obedience.	The exodus
	The Priesthood Numbers 25:10–13	Aaron's descendants would be priests forever.	The Aaronic priesthood
	David 2 Samuel 7:13; 23:5	Salvation would come through David's line through the birth of the Messiah.	David's line continued, and the Messiah was born a descendant of David
	New Covenant Hebrews 8:6–13	Forgiveness and salvation are available through faith in Christ.	Christ's resurrection

---

listed in this chapter: (1) *The Moabites*, descendants of Lot who lived east of the Dead Sea. They posed a constant military and religious threat to Israel (Numbers 25:1–3; Judges 3:12–30; 1 Samuel 14:47). David seemed to have a good relationship with the Moabites at one time; David's great-grandmother Ruth had been from Moab. (2) *King Hadadezer of Zobah*. His defeat at David's hands fulfilled God's promise to Abraham that Israel would control the land as far north as the Euphrates River (Genesis 15:18). (3) *The Edomites*, descendants of Esau (Genesis 36:1) who were also archenemies of Israel (see 2 Kings 8:20; Jeremiah 49:7–22; Ezekiel 25:12–14; and the note on Genesis 36:9).

8:6 The *tribute* was the tax levied on conquered nations. The tax helped to support Israel's government and demonstrated that the conquered nation was under Israel's control.

David's Officials

¹⁵David reigned over all Israel, doing what was just and right for all his people. ¹⁶Joab son of Zeruiah was over the army; Jehoshaphat *ⁱ* son of Ahilud was recorder; ¹⁷Zadok *ʲ* son of Ahitub and Ahimelech son of Abiathar were priests; Seraiah was secretary; ¹⁸Benaiah son of Jehoiada was over the Kerethites *ᵏ* and Pelethites; and David's sons were royal advisers.ᵃ

David and Mephibosheth

9 David asked, "Is there anyone still left of the house of Saul to whom I can show kindness for Jonathan's sake?" *ⁱ*

²Now there was a servant of Saul's household named Ziba. *ᵐ* They called him to appear before David, and the king said to him, "Are you Ziba?"

"Your servant," he replied.

³The king asked, "Is there no one still left of the house of Saul to whom I can show God's kindness?"

Ziba answered the king, "There is still a son of Jonathan; *ⁿ* he is crippled *ᵒ* in both feet."

⁴"Where is he?" the king asked.

Ziba answered, "He is at the house of Makir *ᵖ* son of Ammiel in Lo Debar."

⁵So King David had him brought from Lo Debar, from the house of Makir son of Ammiel.

⁶When Mephibosheth son of Jonathan, the son of Saul, came to David, he bowed down to pay him honor.

David said, "Mephibosheth!"

"Your servant," he replied.

⁷"Don't be afraid," David said to him, "for I will surely show you kindness for the sake of your father Jonathan. I will restore to you all the land that belonged to your grandfather Saul, and you will always eat at my table. *�q*"

⁸Mephibosheth bowed down and said, "What is your servant, that you should notice a dead dog *ʳ* like me?"

ᵃ18 Or *were priests*

8:16
ⁱ1Ki 4:3

8:17
ʲ1Ch 24:3

8:18
ᵏ1Sa 30:14

9:1
ⁱ1Sa 20:14-17,42

9:2
ᵐ2Sa 16:1-4;
19:17,26,29

9:3
ⁿ1Sa 20:14
ᵒ2Sa 4:4

9:4
ᵖ2Sa 17:27-29

9:7
�q2Sa 19:28

9:8
ʳ2Sa 16:9

8:15 David pleased the people (3:36), not because he tried to please them, but because he tried to please God. Often those who try the hardest to become popular never make it. But the praise of people is not that important. Don't spend your time devising ways to become accepted in the public eye. Instead strive to do what is right, and both God and people will respect your convictions.

8:15 King David's reign was characterized by doing what was "just and right." Justice means fairness in interpreting the law, administering punishment with mercy, respect for people's rights, and recognition of people's duty toward God. Is it any wonder

DAVID'S ENEMIES
David wanted to complete the conquest of Canaan begun by Joshua. He defeated the Jebusites at Jerusalem and the Philistines in the vicinity of Gath. The Ammonites, Arameans, and Moabites became his subjects. He put garrisons in Edom and levied a tax upon them.

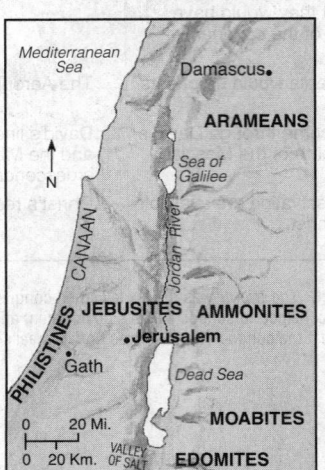

that almost everyone trusted and followed David? Why was it good for David to pursue justice? (1) It was God's command (Deuteronomy 16:18-20) and his character (Deuteronomy 32:4). God's laws were meant to establish a just society. (2) It was in the nation's best interest because times would arise when each individual would need justice. Justice should characterize the way you relate to people. Make sure you are fair in the way you treat them.

9:1ff Most kings in David's day tried to wipe out the families of their rivals in order to prevent any descendants from seeking the throne. But David showed kindness to Mephibosheth, whose father was Jonathan and whose grandfather was King Saul. David was kind, partly because of his loyalty to God's previously anointed king (see the note on 1 Samuel 24:5, 6); partly for political reasons—to unite Judah and Israel (see the notes on 3:13, 14 and 3:29); and mainly because of his vow to show kindness to all of Jonathan's descendants (1 Samuel 20:14-17).

9:3 How Mephibosheth became crippled is recorded in 4:4. Mephibosheth was five years old when Saul and Jonathan died.

9:5, 6 Mephibosheth was afraid to visit the king, who wanted to treat him like a prince. Although Mephibosheth feared for his life and may have felt unworthy, that didn't mean he should refuse David's gifts. When God graciously offers us forgiveness of sins and a place in heaven, we may feel unworthy, but we will receive these gifts if we accept them. A reception even warmer than the one David gave Mephibosheth waits for all who receive God's gifts through trusting Jesus Christ, not because we deserve it, but because of God's promise (Ephesians 2:8, 9).

9:7 His treatment of Mephibosheth shows David's integrity as a leader who accepted his obligation to show love and mercy. His generous provision for Jonathan's son goes beyond any political benefit he might have received. Are you able to forgive those who have wronged you? Can you be generous with those less deserving? Each time we show compassion, our character is strengthened.

9:10
ᵛver 7,11,13;
2Sa 19:28
⁹Then the king summoned Ziba, Saul's servant, and said to him, "I have given your master's grandson everything that belonged to Saul and his family. ¹⁰You and your sons and your servants are to farm the land for him and bring in the crops, so that your master's grandsonˢ may be provided for. And Mephibosheth, grandson of your master, will always eat at my table." (Now Ziba had fifteen sons and twenty servants.)

¹¹Then Ziba said to the king, "Your servant will do whatever my lord the king commands his servant to do." So Mephibosheth ate at David'sᵃ table like one of the king's sons.

¹²Mephibosheth had a young son named Mica, and all the members of Ziba's household were servants of Mephibosheth. ¹³And Mephibosheth lived in Jerusalem, because he always ate at the king's table, and he was crippled in both feet.

David Defeats the Ammonites

10 In the course of time, the king of the Ammonites died, and his son Hanun succeeded him as king. ²David thought, "I will show kindness to Hanun son of Nahash, just as his father showed kindness to me." So David sent a delegation to express his sympathy to Hanun concerning his father.

When David's men came to the land of the Ammonites, ³the Ammonite nobles said to Hanun their lord, "Do you think David is honoring your father by sending men to you to express sympathy? Hasn't David sent them to you to explore the city and spy it out and overthrow it?" ⁴So Hanun seized David's men, shaved off half of each man's beard,ᵗ cut off their garments in the middle at the buttocks,ᵘ and sent them away.

10:4
ᵗIsa 15:2
ᵘIsa 20:4

⁵When David was told about this, he sent messengers to meet the men, for they were greatly humiliated. The king said, "Stay at Jericho till your beards have grown, and then come back."

10:6
ᵛGe 34:30
ʷ2Sa 8:5

⁶When the Ammonites realized that they had become a stenchᵛ in David's nostrils, they hired twenty thousand Arameanʷ foot soldiers from Beth Rehob and Zobah, as well as the king of Maacah with a thousand men, and also twelve thousand men from Tob.

⁷On hearing this, David sent Joab out with the entire army of fighting men. ⁸The Ammonites came out and drew up in battle formation at the entrance to their city gate, while the Arameans of Zobah and Rehob and the men of Tob and Maacah were by themselves in the open country.

⁹Joab saw that there were battle lines in front of him and behind him; so he selected some of the best troops in Israel and deployed them against the Arameans. ¹⁰He put the rest of the men under the command of Abishai his brother and deployed them against the Ammonites. ¹¹Joab said, "If the Arameans are too strong for me, then you are to come to my rescue; but if the Ammonites are too strong for you, then I will come to rescue you. ¹²Be strongˣ and let us fight bravely for our people and the cities of our God. The LORD will do what is good in his sight."ʸ

10:12
ˣDt 31:6; 1Co 16:13
ʸ1Sa 3:18

ᵃ11 Septuagint; Hebrew *my*

10:4, 5 In Israelite culture, all men wore full beards. It was a sign of maturity and authority. Thus when these ambassadors had their beards half shaved, they suffered great indignity. Cutting off their garments also exposed them to ridicule.

10:6 Because Hanun took the wrong advice, he suspected the motives of the ambassadors and humiliated them. Then he realized that David was angry and immediately marshaled his forces for battle. Hanun should have thought through the advice more carefully; but even if he had not, he should have tried to negotiate with David. Instead, he refused to admit any fault and got ready for war. Often we respond angrily and defensively rather than admitting our mistakes, apologizing, and trying to diffuse the other person's anger. Instead of fighting, we should seek peace.

10:12 There must be a balance in life between our actions and our faith in God. David said, "Let us fight bravely." In other words, they should do what they could, using their minds to figure out the best techniques and using their resources. But he also said, "The LORD will do what is good in his sight." He knew that the outcome was in God's hands. We should use our minds and our resources to obey God, while at the same time trusting God for the outcome.

DAVID AND THE AMMONITES
Ammon gathered together its troops from the north; Joab brought the Israelite army to attack them near Rabbah. Joab returned to Jerusalem victorious, but the enemy recruited additional forces and regrouped at Helam. David himself led the next victorious attack.

¹³Then Joab and the troops with him advanced to fight the Arameans, and they fled before him. ¹⁴When the Ammonites saw that the Arameans were fleeing, they fled before Abishai and went inside the city. So Joab returned from fighting the Ammonites and came to Jerusalem.

¹⁵After the Arameans saw that they had been routed by Israel, they regrouped. ¹⁶Hadadezer had Arameans brought from beyond the River*a*; they went to Helam, with Shobach the commander of Hadadezer's army leading them.

¹⁷When David was told of this, he gathered all Israel, crossed the Jordan and went to Helam. The Arameans formed their battle lines to meet David and fought against him. ¹⁸But they fled before Israel, and David killed seven hundred of their charioteers and forty thousand of their foot soldiers. *b* He also struck down Shobach the commander of their army, and he died there. ¹⁹When all the kings who were vassals of Hadadezer saw that they had been defeated by Israel, they made peace with the Israelites and became subject*z* to them.

So the Arameans were afraid to help the Ammonites anymore.

10:19
*z*2Sa 8:6

B. DAVID'S STRUGGLES (11:1—24:25)

After restoring the nation to peace and great military power, David's personal life becomes entangled in sin. He commits adultery with Bathsheba and then orders her husband killed in an attempted cover-up. David deeply regretted what he had done and sought God's forgiveness, but the child of his sinful act died. We may be forgiven by God for our sins, but we will often experience harsh consequences.

1. David and Bathsheba

11 In the spring, *a* at the time when kings go off to war, David sent Joab out with the king's men and the whole Israelite army. *b* They destroyed the Ammonites and besieged Rabbah. But David remained in Jerusalem.

²One evening David got up from his bed and walked around on the roof *c* of the palace. From the roof he saw *d* a woman bathing. The woman was very beautiful, ³and David sent someone to find out about her. The man said, "Isn't this Bathsheba, the daughter of Eliam and the wife of Uriah *e* the Hittite?" ⁴Then David sent messengers to get her. *f* She came to him, and he slept with her. (She had purified herself from her uncleanness.)*g* Then *c* she went back home. ⁵The woman conceived and sent word to David, saying, "I am pregnant."

⁶So David sent this word to Joab: "Send me Uriah the Hittite." And Joab sent him to David. ⁷When Uriah came to him, David asked him how Joab was, how the soldiers were and how the war was going. ⁸Then David said to Uriah, "Go down to your house and wash your feet." So Uriah left the palace, and a gift from the king was sent after him. ⁹But Uriah slept at the entrance to the palace with all his master's servants and did not go down to his house.

¹⁰When David was told, "Uriah did not go home," he asked him, "Haven't you just come from a distance? Why didn't you go home?"

11:1
*a*1Ki 20:22,26
*b*1Ch 20:1

11:2
*c*Dt 22:8
*d*Mt 5:28

11:3
*e*2Sa 23:39

11:4
*f*Ps 51 Title;
Jas 1:14-15
*g*Lev 15:25-30;
18:19

a 16 That is, the Euphrates   *b 18* Some Septuagint manuscripts (see also 1 Chron. 19:18); Hebrew *horsemen*
c 4 Or *with her. When she purified herself from her uncleanness,*

11:1 Winter is the rainy season in Israel, the time when crops are planted. Spring was a good time to go to war because the roads were dry, making travel easier for troop movements, supply wagons, and chariots. In Israel, wheat and barley were ready to be harvested in the spring. These crops were an important food source for traveling armies.

11:1 This successful siege (see 12:26, 27) put an end to the Ammonites' power. From this time on, the Ammonites were subject to Israel.

11:1ff In the episode with Bathsheba, David allowed himself to fall deeper and deeper into sin. (1) David abandoned his purpose by staying home from war (11:1). (2) He focused on his own desires (11:3). (3) When temptation came, he looked into it instead of turning away from it (11:4). (4) He sinned deliberately (11:4). (5) He tried to cover up his sin by deceiving others (11:6–15). (6) He committed murder to continue the cover-up (11:15, 17). Eventually David's sin was exposed (12:9) and punished (12:10–14). (7) The consequences of David's sin were far-reaching, affecting many others (11:17; 12:11, 14, 15).

David could have chosen to stop and turn from evil at any stage along the way. But once sin gets started, it is difficult to

stop (James 1:14, 15). The deeper the mess, the less we want to admit having caused it. It's much easier to stop sliding down a hill when you are near the top than when you are halfway down. The best solution is to stop sin before it starts.

11:3 See 1 Kings 1, p. 495 for Bathsheba's Profile.

11:3, 4 As David looked from the roof of the palace, he saw a beautiful woman bathing, and he was filled with lust. David should have left the roof and fled the temptation. Instead, he entertained the temptation by inquiring about Bathsheba. The results were devastating.

To flee temptation, (1) ask God in earnest prayer to help you stay away from people, places, and situations that may tempt you. (2) Memorize and meditate on portions of Scripture that combat your specific weaknesses. At the root of most temptation is a real need or desire that God can fill, but we must trust in his timing. (3) Find another believer with whom you can openly share your struggles, and call this person for help when temptation strikes.

11:4 The phrase "she had purified herself from her uncleanness" means that Bathsheba had just completed the purification rites following menstruation. Thus she could not have already been pregnant by her own husband when David slept with her. Leviti-

11:11
h 2Sa 7:2

¹¹Uriah said to David, "The ark *h* and Israel and Judah are staying in tents, and my master Joab and my lord's men are camped in the open fields. How could I go to my house to eat and drink and lie with my wife? As surely as you live, I will not do such a thing!"

¹²Then David said to him, "Stay here one more day, and tomorrow I will send you back." So Uriah remained in Jerusalem that day and the next. ¹³At David's invitation, he ate and drank with him, and David made him drunk. But in the evening Uriah went out to sleep on his mat among his master's servants; he did not go home.

11:14
i 1Ki 21:8
11:15
j 2Sa 12:9

¹⁴In the morning David wrote a letter *i* to Joab and sent it with Uriah. ¹⁵In it he wrote, "Put Uriah in the front line where the fighting is fiercest. Then withdraw from him so he will be struck down *j* and die."

¹⁶So while Joab had the city under siege, he put Uriah at a place where he knew the strongest defenders were. ¹⁷When the men of the city came out and fought against Joab, some of the men in David's army fell; moreover, Uriah the Hittite died.

11:21
k Jdg 9:50-54

¹⁸Joab sent David a full account of the battle. ¹⁹He instructed the messenger: "When you have finished giving the king this account of the battle, ²⁰the king's anger may flare up, and he may ask you, 'Why did you get so close to the city to fight? Didn't you know they would shoot arrows from the wall? ²¹Who killed Abimelech son of Jerub-Besheth*a*? Didn't a woman throw an upper millstone on him from the wall,*k* so that he died in Thebez? Why did you get so close to the wall?' If he asks you this, then say to him, 'Also, your servant Uriah the Hittite is dead.'"

²²The messenger set out, and when he arrived he told David everything Joab had sent him to say. ²³The messenger said to David, "The men overpowered us and came out against us in the open, but we drove them back to the entrance to the city gate. ²⁴Then the archers shot arrows at your servants from the wall, and some of the king's men died. Moreover, your servant Uriah the Hittite is dead."

a 21 Also known as *Jerub-Baal* (that is, Gideon)

DAVID'S FAMILY TROUBLES

Wife	Children	What Happened
Michal (Saul's daughter)	She was childless	David gave her five nephews to the Gibeonites to be killed because of Saul's sins
Ahinoam (from Jezreel)	Amnon, David's firstborn	He raped Tamar, his half sister, and was later murdered by Absalom in revenge
Maacah (daughter of King Talmai of Geshur)	Absalom, third son Tamar, the only daughter mentioned by name	Absalom killed Amnon for raping Tamar and then fled to Geshur. Later he returned, only to rebel against David. He set up a tent on the roof and slept with 10 of his father's concubines there. His pride led to his death.
Haggith	Adonijah, fourth son. He was very handsome, but it is recorded that he was never disciplined	He set himself up as king before David's death. His plot was exposed, and David spared his life, but his half brother Solomon later had him executed
Bathsheba	Unnamed son	Died in fulfillment of God's punishment for David and Bathsheba's adultery
Bathsheba	Solomon	Became the next king of Israel. Ironically Solomon's many wives caused his downfall

David's many wives caused him much grief. And as a result of David's sin with Bathsheba, God said that murder would be a constant threat in his family, his family would rebel, and someone else would sleep with his wives. All this happened as the prophet Nathan had predicted. The consequences of sin affect not only us but those we know and love. Remember that the next time you are tempted to sin.

---

cus 15:19–30 gives more information on the purification rites Bathsheba had to perform.

11:15 David put both Bathsheba and Joab in difficult situations. Bathsheba knew it was wrong to commit adultery, but to refuse a king's request could mean punishment or death. Joab did not know why Uriah had to die, but it was obvious the king wanted him killed. We sometimes face situations with only two apparent choices, and both seem wrong. When that happens, we must not lose sight of what God wants. The answer may be to seek out more choices. By doing this, we are likely to find a choice that honors God.

25 David told the messenger, "Say this to Joab: 'Don't let this upset you; the sword devours one as well as another. Press the attack against the city and destroy it.' Say this to encourage Joab."

26 When Uriah's wife heard that her husband was dead, she mourned for him. 27 After the time of mourning was over, David had her brought to his house, and she became his wife and bore him a son. But the thing David had done displeased *l* the LORD.

11:27
l 2Sa 12:9;
Ps 51:4-5

Nathan Rebukes David

12 The LORD sent Nathan to David. *m* When he came to him, *n* he said, "There were two men in a certain town, one rich and the other poor. 2 The rich man had a very large number of sheep and cattle, 3 but the poor man had nothing except one little ewe lamb he had bought. He raised it, and it grew up with him and his children. It shared his food, drank from his cup and even slept in his arms. It was like a daughter to him.

12:1
m Ps 51 Title
n 2Sa 14:4

4 "Now a traveler came to the rich man, but the rich man refrained from taking one of his own sheep or cattle to prepare a meal for the traveler who had come to him. Instead, he took the ewe lamb that belonged to the poor man and prepared it for the one who had come to him."

5 David burned with anger against the man and said to Nathan, "As surely as the LORD lives, the man who did this deserves to die! 6 He must pay for that lamb four times over, *o* because he did such a thing and had no pity."

12:6
o Ex 22:1; Lk 19:8

7 Then Nathan said to David, "You are the man! This is what the LORD, the God of Israel, says: 'I anointed *p* you *q* king over Israel, and I delivered you from the hand of Saul. 8 I gave your master's house to you, and your master's wives into your arms. I gave you the house of Israel and Judah. And if all this had been too little, I would have given you even more. 9 Why did you despise the word of the LORD by doing what is evil in his eyes? You struck down *r* Uriah the Hittite with the sword and took his wife to be your own. You killed him with the sword of the Ammonites. 10 Now, therefore, the sword *s* will never depart from your house, because you despised me and took the wife of Uriah the Hittite to be your own.'

12:7
p 1Sa 16:13
q 1Ki 20:42

12:9
r 2Sa 11:15

12:10
s 2Sa 13:28

11 "This is what the LORD says: 'Out of your own household I am going to bring calamity upon you. *t* Before your very eyes I will take your wives and give them to one who is close to you, and he will lie with your wives in broad daylight. 12 You did it in secret, but I will do this thing in broad daylight *u* before all Israel.'"

12:11
t Dt 28:30;
2Sa 16:21-22

12:12
u 2Sa 16:22

13 Then David said to Nathan, "I have sinned *v* against the LORD."

Nathan replied, "The LORD has taken away your sin. *w* You are not going to die. 14 But because by doing this you have made the enemies of the LORD show utter contempt,*a* *x* the son born to you will die."

12:13
v 1Sa 15:24;
2Sa 24:10
w Pr 28:13;
Mic 7:18-19

12:14
x Isa 52:5; Ro 2:24

a 14 Masoretic Text; an ancient Hebrew scribal tradition *this you have shown utter contempt for the LORD*

11:25 David's response to Uriah's death seems flippant and insensitive. While he grieved deeply for Saul and Abner, his rivals (chapter 1; 3:31–39), he showed no grief for Uriah, a good man with strong spiritual character. Why? David had become callous to his own sin. The only way he could cover up his first sin (adultery) was to sin again, and soon he no longer felt guilty for what he had done. Feelings are not reliable guides for determining right and wrong. Deliberate, repeated sinning had dulled David's sensitivity to God's laws and others' rights. The more you try to cover up a sin, the more insensitive you become toward it. Don't become hardened to sin, as David did. Confess your wrong actions to God before you forget they are sins.

12:1ff As a prophet, Nathan was required to confront sin, even the sin of a king. It took great courage, skill, and tact to speak to David in a way that would make him aware of his wrong actions. When you have to confront someone with unpleasant news, pray for courage, skill, and tact. If you want that person to respond constructively, think through what you are going to say. How you present your message may be as important as what you say. Season your words with wisdom.

12:5, 6 It was a year later, and by then David had become so insensitive to his own sins that he didn't realize he was the villain in Nathan's story. The qualities we condemn in others are often our own character flaws. Which friends, associates, or family members do you find easy to criticize and hard to accept? Instead of trying to change them, ask God to help you understand their feelings and see your own flaws more clearly. You may discover that in condemning others, you have been condemning yourself.

12:10–14 The predictions in these verses came true. Because David murdered Uriah and stole his wife, (1) murder was a constant threat in his family (13:26–30; 18:14, 15; 1 Kings 2:23–25); (2) his household rebelled against him (15:13); (3) his wives were given to another in public view (16:20–23); (4) his first child by Bathsheba died (12:18). If David had known the painful consequences of his sin, he might not have pursued the pleasures of the moment.

12:13 During this incident, David wrote Psalm 51, giving valuable insight into his character and offering hope for us as well. No matter how miserable guilt makes you feel or how terribly you have sinned, you can pour out your heart to God and seek his forgiveness as David did. There is forgiveness for us when we sin. David also wrote Psalm 32 to express the joy he felt after he was forgiven.

12:14 David confessed and repented of his sin (12:13), but God's judgment was that his child would die. The consequences of David's sin were irreversible. Sometimes an apology isn't enough. When God forgives us and restores our relationship with him, he doesn't eliminate all the consequences of our wrong-

12:16
y2Sa 13:31

¹⁵After Nathan had gone home, the Lᴏʀᴅ struck the child that Uriah's wife had borne to David, and he became ill. ¹⁶David pleaded with God for the child. He fasted and went into his house and spent the nights lyingʸ on the ground. ¹⁷The elders of his household stood beside him to get him up from the ground, but he refused, and he would not eat any food with them.

¹⁸On the seventh day the child died. David's servants were afraid to tell him that the child was dead, for they thought, "While the child was still living, we spoke to David but he would not listen to us. How can we tell him the child is dead? He may do something desperate."

¹⁹David noticed that his servants were whispering among themselves and he realized the child was dead. "Is the child dead?" he asked.

"Yes," they replied, "he is dead."

²⁰Then David got up from the ground. After he had washed, put on lotions and changed his clothes, he went into the house of the Lᴏʀᴅ and worshiped. Then he went to his own house, and at his request they served him food, and he ate.

²¹His servants asked him, "Why are you acting this way? While the child was alive, you fasted and wept, but now that the child is dead, you get up and eat!"

NATHAN

This prophet lived up to the meaning of his name, "He [God] has given." He was a necessary and helpful gift from God to David. He served as God's spokesman to David and proved himself a fearless friend and counselor, always willing to speak the truth, even when he knew great pain would result.

In confronting David's multiple sin of coveting, theft, adultery, and murder in his affair with Bathsheba, Nathan was able to help David see his own wrongdoing by showing that he would not have tolerated such actions from anyone else. David's repentance allowed Nathan to comfort him with the reality of God's forgiveness, and at the same time remind him of the painful consequences his sin would bring.

Nathan's approach helps us judge our actions. How often do we make choices that we would condemn others for making? It is helpful to ask ourselves how God and others see our actions. Unfortunately, we have a huge capacity to lie to ourselves. God still provides two safeguards against self-deception: his Word and true friends. In each case, we get a view beyond ourselves. You are holding God's Word. Let it speak to you about yourself, even if the truth is painful. If you don't have a friend like Nathan, ask God for one. And ask God to use you as a suitable Nathan for someone else.

Strengths and accomplishments:	• A trusted adviser to David • A prophet of God • A fearless, but careful confronter • One of God's controls in David's life
Weakness and mistake:	• His eagerness to see David build a temple for God in Jerusalem made him speak without God's instruction
Lessons from his life:	• We should not be afraid to tell the truth to those we care about • A trustworthy companion is one of God's greatest gifts • God cares enough to find a way to communicate to us when we are in the wrong
Vital statistics:	• Occupations: Prophet, royal adviser • Contemporaries: David, Bathsheba, Solomon, Zadok, Adonijah
Key verse:	"Nathan reported to David all the words of this entire revelation" (2 Samuel 7:17).

Nathan's story is told in 2 Samuel 7—1 Kings 1. He is also mentioned in 1 Chronicles 17:15; 2 Chronicles 9:29; 29:25.

---

doing. We may be tempted to say, "If this is wrong, I can always apologize to God," but we must remember that we may set into motion events with irreversible consequences.

12:14 Why did this child have to die? This was not a judgment on the child for being conceived out of wedlock, but a judgment on David for his sin. David and Bathsheba deserved to die, but God spared their lives and took the child instead. God still had work for David to do in building the kingdom. The child's death was a horrible punishment for David and Bathsheba to bear.

It is also possible that had the child lived, God's name would have been dishonored among Israel's pagan neighbors. What would they have thought of a God who rewards murder and adul-

tery by giving a king a new heir? A baby's death is tragic, but despising God brings death to entire nations. While God readily forgave David's sin, he did not negate all its consequences.

12:20–24 David did not continue to dwell on his sin. He returned to God, and God forgave him, opening the way to begin life anew. Even the name God gave Solomon (*Jedidiah*, "loved by the Lᴏʀᴅ"; 12:25) was a reminder of God's grace. When we return to God, accept his forgiveness, and change our ways, he gives us a fresh start. To feel forgiven as David did, admit your sins to God and turn to him. Then move ahead with a new and fresh approach to life.

22 He answered, "While the child was still alive, I fasted and wept. I thought, 'Who knows?[z] The LORD may be gracious to me and let the child live.'[a] 23 But now that he is dead, why should I fast? Can I bring him back again? I will go to him,[b] but he will not return to me."[c]

24 Then David comforted his wife Bathsheba, and he went to her and lay with her. She gave birth to a son, and they named him Solomon.[d] The LORD loved him; 25 and because the LORD loved him, he sent word through Nathan the prophet to name him Jedidiah.[a]

26 Meanwhile Joab fought against Rabbah[e] of the Ammonites and captured the royal citadel. 27 Joab then sent messengers to David, saying, "I have fought against Rabbah and taken its water supply. 28 Now muster the rest of the troops and besiege the city and capture it. Otherwise I will take the city, and it will be named after me."

29 So David mustered the entire army and went to Rabbah, and attacked and captured it. 30 He took the crown[f] from the head of their king[b]—its weight was a talent[c] of gold, and it was set with precious stones—and it was placed on David's head. He took a great quantity of plunder from the city 31 and brought out the people who were there, consigning them to labor with saws and with iron picks and axes, and he made them work at brickmaking.[d] He did this to all the Ammonite towns. Then David and his entire army returned to Jerusalem.

2. Turmoil in David's family
Amnon and Tamar

13 In the course of time, Amnon[g] son of David fell in love with Tamar,[h] the beautiful sister of Absalom son of David.

2 Amnon became frustrated to the point of illness on account of his sister Tamar, for she was a virgin, and it seemed impossible for him to do anything to her.

3 Now Amnon had a friend named Jonadab son of Shimeah,[i] David's brother. Jonadab was a very shrewd man. 4 He asked Amnon, "Why do you, the king's son, look so haggard morning after morning? Won't you tell me?"

Amnon said to him, "I'm in love with Tamar, my brother Absalom's sister."

5 "Go to bed and pretend to be ill," Jonadab said. "When your father comes to see you, say to him, 'I would like my sister Tamar to come and give me something to eat. Let her prepare the food in my sight so I may watch her and then eat it from her hand.'"

6 So Amnon lay down and pretended to be ill. When the king came to see him, Amnon said to him, "I would like my sister Tamar to come and make some special bread in my sight, so I may eat from her hand."

7 David sent word to Tamar at the palace: "Go to the house of your brother Amnon and prepare some food for him." 8 So Tamar went to the house of her brother Amnon, who was lying down. She took some dough, kneaded it, made the bread in his sight and baked it. 9 Then she took the pan and served him the bread, but he refused to eat.

"Send everyone out of here,"[j] Amnon said. So everyone left him. 10 Then Amnon said to Tamar, "Bring the food here into my bedroom so I may eat from your hand." And Tamar took the bread she had prepared and brought it to her brother Amnon in his bedroom. 11 But when she took it to him to eat, he grabbed[k] her and said, "Come to bed with me, my sister."

12 "Don't, my brother!" she said to him. "Don't force me. Such a thing should not be done in Israel![l] Don't do this wicked thing.[m] 13 What about me?[n] Where could I get rid of my disgrace? And what about you? You would be like one of the wicked fools in Israel. Please speak to the king; he will not keep me from being married to you." 14 But he refused to listen to her, and since he was stronger than she, he raped her.[o]

[a] 25 *Jedidiah* means *loved by the LORD.*   [b] 30 Or *of Milcom* (that is, Molech)   [c] 30 That is, about 75 pounds (about 34 kilograms)   [d] 31 The meaning of the Hebrew for this clause is uncertain.

12:22
[z] Jnh 3:9
[a] Isa 38:1-5

12:23
[b] Ge 37:35
[c] Job 7:10

12:24
[d] 1Ch 22:9; Mt 1:6

12:26
[e] Dt 3:11;
1Ch 20:1-3

12:30
[f] 1Ch 20:2

13:1
[g] 2Sa 3:2
[h] 1Ch 3:9

13:3
[i] 1Sa 16:9

13:9
[j] Ge 45:1

13:11
[k] Ge 39:12

13:12
[l] Lev 20:17;
Jdg 20:6
[m] Jdg 19:23

13:13
[n] Lev 18:9

13:14
[o] Dt 22:25

12:22, 23 Perhaps the most bitter experience in life is the death of one's child. For comfort in such difficult circumstances, see Psalms 16:9–11; 17:15; 139; Isaiah 40:11.

12:24 Solomon was the fourth son of David and Bathsheba (1 Chronicles 3:5). Therefore several years passed between the death of their first child and Solomon's birth. Bathsheba may still have been grieving over the child's death.

13:3–5 Amnon was encouraged by his cousin Jonadab to commit sexual sin. We may be more vulnerable to the advice of our relatives because we are close to them. However, we must make sure to evaluate every piece of advice by God's standards, even when it comes from relatives.

13:14, 15 Love and lust are very different. After Amnon raped his half sister, his "love" turned to hate. Although he had claimed to be in love, he was actually overcome by lust. Love is patient; lust requires immediate satisfaction. Love is kind; lust is harsh. Love does not demand its own way; lust does. You can read about the characteristics of real love in 1 Corinthians 13. Lust may feel like love at first, but when physically expressed, it results in self-disgust and hatred of the other person. If you just can't wait, what you feel is not true love.

¹⁵Then Amnon hated her with intense hatred. In fact, he hated her more than he had loved her. Amnon said to her, "Get up and get out!"

¹⁶"No!" she said to him. "Sending me away would be a greater wrong than what you have already done to me."

But he refused to listen to her. ¹⁷He called his personal servant and said, "Get this woman out of here and bolt the door after her." ¹⁸So his servant put her out and bolted the door after her. She was wearing a richly ornamented^a robe,^p for this was the kind of garment the virgin daughters of the king wore. ¹⁹Tamar put ashes^q on her head and tore the ornamented^b robe she was wearing. She put her hand on her head and went away, weeping aloud as she went.

²⁰Her brother Absalom said to her, "Has that Amnon, your brother, been with you? Be quiet now, my sister; he is your brother. Don't take this thing to heart." And Tamar lived in her brother Absalom's house, a desolate woman.

²¹When King David heard all this, he was furious. ²²Absalom never said a word to Amnon, either good or bad;^r he hated^s Amnon because he had disgraced his sister Tamar.

^a 18 The meaning of the Hebrew for this phrase is uncertain.   ^b 19 The meaning of the Hebrew for this word is uncertain.

13:18
^p Ge 37:23

13:19
^q Jos 7:6; 1Sa 4:12; Est 4:1

13:22
^r Ge 31:24
^s Lev 19:17-18; 1Jn 2:9-11

AMNON

Amnon was king David's firstborn son, born and raised during the years between David's rise to fame and his rise to power. He grew into a prince with too much time on his hands and too little control over his thoughts. Amnon set in motion one of the most shameful and destructive series of actions in the royal family. He allowed himself to become obsessed with sexual desire for his half-sister Tamar. When his attempt to seduce Tamar failed, he raped her. Then, his "desire" for her became loathing and he humiliated her. He even made it look like the incest was his sister's fault. Tamar's full brother Absalom later avenged her shame by killing Amnon.

David was an ineffective father. He failed to train or discipline his children. Although he found out and was furious about Amnon's actions, he did nothing. Amnon, like the rest of his siblings, was a child out of control. He was frustrated when he couldn't have his way, yet was disgusted when he did get his way. Without direction, his actions led to self-destruction. The Bible records not even a hint of remorse for what he had done to Tamar.

Family relationships can be sources of strength or systems of dysfunction. We can think about childhood by counting scars and nightmares or by remembering security and dreams. We may be creating in our own children one or the other of these histories. In what specific ways have you been settling the painful issues of the past in your own life? In what ways are you contributing to a better past for your children?

Weaknesses and mistakes:	• Allowed lustful desires to dominate his life • Listened to his cousin Jonadab's bad advice • Raped and then rejected his half-sister, Tamar
Lessons from his life:	• Children who have everything often lack purpose and direction in their lives • Thoughts and impulses turn self-destructive if not controlled or channeled • Parents contribute good or evil by action or inaction in their children's lives • The distance between lust and hatred is very short
Vital statistics:	• Where: Hebron • Occupation: Prince • Relatives: Father: David. Mother: Ahinoam. Many half-brothers including Absalom, Adonijah, and Solomon. Half-sister: Tamar. • Contemporaries: Nathan, Jonadab, Joab, Ahithophel, Hushai
Key verse:	"Then Amnon hated her with intense hatred. In fact, he hated her more than he had loved her. Amnon said to her, 'Get up and get out!'" (2 Samuel 13:15).

Amnon's story is told in 2 Samuel 13:1–39. He is also mentioned in 2 Samuel 3:2 and 1 Chronicles 3:1.

13:16 Rape was strictly forbidden by God (Deuteronomy 22:28, 29). Why was sending Tamar away an even greater crime? By throwing her out, Amnon made it look as if Tamar had made a shameful proposition to him, and there were no witnesses on her behalf because he had gotten rid of the servants. His crime destroyed her chances of marriage—because she was no longer a virgin, she could not be given in marriage.

13:20 Absalom tried to comfort Tamar and persuade her not to turn the incident into a public scandal. Secretly, he planned to take revenge against Amnon himself. This he did two years later

(13:23–33). Absalom told Tamar the crime was only a family matter. But God's standards for moral conduct are not suspended when we deal with family matters.

13:21–24 David was angry with Amnon for raping Tamar, but David did not punish him. David probably hesitated because (1) he didn't want to cross Amnon, who was his firstborn son (1 Chronicles 3:1) and therefore next in line to be king, and (2) David was guilty of a similar sin himself in his adultery with Bathsheba. While David was unsurpassed as a king and military leader, he lacked skill and sensitivity as a husband and father.

Absalom Kills Amnon

23 Two years later, when Absalom's sheepshearers[t] were at Baal Hazor near the border of Ephraim, he invited all the king's sons to come there. 24 Absalom went to the king and said, "Your servant has had shearers come. Will the king and his officials please join me?"

25 "No, my son," the king replied. "All of us should not go; we would only be a burden to you." Although Absalom urged him, he still refused to go, but gave him his blessing.

26 Then Absalom said, "If not, please let my brother Amnon come with us."

The king asked him, "Why should he go with you?" 27 But Absalom urged him, so he sent with him Amnon and the rest of the king's sons.

28 Absalom ordered his men, "Listen! When Amnon is in high[u] spirits from drinking wine and I say to you, 'Strike Amnon down,' then kill him. Don't be afraid. Have not I given you this order? Be strong and brave." 29 So Absalom's men did to Amnon what Absalom had ordered. Then all the king's sons got up, mounted their mules and fled.

30 While they were on their way, the report came to David: "Absalom has struck down all the king's sons; not one of them is left." 31 The king stood up, tore[v] his clothes and lay down on the ground; and all his servants stood by with their clothes torn.

32 But Jonadab son of Shimeah, David's brother, said, "My lord should not think that they killed all the princes; only Amnon is dead. This has been Absalom's expressed intention ever since the day Amnon raped his sister Tamar. 33 My lord the king should not be concerned about the report that all the king's sons are dead. Only Amnon is dead."

34 Meanwhile, Absalom had fled.

Now the man standing watch looked up and saw many people on the road west of him, coming down the side of the hill. The watchman went and told the king, "I see men in the direction of Horonaim, on the side of the hill."[a]

35 Jonadab said to the king, "See, the king's sons are here; it has happened just as your servant said."

36 As he finished speaking, the king's sons came in, wailing loudly. The king, too, and all his servants wept very bitterly.

37 Absalom fled and went to Talmai[w] son of Ammihud, the king of Geshur. But King David mourned for his son every day.

38 After Absalom fled and went to Geshur, he stayed there three years. 39 And the spirit of the king[b] longed to go to Absalom, for he was consoled[x] concerning Amnon's death.

Absalom Returns to Jerusalem

14 Joab son of Zeruiah knew that the king's heart longed for Absalom. 2 So Joab sent someone to Tekoa[y] and had a wise woman brought from there. He said to her, "Pretend you are in mourning. Dress in mourning clothes, and don't use any cosmetic lotions. Act like a woman who has spent many days grieving for the dead. 3 Then go to the king and speak these words to him." And Joab[z] put the words in her mouth.

4 When the woman from Tekoa went[c] to the king, she fell with her face to the ground to pay him honor, and she said, "Help me, O king!"

5 The king asked her, "What is troubling you?"

She said, "I am indeed a widow; my husband is dead. 6 I your servant had two sons. They got into a fight with each other in the field, and no one was there to separate them. One struck the other and killed him. 7 Now the whole clan has risen up against your servant; they

### Cross references (right margin)

13:23
[t] 1Sa 25:7

13:28
[u] Jdg 19:6,9,22; 1Sa 25:36

13:31
[v] 2Sa 1:11; 12:16

13:37
[w] 2Sa 3:3

13:39
[x] 2Sa 12:19-23

14:2
[y] 2Ch 11:6; Am 1:1

14:3
[z] ver 19

14:7
[a] Nu 35:19
[b] Mt 21:38
[c] Dt 19:10-13

---

a 34 Septuagint; Hebrew does not have this sentence.   b 39 Dead Sea Scrolls and some Septuagint manuscripts; Masoretic Text *But* [*the spirit of*] *David the king*   c 4 Many Hebrew manuscripts, Septuagint, Vulgate and Syriac; most Hebrew manuscripts *spoke*

13:37–39 Absalom fled to Geshur because King Talmai was his grandfather (1 Chronicles 3:2), and he would be welcomed.

14:1 Why is so much attention given to Absalom in chapters 13—19? His revenge against Amnon and rebellion against David were beginning the final decline of David's kingdom that had been prophesied in 12:10–12. The cycle of lust and murder had begun with David's adultery with Bathsheba. By killing his half-brother Amnon, Absalom was getting revenge for the rape of his sister Tamar, as well as getting rid of the firstborn son, the one next in line to be king. Clearly he had his sights set on being Israel's king and he did everything in his power to obtain that goal—killing a half-brother and rebelling against his father. Absalom was hand-

some and popular like his father, but lacked his father's heart for God.

What can we learn from this terrible story? (1) Even the highest-ranking and best-equipped people are sinners and rebels at heart. We must guard our own hearts against sin and rebellion. (2) David failed to teach his children God's ways. Even if our children are raised in church, we must teach and exemplify character and obedience to God. (3) David was preoccupied with government, wives, and concubines; he failed to act decisively to correct the evil in his family. At times, his guilt over his own sin caused him to decline to discipline his sons caught in similar sins. That proved to be his family's undoing. Whenever possible, we must say, 'Hand over the one who struck his brother down, so that we may put him to death[a] for the life of his brother whom he killed; then we will get rid of the heir[b] as well.' They would put out the only burning coal I have left,[c] leaving my husband neither name nor descendant on the face of the earth."

8 The king said to the woman, "Go home, and I will issue an order in your behalf."

14:9
[d] 1Sa 25:24
[e] Mt 27:25
[f] 1Ki 2:33

9 But the woman from Tekoa said to him, "My lord the king, let the blame[d] rest on me and on my father's family,[e] and let the king and his throne be without guilt.[f]"

10 The king replied, "If anyone says anything to you, bring him to me, and he will not bother you again."

14:11
[g] Nu 35:12,21
[h] 1Sa 14:45

11 She said, "Then let the king invoke the LORD his God to prevent the avenger[g] of blood from adding to the destruction, so that my son will not be destroyed."

"As surely as the LORD lives," he said, "not one hair of your son's head will fall to the ground.[h]"

12 Then the woman said, "Let your servant speak a word to my lord the king."

"Speak," he replied.

14:13
[i] 2Sa 12:7;
1Ki 20:40
[j] 2Sa 13:38-39
14:14
[k] Heb 9:27
[l] Nu 35:15,25-28;
Job 34:15

13 The woman said, "Why then have you devised a thing like this against the people of God? When the king says this, does he not convict himself,[i] for the king has not brought back his banished son?[j] 14 Like water spilled on the ground, which cannot be recovered, so we must die.[k] But God does not take away life; instead, he devises ways so that a banished person[l] may not remain estranged from him.

15 "And now I have come to say this to my lord the king because the people have made me afraid. Your servant thought, 'I will speak to the king; perhaps he will do what his servant asks. 16 Perhaps the king will agree to deliver his servant from the hand of the man who is trying to cut off both me and my son from the inheritance God gave us.'

14:17
[m] ver 20; 2Sa 19:27

17 "And now your servant says, 'May the word of my lord the king bring me rest, for my lord the king is like an angel[m] of God in discerning good and evil. May the LORD your God be with you.'"

18 Then the king said to the woman, "Do not keep from me the answer to what I am going to ask you."

"Let my lord the king speak," the woman said.

14:19
[n] ver 3

19 The king asked, "Isn't the hand of Joab[n] with you in all this?"

The woman answered, "As surely as you live, my lord the king, no one can turn to the right or to the left from anything my lord the king says. Yes, it was your servant Joab who instructed me to do this and who put all these words into the mouth of your servant. 20 Your

14:20
[o] ver 17; 2Sa 19:27

servant Joab did this to change the present situation. My lord has wisdom like that of an angel of God—he knows everything that happens in the land.[o]"

21 The king said to Joab, "Very well, I will do it. Go, bring back the young man Absalom."

22 Joab fell with his face to the ground to pay him honor, and he blessed the king. Joab said, "Today your servant knows that he has found favor in your eyes, my lord the king, because the king has granted his servant's request."

23 Then Joab went to Geshur and brought Absalom back to Jerusalem. 24 But the king said, "He must go to his own house; he must not see my face." So Absalom went to his own house and did not see the face of the king.

25 In all Israel there was not a man so highly praised for his handsome appearance as Absalom. From the top of his head to the sole of his foot there was no blemish in him. 26 Whenever he cut the hair of his head—he used to cut his hair from time to time when it became too heavy for him—he would weigh it, and its weight was two hundred shekels[a] by the royal standard.

14:27
[p] 2Sa 18:18

27 Three sons[p] and a daughter were born to Absalom. The daughter's name was Tamar, and she became a beautiful woman.

28 Absalom lived two years in Jerusalem without seeing the king's face. 29 Then Absalom sent for Joab in order to send him to the king, but Joab refused to come to him. So he sent a

[a] 26 That is, about 5 pounds (about 2.3 kilograms)

---

break cycles of lust, hatred, and rebellion. To do so, we must stay involved in guiding our children's lives while they are still under our care.

14:11 The law provided for a way to avenge murder. Numbers 35:9–21 records how cities of refuge protected people from revenge and how blood avengers were to pursue murderers.

This woman was asking for the king's protection against any claim against her.

14:27 By naming his daughter Tamar, Absalom was showing his love and respect for his sister Tamar. This was also a reminder to everyone of the Amnon/Tamar incident.

second time, but he refused to come. ³⁰Then he said to his servants, "Look, Joab's field is next to mine, and he has barley there. Go and set it on fire." So Absalom's servants set the field on fire.

³¹Then Joab did go to Absalom's house and he said to him, "Why have your servants set my field on fire?"

³²Absalom said to Joab, "Look, I sent word to you and said, 'Come here so I can send you to the king to ask, "Why have I come from Geshur? It would be better for me if I were still there!"' Now then, I want to see the king's face, and if I am guilty of anything, let him put me to death." ⁹

³³So Joab went to the king and told him this. Then the king summoned Absalom, and he came in and bowed down with his face to the ground before the king. And the king kissed ʳ Absalom.

3. National rebellion against David
Absalom's Conspiracy

15 In the course of time,ˢ Absalom provided himself with a chariotᵗ and horses and with fifty men to run ahead of him. ²He would get up early and stand by the side of the road leading to the city gate. ᵘ Whenever anyone came with a complaint to be placed before the king for a decision, Absalom would call out to him, "What town are you from?" He would answer, "Your servant is from one of the tribes of Israel." ³Then Absalom would say to him, "Look, your claims are valid and proper, but there is no representative of the king to hear you." ⁴And Absalom would add, "If only I were appointed judge in the land!ᵛ Then everyone who has a complaint or case could come to me and I would see that he gets justice."

⁵Also, whenever anyone approached him to bow down before him, Absalom would reach out his hand, take hold of him and kiss him. ⁶Absalom behaved in this way toward all the Israelites who came to the king asking for justice, and so he stole the heartsʷ of the men of Israel.

⁷At the end of fourᵃ years, Absalom said to the king, "Let me go to Hebron and fulfill a vow I made to the LORD. ⁸While your servant was living at Geshurˣ in Aram, I made this vow:ʸ 'If the LORD takes me back to Jerusalem, I will worship the LORD in Hebron.ᵇ'"

⁹The king said to him, "Go in peace." So he went to Hebron.

ᵃ7 Some Septuagint manuscripts, Syriac and Josephus; Hebrew *forty*   ᵇ8 Some Septuagint manuscripts; Hebrew does not have *in Hebron*.

14:32 ⁹1Sa 20:8

14:33 ʳGe 33:4; Lk 15:20

15:1 ˢ2Sa 12:11 ᵗ1Ki 1:5

15:2 ᵘ2Sa 19:8

15:4 ᵛJdg 9:29

15:6 ʷRo 16:18

15:8 ˣ2Sa 13:37-38 ʸGe 28:20

14:30 Already we can see the seeds of rebellion in Absalom. As an independent and scheming young man, he took matters into his own hands and killed his brother (13:22–29). Without his father or anyone else to keep him in check, he probably did whatever he wanted, as evidenced by his setting Joab's field on fire to get his attention (14:30). Undoubtedly his good looks also added to his self-centeredness (14:25). Children need discipline, especially those with natural abilities and beauty. Otherwise, like Absa-lom, they will grow up thinking they can do whatever they want whenever they want to.

14:33 David only made halfhearted efforts to correct his children. He did not punish Amnon for his sin against Tamar, nor did he deal decisively with Absalom's murder of Amnon. Such indecisiveness became David's undoing. When we ignore sin, we experience greater pain than if we deal with it immediately.

15:1ff David wrote several psalms during the days of Absalom's rebellion. Some of them are Psalms 39, 41, 55, 61, and 63.

15:2 The city gate was like city hall and a shopping center combined. Because Jerusalem was the nation's capital, both local and national leaders met there daily to transact business and conduct government affairs. The city gate was the perfect spot for this because government and business transactions needed witnesses to be legitimate, and anyone entering or leaving the city had to enter through the gate. Merchants set up their tent-shops near the gate for the same reason. Absalom, therefore, went to the city gate to win the hearts of Israel's leaders as well as those of the common people.

15:5, 6 Absalom's political strategy was to steal the hearts of the people with his good looks, grand entrances, apparent concern for justice, and friendly embraces. Many were fooled and switched their allegiance. Later, however, Absalom proved to be an evil ruler.

We need to evaluate our leaders to make sure their charisma is not a mask covering graft, deception, or hunger for power. Make sure that underneath their style and charm, they are able to make good decisions and handle people wisely.

15:9 Absalom went to Hebron because it was his hometown (3:2, 3). Hebron was David's first capital as well, and there Absalom could expect to find loyal friends who would be proud of him.

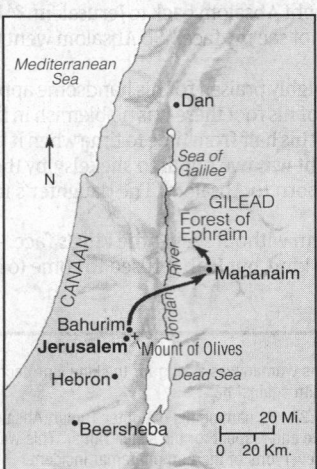

ABSALOM'S REBELLION
Absalom crowned himself king in Hebron. David and his men fled from Jerusalem, crossed the Jordan and went to Mahanaim. Absalom and his army followed, only to be defeated in the forest of Ephraim, where Absalom was killed.

Mediterranean Sea

•Dan

Sea of Galilee

GILEAD Forest of Ephraim

CANAAN

Jordan River

•Mahanaim

Bahurim•
Jerusalem• •Mount of Olives

Hebron•   Dead Sea

•Beersheba

N

0   20 Mi.
0   20 Km.

¹⁰Then Absalom sent secret messengers throughout the tribes of Israel to say, "As soon as you hear the sound of the trumpets, then say, 'Absalom is king in Hebron.'" ¹¹Two hundred men from Jerusalem had accompanied Absalom. They had been invited as guests and went quite innocently, knowing nothing about the matter. ¹²While Absalom was offering sacrifices, he also sent for Ahithophel ^z the Gilonite, David's counselor, to come from Giloh, ^a his hometown. And so the conspiracy gained strength, and Absalom's following kept on increasing. ^b

15:12
^z ver 31,34
^a Jos 15:51
^b Ps 3:1

David Flees

¹³A messenger came and told David, "The hearts of the men of Israel are with Absalom."

15:14
^c Ps 3 Title
^d 2Sa 19:9

¹⁴Then David said to all his officials who were with him in Jerusalem, "Come! We must flee, ^c or none of us will escape from Absalom. ^d We must leave immediately, or he will move quickly to overtake us and bring ruin upon us and put the city to the sword."

¹⁵The king's officials answered him, "Your servants are ready to do whatever our lord the king chooses."

ABSALOM

A father's mistakes are often reflected in the lives of his children. In Absalom, David saw a bitter replay and amplification of many of his own past sins. God had predicted that David's family would suffer because of his sin against Bathsheba and Uriah. David's heart was broken as he realized that God's predictions were coming true. God forgave David, but he did not cancel the consequences of his sin. David was horrified as he saw his son's strengths run wild without the controls God had built into his own life.

By most casual evaluations, Absalom would have made an excellent king, and the people loved him. But he lacked the inner character and control needed in a good leader. His appearance, skill, and position did not make up for his lack of personal integrity.

David's sins took him away from God, but repentance brought him back. In contrast, Absalom sinned and kept on sinning. Although he relied heavily on the advice of others, he was not wise enough to evaluate the counsel he received.

Can you identify with Absalom? Do you find yourself on a fast track toward self-destruction? Absalom wasn't able to say, "I was wrong. I need forgiveness." God offers forgiveness, but we will not experience that forgiveness until we genuinely admit our sins and confess them to God. Absalom rejected his father's love and ultimately God's love. How often do you miss entering back into God's love through the door of forgiveness?

Strengths and accomplishments:	• Was handsome and charismatic like his father, David • Kindly comforted his sister Tamar after she had been raped and allowed her to live with him
Weaknesses and mistakes:	• Avenged the rape of his sister Tamar by killing his half brother Amnon • Plotted against his father to take away the throne • Consistently listened to the wrong advice
Lessons from his life:	• The sins of parents are often repeated and amplified in the children • A smart man gets a lot of advice; a wise man evaluates the advice he gets • Actions against God's plans will fail, sooner or later
Vital statistics:	• Where: Hebron • Occupation: Prince • Relatives: Father: David. Mother: Maacah. Brothers: Amnon, Kileab, Solomon, and others. Sister: Tamar. • Contemporaries: Nathan, Jonadab, Joab, Ahithophel, Hushai
Key verse:	"Then Absalom sent secret messengers throughout the tribes of Israel to say, 'As soon as you hear the sound of the trumpets, then say, "Absalom is king in Hebron"'" (2 Samuel 15:10).

Absalom's story is told in 2 Samuel 3:3; 13—19.

15:14 Had David not escaped from Jerusalem, the ensuing fight might have killed both him and many innocent inhabitants of the city. Some fights that we think necessary can be costly and destructive to those around us. In such cases, it may be wise to back down and save the fight for another day—even if doing so hurts our pride. It takes courage to stand and fight, but it also takes courage to back down for the sake of others.

15:14 Why couldn't David just crush this rebellion? There were several reasons he chose to flee: (1) The rebellion was widespread (15:10–13) and would not have been easily suppressed; (2) David did not want the city of Jerusalem to be destroyed; (3) David still cared for his son and did not want to hurt him. We know that David expected to return to Jerusalem soon because he left ten of his concubines to take care of the palace (15:16).

16The king set out, with his entire household following him; but he left ten concubines[e] to take care of the palace. 17So the king set out, with all the people following him, and they halted at a place some distance away. 18All his men marched past him, along with all the Kerethites[f] and Pelethites; and all the six hundred Gittites who had accompanied him from Gath marched before the king.

19The king said to Ittai[g] the Gittite, "Why should you come along with us? Go back and stay with King Absalom. You are a foreigner, an exile from your homeland. 20You came only yesterday. And today shall I make you wander[h] about with us, when I do not know where I am going? Go back, and take your countrymen. May kindness and faithfulness be with you."

21But Ittai replied to the king, "As surely as the LORD lives, and as my lord the king lives, wherever my lord the king may be, whether it means life or death, there will your servant be."[i]

22David said to Ittai, "Go ahead, march on." So Ittai the Gittite marched on with all his men and the families that were with him.

23The whole countryside wept aloud as all the people passed by. The king also crossed the Kidron Valley, and all the people moved on toward the desert.

24Zadok was there, too, and all the Levites who were with him were carrying the ark of the covenant of God. They set down the ark of God, and Abiathar offered sacrifices[a] until all the people had finished leaving the city.

25Then the king said to Zadok, "Take the ark of God back into the city. If I find favor in the LORD's eyes, he will bring me back and let me see it and his dwelling place[j] again. 26But if he says, 'I am not pleased with you,' then I am ready; let him do to me whatever seems good to him."[k]

27The king also said to Zadok the priest, "Aren't you a seer?[l] Go back to the city in peace, with your son Ahimaaz and Jonathan[m] son of Abiathar. You and Abiathar take your two sons with you. 28I will wait at the fords[n] in the desert until word comes from you to inform me." 29So Zadok and Abiathar took the ark of God back to Jerusalem and stayed there.

30But David continued up the Mount of Olives, weeping as he went; his head[o] was covered and he was barefoot. All the people with him covered their heads too and were weeping as they went up. 31Now David had been told, "Ahithophel[p] is among the conspirators with Absalom." So David prayed, "O LORD, turn Ahithophel's counsel into foolishness."

32When David arrived at the summit, where people used to worship God, Hushai the Arkite[q] was there to meet him, his robe torn and dust on his head. 33David said to him, "If you go with me, you will be a burden[r] to me. 34But if you return to the city and say to Absalom, 'I will be your servant, O king; I was your father's servant in the past, but now I will be your servant,'[s] then you can help me by frustrating Ahithophel's advice. 35Won't the priests Zadok and Abiathar be there with you? Tell them anything you hear in the king's palace.[t] 36Their two sons, Ahimaaz son of Zadok and Jonathan[u] son of Abiathar, are there with them. Send them to me with anything you hear."

37So David's friend Hushai[v] arrived at Jerusalem as Absalom was entering the city.

David and Ziba

16 When David had gone a short distance beyond the summit, there was Ziba,[w] the steward of Mephibosheth, waiting to meet him. He had a string of donkeys saddled and loaded with two hundred loaves of bread, a hundred cakes of raisins, a hundred cakes of figs and a skin of wine.

2The king asked Ziba, "Why have you brought these?"

Ziba answered, "The donkeys are for the king's household to ride on, the bread and fruit are for the men to eat, and the wine is to refresh[x] those who become exhausted in the desert."

3The king then asked, "Where is your master's grandson?"[y]

[a]24 Or *Abiathar went up*

Cross references
15:16 e 2Sa 16:21-22
15:18 f 2Sa 8:18
15:19 g 2Sa 18:2
15:20 h 1Sa 23:13
15:21 i Ru 1:16-17
15:25 j Ps 43:3
15:26 k 1Sa 3:18
15:27 l 1Sa 9:9; m 2Sa 17:17
15:28 n 2Sa 17:16
15:30 o Est 6:12; Isa 20:2-4
15:31 p 2Sa 16:23; 17:14,23
15:32 q Jos 16:2
15:33 r 2Sa 19:35
15:34 s 2Sa 16:19
15:35 t 2Sa 17:15-16
15:36 u ver 27
15:37 v 2Sa 16:16-17; 1Ch 27:33
16:1 w 2Sa 9:1-13
16:2 x 2Sa 17:27-29
16:3 y 2Sa 19:26-27

15:17, 18 David had many loyal non-Israelites in his armed forces. The Gittites, from the Philistine city of Gath, were apparently friends David had acquired while hiding from Saul. The Kerethites and Pelethites were also from Philistine territory. Although Israel was supposed to destroy wicked enemies, the nation was to welcome foreigners who came on friendly terms (Exodus 23:9; Deuteronomy 10:19) and to try to show them the importance of obeying God.

15:24, 25 The priests and Levites were also loyal to David.

15:27–37 David needed spies in Absalom's court to inform him of Absalom's decisions. By sending Hushai to Absalom as a supposed traitor to David, Hushai could offer advice contradictory to Ahithophel's advice. Ahithophel was Absalom's adviser (he was also Bathsheba's grandfather).

16:3 Saul was Mephibosheth's grandfather. Most likely Ziba was lying, hoping to receive a reward from David. (See 19:24–30 for Mephibosheth's side of the story.) For the story of Mephibosheth, see chapter 9.

Ziba said to him, "He is staying in Jerusalem, because he thinks, 'Today the house of Israel will give me back my grandfather's kingdom.'"

[4]Then the king said to Ziba, "All that belonged to Mephibosheth is now yours."

"I humbly bow," Ziba said. "May I find favor in your eyes, my lord the king."

Shimei Curses David

16:5
*z*2Sa 19:16-23;
1Ki 2:8-9,36,44

[5]As King David approached Bahurim, a man from the same clan as Saul's family came out from there. His name was Shimei *z* son of Gera, and he cursed as he came out. [6]He pelted David and all the king's officials with stones, though all the troops and the special guard were on David's right and left. [7]As he cursed, Shimei said, "Get out, get out, you man of blood, you scoundrel! [8]The LORD has repaid you for all the blood you shed in the household of Saul, in whose place you have reigned. The LORD has handed the kingdom over to your son Absalom. You have come to ruin because you are a man of blood!"

[9]Then Abishai son of Zeruiah said to the king, "Why should this dead dog curse my lord the king? Let me go over and cut off his head."

16:10
*a*2Sa 19:22
*b*Ro 9:20

[10]But the king said, "What do you and I have in common, you sons of Zeruiah? *a* If he is cursing because the LORD said to him, 'Curse David,' who can ask, 'Why do you do this?'" *b*

16:11
*c*2Sa 12:11

[11]David then said to Abishai and all his officials, "My son, *c* who is of my own flesh, is trying to take my life. How much more, then, this Benjamite! Leave him alone; let him curse, for the LORD has told him to. [12]It may be that the LORD will see my distress and repay me with

16:12
*d*Dt 23:5; Ro 8:28

good *d* for the cursing I am receiving today."

[13]So David and his men continued along the road while Shimei was going along the hillside opposite him, cursing as he went and throwing stones at him and showering him with dirt. [14]The king and all the people with him arrived at their destination exhausted. And there he refreshed himself.

The Advice of Ahithophel and Hushai

16:15
*e*2Sa 15:37

[15]Meanwhile, Absalom *e* and all the men of Israel came to Jerusalem, and Ahithophel was with him. [16]Then Hushai *f* the Arkite, David's friend, went to Absalom and said to him, "Long

16:16
*f*2Sa 15:37

live the king! Long live the king!"

HIGHS AND LOWS OF DAVID'S LIFE

The Bible calls David a man after God's own heart (1 Samuel 13:14; Acts 13:22), but that didn't mean his life was free of troubles. David's life was full of highs and lows. Some of David's troubles were a result of his sins; some were a result of the sins of others. We can't always control our ups and downs, but we can trust God every day. We can be certain that he will help us through our trials, just as he helped David. In the end, he will reward us for our consistent faith.

16:4 David believed Ziba's charge against Mephibosheth without checking into it or even being skeptical. Don't be hasty to accept someone's condemnation of another, especially when the accuser may profit from the other's downfall. David should have been skeptical of Ziba's comments until he checked them out for himself.

16:5–14 Shimei kept up a steady tirade against David. Although his curses were unjustified because David had had no part in

Saul's death, David and his followers quietly tolerated the abuse. Maintaining your composure in the face of unjustified criticism can be a trying experience and an emotional drain, but if you can't stop criticism, it is best just to ignore it. Remember that God knows what you are enduring, and he will vindicate you if you are in the right.

17Absalom asked Hushai, "Is this the love you show your friend? Why didn't you go with your friend?"[g]

18Hushai said to Absalom, "No, the one chosen by the LORD, by these people, and by all the men of Israel—his I will be, and I will remain with him. 19Furthermore, whom should I serve? Should I not serve the son? Just as I served your father, so I will serve you."[h]

20Absalom said to Ahithophel, "Give us your advice. What should we do?"

21Ahithophel answered, "Lie with your father's concubines whom he left to take care of the palace. Then all Israel will hear that you have made yourself a stench in your father's nostrils, and the hands of everyone with you will be strengthened." 22So they pitched a tent for Absalom on the roof, and he lay with his father's concubines in the sight of all Israel.[i]

23Now in those days the advice Ahithophel gave was like that of one who inquires of God. That was how both David[j] and Absalom regarded all of Ahithophel's advice.

17 Ahithophel said to Absalom, "I would[a] choose twelve thousand men and set out tonight in pursuit of David. 2I would[b] attack him while he is weary and weak.[k] I would[b] strike him with terror, and then all the people with him will flee. I would[b] strike down only the king[l] 3and bring all the people back to you. The death of the man you seek will mean the return of all; all the people will be unharmed." 4This plan seemed good to Absalom and to all the elders of Israel.

5But Absalom said, "Summon also Hushai[m] the Arkite, so we can hear what he has to say." 6When Hushai came to him, Absalom said, "Ahithophel has given this advice. Should we do what he says? If not, give us your opinion."

7Hushai replied to Absalom, "The advice Ahithophel has given is not good this time. 8You know your father and his men; they are fighters, and as fierce as a wild bear robbed of her cubs.[n] Besides, your father is an experienced fighter; he will not spend the night with the troops. 9Even now, he is hidden in a cave or some other place. If he should attack your troops first,[c] whoever hears about it will say, 'There has been a slaughter among the troops who follow Absalom.' 10Then even the bravest soldier, whose heart is like the heart of a lion, will melt[o] with fear, for all Israel knows that your father is a fighter and that those with him are brave.

11"So I advise you: Let all Israel, from Dan to Beersheba—as numerous as the sand on the seashore—be gathered to you, with you yourself leading them into battle. 12Then we will attack him wherever he may be found, and we will fall on him as dew settles on the ground. Neither he nor any of his men will be left alive. 13If he withdraws into a city, then all Israel will bring ropes to that city, and we will drag it down to the valley until not even a piece of it can be found."

14Absalom and all the men of Israel said, "The advice of Hushai the Arkite is better than that of Ahithophel." For the LORD had determined to frustrate[p] the good advice of Ahithophel in order to bring disaster[q] on Absalom.

15Hushai told Zadok and Abiathar, the priests, "Ahithophel has advised Absalom and the elders of Israel to do such and such, but I have advised them to do so and so. 16Now send a message immediately and tell David, 'Do not spend the night at the fords in the desert;[r] cross over without fail, or the king and all the people with him will be swallowed up.'"

17Jonathan[s] and Ahimaaz were staying at En Rogel.[t] A servant girl was to go and inform them, and they were to go and tell King David, for they could not risk being seen entering the city. 18But a young man saw them and told Absalom. So the two of them left quickly and went to the house of a man in Bahurim.[u] He had a well in his courtyard, and they climbed down into it. 19His wife took a covering and spread it out over the opening of the well and scattered grain over it. No one knew anything about it.[v]

20When Absalom's men came to the woman[w] at the house, they asked, "Where are Ahimaaz and Jonathan?"

a1 Or Let me   b2 Or will   c9 Or When some of the men fall at the first attack

---

Cross references

16:17 g 2Sa 19:25
16:19 h 2Sa 15:34
16:22 i 2Sa 12:11-12
16:23 j 2Sa 15:12
17:2 k 2Sa 16:14 l 1Ki 22:31
17:5 m 2Sa 15:32
17:8 n Hos 13:8
17:10 o Jos 2:9,11
17:14 p 2Sa 15:34 q Ps 9:16
17:16 r 2Sa 15:28
17:17 s 2Sa 15:27,36 t Jos 15:7; 18:16
17:18 u 2Sa 16:5
17:19 v Jos 2:6
17:20 w Jos 2:3-5

16:21, 22 This incident fulfilled Nathan's prediction that because of David's sin, another man would sleep with his wives (12:11, 12). (See the note on 3:6, 7 for the cultural significance of this act.)

16:23 Ahithophel was an adviser to Absalom. Most rulers had advisers to help them make decisions about governmental and political matters. They probably arranged the king's marriages as well because these were usually politically motivated unions. But God made Ahithophel's advice seem foolish, just as David had prayed (15:31).

17:11 Hushai appealed to Absalom through flattery, and Absalom's vanity became his own trap. Hushai predicted great glory for Absalom if he personally led the entire army against David. "Pride goes before destruction" (Proverbs 16:18) is an appropriate comment on Absalom's ambitions.

The woman answered them, "They crossed over the brook." a The men searched but found no one, so they returned to Jerusalem.

21After the men had gone, the two climbed out of the well and went to inform King David. They said to him, "Set out and cross the river at once; Ahithophel has advised such and such against you." 22So David and all the people with him set out and crossed the Jordan. By daybreak, no one was left who had not crossed the Jordan.

23When Ahithophel saw that his advice x had not been followed, he saddled his donkey and set out for his house in his hometown. He put his house in order y and then hanged himself. So he died and was buried in his father's tomb.

24David went to Mahanaim, z and Absalom crossed the Jordan with all the men of Israel. 25Absalom had appointed Amasa a over the army in place of Joab. Amasa was the son of a man named Jether,b b an Israelitec who had married Abigail,d the daughter of Nahash and sister of Zeruiah the mother of Joab. 26The Israelites and Absalom camped in the land of Gilead.

27When David came to Mahanaim, Shobi son of Nahash from Rabbah c of the Ammonites, and Makir son of Ammiel from Lo Debar, and Barzillai d the Gileadite from Rogelim 28brought bedding and bowls and articles of pottery. They also brought wheat and barley, flour and roasted grain, beans and lentils, e 29honey and curds, sheep, and cheese from cows' milk for David and his people to eat. For they said, "The people have become hungry and tired and thirsty in the desert. e"

Absalom's Death

18 David mustered the men who were with him and appointed over them commanders of thousands and commanders of hundreds. 2David sent the troops outf—a third under the command of Joab, a third under Joab's brother Abishai son of Zeruiah, and a third under Ittai g the Gittite. The king told the troops, "I myself will surely march out with you."

3But the men said, "You must not go out; if we are forced to flee, they won't care about us. Even if half of us die, they won't care; but you are worth ten thousand of us.f It would be better now for you to give us support from the city." h

4The king answered, "I will do whatever seems best to you."

So the king stood beside the gate while all the men marched out in units of hundreds and of thousands. 5The king commanded Joab, Abishai and Ittai, "Be gentle with the young man Absalom for my sake." And all the troops heard the king giving orders concerning Absalom to each of the commanders.

6The army marched into the field to fight Israel, and the battle took place in the forest i of Ephraim. 7There the army of Israel was defeated by David's men, and the casualties that day were great—twenty thousand men. 8The battle spread out over the whole countryside, and the forest claimed more lives that day than the sword.

9Now Absalom happened to meet David's men. He was riding his mule, and as the mule went under the thick branches of a large oak, Absalom's headj got caught in the tree. He was left hanging in midair, while the mule he was riding kept on going.

10When one of the men saw this, he told Joab, "I just saw Absalom hanging in an oak tree."

11Joab said to the man who had told him this, "What! You saw him? Why didn't you strike him to the ground right there? Then I would have had to give you ten shekelsg of silver and a warrior's belt."

12But the man replied, "Even if a thousand shekelsh were weighed out into my hands, I would not lift my hand against the king's son. In our hearing the king commanded you and

17:23
x2Sa 15:12
y2Ki 20:1; Mt 27:5

17:24
z Ge 32:2; 2Sa 2:8

17:25
a2Sa 19:13
b1Ch 2:13-17

17:27
c2Sa 10:1-2;
12:26,29
d2Sa 19:31-39;
1Ki 2:7

17:29
e2Sa 16:2

18:2
f1Sa 11:11
g2Sa 15:19

18:3
h2Sa 21:17

18:6
iJos 17:18

18:9
j2Sa 14:26

---

a20 Or "They passed by the sheep pen toward the water."   b25 Hebrew Ithra, a variant of Jether   c25 Hebrew and some Septuagint manuscripts; other Septuagint manuscripts (see also 1 Chron. 2:17) Ishmaelite or Jezreelite   d25 Hebrew Abigal, a variant of Abigail   e28 Most Septuagint manuscripts and Syriac; Hebrew lentils, and roasted grain   f3 Two Hebrew manuscripts, some Septuagint manuscripts and Vulgate; most Hebrew manuscripts care; for now there are ten thousand like us   g11 That is, about 4 ounces (about 115 grams)   h12 That is, about 25 pounds (about 11 kilograms)

17:25 Joab and Amasa were David's nephews and Absalom's cousins. Because Joab had left Jerusalem with David (see 18:5, 10ff), Amasa took his place as commander of Israel's troops.

18:1 David took command as he had in former days. In recent years, his life had been characterized by indecisiveness and moral paralysis. At this time he began to take charge and do his duty.

18:12–14 This man had caught Joab in his hypocrisy. He knew Joab would have turned on him for killing the man if the king had

found out about it. Joab could not answer, but only dismissed him. Those about to do evil often do not take the time to consider what they are about to do. They don't care whether or not it is right or lawful. Don't rush into action without thinking. Consider whether what you are about to do is right or wrong.

Abishai and Ittai, 'Protect the young man Absalom for my sake.ᵃ ' ¹³And if I had put my life in jeopardyᵇ—and nothing is hidden from the king—you would have kept your distance from me."

¹⁴Joabᵏ said, "I'm not going to wait like this for you." So he took three javelins in his hand and plunged them into Absalom's heart while Absalom was still alive in the oak tree. ¹⁵And ten of Joab's armor-bearers surrounded Absalom, struck him and killed him.

¹⁶Then Joab *l* sounded the trumpet, and the troops stopped pursuing Israel, for Joab halted them. ¹⁷They took Absalom, threw him into a big pit in the forest and piled upᵐ a large heap of rocksⁿ over him. Meanwhile, all the Israelites fled to their homes.

¹⁸During his lifetime Absalom had taken a pillar and erected it in the King's Valleyᵒ as a monumentᵖ to himself, for he thought, "I have no son�q to carry on the memory of my name." He named the pillar after himself, and it is called Absalom's Monument to this day.

David Mourns

¹⁹Now Ahimaazʳ son of Zadok said, "Let me run and take the news to the king that the Lord has delivered him from the hand of his enemies.ˢ"

²⁰"You are not the one to take the news today," Joab told him. "You may take the news another time, but you must not do so today, because the king's son is dead."

²¹Then Joab said to a Cushite, "Go, tell the king what you have seen." The Cushite bowed down before Joab and ran off.

²²Ahimaaz son of Zadok again said to Joab, "Come what may, please let me run behind the Cushite."

But Joab replied, "My son, why do you want to go? You don't have any news that will bring you a reward."

²³He said, "Come what may, I want to run."

So Joab said, "Run!" Then Ahimaaz ran by way of the plainᶜ and outran the Cushite.

²⁴While David was sitting between the inner and outer gates, the watchman *t* went up to the roof of the gateway by the wall. As he looked out, he saw a man running alone. ²⁵The watchman called out to the king and reported it.

The king said, "If he is alone, he must have good news." And the man came closer and closer.

²⁶Then the watchman saw another man running, and he called down to the gatekeeper, "Look, another man running alone!"

The king said, "He must be bringing good news, too."

²⁷The watchman said, "It seems to me that the first one runs like Ahimaaz son of Zadok."

"He's a good man," the king said. "He comes with good news."

²⁸Then Ahimaaz called out to the king, "All is well!" He bowed down before the king with his face to the ground and said, "Praise be to the Lord your God! He has delivered up the men who lifted their hands against my lord the king."

²⁹The king asked, "Is the young man Absalom safe?"

Ahimaaz answered, "I saw great confusion just as Joab was about to send the king's servant and me, your servant, but I don't know what it was."

³⁰The king said, "Stand aside and wait here." So he stepped aside and stood there.

³¹Then the Cushite arrived and said, "My lord the king, hear the good news! The Lord has delivered you today from all who rose up against you."

³²The king asked the Cushite, "Is the young man Absalom safe?"

The Cushite replied, "May the enemies of my lord the king and all who rise up to harm you be like that young man."ᵘ

³³The king was shaken. He went up to the room over the gateway and wept. As he went, he said: "O my son Absalom! My son, my son Absalom! If only I had diedᵛ instead of you— O Absalom, my son, my son!"ʷ

ᵃ *12* A few Hebrew manuscripts, Septuagint, Vulgate and Syriac; most Hebrew manuscripts may be translated *Absalom, whoever you may be.*   ᵇ *13* Or *Otherwise, if I had acted treacherously toward him*   ᶜ *23* That is, the plain of the Jordan

---

18:14
ᵏ2Sa 14:30

18:16
*l*2Sa 2:28; 20:22

18:17
ᵐJos 7:26
ⁿJos 8:29

18:18
ᵒGe 14:17
ᵖ1Sa 15:12
q2Sa 14:27

18:19
ʳ2Sa 15:36
ˢver 31

18:24
*t*2Sa 19:8; 2Ki 9:17

18:32
ᵘ1Sa 25:26

18:33
ᵛEx 32:32
ʷ2Sa 19:4; Ro 9:3

18:29 Although he reached the city first, Ahimaaz was afraid to tell the king the truth about the death of his son Absalom.

18:33 Why was David so upset over the death of his rebel son? (1) David realized that he, in part, was responsible for Absalom's death. Nathan, the prophet, had said that because David had killed Uriah, his own sons would rebel against him. (2) David was angry at Joab and his officers for killing Absalom against his wishes. (3) David truly loved his son, even though Absalom did nothing to deserve his love. It would have been kinder and more loving to deal with Absalom and his runaway ego when he was younger.

19

Joab was told, "The king is weeping and mourning for Absalom." ²And for the whole army the victory that day was turned into mourning, because on that day the troops heard it said, "The king is grieving for his son." ³The men stole into the city that day as men steal in who are ashamed when they flee from battle. ⁴The king covered his face and cried aloud, "O my son Absalom! O Absalom, my son, my son!"

⁵Then Joab went into the house to the king and said, "Today you have humiliated all your men, who have just saved your life and the lives of your sons and daughters and the lives of your wives and concubines. ⁶You love those who hate you and hate those who love you. You have made it clear today that the commanders and their men mean nothing to you. I see that you would be pleased if Absalom were alive today and all of us were dead. ⁷Now go out and encourage your men. I swear by the LORD that if you don't go out, not a man will be left with you by nightfall. This will be worse for you than all the calamities that have come upon you from your youth till now."

REBELLION
The Bible records many rebellions. Many were against God's chosen leaders. They were doomed for failure. Others were begun by wicked men against wicked men. While these were sometimes successful, the rebel's life usually came to a violent end. Still other rebellions were made by good people against the wicked or unjust actions of others. This kind of rebellion is sometimes good in freeing the common people from oppression and giving them the freedom to turn back to God.

Who rebelled?	Whom they rebelled against	What happened	Reference
Adam and Eve	God	Expelled from Eden	Genesis 3
Israelites	God, Moses	Forced to wander in desert for 40 years	Numbers 14
Korah	Moses	Swallowed by the earth	Numbers 16
Israelites Absalom (David's son)	God	God took away his special promise of protection	Judges 2
Sheba	David	Killed in battle	2 Samuel 15—18
Adonijah (David's son)	David	Killed in battle	2 Samuel 20
Joab	David, Solomon	Killed for treason	1 Kings 1; 2
Ten tribes of Israel	David, Solomon	Supported Adonijah's kingship without seeking God's choice. Killed for treason	1 Kings 1; 2
Baasha, king of Israel	Rehoboam	The kingdom was divided. The 10 tribes forgot about God, sinned, and were eventually taken into captivity	1 Kings 12:16–20
Zimri, king of Israel	Nadab, king of Israel	Overthrew the throne and became king. God destroyed his descendants	1 Kings 15:27—16:7
Jehu, king of Israel	Elah, king of Israel	Overthrew the throne, but killed himself when his rule was not accepted	1 Kings 16:9–16
Joash, king of Judah	Joram, king of Israel Ahaziah, king of Judah	Killed both kings. Later turned from God and his dynasty was wiped out	2 Kings 9; 10
Jehoiada, a priest	Athaliah, queen of Judah	Athaliah, a wicked queen, was overthrown. This was a "good" rebellion	2 Kings 11
Shallum, king of Israel	Zechariah, king of Israel	Overthrew the throne, but then was assassinated	2 Kings 15:8–15
Menahem, king of Israel	Shallum, king of Israel	Overthrew the throne, but then was invaded by Assyrian army	2 Kings 15:16–22
Hoshea, king of Israel	Assyria	The city of Samaria was destroyed, the nation of Israel taken into captivity	2 Kings 17
Zedekiah, king of Judah	Nebuchadnezzar, king of Babylon	The city of Jerusalem was destroyed, the nation of Judah taken into captivity	2 Kings 24; 25

19:4-7 At times we must reprove those in authority over us. Joab knew he was risking the king's displeasure by confronting him, but he saw what had to be done. Joab told David that there would be dreadful consequences if he didn't commend the troops for their victory. Joab's actions are a helpful example to us when personal confrontation is necessary.

8 So the king got up and took his seat in the gateway. When the men were told, "The king is sitting in the gateway,ˣ" they all came before him.

David Returns to Jerusalem

Meanwhile, the Israelites had fled to their homes. 9 Throughout the tribes of Israel, the people were all arguing with each other, saying, "The king delivered us from the hand of our enemies; he is the one who rescued us from the hand of the Philistines.ʸ But now he has fled the country because of Absalom;ᶻ 10 and Absalom, whom we anointed to rule over us, has died in battle. So why do you say nothing about bringing the king back?"

11 King David sent this message to Zadok and Abiathar, the priests: "Ask the elders of Judah, 'Why should you be the last to bring the king back to his palace, since what is being said throughout Israel has reached the king at his quarters? 12 You are my brothers, my own flesh and blood. So why should you be the last to bring back the king?' 13 And say to Amasa,ᵃ 'Are you not my own flesh and blood? May God deal with me, be it ever so severely, if from now on you are not the commander of my army in place of Joab.'"

14 He won over the hearts of all the men of Judah as though they were one man. They sent word to the king, "Return, you and all your men." 15 Then the king returned and went as far as the Jordan.

Now the men of Judah had come to Gilgal ᵇ to go out and meet the king and bring him across the Jordan. 16 Shimeiᶜ son of Gera, the Benjamite from Bahurim, hurried down with the men of Judah to meet King David. 17 With him were a thousand Benjamites, along with Ziba, ᵈ the steward of Saul's household, and his fifteen sons and twenty servants. They rushed to the Jordan, where the king was. 18 They crossed at the ford to take the king's household over and to do whatever he wished.

When Shimei son of Gera crossed the Jordan, he fell prostrate before the king 19 and said to him, "May my lord not hold me guilty. Do not remember how your servant did wrong on the day my lord the king left Jerusalem.ᵉ May the king put it out of his mind. 20 For I your servant know that I have sinned, but today I have come here as the first of the whole house of Joseph to come down and meet my lord the king."

21 Then Abishai son of Zeruiah said, "Shouldn't Shimei be put to death for this? He cursedᶠ the LORD's anointed."

22 David replied, "What do you and I have in common, you sons of Zeruiah?ᵍ This day you have become my adversaries! Should anyone be put to death in Israel today?ʰ Do I not know that today I am king over Israel?" 23 So the king said to Shimei, "You shall not die." And the king promised him on oath.ⁱ

24 Mephibosheth,ʲ Saul's grandson, also went down to meet the king. He had not taken care of his feet or trimmed his mustache or washed his clothes from the day the king left until the day he returned safely. 25 When he came from Jerusalem to meet the king, the king asked him, "Why didn't you go with me,ᵏ Mephibosheth?"

26 He said, "My lord the king, since I your servant am lame, I said, 'I will have my donkey saddled and will ride on it, so I can go with the king.' But Ziba ˡ my servant betrayed me. 27 And he has slandered your servant to my lord the king. My lord the king is like an angelᵐ of God; so do whatever pleases you. 28 All my grandfather's descendants deserved nothing but death from my lord the king, but you gave your servant a place among those who eat at your table.ⁿ So what right do I have to make any more appeals to the king?"

19:8 David sat at the gateway (city gate) because that was where business was conducted and judgment rendered. His presence there showed that he was over his mourning and back in control.

19:8–10 Just a few days before, most of Israel was supporting the rebel ruler Absalom. Now the people wanted David back as their king. Because crowds are often fickle, there must be a higher moral code to follow than the pleasure of the majority. Following the moral principles given in God's Word will help you avoid being swayed by the popular opinions of the crowd.

19:13 David's appointment of Amasa was a shrewd political move. First, Amasa had been commander of Absalom's army; by making Amasa his commander, David would secure the allegiance of the rebel army. Second, by replacing Joab as commander in chief, David punished him for his previous crimes

(3:26–29). Third, Amasa had a great deal of influence over the leaders of Judah (19:14). All of these factors would help to unite the kingdom.

19:19, 20 By admitting his wrong and asking David's forgiveness, Shimei was trying to save his own life. His plan worked for a while. This was a day of celebration, not execution. But we read in 1 Kings 2:8, 9 that David advised Solomon to execute Shimei.

19:21ff David showed tremendous mercy and generosity as he returned to Jerusalem. He spared Shimei, restored Mephibosheth, and rewarded faithful Barzillai. David's fairness sets a standard for government that will be fully realized in Christ's righteous rule in the coming kingdom.

19:24–30 David could not be certain if Mephibosheth or Ziba was in the right, and Scripture leaves the question unanswered. (For the whole story on Mephibosheth, see also 9:1–13 and 16:1–4.)

19:8
ˣ2Sa 15:2

19:9
ʸ2Sa 8:1-14
ᶻ2Sa 15:14

19:13
ᵃ2Sa 17:25

19:15
ᵇJos 5:9

19:16
ᶜ2Sa 16:5-13;
1Ki 2:8

19:17
ᵈ2Sa 16:1-2

19:19
ᵉ1Sa 22:15;
2Sa 16:6-8

19:21
ᶠEx 22:28

19:22
ᵍ2Sa 16:10
ʰ1Sa 11:13

19:23
ⁱ1Ki 2:8,42

19:24
ʲ2Sa 9:6-10

19:25
ᵏ2Sa 16:17

19:26
ˡ2Sa 9:2

19:27
ᵐ2Sa 14:17,20

19:28
ⁿ2Sa 9:7,13

²⁹ The king said to him, "Why say more? I order you and Ziba to divide the fields."

³⁰ Mephibosheth said to the king, "Let him take everything, now that my lord the king has arrived home safely."

³¹ Barzillai ᵒ the Gileadite also came down from Rogelim to cross the Jordan with the king and to send him on his way from there. ³² Now Barzillai was a very old man, eighty years of age. He had provided for the king during his stay in Mahanaim, for he was a very wealthy ᵖ man. ³³ The king said to Barzillai, "Cross over with me and stay with me in Jerusalem, and I will provide for you."

³⁴ But Barzillai answered the king, "How many more years will I live, that I should go up to Jerusalem with the king? ³⁵ I am now eighty �q years old. Can I tell the difference between what is good and what is not? Can your servant taste what he eats and drinks? Can I still hear the voices of men and women singers? Why should your servant be an added burden to my lord the king? ³⁶ Your servant will cross over the Jordan with the king for a short distance, but why should the king reward me in this way? ³⁷ Let your servant return, that I may die in my own town near the tomb of my father ʳ and mother. But here is your servant Kimham. ˢ Let him cross over with my lord the king. Do for him whatever pleases you."

³⁸ The king said, "Kimham shall cross over with me, and I will do for him whatever pleases you. And anything you desire from me I will do for you."

³⁹ So all the people crossed the Jordan, and then the king crossed over. The king kissed Barzillai and gave him his blessing, ᵗ and Barzillai returned to his home.

**Marginal references (left column):**

19:31
ᵒ 1Ki 2:7

19:32
ᵖ 2Sa 17:27

19:35
�q Ps 90:10

19:37
ʳ 1Ki 2:7
ˢ Jer 41:17

19:39
ᵗ Ge 31:55

JOAB

Joab, the great military leader, had two brothers who were also famous soldiers: Abishai and Asahel. Joab proved to be the greatest leader of the three and was the commander of David's army throughout most of David's reign. There is no record that his troops ever lost a battle.

Joab was a fearless fighter like his brothers. Unlike them, he was also a brilliant and ruthless strategist. His plans usually worked, but he was seldom concerned about those hurt or killed by them. He did not hesitate to use treachery or murder to achieve his goals. His career is a story of great accomplishments and shameful acts. He conquered Jerusalem and the surrounding nations, defeated Abner, and reconciled Absalom and David. But he also murdered Abner, Amasa, and Absalom, took part in Uriah's murder, and plotted with Adonijah against Solomon. That plot led to his execution.

Joab set his own standards—he lived by them and died because of them. There is little evidence that Joab ever acknowledged God's standards. On one occasion he confronted David about the danger of taking a census without God's command, but this may have been little more than a move to protect himself. Joab's self-centeredness eventually destroyed him. He was loyal only to himself, even willing to betray his lifelong relationship with David to preserve his power.

Joab's life illustrates the disastrous results of having no source of direction outside oneself. Brilliance and power are self-destructive without God's guidance. Only God can give the direction we need. For that reason, he has made available his Word, the Bible, and he is willing to be personally present in the lives of those who admit their need for him.

Strengths and accomplishments:	• Brilliant planner and strategist • Fearless fighter and resourceful commander • Confident leader who did not hesitate to confront even the king • Helped reconcile David and Absalom • Masterminded the conquest of Jerusalem
Weaknesses and mistakes:	• Was repeatedly ruthless, violent, and vengeful • Carried out David's scheme to have Uriah, Bathsheba's husband, killed • Avenged his brother's murder by murdering Abner • Killed Absalom against David's orders • Plotted with Adonijah against David and Solomon
Lessons from his life:	• Those who live by violence often die by violence • Even brilliant leaders need guidance
Vital statistics:	• Occupation: Commander in chief of David's army • Relatives: Mother: Zeruiah. Brothers: Abishai, Asahel. Uncle: David. • Contemporaries: Saul, Abner, Absalom
Key verse:	"Then the king commanded Benaiah, 'Do as he says. Strike him down and bury him, and so clear me and my father's house of the guilt of the innocent blood that Joab shed'" (1 Kings 2:31).

Joab's story is told in 2 Samuel 2—1 Kings 2. He is also mentioned in 1 Chronicles 2:16; 11:5–9, 20, 26; 19:8–15; 20:1; 21:2–6; 26:28; and in the title of Psalm 60.

⁴⁰When the king crossed over to Gilgal, Kimham crossed with him. All the troops of Judah and half the troops of Israel had taken the king over.

⁴¹Soon all the men of Israel were coming to the king and saying to him, "Why did our brothers, the men of Judah, steal the king away and bring him and his household across the Jordan, together with all his men?"

⁴²All the men of Judah answered the men of Israel, "We did this because the king is closely related to us. Why are you angry about it? Have we eaten any of the king's provisions? Have we taken anything for ourselves?"

⁴³Then the men of Israel answered the men of Judah, "We have ten shares in the king; and besides, we have a greater claim on David than you have. So why do you treat us with contempt? Were we not the first to speak of bringing back our king?"

But the men of Judah responded even more harshly than the men of Israel.

Sheba Rebels Against David

20 Now a troublemaker named Sheba son of Bicri, a Benjamite, happened to be there. He sounded the trumpet and shouted,

> "We have no share in David,ᵘ
>   no part in Jesse's son!ᵛ
> Every man to his tent, O Israel!"

²So all the men of Israel deserted David to follow Sheba son of Bicri. But the men of Judah stayed by their king all the way from the Jordan to Jerusalem.

³When David returned to his palace in Jerusalem, he took the ten concubinesʷ he had left to take care of the palace and put them in a house under guard. He provided for them, but did not lie with them. They were kept in confinement till the day of their death, living as widows.

⁴Then the king said to Amasa,ˣ "Summon the men of Judah to come to me within three days, and be here yourself." ⁵But when Amasa went to summon Judah, he took longer than the time the king had set for him.

⁶David said to Abishai, "Now Sheba son of Bicri will do us more harm than Absalom did. Take your master's men and pursue him, or he will find fortified cities and escape from us." ⁷So Joab's men and the Kerethitesʸ and Pelethites and all the mighty warriors went out under the command of Abishai. They marched out from Jerusalem to pursue Sheba son of Bicri.

⁸While they were at the great rock in Gibeon, Amasa came to meet them. Joab was wearing his military tunic, and strapped over it at his waist was a belt with a dagger in its sheath. As he stepped forward, it dropped out of its sheath.

⁹Joab said to Amasa, "How are you, my brother?" Then Joab took Amasa by the beard with his right hand to kiss him. ¹⁰Amasa was not on his guard against the daggerᶻ in Joab'sᵃ hand, and Joab plunged it into his belly, and his intestines spilled out on the ground. Without being stabbed again, Amasa died. Then Joab and his brother Abishai pursued Sheba son of Bicri.

20:1
ᵘ1Ki 12:16
ᵛ2Ch 10:16

20:3
ʷ2Sa 15:16;
16:21-22

20:4
ˣ2Sa 19:13

20:7
ʸ2Sa 8:18; 1Ki 1:38

20:10
ᶻ2Sa 2:23
ᵃ1Ki 2:5

20:1 Although Israel was a united kingdom, it was still made up of 12 separate tribes. These tribes often had difficulty agreeing on the goals of the nation as a whole. Tribal jealousies had originally kept Israel from completely conquering the promised land (read the book of Joshua), and now tribal jealousies were threatening the stability of David's reign by giving Sheba an opportunity to rebel (20:1ff).

20:7–10 Once again Joab's murderous act went unpunished, just as it did when he killed Abner (3:26, 27). Eventually, however, justice caught up with him (1 Kings 2:28–35). It may seem that sin and treachery often go unpunished, but God's justice is not limited to this life's rewards. Even if Joab had died of old age, he would have to face the day of judgment.

SHEBA'S REBELLION
After defeating Absalom, David returned to Jerusalem from Mahanaim. But Sheba incited a rebellion against David, so David sent Joab, Abishai, and a small army after him. Joab and his troops besieged Abel Beth Maacah, Sheba's hideout, until the people of Abel Beth Maacah killed Sheba themselves.

¹¹One of Joab's men stood beside Amasa and said, "Whoever favors Joab, and whoever is for David, let him follow Joab!" ¹²Amasa lay wallowing in his blood in the middle of the road, and the man saw that all the troops came to a halt there. When he realized that everyone who came up to Amasa stopped, he dragged him from the road into a field and threw a garment over him. ¹³After Amasa had been removed from the road, all the men went on with Joab to pursue Sheba son of Bicri.

¹⁴Sheba passed through all the tribes of Israel to Abel Beth Maacah*a* and through the entire region of the Berites, who gathered together and followed him. ¹⁵All the troops with Joab came and besieged Sheba in Abel Beth Maacah.*b* They built a siege ramp*c* up to the city, and it stood against the outer fortifications. While they were battering the wall to bring it down, ¹⁶a wise woman*d* called from the city, "Listen! Listen! Tell Joab to come here so I can speak to him." ¹⁷He went toward her, and she asked, "Are you Joab?"

"I am," he answered.

She said, "Listen to what your servant has to say."

"I'm listening," he said.

¹⁸She continued, "Long ago they used to say, 'Get your answer at Abel,' and that settled it. ¹⁹We are the peaceful and faithful in Israel. You are trying to destroy a city that is a mother in Israel. Why do you want to swallow up the LORD's inheritance?"*e*

²⁰"Far be it from me!" Joab replied, "Far be it from me to swallow up or destroy! ²¹That is not the case. A man named Sheba son of Bicri, from the hill country of Ephraim, has lifted up his hand against the king, against David. Hand over this one man, and I'll withdraw from the city."

The woman said to Joab, "His head will be thrown to you from the wall."

²²Then the woman went to all the people with her wise advice,*f* and they cut off the head of Sheba son of Bicri and threw it to Joab. So he sounded the trumpet, and his men dispersed from the city, each returning to his home. And Joab went back to the king in Jerusalem.

²³Joab*g* was over Israel's entire army; Benaiah son of Jehoiada was over the Kerethites and Pelethites; ²⁴Adoniram*b h* was in charge of forced labor; Jehoshaphat son of Ahilud was recorder; ²⁵Sheva was secretary; Zadok*i* and Abiathar were priests; ²⁶and Ira the Jairite was David's priest.

4. The later years of David's rule
The Gibeonites Avenged

21 During the reign of David, there was a famine*j* for three successive years; so David sought the face of the LORD. The LORD said, "It is on account of Saul and his blood-stained house; it is because he put the Gibeonites to death."

²The king summoned the Gibeonites*k* and spoke to them. (Now the Gibeonites were not a part of Israel but were survivors of the Amorites; the Israelites had sworn to ⌐spare⌐ them, but Saul in his zeal for Israel and Judah had tried to annihilate them.) ³David asked the Gibeonites, "What shall I do for you? How shall I make amends so that you will bless the LORD's inheritance?"*l*

a 14 Or *Abel, even Beth Maacah*; also in verse 15   *b 24* Some Septuagint manuscripts (see also 1 Kings 4:6 and 5:14); Hebrew *Adoram*

Marginal cross-references

20:15
b 1Ki 15:20;
2Ki 15:29
c 2Ki 19:32

20:16
d 2Sa 14:2

20:19
e 1Sa 26:19;
2Sa 21:3

20:22
f Ecc 9:13

20:23
g 2Sa 8:16-18

20:24
h 1Ki 4:6

20:25
i 2Sa 8:17

21:1
j Ge 12:10

21:2
k Jos 9:15

21:3
l 1Sa 26:19;
2Sa 20:19

20:16ff Joab's men were attacking the city, and it looked as if it would be destroyed. Though women in that society were usually quiet in public, this woman spoke out. She stopped Joab's attack, not with weapons, but with wise words and a plan of action. Often the courage to speak a few sensible words can prevent great disaster.

20:23 Benaiah was the captain of David's bodyguard and a famous member of that special group of mighty men called "the Thirty" (23:24). He remained loyal to David during Absalom's rebellion. Later he helped establish Solomon as king (1 Kings 1:32–40; 2:28–34) and eventually replaced Joab as commander of Israel's army (1 Kings 2:35).

21:1 Farmers relied heavily on spring and fall rains for their crops. If the rains stopped or came at the wrong time, or if the plants became insect infested, there would be drastic food shortages in the coming year. Agriculture at that time was completely dependent upon natural conditions. There were no irrigation

sprinklers, fertilizers, or pesticides. Even moderate variations in rainfall or insect activity could destroy an entire harvest.

21:1ff The next four chapters are an appendix to the book. The events described are not presented in chronological order. They tell of David's exploits at various times during his reign.

21:1–14 Although the Bible does not record Saul's act of vengeance against the Gibeonites, it was apparently a serious crime making him guilty of their blood. Still, why were Saul's sons killed for the murders their father committed? In many Near Eastern cultures, including Israel's, an entire family was held guilty for the crime of the father because the family was considered an indissoluble unit. Saul broke the vow that the Israelites made to the Gibeonites (Joshua 9:16–20). This was a serious offense against God's law (Numbers 30:1, 2). Either David was following the custom of treating the family as a unit, or Saul's sons were guilty of helping Saul kill the Gibeonites.

4 The Gibeonites answered him, "We have no right to demand silver or gold from Saul or his family, nor do we have the right to put anyone in Israel to death."

"What do you want me to do for you?" David asked.

5 They answered the king, "As for the man who destroyed us and plotted against us so that we have been decimated and have no place anywhere in Israel, 6 let seven of his male descendants be given to us to be killed and exposed *m* before the LORD at Gibeah of Saul—the LORD's chosen *n* one."

So the king said, "I will give them to you."

7 The king spared Mephibosheth *o* son of Jonathan, the son of Saul, because of the oath *p* before the LORD between David and Jonathan son of Saul. 8 But the king took Armoni and Mephibosheth, the two sons of Aiah's daughter Rizpah, *q* whom she had borne to Saul, together with the five sons of Saul's daughter Merab, *a* whom she had borne to Adriel son of Barzillai the Meholathite. 9 He handed them over to the Gibeonites, who killed and exposed them on a hill before the LORD. All seven of them fell together; they were put to death during the first days of the harvest, just as the barley harvest was beginning.

10 Rizpah daughter of Aiah took sackcloth and spread it out for herself on a rock. From the beginning of the harvest till the rain poured down from the heavens on the bodies, she did not let the birds of the air touch them by day or the wild animals by night. 11 When David was told what Aiah's daughter Rizpah, Saul's concubine, had done, 12 he went and took the bones of Saul *r* and his son Jonathan from the citizens of Jabesh Gilead. (They had taken them secretly from the public square at Beth Shan, where the Philistines had hung them after they struck Saul down on Gilboa.) 13 David brought the bones of Saul and his son Jonathan from there, and the bones of those who had been killed and exposed were gathered up.

14 They buried the bones of Saul and his son Jonathan in the tomb of Saul's father Kish, at Zela *s* in Benjamin, and did everything the king commanded. After that, *t* God answered prayer *u* in behalf of the land.

Wars Against the Philistines

15 Once again there was a battle between the Philistines and Israel. David went down with his men to fight against the Philistines, and he became exhausted. 16 And Ishbi-Benob, one of the descendants of Rapha, whose bronze spearhead weighed three hundred shekels *b* and who was armed with a new ⌊sword⌋, said he would kill David. 17 But Abishai son of Zeruiah came to David's rescue; he struck the Philistine down and killed him. Then David's men swore to him, saying, "Never again will you go out with us to battle, so that the lamp of Israel will not be extinguished. *v*"

18 In the course of time, there was another battle with the Philistines, at Gob. At that time Sibbecai *w* the Hushathite killed Saph, one of the descendants of Rapha.

19 In another battle with the Philistines at Gob, Elhanan son of Jaare-Oregim *c* the Bethlehemite killed Goliath *d* the Gittite, who had a spear with a shaft like a weaver's rod.

20 In still another battle, which took place at Gath, there was a huge man with six fingers on each hand and six toes on each foot—twenty-four in all. He also was descended from Rapha. 21 When he taunted Israel, Jonathan son of Shimeah, David's brother, killed him.

22 These four were descendants of Rapha in Gath, and they fell at the hands of David and his men.

David's Song of Praise

22 David sang *x* to the LORD the words of this song when the LORD delivered him from the hand of all his enemies and from the hand of Saul. 2 He said:

a 8 Two Hebrew manuscripts, some Septuagint manuscripts and Syriac (see also 1 Samuel 18:19); most Hebrew and Septuagint manuscripts *Michal*   *b* 16 That is, about 7 1/2 pounds (about 3.5 kilograms)   *c* 19 Or *son of Jair the weaver*   *d* 19 Hebrew and Septuagint; 1 Chron. 20:5 *son of Jair killed Lahmi the brother of Goliath*

Cross-references (margin):
21:6 *m* Nu 25:4 *n* 1Sa 10:24
21:7 *o* 2Sa 4:4 *p* 1Sa 18:3; 20:8,15
21:8 *q* 2Sa 3:7
21:12 *r* 1Sa 31:11-13
21:14 *s* Jos 18:28 *t* Jos 7:26 *u* 2Sa 24:25
21:17 *v* 2Sa 18:3
21:18 *w* 1Ch 11:29; 20:4
22:1 *x* Ex 15:1; Jdg 5:1

21:9, 10 The barley harvest was in late April and early May. Barley was similar to wheat but less suitable for breadmaking. Rizpah guarded the men's bodies during the entire harvest season, which lasted from April to October.

21:16–18 By calling these men "descendants of Rapha," the writer was saying that they were giants. For more information on giants, see 1 Samuel 17:4–7 and the note on Genesis 6:4.

22:1ff David was a skilled musician who played his harp for Saul (1 Samuel 16:23), instituted the music programs in the temple (1 Chronicles 25), and wrote more of the book of Psalms than anyone else. Writing a song like this was not unusual for David. This royal hymn of thanksgiving is almost identical to Psalm 18. (For other songs in the Bible, see the chart in Exodus 15, p. 119.)

22:3
y Ge 15:1
z Lk 1:69
a Ps 9:9

"The Lord is my rock, my fortress and my deliverer;
3   my God is my rock, in whom I take refuge,
       my shield*y* and the horn*a z* of my salvation.
He is my stronghold,*a* my refuge and my savior—
       from violent men you save me.
4 I call to the Lord, who is worthy of praise,
       and I am saved from my enemies.

5 "The waves of death swirled about me;
       the torrents of destruction overwhelmed me.

22:6
b Ps 116:3
22:7
c Ps 120:1
d Ps 116:4

6 The cords of the grave*b b* coiled around me;
       the snares of death confronted me.
7 In my distress*c* I called*d* to the Lord;
       I called out to my God.
From his temple he heard my voice;
       my cry came to his ears.

22:8
e Jdg 5:4
f Job 26:11

8 "The earth*e* trembled and quaked,
       the foundations*f* of the heavens*c* shook;
       they trembled because he was angry.

22:9
g Ps 97:3;
Heb 12:29

9 Smoke rose from his nostrils;
       consuming fire*g* came from his mouth,
       burning coals blazed out of it.

22:10
h 1Ki 8:12

10 He parted the heavens and came down;
       dark clouds*h* were under his feet.

a 3 Horn here symbolizes strength. *b 6* Hebrew *Sheol* *c* Hebrew; Vulgate and Syriac (see also Psalm 18:7) *mountains*

ABISHAI

Most great leaders struggle with a few followers who try too hard. For David, Abishai was that kind of follower. His fierce loyalty to David had to be kept from becoming destructive— he was too willing to leap to his leader's defense. David never put down Abishai's eager loyalty. Instead, he patiently tried to direct its powerful energy. This approach, while not completely successful, saved David's life on at least one occasion. At three other times, however, Abishai would have killed for the king if David had not stopped him.

Abishai was an excellent soldier, but he was better at taking orders than giving them. When he wasn't carrying out David's orders, Abishai was usually under the command of his younger brother Joab. The two brothers helped each other accomplish great military feats as well as shameful acts of violence—Abishai helped Joab murder Abner and Amasa. When he was effective as a leader, he led mostly by example. But all too often he did not think before he acted.

We should be challenged by Abishai's admirable qualities of fearlessness and loyalty, but we should be warned by his tendency to act without thinking. It is not enough to be strong and effective; we must also have the self-control and wisdom that God can give us. We are to follow and obey with our hearts and our minds.

Strengths and accomplishments:	• Known as one of the heroes among David's fighting men • A fearless and willing volunteer, fiercely loyal to David • Saved David's life
Weaknesses and mistakes:	• Tended to act without thinking • Helped Joab murder Abner and Amasa
Lessons from his life:	• The most effective followers combine careful thought and action • Blind loyalty can cause great evil
Vital statistics:	• Occupation: Soldier • Relatives: Mother: Zeruiah. Brothers: Joab and Asahel. Uncle: David.
Key verses:	"Abishai the brother of Joab son of Zeruiah was chief of the Three. He raised his spear against three hundred men, whom he killed, and so he became as famous as the Three. Was he not held in greater honor than the Three? He became their commander, even though he was not included among them" (2 Samuel 23:18, 19).

Abishai's story is told in 2 Samuel 2:18—23:19. He is also mentioned in 1 Samuel 26:1–13; 1 Chronicles 2:16; 11:20; 18:12; 19:11, 15.

22:3 David calls God "the horn of my salvation," referring to the strength and defensive protection animals have in their horns. God had helped David overcome his enemies and rescued him from his foes.

11 He mounted the cherubim and flew;
    he soared[a] on the wings of the wind.[i]
12 He made darkness his canopy around him—
    the dark[b] rain clouds of the sky.
13 Out of the brightness of his presence
    bolts of lightning[j] blazed forth.
14 The LORD thundered[k] from heaven;
    the voice of the Most High resounded.
15 He shot arrows and scattered ⌊the enemies⌋,
    bolts of lightning and routed them.
16 The valleys of the sea were exposed
    and the foundations of the earth laid bare
  at the rebuke of the LORD,
    at the blast of breath from his nostrils.

17 "He reached down from on high[l] and took hold of me;
    he drew me out of deep waters.
18 He rescued me from my powerful enemy,
    from my foes, who were too strong for me.
19 They confronted me in the day of my disaster,
    but the LORD was my support.[m]
20 He brought me out into a spacious[n] place;
    he rescued me because he delighted in me.

21 "The LORD has dealt with me according to my righteousness;
    according to the cleanness of my hands[o] he has rewarded me.
22 For I have kept[p] the ways of the LORD;
    I have not done evil by turning from my God.
23 All his laws are before me;[q]
    I have not turned away from his decrees.
24 I have been blameless[r] before him
    and have kept myself from sin.
25 The LORD has rewarded me according to my righteousness,
    according to my cleanness[c] in his sight.

26 "To the faithful you show yourself faithful,
    to the blameless you show yourself blameless,
27 to the pure you show yourself pure,
    but to the crooked you show yourself shrewd.[s]
28 You save the humble,[t]
    but your eyes are on the haughty to bring them low.
29 You are my lamp, O LORD;
    the LORD turns my darkness into light.
30 With your help I can advance against a troop[d];
    with my God I can scale a wall.

31 "As for God, his way is perfect;
    the word of the LORD is flawless.[u]
  He is a shield
    for all who take refuge in him.
32 For who is God besides the LORD?
    And who is the Rock[v] except our God?

22:11 [i] Ps 104:3
22:13 [j] ver 9
22:14 [k] 1Sa 2:10
22:17 [l] Ps 144:7
22:19 [m] Ps 23:4
22:20 [n] Ps 31:8
22:21 [o] Ps 24:4
22:22 [p] Ge 18:19; Ps 128:1
22:23 [q] Dt 6:4-9
22:24 [r] Eph 1:4
22:27 [s] Lev 26:23-24
22:28 [t] Ps 72:12-13
22:31 [u] Ps 12:6
22:32 [v] 1Sa 2:2

a 11 Many Hebrew manuscripts (see also Psalm 18:10); most Hebrew manuscripts *appeared*   b 12 Septuagint and Vulgate (see also Psalm 18:11); Hebrew *massed*   c 25 Hebrew; Septuagint and Vulgate (see also Psalm 18:24) *to the cleanness of my hands*   d 30 Or *can run through a barricade*

22:11 Cherubim are mighty angels.

22:22-24 David was not denying that he had ever sinned. Psalm 51 shows his tremendous anguish over his sin against Uriah and Bathsheba. But David understood God's faithfulness and was writing this hymn from God's perspective. He knew that God had made him clean again—"whiter than snow," (Psalm 51:7) with a "pure heart" (Psalm 51:10). Through the death and resurrection of Jesus Christ, we also are made clean and perfect. God replaces our sin with his purity, and he no longer sees our sin.

22:27 "To the crooked you show yourself shrewd" means that to those who sin, God is a judge who will punish them for their sins. God destroys those who are evil.

33 It is God who arms me with strength[a]
   and makes my way perfect.
34 He makes my feet like the feet of a deer;
   he enables me to stand on the heights.

22:35
w Ps 144:1

35 He trains my hands[w] for battle;
   my arms can bend a bow of bronze.
36 You give me your shield of victory;
   you stoop down to make me great.

22:37
x Pr 4:11

37 You broaden the path[x] beneath me,
   so that my ankles do not turn.

38 "I pursued my enemies and crushed them;
   I did not turn back till they were destroyed.

22:39
y Mal 4:3

39 I crushed[y] them completely, and they could not rise;
   they fell beneath my feet.

22:40
z Ps 44:5

40 You armed me with strength for battle;
   you made my adversaries bow at my feet.[z]

22:41
a Ex 23:27

41 You made my enemies turn their backs[a] in flight,
   and I destroyed my foes.
42 They cried for help, but there was no one to save them—
   to the Lord, but he did not answer.

22:43
b Isa 10:6

43 I beat them as fine as the dust of the earth;
   I pounded and trampled them like mud[b] in the streets.

22:44
c 2Sa 3:1
d Dt 28:13
e Isa 55:3-5

44 "You have delivered[c] me from the attacks of my people;
   you have preserved[d] me as the head of nations.
   People[e] I did not know are subject to me,
45   and foreigners come cringing to me;
   as soon as they hear me, they obey me.

22:46
f Mic 7:17

46 They all lose heart;
   they come trembling[b][f] from their strongholds.

22:47
g Ps 89:26
22:48
h Ps 144:2

47 "The Lord lives! Praise be to my Rock!
   Exalted be God, the Rock, my Savior![g]
48 He is the God who avenges me,[h]
   who puts the nations under me,

22:49
i Ps 140:1,4

49   who sets me free from my enemies.[i]
   You exalted me above my foes;
   from violent men you rescued me.

22:50
j Ro 15:9*

50 Therefore I will praise you, O Lord, among the nations;
   I will sing praises to your name.[j]

22:51
k Ps 144:9-10
l 2Sa 7:13
m Ps 89:24,29

51 He gives his king great victories;[k]
   he shows unfailing kindness to his anointed,
   to David[l] and his descendants forever."[m]

a 33 Dead Sea Scrolls, some Septuagint manuscripts, Vulgate and Syriac (see also Psalm 18:32); Masoretic Text *who is my strong refuge*   b 46 Some Septuagint manuscripts and Vulgate (see also Psalm 18:45); Masoretic Text *they arm themselves.*

| **DAVID REVEALS TRUTHS ABOUT GOD IN HIS SONG OF PRAISE** | David says, "The Lord is my . . ." | Rock, Fortress, Deliverer, Refuge, Shield, Horn of Salvation, Stonghold, Savior, Lamp |
| | David names these characteristics of God. He is . . . | Saving, Worthy of praise, Hearing, Angry (against enemies), Rescuing, Rewarding, Seeing, Faithful, Showing (revealing) himself, Shrewd, Powerful, Strong, Perfect, Pure, Flawless, Shielding (us from enemies), Giving, Gentle, Preserving, Living |

22:47 David praises God wholeheartedly. Praise is not just a song *about* God; it is a song *to* God. In this song, David uses many word pictures such as rock, shield, and fire to portray God's marvelous attributes. Praising God has several aspects to it. We praise God when we: (1) Say thank you to him for each attribute of his divine nature. As you read the Bible, look for other characteristics of God for which to thank him. (2) Focus our hearts on God. Take one attribute of God, such as his mercy, then concentrate on it for an entire week in your meditation and prayer. (3) Thank God for his many gracious gifts to us. Make a list and count your blessings. (4) Thank God for our relationship with him. Through Christ you have been given the gift of salvation. Tell God afresh how much you appreciate it.

The Last Words of David

23 These are the last words of David:

"The oracle of David son of Jesse,
the oracle of the man exalted[n] by the Most High,
the man anointed[o] by the God of Jacob,
Israel's singer of songs[a]:

2 "The Spirit[p] of the LORD spoke through me;
his word was on my tongue.
3 The God of Israel spoke,
the Rock[q] of Israel said to me:
'When one rules over men in righteousness,
when he rules in the fear of God,
4 he is like the light of morning at sunrise[r]
on a cloudless morning,
like the brightness after rain
that brings the grass from the earth.'

5 "Is not my house right with God?
Has he not made with me an everlasting covenant,[s]
arranged and secured in every part?
Will he not bring to fruition my salvation
and grant me my every desire?
6 But evil men are all to be cast aside like thorns,[f]
which are not gathered with the hand.
7 Whoever touches thorns
uses a tool of iron or the shaft of a spear;
they are burned up where they lie."

Marginal references:
23:1 [n] Ps 78:70-71; [o] 1Sa 16:12-13; Ps 89:20
23:2 [p] 2Pe 1:21
23:3 [q] Dt 32:4
23:4 [r] Jdg 5:31
23:5 [s] Ps 89:29
23:6 [f] Mt 13:40-41

David's Mighty Men

8 These are the names of David's mighty men:

Josheb-Basshebeth,[b] a Tahkemonite,[c] was chief of the Three; he raised his spear against eight hundred men, whom he killed[d] in one encounter.

9 Next to him was Eleazar son of Dodai[u] the Ahohite. As one of the three mighty men, he was with David when they taunted the Philistines gathered ⌊at Pas Dammim⌋[e] for battle. Then the men of Israel retreated, 10 but he stood his ground and struck down the Philistines till his hand grew tired and froze to the sword. The LORD brought about a great victory that day. The troops returned to Eleazar, but only to strip the dead.

11 Next to him was Shammah son of Agee the Hararite. When the Philistines banded together at a place where there was a field full of lentils, Israel's troops fled from them. 12 But Shammah took his stand in the middle of the field. He defended it and struck the Philistines down, and the LORD brought about a great victory.

13 During harvest time, three of the thirty chief men came down to David at the cave of Adullam,[v] while a band of Philistines was encamped in the Valley of Rephaim.[w] 14 At that time David was in the stronghold,[x] and the Philistine garrison was at Bethlehem. 15 David longed for water and said, "Oh, that someone would get me a drink of water from the well near the gate of Bethlehem!" 16 So the three mighty men broke through the Philistine lines,

Marginal references:
23:9 [u] 1Ch 27:4
23:13 [v] 1Sa 22:1; [w] 2Sa 5:18
23:14 [x] 1Sa 22:4-5

---

[a]1 Or *Israel's beloved singer* [b]8 Hebrew; some Septuagint manuscripts suggest *Ish-Bosheth,* that is, *Esh-Baal* (see also 1 Chron. 11:11 *Jashobeam*). [c]8 Probably a variant of *Hacmonite* (see 1 Chron. 11:11) [d]8 Some Septuagint manuscripts (see also 1 Chron. 11:11); Hebrew and other Septuagint manuscripts *Three; it was Adino the Eznite who killed eight hundred men* [e]9 See 1 Chron. 11:13; Hebrew *gathered there.*

23:3 In the style of a prophet, David spoke of a just and righteous ruler. This will be fulfilled in Jesus Christ when he returns to rule in perfect justice and peace. For similar prophecies, see Isaiah 11:1–10; Jeremiah 23:5, 6; 33:15–18; Zechariah 9:9, 10. For the fulfillment of some of these prophecies, see Matthew 4:14–16; Luke 24:25–27, 44–49; John 5:45–47; 8:28, 29.

23:8–39 These verses tell of some of the exploits that the special corps of David's army carried out. There were two elite groups of men: "the Thirty" and "the Three" (23:18, 23;

1 Chronicles 11:11–25). To become a member of such a group a man had to show unparalleled courage in battle as well as wisdom in leadership. "The Three" was the most elite group. The list of "the Thirty" actually contains 37 names, but it mentions some warriors known to be dead (Uriah, for example, in 23:39). Apparently, new members were appointed to replace those who had fallen in battle.

23:16 David poured out the water as an offering to God because he was so moved by the sacrifice it represented. When Hebrews drew water from the well near the gate of Bethlehem and carried it back to David. But he refused to drink it; instead, he poured it out before the LORD. [17]"Far be it from me, O LORD, to do this!" he said. "Is it not the blood[y] of men who went at the risk of their lives?" And David would not drink it.

23:17
[y]Lev 17:10-12

Such were the exploits of the three mighty men.

23:18
[z]1Ch 11:20

[18]Abishai[z] the brother of Joab son of Zeruiah was chief of the Three.[a] He raised his spear against three hundred men, whom he killed, and so he became as famous as the Three. [19]Was he not held in greater honor than the Three? He became their commander, even though he was not included among them.

23:20
[a]Jos 15:21

[20]Benaiah son of Jehoiada was a valiant fighter from Kabzeel,[a] who performed great exploits. He struck down two of Moab's best men. He also went down into a pit on a snowy day and killed a lion. [21]And he struck down a huge Egyptian. Although the Egyptian had a spear in his hand, Benaiah went against him with a club. He snatched the spear from the Egyptian's hand and killed him with his own spear. [22]Such were the exploits of Benaiah son of Jehoiada; he too was as famous as the three mighty men. [23]He was held in greater honor than any of the Thirty, but he was not included among the Three. And David put him in charge of his bodyguard.

23:24
[b]2Sa 2:18

[24] Among the Thirty were:
   Asahel[b] the brother of Joab,
   Elhanan son of Dodo from Bethlehem,

23:25
[c]Jdg 7:1;
1Ch 11:27

[25] Shammah the Harodite,[c]
   Elika the Harodite,

[a] 18 Most Hebrew manuscripts (see also 1 Chron. 11:20); two Hebrew manuscripts and Syriac *Thirty*

DAVID'S MIGHTY MEN

One way to understand David's success is to notice the kind of men who followed him. During the time he was being hunted by Saul, David gradually built a fighting force of several hundred men. Some were relatives, others were outcasts of society, many were in trouble with the law. They all had at least one trait in common—complete devotion to David. Their achievements made them famous. Among these men were elite military groups like "the Three" and "the Thirty." They were true heroes.

Scripture gives the impression that these men were motivated to greatness by the personal qualities of their leader. David inspired them to achieve beyond their goals and meet their true potential. Likewise, the leaders we follow and the causes to which we commit ourselves will affect our lives. David's effectiveness was clearly connected with his awareness of God's leading. He was a good leader when he was following *his* Leader. Do you know whom the people you respect most are following? Your answer should help you decide whether they deserve your loyalty. Do you also recognize God's leading in your life? No one can lead you to excellence as your Creator can.

Strengths and accomplishments:	• Able soldiers and military leaders • Shared many special skills • Though frequently outnumbered, were consistently victorious • Loyal to David
Weakness and mistake:	• Often had little in common beyond their loyalty to David and their military expertise
Lessons from their lives:	• Greatness is often inspired by the quality and character of leadership • Even a small force of able and loyal men can accomplish great feats
Vital statistics:	• Where: They came from all over Israel (primarily Judah and Benjamin), and from some of the other surrounding nations as well • Occupations: Various backgrounds—almost all were fugitives
Key verses:	"David left Gath and escaped to the cave of Adullam. When his brothers and his father's household heard about it, they went down to him there. All those who were in distress or in debt or discontented gathered around him, and he became their leader. About four hundred men were with him" (1 Samuel 22:1, 2).

Their stories are told in 1 Samuel 22—2 Samuel 23:39. They are also mentioned in 1 Chronicles 11; 12.

---

offered sacrifices, they never consumed the blood. It represented life, and they poured it out before God. David would not drink this water that represented the lives of his soldiers. Instead, he offered it to God.

26 Helez the Paltite,
　　Ira son of Ikkesh from Tekoa,
27 Abiezer from Anathoth,*d*
　　Mebunnai*a* the Hushathite,
28 Zalmon the Ahohite,
　　Maharai the Netophathite,*e*
29 Heled*b* son of Baanah the Netophathite,
　　Ithai son of Ribai from Gibeah in Benjamin,
30 Benaiah the Pirathonite,
　　Hiddai*c* from the ravines of Gaash,*f*
31 Abi-Albon the Arbathite,
　　Azmaveth the Barhumite,
32 Eliahba the Shaalbonite,
　　the sons of Jashen,
　　Jonathan 33 son of*d* Shammah the Hararite,
　　Ahiam son of Sharar*e* the Hararite,
34 Eliphelet son of Ahasbai the Maacathite,
　　Eliam*g* son of Ahithophel*h* the Gilonite,
35 Hezro the Carmelite,
　　Paarai the Arbite,
36 Igal son of Nathan from Zobah,
　　the son of Hagri,*f*
37 Zelek the Ammonite,
　　Naharai the Beerothite, the armor-bearer of Joab son of Zeruiah,
38 Ira the Ithrite,*i*
　　Gareb the Ithrite
39 and Uriah*j* the Hittite.
　　There were thirty-seven in all.

23:27
d Jos 21:18

23:28
e 2Ki 25:23

23:30
f Jos 24:30

23:34
g 2Sa 11:3
h 2Sa 15:12

23:38
i 1Ch 2:53

23:39
j 2Sa 11:3

David Counts the Fighting Men

24 Again the anger of the LORD burned against Israel, and he incited David against them, saying, "Go and take a census of *k* Israel and Judah."

24:1
k 1Ch 27:23

2 So the king said to Joab and the army commanders*g* with him, "Go throughout the tribes of Israel from Dan to Beersheba*l* and enroll the fighting men, so that I may know how many there are."

24:2
l Jdg 20:1; 2Sa 3:10

3 But Joab replied to the king, "May the LORD your God multiply the troops a hundred times over, and may the eyes of my lord the king see it. But why does my lord the king want to do such a thing?"

4 The king's word, however, overruled Joab and the army commanders; so they left the presence of the king to enroll the fighting men of Israel.

5 After crossing the Jordan, they camped near Aroer,*m* south of the town in the gorge, and then went through Gad and on to Jazer.*n* 6 They went to Gilead and the region of Tahtim Hodshi, and on to Dan Jaan and around toward Sidon.*o* 7 Then they went toward the fortress of Tyre and all the towns of the Hivites and Canaanites. Finally, they went on to Beersheba in the Negev of Judah.

24:5
m Dt 2:36; Jos 13:9
n Nu 21:32

24:6
o Jos 19:28

a27 Hebrew; some Septuagint manuscripts (see also 1 Chron. 11:29) Sibbecai　b29 Some Hebrew manuscripts and Vulgate (see also 1 Chron. 11:30); most Hebrew manuscripts Heleb　c30 Hebrew; some Septuagint manuscripts (see also 1 Chron. 11:32) Hurai　d33 Some Septuagint manuscripts (see also 1 Chron. 11:34); Hebrew does not have son of.　e33 Hebrew; some Septuagint manuscripts (see also 1 Chron. 11:35) Sacar　f36 Some Septuagint manuscripts (see also 1 Chron. 11:38); Hebrew Haggadi　g2 Septuagint (see also verse 4 and 1 Chron. 21:2); Hebrew Joab the army commander

---

24:1 Did God cause David to sin? God does not cause people to sin, but he does allow sinners to reveal the sinfulness of their hearts by their actions. God presented the opportunity to David in order to deal with a disastrous national tendency, and he wanted this desire to show itself. First Chronicles 21:1 says Satan incited David to do it. Hebrew writers do not always distinguish between primary and secondary causes. So if God allowed Satan to tempt David, to them it is as if God did it.

24:1–3 What was wrong with taking a census? A census was commanded in Numbers to prepare an army for conquering the prom-

ised land (Numbers 1:2; 26:2). A census amounted to a draft or conscription for the army. The land was now at peace, so there was no need to enlist troops. Israel had extended its borders and become a recognized power. David's sin was pride and ambition in counting the people so that he could glory in the size of his nation and army, its power and defenses. By doing this, he put his faith in the size of his army rather than in God's ability to protect them regardless of their number. Even Joab knew a census was wrong, but David did not heed his advice. We sin in a similar way when we place our security in money, possessions, or the might of our nation.

8After they had gone through the entire land, they came back to Jerusalem at the end of nine months and twenty days.

24:9
ρ1Ch 21:5

9Joab reported the number of the fighting men to the king: In Israel there were eight hundred thousand able-bodied men who could handle a sword, and in Judah five hundred thousand. ρ

24:10
q1Sa 24:5
r2Sa 12:13
s1Sa 13:13

10David was conscience-stricken q after he had counted the fighting men, and he said to the Lord, "I have sinned r greatly in what I have done. Now, O Lord, I beg you, take away the guilt of your servant. I have done a very foolish thing. s"

24:11
t1Sa 22:5
u1Sa 9:9;
1Ch 29:29

11Before David got up the next morning, the word of the Lord had come to Gad t the prophet, David's seer: u 12"Go and tell David, 'This is what the Lord says: I am giving you three options. Choose one of them for me to carry out against you.'"

13So Gad went to David and said to him, "Shall there come upon you three a years of famine in your land? Or three months of fleeing from your enemies while they pursue you? Or three days of plague in your land? Now then, think it over and decide how I should answer the one who sent me."

24:14
vPs 103:8,13
24:15
w1Ch 27:24
24:16
xGe 6:6; 1Sa 15:11
yEx 12:23

14David said to Gad, "I am in deep distress. Let us fall into the hands of the Lord, for his mercy v is great; but do not let me fall into the hands of men."

15So the Lord sent a plague on Israel from that morning until the end of the time designated, and seventy thousand of the people from Dan to Beersheba died. w 16When the angel stretched out his hand to destroy Jerusalem, the Lord was grieved x because of the calamity and said to the angel who was afflicting the people, "Enough! Withdraw your hand." The angel of the Lord y was then at the threshing floor of Araunah the Jebusite.

17When David saw the angel who was striking down the people, he said to the Lord, "I am the one who has sinned and done wrong. These are but sheep. What have they done? Let your hand fall upon me and my family."

David Builds an Altar

18On that day Gad went to David and said to him, "Go up and build an altar to the Lord on the threshing floor of Araunah the Jebusite." 19So David went up, as the Lord had commanded through Gad. 20When Araunah looked and saw the king and his men coming toward him, he went out and bowed down before the king with his face to the ground.

24:21
zNu 16:44-50

21Araunah said, "Why has my lord the king come to his servant?"

"To buy your threshing floor," David answered, "so I can build an altar to the Lord, that the plague on the people may be stopped." z

24:22
a1Ki 19:21
24:23
bEze 20:40-41

22Araunah said to David, "Let my lord the king take whatever pleases him and offer it up. Here are oxen a for the burnt offering, and here are threshing sledges and ox yokes for the wood. 23O king, Araunah gives b all this to the king." Araunah also said to him, "May the Lord your God accept you."

24But the king replied to Araunah, "No, I insist on paying you for it. I will not sacrifice to the Lord my God burnt offerings that cost me nothing."

So David bought the threshing floor and the oxen and paid fifty shekels b of silver for them. 25David built an altar to the Lord there and sacrificed burnt offerings and fellowship offerings. c Then the Lord answered prayer c in behalf of the land, and the plague on Israel was stopped.

24:25
c2Sa 21:14

a 13 Septuagint (see also 1 Chron. 21:12); Hebrew *seven*   b24 That is, about 1 1/4 pounds (about 0.6 kilogram)
c25 Traditionally *peace offerings*

24:12–14 Both David and the Israelites were guilty of sin (24:1). David's sin was pride, but the Bible does not say why God was angry with the people. Perhaps it was due to their support of the rebellions of Absalom (chapters 15—18) and Sheba (chapter 20), or perhaps they put their security in military and financial prosperity rather than God, as David did. God dealt with the whole nation through David who exemplified the national sin of pride.

God gave David three choices. Each was a form of punishment God had cited for the people's disobedience (disease—Deuteronomy 28:20–22; famine—28:23, 24; war—28:25, 26). David wisely chose the form of punishment that came most directly from God. He knew how brutal men could be, and he also knew God's great mercy. When you sin greatly, turn back to God. To be punished by him is far better than to take your chances without him.

24:18 Many believe that this threshing floor where David built

the altar is the location where Abraham nearly sacrificed Isaac (Genesis 22:1–18). After David's death, Solomon built the temple on this spot. Centuries later, Jesus would teach here.

24:25 The book of 2 Samuel describes David's reign. Since the Israelites first entered the promised land under Joshua, they had been struggling to unite the nation and drive out the wicked inhabitants. Now, after 400 years, Israel was finally at peace. David had accomplished what no leader before him had done. His administration was run on the principle of dedication to God and to the well-being of the people. Yet David also sinned. Despite his sins, the Bible calls David a man after God's own heart (1 Samuel 13:14; Acts 13:22) because when he sinned, he recognized and confessed his sins to God. David committed his life to God and remained loyal to him throughout his lifetime. Psalms gives an even deeper insight into David's love for God.

1 KINGS

VITAL STATISTICS

PURPOSE:
To contrast the lives of those who live for God and those who refuse to do so through the history of the kings of Israel and Judah

AUTHOR:
Unknown. Possibly Jeremiah or a group of prophets

ORIGINAL AUDIENCE:
The people of Israel

SETTING:
The once great nation of Israel turned into a land divided, not only physically, but also spiritually.

KEY VERSES:
"As for you, if you walk before me in integrity of heart and uprightness, as David your father did, and do all I command and observe my decrees and laws, I will establish your royal throne over Israel forever, as I promised David your father when I said, 'You shall never fail to have a man on the throne of Israel'" (9:4, 5).

KEY PEOPLE:
David, Solomon, Rehoboam, Jeroboam, Elijah, Ahab, Jezebel

SPECIAL FEATURE:
The books of 1 and 2 Kings were originally one book.

"I DON'T CARE what anyone says, I'm going to do it!" the boy yells at his mother as he storms out of the house.

This is a familiar scene in our society. The words change, but the essential message is the same: A person is *not* open to advice because his or her mind is closed. Some advice may be sought, but it is heeded only if it reinforces the decision already made or is an easier path to take. It is human nature to reject help and to do things *our* way.

A much wiser approach is to seek, hear, and heed the advice of good counselors. Solomon, the world's wisest man, urges this in Proverbs (see 11:14; 15:22; 24:6). How ironic that his son and successor, Rehoboam, listened instead to foolish advice, with devastating results. At Rehoboam's inauguration, he was petitioned by the people to be a kind and generous ruler. The older men counseled him to "be a servant to these people and serve them and give them a favorable answer" (12:7). But Rehoboam agreed to the cruel advice of his peers who urged him to be harsh. As a result, Rehoboam split the kingdom. Learn from Rehoboam's mistake. Commit yourself to seeking and following wise counsel.

The main events of 1 Kings are David's death, Solomon's reign, the division of the kingdom, and Elijah's ministry. As Solomon ascended the throne, David charged him to obey God's laws and to walk "in his ways" (2:3). This Solomon did; and when given the choice of gifts from God, he humbly asked for discernment (3:9). As a result, Solomon's reign began with great success, including the construction of the temple—his greatest achievement. Unfortunately, Solomon took many pagan wives and concubines who eventually turned his heart away from the Lord to their false gods (11:1–4).

Rehoboam succeeded Solomon and had the opportunity to be a wise, compassionate, and just king. Instead, he accepted the poor advice of his young friends and attempted to rule with an iron hand. But the people rebelled, and the kingdom split with ten tribes in the north (Israel) ruled by Jeroboam, and only Judah and Benjamin remaining with Rehoboam. Both kingdoms wove a path through the reigns of corrupt and idolatrous kings with only the clear voice of the prophets continuing to warn and call the nation back to God.

Elijah is surely one of the greatest prophets, and chapters 17 through 22 feature his conflict with wicked Ahab and Jezebel in Israel. In one of the most dramatic confrontations in history, Elijah defeated the prophets of Baal at Mount Carmel. In spite of incredible opposition, Elijah stood for God and proved that *one plus God* is a majority. If God is on our side, no one can stand against us (Romans 8:31).

So Huram finished all the work he had undertaken for King Solomon in the temple of the LORD:

⁴¹ the two pillars;

the two bowl-shaped capitals on top of the pillars;

the two sets of network decorating the two bowl-shaped capitals on top of the pillars;

⁴² the four hundred pomegranates for the two sets of network (two rows of pomegranates for each network, decorating the bowl-shaped capitals on top of the pillars);

⁴³ the ten stands with their ten basins;

⁴⁴ the Sea and the twelve bulls under it;

⁴⁵ the pots, shovels and sprinkling bowls.

All these objects that Huram made for King Solomon for the temple of the LORD were of burnished bronze. ⁴⁶The king had them cast in clay molds in the plain of the Jordan between Succoth and Zarethan. ᵈ ⁴⁷Solomon left all these things unweighed, because there were so many; the weight of the bronze was not determined.

⁴⁸Solomon also made all the furnishings that were in the LORD's temple:

the golden altar;

the golden table ᵉ on which was the bread of the Presence;

⁴⁹ the lampstands of pure gold (five on the right and five on the left, in front of the inner sanctuary);

the gold floral work and lamps and tongs;

⁵⁰ the pure gold basins, wick trimmers, sprinkling bowls, dishes and censers;

and the gold sockets for the doors of the innermost room, the Most Holy Place, and also for the doors of the main hall of the temple.

⁵¹When all the work King Solomon had done for the temple of the LORD was finished, he brought in the things his father David had dedicated ᶠ—the silver and gold and the furnishings—and he placed them in the treasuries of the LORD's temple.

The Ark Brought to the Temple

8 Then King Solomon summoned into his presence at Jerusalem the elders of Israel, all the heads of the tribes and the chiefs of the Israelite families, to bring up the ark ᵍ of the LORD's covenant from Zion, the City of David. ʰ ²All the men of Israel came together to King Solomon at the time of the festival in the month of Ethanim, the seventh month. ⁱ

³When all the elders of Israel had arrived, the priests took up the ark, ⁴and they brought up the ark of the LORD and the Tent of Meeting ʲ and all the sacred furnishings in it. The priests and Levites carried them up, ⁵and King Solomon and the entire assembly of Israel that had gathered about him were before the ark, sacrificing ᵏ so many sheep and cattle that they could not be recorded or counted.

⁶The priests then brought the ark of the LORD's covenant to its place in the inner sanctuary of the temple, the Most Holy Place, and put it beneath the wings of the cherubim. ˡ ⁷The cherubim spread their wings over the place of the ark and overshadowed the ark and its carrying poles. ⁸These poles were so long that their ends could be seen from the Holy Place in front of the inner sanctuary, but not from outside the Holy Place; and they are still there today. ᵐ ⁹There was nothing in the ark except the two stone tablets ⁿ that Moses had placed in it at Horeb, where the LORD made a covenant with the Israelites after they came out of Egypt.

¹⁰When the priests withdrew from the Holy Place, the cloud ᵒ filled the temple of the LORD. ¹¹And the priests could not perform their service because of the cloud, for the glory of the LORD filled his temple.

7:46
ᵈ Jos 3:16

7:48
ᵉ Ex 37:10

7:51
ᶠ 2Sa 8:11

8:1
ᵍ 2Sa 6:17
ʰ 2Sa 5:7

8:2
ⁱ Lev 23:34

8:4
ʲ 2Ch 1:3

8:5
ᵏ 2Sa 6:13

8:6
ˡ 1Ki 6:19, 27

8:8
ᵐ Ex 25:13-15

8:9
ⁿ Ex 25:21;
Dt 10:2-5; Heb 9:4

8:10
ᵒ Ex 40:34-35

---

worship may change, the purpose of worship should never change—to give honor and praise to God.

8:1ff Solomon gathered the people not just to dedicate the temple, but to rededicate themselves to God's service. Solomon could well be speaking these words to us today: "But your hearts must be fully committed to the LORD our God, to live by his decrees and obey his commands, as at this time" (8:61).

8:1ff What was the difference between the tabernacle and the temple, and why did the Israelites change from one to the other?

As a tent, the tabernacle was a portable place of worship designed for the people as they were traveling toward the promised land. The temple was a permanent place to worship God after the Israelites were at peace in their land. To bring the ark of the Lord's covenant to the temple signified God's actual presence there.

8:6 Cherubim are mighty angels.

12Then Solomon said, "The Lord has said that he would dwell in a dark cloud; 13I have indeed built a magnificent temple for you, a place for you to dwell p forever."

14While the whole assembly of Israel was standing there, the king turned around and blessed q them. 15Then he said:

"Praise be to the Lord, the God of Israel, who with his own hand has fulfilled what he promised with his own mouth to my father David. For he said, 16'Since the day I brought my people Israel out of Egypt, I have not chosen a city in any tribe of Israel to have a temple built for my Name to be there, but I have chosen r David to rule my people Israel.'

17"My father David had it in his heart to build a temple for the Name of the Lord, the God of Israel. 18But the Lord said to my father David, 'Because it was in your heart to build a temple for my Name, you did well to have this in your heart. 19Nevertheless, you s are not the one to build the temple, but your son, who is your own flesh and blood—he is the one who will build the temple for my Name.' t

20"The Lord has kept the promise he made: I have succeeded David my father and now I sit on the throne of Israel, just as the Lord promised, and I have built u the temple for the Name of the Lord, the God of Israel. 21I have provided a place there for the ark, in which is the covenant of the Lord that he made with our fathers when he brought them out of Egypt."

Solomon's Prayer of Dedication

22Then Solomon stood before the altar of the Lord in front of the whole assembly of Israel, spread out his hands v toward heaven 23and said:

"O Lord, God of Israel, there is no God like you in heaven above or on earth below— you who keep your covenant of love w with your servants who continue wholeheartedly in your way. 24You have kept your promise to your servant David my father; with your mouth you have promised and with your hand you have fulfilled it—as it is today.

25"Now Lord, God of Israel, keep for your servant David my father the promises you made to him when you said, 'You shall never fail to have a man to sit before me on the throne of Israel, if only your sons are careful in all they do to walk before me as you have done.' 26And now, O God of Israel, let your word that you promised x your servant David my father come true.

27"But will God really dwell y on earth? The heavens, even the highest heaven, cannot contain z you. How much less this temple I have built! 28Yet give attention to your servant's prayer and his plea for mercy, O Lord my God. Hear the cry and the prayer that your servant is praying in your presence this day. 29May your eyes be open toward this temple night and day, this place of which you said, 'My Name a shall be there,' so that you will hear the prayer your servant prays toward this place. 30Hear the supplication of your servant and of your people Israel when they pray toward this place. Hear from heaven, your dwelling place, and when you hear, forgive.

31"When a man wrongs his neighbor and is required to take an oath and he comes and swears the oath b before your altar in this temple, 32then hear from heaven and act. Judge between your servants, condemning the guilty and bringing down on his own head what he has done. Declare the innocent not guilty, and so establish his innocence. c

33"When your people Israel have been defeated d by an enemy because they have sinned against you, and when they turn back to you and confess your name, praying and making supplication to you in this temple, 34then hear from heaven and forgive the sin of your people Israel and bring them back to the land you gave to their fathers.

8:13
p Ps 132:13

8:14
q 2Sa 6:18

8:16
r 1Sa 16:1

8:19
s 2Sa 7:5
t 2Sa 7:13

8:20
u 1Ch 28:6

8:22
v Ezr 9:5

8:23
w Dt 7:9, 12; Ne 1:5

8:26
x 2Sa 7:25

8:27
y Ac 7:48
z 2Ch 2:6; Isa 66:1; Jer 23:24

8:29
a Dt 12:11

8:31
b Ex 22:11

8:32
c Dt 25:1

8:33
d Lev 26:17; Dt 28:25

8:15–21 For 480 years after Israel's escape from Egypt, God did not ask his people to build a temple for him. Instead he emphasized the importance of his presence among them and their need for spiritual leaders. It is easy to think of a building as the focus of God's presence and power, but God chooses and uses *people* to do his work. Building or enlarging our place of worship may be necessary, but it should never take priority over developing spiritual leaders.

8:24 Solomon was referring to the promise God had made to David in 2 Samuel 7:12–15 that one of David's sons would build the temple.

8:27 In his prayer of dedication, Solomon declared that even the highest heaven cannot contain God. Isn't it amazing that, though the heavens can't contain God, he is willing to live in the hearts of those who love him? The God of the universe takes up residence in his people.

8:33, 34 After Solomon's reign, the people continually turned away from God. The rest of the kingdom era is a vivid fulfillment of Solomon's description in these verses. As a result of the people's sin, God let them be overrun by enemies several times. Then, in desperation, they cried out to God for forgiveness, and God restored them.

8:35
e Lev 26:19

8:36
f 1Sa 12:23
g Ps 27:11

8:37
h Lev 26:26

8:39
i 1Sa 16:7;
1Ch 28:9; Ps 11:4;
Jer 17:10

35 "When the heavens are shut up and there is no rain e because your people have sinned against you, and when they pray toward this place and confess your name and turn from their sin because you have afflicted them, 36 then hear from heaven and forgive the sin of your servants, your people Israel. Teach f them the right way g to live, and send rain on the land you gave your people for an inheritance.

37 "When famine h or plague comes to the land, or blight or mildew, locusts or grasshoppers, or when an enemy besieges them in any of their cities, whatever disaster or disease may come, 38 and when a prayer or plea is made by any of your people Israel— each one aware of the afflictions of his own heart, and spreading out his hands toward this temple— 39 then hear from heaven, your dwelling place. Forgive and act; deal with each man according to all he does, since you know i his heart (for you alone know the hearts of all men), 40 so that they will fear you all the time they live in the land you gave our fathers.

SOLOMON'S TEMPLE
960–586 B.C.
Solomon's temple was a beautiful sight. It took over seven years to build and was a magnificent building containing gold, silver, bronze, and cedar. This house for God was without equal. The description is found in 1 Kings 6—7 and 2 Chronicles 2—4.

Most Holy Place with ark of the covenant

Holy Place (45 feet high) with 10 golden tables for bread of the Presence, 10 gold lampstands, and an altar of incense

Cherubim

Side rooms

Portico

The bronze pillars "Boaz" and "Jakin"

Bronze basins

Curtain, and doors of olive wood

Sea

Altar

© Hugh Claycombe 1986

FURNISHINGS

Cherubim: represented heavenly beings, symbolized God's presence and holiness (gold-plated, 15 feet wide)

Ark of the covenant: contained the law written on two tablets, symbolized God's presence with Israel (wood overlaid with gold)

Curtain: separated the Holy Place from the Most Holy Place (blue, purple, and crimson yarn and fine linen, with cherubim worked into it)

Doors: between Holy Place and Most Holy Place (wood overlaid with gold)

Golden tables (wood overlaid with gold), *gold lampstands* (with seven lamps on each stand), and *altar of incense* (wood overlaid with gold): instruments for priestly functions in the Holy Place

Bronze pillars: named Jakin (meaning "he establishes") and Boaz (meaning "in him is strength")—taken together they could mean "God provides the strength"

Altar: for burning of sacrifices (bronze)

Sea: for priests' washing (had 12,000-gallon capacity)

Bronze basins: for washing the sacrifices (water basins on wheeled bases)

Portico: the entry room

This reconstruction uses known archaeological parallels to supplement the text, and assumes interior dimensions from 1 Kings 6:17-20.
© Hugh Claycombe

41"As for the foreigner who does not belong to your people Israel but has come from a distant land because of your name— 42 for men will hear of your great name and your mighty hand/ and your outstretched arm—when he comes and prays toward this temple, 43 then hear from heaven, your dwelling place, and do whatever the foreigner asks of you, so that all the peoples of the earth may know k your name and fear you, as do your own people Israel, and may know that this house I have built bears your Name.

44"When your people go to war against their enemies, wherever you send them, and when they pray to the LORD toward the city you have chosen and the temple I have built for your Name, 45 then hear from heaven their prayer and their plea, and uphold their cause.

46"When they sin against you—for there is no one who does not sin—and you become angry with them and give them over to the enemy, who takes them captive/ to his own land, far away or near; 47 and if they have a change of heart in the land where they are held captive, and repent and plead m with you in the land of their conquerors and say, 'We have sinned, we have done wrong, we have acted wickedly'; n 48 and if they turn back to you with all their heart and soul in the land of their enemies who took them captive, and pray o to you toward the land you gave their fathers, toward the city you have chosen and the temple I have built for your Name; 49 then from heaven, your dwelling place, hear their prayer and their plea, and uphold their cause. 50 And forgive your people, who have sinned against you; forgive all the offenses they have committed against you, and cause their conquerors to show them mercy; p 51 for they are your people and your inheritance, q whom you brought out of Egypt, out of that iron-smelting furnace. r

52"May your eyes be open to your servant's plea and to the plea of your people Israel, and may you listen to them whenever they cry out to you. 53 For you singled them out from all the nations of the world to be your own inheritance, s just as you declared through your servant Moses when you, O Sovereign LORD, brought our fathers out of Egypt."

54 When Solomon had finished all these prayers and supplications to the LORD, he rose from before the altar of the LORD, where he had been kneeling with his hands spread out toward heaven. 55 He stood and blessed the whole assembly of Israel in a loud voice, saying:

56"Praise be to the LORD, who has given rest t to his people Israel just as he promised. Not one word has failed of all the good promises u he gave through his servant Moses. 57 May the LORD our God be with us as he was with our fathers; may he never leave us nor forsake v us. 58 May he turn our hearts w to him, to walk in all his ways and to keep the commands, decrees and regulations he gave our fathers. 59 And may these words of mine, which I have prayed before the LORD, be near to the LORD our God day and night, that he may uphold the cause of his servant and the cause of his people Israel according to each day's need, 60 so that all the peoples of the earth may know that the LORD is God and that there is no other. 61 But your hearts must be fully committed x to the LORD our God, to live by his decrees and obey his commands, as at this time."

The Dedication of the Temple

62 Then the king and all Israel with him offered sacrifices before the LORD. 63 Solomon offered a sacrifice of fellowship offerings a to the LORD: twenty-two thousand cattle and a hundred and twenty thousand sheep and goats. So the king and all the Israelites dedicated the temple of the LORD.

a 63 Traditionally peace offerings; also in verse 64

8:42
/Dt 3:24

8:43
k 1Sa 17:46

8:46
/Lev 26:33-39

8:47
m Ne 1:6
n Ps 106:6

8:48
o Da 6:10

8:50
p Ps 106:46

8:51
q Dt 9:29
r Jer 11:4

8:53
s Ex 19:5

8:56
t Dt 12:10
u Jos 23:15

8:57
v Jos 1:5

8:58
w Ps 119:36

8:61
x 1Ki 11:4; 2Ki 20:3

8:41–43 God chose Israel to be a blessing to the whole world (Genesis 12:1–3). This blessing found its fulfillment in Jesus— a descendant of Abraham and David (Galatians 3:8, 9)—who became the Messiah for all people, Jews and non-Jews. When the Israelites first entered the promised land, they were ordered to clear out several wicked nations; thus we read in the Old Testament of many wars. But we should not conclude that war was Israel's first duty. After subduing the evil people, Israel was to become a light to the surrounding nations. Sadly, Israel's own sin and spiritual blindness prevented them from reaching out to the rest of the world with God's love. Reaching out to the world

is still the commission of God's people today. Christians need to take every opportunity to spread God's love to the world.

8:46–53 Solomon, who seemed to have prophetic insight into the future captivities of his people (2 Kings 17; 25), asked God to be merciful to them when they cried out to him, to forgive them, and to return them to their homeland. Reference to their return is made in Ezra 1; 2; Nehemiah 1; 2.

8:56–60 Solomon praised the Lord and prayed for the people. His prayer can be a pattern for our prayers. He had five basic requests: (1) for God's presence (8:57); (2) for the desire to do God's will in everything; ("turn our hearts to him," 8:58); (3) for

8:64
y 2Ch 4:1

64 On that same day the king consecrated the middle part of the courtyard in front of the temple of the LORD, and there he offered burnt offerings, grain offerings and the fat of the fellowship offerings, because the bronze altar *y* before the LORD was too small to hold the burnt offerings, the grain offerings and the fat of the fellowship offerings.

8:65
z Nu 34:8
a Ge 15:18

65 So Solomon observed the festival at that time, and all Israel with him—a vast assembly, people from Lebo*a* Hamath*z* to the Wadi of Egypt.*a* They celebrated it before the LORD our God for seven days and seven days more, fourteen days in all. 66 On the following day he sent the people away. They blessed the king and then went home, joyful and glad in heart for all the good things the LORD had done for his servant David and his people Israel.

4. Solomon's greatness and downfall

The LORD Appears to Solomon

9:2
b 1Ki 3:5

9:3
c 2Ki 20:5
d Dt 11:12

9 When Solomon had finished building the temple of the LORD and the royal palace, and had achieved all he had desired to do, 2 the LORD appeared *b* to him a second time, as he had appeared to him at Gibeon. 3 The LORD said to him:

"I have heard *c* the prayer and plea you have made before me; I have consecrated this temple, which you have built, by putting my Name there forever. My eyes *d* and my heart will always be there.

9:5
e 1Ch 22:10
f 2Sa 7:15; 1Ki 2:4

4 "As for you, if you walk before me in integrity of heart and uprightness, as David your father did, and do all I command and observe my decrees and laws, 5 I will establish *e* your royal throne over Israel forever, as I promised David your father when I said, 'You shall never fail *f* to have a man on the throne of Israel.'

9:7
g 2Ki 17:23
h Jer 7:14
i Dt 28:37

9:8
j Dt 29:24;
Jer 22:8-9

6 "But if you *b* or your sons turn away from me and do not observe the commands and decrees I have given you*b* and go off to serve other gods and worship them, 7 then I will cut off Israel from the land *g* I have given them and will reject this temple I have consecrated for my Name. *h* Israel will then become a byword and an object of ridicule *i* among all peoples. 8 And though this temple is now imposing, all who pass by will be appalled and will scoff and say, 'Why has the LORD done such a thing to this land and to this temple?' *j* 9 People will answer, 'Because they have forsaken the LORD their God, who brought their fathers out of Egypt, and have embraced other gods, worshiping and serving them—that is why the LORD brought all this disaster on them.'"

Solomon's Other Activities

10 At the end of twenty years, during which Solomon built these two buildings—the temple of the LORD and the royal palace— 11 King Solomon gave twenty towns in Galilee to Hiram king of Tyre, because Hiram had supplied him with all the cedar and pine and gold he wanted. 12 But when Hiram went from Tyre to see the towns that Solomon had given him, he

a 65 Or from the entrance to   *b 6 The Hebrew is plural.*

SOLOMON'S BUILDING PROJECTS
Solomon became known as one of the great builders in Israel's history. He built Hazor, Megiddo, and Gezer as fortress cities at key points during his reign. He also rebuilt the cities of Lower Beth Horon, Baalath, and Tadmor.

help with each day's need (8:59); (4) for the desire and ability to obey God's decrees and commands (8:58); (5) for the spread of God's kingdom to the entire world (8:60). These prayer requests are just as important today. When you pray for your church or family, you can make these same requests to God.

8:65 A wadi is a stream or dry streambed.

9:4–9 God appeared to Solomon a second time; the first had been at Gibeon (3:4–15). For more on the conditions of God's great promise to David and his descendants, see the note on 2:3, 4.

9:11–14 Was Solomon being unfair to Hiram? It is not clear from these verses whether Solomon gave these towns to Hiram, or they were collateral until he could repay Hiram for the gold he had borrowed. Second Chronicles 8:1, 2 implies that the towns were returned to Solomon. In either case, Hiram probably preferred a piece of land on the coast more suitable for trade (the name he gave these cities, *Cabul*, sounds like the Hebrew word for "good-for-nothing"). In the end, Hiram was repaid many times over through his trade partnerships with Solomon (2 Chronicles 9:10, 21). Because Phoenicia was on friendly terms with Israel and dependent on it for grain and oil, Hiram's relationship with Solomon was more important than a feud over some cities.

was not pleased with them. [13]"What kind of towns are these you have given me, my brother?" he asked. And he called them the Land of Cabul,[a] [k] a name they have to this day. [14]Now Hiram had sent to the king 120 talents[b] of gold.

[15]Here is the account of the forced labor King Solomon conscripted[l] to build the LORD's temple, his own palace, the supporting terraces,[c] [m] the wall of Jerusalem, and Hazor, Megiddo and Gezer. [16](Pharaoh king of Egypt had attacked and captured Gezer. He had set it on fire. He killed its Canaanite inhabitants and then gave it as a wedding gift to his daughter, Solomon's wife. [17]And Solomon rebuilt Gezer.) He built up Lower Beth Horon,[n] [18]Baalath, and Tadmor[d] in the desert, within his land, [19]as well as all his store cities and the towns for his chariots[o] and for his horses[e]—whatever he desired to build in Jerusalem, in Lebanon and throughout all the territory he ruled.

[20]All the people left from the Amorites, Hittites, Perizzites, Hivites and Jebusites (these peoples were not Israelites), [21]that is, their descendants remaining in the land, whom the Israelites could not exterminate[f] [p]—these Solomon conscripted for his slave labor force,[q] as it is to this day. [22]But Solomon did not make slaves[r] of any of the Israelites; they were his fighting men, his government officials, his officers, his captains, and the commanders of his chariots and charioteers. [23]They were also the chief officials in charge of Solomon's projects—550 officials supervising the men who did the work.

[24]After Pharaoh's daughter[s] had come up from the City of David to the palace Solomon had built for her, he constructed the supporting terraces.[t]

[25]Three times a year Solomon sacrificed burnt offerings and fellowship offerings[g] on the altar he had built for the LORD, burning incense before the LORD along with them, and so fulfilled the temple obligations.

[26]King Solomon also built ships[u] at Ezion Geber,[v] which is near Elath in Edom, on the shore of the Red Sea.[h] [27]And Hiram sent his men—sailors[w] who knew the sea—to serve in the fleet with Solomon's men. [28]They sailed to Ophir and brought back 420 talents[i] of gold, which they delivered to King Solomon.

The Queen of Sheba Visits Solomon

10 When the queen of Sheba[x] heard about the fame of Solomon and his relation to the name of the LORD, she came to test him with hard questions. [2]Arriving at Jerusalem with a very great caravan—with camels carrying spices, large quantities of gold, and precious stones—she came to Solomon and talked with him about all that she had on her mind. [3]Solomon answered all her questions; nothing was too hard for the king to explain to her. [4]When the queen of Sheba saw all the wisdom of Solomon and the palace he had built, [5]the food on his table, the seating of his officials, the attending servants in their robes, his cupbearers, and the burnt offerings he made at[j] the temple of the LORD, she was overwhelmed.

[6]She said to the king, "The report I heard in my own country about your achievements and your wisdom is true. [7]But I did not believe these things until I came and saw with my own eyes. Indeed, not even half was told me; in wisdom and wealth you have far exceeded the report I heard. [8]How happy your men must be! How happy your officials, who continually stand before you and hear[y] your wisdom! [9]Praise[z] be to the LORD your God, who has delighted in you and placed you on the throne of Israel. Because of the LORD's eternal love for Israel, he has made you king, to maintain justice[a] and righteousness."

[10]And she gave the king 120 talents[b] of gold, large quantities of spices, and precious stones. Never again were so many spices brought in as those the queen of Sheba gave to King Solomon.

**Cross-references (right margin):**

9:13 [k] Jos 19:27

9:15 [l] 1Ki 5:13 [m] 2Sa 5:9

9:17 [n] Jos 16:3; 2Ch 8:5

9:19 [o] 1Ki 4:26

9:21 [p] Jos 15:63; 17:12 [q] Ezr 2:55, 58

9:22 [r] Lev 25:39

9:24 [s] 1Ki 3:1 [t] 1Ki 11:27; 2Ch 32:5

9:26 [u] 1Ki 22:48 [v] Nu 33:35

9:27 [w] 1Ki 10:11

10:1 [x] Mt 12:42

10:8 [y] Pr 8:34

10:9 [z] 1Ki 5:7 [a] 2Sa 8:15; Ps 72:2

---

a [13] Cabul sounds like the Hebrew for good-for-nothing.　b [14, 10] That is, about 4 1/2 tons (about 4 metric tons)
c [15] Or the Millo; also in verse 24　d [18] The Hebrew may also be read Tamar.　e [19] Or charioteers　f [21] The Hebrew term refers to the irrevocable giving over of things or persons to the LORD, often by totally destroying them.
g [25] Traditionally peace offerings　h [26] Hebrew Yam Suph; that is, Sea of Reeds　i [28] That is, about 16 tons (about 14.5 metric tons)　j [5] Or the ascent by which he went up to

---

9:16 At this time, Israel and Egypt were the major powers in the Near East. For many years Egypt had retained control of Gezer, even though it was in Israelite territory. In Solomon's time the Pharaoh gave the city to his daughter, whom Solomon married, putting Gezer under Israelite control. Intermarriage among royal families was common, but it was not endorsed by God (Deuteronomy 17:17).

10:1–5 The queen of Sheba came to see for herself if everything she had heard about Solomon was true. Contests using riddles or proverbs were often used to test wisdom. The queen may have used some of these as she questioned Solomon (10:1, 3). When she realized the extent of his riches and wisdom, "she was overwhelmed" and no longer questioned his power or wisdom. No longer a competitor, she became an admirer. Her experience was repeated by many kings and foreign dignitaries who paid honor to Solomon (4:34).

10:11
b 1Ki 9:27-28

¹¹(Hiram's ships brought gold from Ophir;*b* and from there they brought great cargoes of almugwood*a* and precious stones. ¹²The king used the almugwood to make supports for the temple of the LORD and for the royal palace, and to make harps and lyres for the musicians. So much almugwood has never been imported or seen since that day.)

¹³King Solomon gave the queen of Sheba all she desired and asked for, besides what he had given her out of his royal bounty. Then she left and returned with her retinue to her own country.

Solomon's Splendor

¹⁴The weight of the gold that Solomon received yearly was 666 talents,*b* ¹⁵not including the revenues from merchants and traders and from all the Arabian kings and the governors of the land.

10:16
c 1Ki 14:26-28
10:17
d 1Ki 7:2

¹⁶King Solomon made two hundred large shields*c* of hammered gold; six hundred bekas*c* of gold went into each shield. ¹⁷He also made three hundred small shields of hammered gold, with three minas*d* of gold in each shield. The king put them in the Palace of the Forest of Lebanon.*d*

¹⁸Then the king made a great throne inlaid with ivory and overlaid with fine gold. ¹⁹The throne had six steps, and its back had a rounded top. On both sides of the seat were armrests, with a lion standing beside each of them. ²⁰Twelve lions stood on the six steps, one at either end of each step. Nothing like it had ever been made for any other kingdom. ²¹All King Solomon's goblets were gold, and all the household articles in the Palace of the Forest of Lebanon were pure gold. Nothing was made of silver, because silver was considered of little value in Solomon's days. ²²The king had a fleet of trading ships*e* at sea along with the ships of Hiram. Once every three years it returned, carrying gold, silver and ivory, and apes and baboons.

a 11 Probably a variant of *algumwood*; also in verse 12   *b 14* That is, about 25 tons (about 23 metric tons)
c 16 That is, about 7 1/2 pounds (about 3.5 kilograms)   *d 17* That is, about 3 3/4 pounds (about 1.7 kilograms)
e 22 Hebrew *of ships of Tarshish*

FRIENDS AND ENEMIES
Solomon's reputation brought acclaim and riches from many nations, but he disobeyed God, marrying pagan women and worshiping their gods. So God raised up enemies like Hadad from Edom and Rezon from Zobah (modern-day Syria). Jeroboam from Zeredah was another enemy who would eventually divide this mighty kingdom.

10:14ff When Solomon asked for wisdom, God promised him riches and honor as well (3:13). These verses show just how extensive his wealth became. Israel was no longer a second-rate nation, but at the height of its power and wealth. Solomon's riches became legendary. Great leaders came from many nations to listen to Israel's powerful king. Jesus would later refer to "Solomon in all his splendor" (Matthew 6:29).

23 King Solomon was greater in riches[e] and wisdom[f] than all the other kings of the earth. 24 The whole world sought audience with Solomon to hear the wisdom God had put in his heart. 25 Year after year, everyone who came brought a gift—articles of silver and gold, robes, weapons and spices, and horses and mules.

26 Solomon accumulated chariots and horses;[g] he had fourteen hundred chariots and twelve thousand horses,[a] which he kept in the chariot cities and also with him in Jerusalem. 27 The king made silver as common in Jerusalem as stones, and cedar as plentiful as sycamore-fig trees in the foothills. 28 Solomon's horses were imported from Egypt[b] and from Kue[c]—the royal merchants purchased them from Kue. 29 They imported a chariot from Egypt for six hundred shekels[d] of silver, and a horse for a hundred and fifty.[e] They also exported them to all the kings of the Hittites and of the Arameans.

Solomon's Wives

11 King Solomon, however, loved many foreign women[h] besides Pharaoh's daughter—Moabites, Ammonites, Edomites, Sidonians and Hittites. 2 They were from nations about which the LORD had told the Israelites, "You must not intermarry[i] with them, because they will surely turn your hearts after their gods." Nevertheless, Solomon held fast to them in love. 3 He had seven hundred wives of royal birth and three hundred concubines, and his wives led him astray. 4 As Solomon grew old, his wives turned his heart after other gods, and his heart was not fully devoted to the LORD his God, as the heart of David his father had been. 5 He followed Ashtoreth[j] the goddess of the Sidonians, and Molech[f] the detestable god of the Ammonites. 6 So Solomon did evil in the eyes of the LORD; he did not follow the LORD completely, as David his father had done.

7 On a hill east[k] of Jerusalem, Solomon built a high place for Chemosh[l] the detestable god of Moab, and for Molech the detestable god of the Ammonites. 8 He did the same for all his foreign wives, who burned incense and offered sacrifices to their gods.

9 The LORD became angry with Solomon because his heart had turned away from the

**Cross references (right margin):**

10:23
e 1Ki 3:13
f 1Ki 4:30

10:26
g 1Ki 4:26;
2Ch 1:14; 9:25

11:1
h Ne 13:26

11:2
i Ex 34:16; Dt 7:3-4

11:5
j Jdg 2:13

11:7
k 2Ki 23:13
l Nu 21:29;
Jdg 11:24

---

a 26 Or charioteers   b 28 Or possibly Muzur, a region in Cilicia; also in verse 29   c 28 Probably Cilicia   d 29 That is, about 15 pounds (about 7 kilograms)   e 29 That is, about 3 3/4 pounds (about 1.7 kilograms)   f 5 Hebrew Milcom; also in verse 33

10:23 Why does the Bible place so much emphasis on Solomon's material possessions? In the Old Testament, riches were considered tangible evidence of God's blessing. Prosperity was seen as a proof of right living. In the books of Ecclesiastes and Job this concept is placed in a broader perspective. In ideal conditions, people prosper when God runs their lives, but prosperity is not guaranteed. Wealth does not prove that a person is living rightly before God, and poverty does not indicate sin.

In fact, a greater evidence that a person is living for God is the presence of suffering and persecution (Mark 10:29–31; 13:13). The most important "treasure" is not earthly, but heavenly (Matthew 6:19–21; 19:21; 1 Timothy 6:17–19). The gift of greatest worth has no price tag—it is the gift of salvation freely offered by God.

10:26—11:3 In accumulating chariots and horses, a huge harem, and incredible wealth, Solomon was violating God's commands for a king (Deuteronomy 17:14–20). God prohibited these actions because he knew how they would hurt the nation both politically and spiritually (1 Samuel 8:11–18). The more luxurious Solomon's court became, the more the people were taxed. Excessive taxation created unrest, and soon conditions became ripe for a revolution. With everything he wanted, Solomon forgot God and allowed pagan influences to enter his court through his pagan wives, thus accelerating the spiritual corruption of the nation.

11:2 Although Solomon had clear instructions from God *not* to marry women from foreign nations, he chose to disregard God's commands. He married not one, but many foreign women, who subsequently led him away from God. God knows our strengths and weaknesses, and his commands are always for our good. When people ignore God's commands, negative consequences inevitably result. It is not enough to know God's Word or even to believe it; we must follow it and apply it to our daily activities and

decisions. Take God's commands seriously. Like Solomon, the wisest man who ever lived, we are not as strong as we may think.

11:3 For all his wisdom, Solomon had some weak spots. He could not say no to compromise or to lustful desires. Whether he married to strengthen political alliances or to gain personal pleasure, these foreign wives led him into idolatry. You may have strong faith, but you also have areas of weakness—and that is where temptation usually strikes. Strengthen and protect yourself where you are weak because a chain is only as strong as its weakest link. If Solomon, the wisest man, could fall, so can you.

11:4 Solomon handled great pressures in running the government, but he could not handle the pressure from his wives who wanted him to worship their gods. In marriage and close friendships, it is difficult to resist pressure to compromise. Our love leads us to identify with the desires of those we care about.

Faced with such pressure, Solomon at first *resisted* it, maintaining pure faith. Then he *tolerated* a more widespread practice of idolatry. Finally he became involved in idolatrous worship, *rationalizing* away the potential danger to himself and to the kingdom. Because we want to please and identify with our loved ones, God asks us not to marry those who do not share our commitment to him.

11:5–8 Ashtoreth was a goddess that symbolized reproductive power—a mistress of the god Baal. Molech was the national god of the Ammonites, called "detestable" because its worship rites included child sacrifice. Chemosh was the Moabites' national god. The Israelites were warned against worshiping all other gods in general and Molech in particular (Exodus 20:1–6; Leviticus 18:21; 20:1–5).

11:9, 10 Solomon didn't turn away from God all at once or in a brief moment. His spiritual coldness started with a minor departure from God's laws (3:1). Over the years, that little sin grew until it resulted in Solomon's downfall. A little sin can be the first step in turning away from God. It is not the sins we don't know about, but

11:9
m 1Ki 3:5; 9:2

11:10
n 1Ki 9:6
o 1Ki 6:12

11:11
p ver 31;
1Ki 12:15-16

11:13
q 2Sa 7:15

11:15
r 2Sa 8:14;
1Ch 18:12

11:23
s 2Sa 8:3

11:24
t 2Sa 10:8, 18

11:26
u 2Sa 20:21;
1Ki 12:2; 2Ch 13:6

11:27
v 1Ki 9:24

11:29
w 1Ki 14:2

Lord, the God of Israel, who had appeared *m* to him twice. 10Although he had forbidden Solomon to follow other gods, *n* Solomon did not keep the Lord's command. *o* 11So the Lord said to Solomon, "Since this is your attitude and you have not kept my covenant and my decrees, which I commanded you, I will most certainly tear *p* the kingdom away from you and give it to one of your subordinates. 12Nevertheless, for the sake of David your father, I will not do it during your lifetime. I will tear it out of the hand of your son. 13Yet I will not tear the whole kingdom from him, but will give him one tribe for the sake *q* of David my servant and for the sake of Jerusalem, which I have chosen."

Solomon's Adversaries

14Then the Lord raised up against Solomon an adversary, Hadad the Edomite, from the royal line of Edom. 15Earlier when David was fighting with Edom, Joab the commander of the army, who had gone up to bury the dead, had struck down all the men in Edom. *r* 16Joab and all the Israelites stayed there for six months, until they had destroyed all the men in Edom. 17But Hadad, still only a boy, fled to Egypt with some Edomite officials who had served his father. 18They set out from Midian and went to Paran. Then taking men from Paran with them, they went to Egypt, to Pharaoh king of Egypt, who gave Hadad a house and land and provided him with food.

19Pharaoh was so pleased with Hadad that he gave him a sister of his own wife, Queen Tahpenes, in marriage. 20The sister of Tahpenes bore him a son named Genubath, whom Tahpenes brought up in the royal palace. There Genubath lived with Pharaoh's own children.

21While he was in Egypt, Hadad heard that David rested with his fathers and that Joab the commander of the army was also dead. Then Hadad said to Pharaoh, "Let me go, that I may return to my own country."

22"What have you lacked here that you want to go back to your own country?" Pharaoh asked.

"Nothing," Hadad replied, "but do let me go!"

23And God raised up against Solomon another adversary, Rezon son of Eliada, who had fled from his master, Hadadezer *s* king of Zobah. 24He gathered men around him and became the leader of a band of rebels when David destroyed the forces*a* ⌊of Zobah⌋; the rebels went to Damascus, *t* where they settled and took control. 25Rezon was Israel's adversary as long as Solomon lived, adding to the trouble caused by Hadad. So Rezon ruled in Aram and was hostile toward Israel.

Jeroboam Rebels Against Solomon

26Also, Jeroboam son of Nebat rebelled *u* against the king. He was one of Solomon's officials, an Ephraimite from Zeredah, and his mother was a widow named Zeruah. 27Here is the account of how he rebelled against the king: Solomon had built the supporting terraces*b* *v* and had filled in the gap in the wall of the city of David his father. 28Now Jeroboam was a man of standing, and when Solomon saw how well the young man did his work, he put him in charge of the whole labor force of the house of Joseph.

29About that time Jeroboam was going out of Jerusalem, and Ahijah *w* the prophet of Shiloh met him on the way, wearing a new cloak. The two of them were alone out in the country,

a24 Hebrew *destroyed them*   *b27* Or *the Millo*

---

the sins we excuse, that cause us the greatest trouble. We must never let any sin go unchallenged. In your life, is an unchallenged sin spreading like a deadly cancer? Don't excuse it. Confess this sin to God and ask him for strength to resist temptation.

11:11-13 Solomon's powerful and glorious kingdom could have been blessed for all time; instead, it was approaching its end. Solomon had God's promises, guidance, and answers to prayer, yet he allowed sin to remain all around him. Eventually it corrupted him so much that he was no longer interested in God. Psalm 127, written by Solomon, says, "Unless the Lord builds the house, its builders labor in vain." Solomon had begun by laying the foundation with God, but he did not follow through in his later years. As a result, he lost everything. It is not enough to get off to a right start in building our marriage, career, or church on God's principles; we must remain faithful to God to the end

(Mark 13:13). God must be in control of our lives from start to finish.

11:14-22 Edom was the kingdom southeast of the Dead Sea. David had added this nation to his empire (2 Samuel 8:13, 14). It was of strategic importance because it controlled the route to the Red Sea. Edom's revolt was disturbing the peace of Solomon's kingdom.

11:29-39 The prophet Ahijah predicted the division of the kingdom of Israel. After Solomon's death, 10 of Israel's 12 tribes would follow Jeroboam. The other two tribes, Judah and the area of Benjamin around Jerusalem, would remain loyal to David. Judah, the largest tribe, and Benjamin, the smallest, were often mentioned as one tribe because they shared the same border. Both Jeroboam and Ahijah were from Ephraim, the most promi-

30 and Ahijah took hold of the new cloak he was wearing and tore ˣ it into twelve pieces. 31 Then he said to Jeroboam, "Take ten pieces for yourself, for this is what the LORD, the God of Israel, says: 'See, I am going to tear ʸ the kingdom out of Solomon's hand and give you ten tribes. 32 But for the sake of my servant David and the city of Jerusalem, which I have chosen out of all the tribes of Israel, he will have one tribe. 33 I will do this because they have ᵃ forsaken me and worshiped ᶻ Ashtoreth the goddess of the Sidonians, Chemosh the god of the Moabites, and Molech the god of the Ammonites, and have not walked in my ways, nor done what is right in my eyes, nor kept my statutes and laws as David, Solomon's father, did.

34 "'But I will not take the whole kingdom out of Solomon's hand; I have made him ruler all the days of his life for the sake of David my servant, whom I chose and who observed my commands and statutes. 35 I will take the kingdom from his son's hands and give you ten tribes. 36 I will give one tribe to his son so that David my servant may always have a lamp ᵃ before me in Jerusalem, the city where I chose to put my Name. 37 However, as for you, I will take you, and you will rule over all that your heart desires; you will be king over Israel. 38 If you do whatever I command you and walk in my ways and do what is right in my eyes by keeping my statutes and commands, as David my servant did, I will be with you. I will build you a dynasty ᵇ as enduring as the one I built for David and will give Israel to you. 39 I will humble David's descendants because of this, but not forever.'"

40 Solomon tried to kill Jeroboam, but Jeroboam fled to Egypt, to Shishak the king, and stayed there until Solomon's death.

Solomon's Death

41 As for the other events of Solomon's reign—all he did and the wisdom he displayed—are they not written in the book of the annals of Solomon? 42 Solomon reigned in Jerusalem over all Israel forty years. 43 Then he rested with his fathers and was buried in the city of David his father. And Rehoboam his son succeeded him as king.

B. THE DIVIDED KINGDOM (12:1—22:53)

After Solomon's death, the northern tribes revolt, forming two separate nations. Each nation experiences disastrous consequences from having evil kings. Elijah appears on the scene, confronting these kings for their sin. God deals with sin in powerful ways. Although judgment may appear to be slow, God will judge evil harshly.

1. Revolt of the northern tribes
Israel Rebels Against Rehoboam

12 Rehoboam went to Shechem, for all the Israelites had gone there to make him king. 2 When Jeroboam son of Nebat heard this (he was still in Egypt, where he had fled ᶜ from King Solomon), he returned from ᵇ Egypt. 3 So they sent for Jeroboam, and he and the

ᵃ33 Hebrew; Septuagint, Vulgate and Syriac *because he has*   ᵇ2 Or *he remained in*

11:30
ˣ1Sa 15:27
11:31
ʸver 11
11:33
ᶻver 5-7

11:36
ᵃ1Ki 15:4; 2Ki 8:19

11:38
ᵇJos 1:5;
2Sa 7:11, 27

12:2
ᶜ1Ki 11:40

---

nent of the 10 rebel tribes. (For more on the divided kingdom, see the note on 12:20.)

11:41 Nothing is known of "the book of the annals of Solomon." See also the note on 14:19.

12:1 Rehoboam was made king at Shechem, about 35 miles north of Jerusalem. It would have been normal to anoint the new king in Jerusalem, the capital city, but Rehoboam saw trouble brewing with Jeroboam and went north to try to maintain good relations with the northern tribes. He probably chose Shechem because it was an ancient location for making covenants (Joshua 24:1). When the kingdom divided, Shechem became the capital of the northern kingdom for a short time (12:25).

THE KINGDOM DIVIDES
Rehoboam's threat of heavier burdens caused a rebellion and divided the nation. Rehoboam ruled the southern kingdom; Jeroboam ruled the northern kingdom. Jeroboam set up idols in Dan and Bethel to discourage worship in Jerusalem. At the same time Aram, Ammon, Moab, and Edom claimed independence from the divided nation.

12:4
d 1Sa 8:11-18

whole assembly of Israel went to Rehoboam and said to him: ⁴"Your father put a heavy yoke *d* on us, but now lighten the harsh labor and the heavy yoke he put on us, and we will serve you."

⁵Rehoboam answered, "Go away for three days and then come back to me." So the people went away.

⁶Then King Rehoboam consulted the elders who had served his father Solomon during his lifetime. "How would you advise me to answer these people?" he asked.

⁷They replied, "If today you will be a servant to these people and serve them and give them a favorable answer, they will always be your servants."

⁸But Rehoboam rejected the advice the elders gave him and consulted the young men who had grown up with him and were serving him. ⁹He asked them, "What is your advice? How should we answer these people who say to me, 'Lighten the yoke your father put on us'?"

¹⁰The young men who had grown up with him replied, "Tell these people who have said to you, 'Your father put a heavy yoke on us, but make our yoke lighter'—tell them, 'My little finger is thicker than my father's waist. ¹¹My father laid on you a heavy yoke; I will make it even heavier. My father scourged you with whips; I will scourge you with scorpions.'"

¹²Three days later Jeroboam and all the people returned to Rehoboam, as the king had said, "Come back to me in three days." ¹³The king answered the people harshly. Rejecting the advice given him by the elders, ¹⁴he followed the advice of the young men and said, "My father made your yoke heavy; I will make it even heavier. My father scourged you with whips; I will scourge you with scorpions." ¹⁵So the king did not listen to the people, for this turn of events was from the Lord, to fulfill the word the Lord had spoken to Jeroboam son of Nebat through Ahijah *e* the Shilonite.

12:15
e 1Ki 11:29

12:16
f 2Sa 20:1

¹⁶When all Israel saw that the king refused to listen to them, they answered the king:

> "What share do we have in David,
>   what part in Jesse's son?
> To your tents, O Israel! *f*
>   Look after your own house, O David!"

TRIBAL JEALOUSIES

Although the kingdom of Israel was "united" under David and Solomon, the tensions between north and south were never resolved. The jealousy and animosity behind this civil war didn't begin with Rehoboam and Jeroboam but had its roots in the days of the judges, when the people were more interested in tribal loyalty than in national unity. Note how easily tension arose between Ephraim, the most prominent tribe in the north, and Judah, the prominent tribe of the south.

- Ephraim claimed the promises in Genesis 48:17–22 and 49:22–26 for its leadership role.
- Joshua, who conquered the promised land, was an Ephraimite (Numbers 13:8).
- Samuel, Israel's greatest judge, was from Ephraim (1 Samuel 1:1ff).
- Ephraim allied with Ish-Bosheth in revolt against David, who was from the tribe of Judah (2 Samuel 2:8–11).
- David, a shepherd from the tribe of Judah, became king over all Israel, including Ephraim, which no longer had a claim to leadership.
- Although David helped to smooth over the bad feelings, the heavy yoke under Solomon and Rehoboam led the northern tribes to the breaking point.

Such tension developed because Ephraim was the key tribe in the north. They resented Judah's role in leadership under David and resented that the nation's capital and center of worship were located in Jerusalem.

12:6–14 Rehoboam asked for advice, but he didn't carefully evaluate what he was told. If he had, he would have realized that the advice offered by the elders was wiser than that of his peers. To evaluate advice, ask if it is realistic, workable, and consistent with Biblical principles. Determine if the results of following the advice will be fair, make improvements, and give a positive solution or direction. Seek counsel from those who are more experienced and wiser. Advice is helpful only if it is consistent with God's standards.

12:15–19 Both Jeroboam and Rehoboam did what was good for themselves, not what was good for their people. Rehoboam

was harsh and did not listen to the people's demands; Jeroboam established new places of worship to keep his people from traveling to Jerusalem, Rehoboam's capital. Both actions backfired. Rehoboam's move divided the nation, and Jeroboam's turned the people from God. Good leaders put the best interests of the "followers" above their own. Making decisions only for yourself will backfire and cause you to lose more than if you had kept the welfare of others in mind.

So the Israelites went home. [17]But as for the Israelites who were living in the towns of Judah,*g* Rehoboam still ruled over them.

[18]King Rehoboam sent out Adoniram,[a] *h* who was in charge of forced labor, but all Israel stoned him to death. King Rehoboam, however, managed to get into his chariot and escape to Jerusalem. [19]So Israel has been in rebellion against the house of David *i* to this day.

[20]When all the Israelites heard that Jeroboam had returned, they sent and called him to the assembly and made him king over all Israel. Only the tribe of Judah remained loyal to the house of David.*j*

[21]When Rehoboam arrived in Jerusalem, he mustered the whole house of Judah and the tribe of Benjamin—a hundred and eighty thousand fighting men—to make war *k* against the house of Israel and to regain the kingdom for Rehoboam son of Solomon.

[22]But this word of God came to Shemaiah the man of God: [23]"Say to Rehoboam son of Solomon king of Judah, to the whole house of Judah and Benjamin, and to the rest of the people, [24]'This is what the LORD says: Do not go up to fight against your brothers, the Israelites. Go home, every one of you, for this is my doing.'" So they obeyed the word of the LORD and went home again, as the LORD had ordered.

Golden Calves at Bethel and Dan

[25]Then Jeroboam fortified Shechem *l* in the hill country of Ephraim and lived there. From there he went out and built up Peniel.[b] *m*

[26]Jeroboam thought to himself, "The kingdom will now likely revert to the house of David. [27]If these people go up to offer sacrifices at the temple of the LORD in Jerusalem,*n* they will again give their allegiance to their lord, Rehoboam king of Judah. They will kill me and return to King Rehoboam."

[28]After seeking advice, the king made two golden calves.*o* He said to the people, "It is too much for you to go up to Jerusalem. Here are your gods, O Israel, who brought you up out of Egypt."*p* [29]One he set up in Bethel,*q* and the other in Dan.*r* [30]And this thing became a sin;*s* the people went even as far as Dan to worship the one there.

[31]Jeroboam built shrines*t* on high places and appointed priests*u* from all sorts of people, even though they were not Levites. [32]He instituted a festival on the fifteenth day of the eighth*v* month, like the festival held in Judah, and offered sacrifices on the altar. This he did in Bethel, sacrificing to the calves he had made. And at Bethel he also installed priests at the high places he had made. [33]On the fifteenth day of the eighth month, a month of his own choosing, he offered sacrifices on the altar he had built at Bethel. So he instituted the festival for the Israelites and went up to the altar to make offerings.

a 18 Some Septuagint manuscripts and Syriac (see also 1 Kings 4:6 and 5:14); Hebrew *Adoram*   *b 25* Hebrew *Penuel,* a variant of *Peniel*

12:17
g 1Ki 11:13, 36
12:18
h 1Ki 4:6; 5:14
12:19
i 2Ki 17:21
12:20
j 1Ki 11:13, 32
12:21
k 2Ch 11:1
12:25
l Jdg 9:45
m Jdg 8:8, 17
12:27
n Dt 12:5-6
12:28
o Ex 32:4
p Ex 32:8
12:29
q Ge 28:19
r Jdg 18:27-31
12:30
s 1Ki 13:34;
2Ki 17:21
12:31
t 1Ki 13:32
u 2Ki 17:32;
2Ch 11:14-15
12:32
v Lev 23:33-34;
Nu 29:12

12:20 This marks the beginning of the division of the kingdom that lasted for centuries. Ten of Israel's 12 tribes followed Jeroboam and called their new nation Israel (the northern kingdom). The other two tribes remained loyal to Rehoboam and called their nation Judah (the southern kingdom). The kingdom did not split overnight. It was already dividing as early as the days of the judges because of tribal jealousies, especially between Ephraim, the most influential tribe of the north, and Judah, the chief tribe of the south.

Before the days of Saul and David, the religious center of Israel was located, for the most part, in the territory of Ephraim. When Solomon built the temple, Jerusalem became the religious center of Israel. This eventually brought tribal rivalries to the breaking point. (For more information on tribal jealousies and how they affected Israel, see Judges 12:1ff; 2 Samuel 2:4ff; 19:41–43.)

12:28 All Jewish men were required to travel to the temple three times each year (Deuteronomy 16:16), but Jeroboam set up his own worship centers and told his people it was too much trouble to travel all the way to Jerusalem. Those who obeyed Jeroboam were disobeying God. Some ideas, though practical, may include suggestions that lead you away from God. Don't let anyone talk you out of doing what is right by telling you that moral actions are not worth the effort. Do what God wants, no matter what the cost in time, energy, reputation, or resources.

12:28, 29 Calves were used as idols to symbolize fertility and

strength. Pagan gods of the Canaanites were often depicted as standing on calves or bulls. Jeroboam shrewdly placed the golden calves in Bethel and Dan, strategic locations. Bethel was just 10 miles north of Jerusalem on the main road, enticing the citizens from the north to stop there instead of traveling the rest of the way to Jerusalem. Dan was the northernmost city in Israel, so people living in the north far from Jerusalem were attracted to its convenient location. As leader of the northern kingdom, Jeroboam wanted to establish his own worship centers; otherwise his people would make regular trips to Jerusalem, and his authority would be undermined. Soon this substitute religion had little in common with true faith in God.

12:30 Jeroboam and his advisers did not learn from Israel's previous disaster with a golden calf (Exodus 32). Perhaps they were ignorant of Scripture, or maybe they knew about the event and decided to ignore it. Study the Bible to become aware of God's acts in history, and then apply the important lessons to your life. If you learn from the past, you will not face disaster as a result of repeating others' mistakes (Isaiah 42:23; 1 Corinthians 10:11).

12:32, 33 Early in Israel's history, the city of Bethel was a symbol of commitment to God because there Jacob had rededicated himself to God (Genesis 28:16–22). But Jeroboam turned the city into Israel's chief religious center, intending it to compete with Jerusalem. Bethel's religion, however, centered on an idol, and this led to Israel's eventual downfall. Bethel developed a

2. Kings of Israel and Judah
The Man of God From Judah

13:1
w 2Ki 23:17

13:2
x 2Ki 23:15-16, 20

13 By the word of the LORD a man of God w came from Judah to Bethel, as Jeroboam was standing by the altar to make an offering. ² He cried out against the altar by the word of the LORD: "O altar, altar! This is what the LORD says: 'A son named Josiah x will be born to the house of David. On you he will sacrifice the priests of the high places who now make offerings here, and human bones will be burned on you.'" ³ That same day the man of God gave a sign: "This is the sign the LORD has declared: The altar will be split apart and the ashes on it will be poured out."

JEROBOAM

Even clear warnings are hard to obey. The Bible is filled with stories of people who had direction from God and yet chose their own way. Their disobedience was rarely due to ignorance of what God wanted; rather, it grew out of stubborn selfishness. Jeroboam was a consistent example of this all-too-human trait.

During his construction activities, Solomon noticed young Jeroboam's natural leadership skills and made him a special project foreman. Shortly after this, God contacted Jeroboam through the prophet Ahijah. He told Jeroboam that God would punish David's dynasty by tearing the kingdom from Solomon's son and that Jeroboam would rule the ten northern tribes. And God made it clear that the same fate would destroy Jeroboam's family if they refused to obey God. Apparently Solomon heard about these events and tried to have Jeroboam killed. The future king escaped to Egypt, where he stayed until Solomon died.

When Rehoboam, Solomon's heir, took the throne, Jeroboam returned. He represented the people in demanding that the new king be more lenient than his father. Rehoboam's unwise choice to reject his people's request led to their rejecting him as king. Only Judah and the annexed tribe of Benjamin remained loyal to David's dynasty. The other ten tribes made Jeroboam king.

Rather than seeing this fulfillment of God's promise as motivation to obey God, Jeroboam decided to do whatever he could to secure his position. He led his kingdom away from the God who had allowed him to reign. God had already warned him of the consequences of this action—his family was eventually wiped out. And Jeroboam set into motion events that would lead to the destruction of the northern kingdom.

Sin's consequences are guaranteed in God's Word, but the timing of those consequences is hard to predict. When we do something directly opposed to God's commands and there isn't immediate disaster, we are often fooled into believing we got away with disobedience. But that is a dangerous assumption. Jeroboam's life should make us recognize our frequent need to admit our disobedience and ask God to forgive us.

Strengths and accomplishments:
- An effective leader and organizer
- First king of the ten tribes of Israel in the divided kingdom
- A charismatic leader with much popular support

Weaknesses and mistakes:
- Erected idols in Israel to keep people away from the temple in Jerusalem
- Appointed priests from outside the tribe of Levi
- Depended more on his own cunning than on God's promises

Lessons from his life:
- Great opportunities are often destroyed by small decisions
- Careless efforts to correct another's errors often lead to the same errors
- Mistakes always occur when we attempt to take over God's role in a situation

Vital statistics:
- Where: The northern kingdom of Israel
- Occupations: Project foreman, king of Israel
- Relatives: Father: Nebat. Mother: Zeruah. Sons: Abijah, Nadab.
- Contemporaries: Solomon, Nathan, Ahijah, Rehoboam

Key verses:
"Even after this, Jeroboam did not change his evil ways, but once more appointed priests for the high places from all sorts of people. Anyone who wanted to become a priest he consecrated for the high places. This was the sin of the house of Jeroboam that led to its downfall and to its destruction from the face of the earth" (1 Kings 13:33, 34).

Jeroboam's story is told in 1 Kings 11:26—14:20. He is also mentioned in 2 Chronicles 10—13.

reputation as a wicked and idolatrous city. The prophets Hosea and Amos recognized the sins of Bethel and condemned the city for its godless ways (Hosea 4:15–17; 10:8; Amos 5:4–6).

13:2 Three hundred years later, this prophecy was fulfilled in every detail when Josiah killed the pagan priests at their own altars. The story is found in 2 Kings 23:1–20.

4 When King Jeroboam heard what the man of God cried out against the altar at Bethel, he stretched out his hand from the altar and said, "Seize him!" But the hand he stretched out toward the man shriveled up, so that he could not pull it back. 5 Also, the altar was split apart and its ashes poured out according to the sign given by the man of God by the word of the LORD.

6 Then the king said to the man of God, "Intercede^y with the LORD your God and pray for me that my hand may be restored." So the man of God interceded with the LORD, and the king's hand was restored and became as it was before.

7 The king said to the man of God, "Come home with me and have something to eat, and I will give you a gift."^z

8 But the man of God answered the king, "Even if you were to give me half your possessions,^a I would not go with you, nor would I eat bread or drink water here. 9 For I was commanded by the word of the LORD: 'You must not eat bread or drink water or return by the way you came.'" 10 So he took another road and did not return by the way he had come to Bethel.

11 Now there was a certain old prophet living in Bethel, whose sons came and told him all that the man of God had done there that day. They also told their father what he had said to the king. 12 Their father asked them, "Which way did he go?" And his sons showed him which road the man of God from Judah had taken. 13 So he said to his sons, "Saddle the donkey for me." And when they had saddled the donkey for him, he mounted it 14 and rode after the man of God. He found him sitting under an oak tree and asked, "Are you the man of God who came from Judah?"

"I am," he replied.

15 So the prophet said to him, "Come home with me and eat."

16 The man of God said, "I cannot turn back and go with you, nor can I eat bread^b or drink water with you in this place. 17 I have been told by the word of the LORD: 'You must not eat bread or drink water there or return by the way you came.'"

18 The old prophet answered, "I too am a prophet, as you are. And an angel said to me by the word of the LORD: 'Bring him back with you to your house so that he may eat bread and drink water.'" (But he was lying to him.) 19 So the man of God returned with him and ate and drank in his house.

20 While they were sitting at the table, the word of the LORD came to the old prophet who had brought him back. 21 He cried out to the man of God who had come from Judah, "This is what the LORD says: 'You have defied the word of the LORD and have not kept the command the LORD your God gave you. 22 You came back and ate bread and drank water in the place where he told you not to eat or drink. Therefore your body will not be buried in the tomb of your fathers.'"

23 When the man of God had finished eating and drinking, the prophet who had brought him back saddled his donkey for him. 24 As he went on his way, a lion^c met him on the road and killed him, and his body was thrown down on the road, with both the donkey and the lion standing beside it. 25 Some people who passed by saw the body thrown down there, with the lion standing beside the body, and they went and reported it in the city where the old prophet lived.

26 When the prophet who had brought him back from his journey heard of it, he said, "It is the man of God who defied the word of the LORD. The LORD has given him over to the lion, which has mauled him and killed him, as the word of the LORD had warned him."

27 The prophet said to his sons, "Saddle the donkey for me," and they did so. 28 Then he went out and found the body thrown down on the road, with the donkey and the lion standing beside it. The lion had neither eaten the body nor mauled the donkey. 29 So the prophet picked up the body of the man of God, laid it on the donkey, and brought it back to his own city to mourn for him and bury him. 30 Then he laid the body in his own tomb, and they mourned over him and said, "Oh, my brother!"^d

13:6
^y Ex 8:8; 9:28;
Ac 8:24

13:7
^z 1Sa 9:7; 2Ki 5:15

13:8
^a Nu 22:18; 24:13

13:16
^b ver 8

13:24
^c 1Ki 20:36

13:30
^d Jer 22:18

13:7-32 This prophet had been given strict orders from God not to eat or drink anything while on his mission (13:9). He died because he listened to a man who claimed to have a message from God, rather than to God himself. This prophet should have followed God's word instead of hearsay. Trust what God's Word says rather than what someone claims is true. And disregard what others claim to be messages from God if their words contradict the Bible.

13:24, 25 Lions are mentioned frequently in the Old Testament. They were common enough to be a threat both to people and to their flocks. Samson (Judges 14:5, 6), David (1 Samuel 17:34-37), and Benaiah (2 Samuel 23:20) all faced wild lions. The fact that the lion and the donkey were standing by the prophet's body showed that this was a divine judgment. Normally, the lion would have attacked the donkey or devoured the man.

13:31
e 2Ki 23:18

13:32
f 1Ki 16:24, 28

13:33
g 1Ki 12:31

13:34
h 1Ki 14:10

14:2
i 1Ki 11:29

14:3
j 1Sa 9:7

14:8
k 1Ki 11:31, 33, 38

14:9
l 2Ch 11:15
m Ps 50:17

³¹After burying him, he said to his sons, "When I die, bury me in the grave where the man of God is buried; lay my bones *e* beside his bones. ³²For the message he declared by the word of the LORD against the altar in Bethel and against all the shrines on the high places in the towns of Samaria *f* will certainly come true."

³³Even after this, Jeroboam did not change his evil ways, but once more appointed priests for the high places from all sorts *g* of people. Anyone who wanted to become a priest he consecrated for the high places. ³⁴This was the sin of the house of Jeroboam that led to its downfall and to its destruction *h* from the face of the earth.

Ahijah's Prophecy Against Jeroboam

14 At that time Abijah son of Jeroboam became ill, ²and Jeroboam said to his wife, "Go, disguise yourself, so you won't be recognized as the wife of Jeroboam. Then go to Shiloh. Ahijah *i* the prophet is there—the one who told me I would be king over this people. ³Take ten loaves of bread *j* with you, some cakes and a jar of honey, and go to him. He will tell you what will happen to the boy." ⁴So Jeroboam's wife did what he said and went to Ahijah's house in Shiloh.

Now Ahijah could not see; his sight was gone because of his age. ⁵But the LORD had told Ahijah, "Jeroboam's wife is coming to ask you about her son, for he is ill, and you are to give her such and such an answer. When she arrives, she will pretend to be someone else."

⁶So when Ahijah heard the sound of her footsteps at the door, he said, "Come in, wife of Jeroboam. Why this pretense? I have been sent to you with bad news. ⁷Go, tell Jeroboam that this is what the LORD, the God of Israel, says: 'I raised you up from among the people and made you a leader over my people Israel. ⁸I tore *k* the kingdom away from the house of David and gave it to you, but you have not been like my servant David, who kept my commands and followed me with all his heart, doing only what was right in my eyes. ⁹You have done more evil than all who lived before you. You have made for yourself other gods, idols *l* made of metal; you have provoked me to anger and thrust me behind your back. *m*

THE APPEAL OF IDOLS	The Appeal of Idols	Modern Parallel
On the surface, the lives of the kings don't make sense. How could they run to idolatry so fast when they had God's Word (at least some of it), prophets, and the example of David? Here are some of the reasons for the enticement of idols:	**Power** The people wanted freedom from the authority of both God and the priests. They wanted their religion to fit their lifestyle, not their lifestyle to fit their religion.	People do not want to answer to a greater authority. Instead of having power *over* others, God wants us to have the Holy Spirit's power to *help* others.
	Pleasure Idol worship exalted sensuality without responsibility or guilt. People acted out the vicious and sensuous personalities of the gods they worshiped, thus gaining approval for their degraded lives.	People deify pleasure, seeking it at the expense of everything else. Instead of seeking pleasure that leads to long-range disaster, God calls us to seek the kind of pleasure that leads to long-range rewards.
	Passion Humanity was reduced to little more than animals. The people did not have to be viewed as unique individuals but could be exploited sexually, politically, and economically.	Like animals, people let physical drives and passion rule them. Instead of seeking passion that exploits others, God calls us to redirect our passions to areas that build others up.
	Praise and Popularity The high and holy nature of God was replaced by gods who were more a reflection of human nature, thus more culturally suitable to the people. These gods no longer required sacrifice, just a token of appeasement.	Sacrifice is seen as self-inflicted punishment, making no sense. Success is to be sought at all costs. Instead of seeking praise for ourselves, God calls us to praise him and those who honor him.

As societies change, they often throw out norms and values no longer considered necessary or acceptable. Believers must be careful not to follow society's example if it discards God's Word. When society does that, only godlessness and evil remain.

13:33, 34 Under penalty of death, God had forbidden anyone to be a priest who was not from the tribe of Levi (Numbers 3:10). Levites were assured of lifetime support from the tithe, so they did not have to spend time farming, worrying about tribal interests, or fearing for their financial futures. Jeroboam's new priests were financed by the king and his fees. They had to mix priestly and secular duties, and they quickly fell into party politics. Because they didn't have job security, these priests were easily corrupted by bribes. Jeroboam's disobedience was the downfall of true religion in the northern kingdom.

¹⁰"'Because of this, I am going to bring disaster on the house of Jeroboam. I will cut off from Jeroboam every last male in Israel—slave or free.ⁿ I will burn up the house of Jeroboam as one burns dung, until it is all gone.ᵒ ¹¹Dogsᵖ will eat those belonging to Jeroboam who die in the city, and the birds of the air will feed on those who die in the country. The Lᴏʀᴅ has spoken!'

¹²"As for you, go back home. When you set foot in your city, the boy will die. ¹³All Israel will mourn for him and bury him. He is the only one belonging to Jeroboam who will be buried, because he is the only one in the house of Jeroboam in whom the Lᴏʀᴅ, the God of Israel, has found anything good.

¹⁴"The Lᴏʀᴅ will raise up for himself a king over Israel who will cut off the family of Jeroboam. This is the day! What? Yes, even now.ᵃ ¹⁵And the Lᴏʀᴅ will strike Israel, so that it will be like a reed swaying in the water. He will uproot Israel from this good land that he gave to their forefathers and scatter them beyond the River,ᵇ because they provokedᑫ the Lᴏʀᴅ to anger by making Asherahʳ poles.ᶜ ¹⁶And he will give Israel up because of the sinsˢ Jeroboam has committed and has caused Israel to commit."

¹⁷Then Jeroboam's wife got up and left and went to Tirzah.ᵗ As soon as she stepped over the threshold of the house, the boy died. ¹⁸They buried him, and all Israel mourned for him, as the Lᴏʀᴅ had said through his servant the prophet Ahijah.

¹⁹The other events of Jeroboam's reign, his wars and how he ruled, are written in the book of the annals of the kings of Israel. ²⁰He reigned for twenty-two years and then rested with his fathers. And Nadab his son succeeded him as king.

Rehoboam King of Judah

²¹Rehoboam son of Solomon was king in Judah. He was forty-one years old when he became king, and he reigned seventeen years in Jerusalem, the city the Lᴏʀᴅ had chosen out of all the tribes of Israel in which to put his Name. His mother's name was Naamah; she was an Ammonite.

²²Judahᵘ did evil in the eyes of the Lᴏʀᴅ. By the sins they committed they stirred up his jealous angerᵛ more than their fathers had done. ²³They also set up for themselves high places, sacred stones and Asherah poles on every high hill and under every spreading tree.ʷ ²⁴There were even male shrine prostitutesˣ in the land; the people engaged in all the detestable practices of the nations the Lᴏʀᴅ had driven out before the Israelites.

²⁵In the fifth year of King Rehoboam, Shishak king of Egypt attackedʸ Jerusalem. ²⁶He carried off the treasures of the temple of the Lᴏʀᴅ and the treasures of the royal palace. He took everything, including all the gold shieldsᶻ Solomon had made. ²⁷So King Rehoboam made bronze shields to replace them and assigned these to the commanders of the guard on duty at the entrance to the royal palace. ²⁸Whenever the king went to the Lᴏʀᴅ's temple, the guards bore the shields, and afterward they returned them to the guardroom.

²⁹As for the other events of Rehoboam's reign, and all he did, are they not written in the book of the annals of the kings of Judah? ³⁰There was continual warfareᵃ between Rehoboam and Jeroboam. ³¹And Rehoboam rested with his fathers and was buried with them in the City of David. His mother's name was Naamah; she was an Ammonite. And Abijahᵈ his son succeeded him as king.

ᵃ14 The meaning of the Hebrew for this sentence is uncertain.   ᵇ15 That is, the Euphrates   ᶜ15 That is, symbols of the goddess Asherah; here and elsewhere in 1 Kings   ᵈ31 Some Hebrew manuscripts and Septuagint (see also 2 Chron. 12:16); most Hebrew manuscripts *Abijam*

14:10
ⁿ Dt 32:36; 2Ki 9:8-9
ᵒ 1Ki 15:29

14:11
ᵖ 1Ki 16:4; 21:24

14:15
ᑫ Jos 23:15-16
ʳ Ex 34:13; Dt 12:3

14:16
ˢ 1Ki 12:30

14:17
ᵗ 1Ki 16:6-9

14:22
ᵘ 2Ch 12:1
ᵛ Dt 32:21

14:23
ʷ Dt 12:2; Isa 57:5

14:24
ˣ Dt 23:17; 2Ki 23:7

14:25
ʸ 2Ch 12:2

14:26
ᶻ 1Ki 10:17

14:30
ᵃ 1Ki 12:21

14:10, 11 These disasters were practical applications to Israel of the specific teachings of Deuteronomy (see Deuteronomy 28:15–19, 36–68; 30:15–20). Ahijah was prophesying the downfall of Israel for its flagrant violation of God's commands.

14:14 Who was this king who would "cut off the family of Jeroboam"? His name was Baasha, and he would kill all of Jeroboam's descendants (15:27–30).

14:15 "Asherah poles" refers to idol worship. Wooden images were used in the worship of Asherah, a Canaanite mother-goddess.

14:19 Three non-biblical books are mentioned in 1 and 2 Kings—the book of the annals of the kings of Israel (14:19), the book of the annals of the kings of Judah (14:29), and the book of the annals of Solomon (11:41). These historical records of Israel and Judah were the main sources of material God directed the author to use to write 1 and 2 Kings. No copies of these books have been found.

14:23 "Sacred stones" were pillars of stone placed next to pagan altars. These pillars were supposed to represent deity.

14:25 When Rehoboam came to power, he inherited a mighty kingdom. Everything he could ever want was given to him. But apparently he did not recognize why he had so much or how it had been obtained. To teach Rehoboam a lesson, God allowed Shishak of Egypt to invade Judah and Israel. Egypt was no longer the world power it had once been, and Shishak, possibly resenting Solomon's enormous success, was determined to change that. Shishak's army was not strong enough to destroy Judah and Israel, but he weakened them so much that they were never the same again.

14:25, 26 Just five years after Solomon died, the temple and palace were ransacked by foreign invaders. How quickly the glory, power, and money disappeared! When the people became

Abijah King of Judah

15 In the eighteenth year of the reign of Jeroboam son of Nebat, Abijah[a] became king of Judah, [2] and he reigned in Jerusalem three years. His mother's name was Maacah[b] daughter of Abishalom.[b]

[3] He committed all the sins his father had done before him; his heart was not fully devoted[c] to the Lord his God, as the heart of David his forefather had been. [4] Nevertheless, for David's sake the Lord his God gave him a lamp[d] in Jerusalem by raising up a son to succeed him and by making Jerusalem strong. [5] For David had done what was right in the eyes of the Lord and had not failed to keep any of the Lord's commands all the days of his life—except in the case of Uriah[e] the Hittite.

[6] There was war[f] between Rehoboam[c] and Jeroboam throughout ⌊Abijah's⌋ lifetime. [7] As for the other events of Abijah's reign, and all he did, are they not written in the book of the annals of the kings of Judah? There was war between Abijah and Jeroboam. [8] And Abijah rested with his fathers and was buried in the City of David. And Asa his son succeeded him as king.

Asa King of Judah

[9] In the twentieth year of Jeroboam king of Israel, Asa became king of Judah, [10] and he reigned in Jerusalem forty-one years. His grandmother's name was Maacah daughter of Abishalom.

**Side references:**
15:2 b2Ch 11:20
15:3 c1Ki 11:4
15:4 d2Ch 21:7
15:5 e2Sa 11:2-27; 12:9
15:6 f1Ki 14:30

a1 Some Hebrew manuscripts and Septuagint (see also 2 Chron. 12:16); most Hebrew manuscripts *Abijam*; also in verses 7 and 8   b2 A variant of *Absalom*; also in verse 10   c6 Most Hebrew manuscripts; some Hebrew manuscripts and Syriac *Abijam* (that is, Abijah)

KINGS TO DATE AND THEIR ENEMIES

ISRAEL

JUDAH

930 **JEROBOAM I** Defeated by Abijah (Judah) 1 Kgs 11:26—14:20 2 Chr 10:12—13:20

909 **NADAB** 1 Kgs 14:20; 15:25-28

908 **BAASHA** Harassed by Asa (Judah) and Ben-Hadad (Aram) 1 Kgs 15:27—16:7 2 Chr 16:1-6

886 **ELAH** Philistines 1 Kgs 16:6-14

885 **ZIMRI** 1 Kgs 16:9-20

885 **TIBNI** 1 Kgs 16:21, 22

885 **OMRI** Philistines 1 Kgs 16:16-28

874 **AHAB** Twice defeated Ben-Hadad II (Aram) and was later killed in battle against Aram 1 Kgs 16:28—22:40 2 Chr 18:1-34

853

930 **REHOBOAM** Defeated by Shishak (Egypt) 1 Kgs 11:43—14:31 2 Chr 9:31—12:16

913 **ABIJAH** Defeated Jeroboam (Israel) 1 Kgs 14:31—15:8 2 Chr 13:1—14:1

910 **ASA** Defeated Zerah (the Cushite) and harassed Baasha 1 Kgs 15:8—24 2 Chr 14:1—16:14

869

All dates are B.C.
For all the kings of Israel and Judah, see the chart at the end of 1 Kings.

spiritually corrupt and immoral (14:24), it was just a short time until they lost everything. Wealth, idol worship, and immorality had become more important to them than God. When God is gone from our lives, everything else becomes useless, no matter how valuable it seems.

15:5 See 2 Samuel 11 for the story of David and Uriah the Hittite.

15:9 See Asa's Profile in 2 Chronicles 14, p. 687 for more information on this king.

[11]Asa did what was right in the eyes of the LORD, as his father David had done. [12]He expelled the male shrine prostitutes[g] from the land and got rid of all the idols his fathers had made. [13]He even deposed his grandmother Maacah from her position as queen mother, because she had made a repulsive Asherah pole. Asa cut the pole down[h] and burned it in the Kidron Valley. [14]Although he did not remove the high places, Asa's heart was fully committed[i] to the LORD all his life. [15]He brought into the temple of the LORD the silver and gold and the articles that he and his father had dedicated.

[16]There was war between Asa and Baasha king of Israel throughout their reigns. [17]Baasha king of Israel went up against Judah and fortified Ramah[j] to prevent anyone from leaving or entering the territory of Asa king of Judah.

[18]Asa then took all the silver and gold that was left in the treasuries of the LORD's temple and of his own palace. He entrusted it to his officials and sent them to Ben-Hadad[k] son of Tabrimmon, the son of Hezion, the king of Aram, who was ruling in Damascus. [19]"Let there be a treaty between me and you," he said, "as there was between my father and your father. See, I am sending you a gift of silver and gold. Now break your treaty with Baasha king of Israel so he will withdraw from me."

[20]Ben-Hadad agreed with King Asa and sent the commanders of his forces against the towns of Israel. He conquered[l] Ijon, Dan, Abel Beth Maacah and all Kinnereth in addition to Naphtali. [21]When Baasha heard this, he stopped building Ramah and withdrew to Tirzah. [22]Then King Asa issued an order to all Judah—no one was exempt—and they carried away from Ramah the stones and timber Baasha had been using there. With them King Asa built up Geba[m] in Benjamin, and also Mizpah.

[23]As for all the other events of Asa's reign, all his achievements, all he did and the cities he built, are they not written in the book of the annals of the kings of Judah? In his old age, however, his feet became diseased. [24]Then Asa rested with his fathers and was buried with them in the city of his father David. And Jehoshaphat[n] his son succeeded him as king.

Nadab King of Israel

[25]Nadab son of Jeroboam became king of Israel in the second year of Asa king of Judah, and he reigned over Israel two years. [26]He did evil in the eyes of the LORD, walking in the ways of his father[o] and in his sin, which he had caused Israel to commit.

[27]Baasha son of Ahijah of the house of Issachar plotted against him, and he struck him down[p] at Gibbethon,[q] a Philistine town, while Nadab and all Israel were besieging it. [28]Baasha killed Nadab in the third year of Asa king of Judah and succeeded him as king.

[29]As soon as he began to reign, he killed Jeroboam's whole family. He did not leave Jeroboam anyone that breathed, but destroyed them all, according to the word of the LORD given through his servant Ahijah the Shilonite— [30]because of the sins Jeroboam had committed and had caused Israel to commit, and because he provoked the LORD, the God of Israel, to anger.

[31]As for the other events of Nadab's reign, and all he did, are they not written in the book of the annals of the kings of Israel? [32]There was war[r] between Asa and Baasha king of Israel throughout their reigns.

Baasha King of Israel

[33]In the third year of Asa king of Judah, Baasha son of Ahijah became king of all Israel in Tirzah, and he reigned twenty-four years. [34]He did evil in the eyes of the LORD, walking in the ways of Jeroboam and in his sin, which he had caused Israel to commit.

16 Then the word of the LORD came to Jehu[s] son of Hanani against Baasha: [2]"I lifted you up from the dust and made you leader[t] of my people Israel, but you walked in the ways of Jeroboam and caused my people Israel to sin and to provoke me to anger by their

15:12 [g]1Ki 14:24
15:13 [h]Ex 32:20
15:14 [i]1Ki 22:43
15:17 [j]Jos 18:25; 1Ki 12:27
15:18 [k]1Ki 11:23-24
15:20 [l]Jdg 18:29; 2Sa 20:14
15:22 [m]Jos 21:17
15:24 [n]Mt 1:8
15:26 [o]1Ki 12:30
15:27 [p]1Ki 14:14 [q]Jos 19:44
15:32 [r]ver 16
16:1 [s]ver 7; 2Ch 19:2; 20:34
16:2 [t]1Ki 14:7-9

15:15 These gifts for the temple were articles devoted to God as sacred offerings that Abijah had taken in his war with Jeroboam (2 Chronicles 13:16, 17) and Asa had taken when he defeated the Cushites (2 Chronicles 14:12, 13).

15:16 Baasha seized the throne from Nadab (15:27, 28), who had replaced his father, Jeroboam, as king.

15:29 See 1 Kings 14:12–14 for Ahijah's prediction of this event.

15:30 All the descendants of Jeroboam were killed because Jeroboam had led Israel into sin. Sin is always judged harshly,

but the worst sinners are those who lead others into doing wrong. Jesus said it would be better if such people had millstones tied around their necks and were thrown into the sea (Mark 9:42). If you have taken the responsibility for leading others, remember the consequences of leading them astray. Teaching the truth is a responsibility that goes with the privilege of leadership.

16:1–7 God had destroyed Jeroboam's descendants for their flagrant sins, and yet Baasha repeated the same mistakes. He did not learn from the example of those who had gone before him; he did not stop to think that his sin would be punished. Make

16:3
u ver 11; 1Ki 14:10

16:4
v 1Ki 14:11

sins. ³So I am about to consume Baasha and his house,*u* and I will make your house like that of Jeroboam son of Nebat. ⁴Dogs *v* will eat those belonging to Baasha who die in the city, and the birds of the air will feed on those who die in the country."

⁵As for the other events of Baasha's reign, what he did and his achievements, are they not written in the book of the annals of the kings of Israel? ⁶Baasha rested with his fathers and was buried in Tirzah. And Elah his son succeeded him as king.

16:7
w ver 1

⁷Moreover, the word of the LORD came through the prophet Jehu *w* son of Hanani to Baasha and his house, because of all the evil he had done in the eyes of the LORD, provoking him to anger by the things he did, and becoming like the house of Jeroboam—and also because he destroyed it.

Elah King of Israel

⁸In the twenty-sixth year of Asa king of Judah, Elah son of Baasha became king of Israel, and he reigned in Tirzah two years.

16:9
x 2Ki 9:30-33

⁹Zimri, one of his officials, who had command of half his chariots, plotted against him. Elah was in Tirzah at the time, getting drunk *x* in the home of Arza, the man in charge of the palace at Tirzah. ¹⁰Zimri came in, struck him down and killed him in the twenty-seventh year of Asa king of Judah. Then he succeeded him as king.

¹¹As soon as he began to reign and was seated on the throne, he killed off Baasha's whole family. He did not spare a single male, whether relative or friend. ¹²So Zimri destroyed the whole family of Baasha, in accordance with the word of the LORD spoken against Baasha

16:13
y Dt 32:21

through the prophet Jehu— ¹³because of all the sins Baasha and his son Elah had committed and had caused Israel to commit, so that they provoked the LORD, the God of Israel, to anger by their worthless idols.*y*

¹⁴As for the other events of Elah's reign, and all he did, are they not written in the book of the annals of the kings of Israel?

Zimri King of Israel

16:15
z 1Ki 15:27

¹⁵In the twenty-seventh year of Asa king of Judah, Zimri reigned in Tirzah seven days. The army was encamped near Gibbethon,*z* a Philistine town. ¹⁶When the Israelites in the camp heard that Zimri had plotted against the king and murdered him, they proclaimed Omri, the commander of the army, king over Israel that very day there in the camp. ¹⁷Then Omri and all the Israelites with him withdrew from Gibbethon and laid siege to Tirzah. ¹⁸When Zimri saw that the city was taken, he went into the citadel of the royal palace and set the palace on fire around him. So he died, ¹⁹because of the sins he had committed, doing evil in the eyes of the LORD and walking in the ways of Jeroboam and in the sin he had committed and had caused Israel to commit.

²⁰As for the other events of Zimri's reign, and the rebellion he carried out, are they not written in the book of the annals of the kings of Israel?

Omri King of Israel

²¹Then the people of Israel were split into two factions; half supported Tibni son of Ginath for king, and the other half supported Omri. ²²But Omri's followers proved stronger than those of Tibni son of Ginath. So Tibni died and Omri became king.

16:24
a 1Ki 13:32

²³In the thirty-first year of Asa king of Judah, Omri became king of Israel, and he reigned twelve years, six of them in Tirzah. ²⁴He bought the hill of Samaria from Shemer for two talents*a* of silver and built a city on the hill, calling it Samaria,*a* after Shemer, the name of the former owner of the hill.

*a*24 That is, about 150 pounds (about 70 kilograms)

---

sure you learn from your past, the experiences of others, and the lives of those whose stories are told in the Bible. Don't repeat mistakes.

16:21, 22 Omri began his reign as political dissension brewed in Israel. After Zimri killed himself, the Israelite army chose Omri, their commander, as the next ruler. Tibni, Omri's chief rival to the throne, died, and Omri then began his evil reign. During his 12-year rule over Israel, he was a shrewd and capable leader. He organized the building of his new capital city, Samaria, while strengthening the nation politically and militarily. But he did not care about the nation's spiritual condition (Micah 6:16), and he

purposely led Israel farther from God in order to put more power in his own hands.

16:24 Omri's new capital, Samaria, offered some political advantages. The city was his personal property, so he had total control over it. Samaria also commanded a hilltop position, which made it easy to defend. Omri died before completing the city. So his son, Ahab, completed it, building not only the beautiful ivory palace (1 Kings 22:39; Amos 3:13–15), but also a temple to the god Baal. Samaria served as the capital city for the rest of Israel's dynasties until it fell to the Assyrians in 722 B.C. (2 Kings 17:5).

25 But Omri did evil[b] in the eyes of the LORD and sinned more than all those before him.
26 He walked in all the ways of Jeroboam son of Nebat and in his sin, which he had caused[c]
Israel to commit, so that they provoked the LORD, the God of Israel, to anger by their worthless idols.

27 As for the other events of Omri's reign, what he did and the things he achieved, are they
not written in the book of the annals of the kings of Israel? 28 Omri rested with his fathers
and was buried in Samaria. And Ahab his son succeeded him as king.

Ahab Becomes King of Israel

29 In the thirty-eighth year of Asa king of Judah, Ahab son of Omri became king of Israel,
and he reigned in Samaria over Israel twenty-two years. 30 Ahab son of Omri did more[d] evil
in the eyes of the LORD than any of those before him. 31 He not only considered it trivial to
commit the sins of Jeroboam son of Nebat, but he also married[e] Jezebel daughter of Ethbaal
king of the Sidonians, and began to serve Baal[f] and worship him. 32 He set up an altar for
Baal in the temple[g] of Baal that he built in Samaria. 33 Ahab also made an Asherah pole[h] and
did more[i] to provoke the LORD, the God of Israel, to anger than did all the kings of Israel before him.

34 In Ahab's time, Hiel of Bethel rebuilt Jericho. He laid its foundations at the cost of his
firstborn son Abiram, and he set up its gates at the cost of his youngest son Segub, in accordance with the word of the LORD spoken by Joshua son of Nun.[j]

3. Elijah's ministry
Elijah Fed by Ravens

17 Now Elijah[k] the Tishbite, from Tishbe[a] in Gilead, said to Ahab, "As the LORD, the God
of Israel, lives, whom I serve, there will be neither dew nor rain[l] in the next few years
except at my word."

2 Then the word of the LORD came to Elijah: 3 "Leave here, turn eastward and hide in the
Kerith Ravine, east of the Jordan. 4 You will drink from the brook, and I have ordered the ravens to feed you there."

5 So he did what the LORD had told him. He went to the Kerith Ravine, east of the Jordan,
and stayed there. 6 The ravens brought him bread and meat in the morning and bread and
meat in the evening, and he drank from the brook.

The Widow at Zarephath

7 Some time later the brook dried up because there had been no rain in the land. 8 Then
the word of the LORD came to him: 9 "Go at once to Zarephath[m] of Sidon and stay there. I

a 1 Or Tishbite, of the settlers

16:25
b Mic 6:16
16:26
c ver 19

16:30
d 1Ki 14:9
16:31
e Dt 7:3
f 2Ki 10:18; 17:16
16:32
g 2Ki 10:21, 27
16:33
h 2Ki 13:6
i 1Ki 21:25
16:34
j Jos 6:26

17:1
k Jas 5:17
l 2Ki 3:14; Lk 4:25

17:9
m Ob 1:20

16:31 Ahab's evil wife, Jezebel, came from the Phoenician city of
Tyre where her father had been a high priest and eventually king.

**ELIJAH HIDES
FROM AHAB**
Elijah prophesied
a drought and
then hid from King
Ahab by the Kerith
Ravine, where he
was fed by ravens.
When the brook
in the ravine dried
up, God sent him
to Zarephath in
Phoenicia where a
widow and her son
fed him and gave
him lodging.

Jezebel worshiped the god Baal. In order to please her, Ahab built
a temple and an altar for Baal (16:32), thus promoting idolatry
and leading the entire nation into sin. (For more about Baal, see
the note on 18:18.)

17:1 Elijah was the first in a long line of important prophets God
sent to Israel and Judah. Israel, the northern kingdom, had no
faithful kings throughout its history. Each king was wicked, actually leading the people in worshiping pagan gods. Few priests
were left from the tribe of Levi (most had gone to Judah), and the
priests appointed by Israel's kings were corrupt and ineffective.
With no king or priests to bring God's word to the people, God
called prophets to try to rescue Israel from its moral and spiritual
decline. For the next 300 years these men and women would play
vital roles in both nations, encouraging the people and leaders to
turn back to God.

17:1 Those who worshiped Baal believed he was the god who
brought the rains and bountiful harvests. So when Elijah walked
into the presence of this Baal-worshiping king and told him there
would be no rain for several years, Ahab was shocked. Ahab had
built a strong military defense, but it would be no help against
drought. He had many priests of Baal, but they could not bring
rain. Elijah bravely confronted the man who led his people into
evil, and he told of a power far greater than any pagan god—the
Lord God of Israel. When rebellion and heresy were at an all-time
high in Israel, God responded not only with words but with action.

17:9
n Lk 4:26

have commanded a widow n in that place to supply you with food." 10 So he went to Zarephath. When he came to the town gate, a widow was there gathering sticks. He called to her and asked, "Would you bring me a little water in a jar so I may have a drink?" 11 As she was going to get it, he called, "And bring me, please, a piece of bread."

17:12
o 2Ki 4:2

12 "As surely as the LORD your God lives," she replied, "I don't have any bread—only a handful of flour in a jar and a little oil o in a jug. I am gathering a few sticks to take home and make a meal for myself and my son, that we may eat it—and die."

ELIJAH

Elijah's single-minded commitment to God shocks and challenges us. He was sent to confront, not comfort, and he spoke God's words to a king who often rejected his message just because he brought it. Elijah chose to carry out his ministry for God alone and paid for that decision by experiencing isolation from others who were also faithful to God.

It is interesting to think about the amazing miracles God accomplished through Elijah, but we would do well to focus on the relationship they shared. All that happened in Elijah's life began with the same miracle that is available to us—he responded to the miracle of being able to know God.

For example, after God worked an overwhelming miracle through Elijah in defeating the prophets of Baal, Queen Jezebel retaliated by threatening Elijah's life. And Elijah ran. He felt afraid, depressed, and abandoned. Despite God's provision of food and shelter in the desert, Elijah wanted to die. So God presented Elijah with an "audio-visual display" and a message he needed to hear. Elijah witnessed a windstorm, an earthquake, and fire. But the Lord was not in any of those powerful things. Instead, God displayed his presence in a gentle whisper.

Elijah, like us, struggled with his feelings even after this comforting message from God. So God confronted Elijah's emotions and commanded action. He told Elijah what to do next and informed him that part of his loneliness was based on ignorance: 7,000 others in Israel were still faithful to God.

Even today, God often speaks through the gentle and obvious rather than the spectacular and unusual. God has work for us to do even when we feel fear and failure. And God always has more resources and people than we know about. Although we might wish to do amazing miracles for God, we should instead focus on developing a relationship with him. The real miracle of Elijah's life was his very personal relationship with God. And that miracle is available to us.

Strengths and accomplishments:	• Was the most famous and dramatic of Israel's prophets • Predicted the beginning and end of a three-year drought • Was used by God to restore a dead child to his mother • Represented God in a showdown with priests of Baal and Asherah • Appeared with Moses and Jesus in the New Testament transfiguration scene
Weaknesses and mistakes:	• Chose to work alone and paid for it with isolation and loneliness • Fled in fear from Jezebel when she threatened his life
Lessons from his life:	• We are never closer to defeat than in our moments of greatest victory • We are never as alone as we may feel; God is always there • God speaks more frequently in persistent whispers than in shouts
Vital statistics:	• Where: Gilead • Occupation: Prophet • Contemporaries: Ahab, Jezebel, Ahaziah, Obadiah, Jehu, Hazael
Key verses:	"At the time of sacrifice, the prophet Elijah stepped forward and prayed: 'O LORD, God of Abraham, Isaac and Israel, let it be known today that you are God in Israel and that I am your servant and have done all these things at your command. Answer me, O LORD, answer me, so these people will know that you, O LORD, are God, and that you are turning their hearts back again.' Then the fire of the LORD fell and burned up the sacrifice, the wood, the stones and the soil, and also licked up the water in the trench" (1 Kings 18:36–38).

Elijah's story is told in 1 Kings 17:1—2 Kings 2:11. He is also mentioned in 2 Chronicles 21:12–15; Malachi 4:5, 6; Matthew 11:14; 16:14; 17:3–13; 27:47–49; Luke 1:17; 4:25, 26; John 1:19–25; Romans 11:2–4; James 5:17, 18.

17:10ff In a nation that was required by law to care for its prophets, it is ironic that God turned to ravens (unclean birds) and a widow (a foreigner from Jezebel's home territory) to care for Elijah. God has help where we least expect it. He provides for us in ways that go beyond our narrow definitions or expectations. No matter how bitter our trials or how seemingly hopeless our situation, we should look for God's caring touch. We may find his providence in some strange places!

¹³Elijah said to her, "Don't be afraid. Go home and do as you have said. But first make a small cake of bread for me from what you have and bring it to me, and then make something for yourself and your son. ¹⁴For this is what the LORD, the God of Israel, says: 'The jar of flour will not be used up and the jug of oil will not run dry until the day the LORD gives rain on the land.'"

¹⁵She went away and did as Elijah had told her. So there was food every day for Elijah and for the woman and her family. ¹⁶For the jar of flour was not used up and the jug of oil did not run dry, in keeping with the word of the LORD spoken by Elijah.

¹⁷Some time later the son of the woman who owned the house became ill. He grew worse and worse, and finally stopped breathing. ¹⁸She said to Elijah, "What do you have against me, man of God? Did you come to remind me of my sin and kill my son?"

¹⁹"Give me your son," Elijah replied. He took him from her arms, carried him to the upper room where he was staying, and laid him on his bed. ²⁰Then he cried out to the LORD, "O LORD my God, have you brought tragedy also upon this widow I am staying with, by causing her son to die?" ²¹Then he stretched ᵖ himself out on the boy three times and cried to the LORD, "O LORD my God, let this boy's life return to him!"

17:21
ᵖ 2Ki 4:34; Ac 20:10

²²The LORD heard Elijah's cry, and the boy's life returned to him, and he lived. ²³Elijah picked up the child and carried him down from the room into the house. He gave him to his mother and said, "Look, your son is alive!"

²⁴Then the woman said to Elijah, "Now I know �q that you are a man of God and that the word of the LORD from your mouth is the truth."

17:24
�q Jn 3:2; 16:30

Elijah and Obadiah

18 After a long time, in the third ʳ year, the word of the LORD came to Elijah: "Go and present yourself to Ahab, and I will send rain ˢ on the land." ²So Elijah went to present himself to Ahab.

18:1
ʳ Lk 4:25; Jas 5:17
ˢ Dt 28:12

Now the famine was severe in Samaria, ³and Ahab had summoned Obadiah, who was in charge of his palace. (Obadiah was a devout believer in the LORD. ⁴While Jezebel was killing off the LORD's prophets, Obadiah had taken a hundred prophets and hidden them in two caves, fifty in each, and had supplied them with food and water.) ⁵Ahab had said to Obadiah, "Go through the land to all the springs and valleys. Maybe we can find some grass to keep the horses and mules alive so we will not have to kill any of our animals." ⁶So they divided the land they were to cover, Ahab going in one direction and Obadiah in another.

⁷As Obadiah was walking along, Elijah met him. Obadiah recognized ᵗ him, bowed down to the ground, and said, "Is it really you, my lord Elijah?"

18:7
ᵗ 2Ki 1:8

⁸"Yes," he replied. "Go tell your master, 'Elijah is here.'"

⁹"What have I done wrong," asked Obadiah, "that you are handing your servant over to Ahab to be put to death? ¹⁰As surely as the LORD your God lives, there is not a nation or kingdom where my master has not sent someone to look ᵘ for you. And whenever a nation or kingdom claimed you were not there, he made them swear they could not find you. ¹¹But

18:10
ᵘ 1Ki 17:3

17:13–16 When the widow of Zarephath met Elijah, she thought she was preparing her last meal. But a simple act of faith produced a miracle. She trusted Elijah and gave all she had to eat to him. Faith is the step between promise and assurance. Miracles seem so out of reach for our feeble faith. But every miracle, large or small, begins with an act of obedience. We may not see the solution until we take the first step of faith.

17:17 Even when God has done a miracle in our lives, our troubles may not be over. The famine was a terrible experience, but the worst was yet to come. God's provision is never given in order to let us rest upon it. We need to depend on him as each new trial faces us.

18:3, 4 Although Elijah was alone in his confrontation with Ahab and Jezebel, he was not the only one in Israel who believed in God. Obadiah had been faithful in hiding 100 prophets still true to the Lord.

Mediterranean Sea
N
Mount Carmel — Kishon Valley
Sea of Galilee
Jezreel
Samaria
Jordan River
ISRAEL
Jerusalem
Dead Sea
JUDAH
0   20 Mi.
0   20 Km.

THE SHOWDOWN AT CARMEL
In a showdown with the false prophets of Baal at Mount Carmel, Elijah set out to prove to evil Ahab that only the Lord is God. Elijah then killed the false prophets in the Kishon Valley and fled back to Jezreel.

18:12
v 2Ki 2:16;
Eze 3:14; Ac 8:39

now you tell me to go to my master and say, 'Elijah is here.' ¹²I don't know where the Spirit ⱽ of the LORD may carry you when I leave you. If I go and tell Ahab and he doesn't find you, he will kill me. Yet I your servant have worshiped the LORD since my youth. ¹³Haven't you heard, my lord, what I did while Jezebel was killing the prophets of the LORD? I hid a hundred of the LORD's prophets in two caves, fifty in each, and supplied them with food and water. ¹⁴And now you tell me to go to my master and say, 'Elijah is here.' He will kill me!"

¹⁵Elijah said, "As the LORD Almighty lives, whom I serve, I will surely present myself to Ahab today."

Elijah on Mount Carmel

18:17
w Jos 7:25;
1Ki 21:20

¹⁶So Obadiah went to meet Ahab and told him, and Ahab went to meet Elijah. ¹⁷When he saw Elijah, he said to him, "Is that you, you troubler ʷ of Israel?"

18:18
x 1Ki 16:31, 33

¹⁸"I have not made trouble for Israel," Elijah replied. "But you ˣ and your father's family have. You have abandoned the LORD's commands and have followed the Baals. ¹⁹Now

18:19
y Jos 19:26

summon the people from all over Israel to meet me on Mount Carmel. ʸ And bring the four hundred and fifty prophets of Baal and the four hundred prophets of Asherah, who eat at Jezebel's table."

²⁰So Ahab sent word throughout all Israel and assembled the prophets on Mount Carmel.

18:21
z Jos 24:15;
2Ki 17:41; Mt 6:24

²¹Elijah went before the people and said, "How long will you waver ᶻ between two opinions? If the LORD is God, follow him; but if Baal is God, follow him."

But the people said nothing.

18:22
a 1Ki 19:10

²²Then Elijah said to them, "I am the only one of the LORD's prophets left, ᵃ but Baal has four hundred and fifty prophets. ²³Get two bulls for us. Let them choose one for themselves, and let them cut it into pieces and put it on the wood but not set fire to it. I will

18:24
b ver 38

prepare the other bull and put it on the wood but not set fire to it. ²⁴Then you call on the name of your god, and I will call on the name of the LORD. The god who answers by fire ᵇ— he is God."

Then all the people said, "What you say is good."

18:26
c Ps 115:4-5;
Jer 10:5

²⁵Elijah said to the prophets of Baal, "Choose one of the bulls and prepare it first, since there are so many of you. Call on the name of your god, but do not light the fire." ²⁶So they took the bull given them and prepared it.

Then they called on the name of Baal from morning till noon. "O Baal, answer us!" they shouted. But there was no response; ᶜ no one answered. And they danced around the altar they had made.

²⁷At noon Elijah began to taunt them. "Shout louder!" he said. "Surely he is a god! Perhaps he is deep in thought, or busy, or traveling. Maybe he is sleeping and must be awak-

---

PROPHETS— FALSE AND TRUE

False Prophets	True Prophets
Worked for political purposes to benefit themselves	Worked for spiritual purposes to serve God and the people
Held positions of great wealth	Owned little or nothing
Gave false messages	Spoke only true messages
Spoke only what the people wanted to hear	Spoke only what God told them to say— no matter how unpopular

The false prophets were an obstacle to bringing God's word to the people. They would bring messages that contradicted the words of the true prophets. They gave "messages" that appealed to the people's sinful nature and comforted their fears. False prophets told people what they wanted to hear. True prophets told God's truth.

18:18 Instead of worshiping the true God, Ahab and his wife Jezebel worshiped Baal, the most popular Canaanite god. Baal idols were often made in the shape of a bull, representing strength and fertility and reflecting lust for power and sexual pleasure.

18:19 Ahab brought 850 pagan prophets to Mount Carmel to match wits and power with Elijah. Evil kings hated God's prophets because they spoke against sin and idolatry and undermined their control over the people. With the wicked kings' backing, many pagan prophets sprang up to counter the words of God's proph-

ets. But Elijah showed the people that speaking a prophecy wasn't enough. One needed the power of a living God to fulfill it.

18:21 Elijah challenged the people to take a stand—to follow whoever was the true God. Why did so many people waver between the two choices? Perhaps some were not sure. Many, however, knew that the Lord was God, but they enjoyed the sinful pleasures and other benefits that came with following Ahab in his idolatrous worship. It is important to take a stand for the Lord. If we just drift along with whatever is pleasant and easy, we will someday discover that we have been worshiping a false god—ourselves.

ened." 28 So they shouted louder and slashed *d* themselves with swords and spears, as was their custom, until their blood flowed. 29 Midday passed, and they continued their frantic prophesying until the time for the evening sacrifice. But there was no response, no one answered, no one paid attention.

30 Then Elijah said to all the people, "Come here to me." They came to him, and he repaired the altar *e* of the LORD, which was in ruins. 31 Elijah took twelve stones, one for each of the tribes descended from Jacob, to whom the word of the LORD had come, saying, "Your name shall be Israel." *f* 32 With the stones he built an altar in the name *g* of the LORD, and he dug a trench around it large enough to hold two seahs *a* of seed. 33 He arranged the wood, cut the bull into pieces and laid it on the wood. Then he said to them, "Fill four large jars with water and pour it on the offering and on the wood."

34 "Do it again," he said, and they did it again.

"Do it a third time," he ordered, and they did it the third time. 35 The water ran down around the altar and even filled the trench.

36 At the time of sacrifice, the prophet Elijah stepped forward and prayed: "O LORD, God of Abraham, Isaac and Israel, let it be known today that you are God in Israel and that I am your servant and have done all these things at your command. *h* 37 Answer me, O LORD, answer me, so these people will know that you, O LORD, are God, and that you are turning their hearts back again."

38 Then the fire *i* of the LORD fell and burned up the sacrifice, the wood, the stones and the soil, and also licked up the water in the trench.

39 When all the people saw this, they fell prostrate and cried, "The LORD—he is God! The LORD—he is God!"

40 Then Elijah commanded them, "Seize the prophets of Baal. Don't let anyone get away!" They seized them, and Elijah had them brought down to the Kishon Valley and slaughtered *j* there.

41 And Elijah said to Ahab, "Go, eat and drink, for there is the sound of a heavy rain." 42 So Ahab went off to eat and drink, but Elijah climbed to the top of Carmel, bent down to the ground and put his face between his knees. *k*

43 "Go and look toward the sea," he told his servant. And he went up and looked.

"There is nothing there," he said.

Seven times Elijah said, "Go back."

44 The seventh time the servant reported, "A cloud as small as a man's hand is rising from the sea."

So Elijah said, "Go and tell Ahab, 'Hitch up your chariot and go down before the rain stops you.'"

a 32 That is, probably about 13 quarts (about 15 liters)

18:28
d Lev 19:28

18:30
e 1Ki 19:10
18:31
f 2Ki 17:34
18:32
g Col 3:17

18:36
h Nu 16:28

18:38
i Lev 9:24;
1Ch 21:26; 2Ch 7:1

18:40
j Dt 13:5; 18:20;
2Ki 10:24-25

18:42
k Jas 5:18

ELIJAH FLEES FROM JEZEBEL
After killing Baal's prophets, Elijah ran from the furious Queen Jezebel. He fled to Beersheba, then into the desert, and finally to Mount Horeb (Sinai). There, like Moses centuries earlier, he talked with God.

18:29 Although the prophets of Baal raved all afternoon, no one answered them. Their god was silent because it was not real. The gods we may be tempted to follow are not idols of wood or stone, but they are just as false and dangerous because they cause us to depend on something other than God. Power, status, appearance, or material possessions can become our gods if we devote our lives to them. But when we reach times of crisis and desperately call out to these gods, there will only be silence. They can offer no true answers, no guidance, and no wisdom.

18:31 Using 12 stones to build the altar took courage. This would have angered some of the people because it was a silent reminder of the split between the tribes. While the 10 tribes of the north called themselves Israel, this name originally was given to all 12 of the tribes together.

18:36-38 God flashed fire from heaven for Elijah. He will also help us accomplish what he commands us to do. The proof may not be as dramatic in our lives as in Elijah's, but God will make resources available to us in creative ways to accomplish his purposes. He will give us the wisdom to raise a family, the courage to take a stand for truth, or the means to provide help for someone in need. Like Elijah, we can have faith that whatever God commands us to do, he will provide what we need to carry it through.

18:46
l 2Ki 4:29

45 Meanwhile, the sky grew black with clouds, the wind rose, a heavy rain came on and Ahab rode off to Jezreel. 46 The power of the LORD came upon Elijah and, tucking his cloak into his belt,*l* he ran ahead of Ahab all the way to Jezreel.

19:1
m 1Ki 18:40

Elijah Flees to Horeb

19:2
n 1Ki 20:10;
2Ki 6:31

19 Now Ahab told Jezebel everything Elijah had done and how he had killed *m* all the prophets with the sword. 2 So Jezebel sent a messenger to Elijah to say, "May the gods

AHAB

The kings of Israel and Judah, both good and evil, had prophets sent by God to advise, confront, and aid them. King David had a faithful friend in God's prophet, Nathan; Ahab could have had an equally faithful friend in Elijah. But while David listened to Nathan and was willing to repent of his sins, Ahab saw Elijah as his enemy. Why? Because Elijah always brought bad news to Ahab, and Ahab refused to acknowledge that it was his own constant disobedience to God and persistent idol worship, not Elijah's prophecies, that brought the evil on his nation. He blamed Elijah for bringing the prophecies of judgment, rather than taking his advice and changing his evil ways.

Ahab was trapped by his own choices, and he was unwilling to take the right action. As king, he was responsible to God and his prophet Elijah, but he was married to an evil woman who drew him into idol worship. He was a childish man who brooded for days if unable to get his own way. He took his evil wife's advice, listened only to the "prophets" who gave good news, and surrounded himself with people who encouraged him to do whatever he wanted. But the value of advice cannot be judged by the number of people for or against it. Ahab consistently chose to follow the majority opinion of those who surrounded him, and that led to his death.

It may seem nice to have someone encourage us to do whatever we want because advice that goes against our wishes is difficult to accept. However, our decisions must be based on the quality of the advice, not its attractiveness or the majority opinion of our peers. God encourages us to get advice from wise counselors, but how can we test the advice we receive? Advice that agrees with the principles in God's Word is reliable. We must always separate advice from our own desires, the majority opinion, or whatever seems best in our limited perspective, and weigh it against God's commands. He will never lead us to do what he has forbidden in his Word—even in principle. Unlike Ahab, we should trust godly counselors and have the courage to stand against those who would have us do otherwise.

Strengths and accomplishments:	• Eighth king of Israel • Capable leader and military strategist
Weaknesses and mistakes:	• Was the most evil king of Israel • Married Jezebel, a pagan woman, and allowed her to promote Baal worship • Brooded about not being able to get a piece of land, and so his wife had its owner, Naboth, killed • Was used to getting his own way, and got depressed when he didn't
Lessons from his life:	• The choice of a spouse will have a significant effect on life—physically, spiritually, and emotionally • Selfishness, left unchecked, can lead to great evil
Vital statistics:	• Where: Northern kingdom of Israel • Occupation: King • Relatives: Wife: Jezebel. Father: Omri. Sons: Ahaziah, Joram. • Contemporaries: Elijah, Naboth, Jehu, Ben-Hadad, Jehoshaphat
Key verses:	"Ahab son of Omri did more evil in the eyes of the LORD than any of those before him . . . He also married Jezebel daughter of Ethbaal king of the Sidonians, and began to serve Baal and worship him. He set up an altar for Baal in the temple of Baal that he built in Samaria. Ahab also made an Asherah pole and did more to provoke the LORD, the God of Israel, to anger than did all the kings of Israel before him" (1 Kings 16:30–33).

Ahab's story is told in 1 Kings 16:28—22:40. He is also mentioned in 2 Chronicles 18—22; Micah 6:16.

18:46 Elijah ran the six miles back to the city in order to give Ahab a last chance to turn from his sin before joining Jezebel in Jezreel. His run also ensured that the correct story of what happened would reach Jezreel.

19:2 Jezebel was enraged about the death of her prophets because they had told her everything *she* wanted to hear, prophesying her future power and glory. Their job was to deify the king and queen and help perpetuate their kingdom. Jezebel was also angry because her supporters had been eliminated and her pride and authority damaged. The money she had invested in these prophets was now lost.

Elijah, who caused the prophets' deaths, was a constant thorn in Jezebel's side because he was always predicting gloom and doom. Since she could not control his actions, Jezebel vowed to kill him. As long as God's prophet was around, she could not carry out all the evil she wanted.

deal with me, be it ever so severely,[n] if by this time tomorrow I do not make your life like that of one of them."

[3] Elijah was afraid[a] and ran for his life. When he came to Beersheba in Judah, he left his servant there, [4] while he himself went a day's journey into the desert. He came to a broom tree, sat down under it and prayed that he might die. "I have had enough, LORD," he said. "Take my life;[o] I am no better than my ancestors." [5] Then he lay down under the tree and fell asleep.

All at once an angel touched him and said, "Get up and eat." [6] He looked around, and there by his head was a cake of bread baked over hot coals, and a jar of water. He ate and drank and then lay down again.

[7] The angel of the LORD came back a second time and touched him and said, "Get up and eat, for the journey is too much for you." [8] So he got up and ate and drank. Strengthened by that food, he traveled forty[p] days and forty nights until he reached Horeb,[q] the mountain of God. [9] There he went into a cave and spent the night.

The LORD Appears to Elijah

And the word of the LORD came to him: "What are you doing here, Elijah?"

[10] He replied, "I have been very zealous for the LORD God Almighty. The Israelites have rejected your covenant, broken down your altars, and put your prophets to death with the sword. I am the only one left,[r] and now they are trying to kill me too."

[11] The LORD said, "Go out and stand on the mountain[s] in the presence of the LORD, for the LORD is about to pass by."

Then a great and powerful wind[t] tore the mountains apart and shattered the rocks before the LORD, but the LORD was not in the wind. After the wind there was an earthquake, but the LORD was not in the earthquake. [12] After the earthquake came a fire, but the LORD was not in the fire. And after the fire came a gentle whisper. [13] When Elijah heard it, he pulled his cloak over his face[u] and went out and stood at the mouth of the cave.

Then a voice said to him, "What are you doing here, Elijah?"

[14] He replied, "I have been very zealous for the LORD God Almighty. The Israelites have rejected your covenant, broken down your altars, and put your prophets to death with the sword. I am the only one left, and now they are trying to kill me too."

[15] The LORD said to him, "Go back the way you came, and go to the Desert of Damascus. When you get there, anoint Hazael[v] king over Aram. [16] Also, anoint Jehu son of Nimshi king over Israel, and anoint Elisha son of Shaphat from Abel Meholah to succeed you as prophet. [17] Jehu will put to death any who escape the sword of Hazael,[w] and Elisha will put to death any who escape the sword of Jehu. [18] Yet I reserve[x] seven thousand in Israel—all whose knees have not bowed down to Baal and all whose mouths have not kissed[y] him."

[a] 3 Or Elijah saw

19:4
[o] Nu 11:15; Jnh 4:8

19:8
[p] Ex 34:28;
Dt 9:9-11, 18;
Mt 4:2
[q] Ex 3:1

19:10
[r] 1Ki 18:4, 22;
Ro 11:3*

19:11
[s] Ex 24:12
[t] Eze 1:4

19:13
[u] Ex 3:6

19:15
[v] 2Ki 8:7-15

19:17
[w] 2Ki 8:12, 29; 9:14;
13:3, 7, 22

19:18
[x] Ro 11:4*
[y] Hos 13:2

19:3ff Elijah experienced the depths of fatigue and discouragement just after his two great spiritual victories: the defeat of the prophets of Baal and the answered prayer for rain. Often discouragement sets in after great spiritual experiences, especially those requiring physical effort or involving great emotion. To lead him out of depression, God first let Elijah rest and eat. Then God confronted him with the need to return to his mission—to speak God's words in Israel. Elijah's battles were not over; he still had work to do. When you feel let down after a great spiritual experience, remember that God's purpose for your life is not yet over.

19:8 When Elijah fled to Mount Horeb, he was returning to the sacred place where God had met Moses and had given his laws to the people. Obviously, God gave Elijah special strength to travel this great distance—over 200 miles—without additional food. Like Moses before him and Jesus after him, Elijah fasted for 40 days and 40 nights (Deuteronomy 9:9; Matthew 4:1, 2). Centuries later, Moses, Elijah, and Jesus would meet together on a mountaintop (Luke 9:28–36).

19:10 Elijah thought he was the only person left who was still true to God. He had seen both the king's court and the priesthood become corrupt. After experiencing great victory at Mount Carmel, he had to run for his life. Lonely and discouraged, he forgot that others had remained faithful during the nation's wickedness. When you are tempted to think that you are the only one remaining faithful to a task, don't stop to feel sorry for yourself. Self-pity will dilute

the good you are doing. Be assured that even if you don't know who they are, others are faithfully obeying God and fulfilling their duties.

19:11–13 Elijah knew that the sound of a gentle whisper was God's voice. He realized that God doesn't reveal himself only in powerful, miraculous ways. To look for God only in something big (rallies, churches, conferences, highly visible leaders) may be to miss him because he is often found gently whispering in the quietness of a humbled heart. Are you listening for God? Step back from the noise and activity of your busy life and listen humbly and quietly for his guidance. It may come when you least expect it.

19:15, 16 God asked Elijah to anoint three different people. The first was Hazael, as king of Aram. Elijah was told to anoint an enemy king because God was going to use Aram as his instrument to punish Israel for its sin. Aram brought Israel's *external* punishment.

Israel's *internal* punishment came from Jehu, the next man Elijah was to anoint. As king of Israel, Jehu would destroy those who worshiped the false god Baal (2 Kings 9; 10).

The third person Elijah was told to anoint was Elisha, the prophet who would succeed him. Elisha's job was to work in Israel, the northern kingdom, to help point the people back to God. At this time, the southern kingdom was ruled by Jehoshaphat, a king devoted to God.

19:18 Kissing Baal meant kissing some object representing him to show loyalty to him.

The Call of Elisha

19:20
z Mt 8:21-22;
Lk 9:61

19So Elijah went from there and found Elisha son of Shaphat. He was plowing with twelve yoke of oxen, and he himself was driving the twelfth pair. Elijah went up to him and threw his cloak around him. 20Elisha then left his oxen and ran after Elijah. "Let me kiss my father and mother good-by," z he said, "and then I will come with you."

"Go back," Elijah replied. "What have I done to you?"

19:21
a 2Sa 24:22

21So Elisha left him and went back. He took his yoke of oxen a and slaughtered them. He burned the plowing equipment to cook the meat and gave it to the people, and they ate. Then he set out to follow Elijah and became his attendant.

Ben-Hadad Attacks Samaria

20:1
b 1Ki 15:18

20 Now Ben-Hadad b king of Aram mustered his entire army. Accompanied by thirty-two kings with their horses and chariots, he went up and besieged Samaria and attacked it. 2He sent messengers into the city to Ahab king of Israel, saying, "This is what Ben-Hadad says: 3'Your silver and gold are mine, and the best of your wives and children are mine.'"

4The king of Israel answered, "Just as you say, my lord the king. I and all I have are yours."

5The messengers came again and said, "This is what Ben-Hadad says: 'I sent to demand your silver and gold, your wives and your children. 6But about this time tomorrow I am going to send my officials to search your palace and the houses of your officials. They will seize everything you value and carry it away.'"

20:7
c 2Ki 5:7

7The king of Israel summoned all the elders of the land and said to them, "See how this man is looking for trouble! c When he sent for my wives and my children, my silver and my gold, I did not refuse him."

8The elders and the people all answered, "Don't listen to him or agree to his demands."

9So he replied to Ben-Hadad's messengers, "Tell my lord the king, 'Your servant will do all you demanded the first time, but this demand I cannot meet.'" They left and took the answer back to Ben-Hadad.

20:10
d 1Ki 19:2

10Then Ben-Hadad sent another message to Ahab: "May the gods deal with me, be it ever so severely, if enough dust d remains in Samaria to give each of my men a handful."

20:11
e Pr 27:1

11The king of Israel answered, "Tell him: 'One who puts on his armor should not boast e like one who takes it off.'"

12Ben-Hadad heard this message while he and the kings were drinking in their tents, a and he ordered his men: "Prepare to attack." So they prepared to attack the city.

a 12 Or in Succoth; also in verse 16

19:19 The cloak was the most important article of clothing a person could own. It was used as protection against the weather, as bedding, as a place to sit, and as luggage. It could be given as a pledge for a debt or torn into pieces to show grief. Elijah put his cloak on Elisha's shoulders to show that he would become Elijah's successor. Later, when the transfer of authority was complete, Elijah left his cloak for Elisha (2 Kings 2:11–14).

GOD DELIVERS AHAB
Despite Ahab's wickedness, God approached him in love. When Samaria was surrounded by Aramean forces, God miraculously delivered the city. But Ahab refused to give God credit. A year later, the Arameans attacked near Aphek. Again God gave Ahab victory, but again the king refused to acknowledge God's help.

19:21 By killing his oxen, Elisha made a strong commitment to follow Elijah. Without them, he could not return to his life as a wealthy farmer. This meal was more than a feast among farmers. It was an offering of thanks to the Lord who chose Elisha to be his prophet.

20:1ff With two evil and two good kings up to this point, the southern kingdom, Judah, wavered between godly and ungodly living. But the northern kingdom, Israel, had eight evil kings in succession. To punish both kingdoms for living their own way instead of following God, God allowed other nations to gain strength and become their enemies. Three main enemies threatened Israel and Judah during the next two centuries—Aram, Assyria, and Babylon. Aram, the first to rise to power, presented an immediate threat to Ahab and Israel.

Ahab Defeats Ben-Hadad

¹³Meanwhile a prophet came to Ahab king of Israel and announced, "This is what the LORD says: 'Do you see this vast army? I will give it into your hand today, and then you will know *f* that I am the LORD.'"

20:13
f ver 28

¹⁴"But who will do this?" asked Ahab.

The prophet replied, "This is what the LORD says: 'The young officers of the provincial commanders will do it.'"

"And who will start the battle?" he asked.

The prophet answered, "You will."

¹⁵So Ahab summoned the young officers of the provincial commanders, 232 men. Then he assembled the rest of the Israelites, 7,000 in all. ¹⁶They set out at noon while Ben-Hadad and the 32 kings allied with him were in their tents getting drunk.*g* ¹⁷The young officers of the provincial commanders went out first.

20:16
g ver 12; 1Ki 16:9

Now Ben-Hadad had dispatched scouts, who reported, "Men are advancing from Samaria." ¹⁸He said, "If they have come out for peace, take them alive; if they have come out for war, take them alive."

¹⁹The young officers of the provincial commanders marched out of the city with the army behind them ²⁰and each one struck down his opponent. At that, the Arameans fled, with the Israelites in pursuit. But Ben-Hadad king of Aram escaped on horseback with some of his horsemen. ²¹The king of Israel advanced and overpowered the horses and chariots and inflicted heavy losses on the Arameans.

²²Afterward, the prophet came to the king of Israel and said, "Strengthen your position and see what must be done, because next spring*h* the king of Aram will attack you again."

20:22
h 2Sa 11:1

²³Meanwhile, the officials of the king of Aram advised him, "Their gods are gods of the hills. That is why they were too strong for us. But if we fight them on the plains, surely we will be stronger than they. ²⁴Do this: Remove all the kings from their commands and replace them with other officers. ²⁵You must also raise an army like the one you lost—horse for horse and chariot for chariot—so we can fight Israel on the plains. Then surely we will be stronger than they." He agreed with them and acted accordingly.

²⁶The next spring Ben-Hadad mustered the Arameans and went up to Aphek*i* to fight against Israel. ²⁷When the Israelites were also mustered and given provisions, they marched out to meet them. The Israelites camped opposite them like two small flocks of goats, while the Arameans covered the countryside.

20:26
i 2Ki 13:17

²⁸The man of God came up and told the king of Israel, "This is what the LORD says: 'Because the Arameans think the LORD is a god of the hills and not a god of the valleys, I will deliver this vast army into your hands, and you will know*j* that I am the LORD.'"

20:28
j ver 13

²⁹For seven days they camped opposite each other, and on the seventh day the battle was joined. The Israelites inflicted a hundred thousand casualties on the Aramean foot soldiers in one day. ³⁰The rest of them escaped to the city of Aphek, where the wall collapsed on twenty-seven thousand of them. And Ben-Hadad fled to the city and hid*k* in an inner room.

20:30
k 1Ki 22:25;
2Ch 18:24

³¹His officials said to him, "Look, we have heard that the kings of the house of Israel are merciful. Let us go to the king of Israel with sackcloth*l* around our waists and ropes around our heads. Perhaps he will spare your life."

20:31
l Ge 37:34

³²Wearing sackcloth around their waists and ropes around their heads, they went to the king of Israel and said, "Your servant Ben-Hadad says: 'Please let me live.'"

The king answered, "Is he still alive? He is my brother."

³³The men took this as a good sign and were quick to pick up his word. "Yes, your brother Ben-Hadad!" they said.

20:13 God defeated the Aramean army for Ahab so that Ahab would know that God alone is the Lord. Despite this great victory and the one to follow on the plains (20:28, 29), Ahab continued to live without God. Evidence of God's greatness surrounds us, but, like Ahab, we can choose to ignore it and go our own way. But when we do, as with this evil king of Israel, disaster will strike. Open your eyes to the evidence— the victories that God is winning for you. Then rededicate yourself to him.

20:23 Since the days of Joshua, Israel's soldiers had a reputation for being superior fighters in the hills, but ineffective in the open plains and valleys because they did not use chariots in battle. Horse-drawn chariots, useless in hilly terrain and dense forests, could easily run down great numbers of foot soldiers on the plains. What Ben-Hadad's officers did not understand was that God, not chariots, made the difference in battle.

20:31 Sackcloth was coarse cloth usually made of goat's hair and was worn as a symbol of mourning for the dead or for natural disaster. Wearing ropes around the head may have been a symbol of putting oneself at another's disposal. In other words, Ahab could have hung them if he wished. Wearing ropes around the head, therefore, showed submission.

"Go and get him," the king said. When Ben-Hadad came out, Ahab had him come up into his chariot.

20:34
m 1Ki 15:20

34 "I will return the cities *m* my father took from your father," Ben-Hadad offered. "You may set up your own market areas in Damascus, as my father did in Samaria."

⌐Ahab said,⌐ "On the basis of a treaty I will set you free." So he made a treaty with him, and let him go.

A Prophet Condemns Ahab

20:35
n 2Ki 2:3-7

35 By the word of the LORD one of the sons of the prophets said to his companion, "Strike me with your weapon," but the man refused. *n*

20:36
o 1Ki 13:24

36 So the prophet said, "Because you have not obeyed the LORD, as soon as you leave me a lion *o* will kill you." And after the man went away, a lion found him and killed him.

37 The prophet found another man and said, "Strike me, please." So the man struck him and wounded him. 38 Then the prophet went and stood by the road waiting for the king. He disguised himself with his headband down over his eyes. 39 As the king passed by, the prophet called out to him, "Your servant went into the thick of the battle, and someone came to me with a captive and said, 'Guard this man. If he is missing, it will be your life for his life, *p* or you must pay a talent *a* of silver.' 40 While your servant was busy here and there, the man disappeared."

20:39
p 2Ki 10:24

"That is your sentence," the king of Israel said. "You have pronounced it yourself."

20:42
q 1Ki 22:31-37

20:43
r 1Ki 21:4

41 Then the prophet quickly removed the headband from his eyes, and the king of Israel recognized him as one of the prophets. 42 He said to the king, "This is what the LORD says: 'You have set free a man I had determined should die. *b* Therefore it is your life for his life, *q* your people for his people.'" 43 Sullen and angry, *r* the king of Israel went to his palace in Samaria.

Naboth's Vineyard

21 Some time later there was an incident involving a vineyard belonging to Naboth the Jezreelite. The vineyard was in Jezreel, close to the palace of Ahab king of Samaria. 2 Ahab said to Naboth, "Let me have your vineyard to use for a vegetable garden, since it is close to my palace. In exchange I will give you a better vineyard or, if you prefer, I will pay you whatever it is worth."

21:3
s Lev 25:23;
Nu 36:7; Eze 46:18

3 But Naboth replied, "The LORD forbid that I should give you the inheritance *s* of my fathers."

4 So Ahab went home, sullen and angry because Naboth the Jezreelite had said, "I will not give you the inheritance of my fathers." He lay on his bed sulking and refused to eat.

5 His wife Jezebel came in and asked him, "Why are you so sullen? Why won't you eat?"

6 He answered her, "Because I said to Naboth the Jezreelite, 'Sell me your vineyard; or if you prefer, I will give you another vineyard in its place.' But he said, 'I will not give you my vineyard.'"

7 Jezebel his wife said, "Is this how you act as king over Israel? Get up and eat! Cheer up. I'll get you the vineyard of Naboth the Jezreelite."

8 So she wrote letters in Ahab's name, placed his seal on them, and sent them to the elders and nobles who lived in Naboth's city with him. 9 In those letters she wrote:

21:10
t Ac 6:11
u Ex 22:28;
Lev 24:15-16

"Proclaim a day of fasting and seat Naboth in a prominent place among the people. 10 But seat two scoundrels *t* opposite him and have them testify that he has cursed *u* both God and the king. Then take him out and stone him to death."

a 39 That is, about 75 pounds (about 34 kilograms)   *b 42* The Hebrew term refers to the irrevocable giving over of things or persons to the LORD, often by totally destroying them.

20:35, 36 The prophet needed a wound so he would look like an injured soldier and could effectively deliver his prophecy to Ahab. The first man was killed by a lion because he refused to obey the Lord's instructions through the prophet.

20:41, 42 It is difficult to explain why Ahab let Ben-Hadad go, especially after all the trouble the Arameans had caused him. God helped Ahab destroy the Aramean army to prove to Ahab and to Aram that he alone was God. But Ahab failed to destroy the king, his greatest enemy. Ben-Hadad was under God's judgment to die, and Ahab had no authority to let him live. For this, God told Ahab that he must now die instead. This prophet's message soon came true when Ahab was killed on the battlefield (22:35).

21:4 After hearing God's judgment (20:42), Ahab went home to pout. Driven by anger and rebellion against God, he had a fit of rage when Naboth refused to sell his vineyard. The same feelings that led him to a career of power grabbing drove him to resent Naboth. Rage turned to hatred and led to murder. Naboth, however, wanted to uphold God's laws: it was considered a duty to keep ancestral land in the family. This incident shows the cruel interplay between Ahab and Jezebel, two of the most wicked leaders in Israel's history.

¹¹So the elders and nobles who lived in Naboth's city did as Jezebel directed in the letters she had written to them. ¹²They proclaimed a fast and seated Naboth in a prominent place among the people. ¹³Then two scoundrels came and sat opposite him and brought charges against Naboth before the people, saying, "Naboth has cursed both God and the king." So they took him outside the city and stoned him to death. ᵛ ¹⁴Then they sent word to Jezebel: "Naboth has been stoned and is dead."

21:13
ᵛ2Ki 9:26

¹⁵As soon as Jezebel heard that Naboth had been stoned to death, she said to Ahab, "Get up and take possession of the vineyard of Naboth the Jezreelite that he refused to sell you. He is no longer alive, but dead." ¹⁶When Ahab heard that Naboth was dead, he got up and went down to take possession of Naboth's vineyard.

¹⁷Then the word of the LORD came to Elijah the Tishbite: ¹⁸"Go down to meet Ahab king of Israel, who rules in Samaria. He is now in Naboth's vineyard, where he has gone to take possession of it. ¹⁹Say to him, 'This is what the LORD says: Have you not murdered a man and seized his property?' Then say to him, 'This is what the LORD says: In the place where dogs licked up Naboth's blood, dogs ʷ will lick up your blood—yes, yours!'"

21:19
ʷ1Ki 22:38

²⁰Ahab said to Elijah, "So you have found me, my enemy!" ˣ

"I have found you," he answered, "because you have sold ʸ yourself to do evil in the eyes of the LORD. ²¹I am going to bring disaster on you. I will consume your descendants and cut off from Ahab every last male ᶻ in Israel—slave or free. ²²I will make your house ᵃ like that of Jeroboam son of Nebat and that of Baasha son of Ahijah, because you have provoked me to anger and have caused Israel to sin.'

21:20
ˣ1Ki 18:17
ʸRo 7:14
21:21
ᶻ1Ki 14:10; 2Ki 9:8
21:22
ᵃ1Ki 15:29

²³"And also concerning Jezebel the LORD says: 'Dogs ᵇ will devour Jezebel by the wall of ᵃ Jezreel.'

21:23
ᵇ2Ki 9:10, 34-36

²⁴"Dogs ᶜ will eat those belonging to Ahab who die in the city, and the birds of the air will feed on those who die in the country."

21:24
ᶜ1Ki 14:11; 16:4

²⁵(There was never a man like Ahab, who sold himself to do evil in the eyes of the LORD, urged on by Jezebel his wife. ²⁶He behaved in the vilest manner by going after idols, like the Amorites ᵈ the LORD drove out before Israel.)

21:26
ᵈGe 15:16

²⁷When Ahab heard these words, he tore his clothes, put on sackcloth and fasted. He lay in sackcloth and went around meekly.

²⁸Then the word of the LORD came to Elijah the Tishbite: ²⁹"Have you noticed how Ahab has humbled himself before me? Because he has humbled himself, I will not bring this disaster in his day, but I will bring it on his house in the days of his son." ᵉ

21:29
ᵉ2Ki 9:26

4. Kings of Israel and Judah

Micaiah Prophesies Against Ahab

22 For three years there was no war between Aram and Israel. ²But in the third year Jehoshaphat king of Judah went down to see the king of Israel. ³The king of Israel had said to his officials, "Don't you know that Ramoth Gilead ᶠ belongs to us and yet we are doing nothing to retake it from the king of Aram?"

22:3
ᶠDt 4:43

⁴So he asked Jehoshaphat, "Will you go with me to fight ᵍ against Ramoth Gilead?"

Jehoshaphat replied to the king of Israel, "I am as you are, my people as your people, my horses as your horses." ⁵But Jehoshaphat also said to the king of Israel, "First seek the counsel of the LORD."

22:4
ᵍ2Ki 3:7

⁶So the king of Israel brought together the prophets—about four hundred men—and asked them, "Shall I go to war against Ramoth Gilead, or shall I refrain?"

ᵃ23 Most Hebrew manuscripts; a few Hebrew manuscripts, Vulgate and Syriac (see also 2 Kings 9:26) *the plot of ground at*

21:13 Jezebel devised a scheme that appeared legal to get the land for her husband. Two witnesses were required to establish guilt, and the punishment for blasphemy was death by stoning. Those who twist the law and legal procedures to get what they want today may be more sophisticated in how they go about it, but they are guilty of the same sin.

21:19, 23 For the fulfillment of these verses, see 22:38 where dogs licked Ahab's blood, and 2 Kings 9:30—10:28 where Jezebel and the rest of Ahab's family were destroyed.

21:20 Ahab still refused to admit his sin against God. Instead he accused Elijah of being his enemy. When we are blinded by envy and hatred, we find it almost impossible to see our own sin.

21:29 Ahab was more wicked than any other king of Israel (16:30; 21:25), but when he repented in deep humility, God took notice and reduced his punishment. The same Lord who was merciful to Ahab wants to be merciful to you. No matter how evil you have been, it is never too late to humble yourself, turn to God, and ask for forgiveness.

22:6 These 400 prophets may have been the 400 Asherah priests left alive by Elijah at Carmel, although 450 prophets of Baal were killed (see 18:19—40).

22:6
h 1Ki 18:19
22:7
i 2Ki 3:11

"Go," *h* they answered, "for the Lord will give it into the king's hand."

7 But Jehoshaphat asked, "Is there not a prophet *i* of the LORD here whom we can inquire of?"

8 The king of Israel answered Jehoshaphat, "There is still one man through whom we can inquire of the LORD, but I hate him because he never prophesies anything good about me, but always bad. He is Micaiah son of Imlah."

"The king should not say that," Jehoshaphat replied.

9 So the king of Israel called one of his officials and said, "Bring Micaiah son of Imlah at once."

10 Dressed in their royal robes, the king of Israel and Jehoshaphat king of Judah were sitting on their thrones at the threshing floor by the entrance of the gate of Samaria, with all the prophets prophesying before them. 11 Now Zedekiah son of Kenaanah had made iron horns *j* and he declared, "This is what the LORD says: 'With these you will gore the Arameans until they are destroyed.'"

22:11
j Dt 33:17;
Zec 1:18-21

12 All the other prophets were prophesying the same thing. "Attack Ramoth Gilead and be victorious," they said, "for the LORD will give it into the king's hand."

JEZEBEL

The Bible is as honest about the lives of its heroes as it is about those who rejected God. Some Bible characters found out what God can do with failures when they turned to him. Many, however, neither admitted their failures nor turned to God.

Jezebel ranks as the most evil woman in the Bible. The Bible even uses her name as an example of people who completely reject God (Revelation 2:20, 21). Many pagan women married into Israel without acknowledging the God their husbands worshiped. They brought their religions with them. But no one was as determined as Jezebel to make all Israel worship *her* gods. To the prophet Elijah, she seemed to have succeeded. He felt he was the only one still faithful to God until God told him there were still 7,000 who had not turned from the faith. Jezebel's one outstanding "success" was in contributing to the cause of the eventual downfall of the northern kingdom—idolatry. God punished the northern tribes for their idolatry by having them carried off into captivity.

Jezebel held great power. She not only managed her husband, Ahab, but she also had 850 assorted pagan priests under her control. She was committed to her gods and to getting what she wanted. She believed that the king had the right to possess anything he wanted. When Naboth refused to sell Ahab his vineyard, Jezebel ruthlessly had Naboth killed and took ownership of the land. Jezebel's plan to wipe out worship of God in Israel led to painful consequences. Before she died, Jezebel suffered the loss of her husband in combat and her son at the hand of Jehu, who took the throne by force. She died in the defiant and scornful way she had lived.

When comparing Jezebel and Elijah, we have to admire each one's strength of commitment. The big difference was *to whom* they were committed. Jezebel was committed to herself and her false gods; Elijah was totally committed to the one true God. In the end, God proved Elijah right. To what or to whom are you most committed? How would God evaluate your commitment?

Weaknesses and mistakes:	• Systematically eliminated the representatives of God in Israel • Promoted and funded Baal worship • Threatened to have Elijah killed • Believed kings and queens could rightfully do or have anything they wanted • Used her strong convictions to get her own way
Lessons from her life:	• It is not enough to be committed or sincere. Where our commitment lies makes a great difference • Rejecting God always leads to disaster
Vital statistics:	• Where: Sidon, Samaria • Occupation: Queen of Israel • Relatives: Husband: Ahab. Father: Ethbaal. Sons: Joram, Ahaziah. • Contemporaries: Elijah, Jehu
Key verse:	"There was never a man like Ahab, who sold himself to do evil in the eyes of the LORD, urged on by Jezebel his wife" (1 Kings 21:25).

Jezebel's story is told in 1 Kings 16:31—2 Kings 9:37. Her name is used as a synonym for great evil in Revelation 2:20.

22:7 Jehoshaphat knew the difference between these pagan prophets and God's prophet, so he asked if a prophet of the Lord was available. Evidently Jehoshaphat wanted to do what was right although Ahab didn't. Both kings disregarded God's message, however, and listened only to the pagan prophets.

22:10 Threshing floors were placed in elevated areas to allow the wind to blow away the discarded hulls of grain.

¹³The messenger who had gone to summon Micaiah said to him, "Look, as one man the other prophets are predicting success for the king. Let your word agree with theirs, and speak favorably."

¹⁴But Micaiah said, "As surely as the Lord lives, I can tell him only what the Lord tells me."[k]

¹⁵When he arrived, the king asked him, "Micaiah, shall we go to war against Ramoth Gilead, or shall I refrain?"

"Attack and be victorious," he answered, "for the Lord will give it into the king's hand."

¹⁶The king said to him, "How many times must I make you swear to tell me nothing but the truth in the name of the Lord?"

¹⁷Then Micaiah answered, "I saw all Israel scattered on the hills like sheep without a shepherd,[l] and the Lord said, 'These people have no master. Let each one go home in peace.'"

¹⁸The king of Israel said to Jehoshaphat, "Didn't I tell you that he never prophesies anything good about me, but only bad?"

¹⁹Micaiah continued, "Therefore hear the word of the Lord: I saw the Lord sitting on his throne[m] with all the host[n] of heaven standing around him on his right and on his left. ²⁰And the Lord said, 'Who will entice Ahab into attacking Ramoth Gilead and going to his death there?'

"One suggested this, and another that. ²¹Finally, a spirit came forward, stood before the Lord and said, 'I will entice him.'

²²"'By what means?' the Lord asked.

"'I will go out and be a lying[o] spirit in the mouths of all his prophets,' he said.

"'You will succeed in enticing him,' said the Lord. 'Go and do it.'

²³"So now the Lord has put a lying spirit in the mouths of all these prophets[p] of yours. The Lord has decreed disaster for you."

²⁴Then Zedekiah son of Kenaanah went up and slapped Micaiah in the face. "Which way did the spirit from[a] the Lord go when he went from me to speak to you?" he asked.

²⁵Micaiah replied, "You will find out on the day you go to hide[q] in an inner room."

²⁶The king of Israel then ordered, "Take Micaiah and send him back to Amon the ruler of the city and to Joash the king's son ²⁷and say, 'This is what the king says: Put this fellow in prison and give him nothing but bread and water until I return safely.'"

²⁸Micaiah declared, "If you ever return safely, the Lord has not spoken[r] through me." Then he added, "Mark my words, all you people!"

Ahab Killed at Ramoth Gilead

²⁹So the king of Israel and Jehoshaphat king of Judah went up to Ramoth Gilead. ³⁰The king of Israel said to Jehoshaphat, "I will enter the battle in disguise,[s] but you wear your royal robes." So the king of Israel disguised himself and went into battle.

³¹Now the king of Aram had ordered his thirty-two chariot commanders, "Do not fight with anyone, small or great, except the king of Israel." ³²When the chariot commanders saw Jehoshaphat, they thought, "Surely this is the king of Israel." So they turned to attack him, but when Jehoshaphat cried out, ³³the chariot commanders saw that he was not the king of Israel and stopped pursuing him.

[a]24 Or *Spirit of*

22:14
[k]Nu 22:18

22:17
[l]Mt 9:36

22:19
[m]Isa 6:1; Da 7:9
[n]Job 1:6

22:22
[o]Jdg 9:23; 2Th 2:11

22:23
[p]Eze 14:9

22:25
[q]1Ki 20:30

22:28
[r]Dt 18:22

22:30
[s]2Ch 35:32

22:15, 16 Why did Micaiah tell Ahab to attack when he had previously vowed to speak only what God had told him? Perhaps he was speaking sarcastically, making fun of the messages from the pagan prophets by showing that they were telling the king only what he wanted to hear. Somehow, Micaiah's tone of voice let everyone know he was mocking the pagan prophets. When confronted, he predicted that the king would die and the battle would be lost. Although Ahab repented temporarily (21:27), he still maintained the system of false prophets. These false prophets would be instrumental in leading him to his own ruin.

22:19-22 The vision Micaiah saw was either a picture of a real incident in heaven, or a parable of what was happening on earth, illustrating that the seductive influence of the false prophets would be part of God's judgment upon Ahab (22:23). Whether or not God sent an angel in disguise, he used the system of false prophets to snare Ahab in his sin. The lying spirit (22:22) symbolized the way of life for these prophets, who told the king only what he wanted to hear.

22:20-22 Does God allow angels to entice people to do evil? To understand evil, we must first understand God. (1) God himself is good (Psalm 11:7). (2) God created a good world that fell because of sin (Romans 5:12). (3) Someday God will recreate the world and it will be good again (Revelation 21:1). (4) God is stronger than evil (Matthew 13:41–43; Revelation 19:11–21). (5) God allows evil, and thus he has control over it. God did not create evil, and he offers help to those who wish to overcome it (Matthew 11:28–30). (6) God uses everything—both good and evil—for his good purposes (Genesis 50:20; Romans 8:28).

The Bible shows us a God who hates all evil and will one day do away with it completely and forever (Revelation 20:10–15). God does not entice anyone to become evil. Those committed to evil, however, may be used by God to sin even more in order to hurry their deserved judgment (Exodus 11:10). We don't need to understand every detail of how God works in order to have perfect confidence in his absolute power over evil and his total goodness toward us.

³⁴But someone drew his bow at random and hit the king of Israel between the sections of his armor. The king told his chariot driver, "Wheel around and get me out of the fighting. I've been wounded." ³⁵All day long the battle raged, and the king was propped up in his chariot facing the Arameans. The blood from his wound ran onto the floor of the chariot, and that evening he died. ³⁶As the sun was setting, a cry spread through the army: "Every man to his town; everyone to his land!"

³⁷So the king died and was brought to Samaria, and they buried him there. ³⁸They washed the chariot at a pool in Samaria (where the prostitutes bathed), ᵃ and the dogs ᵗ licked up his blood, as the word of the LORD had declared.

³⁹As for the other events of Ahab's reign, including all he did, the palace he built and inlaid with ivory, ᵘ and the cities he fortified, are they not written in the book of the annals of the kings of Israel? ⁴⁰Ahab rested with his fathers. And Ahaziah his son succeeded him as king.

22:38
ᵗ1Ki 21:19

22:39
ᵘAm 3:15

Jehoshaphat King of Judah

⁴¹Jehoshaphat son of Asa became king of Judah in the fourth year of Ahab king of Israel. ⁴²Jehoshaphat was thirty-five years old when he became king, and he reigned in Jerusalem

ᵃ38 Or *Samaria and cleaned the weapons*

KINGS TO DATE AND THEIR ENEMIES

874
AHAB
*Twice defeated
Ben-Hadad II
(Aram) and was
later killed in battle
1 Kgs 16:28—22:40
2 Chr 18:1–34*

853
AHAZIAH
*1 Kgs 22:40—
2 Kgs 1:18
2 Chr 20:35–37*

852

I S R A E L

J U D A H

869

853 848 841
JEHORAM
*Lost dominion
over Edom,
assaulted by
Philistines and
Arabs
2 Kgs 8:16–24
2 Chr 21:1–20*

872
JEHOSHAPHAT
*Defeated by Ben-
Hadad II (Aram),
gained miraculous
victory over Moab
and Ammon, and
crushed a rebellion
by Mesha (Moab)
1 Kgs 22:41–50
2 Chr 17:1—21:1
Co-regency
853–848*

910
ASA
*Defeated Zerah
(the Cushite) and
harassed Baasha
1 Kgs 15:8–24
2 Chr 14:1—16:14
Co-regency
872–869*

All dates are B.C.
Solid section of the timeline indicates co-regency.
For all the kings of Israel and Judah, see the chart
at the end of 1 Kings.

22:34 Ahab could not escape God's judgment. The king of Aram sent 32 of his best chariot commanders with the sole purpose of killing Ahab. Thinking he could escape, Ahab tried a disguise, but a random arrow struck him while the chariots chased the wrong king, Jehoshaphat. It was foolish for Ahab to think he could escape by wearing a disguise. Sometimes people try to escape reality by disguising themselves—changing jobs, moving to a new town, even changing spouses. But God sees and evaluates the motives of each person. Any attempted disguise is futile.

22:35 Just as the prophet had predicted (20:42), Ahab was

killed. See Ahab's Profile in chapter 19, p. 531 for more of Ahab's sad story.

22:41–50 For more details on Jehoshaphat, see the other account of his reign in 2 Chronicles 17—20.

twenty-five years. His mother's name was Azubah daughter of Shilhi. [43]In everything he walked in the ways of his father Asa[v] and did not stray from them; he did what was right in the eyes of the LORD. The high places,[w] however, were not removed, and the people continued to offer sacrifices and burn incense there. [44]Jehoshaphat was also at peace with the king of Israel.

[45]As for the other events of Jehoshaphat's reign, the things he achieved and his military exploits, are they not written in the book of the annals of the kings of Judah? [46]He rid the land of the rest of the male shrine prostitutes[x] who remained there even after the reign of his father Asa. [47]There was then no king[y] in Edom; a deputy ruled.

[48]Now Jehoshaphat built a fleet of trading ships[a] to go to Ophir for gold, but they never set sail—they were wrecked at Ezion Geber. [49]At that time Ahaziah son of Ahab said to Jehoshaphat, "Let my men sail with your men," but Jehoshaphat refused.

[50]Then Jehoshaphat rested with his fathers and was buried with them in the city of David his father. And Jehoram his son succeeded him.

Ahaziah King of Israel

[51]Ahaziah son of Ahab became king of Israel in Samaria in the seventeenth year of Jehoshaphat king of Judah, and he reigned over Israel two years. [52]He did evil[z] in the eyes of the LORD, because he walked in the ways of his father and mother and in the ways of Jeroboam son of Nebat, who caused Israel to sin. [53]He served and worshiped Baal and provoked the LORD, the God of Israel, to anger, just as his father[a] had done.

[a]*48 Hebrew of ships of Tarshish*

22:43
[v]2Ch 17:3
[w]1Ki 15:14;
2Ki 12:3

22:46
[x]1Ki 15:12

22:47
[y]2Sa 8:14; 2Ki 3:9

22:52
[z]1Ki 15:26

22:53
[a]1Ki 16:30-32

22:43 Just like his ancestors Solomon and Asa, Jehoshaphat followed God, but he didn't remove the high places—the pagan shrines in the hills (2 Chronicles 20:33). It was against God's laws to worship idols in the shrines (Numbers 33:52), and at first Jehoshaphat attempted to remove them (2 Chronicles 17:6). They were so popular, however, that this proved difficult. In spite of Jehoshaphat's many contributions to the spiritual, moral, and material health of his country, he did not succeed in eradicating the hill shrines.

22:52, 53 The book of 1 Kings begins with a nation united under David, the most devout king in Israel's history. The book ends with a divided kingdom and the death of Ahab, the most wicked king of all. What happened? The people forgot to acknowledge God as their ultimate leader; they appointed human leaders who ignored God; then they conformed to the lifestyles of these evil leaders. Occasional wrongdoing gradually turned into a way of life. Their blatant wickedness could be met only with judgment from God, who allowed enemy nations to arise and defeat Israel and Judah in battle as punishment for their sins. Failing to acknowledge God as our ultimate leader is the first step toward ruin.

NAMES OF GOD

Name of God	Meaning	Reference	Significance
Elohim	God	Genesis 1:1; Numbers 23:19; Psalm 19:1	Refers to God's power and might. He is the only supreme and true God.
Yahweh	The LORD	Genesis 2:4; Exodus 6:2, 3	The proper name of the divine person.
El Elyon	God Most High	Genesis 14:17–20; Numbers 24:16; Psalm 7:17; Isaiah 14:13, 14	He is above all gods; nothing in life is more sacred.
El Roi	God Who Sees	Genesis 16:13	God oversees all creation and the affairs of people.
El Shaddai	God Almighty	Genesis 17:1; Psalm 91:1	God is all-powerful.
Yahweh Yireh	The LORD Will Provide	Genesis 22:13, 14	God will provide our real needs.
Yahweh Nissi	The LORD Is My Banner	Exodus 17:15	We should remember God for helping us.
Adonai	Lord	Deuteronomy 6:4	God alone is the head over all.
Yahweh Elohe Yisrael	LORD God of Israel	Judges 5:3; Psalm 59:5; Isaiah 17:6; Zephaniah 2:9	He is the God of the nation.
Yahweh Shalom	The LORD Is Peace	Judges 6:24	God gives us peace so we need not fear.
Qedosh Yisrael	Holy One of Israel	Isaiah 1:4	God is morally perfect.
Yahweh Sabaoth	LORD of Hosts (*Hosts* refers to armies but also to all the heavenly powers.)	1 Samuel 1:3; Isaiah 6:1–3	God is our savior and protector.
El Olam	The Everlasting God	Isaiah 40:28–31	God is eternal. He will never die.
Yahweh Tsidkenu	The LORD Is Our Righteousness	Jeremiah 23:6; 33:16	God is our standard for right behavior. He alone can make us righteous.
Yahweh Shammah	The LORD Is There	Ezekiel 48:35	God is always present with us.
Attiq Yomin	Ancient of Days	Daniel 7:9, 13	God is the ultimate authority. He will one day judge all nations.

A HARMONY OF THE BOOKS OF KINGS AND CHRONICLES

This chart gives a harmony of the history recorded in 1 & 2 Kings and 1 & 2 Chronicles. It provides you with the names of the kings listed chronologically (showing those in the northern kingdom at the top and the southern kingdom at the bottom), a brief overview of each king's reign, and where you can read about each king. The bold lines above and below the chart give you the names and timelines of prophets who prophesied during the reigns of particular kings.

ELIJAH 875–848

AHIJAH 934–909

930
JEROBOAM I
(22 years)
Fortified a capital city (Shechem), set up two golden calf-idols, led the nation into sin, allowed anyone to be a priest
1 Kgs 11:26—14:34
2 Chr 10:12—13:20

909
NADAB
(2 years)
1 Kgs 15:25–28

908
BAASHA
(24 years)
Led people into idol worship
1 Kgs 15:27—16:7
2 Chr 16:1–6

886
ELAH
(2 years)
Continued idol worship
1 Kgs 16:6–14

885
ZIMRI
(7 days)
1 Kgs 16:9–20

885
TIBNI
(4 years)
1 Kgs 16:21–22

885
OMRI
(12 years)
Built the capital city of Samaria, had great military power, but continued to lead Israel into idolatry
1 Kgs 16:16–28

874
AHAB
(22 years)
Married Jezebel (a non-Jew and extremely wicked woman), worshiped Baal, and suffered three years of famine caused by his consistent disobedience to God
1 Kgs 16:28—22:40
2 Chr 18:1–34

CAPITAL: SHECHEM, THEN TIRZAH, THEN SAMARIA
THE NORTHERN KINGDOM OF ISRAEL (TEN TRIBES)

THE SOUTHERN KINGDOM OF JUDAH (TWO TRIBES)
CAPITAL: JERUSALEM

930
REHOBOAM
(17 years)
Built many fortified cities, strengthened the economy (despite the tribute paid to Egypt), followed God for three years, but then set up idols and shrines to foreign gods
1 Kgs 11:43—14:31
2 Chr 9:31—12:16

913
ABIJAH
(3 years)
Despite his wickedness, he called for God's help to win the battle against Israel
1 Kgs 14:31—15:8
2 Chr 13:1—14:1

910
ASA
(41 years)
Destroyed pagan altars and rebuilt altar of God, built fortified cities, gained much wealth from plunder of foreign conquest, removed the queen mother for worshiping Asherah, led the people to worship God with their hearts, provided peace on home soil, was greatly loved and given a beautiful funeral
1 Kgs 15:8–24
2 Chr 14:1—16:14

872
JEHOSHAPHAT
(25 years)
Arranged for the marriage of his son to a daughter of Ahab (who made trouble later on), had a strong military (kept troops in cities of Israel his father had conquered), collected tribute from the Philistines, worshiped the Lord and destroyed idols, established education, and appointed judges and courts
1 Kgs 15:24; 22:41–50
2 Chr 17:1—21:1

All dates are B.C. The total years of reign sometimes includes years of co-regency.

ELISHA 848–797

JONAH 793–753(?)

841
JEHU
(28 years)
Was responsible for the deaths of Joram (king of Israel), Ahaziah (king of Judah), and Jezebel (wicked mother of Joram); destroyed the priests and temples of Baal but did not consistently follow God
2 Kgs 9:1—10:36
2 Chr 22:7–12

798
JEHOASH
(16 years)
Even though he was evil, he recognized the authority of Elisha as a prophet of God
2 Kgs 13:10—14:16
2 Chr 25:17–24

853
AHAZIAH
(2 years)
Proposed a joint trade venture with Judah
1 Kgs 22:40—
2 Kgs 1:18
2 Chr 20:35–37

852
JORAM
(12 years)
Suffered famine and war during most of his reign
2 Kgs 3:1—8:25
2 Chr 22:5–7

814
JEHOAHAZ
(17 years)
Evil reign included worship of Asherah, usually called "detestable"
2 Kgs 13:1–9

793
JEROBOAM II
(41 years)
Very evil but politically powerful; his nation enjoyed economic prosperity and military peace
2 Kgs 14:16–29

853
JEHORAM
(8 years)
Married a wicked daughter of Ahab, compelled the people to worship idols, and killed all his brothers
2 Kgs 8:16–24
2 Chr 21:1–20

841
AHAZIAH
(1 year)
Friend of Joram of Israel
2 Kgs 8:24—9:29
2 Chr 22:1–10

841
ATHALIAH
(QUEEN)
(6 years)
Killed all her grandchildren except Joash, who was hidden by his nurse for six years, ravaged the temple to furnish Baal's temple
2 Kgs 11:1–20
2 Chr 22:10—23:21

835
JOASH
(40 years)
Was crowned king at the age of seven by Jehoiada (the high priest), promoted peace and prosperity, repaired the temple, and smashed the altars to Baal; abandoned God after Jehoiada died, and even had Jehoiada's son killed
2 Kgs 11:2—12:21
2 Chr 22:11—24:27

796
AMAZIAH
(29 years)
Was basically good but did not completely wipe out idol worship; organized and mustered the army
2 Kgs 14:1–20
2 Chr 25:1–28

792
AZARIAH
(52 years)
Rebuilt a city named Elath, owned many farms and vineyards, constructed water reservoirs and fortified towers, reorganized the army (so powerful that his fame spread to Egypt), but violated God's laws for priestly function—so God struck him with leprosy
2 Kgs 15:1–17
2 Chr 26:1–23

HOSEA 753–715

AMOS 760–750

752
SHALLUM
(1 month)
2 Kgs 15:10–15

742
PEKAHIAH
(2 years)
*Continued idol
worship
2 Kgs 15:22–26*

732
HOSHEA
(9 years)
*Suffered heavy taxa-
tion by Assyria and
eventual conquest—
bringing about
Israelite captivity
and resettlement of
foreigners in Israel
2 Kgs 15:30; 17:1–6*

722
*END OF THE
NORTHERN
KINGDOM—
Israel taken
to Assyria by
Shalmaneser*

740
PEKAH
(8 years)
*During his reign
many of the
people were taken
captive to Assyria
2 Kgs 15:25–31
2 Chr 28:5–8*

753
ZECHARIAH
(6 months)
*Encouraged idol
worship
2 Kgs 14:29—15:11*

752
MENAHEM
(10 years)
*Imposed heavy
taxes and
oppressed his
people
2 Kgs 15:14–22*

ISRAEL

JUDAH

750
JOTHAM
(16 years)
*Rebuilt the Upper
Gate of the Temple,
rebuilt walls and
cities, but still per-
mitted idol worship
2 Kgs 15:32–38
2 Chr 27:1–9*

735
AHAZ
(16 years)
*Sacrificed his own
son to pagan gods,
nailed the Temple
doors shut
2 Kgs 16:1–20
2 Chr 28:1–27*

715
HEZEKIAH
(29 years)
*Was a devoted follower of God,
reopened the Temple doors,
purified the Temple, reinstated
priests and their duties, organized an orchestra to aid worship, destroyed idols (including
the bronze snake of Moses
because people had begun to
worship it), celebrated the
Passover and even invited people
who were living in the north to
participate, constructed large
public waterworks, was given
15 extra years of life, foolishly
showed Babylonian messengers
the wealth in the Temple
2 Kgs 16:20; 18:1—20:21
2 Chr 29:1—32:33*

697
MANASSEH
(55 years)
*Rebuilt all the
pagan shrines,
sacrificed one
of his own sons,
practiced sorcery,
set up an idol
right in the
Temple, murdered
many of his own
people, but
repented during
his Assyrian
captivity
2 Kgs 21:1–18
2 Chr 33:1–20*

MICAH 742–687

ISAIAH 740–681

586
END OF THE SOUTHERN KINGDOM—
carried off captive
to Babylon by
Nebuchadnezzar

642
AMON
(2 years)
2 Kgs 21:18–26
2 Chr 33:20–25

640
JOSIAH
(31 years)
Loved God with all his heart,
repaired the temple, found
a lost scroll of the law (he
promised to obey it, thus God
delayed destruction for Judah
until after his death), personally
oversaw the major project
of destroying idol shrines,
reinstated the priests of God,
celebrated the Passover with
greater zeal than had been
since Samuel's day, was
greatly loved by his people
2 Kgs 21:26—23:30
2 Chr 33:25—35:27

609
JEHOAHAZ
(3 months)
Jailed and taken
to Egypt, where
he died
2 Kgs 23:30–34
2 Chr 36:1–4

609
JEHOIAKIM
(11 years)
Burned part of
God's words given
to Jeremiah, was
a puppet king for
Egypt and then
Babylon, watched
gold and articles
taken from the
temple to Babylon,
saw first exile
(in which Daniel
was taken)
2 Kgs 23:34—24:6
2 Chr 36:5–8

598
JEHOIACHIN
(3 months)
Saw next exile
to Babylon
2 Kgs 24:6–15;
25:27–30
2 Chr 36:8–10

597
ZEDEKIAH
(11 years)
Saw the temple
burned and
Jerusalem
destroyed, was
tortured and carried
away in the final
exile to Babylon
2 Kgs 24:17—25:21
2 Chr 36:10–21

663–654

ZEPHANIAH 640–621

HABAKKUK 612–589

HULDAH 632

OBADIAH 598–580(?)

JEREMIAH 627–586

2 KINGS

VITAL STATISTICS

PURPOSE:
To demonstrate the fate that awaits all who refuse to make God their true leader

AUTHOR:
Unknown. Possibly Jeremiah or a group of prophets

ORIGINAL AUDIENCE:
The people of Israel

SETTING:
The once-united nation of Israel has been divided into two kingdoms, Israel and Judah, for over a century.

KEY VERSES:
"The LORD warned Israel and Judah through all his prophets and seers: 'Turn from your evil ways. Observe my commands and decrees, in accordance with the entire Law that I commanded your fathers to obey and that I delivered to you through my servants the prophets.' But they would not listen and were as stiff-necked as their fathers, who did not trust in the LORD their God" (17:13, 14).

KEY PEOPLE:
Elijah, Elisha, Shunammite woman, Naaman, Jezebel, Jehu, Joash, Hezekiah, Sennacherib, Isaiah, Manasseh, Josiah, Jehoiakim, Zedekiah, Nebuchadnezzar

SPECIAL FEATURES:
The 17 prophetic books at the end of the Old Testament give great insights into the time period of 2 Kings.

SPARKLING as it crashes against boulders along its banks, the river swiftly cascades toward the sea. The current grabs, pushes, and tugs at leaves and logs, carrying them along for the ride. Here and there a sportsman is spotted in a kayak or a canoe, going with the flow. Gravity pulls the water, and the river pulls the rest . . . downward. Suddenly, a silver missile breaks the surface and darts upstream, and then another. Oblivious to the swirling opposition, the shining salmon swim against the stream. They must go upstream, and nothing will stop them from reaching their destination.

The current of society's river is flowing fast and furious, pulling downward everything in its way. It would be easy to float along with the current. But God calls us to swim against the flow. It will not be easy, and we may be alone, but it will be right.

In the book of 2 Kings, we read of evil rulers, rampant idolatry, and a complacent populace—certainly pulling downward. Despite the pressure to conform, to turn from the Lord and to serve only self, a minority of chosen people moved in the opposite direction, toward God. The Bethel prophets and others, as well as two righteous kings, spoke God's word and stood for him. As you read 2 Kings, watch these courageous individuals. Catch the strength and force of Elijah and Elisha and the commitment of Hezekiah and Josiah, and determine to be one who swims against the current!

Second Kings continues the history of Israel, halfway between the death of David and the death of the nation. Israel had been divided (1 Kings 12), and the two kingdoms had begun to slide into idolatry and corruption toward collapse and captivity. Second Kings relates the sordid stories of the 12 kings of the northern kingdom (called Israel) and the 16 kings of the southern kingdom (called Judah). For 130 years Israel endured the succession of evil rulers until they were conquered by Shalmaneser of Assyria and led into captivity in 722 B.C. (17:6). Of all the kings in both the north and south, only two—Hezekiah and Josiah—were called good. Because of their obedience to God and the spiritual revivals during their reigns, Judah stood for an additional 136 years until falling to Nebuchadnezzar and the Babylonians in 586 B.C.

Throughout this dark period, the Bible mentions 30 prophets who proclaimed God's message to the people and their leaders. Most notable of these fearless people of God are Elijah and Elisha. As Elijah neared the end of his earthly ministry, Elisha asked for a double portion of his beloved mentor's spirit (2:9). Soon after, Elijah was taken to heaven in a whirlwind (2:11), and Elisha became God's spokesman to the northern kingdom. Elisha's life was filled with signs, proclamations, warnings, and miracles. Four of the most memorable are the flowing oil (4:1–7), the healing of the Shunammite woman's son (4:8–37), the healing of Naaman's leprosy (5:1–27), and the floating axhead (6:1–7).

Even in the midst of terrible situations, God will have his faithful minority, his remnant (19:31). He desires courageous men and women to proclaim his truth.

THE BLUEPRINT

A. THE DIVIDED KINGDOM
(1:1—17:41)
1. Elisha's ministry
2. Kings of Israel and Judah
3. Israel is exiled to Assyria

B. THE SURVIVING KINGDOM
(18:1—25:30)
1. Kings of Judah
2. Judah is exiled to Babylon

Although Israel had the witness and power of Elisha, the nation turned from God and was exiled to Assyria. Assyria filled the northern kingdom with people from other lands. There has been no return from this captivity—it was permanent. Such is the end of all who shut God out of their lives.

The northern kingdom was destroyed, and prophets were predicting the same fate for Judah. What more could cause the nation to repent? Hezekiah and Josiah were able to stem the tide of evil. They both repaired the temple and gathered the people for the Passover. Josiah eradicated idolatry from the land, but as soon as these good kings were gone, the people returned again to living their own way instead of God's way. Each individual must believe and live for God in his or her family, church, and nation.

MEGATHEMES

THEME	EXPLANATION	IMPORTANCE
Elisha	The purpose of Elisha's ministry was to restore respect for God and his message, and he stood firmly against the evil kings of Israel. By faith, with courage and prayer, he revealed not only God's judgment on sin but also his mercy, love, and tenderness toward faithful people.	Elisha's mighty miracles showed that God controls not only great armies but also events in everyday life. When we listen to and obey God, he shows us his power to transform any situation. God's care is for all who are willing to follow him. He can perform miracles in our lives.
Idolatry	Every evil king in both Israel and Judah encouraged idolatry. These false gods represented war, cruelty, power, and sex. Although they had God's law, priests, and prophets to guide them, these kings sought priests and prophets whom they could manipulate to their own advantage.	An idol is any idea, ability, possession, or person that we regard more highly than God. We condemn Israel and Judah for foolishly worshiping idols, but we also worship other gods—power, money, physical attractiveness. Those who believe in God must resist the lure of these attractive idols.
Evil Kings/ Good Kings	Only 20 percent of Israel and Judah's kings followed God. The evil kings were shortsighted. They thought they could control their nations' destinies by importing other religions, forming alliances with pagan nations, and enriching themselves. The good kings had to spend most of their time undoing the evil done by their predecessors.	Although the evil kings led the people into sin, the priests, princes, heads of families, and military leaders all had to cooperate with the evil plans and practices in order for them to be carried out. We cannot discharge our responsibility to obey God by blaming our leaders. We are responsible to know God's Word and obey it.
God's Patience	God told his people that if they obeyed him, they would live successfully; if they disobeyed, they would be judged and destroyed. God had been patient with the people for hundreds of years. He sent many prophets to guide them. And he gave ample warning of coming destruction. But even God's patience has limits.	God is patient with us. He gives us many chances to hear his message, to turn from sin, and to believe him. His patience does not mean he is indifferent to how we live, nor does it mean we can ignore his warnings. His patience should make us want to come to him now.
Judgment	After King Solomon's reign, Israel lasted 209 years before the Assyrians destroyed it; Judah lasted 345 years before the Babylonians took Jerusalem. After repeated warnings to his people, God used these evil nations as instruments for his justice.	The consequences of rejecting God's commands and purpose for our lives are severe. He will not ignore unbelief or rebellion. We must believe in him and accept Christ's sacrificial death on our behalf, or we will be judged also.

KEY PLACES IN 2 KINGS

The broken lines (— · — ·) indicate modern boundaries.

The history of both Israel and Judah was much affected by the prophet Elisha's ministry. He served Israel for 50 years, fighting the idolatry of its kings and calling its people back to God.

1 Jericho   Elijah's ministry had come to an end. He touched his cloak to the Jordan River, and he and Elisha crossed on dry ground. Elijah was taken by God in a whirlwind, and Elisha returned alone with the cloak. The prophets in Jericho realized that Elisha was Elijah's replacement (1:1—2:25).

2 Desert of Edom   The king of Moab rebelled against Israel, so the nations of Israel, Judah, and Edom decided to attack from the desert of Edom but ran out of water. The kings consulted Elisha, who said God would send both water and victory (3:1—27).

3 Shunem   Elisha cared for individuals and their needs. He helped a woman clear a debt by giving her a supply of oil to

sell. For another family in Shunem, he raised a son from the dead (4:1–37).

4 Gilgal   Elisha cared for the young prophets in Gilgal—he removed poison from a stew, made a small amount of food feed everyone, and even caused an axhead to float so it could be retrieved. It was to Elisha that Naaman, a commander in the Aramean army, came to be healed of leprosy (4:38—6:7).

5 Dothan   Although he cured an Aramean commander's leprosy, Elisha was loyal to Israel. He knew the Aramean army's battle plans and kept Israel's king informed. The Aramean king tracked Elisha down in Dothan and surrounded the city, hoping to kill him. But Elisha prayed that the Arameans would be blinded; then he led the blinded army into Samaria, Israel's capital city (6:8–23).

6 Samaria   But the Arameans didn't learn their lesson. They later besieged Samaria. Ironically, Israel's king thought it was Elisha's fault, but Elisha said food would be available in abundance the next day. True to Elisha's word, the Lord caused panic in the Aramean camp, and the enemy ran, leaving their supplies to Samaria's starving people (6:24—7:20).

7 Damascus   Despite Elisha's loyalty to Israel, he obeyed God and traveled to Damascus, the capital of Aram. King Ben-Hadad was sick, and he sent Hazael to ask Elisha if he would recover. Elisha knew the king would die and told this to Hazael. But Hazael then murdered Ben-Hadad, making himself king. Later, Israel and Judah joined forces to fight this new Aramean threat (8:1–29).

8 Ramoth Gilead   As Israel and Judah warred with Aram, Elisha sent a young prophet to Ramoth Gilead to anoint Jehu as Israel's next king. Jehu set out to destroy the wicked dynasties of Israel and Judah, killing kings Joram and Ahaziah, and wicked Queen Jezebel. He then destroyed King Ahab's family and all the Baal worshipers in Israel (9:1—11:1).

9 Jerusalem   Power-hungry Athaliah became queen of Judah when her son Ahaziah was killed. She had all her grandsons killed except Joash, who was hidden by his aunt. Joash was crowned king at the age of seven and overthrew Athaliah. Meanwhile in Samaria, the Arameans continued to harass Israel. Israel's new king met with Elisha and was told that he would be victorious over Aram three times (11:2—13:19).

Following Elisha's death came a series of evil kings in Israel. Their idolatry and rejection of God caused their downfall. The Assyrian empire captured Samaria and took most of the Israelites into captivity (13:20—17:41). Judah had a short reprieve because of a few good kings who destroyed idols and worshiped God. But many strayed from God. So Jerusalem fell to the next world power, Babylon (18:1—25:30).

A. THE DIVIDED KINGDOM (1:1—17:41)

Elisha begins his ministry to the northern kingdom after Elijah is taken away by a chariot of fire. Elisha performs many miracles and calls Israel to return to God, but they persist in their wickedness. Israel is defeated by Assyria, and the people of the northern kingdom are exiled, never to return. Such is the end of all those who ignore God's warnings and demand their own way in their desire to sin.

The LORD's Judgment on Ahaziah

1 After Ahab's death, Moab[a] rebelled against Israel. ²Now Ahaziah had fallen through the lattice of his upper room in Samaria and injured himself. So he sent messengers,[b] saying to them, "Go and consult Baal-Zebub,[c] the god of Ekron,[d] to see if I will recover[e] from this injury."

³But the angel[f] of the LORD said to Elijah[g] the Tishbite, "Go up and meet the messengers of the king of Samaria and ask them, 'Is it because there is no God in Israel that you are going off to consult Baal-Zebub, the god of Ekron?' ⁴Therefore this is what the LORD says: 'You will not leave[h] the bed you are lying on. You will certainly die!'" So Elijah went.

⁵When the messengers returned to the king, he asked them, "Why have you come back?"

⁶"A man came to meet us," they replied. "And he said to us, 'Go back to the king who sent you and tell him, "This is what the LORD says: Is it because there is no God in Israel that you are sending men to consult Baal-Zebub, the god of Ekron? Therefore you will not leave the bed you are lying on. You will certainly die!"'"

⁷The king asked them, "What kind of man was it who came to meet you and told you this?"

⁸They replied, "He was a man with a garment of hair[i] and with a leather belt around his waist."

The king said, "That was Elijah the Tishbite."

⁹Then he sent to Elijah a captain with his company of fifty men. The captain went up to Elijah, who was sitting on the top of a hill, and said to him, "Man of God, the king says, 'Come down!'"

¹⁰Elijah answered the captain, "If I am a man of God, may fire come down from heaven and consume you and your fifty men!" Then fire[j] fell from heaven and consumed the captain and his men.

¹¹At this the king sent to Elijah another captain with his fifty men. The captain said to him, "Man of God, this is what the king says, 'Come down at once!'"

¹²"If I am a man of God," Elijah replied, "may fire come down from heaven and consume you and your fifty men!" Then the fire of God fell from heaven and consumed him and his fifty men.

¹³So the king sent a third captain with his fifty men. This third captain went up and fell on his knees before Elijah. "Man of God," he begged, "please have respect for my life[k] and the lives of these fifty men, your servants! ¹⁴See, fire has fallen from heaven and consumed the first two captains and all their men. But now have respect for my life!"

¹⁵The angel[l] of the LORD said to Elijah, "Go down with him; do not be afraid[m] of him." So Elijah got up and went down with him to the king.

1:1
[a] 2Sa 8:2; 2Ki 3:5

1:2
[b] ver 16
[c] Mk 3:22
[d] Mt 10:25
[e] 2Ki 8:7-10

1:3
[f] Ge 16:7
[g] 1Ki 17:1

1:4
[h] ver 6, 16

1:8
[i] Zec 13:4; Mt 3:4; Mk 1:6

1:10
[j] 1Ki 18:38; Lk 9:54

1:13
[k] 1Sa 26:21; Ps 72:14

1:15
[l] ver 3
[m] Isa 51:12; Jer 1:17; Eze 2:6

1:1 Because 1 and 2 Kings were originally one book, 2 Kings continues where 1 Kings ends. The once great nation of Israel was split in two because the people forgot God. The book begins with Elijah, a prophet of God, being carried away to heaven. It ends with the people of Israel and Judah being taken into captivity. In 1 Kings, the beautiful temple of God was built. In 2 Kings, it is desecrated and destroyed.

Our world is strikingly similar to the world described in 2 Kings. National and local governments do not seek God, and countries are tormented by war. Many people follow the false gods of technology, materialism, and war. True worship of God is rare on the earth.

In our chaotic and corrupt world, we can turn to examples such as David, Elijah, and Elisha, who were devoted to God's high honor and moral law and who brought about renewal and change in their society. More important, we can look to Jesus Christ, the perfect example. For nations to do God's will, they need individuals who will do God's work. If your heart is committed to God, he can work through you to accomplish the work he has called you to do.

1:2 Baal-Zebub was not the same god as Baal, the Canaanite god worshiped by Ahab and Jezebel (1 Kings 16:31–33). Baal-Zebub was another popular god whose temple was located in the city of Ekron. Because this god was thought to have the power of prophecy, King Ahaziah sent messengers to Ekron to learn of his fate. Supernatural power and mystery were associated with Baal-Zebub. Ahaziah's action showed the king's disrespect for God.

1:8 For more information on Elijah, see his Profile in 1 Kings 18, p. 527.

1:13-15 Notice how the third captain went to Elijah. Although the first two captains called Elijah "man of God," they were not being genuine—God was not in their hearts. The third captain also called him "man of God," but he humbly begged for mercy. His attitude showed respect for God and his power and saved the lives of his men. Effective living begins with a right attitude toward God. Before religious words come to your mouth, make sure they are from your heart. Let respect, humility, and servanthood characterize your attitude toward God and others.

[16]He told the king, "This is what the LORD says: Is it because there is no God in Israel for you to consult that you have sent messengers to consult Baal-Zebub, the god of Ekron? Because you have done this, you will never leave the bed you are lying on. You will certainly die!" [17]So he died, according to the word of the LORD that Elijah had spoken.

Because Ahaziah had no son, Joram[a][n] succeeded him as king in the second year of Jehoram son of Jehoshaphat king of Judah. [18]As for all the other events of Ahaziah's reign, and what he did, are they not written in the book of the annals of the kings of Israel?

1. Elisha's ministry
Elijah Taken Up to Heaven

2 When the LORD was about to take[o] Elijah up to heaven in a whirlwind, Elijah and Elisha[p] were on their way from Gilgal. [2]Elijah said to Elisha, "Stay here; the LORD has sent me to Bethel."

But Elisha said, "As surely as the LORD lives and as you live, I will not leave you."[q] So they went down to Bethel.

[3]The company of the prophets at Bethel came out to Elisha and asked, "Do you know that the LORD is going to take your master from you today?"

"Yes, I know," Elisha replied, "but do not speak of it."

[4]Then Elijah said to him, "Stay here, Elisha; the LORD has sent me to Jericho."

And he replied, "As surely as the LORD lives and as you live, I will not leave you." So they went to Jericho.

[5]The company of the prophets at Jericho went up to Elisha and asked him, "Do you know that the LORD is going to take your master from you today?"

"Yes, I know," he replied, "but do not speak of it."

[6]Then Elijah said to him, "Stay here; the LORD has sent me to the Jordan."[r]

And he replied, "As surely as the LORD lives and as you live, I will not leave you." So the two of them walked on.

[7]Fifty men of the company of the prophets went and stood at a distance, facing the place where Elijah and Elisha had stopped at the Jordan. [8]Elijah took his cloak,[s] rolled it up and struck[t] the water with it. The water divided[u] to the right and to the left, and the two of them crossed over on dry[v] ground.

[9]When they had crossed, Elijah said to Elisha, "Tell me, what can I do for you before I am taken from you?"

"Let me inherit a double portion of your spirit," Elisha replied.

[10]"You have asked a difficult thing," Elijah said, "yet if you see me when I am taken from you, it will be yours—otherwise not."

[11]As they were walking along and talking together, suddenly a chariot of fire[w] and horses of fire appeared and separated the two of them, and Elijah went up to heaven in a whirlwind. [12]Elisha saw this and cried out, "My father! My father! The chariots[x] and horsemen of Israel!" And Elisha saw him no more. Then he took hold of his own clothes and tore them apart.

[a]*17 Hebrew* Jehoram, *a variant of* Joram

1:17
[n]2Ki 3:1; 8:16

2:1
[o]Ge 5:24; Heb 11:5
[p]1Ki 19:16, 21

2:2
[q]Ru 1:16; 1Sa 1:26

2:6
[r]Jos 3:15

2:8
[s]1Ki 19:19
[t]ver 14
[u]Ex 14:21
[v]Ex 14:22, 29

2:11
[w]2Ki 6:17; Ps 104:3, 4

2:12
[x]2Ki 13:14

1:18 The book of the annals of the kings of Israel and the book of the annals of the kings of Judah (8:23) were history books. The inspired writer of 2 Kings selected facts from these books to retell the story of Israel and Judah from God's perspective. God directed the writer's thoughts and selection process to make sure that the truth, God's Word, would be written.

2:3 A "company of the prophets" was similar to a school, a gathering of disciples around a recognized prophet, such as Elijah or Elisha. These companies of prophets, located throughout the country, helped stem the tide of spiritual and moral decline in the nation begun under Jeroboam. The students at Bethel were eyewitnesses to the succession of the prophetic ministry from Elijah to Elisha.

2:8 Elijah's cloak was a symbol of his authority as a prophet.

2:9 Elisha asked for a double portion of Elijah's spirit (prophetic ministry). Deuteronomy 21:17 helps explain Elisha's request. According to custom, the firstborn son would receive a double portion of the father's inheritance (see the note on Genesis 25:31). Elisha was asking to be Elijah's heir, or successor, the one who would continue Elijah's work as leader of the prophets. But the decision to grant this request was up to God. Elijah only told Elisha how he would know if his request had been granted.

2:9 God granted Elisha's request because Elisha's motives were pure. His main goal was not to be better or more powerful than Elijah, but to accomplish more for God. If our motives are pure, we don't have to be afraid to ask great things from God. When we ask God for great power or ability, we need to examine our desires and get rid of any selfishness we find. To have the Holy Spirit's help, we must be willing to ask.

2:11 Elijah was taken to heaven without dying. He is the second person mentioned in Scripture to have this honor. Enoch was the first (Genesis 5:21–24). The other prophets may not have seen God take Elijah, or they may have had a difficult time believing what they had seen. In either case, they wanted to search for Elijah (2:16–18). Finding no physical trace of him would confirm what had happened and strengthen their faith. The only other person taken to heaven in bodily form was Jesus after his resurrection from the dead (Acts 1:9).

2:14
y ver 8

¹³He picked up the cloak that had fallen from Elijah and went back and stood on the bank of the Jordan. ¹⁴Then he took the cloak that had fallen from him and struck ʸ the water with it. "Where now is the Lᴏʀᴅ, the God of Elijah?" he asked. When he struck the water, it divided to the right and to the left, and he crossed over.

2:15
z ver 7

¹⁵The company ᶻ of the prophets from Jericho, who were watching, said, "The spirit of Elijah is resting on Elisha." And they went to meet him and bowed to the ground before him.

2:16
a 1Ki 18:12
b Ac 8:39

¹⁶"Look," they said, "we your servants have fifty able men. Let them go and look for your master. Perhaps the Spirit ᵃ of the Lᴏʀᴅ has picked him up ᵇ and set him down on some mountain or in some valley."

"No," Elisha replied, "do not send them."

¹⁷But they persisted until he was too ashamed to refuse. So he said, "Send them." And they sent fifty men, who searched for three days but did not find him. ¹⁸When they returned to Elisha, who was staying in Jericho, he said to them, "Didn't I tell you not to go?"

Healing of the Water

¹⁹The men of the city said to Elisha, "Look, our lord, this town is well situated, as you can see, but the water is bad and the land is unproductive."

²⁰"Bring me a new bowl," he said, "and put salt in it." So they brought it to him.

2:21
c Ex 15:25;
2Ki 4:41; 6:6

²¹Then he went out to the spring and threw ᶜ the salt into it, saying, "This is what the Lᴏʀᴅ says: 'I have healed this water. Never again will it cause death or make the land unproductive.'" ²²And the water has remained wholesome to this day, according to the word Elisha had spoken.

KINGS TO DATE AND THEIR ENEMIES

852
JORAM
With Judah,
defeated Mesha
(Moab), and was
miraculously
delivered from
Ben-Hadad II
(Aram)
2 Kgs 1:17;
3:1—8:25
2 Chr 22:5–7

853
AHAZIAH
1 Kgs 22:40—
2 Kgs 1:18
2 Chr 20:35–37

841

I S R A E L

J U D A H

872
JEHOSHAPHAT
Defeated by Ben-Hadad II
(Aram), gained miraculous
victory over Moab and
Ammon, and crushed a
rebellion by Mesha
(Moab)
2 Kgs 22:41–50
2 Chr 17:1—21:1
Co-regency 853–848

853
JEHORAM
Lost dominion over
Edom, assaulted by
Philistines and Arabs
2 Kgs 8:16–24
2 Chr 21:1–20

848   841

All dates are B.C.
Solid section of the timeline indicates co-regency.
For all the kings of Israel and Judah, see the chart at the end of 1 Kings.

2:13–25 These three incidents were testimonies to Elisha's commission as a prophet of God. They are recorded to demonstrate Elisha's new power and authority as Israel's chief prophet under God's ultimate power and authority.

2:14 Elisha did not strike the water out of disrespect for God

or Elijah. He was pleading with God to confirm his appointment as Elijah's successor.

Elisha Is Jeered

23 From there Elisha went up to Bethel. As he was walking along the road, some youths came out of the town and jeered at him. "Go on up, you baldhead!" they said. "Go on up, you baldhead!" 24 He turned around, looked at them and called down a curse on them in the name of the LORD. Then two bears came out of the woods and mauled forty-two of the youths. 25 And he went on to Mount Carmel *d* and from there returned to Samaria.

2:25
d 1Ki 18:20

Moab Revolts

3 Joram *a e* son of Ahab became king of Israel in Samaria in the eighteenth year of Jehoshaphat king of Judah, and he reigned twelve years. 2 He did evil in the eyes of the LORD, but not as his father *f* and mother had done. He got rid of the sacred stone of Baal that his father had made. 3 Nevertheless he clung to the sins *g* of Jeroboam son of Nebat, which he had caused Israel to commit; he did not turn away from them.

4 Now Mesha king of Moab raised sheep, and he had to supply the king of Israel with a hundred thousand lambs *h* and with the wool of a hundred thousand rams. 5 But after Ahab died, the king of Moab rebelled *i* against the king of Israel. 6 So at that time King Joram set out from Samaria and mobilized all Israel. 7 He also sent this message to Jehoshaphat king of Judah: "The king of Moab has rebelled against me. Will you go with me to fight *j* against Moab?"

"I will go with you," he replied. "I am as you are, my people as your people, my horses as your horses."

8 "By what route shall we attack?" he asked.

"Through the Desert of Edom," he answered.

9 So the king of Israel set out with the king of Judah and the king of Edom. *k* After a roundabout march of seven days, the army had no more water for themselves or for the animals with them.

3:1
e 2Ki 1:17
3:2
f 1Ki 16:30-32
3:3
g 1Ki 12:28-32
3:4
h Isa 16:1
3:5
i 2Ki 1:1
3:7
j 1Ki 22:4
3:9
k 1Ki 22:47

a 1 Hebrew *Jehoram*, a variant of *Joram*; also in verse 6

2:23, 24 This group of youths was from Bethel, the religious center of idolatry in the northern kingdom, and they probably were warning Elisha not to speak against their immorality as Elijah had done. They were not merely teasing Elisha about his baldness, but showing severe disrespect for Elisha's message and God's power. They may also have jeered because of their disbelief in the chariot of fire that had taken Elijah. When Elisha cursed them, he did not call out the bears himself. God sent them as a judgment for their callous unbelief.

2:23, 24 These young men jeered at God's messenger and paid for it with their lives. Making fun of religious leaders has been a popular sport through the ages. To take a stand for God is to be different from the world and vulnerable to verbal abuse. When we are cynical and sarcastic toward religious leaders, we are in danger of mocking not just the person, but also the spiritual message. While we are not to condone the sin that some leaders commit, we need to pray for them, not laugh at them. True leaders, those who follow God, need to be heard with respect and encouraged in their ministry.

3:1 Although 1:17 says that Jehoram was king of Judah, 3:1 says that Jehoshaphat was Judah's king. As a king grew older, often his son would rule beside him. Jehoshaphat, nearing the end of his reign, appointed his son Jehoram to rule with him. Jehoram served as coruler with Jehoshaphat for five years (853–848 B.C.; he is mentioned again in 8:16–24). Joram, king of Israel, was Ahab's son and Ahaziah's brother (1:17). Both Ahab (1 Kings 16:29—22:40) and Ahaziah (1:2–18) served as kings of Israel before Joram.

3:3 The sins of Israel's kings are often compared to "the sins of Jeroboam," the first ruler of the northern kingdom of Israel. His great sin was to institute idol worship throughout his kingdom, causing people to turn away from God (1 Kings 12:25–33). By ignoring God and allowing idol worship, Joram clung to Jeroboam's sins.

3:4, 5 Israel and Judah held some of the most fertile land and strategic positions in the ancient Near East. It is no wonder that neighboring nations like Moab envied them and constantly attempted to seize the land. Moab lay just southeast of Israel. The country had been under Israel's control for some time due to Ahab's strong military leadership. When Ahab died, Mesha, the Moabite king, took the opportunity to rebel. While Israel's next king, Ahaziah, did nothing about the revolt, his successor, Joram, decided to take action. He joined forces with Jehoshaphat, king of Judah, and went to fight the Moabites. Together, Israel and Judah brought the Moabites to the brink of surrender. But when they saw the Moabite king sacrifice his own son and successor (3:27), they withdrew even though they had won the battle. Moab fought many other battles with both Israel and Judah. Some of them, in fact, were recorded by Mesha (c. 840 B.C.), who carved his exploits on a plaque called the Moabite Stone (discovered in 1868).

WAR AGAINST MOAB
Moab's king rebelled against Israel. So Joram, Israel's king, and Jehoshaphat, Judah's king, attacked Moab. In the parched and rugged Desert of Edom, the armies ran out of water, but Elisha promised that both water and victory would soon come.

¹⁰"What!" exclaimed the king of Israel. "Has the Lord called us three kings together only to hand us over to Moab?"

¹¹But Jehoshaphat asked, "Is there no prophet of the Lord here, that we may inquire *l* of the Lord through him?"

An officer of the king of Israel answered, "Elisha son of Shaphat is here. He used to pour water on the hands of Elijah. *a*"

¹²Jehoshaphat said, "The word of the Lord is with him." So the king of Israel and Jehoshaphat and the king of Edom went down to him.

¹³Elisha said to the king of Israel, "What do we have to do with each other? Go to the prophets of your father and the prophets of your mother."

"No," the king of Israel answered, "because it was the Lord who called us three kings together to hand us over to Moab."

¹⁴Elisha said, "As surely as the Lord Almighty lives, whom I serve, if I did not have respect for the presence of Jehoshaphat king of Judah, I would not look at you or even notice you. ¹⁵But now bring me a harpist." *m*

While the harpist was playing, the hand *n* of the Lord came upon Elisha ¹⁶and he said, "This is what the Lord says: Make this valley full of ditches. ¹⁷For this is what the Lord says: You will see neither wind nor rain, yet this valley will be filled with water, and you, your cattle and your other animals will drink. ¹⁸This is an easy *o* thing in the eyes of the Lord; he will also hand Moab over to you. ¹⁹You will overthrow every fortified city and every major town. You will cut down every good tree, stop up all the springs, and ruin every good field with stones."

²⁰The next morning, about the time *p* for offering the sacrifice, there it was—water flowing from the direction of Edom! And the land was filled with water.

a 11 That is, he was Elijah's personal servant.

3:11
l 1Ki 22:7

3:15
m 1Sa 16:23
n Eze 1:3

3:18
o Ge 18:14;
Jer 32:17, 27;
Mk 10:27

3:20
p Ex 29:39-40

MIRACLES OF ELIJAH & ELISHA

Baal, the false god worshiped by many Israelites, was the god of rain, fire, and farm crops. He also demanded child sacrifice. Elijah's and Elisha's miracles repeatedly show the power of the true God over the purported realm of Baal, as well as the value God places on the life of a child.

Miracle	Reference	Factors
ELIJAH		
1. Food brought by ravens	1 Kings 17:5, 6.	Food
2. Widow's food multiplied	1 Kings 17:12–16.	Flour and oil
3. Widow's son raised to life	1 Kings 17:17–24.	Life of a child
4. Altar and sacrifice consumed	1 Kings 18:16–46.	Fire and water
5. Ahaziah's soldiers consumed	2 Kings 1:9–14.	Fire
6. Jordan River parted	2 Kings 2:6–8.	Water
7. Transported to heaven	2 Kings 2:11, 12.	Fire and wind
ELISHA		
1. Jordan River parted	2 Kings 2:13, 14.	Water
2. Spring purified at Jericho	2 Kings 2:19–22.	Water
3. Widow's oil multiplied	2 Kings 4:1–7.	Oil
4. Dead boy raised to life	2 Kings 4:18–37.	Life of a child
5. Poison in stew purified	2 Kings 4:38–41.	Flour
6. Prophets' food multiplied	2 Kings 4:42–44.	Bread and grain
7. Naaman healed of leprosy	2 Kings 5:1–14.	Water
8. Gehazi became leprous	2 Kings 5:15–27.	Words alone
9. Axhead floated	2 Kings 6:1–7.	Water
10. Aramean army blinded	2 Kings 6:8–23.	Elisha's prayer

3:10 Edom was under Judah's control; thus they marched with them, making three kings.

3:11–20 Jehoshaphat's request for "a prophet of the Lord" shows how true worship and religious experience in both Israel and Judah had declined. In David's day, both the high priest and the prophets gave the king advice. But most of the priests had left Israel (see the first note on 1 Kings 17:1), and God's prophets were seen as messengers of doom (1 Kings 22:18). This miracle predicted by Elisha affirmed God's power and authority and vali-dated Elisha's ministry. In 2 Chronicles 18, King Jehoshaphat of Judah and King Ahab of Israel gave the prophet Micaiah a similar request. But they ignored God's advice—with disastrous results.

3:15 In Old Testament times music often accompanied prophecy (1 Chronicles 25:1).

3:20 The morning sacrifice was one of two sacrifices that the priests were required to offer each day.

²¹Now all the Moabites had heard that the kings had come to fight against them; so every man, young and old, who could bear arms was called up and stationed on the border. ²²When they got up early in the morning, the sun was shining on the water. To the Moabites across the way, the water looked red—like blood. ²³"That's blood!" they said. "Those kings must have fought and slaughtered each other. Now to the plunder, Moab!"

²⁴But when the Moabites came to the camp of Israel, the Israelites rose up and fought them until they fled. And the Israelites invaded the land and slaughtered the Moabites. ²⁵They destroyed the towns, and each man threw a stone on every good field until it was covered. They stopped up all the springs and cut down every good tree. Only Kir Hareseth *q* was left with its stones in place, but men armed with slings surrounded it and attacked it as well.

²⁶When the king of Moab saw that the battle had gone against him, he took with him seven hundred swordsmen to break through to the king of Edom, but they failed. ²⁷Then he took his firstborn *r* son, who was to succeed him as king, and offered him as a sacrifice on the city wall. The fury against Israel was great; they withdrew and returned to their own land.

The Widow's Oil

4 The wife of a man from the company of the prophets cried out to Elisha, "Your servant my husband is dead, and you know that he revered the LORD. But now his creditor *s* is coming to take my two boys as his slaves."

²Elisha replied to her, "How can I help you? Tell me, what do you have in your house?"

"Your servant has nothing there at all," she said, "except a little oil." *t*

³Elisha said, "Go around and ask all your neighbors for empty jars. Don't ask for just a few. ⁴Then go inside and shut the door behind you and your sons. Pour oil into all the jars, and as each is filled, put it to one side."

⁵She left him and afterward shut the door behind her and her sons. They brought the jars to her and she kept pouring. ⁶When all the jars were full, she said to her son, "Bring me another one."

But he replied, "There is not a jar left." Then the oil stopped flowing.

⁷She went and told the man of God, *u* and he said, "Go, sell the oil and pay your debts. You and your sons can live on what is left."

The Shunammite's Son Restored to Life

⁸One day Elisha went to Shunem. *v* And a well-to-do woman was there, who urged him to stay for a meal. So whenever he came by, he stopped there to eat. ⁹She said to her husband,

Margin references:
3:25 *q*ver 19; Isa 16:7; Jer 48:31, 36
3:27 *r*Am 2:1; Mic 6:7
4:1 *s*Lev 25:39-43; Ne 5:3-5
4:2 *t*1Ki 17:12
4:7 *u*1Ki 12:22
4:8 *v*Jos 19:18

4:1 Poor people and debtors were allowed to pay their debts by selling themselves or their children as slaves. God ordered rich people and creditors not to take advantage of these people during their time of extreme need (see Deuteronomy 15:1–18 for an explanation of these practices). This woman's creditor was not acting in the spirit of God's law. Elisha's kind deed demonstrates that God wants us to go beyond simply keeping the law. We must also show compassion.

4:1ff This chapter records four of God's miracles through Elisha: providing money for a poverty-stricken widow (4:1–7); raising a dead boy to life (4:32–37); purifying poisonous food (4:38–41); and providing food for 100 men (4:42–44). These miracles show God's tenderness and care for those who are faithful to him.

When reading the Old Testament, it is easy to focus on God's harsh judgment of the rebellious and to minimize his tender care for those who love and serve him. Seeing God at work providing for his followers helps us keep his severe justice toward the unrepentant in proper perspective.

4:6 The woman and her sons collected jars from their neighbors, pouring oil into them from their one pot. The oil was probably olive oil and was used for cooking, for lamps, and for fuel. The oil stopped pouring only when they ran out of containers. The number of jars they gathered was an indication of their faith. God's provision was as large as their faith and willingness to obey. Beware of limiting God's blessings by a lack of faith and obedience. God is able to do immeasurably more than all we ask or imagine (Ephesians 3:20).

4:9 The Shunammite woman realized that Elisha was a man of God, and so she prepared a room for him to use whenever he was in town. She did this out of kindness and because she sensed a need, not for any selfish motives. Soon, however, her kindness would be rewarded far beyond her wildest dreams. How sensitive are you to those who pass by your home and flow through your life—especially those who teach and preach God's Word? What

THE FAMILY IN SHUNEM
Elisha often stayed with a kind family in Shunem. When the son suddenly died, his mother traveled to Mount Carmel to find Elisha. He returned with her and raised the boy from the dead. Elisha then went to his home in Gilgal.

Map labels: Mediterranean Sea; Mount Carmel; Sea of Galilee; N; Shunem; ISRAEL; Samaria; Jordan River; Gilgal; Jerusalem; Dead Sea; JUDAH; 0 20 Mi.; 0 20 Km.

4:10
wMt 10:41;
Ro 12:13

"I know that this man who often comes our way is a holy man of God. [10]Let's make a small room on the roof and put in it a bed and a table, a chair and a lamp for him. Then he can stay w there whenever he comes to us."

[11]One day when Elisha came, he went up to his room and lay down there. [12]He said to his servant Gehazi, "Call the Shunammite." So he called her, and she stood before him. [13]Elisha said to him, "Tell her, 'You have gone to all this trouble for us. Now what can be done for you? Can we speak on your behalf to the king or the commander of the army?'"

She replied, "I have a home among my own people."

[14]"What can be done for her?" Elisha asked.

Gehazi said, "Well, she has no son and her husband is old."

4:16
xGe 18:10

[15]Then Elisha said, "Call her." So he called her, and she stood in the doorway. [16]"About this time x next year," Elisha said, "you will hold a son in your arms."

"No, my lord," she objected. "Don't mislead your servant, O man of God!"

[17]But the woman became pregnant, and the next year about that same time she gave birth to a son, just as Elisha had told her.

[18]The child grew, and one day he went out to his father, who was with the reapers. [19]"My head! My head!" he said to his father.

His father told a servant, "Carry him to his mother." [20]After the servant had lifted him up and carried him to his mother, the boy sat on her lap until noon, and then he died. [21]She went up and laid him on the bed y of the man of God, then shut the door and went out.

4:21
yver 32

[22]She called her husband and said, "Please send me one of the servants and a donkey so I can go to the man of God quickly and return."

4:23
zNu 10:10;
1Ch 23:31

[23]"Why go to him today?" he asked. "It's not the New Moon z or the Sabbath."

"It's all right," she said.

[24]She saddled the donkey and said to her servant, "Lead on; don't slow down for me unless I tell you." [25]So she set out and came to the man of God at Mount Carmel. a

4:25
a1Ki 18:20;
2Ki 2:25

When he saw her in the distance, the man of God said to his servant Gehazi, "Look! There's the Shunammite! [26]Run to meet her and ask her, 'Are you all right? Is your husband all right? Is your child all right?'"

"Everything is all right," she said.

[27]When she reached the man of God at the mountain, she took hold of his feet. Gehazi came over to push her away, but the man of God said, "Leave her alone! She is in bitter distress, but the LORD has hidden it from me and has not told me why."

[28]"Did I ask you for a son, my lord?" she said. "Didn't I tell you, 'Don't raise my hopes'?"

4:29
b1Ki 18:46; 2Ki 9:1
cEx 4:27

[29]Elisha said to Gehazi, "Tuck your cloak into your belt,b take my staff c in your hand and run. If you meet anyone, do not greet him, and if anyone greets you, do not answer. Lay my staff on the boy's face."

[30]But the child's mother said, "As surely as the LORD lives and as you live, I will not leave you." So he got up and followed her.

[31]Gehazi went on ahead and laid the staff on the boy's face, but there was no sound or response. So Gehazi went back to meet Elisha and told him, "The boy has not awakened."

4:33
d1Ki 17:20; Mt 6:6

[32]When Elisha reached the house, there was the boy lying dead on his couch. [33]He went in, shut the door on the two of them and prayed d to the LORD. [34]Then he got on the bed and lay upon the boy, mouth to mouth, eyes to eyes, hands to hands. As he stretched e himself out upon him, the boy's body grew warm. [35]Elisha turned away and walked back and forth in the room and then got on the bed and stretched out upon him once more. The boy sneezed seven times and opened his eyes. f

4:34
e1Ki 17:21;
Ac 20:10
4:35
f2Ki 8:5

[36]Elisha summoned Gehazi and said, "Call the Shunammite." And he did. When she came, he said, "Take your son." [37]She came in, fell at his feet and bowed to the ground. Then she took her son and went out.

Death in the Pot

4:38
g2Ki 2:1
h2Ki 8:1

[38]Elisha returned to Gilgal g and there was a famine h in that region. While the company of the prophets was meeting with him, he said to his servant, "Put on the large pot and cook some stew for these men."

---

special needs do they have that you could meet? Look for ways to serve and help.

4:32–36 Elisha's prayer and method of raising the dead boy

show God's personal care for hurting people. We must express genuine concern for others as we carry God's message to them. Only then will we faithfully represent our Father in heaven.

39One of them went out into the fields to gather herbs and found a wild vine. He gathered some of its gourds and filled the fold of his cloak. When he returned, he cut them up into the pot of stew, though no one knew what they were. **40**The stew was poured out for the men, but as they began to eat it, they cried out, "O man of God, there is death in the pot!" And they could not eat it.

41Elisha said, "Get some flour." He put it into the pot and said, "Serve it to the people to eat." And there was nothing harmful in the pot. *i*

4:41
*i*Ex 15:25; 2Ki 2:21

Feeding of a Hundred

42A man came from Baal Shalishah,*j* bringing the man of God twenty loaves of barley bread*k* baked from the first ripe grain, along with some heads of new grain. "Give it to the people to eat," Elisha said.

4:42
*j*1Sa 9:4
*k*1Sa 9:7

43"How can I set this before a hundred men?" his servant asked.

But Elisha answered, "Give it to the people to eat. *l* For this is what the LORD says: 'They will eat and have some left over. *m*'" **44**Then he set it before them, and they ate and had some left over, according to the word of the LORD.

4:43
*l*Lk 9:13
*m*Jn 6:12

Naaman Healed of Leprosy

5 Now Naaman was commander of the army of the king of Aram. He was a great man in the sight of his master and highly regarded, because through him the LORD had given victory to Aram. He was a valiant soldier, but he had leprosy. *a n*

5:1
*n*Lk 4:27

2Now bands from Aram had gone out and had taken captive a young girl from Israel, and she served Naaman's wife. **3**She said to her mistress, "If only my master would see the prophet who is in Samaria! He would cure him of his leprosy."

4Naaman went to his master and told him what the girl from Israel had said. **5**"By all means, go," the king of Aram replied. "I will send a letter to the king of Israel." So Naaman left, taking with him ten talents*b* of silver, six thousand shekels*c* of gold and ten sets of clothing. *o* **6**The letter that he took to the king of Israel read: "With this letter I am sending my servant Naaman to you so that you may cure him of his leprosy."

5:5
*o*1Sa 9:7

7As soon as the king of Israel read the letter,*p* he tore his robes and said, "Am I God?*q* Can I kill and bring back to life? *r* Why does this fellow send someone to me to be cured of his leprosy? See how he is trying to pick a quarrel*s* with me!"

5:7
*p*2Ki 19:14
*q*Ge 30:2
*r*Dt 32:39; 1Sa 2:6
*s*1Ki 20:7

8When Elisha the man of God heard that the king of Israel had torn his robes, he sent him this message: "Why have you torn your robes? Have the man come to me and he will know that there is a prophet in Israel." **9**So Naaman went with his horses and chariots and stopped at the door of Elisha's house. **10**Elisha sent a messenger to say to him, "Go, wash *t* yourself seven times in the Jordan, and your flesh will be restored and you will be cleansed."

5:10
*t*Jn 9:7

a 1 The Hebrew word was used for various diseases affecting the skin—not necessarily leprosy; also in verses 3, 6, 7, 11 and 27.   b 5 That is, about 750 pounds (about 340 kilograms)   c 5 That is, about 150 pounds (about 70 kilograms)

4:40 "Death in the pot" means that the food was poisonous. Perhaps a poisonous wild vegetable or herb had been mixed in with the edible plants.

5:1 Leprosy, much like AIDS today, was one of the most feared diseases of the time. Some forms were extremely contagious and, in many cases, incurable. In its worst forms, leprosy led to death. Many lepers were forced out of the cities into quarantined camps. Because Naaman still held his post, he probably had a mild form of the disease, or perhaps it was still in the early stages. In either case, his life would have been tragically shortened by his disease. (For more about leprosy in Bible times, see the note on Leviticus 13:1ff.)

5:2 Aram was Israel's neighbor to the northeast, but the two nations were rarely on friendly terms. Under David, Aram paid tribute to Israel. In Elisha's day, Aram was growing in power and frequently conducted raids on Israel, trying to frustrate the people and bring about political confusion. Israelite captives often would be taken back to Aram after successful raids. Naaman's servant girl was an Israelite, kidnapped from her home and family. Ironically, Naaman's only hope of being cured came from Israel.

5:3, 4 The little girl's faith and Naaman's quest contrast with the stubbornness of Israel's king (5:7). A leader in mighty Aram

sought the God of Israel; Israel's own king would not. We don't know the little girl's name or much about her, but her brief word to her mistress brought healing and faith in God to a powerful Aramean captain. God had placed her for a purpose, and she was faithful. Where has God put you? No matter how humble or small your position, God can use you to spread his Word. Look for opportunities to tell others what God can do. There's no telling who will hear your message!

5:5 The name of Israel's king is not mentioned in this story. The events of 2 Kings 1—8 are mainly about Elisha's ministry and are not intended to be chronological. The king was most likely Jehoram (3:1), but we cannot know for sure.

5:9–15 Naaman, a great hero, was used to getting respect, so he was outraged when Elisha treated him like an ordinary person. A proud man, he expected royal treatment. To wash in a great river would be one thing, but the Jordan was small and dirty. To wash in the Jordan, Naaman thought, was beneath a man of his position. But Naaman had to humble himself and obey Elisha's commands in order to be healed.

Obedience to God begins with humility. We must believe that his way is better than our own. We may not always understand his ways of working, but by humbly obeying, we will receive his blessings. We must remember that (1) God's ways are best;

5:12
u Pr 14:17, 29;
19:11

5:13
v 2Ki 6:21

5:14
w Job 33:25; Lk 4:27

5:15
x Jos 4:24;
1Sa 17:46

5:16
y ver 20, 26;
Ge 14:23

11But Naaman went away angry and said, "I thought that he would surely come out to me and stand and call on the name of the LORD his God, wave his hand over the spot and cure me of my leprosy. **12**Are not Abana and Pharpar, the rivers of Damascus, better than any of the waters of Israel? Couldn't I wash in them and be cleansed?" So he turned and went off in a rage. *u*

13Naaman's servants went to him and said, "My father, *v* if the prophet had told you to do some great thing, would you not have done it? How much more, then, when he tells you, 'Wash and be cleansed'!" **14**So he went down and dipped himself in the Jordan seven times, as the man of God had told him, and his flesh was restored and became clean like that of a young boy. *w*

15Then Naaman and all his attendants went back to the man of God. He stood before him and said, "Now I know *x* that there is no God in all the world except in Israel. Please accept now a gift from your servant."

16The prophet answered, "As surely as the LORD lives, whom I serve, I will not accept a thing." And even though Naaman urged him, he refused. *y*

ELISHA

Few "replacements" in Scripture were as effective as Elisha, who was Elijah's replacement as God's prophet to Israel. But Elisha had a great example to follow in the prophet Elijah. He remained with Elijah until the last moments of his teacher's life on earth. He was willing to follow and learn in order to gain power to do the work to which God had called him.

Both Elijah and Elisha concentrated their efforts on the particular needs of the people around them. The fiery Elijah confronted and exposed idolatry, helping to create an atmosphere where people could freely and publicly worship God. Elisha then moved in to demonstrate God's powerful, yet caring, nature to all who came to him for help. He spent less time in conflict with evil and more in compassionate care of people. The Bible records 18 encounters between Elisha and needy people.

Elisha saw more *in* life than most people because he recognized that with God there was more *to* life. He knew that all we are and have comes to us from God. The miracles that occurred during Elisha's ministry put people in touch with the personal and all-powerful God. Elijah would have been proud of his replacement's work.

We too have great examples to follow—both people in Scripture and those who have positively influenced our lives. We must resist the tendency to think about the limitations that our family background or environment create for us. Instead, we should ask God to use us for his purposes—perhaps, like Elijah, to take a stand against great wrongs or, like Elisha, to show compassion for the daily needs of those around us. Ask him to use you as only he can.

Strengths and accomplishments:	• Was Elijah's successor as a prophet of God • Had a ministry that lasted over 50 years • Had a major impact on four nations: Israel, Judah, Moab, and Aram • Was a man of integrity who did not try to enrich himself at others' expense • Did many miracles to help those in need
Lessons from his life:	• In God's eyes, one measure of greatness is the willingness to serve the poor as well as the powerful • An effective replacement not only learns from his master, but also builds upon his master's achievements
Vital statistics:	• Where: Prophesied to the northern kingdom • Occupations: Farmer, prophet • Relative: Father: Shaphat • Contemporaries: Elijah, Ahab, Jezebel, Jehu
Key verse:	"When they had crossed, Elijah said to Elisha, 'Tell me, what can I do for you before I am taken from you?' 'Let me inherit a double portion of your spirit,' Elisha replied" (2 Kings 2:9).

Elisha's story is told in 1 Kings 19:16—2 Kings 13:20. He is also mentioned in Luke 4:27.

(2) God wants our obedience more than anything else; (3) God can use anything to accomplish his purposes.

5:12 Naaman left in a rage because the cure for his disease seemed too simple. He was a hero, and he expected a heroic cure. Full of pride and self-will, Naaman could not accept the simple cure of faith. Sometimes people react to God's offer of forgiveness in the same way. Just to *believe* in Jesus Christ somehow doesn't seem significant enough to bring eternal life. To obey God's commands doesn't seem heroic. What Naaman

had to do to have his leprosy washed away is similar to what we must do to have our sin washed away—humbly accept God's mercy. Don't let your reaction to the way of faith keep you from the cure you need the most.

5:16 Elisha refused Naaman's money to show that God's favor cannot be purchased. Our money, like Naaman's, is useless when we face death. No matter how much wealth we accumulate in this life, it will evaporate when we stand before God, our Creator. Our faith in Jesus Christ will save us, not our bank accounts.

17"If you will not," said Naaman, "please let me, your servant, be given as much earth z as a pair of mules can carry, for your servant will never again make burnt offerings and sacrifices to any other god but the LORD. 18But may the LORD forgive your servant for this one thing: When my master enters the temple of Rimmon to bow down and he is leaning a on my arm and I bow there also—when I bow down in the temple of Rimmon, may the LORD forgive your servant for this."

19"Go in peace," b Elisha said.

After Naaman had traveled some distance, 20Gehazi, the servant of Elisha the man of God, said to himself, "My master was too easy on Naaman, this Aramean, by not accepting from him what he brought. As surely as the LORD c lives, I will run after him and get something from him."

21So Gehazi hurried after Naaman. When Naaman saw him running toward him, he got down from the chariot to meet him. "Is everything all right?" he asked.

22"Everything is all right," Gehazi answered. "My master sent me to say, 'Two young men from the company of the prophets have just come to me from the hill country of Ephraim. Please give them a talent a of silver and two sets of clothing.'" d

23"By all means, take two talents," said Naaman. He urged Gehazi to accept them, and then tied up the two talents of silver in two bags, with two sets of clothing. He gave them to two of his servants, and they carried them ahead of Gehazi. 24When Gehazi came to the hill, he took the things from the servants and put them away in the house. He sent the men away and they left. 25Then he went in and stood before his master Elisha.

"Where have you been, Gehazi?" Elisha asked.

"Your servant didn't go anywhere," Gehazi answered.

26But Elisha said to him, "Was not my spirit with you when the man got down from his chariot to meet you? Is this the time e to take money, or to accept clothes, olive groves, vineyards, flocks, herds, or menservants and maidservants? 27Naaman's leprosy f will cling to you and to your descendants forever." Then Gehazi went from Elisha's presence and he was leprous, as white as snow. g

An Axhead Floats

6 The company of the prophets said to Elisha, "Look, the place where we meet with you is too small for us. 2Let us go to the Jordan, where each of us can get a pole; and let us build a place there for us to live."

And he said, "Go."

3Then one of them said, "Won't you please come with your servants?"

"I will," Elisha replied. 4And he went with them.

a22 That is, about 75 pounds (about 34 kilograms)

**Side references:**
5:17 z Ex 20:24
5:18 a 2Ki 7:2
5:19 b 1Sa 1:17
5:20 c Ex 20:7
5:22 d ver 5
5:26 e ver 16
5:27 f Nu 12:10 g Ex 4:6

5:18, 19 How could Naaman be forgiven for bowing to a pagan idol? Naaman was not asking for permission to worship the god

ELISHA AND THE ARAMEANS
Elisha knew Aram's battle plans and kept Israel's king informed. The Aramean king tracked down Elisha at Dothan, but Elisha prayed that the Aramean army would be blinded. He then led the blind army into Samaria, Israel's capital city!

Rimmon but to do his civil duty, helping the king get down and up as he bowed. Also known as Hadad, Rimmon, the god of Damascus, was believed to be a god of rain and thunder. Unlike most of his contemporaries, Naaman showed a keen awareness of God's power. Instead of adding God to his nation's collection of idols, he acknowledged that there was only one true God. He did not intend to worship other gods. His asking for pardon in this one area shows the marked contrast between Naaman and the Israelites, who were continually worshiping many idols.

5:20–27 Gehazi saw a perfect opportunity to get rich by selfishly asking for the reward Elisha had refused. Unfortunately, his plan had three problems: (1) he willingly accepted money that had been offered to someone else; (2) he wrongly implied that money could be exchanged for God's free gift of healing and mercy; (3) he lied and tried to cover up his motives for accepting the money. Although Gehazi had been a helpful servant, personal gain had become more important to him than serving God.

This passage is not teaching that money is evil or that ministers should not get paid; instead, it is warning against greed and deceit. True service is motivated by love and devotion to God and seeks no personal gain. As you serve God, check your motives—you can't serve both God and money (Matthew 6:24).

6:1–7 The incident of the floating axhead is recorded to show God's care and provision for those who trust him, even in the insignificant events of everyday life. God is always present.

They went to the Jordan and began to cut down trees. ⁵As one of them was cutting down a tree, the iron axhead fell into the water. "Oh, my lord," he cried out, "it was borrowed!"

6:6
ʰEx 15:25; 2Ki 2:21

⁶The man of God asked, "Where did it fall?" When he showed him the place, Elisha cut a stick and threwʰ it there, and made the iron float. ⁷"Lift it out," he said. Then the man reached out his hand and took it.

Elisha Traps Blinded Arameans

⁸Now the king of Aram was at war with Israel. After conferring with his officers, he said, "I will set up my camp in such and such a place."

6:9
ⁱver 12

⁹The man of God sent word to the kingⁱ of Israel: "Beware of passing that place, because the Arameans are going down there." ¹⁰So the king of Israel checked on the place indicated by the man of God. Time and again Elisha warned the king, so that he was on his guard in such places.

¹¹This enraged the king of Aram. He summoned his officers and demanded of them, "Will you not tell me which of us is on the side of the king of Israel?"

¹²"None of us, my lord the king," said one of his officers, "but Elisha, the prophet who is in Israel, tells the king of Israel the very words you speak in your bedroom."

6:13
ʲGe 37:17

¹³"Go, find out where he is," the king ordered, "so I can send men and capture him." The report came back: "He is in Dothan."ʲ ¹⁴Then he sent horses and chariots and a strong force there. They went by night and surrounded the city.

¹⁵When the servant of the man of God got up and went out early the next morning, an army with horses and chariots had surrounded the city. "Oh, my lord, what shall we do?" the servant asked.

6:16
ᵏ2Ch 32:7;
Ps 55:18; Ro 8:31;
1Jn 4:4

¹⁶"Don't be afraid," the prophet answered. "Those who are with us are moreᵏ than those who are with them."

6:17
ˡ2Ki 2:11, 12;
Ps 68:17; Zec 6:1-7

¹⁷And Elisha prayed, "O LORD, open his eyes so he may see." Then the LORD opened the servant's eyes, and he looked and saw the hills full of horses and chariotsˡ of fire all around Elisha.

6:18
ᵐGe 19:11

¹⁸As the enemy came down toward him, Elisha prayed to the LORD, "Strike these people with blindness."ᵐ So he struck them with blindness, as Elisha had asked.

¹⁹Elisha told them, "This is not the road and this is not the city. Follow me, and I will lead you to the man you are looking for." And he led them to Samaria.

²⁰After they entered the city, Elisha said, "LORD, open the eyes of these men so they can see." Then the LORD opened their eyes and they looked, and there they were, inside Samaria.

6:21
ⁿ2Ki 5:13

²¹When the king of Israel saw them, he asked Elisha, "Shall I kill them, my father?ⁿ Shall I kill them?"

6:22
ᵒDt 20:11;
Ro 12:20

²²"Do not kill them," he answered. "Would you kill men you have capturedᵒ with your own sword or bow? Set food and water before them so that they may eat and drink and then go back to their master." ²³So he prepared a great feast for them, and after they had fin-

6:23
ᵖ2Ki 5:2

ished eating and drinking, he sent them away, and they returned to their master. So the bandsᵖ from Aram stopped raiding Israel's territory.

Famine in Besieged Samaria

²⁴Some time later, Ben-Hadad king of Aram mobilized his entire army and marched up and laid siege to Samaria. ²⁵There was a great famine in the city; the siege lasted so long that

---

Placed in the Bible between the healing of an Aramean general and the deliverance of Israel's army, this miracle also shows Elisha's personal contact with the students in the companies of the prophets. Although he had the respect of kings, Elisha never forgot to care for the faithful. Don't let the importance of your work crowd out your concern for human need.

6:16, 17 Elisha's servant was no longer afraid when he saw God's mighty heavenly army. Faith reveals that God is doing more for his people than we can ever realize through sight alone. When you face difficulties that seem insurmountable, remember that spiritual resources are there even if you can't see them. Look with the eyes of faith and let God show you his resources. If you don't see God working in your life, the problem may be your spiritual eyesight, not God's power.

6:21, 22 Elisha told the king not to kill the Arameans. The king was not to take credit for what God alone had done. In setting

food and water before them, he was heaping "burning coals" on their heads (Proverbs 25:21, 22).

6:23 How long the Arameans stayed away from Israel is not known, but a number of years probably passed before the invasion recorded in 6:24 occurred. The Arameans must have forgotten the time their army had been supernaturally blinded and sent home.

6:24 This was probably Ben-Hadad II, whose father had ruled Aram in the days of Baasha (1 Kings 15:18). Elisha constantly frustrated Ben-Hadad II in his attempts to take control of Israel.

6:25 When a city like Samaria faced famine, it was no small matter. Although its farmers grew enough food to feed the people for a specific season, they did not have enough to maintain them in prolonged times of emergency when all supplies were cut off. This famine was so severe that mothers resorted to eating their children (6:26–30). Deuteronomy 28:49–57 predicted that this would happen when the people of Israel rejected God's leadership.

a donkey's head sold for eighty shekels[a] of silver, and a quarter of a cab[b] of seed pods[c] for five shekels.[d]

26 As the king of Israel was passing by on the wall, a woman cried to him, "Help me, my lord the king!"

27 The king replied, "If the LORD does not help you, where can I get help for you? From the threshing floor? From the winepress?" 28 Then he asked her, "What's the matter?"

She answered, "This woman said to me, 'Give up your son so we may eat him today, and tomorrow we'll eat my son.' 29 So we cooked my son and ate[q] him. The next day I said to her, 'Give up your son so we may eat him,' but she had hidden him."

30 When the king heard the woman's words, he tore his robes. As he went along the wall, the people looked, and there, underneath, he had sackcloth[r] on his body. 31 He said, "May God deal with me, be it ever so severely, if the head of Elisha son of Shaphat remains on his shoulders today!"

32 Now Elisha was sitting in his house, and the elders[s] were sitting with him. The king sent a messenger ahead, but before he arrived, Elisha said to the elders, "Don't you see how this murderer[t] is sending someone to cut off my head? Look, when the messenger comes, shut the door and hold it shut against him. Is not the sound of his master's footsteps behind him?"

33 While he was still talking to them, the messenger came down to him. And ⌊the king⌋ said, "This disaster is from the LORD. Why should I wait[u] for the LORD any longer?"

7 Elisha said, "Hear the word of the LORD. This is what the LORD says: About this time tomorrow, a seah[e] of flour will sell for a shekel[f] and two seahs[g] of barley for a shekel[v] at the gate of Samaria."

2 The officer on whose arm the king was leaning[w] said to the man of God, "Look, even if the LORD should open the floodgates[x] of the heavens, could this happen?"

"You will see it with your own eyes," answered Elisha, "but you will not eat[y] any of it!"

The Siege Lifted

3 Now there were four men with leprosy[h][z] at the entrance of the city gate. They said to each other, "Why stay here until we die? 4 If we say, 'We'll go into the city'—the famine is there, and we will die. And if we stay here, we will die. So let's go over to the camp of the Arameans and surrender. If they spare us, we live; if they kill us, then we die."

5 At dusk they got up and went to the camp of the Arameans. When they reached the edge of the camp, not a man was there, 6 for the Lord had caused the Arameans to hear the sound[a] of chariots and horses and a great army, so that they said to one another, "Look, the king of Israel has hired the Hittite and Egyptian kings to attack us!" 7 So they got up and fled[b] in the dusk and abandoned their tents and their horses and donkeys. They left the camp as it was and ran for their lives.

8 The men who had leprosy reached the edge of the camp and entered one of the tents. They ate and drank, and carried away silver, gold and clothes, and went off and hid them. They returned and entered another tent and took some things from it and hid them also.

### Cross references (margin)

6:29 q Lev 26:29; Dt 28:53-55

6:30 r Ge 37:34; 1Ki 21:27

6:32 s Eze 8:1; 14:1; 20:1 t 1Ki 18:4

6:33 u Job 2:9

7:1 v ver 16

7:2 w 2Ki 5:18 x ver 19; Ge 7:11; Mal 3:10 y ver 17

7:3 z Lev 13:45-46; Nu 5:1-4

7:6 a 2Sa 5:24

7:7 b Ps 48:4-6; Pr 28:1

a 25 That is, about 2 pounds (about 1 kilogram) b 25 That is, probably about 1/2 pint (about 0.3 liter) c 25 Or of doves' dung d 25 That is, about 2 ounces (about 55 grams) e 1 That is, probably about 7 quarts (about 7.3 liters); also in verses 16 and 18 f 1 That is, about 2/5 ounce (about 11 grams); also in verses 16 and 18 g 1 That is, probably about 13 quarts (about 15 liters); also in verses 16 and 18 h 3 The Hebrew word is used for various diseases affecting the skin—not necessarily leprosy; also in verse 8.

6:31–33 Why did the king blame Elisha for the famine and troubles of the siege? Here are some possible reasons: (1) Some commentators say that Elisha must have told the king to trust God for deliverance. The king did this and even wore sackcloth (6:30), but at this point the situation seemed hopeless. Apparently the king thought Elisha had given him bad advice and not even God could help them. (2) For years the kings of Israel and the prophets of God had been in conflict. The prophets often predicted doom because of the kings' evil, so the kings saw them as troublemakers. Thus Israel's king was striking out in frustration at Elisha. (3) The king may have remembered when Elijah helped bring an end to a famine (1 Kings 18:41–46). Knowing Elisha was a man of God, perhaps the king thought he could do any miracle he wanted and was angry that he had not come to Israel's rescue.

7:1, 2 When Elisha prophesied God's deliverance, the king's officer said it couldn't happen. The officer's faith and hope were gone, but God's words came true anyway (7:14–16)! Sometimes we become preoccupied with problems when we should be looking for opportunities. Instead of focusing on the negatives, we should develop an attitude of expectancy. To say that God *cannot* rescue someone or that a situation is *impossible* demonstrates a lack of faith.

7:3 According to the law, lepers were not allowed in the city, but were to depend on charity outside the gate (Leviticus 13:45, 46; Numbers 5:1–4). Because of the famine and the presence of the Aramean army, their situation was desperate.

7:3–10 The lepers discovered the deserted camp and realized that their lives had been spared. At first they kept the good news to themselves, forgetting their fellow citizens who were starving in the city. The Good News about Jesus Christ must be shared too, for no news is more important. We must not forget those who are dying without it. We must not become so preoccupied

9 Then they said to each other, "We're not doing right. This is a day of good news and we are keeping it to ourselves. If we wait until daylight, punishment will overtake us. Let's go at once and report this to the royal palace."

10 So they went and called out to the city gatekeepers and told them, "We went into the Aramean camp and not a man was there—not a sound of anyone—only tethered horses and donkeys, and the tents left just as they were." 11 The gatekeepers shouted the news, and it was reported within the palace.

12 The king got up in the night and said to his officers, "I will tell you what the Arameans have done to us. They know we are starving; so they have left the camp to hide in the countryside, thinking, 'They will surely come out, and then we will take them alive and get into the city.'"

13 One of his officers answered, "Have some men take five of the horses that are left in the city. Their plight will be like that of all the Israelites left here—yes, they will only be like all these Israelites who are doomed. So let us send them to find out what happened."

14 So they selected two chariots with their horses, and the king sent them after the Aramean army. He commanded the drivers, "Go and find out what has happened." 15 They followed them as far as the Jordan, and they found the whole road strewn with the clothing and equipment the Arameans had thrown away in their headlong flight. So the messengers returned and reported to the king. 16 Then the people went out and plundered the camp of the Arameans. So a seah of flour sold for a shekel, and two seahs of barley sold for a shekel,c as the Lord had said.

17 Now the king had put the officer on whose arm he leaned in charge of the gate, and the people trampled him in the gateway, and he died,d just as the man of God had foretold when the king came down to his house. 18 It happened as the man of God had said to the king: "About this time tomorrow, a seah of flour will sell for a shekel and two seahs of barley for a shekel at the gate of Samaria."

19 The officer had said to the man of God, "Look, even if the Lord should open the floodgatese of the heavens, could this happen?" The man of God had replied, "You will see it with your own eyes, but you will not eat any of it!" 20 And that is exactly what happened to him, for the people trampled him in the gateway, and he died.

The Shunammite's Land Restored

8 Now Elisha had said to the woman f whose son he had restored to life, "Go away with your family and stay for a while wherever you can, because the Lord has decreed a famine in the land that will last seven years."g 2 The woman proceeded to do as the man of God said. She and her family went away and stayed in the land of the Philistines seven years.

3 At the end of the seven years she came back from the land of the Philistines and went to the king to beg for her house and land. 4 The king was talking to Gehazi, the servant of the man of God, and had said, "Tell me about all the great things Elisha has done." 5 Just as Gehazi

7:16
c ver 1

7:17
d ver 2

7:19
e ver 2

8:1
f 2Ki 4:8-37
g Ps 105:16;
Hag 1:11

PEOPLE RAISED FROM THE DEAD
God is all-powerful. Nothing in life is beyond his control, not even death.

Elijah raised a boy from the dead	1 Kings 17:22
Elisha raised a boy from the dead	2 Kings 4:34, 35
Elisha's bones raised a man from the dead	2 Kings 13:20, 21
Jesus raised a boy from the dead	Luke 7:14, 15
Jesus raised a girl from the dead	Luke 8:52–56
Jesus raised Lazarus from the dead	John 11:38–44
Peter raised a woman from the dead	Acts 9:40, 41
Paul raised a man from the dead	Acts 20:9–20

---

with our own faith that we neglect sharing it with those around us. Our "good news," like that of the lepers, will not "wait until daylight."

7:19, 20 God, not worthless idols, provides our daily food. Although our faith may be weak or very small, we must avoid becoming skeptical of God's provision. When our resources are low and our doubts are the strongest, remember God can open the floodgates of heaven.

8:1–6 This story must have happened before the events recorded in chapter 5 because the seven-year famine would have ended before Gehazi was struck with leprosy. This shows Elijah's long-term concern for this widow and contrasts his miraculous public ministry with his private ministry to this family. Elisha exemplifies the kind of concern we should have for others.

was telling the king how Elisha had restored[h] the dead to life, the woman whose son Elisha had brought back to life came to beg the king for her house and land.

Gehazi said, "This is the woman, my lord the king, and this is her son whom Elisha restored to life." [6]The king asked the woman about it, and she told him.

Then he assigned an official to her case and said to him, "Give back everything that belonged to her, including all the income from her land from the day she left the country until now."

Hazael Murders Ben-Hadad

[7]Elisha went to Damascus, and Ben-Hadad[i] king of Aram was ill. When the king was told, "The man of God has come all the way up here," [8]he said to Hazael,[j] "Take a gift[k] with you and go to meet the man of God. Consult the LORD through him; ask him, 'Will I recover from this illness?'"

[9]Hazael went to meet Elisha, taking with him as a gift forty camel-loads of all the finest wares of Damascus. He went in and stood before him, and said, "Your son Ben-Hadad king of Aram has sent me to ask, 'Will I recover from this illness?'"

[10]Elisha answered, "Go and say to him, 'You will certainly recover'; but[a] the LORD has revealed to me that he will in fact die." [11]He stared at him with a fixed gaze until Hazael felt ashamed. Then the man of God began to weep.[l]

[12]"Why is my lord weeping?" asked Hazael.

"Because I know the harm[m] you will do to the Israelites," he answered. "You will set fire to their fortified places, kill their young men with the sword, dash their little children to the ground, and rip open[n] their pregnant women."

[13]Hazael said, "How could your servant, a mere dog,[o] accomplish such a feat?"

"The LORD has shown me that you will become king[p] of Aram," answered Elisha.

[14]Then Hazael left Elisha and returned to his master. When Ben-Hadad asked, "What did Elisha say to you?" Hazael replied, "He told me that you would certainly recover." [15]But the next day he took a thick cloth, soaked it in water and spread it over the king's face, so that he died. Then Hazael succeeded him as king.

2. Kings of Israel and Judah
Jehoram King of Judah

[16]In the fifth year of Joram[q] son of Ahab king of Israel, when Jehoshaphat was king of Judah, Jehoram[r] son of Jehoshaphat began his reign as king of Judah. [17]He was thirty-two years old when he became king, and he reigned in Jerusalem eight years. [18]He walked in the ways of the kings of Israel, as the house of Ahab had done, for he married a daughter of Ahab. He did evil in the eyes of the LORD. [19]Nevertheless, for the sake of his servant David, the LORD was not willing to destroy Judah. He had promised to maintain a lamp[s] for David and his descendants forever.

[20]In the time of Jehoram, Edom rebelled against Judah and set up its own king.[t] [21]So Jehoram[b] went to Zair with all his chariots. The Edomites surrounded him and his chariot commanders, but he rose up and broke through by night; his army, however, fled back home. [22]To this day Edom has been in rebellion[u] against Judah. Libnah[v] revolted at the same time.

---

[a]10 The Hebrew may also be read *Go and say, 'You will certainly not recover,' for.* [b]21 Hebrew *Joram*, a variant of *Jehoram*; also in verses 23 and 24

Cross references

8:5 [h]2Ki 4:35

8:7 [i]2Ki 6:24
8:8 [j]1Ki 19:15 [k]1Sa 9:7; 2Ki 1:2

8:11 [l]Lk 19:41

8:12 [m]1Ki 19:17; 2Ki 10:32; 12:17; 13:3, 7 [n]2Ki 15:16

8:13 [o]1Sa 17:43 [p]1Ki 19:15

8:16 [q]2Ki 1:17 [r]2Ch 21:1-4

8:19 [s]2Sa 7:13; 1Ki 11:36

8:20 [t]1Ki 22:47

8:22 [u]Ge 27:40 [v]Jos 21:13

8:12, 13 When Elisha told Hazael he would sin greatly, Hazael protested that he would never do that sort of thing. He did not acknowledge his personal potential for evil. In our enlightened society, we might think that we are above gross sin and can control our actions. We think that we would never sink so low. Instead, we should take a more Biblical and realistic look at ourselves and admit our sinful potential. Then we will ask for God's strength to resist such evil.

8:12–15 Elisha's words about Hazael's treatment of Israel were partially fulfilled in 10:32, 33. Apparently Hazael had known he would be king because Elijah had anointed him (1 Kings 19:15). But he was impatient and, instead of waiting for God's timing, took matters into his own hands, killing Ben-Hadad. God used Hazael as an instrument of judgment against the disobedient Israelites.

8:18 King Jehoshaphat arranged the marriage between Jehoram, his son, and Athaliah, the daughter of wicked Ahab and

Jezebel. Athaliah followed the idolatrous ways of the northern kingdom, bringing Baal worship into Judah and starting the southern kingdom's decline. When Jehoram died, his son Ahaziah became king. Then, when Ahaziah was killed in battle, Athaliah murdered all her grandsons except Joash and made herself queen (11:1–3). Jehoram's marriage may have been politically advantageous, but spiritually it was deadly.

8:20–22 Although Judah and Edom shared a common border and a common ancestor (Isaac), the two nations fought continually. Edom had been a vassal of the united kingdom of Israel and then the southern kingdom of Judah since the days of David (2 Samuel 8:13, 14). Here Edom rebelled against Jehoram and declared independence. Immediately Jehoram marched out to attack Edom, but his ambush failed. Thus Jehoram lost some of his borderlands as punishment for his failure to honor God.

²³As for the other events of Jehoram's reign, and all he did, are they not written in the book of the annals of the kings of Judah? ²⁴Jehoram rested with his fathers and was buried with them in the City of David. And Ahaziah his son succeeded him as king.

Ahaziah King of Judah

²⁵In the twelfth year of Joram son of Ahab king of Israel, Ahaziah son of Jehoram king of Judah began to reign. ²⁶Ahaziah was twenty-two years old when he became king, and he reigned in Jerusalem one year. His mother's name was Athaliah, a granddaughter of Omri king of Israel. ²⁷He walked in the ways of the house of Ahab and did evil in the eyes of the LORD, as the house of Ahab had done, for he was related by marriage to Ahab's family.

²⁸Ahaziah went with Joram son of Ahab to war against Hazael king of Aram at Ramoth Gilead. ʷ The Arameans wounded Joram; ²⁹so King Joram returned to Jezreel ˣ to recover from the wounds the Arameans had inflicted on him at Ramoth ᵃ in his battle with Hazael king of Aram.

Then Ahaziah son of Jehoram king of Judah went down to Jezreel to see Joram son of Ahab, because he had been wounded.

Jehu Anointed King of Israel

9 The prophet Elisha summoned a man from the company of the prophets and said to him, "Tuck your cloak into your belt, ʸ take this flask of oil with you and go to Ramoth Gilead. ᶻ ²When you get there, look for Jehu son of Jehoshaphat, the son of Nimshi. Go to him, get him away from his companions and take him into an inner room. ³Then take the flask and pour the oil on his head and declare, 'This is what the LORD says: I anoint you king over Israel.' Then open the door and run; don't delay!"

⁴So the young man, the prophet, went to Ramoth Gilead. ⁵When he arrived, he found the army officers sitting together. "I have a message for you, commander," he said.

"For which of us?" asked Jehu.

"For you, commander," he replied.

⁶Jehu got up and went into the house. Then the prophet poured the oil ᵃ on Jehu's head and declared, "This is what the LORD, the God of Israel, says: 'I anoint you king over the LORD's people Israel. ⁷You are to destroy the house of Ahab your master, and I will avenge the blood of my servants the prophets and the blood of all the LORD's servants shed by Jezebel. ᵇ ⁸The whole house of Ahab will perish. I will cut off from Ahab every last male ᶜ in Israel—slave or free. ⁹I will make the house of Ahab like the house of Jeroboam ᵈ son of Nebat and like the

8:28
ʷ 1Ki 22:3, 29
8:29
ˣ 2Ki 9:15

9:1
ʸ 2Ki 4:29
ᶻ 2Ki 8:28

9:6
ᵃ 1Ki 19:16;
2Ch 22:7
9:7
ᵇ 1Ki 18:4; 21:15
9:8
ᶜ Dt 32:36;
1Sa 25:22;
1Ki 21:21
9:9
ᵈ 1Ki 14:10; 15:29;
16:3, 11

ᵃ29 Hebrew *Ramah*, a variant of *Ramoth*

8:26 Ahaziah was the only remaining son of Jehoram of Judah. Although he was the youngest son, he took the throne because the rest of his brothers had been taken captive in a raid by the Philistines and Arabs (2 Chronicles 21:16, 17).

8:26, 27 Ahaziah's mother was Athaliah, daughter of Ahab and Jezebel, former king and queen of Israel, and granddaughter of Omri, Ahab's father and predecessor. The evil of Ahab and Jezebel spread to Judah through Athaliah.

8:29 Jezreel was the location of the summer palace of the kings of Israel.

9:1 Tucking the cloak into the belt made it easier to run.

9:3 Elijah had prophesied that many people would be killed when Jehu became king (1 Kings 19:16, 17). Thus Elisha advised the young prophet to get out of the area as soon as he delivered his message, before the slaughter began. Jehu's actions seem harsh, as he hunted down relatives and friends of Ahab (2 Chronicles 22:8, 9), but unchecked Baal worship was destroying the nation. If Israel was to survive, the followers of Baal had to be eliminated. Jehu fulfilled the need of the hour—justice.

9:7 Elisha's statement fulfilled Elijah's prophecy made 20 years earlier that all of Ahab's family would be killed (1 Kings 21:17–24). Jezebel's death, predicted by Elijah, is described in 9:30–37.

9:9 Ahab's dynasty would end as had those of Jeroboam and Baasha. Ahijah had prophesied the end of Jeroboam's dynasty (1 Kings 14:1–11), and this was fulfilled by Baasha (1 Kings 15:29). The prophet Jehu—not King Jehu—then foretold the end of Baasha's family (1 Kings 16:1–7), and this too was fulfilled

(1 Kings 16:11, 12). The end of Ahab's family, therefore, was certain—Elijah had predicted it (1 Kings 21:17–24), and God brought it to pass.

JEHU TAKES OVER ISRAEL Elisha sent a prophet to Ramoth Gilead to anoint Jehu as Israel's new king. Jehu immediately rode to Jezreel to find and kill King Joram of Israel and King Ahaziah of Judah. Jehu killed Joram; Ahaziah fled toward Beth Haggan, where he was wounded. He later died at Megiddo. Back in Jezreel, Jehu had Jezebel killed.

house of Baasha son of Ahijah. [10]As for Jezebel, dogs[e] will devour her on the plot of ground at Jezreel, and no one will bury her.'" Then he opened the door and ran.

[11]When Jehu went out to his fellow officers, one of them asked him, "Is everything all right? Why did this madman[f] come to you?"

"You know the man and the sort of things he says," Jehu replied.

[12]"That's not true!" they said. "Tell us."

Jehu said, "Here is what he told me: 'This is what the LORD says: I anoint you king over Israel.'"

[13]They hurried and took their cloaks and spread[g] them under him on the bare steps. Then they blew the trumpet and shouted, "Jehu is king!"

Jehu Kills Joram and Ahaziah

[14]So Jehu son of Jehoshaphat, the son of Nimshi, conspired against Joram. (Now Joram and all Israel had been defending Ramoth Gilead[h] against Hazael king of Aram, [15]but King Joram[a] had returned to Jezreel to recover[i] from the wounds the Arameans had inflicted on him in the battle with Hazael king of Aram.) Jehu said, "If this is the way you feel, don't let anyone slip out of the city to go and tell the news in Jezreel." [16]Then he got into his chariot and rode to Jezreel, because Joram was resting there and Ahaziah king of Judah had gone down to see him.

[17]When the lookout standing on the tower in Jezreel saw Jehu's troops approaching, he called out, "I see some troops coming."

"Get a horseman," Joram ordered. "Send him to meet them and ask, 'Do you come in peace?'"

[18]The horseman rode off to meet Jehu and said, "This is what the king says: 'Do you come in peace?'"

"What do you have to do with peace?" Jehu replied. "Fall in behind me."

The lookout reported, "The messenger has reached them, but he isn't coming back."

[19]So the king sent out a second horseman. When he came to them he said, "This is what the king says: 'Do you come in peace?'"

Jehu replied, "What do you have to do with peace? Fall in behind me."

[20]The lookout reported, "He has reached them, but he isn't coming back either. The driving is like[j] that of Jehu son of Nimshi—he drives like a madman."

[21]"Hitch up my chariot," Joram ordered. And when it was hitched up, Joram king of Israel and Ahaziah king of Judah rode out, each in his own chariot, to meet Jehu. They met him at the plot of ground that had belonged to Naboth[k] the Jezreelite. [22]When Joram saw Jehu he asked, "Have you come in peace, Jehu?"

"How can there be peace," Jehu replied, "as long as all the idolatry and witchcraft of your mother Jezebel[l] abound?"

[23]Joram turned about and fled, calling out to Ahaziah, "Treachery,[m] Ahaziah!"

[24]Then Jehu drew his bow[n] and shot Joram between the shoulders. The arrow pierced his heart and he slumped down in his chariot. [25]Jehu said to Bidkar, his chariot officer, "Pick him up and throw him on the field that belonged to Naboth the Jezreelite. Remember how you and I were riding together in chariots behind Ahab his father when the LORD made this prophecy[o] about him: [26]'Yesterday I saw the blood of Naboth[p] and the blood of his sons, declares the LORD, and I will surely make you pay for it on this plot of ground, declares the LORD.'[b] Now then, pick him up and throw him on that plot, in accordance with the word of the LORD."

[27]When Ahaziah king of Judah saw what had happened, he fled up the road to Beth Haggan.[c] Jehu chased him, shouting, "Kill him too!" They wounded him in his chariot on the way up to Gur near Ibleam,[q] but he escaped to Megiddo and died there. [28]His servants took him by chariot[r] to Jerusalem and buried him with his fathers in his tomb in the City of David. [29](In the eleventh[s] year of Joram son of Ahab, Ahaziah had become king of Judah.)

[a]15 Hebrew *Jehoram*, a variant of *Joram*; also in verses 17 and 21-24   [b]26 See 1 Kings 21:19.   [c]27 Or *fled by way of the garden house*

9:10
[e]ver 35-36;
1Ki 21:23

9:11
[f]Jer 29:26;
Jn 10:20; Ac 26:24

9:13
[g]Mt 21:8

9:14
[h]2Ki 8:28

9:15
[i]2Ki 8:29

9:20
[j]2Sa 18:27

9:21
[k]1Ki 21:1-7, 15-19

9:22
[l]1Ki 18:19

9:23
[m]2Ki 11:14

9:24
[n]1Ki 22:34

9:25
[o]1Ki 21:19-22, 24-29

9:26
[p]1Ki 21:19

9:27
[q]Jdg 1:27

9:28
[r]2Ki 23:30

9:29
[s]2Ki 8:25

9:18, 19 The horsemen met Jehu and asked if he came in peace. But Jehu responded, "What do you have to do with peace?" Peace, properly understood, comes from God. It is not genuine except when rooted in belief in God and love for him. Jehu knew the men represented a disobedient, wicked king. Don't seek peace and friendship with those who are enemies of the good and the true. Lasting peace can come only from knowing God who gives it to us.

9:26 Joram of Israel was wicked like his father and mother, Ahab and Jezebel; therefore, his body was thrown into the field that his parents had unlawfully taken. Jezebel had arranged the murder of Naboth, the previous owner, because he would not sell his vine-

Jezebel Killed

9:30
t Jer 4:30;
Eze 23:40

9:31
u 1Ki 16:9-10

9:34
v 1Ki 16:31

9:36
w 1Ki 21:23

9:37
x Ps 83:10; Jer 8:2

³⁰Then Jehu went to Jezreel. When Jezebel heard about it, she painted *t* her eyes, arranged her hair and looked out of a window. ³¹As Jehu entered the gate, she asked, "Have you come in peace, Zimri, *u* you murderer of your master?"ᵃ

³²He looked up at the window and called out, "Who is on my side? Who?" Two or three eunuchs looked down at him. ³³"Throw her down!" Jehu said. So they threw her down, and some of her blood spattered the wall and the horses as they trampled her underfoot.

³⁴Jehu went in and ate and drank. "Take care of that cursed woman," he said, "and bury her, for she was a king's daughter."ᵛ ³⁵But when they went out to bury her, they found nothing except her skull, her feet and her hands. ³⁶They went back and told Jehu, who said, "This is the word of the Lord that he spoke through his servant Elijah the Tishbite: On the plot of ground at Jezreel dogs will devour Jezebel's flesh.ᵇ ʷ ³⁷Jezebel's body will be like refuseˣ on the ground in the plot at Jezreel, so that no one will be able to say, 'This is Jezebel.'"

ᵃ31 Or "Did Zimri have peace, who murdered his master?"   ᵇ36 See 1 Kings 21:23.

Jehu had the basic qualities that could have made him a great success. From a human perspective, in fact, he was a successful king. His family ruled the northern kingdom longer than any other. He was used by God as an instrument of punishment to Ahab's evil dynasty, and he fiercely attacked Baal worship. He came close to being God's kind of king, but he recklessly went beyond God's commands and failed to follow through on the obedient actions that began his reign. Within sight of victory, he settled for mediocrity.

Jehu was a man of immediate action but without ultimate purpose. His kingdom moved, bu its destination was unclear. He eliminated one form of idolatry, Baal worship, only to uphold another by continuing to worship the golden calves Jeroboam had set up. He could have accomplished much for God if he had been obedient to the One who made him king. Even when he was carrying out God's directions, Jehu's style showed he was not fully aware of who was directing him.

As he did with Jehu, God gives each person strengths and abilities that will find their greatest usefulness only under his control. Outside that control, however, they don't accomplish what they could and often become tools for evil. One way to make sure this does not happen is to tell God of your willingness to be under his control. With his presence in your life, your natural strengths and abilities will be used to their greatest potential for the greatest good.

Strengths and accomplishments:	• Took the throne from Ahab's family and destroyed his evil influence • Founded the longest-lived dynasty of the northern kingdom • Was anointed by Elijah and confirmed by Elisha • Destroyed Baal worship
Weaknesses and mistakes:	• Had a reckless outlook on life that made him bold and prone to error • Worshiped Jeroboam's golden calves • Was devoted to God only to the point that obedience served his own interests
Lessons from his life:	• Fierce commitment needs control because it can result in recklessness • Obedience involves both action and direction
Vital statistics:	• Where: The northern kingdom of Israel • Occupations: Commander in the army of Joram, king of Israel • Relatives: Grandfather: Nimshi. Father: Jehoshaphat. Son: Jehoahaz. • Contemporaries: Elijah, Elisha, Ahab, Jezebel, Joram, Ahaziah
Key verse:	"Yet Jehu was not careful to keep the law of the Lord, the God of Israel, with all his heart. He did not turn away from the sins of Jeroboam, which he had caused Israel to commit" (2 Kings 10:31).

Jehu's story is told in 1 Kings 19:16—2 Kings 10:36. He is also mentioned in 2 Kings 15:12; 2 Chronicles 22:7–9; Hosea 1:4, 5.

---

yard—which Ahab wanted for a garden (1 Kings 21:1–24). Little did Ahab know that it would become a burial plot for his evil son.

9:31 Why did Jezebel refer to Zimri? Zimri was an army commander who, some 40 years earlier, had killed Elah and then had declared himself king of Israel (1 Kings 16:8–10). Jezebel was accusing Jehu of trying the same treachery.

9:35 Jezebel's skull, feet, and hands were all that remained of

her evil life—no power, no money, no prestige, no royal finery, no family, no spiritual heritage. In the end, her life of luxury and treachery amounted to nothing. Power, health, and wealth may make you feel as if you can live forever. But death strips everyone of all external security. The time to set your life's course is now, while you still have time and before your heart becomes hardened. The end will come soon enough.

Ahab's Family Killed

10 Now there were in Samaria seventy sons of the house of Ahab. So Jehu wrote letters and sent them to Samaria: to the officials of Jezreel,a to the elders and to the guardians of Ahab's children. He said, 2"As soon as this letter reaches you, since your master's sons are with you and you have chariots and horses, a fortified city and weapons, 3choose the best and most worthy of your master's sons and set him on his father's throne. Then fight for your master's house."

4But they were terrified and said, "If two kings could not resist him, how can we?"

5So the palace administrator, the city governor, the elders and the guardians sent this message to Jehu: "We are your servantsy and we will do anything you say. We will not appoint anyone as king; you do whatever you think best."

6Then Jehu wrote them a second letter, saying, "If you are on my side and will obey me, take the heads of your master's sons and come to me in Jezreel by this time tomorrow."

Now the royal princes, seventy of them, were with the leading men of the city, who were rearing them. 7When the letter arrived, these men took the princes and slaughtered all seventyz of them. They put their heads in baskets and sent them to Jehu in Jezreel. 8When the messenger arrived, he told Jehu, "They have brought the heads of the princes."

Then Jehu ordered, "Put them in two piles at the entrance of the city gate until morning."

9The next morning Jehu went out. He stood before all the people and said, "You are innocent. It was I who conspired against my master and killed him, but who killed all these? 10Know then, that not a word the LORD has spoken against the house of Ahab will fail. The LORD has done what he promiseda through his servant Elijah."b 11So Jehu killed everyone in Jezreel who remained of the house of Ahab, as well as all his chief men, his close friends and his priests, leaving him no survivor.

12Jehu then set out and went toward Samaria. At Beth Eked of the Shepherds, 13he met some relatives of Ahaziah king of Judah and asked, "Who are you?"

They said, "We are relatives of Ahaziah,c and we have come down to greet the families of the king and of the queen mother."

14"Take them alive!" he ordered. So they took them alive and slaughtered them by the well of Beth Eked—forty-two men. He left no survivor.

15After he left there, he came upon Jehonadab d son of Recab, e who was on his way to meet him. Jehu greeted him and said, "Are you in accord with me, as I am with you?"

"I am," Jehonadab answered.

"If so," said Jehu, "give me your hand."f So he did, and Jehu helped him up into the chariot. 16Jehu said, "Come with me and see my zealg for the LORD." Then he had him ride along in his chariot.

17When Jehu came to Samaria, he killed all who were left there of Ahab's family;h he destroyed them, according to the word of the LORD spoken to Elijah.

Ministers of Baal Killed

18Then Jehu brought all the people together and said to them, "Ahab servedi Baal a little; Jehu will serve him much. 19Now summon all the prophets of Baal, all his ministers and all his priests. See that no one is missing, because I am going to hold a great sacrifice for Baal. Anyone who fails to come will no longer live." But Jehu was acting deceptively in order to destroy the ministers of Baal.

20Jehu said, "Call an assemblyj in honor of Baal." So they proclaimed it. 21Then he sent word throughout Israel, and all the ministers of Baal came; not one stayed away. They

a 1 Hebrew; some Septuagint manuscripts and Vulgate *of the city*

10:5 y Jos 9:8

10:7 z 1Ki 21:21

10:10 a 2Ki 9:7-10 b 1Ki 21:29

10:13 c 2Ki 8:24, 29; 2Ch 22:8

10:15 d Jer 35:6, 14-19 e 1Ch 2:55 f Ezr 10:19

10:16 g 1Ki 19:10

10:17 h 2Ki 9:8

10:18 i 1Ki 16:31-32

10:20 j Ex 32:5; Joel 1:14

10:7 This fulfilled Elijah's prophecy that not one of Ahab's male descendants would survive (1 Kings 21:17–24).

10:11 In his zeal, Jehu went far beyond the Lord's command with this bloodbath. The prophet Hosea later announced punishment upon Jehu's dynasty for this senseless slaughter (Hosea 1:4, 5). Many times in history, "religious" people have mixed faith with personal ambition, power, or cruelty, without God's consent or blessing. To use God or the Bible to condone oppression is wrong. When people attack Christianity because of atrocities that "Christians" carried out, help them to see that these men and women were using faith to their own political ends and not following Christ.

10:15 Jehonadab was a man who, like Jehu, was zealous in following God. Jehonadab, however, demonstrated his zeal by separating himself and his family from the materialistic, idol-worshiping culture. He founded a group called the Recabites (named after his father Recab), who strove to keep their lives pure by living apart from society's pressures and temptations. Jeremiah 35 gives us an example of their dedication to God. Because of their dedication, God promised that they would always have descendants who would worship him.

crowded into the temple of Baal until it was full from one end to the other. 22And Jehu said to the keeper of the wardrobe, "Bring robes for all the ministers of Baal." So he brought out robes for them.

23Then Jehu and Jehonadab son of Recab went into the temple of Baal. Jehu said to the ministers of Baal, "Look around and see that no servants of the LORD are here with you—only ministers of Baal." 24So they went in to make sacrifices and burnt offerings. Now Jehu had posted eighty men outside with this warning: "If one of you lets any of the men I am placing in your hands escape, it will be your life for his life."k

25As soon as Jehu had finished making the burnt offering, he ordered the guards and officers: "Go in and kill them; let no one escape."l So they cut them down with the sword. The guards and officers threw the bodies out and then entered the inner shrine of the temple of Baal. 26They brought the sacred stonem out of the temple of Baal and burned it. 27They demolished the sacred stone of Baal and tore down the temple of Baal, and people have used it for a latrine to this day.

28So Jehu destroyed Baal worship in Israel. 29However, he did not turn away from the sins of Jeroboam son of Nebat, which he had caused Israel to commit—the worship of the golden calvesn at Bethel and Dan.

30The LORD said to Jehu, "Because you have done well in accomplishing what is right in my eyes and have done to the house of Ahab all I had in mind to do, your descendants will sit on the throne of Israel to the fourth generation."o 31Yet Jehu was not careful to keep the law of the LORD, the God of Israel, with all his heart. He did not turn away from the sins of Jeroboam, which he had caused Israel to commit.

32In those days the LORD began to reduce the size of Israel. Hazaelp overpowered the Israelites throughout their territory 33east of the Jordan in all the land of Gilead (the region of Gad, Reuben and Manasseh), from Aroer by the Arnon Gorge through Gilead to Bashan.

34As for the other events of Jehu's reign, all he did, and all his achievements, are they not written in the book of the annals of the kings of Israel?

35Jehu rested with his fathers and was buried in Samaria. And Jehoahaz his son succeeded him as king. 36The time that Jehu reigned over Israel in Samaria was twenty-eight years.

Athaliah and Joash

11 When Athaliah the mother of Ahaziah saw that her son was dead, she proceeded to destroy the whole royal family. 2But Jehosheba, the daughter of King Jehorama and sister of Ahaziah, took Joashq son of Ahaziah and stole him away from among the royal princes, who were about to be murdered. She put him and his nurse in a bedroom to hide him from Athaliah; so he was not killed. 3He remained hidden with his nurse at the temple of the LORD for six years while Athaliah ruled the land.

4In the seventh year Jehoiada sent for the commanders of units of a hundred, the Caritesr

a2 Hebrew *Joram*, a variant of *Jehoram*

10:24 k 1Ki 20:39

10:25 l 1Ki 18:40

10:26 m 1Ki 14:23

10:29 n 1Ki 12:28-29

10:30 o 2Ki 15:12

10:32 p 2Ki 8:12

11:2 q 2Ki 12:1

11:4 r ver 19

10:24 Israel was supposed to be intolerant of any religion that did not worship the true God. The religions of surrounding nations were evil and corrupt. They were designed to destroy life, not uphold it. Israel was God's special nation, chosen to be an example of what was right. But Israel's kings, priests, and elders first tolerated, then incorporated surrounding pagan beliefs, and thus became apathetic to God's way. We are to be completely intolerant of sin and remove it from our lives. We should be tolerant of people who hold differing views, but we should not condone beliefs or practices that lead people away from God's standards of living.

10:28, 29 Why did Jehu destroy the idols of Baal but not the golden calves in Bethel and Dan? Jehu's motives may have been more political than spiritual. (1) If Jehu had destroyed the golden calves, his people would have traveled to the temple in Jerusalem, in the rival southern kingdom, and worshiped there (which is why Jeroboam set them up in the first place; see 1 Kings 12:25–33). (2) Baal worship was associated with the dynasty of Ahab, so it was politically advantageous to destroy Baal. The golden calves, on the other hand, had a longer history in the northern kingdom and were valued by all political factions. (3) Baal worship was anti-God, but the golden calves were thought by many to be visible representations of God himself, even though God's law stated

clearly that such worship was idolatrous (Exodus 20:3–6). Like Jehu, it is easy for us to denounce the sins of others while excusing sin in our own lives.

10:30, 31 Jehu did much of what the Lord told him to, but he did not obey him with all his heart. He had become God's *instrument* for carrying out justice, but he had not become God's *servant*. As a result, he gave only lip service to God while permitting the worship of the golden calves. Check the condition of your heart toward God. We can be very active in our work for God and still not give the heartfelt obedience he desires.

11:1 This story is continued from 9:27, where Ahaziah, Athaliah's son, had been killed by Jehu. Athaliah's attempt to kill all of Ahaziah's sons was futile because God had promised that the Messiah would be born through David's descendants (2 Samuel 7).

11:2, 3 Jehosheba was the wife of Jehoiada, the high priest, so the temple was a practical and natural place to hide baby Joash. Athaliah, who loved idolatry, would have had no interest in the temple.

11:4 The Carites were mercenary troops possibly associated with the Philistines. Some scholars believe they settled in southern Palestine from Crete.

and the guards and had them brought to him at the temple of the Lord. He made a covenant with them and put them under oath at the temple of the Lord. Then he showed them the king's son. ⁵He commanded them, saying, "This is what you are to do: You who are in the three companies that are going on duty on the Sabbath*s*—a third of you guarding the royal palace, ⁶a third at the Sur Gate, and a third at the gate behind the guard, who take turns guarding the temple— ⁷and you who are in the other two companies that normally go off Sabbath duty are all to guard the temple for the king. ⁸Station yourselves around the king, each man with his weapon in his hand. Anyone who approaches your ranks*a* must be put to death. Stay close to the king wherever he goes."

⁹The commanders of units of a hundred did just as Jehoiada the priest ordered. Each one took his men—those who were going on duty on the Sabbath and those who were going off duty—and came to Jehoiada the priest. ¹⁰Then he gave the commanders the spears and shields*t* that had belonged to King David and that were in the temple of the Lord. ¹¹The guards, each with his weapon in his hand, stationed themselves around the king—near the altar and the temple, from the south side to the north side of the temple.

¹²Jehoiada brought out the king's son and put the crown on him; he presented him with a copy of the covenant *u* and proclaimed him king. They anointed him, and the people clapped their hands and shouted, "Long live the king!" *v*

¹³When Athaliah heard the noise made by the guards and the people, she went to the people at the temple of the Lord. ¹⁴She looked and there was the king, standing by the pillar,*w* as the custom was. The officers and the trumpeters were beside the king, and all the people of the land were rejoicing and blowing trumpets. *x* Then Athaliah tore *y* her robes and called out, "Treason! Treason!"*z*

¹⁵Jehoiada the priest ordered the commanders of units of a hundred, who were in charge of the troops: "Bring her out between the ranks*b* and put to the sword anyone who follows her." For the priest had said, "She must not be put to death in the temple of the Lord." ¹⁶So they seized her as she reached the place where the horses enter the palace grounds, and there she was put to death.

¹⁷Jehoiada then made a covenant *a* between the Lord and the king and people that they would be the Lord's people. He also made a covenant between the king and the people. ¹⁸All the people of the land went to the temple of Baal and tore it down. They smashed*b* the altars and idols to pieces and killed Mattan the priest *c* of Baal in front of the altars.

Then Jehoiada the priest posted guards at the temple of the Lord. ¹⁹He took with him the commanders of hundreds, the Carites, *d* the guards and all the people of the land, and together they brought the king down from the temple of the Lord and went into the palace, entering by way of the gate of the guards. The king then took his place on the royal throne, ²⁰and all the people of the land rejoiced.*e* And the city was quiet, because Athaliah had been slain with the sword at the palace.

²¹Joash*c* was seven years old when he began to reign.

Joash Repairs the Temple

12 In the seventh year of Jehu, Joash*d* became king, and he reigned in Jerusalem forty years. His mother's name was Zibiah; she was from Beersheba. ²Joash did what was right in the eyes of the Lord all the years Jehoiada the priest instructed him. ³The high places,*f* however, were not removed; the people continued to offer sacrifices and burn incense there.

a*8* Or *approaches the precincts*   b*15* Or *out from the precincts*   c*21* Hebrew *Jehoash*, a variant of *Joash*
d*1* Hebrew *Jehoash*, a variant of *Joash*; also in verses 2, 4, 6, 7 and 18

11:5
s1Ch 9:25

11:10
t2Sa 8:7

11:12
uEx 25:16
v1Sa 10:24

11:14
w2Ki 23:3;
2Ch 34:31
x1Ki 1:39
yGe 37:29
z2Ki 9:23

11:17
a2Sa 5:3;
2Ch 15:12; 34:31

11:18
bDt 12:3
c1Ki 18:40;
2Ki 10:25

11:19
dver 4

11:20
ePr 11:10

12:3
f2Ki 14:4; 15:35

11:17 This covenant was in fact a recommitment to a very old covenant—the one set up in the book of Deuteronomy for the righteous rule of the nation. It was meant to function as a constitution for the people. This covenant, however, had been virtually ignored for over 100 years. Unfortunately, with Jehoiada's death, the reforms were discontinued.

11:21 If Joash became king at only seven years of age, who really ran the country? Although the answer is not spelled out in the Bible, Judah was probably run during the first seven years of Joash's reign by the king's mother, the high priest Jehoiada, and other advisers.

12:2ff Joash didn't go far enough in removing sin from the nation, but he did much that was good and right. When we aren't sure if we've gone far enough in correcting our actions, we can ask: (1) Does the Bible expressly prohibit this action? (2) Does this action take me away from loving, worshiping, or serving God? (3) Does it make me its slave? (4) Is it bringing out the best in me, consistent with God's purpose? (5) Does it benefit other believers?

12:3 The Israelites were supposed to offer sacrifices to God only in designated areas under supervision of the priests, not just anywhere (Deuteronomy 12:13, 14). Making sacrifices on the hilltops (high places) copied pagan customs and encouraged

12:4
g 2Ki 22:4
h Ex 35:5
i 1Ch 29:3-9

4 Joash said to the priests, "Collect *g* all the money that is brought as sacred offerings *h* to the temple of the LORD—the money collected in the census, the money received from personal vows and the money brought voluntarily *i* to the temple. 5 Let every priest receive the money from one of the treasurers, and let it be used to repair whatever damage is found in the temple."

6 But by the twenty-third year of King Joash the priests still had not repaired the temple. 7 Therefore King Joash summoned Jehoiada the priest and the other priests and asked them, "Why aren't you repairing the damage done to the temple? Take no more money from your treasurers, but hand it over for repairing the temple." 8 The priests agreed that they would not collect any more money from the people and that they would not repair the temple themselves.

12:9
j Mk 12:41; Lk 21:1

9 Jehoiada the priest took a chest and bored a hole in its lid. He placed it beside the altar, on the right side as one enters the temple of the LORD. The priests who guarded the entrance put into the chest all the money *j* that was brought to the temple of the LORD. 10 Whenever they saw that there was a large amount of money in the chest, the royal secretary and the high priest came, counted the money that had been brought into the temple of the LORD and put it into bags. 11 When the amount had been determined, they gave the money to the men appointed to supervise the work on the temple. With it they paid those who worked on the temple of the LORD—the carpenters and builders, 12 the masons and stonecutters. They purchased timber and dressed stone for the repair of the temple of the LORD, and met all the other expenses of restoring the temple.

12:13
k 1Ki 7:48-51;
2Ch 24:14
12:15
l 2Ki 22:7
12:16
m Nu 18:9
12:17
n 2Ki 8:12
12:18
o 1Ki 15:18

13 The money brought into the temple was not spent for making silver basins, wick trimmers, sprinkling bowls, trumpets or any other articles of gold *k* or silver for the temple of the LORD; 14 it was paid to the workmen, who used it to repair the temple. 15 They did not require an accounting from those to whom they gave the money to pay the workers, because they acted with complete honesty. *l* 16 The money from the guilt offerings *m* and sin offerings was not brought into the temple of the LORD; it belonged to the priests.

17 About this time Hazael *n* king of Aram went up and attacked Gath and captured it. Then he turned to attack Jerusalem. 18 But Joash king of Judah took all the sacred objects dedicated by his fathers—Jehoshaphat, Jehoram and Ahaziah, the kings of Judah—and the gifts he himself had dedicated and all the gold found in the treasuries of the temple of the LORD and of the royal palace, and he sent *o* them to Hazael king of Aram, who then withdrew from Jerusalem.

12:20
p 2Ki 14:5
q 2Ch 24:25

19 As for the other events of the reign of Joash, and all he did, are they not written in the book of the annals of the kings of Judah? 20 His officials *p* conspired against him and assassinated *q* him at Beth Millo, on the road down to Silla. 21 The officials who murdered him were Jozabad son of Shimeath and Jehozabad son of Shomer. He died and was buried with his fathers in the City of David. And Amaziah his son succeeded him as king.

Jehoahaz King of Israel

13:2
r 1Ki 12:26-33

13 In the twenty-third year of Joash son of Ahaziah king of Judah, Jehoahaz son of Jehu became king of Israel in Samaria, and he reigned seventeen years. 2 He did evil *r* in the eyes of the LORD by following the sins of Jeroboam son of Nebat, which he had caused Israel

---

other pagan practices to enter into their worship. By blending in these beliefs, people were custom-making their religion, and it led them far away from God. (For more information on these high places, see the note on 1 Kings 22:43.)

12:4, 5 The temple needed repair because it had been damaged and neglected by previous evil leaders, especially Athaliah (2 Chronicles 24:7). The temple was to be a holy place, set apart for worship of God. Thanks to Joash's fund-raising program, it could be restored. The dirt and filth that had collected inside over the years were cleaned out; joints were remortared; pagan idols and other traces of idol worship were removed; and the gold and bronze were polished. The neglected condition of the temple reveals how far the people had strayed from God.

12:15 What a contrast between the construction supervisors who needed no accounting of their use of the money, and the priests who couldn't be trusted to handle their funds well enough to set some aside for the temple (12:7, 8). As trained men of

God, the Levites should have been responsible and concerned. After all, the temple was their life's work. Though the priests were not dishonest, they did not have the commitment or energy needed to finish the work. Sometimes God's work is better accomplished by devoted laypeople. Don't let your lack of training or position stop you from contributing to God's kingdom. Everyone's energy is needed to carry out God's work.

12:16 To read more about guilt and sin offerings, see Leviticus 4; 5; 6:24—7:10.

12:20 The reasons for the officials' plot against Joash are listed in 2 Chronicles 24:17–26. Joash had begun to worship idols, had killed the prophet Zechariah, and had been conquered by the Arameans. When Joash turned away from God, his life began to unravel. The officials didn't kill Joash because he turned from God; they killed him because his kingdom was out of control. In the end he became an evil man and was killed by evil people.

to commit, and he did not turn away from them. ³So the LORD's anger ˢ burned against Israel, and for a long time he kept them under the power of Hazael king of Aram and Ben-Hadad his son.

⁴Then Jehoahaz sought the LORD's favor, and the LORD listened to him, for he saw ᵗ how severely the king of Aram was oppressing ᵘ Israel. ⁵The LORD provided a deliverer ᵛ for Israel, and they escaped from the power of Aram. So the Israelites lived in their own homes as they had before. ⁶But they did not turn away from the sins of the house of Jeroboam, which he had caused Israel to commit; they continued in them. Also, the Asherah pole ᵃ ʷ remained standing in Samaria.

⁷Nothing had been left of the army of Jehoahaz except fifty horsemen, ten chariots and ten thousand foot soldiers, for the king of Aram had destroyed the rest and made them like the dust at threshing time.

⁸As for the other events of the reign of Jehoahaz, all he did and his achievements, are they not written in the book of the annals of the kings of Israel? ⁹Jehoahaz rested with his fathers and was buried in Samaria. And Jehoash ᵇ his son succeeded him as king.

Jehoash King of Israel

¹⁰In the thirty-seventh year of Joash king of Judah, Jehoash son of Jehoahaz became king of Israel in Samaria, and he reigned sixteen years. ¹¹He did evil in the eyes of the LORD and did not turn away from any of the sins of Jeroboam son of Nebat, which he had caused Israel to commit; he continued in them.

¹²As for the other events of the reign of Jehoash, all he did and his achievements, including his war against Amaziah ˣ king of Judah, are they not written in the book of the annals of the kings of Israel? ¹³Jehoash rested with his fathers, and Jeroboam succeeded him on the throne. Jehoash was buried in Samaria with the kings of Israel.

¹⁴Now Elisha was suffering from the illness from which he died. Jehoash king of Israel went down to see him and wept over him. "My father! My father!" he cried. "The chariots ʸ and horsemen of Israel!"

¹⁵Elisha said, "Get a bow and some arrows," and he did so. ¹⁶"Take the bow in your hands," he said to the king of Israel. When he had taken it, Elisha put his hands on the king's hands.

¹⁷"Open the east window," he said, and he opened it. "Shoot!" Elisha said, and he shot. "The LORD's arrow of victory, the arrow of victory over Aram!" Elisha declared. "You will completely destroy the Arameans at Aphek." ᶻ

¹⁸Then he said, "Take the arrows," and the king took them. Elisha told him, "Strike the ground." He struck it three times and stopped. ¹⁹The man of God was angry with him and said, "You should have struck the ground five or six times; then you would have defeated Aram and completely destroyed it. But now you will defeat it only three times." ᵃ

²⁰Elisha died and was buried.

13:3
ˢ Jdg 2:14

13:4
ᵗ Ex 3:7
ᵘ 2Ki 14:26

13:5
ᵛ ver 25;
2Ki 14:25, 27

13:6
ʷ 1Ki 16:33

13:12
ˣ 2Ki 14:15

13:14
ʸ 2Ki 2:12

13:17
ᶻ 1Ki 20:26

13:19
ᵃ ver 25

ᵃ6 That is, a symbol of the goddess Asherah; here and elsewhere in 2 Kings   ᵇ9 Hebrew *Joash*, a variant of *Jehoash*; also in verses 12-14 and 25

13:4–6 The Lord heard Jehoahaz's prayer for help. God delayed his judgment on Israel when they turned to him, but they did not sustain their dependence on God for long. Although Israel had periodic breaks in their idol worship, they rarely showed genuine faith. It is not enough to say no to sin; we must also say yes to a life of commitment to God. An occasional call for help is not a substitute for a daily life of trust in God.

13:5 Aram, which lay to the north of Israel, was always Israel's enemy. This was partly because Israel blocked most of Aram's trade from the south, and Aram cut off most of Israel's from the north. If one nation could conquer the other, all its trade routes would be open and its economy would flourish. Israel and Aram were so busy fighting each other that they didn't notice the rapidly growing strength of the Assyrians to the far north. Soon both nations would be surprised (16:9; 17:6).

13:9, 10 Jehoash assumed the throne of Israel in 798 B.C. At that time, the king of Judah, Joash, was nearing the end of his reign. In Hebrew, Jehoash and Joash are two forms of the same name. Thus two kings named with the same name, one in the south and one in the north, reigned at approximately the same time. While Joash of Judah began as a good king, Jehoash of Israel was evil.

13:14 Elisha was highly regarded for his prophetic powers and miracles on Israel's behalf. Jehoash called him, "The chariots and horsemen of Israel!" This recalls the title Elijah had given to Elijah (2:12). Jehoash feared Elisha's death because he ascribed the nation's well-being to Elisha rather than to God. Jehoash's fear reveals his lack of spiritual understanding. At least 43 years had passed since Elisha was last mentioned in Scripture (9:1), when he anointed Jehu king (841 B.C.). Jehoash's reign began in 798 B.C.

13:15–19 When Jehoash was told to strike the ground with the arrows, he did it only halfheartedly. As a result, Elisha told the king that his victory over Aram would not be complete. Receiving the full benefits of God's plan for our lives requires us to receive and obey God's commands fully. If we don't follow God's complete instructions, we should not be surprised that we don't receive his full benefits and blessings.

13:20, 21 Elisha was dead, but his good influence remained, even causing miracles. This demonstrated that Elisha was indeed a prophet of God. It also attested to God's power—no pagan idol had ever raised anyone from the dead. This miracle served as one more reminder to Israel that it had rejected God's word as given through Elisha.

13:21
b Mt 27:52

Now Moabite raiders used to enter the country every spring. 21 Once while some Israelites were burying a man, suddenly they saw a band of raiders; so they threw the man's body into Elisha's tomb. When the body touched Elisha's bones, the man came to life b and stood up on his feet.

13:22
c 1Ki 19:17;
2Ki 8:12

13:23
d Ex 2:24

22 Hazael king of Aram oppressed c Israel throughout the reign of Jehoahaz. 23 But the LORD was gracious to them and had compassion and showed concern for them because of his covenant d with Abraham, Isaac and Jacob. To this day he has been unwilling to destroy them or banish them from his presence.

13:25
e ver 18, 19
f 2Ki 10:32

24 Hazael king of Aram died, and Ben-Hadad his son succeeded him as king. 25 Then Jehoash son of Jehoahaz recaptured from Ben-Hadad son of Hazael the towns he had taken in battle from his father Jehoahaz. Three times e Jehoash defeated him, and so he recovered f the Israelite towns.

Amaziah King of Judah

14

In the second year of Jehoash a son of Jehoahaz king of Israel, Amaziah son of Joash king of Judah began to reign. 2 He was twenty-five years old when he became king, and he reigned in Jerusalem twenty-nine years. His mother's name was Jehoaddin; she was from Jerusalem. 3 He did what was right in the eyes of the LORD, but not as his father David had done. In everything he followed the example of his father Joash. 4 The high places, g however, were not removed; the people continued to offer sacrifices and burn incense there.

14:4
g 2Ki 12:3

14:5
h 2Ki 12:20

14:6
i Jer 31:30;
Eze 18:4, 20

5 After the kingdom was firmly in his grasp, he executed the officials h who had murdered his father the king. 6 Yet he did not put the sons of the assassins to death, in accordance with what is written in the Book of the Law of Moses where the LORD commanded: "Fathers shall not be put to death for their children, nor children put to death for their fathers; each is to die for his own sins." b i

14:7
j 2Sa 8:13;
2Ch 25:11

7 He was the one who defeated ten thousand Edomites in the Valley of Salt j and captured Sela in battle, calling it Joktheel, the name it has to this day.

8 Then Amaziah sent messengers to Jehoash son of Jehoahaz, the son of Jehu, king of Israel, with the challenge: "Come, meet me face to face."

14:9
k Jdg 9:8-15

9 But Jehoash king of Israel replied to Amaziah king of Judah: "A thistle k in Lebanon sent a message to a cedar in Lebanon, 'Give your daughter to my son in marriage.' Then a wild beast in Lebanon came along and trampled the thistle underfoot. 10 You have indeed defeated Edom and now you are arrogant. l Glory in your victory, but stay at home! Why ask for trouble and cause your own downfall and that of Judah also?"

14:10
l Dt 8:14;
2Ch 26:16; 32:25

11 Amaziah, however, would not listen, so Jehoash king of Israel attacked. He and Amaziah king of Judah faced each other at Beth Shemesh in Judah. 12 Judah was routed by Israel, and every man fled to his home. 13 Jehoash king of Israel captured Amaziah king of Judah, the

a 1 Hebrew Joash, a variant of Jehoash; also in verses 13, 23 and 27   b 6 Deut. 24:16

GOD OR IDOLS
Why did people continually turn to idols instead of to God?

Idols were:	God is:
Tangible	Intangible—no physical form
Morally similar—had human characteristics	Morally dissimilar—had divine characteristics
Comprehensible	Incomprehensible
Able to be manipulated	Not able to be manipulated
Worshiping idols involved:	*Worshiping God involved:*
Materialism	Sacrifice
Sexual immorality	Purity and commitment
Doing whatever a person wanted	Doing what God wants
Focusing on self	Focusing on others

14:7 Sela was the ancient stronghold of Petra, a city carved into a rock cliff. It was not only a stronghold for Edom, but also a wealthy outpost for trade with India.

14:9, 10 This parable compares Judah to a small thistle. King Amaziah of Judah had become proud after defeating the Edomites. Here he was trying to pick a fight with Israel because he was sure his army was stronger. Jehoash tried to warn

Amaziah not to attack by comparing his army to a thistle and Israel's army to a cedar tree. Amaziah had overrated his strength; his ambition was greater than his ability. He didn't listen to Jehoash and was soundly defeated.

14:13 A broken-down city wall disgraced the citizens and left them defenseless against future invasions.

son of Joash, the son of Ahaziah, at Beth Shemesh. Then Jehoash went to Jerusalem and broke down the wall of Jerusalem from the Ephraim Gate *m* to the Corner Gate *n*—a section about six hundred feet long. *a* ¹⁴He took all the gold and silver and all the articles found in the temple of the LORD and in the treasuries of the royal palace. He also took hostages and returned to Samaria.

¹⁵As for the other events of the reign of Jehoash, what he did and his achievements, including his war *o* against Amaziah king of Judah, are they not written in the book of the annals of the kings of Israel? ¹⁶Jehoash rested with his fathers and was buried in Samaria with the kings of Israel. And Jeroboam his son succeeded him as king.

¹⁷Amaziah son of Joash king of Judah lived for fifteen years after the death of Jehoash son of Jehoahaz king of Israel. ¹⁸As for the other events of Amaziah's reign, are they not written in the book of the annals of the kings of Judah?

¹⁹They conspired against him in Jerusalem, and he fled to Lachish, but they sent men after him to Lachish and killed him there. ²⁰He was brought back by horse and was buried in Jerusalem with his fathers, in the City of David.

²¹Then all the people of Judah took Azariah, *b* who was sixteen years old, and made him king in place of his father Amaziah. ²²He was the one who rebuilt Elath *p* and restored it to Judah after Amaziah rested with his fathers.

Jeroboam II King of Israel

²³In the fifteenth year of Amaziah son of Joash king of Judah, Jeroboam son of Jehoash king of Israel became king in Samaria, and he reigned forty-one years. ²⁴He did evil in the eyes of the LORD and did not turn away from any of the sins of Jeroboam son of Nebat, which he had caused Israel to commit. ²⁵He was the one who restored the boundaries of Israel from Lebo *c* Hamath to the Sea of the Arabah, *d q* in accordance with the word of the LORD, the God of Israel, spoken through his servant Jonah *r* son of Amittai, the prophet from Gath Hepher.

²⁶The LORD had seen how bitterly everyone in Israel, whether slave or free, *s* was suffering; *t* there was no one to help them. ²⁷And since the LORD had not said he would blot out the name of Israel from under heaven, he saved them by the hand of Jeroboam son of Jehoash.

²⁸As for the other events of Jeroboam's reign, all he did, and his military achievements, including how he recovered for Israel both Damascus *u* and Hamath, *v* which had belonged to Yaudi, *e* are they not written in the book of the annals of the kings of Israel? ²⁹Jeroboam rested with his fathers, the kings of Israel. And Zechariah his son succeeded him as king.

Azariah King of Judah

15 In the twenty-seventh year of Jeroboam king of Israel, Azariah *w* son of Amaziah king of Judah began to reign. ²He was sixteen years old when he became king, and he reigned in Jerusalem fifty-two years. His mother's name was Jecoliah; she was from Jerusalem. ³He did what was right in the eyes of the LORD, just as his father Amaziah had done.

a 13 Hebrew *four hundred cubits* (about 180 meters)   *b 21* Also called *Uzziah*   *c 25* Or *from the entrance to*
d 25 That is, the Dead Sea   *e 28* Or *Judah*

Cross references

14:13 *m* Ne 8:16; 12:39; *n* Jer 31:38; Zec 14:10

14:15 *o* 2Ki 13:12

14:22 *p* 2Ki 16:6

14:25 *q* Dt 3:17; *r* Jnh 1:1; Mt 12:39

14:26 *s* Dt 32:36; *t* 2Ki 13:4

14:28 *u* 2Sa 8:5; 1Ki 11:24; *v* 2Ch 8:3

15:1 *w* 2Ki 14:21

14:25 During this period of history, many prophets—such as Hosea, Amos, Jonah, Micah, and Isaiah—began collecting their prophecies and writing them under God's direction. They continued to preach about the worldwide significance of God's work as they looked forward to the future spiritual kingdom. God would use Israel's moral and spiritual decline to prepare the way for the Messiah's coming. Because the kingdom and military power of Israel would be stripped away, many people would be ready to turn to the Good News that Jesus would bring.

14:25 For more information about the prophet Jonah, see the book of Jonah.

14:28 Jeroboam II had no devotion to God, yet under his warlike policies and skillful administration Israel enjoyed more national power and material prosperity than at any time since the days of Solomon. The prophets Amos and Hosea, however, tell us what was really happening within the kingdom (Hosea 13:4–8; Amos 6:11–14). Jeroboam's administration ignored policies of justice and fairness. As a result, the rich became richer, and the poor,

poorer. The people became self-centered, relying more on their power, security, and possessions than on God. The poor were so oppressed that it was hard for them to believe God noticed their plight. Material prosperity is not always an indication of God's blessing. It can also be a result of self-centeredness. If you are experiencing prosperity, remember that God holds us accountable for how we attain success and how we use our wealth. Everything we have really belongs to him. We must use God's gifts with his interests in mind.

15:1 Azariah was also known as Uzziah. His story is given in greater detail in 2 Chronicles 26. He is mentioned in Isaiah 1:1 and 6:1. Before the beginning of Azariah's reign, Israel broke down 200 yards of Jerusalem's walls after defeating Judah and carrying off their king, Amaziah (14:13; 2 Chronicles 25:23, 24). But during Azariah's 52-year reign, Judah rebuilt the wall, refortified the city with anti-siege weapons, and gained independence from Israel. Azariah's devotion to God helped Judah enjoy peace and prosperity such as it had not experienced since the days of Solomon. During this time, however, Israel declined drastically and would soon be overthrown.

⁴The high places, however, were not removed; the people continued to offer sacrifices and burn incense there.

15:5
ˣLev 13:46

⁵The Lᴏʀᴅ afflicted the king with leprosyᵃ until the day he died, and he lived in a separate house.ᵇ ˣ Jotham the king's son had charge of the palace and governed the people of the land.

⁶As for the other events of Azariah's reign, and all he did, are they not written in the book of the annals of the kings of Judah? ⁷Azariah rested with his fathers and was buried near them in the City of David. And Jotham his son succeeded him as king.

Zechariah King of Israel

⁸In the thirty-eighth year of Azariah king of Judah, Zechariah son of Jeroboam became king of Israel in Samaria, and he reigned six months. ⁹He did evil in the eyes of the Lᴏʀᴅ, as his fathers had done. He did not turn away from the sins of Jeroboam son of Nebat, which he had caused Israel to commit.

¹⁰Shallum son of Jabesh conspired against Zechariah. He attacked him in front of the people, ᶜ assassinated him and succeeded him as king. ¹¹The other events of Zechariah's

ᵃ5 The Hebrew word was used for various diseases affecting the skin—not necessarily leprosy.   ᵇ5 Or *in a house where he was relieved of responsibility*   ᶜ10 Hebrew; some Septuagint manuscripts *in Ibleam*

KINGS TO DATE AND THEIR ENEMIES

841	814	798	793
JEHU	**JEHOAHAZ**	**JEHOASH**	**JEROBOAM II**
Lost a large portion	Continually	2 Kgs 13:10—14:16	Recaptured Israel's
of northern Israel to	defeated by	2 Chr 25:17–24	former territories
Hazael (Aram)	Hazael (Aram)	Co-regency 793–782	from Aram
2 Kgs 9:1—10:36	2 Kgs 10:35;		2 Kgs 14:16–29
2 Chr 22:7–9	13:1–9		

ISRAEL

JUDAH

835	796	767
JOASH	**AMAZIAH**	
Averted Hazael's attack	Defeated by	
by paying tribute,	Jehoash and	
and later was defeated	Jeroboam II (Israel)	
by Aram	2 Kgs 14:1–20	
2 Kgs 11:2—12:21	2 Chr 24:27—25:28	
2 Chr 22:11—24:27		

841
AHAZIAH
Hazael (Aram)
2 Kgs 8:24—9:29
2 Chr 22:1–9

841
ATHALIAH (QUEEN)
2 Kgs 11:1–20
2 Chr 22:10—23:21

All dates are B.C.
Solid section of the timeline indicates co-regency.
For all the kings of Israel and Judah, see the chart at the end of 1 Kings.

15:4 Although Azariah accomplished a great deal, he failed to destroy the high places, the location of pagan shrines in Judah, just as his father Amaziah and grandfather Joash had failed to do. Azariah imitated the kings he had heard stories about and had watched while growing up. Although Azariah's father and grandfather were basically good kings, they were poor models in some important areas. To rise above the influence of poor models, we must seek better ones. Christ provides a perfect model. No matter how you were raised or who has influenced your life, you can move beyond those limitations by taking Christ as your example and consciously trying to live as he did.

15:5 For 10 years Jotham was the coruler with his father, Azariah. A father and son would rule together for any of the following reasons: (1) the father was very old and needed help;

(2) the father wanted to train his son in leading the nation; (3) the father was sick or exiled. Many co-regents ruled during the period of the kings—Asa/Jehoshaphat; Jehoshaphat/Jehoram; Azariah/Jotham; Jehoash/Jeroboam II; Hezekiah/Manasseh.

15:8 Zechariah was an evil king because he encouraged Israel to sin by worshiping idols. Sin in our lives is serious. But it is even more serious to encourage others to disobey God. We are responsible for the way we influence others. Beware of double sins: ones that not only hurt us, but also hurt others by encouraging them to sin.

15:10 Zechariah was warned by the prophet Amos of his impending death and the subsequent end of Jeroboam's dynasty (Amos 7:9).

reign are written in the book of the annals of the kings of Israel. [12]So the word of the LORD spoken to Jehu was fulfilled:[y] "Your descendants will sit on the throne of Israel to the fourth generation."[a]

Shallum King of Israel

[13]Shallum son of Jabesh became king in the thirty-ninth year of Uzziah king of Judah, and he reigned in Samaria[z] one month. [14]Then Menahem son of Gadi went from Tirzah[a] up to Samaria. He attacked Shallum son of Jabesh in Samaria, assassinated him and succeeded him as king.

[15]The other events of Shallum's reign, and the conspiracy he led, are written in the book of the annals of the kings of Israel.

[16]At that time Menahem, starting out from Tirzah, attacked Tiphsah[b] and everyone in the city and its vicinity, because they refused to open [c] their gates. He sacked Tiphsah and ripped open all the pregnant women.

Menahem King of Israel

[17]In the thirty-ninth year of Azariah king of Judah, Menahem son of Gadi became king of Israel, and he reigned in Samaria ten years. [18]He did evil in the eyes of the LORD. During his entire reign he did not turn away from the sins of Jeroboam son of Nebat, which he had caused Israel to commit.

[19]Then Pul[b] [d] king of Assyria invaded the land, and Menahem gave him a thousand talents[c] of silver to gain his support and strengthen his own hold on the kingdom. [20]Menahem exacted this money from Israel. Every wealthy man had to contribute fifty shekels[d] of silver to be given to the king of Assyria. So the king of Assyria withdrew and stayed in the land no longer.

[21]As for the other events of Menahem's reign, and all he did, are they not written in the book of the annals of the kings of Israel? [22]Menahem rested with his fathers. And Pekahiah his son succeeded him as king.

Pekahiah King of Israel

[23]In the fiftieth year of Azariah king of Judah, Pekahiah son of Menahem became king of Israel in Samaria, and he reigned two years. [24]Pekahiah did evil in the eyes of the LORD. He did not turn away from the sins of Jeroboam son of Nebat, which he had caused Israel to commit. [25]One of his chief officers, Pekah son of Remaliah, conspired against him. Taking fifty men of Gilead with him, he assassinated Pekahiah, along with Argob and Arieh, in the citadel of the royal palace at Samaria. So Pekah killed Pekahiah and succeeded him as king.

[26]The other events of Pekahiah's reign, and all he did, are written in the book of the annals of the kings of Israel.

Pekah King of Israel

[27]In the fifty-second year of Azariah king of Judah, Pekah[e] son of Remaliah became king of Israel in Samaria, and he reigned twenty years. [28]He did evil in the eyes of the LORD. He did not turn away from the sins of Jeroboam son of Nebat, which he had caused Israel to commit.

[29]In the time of Pekah king of Israel, Tiglath-Pileser[f] king of Assyria came and took Ijon,[g] Abel Beth Maacah, Janoah, Kedesh and Hazor. He took Gilead and Galilee, including all the land of Naphtali, [h] and deported the people to Assyria. [30]Then Hoshea [i] son of Elah conspired against Pekah son of Remaliah. He attacked and assassinated him, and then succeeded him as king in the twentieth year of Jotham son of Uzziah.

15:12	[y]2Ki 10:30
15:13	[z]ver 1, 8
15:14	[a]1Ki 14:17
15:16	[b]1Ki 4:24 [c]2Ki 8:12; Hos 13:16
15:19	[d]1Ch 5:6, 26
15:27	[e]2Ch 28:6; Isa 7:1
15:29	[f]2Ki 17:6; 1Ch 5:26 [g]1Ki 15:20 [h]2Ki 16:9; 17:24; 2Ch 16:4; Isa 9:1
15:30	[i]2Ki 17:1

[a]12 2 Kings 10:30   [b]19 Also called *Tiglath-Pileser*   [c]19 That is, about 37 tons (about 34 metric tons)   [d]20 That is, about 1 1/4 pounds (about 0.6 kilogram)

15:14 Ancient historical documents say that Menahem was the commander in chief of Jeroboam's army (see 14:23–29 for an account of Jeroboam II's reign). After Jeroboam's son was assassinated (15:8–10), Menahem probably saw himself, and not Shallum, as the rightful successor to Israel's throne.

15:18 Menahem, like the kings before him, led his people into sin—"He did evil in the eyes of the LORD." What a horrible epitaph for a leader! Leaders profoundly affect the people they serve. They can either encourage or discourage devotion to God both

by their example and by the structure they give their organization. Good leaders put up no obstacles to faith in God or to right living.

15:19, 20 When King Pul of Assyria (also called Tiglath-Pileser in 15:29) took the throne, the Assyrian empire was becoming a world power, and the nations of Aram, Israel, and Judah were in decline. This is the first mention of Assyria in 2 Kings. Pul's invasion occurred in 743 B.C. Assyria made Israel a vassal, and Menahem was forced to pay tribute to Assyria. This was the first of three Assyrian invasions (15:29 and 17:6 tell of the other ones).

15:30 Hoshea was Israel's last king.

31 As for the other events of Pekah's reign, and all he did, are they not written in the book of the annals of the kings of Israel?

Jotham King of Judah

32 In the second year of Pekah son of Remaliah king of Israel, Jotham son of Uzziah king of Judah began to reign. 33 He was twenty-five years old when he became king, and he reigned in Jerusalem sixteen years. His mother's name was Jerusha daughter of Zadok. 34 He did what was right *j* in the eyes of the LORD, just as his father Uzziah had done. 35 The high places, however, were not removed; the people continued to offer sacrifices and burn incense there. Jotham rebuilt the Upper Gate of the temple of the LORD.

36 As for the other events of Jotham's reign, and what he did, are they not written in the book of the annals of the kings of Judah? 37 (In those days the LORD began to send Rezin *k* king of Aram and Pekah son of Remaliah against Judah.) 38 Jotham rested with his fathers and was buried with them in the City of David, the city of his father. And Ahaz his son succeeded him as king.

Ahaz King of Judah

16 In the seventeenth year of Pekah son of Remaliah, Ahaz son of Jotham king of Judah began to reign. 2 Ahaz was twenty years old when he became king, and he reigned in Jerusalem sixteen years. Unlike David his father, he did not do what was right in the eyes of the LORD his God. 3 He walked in the ways of the kings of Israel and even sacrificed his son *l* in *a* the fire, following the detestable *m* ways of the nations the LORD had driven out before the Israelites. 4 He offered sacrifices and burned incense at the high places, on the hilltops and under every spreading tree. *n*

5 Then Rezin *o* king of Aram and Pekah son of Remaliah king of Israel marched up to fight against Jerusalem and besieged Ahaz, but they could not overpower him. 6 At that time, Rezin king of Aram recovered Elath *p* for Aram by driving out the men of Judah. Edomites then moved into Elath and have lived there to this day.

7 Ahaz sent messengers to say to Tiglath-Pileser *q* king of Assyria, "I am your servant and vassal. Come up and save me out of the hand of the king of Aram and of the king of Israel, who are attacking me." 8 And Ahaz took the silver and gold found in the temple of the LORD and in the treasuries of the royal palace and sent it as a gift *r* to the king of Assyria. 9 The king of Assyria complied by attacking Damascus and capturing it. He deported its inhabitants to Kir *s* and put Rezin to death.

10 Then King Ahaz went to Damascus to meet Tiglath-Pileser king of Assyria. He saw an altar in Damascus and sent to Uriah *t* the priest a sketch of the altar, with detailed plans for its construction. 11 So Uriah the priest built an altar in accordance with all the plans that King Ahaz had sent from Damascus and finished it before King Ahaz returned. 12 When the king came back from Damascus and saw the altar, he approached it and presented offerings *b u* on it. 13 He offered up his burnt offering and grain offering, poured out his drink offering, and

a 3 Or *even made his son pass through*   *b 12* Or *and went up*

**Side references:**

15:34
j ver 3; 2Ch 26:4-5

15:37
k 2Ki 16:5; Isa 7:1

16:3
l Lev 18:21
m Dt 12:31

16:4
n Dt 12:2

16:5
o 2Ki 15:37; Isa 7:1, 4

16:6
p 2Ki 14:22

16:7
q 2Ki 15:29

16:8
r 2Ki 12:18

16:9
s Am 1:5

16:10
t Isa 8:2

16:12
u 2Ch 26:16

15:32 A year after Pekah became king, Uzziah (also called Azariah) of Judah died, and Isaiah the prophet had a vision of God's holiness and Israel's future destruction. See Isaiah 6 for more details on what Isaiah saw.

15:34, 35 Much good can be said of Jotham and his reign as king of Judah, but he failed in a most important area: he didn't destroy the high places, although leaving them clearly violated the first commandment (Exodus 20:3). Like Jotham, we may live basically good lives and yet miss doing what is most important. A lifetime of doing good is not enough if we make the crucial mistake of not following God with all our hearts. A true follower of God puts him first in all areas of life.

16:3 Ahaz was so depraved that he sacrificed his own son to the pagan gods. This was a practice of the Canaanites whom the Israelites were supposed to drive out of the land.

16:5 Israel and Aram were both under Assyria's control. They joined forces against Judah, hoping to force the southern kingdom to join their revolt against Assyria and strengthen their western alliance. But the plan backfired when King Ahaz

of Judah unexpectedly asked Assyria to come to his aid (16:8, 9).

16:10 Ahaz went to Damascus to express gratitude and loyalty to Tiglath-Pileser. Because the Assyrians had captured Damascus, the capital of Aram (732 B.C.), Ahaz was afraid of a southern sweep. But he was relying more on money than on God to keep the powerful king out of his land, and his plan failed. Although Tiglath-Pileser did not conquer Judah, he caused much trouble, and Ahaz regretted asking for his help (2 Chronicles 28:20, 21).

16:10–16 Evil King Ahaz copied pagan religious customs, changed the temple services, and used the temple altar for his personal benefit. In so doing, he demonstrated a callous disregard for God's commands. We condemn Ahaz for his action, but we act the same way if we try to mold God's message to fit our personal preferences. We must worship God for who he is, not what we would selfishly like him to be.

sprinkled the blood of his fellowship offerings[a] on the altar. [14]The bronze altar[v] that stood before the Lord he brought from the front of the temple—from between the new altar and the temple of the Lord—and put it on the north side of the new altar.

[15]King Ahaz then gave these orders to Uriah the priest: "On the large new altar, offer the morning[w] burnt offering and the evening grain offering, the king's burnt offering and his grain offering, and the burnt offering of all the people of the land, and their grain offering and their drink offering. Sprinkle on the altar all the blood of the burnt offerings and sacrifices. But I will use the bronze altar for seeking guidance." [16]And Uriah the priest did just as King Ahaz had ordered.

[17]King Ahaz took away the side panels and removed the basins from the movable stands. He removed the Sea from the bronze bulls that supported it and set it on a stone base.[x] [18]He took away the Sabbath canopy[b] that had been built at the temple and removed the royal entryway outside the temple of the Lord, in deference to the king of Assyria.

[19]As for the other events of the reign of Ahaz, and what he did, are they not written in the book of the annals of the kings of Judah? [20]Ahaz rested with his fathers and was buried with them in the City of David. And Hezekiah his son succeeded him as king.

3. Israel is exiled to Assyria
Hoshea Last King of Israel

17 In the twelfth year of Ahaz king of Judah, Hoshea[y] son of Elah became king of Israel in Samaria, and he reigned nine years. [2]He did evil in the eyes of the Lord, but not like the kings of Israel who preceded him.

[3]Shalmaneser[z] king of Assyria came up to attack Hoshea, who had been Shalmaneser's vassal and had paid him tribute. [4]But the king of Assyria discovered that Hoshea was a traitor, for he had sent envoys to So[c] king of Egypt, and he no longer paid tribute to the king of Assyria, as he had done year by year. Therefore Shalmaneser seized him and put him in prison. [5]The king of Assyria invaded the entire land, marched against Samaria and laid siege to it for three years. [6]In the ninth year of Hoshea, the king of Assyria captured Samaria and deported the Israelites to Assyria. He settled them in Halah, in Gozan on the Habor River and in the towns of the Medes.

a 13 Traditionally peace offerings   b 18 Or the dais of his throne (see Septuagint)   c 4 Or to Sais, to the; So is possibly an abbreviation for Osorkon.

Cross references:
16:14 [v]2Ch 4:1
16:15 [w]Ex 29:38-41
16:17 [x]1Ki 7:27
17:1 [y]2Ki 15:30
17:3 [z]2Ki 18:9-12

16:14–18 Ahaz replaced the altar of burnt offering with a replica of the pagan altar he had seen in Damascus. (The bronze altar was not thrown out, but was kept for use in divination. The sacrifices were washed in the basins. The Sea was a huge reservoir of water for temple use.) This was extremely serious because God had given specific directions on how the altar should look and be used (Exodus 27:1–8). Building this new altar was like installing an idol. But because Judah was Assyria's vassal, Ahaz was eager to please the Assyrian king. Sadly, Ahaz allowed the king of Assyria to

ISRAEL TAKEN CAPTIVE Finally the sins of Israel's people caught up with them. God allowed Assyria to defeat and disperse the people. They were led into captivity, swallowed up by the mighty, evil Assyrian empire. Sin always brings discipline, and the consequences of that sin are sometimes irreversible.

replace God as Judah's leader. No one, no matter how attractive or powerful, should replace God's leadership in our lives.

16:18 Ahaz had become a weak king with a weak and compromising high priest. Judah's religious system was in shambles. It now included pagan customs, and its chief aim was only to please those in power. If we copy others in order to please them, we risk making them more important than God in our lives.

17:3 This was probably Shalmaneser V, who had become king of Assyria after Tiglath-Pileser (727–722 B.C.). He continued to demand heavy tribute from Israel. Israel's King Hoshea decided to rebel against Assyria and join forces with King So of Egypt (17:4). This was not only foolish, but also against God's commands. To destroy this alliance, Shalmaneser attacked and besieged Samaria for three years. Just before Samaria fell, however, Shalmaneser died. His successor, Sargon II, took credit for capturing the city, destroying the nation of Israel, and carrying away its people.

17:5, 6 This was the third and final invasion of Assyria into Israel. (The first two invasions are recorded in 15:19 and 15:29.) The first wave had been merely a warning to Israel—to avoid further attack, pay money and not rebel. The people should have learned their lesson and returned to God. When they didn't, God had allowed Assyria to invade again, this time carrying off some captives from the northern border. But the people still did not realize that they had caused their own troubles. Thus Assyria invaded for the third and final time, destroying Israel completely, carrying away most of the people, and resettling the land with foreigners.

God was doing what he had said he would do (Deuteronomy 28). He had given Israel ample warning; they knew what would come, but they still ignored God. Israel was now no better than the pagan nations it had destroyed in the days of Joshua. The nation

Israel Exiled Because of Sin

17:7
a Jos 23:16

17:8
b Lev 18:3; Dt 18:9

17:9
c 2Ki 18:8

17:10
d Ex 34:13; Mic 5:14
e 1Ki 14:23

7All this took place because the Israelites had sinned a against the LORD their God, who had brought them up out of Egypt from under the power of Pharaoh king of Egypt. They worshiped other gods 8and followed the practices of the nations b the LORD had driven out before them, as well as the practices that the kings of Israel had introduced. 9The Israelites secretly did things against the LORD their God that were not right. From watchtower to fortified city c they built themselves high places in all their towns. 10They set up sacred stones and Asherah poles d on every high hill and under every spreading tree. e 11At every high place they

KINGS TO DATE AND THEIR ENEMIES

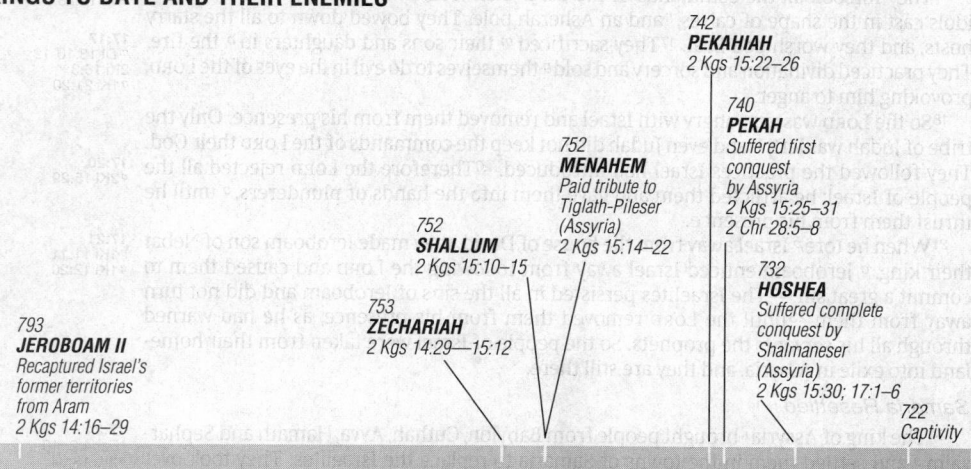

742
PEKAHIAH
2 Kgs 15:22–26

740
PEKAH
Suffered first
conquest
by Assyria
2 Kgs 15:25–31
2 Chr 28:5–8

752
MENAHEM
Paid tribute to
Tiglath-Pileser
(Assyria)
2 Kgs 15:14–22

752
SHALLUM
2 Kgs 15:10–15

732
HOSHEA
Suffered complete
conquest by
Shalmaneser
(Assyria)
2 Kgs 15:30; 17:1–6

753
ZECHARIAH
2 Kgs 14:29—15:12

793
JEROBOAM II
Recaptured Israel's
former territories
from Aram
2 Kgs 14:16–29

722
Captivity

ISRAEL

JUDAH

767   750   740   732   715

796
AMAZIAH
Won battles against
Edom and Selah,
defeated by
Jehoash and
Jeroboam II (Israel)
2 Kgs 14:1–20
2 Chr 24:27—25:28
Co-regency
792–767

792
AZARIAH
Conquered Gath
in Philistia
2 Kgs 15:1–7
2 Chr 26:1–23
Co-regency 750–740

JOTHAM
Won battles against
Ammonites and
Arabs, harassed by
Pekah (Israel) and
Rezin (Aram)
2 Kgs 15:32–38
2 Chr 26:23—27:9
Co-regency 735–732

735
AHAZ
Harassed by
Pekah (Israel),
paid Assyria for
protection against
Rezin (Aram), also
harassed by Edom
and Philistia
2 Kgs 15:38—16:20
2 Chr 27:9—28:27

All dates are B.C.
Solid section of the timeline indicates co-regency.
For all the kings of Israel and Judah, see the chart at the end of 1 Kings.

---

had turned sour and rejected its original purpose—to honor God and be a light to the world.

17:7–17 The Lord judged the people of Israel because they had copied the evil customs of the surrounding nations, worshiping false gods, accommodating pagan customs, and following their own desires. Those who create their own religion tend to live selfishly. And to live for oneself, as Israel learned, brings serious consequences from God. Sometimes following God is difficult and painful, but consider the alternative. You can live for God or die for yourself. Determine to be God's person and do what he says

regardless of the cost. What God thinks of you is infinitely more important than what those around you think. (See Romans 12:1, 2; 1 John 2:15–17.)

17:9 Ruin came upon Israel for both their public sins and their secret sins. Not only did they condone wickedness and idolatry in public, but they committed even worse sins in private. Secret sins are the ones we don't want others to know about because they are embarrassing or incriminating. Sins done in private are not secret to God, and secret defiance of him is just as damaging as open rebellion.

burned incense, as the nations whom the LORD had driven out before them had done. They did wicked things that provoked the LORD to anger. ¹²They worshiped idols, *f* though the LORD had said, "You shall not do this."ᵃ ¹³The LORD warned Israel and Judah through all his prophets and seers: *g* "Turn from your evil ways. *h* Observe my commands and decrees, in accordance with the entire Law that I commanded your fathers to obey and that I delivered to you through my servants the prophets."

¹⁴But they would not listen and were as stiff-necked as their fathers, who did not trust in the LORD their God. ¹⁵They rejected his decrees and the covenant *i* he had made with their fathers and the warnings he had given them. They followed worthless idols*j* and themselves became worthless. They imitated the nations*k* around them although the LORD had ordered them, "Do not do as they do," and they did the things the LORD had forbidden them to do.

¹⁶They forsook all the commands of the LORD their God and made for themselves two idols cast in the shape of calves, *l* and an Asherah pole. They bowed down to all the starry hosts, and they worshiped Baal. ¹⁷They sacrificed *m* their sons and daughters in *b* the fire. They practiced divination and sorcery and sold*n* themselves to do evil in the eyes of the LORD, provoking him to anger.

¹⁸So the LORD was very angry with Israel and removed them from his presence. Only the tribe of Judah was left, ¹⁹and even Judah did not keep the commands of the LORD their God. They followed the practices Israel had introduced. ²⁰Therefore the LORD rejected all the people of Israel; he afflicted them and gave them into the hands of plunderers, *o* until he thrust them from his presence.

²¹When he tore*p* Israel away from the house of David, they made Jeroboam son of Nebat their king. *q* Jeroboam enticed Israel away from following the LORD and caused them to commit a great sin. ²²The Israelites persisted in all the sins of Jeroboam and did not turn away from them ²³until the LORD removed them from his presence, as he had warned through all his servants the prophets. So the people of Israel were taken from their homeland into exile in Assyria, and they are still there.

Samaria Resettled

²⁴The king of Assyria*r* brought people from Babylon, Cuthah, Avva, Hamath and Sepharvaim *s* and settled them in the towns of Samaria to replace the Israelites. They took over Samaria and lived in its towns. ²⁵When they first lived there, they did not worship the LORD;

ᵃ12 Exodus 20:4,5   ᵇ17 Or *They made their sons and daughters pass through*

17:12
f Ex 20:4

17:13
g 1Sa 9:9
h Jer 18:11

17:15
i Dt 29:25
j Dt 32:21
k Dt 12:30-31

17:16
l 1Ki 12:28

17:17
m Dt 18:10-12;
2Ki 16:3
n 1Ki 21:20

17:20
o 2Ki 15:29

17:21
p 1Ki 11:11
q 1Ki 12:20

17:24
r Ezr 4:2, 10
s 2Ki 18:34

17:13–15 The people took on the characteristics of the idols and imitated the godless nations around them. Israel had forgotten the importance and benefits of obeying God's word. The king and the people had become mired in wickedness. Time and again God had sent prophets to warn them of how far they had turned away from him and to call them to turn back.

ISRAEL RESETTLED BY FOREIGNERS   After the Israelites were deported, foreigners from the Assyrian empire were sent to resettle the land. This policy helped Assyria keep peace in conquered territories.

God's patience and mercy are beyond our ability to understand. He will pursue us until we either respond to him or, by our own choice and hardness of heart, make ourselves unreachable. Then God's judgment is swift and sure. The only safe course is to turn to God before our stubbornness puts us out of his reach.

17:16 The "starry hosts" refers to the Canaanite practice of worshiping the sun, moon, and constellations. These were Assyrian gods that were being added to their religion. (See also 21:1–6; 23:4, 5.)

17:17 Divination means witchcraft; and sorcery is consulting evil spirits. Forms of witchcraft, fortune-telling, and black magic were forbidden by God (Deuteronomy 18:9–14). They were wrong because they sought power and guidance totally apart from God, his law, and his Word. Isaiah echoed this law and prophesied of the complete destruction these occult practices would bring to those who participated in them (Isaiah 8:19–22).

17:23 Israel was taken into exile, just as God's prophets had warned. Whatever God predicts will come to pass. This, of course, is good news to those who trust and obey him—they can be confident of his promises; but it is bad news to those who ignore or disobey him. Both the promises and warnings God has given in his Word will surely come true.

17:24 Moving the Israelites out and moving foreigners in was Assyria's resettlement policy to prevent revolt. Spreading the captives across Assyria prevented their uniting, and repopulating Israel with foreign captives made it difficult for the remaining Israelites to unite as well. This mixture of peoples resettled in Israel came to be known as *Samaritans*. They were despised by the Jews, even through the time of Christ (John 4:9).

so he sent lions among them and they killed some of the people. 26 It was reported to the king of Assyria: "The people you deported and resettled in the towns of Samaria do not know what the god of that country requires. He has sent lions among them, which are killing them off, because the people do not know what he requires."

27 Then the king of Assyria gave this order: "Have one of the priests you took captive from Samaria go back to live there and teach the people what the god of the land requires." 28 So one of the priests who had been exiled from Samaria came to live in Bethel and taught them how to worship the LORD.

29 Nevertheless, each national group made its own gods in the several towns where they settled, and set them up in the shrines the people of Samaria had made at the high places. 30 The men from Babylon made Succoth Benoth, the men from Cuthah made Nergal, and the men from Hamath made Ashima; 31 the Avvites made Nibhaz and Tartak, and the Sepharvites burned their children in the fire as sacrifices to Adrammelech and Anammelech, the gods of Sepharvaim. *t* 32 They worshiped the LORD, but they also appointed all sorts *u* of their own people to officiate for them as priests in the shrines at the high places. 33 They worshiped the LORD, but they also served their own gods in accordance with the customs of the nations from which they had been brought.

34 To this day they persist in their former practices. They neither worship the LORD nor adhere to the decrees and ordinances, the laws and commands that the LORD gave the descendants of Jacob, whom he named Israel. *v* 35 When the LORD made a covenant with the Israelites, he commanded them: "Do not worship *w* any other gods or bow down to them, serve them or sacrifice to them. 36 But the LORD, who brought you up out of Egypt with mighty power and outstretched arm, *x* is the one you must worship. To him you shall bow down and to him offer sacrifices. 37 You must always be careful *y* to keep the decrees and ordinances, the laws and commands he wrote for you. Do not worship other gods. 38 Do not forget *z* the covenant I have made with you, and do not worship other gods. 39 Rather, worship the LORD your God; it is he who will deliver you from the hand of all your enemies."

40 They would not listen, however, but persisted in their former practices. 41 Even while these people were worshiping the LORD, they were serving their idols. To this day their children and grandchildren continue to do as their fathers did.

B. THE SURVIVING KINGDOM (18:1—25:30)

After seeing their brothers and sisters carried away into exile, the people of Judah still lapse into sin. Hezekiah and Josiah begin many reforms, but this is not enough to permanently turn the nation back to God. Judah is defeated by the Babylonians, who exile many of them, but they are not scattered, and the land is not repopulated. Sometimes we do not learn from the examples of sin and foolishness around us.

1. Kings of Judah
Hezekiah King of Judah

18 In the third year of Hoshea son of Elah king of Israel, Hezekiah *a* son of Ahaz king of Judah began to reign. 2 He was twenty-five years old when he became king, and he reigned in Jerusalem twenty-nine years. His mother's name was Abijah *a* daughter of Zechariah. 3 He did what was right in the eyes of the LORD, just as his father David had done. 4 He removed *b* the high places, smashed the sacred stones and cut down the Asherah poles. He broke into pieces the bronze snake *c* Moses had made, for up to that time the Israelites had been burning incense to it. (It was called *b* Nehushtan. *c*)

a 2 Hebrew Abi, *a variant of* Abijah   *b 4 Or* He called it   *c 4* Nehushtan *sounds like the Hebrew for* bronze *and* snake *and* unclean thing.

Margin references:
17:31 *t* ver 24
17:32 *u* 1Ki 12:31
17:34 *v* Ge 32:28; 35:10
17:35 *w* Ex 20:5; Jdg 6:10
17:36 *x* Ex 6:6
17:37 *y* Dt 5:32
17:38 *z* Dt 4:23
18:1 *a* 2Ch 28:27
18:4 *b* 2Ch 31:1 *c* Nu 21:9

17:27–29 The new settlers in Israel worshiped God without giving up their pagan customs. They worshiped God to appease him rather than to please him, treating him as a good luck charm or just another idol to add to their collection. A similar attitude is common today. Many people claim to believe in God while refusing to give up attitudes and actions that God denounces. God cannot be added to the values we already have. He must come first, and his Word must shape all our actions and attitudes.

17:29–31 Israel was conquered because it had lost sight of the only true God and the importance of following him. When conquering the land, the Israelites were told to destroy the pagan influences that could lead them away from God. Their failure to do so brought about their ruin. Here they faced an even greater influx of gods from the many pagan peoples moving into the land.

18:4 The bronze snake had been made to cure the Israelites of the bite of venomous snakes (Numbers 21:4–9). It had demonstrated God's presence and power and had reminded the people of his mercy and forgiveness. But it had become an object of worship instead of a reminder of *whom* to worship, so Hezekiah was forced to destroy it. We must be careful that aids to our worship don't become objects of worship themselves. Most objects are not made to be idols—they become idols by the way people use them.

WHO WERE

Who?	When? (B.C.)	Ministered during the reign of these kings	Main message	Significance
AHIJAH	934–909	Jeroboam I of Israel (1 Kings 11:29–39)	Israel would split in two, and God had chosen Jeroboam to lead the 10 tribes. Warned him to remain obedient to God.	We should not take lightly our God-given responsibilities. Jeroboam did and lost his kingdom.
ELIJAH	875–848	Ahab of Israel (1 Kings 17:1—2 Kings 2:11)	In fiery style, urged wicked Ahab to turn back to God. Proved on Mount Carmel who the one true God is (1 Kings 18).	Even giants of faith can't force sinners to change. But those who remain faithful to God have a great impact for him.
MICAIAH	865–853	Ahab of Israel Jehoshaphat of Judah (1 Kings 22:8; 2 Chronicles 18:28)	Ahab would be unsuccessful in fighting the Arameans.	It is foolish to move ahead with plans that are contrary to God's Word.
JEHU	853	Jehoshaphat of Judah (2 Chronicles 19:1–3)	Jehoshaphat should never have allied himself with wicked Ahab.	Partnerships with immoral people can lead us into trouble.
OBADIAH	855–840 (?)	Jehoram of Judah (The book of Obadiah)	God would judge the Edomites for taking advantage of God's people.	Pride is one of the most dangerous sins because it causes us to take advantage of others.
ELISHA	848–797	Joram, Jehu, Jehoahaz, and Jehoash, all of Israel (2 Kings 2:1—9:1; 13:10–21)	Expressed by his actions the importance of helping ordinary people in need.	God is concerned about the everyday needs of his people.
JOEL	835–796 (?)	Joash of Judah (The book of Joel)	Because a plague of locusts had come to punish the nation, called the people to turn back to God before an even greater judgment occurred.	While God judges all people for their sins, he gives eternal salvation only to those who have turned to him.
JONAH	793–753	Jeroboam II of Israel (2 Kings 14:25; the book of Jonah)	Warned Nineveh, the capital of Assyria, to repent of its sins.	God wants all nations to turn to him. His love reaches out to all peoples.
AMOS	760–750	Jeroboam II of Israel (The book of Amos)	Warned those who exploited or ignored the needy. (In Amos's day, Israel was an affluent and materialistic society.)	Believing in God is more than a personal matter. God calls all believers to work against injustices in society and to aid those less fortunate.
HOSEA	753–715	The last seven kings of Israel; Azariah (Uzziah), Jotham, Ahaz, and Hezekiah of Judah (The book of Hosea)	Condemned the people of Israel because they had sinned against God as an adulterous woman sins against her husband.	When we sin, we sever our relationship to God, breaking our commitment to him. While all must answer to God for their sins, those who seek God's forgiveness are spared from eternal judgment.

"The LORD warned Israel and Judah through all his prophets and seers: 'Turn from your evil ways. Observe my commands and decrees . . . '" (2 Kings 17:13). Who were these prophets? Here are some of those who tried to turn people back to God. Predicting the future as revealed by God was just one part of a prophet's job;

THESE PROPHETS?

Who?	When? (B.C.)	Ministered during the reign of these kings	Main message	Significance
MICAH	742–687	Jotham, Ahaz, and Hezekiah of Judah (The book of Micah)	Predicted the fall of both the northern and southern kingdoms. This was God's discipline on the people, actually showing how much he cared for them.	Choosing to live a life apart from God is making a commitment to sin. Sin leads to judgment and death. God alone shows us the way to eternal peace. His discipline often keeps us on the right path.
ISAIAH	740–681	Azariah (Uzziah), Jotham, Ahaz, Hezekiah, and Manasseh of Judah (The book of Isaiah)	Called the people back to a special relationship with God—although judgment through other nations was inevitable.	Sometimes we must suffer judgment and discipline before we are restored to God.
NAHUM	663–654	Manasseh of Judah (The book of Nahum)	The mighty empire of Assyria that oppressed God's people would soon tumble.	Those who do evil and oppress others will one day meet a bitter end.
ZEPHANIAH	640–621	Josiah of Judah (The book of Zephaniah)	A day would come when God, as Judge, would severely punish all nations; but afterward he would show mercy to his people.	We will all be judged for our disobedience to God, but if we remain faithful to him, he will show us mercy.
JEREMIAH	627–586	Josiah, Jehoahaz, Jehoiakim, Jehoiachin, Zedekiah of Judah (The book of Jeremiah)	Repentance would postpone Judah's coming judgment at the hands of Babylon.	Repentance is one of the greatest needs in our world of immorality. God's promises to the faithful shine brightly.
HABAKKUK	612–589	Josiah, Jehoahaz, Jehoiakim, Jehoiachin, Zedekiah of Judah (The book of Habakkuk)	Couldn't understand why God seemed to do nothing about the wickedness in society. Then realized that faith in God alone would one day supply the answer.	Instead of questioning the ways of God, we should realize that he is completely just, and we should have faith that he is in control and that one day evil will be utterly destroyed.
DANIEL	605–536	Prophesied as an exile in Babylon during the reigns of Nebuchadnezzar, Darius the Mede, and Cyrus of Persia (The book of Daniel)	Described both near and distant future events. Through it all, God is sovereign and triumphant.	We should spend less time wondering when the events will happen and more time learning how we should live now so we won't be victims of those events.
EZEKIEL	593–571	Prophesied as an exile in Babylon during the reign of Nebuchadnezzar (The book of Ezekiel)	Sent messages back to Jerusalem urging the people to turn back to God before they were all forced to join him in exile. After Jerusalem fell, he urged his fellow exiles to turn back to God so they could eventually return to their homeland.	God disciplines his people to draw them closer to him.

his main role was to preach God's word to the people—warning, instructing, and encouraging them to live as they ought. (The prophets Haggai, Zechariah, and Malachi were prophets to the people of Judah after they returned from exile. For more information, see the chart in Ezra 6, p. 716.)

⁵Hezekiah trusted *d* in the LORD, the God of Israel. There was no one like him among all the kings of Judah, either before him or after him. ⁶He held fast *e* to the LORD and did not cease to follow him; he kept the commands the LORD had given Moses. ⁷And the LORD was with him; he was successful *f* in whatever he undertook. He rebelled *g* against the king of Assyria and did not serve him. ⁸From watchtower to fortified city, *h* he defeated the Philistines, as far as Gaza and its territory.

⁹In King Hezekiah's fourth year, which was the seventh year of Hoshea son of Elah king of Israel, Shalmaneser king of Assyria marched against Samaria and laid siege to it. ¹⁰At the end of three years the Assyrians took it. So Samaria was captured in Hezekiah's sixth year, which was the ninth year of Hoshea king of Israel. ¹¹The king of Assyria deported Israel to Assyria and settled them in Halah, in Gozan on the Habor River and in towns of the Medes. ¹²This happened because they had not obeyed the LORD their God, but had violated his covenant—all that Moses the servant of the LORD commanded. *i* They neither listened to the commands *j* nor carried them out.

¹³In the fourteenth year of King Hezekiah's reign, Sennacherib king of Assyria attacked all the fortified cities of Judah *k* and captured them. ¹⁴So Hezekiah king of Judah sent this message to the king of Assyria at Lachish: "I have done wrong. Withdraw from me, and I will pay whatever you demand of me." The king of Assyria exacted from Hezekiah king of Judah three hundred talents *a* of silver and thirty talents *b* of gold. ¹⁵So Hezekiah gave *l* him all the silver that was found in the temple of the LORD and in the treasuries of the royal palace.

¹⁶At this time Hezekiah king of Judah stripped off the gold with which he had covered the doors and doorposts of the temple of the LORD, and gave it to the king of Assyria.

Sennacherib Threatens Jerusalem

¹⁷The king of Assyria sent his supreme commander, *m* his chief officer and his field commander with a large army, from Lachish to King Hezekiah at Jerusalem. They came up to Jerusalem and stopped at the aqueduct of the Upper Pool, *n* on the road to the Washerman's Field. ¹⁸They called for the king; and Eliakim *o* son of Hilkiah the palace administrator, Shebna *p* the secretary, and Joah son of Asaph the recorder went out to them.

¹⁹The field commander said to them, "Tell Hezekiah:

"'This is what the great king, the king of Assyria, says: On what are you basing this confidence of yours? ²⁰You say you have strategy and military strength—but you speak only empty words. On whom are you depending, that you rebel against me? ²¹Look now, you are depending on Egypt, *q* that splintered reed of a staff, *r* which pierces a man's hand and wounds him if he leans on it! Such is Pharaoh king of Egypt to all who depend on him. ²²And if you say to me, "We are depending on the LORD our God"— isn't he the one whose high places and altars Hezekiah removed, saying to Judah and Jerusalem, "You must worship before this altar in Jerusalem"?

a 14 That is, about 11 tons (about 10 metric tons) *b 14* That is, about 1 ton (about 1 metric ton)

18:5 "There was no one like him . . . ." In dramatic contrast with his father, Ahaz, Hezekiah followed God more closely and sincerely than any other king of Judah or Israel. This statement refers to the kings after the division of the kingdom and so does not include David, considered the king most devoted to God.

18:7 Judah was sandwiched between two world powers, Egypt and Assyria. Both wanted to control Judah and Israel because they lay at the vital crossroads of all ancient Near East trade. The nation who controlled Judah would have a military and economic advantage over its rivals. When Hezekiah became king, Assyria controlled Judah. Acting with great courage, Hezekiah rebelled against this mighty empire to whom his father had submitted. He placed his faith in God's strength rather than his own, and he obeyed God's commands in spite of the obstacles and dangers that, from a purely human standpoint, looked overwhelming.

18:9–12 These verses flash back to the days just before Israel's destruction. Hezekiah reigned with his father Ahaz for 14 years (729–715 B.C.), by himself for 18 years (715–697 B.C.), and with his son Manasseh for 11 years (697–686 B.C.), a total of 43 years. The 29 years listed in 18:2 indicate only those years in which Hezekiah had complete control of the kingdom. While Hezekiah was on the throne, the nation of Israel to the north

was destroyed (722 B.C.). Knowing Israel's fate probably caused Hezekiah to reform his own nation. (For more on Hezekiah, see 2 Chronicles 29—32 and Isaiah 36—39.)

18:13 This event occurred in 701 B.C., four years after Sennacherib had become Assyria's king. Sennacherib was the son of Sargon II, the king who had deported Israel's people into captivity (see the note on 17:3). To keep Assyria from attacking, the southern kingdom paid tribute annually. But when Sennacherib became king, Hezekiah stopped paying this money, hoping Assyria would ignore him. When Sennacherib and his army retaliated, Hezekiah realized his mistake and paid the tribute money (18:14), but Sennacherib attacked anyway (18:19ff). Although Sennacherib attacked Judah, he was not as war-hungry as the previous Assyrian kings, preferring to spend most of his time building and beautifying his capital city, Nineveh. With less frequent invasions, Hezekiah was able to institute many reforms and strengthen the nation.

18:17 Sending the supreme commander, the chief officer, and the field commander was like sending the vice president, secretary of state, and the head general of the army to speak to the enemy prior to a battle. All of these men were sent in an effort to impress and discourage the Israelites.

**Cross-references (right margin):**

18:5 *d*2Ki 19:10; 23:25

18:6 *e*Dt 10:20

18:7 *f*Ge 39:3; 1Sa 18:14 *g*2Ki 16:7

18:8 *h*2Ki 17:9; Isa 14:29

18:12 *i*Da 9:6, 10 *j*1Ki 9:6

18:13 *k*2Ch 32:1

18:15 *l*1Ki 15:18; 2Ki 16:8

18:17 *m*Isa 20:1 *n*2Ki 20:20

18:18 *o*2Ki 19:2; Isa 22:20 *p*Isa 22:15

18:21 *q*Eze 29:6 *r*Isa 30:5, 7

²³"'Come now, make a bargain with my master, the king of Assyria: I will give you two thousand horses—if you can put riders on them! ²⁴How can you repulse one officer of the least of my master's officials, even though you are depending on Egypt for chariots and horsemenªᵃ? ²⁵Furthermore, have I come to attack and destroy this place without word from the LORD? The LORD himself told me to march against this country and destroy it.'"

²⁶Then Eliakim son of Hilkiah, and Shebna and Joah said to the field commander, "Please speak to your servants in Aramaic,ˢ since we understand it. Don't speak to us in Hebrew in the hearing of the people on the wall."

²⁷But the commander replied, "Was it only to your master and you that my master sent

18:26
ˢEzr 4:7

ᵃ24 Or *charioteers*

HEZEKIAH

The past is an important part of today's actions and tomorrow's plans. The people and kings of Judah had a rich past, filled with God's action, guidance, and commands. But with each passing generation, they also had a growing list of tragedies that occurred when the people forgot that their God, who had cared for them in the past, also cared about the present and the future—and demanded their continued obedience. Hezekiah was one of the few kings of Judah who was constantly aware of God's acts in the past and his interest in the events of every day. The Bible describes him as a king who had a close relationship with God.

As a reformer, Hezekiah was most concerned with present obedience. Judah was filled with visual reminders of the people's lack of trust in God, and Hezekiah boldly cleaned house. Altars, idols, and pagan temples were destroyed. Even the bronze snake Moses had made in the desert was not spared because it had ceased to point the people to God and had also become an idol. The temple in Jerusalem, whose doors had been nailed shut by Hezekiah's own father, was cleaned out and reopened. The Passover was reinstituted as a national holiday, and there was revival in Judah.

Although he had a natural inclination to respond to present problems, Hezekiah's life shows little evidence of concern about the future. He took few actions to preserve the effects of his sweeping reforms. His successful efforts made him proud. His unwise display of wealth to the Babylonian delegation got Judah included on Babylon's "Nations to Conquer" list. When Isaiah informed Hezekiah of the foolishness of his act, the king's answer displayed his persistent lack of foresight—he was thankful that any evil consequences would be delayed until after he died. And the lives of three kings who followed him—Manasseh, Amon, and Josiah—were deeply affected by both Hezekiah's accomplishments *and* his weaknesses.

The past affects your decisions and actions today, and these, in turn, affect the future. There are lessons to learn and errors to avoid repeating. Remember that part of the success of your past will be measured by what you do with it now and how well you use it to prepare for the future.

Strengths and accomplishments:	• Was the king of Judah who instigated civil and religious reforms • Had a personal, growing relationship with God • Developed a powerful prayer life • Noted as the patron of several chapters in the book of Proverbs (Proverbs 25:1)
Weaknesses and mistakes:	• Showed little interest or wisdom in planning for the future and protecting for others the spiritual heritage he enjoyed • Rashly showed all his wealth to messengers from Babylon
Lessons from his life:	• Sweeping reforms are short-lived when little action is taken to preserve them for the future • Past obedience to God does not remove the possibility of present disobedience • Complete dependence on God yields amazing results
Vital statistics:	• Where: Jerusalem • Occupation: 13th king of Judah, the southern kingdom • Relatives: Father: Ahaz. Mother: Abijah. Son: Manasseh. • Contemporaries: Isaiah, Hoshea, Micah, Sennacherib
Key verses:	"Hezekiah trusted in the LORD, the God of Israel. There was no one like him among all the kings of Judah, either before him or after him. He held fast to the LORD and did not cease to follow him; he kept the commands the LORD had given Moses" (2 Kings 18:5, 6).

Hezekiah's story is told in 2 Kings 16:20—20:21; 2 Chronicles 28:27—32:33; Isaiah 36:1—39:8. He is also mentioned in Proverbs 25:1; Isaiah 1:1; Jeremiah 15:4; 26:18, 19; Hosea 1:1; Micah 1:1.

me to say these things, and not to the men sitting on the wall—who, like you, will have to eat their own filth and drink their own urine?'"

28 Then the commander stood and called out in Hebrew: "Hear the word of the great king, the king of Assyria! 29 This is what the king says: Do not let Hezekiah deceive you. He cannot deliver you from my hand. 30 Do not let Hezekiah persuade you to trust in the LORD when he says, 'The LORD will surely deliver us; this city will not be given into the hand of the king of Assyria.'

31 "Do not listen to Hezekiah. This is what the king of Assyria says: Make peace with me and come out to me. Then every one of you will eat from his own vine and fig tree *t* and drink water from his own cistern, 32 until I come and take you to a land like your own, a land of grain and new wine, a land of bread and vineyards, a land of olive trees and honey. Choose life *u* and not death!

"Do not listen to Hezekiah, for he is misleading you when he says, 'The LORD will deliver us.' 33 Has the god *v* of any nation ever delivered his land from the hand of the king of Assyria? 34 Where are the gods of Hamath *w* and Arpad? Where are the gods of Sepharvaim, Hena and Ivvah? Have they rescued Samaria from my hand? 35 Who of all the gods of these countries has been able to save his land from me? How then can the LORD deliver Jerusalem from my hand?"

36 But the people remained silent and said nothing in reply, because the king had commanded, "Do not answer him."

37 Then Eliakim son of Hilkiah the palace administrator, Shebna the secretary and Joah son of Asaph the recorder went to Hezekiah, with their clothes torn, and told him what the field commander had said.

Jerusalem's Deliverance Foretold

19 When King Hezekiah heard this, he tore *x* his clothes and put on sackcloth and went into the temple of the LORD. 2 He sent Eliakim the palace administrator, Shebna the secretary and the leading priests, all wearing sackcloth, to the prophet Isaiah son of Amoz. 3 They told him, "This is what Hezekiah says: This day is a day of distress and rebuke and disgrace, as when children come to the point of birth and there is no strength to deliver them. 4 It may be that the LORD your God will hear all the words of the field commander, whom his master, the king of Assyria, has sent to ridicule *y* the living God, and that he will rebuke *z* him for the words the LORD your God has heard. Therefore pray for the remnant that still survives."

5 When King Hezekiah's officials came to Isaiah, 6 Isaiah said to them, "Tell your master, 'This is what the LORD says: Do not be afraid of what you have heard—those words with which the underlings of the king of Assyria have blasphemed me. 7 Listen! I am going to put such a spirit in him that when he hears a certain report, he will return to his own country, and there I will have him cut down with the sword. *a*'"

8 When the field commander heard that the king of Assyria had left Lachish, *b* he withdrew and found the king fighting against Libnah.

9 Now Sennacherib received a report that Tirhakah, the Cushite *a* king ⌊of Egypt⌋, was marching out to fight against him. So he again sent messengers to Hezekiah with this word: 10 "Say to Hezekiah king of Judah: Do not let the god you depend *c* on deceive you when he says, 'Jerusalem will not be handed over to the king of Assyria.' 11 Surely you have heard what the kings of Assyria have done to all the countries, destroying them completely. And will you be delivered? 12 Did the gods of the nations that were destroyed by my forefathers deliver *d* them: the gods of Gozan, Haran, Rezeph and the people of Eden who were in Tel Assar? 13 Where is the king of Hamath, the king of Arpad, the king of the city of Sepharvaim, or of Hena or Ivvah?" *e*

a9 That is, from the upper Nile region

Margin cross-references

18:31 *t* 1Ki 4:25

18:32 *u* Dt 8:7-9

18:33 *v* 2Ki 19:12

18:34 *w* 2Ki 17:24; 19:13

19:1 *x* Ge 37:34; 1Ki 21:27; 2Ch 32:20-22

19:4 *y* 2Ki 18:35 *z* 2Sa 16:12

19:7 *a* ver 37

19:8 *b* 2Ki 18:14

19:10 *c* 2Ki 18:5

19:12 *d* 2Ki 18:33

19:13 *e* 2Ki 18:34

19:1-7 Sennacherib, whose armies had captured all the fortified cities of Judah, sent a message to Hezekiah to surrender. Realizing the situation was hopeless, Hezekiah went to the temple and prayed. God answered Hezekiah's prayer and delivered Judah by sending an army to attack the Assyrian camp, forcing Sennacherib to leave at once. Prayer should be our first response in any crisis. Don't wait until things are hopeless. Pray daily for his guidance. Our problems are God's opportunities.

19:2 Isaiah the prophet had been working for God since the days of Uzziah—40 years (Isaiah 6:1). Although Assyria was a world power, it could not conquer Judah as long as Isaiah counseled the kings. Isaiah prophesied during the reigns of Uzziah (Azariah), Jotham, Ahaz, and Hezekiah. Ahaz ignored Isaiah, but Hezekiah listened to his advice. To read his prophecies, see the book of Isaiah.

Hezekiah's Prayer

14Hezekiah received the letter from the messengers and read it. Then he went up to the temple of the LORD and spread it out before the LORD. 15And Hezekiah prayed to the LORD: "O LORD, God of Israel, enthroned between the cherubim, you alone are God over all the kingdoms of the earth. You have made heaven and earth. 16Give ear,*f* O LORD, and hear; open your eyes,*g* O LORD, and see; listen to the words Sennacherib has sent to insult the living God.

17"It is true, O LORD, that the Assyrian kings have laid waste these nations and their lands. 18They have thrown their gods into the fire and destroyed them, for they were not gods*h* but only wood and stone, fashioned by men's hands. 19Now, O LORD our God, deliver us from his hand, so that all kingdoms on earth may know*i* that you alone, O LORD, are God."

Isaiah Prophesies Sennacherib's Fall

20Then Isaiah son of Amoz sent a message to Hezekiah: "This is what the LORD, the God of Israel, says: I have heard your prayer concerning Sennacherib king of Assyria. 21This is the word that the LORD has spoken against him:

"'The Virgin Daughter*j* of Zion
　　despises you and mocks you.
The Daughter of Jerusalem
　　tosses her head as you flee.
22 Who is it you have insulted and blasphemed?
　　Against whom have you raised your voice
and lifted your eyes in pride?
　　Against the Holy One of Israel!
23 By your messengers
　　you have heaped insults on the Lord.
And you have said,
　　"With my many chariots*k*
I have ascended the heights of the mountains,
　　the utmost heights of Lebanon.
I have cut down its tallest cedars,
　　the choicest of its pines.
I have reached its remotest parts,
　　the finest of its forests.
24 I have dug wells in foreign lands
　　and drunk the water there.
With the soles of my feet
　　I have dried up all the streams of Egypt."

25 "'Have you not heard?
　　Long ago I ordained it.
In days of old I planned*l* it;
　　now I have brought it to pass,
that you have turned fortified cities
　　into piles of stone.
26 Their people, drained of power,
　　are dismayed and put to shame.
They are like plants in the field,
　　like tender green shoots,
like grass sprouting on the roof,
　　scorched*m* before it grows up.

19:16
f Ps 31:2
g ver 4; 2Ch 6:40

19:18
h Jer 10:3-10
19:19
i Ps 83:18

19:21
j La 2:13

19:23
k Ps 20:7

19:25
l Isa 10:5; 45:7

19:26
m Ps 129:6

19:15 Cherubim are mighty angels.

19:15–19 Although Hezekiah came boldly to God, he did not take God for granted or approach him flippantly. Instead, Hezekiah acknowledged God's sovereignty and Judah's total dependence on him. Hezekiah's prayer provides a good model for us. We should not be afraid to approach God with our prayers, but we must come to him with respect for who he is and what he can do.

19:21–34 God replied to Sennacherib's taunting words (18:19–25), indicting him for arrogance. Sennacherib believed his kingdom had grown because of his own efforts and strength. In reality, said God, he succeeded only because of what God had allowed and caused. It is arrogance to think we are solely responsible for our achievements. God, as Creator, rules over nations and people.

27 "'But I know[n] where you stay
    and when you come and go
    and how you rage against me.
28 Because you rage against me
    and your insolence has reached my ears,
  I will put my hook[o] in your nose
    and my bit in your mouth,
  and I will make you return[p]
    by the way you came.'

29 "This will be the sign[q] for you, O Hezekiah:

"This year you will eat what grows by itself,
    and the second year what springs from that.
  But in the third year sow and reap,
    plant vineyards and eat their fruit.
30 Once more a remnant of the house of Judah
    will take root[r] below and bear fruit above.
31 For out of Jerusalem will come a remnant,
    and out of Mount Zion a band of survivors.

The zeal[s] of the LORD Almighty will accomplish this.

32 "Therefore this is what the LORD says concerning the king of Assyria:

"He will not enter this city
    or shoot an arrow here.
  He will not come before it with shield
    or build a siege ramp against it.
33 By the way that he came he will return;[t]
    he will not enter this city,
                                                        declares the LORD.
34 I will defend[u] this city and save it,
    for my sake and for the sake of David[v] my servant."

35 That night the angel of the LORD went out and put to death a hundred and eighty-five thousand men in the Assyrian camp. When the people got up the next morning—there were all the dead bodies! 36 So Sennacherib king of Assyria broke camp and withdrew. He returned to Nineveh and stayed there.

37 One day, while he was worshiping in the temple of his god Nisroch, his sons Adrammelech and Sharezer cut him down with the sword,[w] and they escaped to the land of Ararat. And Esarhaddon[x] his son succeeded him as king.

Hezekiah's Illness

20 In those days Hezekiah became ill and was at the point of death. The prophet Isaiah son of Amoz went to him and said, "This is what the LORD says: Put your house in order, because you are going to die; you will not recover." 2 Hezekiah turned his face to the wall and prayed to the LORD, 3 "Remember,[y] O LORD, how I have walked before you faithfully and with wholehearted devotion and have done what is good in your eyes." And Hezekiah wept bitterly.

4 Before Isaiah had left the middle court, the word of the LORD came to him: 5 "Go back and tell Hezekiah, the leader of my people, 'This is what the LORD, the God of your father David,

19:27
[n]Ps 139:1-4

19:28
[o]Eze 29:4
[p]ver 33

19:29
[q]Lk 2:12

19:30
[r]2Ch 32:22-23

19:31
[s]Isa 9:7

19:33
[t]ver 28

19:34
[u]2Ki 20:6
[v]1Ki 11:12-13

19:37
[w]ver 7
[x]Ezr 4:2

20:3
[y]Ne 13:22

19:28 The Assyrians treated captives with cruelty. They tortured prisoners for entertainment by blinding them, cutting them, or pulling off strips of their skin until they died. If the Assyrians wished to make a captive a slave, they would often put a hook in his nose. God was saying that the Assyrians would be treated the way they had treated others.

19:31 As long as a tiny spark remains, a fire can be rekindled and fanned into a roaring blaze. Similarly, if just a small remnant of true believers retains the spark of faith, God can rebuild it into a strong nation. And if only a glimmer of faith remains in a heart,

God can use it to restore blazing faith in that believer. If you feel that only a spark of faith remains in you, ask God to use it to rekindle a blazing fire of commitment to him.

20:5, 6 Over a 100-year period of Judah's history (732–640 B.C.), Hezekiah was the only faithful king; but what a difference he made! Because of Hezekiah's faith and prayer, God healed him and saved his city from the Assyrians. You can make a difference too, even if your faith puts you in the minority. Faith and prayer, if they are sincere and directed toward the one true God, can change any situation.

20:5
z 1Sa 9:16; 1Ki 9:3;
2Ki 19:20
a Ps 39:12
20:6
b 2Ki 19:34

says: I have heard z your prayer and seen your tears; a I will heal you. On the third day from now you will go up to the temple of the Lord. 6 I will add fifteen years to your life. And I will deliver you and this city from the hand of the king of Assyria. I will defend b this city for my sake and for the sake of my servant David.'"

7 Then Isaiah said, "Prepare a poultice of figs." They did so and applied it to the boil, and he recovered.

8 Hezekiah had asked Isaiah, "What will be the sign that the Lord will heal me and that I will go up to the temple of the Lord on the third day from now?"

9 Isaiah answered, "This is the Lord's sign to you that the Lord will do what he has promised: Shall the shadow go forward ten steps, or shall it go back ten steps?"

10 "It is a simple matter for the shadow to go forward ten steps," said Hezekiah. "Rather, have it go back ten steps."

11 Then the prophet Isaiah called upon the Lord, and the Lord made the shadow go back the ten steps it had gone down on the stairway of Ahaz.

Envoys From Babylon

12 At that time Merodach-Baladan son of Baladan king of Babylon sent Hezekiah letters and a gift, because he had heard of Hezekiah's illness. 13 Hezekiah received the messengers and showed them all that was in his storehouses—the silver, the gold, the spices and the fine oil—his armory and everything found among his treasures. There was nothing in his palace or in all his kingdom that Hezekiah did not show them.

14 Then Isaiah the prophet went to King Hezekiah and asked, "What did those men say, and where did they come from?"

"From a distant land," Hezekiah replied. "They came from Babylon."

15 The prophet asked, "What did they see in your palace?"

"They saw everything in my palace," Hezekiah said. "There is nothing among my treasures that I did not show them."

20:17
c 2Ki 24:13; 25:13;
Jer 52:17-23
20:18
d 2Ki 24:15;
2Ch 33:11

16 Then Isaiah said to Hezekiah, "Hear the word of the Lord: 17 The time will surely come when everything in your palace, and all that your fathers have stored up until this day, will be carried off to Babylon. c Nothing will be left, says the Lord. 18 And some of your descendants, d your own flesh and blood, that will be born to you, will be taken away, and they will become eunuchs in the palace of the king of Babylon."

19 "The word of the Lord you have spoken is good," Hezekiah replied. For he thought, "Will there not be peace and security in my lifetime?"

20:20
e Ne 3:16

20 As for the other events of Hezekiah's reign, all his achievements and how he made the pool e and the tunnel by which he brought water into the city, are they not written in the book of the annals of the kings of Judah? 21 Hezekiah rested with his fathers. And Manasseh his son succeeded him as king.

20:11 The stairway of Ahaz was a sundial. Egyptian sundials in this period were sometimes made in the form of miniature staircases so that the shadows moved up and down the steps.

20:12–19 Hezekiah had been a good and faithful king. But when Isaiah asked him what he had shown the messengers from Babylon, he replied, "They saw everything in my palace." From the account in 2 Chronicles 32:24–31, it appears that Hezekiah's prosperity, success, and deliverance from sickness had made him proud. Rather than giving credit to God for all his blessings, he tried to impress the foreigners. When God helps us, we must not use his blessings to impress others. A testimony of victory can quickly degenerate into vanity and self-congratulations.

20:14 Babylon, a city that had rebelled against the Assyrian empire, was destroyed by Sennacherib in 689 B.C. This event probably occurred shortly before that date. When Sennacherib died in 681 B.C., his son, Esarhaddon, foolishly rebuilt the city of Babylon. Assyria, whose rulers at that time were weak, allowed Babylon plenty of opportunity to become strong. As the Assyrian army marched off to conquer and oppress faraway lands, the city of Babylon grew and expanded into a small nation. After some years, Babylon was strong enough to rebel

again. It eventually crushed Assyria (612 B.C.) and became the next world power.

20:19 Hezekiah was saying that it was good that these terrible events foretold by Isaiah wouldn't happen during his lifetime. Hezekiah's statement seems selfish, shortsighted, and proud. He knew that his nation would be punished for its sins, so he may have been acknowledging and thanking God for choosing not to destroy Judah during his lifetime.

20:20 The pool and the tunnel refer to a 1,777-foot tunnel built from the Gihon spring to the Pool of Siloam (see 2 Chronicles 32:30). It was from a water source outside the wall of Jerusalem to a secure reservoir inside the city. This was done so the Assyrian army would not cut off the city's water supply.

Manasseh King of Judah

21 Manasseh was twelve years old when he became king, and he reigned in Jerusalem fifty-five years. His mother's name was Hephzibah. ²He did evil in the eyes of the LORD, following the detestable practices*f* of the nations the LORD had driven out before the Israelites. ³He rebuilt the high places*g* his father Hezekiah had destroyed; he also erected altars to Baal*h* and made an Asherah pole, as Ahab king of Israel had done. He bowed down to all the starry hosts*i* and worshiped them. ⁴He built altars*j* in the temple of the LORD, of which the LORD had said, "In Jerusalem I will put my Name."*k* ⁵In both courts of the temple of the LORD, he built altars to all the starry hosts. ⁶He sacrificed his own son*l* in[a] the fire, practiced sorcery and divination, and consulted mediums and spiritists.*m* He did much evil in the eyes of the LORD, provoking him to anger.

⁷He took the carved Asherah pole he had made and put it in the temple, of which the LORD had said to David and to his son Solomon, "In this temple and in Jerusalem, which I have chosen out of all the tribes of Israel, I will put my Name*n* forever. ⁸I will not again*o* make the feet of the Israelites wander from the land I gave their forefathers, if only they will be careful to do everything I commanded them and will keep the whole Law that my servant Moses gave them." ⁹But the people did not listen. Manasseh led them astray, so that they did more evil*p* than the nations the LORD had destroyed before the Israelites.

¹⁰The LORD said through his servants the prophets: ¹¹"Manasseh king of Judah has committed these detestable sins. He has done more evil*q* than the Amorites*r* who preceded him and has led Judah into sin with his idols. ¹²Therefore this is what the LORD, the God of Israel, says: I am going to bring such disaster on Jerusalem and Judah that the ears of everyone who hears of it will tingle.*s* ¹³I will stretch out over Jerusalem the measuring line used against Samaria and the plumb line*t* used against the house of Ahab. I will wipe out Jerusalem as one wipes a dish, wiping it and turning it upside down. ¹⁴I will forsake*u* the remnant*v* of my inheritance and hand them over to their enemies. They will be looted and plundered by all their foes, ¹⁵because they have done evil in my eyes and have provoked me to anger from the day their forefathers came out of Egypt until this day."

¹⁶Moreover, Manasseh also shed so much innocent blood*w* that he filled Jerusalem from end to end—besides the sin that he had caused Judah to commit, so that they did evil in the eyes of the LORD.

¹⁷As for the other events of Manasseh's reign, and all he did, including the sin he committed, are they not written in the book of the annals of the kings of Judah? ¹⁸Manasseh rested with his fathers and was buried in his palace garden, the garden of Uzza. And Amon his son succeeded him as king.

Amon King of Judah

¹⁹Amon was twenty-two years old when he became king, and he reigned in Jerusalem two years. His mother's name was Meshullemeth daughter of Haruz; she was from Jotbah. ²⁰He did evil*x* in the eyes of the LORD, as his father Manasseh had done. ²¹He walked in all the ways of his father; he worshiped the idols his father had worshiped, and bowed down to them. ²²He forsook the LORD, the God of his fathers, and did not walk*y* in the way of the LORD.

a 6 Or He made his own son pass through

**Cross references (margin):**
- 21:2 *f* 2Ki 16:3
- 21:3 *g* 2Ki 18:4; *h* 1Ki 16:32; *i* Dt 17:3; 2Ki 17:16
- 21:4 *j* Jer 32:34; *k* 2Sa 7:13; 1Ki 8:29
- 21:6 *l* Lev 18:21; Dt 18:10; 2Ki 16:3; 17:17; *m* Lev 19:31
- 21:7 *n* 1Ki 8:29; 9:3
- 21:8 *o* 2Sa 7:10
- 21:9 *p* Pr 29:12
- 21:11 *q* 2Ki 24:3-4; *r* 1Ki 21:26
- 21:12 *s* 1Sa 3:11; Jer 19:3
- 21:13 *t* Isa 34:11; Am 7:7-9
- 21:14 *u* Ps 78:58-60; *v* 2Ki 19:4
- 21:16 *w* 2Ki 24:4
- 21:20 *x* ver 2-6
- 21:22 *y* 1Ki 11:33

21:1ff Manasseh followed the example of his grandfather Ahaz more than that of his father. He adopted the wicked practices of the Babylonians and Canaanites including sacrificing his own son (21:6). Manasseh did not listen to the words of God's prophets, but willfully led his people into sin. (See his Profile in 2 Chronicles 33, p. 695 for more information about his life. The "high places" were shrines in the hills for worshiping idols.)

21:6 Manasseh was an evil king, and he angered God with his sin. Listed among Manasseh's sins are occult practices—sorcery and divination, and consulting mediums and spiritists. These acts were strictly forbidden by God (Leviticus 19:31; Deuteronomy 18:9–13) because they demonstrate a lack of faith in him, involve sinful actions, and open the door to demonic influences. Today, many books, television shows, and games emphasize fortune-telling, seances, and other occult practices. Don't let

desire to know the future or the belief that superstition is harmless lead you into condoning occult practices. They are counterfeits of God's power and have at their root a system of beliefs totally opposed to God.

21:7 Asherah was a Canaanite mother-goddess, a mistress of Baal. Her images were made of wood. In Exodus 34:13 and Deuteronomy 12:3, the Israelites were expressly forbidden to associate with Asherah practices in any way.

21:13 The measuring line and the plumb line symbolize the judgment process. These measuring instruments used in construction measured Jerusalem and the city was found lacking. God was saying that he would destroy Jerusalem as he did Samaria and the house of Ahab.

21:16 Tradition says that during Manasseh's massive slaughter, Isaiah was sawed in two when trying to hide in a hollow log (see Hebrews 11:37, 38). Other prophets may also have been killed at this time.

23Amon's officials conspired against him and assassinated the king in his palace. 24Then the people of the land killed all who had plotted against King Amon, and they made Josiah his son king in his place.

25As for the other events of Amon's reign, and what he did, are they not written in the book of the annals of the kings of Judah? 26He was buried in his grave in the garden of Uzza. And Josiah his son succeeded him as king.

The Book of the Law Found

22 Josiah was eight years old when he became king, and he reigned in Jerusalem thirty-one years. His mother's name was Jedidah daughter of Adaiah; she was from Boz-kath.z 2He did what was right in the eyes of the Lord and walked in all the ways of his father David, not turning aside to the righta or to the left.

3In the eighteenth year of his reign, King Josiah sent the secretary, Shaphan son of Azaliah, the son of Meshullam, to the temple of the Lord. He said: 4"Go up to Hilkiah the high priest and have him get ready the money that has been brought into the temple of the Lord, which the doorkeepers have collectedb from the people. 5Have them entrust it to the men appointed to supervise the work on the temple. And have these men pay the workers who repairc the temple of the Lord— 6the carpenters, the builders and the masons. Also have them purchase timber and dressed stone to repair the temple. 7But they need not account for the money entrusted to them, because they are acting faithfully."d

8Hilkiah the high priest said to Shaphan the secretary, "I have found the Book of the Lawe in the temple of the Lord." He gave it to Shaphan, who read it. 9Then Shaphan the secretary went to the king and reported to him: "Your officials have paid out the money that was in the temple of the Lord and have entrusted it to the workers and supervisors at the temple." 10Then Shaphan the secretary informed the king, "Hilkiah the priest has given me a book." And Shaphan read from it in the presence of the king.

11When the king heard the words of the Book of the Law, he tore his robes. 12He gave these orders to Hilkiah the priest, Ahikamf son of Shaphan, Acbor son of Micaiah, Shaphan the secretary and Asaiah the king's attendant: 13"Go and inquire of the Lord for me and for the people and for all Judah about what is written in this book that has been found. Great is the Lord's angerg that burns against us because our fathers have not obeyed the words of this book; they have not acted in accordance with all that is written there concerning us."

14Hilkiah the priest, Ahikam, Acbor, Shaphan and Asaiah went to speak to the prophetess Huldah, who was the wife of Shallum son of Tikvah, the son of Harhas, keeper of the wardrobe. She lived in Jerusalem, in the Second District.

15She said to them, "This is what the Lord, the God of Israel, says: Tell the man who sent you to me, 16'This is what the Lord says: I am going to bring disaster on this place and its people, according to everything written in the bookh the king of Judah has read. 17Because they have forsakeni me and burned incense to other gods and provoked me to anger by all the idols their hands have made,a my anger will burn against this place and will not be quenched.' 18Tell the king of Judah, who sent you to inquire of the Lord, 'This is what the

a17 Or by everything they have done

22:1
z Jos 15:39
22:2
a Dt 5:32

22:4
b 2Ki 12:4-5

22:5
c 2Ki 12:5, 11-14

22:7
d 2Ki 12:15

22:8
e Dt 31:24

22:12
f 2Ki 25:22

22:13
g Dt 29:24-28

22:16
h Dt 29:27; Da 9:11
22:17
i Dt 29:25-27

22:1, 2 In reading the Biblical lists of kings, it is rare to find one who obeyed God completely. Josiah was such a person, and he was only eight years old when he began to reign. For 18 years Josiah reigned obediently; then, when he was 26, he began the reforms based on God's laws. Children are the future leaders of our churches and our world. A person's major work for God may have to wait until he or she is an adult, but no one is ever too young to take God seriously and obey him. Josiah's early years laid the base for his later task of reforming Judah. God can use you, regardless of your age.

22:4 The doorkeepers controlled who entered the temple and supervised the collection of the money.

22:8 This book may have been the entire Pentateuch (Genesis—Deuteronomy) or just the book of Deuteronomy. Because of the long line of evil kings, the record of God's laws had been lost. Josiah, who was about 26 years old at this time, wanted religious reform throughout the nation. When God's Word was found, drastic changes had to be made to bring the kingdom in line with

God's commands. Today you have God's Word at your fingertips. How much change must you make in order to bring your life into line with God's Word?

22:11ff When Josiah heard the law, he tore his robes in despair. He immediately instituted reforms. With just one reading of God's law, he changed the course of the nation. Today many people own Bibles, but few are affected by the truths found in God's Word. The Word of God should cause us, like Josiah, to take action immediately to reform our lives and bring them into harmony with God's will.

22:14 Huldah was a prophetess, as were Miriam (Exodus 15:20) and Deborah (Judges 4:4). God freely selects his servants to carry out his will—rich or poor, male or female, king or slave (Joel 2:28–30). Huldah was obviously highly regarded by the people of her time.

LORD, the God of Israel, says concerning the words you heard: [19]Because your heart was responsive and you humbled[j] yourself before the LORD when you heard what I have spoken against this place and its people, that they would become accursed[k] and laid waste,[l] and because you tore your robes and wept in my presence, I have heard you, declares the LORD. [20]Therefore I will gather you to your fathers, and you will be buried in peace. Your eyes will not see all the disaster I am going to bring on this place.'"

So they took her answer back to the king.

Josiah Renews the Covenant

23 Then the king called together all the elders of Judah and Jerusalem. [2]He went up to the temple of the LORD with the men of Judah, the people of Jerusalem, the priests and the prophets—all the people from the least to the greatest. He read[m] in their hearing all the words of the Book of the Covenant, which had been found in the temple of the LORD. [3]The king stood by the pillar and renewed the covenant[n] in the presence of the LORD—to follow[o] the LORD and keep his commands, regulations and decrees with all his heart and all his soul, thus confirming the words of the covenant written in this book. Then all the people pledged themselves to the covenant.

[4]The king ordered Hilkiah the high priest, the priests next in rank and the doorkeepers to remove from the temple of the LORD all the articles made for Baal and Asherah and all the starry hosts. He burned them outside Jerusalem in the fields of the Kidron Valley and took the ashes to Bethel. [5]He did away with the pagan priests appointed by the kings of Judah to burn incense on the high places of the towns of Judah and on those around Jerusalem—those who burned incense to Baal, to the sun and moon, to the constellations and to all the starry hosts. [6]He took the Asherah pole from the temple of the LORD to the Kidron Valley outside Jerusalem and burned it there. He ground it to powder and scattered the dust over the graves of the common people. [7]He also tore down the quarters of the male shrine prostitutes,[p] which were in the temple of the LORD and where women did weaving for Asherah.

[8]Josiah brought all the priests from the towns of Judah and desecrated the high places, from Geba[q] to Beersheba, where the priests had burned incense. He broke down the shrines[a] at the gates—at the entrance to the Gate of Joshua, the city governor, which is on the left of the city gate. [9]Although the priests of the high places did not serve[r] at the altar of the LORD in Jerusalem, they ate unleavened bread with their fellow priests.

[10]He desecrated Topheth,[s] which was in the Valley of Ben Hinnom, so no one could use it to sacrifice his son[t] or daughter in[b] the fire to Molech. [11]He removed from the entrance to the temple of the LORD the horses that the kings of Judah had dedicated to the sun. They were in the court near the room of an official named Nathan-Melech. Josiah then burned the chariots dedicated to the sun.

[12]He pulled down the altars the kings of Judah had erected on the roof[u] near the upper room of Ahaz, and the altars Manasseh had built in the two courts[v] of the temple of the LORD. He removed them from there, smashed them to pieces and threw the rubble into the Kidron Valley. [13]The king also desecrated the high places that were east of Jerusalem on the south of the Hill of Corruption—the ones Solomon[w] king of Israel had built for Ashtoreth the vile goddess of the Sidonians, for Chemosh the vile god of Moab, and for Molech[c] the detestable god of the people of Ammon. [14]Josiah smashed[x] the sacred stones and cut down the Asherah poles and covered the sites with human bones.

[a]8 Or high places   [b]10 Or to make his son or daughter pass through   [c]13 Hebrew Milcom

---

22:19
[j]1Ki 21:29;
Ps 51:17; Isa 57:15
[k]Jer 26:6
[l]Lev 26:31

23:2
[m]Dt 31:11; 2Ki 22:8

23:3
[n]2Ki 11:14, 17
[o]Dt 13:4

23:7
[p]1Ki 14:24; 15:12;
Eze 16:16

23:8
[q]1Ki 15:22

23:9
[r]Eze 44:10-14

23:10
[s]Isa 30:33;
Jer 7:31, 32
[t]Lev 18:21

23:12
[u]Jer 19:13; Zep 1:5
[v]2Ki 21:5

23:13
[w]1Ki 11:7

23:14
[x]Ex 23:24;
Dt 7:5, 25

22:19 When Josiah realized how corrupt his nation had become, he tore his robes and wept before God. Then God had mercy on him and the nation. Josiah used the customs of his day to show his repentance. Today, we are unlikely to tear our clothing in sorrow for our sin, but weeping, fasting, making restitution or apologies (if our sin has involved others) demonstrate our sincerity when we repent. The hardest part of repentance is changing the attitudes that originally produced the sinful behavior.

23:1, 2 For more about the importance and operation of the temple, see 1 Kings 5—8 and 2 Chronicles 2—7.

23:4-8 When Josiah realized the terrible state of Judah's religious life, he did something about it. It is not enough to say we believe what is right; we must respond with action, doing what faith requires. This is what James was emphasizing when he

wrote, "faith without deeds is useless" (James 2:20). This means acting differently at home, school, work, and church. Simply talking about obedience is not enough.

23:6 This shameful Asherah pole had been set up in God's temple by the evil King Manasseh (21:7). Asherah is most often identified as a sea goddess and the mistress of Baal. She was a chief goddess of the Canaanites. Her worship glorified sex and war and was accompanied by male prostitution.

23:13 The Mount of Olives is here called the Hill of Corruption because it had become a favorite spot to build pagan shrines. Solomon built a pagan shrine and other kings built places of idol worship there. But God-fearing kings such as Hezekiah and Josiah destroyed these pagan worship centers. In New Testament times, Jesus often sat on the Mount of Olives and taught his disciples

23:15
y 1Ki 12:33

23:16
z 1Ki 13:2

23:18
a 1Ki 13:31

23:20
b 2Ki 11:18

¹⁵Even the altar at Bethel, the high place made by Jeroboam ʸ son of Nebat, who had caused Israel to sin—even that altar and high place he demolished. He burned the high place and ground it to powder, and burned the Asherah pole also. ¹⁶Then Josiah ᶻ looked around, and when he saw the tombs that were there on the hillside, he had the bones removed from them and burned on the altar to defile it, in accordance with the word of the LORD proclaimed by the man of God who foretold these things.

¹⁷The king asked, "What is that tombstone I see?"

The men of the city said, "It marks the tomb of the man of God who came from Judah and pronounced against the altar of Bethel the very things you have done to it."

¹⁸"Leave it alone," he said. "Don't let anyone disturb his bonesᵃ." So they spared his bones and those of the prophet who had come from Samaria.

¹⁹Just as he had done at Bethel, Josiah removed and defiled all the shrines at the high places that the kings of Israel had built in the towns of Samaria that had provoked the LORD to anger. ²⁰Josiah slaughteredᵇ all the priests of those high places on the altars and burned human bones on them. Then he went back to Jerusalem.

JOSIAH

Josiah never knew his great-grandfather Hezekiah, but they were alike in many ways. Both had close, personal relationships with God. Both were passionate reformers, making valiant efforts to lead their people back to God. Both were bright flashes of obedience to God among kings with darkened consciences, who seemed bent on outdoing each other in disobedience and evil.

Although Josiah's father and grandfather were exceptionally wicked, his life is an example of God's willingness to provide ongoing guidance to those who set out to be obedient. At a young age, Josiah already understood that there was spiritual sickness in his land. Idols were sprouting in the countryside faster than crops. In a sense, Josiah began his search for God by destroying and cleaning up whatever he recognized as not belonging to the worship of the true God. In the process, God's Word was rediscovered. The king's intentions and the power of God's written revelation were brought together.

As the Book of God's Law was read to Josiah, he was shocked, frightened, and humbled. He realized what a great gap existed between his efforts to lead his people to God and God's expectations for his chosen nation. He was overwhelmed by God's holiness and immediately tried to expose his people to that holiness. The people did respond, but the Bible makes it clear that their renewed worship of God was much more out of respect for Josiah than out of personal understanding of their own guilt before God.

How would you describe your relationship with God? Are your feeble efforts at holiness based mostly on a desire to "go along" with a well-liked leader or popular opinion? Or are you, like Josiah, deeply humbled by God's Word, realizing that great gap between your life and the kind of life God expects, realizing your deep need to be cleansed and renewed by him? Humble obedience pleases God. Good intentions, even reforms, are not enough. You must allow God's Word to truly humble you and change your life.

Strengths and accomplishments:	• Was king of Judah • Sought after God and was open to him • Was a reformer like his great-grandfather Hezekiah • Cleaned out the temple and revived obedience to God's law
Weakness and mistake:	• Became involved in a military conflict that he had been warned against
Lessons from his life:	• God consistently responds to those with repentant and humble hearts • Even sweeping outward reforms are of little lasting value if there are no changes in people's lives
Vital statistics:	• Where: Jerusalem • Occupation: 16th king of Judah, the southern kingdom • Relatives: Father: Amon. Mother: Jedidah. Son: Jehoahaz. • Contemporaries: Jeremiah, Huldah, Hilkiah, Zephaniah
Key verse:	"Neither before nor after Josiah was there a king like him who turned to the LORD as he did—with all his heart and with all his soul and with all his strength, in accordance with all the Law of Moses" (2 Kings 23:25).

Josiah's story is told in 2 Kings 21:24—23:30; 2 Chronicles 33:25—35:26. He is also mentioned in Jeremiah 1:1–3; 22:11, 18.

about serving only God (Matthew 24:3). For more background on Ashtoreth, Chemosh, and Molech, see the note on 1 Kings 11:5–8.

23:16–18 The prophecies mentioned in this passage appear in 1 Kings 13:20–32.

21 The king gave this order to all the people: "Celebrate the Passover *c* to the LORD your God, as it is written in this Book of the Covenant." 22 Not since the days of the judges who led Israel, nor throughout the days of the kings of Israel and the kings of Judah, had any such Passover been observed. 23 But in the eighteenth year of King Josiah, this Passover was celebrated to the LORD in Jerusalem.

24 Furthermore, Josiah got rid of the mediums and spiritists, *d* the household gods, the idols and all the other detestable things seen in Judah and Jerusalem. This he did to fulfill the requirements of the law written in the book that Hilkiah the priest had discovered in the temple of the LORD. 25 Neither before nor after Josiah was there a king like him who turned *e* to the LORD as he did—with all his heart and with all his soul and with all his strength, in accordance with all the Law of Moses.

26 Nevertheless, the LORD did not turn away from the heat of his fierce anger, which burned against Judah because of all that Manasseh *f* had done to provoke him to anger. 27 So the LORD said, "I will remove *g* Judah also from my presence *h* as I removed Israel, and I will reject Jerusalem, the city I chose, and this temple, about which I said, 'There shall my Name be.'*a*"

28 As for the other events of Josiah's reign, and all he did, are they not written in the book of the annals of the kings of Judah?

29 While Josiah was king, Pharaoh Neco king of Egypt went up to the Euphrates River to help the king of Assyria. King Josiah marched out to meet him in battle, but Neco faced him and killed him at Megiddo. 30 Josiah's servants brought his body in a chariot from Megiddo to Jerusalem and buried him in his own tomb. And the people of the land took Jehoahaz son of Josiah and anointed him and made him king in place of his father.

Jehoahaz King of Judah

31 Jehoahaz was twenty-three years old when he became king, and he reigned in Jerusalem three months. His mother's name was Hamutal daughter of Jeremiah; she was from Libnah. 32 He did evil in the eyes of the LORD, just as his fathers had done. 33 Pharaoh Neco put him in chains at Riblah in the land of Hamath *b* so that he might not reign in Jerusalem, and he imposed on Judah a levy of a hundred talents *c* of silver and a talent *d* of gold. 34 Pharaoh Neco made Eliakim *i* son of Josiah king in place of his father Josiah and changed Eliakim's name to Jehoiakim. But he took Jehoahaz and carried him off to Egypt, and there he died. *j* 35 Jehoiakim paid Pharaoh Neco the silver and gold he demanded. In order to do so, he taxed the land and exacted the silver and gold from the people of the land according to their assessments. *k*

a 27 1 Kings 8:29   *b 33* Hebrew; Septuagint (see also 2 Chron. 36:3) *Neco at Riblah in Hamath removed him*
c 33 That is, about 3 3/4 tons (about 3.4 metric tons)   *d 33* That is, about 75 pounds (about 34 kilograms)

23:21
c Ex 12:11; Nu 9:2

23:24
d Dt 18:11

23:25
e 2Ki 18:5

23:26
f 2Ki 21:12; Jer 15:4

23:27
g 2Ki 21:13
h 2Ki 18:11

23:34
i 2Ch 36:5-8
j Jer 22:12;
Eze 19:3-4

23:35
k ver 33

23:21–23 When Josiah rediscovered the Passover in the Book of the Covenant, he ordered everyone to observe the ceremonies exactly as prescribed. This Passover celebration was to have been a yearly holiday celebrated in remembrance of the entire nation's deliverance from slavery in Egypt (Exodus 12), but it had not been kept for many years. As a result, "not since the days of the judges who led Israel, nor throughout the days of the kings of Israel and the kings of Judah, had any such Passover been observed." A common misconception states that God is against celebration, wanting to take all the fun out of life. In reality, God wants to give us life in its fullness (John 10:10), and those who love him have the most to celebrate.

23:25 Josiah is remembered as Judah's most obedient king. His obedience followed this pattern: (1) he recognized sin; (2) he eliminated sinful practices; (3) he attacked the causes of sin. This approach for dealing with sin works. Not only must we remove sinful actions, we must also eliminate causes for sin—those situations, relationships, routines, and patterns of life that lead us to the door of temptation.

23:25 Both Josiah and Hezekiah (18:5) are praised for their reverence toward God. Hezekiah was said to be greatest in trusting God (faith), while Josiah is said to be greatest in following the law of God (obedience). May we follow their example through our trust in God and our obedient actions.

23:29 Pharaoh Neco of Egypt was marching through Judah to Assyria. Egypt and Assyria had formed an alliance to battle Babylon, which was threatening to become the dominant world power. Josiah may have thought that both nations would turn on him after the battle with Babylon, so he tried to stop Egypt's army from marching through his land. But Josiah was killed, his army was defeated, and the nation of Judah became a vassal of Egypt (609 B.C.). A more detailed account of this story is found in 2 Chronicles 35:20–25.

23:31–34 The people appointed Jehoahaz, one of Josiah's sons, to be Judah's next king. But Neco was not happy with their choice, and he exiled Jehoahaz to Egypt, where he died. Neco then installed Eliakim, another of Josiah's sons, king of Judah, changing his name to Jehoiakim. Jehoiakim was little more than a puppet ruler. In 605 B.C., Egypt was defeated by Babylon. Judah then became a vassal of Babylon (24:1).

2. Judah is exiled to Babylon
Jehoiakim King of Judah

36 Jehoiakim was twenty-five years old when he became king, and he reigned in Jerusalem eleven years. His mother's name was Zebidah daughter of Pedaiah; she was from Rumah. 37 And he did evil in the eyes of the LORD, just as his fathers had done.

24:1
*Jer 25:1, 9

24 During Jehoiakim's reign, Nebuchadnezzar *I* king of Babylon invaded the land, and Jehoiakim became his vassal for three years. But then he changed his mind and rebelled against Nebuchadnezzar. 2 The LORD sent Babylonian, a Aramean, Moabite and Ammonite raiders against him. He sent them to destroy Judah, in accordance with the word of the LORD proclaimed by his servants the prophets. 3 Surely these things happened to Judah according

a 2 Or *Chaldean*

KINGS TO DATE AND THEIR ENEMIES

722
Captivity in Assyria

I S R A E L
J U D A H

686

715
HEZEKIAH
Miraculously
delivered from
Sennacherib's
(Assyria) attack,
conquered Gaza
in Philistia
2 Kgs 18:1—20:21
2 Chr 28:27—32:33
Co-regency
697—686

697
MANASSEH
Taken captive
by Assyria,
imprisoned in
Babylon and
later released
2 Kgs 20:21—21:18
2 Chr 32:33—33:20

642
AMON
2 Kgs 21:18—26
2 Chr 33:20—24

609
JEHOAHAZ
Neco (Egypt)
2 Kgs 23:30—34
2 Chr 36:1—4

640
JOSIAH
Died in battle
against Neco
(Egypt)
2 Kgs 22:1—23:30
2 Chr 33:25—35:27

609
JEHOIAKIM
2 Kgs
23:34—24:6
2 Chr 36:4—8

598
JEHOIACHIN
Rebelled against
Babylon and was
taken captive
2 Kgs 24:6—16;
25:27—30
2 Chr 36:8—10

586

597
ZEDEKIAH
Rebelled,
completely
conquered by
Babylon
2 Kgs
24:17—25:21
2 Chr
36:10—20

735
AHAZ
Harassed by
Pekah (Israel),
paid Assyria for
protection against
Rezin (Aram),
also harassed by
Edom and Philistia
2 Kgs 15:38—16:20
2 Chr 27:9—28:27

All dates are B.C.
Solid section of the timeline indicates co-regency.
For all the kings of Israel and Judah, see the chart at the end of 1 Kings.

23:36, 37 Josiah followed God, but Jehoiakim, his son, was evil. He killed the prophet Uriah (Jeremiah 26:20—23) and was dishonest, greedy, and unjust with the people (Jeremiah 22:13—19). Jehoiakim also rebelled against Babylon, switching his allegiance to Egypt. This proved to be a crucial mistake. Nebuchadnezzar crushed Jehoiakim's rebellion and took him to Babylon (2 Chronicles 36:6), but he was eventually allowed to return to Jerusalem, where he died. The Bible does not record the cause of Jehoiakim's death.

23:37 Many good kings had children who did not turn out to follow God. Perhaps it was because of neglect or preoccupation with political and military affairs or because these kings delegated the religious education to others. No doubt many of the children simply rebelled at the way they were raised. Being a strong believer as a parent doesn't guarantee that your children will pick up your beliefs. Children must be taught about faith, and parents dare not leave that task for others to do. Make sure you practice, explain, and teach what you preach.

24:1 Babylon became the new world power after overthrowing Assyria in 612 B.C. and defeating Egypt at the battle of Carchemish in 605 B.C. After defeating Egypt, the Babylonians invaded Judah and brought it under their control. This was the first of three Babylonian invasions of Judah over the next 20 years. The other two invasions occurred in 597 and 586 B.C. With each invasion, captives were taken back to Babylon. Daniel, who wrote the book of Daniel, was one of the captives taken during this first invasion (605 B.C.; Daniel 1:1—6).

24:1 For more information on Nebuchadnezzar, see his Profile in Daniel 4, p. 1375.

24:1—4 Nebuchadnezzar took control as king of Babylon in 605 B.C. Earlier that year Nebuchadnezzar had defeated the Egyptians led by Pharaoh Neco at Carchemish. Thus Babylon had taken control of all Egypt's vassals (including Judah). Later, Nebuchadnezzar invaded the land in order to establish his rule by force.

to the Lord's command, in order to remove them from his presence because of the sins of Manasseh *m* and all he had done, ⁴including the shedding of innocent blood. *n* For he had filled Jerusalem with innocent blood, and the Lord was not willing to forgive.

⁵As for the other events of Jehoiakim's reign, and all he did, are they not written in the book of the annals of the kings of Judah? ⁶Jehoiakim rested *o* with his fathers. And Jehoiachin his son succeeded him as king.

⁷The king of Egypt did not march out from his own country again, because the king of Babylon *p* had taken all his territory, from the Wadi of Egypt to the Euphrates River.

Jehoiachin King of Judah

⁸Jehoiachin was eighteen years old when he became king, and he reigned in Jerusalem three months. His mother's name was Nehushta daughter of Elnathan; she was from Jerusalem. ⁹He did evil in the eyes of the Lord, just as his father had done.

¹⁰At that time the officers of Nebuchadnezzar king of Babylon advanced on Jerusalem and laid siege to it, ¹¹and Nebuchadnezzar himself came up to the city while his officers were besieging it. ¹²Jehoiachin king of Judah, his mother, his attendants, his nobles and his officials all surrendered *q* to him.

In the eighth year of the reign of the king of Babylon, he took Jehoiachin prisoner. ¹³As the Lord had declared, *r* Nebuchadnezzar removed all the treasures *s* from the temple of the Lord and from the royal palace, and took away all the gold articles that Solomon king of Israel had made for the temple of the Lord. ¹⁴He carried into exile *t* all Jerusalem: all the officers and fighting men, and all the craftsmen and artisans—a total of ten thousand. Only the poorest *u* people of the land were left.

¹⁵Nebuchadnezzar took Jehoiachin captive to Babylon. He also took from Jerusalem to Babylon the king's mother, *v* his wives, his officials and the leading men of the land. ¹⁶The king of Babylon also deported to Babylon the entire force of seven thousand fighting men, strong and fit for war, and a thousand craftsmen and artisans. ¹⁷He made Mattaniah, Jehoiachin's uncle, king in his place and changed his name to Zedekiah. *w*

Zedekiah King of Judah

¹⁸Zedekiah *x* was twenty-one years old when he became king, and he reigned in Jerusalem eleven years. His mother's name was Hamutal *y* daughter of Jeremiah; she was from Libnah. ¹⁹He did evil in the eyes of the Lord, just as Jehoiakim had done. ²⁰It was because of the Lord's anger that all this happened to Jerusalem and Judah, and in the end he thrust them from his presence.

The Fall of Jerusalem

Now Zedekiah rebelled against the king of Babylon.

25 So in the ninth year of Zedekiah's reign, on the tenth day of the tenth month, Nebuchadnezzar king of Babylon marched against Jerusalem with his whole army. He

24:3
m 2Ki 23:26
24:4
n 2Ki 21:16

24:6
o Jer 22:19

24:7
p Jer 37:5-7; 46:2

24:12
q Jer 24:1; 29:2
24:13
r 2Ki 20:17
s Isa 39:6

24:14
t Jer 24:1; 52:28
u 2Ki 25:12; Jer 40:7; 52:16

24:15
v Jer 22:24-28

24:17
w 2Ch 36:11; Jer 37:1

24:18
x Jer 52:1
y 2Ki 23:31

24:10 Babylonian troops were already on the march to crush Jehoiakim's rebellion when he died. After Jehoiakim's death, his

JUDAH EXILED Evil permeated Judah, and God's anger flared against his rebellious people. Babylon conquered Assyria and became the new world power. The Babylonian army marched into Jerusalem, burned the temple, tore down the city's massive walls, and carried off the people into captivity.

son Jehoiachin became king of Judah, only to face the mightiest army on earth just weeks after he was crowned (597 B.C.). During this second of three invasions, the Babylonians looted the temple and took most of the leaders captive, including the king. Then Nebuchadnezzar placed Zedekiah, another son of Josiah, on the throne. The Jews, however, didn't recognize him as their true king as long as Jehoiachin was still alive, even though he was a captive in Babylon.

24:14 The Babylonian policy for taking captives was different from that of the Assyrians who moved most of the people out and resettled the land with foreigners (see the note on 17:24). The Babylonians took only the strong and skilled, leaving the poor and weak to rule the land, thus elevating them to positions of authority and winning their loyalty. The leaders were taken to Babylonian cities where they were permitted to live together, find jobs, and become an important part of the society. This policy kept the Jews united and faithful to God throughout the captivity and made it possible for their return in the days of Zerubbabel and Ezra as recorded in the book of Ezra.

25:1 Judah was invaded by the Babylonians three times (24:1; 24:10; 25:1), just as Israel was invaded by the Assyrians three times. Once again, God demonstrated his mercy in the face of

25:1
z Eze 21:22

25:4
a Eze 33:21

25:6
b 2Ki 23:33

25:9
c Ps 74:3-8; Am 2:5

25:10
d Ne 1:3

25:12
e 2Ki 24:14

25:17
f 1Ki 7:15-22

25:18
g 1Ch 6:14; Ezr 7:1
h Jer 21:1; 29:25

25:21
i Dt 28:64; 2Ki 23:27

25:22
j Jer 40:5, 7

25:26
k Jer 43:7

encamped outside the city and built siege works *z* all around it. 2 The city was kept under siege until the eleventh year of King Zedekiah. 3 By the ninth day of the ⌊fourth⌋ *a* month the famine in the city had become so severe that there was no food for the people to eat. 4 Then the city wall was broken through, *a* and the whole army fled at night through the gate between the two walls near the king's garden, though the Babylonians *b* were surrounding the city. They fled toward the Arabah, *c* 5 but the Babylonian *d* army pursued the king and overtook him in the plains of Jericho. All his soldiers were separated from him and scattered, 6 and he was captured. He was taken to the king of Babylon at Riblah, *b* where sentence was pronounced on him. 7 They killed the sons of Zedekiah before his eyes. Then they put out his eyes, bound him with bronze shackles and took him to Babylon.

8 On the seventh day of the fifth month, in the nineteenth year of Nebuchadnezzar king of Babylon, Nebuzaradan commander of the imperial guard, an official of the king of Babylon, came to Jerusalem. 9 He set fire to the temple of the LORD, the royal palace and all the houses of Jerusalem. Every important building he burned down. *c* 10 The whole Babylonian army, under the commander of the imperial guard, broke down the walls *d* around Jerusalem. 11 Nebuzaradan the commander of the guard carried into exile the people who remained in the city, along with the rest of the populace and those who had gone over to the king of Babylon. 12 But the commander left behind some of the poorest people *e* of the land to work the vineyards and fields.

13 The Babylonians broke up the bronze pillars, the movable stands and the bronze Sea that were at the temple of the LORD and they carried the bronze to Babylon. 14 They also took away the pots, shovels, wick trimmers, dishes and all the bronze articles used in the temple service. 15 The commander of the imperial guard took away the censers and sprinkling bowls—all that were made of pure gold or silver.

16 The bronze from the two pillars, the Sea and the movable stands, which Solomon had made for the temple of the LORD, was more than could be weighed. 17 Each pillar *f* was twenty-seven feet *e* high. The bronze capital on top of one pillar was four and a half feet *f* high and was decorated with a network and pomegranates of bronze all around. The other pillar, with its network, was similar.

18 The commander of the guard took as prisoners Seraiah *g* the chief priest, Zephaniah *h* the priest next in rank and the three doorkeepers. 19 Of those still in the city, he took the officer in charge of the fighting men and five royal advisers. He also took the secretary who was chief officer in charge of conscripting the people of the land and sixty of his men who were found in the city. 20 Nebuzaradan the commander took them all and brought them to the king of Babylon at Riblah. 21 There at Riblah, in the land of Hamath, the king had them executed.

So Judah went into captivity, away from her land. *i*

22 Nebuchadnezzar king of Babylon appointed Gedaliah *j* son of Ahikam, the son of Shaphan, to be over the people he had left behind in Judah. 23 When all the army officers and their men heard that the king of Babylon had appointed Gedaliah as governor, they came to Gedaliah at Mizpah—Ishmael son of Nethaniah, Johanan son of Kareah, Seraiah son of Tanhumeth the Netophathite, Jaazaniah the son of the Maacathite, and their men. 24 Gedaliah took an oath to reassure them and their men. "Do not be afraid of the Babylonian officials," he said. "Settle down in the land and serve the king of Babylon, and it will go well with you."

25 In the seventh month, however, Ishmael son of Nethaniah, the son of Elishama, who was of royal blood, came with ten men and assassinated Gedaliah and also the men of Judah and the Babylonians who were with him at Mizpah. 26 At this, all the people from the least to the greatest, together with the army officers, fled to Egypt *k* for fear of the Babylonians.

a 3 See Jer. 52:6.   *b 4* Or *Chaldeans*; also in verses 13, 25 and 26   *c 4* Or *the Jordan Valley*   *d 5* Or *Chaldean*; also in verses 10 and 24   *e 17* Hebrew *eighteen cubits* (about 8.1 meters)   *f 17* Hebrew *three cubits* (about 1.3 meters)

---

deserved judgment by giving the people repeated opportunities to repent.

25:13 The bronze Sea was used to hold the huge reservoir of water for ritual cleansing for the priests. The bronze in the Sea, the pillars, and the movable stands were so valuable that it was broken up and carried off to Babylon.

25:21 Judah, like Israel, was unfaithful to God. So God, as he had warned, allowed Judah to be destroyed and taken away (Deuteronomy 28). The book of Lamentations records the prophet Jeremiah's sorrow at seeing Jerusalem destroyed.

25:22 In place of the king (Zedekiah) who was deported to Babylon, Nebuchadnezzar appointed a governor (Gedaliah) who would faithfully administer the Babylonian policies.

25:22-30 This story shows that Israel's last hope of gaining back its land was gone—even the army officers (now guerrilla rebels) had fled. Judah's earthly kingdom was absolutely demolished. But through prophets like Ezekiel and Daniel, who were also captives, God was able to keep his spiritual kingdom alive in the hearts of many of the exiles.

Jehoiachin Released

27 In the thirty-seventh year of the exile of Jehoiachin king of Judah, in the year Evil-Merodach[a] became king of Babylon, he released Jehoiachin[l] from prison on the twenty-seventh day of the twelfth month. 28 He spoke kindly to him and gave him a seat of honor[m] higher than those of the other kings who were with him in Babylon. 29 So Jehoiachin put aside his prison clothes and for the rest of his life ate regularly at the king's table.[n] 30 Day by day the king gave Jehoiachin a regular allowance as long as he lived.

a27 Also called Amel-Marduk

25:27 /2Ki 24:12;
Jer 52:31-34

25:28
mEzr 5:5; Da 2:48

25:29
n2Sa 9:7

25:27 Evil-Merodach, the son of Nebuchadnezzar, became king of the Babylonian empire in 562 B.C., 24 years after the beginning of the general captivity and 37 years after Jehoiachin was removed from Jerusalem. The new king treated Jehoiachin with kindness, even allowing him to eat at his table (25:29). Evil-Merodach was later killed in a plot by his brother-in-law, Nergal-Sharezer, who succeeded him to the throne.

25:30 The book of 2 Kings opens with Elijah being carried to heaven—the destination awaiting those who follow God. But the book ends with the people of Judah being carried off to foreign lands as humiliated slaves—the result of failing to follow God.

Second Kings is an illustration of what happens when we make anything more important than God, when we make ruinous alliances, when our consciences become desensitized to right and wrong, and when we are no longer able to discern God's purpose for our lives. We may fail, like the people of Judah and Israel, but God's promises do not. He is always available to help us straighten out our lives and start over. And that is just what would happen in the book of Ezra. When the people acknowledged their sins, God was ready and willing to help them return to their land and start again.

KEY PLACES IN 1 CHRONICLES

The broken lines (— ·— ·—) indicate modern boundaries.

1 Hebron Although David had been anointed king years earlier, his reign began when the leaders of Israel accepted him as king at Hebron (11:1–3).

2 Jerusalem David set out to complete the conquest of the land begun by Joshua. He attacked Jerusalem, captured it, and made it his capital (11:4—12:40).

3 Kiriath Jearim The ark of the covenant, which had been captured by the Philistines in battle and returned (1 Samuel 4—6), was in safekeeping in Kiriath Jearim. David summoned all Israel to this city to join in bringing the ark to Jerusalem. Unfortunately, it was not moved according to God's instructions, and as a result, one man died. David left the ark in the home of Obed-Edom until he could discover how to transport it correctly (13:1–14).

4 Tyre David did much building in Jerusalem. King Hiram of Tyre sent workers and supplies to help build David's palace. Cedar, abundant in the mountains north of Israel, was a valuable and hardy wood for the beautiful buildings in Jerusalem (14:1—17:27).

5 Baal Perazim David was not very popular with the Philistines because he had slain Goliath, one of their greatest warriors (1 Samuel 17). When David began to rule over a united Israel, the Philistines set out to capture him. But as David and his army approached Jerusalem, they attacked the Philistines at Baal Perazim. His army defeated the mighty Philistines twice, causing all the surrounding nations to fear David's power (14:11–17). After these battles, David moved the ark to Jerusalem (this time in accordance with God's instructions for transporting the ark). There was great celebration as the ark was brought into Jerusalem (15:1—17:27). David spent the remainder of his life making preparations for the building of the temple, a central place for the worship of God (18:1—29:30).

The genealogies of 1 Chronicles present an overview of Israel's history. The first nine chapters are filled with genealogies tracing the lineages of people from the creation to the exile in Babylon. Saul's death is recorded in chapter 10. Chapter 11 begins the history of David's reign over Israel.

1 CHRONICLES

| Saul becomes king 1050 B.C. (1045 B.C.) | Saul dies; David becomes king over Judah 1010 | David becomes king over all Israel 1003 | David captures Jerusalem 1000 | David captures Rabbah 997(?) |

VITAL STATISTICS

PURPOSE:
To unify God's people, to trace the Davidic line, and to teach that genuine worship ought to be the center of individual and national life

AUTHOR:
Ezra, according to Jewish tradition

ORIGINAL AUDIENCE:
The exiles who returned from captivity

DATE WRITTEN:
Approximately 430 B.C., recording events that occurred from about 1000–960 B.C.

SETTING:
First Chronicles parallels 2 Samuel and serves as a commentary on it. Written after the exile from a priestly point of view, 1 Chronicles emphasizes the religious history of Judah and Israel.

KEY VERSE:
"And David knew that the LORD had established him as king over Israel and that his kingdom had been highly exalted for the sake of his people Israel" (14:2).

KEY PEOPLE:
David, Solomon

KEY PLACES:
Hebron, Jerusalem, the temple

IN THE WIDE shade of the ageless oak, a mother watches her toddler discover acorns, leaves, and dandelions. Nearby, her mother, aunt, and uncle spread the checkerboard cloth over park tables and cover it with bowls and platters of fried chicken, potato salad, baked beans, and assorted family recipes. The clanging of Grandpa's and Dad's horseshoes against stakes regularly pierces the air and mixes with the cheers, laughs, and shouts of teenagers playing a game of touch football. A family reunion—a sunny afternoon filled with four generations of miscellaneous kids, parents, and second cousins once removed.

Reunions are important. They are times for touching and connecting with others from branches of the family tree, tracing one's personal history back through time and culture, seeing physical reminders (her eyes, his nose), recalling warm traditions. Knowing one's genetic and relational path gives a sense of identity, heritage, and destiny.

With this same high purpose, the writer of Chronicles begins his unifying work with an extensive genealogy. He traces the roots of the nation in a literary family reunion from Adam onward, recounting its royal line and the loving plan of a personal God. We read 1 Chronicles and gain a glimpse of God at work through his people for generations. If you are a believer, these people are your ancestors, too. As you approach this part of God's Word, read their names with awe and respect, and gain new security and identity in your relationship with God.

The previous book, 2 Kings, ends with both Israel and Judah in captivity, surely a dark age for God's people. Then follows Chronicles (1 and 2 Chronicles were originally one book). Written after the captivity, it summarizes Israel's history, emphasizing the Jewish people's spiritual heritage in an attempt to unify the nation. The chronicler is selective in his history telling. Instead of writing an exhaustive work, he carefully weaves the narrative, highlighting spiritual lessons and teaching moral truths. In Chronicles the northern kingdom is virtually ignored, David's triumphs—not his sins—are recalled, and the temple is given great prominence as the vital center of national life.

First Chronicles begins with Adam, and for nine chapters, the writer gives us a "Who's Who" of Israel's history with special emphasis on David's royal line. The rest of the book tells the story of David—the great man of God, Israel's king—who served God and laid out the plans for the construction of and worship in the temple.

First Chronicles is an invaluable supplement to 2 Samuel and a strong reminder of the necessity for tracing our roots and thus rediscovering our spiritual foundation. As you read 1 Chronicles, trace your own godly heritage, thank God for your spiritual forefathers, and recommit yourself to passing on God's truth to the next generation.

THE BLUEPRINT

A. THE GENEALOGIES OF ISRAEL
(1:1—9:44)
1. Ancestry of the nation
2. The tribes of Israel
3. Returnees from exile in Babylon

The long list of names that follows presents a history of God's work in the world from Adam through Zerubbabel. Some of these names remind us of stories of great faith, and others, of tragic failure. About most of the people named, however, we know nothing. But those who died unknown to us are known by God. God will also remember us when we die.

B. THE REIGN OF DAVID
(10:1—29:30)
1. David becomes king over all of Israel
2. David brings the ark to Jerusalem
3. David's military exploits
4. David arranges for the building of the temple

David loved the Lord and wanted to build a temple to replace the tabernacle, but God denied his request. David's greatest contribution to the temple would not be the construction but the preparation. We may be unable to see the results of our labors for God in our lifetime, but David's example helps us understand that we serve God so *he* will see *his* results, not so we will see ours.

MEGATHEMES

THEME	EXPLANATION	IMPORTANCE
Israel's History	By retelling Israel's history in the genealogies and the stories of the kings, the writer laid down the true spiritual foundation for the nation. God kept his promises, and we are reminded of them in the historical record of his people, leaders, prophets, priests, and kings.	Israel's past formed a reliable basis for reconstructing the nation after the exile. Because God's promises are revealed in the Bible, we can know God and trust him to keep his word. Like Israel, we should have no higher goal in life than devoted service to God.
God's People	By listing the names of people in Israel's past, God established Israel's true heritage. They were all one family in Adam, one nation in Abraham, one priesthood under Levi, and one kingdom under David. The national and spiritual unity of the people was important to the rebuilding of the nation.	God is always faithful to his people. He protects them in every generation and provides leaders to guide them. Because God has been at work throughout the centuries, his people can trust him to work in the present. You can rely on his presence today.
David, the King	The story of David's life and his relationship with God showed that he was God's appointed leader. David's devotion to God, the law, the temple, true worship, the people, and justice sets the standard for what God's chosen king should be like.	Jesus Christ came to earth as a descendant of David. One day he will rule as king over all the earth. His strength and justice will fulfill God's ideal for the king. He is our hope. We can experience God's kingdom now by giving Christ complete control of our lives.
True Worship	David brought the ark of the covenant to the tabernacle at Jerusalem to restore true worship to the people. God gave the plans for building the temple, and David organized the priests to make worship central to all Israel.	The temple stood as the throne of God on earth, the place of true worship. God's true throne is in the hearts of his people. When we acknowledge him as the true king over our lives, true worship takes place.
The Priests	God ordained the priests and Levites to guide the people in faithful worship according to his law. By leading the people in worship according to God's design, the priests and Levites were an important safeguard to Israel's faith.	For true worship to remain central in our lives, God's people need to take a firm stand for the ways of God recorded in the Bible. Today, all believers are priests for one another, and we should encourage each other to faithful worship.

A. THE GENEALOGIES OF ISRAEL (1:1—9:44)

These genealogies are the official family records of the nation of Israel. They give us an overview of the history of God's work from creation through the captivity of his people. These records served to teach the exiles returning from Babylon about their spiritual heritage as a nation and to inspire them to renew their faithfulness to God. Although these lists show the racial heritage of the Jews, they contain the spiritual heritage for every believer. We are a part of the community of faith that has existed from generation to generation since the dawn of man.

1. Ancestry of the nation

Historical Records From Adam to Abraham

To Noah's Sons

1 Adam, a Seth, Enosh, ²Kenan, b Mahalalel, c Jared, d ³Enoch, e Methuselah, f Lamech, g Noah. h

⁴ The sons of Noah: a i
   Shem, Ham and Japheth. j

The Japhethites

⁵ The sons b of Japheth:
   Gomer, Magog, Madai, Javan, Tubal, Meshech and Tiras.
⁶ The sons of Gomer:
   Ashkenaz, Riphath c and Togarmah.
⁷ The sons of Javan:
   Elishah, Tarshish, the Kittim and the Rodanim.

The Hamites

⁸ The sons of Ham:
   Cush, Mizraim, d Put and Canaan.
⁹ The sons of Cush:
   Seba, Havilah, Sabta, Raamah and Sabteca.
   The sons of Raamah:
   Sheba and Dedan.
¹⁰ Cush was the father e of
   Nimrod, who grew to be a mighty warrior on earth.
¹¹ Mizraim was the father of
   the Ludites, Anamites, Lehabites, Naphtuhites, ¹²Pathrusites, Casluhites (from whom the Philistines came) and Caphtorites.

1:1 aGe 5:1-32; Lk 3:36-38
1:2 bGe 5:9 cGe 5:12 dGe 5:15
1:3 eGe 5:18; Jude 1:14 fGe 5:21 gGe 5:25 hGe 5:29
1:4 iGe 6:10; 10:1 jGe 5:32

a *4 Septuagint; Hebrew does not have this line.*   b *5 Sons may mean* descendants *or* successors *or* nations; *also in verses 6-10, 17 and 20.*   c *6 Many Hebrew manuscripts and Vulgate (see also Septuagint and Gen. 10:3); most Hebrew manuscripts* Diphath   d *8 That is, Egypt; also in verse 11*   e *10 Father may mean* ancestor *or* predecessor *or* founder; *also in verses 11, 13, 18 and 20.*

1:1 This record of names demonstrates that God is interested not only in nations, but also in individuals. Although billions of people have lived since Adam, God knows and remembers the face and name of each person. Each of us is more than a name on a list; we are special persons whom God knows and loves. As we recognize and accept his love, we discover both our uniqueness as individuals and our solidarity with the rest of his family.

1:1ff This long list of names was compiled after the people of Judah, the southern kingdom, were taken captive to Babylon. As the exiles looked forward to the day when they would return to their homeland, one of their biggest fears was that the records of their heritage would be lost. The Jews placed great importance upon their heritage because each person wanted to be able to prove that he was a descendant of Abraham, the father of the Jewish people. Only then could he enjoy the benefits of the special blessings God promised to Abraham and his descendants (see the notes on Genesis 12:1-3 and 17:2-8 for what these special blessings were).

This list reconstructed the family tree for both Judah, the southern kingdom, and Israel, the northern kingdom, before

their captivities and served as proof for those who claimed to be Abraham's descendants. (For more information about why the Bible includes genealogies, read the notes on Genesis 5:1ff, Matthew 1:1, and Luke 3:23–38.)

1:1ff There is more to this long genealogy than meets the eye. It holds importance for us today because it supports the Old Testament promise that Jesus the Messiah would be a descendant of Abraham and David. This promise is recorded in Genesis 12:1-3 and 2 Samuel 7:12, 13.

1:1, 4 Adam's story and Profile are found in Genesis 1—5, p. 9. Noah's story and Profile are found in Genesis 6—9, p. 19.

1:5–9 *Sons* can also mean *descendants;* thus a Biblical genealogy may skip several generations. These lists were not meant to be exhaustive, but to give adequate information about the various family lines.

1:10 Nimrod is also mentioned in Genesis 10:8, 9.

1:11, 12 The Philistines had been Israel's constant enemy from the days of the judges. King David finally weakened them, and by this time they were no longer a threat. (For more information on the Philistines, see the notes on Judges 13:1 and 1 Samuel 4:1.)

13 Canaan was the father of
Sidon his firstborn, a and of the Hittites, 14Jebusites, Amorites, Girgashites,
15Hivites, Arkites, Sinites, 16Arvadites, Zemarites and Hamathites.

The Semites

17 The sons of Shem:
Elam, Asshur, Arphaxad, Lud and Aram.
The sons of Aram:b
Uz, Hul, Gether and Meshech.
18 Arphaxad was the father of Shelah,
and Shelah the father of Eber.
19 Two sons were born to Eber:
One was named Peleg,c because in his time the earth was divided; his brother was
named Joktan.
20 Joktan was the father of
Almodad, Sheleph, Hazarmaveth, Jerah, 21Hadoram, Uzal, Diklah, 22Obal,d Abimael,
Sheba, 23Ophir, Havilah and Jobab. All these were sons of Joktan.

1:24
k Ge 10:21-25;
Lk 3:34-36

24 Shem,k Arphaxad,e Shelah,
25 Eber, Peleg, Reu,
26 Serug, Nahor, Terah
27 and Abram (that is, Abraham).

The Family of Abraham

28 The sons of Abraham:
Isaac and Ishmael.

Descendants of Hagar

29 These were their descendants:
Nebaioth the firstborn of Ishmael, Kedar, Adbeel, Mibsam, 30Mishma, Dumah,
Massa, Hadad, Tema, 31Jetur, Naphish and Kedemah. These were the sons of Ishmael.

Descendants of Keturah

1:32
l Ge 22:24
m Ge 10:7

32 The sons born to Keturah, Abraham's concubine:l
Zimran, Jokshan, Medan, Midian, Ishbak and Shuah.
The sons of Jokshan:
Sheba and Dedan. m
33 The sons of Midian:
Ephah, Epher, Hanoch, Abida and Eldaah.
All these were descendants of Keturah.

Descendants of Sarah

1:34
n Lk 3:34
o Ge 21:2-3; Mt 1:2;
Ac 7:8
p Ge 17:5; 25:25-26

34 Abraham n was the father of Isaac. o
The sons of Isaac:
Esau and Israel.p

a 13 Or *of the Sidonians, the foremost*   b 17 One Hebrew manuscript and some Septuagint manuscripts (see also
Gen. 10:23); most Hebrew manuscripts do not have this line.   c 19 *Peleg* means *division.*   e22 Some Hebrew
manuscripts and Syriac (see also Gen. 10:28); most Hebrew manuscripts *Ebal*   e24 Hebrew; some Septuagint
manuscripts *Arphaxad, Cainan* (see also note at Gen. 11:10)

1:13–16 Canaan was the ancestor of the Canaanites, who inhabited the promised land (also called Canaan) before the Israelites
entered under Joshua's leadership. God helped the Israelites
drive out the Canaanites, a wicked and idolatrous people. The
land's name was then changed to Israel. The book of Joshua
tells that story.

1:19 "The earth was divided" refers to when the earth was
divided into different language groups. At one time, everyone
spoke a single language. But some people became proud of their
accomplishments and gathered to build a monument to themselves—the tower of Babel. The building project was brought to
an abrupt conclusion when God caused the people to speak
different languages. Without the ability to communicate with one
another, the people could not be unified. God showed them that

their great efforts were useless without him. Pride in our achievements must not lead us to conclude that we no longer need God.
This story is told in Genesis 11:1–9.

1:24–27 Abraham's story and Profile are found in Genesis
11:26—25:10, p. 33.

1:28–31 Ishmael's story and Profile are found in Genesis 17
and 21, p. 31.

1:34 Israel is another name for Jacob, given to him by God
(Genesis 32:28). It means "someone who struggles with God."
Israel's (Jacob's) 12 sons became the nation of Israel. Esau's
descendants became the nation of Edom, a constant enemy of
Israel. To learn more about the lives of Isaac and his two sons,
Jacob and Esau, read their stories and Profiles in Genesis 21—
36, p. 51 and 46—49, p. 49.

Esau's Sons

35 The sons of Esau: [q]
   Eliphaz, Reuel,[r] Jeush, Jalam and Korah.
36 The sons of Eliphaz:
   Teman, Omar, Zepho,[a] Gatam and Kenaz;
   by Timna: Amalek.[b] [s]
37 The sons of Reuel:[t]
   Nahath, Zerah, Shammah and Mizzah.

The People of Seir in Edom

38 The sons of Seir:
   Lotan, Shobal, Zibeon, Anah, Dishon, Ezer and Dishan.
39 The sons of Lotan:
   Hori and Homam. Timna was Lotan's sister.
40 The sons of Shobal:
   Alvan,[c] Manahath, Ebal, Shepho and Onam.
   The sons of Zibeon:
   Aiah and Anah.[u]
41 The son of Anah:
   Dishon.
   The sons of Dishon:
   Hemdan,[d] Eshban, Ithran and Keran.
42 The sons of Ezer:
   Bilhan, Zaavan and Akan.[e]
   The sons of Dishan[f]:
   Uz and Aran.

The Rulers of Edom

43 These were the kings who reigned in Edom before any Israelite king reigned[g]:
   Bela son of Beor, whose city was named Dinhabah.
44 When Bela died, Jobab son of Zerah from Bozrah succeeded him as king.
45 When Jobab died, Husham from the land of the Temanites[v] succeeded him as king.
46 When Husham died, Hadad son of Bedad, who defeated Midian in the country of Moab, succeeded him as king. His city was named Avith.
47 When Hadad died, Samlah from Masrekah succeeded him as king.
48 When Samlah died, Shaul from Rehoboth on the river[h] succeeded him as king.
49 When Shaul died, Baal-Hanan son of Acbor succeeded him as king.
50 When Baal-Hanan died, Hadad succeeded him as king. His city was named Pau,[i] and his wife's name was Mehetabel daughter of Matred, the daughter of Me-Zahab.
   51 Hadad also died.

   The chiefs of Edom were:
   Timna, Alvah, Jetheth, 52 Oholibamah, Elah, Pinon, 53 Kenaz, Teman, Mibzar, 54 Magdiel and Iram. These were the chiefs of Edom.

1:35
[q] Ge 36:19
[r] Ge 36:4

1:36
[s] Ex 17:14

1:37
[t] Ge 36:17

1:40
[u] Ge 36:2

1:45
[v] Ge 36:11

a 36 Many Hebrew manuscripts, some Septuagint manuscripts and Syriac (see also Gen. 36:11); most Hebrew manuscripts *Zephi*   b 36 Some Septuagint manuscripts (see also Gen. 36:12); Hebrew *Gatam, Kenaz, Timna and Amalek*   c 40 Many Hebrew manuscripts and some Septuagint manuscripts (see also Gen. 36:23); most Hebrew manuscripts *Alian*   d 41 Many Hebrew manuscripts and some Septuagint manuscripts (see also Gen. 36:26); most Hebrew manuscripts *Hamran*   e 42 Many Hebrew and Septuagint manuscripts (see also Gen. 36:27); most Hebrew manuscripts *Zaavan, Jaakan*   f 42 Hebrew *Dishon*, a variant of *Dishan*   g 43 Or *before an Israelite king reigned over them*   h 48 Possibly the Euphrates   i 50 Many Hebrew manuscripts, some Septuagint manuscripts, Vulgate and Syriac (see also Gen. 36:39); most Hebrew manuscripts *Pai*

1:36 Amalek, Esau's grandson, was the son of his father's concubine (Genesis 36:12). He was the ancestor of the wicked tribe known as Amalekites, the first people to attack the Israelites on their way to the promised land. (For more about the Amalekites, read the note on Exodus 17:8.)

1:43–54 Why are we given information in this genealogy about the descendants of Edom who were Israel's enemies? Esau, ancestor of the Edomites, was Isaac's oldest son and thus a direct descendant of Abraham. As Abraham's first grandson, he deserved a place in the Jewish records. It was through Esau's marriages to pagan women, however, that the nation of Edom began. This genealogy shows the ancestry of enemy nations; they were *not* a part of the direct lineage of King David, and thus of the Messiah. This listing further identified Israel's special identity and role.

Israel's Sons

2 These were the sons of Israel:
Reuben, Simeon, Levi, Judah, Issachar, Zebulun, ²Dan, Joseph, Benjamin, Naphtali, Gad and Asher.

Judah

To Hezron's Sons

2:3
ʷGe 38:2-10

3 The sons of Judah:ʷ
Er, Onan and Shelah. These three were born to him by a Canaanite woman, the daughter of Shua. Er, Judah's firstborn, was wicked in the LORD's sight; so the LORD

2:4
ˣGe 38:29

put him to death. ⁴Tamar, Judah's daughter-in-law, bore him Perezˣ and Zerah. Judah had five sons in all.

2:5
ʸGe 46:12

5 The sons of Perez:ʸ
Hezron and Hamul.
6 The sons of Zerah:
Zimri, Ethan, Heman, Calcol and Dardaᵃ—five in all.

2:7
ᶻJos 7:1
ᵃJos 6:18

7 The son of Carmi:
Achar,ᵇ ᶻ who brought trouble on Israel by violating the ban on taking devoted things.ᶜ ᵃ
8 The son of Ethan:
Azariah.
9 The sons born to Hezron were:
Jerahmeel, Ram and Caleb.ᵈ

From Ram Son of Hezron

10 Ram was the father of
Amminadab, and Amminadab the father of Nahshon, the leader of the people of Judah. ¹¹Nahshon was the father of Salmon,ᵉ Salmon the father of Boaz, ¹²Boaz the father of Obed and Obed the father of Jesse.

2:13
ᵇ1Sa 16:6
2:16
ᶜ2Sa 2:18
2:17
ᵈ2Sa 17:25

13 Jesse was the father of
Eliabᵇ his firstborn; the second son was Abinadab, the third Shimea, ¹⁴the fourth Nethanel, the fifth Raddai, ¹⁵the sixth Ozem and the seventh David. ¹⁶Their sisters were Zeruiah and Abigail. Zeruiah'sᶜ three sons were Abishai, Joab and Asahel. ¹⁷Abigail was the mother of Amasa,ᵈ whose father was Jether the Ishmaelite.

Caleb Son of Hezron

2:19
ᵉver 42, 50
2:20
ᶠEx 31:2

18 Caleb son of Hezron had children by his wife Azubah (and by Jerioth). These were her sons: Jesher, Shobab and Ardon. ¹⁹When Azubah died, Calebᵉ married Ephrath, who bore him Hur. ²⁰Hur was the father of Uri, and Uri the father of Bezalel.ᶠ

ᵃ6 Many Hebrew manuscripts, some Septuagint manuscripts and Syriac (see also 1 Kings 4:31); most Hebrew manuscripts *Dara*   ᵇ7 *Achar* means *trouble*; *Achar* is called *Achan* in Joshua.   ᶜ7 The Hebrew term refers to the irrevocable giving over of things or persons to the LORD, often by totally destroying them.   ᵈ9 Hebrew *Kelubai*, a variant of *Caleb*   ᵉ11 Septuagint (see also Ruth 4:21); Hebrew *Salma*

2:1, 2 The story of Israel's (Jacob's) sons is found in Genesis 29:32—50:26. Profiles, pp. 73, 85, 71 of Reuben, Judah, and Joseph are found in the same section.

2:3 This long genealogy not only lists names, but gives us insights into some of the people. Here, almost as an epitaph, the genealogy states that Er "was wicked in the LORD's sight; so the LORD put him to death." Now, thousands of years later, this is all we know of the man. Each of us is forging a reputation, developing personal qualities by which we will be remembered. How would God summarize your life up to now? Some defiantly claim that how they live is their own business. But Scripture teaches that the way you live today will determine how you will be remembered by others and how you will be judged by God. What you do now *does* matter.

2:7 The plunder referred to in this verse was taken by Achan in direct disobedience to God's instructions following the destruction of Jericho. His greed led to the defeat of Israel at Ai and the death of Achan and his entire family (see Joshua 7).

2:12 Boaz was Ruth's husband and an ancestor of both David and Jesus. Boaz's story and Profile are found in the book of Ruth.

2:15 David is one of the best-known people of the Bible. He was certainly not perfect, but he exemplified what it means to seek God first in all areas of life. God called David "a man after my own heart" (Acts 13:22) because David's greatest desire was to serve and worship God. We can please God in the same way by making God our first consideration in all our desires and plans. David's story is found in 1 Samuel 16:1—1 Kings 2:10 and 1 Chronicles 10:14—29:30. David's Profile is found in 1 Samuel 17, p. 423.

2:16 Joab's story is found in 2 Samuel 2; 3; 10—20; 24; 1 Kings 1—3; 1 Chronicles 11:4-9; 19—21. His Profile is found in 2 Samuel 18, p. 479. Abishai's story is found in 1 Samuel 26; 2 Samuel 2; 3; 10; 15—21; 23; 1 Chronicles 18:12; 19. Abishai's Profile is found in 2 Samuel 21, p. 483.

2:18 This is not the Caleb who spied out the promised land with Joshua. Caleb, the spy, is listed in 4:15.

21 Later, Hezron lay with the daughter of Makir the father of Gilead*g* (he had married her
   when he was sixty years old), and she bore him Segub. 22 Segub was the father of Jair,
   who controlled twenty-three towns in Gilead. 23 (But Geshur and Aram captured
   Havvoth Jair,*a h* as well as Kenath with its surrounding settlements—sixty towns.) All
   these were descendants of Makir the father of Gilead.

24 After Hezron died in Caleb Ephrathah, Abijah the wife of Hezron bore him Ashhur*i*
   the father*b* of Tekoa.

2:21
g Nu 27:1

2:23
h Nu 32:41; Dt 3:14;
Jos 13:30

2:24
i 1Ch 4:5

Jerahmeel Son of Hezron

25 The sons of Jerahmeel the firstborn of Hezron:
   Ram his firstborn, Bunah, Oren, Ozem and*c* Ahijah. 26 Jerahmeel had another wife,
   whose name was Atarah; she was the mother of Onam.
26 The sons of Ram the firstborn of Jerahmeel:
   Maaz, Jamin and Eker.
28 The sons of Onam:
   Shammai and Jada.
   The sons of Shammai:
   Nadab and Abishur.
29 Abishur's wife was named Abihail, who bore him Ahban and Molid.
30 The sons of Nadab:
   Seled and Appaim. Seled died without children.
31 The son of Appaim:
   Ishi, who was the father of Sheshan.
   Sheshan was the father of Ahlai.
32 The sons of Jada, Shammai's brother:
   Jether and Jonathan. Jether died without children.
33 The sons of Jonathan:
   Peleth and Zaza.
   These were the descendants of Jerahmeel.
34 Sheshan had no sons—only daughters.
   He had an Egyptian servant named Jarha. 35 Sheshan gave his daughter in marriage
   to his servant Jarha, and she bore him Attai.
36 Attai was the father of Nathan,
   Nathan the father of Zabad,*j*
37 Zabad the father of Ephlal,
   Ephlal the father of Obed,
38 Obed the father of Jehu,
   Jehu the father of Azariah,
39 Azariah the father of Helez,
   Helez the father of Eleasah,
40 Eleasah the father of Sismai,
   Sismai the father of Shallum,
41 Shallum the father of Jekamiah,
   and Jekamiah the father of Elishama.

2:36
j 1Ch 11:41

The Clans of Caleb

42 The sons of Caleb the brother of Jerahmeel:
   Mesha his firstborn, who was the father of Ziph, and his son Mareshah,*d* who was
   the father of Hebron.
43 The sons of Hebron:
   Korah, Tappuah, Rekem and Shema. 44 Shema was the father of Raham, and Raham
   the father of Jorkeam. Rekem was the father of Shammai. 45 The son of Shammai
   was Maon, and Maon was the father of Beth Zur.
46 Caleb's concubine Ephah was the mother of Haran, Moza and Gazez. Haran was the
   father of Gazez.
47 The sons of Jahdai:
   Regem, Jotham, Geshan, Pelet, Ephah and Shaaph.

a 23 Or captured the settlements of Jair   b 24 Father may mean *civic leader* or *military leader*; also in verses 42, 45,
49-52 and possibly elsewhere.   *c 25 Or Oren and Ozem, by   d 42* The meaning of the Hebrew for this phrase is
uncertain.

⁴⁸ Caleb's concubine Maacah was the mother of Sheber and Tirhanah. ⁴⁹ She also gave birth to Shaaph the father of Madmannah and to Sheva the father of Macbenah and Gibea. Caleb's daughter was Acsah. ⁵⁰ These were the descendants of Caleb.

The sons of Hur the firstborn of Ephrathah:

Shobal the father of Kiriath Jearim, ⁵¹ Salma the father of Bethlehem, and Hareph the father of Beth Gader.

⁵² The descendants of Shobal the father of Kiriath Jearim were:

Haroeh, half the Manahathites, ⁵³ and the clans of Kiriath Jearim: the Ithrites, Puthites, Shumathites and Mishraites. From these descended the Zorathites and Eshtaolites.

⁵⁴ The descendants of Salma:

Bethlehem, the Netophathites, Atroth Beth Joab, half the Manahathites, the Zorites, ⁵⁵ and the clans of scribes a who lived at Jabez: the Tirathites, Shimeathites and Sucathites. These are the Kenites k who came from Hammath, the father of the house of Recab. b l

2:55
k Jdg 1:16
l Jer 35:2-19

The Sons of David

3:1
m Jos 15:56

3 These were the sons of David born to him in Hebron:

The firstborn was Amnon the son of Ahinoam of Jezreel; m
the second, Daniel the son of Abigail of Carmel;
² the third, Absalom the son of Maacah daughter of Talmai king of Geshur;
the fourth, Adonijah the son of Haggith;
³ the fifth, Shephatiah the son of Abital;
and the sixth, Ithream, by his wife Eglah.
⁴ These six were born to David in Hebron, where he reigned seven years and six months. n

3:4
n 2Sa 2:11; 5:5

3:5
o 2Sa 11:3; 12:24

David reigned in Jerusalem thirty-three years, ⁵ and these were the children born to him there:

Shammua,c Shobab, Nathan and Solomon. These four were by Bathshebad o daughter of Ammiel. ⁶ There were also Ibhar, Elishua,e Eliphelet, ⁷ Nogah, Nepheg, Japhia, ⁸ Elishama, Eliada and Eliphelet—nine in all. ⁹ All these were the sons of David, besides his sons by his concubines. And Tamar p was their sister.

3:9
p 2Sa 13:1

The Kings of Judah

3:10
q 1Ki 11:43

¹⁰ Solomon's son was Rehoboam,q
Abijah his son,
Asa his son,
Jehoshaphat his son,
¹¹ Jehoramf r his son,
Ahaziah s his son,
Joash t his son,
¹² Amaziah his son,
Azariah his son,
Jotham u his son,
¹³ Ahaz v his son,
Hezekiah his son,
Manasseh his son,

3:11
r 2Ki 8:16-24;
2Ch 21:1
s 2Ch 22:1-10
t 2Ki 11:1-12:21
3:12
u Isa 1:1; Hos 1:1
3:13
v Isa 7:1

a 55 Or of the Sopherites   b 55 Or father of Beth Recab   c 5 Hebrew Shimea, a variant of Shammua   d 5 One Hebrew manuscript and Vulgate (see also Septuagint and 2 Samuel 11:3); most Hebrew manuscripts Bathshua   e 6 Two Hebrew manuscripts (see also 2 Samuel 5:15 and 1 Chron. 14:5); most Hebrew manuscripts Elishama   f 11 Hebrew Joram, a variant of Jehoram

---

3:1 For more about David's wife Abigail, see 1 Samuel 25; her Profile is in 1 Samuel 26, p. 435.

3:2 David's son Absalom is told about in 2 Samuel 13—18; his Profile is in 2 Samuel 15, p. 471.

3:5 Bathsheba's story is found in 2 Samuel 11; 12; 1 Kings 1, and her Profile is in 1 Kings 1, p. 495. The story of her son, Solomon, who became Israel's third king, is found in 1 Kings 1—11 and 2 Chronicles 1—9. Solomon's Profile is found in 1 Kings 4, p. 503.

3:9 The tragic story of Tamar, David's daughter, is found in 2 Samuel 13; 14.

3:10–14 Many of Solomon's descendants ruled the nation of Judah. For Rehoboam's story and Profile, see 2 Chronicles 10—12, p. 663. For Jehoshaphat's story and Profile, see 2 Chronicles 17—20, p. 671. Azariah's (Uzziah's) story and Profile are found in 2 Chronicles 26, p. 683. Hezekiah's story and Profile are in 2 Kings 18—20, p. 583. For Josiah's story, see 2 Kings 22; 23. His Profile is in 2 Kings 24, p. 591.

14 Amon his son,
Josiah ^w his son.
15 The sons of Josiah:
Johanan the firstborn,
Jehoiakim the second son,
Zedekiah ^x the third,
Shallum the fourth.
16 The successors of Jehoiakim:
Jehoiachin ^{a y} his son,
and Zedekiah. ^z

The Royal Line After the Exile

17 The descendants of Jehoiachin the captive:
Shealtiel his son, ¹⁸Malkiram, Pedaiah, Shenazzar, ^a Jekamiah, Hoshama and Nedabiah.
19 The sons of Pedaiah:
Zerubbabel ^b and Shimei.
The sons of Zerubbabel:
Meshullam and Hananiah.
Shelomith was their sister.
20 There were also five others:
Hashubah, Ohel, Berekiah, Hasadiah and Jushab-Hesed.
21 The descendants of Hananiah:
Pelatiah and Jeshaiah, and the sons of Rephaiah, of Arnan, of Obadiah and of Shecaniah.
22 The descendants of Shecaniah:
Shemaiah and his sons:
Hattush, ^c Igal, Bariah, Neariah and Shaphat—six in all.
23 The sons of Neariah:
Elioenai, Hizkiah and Azrikam—three in all.
24 The sons of Elioenai:
Hodaviah, Eliashib, Pelaiah, Akkub, Johanan, Delaiah and Anani—seven in all.

2. The tribes of Israel
Other Clans of Judah

4 The descendants of Judah: ^d
Perez, Hezron, Carmi, Hur and Shobal.
2 Reaiah son of Shobal was the father of Jahath, and Jahath the father of Ahumai and Lahad. These were the clans of the Zorathites.
3 These were the sons ^b of Etam:
Jezreel, Ishma and Idbash. Their sister was named Hazzelelponi. ⁴Penuel was the father of Gedor, and Ezer the father of Hushah.
These were the descendants of Hur, ^e the firstborn of Ephrathah and father ^c of Bethlehem.
5 Ashhur ^f the father of Tekoa had two wives, Helah and Naarah.
6 Naarah bore him Ahuzzam, Hepher, Temeni and Haahashtari. These were the descendants of Naarah.
7 The sons of Helah:
Zereth, Zohar, Ethnan, ⁸and Koz, who was the father of Anub and Hazzobebah and of the clans of Aharhel son of Harum.

⁹Jabez was more honorable than his brothers. His mother had named him Jabez, ^d saying, "I gave birth to him in pain." ¹⁰Jabez cried out to the God of Israel, "Oh, that you would bless

3:14 ^wJer 1:2; 25:3
3:15 ^xJer 37:1
3:16 ^yMt 1:11 ^z2Ki 24:18
3:18 ^aEzr 1:8
3:19 ^bEzr 5:2
3:22 ^cEzr 8:2-3
4:1 ^dGe 46:12; 1Ch 2:3
4:4 ^e1Ch 2:50
4:5 ^f1Ch 2:24

a 16 Hebrew *Jeconiah*, a variant of *Jehoiachin*; also in verse 17 **b** 3 Some Septuagint manuscripts (see also Vulgate); Hebrew *father* **c** 4 *Father* may mean *civic leader* or *military leader*; also in verses 12, 14, 17, 18 and possibly elsewhere. **d** 9 *Jabez* sounds like the Hebrew for *pain*.

3:15 Jehoiakim's story is found in Jeremiah 22—28; 35; 36. Zedekiah's story is found in Jeremiah 21—39.
3:19, 20 Zerubbabel was the leader of the first exiles to return from Babylon. His story and Profile are found in the book of Ezra.

4:9, 10 Jabez is remembered for a prayer request rather than a heroic act. In his prayer, he asked God to (1) bless him, (2) help him in his work ("enlarge my territory"), (3) be with him in all he did, and (4) keep him from evil and harm. Jabez acknowledged me and enlarge my territory! Let your hand be with me, and keep me from harm so that I will be free from pain." And God granted his request.

¹¹ Kelub, Shuhah's brother, was the father of Mehir, who was the father of Eshton. ¹²Eshton was the father of Beth Rapha, Paseah and Tehinnah the father of Ir Nahash. **a** These were the men of Recah.

a 12 Or of the city of Nahash

WHO'S WHO IN THE BIBLE

Here are some of the people mentioned in this genealogy who are also mentioned elsewhere in the Bible. The writer of Chronicles reproduced a thorough history of Israel in one list of people. Many of the people in this list have exciting stories that can be traced through the Bible. Look up some of the names here that intrigue you. You may be surprised at what you discover!

Name	Key Life Lesson	Reference
Adam (1:1)	Our sins have far greater implications than we realize.	Genesis 2—3
Noah (1:4)	Great rewards come from obeying God.	Genesis 6—9
Abraham (1:27)	Faith alone makes one right in God's eyes.	Genesis 11:26—25:10
Isaac (1:28)	Seeking peace brings true respect.	Genesis 21—35
Esau (1:35)	It is never too late to put away bitterness and forgive.	Genesis 25:20—36:43
Amalek (1:36)	There are evil men and nations who seek to harm God's people.	Exodus 17:8—16
Israel (Jacob) (2:1)	While our sins may haunt us, God will honor our faith.	Genesis 25:20—50:13
Judah (2:3)	God can change the hearts of even the most wicked people.	Genesis 37—50
Tamar (2:4)	God works his purposes even through sinful events.	Genesis 38
Perez (2:5)	Your background does not matter to God.	Genesis 38:27–30
Boaz (2:12)	Those who are kind to others will receive kindness themselves.	The book of Ruth
Jesse (2:13)	Never take lightly the impact you may have on your children.	1 Samuel 16
David (2:15)	True greatness is having a heart for God.	The books of 1 and 2 Samuel
Joab (2:16)	Those who seek power die with nothing.	2 Samuel 2:13—1 Kings 2:34
Amnon (3:1)	Giving in to lust leads only to tragedy.	2 Samuel 13
Absalom (3:2)	Those seeking to oust a God-appointed leader will have a difficult battle.	2 Samuel 13—18
Adonijah (3:2)	God must determine what is rightfully ours.	1 Kings 1—2
Bathsheba (3:5)	One wrong act does not disqualify us from accomplishing things for God.	2 Samuel 11—12; 1 Kings 1—2
Solomon (3:5)	Human wisdom is foolishness without God.	1 Kings 1—11
Reuben (5:1)	What is gained from a moment of passion is only perceived; what is lost is real and permanent.	Genesis 35:22; 37; 49:3, 4
Aaron (6:3)	Don't expect God's leaders to be perfect, but don't let them get away with sin either.	Exodus 4—Numbers 20
Nadab (6:3)	Pretending to be God's representative is dangerous business.	Leviticus 10
Eleazar (6:3)	Those who are consistent in their faith are the best models to follow.	Numbers 20:25–29; 26—34; Joshua 24:33
Korah (6:22)	Rebelling against God's leaders is rebelling against God and will always be unsuccessful.	Numbers 16
Joshua (7:27)	Real courage comes from God.	The book of Joshua
Saul (8:33)	Those who say they follow God but don't live like it waste their God-given potential.	1 Samuel 8—31
Jonathan (8:33)	True friends always think of the other person, not just themselves.	1 Samuel 14—31

God as the true center of his life. When we pray for God's blessing, we should also pray that he will take his rightful position as Lord over our work, our family time, and our recreation. Obeying him in daily responsibilities *is* heroic living.

13 The sons of Kenaz:
> Othniel *g* and Seraiah.

4:13
g Jos 15:17

The sons of Othniel:
> Hathath and Meonothai. **a** 14 Meonothai was the father of Ophrah.

Seraiah was the father of Joab,
> the father of Ge Harashim. **b** It was called this because its people were craftsmen.

15 The sons of Caleb son of Jephunneh:
> Iru, Elah and Naam.

The son of Elah:
> Kenaz.

16 The sons of Jehallelel:
> Ziph, Ziphah, Tiria and Asarel.

17 The sons of Ezrah:
> Jether, Mered, Epher and Jalon. One of Mered's wives gave birth to Miriam, Shammai and Ishbah the father of Eshtemoa. 18 (His Judean wife gave birth to Jered the father of Gedor, Heber the father of Soco, and Jekuthiel the father of Zanoah.) These were the children of Pharaoh's daughter Bithiah, whom Mered had married.

19 The sons of Hodiah's wife, the sister of Naham:
> the father of Keilah the Garmite, and Eshtemoa the Maacathite.

20 The sons of Shimon:
> Amnon, Rinnah, Ben-Hanan and Tilon.

The descendants of Ishi:
> Zoheth and Ben-Zoheth.

21 The sons of Shelah *h* son of Judah:

4:21
h Ge 38:5

> Er the father of Lecah, Laadah the father of Mareshah and the clans of the linen workers at Beth Ashbea, 22 Jokim, the men of Cozeba, and Joash and Saraph, who ruled in Moab and Jashubi Lehem. (These records are from ancient times.) 23 They were the potters who lived at Netaim and Gederah; they stayed there and worked for the king.

Simeon

24 The descendants of Simeon: *i*

4:24
i Ge 29:33
j Nu 26:12

> Nemuel, Jamin, Jarib, *j* Zerah and Shaul;

25 Shallum was Shaul's son, Mibsam his son and Mishma his son.

26 The descendants of Mishma:
> Hammuel his son, Zaccur his son and Shimei his son.

27 Shimei had sixteen sons and six daughters, but his brothers did not have many children; so their entire clan did not become as numerous as the people of Judah. 28 They lived in Beersheba, Moladah, Hazar Shual, 29 Bilhah, Ezem, *k* Tolad, 30 Bethuel, Hormah, Ziklag, 31 Beth Marcaboth, Hazar Susim, Beth Biri and Shaaraim. These were their towns until the reign of David. 32 Their surrounding villages were Etam, Ain, Rimmon, Token and Ashan— five towns— 33 and all the villages around these towns as far as Baalath. *c* These were their settlements. And they kept a genealogical record.

4:29
k Jos 15:29

34 Meshobab, Jamlech, Joshah son of Amaziah, 35 Joel, Jehu son of Joshibiah, the son of Seraiah, the son of Asiel, 36 also Elioenai, Jaakobah, Jeshohaiah, Asaiah, Adiel, Jesimiel, Benaiah, 37 and Ziza son of Shiphi, the son of Allon, the son of Jedaiah, the son of Shimri, the son of Shemaiah.

a 13 Some Septuagint manuscripts and Vulgate; Hebrew does not have *and Meonothai.*   *b 14* Ge Harashim means *valley of craftsmen.*   *c 33* Some Septuagint manuscripts (see also Joshua 19:8); Hebrew *Baal*

4:10 Jabez prayed specifically to be protected from harm and pain. We live in a fallen world filled with sin, and it is important to ask God to keep us safe from the unavoidable evil that comes our way. But we must also avoid evil motives, desires, and actions that begin within us. Therefore, not only must we seek God's protection from evil, but we must also ask God to guard our thoughts and actions. We can begin to utilize his protection by filling our minds with positive thoughts and attitudes.

4:13 Othniel was Israel's first judge. He reformed the nation and brought peace to the land. His story is found in Judges 1:9–15 and 3:5–14.

4:15 Caleb was one of the 12 spies sent into the promised land by Moses. He and Joshua were the only two spies to return with a positive report, believing in God's promise to help the Israelites conquer the land. Caleb's story is told in Numbers 13; 14 and Joshua 14; 15. His Profile is found in Numbers 15, p. 217.

4:40
l Jdg 18:7-10

38 The men listed above by name were leaders of their clans. Their families increased greatly, 39 and they went to the outskirts of Gedor to the east of the valley in search of pasture for their flocks. 40 They found rich, good pasture, and the land was spacious, peaceful and quiet. *l* Some Hamites had lived there formerly.

4:43
m 1Sa 15:8; 30:17;
2Sa 8:12

41 The men whose names were listed came in the days of Hezekiah king of Judah. They attacked the Hamites in their dwellings and also the Meunites who were there and completely destroyed[a] them, as is evident to this day. Then they settled in their place, because there was pasture for their flocks. 42 And five hundred of these Simeonites, led by Pelatiah, Neariah, Rephaiah and Uzziel, the sons of Ishi, invaded the hill country of Seir. 43 They killed the remaining Amalekites *m* who had escaped, and they have lived there to this day.

Reuben

5:1
n Ge 29:32
o Ge 35:22; 49:4
p Ge 48:16, 22

5:2
q Ge 49:10, 12
r Ps 60:7; Mic 5:2;
Mt 2:6

5:3
s Ge 46:9; Ex 6:14;
Nu 26:5-11

5 The sons of Reuben *n* the firstborn of Israel (he was the firstborn, but when he defiled his father's marriage bed, *o* his rights as firstborn were given to the sons of Joseph *p* son of Israel; so he could not be listed in the genealogical record in accordance with his birthright, 2 and though Judah *q* was the strongest of his brothers and a ruler *r* came from him, the rights of the firstborn belonged to Joseph)— 3 the sons of Reuben *s* the firstborn of Israel:

Hanoch, Pallu, Hezron and Carmi.

4 The descendants of Joel:

Shemaiah his son, Gog his son,
Shimei his son, 5 Micah his son,
Reaiah his son, Baal his son,

6 and Beerah his son, whom Tiglath-Pileser *b* king of Assyria took into exile. Beerah was a leader of the Reubenites.

5:7
t ver 17

5:8
u Nu 32:34

5:9
v Jos 22:9

7 Their relatives by clans, *t* listed according to their genealogical records:

Jeiel the chief, Zechariah, 8 and Bela son of Azaz, the son of Shema, the son of Joel. They settled in the area from Aroer *u* to Nebo and Baal Meon. 9 To the east they occupied the land up to the edge of the desert that extends to the Euphrates River, because their livestock had increased in Gilead. *v*

10 During Saul's reign they waged war against the Hagrites, who were defeated at their hands; they occupied the dwellings of the Hagrites throughout the entire region east of Gilead.

Gad

5:11
w Jos 13:24-28
x Jos 13:11

11 The Gadites *w* lived next to them in Bashan, as far as Salecah: *x*
12 Joel was the chief, Shapham the second, then Janai and Shaphat, in Bashan.
13 Their relatives, by families, were:

Michael, Meshullam, Sheba, Jorai, Jacan, Zia and Eber—seven in all.

14 These were the sons of Abihail son of Huri, the son of Jaroah, the son of Gilead, the son of Michael, the son of Jeshishai, the son of Jahdo, the son of Buz.

15 Ahi son of Abdiel, the son of Guni, was head of their family.

16 The Gadites lived in Gilead, in Bashan and its outlying villages, and on all the pasturelands of Sharon as far as they extended.

5:17
y 2Ki 15:32
z 2Ki 14:16, 28

17 All these were entered in the genealogical records during the reigns of Jotham *y* king of Judah and Jeroboam *z* king of Israel.

---

a 41 The Hebrew term refers to the irrevocable giving over of things or persons to the LORD, often by totally destroying them.   *b 6* Hebrew *Tilgath-Pilneser*, a variant of *Tiglath-Pileser*; also in verse 26

5:1 Reuben's sin of incest was recorded for all future generations to read. The purpose of this epitaph was not to smear Reuben's name, but to show that painful memories aren't the only results of sin. The real consequences of sin are ruined lives. As the oldest son, Reuben was the rightful heir to both a double portion of his father's estate and the leadership of Abraham's descendants, who had grown into a large tribe. But his sin stripped away his rights and privileges and ruined his family. Before you give in to temptation, consider the disastrous consequences sin may produce in your life and the lives of others.

5:2 This ruler from the tribe of Judah refers to David and his royal line, and to Jesus the Messiah, David's greatest descendant.

¹⁸The Reubenites, the Gadites and the half-tribe of Manasseh had 44,760 men ready for military service—able-bodied men who could handle shield and sword, who could use a bow, and who were trained for battle. ¹⁹They waged war against the Hagrites, Jetur, *a* Naphish and Nodab. ²⁰They were helped in fighting them, and God handed the Hagrites and all their allies over to them, because they cried *b* out to him during the battle. He answered their prayers, because they trusted in him. ²¹They seized the livestock of the Hagrites—fifty thousand camels, two hundred fifty thousand sheep and two thousand donkeys. They also took one hundred thousand people captive, ²²and many others fell slain, because the battle was God's. And they occupied the land until the exile. *c*

The Half-Tribe of Manasseh

²³The people of the half-tribe of Manasseh were numerous; they settled in the land from Bashan to Baal Hermon, that is, to Senir (Mount Hermon).

²⁴These were the heads of their families: Epher, Ishi, Eliel, Azriel, Jeremiah, Hodaviah and Jahdiel. They were brave warriors, famous men, and heads of their families. ²⁵But they were unfaithful to the God of their fathers and prostituted themselves to the gods of the peoples of the land, whom God had destroyed before them. ²⁶So the God of Israel stirred up the spirit of Pul *d* king of Assyria (that is, Tiglath-Pileser *e* king of Assyria), who took the Reubenites, the Gadites and the half-tribe of Manasseh into exile. He took them to Halah, Habor, Hara and the river of Gozan, where they are to this day.

Levi

6 The sons of Levi: *f*
    Gershon, Kohath and Merari.
² The sons of Kohath:
    Amram, Izhar, Hebron and Uzziel.
³ The children of Amram:
    Aaron, Moses and Miriam.
    The sons of Aaron:
    Nadab, Abihu, *g* Eleazar and Ithamar.
⁴ Eleazar was the father of Phinehas,
    Phinehas the father of Abishua,
⁵ Abishua the father of Bukki,
    Bukki the father of Uzzi,
⁶ Uzzi the father of Zerahiah,
    Zerahiah the father of Meraioth,
⁷ Meraioth the father of Amariah,
    Amariah the father of Ahitub,
⁸ Ahitub the father of Zadok, *h*
    Zadok the father of Ahimaaz,

5:19
a Ge 25:15;
1Ch 1:31
5:20
b 2Ch 14:11;
Ps 22:5
5:22
c 2Ki 15:29; 17:6
5:26
d 2Ki 15:19
e 2Ki 15:29
6:1
f Ge 46:11; Ex 6:16
6:3
g Lev 10:1
6:8
h 2Sa 8:17; 15:27

5:18–22 The armies of Reuben, Gad, and Manasseh succeeded in battle because they trusted God. Although they had instinct and skill as soldiers, they prayed and sought God's direction. The natural and developed abilities God gives us are meant to be used for him, but they should never replace our dependence on him. When we trust in our own cleverness, skill, and strength rather than in God, we open the door for pride. When facing difficult situations, seek God's purpose and ask for his guidance and strength. Psalm 20:7 says, "Some trust in chariots and some in horses, but we trust in the name of the LORD our God."

5:22 The exile mentioned here refers to the exile of the ten northern tribes (the northern kingdom of Israel) to Assyria in 722 B.C. These tribes never returned to their homeland. This story is found in 2 Kings 15:29—17:41.

5:24, 25 As warriors and leaders, these men had established excellent reputations for their great skill and leadership qualities. But in God's eyes they failed in the most important quality— being faithful to God. If you try to measure up to society's standards for fame and success, you may neglect your true purpose—to please and obey God. In the end, God alone examines

our hearts and determines our final standing. How is your present reputation with God?

6:1ff The tribe of Levi was set apart to serve God in the tabernacle (Numbers 3; 4), and later in the temple (1 Chronicles 23—26). Aaron, Levi's descendant (6:3), became Israel's first high priest. God required all future priests to be descendants of Aaron. The rest of the Levites assisted the priests in the various tabernacle or temple duties and assisted the people by teaching them God's word and encouraging them to obey it.

6:3 The people listed here played major roles in the drama of the exodus. Aaron's story is found in the books of Exodus, Leviticus, and Numbers. His Profile is found in Exodus 32, p. 143. Moses was one of the greatest prophets and leaders in Israel's history. His story is found in the books of Exodus, Leviticus, Numbers, and Deuteronomy. His Profile is found in Exodus 14, p. 117. The story of Miriam, Moses' and Aaron's sister, is found in Exodus 2; 15:20, 21; and Numbers 12; 20:1. Her Profile is found in Numbers 13, p. 213. Nadab and Abihu were killed for disobeying God (Leviticus 10). Eleazar became Israel's high priest after Aaron (Numbers 20:24–28), and Ithamar played an important role in organizing the worship services of the tabernacle (Numbers 4:28, 33; 7:8).

⁹ Ahimaaz the father of Azariah,
Azariah the father of Johanan,

6:10
ˡ1Ki 6:1; 2Ch 3:1;
26:17-18

¹⁰ Johanan the father of Azariahˡ (it was he who served as priest in the temple Solomon
built in Jerusalem),

¹¹ Azariah the father of Amariah,
Amariah the father of Ahitub,

¹² Ahitub the father of Zadok,
Zadok the father of Shallum,

6:13
ˡ2Ki 22:1-20

¹³ Shallum the father of Hilkiah,ˡ
Hilkiah the father of Azariah,

6:14
ᵏEzr 2:2; Ne 11:11

¹⁴ Azariah the father of Seraiah,ᵏ
and Seraiah the father of Jehozadak.

6:15
ˡ2Ki 25:18; Hag 1:1,
14; Zec 6:11

¹⁵Jehozadakˡ was deported when the LORD sent Judah and Jerusalem into exile by the hand
of Nebuchadnezzar.

6:16
ᵐGe 29:34; Ex 6:16

¹⁶ The sons of Levi:ᵐ
Gershon,ᵃ Kohath and Merari.

¹⁷ These are the names of the sons of Gershon:
Libni and Shimei.

¹⁸ The sons of Kohath:
Amram, Izhar, Hebron and Uzziel.

6:19
ⁿ1Ch 23:21

¹⁹ The sons of Merari: ⁿ
Mahli and Mushi.

These are the clans of the Levites listed according to their fathers:

²⁰ Of Gershon:
Libni his son, Jehath his son,
Zimmah his son, ²¹Joah his son,
Iddo his son, Zerah his son
and Jeatherai his son.

²² The descendants of Kohath:
Amminadab his son, Korah his son,
Assir his son, ²³Elkanah his son,
Ebiasaph his son, Assir his son,

6:24
ᵒ1Ch 15:5

²⁴ Tahath his son, Urielᵒ his son,
Uzziah his son and Shaul his son.

²⁵ The descendants of Elkanah:
Amasai, Ahimoth,

²⁶ Elkanah his son,ᵇ Zophai his son,
Nahath his son, ²⁷Eliab his son,
Jeroham his son, Elkanah his son
and Samuel his son.ᶜ

6:28
ᵖver 33; 1Sa 8:2

²⁸ The sons of Samuel:
Joelᵈ ᵖ the firstborn
and Abijah the second son.

²⁹ The descendants of Merari:
Mahli, Libni his son,
Shimei his son, Uzzah his son,

³⁰ Shimea his son, Haggiah his son
and Asaiah his son.

ᵃ16 Hebrew *Gershom*, a variant of *Gershon*; also in verses 17, 20, 43, 62 and 71　ᵇ26 Some Hebrew manuscripts,
Septuagint and Syriac; most Hebrew manuscripts *Ahimoth 26and Elkanah. The sons of Elkanah:*　ᶜ27 Some
Septuagint manuscripts (see also 1 Samuel 1:19,20 and 1 Chron. 6:33,34); Hebrew does not have *and Samuel
his son.*　ᵈ28 Some Septuagint manuscripts and Syriac (see also 1 Samuel 8:2 and 1 Chron. 6:33); Hebrew does
not have *Joel.*

6:28 When Samuel became God's leader and spokesman,
Israel was on the brink of collapse. The last few chapters of
the book of Judges give a vivid picture of the moral decay and
the resulting decline of the nation. But with God's help, Samuel
almost single-handedly brought the nation from ruin to revival.
He unified the people by showing them that God was their
common Leader and that any nation that focused on him would

find and fulfill its true purpose. For the rest of Samuel's story,
and to see how he set up rules for governing a nation based
on spiritual principles, read the book of 1 Samuel and his Profile
in chapter 7, p. 403.

The Temple Musicians

31 These are the men David put in charge of the music q in the house of the LORD after the ark came to rest there. 32 They ministered with music before the tabernacle, the Tent of Meeting, until Solomon built the temple of the LORD in Jerusalem. They performed their duties according to the regulations laid down for them.

33 Here are the men who served, together with their sons:

From the Kohathites:

Heman, the musician,
the son of Joel, the son of Samuel,
34 the son of Elkanah, the son of Jeroham,
the son of Eliel, the son of Toah,
35 the son of Zuph, the son of Elkanah,
the son of Mahath, the son of Amasai,
36 the son of Elkanah, the son of Joel,
the son of Azariah, the son of Zephaniah,
37 the son of Tahath, the son of Assir,
the son of Ebiasaph, the son of Korah, r
38 the son of Izhar, the son of Kohath,
the son of Levi, the son of Israel;

39 and Heman's associate Asaph, who served at his right hand:

Asaph son of Berekiah, the son of Shimea,
40 the son of Michael, the son of Baaseiah, a
the son of Malkijah, 41 the son of Ethni,
the son of Zerah, the son of Adaiah,
42 the son of Ethan, the son of Zimmah,
the son of Shimei, 43 the son of Jahath,
the son of Gershon, the son of Levi;

44 and from their associates, the Merarites, at his left hand:

Ethan son of Kishi, the son of Abdi,
the son of Malluch, 45 the son of Hashabiah,
the son of Amaziah, the son of Hilkiah,
46 the son of Amzi, the son of Bani,
the son of Shemer, 47 the son of Mahli,
the son of Mushi, the son of Merari,
the son of Levi.

48 Their fellow Levites were assigned to all the other duties of the tabernacle, the house of God. 49 But Aaron and his descendants were the ones who presented offerings on the altar s of burnt offering and on the altar of incense t in connection with all that was done in the Most Holy Place, making atonement for Israel, in accordance with all that Moses the servant of God had commanded.

50 These were the descendants of Aaron:

Eleazar his son, Phinehas his son,
Abishua his son, 51 Bukki his son,
Uzzi his son, Zerahiah his son,

a 40 Most Hebrew manuscripts; some Hebrew manuscripts, one Septuagint manuscript and Syriac *Maaseiah*

6:31
q 1Ch 15:19

6:37
r Ex 6:24

6:49
s Ex 27:1-8
t Ex 30:1-7, 10

6:31 David did much to bring music into worship. He established songleaders and choirs to perform regularly at the temple (chapter 25). As a young man, David was hired to play the harp for King Saul (1 Samuel 16:15–23). He also wrote many of the songs found in the book of Psalms.

6:31ff The builders and craftsmen had completed the temple, and the priests and Levites had been given their responsibilities for taking care of it. Then it was time for another group of people—the musicians—to exercise their talents for God. Some of those who served with music are recorded here. You don't have to be an ordained minister to have an important place in the body of believers. Builders, craftsmen, worship assistants,

choir members, and songleaders all have significant contributions to make. God has given you a unique combination of talents. Use them to serve and honor him.

6:49 Aaron and his descendants strictly followed the details of worship commanded by God through Moses. They did not choose only those commands they *wanted* to obey. Note what happened to Uzzah when important details in handling the ark of the covenant were neglected (13:6–10). We should not try to obey God selectively, choosing those commands we will obey and those we will ignore. God's Word has authority over every aspect of our lives, not just selected portions.

6:49 For more information on priests, see the note on Leviticus 8:1ff.

52 Meraioth his son, Amariah his son,
Ahitub his son, 53 Zadok his son
and Ahimaaz his son.

54 These were the locations of their settlements allotted as their territory (they were assigned to the descendants of Aaron who were from the Kohathite clan, because the first lot
was for them):

6:56
u Jos 14:13; 15:13

55 They were given Hebron in Judah with its surrounding pasturelands. 56 But the
fields and villages around the city were given to Caleb son of Jephunneh. *u*

6:58
v Jos 10:3

57 So the descendants of Aaron were given Hebron (a city of refuge), and Libnah, *a*
Jattir, Eshtemoa, 58 Hilen, Debir, *v* 59 Ashan, Juttah *b* and Beth Shemesh, together with

6:60
w Jer 1:1

their pasturelands. 60 And from the tribe of Benjamin they were given Gibeon, *c* Geba,
Alemeth and Anathoth, *w* together with their pasturelands.

These towns, which were distributed among the Kohathite clans, were thirteen in all.
61 The rest of Kohath's descendants were allotted ten towns from the clans of half the
tribe of Manasseh.

62 The descendants of Gershon, clan by clan, were allotted thirteen towns from the tribes
of Issachar, Asher and Naphtali, and from the part of the tribe of Manasseh that is in Bashan.

63 The descendants of Merari, clan by clan, were allotted twelve towns from the tribes of
Reuben, Gad and Zebulun.

6:64
x Nu 35:1-8;
Jos 21:3, 41-42

64 So the Israelites gave the Levites these towns *x* and their pasturelands. 65 From the
tribes of Judah, Simeon and Benjamin they allotted the previously named towns.

66 Some of the Kohathite clans were given as their territory towns from the tribe of
Ephraim.

67 In the hill country of Ephraim they were given Shechem (a city of refuge), and

6:68
y Jos 10:10

Gezer, *d* 68 Jokmeam, Beth Horon, *y* 69 Aijalon and Gath Rimmon, together with their
pasturelands.

70 And from half the tribe of Manasseh the Israelites gave Aner and Bileam, together
with their pasturelands, to the rest of the Kohathite clans.

71 The Gershonites received the following:
From the clan of the half-tribe of Manasseh
they received Golan in Bashan and also Ashtaroth, together with their pasturelands;
72 from the tribe of Issachar
they received Kedesh, Daberath, 73 Ramoth and Anem, together with their pasturelands;
74 from the tribe of Asher

6:75
z Nu 13:21

they received Mashal, Abdon, 75 Hukok and Rehob, *z* together with their pasturelands;
76 and from the tribe of Naphtali
they received Kedesh in Galilee, Hammon and Kiriathaim, together with their
pasturelands.

77 The Merarites (the rest of the Levites) received the following:
From the tribe of Zebulun
they received Jokneam, Kartah, *e* Rimmono and Tabor, together with their pasturelands;

*a 57 See Joshua 21:13; Hebrew given the cities of refuge: Hebron, Libnah.   b 59 Syriac (see also Septuagint and
Joshua 21:16); Hebrew does not have Juttah.   c 60 See Joshua 21:17; Hebrew does not have Gibeon.   d 67 See
Joshua 21:21; Hebrew given the cities of refuge: Shechem, Gezer.   e 77 See Septuagint and Joshua 21:34; Hebrew
does not have Jokneam, Kartah.*

6:54 The tribe of Levi was not given a specific area of land as
were the other tribes. Instead, the Levites were to live throughout
the land in order to aid the people of *every* tribe in their worship
of God. Thus the Levites were given towns or pasturelands within
the allotted areas of the other tribes (Joshua 13:14, 33).

6:57ff God had told the tribes to designate specific cities to
be cities of refuge (Numbers 35). These cities were to provide
refuge for a person who accidentally killed someone. This
instruction may have seemed unimportant when it was given—
the Israelites hadn't even entered the promised land. Sometimes
God gives us instructions that do not seem relevant to us at the

moment. But later we can see the importance of those instructions. Don't discard the lessons of the Bible because certain
details seem irrelevant. Obey God now—in the future you will
have a clearer understanding of the reasons for his instructions.

6:61 The Israelites cast lots in order to take the decision-making
process out of human hands and put it into God's hands. Casting
lots was like drawing straws or throwing dice. Lots were cast only
after seeking God's guidance in prayer. (For more information on
casting lots, see the note on Joshua 18:8.)

78 from the tribe of Reuben across the Jordan east of Jericho

they received Bezer in the desert, Jahzah, [79]Kedemoth [a] and Mephaath, together with their pasturelands;

6:79
[a]Dt 2:26

80 and from the tribe of Gad

they received Ramoth in Gilead, Mahanaim, [81]Heshbon and Jazer, together with their pasturelands. [b]

6:81
[b]2Ch 11:14

Issachar

7 The sons of Issachar:[c]

Tola, Puah,[d] Jashub and Shimron—four in all.

7:1
[c]Nu 26:23
[d]Ge 46:13

2 The sons of Tola:

Uzzi, Rephaiah, Jeriel, Jahmai, Ibsam and Samuel—heads of their families. During the reign of David, the descendants of Tola listed as fighting men in their genealogy numbered 22,600.

3 The son of Uzzi:

Izrahiah.

The sons of Izrahiah:

Michael, Obadiah, Joel and Isshiah. All five of them were chiefs. [4]According to their family genealogy, they had 36,000 men ready for battle, for they had many wives and children.

5 The relatives who were fighting men belonging to all the clans of Issachar, as listed in their genealogy, were 87,000 in all.

Benjamin

6 Three sons of Benjamin:[e]

Bela, Beker and Jediael.

7:6
[e]Ge 46:21;
Nu 26:38;
1Ch 8:1-40

7 The sons of Bela:

Ezbon, Uzzi, Uzziel, Jerimoth and Iri, heads of families—five in all. Their genealogical record listed 22,034 fighting men.

8 The sons of Beker:

Zemirah, Joash, Eliezer, Elioenai, Omri, Jeremoth, Abijah, Anathoth and Alemeth. All these were the sons of Beker. [9]Their genealogical record listed the heads of families and 20,200 fighting men.

10 The son of Jediael:

Bilhan.

The sons of Bilhan:

Jeush, Benjamin, Ehud, Kenaanah, Zethan, Tarshish and Ahishahar. [11]All these sons of Jediael were heads of families. There were 17,200 fighting men ready to go out to war.

12 The Shuppites and Huppites were the descendants of Ir, and the Hushites the descendants of Aher.

Naphtali

13 The sons of Naphtali:[f]

Jahziel, Guni, Jezer and Shillem[a]—the descendants of Bilhah.

7:13
[f]Ge 46:24

Manasseh

14 The descendants of Manasseh:

Asriel was his descendant through his Aramean concubine. She gave birth to Makir the father of Gilead. [g] [15]Makir took a wife from among the Huppites and Shuppites. His sister's name was Maacah.

Another descendant was named Zelophehad,[h] who had only daughters.

7:14
[g]Nu 26:30
7:15
[h]Nu 36:1-12

[16]Makir's wife Maacah gave birth to a son and named him Peresh. His brother was named Sheresh, and his sons were Ulam and Rakem.

17 The son of Ulam:

Bedan.

These were the sons of Gilead[i] son of Makir, the son of Manasseh. [18]His sister Hammoleketh gave birth to Ishhod, Abiezer and Mahlah.

7:17
[i]1Sa 12:11

[a]13 Some Hebrew and Septuagint manuscripts (see also Gen. 46:24 and Num. 26:49); most Hebrew manuscripts *Shallum*

¹⁹ The sons of Shemida were:

Ahian, Shechem, Likhi and Aniam.

Ephraim

7:20
j Nu 26:35

²⁰ The descendants of Ephraim:*j*

Shuthelah, Bered his son,

Tahath his son, Eleadah his son,

Tahath his son, ²¹ Zabad his son

and Shuthelah his son.

Ezer and Elead were killed by the native-born men of Gath, when they went down to seize their livestock. ²² Their father Ephraim mourned for them many days, and his relatives came to comfort him. ²³ Then he lay with his wife again, and she became pregnant and gave birth to a son. He named him Beriah,*a* because there had been mis-

7:24
k Jos 16:3, 5

fortune in his family. ²⁴ His daughter was Sheerah, who built Lower and Upper Beth Horon*k* as well as Uzzen Sheerah.

²⁵ Rephah was his son, Resheph his son,*b*

Telah his son, Tahan his son,

²⁶ Ladan his son, Ammihud his son,

Elishama his son, ²⁷ Nun his son

and Joshua his son.

7:28
l Jos 16:7

²⁸ Their lands and settlements included Bethel and its surrounding villages, Naaran to the east, Gezer*l* and its villages to the west, and Shechem and its villages all the way to Ayyah and

7:29
m Jos 17:11

its villages. ²⁹ Along the borders of Manasseh were Beth Shan,*m* Taanach, Megiddo and Dor, together with their villages. The descendants of Joseph son of Israel lived in these towns.

Asher

7:30
n Ge 46:17;
Nu 26:44

³⁰ The sons of Asher:*n*

Imnah, Ishvah, Ishvi and Beriah. Their sister was Serah.

³¹ The sons of Beriah:

Heber and Malkiel, who was the father of Birzaith.

³² Heber was the father of Japhlet, Shomer and Hotham and of their sister Shua.

³³ The sons of Japhlet:

Pasach, Bimhal and Ashvath.

These were Japhlet's sons.

³⁴ The sons of Shomer:

Ahi, Rohgah,*c* Hubbah and Aram.

³⁵ The sons of his brother Helem:

Zophah, Imna, Shelesh and Amal.

³⁶ The sons of Zophah:

Suah, Harnepher, Shual, Beri, Imrah, ³⁷ Bezer, Hod, Shamma, Shilshah, Ithran*d* and Beera.

³⁸ The sons of Jether:

Jephunneh, Pispah and Ara.

³⁹ The sons of Ulla:

Arah, Hanniel and Rizia.

⁴⁰ All these were descendants of Asher—heads of families, choice men, brave warriors and outstanding leaders. The number of men ready for battle, as listed in their genealogy, was 26,000.

The Genealogy of Saul the Benjamite

8:1
o Ge 46:21; 1Ch 7:6

8 Benjamin*o* was the father of Bela his firstborn,

Ashbel the second son, Aharah the third,

² Nohah the fourth and Rapha the fifth.

³ The sons of Bela were:

8:4
p 2Sa 23:9

Addar, Gera, Abihud,*e* ⁴ Abishua, Naaman, Ahoah,*p* ⁵ Gera, Shephuphan and Huram.

---

a 23 Beriah sounds like the Hebrew for *misfortune.*   *b 25* Some Septuagint manuscripts; Hebrew does not have *his son.*   *c 34* Or *of his brother Shomer: Rohgah*   *d 37* Possibly a variant of *Jether*   *e 3* Or *Gera the father of Ehud*

7:27 Joshua was one of Israel's great leaders, leading the people into the promised land. His story is told in the book of Joshua. His Profile is found in Joshua 2, p. 305.

6 These were the descendants of Ehud,q who were heads of families of those living in Geba and were deported to Manahath:

7 Naaman, Ahijah, and Gera, who deported them and who was the father of Uzza and Ahihud.

8 Sons were born to Shaharaim in Moab after he had divorced his wives Hushim and Baara. 9By his wife Hodesh he had Jobab, Zibia, Mesha, Malcam, 10Jeuz, Sakia and Mirmah. These were his sons, heads of families. 11By Hushim he had Abitub and Elpaal.

12 The sons of Elpaal:

Eber, Misham, Shemed (who built Onor and Lod with its surrounding villages), 13and Beriah and Shema, who were heads of families of those living in Aijalon and who drove out the inhabitants of Gath.

14 Ahio, Shashak, Jeremoth, 15Zebadiah, Arad, Eder, 16Michael, Ishpah and Joha were the sons of Beriah.

17 Zebadiah, Meshullam, Hizki, Heber, 18Ishmerai, Izliah and Jobab were the sons of Elpaal.

19 Jakim, Zicri, Zabdi, 20Elienai, Zillethai, Eliel, 21Adaiah, Beraiah and Shimrath were the sons of Shimei.

22 Ishpan, Eber, Eliel, 23Abdon, Zicri, Hanan, 24Hananiah, Elam, Anthothijah, 25Iphdeiah and Penuel were the sons of Shashak.

26 Shamsherai, Shehariah, Athaliah, 27Jaareshiah, Elijah and Zicri were the sons of Jeroham.

28All these were heads of families, chiefs as listed in their genealogy, and they lived in Jerusalem.

29 Jeiela the fatherb of Gibeon lived in Gibeon.

His wife's name was Maacah, 30and his firstborn son was Abdon, followed by Zur, Kish, Baal, Ner,c Nadab, 31Gedor, Ahio, Zeker 32and Mikloth, who was the father of Shimeah. They too lived near their relatives in Jerusalem.

33 Ner was the father of Kish,s Kish the father of Saul,t and Saul the father of Jonathan, Malki-Shua, Abinadab and Esh-Baal.d u

34 The son of Jonathan:v

Merib-Baal,e w who was the father of Micah.

35 The sons of Micah:

Pithon, Melech, Tarea and Ahaz.

36 Ahaz was the father of Jehoaddah, Jehoaddah was the father of Alemeth, Azmaveth and Zimri, and Zimri was the father of Moza. 37Moza was the father of Binea; Raphah was his son, Eleasah his son and Azel his son.

38 Azel had six sons, and these were their names:

Azrikam, Bokeru, Ishmael, Sheariah, Obadiah and Hanan. All these were the sons of Azel.

39 The sons of his brother Eshek:

Ulam his firstborn, Jeush the second son and Eliphelet the third. 40The sons of Ulam were brave warriors who could handle the bow. They had many sons and grandsons—150 in all.

All these were the descendants of Benjamin.

a29 Some Septuagint manuscripts (see also 1 Chron. 9:35); Hebrew does not have Jeiel.   b29 Father may mean civic leader or military leader.   c30 Some Septuagint manuscripts (see also 1 Chron. 9:36); Hebrew does not have Ner.   d33 Also known as Ish-Bosheth   e34 Also known as Mephibosheth

8:6
q1Ch 2:52

8:12
rEzr 2:33; Ne 6:2

8:33
s1Sa 9:1
t1Sa 14:49
u2Sa 2:8

8:34
v2Sa 9:12
w2Sa 4:4

8:8–10 These verses list Shaharaim's children by Hodesh after he had divorced his first two wives, Hushim and Baara. Divorce and polygamy are sometimes recorded in the Old Testament without critical comments. This does not mean that God takes divorce lightly. Malachi 2:15, 16 says, ". . . do not break faith with the wife of your youth. 'I hate divorce,' says the LORD God of Israel . . ." Jesus explained that although divorce was allowed, it was not God's will: "'Moses permitted you to divorce your wives because your hearts were hard. But it was not this way from the beginning'" (Matthew 19:8). Don't assume that God approves of an act because it isn't vigorously condemned in every related Bible reference.

8:33 Saul, Israel's first king, was very inconsistent. His story is found in 1 Samuel 9—31, and his Profile is in 1 Samuel 13, p. 409. Saul's son Jonathan was the opposite. Although Jonathan was the rightful heir to the throne, he realized that David was God's choice to be Israel's next king. Instead of being jealous, Jonathan was David's friend and even helped him escape from Saul's attempts at murder. Jonathan's story is told in 1 Samuel 14—31. His Profile is found in 1 Samuel 20, p. 429.

9 All Israel was listed in the genealogies recorded in the book of the kings of Israel.

3. Returnees from exile in Babylon
The People in Jerusalem

The people of Judah were taken captive to Babylon because of their unfaithfulness. ^x ²Now the first to resettle on their own property in their own towns ^y were some Israelites, priests, Levites and temple servants. ^z

³Those from Judah, from Benjamin, and from Ephraim and Manasseh who lived in Jerusalem were:

⁴ Uthai son of Ammihud, the son of Omri, the son of Imri, the son of Bani, a descendant of Perez son of Judah. ^a

⁵ Of the Shilonites:

Asaiah the firstborn and his sons.

⁶ Of the Zerahites:

Jeuel.

The people from Judah numbered 690.

⁷ Of the Benjamites:

Sallu son of Meshullam, the son of Hodaviah, the son of Hassenuah;

⁸ Ibneiah son of Jeroham; Elah son of Uzzi, the son of Micri; and Meshullam son of Shephatiah, the son of Reuel, the son of Ibnijah.

⁹ The people from Benjamin, as listed in their genealogy, numbered 956. All these men were heads of their families.

¹⁰ Of the priests:

Jedaiah; Jehoiarib; Jakin;

¹¹ Azariah son of Hilkiah, the son of Meshullam, the son of Zadok, the son of Meraioth, the son of Ahitub, the official in charge of the house of God;

¹² Adaiah son of Jeroham, the son of Pashhur, the son of Malkijah; and Maasai son of Adiel, the son of Jahzerah, the son of Meshullam, the son of Meshillemith, the son of Immer.

¹³ The priests, who were heads of families, numbered 1,760. They were able men, responsible for ministering in the house of God.

¹⁴ Of the Levites:

Shemaiah son of Hasshub, the son of Azrikam, the son of Hashabiah, a Merarite; ¹⁵Bakbakkar, Heresh, Galal and Mattaniah son of Mica, the son of Zicri, the son of Asaph; ¹⁶Obadiah son of Shemaiah, the son of Galal, the son of Jeduthun; and Berekiah son of Asa, the son of Elkanah, who lived in the villages of the Netophathites.

¹⁷ The gatekeepers: ^b

Shallum, Akkub, Talmon, Ahiman and their brothers, Shallum their chief ¹⁸being stationed at the King's Gate ^c on the east, up to the present time. These were the gatekeepers belonging to the camp of the Levites. ¹⁹Shallum ^d son of Kore, the son of Ebiasaph, the son of Korah, and his fellow gatekeepers from his family (the Korahites) were responsible for guarding the thresholds of the Tent ^a just as their fathers had

^a*19 That is, the temple; also in verses 21 and 23*

Margin notes:
9:1 ^x1Ch 5:25
9:2 ^yEzr 2:70 ^zEzr 2:43, 58; 8:20; Ne 7:60
9:4 ^aGe 46:12
9:17 ^bver 22
9:18 ^c1Ch 26:14; Eze 46:1
9:19 ^dJer 35:4

9:1 Although not every person in Judah was unfaithful, the entire nation was carried away into captivity. Everyone was affected by the sin of some. Even if we don't participate in a certain widespread wrongdoing, we will still be affected by those who do. It is not enough to say, "I didn't do it." We must speak out against the sins of our society.

9:1ff Chronologically, this chapter could be placed at the end of 2 Chronicles because it records the names of the exiles who returned from the Babylonian captivity. The writer included it here to show his concern for their need, as a nation, to return to what made them great in the first place—obedience to God.

9:10, 11 When we think of doing God's work, usually preaching, teaching, singing, and other kinds of up-front leadership come to mind. Azariah, however, was in charge of the house of God, and he was singled out for special mention. Whatever role you have in church, it is important to God. He appreciates your service and the attitude you have as you do it.

9:17, 18 Gatekeepers guarded the four main entrances to the temple and opened the gates each morning for those who wanted to worship. In addition, they did other day-to-day chores to keep the temple running smoothly—cleaning, preparing the offerings for sacrifice, and accounting for the gifts designated to the temple (9:22–32).

Gatekeepers had to be reliable, honest, and trustworthy. The people in our churches who handle the offerings and care for the materials and functions of the building follow in a great tradition and we should honor them for their reliability and service.

been responsible for guarding the entrance to the dwelling of the LORD. [20]In earlier times Phinehas [e] son of Eleazar was in charge of the gatekeepers, and the LORD was with him. [21]Zechariah [f] son of Meshelemiah was the gatekeeper at the entrance to the Tent of Meeting.

[22]Altogether, those chosen to be gatekeepers at the thresholds numbered 212. They were registered by genealogy in their villages. The gatekeepers had been assigned to their positions of trust by David and Samuel the seer. [23]They and their descendants were in charge of guarding the gates of the house of the LORD—the house called the Tent. [24]The gatekeepers were on the four sides: east, west, north and south. [25]Their brothers in their villages had to come from time to time and share their duties for seven-day [g] periods. [26]But the four principal gatekeepers, who were Levites, were entrusted with the responsibility for the rooms and treasuries in the house of God. [27]They would spend the night stationed around the house of God, [h] because they had to guard it; and they had charge of the key for opening it each morning.

[28]Some of them were in charge of the articles used in the temple service; they counted them when they were brought in and when they were taken out. [29]Others were assigned to take care of the furnishings and all the other articles of the sanctuary, [i] as well as the flour and wine, and the oil, incense and spices. [30]But some [j] of the priests took care of mixing the spices. [31]A Levite named Mattithiah, the firstborn son of Shallum the Korahite, was entrusted with the responsibility for baking the offering bread. [32]Some of their Kohathite brothers were in charge of preparing for every Sabbath the bread set out on the table. [k]

[33]Those who were musicians, [l] heads of Levite families, stayed in the rooms of the temple and were exempt from other duties because they were responsible for the work day and night. [m]

[34]All these were heads of Levite families, chiefs as listed in their genealogy, and they lived in Jerusalem.

The Genealogy of Saul

[35]Jeiel [n] the father [a] of Gibeon lived in Gibeon.

His wife's name was Maacah, [36]and his firstborn son was Abdon, followed by Zur, Kish, Baal, Ner, Nadab, [37]Gedor, Ahio, Zechariah and Mikloth. [38]Mikloth was the father of Shimeam. They too lived near their relatives in Jerusalem.

[39]Ner [o] was the father of Kish, Kish the father of Saul, and Saul the father of Jonathan, Malki-Shua, Abinadab and Esh-Baal. [b]

[40]The son of Jonathan:

Merib-Baal, [c] who was the father of Micah.

[41]The sons of Micah:

Pithon, Melech, Tahrea and Ahaz. [d]

[42]Ahaz was the father of Jadah, Jadah [e] was the father of Alemeth, Azmaveth and Zimri, and Zimri was the father of Moza. [43]Moza was the father of Binea; Rephaiah was his son, Eleasah his son and Azel his son.

[44]Azel had six sons, and these were their names:

Azrikam, Bokeru, Ishmael, Sheariah, Obadiah and Hanan. These were the sons of Azel.

9:20 [e]Nu 25:7-13

9:21 [f]1Ch 26:2, 14

9:25 [g]2Ki 11:5; 2Ch 23:8

9:27 [h]1Ch 23:30-32

9:29 [i]1Ch 23:29
9:30 [j]Ex 30:23-25

9:32 [k]Lev 24:5-8

9:33 [l]1Ch 6:31; 25:1-31
[m]Ps 134:1

9:35 [n]1Ch 8:29

9:39 [o]1Ch 8:33

---

[a]35 *Father* may mean *civic leader* or *military leader.*   [b]39 Also known as *Ish-Bosheth*   [c]40 Also known as *Mephibosheth*   [d]41 Vulgate and Syriac (see also Septuagint and 1 Chron. 8:35); Hebrew does not have *and Ahaz.*   [e]42 Some Hebrew manuscripts and Septuagint (see also 1 Chron. 8:36); most Hebrew manuscripts *Jarah, Jarah*

9:22–32 The priests and Levites put a great deal of time and care into worship. Not only did they perform rather complicated tasks (described in Leviticus 1—9), they also took care of many pieces of equipment. Everything relating to worship was carefully prepared and maintained so they and all the people could enter worship with their minds and hearts focused on God.

In our busy world, it is easy to rush into our one-hour-a-week worship services without preparing ourselves for worship beforehand. We reflect and worry about the week's problems; we pray about whatever comes into our minds; and we do not meditate on the words we are singing. But God wants our worship to be conducted "in a fitting and orderly way" (1 Corinthians 14:40). Just as we prepare to meet a business associate or invited guests, we should carefully prepare to meet our King in worship.

9:33, 34 Worship was the primary focus of many Israelites, whose vocation centered on the house of the Lord. Worship (appreciating God for his nature and worth) should occupy the core of our lives and not just a few minutes once a week. We too can worship at all hours if we stay aware of God's presence and guidance in all situations and if we maintain an attitude of serving him. Build your life around the worship of God rather than making worship just another activity in a busy schedule.

B. THE REIGN OF DAVID (10:1—29:30)

David becomes king over all Israel and captures the city of Jerusalem. God promises blessings to him and the nation, but David is not allowed to build the temple. Instead, he begins to make preparations for its construction. Although stumbling and falling occasionally, David walks step by step with God, sincerely wanting to be obedient. Through David's successes and his failures, we learn the importance of giving our whole heart to God and letting him be the focus of our life, striving each day to be consistent in our obedience to his will.

1. David becomes king over all Israel
Saul Takes His Life

10 Now the Philistines fought against Israel; the Israelites fled before them, and many fell slain on Mount Gilboa. ²The Philistines pressed hard after Saul and his sons, and they killed his sons Jonathan, Abinadab and Malki-Shua. ³The fighting grew fierce around Saul, and when the archers overtook him, they wounded him.

⁴Saul said to his armor-bearer, "Draw your sword and run me through, or these uncircumcised fellows will come and abuse me."

But his armor-bearer was terrified and would not do it; so Saul took his own sword and fell on it. ⁵When the armor-bearer saw that Saul was dead, he too fell on his sword and died. ⁶So Saul and his three sons died, and all his house died together.

⁷When all the Israelites in the valley saw that the army had fled and that Saul and his sons had died, they abandoned their towns and fled. And the Philistines came and occupied them.

⁸The next day, when the Philistines came to strip the dead, they found Saul and his sons fallen on Mount Gilboa. ⁹They stripped him and took his head and his armor, and sent messengers throughout the land of the Philistines to proclaim the news among their idols and their people. ¹⁰They put his armor in the temple of their gods and hung up his head in the temple of Dagon.

¹¹When all the inhabitants of Jabesh Gilead heard of everything the Philistines had done to Saul, ¹²all their valiant men went and took the bodies of Saul and his sons and brought them to Jabesh. Then they buried their bones under the great tree in Jabesh, and they fasted seven days.

¹³Saul died because he was unfaithful *p* to the LORD; he did not keep *q* the word of the LORD and even consulted a medium *r* for guidance, ¹⁴and did not inquire of the LORD. So the LORD put him to death and turned *s* the kingdom *t* over to David son of Jesse.

10:13
p 1Sa 15:23
q 1Sa 13:13
r Lev 19:31;
1Sa 28:7

10:14
s 1Ch 12:23
t 1Sa 15:28

10:1 The chronology of chapters 1—9 covers Israelite history from creation to the exile in Babylon (586 B.C.). At this point, the narrative goes back to the beginning of Israel's kingdom period, picking up with Israel's first king, Saul. 1 Chronicles 10 begins with Saul's death; to learn about his reign, read 1 Samuel.

10:10 Dagon, the most important god of the Philistines, was believed to bring rain and provide rich harvests. The Philistines built temples to him when they settled in the grain-producing land of Canaan. In times of drought, people begged Dagon for pity, even to the point of sacrificing their children in his temples. In times of plenty, the temples were used for twisted forms of entertainment, such as the humiliation of captives (see Judges 16:23–30). But Dagon, like the other pagan gods, was powerless against the one true God (1 Samuel 5:1–7).

10:11, 12 The actions of the valiant warriors who brought back and buried the bodies of King Saul and his sons should encourage us to respect our God-given leaders. David showed respect for Saul's position, even when Saul was chasing him to kill him (1 Samuel 26). How easy it is to be critical of those in authority over us, focusing only on their weaknesses. We cannot excuse sin, but we should respect the positions of those in authority, whether at work, at church, or in government. First Thessalonians 5:12, 13 gives instructions for honoring church leaders. Romans 13:1ff gives instructions for relating to government leaders.

10:13, 14 Saul's unfaithfulness was both active and passive; he not only did wrong, but he also *failed to do right*. He actively disobeyed by attempting murder, ignoring God's instructions, and seeking guidance from a witch. He passively disobeyed by neglecting to ask God for guidance as he ran the kingdom. Obedi-

ence, too, is both passive and active. It is not enough just to avoid what is wrong, we need to actively pursue what is right.

10:13, 14 In the account in 1 Samuel 28, Saul asked the Lord for guidance but received no answer; this account says he "did not inquire of the LORD." The answer to this apparent contradiction lies in understanding Saul's motives and the timing of his request to God. His frantic requests came only when he had tried everything his own way. He never went to God unless there was nowhere else to turn. When he finally asked, God refused to answer. Saul sought God only when it suited him, and God rejected him for his constant stubbornness and rebellion.

10:14 Throughout much of Saul's reign, David was forced to hide from him (1 Samuel 19—30). During this time David had opportunities to kill Saul (1 Samuel 24; 26) and to assume the throne that God had promised him (1 Samuel 16:1–13). But David trusted in God's promise that he would be king in God's good timing. It was not up to David to decide when Saul's reign would end. During this battle, God ended Saul's reign just as he had promised.

10:14 Why does this verse say that the Lord put Saul to death, when Saul took his own life (1 Samuel 31:3, 4)? God had rejected Saul because of his stubbornness and rebellion (1 Samuel 15:22–26) and had judged him for his sins (1 Samuel 28:16–19). God arranged a defeat in battle so that Saul would die and his kingdom would be taken from his family. If Saul had not taken his own life, the Philistine soldiers would have killed him.

David Becomes King Over Israel

11 All Israel came together to David at Hebron and said, "We are your own flesh and blood. 2 In the past, even while Saul was king, you were the one who led Israel on their military campaigns. And the LORD your God said to you, 'You will shepherd *u* my people Israel, and you will become their ruler.'"

3 When all the elders of Israel had come to King David at Hebron, he made a compact with them at Hebron before the LORD, and they anointed *v* David king over Israel, as the LORD had promised through Samuel.

David Conquers Jerusalem

4 David and all the Israelites marched to Jerusalem (that is, Jebus). The Jebusites *w* who lived there 5 said to David, "You will not get in here." Nevertheless, David captured the fortress of Zion, the City of David.

6 David had said, "Whoever leads the attack on the Jebusites will become commander-in-chief." Joab *x* son of Zeruiah went up first, and so he received the command.

7 David then took up residence in the fortress, and so it was called the City of David. 8 He built up the city around it, from the supporting terraces a to the surrounding wall, while Joab restored the rest of the city. 9 And David became more and more powerful, *y* because the LORD Almighty was with him.

David's Mighty Men

10 These were the chiefs of David's mighty men—they, together with all Israel, gave his kingship strong support to extend it over the whole land, as the LORD had promised— 11 this is the list of David's mighty men: *z*

Jashobeam, *b* a Hacmonite, was chief of the officers *c*; he raised his spear against three hundred men, whom he killed in one encounter.

12 Next to him was Eleazar son of Dodai the Ahohite, one of the three mighty men. 13 He was with David at Pas Dammim when the Philistines gathered there for battle. At a place where there was a field full of barley, the troops fled from the Philistines. 14 But they took their stand in the middle of the field. They defended it and struck the Philistines down, and the LORD brought about a great victory.

15 Three of the thirty chiefs came down to David to the rock at the cave of Adullam, while a band of Philistines was encamped in the Valley a of Rephaim. 16 At that time David was in the stronghold, *b* and the Philistine garrison was at Bethlehem. 17 David longed for water and said, "Oh, that someone would get me a drink of water from the well near the gate of Bethlehem!" 18 So the Three broke through the Philistine lines, drew water from the well near the gate of Bethlehem and carried it back to David. But he refused to drink it; instead, he poured it out before the LORD. 19 "God forbid that I should do this!" he said. "Should I drink the blood of these men who went at the risk of their lives?" Because they risked their lives to bring it back, David would not drink it.

a 8 Or *the Millo*   b 11 Possibly a variant of *Jashob-Baal*   c 11 Or *Thirty*; some Septuagint manuscripts *Three* (see also 2 Samuel 23:8)

11:2
u Ps 78:71

11:3
v 1Sa 16:1-13

11:4
w Jdg 1:21; 19:10

11:6
x 2Sa 8:16

11:9
y 2Sa 3:1

11:11
z 2Sa 17:10

11:15
a 1Ch 14:9

11:16
b 2Sa 5:17

11:1, 2 The details of how David came to power are given more completely in 2 Samuel. Chronicles emphasizes that *God* declared David to be the ruler although he used the efforts of many people, even some of Saul's own family. God is still sovereign over history, directing events to accomplish his will. The books of Chronicles demonstrate that no matter what people may do to try to hinder God's work, God still controls all events and works his will in them.

11:3, 4 David was king over Judah for seven and a half years before he captured Jerusalem. When David was finally anointed king over all Israel, 20 years had passed since Samuel had anointed him (1 Samuel 16:1–13). God's promises are worth waiting for, even when his timetable doesn't match our expectations or desires.

11:4 David chose Jerusalem as his capital for both political and military reasons. Jerusalem was near the center of the kingdom and, because it rested on a tribal border, was in neutral territory. Thus its location decreased tribal jealousies. Jerusalem also sat on a high ridge, making it difficult to attack. (For more information on the city of Jerusalem, see the note on 2 Samuel 5:6.)

11:9 David's power increased as a direct result of his consistent

trust in God. In contrast, Saul's power decreased because he wanted all the credit for himself and ignored God (1 Samuel 15:17–26). Those who are concerned about building a name for themselves risk losing the very recognition they crave. Like David, we should be concerned for righteousness, honesty, and excellence, and leave the results to God.

11:12–14 Eleazar's action changed the course of a battle. When everyone around him ran, he held his ground alongside David and was saved by the Lord. In any struggle, fear can keep us from taking a stand for God and from participating in God's victories. Face your fear head on. Find other believers along the way who are worth standing beside through thick and thin. If you are grounded in God, victory will come when you hold that ground.

11:15 The 30 chiefs were the most courageous and highest-ranking officers of David's army.

11:15–19 These three men risked their lives just to serve and please David. David recognized that their loyalty to him was inspired by their devotion to God, so he poured out the water as a drink offering, demonstrating that only God is worthy of such

Such were the exploits of the three mighty men.

11:20
*c*1Sa 26:6

²⁰Abishai *c* the brother of Joab was chief of the Three. He raised his spear against three hundred men, whom he killed, and so he became as famous as the Three. ²¹He was doubly honored above the Three and became their commander, even though he was not included among them.

11:23
*d*1Sa 17:7

²²Benaiah son of Jehoiada was a valiant fighter from Kabzeel, who performed great exploits. He struck down two of Moab's best men. He also went down into a pit on a snowy day and killed a lion. ²³And he struck down an Egyptian who was seven and a half feet*a* tall. Although the Egyptian had a spear like a weaver's rod *d* in his hand, Benaiah went against him with a club. He snatched the spear from the Egyptian's hand and killed him with his own spear. ²⁴Such were the exploits of Benaiah son of Jehoiada; he too was as famous as the three mighty men. ²⁵He was held in greater honor than any of the Thirty, but he was not included among the Three. And David put him in charge of his bodyguard.

11:26
*e*2Sa 2:18

²⁶ The mighty men were:
  Asahel *e* the brother of Joab,
  Elhanan son of Dodo from Bethlehem,
²⁷ Shammoth the Harorite,
  Helez the Pelonite,
²⁸ Ira son of Ikkesh from Tekoa,
  Abiezer from Anathoth,

11:29
*f*2Sa 21:18

²⁹ Sibbecai *f* the Hushathite,
  Ilai the Ahohite,
³⁰ Maharai the Netophathite,
  Heled son of Baanah the Netophathite,
³¹ Ithai son of Ribai from Gibeah in Benjamin,
  Benaiah the Pirathonite,
³² Hurai from the ravines of Gaash,
  Abiel the Arbathite,
³³ Azmaveth the Baharumite,
  Eliahba the Shaalbonite,
³⁴ the sons of Hashem the Gizonite,
  Jonathan son of Shagee the Hararite,
³⁵ Ahiam son of Sacar the Hararite,
  Eliphal son of Ur,
³⁶ Hepher the Mekerathite,
  Ahijah the Pelonite,
³⁷ Hezro the Carmelite,
  Naarai son of Ezbai,
³⁸ Joel the brother of Nathan,
  Mibhar son of Hagri,
³⁹ Zelek the Ammonite,
  Naharai the Berothite, the armor-bearer of Joab son of Zeruiah,
⁴⁰ Ira the Ithrite,
  Gareb the Ithrite,

11:41
*g*2Sa 11:6

⁴¹ Uriah *g* the Hittite,
  Zabad son of Ahlai,
⁴² Adina son of Shiza the Reubenite, who was chief of the Reubenites, and the thirty with him,
⁴³ Hanan son of Maacah,
  Joshaphat the Mithnite,
⁴⁴ Uzzia the Ashterathite,
  Shama and Jeiel the sons of Hotham the Aroerite,
⁴⁵ Jediael son of Shimri,
  his brother Joha the Tizite,

a23 Hebrew *five cubits* (about 2.3 meters)

devotion. They gave the water to David and he, in turn, gave it to God. Just as these men gave of themselves to serve David, we should put aside our own interests to serve other Christians (Romans 12:10). When we serve others, we are also serving God.

46 Eliel the Mahavite,
  Jeribai and Joshaviah the sons of Elnaam,
  Ithmah the Moabite,
47 Eliel, Obed and Jaasiel the Mezobaite.

Warriors Join David

12 These were the men who came to David at Ziklag,[h] while he was banished from the presence of Saul son of Kish (they were among the warriors who helped him in battle; 2 they were armed with bows and were able to shoot arrows or to sling stones right-handed or left-handed;[i] they were kinsmen of Saul from the tribe of Benjamin):

> **12:1**
> h 1Sa 27:2-6
>
> **12:2**
> i Jdg 3:15; 20:16

3 Ahiezer their chief and Joash the sons of Shemaah the Gibeathite; Jeziel and Pelet the sons of Azmaveth; Beracah, Jehu the Anathothite, 4 and Ishmaiah the Gibeonite, a mighty man among the Thirty, who was a leader of the Thirty; Jeremiah, Jahaziel, Johanan, Jozabad the Gederathite, 5 Eluzai, Jerimoth, Bealiah, Shemariah and Shephatiah the Haruphite; 6 Elkanah, Isshiah, Azarel, Joezer and Jashobeam the Korahites; 7 and Joelah and Zebadiah the sons of Jeroham from Gedor.

8 Some Gadites defected to David at his stronghold in the desert. They were brave warriors, ready for battle and able to handle the shield and spear. Their faces were the faces of lions,[j] and they were as swift as gazelles[k] in the mountains.

> **12:8**
> j 2Sa 17:10
> k 2Sa 2:18

9 Ezer was the chief,
  Obadiah the second in command, Eliab the third,
10 Mishmannah the fourth, Jeremiah the fifth,
11 Attai the sixth, Eliel the seventh,
12 Johanan the eighth, Elzabad the ninth,
13 Jeremiah the tenth and Macbannai the eleventh.

14 These Gadites were army commanders; the least was a match for a hundred, and the greatest for a thousand.[l] 15 It was they who crossed the Jordan in the first month when it was overflowing all its banks,[m] and they put to flight everyone living in the valleys, to the east and to the west.

> **12:14**
> l Dt 32:30
>
> **12:15**
> m Jos 3:15

16 Other Benjamites and some men from Judah also came to David in his stronghold. 17 David went out to meet them and said to them, "If you have come to me in peace, to help me, I am ready to have you unite with me. But if you have come to betray me to my enemies when my hands are free from violence, may the God of our fathers see it and judge you." 18 Then the Spirit[n] came upon Amasai,[o] chief of the Thirty, and he said:

> **12:18**
> n Jdg 6:34
> o 2Sa 17:25

12:1 Ziklag was a city in Philistia where David had escaped to hide from Saul. Achish, the Philistine ruler of the area, was happy to have a famous Israelite warrior defect to his land. He did not know, however, that David was only pretending loyalty. Achish gave the city of Ziklag to David, his family, and his army (1 Samuel 27:5–7). David's whereabouts were not a great secret, and many loyal followers joined him there.

12:1ff David surrounded himself with great warriors, the best of the Israelite army. What qualities made them worthy to be David's warriors and servants? (1) They had practiced long and hard to perfect their skills (with bow, sling, and spear); (2) they were mentally tough and determined ("Their faces were the faces of lions," 12:8); (3) they were physically in shape ("as swift as gazelles," 12:8); (4) they were dedicated to serving God and David. Weak leaders are easily threatened by competent subordinates, but strong leaders surround themselves with the best. They are not intimidated by able and competent followers.

12:1–7 All the warriors mentioned here were from the tribe of Benjamin. Even members of Saul's own tribe (1 Samuel 9:1, 2) were deserting him to help David become king over all Israel. It was clear to them that God had chosen David to be Israel's next leader.

12:2 Archers and slingers had special weapons. The sling was unassuming in appearance but deadly in battle. A shallow leather pouch with a cord of leather or goat's hair attached to each side, the sling was whirled around the head. When one side was released, it sent a stone to its target. The bow and arrow had

been in use for thousands of years. Arrowheads were made of stone, wood, or bone because the Philistines still had a monopoly on metalworking (1 Samuel 13:19, 20). Arrow shafts were made of reed or wood, and bowstrings were made of animal gut.

12:8 While the men of Benjamin were expert archers and slingers, the warriors of Gad were experts with the shield and spear. Israelite spears had wood shafts and spearheads of bone or stone and were often thrown through the air toward their mark. Philistine spears had bronze shafts and iron spearheads, and their shields were made of wood and overlaid with leather. Large shields were often carried by an armor-bearer, whose main task was to protect the warrior.

12:18 How did the Holy Spirit work in Old Testament times? When there was an important job to be done, God chose a person to do it, and the Spirit gave that person the needed power and ability. The Spirit gave Bezalel artistic ability (Exodus 31:1–5), Jephthah military prowess (Judges 11:29), David power to rule (1 Samuel 16:13), and Zechariah an authoritative word of prophecy (2 Chronicles 24:20). Here the Holy Spirit came upon Amasai, one of David's warriors. The Spirit came upon individuals in order to accomplish specific goals. Beginning at Pentecost, however, the Spirit came upon all believers, not only to empower them to do God's will, but also to dwell in them day by day (Acts 2:14–21). If you are a believer in Jesus Christ, you will experience the Holy Spirit's ongoing work in your life as well as special times of filling for God's purposes. Expect God's Spirit to work in and through you.

> "We are yours, O David!
>   We are with you, O son of Jesse!
>   Success, success to you,
>   and success to those who help you,
>   for your God will help you."

So David received them and made them leaders of his raiding bands.

^{**12:19**}
^{p 1Sa 29:2-11}

¹⁹Some of the men of Manasseh defected to David when he went with the Philistines to fight against Saul. (He and his men did not help the Philistines because, after consultation, their rulers sent him away. They said, "It will cost us our heads if he deserts to his master Saul.")p ²⁰When David went to Ziklag, these were the men of Manasseh who defected to him: Adnah, Jozabad, Jediael, Michael, Jozabad, Elihu and Zillethai, leaders of units of a thousand in Manasseh. ²¹They helped David against raiding bands, for all of them were brave warriors, and they were commanders in his army. ²²Day after day men came to help David, until he had a great army, like the army of God.a

Others Join David at Hebron

12:23
q 2Sa 2:3-4
r 1Ch 10:14
s 1Sa 16:1

²³These are the numbers of the men armed for battle who came to David at Hebronq to turn r Saul's kingdom over to him, as the Lord had said: s

²⁴men of Judah, carrying shield and spear—6,800 armed for battle;

²⁵men of Simeon, warriors ready for battle—7,100;

12:28
t 2Sa 8:17

²⁶men of Levi—4,600, ²⁷including Jehoiada, leader of the family of Aaron, with 3,700 men, ²⁸and Zadok,t a brave young warrior, with 22 officers from his family;

12:29
u 2Sa 2:8-9

²⁹men of Benjamin, Saul's kinsmen—3,000, mostu of whom had remained loyal to Saul's house until then;

³⁰men of Ephraim, brave warriors, famous in their own clans—20,800;

³¹men of half the tribe of Manasseh, designated by name to come and make David king—18,000;

12:32
v Est 1:13

³²men of Issachar, who understood the times and knew what Israel should dov—200 chiefs, with all their relatives under their command;

³³men of Zebulun, experienced soldiers prepared for battle with every type of weapon, to help David with undivided loyalty—50,000;

³⁴men of Naphtali—1,000 officers, together with 37,000 men carrying shields and spears;

³⁵men of Dan, ready for battle—28,600;

³⁶men of Asher, experienced soldiers prepared for battle—40,000;

³⁷and from east of the Jordan, men of Reuben, Gad and the half-tribe of Manasseh, armed with every type of weapon—120,000.

12:38
w 2Sa 5:1-3

³⁸All these were fighting men who volunteered to serve in the ranks. They came to Hebron fully determined to make David king over all Israel.w All the rest of the Israelites were also of one mind to make David king. ³⁹The men spent three days there with David, eating and drinking, for their families had supplied provisions for them. ⁴⁰Also, their neighbors from as far away as Issachar, Zebulun and Naphtali came bringing food on donkeys, camels, mules and oxen. There were plentiful supplies of flour, fig cakes, raisin x cakes, wine, oil, cattle and sheep, for there was joy in Israel.

12:40
x 1Sa 25:18

a22 Or *a great and mighty army*

12:22 David "had a great army, like the army of God." Men were drawn to David by the reputation of his great warriors, the news of their victories, and their desire to see God's will done in making David king. People are often drawn to a great cause and the brave, determined people who support it. As believers, we have the greatest cause—the salvation of mankind. If we are brave, determined, and faithful, others will be drawn to work with us.

12:26–29 In Numbers 1:47–50, God said that the Levites were to be exempt from military service. Why then are they listed as part of David's army? Although they were exempt from the draft, they strongly supported David and volunteered their services to help install him as king.

12:32 The 200 chiefs from the tribe of Issachar "understood the times." As a result, their knowledge and judgment provided

needed help in making decisions for the nation. For leaders today, it is equally necessary to know what is happening in society in order to plan the best course of action for the church. Knowledge of current events, trends, and needs helps us understand people's thoughts and attitudes. This gives leaders information to help them make wise decisions for the church and make God's message relevant to people's lives.

12:40 The people were ready for change. They had suffered under Saul's leadership because of his disobedience to God (see 10:13). They were so overjoyed with David's coronation that they contributed lavishly to the celebration. It is right and proper to give generously for celebration and joyous worship. God is the author of joy, and he will join us in our celebrations.

2. David brings the ark to Jerusalem
Bringing Back the Ark

13 David conferred with each of his officers, the commanders of thousands and commanders of hundreds. ²He then said to the whole assembly of Israel, "If it seems good to you and if it is the will of the LORD our God, let us send word far and wide to the rest of our brothers throughout the territories of Israel, and also to the priests and Levites who are with them in their towns and pasturelands, to come and join us. ³Let us bring the ark of our God back to us,ʸ for we did not inquire ofᵃ itᵇ during the reign of Saul." ⁴The whole assembly agreed to do this, because it seemed right to all the people.

⁵So David assembled all the Israelites,ᶻ from the Shihor River in Egypt to Leboᶜ Hamath, to bring the ark of God from Kiriath Jearim. ᵃ ⁶David and all the Israelites with him went to Baalahᵇ of Judah (Kiriath Jearim) to bring up from there the ark of God the LORD, who is enthroned between the cherubimᶜ—the ark that is called by the Name.

⁷They moved the ark of God from Abinadab'sᵈ house on a new cart, with Uzzah and Ahio guiding it. ⁸David and all the Israelites were celebrating with all their might before God, with songs and with harps, lyres, tambourines, cymbals and trumpets. ᵉ

⁹When they came to the threshing floor of Kidon, Uzzah reached out his hand to steady the ark, because the oxen stumbled. ¹⁰The LORD's angerᶠ burned against Uzzah, and he struck him downᵍ because he had put his hand on the ark. So he died there before God.

¹¹Then David was angry because the LORD's wrath had broken out against Uzzah, and to this day that place is called Perez Uzzah. ᵈ

¹²David was afraid of God that day and asked, "How can I ever bring the ark of God to me?" ¹³He did not take the ark to be with him in the City of David. Instead, he took it aside to the house of Obed-Edom the Gittite. ¹⁴The ark of God remained with the family of Obed-Edom in his house for three months, and the LORD blessed his householdʰ and everything he had.

ᵃ3 Or *we neglected* ᵇ3 Or *him* ᶜ5 Or *to the entrance to* ᵈ11 *Perez Uzzah* means *outbreak against Uzzah.*

13:3
ʸ1Sa 7:1-2

13:5
ᶻ1Ch 15:3
ᵃ1Sa 6:21; 7:2

13:6
ᵇJos 15:9; 2Sa 6:2
ᶜ2Ki 19:15

13:7
ᵈNu 4:15; 1Sa 7:1

13:8
ᵉ2Sa 6:5

13:10
ᶠ1Ch 15:13, 15
ᵍLev 10:2

13:14
ʰ1Ch 26:4-5

13:1 David took time to confer with all his officers. As king, he had ultimate authority and could have given orders on his own, but he chose to involve others in leadership. Perhaps this is why there was unanimous support for his decisions (13:1–5). When we are in charge, it is tempting to make unilateral decisions, pushing through our own opinions. But effective leaders listen carefully to others' opinions, and they encourage others to participate in making decisions. Of course, we should always consult God first. We can run into big problems if we don't talk to him (see the note on 13:10).

13:1ff The parallel account of moving the ark (2 Samuel 5; 6) shows that David's building projects were completed *before* he brought the ark to Jerusalem. The writer of Chronicles puts the moving of the ark first in order to highlight David's spiritual accomplishments and relationship to God.

13:3 The ark of God is also called the ark of the covenant. The most sacred object of the Hebrew faith, it was a large box containing the stone tablets on which God had written the Ten Commandments (Exodus 25:10–22). David had already made Jerusalem his political capital (11:4–9). At this time, David brought the ark there in order to make Jerusalem the nation's center for worship.

13:3 The ark of God had been in Kiriath Jearim for many years. The neglect of the ark symbolized Israel's neglect of God. Bringing the ark back to the center of Israel's life reflected David's desire to remind the nation of its true foundation—God. Neglecting those things that remind us of God—the Bible, the church, and contact with Christians—will cause us also to neglect God. How would an observer know that God is at the center of your life?

13:6 Cherubim are mighty angels.

13:8 Worship in the Old Testament was more than a sober religious exercise. David's exuberance as he worshiped God with dancing and music is approved in Scripture. Our worship should reflect a healthy balance: sometimes we should be reflective and serious (see Exodus 19:14ff), and sometimes we should show

enthusiasm and jubilation. What do you need—more serious reflection or more joyous celebration?

13:10 Why did Uzzah die? He touched the ark, and that offense was punishable by death. God had given specific instructions about how the ark was to be moved and carried (Numbers 4:5–15), and those instructions had been neglected. The Levites were responsible to move the ark (there is no record that Uzzah was a Levite), and it was to be carried on their shoulders with poles through its rings (Numbers 7:9). It was *never* to be touched. Bringing the ark on a cart followed the Philistines' example (1 Samuel 6:1ff). Uzzah, though sincere in his desire to protect the ark, had to face the consequences of his sin, and David was reminded that his obedience to God's laws was more important than his enthusiasm. Also David had "conferred with each of his officers" (13:1), but he neglected to ask God. The advice of our friends and colleagues is no substitute for God's direction.

13:10–14 Uzzah died instantly for touching the ark, but God blessed Obed-Edom's home where the ark was stored. This demonstrates the two-edged aspect of God's character: he is perfectly loving and perfectly just. Great blessings come to those who obey his commands, but severe punishment comes to those who disobey him. This punishment may come swiftly or over time, but it will come. Sometimes we focus only on the blessings God gives us, while forgetting that when we sin, "It is a dreadful thing to fall into the hands of the living God" (Hebrews 10:31). At other times, however, we concentrate so much on judgment that we miss his blessings. Don't fall into a one-sided view of God. Along with God's blessings comes the responsibility to live up to his demands for fairness, honesty, and justice.

13:11 David was angry at both God and himself. David knew that he had done something wrong in transporting the ark, and he was angry that his plans for the joyous return of the ark had ended in a man's death. Once David's anger cooled, it was replaced by fear as the king realized the importance God placed on the ark, the symbol of his presence and covenant with Israel. David left the ark in Obed-Edom's home until he could consider how to get it to

David's House and Family

14 Now Hiram king of Tyre sent messengers to David, along with cedar logs, stonemasons and carpenters to build a palace for him. 2And David knew that the LORD had established him as king over Israel and that his kingdom had been highly exalted for the sake of his people Israel.

3In Jerusalem David took more wives and became the father of more sons and daughters. 4These are the names of the children born to him there: *i* Shammua, Shobab, Nathan, Solomon, 5Ibhar, Elishua, Elpelet, 6Nogah, Nepheg, Japhia, 7Elishama, Beeliada a and Eliphelet.

David Defeats the Philistines

8When the Philistines heard that David had been anointed king over all Israel, they went up in full force to search for him, but David heard about it and went out to meet them. 9Now the Philistines had come and raided the Valley *j* of Rephaim; 10so David inquired of God: "Shall I go and attack the Philistines? Will you hand them over to me?"

The LORD answered him, "Go, I will hand them over to you."

11So David and his men went up to Baal Perazim, and there he defeated them. He said, "As waters break out, God has broken out against my enemies by my hand." So that place was called Baal Perazim. b 12The Philistines had abandoned their gods there, and David gave orders to burn them in the fire.

13Once more the Philistines raided the valley;*k* 14so David inquired of God again, and God answered him, "Do not go straight up, but circle around them and attack them in front of the balsam trees. 15As soon as you hear the sound of marching in the tops of the balsam trees, move out to battle, because that will mean God has gone out in front of you to strike the Philistine army." 16So David did as God commanded him, and they struck down the Philistine army, all the way from Gibeon to Gezer.

17So David's fame *l* spread throughout every land, and the LORD made all the nations fear *m* him.

The Ark Brought to Jerusalem

15 After David had constructed buildings for himself in the City of David, he prepared a place for the ark of God and pitched *n* a tent for it. 2Then David said, "No one but the Levites *o* may carry the ark of God, because the LORD chose them to carry the ark of the LORD and to minister before him forever."

3David assembled all Israel *p* in Jerusalem to bring up the ark of the LORD to the place he had prepared for it. 4He called together the descendants of Aaron and the Levites:

5 From the descendants of Kohath,
   Uriel the leader and 120 relatives;
6 from the descendants of Merari,
   Asaiah the leader and 220 relatives;

a 7 A variant of *Eliada*   b 11 *Baal Perazim* means *the lord who breaks out.*

Margin references
14:4 *i* 1Ch 3:9
14:9 *j* 1Ch 11:15
14:13 *k* ver 9
14:17 *l* Jos 6:27 *m* Dt 2:25
15:1 *n* 1Ch 16:1
15:2 *o* Nu 4:15; Dt 10:8
15:3 *p* 1Ki 8:1; 1Ch 13:5

Jerusalem. This allowed David to discover God's instructions for transporting the ark. The next trip would be carried out according to God's commands.

14:1 King Hiram also sent lumber and craftsmen to help Solomon build the temple (2 Chronicles 2:1ff).

14:2 God gave David honor and success ("his kingdom had been highly exalted"), but not simply for David's personal gain. David realized that God had prospered him for a special reason—for the sake of God's people! Often we are tempted to use our position or possessions only for our own good. Instead, we must remember that God has placed us where we are and given us all we have so that we may encourage others and give to those in need.

14:3 Accumulating wives and concubines in a harem was the custom of the day among Middle Eastern royalty, but it was not God's ideal (Genesis 2:24). David's marriages brought him greater power and influence, but they also caused strife, jealousy, and even murder within his family. (See the chart in 2 Samuel 11, p. 463 for other consequences of polygamy.)

14:8–16 A map of this battle is in 2 Samuel 5, p. 453.

14:10 Before David went to battle, he inquired of God first, asking

for his presence and guidance. Too often we wait until we are in trouble before turning to God. By then the consequences of our actions are already unfolding. Do you ask for God's help only as a desperate last resort? Instead, go to him first! Like David, you may receive incredible help and avoid serious trouble. Make sure you give God the credit when you see what he does on your behalf.

14:12 David's quick and decisive action against idols helped unify his kingdom and focus the people on worshiping the one true God. He was obeying the law that said, "This is what you are to do to them: Break down their altars, smash their sacred stones, cut down their Asherah poles and burn their idols in the fire" (Deuteronomy 7:5). Most of David's successors failed to destroy idols, and this led to unbelievable moral corruption in Israel.

14:12 Often the soldiers wanted to keep souvenirs from the battle (and 2 Samuel 5:21 states that some of the men kept some of these idols), but David ordered them to burn the idols. The only proper response to sin is to get rid of it completely. You cannot be a follower of God while continuing to hold on to parts of your past life that push God out of the center of your thoughts and actions. Eliminate whatever takes God's rightful place in your life, and follow him with complete devotion.

7 from the descendants of Gershon,[a]
    Joel the leader and 130 relatives;
8 from the descendants of Elizaphan,
    Shemaiah the leader and 200 relatives;
9 from the descendants of Hebron,
    Eliel the leader and 80 relatives;
10 from the descendants of Uzziel,
    Amminadab the leader and 112 relatives.

11 Then David summoned Zadok and Abiathar the priests, and Uriel, Asaiah, Joel, Shemaiah, Eliel and Amminadab the Levites. 12 He said to them, "You are the heads of the Levitical families; you and your fellow Levites are to consecrate yourselves and bring up the ark of the LORD, the God of Israel, to the place I have prepared for it. 13 It was because you, the Levites, did not bring it up the first time that the LORD our God broke out in anger against us. [q] We did not inquire of him about how to do it in the prescribed way." 14 So the priests and Levites consecrated themselves in order to bring up the ark of the LORD, the God of Israel. 15 And the Levites carried the ark of God with the poles on their shoulders, as Moses had commanded [r] in accordance with the word of the LORD.

16 David told the leaders of the Levites to appoint their brothers as singers to sing joyful songs, accompanied by musical instruments: lyres, harps and cymbals. [s]

17 So the Levites appointed Heman [t] son of Joel; from his brothers, Asaph [u] son of Berekiah; and from their brothers the Merarites, [v] Ethan son of Kushaiah; 18 and with them their brothers next in rank: Zechariah, [b] Jaaziel, Shemiramoth, Jehiel, Unni, Eliab, Benaiah, Maaseiah, Mattithiah, Eliphelehu, Mikneiah, Obed-Edom and Jeiel, [c] the gatekeepers.

19 The musicians Heman, Asaph and Ethan were to sound the bronze cymbals; 20 Zechariah, Aziel, Shemiramoth, Jehiel, Unni, Eliab, Maaseiah and Benaiah were to play the lyres according to *alamoth,* [d] 21 and Mattithiah, Eliphelehu, Mikneiah, Obed-Edom, Jeiel and Azaziah were to play the harps, directing according to *sheminith.* [d] 22 Kenaniah the head Levite was in charge of the singing; that was his responsibility because he was skillful at it.

23 Berekiah and Elkanah were to be doorkeepers for the ark. 24 Shebaniah, Joshaphat, Nethanel, Amasai, Zechariah, Benaiah and Eliezer the priests were to blow trumpets [w] before the ark of God. Obed-Edom and Jehiah were also to be doorkeepers for the ark.

25 So David and the elders of Israel and the commanders of units of a thousand went to bring up the ark [x] of the covenant of the LORD from the house of Obed-Edom, with rejoicing. 26 Because God had helped the Levites who were carrying the ark of the covenant of the LORD, seven bulls and seven rams were sacrificed. 27 Now David was clothed in a robe of fine linen, as were all the Levites who were carrying the ark, and as were the singers, and Kenaniah, who was in charge of the singing of the choirs. David also wore a linen ephod. 28 So all Israel brought up the ark of the covenant of the LORD with shouts, with the sounding of rams' horns and trumpets, and of cymbals, and the playing of lyres and harps.

15:13 [q] 2Sa 6:3;
1Ch 13:7-10

15:15 [r] Ex 25:14

15:16 [s] 1Ch 25:1

15:17 [t] 1Ch 6:33
[u] 1Ch 6:39
[v] 1Ch 6:44

15:24 [w] ver 28; 1Ch 16:6

15:25 [x] 1Ch 13:13

[a] 7 Hebrew *Gershom,* a variant of *Gershon*   [b] 18 Three Hebrew manuscripts and most Septuagint manuscripts (see also verse 20 and 1 Chron. 16:5); most Hebrew manuscripts *Zechariah son and* or *Zechariah, Ben and*   [c] 18 Hebrew; Septuagint (see also verse 21) *Jeiel and Azaziah*   [d] 20,21 Probably a musical term

15:12 The priests consecrated themselves so they would be prepared to carry the ark. To *consecrate* literally means to separate, to set apart for sacred purposes, to purify. The priests symbolically separated themselves from sin and evil. This was done by washing themselves and their clothing in a special ceremony (Numbers 8:5–8). While we are not required to carry out such ceremonies today, we can purify ourselves by reading God's Word, thoughtfully applying it to our lives, and preparing our hearts to participate in worship through anticipation, self-examination, and meditation. Just as we "set apart" time for worship, we also "set apart" ourselves to be in God's presence.

15:13 "The first time" refers to the incident recorded in 13:8–11 and 2 Samuel 6:1–11. As the ark was being brought back to Israel on an oxcart, the oxen stumbled. Uzzah, trying to steady the ark with his hand, was killed instantly for touching it. The mistake was not in David's desire to move the ark, but in his method for its return. David either ignored or was unaware of the specific instructions in God's law about how the ark was to be moved. Obviously he had discovered his mistake and was now preparing

to correct it. This incident was a divine object lesson to all Israel that God governed the king and not the other way around. If David had been allowed to handle the ark of God carelessly, what would that have said to the people about their faith?

15:13–15 When David's first attempt to move the ark failed (13:8–14), he learned an important lesson: when God gives specific instructions, it is wise to follow them precisely. This time David saw to it that the Levites carried the ark (Numbers 4:5–15). We may not fully understand the reasons behind God's instructions, but we do know that his wisdom is complete and his judgment infallible. The way to know God's instructions is to know his Word. But just as children do not understand the reasons for all their parents' instructions until they are older, we may not understand all of God's reasons in this life. It is far better to obey God first, and then discover the reasons. We are never free to disobey God just because we don't understand.

15:16–25 The great musical procession was designed as a worthy accompaniment to the great occasion. It heightened the excitement, elevated the people's hearts and minds, and focused their

²⁹As the ark of the covenant of the LORD was entering the City of David, Michal daughter of Saul watched from a window. And when she saw King David dancing and celebrating, she despised him in her heart.

16 They brought the ark of God and set it inside the tent that David had pitched ʸ for it, and they presented burnt offerings and fellowship offerings **a** before God. ²After David had finished sacrificing the burnt offerings and fellowship offerings, he blessed the people in the name of the LORD. ³Then he gave a loaf of bread, a cake of dates and a cake of raisins to each Israelite man and woman.

16:1
ʸ1Ch 15:1

⁴He appointed some of the Levites to minister before the ark of the LORD, to make petition, to give thanks, and to praise the LORD, the God of Israel: ⁵Asaph was the chief, Zechariah second, then Jeiel, Shemiramoth, Jehiel, Mattithiah, Eliab, Benaiah, Obed-Edom and Jeiel. They were to play the lyres and harps, Asaph was to sound the cymbals, ⁶and Benaiah and Jahaziel the priests were to blow the trumpets regularly before the ark of the covenant of God.

David's Psalm of Thanks

⁷That day David first committed to Asaph and his associates this psalm ᶻ of thanks to the LORD:

16:7
ᶻ2Sa 23:1

> ⁸ Give thanks to the LORD, call on his name;
>   make known among the nations ᵃ what he has done.
> ⁹ Sing to him, sing praise to him;
>   tell of all his wonderful acts.
> ¹⁰ Glory in his holy name;
>   let the hearts of those who seek the LORD rejoice.
> ¹¹ Look to the LORD and his strength;
>   seek ᵇ his face always.
> ¹² Remember the wonders he has done,
>   his miracles, ᶜ and the judgments he pronounced,
> ¹³ O descendants of Israel his servant,
>   O sons of Jacob, his chosen ones.

16:8
ᵃ2Ki 19:19

16:11
ᵇPs 24:6

16:12
ᶜPs 78:43

> ¹⁴ He is the LORD our God;
>   his judgments are in all the earth.
> ¹⁵ He remembers ᵇ his covenant forever,
>   the word he commanded, for a thousand generations,
> ¹⁶ the covenant ᵈ he made with Abraham,
>   the oath he swore to Isaac.
> ¹⁷ He confirmed it to Jacob ᵉ as a decree,
>   to Israel as an everlasting covenant:
> ¹⁸ "To you I will give the land of Canaan ᶠ
>   as the portion you will inherit."
> ¹⁹ When they were but few in number, ᵍ
>   few indeed, and strangers in it,

16:16
ᵈGe 17:2; 26:3

16:17
ᵉGe 35:9-12

16:18
ᶠGe 13:14-17

16:19
ᵍGe 34:30

a 1 Traditionally *peace offerings*; also in verse 2   **b** 15 Some Septuagint manuscripts (see also Psalm 105:8); Hebrew *Remember*

---

attention on the event. It also helped seal it in their memory for years to come. Beginning any task by praising God can inspire us to give him our best. Develop the practice of giving praise to God, and you will experience greater joy and strength to face anything.

15:29 David was willing to look foolish in the eyes of some people in order to express his thankfulness to God fully and honestly. In contrast, Michal was so disgusted by his "undignified" actions that she could not rejoice in the ark's return to Jerusalem. Worship had so deteriorated under her father Saul's reign that it had become stilted and ritualistic. Michal could accept David as a military conqueror and as a king, but she could not accept his free and spontaneous expression of praise to God. Some devoted people may look foolish to us in their heartfelt expressions of worship, but we must accept them. In the same way, we should not be afraid to worship God with whatever expressions seem appropriate.

16:4 Certain Levites were appointed to give continual praise and

thanks to God. Praise and thanksgiving should be a regular part of our routine, not reserved only for celebrations. Praise God continually, and you will find that you won't take his blessings for granted.

16:7–36 Four elements of true thanksgiving are found in this song (psalm): (1) *remembering* what God has done, (2) *telling* others about it, (3) *showing* God's glory to others, and (4) *offering* gifts of self, time, and resources. If you are truly thankful, your life will show it.

16:8ff Several parts of this psalm are parallel to songs in the book of Psalms: 16:8–22 with Psalm 105:1–15; 16:23–33 with Psalm 96; 16:34–36 with Psalm 106:1, 47, 48.

16:15–18 This covenant was given to Abraham (Genesis 15:18–21), and then passed on to Isaac (Genesis 26:24, 25) and Jacob (Genesis 28:13–15). God promised to give the land of Canaan (present-day Israel) to their descendants. He also promised that the Messiah would come from their line.

²⁰ they^a wandered from nation to nation,
   from one kingdom to another.
²¹ He allowed no man to oppress them;
   for their sake he rebuked kings:^h
²² "Do not touch my anointed ones;
   do my prophets no harm."

²³ Sing to the LORD, all the earth;
   proclaim his salvation day after day.
²⁴ Declare his glory among the nations,
   his marvelous deeds among all peoples.
²⁵ For great is the LORD and most worthy of praise;
   he is to be fearedⁱ above all gods.
²⁶ For all the gods of the nations are idols,
   but the LORD made the heavens.^j
²⁷ Splendor and majesty are before him;
   strength and joy in his dwelling place.
²⁸ Ascribe to the LORD, O families of nations,
   ascribe to the LORD glory and strength,^k
²⁹   ascribe to the LORD the glory due his name.
  Bring an offering and come before him;
   worship the LORD in the splendor of his^b holiness.
³⁰ Tremble before him, all the earth!
   The world is firmly established; it cannot be moved.
³¹ Let the heavens rejoice, let the earth be glad;^l
   let them say among the nations, "The LORD reigns!"^m
³² Let the sea resound, and all that is in it;ⁿ
   let the fields be jubilant, and everything in them!
³³ Then the trees of the forest will sing,
   they will sing for joy before the LORD,
   for he comes to judge the earth.

³⁴ Give thanks to the LORD, for he is good;
   his love endures forever.^o
³⁵ Cry out, "Save us, O God our Savior;
   gather us and deliver us from the nations,
   that we may give thanks to your holy name,
   that we may glory in your praise."
³⁶ Praise be to the LORD, the God of Israel,^p
   from everlasting to everlasting.

Then all the people said "Amen" and "Praise the LORD."

³⁷ David left Asaph and his associates before the ark of the covenant of the LORD to minister there regularly, according to each day's requirements. ^q ³⁸ He also left Obed-Edom^r and his sixty-eight associates to minister with them. Obed-Edom son of Jeduthun, and also Hosah,^s were gatekeepers.

³⁹ David left Zadok the priest and his fellow priests before the tabernacle of the LORD at the high place in Gibeon ^t ⁴⁰ to present burnt offerings to the LORD on the altar of burnt

**Cross references (margin):**

16:21   ^hGe 12:17; 20:3; Ex 7:15-18
16:25   ⁱPs 89:7
16:26   ^jLev 19:4
16:28   ^kPs 29:1-2
16:31   ^lIsa 49:13; ^mPs 93:1
16:32   ⁿPs 98:7
16:34   ^oEzr 3:11; Ps 136:1-26; Jer 33:11
16:36   ^pDt 27:15; 1Ki 8:15; Ps 72:18-19
16:37   ^q2Ch 8:14
16:38   ^r1Ch 13:13; ^s1Ch 26:10
16:39   ^t1Ki 3:4; 2Ch 1:3

---

^a 18-20 One Hebrew manuscript, Septuagint and Vulgate (see also Psalm 105:12); most Hebrew manuscripts inherit, / ¹⁹ though you are but few in number, / few indeed, and strangers in it." / ²⁰ They   ^b 29 Or LORD with the splendor of

---

16:25 Genuine praise results when we declare God's character and attributes in the presence of others. When we recognize and affirm his goodness we are holding up his perfect moral nature for all to see. Praise benefits us because it takes our minds off our problems and needs and focuses on God's power, mercy, majesty, and love.

16:29 Genuine praise also involves ascribing glory to God. This means that we give credit where credit is due. Remember this in your worship—give God all the glory.

16:37 Asaph and his fellow Levites ministered in the temple, doing each day whatever was needed. To carry out God's work is not merely to engage in religious exercises. It includes other necessary tasks. Even if you don't have the opportunity to teach or preach, God can use you in the ministry. What needs to be done? Cleaning, serving, singing, planning, administering? Look for ways to minister each day.

16:39 David brought the ark to Jerusalem although the tabernacle was still at Gibeon. His plan was to reunite the tabernacle and ark in a new temple at Jerusalem that would then become

16:40
u Ex 29:38;
Nu 28:1-8
16:41
v 2Ch 5:13
16:42
w 2Ch 7:6

offering regularly, morning and evening, in accordance with everything written in the Law *u* of the LORD, which he had given Israel. ⁴¹With them were Heman *v* and Jeduthun and the rest of those chosen and designated by name to give thanks to the LORD, "for his love endures forever." ⁴²Heman and Jeduthun were responsible for the sounding of the trumpets and cymbals and for the playing of the other instruments for sacred song. *w* The sons of Jeduthun were stationed at the gate.

⁴³Then all the people left, each for his own home, and David returned home to bless his family.

God's Promise to David

17 After David was settled in his palace, he said to Nathan the prophet, "Here I am, living in a palace of cedar, while the ark of the covenant of the LORD is under a tent."

²Nathan replied to David, "Whatever you have in mind, do it, for God is with you."

³That night the word of God came to Nathan, saying:

17:4
x 1Ch 28:3

⁴"Go and tell my servant David, 'This is what the LORD says: You *x* are not the one to build me a house to dwell in. ⁵I have not dwelt in a house from the day I brought Israel up out of Egypt to this day. I have moved from one tent site to another, from one dwelling place to another. ⁶Wherever I have moved with all the Israelites, did I ever say to any of their leaders *a* whom I commanded to shepherd my people, "Why have you not built me a house of cedar?"'

17:7
y 2Sa 6:21

⁷"Now then, tell my servant David, 'This is what the LORD Almighty says: I took you from the pasture and from following the flock, to be ruler *y* over my people Israel. ⁸I have been with you wherever you have gone, and I have cut off all your enemies from before you. Now I will make your name like the names of the greatest men of the earth. ⁹And I will provide a place for my people Israel and will plant them so that they can have a home of their own and no longer be disturbed. Wicked people will not oppress them anymore, as they did at the beginning ¹⁰and have done ever since the time I appointed leaders *z* over my people Israel. I will also subdue all your enemies.

17:10
z Jdg 2:16

" 'I declare to you that the LORD will build a house for you: ¹¹When your days are over and you go to be with your fathers, I will raise up your offspring to succeed you, one of your own sons, and I will establish his kingdom. ¹²He is the one who will build a house for me, and I will establish his throne forever. ¹³I will be his father, *a* and he will be my son. *b* I will never take my love away from him, as I took it away from your predecessor. ¹⁴I will set him over my house and my kingdom forever; his throne *c* will be established forever.' "

17:13
a 2Co 6:18
b Heb 1:5*
17:14
c 1Ki 2:12
d Jer 33:17

¹⁵Nathan reported to David all the words of this entire revelation.

a 6 Traditionally *judges*; also in verse 10

Israel's only worship center. The temple, however, was not built until Solomon's time. In the meantime, Israel had two worship centers and two high priests (15:11), one at Gibeon and one at Jerusalem.

17:1 David felt disturbed that the ark, the symbol of God's presence, sat in a tent while he lived in a beautiful palace. David's desire was right, but his timing was wrong. God told David *not* to build a temple (17:3, 4), and David was willing to abide by God's timing. If you live in comparative luxury while God's work, house, or ministers go lacking, perhaps God wants you to change the situation. Like David, take action to correct the imbalance, but be willing to move according to God's timing.

17:3–14 God did not want a warrior to build his temple (28:3; 1 Kings 5:3), and David had shed much blood in unifying the nation. So the honor of building the temple would go to David's son Solomon. David would pass on to Solomon a peaceful and united kingdom, ready to begin work on a beautiful temple.

17:10 God promised to subdue David's enemies. Chapters 18—20 tell how God kept that promise.

17:12–14 Why, after this eternal promise, were the Israelites eventually taken from the promised land into captivity? The promise to David had two parts. The first part was conditional: as long as David's descendants followed God's laws and honored him, they would continually be on the throne of Israel. The second part was unconditional: a son of David would occupy his throne forever. This was Jesus the Messiah. The first part of the promise was based on the faithful obedience of David's descendants. The second part would come true regardless of the way his descendants acted.

David's Prayer

16Then King David went in and sat before the LORD, and he said:

"Who am I, O LORD God, and what is my family, that you have brought me this far? 17And as if this were not enough in your sight, O God, you have spoken about the future of the house of your servant. You have looked on me as though I were the most exalted of men, O LORD God.

18"What more can David say to you for honoring your servant? For you know your servant, 19O LORD. For the sake e of your servant and according to your will, you have done this great thing and made known all these great promises. f

20"There is no one like you, O LORD, and there is no God but you, g as we have heard with our own ears. 21And who is like your people Israel—the one nation on earth whose God went out to redeem h a people for himself, and to make a name for yourself, and to perform great and awesome wonders by driving out nations from before your people, whom you redeemed from Egypt? 22You made your people Israel your very own forever, i and you, O LORD, have become their God.

23"And now, LORD, let the promise you have made concerning your servant and his house be established forever. Do as you promised, 24so that it will be established and that your name will be great forever. Then men will say, 'The LORD Almighty, the God over Israel, is Israel's God!' And the house of your servant David will be established before you.

25"You, my God, have revealed to your servant that you will build a house for him. So your servant has found courage to pray to you. 26O LORD, you are God! You have promised these good things to your servant. 27Now you have been pleased to bless the house of your servant, that it may continue forever in your sight; j for you, O LORD, have blessed it, and it will be blessed forever."

3. David's military exploits

David's Victories

18 In the course of time, David defeated the Philistines and subdued them, and he took Gath and its surrounding villages from the control of the Philistines.

2David also defeated the Moabites, and they became subject to him and brought tribute.

3Moreover, David fought Hadadezer king of Zobah, as far as Hamath, when he went to establish his control along the Euphrates River. 4David captured a thousand of his chariots, seven thousand charioteers and twenty thousand foot soldiers. He hamstrung all but a hundred of the chariot horses.

5When the Arameans of Damascus k came to help Hadadezer king of Zobah, David struck down twenty-two thousand of them. 6He put garrisons in the Aramean kingdom of Damascus, and the Arameans became subject to him and brought tribute. The LORD gave David victory everywhere he went.

7David took the gold shields carried by the officers of Hadadezer and brought them to Jerusalem. 8From Tebah a and Cun, towns that belonged to Hadadezer, David took a great quantity of bronze, which Solomon used to make the bronze Sea, l the pillars and various bronze articles.

a8 Hebrew *Tibhath*, a variant of *Tebah*

17:19
e Isa 37:35
f 2Sa 7:25
17:20
g Ex 9:14; Isa 44:6
17:21
h Ex 6:6
17:22
i Ex 19:5-6

17:27
j Ps 21:6

18:5
k 1Ch 19:6

18:8
l 1Ki 7:23;
2Ch 4:12, 15-16

17:16–20 God told David that Solomon would be given the honor of building the temple. David responded with deep humility, not resentment. This king who had conquered his enemies and was loved by his people said, "Who am I . . . that you have brought me this far?" David recognized that God was the *true* king. God has done just as much for us, and he plans to do even more! Like David, we should humble ourselves and give glory to God, saying, "There is no one like you, O LORD." When God chooses someone else to implement your ideas, will you respond with such humility?

17:16–27 David prayed by humbling himself (17:16–18), praising God (17:19, 20), recognizing God's blessings (17:21, 22), and accepting God's decisions, promises, and commands (17:23, 24). Sometimes we are quick to make requests to God and to tell him our troubles, but these other dimensions of prayer can deepen our spiritual life. Take time to praise God, to count his blessings, and to affirm your commitment to do what he has already said to do.

17:21 David's reference to Israel's exodus from Egypt would have had special significance to the original readers of 1 Chronicles who were either beginning or had just completed a second great exodus back to Israel from captivity in Babylon. Remembering God's promises, mercy, and protection during the first exodus would have encouraged the exiles returning once again to Israel, just as God had promised.

18:2 In 2 Samuel 8:1, 2, it is recorded that David killed two-thirds of the people of Moab. His ancestor Ruth was originally from the land of Moab.

18:6, 14 David was a victorious and just ruler. We see in David's glowing success a hint of what Christ's reign will be like—

⁹When Tou king of Hamath heard that David had defeated the entire army of Hadadezer king of Zobah, ¹⁰he sent his son Hadoram to King David to greet him and congratulate him on his victory in battle over Hadadezer, who had been at war with Tou. Hadoram brought all kinds of articles of gold and silver and bronze.

¹¹King David dedicated these articles to the Lord, as he had done with the silver and gold he had taken from all these nations: Edom and Moab, the Ammonites and the Philistines, and Amalek.

¹²Abishai son of Zeruiah struck down eighteen thousand Edomites*m* in the Valley of Salt. ¹³He put garrisons in Edom, and all the Edomites became subject to David. The Lord gave David victory everywhere he went.

David's Officials

¹⁴David reigned over all Israel,*n* doing what was just and right for all his people. ¹⁵Joab*o* son of Zeruiah was over the army; Jehoshaphat son of Ahilud was recorder; ¹⁶Zadok*p* son of Ahitub and Ahimelech*a q* son of Abiathar were priests; Shavsha was secretary; ¹⁷Benaiah son of Jehoiada was over the Kerethites and Pelethites;*r* and David's sons were chief officials at the king's side.

The Battle Against the Ammonites

19 In the course of time, Nahash king of the Ammonites*s* died, and his son succeeded him as king. ²David thought, "I will show kindness to Hanun son of Nahash, because his father showed kindness to me." So David sent a delegation to express his sympathy to Hanun concerning his father.

When David's men came to Hanun in the land of the Ammonites to express sympathy to him, ³the Ammonite nobles said to Hanun, "Do you think David is honoring your father by sending men to you to express sympathy? Haven't his men come to you to explore and spy out*t* the country and overthrow it?" ⁴So Hanun seized David's men, shaved them, cut off their garments in the middle at the buttocks, and sent them away.

⁵When someone came and told David about the men, he sent messengers to meet them, for they were greatly humiliated. The king said, "Stay at Jericho till your beards have grown, and then come back."

18:12
m 1Ki 11:15

18:14
n 1Ch 11:1

18:15
o 1Ch 11:6

18:16
p 2Sa 8:17
q 1Ch 24:6

18:17
r 2Sa 8:18

19:1
s Ge 19:38

19:3
t Nu 21:32

a 16 Some Hebrew manuscripts, Vulgate and Syriac (see also 2 Samuel 8:17); most Hebrew manuscripts Abimelech

---

complete victory and justice. If David's glory was great, how much greater will Christ's glory be! The great news for us is that we can be rightly related to Jesus Christ through faith. One day we will share in his glory as we reign with him.

18:9–11 When David received gifts from King Tou, he dedicated them to God, realizing that all had come from God and was to be used for him. It is easy to think that our financial and material blessings are the result of our own skill and hard work rather than coming from a loving God (James 1:17). What has God given you? Dedicate all your gifts and resources to him, and use them for his service. He will lead you in the method you should use. The first step is to be willing. The second step is to follow up your willingness with action.

18:13 The list of battles in this chapter shows how God gave David victory after victory. Unbelieving people think that victory comes from their own skill plus a little luck. Just as David acknowledged God's role in his success, so should we. Don't take credit for the work God does.

18:17 The Kerethites and Pelethites were probably a group of foreign soldiers who had joined David during his flight from Saul. They remained loyal to David throughout his reign (2 Samuel 15:17, 18) and became part of his bodyguard.

19:1 The land of Ammon bordered Israel to the east. The nation had a sordid beginning—its founding ancestor, Ben-Ammi, was conceived through incest between Lot and his daughter (Genesis 19:30–38). The Ammonites, who were constant enemies of Israel, reached their greatest strength in the days of the judges. David was the first military leader of Israel to crush them. They were unable to cause further trouble for many years.

19:2, 3 Hanun misread David's intentions. Because he was overly suspicious, he brought disaster upon himself. Because

of past experiences, it is easy to be overly suspicious of others, questioning every move and second-guessing their motives. But while we should be cautious and wise as we deal with others, we should not assume their every action is ill-intended.

19:4, 5 Israelite men always wore beards. To be forcibly shaven was embarrassing enough, but these men were also left half naked. Hanun's actions humiliated these men and insulted Israel.

DAVID SUBDUES HIS ENEMIES David expanded his kingdom as the Lord continued to give him victory. He subdued the Philistines by taking Gath, conquered Moab, won battles as far north as Zobah and Hamath (conquering Aram when they came to help these enemy nations), and subdued the other surrounding nations of Ammon and Amalek.

6 When the Ammonites realized that they had become a stench in David's nostrils, Hanun and the Ammonites sent a thousand talents^a of silver to hire chariots and charioteers from Aram Naharaim,^b Aram Maacah and Zobah.^u 7 They hired thirty-two thousand chariots and charioteers, as well as the king of Maacah with his troops, who came and camped near Medeba,^v while the Ammonites were mustered from their towns and moved out for battle.

19:6
^u1Ch 18:3, 5, 9

19:7
^vNu 21:30;
Jos 13:9, 16

8 On hearing this, David sent Joab out with the entire army of fighting men. 9 The Ammonites came out and drew up in battle formation at the entrance to their city, while the kings who had come were by themselves in the open country.

10 Joab saw that there were battle lines in front of him and behind him; so he selected some of the best troops in Israel and deployed them against the Arameans. 11 He put the rest of the men under the command of Abishai^w his brother, and they were deployed against the Ammonites. 12 Joab said, "If the Arameans are too strong for me, then you are to rescue me; but if the Ammonites are too strong for you, then I will rescue you. 13 Be strong and let us fight bravely for our people and the cities of our God. The LORD will do what is good in his sight."

19:11
^w1Sa 26:6

14 Then Joab and the troops with him advanced to fight the Arameans, and they fled before him. 15 When the Ammonites saw that the Arameans were fleeing, they too fled before his brother Abishai and went inside the city. So Joab went back to Jerusalem.

16 After the Arameans saw that they had been routed by Israel, they sent messengers and had Arameans brought from beyond the River,^c with Shophach the commander of Hadadezer's army leading them.

17 When David was told of this, he gathered all Israel and crossed the Jordan; he advanced against them and formed his battle lines opposite them. David formed his lines to meet the Arameans in battle, and they fought against him. 18 But they fled before Israel, and David killed seven thousand of their charioteers and forty thousand of their foot soldiers. He also killed Shophach the commander of their army.

19 When the vassals of Hadadezer saw that they had been defeated by Israel, they made peace with David and became subject to him.

So the Arameans were not willing to help the Ammonites anymore.

The Capture of Rabbah

20 In the spring, at the time when kings go off to war, Joab led out the armed forces. He laid waste the land of the Ammonites and went to Rabbah^x and besieged it, but David remained in Jerusalem. Joab attacked Rabbah and left it in ruins. 2 David took the crown from the head of their king^d—its weight was found to be a talent^e of gold, and it was set with precious stones—and it was placed on David's head. He took a great quantity of plunder from the city 3 and brought out the people who were there, consigning them to labor with saws and with iron picks and axes. David did this to all the Ammonite towns. Then David and his entire army returned to Jerusalem.

20:1
^x2Sa 12:26

War With the Philistines

4 In the course of time, war broke out with the Philistines, at Gezer. At that time Sibbecai the Hushathite killed Sippai, one of the descendants of the Rephaites, and the Philistines were subjugated.

^a6 That is, about 37 tons (about 34 metric tons)　^b6 That is, Northwest Mesopotamia　^c16 That is, the Euphrates
^d2 Or of Milcom, that is, Molech　^e2 That is, about 75 pounds (about 34 kilograms)

19:6 Rather than admit his mistake and seek forgiveness and reconciliation, Hanun spent an enormous amount of money to cover up his error. His cover-up cost him dearly (20:1–4). It often costs more to cover up an error than to admit it honestly. Rather than compound an error through defensiveness, seek forgiveness and reconciliation as soon as you realize your mistake. You will save yourself and others a lot of pain and trouble.

20:1 David's adultery occurred at this time, while he remained in Jerusalem instead of going to battle (2 Samuel 11; 12). This story may have been excluded from 1 Chronicles because the book was written to focus on God's long-term interest in Israel and on the temple as a symbol of God's presence among them. The story of David and Bathsheba did not fit this purpose. The story of Absa-

lom's rebellion, which occurred between this chapter and the next, was probably omitted for the same reason (2 Samuel 15—18).

20:1 Kings went out to battle following the spring harvest. At this time, farm work eased off, and the armies could live off the land. During the winter, they plotted and planned future conquests. Then, when the fair weather permitted it, their armies went into war. But David ignored this opportunity. He stayed home and sent Joab out to lead the army. It was during this time of inactivity that he sinned with Bathsheba. Look for the "springs" in your life, the times when God wants you to respond, take the initiative, and move out to do his will. It is during these critical times that we may be most sensitive to temptation. Resolve to take the action God has prescribed. Don't give temptation a foothold in your inactivity.

20:1 Rabbah was the capital of the Ammonites and is the site of modern Amman in Jordan.

20:5
y 1Sa 17:7

⁵ In another battle with the Philistines, Elhanan son of Jair killed Lahmi the brother of Goliath the Gittite, who had a spear with a shaft like a weaver's rod. *y*

⁶ In still another battle, which took place at Gath, there was a huge man with six fingers on each hand and six toes on each foot—twenty-four in all. He also was descended from Rapha. ⁷ When he taunted Israel, Jonathan son of Shimea, David's brother, killed him.

⁸ These were descendants of Rapha in Gath, and they fell at the hands of David and his men.

David Numbers the Fighting Men

21:1
z 2Ch 18:21

21:2
a 1Ch 27:23-24

21:3
b Dt 1:11

21 Satan *z* rose up against Israel and incited David to take a census of Israel. ² So David said to Joab and the commanders of the troops, "Go and count *a* the Israelites from Beersheba to Dan. Then report back to me so that I may know how many there are."

³ But Joab replied, "May the LORD multiply his troops a hundred times over. *b* My lord the king, are they not all my lord's subjects? Why does my lord want to do this? Why should he bring guilt on Israel?"

⁴ The king's word, however, overruled Joab; so Joab left and went throughout Israel and then came back to Jerusalem. ⁵ Joab reported the number of the fighting men to David: In all Israel there were one million one hundred thousand men who could handle a sword, including four hundred and seventy thousand in Judah.

⁶ But Joab did not include Levi and Benjamin in the numbering, because the king's command was repulsive to him. ⁷ This command was also evil in the sight of God; so he punished Israel.

21:9
c 1Sa 9:9

⁸ Then David said to God, "I have sinned greatly by doing this. Now, I beg you, take away the guilt of your servant. I have done a very foolish thing."

⁹ The LORD said to Gad, David's seer, *c* ¹⁰ "Go and tell David, 'This is what the LORD says: I am giving you three options. Choose one of them for me to carry out against you.'"

21:12
d Dt 32:24

¹¹ So Gad went to David and said to him, "This is what the LORD says: 'Take your choice: ¹² three years of famine, *d* three months of being swept away *a* before your enemies, with their swords overtaking you, or three days of the sword of the LORD—days of plague in the land, with the angel of the LORD ravaging every part of Israel.' Now then, decide how I should answer the one who sent me."

21:13
e Ps 130:4, 7

¹³ David said to Gad, "I am in deep distress. Let me fall into the hands of the LORD, for his mercy *e* is very great; but do not let me fall into the hands of men."

a 12 Hebrew; Septuagint and Vulgate (see also 2 Samuel 24:13) *of fleeing*

21:1 David's census brought disaster because, unlike the census taken in the book of Numbers (Numbers 1; 2) that God had ordered, this census was taken so David could take pride in the strength of his army. In determining his military strength, he was beginning to trust more in military power than in God. There is a thin line between feeling confident because you rely on God's power and becoming proud because you have been used by God for great purposes.

21:1 The Bible text says Satan *incited* David to take a census. Can Satan force people to do wrong? No, Satan only *tempted* David with the idea, but David *decided to act* on the temptation. Ever since the Garden of Eden, Satan has been tempting people to sin. David's census was not against God's law, but his reason for the census was wrong—pride in his mighty army while forgetting that his real strength came from God. Even Joab, not known for his high moral ideals, recognized the census as sin. From David's example we learn that an action that may not be wrong in itself can be sinful if it is motivated by greed, arrogance, or selfishness. Often our motives, not the action itself, contain the sin. We must constantly weigh our motives before we act.

21:1–3 David fell to Satan's temptation. God provided a way out in Joab's counsel, but David's curiosity was spurred on by arrogance. His faith was in his own strength rather than in God's. If we feel self-sufficient and put confidence in ourselves apart from God, we soon fall to Satan's schemes. Self-sufficiency pulls us away from God. When you are tempted, examine your inner desires to understand why the external temptation is so appealing. (See 1 Corinthians 10:13 for more about escaping temptation.)

21:8 When David realized his sin, he took full responsibility, admitted he was wrong, and asked God to forgive him. Many people want to add God and the benefits of Christianity to their lives without acknowledging their personal sin and guilt. But confession and repentance must come before receiving forgiveness. Like David, we must take full responsibility for our actions and confess them to God before we can expect him to forgive us and continue his work in us.

21:13, 14 Sin has a domino effect; once a sin is committed, a series of consequences follows. God will forgive our sin if we ask him, but the consequences of that sin have already been set in motion. David pled for mercy, and God responded by stopping the angel before his mission of death was complete. The consequences of David's sin, however, had already caused severe damage. God will always forgive our sins and will often intervene to make their bitter consequences less severe, but the scars will remain. Thinking through the possible consequences before we act can stop us and thus save us much sorrow and suffering.

¹⁴So the LORD sent a plague on Israel, and seventy thousand men of Israel fell dead. ᶠ ¹⁵And God sent an angel to destroy Jerusalem. But as the angel was doing so, the LORD saw it and was grievedᵍ because of the calamity and said to the angel who was destroying the people, "Enough! Withdraw your hand." The angel of the LORD was then standing at the threshing floor of Araunahᵃ the Jebusite.

21:14
ᶠ1Ch 27:24
21:15
ᵍGe 6:6; Ex 32:14

¹⁶David looked up and saw the angel of the LORD standing between heaven and earth, with a drawn sword in his hand extended over Jerusalem. Then David and the elders, clothed in sackcloth, fell facedown. ʰ

21:16
ʰNu 14:5

¹⁷David said to God, "Was it not I who ordered the fighting men to be counted? I am the one who has sinned and done wrong. These are but sheep.ⁱ What have they done? O LORD my God, let your hand fall upon me and my family, but do not let this plague remain on your people."

21:17
ⁱ2Sa 7:8; Ps 74:1

¹⁸Then the angel of the LORD ordered Gad to tell David to go up and build an altar to the LORD on the threshing floorʲ of Araunah the Jebusite. ¹⁹So David went up in obedience to the word that Gad had spoken in the name of the LORD.

21:18
ʲ2Ch 3:1

²⁰While Araunah was threshing wheat, he turned and saw the angel; his four sons who were with him hid themselves. ²¹Then David approached, and when Araunah looked and saw him, he left the threshing floor and bowed down before David with his face to the ground.

²²David said to him, "Let me have the site of your threshing floor so I can build an altar to the LORD, that the plague on the people may be stopped. Sell it to me at the full price."

²³Araunah said to David, "Take it! Let my lord the king do whatever pleases him. Look, I will give the oxen for the burnt offerings, the threshing sledges for the wood, and the wheat for the grain offering. I will give all this."

²⁴But King David replied to Araunah, "No, I insist on paying the full price. I will not take for the LORD what is yours, or sacrifice a burnt offering that costs me nothing."

²⁵So David paid Araunah six hundred shekelsᵇ of gold for the site. ²⁶David built an altar to the LORD there and sacrificed burnt offerings and fellowship offerings.ᶜ He called on the LORD, and the LORD answered him with fireᵏ from heaven on the altar of burnt offering.

21:26
ᵏLev 9:24

²⁷Then the LORD spoke to the angel, and he put his sword back into its sheath. ²⁸At that time, when David saw that the LORD had answered him on the threshing floor of Araunah the Jebusite, he offered sacrifices there. ²⁹The tabernacle of the LORD, which Moses had made in the desert, and the altar of burnt offering were at that time on the high place at Gibeon.ˡ ³⁰But David could not go before it to inquire of God, because he was afraid of the sword of the angel of the LORD.

21:29
ˡ1Ki 3:4; 1Ch 16:39

22 Then David said, "The house of the LORD Godᵐ is to be here, and also the altar of burnt offering for Israel."

22:1
ᵐ1Ch 21:18-29;
2Ch 3:1

4. David arranges for the building of the temple
Preparations for the Temple

²So David gave orders to assemble the aliensⁿ living in Israel, and from among them he appointed stonecutters to prepare dressed stone for building the house of God. ³He provided

22:2
ⁿ1Ki 9:21

ᵃ15 Hebrew *Ornan*, a variant of *Araunah*; also in verses 18-28   ᵇ25 That is, about 15 pounds (about 7 kilograms)
ᶜ26 Traditionally *peace offerings*

21:14 Why did 70,000 innocent people die for David's sin? Our society places great emphasis upon the individual. In ancient times, however, the family leaders, tribal leaders, and kings represented the people they led, and all expected to share in their successes as well as in their failures and punishments. David deserved punishment for his sin, but his death could have resulted in political chaos and invasion by enemy armies, leaving hundreds of thousands dead. Instead, God graciously spared David's life. He also put a stop to the plague so that most of the people of Jerusalem were spared.

God made us to work together interdependently. Whether we think it is fair or not, our actions always affect other people whether we want them to or not. We cannot fully know the mind of God in this severe judgment. We don't know where the prophets, the tribal leaders, and the other advisers were during this incident and whether or not they chose to go along with the king. We do know that putting confidence in military might alone is idolatry. To allow anything to take God's place is sinful, and it may cause disastrous consequences.

21:22-24 When David wanted to buy Araunah's land to build an altar, Araunah generously offered it as a gift. But David refused, saying, "I will not take for the LORD what is yours, or sacrifice a burnt offering that costs me nothing." David wanted to offer a sacrifice to God. The word *sacrifice* implies giving something that costs the giver in terms of self, time, or money. To give sacrificially requires more than a token effort or gift. God wants us to give voluntarily, but he wants it to mean something. Giving to God what costs you nothing does not demonstrate commitment.

21:29—22:1 Gibeon was a Benjaminite city about two hours' journey northwest of Jerusalem. Years before, Saul had moved the tabernacle there. In this instance, David didn't go there because he was overwhelmed by God's wrath, as he had been earlier when one person died moving the ark toward Jerusalem. Now 70,000 had died as a result of his pride. The fear David felt was the kind of awe that each of us should have when we consider God's character and God's standards. While we may enjoy God's mercy and acceptance, we dare not take for granted that our God is awesome and holy.

22:1 Out of David's tragic mistake came the purchase of a plot of land that would become the site of God's temple, the symbol of God's presence among his people. Every time the people went

22:3
ᵒver 14

22:4
ᵖ1Ki 5:6

22:5
�q1Ch 29:1

22:7
ʳ1Ch 17:2

22:10
ˢ1Ch 17:12
ᵗ2Sa 7:13

22:11
ᵘver 16

22:12
ᵛ1Ki 3:9-12

22:13
ʷ1Ch 28:7
ˣJos 1:6-9

22:16
ʸver 11

22:17
ᶻ1Ch 28:1-6

22:18
ª1Ch 23:25
ᵇ2Sa 7:1

22:19
ᶜ2Ch 5:7

23:1
ᵈ1Ki 1:33-39;
1Ch 28:5
ᵉ1Ch 29:28

23:3
ᶠNu 4:3-49

23:4
ᵍ2Ch 19:8

a large amount of iron to make nails for the doors of the gateways and for the fittings, and more bronze than could be weighed. ᵒ ⁴He also provided more cedar logsᵖ than could be counted, for the Sidonians and Tyrians had brought large numbers of them to David.

⁵David said, "My son Solomon is young�q and inexperienced, and the house to be built for the LORD should be of great magnificence and fame and splendor in the sight of all the nations. Therefore I will make preparations for it." So David made extensive preparations before his death.

⁶Then he called for his son Solomon and charged him to build a house for the LORD, the God of Israel. ⁷David said to Solomon: "My son, I had it in my heartʳ to build a house for the Name of the LORD my God. ⁸But this word of the LORD came to me: 'You have shed much blood and have fought many wars. You are not to build a house for my Name, because you have shed much blood on the earth in my sight. ⁹But you will have a son who will be a man of peace and rest, and I will give him rest from all his enemies on every side. His name will be Solomon,ª and I will grant Israel peace and quiet during his reign. ¹⁰He is the one who will build a house for my Name.ˢ He will be my son,ᵗ and I will be his father. And I will establish the throne of his kingdom over Israel forever.'

¹¹"Now, my son, the LORD be withᵘ you, and may you have success and build the house of the LORD your God, as he said you would. ¹²May the LORD give you discretion and understand-ingᵛ when he puts you in command over Israel, so that you may keep the law of the LORD your God. ¹³Then you will have success if you are careful to observe the decrees and lawsʷ that the LORD gave Moses for Israel. Be strong and courageous.ˣ Do not be afraid or discouraged.

¹⁴"I have taken great pains to provide for the temple of the LORD a hundred thousand tal-entsᵇ of gold, a million talentsᶜ of silver, quantities of bronze and iron too great to be weighed, and wood and stone. And you may add to them. ¹⁵You have many workmen: stonecutters, ma-sons and carpenters, as well as men skilled in every kind of work ¹⁶in gold and silver, bronze and iron—craftsmenʸ beyond number. Now begin the work, and the LORD be with you."

¹⁷Then David orderedᶻ all the leaders of Israel to help his son Solomon. ¹⁸He said to them, "Is not the LORD your God with you? And has he not granted you restª on every side?ᵇ For he has handed the inhabitants of the land over to me, and the land is subject to the LORD and to his people. ¹⁹Now devote your heart and soul to seeking the LORD your God.ᶜ Begin to build the sanctuary of the LORD God, so that you may bring the ark of the covenant of the LORD and the sacred articles belonging to God into the temple that will be built for the Name of the LORD."

The Levites

23 When David was old and full of years, he made his son Solomon ᵈ king over Israel. ᵉ

²He also gathered together all the leaders of Israel, as well as the priests and Levites. ³The Levites thirty years old or more were counted, and the total number of men was thirty-eight thousand. ᶠ ⁴David said, "Of these, twenty-four thousand are to supervise the work of the

ª9 *Solomon* sounds like and may be derived from the Hebrew for *peace.* ᵇ14 That is, about 3,750 tons (about 3,450 metric tons) ᶜ14 That is, about 37,500 tons (about 34,500 metric tons)

---

to the temple they would remember that God is their true King and that everyone, including their human king, is fallible and subject to sin. God can use our sins for good purposes if we are sorry for them and seek his forgiveness. When we confess our sins, the way is opened for God to bring good from a bad situation.

22:7–10 God told David he would not be the one to build the temple. Instead the task would be left to his son Solomon. David graciously accepted this "no" from God. He was not jealous of the fact that his son would have the honor of building God's temple, but instead made preparations for Solomon to carry out his task. Similarly, we should take steps now to prepare the way for our children to find and fulfill God's purpose. Sooner or later our chil-dren will have to make their own decisions, but we can help by supplying them with the proper tools: showing them how to pray and study God's Word, the difference between right and wrong, and the importance of church involvement.

22:11–16 David made it a point to explain to Solomon exactly why he would be charged with the privilege of building the temple. His instructions to Solomon, including God's reasons for using David in a limited way, must have been memorable moments for

Solomon. The conversations we have with our children deserve our attention, honesty, and vision. Times when we tell our children what we pray God will accomplish in their lives can be some of the best gifts we give them.

23:1 For more information on Solomon's coronation and the attempts to seize his throne, see 1 Kings 1; 2.

23:1ff Although David couldn't build the temple, he could make preparations, and he took that job seriously. He not only gathered funds and materials for God's house, he also planned much of the administration and arranged the worship services. The original readers of Chronicles were rebuilding the temple after it had been destroyed by invading armies, and this information about its proce-dures was invaluable to them. The next five chapters demonstrate that organization is essential for smooth and effective service.

23:3 Why was this census acceptable when the other was not (chapter 21)? This census counted only the Levites—those set apart to serve God—and was used to organize the work in the temple. The census was not based on pride or self-sufficiency as was the previous census of fighting men.

temple of the Lord and six thousand are to be officials and judges.*g* 5 Four thousand are to be gatekeepers and four thousand are to praise the Lord with the musical instruments *h* I have provided for that purpose."

6 David divided *i* the Levites into groups corresponding to the sons of Levi: Gershon, Kohath and Merari.

Gershonites

7 Belonging to the Gershonites:
   Ladan and Shimei.
8 The sons of Ladan:
   Jehiel the first, Zetham and Joel—three in all.
9 The sons of Shimei:
   Shelomoth, Haziel and Haran—three in all.
   These were the heads of the families of Ladan.
10 And the sons of Shimei:
   Jahath, Ziza,*a* Jeush and Beriah.
   These were the sons of Shimei—four in all.
11 Jahath was the first and Ziza the second, but Jeush and Beriah did not have many sons; so they were counted as one family with one assignment.

Kohathites

12 The sons of Kohath:*j*
   Amram, Izhar, Hebron and Uzziel—four in all.
13 The sons of Amram:*k*
   Aaron and Moses.
   Aaron was set apart,*l* he and his descendants forever, to consecrate the most holy things, to offer sacrifices before the Lord, to minister before him and to pronounce blessings in his name forever. 14 The sons of Moses the man of God were counted as part of the tribe of Levi.
15 The sons of Moses:
   Gershom and Eliezer.
16 The descendants of Gershom:*m*
   Shubael was the first.
17 The descendants of Eliezer:
   Rehabiah was the first.
   Eliezer had no other sons, but the sons of Rehabiah were very numerous.
18 The sons of Izhar:
   Shelomith was the first.
19 The sons of Hebron:
   Jeriah the first, Amariah the second, Jahaziel the third and Jekameam the fourth.
20 The sons of Uzziel:
   Micah the first and Isshiah the second.

Merarites

21 The sons of Merari:*n*
   Mahli and Mushi.
   The sons of Mahli:
   Eleazar and Kish.
22 Eleazar died without having sons: he had only daughters. Their cousins, the sons of Kish, married them.
23 The sons of Mushi:
   Mahli, Eder and Jerimoth—three in all.

24 These were the descendants of Levi by their families—the heads of families as they were registered under their names and counted individually, that is, the workers twenty

23:5
*h*1Ch 15:16

23:6
*i*2Ch 8:14

23:12
*j*Ex 6:18

23:13
*k*Ex 6:20; 28:1
*l*Ex 30:7-10

23:16
*m*1Ch 26:24-28

23:21
*n*1Ch 24:26

---

a 10 One Hebrew manuscript, Septuagint and Vulgate (see also verse 11); most Hebrew manuscripts *Zina*

23:14 All that is stated here about Moses is that he was "the man of God." What a profound description of a person! A man or woman of God is one whose life reflects God's presence, priorities, and power.

23:24
ºNu 10:17, 21

23:26
ᵖNu 4:5, 15;
Dt 10:8

23:29
�q Ex 25:30
ʳLev 2:4-7; 6:20-23
ˢLev 19:35-36;
1Ch 9:29, 32

23:31
ᵗLev 23:4;
Isa 1:13-14

23:32
ᵘNu 1:53
ᵛNu 3:6-8, 38

24:1
ʷEx 6:23

24:2
ˣLev 10:1-2; Nu 3:4

years old or more º who served in the temple of the LORD. 25 For David had said, "Since the LORD, the God of Israel, has granted rest to his people and has come to dwell in Jerusalem forever, 26 the Levites no longer need to carry the tabernacle or any of the articles used in its service."ᵖ 27 According to the last instructions of David, the Levites were counted from those twenty years old or more.

28 The duty of the Levites was to help Aaron's descendants in the service of the temple of the LORD: to be in charge of the courtyards, the side rooms, the purification of all sacred things and the performance of other duties at the house of God. 29 They were in charge of the bread set out on the table,�q the flour for the grain offerings,ʳ the unleavened wafers, the baking and the mixing, and all measurements of quantity and size. ˢ 30 They were also to stand every morning to thank and praise the LORD. They were to do the same in the evening 31 and whenever burnt offerings were presented to the LORD on Sabbaths and at New Moon festivals and at appointed feasts.ᵗ They were to serve before the LORD regularly in the proper number and in the way prescribed for them.

32 And so the Levites ᵘ carried out their responsibilities for the Tent of Meeting,ᵛ for the Holy Place and, under their brothers the descendants of Aaron, for the service of the temple of the LORD.

The Divisions of Priests

24 These were the divisions of the sons of Aaron:
The sons of Aaron were Nadab, Abihu, Eleazar and Ithamar.ʷ 2 But Nadab and Abihu died before their father did,ˣ and they had no sons; so Eleazar and Ithamar served as the

---

DUTIES ASSIGNED IN THE TEMPLE

King David charged all these people to do their jobs "for the Name of the LORD" (22:17–19). God needs people of every talent—not just prophets and priests—to obey him.

Administrative Duties	Supervisors	1 Chronicles 23:4, 5
	Officials	1 Chronicles 23:4, 5
	Judges	1 Chronicles 23:4, 5
	Public administrators	1 Chronicles 26:29, 30
Ministerial Duties	Priests	1 Chronicles 24:1
	Prophets	1 Chronicles 25:1
	Assistants for sacrifices	1 Chronicles 23:29–31
	Assistants for purification ceremonies	1 Chronicles 23:28
Service Duties	Bakers of the bread of the Presence	1 Chronicles 23:29
	Those who made the measurements	1 Chronicles 23:29
	Caretakers	1 Chronicles 23:28
Financial Duties	Those who cared for the treasuries	1 Chronicles 26:20
	Those who cared for the dedicated gifts	1 Chronicles 26:26–28
Artistic Duties	Musicians	1 Chronicles 25:6
	Singers	1 Chronicles 25:7
Protective Duties	Gatekeepers	1 Chronicles 26:12–18
Individual Assignments	Chief of the gatekeepers	1 Chronicles 9:19–21
	Scribe	1 Chronicles 24:6
	Seer	1 Chronicles 25:5
	Prophet under the king	1 Chronicles 25:2
	Chief officer of the treasuries	1 Chronicles 26:23, 24

23:28–32 Priests and Levites had different jobs in and around the temple. Priests were authorized to perform the sacrifices. Levites were set apart to help the priests. They did the work of elders, deacons, custodians, assistants, musicians, moving men, and repairmen. Both priests and Levites came from the tribe of Levi, but priests also had to be descendants of Aaron, Israel's first high priest (Exodus 28:1–3). Priests and Levites were supported by Israel's tithes and by revenues from certain cities that had been given to them. Worship in the temple could not have taken place without the combined efforts of the priests and Levites. Their responsibilities were different, but they were equally important to God's plan. No matter what place of service you have in the church, you are important to the healthy functioning of the congregation.

24:1ff The temple service was highly structured, but this did not hinder the Spirit of God. Rather, it provided an orderly context for worship. (Compare 1 Corinthians 14:40.) Sometimes we feel that planning and structure are unspiritual activities that may hinder spontaneity in worship. But order and structure can free us to respond to God. Order brings glory to God as we experience the joy, freedom, and calm that come when we have wisely prepared in advance.

priests. ³With the help of Zadok a descendant of Eleazar and Ahimelech a descendant of Ithamar, David separated them into divisions for their appointed order of ministering. ⁴A larger number of leaders were found among Eleazar's descendants than among Ithamar's, and they were divided accordingly: sixteen heads of families from Eleazar's descendants and eight heads of families from Ithamar's descendants. ⁵They divided them impartially by drawing lots,ʸ for there were officials of the sanctuary and officials of God among the descendants of both Eleazar and Ithamar.

24:5
ʸver 31

⁶The scribe Shemaiah son of Nethanel, a Levite, recorded their names in the presence of the king and of the officials: Zadok the priest, Ahimelechᶻ son of Abiathar and the heads of families of the priests and of the Levites—one family being taken from Eleazar and then one from Ithamar.

24:6
ᶻ1Ch 18:16

⁷ The first lot fell to Jehoiarib,
   the second to Jedaiah,
⁸ the third to Harim,
   the fourth to Seorim,
⁹ the fifth to Malkijah,
   the sixth to Mijamin,
¹⁰ the seventh to Hakkoz,
   the eighth to Abijah,ᵃ
¹¹ the ninth to Jeshua,
   the tenth to Shecaniah,
¹² the eleventh to Eliashib,
   the twelfth to Jakim,
¹³ the thirteenth to Huppah,
   the fourteenth to Jeshebeab,
¹⁴ the fifteenth to Bilgah,
   the sixteenth to Immer,
¹⁵ the seventeenth to Hezir,
   the eighteenth to Happizzez,
¹⁶ the nineteenth to Pethahiah,
   the twentieth to Jehezkel,
¹⁷ the twenty-first to Jakin,
   the twenty-second to Gamul,
¹⁸ the twenty-third to Delaiah
   and the twenty-fourth to Maaziah.

24:10
ᵃNe 12:4, 17;
Lk 1:5

¹⁹This was their appointed order of ministering when they entered the temple of the LORD, according to the regulations prescribed for them by their forefather Aaron, as the LORD, the God of Israel, had commanded him.

The Rest of the Levites

²⁰As for the rest of the descendants of Levi:
   from the sons of Amram: Shubael;
   from the sons of Shubael: Jehdeiah.
²¹ As for Rehabiah,ᵇ from his sons:
   Isshiah was the first.
²² From the Izharites: Shelomoth;
   from the sons of Shelomoth: Jahath.

24:21
ᵇ1Ch 23:17

24:3 This Ahimelech was the son of Abiathar and the grandson of another Ahimelech, one of the priests massacred by Saul (1 Samuel 22:11–18). Abiathar and Zadok were co-high priests under David: one was at Jerusalem where the ark of God was kept, and one was at Gibeon serving at the tabernacle. It appears from 15:11 and 18:16 that Ahimelech began to assume some of Abiathar's duties as his father grew old.

24:4 Eleazar's descendants were divided into 16 groups (as opposed to Ithamar's eight) for three reasons. (1) Eleazar had

received the birthright since his two older brothers, Nadab and Abihu, had been killed (Leviticus 10). The birthright included a double portion of the father's estate. (2) His descendants were greater in number than Ithamar's. (3) His descendants had greater leadership ability. These 24 groups gave order to the functioning of the temple.

24:7–18 Each of these 24 groups of priests served two-week shifts each year at the temple. The rest of the time they served in their hometowns. This system was still in place in Jesus' day (Luke 1:5–9). Zechariah was a member of the Abijah division. During his shift at the temple, an angel appeared to him and predicted that he would have a son, John.

24:23
c 1Ch 23:19

23 The sons of Hebron:c Jeriah the first,a Amariah the second, Jahaziel the third and Jekameam the fourth.

24 The son of Uzziel: Micah;
from the sons of Micah: Shamir.

25 The brother of Micah: Isshiah;
from the sons of Isshiah: Zechariah.

24:26
d 1Ch 6:19; 23:21

26 The sons of Merari: d Mahli and Mushi.
The son of Jaaziah: Beno.

27 The sons of Merari:
from Jaaziah: Beno, Shoham, Zaccur and Ibri.

28 From Mahli: Eleazar, who had no sons.

29 From Kish: the son of Kish:
Jerahmeel.

30 And the sons of Mushi: Mahli, Eder and Jerimoth.

24:31
e ver 5

These were the Levites, according to their families. 31 They also cast lots, e just as their
brothers the descendants of Aaron did, in the presence of King David and of Zadok, Ahimelech, and the heads of families of the priests and of the Levites. The families of the oldest
brother were treated the same as those of the youngest.

The Singers

25:1
f 1Ch 6:39
g 1Ch 6:33
h 1Sa 10:5; 2Ki 3:15
i 1Ch 15:16

25 David, together with the commanders of the army, set apart some of the sons of
Asaph, f Heman g and Jeduthun for the ministry of prophesying, h accompanied by
harps, lyres and cymbals. i Here is the list of the men who performed this service:

a23 Two Hebrew manuscripts and some Septuagint manuscripts (see also 1 Chron. 23:19); most Hebrew
manuscripts *The sons of Jeriah:*

**MUSIC IN
BIBLE TIMES**
Paul clearly puts
forth the Chris-
tian's view that
things are not
good or bad in
and of themselves
(see Romans 14
and 1 Corinthians
14:7, 8, 26). The
point should
always be to
worship the Lord
or help others by
means of the
things of this
world, including
music. Music was
created by God
and can be
returned to him in
praise. Does the
music you play
or listen to have
a negative or
positive impact
upon your relation-
ship with God?

Highlights of Musical Use in Scripture	Reference
Jubal was father of all musicians	Genesis 4:21
Miriam and other women sang and danced to praise God.	Exodus 15:1–21
The priest was to have bells on his robes	Exodus 28:34, 35
Jericho fell to the sound of trumpets	Joshua 6:4–20
Saul experienced the soothing effect of music.	1 Samuel 16:14–23
The king's coronation was accompanied by music	1 Kings 1:39, 40
The ark was accompanied by trumpeters	1 Chronicles 16:6
There were musicians for the king's court	Ecclesiastes 2:8
From David's time on, the use of music in worship was much more organized. Music for the temple became refined	1 Chronicles 15:16–24
	1 Chronicles 16:4–7
	2 Chronicles 5:11–14
Everything was to be used by everyone to praise the Lord	Psalm 150

*In the New Testament, worship continued in the synagogues until the Christians became
unwelcome there, so there was a rich musical heritage already established. The fact that
music is mentioned less often in the New Testament does not mean it was less important.*

Jesus and the disciples sang a hymn.	Matthew 26:30
Paul and Silas sang in jail	Acts 16:25
We are to sing to the Lord as a response to what he has done in our lives.	Ephesians 5:19, 20
	Colossians 3:16
	James 5:13

25:1 There is more to prophesying than predicting the future.
Prophecy also involves singing God's praises and preaching God's
messages (1 Corinthians 14:1ff). Prophets could be musicians,
farmers (Amos 1:1), wives (2 Kings 22:14), or leaders (Deuteronomy 34:10)—anyone who boldly and accurately spoke out for God
and tried to bring people back to worshiping him. From a large
group of musicians David chose those who showed an unusual
ability to tell about God and to encourage others in song.

25:1-7 There were many ways to contribute to the worship in
the tabernacle. Some prophesied (25:1), some led in thanksgiving
and praise (25:3), and others played instruments (25:6, 7). God
wants all his people to participate in worship. You may not be a
master musician, a prophet, or a teacher, but God appreciates
whatever you have to offer. Develop your special gifts to offer
in service to God (Romans 12:3–8; 1 Corinthians 12:29–31).

2 From the sons of Asaph:

Zaccur, Joseph, Nethaniah and Asarelah. The sons of Asaph were under the supervision of Asaph, who prophesied under the king's supervision.

3 As for Jeduthun, from his sons:[j]

Gedaliah, Zeri, Jeshaiah, Shimei,[a] Hashabiah and Mattithiah, six in all, under the supervision of their father Jeduthun, who prophesied, using the harp in thanking and praising the LORD.

4 As for Heman, from his sons:

Bukkiah, Mattaniah, Uzziel, Shubael and Jerimoth; Hananiah, Hanani, Eliathah, Giddalti and Romamti-Ezer; Joshbekashah, Mallothi, Hothir and Mahazioth. 5 All these were sons of Heman the king's seer. They were given him through the promises of God to exalt him.[b] God gave Heman fourteen sons and three daughters.

6 All these men were under the supervision of their fathers[k] for the music of the temple of the LORD, with cymbals, lyres and harps, for the ministry at the house of God. Asaph, Jeduthun and Heman[l] were under the supervision of the king. 7 Along with their relatives—all of them trained and skilled in music for the LORD—they numbered 288. 8 Young and old alike, teacher as well as student, cast lots[m] for their duties.

9 The first lot, which was for Asaph,[n] fell to Joseph,		
his sons and relatives,[c]	12[d]	
the second to Gedaliah,		
he and his relatives and sons,	12	
10 the third to Zaccur,		
his sons and relatives,	12	
11 the fourth to Izri,[e]		
his sons and relatives,	12	
12 the fifth to Nethaniah,		
his sons and relatives,	12	
13 the sixth to Bukkiah,		
his sons and relatives,	12	
14 the seventh to Jesarelah,[f]		
his sons and relatives,	12	
15 the eighth to Jeshaiah,		
his sons and relatives,	12	
16 the ninth to Mattaniah,		
his sons and relatives,	12	
17 the tenth to Shimei,		
his sons and relatives,	12	
18 the eleventh to Azarel,[g]		
his sons and relatives,	12	
19 the twelfth to Hashabiah,		
his sons and relatives,	12	
20 the thirteenth to Shubael,		
his sons and relatives,	12	
21 the fourteenth to Mattithiah,		
his sons and relatives,	12	
22 the fifteenth to Jerimoth,		
his sons and relatives,	12	
23 the sixteenth to Hananiah,		
his sons and relatives,	12	
24 the seventeenth to Joshbekashah,		
his sons and relatives,	12	

Cross references (right margin):

25:3 /1Ch 16:41-42

25:6 k 1Ch 15:16 / 1Ch 15:19

25:8 m 1Ch 26:13

25:9 n 1Ch 6:39

a3 One Hebrew manuscript and some Septuagint manuscripts (see also verse 17); most Hebrew manuscripts do not have *Shimei*.   b5 Hebrew *exalt the horn*   c9 See Septuagint; Hebrew does not have *his sons and relatives*.   d9 See the total in verse 7; Hebrew does not have *twelve*.   e11 A variant of *Zeri*   f14 A variant of *Asarelah*   g18 A variant of *Uzziel*

25:9–31 The musicians were divided into 24 groups to match the 24 groups of Levites (24:7–25). This division of labor gave order to the planning of temple work, promoted excellence by making training easier, gave variety to worship because each group worked a term, and provided opportunities for many to be involved.

²⁵ the eighteenth to Hanani,
        his sons and relatives,   12
²⁶ the nineteenth to Mallothi,
        his sons and relatives,   12
²⁷ the twentieth to Eliathah,
        his sons and relatives,   12
²⁸ the twenty-first to Hothir,
        his sons and relatives,   12
²⁹ the twenty-second to Giddalti,
        his sons and relatives,   12
³⁰ the twenty-third to Mahazioth,
        his sons and relatives,   12
³¹ the twenty-fourth to Romamti-Ezer,
        his sons and relatives,   12

The Gatekeepers

26
The divisions of the gatekeepers:

From the Korahites: Meshelemiah son of Kore, one of the sons of Asaph.
² Meshelemiah had sons:
        Zechariah the firstborn,
        Jediael the second,
        Zebadiah the third,
        Jathniel the fourth,
    ³ Elam the fifth,
        Jehohanan the sixth
        and Eliehoenai the seventh.
    ⁴ Obed-Edom also had sons:
        Shemaiah the firstborn,
        Jehozabad the second,
        Joah the third,
        Sacar the fourth,
        Nethanel the fifth,

26:5
o 2Sa 6:10;
1Ch 13:13

    ⁵ Ammiel the sixth,
        Issachar the seventh
        and Peullethai the eighth.
        (For God had blessed Obed-Edom. *o*)

⁶ His son Shemaiah also had sons, who were leaders in their father's family because they were very capable men. ⁷ The sons of Shemaiah: Othni, Rephael, Obed and Elzabad; his relatives Elihu and Semakiah were also able men. ⁸ All these were descendants of Obed-Edom; they and their sons and their relatives were capable men with the strength to do the work—descendants of Obed-Edom, 62 in all.
⁹ Meshelemiah had sons and relatives, who were able men—18 in all.

¹⁰ Hosah the Merarite had sons: Shimri the first (although he was not the firstborn, his father had appointed him the first), ¹¹Hilkiah the second, Tabaliah the third and Zechariah the fourth. The sons and relatives of Hosah were 13 in all.

26:13
p 1Ch 24:5, 31;
25:8

¹²These divisions of the gatekeepers, through their chief men, had duties for ministering in the temple of the LORD, just as their relatives had. ¹³Lots*p* were cast for each gate, according to their families, young and old alike.

26:1 There were 4,000 gatekeepers (23:4, 5). They were all Levites and did many other jobs as well. Some of their duties included (1) checking out the equipment and utensils used each day and making sure they were returned, (2) storing, ordering, and maintaining the food supplies for the priests and sacrifices, (3) caring for the furniture, (4) mixing the incense that was burned daily, and (5) accounting for the gifts brought. (For more on gatekeepers, see the note on 9:17, 18.)

26:5 "God had blessed Obed-Edom." The status of children in society has fluctuated throughout history; sometimes they are highly esteemed, and sometimes abused and cheated. But Scripture shows no such vacillation—children are called a blessing from God, and God never views them as a burden (Psalm 127:3–5; Mark 10:13–15).

[14] The lot for the East Gate fell to Shelemiah.[a] Then lots were cast for his son Zechariah, a wise counselor, and the lot for the North Gate fell to him. [15] The lot for the South Gate fell to Obed-Edom, and the lot for the storehouse fell to his sons. [16] The lots for the West Gate and the Shalleketh Gate on the upper road fell to Shuppim and Hosah.

Guard was alongside of guard: [17] There were six Levites a day on the east, four a day on the north, four a day on the south and two at a time at the storehouse. [18] As for the court to the west, there were four at the road and two at the court itself.

[19] These were the divisions of the gatekeepers who were descendants of Korah and Merari.

The Treasurers and Other Officials

[20] Their fellow Levites were[b] in charge of the treasuries of the house of God and the treasuries for the dedicated things. [q]

[21] The descendants of Ladan, who were Gershonites through Ladan and who were heads of families belonging to Ladan the Gershonite, [r] were Jehieli, [22] the sons of Jehieli, Zetham and his brother Joel. They were in charge of the treasuries of the temple of the LORD.

[23] From the Amramites, the Izharites, the Hebronites and the Uzzielites:

[24] Shubael,[s] a descendant of Gershom son of Moses, was the officer in charge of the treasuries. [25] His relatives through Eliezer: Rehabiah his son, Jeshaiah his son, Joram his son, Zicri his son and Shelomith [t] his son. [26] Shelomith and his relatives were in charge of all the treasuries for the things dedicated [u] by King David, by the heads of families who were the commanders of thousands and commanders of hundreds, and by the other army commanders. [27] Some of the plunder taken in battle they dedicated for the repair of the temple of the LORD. [28] And everything dedicated by Samuel the seer [v] and by Saul son of Kish, Abner son of Ner and Joab son of Zeruiah, and all the other dedicated things were in the care of Shelomith and his relatives.

[29] From the Izharites: Kenaniah and his sons were assigned duties away from the temple, as officials and judges [w] over Israel.

[30] From the Hebronites: Hashabiah [x] and his relatives—seventeen hundred able men— were responsible in Israel west of the Jordan for all the work of the LORD and for the king's service. [31] As for the Hebronites, [y] Jeriah was their chief according to the genealogical records of their families. In the fortieth year of David's reign a search was made in the records, and capable men among the Hebronites were found at Jazer in Gilead. [32] Jeriah had twenty-seven hundred relatives, who were able men and heads of families, and King David put them in charge of the Reubenites, the Gadites and the half-tribe of Manasseh for every matter pertaining to God and for the affairs of the king.

Army Divisions

27 This is the list of the Israelites—heads of families, commanders of thousands and commanders of hundreds, and their officers, who served the king in all that concerned the army divisions that were on duty month by month throughout the year. Each division consisted of 24,000 men.

[2] In charge of the first division, for the first month, was Jashobeam [z] son of Zabdiel. There were 24,000 men in his division. [3] He was a descendant of Perez and chief of all the army officers for the first month.

[4] In charge of the division for the second month was Dodai [a] the Ahohite; Mikloth was the leader of his division. There were 24,000 men in his division.

[5] The third army commander, for the third month, was Benaiah son of Jehoiada the priest. He was chief and there were 24,000 men in his division. [6] This was the Benaiah who was a mighty man among the Thirty and was over the Thirty. His son Ammizabad was in charge of his division.

[7] The fourth, for the fourth month, was Asahel [b] the brother of Joab; his son Zebadiah was his successor. There were 24,000 men in his division.

[a] 14 A variant of *Meshelemiah* [b] 20 Septuagint; Hebrew *As for the Levites, Ahijah was*

26:20
q1Ch 28:12

26:21
r1Ch 23:7; 29:8

26:24
s1Ch 23:16

26:25
t1Ch 23:18

26:26
u2Sa 8:11

26:28
v1Sa 9:9

26:29
w1Ch 23:4

26:30
x1Ch 27:17

26:31
y1Ch 23:19

27:2
z2Sa 23:8;
1Ch 11:11

27:4
a2Sa 23:9

27:7
b2Sa 2:18;
1Ch 11:26

26:27 War plunder rightfully belonged to the victorious army. These soldiers, however, gave their portion of all the plunder to the temple to express their dedication to God. Like these commanders, we should think of what we *can* give, rather than what we are obligated to give. Is your giving a matter of rejoicing rather than duty? Give as a response of joy and love for God.

⁸ The fifth, for the fifth month, was the commander Shamhuth the Izrahite. There were 24,000 men in his division.

27:9
c 2Sa 23:26;
1Ch 11:28

⁹ The sixth, for the sixth month, was Ira *c* the son of Ikkesh the Tekoite. There were 24,000 men in his division.

27:10
d 2Sa 23:26;
1Ch 11:27

¹⁰ The seventh, for the seventh month, was Helez *d* the Pelonite, an Ephraimite. There were 24,000 men in his division.

27:11
e 2Sa 21:18

¹¹ The eighth, for the eighth month, was Sibbecai *e* the Hushathite, a Zerahite. There were 24,000 men in his division.

27:12
f 2Sa 23:27;
1Ch 11:28

¹² The ninth, for the ninth month, was Abiezer *f* the Anathothite, a Benjamite. There were 24,000 men in his division.

27:13
g 2Sa 23:28;
1Ch 11:30

¹³ The tenth, for the tenth month, was Maharai *g* the Netophathite, a Zerahite. There were 24,000 men in his division.

27:14
h 1Ch 11:31

¹⁴ The eleventh, for the eleventh month, was Benaiah *h* the Pirathonite, an Ephraimite. There were 24,000 men in his division.

¹⁵ The twelfth, for the twelfth month, was Heldai the Netophathite, from the family of Othniel. There were 24,000 men in his division.

Officers of the Tribes

¹⁶ The officers over the tribes of Israel:

over the Reubenites: Eliezer son of Zicri;
over the Simeonites: Shephatiah son of Maacah;

27:17
i 1Ch 26:30

¹⁷ over Levi: Hashabiah *i* son of Kemuel;
over Aaron: Zadok;
¹⁸ over Judah: Elihu, a brother of David;
over Issachar: Omri son of Michael;
¹⁹ over Zebulun: Ishmaiah son of Obadiah;
over Naphtali: Jerimoth son of Azriel;
²⁰ over the Ephraimites: Hoshea son of Azaziah;
over half the tribe of Manasseh: Joel son of Pedaiah;
²¹ over the half-tribe of Manasseh in Gilead: Iddo son of Zechariah;
over Benjamin: Jaasiel son of Abner;
²² over Dan: Azarel son of Jeroham.
These were the officers over the tribes of Israel.

27:23
j Ge 15:5
27:24
k 2Sa 24:15

²³ David did not take the number of the men twenty years old or less, because the LORD had promised to make Israel as numerous as the stars *j* in the sky. ²⁴ Joab son of Zeruiah began to count the men but did not finish. Wrath came on Israel on account of this numbering, *k* and the number was not entered in the book *a* of the annals of King David.

The King's Overseers

²⁵ Azmaveth son of Adiel was in charge of the royal storehouses.
Jonathan son of Uzziah was in charge of the storehouses in the outlying districts, in the towns, the villages and the watchtowers.
²⁶ Ezri son of Kelub was in charge of the field workers who farmed the land.
²⁷ Shimei the Ramathite was in charge of the vineyards.
Zabdi the Shiphmite was in charge of the produce of the vineyards for the wine vats.

27:28
l 1Ki 10:27

²⁸ Baal-Hanan the Gederite was in charge of the olive and sycamore-fig *l* trees in the western foothills.
Joash was in charge of the supplies of olive oil.
²⁹ Shitrai the Sharonite was in charge of the herds grazing in Sharon.
Shaphat son of Adlai was in charge of the herds in the valleys.
³⁰ Obil the Ishmaelite was in charge of the camels.
Jehdeiah the Meronothite was in charge of the donkeys.
³¹ Jaziz the Hagrite was in charge of the flocks.
All these were the officials in charge of King David's property.

a 24 Septuagint; Hebrew *number*

27:24 The book of the annals of King David was a historical document kept in the royal archives with other official records. It no longer exists. See 1 Kings 14:19.

32 Jonathan, David's uncle, was a counselor, a man of insight and a scribe. Jehiel son of Hacmoni took care of the king's sons.

33 Ahithophel *m* was the king's counselor. Hushai *n* the Arkite was the king's friend. 34 Ahithophel was succeeded by Jehoiada son of Benaiah and by Abiathar. *o*

Joab *p* was the commander of the royal army.

27:33
m 2Sa 15:12
n 2Sa 15:37

27:34
o 1Ki 1:7
p 1Ch 11:6

David's Plans for the Temple

28 David summoned all the officials *q* of Israel to assemble at Jerusalem: the officers over the tribes, the commanders of the divisions in the service of the king, the commanders of thousands and commanders of hundreds, and the officials in charge of all the property and livestock belonging to the king and his sons, together with the palace officials, the mighty men and all the brave warriors.

28:1
q 1Ch 27:1-31

2 King David rose to his feet and said: "Listen to me, my brothers and my people. I had it in my heart to build a house as a place of rest for the ark of the covenant of the LORD, for the footstool *r* of our God, and I made plans to build it. 3 But God said to me, 'You are not to build a house for my Name, *s* because you are a warrior and have shed blood.'

28:2
r Ps 132:7

28:3
s 1Ch 22:8

4 "Yet the LORD, the God of Israel, chose me from my whole family *t* to be king over Israel forever. He chose Judah *u* as leader, and from the house of Judah he chose my family, and from my father's sons he was pleased to make me king over all Israel. 5 Of all my sons—and the LORD has given me many *v*—he has chosen my son Solomon *w* to sit on the throne of the kingdom of the LORD over Israel. 6 He said to me: 'Solomon your son is the one who will build my house and my courts, for I have chosen him to be my son, *x* and I will be his father. 7 I will establish his kingdom forever if he is unswerving in carrying out my commands and laws, *y* as is being done at this time.'

28:4
t 1Sa 16:1-13
u Ge 49:10; 1Ch 5:2

28:5
v 1Ch 3:1
w 1Ch 22:9; 23:1

28:6
x 2Sa 7:13

28:7
y 1Ch 22:13

8 "So now I charge you in the sight of all Israel and of the assembly of the LORD, and in the hearing of our God: Be careful to follow all the commands of the LORD your God, that you may possess this good land and pass it on as an inheritance to your descendants forever.

9 "And you, my son Solomon, acknowledge the God of your father, and serve him with wholehearted devotion and with a willing mind, for the LORD searches every heart *z* and understands every motive behind the thoughts. If you seek him, he will be found by you; but if you forsake *a* him, he will reject you forever. 10 Consider now, for the LORD has chosen you to build a temple as a sanctuary. Be strong and do the work."

28:9
z 1Sa 16:7
a 2Ch 15:2

11 Then David gave his son Solomon the plans *b* for the portico of the temple, its buildings, its storerooms, its upper parts, its inner rooms and the place of atonement. 12 He gave him the plans of all that the Spirit had put in his mind for the courts of the temple of the LORD and all the surrounding rooms, for the treasuries of the temple of God and for the treasuries for the dedicated things. *c* 13 He gave him instructions for the divisions *d* of the priests and Levites, and for all the work of serving in the temple of the LORD, as well as for all the articles to be used in its service. 14 He designated the weight of gold for all the gold articles to be used in various kinds of service, and the weight of silver for all the silver articles to be used in various kinds of service: 15 the weight of gold for the gold lampstands *e* and their lamps,

28:11
b Ex 25:9

28:12
c 1Ch 26:20

28:13
d 1Ch 24:1

28:15
e Ex 25:31

27:33, 34 When Absalom rebelled against David, Ahithophel betrayed David and joined the rebellion. Hushai pretended loyalty to Absalom, and his advice caused Absalom's downfall (2 Samuel 15:31—17:23).

28:1 The last two chapters of 1 Chronicles present the transition from David to Solomon as king of Israel. The writer doesn't mention Adonijah's conspiracy or David's frailty (1 Kings 1; 2). Instead, he focuses on the positive—God's plans for Israel and his promise to David's descendants.

28:5 The kingdom of Israel belonged to the Lord, not to David or anyone else. Israel's king, then, was God's deputy, commissioned to carry out God's will for the nation. Thus God could choose the person he wanted as king without following customary lines of succession. David was not Saul's heir, and Solomon was not David's oldest son, but this did not matter because God appointed them.

28:8 David told Solomon to be careful to follow every one of God's commands to ensure Israel's prosperity and the continuation of David's descendants upon the throne. It was the king's

solemn duty to study and obey God's laws. The teachings of Scripture are the keys to security, happiness, and justice, but you'll never discover them unless you search God's Word. If we ignore God's will and neglect his teaching, anything we attempt to build, even if it has God's name on it, will be headed for collapse. Get to know God's commands through regular Bible study, and find ways to apply them consistently.

28:9 "The LORD searches every heart . . . ." Nothing can be hidden from God. He sees and understands everything in our hearts. David found this out the hard way when God sent Nathan to expose David's sins of adultery and murder (2 Samuel 12). David told Solomon to be completely open with God and dedicated to him. It makes no sense to try to hide any thoughts or actions from an all-knowing God. This should cause us joy, not fear, because God knows even the worst about us and loves us anyway.

28:13 Some of the instructions about the work of the priests and Levites are in chapters 23 and 24.

with the weight for each lampstand and its lamps; and the weight of silver for each silver lampstand and its lamps, according to the use of each lampstand; ¹⁶the weight of gold for each table for consecrated bread; the weight of silver for the silver tables; ¹⁷the weight of pure gold for the forks, sprinkling bowls and pitchers; the weight of gold for each gold dish; the weight of silver for each silver dish; ¹⁸and the weight of the refined gold for the altar of incense.ᶠ He also gave him the plan for the chariot,ᵍ that is, the cherubim of gold that spread their wings and shelter ʰ the ark of the covenant of the LORD.

¹⁹"All this," David said, "I have in writing from the hand of the LORD upon me, and he gave me understanding in all the details of the plan."

²⁰David also said to Solomon his son, "Be strong and courageous,ⁱ and do the work. Do not be afraid or discouraged, for the LORD God, my God, is with you. He will not fail you or forsake you until all the work for the service of the temple of the LORD is finished. ²¹The divisions of the priests and Levites are ready for all the work on the temple of God, and every willing man skilledʲ in any craft will help you in all the work. The officials and all the people will obey your every command."

Gifts for Building the Temple

29 Then King David said to the whole assembly: "My son Solomon, the one whom God has chosen, is young and inexperienced. ᵏ The task is great, because this palatial structure is not for man but for the LORD God. ²With all my resources I have provided for the temple of my God—gold for the gold work, silver for the silver, bronze for the bronze, iron for the iron and wood for the wood, as well as onyx for the settings, turquoise,ᵃ ˡ stones of various colors, and all kinds of fine stone and marble—all of these in large quantities.ᵐ ³Besides, in my devotion to the temple of my God I now give my personal treasures of gold and silver for the temple of my God, over and above everything I have provided for this holy temple: ⁴three thousand talentsᵇ of gold (gold of Ophir) and seven thousand talentsᶜ of refined silver,ⁿ for the overlaying of the walls of the buildings, ⁵for the gold work and the silver work, and for all the work to be done by the craftsmen. Now, who is willing to consecrate himself today to the LORD?"

⁶Then the leaders of families, the officers of the tribes of Israel, the commanders of thousands and commanders of hundreds, and the officialsᵒ in charge of the king's work gave willingly. ⁷Theyᵖ gave toward the work on the temple of God five thousand talentsᵈ and ten thousand daricsᵉ of gold, ten thousand talentsᶠ of silver, eighteen thousand

28:18
ᶠ Ex 30:1-10
ᵍ Ex 25:18-22
ʰ Ex 25:20

28:20
ⁱ Dt 31:6; 1Ch 22:13

28:21
ʲ Ex 35:25—36:5

29:1
ᵏ 1Ki 3:7; 1Ch 22:5

29:2
ˡ Isa 54:11
ᵐ 1Ch 22:2-5

29:4
ⁿ 1Ch 22:14

29:6
ᵒ 1Ch 27:1; 28:1

29:7
ᵖ Ne 7:70-71

ᵃ2 The meaning of the Hebrew for this word is uncertain.   ᵇ4 That is, about 110 tons (about 100 metric tons)   ᶜ4 That is, about 260 tons (about 240 metric tons)   ᵈ7 That is, about 190 tons (about 170 metric tons)   ᵉ7 That is, about 185 pounds (about 84 kilograms)   ᶠ7 That is, about 375 tons (about 345 metric tons)

PRINCIPLES TO LIVE BY

King David gave his son Solomon principles to guide him through life (see 1 Chronicles 28:9, 10). These same ideas are ones that any Christian parent would want to present to a child:

1. Get to know God personally.
2. Learn God's commands and discover what he wants you to do.
3. Worship God with wholehearted devotion.
4. Serve God with a willing mind.
5. Be faithful.
6. Don't become discouraged.

28:20 David advised Solomon not to be frightened about the size of his task as king and builder of the temple. Fear can immobilize us. The size of a job, its risks, or the pressure of the situation can cause us to freeze and do nothing. One remedy for fear is found here—don't focus on the fear; instead, get to work. Getting started is often the most difficult and frightening part of a job.

29:1 Solomon became king in 970 B.C.

29:1 It is possible to be obsessed with a church building to the neglect of the real church—the people of God. But the opposite response, neglecting the church building, is also wrong. David makes this point when he says that the temple is not "for man but for the LORD God." Although we should avoid wasteful extravagance, we must remember that every church building can be a visible witness for God. How can your church building be better used to tell the world about God?

29:3–5 David gave from his personal fortune for the temple. He encouraged others to follow his example, and they willingly did. Both the tabernacle (Exodus 35:5—36:7) and the temple were built from the voluntary gifts of the people. Like David, we can acknowledge that all we have comes from God (29:14–16). We may not have David's wealth, but we can develop his willingness to give. It is not what we have that counts with God, but our willingness to give it.

29:6–9 These leaders displayed a right attitude toward their money by giving willingly to God's work. This attitude is described by Paul in 2 Corinthians 9:7: "Each man should give what he has decided in his heart to give, not reluctantly or under compulsion, for God loves a cheerful giver." When we are generous because we are thankful, our attitude can inspire others. Give generously to God's work.

talents[a] of bronze and a hundred thousand talents[b] of iron. [8]Any who had precious stones gave them to the treasury of the temple of the LORD in the custody of Jehiel the Gershonite. [q] [9]The people rejoiced at the willing response of their leaders, for they had given freely and wholeheartedly [r] to the LORD. David the king also rejoiced greatly.

29:8
q 1Ch 26:21

29:9
r 1Ki 8:61; 2Co 9:7

David's Prayer

[10]David praised the LORD in the presence of the whole assembly, saying,

> "Praise be to you, O LORD,
>> God of our father Israel,
>> from everlasting to everlasting.
> [11] Yours, O LORD, is the greatness and the power
>> and the glory and the majesty and the splendor,
>> for everything in heaven and earth is yours.
> Yours, O LORD, is the kingdom;
>> you are exalted as head over all.[s]
> [12] Wealth and honor[t] come from you;
>> you are the ruler of all things.
> In your hands are strength and power
>> to exalt and give strength to all.
> [13] Now, our God, we give you thanks,
>> and praise your glorious name.

29:11
s Rev 5:12-13

29:12
t 2Ch 1:12

[14]"But who am I, and who are my people, that we should be able to give as generously as this? Everything comes from you, and we have given you only what comes from your hand. [15]We are aliens and strangers[u] in your sight, as were all our forefathers. Our days on earth are like a shadow,[v] without hope. [16]O LORD our God, as for all this abundance that we have provided for building you a temple for your Holy Name, it comes from your hand, and all of it belongs to you. [17]I know, my God, that you test the heart and are pleased with integrity. All these things have I given willingly and with honest intent. And now I have seen with joy how willingly your people who are here have given to you.[w] [18]O LORD, God of our fathers Abraham, Isaac and Israel, keep this desire in the hearts of your people forever, and keep their hearts loyal to you. [19]And give my son Solomon the wholehearted devotion[x] to keep your commands, requirements and decrees[y] and to do everything to build the palatial structure for which I have provided."[z]

29:15
u Ps 39:12;
Heb 11:13
v Job 14:2

29:17
w 1Ch 28:9

29:19
x 1Ch 28:9
y Ps 72:1
z 1Ch 22:14

[20]Then David said to the whole assembly, "Praise the LORD your God." So they all praised the LORD, the God of their fathers; they bowed low and fell prostrate before the LORD and the king.

Solomon Acknowledged as King

[21]The next day they made sacrifices to the LORD and presented burnt offerings to him:[a] a thousand bulls, a thousand rams and a thousand male lambs, together with their drink offerings, and other sacrifices in abundance for all Israel. [22]They ate and drank with great joy[b] in the presence of the LORD that day.

Then they acknowledged Solomon son of David as king a second time, anointing him before the LORD to be ruler and Zadok[c] to be priest. [23]So Solomon sat on the throne of the LORD as king in place of his father David. He prospered and all Israel obeyed him. [24]All the officers and mighty men, as well as all of King David's sons, pledged their submission to King Solomon.

29:21
a 1Ki 8:62

29:22
b 1Ch 23:1
c 1Ki 1:33-39

a 7 That is, about 675 tons (about 610 metric tons)   b 7 That is, about 3,750 tons (about 3,450 metric tons)

29:15 David contrasts God's everlasting nature with the fleeting lives of his people. Nothing lasts unless it is rooted in God's unchanging character. If our most impressive deeds fade as dust before God, where should we place our confidence? Only in a relationship with God can we find anything permanent. His love never fades and nothing can take it away.

29:19 "Wholehearted devotion" means to be entirely dedicated to God. This is what David prayed for Solomon—that he would desire, above all else, to serve God. Do you find it hard to do what God wants, or even harder to want to do it? God can give you wholehearted devotion. If you believe in Jesus Christ, this is already happening in you. Paul wrote that God works within us "to will and to act according to his good purpose" (Philippians 2:13). Consider yourself blessed if someone in your life is praying this way for you.

29:21 Drink offerings of wine were poured out as sacrifices to God to acknowledge his role in providing for his people.

29:25
*d*2Ch 1:1, 12
*e*1Ki 3:13

25 The LORD highly exalted Solomon in the sight of all Israel and bestowed on him royal splendor *d* such as no king over Israel ever had before. *e*

The Death of David

29:26
*f*1Ch 18:14
29:27
*g*2Sa 5:4-5;
1Ki 2:11
29:28
*h*Ge 15:15
*i*1Ch 23:1

26 David son of Jesse was king *f* over all Israel. 27 He ruled over Israel forty years—seven in Hebron and thirty-three in Jerusalem. *g* 28 He died *h* at a good old age, having enjoyed long life, wealth and honor. His son Solomon succeeded him as king. *i*

29 As for the events of King David's reign, from beginning to end, they are written in the records of Samuel the seer, the records of Nathan the prophet and the records of Gad the seer, 30 together with the details of his reign and power, and the circumstances that surrounded him and Israel and the kingdoms of all the other lands.

29:25 Solomon surpassed his father's wealth and splendor. David's legacy resulted from his vital relationship with the Lord, and he passed his spiritual values on to Solomon. Any money or power we leave to our children are far less valuable than the spiritual legacy we pass on. What spiritual inheritance will your children receive? In what specific ways are you passing on that legacy today?

29:29 A seer was someone who received messages from God for the nation in visions or dreams.

29:30 First Chronicles vividly illustrates the importance of maintaining a relationship with God. The genealogies in chapters 1—9 emphasize the importance of a spiritual heritage. The second part of the book details the life of David. Few men or women in the Bible were as close to God as David was. His daily contact with God increased his capacity to worship and strengthened his desire to build God's temple. David's life shows us the importance of staying close to God—through studying and obeying his Word and communicating with him daily. Second Chronicles, on the other hand, reveals how quickly our lives can deteriorate (spiritually, mentally, and socially) when we fail to stay well grounded in God.

2 CHRONICLES

| Solomon becomes king 970 B.C. | Temple built 966–959 | The kingdom divides 930 | Asa becomes king of Judah 910 | Jehosha-phat becomes king of Judah 872 | Ahab killed in battle 853 | Athaliah seizes the throne 841 | Uzziah becomes king of Judah 792 |

VITAL STATISTICS

PURPOSE:
To unify the nation around true worship of God by showing his standard for judging kings. The righteous kings of Judah and the religious revivals under their rule are highlighted, and the sins of the evil kings are exposed.

AUTHOR:
Ezra, according to Jewish tradition

ORIGINAL AUDIENCE:
The exiles who returned from captivity

DATE WRITTEN:
Approximately 430 B.C., recording events from the beginning of Solomon's reign (970 B.C.) to the beginning of the Babylonian captivity (586 B.C.)

SETTING:
Second Chronicles parallels 1 and 2 Kings and serves as their commentary. Originally 1 and 2 Chronicles were one book. It was written after the exile from a priestly perspective, highlighting the importance of the temple and the religious revivals in Judah. The northern kingdom, Israel, is virtually ignored in this history.

KEY VERSE:
"If my people who are called by my name, will humble themselves and pray and seek my face and turn from their wicked ways, then will I hear from heaven and will forgive their sin and will heal their land" (7:14).

KEY PEOPLE:
Solomon, the queen of Sheba, Rehoboam, Asa, Jehoshaphat, Jehoram, Joash, Uzziah (Azariah), Ahaz, Hezekiah, Manasseh, Josiah

KEY PLACES:
Jerusalem, the temple

SPECIAL FEATURES:
Includes a detailed record of the temple's construction

THE SLIDE clicks, and our eyes focus on the image flashed onto the screen in the darkened sanctuary. "This idol," explains the missionary, "is made of stone and is worshiped daily. The natives believe that this will guarantee good crops and healthy children." With condescending smiles, we wonder at their ignorance. How could anyone worship an object? Idols are for the naive and the superstitious! But after the presentation, we return home to *our* idols of wealth, prestige, or self-fulfillment. Whatever we put in God's place we worship, despite what we profess.

Our experience parallels Israel's. They were chosen by God to represent him on earth. But too often they forgot the truth and their calling, stumbling blindly after idols as the neighboring nations did. Then prophets, priests, and judgment would push them abruptly back to the one true God. Second Chronicles relates this sordid history of Judah's corrupt and idolatrous kings. Here and there a good king would arise in Judah, and for a time revival would follow, but the downward spiral would continue—ending in chaos, destruction, and captivity.

The chronicler writes this volume to bring the people of Israel back to God by reminding them of their past. Only by following God would they prosper! As you read 2 Chronicles, you will catch a vivid glimpse of Judah's history (the history of Israel, the northern kingdom, is virtually ignored), and you will see the tragic results of idolatry. Learn the lessons of the past: Determine to get rid of any idols in your life and to worship God alone.

Second Chronicles continues the history of 1 Chronicles. David's son Solomon was inaugurated as king. Solomon built the magnificent temple in Jerusalem, thus fulfilling his father's wish and last request (chapters 2—5). Solomon enjoyed a peaceful and prosperous reign of 40 years that made him world famous. After Solomon died, his son Rehoboam assumed the throne, and his immaturity divided the kingdom.

In Judah there were a few good kings and many evil ones. The writer of Chronicles faithfully records their achievements and failures, noting how each king measured up to God's standard for success. Clearly a good king obeyed God's laws, eliminated the places of idol worship, and made no alliances with other nations. Judah's good kings include Asa, Jehoshaphat, Uzziah (Azariah), Hezekiah, and Josiah. Of its many evil ones, Ahaz and Manasseh were perhaps the worst. Eventually the nation was conquered and taken captive, and the temple was destroyed.

The writer's purpose was to reunite the nation around the true worship of God after the captivity. In these pages, he reminds the people of their past. He clearly broadcasts his message through one of the best-known verses in Scripture, "If my people who are called by my name, will humble themselves and pray and seek my face and turn from their wicked ways, then will I hear from heaven and will forgive their sin and will heal their land" (7:14). As you read 2 Chronicles, listen to God's voice and obey him; and receive his redemptive, healing touch.

THE BLUEPRINT

A. THE REIGN OF SOLOMON
   (1:1—9:31)
   1. Solomon asks for wisdom
   2. Solomon builds the temple
   3. Solomon dedicates the temple
   4. Solomon's riches and wisdom

Solomon achieved much in business and government, but most important, he was the man God used to build the glorious temple. This beautiful building was the religious center of the nation. It symbolized the unity of all the tribes, the presence of God among them, and the nation's high calling. We may achieve great things in life, but we must not neglect any effort that will help nurture God's people or bring others into God's kingdom. It is easy for us to get the wrong perspective on what's really important in life.

B. THE KINGDOM OF JUDAH
   (10:1—36:23)
   1. The northern tribes revolt
   2. History of apostasy and reform
   3. Judah is exiled to Babylon

Throughout the reigns of 20 kings, the nation of Judah wavered between obedience to God and apostasy. The reigning king's response to God determined the spiritual climate of the nation and whether or not God would send judgment upon his people. Our personal history is shaped by our response to God. Just as Judah's failure to repent brought them captivity in Babylon, so the abuse of our high calling by sinful living will ultimately bring us catastrophe and destruction.

MEGATHEMES

THEME	EXPLANATION	IMPORTANCE
Temple	The temple was the symbol of God's presence and the place set aside for worship and prayer. Built by Solomon from the plans God gave to David, the temple was the spiritual center of the nation.	As Christians meet together to worship God, they experience the presence of God in a way that no individual believer can, for the dwelling place of God is the people of God. The body of Christ is God's temple.
Peace	As Solomon and his descendants were faithful to God, they experienced victory in battle, success in government, and peace with other nations. Peace was the result of the people being unified and loyal to God and his law.	Only God can bring true peace. God is greater than any enemy, army, or nation. Just as Israel's faithful response was key to her peace and survival as a nation, so our obedience to God as individuals and nations is vital to peace today.
Prayer	After Solomon died, David's kingdom was divided. When a king led the Israelites into idolatry, the nation suffered. When the king and his people prayed to God for deliverance and they turned from their sinful ways, God delivered them.	God still answers prayer today. We have God's promise that if we humble ourselves, seek him, turn from our sin, and pray, God will hear, heal, and forgive us. If we are alert, we can pray for God's guidance before we get into trouble.
Reform	Although idolatry and injustice were common, some kings turned to God and led the people in spiritual revival—renewing their commitment to God and reforming their society. Revival included the destruction of idols, obedience to the law, and the restoration of the priesthood.	We must constantly commit ourselves to obeying God. We are never secure in what others have done before us. Believers in each generation must dedicate themselves to the task of carrying out God's will in their own lives as well as in society.
National Collapse	In 586 B.C. the Babylonians completely destroyed Solomon's beautiful temple. The formal worship of God was ended. The Israelites had abandoned God. As a result, God brought judgment upon his people, and they were carried off into captivity.	Although our disobedience may not be as blatant as Israel's, quite often our commitment to God is insincere and casual. When we forget that all our power, wisdom, and wealth come from God and not ourselves, we are in danger of the same spiritual and moral collapse that Israel experienced.

KEY PLACES IN 2 CHRONICLES

The broken lines (— · — ·) indicate modern boundaries.

Everyone but the tribes of Judah and Benjamin deserted Rehoboam and set up their own kingdom to the north called Israel. Rehoboam returned to Jerusalem as ruler over the southern kingdom called Judah (10:1—12:16). The remainder of 2 Chronicles records the history of Judah.

4 Hill Country of Ephraim   Abijah became the next king of Judah, and soon war broke out between Israel and Judah. When the armies of the two nations arrived for battle in the hill country of Ephraim, Israel had twice as many troops as Judah. It looked like Judah's defeat was certain. But they cried out to God, and God gave them victory over Israel. In their history as separate nations, Judah had a few godly kings, who instituted reforms and brought the people back to God. Israel, however, had a succession of only evil kings (13:1–22).

5 Aram (Syria)   Asa, a godly king, removed every trace of pagan worship from Judah and renewed the people's covenant with God in Jerusalem. But King Baasha of Israel built a fortress to control traffic into Judah. Instead of looking to God for guidance, Asa took the silver and gold from the temple and sent it to the king of Aram, requesting his help against King Baasha. As a result, God became angry with Judah (14:1–16:14).

6 Samaria   Although Jehoshaphat was a godly king, he allied himself with Israel's most evil king, Ahab. Ahab's capital was Samaria. Ahab wanted help fighting against Ramoth Gilead. Jehoshaphat wanted advice, but rather than listening to God's prophet who had promised defeat, he joined Ahab in battle (17:1–18:27).

7 Ramoth Gilead   The alliance with Israel against Ramoth Gilead ended in defeat and Ahab's death. Shaken by his defeat, Jehoshaphat returned to Jerusalem and to God. But his son Jehoram was a wicked king, as was his son Ahaziah, and history repeated itself. Ahaziah formed an alliance with Israel's king Joram to do battle with the Arameans at Ramoth Gilead. This led to the death of both kings (18:28–22:9).

1 Gibeon   David's son Solomon became king over Israel. He summoned the nation's leaders to a ceremony in Gibeon. Here God told Solomon to ask for whatever he desired. Solomon asked for wisdom and knowledge to rule Israel (1:1–12).

2 Jerusalem   After the ceremony in Gibeon, Solomon returned to the capital city, Jerusalem. His reign began a golden age for Israel. Solomon implemented the plans for the temple, which had been drawn up by his father, David. It was a magnificent construction. It symbolized Solomon's wealth and wisdom, which became known worldwide (1:13—9:31).

3 Shechem   After Solomon's death, his son Rehoboam was ready to be crowned in Shechem. However, his promise of higher taxes and harder work for the people led to rebellion.

8 Jerusalem   The rest of Judah's history recorded in 2 Chronicles centers on Jerusalem. Some kings caused Judah to sin by bringing idol worship into their midst. Others cleaned up the idol worship, reopened and restored the temple, and in the case of Josiah, tried to follow God's laws as they were written by Moses. In spite of the few good influences, a series of evil kings sent Judah into a downward spiral that ended with the Babylonian empire overrunning the country. The temple was burned, the walls of the city were broken down, and the people were deported to Babylon.

A. THE REIGN OF SOLOMON (1:1—9:31)

In response to Solomon's request, God gives to Solomon great wisdom. Solomon launches great building programs, including the temple, his greatest achievement. In the midst of the celebration dedicating the temple, fire flashes down from heaven, and God's glory fills the temple, God wants to live among his people and to be central in their lives. Today, our bodies are God's temple, the place where God, through his Holy Spirit, lives and reigns.

1. Solomon asks for wisdom

1:1
a 1Ki 2:12, 26
b Ge 39:2
c 1Ch 29:25

1 Solomon son of David established *a* himself firmly over his kingdom, for the LORD his God was with *b* him and made him exceedingly great. *c*

2 Then Solomon spoke to all Israel—to the commanders of thousands and commanders of hundreds, to the judges and to all the leaders in Israel, the heads of families— 3 and Solomon and the whole assembly went to the high place at Gibeon, for God's Tent of Meeting was there, which Moses the LORD's servant had made in the desert. 4 Now David had brought up the ark of God from Kiriath Jearim to the place he had prepared for it, because he had pitched a tent *d* for it in Jerusalem. 5 But the bronze altar *e* that Bezalel son of Uri, the son of Hur, had made was in Gibeon in front of the tabernacle of the LORD; so Solomon and the assembly inquired of him there. 6 Solomon went up to the bronze altar before the LORD in the Tent of Meeting and offered a thousand burnt offerings on it.

1:4
d 2Sa 6:17

1:5
e Ex 38:2

7 That night God appeared to Solomon and said to him, "Ask for whatever you want me to give you."

1:8
f 1Ch 28:5

8 Solomon answered God, "You have shown great kindness to David my father and have made me *f* king in his place. 9 Now, LORD God, let your promise to my father David be confirmed, for you have made me king over a people who are as numerous as the dust of the earth. 10 Give me wisdom and knowledge, that I may lead *g* this people, for who is able to govern this great people of yours?"

1:10
g Nu 27:17

11 God said to Solomon, "Since this is your heart's desire and you have not asked for wealth, riches or honor, nor for the death of your enemies, and since you have not asked for a long life but for wisdom and knowledge to govern my people over whom I have made you king, 12 therefore wisdom and knowledge will be given you. And I will also give you wealth, riches and honor, such as no king who was before you ever had and none after you will have. *h*"

1:12
h 1Ch 29:25;
2Ch 9:22

13 Then Solomon went to Jerusalem from the high place at Gibeon, from before the Tent of Meeting. And he reigned over Israel.

1:14
i 1Ki 4:26

14 Solomon accumulated chariots *i* and horses; he had fourteen hundred chariots and twelve thousand horses, **a** which he kept in the chariot cities and also with him in Jerusalem. 15 The king made silver and gold as common in Jerusalem as stones, and cedar as plentiful as

a *14 Or charioteers*

1:1 While the book of 1 Chronicles focuses mainly on David's life, 2 Chronicles focuses on the lives of the rest of the kings of Judah, the southern kingdom. Very little is mentioned about Israel, the northern kingdom, because (1) Chronicles was written for Judeans who had returned from captivity in Babylon, and (2) Judah represented David's family, from which the Messiah would come. Israel was in a state of constant turmoil, anarchy, and rebellion against God, but Judah, at least, made sporadic efforts to follow God.

1:1 More details about Solomon's rise to the throne can be read in 1 Kings 1; 2. Solomon's Profile is found in 1 Kings 4, p. 503.

1:2–5 The Tent of Meeting, or tabernacle, that Moses had built centuries earlier (Exodus 35—40) was still in operation although it had been moved several times. When Solomon became king, the tabernacle was located at Gibeon, a town about six miles northwest of Jerusalem. All the tabernacle furniture was kept at Gibeon except the ark of God, which David had moved to Jerusalem (1 Chronicles 13; 15; 16). David wanted the ark, the symbol of God's presence, to reside in the city where he ruled the people. The tabernacle at Gibeon, however, was still considered Israel's main religious center until Solomon built the temple in Jerusalem.

1:10 Wisdom is the ability to make good decisions based on proper discernment and judgment. Knowledge, in this verse, refers to the practical know-how necessary for handling everyday matters. Wisdom applies knowledge. Solomon used his wisdom

and knowledge not only to build the temple from his father's plans, but also to put the nation on firm economic footing.

1:10 God's offer to Solomon stretches the imagination: "Ask for whatever you want me to give you" (1:7). But Solomon put the needs of his people first and asked for wisdom rather than riches. He realized that wisdom would be the most valuable asset he could have as king. Later he wrote, wisdom "is more precious than rubies; nothing you desire can compare with her" (Proverbs 3:15). The same wisdom that was given to Solomon is available to us; the same God offers it. How can we acquire wisdom? First, we must ask God, who "gives generously to all without finding fault" (James 1:5). Second, we must devote ourselves wholeheartedly to studying and applying God's Word, the source of divine wisdom. (For more on Solomon's wisdom, read the notes on 1 Kings 3:6–9 and 3:12.)

1:11, 12 Solomon could have had anything, but he asked for wisdom to rule the nation. Because God approved of the way Solomon ordered his priorities, he gave Solomon wealth, riches, and honor as well. Jesus also spoke about priorities. He said that when we put God first, everything we really need will be given to us as well (Matthew 6:33). This does not guarantee that we will be wealthy and famous like Solomon, but it means that when we put God first, the wisdom he gives will enable us to have richly rewarding lives. When we have a purpose for living and learn to be content with what we have, we will have greater wealth than we could ever accumulate.

sycamore-fig trees in the foothills. [16]Solomon's horses were imported from Egypt [a] and from Kue [b]—the royal merchants purchased them from Kue. [17]They imported a chariot from Egypt for six hundred shekels [c] of silver, and a horse for a hundred and fifty. [d] They also exported them to all the kings of the Hittites and of the Arameans.

2. Solomon builds the temple
Preparations for Building the Temple

2 Solomon gave orders to build a temple for the Name of the Lord and a royal palace for himself. [2]He conscripted seventy thousand men as carriers and eighty thousand as stonecutters in the hills and thirty-six hundred as foremen over them. [j]

[3]Solomon sent this message to Hiram [e] king of Tyre:

"Send me cedar logs [k] as you did for my father David when you sent him cedar to build a palace to live in. [4]Now I am about to build a temple for the Name of the Lord my God and to dedicate it to him for burning fragrant incense [l] before him, for setting out the consecrated bread [m] regularly, and for making burnt offerings every morning and evening and on Sabbaths [n] and New Moons and at the appointed feasts of the Lord our God. This is a lasting ordinance for Israel.

[5]"The temple I am going to build will be great, because our God is greater than all other gods. [o] [6]But who is able to build a temple for him, since the heavens, even the highest heavens, cannot contain him? [p] Who then am I to build a temple for him, except as a place to burn sacrifices before him?

[7]"Send me, therefore, a man skilled to work in gold and silver, bronze and iron, and in purple, crimson and blue yarn, and experienced in the art of engraving, to work in Judah and Jerusalem with my skilled craftsmen, [q] whom my father David provided.

[8]"Send me also cedar, pine and algum [f] logs from Lebanon, for I know that your men are skilled in cutting timber there. My men will work with yours [9]to provide me with plenty of lumber, because the temple I build must be large and magnificent. [10]I will give your servants, the woodsmen who cut the timber, twenty thousand cors [g] of ground wheat, twenty thousand cors of barley, twenty thousand baths [h] of wine and twenty thousand baths of olive oil."

Margin references:
2:2 [j]ver 18
2:3 [k]1Ch 14:1
2:4 [l]Ex 30:7 [m]Ex 25:30 [n]Nu 28:9-10
2:5 [o]1Ch 16:25
2:6 [p]1Ki 8:27
2:7 [q]1Ch 22:16

[a]16 Or possibly *Muzur*, a region in Cilicia; also in verse 17 [b]16 Probably Cilicia [c]17 That is, about 15 pounds (about 7 kilograms) [d]17 That is, about 3 3/4 pounds (about 1.7 kilograms) [e]3 Hebrew *Hiram*, a variant of *Hiram*; also in verses 11 and 12 [f]8 Probably a variant of *almug*; possibly juniper [g]10 That is, probably about 125,000 bushels (about 4,400 kiloliters) [h]10 That is, probably about 115,000 gallons (about 440 kiloliters)

2:1 David had wanted to build a temple for God (2 Samuel 7). God denied his request because David had been a warrior, but God said that David's son Solomon would build the temple. God allowed David to make the plans and preparations for the temple (1 Chronicles 23—26; 28:11–13). David bought the land (2 Samuel 24:18–25; 1 Chronicles 22:1), gathered most of the

construction materials (1 Chronicles 22:14–16), and received the plans from God (1 Chronicles 28:11, 12). It was Solomon's responsibility to make the plans a reality. His job was made easier by his father's exhaustive preparations. God's work can be moved forward when the older generation paves the way for the younger.

2:3–12 Although Hiram was one of David's and Solomon's friendly allies, he was the ruler of a nation that worshiped many different gods. Hiram was happy to send materials for the temple, and both David and Solomon used this occasion to testify about the one true God.

2:5, 6 We should try our best to build beautiful, accessible, and welcoming places of worship to be a testimony and credit to God. In so doing, however, we must remember that God cannot be contained in our building or lovely setting. He is far greater than any structure, so we must focus our praise on him and not merely on the place of worship.

2:7 Why use foreign craftsmen? The Israelites had great knowledge of agriculture, but knew little about metalworking. So they found people who were experts in this area. It is not a sin to obtain secular expertise as we go about God's work. He distributes natural talents as he chooses, and he often decides to give skill to non-Christians. When we hire secular contractors to build or repair our church buildings, we are recognizing that God gives gifts liberally. We may also be gaining an opportunity to tell the workers about God.

2:8, 9 Israel did not have much wood, but Lebanon, a small nation on the seacoast, had some of the finest cedar forests in the ancient Near East. Lebanon also imported a great deal of food

SHIPPING RESOURCES FOR THE TEMPLE
Solomon asked King Hiram of Tyre to provide supplies and skilled workmen to help build God's temple in Jerusalem. The plan was to cut the cedar logs in the mountains of Lebanon, float them by sea to Joppa, then bring them inland to Jerusalem by the shortest and easiest route.

2:11
*r*1Ki 10:9; 2Ch 9:8

[11] Hiram king of Tyre replied by letter to Solomon:

"Because the LORD loves*r* his people, he has made you their king."

2:12
*s*Ps 33:6; 102:25

[12] And Hiram added:

"Praise be to the LORD, the God of Israel, who made heaven and earth!*s* He has given King David a wise son, endowed with intelligence and discernment, who will build a temple for the LORD and a palace for himself.

2:13
*t*1Ki 7:13

[13] "I am sending you Huram-Abi,*t* a man of great skill, [14] whose mother was from Dan and whose father was from Tyre. He is trained to work in gold and silver, bronze and iron, stone and wood, and with purple and blue and crimson yarn and fine linen. He is experienced in all kinds of engraving and can execute any design given to him. He will work with your craftsmen and with those of my lord, David your father.

2:15
*u*ver 10

[15] "Now let my lord send his servants the wheat and barley and the olive oil*u* and wine he promised, [16] and we will cut all the logs from Lebanon that you need and will float them in rafts by sea down to Joppa. You can then take them up to Jerusalem."

2:17
*v*1Ch 22:2

[17] Solomon took a census of all the aliens*v* who were in Israel, after the census his father David had taken; and they were found to be 153,600. [18] He assigned 70,000 of them to be carriers and 80,000 to be stonecutters in the hills, with 3,600 foremen over them to keep the people working.

Solomon Builds the Temple

3:1
*w*1Ch 21:18

3 Then Solomon began to build the temple of the LORD in Jerusalem on Mount Moriah, where the LORD had appeared to his father David. It was on the threshing floor of Araunah*a w* the Jebusite, the place provided by David. [2] He began building on the second day of the second month in the fourth year of his reign.

[3] The foundation Solomon laid for building the temple of God was sixty cubits long and twenty cubits wide*b* (using the cubit of the old standard). [4] The portico at the front of the temple was twenty cubits*c* long across the width of the building and twenty cubits*d* high.

He overlaid the inside with pure gold. [5] He paneled the main hall with pine and covered it with fine gold and decorated it with palm tree and chain designs. [6] He adorned the temple with precious stones. And the gold he used was gold of Parvaim. [7] He overlaid the ceiling beams, doorframes, walls and doors of the temple with gold, and he carved cherubim on the walls.

[8] He built the Most Holy Place, its length corresponding to the width of the temple—twenty cubits long and twenty cubits wide. He overlaid the inside with six hundred talents*e* of fine gold. [9] The gold nails weighed fifty shekels.*f* He also overlaid the upper parts with gold.

3:10
*x*Ex 25:18

[10] In the Most Holy Place he made a pair*x* of sculptured cherubim and overlaid them with gold. [11] The total wingspan of the cherubim was twenty cubits. One wing of the first cherub was five cubits*g* long and touched the temple wall, while its other wing, also five cubits long, touched the wing of the other cherub. [12] Similarly one wing of the second cherub was five cubits long and touched the other temple wall, and its other wing, also five cubits long, touched the wing of the first cherub. [13] The wings of these cherubim extended twenty cubits. They stood on their feet, facing the main hall.*h*

a 1 Hebrew *Ornan,* a variant of *Araunah*   *b 3* That is, about 90 feet (about 27 meters) long and 30 feet (about 9 meters) wide   *c 4* That is, about 30 feet (about 9 meters); also in verses 8, 11 and 13   *d 4* Some Septuagint and Syriac manuscripts; Hebrew *and a hundred and twenty*   *e 8* That is, about 23 tons (about 21 metric tons)   *f 9* That is, about 1 1/4 pounds (about 0.6 kilogram)   *g 11* That is, about 7 1/2 feet (about 2.3 meters); also in verse 15   *h 13* Or *facing inward*

---

from Israel. Thus the two kings made a trade agreement that was beneficial to both nations.

2:17, 18 Why would Solomon force aliens (foreigners) living in Israel to do the work of slaves? These aliens were descendants of the pagan nations who had not been driven out of the land in Joshua's day (Joshua 9:23–27; Judges 1:21–33; 1 Kings 9:20, 21). Scripture has specific laws about treating slaves fairly (Leviticus 25:39–55), so Solomon would not have treated them harshly as other nations might. Solomon's action was probably only in force during the construction of the temple.

3:1 Solomon built a permanent temple on Mount Moriah to replace the movable tabernacle (now at Gibeon) that had accompanied Israel in the desert. Mount Moriah was also the place

where God had stopped Abraham from sacrificing Isaac (Genesis 22:1–18). David purchased the land when it was a threshing floor (see 2 Samuel 24:15–25 and the note on 1 Chronicles 21:22–24).

3:1ff Why was the temple decorated so ornately? Although no one can build God a worthy home (2:6), this temple was going to be the best that humans could design. The care and craftsmanship were acts of worship in themselves. Although a simple chapel is an adequate place to pray and meet God, it is not wrong to want to make a beautiful place of worship.

3:3 The "cubit of the old standard" was equal to 20.5 inches and was the one used by Ezekiel in the temple he envisioned.

3:10 Cherubim are mighty angels.

14He made the curtain[y] of blue, purple and crimson yarn and fine linen, with cherubim worked into it.

15In the front of the temple he made two pillars,[z] which ⌐together⌐ were thirty-five cubits[a] long, each with a capital on top measuring five cubits. 16He made interwoven chains[b] and put them on top of the pillars. He also made a hundred pomegranates[a] and attached them to the chains. 17He erected the pillars in the front of the temple, one to the south and one to the north. The one to the south he named Jakin[c] and the one to the north Boaz. [d]

The Temple's Furnishings

4 He made a bronze altar[b] twenty cubits long, twenty cubits wide and ten cubits high. [e] 2He made the Sea of cast metal, circular in shape, measuring ten cubits from rim to rim and five cubits[f] high. It took a line of thirty cubits[g] to measure around it. 3Below the rim, figures of bulls encircled it—ten to a cubit. [h] The bulls were cast in two rows in one piece with the Sea.

4The Sea stood on twelve bulls, three facing north, three facing west, three facing south and three facing east. The Sea rested on top of them, and their hindquarters were toward the center. 5It was a handbreadth[i] in thickness, and its rim was like the rim of a cup, like a lily blossom. It held three thousand baths.[j]

6He then made ten basins[c] for washing and placed five on the south side and five on the north. In them the things to be used for the burnt offerings were rinsed, but the Sea was to be used by the priests for washing.

7He made ten gold lampstands[d] according to the specifications[e] for them and placed them in the temple, five on the south side and five on the north.

8He made ten tables and placed them in the temple, five on the south side and five on the north. He also made a hundred gold sprinkling bowls.

9He made the courtyard[f] of the priests, and the large court and the doors for the court, and overlaid the doors with bronze. 10He placed the Sea on the south side, at the southeast corner.

11He also made the pots and shovels and sprinkling bowls.

So Huram finished the work he had undertaken for King Solomon in the temple of God:

12 the two pillars;

the two bowl-shaped capitals on top of the pillars;

the two sets of network decorating the two bowl-shaped capitals on top of the pillars;

13 the four hundred pomegranates for the two sets of network (two rows of pomegranates for each network, decorating the bowl-shaped capitals on top of the pillars);

14 the stands[g] with their basins;

15 the Sea and the twelve bulls under it;

16 the pots, shovels, meat forks and all related articles.

All the objects that Huram-Abi[h] made for King Solomon for the temple of the LORD were of polished bronze. 17The king had them cast in clay molds in the plain of the Jordan between Succoth and Zarethan. [k] 18All these things that Solomon made amounted to so much that the weight of the bronze was not determined.

19Solomon also made all the furnishings that were in God's temple:

the golden altar;

the tables[i] on which was the bread of the Presence;

**Side references:**

3:14 [y]Ex 26:31, 33; Heb 9:3

3:15 [z]1Ki 7:15

3:16 [a]1Ki 7:20

4:1 [b]Ex 27:1-2; 2Ki 16:14

4:6 [c]Ex 30:18

4:7 [d]Ex 25:31 [e]Ex 25:40

4:9 [f]1Ki 6:36; 2Ki 21:5

4:14 [g]1Ki 7:27-30

4:16 [h]1Ki 7:13

4:19 [i]Ex 25:23, 30

a 15 That is, about 52 feet (about 16 meters)   b 16 Or possibly made chains in the inner sanctuary; the meaning of the Hebrew for this phrase is uncertain.   c 17 Jakin probably means he establishes.   d 17 Boaz probably means in him is strength.   e 1 That is, about 30 feet (about 9 meters) long and wide, and about 15 feet (about 4.5 meters) high   f 2 That is, about 7 1/2 feet (about 2.3 meters)   g 2 That is, about 45 feet (about 13.5 meters)   h 3 That is, about 1 1/2 feet (about 0.5 meter)   i 5 That is, about 3 inches (about 8 centimeters)   j 5 That is, about 17,500 gallons (about 66 kiloliters)   k 17 Hebrew Zeredatha, a variant of Zarethan

---

4:6 Why was everything in the temple built on such a grand scale? The great size and numbers were necessary to accommodate the huge crowds that would visit for the feasts, such as the Passover (30:13). The numerous daily sacrifices (5:6) required many priests and much equipment.

4:7 The craftsmen followed God's specifications carefully—with spectacular results. When God gives specific instructions, they must be followed to the letter. There is a time to be creative and to put forth our own ideas, but not when the ideas add to, alter,

or contradict any specific directions God has already given to us in the Bible. For best results in your spiritual life, carefully seek and follow God's instructions.

4:11-16 Pots, shovels, and bowls—these are implements of worship unfamiliar to us. Although the articles we use to aid our worship have changed, the purpose of worship remains the same—to give honor and praise to God. We must never let our worship of God be overshadowed by things we use to help us worship him.

4:20
/Ex 25:31

20 the lampstands/ of pure gold with their lamps, to burn in front of the inner sanctuary as prescribed;

21 the gold floral work and lamps and tongs (they were solid gold);

22 the pure gold wick trimmers, sprinkling bowls, dishes and censers; and the gold doors of the temple: the inner doors to the Most Holy Place and the doors of the main hall.

5:1
k 2Sa 8:11

5 When all the work Solomon had done for the temple of the LORD was finished, he brought in the things his father David had dedicated *k*—the silver and gold and all the furnishings—and he placed them in the treasuries of God's temple.

3. Solomon dedicates the temple
The Ark Brought to the Temple

5:2
/2Sa 6:12;
1Ch 15:25

2 Then Solomon summoned to Jerusalem the elders of Israel, all the heads of the tribes and the chiefs of the Israelite families, to bring up the ark/ of the LORD's covenant from Zion, the

---

CAREFUL OBEDIENCE
Solomon and his workers carefully followed God's instructions. As a result, the temple work was blessed by God and completed in every detail. Here are a few examples of people in the Bible who did not carefully follow one of God's instructions, and the resulting consequences. It is *not* enough to obey God halfheartedly.

Who?	God's Instruction	Disobedience	Result
Adam and Eve	Don't eat fruit from the tree of the knowledge of good and evil (Genesis 2:16, 17)	Satan tempted them, and they ate (Genesis 3:1–6)	They were banished from the Garden of Eden, pain and death were inflicted on all people (Genesis 3:24; Romans 5:12)
Nadab and Abihu	Fire for the sacrifice must come from the proper source (Leviticus 6:12, 13)	They used unauthorized fire for their sacrifice (Leviticus 10:1)	They were struck dead (Leviticus 10:2)
Moses	"Speak to that rock . . . it will pour out its water" (Numbers 20:8)	He spoke to the rock, but also struck it with his staff (Numbers 20:11)	He was not allowed to enter the promised land (Numbers 20:12)
Saul	Completely destroy the evil Amalekites (1 Samuel 15:3)	He spared the king and kept some of the plunder (1 Samuel 15:8, 9)	God promised to end his reign (1 Samuel 15:16–26)
Uzzah	Only a priest can touch the holy furnishings and articles (Numbers 4:15)	He touched the ark of the covenant (2 Samuel 6:6)	He died instantly (2 Samuel 6:7)
Uzziah	Only the priests can offer incense in the temple or tabernacle sanctuary (Numbers 16:39, 40; 18:7)	He entered the Holy Place in the temple where only priests were allowed to go (2 Chronicles 26:16–18)	He became a leper (2 Chronicles 26:19)

4:22 All these details about the temple demonstrated the care Israel gave to acts of worship (see the note on 3:1ff). The instructions also served as a manual to the original readers of 2 Chronicles, those who would rebuild a new temple on its original site (Ezra 3:8—6:15) after Solomon's temple was destroyed by the Babylonians (2 Kings 25).

5:1ff Why is there so much emphasis on the temple in the Old Testament?

(1) *It was a symbol of religious authority.* The temple was God's way of centralizing worship at Jerusalem in order to ensure that correct belief would be kept intact through many generations.

(2) *It was a symbol of God's holiness.* The temple's beautiful atmosphere inspired respect and awe for God; it was the setting for many of the great visions of the prophets.

(3) *It was a symbol of God's covenant with Israel.* The temple kept the people focused upon God's law (the tablets of the Ten Commandments were kept in the temple) rather than on the kings' exploits. It was a place where God was especially present to his people.

(4) *It was a symbol of forgiveness.* The temple's design, furni-

ture, and customs were great object lessons for all the people, reminding them of the seriousness of sin, the penalty that sin incurred, and their need of forgiveness.

(5) *It prepared the people for the Messiah.* In the New Testament, Christ said he came to fulfill the law, not destroy it. Hebrews 8:1, 2 and 9:11, 12 use temple customs to explain what Christ did when he died for us.

(6) *It was a testimony to human effort and creativity.* Inspired by the beauty of God's character, people devoted themselves to high achievements in engineering, science, and art in order to praise him.

(7) *It was a place of prayer.* In the temple, people could spend time in prayer to God.

5:1–3 The temple took seven years to build. 1 Kings 6:38 says that the temple was completed in the eighth month (November) of Solomon's eleventh year as king (959 B.C.). Because 5:3 states that the dedication ceremonies were held in the seventh month, they must have occurred either one month before or eleven months after the temple's completion.

City of David. 3And all the men of Israel came together to the king at the time of the festival in the seventh month.

4When all the elders of Israel had arrived, the Levites took up the ark, 5and they brought up the ark and the Tent of Meeting and all the sacred furnishings in it. The priests, who were Levites, carried them up; 6and King Solomon and the entire assembly of Israel that had gathered about him were before the ark, sacrificing so many sheep and cattle that they could not be recorded or counted.

7The priests then brought the ark of the LORD's covenant to its place in the inner sanctuary of the temple, the Most Holy Place, and put it beneath the wings of the cherubim. 8The cherubim spread their wings over the place of the ark and covered the ark and its carrying poles. 9These poles were so long that their ends, extending from the ark, could be seen from in front of the inner sanctuary, but not from outside the Holy Place; and they are still there today. 10There was nothing in the ark except *m* the two tablets *n* that Moses had placed in it at Horeb, where the LORD made a covenant with the Israelites after they came out of Egypt.

11The priests then withdrew from the Holy Place. All the priests who were there had consecrated themselves, regardless of their divisions. *o* 12All the Levites who were musicians *p*— Asaph, Heman, Jeduthun and their sons and relatives—stood on the east side of the altar, dressed in fine linen and playing cymbals, harps and lyres. They were accompanied by 120 priests sounding trumpets. *q* 13The trumpeters and singers joined in unison, as with one voice, to give praise and thanks to the LORD. Accompanied by trumpets, cymbals and other instruments, they raised their voices in praise to the LORD and sang:

> "He is good;
> his love endures forever." *r*

Then the temple of the LORD was filled with a cloud, 14and the priests could not perform *s* their service because of the cloud, for the glory of the LORD filled the temple of God.

6 Then Solomon said, "The LORD has said that he would dwell in a dark cloud; *t* 2I have built a magnificent temple for you, a place for you to dwell forever."

3While the whole assembly of Israel was standing there, the king turned around and blessed them. 4Then he said:

"Praise be to the LORD, the God of Israel, who with his hands has fulfilled what he promised with his mouth to my father David. For he said, 5'Since the day I brought my people out of Egypt, I have not chosen a city in any tribe of Israel to have a temple built for my Name to be there, nor have I chosen anyone to be the leader over my people Israel. 6But now I have chosen Jerusalem for my Name *u* to be there, and I have chosen David *v* to rule my people Israel.'

7"My father David had it in his heart to build a temple for the Name of the LORD, the God of Israel. 8But the LORD said to my father David, 'Because it was in your heart to build a temple for my Name, you did well to have this in your heart. 9Nevertheless, you are not the one to build the temple, but your son, who is your own flesh and blood—he is the one who will build the temple for my Name.'

10"The LORD has kept the promise he made. I have succeeded David my father and now I sit on the throne of Israel, just as the LORD promised, and I have built the temple for the Name of the LORD, the God of Israel. 11There I have placed the ark, in which is the covenant *w* of the LORD that he made with the people of Israel."

5:10
m Heb 9:4
n Dt 10:2

5:11
o 1Ch 24:1

5:12
p 1Ch 25:1
q 1Ch 15:24

5:13
r 1Ch 16:34, 41;
2Ch 7:3

5:14
s Ex 40:35

6:1
t 1Ki 8:12-50

6:6
u 2Ch 12:13
v 1Ch 28:4

6:11
w 2Ch 5:10

5:3 The festival in the seventh month was the Feast of Tabernacles, celebrating God's protection of Israel as they wandered in the desert before entering the promised land. The purpose of this annual festival was to renew Israel's commitment to God and their trust in his guidance and protection. The festival beautifully coincided with the dedication of the temple. As the people remembered the wanderings in the desert when their ancestors had lived in tents, they were even more thankful for the permanence of this glorious temple.

5:9 Under God's inspiration, some books of the Bible were compiled and edited from other sources. Because 1 and 2 Chronicles cover many centuries, they were compiled from several sources by a single person. The phrase "they are still there today" (see also 1 Kings 8:8) was taken from material written before Judah's exile in 586 B.C. Although 1 and 2 Chronicles were compiled after the exile and after Solomon's temple was destroyed, the writer thought it best to leave this phrase in the narrative.

5:7–12 The priests came out of the Holy Place after having placed the ark in the Most Holy Place of the temple. The Holy Place is the outer room, where the bread of the Presence, altar of incense, and lampstand were kept. Ordinarily the Most Holy Place could be entered only once a year by the high priest on the Day of Atonement. On this unique occasion, however, several priests had to enter the Most Holy Place to carry the ark to its new resting place. The Levites praised God when these priests emerged from the Holy Place because they then knew God had accepted this new home for the ark (5:13).

Solomon's Prayer of Dedication

6:14
×Ex 15:11
ʸDt 7:9

6:15
ᶻ1Ch 22:10

6:16
ᵃ2Sa 7:13, 15;
1Ki 2:4; 2Ch 7:18

6:18
ᵇ2Ch 2:6; Isa 66:1;
Ac 7:49

6:20
ᶜPs 34:15
ᵈDt 12:11

6:21
ᵉIsa 43:25; 44:22;
Mic 7:18

6:23
ᶠIsa 3:11

6:26
ᵍ1Ki 17:1

¹²Then Solomon stood before the altar of the LORD in front of the whole assembly of Israel and spread out his hands. ¹³Now he had made a bronze platform, five cubits ᵃ long, five cubits wide and three cubits ᵇ high, and had placed it in the center of the outer court. He stood on the platform and then knelt down before the whole assembly of Israel and spread out his hands toward heaven. ¹⁴He said:

"O LORD, God of Israel, there is no God like you ˣ in heaven or on earth—you who keep your covenant of love ʸ with your servants who continue wholeheartedly in your way. ¹⁵You have kept your promise to your servant David my father; with your mouth you have promised ᶻ and with your hand you have fulfilled it—as it is today.

¹⁶"Now LORD, God of Israel, keep for your servant David my father the promises you made to him when you said, 'You shall never fail ᵃ to have a man to sit before me on the throne of Israel, if only your sons are careful in all they do to walk before me according to my law, as you have done.' ¹⁷And now, O LORD, God of Israel, let your word that you promised your servant David come true.

¹⁸"But will God really dwell on earth with men? The heavens, ᵇ even the highest heavens, cannot contain you. How much less this temple I have built! ¹⁹Yet give attention to your servant's prayer and his plea for mercy, O LORD my God. Hear the cry and the prayer that your servant is praying in your presence. ²⁰May your eyes ᶜ be open toward this temple day and night, this place of which you said you would put your Name ᵈ there. May you hear the prayer your servant prays toward this place. ²¹Hear the supplications of your servant and of your people Israel when they pray toward this place. Hear from heaven, your dwelling place; and when you hear, forgive. ᵉ

²²"When a man wrongs his neighbor and is required to take an oath and he comes and swears the oath before your altar in this temple, ²³then hear from heaven and act. Judge between your servants, repaying ᶠ the guilty by bringing down on his own head what he has done. Declare the innocent not guilty and so establish his innocence.

²⁴"When your people Israel have been defeated by an enemy because they have sinned against you and when they turn back and confess your name, praying and making supplication before you in this temple, ²⁵then hear from heaven and forgive the sin of your people Israel and bring them back to the land you gave to them and their fathers.

²⁶"When the heavens are shut up and there is no rain ᵍ because your people have sinned against you, and when they pray toward this place and confess your name and turn from their sin because you have afflicted them, ²⁷then hear from heaven and forgive the sin of your servants, your people Israel. Teach them the right way to live, and send rain on the land you gave your people for an inheritance.

ᵃ *13* That is, about 7 1/2 feet (about 2.3 meters)   ᵇ *13* That is, about 4 1/2 feet (about 1.3 meters)

5:13 The first service at the temple began with honoring God and acknowledging his presence and goodness. In the same way, our worship should begin by acknowledging God's love. Praise God first; then you will be prepared to present your needs to him. Recalling God's love and mercy will inspire you to worship him daily. Psalm 107 is an example of how David recalled God's enduring love.

6:3 As the people received Solomon's blessing, they stood; as Solomon prayed, he knelt (6:13). Both standing and kneeling are acts of reverence. Acts of reverence make us feel more worshipful, and they let others see that we are honoring God. When you stand or kneel in church or at prayer, make these actions more than mere forms prescribed by tradition. Let them indicate your love for God.

6:12, 13 It was unusual for a king to kneel before someone else in front of his own people because kneeling meant submitting to a higher authority. Solomon demonstrated his great love and respect for God by kneeling before him. His action showed that he acknowledged God as the ultimate king and authority, and it encouraged the people to do the same.

6:18 Solomon marveled that the temple could contain the power of God and that God would be willing to live on earth among sinful people. We marvel that God, through his Son, Jesus, lived

among us in human form to reveal his eternal purposes to us. In doing so, God was reaching out to us in love. God wants us to reach out to him in return in order to know him and to love him with all our hearts. Don't simply marvel at his power; take time to get to know him.

6:19–42 As Solomon led the people in prayer, he asked God to hear their prayers concerning a variety of situations: (1) crime (6:22, 23); (2) enemy attacks (6:24, 25); (3) drought (6:26, 27); (4) famine (6:28–31); (5) the influx of foreigners (6:32, 33); (6) war (6:34, 35); (7) sin (6:36–39). God is concerned with whatever we face, even the difficult consequences we bring upon ourselves. He wants us to turn to him in prayer. When you pray, remember that God hears you. Don't let the extremity of your situation cause you to doubt his care for you.

6:26 Why would Solomon assume that drought would come as a result of sin? Sin is not necessarily the direct cause of natural disasters today, but this was a special case. God had made a specific agreement with the Israelites that drought could be a consequence of their sins (Deuteronomy 28:20–24).

28"When famine*h* or plague comes to the land, or blight or mildew, locusts or grass-hoppers, or when enemies besiege them in any of their cities, whatever disaster or disease may come, 29and when a prayer or plea is made by any of your people Israel—each one aware of his afflictions and pains, and spreading out his hands toward this temple— 30then hear from heaven, your dwelling place. Forgive, and deal with each man according to all he does, since you know his heart (for you alone know the hearts of men),*i* 31so that they will fear you and walk in your ways all the time they live in the land you gave our fathers.

32"As for the foreigner who does not belong to your people Israel but has come from a distant land because of your great name and your mighty hand and your out-stretched arm—when he comes and prays toward this temple, 33then hear from heaven, your dwelling place, and do whatever the foreigner*j* asks of you, so that all the peoples of the earth may know your name and fear you, as do your own people Israel, and may know that this house I have built bears your Name.

34"When your people go to war against their enemies, wherever you send them, and when they pray to you toward this city you have chosen and the temple I have built for your Name, 35then hear from heaven their prayer and their plea, and uphold their cause.

36"When they sin against you—for there is no one who does not sin*k*—and you be-come angry with them and give them over to the enemy, who takes them captive to a land far away or near; 37and if they have a change of heart in the land where they are held captive, and repent and plead with you in the land of their captivity and say, 'We have sinned, we have done wrong and acted wickedly'; 38and if they turn back to you with all their heart and soul in the land of their captivity where they were taken, and pray toward the land you gave their fathers, toward the city you have chosen and to-ward the temple I have built for your Name; 39then from heaven, your dwelling place, hear their prayer and their pleas, and uphold their cause. And forgive your people, who have sinned against you.

40"Now, my God, may your eyes be open and your ears attentive*l* to the prayers offered in this place.

41 "Now arise, O Lord God, and come to your resting place,*m*
       you and the ark of your might.
   May your priests,*n* O Lord God, be clothed with salvation,
       may your saints rejoice in your goodness.
   42 O Lord God, do not reject your anointed one.
       Remember the great love*o* promised to David your servant."

The Dedication of the Temple

7 When Solomon finished praying, fire*p* came down from heaven and consumed the burnt offering and the sacrifices, and the glory of the Lord filled the temple. 2The priests could not enter the temple of the Lord because the glory of the Lord filled it. 3When all the Israelites saw the fire coming down and the glory of the Lord above the temple, they knelt on the pavement with their faces to the ground, and they worshiped and gave thanks to the Lord, saying,

   "He is good;
       his love endures forever."*q*

6:28
*h*2Ch 20:9

6:30
*i*1Sa 16:7; 1Ch 28:9

6:33
*j*2Ch 7:14

6:36
*k*Job 15:14;
Jas 3:1; 1Jn 1:8-10

6:40
*l*2Ch 7:15

6:41
*m*1Ch 28:2
*n*Ps 132:16

6:42
*o*Ps 89:24, 28

7:1
*p*Lev 9:24;
1Ki 18:38
7:3
*q*2Ch 5:13

6:30 Have you ever felt far from God, separated by feelings of failure and personal problems? In his prayer, Solomon under-scored the fact that God stands ready to hear his people, to forgive their sins, and to restore their relationship with him. God is waiting and listening for our confessions of guilt and our recommitment to obey him. He hears us when we pour out our needs and problems to him and is ready to forgive us and restore us to fellowship with him. Don't wait to experience his loving forgiveness.

6:36 "For there is no one who does not sin"—the Bible makes it clear that no one is exempt from sin, not even God's appointed kings. Sin is a condition we all share, and we all should acknowl-edge it as Solomon did. When we realize we have sinned, we should quickly ask God for forgiveness and restoration. Knowing we have a tendency to sin should keep us close to God, seeking his guidance and strength. This truth is also mentioned in Psalm 14:3, Ecclesiastes 7:20, and Romans 3:23.

7:1, 2 God sent fire from heaven to consume the offering and to begin the fire that was to burn continuously under the altar of burnt offering (see Leviticus 6:8–13). This perpetual fire symbolized God's presence. God also sent fire when inaugurat-ing the tabernacle (Leviticus 9:22–24). This was the real dedica-tion of the temple because only God's purifying power can make something holy.

7:6
r 1Ch 15:16
s 2Ch 5:12

4 Then the king and all the people offered sacrifices before the Lord. 5 And King Solomon offered a sacrifice of twenty-two thousand head of cattle and a hundred and twenty thousand sheep and goats. So the king and all the people dedicated the temple of God. 6 The priests took their positions, as did the Levites *r* with the Lord's musical instruments,*s* which King David had made for praising the Lord and which were used when he gave thanks, saying, "His love endures forever." Opposite the Levites, the priests blew their trumpets, and all the Israelites were standing.

7 Solomon consecrated the middle part of the courtyard in front of the temple of the Lord, and there he offered burnt offerings and the fat of the fellowship offerings,*a* because the bronze altar he had made could not hold the burnt offerings, the grain offerings and the fat portions.

7:8
t Ge 15:18
7:9
u Lev 23:36

8 So Solomon observed the festival at that time for seven days, and all Israel with him—a vast assembly, people from Lebo *b* Hamath to the Wadi of Egypt. *t* 9 On the eighth day they held an assembly, for they had celebrated the dedication of the altar for seven days and the festival *u* for seven days more. 10 On the twenty-third day of the seventh month he sent the people to their homes, joyful and glad in heart for the good things the Lord had done for David and Solomon and for his people Israel.

The Lord Appears to Solomon

7:12
v Dt 12:5

11 When Solomon had finished the temple of the Lord and the royal palace, and had succeeded in carrying out all he had in mind to do in the temple of the Lord and in his own palace, 12 the Lord appeared to him at night and said:

"I have heard your prayer and have chosen this place for myself *v* as a temple for sacrifices.

7:14
w 2Ch 6:37
x 2Ch 6:27

13 "When I shut up the heavens so that there is no rain, or command locusts to devour the land or send a plague among my people, 14 if my people, who are called by my name, will humble *w* themselves and pray and seek my face and turn from their wicked ways, then will I hear from heaven and will forgive *x* their sin and will heal their land.

7:15
y 2Ch 6:40

15 Now my eyes will be open and my ears attentive to the prayers offered in this place. *y* 16 I have chosen and consecrated this temple so that my Name may be there forever. My eyes and my heart will always be there.

7:17
z 1Ki 9:4
7:18
a 2Ch 6:16

17 "As for you, if you walk before me *z* as David your father did, and do all I command, and observe my decrees and laws, 18 I will establish your royal throne, as I covenanted with David your father when I said, 'You shall never fail to have a man *a* to rule over Israel.'

7:19
b Dt 28:15
7:20
c Dt 29:28

19 "But if you *c* turn away *b* and forsake the decrees and commands I have given you *c* and go off to serve other gods and worship them, 20 then I will uproot *c* Israel from my land, which I have given them, and will reject this temple I have consecrated for my

a 7 Traditionally *peace offerings*   *b 8* Or *from the entrance to*   *c 19* The Hebrew is plural.

7:4, 5 The temple was dedicated to God, and Solomon and the people prepared to worship him. Dedication means setting apart a place, an object, or a person for an exclusive purpose. The purpose of this dedication was to set apart the temple as a place to worship God. Today, our bodies are God's temple (2 Corinthians 6:16). Solomon's dedication of the temple shows us that we should dedicate ourselves to carry out God's special purpose (Ephesians 1:11, 12).

7:8 A wadi is a stream or dry streambed.

7:12 Months, maybe years, had passed since Solomon's prayer of dedication (chapter 6). Several other building projects had been completed after the temple (7:11; 8:1). Then after all this time, God told Solomon that he had heard Solomon's prayer. How often do we look for immediate answers to our prayers and, when nothing happens, wonder if God has heard us? God does hear, and he will provide for us. We must trust that God will answer at the proper time.

7:14 In chapter 6, Solomon asked God to make provisions for the people when they sinned. God answered with four conditions for forgiveness: (1) humble yourself by admitting your sins, (2) pray to God, asking for forgiveness, (3) seek God continually,

and (4) turn from sinful behavior. True repentance is more than talk—it is changed behavior. Whether we sin individually, as a group, or as a nation, following these steps will lead to forgiveness. God will answer our earnest prayers.

7:17–22 God plainly set forth certain conditions for Solomon to meet if he wanted the kingdom to continue. If Solomon followed God, he and his descendants would prosper; if Solomon did not, he and the nation would be destroyed. In Deuteronomy 27 and 28, these conditions were outlined before all the people.

But sin is deceptively attractive, and Solomon eventually turned from God. As a result, his son and heir lost most of the kingdom. Following God brings benefits and rewards (not necessarily material). Turning away from God brings suffering, punishment, and ultimately destruction. Today, God's conditions are just as clear as they were in Solomon's day. Choose to obey God no matter what happens, knowing that God will eventually bless your efforts.

Name. I will make it a byword and an object of ridicule among all peoples. ²¹And though this temple is now so imposing, all who pass by will be appalled and say,*ᵈ* 'Why has the Lᴏʀᴅ done such a thing to this land and to this temple?' ²²People will answer, 'Because they have forsaken the Lᴏʀᴅ, the God of their fathers, who brought them out of Egypt, and have embraced other gods, worshiping and serving them—that is why he brought all this disaster on them.'"

7:21
*ᵈ*Dt 29:24

4. Solomon's riches and wisdom
Solomon's Other Activities

8 At the end of twenty years, during which Solomon built the temple of the Lᴏʀᴅ and his own palace, ²Solomon rebuilt the villages that Hiram*ᵃ* had given him, and settled Israelites in them. ³Solomon then went to Hamath Zobah and captured it. ⁴He also built up Tadmor in the desert and all the store cities he had built in Hamath. ⁵He rebuilt Upper Beth Horon and Lower Beth Horon as fortified cities, with walls and with gates and bars, ⁶as well as Baalath and all his store cities, and all the cities for his chariots and for his horses*ᵇ*—whatever he desired to build in Jerusalem, in Lebanon and throughout all the territory he ruled.

⁷All the people left from the Hittites, Amorites, Perizzites, Hivites and Jebusites (these peoples were not Israelites), ⁸that is, their descendants remaining in the land, whom the Israelites had not destroyed—these Solomon conscripted for his slave labor force, as it is to this day. ⁹But Solomon did not make slaves of the Israelites for his work; they were his fighting men, commanders of his captains, and commanders of his chariots and charioteers. ¹⁰They were also King Solomon's chief officials—two hundred and fifty officials supervising the men.

¹¹Solomon brought Pharaoh's daughter*ᵉ* up from the City of David to the palace he had built for her, for he said, "My wife must not live in the palace of David king of Israel, because the places the ark of the Lᴏʀᴅ has entered are holy."

8:11
*ᵉ*1Ki 3:1

¹²On the altar of the Lᴏʀᴅ that he had built in front of the portico, Solomon sacrificed burnt offerings to the Lᴏʀᴅ, ¹³according to the daily requirement*ᶠ* for offerings commanded by Moses for Sabbaths, New Moons and the three*ᵍ* annual feasts—the Feast of Unleavened Bread, the Feast of Weeks and the Feast of Tabernacles. ¹⁴In keeping with the ordinance of his father David, he appointed the divisions of the priests for their duties, and the Levites*ʰ* to lead the praise and to assist the priests according to each day's requirement. He also appointed the gatekeepers by divisions for the various gates, because this was what David the man of God*ⁱ* had ordered. ¹⁵They did not deviate from the king's commands to the priests or to the Levites in any matter, including that of the treasuries.

8:13
*ᶠ*Ex 29:38; Nu 28:3
*ᵍ*Ex 23:14
8:14
*ʰ*1Ch 25:1
*ⁱ*Ne 12:24, 36

¹⁶All Solomon's work was carried out, from the day the foundation of the temple of the Lᴏʀᴅ was laid until its completion. So the temple of the Lᴏʀᴅ was finished.

¹⁷Then Solomon went to Ezion Geber and Elath on the coast of Edom. ¹⁸And Hiram sent him ships commanded by his own officers, men who knew the sea. These, with Solomon's men, sailed to Ophir and brought back four hundred and fifty talents*ᶜ* of gold,*ʲ* which they delivered to King Solomon.

8:18
*ʲ*2Ch 9:9

The Queen of Sheba Visits Solomon

9 When the queen of Sheba*ᵏ* heard of Solomon's fame, she came to Jerusalem to test him with hard questions. Arriving with a very great caravan—with camels carrying spices, large quantities of gold, and precious stones—she came to Solomon and talked with him

9:1
*ᵏ*Mt 12:42; Lk 11:31

ᵃ2 Hebrew *Huram*, a variant of *Hiram*; also in verse 18   *ᵇ6* Or *charioteers*   *ᶜ18* That is, about 17 tons (about 16 metric tons)

7:21, 22 Soon after Solomon's reign, the temple was ransacked (12:9). It is difficult for us to imagine that such a great and wise king could become corrupted by idols—symbols of power, prosperity, and sexuality. But even today these idols lure us into their traps. When we allow any desire to rival God's proper place, we have taken the first step toward moral and spiritual decay.

8:11 Solomon married Pharaoh's daughter to secure a military alliance with Egypt. He did not let the woman live in David's palace, however, where the ark of God had once been kept. This implies that Solomon knew his pagan marriage would not please God. Solomon married many other foreign women, and this was contrary to God's law (Deuteronomy 7:3, 4). These women worshiped false gods and were certain to contaminate Israel with

their beliefs and practices. Eventually Solomon's pagan wives caused his downfall (1 Kings 11:1–11).

8:15 Although Solomon carefully followed God's instructions for building the temple and offering sacrifices (8:13), he paid no attention to what God said about marrying pagan women. His sin in marrying a foreign wife (8:11) began his slide away from God. No matter how good or spiritual we are in most areas of life, one unsurrendered area can begin a downfall. Guard carefully *every* area of your life, especially your relationships. Don't give sin any foothold.

9:1–8 The queen of Sheba had heard about Solomon's wisdom, but she was overwhelmed when she saw for herself the fruits of that wisdom. Although Solomon had married Pharaoh's daughter,

9:3
l 1Ki 5:12

about all she had on her mind. [2] Solomon answered all her questions; nothing was too hard for him to explain to her. [3] When the queen of Sheba saw the wisdom of Solomon,*l* as well as the palace he had built, [4] the food on his table, the seating of his officials, the attending servants in their robes, the cupbearers in their robes and the burnt offerings he made at*a* the temple of the LORD, she was overwhelmed.

[5] She said to the king, "The report I heard in my own country about your achievements and your wisdom is true. [6] But I did not believe what they said until I came and saw with my own eyes. Indeed, not even half the greatness of your wisdom was told me; you have far exceeded the report I heard. [7] How happy your men must be! How happy your officials, who continually stand before you and hear your wisdom! [8] Praise be to the LORD your God, who has delighted in you and placed you on his throne*m* as king to rule for the LORD your God. Because of the love of your God for Israel and his desire to uphold them forever, he has made you king*n* over them, to maintain justice and righteousness."

9:8
m 1Ch 28:5; 29:23
n 2Ch 2:11

[9] Then she gave the king 120 talents*b* of gold, large quantities of spices, and precious stones. There had never been such spices as those the queen of Sheba gave to King Solomon.

9:10
o 2Ch 8:18

[10] (The men of Hiram and the men of Solomon brought gold from Ophir;*o* they also brought algumwood*c* and precious stones. [11] The king used the algumwood to make steps for the temple of the LORD and for the royal palace, and to make harps and lyres for the musicians. Nothing like them had ever been seen in Judah.)

[12] King Solomon gave the queen of Sheba all she desired and asked for; he gave her more than she had brought to him. Then she left and returned with her retinue to her own country.

Solomon's Splendor

[13] The weight of the gold that Solomon received yearly was 666 talents,*d* [14] not including the revenues brought in by merchants and traders. Also all the kings of Arabia and the governors of the land brought gold and silver to Solomon.

[15] King Solomon made two hundred large shields of hammered gold; six hundred bekas*e* of hammered gold went into each shield. [16] He also made three hundred small shields of hammered gold, with three hundred bekas*f* of gold in each shield. The king put them in the Palace of the Forest of Lebanon.

[17] Then the king made a great throne inlaid with ivory and overlaid with pure gold. [18] The throne had six steps, and a footstool of gold was attached to it. On both sides of the seat were armrests, with a lion standing beside each of them. [19] Twelve lions stood on the six steps, one at either end of each step. Nothing like it had ever been made for any other kingdom. [20] All King Solomon's goblets were gold, and all the household articles in the Palace of the Forest of Lebanon were pure gold. Nothing was made of silver, because silver was considered of little value in Solomon's day. [21] The king had a fleet of trading ships*g* manned by Hiram's*h* men. Once every three years it returned, carrying gold, silver and ivory, and apes and baboons.

9:22
p 1Ki 3:13; 2Ch 1:12

[22] King Solomon was greater in riches and wisdom than all the other kings of the earth.*p* [23] All the kings of the earth sought audience with Solomon to hear the wisdom God had put in his heart. [24] Year after year, everyone who came brought a gift—articles of silver and gold, and robes, weapons and spices, and horses and mules.

9:25
q 1Ki 4:26
9:26
r 1Ki 4:21
s Ge 15:18-21

[25] Solomon had four thousand stalls for horses and chariots,*q* and twelve thousand horses,*i* which he kept in the chariot cities and also with him in Jerusalem. [26] He ruled*r* over all the kings from the River*j* to the land of the Philistines, as far as the border of Egypt.*s* [27] The king made silver as common in Jerusalem as stones, and cedar as plentiful as sycamore-fig trees in the foothills. [28] Solomon's horses were imported from Egypt*k* and from all other countries.

*a*4 Or *the ascent by which he went up to*   *b*9 That is, about 4 1/2 tons (about 4 metric tons)   *c*10 Probably a variant of *almugwood*   *d*13 That is, about 25 tons (about 23 metric tons)   *e*15 That is, about 7 1/2 pounds (about 3.5 kilograms)   *f*16 That is, about 3 3/4 pounds (about 1.7 kilograms)   *g*21 Hebrew *of ships that could go to Tarshish*   *h*21 Hebrew *Huram*, a variant of *Hiram*   *i*25 Or *charioteers*   *j*26 That is, the Euphrates   *k*28 Or possibly *Muzur*, a region in Cilicia

---

he still sincerely tried to follow God at this stage in his life. When people get to know you and ask hard questions, will your responses reflect God? Your life can be a powerful witness; let others see God at work in you.

9:8 The queen of Sheba marveled at Solomon, claiming that God must love his people greatly to give them such a king. Israel greatly prospered during Solomon's reign, witnessing to God's power and love for his people. The good times show God's love

and faithfulness. But hard times come to believers, too, and our perseverance and steadfast hope during those times will demonstrate our love and faithfulness to God. How we live will help others see our love for God.

9:11 Algumwood was probably sandalwood, a smooth, red-colored wood that accepts a high polish. This beautiful wood was extremely expensive.

Solomon's Death

²⁹As for the other events of Solomon's reign, from beginning to end, are they not written in the records of Nathan the prophet, in the prophecy of Ahijah the Shilonite and in the visions of Iddo the seer concerning Jeroboam son of Nebat? ³⁰Solomon reigned in Jerusalem over all Israel forty years. ³¹Then he rested with his fathers and was buried in the city of David ᵗ his father. And Rehoboam his son succeeded him as king.

9:31
ᵗ 1Ki 2:10

B. THE KINGDOM OF JUDAH (10:1—36:23)

After Solomon's death, the northern tribes revolt, and we read little more about them in 2 Chronicles. The remainder of 2 Chronicles recounts the alternating periods of apostasy and reform in Judah. In the end, Judah would not turn from its sin, and the tragic result was a 70-year captivity in Babylon. Sin in our lives will also lead to judgment and devastation. Although God's judgment may seem slow, it is nevertheless certain.

1. The northern tribes revolt

Israel Rebels Against Rehoboam

10 Rehoboam went to Shechem, for all the Israelites had gone there to make him king. ²When Jeroboam son of Nebat heard this (he was in Egypt, where he had fled ᵘ from King Solomon), he returned from Egypt. ³So they sent for Jeroboam, and he and all Israel went to Rehoboam and said to him: ⁴"Your father put a heavy yoke on us, but now lighten the harsh labor and the heavy yoke he put on us, and we will serve you."

10:2
ᵘ 1Ki 11:40

⁵Rehoboam answered, "Come back to me in three days." So the people went away.

⁶Then King Rehoboam consulted the elders ᵛ who had served his father Solomon during his lifetime. "How would you advise me to answer these people?" he asked.

10:6
ᵛ Job 8:8-9

⁷They replied, "If you will be kind to these people and please them and give them a favorable answer, they will always be your servants."

⁸But Rehoboam rejected the advice the elders ʷ gave him and consulted the young men who had grown up with him and were serving him. ⁹He asked them, "What is your advice? How should we answer these people who say to me, 'Lighten the yoke your father put on us'?"

10:8
ʷ Pr 13:20

¹⁰The young men who had grown up with him replied, "Tell the people who have said to you, 'Your father put a heavy yoke on us, but make our yoke lighter'—tell them, 'My little finger is thicker than my father's waist. ¹¹My father laid on you a heavy yoke; I will make it even heavier. My father scourged you with whips; I will scourge you with scorpions.'"

¹²Three days later Jeroboam and all the people returned to Rehoboam, as the king had said, "Come back to me in three days." ¹³The king answered them harshly. Rejecting the advice of the elders, ¹⁴he followed the advice of the young men and said, "My father made your yoke heavy; I will make it even heavier. My father scourged you with whips; I will scourge you with scorpions." ¹⁵So the king did not listen to the people, for this turn of events was from God,ˣ to fulfill the word the Lord had spoken to Jeroboam son of Nebat through Ahijah the Shilonite.ʸ

10:15
ˣ 2Ch 25:16-20
ʸ 1Ki 11:29

¹⁶When all Israel saw that the king refused to listen to them, they answered the king:

10:16
ᶻ 2Sa 20:1

> "What share do we have in David,ᶻ
> what part in Jesse's son?
> To your tents, O Israel!
> Look after your own house, O David!"

9:29 For the rest of Solomon's story, see 1 Kings 10:26—11:43. In his later years, Solomon turned away from God and led the nation into worshiping idols.

10:1 The crowning of an Israelite king would normally have taken place in Jerusalem, the capital city. But Rehoboam saw that there was the possibility of trouble in the north; so to maintain his hold on the country, he chose Shechem, a city about 35 miles north of Jerusalem. Shechem was an ancient site for making covenants (Joshua 24:1).

10:1–15 Following bad advice can cause disaster. Rehoboam lost the chance to rule a peaceful, united kingdom because he rejected the advice of Solomon's older counselors, preferring the counsel of his peers. Rehoboam made two errors in seeking advice: (1) he did not give extra consideration to the suggestions of those who knew the situation better than he, and (2) he did not ask God for wisdom to discern which was the better option.

It is easy to follow the advice of our peers because they often feel as we do. But their view may be limited. It is important to listen carefully to those who have more experience than we do—they can see the bigger picture.

10:2, 3 Why was Jeroboam in Egypt? Ahijah the prophet had predicted that Israel would split in two and that Jeroboam would become king of the northern section. When Solomon learned of this prophecy, he tried to kill Jeroboam, and Jeroboam was forced to flee to Egypt (1 Kings 11:26–40).

10:14 Rehoboam must have gotten an unbalanced picture of leadership from his father, Solomon. Apparently Rehoboam saw only the difficulty of leading the nation, not the opportunities. He mentioned only the harsher aspects of Solomon's rule, and he himself decided to be very harsh toward the people. As you discuss your responsibilities with your children, be sure that you temper words of complaint with words of joy. Otherwise you

So all the Israelites went home. ¹⁷But as for the Israelites who were living in the towns of Judah, Rehoboam still ruled over them.

¹⁸King Rehoboam sent out Adoniram,ᵃ who was in charge of forced labor, but the Israelites stoned him to death. King Rehoboam, however, managed to get into his chariot and escape to Jerusalem. ¹⁹So Israel has been in rebellion against the house of David to this day.

11:1
ᵃ 1Ki 12:21

11 When Rehoboam arrived in Jerusalem,ᵃ he mustered the house of Judah and Benjamin—a hundred and eighty thousand fighting men—to make war against Israel and to regain the kingdom for Rehoboam.

11:2
ᵇ 2Ch 12:5-7, 15

²But this word of the LORD came to Shemaiah ᵇ the man of God: ³"Say to Rehoboam son of Solomon king of Judah and to all the Israelites in Judah and Benjamin, ⁴'This is what the LORD says: Do not go up to fight against your brothers. Go home, every one of you, for this is my doing.'" So they obeyed the words of the LORD and turned back from marching against Jeroboam.

ᵃ 18 Hebrew *Hadoram,* a variant of *Adoniram*

REHOBOAM

Settling for cheap imitations in exchange for the real thing is a poor way to live. In every area of his life, Rehoboam consistently traded away what was real for what was counterfeit. Given wise and unwise counsel by his advisers at his coronation, he chose to grab for power and control rather than to take patiently the counsel of those older and wiser than he and treat his people with kindness. Although his position came from God, he chose to abandon God. These unwise decisions made him weaker rather than stronger. As a result, he was invaded by the Egyptians and stripped of the riches he had inherited from David and Solomon. To replace them, he had cheap bronze copies made.

Throughout the early part of his reign, Rehoboam fluctuated between obeying God and going his own way. Outward appearances were kept up, but his inward attitudes were evil. Following in the tradition of David gave Rehoboam many opportunities for real greatness. Instead, he ended up with a divided and broken kingdom.

How much of real living have we traded away for the things that do not last? We trade healthy bodies for momentary excitement, personal integrity for fast-fading wealth, honesty for lies, God's wise guidance for our selfish ways. We sin when we willingly give little value to "the real thing" God has already given us.

Our counterfeit lives may fool some people, but they never fool God. Yet in spite of what he sees in us, God offers mercy. Are you a self-managed enterprise, counterfeit at best? Or have you placed yourself in God's care? Do the decisions you must make today need a second consideration in light of Rehoboam's example?

Strengths and accomplishments:	• Fourth and last king of the united nation of Israel, but only for a short time • Fortified his kingdom and achieved a measure of popularity
Weaknesses and mistakes:	• Followed unwise advice and divided his kingdom • Married foreign women, as his father, Solomon, had done • Abandoned the worship of God and allowed idolatry to flourish
Lessons from his life:	• Thoughtless decisions often lead to exchanging what is most valuable for something of far less value • Every choice we make has real and long-lasting consequences
Vital statistics:	• Where: Jerusalem • Occupation: King of the united kingdom of Israel, and later of the southern kingdom of Judah • Relatives: Father: Solomon. Mother: Naamah. Son: Abijah. Wife: Maacah. • Contemporaries: Jeroboam, Shishak, Shemaiah
Key verse:	"After Rehoboam's position as king was established and he had become strong, he and all Israel with him abandoned the law of the LORD" (2 Chronicles 12:1).

Rehoboam's story is told in 1 Kings 11:43—14:31 and 2 Chronicles 9:31—13:7. He is also mentioned in Matthew 1:7.

---

may sour their attitudes toward the work you do and those you serve.

10:16–19 In trying to have it all, Rehoboam lost almost everything. Motivated by greed and power, he pressed too hard and divided his kingdom. He didn't need more money or power because he had inherited the richest kingdom in the world. He didn't need more control because he was the king. His demands were based on selfishness rather than reason or spiritual

discernment. Those who insist on having it all often wind up with little or nothing.

10:16–19 This is the beginning of the divided kingdom. The peaceful united kingdom under Solomon divided into two parts. Ten of the tribes followed Jeroboam and called their nation Israel, or the northern kingdom. The other two tribes, Judah and Benjamin, remained loyal to David's line and accepted Rehoboam's rule. They called their nation Judah, or the southern kingdom.

Rehoboam Fortifies Judah

5 Rehoboam lived in Jerusalem and built up towns for defense in Judah: 6 Bethlehem, Etam, Tekoa, 7 Beth Zur, Soco, Adullam, 8 Gath, Mareshah, Ziph, 9 Adoraim, Lachish, Azekah, 10 Zorah, Aijalon and Hebron. These were fortified cities in Judah and Benjamin. 11 He strengthened their defenses and put commanders in them, with supplies of food, olive oil and wine. 12 He put shields and spears in all the cities, and made them very strong. So Judah and Benjamin were his.

13 The priests and Levites from all their districts throughout Israel sided with him. 14 The Levites *c* even abandoned their pasturelands and property, *d* and came to Judah and Jerusalem because Jeroboam and his sons had rejected them as priests of the LORD. 15 And he appointed *e* his own priests *f* for the high places and for the goat and calf idols he had made. 16 Those from every tribe of Israel *g* who set their hearts on seeking the LORD, the God of Israel, followed the Levites to Jerusalem to offer sacrifices to the LORD, the God of their fathers. 17 They strengthened *h* the kingdom of Judah and supported Rehoboam son of Solomon three years, walking in the ways of David and Solomon during this time.

11:14
c Nu 35:2-5
d 2Ch 13:9

11:15
e 1Ki 13:33
f 1Ki 12:31

11:16
g 2Ch 15:9

11:17
h 2Ch 12:1

2. History of apostasy and reform
Rehoboam's Family

18 Rehoboam married Mahalath, who was the daughter of David's son Jerimoth and of Abihail, the daughter of Jesse's son Eliab. 19 She bore him sons: Jeush, Shemariah and Zaham. 20 Then he married Maacah daughter of Absalom, who bore him Abijah, Attai, Ziza and Shelomith. 21 Rehoboam loved Maacah daughter of Absalom more than any of his other wives and concubines. In all, he had eighteen wives and sixty concubines, twenty-eight sons and sixty daughters.

22 Rehoboam appointed Abijah *i* son of Maacah to be the chief prince among his brothers, in order to make him king. 23 He acted wisely, dispersing some of his sons throughout the districts of Judah and Benjamin, and to all the fortified cities. He gave them abundant provisions and took many wives for them.

11:22
i Dt 21:15-17

Shishak Attacks Jerusalem

12 After Rehoboam's position as king was established and he had become strong, *j* he and all Israel *a* with him had abandoned the law of the LORD. 2 Because they had been unfaithful to the LORD, Shishak king of Egypt attacked Jerusalem in the fifth year of King Rehoboam. 3 With twelve hundred chariots and sixty thousand horsemen and the innumerable troops of Libyans, Sukkites and Cushites *b k* that came with him from Egypt, 4 he captured the fortified cities of Judah and came as far as Jerusalem.

12:1
j 2Ch 11:17

12:3
k 2Ch 16:8

a 1 That is, Judah, as frequently in 2 Chronicles   *b 3* That is, people from the upper Nile region

---

11:1 Rehoboam's foolishness divided his kingdom, and he tried to reunite it by force. True unity, however, cannot be forced—it must be the free response of willing hearts. If you want the loyalty of employees, children, or anyone else in your charge, win their respect through love instead of trying to gain their submission through force.

11:4 Why would God support this rebellion? It was part of the nation's punishment for turning away from God (1 Kings 11:11). It may also have been God's way of saving Rehoboam's smaller kingdom from defeat. In doing so, God preserved David's line and kept intact his plan for the Messiah to be a descendant of David (see 2 Samuel 7:16). When we see division, especially in a church that splits, we wonder what God would have us do. God desires unity, but while we should always work toward reconciliation, we must recognize that only God knows the future. He may allow a division in order to fulfill his greater purposes.

11:13, 14 Before the nation split, the center of worship was in Jerusalem, and people flocked there for the three great annual religious festivals. During the rest of the year, other worship services and rituals were conducted in the tribal territories by priests and Levites who lived throughout the land. They offered sacrifices, taught God's laws, and encouraged the people to continue to follow God and avoid pagan influences.
   After the nation split, Jeroboam, the new king of Israel, saw

these priests and Levites as threats to his new government because they retained loyalty to Jerusalem, now the capital of Judah. So he appointed his own priests, effectively banning the Levites from their duties and forcing them to move to the southern kingdom. Jeroboam's pagan priests encouraged idol worship. With the absence of spiritual leaders, the new northern kingdom was in danger of abandoning God.

11:16 These people obeyed God rather than Jeroboam. By their actions, they preserved their integrity and strengthened the southern kingdom. In the future, most of the people in the northern kingdom would go along with the evil designs of the kings, hoping to benefit by cooperating. Don't follow their example and rationalize away God's teachings in order to gain earthly reward.

12:1, 2 Here "Israel" refers to Judah, the southern kingdom. During his first three years on the throne, Rehoboam made an attempt to obey God, and as a result Judah prospered. But then, at his peak of popularity and power, he abandoned God. The result was destruction because God allowed Judah to be conquered by Egypt. How could this happen? Often it is more difficult to be a believer in good times than in bad. Tough times push us toward God; but easy times can make us feel self-sufficient and self-satisfied. When everything is going right, guard your faith closely.

12:2 A record of this invasion has been found on an Egyptian stone that says Shishak's army penetrated as far north as the Sea

12:5
l 2Ch 11:2

⁵Then the prophet Shemaiah *l* came to Rehoboam and to the leaders of Judah who had assembled in Jerusalem for fear of Shishak, and he said to them, "This is what the LORD says, 'You have abandoned me; therefore, I now abandon you to Shishak.'"

12:6
m Ex 9:27

12:7
n 1Ki 21:29

12:8
o Dt 28:48

⁶The leaders of Israel and the king humbled themselves and said, "The LORD is just." *m*

⁷When the LORD saw that they humbled themselves, this word of the LORD came to Shemaiah: "Since they have humbled themselves, I will not destroy them but will soon give them deliverance. *n* My wrath will not be poured out on Jerusalem through Shishak. ⁸They will, however, become subject *o* to him, so that they may learn the difference between serving me and serving the kings of other lands."

12:9
p 2Ch 9:16

⁹When Shishak king of Egypt attacked Jerusalem, he carried off the treasures of the temple of the LORD and the treasures of the royal palace. He took everything, including the gold shields *p* Solomon had made. ¹⁰So King Rehoboam made bronze shields to replace them and assigned these to the commanders of the guard on duty at the entrance to the royal palace. ¹¹Whenever the king went to the LORD's temple, the guards went with him, bearing the shields, and afterward they returned them to the guardroom.

12:12
q 2Ch 19:3

¹²Because Rehoboam humbled himself, the LORD's anger turned from him, and he was not totally destroyed. Indeed, there was some good *q* in Judah.

12:13
r Dt 12:5

¹³King Rehoboam established himself firmly in Jerusalem and continued as king. He was forty-one years old when he became king, and he reigned seventeen years in Jerusalem, the city the LORD had chosen out of all the tribes of Israel in which to put his Name. *r* His mother's name was Naamah; she was an Ammonite. ¹⁴He did evil because he had not set his heart on seeking the LORD.

12:15
s 2Ch 9:29

¹⁵As for the events of Rehoboam's reign, from beginning to end, are they not written in the records of Shemaiah *s* the prophet and of Iddo the seer that deal with genealogies? There was continual warfare between Rehoboam and Jeroboam. ¹⁶Rehoboam rested with his fathers and was buried in the City of David. And Abijah his son succeeded him as king.

Abijah King of Judah

13:2
t 2Ch 11:20

13 In the eighteenth year of the reign of Jeroboam, Abijah became king of Judah, ²and he reigned in Jerusalem three years. His mother's name was Maacah, *a* a daughter *b* of Uriel of Gibeah.

There was war between Abijah *t* and Jeroboam. ³Abijah went into battle with a force of four hundred thousand able fighting men, and Jeroboam drew up a battle line against him with eight hundred thousand able troops.

13:4
u Jos 18:22
v 1Ch 11:1

13:5
w 2Sa 7:13
x Nu 18:19

13:6
y 1Ki 11:26

⁴Abijah stood on Mount Zemaraim, *u* in the hill country of Ephraim, and said, "Jeroboam and all Israel, *v* listen to me! ⁵Don't you know that the LORD, the God of Israel, has given the kingship of Israel to David and his descendants forever *w* by a covenant of salt? *x* ⁶Yet Jeroboam son of Nebat, an official of Solomon son of David, rebelled *y* against his master. ⁷Some worthless scoundrels gathered around him and opposed Rehoboam son of Solomon when he was young and indecisive and not strong enough to resist them.

a 2 Most Septuagint manuscripts and Syriac (see also 2 Chron. 11:20 and 1 Kings 15:2); Hebrew *Micaiah*
b 2 Or *granddaughter*

---

of Galilee, in the northern kingdom. Egypt was not the world power it had once been, and Shishak wanted to restore his nation to its former greatness. He was not strong enough to conquer both Israel and Judah, but he managed to destroy key cities in Judah in an effort to regain control of the trade routes and strike terror among the people.

12:6–8 God eased his judgment when Israel's leaders confessed their sins, humbled themselves, and recognized God's justice in punishing them. It's never too late to repent, even in the midst of punishment. Regardless of what we have done, God is willing to receive us back into fellowship. Are you struggling and alone because sin has broken your fellowship with God? Confession and humility will open the door to receiving God's mercy.

12:8 "Serving the kings of other lands" was the price Judah had to pay for disobeying God. The nation's leaders thought they could succeed in their own strength, but they were wrong. When we rebel against God, we always pay for it. When we leave God out of our lives, we lose more spiritually than we ever gain financially.

12:10, 11 How ironic that the treasures in Solomon's temple

were removed and the missing royal shields were replaced by cheaper bronze. Rehoboam tried to maintain the trappings and appearance of former glory, but he couldn't measure up. When God is no longer central in our lives, maintaining the appearance of a Christian life becomes superficial. Outer beauty must come from inner strength.

12:14 Rehoboam's story is tragic because he "had not set his heart on seeking the LORD." How tragic a description of the grandson of David, who had been called a man after God's own heart (1 Samuel 13:14). It is dangerous to put off responding to God. God asks us for a firm commitment, and unless we respond by trusting him completely, we will find ourselves alienated from him.

13:1ff 1 Kings 15:3 says Abijah committed many sins, but the Chronicles account has only positive comments about him. For the most part, Abijah was, no doubt, a wicked king. The writer of Chronicles chose to highlight the little good he did in order to show that he was still under God's covenant promise to David. Because of Abijah's fiery speech to Jeroboam (13:4–12), he was spared the immediate consequences of his sin.

⁸"And now you plan to resist the kingdom of the Lord, which is in the hands of David's descendants. You are indeed a vast army and have with you the golden calves ᶻ that Jeroboam made to be your gods. ⁹But didn't you drive out the priests of the Lord,ᵃ the sons of Aaron, and the Levites, and make priests of your own as the peoples of other lands do? Whoever comes to consecrate himself with a young bull and seven rams may become a priest of what are not gods.

¹⁰"As for us, the Lord is our God, and we have not forsaken him. The priests who serve the Lord are sons of Aaron, and the Levites assist them. ¹¹Every morning and eveningᵇ they present burnt offerings and fragrant incense to the Lord. They set out the bread on the ceremonially clean tableᶜ and light the lamps on the gold lampstand every evening. We are observing the requirements of the Lord our God. But you have forsaken him. ¹²God is with us; he is our leader. His priests with their trumpets will sound the battle cry against you.ᵈ Men of Israel, do not fight against the Lord, the God of your fathers, for you will not succeed."

¹³Now Jeroboam had sent troops around to the rear, so that while he was in front of Judah the ambush was behind them. ¹⁴Judah turned and saw that they were being attacked at both front and rear. Then they cried out ᵉ to the Lord. The priests blew their trumpets ¹⁵and the men of Judah raised the battle cry. At the sound of their battle cry, God routed Jeroboam and all Israel before Abijah and Judah. ¹⁶The Israelites fled before Judah, and God delivered ᶠ them into their hands. ¹⁷Abijah and his men inflicted heavy losses on them, so that there were five hundred thousand casualties among Israel's able men. ¹⁸The men of Israel were subdued on that occasion, and the men of Judah were victorious because they reliedᵍ on the Lord, the God of their fathers.

¹⁹Abijah pursued Jeroboam and took from him the towns of Bethel, Jeshanah and Ephron, with their surrounding villages. ²⁰Jeroboam did not regain power during the time of Abijah. And the Lord struck him down and he died.

²¹But Abijah grew in strength. He married fourteen wives and had twenty-two sons and sixteen daughters.

²²The other events of Abijah's reign, what he did and what he said, are written in the annotations of the prophet Iddo.

14 And Abijah rested with his fathers and was buried in the City of David. Asa his son succeeded him as king, and in his days the country was at peace for ten years.

Asa King of Judah

²Asa did what was good and right in the eyes of the Lord his God. ³He removed the foreign altars and the high places, smashed the sacred stones and cut down the Asherah poles.ᵃ ʰ ⁴He commanded Judah to seek the Lord, the God of their fathers, and to obey his laws and commands. ⁵He removed the high places and incense altarsⁱ in every town in Judah, and the kingdom was at peace under him. ⁶He built up the fortified cities of Judah, since the land was at peace. No one was at war with him during those years, for the Lord gave him rest.

⁷"Let us build up these towns," he said to Judah, "and put walls around them, with towers,

ᵃ*3 That is, symbols of the goddess Asherah; here and elsewhere in 2 Chronicles*

13:8
ᶻ1Ki 12:28;
2Ch 11:15

13:9
ᵃ2Ch 11:14-15

13:11
ᵇ2Ch 2:4
ᶜLev 24:5-9

13:12
ᵈNu 10:8-9

13:14
ᵉ2Ch 14:11

13:16
ᶠ2Ch 16:8

13:18
ᵍPs 22:5

14:3
ʰEx 34:13;
1Ki 15:12-14

14:5
ⁱ2Ch 34:4, 7

13:8 Jeroboam's army was cursed because of the golden calves they carried with them. It was as though they had put sin into a physical form so they could haul it around. Consider carefully the things you cherish. If you value anything more than God, it becomes your golden calf and will one day drag you down. Let go of anything that interferes with your relationship with God.

13:9 Abijah criticized Jeroboam's low standards in appointing priests. Anyone is qualified to represent a god that is worthless. To represent the Lord God Almighty, however, a person must live by God's standards, not man's. Those appointed to positions of responsibility in your church should not be selected merely because they volunteer, are influential, or are highly educated. Instead they should demonstrate sound doctrine, dedication to God, and strong spiritual character (see 2 Timothy 3).

13:18, 19 Although outnumbered by Israel, Judah won this conflict by depending on God's help. Some kings in Judah's history focused on God, but not one Israelite king consistently followed God—all followed Jeroboam's idolatry or served Baal. As a result, Israel experienced God's punishment many years before Judah did.

Judah had an advantage—the temple, with its sacrifices and the loyal priests and prophets, was in the southern kingdom. Many of Judah's kings were good, at least for parts of their reigns. Whenever an idolatrous king reigned, his rule was later followed by that of a God-honoring king who reformed religious life. Also, the idolatrous kings usually served for a much shorter time than the good ones. The result was that true faith in God ran stronger and deeper in Judah than in Israel, but it was still not up to God's standards.

14:1–6 Asa's reign was marked by peace because he "did what was good and right in the eyes of the Lord his God." This refrain is often repeated in Chronicles—*obedience* to God leads to *peace* with God and others. In the case of Judah's kings, obedience to God led to national peace, just as God had promised centuries earlier. In our case, obedience may not always bring peace with our enemies, but it will bring peace with God and complete peace in his future kingdom. Obeying God is the first step on the path to peace.

14:3–5 Simply attending worship services is not enough to secure God's peace. Like Asa, we must also actively remove anything that is offensive to God. Becoming more active in church attendance or good deeds will still leave us in turmoil if we have failed to eliminate sinful practices from our lives. We should continually ask God to help us remove any source of temptation from our lives.

14:7 "Rest on every side" means that Judah had peace with all gates and bars. The land is still ours, because we have sought the LORD our God; we sought him and he has given us rest on every side." So they built and prospered.

[8]Asa had an army of three hundred thousand men from Judah, equipped with large shields and with spears, and two hundred and eighty thousand from Benjamin, armed with small shields and with bows. All these were brave fighting men.

[9]Zerah the Cushite[j] marched out against them with a vast army[a] and three hundred chariots, and came as far as Mareshah. [k] [10]Asa went out to meet him, and they took up battle positions in the Valley of Zephathah near Mareshah.

[11]Then Asa called[l] to the LORD his God and said, "LORD, there is no one like you to help the powerless against the mighty. Help us, O LORD our God, for we rely on you, and in your name[m] we have come against this vast army. O LORD, you are our God; do not let man prevail against you."

[12]The LORD struck down[n] the Cushites before Asa and Judah. The Cushites fled, [13]and Asa and his army pursued them as far as Gerar. [o] Such a great number of Cushites fell that they could not recover; they were crushed before the LORD and his forces. The men of Judah carried off a large amount of plunder. [14]They destroyed all the villages around Gerar, for the terror[p] of the LORD had fallen upon them. They plundered all these villages, since there was much booty there. [15]They also attacked the camps of the herdsmen and carried off droves of sheep and goats and camels. Then they returned to Jerusalem.

Asa's Reform

15 The Spirit of God came upon[q] Azariah son of Oded. [2]He went out to meet Asa and said to him, "Listen to me, Asa and all Judah and Benjamin. The LORD is with you[r] when you are with him. [s] If you seek him, he will be found by you, but if you forsake him, he will forsake you. [3]For a long time Israel was without the true God, without a priest to teach[t] and without the law. [4]But in their distress they turned to the LORD, the God of Israel, and sought him,[u] and he was found by them. [5]In those days it was not safe to travel about,[v] for all the inhabitants of the lands were in great turmoil. [6]One nation was being crushed by another and one city by another,[w] because God was troubling them with every kind of distress. [7]But as for you, be strong[x] and do not give up, for your work will be rewarded."

[a]9 Hebrew *with an army of a thousand thousands* or *with an army of thousands upon thousands*

**Margin references:**
14:9
j 2Ch 16:8
k 2Ch 11:8

14:11
l 2Ch 13:14
m 1Sa 17:45

14:12
n 2Ch 13:15
14:13
o Ge 10:19
14:14
p Ge 35:5

15:1
q 2Ch 20:14
15:2
r ver 4, 15
s Jas 4:8
15:3
t Lev 10:11
15:4
u Dt 4:29
15:5
v Jdg 5:6
15:6
w Mt 24:7
15:7
x Jos 1:7, 9

---

her neighbors. Times of peace are not just for resting. They allow us to prepare for times of trouble. King Asa recognized the period of peace as the right time to build his defenses—the moment of attack would be too late. It is also difficult to withstand spiritual attack unless defenses are prepared beforehand. Decisions about how to face temptations must be made with cool heads long before we feel the heat of temptation. Build your defenses now before temptation strikes.

14:11 If you are facing battles you feel you can't possibly win, don't give up. In the face of vast hordes of enemy soldiers, Asa prayed for God's help, recognizing his powerlessness against such a mighty army. The secret of victory is first to admit the futility of unaided human effort and then to trust God to save. His power works best through those who recognize their limitations (2 Corinthians 12:9). It is those who think they can do it all on their own who are in the greatest danger.

15:1, 2 Asa wisely welcomed people who had a close relationship with God, and he listened to their messages. Azariah gave the armies an important warning and encouraged them to stay close to God. Keep in contact with people who are filled with God's Spirit, and you will learn God's counsel. Spend regular time in discussion and prayer with those who can help explain and apply God's message.

15:3 Azariah said that Israel, the northern kingdom, was "without the true God." Eight kings reigned in Israel during the 41-year rule of Asa in Judah, and all eight were evil. Jeroboam, the first ruler of Israel, began this wicked trend by setting up idols and expelling God's priests (11:13–15). Azariah used Israel's problems as an example of the evil that would come to Judah if they turned away from God as their northern brothers and sisters had.

15:7 Azariah encouraged the men of Judah to keep up the good work, "for your work will be rewarded." This is an inspiration for

us too. Recognition and reward are great motivators that have two dimensions: (1) *The temporal dimension.* Living by God's standards may result in acclaim here on earth. (2) *The eternal dimension.* Permanent recognition and reward will be given in the next life. Don't be discouraged if you feel your faith in God is going unrewarded here on earth. The best rewards are not in this life but in the life to come.

ASA'S BATTLES
A huge army from Cush under Zerah advanced toward Mareshah, greatly outnumbering King Asa's army. Asa sent his troops to meet them, and the battle took place in the Valley of Zephathah. Asa prayed to God, and the Cushites were defeated and chased as far as Gerar.

8 When Asa heard these words and the prophecy of Azariah son of[a] Oded the prophet, he took courage. He removed the detestable idols from the whole land of Judah and Benjamin and from the towns he had captured[y] in the hills of Ephraim. He repaired the altar of the LORD that was in front of the portico of the LORD's temple.

9 Then he assembled all Judah and Benjamin and the people from Ephraim, Manasseh and Simeon who had settled among them, for large numbers[z] had come over to him from Israel when they saw that the LORD his God was with him.

10 They assembled at Jerusalem in the third month of the fifteenth year of Asa's reign. 11 At that time they sacrificed to the LORD seven hundred head of cattle and seven thousand sheep and goats from the plunder[a] they had brought back. 12 They entered into a covenant to seek the LORD, the God of their fathers, with all their heart and soul. 13 All who would not seek the LORD, the God of Israel, were to be put to death,[b] whether small or great, man or woman. 14 They took an oath to the LORD with loud acclamation, with shouting and with trumpets and horns. 15 All Judah rejoiced about the oath because they had sworn it wholeheartedly. They sought God eagerly, and he was found by them. So the LORD gave them rest on every side.

16 King Asa also deposed his grandmother Maacah from her position as queen mother, because she had made a repulsive Asherah pole.[c] Asa cut the pole down, broke it up and burned it in the Kidron Valley. 17 Although he did not remove the high places from Israel, Asa's heart was fully committed ⌊to the LORD⌋ all his life. 18 He brought into the temple of God the silver and gold and the articles that he and his father had dedicated.

19 There was no more war until the thirty-fifth year of Asa's reign.

Asa's Last Years

16 In the thirty-sixth year of Asa's reign Baasha[d] king of Israel went up against Judah and fortified Ramah to prevent anyone from leaving or entering the territory of Asa king of Judah.

2 Asa then took the silver and gold out of the treasuries of the LORD's temple and of his own palace and sent it to Ben-Hadad king of Aram, who was ruling in Damascus. 3 "Let there be a treaty between me and you," he said, "as there was between my father and your father. See, I am sending you silver and gold. Now break your treaty with Baasha king of Israel so he will withdraw from me."

4 Ben-Hadad agreed with King Asa and sent the commanders of his forces against the towns of Israel. They conquered Ijon, Dan, Abel Maim[b] and all the store cities of Naphtali. 5 When Baasha heard this, he stopped building Ramah and abandoned his work. 6 Then King Asa brought all the men of Judah, and they carried away from Ramah the stones and timber Baasha had been using. With them he built up Geba and Mizpah.

7 At that time Hanani[e] the seer came to Asa king of Judah and said to him: "Because you relied on the king of Aram and not on the LORD your God, the army of the king of Aram has escaped from your hand. 8 Were not the Cushites[c][f] and Libyans a mighty army with great numbers of chariots and horsemen[d]? Yet when you relied on the LORD, he delivered them into your hand. 9 For the eyes[g] of the LORD range throughout the earth to strengthen those whose hearts are fully committed to him. You have done a foolish[h] thing, and from now on you will be at war."

**Cross references (right margin):**
15:8 y 2Ch 13:19
15:9 z 2Ch 11:16-17
15:11 a 2Ch 14:13
15:13 b Ex 22:20; Dt 13:9-16
15:16 c Ex 34:13; 2Ch 14:2-5
16:1 d Jer 41:9
16:7 e 1Ki 16:1
16:8 f 2Ch 12:3
16:9 g Pr 15:3; Zec 4:10 h 1Sa 13:13

a8 Vulgate and Syriac (see also Septuagint and verse 1); Hebrew does not have *Azariah son of.*   b4 Also known as *Abel Beth Maacah*   c8 That is, people from the upper Nile region   d8 Or *charioteers*

15:14, 15 Many people find it difficult to commit themselves to anything. They are tentative, indecisive, and afraid of responsibility. Asa and his people were different—they had clearly declared themselves for God. Their oath of allegiance was punctuated with shouts and trumpet blasts! This decisive and wholehearted commitment pleased God and resulted in peace for the nation. If you want peace, check to see if there is some area where you lack total commitment to God. Peace comes as a by-product of giving your life wholeheartedly to God.

15:16 The Ten Commandments tell us to honor our fathers and mothers, and yet Asa removed his mother from the throne. While honoring parents is God's command, maintaining loyalty to God is an even higher priority. Jesus warned that respect for parents should never keep us from following him (Luke 14:26). If you

have unbelieving parents, you must respect and honor them, but you must make devotion to God an even higher priority.

16:7–10 Both Judah and Israel suffered from faithless forgetfulness! Although God had delivered them even when they were outnumbered (13:3ff; 14:9ff), they repeatedly sought help from pagan nations rather than from God. That Asa sought help from Aram was evidence of national spiritual decline. With help from God alone, Asa had defeated the Cushites in open battle. But his confidence in God had slipped, and now he sought only a human solution to his problem. When confronted by the prophet Hanani, Asa threw him in prison, revealing the true condition of his heart. It is not sin to use human means to solve our problems, but it is sin to trust them more than God, to think they are better than God's ways, or to leave God completely out of the problem-solving process.

¹⁰Asa was angry with the seer because of this; he was so enraged that he put him in prison. At the same time Asa brutally oppressed some of the people.

¹¹The events of Asa's reign, from beginning to end, are written in the book of the kings of Judah and Israel. ¹²In the thirty-ninth year of his reign Asa was afflicted with a disease in his feet. Though his disease was severe, even in his illness he did not seek help from the Lord,ʲ but only from the physicians. ¹³Then in the forty-first year of his reign Asa died and rested with his fathers. ¹⁴They buried him in the tomb that he had cut out for himself in the City of David. They laid him on a bier covered with spices and various blended perfumes,ʲ and they made a huge fireᵏ in his honor.

16:12
ʲJer 17:5-6

16:14
ʲGe 50:2
ᵏ2Ch 21:19

ASA

God has never accepted the idea that "the ends justify the means." He is just and perfect in all his ways. People, on the other hand, are far from perfect. That a bond can exist between a loving and merciful Creator and a resisting and rebellious creation is as great a miracle as creation itself! As a king, Asa came very close to being good. He traveled a long way with God before getting off track. His sin was not so much deliberate disobedience as choosing the *easy* way rather than the *right* way.

When the odds seemed impossible in the battle with the Cushites, Asa recognized his need to depend on God. Following that victory, God's promise of peace based on obedience spurred the king and people to many years of right living. But Asa was to face a tougher test. Years of animosity between Asa and Israel's king Baasha took an ugly turn. Baasha, king of the rival northern kingdom, was building a fort that threatened both the peace and the economy of Judah. Asa thought he saw a way out—he bribed King Ben-Hadad of Aram to break his alliance with King Baasha. The plan worked brilliantly, but it wasn't God's way. When Asa was confronted by God's prophet Hanani, he flew into a rage, jailed Hanani, and took out his anger on his people. Asa rejected correction and refused to admit his error to God. His greatest failure was missing what God could have done with his life if he had been willing to be humble. His pride ruined the health of his reign. He stubbornly held on to his failure until his death.

Does this attitude sound familiar? Can you identify failures in your life that you have continued to rationalize rather than admit them to God and accept his forgiveness? The ends do not justify the means. Such a belief leads to sin and failure. The stubborn refusal to admit a failure due to sin can become a big problem because it makes you spend time rationalizing rather than learning from your mistakes and moving on.

Strengths and accomplishments:	• Obeyed God during the first ten years of his reign • Carried out a partially successful effort to abolish idolatry • Deposed his idolatrous mother Maacah • Defeated Cush's mighty army
Weaknesses and mistakes:	• Responded with rage when confronted about his sin • Made alliances with foreign nations and evil people
Lessons from his life:	• God not only reinforces good, he confronts evil • Efforts to follow God's plans and rules yield positive results • How well a plan works is no measure of its rightness or approval by God
Vital statistics:	• Where: Jerusalem • Occupation: King of Judah • Relatives: Mother: Maacah. Father: Abijah. Son: Jehoshaphat. • Contemporaries: Hanani, Ben-Hadad, Zerah, Azariah, Baasha
Key verse:	"For the eyes of the Lord range throughout the earth to strengthen those whose hearts are fully committed to him. You have done a foolish thing, and from now on you will be at war" (2 Chronicles 16:9).

Asa's story is told in 1 Kings 15:8–24 and 2 Chronicles 14—16. He is also mentioned in Jeremiah 41:9; Matthew 1:7.

16:12 The criticism of Asa's visit to the physicians was not a general indictment of medicine. Asa's problem was that he completely ignored God's help. The medicine practiced at this time was a mixture of superstition and folk remedies. We should certainly avoid any pseudo-medical treatment derived from occult sources. Asa's experience should also encourage us to follow the New Testament practice of receiving prayer for our sickness (James 5:14) as we seek responsible medical help.

16:14 A bier is the stand or platform on which a coffin or corpse is placed.

Jehoshaphat King of Judah

17 Jehoshaphat his son succeeded him as king and strengthened himself against Israel. ²He stationed troops in all the fortified cities of Judah and put garrisons in Judah and in the towns of Ephraim that his father Asa had captured. *l*

³The LORD was with Jehoshaphat because in his early years he walked in the ways his father David had followed. He did not consult the Baals ⁴but sought *m* the God of his father and followed his commands rather than the practices of Israel. ⁵The LORD established the kingdom under his control; and all Judah brought gifts to Jehoshaphat, so that he had great wealth and honor. *n* ⁶His heart was devoted *o* to the ways of the LORD; furthermore, he removed the high places*p* and the Asherah poles from Judah.

⁷In the third year of his reign he sent his officials Ben-Hail, Obadiah, Zechariah, Nethanel and Micaiah to teach *q* in the towns of Judah. ⁸With them were certain Levites *r*— Shemaiah, Nethaniah, Zebadiah, Asahel, Shemiramoth, Jehonathan, Adonijah, Tobijah and Tob-Adonijah—and the priests Elishama and Jehoram. ⁹They taught throughout Judah, taking with them the Book of the Law *s* of the LORD; they went around to all the towns of Judah and taught the people.

¹⁰The fear *t* of the LORD fell on all the kingdoms of the lands surrounding Judah, so that they did not make war with Jehoshaphat. ¹¹Some Philistines brought Jehoshaphat gifts and silver as tribute, and the Arabs *u* brought him flocks: seven thousand seven hundred rams and seven thousand seven hundred goats.

¹²Jehoshaphat became more and more powerful; he built forts and store cities in Judah ¹³and had large supplies in the towns of Judah. He also kept experienced fighting men in Jerusalem. ¹⁴Their enrollment by families was as follows:

From Judah, commanders of units of 1,000:
Adnah the commander, with 300,000 fighting men;
¹⁵ next, Jehohanan the commander, with 280,000;
¹⁶ next, Amasiah son of Zicri, who volunteered *v* himself for the service of the LORD, with 200,000.
¹⁷ From Benjamin:
Eliada, a valiant soldier, with 200,000 men armed with bows and shields;
¹⁸ next, Jehozabad, with 180,000 men armed for battle.

¹⁹These were the men who served the king, besides those he stationed in the fortified cities throughout Judah.

Micaiah Prophesies Against Ahab

18 Now Jehoshaphat had great wealth and honor, *w* and he allied himself with Ahab by marriage. ²Some years later he went down to visit Ahab in Samaria. Ahab slaughtered many sheep and cattle for him and the people with him and urged him to attack Ramoth Gilead. ³Ahab king of Israel asked Jehoshaphat king of Judah, "Will you go with me against Ramoth Gilead?"

**Margin references:**
17:2 *l* 2Ch 15:8
17:4 *m* 1Ki 12:28; 2Ch 22:9
17:5 *n* 2Ch 18:1
17:6 *o* 2Ch 15:17 *p* 2Ch 19:3; 20:33
17:7 *q* 2Ch 15:3
17:8 *r* 2Ch 19:8
17:9 *s* Dt 6:4-9
17:10 *t* Ge 35:5; 2Ch 14:14
17:11 *u* 2Ch 9:14; 26:8
17:16 *v* Jdg 5:9; 1Ch 29:9
18:1 *w* 2Ch 17:5

17:7–9 The people of Judah were Biblically illiterate. They had never taken time to listen to and discuss God's law and understand how it could change them. Jehoshaphat realized that knowing God's commands was the first step to getting people to live as they should, so he initiated a nationwide religious education program. He reversed the religious decline that had occurred at the end of Asa's reign by putting God first in the people's minds and instilling in them a sense of commitment and mission. Because of this action, the nation began to follow God. Churches and Christian schools today need solid Christian education programs. Exposure to good Bible teaching through church school, church, Bible study, and personal and family devotions is essential for living as God intended.

18:1ff Although Jehoshaphat was deeply committed to God, he arranged for his son to marry Athaliah, the daughter of wicked King Ahab of Israel, and then made a military alliance with him. Jehoshaphat's popularity and power made him attractive to the cunning and opportunistic Ahab. This alliance had three devastating consequences: (1) Jehoshaphat incurred God's wrath (19:2);

(2) when Jehoshaphat died and Athaliah became queen, she seized the throne and almost destroyed all of David's descendants (22:10–12); (3) Athaliah brought the evil practices of Israel into Judah, which eventually led to the nation's downfall.

When believers in leadership positions become allied with unbelievers, values can be compromised and spiritual awareness dulled. The Bible often warns against teaming with unbelievers (2 Corinthians 6:14). (See the note on 20:37 for more on alliances.)

18:3–8 Evil kings did not like God's prophets bringing messages of doom (18:17; Jeremiah 5:13). Many, therefore, hired prophets who told them only what they wanted to hear (Isaiah 30:10, 11; Jeremiah 14:13–16; 23:16, 21, 30–36). These men were false prophets because they extolled the greatness of the king and predicted victory regardless of the real situation.

18:3–8 Wicked Ahab asked Jehoshaphat to join forces with him in battle (18:2, 3). Before making that commitment, Jehoshaphat rightly sought God's advice. However, when God gave his answer through the prophet Micaiah (18:16), Jehoshaphat ignored it (18:28). It does us no good to seek God's advice if we ignore it

Jehoshaphat replied, "I am as you are, and my people as your people; we will join you in the war." ⁴But Jehoshaphat also said to the king of Israel, "First seek the counsel of the Lᴏʀᴅ."

⁵So the king of Israel brought together the prophets—four hundred men—and asked them, "Shall we go to war against Ramoth Gilead, or shall I refrain?"

"Go," they answered, "for God will give it into the king's hand."

⁶But Jehoshaphat asked, "Is there not a prophet of the Lᴏʀᴅ here whom we can inquire of?"

⁷The king of Israel answered Jehoshaphat, "There is still one man through whom we can inquire of the Lᴏʀᴅ, but I hate him because he never prophesies anything good about me, but always bad. He is Micaiah son of Imlah."

"The king should not say that," Jehoshaphat replied.

⁸So the king of Israel called one of his officials and said, "Bring Micaiah son of Imlah at once."

JEHOSHAPHAT

Are children more likely to learn from their parents' mistakes or to simply repeat them? In the lives of the people in the Bible, we find that the effects of parental examples are powerful and long-lasting. For much of his life, Jehoshaphat seems to have been a son who learned from his father Asa's mistakes and followed his positive actions. But on several occasions, his decisions reveal the negative aspects of his father's example.

When the challenges were obvious, like the need for religious education of the people or the threat of war with a vast army, Jehoshaphat turned to God for guidance and made the right choices. His dependence on God was consistent when the odds were clearly against him. It was in depending on God for the day-to-day plans and actions that Jehoshaphat was weak. He allowed his son to marry Athaliah, the daughter of the wicked Ahab and Jezebel of Israel, who did her best to be as evil as her parents. Jehoshaphat was almost killed when, without asking God, he made an alliance with Ahab. Later, he got involved in an unwise ship-building venture with Ahab's son, Ahaziah—a venture that was shipwrecked by God.

God's faithfulness when the issues are clear and the enemy overwhelming is more than enough reason to seek his guidance when the issues are unclear and the enemy unseen. Jehoshaphat knew this, yet he made little use of that knowledge.

We repeat Jehoshaphat's error when we relegate God to the background in the "easy" decisions of life. Then, when things get out of hand, we want him to get us out of the mess we got ourselves into. God wants us to give him not only the major decisions, but also our daily lives—the things we are most often fooled into believing we can control. Perhaps there is nothing major facing you today. Have you paused long enough to give your day to God anyway?

Strengths and accomplishments:	• A bold follower of God, he reminded the people of the early years of his father, Asa • Carried out a national program of religious education • Had many military victories • Developed an extensive legal structure throughout the kingdom
Weaknesses and mistakes:	• Failed to recognize the long-term results of his decisions • Did not completely destroy idolatry in the land • Became entangled with evil King Ahab through alliances • Allowed his son Jehoram to marry Athaliah, Ahab's daughter • Became Ahaziah's business partner in an ill-fated shipping venture
Vital statistics:	• Where: Jerusalem • Occupation: King of Judah • Relatives: Father: Asa. Mother: Azubah. Son: Jehoram. Daughter-in-law: Athaliah. • Contemporaries: Ahab, Jezebel, Micaiah, Ahaziah, Jehu
Key verses:	"He walked in the ways of his father Asa and did not stray from them; he did what was right in the eyes of the Lord. The high places, however, were not removed, and the people still had not set their hearts on the God of their fathers" (2 Chronicles 20:32, 33).

Jehoshaphat's story is told in 1 Kings 15:24—22:50 and 2 Chronicles 17:1—21:1. He is also mentioned in 2 Kings 3:1–14 and Joel 3:2, 12.

when it is given. Real love for God is shown not by merely asking for direction, but by following that direction once it is given.

18:5–16 When you want to please or impress someone, it is tempting to lie to make yourself look good. Ahab's 400 prophets did just that, telling Ahab only what he wanted to hear. They were then rewarded for making Ahab happy. Micaiah, however, told the truth and got arrested (18:25, 26). Obeying God doesn't always protect us from evil consequences. Obedience may, in fact, provoke them. But it is better to suffer from people's displeasure than from God's wrath (Matthew 10:28). If you are ridiculed for being honest, remember that this can be a sign that you are indeed doing what is right in God's eyes (Matthew 5:10–12; Romans 8:17, 35–39).

9 Dressed in their royal robes, the king of Israel and Jehoshaphat king of Judah were sitting on their thrones at the threshing floor by the entrance to the gate of Samaria, with all the prophets prophesying before them. 10 Now Zedekiah son of Kenaanah had made iron horns, and he declared, "This is what the LORD says: 'With these you will gore the Arameans until they are destroyed.'"

11 All the other prophets were prophesying the same thing. "Attack Ramoth Gilead× and be victorious," they said, "for the LORD will give it into the king's hand."

12 The messenger who had gone to summon Micaiah said to him, "Look, as one man the other prophets are predicting success for the king. Let your word agree with theirs, and speak favorably."

13 But Micaiah said, "As surely as the LORD lives, I can tell him only what my God says."ʸ

14 When he arrived, the king asked him, "Micaiah, shall we go to war against Ramoth Gilead, or shall I refrain?"

"Attack and be victorious," he answered, "for they will be given into your hand."

18:11
×2Ch 22:5

18:13
ʸNu 22:18, 20, 35

BIBLE

The Persecuted	The Persecutors	Why the Persecution	Result	Reference
Isaac	The Philistines	God was blessing Isaac, and they envied him	The Philistines could not subdue Isaac, so they made peace with him	Genesis 26:12–33
Moses	Israelites	The Israelites wanted water	God provided water, in answer to Moses' prayer	Exodus 17:1–7
David	Saul and others	David was becoming a powerful leader, threatening Saul's position as king	David endured the persecution and became king	1 Samuel 20—27 Psalms 31:13; 59:1–4
Priests of Nob	Saul and Doeg	Saul and Doeg thought the priests helped David escape	85 priests were killed	1 Samuel 22
Prophets	Jezebel	Jezebel didn't like to have her evil ways pointed out	Many prophets were killed	1 Kings 18:3, 4
Elijah	Ahab and Jezebel	Elijah confronted their sins	Elijah had to flee for his life	1 Kings 18:10—19:2
Micaiah	Ahab	Ahab thought Micaiah was stirring up trouble rather than prophesying from God	Micaiah was thrown into prison	2 Chronicles 18:12–26
Elisha	A king of Israel (probably Joram)	The king thought Elisha had caused the famine	Elisha ignored the threatened persecution and prophesied the famine's end	2 Kings 6:31
Hanani	Asa	Hanani criticized Asa for trusting in Aram's help more than in God's help	Hanani was thrown in prison	2 Chronicles 16:7–10
Zechariah	Joash	Zechariah confronted the people of Judah for disregarding God's commands	Zechariah was executed	2 Chronicles 24:20–22
Uriah	Jehoiakim	Uriah confronted Jehoiakim about his evil ways	Uriah was killed with a sword	Jeremiah 26:20–23
Jeremiah	Zedekiah	Zedekiah thought Jeremiah was a traitor for prophesying Jerusalem's fall	Jeremiah was thrown in prison, then into a muddy cistern	Jeremiah 37:1—38:13
Shadrach, Meshach, Abednego	Nebuchadnezzar	The three men refused to bow down to anyone but God	They were thrown into a fiery furnace, but God miraculously saved them	Daniel 3

18:16
z Nu 27:17

18:21
a Job 1:6; Jn 8:44

15The king said to him, "How many times must I make you swear to tell me nothing but the truth in the name of the LORD?"

16Then Micaiah answered, "I saw all Israel scattered on the hills like sheep without a shepherd,z and the LORD said, 'These people have no master. Let each one go home in peace.'"

17The king of Israel said to Jehoshaphat, "Didn't I tell you that he never prophesies anything good about me, but only bad?"

18Micaiah continued, "Therefore hear the word of the LORD: I saw the LORD sitting on his throne with all the host of heaven standing on his right and on his left. 19And the LORD said, 'Who will entice Ahab king of Israel into attacking Ramoth Gilead and going to his death there?'

"One suggested this, and another that. 20Finally, a spirit came forward, stood before the LORD and said, 'I will entice him.'

"'By what means?' the LORD asked.

21"'I will go and be a lying spirita in the mouths of all his prophets,' he said.

PERSECUTIONS

The Persecuted	The Persecutors	Why the Persecution	Result	Reference
Daniel	National leaders	Daniel was praying	Daniel was thrown into a den of lions, but God miraculously saved him	Daniel 6
Job	Satan	Satan wanted to prove that pain and suffering would make a person abandon God	Job remained faithful to God and was restored	Job 1:8–12; 2:3–7
John the Baptist	Herod and Herodias	John confronted King Herod's adultery	John was beheaded	Matthew 14:3–13
Jesus	Religious leaders	Jesus exposed their sinful motives	Jesus was crucified, but rose again from the dead to show his authority over all evil	Mark 7:1–16; Luke 22:63—24:7
Peter and John	Religious leaders	Peter and John preached that Jesus was God's Son and the only way to salvation	They were thrown into prison, but later released	Acts 4:1–31
Stephen	Religious leaders	Stephen exposed their guilt in crucifying Jesus	Stephen was stoned to death	Acts 6—7
The church	Paul and others	The Christians preached Jesus as the Messiah	Believers faced death, prison, torture, exile	Acts 8:1–3; 9:1–9
James	Herod Agrippa I	To please the Jewish leaders	James was executed	Acts 12:1, 2
Peter	Herod Agrippa I	To please the Jewish leaders	Peter was thrown into prison	Acts 12:3–17
Paul	Jews, city officials	Paul preached about Jesus and confronted those who made money by manipulating others	Paul was stoned; thrown into prison	Acts 14:19; 16:16–24
Timothy	Unknown	Unknown	Timothy was thrown into prison	Hebrews 13:23
John	Probably the Romans	John told others about Jesus	John was sent into exile on a remote island	Revelation 1:9

Micaiah, like thousands of believers before and after him, was persecuted for his faith. The chart shows that persecution comes from a variety of people and is given in a variety of ways. Sometimes God protects us from it; sometimes he doesn't. But as long as we remain faithful to God *alone*, we must expect persecution (see also Luke 6:22; 2 Corinthians 6:4–10; 2 Timothy 2:9–12; Revelation 2:10). God also seems to have a special reward for those who endure such persecution (Revelation 6:9–11; 20:4).

"'You will succeed in enticing him,' said the LORD. 'Go and do it.'

22 "So now the LORD has put a lying spirit in the mouths of these prophets of yours. *b* The LORD has decreed disaster for you."

23 Then Zedekiah son of Kenaanah went up and slapped *c* Micaiah in the face. "Which way did the spirit from *a* the LORD go when he went from me to speak to you?" he asked.

24 Micaiah replied, "You will find out on the day you go to hide in an inner room."

25 The king of Israel then ordered, "Take Micaiah and send him back to Amon the ruler of the city and to Joash the king's son, 26 and say, 'This is what the king says: Put this fellow in prison *d* and give him nothing but bread and water until I return safely.'"

27 Micaiah declared, "If you ever return safely, the LORD has not spoken through me." Then he added, "Mark my words, all you people!"

Ahab Killed at Ramoth Gilead

28 So the king of Israel and Jehoshaphat king of Judah went up to Ramoth Gilead. 29 The king of Israel said to Jehoshaphat, "I will enter the battle in disguise, but you wear your royal robes." So the king of Israel disguised himself and went into battle.

30 Now the king of Aram had ordered his chariot commanders, "Do not fight with anyone, small or great, except the king of Israel." 31 When the chariot commanders saw Jehoshaphat, they thought, "This is the king of Israel." So they turned to attack him, but Jehoshaphat cried out, *e* and the LORD helped him. God drew them away from him, 32 for when the chariot commanders saw that he was not the king of Israel, they stopped pursuing him.

33 But someone drew his bow at random and hit the king of Israel between the sections of his armor. The king told the chariot driver, "Wheel around and get me out of the fighting. I've been wounded." 34 All day long the battle raged, and the king of Israel propped himself up in his chariot facing the Arameans until evening. Then at sunset he died.

19 When Jehoshaphat king of Judah returned safely to his palace in Jerusalem, 2 Jehu the seer, the son of Hanani, went out to meet him and said to the king, "Should you help the wicked and love *b* those who hate the LORD? *f* Because of this, the wrath *g* of the LORD is upon you. 3 There is, however, some good *h* in you, for you have rid the land of the Asherah poles *i* and have set your heart on seeking God."

Jehoshaphat Appoints Judges

4 Jehoshaphat lived in Jerusalem, and he went out again among the people from Beersheba to the hill country of Ephraim and turned them back to the LORD, the God of their fathers.

a 23 Or Spirit of b 2 Or and make alliances with

18:22 Job 12:16; Eze 14:9
18:23 Jer 20:2; Mk 14:65; Ac 23:2
18:26 2Ch 16:10
18:31 2Ch 13:14
19:2 Ps 139:21-22; 2Ch 32:25
19:3 2Ch 12:12; 2Ch 17:6

18:22 God used the seductive influence of false prophets to judge Ahab. They were determined to tell Ahab what he wanted to hear. God confirmed their plans to lie as a means to remove Ahab from the throne. These prophets, supported by Ahab, snared him in his sin. Because he listened to them instead of God, he was killed in battle. The lying spirit is a picture of the prophets' entire way of life—telling the king only what he wanted to hear, not what he needed to hear. Leaders will only find trouble if they surround themselves with advisers whose only thought is to please them.

BATTLE WITH ARAM
King Jehoshaphat made an alliance with evil King Ahab of Israel. Together they decided to attack Ramoth Gilead and rout the Arameans who had occupied the city. But Jehoshaphat first wanted to seek the advice of a prophet. Ahab's prophets predicted victory, but Micaiah predicted defeat. The two kings were defeated, and Ahab was killed.

18:31 Jehoshaphat's troubles began when he joined forces with the evil King Ahab. Almost at once he found himself the target for soldiers who mistakenly identified him as Ahab. He could have accepted this fate because he deserved it, but instead he cried out to God, who miraculously saved him. When we sin and the inevitable consequences follow, we may be tempted to give up. "I chose to sin," we may think, "it's my fault, and I must accept the consequences." While we may deserve what comes to us, that is no reason to avoid calling on God for urgent help. Had Jehoshaphat given up, he might have died. No matter how greatly you have sinned, you can still call upon God.

18:33 Micaiah prophesied death for Ahab (18:16, 27), so Ahab disguised himself to fool the enemy. Apparently the disguise worked, but that didn't change the prophecy. A random Aramean arrow found a crack in his armor and killed him. God fulfills his will despite the defenses people try to erect. God can use anything, even an error, to bring his will to pass. This is good news for God's followers because we can trust him to work his plans and keep his promises no matter how desperate our circumstances are.

19:6
/Dt 1:17; 16:18-20;
17:8-13
19:7
kGe 18:25
/Dt 10:17
19:8
m2Ch 17:8-9
19:10
nDt 17:8-13
19:11
o1Ch 28:20

⁵He appointed judges in the land, in each of the fortified cities of Judah. ⁶He told them, "Consider carefully what you do, because you are not judging for man/ but for the LORD, who is with you whenever you give a verdict. ⁷Now let the fear of the LORD be upon you. Judge carefully, for with the LORD our God there is no injustice k or partiality / or bribery."

⁸In Jerusalem also, Jehoshaphat appointed some of the Levites, priests and heads of Israelite families to administer m the law of the LORD and to settle disputes. And they lived in Jerusalem. ⁹He gave them these orders: "You must serve faithfully and wholeheartedly in the fear of the LORD. ¹⁰In every case that comes before you from your fellow countrymen who live in the cities—whether bloodshed or other concerns of the law, commands, decrees or ordinances—you are to warn them not to sin against the LORD; n otherwise his wrath will come on you and your brothers. Do this, and you will not sin.

¹¹"Amariah the chief priest will be over you in any matter concerning the LORD, and Zebadiah son of Ishmael, the leader of the tribe of Judah, will be over you in any matter concerning the king, and the Levites will serve as officials before you. Act with courage, o and may the LORD be with those who do well."

Jehoshaphat Defeats Moab and Ammon

20 After this, the Moabites and Ammonites with some of the Meunites a came to make war on Jehoshaphat.

20:2
pGe 14:7
20:3
q2Ch 19:3

²Some men came and told Jehoshaphat, "A vast army is coming against you from Edom, b from the other side of the Sea. c It is already in Hazazon Tamar p" (that is, En Gedi). ³Alarmed, Jehoshaphat resolved to inquire of the LORD, and he proclaimed a fast q for all Judah. ⁴The people of Judah came together to seek help from the LORD; indeed, they came from every town in Judah to seek him.

⁵Then Jehoshaphat stood up in the assembly of Judah and Jerusalem at the temple of the LORD in the front of the new courtyard ⁶and said:

20:6
rDt 4:39
s1Ch 29:11-12
20:7
tIsa 41:8

"O LORD, God of our fathers, are you not the God who is in heaven? r You rule over all the kingdoms s of the nations. Power and might are in your hand, and no one can withstand you. ⁷O our God, did you not drive out the inhabitants of this land before your people Israel and give it forever to the descendants of Abraham your friend? t ⁸They have lived in it and have built in it a sanctuary for your Name, saying, ⁹'If calamity comes upon us, whether the sword of judgment, or plague or famine, we will stand in your presence before this temple that bears your Name and will cry out to you in our distress, and you will hear us and save us.'

20:10
uNu 20:14-21
20:11
vPs 83:1-12
20:12
wJdg 11:27
xPs 25:15

¹⁰"But now here are men from Ammon, Moab and Mount Seir, whose territory you would not allow Israel to invade when they came from Egypt; u so they turned away from them and did not destroy them. ¹¹See how they are repaying us by coming to drive us out of the possession v you gave us as an inheritance. ¹²O our God, will you not judge them? w For we have no power to face this vast army that is attacking us. We do not know what to do, but our eyes are upon you. x"

a 1 Some Septuagint manuscripts; Hebrew *Ammonites*   b 2 One Hebrew manuscript; most Hebrew manuscripts, Septuagint and Vulgate *Aram*   c 2 That is, the Dead Sea

---

19:5–10 Jehoshaphat delegated some of the responsibilities for ruling and judging the people, but he warned his appointees that they were accountable to God for the standards they used to judge others. Jehoshaphat's advice is helpful for all leaders: (1) realize you are judging for God (19:6); (2) be impartial and honest (19:7); (3) be faithful (19:9); (4) act only out of fear of God, not people (19:9). God holds us accountable for the authority we exercise.

19:8 Jehoshaphat appointed priests and Levites to help in administering civil laws. Many years earlier, Moses had chosen men who were capable, faithful, and honest to help him judge disputes among the people (Exodus 18:21, 22). Obviously the best kind of leader is one who always acts with reverence for God. Effective leaders get the job done; faithful leaders make sure the job is done in God's way with God's timing. They are careful to instill God's wisdom in future leaders and build God's values into the entire community.

20:3 When the nation was faced with disaster, Jehoshaphat called upon the people to get serious with God by going without

food (fasting) for a designated time. By separating themselves from the daily routine of food preparation and eating, they could devote that extra time to considering their sin and praying to God for help. Hunger pangs would reinforce their feelings of penitence and remind them of their weakness and their dependence upon God. Fasting still can be helpful today as we seek God's will in special situations.

20:6ff Jehoshaphat's prayer had several essential ingredients. (1) He committed the situation to God, acknowledging that only God could save the nation. (2) He sought God's favor because his people were God's people. (3) He acknowledged God's sovereignty over the current situation. (4) He praised God's glory and took comfort in his promises. (5) He professed complete dependence on God, not himself, for deliverance. To be God's kind of leader today, follow Jehoshaphat's example—focus entirely on God's power rather than your own.

13All the men of Judah, with their wives and children and little ones, stood there before the LORD.

14Then the Spirit y of the LORD came upon Jahaziel son of Zechariah, the son of Benaiah, the son of Jeiel, the son of Mattaniah, a Levite and descendant of Asaph, as he stood in the assembly.

20:14
y 2Ch 15:1

15He said: "Listen, King Jehoshaphat and all who live in Judah and Jerusalem! This is what the LORD says to you: 'Do not be afraid or discouraged z because of this vast army. For the battle a is not yours, but God's. 16Tomorrow march down against them. They will be climbing up by the Pass of Ziz, and you will find them at the end of the gorge in the Desert of Jeruel. 17You will not have to fight this battle. Take up your positions; stand firm and see b the deliverance the LORD will give you, O Judah and Jerusalem. Do not be afraid; do not be discouraged. Go out to face them tomorrow, and the LORD will be with you.'"

20:15
z 2Ch 32:7
a 1Sa 17:47

20:17
b Ex 14:13

18Jehoshaphat bowed with his face to the ground, and all the people of Judah and Jerusalem fell down in worship before the LORD. 19Then some Levites from the Kohathites and Korahites stood up and praised the LORD, the God of Israel, with a very loud voice.

20Early in the morning they left for the Desert of Tekoa. As they set out, Jehoshaphat stood and said, "Listen to me, Judah and people of Jerusalem! Have faith c in the LORD your God and you will be upheld; have faith in his prophets and you will be successful." 21After consulting the people, Jehoshaphat appointed men to sing to the LORD and to praise him for the splendor of his a holiness d as they went out at the head of the army, saying:

20:20
c Isa 7:9

20:21
d 1Ch 16:29

> "Give thanks to the LORD,
>   for his love endures forever."

22As they began to sing and praise, the LORD set ambushes e against the men of Ammon and Moab and Mount Seir who were invading Judah, and they were defeated. 23The men of Ammon and Moab rose up against the men from Mount Seir to destroy and annihilate them. After they finished slaughtering the men from Seir, they helped to destroy one another. f

20:22
e 2Ch 13:13

20:23
f Jdg 7:22;
1Sa 14:20

24When the men of Judah came to the place that overlooks the desert and looked toward the vast army, they saw only dead bodies lying on the ground; no one had escaped. 25So Jehoshaphat and his men went to carry off their plunder, and they found among them a great amount of equipment and clothing b and also articles of value—more than they could take away. There was so much plunder that it took three days to collect it. 26On the fourth day they assembled in the Valley of Beracah, where they praised the LORD. This is why it is called the Valley of Beracah c to this day.

27Then, led by Jehoshaphat, all the men of Judah and Jerusalem returned joyfully to Jerusalem, for the LORD had given them cause to rejoice over their enemies. 28They entered Jerusalem and went to the temple of the LORD with harps and lutes and trumpets.

29The fear g of God came upon all the kingdoms of the countries when they heard how the LORD had fought against the enemies of Israel. 30And the kingdom of Jehoshaphat was at peace, for his God had given him rest h on every side.

20:29
g 2Ch 17:10

20:30
h 2Ch 15:15

The End of Jehoshaphat's Reign

31So Jehoshaphat reigned over Judah. He was thirty-five years old when he became king of Judah, and he reigned in Jerusalem twenty-five years. His mother's name was Azubah daughter of Shilhi. 32He walked in the ways of his father Asa and did not stray from them; he did what was right in the eyes of the LORD. 33The high places, i however, were not removed, and the people still had not set their hearts on the God of their fathers.

34The other events of Jehoshaphat's reign, from beginning to end, are written in the annals of Jehu j son of Hanani, which are recorded in the book of the kings of Israel.

20:33
i 2Ch 17:6; 19:3

20:34
j 1Ki 16:1

a 21 Or him with the splendor of   b 25 Some Hebrew manuscripts and Vulgate; most Hebrew manuscripts corpses
c 26 Beracah means praise.

20:15 As the enemy bore down on Judah, God spoke through Jahaziel: "Do not be afraid or discouraged . . . . For the battle is not yours, but God's." We may not fight an enemy army, but every day we battle temptation, pressure, and "rulers . . . of this dark world" (Ephesians 6:12) who want us to rebel against God. Remember, as believers, we have God's Spirit in us. If we ask for God's help when we face struggles, God will fight for us. And God always triumphs.

How do we let God fight for us? (1) By realizing the battle is not ours, but God's; (2) by recognizing human limitations and allowing God's strength to work through our fears and weaknesses; (3) by making sure we are pursuing God's interests and not just our own selfish desires; (4) by asking God for help in our daily battles.

20:33 This summary says that Jehoshaphat did not remove the corrupt high places (idol shrines), while 17:6 and 19:3 say he did remove them. Jehoshaphat destroyed most of the Baal and Asherah idols, but since he did not succeed in wiping out the corrupt religions practiced at the high places, they were probably rebuilt each time he had them removed.

20:37
k 2Ch 9:21

35 Later, Jehoshaphat king of Judah made an alliance with Ahaziah king of Israel, who was guilty of wickedness. 36 He agreed with him to construct a fleet of trading ships.ᵃ After these were built at Ezion Geber, 37 Eliezer son of Dodavahu of Mareshah prophesied against Jehoshaphat, saying, "Because you have made an alliance with Ahaziah, the Lᴏʀᴅ will destroy what you have made." The ships *k* were wrecked and were not able to set sail to trade.ᵇ

21 Then Jehoshaphat rested with his fathers and was buried with them in the City of David. And Jehoram his son succeeded him as king. 2 Jehoram's brothers, the sons of Jehoshaphat, were Azariah, Jehiel, Zechariah, Azariahu, Michael and Shephatiah. All these were sons of Jehoshaphat king of Israel.ᶜ 3 Their father had given them many gifts of silver and gold and articles of value, as well as fortified cities in Judah, but he had given the kingdom to Jehoram because he was his firstborn son.

Jehoram King of Judah

21:4
l Jdg 9:5

21:6
m 1Ki 12:28-30
n 2Ch 18:1

21:7
o 2Sa 7:13
p 1Ki 11:36

21:8
q 2Ch 20:22-23

4 When Jehoram established himself firmly over his father's kingdom, he put all his brothers*l* to the sword along with some of the princes of Israel. 5 Jehoram was thirty-two years old when he became king, and he reigned in Jerusalem eight years. 6 He walked in the ways of the kings of Israel,*m* as the house of Ahab had done, for he married a daughter of Ahab.*n* He did evil in the eyes of the Lᴏʀᴅ. 7 Nevertheless, because of the covenant the Lᴏʀᴅ had made with David,*o* the Lᴏʀᴅ was not willing to destroy the house of David. He had promised to maintain a lamp*p* for him and his descendants forever.

8 In the time of Jehoram, Edom *q* rebelled against Judah and set up its own king. 9 So Jehoram went there with his officers and all his chariots. The Edomites surrounded him and his chariot commanders, but he rose up and broke through by night. 10 To this day Edom has been in rebellion against Judah.

Libnah revolted at the same time, because Jehoram had forsaken the Lᴏʀᴅ, the God of his fathers. 11 He had also built high places on the hills of Judah and had caused the people of Jerusalem to prostitute themselves and had led Judah astray.

21:12
r 2Ch 17:3-6
s 2Ch 14:2

21:13
t 1Ki 16:29-33

12 Jehoram received a letter from Elijah the prophet, which said:

"This is what the Lᴏʀᴅ, the God of your father*r* David, says: 'You have not walked in the ways of your father Jehoshaphat or of Asa*s* king of Judah. 13 But you have walked in the ways of the kings of Israel, and you have led Judah and the people of Jerusalem to prostitute themselves, just as the house of Ahab did.*t* You have also murdered your own brothers, members of your father's house, men who were better than you. 14 So now the Lᴏʀᴅ is about to strike your people, your sons, your wives and everything that is yours, with a heavy blow. 15 You yourself will be very ill with a lingering disease of the bowels, until the disease causes your bowels to come out.'"

ᵃ36 Hebrew *of ships that could go to Tarshish*   ᵇ37 Hebrew *sail for Tarshish*   ᶜ2 That is, Judah, as frequently in 2 Chronicles

---

20:37 Jehoshaphat met disaster when he joined forces with wicked King Ahaziah. He did not learn from his disastrous alliance with Ahab (18:28–34) or from his father's alliance with Aram (16:2–9). The partnership stood on unequal footing because one man served the Lord and the other worshiped idols. We court disaster when we enter into partnership with unbelievers, because our very foundations differ (2 Corinthians 6:14–18). While one serves the Lord, the other does not recognize God's authority. Inevitably, the one who serves God is faced with the temptation to compromise values. When that happens, spiritual disaster results.

Before entering into partnerships, ask: (1) What are my motives? (2) What problems am I avoiding by seeking this partnership? (3) Is this partnership the best solution, or is it only a quick solution to my problem? (4) Have I prayed or asked others to pray for guidance? (5) Are my partner and I really working toward the same goals? (6) Am I willing to settle for less financial gain in order to do what God wants?

21:6 Jehoram, the new king of Judah, married Athaliah, one of the daughters of King Ahab of Israel. She became the mother of Judah's next king, Ahaziah (22:2). Athaliah's mother was Jezebel, the most wicked woman Israel had ever known. Jehoram's marriage to Athaliah was Judah's downfall, for Athaliah brought her mother's wicked influence into Judah, causing the nation to forget God and turn to Baal worship (22:3).

21:7 God promised that a descendant of David would always sit on the throne (2 Samuel 7:8–16). What happened to this promise when the nation was destroyed and carried away? There were two parts to God's promise. (1) In the physical sense, as long as there was an actual throne in Judah, a descendant of David would sit upon it. But this part of the promise depended on the obedience of these kings. When they disobeyed, God was not bound to continue David's temporal line. (2) In the spiritual sense, this promise was completely fulfilled in the coming of Jesus the Messiah, a descendant of David, who would sit on the throne of David forever.

21:8–11 Jehoram's reign was marked by sin and cruelty. He married a woman who worshiped idols; he killed his six brothers; he allowed and even promoted idol worship. Yet he was not killed in battle or by treachery—he died by a lingering and painful disease (21:18, 19). Punishment for sin is not always immediate or dramatic. But if we ignore God's laws, we will eventually suffer the consequences of our sin.

21:12 Chronicles mentions Elijah only here. Much more about this great prophet can be found in 1 Kings 17:1—2 Kings 2:11. Elijah's Profile is found in 1 Kings 18, p. 527.

¹⁶The Lord aroused against Jehoram the hostility of the Philistines and of the Arabs ᵘ who lived near the Cushites. ¹⁷They attacked Judah, invaded it and carried off all the goods found in the king's palace, together with his sons and wives. Not a son was left to him except Ahaziah,ᵃ the youngest.

¹⁸After all this, the Lord afflicted Jehoram with an incurable disease of the bowels. ¹⁹In the course of time, at the end of the second year, his bowels came out because of the disease, and he died in great pain. His people made no fire in his honor,ᵛ as they had for his fathers.

²⁰Jehoram was thirty-two years old when he became king, and he reigned in Jerusalem eight years. He passed away, to no one's regret, and was buried ʷ in the City of David, but not in the tombs of the kings.

Ahaziah King of Judah

22 The people of Jerusalem made Ahaziah, Jehoram's youngest son, king in his place, since the raiders,ˣ who came with the Arabs into the camp, had killed all the older sons. So Ahaziah son of Jehoram king of Judah began to reign.

²Ahaziah was twenty-twoᵇ years old when he became king, and he reigned in Jerusalem one year. His mother's name was Athaliah, a granddaughter of Omri.

³He too walked in the ways of the house of Ahab,ʸ for his mother encouraged him in doing wrong. ⁴He did evil in the eyes of the Lord, as the house of Ahab had done, for after his father's death they became his advisers, to his undoing. ⁵He also followed their counsel when he went with Joramᶜ son of Ahab king of Israel to war against Hazael king of Aram at Ramoth Gilead. The Arameans wounded Joram; ⁶so he returned to Jezreel to recover from the wounds they had inflicted on him at Ramothᵈ in his battle with Hazael king of Aram.

Then Ahaziahᵉ son of Jehoram king of Judah went down to Jezreel to see Joram son of Ahab because he had been wounded.

⁷Through Ahaziah'sᶻ visit to Joram, God brought about Ahaziah's downfall. When Ahaziah arrived, he went out with Joram to meet Jehu son of Nimshi, whom the Lord had anointed to destroy the house of Ahab. ⁸While Jehu was executing judgment on the house of Ahab,ᵃ he found the princes of Judah and the sons of Ahaziah's relatives, who had been attending Ahaziah, and he killed them. ⁹He then went in search of Ahaziah, and his men captured him while he was hiding in Samaria. He was brought to Jehu and put to death. They buried him, for they said, "He was a son of Jehoshaphat, who sought ᵇ the Lord with all his heart." So there was no one in the house of Ahaziah powerful enough to retain the kingdom.

Athaliah and Joash

¹⁰When Athaliah the mother of Ahaziah saw that her son was dead, she proceeded to destroy the whole royal family of the house of Judah. ¹¹But Jehosheba,ᶠ the daughter of King Jehoram, took Joash son of Ahaziah and stole him away from among the royal princes who were about to be murdered and put him and his nurse in a bedroom. Because Jehosheba,ᶠ the daughter of King Jehoram and wife of the priest Jehoiada, was Ahaziah's sister, she hid the child from Athaliah so she could not kill him. ¹²He remained hidden with them at the temple of God for six years while Athaliah ruled the land.

23 In the seventh year Jehoiada showed his strength. He made a covenant with the commanders of units of a hundred: Azariah son of Jeroham, Ishmael son of Jehohanan, Azariah son of Obed, Maaseiah son of Adaiah, and Elishaphat son of Zicri. ²They went throughout Judah and gathered the Levites and the heads of Israelite families from all the towns. When they came to Jerusalem, ³the whole assembly made a covenant with the king at the temple of God.

ᵃ *17* Hebrew *Jehoahaz*, a variant of *Ahaziah*   ᵇ *2* Some Septuagint manuscripts and Syriac (see also 2 Kings 8:26); Hebrew *forty-two*, a variant of *Jehoram*; also in verses 6 and 7   ᵈ *6* Hebrew *Ramah*, a variant of *Ramoth*   ᵉ *6* Some Hebrew manuscripts, Septuagint, Vulgate and Syriac (see also 2 Kings 8:29); most Hebrew manuscripts *Azariah*   ᶠ *11* Hebrew *Jehoshabeath*, a variant of *Jehosheba*

22:4, 5 Although it is wise to seek advice, we must also carefully weigh the advice we receive. Ahaziah had advisers, but the advisers he chose to listen to were wicked and led him to ruin. When you seek advice, listen carefully and use God's Word to "test everything. Hold on to the good" (1 Thessalonians 5:21).

22:7 Jehu's Profile and a more complete story of his reign are found in 2 Kings 9:1—10:36, p. 565.

23:1 After seven years of rule by Athaliah, the queen mother, Jehoiada the priest finally got up his courage and took action to get rid of the idolatrous ruler. To confront the king (or queen) with the demands of God's law was supposed to be the role of every priest in every generation. Tragically, many priests shied away from this duty, and thus only a few made a difference in the nation.

23:1 Although it could have cost him his life, this priest did what was right, restoring the temple worship and anointing the new king. There are times when we must correct a wrong or speak out for what is right. When such a situation arises, gather up your courage and act.

*Cross-references (right margin):*

21:16 ᵘ2Ch 17:10-11; 22:1

21:19 ᵛ2Ch 16:14

21:20 ʷ2Ch 24:25; 28:27; Jer 22:18, 28

22:1 ˣ2Ch 21:16-17

22:3 ʸ2Ch 21:6

22:7 ᶻ2Ch 10:15

22:8 ᵃ2Ki 10:13

22:9 ᵇ2Ch 17:4

23:3
c 2Sa 7:12; 1Ki 2:4;
2Ch 6:16; 21:7

Jehoiada said to them, "The king's son shall reign, as the LORD promised concerning the descendants of David. c 4Now this is what you are to do: A third of you priests and Levites who are going on duty on the Sabbath are to keep watch at the doors, 5a third of you at the royal palace and a third at the Foundation Gate, and all the other men are to be in the court-yards of the temple of the LORD. 6No one is to enter the temple of the LORD except the priests and Levites on duty; they may enter because they are consecrated, but all the other men are to guard what the LORD has assigned to them. a 7The Levites are to station them-selves around the king, each man with his weapons in his hand. Anyone who enters the tem-ple must be put to death. Stay close to the king wherever he goes."

23:8
d 1Ch 24:1

8The Levites and all the men of Judah did just as Jehoiada the priest ordered. Each one took his men—those who were going on duty on the Sabbath and those who were going off duty—for Jehoiada the priest had not released any of the divisions. d 9Then he gave the com-manders of units of a hundred the spears and the large and small shields that had belonged to King David and that were in the temple of God. 10He stationed all the men, each with his weapon in his hand, around the king—near the altar and the temple, from the south side to the north side of the temple.

11Jehoiada and his sons brought out the king's son and put the crown on him; they pre-sented him with a copy of the covenant and proclaimed him king. They anointed him and shouted, "Long live the king!"

12When Athaliah heard the noise of the people running and cheering the king, she went to them at the temple of the LORD. 13She looked, and there was the king, standing by his pil-lar at the entrance. The officers and the trumpeters were beside the king, and all the people of the land were rejoicing and blowing trumpets, and singers with musical instruments were leading the praises. Then Athaliah tore her robes and shouted, "Treason! Treason!"

14Jehoiada the priest sent out the commanders of units of a hundred, who were in charge of the troops, and said to them: "Bring her out between the ranksb and put to the sword any-one who follows her." For the priest had said, "Do not put her to death at the temple of the

23:15
e Ne 3:28; Jer 31:40

LORD." 15So they seized her as she reached the entrance of the Horse Gate e on the palace grounds, and there they put her to death.

23:17
f Dt 13:6-9

16Jehoiada then made a covenant that he and the people and the king c would be the LORD's people. 17All the people went to the temple of Baal and tore it down. They smashed the altars and idols and killed f Mattan the priest of Baal in front of the altars.

23:18
g 1Ch 23:28-32
h 1Ch 23:6

18Then Jehoiada placed the oversight of the temple of the LORD in the hands of the priests, who were Levites, g to whom David had made assignments in the temple, h to present the burnt offerings of the LORD as written in the Law of Moses, with rejoicing and singing, as

23:19
i 1Ch 9:22

David had ordered. 19He also stationed doorkeepers i at the gates of the LORD's temple so that no one who was in any way unclean might enter.

20He took with him the commanders of hundreds, the nobles, the rulers of the people and all the people of the land and brought the king down from the temple of the LORD. They went into the palace through the Upper Gate and seated the king on the royal throne, 21and all the people of the land rejoiced. And the city was quiet, because Athaliah had been slain with the sword.

Joash Repairs the Temple

24:2
j 2Ch 26:5

24 Joash was seven years old when he became king, and he reigned in Jerusalem forty years. His mother's name was Zibiah; she was from Beersheba. 2Joash did what was right in the eyes of the LORDj all the years of Jehoiada the priest. 3Jehoiada chose two wives for him, and he had sons and daughters.

4Some time later Joash decided to restore the temple of the LORD. 5He called together the

a 6 Or to observe the LORD's command ⌊not to enter⌋   b 14 Or out from the precincts   c 16 Or covenant between
⌊the LORD⌋ and the people and the king that they (see 2 Kings 11:17)

23:12–15 Athaliah thought she had it made. After assuming the throne, she killed all potential heirs to it—so she thought. But even the best plans for evil go sour. When the truth was revealed, she was overthrown immediately. It is much safer to live according to the truth, even if it means not obtaining every-thing you want.

23:15–17 Athaliah's life ended as her mother Jezebel's had—by execution. Her life of idolatry and treachery was cut short by God's judgment of her sin. By this time Judah had slipped so far away from God that Baal was worshiped in Jerusalem.

23:18 Jehoiada restored the temple procedures and its wor-ship services according to David's original plans, recorded in 1 Chronicles 24; 25.

24:5 The Levites took their time carrying out the king's order, even though he told them not to delay. A tax for keeping the temple in order was not just the king's wish, but God's command (Exodus 30:11–16). The Levites, therefore, were not only disre-garding the king, but disregarding God. When it comes to follow-ing God's commands, a slow response may be little better than disobedience. Obey God willingly and immediately.

priests and Levites and said to them, "Go to the towns of Judah and collect the money due annually from all Israel, to repair the temple of your God. Do it now." But the Levites did not act at once.

6 Therefore the king summoned Jehoiada the chief priest and said to him, "Why haven't you required the Levites to bring in from Judah and Jerusalem the tax imposed by Moses the servant of the LORD and by the assembly of Israel for the Tent of the Testimony?" k

7 Now the sons of that wicked woman Athaliah had broken into the temple of God and had used even its sacred objects for the Baals.

8 At the king's command, a chest was made and placed outside, at the gate of the temple of the LORD. 9 A proclamation was then issued in Judah and Jerusalem that they should bring to the LORD the tax that Moses the servant of God had required of Israel in the desert. 10 All the officials and all the people brought their contributions gladly, dropping them into the chest until it was full. 11 Whenever the chest was brought in by the Levites to the king's officials and they saw that there was a large amount of money, the royal secretary and the officer of the chief priest would come and empty the chest and carry it back to its place. They did this regularly and collected a great amount of money. 12 The king and Jehoiada gave it to the men who carried out the work required for the temple of the LORD. They hired masons and carpenters to restore the LORD's temple, and also workers in iron and bronze to repair the temple.

13 The men in charge of the work were diligent, and the repairs progressed under them. They rebuilt the temple of God according to its original design and reinforced it. 14 When they had finished, they brought the rest of the money to the king and Jehoiada, and with it were made articles for the LORD's temple: articles for the service and for the burnt offerings, and also dishes and other objects of gold and silver. As long as Jehoiada lived, burnt offerings were presented continually in the temple of the LORD.

15 Now Jehoiada was old and full of years, and he died at the age of a hundred and thirty. 16 He was buried with the kings in the City of David, because of the good he had done in Israel for God and his temple.

The Wickedness of Joash

17 After the death of Jehoiada, the officials of Judah came and paid homage to the king, and he listened to them. 18 They abandoned l the temple of the LORD, the God of their fathers, and worshiped Asherah poles and idols. m Because of their guilt, God's anger n came upon Judah and Jerusalem. 19 Although the LORD sent prophets to the people to bring them back to him, and though they testified against them, they would not listen. o

20 Then the Spirit p of God came upon Zechariah son of Jehoiada the priest. He stood before the people and said, "This is what God says: 'Why do you disobey the LORD's commands? You will not prosper. q Because you have forsaken the LORD, he has forsaken r you.'"

21 But they plotted against him, and by order of the king they stoned s him to death t in the courtyard of the LORD's temple. u 22 King Joash did not remember the kindness Zechariah's father Jehoiada had shown him but killed his son, who said as he lay dying, "May the LORD see this and call you to account." v

23 At the turn of the year,a the army of Aram marched against Joash; it invaded Judah and Jerusalem and killed all the leaders of the people. w They sent all the plunder to their king in

a 23 Probably in the spring

24:6
k Ex 30:12-16

24:18
l ver 4
m Ex 34:13;
1Ki 14:23
n Jos 22:20;
2Ch 19:2

24:19
o Jer 7:25

24:20
p Jdg 3:10;
1Ch 12:18;
2Ch 20:14
q Nu 14:41

24:20
r 2Ch 15:2

24:21
s Ac 7:58-59
t Ne 9:26
u Mt 23:35

24:22
v Ge 9:5

24:23
w 2Ki 12:17-18

24:10 Evidently the Levites weren't convinced that the people would want to contribute to the rebuilding of the temple (24:5), but the people were glad to give of what they had for this project. Don't underestimate people's desire to be faithful to God. When challenged to do God's work, they will often respond willingly and generously.

24:18 If everything went so well in Judah when the people worshiped God, why did they turn away from him? Prosperity can be both a blessing and a curse. While it can be a sign of God's blessing to those who follow him, it carries with it the potential for moral and spiritual decline. Prosperous people are tempted to become self-sufficient and proud—to take God for granted. In our prosperity, we must not forget that God is the source of our blessings. See Deuteronomy 6:10–12; 8:11–14.

24:18-20 When King Joash and the nation of Judah abandoned God, God sent Zechariah to call them to repentance. Before dispensing judgment and punishment, God gave them another chance. In the same way, God does not abandon us or lash out in revenge when we sin. Instead, he aggressively pursues us through his Word, his Spirit in us, the words of others, and sometimes discipline. He does not intend to destroy us, but to urge us to return to him. When you are moving away from God, remember that he is pursuing you. Stop and listen. Allow him to point out your sin so you can repent and follow him again.

24:19 God sent many prophets to Joash and the people to warn them that they were headed for destruction. Joel may have been one of these prophets. Read the book of Joel for more information about the political and spiritual climate of the times.

24:22 Zechariah asked God to call the people to account for their sins. He was not seeking revenge, but pleading for justice. When we feel like despairing over the wickedness around us, we can rest assured that in the end God will bring complete justice to the earth.

24:24
x Lev 26:23-25;
Dt 28:25

Damascus. 24Although the Aramean army had come with only a few men, the LORD delivered into their hands a much larger army. x Because Judah had forsaken the LORD, the God of their fathers, judgment was executed on Joash. 25When the Arameans withdrew, they left Joash severely wounded. His officials conspired against him for murdering the son of Jehoiada the priest, and they killed him in his bed. So he died and was buried in the City of David, but not in the tombs of the kings.

24:26
y 2Ki 12:21

26Those who conspired against him were Zabad,a son of Shimeath an Ammonite woman, and Jehozabad, son of Shimrith b y a Moabite woman. 27The account of his sons, the many prophecies about him, and the record of the restoration of the temple of God are written in the annotations on the book of the kings. And Amaziah his son succeeded him as king.

Amaziah King of Judah

25 Amaziah was twenty-five years old when he became king, and he reigned in Jerusalem twenty-nine years. His mother's name was Jehoaddinc; she was from Jerusalem.

a26 A variant of *Jozabad*   b26 A variant of *Shomer*   c1 Hebrew *Jehoaddan*, a variant of *Jehoaddin*

JOASH

All parents want their children to make the right decisions. But to do this, children must first learn to make *their own* decisions. Making bad ones helps them learn to make good ones. If parents make all the decisions for their children, they leave their children without the skills for wise decision-making when they are on their own. This problem seriously affected Joash. He had great advice, but he never grew up. He became so dependent on what he was told that his effectiveness was limited to the quality of his advisers.

When Joash was one year old, his grandmother Athaliah decided to slaughter all her descendants in a desperate bid for power. Joash was the only survivor, rescued and hidden by his aunt and uncle, Jehosheba and Jehoiada. Jehoiada's work as a priest made it possible to keep Joash hidden in the temple for six years. At that point, Jehoiada arranged for the overthrow of Athaliah and the crowning of Joash. For many years following, Jehoiada made most of the kingdom's decisions for Joash. When the old priest died, he was buried in the royal cemetery as a tribute to his role.

But after Jehoiada's death, Joash didn't know what to do. He listened to counsel that carried him into evil. Within a short time he even ordered the death of Jehoiada's son Zechariah. After a few months, Joash's army had been soundly defeated by the Arameans. Jerusalem was saved only because Joash stripped the temple of its treasures as a bribe. Finally, the king's own officials assassinated him. In contrast to Jehoiada, Joash was not buried among the kings; he is not even listed in Jesus' genealogy in the New Testament.

As dependent as Joash was on Jehoiada, there is little evidence that he ever established a real dependence on the God Jehoiada obeyed. Like many children, Joash's knowledge of God was secondhand. It was a start, but the king needed his own relationship with God that would outlast and overrule the changes in the advice he received.

It would be easy to criticize Joash's failure were it not for the fact that we often fall into the same traps. How often have we acted on poor advice without considering God's Word?

Strengths and accomplishments:	• Carried out extensive repairs on the temple • Was faithful to God as long as Jehoiada lived
Weaknesses and mistakes:	• Allowed idolatry to continue among his people • Used the temple treasures to bribe King Hazael of Aram • Killed Jehoiada's son Zechariah • Allowed his advisers to lead the people away from God
Lessons from his life:	• A good and hopeful start can be ruined by an evil end • Even the best counsel is ineffective if it does not help us make wise decisions • As helpful or hurtful as others may be, we are individually responsible for what we do
Vital statistics:	• Where: Jerusalem • Occupation: King of Judah • Relatives: Father: Ahaziah. Mother: Zibiah. Grandmother: Athaliah. Aunt: Jehosheba. Uncle: Jehoiada. Son: Amaziah. Cousin: Zechariah. • Contemporaries: Jehu, Hazael
Key verses:	"After the death of Jehoiada, the officials of Judah came and paid homage to the king, and he listened to them. They abandoned the temple of the LORD, the God of their fathers, and worshiped Asherah poles and idols. Because of their guilt, God's anger came upon Judah and Jerusalem" (2 Chronicles 24:17, 18).

Joash's story is told in 2 Kings 11:1—14:23 and 2 Chronicles 22:11—25:25.

2He did what was right in the eyes of the LORD, but not wholeheartedly.z 3After the kingdom was firmly in his control, he executed the officials who had murdered his father the king. 4Yet he did not put their sons to death, but acted in accordance with what is written in the Law, in the Book of Moses, where the LORD commanded: "Fathers shall not be put to death for their children, nor children put to death for their fathers; each is to die for his own sins."a a

5Amaziah called the people of Judah together and assigned them according to their families to commanders of thousands and commanders of hundreds for all Judah and Benjamin. He then mustered those twenty years old or more and found that there were three hundred thousand men ready for military service,b able to handle the spear and shield. 6He also hired a hundred thousand fighting men from Israel for a hundred talentsb of silver.

7But a man of God came to him and said, "O king, these troops from Israel must not march with you, for the LORD is not with Israel—not with any of the people of Ephraim. 8Even if you go and fight courageously in battle, God will overthrow you before the enemy, for God has the power to help or to overthrow."c

9Amaziah asked the man of God, "But what about the hundred talents I paid for these Israelite troops?"

The man of God replied, "The LORD can give you much more than that."d

10So Amaziah dismissed the troops who had come to him from Ephraim and sent them home. They were furious with Judah and left for home in a great rage.

11Amaziah then marshaled his strength and led his army to the Valley of Salt, where he killed ten thousand men of Seir. 12The army of Judah also captured ten thousand men alive, took them to the top of a cliff and threw them down so that all were dashed to pieces.

13Meanwhile the troops that Amaziah had sent back and had not allowed to take part in the war raided Judean towns from Samaria to Beth Horon. They killed three thousand people and carried off great quantities of plunder.

14When Amaziah returned from slaughtering the Edomites, he brought back the gods of the people of Seir. He set them up as his own gods,e bowed down to them and burned sacrifices to them. 15The anger of the LORD burned against Amaziah, and he sent a prophet to him, who said, "Why do you consult this people's gods, which could not savef their own people from your hand?"

16While he was still speaking, the king said to him, "Have we appointed you an adviser to the king? Stop! Why be struck down?"

So the prophet stopped but said, "I know that God has determined to destroy you, because you have done this and have not listened to my counsel."

17After Amaziah king of Judah consulted his advisers, he sent this challenge to Jehoashc son of Jehoahaz, the son of Jehu, king of Israel: "Come, meet me face to face."

18But Jehoash king of Israel replied to Amaziah king of Judah: "A thistleg in Lebanon sent a message to a cedar in Lebanon, 'Give your daughter to my son in marriage.' Then a wild beast in Lebanon came along and trampled the thistle underfoot. 19You say to yourself that you have defeated Edom, and now you are arrogant and proud. But stay at home! Why ask for trouble and cause your own downfall and that of Judah also?"

25:2
z ver 14
25:4
a Dt 24:16

25:5
b Nu 1:3

25:8
c 2Ch 14:11; 20:6

25:9
d Dt 8:18; Pr 10:22

25:14
e Ex 20:3; 2Ch 28:23
25:15
f Ps 96:5

25:18
g Jdg 9:8-15

a4 Deut. 24:16   b6 That is, about 3 3/4 tons (about 3.4 metric tons); also in verse 9   c17 Hebrew Joash, a variant of Jehoash; also in verses 18, 21, 23 and 25

25:2 Amaziah did what was right on the outside, but inside he often resented what he had to do. His obedience was at best half-hearted. When the prophet promised God's deliverance, Amaziah first complained about the money that had been lost (25:9). And he valued military success more than God's will. We must search our own hearts and root out any resistance to obeying God. Grudging compliance is not true obedience.

25:9, 10 Amaziah made a financial agreement with Israelite soldiers, offering to pay them to fight for him (25:6). But before they could go to battle, Amaziah sent them home with their pay because of the prophet's warning. Although it cost him plenty, he wisely realized that the money was not worth the ruin the alliance could cause. How would you have reacted? Money must never stand in the way of making right decisions. The Lord's favor is priceless, worth more than any amount of money.

25:14 After the victory, Amaziah returned and sacrificed to idols. We are very susceptible to sin after great victories. It is

then that we feel confident, relaxed, and ready to celebrate. If, in that excitement, we let our defenses down, Satan can attack with all sorts of temptations. When you win, watch out. After the mountain peaks come the valleys.

25:15 Amaziah made a foolish mistake by worshiping the gods of the nation he had just conquered. Impressed by the accomplishments of the Edomites, Amaziah worshiped their idols! How foolish to serve the gods of a defeated enemy. We make the same mistake as Amaziah when we run after money, power, or recognition. By recognizing the emptiness of these worldly pursuits, we can free ourselves from the desire to follow them.

25:18 In this parable, Judah is the thistle and Israel's army is the cedar. Ahaziah was proud after defeating Edom. He wanted to defeat Israel, but Jehoash warned him not to attack. Ahaziah had more ambition than ability, and he paid for it when he was soundly defeated. Don't let ambition and pride into your life, for they will cause you to forget God.

25:20
h 1Ki 12:15;
2Ch 22:7

²⁰Amaziah, however, would not listen, for God so worked that he might hand them over to ⌊Jehoash⌋, because they sought the gods of Edom.ʰ ²¹So Jehoash king of Israel attacked. He and Amaziah king of Judah faced each other at Beth Shemesh in Judah. ²²Judah was routed by Israel, and every man fled to his home. ²³Jehoash king of Israel captured Amaziah king of Judah, the son of Joash, the son of Ahaziah,ᵃ at Beth Shemesh. Then Jehoash brought him to Jerusalem and broke down the wall of Jerusalem from the Ephraim Gate to the Corner Gate—a section about six hundred feetᵇ long. ²⁴He took all the gold and silver and all the articles found in the temple of God that had been in the care of Obed-Edom, together with the palace treasures and the hostages, and returned to Samaria.

²⁵Amaziah son of Joash king of Judah lived for fifteen years after the death of Jehoash son of Jehoahaz king of Israel. ²⁶As for the other events of Amaziah's reign, from beginning to end, are they not written in the book of the kings of Judah and Israel? ²⁷From the time that Amaziah turned away from following the Lord, they conspired against him in Jerusalem and he fled to Lachish, but they sent men after him to Lachish and killed him there. ²⁸He was brought back by horse and was buried with his fathers in the City of Judah.

Uzziah King of Judah

26 Then all the people of Judah took Uzziah,ᶜ who was sixteen years old, and made him king in place of his father Amaziah. ²He was the one who rebuilt Elath and restored it to Judah after Amaziah rested with his fathers.

³Uzziah was sixteen years old when he became king, and he reigned in Jerusalem fifty-two years. His mother's name was Jecoliah; she was from Jerusalem. ⁴He did what was right in the

---

ᵃ*23* Hebrew *Jehoahaz*, a variant of *Ahaziah*   ᵇ*23* Hebrew *four hundred cubits* (about 180 meters)
ᶜ*1* Also called *Azariah*

UZZIAH

We are never closer to failure than during our greatest successes. If we fail to recognize God's part in our achievements, they are no better than failures. Uzziah (also called Azariah) was a remarkably successful king. His achievements brought him fame. He was successful in war and peace, in planning and execution, in building and planting.

Uzziah overestimated his own importance in bringing about the great achievements he experienced. He did so many things well that a consuming pride gradually invaded his life like the leprous disease that finally destroyed his body. In trying to act like a priest, he took on a role that God did not mean for him to have. He had forgotten not only how much God had given him, but also that God had certain roles for others that he needed to respect.

Uzziah's pride was rooted in his lack of thankfulness. We have no accounts of this king's ever showing appreciation to God for the marvelous gifts he received. Our accomplishments may not compare with Uzziah's, but we still owe a debt of thanksgiving to God for our very lives. If God is not getting the credit for your successes, shouldn't you start looking at your life differently?

Strengths and accomplishments:	• Pleased God during his early years as king • Successful warrior and city builder • Skillful in organizing and delegating • Reigned for 52 years
Weaknesses and mistakes:	• Developed a prideful attitude due to his great success • Tried to perform the priests' duties, in direct disobedience to God • Failed to remove many of the symbols of idolatry in the land
Lessons from his life:	• Lack of thankfulness to God can lead to pride • Even successful people must acknowledge the role God has for others in their lives
Vital statistics:	• Where: Jerusalem • Occupation: King of Judah • Relatives: Father: Amaziah. Mother: Jecoliah. Son: Jotham. • Contemporaries: Isaiah, Amos, Hosea, Jeroboam, Zechariah, Azariah
Key verses:	"In Jerusalem he made machines designed by skillful men for use on the towers and on the corner defenses to shoot arrows and hurl large stones. His fame spread far and wide, for he was greatly helped until he became powerful. But after Uzziah became powerful, his pride led to his downfall. He was unfaithful to the Lord his God, and entered the temple of the Lord to burn incense on the altar of incense" (2 Chronicles 26:15, 16).

Uzziah's story is told in 2 Kings 15:1–7 (where he is called Azariah), and in 2 Chronicles 26:1–23. He is also mentioned in Isaiah 1:1; 6:1; 7:1; Hosea 1:1; Amos 1:1; Zechariah 14:5.

eyes of the LORD, just as his father Amaziah had done. [5]He sought God during the days of Zechariah, who instructed him in the fear[a] of God.[i] As long as he sought the LORD, God gave him success.

[6]He went to war against the Philistines[j] and broke down the walls of Gath, Jabneh and Ashdod. He then rebuilt towns near Ashdod and elsewhere among the Philistines. [7]God helped him against the Philistines and against the Arabs[k] who lived in Gur Baal and against the Meunites. [8]The Ammonites[l] brought tribute to Uzziah, and his fame spread as far as the border of Egypt, because he had become very powerful.

[9]Uzziah built towers in Jerusalem at the Corner Gate,[m] at the Valley Gate[n] and at the angle of the wall, and he fortified them. [10]He also built towers in the desert and dug many cisterns, because he had much livestock in the foothills and in the plain. He had people working his fields and vineyards in the hills and in the fertile lands, for he loved the soil.

[11]Uzziah had a well-trained army, ready to go out by divisions according to their numbers as mustered by Jeiel the secretary and Maaseiah the officer under the direction of Hananiah, one of the royal officials. [12]The total number of family leaders over the fighting men was 2,600. [13]Under their command was an army of 307,500 men trained for war, a powerful force to support the king against his enemies. [14]Uzziah provided shields, spears, helmets, coats of armor, bows and slingstones for the entire army. [15]In Jerusalem he made machines designed by skillful men for use on the towers and on the corner defenses to shoot arrows and hurl large stones. His fame spread far and wide, for he was greatly helped until he became powerful.

[16]But after Uzziah became powerful, his pride led to his downfall.[o] He was unfaithful to the LORD his God, and entered the temple of the LORD to burn incense[p] on the altar of incense. [17]Azariah [q] the priest with eighty other courageous priests of the LORD followed him in. [18]They confronted him and said, "It is not right for you, Uzziah, to burn incense to the LORD. That is for the priests,[r] the descendants of Aaron,[s] who have been consecrated to burn incense. Leave the sanctuary, for you have been unfaithful; and you will not be honored by the LORD God."

[19]Uzziah, who had a censer in his hand ready to burn incense, became angry. While he was raging at the priests in their presence before the incense altar in the LORD's temple, leprosy[b] [t] broke out on his forehead. [20]When Azariah the chief priest and all the other priests looked at him, they saw that he had leprosy on his forehead, so they hurried him out. Indeed, he himself was eager to leave, because the LORD had afflicted him.

[21]King Uzziah had leprosy until the day he died. He lived in a separate house[c] [u]—leprous, and excluded from the temple of the LORD. Jotham his son had charge of the palace and governed the people of the land.

[22]The other events of Uzziah's reign, from beginning to end, are recorded by the prophet Isaiah[v] son of Amoz. [23]Uzziah[w] rested with his fathers and was buried near them in a field for burial that belonged to the kings, for people said, "He had leprosy." And Jotham his son succeeded him as king.

Jotham King of Judah

27 Jotham was twenty-five years old when he became king, and he reigned in Jerusalem sixteen years. His mother's name was Jerusha daughter of Zadok. [2]He did what was

---

26:5 *i* 2Ch 24:2; Da 1:17
26:6 *j* Isa 14:29
26:7 *k* 2Ch 21:16
26:8 *l* 2Ch 17:11
26:9 *m* 2Ch 25:23 *n* Ne 3:13
26:16 *o* Dt 32:15; 2Ch 25:19 *p* 2Ki 16:12
26:17 *q* 1Ch 6:10
26:18 *r* Nu 16:39 *s* Ex 30:7
26:19 *t* 2Ki 5:25-27
26:21 *u* Lev 13:46; Nu 5:2
26:22 *v* Isa 1:1
26:23 *w* Isa 6:1

---

a 5 Many Hebrew manuscripts, Septuagint and Syriac; other Hebrew manuscripts *vision*   b 19 The Hebrew word was used for various diseases affecting the skin—not necessarily leprosy; also in verses 20, 21 and 23.   c 21 Or *in a house where he was relieved of responsibilities*

26:15 These machines were similar to the catapults later used by the Romans and were capable of slinging stones or arrows a great distance.

26:16 After God gave Uzziah great prosperity and power, he became proud and corrupt. It is true that "pride goes before destruction" (Proverbs 16:18). If God has given you wealth, influence, popularity, and power, be thankful, but be careful. God hates pride. While it is normal to feel elation when we accomplish something, it is wrong to be disdainful of God or to look down on others. Check your attitudes and remember to give God the credit for what you have. Use your gifts in ways that please him.

26:17-21 When people have power, they often think they can live above the law. But even rulers are subject to God, as Uzziah discovered. No matter what your position in society, God expects you to honor, worship, and obey him.

26:21 For much of his life, Uzziah "did what was right in the eyes of the LORD" (26:4). But Uzziah turned away from God, and he was struck with leprosy and remained leprous until his death. He is remembered more for his arrogant act and subsequent punishment than for his great reforms. God requires lifelong obedience. Spurts of obedience are not enough. Only "he who stands firm to the end" will be rewarded (Mark 13:13). Practice being consistent in your faith every day; that way you will build a lifetime of obedience. Otherwise you, too, may become more famous for your downfall than for your success.

26:23 This was the year that God called Isaiah to be a prophet (Isaiah 6:1).

27:2 Jotham was generally a good king (27:6), but his people remained as corrupt as they had been during his father Uzziah's reign. Those you lead will not always follow your example, but

27:3
ˣ2Ch 33:14;
Ne 3:26

right in the eyes of the LORD, just as his father Uzziah had done, but unlike him he did not enter the temple of the LORD. The people, however, continued their corrupt practices. ³Jotham rebuilt the Upper Gate of the temple of the LORD and did extensive work on the wall at the hill of Ophel. ˣ ⁴He built towns in the Judean hills and forts and towers in the wooded areas.

⁵Jotham made war on the king of the Ammonites and conquered them. That year the Ammonites paid him a hundred talentsᵃ of silver, ten thousand corsᵇ of wheat and ten thousand cors of barley. The Ammonites brought him the same amount also in the second and third years.

27:6
ʸ2Ch 26:5

⁶Jotham grew powerfulʸ because he walked steadfastly before the LORD his God.

⁷The other events in Jotham's reign, including all his wars and the other things he did, are written in the book of the kings of Israel and Judah. ⁸He was twenty-five years old when he became king, and he reigned in Jerusalem sixteen years. ⁹Jotham rested with his fathers and was buried in the City of David. And Ahaz his son succeeded him as king.

Ahaz King of Judah

28:2
ᶻEx 34:17

28:3
ᵃLev 18:21;
2Ch 33:6

28 Ahaz was twenty years old when he became king, and he reigned in Jerusalem sixteen years. Unlike David his father, he did not do what was right in the eyes of the LORD. ²He walked in the ways of the kings of Israel and also made cast idolsᶻ for worshiping the Baals. ³He burned sacrifices in the Valley of Ben Hinnom and sacrificed his sonsᵃ in the

ᵃ5 That is, about 3 3/4 tons (about 3.4 metric tons)   ᵇ5 That is, probably about 62,000 bushels (about 2,200 kiloliters)

Our heritage influences, but doesn't necessarily determine, our life decisions. King Ahaz of Judah illustrates this truth in two ways: He turned away from the good examples of his father Jotham and his grandfather Uzziah, but his poor example seems to have had little effect on his own son Hezekiah, who proved to be a great and godly king.

The circumstances in the life of King Ahaz fall into the general categories of bad and worse. When Judah suffered a debilitating attack from rivals Israel and Aram, the king ignored an opportunity to seek God's help and turned instead to Assyria for assistance. Ahaz's cowardly leadership forced Judah into virtual slavery to the Assyrians.

Soon every evidence that Judah had once been a God-fearing nation was smashed, defaced, or tucked out of sight. Ahaz imported idolatry. He even presented some of his children as offerings to the gods he hoped would rescue him and his nation from their disastrous situation.

We share Ahaz's sin when, from beneath a load of failures and trials, we turn away from good examples and from God. Instead of repenting of any known sin and calling upon God for relief, we, like Ahaz, may appeal to every other source of aid but God—our own abilities, money, or harmful habits. The results only serve to increase our tragic circumstances.

Difficulties and mistakes will either devastate our faith or they will stimulate growth and maturity. The positive differences come when we humbly seek God's help, whatever the situation. Trials that tempt us to turn away from God should, instead, spur us to turn toward God.

Weaknesses and mistakes:	• Failed to trust God • Asked Assyria for help and submitted Judah to crushing domination • Adopted Assyrian religious practices that undermined his people's faith • Sacrificed some of his own children in Baal worship
Lessons from his life:	• Fear is never a good excuse for failing to trust God • Some people or things that seem like obvious sources of help or relief may turn out to be controlling and enslaving instead • Good examples in our lives can't prevent us from making the wrong choices
Vital statistics:	• Where: Jerusalem • Occupation: King of Judah • Relatives: Father: Jotham. Son: Hezekiah.
Key verse:	"In his time of trouble King Ahaz became even more unfaithful to the LORD" (2 Chronicles 28:22).

Ahaz's story is told in 2 Kings 16 and 2 Chronicles 28. Isaiah 7–10 records several amazing prophecies given during his reign.

that should not affect the way you live for God. This sinfulness of Jotham's kingdom is vividly portrayed in Isaiah 1—5.

27:5 The tribute he received amounted to 3 3/4 tons of silver and 62,000 bushels each of wheat and barley.

28:3 Imagine the monstrous evil of a religion that offers young children as sacrifices. God allowed the nation to be conquered in

response to Ahaz's evil practices. Even today the practice hasn't abated. The sacrifice of children to the harsh gods of convenience, economy, and whim continues in sterile medical facilities in numbers that would astound the wicked Ahaz. If we are to allow children to come to Christ (Matthew 19:14), we must first allow them to come into the world.

fire, following the detestable ways of the nations the LORD had driven out before the Israelites. 4 He offered sacrifices and burned incense at the high places, on the hilltops and under every spreading tree.

5 Therefore the LORD his God handed him over to the king of Aram. *b* The Arameans defeated him and took many of his people as prisoners and brought them to Damascus.

He was also given into the hands of the king of Israel, who inflicted heavy casualties on him. 6 In one day Pekah*c* son of Remaliah killed a hundred and twenty thousand soldiers in Judah—because Judah had forsaken the LORD, the God of their fathers. 7 Zicri, an Ephraimite warrior, killed Maaseiah the king's son, Azrikam the officer in charge of the palace, and Elkanah, second to the king. 8 The Israelites took captive from their kinsmen*d* two hundred thousand wives, sons and daughters. They also took a great deal of plunder, which they carried back to Samaria.

9 But a prophet of the LORD named Oded was there, and he went out to meet the army when it returned to Samaria. He said to them, "Because the LORD, the God of your fathers, was angry*e* with Judah, he gave them into your hand. But you have slaughtered them in a rage that reaches to heaven. *f* 10 And now you intend to make the men and women of Judah and Jerusalem your slaves. *g* But aren't you also guilty of sins against the LORD your God? 11 Now listen to me! Send back your fellow countrymen you have taken as prisoners, for the LORD's fierce anger rests on you."

12 Then some of the leaders in Ephraim—Azariah son of Jehohanan, Berekiah son of Meshillemoth, Jehizkiah son of Shallum, and Amasa son of Hadlai—confronted those who were arriving from the war. 13 "You must not bring those prisoners here," they said, "or we will be guilty before the LORD. Do you intend to add to our sin and guilt? For our guilt is already great, and his fierce anger rests on Israel."

14 So the soldiers gave up the prisoners and plunder in the presence of the officials and all the assembly. 15 The men designated by name took the prisoners, and from the plunder they clothed all who were naked. They provided them with clothes and sandals, food and drink,*h* and healing balm. All those who were weak they put on donkeys. So they took them back to their fellow countrymen at Jericho, the City of Palms, *i* and returned to Samaria.

16 At that time King Ahaz sent to the king*a* of Assyria*j* for help. 17 The Edomites had again come and attacked Judah and carried away prisoners, 18 while the Philistines*k* had raided towns in the foothills and in the Negev of Judah. They captured and occupied Beth Shemesh, Aijalon and Gederoth, as well as Soco, Timnah and Gimzo, with their surrounding villages. 19 The LORD had humbled Judah because of Ahaz king of Israel,*b* for he had promoted wickedness in Judah and had been most unfaithful*l* to the LORD. 20 Tiglath-Pileser*c* king of Assyria came to him, but he gave him trouble instead of help. *m* 21 Ahaz took some of the things from the temple of the LORD and from the royal palace and from the princes and presented them to the king of Assyria, but that did not help him.

22 In his time of trouble King Ahaz became even more unfaithful to the LORD. 23 He offered sacrifices to the gods*n* of Damascus, who had defeated him; for he thought, "Since the gods of the kings of Aram have helped them, I will sacrifice to them so they will help me."*o* But they were his downfall and the downfall of all Israel.

24 Ahaz gathered together the furnishings from the temple of God *p* and took them away.*d* He shut the doors*q* of the LORD's temple and set up altars at every street corner in Jerusalem. 25 In every town in Judah he built high places to burn sacrifices to other gods and provoked the LORD, the God of his fathers, to anger.

26 The other events of his reign and all his ways, from beginning to end, are written in the book of the kings of Judah and Israel. 27 Ahaz rested*r* with his fathers and was buried*s* in the city of Jerusalem, but he was not placed in the tombs of the kings of Israel. And Hezekiah his son succeeded him as king.

28:5
b Isa 7:1

28:6
c 2Ki 15:25, 27

28:8
d 2Ch 11:4

28:9
e Isa 47:6
f Ezr 9:6; Rev 18:5

28:10
g Lev 25:39-46

28:15
h 2Ki 6:22
i Dt 34:3

28:16
j 2Ki 16:7

28:18
k Eze 16:27, 57

28:19
l 2Ch 21:2

28:20
m 2Ki 16:7

28:23
n 2Ch 25:14
o Jer 44:17-18

28:24
p 2Ki 16:18
q 2Ch 29:7

28:27
r Isa 14:28-32
s 2Ch 24:25

a 16 One Hebrew manuscript, Septuagint and Vulgate (see also 2 Kings 16:7); most Hebrew manuscripts *kings*
b 19 That is, Judah, as frequently in 2 Chronicles   c 20 Hebrew *Tilgath-Pilneser*, a variant of *Tiglath-Pileser*
d 24 Or *and cut them up*

28:22 Difficulties and struggles can devastate people, or they can stimulate growth and maturity. For Ahaz, deep troubles led to spiritual collapse. We do not need to respond like Ahaz. When facing problems or tragedy, we must remember that rough times give us a chance to grow (James 1:2–4). When you are facing trials, don't turn away from God; turn *to* him. See these times as an opportunity for you to claim God's help.

Hezekiah Purifies the Temple

29:2
*t*2Ch 34:2

29:3
*u*2Ch 28:24
29:5
*v*2Ch 35:6

29:6
*w*Jer 2:27
*x*Eze 8:16

29:8
*y*Dt 28:25;
2Ch 24:18
*z*Jer 25:9, 18
29:9
*a*2Ch 28:5-8, 17
29:10
*b*2Ch 23:16
29:11
*c*Nu 3:6; 8:6, 14

29 Hezekiah was twenty-five years old when he became king, and he reigned in Jerusalem twenty-nine years. His mother's name was Abijah daughter of Zechariah. ²He did what was right in the eyes of the LORD, just as his father David *t* had done.

³In the first month of the first year of his reign, he opened the doors of the temple of the LORD and repaired *u* them. ⁴He brought in the priests and the Levites, assembled them in the square on the east side ⁵and said: "Listen to me, Levites! Consecrate *v* yourselves now and consecrate the temple of the LORD, the God of your fathers. Remove all defilement from the sanctuary. ⁶Our fathers *w* were unfaithful; *x* they did evil in the eyes of the LORD our God and forsook him. They turned their faces away from the LORD's dwelling place and turned their backs on him. ⁷They also shut the doors of the portico and put out the lamps. They did not burn incense or present any burnt offerings at the sanctuary to the God of Israel. ⁸Therefore, the anger of the LORD has fallen on Judah and Jerusalem; he has made them an object of dread and horror *y* and scorn, *z* as you can see with your own eyes. ⁹This is why our fathers have fallen by the sword and why our sons and daughters and our wives are in captivity. *a* ¹⁰Now I intend to make a covenant *b* with the LORD, the God of Israel, so that his fierce anger will turn away from us. ¹¹My sons, do not be negligent now, for the LORD has chosen you to stand before him and serve him, *c* to minister before him and to burn incense."

¹²Then these Levites set to work:

from the Kohathites,
Mahath son of Amasai and Joel son of Azariah;
from the Merarites,
Kish son of Abdi and Azariah son of Jehallelel;
from the Gershonites,
Joah son of Zimmah and Eden son of Joah;
¹³from the descendants of Elizaphan,
Shimri and Jeiel;
from the descendants of Asaph,
Zechariah and Mattaniah;

GREAT REVIVALS IN THE BIBLE	Leader	Reference	How the People Responded
The Bible records several great revivals where people in great numbers turned to God and gave up their sinful ways of living. Each revival was characterized by a *leader* who recognized his nation's spiritual dryness. And in each case, the leader *took action* and was not afraid to make his desires known to the people.	Moses	Exodus 32—33	Accepted God's laws and built the tabernacle
	Samuel	1 Samuel 7:2–13	Promised to make God first in their lives by destroying their idols
	David	2 Samuel 6	Brought the ark of the covenant to Jerusalem; praised God with singing and musical instruments
	Jehoshaphat	2 Chronicles 20	Decided to trust in God alone to help them, and their discouragement turned to joy
	Hezekiah	2 Chronicles 29—31	Purified the temple; got rid of idols; brought tithes to God's house
	Josiah	2 Chronicles 34—35	Made a commitment to obey God's commands and remove sinful influences from their lives
	Ezra	Ezra 9—10 Haggai 1	Stopped associating with those who caused them to compromise their faith; renewed their commitment to God's commands; began rebuilding the temple
	Nehemiah (with Ezra)	Nehemiah 8—10	Fasted, confessed their sins, read God's Word publicly, and promised in writing to again serve God wholeheartedly

---

29:1 Hezekiah's Profile is found in 2 Kings 18, p. 583.

29:11 The Levites, chosen by God to serve in the temple, had been kept from their duties by Ahaz's wickedness (28:24). But Hezekiah called them back into service, reminding them that the Lord had chosen them to minister.

We may not have to face a wicked king, but pressures or responsibilities can render us inactive and ineffective. When you have been given the responsibility to minister, don't neglect your duty. If you have become inactive in Christian service, either by

choice or by circumstance, look for opportunities (and listen to the "Hezekiahs") God will send your way to help you resume your responsibilities. Then, like the Levites, be ready for action (29:12–15).

14 from the descendants of Heman,
     Jehiel and Shimei;
   from the descendants of Jeduthun,
     Shemaiah and Uzziel.

15When they had assembled their brothers and consecrated themselves, they went in to purify *d* the temple of the LORD, as the king had ordered, following the word of the LORD. 16The priests went into the sanctuary of the LORD to purify it. They brought out to the courtyard of the LORD's temple everything unclean that they found in the temple of the LORD. The Levites took it and carried it out to the Kidron Valley. 17They began the consecration on the first day of the first month, and by the eighth day of the month they reached the portico of the LORD. For eight more days they consecrated the temple of the LORD itself, finishing on the sixteenth day of the first month.

18Then they went in to King Hezekiah and reported: "We have purified the entire temple of the LORD, the altar of burnt offering with all its utensils, and the table for setting out the consecrated bread, with all its articles. 19We have prepared and consecrated all the articles *e* that King Ahaz removed in his unfaithfulness while he was king. They are now in front of the LORD's altar."

20Early the next morning King Hezekiah gathered the city officials together and went up to the temple of the LORD. 21They brought seven bulls, seven rams, seven male lambs and seven male goats as a sin offering *f* for the kingdom, for the sanctuary and for Judah. The king commanded the priests, the descendants of Aaron, to offer these on the altar of the LORD. 22So they slaughtered the bulls, and the priests took the blood and sprinkled it on the altar; next they slaughtered the rams and sprinkled their blood on the altar; then they slaughtered the lambs and sprinkled their blood *g* on the altar. 23The goats for the sin offering were brought before the king and the assembly, and they laid their hands *h* on them. 24The priests then slaughtered the goats and presented their blood on the altar for a sin offering to atone *i* for all Israel, because the king had ordered the burnt offering and the sin offering for all Israel.

25He stationed the Levites in the temple of the LORD with cymbals, harps and lyres in the way prescribed by David *j* and Gad *k* the king's seer and Nathan the prophet; this was commanded by the LORD through his prophets. 26So the Levites stood ready with David's instruments, and the priests with their trumpets. *l*

27Hezekiah gave the order to sacrifice the burnt offering on the altar. As the offering began, singing to the LORD began also, accompanied by trumpets and the instruments *m* of David king of Israel. 28The whole assembly bowed in worship, while the singers sang and the trumpeters played. All this continued until the sacrifice of the burnt offering was completed.

29When the offerings were finished, the king and everyone present with him knelt down and worshiped. *n* 30King Hezekiah and his officials ordered the Levites to praise the LORD with the words of David and of Asaph the seer. So they sang praises with gladness and bowed their heads and worshiped.

31Then Hezekiah said, "You have now dedicated yourselves to the LORD. Come and bring sacrifices and thank offerings to the temple of the LORD." So the assembly brought sacrifices and thank offerings, and all whose hearts were willing *o* brought burnt offerings.

32The number of burnt offerings the assembly brought was seventy bulls, a hundred rams and two hundred male lambs—all of them for burnt offerings to the LORD. 33The animals consecrated as sacrifices amounted to six hundred bulls and three thousand sheep and goats. 34The priests, however, were too few to skin all the burnt offerings; so their kinsmen the Levites helped them until the task was finished and until other priests had been consecrated, *p* for the Levites had been more conscientious in consecrating themselves than

29:15 *d* ver 5; 1Ch 23:28; 2Ch 30:12

29:19 *e* 2Ch 28:24

29:21 *f* Lev 4:13-14

29:22 *g* Lev 4:18

29:23 *h* Lev 4:15
29:24 *i* Lev 4:26

29:25 *j* 1Ch 25:6; 2Ch 8:14
k 2Sa 24:11
29:26 *l* 1Ch 15:24; 23:5

29:27 *m* 2Ch 23:18

29:29 *n* 2Ch 20:18

29:31 *o* Ex 35:22

29:34 *p* 2Ch 30:3, 15

29:21 Throughout the Old Testament, the sacrifice was God's appointed way of approaching him and restoring a right relationship with him. The sin offering made by Hezekiah was one such sacrifice, given to ask God's forgiveness for unintentional sins. (For more information on why God required sacrifices and how they were carried out, see the notes in Leviticus 1.)

29:22 The blood sprinkled on the altar represented the innocence of the sacrificed animal taking the place of the guilt of the person making the offering. The animal died so the sinner could

live. This ritual looked forward to the day when Jesus Christ, God's perfect Son, would sacrifice his innocent life on the cross in order that the sinful and guilty human race might be spared the punishment it deserves (Hebrews 10:1–14).

29:30 A seer was someone who received messages from God for the nation through visions or dreams.

29:31 A thank offering, one type of fellowship offering (see Leviticus 7:12–15), was given as an expression of gratitude toward God. As a fellowship offering, it symbolized restored peace and fellowship with God.

29:35
q Lev 3:16
r Nu 15:5-10

the priests had been. ³⁵There were burnt offerings in abundance, together with the fat *q* of the fellowship offerings *a* and the drink offerings *r* that accompanied the burnt offerings. So the service of the temple of the LORD was reestablished. ³⁶Hezekiah and all the people rejoiced at what God had brought about for his people, because it was done so quickly.

Hezekiah Celebrates the Passover

30:2
s Nu 9:10
30:3
t 2Ch 29:34
30:5
u Jdg 20:1

30 Hezekiah sent word to all Israel and Judah and also wrote letters to Ephraim and Manasseh, inviting them to come to the temple of the LORD in Jerusalem and celebrate the Passover to the LORD, the God of Israel. ²The king and his officials and the whole assembly in Jerusalem decided to celebrate *s* the Passover in the second month. ³They had not been able to celebrate it at the regular time because not enough priests had consecrated *t* themselves and the people had not assembled in Jerusalem. ⁴The plan seemed right both to the king and to the whole assembly. ⁵They decided to send a proclamation throughout Israel, from Beersheba to Dan, *u* calling the people to come to Jerusalem and celebrate the Passover to the LORD, the God of Israel. It had not been celebrated in large numbers according to what was written.

⁶At the king's command, couriers went throughout Israel and Judah with letters from the king and from his officials, which read:

"People of Israel, return to the LORD, the God of Abraham, Isaac and Israel, that he may return to you who are left, who have escaped from the hand of the kings of Assyria. ⁷Do not be like your fathers *v* and brothers, who were unfaithful to the LORD, the God of their fathers, so that he made them an object of horror, *w* as you see. ⁸Do not be stiff-necked, *x* as your fathers were; submit to the LORD. Come to the sanctuary, which he has consecrated forever. Serve the LORD your God, so that his fierce anger *y* will turn away from you. ⁹If you return *z* to the LORD, then your brothers and your children will be shown compassion by their captors and will come back to this land, for the LORD your God is gracious and compassionate. *a* He will not turn his face from you if you return to him."

30:7
v Eze 20:18
w 2Ch 29:8
30:8
x Ex 32:9
y 2Ch 29:10
30:9
z Dt 30:2-5; Isa 55:7
a Mic 7:18

30:10
b 2Ch 36:16

¹⁰The couriers went from town to town in Ephraim and Manasseh, as far as Zebulun, but the people scorned and ridiculed *b* them. ¹¹Nevertheless, some men of Asher, Manasseh and Zebulun humbled themselves and went to Jerusalem. ¹²Also in Judah the hand of God was on the people to give them unity of mind to carry out what the king and his officials had ordered, following the word of the LORD.

30:14
c 2Ch 28:24

¹³A very large crowd of people assembled in Jerusalem to celebrate the Feast of Unleavened Bread in the second month. ¹⁴They removed the altars *c* in Jerusalem and cleared away the incense altars and threw them into the Kidron Valley.

a 35 Traditionally *peace offerings*

30:1 The Passover celebration commemorated the time that God spared the lives of Israel's firstborn sons in Egypt. God had promised to send a plague to kill all the firstborn sons except in those homes where the blood of a slain lamb had been painted on the doorframes. The Israelites obeyed, and when the destroyer saw the blood, he "passed over" the house and did not harm anyone in it (Exodus 12:23). After this plague, Pharaoh freed the Israelites from slavery. This celebration was to be a yearly reminder of how God delivered his people. The careful preparations, both in the temple and for the feast, show that this was not a temporary or impulsive revival, but a deep-seated change of heart and life.

30:2, 3 God's law had a provision that, under certain circumstances, the Passover could be celebrated one month later (Numbers 9:10, 11).

30:6–9 Hezekiah was a king dedicated to God and to the spiritual progress of the nation. He sent letters throughout Judah and Israel urging everyone to return to God. He told them not to be stubborn, but to submit to the Lord. To submit means to obey him first, yielding our bodies, minds, wills, and emotions to him. His Holy Spirit must guide and renew every part of us. Only then will we be able to temper our stubborn selfishness.

30:10 The northern kingdom of Israel had recently been conquered by Assyria, and most of the people had been carried away to foreign lands. Hezekiah sent a proclamation to the few people who remained, inviting them to come to the Passover (30:1), but most responded with scorn and ridicule. People may mock you when you try to promote spiritual renewal and growth. Are you prepared to be ridiculed for your faith? When it comes your way, do not waver. Stand strong in your faith, as Hezekiah did, and God will honor you.

30:11 These people invited to the Passover scorned Hezekiah's messengers, but some accepted the invitation. Our efforts to tell others about God often meet with similar reactions. Many people will laugh at an invitation to accept Christ. But this must not stop us from reaching out. If you know and understand that rejecting the gospel is common, you can guard against feelings of personal rejection. Remember that the Holy Spirit convicts and convinces. Our task is to invite others to consider God's actions, his claims, and his promises.

30:14 Just as the priests had consecrated the temple (29:4, 5), so the people cleared the city of pagan idols and then consecrated themselves to prepare for worship (30:17–19). Even the good kings of Judah found it difficult to get rid of the pagan idols and altars in the high places (2 Kings 14:4; 2 Chronicles 20:33). Finally Hezekiah, with the help of his people, completed this task.

[15]They slaughtered the Passover lamb on the fourteenth day of the second month. The priests and the Levites were ashamed and consecrated [d] themselves and brought burnt offerings to the temple of the LORD. [16]Then they took up their regular positions as prescribed in the Law of Moses the man of God. The priests sprinkled the blood handed to them by the Levites. [17]Since many in the crowd had not consecrated themselves, the Levites had to kill [e] the Passover lambs for all those who were not ceremonially clean and could not consecrate their lambs to the LORD. [18]Although most of the many people who came from Ephraim, Manasseh, Issachar and Zebulun had not purified themselves, [f] yet they ate the Passover, contrary to what was written. But Hezekiah prayed for them, saying, "May the LORD, who is good, pardon everyone [19]who sets his heart on seeking God—the LORD, the God of his fathers—even if he is not clean according to the rules of the sanctuary." [20]And the LORD heard Hezekiah and healed the people.

[21]The Israelites who were present in Jerusalem celebrated the Feast of Unleavened Bread[g] for seven days with great rejoicing, while the Levites and priests sang to the LORD every day, accompanied by the LORD's instruments of praise. [a]

[22]Hezekiah spoke encouragingly to all the Levites, who showed good understanding of the service of the LORD. For the seven days they ate their assigned portion and offered fellowship offerings [b] and praised the LORD, the God of their fathers.

[23]The whole assembly then agreed to celebrate [h] the festival seven more days; so for another seven days they celebrated joyfully. [24]Hezekiah king of Judah provided [i] a thousand bulls and seven thousand sheep and goats for the assembly, and the officials provided them with a thousand bulls and ten thousand sheep and goats. A great number of priests consecrated themselves. [25]The entire assembly of Judah rejoiced, along with the priests and Levites and all who had assembled from Israel, including the aliens who had come from Israel and those who lived in Judah. [26]There was great joy in Jerusalem, for since the days of Solomon son of David king of Israel there had been nothing like this in Jerusalem. [27]The priests and the Levites stood to bless [j] the people, and God heard them, for their prayer reached heaven, his holy dwelling place.

31 When all this had ended, the Israelites who were there went out to the towns of Judah, smashed the sacred stones and cut down [k] the Asherah poles. They destroyed the high places and the altars throughout Judah and Benjamin and in Ephraim and Manasseh. After they had destroyed all of them, the Israelites returned to their own towns and to their own property.

Contributions for Worship

[2]Hezekiah assigned the priests and Levites to divisions[l]—each of them according to their duties as priests or Levites—to offer burnt offerings and fellowship offerings, [b] to minister, to give thanks and to sing praises at the gates of the LORD's dwelling. [m] [3]The king contributed from his own possessions for the morning and evening burnt offerings and for the burnt offerings on the Sabbaths, New Moons and appointed feasts as written in the Law of the LORD. [n] [4]He ordered the people living in Jerusalem to give the portion [o] due the priests

30:15 [d]2Ch 29:34

30:17 [e]2Ch 29:34

30:18 [f]Ex 12:43-49

30:21 [g]Ex 12:15, 17; 13:6

30:23 [h]1Ki 8:65

30:24 [i]2Ch 35:7

30:27 [j]Nu 6:23

31:1 [k]2Ki 18:4

31:2 [l]1Ch 24:1 [m]1Ch 23:28-32

31:3 [n]Nu 28:1–29:40

31:4 [o]Nu 18:8; Ne 13:10

[a]21 Or *priests praised the LORD every day with resounding instruments belonging to the LORD* [b]22,2 Traditionally *peace offerings*

30:15 The people were so zealous to celebrate the Passover and bring offerings to the temple that the priests and Levites were ashamed they did not share the same enthusiasm. The zeal of common people's faith motivated the ministers to take action. The devoted faith of laypersons today should motivate professional church staff to rekindle their enthusiasm for God's work. Laypersons should never be shut out of church government or decision-making. The church needs their good examples of faith.

30:22 One important purpose of the fellowship offering was to express gratitude to God for health or for safety in times of crisis.

30:26 It had been more than 200 years since there had been such a celebration in Jerusalem.

31:1ff Why was idol worship so bad? The Israelites had access to the one true God, but they constantly fell into worshiping lifeless idols made of wood or stone. They put aside worshiping the Creator in order to worship the creation. We are just as guilty when God no longer holds first place in our lives. When we think more about wealth, pleasure, prestige, or material possessions

than about God, we are actually worshiping them as gods. Because of idol worship, the people of Judah were eventually sent into captivity in foreign lands (36:14–17). We may not be sent into captivity, but discipline awaits all those who continually put earthly desires above spiritual priorities.

31:2–21 The priests had not been supported by the government during the evil kings' reigns. Now that the temple was repaired, Hezekiah organized the priests and resumed the work of the temple according to a plan originally set up by David (1 Chronicles 23:6–23; 24:3–19).

31:4–8 Hezekiah reinstated the practice of tithing—giving a tenth of one's income to the priests and Levites so they could be free to serve God and minister to the people. The people responded immediately and generously. God's work needs the support of God's people. Does God receive a regular percentage of your income? Generosity makes our giving delightful to us and to God (2 Corinthians 8; 9). How different the church would be today if all believers consistently followed this pattern.

31:5
PNe 13:12

31:6
qLev 27:30
rDt 14:28

31:8
sPs 144:13-15

31:10
tMal 3:10-12

31:15
u2Ch 29:12
vJos 21:9-19

and Levites so they could devote themselves to the Law of the LORD. 5As soon as the order went out, the Israelites generously gave the firstfruits P of their grain, new wine, oil and honey and all that the fields produced. They brought a great amount, a tithe of everything. 6The men of Israel and Judah who lived in the towns of Judah also brought a tithe q of their herds and flocks and a tithe of the holy things dedicated to the LORD their God, and they piled them in heaps. r 7They began doing this in the third month and finished in the seventh month. 8When Hezekiah and his officials came and saw the heaps, they praised the LORD and blessed s his people Israel.

9Hezekiah asked the priests and Levites about the heaps; 10and Azariah the chief priest, from the family of Zadok, answered, "Since the people began to bring their contributions to the temple of the LORD, we have had enough to eat and plenty to spare, because the LORD has blessed his people, and this great amount is left over." t

11Hezekiah gave orders to prepare storerooms in the temple of the LORD, and this was done. 12Then they faithfully brought in the contributions, tithes and dedicated gifts. Conaniah, a Levite, was in charge of these things, and his brother Shimei was next in rank. 13Jehiel, Azaziah, Nahath, Asahel, Jerimoth, Jozabad, Eliel, Ismakiah, Mahath and Benaiah were supervisors under Conaniah and Shimei his brother, by appointment of King Hezekiah and Azariah the official in charge of the temple of God.

14Kore son of Imnah the Levite, keeper of the East Gate, was in charge of the freewill offerings given to God, distributing the contributions made to the LORD and also the consecrated gifts. 15Eden, u Miniamin, Jeshua, Shemaiah, Amariah and Shecaniah assisted him faithfully in the towns v of the priests, distributing to their fellow priests according to their divisions, old and young alike.

16In addition, they distributed to the males three years old or more whose names were in the genealogical records—all who would enter the temple of the LORD to perform the daily duties of their various tasks, according to their responsibilities and their divisions. 17And they distributed to the priests enrolled by their families in the genealogical records and likewise to the Levites twenty years old or more, according to their responsibilities and their divisions. 18They included all the little ones, the wives, and the sons and daughters of the whole community listed in these genealogical records. For they were faithful in consecrating themselves.

19As for the priests, the descendants of Aaron, who lived on the farm lands around their

DAVID'S DYNASTY		
David (40 years, 1 Chr. 10—29)		Uzziah (52 years, 2 Chr. 26)
Solomon (40 years, 2 Chr. 1—9)		Jotham (16 years, 2 Chr. 27)
Rehoboam (17 years, 2 Chr. 10—12)		Ahaz (16 years, 2 Chr. 27)
Abijah (3 years, 2 Chr. 13)		Hezekiah (29 years, 2 Chr. 29—32)
Asa (41 years, 2 Chr. 14—16)		Manasseh (55 years, 2 Chr. 33:1—20)
Jehoshaphat (25 years, 2 Chr. 17—20)		Amon (2 years, 2 Chr. 33:21—25)
Jehoram (8 years, 2 Chr. 21)		Josiah (31 years, 2 Chr. 34—35)
Ahaziah (1 year, 2 Chr. 22:1–9)		Jehoahaz (3 months, 2 Chr. 36:1–4)
Athaliah (6 years, 2 Chr. 22:10—23:21)		Jehoiakim (11 years, 2 Chr. 36:5–8)
Joash (40 years, 2 Chr. 24)		Jehoiachin (3 months, 2 Chr. 36:9–10)
Amaziah (29 years, 2 Chr. 25)		Zedekiah (11 years, 2 Chr. 36:11–16)

The Lord promised David that his kingdom would endure and his throne would be established forever (2 Samuel 7:16). As a partial fulfillment of this promise, David and his descendants ruled Judah for over 400 years. Jesus Christ was a direct descendant of David and was the ultimate fulfillment of this promise (Acts 2:22—36).

31:20, 21 Because Hezekiah did "what was good and right and faithful before the LORD," he led the people of Judah in spiritual renewal. His actions serve as a model of renewal for us: (1) he remembered God's compassion (30:9); (2) he kept going despite ridicule (30:10); (3) he aggressively removed evil influences from his life (30:14; 31:1); (4) he interceded for the people, asking for the Lord's pardon (30:15–20); (5) he was open to spontaneity in worship (30:23); (6) he contributed generously to God's work (31:3). If any of these are lacking in your life, consider how they might apply, and renew your commitment to God.

towns or in any other towns,*w* men were designated by name to distribute portions to every male among them and to all who were recorded in the genealogies of the Levites.

20This is what Hezekiah did throughout Judah, doing what was good and right and faithful*x* before the LORD his God. 21In everything that he undertook in the service of God's temple and in obedience to the law and the commands, he sought his God and worked wholeheartedly. And so he prospered.*y*

Sennacherib Threatens Jerusalem

32 After all that Hezekiah had so faithfully done, Sennacherib*z* king of Assyria came and invaded Judah. He laid siege to the fortified cities, thinking to conquer them for himself. 2When Hezekiah saw that Sennacherib had come and that he intended to make war on Jerusalem, 3he consulted with his officials and military staff about blocking off the water from the springs outside the city, and they helped him. 4A large force of men assembled, and they blocked all the springs*a* and the stream that flowed through the land. "Why should the kings*a* of Assyria come and find plenty of water?" they said. 5Then he worked hard repairing all the broken sections of the wall*b* and building towers on it. He built another wall outside that one and reinforced the supporting terraces*b c* of the City of David. He also made large numbers of weapons and shields.

6He appointed military officers over the people and assembled them before him in the square at the city gate and encouraged them with these words: 7"Be strong and courageous.*d* Do not be afraid or discouraged because of the king of Assyria and the vast army with him, for there is a greater power with us than with him.*e* 8With him is only the arm of flesh,*f* but with us is the LORD our God to help us and to fight our battles."*g* And the people gained confidence from what Hezekiah the king of Judah said.

9Later, when Sennacherib king of Assyria and all his forces were laying siege to Lachish, he sent his officers to Jerusalem with this message for Hezekiah king of Judah and for all the people of Judah who were there:

a 4 Hebrew; Septuagint and Syriac *king*   *b 5* Or *the Millo*

**Cross references (right margin):**
- **31:19** *w*Lev 25:34; Nu 35:2-5
- **31:20** *x*2Ki 20:3
- **31:21** *y*Dt 29:9
- **32:1** *z*2Ki 18:13-19; Isa 36:1
- **32:4** *a*2Ki 20:20
- **32:5** *b*2Ch 25:23 *c*1Ki 9:24
- **32:7** *d*Dt 31:6; 1Ch 22:13 *e*2Ki 6:16
- **32:8** *f*Jer 17:5 *g*2Ch 20:17

32:1 Assyria was a great empire by Hezekiah's time, controlling most of the Middle East. From a small strip of land located in present-day Iran and Iraq, it began to establish its power under Ashurnasirpal II (883–859 B.C.) and his son Shalmaneser III (859–824). Under Tiglath-Pileser III (745–727), Assyria's boundaries extended to the borders of Israel, making it one of the largest empires in ancient history. Shalmaneser V destroyed the northern kingdom in 722, and his grandson, Sennacherib (705–681), tried to bring Judah, the southern kingdom, under his control. Less than a century later, Assyria would lie in ruins (612).

THE ASSYRIAN EMPIRE The mighty Assyrian empire extended from the Persian Gulf, across the Fertile Crescent, and south to Egypt. Shalmaneser III extended the empire toward the Mediterranean Sea by conquering cities as far west as Qarqar. Tiglath-Pileser extended the empire south into Aram, Israel, Judah, and Philistia. It was Shalmaneser V who destroyed Samaria, Israel's capital.

32:1 Sennacherib wanted to "conquer them for himself" so he could force the cities to pay tribute. Forcing captured cities to pay tribute was a way for kings to build their income base. Often Assyria would require an oath of allegiance from a country, including the promise to pay taxes in the form of livestock, wine, battle equipment (horses, chariots, weapons), gold, silver, and anything else that pleased the invading king. Tribute was more important to Assyria than captives because captives cost money. Thus captives were taken only in cases of extreme rebellion or to repopulate cities that had been destroyed.

32:1ff When Hezekiah was confronted with the frightening prospect of an Assyrian invasion, he made two important decisions. He did everything he could to deal with the situation, and he trusted God for the outcome. That is exactly what we must do when faced with difficult or frightening situations. Take all the steps you possibly can to solve the problem or improve the situation. But also commit the situation to God in prayer, trusting him for the solution.

32:3, 4 Cities had to be built near reliable water sources. Natural springs were some of Jerusalem's major sources of water. In a brilliant military move, Hezekiah plugged the springs outside the city and channeled the water through an underground tunnel (32:30); therefore, Jerusalem would have water even through a long siege. Hezekiah's tunnel has been discovered along with an inscription describing how it was built: two groups of workers started digging underground, one in Jerusalem and one at the Gihon spring, and they met in the middle.

32:7, 8 Hezekiah could see with eyes of faith. The number of his opponents meant nothing as long as he was on the Lord's side. Victory is "'not by might nor by power, but by my Spirit,' says the LORD Almighty" (Zechariah 4:6). Hezekiah could confidently encourage his men because he had no doubt about where he stood with God. Are you on the Lord's side? You may never face an enemy army, but the battles you face every day can be won with God's strength.

¹⁰"This is what Sennacherib king of Assyria says: On what are you basing your confidence, that you remain in Jerusalem under siege? ¹¹When Hezekiah says, 'The LORD our God will save us from the hand of the king of Assyria,' he is misleading you, to let you die of hunger and thirst. ¹²Did not Hezekiah himself remove this god's high places and altars, saying to Judah and Jerusalem, 'You must worship before one altar^h and burn sacrifices on it'?

¹³"Do you not know what I and my fathers have done to all the peoples of the other lands? Were the gods of those nations ever able to deliver their land from my hand? ¹⁴Who of all the gods of these nations that my fathers destroyed has been able to save his people from me? How then can your god deliver you from my hand? ¹⁵Now do not let Hezekiah deceive you and mislead you like this. Do not believe him, for no god of any nation or kingdom has been able to deliverⁱ his people from my hand or the hand of my fathers.^j How much less will your god deliver you from my hand!"

¹⁶Sennacherib's officers spoke further against the LORD God and against his servant Hezekiah. ¹⁷The king also wrote letters insulting the LORD, the God of Israel, and saying this against him: "Just as the gods^k of the peoples of the other lands did not rescue their people from my hand, so the god of Hezekiah will not rescue his people from my hand." ¹⁸Then they called out in Hebrew to the people of Jerusalem who were on the wall, to terrify them and make them afraid in order to capture the city. ¹⁹They spoke about the God of Jerusalem as they did about the gods of the other peoples of the world—the work of men's hands.^l

²⁰King Hezekiah and the prophet Isaiah son of Amoz cried out in prayer to heaven about this. ²¹And the LORD sent an angel, who annihilated all the fighting men and the leaders and officers in the camp of the Assyrian king. So he withdrew to his own land in disgrace. And when he went into the temple of his god, some of his sons cut him down with the sword.

²²So the LORD saved Hezekiah and the people of Jerusalem from the hand of Sennacherib king of Assyria and from the hand of all others. He took care of them^a on every side. ²³Many brought offerings to Jerusalem for the LORD and valuable gifts^m for Hezekiah king of Judah. From then on he was highly regarded by all the nations.

Hezekiah's Pride, Success and Death

²⁴In those days Hezekiah became ill and was at the point of death. He prayed to the LORD, who answered him and gave him a miraculous sign. ²⁵But Hezekiah's heart was proudⁿ and he did not respond to the kindness shown him; therefore the LORD's wrath^o was on him and on Judah and Jerusalem. ²⁶Then Hezekiah repented^p of the pride of his heart, as did the people of Jerusalem; therefore the LORD's wrath did not come upon them during the days of Hezekiah.

²⁷Hezekiah had very great riches and honor, and he made treasuries for his silver and gold and for his precious stones, spices, shields and all kinds of valuables. ²⁸He also made buildings to store the harvest of grain, new wine and oil; and he made stalls for various kinds of cattle, and pens for the flocks. ²⁹He built villages and acquired great numbers of flocks and herds, for God had given him very great riches.^q

³⁰It was Hezekiah who blocked the upper outlet of the Gihon^r spring and channeled the water down to the west side of the City of David. He succeeded in everything he undertook. ³¹But

^a22 Hebrew; Septuagint and Vulgate *He gave them rest*

32:12 ^h2Ch 31:1
32:15 ⁱDa 3:15 ^jEx 5:2
32:17 ^k2Ki 19:12
32:19 ^l2Ki 19:18; Ps 115:4-8
32:23 ^m2Ch 17:5
32:25 ⁿ2Ch 26:16 ^o2Ch 24:18
32:26 ^pJer 26:18-19
32:29 ^q1Ch 29:12
32:30 ^r1Ki 1:33

32:31 A test can bring out a person's true character. God tested Hezekiah to see what he was really like and to show him his own shortcomings and the attitude of his heart. God did not totally abandon Hezekiah, nor did he tempt him to sin or trick him. The test was meant to strengthen Hezekiah, develop his character, and prepare him for the tasks ahead. In times of success, most of us can live good lives. But pressure, trouble, or pain will quickly remove our thin veneer of goodness unless our strength comes from God. What are you like under pressure or when everything is going wrong? Do you give in or turn to God? Those who are consistently in touch with God don't have to worry about what pressure may reveal about them.

32:31 Babylon was slowly and quietly rising to become a world power. At the same time, the Assyrian empire was slowly declining due to internal strife and a succession of weak kings. When Assyria was finally crushed in 612 B.C., Babylon under Nebu-chadnezzar moved into its place of prominence. (For more information on Babylon, see the note on 2 Kings 20:14.)

32:31 Why did God leave Hezekiah to himself? After Hezekiah was healed of his sickness, he developed excessive pride. When envoys came to inquire about his miraculous healing, God stepped back to see how Hezekiah would respond. Unfortunately, Hezekiah's actions revealed his runaway pride. He pointed to his own accomplishments rather than to God (see 2 Kings 20:12–19). Pride is any attitude that elevates our effort or abilities above God's, or treats with disdain his work in us. It causes us to congratulate ourselves for our successes and to look down on other people. God does not object to self-confidence, healthy self-esteem, or good feelings about our accomplishments. He objects to the foolish attitude of taking full credit for what he has done or for setting ourselves up as superior to others.

when envoys were sent by the rulers of Babylon[s] to ask him about the miraculous sign that had occurred in the land, God left him to test[t] him and to know everything that was in his heart.

³²The other events of Hezekiah's reign and his acts of devotion are written in the vision of the prophet Isaiah son of Amoz in the book of the kings of Judah and Israel. ³³Hezekiah rested with his fathers and was buried on the hill where the tombs of David's descendants are. All Judah and the people of Jerusalem honored him when he died. And Manasseh his son succeeded him as king.

Manasseh King of Judah

33 Manasseh was twelve years old when he became king, and he reigned in Jerusalem fifty-five years. ²He did evil in the eyes of the LORD, following the detestable[u] practices of the nations the LORD had driven out before the Israelites. ³He rebuilt the high places his father Hezekiah had demolished; he also erected altars to the Baals and made Asherah poles.[v] He bowed down[w] to all the starry hosts and worshiped them. ⁴He built altars in the temple of the LORD, of which the LORD had said, "My Name[x] will remain in Jerusalem forever." ⁵In both courts of the temple of the LORD,[y] he built altars to all the starry hosts. ⁶He sacrificed his sons[z] in[a] the fire in the Valley of Ben Hinnom, practiced sorcery, divination and witchcraft, and consulted mediums and spiritists. He did much evil in the eyes of the LORD, provoking him to anger.

⁷He took the carved image he had made and put it in God's temple, of which God had said to David and to his son Solomon, "In this temple and in Jerusalem, which I have chosen out of all the tribes of Israel, I will put my Name forever. ⁸I will not again make the feet of the Israelites leave the land[a] I assigned to your forefathers, if only they will be careful to do everything I commanded them concerning all the laws, decrees and ordinances given through Moses." ⁹But Manasseh led Judah and the people of Jerusalem astray, so that they did more evil than the nations the LORD had destroyed before the Israelites.

¹⁰The LORD spoke to Manasseh and his people, but they paid no attention. ¹¹So the LORD brought against them the army commanders of the king of Assyria, who took Manasseh prisoner,[b] put a hook in his nose, bound him with bronze shackles and took him to Babylon. ¹²In his distress he sought the favor of the LORD his God and humbled[c] himself greatly before the God of his fathers. ¹³And when he prayed to him, the LORD was moved by his entreaty and listened to his plea; so he brought him back to Jerusalem and to his kingdom. Then Manasseh knew that the LORD is God.

¹⁴Afterward he rebuilt the outer wall of the City of David, west of the Gihon[d] spring in the valley, as far as the entrance of the Fish Gate and encircling the hill of Ophel;[e] he also made it much higher. He stationed military commanders in all the fortified cities in Judah.

¹⁵He got rid of the foreign gods and removed[f] the image from the temple of the LORD, as well as all the altars he had built on the temple hill and in Jerusalem; and he threw them out of the city. ¹⁶Then he restored the altar of the LORD and sacrificed fellowship offerings[b] and thank offerings[g] on it, and told Judah to serve the LORD, the God of Israel. ¹⁷The people, however, continued to sacrifice at the high places, but only to the LORD their God.

¹⁸The other events of Manasseh's reign, including his prayer to his God and the words the seers spoke to him in the name of the LORD, the God of Israel, are written in the annals of the kings of Israel.[c] ¹⁹His prayer and how God was moved by his entreaty, as well as all his sins and unfaithfulness, and the sites where he built high places and set up Asherah poles and idols before he humbled himself—all are written in the records of the seers.[d] ²⁰Manasseh rested with his fathers and was buried[h] in his palace. And Amon his son succeeded him as king.

32:31	s Isa 39:1
	t Dt 8:16
33:2	u Dt 18:9; 2Ch 28:3
33:3	v Dt 16:21-22
	w 2Ch 31:1
33:4	x 2Ch 7:16
33:5	y 2Ch 4:9
33:6	z Lev 18:21; 2Ch 28:3
33:8	a 2Sa 7:10
33:11	b Dt 28:36
33:12	c 2Ch 32:26; 1Pe 5:6
33:14	d 1Ki 1:33
	e 2Ch 27:3
33:15	f ver 3-7
33:16	g Lev 7:11-18
33:20	h 2Ki 21:18

a 6 Or *He made his sons pass through*   b 16 Traditionally *peace offerings*   c 18 That is, Judah, as frequently in 2 Chronicles   d 19 One Hebrew manuscript and Septuagint; most Hebrew manuscripts *of Hozai*

33:6 Sorcery is using power gained from evil spirits. Divination is predicting the future through omens.

33:11 Between 652 and 648 B.C., the city of Babylon rebelled against Assyria. The rebellion was crushed, but Assyria may have suspected that Manasseh supported it. That may explain why Manasseh was taken to Babylon for trial rather than to the Assyrian capital of Nineveh.

33:12, 13 In a list of corrupt kings, Manasseh would rank near the top. His life was a catalog of evil deeds including idol worship, sacrificing his own children, and temple desecration. Eventually, however, he realized his sins and cried out to God for forgiveness.

And God listened. If God can forgive Manasseh, surely he can forgive anyone. Are you burdened by overpowering guilt? Do you doubt that anyone could forgive what you have done? Take heart—until death, no one is beyond the reach of God's forgiveness.

33:17 Although the people worshiped God alone, they worshiped him in the wrong way. God had told them to make their sacrifices only in certain places (Deuteronomy 12:13, 14). This kept them from changing their way of worship and protected them against the dangerous influence of pagan religious practices. Unfortunately, the people continued to use these places of worship, not realizing that (1) they were adopting practices God opposed, and

Amon King of Judah

21Amon was twenty-two years old when he became king, and he reigned in Jerusalem two years. 22He did evil in the eyes of the LORD, as his father Manasseh had done. Amon worshiped and offered sacrifices to all the idols Manasseh had made. 23But unlike his father Manasseh, he did not humble *i* himself before the LORD; Amon increased his guilt.

24Amon's officials conspired against him and assassinated him in his palace. 25Then the people of the land killed all who had plotted against King Amon, and they made Josiah his son king in his place.

Josiah's Reforms

34 Josiah*j* was eight years old when he became king, and he reigned in Jerusalem thirty-one years. 2He did what was right in the eyes of the LORD and walked in the ways of his father David,*k* not turning aside to the right or to the left.

3In the eighth year of his reign, while he was still young, he began to seek the God*l* of his father David. In his twelfth year he began to purge Judah and Jerusalem of high places, Asherah poles, carved idols and cast images. 4Under his direction the altars of the Baals were torn down; he cut to pieces the incense altars that were above them, and smashed the Asherah poles, the idols and the images. These he broke to pieces and scattered over the graves of those who had sacrificed to them.*m* 5He burned*n* the bones of the priests on their altars, and so he purged Judah and Jerusalem. 6In the towns of Manasseh, Ephraim and Simeon, as far as Naphtali, and in the ruins around them, 7he tore down the altars and the

33:23
*i*ver 12

34:1
*j*1Ch 3:14

34:2
*k*2Ch 29:2

34:3
*l*1Ki 13:2; 2Ch 15:2; 33:17, 22

34:4
*m*Ex 32:20; Lev 26:30

34:5
*n*1Ki 13:2

MANASSEH

Even a brief outline of King Manasseh's evil sickens us, and we wonder how God could ever forgive him. Not only did he intentionally offend God by desecrating Solomon's temple with idols, but he also worshiped pagan gods and even sacrificed his children to them! Child sacrifice is a vile act of pagan idolatry, an act against both God and people. Such blatant sins require severe correction.

God showed justice to Manasseh in warning and punishing him. He showed mercy in responding to Manasseh's heartfelt repentance by forgiving and restoring him. Given the nature of Manasseh's rebellion, we are not surprised by God's punishment—defeat and exile at the hands of the Assyrians. But Manasseh's repentance and God's forgiveness are unexpected. Manasseh's life was changed. He was given a new start.

How far has God gone to get your attention? Have you ever, like Manasseh, come to your senses and cried out to God for help? Only your repentance and a prayer for a new attitude stand between you and God's complete forgiveness.

Strengths and accomplishments:	• Despite the bitter consequences of his sins, he learned from them • Humbly repented of his sins before God
Weaknesses and mistakes:	• Challenged God's authority and was defeated • Reversed many of the positive effects of his father Hezekiah's rule • Sacrificed his children to idols
Lessons from his life:	• God will go a long way to get someone's attention • Forgiveness is limited not by the amount of sin, but by our willingness to repent
Vital statistics:	• Where: Jerusalem • Occupation: King of Judah • Relatives: Father: Hezekiah. Mother: Hephzibah. Son: Amon.
Key verses:	"In his distress he sought favor of the LORD his God and humbled himself greatly before the God of his fathers. And when he prayed to him, the LORD was moved by his entreaty and listened to his plea; so he brought him back to Jerusalem and to his kingdom. Then Manasseh knew that the LORD is God" (2 Chronicles 33:12, 13).

Manasseh's story is told in 2 Kings 21:1–18 and 2 Chronicles 32:33—33:20. He is also mentioned in Jeremiah 15:4.

---

(2) these places were against God's law. They were mixing pagan beliefs with worship of God. Blending religious ideas leads to confusion about who God really is. We must take care that subtle secular influences do not distort our worship practices.

34:1 Josiah's Profile is found in 2 Kings 24, p. 591.

34:3 In Josiah's day, boys were considered men at age 12.

By 16, Josiah understood the responsibility of his office. Even at this young age, he showed greater wisdom than many of the older kings who came before him because he had decided to seek the Lord God and his wisdom. Don't let your age disqualify you from serving God.

Asherah poles and crushed the idols to powder ᵒ and cut to pieces all the incense altars throughout Israel. Then he went back to Jerusalem.

⁸In the eighteenth year of Josiah's reign, to purify the land and the temple, he sent Shaphan son of Azaliah and Maaseiah the ruler of the city, with Joah son of Joahaz, the recorder, to repair the temple of the Lᴏʀᴅ his God.

⁹They went to Hilkiah ᵖ the high priest and gave him the money that had been brought into the temple of God, which the Levites who were the doorkeepers had collected from the people of Manasseh, Ephraim and the entire remnant of Israel and from all the people of Judah and Benjamin and the inhabitants of Jerusalem. ¹⁰Then they entrusted it to the men appointed to supervise the work on the Lᴏʀᴅ's temple. These men paid the workers who repaired and restored the temple. ¹¹They also gave money to the carpenters and builders to purchase dressed stone, and timber for joists and beams for the buildings that the kings of Judah had allowed to fall into ruin. �q

¹²The men did the work faithfully. ʳ Over them to direct them were Jahath and Obadiah, Levites descended from Merari, and Zechariah and Meshullam, descended from Kohath. The Levites—all who were skilled in playing musical instruments— ˢ ¹³had charge of the laborers ᵗ and supervised all the workers from job to job. Some of the Levites were secretaries, scribes and doorkeepers.

The Book of the Law Found

¹⁴While they were bringing out the money that had been taken into the temple of the Lᴏʀᴅ, Hilkiah the priest found the Book of the Law of the Lᴏʀᴅ that had been given through Moses. ¹⁵Hilkiah said to Shaphan the secretary, "I have found the Book of the Law in the temple of the Lᴏʀᴅ." He gave it to Shaphan.

¹⁶Then Shaphan took the book to the king and reported to him: "Your officials are doing everything that has been committed to them. ¹⁷They have paid out the money that was in the temple of the Lᴏʀᴅ and have entrusted it to the supervisors and workers." ¹⁸Then Shaphan the secretary informed the king, "Hilkiah the priest has given me a book." And Shaphan read from it in the presence of the king.

¹⁹When the king heard the words of the Law, ᵘ he tore ᵛ his robes. ²⁰He gave these orders to Hilkiah, Ahikam son of Shaphan, Abdon son of Micah, ᵃ Shaphan the secretary and Asaiah the king's attendant: ²¹"Go and inquire of the Lᴏʀᴅ for me and for the remnant in Israel and Judah about what is written in this book that has been found. Great is the Lᴏʀᴅ's anger that is poured out ʷ on us because our fathers have not kept the word of the Lᴏʀᴅ; they have not acted in accordance with all that is written in this book."

²²Hilkiah and those the king had sent with him ᵇ went to speak to the prophetess Huldah, who was the wife of Shallum son of Tokhath, ᶜ the son of Hasrah, ᵈ keeper of the wardrobe. She lived in Jerusalem, in the Second District.

²³She said to them, "This is what the Lᴏʀᴅ, the God of Israel, says: Tell the man who sent you to me, ²⁴'This is what the Lᴏʀᴅ says: I am going to bring disaster on this place and its people ˣ—all the curses ʸ written in the book that has been read in the presence of the king of Judah. ²⁵Because they have forsaken me ᶻ and burned incense to other gods and provoked me to anger by all that their hands have made, ᵉ my anger will be poured out on this place and will not be quenched.' ²⁶Tell the king of Judah, who sent you to inquire of the Lᴏʀᴅ, 'This is what the Lᴏʀᴅ, the God of Israel, says concerning the words you heard: ²⁷Because your heart was responsive ᵃ and you humbled yourself before God when you heard what he spoke against this place and its people, and because you humbled yourself before me and tore your robes and wept in my presence, I have heard you, declares the Lᴏʀᴅ. ²⁸Now I will gather you to your fathers, and you will be buried in peace. Your eyes will not see all the disaster I am going to bring on this place and on those who live here.'"

ᵃ20 Also called Acbor son of Micaiah   ᵇ22 One Hebrew manuscript, Vulgate and Syriac; most Hebrew manuscripts do not have had sent with him.   ᶜ22 Also called Tikvah   ᵈ22 Also called Harhas   ᵉ25 Or by everything they have done

34:7
ᵒ2Ch 31:1

34:9
ᵖ2Ch 35:8

34:11
�q2Ch 33:4-7

34:12
ʳ2Ki 12:15
ˢ1Ch 25:1

34:13
ᵗ1Ch 23:4

34:19
ᵘDt 28:3-68
ᵛJos 7:6

34:21
ʷ2Ch 29:8

34:24
ˣ2Ch 36:14-20
ʸDt 28:15-68

34:25
ᶻ2Ch 33:3-6

34:27
ᵃ2Ch 12:7; 32:26

34:14, 15 The Book of the Law of the Lord that Hilkiah found was probably the book of Deuteronomy that had been lost during the reigns of the evil kings. Now that it was found, Josiah realized that drastic changes had to be made in order to bring the nation back in line with God's commands. This account is also recorded in 2 Kings 22:8–13.

34:19 It is human nature to treat sin lightly—to make excuses, blame somebody else, or minimize the harm done. Not so with Josiah. He was so appalled at the people's neglect of the law that he tore his clothing to express his grief. True understanding of our sins should lead to "godly sorrow" that "brings repentance that leads to salvation" (2 Corinthians 7:10). Are you always excusing your sin, blaming others, and pretending that it's not so bad? God

So they took her answer back to the king. ²⁹Then the king called together all the elders of Judah and Jerusalem. ³⁰He went up to the

34:30
b 2Ki 23:2; Ne 8:1-3

temple of the LORD *b* with the men of Judah, the people of Jerusalem, the priests and the Levites—all the people from the least to the greatest. He read in their hearing all the words of the Book of the Covenant, which had been found in the temple of the LORD. ³¹The king stood by

34:31
c 2Ki 11:14
d 2Ch 23:16

his pillar *c* and renewed the covenant *d* in the presence of the LORD—to follow the LORD and keep his commands, regulations and decrees with all his heart and all his soul, and to obey the words of the covenant written in this book.

³²Then he had everyone in Jerusalem and Benjamin pledge themselves to it; the people of Jerusalem did this in accordance with the covenant of God, the God of their fathers.

³³Josiah removed all the detestable idols from all the territory belonging to the Israelites, and he had all who were present in Israel serve the LORD their God. As long as he lived, they did not fail to follow the LORD, the God of their fathers.

Josiah Celebrates the Passover

35:1
e Ex 12:1-30

35 Josiah celebrated the Passover *e* to the LORD in Jerusalem, and the Passover lamb was slaughtered on the fourteenth day of the first month. ²He appointed the priests to their duties and encouraged them in the service of the LORD's temple. ³He said to the Le-

35:3
f 1Ch 23:26;
2Ch 17:7

vites, who instructed *f* all Israel and who had been consecrated to the LORD: "Put the sacred ark in the temple that Solomon son of David king of Israel built. It is not to be carried about on your shoulders. Now serve the LORD your God and his people Israel. ⁴Prepare yourselves

35:4
g 1Ch 9:10-13;
2Ch 8:14; Ezr 6:18

by families in your divisions, *g* according to the directions written by David king of Israel and by his son Solomon.

⁵"Stand in the holy place with a group of Levites for each subdivision of the families of your fellow countrymen, the lay people. ⁶Slaughter the Passover lambs, consecrate yourselves *h*

35:6
h 2Ch 29:5, 15

and prepare ⌊the lambs⌋ for your fellow countrymen, doing what the LORD commanded through Moses."

35:7
i 2Ch 30:24

⁷Josiah provided for all the lay people who were there a total of thirty thousand sheep and goats for the Passover offerings, *i* and also three thousand cattle—all from the king's own possessions.

⁸His officials also contributed voluntarily to the people and the priests and Levites. Hilkiah, Zechariah and Jehiel, the administrators of God's temple, gave the priests twenty-six hundred Passover offerings and three hundred cattle. ⁹Also Conaniah *j* along with Shemaiah

35:9
j 2Ch 31:12

and Nethanel, his brothers, and Hashabiah, Jeiel and Jozabad, the leaders of the Levites, provided five thousand Passover offerings and five hundred head of cattle for the Levites.

¹⁰The service was arranged and the priests stood in their places with the Levites in their divisions as the king had ordered. ¹¹The Passover lambs were slaughtered, *k* and the priests

35:11
k 2Ch 29:22, 34

sprinkled the blood handed to them, while the Levites skinned the animals. ¹²They set aside the burnt offerings to give them to the subdivisions of the families of the people to offer to the

35:13
l Ex 12:2-11

LORD, as is written in the Book of Moses. They did the same with the cattle. ¹³They roasted the Passover animals over the fire as prescribed, *l* and boiled the holy offerings in pots, caldrons and pans and served them quickly to all the people. ¹⁴After this, they made preparations for themselves and for the priests, because the priests, the descendants of Aaron, were sacrificing the burnt offerings and the fat portions until nightfall. So the Levites made prepara-

35:15
m 1Ch 25:1;
26:12-19

tions for themselves and for the Aaronic priests.

¹⁵The musicians, *m* the descendants of Asaph, were in the places prescribed by David,

---

does not take sin lightly, and he wants us to respond with true remorse as Josiah did.

34:31 When Josiah read the book that Hilkiah discovered (34:14), he responded with repentance and humility and promised to follow God's commands as written in the book. The Bible is God's word to us, "living and active" (Hebrews 4:12), but we cannot know what God wants us to do if we do not read it. And even reading God's Word is not enough; we must be willing to do what it says. There is not much difference between the book hidden in the temple and the Bible hidden on the bookshelf. An unread Bible is as useless as a lost one.

35:3 In Moses' day, one of the duties of the Levites was to carry the ark of the covenant whenever Israel traveled. "Put the sacred ark in the temple" implies that it may have been moved during

the reigns of the previous evil kings, Manasseh and Amon. The ark was now permanently housed in the temple and would no longer be carried about in procession as it was in the desert. Josiah was telling the Levites that they were now free to take on other responsibilities (1 Chronicles 24).

35:15 The temple gatekeepers, who were all Levites, guarded the four main entrances to the temple and opened the gates each morning. They also did other day-to-day chores such as cleaning and preparing the offerings for sacrifice and accounting for the gifts given to the temple. (For more on gatekeepers, see 1 Chronicles 26:1ff.)

Asaph, Heman and Jeduthun the king's seer. The gatekeepers at each gate did not need to leave their posts, because their fellow Levites made the preparations for them.

[16]So at that time the entire service of the LORD was carried out for the celebration of the Passover and the offering of burnt offerings on the altar of the LORD, as King Josiah had ordered. [17]The Israelites who were present celebrated the Passover at that time and observed the Feast of Unleavened Bread for seven days. [18]The Passover had not been observed like this in Israel since the days of the prophet Samuel; and none of the kings of Israel had ever celebrated such a Passover as did Josiah, with the priests, the Levites and all Judah and Israel who were there with the people of Jerusalem. [19]This Passover was celebrated in the eighteenth year of Josiah's reign.

The Death of Josiah

[20]After all this, when Josiah had set the temple in order, Neco king of Egypt went up to fight at Carchemish[n] on the Euphrates, and Josiah marched out to meet him in battle. [21]But Neco sent messengers to him, saying, "What quarrel is there between you and me, O king of Judah? It is not you I am attacking at this time, but the house with which I am at war. God has told me to hurry; so stop opposing God, who is with me, or he will destroy you."

[22]Josiah, however, would not turn away from him, but disguised himself to engage him in battle. He would not listen to what Neco had said at God's command but went to fight him on the plain of Megiddo.

[23]Archers shot King Josiah, and he told his officers, "Take me away; I am badly wounded." [24]So they took him out of his chariot, put him in the other chariot he had and brought him to Jerusalem, where he died. He was buried in the tombs of his fathers, and all Judah and Jerusalem mourned for him.

[25]Jeremiah composed laments for Josiah, and to this day all the men and women singers commemorate Josiah in the laments.[o] These became a tradition in Israel and are written in the Laments.

[26]The other events of Josiah's reign and his acts of devotion, according to what is written in the Law of the LORD— [27]all the events, from beginning to end, are written in the book of

36 the kings of Israel and Judah. [1]And the people of the land took Jehoahaz son of Josiah and made him king in Jerusalem in place of his father.

35:20
[n] Isa 10:9; Jer 46:2

35:25
[o] Jer 22:10, 15-16

35:17 The Feast of Unleavened Bread was a seven-day celebration beginning the day after Passover. Like Passover, it commemorated the exodus from Egypt. For seven days the

THE BATTLE AT CARCHEMISH A world war was brewing in 609 B.C. when Pharaoh Neco of Egypt set out for the city of Carchemish to join the Assyrians in an attempt to defeat the Babylonians, who were rising to great power. Neco marched his armies through Judah, where King Josiah tried to stop him at Megiddo, but was killed. The battle began at Carchemish in 605 B.C., and the Egyptians and Assyrians were soundly defeated, chased to Hamath, and defeated again. Babylon was now the new world power.

people ate bread without yeast, just as their ancestors did while leaving Egypt because it could be made quickly in preparation for their swift departure (Exodus 12:14–20). This feast reminded the people that they had left slavery behind and had come to the land God promised them.

35:20 This event occurred in 609 B.C. Nineveh, the Assyrian capital, had been destroyed three years earlier by the Babylonians. The defeated Assyrians regrouped at Haran and Carchemish, but Babylon sent its army to destroy them once and for all. Pharaoh Neco, who wanted to make Egypt a world power, was worried about Babylon's growing strength, so he marched his army north through Judah to help the Assyrians at Carchemish. But King Josiah of Judah tried to prevent Neco from passing through his land on his way to Carchemish. Josiah was killed, and Judah became subject to Egypt. (2 Kings 23:25–30 helps explain the tragedy. Even though Josiah followed the Lord, God did not turn from his judgment on Judah because of Manasseh's sin and Israel's superficial repentance.) Neco went on to Carchemish and held off the Babylonians for four years, but in 605 he was soundly defeated, and Babylon moved into the spotlight as the dominant world power.

35:21–24 Josiah ignored Neco's message because of who Neco was—king of a pagan nation. The mistaken assumption that Neco could not be part of God's larger plan cost Josiah his life. While not everyone who claims to have a message from God really does, God's messages may come in unexpected ways. God had spoken to pagan kings in the past (Genesis 12:17–20; 20:3–7; see also Daniel 4:1–3). Don't let prejudice or false assumptions blind you to God's message.

35:25 Though Jeremiah recorded these laments for the death of Josiah, they are not the same as the book of Lamentations.

3. Judah is exiled to Babylon

Jehoahaz King of Judah

2 Jehoahaz[a] was twenty-three years old when he became king, and he reigned in Jerusalem three months. 3 The king of Egypt dethroned him in Jerusalem and imposed on Judah a levy of a hundred talents[b] of silver and a talent[c] of gold. 4 The king of Egypt made Eliakim, a brother of Jehoahaz, king over Judah and Jerusalem and changed Eliakim's name to Jehoiakim. But Neco took Eliakim's brother Jehoahaz and carried him off to Egypt.

Jehoiakim King of Judah

5 Jehoiakim[p] was twenty-five years old when he became king, and he reigned in Jerusalem eleven years. He did evil in the eyes of the LORD his God. 6 Nebuchadnezzar king of Babylon attacked him and bound him with bronze shackles to take him to Babylon. [q] 7 Nebuchadnezzar also took to Babylon articles from the temple of the LORD and put them in his temple[d] there. [r]

8 The other events of Jehoiakim's reign, the detestable things he did and all that was found against him, are written in the book of the kings of Israel and Judah. And Jehoiachin his son succeeded him as king.

Jehoiachin King of Judah

9 Jehoiachin was eighteen[e] years old when he became king, and he reigned in Jerusalem three months and ten days. He did evil in the eyes of the LORD. 10 In the spring, King Nebuchadnezzar sent for him and brought him to Babylon, [s] together with articles of value from the temple of the LORD, and he made Jehoiachin's uncle,[f] Zedekiah, king over Judah and Jerusalem.

Zedekiah King of Judah

11 Zedekiah[t] was twenty-one years old when he became king, and he reigned in Jerusalem eleven years. 12 He did evil in the eyes of the LORD his God and did not humble[u] himself before Jeremiah the prophet, who spoke the word of the LORD. 13 He also rebelled against King Nebuchadnezzar, who had made him take an oath in God's name. He became stiff-necked[v] and hardened his heart and would not turn to the LORD, the God of Israel. 14 Furthermore, all the leaders of the priests and the people became more and more unfaithful, following all the detestable practices of the nations and defiling the temple of the LORD, which he had consecrated in Jerusalem.

The Fall of Jerusalem

15 The LORD, the God of their fathers, sent word to them through his messengers again and again,[w] because he had pity on his people and on his dwelling place. 16 But they mocked God's messengers, despised his words and scoffed[x] at his prophets until the wrath[y] of the LORD was aroused against his people and there was no remedy. [z] 17 He brought up against them the king of the Babylonians,[g] who killed their young men with the sword in the sanctuary, and spared neither young man nor young woman, old man or aged. God handed all of them over to Nebuchadnezzar. 18 He carried to Babylon all the articles from the temple of God, both large and small, and the treasures of the LORD's temple and the treasures of the king and his officials. 19 They set fire to God's temple[a] and broke down the wall of Jerusalem; they burned all the palaces and destroyed everything of value there. [b]

36:5
p Jer 26:1; 35:1
36:6
q 2Ch 33:11
36:7
r 2Ki 24:13

36:10
s Jer 22:25; 24:1; 37:1; Eze 17:12

36:11
t Jer 27:1; 28:1
36:12
u 2Ch 33:23; Jer 21:3-7
36:13
v 2Ki 17:14; 2Ch 30:8

36:15
w Jer 7:13, 25; 25:3-4

36:16
x Pr 1:25; Jer 5:13
y Ezr 5:12; Pr 1:30-31
z 2Ch 30:10

36:19
a 1Ki 9:8-9
b Ps 79:1-3

a 2 Hebrew *Joahaz*, a variant of *Jehoahaz*; also in verse 4   b 3 That is, about 3 3/4 tons (about 3.4 metric tons)   c 3 That is, about 75 pounds (about 34 kilograms)   d 7 Or *palace*   e 9 One Hebrew manuscript, some Septuagint manuscripts and Syriac (see also 2 Kings 24:8); most Hebrew manuscripts *eight*   f 10 Hebrew *brother*, that is, relative (see 2 Kings 24:17)   g 17 Or *Chaldeans*

36:6 Nebuchadnezzar was the son of the founder of the new Babylonian empire. In 605 B.C., the year he became king, Nebuchadnezzar won the battle of Carchemish. That loss crushed Assyria (see the note on 35:20). (For more information about Nebuchadnezzar, read his Profile in Daniel 3.)

36:9, 10 In 2 Kings 24:8, Jehoiachin is listed as 18 years old. Many Hebrew manuscripts list him as eight years old. The age given in 2 Kings 24:8 is most likely accurate because he had wives at that time (see 2 Kings 24:15).

36:16 God warned Judah about its sin and continually restored the people to his favor, only to have them turn away. Eventually the situation was beyond remedy. Beware of harboring sin in your heart. The day will come when remedy is no longer possible and God's judgment replaces his mercy. Sin often repeated, but never repented of, invites disaster.

²⁰He carried into exile to Babylon the remnant, who escaped from the sword, and they became servants ᶜ to him and his sons until the kingdom of Persia came to power. ²¹The land enjoyed its sabbath rests; ᵈ all the time of its desolation it rested, until the seventy years ᵉ were completed in fulfillment of the word of the LORD spoken by Jeremiah.

²²In the first year of Cyrus ᶠ king of Persia, in order to fulfill the word of the LORD spoken by Jeremiah, the LORD moved the heart of Cyrus king of Persia to make a proclamation throughout his realm and to put it in writing:

²³"This is what Cyrus king of Persia says:

"'The LORD, the God of heaven, has given me all the kingdoms of the earth and he has appointed me to build a temple for him at Jerusalem in Judah. Anyone of his people among you—may the LORD his God be with him, and let him go up.'"

36:20
ᶜ Jer 27:7
36:21
ᵈ Lev 25:4; 26:34
ᵉ Jer 25:11; 29:10;
Da 9:2
36:22
ᶠ Isa 44:28;
Jer 25:12; 29:10

36:21 Leviticus 26:27–45 strikingly predicts the captivity, telling how God's people would be torn from their land for disobeying

EXILE TO BABYLON Despite Judah's few good kings and timely reforms, the people never truly changed. Their evil continued, and finally God used the Babylonian empire, under Nebuchadnezzar, to conquer Judah, destroy Jerusalem, and take the people captive to Babylon.

him. One of the laws they had ignored stated that one year in every seven the land should lie fallow, resting from producing crops (Exodus 23:10, 11). The 70-year captivity allowed the land to rest, making up for all the years the Israelites had not observed this law. We know that God keeps all his promises—not only his promises of blessing, but also his promises of judgment.

36:22, 23 Cyrus made this proclamation 48 years after the temple was destroyed (36:18, 19), the year after he conquered Babylon. The book of Ezra tells the story of this proclamation and the return of the exiles to Judah.

36:22, 23 Second Chronicles focuses on the rise and fall of the worship of God as symbolized by the Jerusalem temple. David planned the temple; Solomon built it and then put on the greatest dedication service the world had ever seen. Worship in the temple was superbly organized.

But several evil kings defiled the temple and degraded worship so that the people revered idols more highly than God. Finally, King Nebuchadnezzar of Babylon destroyed the temple (36:19). The kings were gone, the temple was destroyed, and the people were removed. The nation was stripped to its very foundation. But fortunately there was a greater foundation—God himself. When everything in life seems stripped away from us, we too still have God—his Word, his presence, and his promises.

EZRA

NAME the truly great men and women of your lifetime. Celebrities, including politicians, war heroes, sports figures, and maybe your parents and special friends come to mind. You remember them because of certain acts or character qualities. Now, name some biblical heroes—figures etched in your mind through countless sermons and church school lessons. This list undoubtedly includes many who served God faithfully and courageously. Does your list include Ezra? Far from being well known, this unheralded man of God deserves to be mentioned in any discussion of greatness.

Ezra was a priest, a scribe, and a great leader. His name means "help," and his whole life was dedicated to serving God and God's people. Tradition says that Ezra wrote most of 1 and 2 Chronicles, Ezra, Nehemiah, and Psalm 119 and that he led the council of 120 men who compiled the Old Testament canon. The narrative of the book of Ezra is centered on God and his promise that the Jews would return to their land, as prophesied by Jeremiah (see the third note on 1:1). This message formed the core of Ezra's life. The last half of the book gives a very personal glimpse of Ezra. His knowledge of Scripture and his God-given wisdom were so obvious to the king that he appointed Ezra to lead the second emigration to Jerusalem, to teach the people God's Word, and to administer national life (7:14–26).

Ezra not only knew God's Word, he believed and obeyed it. Upon learning of the Israelites' sins of intermarriage and idolatry, Ezra fell in humility before God and prayed for the nation (9:1–15). Their disobedience touched him deeply (10:1). His response helped lead the people back to God.

Second Chronicles ends with Cyrus, king of Persia, asking for volunteers to return to Jerusalem to build a house for God. Ezra continues this account (1:1–3 is almost identical to 2 Chronicles 36:22, 23) as two caravans of God's people were returning to Jerusalem. Zerubbabel, the leader of the first trip, was joined by 42,360 pilgrims who journeyed homeward (chapter 2). After arriving, they began to build the altar and the temple foundations (chapter 3). But opposition arose from the local inhabitants, and a campaign of accusations and rumors temporarily halted the project (chapter 4). During this time, the prophets Haggai and Zechariah encouraged the people (chapter 5). Finally, Darius decreed that the work should proceed unhindered (chapter 6).

After a 58-year gap, Ezra led a group of Jews from Persia. Armed with decrees and authority from Artaxerxes I, Ezra's task was to administer the affairs of the land (chapters 7; 8). Upon arriving, he learned of intermarriage between God's people and their pagan neighbors. He wept and prayed for the nation (chapter 9). Ezra's example of humble confession led to national revival (chapter 10). Ezra, a man of God and a true hero, was a model for Israel, and he is a fitting model for us.

Read Ezra, the book, and remember Ezra, the man—a humble, obedient helper. Commit yourself to serving God as he did, with your whole life.

VITAL STATISTICS

PURPOSE:
To show God's faithfulness and the way he kept his promise to restore his people to their land

AUTHOR:
Not stated, but probably Ezra

ORIGINAL AUDIENCE:
The exiles who returned from captivity

DATE WRITTEN:
Around 450 B.C., recording events from about 538–450 B.C. (omitting 516–458 B.C.); possibly begun earlier in Babylon and finished in Jerusalem

SETTING:
Ezra follows 2 Chronicles as a history of the Jewish people, recording their return to the land after the captivity.

KEY VERSES:
"So the Israelites who had returned from the exile ate it [the Passover], together with all who had separated themselves from the unclean practices of their Gentile neighbors in order to seek the LORD, the God of Israel. For seven days they celebrated with joy the Feast of Unleavened Bread, because the LORD had filled them with joy by changing the attitude of the king of Assyria, so that he assisted them in the work on the house of God, the God of Israel" (6:21, 22).

KEY PEOPLE:
Cyrus, Zerubbabel, Haggai, Zechariah, Darius I, Artaxerxes I, Ezra

KEY PLACES:
Babylon, Jerusalem

SPECIAL FEATURES:
Ezra and Nehemiah were one book in the Hebrew Bible, and, with Esther, they comprise the post-captivity historical books. The post-captivity prophetic books are Haggai, Zechariah, and Malachi. Haggai and Zechariah should be studied with Ezra because they prophesied during the period of the reconstruction.

THE BLUEPRINT

A. THE RETURN LED BY ZERUBBABEL
   (1:1—6:22)
   1. The first group of exiles returns
      to the land
   2. The people rebuild the temple

B. THE RETURN LED BY EZRA (7:1—10:44)
   1. The second group of exiles returns
      to the land
   2. Ezra opposes intermarriage

Finally given the chance to return to their homeland, the people started to rebuild the temple, only to be stopped by opposition from their enemies. God's work in the world is not without opposition. We must not get discouraged and quit, as the returning people did at first, but continue on boldly in the face of difficulties, as they did later with encouragement from the prophets.

Ezra returned to Jerusalem almost 80 years after Zerubbabel, only to discover that the people had married pagan or foreign spouses. This polluted the religious purity of the people and endangered the future of the nation. Believers today must be careful not to threaten their walk with God by taking on the practices of unbelievers.

MEGATHEMES

THEME	EXPLANATION	IMPORTANCE
The Jews Return	By returning to the land of Israel from Babylon, the Jews showed their faith in God's promise to restore them as a people. They returned not only to their homeland but also to the place where their forefathers had promised to follow God.	God shows his mercy to every generation. He compassionately restores his people. No matter how difficult our present "captivity," we are never far from his love and mercy. He restores us when we return to him.
Rededication	In 536 B.C., Zerubbabel led the people in rebuilding the altar and laying the temple foundation. They reinstated daily sacrifices and annual feasts, and rededicated themselves to a new spiritual worship of God.	In rededicating the altar, the people were recommitting themselves to God and his service. To grow spiritually, our commitment must be reviewed and renewed often. As we rededicate ourselves to God, our lives become altars to him.
Opposition	Opposition came soon after the altar was built and the temple foundation laid. Enemies of the Jews used deceit to hinder the building for over six years. Finally, there was a decree to stop the building altogether. This opposition severely tested their wavering faith.	There will always be adversaries who oppose God's work. The life of faith is never easy. But God can overrule all opposition to his service. When we face opposition, we must not falter or withdraw, but keep active and patient.
God's Word	When the people returned to the land, they were also returning to the influence of God's Word. The prophets Haggai and Zechariah helped encourage them, while Ezra's preaching of Scripture built them up. God's Word gave them what they needed to do God's work.	We also need the encouragement and direction of God's Word. We must make it the basis for our faith and actions to finish God's work and fulfill our obligations. We must never waver in our commitment to hear and obey his Word.
Faith and Action	The urging of Israel's leaders motivated the people to complete the temple. Over the years they had intermarried with idol worshipers and adopted their pagan practices. Their faith, tested and revived, also led them to remove these sins from their lives.	Faith led them to complete the temple and to remove sin from their society. As we trust God with our hearts and minds, we must also act by completing our daily responsibilities. It is not enough to say we believe; we must make the changes God requires.

A. THE RETURN LED BY ZERUBBABEL (1:1—6:22)

After 70 years in exile, the captives from Judah were allowed to return to their homeland. Nearly 50,000 people made this journey. Upon arrival they began to rebuild the temple, but became discouraged by opposition. After encouragement from Haggai and Zechariah, they returned to the task and completed the temple. The message of the prophets still speaks to us today, encouraging us to continue building up God's church.

1. The first group of exiles returns to the land
Cyrus Helps the Exiles to Return

1 In the first year of Cyrus king of Persia, in order to fulfill the word of the LORD spoken by Jeremiah,[a] the LORD moved the heart[b] of Cyrus king of Persia to make a proclamation throughout his realm and to put it in writing:

1:1
[a] Jer 25:11-12; 29:10-14
[b] 2Ch 36:22, 23

1:1 The book of Ezra opens in 538 B.C., 48 years after Nebuchadnezzar destroyed Jerusalem, defeated the southern kingdom of Judah, and carried the Jews away to Babylon as captives (2 Kings 25; 2 Chronicles 36). Nebuchadnezzar died in 562, and because his

1:2
c Isa 44:28; 45:13
d Ezr 5:13

2 "This is what Cyrus king of Persia says:

"'The LORD, the God of heaven, has given me all the kingdoms of the earth and he has appointed c me to build d a temple for him at Jerusalem in Judah. 3Anyone of his people among you—may his God be with him, and let him go up to Jerusalem in Judah and build the temple of the LORD, the God of Israel, the God who is in Jerusalem. 4And the people of any place where survivors may now be living are to provide him with silver and gold, with goods and livestock, and with freewill offerings for the temple of God in Jerusalem.'"

PROPHECIES FULFILLED BY THE RETURN OF ISRAEL FROM EXILE

Reference	Prophecy	Approximate Date	Fulfillment Date	Significance
Isaiah 44:28	Cyrus would be used by God to guarantee the return of a remnant. Jerusalem would be rebuilt and the temple restored.	688 B.C.	538 B.C.	As God named Cyrus even before he was born, God knows what will happen—he is in control.
Jeremiah 25:12	Babylon would be punished for destroying Jerusalem and exiling God's people.	605 B.C.	539 B.C.	Babylon was conquered by Cyrus the Great. God may seem to allow evil to go unpunished, but consequences for wrongdoing are inevitable. God will punish evil.
Jeremiah 29:10	The people would spend 70 years in Babylon; then God would bring them back to their homeland.	594 B.C.	538 B.C.	The 70 years of captivity passed (see the third note on 1:1), and God provided the opportunity for Zerubbabel to lead the first group of captives home. God's plans may allow for hardship, but his desire is for our good.
Daniel 5:17–30	God had judged the Babylonian empire. It would be given to the Medes and the Persians, forming a new world power.	539 B.C.	539 B.C.	Belshazzar was killed and Babylon was conquered the same night. God's judgment is accurate and swift. God knows the point of no return in each of our lives. Until then, he allows the freedom for us to repent and seek his forgiveness.

God, through his faithful prophets, said that the people of Judah would be taken into captivity because of their sinfulness. But he also promised that they would return to Jerusalem and rebuild the city, the temple, and the nation.

successors were not strong, Babylon was overthrown by Persia in 539, just prior to the events recorded in this book. Both the Babylonians and the Persians had a relaxed policy toward their captives, allowing them to own land and homes and to take ordinary jobs. Many Jews such as Daniel, Mordecai, and Esther rose to prominent positions within the nation. King Cyrus of Persia went a step further: he allowed many groups of exiles, including the Jews, to return to their homelands. By doing this, he hoped to win their loyalty and thus provide buffer zones around the borders of his empire. For the Jews this was a day of hope, a new beginning.

1:1 Cyrus, king of Persia (559–530 B.C.), had already begun his rise to power in the Near East by unifying the Medes and Persians into a strong empire. As he conquered cities, he treated the inhabitants with mercy. Although not a servant of Yahweh, Cyrus was used by God to return the Jews to their homeland. Cyrus may have been shown the prophecy of Isaiah 44:28—45:6, written over a century earlier, which predicted that Cyrus himself would help the Jews return to Jerusalem. Daniel, a prominent government official (Daniel 5:29; 6:28), would have been familiar with the prophecy. The book of Daniel has more to say about Cyrus.

1:1 Jeremiah prophesied that the Jews would remain in captivity for 70 years (Jeremiah 25:11; 29:10). The 70-year period has been

calculated two different ways: (1) from the first captivity in 605 B.C. (2 Kings 24:1) until the altar was rebuilt by the returned exiles in 536 (Ezra 3:1–6), or (2) from the destruction of the temple in 586 until the exiles finished rebuilding it in 516. Many scholars prefer the second approach because the temple was the focus and heartbeat of the nation. Without the temple, the Jews did not consider themselves reestablished as a nation.

1:2 Cyrus was not a Jew, but God worked through him to return the exiled Jews to their homeland. Cyrus gave the proclamation allowing their return, and he gave them protection, money, and the temple articles taken by Nebuchadnezzar. When you face difficult situations and feel surrounded, outnumbered, overpowered, or outclassed, remember that God's power is not limited to your resources. He is able to use anyone to carry out his plans.

1:2–4 This proclamation permitted the Jews to work together to accomplish the huge task of rebuilding the temple. Some did the actual building, while others operated the supply lines. Significant ventures require teamwork, with certain people serving in the forefront and others providing support. Each function is vital to accomplishing the task. When you're asked to serve, do so faithfully as a team member, no matter who gets the credit.

⁵Then the family heads of Judah and Benjamin, and the priests and Levites—everyone whose heart God had moved *e*—prepared to go up and build the house of the Lord in Jerusalem. ⁶All their neighbors assisted them with articles of silver and gold, with goods and livestock, and with valuable gifts, in addition to all the freewill offerings. ⁷Moreover, King Cyrus brought out the articles belonging to the temple of the Lord, which Nebuchadnezzar had carried away from Jerusalem and had placed in the temple of his god.ᵃ ⁸Cyrus king of Persia had them brought by Mithredath the treasurer, who counted them out to Sheshbazzar *g* the prince of Judah.

⁹This was the inventory:

gold dishes	30
silver dishes	1,000
silver pansᵇ	29
¹⁰ gold bowls	30
matching silver bowls	410
other articles	1,000

¹¹In all, there were 5,400 articles of gold and of silver. Sheshbazzar brought all these along when the exiles came up from Babylon to Jerusalem.

The List of the Exiles Who Returned

2 Now these are the people of the province who came up from the captivity of the exiles,*h* whom Nebuchadnezzar king of Babylon *i* had taken captive to Babylon (they returned to

ᵃ7 Or *gods*   ᵇ9 The meaning of the Hebrew for this word is uncertain.

1:5
*e*ver 1; Php 2:13

1:7
*f*2Ki 24:13;
2Ch 36:7, 10;
Ezr 5:14; 6:5

1:8
*g*Ezr 5:14

2:1
*h*2Ch 36:20; Ne 7:6
*i*2Ki 24:16; 25:12

1:5 Cyrus was king over the entire region that had once been Assyria and Babylon. Assyria had deported the Israelites from the northern kingdom (Israel) in 722 B.C. Babylon, the next world power, had taken Israelites captive from the southern kingdom (Judah) in 586 B.C. Therefore, when the Medo-Persian empire came to power, King Cyrus's proclamation of freedom went to all the original 12 tribes, but only Judah and Benjamin responded and returned to rebuild God's temple. The ten tribes of the northern kingdom had been so fractured and dispersed by Assyria, and so much time had elapsed since their captivity, that many might have been unsure of their real heritage. Thus they were unwilling to share in the vision of rebuilding the temple.

1:5 God moved the hearts of the leaders, family heads, priests, and Levites and gave them a great desire to return to Jerusalem to rebuild the temple. Major changes begin on the inside as God works on our attitudes, beliefs, and desires. These inner changes lead to faithful actions. After 48 years of captivity, the arrogant Jewish nation had been humbled. When the people's attitudes and desires changed, God ended their punishment and gave them another opportunity to go home and try again. In the New

Testament, Paul reminds us that "it is God who works in you to will and to act according to his good purpose" (Philippians 2:13). Doing God's will begins with your desires. Are you willing to be humble, to be open to his opportunities, and to move at his direction? Ask God to give you the desire to follow him more closely.

1:5, 6 Many Jews chose to go to Jerusalem, but many more chose to remain in Babylon rather than return to their homeland. The journey back to Jerusalem was difficult, dangerous, and expensive, lasting over four months. Travel conditions were poor; Jerusalem and the surrounding countryside were in ruins; and the people living in the area were hostile.

Persian records indicate that many Jews in captivity had accumulated great wealth. Returning to Jerusalem would have meant giving up everything they had and starting over. Many people couldn't bring themselves to do that; they preferred wealth and security to the sacrifice that God's work would require. Their priorities were upside down (Mark 4:18, 19). We must not let our comfort, security, or material possessions prevent us from doing what God wants.

1:7 When King Nebuchadnezzar ransacked the temple, he took many of the valuable furnishings with him. What he did not take, he burned (2 Chronicles 36:18, 19). Most of the captured items were made of solid gold (1 Kings 7:48–50), and Cyrus kindly returned them to the Jews for the temple they would soon rebuild.

1:8 Either Sheshbazzar was the Babylonian name for Zerubbabel, one of the Jewish leaders during the first return (2:2; 3:8; 4:3), or he was a government official with responsibility for the returning party. The reasons Sheshbazzar may be identified with Zerubbabel are as follows: (1) both were called governors (5:14; Haggai 1:1); (2) both laid the temple foundation (3:8; 5:16); (3) Jews in exile were often given Babylonian names (see Daniel 1:7 where Daniel and his companions were given new names).

1:9–11 Every article of gold and silver was a witness to God's protection and care. Although many years had passed, God delivered these temple articles back to his people. We may be discouraged by events in life, but we must never give up our hope in God's promises to us. The turning point may be just ahead.

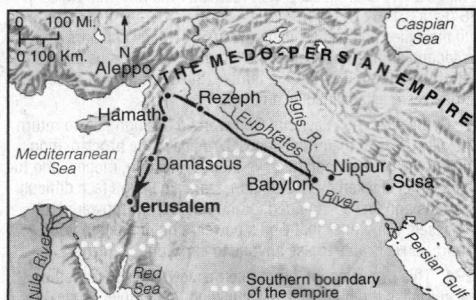

THE JOURNEY HOME The vast Medo-Persian empire included all the area on this map and more. A group of exiles began the long trip back to their homeland. Many exiles, however, preferred the comfort and security they had in Babylon to the dangerous trip back to Jerusalem, and so they decided to stay in Babylon.

Jerusalem and Judah, each to his own town, *i* 2 in company with Zerubbabel, Jeshua, Nehemiah, Seraiah, Reelaiah, Mordecai, Bilshan, Mispar, Bigvai, Rehum and Baanah):

The list of the men of the people of Israel:

3 the descendants of Parosh	2,172
4 of Shephatiah	372
5 of Arah	775
6 of Pahath-Moab (through the line of Jeshua and Joab)	2,812
7 of Elam	1,254
8 of Zattu	945
9 of Zaccai	760
10 of Bani	642
11 of Bebai	623
12 of Azgad	1,222
13 of Adonikam	666
14 of Bigvai	2,056
15 of Adin	454
16 of Ater (through Hezekiah)	98
17 of Bezai	323
18 of Jorah	112
19 of Hashum	223
20 of Gibbar	95
21 the men of Bethlehem	123
22 of Netophah	56
23 of Anathoth	128
24 of Azmaveth	42
25 of Kiriath Jearim, *a* Kephirah and Beeroth	743
26 of Ramah *k* and Geba	621
27 of Micmash	122
28 of Bethel and Ai	223
29 of Nebo	52
30 of Magbish	156

a 25 See Septuagint (see also Neh. 7:29); Hebrew *Kiriath Arim.*

THE RETURN FROM EXILE

Year	Number of People Returned	Persian King	Jewish Leader	Main Accomplishment
538 B.C.	50,000	Cyrus	Zerubbabel	They rebuilt the temple, but only after a 20-year struggle. The work was halted for several years but was finally finished.
458 B.C.	2,000 men and their families	Artaxerxes	Ezra	Ezra confronted the spiritual disobedience of the people, and they repented and established worship at the temple. But the wall of Jerusalem remained in ruins.
445 B.C.	Small group	Artaxerxes	Nehemiah	The city was rebuilt, and a spiritual awakening followed. But the people still struggled with ongoing disobedience.

Babylon, the once-mighty nation that had destroyed Jerusalem and carried the people of Judah into captivity, had itself become a defeated nation. Persia was the new world power, and under its new foreign policy, captured peoples were allowed to return to their homelands. The people of Judah and Israel returned to their land in three successive waves.

2:2 The Nehemiah listed here is a different person from the one who rebuilt Jerusalem's walls 80 years later, and the Mordecai listed here is not the one who appears in the book of Esther.

2:2 This first list is made up of men who were leaders. The same list occurs in Nehemiah 7:7.

2:2–35 These people were from the tribes of Judah and Benjamin (1:5).

2:3–35 This list is the major group of those returning, divided by families (2:3–20) or by cities (2:21–35). Verse 36 begins listing priests, Levites, and other temple servants.

31 of the other Elam	1,254
32 of Harim	320
33 of Lod, Hadid and Ono	725
34 of Jericho*l*	345
35 of Senaah	3,630

2:34
l 1Ki 16:34;
2Ch 28:15

36 The priests:

the descendants of Jedaiah*m* (through the family of Jeshua)	973
37 of Immer*n*	1,052
38 of Pashhur*o*	1,247
39 of Harim*p*	1,017

2:36
m 1Ch 24:7

2:37
n 1Ch 24:14

2:38
o 1Ch 9:12

2:39
p 1Ch 24:8

40 The Levites:

the descendants of Jeshua*q* and Kadmiel (through the line of Hodaviah)	74

2:40
q Ezr 3:9

41 The singers:

the descendants of Asaph	128

42 The gatekeepers of the temple:

the descendants of Shallum, Ater, Talmon, Akkub, Hatita and Shobai	139

43 The temple servants:*r*

the descendants of
Ziha, Hasupha, Tabbaoth,
44 Keros, Siaha, Padon,
45 Lebanah, Hagabah, Akkub,
46 Hagab, Shalmai, Hanan,
47 Giddel, Gahar, Reaiah,
48 Rezin, Nekoda, Gazzam,
49 Uzza, Paseah, Besai,
50 Asnah, Meunim, Nephusim,
51 Bakbuk, Hakupha, Harhur,
52 Bazluth, Mehida, Harsha,
53 Barkos, Sisera, Temah,
54 Neziah and Hatipha

2:43
r 1Ch 9:2

55 The descendants of the servants of Solomon:

the descendants of
Sotai, Hassophereth, Peruda,
56 Jaala, Darkon, Giddel,
57 Shephatiah, Hattil,
Pokereth-Hazzebaim and Ami

58 The temple servants*s* and the descendants of the servants of Solomon	392

2:58
s 1Ch 9:2

59 The following came up from the towns of Tel Melah, Tel Harsha, Kerub, Addon and Immer, but they could not show that their families were descended from Israel:

60 The descendants of Delaiah, Tobiah and Nekoda	652

61 And from among the priests:

The descendants of
Hobaiah, Hakkoz and Barzillai (a man who had married a daughter of Barzillai the Gileadite*t* and was called by that name).

2:61
t 2Sa 17:27

2:59–63 Genealogies were very important credentials to the Hebrew people. If they could not prove they had descended from Abraham, they were not considered true Jews and were excluded from full participation in Jewish community

2:62
u Nu 3:10; 16:39-40
2:63
v Lev 2:3, 10
w Ex 28:30

62 These searched for their family records, but they could not find them and so were excluded from the priesthood u as unclean. 63 The governor ordered them not to eat any of the most sacred food v until there was a priest ministering with the Urim and Thummim. w

64 The whole company numbered 42,360, 65 besides their 7,337 menservants and maidservants; and they also had 200 men and women singers. 66 They had 736 horses, 245 mules, 67 435 camels and 6,720 donkeys.

68 When they arrived at the house of the Lord in Jerusalem, some of the heads of the families gave freewill offerings toward the rebuilding of the house of God on its site. 69 According to their ability they gave to the treasury for this work 61,000 drachmas a of gold, 5,000 minas b of silver and 100 priestly garments.

2:70
x 1Ch 9:2;
Ne 11:3-4

70 The priests, the Levites, the singers, the gatekeepers and the temple servants settled in their own towns, along with some of the other people, and the rest of the Israelites settled in their towns. x

3:1
y Ne 7:73
3:2
z Ezr 2:2
a Hag 1:1
b 1Ch 3:17
c Dt 12:5-6
3:3
d Ezr 4:4
e Nu 28:1-8
3:4
f Ex 23:16;
Nu 29:12-38;
Ne 8:14-18;
Zec 14:16-19
3:5
g Nu 28:3, 11, 14

2. The people rebuild the temple
Rebuilding the Altar

3 When the seventh month came and the Israelites had settled in their towns, y the people assembled as one man in Jerusalem. 2 Then Jeshua z son of Jozadak a and his fellow priests and Zerubbabel son of Shealtiel b and his associates began to build the altar of the God of Israel to sacrifice burnt offerings on it, in accordance with what is written in the Law of Moses c the man of God. 3 Despite their fear d of the peoples around them, they built the altar on its foundation and sacrificed burnt offerings on it to the Lord, both the morning and evening sacrifices. e 4 Then in accordance with what is written, they celebrated the Feast of Tabernacles f with the required number of burnt offerings prescribed for each day. 5 After that, they presented the regular burnt offerings, the New Moon g sacrifices and the sacrifices

a 69 That is, about 1,100 pounds (about 500 kilograms)   b 69 That is, about 3 tons (about 2.9 metric tons)

life. In addition, some privileges were restricted to members of certain tribes. For example, only descendants of Levi (Abraham's great-grandson) could serve in the temple.

2:63 The governor mentioned here was probably Zerubbabel. The Urim and Thummim were two objects, probably shaped like flat stones, originally carried in the garment worn by the high priest. They were used to determine God's will in important matters. (For more on the Urim and Thummim, see the note on Leviticus 8:8.) The "most sacred food" was the food that only the priests could eat. It was their allotted portion of meat that was sacrificed on the altar.

2:68, 69 As the temple reconstruction progressed, everyone contributed freewill offerings according to his or her ability. Some were able to give huge gifts and did so generously. Everyone's effort and cooperation were required, and the people gave as much as they could. Often we limit our giving to ten percent of our income. The Bible, however, emphasizes that we should give from the heart *all* that we are able (2 Corinthians 8:12; 9:6). Let the amount of your gift be decided by God's call to give generously, not by the amount of your leftovers.

2:69 Drachmas and minas were gold and silver coins. The money given was enough to start rebuilding the temple. The people put what resources they had to their best use. They were enthusiastic and sincere, but this temple would never match the splendor of Solomon's. The money David gathered to start the building of Solomon's temple was a thousand times more (1 Chronicles 22:14). Some people wept as they remembered the glorious temple that had been destroyed (3:12).

3:2, 3 The Jews built the altar as one of their first official acts. It symbolized God's presence and protection. It also demonstrated their purpose as a nation and their commitment to serve God alone. Zerubbabel sacrificed burnt offerings as the Law of Moses instructed (Leviticus 1—7). The sacrifices were essential because they demonstrated that the people were seeking God's

guidance, rededicating themselves to living as he commanded, and daily asking him to forgive their sins.

3:3 The Jews were afraid they were going to be attacked by the surrounding people—a mixed group whose ancestors had been conquered by the Assyrians. Foreigners had been forced to resettle in the northern kingdom of Israel after Israel was defeated and her people taken captive in 722 B.C. (4:1, 2). This resettlement procedure was a common tactic of the Assyrians to prevent strong nationalistic uprisings by conquered peoples. Some of the resettled people in Israel had migrated south near Jerusalem, and they might have thought the returning exiles threatened their claim on the land.

3:4 The Feast of Tabernacles lasted seven days. During this time the people lived in temporary dwellings (tents, booths, lean-tos) as their ancestors had done years before as they journeyed through the desert on their way to the promised land. The Feast reminded the people of God's past protection and guidance in the desert and of his continued love for them. The Feast of Tabernacles is described in detail in Leviticus 23:33–36.

3:5 Almost immediately after arriving in the new land, the returning exiles built an altar. The people began worshiping God through sacrifices even before the temple foundations were laid. After many years in captivity, they had learned their lesson—they knew that God does not offer special protection to people who ignore him. They had been carried off by the Babylonians when they were relatively strong; here they were few, weak, and surrounded by enemies. If ever they needed to rely on God's power, it was at this time. They realized the importance of obeying God from the heart, and not merely out of habit. If we want God's help when we undertake large tasks, we must make staying close to him our top priority.

3:5 These sacrifices were originally set up under the Law of Moses in Leviticus 1 and 6:8–13. The feasts are described in Leviticus 23. Every month on the day of the New Moon, they held a special observance (Numbers 10:10).

for all the appointed sacred feasts of the LORD,[h] as well as those brought as freewill offerings to the LORD. [6]On the first day of the seventh month they began to offer burnt offerings to the LORD, though the foundation of the LORD's temple had not yet been laid.

Rebuilding the Temple

[7]Then they gave money to the masons and carpenters, and gave food and drink and oil to the people of Sidon and Tyre, so that they would bring cedar logs by sea from Lebanon to Joppa, as authorized by Cyrus[i] king of Persia.

[8]In the second month of the second year after their arrival at the house of God in Jerusalem, Zerubbabel son of Shealtiel, Jeshua son of Jozadak and the rest of their brothers (the priests and the Levites and all who had returned from the captivity to Jerusalem) began the work, appointing Levites twenty[j] years of age and older to supervise the building of the house of the LORD. [9]Jeshua[k] and his sons and brothers and Kadmiel and his sons (descendants of Hodaviah[a]) and the sons of Henadad and their sons and brothers—all Levites—joined together in supervising those working on the house of God.

[10]When the builders laid the foundation of the temple of the LORD, the priests in their vestments and with trumpets,[l] and the Levites (the sons of Asaph) with cymbals, took their places to praise[m] the LORD, as prescribed by David[n] king of Israel. [11]With praise and thanksgiving they sang to the LORD:

"He is good;
    his love to Israel endures forever."[o]

And all the people gave a great shout[p] of praise to the LORD, because the foundation of the house of the LORD was laid. [12]But many of the older priests and Levites and family heads, who had seen the former temple, wept aloud when they saw the foundation of this temple being laid, while many others shouted for joy. [13]No one could distinguish the sound of the shouts of joy from the sound of weeping, because the people made so much noise. And the sound was heard far away.

Opposition to the Rebuilding

4 When the enemies of Judah and Benjamin heard that the exiles were building a temple for the LORD, the God of Israel, [2]they came to Zerubbabel and to the heads of the families

a9 Hebrew *Yehudah*, probably a variant of *Hodaviah*

3:5
[h] Nu 29:39

3:7
[i] Ezr 1:2-4; 6:3

3:8
[j] 1Ch 23:24

3:9
[k] Ezr 2:40

3:10
[l] 1Ch 16:6
[m] 1Ch 25:1
[n] 1Ch 6:31

3:11
[o] 1Ch 16:34, 41; 2Ch 7:3
[p] Ne 12:24

3:7 When Solomon built the first temple (2 Chronicles 2), he also exchanged food and olive oil—plentiful resources in Israel—for wood, a resource Israel lacked. The wood came from Sidon and Tyre that time too.

3:8 Why was the Lord's temple begun first, even before the city wall? The temple was used for spiritual purposes; the wall, for military and political purposes. God had always been the nation's protector, and the Jews knew that the strongest stone wall would not protect them if God was not with them. They knew that putting their spiritual lives in order was a far higher priority than assuring the national defense.

3:8 It took from September (3:1; September was the seventh month because the year began in March) to June just to *prepare* to build the temple. The exiles took time to make plans because the project was important to them. Preparation may not feel heroic or spiritual, but it is vital to any project meant to be done well.

3:10, 11 David had given clear instructions concerning the use of music in worship services in the temple (1 Chronicles 16; 25).

3:10, 11 Completing the foundation for the temple required great effort on the part of all involved. But no one tried to get praise for himself and his own hard work. Instead, everyone praised God for what had been done. All good gifts come from God—talents, abilities, strength, and leadership. We should thank God for what has been done in and through us!

3:11 The Bible records many songs and musical events. For a list of such events, see the chart in Exodus 16, p. 119.

3:12 Fifty years after its destruction, the temple was being rebuilt (536 B.C.). Some of the older people remembered Solomon's temple, and they wept because the new temple would not

be as glorious as the first one. But the beauty of the building was not nearly as important to God as were the attitudes of the builders and worshipers. God cares more about who we are than what we accomplish. Our world is always changing, and once-magnificent accomplishments decay and disappear. Seek to serve God wholeheartedly. Then you won't need to compare your work with anyone else's.

3:12 Because the new temple was built on the foundation of Solomon's temple, the two structures were not that different in size. But the old temple was far more elaborate and ornate, and was surrounded by many buildings and a vast courtyard. Both temples were constructed of imported cedar wood, but Solomon's was decorated with vast amounts of gold and precious stones. Solomon's temple took over seven years to build; Zerubbabel's took about four years. Solomon's temple was at the hub of a thriving city; Zerubbabel's was surrounded by ruins. No wonder the people wept.

3:13 The celebration after laying the temple foundation was marked by contrasts of emotion—shouts of joy and sounds of weeping. Both were appropriate. The Holy Spirit can stimulate us both to rejoice over the goodness of his grace and to grieve over the sins that required him to correct us. When we come into the presence of Almighty God, we may feel full of joy and thanksgiving, yet at the same time feel sobered by our shortcomings.

4:1-3 The enemies of Judah and Benjamin were people who had been relocated in the northern kingdom when Assyria conquered Israel (see 2 Kings 17 and the note on 3:3). In an attempt to infiltrate and disrupt the project, these people offered to help in the rebuilding project. They wanted to keep a close eye on what the Jews were doing. They were hoping to keep Jerusalem from

ZERUBBABEL

Sometimes God's ownership of a project is only recognized after *our* best efforts have failed. It is dangerous to think of God as responsible for the insignificant details while we take charge of the larger aspects of a project. Instead, it is God who is in control, and we only play a part in his overall plan. When God gives us important jobs to do, it isn't because he needs our help. Zerubbabel learned this lesson.

God's people had been exiled in Babylon for many years. Many had settled into comfortable lifestyles there and wanted to stay. There were, however, almost 60,000 who had not forgotten Judah. When Babylon was defeated in 539 B.C., the Persian ruler, Cyrus, allowed the Jews to return to Jerusalem and rebuild their temple. Zerubbabel led the first and largest group back to the promised land.

Zerubbabel's leadership was by right and recognition. Not only was he a descendant of David, he also had personal leadership qualities. When the people arrived in Judah, they were given time to establish living quarters, and then were called to begin the work. They began not by laying the city walls or constructing government buildings, but by rebuilding the altar, worshiping God together, and celebrating a feast. Under Zerubbabel's leadership, they established a spiritual foundation for their building efforts.

The temple foundation was then quickly completed, and another round of celebration followed. But soon, two problems arose. A few old men remembered Solomon's glorious temple and were saddened at how much smaller and less glorious this one was. Also, some enemies of the Jews tried to infiltrate the work force and stop the building with political pressure. Fear caused the work to grind to a halt. The people went to their homes, and 16 years passed.

We do not know what Zerubbabel did during this time. His discouragement, following those first months of excitement and accomplishment, must have been deep. Those feelings eventually hardened into hopelessness. So God sent the prophets Haggai and Zechariah to be Zerubbabel's encouraging companions. They confronted the people's reluctance and comforted their fears. The work began once again with renewed energy and was completed in four years.

Zerubbabel, like many of us, knew how to start well but found it hard to keep going. His successes depended on the quality of encouragement he received. Zerubbabel let discouragement get the better of him. But when he let God take control, the work was finished. God is always in control. We must not let circumstances or lack of encouragement slow us from doing the tasks God has given us.

Strengths and accomplishments:	• Led the first group of Jewish exiles back to Jerusalem from Babylon • Completed the rebuilding of God's temple • Demonstrated wisdom in the help he accepted and refused • Started his building project with worship as the focal point
Weaknesses and mistakes:	• Needed constant encouragement • Allowed problems and resistance to stop the rebuilding work
Lessons from his life:	• A leader needs to provide not only the initial motivation for a project, but the continued encouragement necessary to keep the project going • A leader must find his/her own dependable source of encouragement • God's faithfulness is shown in the way he preserved David's line
Vital statistics:	• Where: Babylon, Jerusalem • Occupation: Recognized leader of the exiles • Relatives: Father: Shealtiel. Grandfather: Jehoiachin. • Contemporaries: Cyrus, Darius, Zechariah, Haggai
Key verses:	"This is the word of the LORD to Zerubbabel: 'Not by might nor by power, but by my Spirit,' says the LORD Almighty. 'What are you, O mighty mountain? Before Zerubbabel you will become level ground. Then he will bring out the capstone to shouts of "God bless it! God bless it!" '" (Zechariah 4:6, 7).

Zerubbabel's story is told in Ezra 2:2—5:2. He is also mentioned in 1 Chronicles 3:19; Nehemiah 7:7; 12:1, 47; Haggai 1:1, 12, 14; 2:4, 21, 23; Zechariah 4:6–10; Matthew 1:12, 13; Luke 3:27.

---

becoming strong again. The Jews, however, saw through their ploy. Such a partnership with unbelievers would have led God's people to compromise their faith.

4:1–6 Believers can expect opposition when they do God's work (2 Timothy 3:12). Unbelievers and evil spiritual forces are always working against God and his people. The opposition may offer compromising alliances (4:2), attempt to discourage and intimidate us (4:4, 5), or accuse us unjustly (4:6). If you expect these tactics, you won't be halted by them. Move ahead with the work God has planned for you, and trust him to show you how to overcome the obstacles.

4:2 These enemies claimed to worship the same God as Zerubbabel and the rest of the Jews. In one sense, this was true; they worshiped God, but they also worshiped many other gods (see 2 Kings 17:27–29, 32–34, 41). In God's eyes, this was not worship—it was sin and rebellion. True worship involves devotion to God alone (Exodus 20:3–5). To these foreigners, God was just another "idol" to be added to their collection. Their real motive was to disrupt the temple project. Believers today must beware of those who claim to be Christians but whose actions clearly reveal they are using Christianity to serve their own interests.

and said, "Let us help you build because, like you, we seek your God and have been sacrificing to him since the time of Esarhaddon q king of Assyria, who brought us here."

3 But Zerubbabel, Jeshua and the rest of the heads of the families of Israel answered, "You have no part with us in building a temple to our God. We alone will build it for the LORD, the God of Israel, as King Cyrus, the king of Persia, commanded us." r

4 Then the peoples around them set out to discourage the people of Judah and make them afraid to go on building. a s 5 They hired counselors to work against them and frustrate their plans during the entire reign of Cyrus king of Persia and down to the reign of Darius king of Persia.

Later Opposition Under Xerxes and Artaxerxes

6 At the beginning of the reign of Xerxes, b t they lodged an accusation against the people of Judah and Jerusalem.

7 And in the days of Artaxerxes king of Persia, Bishlam, Mithredath, Tabeel and the rest of his associates wrote a letter to Artaxerxes. The letter was written in Aramaic script and in the Aramaic u language. c, d

8 Rehum the commanding officer and Shimshai the secretary wrote a letter against Jerusalem to Artaxerxes the king as follows:

9 Rehum the commanding officer and Shimshai the secretary, together with the rest of their associates—the judges and officials over the men from Tripolis, Persia, e Erech and Babylon, the Elamites of Susa, 10 and the other people whom the great and honorable Ashurbanipal f deported and settled in the city of Samaria and elsewhere in Trans-Euphrates. v

11 (This is a copy of the letter they sent him.)

To King Artaxerxes,

From your servants, the men of Trans-Euphrates:

12 The king should know that the Jews who came up to us from you have gone to Jerusalem and are rebuilding that rebellious and wicked city. They are restoring the walls and repairing the foundations. w

13 Furthermore, the king should know that if this city is built and its walls are restored, no more taxes, tribute or duty x will be paid, and the royal revenues will suffer. 14 Now since we are under obligation to the palace and it is not proper for us to see the king dishonored, we are sending this message to inform the king, 15 so that a search may be made in the archives of your predecessors. In these records you will find that this city is a rebellious city, troublesome to kings and provinces, a place of rebellion from ancient times. That is why this city was destroyed. 16 We inform the king that if this city is built and its walls are restored, you will be left with nothing in Trans-Euphrates.

17 The king sent this reply:

To Rehum the commanding officer, Shimshai the secretary and the rest of their associates living in Samaria and elsewhere in Trans-Euphrates:

4:2 q 2Ki 17:24
4:3 r Ezr 1:1-4; Ne 2:20
4:4 s Ezr 3:3
4:6 t Est 1:1; Da 9:1
4:7 u 2Ki 18:26; Da 2:4
4:10 v ver 17
4:12 w Ezr 5:3, 9
4:13 x Ezr 7:24

---

a 4 Or and troubled them as they built   b 6 Hebrew Ahasuerus, a variant of Xerxes' Persian name   c 7 Or written in Aramaic and translated   d 7 The text of Ezra 4:8—6:18 is in Aramaic.   e 9 Or officials, magistrates and governors over the men from   f 10 Aramaic Osnappar, a variant of Ashurbanipal

---

4:4, 5 Discouragement and fear are two of the greatest obstacles to completing God's work. Most often they come where and when you least expect them. Discouragement eats away at our motivation and fear paralyzes us so we don't act at all. Recognize these common barriers. Remember that God's people in every age have faced these problems and with God's help overcame them. By standing together with other believers, you can overcome fear and discouragement and fulfill God's purposes for your life.

4:6–23 In these verses, Ezra summarizes the entire story of the opposition to building the temple, the walls, and other important buildings in Jerusalem. Chronologically, 4:6 fits between chapters 6 and 7; 4:7–23 refers to the events between Ezra 7 and Nehemiah 1. Ezra grouped them here to highlight the persistent opposition to God's people over the years and God's ability to overcome it.

4:7 This letter sent to King Artaxerxes may have been inscribed on a clay tablet, a fragment of pottery, or sheets of parchment.

4:10 Ashurbanipal (669–627 B.C.) was the Assyrian king who completed the relocation of Israelite captives. He was the last of the strong Assyrian kings. After his death the nation quickly declined. Assyria was conquered by Babylon in 612.

Greetings.

¹⁸The letter you sent us has been read and translated in my presence. ¹⁹I issued an order and a search was made, and it was found that this city has a long history of revolt against kings and has been a place of rebellion and sedition. ²⁰Jerusalem has had powerful kings ruling over the whole of Trans-Euphrates,[y] and taxes, tribute and duty were paid to them. ²¹Now issue an order to these men to stop work, so that this city will not be rebuilt until I so order. ²²Be careful not to neglect this matter. Why let this threat grow, to the detriment of the royal interests?

²³As soon as the copy of the letter of King Artaxerxes was read to Rehum and Shimshai the secretary and their associates, they went immediately to the Jews in Jerusalem and compelled them by force to stop.

²⁴Thus the work on the house of God in Jerusalem came to a standstill until the second year of the reign of Darius king of Persia.

Tattenai's Letter to Darius

5 Now Haggai[z] the prophet and Zechariah[a] the prophet, a descendant of Iddo, prophesied to the Jews in Judah and Jerusalem in the name of the God of Israel, who was over them. ²Then Zerubbabel son of Shealtiel and Jeshua[b] son of Jozadak set to work to rebuild the house of God in Jerusalem. And the prophets of God were with them, helping them.

³At that time Tattenai,[c] governor of Trans-Euphrates, and Shethar-Bozenai and their associates went to them and asked, "Who authorized you to rebuild this temple and restore this structure?"[d] ⁴They also asked, "What are the names of the men constructing this building?"[a] ⁵But the eye of their God[e] was watching over the elders of the Jews, and they were not stopped until a report could go to Darius and his written reply be received.

[a]4 See Septuagint; Aramaic *4We told them the names of the men constructing this building.*

4:20
[y]Ge 15:18-21;
Jos 1:4; 1Ki 4:21;
Ps 72:8-11

5:1
[z]Hag 1:1, 3, 12
[a]Zec 1:1

5:2
[b]Ezr 3:2

5:3
[c]Ezr 6:6
[d]ver 9; Ezr 1:3

5:5
[e]Ezr 7:6, 9, 28;
Ps 33:18

THE PERSIAN KINGS OF EZRA'S DAY	Name	Date of Reign	Relationship to Israel
	Cyrus	559—530 B.C. . .	Conquered Babylon. Established a policy of returning exiles to their homelands. Sent Zerubbabel to Jerusalem, financed his project, and returned the gold and silver articles that Nebuchadnezzar had taken from the temple. He probably knew Daniel.
	Darius	522—486 B.C. . .	Supported construction of the temple in Jerusalem.
	Xerxes (Ahasuerus) . .	486—465 B.C. . .	Was Esther's husband. Allowed the Jews to protect themselves against Haman's attempt to eliminate their people.
	Artaxerxes I	465—424 B.C. . .	Had Nehemiah as his cupbearer. Allowed both Ezra and Nehemiah to return to Jerusalem.

4:19, 20 Artaxerxes said that Jerusalem "has a long history of revolt against kings and has been a place of rebellion and sedition." By reading the historical records, he learned that mighty kings had come from Jerusalem, and he may have feared that another would arise if the city were rebuilt. Solomon had ruled a huge empire (1 Kings 4:21), and Jerusalem's kings had rebelled against mighty powers—for example, Zedekiah rebelled against Nebuchadnezzar despite his oath of loyalty (2 Chronicles 36:13). Artaxerxes did not want to aid the rebuilding of a rebellious city and nation.

4:23 Setbacks and standstills are painful and discouraging to God's workers. These exiles had received a double dose (see 4:1–5 and 4:6–22). Leaders should do everything to keep work from grinding to a halt; yet circumstances sometimes really are beyond our control. When you have been brought to a standstill, remember to still stand strong in the Lord.

4:24 Ezra resumes his chronological account here. It may have been ten years since the Israelites had worked on the temple. It did not begin again until 520 B.C., the second year of Darius's reign (5:1ff).

5:1 More details about the work and messages of Haggai and Zechariah are found in the books of the Bible that bear their names.

5:1, 2 "The prophets of God were with them, helping them." God sometimes sends prophets to encourage and strengthen his people. To accomplish this, Haggai and Zechariah not only preached, but also got involved in the labor. In the church today, God appoints prophetic voices to help us with our work (Ephesians 4:11–13). Their ministry should have the same effect upon us as Haggai's and Zechariah's had on Israel. "But everyone who prophesies speaks to men for their strengthening, encouragement and comfort" (1 Corinthians 14:3). In turn, we should encourage those who bring God's words to us.

5:3–5 The non-Jews who lived nearby attempted to hinder the construction of the temple. But while the legal debate went on and the decision was under appeal, the Jews continued to rebuild. When we are doing God's work, others may try to delay, confuse, or frustrate us, but we can proceed confidently. God will accomplish his purposes in our world, no matter who attempts to block them. Just as he watched over the Jewish elders, he watches over you. Concentrate on God's purpose, and don't be sidetracked by intrigues or slander.

6 This is a copy of the letter that Tattenai, governor of Trans-Euphrates, and Shethar-Bozenai and their associates, the officials of Trans-Euphrates, sent to King Darius. 7 The report they sent him read as follows:

To King Darius:

Cordial greetings.

8 The king should know that we went to the district of Judah, to the temple of the great God. The people are building it with large stones and placing the timbers in the walls. The work is being carried on with diligence and is making rapid progress under their direction.

9 We questioned the elders and asked them, "Who authorized you to rebuild this temple and restore this structure?" 10 We also asked them their names, so that we could write down the names of their leaders for your information.

11 This is the answer they gave us:

"We are the servants of the God of heaven and earth, and we are rebuilding the temple *f* that was built many years ago, one that a great king of Israel built and finished. 12 But because our fathers angered *g* the God of heaven, he handed them over to Nebuchadnezzar the Chaldean, king of Babylon, who destroyed this temple and deported the people to Babylon. *h*

5:11
f 1Ki 6:1

5:12
g 2Ch 36:16
h 2Ki 24:1;
25:8, 9, 11

THE MEDO-PERSIAN EMPIRE

The Medo-Persian empire included the lands of Media and Persia, much of the area shown on this map and more. The Jewish exiles were concentrated in the area around Nippur in the Babylonian province. The decree by King Cyrus that allowed the Israelites to return to their homeland and rebuild the temple was discovered in the palace at Ecbatana.

5:6–17 This letter, in comparison with the previous one (4:11–16), at least stated the facts correctly and asked a fair question. The earlier letter accused the Jews of preparing the foundation for the entire city, rather than reporting that they were doing only what they had been permitted by Cyrus to do. Perhaps the opposition simply thought that sending this letter to Babylon would create enough concern to stop the Jews from rebuilding the temple. God had other plans, however. We can't predict how God will get his purposes accomplished, but we can certainly trust he will succeed!

5:11 While rebuilding the temple, the workers were confronted by the Persia-appointed governor, demanding to know who

gave permission for their construction project (5:3). This could have been intimidating, but, as we learn from the letter, they boldly replied, "We are the servants of the God of heaven and earth."

It is not always easy to speak up for our faith in an unbelieving world, but we must. The way to deal with pressure and intimidation is to recognize that we are workers for God. Our allegiance is to him first, people second. When we contemplate the reactions and criticisms of hostile people, we can become paralyzed with fear. If we try to offend no one or to please everyone, we won't be effective. God is our leader, and his rewards are most important. So don't be intimidated. Let others know by your words and actions whom you really serve.

5:13
l Ezr 1:1

5:14
l Ezr 1:7; 6:5

13"However, in the first year of Cyrus king of Babylon, King Cyrus issued a decree*l* to rebuild this house of God. 14He even removed from the temple*a* of Babylon the gold and silver articles of the house of God, which Nebuchadnezzar had taken from the temple in Jerusalem and brought to the temple*a* in Babylon.*l*

"Then King Cyrus gave them to a man named Sheshbazzar, whom he had appointed governor, 15and he told him, 'Take these articles and go and deposit them in the temple in Jerusalem. And rebuild the house of God on its site.' 16So this Sheshbazzar came and laid the foundations of the house of God*k* in Jerusalem. From that day to the present it has been under construction but is not yet finished."

5:16
k Ezr 3:10; 6:15

5:17
l Ezr 6:1, 2

17Now if it pleases the king, let a search be made in the royal archives*l* of Babylon to see if King Cyrus did in fact issue a decree to rebuild this house of God in Jerusalem. Then let the king send us his decision in this matter.

The Decree of Darius

6:1
m Ezr 5:17

6 King Darius then issued an order, and they searched in the archives*m* stored in the treasury at Babylon. 2A scroll was found in the citadel of Ecbatana in the province of Media, and this was written on it:

Memorandum:

3In the first year of King Cyrus, the king issued a decree concerning the temple of God in Jerusalem:

6:4
n 1Ki 6:36

Let the temple be rebuilt as a place to present sacrifices, and let its foundations be laid. It is to be ninety feet*b* high and ninety feet wide, 4with three courses*n* of large stones and one of timbers. The costs are to be paid by the royal treasury. 5Also, the gold

a 14 Or *palace*   *b* 3 Aramaic *sixty cubits* (about 27 meters)

THE POSTEXILIC PROPHETS

God used these men to confront and comfort his people after their return to their homeland from exile in Babylon.

Who?	When?	Ministered to These Contemporary Leaders	Main Message	Significance
Haggai	520 B.C.	Zerubbabel Joshua	• Encouraged the leaders and the people to continue rebuilding the temple, which God would bless • Challenged the people's careless worship, which God would not bless	Disobedience and careless obedience of God's commands lead to judgment.
Zechariah	520 B.C.	Zerubbabel Joshua	• Emphasized God's command to rebuild his temple • Gave the people another look at God's plan to bless the world through Israel and its coming king—the Messiah (9:9, 10)	Encouragement for today's effort sometimes requires that we remember God has a plan and purpose for tomorrow. Meanwhile the challenge is to live for him today.
Malachi	430 B.C.	The priests are the only leaders mentioned	• Confronted the people and priests with God's promises of judgment on those who reject him and God's blessing on those who live as he desires	God expects our obedience to him to affect our attitude toward him and our treatment of one another.

5:13–17 Cyrus is called king of Persia in 1:1 and king of Babylon in 5:13. Because Persia had just conquered Babylon, Cyrus was king of both nations. Babylon is more important to this story because it was the location of the Hebrews' 70-year captivity. The Babylon in 5:17 may refer to the city of Babylon, which was the capital of the nation of Babylon.

6:1, 2 Many clay and papyrus documents recording business transactions and historical data have been discovered in this area (near present-day Syria). A great library and archives with thousands of such records have been discovered at Ebla in Syria.

and silver articles of the house of God, which Nebuchadnezzar took from the temple in Jerusalem and brought to Babylon, are to be returned to their places in the temple in Jerusalem; they are to be deposited in the house of God. o

6Now then, Tattenai,p governor of Trans-Euphrates, and Shethar-Bozenai and you, their fellow officials of that province, stay away from there. 7Do not interfere with the work on this temple of God. Let the governor of the Jews and the Jewish elders rebuild this house of God on its site.
8Moreover, I hereby decree what you are to do for these elders of the Jews in the construction of this house of God:
The expenses of these men are to be fully paid out of the royal treasury, from the revenues of Trans-Euphrates, so that the work will not stop. 9Whatever is needed—young bulls, rams, male lambs for burnt offerings to the God of heaven, and wheat, salt, wine and oil, as requested by the priests in Jerusalem—must be given them daily without fail, 10so that they may offer sacrifices pleasing to the God of heaven and pray for the well-being of the king and his sons. q
11Furthermore, I decree that if anyone changes this edict, a beam is to be pulled from his house and he is to be lifted up and impaled on it. And for this crime his house is to be made a pile of rubble. r 12May God, who has caused his Name to dwell there, s overthrow any king or people who lifts a hand to change this decree or to destroy this temple in Jerusalem.
I Darius have decreed it. Let it be carried out with diligence.

Completion and Dedication of the Temple

13Then, because of the decree King Darius had sent, Tattenai, governor of Trans-Euphrates, and Shethar-Bozenai and their associates carried it out with diligence. 14So the elders of the Jews continued to build and prosper under the preaching t of Haggai the prophet and Zechariah, a descendant of Iddo. They finished building the temple according to the command of the God of Israel and the decrees of Cyrus, Darius and Artaxerxes, u kings of Persia. 15The temple was completed on the third day of the month Adar, in the sixth year of the reign of King Darius. v
16Then the people of Israel—the priests, the Levites and the rest of the exiles—celebrated the dedication w of the house of God with joy. 17For the dedication of this house of God they offered x a hundred bulls, two hundred rams, four hundred male lambs and, as a sin offering for all Israel, twelve male goats, one for each of the tribes of Israel. 18And they installed the priests in their divisions y and the Levites in their groups for the service of God at Jerusalem, according to what is written in the Book of Moses. z

The Passover

19On the fourteenth day of the first month, the exiles celebrated the Passover. a 20The priests and Levites had purified themselves and were all ceremonially clean. The Levites slaughtered the Passover lamb for all the exiles, for their brothers the priests and for themselves. 21So the Israelites who had returned from the exile ate it, together with all who had separated themselves b from the unclean practices of their Gentile neighbors in order to

6:5
oEzr 1:7; 5:14

6:6
pEzr 5:3

6:10
qEzr 7:23

6:11
rEzr 7:26; Da 2:5;
3:29

6:12
sDt 12:5

6:14
tEzr 5:1
uEzr 7:1

6:15
vZec 1:1; 4:9

6:16
w1Ki 8:63; 2Ch 7:5
6:17
xEzr 8:35
6:18
y1Ch 23:6;
2Ch 35:4
zNu 3:6-9; 8:9-11

6:19
aEx 12:11

6:21
bNe 9:2

6:14 Ezra carefully pointed out that rebuilding the temple was commanded first by God and then by the kings, who were his instruments. How ironic and wonderful that God's work was carried on by the discovery of a lost paragraph in a pagan library. All the opposition of powerful forces was stopped by a clause in a legal document. God's will is supreme over all rulers, all historical events, and all hostile forces. He can deliver us in ways we can't imagine. If we trust in his power and love, no opposition can stop us.

6:15 The temple was completed in 516 B.C.

6:16–22 Feasting and celebration were in order at the great temple dedication. This celebration was similar to the one that

Solomon had when he dedicated the temple in 1 Kings 8:63, although Solomon offered more than 200 times as many cattle and sheep. This Book of Moses was probably Leviticus. The priests and Levites were organized into groups in order to do "the service of God, . . . according to what is written in the Book of Moses." There is time to celebrate, but there is also a time to work. Both are proper and necessary when worshiping God, and both are pleasing to him.

6:19 The Passover was an annual celebration commemorating Israel's deliverance from Egypt. After a series of plagues failed to convince Pharaoh to free the Israelites, God said that he would send the destroying angel to kill the firstborn in every household. But the angel would pass over every home that had the blood of a specified type of lamb on the sides and top of the doorframe. See Exodus 12:1–30 for the story of this event and the establishment of the Passover celebration.

seek the LORD, the God of Israel. ²² For seven days they celebrated with joy the Feast of Unleavened Bread, because the LORD had filled them with joy by changing the attitude c of the king of Assyria, so that he assisted them in the work on the house of God, the God of Israel.

B. THE RETURN LED BY EZRA (7:1—10:44)

Ezra returned to the land with a second group of exiles, 80 years after Zerubbabel. Ezra found the temple rebuilt, but the lives of the people in shambles. Intermarriage with foreigners opposed to God threatened the spiritual future of the nation. So Ezra prayed for guidance and then followed through with action. Christians today must also strive to keep their lives pure, refusing to let the sinful allurements of the world around them compromise their life-style.

It is not personal achievement, but personal commitment to live for God, that is important. Achievements are simply examples of what God can do through someone's life. The most effective leaders spoken of in the Bible had little awareness of the impact their lives had on others. They were too busy obeying God to keep track of their successes. Ezra fits that description.

About 80 years after the rebuilding of the temple under Zerubbabel, Ezra returned to Judah with about 2,000 men and their families. He was given a letter from Artaxerxes instructing him to carry out a program of religious education. Along with the letter came significant power. But long before Ezra's mission began, God had shaped him in three important ways so that he would use the power well. First, as a scribe, Ezra dedicated himself to carefully studying God's Word. Second, he intended to apply and obey personally the commands he discovered in God's Word. Third, he was committed to teaching others both God's Word and its application to life.

Knowing Ezra's priorities, it is not surprising to note his actions when he arrived in Jerusalem. The people had disobeyed God's command not to marry women of foreign nations. On a cold and rainy day, Ezra addressed the people and made it clear they had sinned. Because of the sins of many, all were under God's condemnation. Confession, repentance, and action were needed. The people admitted their sin and devised a plan to deal with the problem.

This initial effort on Ezra's part set the stage for what Nehemiah would later accomplish. Ezra continued his ministry under Nehemiah, and the two were used by God to start a spiritual movement that swept the nation following the rebuilding of Jerusalem.

Ezra achieved great things and made a significant impact because he had the right starting place for his actions and his life: God's Word. He studied it seriously and applied it faithfully. He taught others what he learned. He is, therefore, a great model for anyone who wants to live for God.

Strengths and accomplishments:	• Committed to study, follow, and teach God's Word • Led the second group of exiles from Babylon to Jerusalem • May have written 1 and 2 Chronicles • Concerned about keeping the details of God's commands • Sent by King Artaxerxes to Jerusalem to evaluate the situation, set up a religious education system, and return with a firsthand report • Worked alongside Nehemiah during the last spiritual awakening recorded in the Old Testament
Lessons from his life:	• A person's willingness to know and practice God's Word will have a direct effect on how God uses his/her life • The starting place for serving God is a personal commitment to serve him today, even before knowing what that service will be
Vital statistics:	• Where: Babylon, Jerusalem • Occupations: Scribe among the exiles in Babylon, king's envoy, teacher • Relative: Father: Seriah • Contemporaries: Nehemiah, Artaxerxes
Key verse:	"For Ezra had devoted himself to the study and observance of the Law of the LORD, and to teaching its decrees and laws in Israel" (Ezra 7:10).

Ezra's story is told in Ezra 7:1—10:16 and Nehemiah 8:1—12:36.

6:22 There are many ways to pray for God's help. Have you ever considered that God would change the attitude of a person or group of people? God is infinitely powerful, his insight and wisdom transcend the laws of human nature. While you must always change your attitude as a first step, remember that he can change the attitude of others.

1. The second group of exiles returns to the land
Ezra Comes to Jerusalem

7 After these things, during the reign of Artaxerxes king of Persia, Ezra son of Seraiah, the son of Azariah, the son of Hilkiah, ²the son of Shallum, the son of Zadok, the son of Ahitub, ³the son of Amariah, the son of Azariah, the son of Meraioth, ⁴the son of Zerahiah, the son of Uzzi, the son of Bukki, ⁵the son of Abishua, the son of Phinehas, the son of Eleazar, the son of Aaron the chief priest— ⁶this Ezra came up from Babylon. He was a teacher well versed in the Law of Moses, which the LORD, the God of Israel, had given. The king had granted him everything he asked, for the hand of the LORD his God was on him. ⁷Some of the Israelites, including priests, Levites, singers, gatekeepers and temple servants, also came up to Jerusalem in the seventh year of King Artaxerxes. *d*

7:7
*d*Ezr 8:1

⁸Ezra arrived in Jerusalem in the fifth month of the seventh year of the king. ⁹He had begun his journey from Babylon on the first day of the first month, and he arrived in Jerusalem on the first day of the fifth month, for the gracious hand of his God was on him. ¹⁰For Ezra had devoted himself to the study and observance of the Law of the LORD, and to teaching its decrees and laws in Israel.

King Artaxerxes' Letter to Ezra

¹¹This is a copy of the letter King Artaxerxes had given to Ezra the priest and teacher, a man learned in matters concerning the commands and decrees of the LORD for Israel:

¹²ᵃArtaxerxes, king of kings, *e*

To Ezra the priest, a teacher of the Law of the God of heaven:

Greetings.

7:12
*e*Eze 26:7; Da 2:37

¹³Now I decree that any of the Israelites in my kingdom, including priests and Levites, who wish to go to Jerusalem with you, may go. ¹⁴You are sent by the king and his seven advisers *f* to inquire about Judah and Jerusalem with regard to the Law of your God, which is in your hand. ¹⁵Moreover, you are to take with you the silver and gold that the king and his advisers have freely given to the God of Israel, whose dwelling *g* is in Jerusalem, ¹⁶together with all the silver and gold you may obtain from the province of Babylon, as well as the freewill offerings of the people and priests for the temple of their God in Jerusalem. ¹⁷With this money be sure to buy bulls, rams and male lambs, together with their grain offerings and drink offerings, *h* and sacrifice *i* them on the altar of the temple of your God in Jerusalem.

7:14
*f*Est 1:14

7:15
*g*2Ch 6:2

7:17
*h*Nu 15:5-12
*i*Dt 12:5-11

¹⁸You and your brother Jews may then do whatever seems best with the rest of the silver and gold, in accordance with the will of your God. ¹⁹Deliver to the God of Jerusalem all the articles entrusted to you for worship in the temple of your God. ²⁰And anything else needed for the temple of your God that you may have occasion to supply, you may provide from the royal treasury. *j*

7:20
*j*Ezr 6:4

²¹Now I, King Artaxerxes, order all the treasurers of Trans-Euphrates to provide with diligence whatever Ezra the priest, a teacher of the Law of the God of heaven, may

a 12 The text of Ezra 7:12-26 is in Aramaic.

7:1 There is a gap of almost 60 years between the events of chapters six and seven. The story in the book of Esther occurred during this time, in the reign of Xerxes, who ruled from 486–465 B.C. Artaxerxes, his son, became king in 465, and Ezra returned to Jerusalem in 458.

7:6 Eighty years after the first exiles returned to Jerusalem (2:1), Ezra himself returned. This was his first trip, and it took four months. The temple had been standing for about 58 years. Up to this point in the narrative, Ezra had remained in Babylon, probably compiling a record of the events that had taken place.

Why did he have to ask the king if he could return? Ezra wanted to lead many Jews back to Jerusalem, and he needed a decree from the king stating that any Jew who wanted to return could do so. This decree would be like a passport in case they ran into opposition along the way. The king's generous decree showed that God was blessing Ezra (7:6, 28). It also indicated that Ezra was probably a prominent man in Artaxerxes' kingdom.

He was willing to give up this position in order to return to his homeland and teach the Israelites God's laws.

7:6–10 Ezra demonstrates how a gifted Bible teacher can move God's people forward. He was effective because he was a well-versed student of the Law of the Lord and because he was determined to obey those laws. He taught through both his speaking and his example. Like Ezra, we should determine both to study and to obey God's Word.

7:14 The seven advisers were Artaxerxes' supreme court (see Esther 1:14).

7:14 When Nebuchadnezzar destroyed the temple, he took a vast amount of plunder that may have included a copy of the Book of the Law (2 Chronicles 36:18). It is also possible that this book was brought by the Jews into exile and was confiscated and read by their conquerors. Foreign leaders who worshiped many gods liked to have records of the gods of other nations for military and political reasons.

ask of you—²²up to a hundred talents^a of silver, a hundred cors^b of wheat, a hundred baths^c of wine, a hundred baths^c of olive oil, and salt without limit. ²³Whatever the God of heaven has prescribed, let it be done with diligence for the temple of the God of heaven. Why should there be wrath against the realm of the king and of his sons?^k ²⁴You are also to know that you have no authority to impose taxes, tribute or duty on any of the priests, Levites, singers, gatekeepers, temple servants or other workers at this house of God.

7:23
^k Ezr 6:10

²⁵And you, Ezra, in accordance with the wisdom of your God, which you possess, appoint^l magistrates and judges to administer justice to all the people of Trans-Euphrates—all who know the laws of your God. And you are to teach^m any who do not know them. ²⁶Whoever does not obey the law of your God and the law of the king must surely be punished by death, banishment, confiscation of property, or imprisonment.

7:25
^l Ex 18:21, 26;
Dt 16:18
^m ver 10

²⁷Praise be to the Lord, the God of our fathers, who has put it into the king's heart^n to bring honor to the house of the Lord in Jerusalem in this way ²⁸and who has extended his good favor to me before the king and his advisers and all the king's powerful officials. Because the hand of the Lord my God was on me,^o I took courage and gathered leading men from Israel to go up with me.

7:27
^n Ezr 6:22

7:28
^o Ezr 5:5; 9:9

List of the Family Heads Returning With Ezra

8 These are the family heads and those registered with them who came up with me from Babylon during the reign of King Artaxerxes:

² of the descendants of Phinehas, Gershom;
of the descendants of Ithamar, Daniel;
of the descendants of David, Hattush ³of the descendants of Shecaniah;^p

8:3
^p 1Ch 3:22
^q Ezr 2:3

of the descendants of Parosh,^q Zechariah, and with him were registered 150 men;
⁴ of the descendants of Pahath-Moab, Eliehoenai son of Zerahiah, and with him 200 men;
⁵ of the descendants of Zattu,^d Shecaniah son of Jahaziel, and with him 300 men;
⁶ of the descendants of Adin, Ebed son of Jonathan, and with him 50 men;
⁷ of the descendants of Elam, Jeshaiah son of Athaliah, and with him 70 men;
⁸ of the descendants of Shephatiah, Zebadiah son of Michael, and with him 80 men;
⁹ of the descendants of Joab, Obadiah son of Jehiel, and with him 218 men;
¹⁰ of the descendants of Bani,^e Shelomith son of Josiphiah, and with him 160 men;
¹¹ of the descendants of Bebai, Zechariah son of Bebai, and with him 28 men;
¹² of the descendants of Azgad, Johanan son of Hakkatan, and with him 110 men;

^a 22 That is, about 3 3/4 tons (about 3.4 metric tons)   ^b 22 That is, probably about 600 bushels (about 22 kiloliters)   ^c 22 That is, probably about 600 gallons (about 2.2 kiloliters)   ^d 5 Some Septuagint manuscripts (also 1 Esdras 8:32); Hebrew does not have *Zattu*.   ^e 10 Some Septuagint manuscripts (also 1 Esdras 8:36); Hebrew does not have *Bani*.

7:24 Why did Artaxerxes exempt temple workers from paying taxes? He recognized that the priests and Levites filled an important role in society as spiritual leaders, so he freed them of tax burdens. While the Bible does not teach tax exemption for religious employees, Artaxerxes, a pagan king, recognized and supported the principle. Today, churches have the responsibility to keep worldly burdens off the shoulders of spiritual workers.

7:27 In Ezra's doxology, he acknowledges that God "put it into the king's heart." God can change a king's heart (see Proverbs 21:1). When we face life's challenges, we often must work diligently and with extraordinary effort, realizing that God oversees all our work. Recognize his hand in your success, and remember to praise him for his help and protection.

7:27, 28 Ezra praised God for all that God had done for him and through him. Ezra had honored God throughout his life, and God chose to honor him. Ezra could have assumed that his own greatness and charisma had won over the king and his princes, but he gave the credit to God. We, too, should be grateful to God for our success and not think that we did it in our own power.

7:28 The speaker here is Ezra. He writes in the first person for the remainder of the book.

EZRA'S JOURNEY Ezra led a second group of exiles back to Judah and Jerusalem about 80 years after the first group. He traveled the dangerous route without military escort (8:22), but the people prayed and, under Ezra's godly leadership, arrived safely in Jerusalem after several months.

13 of the descendants of Adonikam, the last ones, whose names were Eliphelet, Jeuel and Shemaiah, and with them 60 men;

14 of the descendants of Bigvai, Uthai and Zaccur, and with them 70 men.

The Return to Jerusalem

15 I assembled them at the canal that flows toward Ahava, *r* and we camped there three days. When I checked among the people and the priests, I found no Levites *s* there. 16 So I summoned Eliezer, Ariel, Shemaiah, Elnathan, Jarib, Elnathan, Nathan, Zechariah and Meshullam, who were leaders, and Joiarib and Elnathan, who were men of learning, 17 and I sent them to Iddo, the leader in Casiphia. I told them what to say to Iddo and his kinsmen, the temple servants *t* in Casiphia, so that they might bring attendants to us for the house of our God. 18 Because the gracious hand of our God was on us, they brought us Sherebiah, a capable man, from the descendants of Mahli son of Levi, the son of Israel, and Sherebiah's sons and brothers, 18 men; 19 and Hashabiah, together with Jeshaiah from the descendants of Merari, and his brothers and nephews, 20 men. 20 They also brought 220 of the temple servants *u*—a body that David and the officials had established to assist the Levites. All were registered by name.

21 There, by the Ahava Canal, *v* I proclaimed a fast, so that we might humble ourselves before our God and ask him for a safe journey for us and our children, with all our possessions. 22 I was ashamed to ask the king for soldiers *w* and horsemen to protect us from enemies on the road, because we had told the king, "The gracious hand of our God is on everyone who looks to him, but his great anger is against all who forsake him. *x*" 23 So we fasted *y* and petitioned our God about this, and he answered our prayer.

24 Then I set apart twelve of the leading priests, together with Sherebiah, Hashabiah and ten of their brothers, 25 and I weighed out *z* to them the offering of silver and gold and the articles that the king, his advisers, his officials and all Israel present there had donated for the house of our God. 26 I weighed out to them 650 talents *a* of silver, silver articles weighing 100 talents, *b* 100 talents *b* of gold, 27 20 bowls of gold valued at 1,000 darics, *c* and two fine articles of polished bronze, as precious as gold.

28 I said to them, "You as well as these articles are consecrated to the LORD. *a* The silver and gold are a freewill offering to the LORD, the God of your fathers. 29 Guard them carefully until you weigh them out in the chambers of the house of the LORD in Jerusalem before the leading priests and the Levites and the family heads of Israel." 30 Then the priests and Levites received the silver and gold and sacred articles that had been weighed out to be taken to the house of our God in Jerusalem.

31 On the twelfth day of the first month we set out from the Ahava Canal to go to Jerusalem. The hand of our God was on us, and he protected us from enemies and bandits along the way. 32 So we arrived in Jerusalem, where we rested three days. *b*

a 26 That is, about 25 tons (about 22 metric tons)   *b 26* That is, about 3 3/4 tons (about 3.4 metric tons)   *c 27* That is, about 19 pounds (about 8.5 kilograms)

8:15 *r* ver 21, 31 *s* Ezr 2:40; 7:7

8:17 *t* Ezr 2:43

8:20 *u* Ezr 2:43

8:21 *v* 2Ch 20:3

8:22 *w* Ezr 7:6, 9, 28 *x* 2Ch 15:2

8:23 *y* 2Ch 33:13

8:25 *z* Ezr 7:15, 16

8:28 *a* Lev 21:6; 22:2-3

8:32 *b* Ne 2:11

8:15 Ezra's progress back to Jerusalem was halted while he waited to recruit Levites. God had called these men to a special service, and yet few were willing to volunteer when their services were needed. God has gifted each of us with abilities so we can make a contribution to his kingdom work (Romans 12:4–8). Don't wait to be recruited, but look for opportunities to volunteer. Don't hinder God's work by holding back. "Each one should use whatever gift he has received to serve others, faithfully administering God's grace in its various forms" (1 Peter 4:10).

8:21 Ezra and the people traveled approximately 900 miles on foot. The trip took them through dangerous and difficult territory and lasted about four months. They prayed that God would give them a safe journey. Our journeys today may not be as difficult and dangerous as Ezra's, but we should recognize our need to ask God for guidance and protection.

8:21–23 Before making all the physical preparations for the journey, Ezra made spiritual preparations. Their prayers and fasting prepared them spiritually by showing their dependence on God for protection, their faith that God was in control, and their affirmation that they were not strong enough to make the trip without

him. When we take time to put God first in any endeavor, we are preparing well for whatever lies ahead.

8:23 Ezra knew God's promises to protect his people, but he didn't take them for granted. He also knew that God's blessings are appropriated through prayer; so Ezra and the people humbled themselves by fasting and praying. And their prayers were answered. Fasting humbled them because going without food was a reminder of their complete dependence on God. Fasting also gave them more time to pray and meditate on God.

Too often we pray glibly and superficially. Serious prayer, by contrast, requires concentration. It puts us in touch with God's will and can really change us. Without serious prayer, we reduce God to a quick-service pharmacist with painkillers for our every ailment.

8:26 Six hundred fifty talents of silver would be about 25 tons. This was a large amount of treasure to transport, with or without a detachment of soldiers for protection.

8:28, 29 Every object used in temple service was consecrated to God; each was considered a holy treasure to be guarded carefully and set apart for his special use. Stewardship means taking special care of whatever God has entrusted to you. This means

³³On the fourth day, in the house of our God, we weighed out the silver and gold and the sacred articles into the hands of Meremoth son of Uriah, the priest. Eleazar son of Phinehas was with him, and so were the Levites Jozabad son of Jeshua and Noadiah son of Binnui. ³⁴Everything was accounted for by number and weight, and the entire weight was recorded at that time.

³⁵Then the exiles who had returned from captivity sacrificed burnt offerings to the God of Israel: twelve bulls for all Israel, ninety-six rams, seventy-seven male lambs and, as a sin offering, twelve male goats. All this was a burnt offering to the LORD. ³⁶They also delivered the king's orders *c* to the royal satraps and to the governors of Trans-Euphrates, who then gave assistance to the people and to the house of God.

8:36
*c*Ezr 7:21-24

2. Ezra opposes intermarriage
Ezra's Prayer About Intermarriage

9:1
*d*Ezr 6:21; Ne 9:2

9 After these things had been done, the leaders came to me and said, "The people of Israel, including the priests and the Levites, have not kept themselves separate *d* from the neighboring peoples with their detestable practices, like those of the Canaanites, Hittites, Perizzites, Jebusites, Ammonites, Moabites, Egyptians and Amorites. ²They have taken some of their daughters as wives for themselves and their sons, and have mingled the holy race *e* with the peoples around them. And the leaders and officials have led the way in this unfaithfulness."

9:2
*e*Ex 22:31

³When I heard this, I tore my tunic and cloak, pulled hair from my head and beard and sat down appalled. ⁴Then everyone who trembled *f* at the words of the God of Israel gathered around me because of this unfaithfulness of the exiles. And I sat there appalled until the evening sacrifice.

9:4
*f*Ezr 10:3

⁵Then, at the evening sacrifice, I rose from my self-abasement, with my tunic and cloak torn, and fell on my knees with my hands spread out to the LORD my God ⁶and prayed:

9:6
*g*2Ch 28:9;
Rev 18:5

"O my God, I am too ashamed and disgraced to lift up my face to you, my God, because our sins are higher than our heads and our guilt has reached to the heavens. *g* ⁷From the days of our forefathers until now, our guilt has been great. Because of our sins, we and our kings and our priests have been subjected to the sword and captivity, to pillage and humiliation *h* at the hand of foreign kings, as it is today.

9:7
*h*Dt 28:37

⁸"But now, for a brief moment, the LORD our God has been gracious in leaving us a remnant and giving us a firm place *i* in his sanctuary, and so our God gives light to our eyes *j* and a little relief in our bondage. ⁹Though we are slaves, *k* our God has not

9:8
*i*Isa 22:23
*j*Ps 13:3

9:9
*k*Ne 9:36

---

considering what God has given to you as being *from* him and *for* his use. What has God entrusted to your care?

8:36 *Satraps* were the equivalent of provincial governors.

9:1, 2 Since the time of the judges, Israelite men had married pagan women and then adopted their religious practices (Judges 3:5–7). Even Israel's great King Solomon was guilty of this sin (1 Kings 11:1–8). Although this practice was forbidden in God's law (Exodus 34:11–16; Deuteronomy 7:1–4), it happened in Ezra's day, and again only a generation after him (Nehemiah 13:23–27). Opposition to mixed marriage was not racial prejudice because Jews and non-Jews of this area were of the same Semitic background. The reasons were strictly spiritual. A person who married a pagan was inclined to adopt that person's pagan beliefs and practices. If the Israelites were insensitive enough to disobey God in something as important as marriage, they wouldn't be strong enough to stand firm against their spouses' idolatry. Until the Israelites finally stopped this practice, idolatry remained a constant problem.

9:2 Some Israelites had married pagan spouses and lost track of God's purpose for them. The New Testament says that believers should not "be yoked together with" unbelievers (2 Corinthians 6:14). Such marriages cannot have unity in the most important issue in life—commitment and obedience to God. Because marriage involves two people becoming one, faith may become an issue, and one spouse may have to compromise beliefs for the sake of unity. Many people discount this problem only to regret it later. Don't allow emotion or passion to blind you to the ulti-

mate importance of marrying someone with whom you can be united spiritually.

9:3–5 Tearing one's clothes or pulling hair from one's head or beard were signs of self-abasement or humility. They expressed sorrow for sin.

9:5–15 After learning about the sins of the people, Ezra fell to his knees in prayer. His heartfelt prayer provides a good perspective on sin. He recognized: (1) that sin is serious (9:6); (2) that no one sins without affecting others (9:7); (3) that he was not sinless, although he didn't have a pagan wife (9:10ff); (4) that God's love and mercy had spared the nation when they did nothing to deserve it (9:8, 9, 15). It is easy to view sin lightly in a world that sees sin as inconsequential, but we should view sin as seriously as Ezra did.

9:5–15 Ezra's prayer confessed the sins of his people. Although he had not sinned in the way his people had, he identified with their sins. With weeping, he expressed shame for sin, fear of the consequences, and desire that the people would come to their senses and repent. His prayer moved the people to tears (10:1). Ezra demonstrated the need for a holy community around the rebuilt temple. We need a holy community in our local churches too. Even when we sin in the worst imaginable way, we can turn to God with prayers of repentance.

9:9 Building a wall was not only a matter of civic pride or architectural beauty, it was essential for security and defense against robbers and marauders (see 9:7). God in his kindness had given them new life and protection.

deserted us in our bondage. He has shown us kindness[i] in the sight of the kings of Persia: He has granted us new life to rebuild the house of our God and repair its ruins, and he has given us a wall of protection in Judah and Jerusalem.

10"But now, O our God, what can we say after this? For we have disregarded the commands 11you gave through your servants the prophets when you said: 'The land you are entering to possess is a land polluted by the corruption of its peoples. By their detestable practices they have filled it with their impurity from one end to the other. 12Therefore, do not give your daughters in marriage to their sons or take their daughters for your sons. Do not seek a treaty of friendship with them[m] at any time, that you may be strong and eat the good things of the land and leave it to your children as an everlasting inheritance.'

13"What has happened to us is a result of our evil deeds and our great guilt, and yet, our God, you have punished us less than our sins have deserved and have given us a remnant like this. 14Shall we again break your commands and intermarry with the peoples who commit such detestable practices? Would you not be angry enough with us to destroy us,[n] leaving us no remnant[o] or survivor? 15O LORD, God of Israel, you are righteous! We are left this day as a remnant. Here we are before you in our guilt, though because of it not one of us can stand[p] in your presence."

The People's Confession of Sin

10 While Ezra was praying and confessing,[q] weeping and throwing himself down before the house of God, a large crowd of Israelites—men, women and children—gathered around him. They too wept bitterly. 2Then Shecaniah son of Jehiel, one of the descendants of Elam, said to Ezra, "We have been unfaithful[r] to our God by marrying foreign women from the peoples around us. But in spite of this, there is still hope for Israel. 3Now let us make a covenant[s] before our God to send away[t] all these women and their children, in accordance with the counsel of my lord and of those who fear the commands of our God. Let it be done according to the Law. 4Rise up; this matter is in your hands. We will support you, so take courage and do it."

5So Ezra rose up and put the leading priests and Levites and all Israel under oath[u] to do what had been suggested. And they took the oath. 6Then Ezra withdrew from before the house of God and went to the room of Jehohanan son of Eliashib. While he was there, he ate no food and drank no water,[v] because he continued to mourn over the unfaithfulness of the exiles.

7A proclamation was then issued throughout Judah and Jerusalem for all the exiles to assemble in Jerusalem. 8Anyone who failed to appear within three days would forfeit all his property, in accordance with the decision of the officials and elders, and would himself be expelled from the assembly of the exiles.

9:9
[i] Ezr 7:28

9:12
[m] Dt 7:3; 23:6

9:14
[n] Dt 9:8
[o] Dt 9:14

9:15
[p] Ne 9:33; Ps 130:3

10:1
[q] 2Ch 20:9; Da 9:20

10:2
[r] Ezr 9:2; Ne 13:27

10:3
[s] 2Ch 34:31
[t] Dt 7:2-3; Ezr 9:4

10:5
[u] Ne 5:12; 13:25

10:6
[v] Dt 9:18

9:15 Ezra recognized that if God gave the people the justice they deserved, they would not be able to stand before him. Often we cry out for justice when we feel abused and unfairly treated. In those moments, we forget the reality of our own sin and the righteous judgment we deserve. How fortunate we are that God gives us mercy and grace rather than only justice. The next time you ask God for fair and just treatment, pause to think what would happen if God gave you what you really deserve. Plead instead for his mercy.

10:1 Ezra set the standard of repentance by his own behavior. His weeping brought others to the point of sorrow. Some may respond when we tell them what to do, but more will follow if we show them what to do and participate ourselves. In this case, Ezra's actions actually motivated a leader to make a significant stand. We can never predict who will follow or benefit from our example.

10:3 Why were the men commanded to send away their wives and children? Although the measure was extreme, intermarriage to pagans was strictly forbidden (Deuteronomy 7:3, 4), and even the priests and Levites had intermarried. This could be compared today to a Christian marrying a devil worshiper. Although a

severe solution, it only involved 113 of the approximately 29,000 families.

Ezra's strong act, though very difficult for some, was necessary to preserve Israel as a nation committed to God. Some of the exiles of the northern kingdom of Israel had lost both their spiritual and physical identity through intermarriage. Their pagan spouses had caused the people to worship idols. Ezra did not want this to happen to the exiles of the southern kingdom of Judah.

10:3, 4, 11 Following Ezra's earnest prayer, the people confessed their sin to God. Then they asked for direction in restoring their relationship with God. True repentance does not end with words of confession—that would be mere lip service. It must lead to corrected behavior and changed attitudes. When you sin and are truly sorry, confess this to God, ask his forgiveness, and accept his grace and mercy. Then, as an act of thankfulness for your forgiveness, make the needed corrections.

10:8 To forfeit one's property meant to be disinherited: to lose one's legal right to own land. This was to ensure that no pagan children would inherit Israel's land. In addition, the person who refused to come to Jerusalem would be expelled from the assembly of the exiles and not allowed to worship in the temple. The Jews considered this a horrible punishment.

⁹Within the three days, all the men of Judah and Benjamin had gathered in Jerusalem. And on the twentieth day of the ninth month, all the people were sitting in the square before the house of God, greatly distressed by the occasion and because of the rain. ¹⁰Then Ezra the priest stood up and said to them, "You have been unfaithful; you have married foreign women, adding to Israel's guilt. ¹¹Now make confession to the LORD, the God of your fathers, and do his will. Separate yourselves from the peoples around you and from your foreign wives."ʷ

¹²The whole assembly responded with a loud voice: "You are right! We must do as you say. ¹³But there are many people here and it is the rainy season; so we cannot stand outside. Besides, this matter cannot be taken care of in a day or two, because we have sinned greatly in this thing. ¹⁴Let our officials act for the whole assembly. Then let everyone in our towns who has married a foreign woman come at a set time, along with the elders and judges of each town, until the fierce angerˣ of our God in this matter is turned away from us." ¹⁵Only Jonathan son of Asahel and Jahzeiah son of Tikvah, supported by Meshullam and Shabbethai the Levite, opposed this.

¹⁶So the exiles did as was proposed. Ezra the priest selected men who were family heads, one from each family division, and all of them designated by name. On the first day of the tenth month they sat down to investigate the cases, ¹⁷and by the first day of the first month they finished dealing with all the men who had married foreign women.

Those Guilty of Intermarriage

¹⁸ Among the descendants of the priests, the following had married foreign women:

From the descendants of Jeshuaʸ son of Jozadak, and his brothers: Maaseiah, Eliezer, Jarib and Gedaliah. ¹⁹(They all gave their handsᶻ in pledge to put away their wives, and for their guilt they each presented a ram from the flock as a guilt offering.)ᵃ

²⁰ From the descendants of Immer:
Hanani and Zebadiah.
²¹ From the descendants of Harim:
Maaseiah, Elijah, Shemaiah, Jehiel and Uzziah.
²² From the descendants of Pashhur:
Elioenai, Maaseiah, Ishmael, Nethanel, Jozabad and Elasah.

²³ Among the Levites:

Jozabad, Shimei, Kelaiah (that is, Kelita), Pethahiah, Judah and Eliezer.
²⁴ From the singers:
Eliashib.
From the gatekeepers:
Shallum, Telem and Uri.

²⁵ And among the other Israelites:

From the descendants of Parosh:ᵇ
Ramiah, Izziah, Malkijah, Mijamin, Eleazar, Malkijah and Benaiah.
²⁶ From the descendants of Elam:
Mattaniah, Zechariah, Jehiel, Abdi, Jeremoth and Elijah.
²⁷ From the descendants of Zattu:
Elioenai, Eliashib, Mattaniah, Jeremoth, Zabad and Aziza.
²⁸ From the descendants of Bebai:
Jehohanan, Hananiah, Zabbai and Athlai.
²⁹ From the descendants of Bani:
Meshullam, Malluch, Adaiah, Jashub, Sheal and Jeremoth.
³⁰ From the descendants of Pahath-Moab:
Adna, Kelal, Benaiah, Maaseiah, Mattaniah, Bezalel, Binnui and Manasseh.
³¹ From the descendants of Harim:
Eliezer, Ishijah, Malkijah, Shemaiah, Shimeon, ³²Benjamin, Malluch and Shemariah.

10:11 As believers in Christ, all our sins are forgiven. His death cleansed us from all sin. Why do we then still confess our sins? Confession is more than appropriating Christ's forgiveness for what we have done wrong, and we do not have to confess again sins that were previously confessed. Confession is agreeing with God that our thoughts, words, and actions are wrong and contrary to his will. It is recommitting ourselves to do his will and to renounce any acts of disobedience. Confession is turning away from sin and asking God for fresh power to live for him.

33 From the descendants of Hashum:

Mattenai, Mattattah, Zabad, Eliphelet, Jeremai, Manasseh and Shimei.

34 From the descendants of Bani:

Maadai, Amram, Uel, 35 Benaiah, Bedeiah, Keluhi, 36 Vaniah, Meremoth, Eliashib, 37 Mattaniah, Mattenai and Jaasu.

38 From the descendants of Binnui:a

Shimei, 39 Shelemiah, Nathan, Adaiah, 40 Macnadebai, Shashai, Sharai, 41 Azarel, Shelemiah, Shemariah, 42 Shallum, Amariah and Joseph.

43 From the descendants of Nebo:

Jeiel, Mattithiah, Zabad, Zebina, Jaddai, Joel and Benaiah.

44 All these had married foreign women, and some of them had children by these wives.b

a 37,38 See Septuagint (also 1 Esdras 9:34); Hebrew *Jaasu* 38 *and Bani and Binnui,* b 44 Or *and they sent them away with their children*

10:44 The book of Ezra opens with God's temple in ruins and the people of Judah captive in Babylon. Ezra tells of the return of God's people, the rebuilding of the temple, and the restoration of the sacrificial worship system. Similarly, God is able to restore and rebuild the lives of people today. No one is so far away from God that he or she cannot be restored. Repentance is all that is required. No matter how far we have strayed or how long it has been since we have worshiped God, he is able to restore our relationship to him and rebuild our lives.

NEHEMIAH

"WHAT this church needs is . . . !" "I can't believe our government officials. If I were there I would . . . !" "Our schools are really in bad shape. Someone ought to do something!"

Gripers, complainers, self-proclaimed prophets, and "armchair quarterbacks" abound. It is easy to analyze, scrutinize, and *talk* about all the problems in the world. But what we really need are people who will not just discuss a situation but who will *do* something about it!

Nehemiah saw a problem and was distressed. Instead of complaining or wallowing in self-pity and grief, he took action. Nehemiah knew that God wanted him to motivate the Jews to rebuild Jerusalem's walls, so he left a responsible position in the Persian government to do what God wanted. Nehemiah knew God could use his talents to get the job done. From the moment he arrived in Jerusalem, everyone knew who was in charge. He organized, managed, supervised, encouraged, met opposition, confronted injustice, and kept going until the walls were built. Nehemiah was a man of action.

The story begins with Nehemiah talking with fellow Jews who reported that the walls and gates of Jerusalem were in disrepair. This was disturbing news, and rebuilding those walls became Nehemiah's burden. At the appropriate time, Nehemiah asked King Artaxerxes for permission to go to Jerusalem to rebuild its fallen walls. The king approved.

Armed with royal letters, Nehemiah traveled to Jerusalem. He organized the people into groups and assigned them to specific sections of the wall (chapter 3). The construction project was not without opposition, however. Sanballat, Tobiah, and others tried to halt the work with insults, ridicule, threats, and sabotage. Some of the workers became fearful; others became weary. In each case, Nehemiah employed a strategy to frustrate the enemies—prayer, encouragement, guard duty, consolidation (chapter 4). But a different problem arose—an internal one. Rich Jews were profiteering off the plight of their working countrymen. Hearing of their oppression and greed, Nehemiah confronted the extortioners face to face (chapter 5). Then, with the walls almost complete, Sanballat, Tobiah, and company tried one last time to stop Nehemiah. But Nehemiah stood firm, and the wall was finished in just 52 days. What a tremendous monument to God's love and faithfulness. Enemies and friends alike knew that God had helped (chapter 6).

After building the walls, Nehemiah continued to organize the people, taking a registration and appointing gatekeepers, Levites, and other officials (chapter 7). Ezra led the city in worship and Bible instruction (chapters 8; 9). This led to a reaffirmation of faith and religious revival as the people promised to serve God faithfully (chapters 10; 11).

Nehemiah closes with the listing of the clans and their leaders, the dedication of the new wall of Jerusalem, and the purging of sin from the land (chapters 12; 13). As you read this book, watch Nehemiah in action—and determine to be a person on whom God can depend to *act* for him in the world.

VITAL STATISTICS

PURPOSE:
Nehemiah is the last of the Old Testament historical books. It records the history of the third return to Jerusalem after captivity, telling how the walls were rebuilt and the people were renewed in their faith.

AUTHOR:
Much of the book is written in the first person, suggesting Nehemiah as the author. Nehemiah probably wrote the book with Ezra serving as editor.

ORIGINAL AUDIENCE:
The exiles who returned from captivity

DATE WRITTEN:
Approximately 445–432 B.C.

SETTING:
Zerubbabel led the first return to Jerusalem in 538 B.C. In 458, Ezra led the second return. Finally, in 445, Nehemiah returned with the third group of exiles to rebuild the city walls.

KEY VERSES:
"So the wall was completed on the twenty-fifth of Elul, in fifty-two days. When all our enemies heard about this, all the surrounding nations were afraid and lost their self-confidence, because they realized that this work had been done with the help of our God" (6:15, 16).

KEY PEOPLE:
Nehemiah, Ezra, Sanballat, Tobiah

KEY PLACE:
Jerusalem

SPECIAL FEATURES:
The book shows the fulfillment of the prophecies of Zechariah and Daniel concerning the rebuilding of Jerusalem's walls.

THE BLUEPRINT

A. REBUILDING THE WALL
   (1:1—7:73)
   1. Nehemiah returns to Jerusalem
   2. Nehemiah leads the people

Nehemiah's life is an example of leadership and organization. Giving up a comfortable and wealthy position in Persia, he returned to the fractured homeland of his ancestors and rallied the people to rebuild Jerusalem's wall. In the face of opposition, he used wise defense measures to care for the people and to keep the project moving. To accomplish more for the sake of God's kingdom, we must pray, persevere, and sacrifice, as did Nehemiah.

B. REFORMING THE PEOPLE
   (7:73—13:31)
   1. Ezra renews the covenant
   2. Nehemiah establishes policies

After the wall was rebuilt, Ezra read the law to the people, bringing about national repentance. Nehemiah and Ezra were very different people, yet God used them both to lead the nation. Remember, there is a place for you in God's work even if you're different from most other people. God uses each person in a unique way to accomplish his purposes.

MEGATHEMES

THEME	EXPLANATION	IMPORTANCE
Vision	Although the Jews completed the temple in 516 B.C., the city walls remained in shambles for the next 70 years. These walls represented power, protection, and beauty to the city of Jerusalem. They were also desperately needed to protect the temple from attack and to ensure the continuity of worship. God put the desire to rebuild the walls in Nehemiah's heart, giving him a vision for the work.	Does God have a vision for us? Are there "walls" that need to be built today? God still wants his people to be united and trained to do his work. As we recognize deep needs in our world, God can give us the vision and desire to "build." With that vision, we can mobilize others to pray and put together a plan of action.
Prayer	Both Nehemiah and Ezra responded to problems with prayer. When Nehemiah began his work, he recognized the problem, immediately prayed, and then acted on the problem.	Prayer is still God's mighty force in solving problems today. Prayer and action go hand in hand. Through prayer, God guides our preparation, teamwork, and diligent efforts to carry out his will.
Leadership	Nehemiah demonstrated excellent leadership. He was spiritually ready to heed God's call. He used careful planning, teamwork, problem solving, and courage to get the work done. Although he had tremendous faith, he never avoided the extra work necessary for good leadership.	Being God's leader is not just gaining recognition, holding a position, or being the boss. It requires planning, hard work, courage, and perseverance. Positive expectations are never a substitute for doing the difficult work. And in order to lead others, you need to listen for God's direction in your own life.
Problems	After the work began, Nehemiah faced scorn, slander, and threats from enemies, as well as fear, conflict, and discouragement from his own workers. Although these problems were difficult, they did not stop Nehemiah from finishing the work.	When difficulties come, there is a tendency for conflict and discouragement to set in. We must recognize that there are no triumphs without troubles. When problems arise, we must face them squarely and press on to complete God's work.
Repentance/ Revival	Although God had enabled them to build the wall, the work wasn't complete until the people rebuilt their lives spiritually. Ezra instructed the people in God's Word. As they listened, they recognized the sin in their lives, admitted it, and took steps to remove it.	Recognizing and admitting sin are not enough; revival must result in reform, or it is merely the expression of enthusiasm. God does not want half-hearted measures. We must not only remove sin from our lives but also ask God to move into the center of all we do.

A. REBUILDING THE WALL (1:1—7:73)

Despite the fact that the returned exiles had been in Jerusalem for many years, the walls of the city remained unrepaired, leaving its people defenseless and vulnerable. Upon hearing this news, Nehemiah seeks permission from the Persian king to go to Jerusalem. Arriving in Jerusalem, he mobilizes the people to begin rebuilding the wall. Faced with opposition, both from without and from within, Nehemiah perseveres until the project is complete and the city resettled. Seemingly impossible tasks can be accomplished when God is helping those who honor him and when their efforts are united.

1. Nehemiah returns to Jerusalem
Nehemiah's Prayer

1 The words of Nehemiah son of Hacaliah:

In the month of Kislev[a] in the twentieth year, while I was in the citadel of Susa, 2 Hanani, one of my brothers, came from Judah with some other men, and I questioned them about the Jewish remnant that survived the exile, and also about Jerusalem.

1:1
[a] Ne 10:1; Zec 7:1

1:3
b Ne 2:3, 13, 17

³ They said to me, "Those who survived the exile and are back in the province are in great trouble and disgrace. The wall of Jerusalem is broken down, and its gates have been burned with fire. *b*"

HOW NEHEMIAH USED PRAYER

Reference	Occasion	Summary of His Prayer	What Prayer Accomplished	Our Prayers
1:4–11	After receiving the bad news about the state of Jerusalem's walls	Recognized God's holiness. Asked for a hearing. Confessed sin. Asked for specific help in approaching the king	Included God in Nehemiah's plans and concerns. Prepared Nehemiah's heart and gave God room to work	How often do you pour out your heart to God? How often do you give him a specific request to answer?
2:4	During his conversation with the king	"Here's where you can help, God!"	Put the expected results in God's hands	Giving God credit for what happens before it happens keeps us from taking more credit than we should.
4:4, 5	After being taunted and ridiculed by Tobiah and Sanballat	"They're mocking you, God. You decide what to do with them."	Expressed anger to God, but Nehemiah did not take matters into his own hands	We are prone to do exactly the opposite— take matters into our hands and not tell God how we feel.
4:9	After threats of attack by enemies	"We are in your hands, God. We'll keep our weapons handy in case you want us to use them."	Showed trust in God even while taking necessary precautions	Trusting God does not mean we do nothing. Action does not mean we do not trust.
6:9	Responding to threats	"O Lord God, please strengthen me!"	Showed Nehemiah's reliance on God for emotional and mental stability	How often do you ask God for help when under pressure?
13:29	Reflecting on the actions of his enemies	Asked God to deal with the enemies and their evil plans	Took away the compulsion to get revenge, and entrusted justice to God	When did you last settle a desire for revenge by turning the matter over to God?
5:19; 13:14, 22, 31	Reflecting on his own efforts to serve God	"Remember me, God."	Kept clear in Nehemiah's mind his own motives for action	How many of your actions today will be done with the purpose of pleasing God?

1:1 Nehemiah wasn't the first of the exiles to return to Jerusalem. Zerubbabel had led the first group back in 538 B.C., more than 90 years earlier (Ezra 1; 2). Ezra followed with a second group in 458 B.C. (Ezra 7), and here Nehemiah was ready to lead the third major return to Jerusalem (445 B.C.). When he arrived after a three-month journey, he saw the completed temple and became acquainted with others who had returned to their homeland.

But Nehemiah also found a disorganized group of people and a defenseless city with no walls to protect it. Before the exile, Israel had its own language, king, army, and identity. At this time it had none of these. What the Jews lacked most was leadership; there was no one to show them where to start and what direction to take as they tried to rebuild their city. As soon as Nehemiah arrived he began a back to the basics program. He helped care for the people's physical needs by setting up a fair system of government and rebuilding Jerusalem's walls. He also cared for their spiritual needs by rebuilding broken lives. Nehemiah is a model of committed, God-honoring leadership, and his book contains many useful lessons for today.

1:2–4 Nehemiah was concerned about Jerusalem because

it was the Jews' holy city. As Judah's capital city, it represented Jewish national identity, and it was blessed with God's special presence in the temple. Jewish history centered around the city from the time of Abraham's gifts to Melchizedek, king of Salem (Genesis 14:17–20), to the days when Solomon built the glorious temple (1 Kings 7:51), and throughout the history of the kings. Nehemiah loved his homeland even though he had lived his whole life in Babylon. He wanted to return to Jerusalem to reunite the Jews and to remove the shame of Jerusalem's broken-down walls. This would bring glory to God and restore the reality and power of God's presence among his people.

4 When I heard these things, I sat down and wept. For some days I mourned and fasted and prayed before the God of heaven. 5 Then I said:

"O LORD, God of heaven, the great and awesome God,*c* who keeps his covenant of love*d* with those who love him and obey his commands, 6 let your ear be attentive and your eyes open to hear the prayer*e* your servant is praying before you day and night for your servants, the people of Israel. I confess the sins we Israelites, including myself and my father's house, have committed against you. 7 We have acted very wickedly*f* toward you. We have not obeyed the commands, decrees and laws you gave your servant Moses.

8 "Remember the instruction you gave your servant Moses, saying, 'If you are unfaithful, I will scatter*g* you among the nations, 9 but if you return to me and obey my commands, then even if your exiled people are at the farthest horizon, I will gather*h* them from there and bring them to the place I have chosen as a dwelling for my Name.'

10 "They are your servants and your people, whom you redeemed by your great strength and your mighty hand.*i* 11 O Lord, let your ear be attentive*j* to the prayer of this your servant and to the prayer of your servants who delight in revering your name. Give your servant success today by granting him favor in the presence of this man."

I was cupbearer to the king.

Artaxerxes Sends Nehemiah to Jerusalem

2 In the month of Nisan in the twentieth year of King Artaxerxes, when wine was brought for him, I took the wine and gave it to the king. I had not been sad in his presence before; 2 so the king asked me, "Why does your face look so sad when you are not ill? This can be nothing but sadness of heart."

**Cross-references (right margin):**
1:5
c Ne 4:14
d Ex 20:6; Da 9:4
1:6
e Da 9:17
1:7
f Dt 28:14-15
1:8
g Lev 26:33
1:9
h Dt 30:4
1:10
i Dt 9:29
1:11
j ver 6

1:4 Nehemiah broke down and wept when he heard that Jerusalem's walls still had not been rebuilt. Why did this upset him? Walls mean little in most present-day cities, but in Nehemiah's day they were as essential as we would consider electrical power or a police force. They offered safety from raids and symbolized strength and peace. Nehemiah also mourned for his people, the Jews, who had been stifled by a previous edict that had kept them from rebuilding their walls (Ezra 4:6–23).

1:4 Nehemiah was deeply grieved about the condition of Jerusalem, but he didn't just brood about it. After his initial grief, he prayed, pouring his heart out to God (1:5–11), and he looked for ways to improve the situation. Nehemiah put all his resources of knowledge, experience, and organization into determining what should be done. When tragic news comes to you, first pray. Then seek ways to move beyond grief to specific action that helps those who need it.

NEHEMIAH GOES TO JERUSALEM Nehemiah worked in Susa as a cupbearer for the king of the vast Medo-Persian empire. When he heard that the rebuilding projects in Jerusalem were progressing slowly, he asked the king if he could go there to help his people complete the task of rebuilding their city's walls. The king agreed to let him go; so he left as soon as possible, traveling along much the same route Ezra had taken.

1:5 God's "covenant of love" refers to God's promise to love the descendants of Abraham. It is also mentioned in Deuteronomy 7:7–9.

1:5ff Nehemiah fasted and prayed for several days, expressing his sorrow for Israel's sin and his desire that Jerusalem would again come alive with the worship of the one true God. Nehemiah demonstrated the elements of effective prayer: (1) praise, (2) thanksgiving, (3) repentance, (4) specific request, and (5) commitment.

Heartfelt prayers like Nehemiah's can help clarify (1) any problem you may be facing, (2) God's great power to help you, and (3) the job you have to do. By the end of his prayer time, Nehemiah knew what action he had to take (1:11). When God's people pray, difficult decisions fall into proper perspective, and appropriate actions follow.

1:11 Nehemiah was in a unique position to speak to the king. He was the trusted cupbearer who ensured the safety and quality of the king's food and drink. Nehemiah was concerned, prayerful, and prepared as he looked for the right opportunity to tell the king about God's people. Each of us is unique and capable of serving no matter what our position. Just as Nehemiah used his place as the king's trusted servant to intercede for his people, we can use our present positions to serve God.

1:11 Nehemiah prayed for success in this venture, not just for the strength to cope with his problems (see also 2:20). Yet the success he prayed for was not for personal advantage, position, or acclaim. He requested success for God's work. When God's purposes are at work, don't hesitate to ask for success.

2:2 The king noticed Nehemiah's sad appearance. It surprised Nehemiah to be singled out for attention and it frightened him because it was dangerous to show sorrow before the king, who could execute anyone who displeased him. In fact, anyone wearing sackcloth (mourning clothes) was barred from the palace (Esther 4:2).

2:2, 3 Nehemiah wasn't ashamed to admit his fear, but he refused to allow fear to stop him from doing what God had called him to do. He acknowledged the king's position and clearly stated the reasons for his own sorrow. When we allow our fears to rule

2:3
k Da 2:4
l Ne 1:3

I was very much afraid, 3 but I said to the king, "May the king live forever!*k* Why should my face not look sad when the city where my fathers are buried lies in ruins, and its gates have been destroyed by fire?*l*"

4 The king said to me, "What is it you want?"

Then I prayed to the God of heaven, 5 and I answered the king, "If it pleases the king and if your servant has found favor in his sight, let him send me to the city in Judah where my fathers are buried so that I can rebuild it."

2:6
m Ne 5:14; 13:6

6 Then the king*m*, with the queen sitting beside him, asked me, "How long will your journey take, and when will you get back?" It pleased the king to send me; so I set a time.

2:7
n Ezr 8:36

2:8
o Ne 7:2
p ver 18; Ezr 7:6

2:9
q Ezr 8:22

7 I also said to him, "If it pleases the king, may I have letters to the governors of Trans-Euphrates,*n* so that they will provide me safe-conduct until I arrive in Judah? 8 And may I have a letter to Asaph, keeper of the king's forest, so he will give me timber to make beams for the gates of the citadel*o* by the temple and for the city wall and for the residence I will occupy?" And because the gracious hand of my God was upon me,*p* the king granted my requests. 9 So I went to the governors of Trans-Euphrates and gave them the king's letters. The king had also sent army officers and cavalry*q* with me.

2:10
r ver 19; Ne 4:1, 7

10 When Sanballat*r* the Horonite and Tobiah the Ammonite official heard about this, they were very much disturbed that someone had come to promote the welfare of the Israelites.

2. Nehemiah leads the people
Nehemiah Inspects Jerusalem's Walls

11 I went to Jerusalem, and after staying there three days 12 I set out during the night with a few men. I had not told anyone what my God had put in my heart to do for Jerusalem. There were no mounts with me except the one I was riding on.

2:13
s Ne 3:13
t Ne 1:3

13 By night I went out through the Valley Gate toward the Jackal*a* Well and the Dung Gate,*s* examining the walls*t* of Jerusalem, which had been broken down, and its gates, which had

a 13 Or Serpent or Fig

---

us, we make fear more powerful than God. Is there a task God wants you to do, but fear is holding you back? God is greater than all your fears. Recognizing why you are afraid is the first step in committing it to God. Realize that if God has called you to a task, he will help you accomplish it.

2:4 With little time to think, Nehemiah immediately prayed. Eight times in this book we read that he prayed spontaneously (2:4; 4:4–5, 9; 5:19; 6:14; 13:14, 22, 29). Nehemiah prayed at any time, even while talking with others. He knew that God is always in charge, is always present, and hears and answers every prayer. Nehemiah could confidently pray throughout the day because he had established an intimate relationship with God during times of extended prayer (1:4–7). If we want to reach God with our emergency prayers, we need to take time to cultivate a strong relationship with God through times of in-depth prayer.

2:6 The king asked Nehemiah how long he would be gone. The Bible does not record Nehemiah's immediate answer, but he ended up staying in Jerusalem for 12 years (5:14; 13:6).

2:7, 8 After his prayer, Nehemiah asked the king for permission to go to Judah. As soon as he got a positive answer, he began asking for additional help. Sometimes when we have needs, we hesitate to ask the right people for help because we are afraid to approach them. Not Nehemiah! He went directly to the person who could help him the most. Don't be reluctant to ask those who are most able to help. They may be more interested and approachable than you think. God's answers to prayer may come as a result of our asking others.

2:8 Nehemiah had position, power, and many good organizational skills, but he acknowledged that God's gracious hand was upon him. He knew that without God's strength, his efforts would be in vain. Do you acknowledge God as your power source and the giver of your gifts?

2:9, 10, 19 When Nehemiah arrived in Judah, opposition greeted him. Opposition to the rebuilding of Jerusalem had been going on

for 90 years by those who settled in the area when the Jews were taken captive. In every generation there are those who hate God's people and try to block God's purpose. When you attempt to do God's work, some will oppose you; some will even hope you fail. If you expect opposition, you will be prepared rather than surprised (1 John 3:13). Knowing that God is behind your task is the best incentive to move ahead in the face of opposition.

2:10 Sanballat was governor of Samaria, and Tobiah was probably governor of Transjordan under the Persians. Why were these government officials so concerned about the arrival of Nehemiah and his small band of exiles? There are several possible reasons. (1) When Zerubbabel first returned with his group (Ezra 1; 2), his refusal to accept help from the Samaritans had caused bad relations. (2) Nehemiah was no ordinary exile; he was the king's personal adviser and cupbearer, arriving in Jerusalem with the king's approval to build and fortify the city. If anyone could rebuild Jerusalem, he could. A rebuilt Jerusalem was a threat to the authority of the Samaritan officials who had been in charge of the land since Judah's exile. (3) This was the third group to return from exile. The increasing number of people in Jerusalem made Sanballat and Tobiah angry. They did not want returned exiles taking control of the land and threatening their secure position.

2:11–17 Nehemiah arrived quietly in Jerusalem and spent several days carefully observing and assessing the damage to the walls. Following this time of thoughtful consideration, he confidently presented his plan. Nehemiah demonstrated an excellent approach to problem solving. He got firsthand information and carefully considered the situation. Then he presented a realistic strategy. Before jumping into a project, follow Nehemiah's example and plan ahead. Check your information to make sure your ideas will work—be realistic. Then you will be able to present your plan with confidence.

been destroyed by fire. ¹⁴Then I moved on toward the Fountain Gate ᵘ and the King's Pool, but there was not enough room for my mount to get through; ¹⁵so I went up the valley by night, examining the wall. Finally, I turned back and reentered through the Valley Gate. ¹⁶The officials did not know where I had gone or what I was doing, because as yet I had said nothing to the Jews or the priests or nobles or officials or any others who would be doing the work.

2:14
ᵘNe 3:15

¹⁷Then I said to them, "You see the trouble we are in: Jerusalem lies in ruins, and its gates have been burned with fire. ᵛ Come, let us rebuild the wall of Jerusalem, and we will no longer be in disgrace." ¹⁸I also told them about the gracious hand of my God upon me ʷ and what the king had said to me.

2:17
ᵛNe 1:3

2:18
ʷ2Sa 2:7

They replied, "Let us start rebuilding." So they began this good work.

¹⁹But when Sanballat the Horonite, Tobiah the Ammonite official and Geshem the Arab heard about it, they mocked and ridiculed us. "What is this you are doing?" they asked. "Are you rebelling against the king?"

²⁰I answered them by saying, "The God of heaven will give us success. We his servants will start rebuilding, but as for you, you have no share ˣ in Jerusalem or any claim or historic right to it."

2:20
ˣEzr 4:3

Builders of the Wall

3 Eliashib the high priest and his fellow priests went to work and rebuilt the Sheep Gate. ʸ They dedicated it and set its doors in place, building as far as the Tower of the Hundred, which they dedicated, and as far as the Tower of Hananel. ᶻ ²The men of Jericho ᵃ built the adjoining section, and Zaccur son of Imri built next to them.

3:1
ʸNe 12:39
ᶻJer 31:38

3:2
ᵃNe 7:36

2:14 The walls were so broken down that Nehemiah's mount couldn't get through, so Nehemiah had to inspect that section on foot.

2:15, 16 Nehemiah kept his mission a secret and surveyed the walls by moonlight to avoid unhealthy gossip about his arrival and to prevent enemies from being alerted to his plans. Only after planning carefully would he be ready to go public with his mission from God. A premature announcement could have caused rivalry among the Jews as to the best way to begin. In this case,

Nehemiah didn't need tedious planning sessions; he needed one plan that would bring quick action.

2:17, 18 Spiritual renewal often begins with one person's vision. Nehemiah had a vision, and he shared it with enthusiasm, inspiring Jerusalem's leaders to rebuild the walls.

We frequently underestimate people and don't challenge them with our dreams for God's work in the world. When God plants an idea in your mind to accomplish something for him, share it with others and trust the Holy Spirit to impress them with similar thoughts. Don't regard yourself as the only one through whom God is working. Often God uses one person to express the vision and others to turn it into reality. When you encourage and inspire others, you put teamwork into action to accomplish God's goals.

2:19 Sanballat and Tobiah labeled the rebuilding of Jerusalem's walls as rebellion against the king, probably threatening to report the builders as traitors. These enemies also ridiculed Nehemiah, saying that the walls could never be rebuilt because the damage was too extensive. Nehemiah did not tell them he already had permission from the king to rebuild. Instead, he simply said he had God's approval—that was enough.

3:1 The high priest is the first person mentioned who pitched in and helped with the work. Spiritual leaders must lead not only by word, but also by action. The Sheep Gate was the gate used to bring sheep into the city to the temple for sacrifices. Nehemiah had the priests repair this gate and section of the wall, respecting the priests' area of interest and at the same time emphasizing the priority of worship.

3:1ff All the citizens of Jerusalem did their part on the huge job of rebuilding the city wall. Similarly, the work of the church requires every member's effort in order for the body of Christ to function effectively (1 Corinthians 12:12–27). The body needs you! Are you doing your part? Find a place to serve God, and start contributing whatever time, talent, and money is needed.

3:1ff Jerusalem was a large city, and because many roads converged there, it required many gates. The wall on each side of these heavy wooden gates was taller and thicker so soldiers could stand guard to defend the gates against attack. Sometimes two stone towers guarded the gate. In times of peace, the city gates were hubs of activity—city council was held there, and shopkeepers set up their wares at the entrance. Building the city walls and gates was not only a military priority, but also a boost for trade and commerce.

THE RESTORATION OF THE CITY WALLS Nehemiah takes us on a counterclockwise tour around Jerusalem (beginning with the Sheep Gate). He describes for us each section, gate, and tower on the wall and who worked to rebuild it.

3:3
*b*Ne 12:39

[3] The Fish Gate *b* was rebuilt by the sons of Hassenaah. They laid its beams and put its doors and bolts and bars in place. [4] Meremoth son of Uriah, the son of Hakkoz, repaired the next section. Next to him Meshullam son of Berekiah, the son of Meshezabel, made repairs, and next to him Zadok son of Baana also made repairs. [5] The next section was repaired by the men of Tekoa, but their nobles would not put their shoulders to the work under their supervisors. *a*

3:6
*c*Ne 12:39
3:7
*d*Ne 2:7
3:8
*e*Ne 12:38

[6] The Jeshanah *b* Gate *c* was repaired by Joiada son of Paseah and Meshullam son of Besodeiah. They laid its beams and put its doors and bolts and bars in place. [7] Next to them, repairs were made by men from Gibeon *d* and Mizpah—Melatiah of Gibeon and Jadon of Meronoth—places under the authority of the governor of Trans-Euphrates. [8] Uzziel son of Harhaiah, one of the goldsmiths, repaired the next section; and Hananiah, one of the perfume-makers, made repairs next to that. They restored *c* Jerusalem as far as the Broad Wall. *e* [9] Rephaiah son of Hur, ruler of a half-district of Jerusalem, repaired the next section. [10] Adjoining this, Jedaiah son of Harumaph made repairs opposite his house, and Hattush son of Hashabneiah made repairs next to him. [11] Malkijah son of Harim and Hasshub son of Pahath-Moab repaired another section and the Tower of the Ovens. *f* [12] Shallum son of Hallohesh, ruler of a half-district of Jerusalem, repaired the next section with the help of his daughters.

3:11
*f*Ne 12:38

3:13
*g*Ne 2:13

[13] The Valley Gate was repaired by Hanun and the residents of Zanoah. They rebuilt it and put its doors and bolts and bars in place. They also repaired five hundred yards *d* of the wall as far as the Dung Gate. *g*

[14] The Dung Gate was repaired by Malkijah son of Recab, ruler of the district of Beth Hakkerem. He rebuilt it and put its doors and bolts and bars in place.

[15] The Fountain Gate was repaired by Shallun son of Col-Hozeh, ruler of the district of Mizpah. He rebuilt it, roofing it over and putting its doors and bolts and bars in place. He also repaired the wall of the Pool of Siloam,*e* by the King's Garden, as far as the steps going down from the City of David. [16] Beyond him, Nehemiah son of Azbuk, ruler of a half-district of Beth Zur, made repairs up to a point opposite the tombs*f* of David, as far as the artificial pool and the House of the Heroes.

[17] Next to him, the repairs were made by the Levites under Rehum son of Bani. Beside him, Hashabiah, ruler of half the district of Keilah, carried out repairs for his district. [18] Next to him, the repairs were made by their countrymen under Binnui*g* son of Henadad, ruler of the other half-district of Keilah. [19] Next to him, Ezer son of Jeshua, ruler of Mizpah, repaired another section, from a point facing the ascent to the armory as far as the angle. [20] Next to him, Baruch son of Zabbai zealously repaired another section, from the angle to the entrance of the house of Eliashib the high priest. [21] Next to him, Meremoth son of Uriah, the son of Hakkoz, repaired another section, from the entrance of Eliashib's house to the end of it.

[22] The repairs next to him were made by the priests from the surrounding region. [23] Beyond them, Benjamin and Hasshub made repairs in front of their house; and next to them, Azariah son of Maaseiah, the son of Ananiah, made repairs beside his house. [24] Next to him, Binnui son of Henadad repaired another section, from Azariah's house to the angle and the corner, [25] and Palal son of Uzai worked opposite the angle and the tower projecting from the upper palace near the court of the guard. *h* Next to him, Pedaiah son of Parosh [26] and the temple servants *i* living on the hill of Ophel made repairs up to a point opposite the Water Gate*j* toward the east and the projecting tower. [27] Next to them, the men of Tekoa repaired another section, from the great projecting tower to the wall of Ophel.

3:25
*h*Jer 32:2; 37:21
3:26
*i*Ne 7:46; 11:21
*j*Ne 8:1, 3, 16

*a*5 Or *their Lord* or *the governor*   *b*6 Or *Old*   *c*8 Or *They left out part of*   *d*13 Hebrew *a thousand cubits* (about 450 meters)   *e*15 Hebrew *Shelah*, a variant of *Shiloah*, that is, Siloam   *f*16 Hebrew; Septuagint, some Vulgate manuscripts and Syriac *tomb*   *g*18 Two Hebrew manuscripts and Syriac (see also Septuagint and verse 24); most Hebrew manuscripts *Bavvai*

3:3 One of the main roads through Jerusalem entered the city through the Fish Gate (2 Chronicles 33:14). The fish market was near the gate, and merchants from Tyre, the Sea of Galilee, and other fishing areas entered this gate to sell their goods.

3:5 The nobles of Tekoa were lazy and wouldn't help. These men were the only ones who did not support the building project in Jerusalem. Every group, even churches, will have those who think they are too wise or important to work hard. Gentle encouragement doesn't seem to help. Sometimes the best policy is to ignore

them. They may think they are getting away with something, but their inactivity will be remembered by all who worked hard.

3:12 Shallum's daughters helped with the difficult work of repairing the city walls. Rebuilding Jerusalem's walls was a matter of national emergency for the Jews, not just a civic beautification project. Nearly everyone was dedicated to the task and willing to work at it.

3:14 The Dung Gate was the gate through which the people carried their garbage to be burned in the Valley of Hinnom.

28Above the Horse Gate,*k* the priests made repairs, each in front of his own house. 29Next to them, Zadok son of Immer made repairs opposite his house. Next to him, Shemaiah son of Shecaniah, the guard at the East Gate, made repairs. 30Next to him, Hananiah son of Shelemiah, and Hanun, the sixth son of Zalaph, repaired another section. Next to them, Meshullam son of Berekiah made repairs opposite his living quarters. 31Next to him, Malkijah, one of the goldsmiths, made repairs as far as the house of the temple servants and the merchants, opposite the Inspection Gate, and as far as the room above the corner; 32and between the room above the corner and the Sheep Gate the goldsmiths and merchants made repairs.

Opposition to the Rebuilding

4 When Sanballat*l* heard that we were rebuilding the wall, he became angry and was greatly incensed. He ridiculed the Jews, 2and in the presence of his associates and the army of Samaria, he said, "What are those feeble Jews doing? Will they restore their wall? Will they offer sacrifices? Will they finish in a day? Can they bring the stones back to life from those heaps of rubble—burned as they are?"

3Tobiah*m* the Ammonite, who was at his side, said, "What they are building—if even a fox climbed up on it, he would break down their wall of stones!"

4Hear us, O our God, for we are despised. *n* Turn their insults back on their own heads. Give them over as plunder in a land of captivity. 5Do not cover up their guilt or blot out their sins from your sight, *o* for they have thrown insults in the face of *a* the builders.

6So we rebuilt the wall till all of it reached half its height, for the people worked with all their heart.

7But when Sanballat, Tobiah, the Arabs, the Ammonites and the men of Ashdod heard that the repairs to Jerusalem's walls had gone ahead and that the gaps were being closed, they were very angry. 8They all plotted together to come and fight against Jerusalem and stir up trouble against it. 9But we prayed to our God and posted a guard day and night to meet this threat.

10Meanwhile, the people in Judah said, "The strength of the laborers is giving out, and there is so much rubble that we cannot rebuild the wall."

a 5 Or have provoked you to anger before

3:28
k 2Ki 11:16;
2Ch 23:15;
Jer 31:40

4:1
l Ne 2:10

4:3
m Ne 2:10

4:4
n Ps 79:12; 123:3-4

4:5
o Ps 69:27-28;
Jer 18:23

3:28 The Horse Gate was at the far eastern point of the wall, facing the Kidron Valley.

3:28 Each priest also repaired the wall in front of his own house, in addition to other sections. If each person was responsible for the part of the wall closest to his own house, (1) he would be more motivated to build it quickly and properly, (2) he wouldn't waste time traveling to more distant parts of the wall, (3) he would defend his own home if the wall were attacked, and (4) he would be able to make the building a family effort. Nehemiah blended self-interest with the group's objectives, helping everyone to feel that the wall project was his own. If you are part of a group working on a large project, make sure each person sees the importance and meaning of the job that he or she has to do. This will ensure high-quality work and personal satisfaction.

3:31 The Inspection Gate was in the northern part of the eastern wall.

4:1 Sanballat was governor of Samaria, the region just north of Judea where Jerusalem was located. Sanballat may have hoped to become governor of Judea as well, but Nehemiah's arrival spoiled his plans. (For his other reasons for opposing Nehemiah, see the note on 2:10.) Sanballat tried to scare Nehemiah away or at least discourage him by scorn (4:2; 6:6), threats (4:8), and bluffs (6:7).

4:1, 2 Almost 300 years before Nehemiah's time, the northern kingdom of Israel was conquered, and most of the people were carried away captive (722 B.C.). Sargon of Assyria repopulated Israel with captives from other lands. These captives eventually intermarried with the few Israelites who remained in the land to form a mixed race of people who became known as Samaritans. The Jews who returned to Jerusalem and the southern region of Judea during the days of Ezra and Nehemiah would have nothing to do with Samaritans, whom they considered to be racially impure.

Relations between both groups grew progressively worse—400 years later, the Jews and Samaritans hated each other (John 4:9).

4:1-5 Ridicule can cut deeply, causing discouragement and despair. Sanballat and Tobiah used ridicule to try to dissuade the Jews from building the wall. Instead of trading insults, however, Nehemiah prayed, and the work continued. When you are mocked for your faith or criticized for doing what you know is right, refuse to respond in the same way or to become discouraged. Tell God how you feel and remember his promise to be with you. This will give you encouragement and strength to carry on.

4:4, 5 Nehemiah is not praying for revenge but that God's justice would be carried out. His prayer is similar to many of David's (see the note in Psalm 7:1-6 and the chart "How Nehemiah Used Prayer").

4:6 The work of rebuilding the wall progressed well because the people had set their hearts and minds on accomplishing the task. They did not lose faith or give up, but they persevered in the work. If God has called you to a task, determine to complete it, even if you face opposition or discouragement. The rewards of work well done will be worth the effort.

4:9 Nehemiah constantly combined prayer with preparation and planning. His people trusted God and at the same time kept vigilant watch over what had been entrusted to them. Too often we pray without looking for what God wants us to do. We show God we are serious when we combine prayer with thought, preparation, and effort.

4:10-14 Accomplishing any large task is tiring. There are always pressures that foster discouragement—the task seems impossible, it can never be finished, or too many factors are working against us. The only cure for fatigue and discouragement is focusing on God's purposes. Nehemiah reminded the workers of their calling,

¹¹Also our enemies said, "Before they know it or see us, we will be right there among them and will kill them and put an end to the work."

¹²Then the Jews who lived near them came and told us ten times over, "Wherever you turn, they will attack us."

¹³Therefore I stationed some of the people behind the lowest points of the wall at the exposed places, posting them by families, with their swords, spears and bows. ¹⁴After I looked

NEHEMIAH

God is in the business of working through his people to accomplish seemingly impossible tasks. God often shapes people with personality characteristics, experiences, and training that prepare them for his purpose, and usually the people have no idea what God has in store for them. God prepared and positioned Nehemiah to accomplish one of the Bible's "impossible" tasks.

Nehemiah was a common man in a unique position. He was secure and successful as cupbearer to the Persian king Artaxerxes. Nehemiah had little power, but he had great influence. He was trusted by the king. He was also a man of God, concerned about the fate of Jerusalem.

Seventy years earlier, Zerubbabel had managed to rebuild God's temple. Thirteen years had passed since Ezra had returned to Jerusalem and helped the people with their spiritual needs. Now Nehemiah was needed. Jerusalem's wall was still in ruins, and the news broke his heart. As he talked to God, a plan began to take form in Nehemiah's mind about his own role in the rebuilding of the city walls. He willingly left the security of his home and job in Persia to follow God on an "impossible" mission. And the rest is history.

From beginning to end, Nehemiah prayed for God's help. He never hesitated to ask God to remember him, closing his autobiography with these words: "Remember me with favor, O my God." Throughout the "impossible" task, Nehemiah displayed unusual leadership. The wall around Jerusalem was rebuilt in record time, despite resistance. Even Israel's enemies grudgingly and fearfully admitted that God was with these builders. Not only that, but God worked through Nehemiah to bring about a spiritual awakening among the people of Judah.

You may not have Nehemiah's unique abilities or feel that you are in a position where you can do anything great for God, but there are two ways you can become useful to God. First, be a person who *talks* to God. Welcome him into your thoughts and share yourself with him—your concerns, feelings, and dreams. Second, be a person who *walks* with God. Put what you learn from his Word into action. God may have an "impossible" mission that he wants to do through you.

Strengths and accomplishments:	• A man of character, persistence, and prayer • Brilliant planner, organizer, and motivator • Under his leadership, the wall around Jerusalem was rebuilt in 52 days • As political leader, led the nation to religious reform and spiritual awakening • Was calm under opposition • Was capable of being bluntly honest with his people when they were sinning
Lessons from his life:	• The first step in any venture is to pray • People under God's direction can accomplish impossible tasks • There are two parts to real service for God: talking with him, and walking with him
Vital statistics:	• Where: Persia, Jerusalem • Occupations: King's cupbearer, city builder, governor of Judah • Relative: Father: Hacaliah • Contemporaries: Ezra, Artaxerxes, Tobiah, Sanballat
Key verse:	"I also told them about the gracious hand of my God upon me and what the king had said to me. They replied, 'Let us start rebuilding.' So they began this good work" (Nehemiah 2:18).

Nehemiah's story is told in the book of Nehemiah.

their goal, and God's protection. If you are overwhelmed by an assignment, tired, and discouraged, remember God's purpose for your life and his special purpose for the project.

4:10-15 The people working on the walls faced the continual threat of terrorist attacks from those who didn't want to see Jerusalem rebuilt. Threats demoralize. The tension created by the possibility of sudden assaults adds to fatigue. Nehemiah took wise, practical steps to counter the threats: (1) he stationed guards at obvious weak points; (2) he reminded the workers to keep weapons close at hand and to fight for God, their families,

and the nation if an attack came; (3) he established duty rotations so that some stood guard while others worked. The preparations for defense and the continuation of the work reversed the effects of terrorism and demoralized the enemies. Obstacles and foes can make us work smarter and live wiser or make us give up our purpose and our way of living. If they accomplish the latter, they have won even if they haven't actually attacked us. But if we adjust our way of living wisely while continuing resolutely to live under God's instructions, the opposition will fail.

things over, I stood up and said to the nobles, the officials and the rest of the people, "Don't be afraid ᵖ of them. Remember the Lord, who is great and awesome, and fight ᵠ for your brothers, your sons and your daughters, your wives and your homes."

¹⁵When our enemies heard that we were aware of their plot and that God had frustrated it,ʳ we all returned to the wall, each to his own work.

¹⁶From that day on, half of my men did the work, while the other half were equipped with spears, shields, bows and armor. The officers posted themselves behind all the people of Judah ¹⁷who were building the wall. Those who carried materials did their work with one hand and held a weapon in the other, ¹⁸and each of the builders wore his sword at his side as he worked. But the man who sounded the trumpet stayed with me.

¹⁹Then I said to the nobles, the officials and the rest of the people, "The work is extensive and spread out, and we are widely separated from each other along the wall. ²⁰Wherever you hear the sound of the trumpet, join us there. Our God will fight ˢ for us!"

²¹So we continued the work with half the men holding spears, from the first light of dawn till the stars came out. ²²At that time I also said to the people, "Have every man and his helper stay inside Jerusalem at night, so they can serve us as guards by night and workmen by day." ²³Neither I nor my brothers nor my men nor the guards with me took off our clothes; each had his weapon, even when he went for water. ᵃ

Nehemiah Helps the Poor

5 Now the men and their wives raised a great outcry against their Jewish brothers. ²Some were saying, "We and our sons and daughters are numerous; in order for us to eat and stay alive, we must get grain."

³Others were saying, "We are mortgaging our fields, our vineyards and our homes to get grain during the famine."

⁴Still others were saying, "We have had to borrow money to pay the king's tax ᵗ on our fields and vineyards. ⁵Although we are of the same flesh and blood as our countrymen and though our sons are as good as theirs, yet we have to subject our sons and daughters to slavery. ᵘ Some of our daughters have already been enslaved, but we are powerless, because our fields and our vineyards belong to others."

⁶When I heard their outcry and these charges, I was very angry. ⁷I pondered them in my mind and then accused the nobles and officials. I told them, "You are exacting usury ᵛ from your own countrymen!" So I called together a large meeting to deal with them ⁸and said: "As far as possible, we have bought ʷ back our Jewish brothers who were sold to the Gentiles. Now you are selling your brothers, only for them to be sold back to us!" They kept quiet, because they could find nothing to say.

⁹So I continued, "What you are doing is not right. Shouldn't you walk in the fear of our

ᵃ*23* The meaning of the Hebrew for this clause is uncertain.

4:14
ᵖNu 14:9; Dt 1:29
ᵠ2Sa 10:12

4:15
ʳ2Sa 17:14; Job 5:12

4:20
ˢEx 14:14; Dt 1:30; 20:4

5:4
ᵗEzr 4:13

5:5
ᵘLev 25:39-43, 47

5:7
ᵛEx 22:25-27; Lev 25:35-37

5:8
ʷLev 25:47

4:16 The workers were spread out along the wall, so Nehemiah devised a plan of defense that would unite and protect his people—half the men worked while the other half stood guard. Christians need to help one another in the same way because we can become so afraid of possible dangers that we can't get anything done. By looking out for each other, we will be free to put forth our best efforts, confident that others are ready to offer help when needed. Don't cut yourself off from others; instead, join together for mutual benefit. You need them as much as they need you.

4:18-20 To further relieve the anxieties of the people, Nehemiah set up a communication system. The man who sounded the trumpet stayed with Nehemiah, and the people knew what to do if they heard it. We have no record that the trumpet was ever used, but simply knowing it would issue a warning when needed was reassuring. The system also put doubt into the minds of those trying to terrorize the workforce since the people on the wall were no longer passive targets. The promise of open, immediate communication helped the group counter the enemy threats and accomplish the reconstruction of the wall in record time.

4:23 Although the exact meaning of the Hebrew phrase, "even when he went for water" is unclear (it has been translated, "in his right hand" or "at his right hand at night"), the point is that each

man always had his weapon close at hand. The guards were prepared and took their responsibilities seriously.

5:1-5 Who were these bitterly resented Jews? They were either (1) Jews who had become wealthy in exile and brought this wealth with them to Jerusalem, or (2) descendants of Jews who had arrived almost a century earlier during the first return under Zerubbabel (Ezra 1; 2) and had established lucrative businesses.

5:7-9 Many of the returned exiles were suffering at the hands of some of their rich countrymen. These people would lend large sums of money; then, when the debtors missed a payment, they would take over their fields. Left with no means of income, the debtors were forced to sell their children into slavery, a common practice of this time. Nehemiah was angry with these Jews who were taking advantage of their own people in order to enrich themselves. Usury is the practice of charging excessive interest. These practices violated the law set forth in Exodus 22:25.

5:9-11 God's concern for the poor is revealed in almost every book of the Bible. Here, Nehemiah insisted that fairness to the poor and oppressed was central to following God. The books of Moses clearly spelled out the Israelites' responsibility to care for the poor (Exodus 22:22–27; Leviticus 25:35–37; Deuteronomy 14:28, 29; 15:7–11). The way we help those in need ought to mirror God's love and concern.

God to avoid the reproach of our Gentile enemies? [10]I and my brothers and my men are also lending the people money and grain. But let the exacting of usury stop! [11]Give back to them immediately their fields, vineyards, olive groves and houses, and also the usury you are charging them—the hundredth part of the money, grain, new wine and oil."

5:12
x Ezr 10:5

[12]"We will give it back," they said. "And we will not demand anything more from them. We will do as you say."

5:13
y Mt 10:14; Ac 18:6

Then I summoned the priests and made the nobles and officials take an oath x to do what they had promised. [13]I also shook y out of the folds of my robe and said, "In this way may God shake out of his house and possessions every man who does not keep this promise. So may such a man be shaken out and emptied!"

At this the whole assembly said, "Amen," and praised the LORD. And the people did as they had promised.

5:14
z Ne 13:6

[14]Moreover, from the twentieth year of King Artaxerxes, z when I was appointed to be their governor in the land of Judah, until his thirty-second year—twelve years—neither I nor my brothers ate the food allotted to the governor. [15]But the earlier governors—those preceding me—placed a heavy burden on the people and took forty shekels a of silver from them in addition to food and wine. Their assistants also lorded it over the people. But out of reverence for God I did not act like that. [16]Instead, I devoted myself to the work on this wall. All my men were assembled there for the work; we b did not acquire any land.

5:18
a 1Ki 4:23

[17]Furthermore, a hundred and fifty Jews and officials ate at my table, as well as those who came to us from the surrounding nations. [18]Each day one ox, six choice sheep and some poultry a were prepared for me, and every ten days an abundant supply of wine of all kinds. In spite of all this, I never demanded the food allotted to the governor, because the demands were heavy on these people.

5:19
b Ne 1:8;
13:14, 22, 31

[19]Remember b me with favor, O my God, for all I have done for these people.

Further Opposition to the Rebuilding

6:1
c Ne 2:10
d Ne 2:19

6 When word came to Sanballat, Tobiah, c Geshem d the Arab and the rest of our enemies that I had rebuilt the wall and not a gap was left in it—though up to that time I had not set the doors in the gates— [2]Sanballat and Geshem sent me this message: "Come, let us meet together in one of the villages c on the plain of Ono. e"

6:2
e 1Ch 8:12

But they were scheming to harm me; [3]so I sent messengers to them with this reply: "I am carrying on a great project and cannot go down. Why should the work stop while I leave it and go down to you?" [4]Four times they sent me the same message, and each time I gave them the same answer.

[5]Then, the fifth time, Sanballat sent his aide to me with the same message, and in his hand was an unsealed letter [6]in which was written:

6:6
f Ne 2:19

"It is reported among the nations—and Geshem d f says it is true—that you and the Jews are plotting to revolt, and therefore you are building the wall. Moreover, according

a 15 That is, about 1 pound (about 0.5 kilogram)   b 16 Most Hebrew manuscripts; some Hebrew manuscripts, Septuagint, Vulgate and Syriac I   c 2 Or in Kephirim   d 6 Hebrew Gashmu, a variant of Geshem

---

5:10 Nehemiah told the rich Jews to stop charging interest ("exacting usury") on their loans to their needy brothers. God never intended people to profit from others' misfortunes. In contrast to the values of this world, God says that caring for one another is more important than personal gain. When a Christian brother or sister suffers, we all suffer (1 Corinthians 12:26). We should help needy believers, not exploit them. The Jerusalem church was praised for working together to eliminate poverty (Acts 4:34, 35). Remember, "He who gives to the poor will lack nothing" (Proverbs 28:27). Make it a practice to help those in need around you.

5:13 This symbolic act was a curse. Nehemiah shook out the fold of his garment and pronounced that anyone who did not keep his promise would likewise be "shaken out and emptied," losing all he had.

5:14, 15 This comment by Nehemiah is a parenthetical statement, comparing his 12 years as governor with the unjust proceedings in the land before he arrived. The governor was appointed by the Persian king, not elected by the people.

5:16 Nehemiah led the entire construction project, but he also worked on the wall alongside the others. He was not a bureaucrat in a well-guarded office, but a leader who got involved in the day-to-day work. He did not use his position to lord it over his people. A good leader keeps in touch with the work to be done. Those who lead best lead by what they do as well as by what they say.

6:1ff Sanballat and Tobiah were desperate. The wall was almost complete, and their efforts to stop its construction were failing. So they tried a new approach, centering their attacks on Nehemiah's character. They attacked him personally with rumors (6:6), deceit (6:10–13), and false reports (6:17). Personal attacks hurt, and when the criticism is unjustified, it is easy to despair. When you are doing God's work, you may receive attacks on your character. Follow Nehemiah's example by trusting God to accomplish the task and by overlooking unjustified abuse.

6:2 The plain of Ono was about 20 miles northwest of Jerusalem. If Sanballat and Geshem could get Nehemiah to agree to meet them there, they could ambush him on the way.

to these reports you are about to become their king [7] and have even appointed prophets to make this proclamation about you in Jerusalem: 'There is a king in Judah!' Now this report will get back to the king; so come, let us confer together."

[8] I sent him this reply: "Nothing like what you are saying is happening; you are just making it up out of your head."

[9] They were all trying to frighten us, thinking, "Their hands will get too weak for the work, and it will not be completed."

⌊But I prayed,⌋ "Now strengthen my hands."

[10] One day I went to the house of Shemaiah son of Delaiah, the son of Mehetabel, who was shut in at his home. He said, "Let us meet in the house of God, inside the temple, and let us close the temple doors, because men are coming to kill you—by night they are coming to kill you."

[11] But I said, "Should a man like me run away? Or should one like me go into the temple to save his life? I will not go!" [12] I realized that God had not sent him, but that he had prophesied against me [g] because Tobiah and Sanballat had hired him. [13] He had been hired to intimidate me so that I would commit a sin by doing this, and then they would give me a bad name to discredit me.

[14] Remember Tobiah and Sanballat, O my God, because of what they have done; remember also the prophetess [h] Noadiah and the rest of the prophets [i] who have been trying to intimidate me.

The Completion of the Wall

[15] So the wall was completed on the twenty-fifth of Elul, in fifty-two days. [16] When all our enemies heard about this, all the surrounding nations were afraid and lost their self-confidence, because they realized that this work had been done with the help of our God.

[17] Also, in those days the nobles of Judah were sending many letters to Tobiah, and replies from Tobiah kept coming to them. [18] For many in Judah were under oath to him, since he was son-in-law to Shecaniah son of Arah, and his son Jehohanan had married the daughter of Meshullam son of Berekiah. [19] Moreover, they kept reporting to me his good deeds and then telling him what I said. And Tobiah sent letters to intimidate me.

7 After the wall had been rebuilt and I had set the doors in place, the gatekeepers [j] and the singers [k] and the Levites [l] were appointed. [2] I put in charge of Jerusalem my brother Hanani, [m] along with [a] Hananiah [n] the commander of the citadel, [o] because he was a man of

a 2 Or Hanani, that is,

6:12
g Eze 13:22-23

6:14
h Eze 13:17-23
i Ne 13:29

7:1
j Ne 6:1, 15
k Ps 68:25
l Ne 8:9

7:2
m Ne 1:2
n Ne 10:23
o Ne 2:8

6:7 During these days, prophets such as Malachi proclaimed the coming of the Messiah (Malachi 3:1–3). Sanballat, with his usual flair for stirring up trouble, tried to turn Nehemiah's people against him by saying that Nehemiah was trying to set himself up as the king. Sanballat also tried to turn the local officials against Nehemiah by threatening to report to the king of Persia that Nehemiah was starting a revolt. The fact that Sanballat had an open, or unsealed, letter delivered to Nehemiah shows that he wanted to make sure the letter's contents were made public. But Sanballat's accusations were untrue and did not divert Nehemiah from his task.

6:9 When opposition builds up against you or God's work, it is tempting to pray, "God, get me out of this situation." But Nehemiah prayed, "Strengthen my hands." He showed tremendous determination and character to remain steadfast in his responsibility. When we pray for strength, God always answers.

6:10 Shemaiah warned Nehemiah of danger and told him to hide in the temple. Nehemiah wisely tested the message, exposing it as another trick of the enemy. People may misuse God's name by saying they know God's will when they have other motives. Examine self-proclaimed messengers from God to see if they stand up to the test of being consistent with what is revealed in God's Word.

6:10–13 Nehemiah did not have the full support of the people. Shemaiah (6:10), Noadiah (6:14), and many of the nobles (6:17) were working against him. When Nehemiah was attacked personally, he refused to give in to fear and flee to the temple. According to God's law, it would have been wrong for Nehemiah to go into the temple to hide because he wasn't a priest (Numbers 18:22). If

he had run for his life, he would have undermined the courage he was trying to instill in the people. Leaders are targets for attacks. Make it a practice to pray for those in authority (1 Timothy 2:1, 2). Request God to give them strength to stand against personal attacks and temptation. They need God-given courage to overcome fear.

6:15 Daniel, who was among the first group of captives taken from Jerusalem to Babylon (605 B.C.), predicted the rebuilding of the city (Daniel 9:25). Here his prophecy comes true. He, like Nehemiah, was a Jew who held a prominent position in the kingdom where he had been exiled (Daniel 5:29—6:3).

6:15 They said it couldn't be done. The job was too big and the problems were too great. But God's men and women, joined together for special tasks, can solve huge problems and accomplish great goals. The vision that Nehemiah saw through humble tears in Persia became a reality with God's help every step of the way. Don't let the size of a task or the length of time needed to accomplish it keep you from doing it. With God's help, it can be done.

7:2 Integrity and fear of God were the key character traits that qualified these men to govern Jerusalem. People of integrity can be trusted to carry out their work; God-fearing people can be expected to do so in line with God's priorities. These men had both qualities. If you are in a position of selecting leaders, look for integrity and reverence as two of the most important qualifications. Although other qualities may seem more impressive, integrity and reverence pass the test of time.

integrity and feared God more than most men do. ³I said to them, "The gates of Jerusalem are not to be opened until the sun is hot. While the gatekeepers are still on duty, have them shut the doors and bar them. Also appoint residents of Jerusalem as guards, some at their posts and some near their own houses."

The List of the Exiles Who Returned

⁴Now the city was large and spacious, but there were few people in it, and the houses had not yet been rebuilt. ⁵So my God put it into my heart to assemble the nobles, the officials and the common people for registration by families. I found the genealogical record of those who had been the first to return. This is what I found written there:

⁶These are the people of the province who came up from the captivity of the ex- iles ᵖ whom Nebuchadnezzar king of Babylon had taken captive (they returned to Jerusalem and Judah, each to his own town, ⁷in company with Zerubbabel, �q Jeshua, Nehemiah, Azariah, Raamiah, Nahamani, Mordecai, Bilshan, Mispereth, Bigvai, Nehum and Baanah):

7:6
ᵖEzr 2:1-70

7:7
�q Ezr 2:2

The list of the men of Israel:

⁸ the descendants of Parosh	2,172
⁹ of Shephatiah	372
¹⁰ of Arah	652
¹¹ of Pahath-Moab (through the line of Jeshua and Joab)	2,818
¹² of Elam	1,254
¹³ of Zattu	845
¹⁴ of Zaccai	760
¹⁵ of Binnui	648
¹⁶ of Bebai	628
¹⁷ of Azgad	2,322
¹⁸ of Adonikam	667
¹⁹ of Bigvai	2,067
²⁰ of Adin	655
²¹ of Ater (through Hezekiah)	98
²² of Hashum	328
²³ of Bezai	324
²⁴ of Hariph	112
²⁵ of Gibeon	95
²⁶ the men of Bethlehem and Netophah	188
²⁷ of Anathoth ʳ	128
²⁸ of Beth Azmaveth	42
²⁹ of Kiriath Jearim, Kephirah and Beeroth	743
³⁰ of Ramah and Geba	621
³¹ of Micmash	122
³² of Bethel and Ai	123
³³ of the other Nebo	52
³⁴ of the other Elam	1,254
³⁵ of Harim	320
³⁶ of Jericho ˢ	345
³⁷ of Lod, Hadid and Ono	721
³⁸ of Senaah	3,930

7:27
ʳ Jos 21:18

7:36
ˢ Ne 3:2

7:3 City gates were usually opened at sunrise, enabling mer- chants to enter and set up their tent-stores. Nehemiah didn't want Jerusalem to be caught unprepared by an enemy attack, so he ordered the gates closed until well after sunrise when the people were sure to be awake and alert.

7:3 The wall was complete, but the work was not finished. Nehemiah assigned each family the task of protecting the section of wall next to their home. It is tempting to relax our guard and rest on past accomplishments after we have completed a large task. But we must continue to serve and to take care of all that

God has entrusted to us. Following through after a project is completed is as vital as doing the project itself.

7:5ff Nehemiah found the genealogical record. Because this genealogy is almost identical to Ezra's (Ezra 2), most likely Ezra's list was stored in the temple archives and was the one Nehemiah found.

39 The priests:

the descendants of Jedaiah (through the family of Jeshua)	973
40 of Immer	1,052
41 of Pashhur	1,247
42 of Harim	1,017

43 The Levites:

the descendants of Jeshua (through Kadmiel through the line of Hodaviah)	74

44 The singers:

the descendants of Asaph	148

45 The gatekeepers:

the descendants of Shallum, Ater, Talmon, Akkub, Hatita and Shobai	138

46 The temple servants:

the descendants of
Ziha, Hasupha, Tabbaoth,
47 Keros, Sia, Padon,
48 Lebana, Hagaba, Shalmai,
49 Hanan, Giddel, Gahar,
50 Reaiah, Rezin, Nekoda,
51 Gazzam, Uzza, Paseah,
52 Besai, Meunim, Nephusim,
53 Bakbuk, Hakupha, Harhur,
54 Bazluth, Mehida, Harsha,
55 Barkos, Sisera, Temah,
56 Neziah and Hatipha

57 The descendants of the servants of Solomon:

the descendants of
Sotai, Sophereth, Perida,
58 Jaala, Darkon, Giddel,
59 Shephatiah, Hattil,
Pokereth-Hazzebaim and Amon

60 The temple servants and the descendants of the servants of Solomon	392

61 The following came up from the towns of Tel Melah, Tel Harsha, Kerub, Addon and Immer, but they could not show that their families were descended from Israel:

62 the descendants of Delaiah, Tobiah and Nekoda	642

63 And from among the priests:

the descendants of
Hobaiah, Hakkoz and Barzillai (a man who had married a daughter of Barzillai the Gileadite and was called by that name).

64 These searched for their family records, but they could not find them and so were excluded from the priesthood as unclean. **65** The governor, therefore, ordered them not to eat any of the most sacred food until there should be a priest ministering with the Urim and Thummim. [f]

7:65
[f] Ex 28:30; Ne 8:9

7:61 Genealogies were greatly valued because it was vitally important for a Jew to be able to prove that he or she was a descendant of Abraham and was, therefore, part of God's people (Genesis 12:1–3; 15; Exodus 19:5, 6; Deuteronomy 11:22–28). A lost genealogy put one's status as a Jew at risk.

7:64, 65 The Urim and Thummim were a means of learning God's will (Exodus 28:30). If someone's name wasn't in the genealogies, he could still be admitted as a priest if the Urim and Thummim proved him to be a Jew and a Levite. It is not clear whether the Urim and Thummim were the originals that had survived the destruction of Jerusalem or if they were new.

66 The whole company numbered 42,360, 67 besides their 7,337 menservants and maidservants; and they also had 245 men and women singers. 68 There were 736 horses, 245 mules,a 69 435 camels and 6,720 donkeys.

70 Some of the heads of the families contributed to the work. The governor gave to the treasury 1,000 drachmasb of gold, 50 bowls and 530 garments for priests. 71 Some of the heads of the families gave to the treasury for the work 20,000 drachmasc of gold and 2,200 minasd of silver. 72 The total given by the rest of the people was 20,000 drachmas of gold, 2,000 minase of silver and 67 garments for priests.

73 The priests, the Levites, the gatekeepers, the singers and the temple servants, along with certain of the people and the rest of the Israelites, settled in their own towns.

7:73
uEzr 3:1

B. REFORMING THE PEOPLE (7:73—13:31)

When Nehemiah arrived in Jerusalem he found more than just broken walls; he found broken lives. In response, Nehemiah gathers the people together to hear Ezra read God's law. The people repent and promise to change their lives by obeying God's words. No matter where we live, backsliding in an ever-present danger. We must constantly check our behavior against God's standards in the Bible so that we do not slide back into sinful ways of living.

1. Ezra renews the covenant
Ezra Reads the Law

8:1
vNe 3:26
wDt 28:61;
2Ch 34:15; Ezr 7:6

8:2
xLev 23:23-25
yDt 31:11

When the seventh month came and the Israelites had settled in their towns, u **8** 1 all the people assembled as one man in the square before the Water Gate. v They told Ezra the scribe to bring out the Book of the Law of Moses, w which the LORD had commanded for Israel.

2 So on the first day of the seventh monthx Ezra the priest brought the Lawy before the assembly, which was made up of men and women and all who were able to understand. 3 He read it aloud from daybreak till noon as he faced the square before the Water Gate in the presence of the men, women and others who could understand. And all the people listened attentively to the Book of the Law.

4 Ezra the scribe stood on a high wooden platform built for the occasion. Beside him on his right stood Mattithiah, Shema, Anaiah, Uriah, Hilkiah and Maaseiah; and on his left were Pedaiah, Mishael, Malkijah, Hashum, Hashbaddanah, Zechariah and Meshullam.

8:5
zJdg 3:20

8:6
aEx 4:31; Ezr 9:5;
1Ti 2:8

8:7
bLev 10:11;
2Ch 17:7

5 Ezra opened the book. All the people could see him because he was standing z above them; and as he opened it, the people all stood up. 6 Ezra praised the LORD, the great God; and all the people lifted their hands a and responded, "Amen! Amen!" Then they bowed down and worshiped the LORD with their faces to the ground.

7 The Levites—Jeshua, Bani, Sherebiah, Jamin, Akkub, Shabbethai, Hodiah, Maaseiah, Kelita, Azariah, Jozabad, Hanan and Pelaiah—instructedb the people in the Law while the people were standing there. 8 They read from the Book of the Law of God, making it clearf and giving the meaning so that the people could understand what was being read.

a68 Some Hebrew manuscripts (see also Ezra 2:66); most Hebrew manuscripts do not have this verse.
b70 That is, about 19 pounds (about 8.5 kilograms)   c71 That is, about 375 pounds (about 170 kilograms); also in verse 72   d71 That is, about 1 1/3 tons (about 1.2 metric tons)   e72 That is, about 1 1/4 tons (about 1.1 metric tons)
f8 Or God, translating it

The "most sacred food" was meat dedicated to God as part of the sacrifice. Only true priests could eat it.

8:1 This is the first mention of Ezra in this book. He had arrived in Jerusalem from Babylon 13 years before Nehemiah (458 B.C., see Ezra 7:6–9). Given the fact that the first seven chapters are taken with the account of Nehemiah's trip to Jerusalem and the three-month monumental construction task, Ezra's appearance at this point in the book emphasizes that the special role he had all along now came to the forefront. Nehemiah led the rebuilding of the wall; Ezra led the spiritual revival of the nation.

8:1 Ezra and Nehemiah were contemporaries (8:9), although Ezra was probably much older. Nehemiah, as governor, was the political leader; and Ezra, as priest and scribe, was the religious leader. A scribe in these days was a combination lawyer, notary public, scholar, and consultant. Scribes were among the most educated people, so they were teachers. No doubt the Jews would have liked to set up the kingdom again as in

the days of David, but this would have signaled rebellion against the king of Persia to whom they were subject. The best alternative was to divide the leadership between Nehemiah and Ezra.

8:1–5 The Book of the Law of Moses was probably the Pentateuch, the first five books of the Bible. The people rose to their feet in respect and anticipation. They listened attentively to Ezra as he read God's Word, and their lives were changed. Because we hear the Bible so often, we can become dulled to its words and immune to its teachings. Instead, we should *listen carefully* to every verse and ask the Holy Spirit to help us answer the question, "How does this apply to *my* life?"

9Then Nehemiah the governor, Ezra the priest and scribe, and the Levites who were instructing the people said to them all, "This day is sacred to the LORD your God. Do not mourn or weep." For all the people had been weeping as they listened to the words of the Law.

10Nehemiah said, "Go and enjoy choice food and sweet drinks, and send some to those who have nothing prepared. This day is sacred to our Lord. Do not grieve, for the joy of the LORD is your strength."

11The Levites calmed all the people, saying, "Be still, for this is a sacred day. Do not grieve."

12Then all the people went away to eat and drink, to send portions of food and to celebrate with great joy, because they now understood the words that had been made known to them.

13On the second day of the month, the heads of all the families, along with the priests and the Levites, gathered around Ezra the scribe to give attention to the words of the Law. 14They found written in the Law, which the LORD had commanded through Moses, that the Israelites were to live in booths during the feast of the seventh month 15and that they should proclaim this word and spread it throughout their towns and in Jerusalem: "Go out into the hill country and bring back branches from olive and wild olive trees, and from myrtles, palms and shade trees, to make booths"—as it is written. a

16So the people went out and brought back branches and built themselves booths on their own roofs, in their courtyards, in the courts of the house of God and in the square by the Water Gate and the one by the Gate of Ephraim. c 17The whole company that had returned from exile built booths and lived in them. From the days of Joshua son of Nun until that day, the Israelites had not celebrated d it like this. And their joy was very great.

18Day after day, from the first day to the last, Ezra read e from the Book of the Law of God. They celebrated the feast for seven days, and on the eighth day, in accordance with the regulation, f there was an assembly.

The Israelites Confess Their Sins

9 On the twenty-fourth day of the same month, the Israelites gathered together, fasting and wearing sackcloth and having dust on their heads. g 2Those of Israelite descent had separated themselves from all foreigners. h They stood in their places and confessed their sins and the wickedness of their fathers. i 3They stood where they were and read from the Book of the Law of the LORD their God for a quarter of the day, and spent another quarter in confession and in worshiping the LORD their God. 4Standing on the stairs were the Levites—Jeshua, Bani, Kadmiel, Shebaniah, Bunni, Sherebiah, Bani and Kenani—who called with loud voices to the LORD their God. 5And the Levites—Jeshua, Kadmiel, Bani, Hashabneiah, Sherebiah, Hodiah, Shebaniah and Pethahiah—said: "Stand up and praise the LORD your God, who is from everlasting to everlasting. b "

"Blessed be your glorious name, and may it be exalted above all blessing and praise.
6You alone are the LORD. You made the heavens, j even the highest heavens, and all

a 15 See Lev. 23:37-40.   b 5 Or God for ever and ever

8:16 c2Ki 14:13; Ne 12:39

8:17 d2Ch 30:21

8:18 eDt 31:11 fLev 23:36, 40; Nu 29:35

9:1 g1Sa 4:12

9:2 hNe 13:3, 30 iEzr 10:11

9:6 j2Ki 19:15

8:9 Ezra, not Nehemiah, was the official religious leader. It is significant that Nehemiah was a layman, not a member of the religious establishment or a prophet. He was motivated by his relationship with God, and he devoted his life to doing God's will in a secular world. Such people are crucial to God's work in all aspects of life. No matter what your work or role in life, view it as God's special calling to serve him. God can accomplish his purposes through you, beginning right where you are.

8:9, 10 The people wept openly when they heard God's laws and realized how far they were from obeying them. But Ezra told them they should be filled with joy because the day was holy. It was time to celebrate and to give gifts to those in need.

Celebration is not to be self-centered. Ezra connected celebration with giving. This gave those in need an opportunity to celebrate as well. Often when we celebrate and give to others (even when we don't feel like it), we are strengthened spiritually and filled with joy. Enter into celebrations that honor God, and allow him to fill you with joy.

8:13ff After Ezra read God's laws to the people, they studied them further and then acted upon them. A careful reading of Scripture always calls for a response to these questions: What should I *do* with this knowledge? How should my life change?

We must *do* something about what we have learned if it is to have real significance for our lives.

8:14–17 During the seven-day Feast of Tabernacles, the people lived in booths made of branches. This practice was instituted as a reminder of their rescue from Egypt and the time spent in shelters in the desert (Leviticus 23:43). They were to think about God's protection and guidance during their years of wandering and the fact that God would still protect and guide them if they obeyed him. This was a time to remember their origins, where they came from. It is helpful to remember our beginnings in order to appreciate where we are today. Think back on your life to see where God has led you. Then thank God for his continuing work to protect you and provide for your needs.

9:1 Fasting, wearing sackcloth, and putting dust on the head were public signs of sorrow and repentance.

9:2, 3 The Hebrews practiced open confession, admitting their sins to one another. Reading and studying God's Word should precede confession (see 8:18) because God can show us where we are sinning. Honest confession should precede worship, because we cannot have a right relationship with God if we hold on to certain sins.

9:6
k Ge 1:1

9:7
l Ge 11:31
m Ge 17:5

9:8
n Ge 15:18-21
o Ge 15:6

9:9
p Ex 14:10-30

9:11
q Ex 14:21
r Ex 15:4-5, 10

9:12
s Ex 13:21

9:13
t Ex 20:1

9:14
u Ex 20:8-11

9:15
v Ex 16:4
w Ex 17:6
x Dt 1:8, 21

9:17
y Nu 14:1-4
z Ps 78:11

9:18
a Ex 32:4

9:20
b Nu 11:17;
Isa 63:11, 14

9:21
c Dt 2:7

9:22
d Nu 21:21

9:25
e Dt 6:10-12
f Dt 32:12-15

9:26
g 1Ki 14:9
h Jdg 2:12-13

9:27
i Jdg 2:14

their starry host, the earth k and all that is on it, the seas and all that is in them. You give life to everything, and the multitudes of heaven worship you.

7 "You are the LORD God, who chose Abram and brought him out of Ur of the Chaldeans l and named him Abraham. m 8 You found his heart faithful to you, and you made a covenant with him to give to his descendants the land of the Canaanites, Hittites, Amorites, Perizzites, Jebusites and Girgashites. n You have kept your promise because you are righteous. o

9 "You saw the suffering of our forefathers in Egypt; you heard their cry at the Red Sea. a p 10 You sent miraculous signs and wonders against Pharaoh, against all his officials and all the people of his land, for you knew how arrogantly the Egyptians treated them. You made a name for yourself, which remains to this day. 11 You divided the sea before them, q so that they passed through it on dry ground, but you hurled their pursuers into the depths, like a stone into mighty waters. r 12 By day you led them with a pillar of cloud, s and by night with a pillar of fire to give them light on the way they were to take.

13 "You came down on Mount Sinai; you spoke to them from heaven. You gave them regulations and laws that are just and right, and decrees and commands that are good. t 14 You made known to them your holy Sabbath u and gave them commands, decrees and laws through your servant Moses. 15 In their hunger you gave them bread from heaven v and in their thirst you brought them water from the rock; w you told them to go in and take possession of the land you had sworn with uplifted hand to give them. x

16 "But they, our forefathers, became arrogant and stiff-necked, and did not obey your commands. 17 They refused to listen and failed to remember the miracles you performed among them. They became stiff-necked and in their rebellion appointed a leader in order to return to their slavery. y But you are a forgiving God, gracious and compassionate, slow to anger and abounding in love. Therefore you did not desert them, z 18 even when they cast for themselves an image of a calf a and said, 'This is your god, who brought you up out of Egypt,' or when they committed awful blasphemies.

19 "Because of your great compassion you did not abandon them in the desert. By day the pillar of cloud did not cease to guide them on their path, nor the pillar of fire by night to shine on the way they were to take. 20 You gave your good Spirit b to instruct them. You did not withhold your manna from their mouths, and you gave them water for their thirst. 21 For forty years you sustained them in the desert; they lacked nothing, c their clothes did not wear out nor did their feet become swollen.

22 "You gave them kingdoms and nations, allotting to them even the remotest frontiers. They took over the country of Sihon b d king of Heshbon and the country of Og king of Bashan. 23 You made their sons as numerous as the stars in the sky, and you brought them into the land that you told their fathers to enter and possess. 24 Their sons went in and took possession of the land. You subdued before them the Canaanites, who lived in the land; you handed the Canaanites over to them, along with their kings and the peoples of the land, to deal with them as they pleased. 25 They captured fortified cities and fertile land; they took possession of houses filled with all kinds of good things, wells already dug, vineyards, olive groves and fruit trees in abundance. They ate to the full and were well-nourished; e they reveled in your great goodness. f

26 "But they were disobedient and rebelled against you; they put your law behind their backs. g They killed your prophets, who had admonished them in order to turn them back to you; they committed awful blasphemies. h 27 So you handed them over to their enemies, i who oppressed them. But when they were oppressed they cried out to you.

a 9 Hebrew *Yam Suph*; that is, Sea of Reeds   b 22 One Hebrew manuscript and Septuagint; most Hebrew manuscripts *Sihon, that is, the country of the*

9:7-38 Many prayers and speeches in the Bible include a long summary of Israel's history because individuals did not have their own copies of the Bible as we do today. This summary of God's past works reminded the people of their great heritage and God's promises.

Remembering our personal history can certainly help us to avoid repeating our mistakes so that we can serve God better. Reviewing our past helps us understand how to improve our behavior. It shows us the pattern to our spiritual growth. Learn from your past so that you will become the kind of person God wants you to be.

9:16-21 Seeing how God continued to be with his people shows that his patience is amazing! In spite of our repeated failings, pride, and stubbornness, he is always ready to forgive (9:17), and his Spirit is always ready to instruct (9:20). Realizing the extent of God's forgiveness helps us forgive those who fail us, even "seventy-seven times" if necessary (Matthew 18:21, 22).

From heaven you heard them, and in your great compassion you gave them deliverers, who rescued them from the hand of their enemies.

28"But as soon as they were at rest, they again did what was evil in your sight. Then you abandoned them to the hand of their enemies so that they ruled over them. And when they cried out to you again, you heard from heaven, and in your compassion you delivered them*j* time after time.

29"You warned them to return to your law, but they became arrogant and disobeyed your commands. They sinned against your ordinances, by which a man will live if he obeys them. *k* Stubbornly they turned their backs on you, became stiff-necked and refused to listen. *l* 30For many years you were patient with them. By your Spirit you admonished them through your prophets. *m* Yet they paid no attention, so you handed them over to the neighboring peoples. 31But in your great mercy you did not put an end to them or abandon them, for you are a gracious and merciful God.

32"Now therefore, O our God, the great, mighty and awesome God, who keeps his covenant of love, do not let all this hardship seem trifling in your eyes—the hardship that has come upon us, upon our kings and leaders, upon our priests and prophets, upon our fathers and all your people, from the days of the kings of Assyria until today. 33In all that has happened to us, you have been just;*n* you have acted faithfully, while we did wrong.*o* 34Our kings, our leaders, our priests and our fathers did not follow your law; they did not pay attention to your commands or the warnings you gave them. 35Even while they were in their kingdom, enjoying your great goodness to them in the spacious and fertile land you gave them, they did not serve you*p* or turn from their evil ways.

36"But see, we are slaves *q* today, slaves in the land you gave our forefathers so they could eat its fruit and the other good things it produces. 37Because of our sins, its abundant harvest goes to the kings you have placed over us. They rule over our bodies and our cattle as they please. We are in great distress.*r*

The Agreement of the People

38"In view of all this, we are making a binding agreement, putting it in writing, and our leaders, our Levites and our priests are affixing their seals to it."

10 Those who sealed it were:

Nehemiah the governor, the son of Hacaliah.

Zedekiah, 2Seraiah, Azariah, Jeremiah,
3 Pashhur, Amariah, Malkijah,
4 Hattush, Shebaniah, Malluch,
5 Harim, Meremoth, Obadiah,
6 Daniel, Ginnethon, Baruch,
7 Meshullam, Abijah, Mijamin,
8 Maaziah, Bilgai and Shemaiah.
These were the priests.

9The Levites:

Jeshua son of Azaniah, Binnui of the sons of Henadad, Kadmiel,
10 and their associates: Shebaniah,
Hodiah, Kelita, Pelaiah, Hanan,

9:28
j Ps 106:43

9:29
k Dt 30:16
l Zec 7:11-12

9:30
m 2Ki 17:13-18

9:33
n Ge 18:25
o Da 9:7-8, 14

9:35
p Dt 28:45-48

9:36
q Dt 28:48; Ezr 9:9

9:37
r Dt 28:33

9:28-31 Israel was devastated by times of intense rebellion and sin. Yet when the people repented and returned to God, he delivered them. God puts no limit on the number of times we can come to him to obtain mercy, but we must *come* in order to obtain it, recognizing our need and asking him for help. This miracle of grace should inspire us to say, "You are a gracious and merciful God!" If there is a recurring problem or difficulty in your life, continue to ask God for help, and be willing and ready to make changes in your attitude and behavior that will correct that situation.

9:35 Sometimes the way we take for granted the very blessings God has showered on us leads us to forget him (9:28). We are often tempted to rely on wealth for security rather than on God who makes it possible. As you see what happened to the Israel-

ites, look at your own life. Do your blessings make you thankful to God and draw you closer to him, or do they make you feel self-sufficient and forgetful of God?

9:36 The Israelites were in the strange position of being slaves in their own land, having to turn over a part of their resources each year to a foreign king. How ironic, since God had given the land to them. This was certainly a bitter reminder of the lasting consequences of sin.

9:38 This binding agreement or covenant between the people and God had six provisions. They agreed to: (1) not marry non-Jewish neighbors (10:30), (2) observe the Sabbath (10:31), (3) observe every seventh year as a sabbath year (10:31), (4) pay a temple tax (10:32, 33), (5) supply wood for the burnt

¹¹ Mica, Rehob, Hashabiah,
¹² Zaccur, Sherebiah, Shebaniah,
¹³ Hodiah, Bani and Beninu.

¹⁴The leaders of the people:

Parosh, Pahath-Moab, Elam, Zattu, Bani,
¹⁵ Bunni, Azgad, Bebai,
¹⁶ Adonijah, Bigvai, Adin,
¹⁷ Ater, Hezekiah, Azzur,
¹⁸ Hodiah, Hashum, Bezai,
¹⁹ Hariph, Anathoth, Nebai,
²⁰ Magpiash, Meshullam, Hezir,
²¹ Meshezabel, Zadok, Jaddua,
²² Pelatiah, Hanan, Anaiah,
²³ Hoshea, Hananiah, Hasshub,
²⁴ Hallohesh, Pilha, Shobek,
²⁵ Rehum, Hashabnah, Maaseiah,
²⁶ Ahiah, Hanan, Anan,
²⁷ Malluch, Harim and Baanah.

10:28
s Ne 9:2

²⁸"The rest of the people—priests, Levites, gatekeepers, singers, temple servants and all who separated themselves from the neighboring peoples ˢ for the sake of the Law of God, together with their wives and all their sons and daughters who are able to understand— ²⁹ all these now join their brothers the nobles, and bind themselves with a curse and an oath to follow the Law of God given through Moses the servant of God and to obey carefully all the commands, regulations and decrees of the LORD our Lord.

GOING HOME: TWO GREAT JOURNEYS OF ISRAEL

What about the Journeys?	The Exodus	The Return from Exile
Where were they?	Egypt (430 years)	Babylon (70 years)
How many?	About 1 million	60,000
How long did the journey take them?	40 years and 2 attempts	100 years and 3 journeys
Who led them?	Moses/Aaron/Joshua	Zerubbabel/Ezra/Nehemiah
What was their purpose?	To reclaim the promised land	To rebuild the temple and city of Jerusalem
What obstacles did they face?	Red Sea/Desert/Enemies	Ruins/Limited Resources/Enemies
What failures did they experience?	Complaining/Disobedience/Retreat—all of which turned a journey of a few weeks into a 40-year ordeal	Fear/Discouragement/Apathy—all of which turned a project of a few months into one that required a century to complete
What successes did they have?	Eventually entered the promised land	Eventually rebuilt Jerusalem's temple and wall
What lessons did they learn?	God will build his nation. God is both faithful and just. God will accomplish great acts to make his promises come true.	God will preserve his nation. God will continue to have a chosen people, a home for them, and a plan to offer himself to them.

---

offerings in the temple (10:34), and (6) give dues to the temple (10:35–38). After years of decadence and exile, the people once again took seriously their responsibility to follow God and keep his laws wholeheartedly.

10:28ff The wall was completed, and the agreement God had made with his people in the days of Moses was restored (Deuteronomy 8). This covenant has principles that are important for us today. Our relationship with God must go far beyond church attendance and regular devotions. It should affect our relationships (10:30), our time (10:31), and our material resources (10:32–39). When you chose to follow God, you promised to serve him in this way. The Israelites had fallen away from their original commitment. We must keep our promise to God in times of adversity or prosperity.

30"We promise not to give our daughters in marriage to the peoples around us or take their daughters for our sons. *t*

31"When the neighboring peoples bring merchandise or grain to sell on the Sabbath, *u* we will not buy from them on the Sabbath or on any holy day. Every seventh year we will forgo working the land *v* and will cancel all debts. *w*

32"We assume the responsibility for carrying out the commands to give a third of a shekel *a* each year for the service of the house of our God: 33 for the bread set out on the table; *x* for the regular grain offerings and burnt offerings; for the offerings on the Sabbaths, New Moon festivals and appointed feasts; for the holy offerings; for sin offerings to make atonement for Israel; and for all the duties of the house of our God.

34"We—the priests, the Levites and the people—have cast lots to determine when each of our families is to bring to the house of our God at set times each year a contribution of wood *y* to burn on the altar of the LORD our God, as it is written in the Law.

35"We also assume responsibility for bringing to the house of the LORD each year the firstfruits *z* of our crops and of every fruit tree. *a*

36"As it is also written in the Law, we will bring the firstborn *b* of our sons and of our cattle, of our herds and of our flocks to the house of our God, to the priests ministering there.

37"Moreover, we will bring to the storerooms of the house of our God, to the priests, the first of our ground meal, of our ⌐grain⌐ offerings, of the fruit of all our trees and of our new wine and oil. *c* And we will bring a tithe *d* of our crops to the Levites, for it is the Levites who collect the tithes in all the towns where we work. 38A priest descended from Aaron is to accompany the Levites when they receive the tithes, and the Levites are to bring a tenth of the tithes *e* up to the house of our God, to the storerooms of the treasury. 39 The people of Israel, including the Levites, are to bring their contributions of grain, new wine and oil to the storerooms where the articles for the sanctuary are kept and where the ministering priests, the gatekeepers and the singers stay.

"We will not neglect the house of our God." *f*

2. Nehemiah establishes policies
The New Residents of Jerusalem

11 Now the leaders of the people settled in Jerusalem, and the rest of the people cast lots to bring one out of every ten to live in Jerusalem, *g* the holy city, *h* while the remaining nine were to stay in their own towns. 2 The people commended all the men who volunteered to live in Jerusalem.

a 32 That is, about 1/8 ounce (about 4 grams)

10:30
t Ex 34:16; Dt 7:3

10:31
u Ne 13:16, 18
v Ex 23:11;
Lev 25:1-7
w Dt 15:1

10:33
x Lev 24:6

10:34
y Ne 13:31

10:35
z Ex 23:19;
Nu 18:12
a Dt 26:1-11

10:36
b Ex 13:2;
Nu 18:14-16

10:37
c Lev 23:17
d Lev 27:30;
Nu 18:21

10:38
e Nu 18:26

10:39
f Dt 12:6;
Ne 13:11, 12

11:1
g Ne 7:4
h ver 18; Isa 48:2

10:30 If God's chosen people were going to witness for him in a pagan world, they needed united, God-fearing families. They also needed to avoid any enticements to worship the idols of the people who lived around them. This was why God prohibited marriage between Israelites and the pagan inhabitants of the land (Deuteronomy 7:3, 4). But Israelites and pagans often intermarried anyway, and the results were disastrous for the families and for the nation. Time after time, marrying foreigners led God's people into idolatry (1 Kings 11:1–11). Whenever the nation turned its back on God, it also lost its prosperity and influence for good.

10:31 The promise to forgive trade inside the city on the Sabbath was an application of the fourth commandment. The people recognized that the lure of money would conflict with the need for a day of rest, keeping the Sabbath holy. By deciding to honor God first, the Israelites were refusing to make money their god. Our culture often makes us choose between convenience and profit on the one hand, and putting God first on the other. Look at your work and worship habits: is God really first?

10:31 Forgoing all debts every seventh year was a part of the law (see Exodus 23:10 and Deuteronomy 15:1, 2). The people were reciting and promising to obey God's law and keep the covenant.

10:32 The temple had been rebuilt under Ezra's leadership about 70 years earlier (Ezra 6:14, 15). So the temple tax, offerings, and feasts had been restored.

10:36 This practice was instituted at the time of the exodus from

Egypt (see the note on Exodus 13:12–14). The people needed to relearn the importance of dedicating the firstfruits of their yield to God. Nehemiah was simply reinstating this practice from the early days of the nation (Exodus 13:1, 2; Numbers 3:40–51). Although this principle was not carried over to New Testament times, the concept of giving God the first portion of our time, treasure, and talent still remains. Do you give God your first and best, or merely what is left over?

10:37–39 According to God's law, the people were to give a tenth of their produce to the temple for the support of the Levites (those who cared for the temple and the religious observances). A tenth of what the Levites received or produced went to the priests for their support. The principle at work was to ensure the support of the house of God and his workers. We must not overlook our responsibility to God's workers today.

11:1ff The exiles who returned were few in number compared to Jerusalem's population in the days of the kings. And because the walls had been rebuilt on their original foundations, the city seemed sparsely populated. Nehemiah asked one-tenth of the people from the outlying areas to move inside the city walls to keep large areas of the city from being vacant. Apparently these people did not want to move into the city. Only a few people volunteered (11:1, 2), and Nehemiah cast lots to determine who among the remaining people would have to move.

Many of them may not have wanted to live in the city because

11:3
i 1Ch 9:2-3; Ezr 2:1

3 These are the provincial leaders who settled in Jerusalem (now some Israelites, priests, Levites, temple servants and descendants of Solomon's servants lived in the towns of Judah, each on his own property in the various towns, *i* **4** while other people from both Judah and Benjamin lived in Jerusalem):

From the descendants of Judah:

Athaiah son of Uzziah, the son of Zechariah, the son of Amariah, the son of Shephatiah, the son of Mahalalel, a descendant of Perez; **5** and Maaseiah son of Baruch, the son of Col-Hozeh, the son of Hazaiah, the son of Adaiah, the son of Joiarib, the son of Zechariah, a descendant of Shelah. **6** The descendants of Perez who lived in Jerusalem totaled 468 able men.

7 From the descendants of Benjamin:

Sallu son of Meshullam, the son of Joed, the son of Pedaiah, the son of Kolaiah, the son of Maaseiah, the son of Ithiel, the son of Jeshaiah, **8** and his followers, Gabbai and Sallai—928 men. **9** Joel son of Zicri was their chief officer, and Judah son of Hassenuah was over the Second District of the city.

10 From the priests:

Jedaiah; the son of Joiarib; Jakin; **11** Seraiah son of Hilkiah, the son of Meshullam, the son of Zadok, the son of Meraioth, the son of Ahitub, supervisor in the house of God, **12** and their associates, who carried on work for the temple—822 men; Adaiah son of Jeroham, the son of Pelaliah, the son of Amzi, the son of Zechariah, the son of Pashhur, the son of Malkijah, **13** and his associates, who were heads of families—242 men; Amashsai son of Azarel, the son of Ahzai, the son of Meshillemoth, the son of Immer, **14** and his[a] associates, who were able men—128. Their chief officer was Zabdiel son of Haggedolim.

15 From the Levites:

Shemaiah son of Hasshub, the son of Azrikam, the son of Hashabiah, the son of Bunni; **16** Shabbethai and Jozabad, two of the heads of the Levites, who had charge of the outside work of the house of God; **17** Mattaniah son of Mica, the son of Zabdi, the son of Asaph, the director who led in thanksgiving and prayer; Bakbukiah, second among his associates; and Abda son of Shammua, the son of Galal, the son of Jeduthun. **18** The Levites in the holy city totaled 284.

19 The gatekeepers:

Akkub, Talmon and their associates, who kept watch at the gates—172 men.

20 The rest of the Israelites, with the priests and Levites, were in all the towns of Judah, each on his ancestral property.

11:21
j Ne 3:26

21 The temple servants*j* lived on the hill of Ophel, and Ziha and Gishpa were in charge of them.

11:22
k 1Ch 9:15

22 The chief officer of the Levites in Jerusalem was Uzzi son of Bani, the son of Hashabiah, the son of Mattaniah, *k* the son of Mica. Uzzi was one of Asaph's descendants, who

11:23
l Ne 7:44

were the singers responsible for the service of the house of God. **23** The singers*l* were under the king's orders, which regulated their daily activity.

11:24
m Ge 38:30

24 Pethahiah son of Meshezabel, one of the descendants of Zerah*m* son of Judah, was the king's agent in all affairs relating to the people.

11:25
n Jos 14:15

25 As for the villages with their fields, some of the people of Judah lived in Kiriath Arba*n* and its surrounding settlements, in Dibon and its settlements, in Jekabzeel and its villages, **26** in

11:27
o Ge 21:14

Jeshua, in Moladah, in Beth Pelet, **27** in Hazar Shual, in Beersheba*o* and its settlements, **28** in

11:28
p 1Sa 27:6

Ziklag,*p* in Meconah and its settlements, **29** in En Rimmon, in Zorah, in Jarmuth, **30** Zanoah,

---

a *14 Most Septuagint manuscripts; Hebrew their*

---

(1) non-Jews attached a stigma to Jerusalem residents, often excluding them from trade because of their religious beliefs; (2) moving into the city meant rebuilding their homes and reestablishing their businesses, a major investment of time and money; (3) living in Jerusalem required stricter obedience to God's word because of greater social pressure and proximity to the temple.

Adullam and their villages, in Lachish *q* and its fields, and in Azekah and its settlements. So they were living all the way from Beersheba to the Valley of Hinnom.

³¹The descendants of the Benjamites from Geba *r* lived in Micmash, *s* Aija, Bethel and its settlements, ³²in Anathoth, *t* Nob and Ananiah, ³³in Hazor, *u* Ramah and Gittaim, ³⁴in Hadid, Zeboim *v* and Neballat, ³⁵in Lod and Ono, and in the Valley of the Craftsmen.

³⁶Some of the divisions of the Levites of Judah settled in Benjamin.

Priests and Levites

12 These were the priests *w* and Levites who returned with Zerubbabel son of Shealtiel and with Jeshua: *x*

Seraiah, Jeremiah, Ezra,

² Amariah, Malluch, Hattush,

³ Shecaniah, Rehum, Meremoth,

⁴ Iddo, Ginnethon, *a* Abijah, *y*

⁵ Mijamin, *b* Moadiah, Bilgah,

⁶ Shemaiah, Joiarib, Jedaiah,

⁷ Sallu, Amok, Hilkiah and Jedaiah.

These were the leaders of the priests and their associates in the days of Jeshua.

⁸The Levites were Jeshua, Binnui, Kadmiel, Sherebiah, Judah, and also Mattaniah, *z* who, together with his associates, was in charge of the songs of thanksgiving. ⁹Bakbukiah and Unni, their associates, stood opposite them in the services.

¹⁰Jeshua was the father of Joiakim, Joiakim the father of Eliashib, Eliashib the father of Joiada, ¹¹Joiada the father of Jonathan, and Jonathan the father of Jaddua.

¹²In the days of Joiakim, these were the heads of the priestly families:

of Seraiah's family, Meraiah;

of Jeremiah's, Hananiah;

¹³ of Ezra's, Meshullam;

of Amariah's, Jehohanan;

¹⁴ of Malluch's, Jonathan;

of Shecaniah's, *c* Joseph;

¹⁵ of Harim's, Adna;

of Meremoth's, *d* Helkai;

¹⁶ of Iddo's, Zechariah;

of Ginnethon's, Meshullam;

¹⁷ of Abijah's, Zicri;

of Miniamin's and of Moadiah's, Piltai;

¹⁸ of Bilgah's, Shammua;

of Shemaiah's, Jehonathan;

¹⁹ of Joiarib's, Mattenai;

of Jedaiah's, Uzzi;

²⁰ of Sallu's, Kallai;

of Amok's, Eber;

²¹ of Hilkiah's, Hashabiah;

of Jedaiah's, Nethanel.

²²The family heads of the Levites in the days of Eliashib, Joiada, Johanan and Jaddua, as well as those of the priests, were recorded in the reign of Darius the Persian. ²³The family heads among the descendants of Levi up to the time of Johanan son of Eliashib were recorded in the book of the annals. ²⁴And the leaders of the Levites were Hashabiah, Sherebiah, Jeshua son of Kadmiel, and their associates, who stood opposite them to give praise and thanksgiving, one section responding to the other, as prescribed by David the man of God.

²⁵Mattaniah, Bakbukiah, Obadiah, Meshullam, Talmon and Akkub were gatekeepers who guarded the storerooms at the gates. ²⁶They served in the days of Joiakim son of Jeshua, the son of Jozadak, and in the days of Nehemiah the governor and of Ezra the priest and scribe.

Dedication of the Wall of Jerusalem

²⁷At the dedication of the wall of Jerusalem, the Levites were sought out from where they lived and were brought to Jerusalem to celebrate joyfully the dedication with songs of

11:30
q Jos 10:3
11:31
r Jos 21:17
s 1Sa 13:2
11:32
t Jos 21:18;
Isa 10:30
11:33
u Jos 11:1
11:34
v 1Sa 13:18
12:1
w Ne 10:1-8
x Ezr 2:2

12:4
y Lk 1:5

12:8
z Ne 11:17

---

a 4 Many Hebrew manuscripts and Vulgate (see also Neh. 12:16); most Hebrew manuscripts *Ginnethoi* *b* 5 A variant of *Miniamin* *c* 14 Very many Hebrew manuscripts, some Septuagint manuscripts and Syriac (see also Neh. 12:3); most Hebrew manuscripts *Shebaniah's* *d* 15 Some Septuagint manuscripts (see also Neh. 12:3); Hebrew *Meraioth's*

12:27
a 1Ch 25:6

12:28
b 1Ch 9:16

thanksgiving and with the music of cymbals, harps and lyres. *a* 28 The singers also were brought together from the region around Jerusalem—from the villages of the Netopha-thites, *b* 29 from Beth Gilgal, and from the area of Geba and Azmaveth, for the singers had built villages for themselves around Jerusalem. 30 When the priests and Levites had purified themselves ceremonially, they purified the people, the gates and the wall.

12:31
c Ne 2:13

31 I had the leaders of Judah go up on top *a* of the wall. I also assigned two large choirs to give thanks. One was to proceed on top *b* of the wall to the right, toward the Dung Gate. *c* 32 Hosha-iah and half the leaders of Judah followed them, 33 along with Azariah, Ezra, Meshullam, 34 Ju-dah, Benjamin, Shemaiah, Jeremiah, 35 as well as some priests with trumpets, and also Zechariah son of Jonathan, the son of Shemaiah, the son of Mattaniah, the son of Micaiah, the son of Zaccur, the son of Asaph, 36 and his associates—Shemaiah, Azarel, Milalai, Gilalai, Maai, Nethanel, Judah and Hanani—with musical instruments ⌞prescribed by⌟ David the man of God. Ezra the scribe led the procession. 37 At the Fountain Gate *d* they continued directly up the steps of the City of David on the ascent to the wall and passed above the house of David to the Water Gate *e* on the east.

12:37
d Ne 2:14; 3:15
e Ne 3:26

12:38
f Ne 3:11
g Ne 3:8

38 The second choir proceeded in the opposite direction. I followed them on top *c* of the wall, together with half the people—past the Tower of the Ovens *f* to the Broad Wall, *g* 39 over the Gate of Ephraim, *h* the Jeshanah *d* Gate, *i* the Fish Gate, *j* the Tower of Hananel *k* and the Tower of the Hundred, as far as the Sheep Gate. At the Gate of the Guard they stopped.

12:39
h 2Ki 14:13; Ne 8:16
i Ne 3:6
j Ne 3:3
k Ne 3:1

40 The two choirs that gave thanks then took their places in the house of God; so did I, to-gether with half the officials, 41 as well as the priests—Eliakim, Maaseiah, Miniamin, Mica-iah, Elioenai, Zechariah and Hananiah with their trumpets— 42 and also Maaseiah, Shemaiah, Eleazar, Uzzi, Jehohanan, Malkijah, Elam and Ezer. The choirs sang under the di-rection of Jezrahiah. 43 And on that day they offered great sacrifices, rejoicing because God had given them great joy. The women and children also rejoiced. The sound of rejoicing in Jerusalem could be heard far away.

12:44
l Ne 13:4, 13

44 At that time men were appointed to be in charge of the storerooms *l* for the contribu-tions, firstfruits and tithes. From the fields around the towns they were to bring into the storerooms the portions required by the Law for the priests and the Levites, for Judah was pleased with the ministering priests and Levites. 45 They performed the service of their God and the service of purification, as did also the singers and gatekeepers, according to the commands of David *m* and his son Solomon. 46 For long ago, in the days of David and Asaph, there had been directors for the singers and for the songs of praise and thanksgiving to God. 47 So in the days of Zerubbabel and of Nehemiah, all Israel contributed the daily portions for the singers and gatekeepers. They also set aside the portion for the other Levites, and the Le-vites set aside the portion for the descendants of Aaron. *n*

12:45
m 1Ch 25:1

12:47
n Nu 18:21; Dt 18:8

Nehemiah's Final Reforms

13:1
o Dt 23:3

13:2
p Nu 22:3-11

13 On that day the Book of Moses was read aloud in the hearing of the people and there it was found written that no Ammonite or Moabite should ever be admitted into the assembly of God, *o* 2 because they had not met the Israelites with food and water but had hired Balaam *p* to call a curse down on them. (Our God, however, turned the curse into a

a 31 Or go alongside   *b 31* Or proceed alongside   *c 38* Or them alongside   *d 39* Or Old

---

12:35, 36 How could the priests have used musical instru-ments? David had instituted music as a part of worship in the temple, and so his instruments had probably been stored there. Although Nebuchadnezzar destroyed the temple, he took many temple items back to Babylon with him (2 Chronicles 36:18). These were most likely preserved in Babylon and given back to the Israelites by Cyrus when they returned to their land (Ezra 1:7–11).

12:35, 36 The trumpet that earlier was a tool to rally the workers against a potential threat (4:18) now became one of the instru-ments used to celebrate the completion of a task, the rededication of the people, and praise to God. Not only had he written powerful psalms, King David also had instituted music as part of worship in the temple. Although Nebuchadnezzar had destroyed the temple, he couldn't destroy worship or the music that served that purpose so well. The reconstruction of the temple and the walls signaled the worship band to start playing again with gusto!

12:44 Further arrangements were made for supporting those who served at the temple. The storerooms were administered by men who made sure the tithes and contributions were collected and distributed appropriately. These storerooms had to be large to hold all the grain presented by the people. This storeroom administration was an important responsibility.

12:44–47 The dedication of the city wall was characterized by joy, praise, and singing (12:24, 27–29, 35, 36, 40–43). Nehemiah repeatedly mentioned David, who began the custom of using choirs in worship. In David's day, Israel was a vigorous, God-fearing nation. These exiles who had returned wanted their rebuilt Jerusalem to be the hub of a renewed nation, strengthened by God; therefore, they dedicated themselves and their city to God.

blessing.)�q ³When the people heard this law, they excluded from Israel all who were of foreign descent.ʳ

⁴Before this, Eliashib the priest had been put in charge of the storeroomsˢ of the house of our God. He was closely associated with Tobiah,ᵗ ⁵and he had provided him with a large room formerly used to store the grain offerings and incense and temple articles, and also the tithesᵘ of grain, new wine and oil prescribed for the Levites, singers and gatekeepers, as well as the contributions for the priests.

⁶But while all this was going on, I was not in Jerusalem, for in the thirty-second year of Artaxerxesᵛ king of Babylon I had returned to the king. Some time later I asked his permission ⁷and came back to Jerusalem. Here I learned about the evil thing Eliashib had done in providing Tobiah a room in the courts of the house of God. ⁸I was greatly displeased and threw all Tobiah's household goods out of the room. ⁹I gave orders to purify the rooms,ʷ and then I put back into them the equipment of the house of God, with the grain offerings and the incense.

¹⁰I also learned that the portions assigned to the Levites had not been given to them, and that all the Levites and singers responsible for the service had gone back to their own fields. ¹¹So I rebuked the officials and asked them, "Why is the house of God neglected?"ˣ Then I called them together and stationed them at their posts.

¹²All Judah brought the tithes of grain, new wine and oil into the storerooms.ʸ ¹³I put Shelemiah the priest, Zadok the scribe, and a Levite named Pedaiah in charge of the storerooms and made Hanan son of Zaccur, the son of Mattaniah, their assistant, because these men were considered trustworthy. They were made responsible for distributing the supplies to their brothers.ᶻ

¹⁴Remember me for this, O my God, and do not blot out what I have so faithfully done for the house of my God and its services.

¹⁵In those days I saw men in Judah treading winepresses on the Sabbath and bringing in grain and loading it on donkeys, together with wine, grapes, figs and all other kinds of loads. And they were bringing all this into Jerusalem on the Sabbath.ᵃ Therefore I warned them against selling food on that day. ¹⁶Men from Tyre who lived in Jerusalem were bringing in fish and all kinds of merchandise and selling them in Jerusalem on the Sabbath to the people of Judah. ¹⁷I rebuked the nobles of Judah and said to them, "What is this wicked thing you are doing—desecrating the Sabbath day? ¹⁸Didn't your forefathers do the same things, so that our God brought all this calamity upon us and upon this city? Now you are stirring up more wrath against Israel by desecrating the Sabbath."ᵇ

¹⁹When evening shadows fell on the gates of Jerusalem before the Sabbath,ᶜ I ordered the doors to be shut and not opened until the Sabbath was over. I stationed some of my own men at the gates so that no load could be brought in on the Sabbath day. ²⁰Once or twice the merchants and sellers of all kinds of goods spent the night outside Jerusalem. ²¹But I warned them and said, "Why do you spend the night by the wall? If you do this again, I will

13:2 qNu 23:11; Dt 23:4-5
13:3 rNe 9:2
13:4 sNe 12:44; tNe 2:10
13:5 uNu 18:21
13:6 vNe 5:14
13:9 w2Ch 29:5
13:11 xNe 10:37-39
13:12 yNe 10:37-39; Mal 3:10
13:13 zNe 12:44
13:15 aEx 20:8-11; Ne 10:31
13:18 bJer 17:21-23
13:19 cLev 23:32

13:3 "All who were of foreign descent" refers to the Ammonites and Moabites, two nations who were bitter enemies of Israel (13:1). God's law clearly stated that these two peoples should never be allowed in the temple (Deuteronomy 23:3–5). This had nothing to do with racial prejudice, because God clearly loved all people, including foreigners (Deuteronomy 10:18). He allowed foreigners to make sacrifices (Numbers 15:15, 16), and he desires all nations to know and love him (Isaiah 42:6). But while God wants all to come to him, he warns believers to stay away from those bent on evil (Proverbs 24:1). The relationships established between Jews and pagans had caused their captivity in the first place. In their celebration and rededication, they had to show they were serious about following God's law.

13:6, 7 Nehemiah had to return to Babylon in 433 B.C., 12 years after he had arrived in Jerusalem. Either he was recalled by Artaxerxes, or he was fulfilling an agreement to return. It is not known exactly how long he remained in Babylon, but when he returned to Jerusalem (13:7), he found that one of his major opponents in rebuilding the wall, Tobiah, had been given his own room at the temple. He was an Ammonite (4:3), and thus forbidden to enter the temple. Eliashib, the priest, had married Tobiah's daughter,

so Tobiah used his influence with his son-in-law to get this special room. Chapters 2, 4, and 6 tell about Tobiah's opposition to Nehemiah and Nehemiah's appropriate action.

13:10 Because the Levites were no longer supported, they had returned to their farms to support themselves, neglecting their temple duties and the spiritual welfare of the people. Spiritual workers deserve their pay, and their support ought to be enough to care for their needs. They shouldn't have to suffer (or leave) because believers don't adequately assess and meet the needs of their ministers.

13:16 Tyre was a large Phoenician city and port on the Mediterranean Sea.

13:17 God had commanded Israel not to work on the Sabbath, but to rest in remembrance of creation and the exodus (Exodus 20:8–11; Deuteronomy 5:12–15). The Sabbath rest, lasting from sunset Friday to sunset Saturday, was to be honored and observed by all Jews, servants, visiting foreigners, and even farm animals. Jerusalem's busy Sabbath trade directly violated God's law, so Nehemiah commanded that the city gates be shut and traders be sent home every Friday afternoon as the Sabbath hours approached.

13:22
*d*Ne 12:30

lay hands on you." From that time on they no longer came on the Sabbath. 22Then I commanded the Levites to purify themselves and go and guard the gates in order to keep the Sabbath day holy.

Remember *d* me for this also, O my God, and show mercy to me according to your great love.

13:23
*e*Ezr 9:1-2

23Moreover, in those days I saw men of Judah who had married *e* women from Ashdod, Ammon and Moab. 24Half of their children spoke the language of Ashdod or the language of one of the other peoples, and did not know how to speak the language of Judah. 25I rebuked them and called curses down on them. I beat some of the men and pulled out their hair. I made them take an oath in God's name and said: "You are not to give your daughters in marriage to their sons, nor are you to take their daughters in marriage for your sons or for

13:26
*f*1Ki 3:13; 2Ch 1:12
*g*2Sa 12:25
*h*1Ki 11:3
13:27
*i*Ezr 10:2

yourselves. 26Was it not because of marriages like these that Solomon king of Israel sinned? Among the many nations there was no king like him. *f* He was loved by his God, *g* and God made him king over all Israel, but even he was led into sin by foreign women. *h* 27Must we hear now that you too are doing all this terrible wickedness and are being unfaithful to our God by marrying *i* foreign women?"

28One of the sons of Joiada son of Eliashib the high priest was son-in-law to Sanballat the Horonite. And I drove him away from me.

13:29
*j*Ne 6:14

29Remember *j* them, O my God, because they defiled the priestly office and the covenant of the priesthood and of the Levites.

13:30
*k*Ne 10:30
13:31
*l*Ne 10:34
*m*ver 14, 22; Ge 8:1

30So I purified the priests and the Levites of everything foreign, *k* and assigned them duties, each to his own task. 31I also made provision for contributions of wood *l* at designated times, and for the firstfruits.

Remember *m* me with favor, O my God.

13:24 Ashdod was on the Mediterranean coast, in the region controlled by the Philistines. Ammon and Moab were across the Jordan to the east. These nations were abhorrent to those who knew Israel's history.

13:25 Nehemiah was filled with righteous indignation at the blatant way the Jews were breaking God's laws and disregarding the covenant they had previously reaffirmed (10:30). The people had promised not to allow their children to marry pagans. But during Nehemiah's absence, the people had been intermarrying, breaking their solemn covenant with God. Nehemiah's severe treatment of these people shows the contrast between his great faithfulness to God and the people's neglect, disobedience, and disloyalty (see also Ezra 10:3).

13:26 Nehemiah used the example of Solomon's mistakes to teach his people. If one of the greatest kings of Israel fell because of the influence of unbelievers, others could too. Nehemiah saw this principle in Solomon's example: your gifts and strengths won't be of much benefit if you fail to deal with your weaknesses. Although Solomon was a great king, his marriages to foreign women brought tragedy to the whole kingdom. A tendency to sin must be recognized and dealt with swiftly; otherwise, it may overpower you and bring you down. One of the strongest reasons for reading the Bible is to learn from the mistakes of God's people.

13:31 "Remember me with favor" means "look favorably upon me for all that I have done."

13:31 Nehemiah's life story provides many principles of effective leadership that are still valid today. (1) *Have a clear purpose and keep evaluating it in light of God's will.* Nothing prevented Nehemiah from staying on track. (2) *Be straightforward and honest.* Everyone knew exactly what Nehemiah needed, and he spoke the truth even when it made his goal harder to achieve. (3) *Live above reproach.* The accusations against Nehemiah were empty and false. (4) *Be a person of constant prayer, deriving power and wisdom from your contact with God.* Everything Nehemiah did glorified God.

Leadership appears glamorous at times, but it is often lonely, thankless, and filled with pressures to compromise values and standards. Nehemiah was able to accomplish a huge task against incredible odds because he learned that there is no success without risk of failure, no reward without hard work, no opportunity without criticism, and no true leadership without trust in God. This book is about rebuilding the wall of a great city, but it is also about spiritual renewal, rebuilding a people's dependence on God. When we take our eyes off God, our lives begin to crumble.

ESTHER

Jerusalem
destroyed;
exiles go to
Babylon
586 B.C.

First
exiles
return to
Jerusalem
538

Temple
completed
516

VITAL STATISTICS

PURPOSE:
To demonstrate God's sovereignty
and his loving care for his people

AUTHOR:
Unknown. Possibly Mordecai (9:29).
Some have suggested Ezra or
Nehemiah because of the similarity
of the writing style.

ORIGINAL AUDIENCE:
The people of Israel

DATE WRITTEN:
Approximately 470 B.C. (Esther
became queen in 479.)

SETTING:
Although Esther follows Nehemiah
in the Bible, its events are about
30 years prior to those recorded in
Nehemiah. The story is set in the
Persian empire, and most of the
action takes place in the king's
palace in Susa, the Persian capital.

KEY VERSE:
"For if you remain silent at this time,
relief and deliverance for the Jews
will arise from another place, but
you and your father's family will
perish. And who knows but that
you have come to royal position
for such a time as this?" (4:14)

KEY PEOPLE:
Esther, Mordecai, King Xerxes I,
Haman

KEY PLACE:
The king's palace in Susa, Persia

SPECIAL FEATURES:
Esther is one of only two books
named for women (Ruth is the
other). The book is unusual in
that in the original version no
name, title, or pronoun for God
appears (see the note on 4:14).
This caused some church fathers
to question the book's inclusion
in Scripture. But God's presence
is clear throughout the book.

DRAMA, power, romance, intrigue—this is the stuff of which best-selling novels are made. But far from a modern piece of fiction, those words describe a true story, lived and written centuries ago. More than entertaining reading, it is a story of the profound interplay of God's sovereignty and human will. God prepared the place and the opportunity, and his people, Esther and Mordecai, chose to act.

The book of Esther begins with Queen Vashti refusing to obey an order from her husband, King Xerxes. She was subsequently banished, and the search began for a new queen. The king sent out a decree to gather together all the beautiful young women in the empire and bring them into the royal harem. Esther, a young Jewish woman, was one of those chosen. King Xerxes was so pleased with Esther that he made her his queen.

Meanwhile, Mordecai, Esther's older cousin, became a government official and during his tenure foiled an assassination plot. But the ambitious and self-serving Haman was appointed second-in-command in the empire. When Mordecai refused to bow in reverence to him, Haman became furious and determined to destroy Mordecai and all the Jews along with him.

To accomplish his vengeful deed, Haman deceived the king and persuaded him to issue an edict condemning the Jews to death. Mordecai told Queen Esther about this edict, and she decided to risk her life to save her people. Esther asked King Xerxes and Haman to be her guests at a banquet. During the feast, the king asked Esther what she really wanted, and he promised to give her anything. Esther simply invited both men to another banquet the next day.

That night, unable to sleep, the king was flipping through some records in the royal archives when he read of the assassination plot that Mordecai had thwarted. Surprised to learn that Mordecai had never been rewarded for this deed, the king asked Haman what should be done to properly thank a hero. Haman thought the king must be talking about him, and so he described a lavish reward. The king agreed, but to Haman's shock and utter humiliation, he learned that Mordecai was the person to be so honored.

During the second banquet, the king again asked Esther what she desired. She replied that someone had plotted to destroy her and her people, and she named Haman as the culprit. Immediately the king sentenced Haman to die on the gallows that he had built for Mordecai.

In the final act of this true-life drama, Mordecai was appointed to Haman's position, and the Jews were guaranteed protection throughout the land. To celebrate this historic occasion, the Feast of Purim was established.

Because of Queen Esther's courageous act, a whole nation was saved. Seeing her God-given opportunity, she seized it! Her life made a difference. Read Esther and watch for God at work in *your* life. Perhaps he has prepared you to act in "such a time as this" (4:14).

Xerxes becomes king of Persia 486		Esther becomes queen 479	Haman's decree to destroy the Jews 474	First Feast of Purim 473

THE BLUEPRINT

1. Esther becomes queen (1:1—2:23)
2. The Jews are threatened (3:1—4:17)
3. Esther intercedes for the Jews (5:1—8:17)
4. The Jews are delivered (9:1—10:3)

The book of Esther is an example of God's divine guidance and care over our lives. God's sovereignty and power are seen throughout this book. Although we may question certain circumstances in our lives, we must have faith that God is in control, working through both the pleasant and difficult times so that we can serve him effectively.

MEGATHEMES

THEME	EXPLANATION	IMPORTANCE
God's Sovereignty	The book of Esther tells of the circumstances that were essential to the survival of God's people in Persia. These "circumstances" were not the result of chance but of God's grand design. God is sovereign over every area of life.	With God in charge, we can take courage. He can guide us through the circumstances we face in our lives. We should expect God to display his power in carrying out his will. As we unite our life's purposes to God's purpose, we benefit from his sovereign care.
Racial Hatred	The Jews in Persia had been a minority since their deportation from Judah 100 years earlier. Haman was a descendant of King Agag, an enemy of the Jews. Lust for power and pride drove Haman to hate Mordecai, Esther's cousin. Haman convinced the king to kill all the Jews.	Racial hatred is always sinful. We must never condone it in any form. Every person on earth has intrinsic worth because God created people in his own image. Therefore, God's people must stand against racism whenever and wherever it occurs.
Deliverance	On February 28th, the Jews celebrate the Feast of Purim, which symbolizes God's deliverance. Purim means "lots," such as those used by Haman to set the date for the extermination of all Jews from Persia. But God overruled, using Queen Esther to intercede on behalf of the Jews.	Because God is in control of history, he is never frustrated by any turn of events or human action. He is able to save us from the evil of this world and deliver us from sin and death. Because we trust God, we are not to fear what people may do to us; instead, we are to be confident in God's control.
Action	Faced with death, Esther and Mordecai set aside their own fear and took action. Esther risked her life by asking King Xerxes to save the Jews.	When outnumbered and powerless, it is natural for us to feel helpless. Esther and Mordecai resisted this temptation and acted with courage. It is not enough to know that God is in control; we must act with self-sacrifice and courage to follow God's guidance.
Wisdom	The Jews were a minority in a world hostile to them. It took great wisdom for Mordecai to survive. Serving as a faithful official of the king, Mordecai took steps to understand and work within the Persian law. Yet he did not compromise his integrity.	It takes great wisdom to survive in a non-believing world. In a setting which is for the most part hostile to Christianity, we can demonstrate wisdom by giving respect to what is true and good and by humbly standing against what is wrong.

1. Esther becomes queen

Queen Vashti Deposed

1 This is what happened during the time of Xerxes,ᵃ ᵃ the Xerxes who ruled over 127 provincesᵇ stretching from India to Cushᵇ: ᶜ ²At that time King Xerxes reigned from his royal throne in the citadel of Susa,ᵈ ³and in the third year of his reign he gave a banquetᵉ for all his nobles and officials. The military leaders of Persia and Media, the princes, and the nobles of the provinces were present.

⁴For a full 180 days he displayed the vast wealth of his kingdom and the splendor and glory of his majesty. ⁵When these days were over, the king gave a banquet, lasting seven days, in the enclosed gardenᶠ of the king's palace, for all the people from the least to the greatest, who were in the citadel of Susa. ⁶The garden had hangings of white and blue linen, fastened with cords of white linen and purple material to silver rings on marble pillars. There were couchesᵍ of gold and silver on a mosaic pavement of porphyry, marble, mother-of-pearl and other costly stones. ⁷Wine was served in goblets of gold, each one different from the other, and the royal wine was abundant, in keeping with the king's liberality.ʰ ⁸By the king's command each guest was allowed to drink in his own way, for the king instructed all the wine stewards to serve each man what he wished.

⁹Queen Vashti also gave a banquet for the women in the royal palace of King Xerxes.

¹⁰On the seventh day, when King Xerxes was in high spiritsⁱ from wine, he commanded the seven eunuchs who served him—Mehuman, Biztha, Harbona,ʲ Bigtha, Abagtha, Zethar and Carcas— ¹¹to bring before him Queen Vashti, wearing her royal crown, in order to display her beauty to the people and nobles, for she was lovely to look at. ¹²But when the attendants delivered the king's command, Queen Vashti refused to come. Then the king became furious and burned with anger.

¹³Since it was customary for the king to consult experts in matters of law and justice, he spoke with the wise men who understood the timesᵏ ¹⁴and were closest to the king—

1:1	ᵃEzr 4:6; Da 9:1
	ᵇEst 9:30
	ᶜEst 8:9
1:2	ᵈNe 1:1
1:3	ᵉEst 2:18
1:5	ᶠEst 7:7-8
1:6	ᵍEze 23:41; Am 6:4
1:7	ʰEst 2:18
1:10	ʲJdg 16:25
	ʲEst 7:9
1:13	ᵏ1Ch 12:32; Jer 10:7; Da 2:12

ᵃ1 Hebrew *Ahasuerus*, a variant of Xerxes' Persian name; here and throughout Esther   ᵇ1 That is, the upper Nile region

---

1:1 Esther's story begins in 483 B.C., 103 years after Nebuchadnezzar had taken the Jews into captivity (2 Kings 25), 54 years after Zerubbabel led the first group of exiles back to Jerusalem (Ezra 1; 2), and 25 years before Ezra led the second group to Jerusalem (Ezra 7). Esther lived in the kingdom of Persia, the dominant kingdom in the Middle East after Babylon's fall in 539 B.C. Esther's parents must have been among those exiles who chose not to return to Jerusalem, even though Cyrus, the Persian king, had issued a decree allowing them to do so. The Jewish exiles had great freedom in Persia, and many remained because they had established themselves there or were fearful of the dangerous journey back to their homeland.

1:1 Xerxes the Great was Persia's fifth king (486–465 B.C.). He was proud and impulsive, as we see from the events in chapter 1. His winter palace was in Susa, where he held the banquet described in 1:3–7. Persian kings often held great banquets before going to war. In 481, Xerxes launched an attack against Greece. After his fleet won a great victory at Thermopylae, he was defeated at Salamis in 480 and had to return to Persia. Esther became queen in 479.

1:2 In this context, "citadel" means "palace."

1:4 The celebration lasted 180 days (about six months) because its real purpose was to plan the battle strategy for invading Greece and to demonstrate that the king had sufficient wealth to carry it out. Waging war was not only for survival; it was a means of acquiring more wealth, territory, and power.

1:5–7 Persia was a world power, and the king, as the center of that power, was one of the wealthiest people in the world. Persian kings loved to flaunt their wealth, even wearing precious gemstones in their beards. Jewelry was a sign of rank for Persian men. Even soldiers wore great amounts of gold jewelry into battle.

1:8 "Each guest was allowed to drink in his own way" means that the guests could drink as much or as little as they wished. (Usually the king controlled how much his guests could drink.)

1:9 Ancient Greek documents call Xerxes' wife Amestris, probably a Greek form of Vashti. Vashti was deposed in 484/483 B.C., but she is mentioned again in ancient records as the queen mother during the reign of her son, Artaxerxes, who succeeded Xerxes. Toward the end of Xerxes' reign, either Esther died or Vashti was able through her son to regain the influence she had lost.

1:10 Some advisers and government officials were castrated in order to prevent them from having children and then rebelling and trying to establish a dynasty of their own. A castrated official was called a eunuch.

1:10, 11 Xerxes made a rash, half-drunk decision, based purely on feelings. His self-restraint and practical wisdom were weakened by too much wine. Poor decisions are made when people don't think clearly. Base your decisions on careful thinking, not on the emotions of the moment. Impulsive decision-making leads to severe complications.

1:12 Queen Vashti refused to parade before the king's all-male party, possibly because it was against Persian custom for a woman to appear before a public gathering of men. This conflict between Persian custom and the king's command put her in a difficult situation, and she chose to refuse her half-drunk husband, hoping he would come to his senses later. Some have suggested that Vashti was pregnant with Artaxerxes, who was born in 483 B.C., and that she did not want to be seen in public in that state.

Whatever the reason, her action was a breach of protocol that also placed Xerxes in a difficult situation. Once he made the command, as a Persian king he could not reverse it (see the note on 1:19). While preparing to invade Greece, Xerxes had invited important officials from all over his land to see his power, wealth, and authority. If it was perceived that he had no authority over his own wife, his military credibility would be damaged—the greatest criterion of success for an ancient king. In addition, King Xerxes was accustomed to getting what he wanted.

1:13–15 Xerxes, like most leaders past and present, kept a handful of advisers whom he consulted on almost all matters.

1:14
l 2Ki 25:19

Carshena, Shethar, Admatha, Tarshish, Meres, Marsena and Memucan, the seven nobles[l] of Persia and Media who had special access to the king and were highest in the kingdom.

¹⁵"According to law, what must be done to Queen Vashti?" he asked. "She has not obeyed the command of King Xerxes that the eunuchs have taken to her."

¹⁶Then Memucan replied in the presence of the king and the nobles, "Queen Vashti has done wrong, not only against the king but also against all the nobles and the peoples of all the provinces of King Xerxes. ¹⁷For the queen's conduct will become known to all the women, and so they will despise their husbands and say, 'King Xerxes commanded Queen Vashti to be brought before him, but she would not come.' ¹⁸This very day the Persian and Median women of the nobility who have heard about the queen's conduct will respond to all the king's nobles in the same way. There will be no end of disrespect and discord.

1:19
m Est 8:8;
Da 6:8, 12

¹⁹"Therefore, if it pleases the king, let him issue a royal decree and let it be written in the laws of Persia and Media, which cannot be repealed,[m] that Vashti is never again to enter the presence of King Xerxes. Also let the king give her royal position to someone else who is better than she. ²⁰Then when the king's edict is proclaimed throughout all his vast realm, all the women will respect their husbands, from the least to the greatest."

²¹The king and his nobles were pleased with this advice, so the king did as Memucan proposed. ²²He sent dispatches to all parts of the kingdom, to each province in its own script and to each people in its own language,[n] proclaiming in each people's tongue that every man should be ruler over his own household.

1:22
n Eph 5:22-24

THE WORLD OF ESTHER'S DAY
Esther lived in the capital of the vast Medo-Persian empire, which incorporated the provinces of Media and Persia, as well as the previous empires of Assyria and Babylon. Esther, a Jew, was chosen by King Xerxes to be his queen. The story of how she saved her people takes place in the palace in Susa.

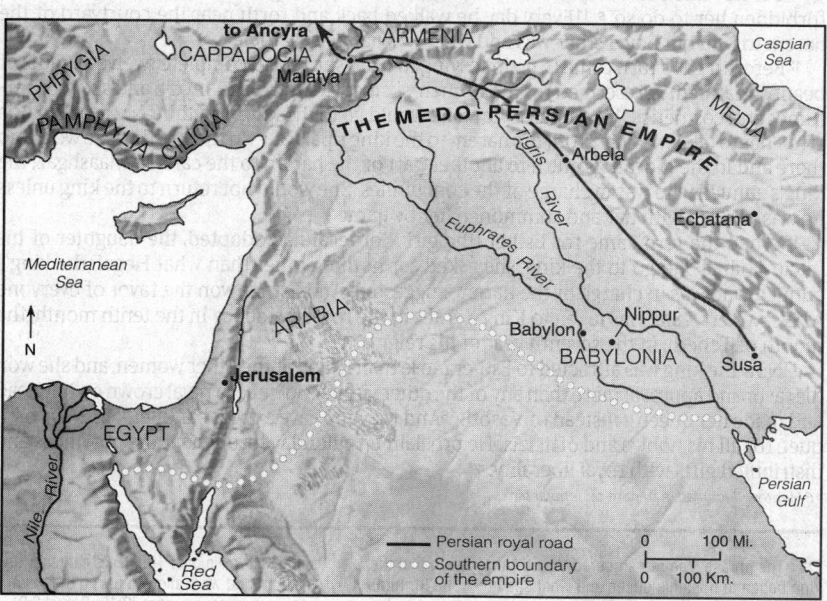

Often a king's success rose or fell on the wisdom of these men. Daniel was such an adviser under Darius and Cyrus (Daniel 6:28).

1:15 Middle Eastern kings often did not have close personal relationships with their wives. Xerxes demonstrates this because (1) he had a harem (2:3); (2) he showed no respect for Vashti's personhood (1:10–12); (3) Esther, when she became queen, did not see him for long periods of time (4:11).

1:16–21 Perhaps the men's thinking had been clouded by drinking. Obviously this law would not cause the women of the country to respect their husbands. Respect between men and women comes from mutual regard and appreciation for each other as those created in God's image, not from legal pronouncements

and orders. Forced obedience is a poor substitute for the love and respect wives and husbands should have for each other.

1:19 A Persian king was thought to be a god by many of his people; therefore, when he issued a law or command, it stood forever (see the notes on 8:8 and Daniel 6:8). The law could never be canceled, even if it was ill-advised; but if necessary, a new law could be issued to neutralize the effects of the old law.

Esther Made Queen

2 Later when the anger of King Xerxes had subsided,[o] he remembered Vashti and what she had done and what he had decreed about her. [2]Then the king's personal attendants proposed, "Let a search be made for beautiful young virgins for the king. [3]Let the king appoint commissioners in every province of his realm to bring all these beautiful girls into the harem at the citadel of Susa. Let them be placed under the care of Hegai, the king's eunuch, who is in charge of the women; and let beauty treatments be given to them. [4]Then let the girl who pleases the king be queen instead of Vashti." This advice appealed to the king, and he followed it.

[5]Now there was in the citadel of Susa a Jew of the tribe of Benjamin, named Mordecai son of Jair, the son of Shimei, the son of Kish,[p] [6]who had been carried into exile from Jerusalem by Nebuchadnezzar king of Babylon, among those taken captive with Jehoiachin[a] [q] king of Judah. [7]Mordecai had a cousin named Hadassah, whom he had brought up because she had neither father nor mother. This girl, who was also known as Esther, was lovely in form and features, and Mordecai had taken her as his own daughter when her father and mother died.

[8]When the king's order and edict had been proclaimed, many girls were brought to the citadel of Susa[r] and put under the care of Hegai. Esther also was taken to the king's palace and entrusted to Hegai, who had charge of the harem. [9]The girl pleased him and won his favor. Immediately he provided her with her beauty treatments and special food. He assigned to her seven maids selected from the king's palace and moved her and her maids into the best place in the harem.

[10]Esther had not revealed her nationality and family background, because Mordecai had forbidden her to do so.[s] [11]Every day he walked back and forth near the courtyard of the harem to find out how Esther was and what was happening to her.

[12]Before a girl's turn came to go in to King Xerxes, she had to complete twelve months of beauty treatments prescribed for the women, six months with oil of myrrh and six with perfumes and cosmetics. [13]And this is how she would go to the king: Anything she wanted was given her to take with her from the harem to the king's palace. [14]In the evening she would go there and in the morning return to another part of the harem to the care of Shaashgaz, the king's eunuch who was in charge of the concubines. She would not return to the king unless he was pleased with her and summoned her by name.

[15]When the turn came for Esther (the girl Mordecai had adopted, the daughter of his uncle Abihail[t]) to go to the king, she asked for nothing other than what Hegai, the king's eunuch who was in charge of the harem, suggested. And Esther won the favor of everyone who saw her. [16]She was taken to King Xerxes in the royal residence in the tenth month, the month of Tebeth, in the seventh year of his reign.

[17]Now the king was attracted to Esther more than to any of the other women, and she won his favor and approval more than any of the other virgins. So he set a royal crown on her head and made her queen[u] instead of Vashti. [18]And the king gave a great banquet,[v] Esther's banquet, for all his nobles and officials. He proclaimed a holiday throughout the provinces and distributed gifts with royal liberality.[w]

[a]6 Hebrew *Jeconiah*, a variant of *Jehoiachin*

2:1 [o]Est 1:19-20; 7:10
2:5 [p]Est 3:2
2:6 [q]2Ki 24:6, 15; 2Ch 36:10, 20
2:8 [r]ver 3, 15
2:10 [s]ver 20
2:15 [t]Est 9:29
2:17 [u]Est 1:11
2:18 [v]Est 1:3 [w]Est 1:7

2:1 The phrase, "he remembered Vashti," may mean that the king began to miss his queen and what she had done for him. But he also remembered that in his anger he had banished her from his presence with a decree that couldn't be rescinded.

2:3, 14–17 Persian kings collected not only vast amounts of jewelry, but also great numbers of women. These young virgins were taken from their homes and were required to live in a separate building near the palace, called a harem. Their sole purpose was to serve the king and to await his call for sexual pleasure. They rarely saw the king, and their lives were restricted and boring. If rejected, Esther would be one of many girls the king had seen once and forgotten. But Esther's presence and beauty pleased the king enough that he crowned her queen in place of Vashti. The queen held a more influential position than a concubine, and she was given more freedom and authority than others in the harem. But even as queen, Esther had few rights—especially because she had been chosen to replace a woman who had become too assertive.

2:5, 6 Mordecai was a Jew. The Jewish population had increased since their exile over 100 years earlier. They had been given great freedom and were allowed to run their own businesses and hold positions in government (2:19; Daniel 6:3).

2:6 The Bible says that Mordecai's family had been carried into exile from Jerusalem by Nebuchadnezzar. If this referred to Mordecai himself, he would have been over 100 years old at the time of this story. Most likely this means that Mordecai's great-grandparents had been carried into captivity, rather than Mordecai himself.

2:10 With virtually no rights and little access to the king, it was better for Esther not to reveal her identity. While boldness in stating our identity as God's people is our responsibility, at times a good strategy is to keep quiet until we have won the right to be heard. This is especially true when dealing with those in authority over us. But we can always let them see the difference God makes in our lives.

2:17 God placed Esther on the throne even before the Jews faced the possibility of complete destruction (3:5ff), so that when trouble came, a person would already be in the position to help.

Mordecai Uncovers a Conspiracy

2:19
x ver 21; Est 3:2

2:20
y ver 10

2:21
z Est 6:2

2:23
a Ps 7:14-16
b Est 6:1; 10:2

¹⁹When the virgins were assembled a second time, Mordecai was sitting at the king's gate.ˣ ²⁰But Esther had kept secret her family background and nationality just as Mordecai had told her to do, for she continued to follow Mordecai's instructions as she had done when he was bringing her up.ʸ

²¹During the time Mordecai was sitting at the king's gate, Bigthanaᵃ and Teresh, two of the king's officersᶻ who guarded the doorway, became angry and conspired to assassinate King Xerxes. ²²But Mordecai found out about the plot and told Queen Esther, who in turn reported it to the king, giving credit to Mordecai. ²³And when the report was investigated and found to be true, the two officials were hangedᵃ on a gallows.ᵇ All this was recorded in the book of the annalsᵇ in the presence of the king.

ᵃ21 Hebrew *Bigthan*, a variant of *Bigthana*   ᵇ23 Or *were hung* (or *impaled*) *on poles*; similarly elsewhere in Esther

---

MORDECAI

Following Jerusalem's last stand against Nebuchadnezzar, Mordecai's family was deported to the Babylonian empire. He was probably born in Susa, a city that became one of Persia's capitals after Cyrus conquered Babylon. Mordecai then inherited an official position among the Jewish captives that kept him around the palace even after the Babylonians were driven out. At one time, when Mordecai overheard plans to assassinate King Xerxes, he reported the plot and saved the king's life.

Mordecai's life was filled with challenges that he turned into opportunities. When his aunt and uncle died, he adopted Esther, their daughter and his young cousin, probably because his own parents were dead and he felt responsible for her. Later, when she was drafted into Xerxes' harem and chosen to be queen, Mordecai continued to advise her. Shortly after this, he found himself in conflict with Xerxes' recently appointed second-in-command, Haman. Although willing to serve the king, Mordecai refused to worship the king's representative. Haman was furious with Mordecai. So he planned to have Mordecai and all the Jews killed. His plan became a law of the Medes and Persians, and it looked as though the Jews were doomed.

Mordecai, willing to be God's servant wherever he was, responded by contacting Esther and telling her that one reason God had allowed her to be queen might well be to save her people from this threat. But God had also placed *him* in the right place years earlier. God revealed to the king through his nighttime reading of historical documents that Mordecai had once saved his life, and the king realized he had never thanked Mordecai. The great honor then given to Mordecai ruined Haman's plan to hang him on the gallows. God had woven an effective counter-strategy against which Haman's plan could not stand.

Later, Mordecai instituted the Jewish feast of Purim. He had a lengthy career of service to the king on behalf of the Jews. In Mordecai's life, God blended both character and circumstances to accomplish great things. He has not changed the way he works. God is using the situations you face each day to weave a pattern of godliness into your character. Pause and ask God to help you respond appropriately to the situations you find yourself in today.

Strengths and accomplishments:	• Exposed an assassination plot against the king • Cared enough to adopt his cousin • Refused to bow to anyone except God • Took Haman's place as second-in-command under Xerxes
Lessons from his life:	• The opportunities we have are more important than the ones we wish we had • We can trust God to weave together the events of life for our best, even though we may not be able to see the overall pattern • The rewards for doing right are sometimes delayed, but they are guaranteed by God himself
Vital statistics:	• Where: Susa, one of several capital cities in Persia • Occupation: Jewish official who became second in rank to Xerxes • Relatives: Adopted daughter: Esther. Father: Jair. • Contemporaries: Xerxes, Haman
Key verse:	"Mordecai the Jew was second in rank to King Xerxes, preeminent among the Jews, and held in high esteem by his many fellow Jews, because he worked for the good of his people and spoke up for the welfare of all the Jews" (Esther 10:3).

Mordecai's story is told in the book of Esther.

No human effort could thwart God's plan to send the Messiah to earth as a Jew. If you are changing jobs, position, or location and can't see God's purpose in your situation, understand that God is in control. He may be placing you in a position so you can help when the need arises.

2. The Jews are threatened
Haman's Plot to Destroy the Jews

3 After these events, King Xerxes honored Haman son of Hammedatha, the Agagite,*c* elevating him and giving him a seat of honor higher than that of all the other nobles. ²All
the royal officials at the king's gate knelt down and paid honor to Haman, for the king had
commanded this concerning him. But Mordecai would not kneel down or pay him honor.

³Then the royal officials at the king's gate asked Mordecai, "Why do you disobey the
king's command?" ⁴Day after day they spoke to him but he refused to comply. Therefore
they told Haman about it to see whether Mordecai's behavior would be tolerated, for he had
told them he was a Jew.

⁵When Haman saw that Mordecai would not kneel down or pay him honor, he was enraged.*d* ⁶Yet having learned who Mordecai's people were, he scorned the idea of killing only
Mordecai. Instead Haman looked for a way to destroy *e* all Mordecai's people, the Jews,
throughout the whole kingdom of Xerxes.

⁷In the twelfth year of King Xerxes, in the first month, the month of Nisan, they cast the
purf (that is, the lot) in the presence of Haman to select a day and month. And the lot fell on*a*
the twelfth month, the month of Adar.

⁸Then Haman said to King Xerxes, "There is a certain people dispersed and scattered
among the peoples in all the provinces of your kingdom whose customs *g* are different from
those of all other people and who do not obey the king's laws; it is not in the king's best interest
to tolerate them.*h* ⁹If it pleases the king, let a decree be issued to destroy them, and I will put ten
thousand talents*b* of silver into the royal treasury for the men who carry out this business."

¹⁰So the king took his signet ring*i* from his finger and gave it to Haman son of Hammedatha, the Agagite, the enemy of the Jews. ¹¹"Keep the money," the king said to Haman, "and do
with the people as you please."

¹²Then on the thirteenth day of the first month the royal secretaries were summoned.
They wrote out in the script of each province and in the language of each people all Haman's
orders to the king's satraps, the govenors of the various provinces and the nobles of the various peoples. These were written in the name of King Xerxes himself and sealed*j* with his

a7 Septuagint; Hebrew does not have *And the lot fell on.*   *b9* That is, about 375 tons (about 345 metric tons)

3:1 *c*Nu 24:7	
3:5 *d*Est 5:9	
3:6 *e*Ps 83:4	
3:7 *f*Est 9:24, 26	
3:8 *g*Ac 16:20-21 *h*Ezr 4:15	
3:10 *i*Ge 41:42; Est 7:6; 8:2	
3:12 *j*1Ki 21:8; Est 8:8-10	

3:2 Mordecai's determination came from his faith in God. He
did not take a poll first to determine the safest or most popular
course of action; he had the courage to stand alone. Doing what
is right will not always make you popular. Those who do right will
be in the minority, but to obey God is more important than to
obey people (Acts 5:29).

3:2–4 Mordecai refused to kneel down before Haman. Jews
did bow down to government authorities, at times, as a sign of
respect (Genesis 23:7; 1 Samuel 24:8), but Haman's ancestors
were ancient enemies of the Jews. Israel had been commanded
by God to "blot out the memory of Amalek from under heaven"
(Deuteronomy 25:17–19; see also Exodus 17:16). Mordecai
was not about to acknowledge Haman as a god. Daniel's three friends had the
same convictions (Daniel 3). We must worship God alone. We
should never let any person, institution, or government take
God's place. When people demand loyalties or duties from you
that do not honor God, don't give in. It may be time to take a
stand.

3:5, 6 Why did Haman want to destroy all Jews just because of
one man's action? (1) Haman was an Agagite (3:1), a descendant
of Agag, king of the Amalekites (1 Samuel 15:20). The Amalekites
were ancient enemies of the Israelites (see Exodus 17:16; Deuteronomy 25:17–19). Haman's hatred was directed not just at
Mordecai, but at all the Jews. (2) As second-in-command in the
Persian empire (3:1), Haman loved his power and authority and
the reverence shown him. The Jews, however, looked to God as
their final authority, not to any man. Haman realized that the only
way to fulfill his self-centered desires was to kill all those who
disregarded his authority. His quest for personal power and his
hatred of the Jewish race consumed him.

3:5, 6 Haman enjoyed the power and prestige of his position,
and he was enraged when Mordecai did not respond with the
expected reverential bow. Haman's anger was not directed just
toward Mordecai, but toward what Mordecai stood for—the
Jews' dedication to God as the only authority worthy of reverence. Haman's attitude was prejudiced: he hated a group of
people because of a difference in belief or culture. Prejudice
grows out of personal pride—considering oneself better than
others. In the end, Haman was punished for his arrogant attitude
(7:9, 10). God will harshly judge those who are prejudiced or
whose pride causes them to look down on others.

3:7 Haman cast lots to determine the best day to carry out his
decree. Little did he know that he was playing into the hands of
God, for the day of death was set for almost a year away, giving
Esther time to make her plea to the king. The Persian word for
lots was *purim*, which became the name for the holiday celebrated by the Jews when they were delivered, not killed, on the
day appointed by Haman.

3:9 Haman must have hoped to acquire this tremendous sum of
money by plundering the homes and businesses of the Jews who
would be killed through his decree. A large number of Jews were
living in the kingdom at this time. Little did Haman know that his
treachery would backfire.

3:10–12 Officials in the ancient world used signet rings as personal signatures. The ring's surface had a raised imprint made
of metal, wood, or bone; Xerxes' was probably made of silver
or gold. Each individual had his own imprint. Letters were sealed
by pressing the ring into soft wax, and official documents were
certified by using the royal signet. By giving Haman his signet
ring, Xerxes gave him his personal signature and with it the
authority to do whatever he wished. Little did the king realize that
his own ring would sign the death warrant for his queen, Esther.

3:13
k Est 8:10-14
l Est 8:11

3:15
m Est 8:15

4:1
n Eze 27:30-31

4:7
o Est 3:9

4:11
p Da 2:9
q Est 5:1, 2; 8:4

own ring. [13]Dispatches were sent by couriers to all the king's provinces with the order to destroy, kill and annihilate all the Jews[k]—young and old, women and little children—on a single day, the thirteenth day of the twelfth month, the month of Adar, and to plunder [l] their goods. [14]A copy of the text of the edict was to be issued as law in every province and made known to the people of every nationality so they would be ready for that day.

[15]Spurred on by the king's command, the couriers went out, and the edict was issued in the citadel of Susa. The king and Haman sat down to drink, but the city of Susa was bewildered.[m]

Mordecai Persuades Esther to Help

4 When Mordecai learned of all that had been done, he tore his clothes, put on sackcloth and ashes,[n] and went out into the city, wailing loudly and bitterly. [2]But he went only as far as the king's gate, because no one clothed in sackcloth was allowed to enter it. [3]In every province to which the edict and order of the king came, there was great mourning among the Jews, with fasting, weeping and wailing. Many lay in sackcloth and ashes.

[4]When Esther's maids and eunuchs came and told her about Mordecai, she was in great distress. She sent clothes for him to put on instead of his sackcloth, but he would not accept them. [5]Then Esther summoned Hathach, one of the king's eunuchs assigned to attend her, and ordered him to find out what was troubling Mordecai and why.

[6]So Hathach went out to Mordecai in the open square of the city in front of the king's gate. [7]Mordecai told him everything that had happened to him, including the exact amount of money Haman had promised to pay into the royal treasury for the destruction of the Jews. [o] [8]He also gave him a copy of the text of the edict for their annihilation, which had been published in Susa, to show to Esther and explain it to her, and he told him to urge her to go into the king's presence to beg for mercy and plead with him for her people.

[9]Hathach went back and reported to Esther what Mordecai had said. [10]Then she instructed him to say to Mordecai, [11]"All the king's officials and the people of the royal provinces know that for any man or woman who approaches the king in the inner court without being summoned the king has but one law:[p] that he be put to death. The only exception to this is for the king to extend the gold scepter[q] to him and spare his life. But thirty days have passed since I was called to go to the king."

GOD BEHIND THE SCENES IN ESTHER
Although God's name is not mentioned in the Hebrew text of Esther, he makes himself known in these ways:

Indirect References	2:17	Esther, who worshiped God, became queen.
	4:14	God's existence and his power over the affairs of people are assumed.
	4:16	Fasting was a distinct spiritual activity usually connected with prayer.
Divine Incidents The book of Esther is filled with divine interventions	2:21, 23	Mordecai overhears a death plot and saves the king's life.
	6:1	Xerxes can't sleep and decides to read a history book.
	6:2	Xerxes reads the exact page needed for the moment, reminding him of an unpaid reward to Mordecai.
	7:9, 10	Haman's plan is exactly reversed—the intended victims are the victors.

Why was God's name hidden in the book of Esther? There were many gods in the Middle East and Persian empire. Usually, their names were mentioned in official documents in order to control the peoples who worshiped those particular gods. The Jews were unique in being the people of one God. A story about them was naturally a story about God, for even the name "Jew" carried with it the connotation of one who worshiped Yahweh.

3:13 Haman's death decree was against all Jews in the Persian empire; thus, it would have included the land of Israel. If his decree had been carried out, all of God's chosen people could have been exterminated, and God's plan to send his Son to earth as a Jew could have been ruined. But God's plans cannot be stopped. Haman was doomed to fail.

4:11—5:2 Esther risked her life by coming before the king. Her courageous act gives us a model to follow in approaching a difficult or dangerous task. Like Esther, we can: (1) *Calculate the cost*. Esther realized her life was at stake. (2) *Set priorities*.

She believed that the safety of the Jewish race was more important than her life. (3) *Prepare*. She gathered support and fasted. (4) *Determine a course of action and move ahead boldly*. She didn't think too long about it, allowing the interlude to lessen her commitment to what she had to do.

Do you have to face a hostile audience, confront a friend on a delicate subject, or talk to your family about changes to be made? Rather than dreading difficult situations or putting them off, take action with confidence by following Esther's inspiring example.

12When Esther's words were reported to Mordecai, 13he sent back this answer: "Do not think that because you are in the king's house you alone of all the Jews will escape. 14For if you remain silent at this time, relief and deliverance for the Jews will arise from another place, but you and your father's family will perish. And who knows but that you have come to royal position for such a time as this?"

15Then Esther sent this reply to Mordecai: 16"Go, gather together all the Jews who are in Susa, and fast for me. Do not eat or drink for three days, night or day. I and my maids will fast as you do. When this is done, I will go to the king, even though it is against the law. And if I perish, I perish."

17So Mordecai went away and carried out all of Esther's instructions.

3. Esther intercedes for the Jews
Esther's Request to the King

5 On the third day Esther put on her royal robes[r] and stood in the inner court of the palace, in front of the king's[s] hall. The king was sitting on his royal throne in the hall, facing the entrance. 2When he saw Queen Esther standing in the court, he was pleased with her and held out to her the gold scepter that was in his hand. So Esther approached and touched the tip of the scepter.[t]

3Then the king asked, "What is it, Queen Esther? What is your request? Even up to half the kingdom,[u] it will be given you."

4"If it pleases the king," replied Esther, "let the king, together with Haman, come today to a banquet I have prepared for him."

5"Bring Haman at once," the king said, "so that we may do what Esther asks."

So the king and Haman went to the banquet Esther had prepared. 6As they were drinking wine, the king again asked Esther, "Now what is your petition? It will be given you. And what is your request? Even up to half the kingdom, it will be granted."[v]

7Esther replied, "My petition and my request is this: 8If the king regards me with favor and if it pleases the king to grant my petition and fulfill my request, let the king and Haman come tomorrow to the banquet I will prepare for them. Then I will answer the king's question."

Haman's Rage Against Mordecai

9Haman went out that day happy and in high spirits. But when he saw Mordecai at the king's gate and observed that he neither rose nor showed fear in his presence, he was filled with rage against Mordecai. 10Nevertheless, Haman restrained himself and went home.

5:1
r Est 4:16
s Est 6:4

5:2
t Est 4:11; 8:4

5:3
u Est 7:2; Mk 6:23

5:6
v Est 7:2

4:13 Although Esther was the queen and shared some of the king's power and wealth, she still needed God's protection and wisdom. No one is secure in his or her own strength in any political system. It is foolish to believe that wealth or position can make us impervious to danger. Deliverance and safety come only from God.

4:13, 14 After the decree to kill the Jews was given, Mordecai and Esther could have despaired, decided to save only themselves, or just waited for God's intervention. Instead, they saw that God had placed them in their positions for a purpose, so they seized the moment and acted. When it is within our reach to save others, we must do so. In a life-threatening situation, don't withdraw, behave selfishly, wallow in despair, or wait for God to fix everything. Instead, ask God for his direction, and *act!* God may have placed you where you are "for such a time as this."

4:14 God is not specifically mentioned in the book of Esther, but it is obvious that Mordecai expected a divine deliverance. While the book of Esther does not mention God by name or title, his presence fills the pages. Esther and Mordecai believed in God's care, and because they acted at the right time, God used them to save his people.

When you face challenges in life, seek to know what God wants you to do, and then do it, confident that he will do his part. You don't know ahead of time how he will accomplish his will. Trust God and prepare to be surprised by the ways he demonstrates his trustworthiness.

4:16 By calling for a fast, Esther was asking the Jews to pray for God's help on her dangerous mission. In the Old Testament,

prayer always accompanies fasting (see Exodus 34:28; Deuteronomy 9:9; Ezra 8:21–23). An important function of a community of believers is mutual support in difficult times. When you are experiencing struggles, turn to fellow believers for support by sharing your trials with them and gaining strength from the bond that unites you. Ask them to pray for you. And when others need your support, give it willingly.

4:16 *Save your own skin* and *Watch out for number one* are mottoes that reflect our world's selfish outlook on life. Esther's attitude stands in bold contrast to this. She knew what she had to do, and she knew it could cost her her life. And yet she responded, "If I perish, I perish." We should have the same commitment to do what is right despite the possible consequences. Do you try to save yourself by remaining silent rather than standing up for what is right? Decide to do what God wants, and trust him for the outcome.

4:17—5:1 God was in control, yet Mordecai and Esther had to act. We cannot understand how both can be true at the same time, and yet they are. God chooses to work through those *willing* to act for him. We should pray as if all depended on God and act as if all depended on us. We should avoid two extremes: doing nothing, and feeling that we must do everything.

5:9 Hatred and bitterness are like weeds with long roots that grow in the heart and corrupt all of life. Haman was so consumed with hatred toward Mordecai that he could not even enjoy the honor of being invited to Esther's party. Hebrews 12:15 warns us to watch out "that no bitter root grows up

5:10
w Est 6:13

5:11
x Est 9:7-10, 13

Calling together his friends and Zeresh,w his wife, 11Haman boasted to them about his vast wealth, his many sons,x and all the ways the king had honored him and how he had elevated him above the other nobles and officials. 12"And that's not all," Haman added. "I'm the only person Queen Esther invited to accompany the king to the banquet she gave. And she has invited me along with the king tomorrow. 13But all this gives me no satisfaction as long as I see that Jew Mordecai sitting at the king's gate."

5:14
y Est 7:9
z Est 6:4

14His wife Zeresh and all his friends said to him, "Have a gallows built, seventy-five feeta high,y and ask the king in the morning to have Mordecai hanged z on it. Then go with the king to the dinner and be happy." This suggestion delighted Haman, and he had the gallows built.

a 14 Hebrew *fifty cubits* (about 23 meters)

We treasure security, even though we know that security in this life carries no guarantees—possessions can be destroyed, beauty fades, relationships can be broken, death is inevitable. Real security, then, must be found beyond this life. Only when our security rests on God and his unchanging nature can we face the challenges that life is sure to bring our way.

Esther's beauty and character won Xerxes' heart, and he made her his queen. Even in her favored position, however, she would risk her life by attempting to see the king when he had not requested her presence. There was no guarantee that the king would even see her. Although she was queen, she was still not secure. But, cautiously and courageously, Esther decided to risk her life by approaching the king on behalf of her people.

She made her plans carefully. The Jews were asked to fast and pray with her before she went to the king. Then on the chosen day she went before him, and he *did* ask her to come forward and speak. But instead of issuing her request directly, she invited him and Haman to a banquet. He was astute enough to realize she had something on her mind, yet she conveyed the importance of the matter by insisting on a second banquet.

In the meantime, God was working behind the scenes. He caused Xerxes to read the historical records of the kingdom late one night, and the king discovered that Mordecai had once saved his life. Xerxes lost no time in honoring Mordecai for that act. During the second banquet, Esther told the king of Haman's plot against the Jews, and Haman was doomed. There is grim justice in Haman's death on the gallows he had built for Mordecai, and it seems fitting that the day on which the Jews were to be slaughtered became the day their enemies died. Esther's risk confirmed that God was the source of her security.

How much of your security lies in your possessions, position, or reputation? God has not placed you in your present position for your own benefit. He put you there *to serve him*. As in Esther's case, this may involve risking your security. Are you willing to let God be your ultimate security?

ESTHER

Strengths and accomplishments:	• Her beauty and character won the heart of Persia's king • She combined courage with careful planning • She was open to advice and willing to act • She was more concerned for others than for her own security
Lessons from her life:	• Serving God often demands that we risk our own security • God has a purpose for the situations in which he places us • Courage, while often vital, does not replace careful planning
Vital statistics:	• Where: Persian empire • Occupation: Xerxes' wife, queen of Persia • Relatives: Cousin: Mordecai. Husband: Xerxes. Father: Abihail.
Key verse:	"Go, gather together all the Jews who are in Susa, and fast for me. Do not eat or drink for three days, night or day. I and my maids will fast as you do. When this is done, I will go to the king, even though it is against the law. And if I perish, I perish" (Esther 4:16).

Esther's story is told in the book of Esther.

---

to cause trouble and defile many." Don't let hatred and its resulting bitterness build in your heart. Like Haman, you will find it backfiring against you (see 6:13; 7:9, 10). If the mere mention of someone's name provokes you to anger, confess your bitterness as sin. Ignoring bitterness, hiding it from others, or making superficial changes in behavior is not enough. If bitterness isn't completely removed, it will grow back, making matters worse.

5:14 Haman's family and friends, who were as arrogant as

he, suggested that the gallows be 75 feet high, probably built on the city wall or some prominent building. They wanted to make sure that all the people of the city saw Mordecai's death and would be reminded of the consequences of disobeying Haman. Ironically, these high gallows allowed everyone to see Haman's death.

Mordecai Honored

6 That night the king could not sleep;[a] so he ordered the book of the chronicles,[b] the record of his reign, to be brought in and read to him. [2]It was found recorded there that Mordecai had exposed Bigthana and Teresh, two of the king's officers who guarded the doorway, who had conspired to assassinate King Xerxes.

[3]"What honor and recognition has Mordecai received for this?" the king asked.

"Nothing has been done for him," his attendants answered.

[4]The king said, "Who is in the court?" Now Haman had just entered the outer court of the palace to speak to the king about hanging Mordecai on the gallows he had erected for him.

[5]His attendants answered, "Haman is standing in the court."

"Bring him in," the king ordered.

[6]When Haman entered, the king asked him, "What should be done for the man the king delights to honor?"

Now Haman thought to himself, "Who is there that the king would rather honor than me?" [7]So he answered the king, "For the man the king delights to honor, [8]have them bring a royal robe the king has worn and a horse[c] the king has ridden, one with a royal crest placed on its head. [9]Then let the robe and horse be entrusted to one of the king's most noble princes. Let them robe the man the king delights to honor, and lead him on the horse through the city streets, proclaiming before him, 'This is what is done for the man the king delights to honor!'[d]"

[10]"Go at once," the king commanded Haman. "Get the robe and the horse and do just as you have suggested for Mordecai the Jew, who sits at the king's gate. Do not neglect anything you have recommended."

[11]So Haman got the robe and the horse. He robed Mordecai, and led him on horseback through the city streets, proclaiming before him, "This is what is done for the man the king delights to honor!"

[12]Afterward Mordecai returned to the king's gate. But Haman rushed home, with his head covered[e] in grief, [13]and told Zeresh[f] his wife and all his friends everything that had happened to him.

His advisers and his wife Zeresh said to him, "Since Mordecai, before whom your downfall has started, is of Jewish origin, you cannot stand against him—you will surely come to ruin!" [14]While they were still talking with him, the king's eunuchs arrived and hurried Haman away to the banquet[g] Esther had prepared.

Haman Hanged

7 So the king and Haman went to dine with Queen Esther, [2]and as they were drinking wine on that second day, the king again asked, "Queen Esther, what is your petition? It will be given you. What is your request? Even up to half the kingdom,[h] it will be granted.[i]"

[3]Then Queen Esther answered, "If I have found favor with you, O king, and if it pleases your majesty, grant me my life—this is my petition. And spare my people—this is my request. [4]For I and my people have been sold for destruction and slaughter and annihilation.[j] If we had merely been sold as male and female slaves, I would have kept quiet, because no such distress would justify disturbing the king.[a]"

[5]King Xerxes asked Queen Esther, "Who is he? Where is the man who has dared to do such a thing?"

[6]Esther said, "The adversary and enemy is this vile Haman."

a4 Or *quiet, but the compensation our adversary offers cannot be compared with the loss the king would suffer*

**Side references:**
6:1 aDa 6:18 bEst 2:23
6:8 c1Ki 1:33
6:9 dGe 41:43
6:12 e2Sa 15:30
6:13 fEst 5:10
6:14 gEst 5:8
7:2 hEst 5:3 iEst 9:12
7:4 jEst 3:9

6:1, 2 Unable to sleep, the king decided to review the history of his reign, and his servants read to him about Mordecai's good deed. This seems coincidental, but God is *always* at work. God has been working quietly and patiently throughout your life as well. The events that have come together for good are not mere coincidence; they are the result of God's sovereign control over the course of people's lives (Romans 8:28).

6:7–9 Haman had wealth, but he craved something even his money couldn't buy—respect. He could buy the trappings of success and power, but his lust for popularity had become an obsession. Don't let your desire for approval, applause, and popularity drive you to immoral actions.

6:10–13 Mordecai had exposed a plot to assassinate Xerxes—thus he had saved the king's life (2:21–23). Although his good deed was recorded in the history books, Mordecai had gone unrewarded. But God was saving Mordecai's reward for the right time. Just as Haman was about to hang Mordecai unjustly, the king was ready to give the reward. Although God promises to reward our good deeds, we sometimes feel our "payoff" is too far away. Be patient. God steps in when it will do the most good.

7:6–10 Haman's hatred and evil plotting turned against him when the king discovered his true intentions. He was hanged on the gallows he had built for someone else. Proverbs 26:27 teaches that a person who digs a pit for others will fall into it himself. What happened to Haman shows the often violent results of setting any kind of trap for others.

7:7
k Est 1:12

Then Haman was terrified before the king and queen. 7 The king got up in a rage,*k* left his wine and went out into the palace garden. But Haman, realizing that the king had already decided his fate, stayed behind to beg Queen Esther for his life.

7:8
l Est 1:6

8 Just as the king returned from the palace garden to the banquet hall, Haman was falling on the couch *l* where Esther was reclining.

The king exclaimed, "Will he even molest the queen while she is with me in the house?"

7:9
m Est 1:10
n Est 5:14
o Ps 7:14-16;
Pr 11:5-6

As soon as the word left the king's mouth, they covered Haman's face. 9 Then Harbona,*m* one of the eunuchs attending the king, said, "A gallows seventy-five feet*a* high *n* stands by Haman's house. He had it made for Mordecai, who spoke up to help the king."

The king said, "Hang him on it!" *o* 10 So they hanged Haman on the gallows he had prepared for Mordecai. Then the king's fury subsided.

a 9 Hebrew *fifty cubits* (about 23 meters)

HAMAN

The most arrogant people are often those who must measure their self-worth by the power or influence they think they have over others. Haman was an extremely arrogant leader. He recognized the king as his superior, but could not accept anyone as an equal. When one man, Mordecai, refused to bow in submission to him, Haman wanted to destroy him. He became consumed with hatred for Mordecai. He was already filled with racial hatred for all the Jewish people because of the long-standing hatred between the Jews and Haman's ancestors, the Amalekites. Mordecai's dedication to God and his refusal to give homage to any human person challenged Haman's self-centered religion. Haman saw the Jews as a threat to his power, and he decided to kill them all.

God was preparing Haman's downfall and the protection of his people long before Haman came to power under Xerxes. Esther, a Jew, became queen, and Mordecai's role in exposing an assassination plot indebted the king to him. Not only was Haman prevented from killing Mordecai, he also had to suffer the humiliation of publicly honoring him. Within hours, Haman died on the gallows he had built to hang Mordecai, and his plan to wipe out the Jews was thwarted. In contrast to Esther, who risked everything for God and won, Haman risked everything for an evil purpose and lost.

Our initial response to the story about Haman is to say that he got what he deserved. But the Bible leads us to ask deeper questions: "How much of Haman is in me?" "Do I desire to control others?" "Am I threatened when others don't appreciate me as I think they should?" "Do I want revenge when my pride is attacked?" Confess these attitudes to God, and ask him to replace them with an attitude of forgiveness. Otherwise, God's justice will settle the matter.

Strength and accomplishment:	• Achieved great power, second in rank to Persia's King Xerxes
Weaknesses and mistakes:	• The desire to control others and receive honor was his highest goal • Was blinded by arrogance and self-importance • Planned to murder Mordecai and built a gallows for him • Orchestrated the plan to slaughter God's people throughout the empire
Lessons from his life:	• Hatred will be punished • God has an amazing record for making evil plans backfire on the planners • Pride and self-importance will be punished • An insatiable thirst for power and prestige is self-destructive
Vital statistics:	• Where: Susa, the capital of Persia • Occupation: Second in rank in the empire • Relative: Wife: Zeresh • Contemporaries: Xerxes, Mordecai, Esther
Key verses:	"When Haman saw that Mordecai would not kneel down or pay him honor, he was enraged. Yet having learned who Mordecai's people were, he scorned the idea of killing only Mordecai. Instead Haman looked for a way to destroy all Mordecai's people, the Jews, throughout the whole kingdom of Xerxes" (Esther 3:5, 6).

Haman's story is told in the book of Esther.

7:8 "They covered Haman's face." A veil was placed over the face of someone condemned to death because Persian kings refused to look upon the face of a condemned person.

The King's Edict in Behalf of the Jews

8 That same day King Xerxes gave Queen Esther the estate of Haman,[p] the enemy of the Jews. And Mordecai came into the presence of the king, for Esther had told how he was related to her. [2]The king took off his signet ring,[q] which he had reclaimed from Haman, and presented it to Mordecai. And Esther appointed him over Haman's estate.

[3]Esther again pleaded with the king, falling at his feet and weeping. She begged him to put an end to the evil plan of Haman the Agagite, which he had devised against the Jews. [4]Then the king extended the gold scepter[r] to Esther and she arose and stood before him.

[5]"If it pleases the king," she said, "and if he regards me with favor and thinks it the right thing to do, and if he is pleased with me, let an order be written overruling the dispatches that Haman son of Hammedatha, the Agagite, devised and wrote to destroy the Jews in all the king's provinces. [6]For how can I bear to see disaster fall on my people? How can I bear to see the destruction of my family?"[s]

[7]King Xerxes replied to Queen Esther and to Mordecai the Jew, "Because Haman attacked the Jews, I have given his estate to Esther, and they have hanged him on the gallows. [8]Now write another decree[t] in the king's name in behalf of the Jews as seems best to you, and seal it with the king's signet ring—for no document written in the king's name and sealed with his ring can be revoked."[u]

[9]At once the royal secretaries were summoned—on the twenty-third day of the third month, the month of Sivan. They wrote out all Mordecai's orders to the Jews, and to the satraps, governors and nobles of the 127 provinces stretching from India to Cush.[a][v] These orders were written in the script of each province and the language of each people and also to the Jews in their own script and language.[w] [10]Mordecai wrote in the name of King Xerxes, sealed the dispatches with the king's signet ring, and sent them by mounted couriers, who rode fast horses especially bred for the king.

[11]The king's edict granted the Jews in every city the right to assemble and protect themselves; to destroy, kill and annihilate any armed force of any nationality or province that might attack them and their women and children; and to plunder the property of their enemies. [12]The day appointed for the Jews to do this in all the provinces of King Xerxes was the thirteenth day of the twelfth month, the month of Adar. [13]A copy of the text of the edict was to be issued as law in every province and made known to the people of every nationality so that the Jews would be ready on that day[x] to avenge themselves on their enemies.

[14]The couriers, riding the royal horses, raced out, spurred on by the king's command. And the edict was also issued in the citadel of Susa.

[15]Mordecai left the king's presence wearing royal garments of blue and white, a large crown of gold and a purple robe of fine linen. And the city of Susa held a joyous celebration. [16]For the Jews it was a time of happiness and joy,[y] gladness and honor. [17]In every province and in every city, wherever the edict of the king went, there was joy and gladness among the Jews, with feasting and celebrating. And many people of other nationalities became Jews because fear of the Jews had seized them.[z]

4. The Jews are delivered
Triumph of the Jews

9 On the thirteenth day of the twelfth month, the month of Adar,[a] the edict commanded by the king was to be carried out. On this day the enemies of the Jews had hoped to overpower them, but now the tables were turned and the Jews got the upper hand over those who hated them.[b] [2]The Jews assembled in their cities in all the provinces of King Xerxes to

[a]9 That is, the upper Nile region

**Cross references (right margin):**

8:1 [p]Est 2:7; 7:6
8:2 [q]Est 3:10
8:4 [r]Est 4:11
8:6 [s]Est 7:4
8:8 [t]Est 3:12-14 [u]Est 1:19
8:9 [v]Est 1:1 [w]Est 1:22
8:13 [x]Est 3:14
8:16 [y]Ps 97:10-12
8:17 [z]Est 9:3
9:1 [a]Est 8:12 [b]Est 3:12-14

8:1–7 While we should not expect earthly rewards for being faithful to God, they often come—and in unexpected ways. Esther and Mordecai were faithful, even to the point of risking their lives to save others. They were willing to give up everything, and God rewarded in proportion to their all-out commitment in ways they could not have foreseen.

8:8 Haman's message had been sealed with the king's signet ring and could not be reversed, even by the king. It was part of the famed "law of the Medes and Persians." Now the king gave permission for whatever other decree Mordecai could devise that would offset the first, without actually canceling it.

8:12 This was the day set by Haman for the extermination of the Jews.

8:15–17 Everyone wants to be a hero and receive praise, honor, and wealth. But few are willing to pay the price. Mordecai served the government faithfully for years, bore Haman's hatred and oppression, and risked his life for his people. He was faithful in obscurity. The price to be paid by God's heroes is long-term commitment, whether or not they receive recognition. Are you ready and willing to pay the price?

9:2
cEst 8:11, 17;
Ps 71:13, 24

9:4
d2Sa 3:1; 1Ch 11:9

9:10
eEst 5:11
fEst 8:11

attack those seeking their destruction. No one could stand against them,c because the people of all the other nationalities were afraid of them. 3And all the nobles of the provinces, the satraps, the governors and the king's administrators helped the Jews, because fear of Mordecai had seized them. 4Mordecai was prominent in the palace; his reputation spread throughout the provinces, and he became more and more powerful. d

5The Jews struck down all their enemies with the sword, killing and destroying them, and they did what they pleased to those who hated them. 6In the citadel of Susa, the Jews killed and destroyed five hundred men. 7They also killed Parshandatha, Dalphon, Aspatha, 8Poratha, Adalia, Aridatha, 9Parmashta, Arisai, Aridai and Vaizatha, 10the ten sonse of Haman son of Hammedatha, the enemy of the Jews. But they did not lay their hands on the plunder. f

11The number of those slain in the citadel of Susa was reported to the king that same day.

HOW GOD WORKS IN THE WORLD	God's Will	What God wants done—he works through . . .		
		➨Natural Order	➨Miracles	➨Providence
	God's Action	➨God set into action through creation a normal working of his universe. He also revealed his expectations of people through his Word and people's consciences.	➨God breaks into the natural order to respond to the expressed needs of people.	➨God overrules the natural order to accomplish an act that people may or may not have requested.
	Examples from Esther	➨God gave Esther natural beauty.	➨God allowed Esther to speak to the king.	➨God allowed Mordecai to overhear a plot.
		➨Esther planned a way to save her people.	➨The people prayed and fasted.	➨Mordecai trusted God to accomplish what was impossible in human terms.
	People's Will	What people want done—we either . . .		
		➨Plan	➨Pray	➨Trust and Obey
	Action We CanTake	➨Can make plans based on the order and dependability of God's creation. Know and obey his words.	➨Can ask God to intervene in certain affairs while realizing that our knowledge and perspective are limited.	➨Can trust that God is in control even when circumstances seem to indicate that he is not.
		or . . .		
	Mistakes We Can Make	➨Disobey	➨Demand	➨Despair
		➨Can violate the natural order, disobey God's commands.	➨Can assume that we understand what is needed and expect God to agree and answer our prayers that way.	➨Can assume God doesn't answer prayer and respond to our needs and live as though there is nothing but the natural order.

9:5–16 Haman had decreed that on the 13th day of the 12th month anyone could kill the Jews and take their property. Mordecai's decree could not reverse Haman's because no law signed by the king could be repealed. Instead, Mordecai had the king sign a new law giving Jews the right to fight back. When the dreaded day arrived, there was much fighting, but the Jews killed only those who wanted to kill them, and they did not take their enemies' possessions, even though they could have (8:11;

9:10, 16). There were no additional riots after the two-day slaughter, so obviously selfish gain or revenge were not primary motives of the Jews. They simply wanted to defend themselves and their families from those who hated them.

9:11 Here the word "citadel" seems to refer to the fortified city of Susa. The king appears to be more concerned about Esther's wishes than the slaughter of his subjects.

12The king said to Queen Esther, "The Jews have killed and destroyed five hundred men and the ten sons of Haman in the citadel of Susa. What have they done in the rest of the king's provinces? Now what is your petition? It will be given you. What is your request? It will also be granted." g

13"If it pleases the king," Esther answered, "give the Jews in Susa permission to carry out this day's edict tomorrow also, and let Haman's ten sons be hanged on gallows."

14So the king commanded that this be done. An edict was issued in Susa, and they hanged the ten sons of Haman. 15The Jews in Susa came together on the fourteenth day of the month of Adar, and they put to death in Susa three hundred men, but they did not lay their hands on the plunder. h

16Meanwhile, the remainder of the Jews who were in the king's provinces also assembled to protect themselves and get relief from their enemies. They killed seventy-five thousand of them but did not lay their hands on the plunder. 17This happened on the thirteenth day of the month of Adar, and on the fourteenth they rested and made it a day of feasting and joy.

Purim Celebrated

18The Jews in Susa, however, had assembled on the thirteenth and fourteenth, and then on the fifteenth they rested and made it a day of feasting and joy.

19That is why rural Jews—those living in villages—observe the fourteenth of the month of Adar as a day of joy and feasting, a day for giving presents to each other. i

20Mordecai recorded these events, and he sent letters to all the Jews throughout the provinces of King Xerxes, near and far, 21to have them celebrate annually the fourteenth and fifteenth days of the month of Adar 22as the time when the Jews got relief from their enemies, and as the month when their sorrow was turned into joy and their mourning into a day of celebration. j He wrote them to observe the days as days of feasting and joy and giving presents of food to one another and gifts to the poor.

23So the Jews agreed to continue the celebration they had begun, doing what Mordecai had written to them. 24For Haman son of Hammedatha, the Agagite, the enemy of all the Jews, had plotted against the Jews to destroy them and had cast the pur k (that is, the lot) for their ruin and destruction. 25But when the plot came to the king's attention, a he issued written orders that the evil scheme Haman had devised against the Jews should come back onto his own head, l and that he and his sons should be hanged on the gallows. m 26(Therefore these days were called Purim, from the word pur. n) Because of everything written in this letter and because of what they had seen and what had happened to them, 27the Jews took it upon themselves to establish the custom that they and their descendants and all who join them should without fail observe these two days every year, in the way prescribed and at the time appointed. 28These days should be remembered and observed in every generation by every family, and in every province and in every city. And these days of Purim should never cease to be celebrated by the Jews, nor should the memory of them die out among their descendants.

29So Queen Esther, daughter of Abihail, o along with Mordecai the Jew, wrote with full authority to confirm this second letter concerning Purim. 30And Mordecai sent letters to all the Jews in the 127 provinces p of the kingdom of Xerxes—words of goodwill and assurance— 31to establish these days of Purim at their designated times, as Mordecai the Jew and Queen Esther had decreed for them, and as they had established for themselves and their descendants in regard to their times of fasting and lamentation. q 32Esther's decree confirmed these regulations about Purim, and it was written down in the records.

a25 Or when Esther came before the king

9:12
gEst 5:6; 7:2

9:15
hEst 8:11

9:19
iver 22; Ne 8:10, 12

9:22
jNe 8:12;
Ps 30:11-12

9:24
kEst 3:7

9:25
lPs 7:16
mEst 7:10
9:26
nver 20

9:29
oEst 2:15
9:30
pEst 1:1
9:31
qEst 4:1-3

9:19–22 People tend to have short memories when it comes to God's faithfulness. To help counter this, Mordecai wrote down these events and encouraged an annual holiday to commemorate the historic days of Purim. Jews still celebrate Purim today. Celebrations of feasting, gladness, and gift-giving are important ways to remember God's specific acts. Today the festivities of Christmas and Easter help us remember the birth and resurrection of Jesus Christ. Don't let the celebration or the exchanging of gifts hide the meaning of these great events.

9:29–31 Among Jews, women were expected to be quiet, to serve in the home, and to stay on the fringe of religious and political life. But Esther was a Jewish woman who broke through the cultural norms, stepping outside her expected role to risk her life to help God's people. Whatever your place in life, God can use you. Be open, available, and ready because God may use you to do what others are afraid even to consider.

The Greatness of Mordecai

10 King Xerxes imposed tribute throughout the empire, to its distant shores. *r* 2 And all his acts of power and might, together with a full account of the greatness of Mordecai *s* to which the king had raised him, are they not written in the book of the annals *t* of the kings of Media and Persia? 3 Mordecai the Jew was second in rank *u* to King Xerxes, *v* preeminent among the Jews, and held in high esteem by his many fellow Jews, because he worked for the good of his people and spoke up for the welfare of all the Jews. *w*

10:1
r Ps 72:10;
Isa 24:15

10:2
s Est 8:15; 9:4
t Est 2:23

10:3
u Ge 41:43
v Ge 41:40
w Ne 2:10

10:3 Mordecai enjoyed a good reputation among the Jews because he was still their friend when he rose to a place of power. Corruption and abuse of authority often characterize those in power. But power used to lift the fallen and ease the burden of the oppressed is power used well. People placed by God in positions of power or political influence must not turn their backs on those in need.

10:3 No archaeological records of Mordecai's being second-in-command have been discovered, but during this time there is a strange gap in ancient Persian records. The records indicate that another man held that position in 465 B.C., about seven years after Mordecai was first appointed. One tablet has been discovered naming Mardukaya as an official in the early years of Xerxes' reign; some believe this was Mordecai.

10:3 In the book of Esther, we clearly see God at work in the lives of individuals and in the affairs of a nation. Even when it looks as if the world is in the hands of evil people, God is still in control, protecting those who are his. Although we may not understand everything happening around us, we must trust in God's protection and retain our integrity by doing what we know is right. Esther, who risked her life appearing before the king, became a hero. Mordecai, who was effectively condemned to death, rose to become the second highest ranking official in the nation. No matter how hopeless our condition, or how much we would like to give up, we need not despair. God is in control of our world.

JOB

TREES snap like toothpicks or fly upward, wrenched from the earth. Whole rooftops sail, cars tumble like toys, houses collapse, and a wall of water obliterates the shore and inundates the land. A hurricane cuts and tears, and only solid foundations survive its unbridled fury. But those foundations can be used for rebuilding after the storm.

For any building, the foundation is critical. It must be deep enough and solid enough to withstand the weight of the building and other stresses. Lives are like buildings, and the quality of each one's foundation will determine the quality of the whole. Too often inferior materials are used, and when tests come, lives crumble.

Job was tested. With a life filled with prestige, possessions, and people, he was suddenly assaulted on every side, devastated, stripped down to his foundation. But his life had been built on God, and he endured.

Job, the book, tells the story of Job, the man of God. It is a gripping drama of riches-to-rags-to-riches, a theological treatise about suffering and divine sovereignty, and a picture of faith that endures. As you read Job, analyze your life and check your foundation. May you be able to say that when all is gone but God, he is enough.

Job was a prosperous farmer living in the land of Uz. He had thousands of sheep, camels, and other livestock, a large family, and many servants. Suddenly, Satan the accuser came before God claiming that Job was trusting God only because he was wealthy and everything was going well for him. And thus the testing of Job's faith began.

Satan was allowed to destroy Job's children, servants, livestock, herdsmen, and home; but Job continued to trust in God. Next Satan attacked Job physically, covering him with painful sores. Job's wife told him to curse God and die (2:9), but Job suffered in silence.

Three of Job's friends, Eliphaz, Bildad, and Zophar, came to visit him. At first they silently grieved with Job. But when they began to talk about the reasons for Job's tragedies, they told him that sin had caused his suffering. They told him to confess his sins and turn back to God. But Job maintained his innocence.

Unable to convince Job of his sin, the three men fell silent (32:1). At this point, another voice—the young Elihu—entered the debate. Although his argument also failed to convince Job, it prepared the way for God to speak.

Finally, God spoke out of a mighty storm. Confronted with the great power and majesty of God, Job fell in humble reverence before him—speechless. God rebuked Job's friends (and Job), and the drama ended with Job restored to happiness and wealth.

It is easy to think that we have all the answers. In reality, only God knows exactly why events unfold as they do, and we must submit to him as our Sovereign. As you read this book, emulate Job and decide to trust God no matter what happens.

THE BLUEPRINT

A. JOB IS TESTED
(1:1—2:13)

Job, a wealthy and upright man, lost his possessions, his children, and his health. Job did not understand why he was suffering. Why does God allow his children to suffer? Although there is an explanation, we may not know it while we are here on earth. In the meantime, we must always be ready for testing in our lives.

B. THREE FRIENDS ANSWER JOB
(3:1—31:40)
1. First round of discussion
2. Second round of discussion
3. Third round of discussion

Job's friends wrongly assumed that suffering always came as a result of sin. With this in mind, they tried to persuade Job to repent of his sin. But the three friends were wrong. Suffering is not always a direct result of personal sin. When we experience severe suffering, it may not be our fault, so we don't have to add to our pain by feeling guilty that some hidden sin is causing our trouble.

C. A YOUNG MAN ANSWERS JOB
(32:1—37:24)

A young man named Elihu, who had been listening to the entire conversation, criticized the three friends for being unable to answer Job. He said that although Job was a good man, he had allowed himself to become proud, and God was punishing him in order to humble him. This answer was partially true because suffering does purify our faith. But God is beyond our comprehension, and we cannot know why he allows each instance of suffering to come into our lives. Our part is simply to remain faithful.

D. GOD ANSWERS JOB
(38:1—41:34)

God himself finally answered Job. God is in control of the world, and only he understands why the good are allowed to suffer. This only becomes clear to us when we see God for who he is. We must courageously accept what God allows to happen in our lives and remain firmly committed to him.

E. JOB IS RESTORED
(42:1–17)

Job finally learned that when nothing else was left, he had God, and that was enough. Through suffering, we learn that God is enough for our lives and our future. We must love God regardless of whether he allows blessing or suffering to come to us. Testing is difficult, but the result is often a deeper relationship with God. Those who endure the testing of their faith will experience God's great rewards in the end.

MEGATHEMES

THEME	EXPLANATION	IMPORTANCE
Suffering	Through no fault of his own, Job lost his wealth, children, and health. Even his friends were convinced that Job had brought this suffering upon himself. For Job, the greatest trial was not the pain or the loss; it was not being able to understand why God allowed him to suffer.	Suffering can be, but is not always, a penalty for sin. In the same way, prosperity is not always a reward for being good. Those who love God are not exempt from trouble. Although we may not be able to understand fully the pain we experience, it can lead us to rediscover God.
Satan's Attacks	Satan attempted to drive a wedge between Job and God by getting Job to believe that God's governing of the world was not just and good. Satan had to ask God for permission to take Job's wealth, children, and health away. Satan was limited to what God allowed.	We must learn to recognize but not fear Satan's attacks because Satan cannot exceed the limits that God sets. Don't let any experience drive a wedge between you and God. Although you can't control how Satan may attack, you can always choose how you will respond when it happens.
God's Goodness	God is all-wise and all-powerful. His will is perfect, yet he doesn't always act in ways that we understand. Job's suffering didn't make sense because everyone believed good people were supposed to prosper. When Job was at the point of despair, God spoke to him, showing him his great power and wisdom.	Although God is present everywhere, at times he may seem far away. This may cause us to feel alone and to doubt his care for us. We should serve God for who he is, not what we feel. He is never insensitive to our suffering. Because God is sufficient, we must hold on to him.

Pride	Job's friends were certain that they were correct in their judgment of him. God rebuked them for their pride and arrogance. Human wisdom is always partial and temporary, so undue pride in our own conclusions is sin.	We must be careful not to judge others who are suffering. We may be demonstrating the sin of pride. We must be cautious in maintaining the certainty of our own conclusions about how God treats us. When we congratulate ourselves for being right, we become proud.
Trusting	God alone knew the purpose behind Job's suffering, and yet he never explained it to Job. In spite of this, Job never gave up on God— even in the midst of suffering. He never placed his hope in his experience, his wisdom, his friends, or his wealth. Job focused on God.	Job showed the kind of trust we are to have. When everything is stripped away, we are to recognize that God is all we ever really had. We should not demand that God explain everything. God gives us himself, but not all the details of his plans. We must remember that this life, with all its pain, is not our final destiny.

A. JOB IS TESTED (1:1—2:13)

Job is portrayed as a wealthy man of upright character who loves God. Yet God allows Satan to destroy his flocks, his possessions, his children, and his health. Job refuses to give up on God, even though he does not understand why this is happening to him. We, too, must trust God when we do not understand the difficulties we face.

Prologue

1 In the land of Uz there lived a man whose name was Job.[a] This man was blameless[b] and upright; he feared God and shunned evil. [2] He had seven sons and three daughters,[c] [3] and he owned seven thousand sheep, three thousand camels, five hundred yoke of oxen and five hundred donkeys, and had a large number of servants. He was the greatest man among all the people of the East.

[4] His sons used to take turns holding feasts in their homes, and they would invite their three sisters to eat and drink with them. [5] When a period of feasting had run its course, Job would send and have them purified. Early in the morning he would sacrifice a burnt offering[d] for each of them, thinking, "Perhaps my children have sinned and cursed God[e] in their hearts." This was Job's regular custom.

Job's First Test

[6] One day the angels[a] came to present themselves before the LORD, and Satan[b] also came with them. [7] The LORD said to Satan, "Where have you come from?"

a6 Hebrew *the sons of God* *b6* Satan means *accuser.*

1:1
a Eze 14:14,20; Jas 5:11
b Ge 6:9; 17:1
1:2
c Job 42:13
1:5
d Ge 8:20
e 1Ki 21:10,13

1:1 As we read the book of Job, we have information that the characters of the story do not. Job, the main character of the book, lost all he had through no fault of his own. As he struggled to understand why all this was happening to him, it became clear that he was not meant to know the reasons. He would have to face life with the answers and explanations held back. Only then would his faith fully develop.

We must experience life as Job did—one day at a time and without complete answers to all of life's questions. Will we, like Job, trust God no matter what? Or will we give in to the temptation to say that God doesn't really care?

1:1 The location of the land of Uz is uncertain. We only know that Uz had plentiful pastures and crops (1:3), was located near a desert (1:19), and was close enough to the Sabeans and Chaldeans to be raided (1:14–17). Uz is also mentioned in Jeremiah 25:19, 20. Most scholars believe Uz was located east of the Jordan River near Canaan (Israel), where the Jews (those to whom God first revealed himself) lived. Job probably knew about God because he knew God's people.

1:1ff As we see calamity and suffering in the book of Job, we must remember that we live in a fallen world where good behavior is not always rewarded and bad behavior is not always punished. When we see a notorious criminal prospering or an innocent child in pain, we say, "That's wrong." And it is. Sin has twisted justice and made our world unpredictable and ugly.

The book of Job shows a good man suffering for no apparent fault of his own. Sadly, our world is like that. But Job's story does not end in despair. Through Job's life we can see that faith

in God is justified even when our situations look hopeless. Faith based on rewards or prosperity is hollow. To be unshakable, faith must be built on the confidence that God's ultimate purpose will come to pass.

1:5 It is not known for sure, but Job probably lived during the days of the patriarchs (Abraham, Isaac, Jacob) before God gave his written law or appointed priests to be religious leaders. During Job's day, the father was the family's religious leader. Because there were no priests to instruct him in God's laws, Job acted as the priest and offered sacrifices to God to ask for forgiveness for sins he and his family had committed. This demonstrated that Job did not consider himself sinless. Job did this out of conviction and love for God, not just because it was his role as head of the house. Do you carry out your spiritual duties because they are expected, or spontaneously from a heart of devotion?

1:5 Job showed deep concern for the spiritual welfare of his children. Fearful that they might have sinned unknowingly, he offered sacrifices for them. Parents today can show the same concern by praying for their children. This means "sacrificing" some time each day to ask God to forgive them, to help them grow, to protect them, and to help them please him.

1:6 The Bible speaks of other heavenly councils where God and the angels plan their activities on earth and where angels are required to give account of themselves (i.e., 1 Kings 22:19–23). Because God is Creator of all angels—both of those who serve him and of those who rebelled—he has complete power and authority over them.

1:6, 7 Satan, originally an angel of God, had become corrupt

1:7
f 1Pe 5:8

Satan answered the Lord, "From roaming through the earth and going back and forth in it." *f*

8 Then the Lord said to Satan, "Have you considered my servant Job? There is no one on earth like him; he is blameless and upright, a man who fears God and shuns evil."

1:10
g Ps 34:7
h Job 29:6;
Ps 128:1-2

9 "Does Job fear God for nothing?" Satan replied. 10 "Have you not put a hedge around him and his household and everything he has? *g* You have blessed the work of his hands, so that his flocks and herds are spread throughout the land. *h* 11 But stretch out your hand and strike everything he has, *i* and he will surely curse you to your face." *j*

1:11
i Job 19:21
j Job 2:5

12 The Lord said to Satan, "Very well, then, everything he has is in your hands, but on the man himself do not lay a finger."

Then Satan went out from the presence of the Lord.

13 One day when Job's sons and daughters were feasting and drinking wine at the oldest brother's house, 14 a messenger came to Job and said, "The oxen were plowing and the donkeys were grazing nearby, 15 and the Sabeans attacked and carried them off. They put the servants to the sword, and I am the only one who has escaped to tell you!"

1:16
k Lev 10:2;
Nu 11:1-3

16 While he was still speaking, another messenger came and said, "The fire of God fell from the sky and burned up the sheep and the servants, *k* and I am the only one who has escaped to tell you!"

1:17
l Ge 11:28,31

17 While he was still speaking, another messenger came and said, "The Chaldeans *l* formed three raiding parties and swept down on your camels and carried them off. They put the servants to the sword, and I am the only one who has escaped to tell you!"

18 While he was still speaking, yet another messenger came and said, "Your sons and daughters were feasting and drinking wine at the oldest brother's house, 19 when suddenly a mighty wind swept in from the desert and struck the four corners of the house. It collapsed on them and they are dead, and I am the only one who has escaped to tell you!"

---

through his own pride. He has been evil since his rebellion against God (1 John 3:8). Satan considers God as his enemy. He tries to hinder God's work in people, but he is limited by God's power and can do only what he is permitted (Luke 22:31, 32; 1 Timothy 1:19, 20; 2 Timothy 2:23–26). Satan is our enemy because he actively looks for people to attack with temptation (1 Peter 5:8, 9) and because he wants to make people hate God. He does this through lies and deception (Genesis 3:1–6). Job, a blameless and upright man who had been greatly blessed, was a perfect target for Satan. Any person who is committed to God should expect Satan's attacks. Satan, who hates God, also hates God's people.

1:6–12 From this conversation, we learn a great deal about Satan. (1) He is accountable to God. All angelic beings, good and evil, are compelled to present themselves before God (1:6). God knew that Satan was intent on attacking Job. (2) Satan can be at only one place at a time (1:6, 7). His demons aid him in his work; but as a created being, he is limited. (3) Satan cannot see into our minds or foretell the future (1:9–11). If he could, he would have known that Job would not break under pressure. (4) Because Satan can do nothing without God's permission (1:12), God's people can overcome his attacks through God's power. (5) God puts limitations on what Satan can do (1:12; 2:6). Satan's response to the Lord's question (1:7) tells us that Satan is real and active on earth. Knowing this about Satan should cause us to remain close to the One who is greater than Satan—God himself.

1:7ff Some people suggest that this dialogue was made up by the author of this book. Could this conversation between God and Satan really have happened? Other Bible passages tell us that Satan does indeed have access to God (see Revelation 12:10). He even went into God's presence to make accusations against Joshua the high priest (Zechariah 3:1, 2). If this conversation didn't take place, then the reasons for Job's suffering become meaningless and the book of Job is reduced to fiction rather than fact.

1:8, 12 Job was a model of trust and obedience to God, yet God permitted Satan to attack him in an especially harsh manner. Although God loves us, believing and obeying him

do not shelter us from life's calamities. Setbacks, tragedies, and sorrows strike Christians and non-Christians alike. But in our tests and trials, God expects us to express our faith to the world. How do you respond to your troubles? Do you ask God, "Why me?" or do you say, "Use me!"?

1:9 Satan attacked Job's motives, saying that Job was blameless and upright only because he had no reason to turn against God. Ever since he had started following God, everything had gone well for Job. Satan wanted to prove that Job worshiped God, not out of love, but because God had given him so much.

Satan accurately analyzed why many people trust God. They are fair-weather believers, following God only when everything is going well or for what they can get. Adversity destroys this superficial faith. But adversity strengthens real faith by causing believers to dig their roots deeper into God in order to withstand the storms. How deep does your faith go? Put the roots of your faith down deep into God so that you can withstand any storm you may face.

1:12 This conversation between God and Satan teaches us an important fact about God—he is fully aware of every attempt by Satan to bring suffering and difficulty upon us. While God may allow us to suffer for a reason beyond our understanding, he is never caught by surprise by our troubles and is always compassionate.

1:15–17 The Sabeans were from southwest Arabia, while the Chaldeans were from the region north of the Persian Gulf.

1:16 "The fire of God" was a poetic way to describe lightning (1 Kings 18:38; 2 Kings 1:10–14). In this case, it had to be unusually powerful to kill 7,000 sheep.

²⁰At this, Job got up and tore his robe^m and shaved his head. Then he fell to the ground in worship^n ²¹and said:

> "Naked I came from my mother's womb,
>   and naked I will depart.^a ^o
> The Lord gave and the Lord has taken away;
>   may the name of the Lord be praised."^p

²²In all this, Job did not sin by charging God with wrongdoing. ^q

Job's Second Test

2 On another day the angels^b came to present themselves before the Lord, and Satan also came with them^r to present himself before him. ²And the Lord said to Satan, "Where have you come from?"

Satan answered the Lord, "From roaming through the earth and going back and forth in it."

³Then the Lord said to Satan, "Have you considered my servant Job? There is no one on earth like him; he is blameless and upright, a man who fears God and shuns evil. And he still maintains his integrity,^s though you incited me against him to ruin him without any reason."^t

⁴"Skin for skin!" Satan replied. "A man will give all he has for his own life. ⁵But stretch out your hand and strike his flesh and bones,^u and he will surely curse you to your face."^v

⁶The Lord said to Satan, "Very well, then, he is in your hands; but you must spare his life."

⁷So Satan went out from the presence of the Lord and afflicted Job with painful sores from the soles of his feet to the top of his head. ⁸Then Job took a piece of broken pottery and scraped himself with it as he sat among the ashes. ^w

⁹His wife said to him, "Are you still holding on to your integrity? Curse God and die!"

¹⁰He replied, "You are talking like a foolish^c woman. Shall we accept good from God, and not trouble?"^x

In all this, Job did not sin in what he said.

Job's Three Friends

¹¹When Job's three friends, Eliphaz the Temanite, Bildad the Shuhite^y and Zophar the Naamathite, heard about all the troubles that had come upon him, they set out from their homes and met together by agreement to go and sympathize with him and comfort him. ^z ¹²When they saw him from a distance, they could hardly recognize him; they began to weep

^a21 Or *will return there*   ^b1 Hebrew *the sons of God*   ^c10 The Hebrew word rendered *foolish* denotes moral deficiency.

1:20
^m Ge 37:29
^n 1Pe 5:6

1:21
^o Ecc 5:15; 1Ti 6:7
^p Job 2:10;
Eph 5:20; 1Th 5:18

1:22
^q Job 2:10

2:1
^r Job 1:6

2:3
^s Job 27:6
^t Job 9:17

2:5
^u Job 19:20
^v Job 1:11

2:8
^w Job 42:6;
Eze 27:30; Mt 11:21

2:10
^x Job 1:21

2:11
^y Ge 25:2
^z Job 42:11

1:20–22 Job did not hide his overwhelming grief. He had not lost his faith in God; instead, his emotions showed that he was human and that he loved his family. God created our emotions, and it is not sinful or inappropriate to express them as Job did. If you have experienced a deep loss, a disappointment, or a heartbreak, admit your feelings to yourself and others, and grieve.

1:20–22 Job had lost his possessions and family in this first of Satan's tests, but he reacted rightly toward God by acknowledging God's sovereign authority over everything God had given him. Satan lost this first round. Job passed the test and proved that people can love God for who he is, not for what he gives.

2:3–6 Can Satan persuade God to change his plans? At first God said he did not want Job harmed physically, but then he decided to allow it. Satan is unable to persuade God to go against his character: God is completely and eternally good. But God was willing to go along with Satan's plan because God knew the eventual outcome of Job's story. God cannot be fooled by Satan. Job's suffering was a test for Job, Satan, and us—not God.

2:4, 5 "Skin for skin" was Satan's comment concerning Job's response to the loss of his family. Satan still held to his opinion that Job was faithful only because of God's blessings. Satan believed that Job was willing to accept the loss of family and property as long as his own skin was safe. Satan's next step was to inflict physical suffering upon Job to prove his original accusation (1:9).

2:6 Again Satan had to seek permission from God to inflict pain upon Job. God limits Satan, and in this case, he did not allow Satan to destroy Job.

2:9 Why was Job's wife spared when the rest of his family was killed? It is possible that her very presence caused Job even more suffering through her chiding or sorrow over all they had lost.

2:10 Many people think that believing in God protects them from trouble, so when calamity comes, they question God's goodness and justice. But the message of Job is that you should not give up on God because he allows you to have bad experiences. Faith in God does not guarantee personal prosperity, and lack of faith does not guarantee troubles in this life. If this were so, people would believe in God simply to get rich. God is capable of rescuing us from suffering, but he may also allow suffering to come for reasons we cannot understand. It is Satan's strategy to get us to doubt God at exactly this moment. Here Job shows a perspective broader than seeking his own personal comfort. If we always knew why we were suffering, our faith would have no room to grow.

2:11 Eliphaz, Bildad, and Zophar were not only Job's friends, they were also known for their wisdom. In the end, however, their wisdom was shown to be narrow-minded and incomplete.

2:11 Upon learning of Job's difficulties, three of his friends came to sympathize with him and comfort him. Later we learn that their words of comfort were not helpful—but at least they came. While God rebuked them for what they said (42:7), he did not rebuke them for what they did—making the effort to come to someone who was in need. Unfortunately, when they came, they did a poor job of comforting Job because they were proud of their own advice and insensitive to Job's needs. When someone is in need, go to that person, but be sensitive in how you comfort him or her.

2:12
a La 2:10;
Eze 27:30

2:13
b Ge 50:10

3:3
c Jer 20:14-18

aloud, and they tore their robes and sprinkled dust on their heads. *a* 13Then they sat on the ground with him for seven days and seven nights. *b* No one said a word to him, because they saw how great his suffering was.

B. THREE FRIENDS ANSWER JOB (3:1—31:40)

Job agonizes over his situation. His three friends explain that he must be suffering because of some terrible sin he committed. They try to persuade Job to repent of his sin. When Job argues that he has not sinned enough to deserve such suffering, his friends respond with even harsher accusations. While there are elements of truth in the speeches of Job's three friends, they are based on wrong assumptions. We must be careful what we assume to be true in the lives of others. We cannot assume that suffering is their own fault or a result of their sin.

1. First round of discussion
Job Speaks

3 After this, Job opened his mouth and cursed the day of his birth. 2He said:

> 3 "May the day of my birth perish,
>   and the night it was said, 'A boy is born!'*c*
> 4 That day—may it turn to darkness;
>   may God above not care about it;
>   may no light shine upon it.
> 5 May darkness and deep shadow*a* claim it once more;
>   may a cloud settle over it;
>   may blackness overwhelm its light.
> 6 That night—may thick darkness seize it;
>   may it not be included among the days of the year
>   nor be entered in any of the months.
> 7 May that night be barren;
>   may no shout of joy be heard in it.
> 8 May those who curse days*b* curse that day,
>   those who are ready to rouse Leviathan.

a5 Or and the shadow of death   b8 Or the sea

THE SOURCES OF SUFFERING	Sources	Who Is Responsible	Who Is Affected	Needed Response
	My sin	I am	Myself and others	Repentance and confession to God
	Others' sin	Person who sinned and others who allowed the sin	Probably many people, including those who sinned	Active resistance to the sinful behavior, while accepting the sinner
	Avoidable physical (or natural) disaster	Persons who ignore the facts or refuse to take precautions	Most of those exposed to the cause	Prevent them if possible; be prepared if they can't be prevented
	Unavoidable physical (or natural) disaster	God, Satan	Most of those present	Ongoing trust in God's faithfulness

When suffering or troubles happen, do they always come from Satan? In Job's story, his series of tragedies did come from Satan, but this is not always the case. The chart above demonstrates the four main causes of suffering. Any one of these or a combination of them may create suffering. If knowing why we are suffering will teach us to avoid the cause, then the causes are worth knowing. However, it is most important to know how to respond during suffering.

2:13 Why did the friends arrive and then just sit quietly? According to Jewish tradition, people who come to comfort someone in mourning should not speak until the mourner speaks. Often the best response to another person's suffering is silence. Job's friends realized that his pain was too deep to be healed with mere words, so they said nothing. (If only they had continued to sit quietly!) Often, we feel we must say something spiritual and insightful to a hurting friend. Perhaps what he or she needs most is just our presence, showing that we care. Pat answers and trite quotations say much less than empathetic silence and loving companionship.

3:1ff Job's response to his second test—physical affliction—contrasts greatly to his attitude after the first test (1:20–22). Job still did not curse God, but he cursed the day of his birth. He felt it would be better never to be born than to be forsaken by God. Job was struggling emotionally, physically, and spiritually; his misery was pervasive and deep. Never underestimate how vulnerable we are during times of suffering and pain. We must hold on to our faith even if there is no relief.

3:8 In Job's day, people were hired to pronounce curses. Job desires that the soothsayers would call up the sea monster, Leviathan, to swallow up the day of Job's birth.

9 May its morning stars become dark;
    may it wait for daylight in vain
    and not see the first rays of dawn,
10 for it did not shut the doors of the womb on me
    to hide trouble from my eyes.

11 "Why did I not perish at birth,
    and die as I came from the womb?*d*
12 Why were there knees to receive me
    and breasts that I might be nursed?
13 For now I would be lying down in peace;
    I would be asleep and at rest
14 with kings and counselors of the earth,
    who built for themselves places now lying in ruins,
15 with rulers who had gold,
    who filled their houses with silver.
16 Or why was I not hidden in the ground like a stillborn child,
    like an infant who never saw the light of day?
17 There the wicked cease from turmoil,
    and there the weary are at rest.
18 Captives also enjoy their ease;
    they no longer hear the slave driver's shout.
19 The small and the great are there,
    and the slave is freed from his master.

20 "Why is light given to those in misery,
    and life to the bitter of soul,
21 to those who long for death that does not come,*e*
    who search for it more than for hidden treasure,
22 who are filled with gladness
    and rejoice when they reach the grave?
23 Why is life given to a man
    whose way is hidden,
    whom God has hedged in?*f*
24 For sighing comes to me instead of food;
    my groans pour out like water.*g*
25 What I feared has come upon me;
    what I dreaded has happened to me.
26 I have no peace, no quietness;
    I have no rest, but only turmoil."

Eliphaz

4 Then Eliphaz the Temanite replied:

2 "If someone ventures a word with you, will you be impatient?
    But who can keep from speaking?

3:11
d Job 10:18

3:21
e Rev 9:6

3:23
f La 3:7

3:24
g Ps 42:3,4

3:11 Job was experiencing extreme physical pain as well as grief over the loss of his family and possessions. He can't be blamed for wishing he were dead. Job's grief placed him at the crossroads of his faith, shattering many misconceptions about God (such as: he makes you rich, always keeps you from trouble and pain, or protects your loved ones). Job was driven back to the basics of his faith in God. He had only two choices: (1) he could curse God and give up, or (2) he could trust God and draw strength from him to continue.

3:23–26 Job had been careful not to worship material possessions but to worship God alone. Here he was overwhelmed by calamities that mocked his caution, and he complained about trials that came despite his right living. All the principles by which he had lived were crumbling, and Job began to lose his perspective. Trials and grief, whether temporary or enduring, do not destroy

the real purpose of life. Life is not given merely for happiness and personal fulfillment, but for us to serve and honor God. The worth and meaning of life is not based on what we feel, but on the one reality no one can take away—God's love for us. Don't assume that because God truly loves you, he will always prevent suffering. The opposite may be true. God's love cannot be measured or limited by how great or how little we may suffer. Romans 8:38, 39 teaches us that nothing can separate us from God's love.

4:1ff Eliphaz claimed to have been given secret knowledge through a special revelation from God (4:12–16), and that he had learned much from personal experience (4:8). He argued that suffering is a direct result of sin, so if Job would only confess his sin, his suffering would end. Eliphaz saw suffering as God's punishment, which should be welcomed in order to bring a person back to God. In some cases, of course, this may be true (Galatians

4:3
h Isa 35:3
4:4
i Isa 35:3;
Heb 12:12
4:5
j Job 19:21
k Job 6:14

3 Think how you have instructed many,
how you have strengthened feeble hands.*h*
4 Your words have supported those who stumbled;
you have strengthened faltering knees.*i*
5 But now trouble comes to you, and you are discouraged;
it strikes*j* you, and you are dismayed.*k*

Children never tire of asking "Why?" Yet the question produces a bitter taste the older we get. Children wonder about everything; adults wonder about suffering. We notice that the world seems to run by a system of cause and effect, yet there are some effects for which we can't find a clear cause, and some causes that don't lead to the expected effects. We would expect Job's wealth and family to give him a very happy life, and, for a while, they did. But the loss and pain he experienced shock us. The first two chapters of his story are more than we can bear. To those so quick to ask "Why?" at the smallest misfortune, Job's faithfulness seems incredible. But even Job had something to learn. We can learn with him.

Our age of "instant" everything has caused us to lose the ability to wait. We expect to learn patience instantly, and in our hurry, we miss the contradiction. Of all that we want now, relief from pain is at the top of our list. We want an instant cure for everything from toothaches to heartbreaks.

Although some pains have been cured, we still live in a world where many people suffer. Job was not expecting instant answers for the intense emotional and physical pain he endured. But in the end, what broke Job's patience was not the suffering, but not knowing *why* he suffered.

When Job expressed his frustration, his friends were ready with their answers. They believed that the law of cause and effect applied to all people's experiences. Their view of life boiled down to this: good things happen to good people, and bad things happen to bad people. Because of this, they felt their role was to help Job admit to whatever sin was causing his suffering.

Job actually looked at life almost the same way as his friends. What he couldn't understand was why he was suffering so much when he was sure he had done nothing to deserve such punishment. The last friend, Elihu, did offer another explanation for the pain by pointing out that God might be allowing it to purify Job. But this was only partly helpful. When God finally spoke, he didn't offer Job an answer. Instead, he drove home the point that it is better to know God than to know answers.

Often we suffer consequences for bad decisions and actions. Job's willingness to repent and confess known wrongs is a good guideline for us. Sometimes suffering shapes us for special service to others. Sometimes suffering is an attack by Satan on our lives. And sometimes we don't know why we suffer. At those times, are we willing to trust God in spite of unanswered questions?

Strengths and accomplishments:	• A man of faith, patience, and endurance • Known as a generous and caring person • Very wealthy
Weakness and mistake:	• Allowed his desire to understand why he was suffering overwhelm him and make him question God
Lessons from his life:	• Knowing God is better than knowing answers • God is not arbitrary or uncaring • Pain is not always punishment
Vital statistics:	• Where: Uz • Occupation: Wealthy landowner and livestock owner • Relatives: Wife and first ten children not named. Daughters from the second set of children: Jemimah, Keziah, Keren-Happuch. • Contemporaries: Eliphaz, Bildad, Zophar, Elihu
Key verses:	"Brothers, as an example of patience in the face of suffering, take the prophets who spoke in the name of the Lord. As you know, we consider blessed those who have persevered. You have heard of Job's perseverance and have seen what the Lord finally brought about. The Lord is full of compassion and mercy" (James 5:10, 11).

Job's story is told in the book of Job. He is also referred to in Ezekiel 14:14, 20 and James 5:11.

6:7, 8), but it was not true with Job. Although Eliphaz had many good and true comments, he made three wrong assumptions: (1) a good and innocent person never suffers; (2) those who suffer are being punished for their past sins; and (3) Job, because he was suffering, had done something wrong in God's eyes. (For more about Eliphaz, see the chart in chapter 28, p. 801. Teman was a trading city in Edom, noted as a place of wisdom; see Jeremiah 49:7.)

6 Should not your piety be your confidence[l]
　　and your blameless[m] ways your hope?

7 "Consider now: Who, being innocent, has ever perished?
　　Where were the upright ever destroyed?[n]

8 As I have observed, those who plow evil
　　and those who sow trouble reap it.[o]

9 At the breath of God[p] they are destroyed;
　　at the blast of his anger they perish.

10 The lions may roar and growl,
　　yet the teeth of the great lions are broken.[q]

11 The lion perishes for lack of prey,[r]
　　and the cubs of the lioness are scattered.

12 "A word was secretly brought to me,
　　my ears caught a whisper[s] of it.

13 Amid disquieting dreams in the night,
　　when deep sleep falls on men,[t]

14 fear and trembling seized me
　　and made all my bones shake.

15 A spirit glided past my face,
　　and the hair on my body stood on end.

16 It stopped,
　　but I could not tell what it was.
　A form stood before my eyes,
　　and I heard a hushed voice:

17 'Can a mortal be more righteous than God?[u]
　　Can a man be more pure than his Maker?[v]

18 If God places no trust in his servants,
　　if he charges his angels with error,[w]

19 how much more those who live in houses of clay,[x]
　　whose foundations[y] are in the dust,
　　who are crushed more readily than a moth!

20 Between dawn and dusk they are broken to pieces;
　　unnoticed, they perish forever.[z]

21 Are not the cords of their tent pulled up,
　　so that they die without wisdom?'[a a]

5　"Call if you will, but who will answer you?
　　To which of the holy ones[b] will you turn?

2 Resentment kills a fool,
　　and envy slays the simple.[c]

a21 Some interpreters end the quotation after verse 17.

4:6
lPr 3:26
mJob 1:1

4:7
nPs 37:25

4:8
oPr 22:8;
Hos 10:13;
Gal 6:7-8

4:9
pIsa 30:33

4:10
qPs 58:6

4:11
rPs 34:10

4:12
sJob 26:14

4:13
tJob 33:15

4:17
uJob 9:2
vJob 35:10

4:18
wJob 15:15

4:19
xJob 10:9
yJob 22:16

4:20
zJob 20:7;
Ps 90:5-6

4:21
aJob 36:12

5:1
bJob 15:15

5:2
cPr 12:16

4:7, 8 Part of what Eliphaz said is true, and part is false. It is true that those who promote sin and trouble eventually will be punished; it is false that anyone who is good and innocent will never suffer.

All the material recorded and quoted in the Bible is there by God's choice. Some is a record of what people said and did but is not an example to follow. The sins, the defeats, the evil thoughts, and misconceptions about God are all part of God's divinely inspired Word, but we should not follow those wrong examples just because they are in the Bible. The Bible gives us teachings and examples of what we *should* do as well as what we *should not* do. Eliphaz's comments are an example of what we should try to avoid—making false assumptions about others based on our own experiences.

4:12, 13 Although Eliphaz claimed that his vision was divinely inspired, it is doubtful that it came from God because later God criticized Eliphaz for misrepresenting him (42:7). Whatever the vision's source, it is summarized in 4:17. On the surface,

this statement is completely true—a mere mortal cannot compare to God and should not try to question God's motives and actions. Eliphaz, however, took this thought and expounded on it later, expressing his own opinions. His conclusion (5:8) reveals a very shallow understanding of Job and his suffering. It is easy for teachers, counselors, and well-meaning friends to begin with a portion of God's truth but then go off on a tangent. Don't limit God to your perspective and finite understanding of life.

4:18, 19 Do angels really make errors? Remember that Eliphaz was speaking, not God, so we must be careful about building our knowledge of the spiritual world from Eliphaz's opinions. In addition, the word translated *error* is used only here, and its meaning is unclear. We could save Eliphaz's credibility by saying he meant fallen angels, but this passage is not meant to teach about angels. Eliphaz was saying that sinful human beings are far beneath God and the angels. Eliphaz was right about God's greatness, but he did not understand God's greater purposes concerning suffering.

5:3
d Jer 12:2

3 I myself have seen a fool taking root,*d*
but suddenly his house was cursed.
4 His children are far from safety,
crushed in court without a defender.
5 The hungry consume his harvest,
taking it even from among thorns,
and the thirsty pant after his wealth.
6 For hardship does not spring from the soil,
nor does trouble sprout from the ground.
7 Yet man is born to trouble
as surely as sparks fly upward.

8 "But if it were I, I would appeal to God;
I would lay my cause before him.
9 He performs wonders that cannot be fathomed,
miracles that cannot be counted.
10 He bestows rain on the earth;
he sends water upon the countryside.

5:11
e Ps 113:7-8

11 The lowly he sets on high,*e*
and those who mourn are lifted to safety.

5:12
f Ne 4:15; Ps 33:10

12 He thwarts the plans*f* of the crafty,
so that their hands achieve no success.

ADVICE FROM JOB'S FRIENDS

Overwhelmed by suffering, Job was not comforted but condemned by his friends. Each of their views represents a well-known way to understand suffering. God proves that each explanation given by Job's friends has less than the whole answer.

Who They Were	Reference	How They Helped	Their Reasoning	Their Advice	Job's Response	God's Response
Eliphaz the Temanite	Job 4—5; 15; 22		Job is suffering because he has sinned.	Go to God and present your case to him. (5:8)	Take back your false accusations. (6:29)	God rebukes Job's friends. (42:7)
Bildad the Shuhite	Job 8; 18; 25	They sat in silence with Job for seven days. (2:11—13)	Job won't admit he sinned, so he's still suffering.	How long will you go on like this? (8:2)	I will say to God, . . . Tell me what charges you have against me. (10:2)	
Zophar the Naamathite	Job 11; 20		Job's sin deserves even more suffering than he's experienced.	Get rid of your sins. (11:13, 14)	I know that I will be justified. (13:18)	
Elihu the Buzite	Job 32—37	Confronted Job with the need to be content even though he didn't know why he was suffering	God is using suffering to mold and train Job.	Keep silent and I will teach you wisdom. (33:33)	No response	God does not directly address Elihu.
God	Job 38—41		Did not explain the reason for the pain	Do you still want to argue with the Almighty? (40:2)	I was talking about things I did not understand. (42:3–5)	

5:8 All three of Job's friends made the mistake of assuming that Job had committed some great sin that had caused his suffering. Neither they nor Job knew of Satan's conversation with God (1:6—2:8). It is human nature to blame people for their own troubles, but Job's story makes it clear that blame cannot always be attached to those whom trouble strikes.

13 He catches the wise in their craftiness,
   and the schemes of the wily are swept away.
14 Darkness comes upon them in the daytime;
   at noon they grope as in the night.
15 He saves the needy*g* from the sword in their mouth;
   he saves them from the clutches of the powerful.
16 So the poor have hope,
   and injustice shuts its mouth.*h*
17 "Blessed is the man whom God corrects;
   so do not despise the discipline*i* of the Almighty.*a**j*
18 For he wounds, but he also binds up;
   he injures, but his hands also heal.
19 From six calamities he will rescue you;
   in seven no harm will befall you.*k*
20 In famine*l* he will ransom you from death,
   and in battle from the stroke of the sword.
21 You will be protected from the lash of the tongue,*m*
   and need not fear when destruction comes.
22 You will laugh at destruction and famine,
   and need not fear the beasts of the earth.*n*
23 For you will have a covenant with the stones of the field,
   and the wild animals will be at peace with you.*o*
24 You will know that your tent is secure;
   you will take stock of your property and find nothing missing.
25 You will know that your children will be many,*p*
   and your descendants like the grass of the earth.*q*
26 You will come to the grave in full vigor,
   like sheaves gathered in season.

27 "We have examined this, and it is true.
   So hear it and apply it to yourself."

Job

 Then Job replied:

2 "If only my anguish could be weighed
   and all my misery be placed on the scales!*r*
3 It would surely outweigh the sand of the seas—
   no wonder my words have been impetuous.
4 The arrows*s* of the Almighty are in me,
   my spirit drinks*t* in their poison;
   God's terrors are marshaled against me.*u*
5 Does a wild donkey bray when it has grass,
   or an ox bellow when it has fodder?

a 17 Hebrew *Shaddai*; here and throughout Job

Cross-references

5:15 *g* Ps 35:10
5:16 *h* Ps 107:42
5:17 *i* Ps 94:12; *j* Heb 12:5-11
5:19 *k* Ps 34:19; 91:10
5:20 *l* Ps 33:19
5:21 *m* Ps 31:20
5:22 *n* Ps 91:13
5:23 *o* Isa 11:6-9
5:25 *p* Ps 112:2; *q* Ps 72:16
6:2 *r* Job 31:6
6:4 *s* Ps 38:2; *t* Job 21:20; *u* Ps 88:15-18

5:13 Paul later quoted part of this verse (1 Corinthians 3:19)—the only time Job is clearly quoted in the New Testament. Although God rebuked Eliphaz for being wrong in his advice to Job (42:7), not all he said was in error. The part Paul quoted was correct—people are often caught in their own traps ("in their craftiness"). This illustrates how Scripture must be used to explain and comment on itself. We must be familiar with the entire scope of God's Word to properly understand the difficult portions of it.

5:17 Eliphaz was correct—it is a blessing to be disciplined by God when we do wrong. Eliphaz's advice, however, did not apply to Job. As we know from the beginning of the book, Job's suffering was not a result of some great sin. We sometimes give people excellent advice only to learn that it does not apply to them and is therefore not very helpful. All who offer counsel from God's Word should take care to thoroughly understand a person's situation *before* giving advice.

5:17–26 Eliphaz's words in 5:17, 18 show a view of discipline that has been almost forgotten: pain can help us grow. These are good words to remember when we face hardship and loss. Because Job did not understand why he suffered, his faith in God had a chance to grow. On the other hand, we must not make Eliphaz's mistake. God does not eliminate all hardship when we are following him closely, and good behavior is not always rewarded by prosperity. Rewards for good and punishment for evil are in God's hands and given out according to his timetable. Satan's ploy is to get us to doubt God's love and faithfulness toward us.

6 Is tasteless food eaten without salt,
> or is there flavor in the white of an egg^a?
7 I refuse to touch it;
> such food makes me ill.

8 "Oh, that I might have my request,
> that God would grant what I hope for,
9 that God would be willing to crush me,
> to let loose his hand and cut me off!

6:10
^vJob 23:12

10 Then I would still have this consolation—
> my joy in unrelenting pain—
> that I had not denied the words^v of the Holy One.

11 "What strength do I have, that I should still hope?
> What prospects, that I should be patient?
12 Do I have the strength of stone?
> Is my flesh bronze?

6:13
^wJob 26:2

13 Do I have any power to help myself,^w
> now that success has been driven from me?

14 "A despairing man should have the devotion of his friends,
> even though he forsakes the fear of the Almighty.

6:15
^xPs 38:11;
Jer 15:18

15 But my brothers are as undependable as intermittent streams,^x
> as the streams that overflow
16 when darkened by thawing ice
> and swollen with melting snow,

6:17
^yJob 24:19

17 but that cease to flow in the dry season,
> and in the heat^y vanish from their channels.
18 Caravans turn aside from their routes;
> they go up into the wasteland and perish.

6:19
^zGe 25:15

19 The caravans of Tema^z look for water,
> the traveling merchants of Sheba look in hope.

6:20
^aJer 14:3

20 They are distressed, because they had been confident;
> they arrive there, only to be disappointed.^a

6:21
^bPs 38:11

21 Now you too have proved to be of no help;
> you see something dreadful and are afraid.^b
22 Have I ever said, 'Give something on my behalf,
> pay a ransom for me from your wealth,
23 deliver me from the hand of the enemy,
> ransom me from the clutches of the ruthless'?

24 "Teach me, and I will be quiet;
> show me where I have been wrong.
25 How painful are honest words!
> But what do your arguments prove?

6:26
^cJob 8:2

26 Do you mean to correct what I say,
> and treat the words of a despairing man as wind?^c

6:27
^dJoel 3:3

27 You would even cast lots^d for the fatherless
> and barter away your friend.

6:28
^eJob 27:4

28 "But now be so kind as to look at me.
> Would I lie to your face?^e

^a6 The meaning of the Hebrew for this phrase is uncertain.

6:6, 7 Job said that Eliphaz's advice was like eating the tasteless white of an egg. When people are going through severe trials, ill-advised counsel is distasteful. They may listen politely, but inside they are upset. Be slow to give advice to those who are hurting. They often need compassion more than they need advice.

6:8, 9 In his grief, Job wanted to give in, to be freed from his discomfort, and to die. But God did not grant Job's request. He had a greater plan for him. Our tendency, like Job's, is to want to give up and get out when the going gets rough. To trust God in the good times is commendable, but to trust him during the difficult times tests us to our limits and exercises our faith. In your struggles, large or small, trust that God is in control and that he will take care of you (Romans 8:28).

29 Relent, do not be unjust;
    reconsider, for my integrity is at stake.a
30 Is there any wickedness on my lips?
    Can my mouth not discernf malice?

7 "Does not man have hard serviceg on earth?
    Are not his days like those of a hired man?h
2 Like a slave longing for the evening shadows,
    or a hired man waiting eagerly for his wages,
3 so I have been allotted months of futility,
    and nights of misery have been assigned to me.
4 When I lie down I think, 'How long before I get up?'i
    The night drags on, and I toss till dawn.
5 My body is clothed with worms and scabs,
    my skin is broken and festering.

6 "My days are swifter than a weaver's shuttle,j
    and they come to an end without hope.k
7 Remember, O God, that my life is but a breath;l
    my eyes will never see happiness again.
8 The eye that now sees me will see me no longer;
    you will look for me, but I will be no more.m
9 As a cloud vanishes and is gone,
    so he who goes down to the graveb n does not return.o
10 He will never come to his house again;
    his place will know him no more.

11 "Therefore I will not keep silent;p
    I will speak out in the anguish of my spirit,
    I will complain in the bitterness of my soul.q
12 Am I the sea, or the monster of the deep,
    that you put me under guard?
13 When I think my bed will comfort me
    and my couch will ease my complaint,r
14 even then you frighten me with dreams
    and terrify me with visions,
15 so that I prefer strangling and death,
    rather than this body of mine.
16 I despise my life;s I would not live forever.
    Let me alone; my days have no meaning.

17 "What is man that you make so much of him,
    that you give him so much attention,t
18 that you examine him every morning
    and test him every moment?
19 Will you never look away from me,
    or let me alone even for an instant?

a29 Or my righteousness still stands   b9 Hebrew Sheol

6:30
f Job 12:11

7:1
g Job 14:14
h Job 14:6

7:4
i Dt 28:67

7:6
j Job 9:25
k Job 13:15

7:7
l Ps 78:39

7:8
m Job 20:7,9,21

7:9
n Job 11:8
o 2Sa 12:23

7:11
p Ps 40:9
q 1Sa 1:10

7:13
r Job 9:27

7:16
s Job 10:1

7:17
t Ps 8:4; 144:3;
Heb 2:6

6:29, 30 Job referred to his own integrity, not because he was sinless, but because he had a right relationship with God. He was not guilty of the sins his friends accused him of (see chapter 31 for his summary of the life he had led). Another rendering of verse 29 could read, "My righteousness still stands." Job was not claiming to be sinless. No one but Jesus Christ has ever been sinless—free from all wrong thoughts and actions. Even Job needed to make some changes in his attitude toward God, as we will see by the end of the book. Nevertheless, Job was righteous (1:8). He carefully obeyed God to the best of his ability in all aspects of his life.

7:11 Job felt deep anguish and bitterness, and he spoke honestly to God about his feelings to let out his frustrations.

If we express our feelings to God, we can deal with them without exploding in harsh words and actions, possibly hurting ourselves and others. The next time strong emotions threaten to overwhelm you, express them openly to God in prayer. This will help you gain an eternal perspective on the situation and give you greater ability to deal with it constructively.

7:12 Job stopped talking to Eliphaz and spoke directly to God. Although Job had lived a blameless life, he was beginning to doubt the value of living in such a way. By doing this, he was coming dangerously close to suggesting that God didn't care about him and was not being fair. Later God reproved Job for this attitude (38:2). Satan always exploits these thoughts to get us to forsake God. Our suffering, like Job's, may not be the result of our sin, but we must be careful not to sin as a result of our suffering.

7:20
u Job 35:6

20 If I have sinned, what have I done to you,u
  O watcher of men?
  Why have you made me your target?
  Have I become a burden to you?a

7:21
v Job 10:14

21 Why do you not pardon my offenses
    and forgive my sins?v
  For I will soon lie down in the dust;
    you will search for me, but I will be no more."

Bildad

8 Then Bildad the Shuhite replied:

2 "How long will you say such things?
    Your words are a blustering wind.

8:3
w Ro 3:5
x Ge 18:25

3 Does God pervert justice?w
    Does the Almighty pervert what is right?x

8:4
y Job 1:19

4 When your children sinned against him,
    he gave them over to the penalty of their sin.y

5 But if you will look to God
    and plead with the Almighty,

6 if you are pure and upright,
    even now he will rouse himself on your behalf
    and restore you to your rightful place.

7 Your beginnings will seem humble,
    so prosperous will your future be.

8:8
z Dt 4:32; 32:7

8 "Ask the former generationsz
    and find out what their fathers learned,

8:9
a Ge 47:9
b 1Ch 29:15

9 for we were born only yesterday and know nothing,a
    and our days on earth are but a shadow.b

10 Will they not instruct you and tell you?
    Will they not bring forth words from their understanding?

11 Can papyrus grow tall where there is no marsh?
    Can reeds thrive without water?

12 While still growing and uncut,
    they wither more quickly than grass.

8:13
c Job 11:20

13 Such is the destiny of all who forget God;
    so perishes the hope of the godless.c

8:14
d Isa 59:5

14 What he trusts in is fragileb;
    what he relies on is a spider's web.d

8:15
e Job 27:18

15 He leans on his web,e but it gives way;
    he clings to it, but it does not hold.

8:16
f Ps 80:11
g Ps 37:35

16 He is like a well-watered plant in the sunshine,
    spreading its shootsf over the garden;g

17 it entwines its roots around a pile of rocks
    and looks for a place among the stones.

a 20 A few manuscripts of the Masoretic Text, an ancient Hebrew scribal tradition and Septuagint; most manuscripts of the Masoretic Text *I have become a burden to myself.*   b 14 The meaning of the Hebrew for this word is uncertain.

7:20 Job referred to God as a watcher or observer of humanity. He was expressing his feeling that God seemed like an enemy to him—someone who mercilessly watched him squirm in his misery. We know that God does watch over everything that happens to us. We must never forget that he sees us with compassion, not merely with critical scrutiny. His eyes are eyes of love.

8:1ff Bildad was upset that Job still claimed innocence while questioning God's justice. The basis of Bildad's argument (the justice of God) was correct, but his idea of God's justice was not. Bildad's argument went like this: God could not be unjust, and God would not punish a just man; therefore Job must be unjust. Bildad felt there were no exceptions to his theory. Like Eliphaz, Bildad wrongly assumed that people suffer only as a result of their sins.

Bildad was even less sensitive and compassionate, saying that Job's children died because of *their* wickedness. (For more information about Bildad, see the chart in chapter 28, p. 801.)

8:14, 15 Bildad wrongly assumed that Job was trusting in something other than God for security, so he pointed out that such supports will collapse ("what he trusts in is fragile"). One of people's basic needs is security, and many will do almost anything to feel secure. Eventually, however, our money, possessions, knowledge, and relationships will fail or be gone. Only God can give lasting security. What have you trusted for your security? How lasting is it? If you have a secure foundation with God, feelings of insecurity will not undermine you.

18 But when it is torn from its spot,
    that place disowns it and says, 'I never saw you.'
19 Surely its life withers away,
    and[a] from the soil other plants grow.

20 "Surely God does not reject a blameless man
    or strengthen the hands of evildoers.
21 He will yet fill your mouth with laughter
    and your lips with shouts of joy.[h]
22 Your enemies will be clothed in shame,[i]
    and the tents of the wicked will be no more."

8:21
[h] Ps 126:2

8:22
[i] Ps 35:26; 109:29

Job

9 Then Job replied:

2 "Indeed, I know that this is true.
    But how can a mortal be righteous before God?[j]
3 Though one wished to dispute with him,
    he could not answer him one time out of a thousand.
4 His wisdom is profound, his power is vast.
    Who has resisted him and come out unscathed?[k]
5 He moves mountains without their knowing it
    and overturns them in his anger.
6 He shakes the earth[l] from its place
    and makes its pillars tremble.
7 He speaks to the sun and it does not shine;
    he seals off the light of the stars.
8 He alone stretches out the heavens
    and treads on the waves of the sea.
9 He is the Maker of the Bear and Orion,
    the Pleiades and the constellations of the south.[m]
10 He performs wonders that cannot be fathomed,
    miracles that cannot be counted.
11 When he passes me, I cannot see him;
    when he goes by, I cannot perceive him.[n]
12 If he snatches away, who can stop him?[o]
    Who can say to him, 'What are you doing?'[p]
13 God does not restrain his anger;
    even the cohorts of Rahab[q] cowered at his feet.

14 "How then can I dispute with him?
    How can I find words to argue with him?
15 Though I were innocent, I could not answer him;[r]
    I could only plead[s] with my Judge for mercy.
16 Even if I summoned him and he responded,
    I do not believe he would give me a hearing.
17 He would crush me[t] with a storm
    and multiply[u] my wounds for no reason.[v]
18 He would not let me regain my breath
    but would overwhelm me with misery.

9:2
[j] Ro 3:20

9:4
[k] 2Ch 13:12

9:6
[l] Isa 2:21;
Heb 12:26

9:9
[m] Ge 1:16

9:11
[n] Job 23:8-9; 35:14

9:12
[o] Job 11:10
[p] Isa 45:9; Ro 9:20

9:13
[q] Job 26:12;
Isa 30:7

9:15
[r] Job 10:15
[s] Job 8:5

9:17
[t] Job 16:12
[u] Job 16:14
[v] Job 2:3

[a] 19 Or Surely all the joy it has / is that

9:1ff Bildad said nothing new to Job. Job knew that the wicked ultimately perish, but his situation confused him. Why, then, was he perishing? Job didn't think his life warranted such suffering, so he wanted his case presented before God (9:32–35). He recognized, however, that arguing with God would be futile and unpro-

ductive (9:4). Job didn't claim to be perfect (7:20, 21; 9:20), but he did claim to be good and faithful (6:29, 30). While Job showed impatience toward God, he did not reject or curse God.

9:9 The Bear, Orion, and Pleiades are constellations of stars.

9:13 Rahab is the name of a legendary sea monster. According to a Babylonian creation myth, Marduk defeated Tiamat (another name for Rahab), then captured her helpers. Job's friends would have known this myth and understood Job's meaning. God is sovereign over all the forces.

¹⁹ If it is a matter of strength, he is mighty!
    And if it is a matter of justice, who will summon him^a?
²⁰ Even if I were innocent, my mouth would condemn me;
    if I were blameless, it would pronounce me guilty.

^a19 See Septuagint; Hebrew *me*.

ELIPHAZ, BILDAD, ZOPHAR

Few people in history have experienced the kind of tragedy that crushed Job. He lost everything. His children were killed, his possessions and wealth were taken, his wife turned her back on him, and his health was broken—all in a matter of days.

Upon learning of Job's difficulties, some of his friends came to help. Eliphaz, Bildad, and Zophar were shocked when they found Job. They wept for him. They tore their clothes and put dust on their heads in acts of sorrow. Then they sat in silence with Job for seven days.

Why did his friends remain silent for so long? One ancient Jewish tradition teaches that people who come to comfort someone in mourning should not speak until the mourner speaks. That is a wise tradition, for often the best response to another person's suffering is to say nothing.

If Job's losses were his first test and his painful boils his second, then his friends provided a third and perhaps most frustrating test. When Job finally vented his grief, each of the friends took turns attempting to explain Job's agony. They heard Job's questions as arrogant claims of not deserving such suffering rather than expressions of deep grief and misunderstanding. They offered answers that only served to make Job's pain go deeper. Eliphaz appealed to personal experience; Bildad pointed to universal wisdom; and Zophar declared what he felt was common sense. They all agreed that Job's problems were his own doing and that questioning God simply made matters worse.

The harder Eliphaz, Bildad, and Zophar tried to explain Job's suffering, the less they helped. Consolation turned to condemnation as the grief-stricken Job rejected their reasoning and demanded a hearing with God. When God finally did speak, he never answered Job's questions. He simply challenged Job to trust, even beyond understanding.

Friendship in grief requires patience. Friends in need don't have to have all their questions answered as much as they need to have someone listen. Some questions are so deep that their best response is silence. Make it a point to be with those in pain, but let your physical presence be your strongest statement of support. Pray for patience. When in doubt about a question, wait. Sit quietly and be the best friend you can be during difficult times.

Strengths and accomplishments:	• Understood the importance of personal contact in sharing grief • Approached Job with silence rather than immediate conversation • Demonstrated a fine understanding of God's justice, but gross ignorance about God's grace
Weaknesses and mistakes:	• Assumed that tragedy and suffering inevitably represent some kind of punishment for sin • Decided to try to explain Job's suffering rather than help him endure it • Heard Job's questions as challenges rather than expressions of grief • Took offense and became abusive when Job did not agree with their assessments or answers
Lessons from their lives:	• Those who wish to comfort people in sorrow should consider silence before speech, empathy before explanations, and patience with their pain • Even the hardest questions that come out of grief do not require instant answers • Genuine friendship includes attentive, compassionate presence in times of sorrow and loss
Vital statistics:	• Where: Uz • Contemporaries: Job, Elihu
Key verse:	"When Job's three friends, Eliphaz the Temanite, Bildad the Shuhite and Zophar the Naamathite, heard about all the troubles that had come upon him, they set out from their homes and met together by agreement to go and sympathize with him and comfort him" (Job 2:11).

Job's interaction with his three friends is found in the book of Job.

9:20, 21 "Even if I were innocent, my mouth would condemn me." Job was saying, "In spite of my good life, God is determined to condemn me." As his suffering continued, he became more impatient. Although Job remained loyal to God, he made statements he would later regret. In times of extended sickness or prolonged pain, it is natural for people to doubt, to despair, or to become impatient. During those times, people need someone to listen to them, to help them work through their feelings and frustrations. Your patience with their impatience will help them.

21 "Although I am blameless,
    I have no concern for myself;
    I despise my own life.w

22 It is all the same; that is why I say,
    'He destroys both the blameless and the wicked.'x

23 When a scourge brings sudden death,
    he mocks the despair of the innocent.

24 When a land falls into the hands of the wicked,y
    he blindfolds its judges.z
    If it is not he, then who is it?

25 "My days are swifter than a runner;a
    they fly away without a glimpse of joy.

26 They skim past like boats of papyrus,
    like eagles swooping down on their prey.b

27 If I say, 'I will forget my complaint,
    I will change my expression, and smile,'

28 I still dread all my sufferings,
    for I know you will not hold me innocent.c

29 Since I am already found guilty,
    why should I struggle in vain?

30 Even if I washed myself with soapa
    and my hands with washing soda,d

31 you would plunge me into a slime pit
    so that even my clothes would detest me.

32 "He is not a man like me that I might answer him,e
    that we might confront each other in court.f

33 If only there were someone to arbitrate between us,g
    to lay his hand upon us both,

34 someone to remove God's rod from me,h
    so that his terror would frighten me no more.

35 Then I would speak up without fear of him,
    but as it now stands with me, I cannot.

10 "I loathe my very life;i
    therefore I will give free rein to my complaint
    and speak out in the bitterness of my soul.j

2 I will say to God: Do not condemn me,
    but tell me what charges you have against me.

3 Does it please you to oppress me,
    to spurn the work of your hands,
    while you smile on the schemes of the wicked?

4 Do you have eyes of flesh?
    Do you see as a mortal sees?k

5 Are your days like those of a mortal
    or your years like those of a man,

6 that you must search out my faults
    and probe after my sin—

7 though you know that I am not guilty
    and that no one can rescue me from your hand?

8 "Your hands shaped me and made me.
    Will you now turn and destroy me?

a 30 Or snow

9:21
w Job 7:16

9:22
x Ecc 9:2,3;
Eze 21:3

9:24
y Job 10:3
z Job 12:6

9:25
a Job 7:6

9:26
b Hab 1:8

9:28
c Job 7:21

9:30
d Jer 2:22

9:32
e Ro 9:20
f Ecc 6:10

9:33
g 1Sa 2:25

9:34
h Ps 39:10

10:1
i 1Ki 19:4
j Job 7:11

10:4
k 1Sa 16:7

10:1 Job began to wallow in self-pity. When we face baffling affliction, our pain lures us toward feeling sorry for ourselves. At this point we are only one step from self-righteousness, where we keep track of life's injustices and say, "Look what happened to me; how unfair it is!" We may feel like blaming God. Remember that life's trials, whether allowed by God or sent by God, can be the means for development and refinement. When facing trials, ask, "What can I learn and how can I grow?" rather than "Who did this to me and how can I get out of it?"

10:9
l Ge 2:7

9 Remember that you molded me like clay.
  Will you now turn me to dust again?*l*
10 Did you not pour me out like milk
  and curdle me like cheese,
11 clothe me with skin and flesh
  and knit me together with bones and sinews?
12 You gave me life and showed me kindness,
  and in your providence watched over my spirit.

13 "But this is what you concealed in your heart,
  and I know that this was in your mind:
14 If I sinned, you would be watching me
  and would not let my offense go unpunished.

10:15
m Job 9:13

15 If I am guilty—woe to me!*m*
  Even if I am innocent, I cannot lift my head,
for I am full of shame
  and drowned in*a* my affliction.

10:16
n Isa 38:13;
La 3:10

16 If I hold my head high, you stalk me like a lion*n*
  and again display your awesome power against me.

10:17
o Job 16:8
p Ru 1:21

17 You bring new witnesses against me*o*
  and increase your anger toward me;*p*
  your forces come against me wave upon wave.

10:18
q Job 3:11

18 "Why then did you bring me out of the womb?*q*
  I wish I had died before any eye saw me.
19 If only I had never come into being,
  or had been carried straight from the womb to the grave!

10:20
r Job 7:16

20 Are not my few days almost over?
  Turn away from me*r* so I can have a moment's joy
21 before I go to the place of no return,
  to the land of gloom and deep shadow,*b*
22 to the land of deepest night,
  of deep shadow and disorder,
  where even the light is like darkness."

Zophar

11 Then Zophar the Naamathite replied:

11:2
s Job 8:2

2 "Are all these words to go unanswered?*s*
  Is this talker to be vindicated?

11:3
t Job 17:2; 21:3

3 Will your idle talk reduce men to silence?
  Will no one rebuke you when you mock?*t*

11:4
u Job 10:7

4 You say to God, 'My beliefs are flawless
  and I am pure*u* in your sight.'
5 Oh, how I wish that God would speak,
  that he would open his lips against you

11:6
v Ezr 9:13

6 and disclose to you the secrets of wisdom,
  for true wisdom has two sides.
  Know this: God has even forgotten some of your sin.*v*

a 15 Or *and aware of*   *b* 21 Or *and the shadow of death*; also in verse 22

10:13, 14 In frustration, Job jumped to the false conclusion that God was out to get him. Wrong assumptions lead to wrong conclusions. We dare not take our limited experiences and jump to conclusions about life in general. If you find yourself doubting God, remember that you don't have all the facts. God wants only the very best for your life. Many people endure great pain, but ultimately they find some greater good came from it. When you're struggling, don't assume the worst.

10:20–22 Job was expressing the view of death common in Old Testament times, that the dead went to a joyless, dark place. There was no punishment or reward there, and no escape from it. (See the note on 19:26 for a broader picture of Job's view of death.)

11:1ff Zophar is the third of Job's friends to speak, and the least courteous. Full of anger, he lashed out at Job, saying that Job deserved more punishment, not less. Zophar took the same position as Eliphaz (chapters 4, 5) and Bildad (chapter 8)—that Job was suffering because of sin—but his speech was by far the most arrogant. Zophar was the kind of person who has an answer for everything; he was totally insensitive to Job's unique situation. (For more on Zophar, see the chart in chapter 28, p. 801.)

7 "Can you fathom *w* the mysteries of God?
   Can you probe the limits of the Almighty?
8 They are higher than the heavens—what can you do?
   They are deeper than the depths of the grave*a*—what can you know?
9 Their measure is longer than the earth
   and wider than the sea.

10 "If he comes along and confines you in prison
   and convenes a court, who can oppose him?*x*
11 Surely he recognizes deceitful men;
   and when he sees evil, does he not take note?*y*
12 But a witless man can no more become wise
   than a wild donkey's colt can be born a man.*b*

13 "Yet if you devote your heart*z* to him
   and stretch out your hands to him,*a*
14 if you put away the sin that is in your hand
   and allow no evil*b* to dwell in your tent,*c*
15 then you will lift up your face without shame;
   you will stand firm and without fear.
16 You will surely forget your trouble,*d*
   recalling it only as waters gone by.
17 Life will be brighter than noonday,*e*
   and darkness will become like morning.
18 You will be secure, because there is hope;
   you will look about you and take your rest*f* in safety.*g*
19 You will lie down, with no one to make you afraid,
   and many will court your favor.
20 But the eyes of the wicked will fail,*h*
   and escape will elude them;
   their hope will become a dying gasp."

Job

12 Then Job replied:

2 "Doubtless you are the people,
   and wisdom will die with you!
3 But I have a mind as well as you;
   I am not inferior to you.
   Who does not know all these things?*i*

4 "I have become a laughingstock to my friends,
   though I called upon God and he answered*j*—
   a mere laughingstock, though righteous and blameless!*k*
5 Men at ease have contempt for misfortune
   as the fate of those whose feet are slipping.
6 The tents of marauders are undisturbed,
   and those who provoke God are secure*l*—
   those who carry their god in their hands.*c*

7 "But ask the animals, and they will teach you,
   or the birds of the air, and they will tell you;

a8 Hebrew *than Sheol*   *b12* Or *wild donkey can be born tame*   *c6* Or *secure / in what God's hand brings them*

11:7
*w*Ecc 3:11

11:10
*x*Job 9:12; Rev 3:7

11:11
*y*Ps 10:14

11:13
*z*1Sa 7:3; Ps 78:8
*a*Ps 88:9

11:14
*b*Ps 101:4
*c*Job 22:23

11:16
*d*Isa 65:16

11:17
*e*Ps 37:6;
Isa 58:8,10

11:18
*f*Ps 3:5
*g*Lev 26:6; Pr 3:24

11:20
*h*Dt 28:65

12:3
*i*Job 13:2

12:4
*j*Ps 91:15
*k*Job 6:29

12:6
*l*Job 9:24

11:11 By calling Job "deceitful," Zophar was accusing Job of hiding secret faults and sins. Although Zophar's assumption was wrong, he explained quite accurately that God knows and sees everything. We are often tempted by the thought, "No one will ever know!" Perhaps we can hide some sin from others, but we can do *nothing* without God knowing about it. Because our very thoughts are known to God, of course he will notice our sins. Job understood this as well as Zophar did, but it didn't apply to his current dilemma.

12:1ff Job answered Zophar's argument with great sarcasm: "Wisdom will die with you." He went on to say that his three friends didn't need to explain God to him—they were saying nothing he didn't already know (12:7–9; 13:1, 2). Job continued to maintain that his friends had completely misunderstood the reason for his suffering. Job did not know it either, but he was certain that his friends' reasons were both narrow-minded and incorrect. Once again Job appealed to God to give him an answer (13:3).

12:10
m Ac 17:28

12:11
n Job 34:3

12:12
o Job 32:7,9

12:13
p Job 9:4

12:14
q Job 19:10

12:15
r 1Ki 8:35
s Ge 7:11

12:16
t Job 13:7,9

12:18
u Ps 116:16

12:20
v Job 32:9

12:22
w 1Co 4:5
x Da 2:22

12:23
y Ps 107:38; Isa 9:3

12:25
z Job 5:14

13:2
a Job 12:3

13:3
b Job 23:3-4

13:4
c Ps 119:69;
Jer 23:32

13:5
d Pr 17:28

8 or speak to the earth, and it will teach you,
  or let the fish of the sea inform you.
9 Which of all these does not know
  that the hand of the Lord has done this?
10 In his hand is the life of every creature
  and the breath of all mankind. m
11 Does not the ear test words
  as the tongue tastes food? n
12 Is not wisdom found among the aged?
  Does not long life bring understanding? o

13 "To God belong wisdom and power; p
  counsel and understanding are his.
14 What he tears down q cannot be rebuilt;
  the man he imprisons cannot be released.
15 If he holds back the waters, r there is drought;
  if he lets them loose, they devastate the land. s
16 To him belong strength and victory;
  both deceived and deceiver are his. t
17 He leads counselors away stripped
  and makes fools of judges.
18 He takes off the shackles u put on by kings
  and ties a loincloth a around their waist.
19 He leads priests away stripped
  and overthrows men long established.
20 He silences the lips of trusted advisers
  and takes away the discernment of elders. v
21 He pours contempt on nobles
  and disarms the mighty.
22 He reveals the deep things of darkness w
  and brings deep shadows into the light. x
23 He makes nations great, and destroys them;
  he enlarges nations, y and disperses them.
24 He deprives the leaders of the earth of their reason;
  he sends them wandering through a trackless waste.
25 They grope in darkness with no light; z
  he makes them stagger like drunkards.

13

  "My eyes have seen all this,
  my ears have heard and understood it.
2 What you know, I also know;
  I am not inferior to you. a
3 But I desire to speak to the Almighty
  and to argue my case with God. b
4 You, however, smear me with lies; c
  you are worthless physicians, all of you!
5 If only you would be altogether silent!
  For you, that would be wisdom. d
6 Hear now my argument;
  listen to the plea of my lips.

a 18 Or *shackles of kings / and ties a belt*

12:24, 25 Job affirmed that no leader has any real wisdom apart from God. No research or report can outweigh God's opinion. No scientific discovery or medical advance takes him by surprise. When we look for guidance for our decisions, we must recognize that God's wisdom is superior to any the world has to offer. Don't let earthly advisers dampen your desire to know God better.

13:4 Job compared his three friends to physicians who did not know what they were doing. They were like eye surgeons trying to perform open-heart surgery. Many of their ideas about God were

true, but they did not apply to Job's situation. They were right to say that God is just. They were right to say God punishes sin. But they were wrong to assume that Job's suffering was a just punishment for his sin. They took a true principle and applied it wrongly, ignoring the vast differences in human circumstances. We must be careful and compassionate in how we apply Biblical condemnations to others; we must be slow to judge.

7 Will you speak wickedly on God's behalf?
    Will you speak deceitfully for him?
8 Will you show him partiality?
    Will you argue the case for God?
9 Would it turn out well if he examined you?
    Could you deceive him as you might deceive men?
10 He would surely rebuke you
    if you secretly showed partiality.
11 Would not his splendor *e* terrify you?   **13:11**
    Would not the dread of him fall on you?   *e* Job 31:23
12 Your maxims are proverbs of ashes;
    your defenses are defenses of clay.

13 "Keep silent and let me speak;
    then let come to me what may.
14 Why do I put myself in jeopardy
    and take my life in my hands?
15 Though he slay me, yet will I hope in him;*f*   **13:15**
    I will surely*a* defend my ways to his face.*g*   *f* Ps 23:4; Pr 14:32
16 Indeed, this will turn out for my deliverance,   *g* Job 27:5
    for no godless man would dare come before him!
17 Listen carefully to my words;
    let your ears take in what I say.
18 Now that I have prepared my case,*h*   **13:18**
    I know I will be vindicated.   *h* Job 23:4
19 Can anyone bring charges against me?*i*   **13:19**
    If so, I will be silent and die.   *i* Isa 50:8

20 "Only grant me these two things, O God,
    and then I will not hide from you:
21 Withdraw your hand far from me,
    and stop frightening me with your terrors.
22 Then summon me and I will answer,*j*   **13:22**
    or let me speak, and you reply.   *j* Job 14:15
23 How many wrongs and sins have I committed?
    Show me my offense and my sin.
24 Why do you hide your face*k*   **13:24**
    and consider me your enemy?*l*   *k* Dt 32:20
                           l Job 19:11; La 2:5
25 Will you torment a windblown leaf?   **13:25**
    Will you chase after dry chaff?*m*   *m* Isa 42:3
26 For you write down bitter things against me **13:26**
    and make me inherit the sins of my youth.*n* *n* Ps 25:7
27 You fasten my feet in shackles;*o*   **13:27**
    you keep close watch on all my paths   *o* Job 33:11
    by putting marks on the soles of my feet.

28 "So man wastes away like something rotten,
    like a garment eaten by moths.

14   "Man born of woman   **14:1**
     is of few days and full of trouble.*p* *p* Ecc 2:23
2 He springs up like a flower and withers away;*q* **14:2**
    like a fleeting shadow,*r* he does not endure. *q* Ps 90:5-6
                               r Job 8:9

a 15 Or He will surely slay me; I have no hope — / yet I will

---

14:1ff Life is brief and full of trouble, Job laments in his closing remarks to this first round of conversation. Sickness, loneliness, disappointment, and death cause Job to say that life is not fair. Some understand verses 14 and 15 to mean that, even in his gloom, Job hoped for the resurrection of the dead. If this is true, then Job understood the one truth that could put his suffering in perspective. God's solution to believers who live in an unfair world is to guarantee life with him forever. No matter how unfair your present world seems, God offers the hope of being in his presence eternally. Have you accepted this offer?

14:3
sPs 144:3

14:4
tPs 51:10
uEph 2:1-3
vJn 3:6; Ro 5:12

14:6
wJob 7:19

14:12
xRev 20:11; 21:1
yAc 3:21

14:15
zJob 13:22

14:16
aPr 5:21; Jer 32:19
bJob 10:6

14:17
cDt 32:34

14:21
dEcc 9:5; Isa 63:16

3 Do you fix your eye on such a one?s
    Will you bring hima before you for judgment?
4 Who can bring what is puret from the impure?u
    No one!v
5 Man's days are determined;
    you have decreed the number of his months
    and have set limits he cannot exceed.
6 So look away from him and let him alone,w
    till he has put in his time like a hired man.

7 "At least there is hope for a tree:
    If it is cut down, it will sprout again,
    and its new shoots will not fail.
8 Its roots may grow old in the ground
    and its stump die in the soil,
9 yet at the scent of water it will bud
    and put forth shoots like a plant.
10 But man dies and is laid low;
    he breathes his last and is no more.
11 As water disappears from the sea
    or a riverbed becomes parched and dry,
12 so man lies down and does not rise;
    till the heavens are no more,x men will not awake
    or be roused from their sleep.y

13 "If only you would hide me in the graveb
    and conceal me till your anger has passed!
    If only you would set me a time
    and then remember me!
14 If a man dies, will he live again?
    All the days of my hard service
    I will wait for my renewalc to come.
15 You will call and I will answer you;z
    you will long for the creature your hands have made.
16 Surely then you will count my stepsa
    but not keep track of my sin.b
17 My offenses will be sealed up in a bag;c
    you will cover over my sin.

18 "But as a mountain erodes and crumbles
    and as a rock is moved from its place,
19 as water wears away stones
    and torrents wash away the soil,
    so you destroy man's hope.
20 You overpower him once for all, and he is gone;
    you change his countenance and send him away.
21 If his sons are honored, he does not know it;
    if they are brought low, he does not see it.d
22 He feels but the pain of his own body
    and mourns only for himself."

a3 Septuagint, Vulgate and Syriac; Hebrew me   b13 Hebrew Sheol   c14 Or release

---

14:7–22 The Old Testament does not say much about the resurrection of the dead. This is not surprising because Jesus had not yet conquered death. Job's pessimism about death is understandable. What is remarkable is his budding hope (14:14). If only God would hide him with the dead and then bring him out again! If only he could die and live again! When we must endure suffering, we have an advantage over Job. We *know* that the dead will rise. Christ arose, and we have hope based on Christ's promise in John 14:19.

14:22 Job's profound speech in this chapter illustrates a great truth: to have a right set of doctrines is not enough. To know what to believe is not all that is required to please God. Truth untested by life's experiences may become static and stagnant. Suffering can bring a dynamic quality to life. Just as drought drives the roots of a tree deeper to find water, so suffering can drive us beyond superficial acceptance of truth to dependence on God for hope and life.

2. Second round of discussion
Eliphaz

15 Then Eliphaz the Temanite replied:

2 "Would a wise man answer with empty notions
    or fill his belly with the hot east wind?
3 Would he argue with useless words,
    with speeches that have no value?
4 But you even undermine piety
    and hinder devotion to God.
5 Your sin prompts your mouth;
    you adopt the tongue of the crafty.
6 Your own mouth condemns you, not mine;
    your own lips testify against you.*e*

7 "Are you the first man ever born?*f*
    Were you brought forth before the hills?*g*
8 Do you listen in on God's council?*h*
    Do you limit wisdom to yourself?
9 What do you know that we do not know?
    What insights do you have that we do not have?*i*
10 The gray-haired and the aged*j* are on our side,
    men even older than your father.
11 Are God's consolations not enough for you,
    words spoken gently to you?
12 Why has your heart carried you away,
    and why do your eyes flash,
13 so that you vent your rage against God
    and pour out such words from your mouth?

14 "What is man, that he could be pure,
    or one born of woman,*k* that he could be righteous?*l*
15 If God places no trust in his holy ones,
    if even the heavens are not pure in his eyes,*m*
16 how much less man, who is vile and corrupt,*n*
    who drinks up evil like water!*o*

17 "Listen to me and I will explain to you;
    let me tell you what I have seen,
18 what wise men have declared,
    hiding nothing received from their fathers*p*
19 (to whom alone the land was given
    when no alien passed among them):
20 All his days the wicked man suffers torment,
    the ruthless through all the years stored up for him.
21 Terrifying sounds fill his ears;
    when all seems well, marauders attack him.*q*
22 He despairs of escaping the darkness;
    he is marked for the sword.
23 He wanders about*r*—food for vultures*a*;
    he knows the day of darkness is at hand.*s*
24 Distress and anguish fill him with terror;
    they overwhelm him, like a king poised to attack,

15:6
e Lk 19:22

15:7
f Job 38:21
g Ps 90:2; Pr 8:25

15:8
h Ro 11:34

15:9
i Job 13:2

15:10
j Job 32:6-7

15:14
k Job 14:4
l Pr 20:9; Ecc 7:20

15:15
m Job 25:5

15:16
n Ps 14:1
o Job 34:7; Pr 19:28

15:18
p Job 8:8

15:21
q 1Th 5:3

15:23
r Ps 109:10
s Job 18:12

---

*a*23 Or *about, looking for food*

15:1ff With the first round of talks concluded, each friend, in the same order, pressed the argument further. Again Job answered each argument (chapters 15—31). This time Eliphaz was more rude, more intense, and more threatening, but he said nothing new. (See his first speech in chapters 4, 5.) He began by saying that Job's words were empty and useless; then he restated his opinion that Job must be a great sinner. According to Eliphaz, the experience and wisdom of their ancestors were more valuable than Job's individual thoughts. Eliphaz assumed that his words were as true as God's. It is easy to spot his arrogance.

15:15, 16 "Even the heavens are not pure in his eyes." Eliphaz was repeating his argument that anything created, whether angels

15:25
*t*Job 36:9

25 because he shakes his fist at God
      and vaunts himself against the Almighty,*t*
26 defiantly charging against him
      with a thick, strong shield.

27 "Though his face is covered with fat
      and his waist bulges with flesh,
28 he will inhabit ruined towns
      and houses where no one lives,
      houses crumbling to rubble.
29 He will no longer be rich and his wealth will not endure,
      nor will his possessions spread over the land.

15:30
*u*Job 22:20

30 He will not escape the darkness;
      a flame*u* will wither his shoots,
      and the breath of God's mouth will carry him away.

15:31
*v*Isa 59:4

31 Let him not deceive himself by trusting what is worthless,*v*
      for he will get nothing in return.

15:32
*w*Job 22:16;
Ps 55:23

32 Before his time he will be paid in full,*w*
      and his branches will not flourish.
33 He will be like a vine stripped of its unripe grapes,
      like an olive tree shedding its blossoms.
34 For the company of the godless will be barren,
      and fire will consume the tents of those who love bribes.

15:35
*x*Ps 7:14; Isa 59:4

35 They conceive trouble and give birth to evil;*x*
      their womb fashions deceit."

Job

16

Then Job replied:

2 "I have heard many things like these;
      miserable comforters are you all!

BIBLE "WAITERS"
In the Bible we find many people who had to "wait on the Lord," just as believers today must patiently wait for Christ's return. We can learn a lesson in patience from these Bible waiters.

Noah waited for God's timing before leaving the ark	Genesis 8:10, 12
Moses waited on God on the mountain	Exodus 24:12
Job waited for God's answers	Job 14:14
Isaiah waited for God to work in Israel	Isaiah 8:17; 25:9; 26:8; 30:18; 33:2; 40:31; 49:23; 59:9, 11; 64:4
Jeremiah understood the need to wait quietly for God's salvation	Lamentations 3:25
Hosea warned the people to return to God and wait for him to work	Hosea 12:6
Micah waited for the God of his salvation	Micah 7:7
Habakkuk warned the people to hold on to their hope and to wait because it would surely come	Habakkuk 2:3
Zephaniah explained that the Lord wanted his people to wait for him	Zephaniah 3:8
Joseph of Arimathea was waiting for God's kingdom	Luke 23:51
The disciples were ordered by Jesus to wait in Jerusalem for the coming of the Holy Spirit	Acts 1:4
Believers are called to wait for heaven, for the promise is sure	Romans 8:23, 25; Galatians 5:5; 1 Thessalonians 1:10; Titus 2:13; 2 Peter 3:12–14

(holy ones) or man, is not a sufficient basis for trust and hope. Only in God can we be sure. (See the note on 4:18, 19.)

16:1ff Job's friends were supposed to be comforting him in his grief. Instead they condemned him for causing his own suffering. Job began his reply to Eliphaz by calling him and his friends "miserable comforters." Job's words reveal several ways to become a better comforter to those in pain: (1) don't talk just for

the sake of talking; (2) don't sermonize by giving pat answers; (3) don't accuse or criticize; (4) put yourself in the other person's place; and (5) offer help and encouragement. Try Job's suggestions, knowing that they are given by a person who needed great comfort. The best comforters are those who know something about personal suffering.

3 Will your long-winded speeches never end?
    What ails you that you keep on arguing?[y]
4 I also could speak like you,
    if you were in my place;
  I could make fine speeches against you
    and shake my head[z] at you.
5 But my mouth would encourage you;
    comfort from my lips would bring you relief.

6 "Yet if I speak, my pain is not relieved;
    and if I refrain, it does not go away.
7 Surely, O God, you have worn me out;[a]
    you have devastated my entire household.
8 You have bound me—and it has become a witness;
    my gauntness[b] rises up and testifies against me.[c]
9 God assails me and tears me in his anger
    and gnashes his teeth at me;[d]
    my opponent fastens on me his piercing eyes.[e]
10 Men open their mouths[f] to jeer at me;
    they strike my cheek[g] in scorn
    and unite together against me.
11 God has turned me over to evil men
    and thrown me into the clutches of the wicked.
12 All was well with me, but he shattered me;
    he seized me by the neck and crushed me.[h]
  He has made me his target;
13   his archers surround me.
  Without pity, he pierces[i] my kidneys
    and spills my gall on the ground.
14 Again and again he bursts upon me;
    he rushes at me like a warrior.[j]

15 "I have sewed sackcloth[k] over my skin
    and buried my brow in the dust.
16 My face is red with weeping,
    deep shadows ring my eyes;
17 yet my hands have been free of violence
    and my prayer is pure.

18 "O earth, do not cover my blood;
    may my cry never be laid to rest![l]
19 Even now my witness[m] is in heaven;
    my advocate is on high.
20 My intercessor is my friend[a]
    as my eyes pour out tears to God;
21 on behalf of a man he pleads with God
    as a man pleads for his friend.

22 "Only a few years will pass
    before I go on the journey of no return.

17   1 My spirit is broken,
    my days are cut short,
    the grave awaits me.[n]
  2 Surely mockers surround me;
    my eyes must dwell on their hostility.

[a]20 Or *My friends treat me with scorn*

16:3
[y] Job 6:26

16:4
[z] Ps 22:7; 109:25;
La 2:15; Mt 27:39

16:7
[a] Job 7:3

16:8
[b] Job 19:20
[c] Job 10:17

16:9
[d] Ps 35:16
[e] Job 13:24

16:10
[f] Ps 22:13
[g] La 3:30; Mic 5:1

16:12
[h] Job 9:17

16:13
[i] Job 20:24

16:14
[j] Joel 2:7

16:15
[k] Ge 37:34

16:18
[l] Ps 66:18-19

16:19
[m] Ro 1:9

17:1
[n] Ps 88:3-4

16:19 Job was afraid that God had abandoned him. Yet he appealed directly to God (his witness and advocate) and to God's knowledge of his innocence. A *witness* is someone who has seen what has happened, and an *advocate* is like a lawyer who speaks on behalf of the plaintiff. By using these terms, Job showed he had cast all his hope for any fair defense upon God in heaven because he would probably die before it happened on earth. In the New Testament we learn that Jesus

17:3
ᵒPs 119:122

3 "Give me, O God, the pledge you demand. ᵒ
   Who else will put up security for me?
4 You have closed their minds to understanding;
   therefore you will not let them triumph.

17:5
ᵖJob 11:20

5 If a man denounces his friends for reward,
   the eyes of his children will fail.ᵖ

17:6
�q Job 30:9

6 "God has made me a byword q to everyone,
   a man in whose face people spit.
7 My eyes have grown dim with grief;
   my whole frame is but a shadow.
8 Upright men are appalled at this;
   the innocent are aroused against the ungodly.

17:9
ʳPr 4:18

9 Nevertheless, the righteous ʳ will hold to their ways,
   and those with clean hands will grow stronger.

10 "But come on, all of you, try again!
   I will not find a wise man among you.

17:11
ˢJob 7:6

11 My days have passed, my plans are shattered,
   and so are the desires of my heart.ˢ
12 These men turn night into day;
   in the face of darkness they say, 'Light is near.'

17:13
ᵗJob 3:13

13 If the only home I hope for is the grave,ᵃ ᵗ
   if I spread out my bed in darkness,
14 if I say to corruption, 'You are my father,'
   and to the worm, 'My mother' or 'My sister,'
15 where then is my hope?
   Who can see any hope for me?

17:16
ᵘJob 3:17-19;
Jnh 2:6

16 Will it go down to the gates of deathᵃ?ᵘ
   Will we descend together into the dust?"

Bildad

18

Then Bildad the Shuhite replied:

2 "When will you end these speeches?
   Be sensible, and then we can talk.

18:3
ᵛPs 73:22

3 Why are we regarded as cattle
   and considered stupid in your sight?ᵛ

18:4
ʷJob 13:14

4 You who tear yourself ʷ to pieces in your anger,
   is the earth to be abandoned for your sake?
   Or must the rocks be moved from their place?

18:5
ˣPr 13:9

5 "The lamp of the wicked is snuffed out;ˣ
   the flame of his fire stops burning.
6 The light in his tent becomes dark;
   the lamp beside him goes out.

ᵃ 13,16 Hebrew *Sheol*

Christ intercedes on our behalf (Hebrews 7:25; 1 John 2:1); therefore, we have nothing to fear.

17:10 Job's three friends had a reputation for being wise, but Job could not find wisdom in any of them. God backed up Job's claim in 42:7, when he condemned these men for their false portrayal of him. Obviously these men had a faulty view of wisdom. They assumed that because they were prosperous and successful, God must be pleased with the way they were living and thinking. Job, however, told his friends that they were starting with the wrong idea because earthly success and prosperity are not proof of faith in God. Likewise, trouble and affliction do not prove faithlessness. The truly wise man knows that wisdom comes from God alone, not from human successes or failures. And the truly wise man never forsakes God. God's wisdom proved superior to Job and to all his friends.

17:15 Job was giving up hope of any future restoration of wealth and family and wrapping himself in thoughts of death and the rest from grief and pain it promised. The rewards that Job's friends described were all related to this present life. They were silent about the possibility of life after death. We must not evaluate life only in terms of this present world because God promises a never-ending, wonderful future to those who are faithful to him.

18:1ff Bildad thought he knew how the universe should be run, and he saw Job as an illustration of the consequences of sin. Bildad rejected Job's side of the story because it did not fit in with his outlook on life. It is easy to condemn Bildad because his errors are obvious; unfortunately, however, we often act the same way when our ideas are threatened.

7 The vigor of his step is weakened;
   his own schemes*y* throw him down.
8 His feet thrust him into a net*z*
   and he wanders into its mesh.
9 A trap seizes him by the heel;
   a snare holds him fast.
10 A noose is hidden for him on the ground;
   a trap lies in his path.
11 Terrors startle him on every side*a*
   and dog his every step.
12 Calamity is hungry*b* for him;
   disaster is ready for him when he falls.
13 It eats away parts of his skin;
   death's firstborn devours his limbs.
14 He is torn from the security of his tent
   and marched off to the king of terrors.
15 Fire resides*a* in his tent;
   burning sulfur is scattered over his dwelling.
16 His roots dry up below*c*
   and his branches wither above.*d*
17 The memory of him perishes from the earth;
   he has no name in the land.*e*
18 He is driven from light into darkness*f*
   and is banished from the world.
19 He has no offspring*g* or descendants*h* among his people,
   no survivor where once he lived.
20 Men of the west are appalled at his fate;
   men of the east are seized with horror.
21 Surely such is the dwelling of an evil man;
   such is the place of one who knows not God."*i*

Job

19 Then Job replied:

2 "How long will you torment me
   and crush me with words?
3 Ten times now you have reproached me;
   shamelessly you attack me.
4 If it is true that I have gone astray,
   my error remains my concern alone.
5 If indeed you would exalt yourselves above me*j*
   and use my humiliation against me,
6 then know that God has wronged me
   and drawn his net*k* around me.

7 "Though I cry, 'I've been wronged!' I get no response;*l*
   though I call for help, there is no justice.

a 15 Or Nothing he had remains

18:7	*y* Job 5:13
18:8	*z* Job 22:10; Ps 9:15; 35:7
18:11	*a* Job 15:21
18:12	*b* Isa 8:21
18:16	*c* Isa 5:24; Am 2:9 *d* Mal 4:1
18:17	*e* Ps 34:16; Pr 10:7
18:18	*f* Job 5:14
18:19	*g* Jer 22:30 *h* Isa 14:22
18:21	*i* 1Th 4:5
19:5	*j* Ps 35:26; 38:16
19:6	*k* Job 18:8
19:7	*l* Job 30:20

18:14 The "king of terrors" is a figure of speech referring to death. Bildad viewed death as a great devourer (18:13), but the Bible teaches that God has the power to devour even death (Psalm 49:15; Isaiah 25:8; 1 Corinthians 15:54–56).

19:3–5 It is easy to point out someone else's faults or sins. Job's friends accused him of sin to make him feel guilty, not to encourage or correct him. If we feel we must admonish some-

one, we should be sure we are confronting that person because we love him, not because we are annoyed, inconvenienced, or seeking to blame him.

19:6 Job felt that God was treating him as an enemy when, in fact, God was his friend and thought highly of him (1:8; 2:3). In his difficulty, Job pointed at the wrong person. It was Satan, not God, who was Job's enemy. Because they stressed ultimate causes, most Israelites believed that both good and evil came from God; they also thought people were responsible for their own destinies. But the evil power loose in this world accounts for much of the suffering we experience. In verse 7, Job continued to cry out to be heard by God.

19:8
m Job 30:26

8 He has blocked my way so I cannot pass;
  he has shrouded my paths in darkness. m
9 He has stripped me of my honor
  and removed the crown from my head.

19:10
n Job 12:14
o Job 7:6

10 He tears me down n on every side till I am gone;
  he uproots my hope o like a tree.

19:11
p Job 16:9
q Job 13:24

11 His anger p burns against me;
  he counts me among his enemies. q
12 His troops advance in force;
  they build a siege ramp against me
  and encamp around my tent.

13 "He has alienated my brothers from me;
  my acquaintances are completely estranged from me.
14 My kinsmen have gone away;
  my friends have forgotten me.
15 My guests and my maidservants count me a stranger;
  they look upon me as an alien.
16 I summon my servant, but he does not answer,
  though I beg him with my own mouth.
17 My breath is offensive to my wife;
  I am loathsome to my own brothers.

19:18
r 2Ki 2:23

18 Even the little boys r scorn me;
  when I appear, they ridicule me.

19:19
s Ps 55:12-13

19 All my intimate friends s detest me;
  those I love have turned against me.

19:20
t Ps 102:5

20 I am nothing but skin and bones; t
  I have escaped with only the skin of my teeth. a

21 "Have pity on me, my friends, have pity,
  for the hand of God has struck me.

19:22
u Ps 69:26

22 Why do you pursue me as God does?
  Will you never get enough of my flesh? u

23 "Oh, that my words were recorded,
  that they were written on a scroll,
24 that they were inscribed with an iron tool on b lead,
  or engraved in rock forever!

19:25
v Ps 78:35;
Isa 43:14
w Job 16:19

25 I know that my Redeemer c v lives, w
  and that in the end he will stand upon the earth. d
26 And after my skin has been destroyed,
  yet e in f my flesh I will see God; x

19:26
x Mt 5:8; 1Co 13:12;
1Jn 3:2

27 I myself will see him
  with my own eyes—I, and not another.
  How my heart yearns within me!

28 "If you say, 'How we will hound him,
  since the root of the trouble lies in him, g '

a 20 Or only my gums   b 24 Or and   c 25 Or defender   d 25 Or upon my grave   e 26 Or And after I awake, / though this ⌊body⌋ has been destroyed, / then   f 26 Or / apart from   g 28 Many Hebrew manuscripts, Septuagint and Vulgate; most Hebrew manuscripts me

---

19:25–27 At the heart of the book of Job comes his ringing affirmation of confidence: "I know that my Redeemer lives." In ancient Israel a *redeemer* was a family member who bought a slave's way to freedom or who took care of a widow (see the note on Ruth 3:1). What tremendous faith Job had, especially in light of the fact that he was unaware of the conference between God and Satan. Job thought that God had brought all these disasters upon him! Faced with death and decay, Job still expected to see God—and he expected to do so in his body. When the book of Job was written, Israel did not have a well-developed doctrine of the resurrection. Although Job struggled with the idea that God

was presently against him, he firmly believed that in the end God would be on his side. This belief was so strong that Job became one of the first to talk about the resurrection of the body (see also Psalm 16:10; Isaiah 26:19; Daniel 12:2, 13).

19:26 Job said: "in my flesh I will see God." In Job's situation, it seemed unlikely to him that he would, in his flesh, see God. And that's just the point of Job's faith! He was confident that God's justice would triumph, even if it would take a miracle like resurrection to accomplish this.

29 you should fear the sword yourselves;
    for wrath will bring punishment by the sword,
    and then you will know that there is judgment.ª"

Zophar

20 Then Zophar the Naamathite replied:

2 "My troubled thoughts prompt me to answer
    because I am greatly disturbed.
3 I hear a rebuke y that dishonors me,
    and my understanding inspires me to reply.

20:3
y Job 19:3

4 "Surely you know how it has been from of old,
    ever since man b was placed on the earth,
5 that the mirth of the wicked is brief,
    the joy of the godless lasts but a moment. z

20:5
z Ps 37:35-36

6 Though his pride reaches to the heavens
    and his head touches the clouds, ª
7 he will perish forever, b like his own dung;
    those who have seen him will say, 'Where is he?'
8 Like a dream c he flies away, no more to be found,
    banished like a vision of the night. d
9 The eye that saw him will not see him again;
    his place will look on him no more. e
10 His children must make amends to the poor;
    his own hands must give back his wealth.
11 The youthful vigor f that fills his bones
    will lie with him in the dust.

20:6
ª Isa 14:13-14;
Ob 1:3-4
20:7
b Job 4:20
20:8
c Ps 73:20
d Ps 90:5
20:9
e Job 7:8

20:11
f Job 13:26

12 "Though evil is sweet in his mouth
    and he hides it under his tongue,
13 though he cannot bear to let it go
    and keeps it in his mouth,
14 yet his food will turn sour in his stomach;
    it will become the venom of serpents within him.
15 He will spit out the riches he swallowed;
    God will make his stomach vomit them up.
16 He will suck the poison of serpents;
    the fangs of an adder will kill him.
17 He will not enjoy the streams,
    the rivers flowing with honey and cream.
18 What he toiled for he must give back uneaten;
    he will not enjoy the profit from his trading.
19 For he has oppressed the poor and left them destitute;
    he has seized houses he did not build.

20 "Surely he will have no respite from his craving; g
    he cannot save himself by his treasure.
21 Nothing is left for him to devour;
    his prosperity will not endure.
22 In the midst of his plenty, distress will overtake him;
    the full force of misery will come upon him.

20:20
g Ecc 5:12-14

a 29 Or / that you may come to know the Almighty   b 4 Or Adam

---

20:1ff Zophar's speech again revealed his false assumption because he based his arguments purely on the idea that Job was an evil hypocrite. Zophar said that although Job had it good for a while, he didn't live righteously, so God took his wealth from him. According to Zophar, Job's calamities *proved* his wickedness.

20:6, 7 Although Zophar was wrong in directing this tirade against Job, he was correct in talking about the final end of evil people. At first, sin seems enjoyable and attractive. Lying, steal-

ing, or oppressing others often brings temporary gain to those who practice these sins. Some live a long time with ill-gotten gain. But in the end, God's justice will prevail. What Zophar missed is that judgment for these sins may not come in the lifetime of the sinner. Punishment may be deferred until the last judgment, when sinners will be eternally cut off from God. We should not be impressed with the success and power of evil people. God's judgment on them is certain.

23 When he has filled his belly,
    God will vent his burning anger against him
    and rain down his blows upon him.
24 Though he flees[h] from an iron weapon,
    a bronze-tipped arrow pierces him.
25 He pulls it out of his back,
    the gleaming point out of his liver.
    Terrors[i] will come over him;[j]
26   total darkness lies in wait for his treasures.
    A fire unfanned will consume him[k]
    and devour what is left in his tent.
27 The heavens will expose his guilt;
    the earth will rise up against him.
28 A flood will carry off his house,
    rushing waters[a] on the day of God's wrath.
29 Such is the fate God allots the wicked,
    the heritage appointed for them by God."[l]

Job

21

Then Job replied:

2 "Listen carefully to my words;
    let this be the consolation you give me.
3 Bear with me while I speak,
    and after I have spoken, mock on.

4 "Is my complaint directed to man?
    Why should I not be impatient?
5 Look at me and be astonished;
    clap your hand over your mouth.[m]
6 When I think about this, I am terrified;
    trembling seizes my body.
7 Why do the wicked live on,
    growing old and increasing in power?[n]
8 They see their children established around them,
    their offspring before their eyes.[o]
9 Their homes are safe and free from fear;
    the rod of God is not upon them.
10 Their bulls never fail to breed;
    their cows calve and do not miscarry.[p]
11 They send forth their children as a flock;
    their little ones dance about.
12 They sing to the music of tambourine and harp;
    they make merry to the sound of the flute.
13 They spend their years in prosperity[q]
    and go down to the grave[b] in peace.[c]
14 Yet they say to God, 'Leave us alone![r]
    We have no desire to know your ways.
15 Who is the Almighty, that we should serve him?
    What would we gain by praying to him?'[s]
16 But their prosperity is not in their own hands,
    so I stand aloof from the counsel of the wicked.

20:24
h Isa 24:18;
Am 5:19

20:25
i Job 18:11;
j Job 16:13

20:26
k Ps 21:9

20:29
l Job 27:13

21:5
m Jdg 18:19;
Job 29:9; 40:4

21:7
n Ps 73:3; Jer 12:1

21:8
o Ps 17:14

21:10
p Ex 23:26

21:13
q Job 36:11

21:14
r Job 22:17

21:15
s Job 34:9

a 28 Or The possessions in his house will be carried off, / washed away   b 13 Hebrew Sheol   c 13 Or in an instant

21:1ff Job refuted Zophar's idea that evil people never experience wealth and happiness, pointing out that in the real world the wicked do indeed prosper. See Psalm 73 for more on the apparent prosperity of evil people. God does as he wills to individuals (21:22–25), and people cannot use their circumstances to measure their own goodness or God's—they are sometimes (but not always) related. Success to Job's friends was based on outward performance; success to God, however, is based on a person's heart.

17 "Yet how often is the lamp of the wicked snuffed out?[t]
   How often does calamity come upon them,
   the fate God allots in his anger?
18 How often are they like straw before the wind,
   like chaff[u] swept away by a gale?
19 ⌊It is said,⌋ 'God stores up a man's punishment for his sons.'[v]
   Let him repay the man himself, so that he will know it!
20 Let his own eyes see his destruction;
   let him drink[w] of the wrath of the Almighty.[a][x]
21 For what does he care about the family he leaves behind
   when his allotted months come to an end?

22 "Can anyone teach knowledge to God,[y]
   since he judges even the highest?
23 One man dies in full vigor,
   completely secure and at ease,
24 his body[b] well nourished,
   his bones rich with marrow.
25 Another man dies in bitterness of soul,
   never having enjoyed anything good.
26 Side by side they lie in the dust,
   and worms cover them both.[z]

27 "I know full well what you are thinking,
   the schemes by which you would wrong me.
28 You say, 'Where now is the great man's house,
   the tents where wicked men lived?'[a]
29 Have you never questioned those who travel?
   Have you paid no regard to their accounts—
30 that the evil man is spared from the day of calamity,[b]
   that he is delivered from[c] the day of wrath?[c]
31 Who denounces his conduct to his face?
   Who repays him for what he has done?
32 He is carried to the grave,
   and watch is kept over his tomb.
33 The soil in the valley is sweet to him;
   all men follow after him,
   and a countless throng goes[d] before him.[d]

34 "So how can you console me with your nonsense?
   Nothing is left of your answers but falsehood!"

3. Third round of discussion
Eliphaz

22 Then Eliphaz the Temanite replied:

2 "Can a man be of benefit to God?[e]
   Can even a wise man benefit him?

**Side notes:**
21:17 [t] Job 18:5
21:18 [u] Ps 1:4
21:19 [v] Ex 20:5
21:20 [w] Isa 51:17 [x] Jer 25:15; Rev 14:10
21:22 [y] Isa 40:13-14; Ro 11:34
21:26 [z] Job 24:20; Ecc 9:2-3
21:28 [a] Job 8:22
21:30 [b] Pr 16:4 [c] Job 20:22,28; 2Pe 2:9
21:33 [d] Job 3:19
22:2 [e] Lk 17:10

---

a 17-20 Verses 17 and 18 may be taken as exclamations and 19 and 20 as declarations.   b 24 The meaning of the Hebrew for this word is uncertain.   c 30 Or *man is reserved for the day of calamity, / that he is brought forth to* d 33 Or / *as a countless throng went*

21:22 Although baffled by the reasons for his suffering, Job affirmed God's superior understanding by asking, "Can anyone teach knowledge to God?" The way you respond to your personal struggles shows your attitude toward God. Rather than becoming angry with God, continue to trust him, no matter what your circumstances may be. Although it is sometimes difficult to see, God *is* in control. We must commit ourselves to him so we will not resent his timing.

21:29-33 If wicked people become wealthy despite their sin, why should we try to be good? The wicked may *seem* to get away

with sin, but there is a higher Judge and a future judgment (Revelation 20:11-15). The final settlement of justice will come not in this life, but in the next. What is important is how a person views God in prosperity or poverty, not the prosperity or poverty itself.

22:1ff This is Eliphaz's third and final speech to Job. When he first spoke to Job (chapters 4, 5), he commended Job's good deeds and gently suggested that Job might need to repent of some sin. While he said nothing new in this speech, he did get more specific. He couldn't shake his belief that suffering is God's punishment for evil deeds, so he suggested several possi-

3 What pleasure would it give the Almighty if you were righteous?
What would he gain if your ways were blameless?

4 "Is it for your piety that he rebukes you
and brings charges against you?
5 Is not your wickedness great?
Are not your sins endless?

22:6
f Ex 22:26

6 You demanded security *f* from your brothers for no reason;
you stripped men of their clothing, leaving them naked.
7 You gave no water to the weary
and you withheld food from the hungry,
8 though you were a powerful man, owning land—
an honored man, living on it.

22:9
g Job 24:3,21

9 And you sent widows away empty-handed *g*
and broke the strength of the fatherless.
10 That is why snares are all around you,
why sudden peril terrifies you,

22:11
h Job 5:14
i Ps 69:1-2

11 why it is so dark *h* you cannot see,
and why a flood of water covers you. *i*

22:12
j Job 11:8

12 "Is not God in the heights of heaven? *j*
And see how lofty are the highest stars!

22:13
k Ps 10:11

13 Yet you say, 'What does God know? *k*
Does he judge through such darkness?

22:14
l Job 26:9

14 Thick clouds *l* veil him, so he does not see us
as he goes about in the vaulted heavens.'
15 Will you keep to the old path
that evil men have trod?

22:16
m Job 15:32
n Mt 7:26-27

16 They were carried off before their time, *m*
their foundations washed away by a flood. *n*
17 They said to God, 'Leave us alone!
What can the Almighty do to us?'
18 Yet it was he who filled their houses with good things,
so I stand aloof from the counsel of the wicked.

22:19
o Ps 58:10; 107:42

19 "The righteous see their ruin and rejoice; *o*
the innocent mock them, saying,
20 'Surely our foes are destroyed,
and fire devours their wealth.'

21 "Submit to God and be at peace with him;
in this way prosperity will come to you.
22 Accept instruction from his mouth
and lay up his words in your heart.

22:23
p Isa 19:22
q Job 11:14

23 If you return to the Almighty, you will be restored: *p*
If you remove wickedness far from your tent *q*
24 and assign your nuggets to the dust,
your gold of Ophir to the rocks in the ravines,
25 then the Almighty will be your gold,
the choicest silver for you.

---

ble sins that Job might have committed. Eliphaz wasn't trying to destroy Job; at the end of his speech he promised that Job would receive peace and restoration if he would only admit his sin and repent.

22:12-14 Eliphaz declared that Job's view of God was too small, and he criticized Job for thinking that God was too far removed from earth to care about him. If Job knew of God's intense, personal interest in him, Eliphaz said, he wouldn't dare take his sins so lightly. Eliphaz had a point—some people do take sin lightly because they think God is far away and doesn't notice all we do. But his point did not apply to Job.

22:21-30 Several times Job's friends showed a partial knowledge of God's truth and character, but they had trouble applying this truth to life. Such was the case with Eliphaz, who gave a beautiful summary of repentance. He was correct in saying that we must ask for God's forgiveness when we sin, but his statement did not apply to Job, who had already sought God's forgiveness (7:20, 21; 9:20; 13:23) and had lived closely in touch with God all along.

26 Surely then you will find delight in the Almighty^r
    and will lift up your face to God.
27 You will pray to him,^s and he will hear you,
    and you will fulfill your vows.
28 What you decide on will be done,
    and light will shine on your ways.
29 When men are brought low and you say, 'Lift them up!'
    then he will save the downcast.^t
30 He will deliver even one who is not innocent,
    who will be delivered through the cleanness of your hands."

Job

23 Then Job replied:

2 "Even today my complaint is bitter;^u
    his hand^a is heavy in spite of^b my groaning.
3 If only I knew where to find him;
    if only I could go to his dwelling!
4 I would state my case before him
    and fill my mouth with arguments.
5 I would find out what he would answer me,
    and consider what he would say.
6 Would he oppose me with great power?^v
    No, he would not press charges against me.
7 There an upright man could present his case before him,^w
    and I would be delivered forever from my judge.

8 "But if I go to the east, he is not there;
    if I go to the west, I do not find him.
9 When he is at work in the north, I do not see him;
    when he turns to the south, I catch no glimpse of him.
10 But he knows the way that I take;
    when he has tested me,^x I will come forth as gold.
11 My feet have closely followed his steps;
    I have kept to his way without turning aside.^y
12 I have not departed from the commands of his lips;
    I have treasured the words of his mouth more than my daily bread.^z

13 "But he stands alone, and who can oppose him?
    He does whatever he pleases.
14 He carries out his decree against me,
    and many such plans he still has in store.^a
15 That is why I am terrified before him;
    when I think of all this, I fear him.
16 God has made my heart faint;
    the Almighty has terrified me.
17 Yet I am not silenced by the darkness,^b
    by the thick darkness that covers my face.

^a2 Septuagint and Syriac; Hebrew / *the hand on me* ^b2 Or *heavy on me in*

22:26
^rJob 27:10;
Isa 58:14
22:27
^sIsa 58:9

22:29
^tMt 23:12; 1Pe 5:5

23:2
^uJob 6:3

23:6
^vJob 9:4
23:7
^wJob 13:3

23:10
^xPs 139:1-3
23:11
^yPs 44:18
23:12
^zJn 4:32,34

23:14
^a1Th 3:3

23:17
^bJob 19:8

23:1—24:25 Job continued his questioning, saying that his suffering would be more bearable if only he knew why it was happening. If there was sin for which he could repent, he would! He knew about the wicked and the fact that they would be punished; he knew God could vindicate him if he so chose. In all his examples of the wicked in the world, his overriding desire was for God to clear his name, prove his righteousness, and explain why he was chosen to receive all this calamity. Job tried to make his friends see that questions about God, life, and justice are not as simple as they assumed.

23:10 In chapter 22, Eliphaz had tried to condemn Job by identifying some secret sin which he may have committed. Here Job declares his confidence in his integrity and God's justice. We are always likely to have hidden sin in our lives, sin we don't even know about because God's standards are so high and our performance is so imperfect. If we are true believers, however, all our sins are forgiven because of what Christ did on the cross in our behalf (Romans 5:1; 8:1). The Bible also teaches that even if we feel guilty, God is greater than our feelings (1 John 3:20). His forgiveness and cleansing are sufficient; they overrule our nagging doubts. The Holy Spirit in us is our proof that we are forgiven in God's eyes even though we may *feel* guilty. If

24

24:1
c Ac 1:7

"Why does the Almighty not set times for judgment?
 Why must those who know him look in vain for such days?c

24:2
d Dt 19:14; 27:17

2 Men move boundary stones;d
  they pasture flocks they have stolen.

3 They drive away the orphan's donkey
  and take the widow's ox in pledge.

24:4
e Pr 28:28

4 They thrust the needy from the path
  and force all the poor of the land into hiding.e

24:5
f Ps 104:23

5 Like wild donkeys in the desert,
   the poor go about their laborf of foraging food;
   the wasteland provides food for their children.

6 They gather fodder in the fields
  and glean in the vineyards of the wicked.

24:7
g Ex 22:27; Job 22:6

7 Lacking clothes, they spend the night naked;
  they have nothing to cover themselves in the cold.g

24:8
h La 4:5

8 They are drenched by mountain rains
  and hugh the rocks for lack of shelter.

9 The fatherless child is snatched from the breast;
  the infant of the poor is seized for a debt.

10 Lacking clothes, they go about naked;
   they carry the sheaves, but still go hungry.

11 They crush olives among the terracesa;
   they tread the winepresses, yet suffer thirst.

24:12
i Job 9:23

12 The groans of the dying rise from the city,
   and the souls of the wounded cry out for help.
   But God charges no one with wrongdoing.i

13 "There are those who rebel against the light,
   who do not know its ways
   or stay in its paths.

24:14
j Ps 10:9

14 When daylight is gone, the murderer rises up
   and kills the poor and needy;
   in the night he steals forth like a thief.j

24:15
k Pr 7:8-9
l Ps 10:11

15 The eye of the adulterer watches for dusk;k
   he thinks, 'No eye will see me,'l
   and he keeps his face concealed.

24:16
m Ex 22:2

16 In the dark, men break into houses,m
   but by day they shut themselves in;
   they want nothing to do with the light.

17 For all of them, deep darkness is their morningb;
   they make friends with the terrors of darkness.c

18 "Yet they are foam on the surface of the water;
   their portion of the land is cursed,
   so that no one goes to the vineyards.

24:19
n Job 6:17

19 As heat and drought snatch away the melted snow,n
   so the graved snatches away those who have sinned.

24:20
o Pr 10:7

20 The womb forgets them,
   the worm feasts on them;
   evil men are no longer rememberedo
   but are broken like a tree.

24:21
p Job 22:9

21 They prey on the barren and childless woman,
   and to the widow show no kindness.p

a 11 Or *olives between the millstones*; the meaning of the Hebrew for this word is uncertain.   b 17 Or *them, their
morning is like the shadow of death*   c 17 Or *of the shadow of death*   d 19 Hebrew *Sheol*

---

we, like Job, are truly seeking God, we can stand up to others' accusations as well as our own nagging doubts. If God has forgiven and accepted us, we are forgiven indeed.

24:18–21 Job suddenly seemed to be arguing on his friends' side. For this reason, some commentators think one of Job's friends said these words. But we shouldn't expect Job to present a unified argument. He was confused. He was not arguing that, in every case, God rewards the wicked and punishes the righteous; he was simply asserting that in his case, a righteous man was suffering.

22 But God drags away the mighty by his power;
　　though they become established, they have no assurance of life.
23 He may let them rest in a feeling of security,
　　but his eyes are on their ways.
24 For a little while they are exalted, and then they are gone;q
　　they are brought low and gathered up like all others;
　　they are cut off like heads of grain.

25 "If this is not so, who can prove me false
　　and reduce my words to nothing?"r

24:24
qPs 37:10

24:25
rJob 6:28

Bildad

25

Then Bildad the Shuhite replied:

2 "Dominion and awe belong to God;s
　　he establishes order in the heights of heaven.
3 Can his forces be numbered?
　　Upon whom does his light not rise?t
4 How then can a man be righteous before God?
　　How can one born of woman be pure?u
5 If even the moon is not bright
　　and the stars are not pure in his eyes,v
6 how much less man, who is but a maggot—
　　a son of man, who is only a worm!"w

25:2
sJob 9:4

25:3
tJas 1:17

25:4
uJob 4:17

25:5
vJob 15:15

25:6
wPs 22:6

Job

26

Then Job replied:

2 "How you have helped the powerless!
　　How you have saved the arm that is feeble!
3 What advice you have offered to one without wisdom!
　　And what great insight you have displayed!
4 Who has helped you utter these words?
　　And whose spirit spoke from your mouth?

5 "The dead are in deep anguish,
　　those beneath the waters and all that live in them.
6 Deatha x is naked before God;
　　Destructionb lies uncovered.y
7 He spreads out the northern ⌊skies⌋ z over empty space;
　　he suspends the earth over nothing.

26:6
xPs 139:8
yHeb 4:13

26:7
zJob 9:8

a6 Hebrew Sheol　b6 Hebrew Abaddon

25:1ff Bildad's final reply was weak. It ignored Job's examples of the prosperity of the wicked. Instead of attempting to refute Job, Bildad accused Job of pride because he was claiming that his suffering was not the result of sin. Job never claimed to be without sin, but only that his sin could not have caused his present trouble.

25:6 It is important to understand that Bildad, not God, was calling man a worm. Human beings are created in God's image (Genesis 1:26, 27). Psalm 8:5 says that man is "a little lower than the heavenly beings." Bildad may have simply been using a poetic description to contrast our worth to the worth and power of God. To come to God, we need not crawl like worms. We can approach him boldly in faith (Hebrews 4:16).

26:1ff Job has the distinction of giving the longest speech in the book—six chapters—weaving together pictures of God's mystery and power in a beautiful poem of trust. Beginning by brushing

off Bildad's latest reply as irrelevant (chapter 25), Job then told Bildad and his friends that they could not possibly know everything about God. Wisdom does not originate from this life or from the human mind—it comes from God (28:27, 28). Job then defended his upright and honest life. He had effectively sought to follow God's way of living. While admitting that he was not perfect, Job maintained that his motives were right.

26:2–4 With great sarcasm, Job attacked Bildad's comments. Theological explanations failed to bring any relief because the friends were unable to turn their knowledge into helpful counsel. When dealing with people, it is more important to love and understand them than to analyze them or give advice. Compassion produces greater results than criticism or blame.

27:6 In the midst of all the accusations, Job was able to declare that his conscience was clear. Only God's forgiveness and the determination to live rightly before God can bring a clear conscience. How important Job's record became as he was being accused. Like Job, we can't claim sinless lives, but we *can* claim forgiven lives. When we confess our sins to God, he forgives us. Then we can live with clear consciences (1 John 1:9).

26:8
a Pr 30:4

26:10
b Job 38:8-11

26:12
c Isa 51:15;
Jer 31:35

26:13
d Isa 27:1

27:2
e Job 34:5

27:3
f Job 32:8; 33:4

27:6
g Job 2:3

27:9
h Job 35:12;
Pr 1:28; Isa 1:15;
Jer 14:12; Mic 3:4

27:10
i Job 22:26

27:13
j Job 20:29

27:14
k Dt 28:41; Hos 9:13
l Job 20:10

27:15
m Ps 78:64

27:17
n Pr 28:8; Ecc 2:26

8 He wraps up the waters *a* in his clouds,
  yet the clouds do not burst under their weight.
9 He covers the face of the full moon,
  spreading his clouds over it.
10 He marks out the horizon on the face of the waters
  for a boundary between light and darkness. *b*
11 The pillars of the heavens quake,
  aghast at his rebuke.
12 By his power he churned up the sea; *c*
  by his wisdom he cut Rahab to pieces.
13 By his breath the skies became fair;
  his hand pierced the gliding serpent. *d*
14 And these are but the outer fringe of his works;
  how faint the whisper we hear of him!
  Who then can understand the thunder of his power?"

27 And Job continued his discourse:

2 "As surely as God lives, who has denied me justice, *e*
  the Almighty, who has made me taste bitterness of soul,
3 as long as I have life within me,
  the breath of God *f* in my nostrils,
4 my lips will not speak wickedness,
  and my tongue will utter no deceit.
5 I will never admit you are in the right;
  till I die, I will not deny my integrity.
6 I will maintain my righteousness and never let go of it;
  my conscience will not reproach me as long as I live. *g*

7 "May my enemies be like the wicked,
  my adversaries like the unjust!
8 For what hope has the godless when he is cut off,
  when God takes away his life?
9 Does God listen to his cry
  when distress comes upon him? *h*
10 Will he find delight in the Almighty? *i*
  Will he call upon God at all times?

11 "I will teach you about the power of God;
  the ways of the Almighty I will not conceal.
12 You have all seen this yourselves.
  Why then this meaningless talk?

13 "Here is the fate God allots to the wicked,
  the heritage a ruthless man receives from the Almighty: *j*
14 However many his children, their fate is the sword; *k*
  his offspring will never have enough to eat. *l*
15 The plague will bury those who survive him,
  and their widows will not weep for them. *m*
16 Though he heaps up silver like dust
  and clothes like piles of clay,
17 what he lays up the righteous will wear, *n*
  and the innocent will divide his silver.
18 The house he builds is like a moth's cocoon,
  like a hut made by a watchman.
19 He lies down wealthy, but will do so no more;
  when he opens his eyes, all is gone.

27:13–23 Job agreed with his friends that the end of the
wicked will be disaster, but he did not agree that *he* was wicked
and deserving of punishment. Most of the punishments Job

listed never happened to him. So he wasn't including himself
as one of the wicked. On the contrary, he continually pleaded
for God to vindicate him.

20 Terrors overtake him like a flood;^o
     a tempest snatches him away in the night.^p
21 The east wind carries him off, and he is gone;
     it sweeps him out of his place.^q
22 It hurls itself against him without mercy^r
     as he flees headlong from its power.
23 It claps its hands in derision
     and hisses him out of his place.

28

"There is a mine for silver
     and a place where gold is refined.
2 Iron is taken from the earth,
     and copper is smelted from ore.
3 Man puts an end to the darkness;^s
     he searches the farthest recesses
     for ore in the blackest darkness.
4 Far from where people dwell he cuts a shaft,
     in places forgotten by the foot of man;
     far from men he dangles and sways.
5 The earth, from which food comes,^t
     is transformed below as by fire;
6 sapphires^a come from its rocks,
     and its dust contains nuggets of gold.
7 No bird of prey knows that hidden path,
     no falcon's eye has seen it.
8 Proud beasts do not set foot on it,
     and no lion prowls there.
9 Man's hand assaults the flinty rock
     and lays bare the roots of the mountains.
10 He tunnels through the rock;
     his eyes see all its treasures.
11 He searches^b the sources of the rivers
     and brings hidden things to light.

12 "But where can wisdom be found?^u
     Where does understanding dwell?
13 Man does not comprehend its worth;^v
     it cannot be found in the land of the living.
14 The deep says, 'It is not in me';
     the sea says, 'It is not with me.'
15 It cannot be bought with the finest gold,
     nor can its price be weighed in silver.^w
16 It cannot be bought with the gold of Ophir,
     with precious onyx or sapphires.
17 Neither gold nor crystal can compare with it,
     nor can it be had for jewels of gold.
18 Coral and jasper are not worthy of mention;
     the price of wisdom is beyond rubies.
19 The topaz of Cush cannot compare with it;
     it cannot be bought with pure gold.

20 "Where then does wisdom come from?
     Where does understanding dwell?

27:20
^oJob 15:21
^pJob 20:8

27:21
^qJob 7:10

27:22
^rJer 13:14;
Eze 5:11

28:3
^sEcc 1:13

28:5
^tPs 104:14

28:12
^uEcc 7:24

28:13
^vPr 3:15

28:15
^wPr 3:13-14;
8:10-11

^a6 Or *lapis lazuli*; also in verse 16   ^b11 Septuagint, Aquila and Vulgate; Hebrew *He dams up*

28:13 Job stated that wisdom cannot be found among the living. It is natural for people who do not understand the importance of God's Word to seek wisdom here on earth. They look to philosophers and other leaders to give them direction for living. Yet Job said that wisdom is not found there. No leader or group of leaders can produce enough knowledge or insight to explain the totality of human experience. The ultimate interpretation of life, of who we are and where we are going, must come from outside and above our mortal life. When looking for guidance, seek God's wisdom as revealed in the Bible. To be lifted above and beyond the boundaries of life, we must know and trust the Lord of life.

28:16 Gold of Ophir was considered the finest gold available. Ophir

²¹ It is hidden from the eyes of every living thing,
    concealed even from the birds of the air.
²² Destruction^a and Death say,
    'Only a rumor of it has reached our ears.'
²³ God understands the way to it
    and he alone knows where it dwells,
²⁴ for he views the ends of the earth
    and sees everything under the heavens.^x
²⁵ When he established the force of the wind
    and measured out the waters,^y
²⁶ when he made a decree for the rain
    and a path for the thunderstorm,
²⁷ then he looked at wisdom and appraised it;
    he confirmed it and tested it.
²⁸ And he said to man,
    'The fear of the Lord—that is wisdom,
    and to shun evil is understanding.^z'"

29

Job continued his discourse:

² "How I long for the months gone by,
    for the days when God watched over me,
³ when his lamp shone upon my head
    and by his light I walked through darkness!
⁴ Oh, for the days when I was in my prime,
    when God's intimate friendship blessed my house,^a
⁵ when the Almighty was still with me
    and my children were around me,
⁶ when my path was drenched with cream^b
    and the rock^c poured out for me streams of olive oil.^d
⁷ "When I went to the gate of the city
    and took my seat in the public square,

^a22 Hebrew *Abaddon*

28:24
^xPr 15:3

28:25
^yPs 135:7

28:28
^zDt 4:6; Pr 1:7

29:4
^aPs 25:14

29:6
^bJob 20:17
^cPs 81:16
^dDt 32:13

WHERE CAN WISDOM BE FOUND?
Job and his friends differed in their ideas of how people become wise.

Person	His Source of Wisdom	Attitude toward God
Eliphaz . . .	Wisdom is learned by observing and experiencing life. He based his advice to Job on his confident, firsthand knowledge (4:7, 8; 5:3, 27).	"I have personally observed how God works and have figured him out."
Bildad	Wisdom is inherited from the past. Trustworthy knowledge is secondhand. He based his advice to Job on traditional proverbs and sayings that he frequently quoted (8:8, 9; 18:5–21).	"Those who have gone before us figured God out, and all we have to do is use that knowledge."
Zophar . . .	Wisdom belongs to the wise. He based his advice on his wisdom that had no other source than himself (11:6; 20:1–29).	"The wise know what God is like, but there aren't many of us around."
Job	God is the source of wisdom, and the first step toward wisdom is to fear God (28:20–28).	"God reveals his wisdom to those who humbly trust him."

---

may have been located in Africa, along the Arabian coast, or in India. Wherever it was, it was a good distance from Israel, for it took Solomon's ships three years to make the voyage (1 Kings 9:28; 10:22).

28:28 "The fear of the Lord" is a key theme in the wisdom literature of the Bible (Job through Song of Songs). It means to have respect and reverence for God and to be in awe of his majesty and power. This is the starting point to finding real wisdom (see Proverbs 1:7–9).

29:6 Cream and olive oil were symbols of material prosperity in an agricultural society. Job's flocks and olive trees were so plentiful that everything seemed to overflow.

29:7ff Job was walking a fine line between bragging about past accomplishments and recalling good deeds in order to answer the

charges against him. Job's one weakness throughout his conversations is that he came dangerously close to pride. Pride is especially deceptive when we are doing right. But it separates us from God by making us think we're better than we really are. Then we trust our own opinions, which leads to other kinds of sin. While it is not wrong to recount past deeds, it is far better to recount God's blessings to us. This will help keep us from inadvertently falling into pride.

29:7–17 Because of this description of Job's work, many commentators believe that Job was a judge. In Job's day, a judge served as both a city councilman and a magistrate, helping to manage the community and settle disputes. In most cases, this was not a full-time position but a part-time post held on the basis of one's respect and standing in the area.

8 the young men saw me and stepped aside
  and the old men rose to their feet;
9 the chief men refrained from speaking
  and covered their mouths with their hands;*e*

29:9
e Job 21:5

10 the voices of the nobles were hushed,
   and their tongues stuck to the roof of their mouths.*f*

29:10
f Ps 137:6

11 Whoever heard me spoke well of me,
   and those who saw me commended me,
12 because I rescued the poor who cried for help,
   and the fatherless*g* who had none to assist him.*h*

29:12
g Job 31:17,21
h Ps 72:12;
Pr 21:13

13 The man who was dying blessed me;
   I made the widow's heart sing.
14 I put on righteousness*i* as my clothing;
   justice was my robe and my turban.

29:14
i Isa 59:17; 61:10;
Eph 6:14

15 I was eyes*j* to the blind
   and feet to the lame.

29:15
j Nu 10:31

16 I was a father to the needy;*k*
   I took up the case of the stranger.

29:16
k Pr 29:7

17 I broke the fangs of the wicked
   and snatched the victims from their teeth.*l*

29:17
l Ps 3:7

18 "I thought, 'I will die in my own house,
   my days as numerous as the grains of sand.*m*

29:18
m Ps 30:6

19 My roots will reach to the water,*n*
   and the dew will lie all night on my branches.

29:19
n Jer 17:8

20 My glory will remain fresh in me,
   the bow*o* ever new in my hand.'*p*

29:20
o Ps 18:34
p Ge 49:24

21 "Men listened to me expectantly,
   waiting in silence for my counsel.
22 After I had spoken, they spoke no more;
   my words fell gently on their ears.*q*

29:22
q Dt 32:2

23 They waited for me as for showers
   and drank in my words as the spring rain.
24 When I smiled at them, they scarcely believed it;
   the light of my face was precious to them.*a*
25 I chose the way for them and sat as their chief;
   I dwelt as a king among his troops;
   I was like one who comforts mourners.

30 "But now they mock me,
   men younger than I,
whose fathers I would have disdained
   to put with my sheep dogs.
2 Of what use was the strength of their hands to me,
   since their vigor had gone from them?
3 Haggard from want and hunger,
   they roamed*b* the parched land
   in desolate wastelands at night.
4 In the brush they gathered salt herbs,
   and their food*c* was the root of the broom tree.
5 They were banished from their fellow men,
   shouted at as if they were thieves.

*a*24 The meaning of the Hebrew for this clause is uncertain.   *b*3 Or *gnawed*   *c*4 Or *fuel*

30:1ff To suffer extreme loss, as Job did, was humiliating. But to face abuse at the hands of young upstarts added insult to injury. Job had lost his family, possessions, health, position, and good name. He was not even respected for suffering bravely. Unfortunately, young people sometimes mock and take advantage of older people and those who are limited in some way. Instead, they should realize that their own physical abilities and attributes are short-lived and that God loves all people equally.

6 They were forced to live in the dry stream beds,
  among the rocks and in holes in the ground.
7 They brayed among the bushes
  and huddled in the undergrowth.
8 A base and nameless brood,
  they were driven out of the land.

30:9
r Ps 69:11
s Job 17:6

9 "And now their sons mock me r in song;
  I have become a byword s among them.
10 They detest me and keep their distance;
  they do not hesitate to spit in my face. t

30:10
t Nu 12:14; Dt 25:9;
Isa 50:6; Mt 26:67

11 Now that God has unstrung my bow and afflicted me,
  they throw off restraint in my presence.

30:12
u Ps 140:4-5
v Job 19:12

12 On my right the tribe a attacks;
  they lay snares for my feet, u
  they build their siege ramps against me. v
13 They break up my road;
  they succeed in destroying me—
  without anyone's helping them. b
14 They advance as through a gaping breach;
  amid the ruins they come rolling in.
15 Terrors overwhelm me;
  my dignity is driven away as by the wind,
  my safety vanishes like a cloud.

30:16
w Ps 42:4

16 "And now my life ebbs away; w
  days of suffering grip me.
17 Night pierces my bones;
  my gnawing pains never rest.
18 In his great power ⌞God⌟ becomes like clothing to me c;
  he binds me like the neck of my garment.
19 He throws me into the mud,
  and I am reduced to dust and ashes.

20 "I cry out to you, O God, but you do not answer;
  I stand up, but you merely look at me.
21 You turn on me ruthlessly;
  with the might of your hand you attack me.

30:22
x Job 27:21
y Job 9:17

22 You snatch me up and drive me before the wind; x
  you toss me about in the storm. y
23 I know you will bring me down to death,
  to the place appointed for all the living.

24 "Surely no one lays a hand on a broken man
  when he cries for help in his distress.

30:25
z Ps 35:13-14;
Ro 12:15

25 Have I not wept for those in trouble?
  Has not my soul grieved for the poor? z

30:26
a Jer 8:15

26 Yet when I hoped for good, evil came;
  when I looked for light, then came darkness. a
27 The churning inside me never stops;
  days of suffering confront me.

30:28
b Ps 42:9

28 I go about blackened, b but not by the sun;
  I stand up in the assembly and cry for help.

30:29
c Mic 1:8

29 I have become a brother of jackals,
  a companion of owls. c

30:30
d Ps 102:3

30 My skin grows black and peels;
  my body burns with fever. d
31 My harp is tuned to mourning,
  and my flute to the sound of wailing.

a 12 The meaning of the Hebrew for this word is uncertain.   b 13 Or me. / 'No one can help him,' ⌞they say⌟.
c 18 Hebrew; Septuagint ⌞God⌟ grasps my clothing

31

"I made a covenant with my eyes
    not to look lustfully at a girl.[e]
2 For what is man's lot from God above,
    his heritage from the Almighty on high?[f]
3 Is it not ruin[g] for the wicked,
    disaster for those who do wrong?
4 Does he not see my ways[h]
    and count my every step?[i]

5 "If I have walked in falsehood
    or my foot has hurried after deceit—
6 let God weigh me in honest scales
    and he will know that I am blameless—
7 if my steps have turned from the path,[j]
    if my heart has been led by my eyes,
    or if my hands have been defiled,
8 then may others eat what I have sown,[k]
    and may my crops be uprooted.

9 "If my heart has been enticed[l] by a woman,
    or if I have lurked at my neighbor's door,
10 then may my wife grind another man's grain,
    and may other men sleep with her.[m]
11 For that would have been shameful,
    a sin to be judged.[n]
12 It is a fire that burns to Destruction[a];
    it would have uprooted my harvest.

13 "If I have denied justice to my menservants and maidservants
    when they had a grievance against me,[o]
14 what will I do when God confronts me?
    What will I answer when called to account?
15 Did not he who made me in the womb make them?
    Did not the same one form us both within our mothers?

16 "If I have denied the desires of the poor
    or let the eyes of the widow[p] grow weary,
17 if I have kept my bread to myself,
    not sharing it with the fatherless—
18 but from my youth I reared him as would a father,
    and from my birth I guided the widow—
19 if I have seen anyone perishing for lack of clothing,
    or a needy man without a garment,
20 and his heart did not bless me
    for warming him with the fleece from my sheep,
21 if I have raised my hand against the fatherless,
    knowing that I had influence in court,
22 then let my arm fall from the shoulder,
    let it be broken off at the joint.[q]
23 For I dreaded destruction from God,
    and for fear of his splendor[r] I could not do such things.

a 12 Hebrew *Abaddon*

Reference	Cross-reference
31:1	[e]Mt 5:28
31:2	[f]Job 20:29
31:3	[g]Job 21:30
31:4	[h]2Ch 16:9 [i]Pr 5:21
31:7	[j]Job 23:11
31:8	[k]Lev 26:16
31:9	[l]Job 24:15
31:10	[m]Jer 8:10
31:11	[n]Ge 38:24
31:13	[o]Dt 24:14-15
31:16	[p]Job 22:9
31:22	[q]Job 38:15
31:23	[r]Job 13:11

31:1-4 Job had not only avoided committing the great sin of adultery; he had not even taken the first step toward that sin by looking at a woman with lust. Job said he was innocent of both outward and inward sins. In chapter 29, Job reviewed his good deeds. Here in chapter 31 he listed sins he had not committed—in his heart (31:1-12), against his neighbors (31:13-23), or against God (31:24-34).

31:24-28 Job affirmed that depending on wealth for happiness is idolatry and denies the God of heaven. We excuse our society's obsession with money and possessions as a necessary evil or "the way it works" in the modern world. But every society in every age has valued the power and prestige that money brings. True believers must purge themselves of the deep-seated desire for more power, prestige, and possessions. They must also not withhold their resources from neighbors near and far who have desperate physical needs.

31:24
s Mt 6:24; Mk 10:24

31:25
t Ps 62:10

31:26
u Eze 8:16

31:28
v Dt 17:2-7

31:29
w Pr 17:5

31:31
x Job 22:7

31:32
y Ge 19:2-3

31:33
z Pr 28:13

31:34
a Ex 23:2

31:35
b Job 19:7; 30:28
c Job 35:14

31:37
d Job 1:3; 29:25

31:39
e 1 Ki 21:19
f Jas 5:4

31:40
g Ge 3:18

24 "If I have put my trust in gold
  or said to pure gold, 'You are my security,' s
25 if I have rejoiced over my great wealth, t
  the fortune my hands had gained,
26 if I have regarded the sun u in its radiance
  or the moon moving in splendor,
27 so that my heart was secretly enticed
  and my hand offered them a kiss of homage,
28 then these also would be sins to be judged, v
  for I would have been unfaithful to God on high.

29 "If I have rejoiced at my enemy's misfortune
  or gloated over the trouble that came to him w—
30 I have not allowed my mouth to sin
  by invoking a curse against his life—
31 if the men of my household have never said,
  'Who has not had his fill of Job's meat?' x—
32 but no stranger had to spend the night in the street,
  for my door was always open to the traveler y—
33 if I have concealed z my sin as men do, a
  by hiding my guilt in my heart
34 because I so feared the crowd a
  and so dreaded the contempt of the clans
  that I kept silent and would not go outside—

35 ("Oh, that I had someone to hear me! b
  I sign now my defense—let the Almighty answer me;
  let my accuser c put his indictment in writing.
36 Surely I would wear it on my shoulder,
  I would put it on like a crown.
37 I would give him an account of my every step;
  like a prince d I would approach him.)—

38 "if my land cries out against me
  and all its furrows are wet with tears,
39 if I have devoured its yield without payment e
  or broken the spirit of its tenants, f
40 then let briers g come up instead of wheat
  and weeds instead of barley."

The words of Job are ended.

C. A YOUNG MAN ANSWERS JOB (32:1—37:24)

Young Elihu rebukes the three friends for being unable to give Job a reasonable answer for why he was suffering. But he only gives a partial answer to Job's question by saying that people cannot understand all that God allows but must trust him. This was the best answer that a human could give, yet it was incomplete. Often the best human answers are incomplete because we do not have all the facts.

32:1
h Job 33:9

32:2
i Ge 22:21

Elihu

32 So these three men stopped answering Job, because he was righteous in his own eyes. h 2 But Elihu son of Barakel the Buzite, i of the family of Ram, became very angry

a 33 Or as Adam did

31:33, 34 Job declared that he did not try to hide his sin as men often do. The fear that our sins will be discovered leads us to patterns of deception. We cover up with lies so that we will appear good to others. But we cannot hide from God. Do you try to keep people from seeing the real you? When you acknowledge your sins, you free yourself to receive forgiveness and a new life.

31:1 If Job was really a good man, his three friends would have to drop their theory that suffering is always God's punishment for evil actions. Instead of considering another viewpoint, however, they cut off the discussion. They were convinced that Job had

some hidden fault or sin, so there was no point in talking if Job would not confess it. But Job knew he had lived uprightly before God and others (chapter 29) and had avoided wrong thoughts and actions (chapter 31). He wasn't about to invent a sin to satisfy his friends!

32:2ff When Eliphaz, Bildad, and Zophar had nothing more to say, Elihu became the fourth person to speak to Job. This was the first and only time he spoke. Apparently he was a bystander and much younger than the others (32:6, 7), but he introduced a new viewpoint. While Job's three friends said he was suffering from with Job for justifying himself rather than God. ³He was also angry with the three friends, because they had found no way to refute Job, and yet had condemned him.ᵃ ⁴Now Elihu had waited before speaking to Job because they were older than he. ⁵But when he saw that the three men had nothing more to say, his anger was aroused.

⁶So Elihu son of Barakel the Buzite said:

> "I am young in years,
>   and you are old;ʲ
> that is why I was fearful,
>   not daring to tell you what I know.

32:6
ʲJob 15:10

⁷ I thought, 'Age should speak;
    advanced years should teach wisdom.'
⁸ But it is the spiritᵇ in a man,
    the breath of the Almighty, that gives him understanding.ᵏ

32:8
ᵏPr 2:6

⁹ It is not only the oldᶜ who are wise,ˡ
    not only the aged who understand what is right.

32:9
ˡ1Co 1:26

¹⁰ "Therefore I say: Listen to me;
    I too will tell you what I know.
¹¹ I waited while you spoke,
    I listened to your reasoning;
while you were searching for words,
¹²   I gave you my full attention.
But not one of you has proved Job wrong;
    none of you has answered his arguments.
¹³ Do not say, 'We have found wisdom;ᵐ
    let God refute him, not man.'

32:13
ᵐJer 9:23

¹⁴ But Job has not marshaled his words against me,
    and I will not answer him with your arguments.

¹⁵ "They are dismayed and have no more to say;
    words have failed them.
¹⁶ Must I wait, now that they are silent,
    now that they stand there with no reply?
¹⁷ I too will have my say;
    I too will tell what I know.
¹⁸ For I am full of words,
    and the spirit within me compels me;
¹⁹ inside I am like bottled-up wine,
    like new wineskins ready to burst.
²⁰ I must speak and find relief;
    I must open my lips and reply.
²¹ I will show partialityⁿ to no one,ᵒ
    nor will I flatter any man;

32:21
ⁿLev 19:15
ᵒMt 22:16

²² for if I were skilled in flattery,
    my Maker would soon take me away.

33   "But now, Job, listen to my words;
            pay attention to everything I say.

ᵃ3 Masoretic Text; an ancient Hebrew scribal tradition *Job, and so had condemned God*   ᵇ8 Or *Spirit*; also in verse 18
ᶜ9 Or *many*; or *great*

---

some past sins, Elihu said Job's suffering would not go away until he realized his *present* sin. He maintained that Job wasn't suffering because of sin, he was sinning because of suffering. Elihu pointed out that Job's attitude had become arrogant as he tried to defend his innocence. Elihu also said that suffering is not meant to punish us as much as it is meant to correct and restore us, to keep us on the right path.

There is much truth in Elihu's speech. He was urging Job to look at his suffering from a different perspective and with a greater purpose in mind. While his speech is on a higher spiritual plateau than the others, Elihu still wrongly assumed that a cor-

rect response to suffering always brings healing and restoration (33:23–30) and that suffering is always in some way connected to sin (34:11).

32:7-9 "The breath of the Almighty, that gives him understanding." It is not enough to recognize a great truth; it must be lived out each day. Elihu recognized the truth that God was the only source of real wisdom, but he did not use God's wisdom to help Job. While he recognized where wisdom came from, he did not seek to acquire it. Becoming wise is an ongoing, lifelong pursuit. Don't be content just to know about wisdom; make it part of your life.

2 I am about to open my mouth;
   my words are on the tip of my tongue.
3 My words come from an upright heart;
   my lips sincerely speak what I know.*p*
4 The Spirit of God has made me;*q*
   the breath of the Almighty*r* gives me life.
5 Answer me then, if you can;
   prepare yourself and confront me.
6 I am just like you before God;
   I too have been taken from clay.
7 No fear of me should alarm you,
   nor should my hand be heavy upon you.

8 "But you have said in my hearing—
   I heard the very words—
9 'I am pure*s* and without sin;
   I am clean and free from guilt.
10 Yet God has found fault with me;
   he considers me his enemy.*t*
11 He fastens my feet in shackles;*u*
   he keeps close watch on all my paths.'

12 "But I tell you, in this you are not right,
   for God is greater than man.
13 Why do you complain to him*v*
   that he answers none of man's words*a*?
14 For God does speak*w*—now one way, now another—
   though man may not perceive it.
15 In a dream,*x* in a vision of the night,
   when deep sleep falls on men
   as they slumber in their beds,
16 he may speak*y* in their ears
   and terrify them with warnings,
17 to turn man from wrongdoing
   and keep him from pride,
18 to preserve his soul from the pit,*b*
   his life from perishing by the sword.*c*
19 Or a man may be chastened on a bed of pain
   with constant distress in his bones,
20 so that his very being finds food*z* repulsive
   and his soul loathes the choicest meal.
21 His flesh wastes away to nothing,
   and his bones, once hidden, now stick out.*a*
22 His soul draws near to the pit,*d*
   and his life to the messengers of death.*e*

23 "Yet if there is an angel on his side
   as a mediator, one out of a thousand,
   to tell a man what is right for him,

a 13 Or *that he does not answer for any of his actions*   *b* 18 Or *preserve him from the grave*   *c* 18 Or *from crossing the River*   *d* 22 Or *He draws near to the grave*   *e* 22 Or *to the dead*

33:3
p Job 6:28; 27:4;
36:4
33:4
q Ge 2:7
r Job 27:3

33:9
s Job 10:7

33:10
t Job 13:24

33:11
u Job 13:27

33:13
v Isa 45:9

33:14
w Ps 62:11
33:15
x Job 4:13

33:16
y Job 36:10,15

33:20
z Ps 107:18

33:21
a Job 16:8

33:13 Being informed brings a sense of security. It's natural to want to know what's happening in our lives. Job wanted to know what was going on, why he was suffering. In previous chapters, we sense his frustration. Elihu claimed to have the answer for Job's biggest question, "Why doesn't God tell me what is happening?" Elihu told Job that God was trying to answer him, but he was not listening. Elihu misjudged God on this point. If God were to answer all our questions, we would not be adequately tested. What if God had said, "Job, Satan's going to test you and afflict you, but in the end you'll be healed and get everything back"?

Job's greatest test was not the pain, but that he did not know *why* he was suffering. Our greatest test may be that we must trust God's goodness even though we don't understand why our lives are going a certain way. We must learn to trust in *God* who is good and not in the goodness of life.

33:14–24 Elihu's point was that God had spoken again and again. He spoke in dreams and visions (33:15–18), through suffering (33:19–22), and by mediating angels (33:23, 24). Job already knew that. Elihu accused Job of not listening to God, which was not true.

24 to be gracious to him and say,
　　'Spare him from going down to the pit[a];
　　I have found a ransom for him'—
25 then his flesh is renewed like a child's;
　　it is restored as in the days of his youth.
26 He prays to God and finds favor with him,
　　he sees God's face and shouts for joy;[b]
　　he is restored by God to his righteous state.
27 Then he comes to men and says,
　　'I sinned, and perverted what was right,[c]
　　but I did not get what I deserved.[d]
28 He redeemed my soul from going down to the pit,[b]
　　and I will live to enjoy the light.'[e]
29 "God does all these things to a man[f]—
　　twice, even three times—
30 to turn back his soul from the pit,[c]
　　that the light of life[g] may shine on him.

31 "Pay attention, Job, and listen to me;
　　be silent, and I will speak.
32 If you have anything to say, answer me;
　　speak up, for I want you to be cleared.
33 But if not, then listen to me;
　　be silent, and I will teach you wisdom."

34 Then Elihu said:

2 "Hear my words, you wise men;
　　listen to me, you men of learning.
3 For the ear tests words
　　as the tongue tastes food.[h]
4 Let us discern for ourselves what is right;
　　let us learn together what is good.

5 "Job says, 'I am innocent,
　　but God denies me justice.
6 Although I am right,
　　I am considered a liar;
　　although I am guiltless,
　　his arrow inflicts an incurable wound.'
7 What man is like Job,
　　who drinks scorn like water?[i]
8 He keeps company with evildoers;
　　he associates with wicked men.
9 For he says, 'It profits a man nothing
　　when he tries to please God.'

10 "So listen to me, you men of understanding.
　　Far be it from God to do evil,
　　from the Almighty to do wrong.[j]
11 He repays a man for what he has done;[k]
　　he brings upon him what his conduct deserves.
12 It is unthinkable that God would do wrong,
　　that the Almighty would pervert justice.[l]

a 24 Or grave　　b 28 Or redeemed me from going down to the grave　　c 30 Or turn him back from the grave

	33:26
	b Job 22:26
	33:27
	c Lk 15:21
	d Ro 6:21
	33:28
	e Job 22:28
	33:29
	f Eph 1:11; Php 2:13
	33:30
	g Ps 56:13
	34:3
	h Job 12:11
	34:7
	i Job 15:16
	34:10
	j Job 8:3
	34:11
	k Ps 62:12; Mt 16:27
	34:12
	l Job 8:3

34:10–15 God doesn't sin and is never unjust, Elihu claimed. Throughout this book, Eliphaz, Bildad, Zophar, and Elihu all have elements of truth in their speeches. Unfortunately, the nuggets of truth are buried under layers of false assumptions and conclusions. Although we might have a wealth of Bible knowledge and life experiences, we must make sure our conclusions are consistent with all of God's Word, not just parts of it.

13 Who appointed him over the earth?
   Who put him in charge of the whole world?*m*

14 If it were his intention
   and he withdrew his spirit*a* and breath,*n*
15 all mankind would perish together
   and man would return to the dust.*o*

16 "If you have understanding, hear this;
   listen to what I say.
17 Can he who hates justice govern?*p*
   Will you condemn the just and mighty One?
18 Is he not the One who says to kings, 'You are worthless,'
   and to nobles, 'You are wicked,'*q*
19 who shows no partiality*r* to princes
   and does not favor the rich over the poor,
   for they are all the work of his hands?
20 They die in an instant, in the middle of the night;*s*
   the people are shaken and they pass away;
   the mighty are removed without human hand.*t*

21 "His eyes are on the ways of men;
   he sees their every step.*u*
22 There is no dark place,*v* no deep shadow,*w*
   where evildoers can hide.
23 God has no need to examine men further,
   that they should come before him for judgment.
24 Without inquiry he shatters the mighty
   and sets up others in their place.*x*
25 Because he takes note of their deeds,
   he overthrows them in the night and they are crushed.
26 He punishes them for their wickedness
   where everyone can see them,
27 because they turned from following him
   and had no regard for any of his ways.*y*
28 They caused the cry of the poor to come before him,
   so that he heard the cry of the needy.*z*
29 But if he remains silent, who can condemn him?
   If he hides his face, who can see him?
   Yet he is over man and nation alike,
30   to keep a godless man from ruling,
      from laying snares for the people.

a 14 Or Spirit

Cross-references (left margin):
34:13 *m* Job 38:4,6
34:14 *n* Ps 104:29
34:15 *o* Ge 3:19
34:17 *p* 2Sa 23:3-4
34:18 *q* Ex 22:28
34:19 *r* Dt 10:17
34:20 *s* Ex 12:29 *t* Job 12:19
34:21 *u* Job 31:4
34:22 *v* Ps 139:12 *w* Am 9:2-3
34:24 *x* Da 2:21
34:27 *y* 1Sa 15:11
34:28 *z* Ex 22:23; Jas 5:4

HOW SUFFERING AFFECTS US

Suffering is helpful when:	Suffering is harmful when:
We turn to God for understanding, endurance, and deliverance	We become hardened and reject God
We ask important questions we might not take time to think about in our normal routine	We refuse to ask any questions and miss any lessons that might be good for us
We are prepared by it to identify with and comfort others who suffer	We allow it to make us self-centered and selfish
We are open to being helped by others who are obeying God	We withdraw from the help others can give
We are ready to learn from a trustworthy God	We reject the fact that God can bring good out of calamity
We realize we can identify with what Christ suffered on the cross for us	We accuse God of being unjust and perhaps lead others to reject him
We are sensitized to the amount of suffering in the world	We refuse to be open to any changes in our lives

31 "Suppose a man says to God,
    'I am guilty but will offend no more.
32 Teach me what I cannot see;
    if I have done wrong, I will not do so again.'
33 Should God then reward you on your terms,
    when you refuse to repent?
You must decide, not I;
    so tell me what you know.

34 "Men of understanding declare,
    wise men who hear me say to me,
35 'Job speaks without knowledge;a
    his words lack insight.'
36 Oh, that Job might be tested to the utmost
    for answering like a wicked man!b
37 To his sin he adds rebellion;
    scornfully he claps his hands among us
    and multiplies his words against God."

35:35
a Job 35:16

34:36
b Job 22:15

35

Then Elihu said:

2 "Do you think this is just?
    You say, 'I will be cleared by God.a'
3 Yet you ask him, 'What profit is it to me,b
    and what do I gain by not sinning?'c

4 "I would like to reply to you
    and to your friends with you.
5 Look up at the heavens and see;
    gaze at the clouds so high above you.d
6 If you sin, how does that affect him?
    If your sins are many, what does that do to him?
7 If you are righteous, what do you give to him,
    or what does he receivee from your hand?f
8 Your wickedness affects only a man like yourself,
    and your righteousness only the sons of men.

9 "Men cry outg under a load of oppression;
    they plead for relief from the arm of the powerful.h
10 But no one says, 'Where is God my Maker,
    who gives songs in the night,i
11 who teachesj more to us than toc the beasts of the earth
    and makes us wiser thand the birds of the air?'
12 He does not answerk when men cry out
    because of the arrogance of the wicked.
13 Indeed, God does not listen to their empty plea;
    the Almighty pays no attention to it.l
14 How much less, then, will he listen
    when you say that you do not see him,
    that your case is before him
    and you must wait for him,
15 and further, that his anger never punishes
    and he does not take the least notice of wickedness.e
16 So Job opens his mouth with empty talk;
    without knowledge he multiplies words."m

35:3
c Job 9:29-31; 34:9

35:5
d Job 22:12

35:7
e Pr 9:12
f Job 22:2-3;
Lk 17:10

35:9
g Ex 2:23
h Job 12:19

35:10
i Ps 42:8; Ac 16:25

35:11
j Ps 94:12

35:12
k Pr 1:28

35:13
l Isa 1:15; Jer 11:11

35:16
m Job 34:35,37

a2 Or *My righteousness is more than God's* b3 Or *you* c11 Or *teaches us by* d11 Or *us wise by* e15 Symmachus,
Theodotion and Vulgate; the meaning of the Hebrew for this word is uncertain.

35:1ff Sometimes we wonder if being faithful to our convictions really does any good at all. Elihu spoke to this very point. His conclusion was that God is still concerned even though he doesn't intervene immediately in every situation. In the broad scope of time God executes justice. We have his promise on that. Don't lose hope. Wait upon God. He notices your right living and your faith.

36

Elihu continued:

2 "Bear with me a little longer and I will show you
    that there is more to be said in God's behalf.
3 I get my knowledge from afar;
    I will ascribe justice to my Maker.
4 Be assured that my words are not false;
    one perfect in knowledge is with you.

5 "God is mighty, but does not despise men;
    he is mighty, and firm in his purpose.
6 He does not keep the wicked alive
    but gives the afflicted their rights.
7 He does not take his eyes off the righteous;[n]
    he enthrones them with kings[o]
    and exalts them forever.
8 But if men are bound in chains,
    held fast by cords of affliction,
9 he tells them what they have done—
    that they have sinned arrogantly.
10 He makes them listen[p] to correction
    and commands them to repent of their evil.
11 If they obey and serve him,[q]
    they will spend the rest of their days in prosperity
    and their years in contentment.
12 But if they do not listen,
    they will perish by the sword[a][r]
    and die without knowledge.

13 "The godless in heart harbor resentment;
    even when he fetters them, they do not cry for help.
14 They die in their youth,
    among male prostitutes of the shrines.
15 But those who suffer he delivers in their suffering;
    he speaks to them in their affliction.

16 "He is wooing[s] you from the jaws of distress
    to a spacious place free from restriction,
    to the comfort of your table[t] laden with choice food.
17 But now you are laden with the judgment due the wicked;
    judgment and justice have taken hold of you.
18 Be careful that no one entices you by riches;
    do not let a large bribe turn you aside.
19 Would your wealth
    or even all your mighty efforts
    sustain you so you would not be in distress?
20 Do not long for the night,[u]
    to drag people away from their homes.[b]
21 Beware of turning to evil,[v]
    which you seem to prefer to affliction.[w]

22 "God is exalted in his power.
    Who is a teacher like him?
23 Who has prescribed his ways for him,[x]
    or said to him, 'You have done wrong'?
24 Remember to extol his work,[y]
    which men have praised in song.[z]
25 All mankind has seen it;
    men gaze on it from afar.

36:7
[n] Ps 33:18
[o] Ps 113:8

36:10
[p] Job 33:16

36:11
[q] Isa 1:19

36:12
[r] Job 15:22

36:16
[s] Hos 2:14
[t] Ps 23:5

36:20
[u] Job 34:20,25

36:21
[v] Ps 66:18
[w] Heb 11:25

36:23
[x] Job 34:13

36:24
[y] Ps 92:5
[z] Rev 15:3

[a] 12 Or will cross the River   [b] 20 The meaning of the Hebrew for verses 18-20 is uncertain.

26 How great is God—beyond our understanding![a]
   The number of his years is past finding out.[b]

27 "He draws up the drops of water,
   which distill as rain to the streams[a];[c]
28 the clouds pour down their moisture
   and abundant showers fall on mankind.
29 Who can understand how he spreads out the clouds,
   how he thunders from his pavilion?
30 See how he scatters his lightning about him,
   bathing the depths of the sea.
31 This is the way he governs[b] the nations[d]
   and provides food in abundance.[e]
32 He fills his hands with lightning
   and commands it to strike its mark.
33 His thunder announces the coming storm;
   even the cattle make known its approach.[c]

37 "At this my heart pounds
       and leaps from its place.
2 Listen! Listen to the roar of his voice,
   to the rumbling that comes from his mouth.
3 He unleashes his lightning beneath the whole heaven
   and sends it to the ends of the earth.
4 After that comes the sound of his roar;
   he thunders with his majestic voice.
   When his voice resounds,
   he holds nothing back.
5 God's voice thunders in marvelous ways;
   he does great things beyond our understanding.[f]
6 He says to the snow,[g] 'Fall on the earth,'
   and to the rain shower, 'Be a mighty downpour.'
7 So that all men he has made may know his work,
   he stops every man from his labor.[d]
8 The animals take cover;
   they remain in their dens.[h]
9 The tempest comes out from its chamber,
   the cold from the driving winds.
10 The breath of God produces ice,
   and the broad waters become frozen.[i]
11 He loads the clouds with moisture;
   he scatters his lightning through them.
12 At his direction they swirl around
   over the face of the whole earth
   to do whatever he commands them.[j]
13 He brings the clouds to punish men,
   or to water his earth[e] and show his love.[k]

14 "Listen to this, Job;
   stop and consider God's wonders.

[a]27 Or distill from the mist as rain   [b]31 Or nourishes   [c]33 Or announces his coming— / the One zealous against evil   [d]7 Or / he fills all men with fear by his power   [e]13 Or to favor them

---

36:26
[a]1Co 13:12
[b]Heb 1:12

36:27
[c]Ps 147:8

36:31
[d]Job 37:13
[e]Ac 14:17

37:5
[f]Job 5:9

37:6
[g]Job 38:22

37:8
[h]Ps 104:22

37:10
[i]Job 38:29-30;
Ps 147:17

37:12
[j]Ps 148:8

37:13
[k]Ex 9:18;
1Ki 18:45;
Job 38:27

36:26 One theme in the poetic literature of the Bible is that God is incomprehensible; we cannot know him completely. We can have some knowledge about him, for the Bible is full of details about who God is, how we can know him, and how we can have an eternal relationship with him. But we can never know enough to answer all of life's questions (Ecclesiastes 3:11), to predict our own future, or to manipulate God for our own ends. Life always creates more questions than we have answers, and we must constantly go to God for fresh insights into life's dilemmas (see 37:19–24).

37:2 Nothing can compare to God. His power and presence are awesome, and when he speaks, we must listen. Too often we presume to speak for God (as did Job's friends), to put words in his mouth, to take him for granted, or to interpret his silence to mean that he is absent or unconcerned. But God cares. He is in control, and he will speak. Be ready to hear his message—in the

15 Do you know how God controls the clouds
  and makes his lightning flash?
16 Do you know how the clouds hang poised,
  those wonders of him who is perfect in knowledge?[l]
17 You who swelter in your clothes
  when the land lies hushed under the south wind,
18 can you join him in spreading out the skies,[m]
  hard as a mirror of cast bronze?

19 "Tell us what we should say to him;
  we cannot draw up our case because of our darkness.
20 Should he be told that I want to speak?
  Would any man ask to be swallowed up?
21 Now no one can look at the sun,
  bright as it is in the skies
  after the wind has swept them clean.
22 Out of the north he comes in golden splendor;
  God comes in awesome majesty.
23 The Almighty is beyond our reach and exalted in power;[n]
  in his justice and great righteousness, he does not oppress.
24 Therefore, men revere him,[o]
  for does he not have regard for all the wise[p] in heart?[a]"

37:16
[l] Job 36:4

37:18
[m] Isa 44:24

37:23
[n] 1Ti 6:16

37:24
[o] Mt 10:28
[p] Mt 11:25

D. GOD ANSWERS JOB (38:1—41:34)

Instead of answering Job's question directly, God asks Job a series of questions that no human could possibly answer. Job responds by recognizing that God's ways are best. During difficult times, we, too, must humbly remember our position before the eternal, holy, incomprehensible God.

[a] 24 Or for he does not have regard for any who think they are wise.

GOD SPEAKS	Whom He Spoke To	What He Said	Reference
On various occasions in the Old Testament, God chose to communicate audibly with individuals. God will always find a way to make contact with those who want to know him. Some of those occasions are listed here.	Adam and Eve	Confronted them about sin	Genesis 3:8–13
	Noah	Gave him directions about building the ark	Genesis 6:13–22; 7:1; 8:15–17
	Abraham	Commanded him to follow God's leading and promised to bless him	Genesis 12:1–9
		Tested his obedience by commanding him to sacrifice his son	Genesis 22:1–14
	Jacob	Permitted him to go to Egypt	Genesis 46:1–4
	Moses	Sent him to lead the people out of Egypt	Exodus 3:1–10
		Gave him the Ten Commandments	Exodus 19:1—20:20
	Moses, Aaron, Miriam	Pronounced judgment on a family conflict	Numbers 12:1–15
	Joshua	Promised to be with him as he was with Moses	Joshua 1:1–9
	Samuel	Chose him to be his spokesman	1 Samuel 3:1–18
	Isaiah	Sent him to the people with his message	Isaiah 6:1–13
	Jeremiah	Encouraged him to be his prophet	Jeremiah 1:4–10
	Ezekiel	Sent him to Israel to warn the nation of coming judgment	Ezekiel 2:1–8

Bible, in your life through the Holy Spirit, and through circumstances and relationships.

37:21–24 Elihu concluded his speech with the tremendous truth that faith in God is far more important than Job's desire for an explanation for his suffering. He came so close to helping Job but then went down the wrong path. Significantly, it is here that God himself breaks into the discussion to draw the right conclusions from this important truth (38:1ff).

37:23 Elihu stressed God's sovereignty over all of nature as a reminder of his sovereignty over our lives. God is in control—he directs, preserves, and maintains his created order. Although we can't see it, God is divinely governing the moral and political affairs of people as well. By spending time observing the majestic and intricate parts of God's creation, we can be reminded of his power in every aspect of our lives.

The LORD Speaks

38 Then the LORD answered Job out of the storm. *q* He said:

38:1
*q*Job 40:6

2 "Who is this that darkens my counsel
   with words without knowledge?
3 Brace yourself like a man;
   I will question you,
   and you shall answer me. *r*

38:3
*r*Job 40:7

4 "Where were you when I laid the earth's foundation? *s*
   Tell me, if you understand.
5 Who marked off its dimensions? Surely you know!
   Who stretched a measuring line across it?

38:4
*s*Ps 104:5; Pr 8:29

6 On what were its footings set,
   or who laid its cornerstone *t*—
7 while the morning stars sang together
   and all the angels *a* shouted for joy?

38:6
*t*Job 26:7

8 "Who shut up the sea behind doors
   when it burst forth from the womb, *u*
9 when I made the clouds its garment
   and wrapped it in thick darkness,

38:8
*u*Ge 1:9-10

10 when I fixed limits for it
   and set its doors and bars in place, *v*

38:10
*v*Job 26:10

11 when I said, 'This far you may come and no farther;
   here is where your proud waves halt'? *w*

38:11
*w*Ps 89:9

12 "Have you ever given orders to the morning,
   or shown the dawn its place,
13 that it might take the earth by the edges
   and shake the wicked *x* out of it?

38:13
*x*Ps 104:35

14 The earth takes shape like clay under a seal;
   its features stand out like those of a garment.
15 The wicked are denied their light,
   and their upraised arm is broken. *y*

38:15
*y*Ps 10:15

16 "Have you journeyed to the springs of the sea
   or walked in the recesses of the deep?
17 Have the gates of death been shown to you?
   Have you seen the gates of the shadow of death *b*?
18 Have you comprehended the vast expanses of the earth?
   Tell me, if you know all this.

19 "What is the way to the abode of light?
   And where does darkness reside?
20 Can you take them to their places?
   Do you know the paths to their dwellings?
21 Surely you know, for you were already born!
   You have lived so many years!

22 "Have you entered the storehouses of the snow
   or seen the storehouses of the hail,

*a*7 Hebrew *the sons of God*   *b*17 Or *gates of deep shadows*

38:1ff Out of a mighty storm, God spoke. Surprisingly, he didn't answer any of Job's questions; Job's questions were not at the heart of the issue. Instead, God used Job's ignorance of the earth's natural order to reveal his ignorance of God's moral order. If Job did not understand the workings of God's physical creation, how could he possibly understand God's mind and character? There is no standard or criterion higher than God himself by which to judge. God himself is the standard. Our only option is to submit to his authority and rest in his care.

38:22, 23 God said he was reserving the storehouses of the snow and hail for times of trouble. God used hail to help Joshua and the Israelites win a battle (Joshua 10:11). Just as armies keep weapons in the armory, God has all the forces of nature in his control. Sometimes he uses them to confound those opposed to him or his people. Job couldn't even begin to know all of God's resources.

38:22–35 God stated that he has all the forces of nature at his command and that he can unleash or restrain them at will.

38:23
z Isa 30:30;
Eze 13:11
a Ex 9:18;
Jos 10:11;
Rev 16:21

23 which I reserve for times of trouble,z
    for days of war and battle?a
24 What is the way to the place where the lightning is dispersed,
    or the place where the east winds are scattered over the earth?
25 Who cuts a channel for the torrents of rain,
    and a path for the thunderstorm,
26 to water a land where no man lives,
    a desert with no one in it,

38:27
b Ps 104:14

27 to satisfy a desolate wasteland
    and make it sprout with grass?b

38:28
c Ps 147:8;
Jer 14:22

28 Does the rain have a father?c
    Who fathers the drops of dew?

38:29
d Ps 147:16-17

29 From whose womb comes the ice?
    Who gives birth to the frost from the heavensd
30 when the waters become hard as stone,
    when the surface of the deep is frozen?

38:31
e Job 9:9; Am 5:8

31 "Can you bind the beautifula Pleiades?
    Can you loose the cords of Orion?e
32 Can you bring forth the constellations in their seasonsb
    or lead out the Bearc with its cubs?
33 Do you know the laws of the heavens?
    Can you set up ⌊God'sd⌋ dominion over the earth?

34 "Can you raise your voice to the clouds
    and cover yourself with a flood of water?
35 Do you send the lightning bolts on their way?
    Do they report to you, 'Here we are'?

38:36
f Job 32:8; Ps 51:6;
Ecc 2:26

36 Who endowed the hearte with wisdom
    or gave understandingf to the minde?
37 Who has the wisdom to count the clouds?
    Who can tip over the water jars of the heavens
38 when the dust becomes hard
    and the clods of earth stick together?

38:39
g Ps 104:21

39 "Do you hunt the prey for the lioness
    and satisfy the hunger of the lionsg

a31 Or the twinkling; or the chains of the   b32 Or the morning star in its season   c32 Or out Leo   d33 Or his; or their
e36 The meaning of the Hebrew for this word is uncertain.

GOD'S JUSTICE   *Wrong View*   *Correct View*

| LAW OF FAIRNESS | | GOD |
| GOD | | JUSTICE |

There is a law of fairness or justice that is higher and more absolute than God. It is binding even for God. God must act in response to that law in order to be fair. Our response is to appeal to that law.

God himself is the standard of justice. He uses his power according to his own moral perfection. Thus, whatever he does is fair, even if we don't understand it. Our response is to appeal directly to him.

No one completely understands such common occurrences as rain or snow, and no one can command them—only God who created them has that power. God's point was that if Job could not explain such common events in nature, how could he possibly explain or question God? And if nature is beyond our grasp, God's moral purposes may not be what we imagine either.

38:31, 32 These are star constellations, and they are all under God's control.

40 when they crouch in their dens
   or lie in wait in a thicket?
41 Who provides food for the raven
   when its young cry out to God
   and wander about for lack of food?[h]

38:41
[h] Ps 147:9; Mt 6:26

39

"Do you know when the mountain goats give birth?
   Do you watch when the doe bears her fawn?
2 Do you count the months till they bear?
   Do you know the time they give birth?
3 They crouch down and bring forth their young;
   their labor pains are ended.
4 Their young thrive and grow strong in the wilds;
   they leave and do not return.

5 "Who let the wild donkey go free?
   Who untied his ropes?
6 I gave him the wasteland[i] as his home,
   the salt flats as his habitat.[j]
7 He laughs at the commotion in the town;
   he does not hear a driver's shout.
8 He ranges the hills for his pasture
   and searches for any green thing.

39:6
[i] Job 24:5; Jer 2:24
[j] Hos 8:9

9 "Will the wild ox[k] consent to serve you?
   Will he stay by your manger at night?
10 Can you hold him to the furrow with a harness?
   Will he till the valleys behind you?
11 Will you rely on him for his great strength?
   Will you leave your heavy work to him?
12 Can you trust him to bring in your grain
   and gather it to your threshing floor?

39:9
[k] Nu 23:22; Dt 33:17

13 "The wings of the ostrich flap joyfully,
   but they cannot compare with the pinions and feathers of the stork.
14 She lays her eggs on the ground
   and lets them warm in the sand,
15 unmindful that a foot may crush them,
   that some wild animal may trample them.
16 She treats her young harshly,[l] as if they were not hers;
   she cares not that her labor was in vain,
17 for God did not endow her with wisdom
   or give her a share of good sense.
18 Yet when she spreads her feathers to run,
   she laughs at horse and rider.

39:16
[l] La 4:3

19 "Do you give the horse his strength
   or clothe his neck with a flowing mane?
20 Do you make him leap like a locust,
   striking terror with his proud snorting?
21 He paws fiercely, rejoicing in his strength,
   and charges into the fray.[m]
22 He laughs at fear, afraid of nothing;
   he does not shy away from the sword.
23 The quiver rattles against his side,
   along with the flashing spear and lance.
24 In frenzied excitement he eats up the ground;
   he cannot stand still when the trumpet sounds.

39:21
[m] Jer 8:6

39:1ff God asked Job several questions about the animal kingdom in order to demonstrate how limited Job's knowledge really
was. God was not seeking answers from Job. Instead, he
was getting Job to recognize and submit to God's power and

25 At the blast of the trumpet he snorts, 'Aha!'
He catches the scent of battle from afar,
the shout of commanders and the battle cry.

26 "Does the hawk take flight by your wisdom
and spread his wings toward the south?

39:27
ⁿOb 1:4

27 Does the eagle soar at your command
and build his nest on high?ⁿ

28 He dwells on a cliff and stays there at night;
a rocky crag is his stronghold.

29 From there he seeks out his food;
his eyes detect it from afar.

39:30
ºMt 24:28; Lk 17:37

30 His young ones feast on blood,
and where the slain are, there is he."º

40:1
ᵖJob 33:13

40 The Lᴏʀᴅ said to Job:ᵖ

2 "Will the one who contends with the Almighty correct him?
Let him who accuses God answer him!"

3 Then Job answered the Lᴏʀᴅ:

40:4
ᑫJob 29:9

4 "I am unworthy—how can I reply to you?
I put my hand over my mouth.ᑫ

5 I spoke once, but I have no answer—
twice, but I will say no more."

40:6
ʳJob 38:1

6 Then the Lᴏʀᴅ spoke to Job out of the storm:ʳ

40:7
ˢJob 42:4

7 "Brace yourself like a man;
I will question you,
and you shall answer me.ˢ

40:8
ᵗRo 3:3

8 "Would you discredit my justice?ᵗ
Would you condemn me to justify yourself?

9 Do you have an arm like God's,
and can your voice thunder like his?

40:10
ᵘPs 93:1; 104:1

10 Then adorn yourself with glory and splendor,
and clothe yourself in honor and majesty.ᵘ

FOUR VIEWS OF SUFFERING

Satan's view	People believe in God only when they are prospering and not suffering. This is wrong.
The view of Job's three friends	Suffering is God's judgment for sin. This is not always true.
Elihu's view	Suffering is God's way to teach, discipline, and refine. This is true, but an incomplete explanation.
God's view	Suffering causes us to trust God for who he is, not what he does.

---

sovereignty. Only then could he hear what God was really saying to him.

40:2-5 How do you contend with or accuse Almighty God? Do you demand answers when things don't go your way, you lose a job, someone close to you is ill or dies, finances are tight, you fail, or unexpected changes occur? The next time you are tempted to complain to God, consider how much he loves you. And remember Job's reaction when he had his chance to speak. Are you worse off than Job or more righteous than he? Give God a chance to reveal his greater purposes for you, but remember that they may unfold over the course of your life and not at the moment you desire.

40:4 Throughout his time of suffering, Job longed to have an opportunity to plead his innocence before God. Here God appeared to Job and gave him that opportunity. But Job decided to remain quiet because it was no longer necessary for him to speak. God had shown Job that, as a limited human being, he had neither the ability to judge the God who created the universe nor the right to ask why. God's actions do not depend on ours. He will do what he knows is best, regardless of what we think is fair. It is important to note, however, that God came to Job, demonstrating his love and care for him.

11 Unleash the fury of your wrath,
   look at every proud man and bring him low,[v]
12 look at every proud man and humble him,[w]
   crush the wicked where they stand.
13 Bury them all in the dust together;
   shroud their faces in the grave.
14 Then I myself will admit to you
   that your own right hand can save you.

15 "Look at the behemoth,[a]
   which I made along with you
   and which feeds on grass like an ox.
16 What strength he has in his loins,
   what power in the muscles of his belly!
17 His tail[b] sways like a cedar;
   the sinews of his thighs are close-knit.
18 His bones are tubes of bronze,
   his limbs like rods of iron.
19 He ranks first among the works of God,[x]
   yet his Maker can approach him with his sword.
20 The hills bring him their produce,[y]
   and all the wild animals play[z] nearby.
21 Under the lotus plants he lies,
   hidden among the reeds in the marsh.
22 The lotuses conceal him in their shadow;
   the poplars by the stream surround him.
23 When the river rages, he is not alarmed;
   he is secure, though the Jordan should surge against his mouth.
24 Can anyone capture him by the eyes,[c]
   or trap him and pierce his nose?

41 "Can you pull in the leviathan[d][a] with a fishhook
   or tie down his tongue with a rope?
2 Can you put a cord through his nose
   or pierce his jaw with a hook?[b]
3 Will he keep begging you for mercy?
   Will he speak to you with gentle words?
4 Will he make an agreement with you
   for you to take him as your slave for life?
5 Can you make a pet of him like a bird
   or put him on a leash for your girls?
6 Will traders barter for him?
   Will they divide him up among the merchants?
7 Can you fill his hide with harpoons
   or his head with fishing spears?
8 If you lay a hand on him,
   you will remember the struggle and never do it again!
9 Any hope of subduing him is false;
   the mere sight of him is overpowering.
10 No one is fierce enough to rouse him.
   Who then is able to stand against me?
11 Who has a claim against me that I must pay?[c]
   Everything under heaven belongs to me.[d]

a 15 Possibly the hippopotamus or the elephant   b 17 Possibly trunk   c 24 Or *by a water hole*   d 1 Possibly
the crocodile

40:11
[v] Isa 2:11,12,17;
Da 4:37
40:12
[w] 1Sa 2:7

40:19
[x] Job 41:33

40:20
[y] Ps 104:14
[z] Ps 104:26

41:1
[a] Ps 104:26;
Isa 27:1
41:2
[b] Isa 37:29

41:11
[c] Ro 11:35
[d] Ex 19:5; Dt 10:14;
1Co 10:26

40:15 The behemoth was a large land animal, possibly an elephant or hippopotamus.

41:1 While *leviathan* usually refers to a seven-headed sea monster in old Canaanite myths, it probably means crocodile here.

41:9–11 It is foolish for people to think they can stand up against God when they are afraid to confront even a crocodile. How much more powerful is God! It is better to submit to God's loving authority than to face his wrath.

12 "I will not fail to speak of his limbs,
   his strength and his graceful form.
13 Who can strip off his outer coat?
   Who would approach him with a bridle?
14 Who dares open the doors of his mouth,
   ringed about with his fearsome teeth?
15 His back has[a] rows of shields
   tightly sealed together;
16 each is so close to the next
   that no air can pass between.
17 They are joined fast to one another;
   they cling together and cannot be parted.
18 His snorting throws out flashes of light;
   his eyes are like the rays of dawn.
19 Firebrands stream from his mouth;
   sparks of fire shoot out.
20 Smoke pours from his nostrils
   as from a boiling pot over a fire of reeds.
21 His breath sets coals ablaze,
   and flames dart from his mouth.
22 Strength resides in his neck;
   dismay goes before him.
23 The folds of his flesh are tightly joined;
   they are firm and immovable.
24 His chest is hard as rock,
   hard as a lower millstone.
25 When he rises up, the mighty are terrified;
   they retreat before his thrashing.
26 The sword that reaches him has no effect,
   nor does the spear or the dart or the javelin.
27 Iron he treats like straw
   and bronze like rotten wood.
28 Arrows do not make him flee;
   slingstones are like chaff to him.
29 A club seems to him but a piece of straw;
   he laughs at the rattling of the lance.
30 His undersides are jagged potsherds,
   leaving a trail in the mud like a threshing sledge.
31 He makes the depths churn like a boiling caldron
   and stirs up the sea like a pot of ointment.
32 Behind him he leaves a glistening wake;
   one would think the deep had white hair.
33 Nothing on earth is his equal—
   a creature without fear.
34 He looks down on all that are haughty;
   he is king over all that are proud."

a 15 Or *His pride is his*

JOB AND JESUS	Subject/Reference in Job	How Jesus Is the Answer
The book of Job is intimately tied to the New Testament because Job's questions and problems are answered perfectly in Jesus Christ.	Someone must help us approach God (9:32, 33)	1 Timothy 2:5
	Is there life after death? (14:14)	John 11:25
	There is one in heaven working on our behalf (16:19)	Hebrews 9:24
	There is one who can save us from judgment (19:25)	Hebrews 7:24, 25
	What is important in life? (21:7–15)	Matthew 16:26; John 3:16
	Where do we find God? (23:3–5)	John 14:9

E. JOB IS RESTORED (42:1–17)

In response to God's speech, Job humbles himself. God rebukes the three friends for adding to Job's suffering by their false assumptions and critical attitudes. Job's material possessions and family are restored, and he receives even greater blessings than he had before. Those who persist in trusting God will be rewarded.

Job

42

Then Job replied to the LORD:

2 "I know that you can do all things;*e*
no plan of yours can be thwarted.

3 ⌊You asked,⌋ 'Who is this that obscures my counsel without knowledge?'*f*
Surely I spoke of things I did not understand,
things too wonderful for me to know.

4 ⌊"You said,⌋ 'Listen now, and I will speak;
I will question you,
and you shall answer me.'*g*

5 My ears had heard of you
but now my eyes have seen you.

6 Therefore I despise myself *h*
and repent in dust and ashes."*i*

42:2
e Ge 18:14;
Mt 19:26

42:3
f Job 38:2

42:4
g Job 38:3; 40:7

42:6
h Job 40:4
i Ezr 9:6

Epilogue

7 After the LORD had said these things to Job, he said to Eliphaz the Temanite, "I am angry with you and your two friends, because you have not spoken of me what is right, as my servant Job has. 8 So now take seven bulls and seven rams*j* and go to my servant Job and sacrifice a burnt offering for yourselves. My servant Job will pray for you, and I will accept his prayer*k* and not deal with you according to your folly. You have not spoken of me what is right, as my servant Job has." 9 So Eliphaz the Temanite, Bildad the Shuhite and Zophar the Naamathite did what the LORD told them; and the LORD accepted Job's prayer.

42:8
j Nu 23:1,29
k Jas 5:15-16;
1Jn 5:16

10 After Job had prayed for his friends, the LORD made him prosperous again*l* and gave him twice as much as he had before. 11 All his brothers and sisters and everyone who had known him before*m* came and ate with him in his house. They comforted and consoled him over all the trouble the LORD had brought upon him, and each one gave him a piece of silver*a* and a gold ring.

42:10
l Ps 14:7

42:11
m Job 19:13

a 11 Hebrew him a kesitah; a kesitah was a unit of money of unknown weight and value.

42:1ff Throughout the book, Job's friends had asked him to admit his sin and ask for forgiveness, and eventually Job did indeed repent. Ironically, Job's repentance was not the kind called for by his friends. He did not ask for forgiveness for committing secret sins, but for questioning God's sovereignty and justice. Job repented of his attitude and acknowledged God's great power and perfect justice. We sin when we angrily ask, "If God is in control, how could he let this happen?" Because we are locked into time, unable to see beyond today, we cannot know the reasons for everything that happens. Will you trust God with your unanswered questions?

42:2–4 Job was quoting the Lord's earlier questions to him (38:2, 3). He openly and honestly faced God and admitted that he was the one who had been foolish. Are you using what you can't understand as an excuse for your lack of trust? Admit to God that you don't even have enough faith to trust him. True faith begins in such humility.

42:7, 8 God made it clear that Job's friends were wrong. The fact that God did not mention any specific sins shows that God confirmed Job's claim to have led a devout and obedient life. Job's friends had made the error of assuming that Job's suffering was caused by some great sin. They were judging Job without knowing what God was doing. We must be careful to avoid making judgments about a person because God may be working in ways we know nothing about.

42:8–10 After receiving much criticism, Job was still able to pray for his three friends. It is difficult to forgive someone who has accused us of wrongdoing, but Job did. Are you praying for those who have hurt you? Can you forgive them? Follow the actions of Job, whom God called a good man, and pray for those who have wronged you.

42:10, 11 Would the message of the book of Job change if God had not restored to Job his former blessings? No. God is still sovereign. Jesus said that anyone who gives up something for the kingdom of God will be repaid (Luke 18:29, 30). Our restoration may or may not be the same kind as Job's, which was both spiritual and material. Our complete restoration may not be in this life—but it *will* happen. God loves us, and he is just. He not only will restore whatever we have lost unjustly, but he also will give us more than we can imagine as we live with him in eternity. Cling tightly to your faith through all your trials, and you too will be rewarded by God—if not now, in the life to come.

¹²The LORD blessed the latter part of Job's life more than the first. He had fourteen thousand sheep, six thousand camels, a thousand yoke of oxen and a thousand donkeys. ¹³And he also had seven sons and three daughters. ¹⁴The first daughter he named Jemimah, the second Keziah and the third Keren-Happuch. ¹⁵Nowhere in all the land were there found women as beautiful as Job's daughters, and their father granted them an inheritance along with their brothers.

42:17
ⁿ Ge 25:8

¹⁶After this, Job lived a hundred and forty years; he saw his children and their children to the fourth generation. ¹⁷And so he died, old and full of years. ⁿ

WHEN WE SUFFER

Here are six questions to ask ourselves when we suffer, and what to do if the answer is yes.

Questions	*Our Response*
Am I being punished by God for sin?	Confess known sin.
Is Satan attacking me as I try to survive as a Christian?	Call on God for strength.
Am I being prepared for a special service, learning to be compassionate to those who suffer?	Resist self-pity. Ask God to open up doors of opportunity and help you discover others who suffer as you do.
Am I specifically selected for testing, like Job?	Accept help from the body of believers. Trust God to work his purpose through you.
Is my suffering a result of natural consequences for which I am not directly responsible?	Recognize that in a sinful world, both good and evil people will suffer. But the good person has a promise from God that his or her suffering will one day come to an end.
Is my suffering due to some unknown reason?	Don't draw inward from the pain. Proclaim your faith in God, know that he cares, and wait patiently for his aid.

42:17 The main question in the book of Job is timely: Why do believers experience troubles and suffering? Through a long debate, Job's supposedly wise friends were unable to answer this question. Job's friends made a serious error for which God rebuked them. They assumed that trouble comes only because people sin. People make the same mistake today when they assert that sickness or lack of material blessing is a sign of unconfessed sin or lack of faith. Though normally (but not always) following God leads to a happier life, and rebelling against God normally (but not always) leads to an unhappy life, *God is in control.* In our world invaded by sin, calamity and suffering may come to good and bad alike.

This does not mean that God is indifferent, uncaring, unjust, or powerless to protect us. Bad things happen because we live in a fallen world where both believers and unbelievers are hit with the tragic consequences of sin. God allows evil for a time although he often turns it around for our good (Romans 8:28). We may have no answers as to why God allows evil, but we can be sure he is all-powerful and knows what he is doing. The next time you face trials and dilemmas, see them as opportunities to turn to God for strength. You will find a God who only desires to show his love and compassion to you. If you can trust him in pain, confusion, and loneliness, you will win the victory and eliminate doubt, one of Satan's greatest footholds in your life. Make God your foundation. You can never be separated from his love.

PSALMS

VITAL STATISTICS

PURPOSE:
To provide poetry for the expression of praise, worship, and confession to God

AUTHORS:
David wrote 73 psalms; Asaph wrote 12; the sons of Korah wrote 9; Solomon wrote 2; Heman (with the sons of Korah), Ethan, and Moses each wrote one; 51 psalms are anonymous. The New Testament ascribes two of the anonymous psalms (Psalms 2 and 95) to David (see Acts 4:25; Hebrews 4:7).

ORIGINAL AUDIENCE:
The people of Israel

DATE WRITTEN:
Between the time of Moses (approximately 1440 B.C.) and the Babylonian captivity (586 B.C.)

SETTING:
For the most part, the psalms were not intended to be narrations of historical events. However, they often parallel events in history, such as David's flight from Saul and his sin with Bathsheba.

KEY VERSE:
"Let everything that has breath praise the LORD. Praise the LORD." (150:6)

KEY PERSON:
David

KEY PLACE:
God's holy temple

"HI, how are you?" "Fine." Not exactly an "in-depth" discussion, this brief interchange is normal as friends and acquaintances pass and briefly touch each other with a cliché or two. Actually, clichés are a way of life, saturating sentences and permeating paragraphs. But if this is the essence of our communication, our relationships will stall on a superficial plateau. Facts and opinions also fill our verbiage. These words go deeper, but the true person still lies hidden beneath them. In reality, only when honest feelings and emotions are shared can real people be known, loved, and helped.

Often, patterns of superficial communication spill over into our talks with God. We easily slide through well-worn lines recited for decades, or we quickly toss a cliché or two at God and call it prayer. Certainly God hears and understands these feeble attempts, but by limiting the depth of our communication, we become shallow in our relationship with him. But God knows us, and he wants to have genuine communication with us.

At the center of the Bible is the book of Psalms. This great collection of songs and prayers expresses the heart and soul of humanity. In them we find the whole range of human experiences expressed. This book holds no clichés. Instead, David and the other writers honestly poured out their true feelings, reflecting a dynamic, powerful, and life-changing friendship with God. The psalmists confess their sins, express their doubts and fears, ask God for help in times of trouble, and praise and worship him.

As you read the book of Psalms, you will hear believers crying out to God from the depths of despair, and you will hear them singing to him in the heights of celebration. But whether the psalm writers are despairing or rejoicing, you will always hear them sharing honest feelings with their God. Because of the honesty expressed by these writers, men and women throughout history have come, again and again, to the book of Psalms for comfort during times of struggle and distress. And through the psalms, they have risen from the depths of despair to new heights of joy and praise as they also discovered the power of God's everlasting love and forgiveness. Let the honesty of the psalms guide you into a deep and genuine relationship with God.

THE BLUEPRINT

BOOK I
PSALMS 1:1—41:13

While the psalms are not organized by topic, it is helpful to compare the dominant themes in each section of the psalms to the five books of Moses. This first collection of psalms, mainly written by David, is similar to the book of Genesis. Just as Genesis tells how mankind was created, fell into sin, and was then promised redemption, many of these psalms discuss humans as blessed, fallen, and redeemed by God.

BOOK II
PSALMS 42:1—72:20

This collection of psalms, mainly written by David and the sons of Korah, is similar to the book of Exodus. Just as Exodus describes the nation of Israel, many of these psalms describe the nation as ruined and then recovered. As God rescued the nation of Israel, he also rescues us. We do not have to work out solutions first, but we can go to God with our problems and ask him to help.

BOOK III
PSALMS 73:1—89:52

This collection of psalms, mainly written by Asaph or Asaph's descendants, is similar to the book of Leviticus. Just as Leviticus discusses the tabernacle and God's holiness, many of these psalms discuss the temple and God's enthronement. Because God is almighty, we can turn to him for deliverance. These psalms praise God because he is holy, and his perfect holiness deserves our worship and reverence.

BOOK IV
PSALMS 90:1—106:48

This collection of psalms, mainly written by unknown authors, is similar to the book of Numbers. Just as Numbers discusses the relationship of the nation of Israel to surrounding nations, these psalms often mention the relationship of God's overruling kingdom to the other nations. Because we are citizens of the kingdom of God, we can keep the events and troubles of earth in their proper perspective.

BOOK V
PSALMS 107:1—150:6

This collection of psalms, mainly written by David, is similar to the book of Deuteronomy. Just as Deuteronomy was concerned with God and his Word, these psalms are anthems of praise and thanksgiving for God and his Word. Most of the psalms were originally set to music and used in worship. We can use these psalms today as they were used in the past, as a hymnbook of praise and worship. This is a book that ought to make our hearts sing.

MEGATHEMES

THEME	EXPLANATION	IMPORTANCE
Praise	Psalms are songs of praise to God as our Creator, Sustainer, and Redeemer. Praise is recognizing, appreciating, and expressing God's greatness.	Focusing our thoughts on God moves us to praise him. The more we know him, the more we can appreciate what he has done for us.
God's Power	God is all-powerful; and he always acts at the right time. He is sovereign over every situation. God's power is shown by the ways he reveals himself in creation, history, and his Word.	When we feel powerless, God can help us. His strength can overcome the despair of any pain or trial. We can always pray that he will deliver, protect, and sustain us.
Forgiveness	Many psalms are intense prayers asking God for forgiveness. God forgives us when we confess our sin and turn from it.	Because God forgives us, we can pray to him honestly and directly. When we receive his forgiveness, we move from alienation to intimacy, from guilt to love.
Thankfulness	We are grateful to God for his personal concern, help, and mercy. Not only does he protect, guide, and forgive us, but his creation provides everything we need.	When we realize how we benefit from knowing God, we can fully express our thanks to him. By thanking him often, we develop spontaneity in our prayer life.
Trust	God is faithful and just. When we put our trust in him, he quiets our hearts. Because he has been faithful throughout history, we can trust him in times of trouble.	People can be unfair and friends may desert us. But we can trust God. Knowing God intimately drives away doubt, fear, and loneliness.

BOOK I   Psalms 1–41

In this book, the psalm writers praise God for his justice, express confidence in God's compassion, recount the depravity of humanity, plead for vindication, ask God to deliver them from their enemies, speak of the blessedness of the forgiven sinner, and portray God as a shepherd. We should worship God with the same sense of adoration found in these psalms.

Theme: Life's two roads. The life of the faithful person is contrasted with the life of the faithless person.

Author: Anonymous

1

1 Blessed is the man
　　who does not walk[a] in the counsel of the wicked
　or stand in the way of sinners
　　or sit[b] in the seat of mockers.
2 But his delight[c] is in the law of the LORD,
　　and on his law he meditates[d] day and night.
3 He is like a tree planted by streams of water,[e]
　　which yields its fruit in season
　and whose leaf does not wither.
　　Whatever he does prospers.[f]

4 Not so the wicked!
　　They are like chaff[g]
　　that the wind blows away.
5 Therefore the wicked will not stand in the judgment,
　　nor sinners in the assembly of the righteous.

6 For the LORD watches over[h] the way of the righteous,
　　but the way of the wicked will perish.

1:1
[a] Pr 4:14
[b] Ps 26:4; Jer 15:17

1:2
[c] Ps 119:16, 35
[d] Jos 1:8

1:3
[e] Jer 17:8
[f] Ge 39:3

1:4
[g] Job 21:18; Isa 17:13

1:6
[h] Ps 37:18; 2Ti 2:19

Theme: God's ultimate rule. A psalm written to celebrate the coronation of an Israelite king, but also written for the coronation of Christ, the eternal King.

Author: David (see Acts 4:25, 26)

2

1 Why do the nations conspire[a]
　　and the peoples plot in vain?

[a] 1 Hebrew; Septuagint rage

1:1 The writer begins his psalm extolling the joys of obeying God and refusing to listen to those who discredit or ridicule him. Our friends and associates can have a profound influence on us, often in very subtle ways. If we insist on friendships with those who mock what God considers important, we might sin by becoming indifferent to God's will. This attitude is the same as mocking. Do your friends build up your faith, or do they tear it down? True friends should help you draw closer to God, not hinder, your relationship with him.

1:1ff God doesn't judge people on the basis of race, sex, or national origin. He judges them on the basis of their faith in him and their response to his revealed will. Those who diligently try to obey God's will are blessed. Their happy condition is like healthy, fruit-bearing trees with strong roots (Jeremiah 17:5–8), and God promises to watch over them. God's wisdom guides their lives. In contrast, those who don't trust and obey God have meaningless lives that blow away like dust.

Only two paths of life lay before us—God's way of obedience or the way of rebellion and destruction. Be sure to choose God's path because the path you choose determines how you will spend eternity.

1:2 You can learn how to follow God by meditating on his Word. Meditating means spending time reading and thinking about what you have read. It means asking yourself how you should change so you will live as God wants. Knowing and meditating on God's Word are the first steps toward applying it to your everyday life. If you want to follow God more closely, you must know what he says.

1:2 This "law of the LORD" means all of Scripture: the first five books of Moses, the Prophets, and the other writings. The more

we know of the whole scope of God's Word, the more resources we will have to guide us in our daily decisions.

1:2, 3 These two verses hold simple wisdom—the more we delight in God's presence, the more fruitful we are. On the other hand, the more we allow those who ridicule God to affect our thoughts and attitudes, the more we separate ourselves from our source of nourishment. We must have contact with unbelievers if we are to witness to them, but we must not join in or imitate their sinful behavior. If you want despair, spend time with mocking sinners; but if you want God's happiness, make friends with those who love God and his Word.

1:3 The phrase, "Whatever he does prospers," does not mean immunity from failure or difficulties. Nor does it guarantee health, wealth, and happiness. What the Bible means by prosperity is this: when we apply God's wisdom, the fruit (results or by-products) we bear will be good and will receive God's approval. Just as a tree soaks up water and bears luscious fruit, we also are to soak up God's Word, producing actions and attitudes that honor God. To achieve anything worthwhile, we must have God's Word in our hearts.

1:4 Chaff is the outer shell (or husk) that must be removed to get at the valuable kernels of grain inside. Chaff was removed by a process called threshing and winnowing. After the plants were cut, they were crushed, and then the pieces were thrown into the air. Chaff is very light and is carried away by even the slightest wind, while the good grain falls back to the earth. Chaff is a symbol of a faithless life that drifts along without direction. Good grain is a symbol of a faithful life that can be used by God. Unlike grain, however, we can choose the direction we will take.

2:1ff Several psalms are called *Messianic* because of their

2:2
i Jn 1:41
j Ac 4:25-26*

2 The kings of the earth take their stand
    and the rulers gather together
against the LORD
    and against his Anointed*i* One.*aj*
3 "Let us break their chains," they say,
    "and throw off their fetters."

2:4
k Ps 37:13

4 The One enthroned in heaven laughs;*k*
    the Lord scoffs at them.
5 Then he rebukes them in his anger
    and terrifies them in his wrath, saying,
6 "I have installed my King*b*
    on Zion, my holy hill."

a2 Or anointed one *b6 Or king*

REASONS TO READ PSALMS

When you want . . .	Read . . .
to find comfort	Psalm 23
to meet God intimately	Psalm 103
to learn a new prayer	Psalm 136
to learn a new song	Psalm 92
to learn more about God	Psalm 24
to understand yourself more clearly	Psalm 8
to know how to come to God each day	Psalm 5
to be forgiven for your sins	Psalm 51
to feel worthwhile	Psalm 139
to understand why you should read the Bible	Psalm 119
to give praise to God	Psalm 145
to know that God is in control	Psalm 146
to give thanks to God	Psalm 136
to please God	Psalm 15
to know why you should worship God	Psalm 104

God's Word was written to be studied, understood, and applied, and the book of Psalms lends itself most directly to application. We understand the psalms best when we "stand under" them and allow them to flow over us like a rain shower. We may turn to Psalms looking for something, but sooner or later we will meet Someone. As we read and memorize the psalms, we will gradually discover how much they are already part of us. They put into words our deepest hurts, longings, thoughts, and prayers. They gently push us toward being what God designed us to be—people loving and living for him.

---

prophetic descriptions of Jesus the Messiah (Christ)—his life, death, resurrection, and future reign. David, who may have written this psalm, was a shepherd, soldier, and king. Clearly he was also a prophet (Acts 2:29, 30) because this psalm describes the rebellion of the nations and the coming of Christ to establish his eternal reign. This psalm is often mentioned in the New Testament (see Acts 4:25, 26; 13:33; Hebrews 1:5, 6; 5:5; Revelation 2:26, 27; 12:5; 19:15).

2:1ff David may have written these words during a conspiracy against Israel by some of the surrounding pagan nations. Chosen and anointed by God, David knew that God would fulfill his promise to bring the Messiah into the world through his bloodline (2 Samuel 7:16; 1 Chronicles 17:11, 12).

2:3 People often think they will be free if they can get away from God. Yet, inevitably, everyone serves somebody or something, whether a human king, an organization, or even one's own selfish desires. Just as a fish is not free when it leaves the water and a tree is not free when it leaves the soil, we are not free when we leave the Lord. We can find the one sure route to freedom by wholeheartedly serving God the Creator. God can set you free to be the person he created you to be.

2:4 God laughs, not at the nations, but at their confused thoughts about power. It is the laughter of a father when his three-year-old boasts that he or she can outrun him or beat him in a wrestling match. The father knows the limited strength of his little child, and God knows the boundaries of power of the nations. Every nation is limited, but God is omnipotent. If you have to choose between confidence in God and confidence in any nation, choose God!

2:4 God is all-powerful. He created the world, and knew about the empires of the earth long before they came into being (Daniel 2:26–45). But pride and power cause nations and leaders to rebel against God and try to break free of him. Many world leaders boast of their power, rant and rave against God and his people, and promise to take over and form their own empires. But God laughs because any power they have comes from him, and he can also take it from them. We need not fear the boasts of tyrants—they are in God's hands and will be judged by him.

⁷ I will proclaim the decree of the LORD:

> He said to me, "You are my Son[a];
> today I have become your Father.[b]/
>
> ⁸ Ask of me,
> and I will make the nations your inheritance,
> the ends of the earth[m] your possession.
> ⁹ You will rule them with an iron scepter[c];
> you will dash them to pieces[n] like pottery.[o]"

¹⁰ Therefore, you kings, be wise;
be warned, you rulers of the earth.
¹¹ Serve the LORD with fear
and rejoice with trembling.
¹² Kiss the Son, lest he be angry
and you be destroyed in your way,
for his wrath[p] can flare up in a moment.
Blessed are all who take refuge in him.

Theme: Confidently trusting God for protection and peace.
Author: David

3

A psalm of David. When he fled from his son Absalom.[q]

¹ O LORD, how many are my foes!
How many rise up against me!
² Many are saying of me,
"God will not deliver him.[r]"   *Selah*[d]

³ But you are a shield[s] around me, O LORD;
you bestow glory on me and lift[e] up my head.[t]
⁴ To the LORD I cry aloud,
and he answers me from his holy hill.   *Selah*

⁵ I lie down and sleep;[u]
I wake again, because the LORD sustains me.
⁶ I will not fear[v] the tens of thousands
drawn up against me on every side.

⁷ Arise, O LORD!
Deliver me, O my God!

**Side references:**

2:7 /Ac 13:33*
2:8 mPs 22:27
2:9 nPs 89:23 oRev 2:27*
2:12 pRev 6:16
3:TITLE q2Sa 15:14
3:2 rPs 71:11
3:3 sGe 15:1; Ps 28:7 tPs 27:6
3:5 uLev 26:6
3:6 vPs 27:3

a7 Or *son*; also in verse 12   b7 Or *have begotten you*   c9 Or *will break them with a rod of iron*   d2 A word of uncertain meaning, occurring frequently in the Psalms; possibly a musical term   e3 Or LORD, / *my Glorious One, who lifts*

2:11, 12 To "kiss the Son" means to surrender fully and submit to him. Christ is not only God's chosen King, he is also the rightful King of our hearts and lives. To be ready for Christ's return, we must submit to his leadership every day.

3:1, 2 David felt like he was in the minority. As many as 10,000 soldiers may have been surrounding him at this time (3:6). Not only did David's enemies view life differently, they actively sought to harm him. As king, David could have trusted his army to defeat Absalom. Instead, he depended upon God's mercy (3:4); therefore, he was at peace with whatever outcome occurred, knowing that God's great purposes would prevail. We can overcome fear by trusting God for his protection in our darkest hour.

3:1–3 David was not sitting on his throne in a place of power; he was running for his life from his rebellious son Absalom and a host of traitors. When circumstances go against us, we may be tempted to think that God also is against us. But David reminds us that the opposite is true. When everything seems to go wrong, God is still for us. If a circumstance has turned against you, don't blame God—seek him!

3:2 The word "Selah" occurs 71 times in Psalms and three times in Habakkuk (3:3, 9, 13). Though its precise use is unknown, the word was most likely a musical sign. Three suggestions for its meaning include: (1) It was a musical direction to the singers and orchestra to play *forte* or *crescendo*. (2) It was a signal to lift up the hands or voice in worship, or to the priest to give a benediction. (3) It was a phrase like "Amen" meaning "so be it," or "Hallelujah" meaning "Praise the Lord."

3:4 God's holy hill was Mount Moriah in Jerusalem, the place where David's son Solomon would build the temple (2 Chronicles 3:1). David knew that God could not be confined to any space, but he wrote poetically, expressing confidence that God would hear him when he prayed. God responds to us when we urgently pray to him.

3:5 Sleep does not come easily during a crisis. David could have had sleepless nights when his son Absalom rebelled and gathered an army to kill him. But he slept peacefully, even during the rebellion. What made the difference? David cried out to the Lord, and the Lord heard him. The assurance of answered prayer brings peace. It is easier to sleep well when we have full assurance that God is in control of circumstances. If you are lying awake at night worrying about what you can't change, pour out your heart to God, and thank him that he is in control. Then sleep will come.

3:7
w Job 16:10

Strike w all my enemies on the jaw;
  break the teeth of the wicked.

3:8
x Isa 43:3, 11

8 From the LORD comes deliverance. x
  May your blessing be on your people.   *Selah*

Theme: Rejoicing in God's protection and peace. We can place our confidence in God because he will listen when we call on him.
Author: David

4

For the director of music. With stringed instruments. A psalm of David.

4:1
y Ps 17:6

1 Answer me when I call to you,
    O my righteous God.
  Give me relief from my distress;
    be merciful to me and hear my prayer. y

2 How long, O men, will you turn my glory into shame a?
  How long will you love delusions and seek false gods b?   *Selah*
3 Know that the LORD has set apart the godly for himself;
  the LORD will hear when I call to him.

a 2 Or you dishonor my Glorious One   b 2 Or seek lies

PSALMS FROM DAVID'S LIFE
Of the more than 70 psalms attributed to David, at least 14 of them are connected with specific events in his life. From them we see an outline of a growing relationship with God. They are listed here, roughly in chronological order.

Event in David's Life	Reference	Psalm	What David Learned about God
When Saul sent men to David's home to kill him	1 Samuel 19	59	God is my fortress.
While running from Saul	1 Samuel 21	34	I will glorify the Lord at all times.
While running from Saul	1 Samuel 21	56	When I am afraid, I will trust in God.
While hiding in the cave of Adullam	1 Samuel 22	142	God is my refuge.
After learning that Doeg had murdered 85 priests and their families	1 Samuel 22	52	God will bring evil people down to everlasting ruin.
When the Ziphites tried to betray him	1 Samuel 23	54	Surely God is my help.
While hiding in a cave	1 Samuel 24	57	I will take refuge in the shadow of God's wings until the disaster has passed.
While hiding in the Desert of En Gedi	1 Samuel 24	63	My soul clings to God; his right hand upholds me.
When Saul's pursuit was over	2 Samuel 22	18	To the faithful, God shows himself faithful.
After being confronted about his adultery with Bathsheba	2 Samuel 12	51	The sacrifices God desires are a broken spirit; a broken and contrite heart he will not despise.
During Absalom's rebellion	2 Samuel 15	3	From the Lord comes deliverance.
During Absalom's rebellion	2 Samuel 15	7	He is a righteous God who searches minds and hearts and can bring to an end the violence of the wicked and make the righteous secure.

3:7 This description of God's anger reveals David's desire for justice against his persecutors. David himself had been slapped and insulted, and here he simply asks for equal treatment for his enemies. He did this, not out of personal revenge, but for the sake of God's justice. Verse 8 shows the humility behind David's words—he realized that faith in God's timing was the answer to his question about the success the wicked had unfairly achieved.

4:1ff This psalm may have been written as David was asking his enemies to reconsider their support of Absalom. Others see this psalm as a prayer for relief from a calamity such as a drought (see 4:7). It was probably written shortly after Psalm 3.

4:3 The godly are those who are faithful and devoted to God.

David knew that God would hear him when he called and would answer him. We too can be confident that God listens to our prayers and answers when we call on him. Sometimes we think that God will not hear us because we have fallen short of his high standards for holy living. But if we have trusted Christ for salvation, God has forgiven us, and he will listen to us. When you feel as though your prayers are bouncing off the ceiling, remember that as a believer you have been set apart by God and that he loves you. He hears and answers, although his answers may not be what you expect. Look at your problems in the light of God's power instead of looking at God in the shadow of your problems.

4 In your anger do not sin;*z*
   when you are on your beds,*a*
   search your hearts and be silent.   *Selah*

5 Offer right sacrifices
   and trust in the LORD.*b*

6 Many are asking, "Who can show us any good?"
   Let the light of your face shine upon us,*c* O LORD.

7 You have filled my heart with greater joy*d*
   than when their grain and new wine abound.

8 I will lie down and sleep*e* in peace,
   for you alone, O LORD,
   make me dwell in safety.*f*

4:4
*z*Eph 4:26*
*a*Ps 77:6

4:5
*b*Dt 33:19; Ps 37:3

4:6
*c*Nu 6:25

4:7
*d*Isa 9:3

4:8
*e*Ps 3:5
*f*Lev 25:18

Theme: The lies of enemies. God is able to defend us from lies spoken against us.
Author: David

5

For the director of music. For flutes. A psalm of David.

1 Give ear to my words, O LORD,
   consider my sighing.

2 Listen to my cry for help,
   my King and my God,
   for to you I pray.

3 In the morning, O LORD, you hear my voice;
   in the morning I lay my requests before you
   and wait in expectation.

4 You are not a God who takes pleasure in evil;
   with you the wicked cannot dwell.

5 The arrogant*g* cannot stand in your presence;
   you hate all who do wrong.

6 You destroy those who tell lies;*h*
   bloodthirsty and deceitful men
   the LORD abhors.

7 But I, by your great mercy,
   will come into your house;
   in reverence will I bow down
   toward your holy temple.

8 Lead me, O LORD, in your righteousness
   because of my enemies—
   make straight your way before me.

9 Not a word from their mouth can be trusted;
   their heart is filled with destruction.

5:5
*g*Ps 73:3

5:6
*h*Ps 55:23

4:5 Worship in David's day included animal sacrifices by the priests in the tabernacle. The animal's blood covered the sins of the one who offered the animal. Specific rules had been given for offering sacrifices, but more important to God than ceremony was the offerer's attitude of submission and obedience (1 Samuel 15:22, 23). Today, a sacrifice offered in the right spirit is still pleasing to God. He wants our obedience and our praise before our gifts (Hebrews 13:15). Offer God your sacrifice of total obedience and heartfelt praise.

4:7 Two kinds of joy are contrasted here—inward joy that comes from knowing and trusting God and happiness that comes as a result of pleasant circumstances. Inward joy is steady as long as we trust God; happiness is unpredictable. Inward joy defeats discouragement; happiness covers it up. Inward joy is lasting; happiness is temporary.

5:1–3 The secret of a close relationship with God is to pray to him earnestly *each morning*. In the morning, our minds are more free from problems and then we can commit the whole day to God. Regular communication helps any friendship and is certainly necessary for a strong relationship with God. We need to communicate with him daily. Do you have a regular time to pray and read God's Word?

5:5 God cannot condone or excuse even the smallest sin. Therefore we cannot excuse ourselves for sinning only a little bit. As we grow spiritually, our sensitivity to sin increases. What is your reaction to sin in your life? Are you insensitive, unconcerned, disappointed, or comfortable? As God makes us aware of sin, we must be intolerant toward it and be willing to change. All believers should strive to be more tolerant of people but less tolerant of the sin in themselves and others.

5:9
i Ro 3:13*

Their throat is an open grave;
 with their tongue they speak deceit.*i*
10 Declare them guilty, O God!
 Let their intrigues be their downfall.
Banish them for their many sins,
 for they have rebelled against you.

5:11
j Ps 69:36

11 But let all who take refuge in you be glad;
 let them ever sing for joy.
Spread your protection over them,
 that those who love your name*j* may rejoice in you.

5:12
k Ps 32:7

12 For surely, O Lord, you bless the righteous;
 you surround them*k* with your favor as with a shield.

Theme: Deliverance in trouble. God is able to rescue us.
Author: David

6 For the director of music. With stringed instruments. According to *sheminith*.*a*
A psalm of David.

1 O Lord, do not rebuke me in your anger
 or discipline me in your wrath.

6:2
l Ps 22:14

2 Be merciful to me, Lord, for I am faint;
 O Lord, heal me, for my bones are in agony.*l*

6:3
m Jn 12:27

3 My soul is in anguish.*m*
 How long, O Lord, how long?

4 Turn, O Lord, and deliver me;
 save me because of your unfailing love.

6:5
n Ps 30:9; Isa 38:18

5 No one remembers you when he is dead.
 Who praises you from the grave*b*?*n*

6 I am worn out from groaning;
 all night long I flood my bed with weeping
 and drench my couch with tears.

6:7
o Ps 31:9

7 My eyes grow weak*o* with sorrow;
 they fail because of all my foes.

6:8
p Ps 119:115

8 Away from me,*p* all you who do evil,
 for the Lord has heard my weeping.

6:9
q Ps 116:1

9 The Lord has heard my cry for mercy;*q*
 the Lord accepts my prayer.
10 All my enemies will be ashamed and dismayed;
 they will turn back in sudden disgrace.

a Title: Probably a musical term *b* 5 Hebrew *Sheol*

6:1ff This is the first of seven "penitential" psalms, where the writer humbly realizes his predicament (usually the result of sin), expresses sorrow over it, and demonstrates a fresh commitment to remain close to God. We don't know the cause of David's pain, but whatever the cause, he sought God for the remedy.

6:1–3 David accepted God's punishment, but he begged God not to discipline him in anger. Jeremiah also asked God to correct him gently and not in anger (Jeremiah 10:24). David recognized that if God treated him with justice alone and not with mercy, he would be wiped out by God's wrath. Often we want God to show mercy to us and justice to everyone else. God in his kindness forgives us instead of giving us what we deserve.

6:6 Pouring out his heart with tears, David was completely honest with God. We can be honest with God even when we are filled with anger or despair because God knows us

thoroughly and wants the very best for us. Anger may result in rash outward acts or turning inward in depression. But because we trust in our all-powerful God, we don't have to be victims of circumstance or be weighed down by the guilt of sin. Be honest with God, and he will help you turn your attention from yourself to him and his mercy.

Theme: A request for justice against those who make slanderous comments. God is the perfect judge and will punish those who persecute the innocent.
Author: David

7

A *shiggaion*[a] of David, which he sang to the LORD concerning Cush, a Benjamite.

1 O LORD my God, I take refuge in you;
  save and deliver me from all who pursue me,[r]
2 or they will tear me like a lion
  and rip me to pieces with no one to rescue me.

3 O LORD my God, if I have done this
  and there is guilt on my hands[s]—
4 if I have done evil to him who is at peace with me
  or without cause have robbed my foe—
5 then let my enemy pursue and overtake me;
  let him trample my life to the ground
  and make me sleep in the dust.   *Selah*

6 Arise,[t] O LORD, in your anger;
  rise up against the rage of my enemies.
  Awake,[u] my God; decree justice.
7 Let the assembled peoples gather around you.
  Rule over them from on high;
8   let the LORD judge the peoples.
Judge me, O LORD, according to my righteousness,[v]
  according to my integrity, O Most High.
9 O righteous God,[w]
  who searches minds and hearts,[x]
bring to an end the violence of the wicked
  and make the righteous secure.

10 My shield[b] is God Most High,
  who saves the upright in heart.[y]
11 God is a righteous judge,
  a God who expresses his wrath every day.
12 If he does not relent,
  he[c] will sharpen his sword;[z]
  he will bend and string his bow.
13 He has prepared his deadly weapons;
  he makes ready his flaming arrows.

14 He who is pregnant with evil
  and conceives trouble gives birth[a] to disillusionment.
15 He who digs a hole and scoops it out
  falls into the pit he has made.[b]

	7:1
	r Ps 31:15
	7:3
	s 1Sa 24:11; Isa 59:3
	7:6
	t Ps 94:2
	u Ps 44:23
	7:8
	v Ps 18:20
	7:9
	w Jer 11:20
	x Rev 2:23
	7:10
	y Ps 125:4
	7:12
	z Dt 32:41
	7:14
	a Isa 59:4; Jas 1:15
	7:15
	b Job 4:8

a Title: Probably a literary or musical term   b 10 Or sovereign   c 12 Or If a man does not repent, / God

---

7 title *Shiggaion* may be a term derived from the verb "to err" or "to wander;" it might also mean "wild" or "ecstatic." It is a poem written with intense feeling, a lament to stir the emotions.

7:1–6 Have you ever been falsely accused or so badly hurt that you wanted revenge? David wrote this psalm in response to the slanderous accusations of those who claimed he was trying to kill Saul and seize the throne (1 Samuel 24:9–11). Instead of taking matters into his own hands and striking back, David cried out to God for justice. The proper response to slander is prayer, not revenge, because God says, "It is mine to avenge; I will repay" (Romans 12:19; see also Deuteronomy 32:35, 36; Hebrews 10:30). Instead of striking back, ask God to take your case, bring justice, and restore your reputation.

7:9 God "searches minds and hearts." Nothing is hidden from God—this can be either terrifying or comforting. Our thoughts are an open book to him. Because God knows even our motives, we have no place to hide, no way to pretend we can get away with sin. But that very knowledge also gives us great comfort. We don't have to impress God or put up a false front. Instead, we can trust God to help us work through our weaknesses in order to serve him as he has planned. When we truly follow God, he rewards our effort.

7:14–16 When allowed to run its course, evil destroys itself. Violent people become victims of violence, and liars become victims of others' deceit (9:15, 16). In the process, however, innocent people are hurt. Sometimes God intervenes and stops evildoers in their tracks in order to protect his followers. At other times, for reasons known only to him, God allows evil to continue

16 The trouble he causes recoils on himself;
   his violence comes down on his own head.

17 I will give thanks to the LORD because of his righteousness
   and will sing praise to the name of the LORD Most High.

Theme: The greatness of God assures the worth of mankind. God, the all-powerful Creator, cares for his most valuable creation—people.
Author: David

8

For the director of music. According to *gittith*.[a] A psalm of David.

1 O LORD, our Lord,
   how majestic is your name in all the earth!

You have set your glory
   above the heavens. [c]

2 From the lips of children and infants
   you have ordained praise[b] [d]
because of your enemies,
   to silence the foe[e] and the avenger.

3 When I consider your heavens,
   the work of your fingers,
the moon and the stars,
   which you have set in place,

4 what is man that you are mindful of him,
   the son of man that you care for him?[f]

5 You made him a little lower than the heavenly beings[c]
   and crowned him with glory and honor.[g]

6 You made him ruler over the works of your hands;
   you put everything under his feet:[h]

7 all flocks and herds,
   and the beasts of the field,

8 the birds of the air,
   and the fish of the sea,
   all that swim the paths of the seas.

9 O LORD, our Lord,
   how majestic is your name in all the earth![i]

8:1 cPs 113:4; 148:13

8:2 dMt 21:16*; ePs 44:16

8:4 fJob 7:17

8:5 gPs 21:5; 103:4

8:6 hHeb 2:6-8*

8:9 iver 1

aTitle: Probably a musical term   b2 Or *strength*   c5 Or *than God*

---

even though innocent people are hurt. It is during these times that we must ask God to protect us. Remember that God will execute final justice, even if it is not during our lifetime.

7:17 During a time of great evil and injustice, David was grateful that God was righteous (see also 7:11). When we wonder if anyone is honest or fair, we can be assured that God will continue to bring justice and fairness when we involve him in our activities. If you ever feel that you are being treated unfairly, ask the one who is always fair and just to be with you. Then thank him for his presence (see Isaiah 42:1–6).

8:1ff Portions of this psalm are quoted in the New Testament and applied to Christ (1 Corinthians 15:27; Hebrews 2:6–8). Jesus became human, just a little lower than the heavenly beings (8:5), and he will raise all who belong to him above the heavenly beings when he comes to reign over the new heaven and new earth. Jesus is the only person who perfectly reflects God's image (Galatians 2:20; Colossians 1:15).

8:2 Children are able to trust and praise God without doubts or reservations. As we get older, many of us find this more and more difficult to do. Ask God to give you childlike faith, removing any barriers to having a closer walk with him. Get in touch with this childlike quality in yourself so that you can be more expressive.

8:3, 4 To respect God's majesty, we must compare ourselves to his greatness. When we look at creation, we often feel small by comparison. This is a healthy way to get back to reality, but God does not want us to dwell on our smallness. Humility means proper respect for God, not self-depreciation.

8:3–5 When we look at the vast expanse of creation, we wonder how God could be concerned for people who constantly disappoint him. Yet God created us only a little lower than himself and the angels! The next time you question your worth as a person, remember that God considers you highly valuable. We have great worth because we bear the stamp of the Creator. (See Genesis 1:26, 27 for the extent of worth God places on all people.) Because God has already declared how valuable we are to him, we can be set free from feelings of worthlessness.

8:6 God gave human beings tremendous authority—to be in charge of the whole earth. But with great authority comes great responsibility. If we own a pet, we have the legal authority to do with it as we wish, but we also have the responsibility to feed and care for it. How do you treat God's creation? Use your resources wisely because God holds you accountable as his steward.

Theme: God never ignores our cries for help.
Author: David, probably written after a victory over the Philistines

9 [a]

For the director of music. To ⌊the tune of⌋ "The Death of the Son." A psalm of David.

¹ I will praise you, O LORD, with all my heart;[j]
  I will tell of all your wonders.
² I will be glad and rejoice[k] in you;
  I will sing praise to your name,[l] O Most High.

³ My enemies turn back;
  they stumble and perish before you.
⁴ For you have upheld my right and my cause;
  you have sat on your throne, judging righteously.
⁵ You have rebuked the nations and destroyed the wicked;
  you have blotted out their name for ever and ever.
⁶ Endless ruin has overtaken the enemy,
  you have uprooted their cities;
  even the memory of them[m] has perished.

⁷ The LORD reigns forever;
  he has established his throne for judgment.
⁸ He will judge the world in righteousness;[n]
  he will govern the peoples with justice.
⁹ The LORD is a refuge for the oppressed,
  a stronghold in times of trouble.[o]
¹⁰ Those who know your name[p] will trust in you,
  for you, LORD, have never forsaken those who seek you.

¹¹ Sing praises to the LORD, enthroned in Zion;
  proclaim among the nations what he has done.[q]
¹² For he who avenges blood[r] remembers;
  he does not ignore the cry of the afflicted.

¹³ O LORD, see how my enemies persecute me!
  Have mercy and lift me up from the gates of death,
¹⁴ that I may declare your praises
  in the gates of the Daughter of Zion
  and there rejoice in your salvation.[s]

¹⁵ The nations have fallen into the pit they have dug;[t]
  their feet are caught in the net they have hidden.

	9:1 [j]Ps 86:12
	9:2 [k]Ps 5:11 [l]Ps 83:18
	9:6 [m]Ps 34:16
	9:8 [n]Ps 96:13
	9:9 [o]Ps 32:7
	9:10 [p]Ps 91:14
	9:11 [q]Ps 105:1
	9:12 [r]Ge 9:5
	9:14 [s]Ps 13:5
	9:15 [t]Ps 7:15-16

[a]Psalms 9 and 10 may have been originally a single acrostic poem, the stanzas of which begin with the successive letters of the Hebrew alphabet. In the Septuagint they constitute one psalm.

9:1ff Praise is expressing to God our appreciation and understanding of his worth. It is saying "thank you" for each aspect of his divine nature. Our inward attitude becomes outward expression. When we praise God, we help ourselves by expanding our awareness of who he is. In each psalm you read, look for an attribute or characteristic of God for which you can thank him.

9:4 God upholds our just cause; he is our vindicator (one who clears us from criticism and justifies us before others). In this life, we may face many injustices: (1) we may be falsely accused and misunderstood by friends and enemies; (2) we may not be truly appreciated by others for the love we show; (3) the true value of our work and service may not be duly rewarded; (4) our ideas may be ignored. But God is to be praised, for he sees and remembers all the good we do, and it is up to him to decide the timing and the appropriateness of our rewards. If we do not trust him to vindicate us, then we will be susceptible to hatred and self-pity. If we do trust him, we can experience God's peace and be free from the worry of how others perceive us and treat us.

9:10 God will never forsake those who seek him. To forsake someone is to abandon that person. God's promise does not mean that if we trust in him we will escape loss or suffering; it means that God himself will never leave us no matter what we face.

9:11 God does not live only in Zion (another name for Mount Moriah, the hill on which the temple was built); he is everywhere all the time. The focal point of Israelite worship, however, came to be Jerusalem and its beautiful temple. God was present in the tabernacle (Exodus 25:8, 9) and in the temple built by Solomon (2 Chronicles 7:16). From this central place of worship, the Jews were to tell the world about the one true God.

9:13, 14 All of us want God to help us when we are in trouble, but often for different reasons. Some want God's help so that they will be successful and other people will like them. Others want God's help so that they will be comfortable and feel good about themselves. David, however, wanted help from God so that justice would be restored to Israel and so that he could show others God's power. When you call to God for help, consider your motive. Is it to save yourself pain and embarrassment or to bring God glory and honor?

9:17
u Job 8:13

9:18
v Pr 23:18

10:1
w Ps 22:1, 11

10:3
x Ps 94:4

10:6
y Rev 18:7

10:7
z Ro 3:14*

10:11
a Job 22:13

16 The LORD is known by his justice;
   the wicked are ensnared by the work of their hands. *Higgaion.*a *Selah*

17 The wicked return to the grave,b
   all the nations that forget God. u

18 But the needy will not always be forgotten,
   nor the hopev of the afflicted ever perish.

19 Arise, O LORD, let not man triumph;
   let the nations be judged in your presence.

20 Strike them with terror, O LORD;
   let the nations know they are but men.   *Selah*

Theme: Why do the wicked succeed? Although God may seem to be hidden at times, we can be assured that he is aware of every injustice.
Author: Anonymous, but probably David. Many ancient manuscripts combine Psalms 9 and 10, and Psalm 9 was written by David.

10 c

1 Why, O LORD, do you stand far off?w
   Why do you hide yourself in times of trouble?

2 In his arrogance the wicked man hunts down the weak,
   who are caught in the schemes he devises.
3 He boastsx of the cravings of his heart;
   he blesses the greedy and reviles the LORD.
4 In his pride the wicked does not seek him;
   in all his thoughts there is no room for God.
5 His ways are always prosperous;
   he is haughty and your laws are far from him;
   he sneers at all his enemies.
6 He says to himself, "Nothing will shake me;
   I'll always be happyy and never have trouble."
7 His mouth is full of cursesz and lies and threats;
   trouble and evil are under his tongue.
8 He lies in wait near the villages;
   from ambush he murders the innocent,
   watching in secret for his victims.
9 He lies in wait like a lion in cover;
   he lies in wait to catch the helpless;
   he catches the helpless and drags them off in his net.
10 His victims are crushed, they collapse;
   they fall under his strength.
11 He says to himself, "God has forgotten;a
   he covers his face and never sees."

a 16 Or *Meditation*; possibly a musical notation   b 17 Hebrew *Sheol*   cPsalms 9 and 10 may have been originally a single acrostic poem, the stanzas of which begin with the successive letters of the Hebrew alphabet. In the Septuagint they constitute one psalm.

9:16 *Higgaion* is a musical direction and probably means to use the quieter instruments.

9:18 The world may ignore the plight of the needy, crushing any earthly hope they may have. But God, the champion of the weak, promises that this will not be the case forever. The wicked nations who forget the Lord and refuse to help their people will be judged by God. He knows our needs, he knows our tendency to despair, and he has promised to care for us (see also 9:9, 12). Even when others forget us, he will remember.

10:1 "Why do you hide yourself in times of trouble?" To the psalm writer, God seemed far away. But even though the writer had honest doubts, he did not stop praying or conclude that God no longer cared. He was not complaining, but simply asking God to hurry to his aid. It is during those times when we feel most alone or oppressed that we need to keep praying, telling God about our troubles.

10:4–6 Some people succeed in everything they do, and they

brag that no one, not even God, can keep them down. We may wonder why God allows these people to amass great wealth while they despise him as they do. But why are we upset when the wicked prosper? Are we angry about the damage they are doing or just jealous of their success? To answer these questions we must gain the right perspective on wickedness and wealth. The wicked will surely be punished because God hates their evil deeds. Wealth is only temporary. It is not necessarily a sign of God's approval on a person's life; nor is lack of it a sign of God's disapproval. Don't let wealth or lack of it become your obsession. See Proverbs 30:7, 8 for a prayer you can pray about money.

10:11 There is an incompatibility between blind arrogance and the presence of God in our hearts. Proud people depend on themselves rather than on God. This causes God's guiding influences to leave their lives. When God's presence is welcome, there is no room for pride because he makes us aware of our true selves.

12 Arise, LORD! Lift up your hand,[b] O God.
   Do not forget the helpless.[c]
13 Why does the wicked man revile God?
   Why does he say to himself,
   "He won't call me to account"?
14 But you, O God, do see trouble and grief;
   you consider it to take it in hand.
   The victim commits himself to you;
   you are the helper[d] of the fatherless.
15 Break the arm of the wicked and evil man;
   call him to account for his wickedness
   that would not be found out.

16 The LORD is King for ever and ever;[e]
   the nations[f] will perish from his land.
17 You hear, O LORD, the desire of the afflicted;
   you encourage them, and you listen to their cry,
18 defending the fatherless and the oppressed,[g]
   in order that man, who is of the earth, may terrify no more.

10:12
[b] Mic 5:9
[c] Ps 9:12

10:14
[d] Ps 68:5

10:16
[e] Ps 29:10
[f] Dt 8:20

10:18
[g] Ps 9:9

Theme: God's rule provides stability in the midst of panic. Because we can trust him, we can face our problems.
Author: David

11

For the director of music. Of David.

1 In the LORD I take refuge.
   How then can you say to me:
   "Flee like a bird to your mountain.
2 For look, the wicked bend their bows;
   they set their arrows[h] against the strings
   to shoot from the shadows
   at the upright in heart.[i]
3 When the foundations[j] are being destroyed,
   what can the righteous do[a]?"

4 The LORD is in his holy temple;[k]
   the LORD is on his heavenly throne.
   He observes the sons of men;
   his eyes examine[l] them.
5 The LORD examines the righteous,[m]
   but the wicked[b] and those who love violence
   his soul hates.[n]
6 On the wicked he will rain
   fiery coals and burning sulfur;
   a scorching wind will be their lot.

11:2
[h] Ps 7:13
[i] Ps 64:3-4

11:3
[j] Ps 82:5

11:4
[k] Ps 18:6
[l] Ps 34:15-16

11:5
[m] Ge 22:1
[n] Ps 5:5

[a] 3 Or *what is the Righteous One doing* [b] 5 Or *The* LORD, *the Righteous One, examines the wicked, /*

10:14 God sees and takes note of each evil deed, encourages us, and listens to our cries (10:17). He is always with us. We can face the wicked because we do not face them alone. God is by our side.

11:1–4 David was forced to flee for safety several times. Being God's anointed king did not make him immune to injustice and hatred from others. He may have written this psalm when he was being hunted by Saul (1 Samuel 18—31) or during the days of Absalom's rebellion (2 Samuel 15—18). In both instances, David fled, but not as if all was lost. He knew God was in control. While David wisely avoided trouble, he did not fearfully run away from his troubles.

11:1–4 David seems to be speaking to those who are advising him to run from his enemies. David's faith contrasted dramatically with the fear of the advisers who tell him to flee. Faith in

God keeps us from losing hope and helps us resist fear. David's advisers were afraid because they saw only frightening circumstances and crumbling foundations. David was comforted and optimistic because he knew God was greater than anything his enemies could bring against him (7:10; 16:1; 31:2, 3).

11:4 When the foundations are shaking and you wish you could hide, remember that God is still in control. His power is not diminished by any turn of events. Nothing happens without his knowledge and permission. When you feel like running away— run to God. He will restore justice and goodness on the earth in his good time.

11:5 God does not shield believers from difficult circumstances, but he tests both the righteous and the wicked. For some, God's tests become a refining fire, while for others, they become an incinerator for destruction. Don't ignore or defy the tests and

11:7
oPs 17:15

7 For the LORD is righteous,
 he loves justice;
 upright men will see his face. o

Theme: The proud and lying words of people versus the true and pure words of God. A call for protection against those who try to manipulate us.
Author: David

12 For the director of music. According to *sheminith*.a A psalm of David.

12:1
pIsa 57:1

1 Help, LORD, for the godly are no more;p
 the faithful have vanished from among men.
2 Everyone lies to his neighbor;
 their flattering lips speak with deception.

3 May the LORD cut off all flattering lips
 and every boastful tongue
4 that says, "We will triumph with our tongues;
 we own our lipsb—who is our master?"

5 "Because of the oppression of the weak
 and the groaning of the needy,
 I will now arise," says the LORD.
 "I will protect them from those who malign them."

12:6
q2Sa 22:31;
Ps 18:30; Pr 30:5

6 And the words of the LORD are flawless,q
 like silver refined in a furnace of clay,
 purified seven times.

7 O LORD, you will keep us safe
 and protect us from such people forever.

12:8
rPs 55:10-11

8 The wicked freely strutr about
 when what is vile is honored among men.

Theme: Praying for relief from despair. We must continue to trust God even when he doesn't answer us immediately.
Author: David

13 For the director of music. A psalm of David.

13:1
sJob 13:24

1 How long, O LORD? Will you forget me forever?
 How long will you hide your faces from me?

aTitle: Probably a musical term   b4 Or / our lips are our plowshares

---

challenges that come your way. Use them as opportunities for you to grow.

12:1 Living for God in a deceitful world can be difficult and lonely. At one time the great prophet Elijah felt so lonely he wanted to die. But God told him that there were 7,000 other faithful servants (1 Kings 19:4, 14, 18). We are never alone in our battle against evil. When you feel alone, seek out other believers for strength and support.

12:2–4 We may be tempted to believe that some lies are relatively harmless, even useful at times. But God does not overlook lies, flattery, deception, or boasting. Each of these sins originates from a bad attitude that is eventually expressed in our speech. The tongue can be our greatest enemy because, though small, it can do great damage (James 3:5). Be careful how you use yours.

12:5 God cares for the weak and the needy. Here he promises to protect the downtrodden and confront their oppressors. We should identify with God's attitude. His work is not done until we care for the needs of the poor.

12:6 Sincerity and truth are extremely valuable because they are so rare. Many people are deceivers, liars, flatterers; they think they will get what they want by deception. As a king, David cer-

tainly faced his share of such people, who hoped to win his favor and gain advancement through flattery. When we feel as though sincerity and truth have nearly gone out of existence, we have one hope—the Word of God. God's Word is as pure and flawless as refined silver. So listen carefully when he speaks to you through his Word.

13:1 Sometimes all we need to do is talk over a problem with a friend to help put it in perspective. In this psalm, the phrase "how long" occurs four times in the first two verses, indicating the depth of David's distress. David expressed his feelings to God and found strength. By the end of his prayer, he was able to profess hope and trust in God. Through prayer we can express our feelings and talk our problems out with God. He helps us regain the right perspective, and this gives us peace (Habakkuk 3:17–19).

13:1–5 David frequently claimed that God was slow to act on his behalf. We often feel this same impatience. It seems that evil and suffering go unchecked, and we wonder when God is going to stop them. David affirmed that he would continue to trust God no matter how long he had to wait for God's justice to be realized. When you feel impatient, remember David's steadfast faith in God's unfailing love.

2 How long must I wrestle with my thoughts[t]
   and every day have sorrow in my heart?
   How long will my enemy triumph over me?

3 Look on me and answer, O LORD my God.
   Give light to my eyes,[u] or I will sleep in death;[v]
4 my enemy will say, "I have overcome him,[w]"
   and my foes will rejoice when I fall.

5 But I trust in your unfailing love;
   my heart rejoices in your salvation.[x]
6 I will sing to the LORD,
   for he has been good to me.

13:2	[t]Ps 42:4
13:3	[u]Ezr 9:8 [v]Jer 51:39
13:4	[w]Ps 25:2
13:5	[x]Ps 9:14

Theme: Only the fool denies God. How foolish it must seem to God when people say there is no God.
Author: David

14

For the director of music. Of David.

1 The fool[a] says in his heart,
   "There is no God."[y]
   They are corrupt, their deeds are vile;
   there is no one who does good.

2 The LORD looks down from heaven[z]
   on the sons of men
   to see if there are any who understand,[a]
   any who seek God.

3 All have turned aside,
   they have together become corrupt;
   there is no one who does good,
   not even one.[b]

4 Will evildoers never learn—
   those who devour my people as men eat bread
   and who do not call on the LORD?[c]
5 There they are, overwhelmed with dread,
   for God is present in the company of the righteous.
6 You evildoers frustrate the plans of the poor,
   but the LORD is their refuge.[d]

14:1	[y]Ps 10:4
14:2	[z]Ps 33:13 [a]Ps 92:6
14:3	[b]Ro 3:10-12*
14:4	[c]Isa 64:7
14:6	[d]Ps 9:9

[a] 1 The Hebrew words rendered *fool* in Psalms denote one who is morally deficient.

13:5, 6 David was faithful to God and trusted wholeheartedly in him, but he felt the pressure of his problems as much as anyone. Instead of giving up or giving in, however, David held on to his faith. In times of despair, it is much harder to hold on than to give up. But if you give up on God, you give in to a life of despair.

14:1–3 The true atheist is either foolish or wicked—foolish because he ignores the evidence that God exists or wicked because he refuses to live by God's truths. We become atheists in practice when we rely more on ourselves than on God. The fools mentioned here are aggressively perverse in their actions. To speak in direct defiance of God is utterly foolish according to the Bible.

14:3 No one but God is perfect; all of us stand guilty before him (see Romans 3:23) and need his forgiveness. No matter how well we perform or how much we achieve compared to others, none of us can boast of his or her goodness when compared to God's standard. God not only expects us to obey his laws, but he wants us to love him with all our heart. No one except Jesus Christ has done that perfectly. Because we all fall short we must turn to Christ to save us (Romans 10:9–11). Have you asked him to save you?

14:3, 4 David applies these observations to his enemies when he says the evildoers "devour my people as men eat bread" (14:4). "They have together become corrupt; there is no one who does good, not even one" (14:3). By contrast, David said, "Though you probe my heart, . . . you will find nothing" (17:3).

There is a clear distinction between those who worship God and those who refuse to worship him. David worshiped God, and under his leadership Israel obeyed God and prospered. Several hundred years later, however, Israel forgot God, and it became difficult to distinguish between God's followers and those who worshiped idols. When Isaiah called Israel to repentance, he, like David, spoke of people who had gone astray (Isaiah 53:6). But Isaiah was talking about the Israelites themselves. Paul quoted Psalm 14 in Romans 3:10–12. He made the image of straying sheep even more general, referring to all people. The whole human race—Jew and Gentile alike—has turned away from God.

14:5 If God is "in the company of the righteous," then those who attack God's followers may be attacking God. To attack God is utterly futile (see 2:4, 5, 10–12). Thus, while we may feel we are losing the battle, we can be absolutely sure that our ultimate victory is in God.

14:7
e Ps 53:6

7 Oh, that salvation for Israel would come out of Zion!
When the LORD restores the fortunes*e* of his people,
let Jacob rejoice and Israel be glad!

Theme: Guidelines for living a blameless life.
Author: David

15 A psalm of David.

15:1
f Ps 24:3-5

1 LORD, who may dwell in your sanctuary?
Who may live on your holy hill?*f*

15:2
g Eph 4:25

2 He whose walk is blameless
and who does what is righteous,
who speaks the truth*g* from his heart

15:3
h Ex 23:1

3 and has no slander*h* on his tongue,
who does his neighbor no wrong
and casts no slur on his fellowman,

15:4
i Ac 28:10

4 who despises a vile man
but honors*i* those who fear the LORD,
who keeps his oath
even when it hurts,

15:5
j Ex 22:25
k 2Pe 1:10

5 who lends his money without usury*j*
and does not accept a bribe against the innocent.

He who does these things
will never be shaken.*k*

TROUBLES AND COMPLAINTS IN PSALMS

We can relate to the psalms because they express our feelings. We all face troubles, as did the psalm writers hundreds of years ago, and we often respond as they did. In Psalm 3, David told God how he felt about the odds against him. But within three verses, the king realized that God's presence and care made the odds meaningless. This experience is repeated in many of the psalms. Usually, the hope and confidence in God outweigh the fear and suffering; sometimes they do not. Still, the psalm writers consistently poured out their thoughts and emotions to God. When they felt abandoned by God, they told him so. When they were impatient with how slowly God seemed to be answering their prayers, they also told him so. Because they recognized the difference between themselves and God, they were free to be human and to be honest with their Creator. That is why so many of the dark psalms end in the light. The psalm writers started by expressing their feelings and ended up remembering to whom they were speaking!

Although we have much in common with these writers, we may differ in two ways: We might not tell God what we are really thinking and feeling; therefore, we also might not recognize, even faintly, who is listening to our prayers!

Notice this pattern as you read Psalms, and put the writers' insights to the test. You may well find that your awareness and appreciation of God will grow as you are honest with him. (See Psalms 3; 6; 13; 31; 37; 64; 77; 102; 121; 142.)

15:1 *Sanctuary* and *holy hill* are interchangeable words describing the focal point of Israelite worship—the dwelling place of God. In Hebrew poetry the repeating pattern is found more in the thought than in the sound or rhythm.

15:1ff God calls his people to be morally upright, and, in this psalm, he gives us ten standards to determine how we are doing. We live among evil people whose standards and morals are eroding. Our standards for living should not come from our evil society, but from God. For other references where righteous conduct is summarized, see Isaiah 33:15; 56:1; Micah 6:8; Habakkuk 2:4; and Mark 12:29–31.

15:2–5 As we grow in our relationship with our Redeemer, we develop a desire to live by his standards. The depth of our eternal relationship with him can often be measured by the way we reflect his standards in our daily activities.

15:3, 4 Words are powerful, and how you use them reflects on your relationship with God. Perhaps nothing so identifies Chris-

tians as their ability to control their speech—speaking the truth, refusing to slander, and keeping oaths (promises). Watch out for what you say. (See James 3:1–12 for more on the importance of controlling your tongue.)

15:5 God was against the Jews' charging interest (usury) or making a profit on loans to needy, fellow Jews (see also Exodus 22:25; Leviticus 25:35–37), although charging interest on loans to foreigners was allowed (Deuteronomy 23:20). Interest was also permitted for business purposes, as long as it wasn't exorbitant (Proverbs 28:8).

15:5 Some people are so obsessed with money that they will change their God-given standards and lifestyle to get it. If money is a controlling force in your life, it must be curbed, or it will harm others and destroy your relationship with God.

Theme: The joys and benefits of a life lived in companionship with God. We enjoy these benefits now and eternally.
Author: David

16 A *miktam*[a] of David.

1 Keep me safe, O God,
    for in you I take refuge.

2 I said to the LORD, "You are my Lord;
    apart from you I have no good thing."[*l*]
3 As for the saints who are in the land,[m]
    they are the glorious ones in whom is all my delight.[b]
4 The sorrows[n] of those will increase
    who run after other gods.
  I will not pour out their libations of blood
    or take up their names[o] on my lips.

5 LORD, you have assigned me my portion and my cup;[p]
    you have made my lot secure.
6 The boundary lines have fallen for me in pleasant places;
    surely I have a delightful inheritance.

7 I will praise the LORD, who counsels me;[q]
    even at night my heart instructs me.
8 I have set the LORD always before me.
    Because he is at my right hand,
    I will not be shaken.

9 Therefore my heart is glad[r] and my tongue rejoices;
    my body also will rest secure,
10 because you will not abandon me to the grave,[c]
    nor will you let your Holy One[d] see decay.
11 You have made[e] known to me the path of life;[s]
    you will fill me with joy in your presence,[t]
    with eternal pleasures at your right hand.

16:2	[*l*] Ps 73:25
16:3	[m] Ps 101:6
16:4	[n] Ps 32:10
	[o] Ex 23:13
16:5	[p] Ps 23:5
16:7	[q] Ps 73:24
16:9	[r] Ps 4:7
16:11	[s] Mt 7:14
	[t] Ac 2:25-28*

Theme: A plea for justice in the face of false accusations and persecution. David urges us to realize the true goal of life—to know God—and the true reward of life—to see God one day.
Author: David, written while he was being persecuted by Saul.

17 A prayer of David.

1 Hear, O LORD, my righteous plea;
    listen to my cry.

[a]Title: Probably a literary or musical term   [b]3 Or *As for the pagan priests who are in the land / and the nobles in whom all delight, I said:*   [c]10 Hebrew *Sheol*   [d]10 Or *your faithful one*   [e]11 Or *You will make*

---

16 title *Miktam* comes from a term that may mean "to cover." It could mean a covering of the lips (a silent prayer), or a prayer that someone might be covered with protection. *Cover* can also mean "atone for." *Miktam* may mean a psalm of atonement.

16:7, 8 It is human nature to make our own plans and *then* ask God to bless them. Instead, we should seek God's will first. By constantly thinking about the Lord and his way of living, we will gain insights that will help us make right decisions and live the way God desires. Communicating with God allows him to counsel us and give us wisdom.

16:8 By saying that he "will not be shaken," David was talking about the unique sense of security felt by believers. God does not exempt believers from the day-to-day circumstances of life. Believers and unbelievers alike experience pain, trouble, and failure at times (Matthew 5:45). Unbelievers have a sense of hopelessness about life and confusion over their true purpose on earth. Those who seek God, however, can move ahead confidently with

what they know is right and important in God's eyes. They know that God will keep them from being moved off of his chosen path.

16:8–11 This psalm is often called a Messianic psalm because it is quoted in the New Testament as referring to the resurrection of Jesus Christ. Both Peter and Paul quoted from this psalm when speaking of Christ's bodily resurrection (see Acts 2:25–28, 31; 13:35–37).

16:9 David's heart was glad—he had found the secret to joy. True joy is far deeper than happiness; we can feel joy in spite of our deepest troubles. Happiness is temporary because it is based on external circumstances, but joy is lasting because it is based on God's presence within us. As we contemplate his daily presence, we will find contentment. As we understand the future he has for us, we will experience joy. Don't base your life on circumstances, but on God.

16:10 David stated confidently that God would not leave him in

17:1
u Isa 29:13

Give ear to my prayer—
  it does not rise from deceitful lips. u
2 May my vindication come from you;
  may your eyes see what is right.

17:3
v Job 23:10

3 Though you probe my heart and examine me at night,
  though you test me, you will find nothing; v
  I have resolved that my mouth will not sin.
4 As for the deeds of men—
  by the word of your lips
  I have kept myself
  from the ways of the violent.

17:5
w Ps 44:18

5 My steps have held to your paths; w
  my feet have not slipped.

17:6
x Ps 116:2

6 I call on you, O God, for you will answer me;
  give ear to me x and hear my prayer.

17:7
y Ps 31:21

7 Show the wonder of your great love, y
  you who save by your right hand
  those who take refuge in you from their foes.

17:8
z Dt 32:10

8 Keep me as the apple of your eye; z
  hide me in the shadow of your wings
9 from the wicked who assail me,
  from my mortal enemies who surround me.

17:10
a Ps 73:7
b 1Sa 2:3
17:11
c Ps 88:17

10 They close up their callous hearts, a
  and their mouths speak with arrogance. b
11 They have tracked me down, they now surround me, c
  with eyes alert, to throw me to the ground.

17:12
d Ps 7:2

12 They are like a lion d hungry for prey,
  like a great lion crouching in cover.

13 Rise up, O LORD, confront them, bring them down;
  rescue me from the wicked by your sword.
14 O LORD, by your hand save me from such men,
  from men of this world whose reward is in this life.

You still the hunger of those you cherish;
  their sons have plenty,
  and they store up wealth for their children.

17:15
e Ps 4:6-7; 16:11;
1Jn 3:2

15 And I—in righteousness I will see your face;
  when I awake, I will be satisfied with seeing your likeness. e

---

the grave. Many people fear death because they can neither control nor understand it. As believers, we can be assured that God will not forget us when we die. He will bring us to life again to live with him forever. This provides *real* security. For other passages about resurrection, see Job 19:25, 26; Isaiah 26:19; Daniel 12:2, 13; Mark 13:27; 1 Corinthians 15:12–58; 1 Thessalonians 4:13–18; Revelation 20:11—21:4.

17:3 Was David saying he was sinless? Far from a proud assumption of purity, David's claim was an understanding of his relationship with God. In Psalms 32 and 51, David freely acknowledged his own sins. Nevertheless, his relationship with God was one of close fellowship and constant repentance and forgiveness. His claim to goodness, therefore, was based on his continual seeking after God.

17:8 Just as we protect our eyes, so God will protect us. We must not conclude, however, that we have somehow missed God's protection if we experience troubles. God's protection has far greater purposes than helping us avoid pain; it is to make us better servants for him. God also protects us by guiding us through painful circumstances, not only by helping us escape them.

17:8 The "shadow of your wings" is a figure of speech symbolizing God's protection. He guards us just as a mother bird protects her young by covering them with her wings. Moses used this same metaphor in Deuteronomy 32:11.

17:13–15 We deceive ourselves when we measure our happiness or contentment in life by the amount of wealth we possess. When we put riches at the top of our value system, we let power, pleasure, and financial security overshadow the eternal value of our relationship with God. We think we will be happy or content when we get riches, only to discover that they don't really satisfy, and the pleasures fade away. The true measurement of happiness or contentment is found in God's love and in doing his will. You will find true happiness if you put your relationship with God above earthly riches.

17:15 The word *awake* shows that David believed in life after death. Although belief in resurrection was not widespread in Old Testament times, several verses show that it was partially understood. Some of these are Job 19:25–27; Psalms 16:10; 49:15; 139:17, 18; Isaiah 26:19; and Daniel 12:2, 13.

Theme: Gratitude for deliverance and victory. The only sure way to be delivered from surrounding evil is to call upon God for help and strength.
Author: David

18 For the director of music. Of David the servant of the LORD. He sang to the LORD the words of this song when the LORD delivered him from the hand of all his enemies and from the hand of Saul. He said:

¹ I love you, O LORD, my strength.

² The LORD is my rock, my fortress and my deliverer;
    my God is my rock, in whom I take refuge.
    He is my shield and the horn[a] of my salvation, my stronghold.

³ I call to the LORD, who is worthy of praise,
    and I am saved from my enemies.

⁴ The cords of death[f] entangled me;
    the torrents[g] of destruction overwhelmed me.

⁵ The cords of the grave[b] coiled around me;
    the snares of death confronted me.

⁶ In my distress I called to the LORD;
    I cried to my God for help.
    From his temple he heard my voice;
    my cry came before him, into his ears.

⁷ The earth trembled and quaked,
    and the foundations of the mountains shook;
    they trembled because he was angry.

⁸ Smoke rose from his nostrils;
    consuming fire came from his mouth,
    burning coals blazed out of it.

⁹ He parted the heavens and came down;[h]
    dark clouds were under his feet.

¹⁰ He mounted the cherubim and flew;
    he soared on the wings of the wind.[i]

¹¹ He made darkness his covering,[j] his canopy around him—
    the dark rain clouds of the sky.

¹² Out of the brightness of his presence[k] clouds advanced,
    with hailstones and bolts of lightning.

¹³ The LORD thundered[l] from heaven;
    the voice of the Most High resounded.[c]

¹⁴ He shot his arrows and scattered ⌊the enemies⌋,
    great bolts of lightning and routed them.[m]

¹⁵ The valleys of the sea were exposed
    and the foundations of the earth laid bare
    at your rebuke,[n] O LORD,
    at the blast of breath from your nostrils.

¹⁶ He reached down from on high and took hold of me;
    he drew me out of deep waters.

18:4
[f] Ps 116:3
[g] Ps 124:4

18:9
[h] Ps 144:5

18:10
[i] Ps 104:3

18:11
[j] Ps 97:2

18:12
[k] Ps 104:2

18:13
[l] Ps 29:3

18:14
[m] Ps 144:6

18:15
[n] Ps 76:6; 106:9

---

[a] *2 Horn* here symbolizes strength.   [b] *5* Hebrew *Sheol*   [c] *13* Some Hebrew manuscripts and Septuagint (see also 2 Samuel 22:14); most Hebrew manuscripts *resounded, / amid hailstones and bolts of lightning*

18:1ff This psalm is almost a duplicate of 2 Samuel 22. It may have been written toward the end of David's life when there was peace. God is praised for his glorious works and blessings through the years.

18:2, 3 God's protection of his people is limitless and can take many forms. David characterized God's care with five military symbols. God is like (1) a *rock* that can't be moved by any who would harm us, (2) a *fortress* or place of safety where the enemy can't follow, (3) a *shield* that comes between us and harm, (4) a *horn* of salvation, a symbol of might and power, (5) a *stronghold* high above our enemies. If you need protection, look to God.

18:10 Cherubim are mighty angels. One of the functions of the cherubim was to serve as guardians. Angels guarded the entrances to both the tree of life (Genesis 3:24) and the Most Holy Place (Exodus 26:31–33). Two cherubim of hammered gold were part of the ark of the covenant (Exodus 25:18–22). The living creatures carrying God's throne in Ezekiel 1 may have been cherubim.

18:13 The "Most High" was an important designation for David to make. Pagan idol worship was deeply rooted in the land, and each region had its own deity. But these images of wood and stone were powerless. David was placing the Lord alone in a superior category: he is by far the Most High.

¹⁷ He rescued me from my powerful enemy,
    from my foes, who were too strong for me.
¹⁸ They confronted me in the day of my disaster,
    but the LORD was my support.

18:19
o Ps 31:8

¹⁹ He brought me out into a spacious place;^o
    he rescued me because he delighted in me.

²⁰ The LORD has dealt with me according to my righteousness;
    according to the cleanness of my hands he has rewarded me.

18:21
p 2Ch 34:33

²¹ For I have kept the ways of the LORD;^p
    I have not done evil by turning from my God.
²² All his laws are before me;
    I have not turned away from his decrees.
²³ I have been blameless before him
    and have kept myself from sin.

18:24
q 1Sa 26:23

²⁴ The LORD has rewarded me according to my righteousness,^q
    according to the cleanness of my hands in his sight.

²⁵ To the faithful you show yourself faithful,
    to the blameless you show yourself blameless,

18:26
r Pr 3:34

²⁶ to the pure you show yourself pure,
    but to the crooked you show yourself shrewd.^r

18:27
s Pr 6:17

²⁷ You save the humble
    but bring low those whose eyes are haughty.^s

18:28
t Job 18:6

²⁸ You, O LORD, keep my lamp burning;
    my God turns my darkness into light.^t
²⁹ With your help I can advance against a troop^a;
    with my God I can scale a wall.

18:30
u Dt 32:4
v Ps 12:6

³⁰ As for God, his way is perfect;^u
    the word of the LORD is flawless.^v
He is a shield
    for all who take refuge in him.

18:31
w Dt 32:39; Ps 86:8;
Isa 45:5, 6, 14, 18,
21
x Dt 32:31

³¹ For who is God besides the LORD?^w
    And who is the Rock^x except our God?
³² It is God who arms me with strength
    and makes my way perfect.

18:33
y Hab 3:19
z Dt 32:13

³³ He makes my feet like the feet of a deer;^y
    he enables me to stand on the heights.^z

18:34
a Ps 144:1

³⁴ He trains my hands for battle;^a
    my arms can bend a bow of bronze.
³⁵ You give me your shield of victory,
    and your right hand sustains me;
    you stoop down to make me great.
³⁶ You broaden the path beneath me,
    so that my ankles do not turn.

a 29 Or can run through a barricade

18:16 Do your troubles, like "deep waters," threaten to drown you? David, helpless and weak, knew that God alone had rescued him from his enemies when he was defenseless. When you wish that God would quickly rescue you from your troubles, remember that he can either deliver you or be your support as you go through them (18:18). Either way, his protection is best for you. When you feel as though you're drowning in troubles, ask God to help you, hold you steady, and protect you. In his care, you are never helpless.

18:30 Some people think that belief in God is a crutch for weak people who cannot make it on their own. God is indeed a shield to protect us when we are too weak to face certain trials by ourselves, but he does not want us to remain weak. He strengthens, protects, and guides us in order to send us back into an evil world

to fight for him. Then he continues to work with us because the strongest person on earth is infinitely weaker than God and needs his help. David was not a coward; he was a mighty warrior who, even with all his armies and weapons, knew that only God could ultimately protect and save him.

18:32–34 God doesn't promise to eliminate challenges; instead, he promises to give us strength to meet those challenges. If he gave us no rough roads to walk, no mountains to climb, and no battles to fight, we would not grow. He does not leave us alone with our challenges, however. Instead he stands beside us, teaches us, and strengthens us to face them.

37 I pursued my enemies and overtook them;
  I did not turn back till they were destroyed.
38 I crushed them so that they could not rise;*b*
  they fell beneath my feet.
39 You armed me with strength for battle;
  you made my adversaries bow at my feet.
40 You made my enemies turn their backs in flight,
  and I destroyed my foes.
41 They cried for help, but there was no one to save them—
  to the LORD, but he did not answer.*c*
42 I beat them as fine as dust borne on the wind;
  I poured them out like mud in the streets.

43 You have delivered me from the attacks of the people;
  you have made me the head of nations;*d*
  people I did not know are subject to me.
44 As soon as they hear me, they obey me;
  foreigners cringe before me.
45 They all lose heart;
  they come trembling from their strongholds.*e*

46 The LORD lives! Praise be to my Rock!
  Exalted be God my Savior!
47 He is the God who avenges me,
  who subdues nations*f* under me,
48   who saves me from my enemies.
  You exalted me above my foes;
  from violent men you rescued me.
49 Therefore I will praise you among the nations, O LORD;
  I will sing*g* praises to your name.*h*
50 He gives his king great victories;
  he shows unfailing kindness to his anointed,
  to David*i* and his descendants forever.

18:38
b Ps 36:12

18:41
c Pr 1:28

18:43
d 2Sa 8:1-14

18:45
e Mic 7:17

18:47
f Ps 47:3

18:49
g Ps 108:1
h Ro 15:9*

18:50
i Ps 144:10

Theme: Both God's creation and his Word reveal his greatness.
Author: David

19

For the director of music. A psalm of David.

1 The heavens*j* declare*k* the glory of God;
  the skies proclaim the work of his hands.
2 Day after day they pour forth speech;
  night after night they display knowledge.*l*
3 There is no speech or language
  where their voice is not heard.*a*

19:1
j Isa 40:22
k Ro 1:19

19:2
l Ps 74:16

*a*3 Or *They have no speech, there are no words; / no sound is heard from them*

18:40–42 David was a merciful man. He spared the lives of Saul (1 Samuel 24:1–8), Nabal (1 Samuel 25:21–35), and Shimei (2 Samuel 16:5–12) and showed great kindness to Mephibosheth (2 Samuel 9). In asking God to destroy his enemies, David was simply asking him to give the wicked the punishment they deserved.

18:43–45 David's great power had become legendary. God had given him victory in every battle. The book of 2 Samuel records victories over the Jebusites (5:6–10), the Philistines (5:17–25; 8:1, 2), Hadadezer of Zobah (8:3, 4), the Arameans (8:5, 6; 10), the Edomites (8:13, 14), and the Ammonites (12:26–31). In addition, the king of Tyre sent supplies and workmen to help David build his palace (5:11). But David did not attribute his victories to himself. He fully realized that the purpose of his position was to bless God's people (1 Chronicles 14:2).

19:1ff In this psalm, David's steps of meditation take him from creation, through God's Word, through David's own sinfulness, to salvation. As God reveals himself through nature (19:1–6), we learn about his power and our finiteness. As God reveals himself through Scripture (19:7–11), we learn about his holiness and our sinfulness. As God reveals himself through daily experiences (19:12–14), we learn about his gracious forgiveness and our salvation.

19:1–6 We are surrounded by fantastic displays of God's craftsmanship—the heavens give dramatic evidence of his existence, his power, his love, his care. To say that the universe happened by chance is absurd. Its design, intricacy, and orderliness point to a personally involved Creator. As you look at God's handiwork in nature and the heavens, thank him for such magnificent beauty and the truth it reveals about the Creator.

19:3, 4 The apostle Paul referred to this psalm when he

19:4
m Ro 10:18*

4 Their voice[a] goes out into all the earth,
  their words to the ends of the world. *m*

In the heavens he has pitched a tent for the sun,
5   which is like a bridegroom coming forth from his pavilion,
  like a champion rejoicing to run his course.

19:6
n Ps 113:3

6 It rises at one end of the heavens
  and makes its circuit to the other;*n*
  nothing is hidden from its heat.

19:7
o Ps 23:3
p Ps 93:5; 111:7

7 The law of the LORD is perfect,
  reviving the soul. *o*
The statutes of the LORD are trustworthy,*p*
  making wise the simple.

19:8
q Ps 119:128

8 The precepts of the LORD are right,*q*
  giving joy to the heart.
The commands of the LORD are radiant,
  giving light to the eyes.
9 The fear of the LORD is pure,
  enduring forever.
The ordinances of the LORD are sure
  and altogether righteous.
10 They are more precious than gold,
  than much pure gold;
they are sweeter than honey,
  than honey from the comb.
11 By them is your servant warned;
  in keeping them there is great reward.

19:12
r Ps 51:2; 90:8

12 Who can discern his errors?
  Forgive my hidden faults.*r*
13 Keep your servant also from willful sins;
  may they not rule over me.
Then will I be blameless,
  innocent of great transgression.

19:14
s Ps 104:34

14 May the words of my mouth and the meditation of my heart
  be pleasing*s* in your sight,
  O LORD, my Rock and my Redeemer.

a 4 Septuagint, Jerome and Syriac; Hebrew *line*

---

explained that everyone knows about God because nature proclaims God's existence and power (Romans 1:19, 20). This does not cancel the need for missions because the message of God's salvation found in his Word, the Bible, must still be told to the ends of the earth. While nature points to the existence of God, the Bible tells us about salvation. God's people must explain to others how they can have a relationship with God. Although people everywhere should already believe in a Creator by just looking at the evidence of nature around them, God needs us to explain his love, mercy, and grace. What are you doing to take God's message to the world?

19:7–11 When we think of statutes, precepts and commands, we often think of rules that keep us from having fun. But here we see the opposite—law that revives us, makes us wise, gives joy to the heart, gives light to the eyes, warns us, and rewards us. That's because God's laws are guidelines and lights for our path, rather than chains on our hands and feet. They point at danger and warn us, and then point at success and guide us.

19:12, 13 Many Christians are plagued by guilt. They worry that they may have committed a sin unknowingly, done something good with selfish intentions, failed to put their whole heart into a task, or neglected what they should have done. Guilt can play an important role in bringing us to Christ and in keeping us behaving properly, but it should not cripple us or make us fearful. God fully and completely forgives us—even for those sins we do unknowingly.

19:14 Would you change the way you live if you knew that every word and thought would be examined by God first? David asks that God approve his words and reflections as though they were offerings brought to the altar. As you begin each day, determine that God's love will guide what you say and how you think.

Theme: A prayer for victory in battle. Such a prayer can help us prepare for any great challenge. David knew that trust should be placed in the Lord more than in human power.
Author: David. The events in 2 Samuel 10 may have prompted this prayer.

20

For the director of music. A psalm of David.

1 May the LORD answer you when you are in distress;
   may the name of the God of Jacob protect you.*t*

2 May he send you help from the sanctuary
   and grant you support from Zion.

3 May he remember all your sacrifices
   and accept your burnt offerings.   **Selah**

4 May he give you the desire of your heart*u*
   and make all your plans succeed.

5 We will shout for joy when you are victorious
   and will lift up our banners in the name of our God.
May the LORD grant all your requests.*v*

6 Now I know that the LORD saves his anointed;*w*
   he answers him from his holy heaven
   with the saving power of his right hand.

7 Some trust in chariots and some in horses,
   but we trust in the name of the LORD our God.*x*

8 They are brought to their knees and fall,
   but we rise up and stand firm.*y*

9 O LORD, save the king!
   Answer*a* us when we call!

20:1	*t* Ps 91:14
20:4	*u* Ps 21:21; 45:16, 19
20:5	*v* 1Sa 1:17
20:6	*w* Ps 28:8
20:7	*x* 2Ch 32:8
20:8	*y* Ps 37:23

Theme: Praising God after victory in battle. When God answers our prayers for victory, we must quickly and openly thank him for his help.
Author: David

21

For the director of music. A psalm of David.

1 O LORD, the king rejoices in your strength.
   How great is his joy in the victories you give!

2 You have granted him the desire of his heart
   and have not withheld the request of his lips.   **Selah**

3 You welcomed him with rich blessings
   and placed a crown of pure gold on his head.

4 He asked you for life, and you gave it to him—
   length of days, for ever and ever.*z*

5 Through the victories you gave, his glory is great;
   you have bestowed on him splendor and majesty.

6 Surely you have granted him eternal blessings
   and made him glad with the joy of your presence.*a*

7 For the king trusts in the LORD;
   through the unfailing love of the Most High
   he will not be shaken.

21:4	*z* Ps 133:3
21:6	*a* 1Ch 17:27

a 9 Or save! / O King, answer

20:6–8 As long as there have been armies and weapons, nations have boasted of their power, but such power does not last. Throughout history, empires and kingdoms have risen to great power only to vanish in the dust. David, however, knew that the true might of his nation was not in weaponry but in worship; not in firepower but in God's power. Because God alone can preserve a nation or an individual, be sure your confidence is in God, who gives eternal victory. Whom do you trust?

21:1–6 David described all that he had as gifts from God: "the desire of his heart," rich blessings, a crown of pure gold, long life,

splendor and majesty, eternal blessings, gladness. We, too, should look upon all we have—position, family, wealth, talent—as gifts from God. Only then will we use them to give glory back to him.

21:7 A good leader trusts the Lord and depends upon his unfailing love. Too often leaders trust in their own cleverness, popular support, or military power. But God is above all these "gods." If you aspire to leadership, keep the Lord God at the center of your life and depend on him. His love will keep you from stumbling.

21:7 Because David trusted in God, God would not let him be

8 Your hand will lay hold[b] on all your enemies;
    your right hand will seize your foes.
9 At the time of your appearing
    you will make them like a fiery furnace.
In his wrath the Lord will swallow them up,
    and his fire will consume them.
10 You will destroy their descendants from the earth,
    their posterity from mankind.
11 Though they plot evil[c] against you
    and devise wicked schemes,[d] they cannot succeed;
12 for you will make them turn their backs
    when you aim at them with drawn bow.

13 Be exalted, O Lord, in your strength;
    we will sing and praise your might.

Theme: A prayer that carries us from great suffering to great joy. Despite apparent rejection by his friends and God, David believed that God would lead him out of despair. He looked forward to that future day when God would rule over the entire earth.
Author: David

22

For the director of music. To ⌊the tune of⌋ "The Doe of the Morning." A psalm of David.

1 My God, my God, why have you forsaken me?[e]
    Why are you so far from saving me,
    so far from the words of my groaning?
2 O my God, I cry out by day, but you do not answer,
    by night,[f] and am not silent.

3 Yet you are enthroned as the Holy One;
    you are the praise of Israel.[a]
4 In you our fathers put their trust;
    they trusted and you delivered them.
5 They cried to you and were saved;
    in you they trusted and were not disappointed.[g]

6 But I am a worm[h] and not a man,
    scorned by men[i] and despised by the people.
7 All who see me mock me;
    they hurl insults,[j] shaking their heads:
8 "He trusts in the Lord;
    let the Lord rescue him.[k]
Let him deliver him,
    since he delights[l] in him."

a3 Or Yet you are holy, / enthroned on the praises of Israel

21:8
b Isa 10:10

21:11
c Ps 2:1
d Ps 10:2

22:1
e Mt 27:46*;
Mk 15:34*

22:2
f Ps 42:3

22:5
g Isa 49:23

22:6
h Job 25:6
i Ps 31:11
22:7
j Mt 27:39, 44

22:8
k Ps 91:14
l Mt 27:43

---

shaken (removed from the throne). When we trust in God, we have permanence and stability. We may lose a great deal—families, jobs, material possessions—but we cannot be shaken from God's favor. He will be our foundation of solid rock. He will never leave or desert us.

21:11 When you see evil schemes unfold, remember that they will not succeed forever. The power of evildoers is only temporary, and God's very presence would send them scattering in a moment. God, according to his plan and purpose, will intervene for his people and give the wicked the judgment they deserve. We should not be dismayed when we see the temporary advantage God's enemies have.

22:1 David gave an amazingly accurate description of the suffering the Messiah would endure hundreds of years later. David was obviously enduring some great trial, but through his suffering he, like the Messiah to come, gained victory. Jesus, the Messiah, quoted this verse while hanging on the cross carrying our burden

of sin (Matthew 27:46). It was not a cry of doubt, but an urgent appeal to God.

22:6 When others despise us and heap scorn upon us, they treat us as less than human. After much degradation, we, like David, could begin to feel like worms. When we feel the sting of rejection, we must keep in mind the hope and victory that God promises us (22:22ff).

9 Yet you brought me out of the womb;[m]
  you made me trust in you
  even at my mother's breast.
10 From birth[n] I was cast upon you;
  from my mother's womb you have been my God.
11 Do not be far from me,
  for trouble is near
  and there is no one to help.

12 Many bulls[o] surround me;
  strong bulls of Bashan encircle me.
13 Roaring lions tearing their prey
  open their mouths wide against me.
14 I am poured out like water,
  and all my bones are out of joint.
  My heart has turned to wax;
  it has melted away[p] within me.
15 My strength is dried up like a potsherd,
  and my tongue sticks to the roof of my mouth;
  you lay me[a] in the dust[q] of death.
16 Dogs have surrounded me;
  a band of evil men has encircled me,
  they have pierced[b][r] my hands and my feet.
17 I can count all my bones;
  people stare[s] and gloat over me.
18 They divide my garments among them
  and cast lots[t] for my clothing.

19 But you, O LORD, be not far off;
  O my Strength, come quickly to help me.
20 Deliver my life from the sword,
  my precious life[u] from the power of the dogs.
21 Rescue me from the mouth of the lions;
  save[c] me from the horns of the wild oxen.

22 I will declare your name to my brothers;
  in the congregation I will praise you.[v]
23 You who fear the LORD, praise him![w]
  All you descendants of Jacob, honor him!
  Revere him, all you descendants of Israel!
24 For he has not despised or disdained
  the suffering of the afflicted one;
  he has not hidden his face from him
  but has listened to his cry for help.[x]

25 From you comes the theme of my praise in the great assembly;[y]
  before those who fear you[d] will I fulfill my vows.

Reference
22:9 [m] Ps 71:6
22:10 [n] Isa 46:3
22:12 [o] Ps 68:30
22:14 [p] Da 5:6
22:15 [q] Ps 104:29
22:16 [r] Isa 53:5; Zec 12:10; Jn 19:34
22:17 [s] Lk 23:35
22:18 [t] Jn 19:24*
22:20 [u] Ps 35:17
22:22 [v] Heb 2:12*
22:23 [w] Ps 135:19
22:24 [x] Heb 5:7
22:25 [y] Ps 35:18

a 15 Or / I am laid   b 16 Some Hebrew manuscripts, Septuagint and Syriac; most Hebrew manuscripts / like the lion,
c 21 Or / you have heard   d 25 Hebrew him

22:9–11 God's loving concern does not begin on the day we are born and conclude on the day we die. It reaches back to those days before we were born, and reaches ahead along the unending path of eternity. Our only sure help comes from a God whose concern for us reaches beyond our earthly existence. When faced with such love, how could anyone reject it?

22:12 The land of Bashan, located east of the Sea of Galilee, was known for its strong and well-fed cattle (Amos 4:1). Because of its grain fields, it was often called the breadbasket of Palestine.

22:15 A "potsherd" is a pottery fragment or a piece of sun-baked clay.

22:18 It is a great insult to human dignity to rob a person of everything, even his clothing, leaving him naked and destitute. Jesus the Messiah would suffer this humiliating experience on the cross (Matthew 27:35). Most of us will never know the shame and suffering of being penniless and virtually naked in a public place, as many of the Jews experienced during the Nazi holocaust, or even the shame of being homeless on the streets of our cities today. But most of us would feel equally exposed and naked when some sin, secret or not-so-secret, would be uncovered. At that time, we will need to cry out with David, "O my Strength, come quickly to help me" (22:19).

22:22 David would praise God in the congregation because his private deliverance deserved a public testimony. God wonderfully

²⁶ The poor will eat and be satisfied;
　　they who seek the LORD will praise him—
　　may your hearts live forever!
²⁷ All the ends of the earth
　　will remember and turn to the LORD,
　and all the families of the nations
　　will bow down before him,
²⁸ for dominion belongs to the LORD
　　and he rules over the nations.

²⁹ All the rich of the earth will feast and worship;
　　all who go down to the dust will kneel before him—
　　those who cannot keep themselves alive.
³⁰ Posterity will serve him;
　　future generations will be told about the Lord.
³¹ They will proclaim his righteousness
　　to a people yet unborn z—
　　for he has done it.

22:31
z Ps 78:6

CHRIST IN THE PSALMS

Both the Jewish and Christian faiths have long believed that many psalms referred as much to the promised Messiah as they did to events at the time. Because the Messiah was to be a descendant of David, it was expected that many of the royal psalms would apply to him. Christians noted how many of the passages seemed to describe in detail events from Christ's life and death. Jesus himself frequently quoted from Psalms. Almost everything that happened at the crucifixion and most of Jesus' words during his final hours were prophesied in Psalms.

The following is a list of the main references in Psalms pertaining to Christ.

Reference in Psalms	Reference to Christ	Fulfillment in the New Testament
2:7	The Messiah will be God's Son	Hebrews 1:5, 6
16:8–10	He will rise from the dead	Luke 24:5–7
22:1–21	He will experience agony on the cross	Matthew 26; 27
22:15	He will thirst while on the cross	John 19:28
22:18	Evil men will cast lots for his clothing	Matthew 27:35; John 19:23, 24
22:22	He will declare God's name	Hebrews 2:12
34:20	His bones will not be broken	John 19:36, 37
40:6–8	He will come to do God's will	Hebrews 10:5–7
41:9	His close friend will betray him	Luke 22:48
45:6, 7	His throne will last forever	Hebrews 1:8, 9
68:18	He will ascend into heaven	Ephesians 4:8–10
69:9	He will be zealous for God	John 2:17
69:21	He will be offered vinegar for his thirst on the cross	Matthew 27:48
89:3, 4, 35, 36	He will be a descendant of David	Luke 1:31–33
96:13	He will return to judge the world	1 Thessalonians 1:10
110:1	He is David's son and David's Lord	Matthew 22:44
110:4	He is the eternal priest-king	Hebrews 6:20
118:22	He is rejected by many but accepted by God	1 Peter 2:7, 8

---

delivers us in the quiet moments when we are hurting, and we must be prepared to offer public praise for his care.

22:30, 31 Unborn generations are depending on our faithfulness today. As we teach our children about the Lord, so they will teach their children and their children's children. If we fail to tell our children about the Lord, we may well be breaking the chain of God's influence in generations to come. We must view our chil-

dren and all the young people we meet as God's future leaders. If we are faithful in opportunities today, we may well be affecting the future.

22:30, 31 If we want our children to serve the Lord, they must hear about him from us. It is not enough to rely on the church or those with more knowledge to provide all their Christian education. We must reinforce the lessons of the Bible in our homes.

Theme: God is seen as a caring shepherd and a dependable guide. We must follow God and obey his commands. He is our only hope for eternal life and security.
Author: David

23 A psalm of David.

1 The LORD is my shepherd,^a I shall not be in want.^b
2 He makes me lie down in green pastures,
 he leads me beside quiet waters,^c
3 he restores my soul.
 He guides me in paths of righteousness^d
 for his name's sake.
4 Even though I walk
 through the valley of the shadow of death,^a
 I will fear no evil,
 for you are with me;^e
 your rod and your staff,
 they comfort me.

5 You prepare a table before me
 in the presence of my enemies.
 You anoint my head with oil;^f
 my cup overflows.
6 Surely goodness and love will follow me
 all the days of my life,
 and I will dwell in the house of the LORD
 forever.

23:1
^aIsa 40:11;
Jn 10:11
^bPhp 4:19

23:2
^cEze 34:14;
Rev 7:17

23:3
^dPs 5:8

23:4
^eIsa 43:2

23:5
^fPs 92:10

Theme: Everything belongs to God—the glorious eternal King. Let us worship him and welcome his glorious reign.
Author: David

24 Of David. A psalm.

1 The earth is the LORD's, and everything in it,
 the world, and all who live in it;
2 for he founded it upon the seas
 and established it upon the waters.

^a4 Or *through the darkest valley*

23:1 In describing the Lord as a shepherd, David wrote out of his own experience because he had spent his early years caring for sheep (1 Samuel 16:10, 11). Sheep are completely dependent on the shepherd for provision, guidance, and protection. The New Testament calls Jesus the good shepherd (John 10:11), the great Shepherd (Hebrews 13:20), and the Chief Shepherd (1 Peter 5:4). As the Lord is the good shepherd, so we are his sheep—not frightened, passive animals, but obedient followers, wise enough to follow one who will lead us in the right places and in right ways. This psalm does not focus on the animal-like qualities of sheep, but on the discipleship qualities of those who follow. When you recognize the good shepherd, follow him!

23:2, 3 When we allow God our shepherd to guide us, we have contentment. When we choose to sin, however, we go our own way and cannot blame God for the environment we create for ourselves. Our shepherd knows the "green pastures" and "quiet waters" that will restore us. We will reach these places only by following him obediently. Rebelling against the shepherd's leading is actually rebelling against our own best interests. We must remember this the next time we are tempted to go our own way rather than the shepherd's way.

23:4 Death casts a frightening shadow over us because we are entirely helpless in its presence. We can struggle with other enemies—pain, suffering, disease, injury—but strength and courage cannot overcome death. It has the final word. Only one person can walk with us through death's dark valley and bring us safely to the other side—the God of life, our shepherd. Because life is uncertain, we should follow this shepherd who offers us eternal comfort.

23:5, 6 In ancient Near Eastern culture, at a banquet it was customary to anoint a person with fragrant oil. Hosts were also expected to protect their guests at all costs. God offers the protection of a host even when enemies surround us. In the final scene of this psalm, we see that believers will dwell with the Lord. God, the perfect shepherd and host, promises to guide and protect us through life to bring us into his house forever.

24:1 Because "the earth is the LORD's," all of us are stewards, or caretakers. We should be committed to the proper management of this world and its resources. We are not to become devoted to anything created or act as sole proprietors, however, because this world will pass away (1 John 2:17).

24:1ff This psalm may have been written to celebrate the moving of the ark of the covenant from Obed-Edom's house to Jerusalem (2 Samuel 6:10–12). Tradition says that this psalm was sung on the first day of each week in the temple services. Verses 1–6 tell who is worthy to join in such a celebration of worship.

24:3
g Ps 15:1

3 Who may ascend the hill of the Lord?
    Who may stand in his holy place?*g*

24:4
h Job 17:9
i Mt 5:8

4 He who has clean hands*h* and a pure heart,*i*
    who does not lift up his soul to an idol
    or swear by what is false.*a*
5 He will receive blessing from the Lord
    and vindication from God his Savior.

24:6
j Ps 27:8

6 Such is the generation of those who seek him,
    who seek your face,*j* O God of Jacob.*b*   *Selah*

24:7
k Isa 26:2

7 Lift up your heads, O you gates;*k*
    be lifted up, you ancient doors,
    that the King of glory may come in.
8 Who is this King of glory?
    The Lord strong and mighty,
    the Lord mighty in battle.
9 Lift up your heads, O you gates;
    lift them up, you ancient doors,
    that the King of glory may come in.
10 Who is he, this King of glory?
    The Lord Almighty—
    he is the King of glory.   *Selah*

Theme: A prayer for defense, guidance, and pardon. As we trust in God, he grants these same requests for us.
Author: David

25 *c*

Of David.

25:1
l Ps 86:4

1 To you, O Lord, I lift up my soul;*l*
2   in you I trust, O my God.
    Do not let me be put to shame,
        nor let my enemies triumph over me.
3 No one whose hope is in you
        will ever be put to shame,
    but they will be put to shame
        who are treacherous without excuse.

4 Show me your ways, O Lord,
    teach me your paths;

*a*4 Or *swear falsely* *b*6 Two Hebrew manuscripts and Syriac (see also Septuagint); most Hebrew manuscripts *face, Jacob* *c*This psalm is an acrostic poem, the verses of which begin with the successive letters of the Hebrew alphabet.

24:4 Swearing by what is false means telling lies under oath. How greatly God values honesty! Dishonesty comes easily, especially when complete truthfulness could cost us something, make us uncomfortable, or put us in an unfavorable light. Dishonest communication hinders relationships. Without honesty, a relationship with God is impossible. If we lie to others, we will begin to deceive ourselves. God cannot hear us or speak to us if we are building a wall of self-deception.

24:7 Who is this King of glory? The King of glory, identified also as the Lord of hosts, or the commander of heaven's armies, is the Messiah himself, eternal, holy, and mighty. This psalm is not only a battle cry for the church, it also looks forward to Christ's future entry into the new Jerusalem to reign forever (Revelation 19:11–21).

24:7–10 This psalm, often set to music, was probably used in corporate worship. It may have been re-enacted many times at the temple. The people outside would call out to the temple gates to open up and let the King of glory in. From inside, the priests or another group would ask, "Who is this King of glory?" Outside, the people would respond in unison, "The Lord strong and mighty, the Lord mighty in battle," proclaiming his great power and strength. The exchange then would be repeated (24:9, 10), and the temple gates would swing open, symbolizing the people's desire to

have God's presence among them. This would have been an important lesson for children who were participating.

25:2 Seventy-two psalms—almost half the book—speak about enemies. Enemies are those who oppose not only us, but also God's way of living. We can view temptations—money, success, prestige, lust—as our enemies. And our greatest enemy is Satan. David asked God to keep his enemies from overcoming him because they opposed what God stood for. If his enemies succeeded, David feared that many would think that living for God was futile. David did not question his own faith—he knew that God would triumph. But he didn't want his enemies' success to be an obstacle to the faith of others.

25:4 David expressed his desire for guidance. How do we receive God's guidance? The first step is to *want* to be guided and to realize that God's primary guidance system is in his Word, the Bible. Psalm 119 tells of the endless knowledge found in God's Word. By reading the Bible and constantly learning from it, we will gain the wisdom to perceive God's direction for our lives. We may be tempted to demand answers from God, but David asked for direction. When we are willing to seek God, learn from his Word, and obey his commands, then will we receive his specific guidance.

⁵ guide me in your truth and teach me,
    for you are God my Savior,
    and my hope is in you all day long.
⁶ Remember, O Lord, your great mercy and love,ᵐ
    for they are from of old.
⁷ Remember not the sins of my youthⁿ
    and my rebellious ways;
  according to your loveᵒ remember me,
    for you are good, O Lord.

⁸ Good and upright is the Lord;
    therefore he instructs sinners in his ways.
⁹ He guides the humble in what is right
    and teaches them his way.
¹⁰ All the ways of the Lord are loving and faithful
    for those who keep the demands of his covenant.ᵖ
¹¹ For the sake of your name, O Lord,
    forgive my iniquity, though it is great.
¹² Who, then, is the man that fears the Lord?
    He will instruct him in the way chosen for him.
¹³ He will spend his days in prosperity,
    and his descendants will inherit the land.
¹⁴ The Lord confides�q in those who fear him;
    he makes his covenant known to them.
¹⁵ My eyes are ever on the Lord,ʳ
    for only he will release my feet from the snare.

¹⁶ Turn to meˢ and be gracious to me,
    for I am lonely and afflicted.
¹⁷ The troubles of my heart have multiplied;
    free me from my anguish.
¹⁸ Look upon my affliction and my distressᵗ
    and take away all my sins.
¹⁹ See how my enemiesᵘ have increased
    and how fiercely they hate me!
²⁰ Guard my lifeᵛ and rescue me;
    let me not be put to shame,
    for I take refuge in you.
²¹ May integrity and uprightness protect me,
    because my hope is in you.

²² Redeem Israel,ʷ O God,
    from all their troubles!

25:6
ᵐPs 103:17;
Isa 63:7, 15
25:7
ⁿJob 13:26
ᵒPs 51:1

25:10
ᵖPs 103:18

25:14
qPr 3:32
25:15
ʳPs 141:8

25:16
ˢPs 69:16

25:18
ᵗ2Sa 16:12

25:19
ᵘPs 3:1

25:20
ᵛPs 86:2

25:22
ʷPs 130:8

25:12 To fear the Lord is to recognize God for who he is: holy, almighty, righteous, pure, all-knowing, all-powerful, and all-wise. When we regard God correctly, we gain a clearer picture of ourselves: sinful, weak, frail, and needy. When we recognize who God is and who we are, we will fall at his feet in humble respect. Only then will he show us how to choose his way.

25:14 "The Lord confides in those who fear him." God offers intimate and lasting friendship to those who revere him, who hold him in highest honor. What relationship could ever compare with having the Lord of all creation for a friend? Your everlasting friendship with God will grow as you respect and honor him.

25:16, 17 Do life's problems always seem to go from bad to worse? God is the only one who can reverse this downward spiral. He can take our problems and turn them into glorious victories. The first and most important step is that we, like David, must cry out, "Turn to me and be gracious to me." When we are willing to do that, God will do his work in us and in our situation. The next step is yours—God has already made his offer.

25:21 We need integrity and honesty to preserve us along life's way. The psalm writer asks for these to protect him step by step. Uprightness says, "This is the Shepherd's way," and integrity says, "I will walk consistently in it."

Theme: Declaring loyalty to God. If we are genuinely committed to God, we can stand up to opposition and examination.

Author: David, possibly written during the days of Absalom's rebellion

26 Of David.

26:1
xPs 7:8
y2Ki 20:3;
Heb 10:23

1 Vindicate me, O Lord,
   for I have led a blameless life;x
I have trusted in the Lord
   without wavering.y

2 Test me, O Lord, and try me,
   examine my heart and my mind;

26:3
z2Ki 20:3

3 for your love is ever before me,
   and I walk continuallyz in your truth.

26:4
aPs 1:1

4 I do not sita with deceitful men,
   nor do I consort with hypocrites;

26:5
bPs 139:21

5 I abhorb the assembly of evildoers
   and refuse to sit with the wicked.

26:6
cPs 73:13

6 I wash my hands in innocence,c
   and go about your altar, O Lord,

26:7
dPs 9:1

7 proclaiming aloud your praise
   and telling of all your wonderful deeds.d

26:8
ePs 27:4

8 I lovee the house where you live, O Lord,
   the place where your glory dwells.

26:9
fPs 28:3

9 Do not take away my soul along with sinners,
   my life with bloodthirsty men,f
10 in whose hands are wicked schemes,
   whose right hands are full of bribes.
11 But I lead a blameless life;
   redeem me and be merciful to me.

26:12
gPs 27:11; 40:2

12 My feet stand on level ground;g
   in the great assembly I will praise the Lord.

PSALMS TO LEARN AND LOVE

Almost everyone, whether religious or not, has heard Psalm 23 because it is quoted so frequently. Many other psalms are also familiar because they are quoted in music, in literature, or in the words of the worship service.

The psalms we know and love are the ones that come into our minds when we need them. They inspire us, comfort us, or correct us just when we need a word from the Lord. If you want to begin memorizing psalms, start with some of these favorites. Memorize the whole psalm or just the verses that speak most directly to you. Or read the psalm aloud several times a day until it is part of you.

26:1–3 In asking God to declare him "blameless," David was not claiming to be sinless—that is impossible for any human being to achieve. Instead, he was pleading with God to clear his name of the false charges made against him by his enemies. We also can ask God to examine us, trusting him to forgive our sins and clear our record according to his mercy.

26:4, 5 Should we stay away from unbelievers? No. Although Christians should avoid some places, Jesus demonstrated that we must go among unbelievers to help them. There is a difference, however, between being *with* unbelievers and being *one of* them. Acting like unbelievers harms our witness for God. Ask about the people you enjoy: If you are with them often, will you become less

obedient to God in outlook or action? If the answer is yes, carefully monitor how you spend your time with these people and their effect on you.

26:8 God's house in this verse refers to either the tabernacle in Gibeon (the one constructed in the days of Moses; see Exodus 40:35) or the temporary dwelling David built to house the ark of the covenant (2 Samuel 6:17). David exclaimed how he loved to worship God at this place. Do you love to worship?

26:12 Too often we complain about our problems to anyone who will listen and praise God only in private. Instead, we ought to complain privately and praise God publicly.

Theme: God offers help for today and hope for the future. Unwavering confidence in God
is our antidote for fear and loneliness.
Author: David

27 Of David.

1 The LORD is my light[h] and my salvation[i]—
    whom shall I fear?
The LORD is the stronghold of my life—
    of whom shall I be afraid?
2 When evil men advance against me
    to devour my flesh,[a]
when my enemies and my foes attack me,
    they will stumble and fall.[j]
3 Though an army besiege me,
    my heart will not fear;[k]
though war break out against me,
    even then will I be confident.

4 One thing[l] I ask of the LORD,
    this is what I seek:
that I may dwell in the house of the LORD
    all the days of my life,[m]
to gaze upon the beauty of the LORD
    and to seek him in his temple.
5 For in the day of trouble
    he will keep me safe in his dwelling;
he will hide me in the shelter of his tabernacle
    and set me high upon a rock.[n]
6 Then my head will be exalted[o]
    above the enemies who surround me;
at his tabernacle will I sacrifice with shouts of joy;
    I will sing and make music to the LORD.

7 Hear my voice when I call, O LORD;
    be merciful to me and answer me.
8 My heart says of you, "Seek his[b] face!"
    Your face, LORD, I will seek.
9 Do not hide your face[p] from me,
    do not turn your servant away in anger;
    you have been my helper.
Do not reject me or forsake me,
    O God my Savior.
10 Though my father and mother forsake me,
    the LORD will receive me.

	27:1
	[h] Isa 60:19
	[i] Ex 15:2
	27:2
	[j] Ps 14:4
	27:3
	[k] Ps 3:6
	27:4
	[l] Ps 90:17
	[m] Ps 26:8
	27:5
	[n] Ps 40:2
	27:6
	[o] Ps 3:3
	27:9
	[p] Ps 69:17

[a] 2 Or *to slander me*   [b] 8 Or *To you, O my heart, he has said, "Seek my*

27:1 Fear is a dark shadow that envelops us and ultimately
imprisons us within ourselves. Everyone has been a prisoner of
fear at one time or another—fear of rejection, misunderstanding,
uncertainty, sickness, or even death. But we can conquer fear
by trusting in the Lord who brings salvation. If we want to dispel
the darkness of fear, let us remember with the psalm writer that
"the LORD is my light and my salvation."

27:4 By the "house of the LORD" and "his temple," David could
be referring to the tabernacle in Gibeon, to the sanctuary he had
built to house the ark of the covenant, or to the temple that his
son Solomon was to build. David probably had the temple in
mind because he made many of the plans for it (1 Chronicles 22).
David may also have used the word *temple* to refer to the presence of the Lord. David's greatest desire was to live in God's
presence each day of his life. Sadly, this is not the greatest desire

of many who claim to be believers. What do you most desire?
Do you look forward to being in the presence of the Lord?

27:7 We often run to God when we experience difficulties. But
David sought God's guiding presence *every day.* When troubles
came his way, he was *already* in God's presence and prepared
to handle any test. Believers can call to God for help at any time,
but how shortsighted to call on God only when troubles come.
Many of our problems could be avoided or handled far more
easily by seeking God's help and direction beforehand.

27:10 Many have had the sad experience of being forsaken by
father or mother. Broken homes, differences of belief, addiction
to drugs or alcohol, even psychological isolation can leave children crippled by this loss. Even as adults, the pain may linger.
God can take that place in our life, fill that void, and heal that
hurt. He can direct us to those who may take the role of father
or mother for us. His love is sufficient for all our needs.

11 Teach me your way, O LORD;
   lead me in a straight path*q*
   because of my oppressors.
12 Do not turn me over to the desire of my foes,
   for false witnesses rise up against me,
   breathing out violence.
13 I am still confident of this:
   I will see the goodness of the LORD
   in the land of the living.
14 Wait for the LORD;
   be strong and take heart
   and wait for the LORD.

Theme: Prayer when surrounded by trouble or wickedness. God is our only real source of safety. Prayer is our best help when trials come our way because it keeps us in communion with God.
Author: David

28 Of David.

1 To you I call, O LORD my Rock;
   do not turn a deaf ear to me.
For if you remain silent,*r*
   I will be like those who have gone down to the pit.*s*
2 Hear my cry for mercy*t*
   as I call to you for help,
as I lift up my hands
   toward your Most Holy Place.*u*

3 Do not drag me away with the wicked,
   with those who do evil,
who speak cordially with their neighbors
   but harbor malice in their hearts.*v*
4 Repay them for their deeds
   and for their evil work;
repay them for what their hands have done
   and bring back upon them what they deserve.*w*
5 Since they show no regard for the works of the LORD
   and what his hands have done,*x*
he will tear them down
   and never build them up again.

6 Praise be to the LORD,
   for he has heard my cry for mercy.
7 The LORD is my strength*y* and my shield;
   my heart trusts*z* in him, and I am helped.
My heart leaps for joy
   and I will give thanks to him in song.

27:11
q Ps 25:4

28:1
r Ps 83:1
s Ps 88:4

28:2
t Ps 138:2
u Ps 5:7

28:3
v Ps 12:2

28:4
w Rev 18:6

28:5
x Isa 5:12

28:7
y Ps 18:1
z Ps 13:5

27:13 The "land of the living" simply means "this life" or "while I am living." David was obviously going through a trial, but he was confident that in this present life God would see him through it.

27:14 David knew from experience what it meant to wait for the Lord. He had been anointed king at age 16, but didn't become king until he was 30. During the interim, he had been chased through the desert by jealous King Saul. David had to wait on God for the fulfillment of his promise to reign. Later, after becoming king, he was chased by his rebellious son, Absalom.

Waiting for God is not easy. Often it seems that he isn't answering our prayers or doesn't understand the urgency of our situation. That kind of thinking implies that God is not in control

or is not fair. But God is worth waiting for. Lamentations 3:24–26 calls us to hope in and wait for the Lord because often God uses waiting to refresh, renew, and teach us. Make good use of your waiting times by discovering what God may be trying to teach you in them.

28:3–5 It's easy to pretend friendship. Wicked people often put on a show of kindness or friendship in order to gain their own ends. David, in his royal position, may have met many who pretended friendship only to meet their own needs. David knew that God would punish these people eventually, but he prayed that their punishment would come swiftly. True believers should be straightforward and sincere in all their relationships.

8 The Lord is the strength of his people,
  a fortress of salvation for his anointed one.*a*

9 Save your people and bless your inheritance;*b*
  be their shepherd and carry them forever.

28:8
a Ps 20:6

28:9
b Dt 9:29

Theme: God reveals his great power in nature. We can trust God to give us both the peace and the strength to weather the storms of life.
Author: David

29

A psalm of David.

1 Ascribe to the Lord,*c* O mighty ones,
  ascribe to the Lord glory and strength.

2 Ascribe to the Lord the glory due his name;
  worship the Lord in the splendor of his*a* holiness.*d*

3 The voice*e* of the Lord is over the waters;
  the God of glory thunders,
  the Lord thunders over the mighty waters.

4 The voice of the Lord is powerful;
  the voice of the Lord is majestic.

5 The voice of the Lord breaks the cedars;
  the Lord breaks in pieces the cedars of Lebanon.

6 He makes Lebanon skip*f* like a calf,
  Sirion*b g* like a young wild ox.

7 The voice of the Lord strikes
  with flashes of lightning.

8 The voice of the Lord shakes the desert;
  the Lord shakes the Desert of Kadesh.*h*

9 The voice of the Lord twists the oaks*c*
  and strips the forests bare.
  And in his temple all cry, "Glory!"

10 The Lord sits*d* enthroned over the flood;
   the Lord is enthroned as King forever.*i*

11 The Lord gives strength to his people;*j*
   the Lord blesses his people with peace.

29:1
c 1Ch 16:28

29:2
d 2Ch 20:21

29:3
e Job 37:5

29:6
f Ps 114:4
g Dt 3:9

29:8
h Nu 13:26

29:10
i Ps 10:16

29:11
j Ps 28:8

Theme: A celebration of God's deliverance. Earthly security is uncertain, but God is always faithful.
Author: David

30

A psalm. A song. For the dedication of the temple.*e* Of David.

1 I will exalt you, O Lord,
  for you lifted me out of the depths
  and did not let my enemies gloat over me.*k*

2 O Lord my God, I called to you for help
  and you healed me.

30:1
k Ps 25:2

a 2 Or Lord with the splendor of   *b* 6 That is, Mount Hermon   *c* 9 Or Lord makes the deer give birth   *d* 10 Or sat
e Title: Or palace

29:5, 6 The cedars of Lebanon were giant trees that could grow to 120 feet tall and 30 feet in circumference. A voice that could break the cedars of Lebanon would be a truly powerful voice—the voice of God. "Sirion" means Mount Hermon. All that was impressive to people was under God's complete control.

29:10, 11 Throughout history, God has revealed his power through mighty miracles over nature, such as the great flood (Genesis 6—9). He promises to continue to reveal his power. Paul urged us to understand how great God's power is (Ephesians 1:18—23). The same power that raised Christ from the dead

is available to help us with our daily problems. When you feel weak and limited, don't despair. Remember that God can give you strength. The power that controls creation and raises the dead is available to you.

30:1ff David may have written this psalm when he dedicated Araunah's threshing floor (which became the future site of the temple) and after God stopped the great plague he had used to discipline David (1 Chronicles 21:1—22:6). The serious illness mentioned in 30:2, 3 may refer to an illness David experienced or to the plague itself.

30:3
l Ps 86:13

3 O Lord, you brought me up from the grave[a];
you spared me from going down into the pit.*l*

4 Sing to the Lord, you saints of his;
praise his holy name.

30:5
m Ps 103:9

5 For his anger[m] lasts only a moment,
but his favor lasts a lifetime;
weeping may remain for a night,
but rejoicing comes in the morning.

6 When I felt secure, I said,
"I will never be shaken."

30:7
n Ps 104:29

7 O Lord, when you favored me,
you made my mountain[b] stand firm;
but when you hid your face,[n]
I was dismayed.

8 To you, O Lord, I called;
to the Lord I cried for mercy:

30:9
o Ps 6:5

9 "What gain is there in my destruction,[c]
in my going down into the pit?
Will the dust praise you?
Will it proclaim your faithfulness?[o]
10 Hear, O Lord, and be merciful to me;
O Lord, be my help."

11 You turned my wailing into dancing;
you removed my sackcloth and clothed me with joy,
12 that my heart may sing to you and not be silent.
O Lord my God, I will give you thanks forever.

Theme: In times of stress, depending upon God requires complete commitment.
Author: David, although some say Jeremiah

31 For the director of music. A psalm of David.

1 In you, O Lord, I have taken refuge;
let me never be put to shame;
deliver me in your righteousness.
2 Turn your ear to me,
come quickly to my rescue;
be my rock of refuge,
a strong fortress to save me.

31:3
p Ps 18:2
q Ps 23:3

3 Since you are my rock and my fortress,[p]
for the sake of your name[q] lead and guide me.

[a] 3 Hebrew *Sheol*   [b] 7 Or *hill country*   [c] 9 Or *there if I am silenced*

30:5 Like a shot given by a doctor, the discomfort of God's anger lasts only a moment, but the good effects go on for a long time. Let God's anger be a sharp pain that warns you to turn from sin.

30:6, 7 Security had made David feel invincible. Although he knew that his riches and power had come from God, they had gone to his head, making him proud. Wealth, power, and fame can be intoxicating, making us feel self-reliant, self-secure, and independent of God. But this false security can be easily shattered. Don't be trapped by the false security of prosperity. Depend on God for your security, and you won't be shaken when worldly possessions disappear.

30:11 *Sackcloth* refers to clothes worn as a sign of mourning.

31:1 David called on the Lord to deliver him. He wanted God to stop those who were unjustly causing trouble. Therefore, David made his request based upon what he knew of God's name,

or character. Because God is righteous and loving, he desires to deliver his people.

31:1–6 We say we have faith in God, but do we really trust him? David's words, "Into your hands I commit my spirit," convey his complete trust in God. Jesus used this phrase as he was dying on the cross—showing his absolute dependence on God the Father (Luke 23:46). Stephen repeated these words as he was being stoned to death (Acts 7:59), confident that in death he was simply passing from God's earthly care to God's eternal care. We should commit our possessions, our families, and our vocations to God. But first and foremost, we should commit *ourselves* completely to him.

⁴ Free me from the trap that is set for me,
　　for you are my refuge.
⁵ Into your hands I commit my spirit;ʳ
　　redeem me, O Lord, the God of truth.

⁶ I hate those who cling to worthless idols;
　　I trust in the Lord.ˢ
⁷ I will be glad and rejoice in your love,
　　for you saw my affliction
　　and knew the anguish of my soul.
⁸ You have not handed me overᵗ to the enemy
　　but have set my feet in a spacious place.

⁹ Be merciful to me, O Lord, for I am in distress;
　　my eyes grow weak with sorrow,ᵘ
　　my soul and my body with grief.
¹⁰ My life is consumed by anguish
　　and my years by groaning;
　　my strength fails because of my affliction,ᵃ
　　and my bones grow weak.
¹¹ Because of all my enemies,
　　I am the utter contempt of my neighbors;
　　I am a dread to my friends—
　　those who see me on the street flee from me.
¹² I am forgotten by them as though I were dead;ᵛ
　　I have become like broken pottery.
¹³ For I hear the slander of many;
　　there is terror on every side;ʷ
　　they conspire against me
　　and plot to take my life.ˣ

¹⁴ But I trust in you, O Lord;
　　I say, "You are my God."
¹⁵ My times are in your hands;
　　deliver me from my enemies
　　and from those who pursue me.
¹⁶ Let your face shineʸ on your servant;
　　save me in your unfailing love.
¹⁷ Let me not be put to shame,ᶻ O Lord,
　　for I have cried out to you;
　　but let the wicked be put to shame
　　and lie silent in the grave.ᵇ
¹⁸ Let their lying lipsᵃ be silenced,
　　for with pride and contempt
　　they speak arrogantlyᵇ against the righteous.

ᵃ10 Or guilt　　ᵇ17 Hebrew Sheol

31:5	ʳLk 23:46
31:6	ˢJnh 2:8
31:8	ᵗDt 32:30
31:9	ᵘPs 6:7
31:12	ᵛPs 88:4
31:13	ʷJer 20:3, 10 ˣMt 27:1
31:16	ʸPs 4:6
31:17	ᶻPs 25:2-3
31:18	ᵃPs 120:2 ᵇPs 94:4

31:6 Why did David suddenly bring up the subject of idol worship? He wanted to contrast his total devotion to God with the diluted worship offered by many Israelites. Pagan religious rituals were never completely banished from Israel and Judah, despite the efforts of David and a few other kings. Obviously a person who clung to idols could not commit his spirit into God's hands. When we put today's idols (wealth, material possessions, success) first in our lives, we cannot expect God's Spirit to guide us. God is our highest authority and requires our first allegiance.

31:8 In David's day, armies needed large areas of land for their military maneuvers. David praised God for the "spacious place"— the open spaces that gave him the freedom to move within God's boundaries. If you feel restrained by God's moral boundaries, remember that God has given you much freedom, far more than you need to move within those boundaries. Use the opportunities

he gives you to make proper decisions. Use them wisely and they will lead to victory.

31:9–13 In describing his feelings, David wrote of the helplessness and hopelessness everyone feels when hated or rejected. But adversity is easier to accept when we recognize our true relationship with the sovereign God (31:14–18). Although our enemies may seem to have the upper hand, they are ultimately the helpless and hopeless ones. Those who know God will be victorious in the end (31:23). We can have courage today because God will preserve us.

31:14, 15 In saying, "My times are in your hands," David was expressing his belief that all of life's circumstances are under God's control. Knowing that God loves and cares for us enables us to keep steady in our faith regardless of our circumstances. It keeps us from sinning foolishly by taking matters into our own hands or resenting God's timetable.

31:19
c Isa 64:4

19 How great is your goodness,
    which you have stored up for those who fear you,
    which you bestow in the sight of men*c*
    on those who take refuge in you.

31:20
d Ps 27:5
e Job 5:21

20 In the shelter of your presence you hide*d* them
    from the intrigues of men;*e*
in your dwelling you keep them safe
    from accusing tongues.

31:21
f Ps 17:7
g 1Sa 23:7

21 Praise be to the LORD,
    for he showed his wonderful love*f* to me
    when I was in a besieged city.*g*

31:22
h Ps 116:11
i La 3:54

22 In my alarm*h* I said,
    "I am cut off from your sight!"
Yet you heard my cry*i* for mercy
    when I called to you for help.

23 Love the LORD, all his saints!
    The LORD preserves the faithful,
    but the proud he pays back in full.

31:24
j Ps 27:14

24 Be strong and take heart,*j*
    all you who hope in the LORD.

Theme: Forgiveness brings true joy. Only when we ask God to forgive our sins will
he give us real happiness and relief from guilt.
Author: David

32 Of David. A *maskil*.*a*

32:1
k Ps 85:2

1 Blessed is he
    whose transgressions are forgiven,
    whose sins are covered.*k*

32:2
l 2Co 5:19
m Jn 1:47

2 Blessed is the man
    whose sin the LORD does not count against him*l*
    and in whose spirit is no deceit.*m*

a Title: Probably a literary or musical term

**CONFESSION,
REPENTANCE,
AND
FORGIVENESS
IN THE PSALMS**

Over the centuries, many believers, overcome by an awareness of their own sins, have found
in the words of the penitential (confession) psalms a ray of hope. The psalm writers shared
with God the depth of their sorrow and repentance, as well as the height of joy at being forgiven. They rejoiced in the knowledge that God would respond to confession and repentance
with complete forgiveness. We who live on the other side of the cross of Christ can rejoice
even more because we understand more. God has shown us that he is willing to forgive
because his judgment on sin was satisfied by Christ's death on the cross.
   As you read these psalms, note the pattern followed by the psalm writers in responding
to God: (1) They recognized their sinfulness and tendency to do wrong; (2) they realized that
sin was rebellion against God himself; (3) they admitted their sins to God; (4) they trusted
in God's willingness to forgive; and (5) they accepted his forgiveness. Use these psalms as
a reminder of how easy it is to drift away from God and fall into sin, and what is needed to
reestablish that fellowship.
   Selected psalms that emphasize these themes are 6; 14; 31; 32; 38; 41; 51; 102; 130; 143.

---

32 title *Maskil* is a term perhaps denoting psalms written to
make a person wise or prudent, to increase a person's success
or skill.

32:1ff Read this psalm in conjunction with Psalm 51—both are
penitential psalms. Here David expressed the joy of forgiveness.
God had forgiven him for the sins he had committed against
Bathsheba and Uriah (2 Samuel 11, 12). This is another of the
penitential (repentance) psalms where the writer confesses his
sin to God.

32:1, 2 God *wants* to forgive sinners. Forgiveness has always
been part of his loving nature. He announced this to Moses
(Exodus 34:7); he revealed it to David; he dramatically showed it
to the world through Jesus Christ. These verses convey several
aspects of God's forgiveness: forgives transgression, covers sin,
and doesn't count our sins against us. Paul quoted these verses
in Romans 4:7, 8 and showed that we can have this joyous experience of forgiveness through faith in Christ.

3 When I kept silent,
    my bones wasted away
    through my groaning all day long.
4 For day and night
    your hand was heavy[n] upon me;
  my strength was sapped
    as in the heat of summer.   *Selah*

32:4
[n] Job 33:7

5 Then I acknowledged my sin to you
    and did not cover up my iniquity.
  I said, "I will confess[o]
    my transgressions to the LORD"—
  and you forgave
    the guilt of my sin.   *Selah*

32:5
[o] Pr 28:13

6 Therefore let everyone who is godly pray to you
    while you may be found;
  surely when the mighty waters rise,
    they will not reach him.
7 You are my hiding place;
    you will protect me from trouble
    and surround me with songs of deliverance.   *Selah*

8 I will instruct you and teach you in the way you should go;
    I will counsel you and watch over you.
9 Do not be like the horse or the mule,
    which have no understanding
  but must be controlled by bit and bridle
    or they will not come to you.
10 Many are the woes of the wicked,[p]
    but the LORD's unfailing love
    surrounds the man who trusts[q] in him.

32:10
[p] Ro 2:9
[q] Pr 16:20

11 Rejoice in the LORD[r] and be glad, you righteous;
    sing, all you who are upright in heart!

32:11
[r] Ps 64:10

Theme: Because God is Creator, Lord, Savior, and Deliverer, he is worthy of our trust and praise. Because he is faithful and his word is dependable, we can rejoice and sing, giving thanks and praise.
Author: Anonymous

33

1 Sing joyfully to the LORD, you righteous;
    it is fitting[s] for the upright[t] to praise him.
2 Praise the LORD with the harp;
    make music to him on the ten-stringed lyre.
3 Sing to him a new song;[u]
    play skillfully, and shout for joy.
4 For the word of the LORD is right and true;
    he is faithful in all he does.

33:1
[s] Ps 147:1
[t] Ps 32:11

33:3
[u] Ps 96:1

32:5 What is confession? To confess our sin is to agree with God, acknowledging that he is right to declare what we have done as sinful, and that we are wrong to desire or to do it. It means affirming our intention of abandoning that sin in order to follow God more faithfully.

32:8, 9 God describes some people as being like horses or mules that have to be controlled by bits and bridles. Rather than letting God guide them step by step, they stubbornly leave God only one option. If God wants to keep them useful for him, he must use discipline and punishment. God longs to guide us with love and wisdom rather than punishment. He

offers to teach us the *best* way to go. Accept the advice written in God's Word and don't let your stubbornness keep you from obeying God.

33:2, 3 David, who some believe wrote this psalm, was an accomplished harpist (1 Samuel 16:15–25). His psalms frequently refer to musical instruments. He undoubtedly composed music for many of the psalms, and he commissioned music for temple worship (1 Chronicles 25).

33:4 All God's words are right and true—they can be trusted. The Bible is reliable because, unlike people, God does not lie, forget, change his words, or leave his promises unfulfilled. We can trust the Bible because it contains the words of a holy, trustworthy, and unchangeable God.

33:5
v Ps 11:7
w Ps 119:64

5 The LORD loves righteousness and justice; v
    the earth is full of his unfailing love. w

6 By the word of the LORD were the heavens made,
    their starry host by the breath of his mouth.
7 He gathers the waters of the sea into jars a;
    he puts the deep into storehouses.
8 Let all the earth fear the LORD;
    let all the people of the world revere him.

33:9
x Ge 1:3

9 For he spoke, and it came to be;
    he commanded, x and it stood firm.

33:10
y Isa 8:10
33:11
z Job 23:13

10 The LORD foils the plans of the nations; y
    he thwarts the purposes of the peoples.
11 But the plans of the LORD stand firm forever,
    the purposes z of his heart through all generations.

33:12
a Ex 19:5; Dt 7:6
33:13
b Job 28:24; Ps 11:4

12 Blessed is the nation whose God is the LORD,
    the people he chose a for his inheritance.
13 From heaven the LORD looks down
    and sees all mankind; b
14 from his dwelling place he watches
    all who live on earth—

33:15
c Jer 32:19

15 he who forms the hearts of all,
    who considers everything they do. c
16 No king is saved by the size of his army;
    no warrior escapes by his great strength.

33:17
d Ps 20:7

17 A horse d is a vain hope for deliverance;
    despite all its great strength it cannot save.
18 But the eyes of the LORD are on those who fear him,
    on those whose hope is in his unfailing love,
19 to deliver them from death
    and keep them alive in famine.

33:20
e Ps 130:6
33:21
f Jn 16:22

20 We wait e in hope for the LORD;
    he is our help and our shield.
21 In him our hearts rejoice, f
    for we trust in his holy name.
22 May your unfailing love rest upon us, O LORD,
    even as we put our hope in you.

a 7 Or sea as into a heap

33:6–9 This is a poetic summary of the first chapter of Genesis. God is not just the coordinator of natural forces, he is the Lord of creation, the almighty God. Because he is all-powerful, we should revere him in all we do.

33:11 "The plans of the LORD stand firm forever." Are you frustrated by inconsistencies you see in others, or even in yourself? God is completely trustworthy—his intentions never change. The Bible promises that good and perfect gifts come to us from the Creator who never changes (James 1:17). When you wonder if there is anyone in whom you can trust, remember that God is completely consistent. Let him counsel you, and trust in his plans for your life.

33:16, 17 *Horse* refers to military strength. Because God rules and overrules every nation, leaders should never put their trust in their physical power. Military might is not the ground of our hope. Our hope is in God and in his gracious offer to save us if we will trust in him.

33:18, 19 This is not an ironclad guarantee that all believers will be delivered from death and starvation. Thousands of Christian saints have been beaten to death, whipped, fed to lions, or executed (Romans 8:35, 36; Hebrews 11:32–40). God can

(and often miraculously does) deliver his followers from pain and death, though sometimes, for purposes known only to him, he chooses not to. When faced with these harsh realities, we must focus on the wise judgments of God. The writer was pleading for God's watchful care and protection. In times of crisis, we can place our hope in God.

Theme: God pays attention to those who call on him. Whether God offers escape from trouble or help in times of trouble, we can be certain that he always hears and acts on behalf of those who love him.
Author: David, after pretending to be insane in order to escape from King Achish (1 Samuel 21:10–15)

34

a Of David. When he pretended to be insane*g* before Abimelech, who drove him away, and he left.

1 I will extol the LORD at all times;
   his praise will always be on my lips.
2 My soul will boast*h* in the LORD;
   let the afflicted hear and rejoice.
3 Glorify the LORD with me;
   let us exalt*i* his name together.

4 I sought the LORD,*j* and he answered me;
   he delivered me from all my fears.
5 Those who look to him are radiant;
   their faces are never covered with shame.
6 This poor man called, and the LORD heard him;
   he saved him out of all his troubles.
7 The angel of the LORD*k* encamps around those who fear him,
   and he delivers them.

8 Taste and see that the LORD is good;*l*
   blessed is the man who takes refuge*m* in him.
9 Fear the LORD, you his saints,
   for those who fear him lack nothing.
10 The lions may grow weak and hungry,
   but those who seek the LORD lack no good thing.*n*

11 Come, my children, listen to me;
   I will teach you the fear of the LORD.
12 Whoever of you loves life*o*
   and desires to see many good days,
13 keep your tongue from evil
   and your lips from speaking lies.
14 Turn from evil and do good;*p*
   seek peace*q* and pursue it.

34:TITLE	*g*1Sa 21:13
34:2	*h*Jer 9:24
34:3	*i*Lk 1:46
34:4	*j*Mt 7:7
34:7	*k*Da 6:22
34:8	*l*1Pe 2:3 *m*Ps 2:12
34:10	*n*Ps 84:11
34:12	*o*1Pe 3:10
34:14	*p*Ps 37:27 *q*Heb 12:14

aThis psalm is an acrostic poem, the verses of which begin with the successive letters of the Hebrew alphabet.

34:1ff God promises great blessings to his people, but many of these blessings require active participation. He will deliver us from fear (34:4), save us out of our troubles (34:6), guard and deliver us (34:7), show us goodness (34:8), supply our needs (34:9), listen when we talk to him (34:15), and redeem us (34:22), but we must do our part. We can appropriate his blessings when we seek him (34:4, 10), cry out to him (34:6, 17), trust him (34:8), fear him (34:7, 9), refrain from lying (34:13), turn from evil, do good and seek peace (34:14), are humble (34:18), and serve him (34:22).

34:8 "Taste and see" does not mean, "Check out God's credentials." Instead it is a warm invitation: "Try this; I know you'll like it." When we take that first step of obedience in following God, we will discover that he is good and kind. When we begin the Christian life, our knowledge of God is partial and incomplete. As we trust him daily, we experience how good he is.

34:9 You say you belong to the Lord, but do you fear him? To fear the Lord means to show deep respect and honor to him. We demonstrate true reverence by our humble attitude and genuine worship. Reverence was shown by Abraham (Genesis 17:2–4), Moses (Exodus 3:5, 6), and the Israelites (Exodus 19:16–24) showed this kind of fear of the Lord.

34:9, 10 At first we may question David's statement, because we seem to lack many good things. This is not a blanket promise that

all Christians will have everything they want. Instead, this is David's praise for God's goodness—all those who call upon God in their need will be answered, sometimes in unexpected ways.

Remember, God knows what we need, and our deepest needs are spiritual. Even though many Christians face unbearable poverty and hardship, they still have enough spiritual nourishment to live for God. David was saying that to have God is to have all you really need. God is enough.

If you feel you don't have everything you need, ask: (1) Is this really a need? (2) Is this really good for me? (3) Is this the best time for me to have what I desire? Even if you answer yes to all three questions, God may allow you to go without to help you grow more dependent on him. He may want you to learn that you need *him* more than having to achieve your immediate desires.

34:11–14 The Bible often connects the fear of the Lord (love and reverence for him) with obedience. "Fear God and keep his commandments" (Ecclesiastes 12:13); "If anyone loves me, he will obey my teaching" (John 14:23). David said that a person who fears the Lord doesn't lie, turns from evil, does good, and promotes peace. Reverence is much more than sitting quietly in church. It includes obeying God in the way we speak and the way we treat others.

34:14 Some may think that peace should come with no effort. But David explained that we are to seek and pursue peace. Paul

34:15
r Job 36:7

15 The eyes of the LORD are on the righteous[r]
　　and his ears are attentive to their cry;

34:16
s Pr 10:7

16 the face of the LORD is against those who do evil,
　　to cut off the memory[s] of them from the earth.

34:17
t Ps 145:19

17 The righteous cry out, and the LORD hears[t] them;
　　he delivers them from all their troubles.

34:18
u Isa 57:15

18 The LORD is close to the brokenhearted[u]
　　and saves those who are crushed in spirit.

34:19
v Pr 24:16

19 A righteous man may have many troubles,
　　but the LORD delivers him from them all;[v]

34:20
w Jn 19:36*

20 he protects all his bones,
　　not one of them will be broken.[w]

34:21
x Ps 94:23

21 Evil will slay the wicked;[x]
　　the foes of the righteous will be condemned.

34:22
y 1Ki 1:29; Ps 71:23

22 The LORD redeems[y] his servants;
　　no one will be condemned who takes refuge in him.

Theme: A prayer to God for help against those who try to inflict injury for no reason. When our enemies are unjust and lie about us, even when we do good to them, we can appeal to God who is always just.

Author: David, possibly written when he was being hunted by Saul (1 Samuel 24)

35 Of David.

1 Contend, O LORD, with those who contend with me;
　　fight against those who fight against me.
2 Take up shield and buckler;
　　arise and come to my aid.
3 Brandish spear and javelin[a]
　　against those who pursue me.
　Say to my soul,
　　"I am your salvation."

35:4
z Ps 70:2

4 May those who seek my life
　　be disgraced[z] and put to shame;
　may those who plot my ruin
　　be turned back in dismay.

35:5
a Job 21:18

5 May they be like chaff[a] before the wind,
　　with the angel of the LORD driving them away;
6 may their path be dark and slippery,
　　with the angel of the LORD pursuing them.

a 3 Or and block the way

---

echoed this thought in Romans 12:18. A person who wants peace cannot be argumentative and contentious. Because peaceful relationships come from our efforts at peacemaking, work hard at living in peace with others each day.

34:18, 19 We often wish we could escape troubles—the pain of grief, loss, sorrow, and failure; or even the small daily frustrations that constantly wear us down. God promises to be "close to the brokenhearted," to be our source of power, courage, and wisdom, helping us through our problems. Sometimes he chooses to deliver us from those problems. When trouble strikes, don't get frustrated with God. Instead, admit that you need God's help and thank him for being by your side.

34:20 This is a prophecy about Christ when he was crucified. Although it was the Roman custom to break the legs of the victim to speed death, not one of Jesus' bones was broken (John 19:32–37). In addition to the prophetic meaning, David was pleading for God's protection in times of crisis.

35:1ff This is one of the "imprecatory" (cursing) psalms that call upon God to deal with enemies. These psalms sound extremely harsh, but we must remember the following: (1) David could not understand why he was forced to flee from men who were unjustly seeking to kill him. He was God's anointed king over a nation called to annihilate the evil people of the land. (2) David's call for justice was sincere; it was not a cover for his own personal vengeance. He truly wanted to seek God's perfect ideal for his nation. (3) David did not say that *he* would take revenge, but he gave the matter to God. These are merely his suggestions. (4) These psalms use hyperbole (or overstatement). They were meant to motivate others to take a strong stand against sin and evil.

Cruelty may be far removed from some people's experience, but it is a daily reality to others. God promises to help the persecuted and to bring judgment on unrepentant sinners. When we pray for justice to be done, we are praying as David did. When Christ returns, the wicked will be punished.

7 Since they hid their net for me without cause
  and without cause dug a pit for me,
8 may ruin overtake them by surprise—[b]
  may the net they hid entangle them,
  may they fall into the pit, to their ruin.
9 Then my soul will rejoice in the LORD
  and delight in his salvation.
10 My whole being will exclaim,
   "Who is like you,[c] O LORD?
  You rescue the poor from those too strong for them,
  the poor and needy from those who rob them."

11 Ruthless witnesses come forward;
   they question me on things I know nothing about.
12 They repay me evil for good[d]
   and leave my soul forlorn.
13 Yet when they were ill, I put on sackcloth
   and humbled myself with fasting.[e]
   When my prayers returned to me unanswered,
14 I went about mourning
   as though for my friend or brother.
   I bowed my head in grief
   as though weeping for my mother.
15 But when I stumbled, they gathered in glee;
   attackers gathered against me when I was unaware.
   They slandered[f] me without ceasing.
16 Like the ungodly they maliciously mocked[a];
   they gnashed their teeth[g] at me.
17 O Lord, how long[h] will you look on?
   Rescue my life from their ravages,
   my precious life[i] from these lions.
18 I will give you thanks in the great assembly;
   among throngs of people I will praise you.

19 Let not those gloat over me
   who are my enemies without cause;
   let not those who hate me without reason[j]
   maliciously wink the eye.[k]
20 They do not speak peaceably,
   but devise false accusations
   against those who live quietly in the land.
21 They gape[l] at me and say, "Aha! Aha!"[m]
   With our own eyes we have seen it."

22 O LORD, you have seen[n] this; be not silent.
   Do not be far[o] from me, O Lord.
23 Awake,[p] and rise to my defense!
   Contend for me, my God and Lord.
24 Vindicate me in your righteousness, O LORD my God;
   do not let them gloat over me.
25 Do not let them think, "Aha, just what we wanted!"
   or say, "We have swallowed him up."[q]

35:8	[b]1Th 5:3
35:10	[c]Ex 15:11
35:12	[d]Jn 10:32
35:13	[e]Job 30:25
35:15	[f]Job 30:1, 8
35:16	[g]La 2:16
35:17	[h]Hab 1:13 [i]Ps 22:20
35:19	[j]Ps 38:19; 69:4 [k]Ps 13:4
35:21	[l]Ps 22:13 [m]Ps 40:15
35:22	[n]Ex 3:7 [o]Ps 10:1; 28:1
35:23	[p]Ps 44:23
35:25	[q]La 2:16

a 16 Septuagint; Hebrew may mean *ungodly circle of mockers.*

35:13 David was sad when his prayers seemed "unanswered." When our deliverance is delayed, we may assume that God hasn't answered our prayers. God hears every prayer, but he answers according to his wisdom. Don't let the absence of an immediate answer cause you to doubt or resent God. Instead let it be an occasion to deepen your faith.

35:21-23 David cried out to God to defend him when people wrongly accused him. If you are unjustly accused, your natural reaction may be to lash out in revenge or to give a detailed defense of your every move. Instead, ask God to fight the battle for you. He will clear your name in the eyes of those who really matter.

²⁶ May all who gloat over my distress
    be put to shame and confusion;
may all who exalt themselves over me
    be clothed with shame and disgrace.
²⁷ May those who delight in my vindication
    shout for joy and gladness;
may they always say, "The LORD be exalted,
    who delights in the well-being of his servant."
²⁸ My tongue will speak of your righteousness
    and of your praises all day long.

Theme: God's faithfulness, justice, and love are contrasted with the sinful hearts of men and women. In spite of our fallen condition, God pours out his love on those who know him.
Author: David

36

For the director of music. Of David the servant of the LORD.

¹ An oracle is within my heart
    concerning the sinfulness of the wicked:^a
There is no fear of God
    before his eyes.^r
² For in his own eyes he flatters himself
    too much to detect or hate his sin.
³ The words of his mouth are wicked and deceitful;
    he has ceased to be wise and to do good.^s
⁴ Even on his bed he plots evil;^t
    he commits himself to a sinful course^u
    and does not reject what is wrong.

⁵ Your love, O LORD, reaches to the heavens,
    your faithfulness to the skies.
⁶ Your righteousness is like the mighty mountains,
    your justice like the great deep.^v
O LORD, you preserve both man and beast.
⁷   How priceless is your unfailing love!
Both high and low among men
    find^b refuge in the shadow of your wings.
⁸ They feast on the abundance of your house;^w
    you give them drink from your river^x of delights.
⁹ For with you is the fountain of life;^y
    in your light we see light.

¹⁰ Continue your love to those who know you,
    your righteousness to the upright in heart.
¹¹ May the foot of the proud not come against me,
    nor the hand of the wicked drive me away.
¹² See how the evildoers lie fallen—
    thrown down, not able to rise!

^a 1 Or heart: / Sin proceeds from the wicked. ^b 7 Or love, O God! / Men find; or love! / Both heavenly beings and men / find

---

36:1
^rRo 3:18*

36:3
^sJer 4:22

36:4
^tPr 4:16
^uIsa 65:2

36:6
^vRo 11:33

36:8
^wPs 65:4
^xJob 20:17;
Rev 22:1

36:9
^yJer 2:13

36:1 Because the wicked have no fear of God, nothing restrains them from sinning. They plunge ahead as if nothing will happen to them. But God is just and is only delaying their punishment. This knowledge should hold us back from sinning. Let the fear of God do its work in you to keep you from sin. In your gratitude for God's love and mercy, don't ignore his justice.

36:5–8 In contrast to evil people and their wicked plots that end in failure, God will triumph. He is faithful, righteous, and just. His love reaches to the heavens; his faithfulness reaches to the skies; his righteousness is as solid as mighty mountains; his judgments

are as full of wisdom as the oceans with water ("the great deep"). We need not fear evil people because we know God loves us, judges evil, and will care for us throughout eternity.

36:9 This vivid image—"fountain of life"—gives us a sense of fresh, cleansing water that gives life to the spiritually thirsty. This same picture is used in Jeremiah 2:13, where God is called the "spring of living water." Jesus spoke of himself as living water that could quench thirst forever and give eternal life (John 4:14).

Theme: Trust in the Lord and wait patiently for him to act. This psalm vividly contrasts the wicked person with the righteous.
Author: David

37 ª   Of David.

1 Do not fret because of evil men
    or be envious*z* of those who do wrong;*a*
2 for like the grass they will soon wither,
    like green plants they will soon die away.*b*

3 Trust in the LORD and do good;
    dwell in the land and enjoy safe pasture.
4 Delight*c* yourself in the LORD
    and he will give you the desires of your heart.

5 Commit your way to the LORD;
    trust in him*d* and he will do this:
6 He will make your righteousness shine like the dawn,*e*
    the justice of your cause like the noonday sun.

7 Be still before the LORD and wait patiently for him;
    do not fret when men succeed in their ways,
    when they carry out their wicked schemes.

8 Refrain from anger and turn from wrath;
    do not fret—it leads only to evil.
9 For evil men will be cut off,
    but those who hope in the LORD will inherit the land.

10 A little while, and the wicked will be no more;*f*
    though you look for them, they will not be found.
11 But the meek will inherit the land*g*
    and enjoy great peace.

12 The wicked plot against the righteous
    and gnash their teeth*h* at them;
13 but the Lord laughs at the wicked,
    for he knows their day is coming.*i*

14 The wicked draw the sword
    and bend the bow
    to bring down the poor and needy,
    to slay those whose ways are upright.
15 But their swords will pierce their own hearts,
    and their bows will be broken.

37:1	*z* Pr 23:17-18
	a Ps 73:3
37:2	*b* Ps 90:6
37:4	*c* Isa 58:14
37:5	*d* Ps 55:22
37:6	*e* Job 11:17
37:10	*f* Job 7:10
37:11	*g* Mt 5:5
37:12	*h* Ps 35:16
37:13	*i* 1Sa 26:10; Ps 2:4

*a*This psalm is an acrostic poem, the stanzas of which begin with the successive letters of the Hebrew alphabet.

37:1 We should never envy evil people, even though some may be extremely popular or excessively rich. No matter how much they have, it will fade and vanish like grass that withers and dies. Those who follow God live differently from the wicked and, in the end, will have far greater treasures in heaven. What the unbeliever gets may last a lifetime, if he is lucky. What you get from following God lasts forever.

37:4, 5 David calls us to take delight in the Lord and to commit everything we have and do (our "way") to him. But how do we do this? To *delight* in someone means to experience great pleasure and joy in his or her presence. This happens only when we know that person well. Thus, to delight in the Lord, we must know him better. Knowledge of God's great love for us will indeed give us delight.

To *commit* ourselves to the Lord means entrusting everything—our lives, families, jobs, possessions—to his control and guidance. To commit ourselves to the Lord means to trust in him (37:5), believing that he can care for us better than we can ourselves. We should be willing to wait patiently (37:7) for him to work out what is best for us.

37:8, 9 Anger and worry (fretting) are two very destructive emotions. They reveal a lack of faith that God loves us and is in control. We should not worry; instead, we should trust in God, giving ourselves to him for his use and safekeeping. When you dwell on your problems, you will become anxious and angry. But if you concentrate on God and his goodness, you will find peace. Where do you focus your attention?

37:11 Meekness hardly seems the proper weapon to deal with enemies. God's warfare must be carried out with calm faith, humility before God, and hope in his deliverance. Jesus also promises a sure reward for those with humble attitudes (Matthew 5:5).

37:16
/Pr 15:16

16 Better the little that the righteous have
    than the wealth/ of many wicked;

37:17
kPs 10:15

17 for the power of the wicked will be broken,k
    but the Lord upholds the righteous.

37:18
lPs 1:6

18 The days of the blameless are known to the Lord,l
    and their inheritance will endure forever.
19 In times of disaster they will not wither;
    in days of famine they will enjoy plenty.

37:20
mPs 102:3

20 But the wicked will perish:
    The Lord's enemies will be like the beauty of the fields,
    they will vanish—vanish like smoke.m

37:21
nPs 112:5

21 The wicked borrow and do not repay,
    but the righteous give generously;n

37:22
oPr 3:33

22 those the Lord blesses will inherit the land,
    but those he curseso will be cut off.

37:23
p1Sa 2:9

23 If the Lord delights in a man's way,
    he makes his steps firm;p

37:24
qPr 24:16

24 though he stumble, he will not fall,q
    for the Lord upholds him with his hand.

25 I was young and now I am old,
    yet I have never seen the righteous forsaken
    or their children begging bread.
26 They are always generous and lend freely;
    their children will be blessed.

37:27
rPs 34:14

27 Turn from evil and do good;r
    then you will dwell in the land forever.

37:28
sPs 21:10

28 For the Lord loves the just
    and will not forsake his faithful ones.

They will be protected forever,
    but the offspring of the wicked will be cut off;s
29 the righteous will inherit the land
    and dwell in it forever.

30 The mouth of the righteous man utters wisdom,
    and his tongue speaks what is just.
31 The law of his God is in his heart;
    his feet do not slip.

37:32
tPs 10:8

37:33
uPs 109:31;
2Pe 2:9

32 The wicked lie in waitt for the righteous,
    seeking their very lives;
33 but the Lord will not leave them in their power
    or let them be condemned when brought to trial.u

37:21 You can tell a lot about a person's character by the way he or she handles money. The wicked person steals under the guise of borrowing. The righteous person gives generously to the needy. Wicked people, therefore, focus on themselves, while righteous people look to the welfare of others.

37:23, 24 The person in whom God delights is one who follows God, trusts him, and tries to do his will. God watches over and makes firm every step that person takes. If you would like to have God direct your way, then seek his advice before you step out.

37:25 Because children starve today, as they did in David's time, what did David mean by these words? David is observing God's provision over a lifetime. Though there are unfortunate exceptions to this general principle, God provides for his own people. The children of the righteous need not go hungry because other believers can help out in their time of need.

In David's day, Israel obeyed God's laws that ensured that the poor were treated fairly and mercifully. As long as Israel was obedient, food would be available for everyone. When Israel forgot God, the rich took care only of themselves, and the poor suffered (Amos 2:6, 7).

When we see a Christian brother or sister suffering today, we can respond in one of three ways: (1) We can say, as Job's friends did, that the afflicted person brought this on himself. (2) We can say that this is a test to help the poor develop more patience and trust in God. (3) We can help the person in need. David would approve of only the last option. Although many governments today have their own programs for helping those in need, this is no excuse for ignoring the poor and needy within our reach.

34 Wait for the LORD[v]
   and keep his way.
He will exalt you to inherit the land;
   when the wicked are cut off, you will see[w] it.

35 I have seen a wicked and ruthless man
   flourishing[x] like a green tree in its native soil,
36 but he soon passed away and was no more;
   though I looked for him, he could not be found.[y]

37 Consider the blameless, observe the upright;
   there is a future[a] for the man of peace.
38 But all sinners will be destroyed;
   the future[b] of the wicked will be cut off.[z]

39 The salvation[a] of the righteous comes from the LORD;
   he is their stronghold in time of trouble.[b]
40 The LORD helps[c] them and delivers[d] them;
   he delivers them from the wicked and saves them,
   because they take refuge in him.

Theme: Sorrow for sin brings hope. God alone is the true source of healing and protection for those who confess their sins to him.
Author: David

38 A psalm of David. A petition.

1 O LORD, do not rebuke me in your anger
   or discipline me in your wrath.[e]
2 For your arrows[f] have pierced me,
   and your hand has come down upon me.
3 Because of your wrath there is no health in my body;
   my bones have no soundness because of my sin.
4 My guilt has overwhelmed me
   like a burden too heavy to bear.[g]
5 My wounds fester and are loathsome
   because of my sinful folly.
6 I am bowed down and brought very low;
   all day long I go about mourning.[h]
7 My back is filled with searing pain;
   there is no health in my body.
8 I am feeble and utterly crushed;
   I groan in anguish of heart.
9 All my longings lie open before you, O Lord;
   my sighing[i] is not hidden from you.
10 My heart pounds, my strength fails me;
   even the light has gone from my eyes.[j]

a 37 Or there will be posterity   b 38 Or posterity

37:34
v Ps 27:14
w Ps 52:6

37:35
x Job 5:3

37:36
y Job 20:5

37:38
z Ps 1:4

37:39
a Ps 3:8
b Ps 9:9

37:40
c 1Ch 5:20
d Isa 31:5

38:1
e Ps 6:1

38:2
f Job 6:4; Ps 32:4

38:4
g Ezr 9:6

38:6
h Ps 35:14

38:9
i Job 3:24

38:10
j Ps 6:7

38:1 As a child might cry to his father, so David cried to God. David was not saying, "Don't punish me," but, "Don't punish me while you are angry." He acknowledged that he deserved to be punished, but he asked that God temper his discipline with mercy. Like children, we are free to ask for mercy, but we should not deny that we deserve punishment.

38:1ff This is called a penitential psalm because David expressed sorrow for his sin (38:18). He stated that his sin led to health problems (38:1–8) and separated him from God and others,

causing extreme loneliness (38:9–14). He then confessed his sin and repented (38:15–22).

38:2–4 David saw his anguish as judgment from God for his sins. Although God does not always send physical illness to punish us for sin, this verse and others in Scripture (Acts 12:21–23; 1 Corinthians 11:30–32) indicate that he does in certain circumstances. Our sin can have physical or mental side effects that can cause great suffering. Sometimes God has to punish his children in order to bring them back to himself (Hebrews 12:5–11). When we repent of our sin, God promises to forgive us. He delivers us from sin's eternal consequences although he does not promise to undo all of sin's earthly consequences.

11 My friends and companions avoid me because of my wounds;
    my neighbors stay far away.
12 Those who seek my life set their traps,
    those who would harm me talk of my ruin;
    all day long they plot deception.

13 I am like a deaf man, who cannot hear,
    like a mute, who cannot open his mouth;
14 I have become like a man who does not hear,
    whose mouth can offer no reply.

38:15
k Ps 39:7

15 I wait k for you, O LORD;
    you will answer, O Lord my God.

38:16
l Ps 35:26

16 For I said, "Do not let them gloat l
    or exalt themselves over me when my foot slips."

17 For I am about to fall,
    and my pain is ever with me.
18 I confess my iniquity;
    I am troubled by my sin.
19 Many are those who are my vigorous enemies;
    those who hate me without reason are numerous.

38:20
m Ps 35:12

20 Those who repay my good with evil m
    slander me when I pursue what is good.

38:21
n Ps 35:22

21 O LORD, do not forsake me;
    be not far n from me, O my God.
22 Come quickly to help me,
    O Lord my Savior.

Theme: Apart from God, life is fleeting and empty. This is an appeal for God's mercy because life is so brief.
Author: David

39

For the director of music. For Jeduthun. A psalm of David.

39:1
o 1Ki 2:4

1 I said, "I will watch my ways o
    and keep my tongue from sin;
  I will put a muzzle on my mouth
    as long as the wicked are in my presence."

39:2
p Ps 38:13

2 But when I was silent p and still,
    not even saying anything good,
    my anguish increased.
3 My heart grew hot within me,
    and as I meditated, the fire burned;
    then I spoke with my tongue:

4 "Show me, O LORD, my life's end
    and the number of my days;
    let me know how fleeting is my life.

38:13, 14 Being silent can be extremely difficult when others tear us down because we want to protect our reputation. We find it difficult to do nothing while they assault something so precious to us. But we don't need to lash back in revenge or justify our position; we can trust God to protect our reputation. Jesus was silent before his accusers (Luke 23:9, 10); he left his case in God's hands (1 Peter 2:21–24). That is a good place to leave our case too!

39:1–3 David resolved to keep his tongue from sin; that is, he decided not to complain to other people about God's treatment of him. David certainly had reason to complain. He was the anointed king of Israel, but he had to wait many years before taking the throne. Then one of his sons tried to kill him and become king

instead. But when David could not keep still any longer, he took his complaints directly to God. We all have complaints about our job, money, or situations, but complaining to others may make them think that God cannot take care of us. It may also look as if we blame God for our troubles. Instead, like David, we should take our complaints directly to God. He can take it.

39:4 Life is short no matter how long we live. If we have something important we want to do, we must not put it off for a better day. Ask yourself, "If I had only six months to live, what would I do?" Tell someone that you love him or her? Deal with an undisciplined area in your life? Tell someone about Jesus? Because life is short, don't neglect what is truly important.

5 You have made my days a mere handbreadth;
    the span of my years is as nothing before you.
    Each man's life is but a breath.   *Selah*

6 Man is a mere phantom as he goes to and fro:
    He bustles about, but only in vain;
    he heaps up wealth, not knowing who will get it.*q*

39:6
*q*Lk 12:20

7 "But now, Lord, what do I look for?
    My hope is in you.

8 Save me from all my transgressions;*r*
    do not make me the scorn of fools.

39:8
*r*Ps 44:13

9 I was silent; I would not open my mouth,*s*
    for you are the one who has done this.

39:9
*s*Job 2:10

10 Remove your scourge from me;
    I am overcome by the blow of your hand.

11 You rebuke and discipline men for their sin;
    you consume their wealth like a moth*t*—
    each man is but a breath.   *Selah*

39:11
*t*Job 13:28

12 "Hear my prayer, O Lord,
    listen to my cry for help;
    be not deaf to my weeping.
    For I dwell with you as an alien,
    a stranger, as all my fathers were.

13 Look away from me, that I may rejoice again
    before I depart and am no more."*u*

39:13
*u*Job 10:21

Theme: Doing God's will sometimes means waiting patiently. While we wait, we can love God, serve others, and tell others about him.
Author: David

40

For the director of music. Of David. A psalm.

1 I waited patiently*v* for the Lord;
    he turned to me and heard my cry.

40:1
*v*Ps 27:14

2 He lifted me out of the slimy pit,
    out of the mud and mire;*w*
  he set my feet on a rock*x*
    and gave me a firm place to stand.

40:2
*w*Ps 69:14
*x*Ps 27:5

3 He put a new song*y* in my mouth,
    a hymn of praise to our God.
  Many will see and fear
    and put their trust in the Lord.

40:3
*y*Ps 33:3

4 Blessed is the man
    who makes the Lord his trust,
  who does not look to the proud,
    to those who turn aside to false gods.*a*

*a*4 Or *to falsehood*

39:5, 6 The brevity of life is a theme throughout the books of Psalms, Proverbs, and Ecclesiastes. Jesus also spoke about it (Luke 12:20). Ironically, people spend so much time securing their lives on earth and spend little or no thought about where they will spend eternity. David realized that amassing riches and busily accomplishing worldly tasks would make no difference in eternity. Few people understand that their only hope is in the Lord. (For other verses on the brevity of life, see Ecclesiastes 2:18 and James 4:14.)

39:10 What did David mean when he asked God to remove the "scourge" because he was overcome by the "blow" of God's hand? It may be a picture of the difficulties David was facing that caused him to feel as if he were being struck. Evidently David thought God was disciplining him, punishing him for his sins. David was expressing his feelings to God, yet David also submitted himself to his powerful and loving heavenly Father.

40:1-4 Waiting for God to help us is not easy, but David received four benefits from waiting: (1) God lifted him out of his despair, (2) God set his feet on a rock, (3) God gave him a firm place to stand, and (4) God put a new song of praise in his mouth. Often blessings cannot be received unless we go through the trial of waiting.

40:5
z Isa 55:8
	5 Many, O Lord my God,
	    are the wonders you have done.
	The things you planned for us
	    no one can recount[z] to you;
	were I to speak and tell of them,
	    they would be too many to declare.

40:6
a 1Sa 15:22
	6 Sacrifice and offering you did not desire,[a]
	    but my ears you have pierced[a,b];
	burnt offerings and sin offerings
	    you did not require.
	7 Then I said, "Here I am, I have come—
	    it is written about me in the scroll.[c]

40:8 *b* Jn 4:34 *c* Ps 37:31	8 I desire to do your will,[b] O my God; your law is within my heart."[c]

40:9
d Ps 22:25
e Ps 119:13
	9 I proclaim righteousness in the great assembly;[d]
	    I do not seal my lips,
	    as you know,[e] O Lord.

40:10
f Ps 89:1
g Ac 20:20
	10 I do not hide your righteousness in my heart;
	    I speak of your faithfulness[f] and salvation.
	I do not conceal your love and your truth
	    from the great assembly.[g]

40:11 *h* Ps 43:3	11 Do not withhold your mercy from me, O Lord; may your love and your truth[h] always protect me.

40:12
i Ps 38:4
j Ps 73:26
	12 For troubles without number surround me;
	    my sins have overtaken me, and I cannot see.[i]
	They are more than the hairs of my head,
	    and my heart fails[j] within me.

	13 Be pleased, O Lord, to save me; O Lord, come quickly to help me.

40:14
k Ps 35:4
	14 May all who seek to take my life
	    be put to shame and confusion;
	may all who desire my ruin[k]
	    be turned back in disgrace.
	15 May those who say to me, "Aha! Aha!"
	    be appalled at their own shame.
	16 But may all who seek you
	    rejoice and be glad in you;

a 6 Hebrew; Septuagint *but a body you have prepared for me* (see also Symmachus and Theodotion)   *b* 6 Or *opened*
c 7 Or *come / with the scroll written for me*

40:6 "Sacrifice and offering you did not desire." The religious ritual of David's day involved sacrificing animals in the tabernacle. David says these acts were meaningless unless done for the right reasons. Today we often make rituals of going to church, taking communion, or paying tithes. These activities are also empty if our reasons for doing them are selfish. God doesn't want these sacrifices and offerings without an attitude of devotion to him. The prophet Samuel told Saul, "To obey is better than sacrifice" (1 Samuel 15:22). Make sure that you give God the obedience and lifelong service he desires from you.

40:7, 8 "I desire to do your will, O my God." Jesus portrayed this attitude of obeying and serving God (John 4:34; 5:30). He came as the prophets foretold, proclaiming the Good News of God's righteousness and forgiveness of sins. In Hebrews 10:5–10, verses 6–8 are applied to Jesus.

40:9, 10 David said he would speak of God's faithfulness and salvation to those around him. When we feel the impact of God's righteousness on our lives, we cannot keep it hidden. We want to tell other people what God has done for us. If God's

faithfulness has changed your life, don't be timid. It is natural to share a good bargain with others or recommend a skillful doctor, so it should also feel natural to share what God has done for us.

40:10 When we think of faithfulness, a friend or a spouse may come to mind. People who are faithful to us accept and love us, even when we are unlovable. Faithful people keep their promises, whether promises of support or promises made in our marriage vows. God's faithfulness is like human faithfulness, only perfect. His love is absolute, and his promises are irrevocable. He loves us in spite of our constant bent toward sin, and he keeps all the promises he has made to us, even when we break our promises to him.

may those who love your salvation always say,
  "The LORD be exalted!"*l*

40:16
l Ps 35:27

17 Yet I am poor and needy;
  may the Lord think of me.
You are my help and my deliverer;
  O my God, do not delay.*m*

40:17
m Ps 70:5

Theme: A prayer for God's mercy when feeling sick or abandoned. When we're sick or when everyone deserts us, God remains at our side.
Author: David

41
For the director of music. A psalm of David.

1 Blessed is he who has regard for the weak;
  the LORD delivers him in times of trouble.
2 The LORD will protect him and preserve his life;
  he will bless him in the land*n*
  and not surrender him to the desire of his foes.*o*

41:2
n Ps 37:22
o Ps 27:12

3 The LORD will sustain him on his sickbed
  and restore him from his bed of illness.

4 I said, "O LORD, have mercy on me;
  heal me, for I have sinned against you."
5 My enemies say of me in malice,
  "When will he die and his name perish?*p*"

41:5
p Ps 38:12

6 Whenever one comes to see me,
  he speaks falsely, while his heart gathers slander;
  then he goes out and spreads it abroad.

7 All my enemies whisper together against me;
  they imagine the worst for me, saying,
8 "A vile disease has beset him;
  he will never get up from the place where he lies."
9 Even my close friend,*q* whom I trusted,
  he who shared my bread,
  has lifted up his heel against me.*r*

41:9
q Ps 55:12
r Job 19:19;
Jn 13:18*

10 But you, O LORD, have mercy on me;
  raise me up, that I may repay them.
11 I know that you are pleased with me,
  for my enemy does not triumph over me.
12 In my integrity you uphold me
  and set me in your presence forever.*s*

41:12
s Job 36:7

13 Praise be to the LORD, the God of Israel,
  from everlasting to everlasting.
          Amen and Amen.*t*

41:13
t Ps 106:48

41:1 The Bible often speaks of God's care for the weak, poor, and needy, and of his blessing those who share this concern. God wants our generosity to reflect his own free giving. As he has blessed us, we should bless others.

41:9 This verse is viewed in the New Testament as a prophecy of Christ's betrayal (John 13:18). Judas, one of Jesus' 12 disciples, had spent three years learning from Jesus, traveling and eating with him (Mark 3:14–19), and handling the finances for the group. Eventually Judas, who knew Jesus extremely well, betrayed him (Matthew 26:14–16, 20–25).

41:13 Psalms is divided into five books, and each one ends with a doxology or an expression of praise to God. The first book of the psalms, chapters 1 through 41, takes us on a journey through suffering, sorrow, and great joy. It teaches us much about God's eternal love and care for us and how we should trust him in the day-to-day experiences of life.

Book II   Psalms 42–72

These psalms include a prayer for rescue, a call to worship, a confession of sin, an encouragement to trust God, a psalm for those hurt by friends, a prayer for those who have been slandered, and a missionary psalm. These psalms can help us retain a sense of wonder in our worship.

Theme: A thirst for God. When you feel lonely or depressed, meditate on God's kindness and love.

Author: The sons of Korah, who were temple musicians and assistants

42 [a]

For the director of music. A *maskil*[b] of the Sons of Korah.

1 As the deer pants for streams of water,
    so my soul pants for you, O God.

42:2
u Ps 63:1

2 My soul thirsts[u] for God, for the living God.
    When can I go and meet with God?

42:3
v Ps 80:5

3 My tears[v] have been my food
    day and night,
while men say to me all day long,
    "Where is your God?"

42:4
w Isa 30:29

4 These things I remember
    as I pour out my soul:
how I used to go with the multitude,
    leading the procession to the house of God,[w]
with shouts of joy and thanksgiving
    among the festive throng.

42:5
x La 3:24

5 Why are you downcast, O my soul?
    Why so disturbed within me?
Put your hope in God,[x]
    for I will yet praise him,
    my Savior and 6 my God.

My[c] soul is downcast within me;
    therefore I will remember you
from the land of the Jordan,
    the heights of Hermon—from Mount Mizar.

42:7
y Ps 88:7

7 Deep calls to deep
    in the roar of your waterfalls;
all your waves and breakers
    have swept over me.[y]

42:8
z Job 35:10

8 By day the LORD directs his love,
    at night[z] his song is with me—
    a prayer to the God of my life.

a In many Hebrew manuscripts Psalms 42 and 43 constitute one psalm.   b Title: Probably a literary or musical term
c 5,6 A few Hebrew manuscripts, Septuagint and Syriac; most Hebrew manuscripts *praise him for his saving help.* /
6 O my God, my

42:1ff Psalms 42—49 were written by the sons of Korah. Korah was a Levite who led a rebellion against Moses (Numbers 16:1–35). He was killed, but his descendants remained faithful to God and continued to serve God in the temple. David appointed men from the clan of Korah to serve as choir leaders (1 Chronicles 6:31–38), and they continued to be temple musicians for hundreds of years (2 Chronicles 20:18, 19).

42:1, 2 As the life of a deer depends upon water, so our lives depend upon God. Those who seek him and long to understand him find never-ending life. Feeling separated from God, this psalmist wouldn't rest until he restored his relationship with God because he knew that his very life depended on it. Do you thirst for God?

42:4, 5 The writer of this psalm was discouraged because he was exiled to a place far from Jerusalem and could not worship in the temple. During these God-given holidays, the nation was

to remember all that God had done for them. Many of these festivals are explained in the chart in Leviticus 23, p. 185.

42:5, 6 Depression is one of the most common emotional ailments. One antidote for depression is to meditate on the record of God's goodness to his people. This will take your mind off the present situation and give hope that it will improve. It will focus your thoughts on God's ability to help you rather than on your inability to help yourself. When you feel depressed, take advantage of this psalm's antidepressant. Read the Bible's accounts of God's goodness, and meditate on them.

42:6 Hermon refers to Mount Hermon. *Mizar* means smallness, so Mount Mizar could be a smaller mountain in that mountain range.

9 I say to God my Rock,
     "Why have you forgotten me?
  Why must I go about mourning,[a]
     oppressed by the enemy?"
10 My bones suffer mortal agony
     as my foes taunt me,
  saying to me all day long,
     "Where is your God?"

11 Why are you downcast, O my soul?
     Why so disturbed within me?
  Put your hope in God,
     for I will yet praise him,
     my Savior and my God.

42:9
[a] Ps 38:6

Theme: Hope in a time of discouragement. In the face of discouragement, our only hope is in God.
Author: The sons of Korah (temple assistants). Psalms 42 and 43 are one psalm in many Hebrew manuscripts.

43 [a]

1 Vindicate me, O God,
     and plead my cause[b] against an ungodly nation;
  rescue me from deceitful and wicked men.
2 You are God my stronghold.
     Why have you rejected me?
  Why must I go about mourning,
     oppressed by the enemy?[c]
3 Send forth your light and your truth,
     let them guide me;
  let them bring me to your holy mountain,
     to the place where you dwell.
4 Then will I go to the altar of God,
     to God, my joy and my delight.
  I will praise you with the harp,
     O God, my God.

5 Why are you downcast, O my soul?
     Why so disturbed within me?
  Put your hope in God,
     for I will yet praise him,
     my Savior and my God.[d]

43:1
[b] Ps 26:1

43:2
[c] Ps 42:9

43:5
[d] Ps 42:6

Theme: A plea for victory by the battle-weary and defeated. When it seems that God has let you down, don't despair. Instead, remember God's past deliverance and be confident that he will restore you.
Author: The sons of Korah (temple assistants)

44

For the director of music. Of the Sons of Korah. A *maskil*.[b]

1 We have heard with our ears, O God;
     our fathers have told us[e]
  what you did in their days,
     in days long ago.

44:1
[e] Ex 12:26; Ps 78:3

[a] In many Hebrew manuscripts Psalms 42 and 43 constitute one psalm.   [b] Title: Probably a literary or musical term

---

43:3 The "holy mountain" is Mount Zion, in Jerusalem, the city that David named as Israel's capital. The temple was built there as the place for the people to meet God in worship and prayer.

43:3, 4 The psalm writer asked God to send his light and truth to guide him to the holy mountain, the temple, where he would meet God. God's truth (see 1 John 2:27) provides the right path

to follow, and God's light (see 1 John 1:5) provides the clear vision to follow it. If you feel surrounded by darkness and uncertainty, follow God's light and truth. He will guide you.

44:1ff This psalm may have been sung at an occasion like the one in 2 Chronicles 20:18, 19, where the faithful Jehoshaphat was surrounded by enemies and the Levites sang to the Lord before the battle.

44:2
f Ex 15:17
g Ps 80:9

2 With your hand you drove out the nations
    and planted f our fathers;
you crushed the peoples
    and made our fathers flourish. g

44:3
h Jos 24:12
i Dt 7:7-8

3 It was not by their sword h that they won the land,
    nor did their arm bring them victory;
it was your right hand, your arm,
    and the light of your face, for you loved i them.

44:4
j Ps 74:12

4 You are my King j and my God,
    who decrees a victories for Jacob.
5 Through you we push back our enemies;
    through your name we trample our foes.

44:6
k Ps 33:16

6 I do not trust in my bow, k
    my sword does not bring me victory;
7 but you give us victory over our enemies,
    you put our adversaries to shame.

44:8
l Ps 34:2

8 In God we make our boast l all day long,
    and we will praise your name forever.   *Selah*

44:9
m Ps 60:1, 10

9 But now you have rejected and humbled us;
    you no longer go out with our armies. m

44:10
n Lev 26:17

10 You made us retreat n before the enemy,
    and our adversaries have plundered us.

44:11
o Dt 28:64

11 You gave us up to be devoured like sheep
    and have scattered us among the nations. o

44:12
p Isa 52:3; Jer 15:13

12 You sold your people for a pittance, p
    gaining nothing from their sale.

13 You have made us a reproach to our neighbors,
    the scorn and derision of those around us.

44:14
q Jer 24:9

14 You have made us a byword among the nations;
    the peoples shake their heads q at us.
15 My disgrace is before me all day long,
    and my face is covered with shame
16 at the taunts of those who reproach and revile me,
    because of the enemy, who is bent on revenge.

17 All this happened to us,
    though we had not forgotten you
or been false to your covenant.

44:18
r Job 23:11

18 Our hearts had not turned r back;
    our feet had not strayed from your path.
19 But you crushed us and made us a haunt for jackals
    and covered us over with deep darkness.

20 If we had forgotten the name of our God
    or spread out our hands to a foreign god,

44:21
s Ps 139:1-2

21 would not God have discovered it,
    since he knows the secrets of the heart? s

a 4 Septuagint, Aquila and Syriac; Hebrew *King, O God; / command*

44:1–3 Driving out the nations refers to the conquest of Canaan (the promised land) described in the book of Joshua. God gave the land to Israel—they were supposed to enter and drive out anyone who was wicked and opposed to God. Israel was told to settle the land and to be a witness to the world of God's power and love. Surrounded by enemies, the psalm writer remembered what God had done for his people and took heart. We can have this same confidence in God when we feel attacked.

44:6, 7 In whom or in what do you trust? Only God is trustworthy—he will never let you down.

44:9–22 Israel had been defeated despite their faith (44:17) and obedience (44:18) to God. The psalm writer could not understand why God allowed this to happen, but he did not give up hope of discovering the answer (44:17–22). Although he felt his suffering was undeserved, he revealed the real reason for it: he suffered because he was *committed to the Lord.* Paul quoted the psalm writer's complaint (Romans 8:36) to show that we must always be ready to face death for the cause of Christ. Thus, our suffering may not be a punishment, but a battle scar that demonstrates our loyalty.

22 Yet for your sake we face death all day long;
   we are considered as sheep to be slaughtered.[t]

44:22
[t] Ro 8:36*

23 Awake,[u] O Lord! Why do you sleep?
   Rouse yourself! Do not reject us forever.

44:23
[u] Ps 7:6

24 Why do you hide your face[v]
   and forget our misery and oppression?

44:24
[v] Job 13:24

25 We are brought down to the dust;[w]
   our bodies cling to the ground.

44:25
[w] Ps 119:25

26 Rise up and help us;
   redeem us because of your unfailing love.

Theme: A poem to the king (possibly Solomon) on the occasion of his wedding. While this psalm was written for a historic occasion, it is also seen as a prophecy about Christ and his bride, the church, who will praise him throughout all generations.
Author: The sons of Korah (temple assistants)

45

For the director of music. To ⌊the tune of⌋ "Lilies." Of the Sons of Korah. A *maskil*.[a] A wedding song.

1 My heart is stirred by a noble theme
   as I recite my verses for the king;
   my tongue is the pen of a skillful writer.

2 You are the most excellent of men
   and your lips have been anointed with grace,[x]
   since God has blessed you forever.

45:2
[x] Lk 4:22

3 Gird your sword upon your side, O mighty one;[y]
   clothe yourself with splendor and majesty.

45:3
[y] Isa 9:6

4 In your majesty ride forth victoriously
   in behalf of truth, humility and righteousness;
   let your right hand display awesome deeds.

5 Let your sharp arrows pierce the hearts of the king's enemies;
   let the nations fall beneath your feet.

6 Your throne, O God, will last for ever and ever;[z]
   a scepter of justice will be the scepter of your kingdom.

45:6
[z] Ps 93:2

7 You love righteousness[a] and hate wickedness;
   therefore God, your God, has set you above your companions
   by anointing you with the oil of joy.[b]

45:7
[a] Ps 33:5
[b] Heb 1:8-9*

8 All your robes are fragrant with myrrh and aloes and cassia;
   from palaces adorned with ivory
   the music of the strings makes you glad.

9 Daughters of kings are among your honored women;
   at your right hand[c] is the royal bride in gold of Ophir.

45:9
[c] 1Ki 2:19

10 Listen, O daughter, consider and give ear:
   Forget your people[d] and your father's house.

45:10
[d] Dt 21:13

[a] Title: Probably a literary or musical term

44:22–26 The writer cried out to God to redeem his people because of his unfailing love. Nothing can separate us from God's love, not even death (Romans 8:36–39). When you fear for your life, ask God for deliverance, and remember that even death cannot separate you from him.

44:23–25 The psalm writer's words suggest that he did not believe God had left him. God was still the Ruler, but he seemed to be asleep, and the writer wondered why. In the New Testament, the disciples wondered why Jesus was asleep when they needed his help during a storm (Mark 4:35–41). In both cases, of course, God was ready to help, but he wished first to build faith in his followers.

45:1ff This is called a Messianic psalm because it prophetically describes the Messiah's future relationship to the church, his body of believers. Verse 2 expresses God's abundant blessing on his Messiah; verses 6–8 find their true fulfillment in Christ (Hebrews 1:8, 9). The church is described as the bride of Christ in Revelation 19:7, 8; 21:9; 22:17.

45:8, 9 Myrrh is a fragrant gum of an Arabian tree, generally used in perfumes. Aloes, a spice, may have come from sandalwood, a close-grained and fragrant wood often used for storage boxes or chests (see also Proverbs 7:14–17; Song of Songs 4:13, 14). Cassia was probably made from flowers of the cinnamon tree. These expensive fragrances were appropriate for a king's wedding. The location of Ophir is unknown, but believed to be in either Arabia or Africa. It was famous as a source of gold.

11 The king is enthralled by your beauty;
     honor him, for he is your lord.
12 The Daughter of Tyre will come with a gift,[a]
     men of wealth will seek your favor.

13 All glorious is the princess within ⌊her chamber⌋;
     her gown is interwoven with gold.

45:14
[e] SS 1:4

14 In embroidered garments she is led to the king;[e]
     her virgin companions follow her
     and are brought to you.

15 They are led in with joy and gladness;
     they enter the palace of the king.

16 Your sons will take the place of your fathers;
     you will make them princes throughout the land.

17 I will perpetuate your memory through all generations;
     therefore the nations will praise you for ever and ever.

Theme: God is always there to help, providing refuge, security, and peace. God's power is complete and his ultimate victory is certain. He will not fail to rescue those who love him.
Author: The sons of Korah (temple assistants)

46

For the director of music. Of the Sons of Korah. According to *alamoth*.[b] A song.

46:1
[f] Dt 4:7

1 God is our refuge and strength,
     an ever-present[f] help in trouble.
2 Therefore we will not fear, though the earth give way
     and the mountains fall into the heart of the sea,

46:3
[g] Ps 93:3

3 though its waters roar[g] and foam
     and the mountains quake with their surging.   *Selah*

46:4
[h] Ps 48:1, 8;
Isa 60:14

4 There is a river whose streams make glad the city of God,[h]
     the holy place where the Most High dwells.

[a] 12 Or *A Tyrian robe is among the gifts*   [b] Title: Probably a musical term

---

PSALMS THAT HAVE INSPIRED HYMNS		
Psalm 23	The King of Love My Shepherd Is	
	My Shepherd Shall Supply My Need	
	The Lord Is My Shepherd	
Psalm 46	A Mighty Fortress Is Our God	
Psalm 61	Hiding in Thee (O safe to the Rock that is higher than I . . .)	
Psalm 87	Glorious Things of Thee Are Spoken	
Psalm 90	O God, Our Help in Ages Past	
Psalm 100	All People That on Earth Do Dwell	
	Before Jehovah's Awful Throne	
Psalm 103	Praise to the Lord, the Almighty	
Psalm 104	O Worship the King, All Glorious Above	
Psalm 126	Bringing in the Sheaves	

45:13–17 This beautiful section of poetry pictures Christ's bride, the church, with the richest blessings as she unites forever with him (see Revelation 19:6–8; 21:2).

46—48 Psalms 46—48 are hymns of praise, celebrating deliverance from some great foe. Psalm 46 may have been written when the Assyrian army invaded the land and surrounded Jerusalem (2 Kings 18:13—19:37).

46:1–3 The fear of mountains or cities suddenly crumbling into the sea as the result of a nuclear blast haunts many people today. But the psalm writer says that even if the world were to end, we need not fear. In the face of utter destruction, the writer expressed a quiet confidence in God's ability to save him. It

seems impossible to consider the end of the world without becoming consumed by fear, but the Bible is clear—God is our refuge even in the face of total destruction. He is not merely a temporary retreat; he is our eternal refuge and can provide strength in any circumstance.

46:4, 5 Many great cities have rivers flowing through them, sustaining people's lives by making agriculture possible and facilitating trade with other cities. Jerusalem had no river, but it had God who, like a river, sustained the people's lives. As long as God lived among the people, the city was invincible. But when the people abandoned him, God no longer protected them, and Jerusalem fell to the Babylonian army.

⁵ God is within her,ⁱ she will not fall;
   God will help her at break of day.
⁶ Nationsʲ are in uproar, kingdoms fall;
   he lifts his voice, the earth melts.

⁷ The LORD Almighty is with us;
   the God of Jacob is our fortress.ᵏ   Selah

⁸ Come and see the works of the LORD,ˡ
   the desolations he has brought on the earth.
⁹ He makes warsᵐ cease to the ends of the earth;
   he breaks the bowⁿ and shatters the spear,
   he burns the shieldsᵃ with fire.ᵒ
¹⁰ "Be still, and know that I am God;
   I will be exaltedᵖ among the nations,
   I will be exalted in the earth."

¹¹ The LORD Almighty is with us;
   the God of Jacob is our fortress.   Selah

Theme: God is still King of the world. All nations of the earth will eventually recognize his lordship.
Author: The sons of Korah (temple assistants)

47

For the director of music. Of the Sons of Korah. A psalm.

¹ Clap your hands, all you nations;
   shout to God with cries of joy.
² How awesome�q is the LORD Most High,
   the great King over all the earth!
³ He subduedʳ nations under us,
   peoples under our feet.
⁴ He chose our inheritanceˢ for us,
   the pride of Jacob, whom he loved.   Selah

⁵ God has ascended amid shouts of joy,
   the LORD amid the sounding of trumpets.
⁶ Sing praises to God, sing praises;
   sing praises to our King, sing praises.

⁷ For God is the King of all the earth;
   sing to him a psalmᵇ ᵗ of praise.
⁸ God reignsᵘ over the nations;
   God is seated on his holy throne.
⁹ The nobles of the nations assemble
   as the people of the God of Abraham,
   for the kingsᶜ of the earth belong to God;ᵛ
   he is greatly exalted.

ᵃ9 Or *chariots*   ᵇ7 Or *a maskil* (probably a literary or musical term)   ᶜ9 Or *shields*

46:5
ⁱIsa 12:6

46:6
ʲPs 2:1

46:7
ᵏPs 9:9

46:8
ˡPs 66:5

46:9
ᵐIsa 2:4
ⁿPs 76:3
ᵒEze 39:9

46:10
ᵖIsa 2:11

47:2
qDt 7:21

47:3
ʳPs 18:39, 47

47:4
ˢ1Pe 1:4

47:7
ᵗCol 3:16

47:8
ᵘ1Ch 16:31

47:9
ᵛPs 89:18

46:10 War and destruction are inevitable, but so is God's final victory. At that time, all will stand quietly before the Lord Almighty. How proper, then, for us to be still now, reverently honoring him and his power and majesty. Take time each day to be still and to exalt God.

47:1ff This psalm may have been written about the same event as Psalm 46—the Assyrian invasion of Judah by Sennacherib (2 Kings 18:13—19:37).

47:2 The Lord Most High is awesome beyond words, but this didn't keep Bible writers from trying to describe him. And it shouldn't keep us from talking about him either. We can't describe God completely, but we can tell others what he has done for us. Don't let the indescribable aspects of God's greatness prevent you from telling others what you know about him.

47:9 Abraham was the father of the Israelite nation. The one true God was sometimes called the "God of Abraham" (Exodus 3:6; 1 Kings 18:36). In a spiritual sense, God's promises to Abraham apply to all who believe in God, Jew or Gentile (Romans 4:11, 12; Galatians 3:7–9). Thus the God of Abraham is our God too.

Theme: God's presence is our joy, security, and salvation. God is praised as the defender of Jerusalem, the holy city of the Jews. He is also our defender and guide forever.

Author: The sons of Korah (temple assistants)

48 A song. A psalm of the Sons of Korah.

48:1
w Ps 96:4
x Mic 4:1; Zec 8:3

1 Great is the LORD,w and most worthy of praise,
    in the city of our God, his holy mountain.x

48:2
y Ps 50:2
z Mt 5:35

2 It is beautifuly in its loftiness,
    the joy of the whole earth.
Like the utmost heights of Zaphona is Mount Zion,
    theb city of the Great King.z
3 God is in her citadels;
    he has shown himself to be her fortress.

48:4
a 2Sa 10:1-19

4 When the kings joined forces,
    when they advanced together,a
5 they saw ⌊her⌋ and were astounded;
    they fled in terror.
6 Trembling seized them there,
    pain like that of a woman in labor.

48:7
b Jer 18:17

7 You destroyed them like ships of Tarshish
    shattered by an east wind.b

8 As we have heard,
    so have we seen
in the city of the LORD Almighty,
    in the city of our God:
    God makes her secure forever. *Selah*

48:9
c Ps 26:3

9 Within your temple, O God,
    we meditate on your unfailing love.c

48:10
d Jos 7:9

10 Like your name,d O God,
    your praise reaches to the ends of the earth;
    your right hand is filled with righteousness.

48:11
e Ps 97:8

11 Mount Zion rejoices,
    the villages of Judah are glad
    because of your judgments.e

12 Walk about Zion, go around her,
    count her towers,

48:13
f Ps 78:6

13 consider well her ramparts,
    view her citadels,
    that you may tell of them to the next generation.f

a 2 Zaphon can refer to a sacred mountain or the direction north. b 2 Or earth, / Mount Zion, on the northern side / of the

---

48:2 Why is Mount Zion—Jerusalem—"the city of the Great King"? Because the temple was located in Jerusalem, the city was seen as the center of God's presence in the world. The Bible pictures Jerusalem as the place where believers will gather in the "last days" (Isaiah 2:2ff), and as the spiritual home of all believers where God will live among them (Revelation 21:2, 3).

48:8 Because Jerusalem has been destroyed several times since this psalm was written, the phrase, "God makes her secure forever" may refer prophetically to the new Jerusalem where God will judge all nations and live with all believers (Revelation 21).

48:11 The people of Judah were from Israel's largest tribe, which settled in the southern part of Canaan where Jerusalem was located (Joshua 15:1–12). David was from Judah, and he made Jerusalem his capital and the center of the nation's worship. Jesus was also a member of the tribe of Judah. The

psalm writer was saying that the day would come when God would bring justice to the land, and God's people would get the respect they deserved.

48:12, 13 After an enemy army had unsuccessfully besieged Jerusalem, the people had to make a tour of the city, inspecting its defenses and praising God for the protection he had given. In times of great joy or after God has brought us through some great trial, we ought to inspect our defenses to make sure that the foundations—faith in God, knowledge of his Word, and the fellowship and prayers of the body of believers—remain strong (Ephesians 2:20–22). Then we should praise God for his protection!

14 For this God is our God for ever and ever;
    he will be our guide even to the end.

Theme: Trusting in worldly possessions is futile. You cannot take possessions with you
when you die, and they cannot buy forgiveness from sin.
Author: The sons of Korah (temple assistants)

49 For the director of music. Of the Sons of Korah. A psalm.

1 Hear this, all you peoples;
    listen, all who live in this world,
2 both low and high,
    rich and poor alike:
3 My mouth will speak words of wisdom;*g*
    the utterance from my heart will give understanding.
4 I will turn my ear to a proverb;*h*
    with the harp I will expound my riddle:
5 Why should I fear*i* when evil days come,
    when wicked deceivers surround me—
6 those who trust in their wealth
    and boast of their great riches?
7 No man can redeem the life of another
    or give to God a ransom for him—
8 the ransom for a life is costly,
    no payment is ever enough—*j*
9 that he should live on*k* forever
    and not see decay.
10 For all can see that wise men die;*l*
    the foolish and the senseless alike perish
    and leave their wealth to others.
11 Their tombs will remain their houses*a* forever,
    their dwellings for endless generations,
    though they had*b* named lands after themselves.
12 But man, despite his riches, does not endure;
    he is*c* like the beasts that perish.
13 This is the fate of those who trust in themselves,
    and of their followers, who approve their sayings.   *Selah*
14 Like sheep they are destined for the grave,*d*
    and death will feed on them.

49:3	*g* Ps 37:30
49:4	*h* Ps 78:2
49:5	*i* Ps 23:4
49:8	*j* Mt 16:26
49:9	*k* Ps 89:48
49:10	*l* Ecc 2:16

a 11 Septuagint and Syriac; Hebrew *In their thoughts their houses will remain*   *b* 11 Or / *for they have*   *c* 12 Hebrew;
Septuagint and Syriac read verse 12 the same as verse 20.   *d* 14 Hebrew *Sheol*; also in verse 15

48:14 We often pray for God's guidance as we struggle with
decisions. What we need is both guidance and a guide—a map
that gives us landmarks and directions and a constant companion who has an intimate knowledge of the way and will make
sure we interpret the map correctly. The Bible will be such a
map, and the Holy Spirit will be the constant companion and
guide. As you make your way through life, use both the map
and your Guide.

49:1ff The futility of worldliness—riches, pride, fame—
resounds from this psalm. Comparable in form to the book
of Ecclesiastes, this psalm is one of the few written more to
instruct than to praise God.

49:7, 8, 15 In the slave market of the ancient world, a slave
had to be redeemed or ransomed (someone had to pay the price)
in order to go free. In Mark 10:45, Ephesians 1:7, and Hebrews

9:12, we learn that Jesus paid such a price so that we could be
set free from slavery to sin in order to begin a new life with him.

There is no way for a person to buy eternal life with God.
Only God can redeem a soul. Don't count on wealth and physical
comforts to keep you happy because you will never have enough
wealth to keep from dying.

49:10–14 The rich and poor have one similarity—when they
die, they leave all they own here on earth. At the moment of
death (and all of us will face that moment), both rich and poor
are naked and empty-handed before God. The only riches we
have at that time are those we have already invested in our eternal heritage. At the time of death, each of us will wish we had
invested less on earth, where we must leave it, and more in
heaven, where we will retain it forever. To have treasure in
heaven, we must place our faith in God, pledge ourselves to
obey him, and utilize our resources for the good of his kingdom.
This is a good time to check up on your investments and see
where you have invested the most. Then do whatever it takes
to place your investments where they really count.

49:14
m Da 7:18; Mal 4:3

The upright will rule*m* over them in the morning;
their forms will decay in the grave,*a*
far from their princely mansions.

49:15
n Hos 13:14

15 But God will redeem my life*b* from the grave;*n*
he will surely take me to himself.

Selah

16 Do not be overawed when a man grows rich,
when the splendor of his house increases;

49:17
o 1Ti 6:7

17 for he will take nothing with him when he dies,
his splendor will not descend with him.*o*

18 Though while he lived he counted himself blessed—
and men praise you when you prosper—

49:19
p Job 33:30

19 he will join the generation of his fathers,
who will never see the light*p* ⌞of life⌟.

20 A man who has riches without understanding
is like the beasts that perish.

Theme: The contrast between true and false faith. God desires sincere thanks, trust, and praise.
Author: Asaph, one of David's chief musicians

50

A psalm of Asaph.

1 The Mighty One, God, the Lord,
speaks and summons the earth
from the rising of the sun to the place where it sets.

2 From Zion, perfect in beauty,
God shines forth.

50:3
q Ps 97:3; Da 7:10

3 Our God comes and will not be silent;
a fire devours before him,*q*
and around him a tempest rages.

50:4
r Dt 4:26

4 He summons the heavens above,
and the earth,*r* that he may judge his people:

50:5
s Ex 24:7

5 "Gather to me my consecrated ones,
who made a covenant*s* with me by sacrifice."

50:6
t Ps 75:7

6 And the heavens proclaim his righteousness,
for God himself is judge.*t*

Selah

50:7
u Ex 20:2

7 "Hear, O my people, and I will speak,
O Israel, and I will testify against you:
I am God, your God.*u*

50:8
v Hos 6:6

8 I do not rebuke you for your sacrifices
or your burnt offerings,*v* which are ever before me.

9 I have no need of a bull from your stall
or of goats from your pens,

10 for every animal of the forest is mine,
and the cattle on a thousand hills.

a 14 Hebrew *Sheol*; also in verse 15   *b* 15 Or *soul*

50:1ff God judges people for treating him lightly. First, he speaks to the superficially religious people who bring their sacrifices but are only going through the motions (50:1–15). They do not honor God with true praise and thankfulness. Second, he chides wicked, hardhearted people for their evil words and immoral lives (50:16–22). He asks the superficially religious for genuine thanksgiving and trust, and he warns the evil people to consider their deeds, lest he destroy them in his anger.

50:1–4 This psalm begins as though God is finally ready to judge the evil people on earth. But surprisingly, we read that God's great fury is leveled against his own people (or at least those who claim to be his). God's judgment must begin with his own people (1 Peter 4:17).

50:5–9 God's perfect moral nature demands that the penalty for sin be death; however, people could offer an animal to God as a substitute for their own lives, symbolizing their faith in the merciful, forgiving God. But, the people were offering sacrifices and forgetting their significance! The very act of sacrifice showed that they had once agreed to follow God wholeheartedly. But at this time their hearts were not in it. We may fall into the same pattern when we participate in religious activities, tithe, or attend church out of habit or conformity rather than out of heartfelt love and obedience. God wants righteousness, not empty ritual. (See the note on 40:6.)

11 I know every bird in the mountains,
   and the creatures of the field are mine.
12 If I were hungry I would not tell you,
   for the world is mine, and all that is in it.
13 Do I eat the flesh of bulls
   or drink the blood of goats?
14 Sacrifice thank offerings^w to God,
   fulfill your vows^x to the Most High,
15 and call upon me in the day of trouble;
   I will deliver you, and you will honor^y me."

16But to the wicked, God says:

   "What right have you to recite my laws
      or take my covenant on your lips?
17 You hate my instruction
   and cast my words behind^z you.
18 When you see a thief, you join^a with him;
   you throw in your lot with adulterers.
19 You use your mouth for evil
   and harness your tongue to deceit.^b
20 You speak continually against your brother
   and slander your own mother's son.
21 These things you have done and I kept silent;^c
   you thought I was altogether^a like you.
   But I will rebuke you
      and accuse^d you to your face.

22 "Consider this, you who forget God,^e
   or I will tear you to pieces, with none to rescue:
23 He who sacrifices thank offerings honors me,
   and he prepares the way
   so that I may show him^b the salvation of God."

Theme: David's plea for mercy, forgiveness, and cleansing. God wants our hearts to be right with him.
Author: David

51

For the director of music. A psalm of David. When the prophet Nathan came to him after David had committed adultery with Bathsheba.

1 Have mercy on me, O God,
   according to your unfailing love;
   according to your great compassion
      blot out my transgressions.^f

^a21 Or thought the 'I AM' was   ^b23 Or and to him who considers his way / I will show

50:14
^wHeb 13:15
^xDt 23:21

50:15
^yPs 22:23

50:17
^zNe 9:26;
Ro 2:21-22

50:18
^aRo 1:32; 1Ti 5:22

50:19
^bPs 52:2

50:21
^cEcc 8:11
^dPs 90:8

50:22
^eJob 8:13; Ps 9:17

51:1
^fIsa 43:25

50:16–22 Some people glibly recite God's laws but are filled with deceit and evil. They claim his promises but refuse to obey him. This is sin, and God will judge people for it. We too are hypocrites when we are not what we claim to be. To let this inconsistency remain shows that we are not true followers of God.

50:21 At times God seems silent. By his silence he is not condoning sin, nor is he indifferent to it. Instead, he is withholding deserved punishment, giving time for people to repent (2 Peter 3:9). God takes no pleasure in the death of the wicked and wants them to turn from evil (Ezekiel 33:11). But his silence does not last forever—a time of punishment will surely come.

51:1ff This psalm expresses one of the clearest examples of repentance in all of Scripture. Countless broken sinners have found in these words an exquisite expression of their deeply felt need for God's mercy and forgiveness. David's confession has helped people examine excuses, half-hearted repentance, and

lack of sorrow over sin that can keep them from experiencing pardon. David's words also demonstrate the place of hope within confession. Use this psalm as a starting point when dealing with a sense of distance or with guilt that is affecting your relationship with God. It will help you identify and rectify sin in your life through confession and repentance.

51:1–7 David was truly sorry for his adultery with Bathsheba and for murdering his husband to cover it up. He knew that his actions had hurt many people. But because David repented of those sins, God mercifully forgave him. No sin is too great to be forgiven! Do you feel that you could never come close to God because you have done something terrible? God can and will forgive you of any sin. While God forgives us, however, he does not always erase the natural consequences of our sin—David's life and family were never the same as a result of what he had done (see 2 Samuel 12:1–23).

51:2
g Heb 9:14

2 Wash away all my iniquity
    and cleanseᵍ me from my sin.

3 For I know my transgressions,
    and my sin is always before me.

51:4
h Ro 3:4*

4 Against you, you only, have I sinned
    and done what is evil in your sight,
so that you are proved right when you speak
    and justified when you judge.ʰ

51:5
i Job 14:4

5 Surely I was sinfulⁱ at birth,
    sinful from the time my mother conceived me.

6 Surely you desire truth in the inner partsᵃ;
    you teachᵇ me wisdom in the inmost place.

51:7
j Lev 14:4; Heb 9:19
k Isa 1:18

7 Cleanse me with hyssop,ʲ and I will be clean;
    wash me, and I will be whiter than snow.ᵏ

8 Let me hear joy and gladness;
    let the bones you have crushed rejoice.

51:9
l Jer 16:17

9 Hide your face from my sinsˡ
    and blot out all my iniquity.

51:10
m Ac 15:9
n Eze 18:31

10 Create in me a pure heart,ᵐ O God,
    and renew a steadfast spirit within me.ⁿ

11 Do not cast me from your presence
    or take your Holy Spirit from me.

12 Restore to me the joy of your salvation
    and grant me a willing spirit, to sustain me.

13 Then I will teach transgressors your ways,
    and sinners will turn back to you.

51:14
o 2Sa 12:9
p Ps 35:28

14 Save me from bloodguilt,ᵒ O God,
    the God who saves me,
    and my tongue will sing of your righteousness.ᵖ

15 O Lord, open my lips,
    and my mouth will declare your praise.

51:16
q 1Sa 15:22;
Ps 40:6

16 You do not delight in sacrifice,�q or I would bring it;
    you do not take pleasure in burnt offerings.

51:17
r Ps 34:18

17 The sacrifices of God areᶜ a broken spirit;
    a broken and contrite heart,ʳ
    O God, you will not despise.

ᵃ6 The meaning of the Hebrew for this phrase is uncertain.   ᵇ6 Or you desired…; / you taught   ᶜ17 Or My sacrifice,
O God, is

51:4 Although David had sinned with Bathsheba, David said that
he had sinned against God. When someone steals, murders, or
slanders, it is against someone else—a victim. According to the
world's standards, extramarital sex between two consenting adults
is acceptable if nobody gets hurt. But people *do* get hurt—in
David's case, a man was murdered, and a baby died. All sin hurts
us and others, but ultimately it offends God because sin in any
form is a rebellion against God's way of living. When tempted to
do wrong, remember that you will be sinning against God. That
may help you avoid the danger.

51:7 Hyssop branches were used by the Israelites in Egypt to
place the blood of a lamb on the doorframes of their homes.
This would keep them safe from death (Exodus 12:22). This
act demonstrated the Israelites' faith and secured their release
from slavery in Egypt. This verse calls for cleansing from sin
and readiness to serve the Lord.

51:10 Because we are born as sinners (51:5), our natural inclination is to please ourselves rather than God. David followed that
inclination when he took another man's wife. We also follow it
when we sin in any way. Like David, we must ask God to cleanse us
from within (51:7), clearing our hearts and spirits for new thoughts

and desires. Right conduct can come only from a clean heart and
spirit. Ask God to create a pure heart and spirit in you.

51:12 Do you ever feel stagnant in your faith, as though you are
just going through the motions? Has sin ever driven a wedge
between you and God, making him seem distant? David felt this
way. He had sinned with Bathsheba and had just been confronted
by Nathan the prophet. In his prayer he cried, "Restore to me the
joy of your salvation." God wants us to be close to him and to
experience his full and complete life. But sin that remains unconfessed makes such intimacy impossible. Confess your sin to God.
You may still have to face some earthly consequences, as David
did, but God will give back the joy of your relationship with him.

51:13 When God forgives our sin and restores us to a relationship with him, we want to reach out to others who need this
forgiveness and reconciliation. The more you have felt God's
forgiveness, the more you will desire to tell others about it.

51:17 God wants a broken spirit and a broken and contrite heart.
You can never please God by outward actions—no matter how
good—if your inward heart attitude is not right. Are you sorry for
your sin? Do you genuinely intend to stop? God is pleased by this
kind of humility.

18 In your good pleasure make Zion prosper;
    build up the walls of Jerusalem.
19 Then there will be righteous sacrifices,*s*
    whole burnt offerings to delight you;
    then bulls will be offered on your altar.

51:19
s Ps 4:5

Theme: God will judge the evildoer. Our anger must not block our confidence in God's ability to defeat evil.
Author: David

52 For the director of music. A *maskil*a of David. When Doeg the Edomite had gone to Saul and told him: "David has gone to the house of Ahimelech."

1 Why do you boast of evil, you mighty man?
    Why do you boast all day long,
        you who are a disgrace in the eyes of God?
2 Your tongue plots destruction;
    it is like a sharpened razor,*t*
    you who practice deceit.
3 You love evil rather than good,
    falsehood*u* rather than speaking the truth.   *Selah*
4 You love every harmful word,
    O you deceitful tongue!

5 Surely God will bring you down to everlasting ruin:
    He will snatch you up and tear you from your tent;
    he will uproot*v* you from the land of the living.   *Selah*
6 The righteous will see and fear;
    they will laugh*w* at him, saying,
7 "Here now is the man
    who did not make God his stronghold
but trusted in his great wealth*x*
    and grew strong by destroying others!"

8 But I am like an olive tree*y*
    flourishing in the house of God;
I trust in God's unfailing love
    for ever and ever.
9 I will praise you forever*z* for what you have done;
    in your name I will hope, for your name is good.*a*
    I will praise you in the presence of your saints.

52:2
t Ps 57:4

52:3
u Jer 9:5

52:5
v Pr 2:22

52:6
w Job 22:19;
Ps 37:34

52:7
x Ps 49:6

52:8
y Jer 11:16

52:9
z Ps 30:12
a Ps 54:6

Theme: All have sinned. Because of sin, no person can find God on his own. Only God can save us.
Author: David

53 For the director of music. According to *mahalath.*b A *maskil*a of David.

1 The fool*b* says in his heart,
    "There is no God."

53:1
b Ro 3:10

aTitle: Probably a literary or musical term   bTitle: Probably a musical term

52:1 This psalm was written about Doeg, the Edomite who had betrayed Ahimelech and David and then killed God's priests (see 1 Samuel 21:7; 22:9–23). Doeg thought he was a great warrior—even boasting about his deed. In reality, his deed was evil, an offense to God. It is easy to mistake "accomplishment" with goodness. Just because something is done well or thoroughly doesn't mean it is good (for example, someone may be a great gambler or a skillful liar). Measure all you do by the rule of God's Word, not by how proficiently you do it.
52:8 With God by his side, David compared himself to an olive tree flourishing in the house of God. Not only is an olive tree

one of the longest-living trees, but a flourishing tree has even greater longevity. David was contrasting God's eternal protection of his faithful servants with the sudden destruction of the wicked (52:5–7).

53:1 Echoing the message of Psalm 14, this psalm proclaims the foolishness of atheism (see also Romans 3:10). People may say there is no God in order to cover their sin, to have an excuse to continue in sin, and/or to ignore the Judge in order to avoid the judgment. A "fool" does not necessarily lack intelligence; many atheists and unbelievers are highly educated. Fools are people who reject God, the only one who can save them.

They are corrupt, and their ways are vile;
   there is no one who does good.

2 God looks down from heaven
      on the sons of men
   to see if there are any who understand,
      any who seek God.
3 Everyone has turned away,
      they have together become corrupt;
   there is no one who does good,
      not even one.

4 Will the evildoers never learn—
      those who devour my people as men eat bread
      and who do not call on God?
5 There they were, overwhelmed with dread,
      where there was nothing to dread. *c*
   God scattered the bones *d* of those who attacked you;
      you put them to shame, for God despised them.

6 Oh, that salvation for Israel would come out of Zion!
      When God restores the fortunes of his people,
      let Jacob rejoice and Israel be glad!

53:5
*c*Lev 26:17
*d*Eze 6:5

Theme: A call for God to overcome enemies. God is our helper, even in times of hurt
and betrayal.
Author: David

54

For the director of music. With stringed instruments. A *maskil*[a] of David. When the
Ziphites had gone to Saul and said, "Is not David hiding among us?"

1 Save me, O God, by your name;
      vindicate me by your might.
2 Hear my prayer, O God;
      listen to the words of my mouth.

3 Strangers are attacking me;*e*
      ruthless men seek my life—
   men without regard for God.   *Selah*

4 Surely God is my help;*f*
      the Lord is the one who sustains me.

5 Let evil recoil on those who slander me;
      in your faithfulness*g* destroy them.

6 I will sacrifice a freewill offering to you;
      I will praise your name, O LORD,
      for it is good.
7 For he has delivered me from all my troubles,
      and my eyes have looked in triumph on my foes.*h*

54:3
*e*Ps 86:14

54:4
*f*Ps 118:7

54:5
*g*Ps 89:49

54:7
*h*Ps 59:10

aTitle: Probably a literary or musical term

53:4, 5 While God is not affected by what we think of him, we
are definitely and eternally affected by what God thinks of us.
This psalm begins with the bold claim that there is no God, but
by this verse, the true reason for rejecting God has become clear.
The reason people reject God has nothing to do with God's existence and everything to do with people's sinfulness. In our desire
to do wrong, we treat God as if he doesn't exist. When God
passes judgment, it will be too late to apologize and admit we
were wrong. Rejection of God will turn into terror of God.

54:3, 4 Many of David's psalms follow the pattern found in these
two verses—a transition from prayer to praise. David was not
afraid to come to God and express his true feelings and needs.

Thus his spirit was lifted, and he praised God, his helper, protector, and friend.

54:5 David asked God to repay evil to his enemies. He simply
stated his confidence in God's promise. Proverbs 26:27 warns
that those who cause trouble will reap trouble. What we have
intended for others may blow up in our own faces. To be honest
and straightforward before God and others is simpler, easier,
and safer in the long run.

Theme: Expressing deep dismay over the treachery of a close friend. When friends hurt us, the burden is too difficult to carry alone.
Author: David

55

For the director of music. With stringed instruments. A *maskil*[a] of David.

1 Listen to my prayer, O God,
    do not ignore my plea;
2 hear me and answer me.
My thoughts trouble me and I am distraught[i]

> **55:2**
> [i]Isa 38:14

3 at the voice of the enemy,
    at the stares of the wicked;
for they bring down suffering upon me[j]
    and revile me in their anger.

> **55:3**
> [j]2Sa 16:6-8

4 My heart is in anguish within me;
    the terrors[k] of death assail me.

> **55:4**
> [k]Ps 116:3

5 Fear and trembling have beset me;
    horror has overwhelmed me.
6 I said, "Oh, that I had the wings of a dove!
    I would fly away and be at rest—
7 I would flee far away
    and stay in the desert;   *Selah*
8 I would hurry to my place of shelter,
    far from the tempest and storm."

9 Confuse the wicked, O Lord, confound their speech,
    for I see violence and strife[l] in the city.

> **55:9**
> [l]Jer 6:7

10 Day and night they prowl about on its walls;
    malice and abuse are within it.
11 Destructive forces are at work in the city;
    threats and lies never leave its streets.

12 If an enemy were insulting me,
    I could endure it;
if a foe were raising himself against me,
    I could hide from him.
13 But it is you, a man like myself,
    my companion, my close friend,[m]

> **55:13**
> [m]Ps 41:9

14 with whom I once enjoyed sweet fellowship
    as we walked with the throng at the house of God.[n]

> **55:14**
> [n]Ps 42:4

15 Let death take my enemies by surprise;
    let them go down alive to the grave,[b][o]
    for evil finds lodging among them.

> **55:15**
> [o]Nu 16:30, 33

16 But I call to God,
    and the LORD saves me.
17 Evening, morning and noon
    I cry out in distress,
    and he hears my voice.

a Title: Probably a literary or musical term   b 15 Hebrew *Sheol*

55:1ff This psalm was most likely written during the time of Absalom's rebellion and Ahithophel's betrayal (2 Samuel 15—17). Some say verses 12–14 are Messianic because they also describe Judas's betrayal of Christ (Matthew 26:14–16, 20–25).

55:6–8 Even those who are especially close to God, as David was, have moments when they want to escape from their problems and pressures.

55:9–11 The city that was supposed to be holy was plagued by internal problems: violence, strife, malice, abuse, destruction, threats, and lies. External enemies, though a constant threat, were not nearly as dangerous as the corruption inside. Even today,

churches often look to defend themselves against troubles from the sinful world while failing to see that their own sins are causing their troubles.

55:12–14 Nothing hurts more than a wound from a friend. At times friends may need to lovingly confront you in order to help you, but betrayal by a friend truly hurts. Betrayal by a friend has caused David great anguish. Real friends stick by you in times of trouble and bring healing, love, acceptance, and understanding. What kind of friend are you? Don't betray those you love.

55:17 Praying evening, morning, and noon is certainly an excellent way to maintain correct priorities throughout every day.

18 He ransoms me unharmed
   from the battle waged against me,
   even though many oppose me.

55:19
p Dt 33:27

19 God, who is enthroned forever,p   *Selah*
   will hear them and afflict them—
   men who never change their ways
   and have no fear of God.

55:20
q Ps 7:4

20 My companion attacks his friends;q
   he violates his covenant.

55:21
r Ps 28:3

21 His speech is smooth as butter,
   yet war is in his heart;
   his words are more soothing than oil,
   yet they are drawn swords.r

55:22
s Ps 37:5
t Ps 37:24

22 Cast your cares on the LORD
   and he will sustain you;s
   he will never let the righteous fall.t

55:23
u Ps 5:6
v Job 15:32;
Pr 10:27

23 But you, O God, will bring down the wicked
   into the pit of corruption;
   bloodthirsty and deceitful menu
   will not live out half their days.v

But as for me, I trust in you.

Theme: Trusting in God's care in the midst of fear. When all seems dark, one truth still shines bright: when God is for us, those against us will never succeed.
Author: David

56

For the director of music. To ⌊the tune of⌋ "A Dove on Distant Oaks." Of David. A *miktam*.a
When the Philistines had seized him in Gath.

56:1
w Ps 57:1-3

1 Be merciful to me, O God, for men hotly pursue me;w
   all day long they press their attack.

56:2
x Ps 57:3

2 My slanderers pursue me all day long;x
   many are attacking me in their pride.

3 When I am afraid,
   I will trust in you.

56:4
y Ps 118:6

4 In God, whose word I praise,
   in God I trust; I will not be afraid.
   What can mortal man do to me?y

5 All day long they twist my words;
   they are always plotting to harm me.

56:6
z Ps 59:3

6 They conspire,z they lurk,
   they watch my steps,
   eager to take my life.

7 On no account let them escape;
   in your anger, O God, bring down the nations.

a Title: Probably a literary or musical term

Daniel followed this pattern (Daniel 6:10), as did Peter (Acts 10:9, 10). The prayers of God's people are effective against the overwhelming evil in the world.

55:22 God wants us to cast our cares on him, but often we continue to bear them ourselves even when we say we are trusting in him. Trust the same strength that sustains you to carry your cares also.

56:1ff This was probably written on the same occasion as Psalm 34, when David fled from Saul to Philistine territory. He had to pretend insanity before Achish when some servants grew suspicious of him (1 Samuel 21:10–15).

56:3, 4 David stated, "What can mortal man do to me?" How much harm can people do to us? They can inflict pain, suffering, and death. But no person can rob us of our souls or our future beyond this life. How much harm can we do to ourselves? The worst thing we can do is to reject God and lose our eternal future. Jesus said, "Do not be afraid of those who kill the body but cannot kill the soul" (Matthew 10:28). Instead, we should fear God, who controls this life and the next.

8 Record my lament;
    list my tears on your scroll[a]—
    are they not in your record?

9 Then my enemies will turn back
    when I call for help.
  By this I will know that God is for me.[a]

10 In God, whose word I praise,
    in the LORD, whose word I praise—

11 in God I trust; I will not be afraid.
    What can man do to me?

12 I am under vows to you, O God;
    I will present my thank offerings to you.

13 For you have delivered me[b] from death[b]
    and my feet from stumbling,
    that I may walk before God
    in the light of life.[c][c]

56:9
[a] Ro 8:31

56:13
[b] Ps 116:8
[c] Job 33:30

Theme: God's faithful help and love in times of trouble. When we face trials, God will quiet our hearts and give us confidence.
Author: David

57 For the director of music. ⌞To the tune of⌟ "Do Not Destroy." Of David. A *miktam*.[d] When he had fled from Saul into the cave.

1 Have mercy on me, O God, have mercy on me,
    for in you my soul takes refuge.[d]
  I will take refuge in the shadow of your wings[e]
    until the disaster has passed.[f]

57:1
[d] Ps 2:12
[e] Ps 17:8
[f] Isa 26:20

2 I cry out to God Most High,
    to God, who fulfills ⌞his purpose⌟ for me.[g]

57:2
[g] Ps 138:8

3 He sends from heaven and saves me,
    rebuking those who hotly pursue me;[h]   *Selah*
  God sends his love and his faithfulness.

57:3
[h] Ps 56:1

4 I am in the midst of lions;[i]
    I lie among ravenous beasts—
  men whose teeth are spears and arrows,
    whose tongues are sharp swords.[j]

57:4
[i] Ps 35:17
[j] Pr 30:14

5 Be exalted, O God, above the heavens;
    let your glory be over all the earth.[k]

57:5
[k] Ps 108:5

6 They spread a net for my feet—
    I was bowed down[l] in distress.
  They dug a pit in my path—
    but they have fallen into it themselves.   *Selah*

57:6
[l] Ps 145:14

7 My heart is steadfast, O God,
    my heart is steadfast;[m]
  I will sing and make music.

57:7
[m] Ps 108:1

[a]8 Or / put my tears in your wineskin   [b]13 Or my soul   [c]13 Or the land of the living   [d]Title: Probably a literary or musical term

---

56:8 Even in our deepest sorrow, God cares! Jesus reminded us further of how much God understands us—he knows even the number of hairs on our heads (Matthew 10:30). Often we waver between faith and fear. When you feel so discouraged that you are sure no one understands, remember that God knows every problem and sees every tear.

57:1ff This psalm was probably written about David's reflections when he was hiding in a cave from Saul (see 1 Samuel 22—24).

57:4 At times, we may be surrounded by people who gossip about us or criticize us. Verbal cruelty can damage us as badly as physical abuse. Rather than answering with hateful words, we, like David, can talk with God about the problem.

57:7 David's firm faith in God contrasted sharply with his enemies' loud lying and boasting. When confronted with verbal attacks, the best defense is simply to be quiet and praise God, realizing that our confidence is in his love and faithfulness (57:10). In times of great suffering, don't turn inward to self-pity or outward to revenge, but upward to God.

57:8
n Ps 16:9

8 Awake, my soul!
Awake, harp and lyre!*n*
I will awaken the dawn.

9 I will praise you, O Lord, among the nations;
I will sing of you among the peoples.

57:10
o Ps 36:5

10 For great is your love, reaching to the heavens;
your faithfulness reaches to the skies.*o*

11 Be exalted, O God, above the heavens;
let your glory be over all the earth.

Theme: A prayer for God's justice. When no justice can be found, rejoice in knowing that justice will triumph because there is a God who will judge with complete fairness.
Author: David, at a time when men in authority were twisting justice

58

For the director of music. ⌐To the tune of⌐ "Do Not Destroy." Of David. A *miktam*.*a*

1 Do you rulers indeed speak justly?
Do you judge uprightly among men?

58:2
p Ps 94:20

2 No, in your heart you devise injustice,
and your hands mete out violence on the earth.*p*

3 Even from birth the wicked go astray;
from the womb they are wayward and speak lies.

4 Their venom is like the venom of a snake,
like that of a cobra that has stopped its ears,

5 that will not heed the tune of the charmer,
however skillful the enchanter may be.

58:6
q Job 4:10

6 Break the teeth in their mouths, O God;
tear out, O Lord, the fangs of the lions!*q*

7 Let them vanish like water that flows away;
when they draw the bow, let their arrows be blunted.

58:8
r Job 3:16

8 Like a slug melting away as it moves along,
like a stillborn child,*r* may they not see the sun.

58:9
s Pr 10:25

9 Before your pots can feel ⌐the heat of⌐ the thorns—
whether they be green or dry—the wicked will be swept away.*b s*

58:10
t Ps 68:23

10 The righteous will be glad when they are avenged,
when they bathe their feet in the blood of the wicked.*t*

11 Then men will say,
"Surely the righteous still are rewarded;
surely there is a God who judges the earth."

a Title: Probably a literary or musical term   *b 9* The meaning of the Hebrew for this verse is uncertain.

57:8 David calls out to his soul and his instruments to prepare for praise. Before a new day begins, he wants to "awaken the dawn" with his song honoring God's faithfulness. Instead of spending a sleepless night worrying about what he cannot change, he uses those wakeful hours to meditate on an expression suitable for the world. David's example shows us how to turn times of stress into times of blessing by considering God's faithfulness in comparison with our fleeting problems. Why worry when you can invest that time in praise?

58:1ff This is called an imprecatory psalm (see the note on 35:1ff). It is a cry for justice so intense that it seems, at first glance, to be a call for revenge.

58:1ff The Old Testament is filled with references to justice, and it is a key topic in the psalms. Unfortunately, many judges and rulers in ancient times took justice into their own hands. They had complete authority with no accountability and the power to make their own laws. When earth's judges are corrupt, there is little hope of justice in this life. But God loves justice, and those who obey him will experience perfect justice in eternity.

58:6–10 Shifting from prayer to prediction, David fervently calls for justice that veers into grisly judgment. Broken teeth and wading in the blood of the wicked convey ugly pictures of the gruesome results of sin. Even uglier pictures of the darkness are often revealed by our own demands for justice and more. This is certainly not the only time David's forceful sense of justice turned back on him (see 2 Samuel 12:1–15). Ironically, David himself would eventually occupy the throne and be subject to the very imprecation he called down on others. We can be grateful that God hears our prayers but we can also be grateful that God doesn't have to abide by our requests.

58:11 Of all people, our national leaders should be just and fair. When they are unjust and unfair, people suffer as politicians wrest power from the people, national morality deteriorates, and God is ignored. When right triumphs at last, "the righteous will be glad" (58:10). Be assured that there will be a day of accountability and that God judges fairly. Be careful never to side with injustice, lest you find yourself standing before an angry Judge.

Theme: Prayer and praise for God's saving help. God's constant love is our place
of safety in a wicked world.
Author: David

59 For the director of music. ⌐To the tune of⌐ "Do Not Destroy." Of David. A *miktam*.ᵃ When
Saul had sent men to watch David's house in order to kill him.

¹ Deliver me from my enemies, O God;ᵘ
  protect me from those who rise up against me.
² Deliver me from evildoers
  and save me from bloodthirsty men. ᵛ

³ See how they lie in wait for me!
  Fierce men conspireʷ against me
  for no offense or sin of mine, O LORD.
⁴ I have done no wrong, yet they are ready to attack me.ˣ
  Arise to help me; look on my plight!
⁵ O LORD God Almighty, the God of Israel,
  rouse yourself to punish all the nations;
  show no mercy to wicked traitors.ʸ   *Selah*

⁶ They return at evening,
  snarling like dogs,ᶻ
  and prowl about the city.
⁷ See what they spew from their mouths—
  they spew out swordsᵃ from their lips,
  and they say, "Who can hear us?"ᵇ
⁸ But you, O LORD, laugh at them;ᶜ
  you scoff at all those nations.

⁹ O my Strength, I watch for you;
  you, O God, are my fortress, ¹⁰ my loving God.

God will go before me
  and will let me gloat over those who slander me.
¹¹ But do not kill them, O Lord our shield,ᵇ
  or my people will forget.ᵈ
In your might make them wander about,
  and bring them down.
¹² For the sins of their mouths,
  for the words of their lips,ᵉ
  let them be caught in their pride.
For the curses and lies they utter,
¹³   consume them in wrath,
  consume them till they are no more.ᶠ
Then it will be known to the ends of the earth
  that God rules over Jacob.   *Selah*

¹⁴ They return at evening,
  snarling like dogs,
  and prowl about the city.
¹⁵ They wander about for food
  and howl if not satisfied.

	59:1 ᵘPs 143:9
	59:2 ᵛPs 139:19
	59:3 ʷPs 56:6
	59:4 ˣPs 35:19, 23
	59:5 ʸJer 18:23
	59:6 ᶻver 14
	59:7 ᵃPs 57:4 ᵇPs 10:11
	59:8 ᶜPs 37:13
	59:11 ᵈDt 4:9
	59:12 ᵉPr 12:13
	59:13 ᶠPs 104:35

ᵃTitle: Probably a literary or musical term ᵇ11 Or *sovereign*

59:7, 8 Vile men curse God as if he cannot hear and will not
respond. But God scoffs at them. Evil people live as if God cannot
see and will not punish. But God watches patiently until that day
when their deeds will rise up to accuse them. As believers we
must be careful not to follow the same foolish practices as evil
people. We must remember that God hears and sees all we do.

59:10 David was hunted by those whose love had turned to jealousy, and this was driving them to try to murder him. Trusted
friends, and even his mentor, the king, had turned against him.
What changeable love! But David knew that God's love for him was
changeless. "His love endures forever" (100:5). God's mercy to all
who trust him is just as permanent as his mercy to David. When
the love of others fails or disappoints us, we can rest in God's
enduring love.

59:16
g Ps 101:1

16 But I will sing of your strength,
in the morning I will sing of your love;*g*
for you are my fortress,
my refuge in times of trouble.

17 O my Strength, I sing praise to you;
you, O God, are my fortress, my loving God.

Theme: Real help comes from God alone. When a situation seems out of control, we can trust God to do mighty things.
Author: David, when Israel was away at war with Aram in the north, and Edom invaded Israel from the south (2 Samuel 8)

60

For the director of music. To ⌊the tune of⌋ "The Lily of the Covenant." A *miktam*ᵃ of David.
For teaching. When he fought Aram Naharaim*b* and Aram Zobah,*c* and when Joab returned and struck down twelve thousand Edomites in the Valley of Salt.

60:1
h Ps 44:9

1 You have rejected us,*h* O God, and burst forth upon us;
you have been angry—now restore us!

60:2
i 2Ch 7:14

60:3
j Ps 71:20

2 You have shaken the land and torn it open;
mend its fractures,*i* for it is quaking.
3 You have shown your people desperate times;*j*
you have given us wine that makes us stagger.

4 But for those who fear you, you have raised a banner
to be unfurled against the bow.   *Selah*

60:5
k Ps 108:6

5 Save us and help us with your right hand,*k*
that those you love may be delivered.

60:6
l Ge 12:6

6 God has spoken from his sanctuary:
"In triumph I will parcel out Shechem*l*
and measure off the Valley of Succoth.

60:7
m Dt 33:17
n Ge 49:10

7 Gilead is mine, and Manasseh is mine;
Ephraim is my helmet,
Judah*m* my scepter.*n*

60:8
o 2Sa 8:1

8 Moab is my washbasin,
upon Edom I toss my sandal;
over Philistia I shout in triumph.*o*"

9 Who will bring me to the fortified city?
Who will lead me to Edom?
10 Is it not you, O God, you who have rejected us
and no longer go out with our armies?

60:11
p Ps 146:3

11 Give us aid against the enemy,
for the help of man is worthless.*p*

60:12
q Nu 24:18

12 With God we will gain the victory,
and he will trample down our enemies.*q*

ᵃTitle: Probably a literary or musical term   bTitle: That is, Arameans of Northwest Mesopotamia   cTitle: That is, Arameans of central Syria

---

59:16 Throughout this psalm, David describes in grim detail the behavior of his enemies. He conveys his own feelings of dread with the desperation and despair that he sees in the lives of those who want to harm him. What a delight, then, in these final verses to read about God's role in David's life as fortress, refuge, and a source of strength. David had learned to turn negative circumstances into reminders of God's faithful presence. What stresses in your life might be transformed today if you made them a starting point for praising God?

60:1ff This psalm gives us information about David's reign not found in the books of 1 and 2 Samuel or 1 and 2 Chronicles. Although the setting of the psalm is found in 2 Samuel 8, that passage makes no reference to the fact that David's forces had met stiff resistance (60:1–3) and apparently even a temporary defeat (60:9, 10). The closer we get to God, the more our enemies will attack us because we threaten their evil and selfish way of living.

60:3 Instead of the wine of blessing, God had given them the cup of his judgment. God's rejection was intended to bring them back to himself.

60:6–10 God said the cities and territories of Israel were his, and he knew the future of each of the nations. When the world seems out of control, we must remind ourselves that God owns the cities and knows the future of every nation. God is in control. In and through him we will gain the victory.

60:8 David mentioned the enemy nations that surrounded Israel. Moab lay directly to the east, Edom to the south, and Philistia to the west. At the time this psalm was written, David was fighting Aram to the north. Although he was surrounded by enemies, David remembered that God had promised triumph over those nations. He knew that Israel's future was closely tied to God's reputation of keeping his promises.

Theme: Prayer for security and assurance. Wherever we are, we can trust that God will be there to answer our cries for help.
Author: David, written when he was forced to escape during the days of Absalom's rebellion (2 Samuel 15—18), or after he had narrowly escaped one of Saul's efforts to kill him while hiding in the desert

61

For the director of music. With stringed instruments. Of David.

1 Hear my cry, O God;[r]
   listen to my prayer.
2 From the ends of the earth I call to you,
   I call as my heart grows faint;
   lead me to the rock that is higher than I.
3 For you have been my refuge,
   a strong tower against the foe.[s]

4 I long to dwell in your tent forever
   and take refuge in the shelter of your wings.[t]
5 For you have heard my vows,[u] O God;
   you have given me the heritage of those who fear your name.

6 Increase the days of the king's life,
   his years for many generations.
7 May he be enthroned in God's presence forever;[v]
   appoint your love and faithfulness to protect him.

8 Then will I ever sing praise to your name
   and fulfill my vows day after day.

Selah

61:1
[r]Ps 64:1

61:3
[s]Pr 18:10

61:4
[t]Ps 91:4

61:5
[u]Ps 56:12

61:7
[v]Ps 41:12

Theme: Placing all hope in God. Knowing that God is in control allows us to wait patiently for him to rescue us. True relief does not come when the problem is resolved because more problems are on the way! True relief comes from an enduring hope in God's ultimate salvation. Only then will all trials be resolved.
Author: David, possibly written during the days of Absalom's rebellion (2 Samuel 15—18)

62

For the director of music. For Jeduthun. A psalm of David.

1 My soul finds rest[w] in God alone;
   my salvation comes from him.
2 He alone is my rock and my salvation;
   he is my fortress, I will never be shaken.

3 How long will you assault a man?
   Would all of you throw him down—
   this leaning wall,[x] this tottering fence?
4 They fully intend to topple him
   from his lofty place;
   they take delight in lies.
   With their mouths they bless,
   but in their hearts they curse.[y]

5 Find rest, O my soul, in God alone;
   my hope comes from him.
6 He alone is my rock and my salvation;
   he is my fortress, I will not be shaken.

Selah

62:1
[w]Ps 33:20

62:3
[x]Isa 30:13

62:4
[y]Ps 28:3

61:1, 2 David must have been far from home when he wrote this psalm. Fortunately, God is not limited to any geographic location. Even when we are among unknown people and surroundings, God never abandons us. A "higher" rock would be a plain of refuge and safety. God's all-surpassing strength is always with us.

61:8 David made a vow to praise God each day. David continually praised God through both the good and difficult times of his life. Do you find something to praise God for each day? As you

do, you will find your heart elevated from daily distractions to lasting confidence.

62:3–6 David expressed his feelings to God and then reaffirmed his faith. Prayer can release our tensions in times of emotional stress. Trusting God to be our rock, salvation, and fortress (62:2) will change our entire outlook on life. No longer must we be held captive by resentment toward others when they hurt us. When we are resting in God's strength, nothing can shake us.

7 My salvation and my honor depend on God[a];
   he is my mighty rock, my refuge.
8 Trust in him at all times, O people;
   pour out your hearts to him,[z]
   for God is our refuge.

Selah

62:8
[z]1Sa 1:15; La 2:19

9 Lowborn men are but a breath,[a]
   the highborn are but a lie;
if weighed on a balance,[b] they are nothing;
   together they are only a breath.
10 Do not trust in extortion
   or take pride in stolen goods;
though your riches increase,
   do not set your heart on them.

62:9
[a]Ps 39:5, 11
[b]Isa 40:15

11 One thing God has spoken,
   two things have I heard:
that you, O God, are strong,
12   and that you, O Lord, are loving.
Surely you will reward each person
   according to what he has done.[c]

62:12
[c]Mt 16:27

Theme: A desire for God's presence, provision, and protection. No matter where we are, our desire should be for God because only he satisfies fully.
Author: David

63 A psalm of David. When he was in the Desert of Judah.

1 O God, you are my God,
   earnestly I seek you;
my soul thirsts for you,[d]
   my body longs for you,
in a dry and weary land
   where there is no water.

63:1
[d]Ps 42:2

2 I have seen you in the sanctuary[e]
   and beheld your power and your glory.
3 Because your love is better than life,
   my lips will glorify you.
4 I will praise you as long as I live,[f]
   and in your name I will lift up my hands.
5 My soul will be satisfied as with the richest of foods;
   with singing lips my mouth will praise you.

63:2
[e]Ps 27:4

63:4
[f]Ps 104:33

6 On my bed I remember you;
   I think of you through the watches of the night.[g]
7 Because you are my help,[h]
   I sing in the shadow of your wings.

63:6
[g]Ps 42:8
63:7
[h]Ps 27:9

[a]7 Or / God Most High is my salvation and my honor

62:9–12 It is tempting to use honor, power, wealth, or prestige to measure people. We may even think that such people are really getting ahead in life. But on God's scales, these people are a "breath," a puff of air. What, then, can tilt the scales when God weighs us? Trusting God and working for him (62:12). Wealth, honor, power, or prestige add nothing to our value in God's eyes, but the faithful work we do for him has eternal value.

63:1ff Psalms 61, 62, and 63 were probably written when David was seeking refuge during Absalom's rebellion (2 Samuel 15—18). David had already lived a full life. David's quiet confidence as stated in these psalms can be seen in the account in 2 Samuel of the events that shook his life. His actions closely paralleled his beliefs during those turbulent days.

63:1–5 Hiding from his enemies in the barren Desert of Judah, David was intensely lonely. He longed for a friend he could trust to ease his loneliness. No wonder he cried out, "O God, . . . my soul thirsts for you, . . . in a dry and weary land." If you are lonely or thirsty for something lasting in your life, remember David's prayer. God alone can satisfy our deepest longings!

63:6 The night was divided into three watches. Someone aware of all three would be having a sleepless night. A cure for sleepless nights is to turn our thoughts to God. There are many reasons we can't sleep—illness, stress, worry—but sleepless nights can be turned into quiet times of reflection and worship. Use them to review how God has guided and helped you.

8 My soul clings to you;
    your right hand upholds me.

9 They who seek my life will be destroyed;
    they will go down to the depths of the earth.*i*

  63:9
  i Ps 55:15

10 They will be given over to the sword
    and become food for jackals.

11 But the king will rejoice in God;
    all who swear by God's name will praise him,*j*
    while the mouths of liars will be silenced.

  63:11
  j Dt 6:13; Isa 45:23

Theme: A complaint against conspiracy. When others conspire against us, we can ask God for protection because he knows everything.
Author: David

64

For the director of music. A psalm of David.

1 Hear me, O God, as I voice my complaint;
    protect my life from the threat of the enemy.*k*

  64:1
  k Ps 140:1

2 Hide me from the conspiracy of the wicked,
    from that noisy crowd of evildoers.

3 They sharpen their tongues like swords
    and aim their words like deadly arrows.*l*

  64:3
  l Ps 58:7

4 They shoot from ambush at the innocent man;
    they shoot at him suddenly, without fear.

5 They encourage each other in evil plans,
    they talk about hiding their snares;
    they say, "Who will see them*a*?"*m*

  64:5
  m Ps 10:11

6 They plot injustice and say,
    "We have devised a perfect plan!"
    Surely the mind and heart of man are cunning.

7 But God will shoot them with arrows;
    suddenly they will be struck down.

8 He will turn their own tongues against them*n*
    and bring them to ruin;
    all who see them will shake their heads in scorn.

  64:8
  n Pr 18:7

9 All mankind will fear;
    they will proclaim the works of God
    and ponder what he has done.

10 Let the righteous rejoice in the LORD
    and take refuge in him;
    let all the upright in heart praise him!*o*

  64:10
  o Ps 32:11

Theme: God provides abundantly. We can be thankful to God for his many blessings.
Author: David

65

For the director of music. A psalm of David. A song.

1 Praise awaits*b* you, O God, in Zion;
    to you our vows will be fulfilled.

a 5 Or us *b 1 Or befits;* the meaning of the Hebrew for this word is uncertain.

64:1ff Evil can come in the form of a secret conspiracy or an ambush because Satan wants to catch us unprepared. He tempts us in our weakest areas when we least expect it. But God himself will strike down our enemies (64:7), whether they are physical or spiritual. Wickedness is widespread and affects us in many ways, but the final victory already belongs to God and those who trust and believe in him.

64:1, 2 We may believe that God wants to hear only certain requests from us. While it is true that we should offer praise,

confession, and respectful petitions, it is true also that God is willing to listen to *anything* we want to tell him. David expressed himself honestly, knowing that God would hear his voice. God will always listen to us, and he will fully understand what we say.

64:3–10 The words spoken against us are among the most painful attacks we may have to face. If we trust in God, these attacks will not hurt us.

65:1, 2 In Old Testament times, vows were taken seriously and fulfilled completely. No one had to make a vow, but once made, it

65:2
p Isa 66:23

2 O you who hear prayer,
    to you all men will come.p
3 When we were overwhelmed by sins,
    you forgavea our transgressions.

65:4
q Ps 4:3; 33:12
r Ps 36:8

4 Blessed are those you chooseq
    and bring near to live in your courts!
  We are filled with the good things of your house,r
    of your holy temple.

5 You answer us with awesome deeds of righteousness,
    O God our Savior,
  the hope of all the ends of the earth
    and of the farthest seas,

65:6
s Ps 93:1

6 who formed the mountains by your power,
    having armed yourself with strength,s

65:7
t Mt 8:26
u Isa 17:12-13

7 who stilled the roaring of the seas,t
    the roaring of their waves,
    and the turmoil of the nations.u
8 Those living far away fear your wonders;
    where morning dawns and evening fades
    you call forth songs of joy.

65:9
v Ps 46:4

9 You care for the land and water it;
    you enrich it abundantly.
  The streams of God are filled with water
    to provide the people with grain,v
    for so you have ordained it.b
10 You drench its furrows
    and level its ridges;
  you soften it with showers
    and bless its crops.
11 You crown the year with your bounty,
    and your carts overflow with abundance.
12 The grasslands of the desert overflow;
    the hills are clothed with gladness.
13 The meadows are covered with flocks
    and the valleys are mantled with grain;
    they shout for joy and sing.

Theme: God answers prayer. Individually and as a body of believers, we should praise and worship God.
Author: Anonymous, written after a great victory in battle.

66 For the director of music. A song. A psalm.

66:1
w Ps 100:1

1 Shout with joy to God, all the earth!w
2   Sing the glory of his name;
     make his praise glorious!

a 3 Or made atonement for   b 9 Or for that is how you prepare the land

was binding (Deuteronomy 23:21–23). The vows mentioned here involved promises to praise God for his answers to prayer.
65:3 Although we may feel overwhelmed by the multitude of our sins, God will forgive them all if we ask sincerely. Do you feel as though God could never forgive you, that your sins are too many, or that some of them are too great? The good news is that God can and will forgive them all. Nobody is beyond redemption, and nobody is so full of sin that he or she cannot be made clean.
65:4 Access to God, the joy of living in the temple courts, was a great honor. God had chosen a special group of Israelites, the tribe of Levi, to serve as priests in the tabernacle (Numbers 3:5–51). They were the only ones who could enter the sacred

rooms where God's presence resided. Because of Jesus' death on the cross, all believers today have personal access to God's presence everywhere and at any time.
65:6-13 This harvest psalm glorifies God the Creator as reflected in the beauty of nature. Nature helps us understand something of God's character. The Jews believed that God's care of nature was a sign of his love and provision for them. Nature shows God's generosity—giving us more than we need or deserve. Understanding God's abundant generosity should make us grateful to God and generous to others.

3 Say to God, "How awesome are your deeds!ˣ
   So great is your power
      that your enemies cringeʸ before you.
4 All the earth bows down to you;
   they sing praise to you,
      they sing praise to your name."   *Selah*

5 Come and see what God has done,
   how awesome his works in man's behalf!
6 He turned the sea into dry land,ᶻ
   they passed through the waters on foot—
      come, let us rejoice in him.
7 He rules forever by his power,
   his eyes watch the nations—
      let not the rebellious rise up against him.   *Selah*

8 Praise our God, O peoples,
   let the sound of his praise be heard;
9 he has preserved our lives
   and kept our feet from slipping.
10 For you, O God, tested us;
   you refined us like silver.ᵃ
11 You brought us into prison
   and laid burdensᵇ on our backs.
12 You let men ride over our heads;ᶜ
   we went through fire and water,
      but you brought us to a place of abundance.ᵈ

13 I will come to your temple with burnt offerings
   and fulfill my vowsᵉ to you—
14 vows my lips promised and my mouth spoke
   when I was in trouble.
15 I will sacrifice fat animals to you
   and an offering of rams;
      I will offer bulls and goats.   *Selah*

16 Come and listen, all you who fear God;
   let me tell you what he has done for me.
17 I cried out to him with my mouth;
   his praise was on my tongue.
18 If I had cherished sin in my heart,
   the Lord would not have listened;ᶠ
19 but God has surely listened
   and heard my voiceᵍ in prayer.
20 Praise be to God,
   who has not rejected my prayer
      or withheld his love from me!

66:3
ˣPs 65:5
ʸPs 18:44

66:6
ᶻEx 14:22

66:10
ᵃPs 17:3;
Isa 48:10;
Zec 13:9;
1Pe 1:6-7

66:11
ᵇLa 1:13

66:12
ᶜIsa 51:23
ᵈIsa 43:2

66:13
ᵉEcc 5:4

66:18
ᶠJas 4:3

66:19
ᵍPs 116:1-2

66:5-7 The writer was remembering God's rescue of the Israelites by parting the Red Sea during the exodus. God saved the Israelites then, and he continues to save his people today.

66:10-12 Just as fire refines silver in the smelting process, trials refine our character. They bring us a new and deeper wisdom, helping us discern truth from falsehood and giving us the discipline to do what we know is right. Above all, these trials help us realize that life is a gift from God to be cherished, not a right to be taken for granted.

66:13-15 People sometimes make bargains with God, saying, "If you heal me (or get me out of this mess), I'll obey you for

the rest of my life." However, soon after they recover, the vow is forgotten and the old lifestyle is resumed. This writer made a promise to God, but he remembered the promise and was prepared to carry it out. God always keeps his promises and wants us to follow his example. Be careful to follow through on whatever you promise to do.

66:18 Our confession of sin must be continual because we continue to do wrong. But true confession requires us to listen to God and to want to stop doing what is wrong. David confessed his sin and prayed, "Forgive my hidden faults. Keep your servant also from willful sins" (19:12, 13). When we *refuse* to repent or when we harbor and cherish certain sins, we place a wall between us and God. We may not be able to remember *every* sin we have ever committed, but our attitude should be one of confession and obedience.

Theme: Joy comes from spreading the news about God around the world.
Author: Anonymous, possibly written for one of the harvest feasts

67

For the director of music. With stringed instruments. A psalm. A song.

1 May God be gracious to us and bless us
  and make his face shine upon us,[h]   *Selah*
2 that your ways may be known on earth,
  your salvation among all nations.[i]

3 May the peoples praise you, O God;
  may all the peoples praise you.
4 May the nations be glad and sing for joy,
  for you rule the peoples justly
  and guide the nations of the earth.   *Selah*
5 May the peoples praise you, O God;
  may all the peoples praise you.

6 Then the land will yield its harvest,[j]
  and God, our God, will bless us.
7 God will bless us,
  and all the ends of the earth will fear him.

67:1 [h] Nu 6:24-26

67:2 [i] Tit 2:11

67:6 [j] Lev 26:4; Ps 85:12; Eze 34:27

Theme: Remembering God's glory and power. Times and cultures change, but God is always majestically present as defender and provider.
Author: David

68

For the director of music. Of David. A psalm. A song.

1 May God arise, may his enemies be scattered;
  may his foes flee[k] before him.
2 As smoke[l] is blown away by the wind,
  may you blow them away;
as wax melts[m] before the fire,
  may the wicked perish before God.
3 But may the righteous be glad
  and rejoice before God;
  may they be happy and joyful.

4 Sing to God, sing praise to his name,
  extol him who rides on the clouds[a]—
his name is the LORD—
  and rejoice before him.
5 A father to the fatherless, a defender of widows,
  is God in his holy dwelling.

68:1 [k] Nu 10:35

68:2 [l] Hos 13:3
[m] Isa 9:18; Mic 1:4

a4 Or / *prepare the way for him who rides through the deserts*

67:2 Could the psalm writer have looked across the years to see the gospel go throughout the earth? This psalm surely speaks of the fulfillment of the Great Commission (Matthew 28:18–20), when Jesus commanded that the gospel be taken to all nations. Count yourself among that great crowd of believers worldwide who know the Savior; praise him for his Good News; and share that gospel so that the harvest will be abundant.

67:7 Every verse in this psalm mentions God's relationship with the entire globe. The intended audience of this message spans the world. God repeatedly spoke to and through his people about his love for all nations. Read this psalm with the realization that it was written for and about you!

68:1ff This psalm begins just like Moses' cry in Numbers 10:35 as the Israelites followed the ark of the covenant. It undoubtedly brought to mind the time when David led a joyous procession that brought the ark from the house of Obed-Edom to Jerusalem (2 Samuel 6:11–15).

68:3–6 With shouts of praise and the sound of trumpets, David and his people took the holy ark toward Mount Zion (2 Samuel 6:15). It was a time to sing praises to the Lord, whose presence brings great joy. Only in God is there hope for the orphans, widows, prisoners, and all other lonely people. If you are lonely or disadvantaged, join David in praise, and discover great joy from loving and praising God.

68:4–6 David praised God for his protection and provision. When we see God's true majesty, our response should be to praise him. This was a song of faith because many of these benefits had not yet come true in David's time. It should also be our song of faith. We must continue to trust God because, in time, he will fulfill all his promises.

6 God sets the lonely in families,[a]
  he leads forth the prisoners[n] with singing;
  but the rebellious live in a sun-scorched land.[o]

7 When you went out[p] before your people, O God,
  when you marched through the wasteland,   *Selah*
8 the earth shook,
  the heavens poured down rain,
  before God, the One of Sinai,
  before God, the God of Israel.
9 You gave abundant showers,[q] O God;
  you refreshed your weary inheritance.
10 Your people settled in it,
  and from your bounty, O God, you provided[r] for the poor.

11 The Lord announced the word,
  and great was the company of those who proclaimed it:
12 "Kings and armies flee in haste;
  in the camps men divide the plunder.
13 Even while you sleep among the campfires,[b]
  the wings of ⌊my⌋ dove are sheathed with silver,
  its feathers with shining gold."
14 When the Almighty[c] scattered[s] the kings in the land,
  it was like snow fallen on Zalmon.

15 The mountains of Bashan are majestic mountains;
  rugged are the mountains of Bashan.
16 Why gaze in envy, O rugged mountains,
  at the mountain where God chooses[t] to reign,
  where the LORD himself will dwell forever?
17 The chariots of God are tens of thousands
  and thousands of thousands;[u]
  the Lord ⌊has come⌋ from Sinai into his sanctuary.
18 When you ascended on high,
  you led captives[v] in your train;
  you received gifts from men,[w]
  even from[d] the rebellious—
  that you,[e] O LORD God, might dwell there.

19 Praise be to the Lord, to God our Savior,
  who daily bears our burdens.   *Selah*
20 Our God is a God who saves;
  from the Sovereign LORD comes escape from death.

21 Surely God will crush the heads of his enemies,
  the hairy crowns of those who go on in their sins.

a6 Or *The desolate in a homeland*   b13 Or *saddlebags*   c14 Hebrew *Shaddai*   d18 Or *gifts for men, / even*
e18 Or *they*

68:6
n Ac 12:6
o Ps 107:34

68:7
p Ex 13:21

68:9
q Dt 11:11

68:10
r Ps 74:19

68:14
s Jos 10:10

68:16
t Dt 12:5

68:17
u Dt 33:2

68:18
v Jdg 5:12
w Eph 4:8*

68:8 Mount Sinai had a prominent role in Israelite history. It was at Mount Sinai that God met Moses and commissioned him to lead Israel out of Egypt (Exodus 3:1–10). It was to Mount Sinai that the nation of Israel returned and received God's laws (Exodus 19:1–3), and God's presence made the entire mountain tremble (Exodus 19:18). This sacred mountain was a constant reminder of God's words and promises.

68:13 The dove is a symbol of God's beloved Israel, who is so protected and blessed that it has taken silver and gold from its enemies, even though it stayed in camp.

68:15, 16 Bashan, the land northeast of Israel, was the home of mighty mountains, including Mount Hermon, the tallest and most awesome mountain in the region. God's choice of Mount Zion, a foothill by comparison, for the site of the temple led the psalm writer to poetically describe the envy of the mountains of Bashan.

68:17 This psalm celebrates the final stages of a journey that began at Mount Sinai with the construction of the ark of the covenant and finally ended at Mount Zion (site of the sanctuary), the chosen dwelling place of God among his people. It may describe the moving of the ark of the covenant into Jerusalem.

68:18 This verse, quoted in Ephesians 4:8, is applied to the ministry of the ascended Christ. It celebrates his victory over evil. It assures all of us who believe in Christ that by trusting him, we can overcome evil.

68:19–21 God sets his people free and crushes his enemies. Salvation is freedom from sin and death. Those who refuse to turn to God will be crushed by sin and death. They will be trapped by the sin they loved and destroyed by the death they feared. How much better it will be for those who love God and fear the consequences of sin.

68:22
x Nu 21:33

22 The Lord says, "I will bring them from Bashan;
  I will bring them from the depths of the sea,*x*

68:23
y Ps 58:10
z 1Ki 21:19

23 that you may plunge your feet in the blood of your foes,*y*
  while the tongues of your dogs*z* have their share."

24 Your procession has come into view, O God,
  the procession of my God and King into the sanctuary.

68:25
a 1Ch 13:8

25 In front are the singers, after them the musicians;
  with them are the maidens playing tambourines.*a*

68:26
b Isa 48:1

26 Praise God in the great congregation;
  praise the LORD in the assembly of Israel.*b*

68:27
c 1Sa 9:21

27 There is the little tribe*c* of Benjamin, leading them,
  there the great throng of Judah's princes,
  and there the princes of Zebulun and of Naphtali.

28 Summon your power, O God*a*;
  show us your strength, O God, as you have done before.

68:29
d Ps 72:10

29 Because of your temple at Jerusalem
  kings will bring you gifts.*d*

68:30
e Ps 22:12

30 Rebuke the beast among the reeds,
  the herd of bulls*e* among the calves of the nations.
  Humbled, may it bring bars of silver.
  Scatter the nations who delight in war.

68:31
f Isa 45:14

31 Envoys will come from Egypt;*f*
  Cush*b* will submit herself to God.

32 Sing to God, O kingdoms of the earth,
  sing praise to the Lord,   *Selah*

68:33
g Ps 18:10

33 to him who rides*g* the ancient skies above,
  who thunders with mighty voice.

68:34
h Ps 29:1

34 Proclaim the power*h* of God,
  whose majesty is over Israel,
  whose power is in the skies.

35 You are awesome, O God, in your sanctuary;
  the God of Israel gives power and strength to his people.

Praise be to God!

Theme: A cry of distress in a sea of trouble. We may have to suffer severely for our
devotion to God, but that should cause us to look forward with joy to the day when evil
and injustice will be gone forever.
Author: David

69

For the director of music. To ⌊the tune of⌋ "Lilies." Of David.

1 Save me, O God,
  for the waters have come up to my neck.

69:2
i Ps 40:2

2 I sink in the miry depths,*i*
  where there is no foothold.
  I have come into the deep waters;
  the floods engulf me.

a 28 Many Hebrew manuscripts, Septuagint and Syriac; most Hebrew manuscripts *Your God has summoned power
for you*   *b 31* That is, the upper Nile region

68:34, 35 When we consider all God has done for us, we
should feel an overwhelming sense of awe as we kneel before
the Lord in his sanctuary. Nature surrounds us with countless
signs of God's wonderful power. His unlimited power and
unspeakable majesty leave us breathless in his presence. How
fortunate we are that God cares for us.

69:1ff This is one of the most quoted psalms in the New Testament, and it is often applied to the ministry and suffering of
Jesus. Verse 4, like John 15:25, speaks of Jesus' many

enemies. The experience of being scorned by his brothers
(69:8) is expressed in John 7:5. Verse 9 portrays David's zeal
for God; Christ showed great zeal when he threw the money
changers out of the temple (John 2:14–17). Paul quoted part
of 69:9 in Romans 15:3. Christ's great suffering is portrayed
in 69:20, 21 (Matthew 27:24; Mark 15:23; Luke 23:36; John
19:28–30). Verses 22 through 28 are quoted in Romans 11:9,
10; and Peter applied 69:25 to Judas (Acts 1:20).

3 I am worn out calling for help;[j]
　　my throat is parched.
My eyes fail,[k]
　　looking for my God.
4 Those who hate me without reason[l]
　　outnumber the hairs of my head;
many are my enemies without cause,[m]
　　those who seek to destroy me.
I am forced to restore
　　what I did not steal.

5 You know my folly, O God;
　　my guilt is not hidden from you.

6 May those who hope in you
　　not be disgraced because of me,
　　O Lord, the LORD Almighty;
may those who seek you
　　not be put to shame because of me,
　　O God of Israel.
7 For I endure scorn for your sake,
　　and shame covers my face.
8 I am a stranger to my brothers,
　　an alien to my own mother's sons;
9 for zeal for your house consumes me,[n]
　　and the insults of those who insult you fall on me.
10 When I weep and fast,[o]
　　I must endure scorn;
11 when I put on sackcloth,
　　people make sport of me.
12 Those who sit at the gate mock me,
　　and I am the song of the drunkards.[p]

13 But I pray to you, O LORD,
　　in the time of your favor;[q]
in your great love, O God,
　　answer me with your sure salvation.
14 Rescue me from the mire,
　　do not let me sink;
deliver me from those who hate me,
　　from the deep waters.[r]
15 Do not let the floodwaters engulf me
　　or the depths swallow me up[s]
　　or the pit close its mouth over me.
16 Answer me, O LORD, out of the goodness of your love;
　　in your great mercy turn to me.
17 Do not hide your face[t] from your servant;
　　answer me quickly, for I am in trouble.
18 Come near and rescue me;
　　redeem me because of my foes.

19 You know how I am scorned,[u] disgraced and shamed;
　　all my enemies are before you.

69:3
[j] Ps 6:6
[k] Ps 119:82;
Isa 38:14

69:4
[l] Jn 15:25*
[m] Ps 35:19

69:9
[n] Jn 2:17*

69:10
[o] Ps 35:13

69:12
[p] Job 30:9

69:13
[q] Isa 49:8

69:14
[r] Ps 144:7

69:15
[s] Nu 16:33

69:17
[t] Ps 27:9

69:19
[u] Ps 22:6

69:3 David cried out until he was physically exhausted, with a parched throat and blurred vision. Yet he still trusted God to save him. When devastated by death or tragedy, we need not collapse or despair because we can turn to God and ask him to save us and help us. The tears will still come, but we will not be crying in vain.

69:13 What problems David faced! He was scoffed at, mocked, insulted, humiliated, and made the object of citywide gossip. But still he prayed. When we are completely beaten down, we are tempted to turn from God, give up, and quit trusting him. When your situation seems hopeless, determine that no matter how bad things become you will continue to pray. God will hear your prayer, and he will rescue you. When others reject us, we need God most. Don't turn from your most faithful friend.

69:20
v Job 16:2
w Isa 63:5

20 Scorn has broken my heart
    and has left me helpless;
I looked for sympathy, but there was none,
    for comforters,v but I found none. w

69:21
x Jn 19:28-30

21 They put gall in my food
    and gave me vinegar for my thirst. x

22 May the table set before them become a snare;
    may it become retribution anda a trap.

69:23
y Ro 11:9-10*

23 May their eyes be darkened so they cannot see,
    and their backs be bent forever. y
24 Pour out your wrath on them;
    let your fierce anger overtake them.

69:25
z Mt 23:38

25 May their place be deserted;z
    let there be no one to dwell in their tents.

69:26
a Isa 53:4

26 For they persecute those you wound
    and talk about the pain of those you hurt.a
27 Charge them with crime upon crime;
    do not let them share in your salvation.

69:28
b Ex 32:32-33;
Php 4:3

28 May they be blotted out of the book of lifeb
    and not be listed with the righteous.

29 I am in pain and distress;
    may your salvation, O God, protect me.

69:30
c Ps 28:7

30 I will praise God's name in songc
    and glorify him with thanksgiving.

69:31
d Ps 50:9-13

31 This will please the LORD more than an ox,
    more than a bull with its horns and hoofs. d

69:32
e Ps 34:2
f Ps 22:26

32 The poor will see and be glade—
    you who seek God, may your hearts live!f
33 The LORD hears the needy
    and does not despise his captive people.

69:34
g Ps 96:11;
Isa 44:23

34 Let heaven and earth praise him,
    the seas and all that move in them,g

69:35
h Ps 51:18;
Isa 44:26

35 for God will save Zion
    and rebuild the cities of Judah. h
Then people will settle there and possess it;

69:36
i Ps 102:28

36   the children of his servants will inherit it,
    and those who love his name will dwell there. i

Theme: An urgent prayer for help. It can be your prayer when you're short on time and long on need.
Author: David

70 For the director of music. Of David. A petition.

1 Hasten, O God, to save me;
    O LORD, come quickly to help me.

70:2
j Ps 35:4
k Ps 35:26

2 May those who seek my lifej
    be put to shame and confusion;
may all who desire my ruin
    be turned back in disgrace. k

a 22 Or snare / and their fellowship become

69:28 The book of life is God's list of those who are in right relationship to him and who remain faithful (1:3; 7:9; 11:7; 34:12; 37:17, 29; 55:22; 75:10; 92:12–14; 140:13). The New Testament use of "book of life" indicates those who will receive eternal life (see Philippians 4:3; Revelation 3:5; 13:8; 20:15).
70:1–5 When others disappoint and threaten us, we feel empty, as though a vital part of ourselves has been stolen. When others break the trust we have placed in them, they also break our spirits. At those empty, broken moments, we must join the writer in begging God to rush to our aid. He alone can fill our lives with his joy (70:4). With the psalm writer we should cry out, "O LORD, do not delay."

3 May those who say to me, "Aha! Aha!"
    turn back because of their shame.
4 But may all who seek you
    rejoice and be glad in you;
may those who love your salvation always say,
    "Let God be exalted!"

5 Yet I am poor and needy;*l*
    come quickly to me, O God.
You are my help and my deliverer;
    O Lᴏʀᴅ, do not delay.

70:5
l Ps 40:17

Theme: God's constant help—from childhood to old age. Our lives are a testimony of what God has done for us.
Author: Anonymous

71

1 In you, O Lᴏʀᴅ, I have taken refuge;
    let me never be put to shame.*m*
2 Rescue me and deliver me in your righteousness;
    turn your ear*n* to me and save me.
3 Be my rock of refuge,
    to which I can always go;
give the command to save me,
    for you are my rock and my fortress.
4 Deliver me, O my God, from the hand of the wicked,*o*
    from the grasp of evil and cruel men.

5 For you have been my hope, O Sovereign Lᴏʀᴅ,
    my confidence*p* since my youth.
6 From birth*q* I have relied on you;
    you brought me forth from my mother's womb.*r*
    I will ever praise*s* you.
7 I have become like a portent*t* to many,
    but you are my strong refuge.*u*
8 My mouth is filled with your praise,
    declaring your splendor*v* all day long.

9 Do not cast me away when I am old;*w*
    do not forsake me when my strength is gone.
10 For my enemies speak against me;
    those who wait to kill me conspire together.
11 They say, "God has forsaken him;
    pursue him and seize him,
    for no one will rescue*x* him."

12 Be not far*y* from me, O God;
    come quickly, O my God, to help*z* me.
13 May my accusers perish in shame;
    may those who want to harm me
    be covered with scorn and disgrace.

14 But as for me, I will always have hope;
    I will praise you more and more.

71:1
m Ps 25:2-3; 31:1

71:2
n Ps 17:6

71:4
o Ps 140:4

71:5
p Jer 17:7

71:6
q Ps 22:10
r Isa 46:3
s Ps 34:1

71:7
t Isa 8:18; 1Co 4:9
u Ps 61:3

71:8
v Ps 35:28

71:9
w ver 18

71:11
x Ps 7:2

71:12
y Ps 35:22
z Ps 70:1

70:4 This short psalm (similar in content to 40:13–17) was David's plea for God to come quickly with his help. Yet even in his moment of panic, he did not forget praise. Praise is important because it helps us remember who God is. Often our prayers are filled with requests for ourselves and others, and we forget to thank God for what he has done and to worship him for who he is. Don't take God for granted and treat him as a vending machine. Even when David was afraid, he praised God.

71:1ff The psalm writer was old and saw his life as a "portent," a solemn sign or testimony to others of all God had done for

him (71:7, 18). Remembering God's lifetime of blessing will help us see the consistency of his grace throughout the years, trust him for the future, and share with others the benefits of following him.

71:14 As we face the sunset years, we recognize that God has been our constant help in the past. As physical powers wane, we need God even more, and we realize he is still our constant help. We must never despair, but keep on expecting his help no matter how severe our limitations. Hope in him helps us to keep going, to keep serving him.

71:15
a Ps 35:28; 40:5

15 My mouth will tell*a* of your righteousness,
    of your salvation all day long,
        though I know not its measure.

71:16
b Ps 106:2

16 I will come and proclaim your mighty acts,*b* O Sovereign LORD;
    I will proclaim your righteousness, yours alone.

71:17
c Ps 26:7

17 Since my youth, O God, you have taught me,
    and to this day I declare your marvelous deeds.*c*
18 Even when I am old and gray,
    do not forsake me, O God,
        till I declare your power to the next generation,
        your might to all who are to come.

71:19
d Ps 57:10
e Ps 35:10

19 Your righteousness reaches to the skies,*d* O God,
    you who have done great things.
        Who, O God, is like you?*e*

71:20
f Ps 60:3
g Hos 6:2

20 Though you have made me see troubles,*f* many and bitter,
    you will restore*g* my life again;
        from the depths of the earth
        you will again bring me up.
21 You will increase my honor
    and comfort me once again.

22 I will praise you with the harp
    for your faithfulness, O my God;
        I will sing praise to you with the lyre,
        O Holy One of Israel.

71:23
h Ps 103:4

23 My lips will shout for joy
    when I sing praise to you—
        I, whom you have redeemed.*h*

71:24
i Ps 35:28

24 My tongue will tell of your righteous acts
    all day long,*i*
        for those who wanted to harm me
        have been put to shame and confusion.

Theme: The perfect king. In this psalm, a king asks God to help his son rule the nation justly and wisely. It looks forward to the endless reign of the Messiah, who alone can rule with perfect justice and whose citizens will enjoy perfect peace.
Author: Solomon

72 Of Solomon.

1 Endow the king with your justice, O God,
    the royal son with your righteousness.

72:2
j Isa 9:7

2 He will*a* judge your people in righteousness,*j*
    your afflicted ones with justice.
3 The mountains will bring prosperity to the people,
    the hills the fruit of righteousness.

72:4
k Isa 11:4

4 He will defend the afflicted among the people
    and save the children of the needy;*k*
        he will crush the oppressor.

5 He will endure*b* as long as the sun,
    as long as the moon, through all generations.

a 2 Or *May he*; similarly in verses 3-11 and 17   *b* 5 Septuagint; Hebrew *You will be feared*

71:18 A person is never too old to serve God, never too old to pray. Though age may stop us from certain physical activities, it need not stifle our desire or limit our opportunities to tell others (especially children) about all we have seen God do in the many years we've lived.

72:1, 2 What qualities do we want most in our leaders? God desires all who rule under him to be righteous and just. Think how the world would change if world leaders would commit themselves to these two qualities. Pray for leaders as you hear about them in the news. Ask God to help them see their need for him; ask God to help them lead with justice and righteousness (see 1 Timothy 2:1, 2).

6 He will be like rain[f] falling on a mown field,
  like showers watering the earth.
7 In his days the righteous will flourish;
  prosperity will abound till the moon is no more.

8 He will rule from sea to sea
  and from the River[a][m] to the ends of the earth.[b][n]
9 The desert tribes will bow before him
  and his enemies will lick the dust.
10 The kings of Tarshish and of distant shores
   will bring tribute to him;
   the kings of Sheba and Seba
   will present him gifts.[o]
11 All kings will bow down to him
   and all nations will serve him.

12 For he will deliver the needy who cry out,
   the afflicted who have no one to help.
13 He will take pity on the weak and the needy
   and save the needy from death.
14 He will rescue them from oppression and violence,
   for precious[p] is their blood in his sight.

15 Long may he live!
   May gold from Sheba be given him.
   May people ever pray for him
   and bless him all day long.
16 Let grain abound throughout the land;
   on the tops of the hills may it sway.
   Let its fruit flourish like Lebanon;
   let it thrive like the grass of the field.
17 May his name endure forever;
   may it continue as long as the sun.[q]

   All nations will be blessed through him,
   and they will call him blessed.[r]

18 Praise be to the LORD God, the God of Israel,[s]
   who alone does marvelous deeds.
19 Praise be to his glorious name forever;
   may the whole earth be filled with his glory.[t]
   Amen and Amen.

20 This concludes the prayers of David son of Jesse.

a8 That is, the Euphrates   b8 Or the end of the land

72:6
f Hos 6:3

72:8
m Ex 23:31
n Zec 9:10

72:10
o 2Ch 9:24

72:14
p Ps 116:15

72:17
q Ps 89:36
r Ge 12:3; Lk 1:48

72:18
s 1Ch 29:10

72:19
t Nu 14:21; Ne 9:5

72:12–14 God cares for the needy, the afflicted, and the weak because they are precious to him. If God feels so strongly about these needy ones and loves them so deeply, how can we ignore their plight? Examine what you are doing to reach out with God's love—are you ignoring their plight or are you helping to meet their needs?

72:17 Solomon, David's son, reigned in Israel's golden age. He built the magnificent temple, and the land rested in peace. This psalm, though written by Solomon, looks beyond Solomon's reign to that of Jesus the Messiah, whose kingdom extends "to the ends of the earth" (72:8) and is greater than any human empire. This will be fulfilled when Christ returns to reign forever (Revelation 11:15). When we anticipate his worldwide rule, it fills our hearts with hope.

72:19, 20 Book II ends with "Amen and Amen," as did Psalm 41, which closed Book I. This last verse does not mean that David wrote this psalm, but that he wrote most of the psalms in Book II.

Book III Psalms 73–89

These psalms celebrate the sovereignty of God, God's hand in history, God's faithfulness, and God's covenant with David. These psalms remind us that our worship should be continual.

Theme: The temporary prosperity of the wicked and the lasting rewards of the righteous. We should live holy lives and trust God for our future rewards.
Author: Asaph, a leader of one of the temple choirs (see 1 Chronicles 25:1)

73 A psalm of Asaph.

¹ Surely God is good to Israel,
  to those who are pure in heart.

² But as for me, my feet had almost slipped;
  I had nearly lost my foothold.

73:3
ᵘPs 37:1

³ For I envied ᵘ the arrogant
  when I saw the prosperity of the wicked.

⁴ They have no struggles;
  their bodies are healthy and strong.ᵃ

73:5
ᵛJob 21:9

⁵ They are free ᵛ from the burdens common to man;
  they are not plagued by human ills.

73:6
ʷPs 109:18

⁶ Therefore pride is their necklace;
  they clothe themselves with violence. ʷ

⁷ From their callous hearts comes iniquityᵇ;
  the evil conceits of their minds know no limits.

73:8
ˣJude 16

⁸ They scoff, and speak with malice;
  in their arroganceˣ they threaten oppression.

⁹ Their mouths lay claim to heaven,
  and their tongues take possession of the earth.

¹⁰ Therefore their people turn to them
  and drink up waters in abundance.ᶜ

¹¹ They say, "How can God know?
  Does the Most High have knowledge?"

¹² This is what the wicked are like—
  always carefree, they increase in wealth.

73:13
ʸJob 34:9
ᶻPs 26:6

¹³ Surely in vainʸ have I kept my heart pure;
  in vain have I washed my hands in innocence.ᶻ

¹⁴ All day long I have been plagued;
  I have been punished every morning.

¹⁵ If I had said, "I will speak thus,"
  I would have betrayed your children.

73:16
ᵃEcc 8:17

¹⁶ When I tried to understandᵃ all this,
  it was oppressive to me

73:17
ᵇPs 77:13
ᶜPs 37:38

¹⁷ till I entered the sanctuaryᵇ of God;
  then I understood their final destiny.ᶜ

73:18
ᵈPs 35:6

¹⁸ Surely you place them on slippery ground;ᵈ
  you cast them down to ruin.

ᵃ4 With a different word division of the Hebrew; Masoretic Text *struggles at their death; / their bodies are healthy*
ᵇ7 Syriac (see also Septuagint); Hebrew *Their eyes bulge with fat*   ᶜ10 The meaning of the Hebrew for this verse is uncertain.

73:1ff Asaph was the leader of one of David's Levitical choirs. He collected Psalms 73—83 but may not have written all of them. In this psalm, Asaph explains that until he entered God's sanctuary, he could not understand the justice in allowing the wicked to thrive while the righteous endured hardship. But when he saw that one day justice would be done, he acknowledged God's wisdom.

73:1-20 Two strong themes wind their way through these verses: (1) the wicked prosper, leaving faithful people wondering why they bother to be good, and (2) the wealth of the wicked looks so inviting that faithful people may wish they could trade places. But these two themes come to unexpected ends, for the wealth of the wicked suddenly loses its power at death and the rewards for the good suddenly take on eternal value. What seemed like wealth is now waste, and what seemed worthless now lasts forever. Don't wish you could trade places with evil people to get their wealth. One day they will wish they could trade places with you and have your eternal wealth.

19 How suddenly are they destroyed,
    completely swept away by terrors!
20 As a dream[e] when one awakes,
    so when you arise, O Lord,
    you will despise them as fantasies.

21 When my heart was grieved
    and my spirit embittered,
22 I was senseless and ignorant;
    I was a brute beast before you.

23 Yet I am always with you;
    you hold me by my right hand.
24 You guide[f] me with your counsel,[g]
    and afterward you will take me into glory.
25 Whom have I in heaven but you?
    And earth has nothing I desire besides you.[h]
26 My flesh and my heart[i] may fail,
    but God is the strength of my heart
    and my portion forever.

27 Those who are far from you will perish;[j]
    you destroy all who are unfaithful to you.
28 But as for me, it is good to be near God.[k]
    I have made the Sovereign LORD my refuge;
    I will tell of all your deeds.

73:20 [e] Job 20:8

73:24 [f] Ps 48:14 [g] Ps 32:8

73:25 [h] Php 3:8

73:26 [i] Ps 84:2

73:27 [j] Ps 119:155

73:28 [k] Heb 10:22

Theme: A plea for God to help his people defend his cause and remember his promises. When we feel devastated or forgotten, we can ask God for help, knowing that he hears.
Author: Asaph (or one of his descendants, since many believe this to have been written after Jerusalem's fall in 586 B.C.)

74 A maskil[a] of Asaph.

1 Why have you rejected us forever,[l] O God?
    Why does your anger smolder against the sheep of your pasture?[m]
2 Remember the people you purchased of old,
    the tribe of your inheritance, whom you redeemed—
    Mount Zion, where you dwelt.[n]
3 Turn your steps toward these everlasting ruins,
    all this destruction the enemy has brought on the sanctuary.

4 Your foes roared[o] in the place where you met with us;
    they set up their standards as signs.
5 They behaved like men wielding axes
    to cut through a thicket of trees.[p]
6 They smashed all the carved paneling
    with their axes and hatchets.
7 They burned your sanctuary to the ground;
    they defiled the dwelling place of your Name.

74:1 [l] Dt 29:20 [m] Ps 95:7

74:2 [n] Ps 68:16

74:4 [o] La 2:7

74:5 [p] Jer 46:22

[a] Title: Probably a literary or musical term

73:20 Asaph realized that the rich who put their hope, joy, and confidence in their wealth live in a dreamworld. A dream exists only in the mind of the dreamer. Don't let your life's goals be so unreal that you awaken too late and miss the reality of God's truth. Happiness and hope can be a reality, but only when they are based on God, not on riches. Because reality is in God, we should get as close to him as we can in order to be realistic about life.

73:23, 24 Asaph declares his confidence in God's presence and guidance. From birth to death God has us continually in his grip.

But far more, we have the hope of the resurrection. Though our courage and strength may fail, we know that one day we will be raised to life to serve him forever. He is our security, and we must cling to him.

74:1, 2 God's anger against Israel had grown hot during the many years of their sin and idolatry. His patience endured for generations, but at last it was set aside for judgment. If you fall into sin and quickly seek God's forgiveness, his mercy may come quickly and his anger may leave quickly. If you persist in sinning against him, don't be surprised when his patience runs out.

74:8
q Ps 83:4

8 They said in their hearts, "We will crush*q* them completely!"
    They burned every place where God was worshiped in the land.
9 We are given no miraculous signs;
    no prophets are left,
    and none of us knows how long this will be.

10 How long will the enemy mock you, O God?
    Will the foe revile your name forever?

74:11
r La 2:3

11 Why do you hold back your hand, your right hand?*r*
    Take it from the folds of your garment and destroy them!

74:12
s Ps 44:4

12 But you, O God, are my king*s* from of old;
    you bring salvation upon the earth.

74:13
t Ex 14:21
u Isa 51:9

13 It was you who split open the sea*t* by your power;
    you broke the heads of the monster*u* in the waters.
14 It was you who crushed the heads of Leviathan
    and gave him as food to the creatures of the desert.

74:15
v Ex 17:6; Nu 20:11
w Jos 3:13

15 It was you who opened up springs*v* and streams;
    you dried up*w* the ever flowing rivers.
16 The day is yours, and yours also the night;
    you established the sun and moon.

74:17
x Ge 8:22

17 It was you who set all the boundaries of the earth;
    you made both summer and winter.*x*

74:18
y Ps 39:8

18 Remember how the enemy has mocked you, O LORD,
    how foolish people*y* have reviled your name.

74:19
z Ps 9:18

19 Do not hand over the life of your dove to wild beasts;
    do not forget the lives of your afflicted*z* people forever.

74:20
a Ge 17:7;
Ps 106:45

20 Have regard for your covenant,*a*
    because haunts of violence fill the dark places of the land.

74:21
b Ps 35:10

21 Do not let the oppressed retreat in disgrace;
    may the poor and needy*b* praise your name.

22 Rise up, O God, and defend your cause;
    remember how fools mock you all day long.
23 Do not ignore the clamor of your adversaries,*c*
    the uproar of your enemies, which rises continually.

74:23
c Ps 65:7

Theme: Because God is the final judge, the tables will be turned upon the wicked. When arrogant people threaten our security, we can be confident that God will ultimately overrule and destroy them.
Author: Asaph

75

For the director of music. ⌐To the tune of⌐ "Do Not Destroy." A psalm of Asaph. A song.

75:1
d Ps 145:18

1 We give thanks to you, O God,
    we give thanks, for your Name is near;*d*
    men tell of your wonderful deeds.

74:8 When enemy armies defeated Israel, they sacked and burned Jerusalem, trying to wipe out every trace of God. This has often been the response of people who hate God. Today many are trying to erase God from traditions in our public life and from subjects taught in our schools. Do what you can to maintain a Christian influence, but don't become discouraged when others appear to make great strides in eliminating all traces of God—they cannot eliminate his presence among believers.

74:10–18 From our perspective, God sometimes seems slow to intervene on our behalf. But what might appear slow to us is good timing from God's perspective. It's easy to become impatient while waiting for God to act, but we must never give up on him. When God is silent and you are in deep anguish, follow the method in this psalm. Review the great acts of God

throughout Biblical history; then review what he has done for you. This will remind you that God is at work, not only in history, but also in your life today.

74:13, 14 "The monster in the waters" recalls the Lord's words to Egypt (Ezekiel 32:2ff). "Leviathan" refers to the Canaanite seven-headed serpent, Lotan. In their legends, Baal defeated these creatures. This psalm praised God for doing in reality what the Canaanite gods could only do in legends.

2 You say, "I choose the appointed time;
  it is I who judge uprightly.
3 When the earth and all its people quake,
  it is I who hold its pillars firm.

Selah

4 To the arrogant I say, 'Boast no more,'
  and to the wicked, 'Do not lift up your horns.*e*
5 Do not lift your horns against heaven;
  do not speak with outstretched neck.'"

6 No one from the east or the west
  or from the desert can exalt a man.
7 But it is God who judges:*f*
  He brings one down, he exalts another.*g*
8 In the hand of the LORD is a cup
  full of foaming wine mixed*h* with spices;
  he pours it out, and all the wicked of the earth
  drink it down to its very dregs.*i*

9 As for me, I will declare this forever;
  I will sing praise to the God of Jacob.
10 I will cut off the horns of all the wicked,
  but the horns of the righteous will be lifted up.*j*

75:4
e Zec 1:21

75:7
f Ps 50:6
g 1Sa 2:7; Da 2:21

75:8
h Pr 23:30
i Jer 25:15

75:10
j 148:14

Theme: A call for God to punish evildoers. Even people's angry revolts will be used by God to bring glory to himself.
Author: Asaph

76

For the director of music. With stringed instruments. A psalm of Asaph. A song.

1 In Judah God is known;
  his name is great in Israel.
2 His tent is in Salem,
  his dwelling place in Zion.
3 There he broke the flashing arrows,
  the shields and the swords, the weapons of war.*k*

Selah

4 You are resplendent with light,
  more majestic than mountains rich with game.
5 Valiant men lie plundered,
  they sleep their last sleep;
  not one of the warriors
  can lift his hands.
6 At your rebuke, O God of Jacob,
  both horse and chariot*l* lie still.
7 You alone are to be feared.
  Who can stand before you when you are angry?*m*
8 From heaven you pronounced judgment,
  and the land feared*n* and was quiet—

76:3
k Ps 46:9

76:6
l Ex 15:1

76:7
m Na 1:6

76:8
n 2Ch 20:29-30

75:2 God will act when he is ready. Children have difficulty grasping the concept of time. "It's not time yet" is not a reason they easily understand because they only comprehend the present. As limited human beings, we can't understand God's perspective about time. We want everything now, unaware that God's timing is better. When God is ready, he will do what needs to be done, not what we would like him to do. We may be as impatient as children, but we must not doubt the wisdom of God's timing. Wait for God to reveal his plan. Don't take matters into your own hands.

75:8 The cup of wine represents God's judgment. The judgment of God is coming against the wicked. God will pour out his fury on his enemies, and they will be forced to drink it. Drinking the cup of God's judgment is a picture used frequently in Scripture

(Isaiah 51:17, 22; Jeremiah 25:15; 49:12; Habakkuk 2:16; Revelation 14:10; 16:19; 18:6). It gives the impression of taking a dose of one's own medicine. To drink it down to the dregs means to be punished completely.

75:10 God will have the last word. He will decide the final outcome, settling all matters that concern both the wicked and the godly. The former will eventually experience his judgment; the latter will experience his faithful love. No matter how dark the days you face, make it your continual practice to acknowledge God's sovereignty over your world. Tell him regularly how grateful you are that he has the final word.

76:1ff This psalm praises God for his awesome power. It was most likely written to celebrate the defeat of Sennacherib's army after it invaded Judah (see 2 Kings 18:13–19, 37).

76:9
o Ps 9:8

9 when you, O God, rose up to judge,o
　　to save all the afflicted of the land.
10 Surely your wrath against men brings you praise,
　　and the survivors of your wrath are restrained.a

Selah

76:11
p Ps 68:29

11 Make vows to the LORD your God and fulfill them;
　　let all the neighboring lands
　　bring giftsp to the One to be feared.
12 He breaks the spirit of rulers;
　　he is feared by the kings of the earth.

Theme: We are comforted through the hard times by remembering God's help in the past. Recalling God's miracles and previous works can give us courage to continue.
Author: Asaph

77

For the director of music. For Jeduthun. Of Asaph. A psalm.

77:1
q Ps 3:4

1 I cried out to Godq for help;
　　I cried out to God to hear me.

77:2
r Ps 50:15; Isa 26:9,
16

2 When I was in distress,r I sought the Lord;
　　at night I stretched out untiring hands
　　and my soul refused to be comforted.

3 I remembered you, O God, and I groaned;
　　I mused, and my spirit grew faint.
4 You kept my eyes from closing;
　　I was too troubled to speak.

Selah

77:5
s Dt 32:7; Ps 143:5;
Isa 51:9

5 I thought about the former days,s
　　the years of long ago;
6 I remembered my songs in the night.
　　My heart mused and my spirit inquired:

77:7
t Ps 85:1

7 "Will the Lord reject forever?
　　Will he never show his favort again?
8 Has his unfailing love vanished forever?
　　Has his promise failed for all time?

77:9
u Isa 49:15

9 Has God forgotten to be merciful?
　　Has he in anger withheld his compassion?u"

Selah

10 Then I thought, "To this I will appeal:
　　the years of the right hand of the Most High."
11 I will remember the deeds of the LORD;
　　yes, I will remember your miracles of long ago.
12 I will meditate on all your works
　　and consider all your mighty deeds.

a 10 Or Surely the wrath of men brings you praise, / and with the remainder of wrath you arm yourself

---

76:10 How can wrath bring praise to God? Hostility to God and his people gives God the opportunity to do great deeds. For example, the Pharaoh of Egypt refused to free the Hebrew slaves (Exodus 5:1, 2) and thus allowed God to work mighty miracles for his people (Exodus 11:9). God turns the tables on evildoers and brings glory to himself from the foolishness of those who deny him or revolt against him. God's wrath expressed in judgment brings praise from those who have been delivered.

76:11, 12 This psalm closes with an invitation to the reader or listener. Having stated the futility of resisting God, the writer shifts to the alternatives. These verses speak of more than surrender to God; they encourage us to actively move toward God, making commitments (vows) to him and carrying them out. What was the last promise you made to God? How much progress have you made in fulfilling it?

77:1ff Asaph cried out to God for courage during a time of deep

distress. The source of Asaph's distress (77:4) was his doubt (77:7–9). He pled, "I cried out to God for help." But in 77:13–20, the "I" is gone. As Asaph expressed his requests to God, his focus changed from thinking of himself to worshiping God: "You are the God who performs miracles" (77:14). Only after he put aside his doubts about God's holiness and care for him (77:13, 14) did he eliminate his distress (77:20). As we pray to God, he shifts our focus from ourselves to him.

77:11, 12 Memories of God's miracles and faithfulness sustained Israel through their difficulties. They knew that God was capable and trustworthy. When you meet new trials, review how good God has been to you, and this will strengthen your faith.

13 Your ways, O God, are holy.
     What god is so great as our God?*v*

14 You are the God who performs miracles;
     you display your power among the peoples.

15 With your mighty arm you redeemed your people,*w*
     the descendants of Jacob and Joseph.   **Selah**

16 The waters*x* saw you, O God,
     the waters saw you and writhed;
     the very depths were convulsed.

17 The clouds poured down water,
     the skies resounded with thunder;
     your arrows flashed back and forth.

18 Your thunder was heard in the whirlwind,
     your lightning lit up the world;
     the earth trembled and quaked.

19 Your path led through the sea,*y*
     your way through the mighty waters,
     though your footprints were not seen.

20 You led your people*z* like a flock*a*
     by the hand of Moses and Aaron.

77:13
v Ex 15:11

77:15
w Ex 6:6; Dt 9:29

77:16
x Ex 14:21, 28

77:19
y Hab 3:15

77:20
z Ex 13:21
a Isa 63:11

Theme: Lessons from history. Asaph retells the history of the Jewish nation from the time of slavery in Egypt to David's reign. It was told over and over to each generation so they would not forget God and make the same mistakes as their ancestors.
Author: Asaph

78 A *maskil*ª of Asaph.

1 O my people, hear my teaching;*b*
     listen to the words of my mouth.

2 I will open my mouth in parables,*c*
     I will utter hidden things, things from of old—

3 what we have heard and known,
     what our fathers have told us.*d*

4 We will not hide them from their children;
     we will tell the next generation
   the praiseworthy deeds of the LORD,
     his power, and the wonders he has done.

5 He decreed statutes for Jacob*e*
     and established the law in Israel,
   which he commanded our forefathers
     to teach their children,

6 so the next generation would know them,
     even the children yet to be born,*f*
     and they in turn would tell their children.

78:1
b Isa 51:4

78:2
c Mt 13:35*

78:3
d Ps 44:1

78:5
e Ps 147:19

78:6
f Ps 102:18

ªTitle: Probably a literary or musical term

77:16–20 These verses refer to the miraculous parting of the Red Sea. This great event is mentioned many times in the Old Testament (Exodus 14:21, 22; Joshua 24:6; Nehemiah 9:9; Psalm 74:13; 106:9; 136:13–15). The story of this incredible miracle was handed down from generation to generation, continually reminding the Israelites of God's power, protection, and love.

78:1ff The people of Israel rebelled and were not faithful to God (78:8); forgot about the wonders God had done (78:11, 12); put God to the test by making demands from him (78:18);

lied to him and tried to flatter him (78:36); and continued to turn away from him even after he did great works on their behalf (78:42–56). God recorded these painful and shameful truths in his Word so that we can avoid the same errors. In 1 Corinthians 10:5–12, Paul used this classic story of Israel's unfaithfulness to warn the early Christians to be faithful.

78:5 God commanded that the stories of his mighty acts in Israel's history and his laws be passed on from parents to children. This shows the purpose and importance of religious education—to help each generation obey God and set their hope on him. It is important to keep children from repeating the same mistakes as their ancestors. What are you doing to pass on the history of God's work to the next generation?

⁷ Then they would put their trust in God
　　and would not forget his deeds
　　but would keep his commands.

78:8
g Ex 32:9

⁸ They would not be like their forefathers—
　　a stubborn*g* and rebellious generation,
　　whose hearts were not loyal to God,
　　whose spirits were not faithful to him.

⁹ The men of Ephraim, though armed with bows,
　　turned back on the day of battle;
¹⁰ they did not keep God's covenant
　　and refused to live by his law.

78:11
h Ps 106:13

¹¹ They forgot what he had done,*h*
　　the wonders he had shown them.

78:12
i Nu 13:22

¹² He did miracles in the sight of their fathers
　　in the land of Egypt, in the region of Zoan.*i*

78:13
j Ex 14:21
k Ex 15:8

¹³ He divided the sea*j* and led them through;
　　he made the water stand firm like a wall.*k*

78:14
l Ex 13:21

¹⁴ He guided them with the cloud by day
　　and with light from the fire all night.*l*

78:15
m Nu 20:11

¹⁵ He split the rocks*m* in the desert
　　and gave them water as abundant as the seas;
¹⁶ he brought streams out of a rocky crag
　　and made water flow down like rivers.

78:17
n Heb 3:16

¹⁷ But they continued to sin*n* against him,
　　rebelling in the desert against the Most High.
¹⁸ They willfully put God to the test
　　by demanding the food they craved.
¹⁹ They spoke against God, saying,
　　"Can God spread a table in the desert?

78:20
o Nu 20:11

²⁰ When he struck the rock, water gushed out,*o*
　　and streams flowed abundantly.
　　But can he also give us food?
　　Can he supply meat for his people?"

78:21
p Nu 11:1

²¹ When the LORD heard them, he was very angry;
　　his fire broke out*p* against Jacob,
　　and his wrath rose against Israel,

78:22
q Heb 3:19

²² for they did not believe in God
　　or trust*q* in his deliverance.

²³ Yet he gave a command to the skies above
　　and opened the doors of the heavens;

78:24
r Jn 6:31*

²⁴ he rained down manna*r* for the people to eat,
　　he gave them the grain of heaven.
²⁵ Men ate the bread of angels;
　　he sent them all the food they could eat.

78:26
s Nu 11:31

²⁶ He let loose the east wind*s* from the heavens
　　and led forth the south wind by his power.
²⁷ He rained meat down on them like dust,
　　flying birds like sand on the seashore.
²⁸ He made them come down inside their camp,
　　all around their tents.

78:29
t Nu 11:20

²⁹ They ate till they had more than enough,*t*
　　for he had given them what they craved.

78:9, 10 Ephraim was the most prominent tribe of Israel from the days of Moses to Saul's time. The tabernacle was set up in its territory. There is no other Biblical record of Ephraim's soldiers turning back from battle, so this is probably a metaphor referring to Ephraim's failure to provide strong leadership during those years. When David became king, the tribe of Judah gained promi-nence. Because of David's faith and obedience, God chose Jerusalem in Judah to be the place for the new temple and rejected Ephraim (78:67). This caused tension between the two tribes. This psalm may have been written because of that tension in order to demonstrate once again why God chose Judah. God works through those who are faithful to him.

30 But before they turned from the food they craved,
    even while it was still in their mouths,
31 God's anger rose against them;
    he put to death the sturdiest among them,
    cutting down the young men of Israel.

32 In spite of all this, they kept on sinning;
    in spite of his wonders, they did not believe.
33 So he ended their days in futility[u]
    and their years in terror.
34 Whenever God slew them, they would seek[v] him;
    they eagerly turned to him again.
35 They remembered that God was their Rock,
    that God Most High was their Redeemer.
36 But then they would flatter him with their mouths,[w]
    lying to him with their tongues;
37 their hearts were not loyal to him,
    they were not faithful to his covenant.
38 Yet he was merciful;
    he forgave[x] their iniquities
    and did not destroy them.
    Time after time he restrained his anger
    and did not stir up his full wrath.
39 He remembered that they were but flesh,[y]
    a passing breeze[z] that does not return.

40 How often they rebelled against him in the desert[a]
    and grieved him in the wasteland!
41 Again and again they put God to the test;
    they vexed the Holy One of Israel.
42 They did not remember his power—
    the day he redeemed them from the oppressor,
43 the day he displayed his miraculous signs in Egypt,
    his wonders in the region of Zoan.
44 He turned their rivers to blood;[b]
    they could not drink from their streams.
45 He sent swarms of flies[c] that devoured them,
    and frogs[d] that devastated them.
46 He gave their crops to the grasshopper,
    their produce to the locust.
47 He destroyed their vines with hail[e]
    and their sycamore-figs with sleet.
48 He gave over their cattle to the hail,
    their livestock to bolts of lightning.
49 He unleashed against them his hot anger,
    his wrath, indignation and hostility—
    a band of destroying angels.
50 He prepared a path for his anger;
    he did not spare them from death
    but gave them over to the plague.
51 He struck down all the firstborn of Egypt,[f]
    the firstfruits of manhood in the tents of Ham.
52 But he brought his people out like a flock;[g]
    he led them like sheep through the desert.

78:33 [u]Nu 14:29, 35

78:34 [v]Hos 5:15

78:36 [w]Eze 33:31

78:38 [x]Isa 48:10

78:39 [y]Ps 103:14
[z]Job 7:7

78:40 [a]Ps 95:8

78:44 [b]Ex 7:20-21

78:45 [c]Ex 8:24;
Ps 105:31
[d]Ex 8:2, 6

78:47 [e]Ex 9:23

78:51 [f]Ex 12:29

78:52 [g]Ps 77:20

78:36, 37 Over and over the children of Israel claimed that they would follow God, but then they turned away from him. The problem was that they made commitments to God with their mouths and not with their hearts; thus their repentance was empty. Talk is cheap. God wants our conduct to back up our spiritual claims and promises.

78:51 This was the Passover described in Exodus 12:29, 30 when all the firstborn of the Egyptians were slain. The "tents of Ham" refers to Noah's second son, who was the ancestor of the Egyptians. Ham is sometimes used as a synonym for Egypt.

78:53
h Ex 14:28

53 He guided them safely, so they were unafraid;
　　but the sea engulfed*h* their enemies.

78:54
i Ps 44:3

54 Thus he brought them to the border of his holy land,
　　to the hill country his right hand*i* had taken.

78:55
i Ps 44:2

55 He drove out nations*i* before them
　　and allotted their lands to them as an inheritance;
　　he settled the tribes of Israel in their homes.

56 But they put God to the test
　　and rebelled against the Most High;
　　they did not keep his statutes.

78:57
k Eze 20:27

57 Like their fathers*k* they were disloyal and faithless,
　　as unreliable as a faulty bow.

58 They angered him with their high places;
　　they aroused his jealousy with their idols.

59 When God heard them, he was very angry;
　　he rejected Israel completely.

60 He abandoned the tabernacle of Shiloh,
　　the tent he had set up among men.

61 He sent ⌊the ark of⌋ his might into captivity,
　　his splendor into the hands of the enemy.

62 He gave his people over to the sword;
　　he was very angry with his inheritance.

78:63
l Jer 7:34

63 Fire consumed their young men,
　　and their maidens had no wedding songs;*l*

78:64
m 1Sa 22:18

64 their priests were put to the sword,*m*
　　and their widows could not weep.

65 Then the Lord awoke as from sleep,
　　as a man wakes from the stupor of wine.

78:66
n 1Sa 5:6

66 He beat back his enemies;
　　he put them to everlasting shame.*n*

67 Then he rejected the tents of Joseph,
　　he did not choose the tribe of Ephraim;

78:68
o Ps 87:2

68 but he chose the tribe of Judah,
　　Mount Zion,*o* which he loved.

69 He built his sanctuary like the heights,
　　like the earth that he established forever.

78:70
p 1Sa 16:1

70 He chose David*p* his servant
　　and took him from the sheep pens;

78:71
q 2Sa 5:2

71 from tending the sheep he brought him
　　to be the shepherd*q* of his people Jacob,
　　of Israel his inheritance.

78:72
r 1Ki 9:4

72 And David shepherded them with integrity of heart;*r*
　　with skillful hands he led them.

78:58 Can God be jealous? According to Scripture, yes (see Deuteronomy 4:24; 5:9; Nahum 1:2). Like everything else about God, his jealousy is perfect. In this case, the offense caused by the ungratefulness and unfaithfulness of his people provoked a just and holy response from God. The shock conveyed in these verses comes not from God's jealousy but from the fact that God, though justified in passing absolute judgment, persistently seasons his responses with grace and patience. God's jealousy over you represents an honor worthy of your deepest gratitude.

78:71, 72 Although David was occupying the throne of Israel when this psalm was written, he is called a shepherd and not a king. Shepherding, a common profession in Biblical times, was a highly responsible job. The flocks were completely dependent upon shepherds for guidance, provision, and protection. David had spent his early years as a shepherd (1 Samuel 16:10, 11). This was a training ground for the future responsibilities God had in store for him. When he was ready, God took him from caring for sheep to caring for Israel, God's people. Don't treat your present situation lightly or irresponsibly; it may be God's training ground for your future.

Theme: When outraged by injustice, cry out to God, not against him. In times of disaster, our mood may be anger, but our trust must remain in God.
Author: Asaph (or one of his descendants), probably written after the Babylonians had leveled Jerusalem (see 2 Kings 25)

79

A psalm of Asaph.

1 O God, the nations have invaded your inheritance;[s]
    they have defiled your holy temple,
    they have reduced Jerusalem to rubble.
2 They have given the dead bodies of your servants
    as food to the birds of the air,
    the flesh of your saints to the beasts of the earth.[t]
3 They have poured out blood like water
    all around Jerusalem,
    and there is no one to bury the dead.
4 We are objects of reproach to our neighbors,
    of scorn and derision to those around us.

5 How long,[u] O Lord? Will you be angry[v] forever?
    How long will your jealousy burn like fire?[w]
6 Pour out your wrath on the nations
    that do not acknowledge[x] you,
  on the kingdoms
    that do not call on your name;
7 for they have devoured Jacob
    and destroyed his homeland.
8 Do not hold against us the sins of the fathers;[y]
    may your mercy come quickly to meet us,
    for we are in desperate need.

9 Help us, O God our Savior,
    for the glory of your name;
  deliver us and forgive our sins
    for your name's sake.[z]
10 Why should the nations say,
    "Where is their God?"[a]
Before our eyes, make known among the nations
    that you avenge the outpoured blood of your servants.
11 May the groans of the prisoners come before you;
    by the strength of your arm
    preserve those condemned to die.

12 Pay back into the laps[b] of our neighbors seven times[c]
    the reproach they have hurled at you, O Lord.
13 Then we your people, the sheep of your pasture,[d]
    will praise you forever;
  from generation to generation
    we will recount your praise.

79:1
[s] Ps 74:2

79:2
[t] Jer 7:33

79:5
[u] Ps 74:10
[v] Ps 74:1
[w] Zep 3:8

79:6
[x] Jer 10:25; 2Th 1:8

79:8
[y] Isa 64:9

79:9
[z] Jer 14:7

79:10
[a] Ps 42:10

79:12
[b] Isa 65:6; Jer 32:18
[c] Ge 4:15

79:13
[d] Ps 74:1; 95:7

79:6 According to the Old Testament, God's wrath and judgment often fell on entire nations because of the sins of people within those nations. Here Asaph pled for judgment on kingdoms that refused to acknowledge God's authority.

Ironically, Asaph's own nation of Judah was being judged by God for refusing to do this very thing (2 Chronicles 36:14–20). These were people who had sworn allegiance to God but were now rejecting him. This made their judgment even worse.

79:10 In the end, God's glory will be evident to all people, but in the meantime, we must endure suffering with patience and allow God to strengthen our character through it. For reasons that we do not know, pagan people often are allowed to scoff at believers. We should be prepared for criticism, jokes, and unkind remarks because God does not place us beyond the attacks of scoffers.

Theme: A prayer for revival and restoration after experiencing destruction. God is our only hope for salvation.

Author: Asaph (or one of his descendants), probably written after the northern kingdom of Israel was defeated and its people deported to Assyria.

80

For the director of music. To ⌊the tune of⌋ "The Lilies of the Covenant." Of Asaph. A psalm.

1 Hear us, O Shepherd of Israel,
    you who lead Joseph like a flock;
  you who sit enthroned between the cherubim, shine forth
2   before Ephraim, Benjamin and Manasseh.
  Awaken your might;
    come and save us.

80:3
e La 5:21
f Nu 6:25

3 Restore[e] us,[f] O God;
    make your face shine upon us,
    that we may be saved.

4 O LORD God Almighty,
    how long will your anger smolder
    against the prayers of your people?

80:5
g Ps 42:3

5 You have fed them with the bread of tears;
    you have made them drink tears by the bowlful.[g]
6 You have made us a source of contention to our neighbors,
    and our enemies mock us.

7 Restore us, O God Almighty;
    make your face shine upon us,
    that we may be saved.

8 You brought a vine out of Egypt;
    you drove out the nations and planted it.

PRAYER IN THE BOOK OF PSALMS

Prayer is human communication with God. Psalms could be described as a collection of song-prayers. Probably the most striking feature of these prayers is their unedited honesty. The words often express our own feelings—feelings that we would prefer no one, much less God, ever knew. Making these psalms our prayers can teach us a great deal about how God wants us to communicate with him. Too often we give God a watered-down version of our feelings, hoping we won't offend him or make him curious about our motives. As we use the psalms to express our feelings, we learn that honesty, openness, and sincerity are valuable to God.

Following are several types of prayers with examples from Psalms. Note that the psalm writers communicated with God in a variety of ways for a variety of reasons. Each of us is invited to communicate with God. Using the psalms will enrich your personal prayer life.

Prayers of:	Psalms:
Praise to God	100; 113; 117
Thanksgiving by a community	67; 75; 136
Thanksgiving by an individual	18; 30; 32
Request by the community	79; 80; 123
Request by an individual	3; 55; 86
Sorrow by the community	44; 74; 137
Sorrow by an individual	5; 6; 120
Anger	35; 109; 140
Confession	6; 32; 51
Faith	11; 16; 23

80:1 Cherubim are mighty angels. That God is "enthroned between the cherubim" is a reminder of his presence on the ark of the Testimony (Exodus 25:17–22).

80:3, 7, 19 Three times the writer calls on God to "restore us." Before restoration must come repentance, turning away from sin.

Repentance involves humbling ourselves and turning to God to receive his forgiveness. As we turn to God, he helps us see ourselves, including our sin, more clearly. Then, as we see our sin, we must repeat the process of repentance. Only then can we constantly be restored to fellowship with God.

9 You cleared the ground for it,
and it took root and filled the land.
10 The mountains were covered with its shade,
the mighty cedars with its branches.
11 It sent out its boughs to the Sea,[a]
its shoots as far as the River.[b]

12 Why have you broken down its walls
so that all who pass by pick its grapes?
13 Boars from the forest ravage it
and the creatures of the field feed on it.

14 Return to us, O God Almighty!
Look down from heaven and see![h]
Watch over this vine,
15   the root your right hand has planted,
the son[c] you have raised up for yourself.

16 Your vine is cut down, it is burned with fire;
at your rebuke[i] your people perish.
17 Let your hand rest on the man at your right hand,
the son of man you have raised up for yourself.
18 Then we will not turn away from you;
revive us, and we will call on your name.

19 Restore us, O LORD God Almighty;
make your face shine upon us,
that we may be saved.

80:14
h Isa 63:15

80:16
i Ps 39:11; 76:6

Theme: A holiday hymn. This hymn celebrates the exodus from Egypt—God's
goodness versus Israel's waywardness. God is our deliverer in spite of our wanderings.
Author: Asaph, probably written to be used during the Feast of Tabernacles

81

For the director of music. According to *gittith*.[d] Of Asaph.

1 Sing for joy to God our strength;
shout aloud to the God of Jacob!
2 Begin the music, strike the tambourine,
play the melodious harp and lyre.

3 Sound the ram's horn at the New Moon,
and when the moon is full, on the day of our Feast;
4 this is a decree for Israel,
an ordinance of the God of Jacob.
5 He established it as a statute for Joseph
when he went out against Egypt,
where we heard a language we did not understand.[e]

6 He says, "I removed the burden from their shoulders;
their hands were set free from the basket.
7 In your distress you called[j] and I rescued you,
I answered[k] you out of a thundercloud;
I tested you at the waters of Meribah.[l]   *Selah*

81:7
j Ex 2:23; Ps 50:15
k Ex 19:19
l Ex 17:7

a 11 Probably the Mediterranean   b 11 That is, the Euphrates   c 15 Or *branch*   d Title: Probably a musical term
e 5 Or / *and we heard a voice we had not known*

80:17 "The man at your right hand" is probably not the Messiah,
but Israel, whom God calls elsewhere his "firstborn son" (Exodus
4:22). The psalm writer is making a plea that God would restore
his mercy to Israel, the people he chose to bring his message into
the world.

81:1–5 Israel's holidays reminded the nation of God's great
miracles. They were times of rejoicing and times to renew one's
strength for life's daily struggles. At Christmas, do your thoughts
revolve mostly around presents? Is Easter only a warm anticipation of spring and Thanksgiving only a good meal? Remember
the spiritual origins of these special days, and use them as opportunities to worship God for his goodness to you, your family, and
your nation.

81:2–4 David instituted music for the temple worship services
(1 Chronicles 25). Music and worship go hand in hand. Worship
should involve the whole person, and music helps lift a person's
thoughts and emotions to God. Through music we can reflect upon
our needs and shortcomings as well as celebrate God's greatness.

81:8
m Ps 50:7

81:9
n Ex 20:3; Dt 32:12; Isa 43:12

81:10
o Ex 20:2

8 "Hear, O my people,m and I will warn you—
    if you would but listen to me, O Israel!
9 You shall have no foreign godn among you;
    you shall not bow down to an alien god.
10 I am the LORD your God,
    who brought you up out of Egypt.o
    Open wide your mouth and I will fill it.

81:12
p Ac 7:42

11 "But my people would not listen to me;
    Israel would not submit to me.
12 So I gave them overp to their stubborn hearts
    to follow their own devices.

81:13
q Dt 5:29; Isa 48:18

13 "If my people would but listen to me,q
    if Israel would follow my ways,
14 how quickly would I subdue their enemies
    and turn my hand against their foes!
15 Those who hate the LORD would cringe before him,
    and their punishment would last forever.

81:16
r Dt 32:14

16 But you would be fed with the finest of wheat;r
    with honey from the rock I would satisfy you."

Theme: A fair judge. God will judge the wicked who have unfairly treated others.
Author: Asaph

82 A psalm of Asaph.

1 God presides in the great assembly;
    he gives judgment among the "gods":

82:2
s Dt 1:17

2 "How long will youa defend the unjust
    and show partialitys to the wicked?

Selah

3 Defend the cause of the weak and fatherless;
    maintain the rights of the poor and oppressed.
4 Rescue the weak and needy;
    deliver them from the hand of the wicked.

82:5
t Mic 3:1
u Ps 11:3

5 "They know nothing, they understand nothing.t
    They walk about in darkness;
    all the foundationsu of the earth are shaken.

82:6
v Jn 10:34*

6 "I said, 'You are "gods";v
    you are all sons of the Most High.'

82:7
w Ps 49:12

7 But you will diew like mere men;
    you will fall like every other ruler."

82:8
x Ps 2:8; Rev 11:15

8 Rise up, O God, judge the earth,
    for all the nations are your inheritance.x

a2 The Hebrew is plural.

81:11, 12 God let the Israelites go on blindly, stubbornly, and selfishly, when they should have been obeying and pursuing God's desires. God sometimes lets us continue in our stubbornness to bring us to our senses. He does not keep us from rebelling, because he wants us to learn the consequences of sin. He uses these experiences to turn people away from greater sin to faith in him.

81:13–16 God had provided in his covenant that he would restore his people if they would listen to him and return to him (Exodus 23:22–27; Leviticus 26:3–13; Deuteronomy 7:12–26; 28:1–14). God remains faithful in our relationship with him (2 Timothy 2:11–13), patiently waiting for our response so he can pour out his blessings. Conduct an inventory of your spiritual life right now. In what ways are you allowing God to affect your daily decisions?

82:1ff God judges human judges. The integrity of the justice system in a nation provides a clear indication of the health of that society. As is the case with all leadership, judges derive their authority ultimately from God and will give an account to God for their verdicts. Believers are commanded to pray for "kings and all those in authority, that we may live peaceful and quiet lives in all godliness and holiness" (1 Timothy 2:2). This psalm reminds us to include judges of every kind in our prayers because we directly benefit from their integrity.

82:6 This psalm calls the rulers and judges of Israel "gods" and "sons of the Most High." They were called gods because they represented God in executing judgment. John 10:34–36 records Jesus using this passage to defend his claims to be God. His argument was as follows: if God would call mere men "gods," why was it blasphemous for him, the true Son of God, to declare himself equal with God?

Theme: Combating God's enemies. This psalm is a prayer for God to do whatever it takes to convince the world that he is indeed God. Someday all will recognize and admit that God is in charge.
Author: Asaph (or one of his descendants)

83 A song. A psalm of Asaph.

1 O God, do not keep silent;[y]
   be not quiet, O God, be not still.
2 See how your enemies are astir,[z]
   how your foes rear their heads.[a]
3 With cunning they conspire against your people;
   they plot against those you cherish.
4 "Come," they say, "let us destroy them as a nation,
   that the name of Israel be remembered no more."

5 With one mind they plot together;
   they form an alliance against you—
6 the tents of Edom and the Ishmaelites,
   of Moab[b] and the Hagrites,
7 Gebal,[a] Ammon and Amalek,
   Philistia, with the people of Tyre.
8 Even Assyria has joined them
   to lend strength to the descendants of Lot.   *Selah*

9 Do to them as you did to Midian,
   as you did to Sisera and Jabin at the river Kishon,
10 who perished at Endor
   and became like refuse on the ground.
11 Make their nobles like Oreb and Zeeb,
   all their princes like Zebah and Zalmunna,[c]
12 who said, "Let us take possession
   of the pasturelands of God."

13 Make them like tumbleweed, O my God,
   like chaff[d] before the wind.
14 As fire consumes the forest
   or a flame sets the mountains ablaze,[e]
15 so pursue them with your tempest
   and terrify them with your storm.
16 Cover their faces with shame
   so that men will seek your name, O Lord.

17 May they ever be ashamed and dismayed;
   may they perish in disgrace.
18 Let them know that you, whose name is the Lord—
   that you alone are the Most High over all the earth.[f]

a 7 That is, Byblos

83:1
[y] Ps 28:1
83:2
[z] Ps 2:1
[a] Ps 81:15

83:6
[b] 2Ch 20:1

83:11
[c] Jdg 8:12, 21

83:13
[d] Ps 35:5; Isa 17:13

83:14
[e] Dt 32:22

83:18
[f] Ps 59:13

83:5–8 This alliance against God may refer to the gathering of certain kings to fight against Jehoshaphat and the people of Judah (2 Chronicles 20). The psalm's author is called Asaph, but this can mean Asaph or one of his descendants. A descendant of Asaph named Jahaziel prophesied victory for Judah in the battle against Jehoshaphat (2 Chronicles 20:13–17). The psalmist says the alliance against Judah is really against God. Thus Jahaziel exclaimed, "The battle is not yours, but God's" (2 Chronicles 20:15). God is "the Most High over all the earth" (83:18), and the enemies of Israel were considered God's enemies.

83:6 The Hagrites may have been the descendants of Hagar (Genesis 21:8–21).

83:8–11 The "descendants of Lot" refers to the Moabites and Ammonites (Genesis 19:36–38). Sisera was the commander of the army of the oppressive Canaanite King Jabin. He was killed by a woman (see Judges 4 for the complete story). (For the story of Oreb and Zeeb, see Judges 7:25; for Zebah and Zalmunna, see Judges 8:21.)

83:13–18 Surrounding Judah were pagan nations that sought Judah's downfall. The writer prayed that God would blow these nations away like chaff before the wind until they recognized that the Lord is supreme over all rulers of the earth. Sometimes we must be humbled by adversity before we will look up and see the Lord; we must be defeated before we can have the ultimate victory. Wouldn't it be better to seek the Lord in times of prosperity than to wait until his judgment is upon us?

Theme: God's living presence is our greatest joy. His radiant presence helps us grow in strength, grace, and glory.
Author: The sons of Korah (temple assistants)

84
For the director of music. According to *gittith*.[a] Of the Sons of Korah. A psalm.

84:1
g Ps 27:4

84:2
h Ps 42:1-2

1 How lovely is your dwelling place,[g]
    O LORD Almighty!
2 My soul yearns,[h] even faints,
    for the courts of the LORD;
my heart and my flesh cry out
    for the living God.

3 Even the sparrow has found a home,
    and the swallow a nest for herself,
    where she may have her young—
a place near your altar,
    O LORD Almighty, my King and my God.
4 Blessed are those who dwell in your house;
    they are ever praising you.
                                   Selah

5 Blessed are those whose strength is in you,
    who have set their hearts on pilgrimage.
6 As they pass through the Valley of Baca,
    they make it a place of springs;
    the autumn rains also cover it with pools.[b]

84:7
i Pr 4:18
j Dt 16:16

7 They go from strength to strength,[i]
    till each appears[j] before God in Zion.

8 Hear my prayer, O LORD God Almighty;
    listen to me, O God of Jacob.
                                     Selah
9 Look upon our shield,[c] O God;
    look with favor on your anointed one.

10 Better is one day in your courts
    than a thousand elsewhere;
I would rather be a doorkeeper in the house of my God
    than dwell in the tents of the wicked.

84:11
k Isa 60:19
l Ge 15:1
m Ps 34:10

11 For the LORD God is a sun[k] and shield;[l]
    the LORD bestows favor and honor;
no good thing does he withhold[m]
    from those whose walk is blameless.

84:12
n Ps 2:12

12 O LORD Almighty,
    blessed[n] is the man who trusts in you.

a Title: Probably a musical term   b 6 Or *blessings*   c 9 Or *sovereign*

84:1, 4 The writer longed to get away from the bustling world to meet God inside his dwelling place, his holy temple. We can meet God anywhere, at any time. But we know that going into a church building can help us step aside from the busy mainstream of life so we can quietly meditate and pray. We find joy not only in the beautiful building but also in the prayers, music, lessons, sermons, and fellowship.

84:5–7 The pilgrimage to the temple passed through the barren Valley of Baca. No specific valley has been identified with Baca. Because *Baca* can mean "weeping," it may have been a symbolic reference to the times of struggles and tears through which people must pass on their way to meet God. Growing strong in God's presence is often preceded by a journey through barren places in our lives. The person who loves to spend time with God will see his or her adversity as an opportunity to experience God's faithfulness even more

deeply. If you are walking through your own Valley of Baca today, be sure your pilgrimage leads toward God, not away from him.

84:11 God does not promise to give us everything *we* think is good, but he will not withhold what is permanently good. He will give us the means to walk along his paths, but we must do the walking. When we obey him, he will not hold anything back that will help us serve him.

Theme: From reverence to restoration. Reverence leads to forgiveness, restoring our love and joy for God.
Author: The sons of Korah (temple assistants)

85

For the director of music. Of the Sons of Korah. A psalm.

1 You showed favor to your land, O Lord;
    you restored the fortunes*o* of Jacob.
2 You forgave the iniquity of your people
    and covered all their sins.
                              Selah
3 You set aside all your wrath
    and turned from your fierce anger.*p*

4 Restore*q* us again, O God our Savior,
    and put away your displeasure toward us.
5 Will you be angry with us forever?*r*
    Will you prolong your anger through all generations?
6 Will you not revive us again,
    that your people may rejoice in you?
7 Show us your unfailing love, O Lord,
    and grant us your salvation.

8 I will listen to what God the Lord will say;
    he promises peace*s* to his people, his saints—
    but let them not return to folly.
9 Surely his salvation*t* is near those who fear him,
    that his glory*u* may dwell in our land.

10 Love and faithfulness meet together;
    righteousness*v* and peace kiss each other.
11 Faithfulness springs forth from the earth,
    and righteousness looks down from heaven.
12 The Lord will indeed give what is good,*w*
    and our land will yield its harvest.
13 Righteousness goes before him
    and prepares the way for his steps.

85:1
o Jer 30:18;
Eze 39:25
85:3
p Dt 13:17
85:4
q Ps 80:3, 7
85:5
r Ps 79:5
85:8
s Zec 9:10
85:9
t Isa 46:13
u Zec 2:5
85:10
v Ps 72:2-3;
Isa 32:17
85:12
w Ps 84:11;
Jas 1:17

Theme: Devoted trust in times of deep trouble.
Author: David

86

A prayer of David.

1 Hear, O Lord, and answer me,
    for I am poor and needy.
2 Guard my life, for I am devoted to you.
    You are my God; save your servant
    who trusts in you.
3 Have mercy*x* on me, O Lord,
    for I call to you all day long.
4 Bring joy to your servant,
    for to you, O Lord,
    I lift*y* up my soul.

5 You are forgiving and good, O Lord,
    abounding in love*z* to all who call to you.

86:3
x Ps 57:1
86:4
y Ps 25:11; 43:8
86:5
z Ps 145:8;
Joel 2:13

85:6, 7 The writer was asking God to revive his people, bringing them back to spiritual life. God is capable of reviving both churches and individuals. He can pour out his love on us, renewing our love for him. If you need revival in your church, family, or personal spiritual life, ask God to give you a fresh touch of his love.

85:9-13 As the writer cries out for God's intervention, he can almost see, taste, and hear God's response. These five verses describe what God can do for those who welcome his herald—righteousness (9:13). This psalm illustrates that the greater the presence of righteousness (obedience to God), the clearer the examples of God's blessings. This principle works equally in the life of a nation or an individual. The more we first seek God's righteousness and his kingdom, as Jesus pointed out, the more we will see everything else taken care of by God (see Matthew 6:25–33).

6 Hear my prayer, O LORD;
　　listen to my cry for mercy.
7 In the day of my trouble I will call to you,
　　for you will answer me.

8 Among the gods there is none like you,*a* O Lord;
　　no deeds can compare with yours.
9 All the nations you have made
　　will come and worship*b* before you, O Lord;
　　they will bring glory to your name.
10 For you are great and do marvelous deeds;*c*
　　you alone*d* are God.

11 Teach me your way,*e* O LORD,
　　and I will walk in your truth;
　give me an undivided heart,
　　that I may fear your name.
12 I will praise you, O Lord my God, with all my heart;
　　I will glorify your name forever.
13 For great is your love toward me;
　　you have delivered me from the depths of the grave.*a*

14 The arrogant are attacking me, O God;
　　a band of ruthless men seeks my life—
　　men without regard for you.
15 But you, O Lord, are a compassionate and gracious God,
　　slow to anger, abounding in love and faithfulness.
16 Turn to me and have mercy on me;
　　grant your strength to your servant
　　and save the son of your maidservant.*b*
17 Give me a sign of your goodness,
　　that my enemies may see it and be put to shame,
　　for you, O LORD, have helped me and comforted me.

Theme: The city of God, where all believers will one day gather.
Author: The sons of Korah (temple assistants)

87 Of the Sons of Korah. A psalm. A song.

1 He has set his foundation on the holy mountain;
2 　the LORD loves the gates of Zion*f*
　　more than all the dwellings of Jacob.

a 13 Hebrew *Sheol*　*b 16* Or *save your faithful son*

86:8
a Ex 15:11; Dt 3:24;
Ps 89:6
86:9
b Rev 15:4

86:10
c Ps 72:18
d Dt 6:4; Mk 12:29
86:11
e Ps 25:5

87:2
f Ps 78:68

86:7 Sometimes our trouble or pain is so great that all we can do is cry out to God, "Guard my life" (86:2). And often, when there is no relief in sight, all we can do is acknowledge the greatness of God and wait for better days ahead. The conviction that God answers prayer will sustain us in such difficult times.

86:8–10 "There is none like you, O Lord." The God of the Bible is unique! He is alive and able to do mighty deeds for those who love him. All human-created deities are powerless because they are merely inventions of the mind, not living beings. The Lord alone is "worthy . . . to receive glory and honor and power" (Revelation 4:11). Although people believe in many gods, you need never fear that God is only one among many or that you may be worshiping the wrong God. The Lord alone is God.

86:11–14 This prayer within a prayer captures a glimpse of vibrant spiritual vitality. Two requests are made: "teach me your way" and "give me an undivided heart." Each request has a God-centered purpose: that the person praying would "walk in your truth" and "fear your name." No matter how well we know and follow God, we can always ask him to increase our awareness

and improve our obedience. Jesus echoed one of these requests in the sixth beatitude, "Blessed are the pure in heart, for they will see God" (Matthew 5:8). Commit this prayer to memory and use it often.

86:17 It is right to pray for a sign of God's goodness. As David found, it may be just what we need. But let us not overlook the signs he has already given: the support of family and friends, the fellowship of other Christians, the light of each new day. And we can be confident that he knows our situation no matter how desperate it becomes, and he cares.

87:1ff Zion (the holy mountain, Jerusalem) and its temple here represent the future community of all believers. This psalm looks ahead to the Holy City of God described in Revelation 21:10–27. The honor of living there will be granted to all whose names are recorded in the Lamb's book of life (Revelation 21:27). It is God's grace that forms and sustains this wonderful community. How could anyone refuse God's offer to be part of this celebration?

3 Glorious things are said of you,
  O city of God:[g]   *Selah*

87:3
[g]Isa 60:1

4 "I will record Rahab[a] and Babylon
   among those who acknowledge me—
  Philistia too, and Tyre, along with Cush[b]—
   and will say, 'This[c] one was born in Zion.'"

5 Indeed, of Zion it will be said,
   "This one and that one were born in her,
   and the Most High himself will establish her."
6 The LORD will write in the register[h] of the peoples:
   "This one was born in Zion."   *Selah*

87:6
[h]Eze 13:9

7 As they make music they will sing,
   "All my fountains are in you."

Theme: When there is no relief in sight. God understands even our deepest misery.
Author: Heman, one of the sons of Korah (possibly the same man mentioned in
1 Chronicles 15:19; 16:41; 25:4, 5 as a musician and the king's seer)

88 A song. A psalm of the Sons of Korah. For the director of music. According to *mahalath
leannoth.*[d] A *maskil*[e] of Heman the Ezrahite.

1 O LORD, the God who saves me,
   day and night I cry out before you.
2 May my prayer come before you;
   turn your ear to my cry.

3 For my soul is full of trouble
   and my life draws near the grave.[f] [i]

88:3
[i]Ps 107:18, 26

4 I am counted among those who go down to the pit;[j]
   I am like a man without strength.

88:4
[j]Ps 28:1

5 I am set apart with the dead,
   like the slain who lie in the grave,
   whom you remember no more,
   who are cut off[k] from your care.

88:5
[k]Isa 53:8

6 You have put me in the lowest pit,
   in the darkest depths.
7 Your wrath lies heavily upon me;
   you have overwhelmed me with all your waves.[l]   *Selah*

88:7
[l]Ps 42:7

8 You have taken from me my closest friends[m]
   and have made me repulsive to them.
   I am confined and cannot escape;

88:8
[m]Job 19:13

9   my eyes are dim with grief.

   I call[n] to you, O LORD, every day;
   I spread out my hands[o] to you.
10 Do you show your wonders to the dead?
   Do those who are dead rise up and praise you?[p]   *Selah*

88:9
[n]Ps 86:3
[o]Ps 143:6

88:10
[p]Ps 6:5

---

a4 A poetic name for Egypt   b4 That is, the upper Nile region   c4 Or "O Rahab and Babylon, / Philistia, Tyre
and Cush, / I will record concerning those who acknowledge me: / 'This   dTitle: Possibly a tune, "The Suffering
of Affliction"   eTitle: Probably a literary or musical term   f3 Hebrew *Sheol*

87:4 Rahab is a name for a monster known in ancient Near
Eastern poetry as an enemy of God. Here the name is used
to represent Egypt, a traditional enemy of God's people.

88:1ff Have you ever felt as though you have hit bottom? The
writer is so low that he even despairs of life itself. Although everything is bad and getting worse, he is able to tell it all to God. This
is one of the few psalms that gives no answer or expression of
hope. Don't think that you must always be cheerful and positive.

Grief and depression take time to heal. No matter how low we
feel, we can always take our problems to God and express our
anguish to him.

88:5 Our feelings may be as obvious and painful as those
expressed by the psalm writer, but they are never the complete
picture. In fact, our feelings are usually very unstable. When we
bring our unedited feelings to God, we allow him to point out
where they are incomplete. We are in trouble whenever we give
our feelings divine authority or assume that God can't handle
what we feel. Praying the psalms teaches us to bring God everything about us and trains us to experience his presence even
when our feelings tell us otherwise.

11 Is your love declared in the grave,
        your faithfulness in Destruction[a]?
12 Are your wonders known in the place of darkness,
        or your righteous deeds in the land of oblivion?

88:13
[q] Ps 5:3

13 But I cry to you for help, O LORD;
        in the morning[q] my prayer comes before you.

88:14
[r] Job 13:24; Ps 13:1

14 Why, O LORD, do you reject me
        and hide your face[r] from me?

88:15
[s] Job 6:4

15 From my youth I have been afflicted and close to death;
        I have suffered your terrors[s] and am in despair.
16 Your wrath has swept over me;
        your terrors have destroyed me.

88:17
[t] Ps 22:16

17 All day long they surround me like a flood;[t]
        they have completely engulfed me.

88:18
[u] Job 19:13

18 You have taken my companions[u] and loved ones from me;
        the darkness is my closest friend.

Theme: God's promise to preserve David's descendants. God's promise is fulfilled in Jesus Christ, who will reign for eternity. The love and kindness promised to David is ours in Christ.
Author: Ethan (a Levite leader and possibly one of the head musicians in the temple, 1 Chronicles 15:17, 19), or one of his descendants

89

A *maskil*[b] of Ethan the Ezrahite.

89:1
[v] Ps 101:1

1 I will sing[v] of the LORD's great love forever;
        with my mouth I will make your faithfulness known through all generations.
2 I will declare that your love stands firm forever,
        that you established your faithfulness in heaven itself.

3 You said, "I have made a covenant with my chosen one,
        I have sworn to David my servant,

89:4
[w] Lk 1:33

4 'I will establish your line forever
        and make your throne firm through all generations.'"[w]   *Selah*

89:5
[x] Ps 19:1

5 The heavens[x] praise your wonders, O LORD,
        your faithfulness too, in the assembly of the holy ones.
6 For who in the skies above can compare with the LORD?
        Who is like the LORD among the heavenly beings?
7 In the council of the holy ones God is greatly feared;
        he is more awesome than all who surround him.
8 O LORD God Almighty, who is like you?
        You are mighty, O LORD, and your faithfulness surrounds you.

89:9
[y] Ps 65:7

9 You rule over the surging sea;
        when its waves mount up, you still them.[y]

89:10
[z] Ps 87:4

10 You crushed Rahab[z] like one of the slain;
        with your strong arm you scattered your enemies.

[a] 11 Hebrew *Abaddon*   [b] Title: Probably a literary or musical term

---

88:13, 14 The writer of this psalm was close to death, perhaps debilitated by disease, and forsaken by friends. But he could still pray. Perhaps you are not so afflicted, but you know someone who is. Consider being a prayer companion for that person. This psalm can be a prayer you can lift to God on his or her behalf.

89:1ff This psalm was written to describe the glorious reign of David. God had promised to make David the mightiest king on earth and to keep his descendants on the throne forever (2 Samuel 7:8–16). But Jerusalem was destroyed, and kings no longer reign there. So these verses can only look forward, prophetically, to the future reign of Jesus Christ, David's

descendant. Verse 27 is a prophecy concerning David's never-ending dynasty, which will reach its fulfillment and highest expression in Christ's future reign over the world (see Revelation 22:5).

89:5 The "assembly of the holy ones" generally refers to angels. In the courts of heaven, a host of angels praise the Lord. This scene is one of majesty and grandeur to show that God is beyond compare. His power and purity place him high above nature and angels. See Deuteronomy 33:2, Luke 2:13, and Hebrews 12:22 for more about angels.

11 The heavens are yours, and yours also the earth;
   you founded the world and all that is in it.
12 You created the north and the south;
   Tabor[a] and Hermon[b] sing for joy at your name.
13 Your arm is endued with power;
   your hand is strong, your right hand exalted.

14 Righteousness and justice are the foundation of your throne;
   love and faithfulness go before you.
15 Blessed are those who have learned to acclaim you,
   who walk in the light of your presence, O LORD.
16 They rejoice in your name all day long;
   they exult in your righteousness.
17 For you are their glory and strength,
   and by your favor you exalt our horn.[a]
18 Indeed, our shield[b] belongs to the LORD,
   our king to the Holy One of Israel.

19 Once you spoke in a vision,
   to your faithful people you said:
   "I have bestowed strength on a warrior;
   I have exalted a young man from among the people.
20 I have found David my servant;
   with my sacred oil I have anointed[c] him.
21 My hand will sustain him;
   surely my arm will strengthen him.
22 No enemy will subject him to tribute;
   no wicked man will oppress[d] him.
23 I will crush his foes before him
   and strike down his adversaries.[e]
24 My faithful love will be with him,
   and through my name his horn[c] will be exalted.
25 I will set his hand over the sea,
   his right hand over the rivers.
26 He will call out to me, 'You are my Father,
   my God, the Rock my Savior.'[f]
27 I will also appoint him my firstborn,
   the most exalted[g] of the kings of the earth.
28 I will maintain my love to him forever,
   and my covenant with him will never fail.
29 I will establish his line forever,
   his throne as long as the heavens endure.[h]

30 "If his sons forsake my law
   and do not follow my statutes,
31 if they violate my decrees
   and fail to keep my commands,
32 I will punish their sin with the rod,
   their iniquity with flogging;
33 but I will not take my love from him,[i]
   nor will I ever betray my faithfulness.

89:12
[a] Jos 19:22
[b] Jos 12:1

89:20
[c] 1Sa 16:1, 12

89:22
[d] 2Sa 7:10

89:23
[e] 2Sa 7:9

89:26
[f] 2Sa 22:47

89:27
[g] Nu 24:7

89:29
[h] Dt 11:21;
Jer 33:17

89:33
[i] 2Sa 7:15

a 17 *Horn* here symbolizes strong one.   b 18 Or *sovereign*   c 24 *Horn* here symbolizes strength.

89:12 This refers to Mount Tabor and Mount Hermon. Mount Tabor, though low in elevation (1,900 feet), was the scene of Deborah's victory in Judges 4. Mount Hermon (9,000 feet) was tall and majestic.

89:14, 15 Righteousness, justice, love, and faithfulness are the foundation of God's throne; they are central characteristics of the way God rules. They summarize his character. As God's ambassadors, we should exhibit the same traits when we deal with people. Make sure your actions flow out of righteousness,

justice, love, and faithfulness because any unfair, unloving, or dishonest action cannot come from God.

89:17, 24 *Horn* refers to the horn of an animal, the symbol of its power. In verse 17, *horn* means our strong one, our hope for the Messiah. In verse 24, David is promised to have God's power to accomplish God's will. Without God's help, we are weak and powerless, inadequate for even the simplest spiritual tasks. But when we are filled with God's Spirit, his power flows through us and our accomplishments will exceed our expectations.

34 I will not violate my covenant
    or alter what my lips have uttered.
35 Once for all, I have sworn by my holiness—
    and I will not lie to David—
36 that his line will continue forever
    and his throne endure before me like the sun;
37 it will be established forever like the moon,
    the faithful witness in the sky."   *Selah*

89:38
j Dt 32:19; 1Ch 28:9

38 But you have rejected,*j* you have spurned,
    you have been very angry with your anointed one.

89:39
k La 5:16

39 You have renounced the covenant with your servant
    and have defiled his crown in the dust.*k*
40 You have broken through all his walls
    and reduced his strongholds to ruins.

89:41
l Ps 44:13

41 All who pass by have plundered him;
    he has become the scorn of his neighbors.*l*
42 You have exalted the right hand of his foes;
    you have made all his enemies rejoice.
43 You have turned back the edge of his sword
    and have not supported him in battle.
44 You have put an end to his splendor
    and cast his throne to the ground.
45 You have cut short the days of his youth;
    you have covered him with a mantle of shame.   *Selah*

89:46
m Ps 79:5

46 How long, O LORD? Will you hide yourself forever?
    How long will your wrath burn like fire?*m*

89:47
n Job 7:7

47 Remember how fleeting is my life.*n*
    For what futility you have created all men!

89:48
o Ps 49:9

48 What man can live and not see death,
    or save himself from the power of the grave*a*?*o*   *Selah*
49 O Lord, where is your former great love,
    which in your faithfulness you swore to David?

89:50
p Ps 69:19

50 Remember, Lord, how your servant has*b* been mocked,*p*
    how I bear in my heart the taunts of all the nations,
51 the taunts with which your enemies have mocked, O LORD,
    with which they have mocked every step of your anointed one.

89:52
q Ps 41:13

52 Praise be to the LORD forever!
    Amen and Amen.*q*

BOOK IV   Psalms 90–106

These psalms include a prayer of Moses, a psalm about oppressors, and a psalm praising God as our King. These psalms remind us that we should remember our place and be submissive before our mighty God.

Theme: God's eternal nature is contrasted with people's frailty. Our time on earth is limited and we are to use it wisely, not living for the moment, but with our eternal home in mind.
Author: Moses, making this the oldest of the psalms

90   A prayer of Moses the man of God.

90:1
r Eze 11:16

1 Lord, you have been our dwelling place*r*
    throughout all generations.

a 48 Hebrew *Sheol*   *b* 50 Or *your servants have*

89:34–37 In light of Israel's continual disobedience throughout history, this is an amazing promise. God promised that David's descendants would always sit on the throne (89:29), but that if the people disobeyed, they would be punished (89:30–32). Yet, even through their disobedience and punishment, God would never break faith with them (89:33). Israel *did* disobey, evil ran rampant, the nation was divided, exile came—but through it all, a remnant of God's people remained faithful. Centuries later, the Messiah arrived, the eternal King from David's line, just as God had promised. All that God promises, he fulfills. He will not take back even one word of what he says. God can also be trusted to save us as he promised he would (Hebrews 6:13–18). God is completely reliable.

2 Before the mountains were born[s]
    or you brought forth the earth and the world,
    from everlasting to everlasting you are God.

3 You turn men back to dust,
    saying, "Return to dust, O sons of men."
4 For a thousand years in your sight
    are like a day that has just gone by,
    or like a watch in the night.[t]
5 You sweep men away[u] in the sleep of death;
    they are like the new grass of the morning—
6 though in the morning it springs up new,
    by evening it is dry and withered.

7 We are consumed by your anger
    and terrified by your indignation.
8 You have set our iniquities before you,
    our secret sins[v] in the light of your presence.
9 All our days pass away under your wrath;
    we finish our years with a moan.
10 The length of our days is seventy years—
    or eighty, if we have the strength;
    yet their span[a] is but trouble and sorrow,
    for they quickly pass, and we fly away.

11 Who knows the power of your anger?
    For your wrath is as great as the fear that is due you.
12 Teach us to number our days[w] aright,
    that we may gain a heart of wisdom.

13 Relent, O LORD! How long will it be?
    Have compassion on your servants.[x]
14 Satisfy us in the morning with your unfailing love,
    that we may sing for joy[y] and be glad all our days.
15 Make us glad for as many days as you have afflicted us,
    for as many years as we have seen trouble.
16 May your deeds be shown to your servants,
    your splendor to their children.[z]

17 May the favor[b] of the Lord our God rest upon us;
    establish the work of our hands for us—
    yes, establish the work of our hands.[a]

90:2	[s] Pr 8:25
90:4	[t] 2Pe 3:8
90:5	[u] Isa 40:6
90:8	[v] Ps 19:12
90:12	[w] Ps 39:4
90:13	[x] Dt 32:36
90:14	[y] Ps 85:6
90:16	[z] Hab 3:2
90:17	[a] Isa 26:12

Theme: God's protection in the midst of danger. God doesn't promise a world free from danger, but he does promise his help whenever we face danger.
Author: Anonymous

91

1 He who dwells in the shelter[b] of the Most High
    will rest in the shadow[c] of the Almighty.[c]

91:1	[b] Ps 31:20
	[c] Ps 17:8

[a] 10 Or yet the best of them   [b] 17 Or beauty   [c] 1 Hebrew Shaddai

---

90:4 Moses reminds us that a thousand years are like a day to the Lord. God is not limited by time. It's easy to get discouraged when years pass and the world doesn't get better. We sometimes wonder if God is able to see the future. But don't assume that God has our limitations. God is completely unrestricted by time. Because he is eternal, we can depend on him.

90:8 God knows all our sins as if they were spread out before him, even the secret ones. We don't need to cover up our sins before him because we can talk openly and honestly with him. But while he knows all that terrible information about us, God still loves us and wants to forgive us. This should encourage us to come to him rather than frighten us into covering up our sin.

90:12 Realizing that life is short helps us use the little time we

have more wisely and for eternal good. Take time to number your days by asking, "What do I want to see happen in my life before I die? What small step could I take toward that purpose today?"

90:17 Because our days are numbered, we want our work to count, to be effective and productive. We desire to see God's eternal plan revealed now and for our work to reflect his permanence. If we feel dissatisfied with this life and all its imperfections, remember our desire to see our work established is placed there by God (see the note on Ecclesiastes 3:11). But our desire can only be satisfied in eternity. Until then we must apply ourselves to loving and serving God.

91:1-6 God is a shelter, a refuge when we are afraid. The writer's faith in the Almighty God as Protector would carry him

91:2
d Ps 142:5

2 I will say[a] of the LORD, "He is my refuge[d] and my fortress,
　　my God, in whom I trust."

91:3
e Ps 124:7

3 Surely he will save you from the fowler's snare[e]
　　and from the deadly pestilence.
4 He will cover you with his feathers,
　　and under his wings you will find refuge;
　　his faithfulness will be your shield and rampart.
5 You will not fear the terror of night,
　　nor the arrow that flies by day,
6 nor the pestilence that stalks in the darkness,
　　nor the plague that destroys at midday.
7 A thousand may fall at your side,
　　ten thousand at your right hand,
　　but it will not come near you.
8 You will only observe with your eyes
　　and see the punishment of the wicked.

9 If you make the Most High your dwelling—
　　even the LORD, who is my refuge—

91:10
f Pr 12:21

10 then no harm[f] will befall you,
　　no disaster will come near your tent.

91:11
g Heb 1:14
h Ps 34:7

11 For he will command his angels[g] concerning you
　　to guard you in all your ways;[h]

91:12
i Mt 4:6*;
Lk 4:10-11*

12 they will lift you up in their hands,
　　so that you will not strike your foot against a stone.[i]
13 You will tread upon the lion and the cobra;
　　you will trample the great lion and the serpent.

14 "Because he loves me," says the LORD, "I will rescue him;
　　I will protect him, for he acknowledges my name.

91:15
j 1Sa 2:30; Ps 50:15

15 He will call upon me, and I will answer him;
　　I will be with him in trouble,
　　I will deliver him and honor him.[j]
16 With long life will I satisfy him
　　and show him my salvation."

Theme: Be thankful and faithful every day. This psalm was used in temple services
on the Sabbath.
Author: Anonymous

92 A psalm. A song. For the Sabbath day.

92:1
k Ps 147:1

1 It is good to praise the LORD
　　and make music to your name,[k] O Most High,
2 to proclaim your love in the morning
　　and your faithfulness at night,

92:3
l Ps 33:2

3 to the music of the ten-stringed lyre
　　and the melody of the harp.[l]

a 2 Or *He says*

---

through all the dangers and fears of life. This should be a picture
of our trust—trading all our fears for faith in him, no matter how
intense our fears. To do this we must "dwell" and "rest" with him
(91:1). By entrusting ourselves to his protection and pledging our
daily devotion to him, we will be kept safe.

91:11 One of the functions of angels is to watch over believers
(Hebrews 1:14). There are examples of guardian angels in Scripture (1 Kings 19:5; Daniel 6:22; Matthew 18:10; Luke 16:22; Acts
12:7), although there is no indication that one angel is assigned
to each believer. Angels can also be God's messengers (Matthew
2:13; Acts 27:23, 24). Angels are not visible, except on special

occasions (Numbers 22:31; Luke 2:9). Verses 11 and 12 were
quoted by Satan when he tempted Jesus (Matthew 4:6; Luke
4:10, 11). It is comforting to know that God watches over us
even in times of great stress and fear.

92:1, 2 During the Thanksgiving holiday, we focus on our blessings and express our gratitude to God for them. But thanks should
be on our lips every day. We can never say thank you enough to
parents, friends, leaders, and especially to God. When thanksgiving becomes an integral part of your life, you will find that your
attitude toward life will change. You will become more positive,
gracious, loving, and humble.

4 For you make me glad by your deeds, O LORD;
   I sing for joy at the works of your hands.

5 How great are your works, O LORD,
   how profound your thoughts!*m*

6 The senseless man*n* does not know,
   fools do not understand,

7 that though the wicked spring up like grass
   and all evildoers flourish,
   they will be forever destroyed.

8 But you, O LORD, are exalted forever.

9 For surely your enemies, O LORD,
   surely your enemies will perish;
   all evildoers will be scattered.*o*

10 You have exalted my horn*a p* like that of a wild ox;
    fine oils*q* have been poured upon me.

11 My eyes have seen the defeat of my adversaries;
    my ears have heard the rout of my wicked foes.*r*

12 The righteous will flourish like a palm tree,
    they will grow like a cedar of Lebanon;*s*

13 planted in the house of the LORD,
    they will flourish in the courts of our God.*t*

14 They will still bear fruit in old age,
    they will stay fresh and green,

15 proclaiming, "The LORD is upright;
    he is my Rock, and there is no wickedness in him."

Theme: God's unchanging and almighty nature. His creation reminds us of his great power.
Author: Anonymous

93

1 The LORD reigns,*u* he is robed in majesty;*v*
   the LORD is robed in majesty
   and is armed with strength.*w*
   The world is firmly established;
   it cannot be moved.*x*

2 Your throne was established long ago;
   you are from all eternity.*y*

3 The seas have lifted up, O LORD,
   the seas have lifted up their voice;
   the seas have lifted up their pounding waves.

4 Mightier than the thunder*z* of the great waters,
   mightier than the breakers of the sea—
   the LORD on high is mighty.

5 Your statutes stand firm;
   holiness adorns your house
   for endless days, O LORD.

a 10 Horn here symbolizes strength.

92:5
m Ps 40:5; Ro 11:33

92:6
n Ps 73:22

92:9
o Ps 68:1

92:10
p Ps 89:17
q Ps 23:5

92:11
r Ps 54:7

92:12
s Ps 52:8; Hos 14:6

92:13
t Ps 100:4

93:1
u Ps 97:1
v Ps 104:1
w Ps 65:6
x Ps 96:10

93:2
y Ps 45:6

93:4
z Ps 65:7

92:12, 13 Palm trees are known for their long life. To flourish like palm trees means to stand tall and to live long. The cedars of Lebanon grew to 120 feet in height and up to 30 feet in circumference; thus, they were solid, strong, and immovable. The writer saw believers as upright, strong, and unmoved by the winds of circumstance. Those who place their faith firmly in God can have this strength and vitality.

92:14 Honoring God is not restricted to young people who seem to have unlimited strength and energy. Even in old age, devoted believers can produce spiritual fruit. There are many faithful older people who continue to have a fresh outlook and can teach us

from a lifetime experience of serving God. Seek out an elderly friend or relative to tell you about his or her experiences with the Lord and challenge you to new heights of spiritual growth.

93:1ff Jewish tradition claims that the next seven psalms (93—99) anticipated some of the works of the Messiah. Psalm 93 is said to have been used in post-captivity temple services and may have been written during Sennacherib's invasion (2 Kings 18:13—19:37).

93:5 The atmosphere of God's eternal reign is holiness. Holiness will be the oxygen of heaven. Meanwhile, God's perfect moral character highlights his glory and can be seen everywhere. God

Theme: God will keep his people from the severe punishment awaiting the wicked. Since God is holy and just, we can be certain that the wicked will not prevail.
Author: Anonymous

94

1 O Lord, the God who avenges,
    O God who avenges, shine forth.
2 Rise up, O Judge[a] of the earth;
    pay back to the proud what they deserve.
3 How long will the wicked, O Lord,
    how long will the wicked be jubilant?

4 They pour out arrogant[b] words;
    all the evildoers are full of boasting.
5 They crush your people, O Lord;
    they oppress your inheritance.
6 They slay the widow and the alien;
    they murder the fatherless.
7 They say, "The Lord does not see;[c]
    the God of Jacob pays no heed."

8 Take heed, you senseless ones among the people;
    you fools, when will you become wise?
9 Does he who implanted the ear not hear?
    Does he who formed the eye not see?[d]
10 Does he who disciplines nations not punish?
    Does he who teaches[e] man lack knowledge?
11 The Lord knows the thoughts of man;
    he knows that they are futile.[f]

12 Blessed is the man you discipline,[g] O Lord,
    the man you teach from your law;
13 you grant him relief from days of trouble,
    till a pit is dug for the wicked.
14 For the Lord will not reject his people;[h]
    he will never forsake his inheritance.
15 Judgment will again be founded on righteousness,
    and all the upright in heart will follow it.

16 Who will rise up for me against the wicked?
    Who will take a stand for me against evildoers?
17 Unless the Lord had given me help,[i]
    I would soon have dwelt in the silence of death.
18 When I said, "My foot is slipping,"[j]
    your love, O Lord, supported me.
19 When anxiety was great within me,
    your consolation brought joy to my soul.

20 Can a corrupt throne be allied with you—
    one that brings on misery by its decrees?
21 They band together against the righteous
    and condemn the innocent[k] to death.
22 But the Lord has become my fortress,
    and my God the rock in whom I take refuge.[l]

94:2 [a]Ge 18:25
94:4 [b]Ps 31:18
94:7 [c]Ps 10:11
94:9 [d]Ex 4:11
94:10 [e]Job 35:11; Isa 28:26
94:11 [f]1Co 3:20*
94:12 [g]Job 5:17; Heb 12:5
94:14 [h]1Sa 12:22; Ro 11:2
94:17 [i]Ps 124:2
94:18 [j]Ps 38:16
94:21 [k]Pr 17:15, 26
94:22 [l]Ps 59:9

---

will never do anything that is not morally perfect. This reassures us that we can trust him, yet it places a demand on us. Our desire to be holy (dedicated to God and morally clean) is our only suitable response. We must never use unholy means to reach a holy goal because God says, "Be holy because I, the Lord your God, am holy" (Leviticus 19:1, 2).

94:12, 13 At times, God must discipline us to help us. This is similar to a loving parent's disciplining his child. The discipline is not very enjoyable to the child, but it is essential to teach him right from wrong. The Bible says that "no discipline seems pleasant at the time, but painful. Later on, however, it produces a harvest of righteousness and peace for those who have been trained by it" (Hebrews 12:11). When you feel God's hand of correction, accept it as proof of his love. Realize that God is urging you to follow his paths instead of stubbornly going your own way.

23 He will repay[m] them for their sins
    and destroy them for their wickedness;
    the LORD our God will destroy them.

Theme: An invitation to worship God.
Author: Anonymous

95

1 Come, let us sing for joy to the LORD;
    let us shout aloud to the Rock of our salvation.
2 Let us come before him with thanksgiving
    and extol him with music and song.

3 For the LORD is the great God,
    the great King above all gods.[n]
4 In his hand are the depths of the earth,
    and the mountain peaks belong to him.
5 The sea is his, for he made it,
    and his hands formed the dry land.

6 Come, let us bow down in worship,
    let us kneel before the LORD our Maker;
7 for he is our God
    and we are the people of his pasture,[o]
    the flock under his care.

    Today, if you hear his voice,
8   do not harden your hearts as you did at Meribah,[a][p]
    as you did that day at Massah[b] in the desert,
9 where your fathers tested[q] and tried me,
    though they had seen what I did.
10 For forty years I was angry with that generation;
    I said, "They are a people whose hearts go astray,
    and they have not known my ways."
11 So I declared on oath in my anger,
    "They shall never enter my rest."[r]

Theme: How to praise God. We can sing about him, tell others about him, worship him, give him glory, bring offerings to him, and live holy lives.
Author: Possibly David because this psalm closely resembles David's hymn of praise in 1 Chronicles 16:23–36

96

1 Sing to the LORD[s] a new song;
    sing to the LORD, all the earth.
2 Sing to the LORD, praise his name;
    proclaim his salvation day after day.

[a]8 Meribah means *quarreling*.   [b]8 Massah means *testing*.

94:23
[m]Ps 7:16

95:3
[n]Ps 96:4

95:7
[o]Ps 79:13

95:8
[p]Ex 17:7

95:9
[q]Ps 78:18;
1Co 10:9

95:11
[r]Heb 4:3*

96:1
[s]1Ch 16:23

95:1–4 Songs, shouts, gratitude, and praise erupted from those gathered to worship the Lord. While there are certainly many examples of stillness and silence in God's presence taught and illustrated in Scripture, there are equally as many examples of raucous worship. Both peaceful silence and enthusiastic praise are appropriate expressions of worship to our great God.

95:8 A hardened heart is as useless as a hardened lump of clay or a hardened loaf of bread. Nothing can restore it and make it useful. The writer warns against hardening our hearts as Israel did in the desert by continuing to resist God's will (Exodus 17:7). The Israelites had been so convinced that God couldn't deliver them that they simply lost their faith in him. When someone's heart becomes hardened, that person is so stubbornly set in his ways that he or she cannot turn to God. This does not happen all at once; it is the result of a series of choices to disregard God's will. If you resist God long enough, God may toss you aside like hardened bread, useless and worthless.

95:8 *Meribah* means "quarreling," and *Massah* means "testing." This refers to the incident at Rephidim (Exodus 17:1–7) when the Israelites complained to Moses because they had no water (see also Numbers 20:1–13).

95:11 What keeps us from God's ultimate blessings (entering his "rest")? Ungrateful hearts (95:2), not worshiping or submitting to him (95:6), hardening our hearts (95:8), testing God because of stubborn doubts (95:9). In Hebrews 4:5–11, we are warned not to harden our hearts, but to reject the glamour of sin and anything else that would lead us away from God.

96:1–4 The psalm writer sings out his praises to God, overwhelmed by all that God has done. If we believe God is great, we cannot help telling others about him. The best witnessing happens when our hearts are full of appreciation for what he has done. God has chosen to use us to "declare . . . his marvelous deeds among all peoples." Praise for our great God overflows from his creation and should overflow from our lips. How well are you doing at telling others about God's greatness?

³ Declare his glory among the nations,
    his marvelous deeds among all peoples.

96:4
ᵗPs 18:3; 145:3
ᵘPs 95:3

⁴ For great is the LORD and most worthy of praise;ᵗ
    he is to be feared above all gods.ᵘ
⁵ For all the gods of the nations are idols,
    but the LORD made the heavens.
⁶ Splendor and majesty are before him;
    strength and glory are in his sanctuary.

96:7
ᵛPs 29:1

⁷ Ascribe to the LORD,ᵛ O families of nations,
    ascribe to the LORD glory and strength.
⁸ Ascribe to the LORD the glory due his name;
    bring an offering and come into his courts.

96:9
ʷPs 29:2

⁹ Worship the LORD in the splendor of hisᵃ holiness;ʷ
    tremble before him, all the earth.

96:10
ˣPs 67:4

¹⁰ Say among the nations, "The LORD reigns."
    The world is firmly established, it cannot be moved;
    he will judge the peoples with equity.ˣ
¹¹ Let the heavens rejoice, let the earth be glad;
    let the sea resound, and all that is in it;
¹²   let the fields be jubilant, and everything in them.
    Then all the trees of the forest will sing for joy;

96:13
ʸRev 19:11

¹³   they will sing before the LORD, for he comes,
    he comes to judgeʸ the earth.
    He will judge the world in righteousness
    and the peoples in his truth.

Theme: God, our awesome Conqueror, is righteous and just.
Author: Anonymous

97:1
ᶻPs 96:10

97

¹ The LORD reigns,ᶻ let the earth be glad;
    let the distant shores rejoice.

97:2
ᵃPs 18:11
ᵇPs 89:14

² Clouds and thick darknessᵃ surround him;
    righteousness and justice are the foundation of his throne.ᵇ

97:3
ᶜPs 18:8

³ Fire goes before him
    and consumesᶜ his foes on every side.
⁴ His lightning lights up the world;
    the earth sees and trembles.

97:5
ᵈMic 1:4

⁵ The mountains meltᵈ like wax before the LORD,
    before the Lord of all the earth.
⁶ The heavens proclaim his righteousness,
    and all the peoples see his glory.

ᵃ9 Or LORD with the splendor of

JUSTICE IN THE BOOK OF PSALMS

Justice is a major theme in Psalms. The Psalmists praise God because he is just; they plead for him to intervene and bring justice where there is oppression and wickedness; they condemn the wicked who trust in their wealth; they extol the righteous who are just toward their neighbors.

Justice in Psalms is more than honesty. It is active intervention on behalf of the helpless, especially the poor. The psalmists do not merely wish the poor could be given what they need, but they plead with God to destroy those nations that are subverting justice and oppressing God's people.

Here are some examples of psalms that speak about justice. As you read them, ask yourself, Who is my neighbor? Does my life-style—my work, my play, my buying habits, my giving—help or hurt people who have less than I do? What one thing could I do this week to help a helpless person?

Selected psalms that emphasize this theme are 7; 9; 15; 37; 50; 72; 75; 82; 94; 145.

97:2 The clouds and thick darkness that surround God symbolize his unapproachable holiness and the inability of people to find him on their own. If he were uncovered, no one could stand before his blazing holiness and glory.

7 All who worship images are put to shame,
    those who boast in idols—
    worship him,^e all you gods!

8 Zion hears and rejoices
    and the villages of Judah are glad
    because of your judgments, O LORD.

9 For you, O LORD, are the Most High over all the earth;^f
    you are exalted^g far above all gods.

10 Let those who love the LORD hate evil,^h
    for he guards the lives of his faithful ones
    and deliversⁱ them from the hand of the wicked.^j
11 Light is shed^k upon the righteous
    and joy on the upright in heart.
12 Rejoice in the LORD, you who are righteous,
    and praise his holy name.^l

97:7
^eHeb 1:6

97:9
^fPs 83:18; 95:3
^gEx 18:11

97:10
^hPs 34:14; Am 5:15
ⁱDa 3:28
^jPs 37:40

97:11
^kJob 22:28

97:12
^lPs 30:4

Theme: A song of joy and victory. Because God is victorious over evil, all those who follow him will be victorious with him when he judges the earth.
Author: Anonymous

98 A psalm.

1 Sing to the LORD a new song,
    for he has done marvelous things;
    his right hand^m and his holy armⁿ
    have worked salvation for him.
2 The LORD has made his salvation known
    and revealed his righteousness to the nations.
3 He has remembered^o his love
    and his faithfulness to the house of Israel;
    all the ends of the earth have seen
    the salvation of our God.

98:1
^mEx 15:6
ⁿIsa 52:10

98:3
^oLk 1:54

4 Shout for joy to the LORD, all the earth,
    burst into jubilant song with music;
5 make music to the LORD with the harp,
    with the harp and the sound of singing,
6 with trumpets^p and the blast of the ram's horn—
    shout for joy before the LORD, the King.

98:6
^pNu 10:10

7 Let the sea resound, and everything in it,
    the world, and all who live in it.
8 Let the rivers clap their hands,
    let the mountains sing together for joy;
9 let them sing before the LORD,
    for he comes to judge the earth.
    He will judge the world in righteousness
    and the peoples with equity.^q

98:9
^qPs 96:10

97:7 People worship all kinds of images and idols. Although God reveals himself and his love through nature and the Bible, there are many who decide to ignore or reject him and pursue goals they believe are more important. The Bible makes it clear that these people are idol worshipers because they give their highest loyalty to something other than God. One day we will stand before God in all his glory and power. Then we will see all our goals and accomplishments for what they really are. How foolish our earthly pursuits will seem then!

97:10 A sincere purpose to please God will result in an alignment of your desires with God's desires. You will love what God loves and hate what God hates. If you love the Lord, you will hate evil. If you do not despise the actions of people who

take advantage of others, if you admire people who only look out for themselves, or if you envy those who get ahead using any means to accomplish their ends, then your primary desire in life is not to please God. Learn to love God's ways and hate evil in every form—not only the obvious sins but also the socially acceptable ones.

98:1ff This is a psalm of praise anticipating the coming of God to rule his people. Jesus fulfilled this anticipation when he came to save all people from their sins (98:2, 3), and he will come again to judge the world (98:8, 9). God is both perfectly loving and perfectly just. He is merciful when he punishes, and he overlooks no sin when he loves. Praise him for his promise to save you and to return again.

Theme: Praise for God's fairness and holiness. Because God is perfectly just and fair, we can trust him completely.
Author: Anonymous

99

99:1
rEx 25:22

1 The LORD reigns,
  let the nations tremble;
he sits enthroned between the cherubim,r
  let the earth shake.

99:2
sPs 97:9

2 Great is the LORD in Zion;
  he is exalteds over all the nations.
3 Let them praise your great and awesome name—
  he is holy.

4 The King is mighty, he loves justice—
  you have established equity;
in Jacob you have done
  what is just and right.
5 Exalt the LORD our God
  and worship at his footstool;
  he is holy.

99:6
tJer 15:1
u1Sa 7:9

6 Moses and Aaron were among his priests,
  Samuelt was among those who called on his name;
they called on the LORD
  and he answeredu them.

99:7
vEx 33:9

7 He spoke to them from the pillar of cloud;v
  they kept his statutes and the decrees he gave them.

99:8
wNu 14:20

8 O LORD our God,
  you answered them;
you were to Israela a forgiving God,w
  though you punished their misdeeds.b
9 Exalt the LORD our God
  and worship at his holy mountain,
  for the LORD our God is holy.

Theme: An invitation to enter joyfully into God's presence. His faithfulness extends to our generation and beyond.
Author: Anonymous

100

A psalm. For giving thanks.

1 Shout for joy to the LORD, all the earth.
2   Worship the LORD with gladness;
    come before him with joyful songs.

a8 Hebrew *them*   b8 Or / *an avenger of the wrongs done to them*

99:1 Cherubim are mighty angels that comprise one of several ranks of angels. (For more on angels, see the note on 91:11.)

99:3 Everyone should praise God's great and awesome name because his name points to his divine nature, his personage, and his reputation. But the name of God is used so often in vulgar conversation that we have lost sight of its holiness. How easy it is to treat God lightly in everyday life. If you claim him as your father, live worthy of the family name. Respect God's name and give him praise by both your *words* and your *life*.

99:5 God's holiness is terribly frightening for sinners, but a wonderful comfort for believers. God is morally perfect and is set apart from people and sin. He has no weaknesses or shortcomings. For sinners, this is frightening because all their inadequacies and evil are exposed by the light of God's holiness.

God cannot tolerate, ignore, or excuse sin. For believers, God's holiness gives comfort because, as we worship him, we are lifted from the mire of sin. As we believe in him and humble ourselves before him, we are made holy.

99:6 The Bible records several instances where Moses, Aaron, and Samuel cried out to God for help (Exodus 15:25; 17:4; Numbers 11:11–15; 12:13; 14:13ff; 16:44–48; 1 Samuel 7:5, 9; 15:11).

3 Know that the LORD is God.ˣ
   It is he who made us, and we are hisᵃ;
   we are his people, the sheep of his pasture.

100:3
ˣPs 46:10

4 Enter his gates with thanksgiving
   and his courts with praise;
   give thanks to him and praise his name.ʸ

100:4
ʸPs 116:17

5 For the LORD is good and his love endures forever;
   his faithfulnessᶻ continues through all generations.

100:5
ᶻPs 119:90

Theme: A prayer for help to walk a blameless path. To live with integrity, both our efforts and God's help are necessary.
Author: David

101 Of David. A psalm.

1 I will sing of your loveᵃ and justice;
   to you, O LORD, I will sing praise.

101:1
ᵃPs 89:1

2 I will be careful to lead a blameless life—
   when will you come to me?

   I will walk in my house
   with blameless heart.

3 I will set before my eyes
   no vile thing.

   The deeds of faithless men I hate;
   they will not cling to me.

4 Men of perverse heartᵇ shall be far from me;
   I will have nothing to do with evil.

101:4
ᵇPr 11:20

5 Whoever slanders his neighbor in secret,
   him will I put to silence;
   whoever has haughty eyesᶜ and a proud heart,
   him will I not endure.

101:5
ᶜPr 6:17

6 My eyes will be on the faithful in the land,
   that they may dwell with me;
   he whose walk is blamelessᵈ
   will minister to me.

101:6
ᵈPs 119:1

7 No one who practices deceit
   will dwell in my house;
   no one who speaks falsely
   will stand in my presence.

ᵃ3 Or and not we ourselves

100:3 David tells us to acknowledge that the Lord is God! How can we do that? We acknowledge him when we shout our praises, appreciate his status as our Creator, accept his authority in every detail of life, enthusiastically agree with the guidance he gives us, and express our thanks for his unfailing love.

100:3 God is our Creator; we did not create ourselves. Many people live as though they are the creator and center of their own little world. This mind-set leads to pride, greed, idolatry, and if everything should be taken away, a loss of hope itself. But when we realize that God created us and gives us all we have, we will want to give to others as God gave to us (2 Corinthians 9:8). Then, if all is lost, we still have God and all he gives us.

100:4 God alone is worthy of being worshiped. What is your attitude toward worship? Do you willingly and joyfully come into God's presence, or are you just going through the motions, reluctantly going to church? This psalm tells us to remember God's goodness and dependability, and then to worship with thanksgiving and praise!

101:1ff David may have written this psalm early in his reign as king as he set down the standards he wanted to follow. David knew that to lead a blameless life he would need God's help (101:2). We can lead blameless lives if we avoid (1) looking at wickedness ("I will set before my eyes no vile thing," 101:3), (2) evil associates ("men of perverse heart," 101:4), (3) slander (101:5), and (4) pride (101:5). While avoiding the wrongs listed above, we must also let God's Word show us the standards by which to live.

101:6 David said that he would keep his eyes "on the faithful in the land." In other words, he would choose as models and as friends those who are godly and truthful. Our friends and associates can have a profound influence on us. Make sure to choose as your closest companions those who are faithful to God and his Word.

101:8
e Jer 21:12
f Ps 75:10
g Ps 118:10-12

8 Every morning[e] I will put to silence
    all the wicked[f] in the land;
I will cut off every evildoer[g]
    from the city of the LORD.

Theme: The cure for distress. Because God is living, eternal, and unchanging, we can trust him to help his people in this generation just as he helped his people in past generations.
Author: Anonymous

102

A prayer of an afflicted man. When he is faint and pours out his lament before the LORD.

1 Hear my prayer, O LORD;
    let my cry for help come to you.

102:2
h Ps 69:17

2 Do not hide your face[h] from me
    when I am in distress.
Turn your ear to me;
    when I call, answer me quickly.

102:3
i Jas 4:14

3 For my days vanish like smoke;[i]
    my bones burn like glowing embers.

102:4
j Ps 37:2

4 My heart is blighted and withered like grass;[j]
    I forget to eat my food.
5 Because of my loud groaning
    I am reduced to skin and bones.

102:6
k Isa 34:11

6 I am like a desert owl,[k]
    like an owl among the ruins.

102:7
l Ps 77:4

7 I lie awake;[l] I have become
    like a bird alone on a roof.
8 All day long my enemies taunt me;
    those who rail against me use my name as a curse.

102:9
m Ps 42:3

9 For I eat ashes as my food
    and mingle my drink with tears[m]
10 because of your great wrath,
    for you have taken me up and thrown me aside.
11 My days are like the evening shadow;
    I wither away like grass.

102:12
n Ps 135:13

12 But you, O LORD, sit enthroned forever;
    your renown endures[n] through all generations.

102:13
o Isa 60:10

13 You will arise and have compassion[o] on Zion,
    for it is time to show favor to her;
    the appointed time has come.
14 For her stones are dear to your servants;
    her very dust moves them to pity.
15 The nations will fear the name of the LORD,
    all the kings of the earth will revere your glory.

102:16
p Isa 60:1-2

16 For the LORD will rebuild Zion
    and appear in his glory.[p]
17 He will respond to the prayer of the destitute;
    he will not despise their plea.

102:3, 4 The writer felt so bad that he forgot to eat. When we face sickness and despair, our days pass blindly and we don't care about even our basic needs. In these times, God alone is our comfort and strength. Even when we are too weak to fight, we can lean on him. It is often when we recognize our weaknesses that God's greatest strength becomes available.

102:6, 7 These birds are pictures of loneliness and desolation. At times we may need to be alone, and solitude may comfort us. But we must be careful not to spurn those who reach out to us.

Don't reject help and conversation. Suffering silently is neither Christian nor particularly healthy. Instead, accept graciously the support and help from family and friends.

102:16–22 Christ's future reign on earth will encompass two events mentioned in these verses. Jerusalem (Zion) will be restored, and the entire world will worship God (Revelation 11:15; 21:1–27).

18 Let this be written*q* for a future generation,
    that a people not yet created*r* may praise the LORD:
19 "The LORD looked down from his sanctuary on high,
    from heaven he viewed the earth,
20 to hear the groans of the prisoners
    and release those condemned to death."
21 So the name of the LORD will be declared*s* in Zion
    and his praise in Jerusalem
22 when the peoples and the kingdoms
    assemble to worship the LORD.

23 In the course of my life*a* he broke my strength;
    he cut short my days.
24 So I said:
    "Do not take me away, O my God, in the midst of my days;
    your years go on*t* through all generations.
25 In the beginning*u* you laid the foundations of the earth,
    and the heavens are the work of your hands.
26 They will perish,*v* but you remain;
    they will all wear out like a garment.
Like clothing you will change them
    and they will be discarded.
27 But you remain the same,*w*
    and your years will never end.
28 The children of your servants*x* will live in your presence;
    their descendants will be established before you."

Theme: God's great love for us. What God does for us tells us what he is really like.
Author: David

103 Of David.

1 Praise the LORD, O my soul;*y*
    all my inmost being, praise his holy name.
2 Praise the LORD, O my soul,
    and forget not all his benefits—
3 who forgives all your sins
    and heals all your diseases,
4 who redeems your life from the pit
    and crowns you with love and compassion,
5 who satisfies your desires with good things
    so that your youth is renewed like the eagle's.

6 The LORD works righteousness
    and justice for all the oppressed.

7 He made known his ways to Moses,
    his deeds to the people of Israel:

a 23 Or *By his power*

**Cross references (right margin):**

102:18
q Ro 15:4
r Ps 22:31

102:21
s Ps 22:22

102:24
t Ps 90:2

102:25
u Heb 1:10-12*

102:26
v Isa 34:4

102:27
w Mal 3:6

102:28
x Ps 69:36

103:1
y Ps 104:1

102:25–27 The writer of this psalm felt rejected and tossed aside because of his great troubles (102:9, 10). Problems and heartaches can overwhelm us and cause us to feel that God has rejected us. But God our Creator is eternally with us and will keep all his promises, even though we may feel alone. The world will perish, but God will remain. Hebrews 1:10-12 quotes these verses to show that Jesus Christ, God's Son, was also present and active at the creation of the world.

103:1ff David's praise focused on the good things God was doing for him. It is easy to complain about life, but David's list gives us plenty for which to praise God—he forgives our sins, heals our diseases, redeems us from death, crowns us with love and com-

passion, satisfies our desires, and gives righteousness and justice. We receive all of these without deserving any of them. No matter how difficult your life's journey, you can always count your blessings—past, present, and future. When you feel as though you have nothing for which to praise God, read David's list.

103:7 God's law was given first to Moses and the people of Israel. God's law presents a clear picture of God's character and his will for his people. It was God's training manual to prepare his people to serve him and to follow his ways. Review the Ten Commandments (Exodus 20) and the history of how they were given, asking God to show you his will and his ways through them.

<table>
<tr><td>

103:8
z Ex 34:6

103:9
a Ps 30:5

103:10
b Ezr 9:13

</td><td>

⁸ The LORD is compassionate and gracious,z
    slow to anger, abounding in love.
⁹ He will not always accuse,
    nor will he harbor his anger forever;a
¹⁰ he does not treat us as our sins deserveb
    or repay us according to our iniquities.

</td></tr>
</table>

103:8 z Ex 34:6	

103:8
z Ex 34:6

⁸ The LORD is compassionate and gracious,z
  slow to anger, abounding in love.

103:9
a Ps 30:5

⁹ He will not always accuse,
  nor will he harbor his anger forever;a

103:10
b Ezr 9:13

¹⁰ he does not treat us as our sins deserveb
  or repay us according to our iniquities.
¹¹ For as high as the heavens are above the earth,
  so great is his love for those who fear him;
¹² as far as the east is from the west,
  so far has he removed our transgressions from us.

103:13
c Mal 3:17

¹³ As a father has compassionc on his children,
  so the LORD has compassion on those who fear him;
¹⁴ for he knows how we are formed,
  he remembers that we are dust.

103:15
d Job 14:2;
1 Pe 1:24

¹⁵ As for man, his days are like grass,
  he flourishes like a flowerd of the field;

103:16
e Job 7:10

¹⁶ the wind blows over it and it is gone,
  and its placee remembers it no more.
¹⁷ But from everlasting to everlasting
  the LORD's love is with those who fear him,
  and his righteousness with their children's children—

103:18
f Dt 7:9

¹⁸ with those who keep his covenant
  and remember to obey his precepts.f

103:19
g Ps 47:2

¹⁹ The LORD has established his throne in heaven,
  and his kingdom rulesg over all.

HOW GOD IS DESCRIBED IN PSALMS

Most of the psalms speak to God or about God. Because they were composed in a variety of situations, various facets of God's character are mentioned. Here is a sample of God's characteristics as understood and experienced by the psalm writers. As you read these psalms, ask yourself if this is the God you know.

God is . . .	Reference
All-knowing and ever present	Psalm 139
Beautiful and desirable	Psalms 27; 36; 45
Creator	Psalms 8; 104; 148
Good and generous	Psalms 34; 81; 107
Great and sovereign	Psalms 33; 89; 96
Holy	Psalms 66; 99; 145
Loving and faithful	Psalms 23; 42; 51
Merciful and forgiving	Psalms 32; 111; 130
Powerful	Psalms 76; 89; 93
Willing to reveal his will, law, and direction	Psalms 1: 19; 119
Righteous and just	Psalms 71; 97; 113
Spirit	Psalms 104; 139; 143

103:12 East and west can never meet. This is a symbolic portrait of God's forgiveness—when he forgives our sin, he separates it from us and doesn't even remember it. We need never wallow in the past, for God forgives and forgets. We tend to dredge up the ugly past, but God has wiped our record clean. If we are to follow God, we must model his forgiveness. When we forgive another, we must also forget the sin. Otherwise, we have not truly forgiven.

103:13 God is like a father—tender and compassionate. Not every child has a tender and compassionate father, however. Too often, sadly, the cycles of abuse and dysfunction rob children of loving fathers. If that is your situation, God offers himself to you to be the Father you never had or perhaps felt you never needed. Of course, you can't "go fishing" with God or be held physically

by him, but you can receive his love in your heart by means of his Holy Spirit (Romans 5:5). God can tenderly heal your deep loss.

103:13, 14 We are fragile, but God's care is eternal. Too often we focus on God as Judge and Lawgiver, ignoring his compassion and concern for us. When God examines our lives, he remembers our human condition. Our weakness should never be used as a justification for sin. His mercy takes everything into account. God will deal with you compassionately. Trust him.

20 Praise the LORD, you his angels,[h]
  you mighty ones who do his bidding,
    who obey his word.
21 Praise the LORD, all his heavenly hosts,
  you his servants who do his will.
22 Praise the LORD, all his works
  everywhere in his dominion.

  Praise the LORD, O my soul.

Theme: Appreciating God through his creation. He not only creates, but maintains his creation. The Lord's care is the source of our joy.
Author: Anonymous

104

1 Praise the LORD, O my soul.

  O LORD my God, you are very great;
    you are clothed with splendor and majesty.
2 He wraps[i] himself in light as with a garment;
  he stretches out the heavens[j] like a tent
3   and lays the beams[k] of his upper chambers on their waters.
  He makes the clouds[l] his chariot
    and rides on the wings of the wind.[m]
4 He makes winds his messengers,[a][n]
  flames of fire his servants.

5 He set the earth on its foundations;
  it can never be moved.
6 You covered it with the deep as with a garment;
  the waters stood above the mountains.
7 But at your rebuke the waters fled,
  at the sound of your thunder they took to flight;
8 they flowed over the mountains,
  they went down into the valleys,
    to the place you assigned for them.
9 You set a boundary they cannot cross;
  never again will they cover the earth.

10 He makes springs pour water into the ravines;
  it flows between the mountains.
11 They give water to all the beasts of the field;
  the wild donkeys quench their thirst.
12 The birds of the air nest by the waters;
  they sing among the branches.
13 He waters the mountains[o] from his upper chambers;
  the earth is satisfied by the fruit of his work.
14 He makes grass grow for the cattle,
  and plants for man to cultivate—
    bringing forth food[p] from the earth:
15 wine[q] that gladdens the heart of man,
  oil to make his face shine,
    and bread that sustains his heart.

a4 Or angels

103:20
hPs 148:2

104:2
iDa 7:9
jIsa 40:22

104:3
kAm 9:6
lIsa 19:1
mPs 18:10

104:4
nHeb 1:7*

104:13
oPs 147:8

104:14
pGe 1:30; Job 28:5

104:15
qJdg 9:13

103:20–22 Everything everywhere is to praise the Lord: all angels—mighty ones and heavenly hosts—and all his works! Praising God means remembering all he has done for us (103:2), fearing him and obeying his commands (103:17, 18), and doing his will (103:21). Does your life praise the Lord?

104:1ff This psalm is a poetic summary of God's creation of the world as found in the first chapter of Genesis. What God created each day is mentioned by the writer as a reason to praise God. On day one, God created light (104:1, 2; Genesis 1:3); day two, the heavens and the waters (104:2, 3; Genesis 1:6); day three,

land and vegetation (104:6–18; Genesis 1:9–13); day four, the sun, moon, and stars (104:19–23; Genesis 1:14–16); day five, fish and birds (104:25, 26; Genesis 1:20–23); and on day six, animals, man, and food to sustain them (104:21–24, 27–30; Genesis 1:24–31). God's act of creation deserves the praise of all people.

104:5 The earth is built on God's foundations. "It can never be moved" by anyone other than God. Even though one day the heavens and the earth will be destroyed (2 Peter 3:10), he will create a new heaven and a new earth that will last forever (Isaiah

¹⁶ The trees of the LORD are well watered,
    the cedars of Lebanon that he planted.
¹⁷ There the birds make their nests;
    the stork has its home in the pine trees.
¹⁸ The high mountains belong to the wild goats;
    the crags are a refuge for the coneys.ᵃ

104:19
ʳGe 1:14

¹⁹ The moon marks off the seasons,ʳ
    and the sun knows when to go down.

104:20
ˢIsa 45:7

²⁰ You bring darkness,ˢ it becomes night,
    and all the beasts of the forest prowl.

104:21
ᵗJob 38:39

²¹ The lions roar for their prey
    and seek their food from God.ᵗ
²² The sun rises, and they steal away;
    they return and lie down in their dens.

104:23
ᵘGe 3:19

²³ Then man goes out to his work,ᵘ
    to his labor until evening.

104:24
ᵛPr 3:19

²⁴ How many are your works, O LORD!
    In wisdom you madeᵛ them all;
    the earth is full of your creatures.
²⁵ There is the sea, vast and spacious,
    teeming with creatures beyond number—
    living things both large and small.

104:26
ʷJob 41:1

²⁶ There the ships go to and fro,
    and the leviathan,ʷ which you formed to frolic there.

104:27
ˣPs 136:25

²⁷ These all look to you
    to give them their foodˣ at the proper time.
²⁸ When you give it to them,
    they gather it up;
when you open your hand,
    they are satisfied with good things.

104:29
ʸJob 34:14;
Ecc 12:7

²⁹ When you hide your face,
    they are terrified;
when you take away their breath,
    they die and return to the dust.ʸ

ᵃ 18 That is, the hyrax or rock badger

HISTORY IN THE BOOK OF PSALMS

For the original hearers, the historical psalms were vivid reminders of God's past acts on behalf of Israel. These history songs were written for passing on important lessons to succeeding generations. They celebrated the many promises God had made and faithfully kept; they also recounted the faithlessness of the people.

We cannot read this ancient history without reflecting on how consistently God's people failed to learn from the past. They repeatedly turned from fresh example of God's faithfulness and forgiveness only to plunge back into sin. God can use these psalms to remind us how often we do exactly the same thing: Having every reason to live for God, we choose instead to live for everything but God. If we paid more attention to "his story," we wouldn't make so many mistakes in our own stories.

Selected historical psalms include: 68; 78; 95; 105; 106; 111; 114; 135; 136; 149.

65:17; Revelation 21:1). The same power that undergirds the world also provides a firm foundation for believers.

104:24 Creation is filled with stunning variety, revealing the rich creativity, goodness, and wisdom of our loving God. As you observe your natural surroundings, thank God for his creativity. Take a fresh look at people, seeing each one as God's unique creation, each with his or her own special talents, abilities, and gifts.

104:26 Here *leviathan* simply means a large and active sea creature.

104:28–30 Psalm 105 expresses God's sovereignty in history;

this psalm tells of his sovereignty over all creation. God has supreme, unlimited power over the entire universe. He creates; he preserves; he governs. As we understand God's power, we realize that he is sufficient to handle our lives.

104:29 Today many people are arrogant enough to think they don't need God. But our every breath depends on the Spirit he has breathed into us (Genesis 2:7; 3:19; Job 33:4; 34:14, 15; Daniel 5:23). Not only do we depend on God for life, but he wants the best for us. We should also desire to learn more of his plans for us each day.

30 When you send your Spirit,
    they are created,
    and you renew the face of the earth.

31 May the glory of the LORD endure forever;
    may the LORD rejoice in his works^z—

104:31
^zGe 1:31

32 he who looks at the earth, and it trembles,
    who touches the mountains, and they smoke.^a

104:32
^aPs 144:5

33 I will sing^b to the LORD all my life;
    I will sing praise to my God as long as I live.

104:33
^bPs 63:4

34 May my meditation be pleasing to him,
    as I rejoice in the LORD.

35 But may sinners vanish from the earth
    and the wicked be no more.

Praise the LORD, O my soul.

Praise the LORD.^a

Theme: God's mighty deeds in bringing Israel to the promised land. Remembering his miracles encourages us to keep living close to him.
Author: David

105

1 Give thanks to the LORD, call on his name;
    make known among the nations what he has done.

2 Sing to him, sing praise to him;
    tell of all his wonderful acts.

3 Glory in his holy name;
    let the hearts of those who seek the LORD rejoice.

4 Look to the LORD and his strength;
    seek his face^c always.

105:4
^cPs 27:8

5 Remember the wonders he has done,
    his miracles, and the judgments he pronounced,^d

105:5
^dPs 77:11

6 O descendants of Abraham his servant,
    O sons of Jacob, his chosen ones.

7 He is the LORD our God;
    his judgments are in all the earth.

8 He remembers his covenant^e forever,
    the word he commanded, for a thousand generations,

105:8
^eLk 1:72

9 the covenant he made with Abraham,^f
    the oath he swore to Isaac.

105:9
^fGe 17:2; 22:16-18

10 He confirmed it to Jacob as a decree,
    to Israel as an everlasting covenant:

11 "To you I will give the land of Canaan^g
    as the portion you will inherit."

105:11
^gGe 13:15; 15:18

12 When they were but few in number,^h
    few indeed, and strangers in it,ⁱ

105:12
^hGe 34:30; Dt 7:7
ⁱHeb 11:9

13 they wandered from nation to nation,
    from one kingdom to another.

^a35 Hebrew *Hallelu Yah*; in the Septuagint this line stands at the beginning of Psalm 105.

105:1ff The first 15 verses of this psalm are also found in 1 Chronicles 16:8–22, where they are sung as part of the celebration of David's bringing the ark of the covenant to Jerusalem. Three other psalms are also hymns recounting Israel's history— 78, 106, and 136.

105:4, 5 If God seems far away, persist in your search for him. God rewards those who sincerely look for him (Hebrews 11:6). Jesus promised, "Seek and you will find" (Matthew 7:7). The writer suggested a valuable way to find God—become familiar with the way he has helped his people in the past. The Bible records the history of God's people. In searching its pages we will discover a loving God who is waiting for us to find him.

105:6–11 The nation Israel, the people through whom God revealed his laws to mankind, is descended from Abraham. God chose Abraham and promised that his descendants would live in the land of Canaan (now called Israel), and that they would be too numerous to count (Genesis 17:6–8). Abraham's son was Isaac; Isaac's son was Jacob. These three men are considered the patriarchs or founders of Israel. God blessed them because of their faith (see Hebrews 11:8–21).

105:14
/Ge 35:5
kGe 12:17-20

14 He allowed no one to oppress/ them;
   for their sake he rebuked kings:k
15 "Do not touch my anointed ones;
   do my prophets no harm."

105:16
/Lev 26:26; Isa 3:1

16 He called down famine/ on the land
   and destroyed all their supplies of food;

105:17
mGe 37:28

17 and he sent a man before them—
   Joseph, sold as a slave.m
18 They bruised his feet with shackles,
   his neck was put in irons,
19 till what he foretold came to pass,
   till the word of the Lord proved him true.

105:20
nGe 41:14

20 The king sent and released him,
   the ruler of peoples set him free.n
21 He made him master of his household,
   ruler over all he possessed,
22 to instruct his princes as he pleased
   and teach his elders wisdom.

105:23
oGe 46:6

23 Then Israel entered Egypt;o
   Jacob lived as an alien in the land of Ham.

105:24
pEx 1:7, 9

24 The Lord made his people very fruitful;
   he made them too numerousp for their foes,
25 whose hearts he turned to hate his people,
   to conspire against his servants.

105:26
qEx 3:10

26 He sent Mosesq his servant,
   and Aaron, whom he had chosen.
27 They performed his miraculous signs among them,
   his wonders in the land of Ham.

105:28
rEx 10:22

28 He sent darknessr and made the land dark—
   for had they not rebelled against his words?

105:29
sEx 7:21

29 He turned their waters into blood,
   causing their fish to die.s

105:30
tEx 8:2, 6

30 Their land teemed with frogs,t
   which went up into the bedrooms of their rulers.

105:31
uEx 8:16-18

31 He spoke, and there came swarms of flies,
   and gnatsu throughout their country.

105:32
vEx 9:22-25

32 He turned their rain into hail,v
   with lightning throughout their land;
33 he struck down their vines and fig trees
   and shattered the trees of their country.
34 He spoke, and the locusts came,
   grasshoppers without number;
35 they ate up every green thing in their land,
   ate up the produce of their soil.
36 Then he struck down all the firstborn in their land,
   the firstfruits of all their manhood.

37 He brought out Israel, laden with silver and gold,
   and from among their tribes no one faltered.
38 Egypt was glad when they left,
   because dread of Israel had fallen on them.

105:39
wEx 13:21

39 He spread out a cloudw as a covering,
   and a fire to give light at night.

105:23–25 Did God cause the Egyptians to hate the Israelites? God is not the author of evil, but the Bible writers don't always distinguish between God's ultimate action and the intermediate steps. Thus by God blessing the Israelites, the Egyptians came to hate them (Exodus 1:8–22). Because God caused the Israelites' blessing, he is also said to have caused the Egyptians to hate them. God used their animosity as a means to lead the Israelites out of Egypt.

⁴⁰ They asked, and he brought them quail^x
    and satisfied them with the bread of heaven.
⁴¹ He opened the rock,^{y} and water gushed out;
    like a river it flowed in the desert.

⁴² For he remembered his holy promise
    given to his servant Abraham.
⁴³ He brought out his people with rejoicing,
    his chosen ones with shouts of joy;
⁴⁴ he gave them the lands of the nations,^{z}
    and they fell heir to what others had toiled for—
⁴⁵ that they might keep his precepts
    and observe his laws.

Praise the LORD.^{a}

105:40
^{x}Ex 16:13

105:41
^{y}1Co 10:4

105:44
^{z}Jos 13:6-7

Theme: A song of national repentance as the people return from captivity. God patiently delivers us, in spite of our forgetfulness and self-willed rebellion.
Author: Anonymous

106

¹ Praise the LORD.^{b}

Give thanks to the LORD, for he is good;
    his love endures forever.
² Who can proclaim the mighty acts of the LORD
    or fully declare his praise?
³ Blessed are they who maintain justice,
    who constantly do what is right.^{a}
⁴ Remember me,^{b} O LORD, when you show favor to your people,
    come to my aid when you save them,
⁵ that I may enjoy the prosperity of your chosen ones,
    that I may share in the joy of your nation
    and join your inheritance in giving praise.

⁶ We have sinned,^{c} even as our fathers did;
    we have done wrong and acted wickedly.
⁷ When our fathers were in Egypt,
    they gave no thought to your miracles;
    they did not remember your many kindnesses,
    and they rebelled by the sea,^{d} the Red Sea.^{e}
⁸ Yet he saved them for his name's sake,^{e}
    to make his mighty power known.
⁹ He rebuked^f the Red Sea, and it dried up;^{g}
    he led them through^h the depths as through a desert.
¹⁰ He saved them^i from the hand of the foe;
    from the hand of the enemy he redeemed them.
¹¹ The waters covered their adversaries;
    not one of them survived.
¹² Then they believed his promises
    and sang his praise.

106:3
^{a}Ps 15:2

106:4
^{b}Ps 119:132

106:6
^{c}Da 9:5

106:7
^{d}Ex 14:11-12

106:8
^{e}Ex 9:16

106:9
^{f}Ps 18:15
^{g}Ex 14:21
^{h}Isa 63:11-14

106:10
^{i}Ex 14:30

^{a}45 Hebrew *Hallelu Yah* ^{b}1 Hebrew *Hallelu Yah*; also in verse 48 ^{c}7 Hebrew *Yam Suph*; that is, Sea of Reeds; also in verses 9 and 22

105:45 God's purpose for saving the Israelites was that they would "keep his precepts and observe his laws." Too often we use our lives and freedom to please ourselves, but we should honor God. That is God's purpose for our lives and why he gave us his Word.

106:1ff While Psalm 105 is a summary of God's faithfulness, Psalm 106 is a summary of man's sinfulness. Psalm 105 covers events up to the exodus from Egypt (Exodus 5—14), and Psalm

106 covers events from the exodus up to what appears to be the Babylonian captivity (2 Kings 25).

106:2 If we ever stopped to list all the mighty acts or miracles in the Bible, we would be astounded. They cover every aspect of life. The more we think about what God has done, the more we can appreciate the miracles he has done for us individually—birth, personality development, loving friends and family, specific guidance, healing, salvation—the list goes on and on. If you think you have never seen a miracle, look closer—you will see God's power and loving intervention on your behalf. God still performs great miracles!

¹³ But they soon forgot what he had done
   and did not wait for his counsel.

106:14
ʲ1Co 10:9

¹⁴ In the desert they gave in to their craving;
   in the wasteland they put God to the test.ʲ

106:15
ᵏNu 11:31
ˡIsa 10:16

¹⁵ So he gave themᵏ what they asked for,
   but sent a wasting diseaseˡ upon them.

106:16
ᵐNu 16:1-3

¹⁶ In the camp they grew enviousᵐ of Moses
   and of Aaron, who was consecrated to the LORD.

106:17
ⁿDt 11:6

¹⁷ The earth openedⁿ up and swallowed Dathan;
   it buried the company of Abiram.
¹⁸ Fire blazed among their followers;
   a flame consumed the wicked.

106:19
ᵒEx 32:4

¹⁹ At Horeb they made a calfᵒ
   and worshiped an idol cast from metal.

106:20
ᵖJer 2:11; Ro 1:23

²⁰ They exchanged their Gloryᵖ
   for an image of a bull, which eats grass.

106:21
�q Ps 78:11

²¹ They forgot the God�q who saved them,
   who had done great things in Egypt,
²² miracles in the land of Ham
   and awesome deeds by the Red Sea.

106:23
ʳEx 32:10

²³ So he said he would destroyʳ them—
   had not Moses, his chosen one,
   stood in the breach before him
   to keep his wrath from destroying them.

106:24
ˢDt 8:7
ᵗHeb 3:18-19

²⁴ Then they despised the pleasant land;ˢ
   they did not believeᵗ his promise.
²⁵ They grumbled in their tents
   and did not obey the LORD.
²⁶ So he swore to them with uplifted hand
   that he would make them fall in the desert,
²⁷ make their descendants fall among the nations
   and scatter them throughout the lands.

²⁸ They yoked themselves to the Baal of Peor
   and ate sacrifices offered to lifeless gods;
²⁹ they provoked the LORD to anger by their wicked deeds,
   and a plague broke out among them.

106:30
ᵘNu 25:8

³⁰ But Phinehas stood up and intervened,
   and the plague was checked.ᵘ
³¹ This was credited to him as righteousness
   for endless generations to come.

106:32
ᵛNu 20:2-13

³² By the waters of Meribahᵛ they angered the LORD,
   and trouble came to Moses because of them;

106:33
ʷNu 20:8-12

³³ for they rebelled against the Spirit of God,
   and rash words came from Moses' lips.ᵃ ʷ

ᵃ33 Or against his spirit, / and rash words came from his lips

---

106:13–15 In the desert, Israel was so intent on getting the food and water *they* wanted that they became blind to what God wanted. They were more concerned about immediate physical gratification than lasting spiritual satisfaction. They did not want what was best for them, and they refused to trust in God's care and provision (Numbers 11:18–33). If you complain enough, God may give you what you ask for, even if it is not the best for you. If you're not getting what you want, perhaps God knows it is not in your best interest. Trust in his care and provision.

106:22 The land of Ham is Egypt.

106:23 "Stood in the breach" means that Moses served as the people's intercessor. This refers to the time when the Lord wanted to destroy the people for worshiping the golden calf (Exodus 32:7–14).

34 They did not destroy[x] the peoples
  as the LORD had commanded them,
35 but they mingled[y] with the nations
  and adopted their customs.
36 They worshiped their idols,[z]
  which became a snare to them.
37 They sacrificed their sons
  and their daughters to demons.
38 They shed innocent blood,
  the blood of their sons[a] and daughters,
whom they sacrificed to the idols of Canaan,
  and the land was desecrated by their blood.
39 They defiled themselves[b] by what they did;
  by their deeds they prostituted[c] themselves.

40 Therefore the LORD was angry with his people
  and abhorred his inheritance.
41 He handed them over[d] to the nations,
  and their foes ruled over them.
42 Their enemies oppressed them
  and subjected them to their power.
43 Many times he delivered them,
  but they were bent on rebellion
  and they wasted away in their sin.

44 But he took note of their distress
  when he heard their cry;[e]
45 for their sake he remembered his covenant
  and out of his great love[f] he relented.
46 He caused them to be pitied[g]
  by all who held them captive.

47 Save us, O LORD our God,
  and gather us from the nations,
that we may give thanks to your holy name
  and glory in your praise.

48 Praise be to the LORD, the God of Israel,
  from everlasting to everlasting.
Let all the people say, "Amen!"[h]

Praise the LORD.

106:34	[x] Jdg 1:21
106:35	[y] Jdg 3:5-6
106:36	[z] Jdg 2:12
106:38	[a] Nu 35:33
106:39	[b] Eze 20:18 [c] Lev 17:7; Nu 15:39
106:41	[d] Jdg 2:14; Ne 9:27
106:44	[e] Jdg 10:10
106:45	[f] Jdg 2:18
106:46	[g] Ezr 9:9; Jer 42:12
106:48	[h] Ps 41:13

106:34-39 Israel constantly turned away from God. How, after the great miracles they saw, could they turn from God and worship the idols of the land? We also have seen God's great miracles, but sometimes find ourselves enticed by the world's gods—power, convenience, fame, sex, and pleasure. As Israel forgot God, so we are susceptible to forgetting him and giving in to the pressures of an evil world. Remember all that God has done for you so you won't be drawn away from him by the world's pleasures.

106:40-42 God allowed trouble to come to the Israelites in order to help them. Our troubles can be helpful because they (1) humble us, (2) wean us from the allurements of the world and drive us back to God, (3) vitalize our prayers, (4) allow us to experience more of God's faithfulness, (5) make us more dependent upon God, (6) encourage us to submit to God's purpose for our lives, and (7) make us more compassionate toward others in trouble.

106:44-46 This is a beautiful picture of God's great love for his people who deserved only judgment. Fortunately, God's compassion and mercy toward us are not limited by our faithfulness to him. God was merciful to us in sending his Son to die for our sins. If he did this while we were captive to sin, how much more merciful will he be now that we are his children?

Book V   Psalms 107–150

These psalms praise God's works, recount the blessing of righteous living, thank God for deliverance, and praise God for his wonderful word. These psalms remind us that the best sacrifice we can offer to God is a faithful and obedient life.

Theme: Thankfulness to God should constantly be on the lips of those whom he has saved. This psalm was written to celebrate the Jews' return from their exile in Babylon.
Author: Anonymous

107

¹ Give thanks to the Lord, for he is good;
    his love endures forever.

² Let the redeemed/ of the Lord say this—
    those he redeemed from the hand of the foe,

³ those he gathered/ from the lands,
    from east and west, from north and south.ᵃ

⁴ Some wandered in desert wastelands,
    finding no way to a city where they could settle.

⁵ They were hungry and thirsty,
    and their lives ebbed away.

⁶ Then they cried outᵏ to the Lord in their trouble,
    and he delivered them from their distress.

⁷ He led them by a straight wayˡ
    to a city where they could settle.

⁸ Let them give thanks to the Lord for his unfailing love
    and his wonderful deeds for men,

⁹ for he satisfiesᵐ the thirsty
    and fills the hungry with good things.

¹⁰ Some sat in darknessⁿ and the deepest gloom,
    prisoners suffering in iron chains,ᵒ

¹¹ for they had rebelled against the words of God
    and despised the counsel of the Most High.

¹² So he subjected them to bitter labor;
    they stumbled, and there was no one to help.ᵖ

¹³ Then they cried to the Lord in their trouble,
    and he saved them from their distress.

¹⁴ He brought them out of darkness and the deepest gloom
    and broke away their chains.�q

¹⁵ Let them give thanks to the Lord for his unfailing love
    and his wonderful deeds for men,

¹⁶ for he breaks down gates of bronze
    and cuts through bars of iron.

107:2
ʲPs 106:10

107:3
ʲPs 106:47

107:6
ᵏPs 50:15

107:7
ˡEzr 8:21

107:9
ᵐLk 1:53

107:10
ⁿLk 1:79
ᵒJob 36:8

107:12
ᵖPs 22:11

107:14
qAc 12:7

ᵃ3 Hebrew *north and the sea*

107:1ff This psalm speaks of four different types of people in distress and how God rescues them: wanderers (107:4–9), prisoners (107:10–16), the sick (107:17–20), and the storm-tossed (107:23–30). No matter how extreme our calamity, God is able to break through to help us. He is loving and kind to those who are distressed.

107:1, 2 "Let the redeemed of the Lord say . . ." God has done so much for us, and we have so much for which to thank him (see Psalm 103). He wants us to tell everyone all that he has done. These verses are not so much a mandate to witness as a declaration that when we live in God's presence we will not be able to keep this glorious experience to ourselves (see also Acts 1:8; 2 Corinthians 5:18–20). What has God done for you? Is there someone you can tell?

107:5–9 Lost, hungry, thirsty, and exhausted, these wanderers typify the Israelites in exile. But they also typify anyone who has not found the satisfaction that comes from knowing God. Anyone who recognizes his or her own lostness can receive the offer of Jesus to satisfy these needs. Jesus is the way (John

14:6), the bread from heaven (John 6:33, 35), the living water (John 4:10–14), and the giver of rest (Matthew 11:28–30). Have you received his life-giving offer?

107:10–16 Do you know anyone who is in prison? Most people think that those in prison deserve whatever misery they experience as punishment for their crimes. But God loves all men and women no matter how far they have fallen. He wants to reach them with his love and dispel the gloom they face (Matthew 25:34–46). Throughout the world, people are imprisoned for their faith; others suffer as victims of injustice. Can you reach out to them? Pray for those in prison. Pray for ministries and Christian chaplains who take God's message of love and forgiveness to prisoners. What can you do to support these efforts?

17 Some became fools through their rebellious ways
   and suffered affliction because of their iniquities.
18 They loathed all food
   and drew near the gates of death.^{r}

107:18
^{r}Job 33:22; Ps 9:13

19 Then they cried to the LORD in their trouble,
   and he saved them from their distress.
20 He sent forth his word^s and healed them;^{t}
   he rescued them from the grave.^{u}

107:20
^{s}Mt 8:8
^{t}Ps 103:3
^{u}Ps 30:3

21 Let them give thanks to the LORD for his unfailing love
   and his wonderful deeds for men.
22 Let them sacrifice thank offerings^v
   and tell of his works^w with songs of joy.

107:22
^{v}Lev 7:12
^{w}Ps 9:11; 73:28;
118:17

23 Others went out on the sea in ships;
   they were merchants on the mighty waters.
24 They saw the works of the LORD,
   his wonderful deeds in the deep.
25 For he spoke and stirred up a tempest^x
   that lifted high the waves.

107:25
^{x}Jnh 1:4

26 They mounted up to the heavens and went down to the depths;
   in their peril their courage melted^y away.

107:26
^{y}Ps 22:14

27 They reeled and staggered like drunken men;
   they were at their wits' end.
28 Then they cried out to the LORD in their trouble,
   and he brought them out of their distress.
29 He stilled the storm^z to a whisper;
   the waves^a of the sea were hushed.

107:29
^{z}Mt 8:26
^{a}Ps 89:9

30 They were glad when it grew calm,
   and he guided them to their desired haven.
31 Let them give thanks to the LORD for his unfailing love
   and his wonderful deeds for men.
32 Let them exalt him in the assembly^b of the people
   and praise him in the council of the elders.

107:32
^{b}Ps 22:22, 25

33 He turned rivers into a desert,
   flowing springs into thirsty ground,
34 and fruitful land into a salt waste,^{c}
   because of the wickedness of those who lived there.

107:34
^{c}Ge 13:10

35 He turned the desert into pools of water
   and the parched ground into flowing springs;
36 there he brought the hungry to live,
   and they founded a city where they could settle.
37 They sowed fields and planted vineyards
   that yielded a fruitful harvest;
38 he blessed them, and their numbers greatly increased,^{d}
   and he did not let their herds diminish.

107:38
^{d}Ge 12:2

39 Then their numbers decreased, and they were humbled
   by oppression, calamity and sorrow;
40 he who pours contempt on nobles
   made them wander in a trackless waste.
41 But he lifted the needy^e out of their affliction
   and increased their families like flocks.

107:41
^{e}1Sa 2:8;
Ps 113:7-9

107:17–20 Fools and rebels surely bring trouble upon themselves. This psalm offers hope for those who have made a mess of their lives. By receiving God's free gift of forgiveness (Micah 7:18–20; 1 John 1:9), anyone can begin a new life and break with the past (see Romans 3:23–26; 2 Corinthians 5:17). By faith in Christ, we can break addictions, heal memories, and restore broken relationships. If we ask Christ to take control of our lives,

he will answer us. His love reaches even those who have rebelled against him.

107:32 Those who have never truly suffered may not appreciate God as much as those who have matured under hardship. Those who have seen God work in times of distress have a deeper insight into his loving-kindness. If you have experienced great trials, you have the potential for great praise.

107:42
f Job 5:16; Ro 3:19

42 The upright see and rejoice,
   but all the wicked shut their mouths.*f*

107:43
g Jer 9:12; Hos 14:9

43 Whoever is wise,*g* let him heed these things
   and consider the great love of the LORD.

Theme: Victory in God's strength. With God's help, we can do more than we think.
Author: David

108 A song. A psalm of David.

1 My heart is steadfast, O God;
   I will sing and make music with all my soul.
2 Awake, harp and lyre!
   I will awaken the dawn.
3 I will praise you, O LORD, among the nations;
   I will sing of you among the peoples.
4 For great is your love, higher than the heavens;
   your faithfulness reaches to the skies.
5 Be exalted, O God, above the heavens,
   and let your glory be over all the earth.

6 Save us and help us with your right hand,
   that those you love may be delivered.
7 God has spoken from his sanctuary:
   "In triumph I will parcel out Shechem
   and measure off the Valley of Succoth.
8 Gilead is mine, Manasseh is mine;
   Ephraim is my helmet,
   Judah my scepter.
9 Moab is my washbasin,
   upon Edom I toss my sandal;
   over Philistia I shout in triumph."

10 Who will bring me to the fortified city?
   Who will lead me to Edom?
11 Is it not you, O God, you who have rejected us
   and no longer go out with our armies?
12 Give us aid against the enemy,
   for the help of man is worthless.
13 With God we will gain the victory,
   and he will trample down our enemies.

Theme: Righteous indignation against liars and slanderers. We can tell God our true feelings and desires.
Author: David

109 For the director of music. Of David. A psalm.

109:1
h Ps 83:1

1 O God, whom I praise,
   do not remain silent,*h*
2 for wicked and deceitful men
   have opened their mouths against me;
   they have spoken against me with lying tongues.

108:1ff The conclusions from two previous psalms have been put together to make this psalm. The first five verses are quoted from Psalm 57:7–11, and the next eight verses (108:6–13) are from Psalm 60:5–12.

108:9 Moab, Edom, and Philistia were Israel's enemies to the east, south, and west, respectively. They despised the Israelites and Israel's God.

108:13 Do our prayers end with requests for help to make it

through stressful situations? David prayed not merely for rescue, but for victory. With God's help we can claim more than mere survival, we can claim victory! Look for ways God can use your distress as an opportunity to show his mighty power.

109:1ff David endured many false accusations (1 Samuel 22:7–13; 2 Samuel 15:3, 4), as did Christ centuries later (Matthew 26:59–61; 27:39–44). Verse 8 is quoted in Acts 1:20 as being fulfilled in Judas's death.

3 With words of hatred*i* they surround me;
  they attack me without cause.

4 In return for my friendship they accuse me,
  but I am a man of prayer.

5 They repay me evil for good,*j*
  and hatred for my friendship.

6 Appoint*a* an evil man*b* to oppose him;
  let an accuser*c k* stand at his right hand.

7 When he is tried, let him be found guilty,
  and may his prayers condemn*l* him.

8 May his days be few;
  may another take his place*m* of leadership.

9 May his children be fatherless
  and his wife a widow.*n*

10 May his children be wandering beggars;
  may they be driven*d* from their ruined homes.

11 May a creditor seize all he has;
  may strangers plunder the fruits of his labor.*o*

12 May no one extend kindness to him
  or take pity on his fatherless children.

13 May his descendants be cut off,*p*
  their names blotted out*q* from the next generation.

14 May the iniquity of his fathers*r* be remembered before the LORD;
  may the sin of his mother never be blotted out.

15 May their sins always remain before the LORD,
  that he may cut off the memory*s* of them from the earth.

16 For he never thought of doing a kindness,
  but hounded to death the poor
  and the needy and the brokenhearted.

17 He loved to pronounce a curse—
  may it*e* come on him;*t*
  he found no pleasure in blessing—
  may it be*f* far from him.

18 He wore cursing as his garment;
  it entered into his body like water,*u*
  into his bones like oil.

19 May it be like a cloak wrapped about him,
  like a belt tied forever around him.

20 May this be the LORD's payment to my accusers,
  to those who speak evil of me.

21 But you, O Sovereign LORD,
  deal well with me for your name's sake;
  out of the goodness of your love, deliver me.

22 For I am poor and needy,
  and my heart is wounded within me.

23 I fade away like an evening shadow;
  I am shaken off like a locust.

	109:3
	i Ps 69:4
	109:5
	j Ps 35:12; 38:20
	109:6
	k Zec 3:1
	109:7
	l Pr 28:9
	109:8
	m Ac 1:20*
	109:9
	n Ex 22:24
	109:11
	o Job 5:5
	109:13
	p Ps 37:28
	q Pr 10:7
	109:14
	r Ex 20:5; Ne 4:5; Jer 18:23
	109:15
	s Ps 34:16
	109:17
	t Pr 14:14
	109:18
	u Nu 5:22

a 6 Or ⌊They say:⌋ "Appoint (with quotation marks at the end of verse 19)   *b* 6 Or the Evil One   *c* 6 Or let Satan
d 10 Septuagint; Hebrew sought   *e* 17 Or curse, / and it has   *f* 17 Or blessing, / and it is

---

109:4 David was angry at being attacked by evil people who slandered him and lied. Yet David remained a friend and a man of prayer. While we must hate evil and work to overcome it, we must love everyone, including those who do evil, because God loves them. We are called to hate the sin, but love the person. Only through God's strength will we be able to follow David's example.

109:6-20 This is another of the imprecatory psalms, a call for God to judge the wicked. (For an explanation of imprecatory psalms, see the note on 35:1ff.) David was not taking vengeance into his own hands, but was asking that God be swift in his promised judgment of evil people. David's words depict the eventual doom of all God's enemies.

109:21 A name is more than a label; it is a representation of character and reputation. David is pleading for God to live up to his name—to his character of love and mercy. "For your name's sake," then, means "in accordance with your character."

109:24
v Heb 12:12

24 My knees give v way from fasting;
    my body is thin and gaunt.

109:25
w Ps 22:6
x Mt 27:39

25 I am an object of scorn w to my accusers;
    when they see me, they shake their heads. x

26 Help me, O LORD my God;
    save me in accordance with your love.

109:27
y Job 37:7

27 Let them know y that it is your hand,
    that you, O LORD, have done it.

109:28
z 2Sa 16:12
a Isa 65:14

28 They may curse, z but you will bless;
    when they attack they will be put to shame,
    but your servant will rejoice. a

109:29
b Ps 35:26

29 My accusers will be clothed with disgrace
    and wrapped in shame b as in a cloak.

30 With my mouth I will greatly extol the LORD;
    in the great throng I will praise him.

109:31
c Ps 16:8

31 For he stands at the right hand c of the needy one,
    to save his life from those who condemn him.

Theme: The credentials for the Messiah. Jesus is the Messiah.
Author: David

110 Of David. A psalm.

110:1
d Mt 22:44*;
Mk 12:36*;
Lk 20:42*; Ac 2:34*
e 1Co 15:25

1 The LORD says d to my Lord:
    "Sit at my right hand
until I make your enemies
    a footstool for your feet." e

2 The LORD will extend your mighty scepter from Zion;
    you will rule in the midst of your enemies.

110:3
f Jdg 5:2; Ps 96:9

3 Your troops will be willing
    on your day of battle.
Arrayed in holy majesty, f
    from the womb of the dawn
    you will receive the dew of your youth. a

4 The LORD has sworn
    and will not change his mind:
"You are a priest forever,
    in the order of Melchizedek."

110:5
g Ps 16:8
h Ps 2:12
i Ps 2:5; Ro 2:5

5 The Lord is at your right hand; g
    he will crush kings h on the day of his wrath. i
6 He will judge the nations, heaping up the dead
    and crushing the rulers of the whole earth.
7 He will drink from a brook beside the way b;
    therefore he will lift up his head.

a 3 Or / your young men will come to you like the dew   b 7 Or / The One who grants succession will set him in authority

110:1 This is one of the most-quoted psalms in the New Testament because of its clear references to the Messiah. In Matthew 22:41–45, Jesus recited the words of this verse and applied them to himself. Verses 1 and 6 look forward to Christ's final and total destruction of the wicked (Revelation 6—9); 110:2 prophesies of Christ's reign on the earth (Revelation 20:1–7); 110:3, 4 tell of Christ's priestly work for his people (Hebrews 5—8); and 110:5, 6 look forward to the final battle on earth when Christ will overcome the forces of evil (Revelation 19:11–21).

110:1–7 Many people have a vague belief in God, but refuse to accept Jesus as anything more than a great human teacher. But the Bible does not allow that option. Both the Old and New Testa-ments proclaim the deity of the One who came to save and to reign. Jesus explained that this psalm spoke of the Messiah as greater than David, Israel's greatest king (Mark 12:35–37). Peter used this psalm to show that Jesus, the Messiah, sits at God's right hand and is Lord over all (Acts 2:32–35). You can't straddle the fence, calling Jesus "just a good teacher," because the Bible clearly calls him Lord.

110:4 For more about Melchizedek, see his Profile at the end of Genesis 16. As a priest like Melchizedek, Christ will never abuse his divine position, and his reign will be forever. Jesus is more fully described as our High Priest in Hebrews 5.

Theme: All that God does is good. Reverence for God is the beginning of wisdom.
Author: Anonymous

111 ^a 1 Praise the LORD.^b

I will extol the LORD with all my heart
in the council of the upright and in the assembly.

2 Great are the works^j of the LORD;
they are pondered by all who delight in them.
3 Glorious and majestic are his deeds,
and his righteousness endures forever.
4 He has caused his wonders to be remembered;
the LORD is gracious and compassionate.
5 He provides food for those who fear him;
he remembers his covenant forever.
6 He has shown his people the power of his works,
giving them the lands of other nations.
7 The works of his hands are faithful and just;
all his precepts are trustworthy.^k
8 They are steadfast for ever and ever,
done in faithfulness and uprightness.
9 He provided redemption^l for his people;
he ordained his covenant forever—
holy and awesome is his name.

10 The fear of the LORD is the beginning of wisdom;
all who follow his precepts have good understanding.
To him belongs eternal praise.

111:2
^jPs 92:5

111:7
^kPs 19:7

111:9
^lLk 1:68

Theme: The advantages of having faith in God. God guards the minds and actions of those who follow his commands.
Author: Anonymous

112 ^a 1 Praise the LORD.^b

Blessed is the man who fears the LORD,
who finds great delight^m in his commands.

2 His children will be mighty in the land;
the generation of the upright will be blessed.
3 Wealth and riches are in his house,
and his righteousness endures forever.
4 Even in darkness light dawns for the upright,
for the gracious and compassionate and righteous man.^c
5 Good will come to him who is generous and lends freely,ⁿ
who conducts his affairs with justice.

112:1
^mPs 119:14, 16, 47, 92

112:5
ⁿPs 37:21, 26

^aThis psalm is an acrostic poem, the lines of which begin with the successive letters of the Hebrew alphabet.
^b1,1 Hebrew *Hallelu Yah* ^c4 Or / for ⌊the LORD⌋ *is gracious and compassionate and righteous*

111—118 Psalms 111—118 are called hallelujah psalms. *Halle-lujah* means "praise the LORD" and expresses the uplifting and optimistic tone of these songs.

111:9 The redemption here pictures the rescue by God of the Israelites from Egypt and the future return from captivity in Babylon (see Deuteronomy 7:8; Jeremiah 31:11). *Redemption* means recovery of something or someone upon payment of a ransom. All people were being held in slavery by sin, until Jesus paid the price to free us—giving his life as a perfect sacrifice. Before Jesus offered himself as a sacrifice for sin, people were not permitted into God's presence (the Most Holy Place); now, all believers can freely approach God's throne through prayer and have God in their lives through the Holy Spirit.

111:10 The only way to become truly wise is to fear (revere) God. This same thought is expressed in Proverbs 1:7–9. Too often people want to skip this step, thinking they can become wise by life experience and academic knowledge alone. But if we do not acknowledge God as the source of wisdom, then our foundation for making wise decisions is shaky, and we are prone to mistakes and foolish choices.

112:1 Many blessings are available to us—honor, prosperity, security, freedom from fear (112:2–9)—if we *fear* the Lord and *delight* in obeying his commands. If you expect God's blessings, you must revere him and gladly obey him.

112:5 Generosity will cure two problems that money can create. The rich man may abuse others in his desire to accumulate wealth. Generosity will eliminate that abuse. Also, the fear of losing money can be a snare. Generosity and respect for God places our trust in him, not our money, for justice and security.

112:6
o Pr 10:7

6 Surely he will never be shaken;
    a righteous man will be remembered° forever.

112:7
p Ps 57:7

7 He will have no fear of bad news;
    his heart is steadfast,ᵖ trusting in the Lᴏʀᴅ.
8 His heart is secure, he will have no fear;
    in the end he will look in triumph on his foes.

112:9
q 2Co 9:9*
r Ps 75:10

9 He has scattered abroad his gifts to the poor,�q
    his righteousness endures forever;
    his hornᵃ will be liftedʳ high in honor.

112:10
s Ps 37:12

10 The wicked man will see and be vexed,
    he will gnash his teethˢ and waste away;
    the longings of the wicked will come to nothing.

Theme: The scope of God's care. God's great mercy is demonstrated by his concern for the poor and the oppressed.
Author: Anonymous

113

1 Praise the Lᴏʀᴅ.ᵇ

Praise, O servants of the Lᴏʀᴅ,
    praise the name of the Lᴏʀᴅ.

113:2
t Da 2:20

2 Let the name of the Lᴏʀᴅ be praised,
    both now and forevermore.ᵗ
3 From the rising of the sun to the place where it sets,
    the name of the Lᴏʀᴅ is to be praised.

113:4
u Ps 99:2
v Ps 8:1

4 The Lᴏʀᴅ is exaltedᵘ over all the nations,
    his glory above the heavens.ᵛ
5 Who is like the Lᴏʀᴅ our God,
    the One who sits enthroned on high,

113:6
w Ps 11:4; 138:6;
Isa 57:15

6 who stoops down to lookʷ
    on the heavens and the earth?

113:7
x 1Sa 2:8
y Ps 107:41

7 He raises the poorˣ from the dust
    and lifts the needyʸ from the ash heap;
8 he seats them with princes,
    with the princes of their people.

113:9
z 1Sa 2:5

9 He settles the barrenᶻ woman in her home
    as a happy mother of children.

Praise the Lᴏʀᴅ.

Theme: The mighty God who delivered Israel from Egypt. We can celebrate God's great work in our life.
Author: Anonymous

114

1 When Israel came out of Egypt,ᵃ
    the house of Jacob from a people of foreign tongue,
2 Judah became God's sanctuary,
    Israel his dominion.

114:1
a Ex 13:3

114:3
b Ex 14:21

3 The sea looked and fled,ᵇ
    the Jordan turned back;

ᵃ9 *Horn* here symbolizes dignity.   ᵇ1 Hebrew *Hallelu Yah*; also in verse 9

112:7, 8 We all want to live without fear; our heroes are fearless people who take on all dangers and overcome them. The writer teaches us that *fear* of God can lead to a *fearless* life. To fear God means to respect and revere him as the almighty Lord. When we trust God completely to take care of us, we will find that our other fears—even of death itself—will subside.

112:9 "His horn will be lifted high in honor" means that God's dignity will be uplifted and those faithful to God will be honored. The horn was a symbol of power and dignity just as the horns of animals represent their strength.

113:5–9 In God's eyes, a person's value has no relationship to his or her wealth or position on the social ladder. Many people who have excelled in God's work began in poverty or humble beginnings. God supersedes the social orders of this world, often choosing his future leaders and ambassadors from among social outcasts. Do you treat the unwanted in society as though they have value? Demonstrate by your actions that all people are valuable and useful in God's eyes.

4 the mountains skipped like rams,
    the hills like lambs.

5 Why was it, O sea, that you fled,
    O Jordan, that you turned back,
6 you mountains, that you skipped like rams,
    you hills, like lambs?

7 Tremble, O earth, at the presence of the Lord,
    at the presence of the God of Jacob,
8 who turned the rock into a pool,
    the hard rock into springs of water.*c*

114:8
c Ex 17:6; Nu 20:11

Theme: God is alive. He is thinking about us and caring for us, and we should put him first in our life.
Author: Anonymous

115

1 Not to us, O LORD, not to us
    but to your name be the glory,
    because of your love and faithfulness.

2 Why do the nations say,
    "Where is their God?"*d*
3 Our God is in heaven;
    he does whatever pleases him.*e*
4 But their idols are silver and gold,
    made by the hands of men.*f*
5 They have mouths, but cannot speak,
    eyes, but they cannot see;
6 they have ears, but cannot hear,
    noses, but they cannot smell;
7 they have hands, but cannot feel,
    feet, but they cannot walk;
    nor can they utter a sound with their throats.
8 Those who make them will be like them,
    and so will all who trust in them.

9 O house of Israel, trust in the LORD—
    he is their help and shield.
10 O house of Aaron, trust in the LORD—
    he is their help and shield.
11 You who fear him, trust in the LORD—
    he is their help and shield.

12 The LORD remembers us and will bless us:
    He will bless the house of Israel,
    he will bless the house of Aaron,

115:2
d Ps 42:3
115:3
e Ps 135:6
115:4
f Jer 10:3-5

114:7 When God gave the law at Mount Sinai, the mountain trembled in God's presence. Even with our great technology, the seas, rivers, and mountains still present us with formidable challenges. But to God, who controls nature, they are as nothing. When observing the power of an ocean wave or the majesty of a mountain peak, think of God's greatness and glory, which are far more awesome than the natural wonders you can see. To tremble at God's presence means to recognize God's complete power and authority and our frailty by comparison.

115—118 Psalms 115—118 were traditionally sung at the Passover meal, commemorating Israel's escape from slavery in Egypt (Exodus 11, 12).

115:1 The writer asked that God's name, not the nation's, be glorified. Too often we ask God to glorify his name *with* ours. For example, we may pray for help to do a good job so that our work will be noticed. Or we may ask that a presentation go well so we

will get applause. There is nothing wrong with looking good or impressing others; the problem comes when we want to look good no matter what happens to God's reputation in the process. Before you pray, ask yourself, "Who will get the credit if God answers my prayer?"

115:4–8 When the psalms were written, many people worshiped idols—statues of wood, stone, or metal. They took pride in what they could see and had contempt for what they couldn't see. Today, we still may value tangible objects (home, clothing, possessions) rather than intangible realities (spiritual growth, salvation, giving to those in need, spending time with loved ones). Those who spend their time obtaining tangible objects are as foolish and empty as the idols themselves. (For more on the foolishness of idols, see Isaiah 44:9–20.)

115:12 "The LORD remembers us," says the psalm writer. What a fantastic truth! There are many times when we feel isolated,

115:13
g Ps 128:1, 4

13 he will bless those who fear g the LORD—
  small and great alike.

14 May the LORD make you increase,
  both you and your children.

115:15
h Ge 1:1; Ps 96:5

15 May you be blessed by the LORD,
  the Maker of heaven h and earth.

16 The highest heavens belong to the LORD,
  but the earth he has given to man.

115:17
i Ps 6:5

17 It is not the dead i who praise the LORD,
  those who go down to silence;

115:18
j Ps 113:2

18 it is we who extol the LORD,
  both now and forevermore. j

Praise the LORD. a

Theme: Praise for being saved from certain death. Worship is a thankful response and not a repayment for what God has done.
Author: Anonymous

116:1
k Ps 18:1

116

1 I love the LORD, k for he heard my voice;
  he heard my cry for mercy.
2 Because he turned his ear to me,
  I will call on him as long as I live.

3 The cords of death entangled me,
  the anguish of the grave b came upon me;
  I was overcome by trouble and sorrow.
4 Then I called on the name of the LORD:
  "O LORD, save me!"

116:5
l Ezr 9:15; Ps 103:8

5 The LORD is gracious and righteous; l
  our God is full of compassion.
6 The LORD protects the simplehearted;
  when I was in great need, he saved me.

116:7
m Mt 11:29
n Ps 13:6

7 Be at rest m once more, O my soul,
  for the LORD has been good n to you.

116:8
o Ps 56:13

8 For you, O LORD, have delivered my soul o from death,
  my eyes from tears,
  my feet from stumbling,

116:9
p Ps 27:13

9 that I may walk before the LORD
  in the land of the living. p

116:10
q 2Co 4:13*

10 I believed; q therefore c I said,
  "I am greatly afflicted."

116:11
r Ro 3:4

11 And in my dismay I said,
  "All men are liars." r

12 How can I repay the LORD
  for all his goodness to me?
13 I will lift up the cup of salvation
  and call on the name of the LORD.

116:14
s Ps 22:25

14 I will fulfill my vows s to the LORD
  in the presence of all his people.

a 18 Hebrew Hallelu Yah   b 3 Hebrew Sheol   c 10 Or believed even when

alone, and abandoned, even by God. In reality, he sees, understands, and thinks about us. When depressed by problems or struggling with self-worth, be encouraged that God keeps you in his thoughts. If he thinks about you, surely his help is near.

116:1, 2 God is so responsive that you can always reach him. He bends down and listens to your voice. This writer's love for

the Lord had grown because he had experienced answers to his prayers. If you are discouraged, remember that God is near, listening carefully to every prayer and answering each prayer in order to give you his best.

15 Precious in the sight[t] of the LORD
    is the death of his saints.
16 O LORD, truly I am your servant;[u]
    I am your servant, the son of your maidservant[a];[v]
    you have freed me from my chains.

17 I will sacrifice a thank offering[w] to you
    and call on the name of the LORD.
18 I will fulfill my vows to the LORD
    in the presence of all his people,
19 in the courts[x] of the house of the LORD—
    in your midst, O Jerusalem.

    Praise the LORD.[b]

	116:15 [t] Ps 72:14
	116:16 [u] Ps 119:125; 143:12 [v] Ps 86:16
	116:17 [w] Ps 50:14
	116:19 [x] Ps 96:8

Theme: Another reason for praise—God's love for the whole world. We should praise God for his unlimited love.
Author: Anonymous

117

1 Praise the LORD, all you nations;[y]
    extol him, all you peoples.
2 For great is his love toward us,
    and the faithfulness of the LORD endures forever.

    Praise the LORD.[b]

117:1
[y] Ro 15:11*

Theme: Confidence in God's eternal love. God's love is unchanging in the midst of changing situations. This gives us security.
Author: Anonymous

118

1 Give thanks to the LORD, for he is good;
    his love endures forever.

2 Let Israel say:[z]
    "His love endures forever."
3 Let the house of Aaron say:
    "His love endures forever."
4 Let those who fear the LORD say:
    "His love endures forever."

5 In my anguish[a] I cried to the LORD,
    and he answered by setting me free.
6 The LORD is with me;[b] I will not be afraid.
    What can man do to me?
7 The LORD is with me; he is my helper.
    I will look in triumph on my enemies.

8 It is better to take refuge in the LORD[c]
    than to trust in man.
9 It is better to take refuge in the LORD
    than to trust in princes.[d]

	118:2 [z] Ps 115:9
	118:5 [a] Ps 120:1
	118:6 [b] Heb 13:6*
	118:8 [c] Ps 40:4
	118:9 [d] Ps 146:3

[a] 16 Or *servant, your faithful son*   [b] 19,2 Hebrew *Hallelu Yah*

116:15 God stays close to us even in death. When someone we love is nearing death, we may become angry and feel abandoned. But believers (saints) are precious to God, and he carefully chooses the time when they will be called into his presence. Let this truth provide comfort when you've lost a loved one. God sees, and each life is valuable to him (see Jesus' statement in Matthew 10:29).

117:1, 2 Not only is Psalm 117 the shortest chapter in the Bible, it is also the middle chapter. Paul quotes from this psalm in Romans 15:11 to show that God's salvation is for *all* people, not just the Jews.

117:1, 2 Have you ever said, "I can't think of anything God has done for me. How can I praise him?" This psalm gives two reasons for praising God: his great love toward us, and his faithfulness that endures forever. If he did nothing else for us, he would still be worthy of our highest praise.

118:8 Pilots put confidence in their planes. Commuters place confidence in trains, cars, or buses. Each day we must put our confidence in something or someone. If you are willing to trust a plane or car to get you to your destination, are you willing to trust God to guide you here on earth and to your eternal destination? Do you trust him more than any human being? How futile it is to trust anything or anyone more than God.

10 All the nations surrounded me,
but in the name of the LORD I cut them off.
11 They surrounded me on every side,
but in the name of the LORD I cut them off.
12 They swarmed around me like bees,[e]
but they died out as quickly as burning thorns;
in the name of the LORD I cut them off.

13 I was pushed back and about to fall,
but the LORD helped me.
14 The LORD is my strength[f] and my song;
he has become my salvation.

15 Shouts of joy and victory
resound in the tents of the righteous:
"The LORD's right hand has done mighty things!
16   The LORD's right hand is lifted high;
the LORD's right hand has done mighty things!"

17 I will not die[g] but live,
and will proclaim[h] what the LORD has done.
18 The LORD has chastened me severely,
but he has not given me over to death.

19 Open for me the gates of righteousness;
I will enter and give thanks to the LORD.
20 This is the gate of the LORD
through which the righteous may enter.[i]
21 I will give you thanks, for you answered me;
you have become my salvation.

22 The stone the builders rejected
has become the capstone;[j]
23 the LORD has done this,
and it is marvelous in our eyes.
24 This is the day the LORD has made;
let us rejoice and be glad in it.

25 O LORD, save us;
O LORD, grant us success.
26 Blessed is he who comes[k] in the name of the LORD.
From the house of the LORD we bless you.[a]
27 The LORD is God,
and he has made his light shine[l] upon us.
With boughs in hand, join in the festal procession
up[b] to the horns of the altar.

28 You are my God, and I will give you thanks;
you are my God,[m] and I will exalt[n] you.

29 Give thanks to the LORD, for he is good;
his love endures forever.

118:12
[e]Dt 1:44

118:14
[f]Ex 15:2

118:17
[g]Hab 1:12
[h]Ps 73:28

118:20
[i]Rev 22:14

118:22
[j]Mt 21:42;
Mk 12:10;
Lk 20:17*; Ac 4:11*

118:26
[k]Mt 21:9*;
Mk 11:9*; Lk 19:38*
118:27
[l]1Pe 2:9

118:28
[m]Isa 25:1
[n]Ex 15:2

[a]26 The Hebrew is plural.   [b]27 Or Bind the festal sacrifice with ropes / and take it

---

118:22, 23 Jesus referred to this verse when he spoke of being rejected by his own people (Matthew 21:42; Mark 12:10, 11; Luke 20:17). Although he was rejected, Jesus is now the "capstone," the most important part of the church (Acts 4:11; Ephesians 2:20; 1 Peter 2:6, 7). The capstone is the center stone in the top of an arch, holding the whole arch together.

118:24 There are days when the last thing we want to do is rejoice. Our mood is down, our situation is out of hand, and our sorrow or guilt is overwhelming. We can relate to the writers of the psalms who often felt this way. But no matter how low the

writers felt, they were always honest with God. And as they talked to God, their prayers ended in praise. When you don't feel like rejoicing, tell God how you truly feel. You will find that God will give you a reason to rejoice. God has given you this day to live and to serve him—be glad!

118:27 The "horns of the altar" were the projections from the four corners of the altar.

Theme: God's word is true and wonderful. Stay true to God and his Word no matter how bad the world becomes. Obedience to God's laws is the only way to achieve real happiness.

Author: Anonymous, some suggest Ezra the priest

119 [a]

א Aleph

1 Blessed are they whose ways are blameless,
  who walk[o] according to the law of the LORD.
2 Blessed are they who keep his statutes
  and seek him with all their heart.
3 They do nothing wrong;[p]
  they walk in his ways.
4 You have laid down precepts
  that are to be fully obeyed.
5 Oh, that my ways were steadfast
  in obeying your decrees!
6 Then I would not be put to shame
  when I consider all your commands.
7 I will praise you with an upright heart
  as I learn your righteous laws.[q]
8 I will obey your decrees;
  do not utterly forsake me.

ב Beth

9 How can a young man keep his way pure?
  By living according to your word.
10 I seek you with all my heart;[r]
  do not let me stray from your commands.
11 I have hidden your word in my heart[s]
  that I might not sin against you.
12 Praise be to you, O LORD;
  teach me your decrees.
13 With my lips I recount
  all the laws that come from your mouth.
14 I rejoice in following your statutes
  as one rejoices in great riches.
15 I meditate on your precepts[t]
  and consider your ways.
16 I delight[u] in your decrees;
  I will not neglect your word.

119:1
[o] Ps 128:1

119:3
[p] 1Jn 3:9; 5:18

119:7
[q] Dt 4:8

119:10
[r] 2Ch 15:15

119:11
[s] Ps 37:31;
Lk 2:19, 51

119:15
[t] Ps 1:2

119:16
[u] Ps 1:2

[a] This psalm is an acrostic poem; the verses of each stanza begin with the same letter of the Hebrew alphabet.

119:1ff This is both the longest psalm and the longest chapter in the Bible. It may have been written by Ezra after the temple was rebuilt (Ezra 6:14, 15) as a repetitive meditation on the beauty of God's Word and how it helps us stay pure and grow in faith. Psalm 119 has 22 carefully constructed sections, each corresponding to a different letter in the Hebrew alphabet and each verse beginning with the letter of its section. Almost every verse mentions God's Word. Such repetition was common in the Hebrew culture. People did not have personal copies of the Scriptures to read as we do, so God's people memorized his Word and passed it along orally. The structure of this psalm allowed for easy memorization. Remember, God's Word, the Bible, is the only sure guide for living a pure life.

119:9 We are drowning in a sea of sexual images and sinful attractions. Everywhere we look we find temptation to fill our minds with thoughts of sexual relationships that God wouldn't approve. The writer asked a question that troubles us all: How

do we stay pure in a contaminating environment? We cannot do this on our own, but must have counsel and strength more dynamic than the tempting influences around us. Where can we find that strength and wisdom? By reading God's Word and doing what it says.

119:11 Hiding (keeping) God's Word in our hearts is a deterrent to sin. This alone should inspire us to memorize Scripture. But memorization alone will not keep us from sin; we must also put God's Word to work in our lives, making it a vital guide for everything we do.

119:12–24 Most of us chafe under rules, for we think they restrict us from doing what we want. At first glance, then, it may seem strange to hear the writer talk of rejoicing in following God's statutes as much as in great riches. But God's laws were given to free us to be all he wants us to be. They restrict us from doing what might cripple us and keep us from being our best. God's guidelines help us follow his path and avoid paths that lead to destruction.

ג Gimel

17 Do good to your servant, and I will live;
   I will obey your word.
18 Open my eyes that I may see
   wonderful things in your law.
19 I am a stranger on earth;v
   do not hide your commands from me.
20 My soul is consumedw with longing
   for your laws at all times.
21 You rebuke the arrogant, who are cursed
   and who stray from your commands.
22 Remove from me scornx and contempt,
   for I keep your statutes.
23 Though rulers sit together and slander me,
   your servant will meditate on your decrees.
24 Your statutes are my delight;
   they are my counselors.

ד Daleth

25 I am laid low in the dust;y
   preserve my life according to your word.
26 I recounted my ways and you answered me;
   teach me your decrees.
27 Let me understand the teaching of your precepts;
   then I will meditate on your wonders.z
28 My soul is weary with sorrow;a
   strengthen me according to your word.
29 Keep me from deceitful ways;
   be gracious to me through your law.
30 I have chosen the way of truth;
   I have set my heart on your laws.
31 I hold fast to your statutes, O LORD;
   do not let me be put to shame.
32 I run in the path of your commands,
   for you have set my heart free.

ה He

33 Teach me, O LORD, to follow your decrees;
   then I will keep them to the end.
34 Give me understanding, and I will keep your law
   and obey it with all my heart.
35 Direct me in the path of your commands,
   for there I find delight.
36 Turn my heart toward your statutes
   and not toward selfish gain.b
37 Turn my eyes away from worthless things;
   preserve my lifec according to your word.a

a 37 Two manuscripts of the Masoretic Text and Dead Sea Scrolls; most manuscripts of the Masoretic Text *life in your way*

119:19 v 1Ch 29:15; Ps 39:12; Heb 11:13
119:20 w Ps 42:2
119:22 x Ps 39:8
119:25 y Ps 44:25
119:27 z Ps 145:5
119:28 a Ps 107:26
119:36 b Lk 12:15
119:37 c Ps 71:20; Isa 33:15

119:19 The writer says that he is a "stranger on earth," and so he needed guidance. Almost any long trip requires a map or guide. As we travel through life, the Bible should be our road map, pointing out safe routes, obstacles to avoid, and our final destination. We must recognize ourselves as pilgrims, travelers here on earth who need to study God's map to learn the way. If we ignore the map, we will wander aimlessly through life and risk missing our real destination.

119:27, 28 Our lives are cluttered with rule books, but the authors never come with us to help us follow the rules. But God does. That is the uniqueness of our Bible. God not only provides the rules and guidelines, but comes with us personally each day to strengthen us so that we can live according to those rules. All we must do is invite him and respond to his direction.

119:36 Today people most often covet financial gain. Money represents power, influence, and success. For many people, money is a god. They think about little else. True, money can buy certain comforts and offer some security. But far more valuable than wealth is obedience to God; it is a heavenly treasure rather than an earthly one (Luke 12:33). We should do what God wants, regardless of the financial implications. Make the writer's prayer your own, asking God to turn your heart toward his statutes and not toward making money; it's in your own best interest in the long run.

38 Fulfill your promise[d] to your servant,
    so that you may be feared.
39 Take away the disgrace I dread,
    for your laws are good.
40 How I long for your precepts!
    Preserve my life in your righteousness.

ו Waw

41 May your unfailing love come to me, O LORD,
    your salvation according to your promise;
42 then I will answer the one who taunts me,
    for I trust in your word.
43 Do not snatch the word of truth from my mouth,
    for I have put my hope in your laws.
44 I will always obey your law,
    for ever and ever.
45 I will walk about in freedom,
    for I have sought out your precepts.
46 I will speak of your statutes before kings[e]
    and will not be put to shame,
47 for I delight in your commands
    because I love them.
48 I lift up my hands to[a] your commands, which I love,
    and I meditate on your decrees.

ז Zayin

49 Remember your word to your servant,
    for you have given me hope.
50 My comfort in my suffering is this:
    Your promise preserves my life.[f]
51 The arrogant mock me without restraint,
    but I do not turn[g] from your law.
52 I remember your ancient laws, O LORD,
    and I find comfort in them.
53 Indignation grips me[h] because of the wicked,
    who have forsaken your law.
54 Your decrees are the theme of my song
    wherever I lodge.
55 In the night I remember[i] your name, O LORD,
    and I will keep your law.
56 This has been my practice:
    I obey your precepts.

ח Heth

57 You are my portion,[j] O LORD;
    I have promised to obey your words.
58 I have sought your face with all my heart;
    be gracious to me according to your promise.
59 I have considered my ways[k]
    and have turned my steps to your statutes.
60 I will hasten and not delay
    to obey your commands.
61 Though the wicked bind me with ropes,
    I will not forget your law.

a48 Or for

119:38
d2Sa 7:25

119:46
eMt 10:18;
Ac 26:1-2

119:50
fRo 15:4

119:51
gJob 23:11

119:53
hEzr 9:3

119:55
iPs 63:6

119:57
jPs 16:5

119:59
kLk 15:17-18

119:44-46 The writer talks about keeping the laws and yet being free. Contrary to what we often expect, obeying God's laws does not inhibit or restrain us. Instead it frees us to be what God designed us to be. By seeking God's salvation and forgiveness, we have freedom from sin and the resulting oppressive guilt. By living God's way, we have freedom to fulfill God's plan for our lives.

62 At midnight I rise to give you thanks
    for your righteous laws.
63 I am a friend to all who fear you,
    to all who follow your precepts.

119:64
l Ps 33:5

64 The earth is filled with your love,*l* O LORD;
    teach me your decrees.

ל Teth

65 Do good to your servant
    according to your word, O LORD.
66 Teach me knowledge and good judgment,
    for I believe in your commands.

119:67
m Jer 31:18-19;
Heb 12:11

67 Before I was afflicted I went astray,*m*
    but now I obey your word.

119:68
n Ps 106:1

68 You are good,*n* and what you do is good;
    teach me your decrees.

119:69
o Job 13:4

69 Though the arrogant have smeared me with lies,*o*
    I keep your precepts with all my heart.

119:70
p Ps 17:10

70 Their hearts are callous*p* and unfeeling,
    but I delight in your law.
71 It was good for me to be afflicted
    so that I might learn your decrees.

119:72
q Ps 19:10;
Pr 8:10-11, 19

72 The law from your mouth is more precious to me
    than thousands of pieces of silver and gold.*q*

י Yodh

119:73
r Job 10:8; Ps 138:8

73 Your hands made me*r* and formed me;
    give me understanding to learn your commands.

119:74
s Ps 34:2

74 May those who fear you rejoice*s* when they see me,
    for I have put my hope in your word.

119:75
t Heb 12:5-11

75 I know, O LORD, that your laws are righteous,
    and in faithfulness*t* you have afflicted me.
76 May your unfailing love be my comfort,
    according to your promise to your servant.
77 Let your compassion come to me that I may live,
    for your law is my delight.
78 May the arrogant be put to shame for wronging me without cause;
    but I will meditate on your precepts.
79 May those who fear you turn to me,
    those who understand your statutes.
80 May my heart be blameless toward your decrees,
    that I may not be put to shame.

כ Kaph

119:81
u Ps 84:2

81 My soul faints*u* with longing for your salvation,
    but I have put my hope in your word.

119:82
v Ps 69:3

82 My eyes fail,*v* looking for your promise;
    I say, "When will you comfort me?"
83 Though I am like a wineskin in the smoke,
    I do not forget your decrees.

119:84
w Ps 39:4; Rev 6:10

84 How long*w* must your servant wait?
    When will you punish my persecutors?

119:85
x Ps 35:7

85 The arrogant dig pitfalls*x* for me,
    contrary to your law.
86 All your commands are trustworthy;
    help me, for men persecute me without cause.
87 They almost wiped me from the earth,
    but I have not forsaken your precepts.

88 Preserve my life according to your love,
　　and I will obey the statutes of your mouth.

ל　Lamedh

89 Your word, O LORD, is eternal;[y]
　　it stands firm in the heavens.
90 Your faithfulness continues through all generations;
　　you established the earth, and it endures.
91 Your laws endure[z] to this day,
　　for all things serve you.
92 If your law had not been my delight,
　　I would have perished in my affliction.
93 I will never forget your precepts,
　　for by them you have preserved my life.
94 Save me, for I am yours;
　　I have sought out your precepts.
95 The wicked are waiting to destroy me,
　　but I will ponder your statutes.
96 To all perfection I see a limit;
　　but your commands are boundless.

מ　Mem

97 Oh, how I love your law!
　　I meditate[a] on it all day long.
98 Your commands make me wiser[b] than my enemies,
　　for they are ever with me.
99 I have more insight than all my teachers,
　　for I meditate on your statutes.
100 I have more understanding than the elders,
　　for I obey your precepts.[c]
101 I have kept my feet[d] from every evil path
　　so that I might obey your word.
102 I have not departed from your laws,
　　for you yourself have taught me.
103 How sweet are your words to my taste,
　　sweeter than honey[e] to my mouth!
104 I gain understanding from your precepts;
　　therefore I hate every wrong path.

נ　Nun

105 Your word is a lamp to my feet
　　and a light[f] for my path.
106 I have taken an oath[g] and confirmed it,
　　that I will follow your righteous laws.
107 I have suffered much;
　　preserve my life, O LORD, according to your word.
108 Accept, O LORD, the willing praise of my mouth,[h]
　　and teach me your laws.
109 Though I constantly take my life in my hands,
　　I will not forget your law.
110 The wicked have set a snare[i] for me,
　　but I have not strayed from your precepts.

119:89
[y]1Pe 1:25

119:91
[z]Jer 33:25

119:97
[a]Ps 1:2

119:98
[b]Dt 4:6

119:100
[c]Job 32:7-9

119:101
[d]Pr 1:15

119:103
[e]Ps 19:10

119:105
[f]Pr 6:23

119:106
[g]Ne 10:29

119:108
[h]Hos 14:2;
Heb 13:15

119:110
[i]Ps 140:5

119:97–104 God's Word makes us wise—wiser than our enemies and wiser than any teachers who ignore it. True wisdom goes beyond amassing knowledge; it is *applying* knowledge in a life-changing way. Intelligent or experienced people are not necessarily wise. Wisdom comes from allowing what God teaches to guide us.
119:105 To walk safely in the woods at night we need a light so we don't trip over tree roots or fall into holes. In this life, we walk through a dark forest of evil. But the Bible can be our light to show us the way ahead so we won't stumble as we walk. It reveals the entangling roots of false values and philosophies. Study the Bible so you will be able to see your way clear enough to stay on the right path.

111 Your statutes are my heritage forever;
　　　they are the joy of my heart.
112 My heart is set on keeping your decrees
　　　to the very end.

ס Samekh

113 I hate double-minded men,
　　　but I love your law.
114 You are my refuge and my shield;
　　　I have put my hope in your word.
115 Away from me,j you evildoers,
　　　that I may keep the commands of my God!
116 Sustain me according to your promise, and I will live;
　　　do not let my hopes be dashed.k
117 Uphold me, and I will be delivered;
　　　I will always have regard for your decrees.
118 You reject all who stray from your decrees,
　　　for their deceitfulness is in vain.
119 All the wicked of the earth you discard like dross;l
　　　therefore I love your statutes.
120 My flesh tremblesm in fear of you;
　　　I stand in awe of your laws.

ע Ayin

121 I have done what is righteous and just;
　　　do not leave me to my oppressors.
122 Ensure your servant's well-being;
　　　let not the arrogant oppress me.
123 My eyes fail, looking for your salvation,
　　　looking for your righteous promise.
124 Deal with your servant according to your love
　　　and teach me your decrees.
125 I am your servant;n give me discernment
　　　that I may understand your statutes.
126 It is time for you to act, O LORD;
　　　your law is being broken.
127 Because I love your commands
　　　more than gold,o more than pure gold,
128 and because I consider all your precepts right,
　　　I hate every wrong path.

פ Pe

129 Your statutes are wonderful;
　　　therefore I obey them.
130 The unfolding of your words gives light;
　　　it gives understanding to the simple.p
131 I open my mouth and pant,
　　　longing for your commands.
132 Turn to me and have mercy on me,
　　　as you always do to those who love your name.

119:115
jPs 6:8; Mt 7:23

119:116
kPs 25:2; Ro 5:5

119:119
lEze 22:18, 19

119:120
mHab 3:16

119:125
nPs 116:16

119:127
oPs 19:10

119:130
pPs 19:7

119:113 Double-minded people cannot make up their minds between good and evil. But when it comes to obeying God, there is no middle ground; you must take a stand. Either you are obeying him or you are not. Either you are doing what he wants or you are undecided. Choose to obey God, and say with the writer, "I love your law."

119:125 The writer asked God for discernment. Faith comes alive when we apply Scripture to our daily tasks and concerns.

We need discernment so we can understand, and we need the desire to apply Scripture where we need help. The Bible is like medicine—it goes to work only when we apply it to the affected areas. As you read the Bible, be alert for lessons, commands, or examples that you can put into practice.

133 Direct my footsteps according to your word;*q*
　　let no sin rule*r* over me.
134 Redeem me from the oppression of men,
　　that I may obey your precepts.
135 Make your face shine*s* upon your servant
　　and teach me your decrees.
136 Streams of tears*t* flow from my eyes,
　　for your law is not obeyed.

119:133
*q*Ps 17:5
*r*Ps 19:13

119:135
*s*Ps 4:6

119:136
*t*Jer 9:1, 18

צ Tsadhe

137 Righteous are you, O Lord,
　　and your laws are right.
138 The statutes you have laid down are righteous;*u*
　　they are fully trustworthy.
139 My zeal wears me out,*v*
　　for my enemies ignore your words.
140 Your promises have been thoroughly tested,*w*
　　and your servant loves them.
141 Though I am lowly and despised,
　　I do not forget your precepts.
142 Your righteousness is everlasting
　　and your law is true.*x*
143 Trouble and distress have come upon me,
　　but your commands are my delight.
144 Your statutes are forever right;
　　give me understanding that I may live.

119:138
*u*Ps 19:7

119:139
*v*Ps 69:9

119:140
*w*Ps 12:6

119:142
*x*Ps 19:7

ק Qoph

145 I call with all my heart; answer me, O Lord,
　　and I will obey your decrees.
146 I call out to you; save me
　　and I will keep your statutes.
147 I rise before dawn*y* and cry for help;
　　I have put my hope in your word.
148 My eyes stay open through the watches of the night,
　　that I may meditate on your promises.
149 Hear my voice in accordance with your love;
　　preserve my life, O Lord, according to your laws.
150 Those who devise wicked schemes are near,
　　but they are far from your law.
151 Yet you are near,*z* O Lord,
　　and all your commands are true.
152 Long ago I learned from your statutes
　　that you established them to last forever.*a*

119:147
*y*Ps 5:3

119:151
*z*Ps 145:18
119:152
*a*Lk 21:33

ר Resh

153 Look upon my suffering and deliver me,
　　for I have not forgotten your law.
154 Defend my cause and redeem me;*b*
　　preserve my life according to your promise.
155 Salvation is far from the wicked,
　　for they do not seek out*c* your decrees.
156 Your compassion is great, O Lord;
　　preserve my life according to your laws.
157 Many are the foes who persecute me,
　　but I have not turned from your statutes.
158 I look on the faithless with loathing,
　　for they do not obey your word.

119:154
*b*1Sa 24:15

119:155
*c*Job 5:4

159 See how I love your precepts;
    preserve my life, O Lord, according to your love.
160 All your words are true;
    all your righteous laws are eternal.

ש Sin and Shin

119:161
d 1Sa 24:11

161 Rulers persecute me*d* without cause,
    but my heart trembles at your word.
162 I rejoice in your promise
    like one who finds great spoil.
163 I hate and abhor falsehood
    but I love your law.
164 Seven times a day I praise you
    for your righteous laws.

119:165
e Pr 3:2; Isa 32:17

165 Great peace*e* have they who love your law,
    and nothing can make them stumble.

119:166
f Ge 49:18

166 I wait for your salvation,*f* O Lord,
    and I follow your commands.
167 I obey your statutes,
    for I love them greatly.

119:168
g Pr 5:21

168 I obey your precepts and your statutes,
    for all my ways are known*g* to you.

ת Taw

169 May my cry come before you, O Lord;
    give me understanding according to your word.
170 May my supplication come before you;
    deliver me according to your promise.
171 May my lips overflow with praise,
    for you teach me your decrees.
172 May my tongue sing of your word,
    for all your commands are righteous.
173 May your hand be ready to help me,
    for I have chosen your precepts.
174 I long for your salvation, O Lord,
    and your law is my delight.
175 Let me live that I may praise you,
    and may your laws sustain me.

119:176
h Isa 53:6

176 I have strayed like a lost sheep.*h*
    Seek your servant,
    for I have not forgotten your commands.

Theme: A prayer for deliverance from false accusers. All believers must live with the tension of being in the world but not belonging to it.
Author: Anonymous, some suggest Hezekiah

120 A song of ascents.

120:1
i Jnh 2:2

1 I call on the Lord in my distress,*i*
    and he answers me.
2 Save me, O Lord, from lying lips
    and from deceitful tongues.

119:160 One of God's characteristics is truthfulness. He embodies perfect truth; therefore, his Word cannot lie. It is true and dependable for guidance and help (see John 17:14–17). The Bible is completely true and trustworthy.

119:165 Modern society longs for peace of mind. Here is clear-cut instruction on how to attain this: if we love God and obey his laws, we will have "great peace." Trust in God, who alone stands above the pressures of daily life and gives us full assurance.

120—134 Psalms 120—134 are called "Pilgrim Psalms" or "Songs of Ascent." They were sung by those who journeyed (and thus "ascended") to the temple for the annual feasts. Each psalm is a "step" along the journey. Psalm 120 begins the journey in a distant land in hostile surroundings; Psalm 122 pictures the pilgrims arriving in Jerusalem; and the rest of the psalms move toward the temple, mentioning various characteristics of God.

3 What will he do to you,
  and what more besides, O deceitful tongue?
4 He will punish you with a warrior's sharp arrows,
  with burning coals of the broom tree.

5 Woe to me that I dwell in Meshech,
  that I live among the tents of Kedar!j
6 Too long have I lived
  among those who hate peace.
7 I am a man of peace;
  but when I speak, they are for war.

120:5
jGe 25:13;
Jer 49:28

Theme: We can depend upon God for help. Pilgrims must travel through lonely country to their destination; they are protected, not by anything created, but by the Creator of everything.
Author: Anonymous, some suggest Hezekiah

121 A song of ascents.

1 I lift up my eyes to the hills—
  where does my help come from?
2 My help comes from the LORD,
  the Maker of heaven and earth.k

121:2
kPs 115:15; 124:8

3 He will not let your foot slip—
  he who watches over you will not slumber;
4 indeed, he who watches over Israel
  will neither slumber nor sleep.

5 The LORD watches overl you—
  the LORD is your shade at your right hand;
6 the sunm will not harm you by day,
  nor the moon by night.

121:5
lIsa 25:4

121:6
mPs 91:5; Isa 49:10

7 The LORD will keep you from all harm—
  he will watch over your life;
8 the LORD will watch over your coming and going
  both now and forevermore.n

121:8
nDt 28:6

Theme: Stepping into the presence of God. What Jerusalem was for the Israelites, the church is to the believer.
Author: David

122 A song of ascents. Of David.

1 I rejoiced with those who said to me,
  "Let us go to the house of the LORD."
2 Our feet are standing
  in your gates, O Jerusalem.

3 Jerusalem is built like a city
  that is closely compacted together.

120:5, 6 Meshech was a nation far to the north of Israel; Kedar a nation to the southeast. Both were known for being warlike and barbarian. Because the writer couldn't have been in two places at one time, he was lamenting that he felt far from home and surrounded by pagan people.

120:7 Peacemaking is not always popular. Some people prefer to fight for what they believe in. The glory of battle is in the hope of winning, but someone must be a loser. The glory of peacemaking is that it may actually produce two winners. Peacemaking is God's way, so we should carefully and prayerfully attempt to be peacemakers.

121:1ff This song expresses assurance and hope in God's protection day and night. He not only made the hills but heaven and earth as well. We should never trust a lesser power than God himself. But not only is he all-powerful, he also watches over us. Nothing diverts or deters him. We are safe. We never outgrow our need for God's untiring watch over our lives.

122:1 Going to God's house can be a chore or a delight. For the writer, it was a delight. As a pilgrim attending one of the three great religious festivals, he rejoiced to worship with God's people in God's house. We may find worship a chore if we have unconfessed sin or if our love for God has cooled. But if we are

4 That is where the tribes go up,
  the tribes of the LORD,
to praise the name of the LORD
  according to the statute given to Israel.
5 There the thrones for judgment stand,
  the thrones of the house of David.

122:6
*o*Ps 51:18

6 Pray for the peace of Jerusalem:
  "May those who love*o* you be secure.
7 May there be peace within your walls
  and security within your citadels."
8 For the sake of my brothers and friends,
  I will say, "Peace be within you."

122:9
*p*Ne 2:10

9 For the sake of the house of the LORD our God,
  I will seek your prosperity.*p*

Theme: Look to God for mercy. We are encouraged to be attentive to God's leading.
Author: Anonymous, some suggest Hezekiah

123 A song of ascents.

123:1
*q*Ps 11:4; 121:1;
141:8

1 I lift up my eyes to you,
  to you whose throne*q* is in heaven.
2 As the eyes of slaves look to the hand of their master,
  as the eyes of a maid look to the hand of her mistress,
so our eyes look to the LORD our God,
  till he shows us his mercy.

3 Have mercy on us, O LORD, have mercy on us,
  for we have endured much contempt.
4 We have endured much ridicule from the proud,
  much contempt from the arrogant.

Theme: God delivers us from those who seek to destroy us. God is on the side of those who seek him.
Author: David, possibly written after his defeat of the Philistines (2 Samuel 5:17–25)

124 A song of ascents. Of David.

124:1
*r*Ps 129:1

1 If the LORD had not been on our side—
  let Israel say*r*—
2 if the LORD had not been on our side
  when men attacked us,
3 when their anger flared against us,
  they would have swallowed us alive;
4 the flood would have engulfed us,
  the torrent would have swept over us,
5 the raging waters
  would have swept us away.

---

close to God and enjoy his presence, we will be eager to worship and praise him. Our attitude toward God will determine our view of worship.

122:5 The "thrones for judgment" are the courts of justice by the town gate. In Bible times, the elders in a town sat to hear cases and administer justice at the gate (Ruth 4:1, 2). Sometimes the king himself would sit at the gate to meet his subjects and make legal decisions (2 Samuel 19:8). Speeches and prophecies were also made at the city gate (Nehemiah 8:1; Jeremiah 17:19, 20).

122:6–9 The writer was not praying for his own peace and prosperity, but for that of his family and friends in Jerusalem. This is intercessory prayer, prayer on behalf of others. Too often we are

quick to pray for our own needs and desires, and omit interceding for others. Will you intercede for someone in need today?

122:6–9 The peace sought in these verses is much more than the mere absence of conflict. It suggests completeness, health, justice, prosperity, and protection. The world cannot provide this peace. Real peace comes from faith in God because he alone embodies all the characteristics of peace. To find peace of mind and peace with others, you must find peace with God.

123:1ff The writer lifted his eyes to God, waiting and watching for God to send his mercy. The more he waited, the more he cried out to God because he knew that the evil and proud offered no help—they had only contempt for God.

6 Praise be to the LORD,
  who has not let us be torn by their teeth.
7 We have escaped like a bird
  out of the fowler's snare;*s*
  the snare has been broken,
  and we have escaped.
8 Our help is in the name of the LORD,
  the Maker of heaven*t* and earth.

124:7
s Ps 91:3; Pr 6:5

124:8
t Ge 1:1; Ps 121:2

Theme: God is our Protector. The mountains around Jerusalem symbolize God's protection for his people.
Author: Anonymous, some suggest Hezekiah

125 A song of ascents.

1 Those who trust in the LORD are like Mount Zion,
  which cannot be shaken but endures forever.
2 As the mountains surround Jerusalem,
  so the LORD surrounds his people
  both now and forevermore.

3 The scepter of the wicked will not remain*u*
  over the land allotted to the righteous,
  for then the righteous might use
  their hands to do evil.

4 Do good, O LORD, to those who are good,
  to those who are upright in heart.
5 But those who turn to crooked ways*v*
  the LORD will banish with the evildoers.

  Peace be upon Israel.*w*

125:3
u Pr 22:8; Isa 14:5

125:5
v Pr 2:15
w Ps 128:6

Theme: God does great things. His power not only releases us from sin's captive hold but brings us back to him.
Author: Anonymous, possibly written to celebrate the exiles' return from captivity (Ezra 1)

126 A song of ascents.

1 When the LORD brought back*x* the captives to*a* Zion,
  we were like men who dreamed.*b*
2 Our mouths were filled with laughter,
  our tongues with songs of joy.*y*
  Then it was said among the nations,
  "The LORD has done great things for them."
3 The LORD has done great things for us,
  and we are filled with joy.

4 Restore our fortunes,*c* O LORD,
  like streams in the Negev.
5 Those who sow in tears
  will reap with songs of joy.

126:1
x Ps 85:1

126:2
y Job 8:21

a 1 Or *LORD restored the fortunes of* *b* 1 Or *men restored to health* *c* 4 Or *Bring back our captives*

124:7, 8 Do you ever feel trapped by overwhelming odds? With God, there is always a way out because he is the Creator of all that exists. No problem is beyond his ability to solve; no circumstance is too difficult for him. We can turn to the Creator for help in our time of need, for he is on our side. God will provide a way out; we need only trust him and look for it. David compared this to a bird escaping the fowler's snare (trap).

125:1 Have you ever known people who were drawn to every new fad or idea? Such people are inconsistent and therefore unreliable. The secret to consistency is to trust in God, because he never

changes. He cannot be shaken by the changes in our world, and he endures forever. The fads and ideas of our world, and our world itself, will not.

125:3 Although the writer said, "The scepter of the wicked will not remain over the land allotted to the righteous," often Israel had to put up with evil rulers. The writer was expressing what will ultimately happen when God executes his final judgment. Human sinfulness often ruins God's ideal on earth, but that doesn't mean God has lost control. Evil prevails only as long as God allows.

126:5, 6 God's ability to restore life is beyond our understanding.

6 He who goes out weeping,
carrying seed to sow,
will return with songs of joy,
carrying sheaves with him.

Theme: Life without God is senseless. All of life's work—building a home, establishing a career, and raising a family—must have God as the foundation.
Author: Solomon

127 A song of ascents. Of Solomon.

127:1
z Ps 121:4

1 Unless the LORD builds the house,
its builders labor in vain.
Unless the LORD watchesᶻ over the city,
the watchmen stand guard in vain.

127:2
a Ge 3:17

2 In vain you rise early
and stay up late,
toiling for foodᵃ to eat—
for he grants sleep toᵃ those he loves.

127:3
b Ge 33:5

3 Sons are a heritage from the LORD,
children a rewardᵇ from him.

127:5
c Pr 27:11

4 Like arrows in the hands of a warrior
are sons born in one's youth.
5 Blessed is the man
whose quiver is full of them.
They will not be put to shame
when they contend with their enemiesᶜ in the gate.

Theme: God, the true head of the home. (This is called the marriage prayer because it was often sung at Israelite marriages.) God will reward your devotion to him with inner peace.
Author: Anonymous, some suggest Hezekiah

128 A song of ascents.

128:1
d Ps 119:1-3

1 Blessed are all who fear the LORD,
who walk in his ways.ᵈ

128:2
e Isa 3:10

2 You will eat the fruit of your labor;ᵉ
blessings and prosperity will be yours.

128:3
f Eze 19:10
g Ps 52:8; 144:12

3 Your wife will be like a fruitful vineᶠ
within your house;
your sons will be like olive shootsᵍ
around your table.

ᵃ2 Or eat— / for while they sleep he provides for

Forests burn down and are able to grow back. Broken bones heal. Even grief is not a permanent condition. Our tears can be seeds that will grow into a harvest of joy because God is able to bring good out of tragedy. When burdened by sorrow, know that your times of grief will end and that you will again find joy. We must be patient as we wait. God's great harvest of joy is coming!

127:1 Families establish homes and watchmen guard cities, but both these activities are futile unless God is with them. A family without God can never experience the spiritual bond God brings to relationships. A city without God will crumble from evil and corruption on the inside. Don't make the mistake of leaving God out of your life—if you do, all your accomplishments will be futile. Make God your highest priority, and let him do the building.

127:2 God is not against human effort. Hard work honors God (Proverbs 31:10–29). But working to the exclusion of rest or to the neglect of family may be a cover-up for an inability to trust God to provide for our needs. We all need adequate rest and times of spiritual refreshment. On the other hand, this verse

is not an excuse to be lazy (Proverbs 18:9). Be careful to maintain a balance: work while trusting God, and also rest while trusting him.

127:3–5 Too often children are seen as liabilities rather than assets. But the Bible calls children "a heritage from the LORD," a reward. We can learn valuable lessons from their inquisitive minds and trusting spirits. Those who view children as a distraction or nuisance should instead see them as an opportunity to shape the future. We dare not treat children as an inconvenience when God values them so highly.

128:1ff A good family life is a reward for following God. The values outlined in God's Word include love, service, honesty, integrity, and prayer. These help all relationships, and they are especially vital to home life. Is your home life heavenly or hectic? Reading and obeying God's Word is a good place to start to make your family all that it should be.

4 Thus is the man blessed
    who fears the LORD.

5 May the LORD bless you from Zion[h]
    all the days of your life;
may you see the prosperity of Jerusalem,
6   and may you live to see your children's children.[i]

Peace be upon Israel.[j]

128:5
hPs 134:3

128:6
iJob 42:16
jPs 125:5

Theme: Confidence in times of persecution. God will bring us through the tough times.
Author: Anonymous, some suggest Hezekiah

129 A song of ascents.

1 They have greatly oppressed me from my youth—
    let Israel say[k]—
2 they have greatly oppressed me from my youth,
    but they have not gained the victory over me.
3 Plowmen have plowed my back
    and made their furrows long.
4 But the LORD is righteous;
    he has cut me free from the cords of the wicked.

5 May all who hate Zion
    be turned back in shame.
6 May they be like grass on the roof,
    which withers[l] before it can grow;
7 with it the reaper cannot fill his hands,
    nor the one who gathers fill his arms.
8 May those who pass by not say,
    "The blessing of the LORD be upon you;
we bless you[m] in the name of the LORD."

129:1
kPs 124:1

129:6
lPs 37:2

129:8
mRu 2:4; Ps 118:26

Theme: Assurance of the Lord's forgiveness. God will surely forgive us if we confess our sins to him.
Author: Anonymous, some suggest Hezekiah

130 A song of ascents.

1 Out of the depths I cry to you, O LORD;
2   O Lord, hear my voice.
Let your ears be attentive
    to my cry for mercy.

3 If you, O LORD, kept a record of sins,
    O Lord, who could stand?
4 But with you there is forgiveness;[n]
    therefore you are feared.[o]

5 I wait for the LORD,[p] my soul waits,
    and in his word[q] I put my hope.
6 My soul waits for the Lord
    more than watchmen wait for the morning,
    more than watchmen wait for the morning.[r]

130:4
nEx 34:7; Jer 33:8
o1Ki 8:40

130:5
pIsa 8:17
qPs 119:81

130:6
rPs 119:147

129:2 The people of Israel were persecuted from their earliest days, but never destroyed completely. The same is true of the church. Christians have faced times of severe persecution, but the church has never been destroyed. As Jesus said to Peter (which means 'rock'), "On this rock I will build my church, and the gates of Hades will not overcome it" (Matthew 16:18). When you face persecution and discrimination, take courage—the church will never be destroyed.

129:3 This verse foreshadowed Jesus' unjust punishment before his death. He endured horrible lashes from the whip of his tormentors, which indeed made "furrows" on his back (John 19:1).

130:1, 2 In the depths of despair, the writer cried out to God. Despair makes us feel isolated and distant from God, but this is precisely when we need God most. Despair over sin should not lead to self-pity, causing us to think more about ourselves than God. Instead, it should lead to confession and then to God's

130:7
s Ps 131:3

7 O Israel, put your hope*s* in the Lord,
  for with the Lord is unfailing love
  and with him is full redemption.
8 He himself will redeem Israel
  from all their sins.

Theme: Trust and contentment. Quiet trust in God is the basis for our contentment.
Author: David

131 A song of ascents. Of David.

131:1
t Ro 12:16

1 My heart is not proud,*t* O Lord,
  my eyes are not haughty;
  I do not concern myself with great matters
  or things too wonderful for me.

131:2
u Mt 18:3;
1Co 14:20

2 But I have stilled and quieted my soul;
  like a weaned child with its mother,
  like a weaned child is my soul*u* within me.

131:3
v Ps 130:7

3 O Israel, put your hope*v* in the Lord
  both now and forevermore.

Theme: Honor God and he will honor you. The psalm writer reflects upon that great day when the ark of the covenant was brought to Jerusalem and praises God for his promise to perpetuate David's line.
Author: Anonymous

132 A song of ascents.

1 O Lord, remember David
  and all the hardships he endured.

132:2
w Ge 49:24

2 He swore an oath to the Lord
  and made a vow to the Mighty One of Jacob:*w*
3 "I will not enter my house
  or go to my bed—
4 I will allow no sleep to my eyes,
  no slumber to my eyelids,

132:5
x Ac 7:46

5 till I find a place*x* for the Lord,
  a dwelling for the Mighty One of Jacob."

132:6
y 1Sa 17:12
z 1Sa 7:2

6 We heard it in Ephrathah,*y*
  we came upon it in the fields of Jaar*a:b z*

132:7
a Ps 5:7

7 "Let us go to his dwelling place;*a*
  let us worship at his footstool—

a6 That is, Kiriath Jearim   *b6 Or heard of it in Ephrathah, / we found it in the fields of Jaar.* (And no quotes around verses 7-9)

---

mercy, forgiveness, and redemption. When we feel overwhelmed by a problem, feeling sorry for ourselves will only increase feelings of hopelessness; but crying out to God will turn our attention to the only One who can really help.

130:3, 4 Keeping a record of sins (or holding a grudge) is like building a wall between you and another person, and it is nearly impossible to talk openly while the wall is there. God doesn't keep a record of our sins; when he forgives, he forgives completely, tearing down any wall between us and him. Therefore, we fear (revere) God, yet we can talk to him about anything. When you pray, realize that God is holding nothing against you. His lines of communication are completely open.

131:1, 2 Pride results from overvaluing ourselves and undervaluing others. It leads to restlessness because it makes us dissatisfied with what we have and concerned about what everyone else is doing. It keeps us always hungering for more attention and

adoration. By contrast, humility puts others first and allows us to be content with God's leading in our lives. Such contentment gives us security so that we no longer have to prove ourselves to others. Let humility and trust affect your perspective and give you the strength and freedom to serve God and others.

132:2–5 This refers to David's desire to build the temple. When David became king, he built a beautiful palace, but he was troubled that the ark of the covenant, the symbol of God's presence among his people (Exodus 25:10–22), remained in a tent (2 Samuel 6:17; 7:1–17). This so bothered David that he couldn't sleep until he corrected the situation. He began to lay the plans for the temple to house the ark. (Eventually the temple was built by his son, Solomon.) We must live so close to God that we become restless until God's will is accomplished through us.

8 arise, O Lord,[b] and come to your resting place,
you and the ark of your might.
9 May your priests be clothed with righteousness;
may your saints sing for joy."

10 For the sake of David your servant,
do not reject your anointed one.

11 The Lord swore an oath to David,[c]
a sure oath that he will not revoke:
"One of your own descendants
I will place on your throne—
12 if your sons keep my covenant
and the statutes I teach them,
then their sons will sit
on your throne for ever and ever."

13 For the Lord has chosen Zion,[d]
he has desired it for his dwelling:
14 "This is my resting place for ever and ever;
here I will sit enthroned, for I have desired it—
15 I will bless her with abundant provisions;
her poor will I satisfy with food.[e]
16 I will clothe her priests with salvation,
and her saints will ever sing for joy.

17 "Here I will make a horn[a] grow[f] for David
and set up a lamp for my anointed one.
18 I will clothe his enemies with shame,
but the crown on his head will be resplendent."

Theme: The joy of harmonious relationships.
Author: David

133

A song of ascents. Of David.

1 How good and pleasant it is
when brothers live together[g] in unity!
2 It is like precious oil poured on the head,
running down on the beard,
running down on Aaron's beard,
down upon the collar of his robes.
3 It is as if the dew of Hermon[h]
were falling on Mount Zion.
For there the Lord bestows his blessing,[i]
even life forevermore.

a *17 Horn here symbolizes strong one, that is, king.*

132:8
b Nu 10:35

132:11
c Ps 89:3-4, 35

132:13
d Ps 48:1-2

132:15
e Ps 147:14

132:17
f Eze 29:21; Lk 1:69

133:1
g Ge 13:8

133:3
h Dt 4:48
i Lev 25:21

132:11, 12 The promise that David's sons would sit on Israel's throne forever is found in 2 Samuel 7:8–29. This promise had two parts: (1) David's descendants would perpetually rule over Israel as long as they followed God, and (2) David's royal line would never end. The first part was conditional; as long as the kings obeyed God ("keep my covenant and the statutes I teach them"), their dynasty continued. The second part of the promise was unconditional. It was fulfilled in Jesus Christ, a descendant of David, who reigns forever.

132:17, 18 The horn to "grow for David" refers to one of his mighty descendants. David's son, Solomon, was indeed a glorious king (1 Kings 3:10–14); but these verses look ahead even further to another descendant of David, Jesus the Messiah (Matthew 1:17). The power, might, and glory of the Messiah will last forever.

133:1–3 David stated that unity is pleasant and precious. Unfortunately, unity does not abound in the church as it should. People disagree and cause division over unimportant issues. Some

delight in causing tension by discrediting others. Unity is important because (1) it makes the church a positive example to the world and helps draw others to us; (2) it helps us cooperate as a body of believers as God meant us to, giving us a foretaste of heaven; (3) it renews and revitalizes ministry because there is less tension to sap our energy.

Living in unity does not mean that we will agree on everything; there will be many opinions just as there are many notes in a musical chord. But we must agree on our purpose in life—to work together for God. Our outward expression of unity will reflect our inward unity of purpose.

133:2 Expensive oil was used by Moses to anoint Aaron as the first high priest of Israel (Exodus 29:7) and to dedicate all the priests to God's service. Brotherly unity, like the anointing oil, shows that we are dedicated to serving God wholeheartedly.

133:3 Mount Hermon is the tallest mountain in Palestine, located northeast of the Sea of Galilee.

Theme: Worship God and experience the joy of his blessings.
Author: Anonymous, some suggest Hezekiah

134

A song of ascents.

¹ Praise the LORD, all you servants^j of the LORD
who minister by night in the house of the LORD.
² Lift up your hands^k in the sanctuary
and praise the LORD.

³ May the LORD, the Maker of heaven^l and earth,
bless you from Zion.

Theme: A hymn of praise. This psalm contrasts the greatness of God with the powerlessness of idols. Pagans worship idols while God's people worship the living God.
Author: Anonymous

135

¹ Praise the LORD.^a

Praise the name of the LORD;
praise him, you servants of the LORD,
² you who minister in the house of the LORD,
in the courts of the house of our God.

³ Praise the LORD, for the LORD is good;^m
sing praise to his name, for that is pleasant.ⁿ
⁴ For the LORD has chosen Jacob to be his own,
Israel to be his treasured possession.^o

⁵ I know that the LORD is great,
that our Lord is greater than all gods.
⁶ The LORD does whatever pleases him,^p
in the heavens and on the earth,
in the seas and all their depths.

⁷ He makes clouds rise from the ends of the earth;
he sends lightning with the rain^q
and brings out the wind from his storehouses.

⁸ He struck down the firstborn^r of Egypt,
the firstborn of men and animals.
⁹ He sent his signs and wonders into your midst, O Egypt,
against Pharaoh and all his servants.^s
¹⁰ He struck down many^t nations
and killed mighty kings—
¹¹ Sihon king of the Amorites,
Og king of Bashan
and all the kings of Canaan^u—
¹² and he gave their land as an inheritance,
an inheritance to his people Israel.

¹³ Your name, O LORD, endures forever,^v
your renown,^w O LORD, through all generations.
¹⁴ For the LORD will vindicate his people
and have compassion on his servants.^x

134:1
j Ps 135:1-2
134:2
k 1Ti 2:8

134:3
l Ps 124:8

135:3
m Ps 119:68
n Ps 147:1
135:4
o Ex 19:5; Dt 7:6

135:6
p Ps 115:3

135:7
q Jer 10:13;
Zec 10:1

135:8
r Ex 12:12

135:9
s Ps 136:10-15
135:10
t Nu 21:21-25;
Ps 136:17-21
135:11
u Jos 12:7-24

135:13
v Ex 3:15
w Ps 102:12
135:14
x Dt 32:36

a 1 Hebrew *Hallelu Yah*; also in verses 3 and 21

134:1–3 This psalm is about a very small group—the Levites who served as temple watchmen ("you servants of the LORD who minister by night"). Singing this psalm, the last of the "songs of ascent" (Psalms 120—134), the worshipers would ascend the hill where the temple sits and see the watchmen who protect it day and night. They saw the watchmen's work as an act of praise to God, done reverently and responsibly. Make your job or your responsibility in the church an act of praise by doing it with reverence to God. Honor him by the quality of your work and the attitude of service you bring to it.

134:3 Zion is another name for Jerusalem.
135:4 That the descendants of Jacob, Israel, were a chosen people reflects God's commission to the nation in Deuteronomy 7:6–8 and in Peter's sermon to the church in 1 Peter 2:9. God treasures us. He gives love and mercy to all those who believe in him.

15 The idols of the nations are silver and gold,
    made by the hands of men.
16 They have mouths, but cannot speak,
    eyes, but they cannot see;
17 they have ears, but cannot hear,
    nor is there breath in their mouths.
18 Those who make them will be like them,
    and so will all who trust in them.

19 O house of Israel, praise the LORD;
    O house of Aaron, praise the LORD;
20 O house of Levi, praise the LORD;
    you who fear him, praise the LORD.
21 Praise be to the LORD from Zion,*y*
    to him who dwells in Jerusalem.

    Praise the LORD.

135:21
y Ps 134:3

Theme: The never-ending story of God's love. God deserves our praise because his endless love never fails.
Author: Anonymous

136

1 Give thanks to the LORD, for he is good.*z*

          His love endures forever.

2 Give thanks to the God of gods.*a*

          His love endures forever.

3 Give thanks to the Lord of lords:

          His love endures forever.

4 to him who alone does great wonders,

          His love endures forever.

5 who by his understanding*b* made the heavens,*c*

          His love endures forever.

6 who spread out the earth*d* upon the waters,

          His love endures forever.

7 who made the great lights*e*—

          His love endures forever.

8 the sun to govern the day,

          His love endures forever.

9 the moon and stars to govern the night;

          His love endures forever.

10 to him who struck down the firstborn*f* of Egypt

          His love endures forever.

11 and brought Israel out*g* from among them

          His love endures forever.

12 with a mighty hand and outstretched arm;

          His love endures forever.

13 to him who divided the Red Sea*a* *h* asunder

          His love endures forever.

14 and brought Israel through the midst of it,

          His love endures forever.

15 but swept Pharaoh and his army into the Red Sea;*i*

          His love endures forever.

136:1
z Ps 106:1
136:2
a Dt 10:17

136:5
b Pr 3:19; Jer 51:15
c Ge 1:1
136:6
d Jer 10:12
136:7
e Ge 1:14, 16

136:10
f Ex 12:29; Ps 135:8
136:11
g Ex 6:6; 12:51

136:13
h Ex 14:21;
Ps 78:13

136:15
i Ex 14:27

a 13 Hebrew *Yam Suph*; that is, Sea of Reeds; also in verse 15

135:15–18 Those who worshiped idols were as blind and insensitive as the idols themselves. They couldn't see or hear what God had to say. In subtle, imperceptible ways we become like the idols we worship. If the true God is your God, you will become more like him as you worship him. What are your goals? What takes priority in your life? Choose carefully because you will take on the characteristics of whatever you worship.

136:1ff Repeated throughout this psalm is the phrase, "His love endures forever." This psalm may have been a responsive reading, with the congregation saying these words in unison after each sentence. The repetition made this important lesson sink in. God's love includes aspects of love, kindness, mercy, and faithfulness. We never have to worry that God will run out of love because it flows from a well that will never run dry.

136:16
j Ex 13:18

16 to him who led his people through the desert,*j*

His love endures forever.

136:17
k Ps 135:9-12

17 who struck down great kings,*k*

His love endures forever.

18 and killed mighty kings—

His love endures forever.

19 Sihon king of the Amorites

His love endures forever.

20 and Og king of Bashan—

His love endures forever.

136:21
l Jos 12:1

21 and gave their land*l* as an inheritance,

His love endures forever.

22 an inheritance to his servant Israel;

His love endures forever.

23 to the One who remembered us in our low estate

His love endures forever.

24 and freed us from our enemies,

His love endures forever.

136:25
m Ps 104:27;
145:15

25 and who gives food*m* to every creature.

His love endures forever.

26 Give thanks to the God of heaven.

His love endures forever.

Theme: A person in exile weeps over the bitterness of captivity. Our sorrow can make it difficult to imagine singing joyful songs again.
Author: Anonymous

137

1 By the rivers of Babylon we sat and wept
    when we remembered Zion.
2 There on the poplars
    we hung our harps,
3 for there our captors asked us for songs,
    our tormentors demanded songs of joy;
    they said, "Sing us one of the songs of Zion!"

4 How can we sing the songs of the LORD
    while in a foreign land?
5 If I forget you, O Jerusalem,
    may my right hand forget ⌊its skill⌋.

137:6
n Eze 3:26

6 May my tongue cling to the roof*n* of my mouth
    if I do not remember you,
if I do not consider Jerusalem
    my highest joy.

137:7
o Jer 49:7;
La 4:21-22

7 Remember, O LORD, what the Edomites*o* did
    on the day Jerusalem fell.
"Tear it down," they cried,
    "tear it down to its foundations!"

137:8
p Isa 13:1, 19;
Jer 25:12, 26;
Rev 18:6

8 O Daughter of Babylon, doomed to destruction,*p*
    happy is he who repays you
    for what you have done to us—
9 he who seizes your infants
    and dashes them against the rocks.

137:7 The Edomites were related to the Israelites, both nations having descended from Isaac and his father Abraham. Although Israel shared its southern border with Edom, there was bitter hatred between the two nations. The Edomites did not come to help when the city of Jerusalem was besieged by the Babylonian army. In fact, they rejoiced when the city was destroyed (Jeremiah 49:7–22; Joel 3:19; Obadiah 1–20).

137:8, 9 God destroyed Babylon and its offspring for their proud assault against God and his kingdom. The Medes and Persians destroyed Babylon in 539 B.C. Many of those who were oppressed lived to see the victory. The phrase about the infants is harsh because the writer is crying out for judgment: "Treat the Babylonians the way they treated us."

Theme: Thanksgiving for answered prayer. God works out his plans for our lives and will bring us through the difficulties we face.
Author: David

138 Of David.

1 I will praise you, O Lord, with all my heart;
    before the "gods" I will sing your praise.
2 I will bow down toward your holy temple[q]
    and will praise your name
      for your love and your faithfulness,
  for you have exalted above all things
    your name and your word.
3 When I called, you answered me;
    you made me bold and stouthearted.

4 May all the kings of the earth[r] praise you, O Lord,
    when they hear the words of your mouth.
5 May they sing of the ways of the Lord,
    for the glory of the Lord is great.

6 Though the Lord is on high, he looks upon the lowly,
    but the proud he knows from afar.
7 Though I walk[s] in the midst of trouble,
    you preserve my life;
  you stretch out your hand against the anger of my foes,
    with your right hand you save me.
8 The Lord will fulfill ⌊his purpose⌋[t] for me;
    your love, O Lord, endures forever—
  do not abandon the works of your hands.[u]

Theme: God is all-seeing, all-knowing, all-powerful, and everywhere present. God knows us, God is with us, and his greatest gift is to allow us to know him.
Author: David

139 For the director of music. Of David. A psalm.

1 O Lord, you have searched me[v]
    and you know[w] me.
2 You know when I sit and when I rise;[x]
    you perceive my thoughts[y] from afar.
3 You discern my going out and my lying down;
    you are familiar with all my ways.[z]
4 Before a word is on my tongue
    you know it completely,[a] O Lord.

5 You hem me in—behind and before;
    you have laid your hand upon me.
6 Such knowledge is too wonderful for me,
    too lofty[b] for me to attain.

138:2
[q] 1Ki 8:29

138:4
[r] Ps 102:15

138:7
[s] Ps 23:4

138:8
[t] Ps 57:2; Php 1:6
[u] Job 10:3, 8

139:1
[v] Ps 17:3
[w] Jer 12:3

139:2
[x] 2Ki 19:27
[y] Mt 9:4

139:3
[z] Job 31:4

139:4
[a] Heb 4:13

139:6
[b] Job 42:3

138:1 "Before the 'gods' " may mean in the presence of subordinate heavenly beings (angels), or, more likely, it may be a statement ridiculing the kings or gods of the pagan nations. God is the highest in the whole earth.

138:1-3 Thanksgiving should be an integral part of our praise to God. This theme is woven throughout the psalms. As we praise and thank God for material and spiritual blessings, we should also thank him for answered prayer. Remember when you asked God for protection, strength, comfort, patience, love, or other special needs, and he supplied them? Beware of taking God's provision and answered prayer for granted.

138:8 Every person dreams and makes plans for the future.

Then they work hard to see those dreams and plans come true. But to make the most of life, we must include God's plan in our plans. He alone knows what is best for us; he alone can fulfill his purpose for us. As you make plans and dream dreams, talk with God about them.

139:1-5 Sometimes we don't let people get to know us completely because we are afraid they will discover something about us that they won't like. But God already knows everything about us, even to the number of hairs on our heads (Matthew 10:30), and still he accepts and loves us. God is with us through every situation, in every trial—protecting, loving, guiding. He knows and loves us completely.

139:7
c Jer 23:24

7 Where can I go from your Spirit?
　　Where can I flee c from your presence?

139:8
d Am 9:2-3
e Pr 15:11

8 If I go up to the heavens, d you are there;
　　if I make my bed e in the depths, a you are there.
9 If I rise on the wings of the dawn,
　　if I settle on the far side of the sea,
10 even there your hand will guide me,
　　your right hand will hold me fast.
11 If I say, "Surely the darkness will hide me
　　and the light become night around me,"

139:12
f Job 34:22

12 even the darkness will not be dark f to you;
　　the night will shine like the day,
　　for darkness is as light to you.

13 For you created my inmost being;
　　you knit me together in my mother's womb.
14 I praise you because I am fearfully and wonderfully made;
　　your works are wonderful,
　　I know that full well.
15 My frame was not hidden from you
　　when I was made in the secret place.
　　When I was woven together in the depths of the earth,
16 　　your eyes saw my unformed body.
All the days ordained for me
　　were written in your book
　　before one of them came to be.

a 8 Hebrew Sheol

ANGER AND VENGEANCE IN THE BOOK OF PSALMS

Several psalms shock those familiar with New Testament teachings. The psalmists didn't hesitate to demand God's justice and make vivid suggestions on how he might carry it out. Apparently, no subject was unsuitable for discussion with God, but our tendency is to avoid the subjects of anger and vengeance in the book of Psalms.

To understand the words of anger and vengeance, we need to understand several things:

(1) The judgments asked for are to be carried out by God and are written out of intense personal and national suffering. The people are unable or unwilling to take revenge themselves and are aking God to intervene. Because few of us have suffered intense cruelty on a personal or national level, we find it difficult to grasp these outbursts.

(2) These writers were intimately aware of God's justice. Some of their words are efforts to vividly imagine what God might allow to happen to those who had harmed his people.

(3) If we dared to write down our thoughts while being unjustly attacked or suffering cruelty, we might be shocked at our own bold desire for vengeance. We would be suprised at how much we have in common with these men of old. The psalmists did not have Jesus' command to pray for one's enemies, but they did point to the right place to start. We are challenged to pay back good for evil, but until we respond to this challenge, we will not know how much we need God's help in order to forgive others.

(4) There is a helpful parallel between the psalms of anger and the psalms of vengeance. The "angry" psalms are intense and graphic, but they are directed at God. He is boldly told how disappointing it is when he turns his back on his people or acts too slowly. But while these thoughts and feelings were sincerely expressed, we know from the psalms themselves that these passing feelings were followed by renewed confidence in God's faithfulness. It is reasonable to expect the same of the "vengeance" psalms. We read, for example, David's angry outburst against Saul's pursuit in Psalm 59, yet we know that David never took personal revenge on Saul. The psalmists freely spoke their minds to God, having confidence that he could sort out what was meant and what was felt. Pray with that same confidence—God can be trusted with your heart.

Selected psalms that emphasize these themes are 10; 23; 28; 35; 59; 69; 109; 137; 139; 140.

139:7 God is omnipresent—he is present everywhere. Because this is so, you can never be lost to his Spirit. This is good news to those who know and love God, because no matter what we do or where we go, we can never be far from God's comforting presence (see Romans 8:35–39).

139:13–15 God's character goes into the creation of every person. When you feel worthless or even begin to hate yourself, remember that God's Spirit is ready and willing to work within you. We should have as much respect for ourselves as our Maker has for us.

17 How precious to[a] me are your thoughts, O God![g]
   How vast is the sum of them!
18 Were I to count them,
   they would outnumber the grains of sand.
   When I awake,
   I am still with you.

19 If only you would slay the wicked,[h] O God!
   Away from me,[i] you bloodthirsty men!
20 They speak of you with evil intent;
   your adversaries misuse your name.[j]
21 Do I not hate those who hate you, O LORD,
   and abhor those who rise up against you?
22 I have nothing but hatred for them;
   I count them my enemies.

23 Search me,[k] O God, and know my heart;
   test me and know my anxious thoughts.
24 See if there is any offensive way in me,
   and lead me[l] in the way everlasting.

139:17
[g] Ps 40:5

139:19
[h] Isa 11:4
[i] Ps 119:115

139:20
[j] Jude 15

139:23
[k] Job 31:6

139:24
[l] Ps 5:8

Theme: Prayer for protection against those who slander or threaten you. Deliverance begins with concentrating on our future life with God.
Author: David

140

For the director of music. A psalm of David.

1 Rescue me, O LORD, from evil men;
   protect me from men of violence,
2 who devise evil plans[m] in their hearts
   and stir up war every day.
3 They make their tongues as sharp as a serpent's;
   the poison of vipers[n] is on their lips.   *Selah*

4 Keep me, O LORD, from the hands of the wicked;[o]
   protect me from men of violence
   who plan to trip my feet.
5 Proud men have hidden a snare for me;
   they have spread out the cords of their net
   and have set traps[p] for me along my path.   *Selah*

6 O LORD, I say to you, "You are my God."
   Hear, O LORD, my cry for mercy.
7 O Sovereign LORD, my strong deliverer,
   who shields my head in the day of battle—
8 do not grant the wicked their desires, O LORD;
   do not let their plans succeed,
   or they will become proud.   *Selah*

9 Let the heads of those who surround me
   be covered with the trouble their lips have caused.[q]

140:2
[m] Ps 56:6

140:3
[n] Ps 58:4

140:4
[o] Ps 71:4

140:5
[p] Ps 31:4

140:9
[q] Ps 7:16

a 17 Or *concerning*

139:21–24 David's hatred for his enemies came from his zeal for God. David regarded his enemies as God's enemies, so his hatred was a desire for God's righteous justice and not for personal vengeance. Is it all right to be angry at people who hate God? Yes, but we must remember that it is God who will deal with them, not us. If we truly love God, then we will be deeply hurt if someone hates him. David asked God to search his heart and mind and point out any wrong motives that may have been behind his strong words. But while we seek justice against evil, we must also pray that God's enemies will turn to him before he judges them (see Matthew 5:44).

139:23, 24 David asked God to search for sin and point it out, even to the level of testing his thoughts. This is exploratory surgery for sin. How are we to recognize sin unless God points it out? Then, when God shows us, we can repent and be forgiven. Make this verse your prayer. If you ask the Lord to search your heart and your thoughts and to reveal your sin, you will be continuing on God's "way everlasting."

140:10
r Ps 11:6

¹⁰ Let burning coals fall upon them;
    may they be thrown into the fire,ʳ
    into miry pits, never to rise.
¹¹ Let slanderers not be established in the land;
    may disaster hunt down men of violence.

140:12
s Ps 9:4

¹² I know that the LORD secures justice for the poor
    and upholds the causeˢ of the needy.
¹³ Surely the righteous will praise your name
    and the upright will live before you.

Theme: A prayer for help when facing temptation. David asks God to protect him and to give him wisdom in accepting criticism. Be open to honest criticism—God may be speaking to you through others.
Author: David

141 A psalm of David.

141:1
t Ps 70:5

¹ O LORD, I call to you; come quicklyᵗ to me.
    Hear my voice when I call to you.

141:2
u Rev 5:8; 8:3
v Ex 29:39, 41

² May my prayer be set before you like incense;ᵘ
    may the lifting up of my hands be like the evening sacrifice.ᵛ

³ Set a guard over my mouth, O LORD;
    keep watch over the door of my lips.

141:4
w Pr 23:6

⁴ Let not my heart be drawn to what is evil,
    to take part in wicked deeds
with men who are evildoers;
    let me not eat of their delicacies.ʷ

141:5
x Pr 9:8

⁵ Let a righteous manᵃ strike me—it is a kindness;
    let him rebuke meˣ—it is oil on my head.
    My head will not refuse it.

    Yet my prayer is ever against the deeds of evildoers;
⁶   their rulers will be thrown down from the cliffs,
    and the wicked will learn that my words were well spoken.
⁷ ⌊They will say,⌋ "As one plows and breaks up the earth,
    so our bones have been scattered at the mouth of the grave.ᵇ"

141:8
y Ps 25:15

⁸ But my eyes are fixedʸ on you, O Sovereign LORD;
    in you I take refuge—do not give me over to death.
⁹ Keep me from the snares they have laid for me,
    from the traps set by evildoers.

141:10
z Ps 35:8

¹⁰ Let the wicked fallᶻ into their own nets,
    while I pass by in safety.

ᵃ5 Or *Let the Righteous One* ᵇ7 Hebrew *Sheol*

140:12 To whom can the poor turn when they are persecuted? They lack the money to get professional help; they may be unable to defend themselves. But there is always someone on their side—the Lord will stand by them and ultimately bring about justice. This should be a comfort for us all. No matter what our situation may be, the Lord is with us. But this truth should also call us to responsibility. As God's people, we are required to defend the rights of the powerless.

141:3 James wrote that "the tongue is a small part of the body, but it makes great boasts" (James 3:5). On the average, a person opens his or her mouth approximately 700 times a day to speak. David wisely asked God to help keep him from speaking evil—sometimes even as he underwent persecution. Jesus himself was silent before his accusers (Matthew 26:63). Knowing the power of the tongue, we would do well to ask God to guard what we say so that our words will bring honor to his name.

141:4 David asked God to guard his heart. Evil acts begin with evil desires. It isn't enough to ask God to keep you away from temptation, make you stronger, or change your circumstances. You must ask him to change you on the inside—at the level of your desires.

141:5 David says that being rebuked by a righteous person is a kindness. Nobody really likes criticism, but everybody can benefit from it when it is given wisely and taken humbly. David suggested how to accept criticism: (1) don't refuse it, (2) consider it a kindness, and (3) keep quiet (don't fight back). Putting these suggestions into practice will help you control how you react to criticism, making it productive rather than destructive, no matter how it was originally intended.

Theme: A prayer when overwhelmed and desperate. When we feel cornered by our enemies, only God can keep us safe.
Author: David

142

A maskil[a] of David. When he was in the cave. A prayer.

1 I cry aloud to the LORD;
    I lift up my voice to the LORD for mercy.[a]

2 I pour out my complaint before him;
    before him I tell my trouble.

3 When my spirit grows faint[b] within me,
    it is you who know my way.
  In the path where I walk
    men have hidden a snare for me.

4 Look to my right and see;
    no one is concerned for me.
  I have no refuge;
    no one cares[c] for my life.

5 I cry to you, O LORD;
    I say, "You are my refuge,
    my portion in the land of the living."[d]

6 Listen to my cry,
    for I am in desperate need;[e]
  rescue me from those who pursue me,
    for they are too strong for me.

7 Set me free from my prison,
    that I may praise your name.

  Then the righteous will gather about me
    because of your goodness to me.[f]

142:1
[a] Ps 30:8

142:3
[b] Ps 140:5; 143:4, 7

142:4
[c] Ps 31:11

142:5
[d] Ps 27:13

142:6
[e] Ps 116:6

142:7
[f] Ps 13:6

Theme: A prayer in the midst of hopelessness and depression. Our prayers should fit into what we know is consistent with God's character and plans.
Author: David

143

A psalm of David.

1 O LORD, hear my prayer,
    listen to my cry for mercy;
  in your faithfulness and righteousness
    come to my relief.

2 Do not bring your servant into judgment,
    for no one living is righteous before you.

3 The enemy pursues me,
    he crushes me to the ground;
  he makes me dwell in darkness
    like those long dead.

4 So my spirit grows faint within me;
    my heart within me is dismayed.

5 I remember[g] the days of long ago;
    I meditate on all your works
    and consider what your hands have done.

6 I spread out my hands[h] to you;
    my soul thirsts for you like a parched land.

143:5
[g] Ps 77:6

143:6
[h] Ps 63:1; 88:9

Selah

[a] Title: Probably a literary or musical term

142:4, 5 Have you ever felt that no one cared what happened to you? David had good reason to feel that way, and he wrote, "I cry to you, O LORD." Through prayer we can pull out of our tailspin and be reminded that God cares for us deeply.

142:7 This psalm was written when David was hiding from Saul in caves like the ones at Adullam (1 Samuel 22) or En Gedi (1 Samuel 24). These may have seemed like prisons to him because of the confinement.

143:7
i Ps 28:1

7 Answer me quickly, O Lᴏʀᴅ;
   my spirit fails.
Do not hide your face*i* from me
   or I will be like those who go down to the pit.

143:8
j Ps 25:1-2

8 Let the morning bring me word of your unfailing love,
   for I have put my trust in you.
Show me the way I should go,
   for to you I lift up my soul.*j*
9 Rescue me from my enemies, O Lᴏʀᴅ,
   for I hide myself in you.

143:10
k Ne 9:20; Ps 25:4-5

10 Teach me to do your will,
   for you are my God;
may your good Spirit
   lead*k* me on level ground.

143:11
l Ps 119:25

11 For your name's sake, O Lᴏʀᴅ, preserve my life;*l*
   in your righteousness, bring me out of trouble.

143:12
m Ps 54:5

12 In your unfailing love, silence my enemies;
   destroy all my foes,*m*
   for I am your servant.

Theme: Rejoicing in God's care. Whether in times of prosperity or adversity, blessed are those whose God is the Lord.
Author: David

144 Of David.

144:1
n Ps 18:2, 34

1 Praise be to the Lᴏʀᴅ my Rock,*n*
   who trains my hands for war,
   my fingers for battle.
2 He is my loving God and my fortress,
   my stronghold and my deliverer,
my shield, in whom I take refuge,
   who subdues peoples*a* under me.

144:3
o Ps 8:4; Heb 2:6

3 O Lᴏʀᴅ, what is man*o* that you care for him,
   the son of man that you think of him?

144:4
p Ps 102:11

4 Man is like a breath;
   his days are like a fleeting shadow.*p*

144:5
q Ps 18:9
r Ps 104:32

5 Part your heavens,*q* O Lᴏʀᴅ, and come down;
   touch the mountains, so that they smoke.*r*

144:6
s Ps 18:14

6 Send forth lightning and scatter the enemies;
   shoot your arrows*s* and rout them.
7 Reach down your hand from on high;
   deliver me and rescue me
from the mighty waters,
   from the hands of foreigners

144:8
t Ps 12:2

8 whose mouths are full of lies,*t*
   whose right hands are deceitful.

a2 Many manuscripts of the Masoretic Text, Dead Sea Scrolls, Aquila, Jerome and Syriac; most manuscripts of the Masoretic Text subdues my people

---

143:7 David was losing hope, caught in paralyzing fear and deep depression. At times, we feel caught in deepening depression, and we are unable to pull ourselves out. At those times, we can come to the Lord and, like David, express our true feelings. Then he will help us as we remember his works (143:5), reach out to him in prayer (143:6), trust him (143:8), and decide to do his will (143:10).

143:10 David's prayer was to be taught to do God's will, not his own. A prayer for guidance is self-centered if it doesn't recognize

God's power to redirect our lives. Asking God to restructure our priorities awakens our minds and stirs our wills.

144:3, 4 Life is short. David reminds us that it is "like a breath" and that our "days are like a fleeting shadow." James says that our lives are "a mist that appears for a little while and then vanishes" (James 4:14). Because life is short, we should live for God while we have the time. Don't waste your life by selecting an inferior purpose that has no lasting value. Live for God—he alone can make your life worthwhile, purposeful, and meaningful.

⁹ I will sing a new song to you, O God;
   on the ten-stringed lyre^u I will make music to you,
¹⁰ to the One who gives victory to kings,
   who delivers his servant David^v from the deadly sword.

¹¹ Deliver me and rescue me
   from the hands of foreigners
whose mouths are full of lies,
   whose right hands are deceitful.

¹² Then our sons in their youth
   will be like well-nurtured plants,^w
and our daughters will be like pillars
   carved to adorn a palace.
¹³ Our barns will be filled
   with every kind of provision.
Our sheep will increase by thousands,
   by tens of thousands in our fields;
¹⁴   our oxen will draw heavy loads.^a
There will be no breaching of walls,
   no going into captivity,
   no cry of distress in our streets.

¹⁵ Blessed are the people^x of whom this is true;
   blessed are the people whose God is the LORD.

Theme: A time will come when all people will join together in recognizing and worshiping God. Because God is full of love, he satisfies all who trust in him.
Author: David

145 ^b

A psalm of praise. Of David.

¹ I will exalt you,^y my God the King;
   I will praise your name for ever and ever.
² Every day I will praise you
   and extol your name for ever and ever.

³ Great is the LORD and most worthy of praise;
   his greatness no one can fathom.^z
⁴ One generation^a will commend your works to another;
   they will tell of your mighty acts.
⁵ They will speak of the glorious splendor of your majesty,
   and I will meditate on your wonderful works.^c
⁶ They will tell of the power of your awesome works,^b
   and I will proclaim^c your great deeds.
⁷ They will celebrate your abundant goodness
   and joyfully sing of your righteousness.

⁸ The LORD is gracious and compassionate,^d
   slow to anger and rich in love.
⁹ The LORD is good to all;
   he has compassion on all he has made.
¹⁰ All you have made will praise you,^e O LORD;
   your saints will extol you.
¹¹ They will tell of the glory of your kingdom
   and speak of your might,
¹² so that all men may know of your mighty acts
   and the glorious splendor of your kingdom.
¹³ Your kingdom is an everlasting kingdom,^f
   and your dominion endures through all generations.

144:9
^uPs 33:2-3

144:10
^vPs 18:50

144:12
^wPs 128:3

144:15
^xPs 33:12

145:1
^yPs 30:1; 34:1

145:3
^zJob 5:9; Ro 11:33

145:4
^aIsa 38:19

145:6
^bPs 66:3
^cDt 32:3

145:8
^dPs 86:15

145:10
^ePs 19:1

145:13
^f2Pe 1:11

^a14 Or *our chieftains will be firmly established*   ^bThis psalm is an acrostic poem, the verses of which (including verse 13b) begin with the successive letters of the Hebrew alphabet.   ^c5 Dead Sea Scrolls and Syriac (see also Septuagint); Masoretic Text *On the glorious splendor of your majesty / and on your wonderful works I will meditate*

The Lord is faithful to all his promises
and loving toward all he has made.a

145:14
*g*Ps 146:8

14 The Lord upholds all those who fall
and lifts up all*g* who are bowed down.

145:15
*h*Ps 104:27

15 The eyes of all look to you,
and you give them their food*h* at the proper time.

16 You open your hand
and satisfy the desires of every living thing.

17 The Lord is righteous in all his ways
and loving toward all he has made.

145:18
*i*Dt 4:7
*j*Jn 4:24

18 The Lord is near*i* to all who call on him,*j*
to all who call on him in truth.

19 He fulfills the desires of those who fear him;
he hears their cry and saves them.

145:20
*k*Ps 31:23

20 The Lord watches over all who love him,*k*
but all the wicked he will destroy.

21 My mouth will speak in praise of the Lord.
Let every creature praise his holy name
for ever and ever.

Theme: The help of people versus the help of God. Help from people is temporal and unstable, but help from God is lasting and complete.
Author: Anonymous

146:1
*l*Ps 103:1

146

1 Praise the Lord.b

Praise the Lord,*l* O my soul.

146:2
*m*Ps 104:33

2 I will praise the Lord all my life;*m*
I will sing praise to my God as long as I live.

146:3
*n*Isa 2:22

3 Do not put your trust in princes,
in mortal men,*n* who cannot save.

146:4
*o*Ecc 12:7

4 When their spirit departs, they return to the ground;*o*
on that very day their plans come to nothing.

5 Blessed is he whose help is the God of Jacob,
whose hope is in the Lord his God,

6 the Maker of heaven and earth,
the sea, and everything in them—
the Lord, who remains faithful forever.

146:7
*p*Ps 103:6
*q*Ps 107:9

7 He upholds the cause of the oppressed*p*
and gives food to the hungry.*q*
The Lord sets prisoners free,

146:8
*r*Mt 9:30

8 the Lord gives sight to the blind,*r*

a 13 One manuscript of the Masoretic Text, Dead Sea Scrolls and Syriac (see also Septuagint); most manuscripts of the Masoretic Text do not have the last two lines of verse 13.   b 1 Hebrew *Hallelu Yah*; also in verse 10

145:14 Sometimes our burdens seem more than we can bear, and we wonder how we can go on. David stands at this bleak intersection of life's road and points toward the Lord, the great burden-bearer. God is able to lift us up because (1) his greatness is unfathomable (145:3); (2) he does mighty acts across many generations (145:4); (3) he is full of glorious splendor and majesty (145:5); (4) he does wonderful and awesome works (145:5, 6); (5) he is righteous (145:7); (6) he is gracious, compassionate, patient, and loving (145:8, 9); (7) he rules over an everlasting kingdom (145:13); (8) he is our source of all our daily needs (145:15, 16); (9) he is righteous and loving in all his dealings (145:17); (10) he remains near to those who call on him (145:18); (11) he hears our cries and saves us (145:19, 20). If you are bending under a burden and feel that you are about to fall, turn to God for help. He is ready to lift you up and bear your burden.

146—150 These last five psalms overflow with praise. Each begins and ends with "Praise the Lord." They show us where, why, and how to praise God. What does praise do? (1) Praise takes our minds off our problems and shortcomings, and focuses them on God. (2) Praise leads us from individual meditation to corporate worship. (3) Praise causes us to consider and appreciate God's character. (4) Praise lifts our perspective from the earthly to the heavenly. (5) Praise prepares our hearts to receive God's love and the power of his Holy Spirit.

146:3–8 The writer portrays man as an inadequate savior, a false hope; even princes cannot deliver (146:3). God is the hope and the help of the needy. Jesus affirms his concern for the poor and afflicted in Luke 4:18–21; 7:21–23. He does not separate the social and spiritual needs of people, but attends to both. While God, not the government, is the hope of the needy, *we* are his instruments to help here on earth.

the LORD lifts up those who are bowed down,
   the LORD loves the righteous.
9 The LORD watches over the alien
   and sustains the fatherless and the widow,
   but he frustrates the ways of the wicked.

10 The LORD reigns[s] forever,
   your God, O Zion, for all generations.

Praise the LORD.

146:10
[s]Ex 15:18;
Ps 10:16

Theme: What gives God joy? Although God created everything, his greatest joy comes from our genuine worship and trust.
Author: Anonymous, written when the exiles returned to Jerusalem

147

1 Praise the LORD.[a]

How good it is to sing praises to our God,
   how pleasant[t] and fitting to praise him![u]

2 The LORD builds up Jerusalem;[v]
   he gathers the exiles[w] of Israel.
3 He heals the brokenhearted
   and binds up their wounds.
4 He determines the number of the stars[x]
   and calls them each by name.
5 Great is our Lord[y] and mighty in power;
   his understanding has no limit.[z]
6 The LORD sustains the humble[a]
   but casts the wicked to the ground.

7 Sing to the LORD with thanksgiving;
   make music to our God on the harp.
8 He covers the sky with clouds;
   he supplies the earth with rain[b]
   and makes grass grow[c] on the hills.
9 He provides food[d] for the cattle
   and for the young ravens when they call.

10 His pleasure is not in the strength of the horse,[e]
   nor his delight in the legs of a man;
11 the LORD delights in those who fear him,
   who put their hope in his unfailing love.

12 Extol the LORD, O Jerusalem;
   praise your God, O Zion,
13 for he strengthens the bars of your gates
   and blesses your people within you.
14 He grants peace to your borders
   and satisfies you[f] with the finest of wheat.

147:1
[t]Ps 135:3
[u]Ps 33:1

147:2
[v]Ps 102:16
[w]Dt 30:3

147:4
[x]Isa 40:26

147:5
[y]Ps 48:1
[z]Isa 40:28

147:6
[a]Ps 146:8-9

147:8
[b]Job 38:26
[c]Ps 104:14

147:9
[d]Ps 104:27-28

147:10
[e]Ps 33:16-17

147:14
[f]Ps 132:15

a 1 Hebrew *Hallelu Yah*; also in verse 20

146:9 God's plans frustrate the "ways of the wicked" because his values are the opposite of society's. Jesus turned society's values upside down when he proclaimed that "many who are first will be last, and many who are last will be first" (Matthew 19:30), and that "whoever wants to save his life will lose it, but whoever loses his life for me will find it" (Matthew 16:25). Don't be surprised when others don't understand your Christian values, but don't give in to theirs.

147:5 Sometimes we feel as if we don't understand ourselves— what we want, how we feel, what's wrong with us, or what we should do about it. But God's understanding has no limit, and

therefore he understands us fully. If you feel troubled and don't understand yourself, remember that God understands you perfectly. Take your mind off yourself and focus it on God. Strive to become more and more like him. The more you learn about God and his ways, the better you will understand yourself.

147:10, 11 We spend much effort trying to sharpen our skills or increase our strength. There is nothing wrong with doing so, and, in fact, our gifts can be used to glorify God. But when we use our skills with no regard for God, they are indeed worth little. It is our *fear* (reverence) and trust that God desires. When he has those, then he will use our skills and strengths in ways far greater than we can imagine.

15 He sends his command to the earth;
  his word runs swiftly.
16 He spreads the snow[g] like wool
  and scatters the frost like ashes.
17 He hurls down his hail like pebbles.
  Who can withstand his icy blast?
18 He sends his word and melts them;
  he stirs up his breezes, and the waters flow.

19 He has revealed his word to Jacob,
  his laws and decrees[h] to Israel.
20 He has done this for no other nation;
  they do not know his laws.

  Praise the LORD.

147:16
g Job 37:6

147:19
h Mal 4:4

Theme: Let all creation praise and worship the Lord.
Author: Anonymous

148
1 Praise the LORD.[a]

Praise the LORD from the heavens,
  praise him in the heights above.
2 Praise him, all his angels,
  praise him, all his heavenly hosts.
3 Praise him, sun and moon,
  praise him, all you shining stars.
4 Praise him, you highest heavens
  and you waters above the skies.[i]
5 Let them praise the name of the LORD,
  for he commanded[j] and they were created.
6 He set them in place for ever and ever;
  he gave a decree[k] that will never pass away.

7 Praise the LORD from the earth,
  you great sea creatures and all ocean depths,
8 lightning and hail, snow and clouds,
  stormy winds that do his bidding,[l]
9 you mountains and all hills,[m]
  fruit trees and all cedars,
10 wild animals and all cattle,
  small creatures and flying birds,

148:4
i Ge 1:7

148:5
j Ge 1:1, 6;
Ps 33:6, 9

148:6
k Ps 89:37;
Jer 33:25

148:8
l Ps 147:15-18

148:9
m Isa 44:23

a 1 Hebrew *Hallelu Yah*; also in verse 14

PRAISE IN THE BOOK OF PSALMS

Most of the psalms are prayers, and most of the prayers include praise to God. Praise expresses admiration, appreciation, and thanks. Praise in the book of Psalms is often directed to God, and just as often the praise is shared with others. Considering all that God has done and does for us, what could be more natural than outbursts of heartfelt praise?

As you read Psalms, note the praise given to God, not only for what he does—his creation, his blessings, his forgiveness—but also for who he is—loving, just, faithful, forgiving, patient. Note also those times when the praise of God is shared with others and they, too, are encouraged to praise him. In what ways have you recently praised God or told others all that he has done for you?

Selected psalms that emphasize this theme are 8; 19; 30; 65; 84; 96; 100; 136; 145; 150.

147:19, 20 The nation of Israel (the descendants of Jacob) was special to God because to its people God brought his laws, and through its people he sent his Son, Jesus Christ. Now any individual who follows God is just as special to him. In fact, the Bible says that the real nation of Israel is not a specific people or geographic place, but the community of all who believe in and obey God (see Galatians 3:28, 29).

148:5–14 All creation is like a majestic symphony or a great

choir composed of many harmonious parts that together offer up songs of praise. Each part (independent, yet part of the whole) is caught up and carried along in the swelling tides of praise. This is a picture of how we as believers should praise God—individually, yet as part of the great choir of believers worldwide. Are you singing your part well in the worldwide choir of praise?

11 kings of the earth and all nations,
   you princes and all rulers on earth,
12 young men and maidens,
   old men and children.

13 Let them praise the name of the LORD,[n]
   for his name alone is exalted;
   his splendor is above the earth and the heavens.[o]
14 He has raised up for his people a horn,[a][p]
   the praise of all his saints,
   of Israel, the people close to his heart.

   Praise the LORD.

148:13
[n] Isa 12:4
[o] Ps 113:4

148:14
[p] Ps 75:10

Theme: A victory celebration. We have the assurance that God truly enjoys his people.
Author: Anonymous

149

1 Praise the LORD.[b][q]

   Sing to the LORD a new song,
   his praise in the assembly of the saints.

2 Let Israel rejoice in their Maker;
   let the people of Zion be glad in their King.
3 Let them praise his name with dancing
   and make music to him with tambourine and harp.[r]
4 For the LORD takes delight[s] in his people;
   he crowns the humble with salvation.[t]
5 Let the saints rejoice in this honor
   and sing for joy on their beds.[u]

6 May the praise of God be in their mouths
   and a double-edged[v] sword in their hands,
7 to inflict vengeance on the nations
   and punishment on the peoples,
8 to bind their kings with fetters,
   their nobles with shackles of iron,
9 to carry out the sentence written against them.
   This is the glory of all his saints.[w]

   Praise the LORD.

149:1
[q] Ps 33:2

149:3
[r] Ps 81:2

149:4
[s] Ps 35:27
[t] Ps 132:16

149:5
[u] Job 35:10

149:6
[v] Heb 4:12;
Rev 1:16

149:9
[w] Ps 148:14

Theme: A closing hymn of praise. God's creation praises him everywhere in every way. We should join this rejoicing song of praise.
Author: Anonymous

150

1 Praise the LORD.[c]

   Praise God in his sanctuary;
   praise him in his mighty heavens.
2 Praise him for his acts of power;[x]
   praise him for his surpassing greatness.
3 Praise him with the sounding of the trumpet,
   praise him with the harp and lyre,[y]

150:2
[x] Dt 3:24

150:3
[y] Ps 149:3

[a] 14 Horn here symbolizes strong one, that is, king.   [b] 1 Hebrew Hallelu Yah; also in verse 9   [c] 1 Hebrew Hallelu Yah; also in verse 6

149:3–5 Although the Bible invites us to praise God, we often aren't sure how to go about it. Here, several ways are suggested—in the dance, with the voice, with musical instruments. God enjoys his people, and we should enjoy praising him.
149:6, 7 The double-edged sword symbolizes the completeness of judgment that will be executed by the Messiah when he returns to punish all evildoers (Revelation 1:16).

150:3–5 Music and song were an integral part of Old Testament worship. David introduced music into the tabernacle and temple services (1 Chronicles 16:4–7). The music must have been loud and joyous as evidenced by the list of instruments and the presence of choirs and songleaders. Music was also important in New Testament worship (Ephesians 5:19; Colossians 3:16).

⁴ praise him with tambourine and dancing,
    praise him with the strings and flute,
⁵ praise him with the clash of cymbals,*z*
    praise him with resounding cymbals.

⁶ Let everything that has breath praise the LORD.

Praise the LORD.

150:5
ᶻ1Ch 15:16

WHERE TO GET HELP IN THE BOOK OF PSALMS

When you feel . . .

Afraid: 3; 4; 27; 46; 49; 56; 91; 118
Alone: 9; 10; 12; 13; 27; 40; 43
"Burned out": 6; 63
Cheated: 41
Confused: 10; 12; 73
Depressed: 27; 34; 42; 43; 88; 143
Distressed: 13; 25; 31; 40; 107
Elated: 19; 96
Guilty: 19; 32; 38; 51
Hateful: 11
Impatient: 13; 27; 37; 40
Insecure: 3; 5; 12; 91
Insulted: 41; 70
Jealous: 37
Like quitting: 29; 43; 145
Lost: 23; 139
Overwhelmed: 25; 69; 142
Penitent/Sorry: 32; 51; 66
Proud: 14; 30; 49
Purposeless: 14; 25; 39; 49; 90
Sad: 13
Self-confident: 24
Tense: 4
Thankful: 118; 136; 138
Threatened: 3; 11; 17
Tired/Weak: 6; 13; 18; 28; 49; 40; 86
Trapped: 7; 17; 42; 88; 142
Unimportant: 8; 90; 139
Vengeful: 3; 7; 109
Worried: 37
Worshipful: 8; 19; 27; 29; 150

When you're facing . . .

Atheists: 10; 14; 19; 52; 53; 115
Competition: 133
Criticism: 35; 56; 120
Danger: 11
Death: 6; 71; 90
Decisions: 1; 119
Discrimination: 54
Doubts: 34; 37; 94
Evil people: 10; 35; 36; 49; 52; 109; 140
Enemies: 3; 25; 35; 41; 56; 59
Heresy: 14
Hypocrisy: 26; 28; 40; 50
Illness: 6; 139
Lies: 5; 12; 120
Old age: 71; 92
Persecution: 1; 3; 7; 56
Poverty: 9; 10; 12
Punishment: 6; 38; 39
Slander/Insults: 7; 15; 35; 43; 120
Slaughter: 6; 46; 83
Sorrow: 23; 34
Success: 18; 112; 127; 128
Temptation: 38; 141
Troubles: 34; 55; 86; 102; 142; 145
Verbal cruelty: 35; 120

When you want . . .

Acceptance: 139
Answers: 4; 17
Confidence: 46; 71
Courage: 11; 42
Fellowship with God: 5; 16; 25; 27; 37; 133
Forgiveness: 32; 38; 40; 51; 69; 86; 103; 130
Friendship: 16
Godliness: 15; 25
Guidance: 1; 5; 15; 19; 25; 32; 48
Healing: 6; 41
Hope: 16; 17; 18; 23; 27
Humility: 19; 147
Illumination: 19
Integrity: 24; 25
Joy: 9; 16; 28; 126
Justice: 2; 7; 14; 26; 37; 49; 58; 82
Knowledge: 2; 8; 18; 19; 25; 29; 97; 103
Leadership: 72
Miracles: 60; 111
Money: 15; 16; 17; 49
Peace: 3; 4
Perspective: 2, 11
Prayer: 5; 17; 27; 61
Protection: 3; 4; 7; 16; 17; 18; 23; 27; 31; 91; 121; 125
Provision: 23
Rest: 23; 27
Salvation: 26; 37; 49; 126
Stability: 11; 33; 46
Vindication: 9; 14; 28; 35; 109
Wisdom: 1; 16; 19; 64; 111a

150:6 How could the message be more clear? The writer was telling the individual listeners to praise God. What a fitting way to end this book of praise—with a direct encouragement for *you* to praise God too. Remember to praise him every day!

150:6 In a way, the book of Psalms parallels our spiritual journey through life. It begins by presenting us with two roads—the way to life and the way to death. If we choose God's way to life, we still face both blessings and troubles, joy and grief,

successes and obstacles. Throughout it all, God is at our side, guiding, encouraging, comforting, and caring. As the wise and faithful person's life draws to an end, he or she realizes clearly that God's road is the right road. Knowing this will cause us to praise God for leading us in the right direction and for assuring our place in the perfect world God has in store for those who have faithfully followed him.

PROVERBS

ALPHABET letters, vowels, and consonants formed into words, sentences, paragraphs, and books—spoken, signed, whispered, written, and printed. From friendly advice to impassioned speeches and from dusty volumes to daily tabloids, messages are sent and received, with each sender trying to impart knowledge . . . and wisdom.

Woven into human fabric is the desire to learn and understand. Our mind sets us apart from animals, and we analyze, conceptualize, theorize, discuss, and debate everything from science to the supernatural. We build schools, institutes, and universities, where learned professors can teach us about the world and about life.

Knowledge is good, but a vast difference stands between "knowledge" (having the facts) and "wisdom" (applying those facts to life). We may amass knowledge, but without wisdom our knowledge is useless. We must learn how to *live out* what we know.

The wisest man who ever lived, Solomon, left us a legacy of written wisdom in three volumes—Proverbs, Ecclesiastes, and Song of Songs. In these books, under the inspiration of the Holy Spirit, he gives practical insights and guidelines for life.

In the first of these three volumes, Solomon passes on his practical advice in the form of proverbs. A proverb is a short, concise sentence that conveys moral truth. The book of Proverbs is a collection of these wise statements. The main theme of Proverbs, as we might expect, is the nature of true wisdom. Solomon writes, "The fear of the LORD is the beginning of knowledge, but fools despise wisdom and discipline" (1:7). He then proceeds to give hundreds of practical examples of how to live according to godly wisdom.

Proverbs covers a wide range of topics, including youth and discipline, family life, self-control and resisting temptation, business matters, words and the tongue, knowing God, marriage, seeking the truth, wealth and poverty, immorality, and, of course, wisdom. These proverbs are short poems (usually in couplet form), containing a holy mixture of common sense and timely warnings. Although they are not meant to teach doctrine, a person who follows their advice will walk closely with God. The word *proverb* comes from a Hebrew word that means "to rule or to govern," and these sayings, reminders, and admonitions provide profound advice for governing our lives.

As you read Proverbs, understand that knowing God is the key to wisdom. Listen to the thoughts and lessons from the world's wisest man, and apply these truths to your life. Don't just read these proverbs; act on them!

THE BLUEPRINT

A. WISDOM FOR YOUNG PEOPLE (1:1—9:18)

Solomon instructed the young people of his day like a father giving advice to his child. While many of these proverbs are directed toward young people, the principles supporting them are helpful to all believers, male and female, young and old. Anyone beginning his or her journey to discover more of wisdom will benefit greatly from these wise sayings.

B. WISDOM FOR ALL PEOPLE (10:1—24:34)

Solomon wanted to impart wisdom to all people, regardless of their age, sex, or position in society. These short, wise sayings give us practical wisdom for daily living. We should study them diligently and integrate them into our lives.

C. WISDOM FOR THE LEADERS
(25:1—31:31)

In addition to the proverbs that Solomon collected, the advisers of Hezekiah collected many proverbs that Solomon and others wrote. While most of these are general in nature, many are directed specifically to the king and those who dealt with the king. These are particularly useful for leaders or those who aspire to be leaders.

MEGATHEMES

THEME	EXPLANATION	IMPORTANCE
Wisdom	God wants his people to be wise. Two kinds of people portray two contrasting paths of life. The fool is the wicked, stubborn person who hates or ignores God. The wise person seeks to know and love God.	When we choose God's way, he grants us wisdom. His Word, the Bible, leads us to live right, have right relationships, and make right decisions.
Relationships	Proverbs gives us advice for developing our personal relationships with friends, family members, and co-workers. In every relationship, we must show love, dedication, and high moral standards.	To relate to people, we need consistency, tact, and discipline to use the wisdom God gives us. If we don't treat others according to the wisdom God gives, our relationships will suffer.
Speech	What we say shows our real attitude toward others. How we talk reveals what we're really like. Our speech is a test of how wise we have become.	To be wise in our speech we need to use self-control. Our words should be honest and well chosen.
Work	God controls the final outcome of all we do. We are accountable to carry out our work with diligence and discipline, not laziness.	Because God evaluates how we live, we should work purposefully. We must never be lax or self-satisfied in using our skills.
Success	Although people work very hard for money and fame, God views success as having a good reputation, moral character, and the spiritual devotion to obey him.	A successful relationship with God counts for eternity. Everything else is perishable. All our resources, time, and talents come from God. We should strive to use them wisely.

A. WISDOM FOR YOUNG PEOPLE (1:1—9:18)

Proverbs begins with a clear statement of its purpose—to impart wisdom for godly living. The first few chapters are Solomon's fatherly advice to young people. Although most of the material in this section is directed toward young people, all who seek wisdom will greatly benefit from these wise words. This is where one can discover the source of wisdom, the value of wisdom, and the benefits of wisdom.

Prologue: Purpose and Theme

1:1
a 1Ki 4:29-34

1 The proverbs of Solomon *a* son of David, king of Israel:

2 for attaining wisdom and discipline;
for understanding words of insight;
3 for acquiring a disciplined and prudent life,
doing what is right and just and fair;

1:4
b Pr 8:5
c Pr 8:12

4 for giving prudence to the simple, *b*
knowledge and discretion *c* to the young—

1:5
d Pr 9:9

5 let the wise listen and add to their learning, *d*
and let the discerning get guidance—

1:1 What the book of Psalms is to prayer and devotional life, the book of Proverbs is to everyday life. Proverbs gives practical suggestions for effective living. This book is not just a collection of homey sayings; it contains deep spiritual insights drawn from experience. A *proverb* is a short, wise, easy-to-learn saying that calls a person to action. It doesn't argue about basic spiritual and moral beliefs; it assumes we already hold them. The book of Proverbs focuses on God—his character, works, and blessings—and it tells how we can live in close relationship to him.

1:1 Solomon, the third king of Israel, son of the great King David, reigned during Israel's golden age. When God said he would give him whatever he wanted, he asked for a discerning heart (1 Kings 3:5–14). God was pleased with this request, and he not only made Solomon wise but also gave him great riches and power and an era of peace. Solomon built the glorious temple in Jerusalem (1 Kings 6) and wrote most of the book of Proverbs. His Profile is found in 1 Kings 4, p. 503.

6 for understanding proverbs and parables,*e*
 the sayings and riddles of the wise.

7 The fear of the LORD*f* is the beginning of knowledge,
 but fools*a* despise wisdom and discipline.

Exhortations to Embrace Wisdom

Warning Against Enticement

8 Listen, my son,*g* to your father's instruction
 and do not forsake your mother's teaching.*h*
9 They will be a garland to grace your head
 and a chain to adorn your neck.

10 My son, if sinners entice you,
 do not give in*i* to them.
11 If they say, "Come along with us;
 let's lie in wait for someone's blood,
 let's waylay some harmless soul;
12 let's swallow them alive, like the grave,*b*
 and whole, like those who go down to the pit;*j*
13 we will get all sorts of valuable things
 and fill our houses with plunder;
14 throw in your lot with us,
 and we will share a common purse"—
15 my son, do not go along with them,
 do not set foot*k* on their paths;*l*
16 for their feet rush into sin,
 they are swift to shed blood.*m*
17 How useless to spread a net
 in full view of all the birds!
18 These men lie in wait for their own blood;
 they waylay only themselves!
19 Such is the end of all who go after ill-gotten gain;
 it takes away the lives of those who get it.

a 7 The Hebrew words rendered *fool* in Proverbs, and often elsewhere in the Old Testament, denote one who is morally deficient.   *b 12* Hebrew *Sheol*

1:6
e Ps 78:2

1:7
f Job 28:28;
Ps 111:10;
Ecc 12:13

1:8
g Pr 4:1
h Pr 6:20

1:10
i Dt 13:8

1:12
j Ps 28:1

1:15
k Ps 119:101
l Ps 1:1

1:16
m Isa 59:7

1:6 Riddles were thought-provoking questions.

1:7 One of the most annoying types of people is a know-it-all, a person who has a dogmatic opinion about everything, is closed to anything new, resents discipline, and refuses to learn. Solomon calls this kind of person a fool. Don't be a know-it-all. Instead, be open to the advice of others, especially those who know you well and can give valuable insight and counsel. Learn how to learn from others. Remember, only God knows it all.

1:7-9 In this age of information, knowledge is plentiful, but wisdom is scarce. Wisdom means far more than simply knowing a lot. It is a basic attitude that affects every aspect of life. The foundation of knowledge is to fear the Lord—to honor and respect God, to live in awe of his power, and to obey his Word.

Faith in God should be the controlling principle for your understanding of the world, your attitudes, and your actions. Trust in God—he will make you truly wise.

1:8 Our actions speak louder than our words. This is especially true in the home. Children learn values, morals, and priorities by observing how their parents act and react every day. If parents exhibit a deep reverence for and dependence on God, the children will catch these attitudes. Let them see your reverence for God. Teach them right living by giving worship an important place in your family life and by reading the Bible together.

1:10-19 Sin is enticing because it offers a quick route to prosperity and makes us feel like one of the crowd. But when we go along with others and refuse to listen to the truth, our own appetites become our masters, and we'll do anything to satisfy them. Sin, even when attractive, is deadly. We must learn to make choices, not on the basis of flashy appeal or short-range pleasure, but in view of the long-range effects. Sometimes this means steering clear of people who want to entice us into activities that we know are wrong. We can't be friendly with sin and expect our lives to remain unaffected.

1:19 Going after "ill-gotten gain" is one of Satan's surest traps. It begins when he plants the suggestion that we can't live without some possession or more money. Then that desire fans its own fire until it becomes an all-consuming obsession. Ask God for wisdom to recognize any greedy desire before it destroys you. God will help you overcome it.

Warning Against Rejecting Wisdom

20 Wisdom calls aloud in the street,
   she raises her voice in the public squares;
21 at the head of the noisy streets[a] she cries out,
   in the gateways of the city she makes her speech:

22 "How long will you simple ones[b] love your simple ways?
   How long will mockers delight in mockery
   and fools hate knowledge?
23 If you had responded to my rebuke,
   I would have poured out my heart to you
   and made my thoughts known to you.
24 But since you rejected me when I called[n]
   and no one gave heed when I stretched out my hand,
25 since you ignored all my advice
   and would not accept my rebuke,
26 I in turn will laugh[o] at your disaster;
   I will mock when calamity overtakes you[p]—
27 when calamity overtakes you like a storm,
   when disaster sweeps over you like a whirlwind,
   when distress and trouble overwhelm you.

28 "Then they will call to me but I will not answer;[q]
   they will look for me but will not find me.[r]
29 Since they hated knowledge
   and did not choose to fear the LORD,
30 since they would not accept my advice
   and spurned my rebuke,[s]
31 they will eat the fruit of their ways
   and be filled with the fruit of their schemes.[t]
32 For the waywardness of the simple will kill them,
   and the complacency of fools will destroy them;

1:24
[n] Isa 65:12; 66:4;
Jer 7:13; Zec 7:11

1:26
[o] Ps 2:4
[p] Pr 10:24

1:28
[q] Isa 1:15; Mic 3:4
[r] Eze 8:18; Zec 7:13

1:30
[s] Ps 81:11

1:31
[t] Job 4:8; Isa 3:11;
Jer 6:19

[a] 21 Hebrew; Septuagint / on the tops of the walls   [b] 22 The Hebrew word rendered *simple* in Proverbs generally denotes one without moral direction and inclined to evil.

UNDER-STANDING PROVERBS Most often, proverbs are written in the form of couplets. These are constructed in three ways:	Type	Description	Key Word(s)	Examples
	Contrasting	Meaning and application come from the differences or contrast between the two statements of the proverb.	"but"	10:6; 15:25, 27
	Comparing	Meaning and application come from the similarities or comparison between the two statements of the proverb.	"as/so" "better/than"	10:26; 15:16, 17; 25:25
	Complementing	Meaning and application come from the way the second statement complements the first.	"and"	10:18; 15:23

1:20 The picture of wisdom calling aloud in the streets is a personification—a literary device to make wisdom come alive for us. Wisdom is not a separate being; it is the mind of God revealed. By reading about Jesus Christ's earthly ministry, we can see wisdom in action. In order to understand how to become wise, we can listen to wisdom calling and instructing us in the book of Proverbs (see the chart in chapter 14, p. 1009). For New Testament calls to wisdom, see 2 Timothy 1:7 and James 1:5. Make sure you don't reject God's offer of wisdom to you.

1:22 In the book of Proverbs, a "simple one" or a fool is not someone with a *mental* deficiency but someone with a *character* deficiency (such as rebellion, laziness, or anger). The fool is not stupid, but he or she is unable to tell right from wrong or good from bad.

1:23–28 God is more than willing to pour out his heart and make known his thoughts to us. To receive his advice, we must be willing to listen, refusing to let pride stand in our way. Pride is thinking more highly of our own wisdom and desires than of God's. If we think we know better than God or feel we have no need of God's direction, we have fallen into foolish and disastrous pride.

1:31, 32 Many proverbs point out that the "fruit of their ways" will be the consequences people will experience in this life. Faced with either choosing God's wisdom or persisting in rebellious independence, many decide to go it alone. The problems such people create for themselves will destroy them. Don't ignore God's advice even if it is painful for the present. It will keep you from greater pain in the future.

33 but whoever listens to me will live in safety[u]
    and be at ease, without fear of harm."

Moral Benefits of Wisdom

2 My son, if you accept my words
    and store up my commands within you,
2 turning your ear to wisdom
    and applying your heart to understanding,
3 and if you call out for insight
    and cry aloud for understanding,
4 and if you look for it as for silver
    and search for it as for hidden treasure,[v]
5 then you will understand the fear of the LORD
    and find the knowledge of God.
6 For the LORD gives wisdom,[w]
    and from his mouth come knowledge and understanding.
7 He holds victory in store for the upright,
    he is a shield to those whose walk is blameless,[x]
8 for he guards the course of the just
    and protects the way of his faithful ones.[y]

9 Then you will understand what is right and just
    and fair—every good path.
10 For wisdom will enter your heart,
    and knowledge will be pleasant to your soul.
11 Discretion will protect you,
    and understanding will guard you.[z]

12 Wisdom will save you from the ways of wicked men,
    from men whose words are perverse,
13 who leave the straight paths
    to walk in dark ways,[a]
14 who delight in doing wrong
    and rejoice in the perverseness of evil,[b]
15 whose paths are crooked[c]
    and who are devious in their ways.

16 It will save you also from the adulteress,
    from the wayward wife with her seductive words,
17 who has left the partner of her youth
    and ignored the covenant she made before God.[a][d]

a 17 Or *covenant of her God*

1:33	[u] Ps 25:12
2:4	[v] Pr 3:14; Mt 13:44
2:6	[w] 1Ki 3:9,12; Jas 1:5
2:7	[x] Ps 84:11
2:8	[y] 1Sa 2:9; Ps 66:9
2:11	[z] Pr 6:22
2:13	[a] Jn 3:19
2:14	[b] Jer 11:15
2:15	[c] Ps 125:5
2:17	[d] Mal 2:14

2:3–6 Wisdom comes in two ways: it is a God-given gift and also the result of an energetic search. Wisdom's starting point is God and his revealed Word, the source of "knowledge and understanding" (2:6). In that sense, wisdom is God's gift to us. But he gives it only to those who earnestly seek it. But because God's wisdom is hidden from the rebellious and foolish, it takes effort to find it and use it. The pathway to wisdom is strenuous. When we are on the path, we discover that true wisdom is God's and that he will guide us and reward our sincere and persistent search.

2:6, 7 God gives us wisdom and victory but not for drifting through life or acting irresponsibly with his gifts and resources. If we are faithful and keep our purpose in life clearly in mind, he will keep us from pride and greed.

2:9, 10 We gain wisdom through a constant process of growing. First, we must trust and honor God. Second, we must realize that the Bible reveals God's wisdom to us. Third, we must make a lifelong series of right choices and avoid moral pitfalls. Fourth, when we make sinful or mistaken choices, we must learn from our errors and recover. People don't develop all aspects of wisdom at once. For example, some people have more insight than discre-

tion; others have more knowledge than common sense. But we can pray for all aspects of wisdom and take the steps to develop them in our lives.

2:11 Discretion is the ability to tell right from wrong. It enables the believer to detect evil motives in men (2:12) and women (2:16). With practice it helps us evaluate courses of action and consequences. For some it is a gift; for most it is developed by using God's truth to make wise choices day by day. Hebrews 5:14 emphasizes that we must train ourselves in order to have discretion.

2:16, 17 An *adulteress* is a seductive woman or a prostitute. Two of the most difficult sins to resist are pride and sexual immorality. Both are seductive. Pride says, "I deserve it"; sexual desire says, "I need it." In combination, their appeal is deadly. In fact, says Solomon, only by relying on God's strength can we overcome them. Pride appeals to the empty head; sexual enticement to the empty heart. By looking to God, we can fill our heads with his wisdom and our hearts with his love. Don't be fooled—remember what God says about who you are and what you were meant to be. Ask him for strength to resist these temptations.

2:18
e Pr 7:27

18 For her house leads down to death
   and her paths to the spirits of the dead. *e*
19 None who go to her return
   or attain the paths of life.

20 Thus you will walk in the ways of good men
   and keep to the paths of the righteous.
2:21
f Ps 37:29
21 For the upright will live in the land, *f*
   and the blameless will remain in it;
22 but the wicked will be cut off from the land,
   and the unfaithful will be torn from it.

Further Benefits of Wisdom

3 My son, do not forget my teaching,
   but keep my commands in your heart,
2 for they will prolong your life many years
   and bring you prosperity.

3 Let love and faithfulness never leave you;
   bind them around your neck,
   write them on the tablet of your heart.
4 Then you will win favor and a good name
   in the sight of God and man.

PEOPLE CALLED "WISE" IN THE BIBLE	The Person	Their Role	Reference	How They Practiced Wisdom
The special description "wise" is used for 12 significant people in the Bible. They can be helpful models in our own pursuit of wisdom.	Joseph	Wise leader	Acts 7:10	Prepared for a major famine; helped rule Egypt
	Moses	Wise leader	Acts 7:20–22	Learned all the Egyptian wisdom, then graduated to God's lessons in wisdom to lead Israel out of Egypt
	Bezalel	Wise artist	Exodus 31:1–5	Designed and supervised the construction of the tabernacle and its utensils in the desert
	Joshua	Wise leader	Deuteronomy 34:9	Learned by observing Moses, obeyed God, led the people into the promised land
	David	Wise leader	2 Samuel 14:20	Never let his failures keep him from the source of wisdom—reverence for God
	Abigail	Wise wife	1 Samuel 25:3	Managed her household sensibly in spite of a surly and mean husband
	Solomon	Wise leader	1 Kings 3:5–14; 4:29–34	Knew what to do even though he often failed to put his own wisdom into action
	Daniel	Wise counselor	Daniel 5:11, 12	Known as a man in touch with God; a solver of complex problems with God's help
	Magi	Wise learners	Matthew 2:1–12	Not only received special knowledge of God's visit to earth but checked it out personally
	Stephen	Wise leader	Acts 6:8–10	Organized the distribution of food to the Grecian widows; preached the gospel to the Jews
	Paul	Wise messenger	2 Peter 3:15, 16	Spent his life communicating God's love to all who would listen
	Christ	Wise youth Wise Savior Wisdom of God	Luke 2:40, 52; 1 Corinthians 1:20–25	Not only lived a perfect life but died on the cross to save us and make God's wise plan of eternal life available to us

3:3 Love and faithfulness are important character qualities. Both involve actions as well as attitudes. A loving person not only feels love; he or she also acts loyally and responsibly. A faithful person not only believes the truth; he or she also works for justice for others. Thoughts and words are not enough—our lives reveal whether we are truly loving and faithful. Do your actions measure up to your attitudes?

⁵ Trust in the LORD⁹ with all your heart
　　and lean not on your own understanding;
⁶ in all your ways acknowledge him,
　　and he will make your pathsʰ straight.ᵃ

⁷ Do not be wise in your own eyes;ⁱ
　　fear the LORD and shun evil.ʲ
⁸ This will bring health to your body
　　and nourishment to your bones.ᵏ

⁹ Honor the LORD with your wealth,
　　with the firstfruits of all your crops;
¹⁰ then your barns will be filledˡ to overflowing,
　　and your vats will brim over with new wine.

¹¹ My son, do not despise the LORD's discipline
　　and do not resent his rebuke,
¹² because the LORD disciplines those he loves,
　　as a fatherᵇ the son he delights in.ᵐ

¹³ Blessed is the man who finds wisdom,
　　the man who gains understanding,
¹⁴ for she is more profitable than silver
　　and yields better returns than gold.ⁿ
¹⁵ She is more precious than rubies;
　　nothing you desire can compare with her.
¹⁶ Long life is in her right hand;
　　in her left hand are riches and honor.
¹⁷ Her ways are pleasant ways,
　　and all her paths are peace.
¹⁸ She is a tree of lifeᵒ to those who embrace her;
　　those who lay hold of her will be blessed.

3:5	9 Ps 37:3,5
3:6	h 1Ch 28:9
3:7	i Ro 12:16 / Pr 16:6
3:8	k Job 21:24
3:10	l Dt 28:8
3:12	m Dt 8:5; Heb 12:5-6*
3:14	n Job 28:15
3:18	o Ge 2:9

ᵃ6 Or *will direct your paths*　ᵇ12 Hebrew; Septuagint */ and he punishes*

3:5, 6 *Leaning* has the sense of putting your whole weight on something, resting on and trusting in that person or thing. When we have an important decision to make, we sometimes feel that we can't trust anyone—not even God. But God knows what is best for us. He is a better judge of what we want than even we are! We must trust him completely in every choice we make. We should not omit careful thinking or belittle our God-given ability to reason; but we should not trust our own ideas to the exclusion of all others. We must not be wise in our own eyes. We should always be willing to listen to and be corrected by God's Word and wise counselors. Bring your decisions to God in prayer; use the Bible as your guide; and then follow God's leading. He will make your paths straight by both guiding and protecting you.

3:6 To receive God's guidance, said Solomon, we must acknowledge God in all our ways. This means turning every area of life over to him. About a thousand years later, Jesus emphasized this same truth (Matthew 6:33). Look at your values and priorities. What is important to you? In what areas have you not acknowledged him? What is his advice? In many areas of your life you may already acknowledge God, but it is in the areas where you attempt to restrict or ignore his influence that will cause you grief. Make him a vital part of everything you do; then he will guide you because you will be working to accomplish his purposes.

3:9, 10 The *firstfruits* refers to the practice of giving to God's use the first and best portion of the harvest (Deuteronomy 26:9–11). Many people give God their leftovers. If they can afford to donate anything, they do so. These people may be sincere and contribute willingly, but their attitude is nonetheless backward. It is better to give God the first part of our income. This demonstrates that God, not possessions, has first place in our lives and that our resources belong to him (we are only managers of God's resources). Giving

to God first helps us conquer greed, helps us properly manage God's resources, and opens us up to receive God's special blessings.

3:11, 12 Since righteous people are not always prosperous, we are to regard adversity as discipline. *Discipline* means "to teach and to train." Discipline sounds negative to many people because some disciplinarians are not loving. God, however, is the source of all love. He doesn't punish us because he enjoys inflicting pain but because he is deeply concerned about our development. He knows that in order to become morally strong and good, we must learn the difference between right and wrong. His loving discipline enables us to do that.

3:11, 12 It's difficult to know when God has been disciplining us until we look back on the situation later. Not every calamity comes directly from God, of course. But if we rebel against God and refuse to repent when God has identified some sin in our lives, he may use guilt, crises, or bad experiences to bring us back to him. Sometimes, however, difficult times come even when we have no flagrant sin. Then, our response should be patience, integrity, and confidence that God will show us what to do.

3:16, 17 Proverbs contains many strong statements about the benefits of wisdom, including long life, wealth, honor, and peace. If you aren't experiencing them, does this mean you are short on wisdom? Not necessarily. Instead of guarantees, these statements are general principles. In a perfect world, wise behavior would always lead to these benefits. Even in our troubled world, living wisely usually results in obvious blessings—but not always. Sometimes sin intervenes, and some blessings must be delayed until Jesus returns to establish his eternal kingdom. That is why we must "live by faith, not by sight" (2 Corinthians 5:7). We can be sure that wisdom ultimately leads to blessing.

3:19
p Ps 104:24

19 By wisdom the LORD laid the earth's foundations,p
   by understanding he set the heavens in place;
20 by his knowledge the deeps were divided,
   and the clouds let drop the dew.

21 My son, preserve sound judgment and discernment,
   do not let them out of your sight;

3:22
q Pr 1:8-9

22 they will be life for you,
   an ornament to grace your neck. q
23 Then you will go on your way in safety,
   and your foot will not stumble;

3:24
r Ps 3:5

24 when you lie down, r you will not be afraid;
   when you lie down, your sleep will be sweet.
25 Have no fear of sudden disaster
   or of the ruin that overtakes the wicked,
26 for the LORD will be your confidence
   and will keep your foot from being snared.

27 Do not withhold good from those who deserve it,
   when it is in your power to act.

3:28
s Lev 19:13

28 Do not say to your neighbor,
   "Come back later; I'll give it tomorrow"—
   when you now have it with you. s

29 Do not plot harm against your neighbor,
   who lives trustfully near you.
30 Do not accuse a man for no reason—
   when he has done you no harm.

3:31
t Ps 37:1

31 Do not envy t a violent man
   or choose any of his ways,

3:32
u Ps 25:14

32 for the LORD detests a perverse man
   but takes the upright into his confidence. u

3:33
v Mal 2:2

33 The LORD's curse v is on the house of the wicked,
   but he blesses the home of the righteous.

3:34
w Jas 4:6*;
1 Pe 5:5*

34 He mocks proud mockers
   but gives grace to the humble. w
35 The wise inherit honor,
   but fools he holds up to shame.

WISDOM: APPLIED TRUTH	Reference	The Person Who Has Wisdom	Benefits of Wisdom
The book of Proverbs tells us about people who have wisdom and enjoy its benefits.	Proverbs 3; 4 A father's instructions	Is loving Is faithful Trusts in the Lord Puts God first Turns away from evil Knows right from wrong Listens and learns Does what is right	Long, prosperous life Favor with God and people Reputation for good judgment Success Health, vitality Riches, honor, pleasure, peace Protection
	Proverbs 8; 9 Wisdom speaks	Possesses knowledge and discretion Hates pride, arrogance, and evil behavior Respects and fears God Gives good advice and has common sense Loves correction and is teachable Knows God	Riches, honor Justice Righteousness Life God's favor Constant learning Understanding

---

3:21 What is the difference between sound judgment and discernment? Discernment (or discretion) is the ability God gives to many people to think and make correct choices. Sound judgment, however, he gives only to those who follow him. Sound judgment includes discernment, but goes beyond it. It also includes the knowledge that comes from instruction, training, and discipline, and the insight that results from knowing and applying God's truths.

3:27, 28 Delaying to do good is inconsiderate and unfair, whether it is repaying a loan, returning a tool, or fulfilling a promise. Withholding destroys trust and creates a great inconvenience. Be as eager to do good as you are to have good done to you.

Wisdom Is Supreme

4 Listen, my sons,[x] to a father's instruction;
pay attention and gain understanding.
2 I give you sound learning,
so do not forsake my teaching.
3 When I was a boy in my father's house,
still tender, and an only child of my mother,
4 he taught me and said,
"Lay hold of my words with all your heart;
keep my commands and you will live.[y]
5 Get wisdom, get understanding;
do not forget my words or swerve from them.
6 Do not forsake wisdom, and she will protect you;[z]
love her, and she will watch over you.
7 Wisdom is supreme; therefore get wisdom.
Though it cost all you have,[a] get understanding.
8 Esteem her, and she will exalt you;
embrace her, and she will honor you.
9 She will set a garland of grace on your head
and present you with a crown of splendor.[a]"

10 Listen, my son, accept what I say,
and the years of your life will be many.[b]
11 I guide you in the way of wisdom
and lead you along straight paths.
12 When you walk, your steps will not be hampered;
when you run, you will not stumble.
13 Hold on to instruction, do not let it go;
guard it well, for it is your life.
14 Do not set foot on the path of the wicked
or walk in the way of evil men.[c]
15 Avoid it, do not travel on it;
turn from it and go on your way.
16 For they cannot sleep till they do evil;[d]
they are robbed of slumber till they make someone fall.
17 They eat the bread of wickedness
and drink the wine of violence.

18 The path of the righteous is like the first gleam of dawn,
shining ever brighter till the full light of day.[e]
19 But the way of the wicked is like deep darkness;[f]
they do not know what makes them stumble.

a 7 Or *Whatever else you get*

4:1
[x] Pr 1:8

4:4
[y] Pr 7:2

4:6
[z] 2Th 2:10

4:9
[a] Pr 1:8-9

4:10
[b] Pr 3:2

4:14
[c] Ps 1:1; Pr 1:15

4:16
[d] Ps 36:4

4:18
[e] 2Sa 23:4

4:19
[f] Job 18:5;
Isa 59:9-10;
Jn 12:35

4:3, 4 One of the greatest responsibilities of parents is to encourage their children to become wise. Here Solomon tells how his father, David, encouraged him to seek wisdom when he was young ("tender," see 1 Kings 2:1–9 and 1 Chronicles 28; 29 for David's charge to his son). This encouragement may have prompted Solomon to ask God for a discerning heart above everything else (1 Kings 3:9). Wisdom can be passed on from parents to children, from generation to generation. Ultimately, of course, all wisdom comes from God; parents can only urge their children to turn to him. If your parents never taught you in this way, God's Word can function as a loving and compassionate mother or father to you. You can learn from the Scriptures and then create a legacy of wisdom as you teach your own children.

4:5–7 If you want wisdom, you must decide to go after it. This will take resolve—a determination not to abandon the search once you begin no matter how difficult the road may become. This is not a once-in-a-lifetime step, but a daily process of choosing

between two paths—the wicked (4:14–17, 19) and the righteous (4:18). Nothing else is more important or more valuable.

4:7 David taught Solomon as a young boy that seeking God's wisdom was the most important choice he could make. Solomon learned the lesson well. When God appeared to Solomon to fulfill any request, Solomon chose wisdom above all else. We should also make God's wisdom our first choice. We don't have to wait for God to appear to us. We can boldly ask him for wisdom today through prayer. James 1:5 assures us that God will grant our request.

4:13–17 Even friends can make you fall. It is difficult for people to accept the fact that friends and acquaintances might be luring them to do wrong. Young people who want to be accepted would never want to confront or criticize a friend for wrong plans or actions. Many other people can't even see how their friends' actions could lead to trouble. While we should be accepting of others, we need a healthy skepticism about human behavior. When you feel yourself being heavily influenced,

20 My son, pay attention to what I say;
    listen closely to my words.

4:21
g Pr 3:21

21 Do not let them out of your sight, *g*
    keep them within your heart;

4:22
h Pr 3:8; 12:18

22 for they are life to those who find them
    and health to a man's whole body. *h*

23 Above all else, guard your heart,
    for it is the wellspring of life.

24 Put away perversity from your mouth;
    keep corrupt talk far from your lips.

25 Let your eyes look straight ahead,
    fix your gaze directly before you.

4:26
i Heb 12:13*

26 Make level *a* paths for your feet *i*
    and take only ways that are firm.

4:27
j Dt 5:32; 28:14

27 Do not swerve to the right or the left; *j*
    keep your foot from evil.

Warning Against Adultery

5

My son, pay attention to my wisdom,
    listen well to my words of insight,

2 that you may maintain discretion
    and your lips may preserve knowledge.

5:3
k Ps 55:21; Pr 2:16

3 For the lips of an adulteress drip honey,
    and her speech is smoother than oil; *k*

5:4
l Ecc 7:26

4 but in the end she is bitter as gall, *l*
    sharp as a double-edged sword.

5:5
m Pr 7:26-27

5 Her feet go down to death;
    her steps lead straight to the grave. *b m*

6 She gives no thought to the way of life;
    her paths are crooked, but she knows it not.

7 Now then, my sons, listen to me;
    do not turn aside from what I say.

8 Keep to a path far from her,
    do not go near the door of her house,

9 lest you give your best strength to others
    and your years to one who is cruel,

a 26 Or *Consider the*   *b* 5 Hebrew *Sheol*

STRATEGY FOR EFFECTIVE LIVING	Begins with . . . God's wisdom	Respecting and appreciating who God is; reverence and awe toward God
	Requires . . . . . Moral application	Trusting in God and his Word; allowing his Word to speak to us personally; being willing to obey
	Requires . . . . . Practical application	Acting on God's direction daily
	Results in . . . . . Effective living	Experiencing what God does with our obedience

---

proceed with caution. Don't let your friends cause you to fall into sin.

4:23-27 Our heart—our feelings of love and desire—dictates to a great extent how we live because we always find time to do what we enjoy. Solomon tells us to guard our heart above all else, making sure we concentrate on those desires that will keep us on the right path. Make sure your affections push you in the right direction. Put boundaries on your desires: don't go after everything you see. Look straight ahead, keep your eyes fixed on your goal, and don't get sidetracked on detours that lead to sin.

5:3 This "adulteress" is a prostitute. Proverbs includes many warnings against illicit sex for several reasons. First, a prostitute's charm is used as an example of any temptation to do

wrong or to leave the pursuit of wisdom. Second, sexual immorality of any kind was and still is extremely dangerous. It destroys family life. It erodes a person's ability to love. It degrades human beings and turns them into objects. It can lead to disease. It can result in unwanted children. Third, sexual immorality is against God's law.

5:3-8 Any person should be on guard against those who use flattery and smooth speech (lips that drip honey) that would lead him or her into sin. The best advice is to take a detour and even avoid conversation with such people.

10 lest strangers feast on your wealth
   and your toil enrich another man's house.
11 At the end of your life you will groan,
   when your flesh and body are spent.
12 You will say, "How I hated discipline!
   How my heart spurned correction!*n*

5:12
n Pr 1:29; 12:1

13 I would not obey my teachers
   or listen to my instructors.
14 I have come to the brink of utter ruin
   in the midst of the whole assembly."

15 Drink water from your own cistern,
   running water from your own well.
16 Should your springs overflow in the streets,
   your streams of water in the public squares?
17 Let them be yours alone,
   never to be shared with strangers.
18 May your fountain be blessed,
   and may you rejoice in the wife of your youth.*o*

5:18
o Mal 2:14

19 A loving doe, a graceful deer*p*—
   may her breasts satisfy you always,
   may you ever be captivated by her love.

5:19
p SS 2:9; 4:5

20 Why be captivated, my son, by an adulteress?
   Why embrace the bosom of another man's wife?

21 For a man's ways are in full view*q* of the LORD,
   and he examines all his paths.*r*

5:21
q Hos 7:2
r Job 31:4; 34:21;
Pr 15:3; Jer 16:17;
Heb 4:13

22 The evil deeds of a wicked man ensnare him;*s*
   the cords of his sin hold him fast.

5:22
s Ps 9:16

23 He will die for lack of discipline,*t*
   led astray by his own great folly.

5:23
t Job 4:21; 36:12

Warnings Against Folly

6 My son, if you have put up security for your neighbor,
   if you have struck hands in pledge*u* for another,

6:1
u Pr 11:15

2 if you have been trapped by what you said,
   ensnared by the words of your mouth,
3 then do this, my son, to free yourself,
   since you have fallen into your neighbor's hands:
   Go and humble yourself;
   press your plea with your neighbor!

5:11-13 At the end of your life, it will be too late to ask for advice. When desire is fully activated, people don't want advice—they want satisfaction. The best time to learn the dangers and foolishness of going after forbidden sex (or anything else that is harmful) is long before the temptation comes. Resistance is easier if the decision has already been made. Don't wait to see what happens. Prepare for temptation by deciding *now* how you will act when you face it.

5:15 "Drink water from your own cistern" is a picture of faithfulness in marriage. It means to enjoy the spouse God has given you. In desert lands, water is precious, and a well is a family's most important possession. In Old Testament times, it was considered a crime to steal water from someone else's well, just as it was a crime to have intercourse with another man's wife. In both cases, the offender endangers the health and security of family.

5:15-21 In contrast to much of what we read, see, and hear today, this passage urges couples to look to each other for life-long satisfaction and companionship. Many temptations entice husbands and wives to leave when marriage becomes dull in order to find excitement and pleasures elsewhere. But God

designed marriage and sanctified it, and only within this covenant relationship can we find real love and fulfillment. Don't let God's best for you be wasted on the illusion of greener pastures somewhere else. Instead, rejoice with your spouse as you give yourselves to God and to each other.

5:18-20 God does not intend faithfulness in marriage to be boring, lifeless, pleasureless, and dull. Sex is a gift God gives to married people for their mutual enjoyment. Real happiness comes when we decide to find pleasure in the relationship God has given or will give us and to commit ourselves to making it pleasurable for our spouse. The real danger is in doubting that God knows and cares for us. We then may resent his timing and carelessly pursue sexual pleasure without his blessing.

5:19 See Song of Songs, chapter 4, for parallels to this frank expression of the joys of sexual pleasure in marriage.

6:1-5 These verses are not a plea against generosity, but against overextending one's financial resources and acting in irresponsible ways that could lead to poverty. It is important to maintain a balance between generosity and good stewardship. God wants us to help our friends and the needy, but he does not promise to cover the costs of every unwise commitment

6:4
ᵛPs 132:4

⁴ Allow no sleep to your eyes,
    no slumber to your eyelids.ᵛ
⁵ Free yourself, like a gazelle from the hand of the hunter,
    like a bird from the snare of the fowler.

⁶ Go to the ant, you sluggard;
    consider its ways and be wise!
⁷ It has no commander,
    no overseer or ruler,
⁸ yet it stores its provisions in summer
    and gathers its food at harvest.

⁹ How long will you lie there, you sluggard?
    When will you get up from your sleep?
¹⁰ A little sleep, a little slumber,
    a little folding of the hands to rest—
¹¹ and poverty will come on you like a bandit
    and scarcity like an armed man.ᵃ

¹² A scoundrel and villain,
    who goes about with a corrupt mouth,
¹³   who winks with his eye,
    signals with his feet
    and motions with his fingers,

6:14
ʷMic 2:1
ˣver 16-19

6:15
ʸ2Ch 36:16

¹⁴   who plots evilʷ with deceit in his heart—
    he always stirs up dissension.ˣ
¹⁵ Therefore disaster will overtake him in an instant;
    he will suddenly be destroyed—without remedy.ʸ

¹⁶ There are six things the Lᴏʀᴅ hates,
    seven that are detestable to him:

6:17
ᶻPs 120:2
ᵃIsa 1:15

¹⁷   haughty eyes,
    a lying tongue,ᶻ
    hands that shed innocent blood,ᵃ

6:18
ᵇGe 6:5

¹⁸   a heart that devises wicked schemes,
    feet that are quick to rush into evil,ᵇ

6:19
ᶜPs 27:12

¹⁹   a false witnessᶜ who pours out lies
    and a man who stirs up dissension among brothers.

ᵃ11 Or *like a vagrant / and scarcity like a beggar*

THINGS GOD HATES
The book of Proverbs notes 14 types of people and actions that God hates. Let these be guidelines of what we are *not* to be and do!

---

we make. We should also act responsibly so that our families do not suffer.

6:6–11 Those last few moments of sleep are delicious—we savor them as we resist beginning another workday. But Proverbs warns against giving in to the temptation of laziness, of sleeping instead of working. This does not mean we should never rest: God gave the Jews the Sabbath, a weekly day of rest and restoration. But we should not rest when we should be working. The ant is used as an example because it utilizes its energy and resources economically. If laziness turns us from our responsibilities, poverty may soon bar us from the legitimate rest we should enjoy. (See also the chart in chapter 28, p. 1037.)

Warning Against Adultery

20 My son, keep your father's commands
and do not forsake your mother's teaching.
21 Bind them upon your heart forever;
fasten them around your neck.[d]
22 When you walk, they will guide you;
when you sleep, they will watch over you;
when you awake, they will speak to you.
23 For these commands are a lamp,
this teaching is a light,[e]
and the corrections of discipline
are the way to life,
24 keeping you from the immoral woman,
from the smooth tongue of the wayward wife.
25 Do not lust in your heart after her beauty
or let her captivate you with her eyes,
26 for the prostitute reduces you to a loaf of bread,
and the adulteress preys upon your very life.[f]
27 Can a man scoop fire into his lap
without his clothes being burned?
28 Can a man walk on hot coals
without his feet being scorched?
29 So is he who sleeps with another man's wife;
no one who touches her will go unpunished.

30 Men do not despise a thief if he steals
to satisfy his hunger when he is starving.
31 Yet if he is caught, he must pay sevenfold,[g]
though it costs him all the wealth of his house.
32 But a man who commits adultery lacks judgment;[h]
whoever does so destroys himself.
33 Blows and disgrace are his lot,
and his shame will never be wiped away;
34 for jealousy arouses a husband's fury,
and he will show no mercy when he takes revenge.
35 He will not accept any compensation;
he will refuse the bribe, however great it is.

Warning Against the Adulteress

7 My son,[i] keep my words
and store up my commands within you.
2 Keep my commands and you will live;[j]
guard my teachings as the apple of your eye.
3 Bind them on your fingers;
write them on the tablet of your heart.[k]
4 Say to wisdom, "You are my sister,"
and call understanding your kinsman;
5 they will keep you from the adulteress,
from the wayward wife with her seductive words.

6:21
[d]Pr 3:3; 7:1-3

6:23
[e]Ps 19:8

6:26
[f]Pr 7:22-23; 29:3

6:31
[g]Ex 22:1-14

6:32
[h]Pr 7:7

7:1
[i]Pr 2:1

7:2
[j]Pr 4:4

7:3
[k]Dt 6:8; Pr 3:3

6:20–23 It is natural and good for children, as they grow toward adulthood, to become increasingly independent of their parents. Young adults, however, should take care not to turn a deaf ear to their parents—to reject their advice just when it is needed most. If you are struggling with a decision or looking for insight, check with your parents or other older adults who know you well. Their extra years of experience may have given them the wisdom you seek.

6:25 Regard lust as a warning sign of danger ahead. When you notice that you are attracted to a person of the opposite sex or preoccupied with thoughts of him or her, your desires may lead you to sin. Ask God to help you change your desires before you are drawn into sin.

6:25–35 Some people argue that it is all right to break God's law against sexual sin if nobody gets hurt. In truth, somebody always gets hurt. Spouses are devastated. Children are scarred. The partners themselves, even if they escape disease and unwanted pregnancy, lose their ability to fulfill commitments, to feel sexual desire, to trust, and to be entirely open with another person. God's laws are not arbitrary. They do not forbid good, clean fun; rather, they warn us against destroying ourselves through unwise actions or running ahead of God's timetable.

6 At the window of my house
   I looked out through the lattice.

7:7
*l*Pr 6:32

7 I saw among the simple,
   I noticed among the young men,
   a youth who lacked judgment.*l*
8 He was going down the street near her corner,
   walking along in the direction of her house

7:9
*m*Job 24:15

9 at twilight,*m* as the day was fading,
   as the dark of night set in.

10 Then out came a woman to meet him,
   dressed like a prostitute and with crafty intent.

7:11
*n*Pr 9:13; 1Ti 5:13

11 (She is loud*n* and defiant,
   her feet never stay at home;
12 now in the street, now in the squares,
   at every corner she lurks.)
13 She took hold of him and kissed him
   and with a brazen face she said:

14 "I have fellowship offerings*a* at home;
   today I fulfilled my vows.
15 So I came out to meet you;
   I looked for you and have found you!
16 I have covered my bed
   with colored linens from Egypt.
17 I have perfumed my bed
   with myrrh, aloes and cinnamon.
18 Come, let's drink deep of love till morning;
   let's enjoy ourselves with love!
19 My husband is not at home;
   he has gone on a long journey.
20 He took his purse filled with money
   and will not be home till full moon."

7:21
*o*Pr 5:3

21 With persuasive words she led him astray;
   she seduced him with her smooth talk.*o*
22 All at once he followed her
   like an ox going to the slaughter,
   like a deer*b* stepping into a noose*c*
23   till an arrow pierces his liver,
   like a bird darting into a snare,
   little knowing it will cost him his life.*p*

7:23
*p*Ecc 9:12

24 Now then, my sons, listen to me;
   pay attention to what I say.
25 Do not let your heart turn to her ways
   or stray into her paths.
26 Many are the victims she has brought down;
   her slain are a mighty throng.

a 14 Traditionally *peace offerings*   *b 22* Syriac (see also Septuagint); Hebrew *fool*   *c 22* The meaning of the Hebrew
for this line is uncertain.

7:6–23 Although this advice is directed toward young men, young women should heed it as well. The person who has no purpose in life is simple-minded (7:7). Without aim or direction, an empty life is unstable, vulnerable to many temptations. Even though the young man in this passage doesn't know where he is going, the adulteress knows where she wants him. Notice her strategies: she is dressed to allure men (7:10); her approach is bold (7:13); she invites him over to her place (7:16–18); she cunningly answers his every objection (7:19, 20); she persuades him with smooth talk (7:21); she traps him (7:23). To combat temptation, make sure your life is full of God's Word and wisdom

(7:4). Recognize the strategies of temptation, and run away from them—fast.

7:25–27 You can take definite steps to avoid sexual sins. First, guard your mind. Don't read books, look at pictures, or encourage fantasies that stimulate the wrong desires. Second, keep away from settings and friends that tempt you to sin. Third, don't think only of the moment—focus on the future. Today's thrill may lead to tomorrow's ruin.

27 Her house is a highway to the grave,a
   leading down to the chambers of death.q

Wisdom's Call

8 Does not wisdom call out?r
   Does not understanding raise her voice?
2 On the heights along the way,
   where the paths meet, she takes her stand;
3 beside the gates leading into the city,
   at the entrances, she cries aloud:
4 "To you, O men, I call out;
   I raise my voice to all mankind.
5 You who are simple, gain prudence;
   you who are foolish, gain understanding.
6 Listen, for I have worthy things to say;
   I open my lips to speak what is right.
7 My mouth speaks what is true,
   for my lips detest wickedness.
8 All the words of my mouth are just;
   none of them is crooked or perverse.
9 To the discerning all of them are right;
   they are faultless to those who have knowledge.
10 Choose my instruction instead of silver,
   knowledge rather than choice gold,
11 for wisdom is more precious s than rubies,
   and nothing you desire can compare with her.t

12 "I, wisdom, dwell together with prudence;
   I possess knowledge and discretion.
13 To fear the LORD is to hate evil;u
   I hate pride and arrogance,
   evil behavior and perverse speech.
14 Counsel and sound judgment are mine;
   I have understanding and power.v
15 By me kings reign
   and rulersw make laws that are just;
16 by me princes govern,
   and all nobles who rule on earth.b
17 I love those who love me,x
   and those who seek me find me.y
18 With me are riches and honor,z
   enduring wealth and prosperity.a
19 My fruit is better than fine gold;
   what I yield surpasses choice silver.b
20 I walk in the way of righteousness,
   along the paths of justice,
21 bestowing wealth on those who love me
   and making their treasuries full.

a27 Hebrew *Sheol*   b16 Many Hebrew manuscripts and Septuagint; most Hebrew manuscripts *and nobles—*
all righteous rulers

7:27
qPr 2:18; 5:5; 9:18

8:1
rPr 1:20; 9:3

8:11
sJob 28:17-19
tPr 3:13-15

8:13
uPr 16:6

8:14
vEcc 7:19

8:15
wDa 2:21; Ro 13:1

8:17
x1Sa 2:30;
Jn 14:21-24
yJas 1:5

8:18
zPr 3:16
aMt 6:33

8:19
bPr 3:13-14

8:1ff Wisdom's call is contrasted to the call of the adulteress in chapter 7. Wisdom is portrayed as a woman who guides us (8:1–13) and makes us succeed (8:14–21). Wisdom was present at the creation and works with the Creator (8:22–31).

God approves of those who listen to wisdom's counsel (8:32–35). Those who hate wisdom love death (8:36). Wisdom should affect every aspect of one's life, from beginning to end. Be sure to open all corners of your life to God's direction and guidance.

8:13 The more a person fears and respects God, the more he or she will hate evil. Love for God and love for sin cannot coexist. Harboring secret sins means that you are tolerating evil within yourself. Make a clean break with sin and commit yourself completely to God.

22 "The LORD brought me forth as the first of his works,[a, b]
    before his deeds of old;
23 I was appointed[c] from eternity,
    from the beginning, before the world began.
24 When there were no oceans, I was given birth,
    when there were no springs abounding with water;
25 before the mountains were settled in place,
    before the hills, I was given birth,
26 before he made the earth or its fields
    or any of the dust of the world.
27 I was there when he set the heavens in place,
    when he marked out the horizon on the face of the deep,
28 when he established the clouds above
    and fixed securely the fountains of the deep,
29 when he gave the sea its boundary[c]
    so the waters would not overstep his command,
   and when he marked out the foundations of the earth.[d]
30   Then I was the craftsman at his side.[e]
   I was filled with delight day after day,
   rejoicing always in his presence,
31 rejoicing in his whole world
    and delighting in mankind.[f]

32 "Now then, my sons, listen to me;
   blessed are[g] those who keep my ways.
33 Listen to my instruction and be wise;
   do not ignore it.
34 Blessed is the man who listens to me,
   watching daily at my doors,
   waiting at my doorway.
35 For whoever finds me finds life
   and receives favor from the LORD.
36 But whoever fails to find me harms himself;
   all who hate me love death."

Invitations of Wisdom and of Folly

9 Wisdom has built[h] her house;
   she has hewn out its seven pillars.
2 She has prepared her meat and mixed her wine;
   she has also set her table.
3 She has sent out her maids, and she calls[i]
   from the highest point of the city.
4 "Let all who are simple come in here!"
   she says to those who lack judgment.[j]
5 "Come, eat my food
   and drink the wine I have mixed.[k]

8:29
[c] Job 38:10
[d] Job 38:5

8:30
[e] Jn 1:1-3

8:31
[f] Ps 16:3

8:32
[g] Lk 11:28

9:1
[h] Eph 2:20-22;
1Pe 2:5

9:3
[i] Pr 8:1-3

9:4
[j] Pr 6:32

9:5
[k] Isa 55:1

[a] 22 Or *way*; or *dominion*   [b] 22 Or *The LORD possessed me at the beginning of his work*; or *The LORD brought me forth at the beginning of his work*   [c] 23 Or *fashioned*

8:22–31 God says that wisdom is primary and fundamental. It is the foundation on which all life is built. Paul and John may have alluded to some of Solomon's statements about wisdom to describe Christ's presence at the creation of the world (Colossians 1:15–17; 2:2, 3; Revelation 3:14).

9:1 The seven pillars are figurative; they do not represent seven principles of wisdom. In the Bible, the number seven represents completeness and perfection. This verse poetically states that wisdom lacks nothing—it is complete and perfect.

9:1ff Wisdom and Folly (foolishness) are portrayed in this chapter as rival young women, each preparing a feast and inviting people to it. But Wisdom is a responsible woman of character,

while Folly is a prostitute serving stolen food. Wisdom appeals first to the mind; Folly to the senses. It is easier to excite the senses, but the pleasures of Folly are temporary. By contrast, the satisfaction that wisdom brings lasts forever.

9:1–5 The banquet described in this chapter has some interesting parallels to the banquet Jesus described in one of his parables (Luke 14:15–24). Many may intend to go, but they never make it because they get sidetracked by other activities that seem more important at the time. Don't let anything become more important than your search for God's wisdom.

6 Leave your simple ways and you will live;
    walk in the way of understanding.

7 "Whoever corrects a mocker invites insult;
    whoever rebukes a wicked man incurs abuse.

8 Do not rebuke a mocker or he will hate you;
    rebuke a wise man and he will love you.[l]

9 Instruct a wise man and he will be wiser still;
    teach a righteous man and he will add to his learning.[m]

10 "The fear of the LORD[n] is the beginning of wisdom,
    and knowledge of the Holy One is understanding.

11 For through me your days will be many,
    and years will be added to your life.[o]

12 If you are wise, your wisdom will reward you;
    if you are a mocker, you alone will suffer."

13 The woman Folly is loud;[p]
    she is undisciplined and without knowledge.

14 She sits at the door of her house,
    on a seat at the highest point of the city,[q]

15 calling out to those who pass by,
    who go straight on their way.

16 "Let all who are simple come in here!"
    she says to those who lack judgment.

17 "Stolen water is sweet;
    food eaten in secret is delicious!"[r]

18 But little do they know that the dead are there,
    that her guests are in the depths of the grave.[a]

9:8
[l] Ps 141:5

9:9
[m] Pr 1:5,7

9:10
[n] Job 28:28; Pr 1:7

9:11
[o] Pr 3:16

9:13
[p] Pr 7:11

9:14
[q] ver 3

9:17
[r] Pr 20:17

B. WISDOM FOR ALL PEOPLE (10:1—24:34)

These short couplets are what we commonly recognize as proverbs. They cover a wide range of topics. The first section was written by Solomon. The next two sections were written by others but collected by Solomon. These sayings give people practical wisdom for godly living at every stage of life.

Proverbs of Solomon

10 The proverbs of Solomon:

A wise son brings joy to his father,[s]
    but a foolish son grief to his mother.

2 Ill-gotten treasures are of no value,
    but righteousness delivers from death.

3 The LORD does not let the righteous go hungry
    but he thwarts the craving of the wicked.

10:1
[s] Pr 15:20

a 18 Hebrew Sheol

9:7–10 Are you a mocker or a wise person? You can tell by the way you respond to criticism. Instead of tossing back a quick putdown or clever retort when rebuked, listen to what is being said. Learn from your critics; this is the path to wisdom. Wisdom begins with knowing God. He gives insight into living because he created life. To know God is not just to know the facts about him, but to stand in awe of him and have a relationship with him. Do you really want to be wise? Get to know God better and better. (See James 1:5; 2 Peter 1:2–4 for more on how to become wise.)

9:14–17 Something is hypnotic and intoxicating about wickedness. One sin leads us to want more; sinful behavior seems more exciting than the Christian life. That is why many people put aside all thought of Wisdom's sumptuous banquet (9:1–5) in order to eat the stolen food of Folly. Don't be deceived—sin is dangerous. Before reaching for forbidden fruit, take a long look

at what happens to those who eat it. (See the chart in chapter 22, pp. 1024-25.)

10:2 Some people bring unhappiness on themselves by choosing ill-gotten treasures. For example, craving satisfaction, they may do something that destroys their chances of ever achieving happiness. God's principles for right living bring lasting happiness because they guide us into long-term right behavior in spite of our ever-changing feelings.

10:3 Proverbs is filled with verses that contrast the righteous person with the wicked. These statements are not intended to apply universally to all people in every situation. For example, some good people do go hungry. Rather, they are intended to communicate the general truth that the life of the person who seeks God is better in the long run than the life of the wicked person—a life that leads to ruin. These statements are not ironclad promises, but general truths. In addition, a proverb like this

10:4
Pr 13:4

⁴ Lazy hands make a man poor,
 but diligent hands bring wealth.*

⁵ He who gathers crops in summer is a wise son,
 but he who sleeps during harvest is a disgraceful son.

⁶ Blessings crown the head of the righteous,
 but violence overwhelms the mouth of the wicked.ᵃ

⁷ The memory of the righteous will be a blessing,
 but the name of the wicked will rot.

⁸ The wise in heart accept commands,
 but a chattering fool comes to ruin.

10:9
u Isa 33:15
v Ps 23:4
w Pr 28:18

⁹ The man of integrityᵘ walks securely,ᵛ
 but he who takes crooked paths will be found out.ʷ

¹⁰ He who winks maliciously causes grief,
 and a chattering fool comes to ruin.

10:11
x Ps 37:30

¹¹ The mouth of the righteous is a fountain of life,ˣ
 but violence overwhelms the mouth of the wicked.

10:12
y 1Pe 4:8

¹² Hatred stirs up dissension,
 but love covers over all wrongs.ʸ

10:13
z Pr 26:3

¹³ Wisdom is found on the lips of the discerning,
 but a rod is for the back of him who lacks judgment.ᶻ

10:14
a Pr 18:6,7

¹⁴ Wise men store up knowledge,
 but the mouth of a fool invites ruin.ᵃ

¹⁵ The wealth of the rich is their fortified city,
 but poverty is the ruin of the poor.

¹⁶ The wages of the righteous bring them life,
 but the income of the wicked brings them punishment.

¹⁷ He who heeds discipline shows the way to life,
 but whoever ignores correction leads others astray.

¹⁸ He who conceals his hatred has lying lips,
 and whoever spreads slander is a fool.

10:19
b Ecc 5:3;
Jas 3:2-12

¹⁹ When words are many, sin is not absent,
 but he who holds his tongue is wise.ᵇ

²⁰ The tongue of the righteous is choice silver,
 but the heart of the wicked is of little value.

²¹ The lips of the righteous nourish many,
 but fools die for lack of judgment.

a 6 Or but the mouth of the wicked conceals violence; also in verse 11

---

assumes a just government that cares for the poor and needy—
the kind of government Israel was intended to have (see Deuteronomy 24:17–22). A corrupt government often thwarts the plans of righteous men and women.

10:3 Proverbs often describes God's care for "the righteous." Being "righteous" does not mean being "like God" in the sense of being perfect. Obviously that is impossible for human beings. Righteous people are those who love the Lord and are seeking to follow him (Psalm 4:3). As Christians, we have been given the power of the Holy Spirit to help us live righteous lives (2 Peter 1:3).

10:4, 5 Every day has 24 hours filled with opportunities to grow, serve, and be productive. Yet it is so easy to waste time, letting life slip from our grasp. Refuse to be a lazy person, sleeping or

frittering away the hours meant for productive work. See time as God's gift and seize your opportunities to live diligently for him.

10:18 By hating another person you may become a liar or a fool. If you try to conceal your hatred, you end up lying. If you slander the other person and are proven wrong, you are a fool. The only way out is to admit your hateful feelings to God. Ask him to change your heart, to help you love instead of hate.

10:20 Words from a good person are valuable ("choice silver"). A lot of poor advice is worth less than a little good advice. It is easy to get opinions from people who will tell us only what they think will please us, but such advice is not helpful. Instead we should look for those who will speak the truth, even when it hurts. Think about the people to whom you go for advice. What do you expect to hear from them?

22 The blessing of the LORD brings wealth,^c → *c*
and he adds no trouble to it.

10:22
^cGe 24:35

23 A fool finds pleasure in evil conduct,^d
but a man of understanding delights in wisdom.

10:23
^dPr 15:21

24 What the wicked dreads will overtake him;
what the righteous desire will be granted.^e

10:24
^ePs 145:17-19;
Mt 5:6; 1Jn 5:14-15

25 When the storm has swept by, the wicked are gone,
but the righteous stand firm^f forever.

10:25
^fPs 15:5

26 As vinegar to the teeth and smoke to the eyes,
so is a sluggard to those who send him.

27 The fear of the LORD adds length to life,^g
but the years of the wicked are cut short.

10:27
^gPr 9:10-11

28 The prospect of the righteous is joy,
but the hopes of the wicked come to nothing.

29 The way of the LORD is a refuge for the righteous,
but it is the ruin of those who do evil.

30 The righteous will never be uprooted,
but the wicked will not remain in the land.

31 The mouth of the righteous brings forth wisdom,^h
but a perverse tongue will be cut out.

10:31
^hPs 37:30

32 The lips of the righteous know what is fitting,
but the mouth of the wicked only what is perverse.

11 The LORD abhors dishonest scales,ⁱ
but accurate weights are his delight.

11:1
ⁱLev 19:36;
Dt 25:13-16

2 When pride comes, then comes disgrace,^j
but with humility comes wisdom.

11:2
^jPr 16:18

3 The integrity of the upright guides them,
but the unfaithful are destroyed by their duplicity.^k

11:3
^kPr 13:6

4 Wealth is worthless in the day of wrath,^l
but righteousness delivers from death.^m

11:4
^lEze 7:19; Zep 1:18
^mGe 7:1

5 The righteousness of the blameless makes a straight way for them,
but the wicked are brought down by their own wickedness.

6 The righteousness of the upright delivers them,
but the unfaithful are trapped by evil desires.

7 When a wicked man dies, his hope perishes;
all he expected from his power comes to nothing.ⁿ

11:7
ⁿPr 10:28

8 The righteous man is rescued from trouble,
and it comes on the wicked instead.

10:22 God supplies most people with the personal and financial abilities to respond to the needs of others. If we all realized how God has blessed us, and if we all used our resources to do God's will, hunger and poverty would be wiped out. Wealth is a blessing only if we use it in the way God intended.

10:24 The wicked person dreads death. Those who do not believe in God usually fear death, and with good reason. By contrast, believers desire eternal life and God's salvation—their hopes will be rewarded. This verse offers a choice: you can have either your fears or your desires come true. You make that choice by rejecting God and living your own way, or by accepting God and following him.

11:4 "The day of wrath" refers to when we die or to the time when God settles accounts with all people. On judgment day, each person will stand alone, accountable for all of his or her deeds. At that time, no amount of riches will buy reconciliation with God. Only our love for God and obedience to him will count.

11:7, 8 These verses, like 10:3, contrast two paths in life, but are not intended to apply universally to all people in all circumstances. God's people are not excluded from problems or struggles. If a person follows God's wisdom, however, God can rescue him or her from trouble. But a wicked person will fall into his or her own traps. Even if good people suffer, they can be sure they will ultimately be rescued from eternal death.

⁹ With his mouth the godless destroys his neighbor,
  but through knowledge the righteous escape.

¹⁰ When the righteous prosper, the city rejoices;
  when the wicked perish, there are shouts of joy.

¹¹ Through the blessing of the upright a city is exalted,
  but by the mouth of the wicked it is destroyed.

¹² A man who lacks judgment derides his neighbor,
  but a man of understanding holds his tongue.

11:13
ᵒLev 19:16;
Pr 20:19

¹³ A gossip betrays a confidence,ᵒ
  but a trustworthy man keeps a secret.

¹⁴ For lack of guidance a nation falls,
  but many advisers make victory sure.

¹⁵ He who puts up security for another will surely suffer,
  but whoever refuses to strike hands in pledge is safe.

¹⁶ A kindhearted woman gains respect,
  but ruthless men gain only wealth.

¹⁷ A kind man benefits himself,
  but a cruel man brings trouble on himself.

11:18
ᵖHos 10:12-13

¹⁸ The wicked man earns deceptive wages,
  but he who sows righteousness reaps a sure reward.ᵖ

¹⁹ The truly righteous man attains life,
  but he who pursues evil goes to his death.

²⁰ The LORD detests men of perverse heart
  but he delights in those whose ways are blameless.

²¹ Be sure of this: The wicked will not go unpunished,
  but those who are righteous will go free.

GOD'S ADVICE ABOUT MONEY

Proverbs gives some practical instruction on the use of money, although sometimes it is advice we would rather not hear. It's more comfortable to continue in our habits than to learn how to use money more wisely. The advice includes:

Be generous in giving. 11:24, 25; 22:9
Place people's needs ahead of profit. 11:26
Be cautious of countersigning for another 17:18; 22:26, 27
Don't accept bribes 17:23
Help the poor 19:17; 21:13
Store up for the future 21:20
Be careful about borrowing 22:7

Other verses to study include 11:15; 20:16; 25:14; 27:13.

11:9 The mouth can be used either as a weapon or a tool, hurting relationships or building them up. Sadly, it is often easier to destroy than to build, and most people have received more destructive comments than those that build up. Every person you meet today is either a demolition site or a construction opportunity. Your words will make a difference. Will they be weapons for destruction or tools for construction?

11:14 A good leader needs and uses wise advisers. One person's perspective and understanding is severely limited; he or she may not have all the facts or may be blinded by bias, emotions, or wrong impressions. To be a wise leader at home, at church, or at work, seek the counsel of others and be open to their advice.

Then, after considering all the facts, make your decision. (See the chart in chapter 29, p. 1039.)

11:19 Righteous people attain life because they live life more fully each day. They also attain life because people usually live longer when they live right, with proper diet, exercise, and rest. In addition, they need not fear death because eternal life is God's gift to them (John 11:25). By contrast, evil people not only find eternal death, but also miss out on real life on earth.

22 Like a gold ring in a pig's snout
    is a beautiful woman who shows no discretion.

23 The desire of the righteous ends only in good,
    but the hope of the wicked only in wrath.

24 One man gives freely, yet gains even more;
    another withholds unduly, but comes to poverty.

25 A generous man will prosper;
    he who refreshes others will himself be refreshed. *q*

11:25
q Mt 5:7; 2Co 9:6-9

26 People curse the man who hoards grain,
    but blessing crowns him who is willing to sell.

27 He who seeks good finds goodwill,
    but evil comes to him who searches for it. *r*

11:27
r Est 7:10;
Ps 7:15-16

28 Whoever trusts in his riches will fall, *s*
    but the righteous will thrive like a green leaf. *t*

11:28
s Mk 10:25; 1Ti 6:17
t Ps 1:3; Jer 17:8

29 He who brings trouble on his family will inherit only wind,
    and the fool will be servant to the wise.

30 The fruit of the righteous is a tree of life, *u*
    and he who wins souls is wise.

11:30
u Jas 5:20

31 If the righteous receive their due on earth,
    how much more the ungodly and the sinner!

12 Whoever loves discipline loves knowledge,
    but he who hates correction is stupid.

2 A good man obtains favor from the LORD,
    but the LORD condemns a crafty man.

3 A man cannot be established through wickedness,
    but the righteous cannot be uprooted. *v*

12:3
v Pr 10:25

4 A wife of noble character is her husband's crown,
    but a disgraceful wife is like decay in his bones. *w*

12:4
w Pr 14:30

11:22 Physical attractiveness without discretion soon wears thin. We are to seek those character strengths that help us make wise decisions, not just those that make us look good. Not everyone who looks good is pleasant to live or work with. While taking good care of our body and appearance is not wrong, we also need to develop our ability to think.

11:24, 25 These two verses present a paradox: that we become richer by being generous. The world says to hold on to as much as possible, but God blesses those who give freely of their possessions, time, and energy. When we give, God supplies us with more so that we can give more. In addition, giving helps us gain a right perspective on our possessions. We realize they were never really ours to begin with, but they were given to us by God to be used to help others. What then do we gain by giving? Freedom from enslavement to our possessions, the joy of helping others, and God's approval.

11:29 One of the greatest resources God gives us is the family. Families provide acceptance, encouragement, guidance, and counsel. Bringing trouble on your family—whether through anger or through an exaggerated desire for independence—is foolish because you cut yourself off from all they provide. In your family, strive for healing, communication, and understanding.

11:30 A wise person is a model of a meaningful life. Like a tree attracts people to its shade, his or her sense of purpose attracts others who want to know how they too can find meaning. Gaining wisdom yourself, then, can be the first step in leading people to

God. Leading people to God is important because it keeps us in touch with God while offering others eternal life.

11:31 Contrary to popular opinion, no one sins and gets away with it. The faithful are rewarded for their faith. The wicked are punished for their sins. Don't think for a moment that "it won't matter" or "nobody will know" or "we won't get caught" (see also 1 Peter 4:18).

12:1 If you don't want to learn, years of schooling will teach you very little. But if you want to be taught, there is no end to what you can learn. This includes being willing to accept discipline and correction and to learn from the wisdom of others. A person who refuses constructive criticism has a problem with pride. Such a person is unlikely to learn very much.

12:3 To be established means to be successful. Real success comes only to those who do what is right. Their efforts stand the test of time. Then, what kind of success does wickedness bring? We all know people who cheated to pass the course or to get a larger tax refund—is this not success? And what about the person who ignores his family commitments and mistreats his workers but gets ahead in business? These apparent successes are only temporary. They are bought at the expense of character. Cheaters grow more and more dishonest, and those who hurt others become callous and cruel. In the long run, evil behavior does not lead to success; it leads only to more evil. Real success maintains personal integrity. If you are not a success by God's standards, you have not achieved true success. (See the chart in chapter 19, p. 1021.)

5 The plans of the righteous are just,
  but the advice of the wicked is deceitful.

12:6
x Pr 14:3

6 The words of the wicked lie in wait for blood,
  but the speech of the upright rescues them.*x*

7 Wicked men are overthrown and are no more,
  but the house of the righteous stands firm.

8 A man is praised according to his wisdom,
  but men with warped minds are despised.

9 Better to be a nobody and yet have a servant
  than pretend to be somebody and have no food.

10 A righteous man cares for the needs of his animal,
  but the kindest acts of the wicked are cruel.

12:11
y Pr 28:19

11 He who works his land will have abundant food,
  but he who chases fantasies lacks judgment.*y*

12 The wicked desire the plunder of evil men,
  but the root of the righteous flourishes.

12:13
z 2Pe 2:9

13 An evil man is trapped by his sinful talk,
  but a righteous man escapes trouble.*z*

12:14
a Pr 13:2
b Isa 3:10-11

14 From the fruit of his lips a man is filled with good things*a*
  as surely as the work of his hands rewards him.*b*

15 The way of a fool seems right to him,
  but a wise man listens to advice.

12:16
c Pr 29:11

16 A fool shows his annoyance at once,
  but a prudent man overlooks an insult.*c*

17 A truthful witness gives honest testimony,
  but a false witness tells lies.

12:18
d Ps 57:4

18 Reckless words pierce like a sword,*d*
  but the tongue of the wise brings healing.

TEACHING AND LEARNING

Good teaching comes from good learning—and Proverbs has more to say to students than to teachers. Proverbs is concerned with the learning of wisdom. The book makes it clear that there are no good alternatives to learning wisdom. We are either becoming wise learners or refusing to learn and becoming foolish failures. Proverbs encourages us to make the right choice.

Wise Learners	Proverb(s)	Foolish Failures
Quietly accept instruction and criticism	10:8; 23:12	Ignore instruction
Love discipline	12:1	Hate correction
Listen to advice	12:15; 21:11; 24:6	Think they need no advice
Accept parents' discipline	13:1	Mock parents
Lead others to life	10:17	Lead others astray
Receive honor	13:18	End in proverty and shame
Profit from constructive rebuke	15:31, 32; 29:1	Sefl-destruct by refusing rebuke

Advice to Teachers:
Help people avoid traps (13:14), use pleasant words (16:21), and speak wise words at the right time (15:23; 18:20).

12:13 Sinful talk is twisting the facts to support your claims. Those who do this are likely to be trapped by their own lies. But for someone who always tells the truth, the facts—plain and unvarnished—give an unshakable defense. If you find that you always have to defend yourself to others, maybe your honesty is less than it should be. (See the chart in chapter 20, p. 1021.)

12:16 When someone annoys or insults you, it is natural to retaliate. But this solves nothing and only encourages trouble. Instead, answer slowly and quietly. Your positive response will achieve positive results. Proverbs 15:1 says, "A gentle answer turns away wrath."

19 Truthful lips endure forever,
   but a lying tongue lasts only a moment.

20 There is deceit in the hearts of those who plot evil,
   but joy for those who promote peace.

21 No harm befalls the righteous,
   but the wicked have their fill of trouble.

22 The Lord detests lying lips,*e*
   but he delights in men who are truthful.

12:22
e Rev 22:15

23 A prudent man keeps his knowledge to himself,*f*
   but the heart of fools blurts out folly.

12:23
f Pr 13:16

24 Diligent hands will rule,
   but laziness ends in slave labor.

25 An anxious heart weighs a man down,*g*
   but a kind word cheers him up.

12:25
g Pr 15:13; Isa 50:4

26 A righteous man is cautious in friendship,*a*
   but the way of the wicked leads them astray.

27 The lazy man does not roast*b* his game,
   but the diligent man prizes his possessions.

28 In the way of righteousness there is life;
   along that path is immortality.

13
A wise son heeds his father's instruction,
   but a mocker does not listen to rebuke.

2 From the fruit of his lips a man enjoys good things,*h*
   but the unfaithful have a craving for violence.

13:2
h Pr 12:14

3 He who guards his lips*i* guards his life,
   but he who speaks rashly will come to ruin.

13:3
i Jas 3:2

4 The sluggard craves and gets nothing,
   but the desires of the diligent are fully satisfied.

5 The righteous hate what is false,
   but the wicked bring shame and disgrace.

6 Righteousness guards the man of integrity,
   but wickedness overthrows the sinner.*j*

13:6
j Pr 11:3,5

a 26 Or *man is a guide to his neighbor*   *b 27* The meaning of the Hebrew for this word is uncertain.

12:19 Truth is always timely; it applies today and in the future. Because it is connected with God's changeless character, it is also changeless. Think for a moment about the centuries that have passed since these proverbs were written. Consider the countless hours that have been spent carefully studying every sentence of Scripture. The Bible has withstood the test of time. Because God is truth, you can trust his Word to guide you.

12:21 This is a general, but not universal, truth. Although harm does befall the righteous, they are able to see opportunities in their problems and move ahead. The wicked, without God's wisdom, are ill-equipped to handle their problems. (See the notes on 3:16, 17; 10:3; 11:7, 8 for more about general truths that are not intended as universal statements.)

12:23 Prudent people have a quiet confidence. Insecure or uncertain people feel the need to prove themselves, but prudent people don't have to prove anything. They know they are capable, so they can get on with their work. Beware of showing off. If you are modest, people may not notice you at first, but they will respect you later.

12:27 The diligent make wise use of their possessions and resources; the lazy waste them. Waste has become a way of life for many who live in a land of plenty. Waste is poor stewardship. Make good use of everything God has given you, and prize it.

12:28 For many, death is a darkened door at the end of life, a passageway to an unknown and feared destiny. But for God's people, death is a bright pathway to a new and better life. So why do we fear death? Is it because of the pain we expect, the separation from loved ones, its surprise? God can help us deal with those fears. He has shown us that death is not final, but is just another step in the eternal life we received when we followed him.

13:3 You have not mastered self-control if you do not control what you say. Words can cut and destroy. James recognized this truth when he stated, "The tongue is a small part of the body, but it makes great boasts" (James 3:5). If you want to be self-controlled, begin with your tongue. Stop and think before you react or speak. If you can control this small but powerful member, you can control the rest of your body. (See the chart in chapter 26, p. 1033.)

13:6 Living right is like posting a guard for your life. Every choice for good sets into motion other opportunities for good.

13:7
k 2Co 6:10

7 One man pretends to be rich, yet has nothing;
　　another pretends to be poor, yet has great wealth. k

8 A man's riches may ransom his life,
　　but a poor man hears no threat.

13:9
l Job 18:5; Pr 24:20

9 The light of the righteous shines brightly,
　　but the lamp of the wicked is snuffed out. l

10 Pride only breeds quarrels,
　　but wisdom is found in those who take advice.

11 Dishonest money dwindles away,
　　but he who gathers money little by little makes it grow.

12 Hope deferred makes the heart sick,
　　but a longing fulfilled is a tree of life.

13:13
m 2Ch 36:16

13 He who scorns instruction will pay for it, m
　　but he who respects a command is rewarded.

13:14
n Pr 10:11

14 The teaching of the wise is a fountain of life, n
　　turning a man from the snares of death.

15 Good understanding wins favor,
　　but the way of the unfaithful is hard. a

13:16
o Pr 12:23

16 Every prudent man acts out of knowledge,
　　but a fool exposes his folly. o

13:17
p Pr 25:13

17 A wicked messenger falls into trouble,
　　but a trustworthy envoy brings healing. p

13:18
q Pr 15:5,31-32

18 He who ignores discipline comes to poverty and shame,
　　but whoever heeds correction is honored. q

19 A longing fulfilled is sweet to the soul,
　　but fools detest turning from evil.

20 He who walks with the wise grows wise,
　　but a companion of fools suffers harm.

a 15 Or *unfaithful does not endure*

Evil choices follow the same pattern, but in the opposite direction. Each decision you make to obey God's Word will bring a greater sense of order to your life, while each decision to disobey will bring confusion and destruction. The right choices you make reflect your integrity. Obedience brings the greatest safety and security.

13:10 "I was wrong" or "I need advice" are difficult phrases to utter because they require humility. Pride is an ingredient in every quarrel. It stirs up conflict and divides people. Humility, by contrast, heals. Guard against pride. If you find yourself constantly arguing, examine your life for pride. Be open to the advice of others, ask for help when you need it, and be willing to admit your mistakes.

13:13 God created us, knows us, and loves us. It only makes sense, then, to listen to his instructions and do what he says. The Bible is his unfailing word to us. It is like an owner's manual for a car. If you obey God's instructions, you will "run right" and find his kind of power to live. If you ignore them, you will have breakdowns, accidents, and failures.

13:17 In Solomon's day, a king had to rely on messengers for information about his country. These messengers had to be trustworthy. Inaccurate information could even lead to bloodshed. Reliable communication is still vital. If the message received is different from the message sent, marriages, businesses, and diplomatic relations can all break down. It is important to choose your words well and to avoid reacting until you clearly understand what the other person means.

13:19 Whether a "longing fulfilled" is good or bad depends on the nature of the desire. It is "sweet to the soul" to achieve worthwhile goals, but not all goals are worth pursuing. When you set your heart on something, you may lose your ability to assess it objectively. With your desire blinding your judgment, you may proceed with an unwise relationship, a wasteful purchase, or a poorly conceived plan. Faithfulness is a virtue, but stubbornness is not.

13:20 The old saying "A rotten apple spoils the barrel" is often applied to friendships, and with good reason. Our friends and associates affect us, sometimes profoundly. Be careful whom you choose as your closest friends. Spend time with people you want to be like—because you and your friends will surely grow to resemble each other.

13:20 When most people need advice, they go to their friends first because friends accept them and usually agree with them. But that is why they may not be able to help them with difficult problems. Our friends are so much like us that they may not have any answers we haven't already heard. Instead, we should seek out older and wiser people to advise us. Wise people have experienced a lot of life—and have succeeded. They are not afraid to tell the truth. Who are the wise, godly people who can warn you of the pitfalls ahead?

21 Misfortune pursues the sinner,
    but prosperity is the reward of the righteous.ʳ

13:21
ʳPs 32:10

22 A good man leaves an inheritance for his children's children,
    but a sinner's wealth is stored up for the righteous.ˢ

13:22
ˢJob 27:17;
Ecc 2:26

23 A poor man's field may produce abundant food,
    but injustice sweeps it away.

24 He who spares the rod hates his son,
    but he who loves him is careful to discipline him.ᵗ

13:24
ᵗPr 19:18; 22:15;
29:15,17

25 The righteous eat to their hearts' content,
    but the stomach of the wicked goes hungry.ᵘ

13:25
ᵘPs 34:10

14 The wise woman builds her house,
    but with her own hands the foolish one tears hers down.

2 He whose walk is upright fears the LORD,
    but he whose ways are devious despises him.

3 A fool's talk brings a rod to his back,
    but the lips of the wise protect them.ᵛ

14:3
ᵛPr 12:6

4 Where there are no oxen, the manger is empty,
    but from the strength of an ox comes an abundant harvest.

5 A truthful witness does not deceive,
    but a false witness pours out lies.ʷ

14:5
ʷPr 6:19; 12:17

6 The mocker seeks wisdom and finds none,
    but knowledge comes easily to the discerning.

7 Stay away from a foolish man,
    for you will not find knowledge on his lips.

8 The wisdom of the prudent is to give thought to their ways,
    but the folly of fools is deception.

9 Fools mock at making amends for sin,
    but goodwill is found among the upright.

10 Each heart knows its own bitterness,
    and no one else can share its joy.

11 The house of the wicked will be destroyed,
    but the tent of the upright will flourish.

13:23 The poor are often victims of an unjust society. A poor man's soil may be good, but unjust laws may rob him of his own produce. This proverb does not take poverty lightly or wink at injustice; it simply describes what often occurs. We should do what we can to fight injustice of every sort. Our efforts may seem inadequate; but it is comforting to know that in the end God's justice will prevail.

13:24 It is not easy for a loving parent to discipline a child, but it is necessary. The greatest responsibility that God gives parents is the nurture and guidance of their children. Lack of discipline puts parents' love in question because it shows a lack of concern for the character development of their children. Disciplining children averts long-range disaster. Without correction, children grow up with no clear understanding of right and wrong and with little direction to their lives. Don't be afraid to discipline your children. It is an act of love. Remember, however, that your efforts cannot make your children wise; they can only encourage your children to seek God's wisdom above all else!

14:4 When a farmer has no oxen for plowing, his food trough for the animals will be empty. The only way to keep your life free of people problems is to keep it free of other people. But if your life is empty of people, it is useless; and if you live only for yourself, your life loses its meaning. Instead of avoiding people, we should serve others, share the faith, and work for justice. Is your life clean, but empty? Or does it give evidence of your serving God wholeheartedly?

14:6 We all know mockers, people who scoff at every word of instruction or advice. They never find wisdom because they don't seek it seriously. Wisdom comes easily to those who pay attention to experienced people and to God. If the wisdom you need does not come easily to you, perhaps your attitude is the barrier.

14:9 How rarely we find goodwill around us today. Angry drivers scowl at each other in the streets. People fight to be first in line. Disgruntled employers and employees both demand their rights. But the common bond of God's people should be goodwill. Those with goodwill think the best of others and assume that others have good motives and intend to do what is right. When someone crosses you, and you feel your blood pressure rising, ask yourself, "How can I show goodwill to this person?"

14:12
xPr 16:25

12 There is a way that seems right to a man,
but in the end it leads to death.x

14:13
yEcc 2:2

13 Even in laughtery the heart may ache,
and joy may end in grief.

14:14
zPr 1:31
aPr 12:14

14 The faithless will be fully repaid for their ways,z
and the good man rewarded for his.a

15 A simple man believes anything,
but a prudent man gives thought to his steps.

14:16
bPr 22:3

16 A wise man fears the LORD and shuns evil,b
but a fool is hotheaded and reckless.

WISDOM AND FOOLISHNESS

The wise and the foolish are often contrasted in Proverbs. The characteristics, reputation, and results of each are worth knowing if wisdom is our goal.

		The Wise	The Foolish	
Characteristics		Help others with good advice	Lack judgment	10:21
		Enjoy wisdom	Enjoy foolishness	10:23
		Cautious with reason	Gullible	14:15
			Avoid the wise	15:12
		Seek knowledge	Feed on foolishness	15:14
		Value wisdom above riches		16:16
		Receive life	Receive punishment	16:22
		Respond to correction	Do not respond to punishment	17:10
		Pursue wisdom	Pursue illusive dreams	17:24
			Blame failure on God	19:3
		Profit from correction	An example to others	19:25
			Proud and arrogant	21:24
			Scorn wise advice	23:9
			Make truth useless	26:7
			Repeat their folly	26:11
		Trust in wisdom	Trust in themselves	28:26
		Control their anger	Unleash their anger	29:11
Reputation		Admired as counselors	Beaten as servants	10:13
		Rewarded with knowledge	Inherit folly	14:18
			Cause strife and quarrels	22:10
			Receive no honor	26:1
		Keep peace	Stir up anger	29:8
Results		Stay on straight paths	Go the wrong way	15:21
			Lash out when discovered in folly	17:12
			Endangered by their words	18:6, 7
		Their wisdom conquers others' strength		21:22
		Avoid wicked paths	Walk a troublesome path	22:5
		Have great advice		24:5
			Will never be chosen as counselors	24:7
			Must be guided by hardship	26:3
			Persist in foolishness	27:22

14:12 The "way that seems right" may offer many options and require few sacrifices. Easy choices, however, should make us take a second look. Is this solution attractive because it allows me to be lazy? Because it doesn't ask me to change my lifestyle? Because it requires no moral restraints? The right choice often requires hard work and self-sacrifice. Don't be enticed by apparent shortcuts that seem right but end in death.

17 A quick-tempered man does foolish things,
   and a crafty man is hated.

18 The simple inherit folly,
   but the prudent are crowned with knowledge.

19 Evil men will bow down in the presence of the good,
   and the wicked at the gates of the righteous.

20 The poor are shunned even by their neighbors,
   but the rich have many friends.*c*

21 He who despises his neighbor sins,
   but blessed is he who is kind to the needy.*d*

22 Do not those who plot evil go astray?
   But those who plan what is good find*a* love and faithfulness.

23 All hard work brings a profit,
   but mere talk leads only to poverty.

24 The wealth of the wise is their crown,
   but the folly of fools yields folly.

25 A truthful witness saves lives,
   but a false witness is deceitful.*e*

26 He who fears the LORD has a secure fortress,
   and for his children it will be a refuge.

27 The fear of the LORD is a fountain of life,
   turning a man from the snares of death.

28 A large population is a king's glory,
   but without subjects a prince is ruined.

29 A patient man has great understanding,
   but a quick-tempered man displays folly.*f*

30 A heart at peace gives life to the body,
   but envy rots the bones.*g*

31 He who oppresses the poor shows contempt for their Maker,*h*
   but whoever is kind to the needy honors God.

32 When calamity comes, the wicked are brought down,
   but even in death the righteous have a refuge.*i*

33 Wisdom reposes in the heart of the discerning*j*
   and even among fools she lets herself be known.*b*

34 Righteousness exalts a nation,
   but sin is a disgrace to any people.

35 A king delights in a wise servant,
   but a shameful servant incurs his wrath.*k*

*a*22 Or *show*   *b*33 Hebrew; Septuagint and Syriac / *but in the heart of fools she is not known*

Ref	
14:20	*c*Pr 19:4,7
14:21	*d*Ps 41:1
14:25	*e*ver 5
14:29	*f*Jas 1:19
14:30	*g*Pr 12:4
14:31	*h*Pr 17:5
14:32	*i*2Ti 4:18
14:33	*j*Pr 2:6-10
14:35	*k*Mt 24:45-51

14:29 A quick temper can be like a fire out of control. It can burn us and everyone else in its path. Anger divides people. It pushes us into hasty decisions that only cause bitterness and guilt. Yet anger, in itself, is not wrong. Anger can be a legitimate reaction to injustice and sin. When you feel yourself getting angry, look for the cause. Are you reacting to an evil situation that you are going to set right? Or are you responding selfishly to a personal insult? Pray that God will help you control your quick temper, channeling your feelings into effective action and conquering selfish anger through humility and repentance.

14:31 God has a special concern for the poor. He insists that people who have material goods should be generous with those who are needy. Providing for the poor is not just a suggestion in the Bible; it is a command that may require a change of attitude (see Leviticus 23:22; Deuteronomy 15:7, 8; Psalms 113:5-9; 146:5-9; Isaiah 58:7; 2 Corinthians 9:9; James 2:1-9).

15

15:1
l Pr 25:15

A gentle answer turns away wrath,*l*
  but a harsh word stirs up anger.

15:2
m Pr 12:23

2 The tongue of the wise commends knowledge,
  but the mouth of the fool gushes folly.*m*

15:3
n Heb 4:13

3 The eyes of the Lord are everywhere,*n*
  keeping watch on the wicked and the good.

4 The tongue that brings healing is a tree of life,
  but a deceitful tongue crushes the spirit.

5 A fool spurns his father's discipline,
  but whoever heeds correction shows prudence.

6 The house of the righteous contains great treasure,
  but the income of the wicked brings them trouble.

7 The lips of the wise spread knowledge;
  not so the hearts of fools.

15:8
o Isa 1:11; Jer 6:20

8 The Lord detests the sacrifice of the wicked,*o*
  but the prayer of the upright pleases him.

15:9
p 1Ti 6:11

9 The Lord detests the way of the wicked
  but he loves those who pursue righteousness.*p*

10 Stern discipline awaits him who leaves the path;
  he who hates correction will die.

15:11
q Job 26:6; Ps 139:8
r 2Ch 6:30

11 Death and Destruction*a* lie open before the Lord*q*—
  how much more the hearts of men!*r*

15:12
s Am 5:10

12 A mocker resents correction;*s*
  he will not consult the wise.

15:13
t Pr 12:25; 17:22

13 A happy heart makes the face cheerful,
  but heartache crushes the spirit.*t*

14 The discerning heart seeks knowledge,
  but the mouth of a fool feeds on folly.

15 All the days of the oppressed are wretched,
  but the cheerful heart has a continual feast.

15:16
u Ps 37:16-17;
1Ti 6:6

16 Better a little with the fear of the Lord
  than great wealth with turmoil.*u*

15:17
v Pr 17:1

17 Better a meal of vegetables where there is love
  than a fattened calf with hatred.*v*

a 11 Hebrew *Sheol* and *Abaddon*

15:1 Have you ever tried to argue in a whisper? It is equally hard to argue with someone who insists on answering gently. On the other hand, a rising voice and harsh words almost always trigger an angry response. To turn away wrath and seek peace, choose gentle words.

15:3 At times it seems that God has let evil run rampant in the world, and we wonder if he even notices it. But God sees everything clearly—both the evil actions and the evil intentions lying behind them (15:11). He is not an indifferent observer. He cares and is active in our world. Right now, his work may be unseen and unfelt, but don't give up. One day he will wipe out evil and punish the evildoers, just as he will establish the good and reward those who do his will.

15:14 What we feed our minds is just as important as what we feed our bodies. The kinds of books we read, the people we talk with, the music we listen to, and the films we watch are all part of our mental diet. Be discerning because what you feed your mind influences your total health and well-being. Thus, a strong desire to discover knowledge is a mark of wisdom.

15:15 Our attitudes color our whole personality. We cannot always choose what happens to us, but we can choose our attitude toward each situation. The secret to a cheerful heart is filling our minds with thoughts that are true, pure, and lovely, with thoughts that dwell on the good things in life (Philippians 4:8). This was Paul's secret as he faced imprisonment, and it can be ours as we face the struggles of daily living. Look at your attitudes and then examine what you allow to enter your mind and what you choose to dwell on. You may need to make some changes.

15:17-19 The "path of the upright" doesn't always seem easy (15:19), but look at the alternatives. Hatred (15:17), dissension (15:18), and laziness (15:19) cause problems that the upright person does not have to face. By comparison, his or her life is a smooth, level road because it is built on a solid foundation of love for God.

18 A hot-tempered man stirs up dissension,ʷ
   but a patient man calms a quarrel.

19 The way of the sluggard is blocked with thorns,
   but the path of the upright is a highway.

20 A wise son brings joy to his father,ˣ
   but a foolish man despises his mother.

21 Folly delights a man who lacks judgment,
   but a man of understanding keeps a straight course.

22 Plans fail for lack of counsel,
   but with many advisers they succeed.

23 A man finds joy in giving an apt reply—
   and how good is a timely word!ʸ

24 The path of life leads upward for the wise
   to keep him from going down to the grave.ᵃ

25 The LORD tears down the proud man's houseᶻ
   but he keeps the widow's boundaries intact.ᵃ

26 The LORD detests the thoughts of the wicked,
   but those of the pure are pleasing to him.

27 A greedy man brings trouble to his family,
   but he who hates bribes will live.

28 The heart of the righteous weighs its answers,ᵇ
   but the mouth of the wicked gushes evil.

29 The LORD is far from the wicked
   but he hears the prayer of the righteous.ᶜ

30 A cheerful look brings joy to the heart,
   and good news gives health to the bones.

31 He who listens to a life-giving rebuke
   will be at home among the wise.

32 He who ignores discipline despises himself,
   but whoever heeds correction gains understanding.

33 The fear of the LORDᵈ teaches a man wisdom,ᵇ
   and humility comes before honor.

16 To man belong the plans of the heart,
   but from the LORD comes the reply of the tongue.

2 All a man's ways seem innocent to him,
   but motives are weighed by the LORD.

15:18
ʷ Pr 26:21

15:20
ˣ Pr 10:1

15:23
ʸ Pr 25:11

15:25
ᶻ Pr 12:7
ᵃ Ps 68:5-6

15:28
ᵇ 1Pe 3:15

15:29
ᶜ Ps 145:18-19

15:33
ᵈ Pr 1:7

ᵃ 24 Hebrew *Sheol*   ᵇ 33 Or *Wisdom teaches the fear of the* LORD

15:22 People with tunnel vision, those who are locked into one way of thinking, are likely to miss the right road because they have closed their minds to any new options. We need the help of those who can enlarge our vision and broaden our perspective. Seek out the advice of those who know you and have a wealth of experience. Build a network of advisers. Then be open to new ideas and be willing to weigh their suggestions carefully. Your plans will be stronger and more likely to succeed.

15:28 The righteous weigh their answers; the wicked don't wait to speak because they don't care about the effects of their words. It is important to have something to say, but it is equally important to weigh it first. Do you carefully plan your words, or do you pour out your thoughts without concern for their impact?

16:1 "From the LORD comes the reply of the tongue" means that the final outcome of the plans we make is in God's hands. If this is so, why make plans? In doing God's will, there must be partnership between our efforts and God's control. He wants us to use our minds, to seek the advice of others, and to plan. Nevertheless, the results are up to him. Planning, then, helps us act God's way. As you live for him, ask for guidance as you plan, and then act on your plan as you trust in him.

16:2 "All a man's ways seem innocent to him." People can rationalize anything if they have no standards for judging right and wrong. We can always prove that we are right. Before putting any plan into action, ask yourself these three questions: (1) Is this plan in harmony with God's truth? (2) Will it work under real-life conditions? (3) Is my attitude pleasing to God?

16:3
ePs 37:5-6

3 Commit to the LORD whatever you do,
and your plans will succeed. *e*

4 The LORD works out everything for his own ends—
even the wicked for a day of disaster.

16:5
fPr 11:20-21

5 The LORD detests all the proud of heart.
Be sure of this: They will not go unpunished. *f*

16:6
gPr 14:16

6 Through love and faithfulness sin is atoned for;
through the fear of the LORD a man avoids evil. *g*

7 When a man's ways are pleasing to the LORD,
he makes even his enemies live at peace with him.

8 Better a little with righteousness
than much gain with injustice.

16:9
hJer 10:23

9 In his heart a man plans his course,
but the LORD determines his steps. *h*

10 The lips of a king speak as an oracle,
and his mouth should not betray justice.

HOW GOD IS DESCRIBED IN PROVERBS

God . . .

is aware of all that happens (15:3)

knows the hearts of all people (15:11; 16:2; 21:2)

controls all things (16:33; 21:30)

is a place of safety (18:10)

rescues good people from danger (11:8, 21)

condemns the wicked (11:31)

hears and delights in our prayers (15:8, 29)

loves those who obey him (15:9; 22:12)

cares for the poor and needy (15:25; 22:22, 23)

tests and purifies hearts (17:3)

hates evil (17:5; 21:27; 28:9)

Our response should be . . .

to fear and revere God (10:27; 14:26, 27; 15:16; 16:6; 19:23; 28:14)

to obey God's Word (13:13; 19:16)

to please God by doing what is right and just (21:3)

to trust in God (22:17–19; 29:25)

Proverbs is a book about wise living. It often focuses on a person's response and attitude toward God, who is the source of wisdom. And a number of proverbs point out aspects of God's character. Knowing God helps us on the way to wisdom.

16:3 There are different ways to fail to commit whatever we do to the Lord. Some people commit their work only superficially. They say the project is being done for the Lord, but in reality they are doing it for themselves. Others give God temporary control of their interests, only to take control back the moment things stop going the way they expect. Still others commit a task fully to the Lord, but put forth no effort themselves, and then they wonder why they do not succeed. We must maintain a delicate balance: trusting God as if everything depended on him, while working as if everything depended on us. Think of a specific effort in which you are involved right now. Have you committed it to the Lord?

16:4 This verse doesn't mean that God created some people to be wicked, but rather that God uses even the activities of wicked people to fulfill his good purposes. God is infinite and we are finite. No matter how great our intellects, we will never be able to understand him completely. But we can accept by faith that he is all-powerful, all-loving, and perfectly good. We can believe that he is not the cause of evil (James 1:13, 17); and we can trust

that there are no loose ends in his system of judgment. Evil is a temporary condition in the universe. One day God will destroy it. In the meantime, he uses even the evil intentions of people for his good purposes (see Genesis 50:20).

16:5 Pride is the inner voice that whispers, "My way is best." It is resisting God's leadership and believing that you are able to live without his help. Whenever you find yourself wanting to do it your way and looking down on other people, you are being pulled by pride. Only when you eliminate pride can God help you become all he meant you to be. (See the chart in chapter 18, p. 1017.)

16:7 We want other people to like us, and sometimes we will do almost anything to win their approval. But God tells us to put our energy into pleasing him instead. Our effort to be peacemakers will usually make us more attractive to those around us, even our enemies. But even if it doesn't, we haven't lost anything. We are still pleasing God, the only one who truly matters.

11 Honest scales and balances are from the LORD;
   all the weights in the bag are of his making.

12 Kings detest wrongdoing,
   for a throne is established through righteousness.*i*

16:12
i Pr 25:5

13 Kings take pleasure in honest lips;
   they value a man who speaks the truth.

14 A king's wrath is a messenger of death,
   but a wise man will appease it.

15 When a king's face brightens, it means life;*j*
   his favor is like a rain cloud in spring.

16:15
j Job 29:24

16 How much better to get wisdom than gold,
   to choose understanding rather than silver!*k*

16:16
k Pr 8:10,19

17 The highway of the upright avoids evil;
   he who guards his way guards his life.

18 Pride goes before destruction,
   a haughty spirit before a fall.*l*

16:18
l Pr 11:2

19 Better to be lowly in spirit and among the oppressed
   than to share plunder with the proud.

20 Whoever gives heed to instruction prospers,
   and blessed is he who trusts in the LORD.*m*

16:20
m Ps 34:8; Jer 17:7

21 The wise in heart are called discerning,
   and pleasant words promote instruction.*a*

22 Understanding is a fountain of life to those who have it,
   but folly brings punishment to fools.

23 A wise man's heart guides his mouth,
   and his lips promote instruction.*b*

24 Pleasant words are a honeycomb,
   sweet to the soul and healing to the bones.

25 There is a way that seems right to a man,
   but in the end it leads to death.*n*

16:25
n Pr 14:12

26 The laborer's appetite works for him;
   his hunger drives him on.

27 A scoundrel plots evil,
   and his speech is like a scorching fire.*o*

16:27
o Jas 3:6

28 A perverse man stirs up dissension,
   and a gossip separates close friends.*p*

16:28
p Pr 17:9

*a*21 Or *words make a man persuasive*   *b*23 Or *mouth / and makes his lips persuasive*

16:11 Whether we buy or sell, make a product or offer a service, we know what is honest and what is dishonest. Sometimes we feel pressure to be dishonest in order to advance ourselves or gain more profit. But if we want to obey God, there is no middle ground: God demands honesty in every business transaction. No amount of rationalizing can cover for a dishonest business practice. Honesty and fairness are not always easy, but they are what God demands. Ask him for discernment and courage to be consistently honest and fair.

16:18 Proud people take little account of their weaknesses and do not anticipate stumbling blocks. They think they are above the frailties of common people. In this state of mind they are easily tripped up. Ironically, proud people seldom realize that pride is their problem, although everyone around them is well aware of it.

Ask someone you trust whether self-satisfaction has blinded you to warning signs. He or she may help you avoid a fall.

16:22 For centuries people sought a fountain of youth, a spring that promised to give eternal life and vitality. It was never found. But God's wisdom is a fountain of life that can make a person happy, healthy, and alive forever. How? When we live by God's Word, he washes away the deadly effects of sin (see Titus 3:4–8), and the hope of eternal life with him gives us a joyful perspective on our present life. The fountain of youth was only a dream, but the fountain of life is reality. The choice is yours. You can be enlightened by God's wisdom, or you can be dragged down by the weight of your own foolishness.

16:26 "The laborer's appetite works for him" means that no matter how much difficulty or drudgery we may find in our work,

16:29
q Pr 1:10

29 A violent man entices his neighbor
   and leads him down a path that is not good. *q*

30 He who winks with his eye is plotting perversity;
   he who purses his lips is bent on evil.

16:31
r Pr 20:29

31 Gray hair is a crown of splendor; *r*
   it is attained by a righteous life.

32 Better a patient man than a warrior,
   a man who controls his temper than one who takes a city.

33 The lot is cast into the lap,
   but its every decision is from the LORD.

17:1
s Pr 15:16,17

17 Better a dry crust with peace and quiet
        than a house full of feasting, *a* with strife. *s*

2 A wise servant will rule over a disgraceful son,
   and will share the inheritance as one of the brothers.

17:3
t Pr 27:21
u Ps 26:2

3 The crucible for silver and the furnace for gold, *t*
   but the LORD tests the heart. *u*

4 A wicked man listens to evil lips;
   a liar pays attention to a malicious tongue.

17:5
v Pr 14:31
w Job 31:29

5 He who mocks the poor shows contempt for their Maker; *v*
   whoever gloats over disaster *w* will not go unpunished.

6 Children's children are a crown to the aged,
   and parents are the pride of their children.

7 Arrogant *b* lips are unsuited to a fool—
   how much worse lying lips to a ruler!

8 A bribe is a charm to the one who gives it;
   wherever he turns, he succeeds.

17:9
x Pr 10:12
y Pr 16:28

9 He who covers over an offense promotes love, *x*
   but whoever repeats the matter separates close friends. *y*

a 1 Hebrew *sacrifices*   *b* 7 Or *Eloquent*

---

our appetite is an incentive to keep going. Hunger makes us work to satisfy that hunger.

16:31 The Hebrews believed that a long life was a sign of God's blessing; therefore, gray hair and old age were good. While young people glory in their strength, old people can rejoice in their years of experience and practical wisdom. Gray hair is not a sign of disgrace to be covered up; it is a crown of splendor. As you deal with older people, treat them with respect.

16:32 Self-control is superior to conquest. Success in business, school, or home life can be ruined by a person who has lost control of his or her temper. So it is a great personal victory to control your temper. When you feel yourself ready to explode, remember that losing control may cause you to forfeit what you want the most.

16:33 The lot was almost always used in ceremonial settings and was the common method for determining God's will. Several important events occurred by lot, including the identification of Achan as the man who had sinned (Joshua 7:14), the division of the promised land among the tribes (Joshua 14:2), and the selection of the first king for the nation (1 Samuel 10:16–26).

17:3 It takes intense heat to purify gold and silver. Similarly, it often takes the heat of trials for the Christian to be purified. Through trials, God shows us what is in us and clears out anything that gets in the way of complete trust in him. Peter says, "These have come so that your faith—of greater worth than gold,

which perishes even though refined by fire—may be proved genuine and may result in praise, glory and honor when Jesus Christ is revealed" (1 Peter 1:7). So when tough times come your way, realize that God wants to use them to refine your faith and purify your heart.

17:5 Few acts are as cruel as making fun of the less fortunate, but many people do this because it makes them feel good to be better off or more successful than someone else. Mocking the poor is mocking the God who made them. We also ridicule God when we mock the weak, those who are different, or anyone else. When you catch yourself putting down others just for fun, stop and think about who created them.

17:8 Solomon is not condoning bribery (see 17:15, 23), but he is making an observation about the way the world operates. Bribes may get people what they want, but the Bible clearly condemns using them (Exodus 23:8; Proverbs 17:23; Matthew 28:11–15).

17:9 This proverb is saying that we should be willing to forgive others' sins against us. Covering over offenses is necessary to any relationship. It is tempting, especially in an argument, to bring up all the mistakes the other person has ever made. Love, however, keeps its mouth shut—difficult though that may be. Try never to bring anything into an argument that is unrelated to the topic being discussed. As we grow to be like Christ, we will acquire God's ability to forget the confessed sins of the past.

10 A rebuke impresses a man of discernment
     more than a hundred lashes a fool.

11 An evil man is bent only on rebellion;
     a merciless official will be sent against him.

12 Better to meet a bear robbed of her cubs
     than a fool in his folly.

13 If a man pays back evil *z* for good,
     evil will never leave his house.

17:13
z Ps 109:4-5;
Jer 18:20

14 Starting a quarrel is like breaching a dam;
     so drop the matter before a dispute breaks out. *a*

17:14
a Pr 20:3

15 Acquitting the guilty and condemning the innocent—
     the Lord detests them both. *b*

17:15
b Ex 23:6-7;
Isa 5:23

16 Of what use is money in the hand of a fool,
     since he has no desire to get wisdom?

17 A friend loves at all times,
     and a brother is born for adversity.

18 A man lacking in judgment strikes hands in pledge
     and puts up security for his neighbor. *c*

17:18
c Pr 6:1-5

19 He who loves a quarrel loves sin;
     he who builds a high gate invites destruction.

20 A man of perverse heart does not prosper;
     he whose tongue is deceitful falls into trouble.

21 To have a fool for a son brings grief;
     there is no joy for the father of a fool. *d*

17:21
d Pr 10:1

22 A cheerful heart is good medicine,
     but a crushed spirit dries up the bones. *e*

17:22
e Ps 22:15

23 A wicked man accepts a bribe *f* in secret
     to pervert the course of justice.

17:23
f Ex 23:8

24 A discerning man keeps wisdom in view,
     but a fool's eyes *g* wander to the ends of the earth.

17:24
g Ecc 2:14

25 A foolish son brings grief to his father
     and bitterness to the one who bore him. *h*

17:25
h Pr 10:1

26 It is not good to punish an innocent man, *i*
     or to flog officials for their integrity.

17:26
i Pr 18:5

27 A man of knowledge uses words with restraint,
     and a man of understanding is even-tempered. *j*

17:27
j Jas 1:19

28 Even a fool is thought wise if he keeps silent,
     and discerning if he holds his tongue. *k*

17:28
k Job 13:5

17:17 What kind of friend are you? There is a vast difference between knowing someone well and being a true friend. The greatest evidence of genuine friendship is loyalty (loving "at all times") (see 1 Corinthians 13:7)—being available to help in times of distress or personal struggles. Too many people are fair-weather friends. They stick around when the friendship helps them and leave when they're not getting anything out of the relationship. Think of your friends and assess your loyalty to them. Be the kind of true friend the Bible encourages.

17:22 To be cheerful is to be ready to greet others with a welcome, a word of encouragement, an enthusiasm for the task at hand, and a positive outlook on the future. Such people are as welcome as pain-relieving medicine.

17:24 While there is something to be said for having big dreams, this proverb points out the folly of chasing fantasies (having eyes that wander "to the ends of the earth," see 12:11). How much better to align your goals with God's, being the kind of person he wants you to be! Such goals (wisdom, honesty, patience, love) may not seem exciting, but they will determine your eternal future. Take time to think about your dreams and goals, and make sure they cover the really important areas of life.

17:27, 28 This proverb highlights several benefits of keeping quiet: (1) it is the best policy if you have nothing worthwhile to say; (2) it allows you the opportunity to listen and learn; (3) it gives you something in common with those who are wiser. Make

18 An unfriendly man pursues selfish ends;
he defies all sound judgment.

2 A fool finds no pleasure in understanding
but delights in airing his own opinions.

3 When wickedness comes, so does contempt,
and with shame comes disgrace.

4 The words of a man's mouth are deep waters,
but the fountain of wisdom is a bubbling brook.

18:5
l Lev 19:15

5 It is not good to be partial to the wicked *l*
or to deprive the innocent of justice.

6 A fool's lips bring him strife,
and his mouth invites a beating.

18:7
m Pr 10:14

7 A fool's mouth is his undoing,
and his lips are a snare to his soul. *m*

8 The words of a gossip are like choice morsels;
they go down to a man's inmost parts.

18:9
n Pr 28:24

9 One who is slack in his work
is brother to one who destroys. *n*

18:10
o 2Sa 22:3

10 The name of the LORD is a strong tower; *o*
the righteous run to it and are safe.

18:11
p Pr 10:15

11 The wealth of the rich is their fortified city; *p*
they imagine it an unscalable wall.

12 Before his downfall a man's heart is proud,
but humility comes before honor.

18:13
q Jn 7:51

13 He who answers before listening—
that is his folly and his shame. *q*

14 A man's spirit sustains him in sickness,
but a crushed spirit who can bear?

HUMILITY AND PRIDE	Results of . . .	Humility	Pride	
		Leads to wisdom	Leads to disgrace	11:2
		Takes advice	Produces quarrels	13:10
		Leads to honor		15:33
			Leads to punishment	16:5
			Leads to destruction	16:18
		Ends in honor	Ends in downfall	18:12
		Brings honor	Brings one low	29:23

Proverbs is direct and forceful in rejecting pride. The proud attitude heads the list of seven things God hates (6:16, 17). The harmful results of pride are constantly contrasted with humility and its benefits.

---

sure to pause to think and to listen so that when you do speak, you will have something important to say.

18:8 It is as hard to refuse to listen to gossip as it is to turn down a delicious dessert. Taking just one morsel of either one creates a taste for more. You can resist rumors the same way a determined dieter resists candy—never even open the box. If you don't nibble on the first bite of gossip, you can't take the second and the third.

18:11 In imagining that their wealth is their strongest defense, rich people are sadly mistaken. Money cannot provide safety— there are too many ways for it to lose its power. The government

may cease to back it; thieves may steal it; inflation may rob it of all value. But God never loses his power. He is always dependable. Where do you look for security and safety—uncertain wealth or God who is always faithful?

18:13, 15, 17 In these concise statements, there are three basic principles for making sound decisions: (1) get the facts before answering; (2) be open to new ideas; (3) make sure you hear both sides of the story before judging. All three principles center around seeking additional information. This is difficult work, but the only alternative is prejudice—judging before getting the facts.

15 The heart of the discerning acquires knowledge;
   the ears of the wise seek it out.

16 A gift *r* opens the way for the giver
   and ushers him into the presence of the great.

17 The first to present his case seems right,
   till another comes forward and questions him.

18 Casting the lot settles disputes *s*
   and keeps strong opponents apart.

19 An offended brother is more unyielding than a fortified city,
   and disputes are like the barred gates of a citadel.

20 From the fruit of his mouth a man's stomach is filled;
   with the harvest from his lips he is satisfied. *t*

21 The tongue has the power of life and death,
   and those who love it will eat its fruit. *u*

22 He who finds a wife finds what is good
   and receives favor from the LORD. *v*

23 A poor man pleads for mercy,
   but a rich man answers harshly.

24 A man of many companions may come to ruin,
   but there is a friend who sticks closer than a brother. *w*

19 Better a poor man whose walk is blameless
   than a fool whose lips are perverse. *x*

2 It is not good to have zeal without knowledge,
   nor to be hasty and miss the way.

3 A man's own folly ruins his life,
   yet his heart rages against the LORD.

4 Wealth brings many friends,
   but a poor man's friend deserts him. *y*

5 A false witness *z* will not go unpunished,
   and he who pours out lies will not go free.

6 Many curry favor with a ruler, *a*
   and everyone is the friend of a man who gives gifts.

7 A poor man is shunned by all his relatives—
   how much more do his friends avoid him!

18:16
r Ge 32:20

18:18
s Pr 16:33

18:20
t Pr 12:14

18:21
u Mt 12:37

18:22
v Pr 19:14

18:24
w Pr 17:17

19:1
x Pr 28:6

19:4
y Pr 14:20

19:5
z Ex 23:1

19:6
a Pr 29:26

18:22 This verse states that it is good to be married. Today's emphasis on individual freedom is misguided. Strong individuals are important, but so are strong marriages. God created marriage for our enjoyment and he pronounced it good. This is one of many passages in the Bible that show marriage as a joyful and good creation of God (Genesis 2:21–25; Proverbs 5:15–19; John 2:1–11).

18:23 This verse does not condone insulting the poor; it is simply recording an unfortunate fact of life. It is wrong for rich people to treat the less fortunate with contempt and arrogance, and God will judge such actions severely (see 14:31).

18:24 Loneliness is everywhere—many people feel cut off and alienated from others. Being in a crowd just makes people more aware of their isolation. We all need friends who will stick close, listen, care, and offer help when it is needed—in good times and bad. It is better to have one such friend than dozens of superficial acquaintances. Instead of wishing you could find a true friend, seek to become one. There are people who need your friendship.

Ask God to reveal them to you, and then take on the challenge of being a true friend.

19:1 A blameless life is far more valuable than wealth, but most people don't act as if they believe this. Afraid of not getting everything they want, they will pay any price to increase their wealth—cheating on their taxes, stealing from stores or employers, withholding tithes, refusing to give. But when we know and love God, we realize that a lower standard of living—or even poverty—is a small price to pay for personal integrity. Do your actions show that you sacrifice your integrity to increase your wealth? What changes do you need to make in order to get your priorities straight?

19:2 We often move hastily through life, rushing headlong into the unknown. Many people marry without knowing what to expect of their partner or of married life. Others try illicit sex or drugs without considering the consequences. Some plunge into jobs without evaluating whether they are suitable to that line of work. Don't rush into the unknown. Be sure you understand what you're getting into and where you want to go before you take the first step. And if it still seems unknown, be sure you are following God.

19:7
b Ps 38:11

Though he pursues them with pleading,
　　they are nowhere to be found.*a b*

19:8
c Pr 16:20

8 He who gets wisdom loves his own soul;
　　he who cherishes understanding prospers.*c*

19:9
d ver 5

9 A false witness will not go unpunished,
　　and he who pours out lies will perish.*d*

10 It is not fitting for a fool to live in luxury—
　　how much worse for a slave to rule over princes!

19:11
e Pr 16:32

11 A man's wisdom gives him patience;*e*
　　it is to his glory to overlook an offense.

19:12
f Pr 16:14-15

12 A king's rage is like the roar of a lion,
　　but his favor is like dew on the grass.*f*

19:13
g Pr 21:9

13 A foolish son is his father's ruin,
　　and a quarrelsome wife is like a constant dripping.*g*

19:14
h 2Co 12:14

14 Houses and wealth are inherited from parents,*h*
　　but a prudent wife is from the LORD.

19:15
i Pr 6:9

15 Laziness brings on deep sleep,
　　and the shiftless man goes hungry.*i*

19:16
j Lk 10:28

16 He who obeys instructions guards his life,
　　but he who is contemptuous of his ways will die.*j*

19:17
k Mt 10:42

17 He who is kind to the poor lends to the LORD,
　　and he will reward him for what he has done.*k*

19:18
l Pr 13:24

18 Discipline your son, for in that there is hope;
　　do not be a willing party to his death.*l*

a 7 The meaning of the Hebrew for this sentence is uncertain.

HOW TO SUCCEED IN GOD'S EYES
Proverbs notes two significant by-products of wise living: success and good reputation. Several verses also point out what causes failure and poor reputation.

Qualities that promote success and a good reputation

Righteousness	10:7; 12:3; 28:12
Hating what is false	13:5
Committing all work to the Lord	16:3
Using words with restraint; being even-tempered	17:27, 28
Loving wisdom and understanding	19:8
Humility and fear of the Lord	22:4
Willingness to confess and renounce sin	28:13

Qualities that prevent success and cause a bad reputation

Wickedness	10:7; 12:3; 28:12
Seeking honor	25:27
Hatred	26:24–26
Praising oneself	27:2
Concealing sin	28:13

Other verses dealing with one's reputation are 11:10, 16; 14:3; 19:10; 22:1; 23:17, 18; 24:13, 14.

19:8 Is it good to love yourself? Yes, when your soul is at stake! This proverb does not condone the self-centered person who loves and protects his or her selfish interests and will do anything to serve them. Instead it encourages those who really care about themselves to seek wisdom.

19:16 The instructions we are told to obey are those found in God's Word—both the Ten Commandments (Exodus 20) and

other passages of instruction. To obey what God teaches in the Bible is self-preserving. To disobey is self-destructive.

19:17 Here God identifies with the poor as Jesus does in Matthew 25:31–46. As our Creator, God values all of us, whether we are poor or rich. When we help the poor, we honor both the Creator and his creation. God accepts our help as if we had offered it directly to him.

19 A hot-tempered man must pay the penalty;
    if you rescue him, you will have to do it again.

20 Listen to advice and accept instruction,
    and in the end you will be wise.

21 Many are the plans in a man's heart,
    but it is the LORD's purpose that prevails.*m*

22 What a man desires is unfailing love*a*;
    better to be poor than a liar.

23 The fear of the LORD leads to life:
    Then one rests content, untouched by trouble.*n*

24 The sluggard buries his hand in the dish;
    he will not even bring it back to his mouth!*o*

25 Flog a mocker, and the simple will learn prudence;
    rebuke a discerning man, and he will gain knowledge.*p*

26 He who robs his father and drives out his mother*q*
    is a son who brings shame and disgrace.

27 Stop listening to instruction, my son,
    and you will stray from the words of knowledge.

28 A corrupt witness mocks at justice,
    and the mouth of the wicked gulps down evil.*r*

29 Penalties are prepared for mockers,
    and beatings for the backs of fools.*s*

20 Wine is a mocker and beer a brawler;
    whoever is led astray by them is not wise.

2 A king's wrath is like the roar of a lion;*t*
    he who angers him forfeits his life.*u*

3 It is to a man's honor to avoid strife,
    but every fool is quick to quarrel.*v*

4 A sluggard does not plow in season;
    so at harvest time he looks but finds nothing.

5 The purposes of a man's heart are deep waters,
    but a man of understanding draws them out.

6 Many a man claims to have unfailing love,
    but a faithful man who can find?*w*

7 The righteous man leads a blameless life;
    blessed are his children after him.*x*

a 22 Or A man's greed is his shame

19:21
m Ps 33:11

19:23
n Pr 12:21

19:24
o Pr 26:15

19:25
p Pr 9:9

19:26
q Pr 28:24

19:28
r Job 15:16

19:29
s Pr 26:3

20:2
t Pr 19:12
u Pr 8:36

20:3
v Pr 17:14

20:6
w Ps 12:1

20:7
x Ps 37:25-26

19:23 Those who fear the Lord are "untouched by trouble" because of their healthy habits, their beneficial lifestyle, and sometimes through God's direct intervention. Nevertheless, the fear of the Lord does not always protect us from trouble in this life: evil things still happen to people who love God. This verse is not a universal promise, but a general guideline. It describes what would happen if this world were sinless, and what will happen in the new earth, when faithful believers will be under God's protection forever. (See the note on 3:16, 17 for more about this concept.)

19:24 "Buries his hand in the dish" refers to the custom of eating where a dish would be passed and people would reach in and get food for themselves. This proverb is saying that some people are so lazy that they won't even feed themselves.

19:25 There is a great difference between the person who learns from criticism and the person who refuses to accept correction.

How we respond to criticism determines whether or not we grow in wisdom. The next time someone criticizes you, listen carefully to all that is said. You might learn something.

20:3 A person who is truly confident of his or her strength does not need to parade it. A truly brave person does not look for chances to prove it. A resourceful woman can find a way out of a fight. A man of endurance will avoid retaliating. Foolish people find it impossible to avoid strife. Men and women of character can. What kind of person are you?

20:4 You've heard similar warnings: if you don't study, you'll fail the test; if you don't save, you won't have money when you need it. God wants us to anticipate future needs and prepare for them. We can't expect him to come to our rescue when we cause our own problems through lack of planning and action. He provides for us, but he also expects us to be responsible.

20:8
y ver 26

8 When a king sits on his throne to judge,
    he winnows out all evil with his eyes.y

20:9
z 1Ki 8:46

9 Who can say, "I have kept my heart pure;
    I am clean and without sin"?z

20:10
a ver 23

10 Differing weights and differing measures—
    the LORD detests them both.a

20:11
b Mt 7:16

11 Even a child is known by his actions,
    by whether his conduct is pureb and right.

12 Ears that hear and eyes that see—
    the LORD has made them both.

20:13
c Pr 6:11

13 Do not love sleep or you will grow poor;c
    stay awake and you will have food to spare.

14 "It's no good, it's no good!" says the buyer;
    then off he goes and boasts about his purchase.

15 Gold there is, and rubies in abundance,
    but lips that speak knowledge are a rare jewel.

16 Take the garment of one who puts up security for a stranger;
    hold it in pledge if he does it for a wayward woman.

20:17
d Pr 9:17

17 Food gained by fraud tastes sweet to a man,d
    but he ends up with a mouth full of gravel.

HONESTY AND DISHONESTY
Proverbs tells us plainly that God despises all forms of dishonesty. Not only does God hate dishonesty, but we are told that it works against us—others no longer trust us, and we cannot even enjoy our dishonest gains. It is wiser to be honest because "a righteous man escapes trouble" (12:13).

20:9 No one is without sin. As soon as we confess our sin and repent, sinful thoughts and actions begin to creep back into our lives. We all need ongoing cleansing, moment by moment. Thank God he provides forgiveness by his mercy when we ask for it. Make confession and repentance a regular part of your talks with God. Rely on him moment by moment for the cleansing you need.

18 Make plans by seeking advice;
　　if you wage war, obtain guidance. *e*

20:18
e Pr 24:6

19 A gossip betrays a confidence; *f*
　　so avoid a man who talks too much.

20:19
f Pr 11:13

20 If a man curses his father or mother,
　　his lamp will be snuffed out in pitch darkness. *g*

20:20
g Job 18:5

21 An inheritance quickly gained at the beginning
　　will not be blessed at the end.

22 Do not say, "I'll pay you back for this wrong!"
　　Wait for the LORD, and he will deliver you. *h*

20:22
h Ro 12:19

23 The LORD detests differing weights,
　　and dishonest scales do not please him. *i*

20:23
i ver 10

24 A man's steps are directed by the LORD.
　　How then can anyone understand his own way?

25 It is a trap for a man to dedicate something rashly
　　and only later to consider his vows. *j*

20:25
j Ecc 5:2,4-5

26 A wise king winnows out the wicked;
　　he drives the threshing wheel over them. *k*

20:26
k ver 8

27 The lamp of the LORD searches the spirit of a man *a*;
　　it searches out his inmost being.

28 Love and faithfulness keep a king safe;
　　through love his throne is made secure.

29 The glory of young men is their strength,
　　gray hair the splendor of the old. *l*

20:29
l Pr 16:31

30 Blows and wounds cleanse away evil,
　　and beatings purge the inmost being.

21

The king's heart is in the hand of the LORD;
　　he directs it like a watercourse wherever he pleases.

a 27 Or The spirit of man is the LORD's lamp

20:23 "Differing weights" refers to the loaded scales a merchant might use in order to cheat the customers. Dishonesty is a difficult sin to avoid. It is easy to cheat if we think no one else is looking. But dishonesty affects the very core of a person. It makes him untrustworthy and untrusting. It eventually makes him unable to know himself or relate to others. Don't take dishonesty lightly. Even the smallest portion of dishonesty contains enough of the poison of deceit to kill your spiritual life. If there is any dishonesty in your life, tell God about it now.

20:24 We are often confused by the events around us. Many things we will never understand; others will fall into place in years to come as we look back and see how God was working. This proverb counsels us not to worry if we don't understand everything as it happens. Instead, we should trust that God knows what he's doing, even if his timing or design is not clear

to us. See Psalm 37:23 for a reassuring promise of God's direction in your life.

20:25 To dedicate something meant that you intended to give it as an offering to God. *Dedicated* means set apart for religious use. This proverb points out the evil of making a vow rashly and then reconsidering it. God takes vows seriously and requires that they be carried out (Deuteronomy 23:21–23). We often make good intentions when making a vow because we want to show God that we are determined to please him. Jesus, however, says it is better not to make promises to God because he knows how difficult they are to keep (Matthew 5:33–37). If you still feel it is important to make a vow, make sure that you weigh the consequences of breaking that vow. (In Judges 11, Jephthah made a rash promise to sacrifice the first thing he saw on his return home. As it happened, he saw his daughter first.) It is better not to make promises than to make them and then later want to change them. It is better still to count the cost beforehand and then to fulfill them. (For a list of other Bible people who made rash vows, see the chart in Judges 11, p. 363.)

21:1 In Solomon's day, kings possessed absolute authority and were often considered to be like gods. This proverb shows that God, not earthly rulers, has ultimate authority over world politics. Although they may not have realized it, the earth's most powerful kings have always been under God's control. (See Isaiah 10:5–8 for an example of a pagan king who was used for God's purposes.)

21:2
m Pr 16:2; 24:12;
Lk 16:15

21:3
n 1Sa 15:22;
Isa 1:11; Mic 6:6-8

21:5
o Pr 10:4

21:11
p Pr 19:25

21:12
q Pr 14:11

21:18
r Pr 11:8

2 All a man's ways seem right to him,
    but the LORD weighs the heart. *m*

3 To do what is right and just
    is more acceptable to the LORD than sacrifice. *n*

4 Haughty eyes and a proud heart,
    the lamp of the wicked, are sin!

5 The plans of the diligent lead to profit *o*
    as surely as haste leads to poverty.

6 A fortune made by a lying tongue
    is a fleeting vapor and a deadly snare. *a*

7 The violence of the wicked will drag them away,
    for they refuse to do what is right.

8 The way of the guilty is devious,
    but the conduct of the innocent is upright.

9 Better to live on a corner of the roof
    than share a house with a quarrelsome wife.

10 The wicked man craves evil;
    his neighbor gets no mercy from him.

11 When a mocker is punished, the simple gain wisdom;
    when a wise man is instructed, he gets knowledge. *p*

12 The Righteous One *b* takes note of the house of the wicked
    and brings the wicked to ruin. *q*

13 If a man shuts his ears to the cry of the poor,
    he too will cry out and not be answered.

14 A gift given in secret soothes anger,
    and a bribe concealed in the cloak pacifies great wrath.

15 When justice is done, it brings joy to the righteous
    but terror to evildoers.

16 A man who strays from the path of understanding
    comes to rest in the company of the dead.

17 He who loves pleasure will become poor;
    whoever loves wine and oil will never be rich.

18 The wicked become a ransom *r* for the righteous,
    and the unfaithful for the upright.

a 6 Some Hebrew manuscripts, Septuagint and Vulgate; most Hebrew manuscripts *vapor for those who seek death*
b 12 Or *The righteous man*

21:2 People can find an excuse for doing almost anything, but God looks behind the excuses to the motives of the heart. We often have to make choices in areas where the right action is difficult to discern. We can help ourselves make such decisions by trying to identify our motives first and then asking, "Would God be pleased with my real reasons for doing this?" God is not pleased when we do good deeds only to receive something in return.

21:3 Sacrifices and offerings are not bribes to make God overlook our character faults. We can't exchange good behavior in one area for bad behavior in another. If our personal and business dealings are not characterized by justice, no amount of generosity when the offering plate is passed will make up for it.

21:5 Faithful completion of mundane tasks is a great accomplishment. Such work is patiently carried out according to

a plan. Diligence does not come naturally to most people; it is a result of strong character. Don't look for quick and easy answers. Be a diligent servant of God.

21:11, 12 It is usually better to learn from the mistakes of others than from our own. We can do this by observing other people's lives and listening to their advice. Take counsel from others instead of plunging ahead and learning the hard way.

21:13 We should work to meet the needs of the poor and protect their rights—we may be in need of such services ourselves someday.

19 Better to live in a desert
    than with a quarrelsome and ill-tempered wife.

20 In the house of the wise are stores of choice food and oil,
    but a foolish man devours all he has.

21 He who pursues righteousness and love
    finds life, prosperity[a] and honor.[s]

22 A wise man attacks the city of the mighty[t]
    and pulls down the stronghold in which they trust.

23 He who guards his mouth[u] and his tongue
    keeps himself from calamity.[v]

24 The proud and arrogant man—"Mocker" is his name;
    he behaves with overweening pride.

25 The sluggard's craving will be the death of him,[w]
    because his hands refuse to work.

26 All day long he craves for more,
    but the righteous give without sparing.

27 The sacrifice of the wicked is detestable[x]—
    how much more so when brought with evil intent!

21:21
sMt 5:6

21:22
tEcc 9:15-16

21:23
uJas 3:2
vPr 12:13

21:25
wPr 13:4

21:27
xJer 6:20

a21 Or *righteousness*

RIGHTEOUSNESS

Proverbs often compares the life-styles of the wicked and the righteous, and makes a strong case for living by God's pattern. The advantages of righteous living and the disadvantages of wicked living are pointed out. The kind of person we decide to be will affect every area of our lives.

	Righteous	Wicked	Reference
Outlook on life	Hopeful	Fearful	10:24
	Concerned about the welfare of God's creation	Even their kindness is cruel	12:10
	Understand justice	Don't understand justice	28:5
Response to life	Covered with blessings	Covered with violence	10:6
		Bent on evil	16:30
	Give thought to their ways	Put up a bold front	21:29
	Persevere against evil	Brought down by calamity	24:15, 16
		Hate those with integrity	29:10
How they are seen by others	Are appreciated	Do not endure	13:15
		Lead others into sin	16:29
	Conduct is upright	Conduct is devious	21:8
	Are not to desire the company of godless people	Plot violence	24:1, 2
	Others are glad when they triumph	Others hide when they rise to power	28:12
	Care for the poor	Unconcerned about the poor	29:7
	Detest the dishonest	Detest the upright	29:27
Quality of life	Stand firm	Swept away	10:25
	Delivered by righteousness	Trapped by evil desires	11:6

21:20 This proverb is about saving for the future. Easy credit has many people living on the edge of bankruptcy. The desire to keep up and to accumulate more pushes them to spend every penny they earn, and they stretch their credit to the limit. But anyone who spends all he has is spending more than he can afford. A wise person puts money aside for when he or she may have less. God approves of foresight and restraint. God's people need to examine their lifestyles to see whether their spending is God-pleasing or merely self-pleasing.

21:27 The kind of worship ("sacrifice") described in this proverb is no better than a bribe. How do people try to bribe God? They may go to church, tithe, or volunteer, not because of their love and devotion to God, but because they hope God will bless them in return. But God has made it very clear that he desires obedience and love more than religious ritual (see 21:3; 1 Samuel 15:22). God does not want our sacrifices of time, energy, and money alone; he wants our hearts—our complete love and devotion. We may be able to bribe people (21:14), but we cannot bribe God.

²⁸ A false witness will perish,
and whoever listens to him will be destroyed forever.^a

²⁹ A wicked man puts up a bold front,
but an upright man gives thought to his ways.

21:30
^y Jer 9:23
^z Isa 8:10; Ac 5:39

³⁰ There is no wisdom,^y no insight, no plan
that can succeed against the LORD.^z

21:31
^a Ps 3:8

³¹ The horse is made ready for the day of battle,
but victory rests with the LORD.^a

22:1
^b Ecc 7:1

22

A good name is more desirable than great riches;
to be esteemed is better than silver or gold.^b

² Rich and poor have this in common:
The LORD is the Maker of them all.

22:3
^c Pr 27:12

³ A prudent man sees danger and takes refuge,
but the simple keep going and suffer for it.^c

⁴ Humility and the fear of the LORD
bring wealth and honor and life.

^a*28 Or / but the words of an obedient man will live on*

AND WICKEDNESS

Quality of life (cont.)	Righteous	Wicked	Reference
	No real harm befalls them	Constant trouble befalls them	
	Income results in treasure	Income results in trouble	12:21
	Avoid evil		15:6
		Fall into constant trouble	16:17
	Are bold as lions	Are fearful constantly	17:20
	Will be safe	Will suddenly fall	28:1
Short-term results	Walk securely	Will be found out	28:18
	Rewarded with prosperity	Pursued by misfortune	10:9
Long-term results	God protects them	God destroys them	13:21
	Evil people will bow to them	Will bow to the righteous	10:29
		Will be punished for rebellion	14:19
Eternal expectations	Never uprooted	Will not remain	17:11
	Earn a sure reward	Earn deceptive wages	10:30
	Attain life	Go to death	11:18
	End only in good	End only in wrath	11:19
	Will stand firm	Will be overthrown	11:23
	Have a refuge when they die	Will be brought down by calamity	12:7
			14:32
God's opinion of them	Delights in the good	Detests the perverse	
			11:20

21:31 This proverb refers to preparing for battle. All our preparation for any task is useless without God. But even with God's help we still must do our part and prepare. His control of the outcome does not negate our responsibilities. God may want you to produce a great book, but you must learn to write. God may want to use you in foreign missions, but you must learn the language. God will accomplish his purposes, and he will be able to use you if you have done your part by being well prepared.

22:4 This is a general observation that would have been especially applicable to an obedient Israelite living in Solomon's God-fearing kingdom. Nevertheless, some have been martyrs at a young age, and some have given away all their wealth for the sake of God's kingdom. The book of Proverbs describes life the way it should be. It does not dwell on the exceptions. (For more on this concept, see the note on 3:16, 17.)

5 In the paths of the wicked lie thorns and snares,^d
    but he who guards his soul stays far from them.

6 Train^a a child in the way he should go,^e
    and when he is old he will not turn from it.

7 The rich rule over the poor,
    and the borrower is servant to the lender.

8 He who sows wickedness reaps trouble,
    and the rod of his fury will be destroyed.

9 A generous man will himself be blessed,^f
    for he shares his food with the poor.

10 Drive out the mocker, and out goes strife;
    quarrels and insults are ended.

11 He who loves a pure heart and whose speech is gracious
    will have the king for his friend.^g

12 The eyes of the LORD keep watch over knowledge,
    but he frustrates the words of the unfaithful.

13 The sluggard says, "There is a lion outside!"^h
    or, "I will be murdered in the streets!"

14 The mouth of an adulteress is a deep pit;ⁱ
    he who is under the LORD's wrath will fall into it.^j

15 Folly is bound up in the heart of a child,
    but the rod of discipline will drive it far from him.^k

16 He who oppresses the poor to increase his wealth
    and he who gives gifts to the rich—both come to poverty.

Sayings of the Wise

17 Pay attention and listen to the sayings of the wise;
    apply your heart to what I teach,
18 for it is pleasing when you keep them in your heart
    and have all of them ready on your lips.
19 So that your trust may be in the LORD,
    I teach you today, even you.
20 Have I not written thirty^b sayings for you,
    sayings of counsel and knowledge,

a6 Or Start   b20 Or not formerly written; or not written excellent

**Cross references (right margin):**

22:5
^dPr 15:19

22:6
^eEph 6:4

22:9
^f2Co 9:6

22:11
^gMt 5:8

22:13
^hPr 26:13

22:14
ⁱPr 2:16; 5:3-5
^jEcc 7:26

22:15
^kPr 13:24

22:6 "In the way he should go" is literally, "according to his the child's way." It is natural to want to bring up all our children alike or train them the same way. This verse implies that parents should discern the individuality and special strengths that God has given each one. While we should not condone or excuse self-will, each child has natural inclinations that parents can develop. By talking to teachers, other parents, and grandparents, we can better discern and develop the individual capabilities of each child.

22:6 Many parents want to make all the choices for their child, but this hurts him or her in the long run. When parents teach a child how to make decisions, they don't have to watch every step he or she takes. They know their children will remain on the right path because they have made the choice themselves. Train your children to choose the right way.

22:7 Does this mean we should never borrow? No, but it warns us never to take on a loan without carefully examining our ability to repay it. A loan we can handle is enabling; a loan we can't handle is enslaving. The borrower must realize that until the loan is repaid, he or she is a servant to the individual or institution that made it.

22:12 "Knowledge" refers to those who have knowledge, those who live right and speak the truth. It takes discipline, determination, and hard work to live God's way, but God protects and rewards those who make the commitment to follow him.

22:13 This proverb refers to an excuse a lazy person might use to avoid going to work. The excuse sounds silly to us, but that's often how our excuses sound to others. Don't rationalize laziness. Take your responsibilities seriously and get to work.

22:15 Young children often do foolish and dangerous things simply because they don't understand the consequences. Wisdom and common sense are not transferred by just being a good example. The wisdom a child learns must be taught consciously. "The rod of discipline" stands for all forms of discipline or training. Just as God trains and corrects us to make us better, so parents must discipline their children to make them learn the difference between right and wrong. To see how God corrects us, read 3:11, 12.

22:21
*l*Lk 1:3-4

21 teaching you true and reliable words,*l*
   so that you can give sound answers
   to him who sent you?

22:22
*m*Zec 7:10
*n*Mal 3:5

22 Do not exploit the poor *m* because they are poor
   and do not crush the needy in court,*n*

22:23
*o*Ps 12:5

23 for the Lord will take up their case*o*
   and will plunder those who plunder them.

24 Do not make friends with a hot-tempered man,
   do not associate with one easily angered,

22:25
*p*1Co 15:33

25 or you may learn his ways
   and get yourself ensnared.*p*

26 Do not be a man who strikes hands in pledge
   or puts up security for debts;
27 if you lack the means to pay,
   your very bed will be snatched from under you.

22:28
*q*Dt 19:14

28 Do not move an ancient boundary stone*q*
   set up by your forefathers.

29 Do you see a man skilled in his work?
   He will serve before kings;
   he will not serve before obscure men.

23 When you sit to dine with a ruler,
   note well what*a* is before you,
2 and put a knife to your throat
   if you are given to gluttony.
3 Do not crave his delicacies,
   for that food is deceptive.

4 Do not wear yourself out to get rich;
   have the wisdom to show restraint.

23:5
*r*Pr 27:24

5 Cast but a glance at riches, and they are gone,
   for they will surely sprout wings
   and fly off to the sky like an eagle.*r*

6 Do not eat the food of a stingy man,
   do not crave his delicacies;
7 for he is the kind of man
   who is always thinking about the cost.*b*

a 1 Or who b 7 Or for as he thinks within himself, / so he is; or for as he puts on a feast, / so he is

---

22:22, 23 This proverb is a message of hope to people who must live and work under unjust authoritarian leaders. It is also a warning to those who enjoy ruling with an iron hand. Sometimes God intervenes and directly destroys tyrants. More often, he uses other rulers to overthrow them or their own oppressed people to rebel against them. If you are in a position of authority at church, work, or home, remember what happens to tyrants. Leadership through kindness is more effective and longer lasting than leadership by force.

22:24, 25 People tend to become like those with whom they spend a lot of time. Even the negative characteristics and habits sometimes rub off. The Bible exhorts us to be cautious in our choice of companions. Choose people with qualities you would like to develop in your own life.

22:26 This verse is saying that it is wise to be slow to countersign a note or to be liable for another person's debt.

22:28 In Joshua 13—21, the land was divided and the boundaries marked out for each tribe. Moses had already warned the people that when they reached the promised land they shouldn't cheat their neighbors by moving one of the landmarks to give themselves more land and their neighbors less (Deuteronomy 19:14; 27:17). "Gerrymandering"—changing political boundaries so that one group of voters benefits and another loses—is a modern form of moving boundary markers.

23:1–3 The point of this proverb is to be careful when eating with an important or influential person because he or she may try to influence or bribe you. Unwary meetings over meals can lead to undermined convictions. No good will come from such meals.

23:4, 5 We have all heard of people who have won millions of dollars and then lost it all. Even the average person can spend an inheritance—or a paycheck—with lightning speed and have little to show for it. Don't spend your time chasing fleeting earthly treasures. Instead store up treasures in heaven, for such treasures will never be lost. (See Luke 12:33, 34 for Jesus' teaching.)

23:6–8 In graphic language, the writer warns us not to envy the lifestyles of those who have become rich by being stingy and miserly, and not to gain their favor by fawning over them. Their "friendship" is phony—they will just use you for their own gain.

"Eat and drink," he says to you,
　　but his heart is not with you.
8 You will vomit up the little you have eaten
　　and will have wasted your compliments.

9 Do not speak to a fool,
　　for he will scorn the wisdom of your words. ᶻ

10 Do not move an ancient boundary stone
　　or encroach on the fields of the fatherless,
11 for their Defender is strong;
　　he will take up their case against you. ᵗ

12 Apply your heart to instruction
　　and your ears to words of knowledge.

13 Do not withhold discipline from a child;
　　if you punish him with the rod, he will not die.
14 Punish him with the rod
　　and save his soul from death. ᵃ

15 My son, if your heart is wise,
　　then my heart will be glad;
16 my inmost being will rejoice
　　when your lips speak what is right.

17 Do not let your heart envy ᵘ sinners,
　　but always be zealous for the fear of the Lᴏʀᴅ.
18 There is surely a future hope for you,
　　and your hope will not be cut off.

19 Listen, my son, and be wise,
　　and keep your heart on the right path.
20 Do not join those who drink too much wine ᵛ
　　or gorge themselves on meat,
21 for drunkards and gluttons become poor, ʷ
　　and drowsiness clothes them in rags.

22 Listen to your father, who gave you life,
　　and do not despise your mother when she is old. ˣ
23 Buy the truth and do not sell it;
　　get wisdom, discipline and understanding. ʸ
24 The father of a righteous man has great joy;
　　he who has a wise son delights in him. ᶻ
25 May your father and mother be glad;
　　may she who gave you birth rejoice!

26 My son, give me your heart
　　and let your eyes keep to my ways,
27 for a prostitute is a deep pit ᵃ
　　and a wayward wife is a narrow well.

ᵃ *14* Hebrew *Sheol*

23:9 ᶻPr 9:7; Mt 7:6

23:11 ᵗPr 22:22-23

23:17 ᵘPs 37:1

23:20 ᵛIsa 5:11,22

23:21 ʷPr 21:17

23:22 ˣPr 1:8; Eph 6:1-2

23:23 ʸPr 4:7

23:24 ᶻver 15-16; Pr 10:1

23:10, 11 The term *Defender* or *redeemer* refers to someone who bought back a family member who had fallen into slavery or who accepted the obligation to marry the widow of a family member (Ruth 4:3–10). God is also called a Redeemer (Exodus 6:6; Job 19:25). (For an explanation of ancient boundary stones, see the note on 22:28.)

23:12 The people most likely to gain knowledge are those who are willing to listen. It is a sign of strength, not weakness, to pay attention to what others have to say. People who are eager to listen continue to learn and grow throughout their lives. If we refuse to become set in our ways, we can always expand the limits of our knowledge.

23:13, 14 The stern tone of discipline here is offset by the affection expressed in verse 15. However, many parents are reluctant to discipline their children at all. Some fear they will forfeit their relationship, that their children will resent them, or that they will stifle their children's development. But correction won't kill children, and it may prevent them from foolish moves that will.

23:17, 18 How easy it is to envy those who get ahead unhampered by Christian responsibility or God's laws. For a time they do seem to get ahead without paying any attention to what God wants. But to those who follow him, God promises a hope and a wonderful future even if we don't achieve it in this life.

23:28
bPr 7:11-12;
Ecc 7:26

28 Like a bandit she lies in wait,b
    and multiplies the unfaithful among men.

29 Who has woe? Who has sorrow?
    Who has strife? Who has complaints?
    Who has needless bruises? Who has bloodshot eyes?

23:30
cPs 75:8; Isa 5:11;
Eph 5:18

30 Those who linger over wine,c
    who go to sample bowls of mixed wine.
31 Do not gaze at wine when it is red,
    when it sparkles in the cup,
    when it goes down smoothly!
32 In the end it bites like a snake
    and poisons like a viper.
33 Your eyes will see strange sights
    and your mind imagine confusing things.
34 You will be like one sleeping on the high seas,
    lying on top of the rigging.
35 "They hit me," you will say, "but I'm not hurt!
    They beat me, but I don't feel it!
    When will I wake up
    so I can find another drink?"

24:1
dPs 37:1; 73:3;
Pr 3:31-32;
23:17-18

24

Do not envyd wicked men,
    do not desire their company;
2 for their hearts plot violence,
    and their lips talk about making trouble.

3 By wisdom a house is built,
    and through understanding it is established;
4 through knowledge its rooms are filled
    with rare and beautiful treasures.

5 A wise man has great power,
    and a man of knowledge increases strength;
6 for waging war you need guidance,
    and for victory many advisers.

7 Wisdom is too high for a fool;
    in the assembly at the gate he has nothing to say.

8 He who plots evil
    will be known as a schemer.
9 The schemes of folly are sin,
    and men detest a mocker.

23:29, 30 The soothing comfort of alcohol is only temporary. Real relief comes from dealing with the cause of the anguish and sorrow and turning to God for peace. Don't lose yourself in alcohol; find yourself in God.

23:29-35 Israel was a wine-producing country. In the Old Testament, winepresses bursting with new wine were considered a sign of blessing (3:10). Wisdom is even said to have set her table with wine (9:2, 5). But the Old Testament writers were alert to the dangers of wine. It dulls the senses; it limits clear judgment (31:1-9); it lowers the capacity for control (4:17); it destroys a person's efficiency (21:17). To make wine an end in itself, a means of self-indulgence, or as an escape from life is to misuse it and invite the consequences of the drunkard.

24:5 The athlete who thinks—who assesses the situation and plans strategies—has an advantage over a physically stronger but unthinking opponent. And wisdom, not muscle, is certainly why God has put people in charge of the animal kingdom. We exercise regularly and eat well to build our strength, but do we take equal pains to develop wisdom? Because wisdom is a vital part of strength, it pays to attain it.

24:6 In any major decision we make concerning college, marriage, career, children, etc., it is not a sign of weakness to ask for advice. Instead, it is foolish not to ask for it. Find good advisers before making any big decision. They can help you expand your alternatives and evaluate your choices.

24:8 Plotting to do evil can be as wrong as doing it because what you think determines what you will do. Left unchecked, wrong desires will lead us to sin. God wants pure lives, free from sin, and planning evil spoils the purity even if the evil action has not yet been committed. Should you say, "Then I might as well go ahead and do it because I've already planned it"? No. You have sinned in your attitude, but you have not yet damaged other people. Stop in your tracks and ask God to forgive you and put you on a different path.

10 If you falter in times of trouble,
    how small is your strength!

11 Rescue those being led away to death;
    hold back those staggering toward slaughter.*e*
12 If you say, "But we knew nothing about this,"
    does not he who weighs*f* the heart perceive it?
Does not he who guards your life know it?
Will he not repay each person according to what he has done?*g*

13 Eat honey, my son, for it is good;
    honey from the comb is sweet to your taste.
14 Know also that wisdom is sweet to your soul;
    if you find it, there is a future hope for you,
    and your hope will not be cut off.

15 Do not lie in wait like an outlaw against a righteous man's house,
    do not raid his dwelling place;
16 for though a righteous man falls seven times, he rises again,
    but the wicked are brought down by calamity.*h*

17 Do not gloat*i* when your enemy falls;
    when he stumbles, do not let your heart rejoice,*j*
18 or the LORD will see and disapprove
    and turn his wrath away from him.

19 Do not fret*k* because of evil men
    or be envious of the wicked,
20 for the evil man has no future hope,
    and the lamp of the wicked will be snuffed out.

21 Fear the LORD and the king,*l* my son,
    and do not join with the rebellious,
22 for those two will send sudden destruction upon them,
    and who knows what calamities they can bring?

Further Sayings of the Wise

23 These also are sayings of the wise:

    To show partiality*m* in judging is not good:
24 Whoever says to the guilty, "You are innocent"—
    peoples will curse him and nations denounce him.
25 But it will go well with those who convict the guilty,
    and rich blessing will come upon them.

26 An honest answer
    is like a kiss on the lips.

27 Finish your outdoor work
    and get your fields ready;
    after that, build your house.

24:11
e Ps 82:4;
Isa 58:6-7
24:12
f Pr 21:2
g Ro 2:6*

24:16
h Mic 7:8

24:17
i Ob 1:12
j Job 31:29

24:19
k Ps 37:1

24:21
l Ro 13:1-5;
1Pe 2:17

24:23
m Lev 19:15

24:10 Times of trouble can be useful. They can show you who you really are, what kind of character you have developed. In addition, they can help you grow stronger. When Jeremiah questioned God because of the trouble he faced, God asked how he ever expected to face big challenges if the little ones tired him out (Jeremiah 12:5). Don't complain about your problems. The trouble you face today is training you to be strong for the more difficult situations you will face in the future.

24:17, 18 David, Solomon's father, refused to gloat over the death of his lifelong enemy Saul (see 2 Samuel 1). On the other hand, the nation of Edom rejoiced over Israel's defeat and was punished by God for their attitude (Obadiah 12). To gloat over others' misfortune is to make yourself the avenger and to put

yourself in the place of God, who alone is the real judge of all the earth (see Deuteronomy 32:35).

24:26 A kiss on the lips was a sign of true friendship. People often think that they should bend the truth to avoid hurting a friend. But one who gives an honest answer is a true friend. To be entrusted with the truth even at the risk of offense, says this proverb, represents a gesture of high honor.

24:27 We should carry out our work in its proper order. If a farmer builds his house in the spring, he will miss the planting season and go a year without food. If a businessman invests his money in a house while his business is struggling to grow, he may lose both. It is possible to work hard and still lose everything if the timing is wrong or the resources to carry it out are not in place.

24:28
ⁿEph 4:25

28 Do not testify against your neighbor without cause,ⁿ
 or use your lips to deceive.

24:29
ᵒPr 20:22;
Mt 5:38-41

29 Do not say, "I'll do to him as he has done to me;
 I'll pay that man back for what he did."ᵒ

24:30
ᵖPr 6:6-11

30 I went past the field of the sluggard,ᵖ
 past the vineyard of the man who lacks judgment;
31 thorns had come up everywhere,
  the ground was covered with weeds,
  and the stone wall was in ruins.
32 I applied my heart to what I observed
 and learned a lesson from what I saw:

24:33
�q Pr 6:10

33 A little sleep, a little slumber,
 a little folding of the hands to restq—
34 and poverty will come on you like a bandit
 and scarcity like an armed man.ᵃ

C. WISDOM FOR THE LEADERS (25:1—31:31)

These proverbs were collected by Hezekiah's advisers. The first section was written by Solomon, and the next two sections were written by others. While we all can learn from these proverbs, many were originally directed toward the king or those who dealt with the king. These are particularly helpful for those who are leaders or aspire to become leaders. The book ends with a description of a truly good wife, who is an example of godly wisdom.

More Proverbs of Solomon

25:1
ʳ1Ki 4:32
ˢPr 1:1

25 These are more proverbs ʳ of Solomon, copied by the men of Hezekiah king of Judah:ˢ

2 It is the glory of God to conceal a matter;
 to search out a matter is the glory of kings.

3 As the heavens are high and the earth is deep,
 so the hearts of kings are unsearchable.

4 Remove the dross from the silver,
 and out comes material forᵇ the silversmith;

25:5
ᵗPr 20:8
ᵘPr 16:12

5 remove the wicked from the king's presence,ᵗ
 and his throne will be established through righteousness.ᵘ

6 Do not exalt yourself in the king's presence,
 and do not claim a place among great men;

25:7
ᵛLk 14:7-10

7 it is better for him to say to you, "Come up here,"ᵛ
 than for him to humiliate you before a nobleman.

25:8
ʷMt 5:25-26

What you have seen with your eyes
8 do not bringᶜ hastily to court,
for what will you do in the end
 if your neighbor puts you to shame?ʷ

ᵃ34 Or like a vagrant / and scarcity like a beggar ᵇ4 Or comes a vessel from ᶜ7,8 Or nobleman / on whom you had set your eyes. / ᵈDo not go

---

24:29 Here is a reverse version of the Golden Rule (see Luke 6:31). Revenge is the way the world operates, but it is not God's way.

25:1 Hezekiah's story is told in 2 Kings 18—20; 2 Chronicles 29—32; and Isaiah 36—39. He was one of the few kings of Judah who honored the Lord. By contrast, his father, Ahaz, actually nailed the temple door shut. Hezekiah restored the temple, destroyed idol worship centers, and earned the respect of surrounding nations, many of whom brought gifts to God because of him. It is not surprising that Hezekiah had these proverbs copied and read, for "in everything that he undertook in the service of God's temple and in obedience to the law and the commands, he sought his God and worked wholeheartedly. And so he prospered" (2 Chronicles 31:21).

25:2–6 These four proverbs all focus on the king. Verse 2 indicates the importance of a king's efforts to discover the truth. This is followed by a parable on the value of a king keeping his own counsel and making up his own mind. Then, because a wise king seeks good advisers, he must be aware of the danger of those who are wicked in places of influence. Last, a warning is issued to those within the court that anyone who makes demands on the king's time treads on dangerous ground. Hezekiah began his collection of wisdom with words for himself.

25:6, 7 Jesus made this proverb into a parable (see Luke 14:7–11). We should not seek honor for ourselves. It is better to quietly and faithfully accomplish the work God has given us to do. As others notice the quality of our lives, then they will draw attention to us.

9 If you argue your case with a neighbor,
　　do not betray another man's confidence,
10 or he who hears it may shame you
　　and you will never lose your bad reputation.

11 A word aptly spoken
　　is like apples of gold in settings of silver.ˣ

25:11
ˣPr 15:23

12 Like an earring of gold or an ornament of fine gold
　　is a wise man's rebuke to a listening ear.ʸ

25:12
ʸPr 15:31

13 Like the coolness of snow at harvest time
　　is a trustworthy messenger to those who send him;
　　he refreshes the spirit of his masters.ᶻ

25:13
ᶻPr 13:17

14 Like clouds and wind without rain
　　is a man who boasts of gifts he does not give.

15 Through patience a ruler can be persuaded,ᵃ
　　and a gentle tongue can break a bone.ᵇ

25:15
ᵃEcc 10:4
ᵇPr 15:1

16 If you find honey, eat just enough—
　　too much of it, and you will vomit.ᶜ

25:16
ᶜver 27

17 Seldom set foot in your neighbor's house—
　　too much of you, and he will hate you.

18 Like a club or a sword or a sharp arrow
　　is the man who gives false testimony against his neighbor.ᵈ

25:18
ᵈPs 57:4; Pr 12:18

19 Like a bad tooth or a lame foot
　　is reliance on the unfaithful in times of trouble.

20 Like one who takes away a garment on a cold day,
　　or like vinegar poured on soda,
　　is one who sings songs to a heavy heart.

21 If your enemy is hungry, give him food to eat;
　　if he is thirsty, give him water to drink.
22 In doing this, you will heap burning coals on his head,
　　and the LORD will reward you.ᵉ

25:22
ᵉ2Sa 16:12;
Ro 12:20*

23 As a north wind brings rain,
　　so a sly tongue brings angry looks.

24 Better to live on a corner of the roof
　　than share a house with a quarrelsome wife.ᶠ

25:24
ᶠPr 21:9

25 Like cold water to a weary soul
　　is good news from a distant land.ᵍ

25:25
ᵍPr 15:30

26 Like a muddied spring or a polluted well
　　is a righteous man who gives way to the wicked.

27 It is not good to eat too much honey,ʰ
　　nor is it honorable to seek one's own honor.ⁱ

25:27
ʰver 16
ⁱPr 27:2

25:13 It is often difficult to find people you can really trust. A faithful employee ("messenger") is punctual, responsible, honest, and hardworking. This person is invaluable as he or she helps take some of the pressure off his or her employer. Find out what your employer needs from you to make his or her job easier, and do it.

25:14 Most churches, missions organizations, and Christian groups depend on the gifts of people to keep their ministries going. But many who promise to give fail to follow through. The Bible is very clear about the effect this has on those involved in the ministry. If you make a pledge, keep your promise.

25:18 Lying ("false testimony") about someone is as vicious as an act of physical violence. Its effects can be as permanent as those of a stab wound. The next time you are tempted to pass

on a bit of gossip, imagine yourself stabbing the victim of your remarks with a sword. This image may shock you into silence.

25:21, 22 God's form of retaliation is most effective and yet difficult to do. Paul quotes this proverb in Romans 12:19–21. In Matthew 5:44, Jesus encourages us to pray for those who hurt us. By returning good for evil, we are acknowledging God as the balancer of all accounts and trusting him to be the judge.

25:26 "Give way to the wicked" means setting aside your standards of right and wrong. No one is helped by someone who compromises with the wicked.

25:27 Dwelling on the honors you deserve can only be harmful. It can make you bitter, discouraged, or angry, and it will not bring you the rewards that you think should be yours. Pining for what you

28 Like a city whose walls are broken down
   is a man who lacks self-control.

26 Like snow in summer or rain*ʲ* in harvest,
   honor is not fitting for a fool.

2 Like a fluttering sparrow or a darting swallow,
   an undeserved curse does not come to rest.*ᵏ*

3 A whip for the horse, a halter for the donkey,*ˡ*
   and a rod for the backs of fools!

4 Do not answer a fool according to his folly,
   or you will be like him yourself.

5 Answer a fool according to his folly,
   or he will be wise in his own eyes.

6 Like cutting off one's feet or drinking violence
   is the sending of a message by the hand of a fool.

7 Like a lame man's legs that hang limp
   is a proverb in the mouth of a fool.

8 Like tying a stone in a sling
   is the giving of honor to a fool.

9 Like a thornbush in a drunkard's hand
   is a proverb in the mouth of a fool.

THE FOUR TONGUES Other verses about our speech include 10:11, 20, 31; 12:6, 17–19; 13:2; 14:3; 19:5, 28; 25:11; 27:2, 5, 14, 17; 29:9.			
	The Controlled Tongue	Those with this speech pattern think before speaking, know when silence is best, and give wise advice.	10:19; 11:12, 13; 12:16; 13:3; 15:1, 4, 28; 16:23; 17:14, 27, 28; 21:23; 24:26
	The Caring Tongue	Those with this speech pattern speak truthfully while seeking to encourage.	10:32, 12:18, 25; 15:23; 16:24; 25:15; 27:9
	The Conniving Tongue	Those with this speech pattern are filled with wrong motives, gossip, slander, and a desire to twist truth.	6:12–14; 8:13; 16:28; 18:8; 25:18; 26:20–28
	The Careless Tongue	Those with this speech pattern are filled with lies, curses, quick-tempered words—which can lead to rebellion and destruction.	10:18, 32; 11:9; 12:16, 18; 15:4; 17:9, 14, 19; 20:19; 25:23

What we say probably affects more people than any other action we take. It is not surprising, then, to find that Proverbs gives special attention to words and how they are used. Four common speech patterns are described in Proverbs. The first two should be copied; the last two should be avoided.

should have received may make you miss the satisfaction of knowing you did your best.

25:28 Even though city walls restricted the inhabitants' movements, people were happy to have them. Without walls, they would have been vulnerable to attack by any passing group of marauders. Self-control limits us, to be sure, but it is necessary. An out-of-control life is open to all sorts of enemy attack. Think of self-control as a wall for defense and protection.

26:2 "An undeserved curse does not come to rest" means that it has no effect.

26:4, 5 These two verses seem to contradict, but they actually are purposely demonstrating the contradiction between reason and folly. A fool remains a fool whether he is answered or not. The wise person has a choice to make depending on what he or she sees is the greatest need of the fool. Some fools don't deserve an answer because they are clearly not in a mood to listen and those who try to answer them will simply stoop to their level. There are other situations where common sense says to answer the fool in order to expose his or her pride and folly.

26:7 Some people are so dulled that they won't sense the wisdom

even if they memorize these proverbs. A mindlessly quoted proverb proves as useless as a paralyzed body part. Only those who want to be wise have the receptive attitude needed to make the most of these wise words. If we want to learn from God, he will respond and pour out his heart to us (1:23).

26:8 Sometimes when someone in a group causes discord or dissension, the leader tries to make that person loyal and productive by giving him or her a place of privilege or responsibility. This usually doesn't work. In fact, it is like tying a stone to the sling of a slingshot—it won't go anywhere and will swing back and hurt you. The dissenter's new power may be just what he or she needs to manipulate the group.

26:9 Normally the first prick of a thorn alerts us, so we remove the thorn before it damages us. A drunk person, however, may not feel the thorn, and so it will work its way into his flesh. Similarly, a fool may not feel the sting of a proverb because he does not see where it touches his life. Instead of taking its point to heart, a fool will apply it to his church, his employer, his spouse, or whomever he is rebelling against. The next time you find yourself saying, "So-and-so should really pay attention to that," stop and ask yourself, "Is there a message in it for me?"

10 Like an archer who wounds at random
    is he who hires a fool or any passer-by.

11 As a dog returns to its vomit,*m*
    so a fool repeats his folly.*n*

26:11
m 2Pe 2:22*
n Ex 8:15

12 Do you see a man wise in his own eyes?*o*
    There is more hope for a fool than for him.*p*

26:12
o Pr 3:7
p Pr 29:20

13 The sluggard says, "There is a lion in the road,
    a fierce lion roaming the streets!"*q*

26:13
q Pr 22:13

14 As a door turns on its hinges,
    so a sluggard turns on his bed.

15 The sluggard buries his hand in the dish;
    he is too lazy to bring it back to his mouth.*r*

26:15
r Pr 19:24

16 The sluggard is wiser in his own eyes
    than seven men who answer discreetly.

17 Like one who seizes a dog by the ears
    is a passer-by who meddles in a quarrel not his own.

18 Like a madman shooting
    firebrands or deadly arrows
19 is a man who deceives his neighbor
    and says, "I was only joking!"

20 Without wood a fire goes out;
    without gossip a quarrel dies down.*s*

26:20
s Pr 22:10

21 As charcoal to embers and as wood to fire,
    so is a quarrelsome man for kindling strife.*t*

26:21
t Pr 15:18

22 The words of a gossip are like choice morsels;
    they go down to a man's inmost parts.*u*

26:22
u Pr 18:8

23 Like a coating of glaze*a* over earthenware
    are fervent lips with an evil heart.

24 A malicious man disguises himself with his lips,
    but in his heart he harbors deceit.
25 Though his speech is charming,*v* do not believe him,
    for seven abominations fill his heart.*w*

26:25
v Ps 28:3
w Jer 9:4-8

26 His malice may be concealed by deception,
    but his wickedness will be exposed in the assembly.

27 If a man digs a pit,*x* he will fall into it;
    if a man rolls a stone, it will roll back on him.*y*

26:27
x Ps 7:15
y Pr 28:10

28 A lying tongue hates those it hurts,
    and a flattering mouth*z* works ruin.

26:28
z Pr 29:5

a 23 With a different word division of the Hebrew; Masoretic Text *of silver dross*

26:13–16 If a person is not willing to work, he or she can find endless excuses to avoid it. But laziness is more dangerous than a prowling lion. The less you do, the less you want to do, and the more useless you become. To overcome laziness, take a few small steps toward change. Set a concrete, realistic goal. Figure out the steps needed to reach it, and follow those steps. Pray for strength and persistence. To keep your excuses from making you useless, stop making useless excuses.

26:17 Seizing the ears of a stray dog is a good way to get bitten, and interfering in arguments is a good way to get hurt. Many times both arguers will turn on the person who interferes. It is best simply to keep out of arguments that are none of your business. If you must become involved, try to wait until the arguers have stopped fighting and cooled off a bit. Then maybe you can help them mend their differences and their relationship.

26:20 Talking about every little irritation or piece of gossip only keeps the fires of anger going. Refusing to discuss them cuts the fuel line and makes the fires die out. Does someone continually irritate you? Decide not to complain about the person, and see if your irritation dies from lack of fuel.

26:24–26 This proverb means that people with hate in their hearts may sound pleasant enough; don't believe what they say.

27:1
ᵃLk 12:19-20;
Jas 4:13-16

27:2
ᵇPr 25:27

27:10
ᶜPr 17:17; 18:24

27:11
ᵈPr 10:1; 23:15-16

27:13
ᵉPr 20:16

27

Do not boast about tomorrow,
　for you do not know what a day may bring forth.ᵃ

2 Let another praise you, and not your own mouth;
　someone else, and not your own lips.ᵇ

3 Stone is heavy and sand a burden,
　but provocation by a fool is heavier than both.

4 Anger is cruel and fury overwhelming,
　but who can stand before jealousy?

5 Better is open rebuke
　than hidden love.

6 Wounds from a friend can be trusted,
　but an enemy multiplies kisses.

7 He who is full loathes honey,
　but to the hungry even what is bitter tastes sweet.

8 Like a bird that strays from its nest
　is a man who strays from his home.

9 Perfume and incense bring joy to the heart,
　and the pleasantness of one's friend springs from his earnest counsel.

10 Do not forsake your friend and the friend of your father,
　and do not go to your brother's house when disasterᶜ strikes you—
　better a neighbor nearby than a brother far away.

11 Be wise, my son, and bring joy to my heart;ᵈ
　then I can answer anyone who treats me with contempt.

12 The prudent see danger and take refuge,
　but the simple keep going and suffer for it.

13 Take the garment of one who puts up security for a stranger;
　hold it in pledge if he does it for a wayward woman.ᵉ

14 If a man loudly blesses his neighbor early in the morning,
　it will be taken as a curse.

15 A quarrelsome wife is like
　a constant dripping on a rainy day;

16 restraining her is like restraining the wind
　or grasping oil with the hand.

17 As iron sharpens iron,
　so one man sharpens another.

27:6 Who would prefer a friend's wounds to an enemy's kisses? Anyone who considers the source. A friend who has your best interests at heart may have to give you unpleasant advice at times, but you know it is for your own good. An enemy, by contrast, may whisper sweet words and happily send you on your way to ruin. We tend to hear what we want to hear, even if an enemy is the only one who will tell us. A friend's advice, no matter how painful, is much more valuable.

27:15, 16 Quarrelsome nagging, a steady stream of unwanted advice, is a form of torture. People nag because they think they're not getting through, but nagging hinders communication more than it helps. When tempted to engage in this destructive habit, stop and examine your motives. Are you more concerned about yourself—getting your way, being right—than about the person you are pretending to help? If you are truly concerned about other people, think of a more effective way to get through to them. Surprise them with words of patience and love, and see what happens.

27:17 Mental sharpness comes from being around good people. And a meeting of minds can help people see their ideas with new clarity, refine them, and shape them into brilliant insights. This requires discussion partners who can challenge one another and stimulate thought—people who focus on the idea without involving their egos in the discussion; people who know how to attack the thought and not the thinker. Two friends who bring their ideas together can help each other become sharper.

18 He who tends a fig tree will eat its fruit,^f
   and he who looks after his master will be honored.^g

27:18
^f1Co 9:7
^gLk 19:12-27

19 As water reflects a face,
   so a man's heart reflects the man.

20 Death and Destruction^a are never satisfied,^h
   and neither are the eyes of man.ⁱ

27:20
^hHab 2:5
ⁱEcc 1:8

21 The crucible for silver and the furnace for gold,^j
   but man is tested by the praise he receives.

27:21
^jPr 17:3

22 Though you grind a fool in a mortar,
   grinding him like grain with a pestle,
   you will not remove his folly from him.

23 Be sure you know the condition of your flocks,
   give careful attention to your herds;
24 for riches do not endure forever,
   and a crown is not secure for all generations.
25 When the hay is removed and new growth appears
   and the grass from the hills is gathered in,
26 the lambs will provide you with clothing,
   and the goats with the price of a field.
27 You will have plenty of goats' milk
   to feed you and your family
   and to nourish your servant girls.

28 The wicked man flees though no one pursues,^k
   but the righteous are as bold as a lion.

28:1
^kLev 26:17; Ps 53:5

2 When a country is rebellious, it has many rulers,
   but a man of understanding and knowledge maintains order.

3 A ruler^b who oppresses the poor
   is like a driving rain that leaves no crops.

4 Those who forsake the law praise the wicked,
   but those who keep the law resist them.

5 Evil men do not understand justice,
   but those who seek the LORD understand it fully.

6 Better a poor man whose walk is blameless
   than a rich man whose ways are perverse.^l

28:6
^lPr 19:1

^a20 Hebrew *Sheol and Abaddon*   ^b3 Or *A poor man*

27:18 With all the problems and concerns a leader has, it can be easy to overlook the very people who most deserve attention—faithful employees or volunteers (those who tend the fig trees). The people who stand behind you, who work hard and help you get the job done, deserve to share in your success. Be sure that in all your worrying, planning, and organizing, you don't forget the people who are helping you the most.

27:21 Praise tests a person, just as high temperatures test metal. How does praise affect you? Do you work to get it? Do you work harder after you've gotten it? Your attitude toward praise tells a lot about your character. People of high integrity are not swayed by praise. They are attuned to their inner convictions, and they do what they should whether or not they are praised for it.

27:23-27 Because life is short and our fortunes uncertain, we should be all the more diligent in what we do with our lives. We should act with foresight, giving responsible attention to our homes, our families, and our careers. We should be responsible stewards, like a farmer with his lands and herds. Thinking ahead is a duty, not an option, for God's people.

28:2 For a government or a society to endure, it needs wise, informed leaders—and these are hard to find. "It has many rulers" may mean that anarchy is prevailing. Each person's selfishness quickly affects others. A selfish employee who steals from his company ruins its productivity. A selfish driver who drinks before taking the wheel makes the state highways unsafe. A selfish spouse who has an adulterous affair often breaks up several families. When enough people live for themselves with little concern for how their actions affect others, the resulting moral rot contaminates the entire nation. Are you part of the problem . . . or the solution?

28:5 Because justice is part of God's character, a person who follows God treats others justly. The beginning of justice is concern for what is happening to others. A Christian cannot be indifferent to human suffering because God isn't. And we certainly must not contribute to human suffering through selfish business practices or unfair government policies. Be sure you are more concerned for justice than merely your own interests. You can't claim to follow God and ignore your neighbor.

28:7
m Pr 23:19-21

7 He who keeps the law is a discerning son,
  but a companion of gluttons disgraces his father. *m*

28:8
n Pr 13:22

8 He who increases his wealth by exorbitant interest
  amasses it for another, *n* who will be kind to the poor.

28:9
o Ps 66:18; Pr 15:8

9 If anyone turns a deaf ear to the law,
  even his prayers are detestable. *o*

28:10
p Pr 26:27

10 He who leads the upright along an evil path
   will fall into his own trap, *p*
   but the blameless will receive a good inheritance.

11 A rich man may be wise in his own eyes,
   but a poor man who has discernment sees through him.

28:12
q Pr 11:10

12 When the righteous triumph, there is great elation;
   but when the wicked rise to power, men go into hiding. *q*

28:13
r Ps 32:1-5

13 He who conceals his sins does not prosper,
   but whoever confesses and renounces them finds mercy. *r*

DILIGENCE AND LAZINESS	The Diligent	The Lazy	Reference
Proverbs makes it clear that diligence—being willing to work hard and do one's best at any job given to him or her— is a vital part of wise living. We work hard, not to become rich, famous, or admired (although those may be by-products), but to serve God with our very best during our lives.	Become rich.	Are soon poor	10:4
	Gather crops early	Sleep during harvest	10:5
		Are an annoyance	10:26
	Have abundant food	Chase fantasies.	12:11
	Gain many rewards		12:14
	Will rule	Will become slaves	12:24
	Prize their possessions	Waste good resources	12:27
	Are fully satisfied	Want much but get little.	13:4
	Bring profit	Experience poverty	14:23
	Have an easy path.	Have trouble all through life.	15:19
		Are like those who destroy	18:9
		Go hungry	19:15
		Won't feed themselves	19:24
		Won't plow in season	20:4
	Stay awake and have food to spare	Love sleep and grow poor.	20:13
	Make careful plans	Make hasty speculations.	21:5
		Love pleasure and become poor.	21:17
	Give without sparing	Desire things but refuse to work for them	21:25, 26
		Are full of excuses for not working	22:13
	Will serve before kings		22:29
		Sleep too much, which leads to poverty	24:30–34
	Reap abundance through hard work	Experience poverty because of laziness.	28:19

28:9 God does not listen to our prayers if we intend to go back to our sin as soon as we get off our knees. If we want to forsake our sin and follow him, however, he willingly listens—no matter how bad our sin has been. What closes his ears is not the depth of our sin, but our secret intention to do it again. God hears our intentions as clearly as he hears our words.

28:11 Rich people often think they are wonderful; depending on no one, they take credit for all they do. But that's a hollow self-esteem. Through dependence on God in their struggles, the poor may develop a richness of spirit that no amount of wealth can provide. The rich person can lose all his material wealth, while no one can take away the poor person's character. Don't be jealous of the rich; money may be all they will ever have.

28:13 It is human nature to hide our sins or overlook our mistakes. But it is hard to learn from a mistake you don't acknowledge making. And what good is a mistake if it doesn't teach you something? To learn from an error you need to admit it, confess it, analyze it, and make adjustments so that it doesn't happen again. Everybody makes mistakes, but only fools repeat them.

28:13 Something in each of us strongly resists admitting we are wrong. That is why we admire people who openly and graciously admit their mistakes and sins. These people have a strong self-image. They do not always have to be right to feel good about themselves. Be willing to reconsider—to admit you are wrong and to change your plans when necessary. And remember, the first step toward forgiveness is confession.

14 Blessed is the man who always fears the LORD,
    but he who hardens his heart falls into trouble.

15 Like a roaring lion or a charging bear
    is a wicked man ruling over a helpless people.

16 A tyrannical ruler lacks judgment,
    but he who hates ill-gotten gain will enjoy a long life.

17 A man tormented by the guilt of murder
    will be a fugitive *s* till death;
    let no one support him.

18 He whose walk is blameless is kept safe,
    but he whose ways are perverse will suddenly fall. *t*

19 He who works his land will have abundant food,
    but the one who chases fantasies will have his fill of poverty. *u*

20 A faithful man will be richly blessed,
    but one eager to get rich will not go unpunished. *v*

21 To show partiality is not good *w*—
    yet a man will do wrong for a piece of bread. *x*

22 A stingy man is eager to get rich
    and is unaware that poverty awaits him.

23 He who rebukes a man will in the end gain more favor
    than he who has a flattering tongue. *y*

24 He who robs his father or mother
    and says, "It's not wrong"—
    he is partner to him who destroys. *z*

25 A greedy man stirs up dissension,
    but he who trusts in the LORD *a* will prosper.

26 He who trusts in himself is a fool,
    but he who walks in wisdom is kept safe.

27 He who gives to the poor will lack nothing,
    but he who closes his eyes to them receives many curses.

28 When the wicked rise to power, people go into hiding;
    but when the wicked perish, the righteous thrive.

29 A man who remains stiff-necked after many rebukes
    will suddenly be destroyed—without remedy. *b*

2 When the righteous thrive, the people rejoice;
    when the wicked rule, the people groan.

3 A man who loves wisdom brings joy to his father, *c*
    but a companion of prostitutes squanders his wealth. *d*

28:17	*s* Ge 9:6
28:18	*t* Pr 10:9
28:19	*u* Pr 12:11
28:20	*v* ver 22; 1Ti 6:9
28:21	*w* Pr 18:5 *x* Eze 13:19
28:23	*y* Pr 27:5-6
28:24	*z* Pr 18:9
28:25	*a* Pr 29:25
29:1	*b* 2Ch 36:16; Pr 6:15
29:3	*c* Pr 10:1 *d* Pr 5:8-10; Lk 15:11-32

28:14 To fear the Lord means to revere and honor him.

28:17, 18 A sinner's conscience will drive him either into guilt resulting in repentance or to death itself because of a refusal to repent. It is no act of kindness to try to make him feel better; the more guilt he feels, the more likely he is to turn to God and repent. If we interfere with the natural consequences of his act, we may make it easier for him to continue in sin.

28:26 For many people, the rugged individualist is a hero. We admire the bold, self-directed men and women who know what they want and fight for it. They are self-reliant, neither giving nor asking advice. What a contrast to God's way. A person can't know the future and can't predict the consequences of his or her choices with certainty. And so the totally self-reliant person is doomed to failure. The wise person depends on God.

28:27 God wants us to identify with the needy, not ignore them. The second part of this proverb could be restated positively: "those who open their eyes to poor people will be blessed." If we help others when they are in trouble, they will do whatever they can to return the favor (see 11:24, 25). Paul promises that God will supply all our needs (Philippians 4:19); he usually does this through other people. What can you do today to help God supply someone's need?

29:1 Warnings rarely come with countdowns. We can't tell when we've had our last chance to change. When we, like the person in this proverb, refuse to consider valid criticism, we leave ourselves open to sudden disaster. The moment we realize that a change is necessary is the best moment to take action. What significant adjustments have been on hold in your life for too long?

⁴ By justice a king gives a country stability,
    but one who is greedy for bribes tears it down.

⁵ Whoever flatters his neighbor
    is spreading a net for his feet.

⁶ An evil man is snared by his own sin,
    but a righteous one can sing and be glad.

29:7
e Job 29:16;
Ps 41:1

⁷ The righteous care about justice for the poor,*e*
    but the wicked have no such concern.

29:8
f Pr 11:11

⁸ Mockers stir up a city,
    but wise men turn away anger.*f*

⁹ If a wise man goes to court with a fool,
    the fool rages and scoffs, and there is no peace.

29:10
g 1Jn 3:12

¹⁰ Bloodthirsty men hate a man of integrity
    and seek to kill the upright.*g*

29:11
h Pr 12:16

¹¹ A fool gives full vent to his anger,
    but a wise man keeps himself under control.*h*

¹² If a ruler listens to lies,
    all his officials become wicked.

¹³ The poor man and the oppressor have this in common:
    The LORD gives sight to the eyes of both.

29:14
i Ps 72:1-5

¹⁴ If a king judges the poor with fairness,
    his throne will always be secure.*i*

29:15
j Pr 13:24

¹⁵ The rod of correction imparts wisdom,
    but a child left to himself disgraces his mother.*j*

29:16
k Ps 37:35-36; 91:8

¹⁶ When the wicked thrive, so does sin,
    but the righteous will see their downfall.*k*

LEADERSHIP
Since many
of the proverbs
came from King
Solomon, it is
natural to expect
some of his
interest to be
directed toward
leadership.
  Other verses
to study: 24:27;
25:13; 27:18.

Qualities of a good leader	Reference
Diligence	12:24
Has trustworthy messengers	13:17
Doesn't penalize people for integrity	17:26
Listens before answering	18:13
Able to discern	18:15
Listens to both sides of the story	18:17
Stands up under adversity	24:10
Stands up under praise	27:21
What happens without good leadership	
Honoring the wrong people backfires	26:8
A wicked ruler is dangerous	28:15
People despair	29:2
A wicked ruler has wicked officials	29:12

29:13 "The LORD gives sight to the eyes of both" means that everyone depends on God for sight. Both the oppressor and the poor have the gift of sight from the same God. God sees and judges both, and his judgment falls on those whose greed or power drives them to oppress the poor.

29:15 Parents of young children often weary of disciplining them. They feel like all they do is nag, scold, and punish. When you're tempted to give up and let your children do what they want, or when you wonder if you've ruined every chance for a loving rela-

tionship with them, remember—kind, firm correction helps them learn, and learning makes them wise. Consistent, loving discipline will ultimately teach them to discipline themselves.

29:16 When the wicked are in leadership, sin prevails. In any organization—whether a church, a business, a family, or a government—the climate comes from the top. The people become like their leaders. What kind of climate are you setting for the people you lead?

17 Discipline your son, and he will give you peace;
    he will bring delight to your soul.

18 Where there is no revelation, the people cast off restraint;
    but blessed is he who keeps the law.*

29:18
l Ps 1:1-21; 19:1-2

19 A servant cannot be corrected by mere words;
    though he understands, he will not respond.

20 Do you see a man who speaks in haste?
    There is more hope for a fool than for him.*

29:20
m Pr 26:12

21 If a man pampers his servant from youth,
    he will bring grief* in the end.

22 An angry man stirs up dissension,
    and a hot-tempered one commits many sins.

23 A man's pride brings him low,
    but a man of lowly spirit gains honor.*

29:23
n Pr 11:2; Isa 66:2;
Mt 23:12

24 The accomplice of a thief is his own enemy;
    he is put under oath and dare not testify.*

29:24
o Lev 5:1

25 Fear of man will prove to be a snare,
    but whoever trusts in the LORD is kept safe.

26 Many seek an audience with a ruler,
    but it is from the LORD that man gets justice.

27 The righteous detest the dishonest;
    the wicked detest the upright.

Sayings of Agur

30 The sayings of Agur son of Jakeh—an oracle*:

    This man declared to Ithiel,
        to Ithiel and to Ucal:*

2 "I am the most ignorant of men;
    I do not have a man's understanding.
3 I have not learned wisdom,
    nor have I knowledge of the Holy One.
4 Who has gone up* to heaven and come down?
    Who has gathered up the wind in the hollow of his hands?
    Who has wrapped up the waters in his cloak?
    Who has established all the ends of the earth?
    What is his name, and the name of his son?
    Tell me if you know!

30:4
p Jn 3:13

5 "Every word of God is flawless;*
    he is a shield to those who take refuge in him.

30:5
q Ps 12:6; 18:30

*a 21 The meaning of the Hebrew for this word is uncertain.   b 1 Or Jakeh of Massa   c 1 Masoretic Text; with
a different word division of the Hebrew declared, "I am weary, O God; / I am weary, O God, and faint.*

29:18 "Revelation" refers to words from God received by prophets. Where there is ignorance or rejection of God, crime and sin run wild. Public morality depends on the knowledge of God, but it also depends on keeping God's laws. In order for both nations and individuals to function well, people must know God's ways and keep his rules. Having God's Word means little if we are not obeying it.

29:24 This proverb is saying that a thief's accomplice may not tell the truth when under oath. Thus, by his participation in the crime and his perjury in the courtroom, he will hurt himself. Further, a witness who refuses to report a crime becomes an accomplice.

29:25 Fear of people can hamper everything you try to do. In extreme forms, it can make you afraid to leave your home. By contrast, fear of God—respect, reverence, and trust—is liberating. Why

fear people who can do no eternal harm? Instead, fear God who can turn the harm intended by others into good for those who trust him.

30:1 The origin of these sayings is not clear. Nothing is known about Agur except that he was a wise teacher who may have come from Lemuel's kingdom (see the note on 31:1).

30:2–4 Because God is infinite, certain aspects of his nature will always remain a mystery. Compare these questions with the questions God asked Job (Job 38—41). Use these questions to probe your own humility and awe before your Creator.

30:4 Some scholars feel that the son referred to is the Son of God, the preincarnate being of the Messiah who, before the foundation of the earth, participated in the creation. Colossians 1:16, 17 teaches that through Christ the world was created.

30:6
r Dt 4:2; Rev 22:18

6 Do not add *r* to his words,
　　or he will rebuke you and prove you a liar.

7 "Two things I ask of you, O Lord;
　　do not refuse me before I die:

30:8
s Mt 6:11

8 Keep falsehood and lies far from me;
　　give me neither poverty nor riches,
　　but give me only my daily bread. *s*

30:9
t Dt 8:10-14;
Hos 13:6

9 Otherwise, I may have too much and disown you
　　and say, 'Who is the Lord?' *t*
Or I may become poor and steal,
　　and so dishonor the name of my God.

10 "Do not slander a servant to his master,
　　or he will curse you, and you will pay for it.

30:11
u Pr 20:20

11 "There are those who curse their fathers
　　and do not bless their mothers; *u*

30:12
v Lk 18:11

12 those who are pure in their own eyes *v*
　　and yet are not cleansed of their filth;

30:13
w Pr 6:17

13 those whose eyes are ever so haughty, *w*
　　whose glances are so disdainful;

30:14
x Job 29:17
y Ps 14:4
z Am 8:4

14 those whose teeth *x* are swords
　　and whose jaws are set with knives
to devour *y* the poor *z* from the earth,
　　the needy from among mankind.

15 "The leech has two daughters.
　　'Give! Give!' they cry.

"There are three things that are never satisfied,
　　four that never say, 'Enough!':

30:16
a Pr 27:20; Hab 2:5

16 the grave, *a a* the barren womb,
　　land, which is never satisfied with water,
　　and fire, which never says, 'Enough!'

17 "The eye that mocks a father,
　　that scorns obedience to a mother,
will be pecked out by the ravens of the valley,
　　will be eaten by the vultures.

18 "There are three things that are too amazing for me,
　　four that I do not understand:

19 the way of an eagle in the sky,
　　the way of a snake on a rock,
the way of a ship on the high seas,
　　and the way of a man with a maiden.

30:20
b Pr 5:6

20 "This is the way of an adulteress:
　　She eats and wipes her mouth
　　and says, 'I've done nothing wrong.' *b*

21 "Under three things the earth trembles,
　　under four it cannot bear up:

30:22
c Pr 19:10

22 a servant who becomes king, *c*
　　a fool who is full of food,

a 16 Hebrew *Sheol*

30:7–9 Having too much money can be dangerous, but so can having too little. Being poor can, in fact, be hazardous to spiritual as well as physical health. On the other hand, being rich is not the answer. As Jesus pointed out, rich people have trouble getting into God's kingdom (Matthew 19:23, 24). Like Paul, we can learn how to live whether we have little or plenty (Philippians 4:12), but our lives are more likely to be effective if we have "neither poverty nor riches."

30:11–14 This sequence of proverbs contains a fourfold description of arrogance. Notice that a life of pride and abuse of others often begins with a lack of appreciation for one's parents. The command to honor one's father and mother does create negative consequences when rejected.

30:15ff "Three things . . . four" is a poetic way of saying the list is not complete. The writer of these proverbs is observing the world with delighted interest. Verses 15–30 are an invitation to look at nature from the perspective of a keen observer.

23 an unloved woman who is married,
   and a maidservant who displaces her mistress.

24 "Four things on earth are small,
   yet they are extremely wise:
25 Ants are creatures of little strength,
   yet they store up their food in the summer;*d*
26 coneys*a* *e* are creatures of little power,
   yet they make their home in the crags;
27 locusts have no king,
   yet they advance together in ranks;
28 a lizard can be caught with the hand,
   yet it is found in kings' palaces.

29 "There are three things that are stately in their stride,
   four that move with stately bearing:
30 a lion, mighty among beasts,
   who retreats before nothing;
31 a strutting rooster, a he-goat,
   and a king with his army around him.*b*

32 "If you have played the fool and exalted yourself,
   or if you have planned evil,
   clap your hand over your mouth!*f*
33 For as churning the milk produces butter,
   and as twisting the nose produces blood,
   so stirring up anger produces strife."

Sayings of King Lemuel

31 The sayings of King Lemuel—an oracle*c* his mother taught him:

2 "O my son, O son of my womb,
   O son of my vows,*d* *g*
3 do not spend your strength on women,
   your vigor on those who ruin kings.*h*

4 "It is not for kings, O Lemuel—
   not for kings to drink wine,*i*
   not for rulers to crave beer,
5 lest they drink and forget what the law decrees,
   and deprive all the oppressed of their rights.
6 Give beer to those who are perishing,
   wine to those who are in anguish;
7 let them drink and forget their poverty
   and remember their misery no more.

8 "Speak*j* up for those who cannot speak for themselves,
   for the rights of all who are destitute.
9 Speak up and judge fairly;
   defend the rights of the poor and needy."*k*

---

a26 That is, the hyrax or rock badger *b31* Or *king secure against revolt* *c1* Or *of Lemuel king of Massa, which*
d2 Or */ the answer to my prayers*

30:25
*d*Pr 6:6-8

30:26
*e*Ps 104:18

30:32
*f*Job 21:5

31:2
*g*Isa 49:15

31:3
*h*Dt 17:17; 1Ki 11:3;
Ne 13:26; Pr 5:1-14

31:4
*i*Pr 20:1; Ecc 10:16-
17; Isa 5:22

31:8
*j*Job 29:12-17

31:9
*k*Lev 19:15;
Dt 1:16; Isa 1:17;
Jer 22:16

30:24–28 Ants can teach us about preparation; coneys (badgers) about wise building; locusts about cooperation and order; and lizards about fearlessness. Compare this to Jesus' teaching in Matthew 6:25–34 that an effective way to resist worry involves a careful observation of the birds and the lilies.

31:1 Little is known about Lemuel except that he was a king who received wise teachings from his mother. His name means "devoted to God." Some believe that Lemuel and Agur were both from the kingdom of Massa in northern Arabia.

31:4–7 Drunkenness might be understandable among dying people in great pain, but it is inexcusable for national leaders. Alco-

hol clouds the mind and can lead to injustice and poor decisions. Leaders have better things to do than anesthetize themselves with alcohol.

31:10–31 Proverbs has a lot to say about women. How fitting that the book ends with a picture of a woman of strong character, great wisdom, many skills, and great compassion.

Some people have the mistaken idea that the ideal woman in the Bible is retiring, servile, and entirely domestic. Not so! This woman is an excellent wife and mother. She is also a manufacturer, importer, manager, realtor, farmer, seamstress, upholsterer, and merchant. Her strength and dignity do not come from

Epilogue: The Wife of Noble Character

31:10
l Ru 3:11; Pr 12:4;
18:22
m Pr 19:14

10aA wife of noble character *l* who can find? *m*
    She is worth far more than rubies.
11 Her husband has full confidence in her
    and lacks nothing of value.
12 She brings him good, not harm,
    all the days of her life.
13 She selects wool and flax
    and works with eager hands.
14 She is like the merchant ships,
    bringing her food from afar.
15 She gets up while it is still dark;
    she provides food for her family
    and portions for her servant girls.
16 She considers a field and buys it;
    out of her earnings she plants a vineyard.
17 She sets about her work vigorously;
    her arms are strong for her tasks.
18 She sees that her trading is profitable,
    and her lamp does not go out at night.
19 In her hand she holds the distaff
    and grasps the spindle with her fingers.

31:20
n Dt 15:11;
Eph 4:28;
Heb 13:16

20 She opens her arms to the poor
    and extends her hands to the needy. *n*
21 When it snows, she has no fear for her household;
    for all of them are clothed in scarlet.
22 She makes coverings for her bed;
    she is clothed in fine linen and purple.

31:23
o Ru 4:1,11;
Pr 12:4

23 Her husband is respected at the city gate,
    where he takes his seat among the elders*o* of the land.
24 She makes linen garments and sells them,
    and supplies the merchants with sashes.
25 She is clothed with strength and dignity;
    she can laugh at the days to come.

31:26
p Pr 10:31

26 She speaks with wisdom,
    and faithful instruction is on her tongue.*p*
27 She watches over the affairs of her household
    and does not eat the bread of idleness.
28 Her children arise and call her blessed;
    her husband also, and he praises her:
29 "Many women do noble things,
    but you surpass them all."
30 Charm is deceptive, and beauty is fleeting;
    but a woman who fears the LORD is to be praised.
31 Give her the reward she has earned,
    and let her works bring her praise at the city gate.

a 10 Verses 10-31 are an acrostic, each verse beginning with a successive letter of the Hebrew alphabet.

---

her amazing achievements, however. They are a result of her reverence for God. In our society where physical appearance counts for so much, it may surprise us to realize that her appearance is never mentioned. Her attractiveness comes entirely from her character.

The woman described in this chapter has outstanding abilities. Her family's social position is high. In fact, she may not be one woman at all—she may be a composite portrait of ideal womanhood. Do not see her as a model to imitate in every detail; your days are not long enough to do everything she does! See her instead as an inspiration to be all you can be. We can't be just like her, but we can learn from her industry, integrity, and resourcefulness.

31:19 The distaff and spindle are two implements used in hand spinning.

31:31 The book of Proverbs begins with the command to fear the Lord (1:7) and ends with the picture of a woman who fulfills this command. Her qualities are mentioned throughout the book: hard work, fear of God, respect for spouse, foresight, encouragement, care for others, concern for the poor, wisdom in handling money. These qualities, when coupled with fear of God, lead to enjoyment, success, honor, and worth. Proverbs is very practical for our day because it shows us how to become wise, make good decisions, and live according to God's ideal.

ECCLESIASTES

VITAL STATISTICS

PURPOSE:
To spare future generations the bitterness of learning through their own experience that life is meaningless apart from God

AUTHOR:
Solomon

ORIGINAL AUDIENCE:
Solomon's subjects in particular, and all people in general

DATE WRITTEN:
Probably around 935 B.C., late in Solomon's life

SETTING:
Solomon was looking back on his life, much of which was lived apart from God.

KEY VERSE:
"Now all has been heard; here is the conclusion of the matter: Fear God and keep his commandments, for this is the whole ⌞duty⌟ of man" (12:13).

THE CHOCOLATE bunny lies in the basket, surrounded by green paper "grass." With Easter morning eyes wide with anticipation, the little boy carefully lifts the candy figure and bites into one of the long ears. But the sweet taste fades quickly, and the child looks again at the candy in his hand. It's hollow!

Empty, futile, hollow, nothing—the words have a ring of disappointment and disillusionment. Yet this is the life experience of many. Grasping the sweet things—possessions, experience, power, and pleasure—they find nothing inside. Life is empty, meaningless—and they sink into despair.

Almost 3,000 years ago, Solomon spoke of this human dilemma; but the insights and applications of his message are relevant to our time. Ecclesiastes, Solomon's written sermon, is an analysis of life's experiences and a critical essay about life's true meaning. In this profound book, Solomon takes us on a reflective journey through his life, explaining how everything he had tried, tested, or tasted had been "meaningless"—useless, irrational, pointless, foolish, and empty—an exercise in futility. And remember, these words are from one who "had it all"— tremendous intellect, power, and wealth. After this biographical tour, Solomon made his triumphant conclusion: "Fear God and keep his commandments, for this is the whole ⌞duty⌟ of man. For God will bring every deed into judgment, including every hidden thing, whether it is good or evil" (12:13, 14).

When Solomon became king, he asked God for wisdom (2 Chronicles 1:7–12), and he became the wisest man in the world (1 Kings 4:29–34). Solomon studied, taught, judged, and wrote. Kings and leaders from other nations came to Jerusalem to learn from him. But with all of his practical insight on life, Solomon failed to heed his own advice, and he began a downward spiral. Near the end of his life, Solomon looked back with an attitude of humility and repentance. He took stock of his life, hoping to spare his readers the bitterness of learning through personal experience that everything apart from God is empty, hollow, and meaningless.

Although the tone of Ecclesiastes is negative and pessimistic, we must not conclude that the only chapter worth reading and applying is the last one, where he draws his conclusions. In reality, the entire book is filled with practical wisdom (how to accomplish things in the world and stay out of trouble) and spiritual wisdom (how to find and know eternal values).

Solomon had a very honest approach. All of his remarks relating to the futility of life are there for a purpose: to lead us to seek fulfillment and happiness in God alone. He was not trying to destroy all hope, but to direct our hopes to the only one who can truly fulfill them and give our life meaning. Solomon affirms the value of knowledge, relationships, work, and pleasure, but only *in their proper place*. Everything temporal must be seen in light of the eternal.

Read Ecclesiastes and learn about life. Hear the stern warnings and dire predictions, and commit yourself to remember your Creator now (12:1).

THE BLUEPRINT

1. Solomon's personal experience (1:1—2:26)
2. Solomon's general observations (3:1—5:20)
3. Solomon's practical counsel (6:1—8:17)
4. Solomon's final conclusion (9:1—12:14)

Ecclesiastes shows that certain paths in life lead to emptiness. This profound book also helps us discover true purpose in life. Such wisdom can spare us from the emptiness that results from a life without God. Solomon teaches that people will not find meaning in life through knowledge, money, pleasure, work, or popularity. True satisfaction comes from knowing that what we are doing is part of God's purpose for our lives. This is a book that can help free us from our scramble for power, approval, and money, and draw us closer to God.

MEGATHEMES

THEME	EXPLANATION	IMPORTANCE
Searching	Solomon searched for satisfaction almost as though he was conducting a scientific experiment. Through this process, he discovered that life without God is a long and fruitless search for enjoyment, meaning, and fulfillment. True happiness is not in our power to attain because we always want more than we can have. In addition, there are circumstances beyond our control that can snatch away our possessions or attainments.	People are still searching. Yet the more they try to get, the more they realize how little they really have. No pleasure or happiness is possible without God. Without him, satisfaction is a lost search. Above everything we should strive to know and love God. He gives wisdom, knowledge, and joy.
Emptiness	Solomon shows how empty it is to pursue the pleasures that this life has to offer rather than seek to have a relationship with the eternal God. The search for pleasure, wealth, and success is ultimately disappointing. Nothing in the world can fill the emptiness and satisfy the deep longings in our restless hearts.	The cure for emptiness is to center on God. His love also can fill the emptiness of human experience. Fear God throughout your life, and fill your life with serving God and others rather than with selfish pleasures.
Work	Solomon tried to shake people's confidence in their own efforts, abilities, and wisdom and to direct them to faith in God as the only sound basis for living. Without God, there is no lasting reward or benefit in hard work.	Work done with the wrong attitude will leave us empty. But work accepted as an assignment from God can be seen as a gift. Examine what you expect from your efforts. God gives you abilities and opportunities to work so that you can use your time well.
Death	The certainty of death makes all human achievements futile. God has a plan for each one of us that goes beyond life and death. The reality of aging and dying reminds each individual of the end to come when God will judge each person's life.	Because life is short, we need wisdom that is greater than this world can offer. We need the words of God so we can live right. If we listen to him, his wisdom spares us the bitterness of futile human experience and gives us a hope that goes beyond death.
Wisdom	Human wisdom doesn't contain all the answers. Knowledge and education have their limits. To understand life and make right choices, we need the wisdom that can be found only in God's Word—the Bible.	When we realize that God will evaluate all that we do, we should learn to live wisely, remembering that he is present each day, and learn to obey his guidelines for living. But in order to have God's wisdom, we must first get to know and honor him.

1. Solomon's personal experience
Everything Is Meaningless

1 The words of the Teacher,[a] [a] son of David, king in Jerusalem:

2 "Meaningless! Meaningless!"
    says the Teacher.
"Utterly meaningless!
    Everything is meaningless."[b]

3 What does man gain from all his labor
    at which he toils under the sun?[c]
4 Generations come and generations go,
    but the earth remains forever. [d]
5 The sun rises and the sun sets,
    and hurries back to where it rises.[e]
6 The wind blows to the south
    and turns to the north;
round and round it goes,
    ever returning on its course.
7 All streams flow into the sea,
    yet the sea is never full.
To the place the streams come from,
    there they return again.
8 All things are wearisome,
    more than one can say.
The eye never has enough of seeing,[f]
    nor the ear its fill of hearing.
9 What has been will be again,
    what has been done will be done again;[g]
there is nothing new under the sun.
10 Is there anything of which one can say,
    "Look! This is something new"?
It was here already, long ago;
    it was here before our time.
11 There is no remembrance of men of old,
    and even those who are yet to come
will not be remembered
    by those who follow.

[a] 1 Or *leader of the assembly*; also in verses 2 and 12

1:1 *ver 12; Ecc 7:27; 12:10*

1:2 *b Ps 39:5-6; 62:9; 144:4; Ecc 12:8*

1:3 *c Ecc 2:11, 22*

1:4 *d Ps 104:5; 119:90*

1:5 *e Ps 19:5-6*

1:8 *f Pr 27:20*

1:9 *g Ecc 3:15*

1:1 The author, Solomon (the "king over Israel in Jerusalem," see 1:12), referred to himself as the Teacher, or leader of the assembly. He was both assembling people to hear a message and gathering wise sayings (proverbs). Solomon, one person in the Bible who had everything (wisdom, power, riches, honor, reputation, God's favor), is the one who discussed the ultimate emptiness of all that this world has to offer. His purpose in this book is to make people realize that their confidence in their own efforts, abilities, and righteousness was meaningless. Instead, their commitment to God is the only reason for living.

1:1–11 Solomon had a purpose for writing skeptically and pessimistically. Near the end of his life, looking back on everything he had done, he saw that most of it seemed meaningless. A common belief was that good people prospered and the wicked suffered, but that hadn't proven true in Solomon's experience. Solomon wrote this book after he had tried everything and achieved much, only to find that nothing apart from God made him happy. He wanted his readers to avoid these same senseless pursuits. If we try to find meaning in our accomplish-

ments rather than in God, we will never be satisfied, and everything we pursue will become wearisome.

1:2 Solomon's kingdom, Israel, was in its golden age, but Solomon wanted the people to understand that success and prosperity don't last long (Psalm 103:14–16; Isaiah 40:6–8; James 4:14). All human accomplishments will one day disappear; we must keep this in mind in order to live wisely. If we don't, we will become either proud and self-sufficient when we succeed or sorely disappointed when we fail. Solomon's goal was to show that earthly possessions and accomplishments are ultimately meaningless. Only the pursuit of God brings real satisfaction. We should honor God in all we say, think, and do.

1:8–11 Many people feel restless and dissatisfied. They wonder: (1) If I am in God's will, why am I so tired and unfulfilled? (2) What is the meaning of life? (3) When I look back on it all, will I be happy with my accomplishments? (4) Why do I feel burned out, disillusioned, dry? (5) What is to become of me? Solomon tests our faith, challenging us to find true and lasting meaning in God alone. As you take a hard look at your life, as Solomon did his, you will see how important serving God is over all other options. Perhaps God is asking you to rethink your purpose and direction in life, just as Solomon did in Ecclesiastes.

Wisdom Is Meaningless

1:12
h ver 1

1:13
i Ecc 3:10

1:15
j Ecc 7:13

1:16
k 1Ki 3:12

1:17
l Ecc 2:3,12

1:18
m Ecc 12:12

12 I, the Teacher,*h* was king over Israel in Jerusalem. 13 I devoted myself to study and to explore by wisdom all that is done under heaven. What a heavy burden God has laid on men!*i* 14 I have seen all the things that are done under the sun; all of them are meaningless, a chasing after the wind.

> 15 What is twisted cannot be straightened;*j*
> what is lacking cannot be counted.

16 I thought to myself, "Look, I have grown and increased in wisdom more than anyone who has ruled over Jerusalem before me;*k* I have experienced much of wisdom and knowledge." 17 Then I applied myself to the understanding of wisdom, and also of madness and folly,*l* but I learned that this, too, is a chasing after the wind.

> 18 For with much wisdom comes much sorrow;
> the more knowledge, the more grief.*m*

Pleasures Are Meaningless

2 I thought in my heart, "Come now, I will test you with pleasure to find out what is good." But that also proved to be meaningless. 2 "Laughter," I said, "is foolish. And what does pleasure accomplish?" 3 I tried cheering myself with wine, and embracing folly—my mind still guiding me with wisdom. I wanted to see what was worthwhile for men to do under heaven during the few days of their lives.

4 I undertook great projects: I built houses for myself and planted vineyards. 5 I made gardens and parks and planted all kinds of fruit trees in them. 6 I made reservoirs to water groves of flourishing trees. 7 I bought male and female slaves and had other slaves who were born in my house. I also owned more herds and flocks than anyone in Jerusalem before me. 8 I amassed silver and gold*n* for myself, and the treasure of kings and provinces. I acquired men and women singers, and a harem*a* as well—the delights of the heart of man. 9 I became greater by far than anyone in Jerusalem before me. In all this my wisdom stayed with me.

2:8
n 1Ki 9:28;
10:10,14, 21

> 10 I denied myself nothing my eyes desired;
> I refused my heart no pleasure.
> My heart took delight in all my work,
> and this was the reward for all my labor.
> 11 Yet when I surveyed all that my hands had done
> and what I had toiled to achieve,

a 8 The meaning of the Hebrew for this phrase is uncertain.

1:12–15 "What is twisted cannot be straightened" refers to the ultimate perplexity and confusion that come to us because of all the unanswered questions in life. Solomon, writing about his own life, discovered that neither his accomplishments nor his wisdom could make him truly happy. True wisdom is found in God, and true happiness comes from pleasing him.

1:16–18 The more you understand, the more pain and difficulty you experience. For example, the more you know, the more imperfection you see around you; and the more you observe, the more evil becomes evident. As you set out with Solomon to find the meaning of life, you must be ready to feel more, think more, question more, hurt more, and do more. Are you ready to pay the price for wisdom?

1:16–18 Solomon highlights two kinds of wisdom in the book of Ecclesiastes: (1) human knowledge, reasoning, or philosophy, and (2) the wisdom that comes from God. In these verses Solomon is talking about human knowledge. When human knowledge ignores God, it only highlights our problems because it can't provide answers without God's eternal perspective and solution.

2:1ff Solomon conducted his search for life's meaning as an experiment. He first tried pursuing pleasure. He undertook great projects, bought slaves and herds and flocks, amassed wealth, acquired singers, added many women to his harem, and became the greatest person in Jerusalem. But none of these gave him satisfaction—"Yet when I surveyed all that my hands had done and what I had toiled to achieve, everything was meaningless, a

chasing after the wind; nothing was gained under the sun" (2:11). Some of the pleasures Solomon sought were wrong and some were worthy, but even the worthy pursuits were futile when he pursued them as an end in themselves. We must look beyond our activities to the reasons we do them and the purpose they fulfill. Is your goal in life to search for meaning or to search for God who gives meaning?

2:4–6 Solomon had built houses, the temple, a kingdom, and a family (see 1 Kings 3—11). In the course of history, they all would be ruined. In Psalm 127:1, Solomon wrote, "Unless the LORD builds the house, its builders labor in vain. Unless the LORD watches over the city, the watchmen stand guard in vain." This book is part of Solomon's testimony to what happens to a kingdom or family that forgets God. As you examine your projects or goals, what is your starting point, your motivation? Without God as your foundation, all you are living for is meaningless.

2:11 Solomon summarized all his attempts at finding life's meaning as "chasing after the wind." We feel the wind as it passes, but we can't catch hold of it or keep it. In all our accomplishments, even the big ones, our good feelings are only temporary. Security and self-worth are not found in these accomplishments, but far beyond them in the love of God. Think about what you consider worthwhile—where you place your time, energy, and money. Will you one day look back and decide that these, too, were a "chasing after the wind"?

everything was meaningless, a chasing after the wind;*o*
nothing was gained under the sun.*p*

2:11
*o*Ecc 1:14
*p*Ecc 1:3

Wisdom and Folly Are Meaningless

12 Then I turned my thoughts to consider wisdom,
and also madness and folly.*q*
What more can the king's successor do
than what has already been done?

2:12
*q*Ecc 1:17

13 I saw that wisdom is better than folly,
just as light is better than darkness.
14 The wise man has eyes in his head,
while the fool walks in the darkness;
but I came to realize
that the same fate overtakes them both.*r*

2:14
*r*Ps 49:10;
Ecc 9:3,11-12

15Then I thought in my heart,

"The fate of the fool will overtake me also.
What then do I gain by being wise?"
I said in my heart,
"This too is meaningless."
16 For the wise man, like the fool, will not be long remembered;
in days to come both will be forgotten.
Like the fool, the wise man too must die!

Toil Is Meaningless

17So I hated life, because the work that is done under the sun was grievous to me. All of it is meaningless, a chasing after the wind. 18I hated all the things I had toiled for under the sun, because I must leave them to the one who comes after me.*s* 19And who knows whether he will be a wise man or a fool? Yet he will have control over all the work into which I have poured my effort and skill under the sun. This too is meaningless. 20So my heart began to despair over all my toilsome labor under the sun. 21For a man may do his work with wisdom, knowledge and skill, and then he must leave all he owns to someone who has not worked for it. This too is meaningless and a great misfortune. 22What does a man get for all the toil and anxious striving with which he labors under the sun?*t* 23All his days his work is pain and grief;*u* even at night his mind does not rest. This too is meaningless.

24A man can do nothing better than to eat and drink*v* and find satisfaction in his work.*w* This too, I see, is from the hand of God,*x* 25for without him, who can eat or find enjoyment? 26To the man who pleases him, God gives wisdom, knowledge and happiness, but to the sinner he gives the task of gathering and storing up wealth*y* to hand it over to the one who pleases God. This too is meaningless, a chasing after the wind.

2:18
*s*Ps 49:10

2:22
*t*Ecc 1:3
2:23
*u*Job 5:7; 14:1
2:24
*v*Ecc 8:15
*w*Ecc 3:22
*x*Ecc 3:12-13;
5:17-19
2:26
*y*Job 27:17

2:16 Solomon realized that wisdom alone cannot guarantee eternal life. Wisdom, riches, and personal achievement matter very little after death—and everyone must die. We must not build our lives on perishable pursuits, but on the solid foundation of God. Then even if everything we have is taken away, we still will have God, who is all we really need anyway. This is the point of the book of Job (see the introduction to Job).

2:16 Is death the ultimate equalizer of all people, no matter what they attained in life? While this appears to be true from an earthly perspective, God makes it clear (as Solomon later points out in 12:14) that what we do here has a great impact upon our eternal reward.

2:17 As king, Solomon had everything a person could want, but here he says that he "hated life." What happened? His marvelous accomplishments left him sour because he pursued them as a means to personal satisfaction. Personal satisfaction, by itself, is empty because we are alone in the enjoyment we receive. What is your attitude about what you do? If your goals are to satisfy only yourself, you will find yourself empty, seeking one thing after another, as Solomon did. If your goal is to serve God and others, then you will experience a full life, one that won't leave you sour.

2:18–23 Solomon continued to show that hard work bears no lasting fruit for those who work solely to earn money and gain possessions. Not only will everything be left behind at death, but it may be left to those who have done nothing to earn it. In addition, it may not be well cared for, and all that was gained may be lost. In fact, Solomon's son, who inherited his throne, immediately made a foolish decision which split the kingdom— see 1 Kings 12. Hard work done with proper motives (caring for your family, serving God) is not wrong. We must work to survive, and, more important, we are responsible for the physical and spiritual well-being of those under our care. But the fruit of hard work done to glorify only ourselves will be passed on to those who may later lose or spoil it all. Such toil often leads to grief, while serving God leads to everlasting joy. Do you know the real reason you are working so hard?

2:24–26 Is Solomon recommending we make life a big, irresponsible party? No, he is encouraging us to take pleasure in what we're doing now and to enjoy life because it comes from God's hand. True enjoyment in life comes only as we follow God's guidelines for living. Without him, satisfaction is a lost search. Those who really know how to enjoy life are the ones

2. Solomon's general observations

A Time for Everything

3:1
z ver 11,17; Ecc 8:6

3
There is a timez for everything,
and a season for every activity under heaven:

2 a time to be born and a time to die,
a time to plant and a time to uproot,
3 a time to kill and a time to heal,
a time to tear down and a time to build,
4 a time to weep and a time to laugh,
a time to mourn and a time to dance,
5 a time to scatter stones and a time to gather them,
a time to embrace and a time to refrain,
6 a time to search and a time to give up,
a time to keep and a time to throw away,
7 a time to tear and a time to mend,
a time to be silent and a time to speak,
8 a time to love and a time to hate,
a time for war and a time for peace.

3:9
a Ecc 1:3
3:10
b Ecc 1:13
3:11
c Ecc 8:17
d Ro 11:33
3:13
e Ecc 2:24

9 What does the worker gain from his toil? a 10 I have seen the burden God has laid on men. b 11 He has made everything beautiful in its time. He has also set eternity in the hearts of men; yet they cannot fathom c what God has done from beginning to end. d 12 I know that there is nothing better for men than to be happy and do good while they live. 13 That everyone may eat and drink, and find satisfaction in all his toil—this is the gift of God. e 14 I know that everything God does will endure forever; nothing can be added to it and nothing taken from it. God does it so that men will revere him.

3:15
f Ecc 1:9

15 Whatever is has already been,
and what will be has been before;f
and God will call the past to account.a

a 15 Or *God calls back the past*

---

who take life each day as a gift from God, thanking him for it and serving him in it. Those without God will have no relief from toil and no direction to guide them through life's complications.

3:1—5:20 Solomon's point in this section is that God has a plan for all people. Thus he provides cycles of life, each with its work for us to do. Although we may face many problems that seem to contradict God's plan, these should not be barriers to believing in him, but rather opportunities to discover that, without God, life's problems have no lasting solutions!

3:1–8 Timing is important. All the experiences listed in these verses are appropriate at certain times. The secret to peace with God is to discover, accept, and appreciate God's perfect timing. The danger is to doubt or resent God's timing. This can lead to despair, rebellion, or moving ahead without his advice.

3:8 When is the time for hating? We shouldn't hate evil people, but we should hate what they do. We should also hate it when people are mistreated, when children are starving, and when God is being dishonored. In addition, we must hate sin in our lives—this is God's attitude (see Psalm 5:5).

3:9–13 Your ability to find satisfaction in your work depends to a large extent upon your attitude. You will become dissatisfied if you lose the sense of purpose God intended for your work. We can enjoy our work if we (1) remember that God has given us work to do (3:10), and (2) realize that the fruit of our labor is a gift from him (3:13). See your work as a way to serve God.

3:11 God has "set eternity in the hearts of men." This means that we can never be completely satisfied with earthly pleasures and pursuits. Because we are created in God's image, (1) we

have a spiritual thirst, (2) we have eternal value, and (3) nothing but the eternal God can truly satisfy us. God has built in us a restless yearning for the kind of perfect world that can only be found in his perfect rule. He has given us a glimpse of the perfection of his creation. But it is only a glimpse; we cannot see into the future or comprehend everything. So we must trust God now and do his work on earth.

3:12 To be happy and do good while we live are worthy goals for life, but we can pursue them the wrong way. God wants us to enjoy life. When we have the proper view of God, we discover that real pleasure is found in enjoying whatever we have as gifts from God, not in what we accumulate.

3:14 What is the purpose of life? It is that we should revere the all-powerful God. To *revere* God means to respect and stand in awe of him because of who he is. Purpose in life starts with *whom* we know, not what we know or how good we are. It is impossible to fulfill your God-given purpose unless you revere God and give him first place in your life.

16And I saw something else under the sun:

In the place of judgment—wickedness was there,
in the place of justice—wickedness was there.

17I thought in my heart,

"God will bring to judgment*g*
both the righteous and the wicked,
for there will be a time for every activity,
a time for every deed."*h*

18I also thought, "As for men, God tests them so that they may see that they are like the animals.*i* 19Man's fate is like that of the animals; the same fate awaits them both: As one dies, so dies the other. All have the same breath*a*; man has no advantage over the animal. Everything is meaningless. 20All go to the same place; all come from dust, and to dust all return.*j* 21Who knows if the spirit of man rises upward*k* and if the spirit of the animal*b* goes down into the earth?"

22So I saw that there is nothing better for a man than to enjoy his work,*l* because that is his lot. For who can bring him to see what will happen after him?

Oppression, Toil, Friendlessness

4 Again I looked and saw all the oppression*m* that was taking place under the sun:

I saw the tears of the oppressed—
and they have no comforter;
power was on the side of their oppressors—
and they have no comforter.
2 And I declared that the dead,
who had already died,
are happier than the living,
who are still alive.
3 But better than both
is he who has not yet been,*n*
who has not seen the evil
that is done under the sun.

4And I saw that all labor and all achievement spring from man's envy of his neighbor. This too is meaningless, a chasing after the wind.

5 The fool folds his hands*o*
and ruins himself.
6 Better one handful with tranquillity
than two handfuls with toil*p*
and chasing after the wind.

a 19 Or *spirit*   *b 21* Or *Who knows the spirit of man, which rises upward, or the spirit of the animal, which*

3:17
g Ro 2:6-8;
2Th 1:6-7
h ver 1

3:18
i Ps 73:22

3:20
j Ge 3:19

3:21
k Ecc 12:7

3:22
l Ecc 2:24

4:1
m Ecc 3:16

4:3
n Job 3:16; Ecc 6:3

4:5
o Pr 6:10

4:6
p Pr 15:16-17; 16:8

3:16 Wickedness sits in the place of justice, thus affecting the legal system. Solomon asked how God's plan can be perfect when so much injustice and oppression exist in the world (4:1). He concluded that God does not ignore injustice, but will bring it to an end at his appointed time (12:13, 14).

3:16ff Solomon reflects on several apparent contradictions in God's control of the world: (1) there is wickedness where there should be justice (3:16, 17); (2) people created in God's image die just like the animals (3:18–21); (3) no one comforts the oppressed (4:1–3); (4) many people are motivated by envy (4:4–6); (5) people are lonely (4:7–12); (6) recognition for accomplishments is temporary (4:13–16). It is easy to use such contradictions as excuses not to believe in God. But Solomon used them to show how we can honestly look at life's problems and still keep our faith. This life is not all there is, yet even in this life we should not pass judgment on God because we don't know everything. God's plan is for us to live forever with him. So live with eternal values in view, realizing that all contradictions will one day be cleared up by the Creator himself (12:14).

3:19–22 Our bodies can't live forever in their present state. In that sense, humans and animals are alike. But Solomon acknowledged that God has given people the hope of eternity (see the note on 3:11), and that we will undergo judgment in the next life (3:17; 12:7, 14)—making us different from animals. Because we have eternity set in our hearts, we have a unique purpose in God's overall plan. Yet we cannot discover God's purpose for our lives by our own efforts—only through building a relationship with him and seeking his guidance. Are you now living as God wants? Do you see life as a gift from him?

4:4–6 Some people are lazy while others are workaholics. Lazy people, seeing the futility of dashing about for success, fold their hands and hurt both themselves and those who depend on them. Workaholics are often driven by envy, greed, and a constant desire to stay ahead of everyone else. Both extremes are foolish and irresponsible. The answer is to work hard but with moderation. Take time to enjoy the other gifts God has given and realize that it is God who gives out the assignments and the rewards, not us.

7Again I saw something meaningless under the sun:

4:8
qPr 27:20

8 There was a man all alone;
  he had neither son nor brother.
There was no end to his toil,
  yet his eyes were not contentq with his wealth.
"For whom am I toiling," he asked,
  "and why am I depriving myself of enjoyment?"
This too is meaningless—
  a miserable business!

9 Two are better than one,
  because they have a good return for their work:
10 If one falls down,
  his friend can help him up.
But pity the man who falls
  and has no one to help him up!
11 Also, if two lie down together, they will keep warm.
  But how can one keep warm alone?
12 Though one may be overpowered,
  two can defend themselves.
A cord of three strands is not quickly broken.

Advancement Is Meaningless

13Better a poor but wise youth than an old but foolish king who no longer knows how to take warning. 14The youth may have come from prison to the kingship, or he may have been born in poverty within his kingdom. 15I saw that all who lived and walked under the sun followed the youth, the king's successor. 16There was no end to all the people who were before them. But those who came later were not pleased with the successor. This too is meaningless, a chasing after the wind.

Stand in Awe of God

5 Guard your steps when you go to the house of God. Go near to listen rather than to offer the sacrifice of fools, who do not know that they do wrong.

5:2
rPr 10:19

2 Do not be quick with your mouth,
  do not be hasty in your heart
  to utter anything before God.
God is in heaven
  and you are on earth,
  so let your words be few.r
3 As a dream comes when there are many cares,
  so the speech of a fool when there are many words.

5:5
sPr 20:25; Ac 5:4

5:7
tEcc 12:13

4When you make a vow to God, do not delay in fulfilling it. He has no pleasure in fools; fulfill your vow. 5It is better not to vow than to make a vow and not fulfill it.s 6Do not let your mouth lead you into sin. And do not protest to the ⌊temple⌋ messenger, "My vow was a mistake." Why should God be angry at what you say and destroy the work of your hands? 7Much dreaming and many words are meaningless. Therefore stand in awe of God. t

---

4:9–12 Cooperating with others has advantages. Life is designed for companionship, not isolation, for intimacy, not loneliness. Some people prefer isolation, thinking they cannot trust anyone. We are not here on earth to serve ourselves, however, but to serve God and others. Don't isolate yourself and try to go it alone. Seek companions; be a team member.

4:13–16 Advancement or getting to the top is meaningless. Position, popularity, and prestige are poor goals for a life's work. Although many pursue them, they are shadows without substance. Many people seek recognition for their accomplishments; but people are fickle, changing quickly and easily. How much better to seek God's approval. His love never changes.

5:1 "Guard your steps" means "be careful." When we enter the house of God, we should have the attitude of being open and ready to listen to God, not to dictate to him what we think he should do.

5:4, 5 Solomon warns his readers about making foolish vows (promises) to God. In Israelite culture, making vows was a serious matter. Vows were voluntary but, once made, were unbreakable (Deuteronomy 23:21–23). It is foolish to make a vow you cannot keep or to play games with God by only partially fulfilling your vow (Proverbs 20:25). It's better not to make a vow than to make a vow to God and break it. It's better still to make a vow and keep it. (See the note on Matthew 5:33ff.)

Riches Are Meaningless

8 If you see the poor oppressed in a district, and justice and rights denied, do not be surprised at such things; for one official is eyed by a higher one, and over them both are others higher still. 9 The increase from the land is taken by all; the king himself profits from the fields.

10 Whoever loves money never has money enough;
  whoever loves wealth is never satisfied with his income.
  This too is meaningless.

11 As goods increase,
  so do those who consume them.
And what benefit are they to the owner
  except to feast his eyes on them?

12 The sleep of a laborer is sweet,
  whether he eats little or much,
but the abundance of a rich man
  permits him no sleep.

13 I have seen a grievous evil under the sun: u

  wealth hoarded to the harm of its owner,
14   or wealth lost through some misfortune,
  so that when he has a son
    there is nothing left for him.
15 Naked a man comes from his mother's womb,
  and as he comes, so he departs. v
He takes nothing from his labor w
  that he can carry in his hand.

16 This too is a grievous evil:

  As a man comes, so he departs,
  and what does he gain,
    since he toils for the wind? x
17 All his days he eats in darkness,
  with great frustration, affliction and anger.

18 Then I realized that it is good and proper for a man to eat and drink, and to find satisfaction in his toilsome labor y under the sun during the few days of life God has given him—for this is his lot. 19 Moreover, when God gives any man wealth and possessions, and enables him to enjoy them, to accept his lot and be happy in his work—this is a gift of God. z 20 He seldom reflects on the days of his life, because God keeps him occupied with gladness of heart.

3. Solomon's practical counsel

6 I have seen another evil under the sun, and it weighs heavily on men: 2 God gives a man wealth, possessions and honor, so that he lacks nothing his heart desires, but God does not enable him to enjoy them, a and a stranger enjoys them instead. This is meaningless, a grievous evil.

Margin references:

5:13
u Ecc 6:1-2

5:15
v Job 1:21
w Ps 49:17; 1Ti 6:7

5:16
x Pr 11:29; Ecc 1:3

5:18
y Ecc 2:10, 24

5:19
z Ecc 2:24; 3:13

6:2
a Ps 17:14

5:10, 11 We always want more than we have. Solomon observed that those who love money and seek it obsessively never find the happiness it promises. Wealth also attracts freeloaders and thieves, causes sleeplessness and fear, and ultimately ends in loss because it must be left behind (Mark 10:23–25; Luke 12:16–21). No matter how much you earn, if you try to create happiness by accumulating wealth, you will never have enough. Money in itself is not wrong, but loving money leads to all sorts of sin. Whatever financial situation you are in, don't depend on money to make you happy. Instead, use what you have for the Lord.

5:19, 20 God wants us to view what we have (whether it is much or little) with the right perspective—our possessions are a gift from God. Although they are not the source of joy, they are a

reason to rejoice because every good thing comes from God. We should focus more on the Giver than the gift. We can be content with what we have when we realize that with God we have everything we need.

6:1—8:15 In this section, Solomon shows that having the right attitude about God can help us deal with present injustices. Prosperity is not always good, and adversity is not always bad. But God is always good; if we live as he wants us to, we will be content.

6:1–6 "God does not enable him to enjoy them" probably means that the person has died without being able to enjoy his wealth and honor. Everyone dies, and both rich and poor end up in the grave. Many people work hard to prolong life and improve their physical

6:3
b Job 3:16; Ecc 4:3

3 A man may have a hundred children and live many years; yet no matter how long he lives, if he cannot enjoy his prosperity and does not receive proper burial, I say that a stillborn *b* child is better off than he. 4 It comes without meaning, it departs in darkness, and in darkness its name is shrouded. 5 Though it never saw the sun or knew anything, it has more rest than does that man— 6 even if he lives a thousand years twice over but fails to enjoy his prosperity. Do not all go to the same place?

6:7
c Pr 16:26

6:8
d Ecc 2:15

7 All man's efforts are for his mouth,
    yet his appetite is never satisfied. *c*
8 What advantage has a wise man
    over a fool? *d*
What does a poor man gain
    by knowing how to conduct himself before others?
9 Better what the eye sees
    than the roving of the appetite.
This too is meaningless,
    a chasing after the wind.

10 Whatever exists has already been named,
    and what man is has been known;
no man can contend
    with one who is stronger than he.
11 The more the words,
    the less the meaning,
    and how does that profit anyone?

6:12
e Ps 39:6

12 For who knows what is good for a man in life, during the few and meaningless days he passes through like a shadow? *e* Who can tell him what will happen under the sun after he is gone?

Wisdom

7:1
f Pr 22:1

7

A good name is better than fine perfume, *f*
    and the day of death better than the day of birth.
2 It is better to go to a house of mourning
    than to go to a house of feasting,
for death is the destiny of every man;
    the living should take this to heart.

7:3
g Pr 14:13

3 Sorrow is better than laughter, *g*
    because a sad face is good for the heart.
4 The heart of the wise is in the house of mourning,
    but the heart of fools is in the house of pleasure.

7:5
h Ps 141:5;
Pr 15:31-32

5 It is better to heed a wise man's rebuke *h*
    than to listen to the song of fools.

---

condition. Yet people don't spend nearly as much time or effort on their spiritual health. How shortsighted it is to work hard to extend this life and not take the steps God requires to gain eternal life.

6:6 "All go to the same place" means that everyone dies.

6:9 "The roving of the appetite" refers to wasting time dreaming and wishing for what one doesn't have.

6:10 God knows and directs everything that happens, and he is in complete control over our lives, even though at times it may not seem that way. How foolish it is for us to contend with our Creator, who knows us completely and can see the future. (See also Jeremiah 18:6; Romans 9:19–24.)

6:12 Solomon is stating the profound truth that we cannot predict what the future holds. The only One who knows what will happen after we're gone is God. No human knows the future, so each day must be lived for its own value. Solomon is arguing against the notion that human beings can take charge of their own destiny. In all our plans we should look up to God, not just ahead to the future.

7:1–4 This seems to contradict Solomon's previous advice to eat, drink, and find satisfaction in one's work—to enjoy what God has given. We are to enjoy what we have while we can, but realize that adversity also strikes. Adversity reminds us that life is short, teaches us to live wisely, and refines our character. Christianity and Judaism see value in suffering and sorrow. The Greeks and Romans despised it; Eastern religions seek to live above it; but Christians and Jews see it as a refining fire. Most would agree that we learn more about God from difficult times than from happy times. Do you try to avoid sorrow and suffering at all costs? See your struggles as great opportunities to learn from God.

7:2, 4 Many people avoid thinking about death, refuse to face it, and are reluctant to attend funerals. Solomon is not encouraging us to think morbidly, but he knows that it is helpful to think clearly about death. It reminds us that we still have time to change, time to examine the direction of our lives, and time to confess our sins and find forgiveness from God. Because everyone will eventually die, it makes sense to plan ahead to experience God's mercy rather than his justice.

6 Like the crackling of thorns under the pot,
    so is the laughter[i] of fools.
    This too is meaningless.

7:6
iEcc 2:2

7 Extortion turns a wise man into a fool,
    and a bribe[j] corrupts the heart.

7:7
jEx 23:8; Dt 16:19

8 The end of a matter is better than its beginning,
    and patience[k] is better than pride.

7:8
kPr 14:29

9 Do not be quickly provoked[l] in your spirit,
    for anger resides in the lap of fools.

7:9
lPr 14:17; Jas 1:19

10 Do not say, "Why were the old days better than these?"
    For it is not wise to ask such questions.

11 Wisdom, like an inheritance, is a good thing
    and benefits those who see the sun.
12 Wisdom is a shelter
    as money is a shelter,
    but the advantage of knowledge is this:
    that wisdom preserves the life of its possessor.

13 Consider what God has done:

Who can straighten
    what he has made crooked?[m]
14 When times are good, be happy;
    but when times are bad, consider:
God has made the one
    as well as the other.
Therefore, a man cannot discover
    anything about his future.

7:13
mEcc 1:15

15 In this meaningless life of mine I have seen both of these:

a righteous man perishing in his righteousness,
    and a wicked man living long in his wickedness.[n]
16 Do not be overrighteous,
    neither be overwise—
    why destroy yourself?
17 Do not be overwicked,
    and do not be a fool—
    why die before your time?[o]
18 It is good to grasp the one
    and not let go of the other.
    The man who fears God will avoid all ⌊extremes⌋.[a]

7:15
nEcc 8:12-14

7:17
oPs 55:23

19 Wisdom makes one wise man more powerful[p]
    than ten rulers in a city.

7:19
pEcc 9:13-18

a 18 Or will follow them both

7:7 Money talks, and it can confuse those who would otherwise judge fairly. We hear about bribes given to judges, police officers, and witnesses. Bribes are given to hurt those who tell the truth and help those who oppose it. People who are involved in extortion or take bribes are indeed fools, no matter how wise they thought they were beforehand. It is said that everyone has a price, but those who are truly wise cannot be bought at any price.

7:8 To finish what we start takes hard work, wise guidance, self-discipline, and patience. Anyone with vision can start a big project. But vision without wisdom will result in unfinished projects and goals.

7:14 God allows both good times and bad times to come to everyone. He blends them in our lives in such a way that we can't predict the future or count on human wisdom and power. We usually give ourselves the credit for the good times. Then in bad

times, we tend to blame God without thanking him for the good that comes out of it. When life appears certain and controllable, don't let self-satisfaction or complacency make you too comfortable, or God may allow bad times to drive you back to him. When life seems uncertain and uncontrollable, don't despair—God is in control and will bring good results out of your struggles.

7:16-18 How can a person be too righteous or too wise? This is a warning against religious conceit—legalism or false righteousness. Solomon was saying that some people become overly righteous or wise *in their own eyes* because they are deluded by their own religious acts. They are so rigid or narrow in their views that they lose their sensitivity to the true reason for being good—to honor God. Balance is important. God created us to be whole people who seek his righteousness and goodness. Thus we should avoid both extremes of legalism and immorality.

7:20
q 1Ki 8:46;
2Ch 6:36; Pr 20:9

20 There is not a righteous man on earth
    who does what is right and never sins.q

21 Do not pay attention to every word people say,
    or you may hear your servant cursing you—
22 for you know in your heart
    that many times you yourself have cursed others.

23All this I tested by wisdom and I said,

"I am determined to be wise"—
    but this was beyond me.

7:24
r Job 28:12

24 Whatever wisdom may be,
    it is far off and most profound—
    who can discover it?r

7:25
s Ecc 1:17

25 So I turned my mind to understand,
    to investigate and to search out wisdom and the scheme of things
and to understand the stupidity of wickedness
    and the madness of folly.s

7:26
t Pr 5:3-5

26 I find more bitter than death
    the woman who is a snare,
whose heart is a trap
    and whose hands are chains.
The man who pleases God will escape her,
    but the sinner she will ensnare.t

27"Look," says the Teacher,a "this is what I have discovered:

"Adding one thing to another to discover the scheme of things—
28   while I was still searching
    but not finding—
I found one ⌊upright⌋ man among a thousand,
    but not one ⌊upright⌋ woman among them all.
29 This only have I found:
    God made mankind upright,
    but men have gone in search of many schemes."

8 Who is like the wise man?
    Who knows the explanation of things?
Wisdom brightens a man's face
    and changes its hard appearance.

Obey the King

2 Obey the king's command, I say, because you took an oath before God. 3 Do not be in a hurry to leave the king's presence. Do not stand up for a bad cause, for he will do whatever he pleases. 4 Since a king's word is supreme, who can say to him, "What are you doing?"

a 27 Or *leader of the assembly*

7:23–25 Solomon, the wisest man in the world, confesses how difficult it has been to act and think wisely. He emphasizes that no matter how much we know, some mysteries we will never understand. So thinking you have enough wisdom is a sure sign that you don't.

7:27, 28 Did Solomon think women were not capable of being upright (wise and good)? No, because in the book of Proverbs he personified wisdom as a responsible woman. The point of Solomon's statement is not that women are unwise, but that hardly anyone, man or woman, is upright before God. In his search, Solomon found that goodness and wisdom were almost as scarce among men as among women, even though men were given a religious education program in his culture and women were not. In effect, the verse is saying, "I have found only one in a thousand people who is wise in God's eyes. No, I have found even fewer than that!"

7:29 God created human beings to live uprightly and do what is right. Instead, they have left God's path to follow their own downward road.

8:1 Wisdom is the ability to see life from God's perspective and then to know the best course of action to take. Most people would agree that wisdom is a valuable asset, but how can we acquire it? Proverbs 9:10 teaches that the fear of the Lord (respect and honor) is the beginning of wisdom. Wisdom comes from knowing and trusting God; it is not merely the way to find God. Knowing God will lead to understanding and then to sharing this knowledge with others.

5 Whoever obeys his command will come to no harm,
  and the wise heart will know the proper time and procedure.
6 For there is a proper time and procedure for every matter,ᵘ
  though a man's misery weighs heavily upon him.

8:6
ᵘEcc 3:1

7 Since no man knows the future,
  who can tell him what is to come?
8 No man has power over the wind to contain itᵃ;
  so no one has power over the day of his death.
  As no one is discharged in time of war,
  so wickedness will not release those who practice it.

⁹All this I saw, as I applied my mind to everything done under the sun. There is a time when a man lords it over others to his ownᵇ hurt. ¹⁰Then too, I saw the wicked buried— those who used to come and go from the holy place and receive praiseᶜ in the city where they did this. This too is meaningless.

¹¹When the sentence for a crime is not quickly carried out, the hearts of the people are filled with schemes to do wrong. ¹²Although a wicked man commits a hundred crimes and still lives a long time, I know that it will go betterᵛ with God-fearing men, who are reverent before God. ¹³Yet because the wicked do not fear God, it will not go well with them, and their days will not lengthen like a shadow.

8:12
ᵛPs 37:11,18-19;
Pr 1:32-33;
Isa 3:10-11

¹⁴There is something else meaningless that occurs on earth: righteous men who get what the wicked deserve, and wicked men who get what the righteous deserve.ʷ This too, I say, is meaningless.ˣ ¹⁵So I commend the enjoyment of life, because nothing is better for a man under the sun than to eat and drink and be glad.ʸ Then joy will accompany him in his work all the days of the life God has given him under the sun.

8:14
ʷPs 73:14
ˣEcc 7:15
8:15
ʸEcc 2:24; 3:12-13;
5:18; 9:7

¹⁶When I applied my mind to know wisdom and to observe man's labor on earth—his eyes not seeing sleep day or night— ¹⁷then I saw all that God has done. No one can comprehend what goes on under the sun. Despite all his efforts to search it out, man cannot discover its meaning. Even if a wise man claims he knows, he cannot really comprehend it.ᶻ

8:17
ᶻEcc 3:11;
Ro 11:33

4. Solomon's final conclusion
A Common Destiny for All

9 So I reflected on all this and concluded that the righteous and the wise and what they do are in God's hands, but no man knows whether love or hate awaits him.ᵃ ²All share a common destiny—the righteous and the wicked, the good and the bad,ᵈ the clean and the unclean, those who offer sacrifices and those who do not.

9:1
ᵃEcc 10:14
9:2
ᵇJob 9:22

As it is with the good man,
  so with the sinner;
as it is with those who take oaths,
  so with those who are afraid to take them.ᵇ

³This is the evil in everything that happens under the sun: The same destiny overtakes all. The hearts of men, moreover, are full of evil and there is madness in their hearts while they live, and afterward they join the dead. ⁴Anyone who is among the living has hopeᵉ—even a live dog is better off than a dead lion!

ᵃ8 Or *over his spirit to retain it*   ᵇ9 Or *to their*   ᶜ10 Some Hebrew manuscripts and Septuagint (Aquila); most Hebrew manuscripts *and are forgotten*   ᵈ2 Septuagint (Aquila), Vulgate and Syriac; Hebrew does not have *and the bad.*
ᵉ4 Or *What then is to be chosen? With all who live, there is hope*

8:10 This verse probably refers to how we quickly forget the evil done by some people after they have died. Returning from the cemetery, we praise them in the very city where they did their evil deeds.

8:11 If God doesn't punish us immediately, we must not assume that he doesn't care or that sin has no consequences. When a young child does something wrong and is not punished, that child will be much more likely to repeat the act. But God knows every wrong we commit, and one day we will have to answer for all that we have done (12:14).

8:15 Solomon recalls the remedy for life's unanswered questions. He recommends joy and contentment as encouragement for us along life's pilgrimage. We must accept each day with its daily measure of work, food, and pleasure. Let us learn to enjoy what God has given us to refresh and strengthen us to continue his work.

8:16, 17 Even if he had access to all the world's wisdom, the wisest man would know very little. No one can fully comprehend God and all that he has done, and there are always more questions than answers. But the unknown should not cast a shadow over our joy, faith, or work because we know that someone greater is in control and that we can put our trust in him. Don't let what you don't know about the future destroy the joy God wants to give you today.

9:2 "All share a common destiny" means that all will eventually die.

9:5
c Job 14:21
d Isa 26:14

⁵ For the living know that they will die,
　　but the dead know nothing;c
they have no further reward,
　　and even the memory of them is forgotten.d
⁶ Their love, their hate
　　and their jealousy have long since vanished;
never again will they have a part
　　in anything that happens under the sun.

9:7
e Ecc 8:15

⁷ Go, eat your food with gladness, and drink your wine with a joyful heart,e for it is now that God favors what you do. ⁸ Always be clothed in white, and always anoint your head with oil. ⁹ Enjoy life with your wife, whom you love, all the days of this meaningless life that God has given you under the sun—all your meaningless days. For this is your lot in life and in your toilsome labor under the sun. ¹⁰ Whatever your hand finds to do, do it with all your might, for in the grave,a where you are going, there is neither working nor planning nor knowledge nor wisdom.

9:11
f Am 2:14-15

¹¹ I have seen something else under the sun:

The race is not to the swift
　　or the battle to the strong,f
nor does food come to the wise
　　or wealth to the brilliant
　　or favor to the learned;
but time and chance happen to them all.

9:12
g Pr 29:6
h Ecc 8:7

¹² Moreover, no man knows when his hour will come:

As fish are caught in a cruel net,
　　or birds are taken in a snare,
so men are trapped by evil timesg
　　that fall unexpectedly upon them.h

Wisdom Better Than Folly

¹³ I also saw under the sun this example of wisdom that greatly impressed me: ¹⁴ There was once a small city with only a few people in it. And a powerful king came against it, surrounded it and built huge siegeworks against it. ¹⁵ Now there lived in that city a man poor but wise, and he saved the city by his wisdom. But nobody remembered that poor man. ¹⁶ So I said, "Wisdom is better than strength." But the poor man's wisdom is despised, and his words are no longer heeded.i

9:16
i Pr 21:22; Ecc 7:19

¹⁷ The quiet words of the wise are more to be heeded
　　than the shouts of a ruler of fools.

a 10 Hebrew *Sheol*

9:5, 10 When Solomon says the dead know nothing and that there is no work, planning, knowledge, or wisdom in death, he is not contrasting life with afterlife, but life with death. After you die, you can't change what you have done. Resurrection to a new life after death was a vague concept for Old Testament believers. It was only made clear after Jesus rose from the dead.

9:7-10 Considering the uncertainties of the future and the certainty of death, Solomon recommends enjoying life as God's gift. He may have been criticizing those who put off all present pleasures in order to accumulate wealth, much like those who get caught up in today's rat race. Solomon asks, "What is your wealth really worth, anyway?" Because the future is so uncertain, we should enjoy God's gifts while we are able.

9:8 Wearing white clothes and having oil on the head were signs of happiness and celebration.

9:9 Solomon also wrote a proverb about marriage. "He who finds a wife finds what is good and receives favor from the LORD" (Proverbs 18:22). How sad it would be to be married and not appreciate the enjoyment and companionship God has given you.

9:10, 11 It isn't difficult to think of cases where the swiftest or the strongest don't win, the wise go hungry, and the intelligent are unrewarded with wealth or honor. Some people see such examples and call life unfair, and they are right. The world is finite, and sin has twisted life, making it what God did not intend. Solomon is trying to reduce our expectations. The book of Proverbs emphasizes how life would go if everyone acted fairly; Ecclesiastes explains what usually happens in our sinful and imperfect world. We must keep our perspective. Don't let the inequities of life keep you from earnest, dedicated work. We serve God, not people (see Colossians 3:23).

9:13-18 Our society honors wealth, attractiveness, and success above wisdom. Yet wisdom is a greater asset than strength, although it is often unrecognized by the masses. Even though it is more effective, wisdom is not always heard, and wise people often go unheeded. From this parable we can learn to be receptive to wisdom, no matter who it comes from.

18 Wisdom/ is better than weapons of war,
    but one sinner destroys much good.

9:18
/ver 16

10 As dead flies give perfume a bad smell,
    so a little folly outweighs wisdom and honor.
2 The heart of the wise inclines to the right,
    but the heart of the fool to the left.
3 Even as he walks along the road,
    the fool lacks sense
    and shows everyone*k* how stupid he is.

10:3
kPr 13:16; 18:2

4 If a ruler's anger rises against you,
    do not leave your post;*l*
    calmness can lay great errors to rest.*m*

10:4
lEcc 8:3
mPr 25:15

5 There is an evil I have seen under the sun,
    the sort of error that arises from a ruler:
6 Fools are put in many high positions,
    while the rich occupy the low ones.
7 I have seen slaves on horseback,
    while princes go on foot like slaves.*n*

10:7
nPr 19:10

8 Whoever digs a pit may fall into it;*o*
    whoever breaks through a wall may be bitten by a snake.

10:8
oPs 7:15; Pr 26:27

9 Whoever quarries stones may be injured by them;
    whoever splits logs may be endangered by them.

10 If the ax is dull
    and its edge unsharpened,
    more strength is needed
    but skill will bring success.

11 If a snake bites before it is charmed,
    there is no profit for the charmer.*p*

10:11
pPs 58:5

12 Words from a wise man's mouth are gracious,*q*
    but a fool is consumed by his own lips.*r*

10:12
qPr 10:32
rPr 10:14

13 At the beginning his words are folly;
    at the end they are wicked madness—
14   and the fool multiplies words.*s*

10:14
sPr 15:2; Ecc 8:7

No one knows what is coming—
    who can tell him what will happen after him?

15 A fool's work wearies him;
    he does not know the way to town.

16 Woe to you, O land whose king was a servant*a t*
    and whose princes feast in the morning.

10:16
tIsa 3:4-5,12

17 Blessed are you, O land whose king is of noble birth
    and whose princes eat at a proper time—
    for strength and not for drunkenness.*u*

10:17
uPr 31:4

a 16 Or king is a child

10:4 This proverb has implications for employer/employee relationships. Employees should ride out the temper tantrums of their employer. If we quietly do our work and don't get upset, the employer will probably get over his or her anger and calm down.

10:5–7 By describing these circumstances that aren't fair or don't make sense, Solomon is saying that wisdom alone can't bring justice. Solomon continues to build to his conclusion that everything we have (from wisdom to riches) is nothing without God. But when God uses what little we have, it becomes all we could ever want or need.

10:10 Trying to do anything without the necessary skills or tools is like chopping wood with a dull ax. If your tool is dull, you should sharpen it to do a better job. Similarly, if you lack skills, you should sharpen them through training and practice. In each situation, sharpening the ax means recognizing where a problem exists, acquiring or honing the skills (or tools) to do the job better, and then going out and doing it. Find the areas of your life where your "ax" is dull, and sharpen your skills so you can be more effective for God's work.

10:16–18 When the Israelites had immature and irresponsible leaders, their nation fell. The books of 1 and 2 Kings describe the decline of the kingdoms when the leaders were concerned only about themselves. These verses pinpoint the basic problems of these leaders—selfishness and laziness.

¹⁸ If a man is lazy, the rafters sag;
　　if his hands are idle, the house leaks.

¹⁹ A feast is made for laughter,
　　and wine makes life merry,
　　but money is the answer for everything.

10:20
ᵛEx 22:28

²⁰ Do not revile the king ᵛ even in your thoughts,
　　or curse the rich in your bedroom,
　　because a bird of the air may carry your words,
　　and a bird on the wing may report what you say.

Bread Upon the Waters

11:1
ʷPr 19:17; Mt 10:42

11 Cast your bread upon the waters,
　　for after many days you will find it again.ʷ
² Give portions to seven, yes to eight,
　　for you do not know what disaster may come upon the land.

³ If clouds are full of water,
　　they pour rain upon the earth.
Whether a tree falls to the south or to the north,
　　in the place where it falls, there will it lie.
⁴ Whoever watches the wind will not plant;
　　whoever looks at the clouds will not reap.

11:5
ˣJn 3:8-10
ʸPs 139:14-16

⁵ As you do not know the path of the wind,ˣ
　　or how the body is formedᵃ in a mother's womb,ʸ
so you cannot understand the work of God,
　　the Maker of all things.

⁶ Sow your seed in the morning,
　　and at evening let not your hands be idle,
for you do not know which will succeed,
　　whether this or that,
　　or whether both will do equally well.

Remember Your Creator While Young

11:7
ᶻEcc 7:11

⁷ Light is sweet,
　　and it pleases the eyes to see the sun.ᶻ
⁸ However many years a man may live,
　　let him enjoy them all.
But let him remember the days of darkness,
　　for they will be many.
　　Everything to come is meaningless.

ᵃ5 Or *know how life* (or *the spirit*) / *enters the body being formed*

10:19 Government leaders, businesses, families, even churches get trapped into thinking money can meet all their needs. We throw money at our problems. But just as the thrill of wine is only temporary, the soothing effect of the last purchase soon wears off and we have to buy more. Scripture recognizes that money is necessary for survival, but it warns against the love of money (see Matthew 6:24; 1 Timothy 6:10; Hebrews 13:5). Money is dangerous because it deceives us into thinking that wealth is the easiest way to get everything we want. The love of money is sinful because we trust money rather than God to solve our problems. Those who pursue its empty promises will one day discover that they have nothing because they are spiritually bankrupt.

11:1–5 In these verses Solomon summarizes that life involves both risk and opportunity. Because life has no guarantees, we must be prepared. Solomon does not support a despairing attitude. Just because life is uncertain does not mean we should do nothing. We need a spirit of trust and adventure, facing life's risks and opportunities with God-directed enthusiasm and faith.

11:4 Waiting for perfect conditions will mean inactivity. This practical insight is especially applicable to our spiritual lives. If we wait for the perfect time and place for personal Bible reading, we will never begin. If we wait for a perfect church, we will never join. If we wait for the perfect ministry, we will never serve. Take steps now to grow spiritually. Don't wait for conditions that may never exist.

11:7, 8 Solomon is no dreary pessimist in 11:7—12:14. He encourages us to rejoice in every day but to remember that eternity is far longer than a person's life span. Psalm 90:12 says, "Teach us to number our days aright, that we may gain a heart of wisdom." The wise person does not just think about the moment and its impact; he or she takes the long-range view toward eternity. Approach your decisions with God's perspective—consider their impact ten years from now and into eternity. Live with the attitude that although our lives are short, we will live with God forever.

9 Be happy, young man, while you are young,
and let your heart give you joy in the days of your youth.
Follow the ways of your heart
and whatever your eyes see,
but know that for all these things
God will bring you to judgment.*a*
10 So then, banish anxiety from your heart
and cast off the troubles of your body,
for youth and vigor are meaningless.

11:9
a Ecc 12:14

12

Remember*b* your Creator
in the days of your youth,
before the days of trouble come
and the years approach when you will say,
"I find no pleasure in them"—
2 before the sun and the light
and the moon and the stars grow dark,
and the clouds return after the rain;
3 when the keepers of the house tremble,
and the strong men stoop,
when the grinders cease because they are few,
and those looking through the windows grow dim;
4 when the doors to the street are closed
and the sound of grinding fades;
when men rise up at the sound of birds,
but all their songs grow faint;
5 when men are afraid of heights
and of dangers in the streets;
when the almond tree blossoms
and the grasshopper drags himself along
and desire no longer is stirred.
Then man goes to his eternal home*c*
and mourners*d* go about the streets.

6 Remember him—before the silver cord is severed,
or the golden bowl is broken;
before the pitcher is shattered at the spring,
or the wheel broken at the well,
7 and the dust returns*e* to the ground it came from,
and the spirit returns to God*f* who gave it.*g*

8 "Meaningless! Meaningless!" says the Teacher.*a*
"Everything is meaningless!"

a 8 Or *the leader of the assembly; also in verses 9 and 10*

12:1
b Ecc 11:8

12:5
c Job 17:13
d Jer 9:17

12:7
e Ge 3:19;
Job 34:15
f Ecc 3:21
g Zec 12:1

11:9, 10 People often say, "It doesn't matter." But many of a person's choices will be irreversible—they will affect that person for a lifetime. What you do when you're young *does* matter. Enjoy life now, but don't do anything physically, morally, or spiritually that will prevent you from enjoying life when you are old.

12:1 A life without God can produce a bitter, lonely, and hopeless old age. A life centered around God is fulfilling; it will make the "days of trouble"—when disabilities, sickness, and handicaps cause barriers to enjoying life—satisfying because of the hope of eternal life. Being young is exciting. But the excitement of youth can become a barrier to closeness with God if it makes young people focus on passing pleasures instead of eternal values. Make your strength available to God when it is still yours—during your youthful years. Don't waste it on evil or meaningless activities that become bad habits and make you callous. Seek God now.

12:6–8 The silver cord, golden bowl, pitcher, and wheel symbolize life's fragility. How easily death comes to us; how swiftly and unexpectedly we can return to the dust from which we came. Therefore, we should recognize life as a precious resource to be used wisely and not squandered frivolously.

12:7, 8 Stripped of God's Spirit, our bodies return to dust. Stripped of God's purpose, our work is in vain. Stripped of God's love, our service is futile. We must put God first over all we do and in all we do because without him we have nothing. Knowing that life is futile without God motivates the wise person to seek God first.

The Conclusion of the Matter

12:9
h 1Ki 4:32

9 Not only was the Teacher wise, but also he imparted knowledge to the people. He pondered and searched out and set in order many proverbs. *h* 10 The Teacher searched to find just the right words, and what he wrote was upright and true.

11 The words of the wise are like goads, their collected sayings like firmly embedded nails—given by one Shepherd. 12 Be warned, my son, of anything in addition to them.

12:12
i Ecc 1:18

Of making many books there is no end, and much study wearies the body. *i*

12:13
j Dt 10:12

13 Now all has been heard;
here is the conclusion of the matter:
Fear God and keep his commandments, *j*
for this is the whole ⌊duty⌋ of man.

12:14
k 1Co 4:5

14 For God will bring every deed into judgment,
including every hidden thing, *k*
whether it is good or evil.

12:11 A goad (also called an oxgoad) was a sharp metal tip attached to a handle and used to keep oxen or cattle moving. Like a goad, a wise word or important truth might be unpleasant when first applied, but it will keep us moving in God's direction.

12:12 There are endless opinions about life and philosophies about how we should live that could be read and studied forever. It is not wrong to study these opinions, but we should spend the majority of our time feeding on the truth of God's Word. Wisdom should lead to action. Wise students of the Bible will understand and do what they are taught. Because our time on earth is so short, we should use it to learn important truths—they affect this life and eternity.

12:13, 14 In his conclusion, Solomon presents his antidotes for the two main ailments presented in this book. Those who lack purpose and direction in life should fear God and keep his commandments. Those who think life is unfair should remember that God will review every person's life to determine how he or she has responded to him, and he will bring every deed into judgment. Have you committed your life to God, both present and future? Does your life measure up to his standards?

12:13, 14 The book of Ecclesiastes cannot be interpreted correctly without reading these final verses. No matter what the mysteries and apparent contradictions of life are, we must work toward the single purpose of knowing God.

In Ecclesiastes, Solomon shows us that we should enjoy life, but this does not exempt us from obeying God's commandments. We should search for purpose and meaning in life, but they cannot be found in human endeavors. We should acknowledge the evil, foolishness, and injustice in life, yet maintain a positive attitude and strong faith in God.

All people will have to stand before God and be judged for what they did in this life. We will not be able to use life's inconsistencies as an excuse for failing to live properly. To live properly, we need to (1) recognize that human effort apart from God is futile; (2) put God first—now; (3) receive everything good as a gift from God; (4) realize that God will judge both evil and good; (5) know that God will judge the quality of every person's life. How strange that people spend their lives striving for the very enjoyment that God gives freely.

SONG OF SONGS

VITAL STATISTICS

PURPOSE:
To tell of the love between a bridegroom (King Solomon) and his bride, to affirm the sanctity of marriage, and to picture God's love for his people

AUTHOR:
Solomon

DATE WRITTEN:
Probably early in Solomon's reign

SETTING:
Israel—the Shulammite woman's garden and the king's palace

KEY VERSE:
"I am my lover's and my lover is mine; he browses among the lilies" (6:3).

KEY PEOPLE:
King Solomon, the Shulammite woman, and friends

SATURATED with stories of sexual escapades, secret rendezvous, and extramarital affairs, today's media teach that immorality means freedom, perversion is natural, and commitment is old-fashioned. Sex, created by God and pronounced good in Eden, has been twisted, exploited, and turned into an urgent, illicit, casual, and self-gratifying activity. Love has turned into lust, giving into getting, and lasting commitment into "no strings attached."

In reality, sexual intercourse, the physical and emotional union of male and female, should be a holy means of celebrating love, producing children, and experiencing pleasure, protected by the commitment of marriage.

God thinks sex is important, and Scripture contains numerous guidelines for its use and warnings about its misuse. And sex is always mentioned in the context of a loving relationship between husband and wife. Perhaps the highlight of this is Song of Songs, the intimate story of a man and a woman, their love, courtship, and marriage. Solomon probably wrote this "song" in his youth, before being overtaken by his own obsession with women, sex, and pleasure.

A moving story, drama, and poem, Song of Songs features the love dialogue between a simple Jewish maiden (the Shulammite woman) and her lover (Solomon, the king). They describe in intimate detail their feelings for each other and their longings to be together. Throughout the dialogue, sex and marriage are put in their proper, God-given perspective.

Much debate has raged over the meaning of this song. Some say it is an allegory of God's love for Israel or for the church. Others say it is a literal story about married love. In reality, it is both—a historical story with two layers of meaning. On one level, we learn about love, marriage, and sex; and on the other level, we see God's overwhelming love for his people. As you read Song of Songs, remember that you are loved by God, and commit yourself to seeing life, sex, and marriage from his point of view.

THE BLUEPRINT

1. The wedding day (1:1—2:7)
2. Memories of courtship (2:8—3:5)
3. Memories of engagement (3:6—5:1)
4. A troubling dream (5:2—6:3)
5. Praising the bride's beauty (6:4—7:9a)
6. The bride's tender appeal (7:9b—8:4)
7. The power of love (8:5–14)

Song of Songs is a wedding song honoring marriage. The most explicit statements on sex in the Bible can be found in this book. It has often been criticized down through the centuries because of its sensuous language. The purity and sacredness of love represented here, however, are greatly needed in our day in which distorted attitudes about love and marriage are commonplace. God created sex and intimacy, and they are holy and good when enjoyed within marriage. A husband and wife honor God when they love and enjoy each other.

MEGATHEMES

THEME	EXPLANATION	IMPORTANCE
Sex	Sex is God's gift to his creatures. He endorses sex but restricts its expression to a man and a woman who are committed to each other in marriage.	God wants sex to be motivated by love and commitment, not lust. It is for mutual pleasure, not selfish enjoyment.

Love	As the relationship developed, the beauty and wonder of a romance unfolded between Solomon and his bride. The intense power of love affected the hearts, minds, and bodies of the two lovers.	Because love is such a powerful expression of feeling and commitment between a man and a woman, it is not to be regarded casually. We are not to manipulate others into loving us, and love should not be prematurely encouraged in a relationship.
Commitment	The power of love requires more than the language of feeling to protect it. Sexual expression is such an integral part of our selfhood that we need the boundary of marriage to safeguard our love. Marriage is the celebration of daily commitment between a husband and wife.	While romance keeps a marriage interesting, commitment keeps romance from dwindling away. The decision to commit yourself to your spouse alone *begins* at the marriage altar. It must be maintained day by day.
Beauty	The two lovers praise the beauty they see in each other. The language they use shows the spontaneity and mystery of love. Praise should not be limited to physical beauty; beautiful personality and moral purity should also be praised.	Our love for someone makes him or her appear beautiful to us. As you consider marriage, don't just look for physical attractiveness in a person. Look for the inner qualities that don't fade with time—spiritual commitment, integrity, sensitivity, and sincerity.
Problems	Over time, feelings of loneliness, indifference, and isolation came between Solomon and his bride. During those times, love grew cold, and barriers were raised.	Through careful communication, lovers can be reconciled, commitment can be renewed, and romance refreshed. Don't let walls come between you and your spouse. Take care of problems while they are still small.

1. The wedding day

1 Solomon's Song of Songs. *a*

1:1
a 1Ki 4:32

Beloved *a*

1:2
b SS 4:10

2 Let him kiss me with the kisses of his mouth—
    for your love *b* is more delightful than wine.
3 Pleasing is the fragrance of your perfumes;
    your name is like perfume poured out.
    No wonder the maidens love you!

1:4
c Ps 45:15

4 Take me away with you—let us hurry!
    Let the king bring me into his chambers. *c*

a Primarily on the basis of the gender of the Hebrew pronouns used, male and female speakers are indicated in the margins by the captions *Lover* and *Beloved* respectively. The words of others are marked *Friends.* In some instances the divisions and their captions are debatable.

1:1 Solomon, a son of King David, became king and was chosen by God to build the temple in Jerusalem. God gave him extraordinary wisdom. Much of Solomon's reign was characterized by wisdom and reverence for God although, toward the end of his life, he became proud and turned from God. Read about Solomon in 1 Kings 1—11 and 1 Chronicles 28—2 Chronicles 9. Solomon wrote and collected more than 3,000 proverbs (see the book of Proverbs) and over 1,000 songs, one of which is this book, Song of Songs. His Profile is found in 1 Kings 4, p. 503.

1:1ff Solomon frequently visited the various parts of his kingdom. One day, as he was visiting some royal vineyards in the north, his royal entourage came by surprise upon a beautiful peasant woman tending the vines. Embarrassed, she ran from them. But Solomon could not forget her. Later, disguised as a shepherd, he returned to the vineyards and won her love. Then, he revealed his true identity and asked her to return to Jerusalem with him. Solomon and his beloved are being married in the palace as this book begins.

The Song of Songs is a series of seven poems, not necessarily in chronological order. It reflects upon the first meeting of Solomon and the peasant woman, their engagement, their wedding, their wedding night, and the growth of their marriage after the wedding.

1:1ff This book features three characters or groups of characters: the girl (the "beloved"), Solomon (the "lover"), and "friends." The girl who caught Solomon's attention may have been from Shunem, a farming community about 60 miles north of Jerusalem. Her tanned skin indicates that she probably worked outside in the vineyards (1:6)—thus she may not have been from the upper class. The friends include either members of Solomon's harem or workers in the palace, as well as the girl's brothers (as in 8:8, 9).

1:1–4 This vivid description of a love relationship begins with a picture of love itself. Love is "more delightful than wine"; it makes the lovers rejoice. Acts 10:9–16 teaches that what God has created and cleansed we should not misuse or call common. We can enjoy love. God created it as a gift to us and a delight for all our senses.

Friends

> We rejoice and delight in you[a];
>> we will praise your love more than wine.

Beloved

> How right they are to adore you!

> 5 Dark am I, yet lovely,
>> O daughters of Jerusalem,
>> dark like the tents of Kedar,
>> like the tent curtains of Solomon.[b]
> 6 Do not stare at me because I am dark,
>> because I am darkened by the sun.
> My mother's sons were angry with me
>> and made me take care of the vineyards;
>> my own vineyard I have neglected.
> 7 Tell me, you whom I love, where you graze your flock
>> and where you rest your sheep at midday.
> Why should I be like a veiled woman
>> beside the flocks of your friends?

Friends

> 8 If you do not know, most beautiful of women,[d]
>> follow the tracks of the sheep
> and graze your young goats
>> by the tents of the shepherds.

1:8
[d]SS 5:9

Lover

> 9 I liken you, my darling, to a mare
>> harnessed to one of the chariots[e] of Pharaoh.
> 10 Your cheeks are beautiful with earrings,
>> your neck with strings of jewels.
> 11 We will make you earrings of gold,
>> studded with silver.

1:9
[e]2Ch 1:17

Beloved

> 12 While the king was at his table,
>> my perfume spread its fragrance.
> 13 My lover is to me a sachet of myrrh
>> resting between my breasts.
> 14 My lover is to me a cluster of henna blossoms
>> from the vineyards of En Gedi.

Lover

> 15 How beautiful you are, my darling!
>> Oh, how beautiful!
>> Your eyes are doves.[f]

1:15
[f]SS 4:1; 5:2,12

a4 The Hebrew is masculine singular.   **b**5 Or *Salma*

1:5 Kedar was a nomadic community in northern Arabia. It was known for its tents that were woven from black goat hair.

1:6 The vineyard mentioned here was apparently owned by Solomon (because he came to visit it) and leased to the girl's step-brothers (her "mother's sons"), who made her take care of the vineyards in the hot sun. Thus she could not take care of her own skin ("my own vineyard I have neglected"). When she was brought to Jerusalem, the young girl was embarrassed about her tanned complexion because the girls in the city had the fair, delicate skin that was considered much more beautiful. But Solomon loved her dark skin.

1:7 The girl felt insecure at being different from the women of

Jerusalem (1:6) and at being alone while her lover was away (1:7). She longed for the security of his presence. The basis of true love is commitment; so in a relationship built on genuine love, there is never any fear of deceit, manipulation, or exploitation.

1:14 En Gedi was an oasis hidden at the base of rugged limestone cliffs west of the Dead Sea. It was known for its fruitful palm trees and fragrant balsam oil. The terrain surrounding En Gedi was some of the most desolate in Palestine and had an extremely hot desert climate. The henna blossoms in En Gedi would have appeared all the more beautiful because of their stark surroundings; thus Solomon was complimenting his beloved's beauty and comparing her favorably with the women she feared.

Beloved

16 How handsome you are, my lover!
   Oh, how charming!
   And our bed is verdant.

Lover

17 The beams of our house are cedars;
   our rafters are firs.

Beloved[a]

2

   I am a rose[b] of Sharon,
      a lily of the valleys.

Lover

2 Like a lily among thorns
   is my darling among the maidens.

Beloved

3 Like an apple tree among the trees of the forest
      is my lover among the young men.
   I delight to sit in his shade,
      and his fruit is sweet to my taste.
4 He has taken me to the banquet hall,
      and his banner over me is love.
5 Strengthen me with raisins,
      refresh me with apples,
   for I am faint with love.
6 His left arm is under my head,
      and his right arm embraces me.[g]
7 Daughters of Jerusalem, I charge you
      by the gazelles and by the does of the field:
   Do not arouse or awaken love
      until it so desires.[h]

2. Memories of courtship

8 Listen! My lover!
   Look! Here he comes,
   leaping across the mountains,
      bounding over the hills.
9 My lover is like a gazelle or a young stag.[i]
   Look! There he stands behind our wall,
      gazing through the windows,
      peering through the lattice.
10 My lover spoke and said to me,
   "Arise, my darling,
      my beautiful one, and come with me.
11 See! The winter is past;
      the rains are over and gone.

2:6
g SS 8:3

2:7
h SS 3:5; 8:4

2:9
i ver 17

aOr *Lover*   b1 Possibly a member of the crocus family

1:16, 17 The lover and his beloved describe their woodland surroundings as a wedding bedroom.

2:1 The rose of Sharon and lily of the valleys were flowers commonly found in Israel. Perhaps the girl was saying, "I'm not so special; I'm just an ordinary flower," to which Solomon replied, "Oh, no, you are extraordinary—a lily among thorns." Solomon used the language of love. Nothing is more vital than encouraging and appreciating the person you love. Be sure to tell your spouse "I love you" every day, and show that love by your actions.

2:7 Feelings of love can create intimacy that overpowers reason. Young people are too often in a hurry to develop an intimate relationship based on their strong feelings. But feelings aren't enough to support a lasting relationship. This verse encourages us not to force romance lest the feelings of love grow faster than the commitment needed to make love last. Patiently wait for feelings of love and commitment to develop together.

2:8—3:5 In this section Solomon's beloved reflects on her courtship with Solomon, remembering the first day they met and recalling one of her dreams about their being together.

12 Flowers appear on the earth;
    the season of singing has come,
the cooing of doves
    is heard in our land.
13 The fig tree forms its early fruit;
    the blossoming vines spread their fragrance.
Arise, come, my darling;
    my beautiful one, come with me."

Lover

14 My dove in the clefts of the rock,
    in the hiding places on the mountainside,
show me your face,
    let me hear your voice;
for your voice is sweet,
    and your face is lovely.*j*
15 Catch for us the foxes,
    the little foxes
that ruin the vineyards,
    our vineyards that are in bloom.

Beloved

16 My lover is mine and I am his;*k*
    he browses among the lilies.*l*
17 Until the day breaks
    and the shadows flee,
turn, my lover,
    and be like a gazelle
or like a young stag*m*
    on the rugged hills.*a*

3 All night long on my bed
    I looked for the one my heart loves;
    I looked for him but did not find him.
2 I will get up now and go about the city,
    through its streets and squares;
I will search for the one my heart loves.
    So I looked for him but did not find him.
3 The watchmen found me
    as they made their rounds in the city.*n*
"Have you seen the one my heart loves?"
4 Scarcely had I passed them
    when I found the one my heart loves.
I held him and would not let him go
    till I had brought him to my mother's house,
    to the room of the one who conceived me.
5 Daughters of Jerusalem, I charge you*o*
    by the gazelles and by the does of the field:
Do not arouse or awaken love
    until it so desires.*p*

2:14
*j*SS 1:5; 8:13

2:16
*k*SS 7:10
*l*SS 6:3

2:17
*m*ver 9

3:3
*n*SS 5:7

3:5
*o*SS 2:7
*p*SS 8:4

a 17 Or *the hills of Bether*

2:12, 13 The lovers celebrated their joy in the creation and in their love. God created the world, the beauty we see, the joy of love and sex, and he gave us senses to enjoy them. Never let problems, conflicts, or the ravages of time ruin your ability to enjoy God's gifts. Take time to enjoy the world God has created.

2:15 "The little foxes" are an example of the kinds of problems that can disturb or destroy a relationship. The lovers wanted anything that could potentially cause problems between them to be removed. Often the "little foxes" cause the biggest prob-

lems in marriage. These irritations must not be minimized or ignored, but identified so that, together, the couple can deal with them.

3:1–4 Many scholars agree that in these verses the girl is recalling a dream that caused her to become so concerned about her lover's whereabouts that she arose in the middle of the night to search for him. When you love someone, you will do all you can to ensure the safety of that person and care for his or her needs, even at a cost to your personal comfort. This

3. Memories of engagement

3:6
qSS 8:5

6 Who is this coming up from the desert q
   like a column of smoke,
perfumed with myrrh and incense
   made from all the spices of the merchant?
7 Look! It is Solomon's carriage,
   escorted by sixty warriors,
   the noblest of Israel,
8 all of them wearing the sword,
   all experienced in battle,
each with his sword at his side,
   prepared for the terrors of the night.
9 King Solomon made for himself the carriage;
   he made it of wood from Lebanon.
10 Its posts he made of silver,
   its base of gold.
Its seat was upholstered with purple,
   its interior lovingly inlaid
by a the daughters of Jerusalem.
11 Come out, you daughters of Zion,
   and look at King Solomon wearing the crown,
   the crown with which his mother crowned him
on the day of his wedding,
   the day his heart rejoiced.

Lover

4

4:1
rSS 1:15; 5:12
sSS 6:5

How beautiful you are, my darling!
   Oh, how beautiful!
   Your eyes behind your veil are doves. r
Your hair is like a flock of goats
   descending from Mount Gilead. s

4:2
tSS 6:6

2 Your teeth are like a flock of sheep just shorn,
   coming up from the washing.
Each has its twin;
   not one of them is alone. t

4:3
uSS 6:7

3 Your lips are like a scarlet ribbon;
   your mouth is lovely.
Your temples behind your veil
   are like the halves of a pomegranate. u

4:4
vSS 7:4

4 Your neck is like the tower v of David,
   built with elegance b;
on it hang a thousand shields,
   all of them shields of warriors.

4:5
wSS 7:3

5 Your two breasts w are like two fawns,
   like twin fawns of a gazelle
   that browse among the lilies.

a 10 Or *its inlaid interior a gift of love / from*   b 4 The meaning of the Hebrew for this word is uncertain.

---

shows up most often in small actions—walking upstairs to get your spouse a glass of water, leaving work early to attend some function your child is involved in, or sacrificing your personal comfort to tend to the needs of a friend.

3:6—5:1 Here the scene changes. Some believe that the wedding procession is described in 3:6–11, the wedding night in 4:1—5:1, and the consummation of the marriage in 4:16—5:1. Another possible explanation is that the period of Solomon's engagement to the girl is being remembered. In the previous section (2:8—3:5), Solomon and the girl fell in love. In this section, Solomon returns to the girl in all his royal splendor (3:6–11), expresses his great love for her (4:1–5), and then

proposes (4:7–15). The girl accepts (4:16), and Solomon responds to her acceptance (5:1).

3:7, 9 Solomon's carriage was probably a covered and curtained couch used for carrying a single passenger on the shoulders of men.

4:1–7 We feel like awkward onlookers when we read this intensely private and intimate exchange. In the ecstasy of their love, the lovers praise each other using beautiful imagery. Their words may seem strange to readers from a different culture, but their intense feelings of love and admiration are universal. Communicating love and expressing admiration in both words and actions can enhance every marriage.

6 Until the day breaks
 and the shadows flee,^x
I will go to the mountain of myrrh
 and to the hill of incense.
7 All beautiful you are, my darling;
 there is no flaw in you.

8 Come with me from Lebanon, my bride,
 come with me from Lebanon.
Descend from the crest of Amana,
 from the top of Senir,^y the summit of Hermon,
from the lions' dens
 and the mountain haunts of the leopards.
9 You have stolen my heart, my sister, my bride;
 you have stolen my heart
with one glance of your eyes,
 with one jewel of your necklace.
10 How delightful is your love, my sister, my bride!
 How much more pleasing is your love than wine,
 and the fragrance of your perfume than any spice!
11 Your lips drop sweetness as the honeycomb, my bride;
 milk and honey are under your tongue.
 The fragrance of your garments is like that of Lebanon.
12 You are a garden locked up, my sister, my bride;
 you are a spring enclosed, a sealed fountain.
13 Your plants are an orchard of pomegranates
 with choice fruits,
 with henna and nard,
14 nard and saffron,
 calamus and cinnamon,
 with every kind of incense tree,
 with myrrh and aloes
 and all the finest spices.
15 You are^a a garden fountain,
 a well of flowing water
 streaming down from Lebanon.

Beloved

16 Awake, north wind,
 and come, south wind!
Blow on my garden,
 that its fragrance may spread abroad.
Let my lover come into his garden
 and taste its choice fruits.^z

Lover

5 I have come into my garden, my sister, my bride;
 I have gathered my myrrh with my spice.
I have eaten my honeycomb and my honey;
 I have drunk my wine and my milk.^a

^a 15 Or I am (spoken by the Beloved)

4:6
^xSS 2:17

4:8
^yDt 3:9

4:16
^zSS 5:1

5:1
^aSS 4:11

4:12 In comparing his bride to a locked garden, Solomon is praising her virginity. Virginity, considered old-fashioned by many in today's culture, has always been God's plan for unmarried people—and with good reason. Sex without marriage is cheap. It cannot compare with the joy of giving yourself completely to the one who is totally committed to you.

4:15 Solomon's bride was as refreshing to him as a fountain. Could your spouse say the same about you? Sometimes the familiarity that comes with marriage causes us to forget the over-whelming feelings of love and refreshment we shared at the beginning. Many marriages could use a course in "refreshing." Do you refresh your spouse, or are you a burden of complaints, sorrows, and problems? Partners in marriage should continually work at refreshing each other by an encouraging word, an unexpected gift, a change of pace, a surprise call or note, or even a withholding of a discussion of some problem until the proper time. Your spouse needs you to be a haven of refreshment because the rest of the world usually isn't.

Friends

Eat, O friends, and drink;
   drink your fill, O lovers.

4. A troubling dream
Beloved

2 I slept but my heart was awake.
   Listen! My lover is knocking:
"Open to me, my sister, my darling,
   my dove, my flawless one.
My head is drenched with dew,
   my hair with the dampness of the night."
3 I have taken off my robe—
   must I put it on again?
I have washed my feet—
   must I soil them again?
4 My lover thrust his hand through the latch-opening;
   my heart began to pound for him.
5 I arose to open for my lover,
   and my hands dripped with myrrh,
my fingers with flowing myrrh,
   on the handles of the lock.

5:6
*b*SS 3:1

6 I opened for my lover,
   but my lover had left; he was gone.
   My heart sank at his departure.*a*
I looked*b* for him but did not find him.
   I called him but he did not answer.

5:7
*c*SS 3:3

7 The watchmen found me
   as they made their rounds in the city.*c*
They beat me, they bruised me;
   they took away my cloak,
   those watchmen of the walls!
8 O daughters of Jerusalem, I charge you—
   if you find my lover,
what will you tell him?
   Tell him I am faint with love.

Friends

5:9
*d*SS 1:8

9 How is your beloved better than others,
   most beautiful of women?*d*
How is your beloved better than others,
   that you charge us so?

Beloved

10 My lover is radiant and ruddy,
   outstanding among ten thousand.

*a*6 Or *heart had gone out to him when he spoke*

5:2ff This new section tells how the couple's marriage grew and matured in spite of problems. Some time had passed since the wedding, and the girl felt as though some indifference had developed in their relationship. She had become cool to her husband's advances, and by the time she changed her mind and responded to him, he had left. Her self-centeredness and impatience, though brief, caused separation. But she quickly moved to correct the problem by searching for her husband (5:6–8).

5:2–8 Inevitably, with the passing of time and the growth of familiarity, a marriage will start to lose its initial sparkle. Glances and touches no longer produce the same emotional response. Conflicts and pressures may creep in, causing you to lose your

tenderness toward your spouse. The world is not a haven for lovers; in fact, external stress often works against the marriage relationship. But spouses can learn to be havens for each other. If intimacy and passion decline, remember that they can be renewed and regenerated. Take time to remember those first thrills, the excitement of sex, your spouse's strengths, and the commitment you made. When you focus on the positives, reconciliation and renewal can result.

5:7 The girl was alone outside during the night. In Old Testament times, she would have been looked upon as a criminal or a prostitute and treated as such. This image symbolizes the pain she felt at being separated from her lover.

11 His head is purest gold;
 his hair is wavy
 and black as a raven.
12 His eyes are like doves *e*
 by the water streams,
washed in milk,
 mounted like jewels.
13 His cheeks are like beds of spice
 yielding perfume.
His lips are like lilies
 dripping with myrrh.
14 His arms are rods of gold
 set with chrysolite.
His body is like polished ivory
 decorated with sapphires. *a*
15 His legs are pillars of marble
 set on bases of pure gold.
His appearance is like Lebanon,
 choice as its cedars.
16 His mouth is sweetness itself;
 he is altogether lovely.
This is my lover, this my friend,
 O daughters of Jerusalem.

Friends

6

Where has your lover gone,
 most beautiful of women? *f*
Which way did your lover turn,
 that we may look for him with you?

Beloved

2 My lover has gone down to his garden,
 to the beds of spices,
to browse in the gardens
 and to gather lilies.
3 I am my lover's and my lover is mine; *g*
 he browses among the lilies. *h*

5. Praising the bride's beauty

Lover

4 You are beautiful, my darling, as Tirzah,
 lovely as Jerusalem,
 majestic as troops with banners. *i*
5 Turn your eyes from me;
 they overwhelm me.
Your hair is like a flock of goats
 descending from Gilead. *j*
6 Your teeth are like a flock of sheep
 coming up from the washing.
Each has its twin,
 not one of them is alone. *k*

5:12
e SS 1:15; 4:1

6:1
f SS 1:8

6:3
g SS 7:10
h SS 2:16

6:4
i ver 10

6:5
j SS 4:1

6:6
k SS 4:2

---

a 14 Or lapis lazuli

5:16 The girl calls Solomon her "friend." In a healthy marriage, lovers are also good friends. Too often people are driven into marriage by the exciting feelings of love and passion before they take the time to develop a deep friendship. This involves listening, sharing, and showing understanding for the other's likes and dislikes. Friendship takes time, but it makes a love relationship much deeper and far more satisfying.

6:3 The girl said that she and her lover belonged to each other—

they had given themselves to each other unreservedly. No matter how close we may be to our parents or our best friends, only in marriage can we realize complete union of mind, heart, and body.

6:4 Tirzah was a city about 35 miles northeast of Jerusalem. Its name means "pleasure" or "beauty." Jeroboam made Tirzah the first capital of the divided northern kingdom (1 Kings 14:17). "Majestic as troops with banners" means that the beloved must have had awe-inspiring beauty, like a mighty army readying for battle.

6:7
*l*SS 4:3

7 Your temples behind your veil
   are like the halves of a pomegranate.*l*
8 Sixty queens there may be,
   and eighty concubines,
   and virgins beyond number;
9 but my dove, my perfect one, is unique,
   the only daughter of her mother,
   the favorite of the one who bore her.
The maidens saw her and called her blessed;
   the queens and concubines praised her.

Friends

10 Who is this that appears like the dawn,
   fair as the moon, bright as the sun,
   majestic as the stars in procession?

Lover

6:11
*m*SS 7:12

11 I went down to the grove of nut trees
   to look at the new growth in the valley,
to see if the vines had budded
   or the pomegranates were in bloom.*m*
12 Before I realized it,
   my desire set me among the royal chariots of my people.*a*

Friends

13 Come back, come back, O Shulammite;
   come back, come back, that we may gaze on you!

Lover

Why would you gaze on the Shulammite
   as on the dance of Mahanaim?

7:1
*n*Ps 45:13

7

How beautiful your sandaled feet,
   O prince's*n* daughter!
Your graceful legs are like jewels,
   the work of a craftsman's hands.

7:3
*o*SS 4:5

7:4
*p*SS 4:4

2 Your navel is a rounded goblet
   that never lacks blended wine.
Your waist is a mound of wheat
   encircled by lilies.
3 Your breasts*o* are like two fawns,
   twins of a gazelle.
4 Your neck is like an ivory tower.*p*
Your eyes are the pools of Heshbon
   by the gate of Bath Rabbim.
Your nose is like the tower of Lebanon
   looking toward Damascus.

7:5
*q*Isa 35:2

5 Your head crowns you like Mount Carmel.*q*
Your hair is like royal tapestry;
   the king is held captive by its tresses.

7:6
*r*SS 1:15

6 How beautiful*r* you are and how pleasing,
   O love, with your delights!

a 12 Or *among the chariots of Amminadab;* or *among the chariots of the people of the prince*

6:8, 9 Solomon did indeed have many queens (wives) and concubines (1 Kings 11:3). Polygamy, though not condoned, was common in Old Testament days. Solomon says that his love for this woman has not diminished since their wedding night, even though many other women are available to him.

7:1 *Graceful* can mean "curvaceous."

7:4, 5 The phrase "your eyes are the pools of Heshbon"

suggests sparkling eyes. Heshbon was the ancient capital of the Amorites. Bath Rabbim may have been a gate of Heshbon. The "tower of Lebanon" may have been a watchtower (evidently a prominent one and seen as very beautiful). Some suggest that this refers to the Lebanon mountain range. Mount Carmel overlooks the Mediterranean Sea and Palestine.

7 Your stature is like that of the palm,
    and your breasts like clusters of fruit.
8 I said, "I will climb the palm tree;
    I will take hold of its fruit."
May your breasts be like the clusters of the vine,
    the fragrance of your breath like apples,[s]
9   and your mouth like the best wine.

6. The bride's tender appeal

Beloved

May the wine go straight to my lover,
    flowing gently over lips and teeth.[a]
10 I belong to my lover,
    and his desire[t] is for me.[u]
11 Come, my lover, let us go to the countryside,
    let us spend the night in the villages.[b]
12 Let us go early to the vineyards
    to see if the vines have budded,
if their blossoms have opened,
    and if the pomegranates are in bloom[v]—
there I will give you my love.
13 The mandrakes[w] send out their fragrance,
    and at our door is every delicacy,
both new and old,
    that I have stored up for you, my lover.

8   If only you were to me like a brother,
    who was nursed at my mother's breasts!
Then, if I found you outside,
    I would kiss you,
    and no one would despise me.
2 I would lead you
    and bring you to my mother's house—
    she who has taught me.
I would give you spiced wine to drink,
    the nectar of my pomegranates.
3 His left arm is under my head
    and his right arm embraces me.[x]
4 Daughters of Jerusalem, I charge you:
    Do not arouse or awaken love
    until it so desires.[y]

7. The power of love

Friends

5 Who is this coming up from the desert[z]
    leaning on her lover?

Beloved

Under the apple tree I roused you;
    there your mother conceived you,
    there she who was in labor gave you birth.
6 Place me like a seal over your heart,
    like a seal on your arm;

7:8
[s] SS 2:5

7:10
[t] Ps 45:11
[u] SS 2:16; 6:3

7:12
[v] SS 6:11

7:13
[w] Ge 30:14

8:3
[x] SS 2:6
8:4
[y] SS 2:7; 3:5

8:5
[z] SS 3:6

---

[a] 9 Septuagint, Aquila, Vulgate and Syriac; Hebrew *lips of sleepers*   [b] 11 Or *henna bushes*

7:10–13 As a marriage matures, love and freedom between marriage partners should increase. Here the girl takes the initiative in lovemaking. Many cultures have stereotypes of the roles men and women play in lovemaking, but the security of true love gives both marriage partners the freedom to initiate acts of love.

7:13 Mandrakes were a somewhat rare plant often thought to

increase fertility. Mandrakes are also mentioned in Genesis 30:14–17.

8:1 In the ancient Near East, it was improper to show public affection except between family members. The girl is wishing that she could freely show affection to her lover, even in public.

8:6, 7 In this final description of their love, the girl includes

for love is as strong as death,
    its jealousy[a] unyielding as the grave.[b]
It burns like blazing fire,
    like a mighty flame.[c]

8:7
[a] Pr 6:35

7 Many waters cannot quench love;
    rivers cannot wash it away.
If one were to give
    all the wealth of his house for love,
it[d] would be utterly scorned.[a]

Friends

8 We have a young sister,
    and her breasts are not yet grown.
What shall we do for our sister
    for the day she is spoken for?
9 If she is a wall,
    we will build towers of silver on her.
If she is a door,
    we will enclose her with panels of cedar.

Beloved

10 I am a wall,
    and my breasts are like towers.
Thus I have become in his eyes
    like one bringing contentment.

8:11
[b] Ecc 2:4
[c] Isa 7:23

11 Solomon had a vineyard[b] in Baal Hamon;
    he let out his vineyard to tenants.
Each was to bring for its fruit
    a thousand shekels[e] [c] of silver.
12 But my own vineyard is mine to give;
    the thousand shekels are for you, O Solomon,
and two hundred[f] are for those who tend its fruit.

Lover

13 You who dwell in the gardens
    with friends in attendance,
let me hear your voice!

Beloved

8:14
[d] SS 2:9
[e] SS 2:8,17

14 Come away, my lover,
    and be like a gazelle
or like a young stag[d]
    on the spice-laden mountains.[e]

[a] 6 Or *ardor* [b] 6 Hebrew *Sheol* [c] 6 Or / *like the very flame of the LORD* [d] 7 Or *he* [e] 11 That is, about 25 pounds (about 11.5 kilograms); also in verse 12 [f] 12 That is, about 5 pounds (about 2.3 kilograms)

---

some of its significant characteristics (see also 1 Corinthians 13). Love is as strong as death; it cannot be killed by time or disaster. Love is priceless; even the richest king cannot buy it. Love must be accepted as a gift from God and shared within the guidelines God provides. Accept the love of your spouse as God's gift, and strive to make your love a reflection of God's perfect love.

8:8, 9 The girl is reflecting on the days when she was younger and under the care of her brothers, who wondered how to help her prepare for marriage. They decided that if she remained a virgin before marriage, standing firm like a wall against sexual temptation, they would praise her. But if she was like a door, open to immorality, they would take steps to guard her from doing something foolish. In 8:10, she testifies that she has been persistent in her morality and thus has found favor in Solomon's eyes.

8:11, 12 Solomon could demand rent from the tenants for his vineyard, but the girl had her own vineyard and it was her right to assign it. But she willingly gave Solomon its fruit. In a good

marriage, there is no private property, for everything is shared between the partners. Note: Baal Hamon is mentioned only here in the Bible, and its location is unknown.

8:14 The love between Solomon and his bride did not diminish in intensity after their wedding night. The lovers relied on each other and kept no secrets from each other. Devotion and commitment were the keys to their relationship. The faithfulness of our marital love should reflect God's perfect faithfulness to us.

Paul shows how marriage represents Christ's relationship to his church (Ephesians 5:22–33), and John pictures the second coming as a great marriage feast for Christ and his bride, his faithful followers (Revelation 19:7, 8; 21:1, 2). Many theologians have thought that Song of Songs is an allegory showing Christ's love for his church. It makes even better sense to say that it is a love poem about a real human love relationship, and that all loving, committed marriages are reflections of God's love.

ISAIAH

Amos becomes a prophet 760 B.C.	Hosea becomes a prophet 753	Micah becomes a prophet 742	Isaiah becomes a prophet 740	Ahaz becomes king of Judah 735	Hoshea becomes king of Israel 732	Israel falls to the Assyrians 722	Hezekiah becomes king of Judah 715

VITAL STATISTICS

PURPOSE:
To call the nation of Judah back to God and to tell of God's salvation through the Messiah

AUTHOR:
The prophet Isaiah son of Amoz

DATE WRITTEN:
The events of chapters 1—39 occurred during Isaiah's ministry, so they were probably written about 700 B.C. Chapters 40—66, however, may have been written near the end of his life, about 681 B.C.

SETTING:
Isaiah is speaking and writing mainly in Jerusalem

KEY VERSE:
"But he was pierced for our transgressions, he was crushed for our iniquities; the punishment that brought us peace was upon him, and by his wounds we are healed" (53:5).

KEY PEOPLE:
Isaiah; his two sons, Shear-Jashub and Maher-Shalal-Hash-Baz

SPECIAL FEATURES:
The book of Isaiah contains both prose and poetry and uses personification (attributing personal qualities to divine beings or inanimate objects). Also, many of the prophecies in Isaiah contain predictions that foretell a soon-to-occur event and a distant future event at the same time.

SLOWLY he rose, and the crowd fell silent. Those at the back leaned forward, straining to hear. The atmosphere was electric. He spoke, and his carefully chosen words flew like swift arrows and found their mark. The great man, a spokesman for God, was warning—and condemning. The crowd became restless—shifting positions, clenching fists, and murmuring. Some agreed with his message, nodding their heads and weeping softly. But most were angry, and they began to shout back insults and threats.

Such was the life of a prophet.

The "office" of prophet was instituted during the days of Samuel, the last of the judges. Prophets stood with the priests as God's special representatives. The prophet's role was to speak for God, confronting the people and their leaders with God's commands and promises. Because of this confrontational stance and the continuing tendency of people to disobey God, true prophets usually were not very popular. But though their message often went unheeded, they faithfully and forcefully proclaimed the truth.

The book of Isaiah is the first of the writings of the prophets in the Bible, and Isaiah, the author, is generally considered to be the greatest prophet. He was probably reared in an aristocratic home and was married to a prophet. In the beginning of his ministry he was well liked. But, like most prophets, he soon became unpopular because his messages were so difficult to hear. He called the people to turn from their lives of sin and warned them of God's judgment and punishment. Isaiah had an active ministry for 60 years before he was executed during Manasseh's reign (according to tradition). As God's special messenger to Judah, Isaiah prophesied during the reigns of several of its rulers. Many of those messages are recorded in his book: Uzziah and Jotham, chapters 1—6; Ahaz, chapters 7—14; and Hezekiah, chapters 15—39.

The first half of the book of Isaiah (chapters 1—39) contains scathing denunciations and pronouncements as he calls Judah, Israel, and the surrounding nations to repent of their sins. The last 27 chapters (40—66), however, are filled with consolation and hope as Isaiah unfolds God's promise of future blessings through his Messiah.

As you read Isaiah, imagine this strong and courageous man of God, fearlessly proclaiming God's word, and listen to his message in relation to your own life—*return, repent, and be renewed*. Then trust in God's *redemption* through Christ and *rejoice*. Your Savior has come, and he's coming again!

THE BLUEPRINT

A. WORDS OF JUDGMENT (1:1—39:8)
1. The sins of Israel and Judah
2. Judgment against pagan nations
3. God's purpose in judgment
4. Jerusalem's true and false hopes
5. Events during the reign of Hezekiah

The 39 chapters in the first half of Isaiah generally carry the message of judgment for sin. Isaiah brings the message of judgment to Judah, Israel, and the surrounding pagan nations. The people of Judah had a form of godliness, but in their hearts they were corrupt. Isaiah's warnings were intended to purify the people by helping them understand God's true nature and message. However, they ignored the repeated warnings that Isaiah brought. We need to heed the prophetic voice and not repeat their error.

B. WORDS OF COMFORT (40:1—66:24)
1. Israel's release from captivity
2. The future Redeemer
3. The future kingdom

The 27 chapters in the second half of Isaiah generally bring a message of forgiveness, comfort, and hope. This message of hope looks forward to the coming of the Messiah. Isaiah speaks more about the Messiah than does any other Old Testament prophet. He describes the Messiah as both a suffering Servant and a sovereign Lord. The fact that the Messiah was to be both a suffering Servant and a sovereign Lord could not be understood clearly until New Testament times. Based on what Jesus Christ has done, God freely offers forgiveness to all who turn to him in faith. This is God's message of comfort to us because those who heed it find eternal peace and fellowship with him.

MEGATHEMES

THEME	EXPLANATION	IMPORTANCE
Holiness	God is highly exalted above all his creatures. His moral perfection stands in contrast to evil people and nations. God is perfect and sinless in all his motives and actions, so he is in perfect control of his power, judgment, love, and mercy. His holy nature is our standard for morality.	Because God is without sin, he alone can help us with our sin. It is only right that we regard him as supreme in power and moral perfection. We must never treat God as common or ordinary. He alone deserves our devotion and praise. He is always truthful, fair, and just.
Punishment	Because God is holy, he requires his people to treat others justly. He promised to punish Israel, Judah, and other nations for faithless immorality and idolatry. True faith had degenerated into national pride and empty religious rituals.	We must trust in God alone and fulfill his commands. We cannot forsake justice nor give in to selfishness. If we harden our hearts against his message, punishment will surely come to us.
Salvation	Because God's judgment is coming, we need a Savior. No person or nation can be saved without God's help. Christ's perfect sacrifice for our sins is foretold and portrayed in Isaiah. All who trust God can be freed from their sin and restored to him.	Christ died to save us from our sin. We cannot save ourselves. He is willing to save all those who turn from their sin and come to him. Salvation is from God alone. No amount of good works can earn it.
Messiah	God will send the Messiah to save his people. He will set up his own Kingdom as the faithful Prince of Peace, who rules with righteousness. He will come as sovereign Lord, but he will do so as a servant who will die to take away sins.	Our trust must be in the Messiah, not in ourselves or in any nation or power. There is no hope unless we believe in him. Trust Christ fully and let him rule in your life as your sovereign Lord.
Hope	God promises comfort, deliverance, and restoration in his future Kingdom. The Messiah will rule over his faithful followers in the age to come. Hope is possible because Christ is coming.	We can be refreshed because there is compassion for those who repent. No matter how bleak our situation or how evil the world is, we must continue to be God's faithful people who hope for his return.

A. WORDS OF JUDGMENT (1:1—39:8)

Isaiah begins by bringing a message of divine judgment for both Israel and Judah. Although the advance of the Assyrians poses a problem for Judah, God foretells the destruction of Assyria and other evil surrounding nations through the prophet Isaiah. The section ends with the Assyrian invasion being held off, demonstrating the clear unfolding of God's plan and promises for the nation at this time.

1. The sins of Israel and Judah

1 The vision concerning Judah and Jerusalem that Isaiah son of Amoz saw[a] during the reigns of Uzziah, Jotham, Ahaz[b] and Hezekiah, kings of Judah.

1:1 [a] Isa 2:1 [b] 2Ki 16:1

A Rebellious Nation

2 Hear, O heavens! Listen, O earth!
   For the LORD has spoken:
   "I reared children and brought them up,
     but they have rebelled against me.
3 The ox knows his master,
     the donkey his owner's manger,
   but Israel does not know,[c]
     my people do not understand."

1:3 [c] Jer 9:3, 6

4 Ah, sinful nation,
     a people loaded with guilt,
   a brood of evildoers,[d]
     children given to corruption!
   They have forsaken the LORD;
     they have spurned the Holy One[e] of Israel
     and turned their backs on him.

1:4 [d] Isa 14:20 [e] Isa 5:19, 24

5 Why should you be beaten anymore?
     Why do you persist in rebellion?[f]
   Your whole head is injured,
     your whole heart afflicted.[g]
6 From the sole of your foot to the top of your head
     there is no soundness[h]—
   only wounds and welts
     and open sores,
   not cleansed or bandaged
     or soothed with oil.

1:5 [f] Isa 31:6 [g] Isa 33:6, 24

1:6 [h] Ps 38:3

7 Your country is desolate,
     your cities burned with fire;
   your fields are being stripped by foreigners
     right before you,
   laid waste as when overthrown by strangers.

1:1 Isaiah was a prophet during the time when the original nation of Israel had been divided into two kingdoms—Israel in the north, and Judah in the south. The northern kingdom had sinned greatly against God, and the southern kingdom was headed in the same direction—perverting justice, oppressing the poor, turning from God to idols, and looking for military aid from pagan nations rather than help from God. Isaiah came primarily as a prophet to Judah, but his message was also for the northern kingdom. Sometimes "Israel" refers to both kingdoms. Isaiah lived to see the destruction and captivity of the northern kingdom in 722 B.C.; thus, his ministry began with warning the northern kingdom.

1:2-4 Here "Israel" means the southern kingdom, Judah. The people of Judah were sinning greatly and refused to know and understand God. God brought charges against them through Isaiah because they had rebelled and had forsaken the Lord. By these acts, they had broken their moral and spiritual covenant with God (see Deuteronomy 28). By breaking their agreement, they were bringing God's punishment upon themselves. First God

gave them prosperity, but they didn't serve him. Then God sent them warnings, but they refused to listen. Finally, he would bring the fire of his judgment (see 1:7).

1:4-9 As long as the people of Judah continued to sin, they cut themselves off from God's help and isolated themselves. When you feel lonely and separated from God, remember that God does not abandon you. Our sins cut us off from him. The only sure cure for this kind of loneliness is to restore a meaningful relationship with God by confessing your sin, obeying his instructions, and communicating regularly with him (see Psalm 140:13; Isaiah 1:16-19; 1 John 1:9).

1:7 Was this destruction taking place at that time? Judah was attacked many times during Isaiah's lifetime. To be stripped (devastated) by foreigners was the worst kind of judgment. This verse could be a picture of the results of these invasions or a prediction of the coming invasion of Israel by Assyria. But most likely it pointed to Babylon's future invasion of Judah and the fall of Jerusalem in 586 B.C. as well.

1:8
i Job 27:18

8 The Daughter of Zion is left
    like a shelter in a vineyard,
    like a hut *i* in a field of melons,
    like a city under siege.

1:9
j Ge 19:24; Ro 9:29*

9 Unless the LORD Almighty
    had left us some survivors,
  we would have become like Sodom,
    we would have been like Gomorrah. *j*

1:10
k Isa 28:14
l Eze 16:49;
Rev 11:8

10 Hear the word of the LORD, *k*
    you rulers of Sodom; *l*
  listen to the law of our God,
    you people of Gomorrah!

1:11
m 1Sa 15:22

11 "The multitude of your sacrifices—
    what are they to me?" says the LORD.
  "I have more than enough of burnt offerings,
    of rams and the fat of fattened animals;
  I have no pleasure
    in the blood of bulls and lambs and goats. *m*

1:12
n Ex 23:17

12 When you come to appear before me,
    who has asked this of you, *n*
    this trampling of my courts?

1:13
o Isa 66:3
p Jer 7:9
q 1Ch 23:31

13 Stop bringing meaningless offerings! *o*
    Your incense *p* is detestable to me.
  New Moons, Sabbaths and convocations *q*—
    I cannot bear your evil assemblies.

1:14
r Nu 28:11–29:39
s Isa 43:22, 24

14 Your New Moon festivals and your appointed feasts *r*
    my soul hates.
  They have become a burden to me;
    I am weary *s* of bearing them.
15 When you spread out your hands in prayer,
    I will hide my eyes from you;

ISAIAH served as a prophet to Judah from 740–681 B.C.	Climate of the times	Society was in a great upheaval. Under King Ahaz and King Manasseh, the people reverted to idolatry, and there was even child sacrifice.
	Main message.	Although judgment from other nations was inevitable, the people could still have a special relationship with God.
	Importance of message. . . .	Sometimes we must suffer judgment and discipline before we are restored to God.
	Contemporary prophets . . .	Hosea (753–715 B.C.), Micah (742–687 B.C.)

1:9 Sodom and Gomorrah were two cities that God completely destroyed for their great wickedness (Genesis 19:1–25). They are mentioned elsewhere in the Bible as examples of God's judgment against sin (Jeremiah 50:40; Ezekiel 16:46–63; Matthew 11:23, 24; Jude 7). "Some survivors" from Judah were spared by God because they were faithful.

1:10 Isaiah compared the rulers and people of Judah to the rulers and people of Sodom and Gomorrah. To hear what God wanted to say, the people had to listen and be willing to obey. When we can't hear God's message, perhaps we are not listening carefully or we are not truly willing to do what he says.

1:10–14 God was unhappy with their sacrifices, but he was not revoking the system of sacrifices he had initiated with Moses. Instead, God was calling for sincere faith and devotion. The leaders were carefully making the traditional sacrifices and offerings at holy celebrations, but they were still unfaithful to God in their hearts. Sacrifices were to be an outward sign of their inward faith in God, but the outward signs became empty because no inward faith existed. Why, then, did they continue to offer sacrifices?

Like many people today, they had come to place more faith in the rituals of their religion than in the God they worshiped. Examine your own worship experience: Is it just entertainment as you enjoy the music and go along with what others do? Or is it genuine heartfelt praise to God? God does not take pleasure in our outward expressions if our inward faith is missing (see Deuteronomy 10:12–16; 1 Samuel 15:22, 23; Psalm 51:16–19; Hosea 6:6).

1:13 "New Moons" and "Sabbaths" refer to monthly offerings (Numbers 28:11–14) and weekly and special annual Sabbaths on the Day of Atonement and Feast of Tabernacles (Leviticus 16:34, 39). For all the feasts, see the chart in Leviticus 23, p. 185. Although the people did not feel sorry for their sins, they continued to offer sacrifices for forgiveness. Gifts and sacrifices mean nothing to God when they come from someone with a corrupt heart. God wants us to love him, trust him, and turn from our sin; after that, he will be pleased with our "sacrifices" of time, money, or service.

even if you offer many prayers,
    I will not listen.
Your hands are full of blood;[t]

16   wash and make yourselves clean.
Take your evil deeds
    out of my sight!
Stop doing wrong,[u]

17   learn to do right!
Seek justice,
    encourage the oppressed.[a]
Defend the cause of the fatherless,[v]
    plead the case of the widow.

18 "Come now, let us reason together,"[w]
    says the LORD.
"Though your sins are like scarlet,
    they shall be as white as snow;[x]
though they are red as crimson,
    they shall be like wool.

19 If you are willing and obedient,
    you will eat the best from the land;[y]

20 but if you resist and rebel,
    you will be devoured by the sword."[z]

For the mouth of the LORD has spoken.

21 See how the faithful city
    has become a harlot![a]
She once was full of justice;
    righteousness used to dwell in her—
    but now murderers!

22 Your silver has become dross,
    your choice wine is diluted with water.

23 Your rulers are rebels,
    companions of thieves;
they all love bribes
    and chase after gifts.
They do not defend the cause of the fatherless;
    the widow's case does not come before them.[b]

24 Therefore the Lord, the LORD Almighty,
    the Mighty One of Israel, declares:
"Ah, I will get relief from my foes
    and avenge[c] myself on my enemies.

25 I will turn my hand against you;
    I will thoroughly purge away your dross
    and remove all your impurities.[d]

1:15
[t] Isa 59:3
1:16
[u] Isa 55:7
1:17
[v] Ps 82:3
1:18
[w] Isa 43:9, 26
[x] Ps 51:7; Rev 7:14
1:19
[y] Dt 30:15-16
1:20
[z] Isa 3:25
1:21
[a] Jer 2:20
1:23
[b] Jer 5:28
1:24
[c] Isa 35:4
1:25
[d] Mal 3:3

a 17 Or / rebuke the oppressor

1:18 Scarlet, or crimson, was the color of a deep-red permanent dye, and its deep stain was virtually impossible to remove from clothing. The bloodstained hands of the murderers are probably in view here (see 1:15, 21). The stain of sin seems equally permanent, but God can remove sin's stain from our lives as he promised to do for the Israelites. We don't have to go through life permanently soiled. God's Word assures us that if we are willing and obedient, Christ will forgive and remove our most indelible stains (Psalm 51:1–7). Will you ask him to make you clean?

1:21, 22 "The faithful city" refers to Jerusalem, representing all of Judah. God compares the actions of his people to a harlot. The people had turned from the worship of the true God to

worshiping idols. Their faith was defective, impure, and diluted. Idolatry, outward or inward, is spiritual adultery, breaking our commitment to God in order to love something else. Jesus described the people of his day as adulterous, even though they were religiously strict. As the church, we are the "bride" of Christ (Revelation 19:7), and, by faith, we can be clothed in his righteousness. Has your faith become impure or watered down? Ask God to restore you. Keep your devotion to him strong and pure.

1:25 God promised to refine his people similar to the way that metal is purged with lye in a smelting pot. This process involves melting the metal and skimming off the impure dross until the worker can see his own image in the liquid metal. We must be willing to submit to God, allowing him to remove our sin so that we might reflect his image.

1:26
e Jer 33:7, 11
f Zec 8:3

26 I will restore your judges as in days of old, *e*
    your counselors as at the beginning.
Afterward you will be called
    the City of Righteousness, *f*
    the Faithful City."

27 Zion will be redeemed with justice,
    her penitent ones with righteousness.

1:28
g Ps 9:5; 2Th 1:8-9

28 But rebels and sinners will both be broken,
    and those who forsake the Lord will perish. *g*

1:29
h Isa 57:5
i Isa 65:3

29 "You will be ashamed because of the sacred oaks *h*
    in which you have delighted;
    you will be disgraced because of the gardens *i*
    that you have chosen.
30 You will be like an oak with fading leaves,
    like a garden without water.
31 The mighty man will become tinder
    and his work a spark;
    both will burn together,
    with no one to quench the fire."

The Mountain of the Lord

2 This is what Isaiah son of Amoz saw concerning Judah and Jerusalem:

2:2
j Mic 4:7

2 In the last days

    the mountain *j* of the Lord's temple will be established
        as chief among the mountains;
    it will be raised above the hills,
        and all nations will stream to it.

2:3
k Lk 24:47

3 Many peoples will come and say,

    "Come, let us go up to the mountain of the Lord,
        to the house of the God of Jacob.
    He will teach us his ways,
        so that we may walk in his paths."
    The law will go out from Zion,
        the word of the Lord from Jerusalem. *k*
4 He will judge between the nations
        and will settle disputes for many peoples.
    They will beat their swords into plowshares
        and their spears into pruning hooks.

1:26 Isaiah often speaks with both the near present and far future in mind. His prophecies do not necessarily apply to one event, but may apply to a series of present and future events.

1:29, 30 Throughout history, the oak tree has been a symbol of strength, but the people were worshiping "sacred oaks." Ezekiel mentions that groves of oak trees were used as places for idol worship (Ezekiel 6:13). Are you devoted to symbols of strength and power that rival God's place in your life? Do you have interests and commitments where your love for them borders on worship? Make God your first loyalty; everything else will fade in time and burn away under his scrutiny.

1:31 A spark set to tinder ignites a quick, devouring fire. God compares mighty people whose evil deeds devour them to a roaring fire. Our lives can be destroyed quickly by a small but deadly spark of evil. What potential "fire hazards" do you need to remove?

2:2 The temple was built on the mountain of the Lord, Mount Moriah, highly visible to all the people of Jerusalem. For more on the significance of the temple, see the note on 2 Chronicles 5:1ff. In the last days the temple will attract the nations, not because of

its architecture and prominence, but because of God's presence and influence.

2:2–4 God gave Isaiah the gift of seeing the future. At this time, God showed Isaiah what would eventually happen to Jerusalem. Revelation 21 depicts the glorious fulfillment of this prophecy in the new Jerusalem, where only those whose names are written in the Lamb's book of life will be allowed to enter. God made a covenant (promise) with his people and will never break it. God's faithfulness gives us hope for the future. Ask God to help you spread his word.

2:4, 5 This describes a wonderful future of peace when instruments of war will be converted to instruments of farming, when we will be taught God's laws and will obey them. Although we know that eventually God will remove all sin and thus the causes of war, conflicts, and other problems, we should not wait for him to act before we begin to obey him. Just as Judah was told in 2:5, we should walk in his light now. Though our eternal reward awaits us, we already can enjoy many benefits of obedience now as we apply God's Word to our lives.

Nation will not take up sword against nation,[l]
    nor will they train for war anymore.
5 Come, O house of Jacob,[m]
    let us walk in the light of the LORD.

The Day of the LORD

6 You have abandoned[n] your people,
    the house of Jacob.
They are full of superstitions from the East;
    they practice divination like the Philistines
    and clasp hands with pagans.[o]
7 Their land is full of silver and gold;
    there is no end to their treasures.
Their land is full of horses;[p]
    there is no end to their chariots.
8 Their land is full of idols;
    they bow down to the work of their hands,
    to what their fingers[q] have made.
9 So man will be brought low
    and mankind humbled—
    do not forgive them.[a]

10 Go into the rocks,
    hide in the ground
from dread of the LORD
    and the splendor of his majesty![r]
11 The eyes of the arrogant man will be humbled
    and the pride[s] of men brought low;
the LORD alone will be exalted in that day.

12 The LORD Almighty has a day in store
    for all the proud and lofty,
    for all that is exalted[t]
    (and they will be humbled),
13 for all the cedars of Lebanon, tall and lofty,
    and all the oaks of Bashan,[u]
14 for all the towering mountains
    and all the high hills,[v]
15 for every lofty tower
    and every fortified wall,
16 for every trading ship[b]
    and every stately vessel.
17 The arrogance of man will be brought low
    and the pride of men humbled;

a 9 Or *not raise them up*   b 16 Hebrew *every ship of Tarshish*

Cross references:

2:4 [l]Isa 32:18; Hos 2:18

2:5 [m]Isa 58:1

2:6 [n]Dt 31:17 [o]2Ki 16:7

2:7 [p]Dt 17:16

2:8 [q]Isa 17:8

2:10 [r]2Th 1:9; Rev 6:15-16

2:11 [s]Isa 5:15

2:12 [t]Isa 24:4, 21

2:13 [u]Zec 11:2

2:14 [v]Isa 30:25

2:6 The people were following practices of the Assyrian empire. "Divination like the Philistines" meant that they were claiming to know and control the future by the power of demons or by interpreting omens. These practices were forbidden by God (see Leviticus 19:26; Deuteronomy 18:10, 14). The Philistines worshiped Dagon, Ashtoreth, and Baal-Zebub. During the more sinful periods of their history, the people of Israel worshiped these pagan gods along with Yahweh, and even gave them Hebrew names.

2:8, 9 Under the reign of evil kings, idol worship flourished in both Israel and Judah. A few good kings in Judah stopped it during their reigns. Though very few people worship carved or molded images today, worshiping objects that symbolize power continues. We pay homage to cars, homes, sports stars, celebrities, money, etc. Idol worship is evil because (1) it insults God when we worship something he created rather than worshiping him; (2) it keeps us from knowing and serving God when we put our confidence in anything other than him; (3) it causes us to rely on our own efforts rather than on God. (See also Deuteronomy 27:15.)

2:12 The "day" of the Lord Almighty is the day of judgment, the time when God will judge both evil and good. That day will come, and we will want a proper relationship with God when it does. Pride, however, will cripple us. God alone must be exalted (2:11, 17) as the first step toward developing that relationship with him.

2:15-17 Lofty towers were part of a city or nation's defenses. This phrase refers to security based on military fortresses. "Every trading ship" pictures economic prosperity; and a "stately vessel" reveals pleasure and enjoyment. Nothing can compare with or rival the place God must have in our hearts and minds. To place our hope elsewhere is nothing but false pride. Place your confidence in God alone.

2:18
w Isa 21:9

the LORD alone will be exalted in that day,
18 and the idols will totally disappear. w

2:19
x Heb 12:26

19 Men will flee to caves in the rocks
and to holes in the ground
from dread of the LORD
and the splendor of his majesty,
when he rises to shake the earth. x
20 In that day men will throw away
to the rodents and bats
their idols of silver and idols of gold,
which they made to worship.

2:21
y ver 19

21 They will flee to caverns in the rocks
and to the overhanging crags
from dread of the LORD
and the splendor of his majesty,
when he rises to shake the earth. y

2:22
z Ps 146:3
a Jas 4:14

22 Stop trusting in man, z
who has but a breath in his nostrils.
Of what account is he? a

Judgment on Jerusalem and Judah

3:1
b Lev 26:26

3 See now, the Lord,
the LORD Almighty,
is about to take from Jerusalem and Judah
both supply and support:
all supplies of food b and all supplies of water,
2 the hero and warrior,
the judge and prophet,
the soothsayer and elder,
3 the captain of fifty and man of rank,
the counselor, skilled craftsman and clever enchanter.

3:4
c Ecc 10:16 fn

3:5
d Mic 7:2, 6

4 I will make boys their officials;
mere children will govern them. c
5 People will oppress each other—
man against man, neighbor against neighbor. d
The young will rise up against the old,
the base against the honorable.

6 A man will seize one of his brothers
at his father's home, and say,
"You have a cloak, you be our leader;
take charge of this heap of ruins!"

3:7
e Eze 34:4

7 But in that day he will cry out,
"I have no remedy. e
I have no food or clothing in my house;
do not make me the leader of the people."

2:19 See Revelation 6:15–17 for a description of the dread in God's enemies on the day of his wrath. The Bible talks of two kinds of fear. In this verse, fear is the panic and peril unbelievers feel at the judgment of God. The right kind of fear means to revere and stand in awe of God. Proverbs 1:7 says, "The fear of the LORD is the beginning of knowledge." Those who honor and respect God need not fear God's wrath.

2:22 "But a breath in his nostrils" refers to mankind's mortality. People are very limited when compared to God. They can be unreliable, selfish, and shortsighted. Yet we trust our lives and futures more readily to mortal human beings than to the all-knowing God. Beware of people who want you to trust them instead of God.

Remember that only God is completely reliable. He is perfect and we can rely on his enduring love (Psalm 100:5).

3:1–3 Jerusalem besieged, her leaders destroyed—this unhappy picture would soon become a reality. Disobedience would bring serious affliction and great destruction, as God had warned (Deuteronomy 28).

3:2 Isaiah was not condoning the use of soothsayers (diviners) by including them on this list. He was showing how far the nation had sunk. See the note on 2:6.

3:4–9 This section describes what happens when a nation loses its leadership.

8 Jerusalem staggers,
    Judah is falling;[f]
their words and deeds are against the LORD,
    defying his glorious presence.
9 The look on their faces testifies against them;
    they parade their sin like Sodom;[g]
    they do not hide it.
Woe to them!
    They have brought disaster upon themselves.

10 Tell the righteous it will be well with them,
    for they will enjoy the fruit of their deeds.
11 Woe to the wicked! Disaster is upon them!
    They will be paid back for what their hands have done.

12 Youths[h] oppress my people,
    women rule over them.
O my people, your guides lead you astray;[i]
    they turn you from the path.

13 The LORD takes his place in court;
    he rises to judge[j] the people.
14 The LORD enters into judgment
    against the elders and leaders of his people:
"It is you who have ruined my vineyard;
    the plunder[k] from the poor is in your houses.
15 What do you mean by crushing my people
    and grinding the faces of the poor?"
        declares the Lord, the LORD Almighty.

16 The LORD says,
    "The women of Zion are haughty,
walking along with outstretched necks,
    flirting with their eyes,
tripping along with mincing steps,
    with ornaments jingling on their ankles.
17 Therefore the Lord will bring sores on the heads of the women of Zion;
    the LORD will make their scalps bald."

18 In that day the Lord will snatch away their finery: the bangles and headbands and crescent necklaces,[l] 19 the earrings and bracelets and veils, 20 the headdresses[m] and ankle chains and sashes, the perfume bottles and charms, 21 the signet rings and nose rings, 22 the fine robes and the capes and cloaks, the purses 23 and mirrors, and the linen garments and tiaras and shawls.

3:8
[f]Isa 1:7

3:9
[g]Ge 13:13

3:12
[h]ver 4
[i]Isa 9:16

3:13
[j]Mic 6:2

3:14
[k]Jas 2:6

3:18
[l]Jdg 8:21

3:20
[m]Ex 39:28

3:9–11 The people would be proud of their sins, parading them out in the open. But sin is self-destructive. In today's world, sinful living often appears glamorous, exciting, and clever. But sin is wrong regardless of how society perceives it, and, in the long run, sin will make us miserable and destroy us. God tries to protect us by warning us about the harm we will cause ourselves by sinning. Those who are proud of their sins will receive the punishment from God they deserve. Having rejected God's path to life (see Psalm 1), the only alternative is the path to destruction.

3:10, 11 In the middle of this gloomy message, God gives hope—eventually the righteous will receive God's reward and the wicked will receive their punishment. It is disheartening to see the wicked prosper while we struggle to obey God and follow his plan. Yet we keep holding on to God's truth and take heart! God will bring about justice in the end, and he will reward those who have been faithful.

3:14 The elders and leaders were responsible to help people, but instead they stole from the poor. Because they were unjust, Isaiah said the leaders would be the first to receive God's judgment.

Leaders will be held accountable. If you are in a position of leadership, you must lead according to God's just commands. Put the needs of others before your own. Fulfill the purpose God intended. Don't seek your own advantage. Corruption will bring God's wrath, especially if others follow your example.

3:14 Why is justice so important in the Bible? (1) Justice is part of God's nature; it is the way he runs the universe. (2) It is a natural desire in every person. Even as sinners, we all want justice for ourselves. (3) When government and church leaders are unjust, the poor and powerless suffer. Thus they are hindered from worshiping God. (4) God holds the poor in high regard. They are the ones most likely to turn to him for help and comfort. Injustice, then, attacks God's children. When we do nothing to help the oppressed, we are in fact joining with the oppressor. Because we follow a just God, we must uphold justice.

3:16–26 The women of Judah had placed their emphasis on clothing and jewelry rather than on God. They dressed to be noticed, to gain approval, and to be fashionable. Yet they ignored the real purpose for their lives. Instead of being concerned about

3:24
n Isa 22:12

24 Instead of fragrance there will be a stench;
  instead of a sash, a rope;
  instead of well-dressed hair, baldness;*n*
  instead of fine clothing, sackcloth;
  instead of beauty, branding.

3:25
o Isa 1:20

25 Your men will fall by the sword,*o*
  your warriors in battle.

3:26
p Jer 14:2
q La 2:10

26 The gates of Zion will lament and mourn;*p*
  destitute, she will sit on the ground.*q*

4:1
r Isa 13:12
s 2Th 3:12

4

1 In that day seven women
  will take hold of one man*r*
and say, "We will eat our own food*s*
  and provide our own clothes;
only let us be called by your name.
  Take away our disgrace!"

The Branch of the LORD

4:2
t Jer 23:5-6

4:3
u Isa 60:21
v Lk 10:20

4:4
w Isa 28:6

4:5
x Ex 13:21

4:6
y Isa 25:4

2 In that day the Branch of the LORD*t* will be beautiful and glorious, and the fruit of the land will be the pride and glory of the survivors in Israel. 3 Those who are left in Zion, who remain in Jerusalem, will be called holy,*u* all who are recorded*v* among the living in Jerusalem. 4 The Lord will wash away the filth of the women of Zion; he will cleanse the bloodstains from Jerusalem by a spirit*a* of judgment*w* and a spirit*a* of fire. 5 Then the LORD will create over all of Mount Zion and over those who assemble there a cloud of smoke by day and a glow of flaming fire by night;*x* over all the glory will be a canopy. 6 It will be a shelter and shade from the heat of the day, and a refuge*y* and hiding place from the storm and rain.

The Song of the Vineyard

5:1
z Ps 80:8-9

5

I will sing for the one I love
  a song about his vineyard:*z*
My loved one had a vineyard
  on a fertile hillside.

5:2
a Jer 2:21
b Lk 13:6

2 He dug it up and cleared it of stones
  and planted it with the choicest vines.*a*
He built a watchtower in it
  and cut out a winepress as well.
Then he looked for a crop of good grapes,
  but it yielded only bad fruit.*b*

5:3
c Mt 21:40

3 "Now you dwellers in Jerusalem and men of Judah,
  judge between me and my vineyard.*c*

5:4
d Mt 23:37

4 What more could have been done for my vineyard
  than I have done for it?*d*
When I looked for good grapes,
  why did it yield only bad?
5 Now I will tell you
  what I am going to do to my vineyard:

a 4 Or *the Spirit*

---

the oppression around them (3:14, 15), they were self-serving and self-centered. People who abuse their possessions will end up with nothing. These verses are not an indictment against clothing and jewelry, but a judgment on those who use them lavishly while remaining blind to the needs of others. When God blesses you with money or position, don't flaunt it. Use what you have to help others, not impress them.

4:2–4 The "Branch of the LORD" probably refers to the Messiah, although some believe it refers to Judah. The point is that during the distress predicted by Isaiah, some people will be protected by God's loving grace. Those protected will be set apart to serve God when Messiah rules the earth (Jeremiah 23:5, 6; Zechariah 6:12, 13). Their distinctive mark will be their holiness, not wealth or prestige. This holiness comes from a sincere desire to obey God's

moral standards and from their wholehearted devotion to him. Evil will not always continue as it does now. The time will come when God will put an end to all evil, and his faithful followers will share in his glorious reign.

5:1–7 The lesson of the song of the vineyard shows that God's chosen nation was to bear fruit—to carry out his work, to uphold justice. It did bear fruit, but the fruit was bad. Jesus said, "By their fruit you will recognize them" (Matthew 7:20). Have you examined your own "fruit" lately? Is it good or bad—useful or wild?

I will take away its hedge,
    and it will be destroyed;
I will break down its wall,*e*
    and it will be trampled.*f*
6 I will make it a wasteland,
    neither pruned nor cultivated,
    and briers and thorns will grow there.
I will command the clouds
    not to rain on it."

7 The vineyard*g* of the LORD Almighty
    is the house of Israel,
and the men of Judah
    are the garden of his delight.
And he looked for justice, but saw bloodshed;
    for righteousness, but heard cries of distress.

Woes and Judgments

8 Woe to you who add house to house
    and join field to field*h*
till no space is left
    and you live alone in the land.

9 The LORD Almighty has declared in my hearing:*i*

"Surely the great houses will become desolate,
    the fine mansions left without occupants.
10 A ten-acre*a* vineyard will produce only a bath*b* of wine,
    a homer*c* of seed only an ephah*d* of grain."

11 Woe to those who rise early in the morning
    to run after their drinks,
who stay up late at night
    till they are inflamed with wine.*j*
12 They have harps and lyres at their banquets,
    tambourines and flutes and wine,
but they have no regard*k* for the deeds of the LORD,
    no respect for the work of his hands.*l*
13 Therefore my people will go into exile
    for lack of understanding;
their men of rank will die of hunger
    and their masses will be parched with thirst.
14 Therefore the grave*e* enlarges its appetite
    and opens its mouth without limit;
into it will descend their nobles and masses
    with all their brawlers and revelers.
15 So man will be brought low
    and mankind humbled,*m*
    the eyes of the arrogant*n* humbled.

5:5
e Ps 80:12
f Lk 21:24

5:7
g Ps 80:8

5:8
h Mic 2:2

5:9
i Isa 22:14

5:11
j Pr 23:29-30

5:12
k Job 34:27
l Ps 28:5; Am 6:5-6

5:15
m Isa 2:9
n Isa 2:11

a 10 Hebrew *ten-yoke*, that is, the land plowed by 10 yoke of oxen in one day   *b* 10 That is, probably about 6 gallons (about 22 liters)   *c* 10 That is, probably about 6 bushels (about 220 liters)   *d* 10 That is, probably about 3/5 bushel (about 22 liters)   *e* 14 Hebrew *Sheol*

5:8-25 In this section, God condemns six sins: (1) exploiting others (5:8–10); (2) drunkenness (5:11, 12); (3) taking sarcastic pride in sin (5:18, 19); (4) confusing moral standards (5:20); (5) being conceited (5:21); (6) perverting justice (5:22–24). Because of these sins, God punished Israel with destruction by Assyria (5:25–30). A similar fate was awaiting Judah if they didn't turn from these sins.

5:11-13 These people spent many hours drinking and partying, but Isaiah predicted that eventually many would die of hunger and thirst. Ironically, our pleasures—if they do not have God's bless-

ing—may destroy us. Leaving God out of our lives allows sin to come in. Pursuing our own pleasure while ignoring or exploiting the needs of others leaves us empty and under God's anger. God wants us to enjoy life (1 Timothy 6:17) but to avoid those activities that could lead us away from him.

5:13 The nation's heroes—the "men of rank"—would suffer the same humiliation as the common people. Why? Because they lived by their own values rather than God's. Many of today's media, business, and sports heroes are idolized because of their ability to live as they please. Are your heroes

5:16
o Isa 29:23

16 But the LORD Almighty will be exalted by his justice,
and the holy God will show himself holy*o* by his righteousness.
17 Then sheep will graze as in their own pasture;
lambs will feed*a* among the ruins of the rich.

5:18
p Isa 59:4-8

18 Woe to those who draw sin along with cords of deceit,
and wickedness*p* as with cart ropes,

5:19
q Eze 12:22;
2Pe 3:4

19 to those who say, "Let God hurry,
let him hasten his work
so we may see it.
Let it approach,
let the plan of the Holy One of Israel come,
so we may know it."*q*

5:20
r Mt 6:22-23

20 Woe to those who call evil good
and good evil,
who put darkness for light
and light for darkness,*r*
who put bitter for sweet
and sweet for bitter.

5:21
s Ro 12:16

21 Woe to those who are wise in their own eyes*s*
and clever in their own sight.

22 Woe to those who are heroes at drinking wine
and champions at mixing drinks,

5:23
t Ps 94:21

23 who acquit the guilty for a bribe,
but deny justice to the innocent.*t*

5:24
u Job 18:16

24 Therefore, as tongues of fire lick up straw
and as dry grass sinks down in the flames,
so their roots will decay*u*
and their flowers blow away like dust;
for they have rejected the law of the LORD Almighty
and spurned the word of the Holy One of Israel.

5:25
v 2Ki 22:13
w Isa 9:12, 17, 21

25 Therefore the LORD's anger*v* burns against his people;
his hand is raised and he strikes them down.
The mountains shake,
and the dead bodies are like refuse in the streets.

Yet for all this, his anger is not turned away,
his hand is still upraised.*w*

5:26
x Isa 7:18
y Dt 28:49

26 He lifts up a banner for the distant nations,
he whistles*x* for those at the ends of the earth.*y*
Here they come,
swiftly and speedily!

a 17 Septuagint; Hebrew / *strangers will eat*

---

those who defy God, or those who defy the world in order to serve God?

5:18, 19 Some people drag their sins around with them. Some do so arrogantly, but for others, their sins have become a burden that wears them out. Are you dragging around a cartload of sins that you refuse to give up? Before you find yourself worn out and useless, turn to the One who promises to take away your burden of sin and replace it with a purpose for living that is a joy to fulfill (see Matthew 11:28–30).

5:20 When people do not carefully observe the distinction between good and evil, destruction soon follows. It is easy for people to say, "No one can decide for anyone else what is really right or wrong." They may think getting drunk can't hurt them, extramarital sex isn't really wrong, or money doesn't control them. But when we make excuses for our actions, we break down the distinction between right and wrong. If we do not take God's

Word, the Bible, as our standard, soon all moral choices will appear fuzzy. Without God, we are headed for a breakdown and much suffering.

5:24 The people suffered because they rejected God's law. It is sad to see so many people today searching for meaning in life while spurning God's Word. We can avoid the error of Israel and Judah by making not only reading the Bible, but also understanding and obeying it, a high priority in our lives.

5:26–30 This passage describes what God would do if the people disobeyed him (Deuteronomy 28). Assyria began to torment Israel during the reign of Ahaz (735–715 B.C.). This powerful aggressor destroyed the northern kingdom in 722 B.C. and scattered the people throughout its own empire. Sin has consequences. Although this judgment was not immediate, eventually Israel was punished.

27 Not one of them grows tired or stumbles,
    not one slumbers or sleeps;
  not a belt is loosened at the waist,
    not a sandal thong is broken.z

28 Their arrows are sharp,
    all their bowsa are strung;
  their horses' hoofs seem like flint,
    their chariot wheels like a whirlwind.

29 Their roar is like that of the lion,b
    they roar like young lions;
  they growl as they seizec their prey
    and carry it off with no one to rescue.d

30 In that day they will roar over it
    like the roaring of the sea.
  And if one looks at the land,
    he will see darkness and distress;e
    even the light will be darkened by the clouds.

5:27
z Joel 2:7-8

5:28
a Ps 7:12

5:29
b Jer 51:38
c Isa 10:6
d Isa 42:22

5:30
e Isa 8:22

Isaiah's Commission

6 In the year that King Uzziah died,f I saw the Lordg seated on a throne, high and exalted, and the train of his robe filled the temple. 2Above him were seraphs, each with six wings: With two wings they covered their faces, with two they covered their feet, and with two they were flying. 3And they were calling to one another:

6:1
f 2Ki 15:7
g Jn 12:41

6:3
h Ps 72:19; Rev 4:8

"Holy, holy, holy is the LORD Almighty;
    the whole earth is full of his glory."h

4At the sound of their voices the doorposts and thresholds shook and the temple was filled with smoke.

5"Woe to me!" I cried. "I am ruined! For I am a man of unclean lips, and I live among a people of unclean lips, and my eyes have seen the King, the LORD Almighty."

6Then one of the seraphs flew to me with a live coal in his hand, which he had taken with tongs from the altar. 7With it he touched my mouth and said, "See, this has touched your lips;i your guilt is taken away and your sin atoned for."

6:7
i Jer 1:9

8Then I heard the voice of the Lord saying, "Whom shall I send? And who will go for us?"
And I said, "Here am I. Send me!"
9He said, "Go and tell this people:

6:1 The year that King Uzziah died was approximately 740 B.C. He remained leprous until he died because he tried to take over the high priest's duties (2 Chronicles 26:18–21). Although Uzziah was generally a good king with a long and prosperous reign, many of his people turned away from God.

6:1ff Isaiah's vision was his commission to be God's messenger to his people. Isaiah was given a difficult mission. He had to tell people who believed they were blessed by God that instead God was going to destroy them because of their disobedience.

6:1ff Isaiah's lofty view of God in 6:1–4 gives us a sense of God's greatness, mystery, and power. Isaiah's example of recognizing his sinfulness before God encourages us to confess our sin. His picture of forgiveness reminds us that we, too, are forgiven. When we recognize how great our God is, how sinful we are, and the extent of God's forgiveness, we receive power to do his work. How does your concept of the greatness of God measure up to Isaiah's?

6:1–3 The throne, the attending seraphs (angels), and the threefold *holy* all stressed God's holiness. Seraphs were a type of angel whose name is derived from the word for "burn," perhaps indicating their purity as God's ministers. In a time when moral and spiritual decay had peaked, it was important for Isaiah to see God in his holiness. Holiness means morally perfect, pure, and set apart from all sin. We also need to discover God's holiness. Our daily frustrations, society's pres-

sures, and our shortcomings reduce and narrow our view of God. We need the Bible's view of God as high and lifted up to empower us to deal with our problems and concerns. God's moral perfection, properly seen, will purify us from sin, cleanse our minds from our problems, and enable us to worship and to serve.

6:5–8 Seeing the Lord and listening to the praise of the angels, Isaiah realized that he was unclean before God, with no hope of measuring up to God's standard of holiness. When Isaiah's lips were touched with a live burning coal, however, he was told that his sins were forgiven. It wasn't the coal that cleansed him, but God. In response Isaiah submitted himself entirely to God's service. No matter how difficult his task would be, he said, "Here am I. Send me!" The painful cleansing process was necessary before Isaiah could fulfill the task to which God was calling him. Before we accept God's call to speak for him to those around us, we must be cleansed as Isaiah was, confessing our sins and submitting to God's control. Letting God purify us may be painful, but we must be purified so that we can truly represent God, who is pure and holy.

6:8 The more clearly Isaiah saw God (6:5), the more aware Isaiah became of his own powerlessness and inadequacy to do anything of lasting value without God. But he was willing to be God's spokesman. When God calls, will you also say, "Here am I. Send me!"?

6:9–13 God told Isaiah that the people would listen but not

6:9
/Mt 13:15*

6:10
kPs 119:70
/Jer 5:21
mMk 4:12*;
Ac 28:26-27*

> "'Be ever hearing, but never understanding;
>   be ever seeing, but never perceiving.'/
> 10 Make the heart of this people calloused;k
>   make their ears dull
>   and close their eyes.a
> Otherwise they might see with their eyes,
>   hear with their ears,/
>   understand with their hearts,
> and turn and be healed."m

a9,10 Hebrew; Septuagint 'You will be ever hearing, but never understanding; / you will be ever seeing, but never perceiving.' / 10This people's heart has become calloused; / they hardly hear with their ears, / and they have closed their eyes

ISAIAH

Trees and prophets share at least one important characteristic—both are planted for the future. Yet seedlings are often overlooked and prophets often ignored. Isaiah is one of the best examples of this. The people of his time could have been rescued by his words. Instead, they refused to believe him. With the passing of centuries, however, Isaiah's words have cast a shadow on all of history.

Isaiah was active as a prophet during the reigns of five kings, but he did not set out to be a prophet. By the time King Uzziah died, Isaiah may have been established as a scribe in the royal palace in Jerusalem. It was a respectable career, but God had other plans for his servant. Isaiah's account of God's call leaves little doubt about what motivated the prophet for the next half century. His vision of God was unforgettable.

The encounter with God permanently affected Isaiah's character. He reflected the God he represented. Isaiah's messages—some comforting, some confronting—are so distinct that some have guessed they came from different authors. Isaiah's testimony is that the messages came from the only One capable of being perfect in justice as well as in mercy—God himself.

When he called Isaiah as a prophet, God did not encourage him with predictions of great success. God told Isaiah that the people would not listen. But he was to speak and write his messages anyway because eventually some *would* listen. God compared his people to a tree that would have to be cut down so that a new tree could grow from the old stump (Isaiah 6:13).

We who are part of that future can see that many of the promises God gave through Isaiah have been fulfilled in Jesus Christ. We also gain the hope of knowing that God is active in all of history, including our own.

Strengths and accomplishments:	• Considered the greatest Old Testament prophet • Quoted at least 50 times in the New Testament • Had powerful messages of both judgment and hope • Carried out a consistent ministry even though there was little positive response from his listeners • His ministry spanned the reigns of five kings of Judah
Lessons from his life:	• God's help is needed in order to effectively confront sin while comforting people • One result of experiencing forgiveness is the desire to share that forgiveness with others • God is purely and perfectly holy, just, and loving
Vital statistics:	• Where: Jerusalem • Occupations: Scribe, prophet • Relatives: Father: Amoz. Sons: Shear-Jashub, Maher-Shalal-Hash-Baz. • Contemporaries: Uzziah, Jotham, Ahaz, Hezekiah, Manasseh, Micah
Key verse:	"Then I heard the voice of the Lord saying, 'Whom shall I send? And who will go for us?' And I said, 'Here am I. Send me!' " (Isaiah 6:8).

Isaiah's story is told in 2 Kings 19:2—20:19. He is also mentioned in 2 Chronicles 26:22; 32:20, 32; Matthew 3:3; 8:17; 12:17–21; John 12:38–41; Romans 10:16, 20, 21.

learn from his message because their hearts had become calloused (hardened) beyond repentance. God's patience with their chronic rebellion was finally exhausted. His judgment was to abandon them to their rebellion and hardness of heart. Why did God send Isaiah if he knew the people wouldn't listen? Although the nation itself would not repent and would reap judgment, some individuals would listen. In 6:13 God explains

his plan for a remnant (holy seed) of faithful followers. God is merciful even when he judges. We can gain encouragement from God's promise to preserve his people. If we are faithful to him we can be sure of his mercy.

11 Then I said, "For how long, O Lord?"
And he answered:

> "Until the cities lie ruined
>   and without inhabitant,
> until the houses are left deserted
>   and the fields ruined and ravaged,
> 12 until the LORD has sent everyone far away
>   and the land is utterly forsaken. n
> 13 And though a tenth remains in the land,
>   it will again be laid waste.
> But as the terebinth and oak
>   leave stumps when they are cut down,
>   so the holy seed will be the stump in the land."

6:12
n Jer 4:29

The Sign of Immanuel

7 When Ahaz son of Jotham, the son of Uzziah, was king of Judah, King Rezin o of Aram and Pekah son of Remaliah king of Israel marched up to fight against Jerusalem, but they could not overpower it.

7:1
o 2Ki 15:37

2 Now the house of David p was told, "Aram has allied itself with a Ephraim"; so the hearts of Ahaz and his people were shaken, as the trees of the forest are shaken by the wind.

7:2
p ver 13

3 Then the LORD said to Isaiah, "Go out, you and your son Shear-Jashub, b to meet Ahaz at the end of the aqueduct of the Upper Pool, on the road to the Washerman's Field. q 4 Say to him, 'Be careful, keep calm r and don't be afraid. Do not lose heart because of these two smoldering stubs of firewood—because of the fierce anger s of Rezin and Aram and of the son of Remaliah. 5 Aram, Ephraim and Remaliah's son have plotted your ruin, saying, 6 "Let us invade Judah; let us tear it apart and divide it among ourselves, and make the son of Tabeel king over it." 7 Yet this is what the Sovereign LORD says:

7:3
q 2Ki 18:17
7:4
r Isa 30:15
s Isa 10:24

> "'It will not take place,
>   it will not happen, t
> 8 for the head of Aram is Damascus,
>   and the head of Damascus is only Rezin.
> Within sixty-five years
>   Ephraim will be too shattered u to be a people.
> 9 The head of Ephraim is Samaria,
>   and the head of Samaria is only Remaliah's son.
> If you do not stand firm in your faith, v
>   you will not stand at all.'"

7:7
t Isa 8:10

7:8
u Isa 17:1-3

7:9
v 2Ch 20:20

a 2 Or has set up camp in   b 3 Shear-Jashub means a remnant will return.

6:11–13 When would the people listen? Only after they had come to the end and had nowhere to turn but to God. This would happen when the land was destroyed by invading armies and the people taken into captivity. The "tenth" refers either to those who remained in the land after the captivity, or those who returned from Babylon to rebuild the land. Each group was about a tenth of the total population. When will we listen to God? Must we, like Judah, go through calamities before we will listen to God's words? Consider what God may be telling you, and obey him before time runs out.

7:1 The year was 734 B.C. Ahaz, king of Judah in Jerusalem, was about to be attacked by an alliance of the northern kingdom of Israel and Aram. He was frightened by the possible end of his reign and by the invading armies who killed many people or took them as captives (2 Chronicles 28:5–21). But, as Isaiah predicted, the kingdom of Judah did not come to an end at this time. The sign of Immanuel would be a sign of deliverance.

7:2 "The house of David" refers to Judah, the southern kingdom. "Ephraim," the dominant tribe in the north, is a reference to Israel, the northern kingdom.

7:3 Shear-Jashub means "a remnant will return." God told Isaiah to give his son this name as a reminder of his plan for mercy.

From the beginning of God's judgment he planned to restore a remnant of his people. Shear-Jashub was a reminder to the people of God's faithfulness to them.

7:3 The "aqueduct of the Upper Pool" may have been the site of the Gihon spring, located east of Jerusalem. The Gihon spring was the main source of water for the holy city, and was also the spring that emptied into Hezekiah's famous water tunnel (2 Chronicles 32:30). The "Washerman's Field" was a well-known place where clothing or newly woven cloth was laid in the sun to dry and whiten (see 36:2).

7:4—8:15 Isaiah predicted the breakup of Israel's alliance with Aram (7:4–9). Because of this alliance, Israel would be destroyed; Assyria would be the instrument God would use to destroy them (7:8–25) and to punish Judah. But God would not let Assyria destroy Judah (8:1–15). They would be spared because God's gracious plans cannot be thwarted.

7:8 Ahaz, one of Judah's worst kings, refused God's help and instead, he tried to buy aid from the Assyrians with silver and gold from the temple (2 Kings 16:8). When the Assyrians came, they brought further trouble instead of help. In 722 B.C., Samaria, the capital of Ephraim (another name for Israel, the northern kingdom), fell to the Assyrian armies, thus ending the northern kingdom.

¹⁰Again the LORD spoke to Ahaz, ¹¹"Ask the LORD your God for a sign, whether in the deepest depths or in the highest heights."

¹²But Ahaz said, "I will not ask; I will not put the LORD to the test."

¹³Then Isaiah said, "Hear now, you house of David! Is it not enough to try the patience of men? Will you try the patience of my God also? ¹⁴Therefore the Lord himself will give youᵃ a sign: The virgin will be with child and will give birth to a son, and ᵇ will call him Immanuel.ᶜ ʷ ¹⁵He will eat curds and honey when he knows enough to reject the wrong and choose the right. ¹⁶But before the boy knowsˣ enough to reject the wrong and choose the right, the land of the two kings you dread will be laid waste. ¹⁷The LORD will bring on you and on your people and on the house of your father a time unlike any since Ephraim broke awayʸ from Judah—he will bring the king of Assyria. ᶻ"

¹⁸In that day the LORD will whistleᵃ for flies from the distant streams of Egypt and for bees from the land of Assyria. ¹⁹They will all come and settle in the steep ravines and in the crevices in the rocks, on all the thornbushes and at all the water holes. ²⁰In that day the Lord will useᵇ a razor hired from beyond the Riverᵈ—the king of Assyria—to shave your head and the hair of your legs, and to take off your beards also. ²¹In that day, a man will keep alive a young cow and two goats. ²²And because of the abundance of the milk they give, he will have curds to eat. All who remain in the land will eat curds and honey. ²³In that day, in every place where there were a thousand vines worth a thousand silver shekels,ᵉ there will be only briers and thorns. ᶜ ²⁴Men will go there with bow and arrow, for the land will be covered with briers and thorns. ²⁵As for all the hills once cultivated by the hoe, you will no longer go there for fear of the briers and thorns; they will become places where cattle are turned loose and where sheep run.

Assyria, the LORD's Instrument

8 The LORD said to me, "Take a large scroll and write on it with an ordinary pen: Maher-Shalal-Hash-Baz.ᶠ ²And I will call in Uriahᵈ the priest and Zechariah son of Jeberekiah as reliable witnesses for me."

³Then I went to the prophetess, and she conceived and gave birth to a son. And the LORD said to me, "Name him Maher-Shalal-Hash-Baz. ⁴Before the boy knowsᵉ how to say 'My father' or 'My mother,' the wealth of Damascus and the plunder of Samaria will be carried off by the king of Assyria."

⁵The LORD spoke to me again:

ᵃ14 The Hebrew is plural.   ᵇ14 Masoretic Text; Dead Sea Scrolls *and he* or *and they*   ᶜ14 *Immanuel* means *God with us.*   ᵈ20 That is, the Euphrates   ᵉ23 That is, about 25 pounds (about 11.5 kilograms)   ᶠ1 *Maher-Shalal-Hash-Baz* means *quick to the plunder, swift to the spoil*; also in verse 3.

7:14
ʷIsa 8:8, 10;
Mt 1:23*

7:16
ˣIsa 8:4

7:17
ʸ1Ki 12:16
ᶻ2Ch 28:20

7:18
ᵃIsa 5:26

7:20
ᵇIsa 10:15

7:23
ᶜIsa 5:6

8:2
ᵈ2Ki 16:10

8:4
ᵉIsa 7:16

7:12 Ahaz appeared righteous by saying he would not test God with a sign ("I will not ask; I will not put the LORD to the test"). In fact, God had told him to ask, but Ahaz didn't really want to know what God would say. Often we use some excuse—such as not wanting to bother God or blaming some theological question that concerns us—to keep us from communicating with him. Don't let anything keep you from hearing and obeying God.

7:14–16 *Virgin* is translated from a Hebrew word used for an unmarried woman old enough to be married, one who is sexually mature (see Genesis 24:43; Exodus 2:8; Psalm 68:25; Proverbs 30:19; Song of Songs 1:3; 6:8). Some have compared this young woman to Isaiah's young wife and newborn son (8:1–4). This is not likely because she had a child, Shear-Jashub, and her second child was not named Immanuel. Some believe that Isaiah's first wife may have died, and so this is his second wife. It is more likely that this prophecy had a double fulfillment. (1) A young woman from the house of Ahaz who was not married would marry and have a son. Before three years passed (one year for pregnancy and two for the child to be old enough to talk), the two invading kings would be destroyed. (2) Matthew 1:23 quotes Isaiah 7:14 to show a further fulfillment of this prophecy in that a virgin named Mary conceived and bore a son, Immanuel, the Christ.

7:18 Flies and bees are symbols of God's judgment (see Exodus 23:28). Egypt and Assyria did not at this time devastate Judah. Hezekiah followed Ahaz as king, and he honored God; therefore God held back his hand of judgment. Two more evil kings reigned before Josiah, of whom it was said that no other king turned so completely to the Lord (2 Kings 23:25). However, Judah's doom had been sealed by the extreme evil of Josiah's father, Amon. During Josiah's reign, Egypt marched against the Assyrians. Josiah then declared war on Egypt, though God told him not to. After Josiah was killed (2 Chronicles 35:20–27), only weak kings reigned in Judah. The Egyptians carried off Josiah's son, Jehoahaz, after three months. The next king, Jehoiakim, was taken by Nebuchadnezzar to Babylon. Egypt and Assyria had dealt death blows to Judah.

7:20 Hiring Assyria to save them would be Judah's downfall (2 Kings 16:7, 8). To "shave" Judah's hair was symbolic of total humiliation. Numbers 6:9 explains that after being defiled, a person who had been set apart for the Lord had to shave his head as part of the cleansing process. Shaving bodily hair was an embarrassment—an exposure of nakedness. For a Hebrew man, having his beard shaved was humiliating (2 Samuel 10:4, 5).

7:21–25 Judah's rich farmland would be trampled until it became pastureland fit only for grazing. No longer would it be a place of agricultural abundance, a land "flowing with milk and honey" (Exodus 3:8), but a land with only curds, briers, and thorns.

8:1–4 These verses predict the fall of Israel and Aram. Aram fell to Assyria in 732 B.C., and Israel followed in 722 B.C. Isaiah put his message on a large scroll in a public place. God was warning all his people. The name of the child means "swift to plunder and quick to spoil."

6 "Because this people has rejected
    the gently flowing waters of Shiloah
and rejoices over Rezin
    and the son of Remaliah,[f]
7 therefore the Lord is about to bring against them
    the mighty floodwaters of the River[a]—
    the king of Assyria with all his pomp.
It will overflow all its channels,
    run over all its banks
8 and sweep on into Judah, swirling over it,
    passing through it and reaching up to the neck.
Its outspread wings will cover the breadth of your land,
    O Immanuel[b]!"[g]

9 Raise the war cry,[c] you nations, and be shattered!
    Listen, all you distant lands.
Prepare for battle, and be shattered!
Prepare for battle, and be shattered!
10 Devise your strategy, but it will be thwarted;[h]
    propose your plan, but it will not stand,[i]
for God is with us.[d][j]

Fear God

11 The LORD spoke to me with his strong hand upon me, warning me not to follow the way of this people. He said:

12 "Do not call conspiracy[k]
    everything that these people call conspiracy[e];
do not fear what they fear,
    and do not dread it.[l]
13 The LORD Almighty is the one you are to regard as holy,[m]
    he is the one you are to fear,
    he is the one you are to dread,
14 and he will be a sanctuary;[n]
    but for both houses of Israel he will be
a stone that causes men to stumble
    and a rock that makes them fall.[o]
And for the people of Jerusalem he will be
    a trap and a snare.
15 Many of them will stumble;[p]
    they will fall and be broken,
    they will be snared and captured."

16 Bind up the testimony
    and seal up the law among my disciples.

8:6 [f] Isa 7:1

8:8 [g] Isa 7:14

8:10 [h] Job 5:12 [i] Isa 7:7 [j] Ro 8:31

8:12 [k] Isa 7:2 [l] 1Pe 3:14*

8:13 [m] Nu 20:12

8:14 [n] Eze 11:16 [o] Lk 2:34; Ro 9:33*; 1Pe 2:8*

8:15 [p] Lk 20:18

[a]7 That is, the Euphrates   [b]8 *Immanuel* means *God with us.*   [c]9 Or *Do your worst*   [d]10 Hebrew *Immanuel*
[e]12 Or *Do not call for a treaty / every time these people call for a treaty*

8:6–8 "The gently flowing waters of Shiloah" refers to God's gentle and sustaining care. Because Judah rejected God's kindness, choosing instead to seek help from other nations, God would punish them. We see two distinct attributes of God—his love and his wrath. To ignore his love and guidance results in sin and invites his wrath. We must recognize the consequences of our choices. God wants to protect us from bad choices, but he still gives us the freedom to make them.

8:7, 8 The heart of the Assyrian empire was located between the Tigris and Euphrates Rivers. This flood is a poetic way of describing the overwhelming force of the Assyrian army.

8:9 To "be shattered" means to lose courage by the pressure of sudden fear.

8:11 Isaiah, along with most of the prophets, was viewed as a traitor because he did not support Judah's national policies. He

called the people to commit themselves first to God, and then to the king. He even predicted the overthrow of the government.

8:11–15 For the people of Judah, fear of invasion was a constant threat. They had powerful enemies on their doorstep. Yet Isaiah said, "The LORD Almighty . . . is the one you are to fear . . . he will be a sanctuary." Fear is a powerful enemy of our faith and a strong deterrent to the believer's peace of mind. Fear of war, terrorist attacks, disease, and pollution can rob us of our trust in God. God is our shelter and hiding place (4:6). Ask him to drive inappropriate fear from your heart and to help you fear only him.

8:16 "Bind up the testimony" and "seal up the law" mean that the words would be written down and preserved for future generations. Because some people faithfully preserved the teaching of God and passed on these words from generation to generation, we have the book of Isaiah today. Each of us needs to accept the

¹⁷ I will wait for the LORD,
    who is hiding his face from the house of Jacob.
    I will put my trust in him.

8:18
*q*Heb 2:13*

¹⁸Here am I, and the children the LORD has given me.*q* We are signs and symbols in Israel from the LORD Almighty, who dwells on Mount Zion.

8:19
*r*1Sa 28:8

¹⁹When men tell you to consult*r* mediums and spiritists, who whisper and mutter, should not a people inquire of their God? Why consult the dead on behalf of the living? ²⁰To the law*s*

8:20
*s*Lk 16:29
*t*Mic 3:6

and to the testimony! If they do not speak according to this word, they have no light*t* of dawn. ²¹Distressed and hungry, they will roam through the land; when they are famished, they will become enraged and, looking upward, will curse their king and their God. ²²Then they will

8:22
*u*Isa 5:30

look toward the earth and see only distress and darkness and fearful gloom, and they will be thrust into utter darkness. *u*

To Us a Child Is Born

9:1
*v*2Ki 15:29

9 Nevertheless, there will be no more gloom for those who were in distress. In the past he humbled the land of Zebulun and the land of Naphtali, *v* but in the future he will honor Galilee of the Gentiles, by the way of the sea, along the Jordan—

9:2
*w*Eph 5:8
*x*Mt 4:15-16*

    ² The people walking in darkness
       have seen a great light;*w*
    on those living in the land of the shadow of death*a*
       a light has dawned.*x*
    ³ You have enlarged the nation
       and increased their joy;
    they rejoice before you
       as people rejoice at the harvest,
    as men rejoice
       when dividing the plunder.

*a*2 Or *land of darkness*

NAMES FOR MESSIAH

Wonderful Counselor	He is exceptional, distinguished, and without peer, the one who gives the right advice.
Mighty God	He is God himself.
Everlasting Father.	He is timeless; he is God our Father.
Prince of Peace.	His government is one of justice and peace.

Isaiah uses four names in 9:6 to describe the Messiah. These names have special meaning to us.

---

responsibility to pass on God's Word to our children and grandchildren, encouraging them to love the Bible, read it, and learn from it. Then they will faithfully pass it on to their children and grandchildren.

8:17 Isaiah decided to wait for the Lord, though God was "hiding his face from the house of Jacob." For some believers, patient waiting becomes the most difficult testing they must face: waiting for illness to pass, for a child to return to God and the church, or for God to make matters right in a particular situation. Many of the prophecies God gave through the prophets would not come true for 700 years; others still haven't been fulfilled in our lifetime. Are you willing to accept the Lord's timing, not yours?

8:19 The people would consult mediums and spiritists to seek answers from dead people instead of consulting the living God. God alone knows the future, and only he is eternal. We can trust God to guide us.

8:21 After rejecting God's plan for them, the people of Judah would blame God for their trials. People continually blame God for their self-induced problems. How do you respond to the unpleasant results of your own choices? Where do you fix the blame? Instead of blaming God, look for ways to grow through your failures.

9:1 In our gloom and despair, we fear that our sorrows and troubles will never end. But we can take comfort in this certainty: although the Lord may not always take us around our troubles, if we follow him wholeheartedly, he will lead us safely through them.

9:1–7 This child who would become their deliverer is the Messiah, Jesus. Matthew quotes these verses in describing Christ's ministry (Matthew 4:15, 16). The territories of Zebulun and Naphtali represent the northern kingdom as a whole. These were also the territories where Jesus grew up and often ministered; this is why they would see "a great light."

9:2 The apostle John also referred to Jesus as the "light" (John 1:9). Jesus referred to himself as "the light of the world" (John 8:12). Whenever we see the lights of Christmas, let them remind us that they recall Christ, our true Light.

9:2–6 In a time of great darkness, God promised to send a light who would shine on everyone living in the shadow of death. He is both "Wonderful Counselor" and "Mighty God." This message of hope was fulfilled in the birth of Christ and the establishment of his eternal kingdom. He came to deliver all people from their slavery to sin.

4 For as in the day of Midian's defeat,
   you have shattered
the yoke that burdens them,
   the bar across their shoulders,*y*
   the rod of their oppressor.*z*
5 Every warrior's boot used in battle
   and every garment rolled in blood
will be destined for burning,
   will be fuel for the fire.
6 For to us a child is born,*a*
   to us a son is given,*b*
   and the government*c* will be on his shoulders.
And he will be called
   Wonderful Counselor,*a* Mighty God,*d*
   Everlasting Father, Prince of Peace.
7 Of the increase of his government and peace
   there will be no end.*e*
He will reign on David's throne
   and over his kingdom,
establishing and upholding it
   with justice*f* and righteousness
   from that time on and forever.
The zeal*g* of the LORD Almighty
   will accomplish this.

The LORD's Anger Against Israel

8 The Lord has sent a message against Jacob;
   it will fall on Israel.
9 All the people will know it—
   Ephraim and the inhabitants of Samaria—
who say with pride
   and arrogance*h* of heart,
10 "The bricks have fallen down,
   but we will rebuild with dressed stone;
the fig trees have been felled,
   but we will replace them with cedars."
11 But the LORD has strengthened Rezin's*i* foes against them
   and has spurred their enemies on.
12 Arameans from the east and Philistines*j* from the west
   have devoured Israel with open mouth.

Yet for all this, his anger is not turned away,
   his hand is still upraised.

13 But the people have not returned to him who struck*k* them,
   nor have they sought the LORD Almighty.
14 So the LORD will cut off from Israel both head and tail,
   both palm branch and reed in a single day;*l*
15 the elders and prominent men are the head,
   the prophets who teach lies are the tail.
16 Those who guide this people mislead them,
   and those who are guided are led astray.*m*
17 Therefore the Lord will take no pleasure in the young men,
   nor will he pity the fatherless and widows,

a 6 Or *Wonderful, Counselor*

9:4
y Isa 10:27
z Isa 14:4

9:6
a Lk 2:11
b Jn 3:16
c Mt 28:18
d Isa 10:21

9:7
e Da 2:44; Lk 1:33
f Isa 11:4
g Isa 37:32

9:9
h Isa 46:12

9:11
i Isa 7:8

9:12
j 2Ch 28:18

9:13
k Jer 5:3

9:14
l Rev 18:8

9:16
m Isa 3:12

9:8–10 Pride made Israel think it would recover and rebuild in its own strength. Even though God made Israel a nation and gave them the land they occupied, the people put their trust in themselves rather than in him. Too often we take pride in our accomplishments, forgetting that it is God who has given us our every resource and ability. We may even become proud of our unique status as Christians. God is not pleased with *any* pride or trust in ourselves because it cuts off our contact with him.

9:17
n Isa 10:6
o Isa 5:25

for everyone is ungodly[n] and wicked,
  every mouth speaks vileness.

Yet for all this, his anger is not turned away,
  his hand is still upraised.[o]

9:18
p Mal 4:1

18 Surely wickedness burns like a fire;[p]
  it consumes briers and thorns,
it sets the forest thickets ablaze,
  so that it rolls upward in a column of smoke.

9:19
q Mic 7:2, 6

19 By the wrath of the LORD Almighty
  the land will be scorched
and the people will be fuel for the fire;
  no one will spare his brother.[q]

9:20
r Isa 49:26

20 On the right they will devour,
  but still be hungry;
on the left they will eat,[r]
  but not be satisfied.
Each will feed on the flesh of his own offspring[a]:

9:21
s Isa 5:25

21 Manasseh will feed on Ephraim, and Ephraim on Manasseh;
  together they will turn against Judah.

Yet for all this, his anger is not turned away,
  his hand is still upraised.[s]

10
Woe to those who make unjust laws,
  to those who issue oppressive decrees,
2 to deprive the poor of their rights
  and withhold justice from the oppressed of my people,
making widows their prey
  and robbing the fatherless.

10:3
t Job 31:14; Hos 9:7
u Lk 19:44
v Isa 20:6

3 What will you do on the day of reckoning,[t]
  when disaster[u] comes from afar?
To whom will you run for help?[v]
  Where will you leave your riches?

10:4
w Isa 5:25

4 Nothing will remain but to cringe among the captives
  or fall among the slain.

Yet for all this, his anger is not turned away,[w]
  his hand is still upraised.

God's Judgment on Assyria

10:5
x Jer 51:20

5 "Woe to the Assyrian, the rod of my anger,
  in whose hand is the club[x] of my wrath!

10:6
y Isa 9:17
z Isa 5:29

6 I send him against a godless[y] nation,
  I dispatch him against a people who anger me,
to seize loot and snatch plunder,[z]
  and to trample them down like mud in the streets.

10:7
a Ge 50:20

7 But this is not what he intends,[a]
  this is not what he has in mind;
his purpose is to destroy,
  to put an end to many nations.

a 20 Or arm

9:21 Ephraim and Manasseh were tribes in the northern kingdom descended from Joseph's two sons. They fought a civil war because of their selfishness and wickedness (see Judges 12:4).

10:1 God will judge crooked judges and those who make unjust laws. Those who oppress others will be oppressed themselves. It is not enough to live in a land founded on justice; each individual must deal justly with the poor and the powerless. Don't pass your responsibility off to your nation or even your church. You are accountable to God for what you do for the poor.

10:7 Although Assyria did not know it was part of God's plan, God used this nation to judge his people. God accomplishes his plans in history despite people or nations who reject him. He did not merely set the world in motion and let it go! Because our all-powerful, sovereign God is still in control today, we have security even in a rapidly changing world.

8 'Are not my commanders all kings?' he says.
9 'Has not Calno fared like Carchemish?[b]
Is not Hamath like Arpad,
and Samaria like Damascus?[c]
10 As my hand seized the kingdoms of the idols,[d]
kingdoms whose images excelled those of Jerusalem and Samaria—
11 shall I not deal with Jerusalem and her images
as I dealt with Samaria and her idols?'"

12 When the Lord has finished all his work against Mount Zion[e] and Jerusalem, he will say, "I will punish the king of Assyria for the willful pride of his heart and the haughty look in his eyes. 13 For he says:

"'By the strength of my hand I have done this,[f]
and by my wisdom, because I have understanding.
I removed the boundaries of nations,
I plundered their treasures;[g]
like a mighty one I subdued[a] their kings.
14 As one reaches into a nest,
so my hand reached for the wealth[h] of the nations;
as men gather abandoned eggs,
so I gathered all the countries;
not one flapped a wing,
or opened its mouth to chirp.'"

15 Does the ax raise itself above him who swings it,
or the saw boast against him who uses it?[i]
As if a rod were to wield him who lifts it up,
or a club brandish him who is not wood!
16 Therefore, the Lord, the LORD Almighty,
will send a wasting disease[j] upon his sturdy warriors;
under his pomp a fire will be kindled
like a blazing flame.
17 The Light of Israel will become a fire,
their Holy One[k] a flame;
in a single day it will burn and consume
his thorns and his briers.
18 The splendor of his forests and fertile fields
it will completely destroy,
as when a sick man wastes away.
19 And the remaining trees of his forests will be so few
that a child could write them down.

a 13 Or / I subdued the mighty,

10:9	b 2Ch 35:20
	c 2Ki 16:9
10:10	d 2Ki 19:18
10:12	e 2Ki 19:31
10:13	f Isa 37:24; Da 4:30
	g Eze 28:4
10:14	h Job 31:25
10:15	i Ro 9:20-21
10:16	j Isa 17:4
10:17	k Isa 37:23

10:9 Calno, Carchemish, Hamath, Arpad, Samaria, and Damascus were cities conquered by Assyria. Assured of great victories that would enlarge the empire, the king of Assyria gave an arrogant speech. Already Assyria had conquered several cities and thought Judah would be defeated along with the others. Little did they know that they were under the mightier hand of God.

10:10 Samaria and Jerusalem were filled with idols that were powerless against the Assyrian military machine. Only the God of the universe could and would overthrow Assyria, but not until he had used the Assyrians for his purposes.

10:12 The predicted punishment of the Assyrians soon took place. In 701 B.C., 185,000 Assyrian soldiers were slain by the angel of the Lord (37:36, 37). Later, the Assyrian empire fell to Babylon, never to rise again as a world power.

10:12 The Assyrians were haughty. They thought they had accomplished everything in their own power. Our perspective can become distorted by our accomplishments if we fail to recognize God working his purposes through us. When we think we are strong enough for anything, we are bound to fail because pride has blinded us to the reality that God is ultimately in control.

10:15 No instrument or tool accomplishes its purposes without a greater power. The Assyrians were a tool in God's hands, but they failed to recognize it. When a tool boasts of greater power than the one who uses it, it is in danger of being discarded. We are useful only to the extent that we allow God to use us. If God has given us resources and special talents, we must not regard them as our own creation or special privilege.

10:17 Assyria's downfall came in 612 B.C. when Nineveh, the capital city, was destroyed. Assyria had been God's instrument of judgment against Israel, but it too would be judged for its wickedness. No one escapes God's judgment against sin, not even the most powerful of nations (Psalm 2).

The Remnant of Israel

10:20
l 2Ki 16:7

20 In that day the remnant of Israel,
        the survivors of the house of Jacob,
    will no longer rely*l* on him
        who struck them down
    but will truly rely on the LORD,
        the Holy One of Israel.
21 A remnant will return,*a* a remnant of Jacob
        will return to the Mighty God.

10:22
m Isa 28:22

22 Though your people, O Israel, be like the sand by the sea,
        only a remnant will return.
    Destruction has been decreed,*m*
        overwhelming and righteous.

10:23
n Ro 9:27-28*

23 The Lord, the LORD Almighty, will carry out
        the destruction decreed upon the whole land.*n*

10:24
o Ps 87:5-6

24 Therefore, this is what the Lord, the LORD Almighty, says:

    "O my people who live in Zion,*o*
        do not be afraid of the Assyrians,
    who beat you with a rod
        and lift up a club against you, as Egypt did.
25 Very soon my anger against you will end
        and my wrath will be directed to their destruction."

10:26
p Isa 37:36-38
q Ex 14:16

26 The LORD Almighty will lash*p* them with a whip,
        as when he struck down Midian at the rock of Oreb;
    and he will raise his staff over the waters,*q*
        as he did in Egypt.
27 In that day their burden will be lifted from your shoulders,
        their yoke from your neck;
    the yoke will be broken
        because you have grown so fat.*b*

10:28
r 1Sa 14:2
s 1Sa 13:2

28 They enter Aiath;
        they pass through Migron;*r*
        they store supplies at Micmash.*s*
29 They go over the pass, and say,
        "We will camp overnight at Geba."
    Ramah trembles;
        Gibeah of Saul flees.

10:30
t 1Sa 25:44

30 Cry out, O Daughter of Gallim!*t*
        Listen, O Laishah!
        Poor Anathoth!
31 Madmenah is in flight;
        the people of Gebim take cover.

10:32
u 1Sa 21:1

32 This day they will halt at Nob;*u*
        they will shake their fist
    at the mount of the Daughter of Zion,
        at the hill of Jerusalem.

a 21 Hebrew *shear-jashub*; also in verse 22   *b* 27 Hebrew; Septuagint *broken / from your shoulders*

10:20, 21 Once Assyria's army was destroyed, a small group of God's people would stop relying on Assyria and start trusting God. This remnant would be but a fraction of Israel's former population: see Ezra 2:64, 65 for the small number who returned to Judah (see also 11:10–16).

10:20, 21 Those who remained faithful to God despite the horrors of the invasion are called the remnant. The key to being a part of the remnant was *faith*. Being a descendant of Abraham, living in the promised land, having trusted God at one time—

none of these were good enough. Are you relying on your Christian heritage, your participation in church, or a past experience to put you in a right relationship with God? The key to being a true Christian is faith in the mighty God.

10:28–34 The way these cities are listed approximates the route the Assyrians would take in their invasion of Judah in 701 B.C. They would go from Aiath (probably Ai) at the northern border to Nob (only two miles from Jerusalem).

33 See, the Lord, the LORD Almighty,
    will lop off the boughs with great power.
The lofty trees will be felled,
    the tall^v ones will be brought low.
34 He will cut down the forest thickets with an ax;
    Lebanon will fall before the Mighty One.

The Branch From Jesse

11 A shoot will come up from the stump of Jesse;^w
    from his roots a Branch^x will bear fruit.
2 The Spirit^y of the LORD will rest on him—
    the Spirit of wisdom and of understanding,
    the Spirit of counsel and of power,
    the Spirit of knowledge and of the fear of the LORD—
3 and he will delight in the fear of the LORD.

He will not judge by what he sees with his eyes,^z
    or decide by what he hears with his ears;^a
4 but with righteousness he will judge the needy,
    with justice he will give decisions for the poor of the earth.
He will strike^b the earth with the rod of his mouth;
    with the breath^c of his lips he will slay the wicked.
5 Righteousness will be his belt
    and faithfulness the sash around his waist.^d

6 The wolf will live with the lamb,^e
    the leopard will lie down with the goat,
the calf and the lion and the yearling^a together;
    and a little child will lead them.
7 The cow will feed with the bear,
    their young will lie down together,
    and the lion will eat straw like the ox.
8 The infant will play near the hole of the cobra,
    and the young child put his hand into the viper's nest.
9 They will neither harm nor destroy^f
    on all my holy mountain,
for the earth will be full of the knowledge^g of the LORD
    as the waters cover the sea.

10 In that day the Root of Jesse will stand as a banner for the peoples; the nations^h will rally to him,ⁱ and his place of rest will be glorious. 11 In that day the Lord will reach out his hand a second time to reclaim the remnant that is left of his people from Assyria,^j from Lower Egypt, from Upper Egypt,^b from Cush,^c from Elam, from Babylonia,^d from Hamath and from the islands of the sea.

^a6 Hebrew; Septuagint *lion will feed*   ^b11 Hebrew *from Pathros*   ^c11 That is, the upper Nile region
^d11 Hebrew *Shinar*

**Cross references (right margin):**

10:33
^vAm 2:9

11:1
^wRev 5:5
^xIsa 4:2

11:2
^yIsa 61:1; Mt 3:16;
Jn 1:32-33

11:3
^zJn 7:24
^aJn 2:25

11:4
^bMal 4:6
^cJob 4:9; 2Th 2:8

11:5
^dEph 6:14

11:6
^eIsa 65:25

11:9
^fJob 5:23
^gHab 2:14

11:10
^hLk 2:32
ⁱRo 15:12*

11:11
^jMic 7:12;
Zec 10:10

11:1–9 Assyria would be like a tree cut down at the height of its power (10:33, 34), never to rise again. Judah (the royal line of David) would be like a tree chopped down to a stump. But from that stump a new shoot would grow—the Messiah. He would be greater than the original tree and would bear much fruit. The Messiah is the fulfillment of God's promise that a descendant of David would rule forever (2 Samuel 7:16).

11:3–5 God will judge with righteousness and justice. How we long for fair treatment from others, but do we give it? We hate those who base their judgments on appearance, false evidence, or hearsay, but are we quick to judge others using those same standards? Only Christ can be the perfectly fair judge. Only as he governs our hearts can we learn to be as fair in our treatment of others as we expect others to be toward us.

11:4, 5 Judah had become corrupt and was surrounded by hostile, foreign powers. The nation desperately needed a revival of righteousness, justice, and faithfulness. They needed to turn from selfishness and give justice to the poor and the oppressed. The righteousness that God values is more than refraining from sin. It is actively turning toward others and offering them the help they need.

11:6–10 A golden age is yet to come, a time of peace when children could play safely with formerly dangerous animals. Not all of this was fulfilled at Christ's first coming. For example, nature has not returned to its intended balance and harmony (see Romans 8:9–22). Such perfect tranquility will be possible only when Christ reigns over the earth.

11:11 When will this remnant of God's people be returned to their land? Old Testament prophecy is often applied both to the near future and the distant future. Judah would soon be exiled to Babylon, and a remnant would return to Jerusalem in 537 B.C. at Cyrus's decree. In the ages to come, however, God's people

12 He will raise a banner for the nations
and gather the exiles of Israel;
he will assemble the scattered people of Judah
from the four quarters of the earth.

11:13
k Jer 3:18;
Eze 37:16-17, 22

13 Ephraim's jealousy will vanish,
and Judah's enemies[a] will be cut off;
Ephraim will not be jealous of Judah,
nor Judah hostile toward Ephraim. k

11:14
l Da 11:41

14 They will swoop down on the slopes of Philistia to the west;
together they will plunder the people to the east.
They will lay hands on Edom l and Moab,
and the Ammonites will be subject to them.
15 The LORD will dry up
the gulf of the Egyptian sea;
with a scorching wind he will sweep his hand
over the Euphrates River.[b]
He will break it up into seven streams
so that men can cross over in sandals.

11:16
m Isa 19:23
n Ex 14:26-31

16 There will be a highway m for the remnant of his people
that is left from Assyria,
as there was for Israel
when they came up from Egypt. n

Songs of Praise

12 In that day you will say:

"I will praise you, O LORD.
Although you were angry with me,
your anger has turned away
and you have comforted me.

12:2
o Ex 15:2;
Ps 118:14

2 Surely God is my salvation;
I will trust and not be afraid.
The LORD, the LORD, is my strength and my song;
he has become my salvation. o"

12:3
p Jn 4:10, 14

3 With joy you will draw water p
from the wells of salvation.

12:4
q Ps 105:1

4 In that day you will say:

"Give thanks to the LORD, call on his name;q
make known among the nations what he has done,
and proclaim that his name is exalted.

12:5
r Ex 15:1
s Ps 98:1

5 Sing r to the LORD, for he has done glorious things;s
let this be known to all the world.

12:6
t Zep 3:14-17

6 Shout aloud and sing for joy, people of Zion,
for great is the Holy One of Israel among you. t"

a 13 Or *hostility*   b 15 Hebrew *the River*

---

would be dispersed throughout the world. These cities represent the four corners of the known world—Hamath in the north, Egypt in the south, Assyria and Babylonia in the east, the islands of the sea in the west. Ultimately God's people will be regathered when Christ comes to reign over the earth.

11:13 Ephraim, the dominant tribe of the north, is used as another name for Israel, the northern kingdom.

11:14 Edom, Moab, and Ammon were three countries bordering Judah (along with Philistia). They were the nations who, when Judah was defeated, rejoiced and took their land.

11:15, 16 Isaiah is talking about a new or second exodus when God will bring his scattered people back to Judah and the Messiah will come to rule the world. The Lord dried up the Red

Sea so the Israelites could walk through it on their way to the promised land (Exodus 14). He dried up the Jordan River so the nation could cross into the land (Joshua 3). God will again provide the way of return for his people.

12:1ff This chapter is a hymn of praise—another graphic description of the people's joy when Jesus Christ comes to reign over the earth. Even now we need to express our gratitude to God—thanking him, praising him, and telling others about him. From the depths of our gratitude, we must praise him. And we should share the Good News with others.

2. Judgment against pagan nations
A Prophecy Against Babylon

13 An oracle concerning Babylon that Isaiah son of Amoz saw:

2 Raise a banner [u] on a bare hilltop,
   shout to them;
   beckon to them
      to enter the gates of the nobles.

3 I have commanded my holy ones;
   I have summoned my warriors [v] to carry out my wrath—
      those who rejoice [w] in my triumph.

4 Listen, a noise on the mountains,
      like that of a great multitude!
   Listen, an uproar among the kingdoms,
      like nations massing together!
   The LORD Almighty is mustering
      an army for war.

5 They come from faraway lands,
      from the ends of the heavens [x]—
   the LORD and the weapons of his wrath—
      to destroy [y] the whole country.

6 Wail, for the day [z] of the LORD is near;
      it will come like destruction from the Almighty.[a]

7 Because of this, all hands will go limp,
      every man's heart will melt.[a]

8 Terror will seize them,
      pain and anguish will grip them;
      they will writhe like a woman in labor.
   They will look aghast at each other,
      their faces aflame.

9 See, the day of the LORD is coming
      —a cruel day, with wrath and fierce anger—
   to make the land desolate
      and destroy the sinners within it.

10 The stars of heaven and their constellations
      will not show their light.
   The rising sun will be darkened [b]
      and the moon will not give its light.[c]

11 I will punish the world for its evil,
      the wicked for their sins.
   I will put an end to the arrogance of the haughty
      and will humble the pride of the ruthless.

12 I will make man [d] scarcer than pure gold,
      more rare than the gold of Ophir.

13 Therefore I will make the heavens tremble;[e]
      and the earth will shake from its place
   at the wrath of the LORD Almighty,
      in the day of his burning anger.

[a] 6 Hebrew *Shaddai*

13:2
[u] Jer 51:27

13:3
[v] Joel 3:11
[w] Ps 149:2

13:5
[x] Isa 5:26
[y] Isa 24:1

13:6
[z] Joel 1:15

13:7
[a] Eze 21:7

13:10
[b] Isa 5:30
[c] Eze 32:7;
Mt 24:29*;
Mk 13:24*

13:12
[d] Isa 4:1

13:13
[e] Isa 34:4; 51:6;
Hag 2:6

13:1ff Chapters 1—12 speak of judgment against the southern kingdom and, to a lesser extent, against the northern kingdom. Chapters 13—23 are about the judgment on other nations. Chapter 13 is an oracle or message from God concerning Babylon. Long before Babylon became a world power and threatened Judah, Isaiah spoke of its destruction. Babylon was the rallying point of rebellion against God after the flood (Genesis 11).

Revelation 17 and 18 use Babylon as a symbol of God's enemies. At the time of this oracle, Babylon was still part of the Assyrian empire. Isaiah communicated a message of challenge and hope to God's people, telling them not to rely on other nations but to rely on God alone. And he let them know that their greatest enemies would receive from God the punishment they deserve.

13:12 Ophir was known for its rare and valuable gold. It is thought to have been located on the southwestern coast of Arabia.

13:14
f Jer 50:16

14 Like a hunted gazelle,
   like sheep without a shepherd,
each will return to his own people,
   each will flee to his native land. *f*

13:15
g Isa 14:19

15 Whoever is captured will be thrust through;
   all who are caught will fall by the sword. *g*

13:16
h Ps 137:9

16 Their infants *h* will be dashed to pieces before their eyes;
   their houses will be looted and their wives ravished.

17 See, I will stir up against them the Medes,
   who do not care for silver
   and have no delight in gold.
18 Their bows will strike down the young men;
   they will have no mercy on infants
   nor will they look with compassion on children.

13:19
i Da 4:30
j Ge 19:24

19 Babylon, the jewel of kingdoms,
   the glory *i* of the Babylonians' **a** pride,
will be overthrown by God
   like Sodom and Gomorrah. *j*
20 She will never be inhabited
   or lived in through all generations;
no Arab will pitch his tent there,
   no shepherd will rest his flocks there.
21 But desert creatures will lie there,
   jackals will fill her houses;
there the owls will dwell,
   and there the wild goats will leap about.

13:22
k Jer 51:33

22 Hyenas will howl in her strongholds,
   jackals in her luxurious palaces.
Her time is at hand, *k*
   and her days will not be prolonged.

14:1
l Ps 102:13
m Zec 1:17; 2:12
n Eph 2:12-19

14
The LORD will have compassion *l* on Jacob;
   once again he will choose *m* Israel
and will settle them in their own land.
Aliens *n* will join them
   and unite with the house of Jacob.

14:2
o Isa 60:9
p Isa 49:7, 23
q Isa 60:14

2 Nations will take them
   and bring *o* them to their own place.
And the house of Israel will possess the nations *p*
   as menservants and maidservants in the LORD's land.
They will make captives of their captors
   and rule over their oppressors. *q*

14:4
r Hab 2:6

3 On the day the LORD gives you relief from suffering and turmoil and cruel bondage, 4 you will take up this taunt *r* against the king of Babylon:

How the oppressor has come to an end!
   How his fury **b** has ended!

a 19 Or *Chaldeans'*   **b** 4 Dead Sea Scrolls, Septuagint and Syriac; the meaning of the word in the Masoretic Text is uncertain.

13:20 Even before Babylon became a world power, Isaiah prophesied that, though it would shine for a while, Babylon's destruction would be so complete that the land would never again be inhabited. Babylon, in present-day Iraq, still lies in utter ruin, burned under mounds of dirt and sand.

14:1 A prominent theme in Isaiah is that aliens (non-Israelites) would join the returning Israelites (56:6, 7; 60:10; 61:5). God's intention was that through his faithful people all the world would be blessed (Genesis 12:3). Through the family of David, the whole world could be saved by Christ. God's Word must be avail-

able to all people groups in their own languages. We must not limit God's love to our own people. God loves the whole world. We must support and help those missions that are reaching out to people who haven't heard the Good News of salvation.

14:4–11 These verses could have both present and future significance in reference to Babylon. The historical city and empire would be permanently destroyed. Babylon has also been used as a picture of all those who oppose God. Thus, in the end times, all who oppose God will be destroyed and all evil will be removed from the earth forever.

5 The Lord has broken the rod of the wicked,
　　the scepter of the rulers,
6 which in anger struck down peoples[s]
　　with unceasing blows,
　and in fury subdued nations
　　with relentless aggression.[t]
7 All the lands are at rest and at peace;
　　they break into singing.
8 Even the pine trees[u] and the cedars of Lebanon
　　exult over you and say,
　"Now that you have been laid low,
　　no woodsman comes to cut us down."

9 The grave[a][v] below is all astir
　　to meet you at your coming;
　it rouses the spirits of the departed to greet you—
　　all those who were leaders in the world;
　it makes them rise from their thrones—
　　all those who were kings over the nations.
10 They will all respond,
　　they will say to you,
　"You also have become weak, as we are;
　　you have become like us."
11 All your pomp has been brought down to the grave,
　　along with the noise of your harps;
　maggots are spread out beneath you
　　and worms cover you.

12 How you have fallen[w] from heaven,
　　O morning star, son of the dawn!
　You have been cast down to the earth,
　　you who once laid low the nations!
13 You said in your heart,
　　"I will ascend[x] to heaven;
　I will raise my throne[y]
　　above the stars of God;
　I will sit enthroned on the mount of assembly,
　　on the utmost heights of the sacred mountain.[b]
14 I will ascend above the tops of the clouds;
　　I will make myself like the Most High."[z]
15 But you are brought down to the grave,
　　to the depths[a] of the pit.

16 Those who see you stare at you,
　　they ponder your fate:
　"Is this the man who shook the earth
　　and made kingdoms tremble,
17 the man who made the world a desert,[b]
　　who overthrew its cities
　　and would not let his captives go home?"

a 9 Hebrew *Sheol*; also in verses 11 and 15　　b 13 Or *the north*; Hebrew *Zaphon*

14:6	
s Isa 10:14	
t Isa 47:6	

14:8
u Eze 31:16

14:9
v Eze 32:21

14:12
w Isa 34:4;
Lk 10:18

14:13
x Da 8:10
y Eze 28:2

14:14
z Isa 47:8; 2Th 2:4

14:15
a Mt 11:23

14:17
b Joel 2:3

14:5, 6 Power fades quickly. God permitted Babylon to have temporary power for a purpose—to punish his wayward people. When the purpose ended, so did the power. Beware of placing confidence in human power because one day it will fade, no matter how strong it appears now.

14:12 "Morning star, son of the dawn" could be names used to worship the kings of Assyria and Babylon. More likely, it means that they will fade like the morning star when the sun rises.

14:12-14 There are several interpretations for the fallen one in these verses. (1) He is Satan, because the person here is too powerful to be any human king. Although Satan may fit verses 12–14, he does not fit well with the rest of the chapter. (2) This could be Sennacherib or Nebuchadnezzar, kings with supreme power. Their people looked upon them as gods. These kings wanted to rule the world. (3) This could refer to both Satan and a great human king, possibly Nebuchadnezzar, because Babylon is pictured as the seat of evil in Revelation 17; 18. Pride was Satan's sin as well as Babylon's. Common to all three viewpoints is the

18 All the kings of the nations lie in state,
   each in his own tomb.

14:19
cIsa 22:16-18

19 But you are cast out c of your tomb
   like a rejected branch;
you are covered with the slain,
   with those pierced by the sword,
   those who descend to the stones of the pit.
Like a corpse trampled underfoot,

14:20
dJob 18:19
ePs 21:10

20   you will not join them in burial,
   for you have destroyed your land
   and killed your people.

The offspring d of the wicked
   will never be mentioned e again.

14:21
fEx 20:5

21 Prepare a place to slaughter his sons
   for the sins of their forefathers; f
they are not to rise to inherit the land
   and cover the earth with their cities.

14:22
gJob 18:19

22 "I will rise up against them,"
   declares the LORD Almighty.
"I will cut off from Babylon her name and survivors,
   her offspring and descendants, g"

declares the LORD.

14:23
hIsa 34:11-15;
Zep 2:14

23 "I will turn her into a place for owls h
   and into swampland;
I will sweep her with the broom of destruction,"
   declares the LORD Almighty.

A Prophecy Against Assyria

14:24
iAc 4:28

24 The LORD Almighty has sworn,

"Surely, as I have planned, so it will be,
   and as I have purposed, so it will stand. i

14:25
jIsa 10:5, 12
kIsa 10:27

25 I will crush the Assyrian j in my land;
   on my mountains I will trample him down.
His yoke will be taken from my people,
   and his burden removed from their shoulders. k"

14:26
lEx 15:12

26 This is the plan determined for the whole world;
   this is the hand l stretched out over all nations.

14:27
m2Ch 20:6;
Isa 43:13; Da 4:35

27 For the LORD Almighty has purposed, and who can thwart him?
   His hand is stretched out, and who can turn it back? m

A Prophecy Against the Philistines

14:28
n2Ki 16:20

28 This oracle came in the year King Ahaz n died:

14:29
o2Ch 26:6

29 Do not rejoice, all you Philistines, o
   that the rod that struck you is broken;
from the root of that snake will spring up a viper,
   its fruit will be a darting, venomous serpent.

14:30
pIsa 3:15

30 The poorest of the poor will find pasture,
   and the needy p will lie down in safety.
But your root I will destroy by famine;
   it will slay your survivors.

---

truth that pride willfully opposes God and will result in judgment.
Israel made the mistake of being too proud to depend on God,
and we are vulnerable to that same mistake.
14:24–27 This prophecy came true as Isaiah predicted (see
2 Kings 19 and Isaiah 37:21–38).

14:28–31 Isaiah received this message from the Lord in 715 B.C.,
the year that King Ahaz of Judah died. "The rod that struck you"
(14:29) was not Ahaz but Shalmaneser V or Sargon of Assyria.
The "cloud of smoke" from the north (14:31) refers to the soldiers
of Sargon of Assyria.

31 Wail, O gate! Howl, O city!
　　Melt away, all you Philistines!
　A cloud of smoke comes from the north,q
　　and there is not a straggler in its ranks.

32 What answer shall be given
　　to the envoys of that nation?
　"The LORD has established Zion,r
　　and in her his afflicted people will find refuge."

14:31
q Jer 1:14

14:32
r Ps 87:2, 5

A Prophecy Against Moab

15

An oracle concerning Moab:

　Ar in Moab is ruined,
　　destroyed in a night!
　Kir in Moab is ruined,
　　destroyed in a night!
2 Dibon goes up to its temple,
　　to its high places to weep;
　Moab wails over Nebo and Medeba.
　Every head is shaveds
　　and every beard cut off.
3 In the streets they wear sackcloth;
　　on the roofs and in the public squarest
　they all wail,
　　prostrate with weeping.
4 Heshbon and Elealeh cry out,
　　their voices are heard all the way to Jahaz.
　Therefore the armed men of Moab cry out,
　　and their hearts are faint.

5 My heart cries out over Moab;
　　her fugitives flee as far as Zoar,
　　as far as Eglath Shelishiyah.
　They go up the way to Luhith,
　　weeping as they go;
　on the road to Horonaim
　　they lament their destruction.u
6 The waters of Nimrim are dried up
　　and the grass is withered;v
　the vegetation is gone
　　and nothing green is left.
7 So the wealth they have acquired w and stored up
　　they carry away over the Ravine of the Poplars.
8 Their outcry echoes along the border of Moab;
　　their wailing reaches as far as Eglaim,
　　their lamentation as far as Beer Elim.
9 Dimon'sa waters are full of blood,
　　but I will bring still more upon Dimona—
　a lionx upon the fugitives of Moab
　　and upon those who remain in the land.

15:2
s Lev 21:5

15:3
t Jer 48:38

15:5
u Jer 48:5

15:6
v Joel 1:12

15:7
w Isa 30:6

15:9
x 2Ki 17:25

16

Send lambsy as tribute
　　to the ruler of the land,
from Sela,z across the desert,
　　to the mount of the Daughter of Zion.

16:1
y 2Ki 3:4
z 2Ki 14:7

a 9 Masoretic Text; Dead Sea Scrolls, some Septuagint manuscripts and Vulgate Dibon

---

15:1 Moab was east of the Dead Sea. The Moabites were descendants of Lot through his incestuous relationship with his older daughter (Genesis 19:31–38). Moab had always been Israel's enemy. They oppressed Israel and invaded their land (Judges 3:12–14), fought against Saul (1 Samuel 14:47) and against David (2 Samuel 8:2, 11, 12). Moab would be punished for treating Israel harshly.

16:1ff Attacked by the Assyrians, Moabite refugees would flee

16:2
a Nu 21:13-14

2 Like fluttering birds
        pushed from the nest,
    so are the women of Moab
        at the fords of the Arnon.*a*

3 "Give us counsel,
        render a decision.
    Make your shadow like night—
        at high noon.
    Hide the fugitives,
        do not betray the refugees.

16:4
b Isa 9:4

4 Let the Moabite fugitives stay with you;
        be their shelter from the destroyer."

    The oppressor*b* will come to an end,
        and destruction will cease;
    the aggressor will vanish from the land.

16:5
c Da 7:14; Mic 4:7
d Lk 1:32

5 In love a throne*c* will be established;
        in faithfulness a man will sit on it—
    one from the house*a* of David*d*—
    one who in judging seeks justice
        and speeds the cause of righteousness.

6 We have heard of Moab's pride—
        her overweening pride and conceit,
    her pride and her insolence—
        but her boasts are empty.

16:7
e 2Ki 3:25

7 Therefore the Moabites wail,
        they wail together for Moab.
    Lament and grieve
        for the men*b* of Kir Hareseth.*e*

8 The fields of Heshbon wither,
        the vines of Sibmah also.
    The rulers of the nations
        have trampled down the choicest vines,
    which once reached Jazer
        and spread toward the desert.
    Their shoots spread out
        and went as far as the sea.

16:9
f Isa 15:3
g Jer 40:12

9 So I weep,*f* as Jazer weeps,
        for the vines of Sibmah.
    O Heshbon, O Elealeh,
        I drench you with tears!
    The shouts of joy over your ripened fruit
        and over your harvests*g* have been stilled.

16:10
h Isa 24:7-8

10 Joy and gladness are taken away from the orchards;*h*
        no one sings or shouts in the vineyards;
    no one treads out wine at the presses,
        for I have put an end to the shouting.

16:11
i Isa 63:15

11 My heart laments for Moab like a harp,
        my inmost being*i* for Kir Hareseth.

a5 Hebrew *tent*   *b7* Or *"raisin cakes,"* a wordplay

---

to Sela, which lay in the country of Edom to the south.
Desperate Moabites would send a tribute of lambs to Jerusalem asking for Judah's protection. Jerusalem would be a
safe refuge for a while. Isaiah advised Judah to accept these
refugees as a sign of compassion during the enemy's time
of devastation.

16:10 The treading of grapes (squeezing the juice from grapes
by mashing them with bare feet) was the climax of the harvest

season, a time of great joy in the vineyards. But the joy of
harvest would soon be ended because the people in their pride
ignored God and rebelled against him.

¹² When Moab appears at her high place,
 she only wears herself out;
when she goes to her shrine*ʲ* to pray,
 it is to no avail.

¹³This is the word the LORD has already spoken concerning Moab. ¹⁴But now the LORD says: "Within three years, as a servant bound by contract would count them, Moab's splendor and all her many people will be despised, and her survivors will be very few and feeble."*ᵏ*

An Oracle Against Damascus

17 An oracle concerning Damascus:*ˡ*

 "See, Damascus will no longer be a city
  but will become a heap of ruins.*ᵐ*
² The cities of Aroer will be deserted
  and left to flocks, which will lie down,
 with no one to make them afraid.*ⁿ*
³ The fortified city will disappear from Ephraim,
  and royal power from Damascus;
 the remnant of Aram will be
  like the glory of the Israelites,"*ᵒ*

 declares the LORD Almighty.

⁴ "In that day the glory of Jacob will fade;
  the fat of his body will waste*ᵖ* away.
⁵ It will be as when a reaper gathers the standing grain
  and harvests*�q* the grain with his arm—
 as when a man gleans heads of grain
  in the Valley of Rephaim.
⁶ Yet some gleanings will remain,*ʳ*
  as when an olive tree is beaten,
 leaving two or three olives on the topmost branches,
  four or five on the fruitful boughs,"

 declares the LORD, the God of Israel.

⁷ In that day men will look to their Maker
  and turn their eyes to the Holy One*ˢ* of Israel.
⁸ They will not look to the altars,
  the work of their hands,
 and they will have no regard for the Asherah poles*ᵃ*
  and the incense altars their fingers have made.

⁹ In that day their strong cities, which they left because of the Israelites, will be like places abandoned to thickets and undergrowth. And all will be desolation.

ᵃ 8 That is, symbols of the goddess Asherah

16:12	ʲIsa 15:2
16:14	ᵏIsa 21:17
17:1	ˡJer 49:23 / ᵐAm 1:3; Zec 9:1
17:2	ⁿJer 7:33
17:3	ᵒIsa 7:8, 16; 8:4
17:4	ᵖIsa 10:16
17:5	qJer 51:33
17:6	ʳIsa 24:13
17:7	ˢMic 7:7

16:12 When the people of Moab experienced God's wrath, they sought their own idols and gods. Nothing happened, however, because there was no one there to save them. When we seek our own ways of escape in order to get through our daily troubles, the effect is the same: no pleasure, pastime, or man-made religious idea will come to save us. Our hope lies in God, the only One who can hear and help.

16:13, 14 Tiglath-Pileser III invaded Moab in 732 B.C.; Sennacherib invaded Moab the same year that he invaded Judah, 701 B.C. The earlier event occurred three years after Isaiah's prediction, marking Isaiah as a true prophet. In these events, the people of Israel saw prophecy fulfilled before their very eyes.

17:1ff The northern kingdom and Aram made an alliance to fight against Assyria. But Tiglath-Pileser III captured Damascus, the capital of Aram, in 732 B.C. and annexed the northern kingdom to the Assyrian empire. Ahaz, king of Judah, paid tribute to Tiglath-Pileser III (2 Kings 16:1–14).

17:7–11 God's message to Damascus is that it will be com-

pletely destroyed. The Arameans had turned from the God who could save them, depending instead on their idols and their own strength. No matter how successful they were, God's judgment was sure. Often we depend on the trappings of success (expensive cars, pastimes, clothes, homes) to give us fulfillment. But God says we will reap grief and pain if we have depended on temporal things to give us eternal security. If we don't want the same treatment Damascus received, we must turn from these false allurements and trust in God.

17:8 The Asherah poles were images of Asherah, a Canaanite goddess who was the female consort of Baal. Queen Jezebel may have brought the worship of Asherah into the northern kingdom. The cult encouraged immoral sexual practices and attracted many people. The Bible warns against worshiping Asherah poles (Exodus 34:13; Deuteronomy 12:3; 16:21), and Manasseh was condemned for putting up an Asherah pole in the temple (2 Kings 21:7).

Asherah poles are not a problem in our world, but a religion based on sexuality is. Pornography has become an addiction for

17:10
t Ps 68:19

10 You have forgotten God your Savior;*t*
    you have not remembered the Rock, your fortress.
Therefore, though you set out the finest plants
    and plant imported vines,

17:11
u Ps 90:6
v Job 4:8

11 though on the day you set them out, you make them grow,
    and on the morning*u* when you plant them, you bring them to bud,
yet the harvest will be as nothing
    in the day of disease and incurable pain.*v*

17:12
w Jer 6:23

12 Oh, the raging of many nations—
    they rage like the raging sea!*w*
Oh, the uproar of the peoples—
    they roar like the roaring of great waters!

17:13
x Ps 9:5

13 Although the peoples roar like the roar of surging waters,
    when he rebukes*x* them they flee far away,
driven before the wind like chaff on the hills,
    like tumbleweed before a gale.

17:14
y 2Ki 19:35

14 In the evening, sudden terror!
    Before the morning, they are gone!*y*
This is the portion of those who loot us,
    the lot of those who plunder us.

A Prophecy Against Cush

18:1
z Isa 20:3-5;
Eze 30:4-5, 9;
Zep 2:12; 3:10

18:2
a ver 7

18 Woe to the land of whirring wings*a*
        along the rivers of Cush,*b z*
    2 which sends envoys by sea
        in papyrus boats over the water.

Go, swift messengers,
to a people tall and smooth-skinned,
    to a people feared far and wide,
an aggressive nation of strange speech,
    whose land is divided by rivers.*a*

3 All you people of the world,
    you who live on the earth,

a 1 Or of locusts   b 1 That is, the upper Nile region

**ALLIANCES
TODAY**

Government. . . . . We rely on government legislation to protect the moral decisions
                          we want made, but legislation cannot change people's hearts.

Science . . . . We enjoy the benefits of science and technology. We look to
                          scientific predictions and analysis before we look to the Bible.

Education . . . . We act as though education and degrees can guarantee our future
                          and success without considering what God plans for our future.

Medical care . . . . We regard medicine as the way to prolong life and preserve its
                          quality—quite apart from faith and moral living.

Financial systems . . . . . We place our faith in financial "security"—making as much money
                          as we can for ourselves—forgetting that, while being wise with our
                          money, we must trust God for our needs.

Isaiah warned Judah not to ally with Egypt (20:5; 30:1, 2; 31:1). He knew that trust in any
nation or any military might was futile. Judah's only hope was to trust in God. Although we
don't consciously put our hope for deliverance in political alliances in quite the same way,
we often put our hope in other places.

---

many people. Media and entertainment industries feed our society's obsession with sex. The runaway desire for stimulation and gratification often comes from an empty, lonely heart. God offers real joy and lasting love. Be on the alert for how sexual images divert us from God.

18:1ff This prophecy was probably given in the days of Hezekiah (2 Kings 19; 20). The "land of whirring wings" refers to locusts, and probably pictures the armies of Cush. The king of Cush had

heard that Assyria's great army was marching south toward them. He sent messengers up the Nile asking the surrounding nations to form an alliance. Judah was also asked, but Isaiah told the messengers to return home because Judah needed only God's help to repel the Assyrians. Isaiah prophesied that Assyria would be destroyed at the proper time (37:21–38).

18:3 This is a signal of the doom of Cush and Assyria's victory over Cush (see 20:1–6).

when a banner is raised on the mountains,
    you will see it,
and when a trumpet sounds,
    you will hear it.
4 This is what the LORD says to me: 18:4
    "I will remain quiet and will look on from my dwelling place,   *b* Isa 26:19
like shimmering heat in the sunshine,
    like a cloud of dew*b* in the heat of harvest."
5 For, before the harvest, when the blossom is gone
    and the flower becomes a ripening grape,
he will cut off the shoots with pruning knives,
    and cut down and take away the spreading branches.
6 They will all be left to the mountain birds of prey   18:6
    and to the wild animals;*c*   *c* Jer 7:33
the birds will feed on them all summer,
    the wild animals all winter.

7 At that time gifts will be brought to the LORD Almighty   18:7
                                                                  d Ps 68:31
    from a people tall and smooth-skinned,
    from a people feared far and wide,
an aggressive nation of strange speech,
    whose land is divided by rivers—

the gifts will be brought to Mount Zion, the place of the Name of the LORD Almighty. *d*

A Prophecy About Egypt

19 An oracle*e* concerning Egypt:*f*   19:1
                                                                  e Jer 43:12
See, the LORD rides on a swift cloud*g*   *f* Ex 12:12
    and is coming to Egypt.   *g* Ps 18:10; 104:3
The idols of Egypt tremble before him,
    and the hearts of the Egyptians melt within them.

2 "I will stir up Egyptian against Egyptian—   19:2
    brother will fight against brother,*h*   *h* Jdg 7:22
neighbor against neighbor,   *i* 2Ch 20:23
    city against city,
    kingdom against kingdom.*i*
3 The Egyptians will lose heart,   19:3
    and I will bring their plans to nothing;   *j* Isa 8:19
they will consult the idols and the spirits of the dead,
    the mediums and the spiritists.*j*
4 I will hand the Egyptians over   19:4
    to the power of a cruel master,   *k* Isa 20:4;
and a fierce king*k* will rule over them,"   Jer 46:26;
    declares the Lord, the LORD Almighty.   Eze 29:19

5 The waters of the river will dry up,*l*   19:5
    and the riverbed will be parched and dry.   *l* Jer 51:36
6 The canals will stink;   19:6
    the streams of Egypt will dwindle and dry up.*m*   *m* Eze 30:12
The reeds and rushes will wither,
7   also the plants along the Nile,
    at the mouth of the river.
Every sown field along the Nile
    will become parched, will blow away and be no more.

19:1 Egypt, the nation where God's people were enslaved for 400 years (Exodus 1), was hated by the people of Israel. Yet Judah was considering an alliance with Egypt against Assyria (2 Kings 18:17ff). But Isaiah warned against this alliance because God would destroy Assyria in his time.

⁸ The fishermen will groan and lament,
 all who cast hooks into the Nile;
 those who throw nets on the water
  will pine away.
⁹ Those who work with combed flax will despair,
 the weavers of fine linenⁿ will lose hope.
¹⁰ The workers in cloth will be dejected,
 and all the wage earners will be sick at heart.

¹¹ The officials of Zoan^o are nothing but fools;
 the wise counselors of Pharaoh give senseless advice.
How can you say to Pharaoh,
 "I am one of the wise men,
 a disciple of the ancient kings"?

¹² Where are your wise men now?
 Let them show you and make known
what the Lord Almighty
 has planned against Egypt.
¹³ The officials of Zoan have become fools,
 the leaders of Memphis^{a p} are deceived;
the cornerstones of her peoples
 have led Egypt astray.
¹⁴ The Lord has poured into them
 a spirit of dizziness;
they make Egypt stagger in all that she does,
 as a drunkard staggers around in his vomit.
¹⁵ There is nothing Egypt can do—
 head or tail, palm branch or reed.^q

¹⁶In that day the Egyptians will be like women. They will shudder with fear at the uplifted hand^r that the Lord Almighty raises against them. ¹⁷And the land of Judah will bring terror to the Egyptians; everyone to whom Judah is mentioned will be terrified, because of what the Lord Almighty is planning against them.

¹⁸In that day five cities in Egypt will speak the language of Canaan and swear allegiance to the Lord Almighty. One of them will be called the City of Destruction.^b

¹⁹In that day there will be an altar^s to the Lord in the heart of Egypt, and a monument^t to the Lord at its border. ²⁰It will be a sign and witness to the Lord Almighty in the land of Egypt. When they cry out to the Lord because of their oppressors, he will send them a savior and defender, and he will rescue^u them. ²¹So the Lord will make himself known to the Egyptians, and in that day they will acknowledge the Lord. They will worship with sacrifices and grain offerings; they will make vows to the Lord and keep them. ²²The Lord will strike Egypt with a plague; he will strike them and heal them. They will turn^v to the Lord, and he will respond to their pleas and heal them.

²³In that day there will be a highway^w from Egypt to Assyria. The Assyrians will go to Egypt and the Egyptians to Assyria. The Egyptians and Assyrians will worship^x together. ²⁴In that day Israel will be the third, along with Egypt and Assyria, a blessing on the earth. ²⁵The Lord Almighty will bless them, saying, "Blessed be Egypt my people,^y Assyria my handiwork,^z and Israel my inheritance.^a"

19:9
ⁿPr 7:16

19:11
^oNu 13:22

19:13
^pJer 2:16

19:15
^qIsa 9:14

19:16
^rIsa 11:15

19:19
^sJos 22:10
^tGe 28:18

19:20
^uIsa 49:24-26

19:22
^vIsa 45:14

19:23
^wIsa 11:16
^xIsa 27:13

19:25
^yPs 100:3
^zIsa 29:23;
Eph 2:10
^aHos 2:23

^a 13 Hebrew *Noph*   ^b 18 Most manuscripts of the Masoretic Text; some manuscripts of the Masoretic Text, Dead Sea Scrolls and Vulgate *City of the Sun* (that is, Heliopolis)

19:11–15 Egypt was noted for its wisdom, but here its wise men and officials were deceived and foolish. True wisdom can come only from God. We must ask him for wisdom to guide our decisions, or we will also be uncertain and misdirected. Are you confused about something now? Ask God for wisdom to deal with it.

19:19, 23 After Egypt's chastening, it would turn from idols and worship the one true God. Even more amazing is Isaiah's prophecy that the two chief oppressors of Israel, Egypt and Assyria, would unite in worship. This prophecy will come true "in that day," the future day of Christ's reign.

19:20 When Egypt calls to God for help, he will send a savior to deliver them. Our Savior, Jesus Christ, is available to all who call upon him. We too can pray and receive his saving power (John 1:12).

19:23–25 In Jesus Christ, former enemies may unite in love. In Christ, people and nations that are poles apart politically will bow at his feet as brothers and sisters. Christ breaks down every barrier that threatens relationships (see Ephesians 2:13–19).

A Prophecy Against Egypt and Cush

20 In the year that the supreme commander,[b] sent by Sargon king of Assyria, came to Ashdod and attacked and captured it— [2] at that time the LORD spoke through Isaiah son of Amoz. He said to him, "Take off the sackcloth[c] from your body and the sandals from your feet." And he did so, going around stripped[d] and barefoot.[e]

[3] Then the LORD said, "Just as my servant Isaiah has gone stripped and barefoot for three years, as a sign[f] and portent against Egypt and Cush,[a] [4] so the king of Assyria will lead away stripped and barefoot the Egyptian captives and Cushite exiles, young and old, with buttocks bared—to Egypt's shame. [5] Those who trusted in Cush and boasted in Egypt[g] will be afraid and put to shame. [6] In that day the people who live on this coast will say, 'See what has happened to those we relied on, those we fled to for help and deliverance from the king of Assyria! How then can we escape?'"

A Prophecy Against Babylon

21 An oracle concerning the Desert by the Sea:

Like whirlwinds sweeping through the southland,[h]
    an invader comes from the desert,
    from a land of terror.

[2] A dire vision has been shown to me:
    The traitor betrays,[i] the looter takes loot.
    Elam,[j] attack! Media, lay siege!
    I will bring to an end all the groaning she caused.

[3] At this my body is racked with pain,
    pangs seize me, like those of a woman in labor;
I am staggered by what I hear,
    I am bewildered by what I see.
[4] My heart falters,
    fear makes me tremble;
the twilight I longed for
    has become a horror to me.

[5] They set the tables,
    they spread the rugs,
    they eat, they drink!
Get up, you officers,
    oil the shields!

[6] This is what the Lord says to me:

"Go, post a lookout
    and have him report what he sees.
[7] When he sees chariots[k]
    with teams of horses,
riders on donkeys
    or riders on camels,
let him be alert,
    fully alert."

a3 That is, the upper Nile region; also in verse 5

Cross-references
20:1 b 2Ki 18:17
20:2 c Zec 13:4 · d 1Sa 19:24 · e Mic 1:8
20:3 f Isa 8:18
20:5 g 2Ki 18:21
21:1 h Zec 9:14
21:2 i Isa 33:1 · j Jer 49:34
21:7 k ver 9

20:1ff Sargon II was king of Assyria from 722–705 B.C., and this event happened in 711 B.C. Isaiah graphically reminds Judah that they should not count on foreign alliances to protect them.

20:2 God's command to Isaiah was to walk about naked for three years, a humiliating experience. God was using Isaiah to demonstrate the humiliation that Egypt and Cush would experience at the hands of Assyria. But the message was really for Judah: Don't put your trust in foreign governments, or you will experience this kind of shame from your captors. Human governments and institutions can never take God's place.

20:2 God asked Isaiah to do something that seemed shameful and illogical. At times, God may ask us to take steps we don't understand. We must obey God in complete faith, for he will never ask us to do something wrong.

21:1ff "The Desert by the Sea" is Babylon by the Persian Gulf. Some scholars say this prophecy was fulfilled at Babylon's fall in 539 B.C. (see Daniel 5). But others say this was a prophecy of Babylon's revolt against Assyria around 700 B.C.

21:5 If the prophecy refers to the fall of Babylon in 539 B.C., this may picture the feast in Daniel 5.

21:6, 7 Lookouts (watchmen on the city walls) often appear in prophetic visions of destruction. They are the first to see trouble

21:8
*Hab 2:1

[8]And the lookout[a] *l* shouted,

> "Day after day, my lord, I stand on the watchtower;
>   every night I stay at my post.

21:9
m Rev 14:8
n Jer 51:8; Rev 18:2
o Isa 46:1; Jer 50:2;
51:44

> [9] Look, here comes a man in a chariot
>   with a team of horses.
> And he gives back the answer:
>   'Babylon[m] has fallen,[n] has fallen!
> All the images of its gods[o]
>   lie shattered on the ground!'"

21:10
p Jer 51:33

> [10] O my people, crushed on the threshing floor,[p]
>   I tell you what I have heard
> from the LORD Almighty,
>   from the God of Israel.

A Prophecy Against Edom

[11]An oracle concerning Dumah[b]:

> Someone calls to me from Seir,
>   "Watchman, what is left of the night?
>   Watchman, what is left of the night?"
> [12] The watchman replies,
>   "Morning is coming, but also the night.
> If you would ask, then ask;
>   and come back yet again."

A Prophecy Against Arabia

[13]An oracle concerning Arabia:

> You caravans of Dedanites,
>   who camp in the thickets of Arabia,
> [14]   bring water for the thirsty;
> you who live in Tema,
>   bring food for the fugitives.
> [15] They flee from the sword,
>   from the drawn sword,
> from the bent bow
>   and from the heat of battle.

21:16
q Isa 16:14
r Ps 120:5; Isa 60:7

[16]This is what the Lord says to me: "Within one year, as a servant bound by contract[q] would count it, all the pomp of Kedar[r] will come to an end. [17]The survivors of the bowmen, the warriors of Kedar, will be few." The LORD, the God of Israel, has spoken.

[a]*8 Dead Sea Scrolls and Syriac; Masoretic Text A lion*   [b]*11 Dumah means silence or stillness, a wordplay on Edom.*

---

coming. The prophet Habakkuk was a watchman (Habakkuk 2:1). The vision of the riders on horses could represent the Medes and Persians attacking Babylon in 539 B.C.

21:8, 9 Babylon was not only a great and powerful city, it was also filled with horrible sin (idolatry, witchcraft, and temple prostitution). Babylon was, and remains, a symbol of all that stands against God. Despite all its glory and power, Babylon would be destroyed, along with all its idols. They would give no help in time of trouble.

21:10 Threshing and winnowing were two steps in ancient Israel's farming process. The heads of wheat (often used to symbolize Israel) were first trampled to break open the seeds and expose the valued grain inside (threshing). The seeds were then thrown into the air, and the worthless chaff blew away while the grain fell back to the ground (winnowing). Israel would experience this same kind of process—the worthless, sinful, rebellious people would be taken away, but God would keep the good "grain" to replenish Israel.

21:11 Dumah, or Edom, had been a constant enemy of God's people. They rejoiced when Israel fell to the Assyrians, and this sealed Edom's doom (34:8ff; 63:4). Seir was another name for Edom because the hill country of Seir was given to Esau and his descendants (see Joshua 24:4). Obadiah foretells, in great detail, the destruction of Edom.

21:13ff The places listed here are all in Arabia. They are border cities that controlled the trade routes through the land. This is Isaiah's prediction of disaster.

A Prophecy About Jerusalem

22 An oracle concerning the Valley[s] of Vision:

> What troubles you now,
>> that you have all gone up on the roofs,
> 2 O town full of commotion,
>> O city of tumult and revelry?[t]
> Your slain were not killed by the sword,
>> nor did they die in battle.
> 3 All your leaders have fled together;
>> they have been captured without using the bow.
> All you who were caught were taken prisoner together,
>> having fled while the enemy was still far away.
> 4 Therefore I said, "Turn away from me;
>> let me weep bitterly.
> Do not try to console me
>> over the destruction of my people."[u]

> 5 The Lord, the LORD Almighty, has a day
>> of tumult and trampling and terror[v]
>> in the Valley of Vision,
> a day of battering down walls
>> and of crying out to the mountains.
> 6 Elam takes up the quiver,[w]
>> with her charioteers and horses;
> Kir[x] uncovers the shield.
> 7 Your choicest valleys are full of chariots,
>> and horsemen are posted at the city gates;
> 8   the defenses of Judah are stripped away.

> And you looked in that day
>> to the weapons in the Palace of the Forest;[y]
> 9 you saw that the City of David
>> had many breaches in its defenses;
> you stored up water
>> in the Lower Pool.
> 10 You counted the buildings in Jerusalem
>> and tore down houses to strengthen the wall.
> 11 You built a reservoir between the two walls[z]
>> for the water of the Old Pool,[a]
> but you did not look to the One who made it,
>> or have regard for the One who planned it long ago.

> 12 The Lord, the LORD Almighty,
>> called you on that day
> to weep and to wail,
>> to tear out your hair[b] and put on sackcloth.[c]

22:1 [s] Joel 3:2, 12, 14

22:2 [t] Isa 32:13

22:4 [u] Jer 9:1

22:5 [v] La 1:5

22:6 [w] Jer 49:35 [x] 2Ki 16:9

22:8 [y] 1Ki 7:2

22:11 [z] 2Ki 25:4 [a] 2Ch 32:4

22:12 [b] Mic 1:16 [c] Joel 1:13

22:1–13 "The Valley of Vision" refers to the city of Jerusalem, where God revealed himself. Jerusalem would be attacked unless God's people returned to him. Instead they used every means of protection possible except asking God for help. They wanted to trust in their ingenuity, their weapons, and even their pagan neighbors (see 2 Chronicles 32 for the description of a siege of Jerusalem).

22:4 Isaiah had warned his people, but they did not repent; thus they would experience God's judgment. Because of his care for them, Isaiah was hurt by their punishment and mourned deeply for them. Sometimes people we care for ignore our attempts to

help, so they suffer the very grief we wanted to spare them. At times like that we grieve because of our concern. God expects us to be involved with others, and this may sometimes require us to suffer with them.

22:6, 7 Elam and Kir were under Assyrian rule. The entire Assyrian army, including its vassals, joined in the attack against Jerusalem.

22:8–11 The leaders of Judah did what they could to prepare for war: they got weapons, inspected the walls, and stored up water in a reservoir. But all their work was pointless because they never asked God for help. Too often we take steps that, though good in themselves, really won't give us the help we need. We must get the weapons and inspect the walls, but God must guide the work.

22:13
d Isa 56:12
e 1Co 15:32*

13 But see, there is joy and revelry,
　　slaughtering of cattle and killing of sheep,
　　eating of meat and drinking of wine! *d*
"Let us eat and drink," you say,
　　"for tomorrow we die!" *e*

22:14
f Isa 5:9

14 The LORD Almighty has revealed this in my hearing: *f* "Till your dying day this sin will not be atoned for," says the Lord, the LORD Almighty.

22:15
g 2Ki 18:18; Isa 36:3

15 This is what the Lord, the LORD Almighty, says:

"Go, say to this steward,
　　to Shebna, *g* who is in charge of the palace:

22:16
h Mt 27:60

16 What are you doing here and who gave you permission
　　to cut out a grave *h* for yourself here,
hewing your grave on the height
　　and chiseling your resting place in the rock?

17 "Beware, the LORD is about to take firm hold of you
　　and hurl you away, O you mighty man.

22:18
i Isa 17:13

18 He will roll you up tightly like a ball
　　and throw *i* you into a large country.
There you will die
　　and there your splendid chariots will remain—
　　you disgrace to your master's house!
19 I will depose you from your office,
　　and you will be ousted from your position.

22:20
j 2Ki 18:18
22:22
k Rev 3:7
l Job 12:14
22:23
m Ezr 9:8
n Job 36:7

20 "In that day I will summon my servant, Eliakim *j* son of Hilkiah. 21 I will clothe him with your robe and fasten your sash around him and hand your authority over to him. He will be a father to those who live in Jerusalem and to the house of Judah. 22 I will place on his shoulder the key *k* to the house of David; what he opens no one can shut, and what he shuts no one can open. *l* 23 I will drive him like a peg into a firm place; *m* he will be a seat *a* of honor *n* for the house of his father. 24 All the glory of his family will hang on him: its offspring and off-shoots—all its lesser vessels, from the bowls to all the jars.

22:25
o ver 23
p Isa 46:11

25 "In that day," declares the LORD Almighty, "the peg *o* driven into the firm place will give way; it will be sheared off and will fall, and the load hanging on it will be cut down." The LORD has spoken. *p*

A Prophecy About Tyre

23:1
q Jer 47:4; Eze 26;
27; 28; Zec 9:2-4

23
An oracle concerning Tyre: *q*

Wail, O ships of Tarshish!
For Tyre is destroyed
　　and left without house or harbor.
From the land of Cyprus *b*
　　word has come to them.

a 23 Or *throne*　　*b* 1 Hebrew *Kittim*

22:13, 14 The people said, "Let us eat and drink," because they had given up hope. Attacked on every side (22:7), they should have repented (22:12), but they chose to feast instead. The root problem was that Judah did not trust God's power or his promises (see 56:12; 1 Corinthians 15:32). When you face difficulties, turn to God. Today we still see people giving up hope. There are two common responses to hopelessness: despair and self-indulgence. But this life is not all there is, so we are not to act as if we had no hope. Our proper response should be to trust God and his promise to include us in the perfect and just new world that he will create.

22:15–25 Shebna, a high court steward or official, was just as materialistic as the rest of the people in Jerusalem (22:13). He may have been in the group favoring an alliance with foreigners,

thus ignoring Isaiah's advice. The Lord revealed that Shebna would lose his position and be replaced by Eliakim (22:21). Eliakim would be the "peg" driven into "a firm place" (22:23). Unfortunately, Eliakim too would fall (22:25).

23:1ff Isaiah's prophecies against other nations began in the east with Babylon (chapter 13) and ended in the west with Tyre in Phoenicia. Tyre was one of the most famous cities of the ancient world. A major trading center with a large seaport, Tyre was very wealthy and very evil. Tyre was rebuked by Jeremiah (Jeremiah 25:22, 27; 47:4), Ezekiel (Ezekiel 26—28), Joel (Joel 3:4–8), Amos (Amos 1:9, 10), and Zechariah (Zechariah 9:3, 4). This is another warning against political alliances with unstable neighbors.

² Be silent, you people of the island
    and you merchants of Sidon,
    whom the seafarers have enriched.
³ On the great waters
    came the grain of the Shihor;
    the harvest of the Nile[a] was the revenue of Tyre,[r]
    and she became the marketplace of the nations.

⁴ Be ashamed, O Sidon, and you, O fortress of the sea,
    for the sea has spoken:
"I have neither been in labor nor given birth;
    I have neither reared sons nor brought up daughters."
⁵ When word comes to Egypt,
    they will be in anguish at the report from Tyre.

⁶ Cross over to Tarshish;
    wail, you people of the island.
⁷ Is this your city of revelry,[s]
    the old, old city,
    whose feet have taken her
    to settle in far-off lands?
⁸ Who planned this against Tyre,
    the bestower of crowns,
    whose merchants are princes,
    whose traders are renowned in the earth?
⁹ The LORD Almighty planned it,
    to bring low[t] the pride of all glory
    and to humble all who are renowned[u] on the earth.

¹⁰ Till[b] your land as along the Nile,
    O Daughter of Tarshish,
    for you no longer have a harbor.
¹¹ The LORD has stretched out his hand over the sea
    and made its kingdoms tremble.
He has given an order concerning Phoenicia[c]
    that her fortresses be destroyed.[v]
¹² He said, "No more of your reveling,[w]
    O Virgin Daughter of Sidon, now crushed!

"Up, cross over to Cyprus[d];
    even there you will find no rest."
¹³ Look at the land of the Babylonians,[e]
    this people that is now of no account!
The Assyrians[x] have made it
    a place for desert creatures;
they raised up their siege towers,
    they stripped its fortresses bare
    and turned it into a ruin.[y]

¹⁴ Wail, you ships of Tarshish;
    your fortress is destroyed!

¹⁵At that time Tyre[z] will be forgotten for seventy years, the span of a king's life. But at the
end of these seventy years, it will happen to Tyre as in the song of the prostitute:

23:3
[r] Eze 27:3

23:7
[s] Isa 22:2; 32:13

23:9
[t] Job 40:11
[u] Isa 5:13

23:11
[v] Isa 25:2

23:12
[w] Rev 18:22

23:13
[x] Isa 10:5
[y] Isa 10:7

23:15
[z] Jer 25:22

[a] 2,3 Masoretic Text; one Dead Sea Scroll *Sidon, / who cross over the sea; / your envoys* ³*are on the great waters. /
The grain of the Shihor, / the harvest of the Nile,* [b] 10 Dead Sea Scrolls and some Septuagint manuscripts;
Masoretic Text *Go through* [c] 11 Hebrew *Canaan* [d] 12 Hebrew *Kittim* [e] 13 Or *Chaldeans*

23:5 Why would Egypt be "in anguish" when Tyre fell? Egypt
depended on Tyre's shipping expertise to promote and carry their
products around the world. Egypt would lose an important trading
partner with the fall of Tyre.
23:9 God would destroy Tyre because he hated its people's
pride. Pride separates people from God, and he will not tolerate it.

We must examine our lives and remember that all true accomplishment comes from our Creator. We have no reason for pride
in ourselves.
23:15, 16 Some scholars believe this is a literal 70 years; some
say it is symbolic of a long period of time. If it is literal, this
may have occurred between 700–630 B.C. during the Assyrian

16 "Take up a harp, walk through the city,
    O prostitute forgotten;
  play the harp well, sing many a song,
    so that you will be remembered."

¹⁷At the end of seventy years, the LORD will deal with Tyre. She will return to her hire as a prostitute ^a and will ply her trade with all the kingdoms on the face of the earth. ¹⁸Yet her profit and her earnings will be set apart for the LORD; they will not be stored up or hoarded. Her profits will go to those who live before the LORD,^b for abundant food and fine clothes.

23:17
^aEze 16:26;
Rev 17:1
23:18
^bIsa 60:5-9

3. God's purpose in judgment
The LORD's Devastation of the Earth

24

See, the LORD is going to lay waste the earth
    and devastate it;
  he will ruin its face
    and scatter its inhabitants—
² it will be the same
    for priest as for people,^c
    for master as for servant,
    for mistress as for maid,
    for seller as for buyer,
    for borrower as for lender,
    for debtor as for creditor.^d
³ The earth will be completely laid waste
    and totally plundered.

24:2
^cHos 4:9
^dDt 23:19-20

The LORD has spoken this word.

⁴ The earth dries up and withers,
    the world languishes and withers,
    the exalted of the earth languish.
⁵ The earth is defiled ^e by its people;
    they have disobeyed the laws,
  violated the statutes
    and broken the everlasting covenant.
⁶ Therefore a curse consumes the earth;
    its people must bear their guilt.
  Therefore earth's inhabitants are burned up,
    and very few are left.
⁷ The new wine dries up and the vine withers;^f
    all the merrymakers groan.^g
⁸ The gaiety of the tambourines is stilled,
    the noise^h of the revelers has stopped,
    the joyful harpⁱ is silent.^j
⁹ No longer do they drink wine with a song;
    the beer is bitter^k to its drinkers.
¹⁰ The ruined city lies desolate;
    the entrance to every house is barred.
¹¹ In the streets they cry out for wine;
    all joy turns to gloom,
    all gaiety is banished from the earth.

24:5
^eGe 3:17; Nu 35:33

24:7
^fJoel 1:10-12
^gIsa 16:8-10
24:8
^hHos 2:11
ⁱRev 18:22
^jEze 26:13
24:9
^kIsa 5:20

---

captivity of Israel, or it may have been during the 70-year captivity of the Jews in Babylon (605–536 B.C.). During the 70 years, the Jews would forget about Tyre. But when they returned from captivity, they would once again trade with Tyre.

24—27 These four chapters are often called "Isaiah's Apocalypse." They discuss God's judgment on the entire world for its sin. Isaiah's prophecies were first directed to Judah, then to Israel, then to the surrounding nations, and finally to the whole world. These chapters describe the last days when God will judge the whole world. At that time he will finally and permanently remove evil.

24:4, 5 Not only the people suffered from their sins; even the land suffered the effects of evil and lawbreaking. Today we see the results of sin in our own land—pollution, crime, addiction, poverty. Sin affects every aspect of society so extensively that even those faithful to God suffer. We cannot blame God for these conditions because human sin has brought them about. The more we who are believers renounce sin, speak against immoral practices, and share God's Word with others, the more we slow our society's deterioration. We must not give up: sin is rampant, but we can make a difference.

¹² The city is left in ruins,
    its gate is battered to pieces.
¹³ So will it be on the earth
    and among the nations,
  as when an olive tree is beaten,¹
    or as when gleanings are left after the grape harvest.

¹⁴ They raise their voices, they shout for joy;
    from the west they acclaim the LORD's majesty.
¹⁵ Therefore in the east give glory to the LORD;
    exalt[m] the name of the LORD, the God of Israel,
  in the islands of the sea.
¹⁶ From the ends of the earth we hear singing:
    "Glory to the Righteous One."

  But I said, "I waste away, I waste away!
    Woe to me!
  The treacherous betray!
    With treachery the treacherous betray![n]"
¹⁷ Terror and pit and snare[o] await you,
    O people of the earth.
¹⁸ Whoever flees at the sound of terror
    will fall into a pit;
  whoever climbs out of the pit
    will be caught in a snare.

  The floodgates of the heavens[p] are opened,
    the foundations of the earth shake.[q]
¹⁹ The earth is broken up,
    the earth is split asunder,
    the earth is thoroughly shaken.
²⁰ The earth reels like a drunkard,[r]
    it sways like a hut in the wind;
  so heavy upon it is the guilt of its rebellion
    that it falls—never to rise again.

²¹ In that day the LORD will punish[s]
    the powers in the heavens above
    and the kings on the earth below.
²² They will be herded together
    like prisoners bound in a dungeon;
  they will be shut up in prison
    and be punished[a] after many days.
²³ The moon will be abashed, the sun[t] ashamed;
    for the LORD Almighty will reign
  on Mount Zion[u] and in Jerusalem,
    and before its elders, gloriously.[v]

Praise to the LORD

25 O LORD, you are my God;
    I will exalt you and praise your name,
  for in perfect faithfulness
    you have done marvelous things,[w]
      things planned long ago.

ᵃ22 Or *released*

24:13	
¹Isa 17:6	
24:15	
ᵐMal 1:11	
24:16	
ⁿJer 5:11	
24:17	
ᵒJer 48:43	
24:18	
ᵖGe 7:11	
�q Ps 18:7	
24:20	
ʳIsa 19:14	
24:21	
ˢIsa 10:12	
24:23	
ᵗIsa 13:10	
ᵘHeb 12:22	
ᵛIsa 60:19	
25:1	
ʷPs 98:1	

24:14–16 The believers who are left behind after God judges Judah will sing to the glory of God's righteousness. Isaiah grieved because of his world's condition. We too can become depressed by the evil all around us. At those times we need to hold on to God's promises for the future and look forward to singing praises to him when he restores heaven and earth.

24:21 "The powers in the heavens above" refer to spiritual forces opposed to God. Nobody, not even the fallen angels, will escape due punishment.

25:1 Isaiah honored and praised God because he realized

25:2
x Isa 17:1
y Isa 13:22

2 You have made the city a heap of rubble,x
    the fortified town a ruin,
the foreigners' strongholdy a city no more;
    it will never be rebuilt.
3 Therefore strong peoples will honor you;
    cities of ruthless nations will revere you.

25:4
z Isa 4:6

4 You have been a refugez for the poor,
    a refuge for the needy in his distress,
a shelter from the storm
    and a shade from the heat.
For the breath of the ruthless
    is like a storm driving against a wall

25:5
a Jer 51:55

5   and like the heat of the desert.
You silencea the uproar of foreigners;
    as heat is reduced by the shadow of a cloud,
    so the song of the ruthless is stilled.

25:6
b Isa 2:2
c Mt 8:11; 22:4
d Pr 9:2

6 On this mountainb the LORD Almighty will prepare
    a feastc of rich food for all peoples,
a banquet of aged wine—
    the best of meats and the finest of wines.d

25:7
e 2Co 3:15-16

7 On this mountain he will destroy
    the shroude that enfolds all peoples,
the sheet that covers all nations;

25:8
f Hos 13:14;
1Co 15:54-55*
g Rev 7:17; 21:4

8   he will swallow up deathf forever.
The Sovereign LORD will wipe away the tearsg
    from all faces;
he will remove the disgrace of his people
    from all the earth.

                              The LORD has spoken.

25:9
h Isa 40:9
i Ps 20:5; Isa 33:22

9 In that day they will say,

"Surely this is our God;h
    we trusted in him, and he savedi us.
This is the LORD, we trusted in him;
    let us rejoice and be glad in his salvation."

10 The hand of the LORD will rest on this mountain;
    but Moab will be trampled under him
as straw is trampled down in the manure.
11 They will spread out their hands in it,
    as a swimmer spreads out his hands to swim.
God will bring down their pride
    despite the clevernessa of their hands.

a 11 The meaning of the Hebrew for this word is uncertain.

---

that God completes his plans as promised. God also fulfills his promises to you. Think of the prayers he has answered, and praise him for his goodness and faithfulness.

25:4 The poor suffered because ruthless people oppressed them. But God is concerned for the poor and is a refuge for them. When we are disadvantaged or oppressed, we can turn to God for comfort and help. Jesus states that the kingdom of God belongs to the poor (Luke 6:20).

25:6 Here is a marvelous prophecy of "all peoples"—Gentiles and Jews together—at God's Messianic feast, celebrating the overthrow of evil and the joy of eternity with God. It shows that God intended his saving message to go out to the whole world, not just to the Jews. During the feast, God will end death forever (25:7, 8). The people who participate in this great feast will be those who have been living by faith. That is why they say, "Surely this is our God; we trusted in him, and he saved us"

(25:9). See also chapter 55 for another presentation of this great banquet.

25:8 When the Lord speaks, he does what he says. It is comforting to know that God's plans and activities are closely tied to his word. When we pray according to God's will (as expressed in the Bible) and claim his promises (as recorded in the Bible), he hears us and answers our requests.

25:8 Part of this verse is quoted in 1 Corinthians 15:54 to describe Christ's victory over death. God's ultimate victory is seen when death, our ultimate enemy, is defeated (see also Hosea 13:14). Another part of this verse is quoted in Revelation 21:4, which describes the glorious scene of God's presence with his people.

25:10 Moab was a symbol of all who oppose God and are rebellious to the end. Moab was Israel's enemy for years (see the note on 15:1).

¹² He will bring down your high fortified walls
and lay them low;
he will bring them down to the ground,
to the very dust.

A Song of Praise

26 In that day this song will be sung in the land of Judah:

26:1
j Isa 60:18

We have a strong city;
God makes salvation
its walls*j* and ramparts.
² Open the gates
that the righteous nation may enter,
the nation that keeps faith.
³ You will keep in perfect peace
him whose mind is steadfast,
because he trusts in you.
⁴ Trust in the LORD forever,
for the LORD, the LORD, is the Rock eternal.
⁵ He humbles those who dwell on high,
he lays the lofty city low;

26:5
k Isa 25:12

he levels it to the ground*k*
and casts it down to the dust.
⁶ Feet trample it down—
the feet of the oppressed,
the footsteps of the poor.*l*

26:6
l Isa 3:15

⁷ The path of the righteous is level;
O upright One, you make the way of the righteous smooth.
⁸ Yes, LORD, walking in the way of your laws,*a m*
we wait for you;

26:8
m Isa 56:1

your name and renown
are the desire of our hearts.
⁹ My soul yearns for you in the night;
in the morning my spirit longs*n* for you.

26:9
n Isa 55:6

When your judgments come upon the earth,
the people of the world learn righteousness.
¹⁰ Though grace is shown to the wicked,
they do not learn righteousness;

26:10
o Isa 22:12-13

even in a land of uprightness they go on doing evil
and regard*o* not the majesty of the LORD.
¹¹ O LORD, your hand is lifted high,
but they do not see it.
Let them see your zeal for your people and be put to shame;
let the fire reserved for your enemies consume them.

¹² LORD, you establish peace for us;
all that we have accomplished you have done for us.

a 8 Or *judgments*

26:1ff People will praise God on the day of the Lord when Christ establishes his kingdom (see chapter 12). Chapter 26 is a psalm of trust, praise, and meditation. Once more, God revealed the future to Isaiah.

26:3 We can never avoid strife in the world around us, but with God we can know perfect peace even in turmoil. When we are devoted to him, our whole attitude is steady and stable. Supported by God's unchanging love and mighty power, we are not shaken by the surrounding chaos (see Philippians 4:7). Do you want peace? Keep your thoughts on and your trust in God.

26:7, 8 At times the "path of the righteous" doesn't seem

smooth and it isn't easy to do God's will, but we are never alone when we face tough times. God is there to help us through difficulties, to comfort us, and to lead us. God does this by giving us a purpose (keeping our mind centered on him, 26:3) and giving us provisions as we travel. God provides us with relationships of family, friends, and mentors. God gives us wisdom to make decisions and faith to trust him. Don't despair; stay on God's path.

26:10 Even wicked people receive God's benefits, but that doesn't teach them to do what is right. Sometimes God's judgment teaches us more than God's good gifts. If you have been enriched by God's goodness and grace, respond to him with your grateful devotion.

26:13
p Isa 2:8; 10:5, 11

13 O LORD, our God, other lords*p* besides you have ruled over us,
  but your name alone do we honor.
14 They are now dead, they live no more;
  those departed spirits do not rise.
You punished them and brought them to ruin;
  you wiped out all memory of them.

26:15
q Isa 33:17

15 You have enlarged the nation, O LORD;
  you have enlarged the nation.
You have gained glory for yourself;
  you have extended all the borders*q* of the land.

26:16
r Hos 5:15

16 LORD, they came to you in their distress;*r*
  when you disciplined them,
  they could barely whisper a prayer.*a*

26:17
s Jn 16:21

17 As a woman with child and about to give birth*s*
  writhes and cries out in her pain,
  so were we in your presence, O LORD.

26:18
t Ps 17:14

18 We were with child, we writhed in pain,
  but we gave birth to wind.
We have not brought salvation*t* to the earth;
  we have not given birth to people of the world.

26:19
u Eze 37:1-14;
Da 12:2

19 But your dead will live;
  their bodies will rise.
You who dwell in the dust,
  wake up and shout for joy.
Your dew is like the dew of the morning;
  the earth will give birth to her dead.*u*

26:20
v Ex 12:23
w Ps 30:5;
Isa 54:7-8

20 Go, my people, enter your rooms
  and shut the doors*v* behind you;
hide yourselves for a little while
  until his wrath has passed by.*w*

26:21
x Jude 1:14
y Mic 1:3

21 See, the LORD is coming*x* out of his dwelling*y*
  to punish the people of the earth for their sins.
The earth will disclose the blood shed upon her;
  she will conceal her slain no longer.

Deliverance of Israel

27:1
z Ps 74:13

27 In that day,

  the LORD will punish with his sword,
    his fierce, great and powerful sword,
  Leviathan the gliding serpent,
  Leviathan the coiling serpent;
  he will slay the monster*z* of the sea.

a 16 The meaning of the Hebrew for this clause is uncertain.

26:16-19 The people realized the pain of being away from God's presence, and yet they are assured that they will live again. God turned his back on his people when they disobeyed, but a small number never lost hope and continued to seek him. No matter how difficult times may be, we have hope when we keep our trust in him. Can you wait patiently for God to act?

26:19 Some people say there is no life after death. Others believe that there is, but it is not physical life. But Isaiah tells us that our bodies shall rise again. According to 1 Corinthians 15:50–53, all the dead believers will arise with new imperishable bodies—bodies like the one Jesus had when he was resurrected (see Philippians 3:21). Isaiah 26:19 is not the only Old Testament verse to speak about the resurrection; see also Job 19:26; Psalm 16:10; Daniel 12:2, 13.

26:20, 21 When God comes to judge the earth, the guilty will find no place to hide. Jesus said that the hidden will be made known because his truth, like a light shining in a dark corner, will reveal it (Matthew 10:26). Instead of trying to hide your shameful thoughts and actions from God, confess them to him and receive his forgiveness.

27:1 "That day" is a reference to the end of the evil world as we know it. In ancient Aramean (Ugaritic) literature, Leviathan was a seven-headed monster, the enemy of God's created order. Thus Isaiah is comparing God's slaughter of the wicked to the conquering of a great enemy. Although evil is a powerful foe, God will crush it and abolish it from the earth forever.

2 In that day—

"Sing about a fruitful vineyard:[a]
3   I, the LORD, watch over it;
      I water it continually.
   I guard it day and night
      so that no one may harm it.
4   I am not angry.
   If only there were briers and thorns confronting me!
      I would march against them in battle;
      I would set them all on fire.
5   Or else let them come to me for refuge;[b]
      let them make peace[c] with me,
      yes, let them make peace with me."

6 In days to come Jacob will take root,
      Israel will bud and blossom[d]
      and fill all the world with fruit.[e]

7 Has ⌊the LORD⌋ struck her
      as he struck down those who struck her?
   Has she been killed
      as those were killed who killed her?
8 By warfare[a] and exile you contend with her—
      with his fierce blast he drives her out,
      as on a day the east wind blows.
9 By this, then, will Jacob's guilt be atoned for,
      and this will be the full fruitage of the removal of his sin:[f]
   When he makes all the altar stones
      to be like chalk stones crushed to pieces,
   no Asherah poles[b] or incense altars
      will be left standing.
10 The fortified city stands desolate,[g]
      an abandoned settlement, forsaken like the desert;
   there the calves graze,
      there they lie down;[h]
      they strip its branches bare.
11 When its twigs are dry, they are broken off
      and women come and make fires with them.
   For this is a people without understanding;[i]
      so their Maker has no compassion on them,
      and their Creator[j] shows them no favor.

12 In that day the LORD will thresh from the flowing Euphrates[c] to the Wadi of Egypt, and you, O Israelites, will be gathered up one by one. 13 And in that day a great trumpet[k] will sound. Those who were perishing in Assyria and those who were exiled in Egypt will come and worship the LORD on the holy mountain in Jerusalem.

a 8 See Septuagint; the meaning of the Hebrew for this word is uncertain.   b 9 That is, symbols of the goddess Asherah   c 12 Hebrew River

27:2
a Jer 2:21

27:5
b Isa 25:4
c Job 22:21

27:6
d Hos 14:5-6
e Isa 37:31

27:9
f Ro 11:27*

27:10
g Isa 32:14
h Isa 17:2

27:11
i Dt 32:28; Isa 1:3; Jer 8:7
j Dt 32:18; Isa 43:1, 7, 15; 44:1-2, 21, 24

27:13
k Lev 25:9; Mt 24:31

27:2-6 The trampled vineyard of chapter 5 will be restored in God's new earth. God will protect and care for the vineyard, his people. It will no longer produce worthless fruit but will produce enough good fruit for the whole world. Gentiles will come to know God through Israel.

27:9 Only God can take away sin, but to be driven out of the land was considered the penalty that would purify God's people.

Deuteronomy 28:49-52, 64 explains God's warning about these consequences.

27:11 Isaiah compares the state of Israel's spiritual life with dry twigs that are broken off and used to make fires. Trees in Scripture often represent spiritual life. The trunk is the channel of strength from God; the branches are the people who serve him. Tree branches sometimes waver and blow in the wind. Like Israel, they may dry up from internal rottenness and become useless for anything except building a fire. What kind of branch are you? If you are withering spiritually, check to see if you are firmly attached to God.

27:12 A wadi is a stream or dry streambed.

4. Jerusalem's true and false hopes
Woe to Ephraim

28 Woe to that wreath, the pride of Ephraim's drunkards,
　　to the fading flower, his glorious beauty,
set on the head of a fertile valley—
　　to that city, the pride of those laid low by wine!
2 See, the Lord has one who is powerful and strong.
　　Like a hailstorm*l* and a destructive wind,
like a driving rain and a flooding downpour,
　　he will throw it forcefully to the ground.
3 That wreath, the pride of Ephraim's drunkards,
　　will be trampled underfoot.
4 That fading flower, his glorious beauty,
　　set on the head of a fertile valley,
will be like a fig*m* ripe before harvest—
　　as soon as someone sees it and takes it in his hand,
　　he swallows it.

5 In that day the LORD Almighty
　　will be a glorious crown,*n*
a beautiful wreath
　　for the remnant of his people.
6 He will be a spirit of justice*o*
　　to him who sits in judgment,
a source of strength
　　to those who turn back the battle at the gate.

7 And these also stagger from wine
　　and reel*p* from beer:
Priests and prophets stagger from beer
　　and are befuddled with wine;
they reel from beer,
　　they stagger when seeing visions,*q*
　　they stumble when rendering decisions.
8 All the tables are covered with vomit*r*
　　and there is not a spot without filth.

9 "Who is it he is trying to teach?
　　To whom is he explaining his message?
To children weaned*s* from their milk,
　　to those just taken from the breast?
10 For it is:
　　Do and do, do and do,
　　rule on rule, rule on rule*a*;
　　a little here, a little there."

11 Very well then, with foreign lips and strange tongues
　　God will speak to this people,*t*
12 to whom he said,
　　"This is the resting place, let the weary rest";*u*
and, "This is the place of repose"—
　　but they would not listen.

Cross references

28:2
l Isa 30:30;
Eze 13:11

28:4
m Hos 9:10

28:5
n Isa 62:3

28:6
o Isa 11:2-4

28:7
p Isa 56:10-12
q Hos 4:11

28:8
r Jer 48:26

28:9
s Ps 131:2

28:11
t 1Co 14:21*

28:12
u Mt 11:28-29

a 10 Hebrew */ sav lasav sav lasav / kav lakav kav lakav* (possibly meaningless sounds; perhaps a mimicking of the prophet's words); also in verse 13

28:1 Ephraim represents the northern kingdom of Israel, ruled by a line of evil kings. When Israel split into two kingdoms after Solomon's reign, Jerusalem ended up in the southern kingdom. Leaders in the northern kingdom, wishing to stay entirely separate from their relatives to the south, set up idols to keep the people from going to the temple in Jerusalem to worship (see 1 Kings 12). Thus the people in the northern kingdom were led into idolatry. Isaiah gave this message to Israel to warn them, as well as to Judah to encourage them to repent before being punished as the northern kingdom would be only a few years later.

28:9–14 These verses characterize the people's reaction to Isaiah. In effect, they were saying, "He's speaking to us like a school teacher speaks to small children. We don't need to be taught. We'll make up our own minds." For this attitude, Isaiah prophesied that the Assyrians would teach them in a way they would like even less.

13 So then, the word of the LORD to them will become:
    Do and do, do and do,
    rule on rule, rule on rule;
    a little here, a little there—
so that they will go and fall backward,
    be injured and snared and captured.

14 Therefore hear the word of the LORD, you scoffers
    who rule this people in Jerusalem.
15 You boast, "We have entered into a covenant with death,
    with the grave[a] we have made an agreement.
When an overwhelming scourge sweeps by,[v]
    it cannot touch us,
for we have made a lie our refuge
    and falsehood[b] our hiding place.[w]"

16 So this is what the Sovereign LORD says:

    "See, I lay a stone in Zion,
        a tested stone,[x]
    a precious cornerstone for a sure foundation;
        the one who trusts will never be dismayed.[y]
17 I will make justice[z] the measuring line
        and righteousness the plumb line;
    hail will sweep away your refuge, the lie,
        and water will overflow your hiding place.
18 Your covenant with death will be annulled;
        your agreement with the grave will not stand.
    When the overwhelming scourge sweeps by,[a]
        you will be beaten down by it.
19 As often as it comes it will carry you away;
        morning after morning, by day and by night,
    it will sweep through."

    The understanding of this message
        will bring sheer terror.
20 The bed is too short to stretch out on,
        the blanket too narrow to wrap around you.
21 The LORD will rise up as he did at Mount Perazim,[b]
        he will rouse himself as in the Valley of Gibeon[c]—
    to do his work, his strange work,
        and perform his task, his alien task.
22 Now stop your mocking,
        or your chains will become heavier;
    the Lord, the LORD Almighty, has told me
        of the destruction decreed[d] against the whole land.[e]

23 Listen and hear my voice;
        pay attention and hear what I say.

a 15 Hebrew *Sheol*; also in verse 18   b 15 Or *false gods*

28:15
v ver 2, 18
w Isa 29:15

28:16
x Ps 118:22;
Mt 21:42; Ac 4:11;
Eph 2:20
y Ro 9:33*; 10:11*;
1Pe 2:6*

28:17
z Isa 5:16

28:18
a ver 15

28:21
b 1Ch 14:11
c Jos 10:10, 12;
1Ch 14:16

28:22
d Isa 10:22
e Isa 10:23

28:15 Judah was afraid of the Assyrians, the "overwhelming scourge." Instead of trusting God, the Judeans turned to other sources for security. God accused them of making a covenant with death. It is used to mean the grave or state of being dead. This passage may refer to Hezekiah's alliance with Pharaoh Tirhakah against Assyria (2 Kings 19:9; Isaiah 37:9). God would cancel this agreement—Egypt would be of no help when Assyria attacked. Is it worth selling out what you believe in for temporary protection against an enemy? If you want lasting protection, turn to the only one able to deliver you from *eternal* death—God.

28:16 If you're building anything, you need a firm base. Isaiah speaks of a foundation stone, a *cornerstone*, that will be laid in

Zion. This cornerstone is the Messiah, the foundation on whom we build our lives. Is your life built on the flimsy base of your own successes or dreams? Or is it set on a firm foundation (see Psalm 118:22; 1 Peter 2:8)?

28:21 God fought on Joshua's side at the Valley of Gibeon (Joshua 10:1–14) and on David's side at Mount Perazim (2 Samuel 5:20). But here he would fight *against* Israel, his own people, in these same places.

28:23–29 The farmer uses special tools to plant and harvest tender herbs so he will not destroy them. He takes into account how fragile they are. In the same way God takes all our individual circumstances and weaknesses into account. He deals with

24 When a farmer plows for planting, does he plow continually?
Does he keep on breaking up and harrowing the soil?
25 When he has leveled the surface,
does he not sow caraway and scatter cummin?
Does he not plant wheat in its place,a
barley in its plot,a
and spelt in its field?
26 His God instructs him
and teaches him the right way.

27 Caraway is not threshed with a sledge,
nor is a cartwheel rolled over cummin;
caraway is beaten out with a rod,
and cummin with a stick.
28 Grain must be ground to make bread;
so one does not go on threshing it forever.
Though he drives the wheels of his threshing cart over it,
his horses do not grind it.

28:29
f Isa 9:6
g Ro 11:33

29 All this also comes from the LORD Almighty,
wonderful in counself and magnificent in wisdom.g

Woe to David's City

29:1
h 2Sa 5:9

29 Woe to you, Ariel, Ariel,h
the city where David settled!
Add year to year
and let your cycle of festivals go on.

29:2
i Isa 3:26; La 2:5

2 Yet I will besiege Ariel;
she will mourn and lament,i
she will be to me like an altar hearth.b

29:3
j Lk 19:43-44

3 I will encamp against you all around;
I will encirclej you with towers
and set up my siege works against you.

29:4
k Isa 8:19

4 Brought low, you will speak from the ground;
your speech will mumblek out of the dust.
Your voice will come ghostlike from the earth;
out of the dust your speech will whisper.

29:5
l Isa 17:14

5 But your many enemies will become like fine dust,
the ruthless hordes like blown chaff.
Suddenly,l in an instant,
6 the LORD Almighty will come
with thunder and earthquake and great noise,
with windstorm and tempest and flames of a devouring fire.

29:7
m Job 20:8

7 Then the hordes of all the nations that fight against Ariel,
that attack her and her fortress and besiege her,
will be as it is with a dream,m
with a vision in the night—
8 as when a hungry man dreams that he is eating,
but he awakens, and his hunger remains;
as when a thirsty man dreams that he is drinking,
but he awakens faint, with his thirst unquenched.
So will it be with the hordes of all the nations
that fight against Mount Zion.

a 25 The meaning of the Hebrew for this word is uncertain.   b 2 The Hebrew for *altar hearth* sounds like the Hebrew for *Ariel.*

each of us sensitively. We should follow his example when we deal with others. Different people require different treatment. Be sensitive to the needs of those around you and the special treatment they may need.

29:1 *Ariel* is a special name for Jerusalem, David's city. It may mean "lion of God" (Jerusalem is strong as a lion) or "altar hearth." (Jerusalem is the place of the altar in the temple. See 29:2; Ezekiel 43:15, 16.)

9 Be stunned and amazed,
    blind yourselves and be sightless;
be drunk, but not from wine,[n]
    stagger, but not from beer.

10 The LORD has brought over you a deep sleep:
    He has sealed your eyes[o] (the prophets);
    he has covered your heads (the seers).

11 For you this whole vision is nothing but words sealed[p] in a scroll. And if you give the scroll to someone who can read, and say to him, "Read this, please," he will answer, "I can't; it is sealed." 12 Or if you give the scroll to someone who cannot read, and say, "Read this, please," he will answer, "I don't know how to read."

13 The Lord says:

"These people come near to me with their mouth
    and honor me with their lips,
    but their hearts are far from me.[q]
Their worship of me
    is made up only of rules taught by men.[a][r]

14 Therefore once more I will astound these people
    with wonder upon wonder;[s]
the wisdom of the wise[t] will perish,
    the intelligence of the intelligent will vanish.[u]"

15 Woe to those who go to great depths
    to hide their plans from the LORD,
who do their work in darkness and think,
    "Who sees us?[v] Who will know?"

16 You turn things upside down,
    as if the potter were thought to be like the clay!
Shall what is formed say to him who formed it,
    "He did not make me"?
Can the pot say of the potter,[w]
    "He knows nothing"?

17 In a very short time, will not Lebanon be turned into a fertile field
    and the fertile field seem like a forest?[x]

18 In that day the deaf will hear the words of the scroll,
    and out of gloom and darkness
    the eyes of the blind will see.[y]

19 Once more the humble[z] will rejoice in the LORD;
    the needy[a] will rejoice in the Holy One of Israel.

20 The ruthless will vanish,
    the mockers will disappear,
    and all who have an eye for evil will be cut down—

21 those who with a word make a man out to be guilty,
    who ensnare the defender in court[b]
    and with false testimony deprive the innocent of justice.

[a] 13 Hebrew; Septuagint *They worship me in vain; / their teachings are but rules taught by men*

29:13, 14 The people claimed to be close to God, but they were disobedient and merely went through the motions; therefore, God would bring judgment upon them. Religion had become routine instead of real. Jesus quoted Isaiah's condemnation of Israel's hypocrisy when he spoke to the Pharisees, the religious leaders of his day (Matthew 15:7–9; Mark 7:6, 7). We are all capable of hypocrisy. Often we slip into routine patterns when we worship and we neglect to give God our love and devotion. If we want to be called God's people, we must be obedient and worship him honestly and sincerely.

29:15 Thinking God couldn't see them and didn't know what was happening, the people of Jerusalem tried to hide their plans from him. How strange that so many people think they can hide from God. In Psalm 139 we learn that God has examined us and knows everything about us. Would you be embarrassed if your best friends knew your personal thoughts? Remember that God knows all of them.

29:17–24 The world described here, under Christ's rule, will be far different from the one we live in today. There will be no more

²² Therefore this is what the Lord, who redeemed Abraham, says to the house of Jacob:

> "No longer will Jacob be ashamed;
>   no longer will their faces grow pale.
> ²³ When they see among them their children,
>   the work of my hands,
> they will keep my name holy;
>   they will acknowledge the holiness of the Holy One of Jacob,
>   and will stand in awe of the God of Israel.

29:24
c Isa 28:7

> ²⁴ Those who are wayward *c* in spirit will gain understanding;
>   those who complain will accept instruction."

Woe to the Obstinate Nation

30:1
d Isa 29:15

30

> "Woe *d* to the obstinate children,"
>   declares the Lord,
> "to those who carry out plans that are not mine,
>   forming an alliance, but not by my Spirit,
>   heaping sin upon sin;

30:2
e Isa 31:1

> ² who go down to Egypt *e*
>   without consulting me;
> who look for help to Pharaoh's protection,
>   to Egypt's shade for refuge.

30:3
f Isa 20:4-5

> ³ But Pharaoh's protection will be to your shame,
>   Egypt's shade will bring you disgrace. *f*

30:4
g Isa 19:11

> ⁴ Though they have officials in Zoan *g*
>   and their envoys have arrived in Hanes,

30:5
h ver 7

> ⁵ everyone will be put to shame
>   because of a people *h* useless to them,
> who bring neither help nor advantage,
>   but only shame and disgrace."

30:6
i Isa 15:7

> ⁶ An oracle concerning the animals of the Negev:

> Through a land of hardship and distress,
>   of lions and lionesses,
>   of adders and darting snakes,
> the envoys carry their riches on donkeys' backs,
>   their treasures *i* on the humps of camels,
> to that unprofitable nation,
> ⁷   to Egypt, whose help is utterly useless.
> Therefore I call her
>   Rahab the Do-Nothing.

> ⁸ Go now, write it on a tablet for them,
>   inscribe it on a scroll,
> that for the days to come
>   it may be an everlasting witness.

30:9
j Isa 28:15

> ⁹ These are rebellious people, deceitful *j* children,
>   children unwilling to listen to the Lord's instruction.

---

violence or gloom. This new world will be characterized by joy, understanding, justice, and praise to God.

30:1 The obstinate children are the people of Judah (see 1:2), those who have rebelled against God. The negotiations for an alliance were underway, and Isaiah condemned their twisted plans. The people of Judah sought advice from everyone but God. When we are driven by fear, we tend to search everywhere for comfort, advice, and relief, hoping to find an easy way out of our troubles. Instead, we should consult God. Although he gives emergency help in a crisis, he prefers to be our Guide throughout our lives. By reading his Word and actively seeking to do his will, we can maintain our bond with him who provides stability no matter what the crisis.

30:2ff Hezekiah had been seeking a defensive alliance with Egypt against Sennacherib of Assyria (see 2 Kings 18:21).

30:6 This oracle is titled "concerning the animals of the Negev," but is directed to those who carried bribes to Egypt through the desert in the Negev region.

30:7 Rahab was a mythological female sea monster associated with Leviathan (see the note on 27:1; also Job 9:13; 26:12). It was a name associated with Egypt, where hippopotamuses, perhaps a likeness to Rahab, sat on the Nile River and did nothing.

10 They say to the seers,
  "See no more visions!"
and to the prophets,
  "Give us no more visions of what is right!
Tell us pleasant things,
  prophesy illusions.
11 Leave this way,
  get off this path,
and stop confronting[k] us
  with the Holy One of Israel!"

30:11
k Job 21:14

12 Therefore, this is what the Holy One of Israel says:

"Because you have rejected this message,
  relied on oppression
  and depended on deceit,
13 this sin will become for you
  like a high wall,[l] cracked and bulging,
  that collapses suddenly,[m] in an instant.
14 It will break in pieces like pottery,[n]
  shattered so mercilessly
that among its pieces not a fragment will be found
  for taking coals from a hearth
  or scooping water out of a cistern."

30:13
l Ps 62:3
m Isa 29:5

30:14
n Ps 2:9;
Jer 19:10-11

15 This is what the Sovereign Lord, the Holy One of Israel, says:

"In repentance and rest is your salvation,
  in quietness and trust[o] is your strength,
  but you would have none of it.
16 You said, 'No, we will flee on horses.'[p]
  Therefore you will flee!
You said, 'We will ride off on swift horses.'
  Therefore your pursuers will be swift!
17 A thousand will flee
  at the threat of one;
at the threat of five[q]
  you will all flee[r] away,
till you are left
  like a flagstaff on a mountaintop,
  like a banner on a hill."

30:15
o Isa 32:17

30:16
p Isa 31:1, 3

30:17
q Lev 26:8;
Jos 23:10
r Dt 28:25

18 Yet the Lord longs[s] to be gracious to you;
  he rises to show you compassion.
For the Lord is a God of justice.[t]
  Blessed are all who wait for him!

30:18
s Isa 42:14
t Isa 5:16

19 O people of Zion, who live in Jerusalem, you will weep no more. How gracious he will be when you cry for help! As soon as he hears, he will answer you. 20 Although the Lord gives you the bread[u] of adversity and the water of affliction, your teachers will be hidden[v] no more;

30:20
u 1Ki 22:27
v Ps 74:9; Am 8:11

30:10, 11 Some people in Judah may have sought refuge in Egypt. In their desire to find security, they wanted to hear only good news. They did not welcome the truth from God's prophets. Often the truth makes us uncomfortable. We prefer lies and illusions when they make us feel more secure. It is much better to face reality than to live a lie. Don't settle for something that makes you feel comfortable but is not true.

30:15 God warned Judah that turning to Egypt and other nations for military might could not save them. Only God could do that. They must wait for him in "quietness and trust." No amount of fast talking or hasty activity could speed up God's grand design. We have nothing to say to God but thank you. Salvation comes

from God alone. Because he has saved us, we can trust him and be peacefully confident that he will give us strength to face our difficulties. We should lay aside our busy care and endless effort and allow him to act.

30:20 The Lord gave his people the bread of adversity and the water of affliction, but he promised to be with them, teach them, and guide them during hard times. God expects a lot from us, and many times following him can be painful; but he always acts out of his love for us. The next time you go through a difficult time, try to appreciate the experience and grow from it, learning what God wants to teach you. God may be showing you his love by patiently walking with you through adversity.

with your own eyes you will see them. ²¹Whether you turn to the right or to the left, your ears will hear a voice behind you, saying, "This is the way; walk in it." ²²Then you will defile your idols overlaid with silver and your images covered with gold; you will throw them away like a menstrual cloth and say to them, "Away with you!"

30:23
ʷPs 65:13

²³He will also send you rain for the seed you sow in the ground, and the food that comes from the land will be rich and plentiful. In that day your cattle will graze in broad meadows. ʷ ²⁴The oxen and donkeys that work the soil will eat fodder and mash, spread out with fork and shovel. ²⁵In the day of great slaughter, when the towers fall, streams of water will flow on every high mountain and every lofty hill. ²⁶The moon will shine like the sun, ˣ and the sunlight will be seven times brighter, like the light of seven full days, when the LORD binds up the bruises of his people and heals ʸ the wounds he inflicted.

30:26
ˣIsa 60:19-20;
Rev 21:23
ʸIsa 1:5

30:27
ᶻIsa 59:19

²⁷ See, the Name ᶻ of the LORD comes from afar,
    with burning anger and dense clouds of smoke;
  his lips are full of wrath,
    and his tongue is a consuming fire.

30:28
ᵃIsa 11:4
ᵇIsa 8:8
ᶜ2Ki 19:28;
Isa 37:29

²⁸ His breath ᵃ is like a rushing torrent,
    rising up to the neck. ᵇ
  He shakes the nations in the sieve of destruction;
    he places in the jaws of the peoples
    a bit ᶜ that leads them astray.

30:29
ᵈPs 42:4

²⁹ And you will sing
    as on the night you celebrate a holy festival;
  your hearts will rejoice
    as when people go up with flutes
  to the mountain ᵈ of the LORD,
    to the Rock of Israel.

³⁰ The LORD will cause men to hear his majestic voice
    and will make them see his arm coming down
  with raging anger and consuming fire,
    with cloudburst, thunderstorm and hail.

30:31
ᵉIsa 10:5, 12

³¹ The voice of the LORD will shatter Assyria; ᵉ
    with his scepter he will strike them down.

30:32
ᶠEze 32:10

³² Every stroke the LORD lays on them
    with his punishing rod
  will be to the music of tambourines and harps,
    as he fights them in battle with the blows of his arm. ᶠ

³³ Topheth has long been prepared;
    it has been made ready for the king.
  Its fire pit has been made deep and wide,
    with an abundance of fire and wood;
  the breath of the LORD,
    like a stream of burning sulfur,
    sets it ablaze.

Woe to Those Who Rely on Egypt

31:1
ᵍIsa 30:2, 5

31 Woe to those who go down to Egypt ᵍ for help,
    who rely on horses,

30:21 When the people of Jerusalem left God's path, he would correct them. He will do the same for us. But when we hear his voice of correction, we must be willing to follow it!

30:27 The judgment of God will be accompanied by thick, rising smoke and words that consume like fire (see 33:14; Luke 12:49; Hebrews 12:29). People who were brought up in a church but dropped out often complain about the preaching of the wrath of God. Yet his wrath and anger are very real and are designed for the rebellious and for those who hate God, not for those who are humble and love him. Are you one of God's people? Help others discover God's love so that his wrath will never be an issue for them.

31:1 It was wrong for Judah to look to other nations for military help. (1) They were trusting in human beings instead of God. Judah sought protection from those who were powerless compared to God. Both Egypt and Judah would fall as a result of their arrogance. (2) They were serving their own interests instead of God's, and thus they did not even consult him. They violated God's stipulation in Deuteronomy 17:16. (3) They did not want to pay the price of looking to God and repenting of their sinful ways. When we have problems, it is good to seek help, but we must never bypass God or his previous directions to us.

who trust in the multitude of their chariots
    and in the great strength of their horsemen,
but do not look to the Holy One of Israel,
    or seek help from the LORD.^h

2 Yet he too is wise and can bring disaster;
    he does not take back his words.ⁱ
He will rise up against the house of the wicked,
    against those who help evildoers.

3 But the Egyptians are men and not God;^j
    their horses are flesh and not spirit.
When the LORD stretches out his hand,
    he who helps will stumble,
    he who is helped^k will fall;
    both will perish together.

4 This is what the LORD says to me:

"As a lion^l growls,
    a great lion over his prey—
and though a whole band of shepherds
    is called together against him,
he is not frightened by their shouts
    or disturbed by their clamor—
so the LORD Almighty will come down^m
    to do battle on Mount Zion and on its heights.

5 Like birds hovering overhead,
    the LORD Almighty will shieldⁿ Jerusalem;
he will shield it and deliver it,
    he will 'pass over' it and will rescue it."

6 Return to him you have so greatly revolted against, O Israelites. 7 For in that day every one of you will reject the idols of silver and gold ^o your sinful hands have made.

8 "Assyria^p will fall by a sword that is not of man;
    a sword, not of mortals, will devour them.
They will flee before the sword
    and their young men will be put to forced labor.

9 Their stronghold^q will fall because of terror;
    at sight of the battle standard their commanders will panic,"
declares the LORD,
    whose fire^r is in Zion,
    whose furnace is in Jerusalem.

The Kingdom of Righteousness

32 See, a king will reign in righteousness
    and rulers will rule with justice.^s
2 Each man will be like a shelter ^t from the wind
    and a refuge from the storm,
like streams of water in the desert
    and the shadow of a great rock in a thirsty land.

3 Then the eyes of those who see will no longer be closed,^u
    and the ears of those who hear will listen.

31:1 [h] Ps 20:7; Da 9:13
31:2 [i] Nu 23:19
31:3 [j] Eze 28:9 [k] Isa 30:5-7
31:4 [l] Am 3:8 [m] Isa 42:13
31:5 [n] Ps 91:4
31:7 [o] Isa 2:20
31:8 [p] Isa 10:12
31:9 [q] Dt 32:31, 37 [r] Isa 10:17
32:1 [s] Isa 9:7
32:2 [t] Isa 4:6
32:3 [u] Isa 29:18

31:7 Someday these people would throw their idols away, recognizing that they are nothing but man-made objects. Idols such as money, fame, or success are seductive. Instead of contributing to our spiritual development, they rob us of our time, energy, and devotion that ought to be directed toward God. At first our idols seem exciting and promise to take us places, but in the end we will find that we have become their slaves. We need to recognize their worthlessness now, before they rob us of our freedom.

32:1 Having suffered much injustice from evil rulers, many in Judah were hungry for a strong king who would rule with justice. This desire will be fulfilled when Christ reigns. Evil will be banished, and the King will reign in righteousness and rule with justice. In the immediate future, Judah would be destroyed and taken into captivity. But one day, God's Son, the King unlike any other king, will reign in righteousness.

4 The mind of the rash will know and understand,
  and the stammering tongue will be fluent and clear.

32:5
v 1Sa 25:25

5 No longer will the fool v be called noble
  nor the scoundrel be highly respected.

32:6
w Isa 3:15

6 For the fool speaks folly,
  his mind is busy with evil:
He practices ungodliness
  and spreads error concerning the LORD;
the hungry he leaves empty w
  and from the thirsty he withholds water.

32:7
x Jer 5:26-28

7 The scoundrel's methods are wicked, x
he makes up evil schemes
  to destroy the poor with lies,
  even when the plea of the needy is just.

8 But the noble man makes noble plans,
  and by noble deeds he stands.

The Women of Jerusalem

32:9
y Isa 28:23

9 You women who are so complacent,
  rise up and listen y to me;
you daughters who feel secure,
  hear what I have to say!

32:10
z Isa 5:5-6

10 In little more than a year
  you who feel secure will tremble;
the grape harvest will fail, z
  and the harvest of fruit will not come.

32:11
a Isa 47:2

11 Tremble, you complacent women;
  shudder, you daughters who feel secure!
Strip off your clothes, a
  put sackcloth around your waists.

32:12
b Na 2:7

12 Beat your breasts b for the pleasant fields,
  for the fruitful vines

32:13
c Isa 22:2

13 and for the land of my people,
  a land overgrown with thorns and briers—
yes, mourn for all houses of merriment
  and for this city of revelry. c

32:14
d Isa 13:22

14 The fortress d will be abandoned,
  the noisy city deserted;
citadel and watchtower will become a wasteland forever,
  the delight of donkeys, a pasture for flocks,

32:15
e Joel 2:28
f Isa 29:17

15 till the Spirit e is poured upon us from on high,
  and the desert becomes a fertile field,
  and the fertile field seems like a forest. f

16 Justice will dwell in the desert
  and righteousness live in the fertile field.

32:17
g Jas 3:18
h Isa 30:15

17 The fruit of righteousness will be peace; g
  the effect of righteousness will be quietness and confidence h forever.

32:5, 6 When the righteous King comes, people's motives will become transparent. Fools will not be regarded as noble. Those who have opposed God's standards of living will be unable to maintain their deception. In the blazing light of the holy Savior, sin cannot disguise itself and appear good. Christ's revealing light shines into the darkest corners of our hearts, showing sin clearly for what it is. When King Jesus reigns in your heart, there is no place for sin, no matter how well hidden you may think it is.

32:9–13 The people turned their backs on God and concentrated on their own pleasures. This warning is not just to the women of Jerusalem (see 3:16—4:1), but to all who sit back in their thoughtless complacency, enjoying crops, clothes, land, and cities while an enemy approaches. Wealth and luxury bring false security,

lulling us into thinking all is well when disaster is around the corner. By abandoning God's purpose for our lives, we also abandon his help.

32:15–17 God acts from above to change man's condition here on earth. Only when God's Spirit is among us can we achieve true peace and fruitfulness (Ezekiel 36:22–38; Galatians 5:22, 23). This will happen in the end times. We can also have God's Spirit with us now, for he is available to all believers through Christ (John 15:26). But the outpouring mentioned here happens when the worldwide kingdom of God is established for all eternity (see Joel 2:28, 29).

¹⁸ My people will live in peaceful dwelling places,
  in secure homes,
    in undisturbed places of rest.
¹⁹ Though hail *i* flattens the forest *j*
    and the city is leveled completely,
²⁰ how blessed you will be,
    sowing your seed by every stream,
    and letting your cattle and donkeys range free. *k*

32:19
i Isa 30:30
j Zec 11:2
32:20
k Isa 30:24

Distress and Help

33 Woe to you, O destroyer,
    you who have not been destroyed!
Woe to you, O traitor,
    you who have not been betrayed!
When you stop destroying,
    you will be destroyed; *l*
when you stop betraying,
    you will be betrayed. *m*

33:1
l Hab 2:8
m Isa 21:2

² O LORD, be gracious to us;
    we long for you.
Be our strength every morning,
    our salvation *n* in time of distress.
³ At the thunder of your voice, the peoples flee;
    when you rise up, the nations scatter.
⁴ Your plunder, O nations, is harvested as by young locusts;
    like a swarm of locusts men pounce on it.

33:2
n Isa 25:9

⁵ The LORD is exalted, *o* for he dwells on high;
    he will fill Zion with justice and righteousness.
⁶ He will be the sure foundation for your times,
    a rich store of salvation and wisdom and knowledge;
    the fear *p* of the LORD is the key to this treasure. *a*

33:5
o Ps 97:9
33:6
p Mt 6:33

⁷ Look, their brave men cry aloud in the streets;
    the envoys *q* of peace weep bitterly.
⁸ The highways are deserted,
    no travelers are on the roads.
The treaty is broken,
    its witnesses *b* are despised,
    no one is respected.

33:7
q 2Ki 18:37

⁹ The land mourns *c* and wastes away,
    Lebanon *r* is ashamed and withers; *s*
Sharon is like the Arabah,
    and Bashan and Carmel drop their leaves.

33:9
r Isa 2:13
s Isa 24:4

¹⁰ "Now will I arise," *t* says the LORD.
    "Now will I be exalted;
    now will I be lifted up.

33:10
t Ps 12:5

a 6 Or is a treasure from him   *b 8 Dead Sea Scrolls; Masoretic Text / the cities*   *c 9 Or dries up*

33:1 The "destroyer" is Assyria. Assyria continually broke its promises, but demanded that others keep theirs. It is easy to put ourselves in the same selfish position, demanding our rights while ignoring the rights of others. Broken promises shatter trust and destroy relationships. Determine to keep your promises; at the same time, ask forgiveness for past promises you have broken. Treat others with the same fairness that you demand for yourself.

33:2 These are the words of the righteous remnant who were waiting for God to deliver them from their oppression.

33:4 See 2 Kings 19:20–37 and Isaiah 37:21–38 for a description of the victory over Assyria described here.

33:5 When Christ's kingdom is established, Zion—Jerusalem—will be the home of justice and righteousness because the Messiah will reign there. As a light to the world, the new Jerusalem will be the Holy City (Revelation 21:2).

33:8 The Assyrians broke their peace treaty (2 Kings 18:14–17).

33:9 These fruitful, productive areas would become deserts. Lebanon was known for its huge cedars. Sharon was very fertile. Bashan was very productive in grain and cattle. Carmel was thickly forested.

33:11
u Ps 7:14; Isa 59:4

11 You conceive[u] chaff,
    you give birth to straw;
    your breath is a fire that consumes you.
12 The peoples will be burned as if to lime;
    like cut thornbushes they will be set ablaze."

33:13
v Ps 49:1

13 You who are far away,[v] hear what I have done;
    you who are near, acknowledge my power!
14 The sinners in Zion are terrified;
    trembling grips the godless:
    "Who of us can dwell with the consuming fire?
    Who of us can dwell with everlasting burning?"

33:15
w Ps 15:2; 24:4
x Ps 119:37

15 He who walks righteously
    and speaks what is right,[w]
    who rejects gain from extortion
    and keeps his hand from accepting bribes,
    who stops his ears against plots of murder
    and shuts his eyes[x] against contemplating evil—

33:16
y Isa 25:4

16 this is the man who will dwell on the heights,
    whose refuge[y] will be the mountain fortress.
    His bread will be supplied,
    and water will not fail him.

33:17
z Isa 26:15

17 Your eyes will see the king in his beauty
    and view a land that stretches afar.[z]

33:18
a Isa 17:14

18 In your thoughts you will ponder the former terror:[a]
    "Where is that chief officer?
    Where is the one who took the revenue?
    Where is the officer in charge of the towers?"

33:19
b Jer 5:15

19 You will see those arrogant people no more,
    those people of an obscure speech,
    with their strange, incomprehensible tongue.[b]

33:20
c Ps 46:5; 125:1-2

20 Look upon Zion, the city of our festivals;
    your eyes will see Jerusalem,
    a peaceful abode, a tent that will not be moved;[c]
    its stakes will never be pulled up,
    nor any of its ropes broken.
21 There the LORD will be our Mighty One.
    It will be like a place of broad rivers and streams.
    No galley with oars will ride them,
    no mighty ship will sail them.

33:22
d Jas 4:12

22 For the LORD is our judge,
    the LORD is our lawgiver,[d]
    the LORD is our king;
    it is he who will save us.

23 Your rigging hangs loose:
    The mast is not held secure,
    the sail is not spread.
    Then an abundance of spoils will be divided
    and even the lame will carry off plunder.

33:24
e Jer 50:20

24 No one living in Zion will say, "I am ill";
    and the sins of those who dwell there will be forgiven.[e]

33:14-16 These sinners realized that they could not live in the presence of the holy God, for he is like a fire that consumes evil. Only those who walk righteously and speak what is right can live with God. Isaiah gives examples of how to demonstrate our righteousness and uprightness: we can reject gain from extortion and bribes, refuse to listen to plots of wrong actions, and shut our eyes to evil. If we are fair and honest in our relationships, we will dwell with God, and he will supply our needs.

Judgment Against the Nations

34
Come near, you nations, and listen;
    pay attention, you peoples!
Let the earth*f* hear, and all that is in it,
    the world, and all that comes out of it!*g*

2 The Lord is angry with all nations;
    his wrath is upon all their armies.
He will totally destroy*a* them,
    he will give them over to slaughter.
3 Their slain will be thrown out,
    their dead bodies will send up a stench;*h*
    the mountains will be soaked with their blood.
4 All the stars of the heavens will be dissolved*i*
    and the sky rolled up*j* like a scroll;
all the starry host will fall*k*
    like withered leaves from the vine,
    like shriveled figs from the fig tree.

5 My sword*l* has drunk its fill in the heavens;
    see, it descends in judgment on Edom,
    the people I have totally destroyed.*m*
6 The sword of the Lord is bathed in blood,
    it is covered with fat—
the blood of lambs and goats,
    fat from the kidneys of rams.
For the Lord has a sacrifice in Bozrah
    and a great slaughter in Edom.
7 And the wild oxen will fall with them,
    the bull calves and the great bulls.
Their land will be drenched with blood,
    and the dust will be soaked with fat.

8 For the Lord has a day of vengeance,*n*
    a year of retribution, to uphold Zion's cause.
9 Edom's streams will be turned into pitch,
    her dust into burning sulfur;
    her land will become blazing pitch!
10 It will not be quenched night and day;
    its smoke will rise forever.*o*
From generation to generation it will lie desolate;
    no one will ever pass through it again.
11 The desert owl*b* *p* and screech owl*b* will possess it;
    the great owl*b* and the raven will nest there.
God will stretch out over Edom
    the measuring line of chaos
    and the plumb line*q* of desolation.
12 Her nobles will have nothing there to be called a kingdom,
    all her princes will vanish away.
13 Thorns will overrun her citadels,
    nettles and brambles her strongholds.*r*
She will become a haunt for jackals,
    a home for owls.
14 Desert creatures will meet with hyenas,*s*
    and wild goats will bleat to each other;

34:1
*f*Ps 49:1
*g*Dt 32:1

34:3
*h*Joel 2:20

34:4
*i*2Pe 3:10
*j*Eze 32:7-8
*k*Joel 2:31;
Mt 24:29*; Rev 6:13

34:5
*l*Jer 46:10
*m*Mal 1:4

34:8
*n*Isa 63:4

34:10
*o*Rev 14:10-11;
19:3

34:11
*p*Zep 2:14
*q*2Ki 21:13; La 2:8

34:13
*r*Isa 13:22; 32:13

34:14
*s*Isa 13:22

---

*a*2 The Hebrew term refers to the irrevocable giving over of things or persons to the Lord, often by totally destroying them; also in verse 5.   *b*11 The precise identification of these birds is uncertain.

34:5 The Edomites shared a common ancestry with Israel. The Israelites were descended from Jacob; the Edomites from Jacob's twin brother, Esau. Edom was always Israel's bitter enemy. The destruction of Edom mentioned here is a picture of the ultimate end of all who oppose God and his people.

there the night creatures will also repose
and find for themselves places of rest.
15 The owl will nest there and lay eggs,
she will hatch them, and care for her young under the shadow of her wings;
there also the falcons will gather,
each with its mate.

16Look in the scroll of the LORD and read:

None of these will be missing,
not one will lack her mate.
For it is his mouth that has given the order,
and his Spirit will gather them together.

34:17
t Jer 13:25

17 He allots their portions;*t*
his hand distributes them by measure.
They will possess it forever
and dwell there from generation to generation.

Joy of the Redeemed

35 The desert and the parched land will be glad;
the wilderness will rejoice and blossom.
Like the crocus, 2 it will burst into bloom;
it will rejoice greatly and shout for joy.*u*
The glory of Lebanon*v* will be given to it,
the splendor of Carmel and Sharon;
they will see the glory of the LORD,
the splendor of our God.

35:2
u Isa 55:12
v Isa 32:15

35:3
w Job 4:4;
Heb 12:12

3 Strengthen the feeble hands,
steady the knees*w* that give way;
4 say to those with fearful hearts,
"Be strong, do not fear;
your God will come,
he will come with vengeance;
with divine retribution
he will come to save you."

35:5
x Mt 11:5; Jn 9:6-7
y Isa 29:18

5 Then will the eyes of the blind be opened*x*
and the ears of the deaf*y* unstopped.

35:6
z Mt 15:30; Jn 5:8-9
a Mt 9:32-33
b Isa 41:18; Jn 7:38

6 Then will the lame*z* leap like a deer,
and the mute tongue*a* shout for joy.
Water will gush forth in the wilderness
and streams*b* in the desert.
7 The burning sand will become a pool,
the thirsty ground bubbling springs.
In the haunts where jackals once lay,
grass and reeds and papyrus will grow.

34:16 Isaiah referred to the prophecies that God commanded him to write down as the "scroll of the LORD." Whoever lived to see the time of Edom's destruction would have only to look to these prophecies to find agreement between what happened and what was predicted. Prophecy predicts and history reveals what has been in God's mind for all time.

35:1ff In chapters 1—34, Isaiah has delivered a message of judgment on all nations, including Israel and Judah, for rejecting God. Although there have been glimpses of relief and restoration for the remnant of faithful believers, the climate of wrath, fury, judgment, and destruction has prevailed. Now Isaiah breaks through with a vision of beauty and encouragement. God is just as thorough in his mercy as he is severe in his judgment. God's complete moral perfection is revealed by his hatred of all sin, and this leads to judgment. This same moral perfection is revealed in

his love for all he has created. This leads to mercy for those who have sinned but who have sincerely loved Jesus and put their trust in him.

35:1ff This chapter is a beautiful picture of the final kingdom in which God will establish his justice and destroy all evil. This is the world the redeemed can anticipate after the judgment when creation itself will rejoice in God. Chapter 34 spoke of great distress when God will judge all people for their actions. Chapter 35 pictures the days when life will be peaceful at last and everything will be made right. Carmel and Sharon were regions of thick vegetation and fertile soil. They were symbols of productivity and plenty.

8 And a highway[c] will be there;
    it will be called the Way of Holiness.
The unclean will not journey on it;
    it will be for those who walk in that Way;
    wicked fools will not go about on it.[a]
9 No lion will be there,
    nor will any ferocious beast get up on it;
    they will not be found there.
But only the redeemed will walk there,
10   and the ransomed of the LORD will return.
They will enter Zion with singing;
    everlasting joy will crown their heads.
Gladness and joy will overtake them,
    and sorrow and sighing will flee away.[d]

35:8
[c] Mt 7:13-14

35:10
[d] Isa 51:11;
Rev 7:17; 21:4

5. Events during the reign of Hezekiah
Sennacherib Threatens Jerusalem

36 In the fourteenth year of King Hezekiah's reign, Sennacherib[e] king of Assyria attacked all the fortified cities of Judah and captured them. 2 Then the king of Assyria sent his field commander with a large army from Lachish to King Hezekiah at Jerusalem. When the commander stopped at the aqueduct of the Upper Pool, on the road to the Washerman's Field, 3 Eliakim[f] son of Hilkiah the palace administrator, Shebna the secretary, and Joah son of Asaph the recorder went out to him.

4 The field commander said to them, "Tell Hezekiah,

"'This is what the great king, the king of Assyria, says: On what are you basing this confidence of yours? 5 You say you have strategy and military strength—but you speak only empty words. On whom are you depending, that you rebel against me? 6 Look now, you are depending on Egypt,[g] that splintered reed[h] of a staff, which pierces a man's hand and wounds him if he leans on it! Such is Pharaoh king of Egypt to all who depend on him. 7 And if you say to me, "We are depending on the LORD our God"—isn't he the one whose high places and altars Hezekiah removed,[i] saying to Judah and Jerusalem, "You must worship before this altar"?

8 "'Come now, make a bargain with my master, the king of Assyria: I will give you two thousand horses—if you can put riders on them! 9 How then can you repulse one officer of the least of my master's officials, even though you are depending on Egypt for chariots and horsemen?[j] 10 Furthermore, have I come to attack and destroy this land without the LORD? The LORD himself told me to march against this country and destroy it.'"

36:1
[e] 2Ch 32:1

36:3
[f] Isa 22:20-21

36:6
[g] Isa 30:2, 5
[h] Eze 29:6-7

36:7
[i] 2Ki 18:4

36:9
[j] Isa 30:2-5

[a] 8 Or / *the simple will not stray from it*

35:8-10 This highway, the "Way of Holiness," is the way that righteous pilgrims will take from the desert of suffering to Zion (Jerusalem). It is found only by following God. Only the redeemed will travel God's highway; they will be protected from wicked travelers and harmful animals. God is preparing a way for his people (those who walk in his ways) to travel to his home, and he will walk with us. God never stops at simply pointing the way; he is always beside us as we go.

36:4-6 Chapter 19 describes Isaiah's prophecy of judgment upon Egypt, while chapters 30 and 31 pronounce woe on those from Judah who would ally themselves with Egypt in the face of Assyria's impending attack. Sennacherib of Assyria was taunting Judah for trusting in Egypt. Even the Assyrians knew that Egypt could not help Judah.

36:5 Hezekiah put great trust in Pharaoh's promise to help Israel against the Assyrians, but promises are only as good as the credibility of the person making them. It was Pharaoh's word against God's. How quickly we organize our lives around human advice when dealing with our problems while we neglect God's eternal promises. When choosing between God's word and someone else's, whose will you believe?

36:7 The field commander from Assyria claimed that Hezekiah had insulted God by tearing down his altars and making the people worship only in Jerusalem. But Hezekiah's reform sought to eliminate idol worship (which occurred mainly on high hills) so that the people worshiped only the true God. Either the Assyrians didn't know about the religion of the true God, or they wanted to deceive the people into thinking they had angered a powerful god.

In the same way, Satan tries to confuse or deceive us. People don't necessarily need to be sinful to be ineffective for God; they need only be confused about what God wants. To avoid Satan's deceit, study God's Word carefully and regularly. When you know what God says, you will not fall for Satan's lies.

36:10 Sennacherib continued his demoralization campaign by sending the field commander to try to convince the people of Judah that God had turned against them. The Assyrians hoped to convince the people of Judah to surrender without fighting. But Isaiah had already said that the Assyrians *would not* destroy Jerusalem, so the people did not need to be afraid of them (10:24-27; 29:5-8).

36:11
k Ezr 4:7

¹¹Then Eliakim, Shebna and Joah said to the field commander, "Please speak to your servants in Aramaic,ᵏ since we understand it. Don't speak to us in Hebrew in the hearing of the people on the wall."

¹²But the commander replied, "Was it only to your master and you that my master sent me to say these things, and not to the men sitting on the wall—who, like you, will have to eat their own filth and drink their own urine?"

36:13
l 2Ch 32:18

¹³Then the commander stood and called out in Hebrew,ˡ "Hear the words of the great king, the king of Assyria! ¹⁴This is what the king says: Do not let Hezekiah deceive you. He cannot deliver you! ¹⁵Do not let Hezekiah persuade you to trust in the LORD when he says, 'The LORD will surely deliver us; this city will not be given into the hand of the king of Assyria.'

36:16
m Zec 3:10
n Pr 5:15

¹⁶"Do not listen to Hezekiah. This is what the king of Assyria says: Make peace with me and come out to me. Then every one of you will eat from his own vine and fig tree ᵐ and drink water from his own cistern,ⁿ ¹⁷until I come and take you to a land like your own—a land of grain and new wine, a land of bread and vineyards.

¹⁸"Do not let Hezekiah mislead you when he says, 'The LORD will deliver us.' Has the god of any nation ever delivered his land from the hand of the king of Assyria? ¹⁹Where are the gods of Hamath and Arpad? Where are the gods of Sepharvaim? Have they rescued Samaria from my hand? ²⁰Who of all the gods º of these countries has been able to save his land from me? How then can the LORD deliver Jerusalem from my hand?"

36:20
º 1Ki 20:23

²¹But the people remained silent and said nothing in reply, because the king had commanded, "Do not answer him."

ASSYRIA ADVANCES
As Sennacherib beautified his capital city, Nineveh, Hezekiah withheld tribute and prepared for battle. The Assyrians advanced toward their rebellious western border, attacking swiftly down the Mediterranean coast. From Lachish, Sennacherib threatened to take Jerusalem, but Isaiah knew his threats would die with him on his return to Nineveh.

36:11 Aramaic was an international language at this time. See also 22:15–25 for Isaiah's prophecies concerning Eliakim and Shebna.

36:17 Sennacherib's commander tried yet another ploy to demoralize the people. He appealed to the starving city under siege by offering to take them to a land with plenty of food if they surrendered. The Assyrian policy for dealing with conquered nations was to resettle the inhabitants and then to move other conquered peoples into the recently conquered area. This provided manpower for their armies and prevented revolts in conquered territories.

36:19, 20 The field commander said that the gods of the other cities he had conquered had not been able to save their people, so how could the God of Jerusalem save them? The Lord was supposedly the God of Samaria (the northern kingdom), and it fell. But the Lord was the God of Samaria in name only because the people were not worshiping him. That is why prophets foretold the fall of Samaria. But for the Lord's own sake and for the sake of David, the Lord would rescue them from the Assyrian army (37:35).

22 Then Eliakim son of Hilkiah the palace administrator, Shebna the secretary, and Joah son of Asaph the recorder went to Hezekiah, with their clothes torn, and told him what the field commander had said.

Jerusalem's Deliverance Foretold

37 When King Hezekiah heard this, he tore his clothes and put on sackcloth and went into the temple of the LORD. 2 He sent Eliakim the palace administrator, Shebna the secretary, and the leading priests, all wearing sackcloth, to the prophet Isaiah son of Amoz. 3 They told him, "This is what Hezekiah says: This day is a day of distress and rebuke and disgrace, as when children come to the point of birth*p* and there is no strength to deliver them. 4 It may be that the LORD your God will hear the words of the field commander, whom his master, the king of Assyria, has sent to ridicule the living God, and that he will rebuke him for the words the LORD your God has heard.*q* Therefore pray for the remnant that still survives."

5 When King Hezekiah's officials came to Isaiah, 6 Isaiah said to them, "Tell your master, 'This is what the LORD says: Do not be afraid *r* of what you have heard—those words with which the underlings of the king of Assyria have blasphemed me. 7 Listen! I am going to put a spirit in him so that when he hears a certain report,*s* he will return to his own country, and there I will have him cut down with the sword.'"

8 When the field commander heard that the king of Assyria had left Lachish, he withdrew and found the king fighting against Libnah.

9 Now Sennacherib received a report *t* that Tirhakah, the Cushite *a* king ⌞of Egypt⌟, was marching out to fight against him. When he heard it, he sent messengers to Hezekiah with this word: 10 "Say to Hezekiah king of Judah: Do not let the god you depend on deceive you when he says, 'Jerusalem will not be handed over to the king of Assyria.'*u* 11 Surely you have heard what the kings of Assyria have done to all the countries, destroying them completely. And will you be delivered?*v* 12 Did the gods of the nations that were destroyed by my forefathers deliver them—the gods of Gozan, Haran,*w* Rezeph and the people of Eden who were in Tel Assar? 13 Where is the king of Hamath, the king of Arpad, the king of the city of Sepharvaim, or of Hena or Ivvah?"

Hezekiah's Prayer

14 Hezekiah received the letter from the messengers and read it. Then he went up to the temple of the LORD and spread it out before the LORD. 15 And Hezekiah prayed to the LORD: 16 "O LORD Almighty, God of Israel, enthroned between the cherubim, you alone are God *x* over all the kingdoms of the earth. You have made heaven and earth. 17 Give ear, O LORD, and hear; open your eyes, O LORD, and see;*y* listen to all the words Sennacherib has sent to insult the living God.

18 "It is true, O LORD, that the Assyrian kings have laid waste all these peoples and their lands. *z* 19 They have thrown their gods into the fire and destroyed them, for they were not gods but only wood and stone, fashioned by human hands. 20 Now, O LORD our God, deliver us from his hand, so that all kingdoms on earth may know that you alone, O LORD, are God.*b a*"

Sennacherib's Fall

21 Then Isaiah son of Amoz sent a message to Hezekiah: "This is what the LORD, the God of Israel, says: Because you have prayed to me concerning Sennacherib king of Assyria, 22 this is the word the LORD has spoken against him:

> "The Virgin Daughter of Zion
> despises and mocks you.

a 9 That is, from the upper Nile region   *b 20* Dead Sea Scrolls (see also 2 Kings 19:19); Masoretic Text *alone are the* LORD

37:3 *p* Isa 26:18

37:4 *q* Isa 36:13, 18-20

37:6 *r* Isa 7:4

37:7 *s* ver 9

37:9 *t* ver 7

37:10 *u* Isa 36:15

37:11 *v* Isa 36:18-20

37:12 *w* Ge 11:31

37:16 *x* Dt 10:17

37:17 *y* Da 9:18

37:18 *z* 2Ki 15:29

37:20 *a* Ps 46:10

37:3 Judah is compared to a woman who is trying to give birth to a child but is too weak to deliver. When the situation seemed hopeless, Hezekiah didn't give up. Instead, he asked the prophet Isaiah to pray that God would help his people. No matter how bad your circumstances seem, don't despair. Turn to God.

37:4 Hezekiah did exactly what Isaiah had been calling the people to do (chapters 1—35). He turned to God and watched him come to Judah's aid. Turning to God means believing that God is there and that he is able to help us.

37:8–10 Although the answer to Hezekiah's prayer was already in motion because Tirhakah was poised to attack, Hezekiah did not know it. He persisted in prayer and faith even though he could not see the answer coming. When we pray, we must have faith that God has already prepared the best answer. Our task is to ask in faith and wait in humility.

37:16 Cherubim are mighty angels. "Enthroned between the cherubim" refers to the atonement cover on the ark of the covenant in the Jerusalem temple. This is a description of God's holiness, power, and sovereignty.

The Daughter of Jerusalem
tosses her head[b] as you flee.

23 Who is it you have insulted and blasphemed?
Against whom have you raised your voice
and lifted your eyes in pride?[c]
Against the Holy One of Israel!

24 By your messengers
you have heaped insults on the Lord.
And you have said,
'With my many chariots
I have ascended the heights of the mountains,
the utmost heights of Lebanon.[d]
I have cut down its tallest cedars,
the choicest of its pines.
I have reached its remotest heights,
the finest of its forests.

25 I have dug wells in foreign lands[a]
and drunk the water there.
With the soles of my feet
I have dried up all the streams of Egypt.'

26 "Have you not heard?
Long ago I ordained[e] it.
In days of old I planned it;
now I have brought it to pass,
that you have turned fortified cities
into piles of stone.

27 Their people, drained of power,
are dismayed and put to shame.
They are like plants in the field,
like tender green shoots,
like grass sprouting on the roof,[f]
scorched[b] before it grows up.

28 "But I know where you stay
and when you come and go
and how you rage against me.

29 Because you rage against me
and because your insolence[g] has reached my ears,
I will put my hook in your nose[h]
and my bit in your mouth,
and I will make you return
by the way you came.[i]

30 "This will be the sign for you, O Hezekiah:

"This year you will eat what grows by itself,
and the second year what springs from that.
But in the third year sow and reap,
plant vineyards and eat their fruit.

31 Once more a remnant of the house of Judah
will take root below and bear fruit[j] above.

32 For out of Jerusalem will come a remnant,
and out of Mount Zion a band of survivors.

37:22
[b] Job 16:4
37:23
[c] Isa 2:11
37:24
[d] Isa 14:8
37:26
[e] Ac 2:23
37:27
[f] Ps 129:6
37:29
[g] Isa 10:12
[h] Isa 30:28;
Eze 38:4
[i] ver 34
37:31
[j] Isa 27:6

[a]25 Dead Sea Scrolls (see also 2 Kings 19:24); Masoretic Text does not have *in foreign lands*.   [b]27 Some manuscripts of the Masoretic Text, Dead Sea Scrolls and some Septuagint manuscripts (see also 2 Kings 19:26); most manuscripts of the Masoretic Text *roof / and terraced fields*

37:29   This was a common torture the Assyrians used on their captives. They were often led away with hooks in their noses or bits in their mouths as signs of humiliation.

The zeal[k] of the LORD Almighty
    will accomplish this.

33 "Therefore this is what the LORD says concerning the king of Assyria:

"He will not enter this city
    or shoot an arrow here.
He will not come before it with shield
    or build a siege ramp against it.
34 By the way that he came he will return;
    he will not enter this city,"

                          declares the LORD.

35 "I will defend[l] this city and save it,
    for my sake and for the sake of David[m] my servant!"

36 Then the angel of the LORD went out and put to death a hundred and eighty-five thousand men in the Assyrian camp. When the people got up the next morning—there were all the dead bodies! 37 So Sennacherib king of Assyria broke camp and withdrew. He returned to Nineveh and stayed there.

38 One day, while he was worshiping in the temple of his god Nisroch, his sons Adrammelech and Sharezer cut him down with the sword, and they escaped to the land of Ararat.[n] And Esarhaddon his son succeeded him as king.

Hezekiah's Illness

38 In those days Hezekiah became ill and was at the point of death. The prophet Isaiah son of Amoz went to him and said, "This is what the LORD says: Put your house in order,[o] because you are going to die; you will not recover."

2 Hezekiah turned his face to the wall and prayed to the LORD, 3 "Remember, O LORD, how I have walked[p] before you faithfully and with wholehearted devotion and have done what is good in your eyes." And Hezekiah wept bitterly.

4 Then the word of the LORD came to Isaiah: 5 "Go and tell Hezekiah, 'This is what the LORD, the God of your father David, says: I have heard your prayer and seen your tears; I will add fifteen years[q] to your life. 6 And I will deliver you and this city from the hand of the king of Assyria. I will defend[r] this city.

7 "'This is the LORD's sign[s] to you that the LORD will do what he has promised: 8 I will make the shadow cast by the sun go back the ten steps it has gone down on the stairway of Ahaz.'" So the sunlight went back the ten steps it had gone down.

9 A writing of Hezekiah king of Judah after his illness and recovery:

10 I said, "In the prime of my life[t]
    must I go through the gates of death[a]
    and be robbed of the rest of my years?[u]"
11 I said, "I will not again see the LORD,
    the LORD, in the land of the living;[v]
no longer will I look on mankind,
    or be with those who now dwell in this world.[b]
12 Like a shepherd's tent my house
    has been pulled down and taken from me.
Like a weaver I have rolled[w] up my life,
    and he has cut me off from the loom;[x]
    day and night you made an end of me.

---

a 10 Hebrew *Sheol*   *b 11* A few Hebrew manuscripts; most Hebrew manuscripts *in the place of cessation*

37:32
[k] Isa 9:7

37:35
[l] Isa 38:6
[m] 2Ki 20:6

37:38
[n] Jer 51:27

38:1
[o] 2Sa 17:23

38:3
[p] Ne 13:14

38:5
[q] 2Ki 18:2

38:6
[r] Isa 37:35

38:7
[s] Isa 7:11, 14

38:10
[t] Ps 102:24
[u] Job 17:11

38:11
[v] Ps 27:13; 116:9

38:12
[w] Heb 1:12
[x] Job 7:6

37:35 God would defend Jerusalem for the sake of his honor and for David's sake in remembrance of his promise to David. Assyria had insulted God. They would not be his instrument to punish Jerusalem. What Jerusalem could not possibly do, God would do for them. God is prepared to do the impossible if we trust him enough to ask.

37:38 The death of Sennacherib was prophesied by Isaiah in 10:12, 33, 34 and in 37:7. His death is also recorded in 2 Kings 19.

38:1ff The events of chapters 38 and 39 happened before those of chapters 36 and 37.

38:1-5 When Isaiah went to Hezekiah, who was extremely ill, and told him of his impending death, Hezekiah immediately turned to God. God responded to his prayer, allowing Hezekiah to live another 15 years. In response to fervent prayer, God may change the course of our lives too. Never hesitate to ask God for radical changes if you will honor him with those changes.

38:1-6 According to 2 Chronicles 32:24-26, Hezekiah had a

38:13
y Job 10:16

13 I waited patiently till dawn,
   but like a lion he broke all my bones;y
   day and night you made an end of me.

38:14
z Isa 59:11

14 I cried like a swift or thrush,
   I moaned like a mourning dove.z
   My eyes grew weak as I looked to the heavens.
   I am troubled; O Lord, come to my aid!"

38:15
a 1Ki 21:27
b Job 7:11

15 But what can I say?
   He has spoken to me, and he himself has done this.
   I will walk humblya all my years
   because of this anguish of my soul.b

16 Lord, by such things men live;
   and my spirit finds life in them too.
   You restored me to health
   and let me live.

38:17
c Ps 30:3

17 Surely it was for my benefit
   that I suffered such anguish.
   In your love you kept me
   from the pitc of destruction;
   you have put all my sins
   behind your back.

38:18
d Ecc 9:10
e Ps 6:5; 88:10-11

18 For the gravea d cannot praise you,
   death cannot sing your praise;e
   those who go down to the pit
   cannot hope for your faithfulness.

38:19
f Dt 6:7

19 The living, the living—they praisef you,
   as I am doing today;
   fathers tell their children
   about your faithfulness.

38:20
g Ps 33:2
h Ps 116:17-19

20 The LORD will save me,
   and we will sing with stringed instrumentsg
   all the days of our lives
   in the templeh of the LORD.

21 Isaiah had said, "Prepare a poultice of figs and apply it to the boil, and he will recover."
22 Hezekiah had asked, "What will be the sign that I will go up to the temple of the LORD?"

Envoys From Babylon

39:2
i 2Ch 32:31
j 2Ki 18:15

39 At that time Merodach-Baladan son of Baladan king of Babylon sent Hezekiah letters and a gift, because he had heard of his illness and recovery. 2 Hezekiah received the envoys i gladly and showed them what was in his storehouses—the silver, the gold,j the spices, the fine oil, his entire armory and everything found among his treasures. There was nothing in his palace or in all his kingdom that Hezekiah did not show them.

3 Then Isaiah the prophet went to King Hezekiah and asked, "What did those men say, and where did they come from?"

a 18 Hebrew Sheol

---

problem with pride even after this double miracle of healing and deliverance. Eventually he and his subjects humbled themselves, so God's judgment was put off for several more generations.

38:16–18 Hezekiah realized that his prayer brought deliverance and forgiveness. His words "the grave cannot praise you" may reveal that he was unaware of the blessedness of the future life for those who trust in God (57:1, 2), or he may have meant that dead bodies cannot praise God. In either case, Hezekiah knew that God had spared his life, so in his poem Hezekiah praises God. Hezekiah recognized the good that came from his bitter experience. The next time you have difficult struggles, pray for God's help to gain something beneficial from them.

38:19 Hezekiah spoke of the significance of passing the joy of

the Lord from father to child, from generation to generation. The heritage of our faith has come to us because of faithful men and women who have carried God's message to us across the centuries. Do you share with your children or other young people the excitement of your relationship with God?

39:1ff Merodach-Baladan, a Babylonian prince, was planning a revolt against Assyria and was forming an alliance. He probably hoped to convince Hezekiah to join this alliance against Assyria. Hezekiah, feeling honored by this attention and perhaps feeling some sympathy for their proposal, showed the Babylonian envoys his treasures. But Isaiah warned the king not to trust Babylon. Someday they would turn on Judah and devour Jerusalem's wealth.

"From a distant land," Hezekiah replied. "They came to me from Babylon."

4 The prophet asked, "What did they see in your palace?"

"They saw everything in my palace," Hezekiah said. "There is nothing among my treasures that I did not show them."

5 Then Isaiah said to Hezekiah, "Hear the word of the Lord Almighty: 6 The time will surely come when everything in your palace, and all that your fathers have stored up until this day, will be carried off to Babylon. *k* Nothing will be left, says the Lord. 7 And some of your descendants, your own flesh and blood who will be born to you, will be taken away, and they will become eunuchs in the palace of the king of Babylon. *l*"

8 "The word of the Lord you have spoken is good," Hezekiah replied. For he thought, "There will be peace and security in my lifetime. *m*"

39:6
k Jer 20:5

39:7
l Da 1:1-7

39:8
m 2Ch 32:26

B. WORDS OF COMFORT (40:1—66:24)

Isaiah now speaks of events that will occur after the captivity. This includes the decree by Cyrus to release the remnant captives and allow them to return to Jerusalem after he conquered Babylon. But Isaiah also foretells the coming of the suffering Servant, Jesus Christ, and describes his life and death with incredible detail. Isaiah also speaks about the coming of the new heavens and earth, when God's people will be completely restored. Because all believers will participate in this new world to come, we can have confident hope in the future.

1. Israel's release from captivity
Comfort for God's People

40   Comfort, comfort *n* my people,
         says your God.
2 Speak tenderly *o* to Jerusalem,
      and proclaim to her
   that her hard service has been completed, *p*
      that her sin has been paid for,
   that she has received from the Lord's hand
      double for all her sins.

3 A voice of one calling:
   "In the desert prepare
      the way *q* for the Lord *a*;
   make straight in the wilderness
      a highway for our God. *b r*
4 Every valley shall be raised up,
      every mountain and hill made low;

40:1
n Isa 12:1

40:2
o Isa 35:4
p Isa 41:11-13

40:3
q Mal 3:1
r Mt 3:3*

a 3 Or A voice of one calling in the desert: / "Prepare the way for the Lord   *b 3 Hebrew; Septuagint make straight the paths of our God*

39:4–7 What was so wrong about showing these Babylonians around? Hezekiah failed to see that the Babylonians would become his next threat, and that they, not the Assyrians, would conquer his city. When Isaiah told him that Babylon would someday carry it all away, this was an amazing prophecy because Babylon was struggling for independence under Assyria. Hezekiah's self-satisfied display of his earthly treasures brought its own consequences (2 Kings 25; Daniel 1:1, 2). His response (39:8) may seem a bit shortsighted, but he simply was expressing gratitude for the blessing from God that peace would reign during his lifetime and that God's judgment would not be more severe.

39:8 Hezekiah, one of Judah's most faithful kings, worked hard throughout his reign to stamp out idol worship and to purify the worship of the true God at the Jerusalem temple. Nevertheless, he knew his kingdom was not pure. Powerful undercurrents of evil invited destruction, and only God's miraculous interventions preserved Judah from its enemies. Here Hezekiah was grateful that God would preserve peace during his reign. As soon as Hezekiah died, the nation rushed back to its sinful ways under the leadership of Manasseh, Hezekiah's son. He actually rebuilt the centers of idolatry his father had destroyed.

40:1ff The book of Isaiah makes a dramatic shift at this point. The following chapters discuss the majesty of God, who is coming to rule the earth and judge all people. God will reunite

Israel and Judah and restore them to glory. Instead of warning the people of impending judgment, Isaiah here comforts them. Chapter 40 refers to the restoration after the exile. Cyrus is the instrument of their deliverance from Babylon. Secondarily, it looks to the end of time when "Babylon"—the future evil world system—will be destroyed and the persecution of God's people will end.

40:1, 2 Judah still had 100 years of trouble before Jerusalem would fall, then 70 years of exile. So God tells Isaiah to speak tenderly and to comfort Jerusalem.

The seeds of comfort may take root in the soil of adversity. When your life seems to be falling apart, ask God to comfort you. You may not escape adversity, but you may find God's comfort as you face it. Sometimes, however, the only comfort we have is in the knowledge that someday we will be with God. Appreciate the comfort and encouragement found in his Word, his presence, and his people.

40:3–5 Preparing a straight highway means removing obstacles and rolling out the red carpet for the coming of the Lord. The desert is a picture of life's trials and sufferings. We are not immune to these, but our faith need not be hindered by them. Isaiah told people to prepare to see God work. John the Baptist used these words as he challenged the people to prepare for the coming Messiah (Matthew 3:3).

the rough ground shall become level,
    the rugged places a plain.

40:5
sIsa 52:10;
Lk 3:4-6*
5 And the glory of the LORD will be revealed,
    and all mankind together will see it.s

                    For the mouth of the LORD has spoken."

40:6
tJob 14:2
6 A voice says, "Cry out."
    And I said, "What shall I cry?"

"All men are like grass,t
    and all their glory is like the flowers of the field.
7 The grass withers and the flowers fall,
    because the breath of the LORD blows on them.
    Surely the people are grass.

40:8
uIsa 55:11
vMt 5:18;
1Pe 1:24-25*
8 The grass withers and the flowers fall,
    but the wordu of our God stands forever.v

40:9
wIsa 52:7-10
9 You who bring good tidingsw to Zion,
    go up on a high mountain.
You who bring good tidings to Jerusalem,a
    lift up your voice with a shout,
lift it up, do not be afraid;
    say to the towns of Judah,
    "Here is your God!"

40:10
xIsa 59:16
yIsa 62:11;
Rev 22:12
10 See, the Sovereign LORD comes with power,
    and his armx rules for him.
See, his rewardy is with him,
    and his recompense accompanies him.

40:11
zEze 34:23;
Jn 10:11
11 He tends his flock like a shepherd:z
    He gathers the lambs in his arms
and carries them close to his heart;
    he gently leads those that have young.

12 Who has measured the waters in the hollow of his hand,
    or with the breadth of his hand marked off the heavens?
Who has held the dust of the earth in a basket,
    or weighed the mountains on the scales
    and the hills in a balance?

40:13
a1Co 2:16*
13 Who has understood the mindb of the LORD,
    or instructed him as his counselor?a

40:14
bJob 21:22
14 Whom did the LORD consult to enlighten him,
    and who taught him the right way?
Who was it that taught him knowledgeb
    or showed him the path of understanding?

15 Surely the nations are like a drop in a bucket;
    they are regarded as dust on the scales;
    he weighs the islands as though they were fine dust.

a9 Or O Zion, bringer of good tidings, / go up on a high mountain. / O Jerusalem, bringer of good tidings
b13 Or Spirit; or spirit

40:6–8 People are compared here to grass and flowers that wither away. We are mortal, but God's Word is eternal and unfailing. Public opinion changes and is unreliable, but God's Word is constant. Only in God's eternal Word will we find lasting solutions to our problems and needs.

40:11 God is often pictured as a shepherd, gently caring for and guiding his flock. He is powerful (40:10), yet careful and gentle. He is called a shepherd (Psalm 23); the good shepherd (John 10:11, 14); the great Shepherd (Hebrews 13:20); and the Chief Shepherd (1 Peter 5:4). Note that the shepherd is caring for the most defenseless members of his society: children and those caring for them. This reinforces the prophetic theme that the truly

powerful nation is not the one with a strong military, but rather the one that relies on God's caring strength.

40:12–31 Isaiah describes God's power to create, his provision to sustain, and his presence to help. God is almighty and all-powerful; but even so, he cares for each of us personally. No person or thing can be compared to God (40:25). We describe God as best we can with our limited knowledge and language, but we only limit our understanding of him and his power when we compare him to what we experience on earth. What is your concept of God, especially as revealed in his Son, Jesus Christ? Don't limit his work in your life by underestimating him.

16 Lebanon is not sufficient for altar fires,
   nor its animals enough for burnt offerings.
17 Before him all the nations are as nothing;
   they are regarded by him as worthless
   and less than nothing.

18 To whom, then, will you compare God? c
   What image d will you compare him to?
19 As for an idol, a craftsman casts it,
   and a goldsmith e overlays it with gold
   and fashions silver chains for it.
20 A man too poor to present such an offering
   selects wood that will not rot.
   He looks for a skilled craftsman
   to set up an idol that will not topple.

21 Do you not know?
   Have you not heard?
   Has it not been told f you from the beginning?
   Have you not understood g since the earth was founded?
22 He sits enthroned above the circle of the earth,
   and its people are like grasshoppers. h
   He stretches out the heavens like a canopy,
   and spreads them out like a tent to live in.
23 He brings princes to naught
   and reduces the rulers of this world to nothing. i
24 No sooner are they planted,
   no sooner are they sown,
   no sooner do they take root in the ground,
   than he blows on them and they wither,
   and a whirlwind sweeps them away like chaff.

25 "To whom will you compare me? j
   Or who is my equal?" says the Holy One.
26 Lift your eyes and look to the heavens: k
   Who created all these?
   He who brings out the starry host l one by one,
   and calls them each by name.
   Because of his great power and mighty strength,
   not one of them is missing.

27 Why do you say, O Jacob,
   and complain, O Israel,
   "My way is hidden from the LORD;
   my cause is disregarded by my God"?
28 Do you not know?
   Have you not heard?
   The LORD is the everlasting m God,
   the Creator of the ends of the earth.
   He will not grow tired or weary,
   and his understanding no one can fathom. n
29 He gives strength to the weary o
   and increases the power of the weak.
30 Even youths grow tired and weary,
   and young men stumble and fall;

40:18
c Isa 46:5
d Ac 17:29

40:19
e Isa 41:7

40:21
f Ps 19:1; Ac 14:17
g Ro 1:19

40:22
h Ps 104:2; Isa 42:5

40:23
i Job 12:21;
Ps 107:40

40:25
j ver 18

40:26
k Isa 51:6
l Ps 147:4

40:28
m Ps 90:2
n Ps 147:5;
Ro 11:33

40:29
o Jer 31:25

40:29–31 Even the strongest people get tired at times, but God's power and strength never diminish. He is never too tired or too busy to help and listen. His strength is our source of strength. When you feel all of life crushing you and cannot go another step, remember that you can call upon God to renew your strength.

40:31
p Ps 103:5

31 but those who hope in the LORD
   will renew their strength.
They will soar on wings like eagles;p
   they will run and not grow weary,
   they will walk and not be faint.

The Helper of Israel

41:1
q Zec 2:13
r Isa 34:1

41

"Be silentq before me, you islands!
   Let the nations renew their strength!
Let them come forward and speak;
   let us meet togetherr at the place of judgment.

41:2
s Isa 45:1, 13

2 "Who has stirred up one from the east,s
   calling him in righteousness to his servicea?
He hands nations over to him
   and subdues kings before him.
He turns them to dust with his sword,
   to windblown chaff with his bow.
3 He pursues them and moves on unscathed,
   by a path his feet have not traveled before.

41:4
t Isa 44:6; Rev 1:8,
17; 22:13

4 Who has done this and carried it through,
   calling forth the generations from the beginning?
I, the LORD—with the first of them
   and with the lastt—I am he."

5 The islands have seen it and fear;
   the ends of the earth tremble.
They approach and come forward;
6   each helps the other
   and says to his brother, "Be strong!"
7 The craftsman encourages the goldsmith,
   and he who smooths with the hammer
   spurs on him who strikes the anvil.
He says of the welding, "It is good."
   He nails down the idol so it will not topple.

41:8
u 2Ch 20:7;
Jas 2:23

8 "But you, O Israel, my servant,
   Jacob, whom I have chosen,
   you descendants of Abraham my friend,u
9 I took you from the ends of the earth,
   from its farthest corners I called you.
I said, 'You are my servant';
   I have chosen you and have not rejected you.

a 2 Or / whom victory meets at every step

40:31 Hoping in the Lord is expecting that his promise of strength will help us to rise above life's distractions and difficulties. Do you believe God loves you and wants the best for you? Can you relax, confident that his purposes are right? Are you convinced that he has the power to control all of life—and your life as well? Though your faith may be struggling or weak, accept his provisions and care for you.

41:1ff The "one from the east" is Cyrus II of Persia, who would be king within a century and a half (he is also mentioned by name in 44:28). He conquered Babylon in 539 B.C. and was responsible for the decree releasing the exiled Jews to return to Jerusalem. God could even use a pagan ruler to protect and care for Israel, because God is in control of all world empires and politics.

41:4 Each generation gets caught up in its own problems, but God's plan embraces all generations. When your great-grandparents lived, God worked personally in the lives of his people. When your great-grandchildren live, God will still work person-

ally in the lives of his people. He is the only one who sees 100 years from now as clearly as 100 years ago. When you are concerned about the future, talk with God, who knows the generations of the future as well as he knows the generations of the past.

41:8-10 God chose Israel through Abraham because he wanted to, not because the people deserved it (Deuteronomy 7:6-8; 9:4-6). Although God chose the Israelites to represent him to the world, they failed to do this; so God punished them and sent them into captivity. Now all believers are God's chosen people, and all share the responsibility of representing him to the world. One day God will bring all his faithful people together. We need not fear because (1) God is with us ("I am with you"), (2) God has established a relationship with us ("I am your God"), and (3) God gives us assurance of his strength, help, and victory over sin and death. Have you realized all the ways God has helped you?

10 So do not fear, for I am with you;ᵛ
    do not be dismayed, for I am your God.
  I will strengthen you and help you;
    I will uphold you with my righteous right hand.

41:10
ᵛIsa 43:2, 5

11 "All who rage against you
    will surely be ashamed and disgraced;ʷ
  those who oppose you
    will be as nothing and perish.

41:11
ʷIsa 45:24

12 Though you search for your enemies,
    you will not find them.
  Those who wage war against you
    will be as nothingˣ at all.

41:12
ˣIsa 17:14

13 For I am the Lord, your God,
    who takes hold of your right hand
  and says to you, Do not fear;
    I will help you.

14 Do not be afraid, O worm Jacob,
    O little Israel,
  for I myself will help you," declares the Lord,
    your Redeemer, the Holy One of Israel.

15 "See, I will make you into a threshing sledge,ʸ
    new and sharp, with many teeth.
  You will thresh the mountains and crush them,
    and reduce the hills to chaff.

41:15
ʸMic 4:13

16 You will winnowᶻ them, the wind will pick them up,
    and a gale will blow them away.
  But you will rejoice in the Lord
    and glory in the Holy One of Israel.

41:16
ᶻJer 51:2

17 "The poor and needy search for water,
    but there is none;
    their tongues are parched with thirst.
  But I the Lord will answer them;
    I, the God of Israel, will not forsake them.

18 I will make rivers flow on barren heights,
    and springs within the valleys.
  I will turn the desertᵃ into pools of water,
    and the parched ground into springs.ᵇ

41:18
ᵃIsa 43:19
ᵇIsa 35:7

19 I will put in the desert
    the cedar and the acacia, the myrtle and the olive.
  I will set pines in the wasteland,
    the fir and the cypress together,

20 so that people may see and know,
    may consider and understand,
  that the hand of the Lord has done this,
    that the Holy One of Israel has created it.

21 "Present your case," says the Lord.
    "Set forth your arguments," says Jacob's King.

22 "Bring in ⌊your idols⌋ to tell us
    what is going to happen.ᶜ
  Tell us what the former things were,
    so that we may consider them
    and know their final outcome.
  Or declare to us the things to come,

41:22
ᶜIsa 45:21

41:21–24 Israel was surrounded by many nations whose gods supposedly had special powers, such as raising crops and providing victories in war. These gods, however, failed to deliver. A god with limited or no power at all is not really a god.

When we are tempted to put our trust in something other than the living God—money, career, family, or even military power—we should stop and ask some serious questions. Will it come through? Will it unfailingly provide what I am looking for? God

41:23
d Isa 42:9; 44:7-8
e Jer 10:5

23 tell us what the future holds,
  so we may know[d] that you are gods.
 Do something, whether good or bad,[e]
  so that we will be dismayed and filled with fear.

41:24
f Isa 44:9; 1Co 8:4
g Ps 115:8

24 But you are less than nothing[f]
  and your works are utterly worthless;
  he who chooses you is detestable.[g]

41:25
h ver 2

25 "I have stirred up one from the north,[h] and he comes—
  one from the rising sun who calls on my name.
 He treads on rulers as if they were mortar,
  as if he were a potter treading the clay.

41:26
i Hab 2:18-19

26 Who told of this from the beginning, so we could know,
  or beforehand, so we could say, 'He was right'?
 No one told of this,
  no one foretold it,
  no one heard any words[i] from you.

41:27
j Isa 40:9

27 I was the first to tell Zion, 'Look, here they are!'
  I gave to Jerusalem a messenger of good tidings.[j]

41:28
k Isa 63:5

28 I look but there is no one[k]—
  no one among them to give counsel,
  no one to give answer when I ask them.

41:29
l ver 24
m Jer 5:13

29 See, they are all false!
  Their deeds amount to nothing;[l]
  their images are but wind[m] and confusion.

The Servant of the LORD

42:1
n Isa 43:10
o Mt 3:16-17

42 "Here is my servant, whom I uphold,
  my chosen one[n] in whom I delight;
 I will put my Spirit[o] on him
  and he will bring justice to the nations.
2 He will not shout or cry out,
  or raise his voice in the streets.
3 A bruised reed he will not break,
  and a smoldering wick he will not snuff out.
 In faithfulness he will bring forth justice;

42:4
p Mt 12:18-21*

4 he will not falter or be discouraged
 till he establishes justice on earth.
  In his law the islands will put their hope."[p]

42:5
q Ac 17:25

5 This is what God the LORD says—
 he who created the heavens and stretched them out,
  who spread out the earth and all that comes out of it,
 who gives breath[q] to its people,
  and life to those who walk on it:

**THE SERVANT
IN ISAIAH**

The nation Israel is called the servant: 41:8; 42:19; 43:10; 44:1, 2, 21; 45:4; 48:20
The Messiah is called the Servant: 42:1–17; 49:5–7; 50:10; 52:13; 53:11

The nation was given a mission to serve God, to be custodian of his word, and to be a light to the Gentile nations. Because of sin and rebellion, they failed. God sent his Son, Christ, as Messiah to fulfill that mission on earth.

---

delivers. When he makes a promise, he keeps it. He is the only completely trustworthy God.

42:1–4 These verses are quoted in Matthew 12:18–21 with reference to Christ. The chosen servant reveals a character of gentleness, encouragement, justice, and truth. When you feel broken and bruised or burned out in your spiritual life, God won't step on you or toss you aside as useless, but will gently pick you up. God's loving attributes are desperately needed in the world today.

Through God's Spirit, we can show such sensitivity to people around us, reflecting God's goodness and honesty to them.

42:1–9 Sometimes called the Servant Song, these verses are about the Servant-Messiah, not the servant Cyrus (described in chapter 41). Israel and the Messiah are both often called servant. Israel, as God's servant, was to help bring the world to a knowledge of God. The Messiah, Jesus, would fulfill this task and show God himself to the world.

6 "I, the LORD, have called you in righteousness;
    I will take hold of your hand.
I will keep you and will make you
    to be a covenant[r] for the people
    and a light for the Gentiles,[s]
7 to open eyes that are blind,[t]
    to free[u] captives from prison
    and to release from the dungeon those who sit in darkness.

8 "I am the LORD; that is my name!
    I will not give my glory to another[v]
    or my praise to idols.
9 See, the former things have taken place,
    and new things I declare;
before they spring into being
    I announce them to you."

Song of Praise to the LORD

10 Sing to the LORD a new song,[w]
    his praise from the ends of the earth,
you who go down to the sea, and all that is in it,
    you islands, and all who live in them.
11 Let the desert and its towns raise their voices;
    let the settlements where Kedar lives rejoice.
Let the people of Sela sing for joy;
    let them shout from the mountaintops.
12 Let them give glory[x] to the LORD
    and proclaim his praise in the islands.
13 The LORD will march out like a mighty[y] man,
    like a warrior he will stir up his zeal;
with a shout he will raise the battle cry
    and will triumph over his enemies.[z]

14 "For a long time I have kept silent,
    I have been quiet and held myself back.
But now, like a woman in childbirth,
    I cry out, I gasp and pant.
15 I will lay waste the mountains and hills
    and dry up all their vegetation;
I will turn rivers into islands
    and dry up the pools.
16 I will lead the blind by ways they have not known,
    along unfamiliar paths I will guide them;
I will turn the darkness into light before them
    and make the rough places smooth.[a]
These are the things I will do;
    I will not forsake them.
17 But those who trust in idols,
    who say to images, 'You are our gods,'
    will be turned back in utter shame.[b]

Israel Blind and Deaf

18 "Hear, you deaf;
    look, you blind, and see!

42:6
[r] Isa 49:8
[s] Lk 2:32; Ac 13:47

42:7
[t] Isa 35:5
[u] Isa 61:1

42:8
[v] Isa 48:11

42:10
[w] Ps 33:3; 40:3; 98:1

42:12
[x] Isa 24:15

42:13
[y] Isa 9:6
[z] Isa 66:14

42:16
[a] Lk 3:5

42:17
[b] Ps 97:7; Isa 1:29; 44:11; 45:16

42:6, 7 Part of Christ's mission on earth was to demonstrate God's righteousness and to be a light for the Gentiles (to all nations). Through Christ, all people have the opportunity to share in his mission. God calls us to be servants of his Son, demonstrating God's righteousness and bringing his light. What a rare privilege it is to help the Messiah fulfill his mission! But

we must seek his righteousness (Matthew 6:33) before we demonstrate it to others, and let his light shine in us before we can be lights ourselves (Matthew 5:16; 2 Corinthians 4:6).
42:10 Look at all that the Lord will do for us and through us (42:6–9)! Majestic works prompt majestic responses. Do you really appreciate the good that God does for you

42:19
c Isa 43:8

19 Who is blind c but my servant,
and deaf like the messenger I send?
Who is blind like the one committed to me,
blind like the servant of the LORD?
20 You have seen many things, but have paid no attention;
your ears are open, but you hear nothing."
21 It pleased the LORD
for the sake of his righteousness
to make his law great and glorious.

42:22
d Isa 24:18

22 But this is a people plundered and looted,
all of them trapped in pits d
or hidden away in prisons.
They have become plunder,
with no one to rescue them;
they have been made loot,
with no one to say, "Send them back."

23 Which of you will listen to this
or pay close attention in time to come?

42:24
e Isa 30:15

24 Who handed Jacob over to become loot,
and Israel to the plunderers?
Was it not the LORD,
against whom we have sinned?
For they would not follow e his ways;
they did not obey his law.

42:25
f 2Ki 25:9
g Hos 7:9

25 So he poured out on them his burning anger,
the violence of war.
It enveloped them in flames, f yet they did not understand;
it consumed them, but they did not take it to heart. g

Israel's Only Savior

43:1
h Isa 44:21
i Isa 44:2, 6
j Isa 45:3-4

43 But now, this is what the LORD says—
he who created you, O Jacob, h
he who formed you, O Israel: h
"Fear not, for I have redeemed i you;
I have summoned you by name; j you are mine.

43:2
k Dt 31:6, 8
l Ps 66:12;
Da 3:25-27

2 When you pass through the waters,
I will be with you; k
and when you pass through the rivers,
they will not sweep over you.
When you walk through the fire,
you will not be burned;
the flames will not set you ablaze. l

---

and through you? If so, let your praise to him reflect how you really feel.

42:19, 20 How could Israel and Judah be God's servants and yet be so blind? How could they be so close to God and see so little? Jesus condemned the religious leaders of his day for the same disregard of God (John 9:39–41). Yet do we not fail in the same way? Sometimes partial blindness—seeing but not understanding, or knowing what is right but not doing it—can be worse than not seeing at all.

42:23 We may condemn our predecessors for their failures, but we are twice as guilty if we repeat the same mistakes that we recognize as failures. We may be so ready to direct God's message at others that we can't see how it touches our own lives. Make sure you are willing to take your own advice as you teach or lead.

43:1ff Chapter 42 ends with God's sorrow over the spiritual decay of his people. In chapter 43, God says that despite the

people's spiritual failure, he will show them mercy, bring them back from captivity, and restore them. He would give them an outpouring of love, not wrath. Then the world would know that God alone had done this.

43:1–4 God created Israel and made it special to him. God redeemed Israel and summoned them by name to be those who belong to him. God protected Israel in times of trouble. We are important to God, and he also summons us by name and gives us his name (43:7)! When we bear God's wonderful name, we must never do anything that would bring shame to it.

43:2 Going through rivers of difficulty will either cause you to drown or force you to grow stronger. If you go in your own strength, you are more likely to drown. If you invite the Lord to go with you, he will protect you.

3 For I am the LORD, your God,
    the Holy One of Israel, your Savior;
I give Egypt for your ransom,
    Cush[a] and Seba in your stead.
4 Since you are precious and honored in my sight,
    and because I love you,
I will give men in exchange for you,
    and people in exchange for your life.
5 Do not be afraid, for I am with you;
    I will bring your children from the east
    and gather you from the west.
6 I will say to the north, 'Give them up!'
    and to the south, 'Do not hold them back.'
Bring my sons from afar
    and my daughters from the ends of the earth—
7 everyone who is called by my name,
    whom I created for my glory,
    whom I formed and made.[m]"

8 Lead out those who have eyes but are blind,[n]
    who have ears but are deaf.[o]
9 All the nations gather together
    and the peoples assemble.
Which of them foretold[p] this
    and proclaimed to us the former things?
Let them bring in their witnesses to prove they were right,
    so that others may hear and say, "It is true."
10 "You are my witnesses," declares the LORD,
    "and my servant whom I have chosen,
so that you may know and believe me
    and understand that I am he.
Before me no god[q] was formed,
    nor will there be one after me.
11 I, even I, am the LORD,
    and apart from me there is no savior.[r]
12 I have revealed and saved and proclaimed—
    I, and not some foreign god[s] among you.
You are my witnesses,[t]" declares the LORD, "that I am God.
13   Yes, and from ancient days[u] I am he.
No one can deliver out of my hand.
    When I act, who can reverse it?"[v]

God's Mercy and Israel's Unfaithfulness

14 This is what the LORD says—
    your Redeemer, the Holy One of Israel:
"For your sake I will send to Babylon
    and bring down as fugitives all the Babylonians,[b]
    in the ships in which they took pride.
15 I am the LORD, your Holy One,
    Israel's Creator, your King."

a 3 That is, the upper Nile region   b 14 Or Chaldeans

Cross references

43:7
m Ps 100:3;
Eph 2:10

43:8
n Isa 6:9-10
o Isa 42:20;
Eze 12:2

43:9
p Isa 41:26

43:10
q Isa 44:6, 8

43:11
r Isa 45:21

43:12
s Dt 32:12; Ps 81:9
t Isa 44:8

43:13
u Ps 90:2
v Isa 14:27

43:3 God gave other nations to Persia in exchange for returning the Jews to their homeland. Egypt, Cush, and parts of Arabia (Seba) had attacked Persia, and the Persians defeated them.

43:5, 6 Isaiah was speaking primarily of Israel's return from Babylon. But there is a broader meaning: all God's people will be regathered when Christ comes to rule in peace over the earth.

43:10, 11 Israel's task was to be a witness (44:8), telling the world who God is and what he has done. Believers today share

the responsibility of being God's witnesses. Do people know what God is like through your words and example? They cannot see God directly, but they can see him reflected in you.

43:15–21 This section pictures a new exodus for a people once again oppressed, as the Israelites had been as slaves in Egypt before the exodus. They would cry to God, and again he would hear and deliver them. A new exodus would take place through a new desert. The past miracles were nothing compared to what God would do for his people in the future.

43:16
w Ps 77:19;
Isa 51:10

16 This is what the Lord says—
   he who made a way through the sea,
   a path through the mighty waters,w
17 who drew out the chariots and horses,
   the army and reinforcements together,
   and they lay there, never to rise again,
   extinguished, snuffed out like a wick:
18 "Forget the former things;
   do not dwell on the past.

43:19
x 2Co 5:17
y Ex 17:6; Nu 20:11

19 See, I am doing a new thing!x
   Now it springs up; do you not perceive it?
   I am making a way in the deserty
   and streams in the wasteland.

43:20
z Isa 48:21

20 The wild animals honor me,
   the jackals and the owls,
   because I provide waterz in the desert
   and streams in the wasteland,
   to give drink to my people, my chosen,

43:21
a Ps 102:18

21   the people I formed for myself
      that they may proclaim my praise.a

22 "Yet you have not called upon me, O Jacob,
   you have not wearied yourselves for me, O Israel.

43:23
b Am 5:25

23 You have not brought me sheep for burnt offerings,
   nor honored me with your sacrifices.b
   I have not burdened you with grain offerings
   nor wearied you with demands for incense.

43:24
c Isa 1:14
d Mal 2:17

24 You have not bought any fragrant calamus for me,
   or lavished on me the fat of your sacrifices.
   But you have burdened me with your sins
   and weariedc me with your offenses.d

43:25
e Eze 36:22
f Jer 31:34

25 "I, even I, am he who blots out
   your transgressions, for my own sake,e
   and remembers your sins no more.f
26 Review the past for me,
   let us argue the matter together;
   state the case for your innocence.
27 Your first father sinned;
   your spokesmen rebelled against me.
28 So I will disgrace the dignitaries of your temple,
   and I will consign Jacob to destructiona
   and Israel to scorn.

Israel the Chosen

44:1
g ver 21; Jer 30:10;
46:27-28

44 "But now listen, O Jacob, my servant,g
       Israel, whom I have chosen.
   2 This is what the Lord says—
     he who made you, who formed you in the womb,
     and who will help you:

a28 The Hebrew term refers to the irrevocable giving over of things or persons to the Lord, often by totally destroying them.

43:22–24 Calamus may have been an ingredient in the incense used in worship. A sacrifice required both giving up a valuable animal and pleading with God for forgiveness. But the people presented God with sins instead of sacrifices. Can you imagine bringing the best of your sins to God's altar? This ironic picture shows the depths to which Israel had sunk. What do you present to God—your sins, or a plea for his forgiveness?

43:25 How tempting it is to remind someone of a past offense! But when God forgives our sins he totally forgets them. We never have to fear that he will remind us of them later. Because God forgives our sin, we need to forgive others.

44:2 Jeshurun ("the upright one") is a poetic name for Israel (Deuteronomy 32:15; 33:5, 26).

Do not be afraid, O Jacob, my servant,
  Jeshurun,[h] whom I have chosen.
3 For I will pour water on the thirsty land,
  and streams on the dry ground;
I will pour out my Spirit[i] on your offspring,
  and my blessing on your descendants.
4 They will spring up like grass in a meadow,
  like poplar trees by flowing streams.
5 One will say, 'I belong to the LORD';
  another will call himself by the name of Jacob;
still another will write on his hand, 'The LORD's,'
  and will take the name Israel.

The LORD, Not Idols

6 "This is what the LORD says—
  Israel's King and Redeemer, the LORD Almighty:
I am the first and I am the last;[j]
  apart from me there is no God.
7 Who then is like me? Let him proclaim it.
  Let him declare and lay out before me
what has happened since I established my ancient people,
  and what is yet to come—
  yes, let him foretell[k] what will come.
8 Do not tremble, do not be afraid.
  Did I not proclaim this and foretell it long ago?
You are my witnesses. Is there any God[l] besides me?
  No, there is no other Rock;[m] I know not one."

9 All who make idols are nothing,
  and the things they treasure are worthless.
Those who would speak up for them are blind;
  they are ignorant, to their own shame.
10 Who shapes a god and casts an idol,
  which can profit him nothing?[n]
11 He and his kind will be put to shame;
  craftsmen are nothing but men.
Let them all come together and take their stand;
  they will be brought down to terror and infamy.[o]

12 The blacksmith[p] takes a tool
  and works with it in the coals;
he shapes an idol with hammers,
  he forges it with the might of his arm.[q]
He gets hungry and loses his strength;
  he drinks no water and grows faint.
13 The carpenter[r] measures with a line
  and makes an outline with a marker;
he roughs it out with chisels
  and marks it with compasses.
He shapes it in the form of man,
  of man in all his glory,
  that it may dwell in a shrine.

44:2
[h] Dt 32:15
44:3
[i] Joel 2:28

44:6
[j] Isa 41:4; Rev 1:8, 17; 22:13

44:7
[k] Isa 41:22, 26

44:8
[l] Isa 43:10
[m] Dt 4:35; 1Sa 2:2

44:10
[n] Jer 10:5

44:11
[o] Isa 42:17

44:12
[p] Isa 40:19
[q] Jer 10:3-5

44:13
[r] Isa 41:7

44:5 The time will come when Israel will be proud of belonging to God. If we are truly God's, we should be unashamed and delighted to let everyone know about our relationship with him (44:8).

44:8, 9 The manufactured idols were guilty of false advertising. They made big promises, but they were worthless and helpless. In contrast, God fulfills his claims and delivers on all his promises. God challenges us to be his witnesses. When we share our faith with those who can find no meaning in life or have no hope of eternal life, we are not proclaiming anything shoddy or unreliable. God is real and life with him is best. Pray for boldness in your life to share your faith in Christ with friends, relatives, and neighbors.

44:9-20 Here Isaiah describes how people make their own gods. How absurd to make a god from the same tree that gives firewood. Do we make our own gods—money, fame, or power? If we make a god of our own choosing, we deceive ourselves. We cannot expect it to empower our lives.

14 He cut down cedars,
      or perhaps took a cypress or oak.
   He let it grow among the trees of the forest,
      or planted a pine, and the rain made it grow.

44:15
*s*2Ch 25:14

15 It is man's fuel for burning;
      some of it he takes and warms himself,
      he kindles a fire and bakes bread.
   But he also fashions a god and worships it;
      he makes an idol and bows*s* down to it.

16 Half of the wood he burns in the fire;
      over it he prepares his meal,
      he roasts his meat and eats his fill.
   He also warms himself and says,
      "Ah! I am warm; I see the fire."

44:17
*t*1Ki 18:26

17 From the rest he makes a god, his idol;
      he bows down to it and worships.
   He prays*t* to it and says,
      "Save me; you are my god."

44:18
*u*Isa 6:9-10

18 They know nothing, they understand nothing;
      their eyes*u* are plastered over so they cannot see,
      and their minds closed so they cannot understand.

44:19
*v*Isa 45:20
*w*Dt 27:15

19 No one stops to think,
      no one has the knowledge or understanding*v* to say,
   "Half of it I used for fuel;
      I even baked bread over its coals,
      I roasted meat and I ate.
   Shall I make a detestable*w* thing from what is left?
      Shall I bow down to a block of wood?"

44:20
*x*Ps 102:9
*y*Job 15:31;
Ro 1:21-23, 28;
2Th 2:11

20 He feeds on ashes,*x* a deluded*y* heart misleads him;
      he cannot save himself, or say,
      "Is not this thing in my right hand a lie?"

44:21
*z*Isa 46:8
*a*Isa 49:15

21 "Remember*z* these things, O Jacob,
      for you are my servant, O Israel.
   I have made you, you are my servant;
      O Israel, I will not forget you.*a*

22 I have swept away your offenses like a cloud,
      your sins like the morning mist.
   Return to me,
      for I have redeemed you."

44:23
*b*Isa 61:3

23 Sing for joy, O heavens, for the LORD has done this;
      shout aloud, O earth beneath.
   Burst into song, you mountains,
      you forests and all your trees,
   for the LORD has redeemed Jacob,
      he displays his glory*b* in Israel.

TODAY'S IDOLATRY

Isaiah tells us, "Who shapes a god and casts an idol, which can profit him nothing?" (44:10). We think of idols as statues of wood or stone, but in reality an idol is anything natural that is given sacred value and power. If your answer to any of the following questions is anything or anyone other than God, you may need to check out who or what you are worshiping.

- Who created me?
- Whom do I ultimately trust?
- Whom do I look to for ultimate truth?
- Whom do I look to for security and happiness?
- Who is in charge of my future?

44:21 God said that we should serve our Creator (17:7; 40:28; 43:15; 45:9). Idolaters do the opposite—serving or worshiping what they have made rather than the One who made them. Our Creator paid the price to set us free from our sins against him.

By contrast, no idol ever created anybody, and no idol can redeem us from our sins.

Jerusalem to Be Inhabited

24 "This is what the LORD says—
     your Redeemer,*c* who formed you in the womb:

I am the LORD,
   who has made all things,
   who alone stretched out the heavens,
   who spread out the earth by myself,

25 who foils the signs of false prophets
     and makes fools of diviners,
   who overthrows the learning of the wise*d*
     and turns it into nonsense,

26 who carries out the words*e* of his servants
     and fulfills the predictions of his messengers,

who says of Jerusalem, 'It shall be inhabited,'
   of the towns of Judah, 'They shall be built,'
   and of their ruins, 'I will restore them,'

27 who says to the watery deep, 'Be dry,
     and I will dry up your streams,'

28 who says of Cyrus,*f* 'He is my shepherd
     and will accomplish all that I please;
   he will say of Jerusalem, "Let it be rebuilt,"
     and of the temple,*g* "Let its foundations be laid."'

45 "This is what the LORD says to his anointed,
     to Cyrus, whose right hand I take hold*h* of
   to subdue nations before him
     and to strip kings of their armor,
   to open doors before him
     so that gates will not be shut:

2 I will go before you
     and will level*i* the mountains*a*;
   I will break down gates of bronze
     and cut through bars of iron.*j*

3 I will give you the treasures of darkness,
     riches stored in secret places,
   so that you may know that I am the LORD,
     the God of Israel, who summons you by name.*k*

4 For the sake of Jacob my servant,
     of Israel my chosen,
   I summon you by name
     and bestow on you a title of honor,
     though you do not acknowledge me.

5 I am the LORD, and there is no other;*l*
     apart from me there is no God.

a2 Dead Sea Scrolls and Septuagint; the meaning of the word in the Masoretic Text is uncertain.

	44:24 *c* Isa 43:14
	44:25 *d* 1Co 1:27
	44:26 *e* Zec 1:6
	44:28 *f* 2Ch 36:22 *g* Ezr 1:2-4
	45:1 *h* Isa 41:13
	45:2 *i* Isa 40:4 *j* Ps 107:16
	45:3 *k* Ex 33:12
	45:5 *l* Isa 44:8

44:25, 26 False prophets were people who claimed to bring messages from the gods. Diviners were people who would fake omens for their own benefit. Because God is truth, he is the standard for all teachings. We can always trust his Word as absolute truth. His Word is completely accurate, and against it we can measure all other teachings. If you are unsure about a teaching, *test it against God's Word.* God condemned the false prophets because they gave advice opposite to his.

44:28 Isaiah, who prophesied from about 740—681 B.C., called Cyrus by name almost 150 years before he ruled (559—530 B.C.)! Later historians said that Cyrus read this prophecy and was so moved that he carried it out. Isaiah also predicted that Jerusalem would fall more than 100 years before it happened (586 B.C.) and

that the temple would be rebuilt about 200 years before it happened. It is clear these prophecies came from a God who knows the future.

45:1-8 This is the only place in the Bible where a Gentile ruler is said to be "anointed." God is the power over all powers, and he anoints whom he chooses for his special tasks. Cyrus's kingdom spread across 2,000 miles (the largest of any empire then known), including the territories of both the Assyrian and the Babylonian empires. Why did God anoint Cyrus? Because God had a special task for him to do for Israel. Cyrus would allow God's city, Jerusalem, to be rebuilt, and he would set the exiles free without expecting anything in return. Few kings of Israel or Judah had done as much for God's people as Cyrus would.

I will strengthen you,
    though you have not acknowledged me,

45:6
m Mal 1:11

6 so that from the rising of the sun
    to the place of its setting*m*
men may know there is none besides me.
    I am the LORD, and there is no other.

45:7
n Am 3:6

7 I form the light and create darkness,
    I bring prosperity and create disaster;*n*
    I, the LORD, do all these things.

45:8
o Ps 72:6
p Ps 85:11

8 "You heavens above, rain *o* down righteousness;*p*
    let the clouds shower it down.
Let the earth open wide,
    let salvation spring up,
let righteousness grow with it;
    I, the LORD, have created it.

45:9
q Isa 29:16;
Ro 9:20-21*

9 "Woe to him who quarrels with his Maker,
    to him who is but a potsherd among the potsherds on the ground.
Does the clay say to the potter,*q*
    'What are you making?'
Does your work say,
    'He has no hands'?
10 Woe to him who says to his father,
    'What have you begotten?'
or to his mother,
    'What have you brought to birth?'

11 "This is what the LORD says—
    the Holy One of Israel, and its Maker:
Concerning things to come,
    do you question me about my children,
    or give me orders about the work of my hands?

45:12
r Ge 2:1; Isa 42:5

12 It is I who made the earth
    and created mankind upon it.
My own hands stretched out the heavens;*r*
    I marshaled their starry hosts.

45:13
s Isa 41:2
t Isa 52:3

13 I will raise up Cyrus*a* *s* in my righteousness:
    I will make all his ways straight.
He will rebuild my city
    and set my exiles free,
but not for a price or reward,*t*
    says the LORD Almighty."

45:14
u Isa 14:1-2

14 This is what the LORD says:

"The products of Egypt and the merchandise of Cush,*b*
    and those tall Sabeans—
they will come over to you
    and will be yours;
they will trudge behind you,
    coming over to you in chains.*u*
They will bow down before you
    and plead with you, saying,

a 13 Hebrew *him*   *b* 14 That is, the upper Nile region

45:7 God is ruler over light and darkness, over prosperity and disaster. Our lives are sprinkled with both types of experiences, and both are needed for us to grow spiritually. When good times come, thank God and use your prosperity for him. When bad times come, don't resent them, but ask what you can learn from this refining experience to make you a better servant of God.

45:9 A potsherd is a broken piece of pottery, essentially worthless.

45:14 The Sabeans were people from Seba in southern Arabia.

'Surely God is with you,^{v} and there is no other;
  there is no other god.'"

¹⁵ Truly you are a God who hides himself,
  O God and Savior of Israel.
¹⁶ All the makers of idols will be put to shame and disgraced;^{w}
  they will go off into disgrace together.
¹⁷ But Israel will be saved by the LORD
  with an everlasting salvation;^{x}
you will never be put to shame or disgraced,
  to ages everlasting.

¹⁸ For this is what the LORD says—
he who created the heavens,
  he is God;
he who fashioned and made the earth,
  he founded it;
he did not create it to be empty,^{y}
  but formed it to be inhabited^z—
he says:
"I am the LORD,
  and there is no other.^{a}
¹⁹ I have not spoken in secret,
  from somewhere in a land of darkness;
I have not said to Jacob's descendants,^{b}
  'Seek me in vain.'
I, the LORD, speak the truth;
  I declare what is right.

²⁰ "Gather together and come;
  assemble, you fugitives from the nations.
Ignorant are those who carry^c about idols of wood,
  who pray to gods that cannot save.^{d}
²¹ Declare what is to be, present it—
  let them take counsel together.
Who foretold this long ago,
  who declared it from the distant past?
Was it not I, the LORD?
  And there is no God apart from me,
a righteous God and a Savior;
  there is none but me.

²² "Turn to me and be saved,
  all you ends of the earth;
for I am God, and there is no other.
²³ By myself I have sworn,
  my mouth has uttered in all integrity^e
a word that will not be revoked:
Before me every knee will bow;
  by me every tongue will swear.^{f}
²⁴ They will say of me, 'In the LORD alone
  are righteousness and strength.'"
All who have raged against him
  will come to him and be put to shame.^{g}

	45:14 ^{v}1Co 14:25
	45:16 ^{w}Isa 44:9, 11
	45:17 ^{x}Isa 26:4
	45:18 ^{y}Ge 1:2 ^{z}Isa 42:5 ^{a}ver 5
	45:19 ^{b}Isa 41:8
	45:20 ^{c}Jer 10:5 ^{d}Isa 46:6-7
	45:23 ^{e}Heb 6:13 ^{f}Ro 14:11*
	45:24 ^{g}Isa 41:11

45:17 Until this time, Israel had anticipated temporal salvation—God would save them from their enemies. Here Isaiah tells of everlasting salvation with God.

45:18, 19 God's promises are public, and their fulfillment is sure. So why do we ever doubt him? We never have to be uncertain when we have a God of truth and righteousness.

45:22 Salvation is for all nations, not just the Israelites. Many times it seems as though Israel had an inside track on salvation. But God makes it clear that his people include *all* those who follow him. Israel was to be the means through which the whole world would come to know God. Jesus, the Messiah, fulfilled Israel's role and gave all people the opportunity to follow God. (See also Romans 11:11; Galatians 3:28; Ephesians 3:6; Philippians 2:10.)

25 But in the Lord all the descendants of Israel
   will be found righteous and will exult.

Gods of Babylon

46:1
ʰIsa 21:9; Jer 50:2

46

Bel ʰ bows down, Nebo stoops low;
   their idols are borne by beasts of burden. ᵃ
The images that are carried about are burdensome,
   a burden for the weary.
2 They stoop and bow down together;
   unable to rescue the burden,
   they themselves go off into captivity.

46:3
ⁱver 12

3 "Listen ⁱ to me, O house of Jacob,
   all you who remain of the house of Israel,
you whom I have upheld since you were conceived,
   and have carried since your birth.
4 Even to your old age and gray hairs
   I am he, I am he who will sustain you.
I have made you and I will carry you;
   I will sustain you and I will rescue you.

46:5
ʲIsa 40:18, 25
46:6
ᵏIsa 40:19
ˡIsa 44:17

5 "To whom will you compare me or count me equal?
   To whom will you liken me that we may be compared? ʲ
6 Some pour out gold from their bags
   and weigh out silver on the scales;
they hire a goldsmith ᵏ to make it into a god,
   and they bow down and worship it. ˡ

46:7
ᵐIsa 45:20

7 They lift it to their shoulders and carry it;
   they set it up in its place, and there it stands.
   From that spot it cannot move.
Though one cries out to it, it does not answer;
   it cannot save ᵐ him from his troubles.

46:8
ⁿIsa 44:21

8 "Remember ⁿ this, fix it in mind,
   take it to heart, you rebels.

ᵃ 1 Or *are but beasts and cattle*

MAJOR IDOLS MENTIONED IN THE BIBLE	Name	Where they were worshiped	What they stood for	What the worship included
	Bel (Marduk)	Babylon	Weather, war, sun god	Prostitution, child sacrifice
	Nebo (son of Marduk)	Babylon	Learning, astronomy, science	
	Ashtoreth (Asherah)	Canaan	Goddess of love, childbirth, and fertility	Prostitution
	Chemosh	Moab		Child sacrifice
	Molech	Ammon	National god	Child sacrifice
	Baal	Canaan	Rain, harvest, symbolized strength and fertility	Prostitution
	Dagon	Philistia	Harvest, grain, success in farming	Child sacrifice

---

46:1–4 Cyrus would carry out God's judgment against Babylon. Bel was the chief deity of the Babylonians; Nebo was the god of science and learning. These "gods," however, needed animals and people to carry them around and could not even save themselves from being taken into captivity. They had no power at all. In contrast to gods who must be hauled around by people, our God created us and cares for us. His love is so enduring that he will care for us throughout our lifetime and even through death.

46:8–11 Israel was tempted to waver between the Lord God and pagan gods. Isaiah affirms the sole lordship of God. God is unique in his knowledge and in his control of the future. His consistent purpose is to carry out what he has planned. When we are tempted to pursue anything that promises pleasure, comfort, peace, or security apart from God, we must remember our commitment to God.

9 Remember the former things, those of long ago;
    I am God, and there is no other;
    I am God, and there is none like me.*o*

10 I make known the end from the beginning,
    from ancient times,*p* what is still to come.
    I say: My purpose will stand,*q*
    and I will do all that I please.

11 From the east I summon a bird of prey;
    from a far-off land, a man to fulfill my purpose.
    What I have said, that will I bring about;
    what I have planned, that will I do.

12 Listen*r* to me, you stubborn-hearted,
    you who are far from righteousness.*s*

13 I am bringing my righteousness near,
    it is not far away;
    and my salvation will not be delayed.
    I will grant salvation to Zion,
    my splendor*t* to Israel.

The Fall of Babylon

47 "Go down, sit in the dust,
    Virgin Daughter of Babylon;
    sit on the ground without a throne,
    Daughter of the Babylonians.*a u*
    No more will you be called
    tender or delicate.

2 Take millstones*v* and grind flour;
    take off your veil.
    Lift up your skirts, bare your legs,
    and wade through the streams.

3 Your nakedness*w* will be exposed
    and your shame uncovered.
    I will take vengeance;
    I will spare no one."

4 Our Redeemer—the LORD Almighty is his name—
    is the Holy One of Israel.

5 "Sit in silence, go into darkness,*x*
    Daughter of the Babylonians;
    no more will you be called
    queen of kingdoms.*y*

6 I was angry with my people
    and desecrated my inheritance;
    I gave them into your hand,
    and you showed them no mercy.
    Even on the aged
    you laid a very heavy yoke.

7 You said, 'I will continue forever—
    the eternal queen!'

a 1 Or Chaldeans; also in verse 5

46:9 *o* Isa 45:5, 21

46:10 *p* Isa 45:21
q Ac 5:39

46:12 *r* ver 3
s Jer 2:5

46:13 *t* Isa 44:23

47:1 *u* Jer 51:33

47:2 *v* Ex 11:5; Mt 24:41

47:3 *w* Eze 16:37

47:5 *x* Isa 13:10
y Isa 13:19

46:13 Much of the book of Isaiah speaks of a future deliverance when we will all live with God in perfect peace. God offers not only this future hope but also help for our present needs. His righteousness is near us, and we do not have to wait for his salvation.

47:1ff Here Isaiah predicted the fall of Babylon more than 150 years before it happened. At this time, Babylon had not yet emerged as the mightiest force on earth, the proud empire that would destroy Judah and Jerusalem. But the Babylonians, Judah's captors, would become captives themselves in 539 B.C. God, not Babylon, has the ultimate power. He used Babylon to

punish his sinful people; he would use Medo-Persia to destroy Babylon and free his people.

47:8, 9 Caught up in the pursuit of power and pleasure, Babylon believed in its own greatness and claimed to be the *only* power on earth. Babylon felt completely secure, and Nebuchadnezzar, its king, exalted himself as a "god." But the true God taught Nebuchadnezzar a powerful lesson by taking everything away from him (Daniel 4:28–37). Our society is addicted to pleasure and power, but these can quickly pass away. Look at your own life and ask yourself how you can be more responsible with the

47:7
z Dt 32:29

47:8
a Isa 32:9
b Zep 2:15
c Rev 18:7

47:9
d 1Th 5:3
e Na 3:4

47:10
f Ps 52:7
g Isa 29:15

47:11
h 1Th 5:3

47:13
i Isa 57:10

47:14
j Na 1:10

47:15
k Rev 18:11

But you did not consider these things
　or reflect on what might happen. z

8 "Now then, listen, you wanton creature,
　　lounging in your security a
and saying to yourself,
　'I am, and there is none besides me. b
I will never be a widow c
　or suffer the loss of children.'

9 Both of these will overtake you
　　in a moment, d on a single day:
　loss of children and widowhood.
They will come upon you in full measure,
　in spite of your many sorceries e
　and all your potent spells.

10 You have trusted f in your wickedness
　　and have said, 'No one sees me.' g
Your wisdom and knowledge mislead you
　when you say to yourself,
　'I am, and there is none besides me.'

11 Disaster will come upon you,
　　and you will not know how to conjure it away.
A calamity will fall upon you
　　that you cannot ward off with a ransom;
a catastrophe you cannot foresee
　will suddenly h come upon you.

12 "Keep on, then, with your magic spells
　　and with your many sorceries,
　which you have labored at since childhood.
Perhaps you will succeed,
　perhaps you will cause terror.

13 All the counsel you have received has only worn you out! i
　　Let your astrologers come forward,
those stargazers who make predictions month by month,
　let them save you from what is coming upon you.

14 Surely they are like stubble; j
　　the fire will burn them up.
They cannot even save themselves
　from the power of the flame.
Here are no coals to warm anyone;
　here is no fire to sit by.

15 That is all they can do for you—
　　these you have labored with
　and trafficked k with since childhood.
Each of them goes on in his error;
　there is not one that can save you.

Stubborn Israel

48

"Listen to this, O house of Jacob,
　you who are called by the name of Israel
　and come from the line of Judah,

---

talents and possessions God has given you. How can you use your life for God's honor rather than your own?

47:12-15 The people of Babylon sought advice and help from astrologers and stargazers. But like the idols of wood or gold, astrologers could not even deliver themselves from what was to come from the hand of God. Why rely on those who are powerless? The helpless cannot help us. Alternatives to God are destined to fail. If you want help, find it in God, who has proven his power in creation and in history.

48:1 The people of Judah felt confident because they lived in Jerusalem, the city with God's temple. They depended on their heritage, their city, and their temple—but this was false security because they did not depend on God. Do you feel secure because you go to church or live in a Christian country? Heritage, buildings, or nations cannot give us a relationship with God; we must truly depend on him personally, with all our hearts and minds.

you who take oaths in the name of the LORD
　　and invoke the God of Israel—
　　but not in truth[l] or righteousness—
2 you who call yourselves citizens of the holy city[m]
　　and rely[n] on the God of Israel—
　　the LORD Almighty is his name:
3 I foretold the former things long ago,
　　my mouth announced them and I made them known;
　　then suddenly I acted, and they came to pass.
4 For I knew how stubborn[o] you were;
　　the sinews of your neck[p] were iron,
　　your forehead was bronze.
5 Therefore I told you these things long ago;
　　before they happened I announced them to you
so that you could not say,
　　'My idols did them;
　　my wooden image and metal god ordained them.'
6 You have heard these things; look at them all.
　　Will you not admit them?

"From now on I will tell you of new things,
　　of hidden things unknown to you.
7 They are created now, and not long ago;
　　you have not heard of them before today.
So you cannot say,
　　'Yes, I knew of them.'
8 You have neither heard nor understood;
　　from of old your ear has not been open.
Well do I know how treacherous you are;
　　you were called a rebel[q] from birth.
9 For my own name's sake I delay my wrath;[r]
　　for the sake of my praise I hold it back from you,
　　so as not to cut you off.
10 See, I have refined you, though not as silver;
　　I have tested you in the furnace of affliction.
11 For my own sake, for my own sake, I do this.
　　How can I let myself be defamed?[s]
　　I will not yield my glory to another.[t]

Israel Freed

12 "Listen to me, O Jacob,
　　Israel, whom I have called:
I am he;
　　I am the first and I am the last.[u]
13 My own hand laid the foundations of the earth,
　　and my right hand spread out the heavens;
when I summon them,
　　they all stand up together.[v]

14 "Come together, all of you, and listen:
　　Which of ₍the idols₎ has foretold these things?

48:1
[l] Jer 4:2
48:2
[m] Isa 52:1
[n] Mic 3:11; Ro 2:17

48:4
[o] Dt 31:27
[p] Ex 32:9

48:8
[q] Ps 58:3

48:9
[r] Ps 78:38

48:11
[s] Dt 32:27;
Eze 20:9, 14,
22, 44
[t] Isa 42:8

48:12
[u] Rev 1:17; 22:13

48:13
[v] Isa 40:26

48:9–11 There was nothing in Israel's actions, attitudes, or accomplishments to compel God to love and to save them. But for his own sake, to show who he is and what he can do, he saved them. God does not save us because we are good but because he loves us and because of his forgiving nature.

48:10 Do you find it easy to complain when your life becomes complicated or difficult? Why would a loving God allow all kinds of unpleasant experiences to come to his children? This verse shows us plainly that God tests us in the "furnace of affliction."

Rather than complain, our response should be to turn to God in faith for the strength to endure, and rejoice in our sufferings (see Romans 5:3; James 1:2–4). For without the testing, we would never know what we are capable of doing, nor would we grow. And without the refining, we will not become more pure and more like Christ. If you are facing adversity or suffering, seek God and his refining work in your life.

48:14, 15 "The LORD's chosen ally" refers to Cyrus—and this must have shocked his audience. How could the Lord choose a

The Lord's chosen ally
　　will carry out his purpose against Babylon;
　　his arm will be against the Babylonians.ᵃ

48:15
ʷ Isa 45:1

¹⁵ I, even I, have spoken;
　　yes, I have calledʷ him.
I will bring him,
　　and he will succeed in his mission.

48:16
ˣ Isa 45:19
ʸ Zec 2:9, 11

¹⁶"Come near me and listen to this:

　　"From the first announcement I have not spoken in secret;ˣ
　　　at the time it happens, I am there."

And now the Sovereign Lord has sentʸ me,
　　with his Spirit.

48:17
ᶻ Isa 43:14
ᵃ Ps 32:8

¹⁷ This is what the Lord says—
　　your Redeemer, the Holy Oneᶻ of Israel:
"I am the Lord your God,
　　who teaches you what is best for you,
　　who directs you in the wayᵃ you should go.

48:18
ᵇ Dt 32:29
ᶜ Ps 119:165

¹⁸ If only you had paid attentionᵇ to my commands,
　　your peaceᶜ would have been like a river,
　　your righteousness like the waves of the sea.

48:19
ᵈ Ge 22:17

¹⁹ Your descendants would have been like the sand,
　　your children like its numberless grains;ᵈ
their name would never be cut off
　　nor destroyed from before me."

48:20
ᵉ Jer 50:8

²⁰ Leave Babylon,
　　fleeᵉ from the Babylonians!
Announce this with shouts of joy
　　and proclaim it.
Send it out to the ends of the earth;
　　say, "The Lord has redeemed his servant Jacob."

48:21
ᶠ Ex 17:6; Nu 20:11

²¹ They did not thirst when he led them through the deserts;
　　he made water flow for them from the rock;
he split the rock
　　and water gushed out.ᶠ

48:22
ᵍ Isa 57:21

²² "There is no peace," says the Lord, "for the wicked."ᵍ

2. The future Redeemer
The Servant of the LORD

49

Listen to me, you islands;
　　hear this, you distant nations:

ᵃ 14 Or *Chaldeans*; also in verse 20

---

pagan king, an enemy? But it was Cyrus whom God would use to free his people from their captivity in Babylon. Cyrus's mission was to set Israel free by conquering Babylon, then to decree that all Jews could return to their homeland. Who but a prophet of God could tell such an inconceivable but true story almost 200 years before it happened?

48:17, 18 Like a loving parent, God teaches and directs us. We should listen to him because peace and righteousness come to us as we obey his Word. Refusing to pay attention to God's commands invites punishment and threatens that peace and righteousness.

48:20 Do you see the captives leaving Babylon many years later? No wonder they are shouting with joy, as their ancestors shouted joyfully after they crossed the Red Sea, free from slavery at last! What is holding you captive? Be free! The Lord has redeemed his servants from the slavery of sin. When you let him free you from your captivity, you will feel like shouting with joy.

48:22 Many people cry out for comfort, security, and relief, but they haven't taken the first steps to turn away from sin and open the channels to God. They have not repented and trusted in him. If you want true peace, seek God first. Then he will give you his peace.

49:1–7 Before the servant, the Messiah, was born, God had chosen him to bring the light of the gospel (the message of salvation) to the world (see Acts 13:47). Christ offered salvation to all nations, and his apostles began the missionary movement to take this gospel to the ends of the earth. Missionary work today continues Jesus' Great Commission (Matthew 28:18–20), taking the light of the gospel to all nations. Do you support evangelism and missionary efforts with your money? Do you have talent or other resources to help spread the message of Christ? God wants you to be involved. How can you help?

Before I was born[h] the LORD called me;
    from my birth he has made mention of my name.
2 He made my mouth like a sharpened sword,[i]
    in the shadow of his hand he hid me;
he made me into a polished arrow
    and concealed me in his quiver.
3 He said to me, "You are my servant,[j]
    Israel, in whom I will display my splendor."
4 But I said, "I have labored to no purpose;
    I have spent my strength in vain and for nothing.
Yet what is due me is in the LORD's hand,
    and my reward is with my God."

5 And now the LORD says—
    he who formed me in the womb to be his servant
to bring Jacob back to him
    and gather Israel to himself,
for I am honored[k] in the eyes of the LORD
    and my God has been my strength—
6 he says:
"It is too small a thing for you to be my servant
    to restore the tribes of Jacob
    and bring back those of Israel I have kept.
I will also make you a light for the Gentiles,[l]
    that you may bring my salvation to the ends of the earth."[m]

7 This is what the LORD says—
    the Redeemer and Holy One of Israel—
to him who was despised and abhorred by the nation,
    to the servant of rulers:
"Kings[n] will see you and rise up,
    princes will see and bow down,
because of the LORD, who is faithful,
    the Holy One of Israel, who has chosen you."

Restoration of Israel

8 This is what the LORD says:

"In the time of my favor[o] I will answer you,
    and in the day of salvation I will help you;[p]
I will keep you and will make you
    to be a covenant for the people,[q]
to restore the land
    and to reassign its desolate inheritances,
9 to say to the captives,[r] 'Come out,'
    and to those in darkness, 'Be free!'

"They will feed beside the roads
    and find pasture on every barren hill.
10 They will neither hunger nor thirst,
    nor will the desert heat or the sun beat upon them.[s]
He who has compassion on them will guide them
    and lead them beside springs of water.
11 I will turn all my mountains into roads,
    and my highways will be raised up.[t]
12 See, they will come from afar[u]—
    some from the north, some from the west,
    some from the region of Aswan.[a]"

a 12 Dead Sea Scrolls; Masoretic Text *Sinim*

Cross references:
49:1 [h] Isa 44:24
49:2 [i] Rev 1:16
49:3 [j] Zec 3:8
49:5 [k] Isa 43:4
49:6 [l] Lk 2:32; [m] Ac 13:47*
49:7 [n] Isa 52:15
49:8 [o] Ps 69:13; [p] 2Co 6:2*; [q] Isa 42:6
49:9 [r] Isa 42:7
49:10 [s] Ps 121:6; Rev 7:16
49:11 [t] Isa 40:4
49:12 [u] Isa 43:5-6

49:12 The region of Aswan is in southern Egypt (see Ezekiel 29:10).

49:13
v Isa 44:23
w Isa 40:1

13 Shout for joy, O heavens;
    rejoice, O earth;
    burst into song, O mountains!v
For the Lord comfortsw his people
    and will have compassion on his afflicted ones.

14 But Zion said, "The Lord has forsaken me,
    the Lord has forgotten me."

49:15
x Isa 44:21

15 "Can a mother forget the baby at her breast
    and have no compassion on the child she has borne?
Though she may forget,
    I will not forget you!x

49:16
y SS 8:6

16 See, I have engravedy you on the palms of my hands;
    your walls are ever before me.

17 Your sons hasten back,
    and those who laid you waste depart from you.

49:18
z Isa 60:4
a Isa 52:1

18 Lift up your eyes and look around;
    all your sons gatherz and come to you.
As surely as I live," declares the Lord,
    "you will weara them all as ornaments;
    you will put them on, like a bride.

49:19
b Isa 54:1, 3
c Zec 10:10

19 "Though you were ruined and made desolateb
    and your land laid waste,
now you will be too small for your people,c
    and those who devoured you will be far away.

49:20
d Isa 54:1-3

20 The children born during your bereavement
    will yet say in your hearing,
'This place is too small for us;
    give us more space to live in.'d

21 Then you will say in your heart,
    'Who bore me these?
I was bereaved and barren;
    I was exiled and rejected.
    Who brought these up?
I was left all alone,
    but these—where have they come from?'"

49:22
e Isa 60:4

22 This is what the Sovereign Lord says:

"See, I will beckon to the Gentiles,
    I will lift up my banner to the peoples;
they will bring your sons in their arms
    and carry your daughters on their shoulders.e

49:23
f Isa 60:16
g Ps 72:9
h Mic 7:17

23 Kings will be your foster fathers,
    and their queens your nursing mothers.f
They will bow down before you with their faces to the ground;
    they will lick the dustg at your feet.
Then you will know that I am the Lord;h
    those who hope in me will not be disappointed."

49:24
i Mt 12:29

24 Can plunder be taken from warriors,i
    or captives rescued from the fiercea?

a 24 Dead Sea Scrolls, Vulgate and Syriac (see also Septuagint and verse 25); Masoretic Text *righteous*

49:14, 15 The people of Israel felt that God had forsaken them in Babylon; but Isaiah pointed out that God would never forget them, as a loving mother would not forget her little child. When we feel that God has forsaken us, we must ask if we have forsaken and forgotten God (see Deuteronomy 31:6).

49:24, 25 God would prove to the world that he is God by doing the impossible—causing warriors to set their captives free; and these warriors would even return the plunder they had taken from the captives! God had done this before at the exodus and would do it again when the exiles returned to Israel. Never should we doubt that God will fulfill his promises. He will even do the impossible to make them come true.

25 But this is what the LORD says:

"Yes, captives will be taken from warriors,
    and plunder retrieved from the fierce;
I will contend with those who contend with you,
    and your children I will save.[j]
26 I will make your oppressors eat[k] their own flesh;
    they will be drunk on their own blood, as with wine.
Then all mankind will know
    that I, the LORD, am your Savior,
    your Redeemer, the Mighty One of Jacob."

Israel's Sin and the Servant's Obedience

50 This is what the LORD says:

"Where is your mother's certificate of divorce[l]
    with which I sent her away?
Or to which of my creditors
    did I sell you?
Because of your sins you were sold;[m]
    because of your transgressions your mother was sent away.
2 When I came, why was there no one?
    When I called, why was there no one to answer?
Was my arm too short[n] to ransom you?
    Do I lack the strength to rescue you?
By a mere rebuke I dry up the sea,[o]
    I turn rivers into a desert;
their fish rot for lack of water
    and die of thirst.
3 I clothe the sky with darkness
    and make sackcloth[p] its covering."

4 The Sovereign LORD has given me an instructed tongue,
    to know the word that sustains the weary.
He wakens me morning by morning,
    wakens my ear to listen like one being taught.
5 The Sovereign LORD has opened my ears,
    and I have not been rebellious;[q]
    I have not drawn back.
6 I offered my back to those who beat[r] me,
    my cheeks to those who pulled out my beard;
I did not hide my face
    from mocking and spitting.[s]
7 Because the Sovereign LORD helps me,
    I will not be disgraced.
Therefore have I set my face like flint,[t]
    and I know I will not be put to shame.
8 He who vindicates me is near.
    Who then will bring charges against me?[u]
    Let us face each other!
Who is my accuser?
    Let him confront me!
9 It is the Sovereign LORD who helps[v] me.
    Who is he that will condemn me?
They will all wear out like a garment;
    the moths[w] will eat them up.

49:25
j Isa 25:9

49:26
k Isa 9:20

50:1
l Dt 24:1
m Isa 52:3

50:2
n Nu 11:23
o Ex 14:22; Jos 3:16

50:3
p Rev 6:12

50:5
q Mt 26:39; Jn 14:31

50:6
r Lk 22:63
s Mt 26:67

50:7
t Eze 3:8-9

50:8
u Ro 8:32-34

50:9
v Isa 41:10
w Job 13:28

50:1, 2 God promised to fight for Israel, but Israel sold itself into sin. Israel had caused its own problems. "Was my arm too short?" means "Am I powerless to help?" The people of Israel forgot God and trusted in other countries to help them. God had not rejected Israel, but Israel had rejected God.

¹⁰ Who among you fears the LORD
    and obeys the word of his servant?
Let him who walks in the dark,
    who has no light,
trust in the name of the LORD
    and rely on his God.
¹¹ But now, all you who light fires
    and provide yourselves with flaming torches,
go, walk in the light of your fires
    and of the torches you have set ablaze.
This is what you shall receive from my hand:
    You will lie down in torment.*x*

50:11
x Isa 65:13-15

Everlasting Salvation for Zion

51 "Listen to me, you who pursue righteousness
    and who seek the LORD:
Look to the rock from which you were cut
    and to the quarry from which you were hewn;
² look to Abraham,*y* your father,
    and to Sarah, who gave you birth.
When I called him he was but one,
    and I blessed him and made him many.*z*
³ The LORD will surely comfort Zion
    and will look with compassion on all her ruins;*a*
he will make her deserts like Eden,
    her wastelands like the garden of the LORD.
Joy and gladness will be found in her,
    thanksgiving and the sound of singing.

51:2
y Heb 11:11
z Ge 12:2

51:3
a Isa 52:9

⁴ "Listen to me, my people;
    hear me, my nation:
The law will go out from me;
    my justice*b* will become a light to the nations.*c*
⁵ My righteousness draws near speedily,
    my salvation is on the way,*d*
and my arm will bring justice to the nations.
    The islands will look to me
    and wait in hope for my arm.
⁶ Lift up your eyes to the heavens,
    look at the earth beneath;
the heavens will vanish like smoke,*e*
    the earth will wear out like a garment
    and its inhabitants die like flies.
But my salvation will last forever,
    my righteousness will never fail.

51:4
b Isa 2:4
c Isa 42:4, 6

51:5
d Isa 46:13

51:6
e Mt 24:35;
2Pe 3:10

⁷ "Hear me, you who know what is right,*f*
    you people who have my law in your hearts:*g*
Do not fear the reproach of men
    or be terrified by their insults.*h*

51:7
f ver 1
g Ps 37:31
h Ac 5:41

50:10, 11 If we walk by our own light and reject God's, we become self-sufficient, and the result of self-sufficiency is torment. When we place confidence in our own intelligence, appearance, or accomplishments instead of in God, we risk torment later when these strengths fade.

51:1, 2 The faithful remnant may have felt alone because they were few. But God reminded them of their ancestors, the source of their spiritual heritage—Abraham and Sarah. Abraham was only one person, but much came from his faithfulness. If the faithful few would remain faithful, even more could come from

them. If we Christians, even a faithful few, remain faithful, think what God can do through us!

51:7 Isaiah encouraged those who follow God's laws. He gave them hope when they faced people's reproach or insults because of their faith. We need not fear when people insult us for our faith because God is with us and truth will prevail. If people make fun of you or dislike you because you believe in God, remember that they are not against you personally but against God. God will deal with them; you should concentrate on loving and obeying him.

8 For the moth will eat them up like a garment;
    the worm will devour them like wool.
But my righteousness will last forever,
    my salvation through all generations."

9 Awake, awake! Clothe yourself with strength,
    O arm of the LORD;
awake, as in days gone by,
    as in generations of old.
Was it not you who cut Rahab to pieces,
    who pierced that monster[i] through?
10 Was it not you who dried up the sea,
    the waters of the great deep,
who made a road in the depths of the sea
    so that the redeemed might cross over?
11 The ransomed[j] of the LORD will return.
    They will enter Zion with singing;
everlasting joy will crown their heads.
Gladness and joy will overtake them,
    and sorrow and sighing will flee away.[k]

12 "I, even I, am he who comforts you.
    Who are you that you fear mortal men,[l]
    the sons of men, who are but grass,[m]
13 that you forget[n] the LORD your Maker,
    who stretched out the heavens[o]
    and laid the foundations of the earth,
that you live in constant terror every day
    because of the wrath of the oppressor,
    who is bent on destruction?
For where is the wrath of the oppressor?
14   The cowering prisoners will soon be set free;
they will not die in their dungeon,
    nor will they lack bread.[p]
15 For I am the LORD your God,
    who churns up the sea[q] so that its waves roar—
    the LORD Almighty is his name.
16 I have put my words in your mouth[r]
    and covered you with the shadow of my hand—
I who set the heavens in place,
    who laid the foundations of the earth,
    and who say to Zion, 'You are my people.'"

The Cup of the LORD's Wrath

17 Awake, awake![s]
    Rise up, O Jerusalem,
you who have drunk from the hand of the LORD
    the cup of his wrath,[t]
you who have drained to its dregs
    the goblet that makes men stagger.

51:9
[i]Ps 74:13

51:11
[j]Isa 35:9
[k]Rev 7:17

51:12
[l]Ps 118:6
[m]1Pe 1:24

51:13
[n]Isa 17:10
[o]Ps 104:2

51:14
[p]Isa 49:10

51:15
[q]Jer 31:35

51:16
[r]Dt 18:18; Isa 59:21

51:17
[s]Isa 52:1
[t]Job 21:20

51:9, 10 "Rahab" was a derogatory term used for Egypt (see the note on 30:7). God had performed many powerful miracles in founding Israel, perhaps none more exciting than the drying up of the sea (the Red Sea, see Exodus 14). Our God is the same God who made a road in the depths of the sea. His methods may change, but his love and care do not.

51:12-16 God's people feared Babylon, but not God. They had reason to fear Babylon for the harm it wanted to do, but they should also have realized that God's power is much greater than Babylon's. Babylon was interested in making the people

captives; God was interested in setting them free. The people had misplaced their fear and their love. Jerusalem should have feared God's power and loved his mercy.

51:17—52:10 Jerusalem was God's holy city, the city with God's temple. But the people of Judah experienced ruin instead of prosperity, destruction instead of liberty. Because of their sins, the people suffered. But God promised to restore Jerusalem as a holy city where sinners cannot enter. "Lay bare his holy arm" (52:10) means that God has revealed his holy power and justice. God reigns. Put your entire faith and confidence in his ability to control the course of history—and your life.

51:20
u Isa 5:25

18 Of all the sons she bore
  there was none to guide her;
of all the sons she reared
  there was none to take her by the hand.
19 These double calamities have come upon you—
  who can comfort you?—
ruin and destruction, famine and sword—
  who can[a] console you?
20 Your sons have fainted;
  they lie at the head of every street,[u]
  like antelope caught in a net.
They are filled with the wrath of the LORD
  and the rebuke of your God.

21 Therefore hear this, you afflicted one,
  made drunk, but not with wine.
22 This is what your Sovereign LORD says,
  your God, who defends his people:
"See, I have taken out of your hand
  the cup that made you stagger;
from that cup, the goblet of my wrath,
  you will never drink again.

51:23
v Jer 25:15-17, 26,
28; 49:12
w Zec 12:2

23 I will put it into the hands of your tormentors,[v]
  who said to you,
  'Fall prostrate[w] that we may walk over you.'
And you made your back like the ground,
  like a street to be walked over."

52:1
x Isa 51:17
y Ne 11:1; Mt 4:5
z Rev 21:27

52 Awake, awake,[x] O Zion,
  clothe yourself with strength.
Put on your garments of splendor,
  O Jerusalem, the holy city.[y]
The uncircumcised and defiled
  will not enter you again.[z]
2 Shake off your dust;
  rise up, sit enthroned, O Jerusalem.
Free yourself from the chains on your neck,
  O captive Daughter of Zion.

52:3
a Ps 44:12

3 For this is what the LORD says:

"You were sold for nothing,[a]
  and without money you will be redeemed."

52:4
b Ge 46:6

4 For this is what the Sovereign LORD says:

"At first my people went down to Egypt[b] to live;
  lately, Assyria has oppressed them.

52:5
c Eze 36:20;
Ro 2:24*

5 "And now what do I have here?" declares the LORD.

"For my people have been taken away for nothing,
  and those who rule them mock,[b]"

                                            declares the LORD.

"And all day long
  my name is constantly blasphemed.[c]
6 Therefore my people will know my name;
  therefore in that day they will know
that it is I who foretold it.
  Yes, it is I."

a 19 Dead Sea Scrolls, Septuagint, Vulgate and Syriac; Masoretic Text / how can I   b 5 Dead Sea Scrolls and Vulgate;
Masoretic Text wail

7 How beautiful on the mountains
   are the feet of those who bring good news,*d*
who proclaim peace,
   who bring good tidings,
   who proclaim salvation,
who say to Zion,
   "Your God reigns!"*e*
8 Listen! Your watchmen lift up their voices;
   together they shout for joy.
When the LORD returns to Zion,
   they will see it with their own eyes.
9 Burst into songs of joy together,
   you ruins of Jerusalem,
for the LORD has comforted his people,
   he has redeemed Jerusalem.*f*
10 The LORD will lay bare his holy arm
   in the sight of all the nations,
and all the ends of the earth will see
   the salvation*g* of our God.

11 Depart, depart, go out from there!
   Touch no unclean thing!*h*
Come out from it and be pure,
   you who carry the vessels of the LORD.
12 But you will not leave in haste
   or go in flight;
for the LORD will go before you,
   the God of Israel will be your rear guard.

The Suffering and Glory of the Servant

13 See, my servant*i* will act wisely*a*;
   he will be raised and lifted up and highly exalted.*j*
14 Just as there were many who were appalled at him*b*—
   his appearance was so disfigured beyond that of any man
   and his form marred beyond human likeness—
15 so will he sprinkle many nations,*c*
   and kings will shut their mouths because of him.
For what they were not told, they will see,
   and what they have not heard, they will understand.*k*

53
Who has believed our message*l*
   and to whom has the arm of the LORD been revealed?*m*
2 He grew up before him like a tender shoot,
   and like a root out of dry ground.
He had no beauty or majesty to attract us to him,
   nothing in his appearance*n* that we should desire him.

a 13 Or *will prosper*   *b 14* Hebrew *you*   *c 15* Hebrew; Septuagint *so will many nations marvel at him*

52:7
d Ro 10:15*
e Ps 93:1

52:9
f Isa 48:20

52:10
g Ps 98:2-3; Lk 3:6

52:11
h 2Co 6:17*

52:13
i Isa 42:1
j Php 2:9

52:15
k Ro 15:21*

53:1
l Ro 10:16*
m Jn 12:38*

53:2
n Isa 52:14

52:7 God says that the feet of those who bring good news are "beautiful." It is a wonderful privilege to be able to share God's Good News with others, his news of redemption, salvation, and peace. To whom do you need to give the Good News?

52:12 The people did not have to leave in fearful haste because Cyrus, God's anointed (45:1), decreed that the Jewish exiles could return safely to Jerusalem (Ezra 1:1–4). They had the king's approval, his guaranteed protection. More important, the Lord would go ahead to point the way and be behind to protect them.

52:13 The "servant," as the term is used here, is the Messiah, our Lord Jesus. He would be highly exalted because of his sacrifice, described in chapter 53.

52:14, 15 This servant, Christ, would be "marred beyond human likeness"; but through his suffering, he would cleanse the nations (Hebrews 10:14; 1 Peter 1:2).

53:1ff This chapter continues to speak of the Messiah, Jesus, who would suffer for the sins of all people. Such a prophecy is astounding! Who would believe that God would choose to save the world through a humble, suffering servant rather than a glorious king? The idea is contrary to human pride and worldly ways. But God often works in ways we don't expect. The Messiah's strength is shown by humility, suffering, and mercy.

53:2 There was nothing beautiful or majestic in the physical appearance of this servant. Israel would miscalculate the servant's importance—they would consider him an ordinary man. But even though Jesus would not attract a large following based on his

53:3
oPs 22:6;
Jn 1:10-11

3 He was despised and rejected by men,
  a man of sorrows, and familiar with suffering.
Like one from whom men hide their faces
  he was despised,o and we esteemed him not.

53:4
pMt 8:17*

4 Surely he took up our infirmities
  and carried our sorrows,p
yet we considered him stricken by God,
  smitten by him, and afflicted.

53:5
qRo 4:25
r1Pe 2:24-25

5 But he was pierced for our transgressions,q
  he was crushed for our iniquities;
the punishment that brought us peace was upon him,
  and by his wounds we are healed.r

6 We all, like sheep, have gone astray,
  each of us has turned to his own way;
and the LORD has laid on him
  the iniquity of us all.

53:7
sMk 14:61

7 He was oppressed and afflicted,
  yet he did not open his mouth;s
he was led like a lamb to the slaughter,
  and as a sheep before her shearers is silent,
  so he did not open his mouth.

53:8
tAc 8:32-33*

8 By oppressiona and judgment he was taken away.
  And who can speak of his descendants?
For he was cut off from the land of the living;t
  for the transgression of my people he was stricken.b

53:9
uMt 27:57-60
v1Pe 2:22*

9 He was assigned a grave with the wicked,
  and with the richu in his death,
though he had done no violence,
  nor was any deceit in his mouth.v

53:10
wIsa 46:10

10 Yet it was the LORD's willw to crush him and cause him to suffer,
  and though the LORD makesc his life a guilt offering,
he will see his offspring and prolong his days,
  and the will of the LORD will prosper in his hand.

53:11
xJn 10:14-18
yRo 5:18-19

11 After the sufferingx of his soul,
  he will see the light ⌊of life⌋d and be satisfiede;
by his knowledgef my righteous servant will justifyy many,
  and he will bear their iniquities.

12 Therefore I will give him a portion among the great,g
  and he will divide the spoils with the strong,h

---

a8 Or From arrest   b8 Or away. / Yet who of his generation considered / that he was cut off from the land of the living / for the transgression of my people, / to whom the blow was due?   c10 Hebrew though you make   d11 Dead Sea Scrolls (see also Septuagint); Masoretic Text does not have the light ⌊of life⌋.   e11 Or (with Masoretic Text) 11He will see the result of the suffering of his soul / and be satisfied   f11 Or by knowledge of him   g12 Or many   h12 Or numerous

---

physical appearance, he would bring salvation and healing. Many people miscalculate the importance of Jesus' life and work, and they need faithful Christians to point out his extraordinary nature.

53:4, 5 How could an Old Testament person understand the idea of Christ dying for our sins (our transgressions and iniquities)— actually bearing the punishment that we deserved? The sacrifices suggested this idea, but it is one thing to kill a lamb, and something quite different to think of God's chosen servant as that Lamb. But God was pulling aside the curtain of time to let the people of Isaiah's day look ahead to the suffering of the future Messiah and the resulting forgiveness made available to all mankind.

53:6 Isaiah speaks of Israel straying from God and compares them to wandering sheep. Yet God would send the Messiah to bring them back into the fold. We have the hindsight to see and know the identity of the promised Messiah who has come and died for our sins. But if we can see all that Jesus did and still reject him, our sin is much greater than that of the ancient Israel-

ites who could not see what we have seen. Have you given your life to Jesus Christ, the "good shepherd" (John 10:11–16), or are you still going your own way like a wandering sheep?

53:7–12 In the Old Testament, people offered animals as sacrifices for their sins. Here, the sinless servant of the Lord offers himself for our sins. He is the Lamb (53:7) offered for the sins of all people (John 1:29; Revelation 5:6–14). The Messiah suffered for our sakes, bearing our sins to make us acceptable to God. What can we say to such love? How will we respond to him?

53:11 "My righteous servant will justify many" tells of the enormous family of believers who will become righteous, not by their own works, but by the Messiah's great work on the cross. They are justified because they have claimed Christ, the righteous servant, as their Savior and Lord (see Romans 10:9; 2 Corinthians 5:21). Their life of sin is stripped away, and they are clothed with Christ's goodness (Ephesians 4:22–24).

because he poured out his life unto death,[z]
and was numbered with the transgressors.[a]
For he bore the sin of many,
and made intercession for the transgressors.

53:12
[z] Mt 26:28, 38,
39, 42
[a] Lk 22:37*

The Future Glory of Zion

54 "Sing, O barren woman,
you who never bore a child;
burst into song, shout for joy,
you who were never in labor;
because more are the children of the desolate woman
than of her who has a husband,[b]"

says the LORD.

54:1
[b] Gal 4:27*

2 "Enlarge the place of your tent,[c]
stretch your tent curtains wide,
do not hold back;
lengthen your cords,
strengthen your stakes.

54:2
[c] Isa 49:19-20

3 For you will spread out to the right and to the left;
your descendants will dispossess nations
and settle in their desolate[d] cities.

54:3
[d] Isa 49:19

4 "Do not be afraid; you will not suffer shame.
Do not fear disgrace; you will not be humiliated.
You will forget the shame of your youth
and remember no more the reproach of your widowhood.

5 For your Maker is your husband[e]—
the LORD Almighty is his name—
the Holy One of Israel is your Redeemer;[f]
he is called the God of all the earth.

54:5
[e] Jer 3:14
[f] Isa 48:17

6 The LORD will call you back
as if you were a wife deserted[g] and distressed in spirit—
a wife who married young,
only to be rejected," says your God.

54:6
[g] Isa 62:4, 12

7 "For a brief moment[h] I abandoned you,
but with deep compassion I will bring you back.

54:7
[h] Isa 26:20

8 In a surge of anger[i]
I hid my face from you for a moment,
but with everlasting kindness
I will have compassion on you,"
says the LORD your Redeemer.

54:8
[i] Isa 60:10

9 "To me this is like the days of Noah,
when I swore that the waters of Noah would never again cover the earth.
So now I have sworn not to be angry[j] with you,
never to rebuke you again.

54:9
[j] Isa 12:1

10 Though the mountains be shaken
and the hills be removed,
yet my unfailing love for you will not be shaken[k]
nor my covenant[l] of peace be removed,"
says the LORD, who has compassion on you.

54:10
[k] Isa 51:6
[l] Ps 89:34

54:1 To be childless ("barren") at that time was a woman's great shame, a disgrace. Families depended on children for survival, especially when the parents became elderly. Israel (Zion) was unfruitful, like a childless woman, but God would permit her to have many children and would change her mourning into singing.

54:6-8 God said that he had abandoned Israel for a brief moment, so the nation was like a young wife rejected by her husband. But God still called Israel his own. The God we serve is holy, and he cannot tolerate sin. When his people blatantly sinned, God in his anger chose to punish them. Sin separates

us from God and brings us pain and suffering. But if we confess our sin and repent, then God will forgive us. Have you ever been separated from a loved one and then experienced joy when that person returned? That is like the joy God experiences when you repent and return to him.

54:9-13 God made a covenant with Noah that he has never broken (Genesis 9:8-17). Likewise, God made a covenant of peace with the people of Israel that the time would come when he would stop rebuking them, would restore their wealth, and would personally teach their children.

54:11
m 1Ch 29:2;
Rev 21:18

11 "O afflicted city, lashed by storms and not comforted,
    I will build you with stones of turquoise,[a] [m]
    your foundations with sapphires.[b]
12 I will make your battlements of rubies,
    your gates of sparkling jewels,
    and all your walls of precious stones.

54:13
n Jn 6:45*

13 All your sons will be taught by the LORD,[n]
    and great will be your children's peace.

54:14
o Isa 9:4

14 In righteousness you will be established:
    Tyranny[o] will be far from you;
    you will have nothing to fear.
    Terror will be far removed;
    it will not come near you.

54:15
p Isa 41:11-16

15 If anyone does attack you, it will not be my doing;
    whoever attacks you will surrender[p] to you.

16 "See, it is I who created the blacksmith
    who fans the coals into flame
    and forges a weapon fit for its work.
    And it is I who have created the destroyer to work havoc;

54:17
q Isa 29:8
r Isa 45:24-25

17   no weapon forged against you will prevail,[q]
    and you will refute[r] every tongue that accuses you.
    This is the heritage of the servants of the LORD,
    and this is their vindication from me,"

                     declares the LORD.

Invitation to the Thirsty

55:1
s Jn 4:14
t Rev 3:18

55

"Come, all you who are thirsty,[s]
    come to the waters;
and you who have no money,
    come, buy[t] and eat!
Come, buy wine and milk
    without money and without cost.
2 Why spend money on what is not bread,
    and your labor on what does not satisfy?
Listen, listen to me, and eat what is good,
    and your soul will delight in the richest of fare.

55:3
u Isa 61:8
v Ac 13:34*

3 Give ear and come to me;
    hear me, that your soul may live.
I will make an everlasting covenant[u] with you,
    my faithful love promised to David.[v]

55:4
w Jer 30:9;
Eze 34:23-24

4 See, I have made him a witness to the peoples,
    a leader and commander[w] of the peoples.

55:5
x Isa 60:9

5 Surely you will summon nations you know not,
    and nations that do not know you will hasten to you,
because of the LORD your God,
    the Holy One of Israel,
    for he has endowed you with splendor."[x]

55:6
y Ps 32:6;
2Co 6:1-2

6 Seek the LORD while he may be found;[y]
    call on him while he is near.

  a 11 The meaning of the Hebrew for this word is uncertain. **b** 11 Or *lapis lazuli*

55:1–6 Food costs money, lasts only a short time, and meets only physical needs. But God offers us *free* nourishment that feeds our soul. How do we get it? We come (55:1), listen (55:2), seek, and call on God (55:6). God's salvation is freely offered, but to nourish our souls we must eagerly receive it. We will starve spiritually without this food as surely as we will starve physically without our daily bread.

55:3 God's covenant with David promised a permanent homeland for the Israelites, no threat from pagan nations, and no wars (2 Samuel 7:10, 11). But Israel did not fulfill its part of the covenant

by obeying God and staying away from idols. Even so, God was ready to renew his covenant again. He is a forgiving God!

55:6 Isaiah tells us to call on the Lord while he is near. God is not planning to move away from us, but we often move far from him or erect a barrier between ourselves and him. Don't wait until you have drifted far away from God to seek him. Later in life turning to him may be far more difficult. Or God may come to judge the earth before you decide to turn to him. Seek God now, while you can, before it is too late.

7 Let the wicked forsake his way
　　and the evil man his thoughts.
Let him turnz to the Lord, and he will have mercy on him,
　　and to our God, for he will freely pardon.

8 "For my thoughts are not your thoughts,
　　neither are your ways my ways,"

declares the Lord.

9 "As the heavens are higher than the earth,a
　　so are my ways higher than your ways
　　and my thoughts than your thoughts.
10 As the rainb and the snow
　　come down from heaven,
and do not return to it
　　without watering the earth
and making it bud and flourish,
　　so that it yields seed for the sower and bread for the eater,c
11 so is my word that goes out from my mouth:
　　It will not return to me empty,
but will accomplish what I desire
　　and achieve the purpose for which I sent it.
12 You will go out in joy
　　and be led forth in peace;d
the mountains and hills
　　will burst into song before you,
and all the treese of the field
　　will clap their hands.
13 Instead of the thornbush will grow the pine tree,
　　and instead of briers the myrtlef will grow.
This will be for the Lord's renown,g
　　for an everlasting sign,
　　which will not be destroyed."

Salvation for Others

56 This is what the Lord says:

"Maintain justice
　　and do what is right,
for my salvation is close at hand
　　and my righteousness will soon be revealed.
2 Blessed is the man who does this,
　　the man who holds it fast,
who keeps the Sabbathh without desecrating it,
　　and keeps his hand from doing any evil."

3 Let no foreigner who has bound himself to the Lord say,
　　"The Lord will surely exclude me from his people."
And let not any eunuchi complain,
　　"I am only a dry tree."

4 For this is what the Lord says:

"To the eunuchs who keep my Sabbaths,
　　who choose what pleases me
　　and hold fast to my covenant—

55:7
z Isa 44:22

55:9
a Ps 103:11

55:10
b Isa 30:23
c 2Co 9:10

55:12
d Isa 54:10, 13
e 1Ch 16:33

55:13
f Isa 41:19
g Isa 63:12

56:2
h Isa 58:13

56:3
i Ac 8:27

55:8, 9 The people of Israel were foolish to act as if they knew what God was thinking and planning. His knowledge and wisdom are far greater than man's. We are foolish to try to fit God into our mold—to make his plans and purposes conform to ours. Instead, we must strive to fit into *his* plans.

56:2 God commanded his people to rest and honor him on the Sabbath (Exodus 20:8–11). He wants us to serve him every day,

but he wants us to make one day special when we rest and focus our thoughts on him. For the Israelites, this special day was the Sabbath (Saturday). Some Christians set Saturday aside as this special day, but many accept Sunday (the day of the week that Jesus rose from the dead) as the "Lord's Day," a day of rest and honor to God. Do you make Sunday special?

56:3 Isaiah clearly proclaims the radical message that God's

56:5
Isa 48:19

⁵ to them I will give within my temple and its walls
    a memorial and a name
    better than sons and daughters;
I will give them an everlasting name
    that will not be cut off.ʲ

56:6
k Isa 60:7, 10

⁶ And foreigners who bind themselves to the LORD
    to serveᵏ him,
to love the name of the LORD,
    and to worship him,
all who keep the Sabbath without desecrating it
    and who hold fast to my covenant—

56:7
l Heb 13:15
m Mt 21:13*

⁷ these I will bring to my holy mountain
    and give them joy in my house of prayer.
Their burnt offerings and sacrificesˡ
    will be accepted on my altar;
for my house will be called
    a house of prayer for all nations.ᵐ"

56:8
n Isa 11:12;
Jn 10:16

⁸ The Sovereign LORD declares—
    he who gathers the exiles of Israel:
"I will gatherⁿ still others to them
    besides those already gathered."

God's Accusation Against the Wicked

56:9
o Jer 12:9

⁹ Come, all you beasts of the field,ᵒ
    come and devour, all you beasts of the forest!
¹⁰ Israel's watchmen are blind,
    they all lack knowledge;
they are all mute dogs,
    they cannot bark;
they lie around and dream,
    they love to sleep.

56:11
p Mic 3:11

¹¹ They are dogs with mighty appetites;
    they never have enough.
They are shepherds who lack understanding;
    they all turn to their own way,
    each seeks his own gain.ᵖ

56:12
q Lk 12:18-19

¹² "Come," each one cries, "let me get wine!
    Let us drink our fill of beer!
And tomorrow will be like today,
    or even far better."�q

57:1
r Ps 12:1

57

The righteous perish,ʳ
    and no one ponders it in his heart;
devout men are taken away,
    and no one understands
that the righteous are taken away
    to be spared from evil.

57:2
s Isa 26:7

² Those who walk uprightlyˢ
    enter into peace;
they find rest as they lie in death.

---

blessings are for *all* people, even foreigners and eunuchs, who
were often excluded from worship and not even considered
citizens in Israel. Whatever your race, social position, work,
or financial situation, God's blessings are as much for you as
for anyone else. No one must exclude in any way those God
chooses to include.

56:7 Jesus quoted from this verse when he threw the money
changers out of the temple (Mark 11:17). See the second note
on Mark 11:15–17.

56:9–11 The "watchmen" were the nation's leaders. The leaders
of Israel were blind to every danger and thus did not warn when
danger was coming. Apathetic about their people's needs, they
were more concerned about satisfying their own greed. Leadership's special privileges can cause leaders either to sacrifice for
the good of their people or to sacrifice their people for their own
greed. If you are in a leadership position, use it for the good of
your people.

3 "But you—come here, you sons of a sorceress,
    you offspring of adulterers[t] and prostitutes!
4 Whom are you mocking?
        At whom do you sneer
        and stick out your tongue?
    Are you not a brood of rebels,
        the offspring of liars?
5 You burn with lust among the oaks
        and under every spreading tree;[u]
    you sacrifice your children in the ravines
        and under the overhanging crags.
6 ⌊The idols⌋ among the smooth stones of the ravines are your portion;
        they, they are your lot.
    Yes, to them you have poured out drink offerings[v]
        and offered grain offerings.
        In the light of these things, should I relent?
7 You have made your bed on a high and lofty hill;[w]
        there you went up to offer your sacrifices.
8 Behind your doors and your doorposts
        you have put your pagan symbols.
    Forsaking me, you uncovered your bed,
        you climbed into it and opened it wide;
    you made a pact with those whose beds you love,[x]
        and you looked on their nakedness.
9 You went to Molech[a] with olive oil
        and increased your perfumes.
    You sent your ambassadors[b][y] far away;
        you descended to the grave[c] itself!
10 You were wearied by all your ways,
        but you would not say, 'It is hopeless.'[z]
    You found renewal of your strength,
        and so you did not faint.

11 "Whom have you so dreaded and feared
        that you have been false to me,
    and have neither remembered me
        nor pondered this in your hearts?
    Is it not because I have long been silent[a]
        that you do not fear me?
12 I will expose your righteousness and your works,
        and they will not benefit you.
13 When you cry out for help,
        let your collection ⌊of idols⌋ save you!
    The wind will carry all of them off,
        a mere breath will blow them away.
    But the man who makes me his refuge
        will inherit the land
        and possess my holy mountain."

a 9 Or *to the king*   b 9 Or *idols*   c 9 Hebrew *Sheol*

57:3
[t] Mt 16:4

57:5
[u] 2Ki 16:4

57:6
[v] Jer 7:18

57:7
[w] Eze 16:16

57:8
[x] Eze 16:26

57:9
[y] Eze 23:16, 40

57:10
[z] Jer 2:25

57:11
[a] Ps 50:21

57:7, 8 Marriage is an exclusive relationship where a man and a woman become one. Adultery breaks this beautiful bond of unity. When the people turned from God and gave their love to idols, God said they were committing spiritual adultery—breaking their exclusive commitment to God. How could people give their love to worthless wood and stone instead of to the God who made them and loved them so very much?

57:9 Molech was an Ammonite god whose worship included child sacrifice.

57:12 God says that he will expose their righteousness and works for what they really were—mere pretensions of doing good. Isaiah warned these people that their righteousness and works would not save them any more than their weak, worthless idols. We cannot gain our salvation through good deeds because our best deeds are not good enough to outweigh our sins. Salvation is a gift from God, received only through faith in Christ, not good deeds (Ephesians 2:8, 9).

Comfort for the Contrite

¹⁴And it will be said:

> "Build up, build up, prepare the road!
>> Remove the obstacles out of the way of my people."[b]
> ¹⁵ For this is what the high and lofty One says—
>> he who lives forever, whose name is holy:
> "I live in a high and holy place,
>> but also with him who is contrite and lowly in spirit,[c]
> to revive the spirit of the lowly
>> and to revive the heart of the contrite.[d]
> ¹⁶ I will not accuse forever,
>> nor will I always be angry,[e]
> for then the spirit of man would grow faint before me—
>> the breath of man that I have created.
> ¹⁷ I was enraged by his sinful greed;
>> I punished him, and hid my face in anger,
> yet he kept on in his willful ways.[f]
> ¹⁸ I have seen his ways, but I will heal him;
>> I will guide him and restore comfort[g] to him,
> ¹⁹   creating praise on the lips[h] of the mourners in Israel.
> Peace, peace,[i] to those far and near,"[j]
>> says the Lord. "And I will heal them."
> ²⁰ But the wicked are like the tossing sea,
>> which cannot rest,
> whose waves cast up mire and mud.
> ²¹ "There is no peace," says my God, "for the wicked."[k]

True Fasting

58 "Shout it aloud, do not hold back.
>> Raise your voice like a trumpet.
> Declare to my people their rebellion
>> and to the house of Jacob their sins.
> ² For day after day they seek[l] me out;
>> they seem eager to know my ways,
> as if they were a nation that does what is right
>> and has not forsaken the commands of its God.
> They ask me for just decisions
>> and seem eager for God to come near them.
> ³ 'Why have we fasted,' they say,
>> 'and you have not seen it?
> Why have we humbled ourselves,
>> and you have not noticed?'[m]
>
> "Yet on the day of your fasting, you do as you please
>> and exploit all your workers.
> ⁴ Your fasting ends in quarreling and strife,[n]
>> and in striking each other with wicked fists.
> You cannot fast as you do today
>> and expect your voice to be heard on high.
> ⁵ Is this the kind of fast[o] I have chosen,
>> only a day for a man to humble himself?
> Is it only for bowing one's head like a reed
>> and for lying on sackcloth and ashes?

**Cross references (left margin):**

57:14
[b] Jer 18:15

57:15
[c] Ps 34:18; 51:17
[d] Isa 61:1

57:16
[e] Ps 85:5; 103:9;
Mic 7:18

57:17
[f] Isa 1:4

57:18
[g] Isa 61:1-3

57:19
[h] Heb 13:15
[i] Eph 2:17
[j] Ac 2:39

57:21
[k] Isa 48:22

58:2
[l] Isa 48:1

58:3
[m] Mal 3:14

58:4
[n] 1Ki 21:9-13

58:5
[o] Zec 7:5

57:14–21 Verses 1–13 speak of pride and lust; verses 14–21 tell how God relates to those who are humble and repentant ("contrite"). The high and holy God came down to our level to save us because it is impossible for us to go up to his level to save ourselves (see 2 Chronicles 6:18; Psalm 51:1–7; Philippians 2).

58:1ff True worship was more than religious ritual, going to the temple every day, fasting, and listening to Scripture readings. These people missed the point of a living, vital relationship with God. He doesn't want us acting pious when we have unforgiven sin in our hearts and perform sinful practices with our hands. More important even than correct worship and doctrine is genuine compassion for the poor, the helpless, and the oppressed.

Is that what you call a fast,
a day acceptable to the Lord?

6 "Is not this the kind of fasting I have chosen:
to loose the chains of injustice^p
and untie the cords of the yoke,
to set the oppressed^q free
and break every yoke?

58:6
p Ne 5:10-11
q Jer 34:9

7 Is it not to share your food with the hungry
and to provide the poor wanderer with shelter—
when you see the naked, to clothe^r him,
and not to turn away from your own flesh and blood?^s

58:7
r Job 31:19-20;
Mt 25:36
s Ge 29:14

8 Then your light will break forth like the dawn,
and your healing will quickly appear;
then your righteousness^a will go before you,
and the glory of the Lord will be your rear guard.^t

58:8
t Ex 14:19

9 Then you will call, and the Lord will answer;
you will cry for help, and he will say: Here am I.

58:9
u Ps 12:2

"If you do away with the yoke of oppression,
with the pointing finger and malicious talk,^u

10 and if you spend yourselves in behalf of the hungry
and satisfy the needs of the oppressed,
then your light will rise in the darkness,
and your night will become like the noonday.

11 The Lord will guide you always;
he will satisfy your needs in a sun-scorched land
and will strengthen your frame.
You will be like a well-watered garden,
like a spring^v whose waters never fail.

58:11
v Jn 4:14

12 Your people will rebuild the ancient ruins^w
and will raise up the age-old foundations;
you will be called Repairer of Broken Walls,
Restorer of Streets with Dwellings.

58:12
w Isa 49:8

13 "If you keep your feet from breaking the Sabbath^x
and from doing as you please on my holy day,
if you call the Sabbath a delight
and the Lord's holy day honorable,
and if you honor it by not going your own way
and not doing as you please or speaking idle words,

58:13
x Isa 56:2

14 then you will find your joy in the Lord,
and I will cause you to ride on the heights^y of the land
and to feast on the inheritance of your father Jacob."
The mouth of the Lord has spoken.^z

58:14
y Dt 32:13
z Isa 1:20

Sin, Confession and Redemption

59 Surely the arm of the Lord is not too short^a to save,
nor his ear too dull to hear.
2 But your iniquities have separated
you from your God;

59:1
a Nu 11:23; Isa 50:2

^a 8 Or *your righteous One*

58:6–12 We cannot be saved by deeds of service without faith in Christ, but our faith lacks sincerity if it doesn't reach out to others. Fasting can be beneficial spiritually and physically, but at its best fasting helps only the person doing it. God says he wants our service to go beyond our own personal growth to acts of kindness, charity, justice, and generosity. True fasting is more than what we don't eat; it is pleasing God by applying his Word to our society.

58:13, 14 The day of rest should be observed and regarded not only because Sabbath-keeping is a commandment but also

because it is best for us and because it honors God. Keeping the Sabbath shows proper respect to God, our Creator, who also rested on the seventh day (Genesis 2:3). It also unifies our family and sets priorities for them. Our day of rest refreshes us spiritually and physically—providing time when we can gather together for worship and when we can reflect on God without the stress of our everyday activities.

59:1–14 Sin offends our holy God and separates us from him. Because God is holy, he cannot ignore, excuse, or tolerate sin as

59:2
b Isa 1:15; 58:4
59:3
c Isa 1:15

your sins have hidden his face from you,
so that he will not hear.*b*
3 For your hands are stained with blood,*c*
your fingers with guilt.
Your lips have spoken lies,
and your tongue mutters wicked things.

59:4
d Job 15:35; Ps 7:14

4 No one calls for justice;
no one pleads his case with integrity.
They rely on empty arguments and speak lies;
they conceive trouble and give birth to evil.*d*

59:5
e Job 8:14

5 They hatch the eggs of vipers
and spin a spider's web.*e*
Whoever eats their eggs will die,
and when one is broken, an adder is hatched.

59:6
f Isa 28:20
g Isa 58:4

6 Their cobwebs are useless for clothing;
they cannot cover themselves with what they make.*f*
Their deeds are evil deeds,
and acts of violence*g* are in their hands.

59:7
h Ro 3:15-17*

7 Their feet rush into sin;
they are swift to shed innocent blood.
Their thoughts are evil thoughts;
ruin and destruction mark their ways.*h*
8 The way of peace they do not know;
there is no justice in their paths.
They have turned them into crooked roads;
no one who walks in them will know peace.

59:9
i Isa 5:30

9 So justice is far from us,
and righteousness does not reach us.
We look for light, but all is darkness;*i*
for brightness, but we walk in deep shadows.

59:10
j Dt 28:29
k Isa 8:15

10 Like the blind*j* we grope along the wall,
feeling our way like men without eyes.
At midday we stumble*k* as if it were twilight;
among the strong, we are like the dead.

59:11
l Isa 38:14;
Eze 7:16

11 We all growl like bears;
we moan mournfully like doves.*l*
We look for justice, but find none;
for deliverance, but it is far away.

12 For our offenses are many in your sight,
and our sins testify against us.
Our offenses are ever with us,
and we acknowledge our iniquities:

59:13
m Tit 1:16

13 rebellion and treachery against the LORD,
turning our backs*m* on our God,
fomenting oppression and revolt,
uttering lies our hearts have conceived.

59:14
n Isa 1:21

14 So justice is driven back,
and righteousness*n* stands at a distance;
truth has stumbled in the streets,
honesty cannot enter.
15 Truth is nowhere to be found,
and whoever shuns evil becomes a prey.

---

though it didn't matter. Sin cuts people off from him, forming a wall to isolate God from the people he loves. No wonder this long list of wretched sins makes God angry and forces him to look the other way. People who die with their life of sin unforgiven separate themselves eternally from God. God wants them to live with him forever, but he cannot take them into his holy presence unless

their sin is removed. Have you confessed your sin to God, allowing him to remove it? The Lord can save you if you turn to him.

59:15 Because of Israel's willful, persistent rebellion (chapters 56—59), the nation became unable to take action against its sins. Sin fills the vacuum left when God's truth no longer fills our lives. Only God can defeat sin.

The LORD looked and was displeased
  that there was no justice.
16 He saw that there was no one,
  he was appalled that there was no one to intervene;
so his own arm worked salvation[o] for him,
  and his own righteousness sustained him.
17 He put on righteousness as his breastplate,[p]
  and the helmet[q] of salvation on his head;
he put on the garments of vengeance
  and wrapped himself in zeal as in a cloak.
18 According to what they have done,
  so will he repay
wrath to his enemies
  and retribution to his foes;
  he will repay the islands their due.
19 From the west, men will fear the name of the LORD,
  and from the rising of the sun,[r] they will revere his glory.
For he will come like a pent-up flood
  that the breath of the LORD drives along.[a]

20 "The Redeemer will come to Zion,
  to those in Jacob who repent of their sins,"[s]

                     declares the LORD.

21 "As for me, this is my covenant with them," says the LORD. "My Spirit, who is on you, and my words that I have put in your mouth will not depart from your mouth, or from the mouths of your children, or from the mouths of their descendants from this time on and forever," says the LORD.

3. The future kingdom
The Glory of Zion

60   "Arise, shine, for your light[t] has come,
    and the glory of the LORD rises upon you.
2 See, darkness covers the earth
  and thick darkness[u] is over the peoples,
but the LORD rises upon you
  and his glory appears over you.
3 Nations will come to your light,
  and kings[v] to the brightness of your dawn.

4 "Lift up your eyes and look about you:
  All assemble and come to you;
your sons come from afar,
  and your daughters are carried on the arm.[w]
5 Then you will look and be radiant,
  your heart will throb and swell with joy;
the wealth on the seas will be brought to you,
  to you the riches of the nations will come.
6 Herds of camels will cover your land,
  young camels of Midian and Ephah.[x]

[a] 19 Or *When the enemy comes in like a flood, / the Spirit of the LORD will put him to flight*

59:16	o Ps 98:1; Isa 63:5
59:17	p Eph 6:14
	q 1 Th 5:8
59:19	r Ps 113:3
59:20	s Ro 11:26-27*
60:1	t Eph 5:14
60:2	u Col 1:13
60:3	v Isa 49:23
60:4	w Isa 49:20-22
60:6	x Ge 25:4

59:16, 17 God would, in fact, act to rescue the nation from enemy armies (Assyria and Babylon) and to punish wicked Israelites as well. He would also rescue his people from sin. Because this is an impossible task for any human, God himself, as the Messiah, would personally step in to help (Romans 11:26, 27). Whether we sin once or many times, out of rebellion or out of ignorance, our sin separates us from God and will continue to separate us until God forgives us and removes it.

59:21 When the Holy Spirit dwells within his people, they change. Their former desires no longer entice them; now their

chief aim is to please God. We who are Christians today are the heirs of this prophecy; we are able to respond to God's will and distinguish between good and evil because the Holy Spirit dwells within us (John 14:26; Philippians 2:13; Hebrews 5:14).

60:1ff As we read these promises, we long for their fulfillment. But we must patiently wait for God's timing. He is in control of history, and he weaves together all our lives into his plan.

60:6, 7 The places mentioned belonged to obscure tribes in the Arabian desert hundreds of miles from Israel. All people would come to Jerusalem because God would be living there and they

60:6
y Ps 72:10

And all from Sheba[y] will come,
  bearing gold and incense
  and proclaiming the praise of the LORD.

60:7
z Ge 25:13
a Hag 2:3, 7, 9

[7] All Kedar's[z] flocks will be gathered to you,
  the rams of Nebaioth will serve you;
they will be accepted as offerings on my altar,
  and I will adorn my glorious temple.[a]

[8] "Who are these that fly along like clouds,
  like doves to their nests?

60:9
b Isa 55:5

[9] Surely the islands look to me;
  in the lead are the ships of Tarshish,[a]
bringing your sons from afar,
  with their silver and gold,
to the honor of the LORD your God,
  the Holy One of Israel,
  for he has endowed you with splendor.[b]

60:10
c Isa 49:23;
Rev 21:24
d Isa 54:8

[10] "Foreigners will rebuild your walls,
  and their kings[c] will serve you.
Though in anger I struck you,
  in favor I will show you compassion.[d]

60:11
e Ps 149:8

[11] Your gates will always stand open,
  they will never be shut, day or night,
so that men may bring you the wealth of the nations—
  their kings[e] led in triumphal procession.

[12] For the nation or kingdom that will not serve you will perish;
  it will be utterly ruined.

60:13
f Isa 35:2
g 1Ch 28:2;
Ps 132:7

[13] "The glory of Lebanon[f] will come to you,
  the pine, the fir and the cypress together,
to adorn the place of my sanctuary;
  and I will glorify the place of my feet.[g]

60:14
h Isa 49:23; Rev 3:9
i Heb 12:22

[14] The sons of your oppressors will come bowing before you;
  all who despise you will bow down[h] at your feet
and will call you the City of the LORD,
  Zion[i] of the Holy One of Israel.

[15] "Although you have been forsaken and hated,
  with no one traveling through,
I will make you the everlasting pride
  and the joy of all generations.

60:16
j Isa 49:23

[16] You will drink the milk of nations
  and be nursed[j] at royal breasts.
Then you will know that I, the LORD, am your Savior,
  your Redeemer, the Mighty One of Jacob.

[17] Instead of bronze I will bring you gold,
  and silver in place of iron.
Instead of wood I will bring you bronze,
  and iron in place of stones.
I will make peace your governor
  and righteousness your ruler.

60:18
k Isa 26:1

[18] No longer will violence be heard in your land,
  nor ruin or destruction within your borders,
but you will call your walls Salvation[k]
  and your gates Praise.

[a]9 Or *the trading ships*

---

would be attracted to his light. Don't be discouraged when you look around and see so few people turning to God; one day people throughout the earth will recognize him as the one true God.

19 The sun will no more be your light by day,
    nor will the brightness of the moon shine on you,
for the LORD will be your everlasting light,
    and your God will be your glory.*l*

60:19
l Zec 2:5; Rev 21:23

20 Your sun will never set again,
    and your moon will wane no more;
the LORD will be your everlasting light,
    and your days of sorrow will end.

21 Then will all your people be righteous
    and they will possess*m* the land forever.
They are the shoot I have planted,
    the work of my hands,*n*
    for the display of my splendor.

60:21
m Ps 37:11, 22
n Isa 29:23

22 The least of you will become a thousand,
    the smallest a mighty nation.
I am the LORD;
    in its time I will do this swiftly."

The Year of the LORD's Favor

61

The Spirit of the Sovereign LORD is on me,
    because the LORD has anointed me
    to preach good news to the poor.*o*
He has sent me to bind up*p* the brokenhearted,
    to proclaim freedom for the captives*q*
    and release from darkness for the prisoners,*a*

61:1
o Mt 11:5
p Isa 57:15
q Isa 42:7

2 to proclaim the year of the LORD's favor*r*
    and the day of vengeance*s* of our God,
to comfort*t* all who mourn,
3   and provide for those who grieve in Zion—
to bestow on them a crown of beauty
    instead of ashes,
the oil of gladness
    instead of mourning,
and a garment of praise
    instead of a spirit of despair.
They will be called oaks of righteousness,
    a planting of the LORD
    for the display of his splendor.*u*

61:2
r Lk 4:18-19*
s Isa 34:8
t Isa 57:18; Mt 5:4
61:3
u Isa 60:20-21

4 They will rebuild the ancient ruins*v*
    and restore the places long devastated;
they will renew the ruined cities
    that have been devastated for generations.
5 Aliens will shepherd your flocks;
    foreigners will work your fields and vineyards.
6 And you will be called priests of the LORD,
    you will be named ministers of our God.
You will feed on the wealth of nations,
    and in their riches you will boast.

61:4
v Isa 49:8;
Eze 36:33

7 Instead of their shame
    my people will receive a double*w* portion,

61:7
w Isa 40:2; Zec 9:12

a 1 Hebrew; Septuagint *the blind*

60:19, 20 See Revelation 21:23, 24 and 22:5, where this beautiful reality is also promised.

61:1, 2 Jesus quoted these words in Luke 4:18, 19. As he read to the people in the synagogue, he stopped in the middle of 61:2 after the words, "to proclaim the year of the LORD's favor." Rolling up the scroll, he said, "Today this scripture is fulfilled in your hearing" (Luke 4:21). The next phrase in 61:2, "and the day of vengeance of our God," will come true when Jesus returns to earth again. We are now under God's favor; his wrath is yet to come.

61:6 Under the old covenant, God ordained the priests of Israel to stand between him and his people. They brought God's word to the people and the people's needs and sins to God. Under the new covenant, all believers are priests of the Lord (1 Peter 2:5),

and instead of disgrace
    they will rejoice in their inheritance;
and so they will inherit a double portion in their land,
    and everlasting joy will be theirs.

61:8
x Isa 55:3

8 "For I, the LORD, love justice;
    I hate robbery and iniquity.
In my faithfulness I will reward them
    and make an everlasting covenant*x* with them.
9 Their descendants will be known among the nations
    and their offspring among the peoples.
All who see them will acknowledge
    that they are a people the LORD has blessed."

61:10
y Isa 49:18;
Rev 21:2

10 I delight greatly in the LORD;
    my soul rejoices in my God.
For he has clothed me with garments of salvation
    and arrayed me in a robe of righteousness,
as a bridegroom adorns his head like a priest,
    and as a bride*y* adorns herself with her jewels.

61:11
z Ps 85:11

11 For as the soil makes the sprout come up
    and a garden causes seeds to grow,
so the Sovereign LORD will make righteousness*z* and praise
    spring up before all nations.

Zion's New Name

62

For Zion's sake I will not keep silent,
    for Jerusalem's sake I will not remain quiet,
till her righteousness shines out like the dawn,
    her salvation like a blazing torch.

62:2
a Isa 60:3
b ver 4, 12

2 The nations*a* will see your righteousness,
    and all kings your glory;
you will be called by a new name*b*
    that the mouth of the LORD will bestow.

62:3
c Zec 9:16

3 You will be a crown*c* of splendor in the LORD's hand,
    a royal diadem in the hand of your God.

62:4
d Isa 54:6

4 No longer will they call you Deserted,*d*
    or name your land Desolate.
But you will be called Hephzibah,*a*
    and your land Beulah*b*;
for the LORD will take delight in you,
    and your land will be married.

62:5
e Isa 65:19

5 As a young man marries a maiden,
    so will your sons*c* marry you;
as a bridegroom rejoices over his bride,
    so will your God rejoice*e* over you.

62:6
f Isa 52:8; Eze 3:17

6 I have posted watchmen*f* on your walls, O Jerusalem;
    they will never be silent day or night.

*a*4 *Hephzibah means* my delight is in her.   *b*4 *Beulah means* married.   *c*5 Or *Builder*

---

reading God's Word and seeking to understand it, confessing their sins directly to God, and ministering to others.

61:8 We suffer for many reasons—our own mistakes, someone else's mistakes, injustice. When we suffer for our own mistakes, we get what we deserve. When we suffer because of others or because of injustice, God is angry. God in his mercy says that his people have suffered enough. God will reward those who suffer because of injustice. He will settle all accounts.

61:10 "Me" could refer to the Messiah, the person anointed with the Spirit of the Lord (61:1), or to Zion (62:1), which symbolizes God's people. The imagery of the bridegroom is often used in

Scripture to depict the Messiah (see Matthew 9:15), while the imagery of the bride is used to depict God's people (see Revelation 19:6–8). We too can put on our new clothes—right relationship with God—by putting our trust in Christ (2 Corinthians 5:21).

62:1–7 Many commentators believe Isaiah is speaking in verse 1. If so, Isaiah's zeal for his people and his desire to see the work of salvation completed caused him to pray without resting, hoping that Israel would be saved. We should have Isaiah's zeal to see God's will done. This is what we mean when we pray, "Your kingdom come, your will be done on earth as it is in heaven" (Matthew 6:10). It is good to keep praying persistently for others.

You who call on the LORD,
  give yourselves no rest,
7 and give him no rest till he establishes Jerusalem
  and makes her the praise of the earth.

8 The LORD has sworn by his right hand
  and by his mighty arm:
"Never again will I give your grain*g*
  as food for your enemies,
and never again will foreigners drink the new wine
  for which you have toiled;
9 but those who harvest it will eat it
  and praise the LORD,
and those who gather the grapes will drink it
  in the courts of my sanctuary."

62:8
g Dt 28:30-33;
Jer 5:17

10 Pass through, pass through the gates!
  Prepare the way for the people.
Build up, build up the highway!*h*
  Remove the stones.
Raise a banner for the nations.

62:10
h Isa 57:14

11 The LORD has made proclamation
  to the ends of the earth:
"Say to the Daughter of Zion,*i*
  'See, your Savior comes!
See, his reward is with him,
  and his recompense accompanies him.'"*j*
12 They will be called *k* the Holy People,
  the Redeemed of the LORD;
and you will be called Sought After,
  the City No Longer Deserted.

62:11
i Zec 9:9; Mt 21:5
j Isa 40:10

62:12
k ver 4

God's Day of Vengeance and Redemption

63 Who is this coming from Edom,
  from Bozrah,*l* with his garments stained crimson?
Who is this, robed in splendor,
  striding forward in the greatness of his strength?

"It is I, speaking in righteousness,
  mighty to save."

63:1
l Am 1:12

2 Why are your garments red,
  like those of one treading the winepress?

3 "I have trodden the winepress*m* alone;
  from the nations no one was with me.
I trampled them in my anger
  and trod them down in my wrath;
their blood spattered my garments,
  and I stained all my clothing.
4 For the day of vengeance was in my heart,
  and the year of my redemption has come.
5 I looked, but there was no one to help,
  I was appalled that no one gave support;

63:3
m Rev 14:20; 19:15

62:12 The people of Jerusalem (Zion) will have new names—
"the Holy People" and "the Redeemed of the LORD." Believers
today also have new names—Christians. In 1 Peter 2:5, we are
called "a holy priesthood."

63:1–4 Edom was a constant enemy of Israel despite its
common ancestry in Isaac (Genesis 25:23). Edom rejoiced

at any trouble Israel faced. The imagery in this passage is
of a watchman on the wall of Jerusalem, seeing Edom
approaching and fearing that the Edomite king in his crimson
garment is leading an attack. But it turns out to be the Lord,
in bloodstained clothes, who has trampled and destroyed Edom.
Bozrah is a city in Edom. (For other prophecies against Edom,
see Amos 1:11, 12; Obadiah 10, 11; Malachi 1:2–4.)

63:5
n Isa 59:16

so my own arm worked salvation for me,
    and my own wrath sustained me. n

63:6
o Isa 34:3

⁶ I trampled the nations in my anger;
    in my wrath I made them drunk
    and poured their blood o on the ground."

Praise and Prayer

63:7
p Isa 54:8
q Ps 51:1

⁷ I will tell of the kindnesses p of the Lord,
    the deeds for which he is to be praised,
    according to all the Lord has done for us—
yes, the many good things he has done
    for the house of Israel,
    according to his compassion q and many kindnesses.
⁸ He said, "Surely they are my people,
    sons who will not be false to me";
    and so he became their Savior.

63:9
r Dt 7:7-8

⁹ In all their distress he too was distressed,
    and the angel of his presence saved them.
In his love and mercy he redeemed r them;
    he lifted them up and carried them
    all the days of old.

63:10
s Ps 78:40
t Ps 51:11; Ac 7:51;
Eph 4:30

¹⁰ Yet they rebelled s
    and grieved his Holy Spirit. t
So he turned and became their enemy
    and he himself fought against them.

63:11
u Ex 14:22, 30
v Nu 11:17

¹¹ Then his people recalled a the days of old,
    the days of Moses and his people—
where is he who brought them through the sea, u
    with the shepherd of his flock?
Where is he who set
    his Holy Spirit v among them,
¹² who sent his glorious arm of power
    to be at Moses' right hand,
who divided the waters before them,
    to gain for himself everlasting renown,
¹³ who led them through the depths?
Like a horse in open country,
    they did not stumble;

a 11 Or *But may he recall*

THE SPIRIT IN ISAIAH	Reference	Main Teaching
	11:2	The Spirit of the Lord brings wisdom, understanding, knowledge, and the fear of the Lord.
	32:15	The Spirit of the Lord brings abundance.
	34:16	The Spirit of the Lord carries out God's word.
	40:13	The Spirit of the Lord is the Master Counselor.
	42:1	The Messiah, God's Servant, will be given the Spirit.
	44:3–5	Through the Spirit, God's true children will thrive.
	48:16	The Spirit of the Lord sent Isaiah to prophesy.
	61:1	God's servants (Isaiah and then Jesus) were appointed by the Spirit to proclaim the Good News.
	63:10, 11	The Spirit of the Lord was grieved because of God's people.
	63:14	The Spirit of the Lord gives rest.

63:10 Grieving the Holy Spirit is willfully thwarting his leading by disobedience or rebellion. Isaiah mentions the work of the Holy Spirit more than any other Old Testament writer. See the note on Ephesians 4:28–32 for more on grieving the Holy Spirit.

¹⁴ like cattle that go down to the plain,
    they were given rest by the Spirit of the LORD.
This is how you guided your people
    to make for yourself a glorious name.

¹⁵ Look down from heaven^w and see
    from your lofty throne, holy and glorious.
Where are your zeal and your might?
    Your tenderness and compassion^x are withheld from us.
¹⁶ But you are our Father,
    though Abraham does not know us
    or Israel acknowledge us;
you, O LORD, are our Father,
    our Redeemer from of old is your name.
¹⁷ Why, O LORD, do you make us wander from your ways
    and harden our hearts so we do not revere^y you?
Return for the sake of your servants,
    the tribes that are your inheritance.
¹⁸ For a little while your people possessed your holy place,
    but now our enemies have trampled down your sanctuary.^z
¹⁹ We are yours from of old;
    but you have not ruled over them,
    they have not been called by your name.^a

64   Oh, that you would rend the heavens^a and come down,
    that the mountains would tremble before you!
² As when fire sets twigs ablaze
    and causes water to boil,
come down to make your name known to your enemies
    and cause the nations to quake^b before you!
³ For when you did awesome^c things that we did not expect,
    you came down, and the mountains trembled before you.
⁴ Since ancient times no one has heard,
    no ear has perceived,
no eye has seen any God besides you,
    who acts on behalf of those who wait for him.^d
⁵ You come to the help of those who gladly do right,
    who remember your ways.
But when we continued to sin against them,
    you were angry.
    How then can we be saved?
⁶ All of us have become like one who is unclean,
    and all our righteous^e acts are like filthy rags;
we all shrivel up like a leaf,^f
    and like the wind our sins sweep us away.
⁷ No one calls on your name
    or strives to lay hold of you;
for you have hidden your face from us
    and made us waste away because of our sins.

^a 19 Or *We are like those you have never ruled, / like those never called by your name*

63:15
^wDt 26:15;
Ps 80:14
^xJer 31:20;
Hos 11:8

63:17
^yIsa 29:13

63:18
^zPs 74:3-8

64:1
^aPs 144:5

64:2
^bJer 5:22

64:3
^cPs 65:5

64:4
^d1Co 2:9*

64:6
^eIsa 46:12
^fPs 90:5-6

63:15—64:7 On behalf of the faithful remnant, Isaiah asks God for two favors: to show tenderness and compassion to them and to punish their enemies. Before making these requests, Isaiah recited the Lord's past favors, reminding him of his compassion in former days (63:7–14).

64:1-6 God's appearance is so intense that it is like a consuming fire that burns everything in its path. If we are so impure, how can we be saved? Only by God's mercy. The Israelites had experienced God's appearance at Mount Sinai (Exodus 19:16–19). When God met with Moses there was a thunder-

storm, smoke, and an earthquake. If God were to meet us today, his glory would overwhelm us, especially when we look at our "filthy rags" (64:6).

64:6 Sin makes us unclean so that we cannot approach God (6:5; Romans 3:23) any more than a beggar in rotten rags could dine at a king's table. Our best efforts are still infected with sin. Our only hope, therefore, is faith in Jesus Christ, who can cleanse us and bring us into God's presence (read Romans 3).

    This passage can easily be misunderstood. It doesn't mean that God will reject us if we come to him in faith, nor that he

64:8
g Isa 63:16
h Isa 29:16

8 Yet, O LORD, you are our Father.*g*
   We are the clay, you are the potter;*h*
   we are all the work of your hand.
9 Do not be angry beyond measure, O LORD;
   do not remember our sins forever.
   Oh, look upon us, we pray,
   for we are all your people.
10 Your sacred cities have become a desert;
   even Zion is a desert, Jerusalem a desolation.

64:11
i Ps 74:3-7

11 Our holy and glorious temple, *i* where our fathers praised you,
   has been burned with fire,
   and all that we treasured lies in ruins.

64:12
j Isa 42:14

12 After all this, O LORD, will you hold yourself back?*j*
   Will you keep silent and punish us beyond measure?

Judgment and Salvation

65:1
k Ro 10:20*

65 "I revealed myself to those who did not ask for me;
   I was found by those who did not seek me. *k*
   To a nation that did not call on my name,
   I said, 'Here am I, here am I.'

65:2
l Ro 10:21*

2 All day long I have held out my hands
   to an obstinate people,*l*
   who walk in ways not good,
   pursuing their own imaginations—
3 a people who continually provoke me
   to my very face,
   offering sacrifices in gardens
   and burning incense on altars of brick;

65:4
m Lev 11:7

4 who sit among the graves
   and spend their nights keeping secret vigil;
   who eat the flesh of pigs,*m*
   and whose pots hold broth of unclean meat;

65:5
n Mt 9:11;
Lk 18:9-12

5 who say, 'Keep away; don't come near me,
   for I am too sacred*n* for you!'
   Such people are smoke in my nostrils,
   a fire that keeps burning all day.

65:6
o Ps 50:3
p Jer 16:18

6 "See, it stands written before me:
   I will not keep silent*o* but will pay back*p* in full;
   I will pay it back into their laps—

65:7
q Isa 57:7

7 both your sins and the sins of your fathers,"
   says the LORD.
"Because they burned sacrifices on the mountains
   and defied me on the hills,*q*
I will measure into their laps
   the full payment for their former deeds."

despises our efforts to please him. It means that if we come to him demanding acceptance on the basis of our "good" conduct, God will point out that our righteousness is nothing compared to his infinite righteousness. This message is primarily for the unrepentant person, not the true follower of God.

65:1 Israel considered itself to be the only people of God, but the time would come when other nations would seek him. Paul mentions Isaiah's statement in Romans 10:20 and points out that these other nations were the Gentiles. God's people today are those who accept Jesus as Savior and Lord, whether they are Jews or Gentiles. The gospel is for every person. Do not ignore or reject anyone when you share the gospel. You may be surprised at how many are sincerely searching for God.

65:3–5 God said these people directly disobeyed his laws when they worshiped and sacrificed to idols (Exodus 20:1–6), consulted the dead and evil spirits (Leviticus 19:31), and ate forbidden foods (Leviticus 11). But they were so perverse that they still thought they were spiritually superior to others. Jesus called such people hypocrites (Matthew 23:13–36).

65:6 God said he would pay back the people for their sins. Judgment is not our job but God's because he alone is just. Who else knows our hearts and minds? Who else knows what is a completely fair reward or punishment? Leave judgment of others up to God. If he gave *us* what we deserve, he might wipe us out. Instead, pray for his mercy.

8 This is what the LORD says:

> "As when juice is still found in a cluster of grapes
> and men say, 'Don't destroy it,
> there is yet some good in it,'
> so will I do in behalf of my servants;
> I will not destroy them all.

9 I will bring forth descendants from Jacob,
> and from Judah those who will possess my mountains;
> my chosen people will inherit them,
> and there will my servants live.[r]

65:9
[r] Isa 32:18

10 Sharon[s] will become a pasture for flocks,
> and the Valley of Achor a resting place for herds,
> for my people who seek me.

65:10
[s] Isa 35:2

11 "But as for you who forsake[t] the LORD
> and forget my holy mountain,
> who spread a table for Fortune
> and fill bowls of mixed wine for Destiny,

65:11
[t] Dt 29:24-25

12 I will destine you for the sword,
> and you will all bend down for the slaughter;
> for I called but you did not answer,[u]
> I spoke but you did not listen.[v]
> You did evil in my sight
> and chose what displeases me."

65:12
[u] Pr 1:24-25
[v] 2Ch 36:15-16;
Jer 7:13

13 Therefore this is what the Sovereign LORD says:

> "My servants will eat,[w]
> but you will go hungry;
> my servants will drink,
> but you will go thirsty;
> my servants will rejoice,
> but you will be put to shame.

65:13
[w] Isa 1:19

14 My servants will sing
> out of the joy of their hearts,
> but you will cry out[x]
> from anguish of heart
> and wail in brokenness of spirit.

65:14
[x] Mt 8:12

15 You will leave your name
> to my chosen ones as a curse;[y]
> the Sovereign LORD will put you to death,
> but to his servants he will give another name.

65:15
[y] Zec 8:13

16 Whoever invokes a blessing in the land
> will do so by the God of truth;[z]
> he who takes an oath in the land
> will swear by the God of truth.
> For the past troubles will be forgotten
> and hidden from my eyes.

65:16
[z] Ps 31:5

New Heavens and a New Earth

17 "Behold, I will create
> new heavens and a new earth.[a]
> The former things will not be remembered,[b]
> nor will they come to mind.

65:17
[a] 2Pe 3:13
[b] Isa 43:18

65:8, 9 God will always preserve a faithful remnant of his people. No matter how bad the world is, there are always a few who remain loyal to him. Jesus made this point in Matthew 13:36–43.

65:10 Sharon is a plain in the western part of Israel. The Valley of Achor is in the east, near Jericho. The Valley of Achor was also called the Valley of Trouble because Achan was executed

there for hiding the devoted goods of battle (Joshua 7:10–26). Even in this valley there will be peace: the coming restoration will be complete.

65:17–25 In 65:17–19 we have a pictorial description of the new heavens and the new earth. They are eternal, and in them safety, peace, and plenty will be available to all (see also 66:22,

¹⁸ But be glad and rejoice forever
      in what I will create,
   for I will create Jerusalem to be a delight
      and its people a joy.

65:19
ᶜIsa 35:10; 62:5
ᵈRev 7:17

¹⁹ I will rejoiceᶜ over Jerusalem
      and take delight in my people;
   the sound of weeping and of cryingᵈ
      will be heard in it no more.

65:20
ᵉEcc 8:13

²⁰ "Never again will there be in it
      an infant who lives but a few days,
      or an old man who does not live out his years;ᵉ
   he who dies at a hundred
      will be thought a mere youth;
   he who fails to reachᵃ a hundred
      will be considered accursed.
²¹ They will build houses and dwell in them;
      they will plant vineyards and eat their fruit.

65:22
ᶠPs 92:12-14

²² No longer will they build houses and others live in them,
      or plant and others eat.
   For as the days of a tree,ᶠ
      so will be the days of my people;
   my chosen ones will long enjoy
      the works of their hands.

65:23
ᵍIsa 61:9

²³ They will not toil in vain
      or bear children doomed to misfortune;
   for they will be a people blessedᵍ by the Lᴏʀᴅ,
      they and their descendants with them.

65:24
ʰDa 9:20-23

²⁴ Before they call I will answer;
      while they are still speakingʰ I will hear.

65:25
ⁱIsa 11:6
ʲGe 3:14

²⁵ The wolf and the lambⁱ will feed together,
      and the lion will eat straw like the ox,
      but dust will be the serpent'sʲ food.
   They will neither harm nor destroy
      on all my holy mountain,"

                                                                    says the Lᴏʀᴅ.

Judgment and Hope

66:1
ᵏ1Ki 8:27;
Mt 5:34-35

66 This is what the Lᴏʀᴅ says:

   "Heaven is my throne,
      and the earth is my footstool.ᵏ
   Where is the house you will build for me?
      Where will my resting place be?

66:2
ˡAc 7:50*

² Has not my hand made all these things,ˡ
      and so they came into being?"

                                                                    declares the Lᴏʀᴅ.

ᵃ20 Or / the sinner who reaches

23; 2 Peter 3:13; Revelation 21:1). Verses 20–25 may refer to the reign of Christ on earth because sin and death have not yet been finally destroyed.

66:1 Even the beautiful temple in Jerusalem was woefully inadequate for a God who is present everywhere. God cannot be confined to any human structure (see 2 Chronicles 6:18; Acts 7:49, 50). This chapter is a fitting climax to the book. God will lift up the humble, judge all people, destroy the wicked, bring all believers together, and establish the new heavens and the new earth. Let this hope encourage you each day.

66:2, 3 These key verses summarize Isaiah's message. He contrasted two ways of living: that of humble persons who have

a profound reverence for God's messages and their application to life, and that of those who choose their own way. The sacrifices of the arrogant were only external compliance. In their hearts they were murderers, perverts, and idolaters. God shows mercy to the humble, but he curses the proud and self-sufficient (see Luke 1:51–53). Our society urges us to be assertive and to affirm ourselves. Don't let your freedom and right to choose lead you away from God's pathway to eternal life.

"This is the one I esteem:
    he who is humble and contrite in spirit,*m*
    and trembles at my word.
3 But whoever sacrifices a bull*n*
    is like one who kills a man,
and whoever offers a lamb,
    like one who breaks a dog's neck;
whoever makes a grain offering
    is like one who presents pig's blood,
and whoever burns memorial incense,
    like one who worships an idol.
They have chosen their own ways,
    and their souls delight in their abominations;
4 so I also will choose harsh treatment for them
    and will bring upon them what they dread.
For when I called, no one answered,*o*
    when I spoke, no one listened.
They did evil in my sight
    and chose what displeases me."*p*

5 Hear the word of the LORD,
    you who tremble at his word:
"Your brothers who hate you,
    and exclude you because of my name, have said,
'Let the LORD be glorified,
    that we may see your joy!'
Yet they will be put to shame.*q*
6 Hear that uproar from the city,
    hear that noise from the temple!
It is the sound of the LORD
    repaying*r* his enemies all they deserve.

7 "Before she goes into labor,
    she gives birth;
before the pains come upon her,
    she delivers a son.
8 Who has ever heard of such a thing?
    Who has ever seen*s* such things?
Can a country be born in a day
    or a nation be brought forth in a moment?
Yet no sooner is Zion in labor
    than she gives birth to her children.
9 Do I bring to the moment of birth
    and not give delivery?" says the LORD.
"Do I close up the womb
    when I bring to delivery?" says your God.
10 "Rejoice with Jerusalem and be glad for her,
    all you who love*t* her;
rejoice greatly with her,
    all you who mourn over her.
11 For you will nurse*u* and be satisfied
    at her comforting breasts;
you will drink deeply
    and delight in her overflowing abundance."

12 For this is what the LORD says:

"I will extend peace to her like a river,*v*

66:2
m Isa 57:15

66:3
n Isa 1:11

66:4
o Pr 1:24; Jer 7:13
p Isa 65:12

66:5
q Lk 13:17

66:6
r Isa 65:6

66:8
s Isa 64:4

66:10
t Ps 26:8

66:11
u Isa 60:16

66:12
v Isa 48:18
w Isa 60:5
x Isa 60:4

66:7-9 God will not leave his work of national restoration unfinished. In this image of birth, God shows that he will accomplish what he has promised. It is as unstoppable as the birth of a baby. When all the pain is over, the joy begins.

and the wealth[w] of nations like a flooding stream;
you will nurse and be carried[x] on her arm
and dandled on her knees.

66:13
y 2Co 1:4

13 As a mother comforts her child,
so will I comfort[y] you;
and you will be comforted over Jerusalem."

14 When you see this, your heart will rejoice
and you will flourish like grass;
the hand of the LORD will be made known to his servants,
but his fury will be shown to his foes.

15 See, the LORD is coming with fire,
and his chariots are like a whirlwind;
he will bring down his anger with fury,
and his rebuke with flames of fire.

66:16
z Isa 30:30

16 For with fire[z] and with his sword
the LORD will execute judgment upon all men,
and many will be those slain by the LORD.

66:17
a Ps 37:20

17 "Those who consecrate and purify themselves to go into the gardens, following the one in the midst of[a] those who eat the flesh of pigs and rats and other abominable things—they will meet their end[a] together," declares the LORD.

18 "And I, because of their actions and their imaginations, am about to come[b] and gather all nations and tongues, and they will come and see my glory.

66:19
b Eze 27:10

19 "I will set a sign among them, and I will send some of those who survive to the nations—to Tarshish, to the Libyans[c] and Lydians[b] (famous as archers), to Tubal and Greece, and to the distant islands that have not heard of my fame or seen my glory. They will proclaim my glory among the nations. 20And they will bring all your brothers, from all the nations, to my holy mountain in Jerusalem as an offering to the LORD—on horses, in chariots and wagons, and on mules and camels," says the LORD. "They will bring them, as the Israelites bring their grain offerings, to the temple of the LORD in ceremonially clean vessels. 21And I will select some of them also to be priests[c] and Levites," says the LORD.

66:21
c Ex 19:6; Isa 61:6;
1Pe 2:5, 9

66:22
d Isa 65:17;
2Pe 3:13; Rev 21:1

22 "As the new heavens and the new earth[d] that I make will endure before me," declares the LORD, "so will your name and descendants endure. 23From one New Moon to another and from one Sabbath to another, all mankind will come and bow down before me," says the LORD. 24 "And they will go out and look upon the dead bodies of those who rebelled against me; their worm will not die, nor will their fire be quenched,[e] and they will be loathsome to all mankind."

66:24
e Isa 1:31; Mk 9:48*

a 17 Or *gardens behind one of your temples, and* 　 *b* 18 The meaning of the Hebrew for this clause is uncertain.
c 19 Some Septuagint manuscripts *Put* (Libyans); Hebrew *Pul*

66:15–17 This is a vivid picture of the great judgment that will occur at Christ's second coming (2 Thessalonians 1:7–9).

66:19 God's people will go out as missionaries to all parts of the earth—to Tarshish (Spain), to the Libyans in northern Africa, to the Lydians in western Asia Minor, to northeastern Asia Minor (Tubal), and to Greece.

66:22–24 Isaiah brings his book to a close with great drama. For the faithless there is a sobering portrayal of judgment. For

the faithful, there is a glorious picture of rich reward—"so will your name and descendants endure." The contrast is so striking that it would seem that everyone would want to be God's follower. But we are often just as rebellious, foolish, and reluctant to change as the Israelites. We are just as negligent in feeding the hungry, working for justice, obeying God's Word, and taking up his causes. Make sure you are among those who will be richly blessed.

JEREMIAH

Zephaniah
becomes
a prophet
640 B.C.

Jeremiah
becomes
a prophet
627

King
Josiah
killed
in battle
609

Daniel
taken
captive
605

VITAL STATISTICS

PURPOSE:
To urge God's people to turn from their sins and back to God

AUTHOR:
Jeremiah

ORIGINAL AUDIENCE:
Judah (the southern kingdom) and its capital city, Jerusalem

DATE WRITTEN:
During Jeremiah's ministry, approximately 627–586 B.C.

SETTING:
Jeremiah ministered under Judah's last five kings—Josiah, Jehoahaz, Jehoiakim, Jehoiachin, and Zedekiah. The nation was sliding quickly toward destruction and was eventually conquered by Babylon in 586 B.C. (see 2 Kings 21—25). The prophet Zephaniah preceded Jeremiah, and Habakkuk was Jeremiah's contemporary.

KEY VERSE:
"'Your wickedness will punish you; your backsliding will rebuke you. Consider then and realize how evil and bitter it is for you when you forsake the LORD your God and have no awe of me,' declares the Lord, the LORD Almighty" (2:19).

KEY PEOPLE:
Judah's kings (listed above), Baruch, Ebed-Melech, King Nebuchadnezzar, the Recabites

KEY PLACES:
Anathoth, Jerusalem, Ramah, Egypt

SPECIAL FEATURES:
This book is a combination of history, poetry, and biography. Jeremiah often used symbolism to communicate his message.

WHAT is success? Most definitions include references to achieving goals and acquiring wealth, prestige, favor, and power. "Successful" people enjoy the good life—being financially and emotionally secure, being surrounded by admirers, and enjoying the fruits of their labors. They are leaders, opinion makers, and trendsetters. Their example is emulated; their accomplishments are noticed. They know who they are and where they are going, and they stride confidently to meet their goals.

By these standards, Jeremiah was a miserable failure. For 40 years he served as God's spokesman to Judah, but when Jeremiah spoke, nobody listened. Consistently and passionately he urged them to act, but nobody moved. And he certainly did not attain material success. He was poor and underwent severe deprivation to deliver his prophecies. He was thrown into prison (chapter 37) and into a cistern (chapter 38), and he was taken to Egypt against his will (chapter 43). He was rejected by his neighbors (11:19–21), his family (12:6), the false priests and prophets (20:1, 2; 28:1–17), friends (20:10), his audience (26:8), and the kings (36:23). Throughout his life, Jeremiah stood alone, declaring God's messages of doom, announcing the new covenant, and weeping over the fate of his beloved country. In the eyes of the world, Jeremiah was not a success.

But in God's eyes, Jeremiah was one of the most successful people in all of history. Success, as measured by God, involves obedience and faithfulness. Regardless of opposition and personal cost, Jeremiah courageously and faithfully proclaimed the word of God. He was obedient to his calling. Jeremiah's book begins with his call to be a prophet. The next 38 chapters are prophecies about Israel (the nation united) and Judah (the southern kingdom). Chapters 2—20 are general and undated, and chapters 21—39 are particular and dated. The basic theme of Jeremiah's message is simple: "Repent and turn to God, or he will punish." Because the people rejected this warning, Jeremiah then began predicting the destruction of Jerusalem. This terrible event is described in chapter 39. Chapters 40—45 describe events following Jerusalem's fall. The book concludes with prophecies concerning a variety of nations (chapters 46—52).

As you read Jeremiah, feel with him as he agonizes over the message he must deliver, pray with him for those who refuse to respond to the truth, and watch his example of faith and courage. Then commit yourself to being successful in God's eyes.

THE BLUEPRINT

A. GOD'S JUDGMENT ON JUDAH (1:1—45:5)
1. The call of Jeremiah
2. Jeremiah condemns Judah for its sins
3. Jeremiah prophesies destruction
4. Jeremiah accuses Judah's leaders
5. Restoration is promised
6. God's promised judgment arrives

Jeremiah confronts many people with their sins: kings, false prophets, those at the temples, and those at the gates. A lack of response made Jeremiah wonder if he was doing any good at all. He often felt discouraged and sometimes bitter. To bring such gloomy messages to these people was a hard task. We, too, have a responsibility to bring this news to a fallen world: Those who continue in their sinful ways are eternally doomed. Although we may feel discouraged at the lack of response, we must press on to tell others about the consequences of sin and the hope that God offers. Those who tell people only what they want to hear are being unfaithful to God's message.

B. GOD'S JUDGMENT ON THE NATIONS (46:1—52:34)
1. Prophecies about foreign nations
2. The fall of Jerusalem

Jeremiah lived to see many of his prophecies come true—most notably the fall of Jerusalem. The fulfillment of this and other prophecies against the foreign nations came as a result of sin. Those who refuse to confess their sin bring judgment upon themselves.

MEGATHEMES

THEME	EXPLANATION	IMPORTANCE
Sin	King Josiah's reformation failed because the people's repentance was shallow. They continued in their selfishness and worship of idols. All the leaders rejected God's law and will for the people. Jeremiah lists all their sins, predicts God's judgment, and begs for repentance.	Judah's deterioration and disaster came from a callous disregard and disobedience of God. When we ignore sin and refuse to listen to God's warning, we invite disaster. Don't settle for half measures in removing sin.
Punishment	Because of sin, Jerusalem was destroyed, the temple was ruined, and the people were captured and carried off to Babylon. The people were responsible for their destruction and captivity because they refused to listen to God's message.	Unconfessed sin brings God's full punishment. It is useless to blame anyone else for our sin; we are accountable to God before anyone else. We must answer to him for how we live.
God Is Lord of All	God is the righteous Creator. He is accountable to no one but himself. He wisely and lovingly directs all creation to fulfill his plans, and he brings events to pass according to his timetable. He is Lord over all the world.	Because of God's majestic power and love, our only duty is to submit to his authority. By following his plans, not our own, we can have a loving relationship with him and serve him with our whole heart.
New Hearts	Jeremiah predicted that after the destruction of the nation, God would send a new shepherd, the Messiah. He would lead them into a new future, a new covenant, and a new day of hope. He would accomplish this by changing their sinful hearts into hearts of love for God.	God still transforms people by changing their hearts. His love can eliminate the problems created by sin. We can have assurance of a new heart by loving God, trusting Christ to save us, and repenting of our sin.
Faithful Service	Jeremiah served God faithfully for 40 years. During that time the people ignored, rejected, and persecuted him. Jeremiah's preaching was unsuccessful by human standards, yet he did not fail in his task. He remained faithful to God.	People's acceptance or rejection of us is not the measure of our success. God's approval alone should be our standard for service. We must bring God's message to others even when we are rejected. We must do God's work even if it means suffering for it.

A. GOD'S JUDGMENT ON JUDAH (1:1—45:5)

Jeremiah was called by God to be a prophet to Judah (the southern kingdom). He faithfully confronted the leaders and the people with their sin, prophesied both their 70-year captivity in Babylon and their eventual return from exile. After surviving the fall of Jerusalem, Jeremiah was forcefully taken to Egypt. Yet Jeremiah remained faithful in spite of Jerusalem's destruction. Years of obedience had made him strong and courageous. May we be able to stand through difficult times as did Jeremiah.

1. The call of Jeremiah

1 The words of Jeremiah son of Hilkiah, one of the priests at Anathoth[a] in the territory of Benjamin. [2] The word of the LORD came to him in the thirteenth year of the reign of Josiah son of Amon king of Judah, [3] and through the reign of Jehoiakim son of Josiah king of Judah, down to the fifth month of the eleventh year of Zedekiah[b] son of Josiah king of Judah, when the people of Jerusalem went into exile.

The Call of Jeremiah

[4] The word of the LORD came to me, saying,

> [5] "Before I formed you in the womb I knew[a] you,
>   before you were born[c] I set you apart;
>   I appointed you as a prophet to the nations."

[6] "Ah, Sovereign LORD," I said, "I do not know how to speak;[d] I am only a child." [7] But the LORD said to me, "Do not say, 'I am only a child.' You must go to everyone I send you to and say whatever I command you. [8] Do not be afraid[e] of them, for I am with you[f] and will rescue you," declares the LORD.

[9] Then the LORD reached out his hand and touched[g] my mouth and said to me, "Now, I have put my words in your mouth. [10] See, today I appoint you over nations and kingdoms to uproot and tear down, to destroy and overthrow, to build and to plant."[h]

[11] The word of the LORD came to me: "What do you see, Jeremiah?"

"I see the branch of an almond tree," I replied.

[12] The LORD said to me, "You have seen correctly, for I am watching[b] to see that my word is fulfilled."

[13] The word of the LORD came to me again: "What do you see?"

"I see a boiling pot, tilting away from the north," I answered.

[a]5 Or *chose*   [b]12 The Hebrew for *watching* sounds like the Hebrew for *almond tree*.

1:1
[a]Jos 21:18;
1Ch 6:60;
Jer 32:7-9

1:3
[b]Jer 39:2

1:5
[c]Isa 49:1

1:6
[d]Ex 4:10

1:8
[e]Eze 2:6
[f]Jer 15:20

1:9
[g]Isa 6:7

1:10
[h]Jer 18:7-10

1:1, 2 After King Solomon's death, the united kingdom of Israel had split into rival northern and southern kingdoms. The northern kingdom was called Israel; the southern, Judah. Jeremiah was from Anathoth, four miles north of Jerusalem in the southern kingdom. He lived and prophesied during the reigns of the last five kings of Judah. This was a chaotic time politically, morally, and spiritually. As Babylon, Egypt, and Assyria battled for world supremacy, Judah found itself caught in the middle of the triangle. Although Jeremiah prophesied for 40 years, he never saw his people heed his words and turn from their sins.

1:5 God knew you, as he knew Jeremiah, long before you were born or even conceived. He thought about you and planned for you. When you feel discouraged or inadequate, remember that God has always thought of you as valuable and that he has a purpose in mind for you.

1:5 Jeremiah was "appointed" by God "as a prophet to the nations." God has a purpose for each Christian, but some people are appointed by God for specific kinds of work. Samson (Judges 13:3–5), David (1 Samuel 16:12, 13), John the Baptist (Luke 1:13–17), and Paul (Galatians 1:15, 16) were also called to do particular jobs for God. Whatever work you do should be done for the glory of God (Philippians 1:11). If God gives you a specific task, accept it cheerfully and do it with diligence. If God has not given you a specific call or assignment, then seek to fulfill the mission common to all believers—to love, obey, and serve God—until his guidance becomes more clear.

1:6–8 Often people struggle with new challenges because they lack self-confidence, feeling that they have inadequate ability, training, or experience. Jeremiah thought he was "only

a child"—too young and inexperienced to be God's spokesman to the world. But God promised to be with him. We should not allow feelings of inadequacy to keep us from obeying God's call. He will *always* be with us. When you find yourself avoiding something you know you should do, be careful not to use lack of self-confidence as an excuse. If God gives you a job to do, he will provide all you need to do it.

1:8 God promised to "rescue" Jeremiah from trouble, not to keep trouble from coming. God did not insulate him from imprisonment, deportation, or insults. God does not keep us from encountering life's storms, but he will see us through them. In fact, God walks through these storms with us and rescues us.

1:10 God appointed Jeremiah to bring his word to "nations and kingdoms." Jeremiah's work was to warn not only the Jews but all the nations of the world about God's judgment on sin. Don't forget in reading the Old Testament that, while God was consistently working through the people of Judah and Israel, his plan was to communicate to every nation and person. We are included in Jeremiah's message of judgment and hope, and as believers we are to share God's desire to reach the whole world for him.

1:11–14 The vision of the branch from an almond tree revealed the beginning of God's judgment because the almond tree is among the first to blossom in the spring. God saw the sins of Judah and the nations, and he would carry out swift and certain judgment. The boiling pot tilting away from the north and spilling over Judah pictured Babylon delivering God's scalding judgment against Judah's people.

14The Lord said to me, "From the north disaster will be poured out on all who live in the land. **15**I am about to summon all the peoples of the northern kingdoms," declares the Lord.

"Their kings will come and set up their thrones
　in the entrance of the gates of Jerusalem;
they will come against all her surrounding walls
　and against all the towns of Judah.
16 I will pronounce my judgments on my people
　because of their wickedness*i* in forsaking me,*j*
in burning incense to other gods
　and in worshiping what their hands have made.

1:16
*i*Dt 28:20
*j*Jer 17:13

17"Get yourself ready! Stand up and say to them whatever I command you. Do not be terrified*k* by them, or I will terrify you before them. **18**Today I have made you a fortified city, an iron pillar and a bronze wall to stand against the whole land—against the kings of Judah, its officials, its priests and the people of the land. **19**They will fight against you but will not overcome you, for I am with you and will rescue*l* you," declares the Lord.

1:17
*k*Eze 2:6

1:19
*l*ver 8

2. Jeremiah condemns Judah for her sins
Israel Forsakes God

2:2
*m*Eze 16:8-14, 60
*n*Dt 2:7

2 The word of the Lord came to me: **2**"Go and proclaim in the hearing of Jerusalem:

"'I remember the devotion of your youth,*m*
　how as a bride you loved me
and followed me through the desert,*n*
　through a land not sown.
3 Israel was holy to the Lord,*o*
　the firstfruits of his harvest;
all who devoured her were held guilty,*p*
　and disaster overtook them,'"

2:3
*o*Ex 19:6
*p*Jer 50:7

declares the Lord.

JEREMIAH served as a prophet to Judah from 627 B.C. until the exile in 586 B.C.

Climate of the times	Society was deteriorating economically, politically, spiritually. Wars and captivity dominated the world scene. God's word was deemed offensive.
Main message..........	Repentance from sin would postpone Judah's coming judgment at the hands of Babylon.
Importance of message....	Repentance is one of the greatest needs in our immoral world. God's promises to the faithful shine brightly by bringing hope for tomorrow and strength for today.
Contemporary prophets ...	Habakkuk (612–588 B.C.), Zephaniah (640–621 B.C.)

1:14-19 The problems we face may not seem as ominous as Jeremiah's, but they are critical to us and may overwhelm us! God's promise to Jeremiah and to us is that nothing will defeat us completely; he will help us through the most agonizing problems. Face each day with the assurance that God will be with you and see you through.

1:16 The people of Judah sinned greatly by continuing to burn incense to and worship other gods. God had commanded them specifically against this (Exodus 20:3–6) because idolatry places trust in created things rather than the Creator. Although these people belonged to God, they chose to follow false gods. Many "gods" entice us to turn away from God. Material possessions, dreams for the future, approval of others, and vocational goals compete for our total commitment. Striving after these at the expense of our commitment to God puts our heart where Judah's was—and God severely punished them.

2:1—3:5 In this section, the marriage analogy sharply contrasts God's love for his people with their love for other gods and reveals Judah's faithlessness. Jeremiah condemned Judah (he sometimes called Judah "Jerusalem," the name of its capital city) for seeking

security in worthless, changeable things rather than the unchangeable God. We may be tempted to seek security from possessions, people, or our own abilities, but these will fail us. There is no lasting security apart from the eternal God.

2:2 We appreciate a friend who remains true to his or her commitment, and we are disappointed with someone who fails to keep a promise. God was pleased when his people obeyed initially, but he became angry with them when they refused to keep their commitment. Temptations distract us from God. Think about your original commitment to obey God, and ask yourself if you are remaining truly devoted.

2:3 The phrase, "Israel was ... the firstfruits of his harvest" is a comparison with the firstfruits (first part) of the harvest. Both were to be set apart for God (Deuteronomy 26:1–11). That's how God's people had declared their allegiance to him in years gone by. Israel had been as eager to please God as if she were his young bride, a holy, devoted people. This contrasted greatly with the situation in Jeremiah's time.

4 Hear the word of the LORD, O house of Jacob,
    all you clans of the house of Israel.

5 This is what the LORD says:

    "What fault did your fathers find in me,
      that they strayed so far from me?
    They followed worthless idols
      and became worthless*q* themselves.
6 They did not ask, 'Where is the LORD,
    who brought us up out of Egypt
    and led us through the barren wilderness,
      through a land of deserts*r* and rifts,*s*
    a land of drought and darkness,*a*
    a land where no one travels and no one lives?'
7 I brought you into a fertile land
    to eat its fruit and rich produce.*t*
    But you came and defiled my land
    and made my inheritance detestable.
8 The priests did not ask,
    'Where is the LORD?'
    Those who deal with the law did not know me;
      the leaders rebelled against me.
    The prophets prophesied by Baal,*u*
      following worthless idols.

9 "Therefore I bring charges*v* against you again,"
                declares the LORD.

    "And I will bring charges against your children's children.
10 Cross over to the coasts of Kittim*b* and look,
    send to Kedar*c* and observe closely;
    see if there has ever been anything like this:
11 Has a nation ever changed its gods?
    (Yet they are not gods*w* at all.)
    But my people have exchanged their*d* Glory*x*
      for worthless idols.
12 Be appalled at this, O heavens,
    and shudder with great horror,"
                declares the LORD.

13 "My people have committed two sins:
    They have forsaken me,
      the spring of living water,*y*
    and have dug their own cisterns,
      broken cisterns that cannot hold water.

2:5
*q*2Ki 17:15

2:6
*r*Dt 8:15
*s*Dt 32:10

2:7
*t*Nu 13:27

2:8
*u*Jer 23:13

2:9
*v*Eze 20:35-36

2:11
*w*Isa 37:19
*x*Ps 106:20;
Ro 1:23

2:13
*y*Ps 36:9; Jn 4:14

a 6 Or *and the shadow of death*   *b 10* That is, Cyprus and western coastlands   *c 10* The home of Bedouin tribes in the Syro-Arabian desert   *d 11* Masoretic Text; an ancient Hebrew scribal tradition *my*

2:4–8 The united nation of Israel included both the "house of Israel" and the "house of Jacob" (Judah). Jeremiah knew Israel's history well. The prophets recited history to the people for several reasons: (1) to remind them of God's faithfulness; (2) to make sure the people wouldn't forget (they didn't have Bibles to read); (3) to emphasize God's love for them; (4) to remind the people that there was a time when they *were* close to God. We should learn from history so we can build on the successes and avoid repeating the failures of others.

2:8 Baal was the chief male god of the Canaanite religion. Baal was the god of fertility. Worship of Baal included animal sacrifice and sacred prostitution (male and female) in the high places. Jezebel, the wife of King Ahab, introduced Baal worship into the northern kingdom, and eventually it spread to Judah. The sexual orientation of this worship was a constant temptation to the Israelites, who were called to be holy.

2:10 God was saying that even pagan nations like Kittim (Cyprus, in the west) and Kedar (the home of Arab tribes living in the desert east of Palestine) remained loyal to their national gods. But Israel had abandoned the one and only God for a completely worthless object of worship.

2:13 Who would set aside a sparkling spring of water for a cistern, a pit that collected rainwater? God told the Israelites they were doing that very thing when they turned from him, the spring of living water, to the worship of idols. Not only that, but the cisterns they chose were broken and empty. The people had built religious systems in which to store truth, but those systems were worthless. Why should we cling to the broken promises of unstable "cisterns" (money, power, religious systems, or whatever transitory thing we are putting in place of God) when God promises to constantly refresh us with himself, the living water (John 4:10)?

2:15
z Jer 4:7

2:17
a Jer 4:18

14 Is Israel a servant, a slave by birth?
   Why then has he become plunder?
15 Lions^z have roared;
   they have growled at him.
They have laid waste his land;
   his towns are burned and deserted.
16 Also, the men of Memphis^a and Tahpanhes
   have shaved the crown of your head.^b
17 Have you not brought this on yourselves^a
   by forsaking the LORD your God
   when he led you in the way?

a 16 Hebrew *Noph*   b 16 Or *have cracked your skull*

JEREMIAH

Endurance is not a common quality. Many people lack the long-term commitment, caring, and willingness that are vital to sticking with a task against all odds. But Jeremiah was a prophet who endured.

Jeremiah's call by God teaches how intimately God knows us. He valued us before anyone else knew we would exist. He cared for us while we were in our mother's womb. He planned our lives while our bodies were still being formed. He values us more highly than we value ourselves.

Jeremiah had to depend on God's love as he developed endurance. His audiences were usually antagonistic or apathetic to his messages. He was ignored; his life was often threatened. He saw both the excitement of a spiritual awakening and the sorrow of a national return to idolatry. With the exception of the good King Josiah, Jeremiah watched king after king ignore his warnings and lead the people away from God. He saw fellow prophets murdered. He himself was severely persecuted. Finally, he watched Judah's defeat at the hands of the Babylonians.

Jeremiah responded to all this with God's message and human tears. He felt firsthand God's love for his people and the people's rejection of that love. But even when he was angry with God and tempted to give up, Jeremiah knew he had to keep going. God had called him to endure. He expressed intense feelings, but he also saw beyond the feelings to the God who was soon to execute justice, but who afterward would administer mercy.

It may be easy for us to identify with Jeremiah's frustrations and discouragement, but we need to realize that this prophet's life is also an encouragement to faithfulness.

Strengths and accomplishments:	• Wrote two Old Testament books, Jeremiah and Lamentations • Ministered during the reigns of the last five kings of Judah • Was a catalyst for the great spiritual reformation under King Josiah • Acted as God's faithful messenger in spite of many attempts on his life • Was so deeply sorrowful for the fallen condition of Judah that he earned the title "weeping prophet"
Lessons from his life:	• The majority opinion is not necessarily God's will • Although punishment for sin is severe, there is hope in God's mercy • God will not accept empty or insincere worship • Serving God does not guarantee earthly security
Vital statistics:	• Where: Anathoth • Occupation: Prophet • Relative: Father: Hilkiah • Contemporaries: Josiah, Jehoahaz, Jehoiakim, Jehoiachin, Zedekiah, Baruch
Key verses:	"'Ah, Sovereign LORD,' I said, 'I do not know how to speak; I am only a child.' But the LORD said to me, 'Do not say, "I am only a child." You must go to everyone I send you to and say whatever I command you. Do not be afraid of them, for I am with you and will rescue you,' declares the LORD" (Jeremiah 1:6–8).

Jeremiah's story is told in the book of Jeremiah. He is also mentioned in Ezra 1:1; Daniel 9:2; Matthew 2:17; 16:14; 27:9. See also 2 Chronicles 34, 35 for the story of the spiritual revival under Josiah.

2:16, 17 Memphis was near modern Cairo's present location in lower Egypt, and Tahpanhes was in northeastern Egypt. Jeremiah could be speaking of Pharaoh Shishak's previous invasion of Judah in 926 B.C. (1 Kings 14:25), or he may have been predicting Pharaoh Neco's invasion in 609 B.C. when King Josiah of Judah would be killed (2 Kings 23:29, 30). Jeremiah's point is that the people brought this on themselves by rebelling against God.

18 Now why go to Egypt[b]
    to drink water from the Shihor[a]?[c]
And why go to Assyria
    to drink water from the River[b]?
19 Your wickedness will punish you;
    your backsliding will rebuke you.
Consider then and realize
    how evil and bitter it is for you
when you forsake the Lord your God
    and have no awe of me,"

           declares the Lord, the Lord Almighty.

20 "Long ago you broke off your yoke
    and tore off your bonds;
    you said, 'I will not serve you!'
Indeed, on every high hill
    and under every spreading tree[d]
    you lay down as a prostitute.
21 I had planted[e] you like a choice vine
    of sound and reliable stock.
How then did you turn against me
    into a corrupt,[f] wild vine?
22 Although you wash yourself with soda
    and use an abundance of soap,
    the stain of your guilt is still before me,"

           declares the Sovereign Lord.

23 "How can you say, 'I am not defiled;[g]
    I have not run after the Baals'?
See how you behaved in the valley;[h]
    consider what you have done.
You are a swift she-camel
    running here and there,
24 a wild donkey[i] accustomed to the desert,
    sniffing the wind in her craving—
    in her heat who can restrain her?
Any males that pursue her need not tire themselves;
    at mating time they will find her.
25 Do not run until your feet are bare
    and your throat is dry.
But you said, 'It's no use!
    I love foreign gods,
    and I must go after them.'

26 "As a thief is disgraced[j] when he is caught,
    so the house of Israel is disgraced—
they, their kings and their officials,
    their priests and their prophets.
27 They say to wood, 'You are my father,'
    and to stone, 'You gave me birth.'
They have turned their backs to me
    and not their faces;

a 18 That is, a branch of the Nile   b 18 That is, the Euphrates

2:18
b Isa 30:2
c Jos 13:3

2:20
d Dt 12:2

2:21
e Ex 15:17
f Isa 5:4

2:23
g Pr 30:12
h Jer 7:31

2:24
i Jer 14:6

2:26
j Jer 48:27

2:22 The stain of sin is more than skin-deep. Israel had stains that could not be washed out, even with the strongest cleansers. Spiritual cleansing must reach deep into the heart—and this is a job that God alone can do. We cannot ignore the effects of sin and hope they will go away. Your sin has caused a deep stain that God can and will remove if you are willing to let him cleanse you (Isaiah 1:18; Ezekiel 36:25).

2:23-27 The people are compared to animals who search for mates in mating season. Unrestrained, they rush for power, money, alliances with foreign powers, and other gods. The idols did not seek the people; the people sought the idols and then ran wildly after them. Then they became so comfortable in their sin that they could not think of giving it up. Their only shame was in getting caught. If we desire something so much that we'll do anything to get it, this is a sign that we are addicted to it and out of tune with God.

2:27
k Isa 26:16

    yet when they are in trouble,k they say,
      'Come and save us!'

2:28
l Isa 45:20
m Jer 11:13

28 Where then are the godsl you made for yourselves?
    Let them come if they can save you
      when you are in trouble!
    For you have as many gods
      as you have towns,m O Judah.

29 "Why do you bring charges against me?
    You have all rebelled against me,"

                                           declares the LORD.

2:30
n Ac 7:52

30 "In vain I punished your people;
    they did not respond to correction.
    Your sword has devoured your prophetsn
      like a ravening lion.

2:31
o Isa 45:19

31 "You of this generation, consider the word of the LORD:

    "Have I been a desert to Israel
      or a land of great darkness?o
    Why do my people say, 'We are free to roam;
      we will come to you no more'?
32 Does a maiden forget her jewelry,
      a bride her wedding ornaments?
    Yet my people have forgotten me,
      days without number.
33 How skilled you are at pursuing love!
      Even the worst of women can learn from your ways.

2:34
p Ex 22:2

34 On your clothes men find
      the lifeblood of the innocent poor,
    though you did not catch them breaking in.p
    Yet in spite of all this
35   you say, 'I am innocent;
      he is not angry with me.'
    But I will pass judgment on you
      because you say, 'I have not sinned.'

THE KINGS OF JEREMIAH'S LIFETIME	King	Story of his reign	Dates of his reign	Character of reign	Jeremiah's message to the king
	Josiah	2 Kings 22:1—23:30	640–609 B.C.	Mostly good	3:6–25
	Jehoahaz	2 Kings 23:31–33	609 B.C.	Evil	22:11–17
	Jehoiakim	2 Kings 23:34—24:7	609–598 B.C.	Evil	22:18–23; 25:1–38; 26:1–24; 27:1–11; 35:1–19; 36:1–32
	Jehoiachin	2 Kings 24:8–17	598–597 B.C.	Evil	13:18–27; 22:24–30
	Zedekiah	2 Kings 24:18—25:26	597–586 B.C.	Evil	21:1–14; 24:8–10; 27:12–22; 32:1–5; 34:1–22; 37:1–21; 38:1–28; 51:59–64

2:30 Being a prophet in Jeremiah's day was risky business. Prophets had to criticize the policies of evil kings, and this made them appear to be traitors. The kings hated the prophets for standing against their policies, and the people often hated the prophets for preaching against their idolatrous lifestyles (see Acts 7:52).

2:31, 32 Forgetting can be dangerous, whether it is intentional or an oversight. Israel deliberately ignored God by focusing its affections on the allurements of the world. The more we focus

on the passing pleasures of this life, the easier it becomes to forget God's care, his love, his dependability, his guidance, and most of all, God himself. What pleases you most? Have you been forgetting God lately?

36 Why do you go about so much,
　　changing your ways?
　You will be disappointed by Egypt^q
　　as you were by Assyria.
37 You will also leave that place
　　with your hands on your head,^r
　for the LORD has rejected those you trust;
　　you will not be helped by them.

2:36
q Isa 30:2, 3, 7

2:37
r 2Sa 13:19

3 "If a man divorces^s his wife
　　and she leaves him and marries another man,
　should he return to her again?
　　Would not the land be completely defiled?
　But you have lived as a prostitute with many lovers^t—
　　would you now return to me?"

declares the LORD.

3:1
s Dt 24:1-4
t Jer 2:20, 25;
Eze 16:26, 29

2 "Look up to the barren heights and see.
　　Is there any place where you have not been ravished?
　By the roadside you sat waiting for lovers,
　　sat like a nomad^a in the desert.
　You have defiled the land^u
　　with your prostitution and wickedness.
3 Therefore the showers have been withheld,^v
　　and no spring rains have fallen.
　Yet you have the brazen look of a prostitute;
　　you refuse to blush with shame.^w
4 Have you not just called to me:
　　'My Father, my friend from my youth,
5 will you always be angry?^x
　　Will your wrath continue forever?'
　This is how you talk,
　　but you do all the evil you can."

3:2
u Jer 2:7

3:3
v Lev 26:19
w Jer 6:15

3:5
x Ps 103:9;
Isa 57:16

Unfaithful Israel

6 During the reign of King Josiah, the LORD said to me, "Have you seen what faithless Israel has done? She has gone up on every high hill and under every spreading tree and has committed adultery there. 7 I thought that after she had done all this she would return to me but she did not, and her unfaithful sister^y Judah saw it. 8 I gave faithless Israel her certificate of divorce and sent her away because of all her adulteries. Yet I saw that her unfaithful sister Judah had no fear;^z she also went out and committed adultery. 9 Because Israel's immorality mattered so little to her, she defiled the land and committed adultery with stone and wood.^a 10 In spite of all this, her unfaithful sister Judah did not return to me with all her heart, but only in pretense," declares the LORD.

3:7
y Eze 16:46

3:8
z Eze 23:11

3:9
a Jer 2:27

a 2 Or an Arab

2:36 God is not against alliances or working partnerships, but he is against people trusting others for the help that should come from him. This was the problem in Jeremiah's time. After the days of David and Solomon, Israel fell apart because the leaders turned to other nations and gods instead of the true God. They played power politics, thinking that their strong neighbors could protect them. But Judah would soon learn that its alliance with Egypt would be just as disappointing as its former alliance with Assyria (2 Kings 16:8, 9; Isaiah 7:13–25).

3:1 This law, found in Deuteronomy 24:1–4, says that a divorced woman who remarries can never be reunited with her first husband. Judah "divorced" God and "married" other gods. God had every right to permanently disown his wayward people, but in his mercy he was willing to take them back again.

3:2 "Like a nomad in the desert" means that Judah anticipated idolatry as a thief might hide in the wilderness to plunder a passing caravan.

3:4, 5 In spite of their great sin, the people of Israel continued to talk like they were God's children. The only way they could do this was to minimize their sin. When we know we've done something wrong, we want to downplay the error and relieve some of the guilt we feel. As we minimize our sinfulness, we naturally shy away from making changes, and so we keep on sinning. But if we view every wrong attitude and action as a serious offense against God, we will begin to understand what living for God is all about. Is there any sin in your life that you've written off as too small to worry about? God says that we must confess and turn away from *every* sin.

3:6—6:30 The northern kingdom, Israel, had fallen to Assyria, and its people had been taken into captivity. The tragic lesson of their fall should have caused the southern kingdom, Judah, to return to God, but Judah paid no attention. Jeremiah urged Judah to return to God to avoid certain disaster. This message came between 627 and 621 B.C., during Josiah's reign.

3:11
b Eze 16:52
3:12
c Ps 86:15

¹¹The Lord said to me, "Faithless Israel is more righteous *b* than unfaithful Judah. ¹²Go, proclaim this message toward the north:

> "'Return, faithless Israel,' declares the Lord,
>   'I will frown on you no longer,
> for I am merciful,' declares the Lord,
>   'I will not be angry *c* forever.

3:13
d Dt 30:1-3
e Jer 2:25
f Dt 12:2

> ¹³ Only acknowledge *d* your guilt—
>   you have rebelled against the Lord your God,
> you have scattered your favors to foreign gods *e*
>   under every spreading tree, *f*
>   and have not obeyed me,'"
>
>   declares the Lord.

3:14
g Hos 2:19
3:15
h Ac 20:28
3:16
i Isa 65:17

¹⁴"Return, *g* faithless people," declares the Lord, "for I am your husband. I will choose you—one from a town and two from a clan—and bring you to Zion. ¹⁵Then I will give you shepherds *h* after my own heart, who will lead you with knowledge and understanding. ¹⁶In those days, when your numbers have increased greatly in the land," declares the Lord, "men will no longer say, 'The ark of the covenant of the Lord.' It will never enter their minds or be remembered; *i* it will not be missed, nor will another one be made. ¹⁷At that time they will

3:17
j Isa 60:9
k Jer 11:8
3:18
l Hos 1:11
m Isa 11:13
n Jer 31:8
o Am 9:15

call Jerusalem The Throne of the Lord, and all nations will gather in Jerusalem to honor *j* the name of the Lord. No longer will they follow the stubbornness of their evil hearts. *k* ¹⁸In those days the house of Judah will join the house of Israel, *l* and together *m* they will come from a northern *n* land to the land *o* I gave your forefathers as an inheritance.

¹⁹"I myself said,

3:19
p Isa 63:16

> "'How gladly would I treat you like sons
>   and give you a desirable land,
>   the most beautiful inheritance of any nation.'
> I thought you would call me 'Father' *p*
>   and not turn away from following me.
> ²⁰ But like a woman unfaithful to her husband,
>   so you have been unfaithful to me, O house of Israel,"
>
>   declares the Lord.
>
> ²¹ A cry is heard on the barren heights,
>   the weeping and pleading of the people of Israel,
> because they have perverted their ways
>   and have forgotten the Lord their God.

Although Josiah obeyed God's commands, his example apparently did not penetrate the hearts of the people. If the people refused to repent, God said he would destroy the nation because of the evils of Josiah's grandfather, King Manasseh (2 Kings 23:25–27).

3:11–13 Israel was not even trying to look as if it were obeying God, but Judah maintained the appearance of right faith without a true heart. Believing the right doctrines without heartfelt commitment is like offering sacrifices without true repentance. Judah's false repentance brought Jeremiah's words of condemnation. To live without faith is hopeless; to express sorrow without change is treacherous and unfaithful. Being sorry for sin is not enough. Repentance demands a change of mind and heart that results in changed behavior.

3:12–18 The northern kingdom, Israel, was in captivity, being punished for its sins. The people of Judah undoubtedly looked down on these northern neighbors for their blatant heresy and degraded morals. Even so, Jeremiah promised the remnant of Israel God's blessings if they would turn to him. Judah, still secure in its own mind, should have turned to God after seeing the destruction of Israel. But the people of Judah refused, so Jeremiah startled them by reaffirming God's promise to Israel's remnant if they would repent.

3:15 God promised to give his people leaders ("shepherds"

after his own heart) who would follow him, filled with knowledge (wisdom) and understanding. God saw Israel's lack of direction, so he promised to provide the right kind of leadership. We look to and trust our leaders for guidance and direction. But if they do not follow God, they will lead us astray. Pray for God-honoring leaders in our nations, communities, and churches—those who will be good examples and bring us God's wisdom.

3:16, 17 In the days of Solomon's reign over a united Israel, the people had a beautiful temple where they worshiped God. The temple housed the ark of the covenant, the symbol of God's presence with the people. The ark held the tablets of the Ten Commandments (see Exodus 25:10–22). Those days with the ark wouldn't be missed in the future kingdom because God's presence by the Holy Spirit would be there personally among his people.

22 "Return,*q* faithless people;
　　I will cure*r* you of backsliding."

"Yes, we will come to you,
　　for you are the LORD our God.
23 Surely the ⌊idolatrous⌋ commotion on the hills
　　and mountains is a deception;
surely in the LORD our God
　　is the salvation*s* of Israel.
24 From our youth shameful gods have consumed
　　the fruits of our fathers' labor—
their flocks and herds,
　　their sons and daughters.
25 Let us lie down in our shame,*t*
　　and let our disgrace cover us.
We have sinned against the LORD our God,
　　both we and our fathers;
from our youth*u* till this day
　　we have not obeyed the LORD our God."

4 "If you will return*v*, O Israel,
　　return to me,"
　　　　　　　　　　　　　　　　　　declares the LORD.

"If you put your detestable idols out of my sight
　　and no longer go astray,
2 and if in a truthful, just and righteous way
　　you swear,*w* 'As surely as the LORD lives,'
then the nations will be blessed*x* by him
　　and in him they will glory."

3 This is what the LORD says to the men of Judah and to Jerusalem:

"Break up your unplowed ground*y*
　　and do not sow among thorns.*z*
4 Circumcise yourselves to the LORD,
　　circumcise your hearts,*a*
you men of Judah and people of Jerusalem,
　　or my wrath will break out and burn like fire
because of the evil you have done—
　　burn with no one to quench it.

Disaster From the North

5 "Announce in Judah and proclaim in Jerusalem and say:
　　'Sound the trumpet throughout the land!'
Cry aloud and say:
　　'Gather together!
　　Let us flee to the fortified cities!'*b*

3:22
q Hos 14:4
r Hos 6:1

3:23
s Ps 3:8

3:25
t Ezr 9:6
u Jer 22:21

4:1
v Jer 3:1, 22;
Joel 2:12

4:2
w Dt 10:20;
Isa 65:16
x Ge 22:18; Gal 3:8

4:3
y Hos 10:12
z Mk 4:18

4:4
a Dt 10:16; Jer 9:26

4:5
b Jer 8:14

3:22–25 Jeremiah predicted a day when the nation would be reunited, true worship would be reinstated, and sin would be seen for what it is. Our world glorifies the thrill that comes from wealth, competition, and sexual pleasure, and it ignores the sin that is so often associated with these thrills. It is sad that so few see sin as it really is—a deception. Most people can't see this until they are destroyed by the sin they pursue. The advantage of believing God's Word is that we don't have to learn by hard experience the destructive results of sin.

4:1, 2 Throughout the Old Testament, God consistently revealed his intentions to bless the nations of the world. His global vision included a central role for the people of Israel as the channel through which God would pour out his blessings on all nations.

But their privilege as the chosen people was in jeopardy as long as they insisted on disobedience and idolatry.

4:3 Jeremiah told the people to break up the hardness of their hearts as a plow breaks up unplowed ground—soil that has not been tilled for a season. Good kings like Josiah had tried to turn the people back to God, but the people had continued to worship their idols in secret. Their hearts had become hardened to God's will. Unless their hearts were broken and cleaned up, the good seed of God's commands could not take root. Old habits and hidden sins had to be uprooted and rejected. Likewise we must remove our heart-hardening sin if we expect God's Word to take root and grow in our life.

4:6, 7 The disaster from the north would come from Babylon when Nabopolassar and Nebuchadnezzar II attacked (see 2 Chronicles 36).

4:6
c Jer 1:13-15

6 Raise the signal to go to Zion!
  Flee for safety without delay!
For I am bringing disaster from the north,c
  even terrible destruction."

4:7
d Isa 1:7
e Jer 25:9

7 A lion has come out of his lair;
  a destroyer of nations has set out.
He has left his place
  to lay wasted your land.
Your towns will lie in ruinse
  without inhabitant.

4:8
f Isa 22:12

8 So put on sackcloth,f
  lament and wail,
for the fierce anger of the Lord
  has not turned away from us.

9 "In that day," declares the Lord,
  "the king and the officials will lose heart,
the priests will be horrified,
  and the prophets will be appalled."

4:10
g 2Th 2:11
h Jer 14:13

10 Then I said, "Ah, Sovereign Lord, how completely you have deceivedg this people and
Jerusalem by saying, 'You will have peace,'h when the sword is at our throats."

4:11
i Eze 17:10

11 At that time this people and Jerusalem will be told, "A scorching windi from the barren
heights in the desert blows toward my people, but not to winnow or cleanse; 12a wind too
strong for that comes from me.a Now I pronounce my judgments against them."

4:13
j Isa 5:28

13 Look! He advances like the clouds,
  his chariots come like a whirlwind,j
his horses are swifter than eagles.
  Woe to us! We are ruined!

4:14
k Jas 4:8

14 O Jerusalem, washk the evil from your heart and be saved.
  How long will you harbor wicked thoughts?
15 A voice is announcing from Dan,
  proclaiming disaster from the hills of Ephraim.
16 "Tell this to the nations,
  proclaim it to Jerusalem:
'A besieging army is coming from a distant land,
  raising a war cry against the cities of Judah.

4:17
l 2Ki 25:1, 4

17 They surroundl her like men guarding a field,
  because she has rebelled against me,'"

                                                          declares the Lord.

4:18
m Ps 107:17;
Isa 50:1
n Jer 2:17
o Jer 2:19

18 "Your own conduct and actionsm
  have brought this upon you.n
This is your punishment.
  How bittero it is!
  How it pierces to the heart!"

19 Oh, my anguish, my anguish!
  I writhe in pain.

a 12 Or *comes at my command*

4:10 Jeremiah, deeply moved by God's words, expressed his
sorrow and confusion to God. Jeremiah was intercessor for the
people. These people had false expectations because of the past
promises of blessings, their blindness to their own sin, and the
false prophets who kept telling them that all was well.

4:15 Disaster was announced first from Dan and then on to the
hills of Ephraim because Dan was located at the northern border
of Israel. Thus the Danites would be the first to see the approaching armies as they invaded from the north. No one would be able
to stop the armies because they would be coming as punishment
for the people's sin.

4:19-31 Jeremiah was anguished by the sure devastation of the
coming judgment. This judgment would continue until the people
turned from their sin and listened to God. Although this prophecy
refers to the future destruction by Babylon, it could also describe
the judgment of all sinners at the end of the world. These verses
also speak to those in an age of terrorism about overwhelming
feelings of dread and the importance of recognizing God's ultimate control over the events of history.

Oh, the agony of my heart!
    My heart pounds within me,
    I cannot keep silent.
For I have heard the sound of the trumpet;
    I have heard the battle cry.
20 Disaster follows disaster;
    the whole land lies in ruins.
In an instant my tents^p are destroyed,
    my shelter in a moment.
21 How long must I see the battle standard
    and hear the sound of the trumpet?

22 "My people are fools;
    they do not know me.
They are senseless children;
    they have no understanding.
They are skilled in doing evil;
    they know not how to do good."

23 I looked at the earth,
    and it was formless and empty;^q
and at the heavens,
    and their light was gone.
24 I looked at the mountains,
    and they were quaking;
    all the hills were swaying.
25 I looked, and there were no people;
    every bird in the sky had flown away.^r
26 I looked, and the fruitful land was a desert;
    all its towns lay in ruins
    before the LORD, before his fierce anger.

27 This is what the LORD says:

    "The whole land will be ruined,
    though I will not destroy^s it completely.
28 Therefore the earth will mourn^t
    and the heavens above grow dark,
because I have spoken and will not relent,^u
    I have decided and will not turn back."

29 At the sound of horsemen and archers
    every town takes to flight.
Some go into the thickets;
    some climb up among the rocks.
All the towns are deserted;
    no one lives in them.

30 What are you doing, O devastated one?
    Why dress yourself in scarlet
    and put on jewels of gold?
Why shade your eyes with paint?^v
    You adorn yourself in vain.
Your lovers despise you;
    they seek your life.

4:20
p Jer 10:20

4:23
q Ge 1:2

4:25
r Zep 1:3

4:27
s Jer 5:10, 18;
30:11; 46:28

4:28
t Hos 4:3
u Nu 23:19

4:30
v 2Ki 9:30

4:22 Judah was skilled in doing evil and did not know how to do good. Right living is more than simply avoiding sin. It requires decision and discipline. We must develop skills in right living because our behavior attracts attention to our God. We should pursue excellence in Christian living with as much effort as we pursue excellence at work.

4:27 God warned that destruction was certain, but he promised that the faithful remnant would be spared. God is committed to preserving those who are faithful to him.

4:31
w Isa 1:15; La 1:17

31 I hear a cry as of a woman in labor,
   a groan as of one bearing her first child—
the cry of the Daughter of Zion gasping for breath,
   stretching out her hands w and saying,
"Alas! I am fainting;
   my life is given over to murderers."

Not One Is Upright

5:1
x Eze 22:30
y Ge 18:32

5

"Go up and down x the streets of Jerusalem,
   look around and consider,
   search through her squares.
If you can find but one person y
   who deals honestly and seeks the truth,
   I will forgive this city.

5:2
z Jer 4:2

2 Although they say, 'As surely as the LORD lives,' z
   still they are swearing falsely."

5:3
a Isa 9:13

3 O LORD, do not your eyes look for truth?
   You struck a them, but they felt no pain;
   you crushed them, but they refused correction.
They made their faces harder than stone
   and refused to repent.
4 I thought, "These are only the poor;
   they are foolish,
for they do not know the way of the LORD,
   the requirements of their God.

5:5
b Mic 3:1, 9

5 So I will go to the leaders b
   and speak to them;
surely they know the way of the LORD,
   the requirements of their God."
But with one accord they too had broken off the yoke
   and torn off the bonds.

5:6
c Hos 13:7

6 Therefore a lion from the forest will attack them,
   a wolf from the desert will ravage them,
a leopard c will lie in wait near their towns
   to tear to pieces any who venture out,
for their rebellion is great
   and their backslidings many.

5:7
d Jos 23:7
e Dt 32:21; Gal 4:8

7 "Why should I forgive you?
   Your children have forsaken me
   and sworn d by gods that are not gods. e
I supplied all their needs,
   yet they committed adultery
   and thronged to the houses of prostitutes.

5:8
f Eze 22:11

8 They are well-fed, lusty stallions,
   each neighing for another man's wife. f

5:1 Jerusalem was the capital city and center of worship for Judah, but God challenged anyone to find *one* honest and truthful person in the entire city. God was willing to spare the city if one upright person could be found (he made a similar statement about Sodom; see Genesis 18:32). Think how significant your testimony may be in your city or community. You may represent the only witness for God to many people. Are you faithful to that opportunity?

5:3 Nothing but truth is acceptable to God. When we pray, sing, speak, or serve, nothing closes the door of God's acceptance more than hypocrisy, lying, or pretense. God sees through us and refuses to listen. To be close to God, be honest with him.

5:4, 5 Even the leaders who knew God's laws and understood his words of judgment had rejected him. They were supposed to

teach and guide the people, but instead they led them into sin. Jeremiah observed the poor and foolish (ignorant)—those who were uninformed of God's ways—and realized they were not learning God's laws from their leaders. Thus God's search in Jerusalem was complete. There were no true followers in any level of society.

5:7 God held these people responsible for the sins of their children because the children had followed their parents' example. The sin of leading others, especially our children, astray by our example is one for which God will hold us accountable.

9 Should I not punish them for this?"*g*
    declares the LORD.
  "Should I not avenge myself
    on such a nation as this?

10 "Go through her vineyards and ravage them,
    but do not destroy them completely.
  Strip off her branches,
    for these people do not belong to the LORD.
11 The house of Israel and the house of Judah
    have been utterly unfaithful*h* to me,"

declares the LORD.

12 They have lied about the LORD;
    they said, "He will do nothing!
  No harm will come to us;
    we will never see sword or famine.*i*
13 The prophets are but wind
    and the word is not in them;
    so let what they say be done to them."

14 Therefore this is what the LORD God Almighty says:

  "Because the people have spoken these words,
    I will make my words in your mouth*j* a fire
    and these people the wood it consumes.
15 O house of Israel," declares the LORD,
    "I am bringing a distant nation*k* against you—
  an ancient and enduring nation,
    a people whose language you do not know,
    whose speech you do not understand.
16 Their quivers are like an open grave;
    all of them are mighty warriors.
17 They will devour*l* your harvests and food,
    devour*m* your sons and daughters;
  they will devour*n* your flocks and herds,
    devour your vines and fig trees.
  With the sword they will destroy
    the fortified cities in which you trust.

18 "Yet even in those days," declares the LORD, "I will not destroy you completely. 19 And when the people ask,*o* 'Why has the LORD our God done all this to us?' you will tell them, 'As you have forsaken me and served foreign gods in your own land, so now you will serve foreigners*p* in a land not your own.'

20 "Announce this to the house of Jacob
    and proclaim it in Judah:
21 Hear this, you foolish and senseless people,
    who have eyes*q* but do not see,
    who have ears but do not hear:*r*
22 Should you not fear me?" declares the LORD.
    "Should you not tremble in my presence?

5:9	*g* Jer 9:9
5:11	*h* Jer 3:20
5:12	*i* Jer 14:13
5:14	*j* Jer 1:9
5:15	*k* Dt 28:49; Isa 5:26; Jer 4:16
5:17	*l* Lev 26:16 *m* Dt 28:32 *n* Dt 28:31
5:19	*o* Dt 29:24-26; 1Ki 9:9 *p* Dt 28:48
5:21	*q* Isa 6:10; Eze 12:2 *r* Mt 13:15

5:15 Babylon was indeed an ancient nation. The old Babylonian empire had lasted from about 1900 B.C. to 1550 B.C., and earlier kingdoms had been on her soil as early as 3000 B.C. Babylon in Jeremiah's day would shortly rebel against Assyrian domination, form its own army, conquer Assyria, and become the next dominant world power.

5:21 Have you spoken to someone, only to realize that the person hasn't heard a word you were saying? Jeremiah told the people that their eyes and ears did them no good because they refused to see or hear God's message. The people of Judah and Israel were foolishly deaf when God promised blessings for obedience and destruction for disobedience. When God speaks through his Word or his messengers, we harm ourselves if we fail to listen. God's message will never change us unless we listen to it.

5:22–24 What is your attitude when you come into God's presence? We should come with fear and trembling (that is, awe and respect) because God sets the boundaries of the roaring ocean and establishes the rains and harvests. God had to strip away all the benefits that Judah and Israel had grown to expect from him and give the people another opportunity to turn back to him. God

I made the sand a boundary for the sea,
an everlasting barrier it cannot cross.
The waves may roll, but they cannot prevail;
they may roar, but they cannot cross it.

23 But these people have stubborn and rebellious hearts;
they have turned aside and gone away.

5:24
s Ge 8:22

24 They do not say to themselves,
'Let us fear the LORD our God,
who gives autumn and spring rains in season,
who assures us of the regular weeks of harvest.'*s*

25 Your wrongdoings have kept these away;
your sins have deprived you of good.

26 "Among my people are wicked men
who lie in wait like men who snare birds
and like those who set traps to catch men.

27 Like cages full of birds,
their houses are full of deceit;
they have become rich and powerful

5:28
t Dt 32:15
u Zec 7:10
v Isa 1:23

28 and have grown fat*t* and sleek.
Their evil deeds have no limit;
they do not plead the case of the fatherless*u* to win it,
they do not defend the rights of the poor.*v*

29 Should I not punish them for this?"
declares the LORD.
"Should I not avenge myself
on such a nation as this?

5:30
w Hos 6:10

30 "A horrible*w* and shocking thing
has happened in the land:

5:31
x Eze 13:6; Mic 2:11

31 The prophets prophesy lies,*x*
the priests rule by their own authority,
and my people love it this way.
But what will you do in the end?

Jerusalem Under Siege

6:1
y Ne 3:14
z Jer 4:6

6

1 "Flee for safety, people of Benjamin!
Flee from Jerusalem!
Sound the trumpet in Tekoa!
Raise the signal over Beth Hakkerem!*y*
For disaster looms out of the north,*z*
even terrible destruction.

2 I will destroy the Daughter of Zion,
so beautiful and delicate.

6:3
a 2Ki 25:4

3 Shepherds with their flocks will come against her;
they will pitch their tents around*a* her,
each tending his own portion."

4 "Prepare for battle against her!
Arise, let us attack at noon!
But, alas, the daylight is fading,
and the shadows of evening grow long.

---

still sometimes uses the same method of blessing or withholding blessing to get our attention. Don't wait until God removes your cherished resources before committing yourself to him as you should.

5:28, 29 People and nations who please God treat the fatherless (orphans) justly and care for the poor. Wicked men in Israel treated the defenseless unjustly, which displeased God greatly. Some defenseless people—orphans, the poor, the homeless, and

the lonely—are within your reach. What action can you take to help at least one of them?

6:1 The Lord warned Jeremiah's own tribe of Benjamin to flee, not to the security of the great walled city of Jerusalem because it would be under siege, but toward Tekoa, a town about 12 miles south of Jerusalem. The warning smoke signal was lit at Beth Hakkerem, halfway between Jerusalem and Bethlehem.

6:3 The shepherds were the leaders of Babylon's armies.

5 So arise, let us attack at night
and destroy her fortresses!"

6 This is what the LORD Almighty says:

"Cut down the trees
and build siege ramps against Jerusalem.
This city must be punished;
it is filled with oppression.
7 As a well pours out its water,
so she pours out her wickedness.
Violence[b] and destruction[c] resound in her;
her sickness and wounds are ever before me.
8 Take warning, O Jerusalem,
or I will turn away[d] from you
and make your land desolate
so no one can live in it."

9 This is what the LORD Almighty says:

"Let them glean the remnant of Israel
as thoroughly as a vine;
pass your hand over the branches again,
like one gathering grapes."

10 To whom can I speak and give warning?
Who will listen to me?
Their ears are closed[a] [e]
so they cannot hear.
The word[f] of the LORD is offensive to them;
they find no pleasure in it.
11 But I am full of the wrath of the LORD,
and I cannot hold it in.

"Pour it out on the children in the street
and on the young men gathered together;
both husband and wife will be caught in it,
and the old, those weighed down with years.
12 Their houses will be turned over to others,[g]
together with their fields and their wives,[h]
when I stretch out my hand
against those who live in the land,"

declares the LORD.

13 "From the least to the greatest,
all are greedy for gain;[i]
prophets and priests alike,
all practice deceit.[j]
14 They dress the wound of my people
as though it were not serious.
'Peace, peace,' they say,
when there is no peace.[k]

a 10 Hebrew *uncircumcised*

6:7	[b] Ps 55:9; Eze 7:11, 23 [c] Jer 20:8
6:8	[d] Hos 9:12
6:10	[e] Ac 7:51 [f] Jer 20:8
6:12	[g] Dt 28:30 [h] Jer 8:10
6:13	[i] Isa 56:11 [j] Jer 8:10
6:14	[k] Jer 8:11; Eze 13:10

6:9 The remnant mentioned here is not to be confused with the righteous remnant. This remnant is those left after the first wave of destruction. Like a grape-gatherer, Babylon wouldn't be satisfied until every person was taken. Babylonians invaded Judah three times until they destroyed the nation and its temple completely (2 Kings 24; 25).

6:10 The people became angry and closed their ears. They wanted no part of God's commands because living for God did not appear very exciting. As in Jeremiah's day, people today dislike God's demand for disciplined living. As unsettling as people's responses might be, we must continue to share God's word. Our responsibility is to present God's word; their responsibility is to accept it. We must not let what people want to hear determine what we say.

6:14 "Ignore it and maybe it will go away!" Sound familiar? This was Israel's response to Jeremiah's warnings. They kept listening to predictions of peace because they did not like Jeremiah's condemnation of their sin. But denying the truth never

6:15
Jer 3:3

15 Are they ashamed of their loathsome conduct?
  No, they have no shame at all;
  they do not even know how to blush.*
So they will fall among the fallen;
  they will be brought down when I punish them,"

says the Lord.

6:16
m Jer 18:15
n Mt 11:29

16 This is what the Lord says:

"Stand at the crossroads and look;
  ask for the ancient paths,*m*
ask where the good way is, and walk in it,
  and you will find rest*n* for your souls.
  But you said, 'We will not walk in it.'
17 I appointed watchmen over you and said,
  'Listen to the sound of the trumpet!'
  But you said, 'We will not listen.'
18 Therefore hear, O nations;
  observe, O witnesses,
  what will happen to them.

6:19
o Pr 1:31

19 Hear, O earth:
I am bringing disaster on this people,
  the fruit of their schemes,*o*
because they have not listened to my words
  and have rejected my law.

6:20
p Am 5:22
q Mic 6:7-8
r Isa 1:11

20 What do I care about incense from Sheba
  or sweet calamus from a distant land?
Your burnt offerings are not acceptable;*p*
  your sacrifices*q* do not please me."*r*

21 Therefore this is what the Lord says:

"I will put obstacles before this people.
  Fathers and sons alike will stumble over them;
  neighbors and friends will perish."

22 This is what the Lord says:

"Look, an army is coming
  from the land of the north;
a great nation is being stirred up
  from the ends of the earth.
23 They are armed with bow and spear;
  they are cruel and show no mercy.
They sound like the roaring sea
  as they ride on their horses;
they come like men in battle formation
  to attack you, O Daughter of Zion."

6:24
s Jer 4:31;
50:41-43

24 We have heard reports about them,
  and our hands hang limp.
Anguish has gripped us,
  pain like that of a woman in labor.*s*

---

changes it; what God says always happens. Sin is never removed by denying its existence. We must confess to God that we have sinned and ask him to forgive us.

6:16 The right path for living is ancient and has been marked out by God. But the people refused to take God's path, going their own way instead. We face the same decision today, going God's old but true way, or following a new path of our own choosing. Don't be misled. The only way to find peace and "rest for your souls" is to walk on God's path.

6:20 Sheba, located in southwest Arabia, was a center of trade in incense and spices used in pagan religious rituals.

25 Do not go out to the fields
   or walk on the roads,
for the enemy has a sword,
   and there is terror on every side.
26 O my people, put on sackcloth[t]
   and roll in ashes;[u]
mourn with bitter wailing
   as for an only son,[v]
for suddenly the destroyer
   will come upon us.

6:26
[t]Jer 4:8
[u]Jer 25:34
[v]Zec 12:10

27 "I have made you a tester of metals
   and my people the ore,
that you may observe
   and test their ways.
28 They are all hardened rebels,
   going about to slander.
They are bronze and iron;[w]
   they all act corruptly.

6:28
[w]Eze 22:18

29 The bellows blow fiercely
   to burn away the lead with fire,
but the refining goes on in vain;
   the wicked are not purged out.
30 They are called rejected silver,
   because the LORD has rejected them."

False Religion Worthless

7 This is the word that came to Jeremiah from the LORD: 2 "Stand at the gate of the LORD's house and there proclaim this message:

"'Hear the word of the LORD, all you people of Judah who come through these gates to worship the LORD. 3 This is what the LORD Almighty, the God of Israel, says: Reform your ways[x] and your actions, and I will let you live in this place. 4 Do not trust in deceptive[y] words and say, "This is the temple of the LORD, the temple of the LORD, the temple of the LORD!" 5 If you really change your ways and your actions and deal with each other justly,[z] 6 if you do not oppress the alien, the fatherless or the widow and do not shed innocent blood in this place, and if you do not follow other gods[a] to your own harm, 7 then I will let you live in this place, in the land I gave your forefathers for ever and ever. 8 But look, you are trusting in deceptive words that are worthless.

9 "'Will you steal and murder, commit adultery and perjury,[a] burn incense to Baal and follow other gods[b] you have not known, 10 and then come and stand before me in this house,[c] which bears my Name, and say, "We are safe"—safe to do all these detestable things?

[a]9 Or and swear by false gods

7:3
[x]Jer 18:11; 26:13
7:4
[y]Mic 3:11
7:5
[z]Jer 22:3
7:6
[a]Dt 8:19

7:9
[b]Ex 20:3
7:10
[c]Jer 32:34;
Eze 23:38-39

6:25 Ominous travel warnings, increased threat levels, and tight security were as much a part of life in ancient Israel as they are in the world today. Terrorism, in one form or another, has been a tactic throughout history. The question raised about such real or potential dangers forces us to examine our sense of ultimate security. Whether the outlook is bleak or hopeful, do we actually trust in God? Or does our trust last only as long as the threat seems distant?

6:29, 30 Metal is purified by fire. As it is heated, impurities are burned away and only the pure metal remains. As God tested the people of Judah, however, he could find no purity in their lives. They continued in their sinful ways. Do you see impurities in your life that should be burned away? Confess these to God and allow him to purify you as he sees fit. Take time right now to reflect on the areas of your life that he has already refined; then thank him for what he is doing.

7:1—10:25 As this section opens, God sends Jeremiah to the temple gates to confront the false belief that God will not let harm come to the temple and those who live near it. Jeremiah rebukes

the people for their false and worthless religion, their idolatry, and the shameless behavior of the people and their leaders. Judah, he says, is ripe for judgment and exile. This happened during the reign of Jehoiakim, a puppet of Egypt. The nation, in shock over the death of Josiah, was going through a spiritual reversal that removed much of the good Josiah had done. The themes of this section are false religion, idolatry, and hypocrisy. Jeremiah was almost put to death for this sermon, but he was saved by the officials of Judah (see chapter 26).

7:2, 3 The people followed a worship ritual but maintained a sinful lifestyle. It was religion without personal commitment to God. We can easily do the same. Attending church, taking communion, teaching church school, singing in the choir—all are empty exercises unless we are truly doing them for God. It is good to do these activities, not because we ought to do them for the church, but because we want to do them for God.

7:9–11 There are several parallels between how the people of Judah viewed their temple and how many today view their churches. (1) *They didn't make the temple part of their daily*

7:11
dMt 21:13*

7:12
eJos 18:1
f1Sa 4:10-11, 22

7:13
gIsa 65:12

7:15
hPs 78:67

7:16
iEx 32:10

7:21
jIsa 1:11;
Am 5:21-22
kHos 8:13

7:22
l1Sa 15:22;
Ps 51:16; Hos 6:6

7:23
mLev 26:12

7:26
nJer 16:12

7:27
oEze 2:7

7:29
pJob 1:20

[11] Has this house, which bears my Name, become a den of robbers [d] to you? But I have been watching! declares the LORD.

[12] "'Go now to the place in Shiloh [e] where I first made a dwelling for my Name, and see what I did [f] to it because of the wickedness of my people Israel. [13] While you were doing all these things, declares the LORD, I spoke to you again and again, but you did not listen; [g] I called you, but you did not answer. [14] Therefore, what I did to Shiloh I will now do to the house that bears my Name, the temple you trust in, the place I gave to you and your fathers. [15] I will thrust you from my presence, just as I did all your brothers, the people of Ephraim.' [h]

[16] "So do not pray for this people nor offer any plea [i] or petition for them; do not plead with me, for I will not listen to you. [17] Do you not see what they are doing in the towns of Judah and in the streets of Jerusalem? [18] The children gather wood, the fathers light the fire, and the women knead the dough and make cakes of bread for the Queen of Heaven. They pour out drink offerings to other gods to provoke me to anger. [19] But am I the one they are provoking? declares the LORD. Are they not rather harming themselves, to their own shame?

[20] "Therefore this is what the Sovereign LORD says: My anger and my wrath will be poured out on this place, on man and beast, on the trees of the field and on the fruit of the ground, and it will burn and not be quenched.

[21] "This is what the LORD Almighty, the God of Israel, says: Go ahead, add your burnt offerings to your other sacrifices [j] and eat [k] the meat yourselves! [22] For when I brought your forefathers out of Egypt and spoke to them, I did not just give them commands about burnt offerings and sacrifices, [l] [23] but I gave them this command: Obey me, and I will be your God and you will be my people. [m] Walk in all the ways I command you, that it may go well with you. [24] But they did not listen or pay attention; instead, they followed the stubborn inclinations of their evil hearts. They went backward and not forward. [25] From the time your forefathers left Egypt until now, day after day, again and again I sent you my servants the prophets. [26] But they did not listen to me or pay attention. They were stiff-necked and did more evil than their forefathers.' [n]

[27] "When you tell [o] them all this, they will not listen to you; when you call to them, they will not answer. [28] Therefore say to them, 'This is the nation that has not obeyed the LORD its God or responded to correction. Truth has perished; it has vanished from their lips. [29] Cut off [p] your hair and throw it away; take up a lament on the barren heights, for the LORD has rejected and abandoned this generation that is under his wrath.

---

living. We go to beautiful churches well-prepared for worship, but often we don't take the presence of God with us through the week. (2) *The image of the temple became more important than the substance of faith.* The image of going to church and belonging to a group can become more important than a life changed for God. (3) *The people used their temple as a sanctuary.* Many use religious affiliation as a hideout, thinking it will protect them from evil and problems.

7:11, 12 Jesus used these words from 7:11 in clearing the temple (Mark 11:17; Luke 19:46). This passage applied to the evil in the temple in Jesus' day as well as in Jeremiah's. God's tabernacle had been at Shiloh, but Shiloh had been abandoned (Psalm 78:60; Jeremiah 26:6). If God did not preserve Shiloh because the tabernacle was there, why would he preserve Jerusalem because of the temple?

7:15 Ephraim is another name for Israel, the northern kingdom, which had been taken into captivity by Assyria in 722 B.C.

7:18 The Queen of Heaven was a name for Ishtar, the Mesopotamian goddess of love and fertility. After the fall of Jerusalem, the refugees from Judah who fled to Egypt continued to worship her (44:17). A papyrus dating from the 5th century B.C., found at Hermopolis in Egypt, mentions the Queen of Heaven among the gods honored by the Jewish community living there.

7:19 This verse answers the question, "Who gets hurt when we turn away from God?" We do! Separating ourselves from God is like keeping a green plant away from sunlight or water.

God is our only source of spiritual strength. Cut yourself off from him, and you cut off life itself.

7:21-23 God had set up a system of sacrifices to encourage the people to joyfully obey him (see the book of Leviticus). He required the people to make these sacrifices, not because the sacrifices themselves pleased him, but because they caused the people to recognize their sin and refocus on living for God. They faithfully made the sacrifices but forgot the reason they were offering them, and thus they disobeyed God. Jeremiah reminded the people that acting out religious rituals was meaningless unless they were prepared to obey God in all areas of life. (See the chart in Hosea 7, p. 1403.)

7:25 From the time of Moses to the end of the Old Testament period, God sent many prophets to Israel and Judah. No matter how bad the circumstances were, God always raised up a prophet to speak against their stubborn spiritual attitudes.

7:27 Why did God instruct Jeremiah to prophesy and proclaim if the effort would be fruitless? God demonstrates his consistent faithfulness even in the face of human resistance. God was also "going on record" for those beyond Jeremiah's generation. See 1 Corinthians 10:1-11 for an explanation of God's detailed recording of the past failures of his people. The stories are intended to guide us and prevent us from making the same mistakes.

The Valley of Slaughter

30 "'The people of Judah have done evil in my eyes, declares the LORD. They have set up their detestable idols *q* in the house that bears my Name and have defiled it. 31 They have built the high places of Topheth *r* in the Valley of Ben Hinnom to burn their sons and daughters in the fire—something I did not command, nor did it enter my mind. 32 So beware, the days are coming, declares the LORD, when people will no longer call it Topheth or the Valley of Ben Hinnom, but the Valley of Slaughter, *s* for they will bury *t* the dead in Topheth until there is no more room. 33 Then the carcasses of this people will become food for the birds of the air and the beasts of the earth, and there will be no one to frighten them away. 34 I will bring an end to the sounds *u* of joy and gladness and to the voices of bride and bridegroom *v* in the towns of Judah and the streets of Jerusalem, for the land will become desolate.

8 "'At that time, declares the LORD, the bones of the kings and officials of Judah, the bones of the priests and prophets, and the bones of the people of Jerusalem will be removed from their graves. 2 They will be exposed to the sun and the moon and all the stars of the heavens, which they have loved and served and which they have followed and consulted and worshiped. They will not be gathered up or buried, but will be like refuse lying on the ground. 3 Wherever I banish them, all the survivors of this evil nation will prefer death to life, *w* declares the LORD Almighty.'

Sin and Punishment

4 "Say to them, 'This is what the LORD says:

"'When men fall down, do they not get up?
    When a man turns away, does he not return?
5 Why then have these people turned away?
    Why does Jerusalem always turn away?
They cling to deceit;
    they refuse to return.
6 I have listened attentively,
    but they do not say what is right.
No one repents of his wickedness,
    saying, "What have I done?"
Each pursues his own course
    like a horse charging into battle.
7 Even the stork in the sky
    knows her appointed seasons,
and the dove, the swift and the thrush
    observe the time of their migration.
But my people do not know *x*
    the requirements of the LORD.

8 "'How can you say, "We are wise,
    for we have the law *y* of the LORD,"
when actually the lying pen of the scribes
    has handled it falsely?
9 The wise will be put to shame;
    they will be dismayed and trapped.
Since they have rejected the word of the LORD,
    what kind of wisdom do they have?

7:30
q Eze 7:20-22
7:31
r 2Ki 23:10
7:32
s Jer 19:6
t Jer 19:11

7:34
u Isa 24:8
v Rev 18:23

8:3
w Job 3:22; Rev 9:6

8:7
x Isa 1:3; Jer 5:4-5

8:8
y Ro 2:17

7:31, 32 The high places (or altars) of Topheth (meaning "fireplace") were set up in the Valley of Ben Hinnom, where debris and rubbish from the city were thrown away. This altar was used to worship Molech—a god who required child sacrifice (2 Kings 23:10). Their valley of sacrifice would become their valley of slaughter by the Babylonians. At the place where the people had killed their children in sinful idol worship, they themselves would be slaughtered.

8:1, 2 The threat that the graves of Judah's people would be opened was horrible to a people who highly honored the dead and believed that it was the highest desecration to open graves.

This would be an ironic punishment for idol worshipers: their bones would be laid out before the sun, moon, and stars—the gods they thought could save them.

8:4–6 When people fall down or realize that they are headed in the wrong direction, it only makes sense for them to get up or change directions. But as God watched the nation, he saw people living sinful lives by choice, deceiving themselves that there would be no consequences. They had lost perspective concerning God's will for their lives and were trying to minimize their sin. Are there some indicators that you have fallen down or are heading the wrong way? What are you doing to get back on the right path?

8:10
z Isa 56:11

10 Therefore I will give their wives to other men
and their fields to new owners.
From the least to the greatest,
all are greedy for gain;z
prophets and priests alike,
all practice deceit.

8:11
a Jer 6:14

11 They dress the wound of my people
as though it were not serious.
"Peace, peace," they say,
when there is no peace.a

8:12
b Jer 3:3

12 Are they ashamed of their loathsome conduct?
No, they have no shameb at all;
they do not even know how to blush.
So they will fall among the fallen;
they will be brought down when they are punished,

says the LORD.

8:13
c Joel 1:7
d Mt 21:19

13 "'I will take away their harvest,

declares the LORD.

There will be no grapes on the vine.c
There will be no figs on the tree,
and their leaves will wither.d
What I have given them
will be taken from them.a'"

8:14
e Jer 4:5
f Jer 9:15
g Jer 14:7, 20

14 "Why are we sitting here?
Gather together!
Let us flee to the fortified citiese
and perish there!
For the LORD our God has doomed us to perish
and given us poisoned waterf to drink,
because we have sinnedg against him.

8:15
h Jer 14:19

15 We hoped for peace
but no good has come,
for a time of healing
but there was only terror.h

8:16
i Jer 4:15

16 The snorting of the enemy's horses
is heard from Dan;i
at the neighing of their stallions
the whole land trembles.
They have come to devour
the land and everything in it,
the city and all who live there."

8:17
j Ps 58:5

17 "See, I will send venomous snakes among you,
vipers that cannot be charmed,j
and they will bite you,"

declares the LORD.

18 O my Comforterb in sorrow,
my heart is faint within me.
19 Listen to the cry of my people
from a land far away:
"Is the LORD not in Zion?
Is her King no longer there?"

a 13 The meaning of the Hebrew for this sentence is uncertain.   b 18 The meaning of the Hebrew for this word is uncertain.

8:16 Dan was the northernmost tribe in Israel.
8:18, 19 Jeremiah was pleading with God to save his people.

"Why have they provoked me to anger with their images,
 with their worthless foreign idols?"

20 "The harvest is past,
 the summer has ended,
 and we are not saved."

21 Since my people are crushed, I am crushed;
 I mourn, and horror grips me.
22 Is there no balm in Gilead?[k]
 Is there no physician there?
Why then is there no healing
 for the wound of my people?

9
1 Oh, that my head were a spring of water
 and my eyes a fountain of tears!
I would weep day and night
 for the slain of my people.[l]
2 Oh, that I had in the desert
 a lodging place for travelers,
so that I might leave my people
 and go away from them;
for they are all adulterers,[m]
 a crowd of unfaithful people.

3 "They make ready their tongue
 like a bow, to shoot lies;[n]
it is not by truth
 that they triumph[a] in the land.
They go from one sin to another;
 they do not acknowledge me,"

      declares the LORD.

4 "Beware of your friends;
 do not trust your brothers.[o]
For every brother is a deceiver,[b]
 and every friend a slanderer.
5 Friend deceives friend,
 and no one speaks the truth.
They have taught their tongues to lie;
 they weary themselves with sinning.
6 You[c] live in the midst of deception;[p]
 in their deceit they refuse to acknowledge me,"

      declares the LORD.

7 Therefore this is what the LORD Almighty says:

"See, I will refine[q] and test them,
 for what else can I do
 because of the sin of my people?
8 Their tongue is a deadly arrow;
 it speaks with deceit.

8:22
[k] Ge 37:25

9:1
[l] Isa 22:4

9:2
[m] Jer 5:7-8

9:3
[n] Ps 64:3

9:4
[o] Mic 7:5-6

9:6
[p] Jer 5:27

9:7
[q] Isa 1:25

[a] 3 Or lies; / they are not valiant for truth [b] 4 Or a deceiving Jacob [c] 6 That is, Jeremiah (the Hebrew is singular)

8:20-22 These words vividly portray Jeremiah's emotion as he watched his people reject God. He responded with anguish to a world dying in sin. We watch that same world still dying in sin, still rejecting God. But how often is our heart broken for our lost friends and neighbors, our lost world? Only when we have Jeremiah's kind of passionate concern will we be moved to help. We must begin by asking God to break our hearts for the world he loves.

8:22 Gilead was famous for its healing balm (medicine). This is a rhetorical question. The obvious answer is, "Yes—God," but Israel was not applying the "balm"; they were not obeying

the Lord. Although the people's spiritual sickness was still very deep, it could be healed. But the people refused the medicine. God could heal their self-inflicted wounds, but he would not force his healing on them.

9:1-6 Jeremiah felt conflicting emotions concerning his people. Lying, deceit, treachery, adultery, and idolatry had become common sins. He was angered by their sin, but he had compassion too. He was set apart from them by his mission for God, but he was also one of them. Jesus had similar feelings when he stood before Jerusalem, the city that would reject him (Matthew 23:37).

With his mouth each speaks cordially to his neighbor,
　　but in his heart he sets a trap for him.

9:9
r Jer 5:9, 29

⁹ Should I not punish them for this?"
　　declares the LORD.
"Should I not avenge*r* myself
　　on such a nation as this?"

9:10
s Jer 4:25; Hos 4:3

¹⁰ I will weep and wail for the mountains
　　and take up a lament concerning the desert pastures.
They are desolate and untraveled,
　　and the lowing of cattle is not heard.
The birds of the air*s* have fled
　　and the animals are gone.

9:11
t Isa 34:13
u Isa 25:2

¹¹ "I will make Jerusalem a heap of ruins,
　　a haunt of jackals;*t*
and I will lay waste the towns of Judah
　　so no one can live there."*u*

¹²What man is wise enough to understand this? Who has been instructed by the LORD and can explain it? Why has the land been ruined and laid waste like a desert that no one can cross?

¹³The LORD said, "It is because they have forsaken my law, which I set before them; they have not obeyed me or followed my law. ¹⁴Instead, they have followed the stubbornness of their hearts; they have followed the Baals, as their fathers taught them." ¹⁵Therefore, this is what the LORD Almighty, the God of Israel, says: "See, I will make this people eat bitter food and drink poisoned water.*v* ¹⁶I will scatter them among nations*w* that neither they nor their fathers have known,*x* and I will pursue them with the sword*y* until I have destroyed them."*z*

9:15
v Jer 8:14

9:16
w Lev 26:33
x Dt 28:64
y Eze 5:2
z Jer 44:27

¹⁷This is what the LORD Almighty says:

9:17
a Ecc 12:5; Am 5:16

"Consider now! Call for the wailing women*a* to come;
　　send for the most skillful of them.

9:18
b Jer 14:17

¹⁸ Let them come quickly
　　and wail over us
till our eyes overflow with tears
　　and water streams from our eyelids.*b*
¹⁹ The sound of wailing is heard from Zion:
　　'How ruined we are!
How great is our shame!

OLD TESTAMENT TESTS FOR FALSE PROPHETS

In the Old Testament, various signs or works pointed to a true or false prophet. Many of these can be applied today.

1. Does the prophet use fortune-telling?
Divination was expressly forbidden by God (Deuteronomy 18:9–14). No true teacher or prophet would use fortune-telling or have any dealings with spirits of the dead (Jeremiah 14:14; Ezekiel 12:24; Micah 3:7).

2. Have the prophet's short-term prophecies been fulfilled?
Deuteronomy 18:22 used this as a test. Do predictions come to pass?

3. Is the prophet marked by a desire to say only what pleases people?
Many false prophets told people what they wanted to hear. A true prophet serves God, not people (Jeremiah 8:11; 14:13; 23:17; Ezekiel 13:10; Micah 3:5).

4. Does the prophet draw people away from God?
Many teachers draw people to themselves or to the system or organization they have built (Deuteronomy 13:1–3).

5. Does the prophet's prophecy confirm the Bible's main teaching?
If a prophecy is inconsistent with or contradictory to Scripture, it is not to be believed.

6. What is the prophet's moral character?
False prophets were charged with lying (Jeremiah 8:10; 14:14), drunkenness (Isaiah 28:7), and immorality (Jeremiah 23:14).

7. Do other Spirit-led people discern authenticity in this prophet?
Discernment by others who are led of the Spirit is a key test (1 Kings 22:7). The New Testament speaks of this a great deal (John 10:4–15; 1 Corinthians 2:14; 14:29, 32; 1 John 4:1).

We must leave our land
  because our houses are in ruins.'"

20 Now, O women, hear the word of the Lord;
  open your ears to the words of his mouth.
Teach your daughters how to wail;
  teach one another a lament.
21 Death has climbed in through our windows
  and has entered our fortresses;
it has cut off the children from the streets
  and the young men from the public squares.

22 Say, "This is what the Lord declares:

"' The dead bodies of men will lie
  like refuse[c] on the open field,
like cut grain behind the reaper,
  with no one to gather them.'"

23 This is what the Lord says:

"Let not the wise man boast of his wisdom[d]
  or the strong man boast of his strength
  or the rich man boast of his riches,
24 but let him who boasts boast[e] about this:
  that he understands and knows me,
that I am the Lord,[f] who exercises kindness,[g]
  justice and righteousness on earth,
  for in these I delight,"

                             declares the Lord.

25 "The days are coming," declares the Lord, "when I will punish all who are circumcised only in the flesh[h] — 26 Egypt, Judah, Edom, Ammon, Moab and all who live in the desert in distant places.[a][i] For all these nations are really uncircumcised, and even the whole house of Israel is uncircumcised in heart.[j]"

God and Idols

10 Hear what the Lord says to you, O house of Israel. 2 This is what the Lord says:

"Do not learn the ways of the nations[k]
  or be terrified by signs in the sky,
  though the nations are terrified by them.
3 For the customs of the peoples are worthless;
  they cut a tree out of the forest,
  and a craftsman[l] shapes it with his chisel.
4 They adorn it with silver and gold;
  they fasten it with hammer and nails
  so it will not totter.[m]
5 Like a scarecrow in a melon patch,
  their idols cannot speak;[n]
they must be carried
  because they cannot walk.[o]

a 26 Or *desert and who clip the hair by their foreheads*

9:22	
c Jer 8:2	
9:23	
d Ecc 9:11	
9:24	
e 1Co 1:31*	
f 2Co 10:17*	
g Ps 51:1; Mic 7:18	
9:25	
h Ro 2:8-9	
9:26	
i Jer 25:23	
j Lev 26:41; Ro 2:28	
10:2	
k Lev 20:23	
10:3	
l Isa 40:19	
10:4	
m Isa 41:7	
10:5	
n 1Co 12:2	
o Ps 115:5, 7	

9:23, 24 People tend to admire four qualities in others: human wisdom, power, kindness, and riches. But God puts a higher priority on knowing him personally and living a life that reflects his justice, righteousness, and love. What do you want people to admire most about you?

9:25, 26 Circumcision went back to the time of Abraham. For the people of Israel it was a symbol of their covenant relationship to God (Genesis 17:9–14). Circumcision was also practiced by pagan nations, but not as the sign of a covenant with God. By Jeremiah's time, the Israelites had forgotten the spiritual significance of circumcision even though they continued to do the physical ritual.

10:2, 3 Most people would like to know the future. Decisions would be easier, certain failures avoided, and some successes assured. The people of Judah wanted to know the future too, and they tried to discern it through reading the signs in the sky. Jeremiah's response applies today: God made the earth and the heavens, including stars that people consult and worship (10:12). No one will discover the future in made-up charts of God's stars. But God, who promises to guide you, knows your future and will be with you all the way. He may not reveal your future to you, but he will walk with you as the future unfolds. Don't trust the stars; trust the One who made the stars.

10:5
p Isa 41:24; 46:7

Do not fear them;
    they can do no harm
    nor can they do any good."p

6 No one is like you, O Lord;
    you are great,
    and your name is mighty in power.
7 Who should not revere you,
    O King of the nations?
    This is your due.
Among all the wise men of the nations
    and in all their kingdoms,
    there is no one like you.
8 They are all senseless and foolish;
    they are taught by worthless wooden idols.

10:9
q Ps 115:4

9 Hammered silver is brought from Tarshish
    and gold from Uphaz.
What the craftsman and goldsmith have madeq
    is then dressed in blue and purple—
    all made by skilled workers.
10 But the Lord is the true God;
    he is the living God, the eternal King.
When he is angry, the earth trembles;
    the nations cannot endure his wrath.

10:11
r Ps 96:5; Isa 2:18

11 "Tell them this: 'These gods, who did not make the heavens and the earth, will perish r
from the earth and from under the heavens.'" a

10:12
s Ge 1:1, 8;
Isa 40:22

12 But God made the earth by his power;
    he founded the world by his wisdom
    and stretched out the heavens s by his understanding.

10:13
t Ps 135:7

13 When he thunders, the waters in the heavens roar;
    he makes clouds rise from the ends of the earth.
He sends lightning with the rain t
    and brings out the wind from his storehouses.

14 Everyone is senseless and without knowledge;
    every goldsmith is shamed by his idols.
His images are a fraud;
    they have no breath in them.
15 They are worthless, the objects of mockery;
    when their judgment comes, they will perish.

10:16
u Dt 32:9

16 He who is the Portion u of Jacob is not like these,
    for he is the Maker of all things,
including Israel, the tribe of his inheritance—
    the Lord Almighty is his name.

Coming Destruction

10:17
v Eze 12:3-12

17 Gather up your belongings v to leave the land,
    you who live under siege.

10:18
w 1Sa 25:29

18 For this is what the Lord says:
    "At this time I will hurl w out
    those who live in this land;

a 11 The text of this verse is in Aramaic.

10:8 Those who put their trust in a chunk of wood, even though it is carved well and clothed beautifully, are foolish. The simplest person who worships God is wiser than the wisest person who worships a worthless substitute, because this simple person has discerned who God really is. In what or whom do you place your trust?

10:9 Tarshish was located at the westward limit of the ancient world, perhaps in what is now Spain (see Jonah 1:3). It was a source of silver, tin, lead, and iron for Tyre (Ezekiel 27:12). The location of Uphaz is unknown. Instead, it may be a metallurgical term for "refined gold." No matter how well made or how beautiful idols are, they can never have the power and life of the true and living God.

I will bring distress on them
   so that they may be captured."

19 Woe to me because of my injury!
   My wound is incurable!
Yet I said to myself,
   "This is my sickness, and I must endure^x it."

10:19
ˣMic 7:9

20 My tent^y is destroyed;
   all its ropes are snapped.
My sons are gone from me and are no more;
   no one is left now to pitch my tent
   or to set up my shelter.

10:20
ʸJer 4:20

21 The shepherds are senseless
   and do not inquire of the LORD;
so they do not prosper
   and all their flock is scattered.^z

10:21
ᶻJer 23:2

22 Listen! The report is coming—
   a great commotion from the land of the north!
It will make the towns of Judah desolate,
   a haunt of jackals.^a

10:22
ᵃJer 9:11

Jeremiah's Prayer

23 I know, O LORD, that a man's life is not his own;
   it is not for man to direct his steps.
24 Correct me, LORD, but only with justice—
   not in your anger,^b
   lest you reduce me to nothing.

10:24
ᵇPs 6:1

25 Pour out your wrath on the nations
   that do not acknowledge you,
on the peoples who do not call on your name.
For they have devoured^c Jacob;
   they have devoured him completely
   and destroyed his homeland.^d

10:25
ᶜJer 8:16
ᵈPs 79:6-7

3. Jeremiah prophesies destruction
The Covenant Is Broken

11 This is the word that came to Jeremiah from the LORD: ²"Listen to the terms of this covenant and tell them to the people of Judah and to those who live in Jerusalem. ³Tell them that this is what the LORD, the God of Israel, says: 'Cursed^e is the man who does not obey the terms of this covenant— ⁴the terms I commanded your forefathers when I brought them out of Egypt, out of the iron-smelting furnace. ^f' I said, 'Obey^g me and do everything I command you, and you will be my people,^h and I will be your God. ⁵Then I will fulfill the oath I sworeⁱ to your forefathers, to give them a land flowing with milk and honey'—the land you possess today."

I answered, "Amen, LORD."

⁶The LORD said to me, "Proclaim all these words in the towns of Judah and in the streets of Jerusalem: 'Listen to the terms of this covenant and follow^j them. ⁷From the time I brought your forefathers up from Egypt until today, I warned them again and again, saying, "Obey me." ⁸But they did not listen or pay attention; instead, they followed the stubbornness of their evil hearts. So I brought on them all the curses of the covenant I had commanded them to follow but that they did not keep.'"

11:3
ᵉDt 27:26
11:4
ᶠDt 4:20
ᵍEx 24:8
ʰJer 7:23
11:5
ⁱDt 7:12

11:6
ʲDt 15:5; Ro 2:13; Jas 1:22

10:19–21 In this section, Jeremiah uses the picture of nomads wandering in the desert trying to pitch their tents. The shepherds of the nation are the evil leaders responsible for the distress. The flock is the people of Judah. Instead of guiding the people to God, the leaders were leading them astray.

10:23, 24 God's ability to direct our lives well is infinitely beyond our ability. Sometimes we are afraid of God's power and God's plans because we know his power would easily crush us if he

used it against us. Don't be afraid to let God correct your plans. He will give you wisdom if you are willing.

11:1—13:27 This section concerns the broken covenant, and a rebuke for those who returned to idols after Josiah's reform. Jeremiah's rebuke prompted a threat against his life by his own countrymen. As Jeremiah suffered, he pondered the prosperity of the wicked. As he brought these words to a close, he used a ruined linen belt and filled wineskins as object lessons of God's coming judgment (see the note on 13:1–11).

11:9
k Eze 22:25

11:10
l Jdg 2:12-13

11:11
m Jer 14:12

11:12
n Dt 32:37

⁹Then the LORD said to me, "There is a conspiracy[k] among the people of Judah and those who live in Jerusalem. ¹⁰They have returned to the sins of their forefathers, who refused to listen to my words. They have followed other gods[l] to serve them. Both the house of Israel and the house of Judah have broken the covenant I made with their forefathers. ¹¹Therefore this is what the LORD says: 'I will bring on them a disaster they cannot escape. Although they cry[m] out to me, I will not listen to them. ¹²The towns of Judah and the people of Jerusalem will go and cry out to the gods to whom they burn incense, but they will not help them at all when disaster[n] strikes. ¹³You have as many gods as you have towns, O Judah; and the altars you have set up to burn incense to that shameful god Baal are as many as the streets of Jerusalem.'

11:14
o Ex 32:10

¹⁴"Do not pray[o] for this people nor offer any plea or petition for them, because I will not listen when they call to me in the time of their distress.

¹⁵ "What is my beloved doing in my temple
    as she works out her evil schemes with many?
    Can consecrated meat avert ⌐your punishment⌐?
When you engage in your wickedness,
    then you rejoice.[a] "

11:16
p Jer 21:14

¹⁶ The LORD called you a thriving olive tree
    with fruit beautiful in form.
But with the roar of a mighty storm
    he will set it on fire,[p]
    and its branches will be broken.

11:17
q Isa 5:2

¹⁷The LORD Almighty, who planted[q] you, has decreed disaster for you, because the house of Israel and the house of Judah have done evil and provoked me to anger by burning incense to Baal.

Plot Against Jeremiah

11:19
r Ps 83:4

¹⁸Because the LORD revealed their plot to me, I knew it, for at that time he showed me what they were doing. ¹⁹I had been like a gentle lamb led to the slaughter; I did not realize that they had plotted against me, saying,

"Let us destroy the tree and its fruit;
    let us cut him off from the land of the living,
    that his name be remembered[r] no more."

11:20
s Ps 7:9

²⁰ But, O LORD Almighty, you who judge righteously
    and test the heart and mind,[s]
let me see your vengeance upon them,
    for to you I have committed my cause.

11:21
t Jer 12:6

²¹"Therefore this is what the LORD says about the men of Anathoth who are seeking your life[t] and saying, 'Do not prophesy in the name of the LORD or you will die by our hands'—

11:22
u Jer 18:21

11:23
v Jer 23:12

²²therefore this is what the LORD Almighty says: 'I will punish them. Their young men[u] will die by the sword, their sons and daughters by famine. ²³Not even a remnant will be left to them, because I will bring disaster on the men of Anathoth in the year of their punishment.[v]' "

a 15 Or *Could consecrated meat avert your punishment? / Then you would rejoice*

11:14 At first glance this command is shocking—God tells Jeremiah not to pray for the people and says he won't listen to the people if they pray. A time comes when God must dispense justice. Sin brings its own bitter reward. If the people were unrepentant and continued in their sin, neither their prayers nor Jeremiah's would prevent God's judgment. Their only hope was repentance—sorrow for sin, turning from it, and turning to God. How can we keep praying for God's help if we haven't committed our lives to him? God's blessings come when we are committed to him, not when we selfishly hang on to our sinful ways.

11:18-23 To Jeremiah's surprise, the people of Anathoth, his hometown, were plotting to kill him. They wanted to silence Jere-

miah's message for several reasons: (1) economic—his condemnation of idol worship would hurt the business of the idol-makers; (2) religious—the message of doom and gloom made the people feel depressed and guilty; (3) political—he openly rebuked their hypocritical politics; and (4) personal—the people hated him for showing them that they were wrong. Jeremiah had two options: run and hide, or call on God. Jeremiah called, and God answered. Like Jeremiah, we can either run and hide when we face threats because of our faithfulness to God, or we can call on God for help. Hiding compromises our message; calling on God lets him reinforce it.

Jeremiah's Complaint

12 You are always righteous, O LORD,
    when I bring a case before you.
Yet I would speak with you about your justice:
    Why does the way of the wicked prosper?[w]
    Why do all the faithless live at ease?

2 You have planted[x] them, and they have taken root;
    they grow and bear fruit.
You are always on their lips
    but far from their hearts.

3 Yet you know me, O LORD;
    you see me and test[y] my thoughts about you.
Drag them off like sheep to be butchered!
    Set them apart for the day of slaughter!

4 How long will the land lie parched[a]
    and the grass in every field be withered?[z]
Because those who live in it are wicked,
    the animals and birds have perished.
Moreover, the people are saying,
    "He will not see what happens to us."

God's Answer

5 "If you have raced with men on foot
    and they have worn you out,
    how can you compete with horses?
If you stumble in safe country,[b]
    how will you manage in the thickets by[c] the Jordan?

6 Your brothers, your own family—
    even they have betrayed you;
    they have raised a loud cry against you.[a]
Do not trust them,
    though they speak well of you.

7 "I will forsake my house,
    abandon my inheritance;
I will give the one I love
    into the hands of her enemies.

8 My inheritance has become to me
    like a lion in the forest.
She roars at me;
    therefore I hate her.[b]

9 Has not my inheritance become to me
    like a speckled bird of prey
    that other birds of prey surround and attack?
Go and gather all the wild beasts;
    bring them to devour.[c]

10 Many shepherds will ruin my vineyard
    and trample down my field;

12:1
[w] Jer 5:27-28

12:2
[x] Jer 11:17

12:3
[y] Ps 139:1-4;
Jer 11:20

12:4
[z] Joel 1:10-12

12:6
[a] Pr 26:24-25;
Jer 9:4

12:8
[b] Hos 9:15

12:9
[c] Isa 56:9

---

[a]4 Or *land mourn* [b]5 Or *If you put your trust in a land of safety* [c]5 Or *the flooding of*

12:1-6 Many people have asked, "Why does the way of the wicked prosper?" (See, for example, Job 21:4–21 and Habakkuk 1:1–4.) Jeremiah knew that God's justice would ultimately come, but he was impatient because he wanted justice to come quickly. God didn't give a doctrinal answer; instead he gave a challenge—if Jeremiah couldn't handle this, how would he handle the injustices ahead? It is natural for us to demand fair play and cry for justice against those who take advantage of others. But when we call for justice, we must realize that we ourselves would be in big trouble if God gave each of us what we truly deserve.

12:5, 6 Life was extremely difficult for Jeremiah despite his love for and obedience to God. When he called to God for relief, God's reply in effect was, "If you think this is bad, how are you going to cope when it gets really tough?" Not all of God's answers to prayer are nice or easy to handle. Any Christian who has experienced war, bereavement, or a serious illness knows this. But we are to be committed to God even when the going gets tough and when his answers to our prayers don't bring immediate relief.

12:10
d Isa 5:1-7

they will turn my pleasant field
into a desolate wasteland. *d*

12:11
e Isa 42:25

11 It will be made a wasteland,
parched and desolate before me; *e*
the whole land will be laid waste
because there is no one who cares.
12 Over all the barren heights in the desert
destroyers will swarm,
for the sword of the Lord will devour
from one end of the land to the other;
no one will be safe.

12:13
f Lev 26:20;
Dt 28:38; Mic 6:15

13 They will sow wheat but reap thorns;
they will wear themselves out but gain nothing. *f*
So bear the shame of your harvest
because of the Lord's fierce anger."

12:14
g Zec 2:7-9

14 This is what the Lord says: "As for all my wicked neighbors who seize the inheritance I gave my people Israel, I will uproot *g* them from their lands and I will uproot the house of Judah from among them.

12:15
h Am 9:14-15

12:16
i Jer 4:2

12:17
j Isa 60:12

15 But after I uproot them, I will again have compassion and will bring *h* each of them back to his own inheritance and his own country. 16 And if they learn well the ways of my people and swear by my name, saying, 'As surely as the Lord lives' *i*—even as they once taught my people to swear by Baal—then they will be established among my people. 17 But if any nation does not listen, I will completely uproot and destroy *j* it," declares the Lord.

A Linen Belt

13 This is what the Lord said to me: "Go and buy a linen belt and put it around your waist, but do not let it touch water." 2 So I bought a belt, as the Lord directed, and put it around my waist.

3 Then the word of the Lord came to me a second time: 4 "Take the belt you bought and are wearing around your waist, and go now to Perath *a* and hide it there in a crevice in the

13:5
k Ex 40:16

rocks." 5 So I went and hid it at Perath, as the Lord told me. *k*

6 Many days later the Lord said to me, "Go now to Perath and get the belt I told you to hide there." 7 So I went to Perath and dug up the belt and took it from the place where I had hidden it, but now it was ruined and completely useless.

13:9
l Lev 26:19

13:10
m Jer 11:8; 16:12
n Jer 9:14

13:11
o Jer 32:20; 33:9
p Ex 19:5-6

8 Then the word of the Lord came to me: 9 "This is what the Lord says: 'In the same way I will ruin the pride of Judah and the great pride *l* of Jerusalem. 10 These wicked people, who refuse to listen to my words, who follow the stubbornness of their hearts *m* and go after other gods *n* to serve and worship them, will be like this belt—completely useless! 11 For as a belt is bound around a man's waist, so I bound the whole house of Israel and the whole house of Judah to me,' declares the Lord, 'to be my people for my renown *o* and praise and honor. *p* But they have not listened.'

Wineskins

13:13
q Isa 51:17; 63:6

13:14
r Jer 16:5

12 "Say to them: 'This is what the Lord, the God of Israel, says: Every wineskin should be filled with wine.' And if they say to you, 'Don't we know that every wineskin should be filled with wine?' 13 then tell them, 'This is what the Lord says: I am going to fill with drunkenness *q* all who live in this land, including the kings who sit on David's throne, the priests, the prophets and all those living in Jerusalem. 14 I will smash them one against the other, fathers and sons alike, declares the Lord. I will allow no pity or mercy or compassion *r* to keep me from destroying them.'"

a 4 Or possibly *the Euphrates*; also in verses 5-7

12:14–17 God chose a people through whom to demonstrate his care for the world. The nation of Israel was given much; thus, much was required of her. But she repeatedly failed. The fate of other nations depended on their willingness to demonstrate faith in God whether or not God's chosen people accomplished their task of witness. God's love extends to reach every square inch of the globe.

13:1 A linen belt was one of the more intimate pieces of clothing, clinging close to the body. It was like underwear. Jeremiah's

action showed how God would ruin Judah just as Jeremiah had ruined the linen belt.

13:1–11 Actions speak louder than words. Jeremiah often used vivid object lessons to arouse the people's curiosity and get his point across. This lesson of the linen belt illustrated Judah's destiny. Although the people had once been close to God, their pride had made them useless. Proud people may look important, but God says their pride makes them good for nothing, completely useless. Pride rots our hearts until we lose our usefulness to God.

Threat of Captivity

15 Hear and pay attention,
   do not be arrogant,
   for the LORD has spoken.
16 Give glory to the LORD your God
   before he brings the darkness,
   before your feet stumble
   on the darkening hills.
   You hope for light,
   but he will turn it to thick darkness
   and change it to deep gloom. *s*

17 But if you do not listen,
   I will weep in secret
   because of your pride;
   my eyes will weep bitterly,
   overflowing with tears, *t*
   because the LORD's flock will be taken captive. *u*

18 Say to the king and to the queen mother,
   "Come down from your thrones,
   for your glorious crowns
   will fall from your heads."
19 The cities in the Negev will be shut up,
   and there will be no one to open them.
   All Judah *v* will be carried into exile,
   carried completely away.

20 Lift up your eyes and see
   those who are coming from the north. *w*
   Where is the flock that was entrusted to you,
   the sheep of which you boasted?
21 What will you say when ˌthe LORDˌ sets over you
   those you cultivated as your special allies?
   Will not pain grip you
   like that of a woman in labor?
22 And if you ask yourself,
   "Why has this happened to me?"—
   it is because of your many sins *x*
   that your skirts have been torn off
   and your body mistreated. *y*
23 Can the Ethiopian *a* change his skin
   or the leopard its spots?
   Neither can you do good
   who are accustomed to doing evil.

24 "I will scatter you like chaff
   driven by the desert wind.

a23 Hebrew *Cushite* (probably a person from the upper Nile region)

13:16
s Isa 59:9

13:17
t Jer 9:1
u Jer 14:18

13:19
v Jer 20:4

13:20
w Jer 6:22

13:22
x Jer 16:10-12
y Eze 16:37;
Na 3:5-6

13:15 While it is good to respect our country and our church, our loyalties always carry a hidden danger—arrogance. When is pride harmful? When it causes us to (1) look down on others; (2) be selfish with our resources; (3) force our solutions on others' problems; (4) think God is blessing us because of our own merits; (5) be content with our plans rather than seeking God's plans.

13:18 The king was Jehoiachin, and his mother was Nehushta. The king's father, Jehoiakim, had surrendered to Nebuchadnezzar but later rebelled. During Jehoiachin's reign, Nebuchadnezzar's armies besieged Jerusalem, and both Jehoiachin and Nehushta

surrendered. Jehoiachin was sent to Babylon and imprisoned (2 Kings 24:1–12). Jeremiah's prophecy came true.

13:19 The Negev region is the dry wasteland stretching south from Beersheba. The towns in this area would be closed to any refugees fleeing the invading army.

13:23 Not even the threat of captivity could move the people to repent. The people had become so accustomed to doing evil that they had lost their ability to change. God never rejects those who sincerely turn to him. God is warning them to repent before it becomes impossible to change. We must never put off until tomorrow those changes God wants us to make. Our attitudes and patterns for living can become so set that we will lose all desire to change and will no longer fear the consequences.

13:25
z Job 20:29

25 This is your lot,
  the portion[z] I have decreed for you,"

declares the LORD,

"because you have forgotten me
  and trusted in false gods.

13:26
a La 1:8

26 I will pull up your skirts over your face
  that your shame may be seen[a]—

13:27
b Jer 2:20

27 your adulteries and lustful neighings,
  your shameless prostitution![b]
I have seen your detestable acts
  on the hills and in the fields.
Woe to you, O Jerusalem!
  How long will you be unclean?"

Drought, Famine, Sword

14 This is the word of the LORD to Jeremiah concerning the drought:

14:2
c Isa 3:26; Jer 8:21

2 "Judah mourns,[c]
  her cities languish;
they wail for the land,
  and a cry goes up from Jerusalem.

14:3
d 2Ki 18:31
e 2Sa 15:30

3 The nobles send their servants for water;
  they go to the cisterns
  but find no water.[d]
They return with their jars unfilled;
  dismayed and despairing,
  they cover their heads.[e]

4 The ground is cracked
  because there is no rain in the land;
the farmers are dismayed
  and cover their heads.

14:5
f Isa 15:6

5 Even the doe in the field
  deserts her newborn fawn
  because there is no grass.[f]

14:6
g Jer 2:24

6 Wild donkeys stand on the barren heights[g]
  and pant like jackals;
their eyesight fails
  for lack of pasture."

7 Although our sins testify against us,
  O LORD, do something for the sake of your name.
For our backsliding is great;
  we have sinned against you.

14:8
h Jer 17:13

8 O Hope[h] of Israel,
  its Savior in times of distress,
why are you like a stranger in the land,
  like a traveler who stays only a night?
9 Why are you like a man taken by surprise,
  like a warrior powerless to save?
You are among us, O LORD,
  and we bear your name;
  do not forsake us!

14:10
i Jer 2:25

10 This is what the LORD says about this people:

"They greatly love to wander;
  they do not restrain their feet.[i]

14:1—15:21 This section opens with God sending a drought on Judah and refusing to answer their prayers for rain. It continues with Jeremiah's description of judgment to come.
14:1ff Drought was a judgment with devastating consequences.

As usual, when their backs were to the wall, the people cried out to God. But God rejected their plea because they did not repent; they merely wanted his rescue. Not even Jeremiah's prayers on their behalf would help. Their only hope was to turn to God.

So the LORD does not accept them;
    he will now remember their wickedness
    and punish them for their sins."[j]

14:10
j Hos 8:13

11Then the LORD said to me, "Do not pray[k] for the well-being of this people. 12Although they fast, I will not listen to their cry;[l] though they offer burnt offerings[m] and grain offerings, I will not accept[n] them. Instead, I will destroy them with the sword, famine and plague."

14:11
k Ex 32:10
14:12
l Isa 1:15
m Jer 7:21
n Jer 6:20

13But I said, "Ah, Sovereign LORD, the prophets keep telling them, 'You will not see the sword or suffer famine.[o] Indeed, I will give you lasting peace in this place.'"

14:13
o Jer 5:12

14Then the LORD said to me, "The prophets are prophesying lies in my name. I have not sent them or appointed them or spoken to them. They are prophesying to you false visions, divinations, idolatries[a] and the delusions of their own minds. 15Therefore, this is what the LORD says about the prophets who are prophesying in my name: I did not send them, yet they are saying, 'No sword or famine will touch this land.' Those same prophets will perish by sword and famine.[p] 16And the people they are prophesying to will be thrown out into the streets of Jerusalem because of the famine and sword. There will be no one to bury them or their wives, their sons or their daughters. I will pour out on them the calamity they deserve.

14:15
p Jer 5:12-13

17"Speak this word to them:

14:17
q Jer 9:1

    "' Let my eyes overflow with tears[q]
      night and day without ceasing;
    for my virgin daughter—my people—
      has suffered a grievous wound,
      a crushing blow.
18 If I go into the country,
    I see those slain by the sword;
if I go into the city,
    I see the ravages of famine.[r]
Both prophet and priest
    have gone to a land they know not.'"

14:18
r Eze 7:15

19 Have you rejected Judah completely?
    Do you despise Zion?
Why have you afflicted us
    so that we cannot be healed?[s]
We hoped for peace
    but no good has come,
for a time of healing
    but there is only terror.[t]
20 O LORD, we acknowledge our wickedness
    and the guilt of our fathers;
    we have indeed sinned against you.
21 For the sake of your name do not despise us;
    do not dishonor your glorious throne.[u]
Remember your covenant with us
    and do not break it.
22 Do any of the worthless idols of the nations bring rain?
    Do the skies themselves send down showers?
No, it is you, O LORD our God.
    Therefore our hope is in you,
    for you are the one who does all this.

14:19
s Jer 30:12-13
t Jer 8:15

14:21
u Jer 3:17

a 14 Or visions, worthless divinations

14:14 What made the people listen to and support the false prophets? These "prophets" said what the people wanted to hear. False teachers earn fame and money by telling people what they want to hear, but they lead people away from God. If we encourage false teachers, we are as guilty as they are.

14:19-22 Interceding for the people, Jeremiah asked God if Judah's repentance would bring his help. But God refused to come to their aid (15:1) because the people were insincere, wicked, and stubborn. They knew he wanted to bless them, and they knew what they needed to do to receive that blessing. They wanted God to do his part, but they did not want to do theirs. It's easy to express sorrow for wrong actions, especially when we want something, but we must be willing to stop doing what is wrong. God will forgive those who are truly repentant, but hypocrites will be severely punished.

15:1
vEx 32:11
w1Sa 7:9
xJer 7:16;
Eze 14:14, 20

15 Then the LORD said to me: "Even if Moses[v] and Samuel[w] were to stand before me, my heart would not go out to this people.[x] Send them away from my presence! Let them go! [2]And if they ask you, 'Where shall we go?' tell them, 'This is what the LORD says:

"'Those destined for death, to death;
those for the sword, to the sword;
those for starvation, to starvation;
those for captivity, to captivity.'

15:3
yLev 26:16
zDt 28:26
15:4
aDt 28:25
b2Ki 23:26-27

[3]"I will send four kinds of destroyers[y] against them," declares the LORD, "the sword to kill and the dogs to drag away and the birds[z] of the air and the beasts of the earth to devour and destroy. [4]I will make them abhorrent to all the kingdoms of the earth[a] because of what Manasseh[b] son of Hezekiah king of Judah did in Jerusalem.

15:5
cIsa 51:19

[5]"Who will have pity[c] on you, O Jerusalem?
Who will mourn for you?
Who will stop to ask how you are?

15:6
dJer 6:19; 7:24

[6]You have rejected[d] me," declares the LORD.
"You keep on backsliding.
So I will lay hands on you and destroy you;
I can no longer show compassion.

15:7
eJer 18:21

[7]I will winnow them with a winnowing fork
at the city gates of the land.
I will bring bereavement and destruction on my people,[e]
for they have not changed their ways.
[8]I will make their widows more numerous
than the sand of the sea.
At midday I will bring a destroyer
against the mothers of their young men;
suddenly I will bring down on them
anguish and terror.

15:9
f1Sa 2:5

[9]The mother of seven will grow faint[f]
and breathe her last.
Her sun will set while it is still day;
she will be disgraced and humiliated.
I will put the survivors to the sword
before their enemies,"

declares the LORD.

15:10
gJob 3:1

[10]Alas, my mother, that you gave me birth,[g]
a man with whom the whole land strives and contends!
I have neither lent nor borrowed,
yet everyone curses me.

[11]The LORD said,

"Surely I will deliver you for a good purpose;
surely I will make your enemies plead with you
in times of disaster and times of distress.

[12]"Can a man break iron—
iron from the north—or bronze?

15:13
hPs 44:12

[13]Your wealth and your treasures
I will give as plunder, without charge,[h]
because of all your sins
throughout your country.

15:1 Moses and Samuel were two of God's greatest prophets. Like Jeremiah, both interceded between God and the people (Exodus 32:11; Numbers 14:11–20; 1 Samuel 7:9; 12:17; Psalm 99:6). Intercession is often effective. In this case, however, the people were so wicked and stubborn that God knew they would not turn to him.

15:3, 4 The goal of these destroyers was to destroy the living and devour the dead. This would happen because of Manasseh's evil reign and the people's sin (2 Kings 21:1–16; 23:26; 24:3), and the destruction would be complete. The people may have argued that they should not be responsible for Manasseh's sins, but they continued what Manasseh began. If we follow corrupt leaders knowingly, we can't excuse ourselves by blaming their bad example.

14 I will enslave you to your enemies
    in[a] a land you do not know,[i]
for my anger will kindle a fire[j]
    that will burn against you."

15 You understand, O Lord;
    remember me and care for me.
Avenge me on my persecutors.[k]
You are long-suffering—do not take me away;
    think of how I suffer reproach for your sake.[l]

16 When your words came, I ate[m] them;
    they were my joy and my heart's delight,
for I bear your name,
    O Lord God Almighty.

17 I never sat[n] in the company of revelers,
    never made merry with them;
I sat alone because your hand was on me
    and you had filled me with indignation.

18 Why is my pain unending
    and my wound grievous and incurable?[o]
Will you be to me like a deceptive brook,
    like a spring that fails?

19 Therefore this is what the Lord says:

"If you repent, I will restore you
    that you may serve me;
if you utter worthy, not worthless, words,
    you will be my spokesman.
Let this people turn to you,
    but you must not turn to them.
20 I will make you a wall to this people,
    a fortified wall of bronze;
they will fight against you
    but will not overcome you,
for I am with you
    to rescue and save you,"[p]

declares the Lord.

21 "I will save you from the hands of the wicked
    and redeem you from the grasp of the cruel."

Day of Disaster

16 Then the word of the Lord came to me: 2"You must not marry and have sons or daughters in this place." 3For this is what the Lord says about the sons and daughters born in this land and about the women who are their mothers and the men who are their fathers: 4"They will die of deadly diseases. They will not be mourned or buried but will be like refuse lying on the ground. 9 They will perish by sword and famine, and their dead bodies will become food for the birds of the air and the beasts of the earth."[r]

a 14 Some Hebrew manuscripts, Septuagint and Syriac (see also Jer. 17:4); most Hebrew manuscripts *I will cause your enemies to bring you* / *into*

**Marginal references:**

15:14 [i] Jer 16:13; [j] Dt 32:22
15:15 [k] Jer 12:3; [l] Ps 69:7-9
15:16 [m] Eze 3:3
15:17 [n] Ps 1:1; 26:4-5; Jer 16:8
15:18 [o] Jer 30:15
15:20 [p] Jer 20:11
16:4 [q] Ps 83:10; [r] Jer 15:3; 34:20

15:17-21 Jeremiah accused God of not helping him when he really needed it. Jeremiah had taken his eyes off God's purposes and was feeling sorry for himself. He was angry, hurt, and afraid. In response, God didn't get angry at Jeremiah; he answered by rearranging Jeremiah's priorities. As God's mouthpiece, he was to influence the people, not let them influence him. There are three important lessons in this passage: (1) in prayer we can reveal our deepest thoughts to God; (2) God expects us to trust him, no matter what; (3) we are here to influence others for God.

16:1—17:18 This section portrays the coming day of disaster. It begins by showing Jeremiah's loneliness. He is a social outcast because of his harsh messages and his celibate lifestyle. He must not marry, have children, or take part in funerals or festivals. The section concludes with another appeal to avoid judgment by turning to God. The people did not heed Jeremiah's words, however, and the first wave of destruction came almost immediately, in 605 B.C. (2 Kings 24:8–12). The second wave came in 597 B.C., and Judah was completely destroyed in 586 B.C.

5 For this is what the LORD says: "Do not enter a house where there is a funeral meal; do not go to mourn or show sympathy, because I have withdrawn my blessing, my love and my pity from this people," declares the LORD. 6 "Both high and low will die in this land. They will not be buried or mourned, and no one will cut himself or shave *s* his head for them. 7 No one will offer food to comfort those who mourn for the dead—not even for a father or a mother—nor will anyone give them a drink to console them.

8 "And do not enter a house where there is feasting and sit down to eat and drink. 9 For this is what the LORD Almighty, the God of Israel, says: Before your eyes and in your days I will bring an end to the sounds *t* of joy and gladness and to the voices of bride and bridegroom in this place. *u*

10 "When you tell these people all this and they ask you, 'Why has the LORD decreed such a great disaster against us? What wrong have we done? What sin have we committed against the LORD our God?' *v* 11 then say to them, 'It is because your fathers forsook me,' declares the LORD, 'and followed other gods and served and worshiped them. They forsook me and did not keep my law. *w* 12 But you have behaved more wickedly than your fathers. *x* See how each of you is following the stubbornness of his evil heart *y* instead of obeying me. 13 So I will throw you out of this land into a land neither you nor your fathers have known, *z* and there you will serve other gods day and night, for I will show you no favor.'

14 "However, the days are coming," declares the LORD, "when men will no longer say, 'As surely as the LORD lives, who brought the Israelites up out of Egypt,' *a* 15 but they will say, 'As surely as the LORD lives, who brought the Israelites up out of the land of the north and out of all the countries where he had banished them.' For I will restore *b* them to the land I gave their forefathers.

16 "But now I will send for many fishermen," declares the LORD, "and they will catch them. *c* After that I will send for many hunters, and they will hunt them down on every mountain and hill and from the crevices of the rocks. 17 My eyes are on all their ways; they are not hidden from me, nor is their sin concealed from my eyes. 18 I will repay them double for their wickedness and their sin, because they have defiled my land with the lifeless forms of their vile images and have filled my inheritance with their detestable idols."

19 O LORD, my strength and my fortress,
   my refuge in time of distress,
to you the nations will come
   from the ends of the earth and say,
"Our fathers possessed nothing but false gods,
   worthless idols that did them no good.
20 Do men make their own gods?
   Yes, but they are not gods!" *d*

21 "Therefore I will teach them—
   this time I will teach them
   my power and might.
Then they will know
   that my name is the LORD.

16:6
s Jer 41:5; 47:5

16:9
t Hos 2:11
u Rev 18:23

16:10
v Dt 29:24; Jer 5:19

16:11
w Jer 22:9

16:12
x Jer 7:26
y Jer 13:10

16:13
z Dt 28:36

16:14
a Jer 23:7-8

16:15
b Jer 24:6

16:16
c Am 4:2;
Hab 1:14-15

16:20
d Isa 37:19; Jer 2:11

16:5–7 In Jeremiah's culture, it was unthinkable not to show grief publicly. The absence of mourning showed the people how complete their devastation would be. So many people would die that it would be impossible to carry out mourning rituals for all of them.

16:8–13 Jeremiah was also told not to participate in parties or other joyful events to show how seriously God took the nation's sins. In both cases (no public grief or joy), Jeremiah's life was to be an attention-getter and an illustration of God's truth. Sometimes we think that the only way to communicate is through speaking or teaching, but God can use a wide variety of means to bring his message. Use your creativity.

16:14, 15 The book of Exodus records God's miraculous rescue of his people from Egyptian slavery (Exodus 1—15). The people's return from exile would be so momentous that it would overshadow even the exodus from Egypt. Even though his people had been so stubborn, God would once again show his great mercy.

16:17 Small children think that if they can't see you, then you can't see them. The people of Israel may have wished that hiding from God were as simple as closing their eyes. Although they closed their eyes to their sinful ways, their sins certainly weren't hidden from God. He who sees everything cannot be deceived. Do you have a sinful attitude or action that you hope God won't notice? He knows about it. The first step of repentance is to acknowledge that God knows about your sins.

16:19 In this prayer, Jeremiah approached God with three descriptive names: strength, fortress, and refuge. Each name gives a slightly different glimpse of how Jeremiah experienced God's presence, and each is a picture of security and protection. Let God be your strength when you feel weak, your fortress when enemies come against you, and your refuge when you need to retreat from life's pressures.

17

"Judah's sin is engraved with an iron tool,[e]
   inscribed with a flint point,
on the tablets of their hearts[f]
   and on the horns of their altars.
2 Even their children remember
      their altars and Asherah poles[a]
   beside the spreading trees
      and on the high hills.
3 My mountain in the land
      and your[b] wealth and all your treasures
   I will give away as plunder,
      together with your high places,
      because of sin throughout your country.
4 Through your own fault you will lose
      the inheritance I gave you.
   I will enslave you to your enemies
      in a land you do not know,
   for you have kindled my anger,
      and it will burn[g] forever."

5 This is what the LORD says:

"Cursed is the one who trusts in man,[h]
      who depends on flesh for his strength
      and whose heart turns away from the LORD.
6 He will be like a bush in the wastelands;
      he will not see prosperity when it comes.
   He will dwell in the parched places of the desert,
      in a salt[i] land where no one lives.

7 "But blessed is the man who trusts[j] in the LORD,
      whose confidence is in him.
8 He will be like a tree planted by the water
      that sends out its roots by the stream.
   It does not fear when heat comes;
      its leaves are always green.
   It has no worries in a year of drought
      and never fails to bear fruit."[k]

9 The heart is deceitful above all things
      and beyond cure.
   Who can understand it?

10 "I the LORD search the heart[l]
      and examine the mind,[m]
   to reward[n] a man according to his conduct,
      according to what his deeds deserve."[o]

17:1
   [e] Job 19:24
   [f] Pr 3:3; 2Co 3:3

17:4
   [g] Jer 15:14

17:5
   [h] Isa 30:1-3

17:6
   [i] Dt 29:23

17:7
   [j] Ps 34:8; Pr 16:20

17:8
   [k] Ps 1:3

17:10
   [l] 1Sa 16:7
   [m] Jer 20:12; Ro 8:27
   [n] Jer 32:19
   [o] Ro 2:6

[a] 2 That is, symbols of the goddess Asherah   [b] 2,3 Or hills / 3 and the mountains of the land. / Your

---

17:1 God's people continued to sin even though they had the law, the prophets of God, and history filled with God's miracles. How could they do that? Why do we continue to cherish sin even though we understand the eternal consequences? Jeremiah says the heart is deceitful (17:9), and "Judah's sin is engraved . . . on the tablets of their hearts." The Hebrews symbolized the various aspects of a person by locating them in certain physical organs. The heart was the organ of reason, intelligence, and will. So deep is our tendency to sin that only God's redemption can deliver us.

17:5-8 Two kinds of people are contrasted here: those who trust in human beings and those who trust in the Lord. The people of Judah were trusting in false gods and military alliances instead of God, and thus they were barren and unfruitful. In contrast, those

who trust in the Lord flourish like trees planted by water (see Psalm 1). In times of trouble, those who trust in human beings will be impoverished and spiritually weak, so they will have no strength to draw on. But those who trust in the Lord will have abundant strength, not only for their own needs, but even for the needs of others. Are you satisfied with being unfruitful, or do you, like a well-watered tree, have strength for the time of crisis and even some to share as you bear fruit for the Lord?

17:9, 10 God makes it clear why we sin—it's a matter of the heart. Our hearts have been inclined toward sin from the time we were born. It is easy to fall into the routine of forgetting and forsaking God. But we can still choose whether or not to continue in sin. We can yield to a specific temptation, or we can ask God to help us resist temptation when it comes.

11 Like a partridge that hatches eggs it did not lay
    is the man who gains riches by unjust means.
When his life is half gone, they will desert him,
    and in the end he will prove to be a fool.

12 A glorious throne, exalted from the beginning,
    is the place of our sanctuary.

17:13
p Jer 14:8
q Isa 1:28

13 O LORD, the hope^p of Israel,
    all who forsake^q you will be put to shame.
Those who turn away from you will be written in the dust
    because they have forsaken the LORD,
    the spring of living water.

17:14
r Ps 109:1

14 Heal me, O LORD, and I will be healed;
    save me and I will be saved,
    for you are the one I praise.^r

17:15
s Isa 5:19

15 They keep saying to me,
    "Where is the word of the LORD?
    Let it now be fulfilled!"^s
16 I have not run away from being your shepherd;
    you know I have not desired the day of despair.
    What passes my lips is open before you.

17:17
t Jer 16:19

17 Do not be a terror to me;
    you are my refuge^t in the day of disaster.

17:18
u Ps 35:1-8

18 Let my persecutors be put to shame,
    but keep me from shame;
let them be terrified,
    but keep me from terror.
Bring on them the day of disaster;
    destroy them with double destruction.^u

Keeping the Sabbath Holy

19 This is what the LORD said to me: "Go and stand at the gate of the people, through which the kings of Judah go in and out; stand also at all the other gates of Jerusalem. 20 Say to them, 'Hear the word of the LORD, O kings of Judah and all people of Judah and everyone living in Jerusalem who come through these gates. 21 This is what the LORD says: Be careful not to carry a load on the Sabbath^v day or bring it through the gates of Jerusalem. 22 Do not bring a load out of your houses or do any work on the Sabbath, but keep the Sabbath day holy, as I commanded your forefathers. ^w 23 Yet they did not listen or pay attention;^x they were stiff-necked and would not listen or respond to discipline. 24 But if you are careful to obey me, declares the LORD, and bring no load through the gates of this city on the Sabbath, but keep the Sabbath day holy by not doing any work on it, 25 then kings who sit on David's throne^y will come through the gates of this city with their officials. They and their officials will come riding in chariots and on horses, accompanied by the men of Judah and those living in Jerusalem, and this city will be inhabited forever. 26 People will come from the towns of Judah and the villages around Jerusalem, from the territory of Benjamin and the western foothills, from the hill country and the Negev, ^z bringing burnt offerings and sacrifices, grain offerings, incense and thank offerings to the house of the LORD. 27 But if you do not obey me to keep the Sabbath day holy by not carrying any load as you come through the gates of Jerusalem on the Sabbath day, then I will kindle an unquenchable fire in the gates of Jerusalem that will consume her fortresses.'" ^a

17:21
v Nu 15:32-36;
Ne 13:15-21

17:22
w Ex 20:8

17:23
x Jer 7:26

17:25
y Jer 22:2, 4

17:26
z Zec 7:7

17:27
a 2Ki 25:9

17:11 There is a right way and a wrong way to do any task. Jeremiah says that the man who becomes rich by unjust means will end up foolish and poor. Whether at work, school, or play, we should strive to be honest in all our dealings. Getting a promotion, passing an exam, or gaining prestige unjustly will never bring God's blessing or lasting happiness.

17:19–27 The people were working on the Sabbath, their day of rest (Exodus 20:8–11). Instead of entering the gates of the city on their way to worship, they continued the hustle and

bustle of business like any other day. They considered making money more important than keeping God's law. If they would repent and put God first in their lives, God promised them honor among the nations. Over a century later, when Nehemiah led the exiles on their return to Jerusalem, one of his most important reforms was to reinstitute Sabbath observance (Nehemiah 13:15–22).

17:26 The Negev is the southern part of Judah.

At the Potter's House

18 This is the word that came to Jeremiah from the LORD: 2 "Go down to the potter's house, and there I will give you my message." 3 So I went down to the potter's house, and I saw him working at the wheel. 4 But the pot he was shaping from the clay was marred in his hands; so the potter formed it into another pot, shaping it as seemed best to him.

5 Then the word of the LORD came to me: 6 "O house of Israel, can I not do with you as this potter does?" declares the LORD. "Like clay[b] in the hand of the potter, so are you in my hand, O house of Israel. 7 If at any time I announce that a nation or kingdom is to be uprooted,[c] torn down and destroyed, 8 and if that nation I warned repents of its evil, then I will relent[d] and not inflict on it the disaster I had planned. 9 And if at another time I announce that a nation or kingdom is to be built up and planted, 10 and if it does evil[e] in my sight and does not obey me, then I will reconsider the good I had intended to do for it.

11 "Now therefore say to the people of Judah and those living in Jerusalem, 'This is what the LORD says: Look! I am preparing a disaster for you and devising a plan against you. So turn[f] from your evil ways, each one of you, and reform your ways and your actions.' 12 But they will reply, 'It's no use.[g] We will continue with our own plans; each of us will follow the stubbornness of his evil heart.'"

13 Therefore this is what the LORD says:

> "Inquire among the nations:
>   Who has ever heard anything like this?
> A most horrible[h] thing has been done
>   by Virgin Israel.
> 14 Does the snow of Lebanon
>   ever vanish from its rocky slopes?
> Do its cool waters from distant sources
>   ever cease to flow?[a]
> 15 Yet my people have forgotten me;
>   they burn incense to worthless idols,
> which made them stumble in their ways
>   and in the ancient paths.[i]
> They made them walk in bypaths
>   and on roads not built up.
> 16 Their land will be laid waste,
>   an object of lasting scorn;
> all who pass by will be appalled
>   and will shake their heads.
> 17 Like a wind[j] from the east,
>   I will scatter them before their enemies;
> I will show them my back and not my face[k]
>   in the day of their disaster."

18 They said, "Come, let's make plans[l] against Jeremiah; for the teaching of the law by the priest[m] will not be lost, nor will counsel from the wise, nor the word from the prophets. So come, let's attack him with our tongues and pay no attention to anything he says."

a 14 The meaning of the Hebrew for this sentence is uncertain.

18:6	b Isa 45:9; Ro 9:20-21
18:7	c Jer 1:10
18:8	d Jer 26:13; Jnh 3:8-10
18:10	e Eze 33:18
18:11	f 2Ki 17:13
18:12	g Isa 57:10; Jer 2:25
18:13	h Jer 5:30
18:15	i Jer 6:16
18:17	j Jer 13:24 k Jer 2:27
18:18	l Jer 11:19 m Mal 2:7

18:1—19:15 The parables in these chapters, probably written during the early years of Jehoiakim's reign, illustrate God's sovereignty over the nation. God has power over the clay (Judah), and he continues to work with it to make it a useful vessel. But Judah must soon repent, or the clay will harden the wrong way. Then it will be worth nothing and will be broken and destroyed.

18:6 As the potter molded or shaped a clay pot on the potter's wheel, defects often appeared. The potter had power over the clay, to permit the defects to remain or to reshape the pot. Likewise, God had power to reshape the nation to conform to his purposes. Our strategy should not be to become mindless and passive—one aspect of clay—but to be willing and receptive to God's impact on us. As we yield to God, he begins reshaping us into valuable vessels.

18:12 Our society admires assertiveness, independence, and defiance of authority. In a relationship with God these qualities become stubbornness, self-importance, and refusal to listen or change. Left unchecked, stubbornness becomes a way of life hostile to God.

18:18 Jeremiah's words and actions challenged the people's social and moral behavior. He had openly spoken against the king, the officials, the priests and prophets, the scribes, and the wise (4:9; 8:8, 9). He wasn't afraid to give unpopular criticism. The people could either obey him or silence him. They chose the latter. They did not think they needed Jeremiah; their false prophets told them what they wanted to hear. How do you respond to criticism? Listen carefully—God may be trying to tell you something.

¹⁹ Listen to me, O Lᴏʀᴅ;
  hear what my accusers are saying!

18:20
n Ps 35:7

²⁰ Should good be repaid with evil?
  Yet they have dug a pit*ⁿ* for me.
Remember that I stood before you
  and spoke in their behalf
  to turn your wrath away from them.

18:21
o Ps 109:9

²¹ So give their children over to famine;
  hand them over to the power of the sword.
Let their wives be made childless and widows;*ᵒ*
  let their men be put to death,
  their young men slain by the sword in battle.

²² Let a cry be heard from their houses
  when you suddenly bring invaders against them,
for they have dug a pit to capture me
  and have hidden snares for my feet.

²³ But you know, O Lᴏʀᴅ,
  all their plots to kill me.
Do not forgive their crimes
  or blot out their sins from your sight.
Let them be overthrown before you;
  deal with them in the time of your anger.

19:2
p Jos 15:8

19:3
q Jer 17:20
r 1Sa 3:11

19:4
s Isa 65:11
t 2Ki 21:16

19:5
u Lev 18:21

19:6
v Jos 15:8

19 This is what the Lᴏʀᴅ says: "Go and buy a clay jar from a potter. Take along some of the elders of the people and of the priests ²and go out to the Valley of Ben Hinnom,*ᵖ* near the entrance of the Potsherd Gate. There proclaim the words I tell you, ³and say, 'Hear the word of the Lᴏʀᴅ, O kings*q* of Judah and people of Jerusalem. This is what the Lᴏʀᴅ Almighty, the God of Israel, says: Listen! I am going to bring a disaster on this place that will make the ears of everyone who hears of it tingle.*ʳ* ⁴For they have forsaken*ˢ* me and made this a place of foreign gods; they have burned sacrifices in it to gods that neither they nor their fathers nor the kings of Judah ever knew, and they have filled this place with the blood of the innocent.*ᵗ* ⁵They have built the high places of Baal to burn their sons*ᵘ* in the fire as offerings to Baal—something I did not command or mention, nor did it enter my mind. ⁶So beware, the days are coming, declares the Lᴏʀᴅ, when people will no longer call this place Topheth or the Valley of Ben Hinnom,*ᵛ* but the Valley of Slaughter.

GOD'S OBJECT LESSONS IN JEREMIAH	Reference	Object Lesson	Significance
	1:11, 12	Branch of an almond tree	God will carry out his threats of punishment.
	1:13	Boiling pot, tilting away from the north	God will punish Judah.
	13:1–11	A ruined linen belt	Because the people refused to listen to God, they had become useless, good for nothing, like a ruined linen belt.
	18:1–17	Potter's clay	God could destroy his sinful people if he so desired. This is a warning to them to repent before he is forced to bring judgment.
	19:1–12	Broken clay jars	God would smash Judah just as Jeremiah smashed the clay jars.
	24:1–10	Two baskets of figs	Good figs represent God's remnant. Poor figs are the people left behind.
	27:2–11	Yoke	Any nation who refused to submit to Babylon's yoke of control would be punished.
	43:8–13	Large stones	The stones marked the place where Nebuchadnezzar would set his throne when God allowed him to conquer Egypt.
	51:59–64	Scroll sunk in the river	Babylon would sink to rise no more.

19:6 The Valley of Ben Hinnom was the garbage dump of Jerusalem and the place where children were sacrificed to the god Molech. It is also mentioned in 7:31, 32. Topheth was located in the valley and means "fireplace." God declared that the place of sacrifice would become a place of slaughter. The killers of the innocent would be judged by losing their own lives.

7"'In this place I will ruin^a the plans of Judah and Jerusalem. I will make them fall by the sword before their enemies, at the hands of those who seek their lives, and I will give their carcasses^w as food to the birds of the air and the beasts of the earth. 8I will devastate this city and make it an object of scorn;^x all who pass by will be appalled and will scoff because of all its wounds. 9I will make them eat^y the flesh of their sons and daughters, and they will eat one another's flesh during the stress of the siege imposed on them by the enemies who seek their lives.'

10"Then break the jar while those who go with you are watching, 11and say to them, 'This is what the LORD Almighty says: I will smash^z this nation and this city just as this potter's jar is smashed and cannot be repaired. They will bury^a the dead in Topheth until there is no more room. 12This is what I will do to this place and to those who live here, declares the LORD. I will make this city like Topheth. 13The houses in Jerusalem and those of the kings of Judah will be defiled like this place, Topheth—all the houses where they burned incense on the roofs to all the starry hosts and poured out drink offerings to other gods.'"

14Jeremiah then returned from Topheth, where the LORD had sent him to prophesy, and stood in the court^b of the LORD's temple and said to all the people, 15"This is what the LORD Almighty, the God of Israel, says: 'Listen! I am going to bring on this city and the villages around it every disaster I pronounced against them, because they were stiff-necked^c and would not listen to my words.'"

Jeremiah and Pashhur

20 When the priest Pashhur son of Immer,^d the chief officer in the temple of the LORD, heard Jeremiah prophesying these things, 2he had Jeremiah the prophet beaten and put in the stocks at the Upper Gate of Benjamin at the LORD's temple. 3The next day, when Pashhur released him from the stocks, Jeremiah said to him, "The LORD's name for you is not Pashhur, but Magor-Missabib.^b 4For this is what the LORD says: 'I will make you a terror to yourself and to all your friends; with your own eyes^e you will see them fall by the sword of their enemies. I will hand all Judah over to the king of Babylon, who will carry them away to Babylon or put them to the sword. 5I will hand over to their enemies all the wealth of this city—all its products, all its valuables and all the treasures of the kings of Judah. They will take it away^f as plunder and carry it off to Babylon. 6And you, Pashhur, and all who live in your house will go into exile to Babylon. There you will die and be buried, you and all your friends to whom you have prophesied^g lies.'"

Jeremiah's Complaint

7 O LORD, you deceived^c me, and I was deceived^c;
  you overpowered me and prevailed.
I am ridiculed all day long;
  everyone mocks me.
8 Whenever I speak, I cry out
  proclaiming violence and destruction.^h

^a7 The Hebrew for *ruin* sounds like the Hebrew for *jar* (see verses 1 and 10). ^b3 Magor-Missabib means *terror on every side.* ^c7 Or *persuaded*

**Cross references (right margin):**
19:7 ^wJer 16:4
19:8 ^xJer 18:16
19:9 ^yDt 28:49-57; La 4:10
19:11 ^zPs 2:9; Isa 30:14 ^aJer 7:32
19:14 ^b2Ch 20:5
19:15 ^cJer 7:26; 17:23
20:1 ^d1Ch 24:14
20:4 ^eJer 29:21
20:5 ^f2Ki 20:17
20:6 ^gJer 14:15
20:8 ^hJer 6:7

19:7–13 The horrible carnage that Jeremiah predicted happened twice, in 586 B.C. during the Babylonian invasion under Nebuchadnezzar, and in A.D. 70 when Titus destroyed Jerusalem. During the Babylonian siege, food became so scarce that people became cannibals, even eating their own children. (See Leviticus 26:29 and Deuteronomy 28:53–57 for prophecies concerning this; and see 2 Kings 6:28, 29; Lamentations 2:20; 4:10 for accounts of actual occurrences.)

20:1ff This event took place during the reign of Jehoiakim of Judah. Jeremiah preached at the Valley of Ben Hinnom, the center of idolatry in the city. He also preached in the temple, which should have been the center of true worship. Both places attracted many people; both were places of false worship.

20:1–3 Pashhur was the official in charge of maintaining order in the temple (see 29:26 for a description of the responsibility). He was also a priest and had pretended to be a prophet. After hearing Jeremiah's words, Pashhur had him beaten and put in the stocks (locked up) instead of taking his message to heart and

acting on it. The truth sometimes stings, but our reaction to the truth shows what we are made of. We can deny the charges and destroy evidence of our misdeeds, or we can take the truth humbly to heart and let it change us. Pashhur may have thought he was a strong leader, but he was really a coward.

20:4–6 This prophecy of destruction came true in three waves of invasion by Babylon. The first wave happened within the year (605 B.C.). Pashhur was probably exiled to Babylon during the second wave in 597 B.C. when Jehoiachin was taken captive. The third invasion occurred in 586 B.C.

20:7–18 Jeremiah cried out in despair mixed with praise, unburdening his heart to God. He had faithfully proclaimed God's word and had received nothing in return but persecution and sorrow. Yet when he withheld God's word for a while, it became fire in his bones until he could hold it back no longer. When God's living message of forgiveness becomes fire in your bones, you also will feel compelled to share it with others, regardless of the results.

So the word of the LORD has brought me
   insult and reproach all day long.
9 But if I say, "I will not mention him
   or speak any more in his name,"
his word is in my heart like a fire,[i]
   a fire shut up in my bones.
I am weary of holding it in;[j]
   indeed, I cannot.

20:9
[i] Ps 39:3
[j] Job 32:18-20;
Ac 4:20

10 I hear many whispering,
   "Terror on every side!
   Report him! Let's report him!"
All my friends
   are waiting for me to slip,[k] saying,
"Perhaps he will be deceived;
   then we will prevail over him
   and take our revenge on him."

20:10
[k] Lk 11:53-54

11 But the LORD is with me like a mighty warrior;
   so my persecutors[l] will stumble and not prevail.[m]
They will fail and be thoroughly disgraced;
   their dishonor will never be forgotten.

20:11
[l] Jer 17:18
[m] Jer 15:20

12 O LORD Almighty, you who examine the righteous
   and probe the heart and mind,[n]
let me see your vengeance upon them,
   for to you I have committed[o] my cause.

20:12
[n] Jer 17:10
[o] Jer 11:20

13 Sing to the LORD!
   Give praise to the LORD!
He rescues the life of the needy
   from the hands of the wicked.

14 Cursed be the day I was born![p]
   May the day my mother bore me not be blessed!
15 Cursed be the man who brought my father the news,
   who made him very glad, saying,
   "A child is born to you—a son!"

20:14
[p] Job 3:3;
Jer 15:10

16 May that man be like the towns[q]
   the LORD overthrew without pity.
May he hear wailing in the morning,
   a battle cry at noon.

20:16
[q] Ge 19:25

17 For he did not kill me in the womb,[r]
   with my mother as my grave,
   her womb enlarged forever.
18 Why did I ever come out of the womb
   to see trouble and sorrow
   and to end my days in shame?

20:17
[r] Job 10:18-19

20:14–18 Probably as troubling as the self-loathing that oozes from these verses is the stark contrast between the exuberant confidence of the previous paragraph and the sudden inward turn of revulsion. In Jeremiah's honestly recorded moments of despair, however, we can find hope. If someone with such intimate awareness of God's presence struggled with insecurity, we ought not to be surprised over our own failures and weaknesses. Jeremiah doesn't give us an excuse, but an example. No matter how we may feel about ourselves at any moment, God remains unchanged, loving, and present in our lives.

21:1 Chapters 21—28 are Jeremiah's messages concerning Nebuchadnezzar's attacks on Jerusalem between 588 and 586 B.C. (see also 2 Kings 25). King Zedekiah decided to rebel against Nebuchadnezzar (2 Kings 24:20), and the nobles advised allying with Egypt. Jeremiah pronounced judgment on the kings (21:1—23:8) and false prophets (23:9–40) for leading the people astray.

4. Jeremiah accuses Judah's leaders
God Rejects Zedekiah's Request

21 The word came to Jeremiah from the LORD when King Zedekiah[s] sent to him Pashhur son of Malkijah and the priest Zephaniah[t] son of Maaseiah. They said: 2"Inquire now of the LORD for us because Nebuchadnezzar[a] king of Babylon is attacking us. Perhaps the LORD will perform wonders for us as in times past so that he will withdraw from us."

3But Jeremiah answered them, "Tell Zedekiah, 4'This is what the LORD, the God of Israel, says: I am about to turn against you the weapons of war that are in your hands, which you are using to fight the king of Babylon and the Babylonians[b] who are outside the wall besieging you. And I will gather them inside this city. 5I myself will fight against you with an outstretched hand and a mighty arm in anger and fury and great wrath. 6I will strike down those who live in this city—both men and animals—and they will die of a terrible plague. [u] 7After that, declares the LORD, I will hand over Zedekiah[v] king of Judah, his officials and the people in this city who survive the plague, sword and famine, to Nebuchadnezzar king of Babylon[w] and to their enemies who seek their lives. He will put them to the sword; he will show them no mercy or pity or compassion.'[x]

8"Furthermore, tell the people, 'This is what the LORD says: See, I am setting before you the way of life and the way of death. 9Whoever stays in this city will die by the sword, famine or plague.[y] But whoever goes out and surrenders to the Babylonians who are besieging you will live; he will escape with his life. [z] 10I have determined to do this city harm [a] and not good, declares the LORD. It will be given into the hands [b] of the king of Babylon, and he will destroy it with fire.'[c]

11"Moreover, say to the royal house of Judah, 'Hear the word of the LORD; 12O house of David, this is what the LORD says:

"'Administer justice every morning;
    rescue from the hand of his oppressor
    the one who has been robbed,
or my wrath will break out and burn like fire
    because of the evil you have done—
    burn with no one to quench it.
13 I am against[d] you, Jerusalem,
    you who live above this valley
    on the rocky plateau,
                                        declares the LORD—
you who say, "Who can come against us?
    Who can enter our refuge?"[e]
14 I will punish you as your deeds[f] deserve,
                                        declares the LORD.

I will kindle a fire[g] in your forests
    that will consume everything around you.'"

Judgment Against Evil Kings

22 This is what the LORD says: "Go down to the palace of the king of Judah and proclaim this message there: 2'Hear the word of the LORD, O king of Judah, you who sit on David's throne—you, your officials and your people who come through these gates. 3This is

21:1
s2Ki 24:18
t2Ki 25:18

21:6
uJer 14:12

21:7
vJer 52:9
wJer 37:17; 39:5
x2Ch 36:17

21:9
yJer 14:12
zJer 38:2, 17; 39:18; 45:5

21:10
aJer 44:11, 27
bJer 38:2-3
cJer 52:13

21:13
dEze 13:8
eJer 49:4

21:14
fIsa 3:10-11
g2Ch 36:19

[a]2 Hebrew *Nebuchadrezzar*, of which *Nebuchadnezzar* is a variant; here and often in Jeremiah and Ezekiel
[b]4 Or *Chaldeans*; also in verse 9

21:1, 2 King Zedekiah probably was referring to God's deliverance of Jerusalem from Sennacherib, king of Assyria, in the days of Hezekiah (Isaiah 36; 37). But Zedekiah's hopes were dashed. He was Judah's last ruler during the time of the exile of 586 B.C.

21:1, 2 Pashhur came to the prophet for help. (This is not the same Pashhur as in 20:1.) God still had work for Jeremiah to do. In living out our faith, we may find that rejection, disappointment, or hard work has brought us to the point of despondency. But we are still needed. God has important work for us as well.

21:1–14 Jeremiah had foretold Jerusalem's destruction. The city's leaders had denied his word and mocked his announcements. In desperation, King Zedekiah turned to God for help, but

without acknowledging God's warnings or admitting his sin. Too often we expect God to help us in our time of trouble even though we have ignored him in our time of prosperity. But God wants a lasting relationship. Are you trying to build a lasting friendship with God, or are you merely using him occasionally to escape trouble? What would you think of your family or friends if they thought of you only as a temporary resource?

21:13 Jerusalem was built on a plateau with valleys on three sides. Because of its strategic location, the inhabitants thought they were safe.

22:1ff Chapters 22—25 may not be in chronological order. In 21:8–10 God implied that it was too late for repentance. In 22:4,

22:3
h Jer 21:12

22:4
i Jer 17:25

22:5
j Jer 17:27
k Heb 6:13

what the LORD says: Do what is just and right. Rescue from the hand of his oppressor h the one who has been robbed. Do no wrong or violence to the alien, the fatherless or the widow, and do not shed innocent blood in this place. 4 For if you are careful to carry out these commands, then kings i who sit on David's throne will come through the gates of this palace, riding in chariots and on horses, accompanied by their officials and their people. 5 But if you do not obey j these commands, declares the LORD, I swear k by myself that this palace will become a ruin.'"

6 For this is what the LORD says about the palace of the king of Judah:

> "Though you are like Gilead to me,
>   like the summit of Lebanon,
> I will surely make you like a desert,
>   like towns not inhabited.

22:7
l Isa 10:34

> 7 I will send destroyers against you,
>   each man with his weapons,
> and they will cut l up your fine cedar beams
>   and throw them into the fire.

22:8
m Dt 29:25-26;
1Ki 9:8-9
22:9
n 2Ki 22:17

8 "People from many nations will pass by this city and will ask one another, 'Why has the LORD done such a thing to this great city?' m 9 And the answer will be: 'Because they have forsaken the covenant of the LORD their God and have worshiped and served other gods.' n '"

> 10 Do not weep for the dead ⌊king⌋ or mourn his loss;
>   rather, weep bitterly for him who is exiled,
> because he will never return
>   nor see his native land again.

22:11
o 2Ki 23:31

11 For this is what the LORD says about Shallum a o son of Josiah, who succeeded his father as king of Judah but has gone from this place: "He will never return. 12 He will die in the place where they have led him captive; he will not see this land again."

22:13
p Mic 3:10; Hab 2:9
q Jas 5:4

> 13 "Woe to him who builds p his palace by unrighteousness,
>   his upper rooms by injustice,
> making his countrymen work for nothing,
>   not paying q them for their labor.

22:14
r Isa 5:8-9

> 14 He says, 'I will build myself a great palace r
>   with spacious upper rooms.'
> So he makes large windows in it,
>   panels it with cedar
>   and decorates it in red.

22:15
s Isa 3:10

> 15 "Does it make you a king
>   to have more and more cedar?
> Did not your father have food and drink?
>   He did what was right and just,
>   so all went well s with him.

22:16
t Ps 72:1-4, 12-13

> 16 He defended the cause of the poor and needy, t
>   and so all went well.
> Is that not what it means to know me?"
>   declares the LORD.

a 11 Also called Jehoahaz

---

however, God said that there was still time to change. The events to which this chapter refers occurred before those of chapter 21.

22:3 God gave the king the basis for rebuilding the nation—turn from evil and do right. Doing what is right is more than simply believing all the right doctrines about God. It means living obediently to God. Good deeds do not save us, but they display our faith (James 2:17–26).

22:10–12 Good King Josiah had died at the battle of Megiddo (2 Kings 23:29); his son Shallum (Jehoahaz) reigned for only three months in 609 B.C. before being taken away to Egypt by Pharaoh Neco. He would be the first ruler to die in exile. The people were told not to waste their tears on the death of Josiah,

but to cry for the king who was taken into exile and would never return.

22:15, 16 God passed judgment on King Jehoiakim. His father, Josiah, had been one of Judah's great kings, but Jehoiakim was evil. Josiah had been faithful to his responsibility to be a model of right living, but Jehoiakim had been unfaithful to his responsibility to imitate his father. God's judgment was on unfaithful Jehoiakim. He could not claim his father's blessings when he had not followed his father's God. We may inherit our parents' money, but we cannot inherit their faith. A great heritage, a good education, or a beautiful home doesn't guarantee strong character. We must have our own relationship with God.

17 "But your eyes and your heart
          are set only on dishonest gain,
     on shedding innocent blood
          and on oppression and extortion."

18 Therefore this is what the LORD says about Jehoiakim son of Josiah king of Judah:

     "They will not mourn for him:
          'Alas, my brother! Alas, my sister!'
     They will not mourn for him:
          'Alas, my master! Alas, his splendor!'
19 He will have the burial of a donkey—
          dragged away and thrown[u]
          outside the gates of Jerusalem."

20 "Go up to Lebanon and cry out,
          let your voice be heard in Bashan,
     cry out from Abarim,
          for all your allies are crushed.
21 I warned you when you felt secure,
          but you said, 'I will not listen!'
     This has been your way from your youth;[v]
          you have not obeyed me.
22 The wind will drive all your shepherds away,
          and your allies will go into exile.
     Then you will be ashamed and disgraced
          because of all your wickedness.
23 You who live in 'Lebanon,[a]'
          who are nestled in cedar buildings,
     how you will groan when pangs come upon you,
          pain[w] like that of a woman in labor!

24 "As surely as I live," declares the LORD, "even if you, Jehoiachin[b] son of Jehoiakim king of Judah, were a signet ring on my right hand, I would still pull you off. 25 I will hand you over[x] to those who seek your life, those you fear—to Nebuchadnezzar king of Babylon and to the Babylonians. c 26 I will hurl[y] you and the mother who gave you birth into another country, where neither of you was born, and there you both will die. 27 You will never come back to the land you long to return to."

28 Is this man Jehoiachin a despised, broken pot,[z]
          an object no one wants?
     Why will he and his children be hurled out,
          cast into a land they do not know?
29 O land,[a] land, land,
          hear the word of the LORD!
30 This is what the LORD says:
     "Record this man as if childless,[b]
          a man who will not prosper in his lifetime,
     for none of his offspring will prosper,
          none will sit on the throne of David
          or rule anymore in Judah."

22:19 [u] Jer 36:30

22:21 [v] Jer 3:25

22:23 [w] Jer 4:31

22:25 [x] Jer 34:20

22:26 [y] 2Ki 24:8; 2Ch 36:10

22:28 [z] Ps 31:12; Jer 48:38; Hos 8:8

22:29 [a] Jer 6:19

22:30 [b] 1Ch 3:18; Mt 1:12

a23 That is, the palace in Jerusalem (see 1 Kings 7:2)   b24 Hebrew *Coniah*, a variant of *Jehoiachin*; also in verse 28   c25 Or *Chaldeans*

22:21 Jehoiakim had been hardheaded and hardhearted since childhood. God warned him, but he refused to listen. His prosperity always took a higher priority than his relationship with God. If you ever find yourself so comfortable that you don't have time for God, stop and ask which is more important—the comforts of this life or a close relationship with God.

22:24, 25 A signet ring was extremely valuable because a king used it to authenticate important documents. Jehoiachin's sins spoiled his usefulness to God. Even if he were God's own signet ring, God would depose him because of his sins (see 24:1).

22:30 Zedekiah reigned after Jehoiachin but died before him (52:10, 11). Jehoiachin was the last king of David's line to sit on the throne in Judah (1 Chronicles 3:15–20). He had seven sons, but not one served as king. Jehoiachin's grandson Zerubbabel ruled after the return from exile (Ezra 2:2). He was only a governor, not a king.

The Righteous Branch

23:1
c Jer 10:21

23

"Woe to the shepherds [c] who are destroying and scattering the sheep of my pasture!" declares the LORD. [2] Therefore this is what the LORD, the God of Israel, says to the shepherds who tend my people: "Because you have scattered my flock and driven them away and have not bestowed care on them, I will bestow punishment on you for the evil you have

23:3
d Jer 32:37
23:4
e Jer 3:15;
Eze 34:23
f Jer 30:10

done," declares the LORD. [3] "I myself will gather the remnant [d] of my flock out of all the countries where I have driven them and will bring them back to their pasture, where they will be fruitful and increase in number. [4] I will place shepherds [e] over them who will tend them, and they will no longer be afraid [f] or terrified, nor will any be missing," declares the LORD.

23:5
g Isa 4:2
h Isa 9:7
i Isa 11:1; Zec 6:12

[5] "The days are coming," declares the LORD,
   "when I will raise up to David [a] a righteous Branch, [g]
a King who will reign [h] wisely
   and do what is just and right [i] in the land.

23:6
j Jer 33:16
k 1Co 1:30

[6] In his days Judah will be saved
   and Israel will live in safety.
This is the name [j] by which he will be called:
   The LORD Our Righteousness. [k]

23:7
l Jer 16:14

[7] "So then, the days are coming," declares the LORD, "when people will no longer say, 'As surely as the LORD lives, who brought the Israelites up out of Egypt,' [l] [8] but they will say, 'As surely as the LORD lives, who brought the descendants of Israel up out of the land of the north and out of all the countries where he had banished them.' Then they will live in their own land."

Lying Prophets

[9] Concerning the prophets:

My heart is broken within me;
   all my bones tremble.
I am like a drunken man,
   like a man overcome by wine,
because of the LORD
   and his holy words.

23:10
m Jer 9:10

[10] The land is full of adulterers;
   because of the curse [b] the land lies parched [c]
   and the pastures [m] in the desert are withered.
The ⌊prophets⌋ follow an evil course
   and use their power unjustly.

23:11
n Jer 6:13; Zep 3:4

[11] "Both prophet and priest are godless; [n]
   even in my temple I find their wickedness,"
                                                            declares the LORD.

23:12
o Jer 13:16
p Jer 11:23

[12] "Therefore their path will become slippery; [o]
   they will be banished to darkness
   and there they will fall.
I will bring disaster on them
   in the year they are punished. [p]"
                                                            declares the LORD.

a 5 Or *up from David's line*   b 10 Or *because of these things*   c 10 Or *land mourns*

23:1–4 Those responsible to lead Israel in God's path were the very ones responsible for Israel's present plight, and so God had decreed harsh judgment against them. Leaders are held responsible for those entrusted to their care. Whom has God placed in your care? Remember that you are accountable to God for those you influence and lead.

23:5, 6 Jeremiah contrasted the present corrupt leaders with the coming Messiah, the perfect King who would come from David's line to reign over Israel.

23:9–14 How did the nation become so corrupt? A major factor was false prophecy. The false prophets had a large, enthusiastic

audience and were very popular because they made the people believe that all was well. By contrast, Jeremiah's message from God was unpopular because it showed the people how bad they were.

There are four warning signs of false prophets—characteristics we need to watch for even today. (1) They may appear to speak God's message, but they do not live according to his principles. (2) They water down God's message in order to make it more palatable. (3) They encourage their listeners, often subtly, to disobey God. (4) They tend to be arrogant and self-serving, appealing to the desires of their audience instead of being true to God's Word.

13 "Among the prophets of Samaria
    I saw this repulsive thing:
They prophesied by Baal
    and led my people Israel astray.
14 And among the prophets of Jerusalem
    I have seen something horrible:
They commit adultery and live a lie. q
They strengthen the hands of evildoers,
    so that no one turns from his wickedness.
They are all like Sodom to me;
    the people of Jerusalem are like Gomorrah."

23:14
q Jer 29:23

15Therefore, this is what the LORD Almighty says concerning the prophets:

"I will make them eat bitter food
    and drink poisoned water,
because from the prophets of Jerusalem
    ungodliness has spread throughout the land."

16This is what the LORD Almighty says:

23:16
r Jer 14:14

"Do not listen to what the prophets are prophesying to you;
    they fill you with false hopes.
They speak visions r from their own minds,
    not from the mouth of the LORD.
17 They keep saying to those who despise me,
    'The LORD says: You will have peace.'
And to all who follow the stubbornness of their hearts
    they say, 'No harm s will come to you.'
18 But which of them has stood in the council of the LORD
    to see or to hear his word?
    Who has listened and heard his word?
19 See, the storm t of the LORD
    will burst out in wrath,
a whirlwind swirling down
    on the heads of the wicked.
20 The anger of the LORD will not turn back
    until he fully accomplishes
    the purposes of his heart.
In days to come
    you will understand it clearly.
21 I did not send u these prophets,
    yet they have run with their message;
I did not speak to them,
    yet they have prophesied.
22 But if they had stood in my council,
    they would have proclaimed my words to my people
and would have turned them from their evil ways
    and from their evil deeds.

23:17
s Jer 5:12; Mic 3:11

23:19
t Jer 25:32; 30:23

23:21
u Jer 14:14

23 "Am I only a God nearby, v"

23:23
v Ps 139:1-10

declares the LORD,

    "and not a God far away?

23:14 Sodom and Gomorrah were sinful cities destroyed by God (Genesis 19:23, 24). In the Bible they typify the ultimate in degrading, sinful behavior and rebellion against God.

23:20 "In days to come you will understand it clearly" means that the people would see the truth of this prophecy when Jerusalem fell.

23:21–24 In Jeremiah's time, those who claimed to speak for God were often guilty of representing a deity they thought of as limited and localized—a neighborhood god. Their gods frequently had limited interests and shortsighted awareness. God declares his omnipresence with a question: "Do not I fill heaven and earth?" We make the same mistake those would-be prophets made when we assume God doesn't know or care about the situations in our lives or when we question his ability to handle things beyond our control. How big is the God you worship?

23:24
w 1Ki 8:27

24 Can anyone hide in secret places
so that I cannot see him?"

declares the LORD.

"Do not I fill heaven and earth?"w

declares the LORD.

23:25
x Jer 14:14

25 "I have heard what the prophets say who prophesy lies x in my name. They say, 'I had a dream! I had a dream!' 26 How long will this continue in the hearts of these lying prophets,

23:27
y Jdg 3:7

who prophesy the delusions of their own minds? 27 They think the dreams they tell one another will make my people forget my name, just as their fathers forgot y my name through Baal worship. 28 Let the prophet who has a dream tell his dream, but let the one who has my word speak it faithfully. For what has straw to do with grain?" declares the LORD. 29 "Is not my word like fire," declares the LORD, "and like a hammer that breaks a rock in pieces?

23:30
z Dt 18:20

30 "Therefore," declares the LORD, "I am against the prophets z who steal from one another words supposedly from me. 31 Yes," declares the LORD, "I am against the prophets who wag their own tongues and yet declare, 'The LORD declares.' 32 Indeed, I am against those who prophesy false dreams," declares the LORD. "They tell them and lead my people astray with their reckless lies, yet I did not send or appoint them. They do not benefit these people in the least," declares the LORD.

False Oracles and False Prophets

23:33
a Mal 1:1
b ver 39
23:34
c La 2:14
23:35
d Jer 33:3

33 "When these people, or a prophet or a priest, ask you, 'What is the oracle a a of the LORD?' say to them, 'What oracle?b I will forsake b you, declares the LORD.' 34 If a prophet or a priest or anyone else claims, 'This is the oracle c of the LORD,' I will punish that man and his household. 35 This is what each of you keeps on saying to his friend or relative: 'What is the LORD's answer?' d or 'What has the LORD spoken?' 36 But you must not mention 'the oracle of the LORD' again, because every man's own word becomes his oracle and so you distort the words of the living God, the LORD Almighty, our God. 37 This is what you keep saying to a prophet: 'What is the LORD's answer to you?' or 'What has the LORD spoken?' 38 Although you claim, 'This is the oracle of the LORD,' this is what the LORD says: You used the words, 'This is the oracle of the LORD,' even though I told you that you must not claim, 'This is the oracle of the LORD.' 39 Therefore, I will surely forget you and cast you out of my presence along with the

23:40
e Jer 20:11

city I gave to you and your fathers. 40 I will bring upon you everlasting disgrace e—everlasting shame that will not be forgotten."

Two Baskets of Figs

24:1
f 2Ch 36:9; Jer 29:2
g Am 8:1-2

24 After Jehoiachin c f son of Jehoiakim king of Judah and the officials, the craftsmen and the artisans of Judah were carried into exile from Jerusalem to Babylon by Nebuchadnezzar king of Babylon, the LORD showed me two baskets of figs g placed in front of the temple of the LORD. 2 One basket had very good figs, like those that ripen early; the other basket had very poor figs, so bad they could not be eaten.

a 33 Or burden (see Septuagint and Vulgate)   b 33 Hebrew; Septuagint and Vulgate 'You are the burden. (The Hebrew for oracle and burden is the same.)   c 1 Hebrew Jeconiah, a variant of Jehoiachin

---

23:28 True prophets and false prophets are as different as straw and grain. Straw is useless for food and cannot compare to nourishing grain. To share the gospel is a great responsibility because the way we present it and live it will encourage people either to accept it or reject it. Whether we speak from a pulpit, teach in a class, or share with friends, we are entrusted with accurately communicating and living out God's Word. As you share God's Word with friends and neighbors, they will look for its effectiveness in your life. Unless it has changed you, why should they let it change them? If you preach it, make sure you live it!

23:33–40 People mocked Jeremiah by saying sarcastically, "What is the oracle of the LORD?" (oracle meaning "utterance" or "burden"). The people mocked Jeremiah and God because it seemed that Jeremiah brought nothing but God's sad news of condemnation. But this sad news was the truth. If they had accepted it, they would have had to repent and turn to God. Because they did not want to do this, they rejected Jeremiah's message. Have you ever rejected a message or made fun of it because it would require you to change your ways? Before dismissing someone who brings sad news, look carefully at your motives.

24:1 This happened in 597 B.C. Jehoiachin was taken to Babylon, and Zedekiah became king. Often royal officials were exiled to keep them from exerting power and starting a rebellion. Skilled craftsmen and artisans were taken because they were valuable for Babylon's building program. Jeremiah foretold this event in 22:24–28.

24:2–10 The good figs represented the exiles to Babylon—not because they themselves were good, but because their hearts would respond to God. He would preserve them and bring them back to the land. The poor figs represented those who remained in Judah or ran away to Egypt. Those people may have arrogantly believed they would be blessed if they remained in the land or escaped to Egypt, but the opposite was true because God would use the captivity to refine the exiles. We may assume we are blessed when life goes well and cursed when it does not. But trouble is a blessing when it makes us stronger, and prosperity is a curse if it entices us away from God. If you are facing trouble, ask God to help you grow stronger for him. If things are going your way, ask God to help you use your prosperity for him.

3 Then the LORD asked me, "What do you see,[h] Jeremiah?"

"Figs," I answered. "The good ones are very good, but the poor ones are so bad they cannot be eaten."

4 Then the word of the LORD came to me: 5 "This is what the LORD, the God of Israel, says: 'Like these good figs, I regard as good the exiles from Judah, whom I sent away from this place to the land of the Babylonians.[a] 6 My eyes will watch over them for their good, and I will bring them back[i] to this land. I will build[j] them up and not tear them down; I will plant them and not uproot them. 7 I will give them a heart to know me, that I am the LORD. They will be my people,[k] and I will be their God, for they will return[l] to me with all their heart.

8 "But like the poor[m] figs, which are so bad they cannot be eaten,' says the LORD, 'so will I deal with Zedekiah king of Judah, his officials and the survivors from Jerusalem, whether they remain in this land or live in Egypt. 9 I will make them abhorrent[n] and an offense to all the kingdoms of the earth, a reproach and a byword,[o] an object of ridicule and cursing,[p] wherever I banish them. 10 I will send the sword, famine and plague against them until they are destroyed from the land I gave to them and their fathers.'"

Seventy Years of Captivity

25 The word came to Jeremiah concerning all the people of Judah in the fourth year of Jehoiakim[q] son of Josiah king of Judah, which was the first year of Nebuchadnezzar king of Babylon. 2 So Jeremiah the prophet said to all the people of Judah and to all those living in Jerusalem: 3 For twenty-three years—from the thirteenth year of Josiah[r] son of Amon king of Judah until this very day—the word of the LORD has come to me and I have spoken to you again and again, but you have not listened.

4 And though the LORD has sent all his servants the prophets to you again and again, you have not listened or paid any attention. 5 They said, "Turn now, each of you, from your evil ways and your evil practices, and you can stay in the land the LORD gave to you and your fathers for ever and ever. 6 Do not follow other gods to serve and worship them; do not provoke me to anger with what your hands have made. Then I will not harm you."

7 "But you did not listen to me," declares the LORD, "and you have provoked me with what your hands have made, and you have brought harm to yourselves."

8 Therefore the LORD Almighty says this: "Because you have not listened to my words, 9 I will summon all the peoples of the north[s] and my servant[t] Nebuchadnezzar king of Babylon," declares the LORD, "and I will bring them against this land and its inhabitants and against all the surrounding nations. I will completely destroy[b] them and make them an object of horror and scorn,[u] and an everlasting ruin. 10 I will banish from them the sounds of joy and gladness, the voices of bride and bridegroom, the sound of millstones and the light of the lamp.[v] 11 This whole country will become a desolate wasteland, and these nations will serve the king of Babylon seventy years.

12 "But when the seventy years are fulfilled, I will punish the king of Babylon and his nation, the land of the Babylonians,[a] for their guilt," declares the LORD, "and will make it desolate forever. 13 I will bring upon that land all the things I have spoken against it, all that are written in this book and prophesied by Jeremiah against all the nations. 14 They themselves will be enslaved by many nations[w] and great kings; I will repay[x] them according to their deeds and the work of their hands."

a 5, 12 Or *Chaldeans*   b 9 The Hebrew term refers to the irrevocable giving over of things or persons to the LORD, often by totally destroying them.

24:3
h Jer 1:11

24:6
i Jer 29:10
j Jer 33:7; 42:10

24:7
k Jer 31:33;
Heb 8:10
l Jer 32:40

24:8
m Jer 29:17

24:9
n Jer 15:4; 34:17
o 1Ki 9:7
p Jer 29:18

25:1
q 2Ki 24:2; Jer 36:1

25:3
r Jer 1:2

25:9
s Jer 1:15
t Jer 27:6
u Jer 18:16

25:10
v Rev 18:22-23

25:14
w Jer 50:9; 51:27-28
x Jer 51:6

24:6 The exiles in Babylon were cared for by the Lord. Although they were moved to a foreign land, their captivity was not enslavement. The people could function in business and own homes. Some, like Daniel, even held high positions in the government (see Daniel 2:48).

25:1ff Jeremiah gave this message in 605 B.C., the year Nebuchadnezzar came to power. From verse 3 we learn that the beginning of Jeremiah's ministry was in 627 B.C. He predicted the 70 years of captivity a full 20 years before it began.

25:2–6 Imagine preaching the same message for 23 years and continually being rejected! Jeremiah faced this; but because he had committed his life to God, he continued to proclaim the message: "Turn now, each of you, from your evil ways and your evil practices." Regardless of the people's response, Jeremiah did not give up. God never stops loving us, even when we reject him. We can thank God that he won't give up on us, and, like Jeremiah, we can commit ourselves to never forsaking him. No matter how people respond when you tell them about God, remain faithful to God's high call and continue to witness for him.

25:12 This event is further described in Daniel 5. The troops of Cyrus the Great entered Babylon in 539 B.C. and killed Belshazzar, the last Babylonian ruler.

The Cup of God's Wrath

25:15
ʸIsa 51:17; Ps 75:8

¹⁵This is what the LORD, the God of Israel, said to me: "Take from my hand this cupʸ filled with the wine of my wrath and make all the nations to whom I send you drink it. ¹⁶When they drink it, they will stagger and go mad because of the sword I will send among them."

25:17
ᶻJer 1:10
25:18
ᵃJer 24:9

¹⁷So I took the cup from the LORD's hand and made all the nations to whom he sentᶻ me drink it: ¹⁸Jerusalem and the towns of Judah, its kings and officials, to make them a ruin and an object of horror and scorn and cursing,ᵃ as they are today; ¹⁹Pharaoh king of Egypt, his attendants, his officials and all his people, ²⁰and all the foreign people there; all the kings of Uz; all the kings of the Philistines (those of Ashkelon, Gaza, Ekron, and the people left at

25:21
ᵇJer 49:1
25:23
ᶜJer 9:26
25:26
ᵈJer 50:3, 9

Ashdod); ²¹Edom, Moab and Ammon;ᵇ ²²all the kings of Tyre and Sidon; the kings of the coastlands across the sea; ²³Dedan, Tema, Buz and all who are in distant placesᵃ;ᶜ ²⁴all the kings of Arabia and all the kings of the foreign people who live in the desert; ²⁵all the kings of Zimri, Elam and Media; ²⁶and all the kings of the north,ᵈ near and far, one after the other—all the kingdoms on the face of the earth. And after all of them, the king of Sheshachᵇ will drink it too.

25:27
ᵉHab 2:16
ᶠEze 21:4

²⁷"Then tell them, 'This is what the LORD Almighty, the God of Israel, says: Drink, get drunkᵉ and vomit, and fall to rise no more because of the swordᶠ I will send among you.' ²⁸But if they refuse to take the cup from your hand and drink, tell them, 'This is what the LORD Almighty says: You must drink it! ²⁹See, I am beginning to bring disaster on the city that bears my Name, and will you indeed go unpunished? You will not go unpunished, for I am calling down a sword upon all who live on the earth, declares the LORD Almighty.'

25:30
ᵍIsa 16:10; 42:13

³⁰"Now prophesy all these words against them and say to them:

> "'The LORD will roarᵍ from on high;
> he will thunder from his holy dwelling
> and roar mightily against his land.
> He will shout like those who tread the grapes,
> shout against all who live on the earth.

25:31
ʰHos 4:1

> ³¹ The tumult will resound to the ends of the earth,
> for the LORD will bring chargesʰ against the nations;
> he will bring judgment on all mankind
> and put the wicked to the sword,'"

declares the LORD.

25:32
ⁱIsa 34:2
ʲJer 23:19

³²This is what the LORD Almighty says:

> "Look! Disaster is spreading
> from nation to nation;ⁱ
> a mighty stormʲ is rising
> from the ends of the earth."

25:33
ᵏIsa 66:16
ˡJer 16:4
ᵐPs 79:3

³³At that time those slainᵏ by the LORD will be everywhere—from one end of the earth to the other. They will not be mourned or gatheredˡ up or buried,ᵐ but will be like refuse lying on the ground.

25:34
ⁿJer 6:26
ᵒIsa 34:6

> ³⁴ Weep and wail, you shepherds;
> rollⁿ in the dust, you leaders of the flock.
> For your time to be slaughteredᵒ has come;
> you will fall and be shattered like fine pottery.
> ³⁵ The shepherds will have nowhere to flee,
> the leaders of the flock no place to escape.
> ³⁶ Hear the cry of the shepherds,
> the wailing of the leaders of the flock,
> for the LORD is destroying their pasture.
> ³⁷ The peaceful meadows will be laid waste
> because of the fierce anger of the LORD.

ᵃ23 Or *who clip the hair by their foreheads*   ᵇ26 *Sheshach* is a cryptogram for Babylon.

25:15–38 Judah would not be the only nation to drink the cup of God's wrath. Here Jeremiah listed other wicked nations who would experience God's wrath at the hand of Babylon. Finally, Babylon itself (called Sheshach in 25:26) would be destroyed because of its sin.

38 Like a lion[p] he will leave his lair,
    and their land will become desolate
because of the sword[a] of the oppressor
    and because of the LORD's fierce anger.

25:38
p Jer 4:7

Jeremiah Threatened With Death

26 Early in the reign of Jehoiakim[q] son of Josiah king of Judah, this word came from the LORD: 2 "This is what the LORD says: Stand in the courtyard[r] of the LORD's house and speak to all the people of the towns of Judah who come to worship in the house of the LORD. Tell[s] them everything I command you; do not omit[t] a word. 3 Perhaps they will listen and each will turn from his evil way. Then I will relent[u] and not bring on them the disaster I was planning because of the evil they have done. 4 Say to them, 'This is what the LORD says: If you do not listen[v] to me and follow my law, which I have set before you, 5 and if you do not listen to the words of my servants the prophets, whom I have sent to you again and again (though you have not listened[w]), 6 then I will make this house like Shiloh and this city an object of cursing among all the nations of the earth.'"

7 The priests, the prophets and all the people heard Jeremiah speak these words in the house of the LORD. 8 But as soon as Jeremiah finished telling all the people everything the LORD had commanded him to say, the priests, the prophets and all the people seized him and said, "You must die! 9 Why do you prophesy in the LORD's name that this house will be like Shiloh and this city will be desolate and deserted?"[x] And all the people crowded around Jeremiah in the house of the LORD.

10 When the officials of Judah heard about these things, they went up from the royal palace to the house of the LORD and took their places at the entrance of the New Gate of the LORD's house. 11 Then the priests and the prophets said to the officials and all the people, "This man should be sentenced to death[y] because he has prophesied against this city. You have heard it with your own ears!"

12 Then Jeremiah said to all the officials and all the people: "The LORD sent me to prophesy against this house and this city all the things you have heard. 13 Now reform[z] your ways and your actions and obey the LORD your God. Then the LORD will relent and not bring the disaster he has pronounced against you. 14 As for me, I am in your hands;[a] do with me whatever you think is good and right. 15 Be assured, however, that if you put me to death, you will bring the guilt of innocent blood on yourselves and on this city and on those who live in it, for in truth the LORD has sent me to you to speak all these words in your hearing."

16 Then the officials and all the people said to the priests and the prophets, "This man should not be sentenced to death![b] He has spoken to us in the name of the LORD our God."

17 Some of the elders of the land stepped forward and said to the entire assembly of people, 18 "Micah[c] of Moresheth prophesied in the days of Hezekiah king of Judah. He told all the people of Judah, 'This is what the LORD Almighty says:

26:1
q 2Ki 23:36
26:2
r Jer 19:14
s Jer 1:17; Ac 20:27
t Dt 4:2
26:3
u Jer 18:8
26:4
v Lev 26:14
26:5
w Jer 25:4

26:9
x Jer 9:11

26:11
y Jer 38:4; Mt 26:66

26:13
z Jer 7:5;
Joel 2:12-14
26:14
a Jer 38:5

26:16
b Ac 5:34-39; 23:29

26:18
c Mic 1:1

a 38 Some Hebrew manuscripts and Septuagint (see also Jer. 46:16 and 50:16); most Hebrew manuscripts *anger*

26:1ff The events described in this chapter took place in 609–608 B.C., before the events described in chapter 25. Jehoiakim was a materialistic and self-centered king who persecuted and murdered innocent people (36:22–32; 2 Kings 23:36—24:6). Chapter 26 describes how and why Jeremiah was on trial for his life.

26:2 God reminded Jeremiah that he wanted his entire message given—"Do not omit a word." Jeremiah may have been tempted to leave out the parts that would turn his audience against him, would sound too harsh, or would make him sound like a traitor. But by God's command, he was not to delete parts of God's message to suit himself, his audience, or the circumstances in which he found himself. Like Jeremiah, we must never ignore or repress important parts of God's Word to please anyone.

26:2–9 Shiloh was where the tabernacle had been set up after the conquest of Canaan (Joshua 18:1). It was destroyed in 1050 B.C. by the Philistines. "I will make this house like Shiloh" means that Jerusalem and the temple would be destroyed. When Jeremiah said that Jerusalem, the city of God, would become an

object of cursing and the temple would be destroyed (26:6), the priests and false prophets were infuriated. The temple was important to them because the people's reverence for it brought them power. By saying that the temple would be destroyed, Jeremiah undermined their authority. Jesus also infuriated the religious leaders of his time by foretelling the destruction of Jerusalem and the temple (Matthew 24:2).

26:11 Jeremiah was branded a traitor because he prophesied the destruction of the city and the temple. But the "courageous" people advocated a foreign alliance to fight Babylon and retain their independence. The accusations they leveled at Jeremiah were actually true of themselves—they were the traitors because they had turned away from God.

26:17–19 The elders remembered the words of the prophet Micah (Micah 3:12), which was similar to the words Jeremiah spoke. When Micah called the people to repent, they turned from their wickedness. Although these people did not kill Jeremiah, they missed the main point—that the application of the story was for them. They spared Jeremiah, but they did not spare themselves by repenting of their sins. As you recall a great story of the Bible, ask how it can be applied to *your* life.

26:18
d Zec 8:3

"'Zion will be plowed like a field,
  Jerusalem will become a heap of rubble,
  the temple hill*d* a mound overgrown with thickets.'*a*

26:19
e 2Ch 32:24-26

19"Did Hezekiah king of Judah or anyone else in Judah put him to death? Did not Hezekiah*e* fear the Lord and seek his favor? And did not the Lord relent, so that he did not bring the disaster he pronounced against them? We are about to bring a terrible disaster on ourselves!"

26:20
f Jos 9:17

20(Now Uriah son of Shemaiah from Kiriath Jearim*f* was another man who prophesied in the name of the Lord; he prophesied the same things against this city and this land as Jeremiah did. 21When King Jehoiakim and all his officers and officials heard his words, the king sought to put him to death. But Uriah heard of it and fled*g* in fear to Egypt. 22King Jehoiakim, however, sent Elnathan*h* son of Acbor to Egypt, along with some other men. 23They brought Uriah out of Egypt and took him to King Jehoiakim, who had him struck down with a sword and his body thrown into the burial place of the common people.)

26:21
g Mt 10:23
26:22
h Jer 36:12, 25

26:24
i 2Ki 22:12

24Furthermore, Ahikam*i* son of Shaphan supported Jeremiah, and so he was not handed over to the people to be put to death.

Judah to Serve Nebuchadnezzar

27:2
j Jer 28:10, 13

27 Early in the reign of Zedekiah*b* son of Josiah king of Judah, this word came to Jeremiah from the Lord: 2This is what the Lord said to me: "Make a yoke*j* out of straps and crossbars and put it on your neck. 3Then send word to the kings of Edom, Moab, Ammon, Tyre and Sidon through the envoys who have come to Jerusalem to Zedekiah king of Judah. 4Give them a message for their masters and say, 'This is what the Lord Almighty, the God of Israel, says: "Tell this to your masters: 5With my great power and outstretched arm I made the earth and its people and the animals that are on it, and I give*k* it to anyone I please. 6Now I will hand all your countries over to my servant*l* Nebuchadnezzar*m* king of Babylon; I will make even the wild animals subject to him.*n* 7All nations will serve him and his son and his grandson until the time*o* for his land comes; then many nations and great kings will subjugate him.

27:5
k Ps 115:16
27:6
l Jer 25:9
m Eze 29:18-20
n Jer 28:14
27:7
o Jer 25:12

27:9
p Dt 18:11
27:10
q Jer 23:25
27:11
r Jer 21:9

8"'"If, however, any nation or kingdom will not serve Nebuchadnezzar king of Babylon or bow its neck under his yoke, I will punish that nation with the sword, famine and plague, declares the Lord, until I destroy it by his hand. 9So do not listen to your prophets, your diviners, your interpreters of dreams, your mediums*p* or your sorcerers who tell you, 'You will not serve the king of Babylon.' 10They prophesy lies*q* to you that will only serve to remove you far from your lands; I will banish you and you will perish. 11But if any nation will bow its neck under the yoke*r* of the king of Babylon and serve him, I will let that nation remain in its own land to till it and to live there, declares the Lord."'"

27:13
s Eze 18:31

27:14
t Jer 14:14
27:15
u Jer 6:15

12I gave the same message to Zedekiah king of Judah. I said, "Bow your neck under the yoke of the king of Babylon; serve him and his people, and you will live. 13Why will you and your people die*s* by the sword, famine and plague with which the Lord has threatened any nation that will not serve the king of Babylon? 14Do not listen to the words of the prophets who say to you, 'You will not serve the king of Babylon,' for they are prophesying lies*t* to you. 15'I have not sent them,' declares the Lord. 'They are prophesying lies in my name. Therefore, I will banish you and you will perish,*u* both you and the prophets who prophesy to you.'"

a 18 Micah 3:12   *b 1* A few Hebrew manuscripts and Syriac (see also Jer. 27:3,12 and 28:1); most Hebrew manuscripts *Jehoiakim* (Most Septuagint manuscripts do not have this verse.)

26:20-23 Uriah is an otherwise unknown prophet who was executed for faithfully proclaiming God's words. This shows us that God has had other prophets whose words are not included in the Bible.

27:1ff The year was 593 B.C., and Nebuchadnezzar had already invaded Judah once and had taken many captives. Jeremiah wore a yoke (a wooden frame used to fasten a team of animals to a plow) as a symbol of bondage. This was an object lesson, telling the people they must put themselves under Babylon's yoke or be destroyed.

27:5, 6 God punished the people of Judah in an unusual way, by appointing a foreign ruler to be his "servant." Nebuchadnezzar was not employed to proclaim God's message, but to fulfill God's promise of judgment on sin. Because God is in control

of all events, he uses whomever he wants. God may use unlikely people or circumstances to teach you. Be ready to accept God's correction, even if it comes from unexpected sources.

27:12-18 Zedekiah was in a tough spot. Jeremiah called on him to surrender to Nebuchadnezzar at a time when many of the other leaders wanted him to form an alliance and fight. It would be disgraceful for a king to surrender, and he would look like a coward. This was a great opportunity for the false prophets, who kept saying that the Babylonians would not defeat the great city of Jerusalem and that God would never allow the magnificent, holy temple to be destroyed.

¹⁶Then I said to the priests and all these people, "This is what the LORD says: Do not listen to the prophets who say, 'Very soon now the articles ᵛ from the LORD's house will be brought back from Babylon.' They are prophesying lies to you. ¹⁷Do not listen to them. Serve the king of Babylon, and you will live. Why should this city become a ruin? ¹⁸If they are prophets and have the word of the LORD, let them plead with the LORD Almighty that the furnishings remaining in the house of the LORD and in the palace of the king of Judah and in Jerusalem not be taken to Babylon. ¹⁹For this is what the LORD Almighty says about the pillars, the Sea, ʷ the movable stands and the other furnishings ˣ that are left in this city, ²⁰which Nebuchadnezzar king of Babylon did not take away when he carried ʸ Jehoiachin ᵃ son of Jehoiakim king of Judah into exile from Jerusalem to Babylon, along with all the nobles of Judah and Jerusalem— ²¹yes, this is what the LORD Almighty, the God of Israel, says about the things that are left in the house of the LORD and in the palace of the king of Judah and in Jerusalem: ²²'They will be taken to Babylon and there they will remain until the day I come for them,' declares the LORD. 'Then I will bring ᶻ them back and restore them to this place.'"

The False Prophet Hananiah

28 In the fifth month of that same year, the fourth year, early in the reign of Zedekiah ᵃ king of Judah, the prophet Hananiah son of Azzur, who was from Gibeon, said to me in the house of the LORD in the presence of the priests and all the people: ²"This is what the LORD Almighty, the God of Israel, says: 'I will break the yoke ᵇ of the king of Babylon. ³Within two years I will bring back to this place all the articles ᶜ of the LORD's house that Nebuchadnezzar king of Babylon removed from here and took to Babylon. ⁴I will also bring back to this place Jehoiachin ᵃ ᵈ son of Jehoiakim king of Judah and all the other exiles from Judah who went to Babylon,' declares the LORD, 'for I will break the yoke of the king of Babylon.'"

⁵Then the prophet Jeremiah replied to the prophet Hananiah before the priests and all the people who were standing in the house of the LORD. ⁶He said, "Amen! May the LORD do so! May the LORD fulfill the words you have prophesied by bringing the articles of the LORD's house and all the exiles back to this place from Babylon. ⁷Nevertheless, listen to what I have to say in your hearing and in the hearing of all the people: ⁸From early times the prophets who preceded you and me have prophesied war, disaster and plague against many countries and great kingdoms. ⁹But the prophet who prophesies peace will be recognized as one truly sent by the LORD only if his prediction comes true. ᵉ"

¹⁰Then the prophet Hananiah took the yoke ᶠ off the neck of the prophet Jeremiah and broke it, ¹¹and he said before all the people, "This is what the LORD says: 'In the same way will I break the yoke of Nebuchadnezzar king of Babylon off the neck of all the nations within two years.'" At this, the prophet Jeremiah went on his way.

¹²Shortly after the prophet Hananiah had broken the yoke off the neck of the prophet Jeremiah, the word of the LORD came to Jeremiah: ¹³"Go and tell Hananiah, 'This is what the LORD says: You have broken a wooden yoke, but in its place you will get a yoke of iron. ¹⁴This is what the LORD Almighty, the God of Israel, says: I will put an iron yoke ᵍ on the necks of all these nations to make them serve Nebuchadnezzar king of Babylon, and they will serve him. I will even give him control over the wild animals. ʰ'"

¹⁵Then the prophet Jeremiah said to Hananiah the prophet, "Listen, Hananiah! The LORD has not sent you, yet you have persuaded this nation to trust in lies. ⁱ ¹⁶Therefore, this is what the LORD says: 'I am about to remove you from the face of the earth. This very year you are going to die, because you have preached rebellion ʲ against the LORD.'"

¹⁷In the seventh month of that same year, Hananiah the prophet died.

ᵃ 20,4 Hebrew *Jeconiah*, a variant of *Jehoiachin*

27:16
ᵛ2Ch 36:7, 10;
Jer 28:3; Da 1:2

27:19
ʷ2Ki 25:13
ˣJer 52:17-23

27:20
ʸJer 24:1

27:22
ᶻEzr 1:7; 7:19

28:1
ᵃJer 27:1, 3

28:2
ᵇJer 27:12

28:3
ᶜ2Ki 24:13

28:4
ᵈJer 22:24-27

28:9
ᵉDt 18:22

28:10
ᶠJer 27:2

28:14
ᵍDt 28:48
ʰJer 27:6

28:15
ⁱEze 13:6

28:16
ʲDt 13:5; Jer 29:32

27:19–22 When Nebuchadnezzar invaded Judah, first in 605 and then in 597 B.C., he took away many important people living in Jerusalem—including Daniel and Ezekiel. Although these men were captives, they had a profound impact on the exiles and leaders in Babylon. Jeremiah predicted that more people and even the precious objects in the temple would be taken. This happened in 586 B.C. during Babylon's third and last invasion.

28:6–9 Hananiah had just come up with a prophecy everyone liked. He declared that God would soon bring relief from all their problems and oppressors. Jeremiah had to admit that Hananiah's words echoed his own wishes. He sincerely hoped Hananiah was right. But unfortunately, Hananiah's words were not from God.

Positive or negative, God's words are exactly true. We, like Jeremiah, may honestly wish for results or benefits outside God's plans. But if we are going to be faithful to God, there will be times when we must disagree with our own wishes in order to speak the truth and be obedient to God.

28:8–17 Jeremiah spoke the truth, but it was unpopular; Hananiah spoke lies, but his deceitful words brought false hope and comfort to the people. God had already outlined the marks of a true prophet (Deuteronomy 13; 18:20–22): a true prophet's predictions always come true and his words never contradict previous revelation. Jeremiah's predictions were already coming true, from Hananiah's death to the Babylonian invasions. But the

A Letter to the Exiles

29 This is the text of the letter that the prophet Jeremiah sent from Jerusalem to the surviving elders among the exiles and to the priests, the prophets and all the other people Nebuchadnezzar had carried into exile from Jerusalem to Babylon. ²(This was after King Jehoiachin^a ^k and the queen mother, the court officials and the leaders of Judah and Jerusalem, the craftsmen and the artisans had gone into exile from Jerusalem.) ³He entrusted the letter to Elasah son of Shaphan and to Gemariah son of Hilkiah, whom Zedekiah king of Judah sent to King Nebuchadnezzar in Babylon. It said:

⁴This is what the LORD Almighty, the God of Israel, says to all those I carried^l into exile from Jerusalem to Babylon: ⁵"Build houses and settle down; plant gardens and eat what they produce. ⁶Marry and have sons and daughters; find wives for your sons and give your daughters in marriage, so that they too may have sons and daughters. Increase in number there; do not decrease. ⁷Also, seek the peace and prosperity of the city to which I have carried you into exile. Pray^m to the LORD for it, because if it prospers, you too will prosper." ⁸Yes, this is what the LORD Almighty, the God of Israel, says: "Do not let the prophets and diviners among you deceive you. Do not listen to the dreams you encourage them to have. ⁹They are prophesying liesⁿ to you in my name. I have not sent them," declares the LORD.

¹⁰This is what the LORD says: "When seventy years^o are completed for Babylon, I will come to you and fulfill my gracious promise to bring you back^p to this place. ¹¹For I know the plans I have for you," declares the LORD, "plans to prosper you and not to harm you, plans to give you hope and a future. ¹²Then you will call upon me and come and pray to me, and I will listen^q to you. ¹³You will seek me and find me when you seek me with all your heart.^r ¹⁴I will be found by you," declares the LORD, "and will bring you back from captivity.^b I will gather you from all the nations and places where I have banished you," declares the LORD, "and will bring you back to the place from which I carried you into exile."

¹⁵You may say, "The LORD has raised up prophets for us in Babylon," ¹⁶but this is what the LORD says about the king who sits on David's throne and all the people who remain in this city, your countrymen who did not go with you into exile— ¹⁷yes, this is what the LORD Almighty says: "I will send the sword, famine and plague against them and I will make them like poor figs^s that are so bad they cannot be eaten. ¹⁸I will pursue them with the sword, famine and plague and will make them abhorrent to all the kingdoms of the earth and an object of cursing and horror,^t of scorn and reproach, among all the nations where I drive them. ¹⁹For they have not listened to my words," declares the LORD, "words that I sent to them again and again by my servants the prophets.^u And you exiles have not listened either," declares the LORD.

### Cross references (margin)

29:2
k 2Ki 24:12;
Jer 22:24-28

29:4
l Jer 24:5

29:7
m Ezr 6:10;
1Ti 2:1-2

29:9
n Jer 14:14

29:10
o 2Ch 36:21;
Jer 25:12; Da 9:2
p Jer 21:22

29:12
q Ps 145:19

29:13
r Jer 24:7

29:17
s Jer 24:8-10

29:18
t Dt 28:25;
Jer 42:18

29:19
u Jer 25:4

---

^a2 Hebrew *Jeconiah*, a variant of *Jehoiachin*   ^b14 Or *will restore your fortunes*

---

people still preferred to listen to comforting lies rather than painful truth.

29:4–7 Jeremiah wrote to the captives in Babylon (29:4–23 is the letter) instructing them to move ahead with their lives and to pray for the pagan nation that enslaved them. Life cannot grind to a halt during troubled times. In an unpleasant or distressing situation, we must adjust and keep moving. You may find it difficult to pray for those in authority if they are evil, but that is when your prayers are most needed (1 Timothy 2:1, 2). When you enter times of trouble or sudden change, pray diligently and move ahead, doing whatever you can rather than giving up because of fear and uncertainty.

29:10 Scholars differ on the exact dates of this 70-year period in Babylon. Some say it refers to the years 605–538 B.C., from the first deportation to Babylon to the arrival of the first exiles back in Jerusalem after Cyrus's freedom decree. Others point to the years 586–516 B.C., from the last deportation to Babylon and the destruction of the temple until its rebuilding. A third possibility is that 70 years is an approximate number meaning a lifetime. All agree that God sent his people to Babylon for a long time, not the short captivity predicted by the false prophets.

29:11 We're all encouraged by a leader who stirs us to move

ahead, someone who believes we can do the task he has given and who will be with us all the way. God is that kind of leader. He knows the future, and his plans for us are good and full of hope. As long as God, who knows the future, provides our agenda and goes with us as we fulfill his mission, we can have boundless hope. This does not mean that we will be spared pain, suffering, or hardship, but that God will see us through to a glorious conclusion.

29:12–14 God did not forget his people, even though they were captive in Babylon. He planned to give them a new beginning with a new purpose—to turn them into new people. In times of deep trouble, it may appear as though God has forgotten you. But God may be preparing you, as he did the people of Judah, for a new beginning with him at the center.

29:13 According to God's wise plan, his people were to have hope and a future; consequently they could call upon him in confidence. Although the exiles were in a difficult place and time, they should not despair because they had God's presence, the privilege of prayer, and God's grace. God can be sought and found when we seek him wholeheartedly. Neither strange lands, sorrows, frustration, nor physical problems can break that communion.

²⁰Therefore, hear the word of the LORD, all you exiles whom I have sent away from Jerusalem to Babylon. ²¹This is what the LORD Almighty, the God of Israel, says about Ahab son of Kolaiah and Zedekiah son of Maaseiah, who are prophesying lies to you in my name: "I will hand them over to Nebuchadnezzar king of Babylon, and he will put them to death before your very eyes. ²²Because of them, all the exiles from Judah who are in Babylon will use this curse: 'The LORD treat you like Zedekiah and Ahab, whom the king of Babylon burned in the fire.' ²³For they have done outrageous things in Israel; they have committed adultery with their neighbors' wives and in my name have spoken lies, which I did not tell them to do. I know it and am a witness to it," declares the LORD.

Message to Shemaiah

²⁴Tell Shemaiah the Nehelamite, ²⁵"This is what the LORD Almighty, the God of Israel, says: You sent letters in your own name to all the people in Jerusalem, to Zephaniah ᵛ son of Maaseiah the priest, and to all the other priests. You said to Zephaniah, ²⁶'The LORD has appointed you priest in place of Jehoiada to be in charge of the house of the LORD; you should put any madman who acts like a prophet into the stocks ʷ and neck-irons. ²⁷So why have you not reprimanded Jeremiah from Anathoth, who poses as a prophet among you? ²⁸He has sent this message to us in Babylon: It will be a long time. Therefore build ˣ houses and settle down; plant gardens and eat what they produce.'"

²⁹Zephaniah the priest, however, read the letter to Jeremiah the prophet. ³⁰Then the word of the LORD came to Jeremiah: ³¹"Send this message to all the exiles: 'This is what the LORD says about Shemaiah the Nehelamite: Because Shemaiah has prophesied to you, even though I did not send ʸ him, and has led you to believe a lie, ³²this is what the LORD says: I will surely punish Shemaiah the Nehelamite and his descendants. He will have no one left among this people, nor will he see the good things I will do for my people, declares the LORD, because he has preached rebellion ᶻ against me.'"

5. Restoration is promised
Restoration of Israel

30 This is the word that came to Jeremiah from the LORD: ²"This is what the LORD, the God of Israel, says: 'Write in a book all the words I have spoken to you. ³The days are coming,' declares the LORD, 'when I will bring my people Israel and Judah back from captivityᵃ and restore them to the land I gave their forefathers to possess,' says the LORD."

⁴These are the words the LORD spoke concerning Israel and Judah: ⁵"This is what the LORD says:

> "'Cries of fear are heard—
> terror, not peace.
> ⁶ Ask and see:
> Can a man bear children?
> Then why do I see every strong man
> with his hands on his stomach like a woman in labor,ᵃ
> every face turned deathly pale?
> ⁷ How awful that dayᵇ will be!
> None will be like it.

ᵃ3 Or *will restore the fortunes of my people Israel and Judah*

29:25
ᵛ2Ki 25:18

29:26
ʷJer 20:2

29:28
ˣver 5

29:31
ʸJer 14:14; 28:15

29:32
ᶻJer 28:16

30:6
ᵃJer 4:31

30:7
ᵇJoel 2:11

29:20–23 Why would Nebuchadnezzar decide to execute these two false prophets? In contrast to Jeremiah's message from God that the people should settle in Babylon and wait faithfully for seventy years to pass, the false prophets were inciting false hopes for a quick return to Jerusalem. This would have sounded like rebellion to the Babylonian king, who would have had little hesitation over killing uncooperative refugees.

29:21 These false prophets, Ahab and Zedekiah, should not be confused with the kings who had the same names. Their family connections clearly identify them.

29:24–28 These verses describe the reaction of Shemaiah, a false prophet exiled in 597 B.C. who had protested about

Jeremiah's letter. To discredit Jeremiah, Shemaiah accused him of false prophecy. Although Jeremiah's message was true and his words were from God, the people hated him because he told them to make the most of the exile. But Jeremiah's truth from God offered temporary correction and long-range benefit, while the false teachers' lies offered only temporary comfort and long-range punishment.

30:1ff Chapters 30 and 31 show that Jeremiah spoke of hope and consolation as well as trouble and gloom. The people would one day be restored to their land, and God would make a new covenant with them to replace the one they broke. Where once they sinned and disobeyed, eventually they would repent and obey.

It will be a time of trouble for Jacob,
　　but he will be saved out of it.

8 "'In that day,' declares the LORD Almighty,
　　'I will break the yoke off their necks
　　and will tear off their bonds;
　　no longer will foreigners enslave them.
9 Instead, they will serve the LORD their God
　　and David[c] their king,[d]
　　whom I will raise up for them.

10 "'So do not fear,[e] O Jacob my servant;[f]
　　do not be dismayed, O Israel,'
　　　　　　　　　　　　　　　　　　declares the LORD.

'I will surely save you out of a distant place,
　　your descendants from the land of their exile.
Jacob will again have peace and security,
　　and no one will make him afraid.
11 I am with you and will save you,'
　　declares the LORD.
'Though I completely destroy all the nations
　　among which I scatter you,
　　I will not completely destroy[g] you.
I will discipline[h] you but only with justice;
　　I will not let you go entirely unpunished.'

12 "This is what the LORD says:

"'Your wound is incurable,
　　your injury beyond healing.
13 There is no one to plead your cause,
　　no remedy for your sore,
　　no healing for you.
14 All your allies[i] have forgotten you;
　　they care nothing for you.
I have struck you as an enemy would
　　and punished you as would the cruel,
because your guilt is so great
　　and your sins[j] so many.
15 Why do you cry out over your wound,
　　your pain that has no cure?
Because of your great guilt and many sins
　　I have done these things to you.

16 "'But all who devour[k] you will be devoured;
　　all your enemies will go into exile.
Those who plunder you will be plundered;
　　all who make spoil of you I will despoil.
17 But I will restore you to health
　　and heal your wounds,'
　　　　　　　　　　　　　　　　　　declares the LORD,

30:9
c Isa 55:3-4;
Lk 1:69; Ac 2:30;
13:23
d Eze 34:23-24;
37:24; Hos 3:5

30:10
e Isa 43:5
f Isa 44:2

30:11
g Jer 4:27; 46:28
h Jer 10:24

30:14
i La 1:2
j Jer 5:6

30:16
k Isa 33:1;
Jer 10:25

30:8, 9 Like Isaiah, Jeremiah associated events of the near future and those of the distant future. Reading these prophecies is like looking at several mountain peaks in a range. From a distance they look as though they are next to each other, when actually they are miles apart. Jeremiah presents near and distant events as if they will all happen soon. He sees the exile, but he sees also the future day when Christ will reign forever. The reference to David is not to King David, but to his famous descendant, the Messiah (Luke 1:69).

30:12, 13, 17 The medical language here conveys the idea that sin is terminal. Sinful people cannot be cured by being good or

being religious. Beware of putting your confidence in useless cures while your sin spreads and causes you pain. God alone can cure the disease of sin, but you must be willing to let him do it.

30:15 Judah protested its punishment, even though the sin that caused the pain was scandalous. But punishment is an opportunity for growth because it makes us aware of sin's consequences. The people should have asked how they could profit from their mistakes. Remember this the next time you are corrected.

'because you are called an outcast,
  Zion for whom no one cares.'

18"This is what the LORD says:

"'I will restore the fortunes[l] of Jacob's tents
    and have compassion[m] on his dwellings;
the city will be rebuilt on her ruins,
    and the palace will stand in its proper place.
19 From them will come songs of thanksgiving
    and the sound of rejoicing.
I will add to their numbers,
    and they will not be decreased;
I will bring them honor,
    and they will not be disdained.
20 Their children will be as in days of old,
    and their community will be established[n] before me;
    I will punish all who oppress them.
21 Their leader will be one of their own;
    their ruler will arise from among them.
I will bring him near[o] and he will come close to me,
    for who is he who will devote himself
    to be close to me?'

                                                    declares the LORD.

22 "'So you will be my people,
    and I will be your God.'"

23 See, the storm[p] of the LORD
    will burst out in wrath,
a driving wind swirling down
    on the heads of the wicked.
24 The fierce anger of the LORD will not turn back
    until he fully accomplishes
    the purposes of his heart.
In days to come
    you will understand this.

31

"At that time," declares the LORD, "I will be the God[q] of all the clans of Israel, and they will be my people."
2 This is what the LORD says:

"The people who survive the sword
    will find favor[r] in the desert;
I will come to give rest to Israel."

3 The LORD appeared to us in the past,[a] saying:

"I have loved you with an everlasting love;
    I have drawn[s] you with loving-kindness.
4 I will build you up again
    and you will be rebuilt, O Virgin Israel.
Again you will take up your tambourines
    and go out to dance with the joyful.[t]

a3 Or LORD has appeared to us from afar

30:18 | Jer 31:23
m Ps 102:13

30:20 n Isa 54:14

30:21 o Nu 16:5

30:23 p Jer 23:19

31:1 q Jer 30:22

31:2 r Nu 14:20

31:3 s Hos 11:4

31:4 t Jer 30:19

30:18 This prophecy that Jerusalem would be rebuilt was not completely fulfilled by the work of Ezra, Nehemiah, and Zerubbabel. The city was indeed rebuilt after the captivity, but the final restoration will occur when all believers are gathered in Christ's kingdom. This restoration will include buildings (30:18), people (30:19), and rulers (30:21).

30:21 This verse refers to the restoration after the Babylonian captivity, as well as to the final restoration under Christ.

31:1 This promise is to all the clans (tribes) of Israel, not only to the tribe of Judah. The restoration will include all people who trust God.

31:3 God reaches toward his people with kindness motivated by deep and everlasting love. He is eager to do the best for them if they will only let him. After many words of warning about sin, this reminder of God's magnificent love is a breath of fresh air. Rather than thinking of God with dread, look carefully and see him lovingly drawing us toward himself.

31:5
uIsa 65:21;
Am 9:14

5 Again you will plant vineyards
  on the hills of Samaria;
the farmers will plant them
  and enjoy their fruit.u

31:6
vIsa 2:3; Mic 4:2

6 There will be a day when watchmen cry out
  on the hills of Ephraim,
'Come, let us go up to Zion,
  to the LORD our God.'"v

31:7
wDt 28:13

7 This is what the LORD says:

"Sing with joy for Jacob;
  shout for the foremostw of the nations.
Make your praises heard, and say,
  'O LORD, save your people,
  the remnant of Israel.'

31:8
xJer 3:18; 23:8
yIsa 42:16

8 See, I will bring them from the land of the northx
  and gather them from the ends of the earth.
Among them will be the blindy and the lame,
  expectant mothers and women in labor;
  a great throng will return.

31:9
zIsa 49:11

9 They will come with weeping;
  they will pray as I bring them back.
I will lead them beside streams of water
  on a levelz path where they will not stumble,
because I am Israel's father,
  and Ephraim is my firstborn son.

31:10
aIsa 40:11

10 "Hear the word of the LORD, O nations;
  proclaim it in distant coastlands:
'He who scattered Israel will gather them
  and will watch over his flock like a shepherd.'a

31:11
bIsa 44:23; 48:20

11 For the LORD will ransom Jacob
  and redeemb them from the hand of those stronger than they.

31:12
cEze 17:23

12 They will come and shout for joy on the heightsc of Zion;
  they will rejoice in the bounty of the LORD—
the grain, the new wine and the oil,
  the young of the flocks and herds.
They will be like a well-watered garden,
  and they will sorrow no more.

31:13
dIsa 51:11

13 Then maidens will dance and be glad,
  young men and old as well.
I will turn their mourning into gladness;
  I will give them comfort and joyd instead of sorrow.

14 I will satisfy the priests with abundance,
  and my people will be filled with my bounty,"

declares the LORD.

31:15
eJos 18:25
fMt 2:17-18*

15 This is what the LORD says:

"A voice is heard in Ramah,e
  mourning and great weeping,
Rachel weeping for her children
  and refusing to be comforted,
  because her children are no more."f

31:14 This means that many sacrifices will be made at the temple so that the priests will have a feast with their portion. It is also a symbol of life and prosperity (Psalm 36:8; 63:5; Isaiah 55:2).

31:15 Rachel, Jacob's favorite wife, was the symbolic mother of the northern tribes, who were taken away by the Assyrians as slaves. Rachel is pictured crying for the exiles at Ramah, a stag-

ing point of deportation. This verse is quoted in Matthew 2:18 to describe the sadness of the mothers of Bethlehem as the male children were killed. The weeping was great in both cases.

¹⁶This is what the LORD says:

31:16
⁹Eze 11:17

> "Restrain your voice from weeping
>   and your eyes from tears,
> for your work will be rewarded,"

declares the LORD.

> "They will return⁹ from the land of the enemy.
> ¹⁷ So there is hope for your future,"

declares the LORD.

> "Your children will return to their own land.

¹⁸ "I have surely heard Ephraim's moaning:
>   'You disciplinedʰ me like an unruly calf,
>   and I have been disciplined.
> Restore me, and I will return,
>   because you are the LORD my God.

31:18
ʰJob 5:17

¹⁹ After I strayed,
>   I repented;
> after I came to understand,
>   I beat my breast.
> I was ashamed and humiliated
>   because I bore the disgrace of my youth.'

²⁰ Is not Ephraim my dear son,
>   the child in whom I delight?
> Though I often speak against him,
>   I still rememberⁱ him.
> Therefore my heart yearns for him;
>   I have great compassionʲ for him,"

31:20
ⁱHos 4:4; 11:8
ʲIsa 63:15

declares the LORD.

²¹ "Set up road signs;
>   put up guideposts.
> Take note of the highway,ᵏ
>   the road that you take.
> Return, O Virgin Israel,
>   return to your towns.

31:21
ᵏJer 50:5

²² How long will you wander,
>   O unfaithful daughter?
> The LORD will create a new thing on earth—
>   a woman will surroundᵃ a man."

²³This is what the LORD Almighty, the God of Israel, says: "When I bring them back from captivity,ᵇ the people in the land of Judah and in its towns will once again use these words: 'The LORD bless you, O righteous dwelling,ˡ O sacred mountain.'ᵐ ²⁴ People will live together in Judah and all its towns—farmers and those who move about with their flocks. ²⁵ I will refresh the weary and satisfy the faint."

31:23
ˡIsa 1:26
ᵐZec 8:3

²⁶At this I awoke and looked around. My sleep had been pleasant to me.

²⁷"The days are coming," declares the LORD, "when I will plantⁿ the house of Israel and the house of Judah with the offspring of men and of animals. ²⁸Just as I watched over them to uproot and tear down, and to overthrow, destroy and bring disaster,ᵒ so I will watch over them to build and to plant,"ᵖ declares the LORD. ²⁹"In those days people will no longer say,

31:27
ⁿEze 36:9-11;
Hos 2:23
31:28
ᵒJer 44:27
ᵖJer 1:10

> 'The fathers have eaten sour grapes,
>   and the children's teeth are set on edge.'ᵍ

31:29
ᵍEze 18:2

ᵃ22 Or *will go about* ⌊*seeking*⌋; or *will protect*   ᵇ23 Or *I restore their fortunes*

31:18–20 "I beat my breast" was an expression picturing grief and mourning. Ephraim was one of the major tribes of the northern kingdom. Although the northern kingdom had sunk into the most degrading sins, God still loved the people. A remnant would turn to God, repenting of their sins, and God would forgive. God still loves you, despite anything you may have done. He will forgive you if you turn back to him.

31:29, 30 The people tried to blame God's judgment on the sins of their fathers. One person's sin does indeed affect other people, but all people are still held personally accountable for the sin in

30Instead, everyone will die for his own sin; whoever eats sour grapes—his own teeth will be set on edge.

31:31
r Jer 32:40;
Heb 8:8-12*

31 "The time is coming," declares the LORD,
   "when I will make a new covenant*r*
with the house of Israel
   and with the house of Judah.
32 It will not be like the covenant
   I made with their forefathers
when I took them by the hand
   to lead them out of Egypt,
because they broke my covenant,
   though I was a husband to*a* them,*b*"

declares the LORD.

31:33
s Jer 24:7

33 "This is the covenant I will make with the house of Israel
   after that time," declares the LORD.
"I will put my law in their minds
   and write it on their hearts.
I will be their God,
   and they will be my people.*s*

31:34
t Jn 6:45
u Isa 54:13
v Mic 7:19;
Heb 10:17*

34 No longer will a man teach his neighbor,
   or a man his brother, saying, 'Know the LORD,'
because they will all know*t* me,
   from the least of them to the greatest,"

declares the LORD.

"For I will forgive*u* their wickedness
   and will remember their sins*v* no more."

31:35
w Ge 1:16
x Jer 10:16

35 This is what the LORD says,

he who appoints the sun
   to shine by day,
who decrees the moon and stars
   to shine by night,*w*
who stirs up the sea
   so that its waves roar—
the LORD Almighty is his name:*x*

31:36
y Jer 33:20-26

36 "Only if these decrees*y* vanish from my sight,"
   declares the LORD,
"will the descendants of Israel ever cease
   to be a nation before me."

31:37
z Jer 33:22

37 This is what the LORD says:

"Only if the heavens above can be measured*z*
   and the foundations of the earth below be searched out
will I reject all the descendants of Israel
   because of all they have done,"

declares the LORD.

a32 Hebrew; Septuagint and Syriac / *and I turned away from*   *b32* Or *was their master*

---

their own lives (Deuteronomy 24:16; Ezekiel 18:2). What excuses do you use for your sins?

31:33 God would write his law on their hearts rather than on tablets of stone, as he did the Ten Commandments. In 17:1 their sin was engraved on their hearts so that they wanted above all to disobey. This change seems to describe an experience very much like the new birth, with God taking the initiative. When we turn our lives over to God, he, by his Holy Spirit, builds into us the desire to obey him.

31:33 The old covenant, broken by the people, would be replaced by a new covenant. The foundation of this new covenant is Christ (Hebrews 8:6). It is revolutionary, involving not only

Israel and Judah, but even the Gentiles. It offers a unique personal relationship with God himself, with his laws written on individuals' hearts instead of on stone. Jeremiah looked forward to the day when Jesus would come to establish this covenant. But for us today, this covenant is here. We have the wonderful opportunity to make a fresh start and establish a permanent, personal relationship with God (see 29:11; 32:38–40).

31:35–37 God has the power to do away with the decrees of nature or even to do away with his people. But he will do neither. This is not a prediction; it is a promise. This is God's way of saying that he will not reject Israel any more than he will do away with nature's laws. Neither will happen!

38"The days are coming," declares the LORD, "when this city will be rebuilt for me from the Tower of Hananel a to the Corner Gate. 39 The measuring line will stretch from there straight to the hill of Gareb and then turn to Goah. 40 The whole valley where dead bodies and ashes are thrown, and all the terraces out to the Kidron Valley on the east as far as the corner of the Horse Gate, will be holy b to the LORD. The city will never again be uprooted or demolished."

Jeremiah Buys a Field

32 This is the word that came to Jeremiah from the LORD in the tenth c year of Zedekiah king of Judah, which was the eighteenth year of Nebuchadnezzar. 2 The army of the king of Babylon was then besieging Jerusalem, and Jeremiah the prophet was confined in the courtyard of the guard d in the royal palace of Judah.

3 Now Zedekiah king of Judah had imprisoned him there, saying, "Why do you prophesy as you do? You say, 'This is what the LORD says: I am about to hand this city over to the king of Babylon, and he will capture e it. 4 Zedekiah king of Judah will not escape f out of the hands of the Babylonians a but will certainly be handed over to the king of Babylon, and will speak with him face to face and see him with his own eyes. 5 He will take Zedekiah to Babylon, where he will remain until I deal with him, declares the LORD. If you fight against the Babylonians, you will not succeed.'"

6 Jeremiah said, "The word of the LORD came to me: 7 Hanamel son of Shallum your uncle is going to come to you and say, 'Buy my field at Anathoth, because as nearest relative it is your right and duty g to buy it.'

8 "Then, just as the LORD had said, my cousin Hanamel came to me in the courtyard of the guard and said, 'Buy my field at Anathoth in the territory of Benjamin. Since it is your right to redeem it and possess it, buy it for yourself.'

"I knew that this was the word of the LORD; 9 so I bought the field at Anathoth from my cousin Hanamel and weighed out for him seventeen shekels b of silver. h 10 I signed and sealed the deed, had it witnessed, and weighed out the silver on the scales. 11 I took the deed of purchase—the sealed copy containing the terms and conditions, as well as the unsealed copy— 12 and I gave this deed to Baruch i son of Neriah, the son of Mahseiah, in the presence of my cousin Hanamel and of the witnesses who had signed the deed and of all the Jews sitting in the courtyard of the guard.

13 "In their presence I gave Baruch these instructions: 14 'This is what the LORD Almighty, the God of Israel, says: Take these documents, both the sealed and unsealed copies of the deed of purchase, and put them in a clay jar so they will last a long time. 15 For this is what the LORD Almighty, the God of Israel, says: Houses, fields and vineyards will again be bought in this land.'

16 "After I had given the deed of purchase to Baruch son of Neriah, I prayed to the LORD:

17 "Ah, Sovereign LORD, you have made the heavens and the earth by your great power and outstretched arm. j Nothing is too hard for you. 18 You show love to thousands but bring the punishment for the fathers' sins into the laps of their children k after them. O great and powerful God, whose name is the LORD Almighty, l 19 great are your purposes and mighty are your deeds. m Your eyes are open to all the ways of men; n you reward everyone according to his conduct and as his deeds deserve. o 20 You performed

31:38	a Ne 3:1
31:40	b Joel 3:17
32:1	c 2Ki 25:1
32:2	d Ne 3:25
32:3	e Jer 34:2-3
32:4	f Jer 38:18, 23; 39:5-7
32:7	g Lev 25:24-25; Ru 4:3-4
32:9	h Ge 23:16
32:12	i Jer 36:4
32:17	j 2Ki 19:15
32:18	k Ex 20:5 l Jer 10:16
32:19	m Isa 28:29 n Jer 16:17 o Jer 17:10

a 4 Or *Chaldeans*; also in verses 5, 24, 25, 28, 29 and 43   b 9 That is, about 7 ounces (about 200 grams)

31:38-40 These points mark the boundaries of restored Jerusalem in the days of Nehemiah. Gareb and Goah are unknown. The valley of the dead bodies and ashes probably refer to the Valley of Ben Hinnom where children were sacrificed in pagan worship.

32:1-12 God told Jeremiah to buy a field outside Jerusalem. The city had been under siege for a year, and Jeremiah bought land that the soldiers occupied—certainly a poor investment. In addition, Jeremiah was a prisoner in the palace. But Jeremiah was demonstrating his faith in God's promises to bring his people back and to rebuild Jerusalem.

32:6-17 Trust doesn't come easy. It wasn't easy for Jeremiah to publicly buy land already captured by the enemy. But he trusted God. It wasn't easy for David to believe that he would become king, even after he was anointed. But he trusted God (1 Samuel 16—31). It wasn't easy for Moses to believe that he and his people would escape Egypt, even after God spoke to him from a burning bush. But he trusted God (Exodus 3:1—4:20). It isn't easy for us to believe that God can fulfill his "impossible" promises either, but we must trust him. God, who worked in the lives of Biblical heroes, will work in our lives too, if we will let him.

32:17-25 After Jeremiah bought the field, he began to wonder if such a move was wise. He sought relief in prayer from his nagging doubts. In this prayer, Jeremiah affirmed that God is Creator (32:17), the wise Judge of all the ways of people (32:19), and Redeemer (32:21). God loves us and sees our situation. Whenever we doubt God's wisdom or wonder if it is practical to obey him, we can review what we already know about him. Such thoughts and prayers will quiet our doubts and calm our fears.

32:20
p Ex 9:16

32:21
q Ex 6:6; Da 9:15

32:22
r Ex 3:8

32:23
s Jer 11:8

miraculous signs and wonders in Egypt*p* and have continued them to this day, both in Israel and among all mankind, and have gained the renown that is still yours. *21* You brought your people Israel out of Egypt with signs and wonders, by a mighty hand*q* and an outstretched arm and with great terror. *22* You gave them this land you had sworn to give their forefathers, a land flowing with milk and honey.*r* *23* They came in and took possession of it, but they did not obey you or follow your law;*s* they did not do what you commanded them to do. So you brought all this disaster upon them.

24 "See how the siege ramps are built up to take the city. Because of the sword, famine and plague, the city will be handed over to the Babylonians who are attacking it. What you said has happened, as you now see. *25* And though the city will be handed over to the Babylonians, you, O Sovereign LORD, say to me, 'Buy the field with silver and have the transaction witnessed.'"

32:27
t Nu 16:22

32:29
u Jer 21:10; 52:13
v Jer 19:13

26 Then the word of the LORD came to Jeremiah: *27* "I am the LORD, the God of all mankind.*t* Is anything too hard for me? *28* Therefore, this is what the LORD says: I am about to hand this city over to the Babylonians and to Nebuchadnezzar king of Babylon, who will capture it. *29* The Babylonians who are attacking this city will come in and set it on fire; they will burn it down,*u* along with the houses*v* where the people provoked me to anger by burning incense on the roofs to Baal and by pouring out drink offerings to other gods.

32:32
w Da 9:8

32:33
x Jer 2:27

32:35
y Lev 18:21
z Jer 19:5

30 "The people of Israel and Judah have done nothing but evil in my sight from their youth; indeed, the people of Israel have done nothing but provoke me with what their hands have made, declares the LORD. *31* From the day it was built until now, this city has so aroused my anger and wrath that I must remove it from my sight. *32* The people of Israel and Judah have provoked me by all the evil*w* they have done—they, their kings and officials, their priests and prophets, the men of Judah and the people of Jerusalem. *33* They turned their backs*x* to me and not their faces; though I taught them again and again, they would not listen or respond to discipline. *34* They set up their abominable idols in the house that bears my Name and defiled it. *35* They built high places for Baal in the Valley of Ben Hinnom to sacrifice their sons and daughters*a* to Molech,*y* though I never commanded, nor did it enter my mind,*z* that they should do such a detestable thing and so make Judah sin.

32:37
a Jer 23:3, 6
b Dt 30:3

32:38
c 2Co 6:16*

32:40
d Isa 55:3

32:41
e Dt 30:9
f Am 9:15

32:42
g Jer 31:28

32:43
h ver 15

32:44
i Jer 17:26

36 "You are saying about this city, 'By the sword, famine and plague it will be handed over to the king of Babylon'; but this is what the LORD, the God of Israel, says: *37* I will surely gather*a* them from all the lands where I banish them in my furious anger and great wrath; I will bring them back to this place and let them live in safety.*b* *38* They will be my people,*c* and I will be their God. *39* I will give them singleness of heart and action, so that they will always fear me for their own good and the good of their children after them. *40* I will make an everlasting covenant*d* with them: I will never stop doing good to them, and I will inspire them to fear me, so that they will never turn away from me. *41* I will rejoice in doing them good*e* and will assuredly plant*f* them in this land with all my heart and soul.

42 "This is what the LORD says: As I have brought all this great calamity on this people, so I will give them all the prosperity I have promised*g* them. *43* Once more fields will be bought*h* in this land of which you say, 'It is a desolate waste, without men or animals, for it has been handed over to the Babylonians.' *44* Fields will be bought for silver, and deeds will be signed, sealed and witnessed in the territory of Benjamin, in the villages around Jerusalem, in the towns of Judah and in the towns of the hill country, of the western foothills and of the Negev,*i* because I will restore their fortunes,*b* declares the LORD."

a35 Or *to make their sons and daughters pass through* ⌊*the fire*⌋   *b44* Or *will bring them back from captivity*

32:35 These high places were where the most important and grotesque part of Molech worship took place. Children were offered in sacrifice to this pagan god.

32:36–42 God uses his power to accomplish *his* purposes through *his* people. God doesn't give you power to be all you want to be, but he gives you power to be all *he* wants you to be. The people of Israel had to learn that trusting God meant radically realigning their purposes and desires toward him. God gave them "singleness of heart" toward him (32:39). We must develop that singleness of heart and action to love God above anything else.

32:44 The hill country is in western Palestine. The Negev is the southern part of Judah.

Promise of Restoration

33 While Jeremiah was still confined in the courtyard of the guard, the word of the LORD came to him a second time: [2] "This is what the LORD says, he who made the earth, the LORD who formed it and established it—the LORD is his name:[j] [3] 'Call[k] to me and I will answer you and tell you great and unsearchable things you do not know.' [4] For this is what the LORD, the God of Israel, says about the houses in this city and the royal palaces of Judah that have been torn down to be used against the siege ramps and the sword [5] in the fight with the Babylonians[a]: 'They will be filled with the dead bodies of the men I will slay in my anger and wrath. I will hide my face from this city because of all its wickedness.

[6] "'Nevertheless, I will bring health and healing to it; I will heal my people and will let them enjoy abundant peace and security. [7] I will bring Judah[l] and Israel back from captivity[b] and will rebuild them as they were before. [8] I will cleanse[m] them from all the sin they have committed against me and will forgive all their sins of rebellion against me. [9] Then this city will bring me renown, joy, praise and honor before all nations on earth that hear of all the good things I do for it; and they will be in awe and will tremble at the abundant prosperity and peace I provide for it.'

[10] "This is what the LORD says: 'You say about this place, "It is a desolate waste, without men or animals."[n] Yet in the towns of Judah and the streets of Jerusalem that are deserted, inhabited by neither men nor animals, there will be heard once more [11] the sounds of joy and gladness, the voices of bride and bridegroom, and the voices of those who bring thank offerings[o] to the house of the LORD, saying,

"Give thanks to the LORD Almighty,
    for the LORD is good;
    his love endures forever."[p]

For I will restore the fortunes of the land as they were before,' says the LORD.

[12] "This is what the LORD Almighty says: 'In this place, desolate and without men or animals—in all its towns there will again be pastures for shepherds to rest their flocks. [q] [13] In the towns of the hill country, of the western foothills and of the Negev,[r] in the territory of Benjamin, in the villages around Jerusalem and in the towns of Judah, flocks will again pass under the hand[s] of the one who counts them,' says the LORD.

[14] "'The days are coming,' declares the LORD, 'when I will fulfill the gracious promise I made to the house of Israel and to the house of Judah.

[15] "'In those days and at that time
    I will make a righteous Branch[t] sprout from David's line;
    he will do what is just and right in the land.
[16] In those days Judah will be saved
    and Jerusalem will live in safety.
This is the name by which it[c] will be called:
    The LORD Our Righteousness.'

[17] For this is what the LORD says: 'David will never fail[u] to have a man to sit on the throne of the house of Israel, [18] nor will the priests, who are Levites, ever fail to have a man to stand before me continually to offer burnt offerings, to burn grain offerings and to present sacrifices.'"

a 5 Or *Chaldeans*   b 7 Or *will restore the fortunes of Judah and Israel*   c 16 Or *he*

33:2
j Ex 15:3

33:3
k Jer 29:12

33:7
l Jer 32:44

33:8
m Heb 9:13-14

33:10
n Jer 32:43

33:11
o Lev 7:12
p 2Ch 5:13

33:12
q Isa 65:10

33:13
r Jer 17:26
s Lev 27:32

33:15
t Isa 4:2

33:17
u 2Sa 7:13; 1Ki 2:4

33:1ff God would restore Jerusalem, not because the people cried, but because it was part of his ultimate plan. The Babylonian disaster did not change God's purposes for his people. Although Jerusalem would be destroyed, it would be restored (after the 70-year captivity and in the end times when the Messiah will rule). God's justice is always tempered by his mercy.

33:3 God assured Jeremiah that he had only to call to God and God would answer (see also Psalm 145:18; Isaiah 58:9; Matthew 7:7). God is ready to answer our prayers, but we must ask for his assistance. Surely God could take care of our needs without our asking. But when we ask, we are acknowledging that he alone is God and that we cannot accomplish in our own strength all that

is his domain to do. When we ask, we must humble ourselves, lay aside our willfulness and worry, and determine to obey him.

33:15, 16 These verses refer to both the first and second comings of Christ. At his first coming he would set up his reign in the hearts of believers; at his second coming he will execute justice and righteousness throughout the whole earth. Christ is the "righteous Branch" sprouting from David, the man after God's own heart.

33:18 As Christ fulfills the role of King, he also fulfills the role of Priest, maintaining constant fellowship with God and mediating for the people (see the note on 22:30). This verse does not mean that actual priests will perform sacrifices, for sacrifices will no longer be necessary (Hebrews 7:24, 25). Now that Christ is our High Priest, all believers are priests of God, and we can come before him personally.

¹⁹The word of the LORD came to Jeremiah: ²⁰"This is what the LORD says: 'If you can break my covenant with the day and my covenant with the night, so that day and night no longer come at their appointed time, ²¹then my covenant with David my servant—and my covenant with the Levites who are priests ministering before me—can be broken and David will no longer have a descendant to reign on his throne. ²²I will make the descendants of David my servant and the Levites who minister before me as countless ^v as the stars of the sky and as measureless as the sand on the seashore.'"

²³The word of the LORD came to Jeremiah: ²⁴"Have you not noticed that these people are saying, 'The LORD has rejected the two kingdoms^a he chose'? So they despise my people and no longer regard them as a nation. ²⁵This is what the LORD says: 'If I have not established my covenant with day and night ^w and the fixed laws of heaven and earth,^x ²⁶then I will reject^y the descendants of Jacob and David my servant and will not choose one of his sons to rule over the descendants of Abraham, Isaac and Jacob. For I will restore their fortunes ^b and have compassion on them.'"

6. God's promised judgment arrives
Warning to Zedekiah

34 While Nebuchadnezzar king of Babylon and all his army and all the kingdoms and peoples in the empire he ruled were fighting against Jerusalem ^z and all its surrounding towns, this word came to Jeremiah from the LORD: ²"This is what the LORD, the God of Israel, says: Go to Zedekiah king of Judah and tell him, 'This is what the LORD says: I am about to hand this city over to the king of Babylon, and he will burn it down.^a ³You will not escape from his grasp but will surely be captured and handed over^b to him. You will see the king of Babylon with your own eyes, and he will speak with you face to face. And you will go to Babylon.

⁴"'Yet hear the promise of the LORD, O Zedekiah king of Judah. This is what the LORD says concerning you: You will not die by the sword; ⁵you will die peacefully. As people made a funeral fire^c in honor of your fathers, the former kings who preceded you, so they will make a fire in your honor and lament, "Alas,^d O master!" I myself make this promise, declares the LORD.'"

⁶Then Jeremiah the prophet told all this to Zedekiah king of Judah, in Jerusalem, ⁷while the army of the king of Babylon was fighting against Jerusalem and the other cities of Judah that were still holding out—Lachish and Azekah.^e These were the only fortified cities left in Judah.

Freedom for Slaves

⁸The word came to Jeremiah from the LORD after King Zedekiah had made a covenant with all the people in Jerusalem to proclaim freedom^f for the slaves. ⁹Everyone was to free his Hebrew slaves, both male and female; no one was to hold a fellow Jew in bondage.^g ¹⁰So all the officials and people who entered into this covenant agreed that they would free their male and female slaves and no longer hold them in bondage. They agreed, and set them

^a24 Or *families*   ^b26 Or *will bring them back from captivity*

**Cross-references (left margin):**

33:22
^vGe 15:5

33:25
^wJer 31:35-36
^xPs 74:16-17

33:26
^yJer 31:37

34:1
^z2Ki 25:1; Jer 39:1

34:2
^aJer 32:29

34:3
^bJer 32:4

34:5
^c2Ch 16:14
^dJer 22:18

34:7
^e2Ch 11:9

34:8
^fEx 21:2

34:9
^gLev 25:39-46

BABYLON ATTACKS JUDAH

Zedekiah incurred Babylon's wrath in allying with Egypt (37:5) and not surrendering as God told him through Jeremiah (38:17). Nebuchadnezzar attacked Judah for the third and final time, moving systematically until all its cities fell. Jerusalem withstood siege for several months but was burned, as Jeremiah predicted (chapter 39).

34:1ff This chapter describes the fulfillment of many of Jeremiah's predictions. In the book of Jeremiah, many prophecies were both given and quickly fulfilled.

34:8, 9 Babylon had laid siege to Jerusalem, and the city was about to fall. Zedekiah finally decided to listen to Jeremiah and try to appease God—so he freed the slaves. He thought he could win God's favor with a kind act, but what he needed was a change of heart. The people had been disobeying God's law from the beginning (Exodus 21:2–11; Leviticus 25:39–55; Deuteronomy 15:12–18). When the siege was temporarily lifted, the people became bold and returned to their sins (34:11–17; 37:5, 11).

free. ¹¹But afterward they changed their minds and took back the slaves they had freed and enslaved them again.

¹²Then the word of the LORD came to Jeremiah: ¹³"This is what the LORD, the God of Israel, says: I made a covenant with your forefathers when I brought them out of Egypt, out of the land of slavery. I said, ¹⁴'Every seventh year each of you must free any fellow Hebrew who has sold himself to you. After he has served you six years, you must let him go free.'ᵃ ʰ Your fathers, however, did not listen to me or pay attentionⁱ to me. ¹⁵Recently you repented and did what is right in my sight: Each of you proclaimed freedom to his countrymen. You even made a covenant before me in the house that bears my Name.ʲ ¹⁶But now you have turned around and profanedᵏ my name; each of you has taken back the male and female slaves you had set free to go where they wished. You have forced them to become your slaves again.

¹⁷"Therefore, this is what the LORD says: You have not obeyed me; you have not proclaimed freedom for your fellow countrymen. So I now proclaim 'freedom' for you,ˡ declares the LORD—'freedom' to fall by the sword, plague and famine. I will make you abhorrent to all the kingdoms of the earth.ᵐ ¹⁸The men who have violated my covenant and have not fulfilled the terms of the covenant they made before me, I will treat like the calf they cut in two and then walked between its pieces.ⁿ ¹⁹The leaders of Judah and Jerusalem, the court officials, the priests and all the people of the land who walked between the pieces of the calf, ²⁰I will hand over to their enemies who seek their lives. Their dead bodies will become food for the birds of the air and the beasts of the earth.ᵒ

²¹"I will hand Zedekiah king of Judah and his officials over to their enemies who seek their lives, to the army of the king of Babylon, which has withdrawnᵖ from you. ²²I am going to give the order, declares the LORD, and I will bring them back to this city. They will fight against it, take it and burn it down. And I will lay waste the towns of Judah so no one can live there."

The Recabites

35 This is the word that came to Jeremiah from the LORD during the reign of Jehoiakim son of Josiah king of Judah: ²"Go to the Recabite�q family and invite them to come to one of the side roomsʳ of the house of the LORD and give them wine to drink."

³So I went to get Jaazaniah son of Jeremiah, the son of Habazziniah, and his brothers and all his sons—the whole family of the Recabites. ⁴I brought them into the house of the LORD, into the room of the sons of Hanan son of Igdaliah the man of God. It was next to the room of the officials, which was over that of Maaseiah son of Shallumˢ the doorkeeper. ⁵Then I set bowls full of wine and some cups before the men of the Recabite family and said to them, "Drink some wine."

⁶But they replied, "We do not drink wine, because our forefather Jonadabᵗ son of Recab gave us this command: 'Neither you nor your descendants must ever drink wine. ⁷Also you must never build houses, sow seed or plant vineyards; you must never have any of these things, but must always live in tents. Then you will live a long time in the landᵘ where you are nomads.' ⁸We have obeyed everything our forefather Jonadab son of Recab commanded us. Neither we nor our wives nor our sons and daughters have ever drunk wine ⁹or built houses to live in or had vineyards, fields or crops. ¹⁰We have lived in tents and have fully obeyed everything our forefather Jonadab commanded us. ¹¹But when Nebuchadnezzar king of Babylon invaded this land, we said, 'Come, we must go to Jerusalem to escape the Babylonianᵇ and Aramean armies.' So we have remained in Jerusalem."

ᵃ*14* Deut. 15:12   ᵇ*11* Or *Chaldean*

34:14
ʰEx 21:2
ⁱDt 15:12

34:15
ʲJer 7:10-11

34:16
ᵏEx 20:7;
Lev 19:12

34:17
ˡMt 7:2
ᵐDt 28:25, 64

34:18
ⁿGe 15:10

34:20
ᵒJer 7:33; 19:7

34:21
ᵖJer 37:5

35:2
qʰ2Ki 10:15;
1Ch 2:55
ʳ1Ki 6:5

35:4
ˢ1Ch 9:19

35:6
ᵗ2Ki 10:15

35:7
ᵘEx 20:12;
Eph 6:2-3

34:15, 16 The people of Israel had a hard time keeping their promises to God. In the temple, they would solemnly promise to obey God, but back in their homes and at work they wouldn't do it. God expressed his great displeasure. If you want to please God, make sure you keep your promises. God wants promises lived out, not just piously made.

34:18–20 Cutting a calf in two and walking between the halves was a customary way to ratify a contract (Genesis 15:9, 10). This action symbolized the judgment on anyone who broke the contract. God was saying, "You have broken the contract you made with me, so you know the judgment awaiting you!"

35:1ff The Recabites' code of conduct resembled that of the Nazirites, who took a special vow of dedication to God (Numbers 6). For 200 years, they had obeyed their ancestors' vow to abstain from wine. While the rest of the nation was breaking its covenant with God, these people were steadfast in their commitment. God wanted the rest of his people to remain as committed to their covenant with him as the Recabites were to their vow. God had Jeremiah tempt the Recabites with wine to demonstrate their commitment and dedication. God knew they wouldn't break their vow.

35:6 Jonadab son of Recab had joined Jehu in purging the northern kingdom of Baal worship (2 Kings 10:15–28).

35:13
v Jer 32:33

35:14
w Jer 7:13

35:15
x Jer 18:11

35:17
y Pr 1:24
z Isa 65:12; 66:4;
Jer 7:13

35:19
a Jer 15:19

¹²Then the word of the LORD came to Jeremiah, saying: ¹³"This is what the LORD Almighty, the God of Israel, says: Go and tell the men of Judah and the people of Jerusalem, 'Will you not learn a lesson v and obey my words?' declares the LORD. ¹⁴'Jonadab son of Recab ordered his sons not to drink wine and this command has been kept. To this day they do not drink wine, because they obey their forefather's command. But I have spoken to you again and again, w yet you have not obeyed me. ¹⁵Again and again I sent all my servants the prophets to you. They said, "Each of you must turn from your wicked ways and reform x your actions; do not follow other gods to serve them. Then you will live in the land I have given to you and your fathers." But you have not paid attention or listened to me. ¹⁶The descendants of Jonadab son of Recab have carried out the command their forefather gave them, but these people have not obeyed me.'

¹⁷"Therefore, this is what the LORD God Almighty, the God of Israel, says: 'Listen! I am going to bring on Judah and on everyone living in Jerusalem every disaster I pronounced against them. I spoke to them, but they did not listen; y I called to them, but they did not answer.'" z

¹⁸Then Jeremiah said to the family of the Recabites, "This is what the LORD Almighty, the God of Israel, says: 'You have obeyed the command of your forefather Jonadab and have followed all his instructions and have done everything he ordered.' ¹⁹Therefore, this is what the LORD Almighty, the God of Israel, says: 'Jonadab son of Recab will never fail to have a man to serve a me.'"

Jehoiakim Burns Jeremiah's Scroll

36:2
b Jer 30:2
c Jer 25:3

36:3
d ver 7
e Mk 4:12
f Jer 26:3; Jnh 3:8;
Ac 3:19
g Jer 18:8

36:4
h Jer 32:12
i ver 18
j Eze 2:9

36:10
k Jer 26:10

36 In the fourth year of Jehoiakim son of Josiah king of Judah, this word came to Jeremiah from the LORD: ²"Take a scroll b and write on it all the words I have spoken to you concerning Israel, Judah and all the other nations from the time I began speaking to you in the reign of Josiah c till now. ³Perhaps d when the people of Judah hear e about every disaster I plan to inflict on them, each of them will turn f from his wicked way; then I will forgive g their wickedness and their sin."

⁴So Jeremiah called Baruch h son of Neriah, and while Jeremiah dictated i all the words the LORD had spoken to him, Baruch wrote them on the scroll. j ⁵Then Jeremiah told Baruch, "I am restricted; I cannot go to the LORD's temple. ⁶So you go to the house of the LORD on a day of fasting and read to the people from the scroll the words of the LORD that you wrote as I dictated. Read them to all the people of Judah who come in from their towns. ⁷Perhaps they will bring their petition before the LORD, and each will turn from his wicked ways, for the anger and wrath pronounced against this people by the LORD are great."

⁸Baruch son of Neriah did everything Jeremiah the prophet told him to do; at the LORD's temple he read the words of the LORD from the scroll. ⁹In the ninth month of the fifth year of Jehoiakim son of Josiah king of Judah, a time of fasting before the LORD was proclaimed for all the people in Jerusalem and those who had come from the towns of Judah. ¹⁰From the room of Gemariah son of Shaphan the secretary, which was in the upper courtyard at the entrance of the New Gate k of the temple, Baruch read to all the people at the LORD's temple the words of Jeremiah from the scroll.

35:13–17 There is a vivid contrast between the Recabites and the other Israelites. (1) The Recabites kept their vows to a fallible human leader; the people of Israel broke their covenant with their infallible divine Leader. (2) Jonadab told his family one time not to drink, and they obeyed; God commanded Israel constantly to turn from sin, and they refused. (3) The Recabites obeyed laws that dealt with temporal issues; Israel refused to obey God's laws that dealt with eternal issues. (4) The Recabites had obeyed for hundreds of years; Israel had disobeyed for hundreds of years. (5) The Recabites would be rewarded; Israel would be punished. We often are willing to observe customs merely for the sake of tradition; how much more should we obey God's Word because it is eternal.

36:1ff This happened in the summer of 605 B.C., shortly after Nebuchadnezzar's victory over the Egyptian army at Carchemish, before the events recorded in chapters 34 and 35.

36:2–4 Most people in ancient times could neither read nor write, so those who could were extremely valuable. These scribes held positions of great importance and were very respected for their knowledge. Baruch was Jeremiah's scribe. Writing was often done on vellum or papyrus sheets that were sewn or glued together and stored in long rolls called scrolls. After the exile, scribes became teachers of the law. In New Testament times, the scribes formed a powerful political party.

36:9 A time of fasting (when people abstained from eating food to show their humility and repentance) was often called during times of national emergency. Babylon was destroying city after city and closing in on Jerusalem. As the people came to the temple, Baruch told them how to avert the coming tragedy. But they refused to listen.

36:10–32 God told Jeremiah to write his words on a scroll. Because he was not allowed to go to the temple, Jeremiah asked his scribe, Baruch, to whom he had dictated the scroll to read it to the people gathered there. Baruch then read it to the officials, and finally Jehudi read it to the king himself. Although the king burned the scroll, he could not destroy the word of God. Today many people try to put God's Word aside or say that it contains errors and therefore cannot be trusted. People may reject God's Word, but they cannot destroy it. God's Word will stand forever (Psalm 119:89).

11When Micaiah son of Gemariah, the son of Shaphan, heard all the words of the Lord from the scroll, 12he went down to the secretary's room in the royal palace, where all the officials were sitting: Elishama the secretary, Delaiah son of Shemaiah, Elnathan *l* son of Acbor, Gemariah son of Shaphan, Zedekiah son of Hananiah, and all the other officials. 13After Micaiah told them everything he had heard Baruch read to the people from the scroll, 14all the officials sent Jehudi son of Nethaniah, the son of Shelemiah, the son of Cushi, to say to Baruch, "Bring the scroll from which you have read to the people and come." So Baruch son of Neriah went to them with the scroll in his hand. 15They said to him, "Sit down, please, and read it to us."

So Baruch read it to them. 16When they heard all these words, they looked at each other in fear and said to Baruch, "We must report all these words to the king." 17Then they asked Baruch, "Tell us, how did you come to write all this? Did Jeremiah dictate it?"

18"Yes," Baruch replied, "he dictated *m* all these words to me, and I wrote them in ink on the scroll."

19Then the officials said to Baruch, "You and Jeremiah, go and hide. Don't let anyone know where you are."

20After they put the scroll in the room of Elishama the secretary, they went to the king in the courtyard and reported everything to him. 21The king sent Jehudi to get the scroll, and Jehudi brought it from the room of Elishama the secretary and read it to the king and all the officials standing beside him. 22It was the ninth month and the king was sitting in the winter apartment, *n* with a fire burning in the firepot in front of him. 23Whenever Jehudi had read three or four columns of the scroll, the king cut them off with a scribe's knife and threw them into the firepot, until the entire scroll was burned in the fire. 24The king and all his attendants who heard all these words showed no fear, nor did they tear their clothes. *o* 25Even though Elnathan, Delaiah and Gemariah urged the king not to burn the scroll, he would not listen to them. 26Instead, the king commanded Jerahmeel, a son of the king, Seraiah son of Azriel and Shelemiah son of Abdeel to arrest Baruch the scribe and Jeremiah the prophet. But the Lord had hidden them.

27After the king burned the scroll containing the words that Baruch had written at Jeremiah's dictation,*p* the word of the Lord came to Jeremiah: 28"Take another scroll and write on it all the words that were on the first scroll, which Jehoiakim king of Judah burned up. 29Also tell Jehoiakim king of Judah, 'This is what the Lord says: You burned that scroll and said, "Why did you write on it that the king of Babylon would certainly come and destroy this land and cut off both men and animals from it?" *q* 30Therefore, this is what the Lord says about Jehoiakim king of Judah: He will have no one to sit on the throne of David; his body will be thrown out *r* and exposed to the heat by day and the frost by night. 31I will punish him and his children and his attendants for their wickedness; I will bring on them and those living in Jerusalem and the people of Judah every disaster I pronounced against them, because they have not listened.'"

32So Jeremiah took another scroll and gave it to the scribe Baruch son of Neriah, and as Jeremiah dictated,*s* Baruch wrote on it all the words of the scroll that Jehoiakim king of Judah had burned in the fire. And many similar words were added to them.

Jeremiah in Prison

37 Zedekiah*t* son of Josiah was made king of Judah by Nebuchadnezzar king of Babylon; he reigned in place of Jehoiachin*a u* son of Jehoiakim. 2Neither he nor his attendants

a 1 Hebrew Coniah, a variant of Jehoiachin

### Cross-references (margin)

36:12 *l* Jer 26:22

36:18 *m* ver 4

36:22 *n* Am 3:15

36:24 *o* 2Ki 22:11; Isa 37:1

36:27 *p* ver 4

36:29 *q* Isa 30:10

36:30 *r* Jer 22:19

36:32 *s* ver 4

37:1 *t* 2Ki 24:17 *u* 2Ch 36:10; Jer 22:24

36:22 A firepot is a pan for holding burning coals, used to heat a room.

36:25 Only three leaders protested this evil act of burning the scroll containing God's word. This shows how complacent and insensitive to God the people had become. Not only did the king reject God's word, he tried to destroy it. Speaking out against these actions took courage. Anyone who decides to live for God must be willing to stand for right even if almost everyone else turns away. It is in the climate of darkness and sin that genuine faith shines most brightly.

36:30 Jehoiakim's son, Jehoiachin, was king for three months before he was taken into captivity, but this did not qualify as sitting

"on the throne of David"—an expression that implied permanence. Jehoiakim did not secure a dynasty. Zedekiah, the next ruler, was Jehoiachin's uncle. Thus the line of mortal human kings descended from David's son Solomon was finished, but in less than 600 years the eternal King would come through the descendants of Solomon's brother Nathan (see also the note on 22:30).

37:1ff King Jehoiakim died on the way to Babylon (2 Chronicles 36:6), and his son Jehoiachin was appointed king, but Jehoiachin was taken captive to Babylon three months later. Nebuchadnezzar then appointed Zedekiah as his vassal in Judah.

37:2, 3 King Zedekiah and his officials did not want to listen to Jeremiah's words, but they wanted the blessings of his prayers.

37:2
v 2Ch 36:12, 14

37:3
w Jer 29:25; 52:24
x Jer 21:1-2

37:4
y ver 15

37:5
z Eze 17:15
a 2Ki 24:7

37:8
b Jer 34:22

37:14
c Jer 40:4

37:21
d Jer 38:9
e Jer 52:6
f Jer 32:2;
38:6, 13, 28

38:1
g Jer 37:3

38:2
h Jer 21:9

38:3
i Jer 21:4, 10; 32:3

38:4
j Jer 26:11

nor the people of the land paid any attention v to the words the LORD had spoken through Jeremiah the prophet.

3 King Zedekiah, however, sent Jehucal son of Shelemiah with the priest Zephaniah w son of Maaseiah to Jeremiah the prophet with this message: "Please pray x to the LORD our God for us."

4 Now Jeremiah was free to come and go among the people, for he had not yet been put in prison. y 5 Pharaoh's army had marched out of Egypt, z and when the Babylonians a who were besieging Jerusalem heard the report about them, they withdrew from Jerusalem. a

6 Then the word of the LORD came to Jeremiah the prophet: 7 "This is what the LORD, the God of Israel, says: Tell the king of Judah, who sent you to inquire of me, 'Pharaoh's army, which has marched out to support you, will go back to its own land, to Egypt. 8 Then the Babylonians will return and attack this city; they will capture it and burn b it down.'

9 "This is what the LORD says: Do not deceive yourselves, thinking, 'The Babylonians will surely leave us.' They will not! 10 Even if you were to defeat the entire Babylonian b army that is attacking you and only wounded men were left in their tents, they would come out and burn this city down."

11 After the Babylonian army had withdrawn from Jerusalem because of Pharaoh's army, 12 Jeremiah started to leave the city to go to the territory of Benjamin to get his share of the property among the people there. 13 But when he reached the Benjamin Gate, the captain of the guard, whose name was Irijah son of Shelemiah, the son of Hananiah, arrested him and said, "You are deserting to the Babylonians!"

14 "That's not true!" Jeremiah said. "I am not deserting to the Babylonians." But Irijah would not listen to him; instead, he arrested c Jeremiah and brought him to the officials. 15 They were angry with Jeremiah and had him beaten and imprisoned in the house of Jonathan the secretary, which they had made into a prison.

16 Jeremiah was put into a vaulted cell in a dungeon, where he remained a long time. 17 Then King Zedekiah sent for him and had him brought to the palace, where he asked him privately, "Is there any word from the LORD?"

"Yes," Jeremiah replied, "you will be handed over to the king of Babylon."

18 Then Jeremiah said to King Zedekiah, "What crime have I committed against you or your officials or this people, that you have put me in prison? 19 Where are your prophets who prophesied to you, 'The king of Babylon will not attack you or this land'? 20 But now, my lord the king, please listen. Let me bring my petition before you: Do not send me back to the house of Jonathan the secretary, or I will die there."

21 King Zedekiah then gave orders for Jeremiah to be placed in the courtyard of the guard and given bread from the street of the bakers each day until all the bread d in the city was gone. e So Jeremiah remained in the courtyard of the guard. f

Jeremiah Thrown Into a Cistern

38 Shephatiah son of Mattan, Gedaliah son of Pashhur, Jehucal c g son of Shelemiah, and Pashhur son of Malkijah heard what Jeremiah was telling all the people when he said, 2 "This is what the LORD says: 'Whoever stays in this city will die by the sword, famine or plague, but whoever goes over to the Babylonians d will live. He will escape with his life; he will live.' h 3 And this is what the LORD says: 'This city will certainly be handed over to the army of the king of Babylon, who will capture it.'" i

4 Then the officials said to the king, "This man should be put to death. j He is discouraging

a 5 Or *Chaldeans*; also in verses 8, 9, 13 and 14   b 10 Or *Chaldean*; also in verse 11   c 1 Hebrew *Jucal*, a variant of *Jehucal*   d 2 Or *Chaldeans*; also in verses 18, 19 and 23

They wanted a superficial religion that wouldn't cost anything. But God is not pleased with those who come to him only for what they can get rather than seeking to establish or deepen a relationship with him. We would not accept that kind of relationship with someone else, and we shouldn't expect God to accept it from us.

37:5 When Nebuchadnezzar besieged Jerusalem in 589 B.C., Pharaoh Hophra marched against him at Zedekiah's invitation. Jerusalem looked to Egypt for help in spite of Jeremiah's warnings. But the Egyptians were no help, for as soon as the Babylonians turned on them, they retreated. Jeremiah's warnings had been correct.

37:17 Zedekiah teetered between surrender and resistance.

Too frightened and weak to exercise authority, he asked Jeremiah to come secretly to the palace, perhaps hoping for some better news from God. Zedekiah was desperate; he wanted to hear a word from the Lord, but he feared the political ramifications of being caught talking to Jeremiah.

38:4, 5 No wonder Judah was in turmoil: the king agreed with everybody. He listened to Jeremiah (37:21); then he agreed Jeremiah should be killed (38:5); and finally he rescued Jeremiah (38:10). Jeremiah was not popular; his words undermined the morale of the army and the people. Zedekiah couldn't decide between public opinion and God's will. What is most influential in your life—what others say and think or what God wants?

the soldiers who are left in this city, as well as all the people, by the things he is saying to them. This man is not seeking the good of these people but their ruin."

⁵"He is in your hands," King Zedekiah answered. "The king can do nothing to oppose you."

⁶So they took Jeremiah and put him into the cistern of Malkijah, the king's son, which was in the courtyard of the guard. ᵏ They lowered Jeremiah by ropes into the cistern; it had no water in it, only mud, and Jeremiah sank down into the mud.

38:6
ᵏ Jer 37:21

⁷But Ebed-Melech, ᴵ a Cushite,ᵃ an officialᵇ in the royal palace, heard that they had put Jeremiah into the cistern. While the king was sitting in the Benjamin Gate, ⁸Ebed-Melech went out of the palace and said to him, ⁹"My lord the king, these men have acted wickedly in all they have done to Jeremiah the prophet. They have thrown him into a cistern, where he will starve to death when there is no longer any bread ᵐ in the city."

38:7
ᴵ Jer 39:16
38:9
ᵐ Jer 37:21

¹⁰Then the king commanded Ebed-Melech the Cushite, "Take thirty men from here with you and lift Jeremiah the prophet out of the cistern before he dies."

¹¹So Ebed-Melech took the men with him and went to a room under the treasury in the palace. He took some old rags and worn-out clothes from there and let them down with ropes to Jeremiah in the cistern. ¹²Ebed-Melech the Cushite said to Jeremiah, "Put these old rags and worn-out clothes under your arms to pad the ropes." Jeremiah did so, ¹³and they pulled him up with the ropes and lifted him out of the cistern. And Jeremiah remained in the courtyard of the guard. ⁿ

38:13
ⁿ Jer 37:21

Zedekiah Questions Jeremiah Again

¹⁴Then King Zedekiah sent for Jeremiah the prophet and had him brought to the third entrance to the temple of the LORD. "I am going to ask you something," the king said to Jeremiah. "Do not hide anything from me."

¹⁵Jeremiah said to Zedekiah, "If I give you an answer, will you not kill me? Even if I did give you counsel, you would not listen to me."

¹⁶But King Zedekiah swore this oath secretly ᵒ to Jeremiah: "As surely as the LORD lives, who has given us breath,ᵖ I will neither kill you nor hand you over to those who are seeking your life."

38:16
ᵒ Jer 37:17
ᵖ Isa 57:16

¹⁷Then Jeremiah said to Zedekiah, "This is what the LORD God Almighty, the God of Israel, says: 'If you surrender to the officers of the king of Babylon, your life will be spared and this city will not be burned down; you and your family will live.�q ¹⁸But if you will not surrender to the officers of the king of Babylon, this city will be handed overʳ to the Babylonians and they will burn it down; you yourself will not escapeˢ from their hands.'"

38:17
q 2Ki 24:12
38:18
ʳ Jer 34:3
ˢ Jer 32:4

¹⁹King Zedekiah said to Jeremiah, "I am afraidᵗ of the Jews who have gone over to the Babylonians, for the Babylonians may hand me over to them and they will mistreat me."

38:19
ᵗ Isa 51:12

²⁰"They will not hand you over," Jeremiah replied. "Obeyᵘ the LORD by doing what I tell you. Then it will go well with you, and your life will be spared. ²¹But if you refuse to surrender, this is what the LORD has revealed to me: ²²All the women ᵛ left in the palace of the king of Judah will be brought out to the officials of the king of Babylon. Those women will say to you:

38:20
ᵘ Jer 11:4
38:22
ᵛ Jer 6:12

ᵃ 7 Probably from the upper Nile region   ᵇ 7 Or *a eunuch*

38:6 Officials put Jeremiah in a cistern to kill him. A cistern was a large hole in the ground lined with rocks to collect rainwater. The bottom would have been dark, damp, and, in this case, full of mud. Jeremiah could drown, die of exposure, or starve to death in the cistern.

38:6 Judah's leaders persecuted Jeremiah repeatedly for faithfully proclaiming God's messages. For 40 years of faithful ministry, he received no acclaim, no love, no popular following. He was beaten, jailed, threatened, and even forced to leave his homeland. Only the pagan Babylonians showed him any respect (39:11, 12). God does not guarantee that his servants will escape persecution, even when they are faithful. But God does promise that he will be with them and will give them strength to endure (2 Corinthians 1:3–7). As you minister to others, recog-

nize that your service is for God and not just for human approval. God rewards our faithfulness, but not always during our stay on earth.

38:7, 8 The Benjamin Gate was one of Jerusalem's city gates where legal matters were handled. A palace official, Ebed-Melech, had access to the king. When Ebed-Melech heard of Jeremiah's plight, he went immediately to deal with the injustice.

38:9–13 Ebed-Melech feared God more than people. He alone among the palace officials stood up against the murder plot. His obedience could have cost him his life. Because he obeyed, however, he was spared when Jerusalem fell (39:15–18). You can either go along with the crowd or speak up for God. When someone is treated unkindly or unjustly, for example, reach out to that person with God's love. You may be the only one who does. And, when you are being treated unkindly yourself, be sure to thank God when he sends an "Ebed-Melech" your way.

"'They misled you and overcame you—
those trusted friends of yours.
Your feet are sunk in the mud;
your friends have deserted you.'

38:23
w Jer 41:10

23 "All your wives and children will be brought out to the Babylonians. You yourself will not escape from their hands but will be captured w by the king of Babylon; and this city will a be burned down."

24 Then Zedekiah said to Jeremiah, "Do not let anyone know about this conversation, or you may die. 25 If the officials hear that I talked with you, and they come to you and say, 'Tell us what you said to the king and what the king said to you; do not hide it from us or we will kill you,' 26 then tell them, 'I was pleading with the king not to send me back to Jonathan's house x to die there.'"

38:26
x Jer 37:15

27 All the officials did come to Jeremiah and question him, and he told them everything the king had ordered him to say. So they said no more to him, for no one had heard his conversation with the king.

38:28
y Jer 37:21; 39:14

28 And Jeremiah remained in the courtyard of the guard y until the day Jerusalem was captured.

a 23 Or *and you will cause this city to*

EBED-MELECH

During one of the bleakest moments in Jeremiah's life, God demonstrated his power by providing help from an unexpected source. Ebed-Melech, a high-ranking African official in Zedekiah's court, risked his career and perhaps his life to rescue Jeremiah from a muddy cistern. This unsung Ethiopian represents a crowd of quiet heroes throughout Bible history who showed real courage and character. He made the most of his position in life by using it to serve God.

Spineless King Zedekiah had agreed to let Jeremiah's enemies arrange for the prophet's death. Though he had previously consulted with Jeremiah and even arranged for less harsh imprisonment, Zedekiah wavered under pressure. When certain influential voices demanded Jeremiah's life, Zedekiah offered no resistance. The plan involved lowering Jeremiah into an empty cistern and leaving him to die of starvation.

Ebed-Melech's response shows us a radical and almost reckless pursuit of justice. He appealed directly to the king who was holding court in a public place. His boldness prodded Zedekiah to reverse his previous decision. Ebed-Melech took the king's men, gathered the padding and ropes he would need, and hauled the shivering and slimy prophet out of the pit. The picture wasn't pretty, but the mission succeeded. Jeremiah later had the privilege of informing his Ethiopian rescuer that God would keep him safe during the fall and destruction of Jerusalem.

In whatever place you find yourself in life, continually ask God to help you see and respond to needs that you are uniquely placed to meet. Like Ebed-Melech, you may experience fear along the way. But better to fear and act anyway than to live with the disappointment that fear prevented you from serving God and his people.

Strengths and accomplishments:	• Took Jeremiah's case before the king and secured his rescue • Organized the extraction of the prophet from the quagmire-filled cistern • Received God's guarantee of safety during the Babylonian destruction of Jerusalem
Lessons from his life:	• The places we serve in life can often provide us with unique opportunities to serve God and his people • We can trust God and act in spite of our fear • God does not forget those who take a stand for him • One bold person's actions may stem a tide of evil
Vital statistics:	• Where: From Ethiopia, lived in Judah • Occupation: Palace official in Judah • Contemporaries: Jeremiah, Baruch, Zedekiah
Key verse:	"I will save you; you will not fall by the sword but will escape with your life, because you trust in me, declares the LORD" (Jeremiah 39:18).

Ebed-Melech's story is told in Jeremiah 38—39.

38:27 The officials wanted accurate information, but not God's truth. They wanted to use this information against God, his prophet, and the king. But Jeremiah told the officials only what the king ordered him to say. We must not withhold God's truth from others, but we should withhold information that will be used to bring evil to God's people.

The Fall of Jerusalem

39 This is how Jerusalem was taken: [1] In the ninth year of Zedekiah king of Judah, in the tenth month, Nebuchadnezzar king of Babylon marched against Jerusalem with his whole army and laid siege [z] to it. [2] And on the ninth day of the fourth month of Zedekiah's eleventh year, the city wall was broken through. [3] Then all the officials of the king of Babylon came and took seats in the Middle Gate: Nergal-Sharezer of Samgar, Nebo-Sarsekim [a] a chief officer, Nergal-Sharezer a high official and all the other officials of the king of Babylon. [4] When Zedekiah king of Judah and all the soldiers saw them, they fled; they left the city at night by way of the king's garden, through the gate between the two walls, and headed toward the Arabah. [b]

[5] But the Babylonian [c] army pursued them and overtook Zedekiah [a] in the plains of Jericho. They captured him and took him to Nebuchadnezzar king of Babylon at Riblah [b] in the land of Hamath, where he pronounced sentence on him. [6] There at Riblah the king of Babylon slaughtered the sons of Zedekiah before his eyes and also killed all the nobles of Judah. [7] Then he put out Zedekiah's eyes [c] and bound him with bronze shackles to take him to Babylon. [d]

[8] The Babylonians [d] set fire [e] to the royal palace and the houses of the people and broke down the walls of Jerusalem. [9] Nebuzaradan commander of the imperial guard carried into exile to Babylon the people who remained in the city, along with those who had gone over to him, and the rest of the people. [10] But Nebuzaradan the commander of the guard left behind in the land of Judah some of the poor people, who owned nothing; and at that time he gave them vineyards and fields.

[11] Now Nebuchadnezzar king of Babylon had given these orders about Jeremiah through Nebuzaradan commander of the imperial guard: [12] "Take him and look after him; don't harm him but do for him whatever he asks." [13] So Nebuzaradan the commander of the guard, Nebushazban a chief officer, Nergal-Sharezer a high official and all the other officers of the king of Babylon [14] sent and had Jeremiah taken out of the courtyard of the guard. [f] They turned him over to Gedaliah son of Ahikam, the son of Shaphan, to take him back to his home. So he remained among his own people.

[15] While Jeremiah had been confined in the courtyard of the guard, the word of the LORD came to him: [16] "Go and tell Ebed-Melech [g] the Cushite, 'This is what the LORD Almighty, the God of Israel, says: I am about to fulfill my words against this city through disaster, [h] not prosperity. At that time they will be fulfilled before your eyes. [17] But I will rescue you on that day, declares the LORD; you will not be handed over to those you fear. [18] I will save you; you will not fall by the sword [i] but will escape with your life, [j] because you trust in me, declares the LORD.'"

Jeremiah Freed

40 The word came to Jeremiah from the LORD after Nebuzaradan commander of the imperial guard had released him at Ramah. He had found Jeremiah bound in chains among all the captives from Jerusalem and Judah who were being carried into exile to

39:1 [z] 2Ki 25:1

39:5 [a] Jer 32:4 [b] 2Ki 23:33

39:7 [c] Eze 12:13 [d] Jer 32:5

39:8 [e] Jer 38:18

39:14 [f] Jer 38:28

39:16 [g] Jer 38:7 [h] Da 9:12

39:18 [i] Jer 45:5 [j] Jer 21:9

[a] 3 Or *Nergal-Sharezer, Samgar-Nebo, Sarsekim* [b] 4 Or *the Jordan Valley* [c] 5 Or *Chaldean* [d] 8 Or *Chaldeans*

39:1ff Zedekiah, son of Josiah and last king of Judah, ruled 11 years, from 597 to 586 B.C. Zedekiah's two older brothers, Jehoahaz and Jehoiakim, and his nephew Jehoiachin ruled before him. When Jehoiachin was exiled to Babylon, Nebuchadnezzar made 21-year-old Mattaniah the king, changing his name to Zedekiah. Zedekiah rebelled against Nebuchadnezzar, who captured him, killed his sons in front of him, and then blinded him and took him back to Babylon where he later died (see 2 Kings 24; 25; 2 Chronicles 36; and Jeremiah 52).

39:5 Riblah was 200 miles north of Jerusalem. This was the Babylonian headquarters for ruling the region.

39:10 Babylon had a shrewd foreign policy toward conquered lands. They deported the rich and powerful, leaving only the very poor in charge, thus making them grateful to their conquerors. This policy assured that conquered populations would be too loyal and too weak to revolt.

39:11, 12 God had promised to rescue Jeremiah from his trouble (1:8). The superstitious Babylonians, who highly respected magicians and fortune-tellers, treated Jeremiah as a seer. Because he had been imprisoned by his own people, they assumed he was a traitor and on their side. They undoubtedly knew he had counseled cooperation with Babylon and predicted a Babylonian victory. So the Babylonians freed Jeremiah and protected him.

39:13, 14 What a difference there is between Jeremiah's fate and Zedekiah's! Jeremiah was freed; Zedekiah was imprisoned. Jeremiah was saved because of his faith; Zedekiah was destroyed because of his fear. Jeremiah was treated with respect; Zedekiah was treated with contempt. Jeremiah was concerned for the people; Zedekiah was concerned for himself.

39:17, 18 Ebed-Melech had risked his life to save God's prophet Jeremiah (38:7–13). When Babylon conquered Jerusalem, God protected Ebed-Melech from the Babylonians. God has special rewards for his faithful people, but not everyone will receive them in this life (see the note on 38:6).

40—45 These six chapters cover events following Jerusalem's fall to Babylon.

40:2
k Jer 50:7

40:3
l Da 9:11

40:4
m Jer 39:11-12

40:5
n Jer 39:14

40:6
o Jdg 20:1

40:7
p Jer 39:10

40:8
q Jer 41:1, 2

40:9
r Jer 27:11
s Jer 38:20

40:12
t Jer 43:5

40:14
u Jer 41:10

41:1
v Jer 40:8

41:2
w Jer 40:5

Babylon. ²When the commander of the guard found Jeremiah, he said to him, "The LORD your God decreed this disaster for this place. *k* ³And now the LORD has brought it about; he has done just as he said he would. All this happened because you people sinned *l* against the LORD and did not obey him. ⁴But today I am freeing you from the chains on your wrists. Come with me to Babylon, if you like, and I will look after you; but if you do not want to, then don't come. Look, the whole country lies before you; go wherever you please." *m* ⁵However, before Jeremiah turned to go, *a* Nebuzaradan added, "Go back to Gedaliah son of Ahikam, the son of Shaphan, whom the king of Babylon has appointed over the towns of Judah, and live with him among the people, or go anywhere else you please." *n*

Then the commander gave him provisions and a present and let him go. ⁶So Jeremiah went to Gedaliah son of Ahikam at Mizpah *o* and stayed with him among the people who were left behind in the land.

Gedaliah Assassinated

⁷When all the army officers and their men who were still in the open country heard that the king of Babylon had appointed Gedaliah son of Ahikam as governor over the land and had put him in charge of the men, women and children who were the poorest *p* in the land and who had not been carried into exile to Babylon, ⁸they came to Gedaliah at Mizpah—Ishmael *q* son of Nethaniah, Johanan and Jonathan the sons of Kareah, Seraiah son of Tanhumeth, the sons of Ephai the Netophathite, and Jaazaniah *b* the son of the Maacathite, and their men. ⁹Gedaliah son of Ahikam, the son of Shaphan, took an oath to reassure them and their men. "Do not be afraid to serve *r* the Babylonians, *c*" he said. "Settle down in the land and serve the king of Babylon, and it will go well with you. *s* ¹⁰I myself will stay at Mizpah to represent you before the Babylonians who come to us, but you are to harvest the wine, summer fruit and oil, and put them in your storage jars, and live in the towns you have taken over."

¹¹When all the Jews in Moab, Ammon, Edom and all the other countries heard that the king of Babylon had left a remnant in Judah and had appointed Gedaliah son of Ahikam, the son of Shaphan, as governor over them, ¹²they all came back to the land of Judah, to Gedaliah at Mizpah, from all the countries where they had been scattered. *t* And they harvested an abundance of wine and summer fruit.

¹³Johanan son of Kareah and all the army officers still in the open country came to Gedaliah at Mizpah ¹⁴and said to him, "Don't you know that Baalis king of the Ammonites *u* has sent Ishmael son of Nethaniah to take your life?" But Gedaliah son of Ahikam did not believe them.

¹⁵Then Johanan son of Kareah said privately to Gedaliah in Mizpah, "Let me go and kill Ishmael son of Nethaniah, and no one will know it. Why should he take your life and cause all the Jews who are gathered around you to be scattered and the remnant of Judah to perish?"

¹⁶But Gedaliah son of Ahikam said to Johanan son of Kareah, "Don't do such a thing! What you are saying about Ishmael is not true."

41 In the seventh month Ishmael *v* son of Nethaniah, the son of Elishama, who was of royal blood and had been one of the king's officers, came with ten men to Gedaliah son of Ahikam at Mizpah. While they were eating together there, ²Ishmael son of Nethaniah and the ten men who were with him got up and struck down Gedaliah son of Ahikam, the son of Shaphan, with the sword, killing the one whom the king of Babylon had appointed *w* as governor over the land. ³Ishmael also killed all the Jews who were with Gedaliah at Mizpah, as well as the Babylonian *d* soldiers who were there.

a 5 Or *Jeremiah answered*   *b* 8 Hebrew *Jezaniah,* a variant of *Jaazaniah*   *c* 9 Or *Chaldeans;* also in verse 10
d 3 Or *Chaldean*

40:2, 3 The Babylonian commander, who did not know God, acknowledged that God had given the Babylonians victory. It is strange when people recognize that God exists and does miracles, but still they do not personally accept him. Knowing God is more than knowing about him. Be sure you know him personally.

40:4 Jeremiah was free to go anywhere. In Babylon he would have had great comfort and power. In Judah he would continue to face hardship. In Babylon Jeremiah would have been favored by the Babylonians, but hated by the Judean exiles. In Judah he would remain poor and unwanted, but the Judean remnant would know he was not a traitor. Jeremiah returned to Judah.

40:6 Mizpah was a few miles north of Jerusalem. Not thoroughly destroyed by the Babylonians, Mizpah served as a refuge after the destruction of Jerusalem.

40:13—41:3 Gedaliah, appointed governor of Judah, foolishly ignored the warnings of assassination. Ishmael, in the line of David, may have been angry that he had been passed over for leadership. This is similar to the chaotic political situation that Ezra and Nehemiah faced when they returned to rebuild the temple and the city.

⁴The day after Gedaliah's assassination, before anyone knew about it, ⁵eighty men who had shaved off their beards,ˣ torn their clothes and cut themselves came from Shechem, Shiloh and Samaria,ʸ bringing grain offerings and incense with them to the house of the LORD. ᶻ ⁶Ishmael son of Nethaniah went out from Mizpah to meet them, weeping as he went. When he met them, he said, "Come to Gedaliah son of Ahikam." ⁷When they went into the city, Ishmael son of Nethaniah and the men who were with him slaughtered them and threw them into a cistern. ⁸But ten of them said to Ishmael, "Don't kill us! We have wheat and barley, oil and honey, hidden in a field." So he let them alone and did not kill them with the others. ⁹Now the cistern where he threw all the bodies of the men he had killed along with Gedaliah was the one King Asaᵃ had made as part of his defense against Baasha king of Israel. Ishmael son of Nethaniah filled it with the dead.

¹⁰Ishmael made captives of all the rest of the people who were in Mizpah—the king's daughters along with all the others who were left there, over whom Nebuzaradan commander of the imperial guard had appointed Gedaliah son of Ahikam. Ishmael son of Nethaniah took them captive and set out to cross over to the Ammonites. ᵇ

¹¹When Johanan ᶜ son of Kareah and all the army officers who were with him heard about all the crimes Ishmael son of Nethaniah had committed, ¹²they took all their men and went to fight Ishmael son of Nethaniah. They caught up with him near the great pool ᵈ in Gibeon. ¹³When all the people Ishmael had with him saw Johanan son of Kareah and the army officers who were with him, they were glad. ¹⁴All the people Ishmael had taken captive at Mizpah turned and went over to Johanan son of Kareah. ¹⁵But Ishmael son of Nethaniah and eight of his men escaped from Johanan and fled to the Ammonites.

Flight to Egypt

¹⁶Then Johanan son of Kareah and all the army officers who were with him led away all the survivors from Mizpah whom he had recovered from Ishmael son of Nethaniah after he had assassinated Gedaliah son of Ahikam: the soldiers, women, children and court officials he had brought from Gibeon. ¹⁷And they went on, stopping at Geruth Kimhamᵉ near Bethlehem on their way to Egypt ¹⁸to escape the Babylonians.ᵃ They were afraid of them because Ishmael son of Nethaniah had killed Gedaliah ᶠ son of Ahikam, whom the king of Babylon had appointed as governor over the land.

42 Then all the army officers, including Johananᵍ son of Kareah and Jezaniahᵇ son of Hoshaiah, and all the people from the least to the greatest approached ²Jeremiah the prophet and said to him, "Please hear our petition and pray to the LORD your God for this entire remnant. For as you now see, though we were once many, now only a few are left. ³Pray that the LORD your God will tell us where we should go and what we should do."

⁴"I have heard you," replied Jeremiah the prophet. "I will certainly pray to the LORD your God as you have requested; I will tell you everything the LORD says and will keep nothing back from you."ʰ

⁵Then they said to Jeremiah, "May the LORD be a true and faithful witnessⁱ against us if we do not act in accordance with everything the LORD your God sends you to tell us. ⁶Whether it is favorable or unfavorable, we will obey the LORD our God, to whom we are sending you, so that it will go wellʲ with us, for we will obey the LORD our God."

⁷Ten days later the word of the LORD came to Jeremiah. ⁸So he called together Johanan son of Kareah and all the army officers who were with him and all the people from the least to the greatest. ⁹He said to them, "This is what the LORD, the God of Israel, to whom you sent me to present your petition, says: ¹⁰'If you stay in this land, I will buildᵏ you up and not tear you down; I will plantˡ you and not uproot you, for I am grieved over the disaster I have inflicted on you. ¹¹Do not be afraid of the king of Babylon, whom you now fear. Do not be afraid of him, declares the LORD, for I am with you and will saveᵐ you and deliver you from his hands.ⁿ ¹²I will show you compassion so that he will have compassion on you and restore you to your land.'ᵒ

ᵃ18 Or *Chaldeans*   ᵇ1 Hebrew; Septuagint (see also 43:2) *Azariah*

41:5 ˣLev 19:27; ʸ1Ki 16:24; ᶻ2Ki 25:9

41:9 ᵃ1Ki 15:22; 2Ch 16:6

41:10 ᵇJer 40:14

41:11 ᶜJer 40:8

41:12 ᵈ2Sa 2:13

41:17 ᵉ2Sa 19:37

41:18 ᶠJer 40:5

42:1 ᵍJer 40:13; 41:11

42:4 ʰ1Ki 22:14; 1Sa 3:17

42:5 ⁱGe 31:50

42:6 ʲDt 6:3; Jer 7:23

42:10 ᵏJer 24:6; ˡJer 31:28

42:11 ᵐIsa 43:5; ⁿRo 8:31

42:12 ᵒPs 106:44-46

41:4–9 The 80 men came from three cities of the northern kingdom to worship in Jerusalem. Ishmael probably killed them for the money and food they were carrying. Without a king, with no law and no loyalty to God, Judah was subjected to complete anarchy. **41:16, 17** Johanan and his group were already on their way to Egypt, headed south from Gibeon, stopping first at Geruth Kimham, near Bethlehem. Their visit to Jeremiah (42:1–6) was hypocritical, as Jeremiah later told them (42:20).

42:5, 6 Johanan and his associates spoke their own curse; Jeremiah merely elaborated on it. It was a tragic mistake to ask for God's guidance with no intention of following it. Be sure never to ask God for something that you know in your heart you

42:13
P Jer 44:16

13"However, if you say, 'We will not stay in this land,' and so disobey^p the Lord your God, 14and if you say, 'No, we will go and live in Egypt, where we will not see war or hear the trumpet or be hungry for bread,' 15then hear the word of the Lord, O remnant of Judah. This is what the Lord Almighty, the God of Israel, says: 'If you are determined to go to Egypt and you do go to settle there, 16then the sword you fear will overtake you there, and the famine you dread will follow you into Egypt, and there you will die. 17Indeed, all who are determined to go to Egypt to settle there will die by the sword, famine and plague;^q not one of them will survive or escape the disaster I will bring on them.' 18This is what the Lord Almighty, the God of Israel, says: 'As my anger and wrath^r have been poured out on those who lived in Jerusalem, so will my wrath be poured out on you when you go to Egypt. You will be an object of cursing and horror,^s of condemnation and reproach; you will never see this place again.'

42:17
q Jer 44:13
42:18
r Jer 7:20
s Jer 29:18

42:19
t Dt 17:16

19"O remnant of Judah, the Lord has told you, 'Do not go to Egypt.'^t Be sure of this: I warn you today 20that you made a fatal mistake^a when you sent me to the Lord your God and said, 'Pray to the Lord our God for us; tell us everything he says and we will do it.' 21I have told you today, but you still have not obeyed the Lord your God in all he sent me to tell you. 22So now, be sure of this: You will die by the sword, famine and plague in the place where you want to go to settle."

43 When Jeremiah finished telling the people all the words of the Lord their God— everything the Lord had sent him to tell them— 2Azariah son of Hoshaiah and Johanan^u son of Kareah and all the arrogant men said to Jeremiah, "You are lying! The Lord our God has not sent you to say, 'You must not go to Egypt to settle there.' 3But Baruch son of Neriah is inciting you against us to hand us over to the Babylonians,^b so they may kill us or carry us into exile to Babylon."

43:2
u Jer 42:1

4So Johanan son of Kareah and all the army officers and all the people disobeyed the Lord's command to stay in the land of Judah. 5Instead, Johanan son of Kareah and all the army officers led away all the remnant of Judah who had come back to live in the land of Judah from all the nations where they had been scattered.^v 6They also led away all the men, women and children and the king's daughters whom Nebuzaradan commander of the imperial guard had left with Gedaliah son of Ahikam, the son of Shaphan, and Jeremiah the prophet and Baruch son of Neriah. 7So they entered Egypt in disobedience to the Lord and went as far as Tahpanhes.^w

43:5
v Jer 40:12

43:7
w Jer 44:1

8In Tahpanhes the word of the Lord came to Jeremiah: 9"While the Jews are watching, take some large stones with you and bury them in clay in the brick pavement at the entrance to Pharaoh's palace in Tahpanhes. 10Then say to them, 'This is what the Lord Almighty, the God of Israel, says: I will send for my servant^x Nebuchadnezzar king of Babylon, and I will set his throne over these stones I have buried here; he will spread his royal canopy above them. 11He will come and attack Egypt,^y bringing death to those destined for death, captivity to those destined for captivity, and the sword to those destined for the sword.^z 12He^c will set fire to the temples of the gods^a of Egypt; he will burn their temples and take their gods captive. As a shepherd wraps his garment around him, so will he wrap Egypt around himself and depart from there unscathed. 13There in the temple of the sun^d in Egypt he will demolish the sacred pillars and will burn down the temples of the gods of Egypt.'"

43:10
x Jer 25:9; 27:6

43:11
y Jer 46:13-26
z Jer 15:2; 44:13

43:12
a Jer 46:25

^a20 Or you erred in your hearts   ^b3 Or Chaldeans   ^c12 Or I   ^d13 Or in Heliopolis

---

really do not want. It is better not to pray than to pray hypocritically. God cannot be deceived.

43:1–3 Johanan and his tiny band had come to Jeremiah for God's approval of their plan, not for God's direction. This is a recurring problem for most of us—seeking God's approval of our desires rather than asking him for guidance. It's not good to make plans unless we are willing to have God change them, and it is not good to pray unless we are willing to accept God's answer.

43:4–7 Afraid to obey the Lord, the people headed for Egypt, even forcing Jeremiah to go with them. (They thought that perhaps God would spare them if Jeremiah was with them.) Jeremiah had served as a prophet for 40 years. Many of his words had already come true, and he had turned down an offer to live comfortably in Babylon, returning instead to his beloved people. But the people still rejected Jeremiah's advice. The response of

our audience is not necessarily a measure of our success. Jeremiah was doing all God asked, but he had been called to minister to a very stubborn group of people.

43:10–13 Nebuchadnezzar invaded Egypt in 568–567 B.C. Like Judah, Egypt rebelled against him and was quickly crushed. So much for the great empire on which Judah had constantly placed its hopes!

Disaster Because of Idolatry

44 This word came to Jeremiah concerning all the Jews living in Lower Egypt—in Migdol, Tahpanhes *b* and Memphis *a* *c*—and in Upper Egypt *b*: *d* 2"This is what the Lord Almighty, the God of Israel, says: You saw the great disaster I brought on Jerusalem and on all the towns of Judah. Today they lie deserted and in ruins *e* 3because of the evil they have done. They provoked me to anger by burning incense and by worshiping other gods *f* that neither they nor you nor your fathers *g* ever knew. 4Again and again I sent my servants the prophets, *h* who said, 'Do not do this detestable thing that I hate!' 5But they did not listen or pay attention; they did not turn from their wickedness or stop burning incense to other gods. 6Therefore, my fierce anger was poured out; it raged against the towns of Judah and the streets of Jerusalem and made them the desolate ruins they are today.

7"Now this is what the Lord God Almighty, the God of Israel, says: Why bring such great disaster on yourselves by cutting off from Judah the men and women, the children and infants, and so leave yourselves without a remnant? 8Why provoke me to anger with what your hands have made, *i* burning incense to other gods in Egypt, where you have come to live? You will destroy yourselves and make yourselves an object of cursing and reproach *j* among all the nations on earth. 9Have you forgotten the wickedness committed by your fathers and by the kings and queens of Judah and the wickedness committed by you and your wives in the land of Judah and the streets of Jerusalem? 10To this day they have not humbled themselves or shown reverence, nor have they followed my law and the decrees I set before you and your fathers.

11"Therefore, this is what the Lord Almighty, the God of Israel, says: I am determined to bring disaster *k* on you and to destroy all Judah. 12I will take away the remnant of Judah who were determined to go to Egypt to settle there. They will all perish in Egypt; they will fall by the sword or die from famine. From the least to the greatest, they will die by sword or famine. They will become an object of cursing and horror, of condemnation and reproach. *l* 13I will punish those who live in Egypt with the sword, famine and plague, as I punished Jerusalem. 14None of the remnant of Judah who have gone to live in Egypt will escape or survive to return to the land of Judah, to which they long to return and live; none will return except a few fugitives." *m*

15Then all the men who knew that their wives were burning incense to other gods, along with all the women who were present—a large assembly—and all the people living in Lower and Upper Egypt, *c* said to Jeremiah, 16"We will not listen to the message you have spoken to us in the name of the Lord! 17We will certainly do everything we said we would: *n* We will burn incense to the Queen of Heaven *o* and will pour out drink offerings to her just as we and our fathers, our kings and our officials did in the towns of Judah and in the streets of Jerusalem. At that time we had plenty of food and were well off and suffered no harm. 18But ever

a 1 Hebrew *Noph*   *b* 1 Hebrew *in Pathros*   *c* 15 Hebrew *in Egypt and Pathros*

44:1
b Jer 43:7, 8
c Isa 19:13
d Jer 46:14

44:2
e Jer 9:11; 34:22

44:3
f Dt 13:6-11
g Dt 32:17; Jer 19:4

44:4
h Jer 7:25; 25:4; 26:5

44:8
i Jer 25:6-7
j Jer 42:18

44:11
k Jer 21:10; Am 9:4

44:12
l Jer 42:15-18

44:14
m ver 28;
Jer 22:24-27

44:17
n Dt 23:23
o Jer 7:18

ESCAPE TO EGYPT

With Judah in turmoil after the murder of Gedaliah, the people turned to Jeremiah for guidance. Jeremiah had God's answer, "Stay in this land." But the leaders disobeyed and went to Egypt, taking Jeremiah with them. In Egypt, Jeremiah told them they were in grave danger.

44:1ff This message, given in 580 B.C. while Jeremiah was in Egypt against his will, reminded the people that their following other gods had brought destruction on their land. Jeremiah told them that they would never return to Judah because the escape to Egypt had been against God's advice (42:9ff). But the people refused to learn any lessons from all the destruction their sins had caused.

44:9, 10 When we forget a lesson or refuse to learn it, we risk repeating our mistakes. The people of Judah struggled with this; to forget their former sins was to repeat them. To fail to learn from failure is to assure future failure. Your past is your school of experience. Let your past mistakes point you to God's way.

44:15–18 The farther we drift from God, the more confused our thinking becomes. Whatever spiritual life was left in the Israelites when they went to Egypt was lost as they sank into the depths of idolatry. (For more information on the "Queen of Heaven," see the note on 7:18.) The escape to Egypt had brought a change in their pagan worship habits, and they blamed their troubles on their neglect of their idols. But idol worship had started all their problems in the first place. The people refused to recognize the true source of their problems—departure from since we stopped burning incense to the Queen of Heaven and pouring out drink offerings to her, we have had nothing and have been perishing by sword and famine."

44:19
P Jer 7:18

19 The women added, "When we burned incense to the Queen of Heaven*p* and poured out drink offerings to her, did not our husbands know that we were making cakes like her image and pouring out drink offerings to her?"

20 Then Jeremiah said to all the people, both men and women, who were answering him, 21 "Did not the LORD remember and think about the incense burned in the towns of Judah and the streets of Jerusalem by you and your fathers, your kings and your officials and the

44:22
q Jer 25:18
44:23
r Da 9:11-12

people of the land? 22 When the LORD could no longer endure your wicked actions and the detestable things you did, your land became an object of cursing*q* and a desolate waste without inhabitants, as it is today. 23 Because you have burned incense and have sinned against the LORD and have not obeyed him or followed his law or his decrees or his stipulations, this disaster has come upon you, as you now see."*r*

44:24
s ver 15
t Jer 43:7

24 Then Jeremiah said to all the people, including the women, *s* "Hear the word of the LORD, all you people of Judah in Egypt. *t* 25 This is what the LORD Almighty, the God of Israel, says: You and your wives have shown by your actions what you promised when you said, 'We will certainly carry out the vows we made to burn incense and pour out drink offerings to the Queen of Heaven.'

44:26
u Ge 22:16

"Go ahead then, do what you promised! Keep your vows! 26 But hear the word of the LORD, all Jews living in Egypt: 'I swear*u* by my great name,' says the LORD, 'that no one from Judah living anywhere in Egypt will ever again invoke my name or swear, "As surely as the

44:27
v Jer 31:28
44:28
w ver 13-14

Sovereign LORD lives." 27 For I am watching over them for harm, *v* not for good; the Jews in Egypt will perish by sword and famine until they are all destroyed. 28 Those who escape the sword and return to the land of Judah from Egypt will be very few. *w* Then the whole remnant of Judah who came to live in Egypt will know whose word will stand—mine or theirs.

44:30
x Jer 46:26;
Eze 30:21
y Jer 39:5

29 "'This will be the sign to you that I will punish you in this place,' declares the LORD, 'so that you will know that my threats of harm against you will surely stand.' 30 This is what the LORD says: 'I am going to hand Pharaoh*x* Hophra king of Egypt over to his enemies who seek his life, just as I handed Zedekiah king of Judah over to Nebuchadnezzar king of Babylon, the enemy who was seeking his life.'"*y*

A Message to Baruch

45:1
z Jer 36:4, 18, 32

45 This is what Jeremiah the prophet told Baruch*z* son of Neriah in the fourth year of Jehoiakim son of Josiah king of Judah, after Baruch had written on a scroll the words Jeremiah was then dictating: 2 "This is what the LORD, the God of Israel, says to you, Baruch: 3 You said, 'Woe to me! The LORD has added sorrow to my pain; I am worn out with groaning and find no rest.'"

45:4
a Isa 5:5-7
45:5
b Jer 21:9; 38:2;
39:18

4 ⌊The LORD said,⌋ "Say this to him: 'This is what the LORD says: I will overthrow what I have built and uproot what I have planted, throughout the land. *a* 5 Should you then seek great things for yourself? Seek them not. For I will bring disaster on all people, declares the LORD, but wherever you go I will let you escape with your life.'"*b*

God's leading. When calamity forces you to examine your life, take a close look at God's instructions for you and be willing to humbly apply what you find there.

44:28 After Jeremiah's forced move to Egypt, there is no word in the Bible about the events in the rest of his life.

44:30 Pharaoh Hophra ruled Egypt from 588 to 569 B.C. and was killed by Ahmose, one of his generals, who was then crowned in his place.

45:1ff The event relating to this chapter is recorded in 36:1–8. The chapter was written in 605–604 B.C. Baruch was the scribe who recorded Jeremiah's words on a scroll.

45:5 Baruch had long been serving this unpopular prophet, writing his book of struggles and judgments, and now he was upset. God told Baruch to take his eyes off himself and whatever rewards he thought he deserved. If Baruch did this, God would protect him. It is easy to lose the joy of serving our God when we take our eyes off him. The more we look away from God's purposes toward our own sacrifices, the more frustrated we

will become. As you serve God, beware of focusing on what you are giving up. When this happens, ask God's forgiveness; then redirect your attention to the incomparable privilege of serving God.

B. GOD'S JUDGMENT ON THE NATIONS (46:1—52:34)

All of Jeremiah's prophecies against foreign nations have been grouped together. Many of the people in these nations assumed that they were free from judgment and punishment for their sin. Following these prophecies is a historical appendix recounting the fall of Jerusalem. Just as Jerusalem received its punishment, these nations were certain to receive theirs as well. Those today who think that judgment will never touch them are forewarned.

1. Prophecies about foreign nations

A Message About Egypt

46 This is the word of the LORD that came to Jeremiah the prophet concerning the nations: c

46:1
c Jer 25:15-38

² Concerning Egypt:

This is the message against the army of Pharaoh Neco d king of Egypt, which was defeated at Carchemish e on the Euphrates River by Nebuchadnezzar king of Babylon in the fourth year of Jehoiakim son of Josiah king of Judah:

46:2
d 2Ki 23:29
e 2Ch 35:20

³ "Prepare your shields, f both large and small,
  and march out for battle!

46:3
f Jer 51:11-12

⁴ Harness the horses,
  mount the steeds!
Take your positions
  with helmets on!
Polish your spears,
  put on your armor!

⁵ What do I see?
  They are terrified,
they are retreating,
  their warriors are defeated.
They flee in haste
  without looking back,
and there is terror g on every side,"

46:5
g Jer 49:29

declares the LORD.

⁶ "The swift cannot flee
  nor the strong escape.
In the north by the River Euphrates
  they stumble and fall. h

46:6
h Da 11:19

⁷ "Who is this that rises like the Nile,
  like rivers of surging waters? i

46:7
i Jer 47:2

⁸ Egypt rises like the Nile,
  like rivers of surging waters.
She says, 'I will rise and cover the earth;
  I will destroy cities and their people.'

⁹ Charge, O horses!
  Drive furiously, O charioteers!
March on, O warriors—
  men of Cush a and Put who carry shields,
  men of Lydia j who draw the bow.

46:9
j Isa 66:19

¹⁰ But that day k belongs to the Lord, the LORD Almighty—
  a day of vengeance, for vengeance on his foes.

46:10
k Joel 1:15

a 9 That is, the upper Nile region

46:1ff In this chapter, we gain several insights about God and his plan for this world. (1) Although God chose Israel for a special purpose, he loves all people and wants all to come to him. (2) God is holy and will not tolerate sin. (3) God's judgments are not based on prejudice and a desire for revenge, but on fairness and justice. (4) God does not delight in judgment, but in salvation. (5) God is impartial—he judges everyone by the same standard.

46:2 At the battle of Carchemish in 605 B.C., Babylon and

Egypt, the two major world powers after Assyria's fall, clashed. The Babylonians entered Carchemish by surprise and defeated Egypt. This battle, which passed world leadership to Babylon, was Nebuchadnezzar's first victory, establishing him in his new position as king of the Babylonian empire. With Egypt's power declining, it was both poor strategy and disobedience to God for Judah to form an alliance with Egypt.

46:9 The soldiers from Cush and Put were from eastern and northern Africa. The men of Lydia may have been from Greece.

The sword will devour till it is satisfied,
   till it has quenched its thirst with blood.
46:10
l Zep 1:7
For the Lord, the Lᴏʀᴅ Almighty, will offer sacrifice*l*
   in the land of the north by the River Euphrates.

46:11
m Jer 8:22
n Isa 47:1
11 "Go up to Gilead and get balm,*m*
   O Virgin*n* Daughter of Egypt.
But you multiply remedies in vain;
   there is no healing for you.
12 The nations will hear of your shame;
   your cries will fill the earth.
One warrior will stumble over another;
   both will fall down together."

46:13
o Isa 19:1
13 This is the message the Lᴏʀᴅ spoke to Jeremiah the prophet about the coming of Nebuchadnezzar king of Babylon to attack Egypt: *o*

14 "Announce this in Egypt, and proclaim it in Migdol;
   proclaim it also in Memphis*a* and Tahpanhes:
'Take your positions and get ready,
   for the sword devours those around you.'
15 Why will your warriors be laid low?
   They cannot stand, for the Lᴏʀᴅ will push them down.
46:16
p Lev 26:37
16 They will stumble*p* repeatedly;
   they will fall over each other.
They will say, 'Get up, let us go back
   to our own people and our native lands,
   away from the sword of the oppressor.'
17 There they will exclaim,
   'Pharaoh king of Egypt is only a loud noise;
   he has missed his opportunity.'

46:18
q Jer 48:15
18 "As surely as I live," declares the King,*q*
   whose name is the Lᴏʀᴅ Almighty,
"one will come who is like Tabor among the mountains,
   like Carmel by the sea.
46:19
r Isa 20:4
19 Pack your belongings for exile,*r*
   you who live in Egypt,
for Memphis will be laid waste
   and lie in ruins without inhabitant.

20 "Egypt is a beautiful heifer,
   but a gadfly is coming
   against her from the north.
46:21
s Ps 37:13
21 The mercenaries in her ranks
   are like fattened calves.
They too will turn and flee together,
   they will not stand their ground,
for the day*s* of disaster is coming upon them,
   the time for them to be punished.
22 Egypt will hiss like a fleeing serpent
   as the enemy advances in force;
they will come against her with axes,
   like men who cut down trees.
23 They will chop down her forest,"

                        declares the Lᴏʀᴅ,
"dense though it be.

a 14 Hebrew *Noph*; also in verse 19

46:17 The Egyptian pharaoh was a "loud noise" who "missed his opportunity" because, although he had come to help Jerusalem, he beat a hasty retreat when the Babylonians turned on him. Jeremiah had prophesied that Pharaoh Hophra would be killed by his enemies (44:30). This was fulfilled nearly 20 years later when his co-regent Ahmose led a revolt.

They are more numerous than locusts,
they cannot be counted.
24 The Daughter of Egypt will be put to shame,
handed over to the people of the north.*"

46:24
*Jer 1:15

25 The LORD Almighty, the God of Israel, says: "I am about to bring punishment on Amon god of Thebes,ᵃ ᵘ on Pharaoh, on Egypt and her godsᵛ and her kings, and on those who rely on Pharaoh. 26 I will hand them over to those who seek their lives, to Nebuchadnezzar kingʷ of Babylon and his officers. Later, however, Egypt will be inhabitedˣ as in times past," declares the LORD.

46:25
ᵘEze 30:14
ᵛJer 43:12
46:26
ʷEze 32:11
ˣEze 29:11-16

27 "Do not fear,ʸ O Jacob my servant;
do not be dismayed, O Israel.
I will surely save you out of a distant place,
your descendants from the land of their exile.
Jacob will again have peace and security,
and no one will make him afraid.
28 Do not fear, O Jacob my servant,
for I am with you," declares the LORD.
"Though I completely destroyᶻ all the nations
among which I scatter you,
I will not completely destroy you.
I will discipline you but only with justice;
I will not let you go entirely unpunished."

46:27
ʸIsa 41:13; 43:5

46:28
ᶻJer 4:27

A Message About the Philistines

47 This is the word of the LORD that came to Jeremiah the prophet concerning the Philistines before Pharaoh attacked Gaza:ᵃ

47:1
ᵃAm 1:6; Zec 9:5-7

2 This is what the LORD says:

47:2
ᵇIsa 8:7

"See how the waters are rising in the north;ᵇ
they will become an overflowing torrent.
They will overflow the land and everything in it,
the towns and those who live in them.
The people will cry out;
all who dwell in the land will wail
3 at the sound of the hoofs of galloping steeds,
at the noise of enemy chariots
and the rumble of their wheels.
Fathers will not turn to help their children;
their hands will hang limp.
4 For the day has come
to destroy all the Philistines
and to cut off all survivors
who could help Tyre and Sidon.
The LORD is about to destroy the Philistines,ᶜ
the remnant from the coasts of Caphtor.ᵇ
5 Gaza will shaveᵈ her head in mourning;
Ashkelonᵉ will be silenced.
O remnant on the plain,
how long will you cut yourselves?

47:4
ᶜGe 10:14

47:5
ᵈMic 1:16
ᵉJer 25:20

6 "'Ah, swordᶠ of the LORD,' ⌐you cry,⌐
'how long till you rest?

47:6
ᶠJer 12:12

ᵃ25 Hebrew *No*   ᵇ4 That is, Crete

46:28 God punished his people in order to bring them back to himself, and he punishes us to correct and purify us. No one welcomes punishment, but we should all welcome its results: correction and purity.

47:1 Located on the coastal plain next to Judah, Philistia had always been a thorn in Israel's side. The two nations battled constantly. Other prophets who spoke against Philistia include Isaiah (14:28–32), Ezekiel (25:15–17), Amos (1:6–8), and Zephaniah (2:4–7).

Return to your scabbard;
cease and be still.'
7 But how can it rest
when the LORD has commanded it,
when he has ordered it
to attack Ashkelon and the coast?"

A Message About Moab

48 Concerning Moab:

48:1
g Nu 32:37

This is what the LORD Almighty, the God of Israel, says:

"Woe to Nebo, for it will be ruined.
Kiriathaim*g* will be disgraced and captured;
the stronghold*a* will be disgraced and shattered.

48:2
h Isa 16:14

2 Moab will be praised*h* no more;
in Heshbon*b* men will plot her downfall:
'Come, let us put an end to that nation.'
You too, O Madmen,*c* will be silenced;
the sword will pursue you.
3 Listen to the cries from Horonaim,
cries of great havoc and destruction.
4 Moab will be broken;
her little ones will cry out.*d*

48:5
i Isa 15:5

5 They go up the way to Luhith,*i*
weeping bitterly as they go;
on the road down to Horonaim
anguished cries over the destruction are heard.
6 Flee! Run for your lives;
become like a bush*e* in the desert.

48:7
j Nu 21:29

7 Since you trust in your deeds and riches,
you too will be taken captive,
and Chemosh*j* will go into exile,
together with his priests and officials.
8 The destroyer will come against every town,
and not a town will escape.
The valley will be ruined
and the plateau destroyed,
because the LORD has spoken.
9 Put salt on Moab,
for she will be laid waste*f*;
her towns will become desolate,
with no one to live in them.

48:10
k 1Ki 20:42

10 "A curse on him who is lax in doing the LORD's work!
A curse on him who keeps his sword from bloodshed!*k*

48:11
l Zep 1:12

11 "Moab has been at rest from youth,
like wine left on its dregs,*l*
not poured from one jar to another—
she has not gone into exile.

a1 Or / *Misgab*   *b2* The Hebrew for *Heshbon* sounds like the Hebrew for *plot*.   *c2* The name of the Moabite town
Madmen sounds like the Hebrew for *be silenced*.   *d4* Hebrew; Septuagint / *proclaim it to Zoar*   *e6* Or *like Aroer*
f9 Or *Give wings to Moab, / for she will fly away*

48:1 The Moabites were descendants of Lot through an incestuous relationship with one of his daughters (Genesis 19:30–37).
They led the Israelites into idolatry (Numbers 25:1–3) and joined
the bands of raiders Nebuchadnezzar sent into Judah in 602 B.C.
They were later conquered by Babylon and disappeared as a nation.
48:7 Chemosh was the main god of the nation of Moab (Numbers
21:29), and child sacrifice was an important part of his worship

(2 Kings 3:26, 27). God's judgment made it clear that human-made
resources and gods are no match for the Lord Almighty.
48:9 Putting salt on a city was a symbolic act to show that it was
totally destroyed (see Judges 9:45). Salt in the fields would make
them unfit for crops.

So she tastes as she did,
   and her aroma is unchanged.
12 But days are coming,"
   declares the LORD,
"when I will send men who pour from jars,
   and they will pour her out;
they will empty her jars
   and smash her jugs.
13 Then Moab will be ashamed of Chemosh,
   as the house of Israel was ashamed
   when they trusted in Bethel.

14 "How can you say, 'We are warriors,
   men valiant in battle'?
15 Moab will be destroyed and her towns invaded;
   her finest young men will go down in the slaughter,*m*"
   declares the King,*n* whose name is the LORD Almighty.
16 "The fall of Moab is at hand;
   her calamity will come quickly.
17 Mourn for her, all who live around her,
   all who know her fame;
say, 'How broken is the mighty scepter,
   how broken the glorious staff!'

18 "Come down from your glory
   and sit on the parched ground,*o*
   O inhabitants of the Daughter of Dibon,
for he who destroys Moab
   will come up against you
   and ruin your fortified cities.
19 Stand by the road and watch,
   you who live in Aroer.*p*
Ask the man fleeing and the woman escaping,
   ask them, 'What has happened?'
20 Moab is disgraced, for she is shattered.
   Wail and cry out!
Announce by the Arnon*q*
   that Moab is destroyed.
21 Judgment has come to the plateau—
   to Holon, Jahzah and Mephaath,*r*
22   to Dibon, Nebo and Beth Diblathaim,
23   to Kiriathaim, Beth Gamul and Beth Meon,
24   to Kerioth*s* and Bozrah—
   to all the towns of Moab, far and near.
25 Moab's horn*a t* is cut off;
   her arm is broken,"

                          declares the LORD.

26 "Make her drunk,*u*
   for she has defied the LORD.
Let Moab wallow in her vomit;
   let her be an object of ridicule.
27 Was not Israel the object of your ridicule?*v*
   Was she caught among thieves,
that you shake your head in scorn
   whenever you speak of her?

*a*25 *Horn* here symbolizes strength.

48:15
m Jer 50:27
n Jer 46:18

48:18
o Isa 47:1

48:19
p Dt 2:36

48:20
q Nu 21:13

48:21
r Jos 13:18

48:24
s Am 2:2

48:25
t Ps 75:10

48:26
u Jer 25:16, 27

48:27
v Jer 2:26

48:13 After Israel divided into northern and southern kingdoms, the northern kingdom set up golden calf-idols in Bethel and Dan to keep people from going to worship in Jerusalem, capital of the southern kingdom (1 Kings 12:25–29).

28 Abandon your towns and dwell among the rocks,
   you who live in Moab.
Be like a dove that makes its nest
   at the mouth of a cave.

48:29
w Isa 16:6

29 "We have heard of Moab's pride*w*—
   her overweening pride and conceit,
her pride and arrogance
   and the haughtiness of her heart.
30 I know her insolence but it is futile,"

declares the LORD,

   "and her boasts accomplish nothing.

48:31
x Isa 15:5-8

31 Therefore I wail*x* over Moab,
   for all Moab I cry out,
   I moan for the men of Kir Hareseth.
32 I weep for you, as Jazer weeps,
   O vines of Sibmah.
Your branches spread as far as the sea;
   they reached as far as the sea of Jazer.
The destroyer has fallen
   on your ripened fruit and grapes.

48:33
y Joel 1:12

33 Joy and gladness are gone
   from the orchards and fields of Moab.
I have stopped the flow of wine from the presses;
   no one treads them with shouts of joy.*y*
Although there are shouts,
   they are not shouts of joy.

48:34
z Isa 15:4
a Isa 15:5
b Isa 15:6

34 "The sound of their cry rises
   from Heshbon to Elealeh and Jahaz,*z*
from Zoar as far as Horonaim*a* and Eglath Shelishiyah,
   for even the waters of Nimrim are dried up.*b*

48:35
c Isa 15:2; 16:12

35 In Moab I will put an end
   to those who make offerings on the high places*c*
   and burn incense to their gods,"

declares the LORD.

48:36
d Isa 15:7

36 "So my heart laments for Moab like a flute;
   it laments like a flute for the men of Kir Hareseth.
   The wealth they acquired*d* is gone.

48:37
e Isa 15:2

37 Every head is shaved*e*
   and every beard cut off;
every hand is slashed
   and every waist is covered with sackcloth.

48:38
f Jer 22:28

38 On all the roofs in Moab
   and in the public squares
there is nothing but mourning,
   for I have broken Moab
   like a jar*f* that no one wants,"

declares the LORD.

39 "How shattered she is! How they wail!
   How Moab turns her back in shame!
Moab has become an object of ridicule,
   an object of horror to all those around her."

48:29 Moab was condemned for its pride. God cannot tolerate pride because pride is taking personal credit for what God has done or looking down on others. God does not condemn our taking satisfaction in what we do (Ecclesiastes 3:22), but he stands against overestimates of our own importance. Romans 12:3 teaches us to have an honest estimate of ourselves.

48:31 Kir Hareseth was a stronghold city in Moab. God's compassion reaches to all creation, even to his enemies.

40 This is what the LORD says:

> "Look! An eagle is swooping down,
>> spreading its wings[g] over Moab.
> 41 Kerioth[a] will be captured
>> and the strongholds taken.
> In that day the hearts of Moab's warriors
>> will be like the heart of a woman in labor.[h]
> 42 Moab will be destroyed as a nation
>> because she defied the LORD.
> 43 Terror and pit and snare[i] await you,
>> O people of Moab,"

declares the LORD.

> 44 "Whoever flees from the terror
>> will fall into a pit,
> whoever climbs out of the pit
>> will be caught in a snare;
> for I will bring upon Moab
>> the year of her punishment,"

declares the LORD.

> 45 "In the shadow of Heshbon
>> the fugitives stand helpless,
> for a fire has gone out from Heshbon,
>> a blaze from the midst of Sihon;[j]
> it burns the foreheads of Moab,
>> the skulls[k] of the noisy boasters.
> 46 Woe to you, O Moab![l]
>> The people of Chemosh are destroyed;
> your sons are taken into exile
>> and your daughters into captivity.

> 47 "Yet I will restore[m] the fortunes of Moab
>> in days to come,"

declares the LORD.

Here ends the judgment on Moab.

A Message About Ammon

49

Concerning the Ammonites:[n]

This is what the LORD says:

> "Has Israel no sons?
>> Has she no heirs?
> Why then has Molech[b] taken possession of Gad?
>> Why do his people live in its towns?
> 2 But the days are coming,"
>> declares the LORD,
> "when I will sound the battle cry[o]
>> against Rabbah of the Ammonites;
> it will become a mound of ruins,
>> and its surrounding villages will be set on fire.
> Then Israel will drive out
>> those who drove her out,[p]"

says the LORD.

48:40	[g] Isa 8:8
48:41	[h] Isa 21:3
48:43	[i] Isa 24:17
48:45	[j] Nu 21:21, 26-28 [k] Nu 24:17
48:46	[l] Nu 21:29
48:47	[m] Jer 49:6, 39
49:1	[n] Am 1:13; Zep 2:8-9
49:2	[o] Jer 4:19 [p] Eze 21:28-32; 25:2-11

---

[a] 41 Or *The cities*   [b] 1 Or *their king*; Hebrew *malcam*; also in verse 3

49:1 The Ammonites were descendants of Lot through an incestuous relationship with one of his daughters (as were the Moabites; see Genesis 19:30–38). They were condemned for stealing land from God's people and for worshiping the idol Molech, to whom they sacrificed children.

49:3
q Jer 48:7

3 "Wail, O Heshbon, for Ai is destroyed!
　　Cry out, O inhabitants of Rabbah!
　Put on sackcloth and mourn;
　　rush here and there inside the walls,
　for Molech will go into exile,q
　　together with his priests and officials.
4 Why do you boast of your valleys,
　　boast of your valleys so fruitful?
　O unfaithful daughter,
　　you trust in your riches and say,
　　'Who will attack me?'
5 I will bring terror on you
　　from all those around you,"

　　　　　　　　　　　　　　declares the Lord, the LORD Almighty.

　"Every one of you will be driven away,
　　and no one will gather the fugitives.

49:6
r ver 39; Jer 48:47

6 "Yet afterward, I will restore r the fortunes of the Ammonites,"

　　　　　　　　　　　　　　　　　　declares the LORD.

A Message About Edom

49:7
s Eze 25:12

7 Concerning Edom: s

This is what the LORD Almighty says:

　"Is there no longer wisdom in Teman?
　　Has counsel perished from the prudent?
　　Has their wisdom decayed?
8 Turn and flee, hide in deep caves,
　　you who live in Dedan,
　for I will bring disaster on Esau
　　at the time I punish him.
9 If grape pickers came to you,
　　would they not leave a few grapes?
　If thieves came during the night,
　　would they not steal only as much as they wanted?
10 But I will strip Esau bare;
　　I will uncover his hiding places,
　　so that he cannot conceal himself.
　His children, relatives and neighbors will perish,
　　and he will be no more.
11 Leave your orphans; I will protect their lives.
　　Your widows too can trust in me."

49:12
t Jer 25:28-29
49:13
u Ge 22:16
v Isa 34:6

12 This is what the LORD says: "If those who do not deserve to drink the cup must drink it, why should you go unpunished? t You will not go unpunished, but must drink it. 13 I swear u by myself," declares the LORD, "that Bozrah v will become a ruin and an object of horror, of reproach and of cursing; and all its towns will be in ruins forever."

14 I have heard a message from the LORD:
　　An envoy was sent to the nations to say,
　"Assemble yourselves to attack it!
　　Rise up for battle!"

49:7 Because the Israelites descended from Jacob and the Edomites from his twin brother, Esau, both nations descended from their father, Isaac. There was constant conflict between these nations, and Edom rejoiced at the fall of Jerusalem (see the book of Obadiah). Teman, a town in the northern part of Edom, was known for its wisdom and was the hometown of Eliphaz, one of Job's friends (Job 2:11). But even the wisdom of Teman could not save Edom from God's wrath.

49:8 Dedan was a flourishing city that supported caravan travel. God told its inhabitants to flee to the caves or they would also be destroyed. Teman and Dedan were at opposite ends of the country, so this shows the completeness of God's destruction of Edom. Bozrah (49:13) was a town in northern Edom.

15 "Now I will make you small among the nations,
       despised among men.
16 The terror you inspire
       and the pride of your heart have deceived you,
   you who live in the clefts of the rocks,
       who occupy the heights of the hill.
   Though you build your nest[w] as high as the eagle's,
       from there I will bring you down,"

declares the LORD.

17 "Edom will become an object of horror;
       all who pass by will be appalled and will scoff
       because of all its wounds.[x]
18 As Sodom and Gomorrah[y] were overthrown,
       along with their neighboring towns,"

says the LORD,

   "so no one will live there;
       no man will dwell in it.

19 "Like a lion coming up from Jordan's thickets[z]
       to a rich pastureland,
   I will chase Edom from its land in an instant.
       Who is the chosen one I will appoint for this?
   Who is like me and who can challenge me?[a]
       And what shepherd can stand against me?"
20 Therefore, hear what the LORD has planned against Edom,
       what he has purposed against those who live in Teman:
   The young of the flock[b] will be dragged away;
       he will completely destroy[c] their pasture because of them.
21 At the sound of their fall the earth will tremble;
       their cry[d] will resound to the Red Sea.[a]
22 Look! An eagle will soar and swoop down,
       spreading its wings over Bozrah.
   In that day the hearts of Edom's warriors
       will be like the heart of a woman in labor.[e]

A Message About Damascus

23 Concerning Damascus:

   "Hamath[f] and Arpad are dismayed,
       for they have heard bad news.
   They are disheartened,
       troubled like[b] the restless sea.[g]
24 Damascus has become feeble,
       she has turned to flee
       and panic has gripped her;
   anguish and pain have seized her,
       pain like that of a woman in labor.
25 Why has the city of renown not been abandoned,
       the town in which I delight?
26 Surely, her young men will fall in the streets;
       all her soldiers will be silenced[h] in that day,"

declares the LORD Almighty.

Cross-references (right margin):
49:16 w Job 39:27; Am 9:2
49:17 x Jer 50:13
49:18 y Ge 19:24; Dt 29:23
49:19 z Jer 12:5; a Jer 50:44
49:20 b Jer 50:45; c Mal 1:3-4
49:21 d Jer 50:46
49:22 e Jer 48:40-41
49:23 f Isa 10:9; g Isa 57:20
49:26 h Jer 50:30

a21 Hebrew *Yam Suph*; that is, Sea of Reeds   b23 Hebrew *on* or *by*

49:16 Edom was located in a rock fortress that today is known as Petra, in southern Jordan. Edom thought it was invincible because of its location. Edom was destroyed because of her pride. Pride destroys individuals as well as nations. It makes us think we can take care of ourselves without God's help. Even serving God and others can lead us into pride. Take inventory of your life and service for God; ask God to point out and remove any pride you may be harboring.

49:23-26 Damascus was the capital of Aram, north of Israel. This city was defeated by both Assyria and Babylon. Nebuchadnezzar attacked and defeated Damascus in 605 B.C. (Amos 1:4, 5). It is difficult to attribute the defeat of the army to a particular event, but God utterly destroyed Aram.

49:27
i Am 1:4
j 1Ki 15:18

27 "I will set fire[i] to the walls of Damascus;
    it will consume the fortresses of Ben-Hadad.[j]"

A Message About Kedar and Hazor

28 Concerning Kedar and the kingdoms of Hazor, which Nebuchadnezzar king of Babylon attacked:

This is what the LORD says:

"Arise, and attack Kedar
    and destroy the people of the East.

49:29
k Jer 6:25; 46:5

29 Their tents and their flocks will be taken;
    their shelters will be carried off
    with all their goods and camels.
Men will shout to them,
    'Terror[k] on every side!'

30 "Flee quickly away!
    Stay in deep caves, you who live in Hazor,"

declares the LORD.

"Nebuchadnezzar king of Babylon has plotted against you;
    he has devised a plan against you.

49:31
l Eze 38:11

31 "Arise and attack a nation at ease,
    which lives in confidence,"

declares the LORD,

"a nation that has neither gates nor bars;[l]
    its people live alone.

49:32
m Jer 9:26

32 Their camels will become plunder,
    and their large herds will be booty.
I will scatter to the winds those who are in distant places[a] [m]
    and will bring disaster on them from every side,"

declares the LORD.

49:33
n Jer 10:22

33 "Hazor will become a haunt of jackals,
    a desolate[n] place forever.
No one will live there;
    no man will dwell in it."

A Message About Elam

34 This is the word of the LORD that came to Jeremiah the prophet concerning Elam, early in the reign of Zedekiah king of Judah:

49:35
o Isa 22:6

35 This is what the LORD Almighty says:

"See, I will break the bow[o] of Elam,
    the mainstay of their might.
36 I will bring against Elam the four winds
    from the four quarters of the heavens;
I will scatter them to the four winds,
    and there will not be a nation
    where Elam's exiles do not go.

49:37
p Jer 9:16

37 I will shatter Elam before their foes,
    before those who seek their lives;
I will bring disaster upon them,
    even my fierce anger,"

declares the LORD.

"I will pursue them with the sword[p]
    until I have made an end of them.

a 32 Or *who clip the hair by their foreheads*

49:28 Kedar and Hazor were nomadic tribes east of Israel and south of Aram, in the desert. In 599 B.C. Nebuchadnezzar destroyed them.

49:34 Elam lay east of Babylon and was attacked by Nebuchadnezzar in 597 B.C. Later Elam became the nucleus of the Persian empire (Daniel 8:2) and the residence of Darius.

38 I will set my throne in Elam
    and destroy her king and officials,"

                                                        declares the LORD.

39 "Yet I will restore*q* the fortunes of Elam   **49:39**
    in days to come,"   *q* Jer 48:47

                                                        declares the LORD.

A Message About Babylon

50 This is the word the LORD spoke through Jeremiah the prophet concerning Babylon*r*   **50:1**
       and the land of the Babylonians*a*:   *r* Ge 10:10; Isa 13:1

2 "Announce and proclaim among the nations,   **50:2**
    lift up a banner and proclaim it;   *s* Isa 46:1
    keep nothing back, but say,
  'Babylon will be captured;
    Bel*s* will be put to shame,
    Marduk filled with terror.
  Her images will be put to shame
    and her idols filled with terror.'
3 A nation from the north will attack her
    and lay waste her land.
  No one will live in it;
    both men and animals will flee away.

4 "In those days, at that time,"   **50:4**
    declares the LORD,   *t* Hos 1:11
  "the people of Israel and the people of Judah together*t*   *u* Ezr 3:12; Jer 31:9
    will go in tears*u* to seek*v* the LORD their God.   *v* Hos 3:5
5 They will ask the way to Zion
    and turn their faces toward it.
  They will come and bind themselves to the LORD
    in an everlasting covenant
    that will not be forgotten.

6 "My people have been lost sheep;*w*   **50:6**
    their shepherds have led them astray   *w* Isa 53:6
    and caused them to roam on the mountains.   *x* Jer 3:6
  They wandered over mountain and hill*x*
    and forgot their own resting place.
7 Whoever found them devoured them;
    their enemies said, 'We are not guilty,
  for they sinned against the LORD, their true pasture,
    the LORD, the hope of their fathers.'

8 "Flee*y* out of Babylon;   **50:8**
    leave the land of the Babylonians,   *y* Isa 48:20;
    and be like the goats that lead the flock.   Jer 51:6; Rev 18:4
9 For I will stir up and bring against Babylon
    an alliance of great nations from the land of the north.
  They will take up their positions against her,
    and from the north she will be captured.

a 1 Or *Chaldeans*; also in verses 8, 25, 35 and 45

49:38 The throne represents God's judgment and sovereignty. God would preside over Elam's destruction. He is the King over all kings, including Elam's.

50:1ff At the height of its power, the Babylonian empire seemed invincible. But when Babylon had finished serving God's purpose of punishing Judah for her sins, it would be punished and crushed for its own. Babylon was destroyed in 539 B.C. by the Medo-Persians (Daniel 5:30, 31). Babylon is also used in Scripture as a symbol of all evil. This message can thus apply to the end times when God wipes out all evil, once and for all.

50:3 The nation from the north was Medo-Persia, an alliance of Media and Persia that would become the next world power. Cyrus took the city of Babylon by surprise and brought the nation to its knees in 539 B.C. (Daniel 5:30, 31). The complete destruction of the city was accomplished by later Persian kings.

Their arrows will be like skilled warriors
    who do not return empty-handed.
¹⁰ So Babylonia*a* will be plundered;
    all who plunder her will have their fill,"

declares the LORD.

50:11
z Isa 47:6

¹¹ "Because you rejoice and are glad,
    you who pillage my inheritance,*z*
because you frolic like a heifer threshing grain
    and neigh like stallions,
¹² your mother will be greatly ashamed;
    she who gave you birth will be disgraced.
She will be the least of the nations—
    a wilderness, a dry land, a desert.

50:13
a Jer 49:17

¹³ Because of the LORD's anger she will not be inhabited
    but will be completely desolate.
All who pass Babylon will be horrified and scoff
    because of all her wounds.*a*

¹⁴ "Take up your positions around Babylon,
    all you who draw the bow.
Shoot at her! Spare no arrows,
    for she has sinned against the LORD.

50:15
b Jer 51:14
c Jer 51:44, 58

¹⁵ Shout*b* against her on every side!
    She surrenders, her towers fall,
    her walls*c* are torn down.
Since this is the vengeance of the LORD,
    take vengeance on her;
    do to her as she has done to others.
¹⁶ Cut off from Babylon the sower,
    and the reaper with his sickle at harvest.
Because of the sword of the oppressor
    let everyone return to his own people,
    let everyone flee to his own land.

50:17
d Jer 2:15
e 2Ki 17:6
f 2Ki 24:10, 14

¹⁷ "Israel is a scattered flock
    that lions*d* have chased away.
The first to devour him
    was the king*e* of Assyria;
the last to crush his bones
    was Nebuchadnezzar*f* king of Babylon."

¹⁸Therefore this is what the LORD Almighty, the God of Israel, says:

"I will punish the king of Babylon and his land
    as I punished the king of Assyria.

50:19
g Jer 33:12

¹⁹ But I will bring Israel back to his own pasture
    and he will graze on Carmel and Bashan;
his appetite will be satisfied
    on the hills*g* of Ephraim and Gilead.
²⁰ In those days, at that time,"
    declares the LORD,
"search will be made for Israel's guilt,
    but there will be none,

a 10 Or *Chaldea*

50:17-20 God would punish wicked Babylon as he punished
Assyria for what they had done to Israel. Assyria was crushed
by Babylon, which Assyria had once ruled over. Babylon in turn
would be crushed by Medo-Persia, which was formerly under
Babylon's authority. These verses also look to the time when the
Messiah will rule and Israel will be fully restored. No sin will then
be found in Israel because those who sought God will be
forgiven.

and for the sins of Judah,
    but none will be found,
for I will forgive[h] the remnant[i] I spare.

50:20
h Jer 31:34
i Isa 1:9

21 "Attack the land of Merathaim
    and those who live in Pekod.[j]
Pursue, kill and completely destroy[a] them,"

50:21
j Eze 23:23

                          declares the LORD.

   "Do everything I have commanded you.
22 The noise[k] of battle is in the land,
    the noise of great destruction!
23 How broken and shattered
    is the hammer of the whole earth!
How desolate is Babylon
    among the nations!

50:22
k Jer 51:54

24 I set a trap[l] for you, O Babylon,
    and you were caught before you knew it;
you were found and captured[m]
    because you opposed the LORD.
25 The LORD has opened his arsenal
    and brought out the weapons[n] of his wrath,
for the Sovereign LORD Almighty has work to do
    in the land of the Babylonians.

50:24
l Da 5:30-31
m Jer 51:31

50:25
n Isa 13:5

26 Come against her from afar.
    Break open her granaries;
    pile her up like heaps of grain.
Completely destroy her
    and leave her no remnant.
27 Kill all her young bulls;
    let them go down to the slaughter!
Woe to them! For their day has come,
    the time for them to be punished.
28 Listen to the fugitives and refugees from Babylon
    declaring in Zion[o]
how the LORD our God has taken vengeance,
    vengeance for his temple.

50:28
o Jer 51:10

29 "Summon archers against Babylon,
    all those who draw the bow.
Encamp all around her;
    let no one escape.
Repay[p] her for her deeds;[q]
    do to her as she has done.
For she has defied the LORD,
    the Holy One of Israel.

50:29
p Rev 18:6
q Jer 51:56

30 Therefore, her young men[r] will fall in the streets;
    all her soldiers will be silenced in that day,"

50:30
r Jer 49:26

                          declares the LORD.

31 "See, I am against you, O arrogant one,"
    declares the Lord, the LORD Almighty,
"for your day has come,
    the time for you to be punished.
32 The arrogant one will stumble and fall
    and no one will help her up;

a 21 The Hebrew term refers to the irrevocable giving over of things or persons to the LORD, often by totally destroying them; also in verse 26.

50:21 Merathaim was located in southern Babylonia; Pekod was in eastern Babylonia.

50:32 Pride (arrogance) was Babylon's characteristic sin. Pride comes from feeling self-sufficient or believing that we don't need God. Proud nations or persons, however, will eventually fail

50:32
s Jer 21:14; 49:27

I will kindle a fire[s] in her towns
 that will consume all who are around her."

33 This is what the LORD Almighty says:

"The people of Israel are oppressed,
 and the people of Judah as well.
All their captors hold them fast,
 refusing to let them go.
 34 Yet their Redeemer is strong;
  the LORD Almighty is his name.
He will vigorously defend their cause
 so that he may bring rest to their land,
 but unrest to those who live in Babylon.

35 "A sword against the Babylonians!"
 declares the LORD—
"against those who live in Babylon
 and against her officials and wise men!
36 A sword against her false prophets!
 They will become fools.
A sword against her warriors!
 They will be filled with terror.

50:37
t Jer 51:30; Na 3:13

37 A sword against her horses and chariots
 and all the foreigners in her ranks!
 They will become women.[t]
A sword against her treasures!
 They will be plundered.

50:38
u Jer 51:36

38 A drought on[a] her waters!
 They will dry[u] up.
For it is a land of idols,
 idols that will go mad with terror.

50:39
v Isa 13:19-22

39 "So desert creatures and hyenas will live there,
 and there the owl will dwell.
It will never again be inhabited
 or lived in from generation to generation.[v]

50:40
w Ge 19:24

40 As God overthrew Sodom and Gomorrah[w]
 along with their neighboring towns,"
          declares the LORD,
"so no one will live there;
 no man will dwell in it.

50:41
x Jer 6:22

41 "Look! An army is coming from the north;[x]
 a great nation and many kings
 are being stirred up from the ends of the earth.

50:42
y Isa 13:18
z Isa 5:30
a Jer 6:23

42 They are armed with bows and spears;
 they are cruel and without mercy.[y]
They sound like the roaring sea[z]
 as they ride on their horses;
they come like men in battle formation
 to attack you, O Daughter of Babylon.[a]
43 The king of Babylon has heard reports about them,
 and his hands hang limp.

a 38 Or A sword against

---

because they refuse to recognize God as the ultimate power. Getting rid of pride is not easy, but we can admit that it often rules us and ask God to forgive us and help us overcome it. The best antidote to pride is to focus our attention on the greatness and goodness of God.

50:39 Babylon remains a wasteland to this day. See also Isaiah 13:19–22.

Anguish has gripped him,
    pain like that of a woman in labor.
44 Like a lion coming up from Jordan's thickets
    to a rich pastureland,
I will chase Babylon from its land in an instant.
    Who is the chosen one I will appoint for this?
Who is like me and who can challenge me?[b]
    And what shepherd can stand against me?"
45 Therefore, hear what the LORD has planned against Babylon,
    what he has purposed[c] against the land of the Babylonians:
The young of the flock will be dragged away;
    he will completely destroy their pasture because of them.
46 At the sound of Babylon's capture the earth will tremble;
    its cry will resound among the nations.

51 This is what the LORD says:

    "See, I will stir up the spirit of a destroyer
       against Babylon and the people of Leb Kamai.[a]
2 I will send foreigners to Babylon
    to winnow[d] her and to devastate her land;
they will oppose her on every side
    in the day of her disaster.
3 Let not the archer string his bow,
    nor let him put on his armor.
Do not spare her young men;
    completely destroy[b] her army.
4 They will fall down slain in Babylon,[c]
    fatally wounded in her streets.[e]
5 For Israel and Judah have not been forsaken
    by their God, the LORD Almighty,
though their land[d] is full of guilt
    before the Holy One of Israel.

6 "Flee[f] from Babylon!
    Run for your lives!
    Do not be destroyed because of her sins.[g]
It is time for the LORD's vengeance;[h]
    he will pay[i] her what she deserves.
7 Babylon was a gold cup[j] in the LORD's hand;
    she made the whole earth drunk.
The nations drank her wine;
    therefore they have now gone mad.
8 Babylon will suddenly fall[k] and be broken.
    Wail over her!
Get balm for her pain;
    perhaps she can be healed.

9 "'We would have healed Babylon,
    but she cannot be healed;
let us leave[l] her and each go to his own land,

50:44	*b* Job 41:10; Jer 49:19
50:45	*c* Isa 14:24; Jer 51:11
51:2	*d* Jer 15:7
51:4	*e* Jer 49:26; 50:30
51:6	*f* Jer 50:8 *g* Rev 18:4 *h* Jer 50:15 *i* Jer 25:14
51:7	*j* Jer 25:15-16; Rev 14:8-10; 17:4
51:8	*k* Isa 21:9; Rev 14:8
51:9	*l* Isa 13:14; Jer 50:16

---

a 1 Leb Kamai is a cryptogram for Chaldea, that is, Babylonia.   *b 3* The Hebrew term refers to the irrevocable giving over of things or persons to the LORD, often by totally destroying them.   *c 4* Or Chaldea   *d 5* Or / and the land ⌊of the Babylonians⌋

50:44–46 This invader was Cyrus, who attacked Babylon by surprise and overthrew it. The world was shocked that its greatest empire was overthrown so quickly. No earthly power, no matter how great, can last forever.

51:2 To winnow is to separate the wheat from the chaff. When winnowers threw the mixture into the air, the wind blew away the worthless chaff while the wheat settled to the floor. Babylon would be blown away like chaff in the wind. (See also Matthew 3:12 where John the Baptist says Jesus will separate the wheat from the chaff.)

51:9
m Rev 18:4-5

for her judgment *m* reaches to the skies,
it rises as high as the clouds.'

51:10
n Jer 50:28

10 "'The Lord has vindicated us;
come, let us tell in Zion
what the Lord our God has done.'*n*

51:11
o Jer 46:4
p Jer 50:28

11 "Sharpen the arrows,
take up the shields!*o*
The Lord has stirred up the kings of the Medes,
because his purpose is to destroy Babylon.
The Lord will take vengeance,
vengeance for his temple.*p*
12 Lift up a banner against the walls of Babylon!
Reinforce the guard,
station the watchmen,
prepare an ambush!
The Lord will carry out his purpose,
his decree against the people of Babylon.

51:13
q Rev 17:1, 15

13 You who live by many waters*q*
and are rich in treasures,
your end has come,
the time for you to be cut off.

51:14
r Na 3:15

14 The Lord Almighty has sworn by himself:
I will surely fill you with men, as with a swarm of locusts,*r*
and they will shout in triumph over you.

51:15
s Ge 1:1

15 "He made the earth by his power;
he founded the world by his wisdom
and stretched*s* out the heavens by his understanding.

51:16
t Ps 135:7

16 When he thunders, the waters in the heavens roar;
he makes clouds rise from the ends of the earth.
He sends lightning with the rain
and brings out the wind from his storehouses.*t*

17 "Every man is senseless and without knowledge;
every goldsmith is shamed by his idols.
His images are a fraud;
they have no breath in them.
18 They are worthless, the objects of mockery;
when their judgment comes, they will perish.
19 He who is the Portion of Jacob is not like these,
for he is the Maker of all things,
including the tribe of his inheritance—
the Lord Almighty is his name.

51:20
u Isa 10:5

20 "You are my war club,*u*
my weapon for battle—
with you I shatter nations,
with you I destroy kingdoms,
21 with you I shatter horse and rider,
with you I shatter chariot and driver,

51:22
v 2Ch 36:17;
Isa 13:17-18

22 with you I shatter man and woman,
with you I shatter old man and youth,
with you I shatter young man and maiden,*v*

51:11 Cyrus, king of Persia, had allied with Babylon to defeat Nineveh (capital of the Assyrian empire) in 612 B.C. Then the Medes joined Persia to defeat Babylon (539 B.C.).
51:17–19 It is foolish to trust in man-made images rather than in God. It is easy to think that the things we see and

touch will bring us more security than God. But things rust, rot, and decay. God is eternal. Why put your trust in something that will disappear within a few years?

23 with you I shatter shepherd and flock,
    with you I shatter farmer and oxen,
    with you I shatter governors and officials.

24 "Before your eyes I will repay^w Babylon and all who live in Babylonia^a for all the wrong
they have done in Zion," declares the LORD.

51:24
^w Jer 50:15

25 "I am against you, O destroying mountain,
    you who destroy the whole earth,"

51:25
^x Zec 4:7

                                                  declares the LORD.

    "I will stretch out my hand against you,
       roll you off the cliffs,
    and make you a burned-out mountain.^x
26 No rock will be taken from you for a cornerstone,
    nor any stone for a foundation,
    for you will be desolate forever,"

                                                  declares the LORD.

27 "Lift up a banner^y in the land!
    Blow the trumpet among the nations!
    Prepare the nations for battle against her;
       summon against her these kingdoms:
       Ararat, Minni and Ashkenaz.
    Appoint a commander against her;
       send up horses like a swarm of locusts.

51:27
^y Isa 13:2

28 Prepare the nations for battle against her—
    the kings of the Medes,^z
    their governors and all their officials,
    and all the countries they rule.

51:28
^z ver 11

29 The land trembles and writhes,
    for the LORD's purposes against Babylon stand—
    to lay waste the land of Babylon
    so that no one will live there.
30 Babylon's warriors^a have stopped fighting;
    they remain in their strongholds.
    Their strength is exhausted;
    they have become like women.
    Her dwellings are set on fire;
    the bars^b of her gates are broken.
31 One courier follows another
    and messenger follows messenger
    to announce to the king of Babylon
    that his entire city is captured,
32 the river crossings seized,
    the marshes set on fire,
    and the soldiers terrified."

51:30
^a Jer 50:36
^b La 2:9; Na 3:13

33 This is what the LORD Almighty, the God of Israel, says:

    "The Daughter of Babylon is like a threshing floor^c
    at the time it is trampled;
    the time to harvest^d her will soon come."

51:33
^c Isa 21:10
^d Isa 17:5; Hos 6:11

34 "Nebuchadnezzar^e king of Babylon has devoured us,
    he has thrown us into confusion,
    he has made us an empty jar.

51:34
^e Jer 50:17

^a 24 Or *Chaldea*; also in verse 35

51:33 Grain was threshed on a threshing floor, where sheaves were brought from the field. The stalks of grain were distributed on the floor, a large level section of hard ground. There the grain was crushed to separate the kernels from the stalk; then the kernels were beaten with a wooden tool. Sometimes a wooden sledge was pulled over the grain by animals to break the kernels loose. Babylon would soon be "threshed" as God judged it for its sins.

> Like a serpent he has swallowed us
> and filled his stomach with our delicacies,
> and then has spewed us out.
> 35 May the violence done to our flesh[a] be upon Babylon,"
> say the inhabitants of Zion.
> "May our blood be on those who live in Babylonia,"
> says Jerusalem.

51:36
f Jer 50:38

36 Therefore, this is what the LORD says:

> "See, I will defend your cause
> and avenge you;
> I will dry up[f] her sea
> and make her springs dry.

51:37
g Rev 18:2

> 37 Babylon will be a heap of ruins,
> a haunt[g] of jackals,
> an object of horror and scorn,
> a place where no one lives.
> 38 Her people all roar like young lions,
> they growl like lion cubs.
> 39 But while they are aroused,
> I will set out a feast for them
> and make them drunk,
> so that they shout with laughter—
> then sleep forever and not awake,"

> declares the LORD.

> 40 "I will bring them down
> like lambs to the slaughter,
> like rams and goats.

51:41
h Jer 25:26

> 41 "How Sheshach[b] [h] will be captured,
> the boast of the whole earth seized!
> What a horror Babylon will be
> among the nations!

51:42
i Isa 8:7

> 42 The sea will rise over Babylon;
> its roaring waves[i] will cover her.
> 43 Her towns will be desolate,
> a dry and desert land,
> a land where no one lives,
> through which no man travels.

51:44
j Isa 46:1
k ver 58

> 44 I will punish Bel[j] in Babylon
> and make him spew out what he has swallowed.
> The nations will no longer stream to him.
> And the wall[k] of Babylon will fall.

51:45
l Rev 18:4
m ver 6; Jer 50:8

> 45 "Come out[l] of her, my people!
> Run[m] for your lives!
> Run from the fierce anger of the LORD.

51:46
n 2Ki 19:7

> 46 Do not lose heart or be afraid
> when rumors[n] are heard in the land;
> one rumor comes this year, another the next,
> rumors of violence in the land
> and of ruler against ruler.

51:47
o ver 52

> 47 For the time will surely come
> when I will punish the idols[o] of Babylon;

a 35 Or *done to us and to our children*   b 41 *Sheshach* is a cryptogram for Babylon.

51:36 This verse may refer to an event accomplished by Cyrus, who took Babylon by surprise by diverting the river that ran through the city far upstream and walking in on the dry riverbed. More likely it is saying that Babylon will be deprived of life-giving water. Unlike Jerusalem, Babylon will not be restored.

51:44 Bel is one of the names of Marduk, the chief god of the city of Babylon.

her whole land will be disgraced
and her slain will all lie fallen within her.
48 Then heaven and earth and all that is in them
will shout[p] for joy over Babylon,
for out of the north
destroyers will attack her,"

                                  declares the LORD.

51:48
[p] Isa 44:23

49 "Babylon must fall because of Israel's slain,
just as the slain in all the earth
have fallen because of Babylon.[q]
50 You who have escaped the sword,
leave and do not linger!
Remember the LORD in a distant land,
and think on Jerusalem."

51:49
[q] Jer 50:29

51 "We are disgraced,[r]
for we have been insulted
and shame covers our faces,
because foreigners have entered
the holy places of the LORD's house."

51:51
[r] Ps 44:13-16

52 "But days are coming," declares the LORD,
"when I will punish her idols,
and throughout her land
the wounded will groan.
53 Even if Babylon reaches the sky[s]
and fortifies her lofty stronghold,
I will send destroyers[t] against her,"

                                  declares the LORD.

51:53
[s] Isa 14:13-14
[t] Jer 49:16

54 "The sound of a cry comes from Babylon,
the sound of great destruction[u]
from the land of the Babylonians.[a]
55 The LORD will destroy Babylon;
he will silence her noisy din.
Waves ⌊of enemies⌋ will rage like great waters;
the roar of their voices will resound.
56 A destroyer will come against Babylon;
her warriors will be captured,
and their bows will be broken.
For the LORD is a God of retribution;
he will repay[v] in full.
57 I will make her officials and wise men drunk,
her governors, officers and warriors as well;
they will sleep[w] forever and not awake,"
declares the King,[x] whose name is the LORD Almighty.

51:54
[u] Jer 50:22

51:56
[v] ver 6; Ps 94:1-2

51:57
[w] Ps 76:5
[x] Jer 46:18; 48:15

58 This is what the LORD Almighty says:

"Babylon's thick wall will be leveled
and her high gates set on fire;
the peoples exhaust themselves for nothing,
the nations' labor is only fuel for the flames."[y]

51:58
[y] Hab 2:13

59 This is the message Jeremiah gave to the staff officer Seraiah son of Neriah, the son
of Mahseiah, when he went to Babylon with Zedekiah king of Judah in the fourth[z] year of

51:59
[z] Jer 28:1

a 54 Or Chaldeans

51:51 The people were paralyzed with guilt over their past. The
Babylonian armies had desecrated the temple, and the people were
ashamed to return to Jerusalem. But God told them to return to
the city because he would destroy Babylon for its sins.
51:59 Jeremiah could not visit Babylon, so he sent the message

51:60
ᵃ Jer 30:2
51:62
ᵇ Jer 50:13, 39

51:64
ᶜ ver 58

his reign. ⁶⁰Jeremiah had written on a scrollᵃ about all the disasters that would come upon Babylon—all that had been recorded concerning Babylon. ⁶¹He said to Seraiah, "When you get to Babylon, see that you read all these words aloud. ⁶²Then say, 'O LORD, you have said you will destroy this place, so that neither man nor animal will live in it; it will be desolateᵇ forever.' ⁶³When you finish reading this scroll, tie a stone to it and throw it into the Euphrates. ⁶⁴Then say, 'So will Babylon sink to rise no more because of the disaster I will bring upon her. And her peopleᶜ will fall.'"

The words of Jeremiah end here.

2. The fall of Jerusalem

52:1
ᵈ 2Ki 24:17

52:3
ᵉ Isa 3:1

52:4
ᶠ Zec 8:19
ᵍ 2Ki 25:1-7;
Jer 39:1

52:9
ʰ Jer 32:4

52:11
ⁱ Eze 12:13

52:12
ʲ Jer 39:9

52:13
ᵏ 2Ch 36:19

52:17
ˡ 1Ki 7:15
ᵐ 1Ki 7:27-37
ⁿ Jer 27:19-22
52:19
ᵒ 1Ki 7:50

52 Zedekiahᵈ was twenty-one years old when he became king, and he reigned in Jerusalem eleven years. His mother's name was Hamutal daughter of Jeremiah; she was from Libnah. ²He did evil in the eyes of the LORD, just as Jehoiakim had done. ³It was because of the LORD's anger that all this happened to Jerusalem and Judah,ᵉ and in the end he thrust them from his presence.

Now Zedekiah rebelled against the king of Babylon.

⁴So in the ninth year of Zedekiah's reign, on the tenthᶠ day of the tenth month, Nebuchadnezzar king of Babylon marched against Jerusalem ᵍ with his whole army. They camped outside the city and built siege works all around it. ⁵The city was kept under siege until the eleventh year of King Zedekiah.

⁶By the ninth day of the fourth month the famine in the city had become so severe that there was no food for the people to eat. ⁷Then the city wall was broken through, and the whole army fled. They left the city at night through the gate between the two walls near the king's garden, though the Babyloniansᵃ were surrounding the city. They fled toward the Arabah,ᵇ ⁸but the Babylonianᶜ army pursued King Zedekiah and overtook him in the plains of Jericho. All his soldiers were separated from him and scattered, ⁹and he was captured. ʰ

He was taken to the king of Babylon at Riblah in the land of Hamath, where he pronounced sentence on him. ¹⁰There at Riblah the king of Babylon slaughtered the sons of Zedekiah before his eyes; he also killed all the officials of Judah. ¹¹Then he put out Zedekiah's eyes, bound him with bronze shackles and took him to Babylon, where he put him in prison till the day of his death. ⁱ

¹²On the tenth day of the fifth month, in the nineteenth year of Nebuchadnezzar king of Babylon, Nebuzaradanʲ commander of the imperial guard, who served the king of Babylon, came to Jerusalem. ¹³He set fire ᵏ to the temple of the LORD, the royal palace and all the houses of Jerusalem. Every important building he burned down. ¹⁴The whole Babylonian army under the commander of the imperial guard broke down all the walls around Jerusalem. ¹⁵Nebuzaradan the commander of the guard carried into exile some of the poorest people and those who remained in the city, along with the rest of the craftsmenᵈ and those who had gone over to the king of Babylon. ¹⁶But Nebuzaradan left behind the rest of the poorest people of the land to work the vineyards and fields.

¹⁷The Babylonians broke up the bronze pillars,ˡ the movable standsᵐ and the bronze Sea that were at the temple of the LORD and they carried all the bronze to Babylon. ⁿ ¹⁸They also took away the pots, shovels, wick trimmers, sprinkling bowls, dishes and all the bronze articles used in the temple service. ¹⁹The commander of the imperial guard took away the basins, censers,ᵒ sprinkling bowls, pots, lampstands, dishes and bowls used for drink offerings—all that were made of pure gold or silver.

²⁰The bronze from the two pillars, the Sea and the twelve bronze bulls under it, and the movable stands, which King Solomon had made for the temple of the LORD, was more than

ᵃ7 Or *Chaldeans*; also in verse 17   ᵇ7 Or *the Jordan Valley*   ᶜ8 Or *Chaldean*; also in verse 14   ᵈ15 Or *populace*

---

with Seraiah, the officer who cared for the comforts of the army. Seraiah was probably Baruch's brother (32:12).

51:60–64 In this last of Jeremiah's messages, we find again the twin themes of God's sovereignty and his judgment. Babylon had been allowed to oppress the people of Israel, but Babylon itself would be judged. Although God brings good out of evil, he does not allow evil to remain unpunished. The wicked may succeed for a while, but resist the temptation to follow them or you may share in their judgment.

52:1ff This chapter provides more detail about the destruction of Jerusalem recorded in chapter 39 (similar material is found in 2 Kings 24:18—25:21). This appendix shows that Jeremiah's prophecies concerning the destruction of Jerusalem and the Babylonian captivity happened just as he predicted. For more information on Zedekiah, see the note on 39:1ff.

52:8, 9 Riblah was 200 miles north of Jerusalem. This was the Babylonian headquarters for ruling the region. Hamath was the district of Aram containing the nation's capital.

could be weighed. ᵖ ²¹Each of the pillars was eighteen cubits high and twelve cubits in circumference ᵃ; each was four fingers thick, and hollow. ᑫ ²²The bronze capital on top of the one pillar was five cubits ᵇ high and was decorated with a network and pomegranates of bronze all around. The other pillar, with its pomegranates, was similar. ²³There were ninety-six pomegranates on the sides; the total number of pomegranates ʳ above the surrounding network was a hundred.

²⁴The commander of the guard took as prisoners Seraiah ˢ the chief priest, Zephaniah ᵗ the priest next in rank and the three doorkeepers. ²⁵Of those still in the city, he took the officer in charge of the fighting men, and seven royal advisers. He also took the secretary who was chief officer in charge of conscripting the people of the land and sixty of his men who were found in the city. ²⁶Nebuzaradan the commander took them all and brought them to the king of Babylon at Riblah. ²⁷There at Riblah, in the land of Hamath, the king had them executed.

So Judah went into captivity, away from her land. ²⁸This is the number of the people Nebuchadnezzar carried into exile: ᵘ

in the seventh year, 3,023 Jews;
²⁹ in Nebuchadnezzar's eighteenth year,
832 people from Jerusalem;
³⁰ in his twenty-third year,
745 Jews taken into exile by Nebuzaradan the commander of the imperial guard.
There were 4,600 people in all.

Jehoiachin Released

³¹In the thirty-seventh year of the exile of Jehoiachin king of Judah, in the year Evil-Merodach ᶜ became king of Babylon, he released Jehoiachin king of Judah and freed him from prison on the twenty-fifth day of the twelfth month. ³²He spoke kindly to him and gave him a seat of honor higher than those of the other kings who were with him in Babylon. ³³So Jehoiachin put aside his prison clothes and for the rest of his life ate regularly at the king's table. ᵛ ³⁴Day by day the king of Babylon gave Jehoiachin a regular allowance ʷ as long as he lived, till the day of his death.

ᵃ21 That is, about 27 feet (about 8.1 meters) high and 18 feet (about 5.4 meters) in circumference   ᵇ22 That is, about 7 1/2 feet (about 2.3 meters)   ᶜ31 Also called *Amel-Marduk*

52:20
ᵖ1Ki 7:47

52:21
ᑫ1Ki 7:15

52:23
ʳ1Ki 7:20

52:24
ˢ2Ki 25:18
ᵗJer 21:1; 37:3

52:28
ᵘ2Ki 24:14-16

52:33
ᵛ2Sa 9:7

52:34
ʷ2Sa 9:10

52:21 A cubit was a standard of measure about 17 to 20 inches long.

52:31 Babylon's king showed kindness to Jehoiachin. In 561 B.C. Jehoiachin was released from prison and allowed to eat with the king. God continued to show kindness to the descendants of King David, even in exile.

52:34 In the world's eyes, Jeremiah looked totally unsuccessful. He had no money, family, or friends. He prophesied the destruction of the nation, the capital city, and the temple, but the political and religious leaders would not accept or follow his advice. No group of people liked him or listened to him. Yet as we look back, we see that he successfully completed the work God gave him to do. Success must never be measured by popularity, fame, or fortune, for these are temporal measures. King Zedekiah, for example, lost everything by pursuing selfish goals. God measures our success with the yardsticks of obedience, faithfulness, and righteousness. If you are faithfully doing the work God gives you, you are successful in his eyes.

LAMENTATIONS

TEARS are defined simply as "drops of salty fluid flowing from the eyes." They can be caused by irritation or laughter but are usually associated with weeping, sorrow, and grief. When we cry, friends wonder what's wrong and try to console us. Babies cry for food; children cry a the loss of a pet; adults cry when confronted with trauma and death.

Jeremiah's grief ran deep. He is remembered as the "weeping prophet," and his tears flowed from a broken heart. As God's spokesman, he knew what lay ahead for Judah, his country, and for Jerusalem, the capital and "the city of God." God's judgment would fall and destruction would come. So Jeremiah wept. His tears were not self-centered, mourning over personal suffering or loss. He wept because the people had rejected their God—the God who had made them, loved them, and sought repeatedly to bless them. Jeremiah's heart was broken because he knew that the selfishness and sinfulness of the people would bring them much suffering and an extended exile. Jeremiah's tears were tears of empathy and sympathy. His heart was broken with those things that break God's heart.

Jeremiah's two books focus on one event—the destruction of Jerusalem. The book of Jeremiah predicts it, and Lamentations looks back on it. Known as the book of tears, Lamentations is a dirge, a funeral song written for the fallen city of Jerusalem.

What makes a person cry says a lot about that person—whether he or she is self-centered or God-centered. The book of Lamentations allows us to see what made Jeremiah sorrowful. As one of God's choice servants, he stands alone in the depth of his emotions, broken by his care for the people, his love for the nation, and his devotion to God.

What causes your tears? Do you weep because your selfish pride has been wounded or because the people around you lead sinful lives and reject the God who loves them dearly? Do you weep because you have lost something of value or because people all around you will suffer for their sinfulness? Our world is filled with injustice, poverty, war, and rebellion against God, all of which should move us to tears and to action. Read Lamentations and learn what it means to grieve with God.

VITAL STATISTICS

PURPOSE:
To teach people that to disobey God is to invite disaster, and to show that God suffers when his people suffer

AUTHOR:
Jeremiah

ORIGINAL AUDIENCE:
The exiled people of Judah

DATE WRITTEN:
Soon after the fall of Jerusalem in 586 B.C.

SETTING:
Jerusalem had been destroyed by Babylon and her people killed, tortured, or taken captive.

KEY VERSE:
"My eyes fail from weeping, I am in torment within, my heart is poured out on the ground because my people are destroyed, because children and infants faint in the streets of the city" (2:11).

KEY PEOPLE:
Jeremiah, the people of Jerusalem

KEY PLACE:
Jerusalem

SPECIAL FEATURES:
Three strands of Hebrew thought meet in Lamentations—prophecy, ritual, and wisdom. Lamentations is written in the rhythm and style of ancient Jewish funeral songs or chants. It contains five poems corresponding to the five chapters (see the second note on 3:1ff).

THE BLUEPRINT

1. Jeremiah mourns for Jerusalem (1:1–22)
2. God's anger at sin (2:1–22)
3. Hope in the midst of affliction (3:1–66)
4. God's anger is satisfied (4:1–22)
5. Jeremiah pleads for restoration (5:1–22)

Jeremiah grieves deeply because of the destruction of Jerusalem and the devastation of his nation. But in the middle of the book, in the depths of his grief, there shines a ray of hope. God's compassion is ever present. His faithfulness is great. Jeremiah realizes that it is only the Lord's mercy that has prevented total annihilation. This book shows us the serious consequences of sin and how we can still have hope in the midst of tragedy because God is able to turn it around for good. We see the timeless importance of prayer and confession of sin. We will all face tragedy in our life. But in the midst of our afflictions, there is hope in God.

MEGATHEMES

THEME	EXPLANATION	IMPORTANCE
Destruction of Jerusalem	Lamentations is a sad funeral song for the great capital city of the Jews. The temple has been destroyed, the king is gone, and the people are in exile. God had warned that he would destroy them if they abandoned him. Now, afterward, the people realize their condition and confess their sin.	God's warnings are justified. He does what he says he will do. His punishment for sin is certain. Only by confessing and renouncing our sin can we turn to him for deliverance. How much better to do so before his warnings are fulfilled.
God's Mercy	God's compassion was at work even when the Israelites were experiencing the affliction of their Babylonian conquerors. Although the people had been unfaithful, God's faithfulness was great. He used this affliction to bring his people back to him.	God will always be faithful to his people. His merciful, refining work is evident even in affliction. At those times, we must pray for forgiveness and then turn to him for deliverance.
Sin's Consequences	God was angry at the prolonged rebellion by his people. Sin was the cause of their misery, and destruction was the result of their sin. The destruction of the nation shows the vanity of human glory and pride.	To continue in rebellion against God is to invite disaster. We must never trust our own leadership, resources, intelligence, or power more than God. If we do, we will experience consequences similar to Jerusalem's.
Hope	God's mercy in sparing some of the people offers hope for better days. One day, the people will be restored to a true and fervent relationship with God.	Only God can deliver us from sin. Without him there is no comfort or hope for the future. Because of Christ's death for us and his promise to return, we have a bright hope for tomorrow.

1. Jeremiah mourns for Jerusalem

1 ^a
How deserted lies the city,
    once so full of people!
How like a widow[a] is she,
    who once was great among the nations!
She who was queen among the provinces
    has now become a slave.[b]

2 Bitterly she weeps at night,
    tears are upon her cheeks.
Among all her lovers
    there is none to comfort her.
All her friends have betrayed her;
    they have become her enemies.

3 After affliction and harsh labor,
    Judah has gone into exile.[c]
She dwells among the nations;
    she finds no resting place.
All who pursue her have overtaken her
    in the midst of her distress.

4 The roads to Zion mourn,
    for no one comes to her appointed feasts.
All her gateways are desolate,
    her priests groan,

1:1
a Isa 47:8
b Isa 3:26

1:3
c Jer 13:19

aThis chapter is an acrostic poem, the verses of which begin with the successive letters of the Hebrew alphabet.

1:1 This is the prophet Jeremiah's song of sorrow for Jerusalem's destruction. The nation of Judah had been utterly defeated, the temple destroyed, and captives taken away to Babylon. Jeremiah's tears were for the suffering and humiliation of the people, but those tears penetrated even deeper into his heart. He wept because God had rejected the people for their rebellious ways.

Each year this book was read aloud to remind all the Jews that their great city fell because of their stubborn sinfulness.
1:2 The term *lovers* refers to nations such as Egypt, to whom Judah kept turning for help. As the Babylonians closed in on Jerusalem, the nation of Judah turned away from God and sought help and protection from other nations instead.

1:4
d Joel 1:8-13

her maidens grieve,
  and she is in bitter anguish.*d*

1:5
e Jer 52:28-30

5 Her foes have become her masters;
    her enemies are at ease.
The LORD has brought her grief
    because of her many sins.
Her children have gone into exile,*e*
    captive before the foe.

1:6
f Jer 13:18

6 All the splendor has departed
    from the Daughter of Zion.*f*
Her princes are like deer
    that find no pasture;
in weakness they have fled
    before the pursuer.

1:7
g Jer 37:7

7 In the days of her affliction and wandering
    Jerusalem remembers all the treasures
    that were hers in days of old.
When her people fell into enemy hands,
    there was no one to help her.*g*
Her enemies looked at her
    and laughed at her destruction.

1:8
h Jer 13:22, 26

8 Jerusalem has sinned greatly
    and so has become unclean.
All who honored her despise her,
    for they have seen her nakedness;*h*
she herself groans
    and turns away.

1:9
i Dt 32:28-29;
Isa 47:7

9 Her filthiness clung to her skirts;
    she did not consider her future.*i*
Her fall was astounding;
    there was none to comfort her.
"Look, O LORD, on my affliction,
    for the enemy has triumphed."

1:10
j Isa 64:11
k Jer 51:51
l Dt 23:3

10 The enemy laid hands
    on all her treasures;*j*
she saw pagan nations
    enter her sanctuary*k*—
those you had forbidden*l*
    to enter your assembly.

1:11
m Jer 52:6

11 All her people groan
    as they search for bread;*m*
they barter their treasures for food
    to keep themselves alive.
"Look, O LORD, and consider,
    for I am despised."

1:12
n Jer 18:16
o Jer 30:24

12 "Is it nothing to you, all you who pass by?*n*
    Look around and see.
Is any suffering like my suffering
    that was inflicted on me,
that the LORD brought on me
    in the day of his fierce anger?*o*

1:9 The warning was loud and clear: If Judah played with fire, its people would get burned. Jerusalem foolishly took a chance and lost, refusing to believe that immoral living brings God's punishment. The ultimate consequence of sin is punishment (Romans 6:23). We can choose to ignore God's warnings, but as surely as judgment came upon Jerusalem, so will it come upon those who defy God. Are you listening to God's Word? Are you obeying it? Obedience is a sure sign of your love for God.

¹³ "From on high he sent fire,
　　sent it down into my bones.
He spread a net for my feet
　　and turned me back.
He made me desolate,ᵖ
　　faint all the day long.

1:13
ᵖ Jer 44:6

¹⁴ "My sins have been bound into a yokeᵃ;�q
　　by his hands they were woven together.
They have come upon my neck
　　and the Lord has sapped my strength.
He has handed me over
　　to those I cannot withstand.

1:14
q Dt 28:48

¹⁵ "The Lord has rejected
　　all the warriors in my midst;
he has summoned an armyʳ against me
　　toᵇ crush my young men.
In his winepress the Lord has trampled
　　the Virgin Daughter of Judah.

1:15
ʳ Isa 41:2

¹⁶ "This is why I weep
　　and my eyes overflow with tears.ˢ
No one is near to comfort me,
　　no one to restore my spirit.
My children are destitute
　　because the enemy has prevailed."ᵗ

1:16
ˢ La 2:11, 18
ᵗ Jer 13:17

¹⁷ Zion stretches out her hands,ᵘ
　　but there is no one to comfort her.
The Lᴏʀᴅ has decreed for Jacob
　　that his neighbors become his foes;
Jerusalem has become
　　an unclean thing among them.

1:17
ᵘ Jer 4:31

¹⁸ "The Lᴏʀᴅ is righteous,
　　yet I rebelledᵛ against his command.
Listen, all you peoples;
　　look upon my suffering.
My young men and maidens
　　have gone into exile.

1:18
ᵛ 1Sa 12:14

¹⁹ "I called to my allies
　　but they betrayed me.
My priests and my elders
　　perishedʷ in the city
while they searched for food
　　to keep themselves alive.

1:19
ʷ La 2:20

²⁰ "See, O Lᴏʀᴅ, how distressedˣ I am!
　　I am in tormentʸ within,
and in my heart I am disturbed,
　　for I have been most rebellious.

1:20
ˣ Jer 4:19
ʸ La 2:11

ᵃ 14 Most Hebrew manuscripts; Septuagint *He kept watch over my sins*   ᵇ 15 Or *has set a time for me / when he will*

1:14 At first, sin seems to offer freedom. But the liberty to do anything we want gradually becomes a desire to do everything. Then we become captive to sin, bound by its "yoke." Freedom from sin's captivity comes only from God. He gives us freedom, not to do anything we want, but to do what he knows is best for us. Strange as it may seem, true freedom comes in obeying God—following his guidance so that we can receive his best.

1:16 Jeremiah's sorrow expresses the sorrow of the nation. God is the comforter, but because of the people's sins, he had to turn away from them and become their judge. When we suffer the consequences of sin, repentance from the sin that caused the problem is the first and most important way to find relief.

1:19 Jerusalem's allies could not come to help because, like Jerusalem, they failed to seek God. Though these allies appeared strong, they were actually weak because God was not with them. Dependable assistance can come only from an ally whose power is from God. When you seek wise counsel, go to Christians who get their wisdom from the all-knowing God.

1:20
z Eze 7:15

Outside, the sword bereaves;
  inside, there is only death.*z*

1:21
a La 2:15
b Jer 30:16

21 "People have heard my groaning,
    but there is no one to comfort me.
  All my enemies have heard of my distress;
    they rejoice*a* at what you have done.
  May you bring the day*b* you have announced
    so they may become like me.

22 "Let all their wickedness come before you;
    deal with them
  as you have dealt with me
    because of all my sins.
  My groans are many
    and my heart is faint."

2. God's anger at sin

2:1
c Ps 99:5

2 *a*   How the Lord has covered the Daughter of Zion
              with the cloud of his anger*b*!
        He has hurled down the splendor of Israel
          from heaven to earth;
        he has not remembered his footstool*c*
          in the day of his anger.

2:2
d Ps 89:39-40
e Isa 25:12

2 Without pity the Lord has swallowed up
    all the dwellings of Jacob;
  in his wrath he has torn down
    the strongholds*d* of the Daughter of Judah.
  He has brought her kingdom and its princes
    down to the ground*e* in dishonor.

2:3
f Ps 74:11

3 In fierce anger he has cut off
    every horn*c* of Israel.
  He has withdrawn his right hand*f*
    at the approach of the enemy.
  He has burned in Jacob like a flaming fire
    that consumes everything around it.

2:4
g La 3:12-13
h Eze 24:16, 25

4 Like an enemy he has strung his bow;*g*
    his right hand is ready.
  Like a foe he has slain
    all who were pleasing to the eye;*h*
  he has poured out his wrath like fire
    on the tent of the Daughter of Zion.

2:5
i Jer 9:17-20

5 The Lord is like an enemy;
    he has swallowed up Israel.
  He has swallowed up all her palaces
    and destroyed her strongholds.
  He has multiplied mourning and lamentation
    for the Daughter of Judah.*i*

2:6
j Jer 52:13

6 He has laid waste his dwelling like a garden;
    he has destroyed his place of meeting.*j*

a This chapter is an acrostic poem, the verses of which begin with the successive letters of the Hebrew alphabet.
b 1 Or *How the Lord in his anger / has treated the Daughter of Zion with contempt*   *c* 3 Or */ all the strength*; or *every king*; *horn* here symbolizes strength.

1:22 Babylon, although sinful, was God's instrument for punishing Judah and its capital, Jerusalem. The people of Jerusalem were pleading for God to punish sinful Babylon as he had punished them ("deal with them as you have dealt with me"). God would do this, for he had already passed judgment on Babylon (see Jeremiah 50:1–27).

2:6 King Solomon's temple (here called God's "dwelling" and "place of meeting") in Jerusalem represented God's presence with the people (1 Kings 8:1–11). The temple was the central place of worship. Many in Jeremiah's day assumed that God would never allow his temple to be harmed. Its destruction symbolized God's rejection of his people—that he no longer lived among them.

The LORD has made Zion forget
   her appointed feasts and her Sabbaths;[k]
in his fierce anger he has spurned
   both king and priest.

7 The Lord has rejected his altar
   and abandoned his sanctuary.
He has handed over to the enemy
   the walls of her palaces;[l]
they have raised a shout in the house of the LORD
   as on the day of an appointed feast.

8 The LORD determined to tear down
   the wall around the Daughter of Zion.
He stretched out a measuring line[m]
   and did not withhold his hand from destroying.
He made ramparts and walls lament;
   together they wasted away.

9 Her gates have sunk into the ground;
   their bars he has broken and destroyed.
Her king and her princes are exiled[n] among the nations,
   the law is no more,
and her prophets no longer find
   visions from the LORD.

10 The elders of the Daughter of Zion
   sit on the ground in silence;
they have sprinkled dust on their heads[o]
   and put on sackcloth.[p]
The young women of Jerusalem
   have bowed their heads to the ground.[q]

11 My eyes fail from weeping,[r]
   I am in torment within,
my heart is poured out[s] on the ground
   because my people are destroyed,
because children and infants faint
   in the streets of the city.

12 They say to their mothers,
   "Where is bread and wine?"
as they faint like wounded men
   in the streets of the city,
as their lives ebb away
   in their mothers' arms.

13 What can I say for you?
   With what can I compare you,
   O Daughter of Jerusalem?

2:6
[k] Zep 3:18

2:7
[l] Jer 33:4-5

2:8
[m] 2Ki 21:13;
Isa 34:11

2:9
[n] Dt 28:36

2:10
[o] Job 2:12
[p] Isa 15:3
[q] Job 2:13; Isa 3:26

2:11
[r] La 3:48-51
[s] Ps 22:14

2:7 Our place of worship is not as important to God as our priorities in worship. A church building may be beautiful, but if its people don't sincerely follow God, the church will decay from within. The people of Judah, despite their stunning temple, had rejected in their daily lives what they proclaimed in their worship rituals. Thus their worship had turned into a mocking lie. When you worship, are you saying words you don't really mean? Do you pray for help you don't really believe will come? Do you express love for God you don't really have? Earnestly seek God and catch a fresh vision of his love and care. Then worship him wholeheartedly.

2:9 Four powerful symbols and sources of security were lost: the protection of the "gates," the leadership of the "king" and "princes," the guidance of the "law," and the vision of the "prophets." With those four factors present, the people were lulled into a false sense of security and felt comfortable with their sins. But after each was removed, the people were confronted with the choice of repenting and returning to God or continuing on this path of suffering. Don't substitute symbols, even good ones, for the reality of a living, personal relationship with God himself.

2:11 Jeremiah's tears were sincere and full of compassion. Sorrow does not mean that we lack faith or strength. There is nothing wrong with crying—Jesus himself felt sorrow and even wept (John 11:35). How do we react to the tearing down of our society and to moral degradation? This may not be as obvious as an invading enemy army, but the destruction is just as certain. We too should be deeply moved when we see the moral decay that surrounds us.

To what can I liken you,
    that I may comfort you,
    O Virgin Daughter of Zion?

2:13
t La 1:12

Your wound is as deep as the sea.*t*
    Who can heal you?

14 The visions of your prophets
    were false and worthless;
    they did not expose your sin
    to ward off your captivity.
    The oracles they gave you
    were false and misleading.

2:15
u Eze 25:6
v Ps 48:2

15 All who pass your way
    clap their hands at you;*u*
    they scoff and shake their heads
    at the Daughter of Jerusalem:
    "Is this the city that was called
    the perfection of beauty,
    the joy of the whole earth?"*v*

2:16
w Ps 56:2; La 3:46

16 All your enemies open their mouths
    wide against you;*w*
    they scoff and gnash their teeth
    and say, "We have swallowed her up.
    This is the day we have waited for;
    we have lived to see it."

2:17
x Dt 28:15-45

17 The Lᴏʀᴅ has done what he planned;
    he has fulfilled his word,
    which he decreed long ago.*x*
    He has overthrown you without pity,
    he has let the enemy gloat over you,
    he has exalted the horn*a* of your foes.

2:18
y La 1:16

18 The hearts of the people
    cry out to the Lord.
    O wall of the Daughter of Zion,
    let your tears*y* flow like a river
    day and night;
    give yourself no relief,
    your eyes no rest.

2:19
z Ps 62:8

19 Arise, cry out in the night,
    as the watches of the night begin;
    pour out your heart*z* like water
    in the presence of the Lord.
    Lift up your hands to him
    for the lives of your children,

a 17 *Horn* here symbolizes strength.

2:14 False prophets were everywhere in Jeremiah's day. They gave counterfeit and misleading "oracles" (messages to people from God). While Jeremiah warned the people of coming destruction and lengthy captivity, the false prophets said that all was well and so the people need not fear. All of Jeremiah's words came true because he was a true prophet of God (Jeremiah 14:14–16).

2:15 Clapping hands, scoffing, and shaking heads were all signs of derision and mockery. They were contemptuous gestures.

2:19 Chapter 1 describes Jerusalem's desolation and calls for God's revenge on his enemies. Chapter 2 includes a call for God's people to pour out their hearts in the Lord's presence. The people must turn from their sins; they must sincerely mourn over their wrongs against God (3:40–42). The people had much to cry about. Because of their stubborn rebellion against God, they had brought great suffering to all, especially the innocent. Was this suffering God's fault? No, it was the fault of the wayward people. Sinful people brought destruction on themselves, but tragically, sin's consequences affected everyone—good and evil alike.

2:19 The people's suffering and sin should have brought them to the Lord, weeping for forgiveness. Only when our prideful, independent hearts are broken over sin can God come to our rescue. Just feeling sorry about experiencing sin's consequences does not bring forgiveness. But if we cry out to God in repentance, he will forgive us.

who faint*a* from hunger
    at the head of every street.

20 "Look, O LORD, and consider:
    Whom have you ever treated like this?
Should women eat their offspring,*b*
    the children they have cared for?
Should priest and prophet be killed
    in the sanctuary of the Lord?

21 "Young and old lie together
    in the dust of the streets;
my young men and maidens
    have fallen by the sword.*c*
You have slain them in the day of your anger;
    you have slaughtered them without pity.

22 "As you summon to a feast day,
    so you summoned against me terrors*d* on every side.
In the day of the LORD's anger
    no one escaped or survived;
those I cared for and reared,
    my enemy has destroyed."

2:19
a Isa 51:20

2:20
b Jer 19:9

2:21
c 2Ch 36:17

2:22
d Ps 31:13

3. Hope in the midst of affliction

3 *a* I am the man who has seen affliction
        by the rod of his wrath.
2 He has driven me away and made me walk
    in darkness rather than light;
3 indeed, he has turned his hand against me
    again and again, all day long.

4 He has made my skin and my flesh grow old
    and has broken my bones.*e*
5 He has besieged me and surrounded me
    with bitterness and hardship.
6 He has made me dwell in darkness
    like those long dead.*f*

7 He has walled me in so I cannot escape;
    he has weighed me down with chains.
8 Even when I call out or cry for help,
    he shuts out my prayer.*g*
9 He has barred my way with blocks of stone;
    he has made my paths crooked.

10 Like a bear lying in wait,
    like a lion in hiding,
11 he dragged me from the path and mangled*h* me
    and left me without help.

3:4
e Ps 51:8; Isa 38:13

3:6
f Ps 88:5-6

3:8
g Job 30:20

3:11
h Hos 6:1

a This chapter is an acrostic poem; the verses of each stanza begin with the successive letters of the Hebrew alphabet, and the verses within each stanza begin with the same letter.

2:21, 22 This horrible scene could have been avoided. Jeremiah had warned the people for years that this day of destruction would come, and it broke his heart to see it fulfilled. We are always shocked when we hear of tragedy striking the innocent. But often innocent bystanders are victims of judgment on a nation. Sin has a way of causing great sorrow and devastation to many.

3:1ff In Jeremiah's darkest moment, his hope was strengthened with this assurance: God had been faithful and would continue to be faithful. Jeremiah saw both God's judgment and God's

steadfast love. In the time of judgment, Jeremiah could still cling to God's love just as in times of prosperity he had warned of God's judgment.

3:1ff In the original Hebrew, the first four chapters in Lamentations are acrostic poems. Each verse in each chapter begins with a successive letter of the Hebrew alphabet. Chapter 3 has 66 verses rather than 22 because it is a triple acrostic: the first three verses begin with the equivalent of *A*, the next three with *B*, and so on (see the NIV text note). This was a typical form of Hebrew poetry. Other examples of acrostics are Psalms 37, 119, and 145, and Proverbs 31:10–31.

3:12
i Job 7:20

12 He drew his bow
    and made me the target*i* for his arrows.

13 He pierced my heart
    with arrows from his quiver.

3:14
j Jer 20:7
k Job 30:9

14 I became the laughingstock*j* of all my people;
    they mock me in song*k* all day long.

3:15
l Jer 9:15

15 He has filled me with bitter herbs
    and sated me with gall.*l*

3:16
m Pr 20:17

16 He has broken my teeth with gravel;*m*
    he has trampled me in the dust.

17 I have been deprived of peace;
    I have forgotten what prosperity is.

18 So I say, "My splendor is gone
    and all that I had hoped from the LORD."

19 I remember my affliction and my wandering,
    the bitterness and the gall.

20 I well remember them,
    and my soul is downcast within me.

21 Yet this I call to mind
    and therefore I have hope:

3:22
n Mal 3:6

22 Because of the LORD's great love we are not consumed,
    for his compassions never fail.*n*

23 They are new every morning;
    great is your faithfulness.

24 I say to myself, "The LORD is my portion;
    therefore I will wait for him."

25 The LORD is good to those whose hope is in him,
    to the one who seeks him;

3:26
o Ps 37:7

26 it is good to wait quietly
    for the salvation of the LORD.*o*

27 It is good for a man to bear the yoke
    while he is young.

3:28
p Jer 15:17

28 Let him sit alone in silence,*p*
    for the LORD has laid it on him.

29 Let him bury his face in the dust—
    there may yet be hope.

3:30
q Isa 50:6

30 Let him offer his cheek to one who would strike him,*q*
    and let him be filled with disgrace.

3:31
r Ps 94:14

31 For men are not cast off
    by the Lord forever.*r*

32 Though he brings grief, he will show compassion,
    so great is his unfailing love.

3:33
s Eze 33:11

33 For he does not willingly bring affliction
    or grief to the children of men.*s*

3:21, 22 Jeremiah saw one ray of hope in all the sin and sorrow surrounding him: "Because of the LORD's great love we are not consumed, for his compassions never fail." God willingly responds with help when we ask. Perhaps there is some sin in your life that you thought God would not forgive. God's steadfast love and mercy are greater than any sin, and he promises forgiveness.

3:23 Jeremiah knew from personal experience about God's faithfulness. God had promised that punishment would follow disobedience, and it did. But God also had promised future restoration and blessing, and Jeremiah knew that God would keep that promise also. Trusting in God's faithfulness day by day makes us confident in his great promises for the future.

3:27–33 To "bear the yoke" means to willingly come under God's discipline and learn what he wants to teach. This involves several important factors: (1) silent reflection on what God wants, (2) repentant humility, (3) self-control in the face of adversity, and (4) confident patience, depending on the divine Teacher to bring about loving lessons in our lives. God has several long-term and short-term lessons for you right now. Are you doing your homework?

3:30 To "offer his cheek to one who would strike him" means to submit to physical abuse without defending yourself or fighting back. Jesus taught his followers to turn the other cheek (Matthew 5:39), and he exemplified this at the highest level just before his crucifixion (Matthew 27:27–31; Luke 22:64; John 18:22; 19:3).

34 To crush underfoot
    all prisoners in the land,
35 to deny a man his rights
    before the Most High,
36 to deprive a man of justice—
    would not the Lord see such things?*t*

37 Who can speak and have it happen
    if the Lord has not decreed it?*u*
38 Is it not from the mouth of the Most High
    that both calamities and good things come?*v*
39 Why should any living man complain
    when punished for his sins?*w*

40 Let us examine our ways and test them,
    and let us return to the LORD.*x*
41 Let us lift up our hearts and our hands
    to God in heaven, and say:
42 "We have sinned and rebelled*y*
    and you have not forgiven.

43 "You have covered yourself with anger and pursued us;
    you have slain without pity.
44 You have covered yourself with a cloud
    so that no prayer*z* can get through.
45 You have made us scum*a* and refuse
    among the nations.

46 "All our enemies have opened their mouths
    wide against us.*b*
47 We have suffered terror and pitfalls,
    ruin and destruction.*c*"
48 Streams of tears flow from my eyes
    because my people are destroyed.

49 My eyes will flow unceasingly,
    without relief,*d*
50 until the LORD looks down
    from heaven and sees.*e*
51 What I see brings grief to my soul
    because of all the women of my city.

52 Those who were my enemies without cause
    hunted me like a bird.*f*
53 They tried to end my life in a pit*g*
    and threw stones at me;
54 the waters closed over my head,*h*
    and I thought I was about to be cut off.

55 I called on your name, O LORD,
    from the depths of the pit.*i*
56 You heard my plea: "Do not close your ears
    to my cry for relief."
57 You came near when I called you,
    and you said, "Do not fear."*j*

3:36
*t*Hab 1:13

3:37
*u*Ps 33:9-11

3:38
*v*Job 2:10

3:39
*w*Mic 7:9

3:40
*x*Ps 119:59

3:42
*y*Da 9:5

3:44
*z*ver 8

3:45
*a*1Co 4:13

3:46
*b*La 2:16

3:47
*c*Isa 24:17-18

3:49
*d*Jer 14:17

3:50
*e*Isa 63:15

3:52
*f*Ps 35:7

3:53
*g*Jer 37:16

3:54
*h*Ps 69:2

3:55
*i*Jnh 2:2

3:57
*j*Isa 41:10

3:39–42 Parents discipline children to produce right behavior. God disciplined Judah to produce right living and genuine worship. We must not complain about corrective or instructive discipline in our lives but learn from it, trusting God and being willing to change. We must allow God's correction to bring about the kind of behavior in our lives that pleases him.

3:52–57 At one point in his ministry, Jeremiah was thrown into an empty cistern, and he was left to die in the mire at the bottom (Jeremiah 38:6–13). But God rescued him. Jeremiah used this experience as a picture of the nation sinking into sin. If they turned to God, he would rescue them.

58 O Lord, you took up my case;
    you redeemed my life.
59 You have seen, O Lord, the wrong done to me.
    Uphold my cause!

3:60
k Jer 11:20

60 You have seen the depth of their vengeance,
    all their plots against me.*k*

61 O Lord, you have heard their insults,
    all their plots against me—
62 what my enemies whisper and mutter
    against me all day long.
63 Look at them! Sitting or standing,
    they mock me in their songs.

3:64
l Ps 28:4

64 Pay them back what they deserve, O Lord,
    for what their hands have done.*l*

3:65
m Isa 6:10

65 Put a veil over their hearts,*m*
    and may your curse be on them!
66 Pursue them in anger and destroy them
    from under the heavens of the Lord.

4. God's anger is satisfied

4 *a* How the gold has lost its luster,
    the fine gold become dull!
The sacred gems are scattered
    at the head of every street.

2 How the precious sons of Zion,
    once worth their weight in gold,
are now considered as pots of clay,
    the work of a potter's hands!

3 Even jackals offer their breasts
    to nurse their young,
but my people have become heartless
    like ostriches in the desert.

4:4
n La 2:11, 12

4 Because of thirst the infant's tongue
    sticks to the roof of its mouth;
the children beg for bread,
    but no one gives it to them.*n*

5 Those who once ate delicacies
    are destitute in the streets.
Those nurtured in purple
    now lie on ash heaps.

4:6
o Ge 19:25

6 The punishment of my people
    is greater than that of Sodom,*o*

a This chapter is an acrostic poem, the verses of which begin with the successive letters of the Hebrew alphabet.

4:1ff This chapter contrasts the situation before the siege of Jerusalem with the situation after the siege. The sights and sounds of prosperity were gone because of the people's sin. This chapter warns us not to assume that when life is going well, it will always stay that way. We must be careful not to glory in our prosperity or we will fall into spiritual poverty.

4:1–10 When a city was under siege, the city wall—built for protection—sealed the people inside. They could not get out to the fields to get food and water because the enemy was camped around the city. As food in the city ran out, the people watched their enemies harvest and eat the food in the fields. The siege was a test of wills to see which army could outlast the other. Jerusalem was under siege for two years. Life became so harsh

that people even ate their own children, and dead bodies were left to rot in the streets. All hope was gone.

4:6 The city of Sodom, destroyed by burning sulfur from heaven because of its wickedness (Genesis 18:20—19:29), became a symbol of God's ultimate judgment. Yet the guilt of Jerusalem was even greater than that of Sodom! Jeremiah wasn't comparing sins but acknowledging that Sodom had few of the advantages and blessings that the people of Jerusalem had enjoyed from God. Jerusalem's greater guilt was in turning away in spite of the city's countless God-given benefits.

which was overthrown in a moment
    without a hand turned to help her.

7 Their princes were brighter than snow
      and whiter than milk,
  their bodies more ruddy than rubies,
      their appearance like sapphires.ᵃ

8 But now they are blacker than soot;
      they are not recognized in the streets.
  Their skin has shriveled on their bones;ᵖ
      it has become as dry as a stick.

	4:8
	ᵖPs 102:3-5

9 Those killed by the sword are better off
      than those who die of famine;
  racked with hunger, they waste away
      for lack of food from the field.

10 With their own hands compassionate women
       have cooked their own children,q
   who became their food
       when my people were destroyed.

	4:10
	qDt 28:53-57;
	La 2:20

11 The Lᴏʀᴅ has given full vent to his wrath;
       he has poured out his fierce anger.
   He kindled a fire in Zion
       that consumed her foundations.r

	4:11
	rDt 32:22; Jer 7:20

12 The kings of the earth did not believe,
       nor did any of the world's people,
   that enemies and foes could enter
       the gates of Jerusalem.

13 But it happened because of the sins of her prophets
       and the iniquities of her priests,s
   who shed within her
       the blood of the righteous.

	4:13
	sJer 6:13;
	Eze 22:28

14 Now they grope through the streets
       like men who are blind.
   They are so defiled with bloodt
       that no one dares to touch their garments.

	4:14
	tJer 2:34; 19:4

15 "Go away! You are unclean!" men cry to them.
       "Away! Away! Don't touch us!"
   When they flee and wander about,
       people among the nations say,
       "They can stay here no longer."u

	4:15
	uLev 13:46

16 The Lᴏʀᴅ himself has scattered them;
       he no longer watches over them.
   The priests are shown no honor,
       the elders no favor.

17 Moreover, our eyes failed,
       looking in vain for help;

ᵃ 7 Or *lapis lazuli*

4:13-15 To be defiled or unclean meant to be unfit to enter the temple or to worship before God. The priests and prophets should have been the most careful to maintain ceremonial purity so that they could continue to perform their duties before God. But many priests and prophets did evil and were defiled. As the nation's leaders, their example led the people into sin and caused the ultimate downfall of the nation and its capital city, Jerusalem.

4:17 Judah had asked Egypt to help them fight the Babylonian army. Egypt gave Judah false hope—they started to help, but then retreated (Jeremiah 37:5-7). Jeremiah warned Judah not to ally itself with Egypt. He told the leaders to rely on God, but they refused to listen.

4:17
v Jer 37:7

from our towers we watched
for a nation v that could not save us.

4:18
w Eze 7:2-12

18 Men stalked us at every step,
so we could not walk in our streets.
Our end was near, our days were numbered,
for our end had come. w

19 Our pursuers were swifter
than eagles in the sky;
they chased us over the mountains
and lay in wait for us in the desert.

4:20
x 2Sa 19:21

20 The LORD's anointed, x our very life breath,
was caught in their traps.
We thought that under his shadow
we would live among the nations.

21 Rejoice and be glad, O Daughter of Edom,
you who live in the land of Uz.
But to you also the cup will be passed;
you will be drunk and stripped naked.

4:22
y Isa 40:2

22 O Daughter of Zion, your punishment will end; y
he will not prolong your exile.
But, O Daughter of Edom, he will punish your sin
and expose your wickedness.

5. Jeremiah pleads for restoration

5:1
z Ps 44:13-16

5 Remember, O LORD, what has happened to us;
look, and see our disgrace. z
2 Our inheritance has been turned over to aliens,
our homes to foreigners.

5:3
a Jer 15:8

3 We have become orphans and fatherless,
our mothers like widows. a
4 We must buy the water we drink;
our wood can be had only at a price.

5:5
b Ne 9:37

5 Those who pursue us are at our heels;
we are weary b and find no rest.
6 We submitted to Egypt and Assyria
to get enough bread.

5:7
c Jer 14:20

7 Our fathers sinned and are no more,
and we bear their punishment. c

5:8
d Zec 11:6

8 Slaves rule over us,
and there is none to free us from their hands. d
9 We get our bread at the risk of our lives
because of the sword in the desert.
10 Our skin is hot as an oven,
feverish from hunger.

5:11
e Zec 14:2

11 Women have been ravished e in Zion,
and virgins in the towns of Judah.

4:20 King Zedekiah, although called "the LORD's anointed," had little spiritual depth and leadership power. Instead of putting his faith in God and listening to God's true prophet, Jeremiah, he listened to the false prophets. To make matters worse, the people chose to follow and trust in their king (2 Chronicles 36:11–23). They chose the path of false confidence and complacency, wanting to feel secure rather than to follow the directives God was giving his people through Jeremiah. But the object of their confidence—King Zedekiah—was captured.

4:21, 22 Edom was Judah's archenemy, even though they had a common ancestor, Isaac (see Genesis 25:19–26; 36:1). Edom had actively aided Babylon in the siege of Jerusalem. As a reward, Nebuchadnezzar gave the outlying lands of Judah to Edom. Jeremiah said that the nation of Edom would be judged for treachery against Judah—in essence, against its own relatives. (See also Jeremiah 49:7–22; Ezekiel 25:12–14; Amos 9:12; Obadiah 1–21.)

5:1ff After expressing the full extent of his or her grief, the true believer should turn to God in prayer. Here Jeremiah prayed for mercy for his people. At the end of his prayer he wondered if God was "angry with us beyond measure." But God would not stay angry with them forever—as it says in Micah 7:18, "You do not stay angry forever but delight in showing unfailing love."

12 Princes have been hung up by their hands;
    elders are shown no respect.
13 Young men toil at the millstones;
    boys stagger under loads of wood.
14 The elders are gone from the city gate;
    the young men have stopped their music.*f*   **5:14**
                                                        f Jer 7:34
15 Joy is gone from our hearts;
    our dancing has turned to mourning.
16 The crown*g* has fallen from our head.   **5:16**
    Woe to us, for we have sinned!   *g* Ps 89:39
17 Because of this our hearts*h* are faint,   **5:17**
    because of these things our eyes grow dim   *h* Isa 1:5
18 for Mount Zion, which lies desolate,
    with jackals prowling over it.

19 You, O Lord, reign forever;   **5:19**
    your throne endures*i* from generation to generation.   *i* Ps 45:6
20 Why do you always forget us?*j*   **5:20**
    Why do you forsake us so long?   *j* Ps 13:1
21 Restore us to yourself, O Lord, that we may return;
    renew our days as of old
22 unless you have utterly rejected us
    and are angry with us beyond measure.

5:14 During peace and prosperity, the leaders and elders of the city would sit at the city gate and talk over politics, theology, and philosophy, and conduct business. As Jeremiah prayed, he saw fewer and fewer evidences of either the healthy interaction or the lighthearted dancing of their former lives under God's blessing. They had lost even the everyday events they had assumed would always be there. A lack of continual gratefulness to God often indicates that we are taking the goodness of life for granted.

5:22 A high calling flouted by low living results in deep suffering. Lamentations gives us a portrait of the bitter suffering the

people of Jerusalem experienced when sin caught up with them and God turned his back on them. Every material goal they had lived for collapsed. But although God turned away from them because of their sin, he did not abandon them—that was their great hope. Despite their sinful past, God would restore them if they returned to him. Hope is found only in the Lord. Thus our grief should turn us toward him, not away from him.

EZEKIEL

| Jeremiah becomes a prophet to Judah 627 B.C. | Daniel taken captive to Babylon 605 | Ezekiel taken captive to Babylon 597 | Ezekiel becomes a prophet to exiles 593 | Judah falls; Jerusalem destroyed 586 | Ezekiel's ministry ends 571 | | Babylon overthrown by Cyrus 539 | First exiles return to Judah 538 |

A COMPUTER can be programmed to respond at your command. And by conditioning a dog with rewards and punishments, you can teach it to obey. But as every parent knows, children are not so easily taught. People have wills and must choose to submit, to follow the instructions of those who have authority over them. Surely discipline is part of the process—boys and girls should know that they will reap the consequences of disobedience.

God's children must learn to obey their heavenly Father. Created in his image, they have a choice, and God allows them to choose.

Ezekiel was a man who chose to obey God. Although he was a priest (1:3), he served as a Jewish "street preacher" in Babylon for 22 years, telling everyone about God's judgment and salvation, and calling them to repent and obey. And Ezekiel *lived* what he preached. During his ministry God told him to illustrate his messages with dramatic object lessons. Some of these acts included (1) lying on his side for 390 days during which he could eat only one eight-ounce meal a day cooked over manure, (2) shaving his head and beard, and (3) showing no sorrow when his wife died. He obeyed and faithfully proclaimed God's word.

God may not ask you to do anything quite so dramatic or difficult; but if he did, would you do it?

The book of Ezekiel chronicles the prophet's life and ministry. Beginning with his call as a prophet and commissioning as a "watchman for the house of Israel" (chapters 1—3), Ezekiel immediately began to preach and demonstrate God's truth, as he predicted the approaching siege and destruction of Jerusalem (chapters 4—24). This devastation would be God's judgment for the people's idolatry. Ezekiel challenged them to turn from their wicked ways. In the next section, he spoke to the surrounding nations, prophesying that God would judge them for their sins as well (chapters 25—32). The book concludes with a message of hope, as Ezekiel proclaimed the faithfulness of God and foretold the future blessings for God's people (chapters 33—48).

As you read this exciting record, observe how Ezekiel fearlessly preached the word of God to the exiled Jews in the streets of Babylon, and hear the timeless truth of God's love and power. Think about each person's responsibility to trust God and about the inevitability of God's judgment against idolatry, rebellion, and indifference. Then commit yourself to obey God, whatever, wherever, and whenever he asks.

VITAL STATISTICS

PURPOSE:
To announce God's judgment on Israel and other nations and to foretell the eventual salvation of God's people

AUTHOR:
Ezekiel son of Buzi, a Zadokite priest

ORIGINAL AUDIENCE:
The Jews in captivity in Babylonia

DATE WRITTEN:
Approximately 571 B.C.

SETTING:
Ezekiel was a younger contemporary of Jeremiah. While Jeremiah ministered to the people still in Judah, Ezekiel prophesied to those already exiled in Babylonia after the defeat of Jehoiachin. He was taken there in 597 B.C.

KEY VERSES:
"For I will take you out of the nations; I will gather you from all the countries and bring you back into your own land. I will sprinkle clean water on you, and you will be clean; I will cleanse you from all your impurities and from all your idols. I will give you a new heart and put a new spirit in you; I will remove from you your heart of stone and give you a heart of flesh" (36:24—26).

KEY PEOPLE:
Ezekiel, Israel's leaders, Ezekiel's wife, Nebuchadnezzar, "the prince"

KEY PLACES:
Jerusalem, Babylon, and Egypt

THE BLUEPRINT

A. MESSAGES OF DOOM
  (1:1—24:27)
  1. Ezekiel's call and commission
  2. Visions of sin and judgment
  3. Punishment is certain

While Jeremiah was prophesying in Jerusalem that the city would soon fall to the Babylonians, Ezekiel was giving the same message to the captives who were already in Babylon. Like those in Jerusalem, the captives stubbornly believed that Jerusalem would not fall and that they would soon return to their land. Ezekiel warned them that punishment was certain because of their sins and that God was purifying his people. God will always punish sin, whether we believe it or not.

B. MESSAGES AGAINST
  FOREIGN NATIONS
  (25:1—32:32)

Ezekiel condemns the sinful actions of seven nations. The people in these nations were saying that God was obviously too weak to defend his people and the city of Jerusalem. But God was allowing his people to be defeated in order to punish them for their sins. These pagan nations, however, would face a similar fate, and then they would know that God is all-powerful. Those who dare to mock God today will also face a terrible fate.

C. MESSAGES OF HOPE
  (33:1—48:35)
  1. Restoring the people of God
  2. Restoring the worship of God

After the fall of Jerusalem, Ezekiel delivered messages of future restoration and hope for the people. God is holy, but Jerusalem and the temple had become defiled. The nation had to be cleansed through 70 years of captivity. Ezekiel gives a vivid picture of the unchangeable holiness of God. We, too, must gain a vision of the glory of God, a fresh sense of his greatness, as we face the struggles of daily life.

MEGATHEMES

THEME	EXPLANATION	IMPORTANCE
God's Holiness	Ezekiel saw a vision that revealed God's absolute moral perfection. God was spiritually and morally superior to members of Israel's corrupt and compromising society. Ezekiel wrote to let the people know that God in his holiness was also present in Babylon, not just in Jerusalem.	Because God is morally perfect, he can help us live above our tendency to compromise with this world. When we focus on his greatness, he gives us the power to overcome sin and to reflect his holiness.
Sin	Israel had sinned, and God's punishment came. The fall of Jerusalem and the Babylonian exile were used by God to correct the rebels and draw them back from their sinful way of life. Ezekiel warned them that not only was the nation responsible for sin but each individual was also accountable to God.	We cannot excuse ourselves from our responsibilities before God. We are accountable to God for our choices. Rather than neglect him, we must recognize sin for what it is—rebellion against God—and choose to follow him instead.
Restoration	Ezekiel consoles the people by telling them that the day will come when God will restore those who turn from sin. God will be their King and Shepherd. He will give his people a new heart to worship him, and he will establish a new government and a new temple.	The certainty of future restoration encourages believers in times of trial. But we must be faithful to God because we love him, not merely for what he can do for us. Is our faith in *him* or merely in our future benefits?
Leaders	Ezekiel condemned the shepherds (unfaithful priests and leaders), who led the people astray. By contrast, he served as a caring shepherd and a faithful watchman to warn the people about their sin. One day God's perfect Shepherd, the Messiah, will lead his people.	Jesus is our perfect leader. If we truly want him to lead us, our devotion must be more than talk. If we are given the responsibility of leading others, we must take care of them even if it means sacrificing personal pleasure, happiness, time, or money. We are responsible for those we lead.
Worship	An angel gave Ezekiel a vision of the temple in great detail. God's holy presence had departed from Israel and the temple because of sin. The building of a future temple portrays the return of God's glory and presence. God will cleanse his people and restore true worship.	All of God's promises will be fulfilled under the rule of the Messiah. The faithful followers will be restored to perfect fellowship with God and with one another. To be prepared for this time, we must focus on God. We do this through regular worship. Through worship we learn about God's holiness and the changes we must make in how we live.

A. MESSAGES OF DOOM (1:1—24:27)

Ezekiel prophesied to the exiles in Babylon. He had to dispel the false hope that Israel's captivity would be short, explain the reasons for the severe judgments on their nation, and bring a message of future hope. Although the people did not respond positively, they heard the messages and knew the truth. God's people were not left without explanation and direction, and neither are we.

1. Ezekiel's call and commission
The Living Creatures and the Glory of the LORD

1:1
a Mt 3:16; Ac 7:56

1:3
b 2Ki 3:15

1:5
c Rev 4:6

1:7
d Rev 1:15

1:8
e Eze 10:8

1 In the*a* thirtieth year, in the fourth month on the fifth day, while I was among the exiles by the Kebar River, the heavens were opened*a* and I saw visions of God.

2 On the fifth of the month—it was the fifth year of the exile of King Jehoiachin— 3 the word of the LORD came to Ezekiel the priest, the son of Buzi,*b* by the Kebar River in the land of the Babylonians.*c* There the hand of the LORD was upon him.*b*

4 I looked, and I saw a windstorm coming out of the north—an immense cloud with flashing lightning and surrounded by brilliant light. The center of the fire looked like glowing metal, 5 and in the fire was what looked like four living creatures.*c* In appearance their form was that of a man, 6 but each of them had four faces and four wings. 7 Their legs were straight; their feet were like those of a calf and gleamed like burnished bronze.*d* 8 Under their wings on their four sides they had the hands of a man.*e* All four of them had faces and

a 1 Or ⌊my⌋   b 3 Or Ezekiel son of Buzi the priest   c 3 Or Chaldeans

---

EZEKIEL
served as a
prophet to
the exiles in
Babylon from
593–571 B.C.

Climate of the times	Ezekiel and his people are taken to Babylon as captives. The Jews become foreigners in a strange land ruled by an authoritarian government.
Main message.	Because of the people's sins, God allowed the nation of Judah to be destroyed. But there was still hope—God promised to restore the land to those who remained faithful to him.
Importance of message. . . .	God never forgets those who faithfully seek to obey him. They have a glorious future ahead.
Contemporary prophets . . .	Daniel (605–536 B.C.), Habakkuk (612–589 B.C.), Jeremiah (627–586 B.C.).

1:1 Ezekiel, born and raised in the land of Judah, was preparing to become a priest in God's temple when the Babylonians attacked in 597 B.C. and carried him away along with 10,000 other captives (2 Kings 24:10–14). The nation was on the brink of complete destruction. Four to five years later, when Ezekiel was 30 (the normal age for becoming a priest), God called him to be a prophet. During the first six years when Ezekiel ministered in the land of the Babylonians (1:3), Jeremiah was preaching to the Jews still in Judah, and Daniel was serving in Nebuchadnezzar's court. The Kebar River connected to the Euphrates in Babylonia and was the location of a Jewish settlement of exiles.

1:1 Why did the Jewish exiles in Babylonia need a prophet? God wanted Ezekiel to: (1) help the exiles understand why they had been taken captive, (2) dispel the false hope that the captivity was going to be short, (3) bring a new message of hope, and (4) call the people to a new awareness of their dependence upon God.

1:1ff Ezekiel's latest dated message from God (29:17) was given in 571 B.C. He was taken captive during the second Babylonian invasion of Judah in 597 B.C. The Babylonians invaded Judah a third and final time in 586 B.C., completely destroying Jerusalem, burning the temple, and deporting the rest of the people (see 2 Kings 25). Ezekiel dates all his messages from the year he was taken captive (597). His first prophecy to the exiles occurred four to five years after he arrived in Babylonia (593 B.C.).

1:1 God communicated to Ezekiel in visions. A vision is a miraculous revelation of God's truth. These visions seem strange to us because they are *apocalyptic*. This means that Ezekiel saw symbolic pictures that vividly conveyed an idea. Daniel and John were other Bible writers who used apocalyptic imagery. The people in exile had lost their perspective of God's purpose and presence, and Ezekiel came to them with a vision from God to show God's

awesome glory and holiness and to warn the exiles of sin's consequences before it was too late.

1:3 The name *Ezekiel* means "God is strong" or "God strengthens." In a very real sense, this sums up the basic message of the book—that in spite of the captivity, God's sovereign strength prevails, and he will judge his enemies and restore his true people.

1:4ff In this first vision, God called Ezekiel to be a prophet (see 2:5). Nothing in Ezekiel's previous experience had prepared him for such a display of God's glorious presence and power. The immense cloud flashed with lightning and was surrounded by a brilliant light. From the fire in the cloud came four living creatures. They showed Ezekiel that Jerusalem's coming destruction was God's punishment of Judah for its sins. (These living creatures are also seen in Revelation 4:6, 7.)

When Ezekiel received this vision, he was far away from the temple in Jerusalem, the physical symbol of God's presence. Through this vision, he learned that God is present everywhere and that God's activities in heaven are shaping the events on earth.

1:5 Each of the four living creatures had four faces, symbolizing God's perfect nature. Some believe that the lion represented strength; the ox, diligent service; the man, intelligence; and the eagle, divinity. Others see these as the most majestic of God's creatures and say that they therefore represented God's whole creation. The early church fathers saw a connection between these beings and the four Gospels: the lion with Matthew, presenting Christ as the Lion of Judah; the ox with Mark, portraying Christ as the Servant; the human with Luke, portraying Christ as the perfect human; the eagle with John, portraying Christ as the Son of God, exalted and divine. The vision of John in Revelation 4 parallels Ezekiel's vision.

wings, 9 and their wings touched one another. Each one went straight ahead; they did not turn as they moved.

10 Their faces looked like this: Each of the four had the face of a man, and on the right side each had the face of a lion, and on the left the face of an ox; each also had the face of an eagle. *f* 11 Such were their faces. Their wings *g* were spread out upward; each had two wings, one touching the wing of another creature on either side, and two wings covering its body. 12 Each one went straight ahead. Wherever the spirit would go, they would go, without turning as they went. 13 The appearance of the living creatures was like burning coals of fire or like torches. Fire moved back and forth among the creatures; it was bright, and lightning *h* flashed out of it. 14 The creatures sped back and forth like flashes of lightning.

15 As I looked at the living creatures, I saw a wheel on the ground beside each creature with its four faces. 16 This was the appearance and structure of the wheels: They sparkled like chrysolite, *i* and all four looked alike. Each appeared to be made like a wheel intersecting a wheel. 17 As they moved, they would go in any one of the four directions the creatures faced; the wheels did not turn about *a* as the creatures went. 18 Their rims were high and awesome, and all four rims were full of eyes *j* all around.

19 When the living creatures moved, the wheels beside them moved; and when the living creatures rose from the ground, the wheels also rose. 20 Wherever the spirit would go, they would go, *k* and the wheels would rise along with them, because the spirit of the living creatures was in the wheels. 21 When the creatures moved, they also moved; when the creatures stood still, they also stood still; and when the creatures rose from the ground, the wheels rose along with them, because the spirit of the living creatures was in the wheels. *l*

22 Spread out above the heads of the living creatures was what looked like an expanse, *m* sparkling like ice, and awesome. 23 Under the expanse their wings were stretched out one toward the other, and each had two wings covering its body. 24 When the creatures moved, I heard the sound of their wings, like the roar of rushing waters, like the voice *n* of the Almighty, *b* like the tumult of an army. When they stood still, they lowered their wings.

25 Then there came a voice from above the expanse over their heads as they stood with lowered wings. 26 Above the expanse over their heads was what looked like a throne of sapphire, *c o* and high above on the throne was a figure like that of a man. 27 I saw that from what appeared to be his waist up he looked like glowing metal, as if full of fire, and that from there down he looked like fire; and brilliant light surrounded him. *p* 28 Like the appearance of a rainbow *q* in the clouds on a rainy day, so was the radiance around him. *r*

This was the appearance of the likeness of the glory of the Lord. When I saw it, I fell facedown, and I heard the voice of one speaking.

a 17 Or *aside*   b 24 Hebrew *Shaddai*   c 26 Or *lapis lazuli*

1:10 *f* Rev 4:7

1:11 *g* Isa 6:2

1:13 *h* Rev 4:5

1:16 *i* Eze 10:9-11

1:18 *j* Eze 10:12; Rev 4:6

1:20 *k* ver 12

1:21 *l* Eze 10:17

1:22 *m* Eze 10:1

1:24 *n* Eze 10:5; 43:2; Rev 1:15

1:26 *o* Ex 24:10

1:27 *p* Eze 8:2

1:28 *q* Rev 10:1 *r* Rev 4:2

1:16–18 The "wheel intersecting a wheel" was probably two wheels at right angles to each other, one on a north-south axis and the other on an east-west axis. Able to move anywhere, these wheels show that God is present everywhere and is able to see all things (1:18). God is not restricted to Jerusalem, but rules all of life and history. Though the exiles had experienced great change, God was still in control.

1:26 This "figure like that of a man" revealed God's holiness and prepared Ezekiel for what God was about to tell him. The figure represented God himself on the throne. In a similar way, Christ revealed God in human form and prepared us for his message of salvation. Christ came into history in a real, human body.

1:27, 28 The glory of the Lord appeared like fire and brilliant light to Ezekiel. Ezekiel fell facedown, overwhelmed by the contrast between God's holiness and his own sinfulness and insignificance. Eventually every person will fall before God, either out of reverence and awe for his mercy or out of fear of his judgment. Based on the way you are living today, how will you respond to God's holiness?

1:27, 28 The four living creatures and the four wheels are powerful pictures of judgment, yet the rainbow over the throne symbolizes God's never-ending faithfulness to his people. Just as God sent a rainbow to Noah to symbolize his promise never again to destroy the earth by a flood (Genesis 9:8–17), so this rainbow symbolizes God's promise to preserve those who remain faithful to him. The purpose of God's judgment is to correct us and, ultimately, to allow perfect peace and righteousness to reign on the earth forever.

EXILE IN BABYLON Ezekiel worked for God right where he was—among the exiles in various colonies near the Kebar River in Babylonia. Jerusalem and its temple lay over 500 miles away, but Ezekiel helped the people understand that, although they were far from home, they did not need to be far from God.

Ezekiel's Call

2:1
sDa 10:11

2:2
tEze 3:24

2:3
uJer 3:25;
Eze 20:8-24

2:4
vEze 3:7

2:5
wEze 3:11
xEze 3:27
yEze 33:33

2:6
zMic 7:4

2:7
aJer 1:7

2:8
bRev 10:9

2:9
cEze 8:3

2 He said to me, "Son of man, stand *s* up on your feet and I will speak to you." ²As he spoke, the Spirit came into me and raised me *t* to my feet, and I heard him speaking to me.

³He said: "Son of man, I am sending you to the Israelites, to a rebellious nation that has rebelled against me; they and their fathers have been in revolt against me to this very day. *u* ⁴The people to whom I am sending you are obstinate and stubborn. *v* Say to them, 'This is what the Sovereign LORD says.' ⁵And whether they listen or fail to listen *w*—for they are a rebellious house *x*—they will know that a prophet has been among them. *y* ⁶And you, son of man, do not be afraid of them or their words. Do not be afraid, though briers and thorns *z* are all around you and you live among scorpions. Do not be afraid of what they say or terrified by them, though they are a rebellious house. ⁷You must speak my words to them, whether they listen or fail to listen, for they are rebellious. *a* ⁸But you, son of man, listen to what I say to you. Do not rebel like that rebellious house; open your mouth and eat *b* what I give you."

⁹Then I looked, and I saw a hand *c* stretched out to me. In it was a scroll, ¹⁰which he unrolled before me. On both sides of it were written words of lament and mourning and woe.

3:3
dJer 15:16
ePs 19:10;
Rev 10:9-10

3 And he said to me, "Son of man, eat what is before you, eat this scroll; then go and speak to the house of Israel." ²So I opened my mouth, and he gave me the scroll to eat.

³Then he said to me, "Son of man, eat this scroll I am giving you and fill your stomach with it." So I ate *d* it, and it tasted as sweet as honey *e* in my mouth.

⁴He then said to me: "Son of man, go now to the house of Israel and speak my words to them. ⁵You are not being sent to a people of obscure speech and difficult language, but to the house of Israel— ⁶not to many peoples of obscure speech and difficult language, whose words you cannot understand. Surely if I had sent you to them, they would have listened to you. ⁷But the house of Israel is not willing to listen to you because they are not willing to listen to me, for the whole house of Israel is hardened and obstinate. ⁸But I will make you as unyielding and hardened as they are. ⁹I will make your forehead like the hardest stone, harder than flint. Do not be afraid of them or terrified by them, though they are a rebellious house."

2:1 The immortal God addressed Ezekiel by calling him "Son of man," emphasizing the distance between them. It is amazing that God chooses to work his divine will on earth through finite, imperfect beings. We are made from the dust of the ground, yet God chooses to place within us his life and breath and to ask us to serve him.

2:2 We can only imagine what it was like for Ezekiel to experience this vision. Certainly there was much he did not understand, but Ezekiel knew that each part had significance because it came from God. When God saw Ezekiel's open and obedient attitude, he filled Ezekiel with his Spirit and gave him power for the job ahead. God doesn't expect us to understand everything about him, but to be willing and obedient servants, faithful to what we know is true and right.

2:3–5 The business world defines success in terms of giving customers what they want. Ezekiel, however, was called to give God's message to the people, whether they would listen or not. The measure of Ezekiel's success would not be how well the people responded, but how well he obeyed God and thus fulfilled God's purpose for him. Isaiah and Jeremiah also prophesied with little positive response (see Isaiah 6:9–12; Jeremiah 1:17–19). God's truth does not depend on how people respond. God will not judge us for how well others respond to our witness to our faith, but for how faithful we have been. God always gives us the strength to accomplish what he asks us to do.

2:4, 5 God called the people "obstinate and stubborn" because they refused to admit their sin. Rebelliousness was the nation's primary characteristic at this time. Even when God pointed out their wrongdoing, the people ignored the truth. Is God pointing at some sin in your life? Don't be stubborn—confess your sin and begin to live for God. By obeying him now you will be ready for God's final review of your life (Matthew 25:31–46).

2:6–8 God gave Ezekiel the difficult responsibility of presenting his message to ungrateful and abusive people. Sometimes we must be an example to or share our faith with unkind people. The Lord told Ezekiel to be afraid and rebel, but to speak his words, whether or not the people would listen. He also wants us to tell the Good News, whether it's convenient or not (2 Timothy 4:2).

2:6–10 Three times God told Ezekiel not to be afraid. When God's Spirit is within us, we can lay aside our fears of rejection or ridicule. God's strength is powerful enough to help us live for him even under the heaviest criticism.

2:9, 10 Ancient books were usually scrolls, one page (up to 30 feet long) rolled up simultaneously from both ends. Normally, scrolls had writing on only one side. But in this case, the warnings overflowed to the scroll's other side, showing the full measure of judgment about to descend on Judah.

3:1–3 In his vision, Ezekiel ate God's message and found this spiritual food not only good for him, but also sweet as honey (see Revelation 10:8–10 for a similar use of this image). If you "digest" God's Word, you will find that not only does it make you stronger in your faith, but its wisdom also sweetens your life. You need to feed yourself spiritually just as you do physically. This means doing more than simply giving God's message a casual glance. You must make digesting God's Word a regular part of your life.

3:8, 9 Belief in God is not a crutch for those too weak to stand on their own. God makes his followers strong enough to stand against anything or anyone, including those who hate what is right. Just as God gave Ezekiel tough faith ("harder than flint"), he wants to give you the stability, perseverance, and insight you need to live up to the great task he has given you. Give yourself over to God's conditioning and let him get your life in shape.

10And he said to me, "Son of man, listen carefully and take to heart all the words I speak to you. 11Go now to your countrymen in exile and speak to them. Say to them, 'This is what the Sovereign LORD says,' whether they listen or fail to listen."

12Then the Spirit lifted me up,*f* and I heard behind me a loud rumbling sound—May the glory of the LORD be praised in his dwelling place!— 13the sound of the wings of the living creatures brushing against each other and the sound of the wheels beside them, a loud rumbling sound. 14The Spirit then lifted me up and took me away, and I went in bitterness and in the anger of my spirit, with the strong hand of the LORD upon me. 15I came to the exiles who lived at Tel Abib near the Kebar River. And there, where they were living, I sat among them for seven days—overwhelmed.

Warning to Israel

16At the end of seven days the word of the LORD came to me: 17"Son of man, I have made you a watchman*g* for the house of Israel; so hear the word I speak and give them warning from me. 18When I say to a wicked man, 'You will surely die,' and you do not warn him or speak out to dissuade him from his evil ways in order to save his life, that wicked man will die for*a* his sin, and I will hold you accountable for his blood. 19But if you do warn the wicked man and he does not turn from his wickedness or from his evil ways, he will die for his sin; but you will have saved yourself.*h*

20"Again, when a righteous man turns from his righteousness and does evil, and I put a stumbling block before him, he will die. Since you did not warn him, he will die for his sin. The righteous things he did will not be remembered, and I will hold you accountable for his blood.*i* 21But if you do warn the righteous man not to sin and he does not sin, he will surely live because he took warning, and you will have saved yourself."

22The hand of the LORD was upon me there, and he said to me, "Get up and go*j* out to the plain, and there I will speak to you." 23So I got up and went out to the plain. And the glory of the LORD was standing there, like the glory I had seen by the Kebar River,*k* and I fell facedown. 24Then the Spirit came into me and raised me*l* to my feet. He spoke to me and said: "Go, shut yourself inside your house. 25And you, son of man, they will tie with ropes; you will be

a 18 Or *in*; also in verses 19 and 20

Cross-references:
- 3:12 *f* Eze 8:3
- 3:17 *g* Isa 52:8
- 3:19 *h* Ac 20:26
- 3:20 *i* Eze 18:24
- 3:22 *j* Ac 9:6
- 3:23 *k* Eze 1:1
- 3:24 *l* Eze 2:2

3:10, 11 Ezekiel needed to take God's words to heart before preaching them to others. God's message must sink deep into your heart and show in your actions before you can effectively help others understand and apply the gospel.

3:14, 15 Ezekiel was bitter and angry, not at God, but at the sins and attitudes of the people. Ezekiel's extraordinary vision had ended, and he had to begin the tedious job of prophesying among his people, who cared little about God's messages. Before the exile, the people had heard Jeremiah, but they would not listen. Here Ezekiel had to give a similar message, and he expected to be rejected as well. But Ezekiel had the vision of the living creatures and the rumbling wheels on his side. He had nothing to fear because God was with him. Despite knowing the probable outcome, Ezekiel obeyed God.

As we grow, we will have times of great joy when we feel close to God, and times when sins, struggles, or everyday tasks overwhelm us. Like Ezekiel, we should obey God even when we don't feel like it. Don't let feelings hinder your obedience.

3:15 Ezekiel sat quietly among the people for seven days. This was the customary period of mourning for the dead (Genesis 50:10; 1 Samuel 31:13; Job 2:13). Ezekiel was mourning for those who were spiritually dead. Tel Abib was the location of the settlement of Jews who were exiled from Jerusalem.

3:17, 18 A watchman's job was to stand on the city wall and warn the people of approaching danger. Ezekiel's role was to be a spiritual watchman, warning the people of the judgment to come. Some think that the phrase "accountable for his blood" means that just as a watchman on the wall would pay with his life if he failed to warn the city of approaching enemies, Ezekiel would have been held accountable if he had refused to warn the people of coming judgment. Others believe this phrase simply means that God would hold Ezekiel responsible.

3:18, 19 God had already told Ezekiel that the people would not listen, so why should he bother to tell them God's message? God wanted the people to know they had been warned. Ezekiel's job was to obey God. We are responsible to tell others about God's judgment and his message of salvation, although we are not held responsible for how they respond. If we refuse to tell others what we know, however, God will judge us. Remember God's words to Ezekiel when you are tempted to remain silent among those who don't believe.

3:18–21 In these verses, God is not talking about loss of salvation but rather about physical death. If the people back in Judah continued in their sins, they and their land and cities would be destroyed by Nebuchadnezzar's armies. If, on the other hand, the people would turn to God, God would spare them. God would hold Ezekiel responsible for his fellow Jews if he failed to warn them of the consequences of their sins. All people are individually responsible to God, but believers have a special responsibility to warn unbelievers of the consequences of rejecting God. If we fail to do this, God will hold us responsible for what happens to them. This should motivate us to begin sharing our faith with others—by both word and deed—and to avoid becoming callous or unconcerned in our attitude.

3:23 Ezekiel recognized his helplessness before God and fell facedown in his presence. Sometimes our prosperity, popularity, or physical strength blind us to our spiritual helplessness. But nothing we do on our own can accomplish much for God. Only when God is in control of our wills can we accomplish great tasks for him. The first step to being God's person is to admit that you need his help; then you can begin to see what God can really do in your life.

3:24–27 Ezekiel was allowed to speak only when God had a message for the people. Thus the people knew that whatever Ezekiel said was God's message. They did not have to wonder whether Ezekiel was speaking by God's authority or his own.

3:25
m Eze 4:8

3:26
n Eze 24:27

3:27
o Eze 24:27; 33:22

bound so that you cannot go out among the people. m 26 I will make your tongue stick to the roof of your mouth so that you will be silent and unable to rebuke them, though they are a rebellious house. n 27 But when I speak to you, I will open your mouth and you shall say to them, 'This is what the Sovereign LORD says.' Whoever will listen let him listen, and whoever will refuse let him refuse; for they are a rebellious house. o

2. Visions of sin and judgment
Siege of Jerusalem Symbolized

4:3
p Eze 12:3-6

4 "Now, son of man, take a clay tablet, put it in front of you and draw the city of Jerusalem on it. 2 Then lay siege to it: Erect siege works against it, build a ramp up to it, set up camps against it and put battering rams around it. 3 Then take an iron pan, place it as an iron wall between you and the city and turn your face toward it. It will be under siege, and you shall besiege it. This will be a sign p to the house of Israel.

Although Ezekiel's visions and prophecies were clear and vivid, very little is known about the prophet's personal life. He was among the thousands of young men deported from Judah to Babylon when King Jehoiakim surrendered. Until those tragic days, Ezekiel was being trained for the priesthood. But during the exile in Babylon, God called Ezekiel to be his prophet during one of Israel's darkest times.

Ezekiel experienced the same kind of shocking encounter with God that Isaiah had reported 150 years earlier. Like Isaiah, Ezekiel was never the same after his personal encounter with God. Although God's messages through both these prophets had many points in common, the conditions in which they lived were very different. Isaiah warned of the coming storm; Ezekiel spoke in the midst of the storm of national defeat that devastated his people. He announced that even Jerusalem would not escape destruction. In addition, during this time Ezekiel had to endure the pain of his wife's death.

God's description of Ezekiel as a watchman on the walls of the city captures the personal nature of his ministry. A watchman's job was dangerous. If he failed at his post, he and the entire city might be destroyed. His own safety depended on the quality of his work. The importance of each person's accountability before God was a central part of Ezekiel's message. He taught the exiles that God expected personal obedience and worship from each of them.

As in Ezekiel's day, it is easy for us today to forget that God has a personal interest in each one of us. We may feel insignificant or out of control when we look at world events. But knowing that God is ultimately in control, that he cares, and that he is willing to be known by us can bring a new sense of purpose to our lives. How do you measure your worth? Are you valuable because of your achievements and potential, or because God, your Creator and Designer, declares you valuable?

Strengths and accomplishments:	• Was a priest by training, a prophet by God's call • Received vivid visions and delivered powerful messages • Served as God's messenger during Israel's captivity in Babylon • God shaped his character to fit his mission—a tough and courageous man to reach a hard and stubborn people (Ezekiel 3:8)
Lessons from his life:	• Even the repeated failures of his people will not prevent God's plan for the world from being fulfilled • Each person's response to God determines his or her eternal destiny • In seemingly hopeless situations God still has people through whom he can work
Vital statistics:	• Where: Babylon • Occupation: Prophet to the captives in Babylon • Relatives: Father: Buzi. Wife: Unknown. • Contemporaries: Jehoiachin, Jeremiah, Jehoiakim, Nebuchadnezzar
Key verses:	"And he said to me, 'Son of man, listen carefully and take to heart all the words I speak to you. Go now to your countrymen in exile and speak to them. Say to them, 'This is what the Sovereign LORD says,' whether they listen or fail to listen' " (Ezekiel 3:10, 11).

Ezekiel's story is told in the book of Ezekiel and 2 Kings 24:10–17.

4:1ff Ezekiel acted out the coming siege and fall of Jerusalem before it actually happened. God gave Ezekiel specific instructions about what to do and say and how to do and say it. Each detail had a specific meaning. Often we ignore or disregard the smaller details of God's Word, thinking God probably doesn't care. Like Ezekiel, we should want to obey God completely, even in the details.

4"Then lie on your left side and put the sin of the house of Israel upon yourself.ª You are to bear their sin for the number of days you lie on your side. 5I have assigned you the same number of days as the years of their sin. So for 390 days you will bear the sin of the house of Israel.

6"After you have finished this, lie down again, this time on your right side, and bear the sin of the house of Judah. I have assigned you 40 days, a day for each year. 7Turn your face toward the siege of Jerusalem and with bared arm prophesy against her. 8I will tie you up with ropes so that you cannot turn from one side to the other until you have finished the days of your siege. q

9"Take wheat and barley, beans and lentils, millet and spelt; put them in a storage jar and use them to make bread for yourself. You are to eat it during the 390 days you lie on your side. 10Weigh out twenty shekelsᵇ of food to eat each day and eat it at set times. 11Also measure out a sixth of a hinᶜ of water and drink it at set times. 12Eat the food as you would a barley cake; bake it in the sight of the people, using human excrement for fuel." 13The LORD said, "In this way the people of Israel will eat defiled food among the nations where I will drive them."ʳ

14Then I said, "Not so, Sovereign LORD! I have never defiled myself. From my youth until now I have never eaten anything found dead or torn by wild animals. No unclean meat has ever entered my mouth."

15"Very well," he said, "I will let you bake your bread over cow manure instead of human excrement."

16He then said to me: "Son of man, I will cut off the supply of food in Jerusalem. The people will eat rationed food in anxiety and drink rationed water in despair,ˢ 17for food and water will be scarce. They will be appalled at the sight of each other and will waste away because of ᵈ their sin.ᵗ

5 "Now, son of man, take a sharp sword and use it as a barber's razor to shaveᵘ your head and your beard. ᵛ Then take a set of scales and divide up the hair. 2When the days of your siege come to an end, burn a third of the hair with fire inside the city. Take a third and strike it with the sword all around the city. And scatter a third to the wind. For I will pursue them with drawn sword. 3But take a few strands of hair and tuck them away in the folds of your garment. 4Again, take a few of these and throw them into the fire and burn them up. A fire will spread from there to the whole house of Israel.

5"This is what the Sovereign LORD says: This is Jerusalem, which I have set in the center of the nations, with countries all around her. 6Yet in her wickedness she has rebelled against my laws and decrees more than the nations and countries around her. She has rejected my laws and has not followed my decrees. ʷ

7"Therefore this is what the Sovereign LORD says: You have been more unruly than the nations around you and have not followed my decrees or kept my laws. You have not evenᵉ conformed to the standards of the nations around you.ˣ

ª4 Or your side   ᵇ10 That is, about 8 ounces (about 0.2 kilogram)   ᶜ11 That is, about 2/3 quart (about 0.6 liter)
ᵈ17 Or away in   ᵉ7 Most Hebrew manuscripts; some Hebrew manuscripts and Syriac You have

---

4:8
qEze 3:25

4:13
rHos 9:3

4:16
sver 10-11;
Lev 26:26; Isa 3:1;
Eze 12:19
4:17
tLev 26:39;
Eze 24:23

5:1
uEze 44:20
vLev 21:5

5:6
wZec 7:11

5:7
xEze 16:47

4:4–17 Ezekiel's unusual actions symbolically portrayed the fate of Jerusalem. He lay on his left side for 390 days to show that Israel would be punished for 390 years; then he lay on his right side for 40 days to show that Judah would be punished for 40 years. Ezekiel was not allowed to move, symbolizing the fact that the people of Jerusalem would be imprisoned within the walls of the city. We know that Ezekiel did not have to lie on his side all day because these verses tell of other tasks God asked him to do during this time. The small amount of food he was allowed to eat represented the normal ration provided to those living in a city under siege by enemy armies. The food that was to be cooked over dried human excrement was a symbol of Judah's spiritual uncleanness.

Certainly many people saw these spectacles and, in the process, heard Ezekiel's occasional speeches (3:27). How many would be willing to so dramatically portray the sins of our nation? We need to pray for greater boldness in our witness.

4:12–14 Ezekiel asked God not to make him use human excrement for fuel because it violated the laws for purity (Leviticus 21; 22; Deuteronomy 23:12–14). As a priest, Ezekiel would have been careful to keep all these laws. To use human excrement for fuel would paint a dramatic picture of ruin. If nothing was left in the

city that could be burned, it would be impossible to continue to follow God's laws for sacrifices.

5:1–10 Shaving one's head and beard signified mourning, humiliation, and repentance. God told Ezekiel to shave his head and beard and then to divide the hair into three parts, symbolizing what was going to happen to the people in Jerusalem (see 5:12). Along with verbal prophecies, God asked Ezekiel to use dramatic visual images to command the people's attention and to burn an indelible impression on their minds. Just as God gave Ezekiel creative ways to communicate his message to the exiles, we can creatively communicate the Good News about God to a lost generation.

5:3, 4 The few strands of hair Ezekiel put in his garment symbolized the small remnant of faithful people whom God would preserve. But even some from this remnant would be judged and destroyed because their faith was not genuine. Where will you stand in the coming judgment? Matthew 7:22, 23 warns that many who believe they are safe are not. Make sure your commitment is vital and heartfelt.

5:7 The people's wickedness was so great that they couldn't even keep the laws of the pagan nations around them, not to mention God's laws.

5:9
y Da 9:12

5:10
z Lev 26:29
a Eze 12:14;
Zec 2:6

5:12
b Eze 12:14

5:14
c Ne 2:17

5:15
d Eze 25:17

5:16
e Dt 32:24

5:17
f Eze 38:22
g Eze 14:21

6:2
h Eze 36:1

6:3
i Lev 26:30

8"Therefore this is what the Sovereign Lord says: I myself am against you, Jerusalem, and I will inflict punishment on you in the sight of the nations. 9Because of all your detestable idols, I will do to you what I have never done before and will never do again. y 10Therefore in your midst fathers will eat their children, and children will eat their fathers. z I will inflict punishment on you and will scatter all your survivors to the winds. a 11Therefore as surely as I live, declares the Sovereign Lord, because you have defiled my sanctuary with all your vile images and detestable practices, I myself will withdraw my favor; I will not look on you with pity or spare you. 12A third of your people will die of the plague or perish by famine inside you; a third will fall by the sword outside your walls; and a third I will scatter to the winds and pursue with drawn sword. b

13"Then my anger will cease and my wrath against them will subside, and I will be avenged. And when I have spent my wrath upon them, they will know that I the Lord have spoken in my zeal.

14"I will make you a ruin and a reproach among the nations around you, in the sight of all who pass by. c 15You will be a reproach and a taunt, a warning and an object of horror to the nations around you when I inflict punishment on you in anger and in wrath and with stinging rebuke. I the Lord have spoken. d 16When I shoot at you with my deadly and destructive arrows of famine, I will shoot to destroy you. I will bring more and more famine upon you and cut off your supply of food. e 17I will send famine and wild beasts against you, and they will leave you childless. Plague and bloodshed f will sweep through you, and I will bring the sword against you. I the Lord have spoken. g"

A Prophecy Against the Mountains of Israel

6 The word of the Lord came to me: 2"Son of man, set your face against the mountains h of Israel; prophesy against them 3and say: 'O mountains of Israel, hear the word of the Sovereign Lord. This is what the Sovereign Lord says to the mountains and hills, to the ravines and valleys: I am about to bring a sword against you, and I will destroy your high places. i 4Your altars will be demolished and your incense altars will be smashed; and I will slay your

EZEKIEL'S ACTS OF OBEDIENCE		
2:1	. . . .	Stood and received God's message
3:24–27	. . . .	Shut himself inside his house
3:27	. . . .	Faithfully proclaimed God's message
4:1ff	. . . .	Drew city of Jerusalem on a clay tablet
4:4, 5	. . . .	Lay on his left side for 390 days
4:6	. . . .	Lay on his right side for 40 days
4:9–17	. . . .	Followed specific cooking instructions
5:1–4	. . . .	Shaved his head and beard
12:3–7	. . . .	Left home to demonstrate exile
13:1ff	. . . .	Spoke against false prophets
19:1ff	. . . .	Sang a lament concerning the leaders
21:2	. . . .	Prophesied against Israel and the temple
21:19–23	. . . .	Marked out two roads for Babylon's king
24:16, 17	. . . .	Did not mourn his wife's death

5:11 It was a serious sin to defile the temple, God's sanctuary, by worshiping idols and practicing evil within its very walls. In the New Testament, we learn that God now makes his home *within* those who are his. Our bodies are God's temple (see 1 Corinthians 6:19). We defile God's temple today by allowing gossiping, bitterness, love of money, lying, or any other wrong actions or attitudes to be a part of our lives. By asking the Holy Spirit's help, we can keep from defiling his temple, our bodies.

5:13 Have you ever seen someone try to discipline a child by saying, "If you do that one more time . . ."? If the parent doesn't follow through, the child learns not to listen. Empty threats backfire. God was going to punish the Israelites for their blatant sins, and he wanted them to know that he would do what he said. The

people learned the hard way that God always follows through on his word. Too many people ignore God's warnings, treating them as empty threats. But what God threatens, he does. Don't make the mistake of thinking God doesn't really mean what he says.

6:1ff This is the beginning of a two-part message. Remember that Ezekiel could speak only when giving messages from God. The message in chapter 6 is that Judah's idolatry will surely call down God's judgment. The message in chapter 7 describes the nature of that judgment—utter destruction of the nation. Nevertheless, God in his mercy saved a remnant. Ezekiel prophesies against the mountains of Israel because mountains were sites of the "high places" used to worship idols.

people in front of your idols. ⁵I will lay the dead bodies of the Israelites in front of their idols, and I will scatter your bones ʲ around your altars. ⁶Wherever you live, the towns will be laid waste and the high places demolished, so that your altars will be laid waste and devastated, your idols ᵏ smashed and ruined, your incense altars broken down, and what you have made wiped out. ⁷Your people will fall slain among you, and you will know that I am the Lᴏʀᴅ.

⁸"'But I will spare some, for some of you will escape ˡ the sword when you are scattered among the lands and nations. ᵐ ⁹Then in the nations where they have been carried captive, those who escape will remember me—how I have been grieved ⁿ by their adulterous hearts, which have turned away from me, and by their eyes, which have lusted after their idols. They will loathe themselves for the evil they have done and for all their detestable practices.ᵒ ¹⁰And they will know that I am the Lᴏʀᴅ; I did not threaten in vain to bring this calamity on them.

¹¹"'This is what the Sovereign Lᴏʀᴅ says: Strike your hands together and stamp your feet and cry out "Alas!" because of all the wicked and detestable practices of the house of Israel, for they will fall by the sword, famine and plague. ᵖ ¹²He that is far away will die of the plague, and he that is near will fall by the sword, and he that survives and is spared will die of famine. So will I spend my wrath upon them. ᑫ ¹³And they will know that I am the Lᴏʀᴅ, when their people lie slain among their idols around their altars, on every high hill and on all the mountaintops, under every spreading tree and every leafy oak ʳ—places where they offered fragrant incense to all their idols.ˢ ¹⁴And I will stretch out my hand against them and make the land a desolate waste from the desert to Diblah ᵃ—wherever they live. Then they will know that I am the Lᴏʀᴅ.'"

The End Has Come

7 The word of the Lᴏʀᴅ came to me: ²"Son of man, this is what the Sovereign Lᴏʀᴅ says to the land of Israel: The end! ᵗ The end has come upon the four corners of the land. ³The end is now upon you and I will unleash my anger against you. I will judge you according to your conduct and repay you for all your detestable practices. ⁴I will not look on you with pity ᵘ or spare you; I will surely repay you for your conduct and the detestable practices among you. Then you will know that I am the Lᴏʀᴅ.

⁵"This is what the Sovereign Lᴏʀᴅ says: Disaster! ᵛ An unheard-of ᵇ disaster is coming. ⁶The end has come! The end has come! It has roused itself against you. It has come! ⁷Doom has come upon you—you who dwell in the land. The time has come, the day is near; there is panic, not joy, upon the mountains. ⁸I am about to pour out my wrath on you and spend my anger against you; I will judge you according to your conduct and repay you for all your detestable practices. ʷ ⁹I will not look on you with pity or spare you; I will repay you in accordance with your conduct and the detestable practices among you. Then you will know that it is I the Lᴏʀᴅ who strikes the blow.

¹⁰"The day is here! It has come! Doom has burst forth, the rod ˣ has budded, arrogance has blossomed! ¹¹Violence has grown into ᶜ a rod to punish wickedness; none of the people will be left, none of that crowd—no wealth, nothing of value.ʸ ¹²The time has come, the day

---

6:5
ʲJer 8:1-2
6:6
ᵏZec 13:2

6:8
ˡJer 44:28
ᵐEze 14:22
6:9
ⁿPs 78:40; Isa 7:13
ᵒEze 20:43

6:11
ᵖEze 5:12; 21:14, 17
6:12
ᑫEze 5:12
6:13
ʳIsa 57:5
ˢJer 2:20; Hos 4:13

7:2
ᵗAm 8:2, 10

7:4
ᵘEze 5:11

7:5
ᵛ2Ki 21:12

7:8
ʷEze 20:8, 21

7:10
ˣIsa 10:5
7:11
ʸJer 16:6

ᵃ *14* Most Hebrew manuscripts; a few Hebrew manuscripts *Riblah*   ᵇ *5* Most Hebrew manuscripts; some Hebrew manuscripts and Syriac *Disaster after*   ᶜ *11 Or The violent one has become*

6:8–10 A ray of light appears in this prophecy of darkness—God would spare a small group—a remnant—of people, but only after they had learned some hard lessons. God sometimes has to break a person in order to bring him or her to true repentance. The people needed new attitudes, but they wouldn't change until God broke their hearts with humiliation, pain, suffering, and defeat. Does your heart long for God enough to change those areas displeasing him? Or will God have to break your heart?

6:11 Prophets often used this threefold description of judgment upon Jerusalem—sword, famine, and plague—as a way of saying that the destruction would be complete. The sword meant death in battle; famine came when enemies besieged a city; plague was always a danger during famine. Don't make the mistake of underestimating the extent of God's judgment. If you ignore the Biblical warnings and turn away from God, his punishment awaits you.

6:14 The phrase "then they will know that I am the Lᴏʀᴅ" (or a variation on this phrase) occurs 65 times in the book of Ezekiel. The purpose of all God's punishment was not to take revenge, but

to impress upon the people the truth that the Lord is the only true and living God. People in Ezekiel's day were worshiping human-made idols and calling them gods. Today money, sex, and power have become idols for many. Punishment will come upon all who put other things ahead of God. It is easy to forget that the Lord alone is God, the supreme authority and the only source of eternal love and life. Remember that God may use the difficulties of your life to teach you that he alone is God.

7:10, 11 In chapter 7, Ezekiel predicts the complete destruction of Judah. The wicked and proud will finally get what they deserve. If it seems as though God ignores the evil and proud people of our day, be assured that a day of judgment will come, just as it came for the people of Judah. God is waiting patiently for sinners to repent (see 2 Peter 3:9), but when his judgment comes, "none of the people will be left." What you decide about God now will determine your fate then.

7:12, 13 The nation of Judah trusted in its prosperity and possessions instead of in God. So God planned to destroy the basis of its prosperity. Whenever we begin to trust in jobs, the has arrived. Let not the buyer rejoice nor the seller grieve, for wrath is upon the whole crowd. 13The seller will not recover the land he has sold as long as both of them live, for the vision concerning the whole crowd will not be reversed. Because of their sins, not one of them will preserve his life. 14Though they blow the trumpet and get everything ready, no one will go into battle, for my wrath is upon the whole crowd.

15"Outside is the sword, inside are plague and famine; those in the country will die by the sword, and those in the city will be devoured by famine and plague. z 16All who survive and escape will be in the mountains, moaning like doves of the valleys, each because of his sins. a 17Every hand will go limp, and every knee will become as weak as water. 18They will put on sackcloth and be clothed with terror. Their faces will be covered with shame and their heads will be shaved. b 19They will throw their silver into the streets, and their gold will be an unclean thing. Their silver and gold will not be able to save them in the day of the Lord's wrath. c They will not satisfy their hunger or fill their stomachs with it, for it has made them stumble into sin. d 20They were proud of their beautiful jewelry and used it to make their detestable idols and vile images. Therefore I will turn these into an unclean thing for them. 21I will hand it all over as plunder to foreigners and as loot to the wicked of the earth, and they will defile it. 22I will turn my face away from them, and they will desecrate my treasured place; robbers will enter it and desecrate it.

23"Prepare chains, because the land is full of bloodshed e and the city is full of violence. 24I will bring the most wicked of the nations to take possession of their houses; I will put an end to the pride of the mighty, and their sanctuaries f will be desecrated. 25When terror comes, they will seek peace, but there will be none. 26Calamity upon calamity g will come, and rumor upon rumor. They will try to get a vision from the prophet; the teaching of the law by the priest will be lost, as will the counsel of the elders. 27The king will mourn, the prince will be clothed with despair, h and the hands of the people of the land will tremble. I will deal with them according to their conduct, and by their own standards I will judge them. Then they will know that I am the Lord."

Idolatry in the Temple

8 In the sixth year, in the sixth month on the fifth day, while I was sitting in my house and the elders i of Judah were sitting before me, the hand of the Sovereign Lord came upon me there. 2I looked, and I saw a figure like that of a man. a From what appeared to be his waist down he was like fire, and from there up his appearance was as bright as glowing metal. j 3He stretched out what looked like a hand and took me by the hair of my head. The Spirit lifted me up k between earth and heaven and in visions of God he took me to Jerusalem, to the entrance to the north gate of the inner court, where the idol that provokes to jealousy stood. 4And there before me was the glory l of the God of Israel, as in the vision I had seen in the plain.

a2 Or saw a fiery figure

Cross references
7:15 zDt 32:25
7:16 aEze 6:8
7:18 bIsa 15:2-3; Am 8:10
7:19 cZep 1:7, 18 dPr 11:4
7:23 e2Ki 21:16
7:24 fEze 24:21
7:26 gJer 4:20
7:27 hEze 26:16
8:1 iEze 14:1
8:2 jEze 1:4, 26-27
8:3 kEze 11:1
8:4 lEze 1:28

---

economy, a political system, or military might for our security, we put God in the back seat.

7:19 God's people had allowed their love of money to lead them into sin. For this, God would destroy them. Money has a strange power to lead people into sin. Paul said that "the love of money is a root of all kinds of evil" (1 Timothy 6:10). It is ironic that we use a gift of God—money—to buy things that separate us from him. It is tragic that we spend so much money seeking to satisfy ourselves, and so little time seeking God, the true source of satisfaction.

7:20 God gave the people silver and gold, but they used that silver and gold to make idols. The resources God gives us should be used to do his work and carry out his will, but too often we use them to satisfy our own desires. When we abuse God's gifts or use resources selfishly, we miss the real purpose God had in mind. This is as shortsighted as idolatry.

7:24 The people of Jerusalem took great pride in their buildings. The temple itself was a source of pride (see 24:20, 21). This pride would be crushed when the evil and godless Babylonians destroyed Jerusalem's houses and holy places. If you are going through a humiliating experience, God may be using that experience to weed out pride in your life.

8:1ff This prophecy's date corresponds to 592 B.C. The message of chapters 8—11 is directed specifically toward Jerusalem and its leaders. Chapter 8 records Ezekiel being taken in a vision from Babylon to the temple in Jerusalem to see the great wickedness being practiced there. The people and their religious leaders were thoroughly corrupt. While Ezekiel's first vision (chapters 1—3) showed that judgment was from God, this vision showed that their sin was the reason for judgment.

8:2 This figure could have been an angel or a manifestation of God himself. In Ezekiel's previous vision, a man with a similar appearance was pictured as God on his throne (1:26–28).

8:3–5 This "idol that provokes to jealousy" could be an image of Asherah, the Canaanite goddess of fertility, whose character encouraged sexual immorality and self-gratification. King Manasseh had placed such an idol in the temple (2 Kings 21:7). King Josiah had burned the Asherah pole (2 Kings 23:6), but there were certainly many other idols around.

⁵Then he said to me, "Son of man, look toward the north." So I looked, and in the entrance north of the gate of the altar I saw this idol of jealousy.

⁶And he said to me, "Son of man, do you see what they are doing—the utterly detestable things the house of Israel is doing here, things that will drive me far from my sanctuary? But you will see things that are even more detestable."

⁷Then he brought me to the entrance to the court. I looked, and I saw a hole in the wall. ⁸He said to me, "Son of man, now dig into the wall." So I dug into the wall and saw a doorway there.

⁹And he said to me, "Go in and see the wicked and detestable things they are doing here." ¹⁰So I went in and looked, and I saw portrayed all over the walls all kinds of crawling things and detestable animals and all the idols of the house of Israel. ¹¹In front of them stood seventy elders of the house of Israel, and Jaazaniah son of Shaphan was standing among them. Each had a censer in his hand, and a fragrant cloud of incense was rising.

¹²He said to me, "Son of man, have you seen what the elders of the house of Israel are doing in the darkness, each at the shrine of his own idol? They say, 'The Lord does not see[m] us; the Lord has forsaken the land.'" ¹³Again, he said, "You will see them doing things that are even more detestable."

8:12
[m] Eze 9:9

¹⁴Then he brought me to the entrance to the north gate of the house of the Lord, and I saw women sitting there, mourning for Tammuz. ¹⁵He said to me, "Do you see this, son of man? You will see things that are even more detestable than this."

¹⁶He then brought me into the inner court of the house of the Lord, and there at the entrance to the temple, between the portico and the altar, were about twenty-five men. With their backs toward the temple of the Lord and their faces toward the east, they were bowing down to the sun in the east.[n]

8:16
[n] Dt 4:19; Jer 2:27

¹⁷He said to me, "Have you seen this, son of man? Is it a trivial matter for the house of Judah to do the detestable things they are doing here? Must they also fill the land with violence[o] and continually provoke me to anger? Look at them putting the branch to their nose! ¹⁸Therefore I will deal with them in anger; I will not look on them with pity or spare them. Although they shout in my ears, I will not listen[p] to them."

8:17
[o] Eze 9:9
8:18
[p] Isa 1:15;
Jer 11:11; Mic 3:4;
Zec 7:13

Idolaters Killed

9 Then I heard him call out in a loud voice, "Bring the guards of the city here, each with a weapon in his hand." ²And I saw six men coming from the direction of the upper gate, which faces north, each with a deadly weapon in his hand. With them was a man clothed in linen who had a writing kit at his side. They came in and stood beside the bronze altar.

³Now the glory[q] of the God of Israel went up from above the cherubim,[r] where it had been, and moved to the threshold of the temple. Then the Lord called to the man clothed in linen who had the writing kit at his side ⁴and said to him, "Go throughout the city of Jerusalem

9:3
[q] Eze 10:4
[r] Eze 11:22

8:6ff In scene after scene, God revealed to Ezekiel the extent to which the people had embraced idolatry and wickedness. God's Spirit works within us in a similar way, revealing sin that lurks in our lives. How comfortable would you feel if God held an open house in your life today?

8:14 Tammuz was the Babylonian god of spring. He was the husband or lover of the goddess Ishtar. The followers of this cult believed that the green vegetation shriveled and died in the hot summer because Tammuz had died and descended into the underworld. Thus, the worshipers wept and mourned his death. In the springtime, when the new vegetation appeared, they rejoiced, believing that Tammuz had come back to life. God was showing Ezekiel that many people were no longer worshiping the *true* God of life and vegetation. We must also be careful not to spend so much time thinking about the benefits of creation that we lose sight of the Creator.

8:17 The branch to the nose could refer either to a cultic worship practice, or to the fact that Judah's sins had become a stench to God.

9:1ff This chapter presents a picture of coming judgment. After Ezekiel had seen how corrupt Jerusalem had become, God called one man to spare the small minority who had been faithful. Then he called six men to slaughter the wicked people in the city. This judgment was ordered by God himself (9:5–7).

9:2 The writing kit was a common object in Ezekiel's day. It included a long narrow board with a groove to hold the reed brush that was used to write on parchment, papyrus, or dried clay. The board had hollowed out areas for holding cakes of black and red ink that had to be moistened before use.

9:3 What is God's glory? It is the manifestation of God's character—his ultimate power, transcendence, and moral perfection. God is completely above man and his limitations. Yet God reveals himself to us so that we can worship and follow him.

9:3 Cherubim ("cherub" is singular) are an order of powerful angelic beings created to glorify God. They are associated with God's absolute holiness and moral perfection. God placed cherubim at the entrance of Eden to keep Adam and Eve out after they sinned (Genesis 3:24). Representations of cherubim were used to decorate the tabernacle and temple. The lid of the ark of the covenant, called the atonement cover, was adorned with two gold cherubim (Exodus 37:6–9). It was a symbol of the very presence of God. The cherubim seen by Ezekiel left the temple along with the glory of God (chapter 10). Ezekiel then recognized them as the living creatures he had seen in his first vision (see chapter 1).

9:4, 5 God told the man with the writing kit to put a mark on those who were faithful to God. Their faithfulness was determined by their sensitivity to and sorrow over their nation's sin. Those with the mark were spared when the six men began to destroy the

9:4
s Ex 12:7;
Rev 7:3; 9:4
t Ps 119:136
u Ps 119:53

9:6
v 2Ch 36:17;
Jer 25:29

9:8
w Eze 11:13

9:9
x Eze 8:12

9:10
y Eze 7:4; 8:18
z Eze 11:21

10:1
a Eze 1:22
10:2
b Rev 8:5

10:4
c Eze 1:28; 9:3

10:5
d Eze 1:24

10:9
e Eze 1:15-16

10:14
f Eze 1:6
g Eze 1:10

and put a mark s on the foreheads of those who grieve and lament t over all the detestable things that are done in it. u”

5 As I listened, he said to the others, “Follow him through the city and kill, without showing pity or compassion. 6 Slaughter old men, young men and maidens, women and children, but do not touch anyone who has the mark. Begin at my sanctuary.” So they began with the elders who were in front of the temple. v

7 Then he said to them, “Defile the temple and fill the courts with the slain. Go!” So they went out and began killing throughout the city. 8 While they were killing and I was left alone, I fell facedown, crying out, “Ah, Sovereign Lord! Are you going to destroy the entire remnant of Israel in this outpouring of your wrath on Jerusalem? w”

9 He answered me, “The sin of the house of Israel and Judah is exceedingly great; the land is full of bloodshed and the city is full of injustice. They say, ‘The Lord has forsaken the land; the Lord does not see.’ x 10 So I will not look on them with pity y or spare them, but I will bring down on their own heads what they have done. z”

11 Then the man in linen with the writing kit at his side brought back word, saying, “I have done as you commanded.”

The Glory Departs From the Temple

10 I looked, and I saw the likeness of a throne of sapphire a above the expanse a that was over the heads of the cherubim. 2 The Lord said to the man clothed in linen, “Go in among the wheels beneath the cherubim. Fill b your hands with burning coals from among the cherubim and scatter them over the city.” And as I watched, he went in.

3 Now the cherubim were standing on the south side of the temple when the man went in, and a cloud filled the inner court. 4 Then the glory of the Lord c rose from above the cherubim and moved to the threshold of the temple. The cloud filled the temple, and the court was full of the radiance of the glory of the Lord. 5 The sound of the wings of the cherubim could be heard as far away as the outer court, like the voice d of God Almighty b when he speaks.

6 When the Lord commanded the man in linen, “Take fire from among the wheels, from among the cherubim,” the man went in and stood beside a wheel. 7 Then one of the cherubim reached out his hand to the fire that was among them. He took up some of it and put it into the hands of the man in linen, who took it and went out. 8 (Under the wings of the cherubim could be seen what looked like the hands of a man.)

9 I looked, and I saw beside the cherubim four wheels, one beside each of the cherubim; the wheels sparkled like chrysolite. e 10 As for their appearance, the four of them looked alike; each was like a wheel intersecting a wheel. 11 As they moved, they would go in any one of the four directions the cherubim faced; the wheels did not turn about e as the cherubim went. The cherubim went in whatever direction the head faced, without turning as they went. 12 Their entire bodies, including their backs, their hands and their wings, were completely full of eyes, as were their four wheels. 13 I heard the wheels being called “the whirling wheels.” 14 Each of the cherubim had four faces: f One face was that of a cherub, the second the face of a man, the third the face of a lion, and the fourth the face of an eagle. g

a 1 Or lapis lazuli   b 5 Hebrew El-Shaddai   c 11 Or aside

---

wicked people. During the exodus, the Israelites put a mark of blood on their doorframes to save them from death. In the final days, God will mark the foreheads of those destined for salvation (Revelation 7:3), and Satan will mark his followers (Revelation 13:16, 17), who, like him, are destined for destruction. When God punishes sin, he won’t forget his promise to preserve his people.

9:6 The spiritual leaders (“elders”) of Israel blatantly promoted their idolatrous beliefs, and the people abandoned God and followed them. Spiritual leaders are especially accountable to God because they are entrusted with the task of teaching the truth (see James 3:1). When they pervert the truth, they can lead countless people away from God and even cause a nation to fall. It is not surprising, then, that when God began to judge the nation, he started at the temple and worked outward (see 1 Peter 4:17). How sad it is that in the temple, the one place where they should have been teaching God’s truth, these men were teaching lies.

9:9, 10 The people said that the Lord had forsaken the land and wouldn’t see their sin. People have many convenient explanations

to make it easier to sin: “It doesn’t matter,” “Everybody’s doing it,” or “Nobody will ever know.” Do you find yourself making excuses for sin? Rationalizing sin makes it easier to commit, but rationalization does not convince God or cancel the punishment.

10:1ff Chapters 8—11 depict God’s glory departing from the temple. In 8:3, 4, his glory was over the northern gate. It then moved to the door (the “threshold,” 9:3), the south side of the temple (10:3, 4), the eastern gate (10:18, 19; 11:1), and finally the mountain east of the temple (11:23), probably the Mount of Olives. Because of the nation’s sins, God’s glory had departed.

10:2 God’s perfect holiness demands judgment for sin. The cherubim are mighty angels. The burning coals scattered over the city represent the purging of sin. For Jerusalem, this meant the destruction of all the people who blatantly sinned and refused to repent. Shortly after this prophecy, the Babylonians destroyed Jerusalem by fire (2 Kings 25:9; 2 Chronicles 36:19).

15Then the cherubim rose upward. These were the living creatures[h] I had seen by the Kebar River. 16When the cherubim moved, the wheels beside them moved; and when the cherubim spread their wings to rise from the ground, the wheels did not leave their side. 17When the cherubim stood still, they also stood still; and when the cherubim rose, they rose with them, because the spirit of the living creatures was in them.[i]

18Then the glory of the LORD departed from over the threshold of the temple and stopped above the cherubim. 19While I watched, the cherubim spread their wings and rose from the ground, and as they went, the wheels went with them.[j] They stopped at the entrance to the east gate of the LORD's house, and the glory of the God of Israel was above them.

20These were the living creatures I had seen beneath the God of Israel by the Kebar River, and I realized that they were cherubim. 21Each had four faces and four wings,[k] and under their wings was what looked like the hands of a man. 22Their faces had the same appearance as those I had seen by the Kebar River. Each one went straight ahead.

Judgment on Israel's Leaders

11 Then the Spirit lifted me up and brought me to the gate of the house of the LORD that faces east. There at the entrance to the gate were twenty-five men, and I saw among them Jaazaniah son of Azzur and Pelatiah son of Benaiah, leaders of the people. 2The LORD said to me, "Son of man, these are the men who are plotting evil and giving wicked advice in this city. 3They say, 'Will it not soon be time to build houses?[a] This city is a cooking pot,[l] and we are the meat.' 4Therefore prophesy against them; prophesy, son of man."

5Then the Spirit of the LORD came upon me, and he told me to say: "This is what the LORD says: That is what you are saying, O house of Israel, but I know what is going through your mind. 6You have killed many people in this city and filled its streets with the dead.[m]

7"Therefore this is what the Sovereign LORD says: The bodies you have thrown there are the meat and this city is the pot, but I will drive you out of it.[n] 8You fear the sword, and the sword is what I will bring against you, declares the Sovereign LORD. 9I will drive you out of the city and hand you over to foreigners and inflict punishment on you.[o] 10You will fall by the sword, and I will execute judgment on you at the borders of Israel.[p] Then you will know that I am the LORD. 11This city will not be a pot for you, nor will you be the meat in it; I will execute judgment on you at the borders of Israel. 12And you will know that I am the LORD, for you have not followed my decrees or kept my laws but have conformed to the standards of the nations around you.[q]"

13Now as I was prophesying, Pelatiah son of Benaiah died. Then I fell facedown and cried out in a loud voice, "Ah, Sovereign LORD! Will you completely destroy the remnant of Israel?[r]"

14The word of the LORD came to me: 15"Son of man, your brothers—your brothers who are your blood relatives[b] and the whole house of Israel—are those of whom the people of Jerusalem have said, 'They are[c] far away from the LORD; this land was given to us as our possession.'

a 3 Or This is not the time to build houses.   b 15 Or are in exile with you (see Septuagint and Syriac)   c 15 Or those to whom the people of Jerusalem have said, 'Stay

**Cross references (right margin):**

10:15 h Eze 1:3, 5

10:17 i Eze 1:20-21

10:19 j Eze 11:1, 22

10:21 k Eze 1:6

11:3 l Jer 1:13; Eze 24:3

11:6 m Eze 7:23

11:7 n Eze 24:3-13; Mic 3:2-3

11:9 o Eze 5:8

11:10 p 2Ki 14:25

11:12 q Eze 8:10

11:13 r Eze 9:8

10:18 God's glory departed from the temple and was never completely present again until Christ himself visited it in New Testament times. God's holiness required that he leave the temple because the people had so defiled it. God had to completely destroy what people had perverted in order for true worship to be revived. We must commit ourselves, our families, our churches, and our nation to follow God faithfully so that we never have to experience God abandoning us.

11:1-4 God had abandoned his altar and temple (chapters 9—11); here his judgment was complete as his glory stopped above the mountain east of the city (11:23). The city gate was where merchants and politicians conducted business, so the 25 men may have represented the nation's rulers. Because of their leadership positions, they were responsible for leading the people astray. They had wrongly said that they were secure from another attack by the Babylonians. "This city is a cooking pot, and we are the meat" means they believed that they were the elite, the influential, the ones who would be protected from all harm. Without God, however, our situation is always precarious.

11:5 God knew everything about the Israelites, even their thoughts. He also knows everything about us, even the sins we try to hide. Instead of worrying about people noticing how we look or what we do, we should care about what God thinks, for he sees everything. Trying to hide our thoughts and actions from God is futile. "Secret" sins are never secret from God. The only effective way to deal with sin is to confess it and ask God to help us overcome it.

11:12 From the time they entered the promised land, the Israelites were warned not to copy the customs and religious practices of other nations. Disobeying this command and following pagan customs instead of God's laws always got them into trouble. Today, believers are still tempted to conform to the ways of the world. But we must get our standards of right and wrong from God, not from the popular trends of society.

11:14ff God promised the exiles in Babylonia that he would continue to be with them even though they were not in Jerusalem. This was a major concern to the Jews because they believed that God was present primarily in the temple. But God assured them that he would continue to be their God regardless of where they were. In the midst of Ezekiel's burning message of judgment stands a cool oasis—God's promise to restore the faithful few to their homeland. God's arms are now open to receive those who will repent of their sins.

11:15-21 God's messages through Ezekiel are full of irony. Here God says that the Jews in captivity are the faithful ones, and those in

Promised Return of Israel

11:16
s Isa 8:14

16"Therefore say: 'This is what the Sovereign Lord says: Although I sent them far away among the nations and scattered them among the countries, yet for a little while I have been a sanctuary s for them in the countries where they have gone.'

11:17
t Jer 24:5-6

17"Therefore say: 'This is what the Sovereign Lord says: I will gather you from the nations and bring you back from the countries where you have been scattered, and I will give you back the land of Israel again.' t

11:18
u Eze 37:23

11:19
v Jer 32:39
w Eze 18:31; 36:26

11:20
x Ps 105:45
y Eze 14:11

11:21
z Eze 9:10

11:22
a Eze 10:19

11:23
b Eze 8:4
c Zec 14:4

18"They will return to it and remove all its vile images and detestable idols. u 19I will give them an undivided heart v and put a new spirit in them; I will remove from them their heart of stone and give them a heart of flesh. w 20Then they will follow my decrees and be careful to keep my laws. x They will be my people, and I will be their God. y 21But as for those whose hearts are devoted to their vile images and detestable idols, I will bring down on their own heads what they have done, declares the Sovereign Lord. z"

22Then the cherubim, with the wheels beside them, spread their wings, and the glory of the God of Israel was above them. a 23The glory b of the Lord went up from within the city and stopped above the mountain c east of it. 24The Spirit lifted me up and brought me to the exiles in Babylonia a in the vision given by the Spirit of God.

Then the vision I had seen went up from me, 25and I told the exiles everything the Lord had shown me.

3. Punishment is certain
The Exile Symbolized

12:2
d Mt 13:15

12 The word of the Lord came to me: 2"Son of man, you are living among a rebellious people. They have eyes to see but do not see and ears to hear but do not hear, for they are a rebellious people. d

3"Therefore, son of man, pack your belongings for exile and in the daytime, as they watch, set out and go from where you are to another place. Perhaps they will understand, though they are a rebellious house. 4During the daytime, while they watch, bring out your belongings packed for exile. Then in the evening, while they are watching, go out like those who go into exile. 5While they watch, dig through the wall and take your belongings out through it. 6Put them on your shoulder as they are watching and carry them out at dusk. Cover your face so that you cannot see the land, for I have made you a sign e to the house of Israel."

12:6
e Isa 8:18; Eze 4:3; 24:24

7So I did as I was commanded. During the day I brought out my things packed for exile. Then in the evening I dug through the wall with my hands. I took my belongings out at dusk, carrying them on my shoulders while they watched.

12:9
f Eze 17:12; 24:19

8In the morning the word of the Lord came to me: 9"Son of man, did not that rebellious house of Israel ask you, 'What are you doing?' f

a 24 Or *Chaldea*

Jerusalem are the sinful and wicked ones. This was the opposite of the people's perception. Appearances can be deceiving. God will evaluate your life by your faith and obedience, not by your apparent earthly success. Furthermore, we should not judge others by outward appearances.

11:16 God was a sanctuary for the righteous remnant. Idolatrous people, even though they worshiped in the Jerusalem temple (11:15), would find no true sanctuary; but the faithful exiles, though they were far from home, would be protected by God. Likewise, our external circumstances do not truly indicate our standing with God. Those who appear safe and secure may be far from him, while those going through difficult times may be safely under God's spiritual protection. We can depend on God to keep us safe if we pledge ourselves to his care.

11:18, 19 "Undivided heart" indicates a unanimous singleness of purpose. No longer will God's people seek many gods; they will be content with God. Their stony, stubborn hearts will be radically transplanted with tender, responsive hearts (see Jeremiah 32:39; Ezekiel 18:31; 36:26). This new life can only be the work of the Holy Spirit. It is God's work, but we must recognize and turn from our sin. When we do, God will give us new motives, new guidelines, and new purpose. Have you received your new heart?

11:23 God's glory left Jerusalem and stood above a mountain on the east side of the city—almost certainly the Mount of Olives. Ezekiel 43:1–4 implies that God will return the same way he left when he comes back to earth to set up his perfect kingdom.

12:1ff Ezekiel played the role of a captive being led away to exile, portraying what was about to happen to King Zedekiah and the people remaining in Jerusalem. The exiles knew exactly what Ezekiel was doing because only six years earlier they had made similar preparations as they left Jerusalem for Babylonia. This was to show the people that they should not trust the king or the capital city to save them from the Babylonian army—only God could do that. And the exiles who hoped for an early return from exile would be disappointed. Ezekiel's graphic demonstration was proven correct to the last detail. But when he warned them, many refused to listen.

¹⁰"Say to them, 'This is what the Sovereign LORD says: This oracle concerns the prince in Jerusalem and the whole house of Israel who are there.' ¹¹Say to them, 'I am a sign to you.'

"As I have done, so it will be done to them. They will go into exile as captives.

¹²"The prince among them will put his things on his shoulder at dusk *g* and leave, and a hole will be dug in the wall for him to go through. He will cover his face so that he cannot see the land. ¹³I will spread my net for him, and he will be caught in my snare; I will bring him to Babylonia, the land of the Chaldeans, but he will not see it, and there he will die. *h* ¹⁴I will scatter to the winds all those around him—his staff and all his troops—and I will pursue them with drawn sword. *i*

¹⁵"They will know that I am the LORD, when I disperse them among the nations and scatter them through the countries. ¹⁶But I will spare a few of them from the sword, famine and plague, so that in the nations where they go they may acknowledge all their detestable practices. Then they will know that I am the LORD."

¹⁷The word of the LORD came to me: ¹⁸"Son of man, tremble as you eat your food, *j* and shudder in fear as you drink your water. ¹⁹Say to the people of the land: 'This is what the Sovereign LORD says about those living in Jerusalem and in the land of Israel: They will eat their food in anxiety and drink their water in despair, for their land will be stripped of everything *k* in it because of the violence of all who live there. ²⁰The inhabited towns will be laid waste and the land will be desolate. Then you will know that I am the LORD.'"

²¹The word of the LORD came to me: ²²"Son of man, what is this proverb you have in the land of Israel: 'The days go by and every vision comes to nothing'? *l* ²³Say to them, 'This is what the Sovereign LORD says: I am going to put an end to this proverb, and they will no longer quote it in Israel.' Say to them, 'The days are near when every vision will be fulfilled. *m* ²⁴For there will be no more false visions or flattering divinations *n* among the people of Israel. ²⁵But I the LORD will speak what I will, and it shall be fulfilled without delay. For in your days, you rebellious house, I will fulfill whatever I say, declares the Sovereign LORD.'"

²⁶The word of the LORD came to me: ²⁷"Son of man, the house of Israel is saying, 'The vision he sees is for many years from now, and he prophesies about the distant future.'

²⁸"Therefore say to them, 'This is what the Sovereign LORD says: None of my words will be delayed any longer; whatever I say will be fulfilled, declares the Sovereign LORD.'"

False Prophets Condemned

13 The word of the LORD came to me: ²"Son of man, prophesy against the prophets of Israel who are now prophesying. Say to those who prophesy out of their own imagination: 'Hear the word of the LORD! ³This is what the Sovereign LORD says: Woe to the foolish *a* prophets who follow their own spirit and have seen nothing! ⁴Your prophets, O Israel, are like jackals among ruins. ⁵You have not gone up to the breaks in the wall to repair *o* it for the house of Israel so that it will stand firm in the battle on the day of the LORD. ⁶Their visions are false and their divinations a lie. They say, "The LORD declares," when the LORD has not sent them; yet they expect their words to be fulfilled. *p* ⁷Have you not seen false visions and uttered lying divinations when you say, "The LORD declares," though I have not spoken?

*a*3 Or *wicked*

12:12
*g*Jer 39:4

12:13
*h*Jer 52:11

12:14
*i*2Ki 25:5;
Eze 5:10, 12

12:18
*j*Eze 4:16

12:19
*k*Zec 7:14

12:22
*l*Eze 11:3; Am 6:3;
2Pe 3:4

12:23
*m*Joel 2:1;
Zep 1:14

12:24
*n*Eze 13:23

13:5
*o*Eze 22:30

13:6
*p*Eze 22:28

12:10-12 Zedekiah, Judah's last king (597–586 B.C.), was reigning in Jerusalem when Ezekiel gave these oracles or messages from God. Ezekiel showed the people what would happen to Zedekiah. Jerusalem would be attacked again, and Zedekiah would join the exiles already in Babylon. Zedekiah would be unable to see because Nebuchadnezzar would have his eyes gouged out (2 Kings 25:3–7; Jeremiah 52:10, 11).

12:21-28 These two short messages were warnings that God's words would come true—*soon!* Less than six years later, Jerusalem would be destroyed. Yet the people were skeptical. Unbelief and false security led them to believe it would never happen. The apostle Peter dealt with this problem in the church (2 Peter 3:9). It is dangerous to say Christ will never return or to regard his coming as so far in the future as to be irrelevant today. All that

God says is sure to happen. Don't dare assume that you have plenty of time to get right with God.

13:1ff This warning was directed against false prophets whose messages were not from God, but were lies intended to win popularity by saying whatever made the people happy. False prophets did not care about the truth as Ezekiel did. They lulled people into a false sense of security, making Ezekiel's job even more difficult. Beware of people who bend the truth in their quest for popularity and power.

13:2, 3 The false prophets had a large following because they comforted the people and approved of their sinful actions. Lies are often attractive, and liars may have large followings. Today, for example, some spiritual leaders assure us that God promises his followers health and material success. This is comforting, but is it true? God's own Son did not have an easy life on earth. Make sure the messages you believe are consistent with what God teaches in his Word.

8"'Therefore this is what the Sovereign Lord says: Because of your false words and lying visions, I am against you, declares the Sovereign Lord. 9My hand will be against the prophets who see false visions and utter lying divinations. They will not belong to the council of my people or be listed in the records of the house of Israel, nor will they enter the land of Israel. Then you will know that I am the Sovereign Lord.

10"'Because they lead my people astray, saying, "Peace," when there is no peace, and because, when a flimsy wall is built, they cover it with whitewash, q 11therefore tell those who cover it with whitewash that it is going to fall. Rain will come in torrents, and I will send hailstones hurtling down, and violent winds will burst forth. r 12When the wall collapses, will people not ask you, "Where is the whitewash you covered it with?"

13"'Therefore this is what the Sovereign Lord says: In my wrath I will unleash a violent wind, and in my anger hailstones and torrents of rain will fall with destructive fury. s 14I will tear down the wall you have covered with whitewash and will level it to the ground so that its foundation will be laid bare. When it a falls, you will be destroyed in it; and you will know that I am the Lord. 15So I will spend my wrath against the wall and against those who covered it with whitewash. I will say to you, "The wall is gone and so are those who whitewashed it, 16those prophets of Israel who prophesied to Jerusalem and saw visions of peace for her when there was no peace, declares the Sovereign Lord. t"'

17"Now, son of man, set your face against the daughters of your people who prophesy out of their own imagination. Prophesy against them u 18and say, 'This is what the Sovereign Lord says: Woe to the women who sew magic charms on all their wrists and make veils of various lengths for their heads in order to ensnare people. Will you ensnare the lives of my people but preserve your own? 19You have profaned me among my people for a few handfuls of barley and scraps of bread. By lying to my people, who listen to lies, you have killed those who should not have died and have spared those who should not live. v

20"'Therefore this is what the Sovereign Lord says: I am against your magic charms with which you ensnare people like birds and I will tear them from your arms; I will set free the people that you ensnare like birds. 21I will tear off your veils and save my people from your hands, and they will no longer fall prey to your power. Then you will know that I am the Lord. 22Because you disheartened the righteous with your lies, when I had brought them no grief, and because you encouraged the wicked not to turn from their evil ways and so save their lives, w 23therefore you will no longer see false visions or practice divination. x I will save my people from your hands. And then you will know that I am the Lord. y'"

Idolaters Condemned

14 Some of the elders of Israel came to me and sat down in front of me. z 2Then the word of the Lord came to me: 3"Son of man, these men have set up idols in their hearts and put wicked stumbling blocks a before their faces. Should I let them inquire of me at all? 4Therefore speak to them and tell them, 'This is what the Sovereign Lord says: When any Israelite sets up idols in his heart and puts a wicked stumbling block before his face and then goes to a prophet, I the Lord will answer him myself in keeping with his great idolatry. 5I will do this to recapture the hearts of the people of Israel, who have all deserted b me for their idols.'

a 14 Or the city

**Cross references (left margin):**

13:10
q Eze 22:28
13:11
r Eze 38:22

13:13
s Isa 30:30

13:16
t Isa 57:21

13:17
u ver 2

13:19
v Pr 28:21

13:22
w Jer 23:14
13:23
x ver 6; Eze 12:24
y Mic 3:6

14:1
z Eze 8:1; 20:1
14:3
a Eze 7:19

14:5
b Zec 11:8

13:10–12 These false prophets covered their lies (a "flimsy wall") with "whitewash"—a pleasing front. Such superficiality can't hold up under God's scrutiny.

13:17 In the Bible, the gift of prophecy was given to women as well as men. Miriam (Exodus 15:20), Deborah (Judges 4:4), and Huldah (2 Kings 22:14) were prophetesses. But the women mentioned here are more like the witch of 1 Samuel 28:7, and they are condemned for disheartening the righteous (13:22).

13:18 These magic charms and veils were used in witchcraft practices. They were advertised as good luck charms, but were used to ensnare the people in idolatry.

14:3 God condemned the elders for worshiping idols in their hearts and then daring to come to God's prophet for advice. On the outside, they appeared to worship God, making regular visits to the temple to offer sacrifices. But they were not sincere. It is easy for us to criticize the Israelites for worshiping idols when

they so clearly needed God instead. But we have idols in our hearts when we pursue reputation, acceptance, wealth, or sensual pleasure with the intensity and commitment that should be reserved for serving God.

14:3–5 For Hebrew writers, important functions of life were assigned to different physical organs. The heart was considered the core of a person's intellectual and spiritual function. Because all people have someone or something as the object of their heart's devotion, they have the potential for idolatry within them. God wants to recapture the hearts of his people. We must never let anything captivate our allegiance or imagination in such a way to replace or weaken our devotion to God.

6"Therefore say to the house of Israel, 'This is what the Sovereign LORD says: Repent! Turn from your idols and renounce all your detestable practices! c

7"'When any Israelite or any alien living in Israel separates himself from me and sets up idols in his heart and puts a wicked stumbling block before his face and then goes to a prophet to inquire of me, I the LORD will answer him myself. 8 I will set my face against d that man and make him an example and a byword. e I will cut him off from my people. Then you will know that I am the LORD.

9"'And if the prophet is enticed f to utter a prophecy, I the LORD have enticed that prophet, and I will stretch out my hand against him and destroy him from among my people Israel. 10 They will bear their guilt—the prophet will be as guilty as the one who consults him. 11 Then the people of Israel will no longer stray from me, nor will they defile themselves anymore with all their sins. They will be my people, and I will be their God, declares the Sovereign LORD. g '"

Judgment Inescapable

12 The word of the LORD came to me: 13"Son of man, if a country sins against me by being unfaithful and I stretch out my hand against it to cut off its food supply h and send famine upon it and kill its men and their animals, 14 even if these three men—Noah, Daniel a and Job—were in it, they could save only themselves by their righteousness, i declares the Sovereign LORD.

15"Or if I send wild beasts j through that country and they leave it childless and it becomes desolate so that no one can pass through it because of the beasts, 16 as surely as I live, declares the Sovereign LORD, even if these three men were in it, they could not save their own sons or daughters. They alone would be saved, but the land would be desolate.

17"Or if I bring a sword k against that country and say, 'Let the sword pass throughout the land,' and I kill its men and their animals, l 18 as surely as I live, declares the Sovereign LORD, even if these three men were in it, they could not save their own sons or daughters. They alone would be saved.

19"Or if I send a plague into that land and pour out my wrath upon it through bloodshed, killing its men and their animals, m 20 as surely as I live, declares the Sovereign LORD, even if Noah, Daniel and Job were in it, they could save neither son nor daughter. They would save only themselves by their righteousness.

21"For this is what the Sovereign LORD says: How much worse will it be when I send against Jerusalem my four dreadful judgments—sword and famine and wild beasts and plague—to kill its men and their animals! n 22 Yet there will be some survivors—sons and daughters who will be brought out of it. They will come to you, and when you see their conduct and their actions, you will be consoled regarding the disaster I have brought upon Jerusalem—every disaster I have brought upon it. 23 You will be consoled when you see their conduct and their actions, for you will know that I have done nothing in it without cause, declares the Sovereign LORD. o "

Jerusalem, A Useless Vine

15 The word of the LORD came to me: 2"Son of man, how is the wood of a vine p better than that of a branch on any of the trees in the forest? 3 Is wood ever taken from it to make anything useful? Do they make pegs from it to hang things on? 4 And after it is thrown

a 14 Or Danel; the Hebrew spelling may suggest a person other than the prophet Daniel; also in verse 20.

**Cross references (right margin):**
14:6 c Isa 2:20
14:8 d Eze 15:7 e Eze 5:15
14:9 f Jer 4:10
14:11 g Eze 11:19-20
14:13 h Lev 26:26
14:14 i Jer 15:1
14:15 j Eze 5:17
14:17 k Eze 5:12; 21:3-4 l Eze 25:13
14:19 m Eze 38:22
14:21 n Eze 5:17
14:23 o Jer 22:8-9
15:2 p Hos 10:1

14:6–11 The people of Judah, though eager to accept the messages of false prophets, considered the presence of a few God-fearing men in the nation an insurance policy against disaster. In a pinch, they could always ask God's prophets for advice. But merely having God's people around doesn't help. We must remember that the relationship our pastor, family, or friends have with God will not protect us from the consequences of our own sins. Each person is responsible for his or her own relationship with God. Is your faith personal and real, or are you resting in what others have done?

14:14–19 Noah, Daniel, and Job were great men in Israel's history, renowned for their relationships with God and for their wisdom (see Genesis 6:8, 9; Daniel 2:47, 48; Job 1:1). Daniel had been taken into captivity during Babylon's first invasion of

Judah in 605 B.C., eight years before Ezekiel was taken captive. At the time of Ezekiel's message, Daniel occupied a high government position in Babylon. But even these great men of God could not have saved the people of Judah because God had already passed judgment on the nation's pervasive evil.

15:1ff The messages given to Ezekiel in chapters 15—17 provided further evidence that God was going to destroy Jerusalem. The first message was about a vine, useless at first and even more useless after being burned. The people of Jerusalem were useless to God because of their idol worship, and so they would be destroyed and their cities burned. Isaiah also compared the nation of Israel to a vineyard (see Isaiah 5:1–8). Have you also become dormant and unfruitful to God? How can you begin fulfilling his plan for you?

15:4
*q*Jn 15:6

on the fire as fuel and the fire burns both ends and chars the middle, is it then useful for anything? *q* 5If it was not useful for anything when it was whole, how much less can it be made into something useful when the fire has burned it and it is charred?

6"Therefore this is what the Sovereign Lord says: As I have given the wood of the vine among the trees of the forest as fuel for the fire, so will I treat the people living in Jerusalem. 7I will set my face against*r* them. Although they have come out of the fire, the fire will yet consume them. And when I set my face against them, you will know that I am the Lord. *s* 8I will make the land desolate because they have been unfaithful, declares the Sovereign Lord."

15:7
*r*Eze 14:8
*s*Isa 24:18

An Allegory of Unfaithful Jerusalem

16:2
*t*Eze 20:4; 22:2

16 The word of the Lord came to me: 2"Son of man, confront Jerusalem with her detestable practices*t* 3and say, 'This is what the Sovereign Lord says to Jerusalem: Your ancestry and birth were in the land of the Canaanites; your father was an Amorite and your mother a Hittite. 4On the day you were born *u* your cord was not cut, nor were you washed with water to make you clean, nor were you rubbed with salt or wrapped in cloths. 5No one looked on you with pity or had compassion enough to do any of these things for you. Rather, you were thrown out into the open field, for on the day you were born you were despised.

16:4
*u*Hos 2:3

16:7
*v*Ex 1:7

6"'Then I passed by and saw you kicking about in your blood, and as you lay there in your blood I said to you, "Live!"*a* 7I made you grow like a plant of the field. You grew up and developed and became the most beautiful of jewels. *b* Your breasts were formed and your hair grew, you who were naked and bare. *v*

16:8
*w*Ru 3:9
*x*Jer 2:2

8"'Later I passed by, and when I looked at you and saw that you were old enough for love, I spread the corner of my garment*w* over you and covered your nakedness. I gave you my solemn oath and entered into a covenant with you, declares the Sovereign Lord, and you became mine. *x*

9"'I bathed*c* you with water and washed the blood from you and put ointments on you. 10I clothed you with an embroidered dress and put leather sandals on you. I dressed you in fine linen and covered you with costly garments. 11I adorned you with jewelry: *y* I put bracelets on your arms and a necklace around your neck, 12and I put a ring on your nose,*z* earrings on your ears and a beautiful crown on your head. 13So you were adorned with gold and silver; your clothes were of fine linen and costly fabric and embroidered cloth. Your food was fine flour, honey and olive oil. *a* You became very beautiful and rose to be a queen. *b* 14And your fame spread among the nations on account of your beauty, *c* because the splendor I had given you made your beauty perfect, declares the Sovereign Lord.

16:11
*y*Eze 23:40

16:12
*z*Isa 3:21

16:13
*a*1Sa 10:1
*b*Dt 32:13-14

16:14
*c*La 2:15

16:15
*d*Isa 57:8; Jer 2:20

15"'But you trusted in your beauty and used your fame to become a prostitute. You lavished your favors on anyone who passed by and your beauty became his.*d* *d* 16You took some of your garments to make gaudy high places, where you carried on your prostitution. Such things should not happen, nor should they ever occur. 17You also took the fine jewelry I gave you, the jewelry made of my gold and silver, and you made for yourself male idols and engaged in prostitution with them. 18And you took your embroidered clothes to put on them, and you offered my oil and incense before them. 19Also the food I provided for you—the fine flour, olive oil and honey I gave you to eat—you offered as fragrant incense before them. That is what happened, declares the Sovereign Lord. *e*

16:19
*e*Hos 2:8

*a*6 A few Hebrew manuscripts, Septuagint and Syriac; most Hebrew manuscripts *"Live!" And as you lay there in your blood I said to you, "Live!"* *b*7 Or *became mature* *c*9 Or *I had bathed* *d*15 Most Hebrew manuscripts; one Hebrew manuscript (see some Septuagint manuscripts) *by. Such a thing should not happen*

16:1ff This message reminded Jerusalem of its former despised status among the Canaanite nations. Using the imagery of a young baby growing to mature womanhood, God reminded Jerusalem that he raised her from a lowly state to great glory as his bride. She betrayed God's trust and prostituted herself, however, by seeking alliances with pagan nations and adopting their customs. If we push God aside for anything, even education, family, career, or pleasure, we are abandoning him in the same way.

16:3 *Canaan* was the ancient name of the territory taken over by the children of Israel and *Canaanites* were the people who lived there. The Bible often uses this name to refer to all the corrupt pagan nations of the region. The Amorites and Hittites, two Canaanite peoples, were known for their wickedness.

But here God implies that his people are no better than the Canaanites.

16:15 God cared for and loved Judah, only to have her turn away to other nations and their false gods. The nation had grown to maturity and became famous, but it forgot who had given them their life (16:22). This is a picture of spiritual adultery (called apostasy—turning from the one true God). As you become wise and more mature, don't turn away from the One who truly loves you.

20"'And you took your sons and daughters whom you bore to me and sacrificed them as food to the idols. Was your prostitution not enough?[f] 21You slaughtered my children and sacrificed them[a] to the idols. 22In all your detestable practices and your prostitution you did not remember the days of your youth,[g] when you were naked and bare, kicking about in your blood.[h]

23"'Woe! Woe to you, declares the Sovereign LORD. In addition to all your other wickedness, 24you built a mound for yourself and made a lofty shrine[i] in every public square. 25At the head of every street you built your lofty shrines and degraded your beauty, offering your body with increasing promiscuity to anyone who passed by.[j] 26You engaged in prostitution with the Egyptians, your lustful neighbors, and provoked[k] me to anger with your increasing promiscuity. 27So I stretched out my hand against you and reduced your territory; I gave you over to the greed of your enemies, the daughters of the Philistines,[l] who were shocked by your lewd conduct. 28You engaged in prostitution with the Assyrians[m] too, because you were insatiable; and even after that, you still were not satisfied. 29Then you increased your promiscuity to include Babylonia,[b] a land of merchants, but even with this you were not satisfied.

30"'How weak-willed you are, declares the Sovereign LORD, when you do all these things, acting like a brazen prostitute![n] 31When you built your mounds at the head of every street and made your lofty shrines in every public square, you were unlike a prostitute, because you scorned payment.

32"'You adulterous wife! You prefer strangers to your own husband! 33Every prostitute receives a fee, but you give gifts to all your lovers, bribing them to come to you from everywhere for your illicit favors.[o] 34So in your prostitution you are the opposite of others; no one runs after you for your favors. You are the very opposite, for you give payment and none is given to you.

35"'Therefore, you prostitute, hear the word of the LORD! 36This is what the Sovereign LORD says: Because you poured out your wealth[c] and exposed your nakedness in your promiscuity with your lovers, and because of all your detestable idols, and because you gave them your children's blood,[p] 37therefore I am going to gather all your lovers, with whom you found pleasure, those you loved as well as those you hated. I will gather them against you from all around and will strip you in front of them, and they will see all your nakedness. 38I will sentence you to the punishment of women who commit adultery and who shed blood;[q] I will bring upon you the blood vengeance of my wrath and jealous anger. 39Then I will hand you over to your lovers, and they will tear down your mounds and destroy your lofty shrines. They will strip you of your clothes and take your fine jewelry and leave you naked and bare.[r] 40They will bring a mob against you, who will stone you and hack you to pieces with their swords. 41They will burn down your houses and inflict punishment on you in the sight of many women. I will put a stop[s] to your prostitution, and you will no longer pay your lovers. 42Then my wrath against you will subside and my jealous anger will turn away from you; I will be calm and no longer angry.[t]

43"'Because you did not remember[u] the days of your youth but enraged me with all these things, I will surely bring down[v] on your head what you have done, declares the Sovereign LORD. Did you not add lewdness to all your other detestable practices?[w]

44"'Everyone who quotes proverbs will quote this proverb about you: "Like mother, like daughter." 45You are a true daughter of your mother, who despised her husband and her children; and you are a true sister of your sisters, who despised their husbands and their children. Your mother was a Hittite and your father an Amorite. 46Your older sister was Samaria, who lived to the north of you with her daughters; and your younger sister, who lived to the south of you with her daughters, was Sodom. 47You not only walked in their ways and copied

a 21 Or and made them pass through ⌊the fire⌋   b 29 Or Chaldea   c 36 Or lust

16:20
[f] Ps 106:37-38

16:22
[g] Jer 2:2
[h] ver 6

16:24
[i] Isa 57:7

16:25
[j] Pr 9:14

16:26
[k] Eze 8:17

16:27
[l] 2Ch 28:18

16:28
[m] 2Ki 16:7

16:30
[n] Jer 3:3

16:33
[o] Hos 8:9-10

16:36
[p] Jer 19:5

16:38
[q] Eze 23:45

16:39
[r] Eze 23:26

16:41
[s] Eze 23:27, 48

16:42
[t] Eze 5:13
[u] Ps 78:42

16:43
[v] Eze 22:31
[w] ver 22; Eze 11:21

16:20, 21 Child sacrifice had been practiced by the Canaanites long before Israel invaded their land, but it was strictly forbidden by God (Leviticus 20:1–3). By Ezekiel's time, however, the people were openly sacrificing their own children (2 Kings 16:3; 21:6). Jeremiah confirmed that this was a common practice (Jeremiah 7:31; 32:35). Because of such vile acts among the people and priesthood, the temple became unfit for God to inhabit. When God left the temple, he was no longer Judah's guide and protector.

16:27 The conduct of the Jews was so disgusting that even those who worshiped other gods, including their great enemy

the Philistines, would have been ashamed to behave that way. The Jews outdid them in doing evil.

16:44–52 The city of Sodom, a symbol of total corruption, was completely destroyed by God for its wickedness (Genesis 19:24, 25). Samaria, the capital of what had been the northern kingdom (Israel), was despised and rejected by the Jews in Judah. To be called a sister of Samaria and Sodom was bad enough, but to be called *more depraved* than that meant that Judah's sins were an unspeakable abomination and that its doom was inevitable. The reason it was considered worse was not necessarily that Judah's

16:47
x2Ki 21:9; Eze 5:7

16:48
yMt 10:15;
11:23-24

16:49
zGe 13:13

16:51
aJer 3:8-11

16:54
bEze 14:22

16:57
c2Ki 16:6

16:58
dEze 23:49

16:60
eJer 32:40

16:62
fEze 20:37, 43-44

16:63
gRo 3:19

17:2
hEze 20:49

17:3
iJer 22:23

17:5
jDt 8:7-9; Isa 44:4

their detestable practices, but in all your ways you soon became more depraved than they. x ⁴⁸As surely as I live, declares the Sovereign LORD, your sister Sodom and her daughters never did what you and your daughters have done. y

⁴⁹"'Now this was the sin of your sister Sodom: z She and her daughters were arrogant, overfed and unconcerned; they did not help the poor and needy. ⁵⁰They were haughty and did detestable things before me. Therefore I did away with them as you have seen. ⁵¹Samaria did not commit half the sins you did. You have done more detestable things than they, and have made your sisters seem righteous by all these things you have done. a ⁵²Bear your disgrace, for you have furnished some justification for your sisters. Because your sins were more vile than theirs, they appear more righteous than you. So then, be ashamed and bear your disgrace, for you have made your sisters appear righteous.

⁵³"However, I will restore the fortunes of Sodom and her daughters and of Samaria and her daughters, and your fortunes along with them, ⁵⁴so that you may bear your disgrace b and be ashamed of all you have done in giving them comfort. ⁵⁵And your sisters, Sodom with her daughters and Samaria with her daughters, will return to what they were before; and you and your daughters will return to what you were before. ⁵⁶You would not even mention your sister Sodom in the day of your pride, ⁵⁷before your wickedness was uncovered. Even so, you are now scorned by the daughters of Edom a c and all her neighbors and the daughters of the Philistines—all those around you who despise you. ⁵⁸You will bear the consequences of your lewdness and your detestable practices, declares the LORD. d

⁵⁹"'This is what the Sovereign LORD says: I will deal with you as you deserve, because you have despised my oath by breaking the covenant. ⁶⁰Yet I will remember the covenant I made with you in the days of your youth, and I will establish an everlasting covenant e with you. ⁶¹Then you will remember your ways and be ashamed when you receive your sisters, both those who are older than you and those who are younger. I will give them to you as daughters, but not on the basis of my covenant with you. ⁶²So I will establish my covenant with you, and you will know that I am the LORD. f ⁶³Then, when I make atonement for you for all you have done, you will remember and be ashamed and never again open your mouth g because of your humiliation, declares the Sovereign LORD.'"

Two Eagles and a Vine

17 The word of the LORD came to me: ²"Son of man, set forth an allegory and tell the house of Israel a parable. h ³Say to them, 'This is what the Sovereign LORD says: A great eagle with powerful wings, long feathers and full plumage of varied colors came to Lebanon. i Taking hold of the top of a cedar, ⁴he broke off its topmost shoot and carried it away to a land of merchants, where he planted it in a city of traders.

⁵"'He took some of the seed of your land and put it in fertile soil. He planted it like a willow by abundant water, j ⁶and it sprouted and became a low, spreading vine. Its branches turned toward him, but its roots remained under it. So it became a vine and produced branches and put out leafy boughs.

a57 Many Hebrew manuscripts and Syriac; most Hebrew manuscripts, Septuagint and Vulgate *Aram*

---

sins were worse, but that Judah knew better. In that light, we who live in an age when God's message is made clear to us through the Bible are worse than Judah if we continue in sin! (See also Matthew 11:20–24.)

16:49 It is easy to judge and condemn Sodom, especially for its terrible sexual sins. Ezekiel reminded Judah, however, that Sodom was destroyed because its people were arrogant, overfed, and unconcerned about the needy people within their reach. It is easy to be selective in what we consider gross sin. If we do not commit such horrible sins as adultery, homosexuality, stealing, and murder, we may think we are living good enough lives. But what about sins like arrogance, gluttony, and indifference to the needy? These sins may not be as shocking to you as the others, but they are also forbidden by God.

16:59–63 Although the people had broken their promises and did not deserve anything but punishment, God would not break his promises. If the people turned back to him, he would again forgive them and renew his covenant. This covenant was put into effect when Jesus paid for the sins of all mankind by his death on the cross (Hebrews 10:8–10). No one is beyond the reach of

God's forgiveness. Although we don't deserve anything but punishment for our sins, God's arms are still outstretched. He will not break his promise to give us salvation and forgiveness if we repent and turn to him.

17:1ff The first eagle in this chapter represents King Nebuchadnezzar of Babylon (see 17:12), who appointed or "planted" Zedekiah as king in Jerusalem. Zedekiah rebelled against this arrangement and tried to ally with Egypt, the second eagle, to battle against Babylon. This took place while Ezekiel, miles away in Babylon, was describing these events (explained in verses 10–21). Jeremiah, a prophet in Judah, was also warning Zedekiah not to form this alliance (Jeremiah 2:36, 37). Although many miles apart, the prophets had the same message because both spoke for God. God still directs his chosen spokesmen to speak his truth all around the world.

⁷"'But there was another great eagle with powerful wings and full plumage. The vine now sent out its roots toward him from the plot where it was planted and stretched out its branches to him for water. ⁸It had been planted in good soil by abundant water so that it would produce branches, bear fruit and become a splendid vine.'

⁹"Say to them, 'This is what the Sovereign LORD says: Will it thrive? Will it not be up-rooted and stripped of its fruit so that it withers? All its new growth will wither. It will not take a strong arm or many people to pull it up by the roots. ¹⁰Even if itᵏ is transplanted, will it thrive? Will it not wither completely when the east wind strikes it—wither away in the plot where it grew?'"

¹¹Then the word of the LORD came to me: ¹²"Say to this rebellious house, 'Do you not know what these things mean?ˡ' Say to them: 'The king of Babylon went to Jerusalem and carried off her king and her nobles, bringing them back with him to Babylon. ¹³Then he took a member of the royal family and made a treaty with him, putting him under oath.ᵐ He also carried away the leading men of the land, ¹⁴so that the kingdom would be brought low,ⁿ unable to rise again, surviving only by keeping his treaty. ¹⁵But the king rebelled against him by sending his envoys to Egypt to get horses and a large army. Will he succeed? Will he who does such things escape? Will he break the treaty and yet escape?

¹⁶"'As surely as I live, declares the Sovereign LORD, he shall dieᵒ in Babylon, in the land of the king who put him on the throne, whose oath he despised and whose treaty he broke. ¹⁷Pharaohᵖ with his mighty army and great horde will be of no help to him in war, when ramps are built and siege works erected to destroy many lives.�q ¹⁸He despised the oath by breaking the covenant. Because he had given his hand in pledgeʳ and yet did all these things, he shall not escape.

¹⁹"'Therefore this is what the Sovereign LORD says: As surely as I live, I will bring down on his head my oath that he despised and my covenant that he broke. ²⁰I will spread my netˢ for him, and he will be caught in my snare. I will bring him to Babylon and execute judgmentᵗ upon him there because he was unfaithful to me. ²¹All his fleeing troops will fall by the sword,ᵘ and the survivors will be scattered to the winds. Then you will know that I the LORD have spoken.

²²"'This is what the Sovereign LORD says: I myself will take a shoot from the very top of a cedar and plant it; I will break off a tender sprig from its topmost shoots and plant it on a high and lofty mountain.ᵛ ²³On the mountain heights of Israel I will plant it; it will produce branches and bear fruit and become a splendid cedar. Birds of every kind will nest in it; they will find shelter in the shade of its branches. ²⁴All the trees of the fieldʷ will know that I the LORD bring down the tall tree and make the low tree grow tall. I dry up the green tree and make the dry tree flourish.

"'I the LORD have spoken, and I will do it.'"

The Soul Who Sins Will Die

18 The word of the LORD came to me: ²"What do you people mean by quoting this proverb about the land of Israel:

"'The fathers eat sour grapes,
    and the children's teeth are set on edge'?ˣ

17:10   ᵏHos 13:15

17:12   ˡEze 12:9

17:13   ᵐ2Ch 36:13

17:14   ⁿEze 29:14

17:16   ᵒEze 12:13

17:17   ᵖJer 37:7
   qEze 29:6-7

17:18   ʳ1Ch 29:24

17:20   ˢEze 12:13
   ᵗEze 20:36

17:21   ᵘEze 12:14

17:22   ᵛJer 23:5

17:24   ʷPs 96:12

18:2   ˣJer 31:29

17:10 This east wind was the hot, dry wind blowing off the desert, a wind that could wither a flourishing crop. The hot wind of Nebuchadnezzar's armies was about to overcome the nation of Judah.

17:22, 23 Ezekiel's prophecy of judgment ends in hope. When the people put their hope in foreign alliances, they were disappointed. Only God could give them true hope. God said he would plant a tender sprig, the Messiah, whose kingdom would grow and become a shelter for all who come to him (see Isaiah 11:1–5). This prophecy was fulfilled at the coming of Jesus Christ.

18:1ff The people of Judah believed they were being punished for the sins of their ancestors, not their own. They thought this way because this was the teaching of the Ten Commandments

(Exodus 20:5). Instead, Ezekiel taught that the destruction of Jerusalem was due to the spiritual decay in previous generations. But this belief in the corporate life of Israel led to fatalism and irresponsibility. So Ezekiel gave God's new policy for this new land because the people had misconstrued the old one. God judges each person individually. Although we often suffer from the effects of sins committed by those who came before us, God does not punish us for someone else's sins, and we can't use their mistakes as an excuse for our sins. Each person is accountable to God for his or her actions.

In addition, some people of Judah used the corporate umbrella of God's blessing as an excuse for disobeying God. They thought that because of their righteous ancestors (18:5–9) they would live. God told them that they would not; they were the evil sons of righteous parents and, as such, would die (18:10–13). If, however, anyone returned to God, he or she would live (18:14–18).

³"As surely as I live, declares the Sovereign Lᴏʀᴅ, you will no longer quote this proverb in Israel. ⁴For every living soul belongs to me, the father as well as the son—both alike belong to me. The soul who sins is the one who will die. ʸ

18:4
ʸ Ro 6:23

⁵ "Suppose there is a righteous man
　　who does what is just and right.
⁶ He does not eat at the mountain ᶻ shrines
　　or look to the idols of the house of Israel.
He does not defile his neighbor's wife
　　or lie with a woman during her period.
⁷ He does not oppress ᵃ anyone,
　　but returns what he took in pledge ᵇ for a loan.
He does not commit robbery
　　but gives his food to the hungry
　　and provides clothing for the naked.
⁸ He does not lend at usury
　　or take excessive interest. ᵃ ᶜ
He withholds his hand from doing wrong
　　and judges fairly ᵈ between man and man.
⁹ He follows my decrees
　　and faithfully keeps my laws.
That man is righteous;
　　he will surely live, ᵉ

18:6
ᶻ Eze 22:9

18:7
ᵃ Ex 22:21
ᵇ Dt 24:12

18:8
ᶜ Ex 22:25;
Lev 25:35-37;
Dt 23:19-20
ᵈ Zec 8:16

18:9
ᵉ Am 5:4

　　　　　　　　　　　　　　　　　　declares the Sovereign Lᴏʀᴅ.

¹⁰"Suppose he has a violent son, who sheds blood or does any of these other things ᵇ ¹¹(though the father has done none of them):

"He eats at the mountain shrines.
He defiles his neighbor's wife.
¹² He oppresses the poor ᶠ and needy.
He commits robbery.
He does not return what he took in pledge.
He looks to the idols.
He does detestable things. ᵍ
¹³ He lends at usury and takes excessive interest.

18:12
ᶠ Am 4:1
ᵍ Isa 59:6-7;
Eze 8:6, 17

Will such a man live? He will not! Because he has done all these detestable things, he will surely be put to death and his blood will be on his own head.

¹⁴"But suppose this son has a son who sees all the sins his father commits, and though he sees them, he does not do such things:

¹⁵ "He does not eat at the mountain shrines
　　or look to the idols of the house of Israel.
He does not defile his neighbor's wife.
¹⁶ He does not oppress anyone
　　or require a pledge for a loan.
He does not commit robbery
　　but gives his food to the hungry
　　and provides clothing for the naked.
¹⁷ He withholds his hand from sin ᶜ
　　and takes no usury or excessive interest.
He keeps my laws and follows my decrees.

ᵃ 8 Or *take interest*; similarly in verses 13 and 17　ᵇ 10 Or *things to a brother*　ᶜ 17 Septuagint (see also verse 8); Hebrew *from the poor*

18:8 The Law of Moses had rules about charging interest (Exodus 22:25; Leviticus 25:36; Deuteronomy 23:19, 20) to prevent God's people from taking advantage of the poor or of fellow Israelites.

18:12 Returning what one took in pledge referred to the lender letting the debtor use the cloak each night that he has placed as

security on his loan. Without the cloak, the debtor would be cold at night. (See Exodus 22:26 and Deuteronomy 24:10–13 for the giving of this law.)

He will not die for his father's sin; he will surely live. [18]But his father will die for his own sin, because he practiced extortion, robbed his brother and did what was wrong among his people.

[19]"Yet you ask, 'Why does the son not share the guilt of his father?' Since the son has done what is just and right and has been careful to keep all my decrees, he will surely live. [h] [20]The soul who sins is the one who will die. The son will not share the guilt of the father, nor will the father share the guilt of the son. The righteousness of the righteous man will be credited to him, and the wickedness of the wicked will be charged against him. [i]

[21]"But if a wicked man turns away from all the sins he has committed and keeps all my decrees and does what is just and right, he will surely live; he will not die. [j] [22]None of the offenses he has committed will be remembered against him. Because of the righteous things he has done, he will live. [k] [23]Do I take any pleasure in the death of the wicked? declares the Sovereign LORD. Rather, am I not pleased when they turn from their ways and live? [l]

[24]"But if a righteous man turns from his righteousness and commits sin and does the same detestable things the wicked man does, will he live? None of the righteous things he has done will be remembered. Because of the unfaithfulness he is guilty of and because of the sins he has committed, he will die. [m]

[25]"Yet you say, 'The way of the Lord is not just.' Hear, O house of Israel: Is my way unjust? [n] Is it not your ways that are unjust? [26]If a righteous man turns from his righteousness and commits sin, he will die for it; because of the sin he has committed he will die. [27]But if a wicked man turns away from the wickedness he has committed and does what is just and right, he will save his life. [28]Because he considers all the offenses he has committed and turns away from them, he will surely live; he will not die. [29]Yet the house of Israel says, 'The way of the Lord is not just.' Are my ways unjust, O house of Israel? Is it not your ways that are unjust?

[30]"Therefore, O house of Israel, I will judge you, each one according to his ways, declares the Sovereign LORD. Repent! Turn away from all your offenses; then sin will not be your downfall. [o] [31]Rid yourselves of all the offenses you have committed, and get a new heart and a new spirit. Why will you die, O house of Israel? [p] [32]For I take no pleasure in the death of anyone, declares the Sovereign LORD. Repent and live!

A Lament for Israel's Princes

19 "Take up a lament concerning the princes of Israel [2]and say:

> "'What a lioness was your mother
> among the lions!
> She lay down among the young lions
> and reared her cubs.
> [3] She brought up one of her cubs,
> and he became a strong lion.
> He learned to tear the prey
> and he devoured men.
> [4] The nations heard about him,
> and he was trapped in their pit.
> They led him with hooks
> to the land of Egypt. [q]

18:19
[h] Ex 20:5

18:20
[i] Dt 24:16; Isa 3:11;
Ro 2:9

18:21
[j] Eze 33:12, 19

18:22
[k] Ps 18:20-24

18:23
[l] Eze 33:11

18:24
[m] Eze 3:20

18:25
[n] Eze 33:17

18:30
[o] Eze 7:3

18:31
[p] Eze 11:19; 36:26

19:4
[q] 2Ki 23:33-34;
2Ch 36:4

18:23 God is perfect love, but he also dispenses perfect justice. His perfect love causes him to be merciful to those who recognize their sin and turn back to him, but he cannot overlook those who willfully sin. Wicked people die both physically and spiritually. God takes no joy in their deaths; he would prefer that they turn to him and have eternal life. Likewise, we should not rejoice in the misfortunes of nonbelievers. Instead, we should do all in our power to bring them to faith.

18:25 A typical childish response to punishment is to say, "That isn't fair!" In reality, God is fair, but *we* have broken the rules. It is not God who must live up to our ideas of fairness; instead, we must live up to his. Don't spend your time looking for the loopholes in God's law. Instead, live up to God's standards.

18:30–32 Ezekiel's solution to the problem of inherited guilt is for each person to have a changed life. This is God's work in us and not something we can do for ourselves. The Holy Spirit does

it (Psalm 51:10–12). If we renounce our life's direction of sin and rebellion and turn to God, he will give us a new direction, a new love, and a new power to change. You can begin by faith, trusting in God's power to change your heart and mind. Then determine to live each day with him in control (Ephesians 4:22–24).

19:1ff Ezekiel used illustrations to communicate many of his messages. With the picture of the lioness and her cubs, he raised the curiosity of his listeners. The lioness symbolized the nation of Judah, and the two cubs were two of its kings. The first cub was King Jehoahaz, who had been taken captive to Egypt in 609 B.C. by Pharaoh Neco (2 Kings 23:31–33). The second cub was either King Jehoiachin, who had already been taken into captivity in Babylon (2 Kings 24:8ff), or King Zedekiah, who soon would be taken (2 Kings 25:7). This illustration showed that for Judah, there was no hope for a quick return from exile, and no escape from the approaching Babylonian armies.

5 "'When she saw her hope unfulfilled,
 her expectation gone,
 she took another of her cubs
 and made him a strong lion.
6 He prowled among the lions,
 for he was now a strong lion.
 He learned to tear the prey
 and he devoured men.
7 He broke down[a] their strongholds
 and devastated their towns.
 The land and all who were in it
 were terrified by his roaring.

19:8
r 2Ki 24:2

8 Then the nations[r] came against him,
 those from regions round about.
 They spread their net for him,
 and he was trapped in their pit.

19:9
s 2Ch 36:6

9 With hooks they pulled him into a cage
 and brought him to the king of Babylon.[s]
 They put him in prison,
 so his roar was heard no longer
 on the mountains of Israel.

10 "'Your mother was like a vine in your vineyard[b]
 planted by the water;
 it was fruitful and full of branches
 because of abundant water.

19:11
t Eze 31:3

11 Its branches were strong,
 fit for a ruler's scepter.
 It towered high
 above the thick foliage,
 conspicuous for its height
 and for its many branches.[t]

19:12
u Eze 17:10
v Hos 13:15

12 But it was uprooted[u] in fury
 and thrown to the ground.
 The east wind made it shrivel,
 it was stripped of its fruit;
 its strong branches withered
 and fire consumed them.[v]
13 Now it is planted in the desert,
 in a dry and thirsty land.

19:14
w Eze 15:4

14 Fire spread from one of its main[c] branches
 and consumed its fruit.
 No strong branch is left on it
 fit for a ruler's scepter.'[w]

This is a lament and is to be used as a lament."

Rebellious Israel

20:1
x Eze 8:1

20 In the seventh year, in the fifth month on the tenth day, some of the elders of Israel came to inquire of the LORD, and they sat down in front of me.[x]
2 Then the word of the LORD came to me: 3 "Son of man, speak to the elders of Israel and

---

a 7 Targum (see Septuagint); Hebrew *He knew*   *b* 10 Two Hebrew manuscripts; most Hebrew manuscripts *your blood*
c 14 Or *from under its*

19:11, 12 Not even the political and military might of Judah's kings could save the nation. Like branches of a vine, they would be cut off and uprooted by "the east wind"—the powerful Babylonian army.

20:1ff Here Ezekiel gives a panoramic view of Israel's history of rebellion. The emphasis is on God's attempts to bring the nation back to himself and on God's mercy for his constantly rebellious

and disobedient people. Ezekiel gives the message that the people alone are responsible for the troubles and judgments they have experienced. Those who persist in rebellion God will "purge" (20:38), while he will bring the faithful "into the land of Israel, the land I had sworn with uplifted hand to give to your fathers." The reason: that "you will know that I am the LORD" (20:42).

say to them, 'This is what the Sovereign LORD says: Have you come to inquire *y* of me? As surely as I live, I will not let you inquire of me, declares the Sovereign LORD.'

⁴"Will you judge them? Will you judge them, son of man? Then confront them with the detestable practices of their fathers *z* ⁵and say to them: 'This is what the Sovereign LORD says: On the day I chose Israel, I swore with uplifted hand to the descendants of the house of Jacob and revealed myself to them in Egypt. With uplifted hand I said to them, "I am the LORD your God. *a*" ⁶On that day I swore to them that I would bring them out of Egypt into a land I had searched out for them, a land flowing with milk and honey,*b* the most beautiful of all lands.*c* ⁷And I said to them, "Each of you, get rid of the vile images you have set your eyes on, and do not defile yourselves with the idols of Egypt. I am the LORD your God. *d*"

⁸"'But they rebelled against me and would not listen to me; they did not get rid of the vile images they had set their eyes on, nor did they forsake the idols of Egypt. *e* So I said I would pour out my wrath on them and spend my anger against them in Egypt. ⁹But for the sake of my name I did what would keep it from being profaned in the eyes of the nations they lived among and in whose sight I had revealed myself to the Israelites by bringing them out of Egypt. *f* ¹⁰Therefore I led them out of Egypt and brought them into the desert. ¹¹I gave them my decrees and made known to them my laws, for the man who obeys them will live by them. *g* ¹²Also I gave them my Sabbaths as a sign between us, so they would know that I the LORD made them holy.

¹³"'Yet the people of Israel rebelled *h* against me in the desert. They did not follow my decrees but rejected my laws—although the man who obeys them will live by them—and they utterly desecrated my Sabbaths. So I said I would pour out my wrath on them and destroy them in the desert. ¹⁴But for the sake of my name I did what would keep it from being profaned in the eyes of the nations in whose sight I had brought them out. ¹⁵Also with uplifted hand I swore to them in the desert that I would not bring them into the land I had given them—a land flowing with milk and honey, most beautiful of all lands *i*— ¹⁶because they rejected my laws and did not follow my decrees and desecrated my Sabbaths. For their hearts were devoted to their idols. *j* ¹⁷Yet I looked on them with pity and did not destroy them or put an end to them in the desert. ¹⁸I said to their children in the desert, "Do not follow the statutes of your fathers or keep their laws or defile yourselves with their idols. ¹⁹I am the LORD your God; follow my decrees and be careful to keep my laws. *k* ²⁰Keep my Sabbaths holy, that they may be a sign between us. Then you will know that I am the LORD your God."

²¹"'But the children rebelled against me: They did not follow my decrees, they were not careful to keep my laws—although the man who obeys them will live by them—and they desecrated my Sabbaths. So I said I would pour out my wrath on them and spend my anger against them in the desert. ²²But I withheld *l* my hand, and for the sake of my name I did what would keep it from being profaned in the eyes of the nations in whose sight I had brought them out. ²³Also with uplifted hand I swore to them in the desert that I would disperse them among the nations and scatter *m* them through the countries, ²⁴because they had not obeyed my laws but had rejected my decrees and desecrated my Sabbaths, and their eyes ⌊lusted⌋ after *n* their fathers' idols. ²⁵I also gave them over *o* to statutes that were not good and laws they could not live by; ²⁶I let them become defiled through their gifts—the sacrifice of every firstborn *a*—that I might fill them with horror so they would know that I am the LORD.'

a 26 Or *—making every firstborn pass through* ⌊*the fire*⌋

Cross references

20:3 *y* Eze 14:3

20:4 *z* Eze 16:2; 22:2

20:5 *a* Ex 6:7

20:6 *b* Ex 3:8; Jer 32:22 *c* Dt 8:7; Ps 48:2

20:7 *d* Dt 29:18

20:8 *e* Eze 7:8

20:9 *f* Eze 36:22

20:11 *g* Lev 18:5

20:13 *h* Ps 78:40

20:15 *i* Ps 95:11

20:16 *j* Am 5:26

20:19 *k* Dt 5:32-33

20:22 *l* Ps 78:38

20:23 *m* Lev 26:33; Dt 28:64

20:24 *n* Eze 6:9

20:25 *o* Ps 81:12

20:12, 13 The Sabbath, instituted by God at creation, was entrusted to Israel as a sign that God had created and redeemed them (Exodus 20:8–11; Deuteronomy 5:12–15). This day of rest was a gift from a loving God, not a difficult obligation. But the people repeatedly desecrated the Sabbath and ignored their God (see also 20:20, 21). It was meant to be a memory device but they ignored it. Today, many Christians celebrate the Lord's Day, Sunday, as their Sabbath. Whatever the day, we must be careful to fulfill God's purpose for the Sabbath. He wants us to rest, to refocus, and to remember him.

20:23, 24 At the very beginning of Israel's history, God clearly warned the people about the consequences of disobedience (Deuteronomy 28:15ff). When the people disobeyed, God let

them experience those devastating consequences to remind them of the seriousness of their sins. If you choose to live for yourself, apart from God, you may experience similar destructive consequences. Even through such consequences, however, God may be drawing you to himself. Let your misfortunes bring you to your senses and to the merciful God before it is too late.

20:25 Why would God give them laws that weren't good? This isn't talking about any aspect of the Law of Moses—Ezekiel reinforces that law (20:11, 13, 21). Evidently the Jews had taken Exodus 13:12 and 22:29, the dedication of firstborn animals and children, as a justification for child sacrifice to the Canaanite god Molech. God gave them over to this delusion to get them to acknowledge him, to jar their consciences, and to revitalize their faith (20:26).

20:27
p Ro 2:24
20:28
q Eze 6:13

27 "Therefore, son of man, speak to the people of Israel and say to them, 'This is what the Sovereign LORD says: In this also your fathers blasphemed p me by forsaking me: 28 When I brought them into the land I had sworn to give them and they saw any high hill or any leafy tree, there they offered their sacrifices, made offerings that provoked me to anger, presented their fragrant incense and poured out their drink offerings. q 29 Then I said to them: What is this high place you go to?'" (It is called Bamah a to this day.)

Judgment and Restoration

20:30
r Jer 16:12
20:31
s Eze 16:20
t Ps 106:37-39

30 "Therefore say to the house of Israel: 'This is what the Sovereign LORD says: Will you defile yourselves the way your fathers did and lust after their vile images? r 31 When you offer your gifts—the sacrifice of your sons s in b the fire—you continue to defile yourselves with all your idols to this day. Am I to let you inquire of me, O house of Israel? As surely as I live, declares the Sovereign LORD, I will not let you inquire of me. t

20:33
u Jer 21:5
20:34
v Jer 44:6

32 "'You say, "We want to be like the nations, like the peoples of the world, who serve wood and stone." But what you have in mind will never happen. 33 As surely as I live, declares the Sovereign LORD, I will rule over you with a mighty hand and an outstretched arm and with outpoured wrath. u 34 I will bring you from the nations and gather you from the countries where you have been scattered—with a mighty hand and an outstretched arm and with outpoured wrath. v 35 I will bring you into the desert of the nations and there, face to face, I will execute judgment upon you. 36 As I judged your fathers in the desert of the land of Egypt, so I will judge you, declares the Sovereign LORD. 37 I will take note of you as you pass under my rod, w and I will bring you into the bond of the covenant. 38 I will purge x you of those who revolt and rebel against me. Although I will bring them out of the land where they are living, yet they will not enter the land of Israel. Then you will know that I am the LORD.

20:37
w Lev 27:32;
Jer 33:13
20:38
x Eze 34:17-22
20:39
y Isa 1:13
20:40
z Isa 60:7
a Isa 56:7

39 "'As for you, O house of Israel, this is what the Sovereign LORD says: Go and serve your idols, every one of you! But afterward you will surely listen to me and no longer profane my holy name with your gifts and idols. y 40 For on my holy mountain, the high mountain of Israel, declares the Sovereign LORD, there in the land the entire house of Israel will serve me, and there I will accept them. There I will require your offerings z and your choice gifts, c along with all your holy sacrifices. a 41 I will accept you as fragrant incense when I bring you out from the nations and gather you from the countries where you have been scattered, and I will show myself holy among you in the sight of the nations. 42 Then you will know that I am the LORD, when I bring you into the land of Israel, b the land I had sworn with uplifted hand to give to your fathers. 43 There you will remember your conduct and all the actions by which you have defiled yourselves, and you will loathe yourselves for all the evil you have done. c 44 You will know that I am the LORD, when I deal with you for my name's sake d and not according to your evil ways and your corrupt practices, O house of Israel, declares the Sovereign LORD. e'"

20:42
b Eze 34:13
20:43
c Eze 16:61;
Hos 5:15
20:44
d Eze 36:22
e Eze 24:24

Prophecy Against the South

20:46
f Eze 21:2

45 The word of the LORD came to me: 46 "Son of man, set your face toward the south; preach against the south and prophesy against f the forest of the southland. 47 Say to the southern forest: 'Hear the word of the LORD. This is what the Sovereign LORD says: I am about to set fire to you, and it will consume all your trees, both green and dry. The blazing

a 29 Bamah means *high place.*   b 31 Or *—making your sons pass through*   c 40 Or *and the gifts of your firstfruits*

20:35, 36 When the Israelites disobeyed God by refusing to enter the promised land the first time, God chose to purify his people by forcing them to wander in the desert until that entire generation died (Numbers 14:26–35). Here he promised to purge the nation of its rebellious people again as they cross the vast desert from their captivity in Babylon. Only those who faithfully followed God would be able to return to their land. The purpose of this desert judgment would be to purge all those who worship idols and to restore all those faithful to God.

20:39 The Israelites were worshiping idols and giving gifts to God at the same time! They did not believe in their God as the one true God; instead, they worshiped him along with the other gods of the land. Perhaps they enjoyed the immoral pleasures of idol worship; or perhaps they didn't want to miss out on the benefits the idols might give them. Often people believe in God

and give him gifts of church attendance or service, while still holding on to their idols of money, power, or pleasure, not wanting to miss out on any possible benefits. But God wants all of our lives and all of our devotion; he will not share it because devotion to anything else is idol worship. Beware of trying to keep God pleased while you also pursue the pleasures of sin. You must choose one or the other.

20:45–47 "Toward the south" refers to Jerusalem and Judah. "The southland" is the region of the Negev, which is compared to a forest about to be destroyed by fire.

flame will not be quenched, and every face from south to north will be scorched by it. *g* **20:47**
g Jer 21:14
48 Everyone will see that I the LORD have kindled it; it will not be quenched. *h*'"

20:48
h Jer 7:20
49 Then I said, "Ah, Sovereign LORD! They are saying of me, 'Isn't he just telling parables?'"

Babylon, God's Sword of Judgment

21 The word of the LORD came to me: 2 "Son of man, set your face against Jerusalem and preach against the sanctuary. Prophesy against *i* the land of Israel 3 and say to her: 'This is what the LORD says: I am against you. I will draw my sword from its scabbard and cut off from you both the righteous and the wicked. 4 Because I am going to cut off the righteous and the wicked, my sword will be unsheathed against everyone from south to north. *j* 5 Then all people will know that I the LORD have drawn my sword from its scabbard; it will not return again.'

21:2
i Eze 20:46

21:4
j Eze 20:47

6 "Therefore groan, son of man! Groan before them with broken heart and bitter grief. *k* 7 And when they ask you, 'Why are you groaning?' you shall say, 'Because of the news that is coming. Every heart will melt and every hand go limp; *l* every spirit will become faint and every knee become as weak as water.' It is coming! It will surely take place, declares the Sovereign LORD."

21:6
k Isa 22:4
21:7
l Eze 7:17

8 The word of the LORD came to me: 9 "Son of man, prophesy and say, 'This is what the Lord says:

"'A sword, a sword,
    sharpened and polished—
10 sharpened for the slaughter, *m*
    polished to flash like lightning!

21:10
m Isa 34:5-6

"'Shall we rejoice in the scepter of my son ⌊Judah⌋? The sword despises every such stick.

11 "'The sword is appointed to be polished,
    to be grasped with the hand;
it is sharpened and polished,
    made ready for the hand of the slayer.
12 Cry out and wail, son of man,
    for it is against my people;
    it is against all the princes of Israel.
They are thrown to the sword
    along with my people.
Therefore beat your breast. *n*

21:12
n Jer 31:19

13 "'Testing will surely come. And what if the scepter ⌊of Judah⌋, which the sword despises, does not continue? declares the Sovereign LORD.'

14 "So then, son of man, prophesy
    and strike your hands *o* together.
Let the sword strike twice,
    even three times.
It is a sword for slaughter—
    a sword for great slaughter,
    closing in on them from every side.
15 So that hearts may melt
    and the fallen be many,
I have stationed the sword for slaughter*a*
    at all their gates.

21:14
o Nu 24:10

a 15 Septuagint; the meaning of the Hebrew for this word is uncertain.

20:49 Ezekiel was exasperated and discouraged. Many Israelites were complaining that he spoke only in riddles ("parables"), so they refused to listen. No matter how important our work or how significant our ministry, we will have moments of discouragement. Apparently God did not answer Ezekiel's plea; instead, he gave Ezekiel another message to proclaim. What has been discouraging you? Have you felt like giving up? Instead, continue doing what God has told you to do. He promises to reward the faithful (Mark 13:13). God's cure for discouragement may be another assignment. In serving others, we may find the renewal we need.

21:1ff The short message in 20:45–48 introduces the first of three messages about the judgments that would come upon Jerusalem: (1) the sword of the Lord (21:1–7); (2) the sharpened sword (21:8–17); (3) the sword of Nebuchadnezzar (21:18–22). The city would be destroyed because it was defiled. According to Jewish law, defiled objects were to be passed through fire in order to purify them (see Numbers 31:22, 23; Psalm 66:10–12; Proverbs 17:3). God's judgment is designed to purify; destruction is often a necessary part of that process.

21:12 Beating the breast was a gesture of grief.

Oh! It is made to flash like lightning,
    it is grasped for slaughter.
16 O sword, slash to the right,
    then to the left,
    wherever your blade is turned.
17 I too will strike my hands[p] together,
    and my wrath will subside.
I the Lord have spoken."

18 The word of the Lord came to me: 19 "Son of man, mark out two roads for the sword of the king of Babylon to take, both starting from the same country. Make a signpost where the road branches off to the city. 20 Mark out one road for the sword to come against Rabbah of the Ammonites[q] and another against Judah and fortified Jerusalem. 21 For the king of Babylon will stop at the fork in the road, at the junction of the two roads, to seek an omen: He will cast lots[r] with arrows, he will consult his idols, he will examine the liver.[s] 22 Into his right hand will come the lot for Jerusalem, where he is to set up battering rams, to give the command to slaughter, to sound the battle cry, to set battering rams against the gates, to build a ramp and to erect siege works.[t] 23 It will seem like a false omen to those who have sworn allegiance to him, but he will remind them of their guilt and take them captive.

24 "Therefore this is what the Sovereign Lord says: 'Because you people have brought to mind your guilt by your open rebellion, revealing your sins in all that you do—because you have done this, you will be taken captive.

25 "'O profane and wicked prince of Israel, whose day has come, whose time of punishment has reached its climax, 26 this is what the Sovereign Lord says: Take off the turban, remove the crown.[u] It will not be as it was: The lowly will be exalted and the exalted will be brought low. 27 A ruin! A ruin! I will make it a ruin! It will not be restored until he comes to whom it rightfully belongs; to him I will give it.'[v]

28 "And you, son of man, prophesy and say, 'This is what the Sovereign Lord says about the Ammonites and their insults:

"'A sword, a sword,
    drawn for the slaughter,
    polished to consume
    and to flash like lightning!
29 Despite false visions concerning you
    and lying divinations about you,
    it will be laid on the necks
    of the wicked who are to be slain,
    whose day has come,
    whose time of punishment has reached its climax.[w]
30 Return the sword to its scabbard.[x]
    In the place where you were created,
    in the land of your ancestry,
    I will judge you.
31 I will pour out my wrath upon you
    and breathe out my fiery anger[y] against you;
I will hand you over to brutal men,
    men skilled in destruction.

21:18–23 Ammon evidently rebelled against Babylon about the same time as King Zedekiah of Judah. In 589 B.C. the nations of Judah and Ammon were among those who conspired against Babylon (Jeremiah 27:3). Ezekiel gave this message to the exiles who had heard the news and were again filled with hope of returning to their homeland. Ezekiel said that Babylon's king would march his armies into the region to stop the rebellion. Traveling from the north, he would stop at a fork in the road, one leading to Rabbah, the capital of Ammon, and the other leading to Jerusalem, the capital of Judah. He had to decide which city to destroy. Just as Ezekiel predicted, King Nebuchadnezzar went to Jerusalem and besieged it.

21:21 Nebuchadnezzar had three ways to get advice on the future. One was shaking the arrows, much like drawing straws, to see which course of action was right; the second was consulting an idol to see if some spirit might direct him; the third was having priests inspect the liver of a sacrificed animal to see if its shape and size would indicate a decision.

21:28 The Ammonites and Israelites were usually fighting with each other. God told the Israelites not to ally with foreign nations, but Judah and Ammon united against Babylon in 589 B.C. (Jeremiah 27:3). God first judged Judah when Nebuchadnezzar first went to Jerusalem (21:22); but Ammon will also be judged, not for allying with Judah, but for watching Jerusalem's destruction with insulting delight.

32 You will be fuel for the fire,
   your blood will be shed in your land,
you will be remembered^z no more;
   for I the LORD have spoken.'"

21:32
z Eze 25:10

Jerusalem's Sins

22 The word of the LORD came to me: 2 "Son of man, will you judge her? Will you judge this city of bloodshed?^a Then confront her with all her detestable practices 3 and say: 'This is what the Sovereign LORD says: O city that brings on herself doom by shedding blood in her midst and defiles herself by making idols, 4 you have become guilty because of the blood you have shed ^b and have become defiled by the idols you have made. You have brought your days to a close, and the end of your years has come. Therefore I will make you an object of scorn to the nations and a laughingstock to all the countries. 5 Those who are near and those who are far away will mock you, O infamous city, full of turmoil.

22:2
a Na 3:1

22:4
b 2Ki 21:16

6 "'See how each of the princes of Israel who are in you uses his power to shed blood.^c 7 In you they have treated father and mother with contempt;^d in you they have oppressed the alien and mistreated the fatherless and the widow.^e 8 You have despised my holy things and desecrated my Sabbaths. 9 In you are slanderous men bent on shedding blood; in you are those who eat at the mountain shrines and commit lewd acts. 10 In you are those who dishonor their fathers' bed; in you are those who violate women during their period, when they are ceremonially unclean.^f 11 In you one man commits a detestable offense with his neighbor's wife, another shamefully defiles his daughter-in-law,^g and another violates his sister, his own father's daughter. 12 In you men accept bribes to shed blood; you take usury and excessive interest^a and make unjust gain from your neighbors by extortion. And you have forgotten me, declares the Sovereign LORD.

22:6
c Isa 1:23
22:7
d Dt 27:16
e Ex 22:21-22
22:10
f Lev 18:8, 19
22:11
g Lev 18:15

13 "'I will surely strike my hands together at the unjust gain you have made and at the blood you have shed in your midst. 14 Will your courage endure or your hands be strong in the day I deal with you? I the LORD have spoken, and I will do it.^h 15 I will disperse you among the nations and scatterⁱ you through the countries; and I will put an end to your uncleanness.^j 16 When you have been defiled^b in the eyes of the nations, you will know that I am the LORD.'"

22:14
h Eze 21:7
22:15
i Dt 4:27
j Eze 23:27

17 Then the word of the LORD came to me: 18 "Son of man, the house of Israel has become dross^k to me; all of them are the copper, tin, iron and lead left inside a furnace. They are but the dross of silver.^l 19 Therefore this is what the Sovereign LORD says: 'Because you have all become dross, I will gather you into Jerusalem. 20 As men gather silver, copper, iron, lead and tin into a furnace to melt it with a fiery blast, so will I gather you in my anger and my wrath and put you inside the city and melt you. 21 I will gather you and I will blow on you with my fiery wrath, and you will be melted inside her. 22 As silver is melted in a furnace, so you will be melted inside her, and you will know that I the LORD have poured out my wrath upon you.'"^m

22:18
k Isa 1:22
l Jer 6:28-30
22:22
m Eze 20:8, 33

23 Again the word of the LORD came to me: 24 "Son of man, say to the land, 'You are a land that has had no rain or showers ^c in the day of wrath.' 25 There is a conspiracy of her princes^d within her like a roaring lion tearing its prey; they devour people,ⁿ take treasures and precious things and make many widows within her. 26 Her priests do violence to my law and profane my holy things; they do not distinguish between the holy and the common; they teach that there is no difference between the unclean and the clean;^o and they shut their

22:25
n Hos 6:9
22:26
o Lev 10:10

a 12 Or usury and interest   b 16 Or When I have allotted you your inheritance   c 24 Septuagint; Hebrew has not been cleansed or rained on   d 25 Septuagint; Hebrew prophets

---

22:1ff Chapter 22 explains why Jerusalem's judgment would come (22:2–16), how it would come (22:17–22), and who would be judged by it (22:23–31).

22:6–13 The leaders were especially responsible for the moral climate of the nation because God chose them to lead. The same is true today (see James 3:1). Unfortunately, many of the sins mentioned here have been committed in recent years by Christian leaders. We are living in a time of unprecedented attacks by Satan. We must uphold our leaders in prayer, and leaders must seek accountability to help them keep their moral and spiritual integrity.

22:17–22 Precious metals are refined with intense heat to remove the impurities. When heated, the dross (impurities) rises to the top of the molten metal and is skimmed off and thrown away. The purpose of the invasion of Jerusalem was to refine the people, but the refining process showed that the people, like worthless dross, had nothing good in them.

22:26 The priests were supposed to keep God's worship pure and teach the people right living. But the worship of God had become commonplace to them; they ignored the Sabbath, and they refused to teach the people. They no longer carried out their God-given duties (Leviticus 10:10, 11; Ezekiel 44:23). When doing God's work becomes no more important than any mundane task, we are no longer giving God the reverence he deserves. Instead of bringing God down to our level, we should live up to his level.

22:27
p Isa 1:23

22:28
q Eze 13:2, 6-7

22:29
r Ex 23:9

22:30
s Eze 13:5
t Ps 106:23; Jer 5:1

22:31
u Eze 9:10

eyes to the keeping of my Sabbaths, so that I am profaned among them. ²⁷Her officials within her are like wolves tearing their prey; they shed blood and kill people to make unjust gain. *p* ²⁸Her prophets whitewash these deeds for them by false visions and lying divinations. They say, 'This is what the Sovereign LORD says'—when the LORD has not spoken. *q* ²⁹The people of the land practice extortion and commit robbery; they oppress the poor and needy and mistreat the alien, *r* denying them justice.

³⁰"I looked for a man among them who would build up the wall *s* and stand before me in the gap on behalf of the land so I would not have to destroy it, but I found none. *t* ³¹So I will pour out my wrath on them and consume them with my fiery anger, bringing down on their own heads all they have done, declares the Sovereign LORD. *u*"

Two Adulterous Sisters

23 The word of the LORD came to me: ²"Son of man, there were two women, daughters of the same mother. ³They became prostitutes in Egypt, engaging in prostitution from their youth. In that land their breasts were fondled and their virgin bosoms caressed. ⁴The older was named Oholah, and her sister was Oholibah. They were mine and gave birth to sons and daughters. Oholah is Samaria, and Oholibah is Jerusalem.

23:5
v Hos 8:9

23:7
w Hos 5:3

23:8
x Ex 32:4

⁵"Oholah engaged in prostitution while she was still mine; and she lusted after her lovers, the Assyrians—warriors *v* ⁶clothed in blue, governors and commanders, all of them handsome young men, and mounted horsemen. ⁷She gave herself as a prostitute to all the elite of the Assyrians and defiled herself with all the idols of everyone she lusted after. *w* ⁸She did not give up the prostitution she began in Egypt, *x* when during her youth men slept with her, caressed her virgin bosom and poured out their lust upon her.

23:10
y Eze 16:36

⁹"Therefore I handed her over to her lovers, the Assyrians, for whom she lusted. ¹⁰They stripped her naked, took away her sons and daughters and killed her with the sword. She became a byword among women, and punishment was inflicted on her. *y*

23:11
z Jer 3:8-11

23:12
a 2Ki 16:7-15

23:14
b Eze 8:10

¹¹"Her sister Oholibah saw this, yet in her lust and prostitution she was more depraved than her sister. *z* ¹²She too lusted after the Assyrians—governors and commanders, warriors in full dress, mounted horsemen, all handsome young men. *a* ¹³I saw that she too defiled herself; both of them went the same way.

¹⁴"But she carried her prostitution still further. She saw men portrayed on a wall, *b* figures of Chaldeans*a* portrayed in red, ¹⁵with belts around their waists and flowing turbans on their heads; all of them looked like Babylonian chariot officers, natives of Chaldea. *b* ¹⁶As soon as she saw them, she lusted after them and sent messengers to them in Chaldea. ¹⁷Then the Babylonians came to her, to the bed of love, and in their lust they defiled her. After she had been defiled by them, she turned away from them in disgust. ¹⁸When she carried on her prostitution openly and exposed her nakedness, I turned away*c* from her in disgust, just as I

23:18
c Jer 6:8

a 14 Or *Babylonians*   *b 15* Or *Babylonia*; also in verse 16

22:30 The wall spoken of here is not made of stones, but of faithful people united in their efforts to resist evil. This wall was in disrepair because there was no one who could lead the people back to God. The feeble attempts to repair the gap—through religious rituals or messages based on opinion rather than God's will—were as worthless as whitewash, only covering the real problems. What the people really needed was total spiritual reconstruction! When we give the appearance of loving God without living his way, we are covering up sins that could eventually damage us beyond repair. Don't use religion as a whitewash; repair your life by applying the principles of God's Word. Then you can join with others to stand "in the gap" and make a difference for God in the world.

23:1ff Ezekiel continued his discussion of the reasons for God's judgment by telling a further allegory. He compared the northern and southern kingdoms to two sisters who became prostitutes. The proud citizens of Jerusalem had long scorned their sister city of Samaria, thinking that they of Jerusalem were superior. But God called both of these cities prostitutes—a shock to the people of Jerusalem who thought they were righteous. Just as the imagery of this message was shocking and distasteful to the people, so our sins are repugnant to God.

23:4–6 Oholah (meaning, "her tent"), the northern kingdom of Israel, was lured away from God by the dashing Assyrians—their

fashionable clothes and powerful positions. The people coveted youth, strength, power, wealth, and pleasure—the same qualities people think will bring happiness today. But the charming Assyrians drew Israel away from God.

23:11ff Oholibah (meaning, "my tent is in her") was shown to be worse because she did not learn from the judgment upon her sister, but continued in her lust for the Assyrians and Babylonians. Therefore, her judgment was equally certain. Just as Oholibah was privileged and should have known better, so we are privileged because we know about Christ. We need to be doubly sure that we follow him.

23:12 "She too lusted after the Assyrians" may mean excessively trying to please and probably refers to Ahaz paying protection money to Tiglath-Pileser III (2 Kings 16:7, 8).

23:16 An invitation to Chaldea (Babylon) was given by Hezekiah to the envoys from Babylon (2 Kings 20:12ff; Isaiah 38; 39).

23:17 At first, Judah made an alliance with Babylonia (Chaldea), but then changed its mind. During the reigns of the last two Judean kings, Jehoiakim and Zedekiah, Judah looked to Egypt for help. Judah's unfaithfulness (its alliances with godless nations) cost it the only real protection it ever had—God.

had turned away from her sister. [19]Yet she became more and more promiscuous as she recalled the days of her youth, when she was a prostitute in Egypt. [20]There she lusted after her lovers, whose genitals were like those of donkeys and whose emission was like that of horses. [21]So you longed for the lewdness of your youth, when in Egypt your bosom was caressed and your young breasts fondled. [a]

[22]"Therefore, Oholibah, this is what the Sovereign Lord says: I will stir up your lovers against you, those you turned away from in disgust, and I will bring them against you from every side— [23]the Babylonians and all the Chaldeans, the men of Pekod [e] and Shoa and Koa, and all the Assyrians with them, handsome young men, all of them governors and commanders, chariot officers and men of high rank, all mounted on horses. [24]They will come against you with weapons, [b] chariots and wagons and with a throng of people; they will take up positions against you on every side with large and small shields and with helmets. I will turn you over to them for punishment, [f] and they will punish you according to their standards. [25]I will direct my jealous anger against you, and they will deal with you in fury. They will cut off your noses and your ears, and those of you who are left will fall by the sword. They will take away your sons and daughters, [g] and those of you who are left will be consumed by fire. [26]They will also strip you of your clothes and take your fine jewelry. [h] [27]So I will put a stop [i] to the lewdness and prostitution you began in Egypt. You will not look on these things with longing or remember Egypt anymore.

[28]"For this is what the Sovereign Lord says: I am about to hand you over to those you hate, to those you turned away from in disgust. [29]They will deal with you in hatred and take away everything you have worked for. They will leave you naked and bare, and the shame of your prostitution will be exposed. Your lewdness and promiscuity [30]have brought this upon you, because you lusted after the nations and defiled yourself with their idols. [j] [31]You have gone the way of your sister; so I will put her cup into your hand.

[32]"This is what the Sovereign Lord says:

> "You will drink your sister's cup,
>   a cup large and deep;
> it will bring scorn and derision,
>   for it holds so much. [k]
> [33]You will be filled with drunkenness and sorrow,
>   the cup of ruin and desolation,
>   the cup of your sister Samaria.
> [34]You will drink it [l] and drain it dry;
>   you will dash it to pieces
>   and tear your breasts.

I have spoken, declares the Sovereign Lord.

[35]"Therefore this is what the Sovereign Lord says: Since you have forgotten [m] me and thrust me behind your back, [n] you must bear the consequences of your lewdness and prostitution."

[36]The Lord said to me: "Son of man, will you judge Oholah and Oholibah? Then confront them with their detestable practices, [o] [37]for they have committed adultery and blood is on their hands. They committed adultery with their idols; they even sacrificed their children, whom they bore to me, [c] as food for them. [38]They have also done this to me: At that same time they defiled my sanctuary and desecrated my Sabbaths. [39]On the very day they sacrificed their children to their idols, they entered my sanctuary and desecrated it. That is what they did in my house.

---

[a]21 Syriac (see also verse 3); Hebrew *caressed because of your young breasts*   [b]24 The meaning of the Hebrew for this word is uncertain.   [c]37 Or *even made the children they bore to me pass through* ⌊*the fire*⌋

23:22
[d]Eze 16:37

23:23
[e]Jer 50:21

23:24
[f]Jer 39:5-6

23:25
[g]ver 47

23:26
[h]Eze 16:39

23:27
[i]Eze 16:41

23:30
[j]Eze 6:9

23:32
[k]Isa 51:17;
Jer 25:15

23:34
[l]Isa 51:17

23:35
[m]Jer 3:21
[n]1Ki 14:9

23:36
[o]Isa 58:1

23:21 "Lewdness" is promiscuity (see also 23:27, 49)—giving sexual favors instead of being faithful to a spouse or to God. We don't think of ourselves as being spiritually promiscuous, but we often spend more time seeking advice from magazines, television commercials, and non-Christian experts than we do from God and his Word.

23:22–26 This predicts the last attack on Jerusalem that would destroy the city and bring to Babylonia the third wave of captives

in 586 B.C. (2 Kings 25; Jeremiah 52). The first attack came in 605 B.C., the second in 597 B.C. Pekod, Shoa, and Koa were Babylonian allies.

23:39 The Israelites went so far as to sacrifice their own children to idols and then to sacrifice to the Lord the same day. This made a mockery of worship. We cannot praise God and willfully sin at the same time. That would be like a person going to bed with a neighbor and then celebrating his or her wedding anniversary.

23:40
p 2Ki 9:30
q Jer 4:30

23:41
r Est 1:6; Am 6:4

23:45
s Eze 16:38

23:47
t 2Ch 36:19
u Eze 16:40-41

23:48
v 2Pe 2:6

24:2
w 2Ki 25:1; Jer 39:1;
52:4

24:3
x Eze 17:2
y Jer 1:13; Eze 11:3

24:6
z Eze 22:2

24:7
a Lev 17:13

40 "They even sent messengers for men who came from far away, and when they arrived you bathed yourself for them, painted your eyes p and put on your jewelry. q 41 You sat on an elegant couch, r with a table spread before it on which you had placed the incense and oil that belonged to me.

42 "The noise of a carefree crowd was around her; Sabeans a were brought from the desert along with men from the rabble, and they put bracelets on the arms of the woman and her sister and beautiful crowns on their heads. 43 Then I said about the one worn out by adultery, 'Now let them use her as a prostitute, for that is all she is.' 44 And they slept with her. As men sleep with a prostitute, so they slept with those lewd women, Oholah and Oholibah. 45 But righteous men will sentence them to the punishment of women who commit adultery and shed blood, because they are adulterous and blood is on their hands. s

46 "This is what the Sovereign LORD says: Bring a mob against them and give them over to terror and plunder. 47 The mob will stone them and cut them down with their swords; they will kill their sons and daughters and burn t down their houses. u

48 "So I will put an end to lewdness in the land, that all women may take warning and not imitate you. v 49 You will suffer the penalty for your lewdness and bear the consequences of your sins of idolatry. Then you will know that I am the Sovereign LORD."

The Cooking Pot

24 In the ninth year, in the tenth month on the tenth day, the word of the LORD came to me: 2 "Son of man, record this date, this very date, because the king of Babylon has laid siege to Jerusalem this very day. w 3 Tell this rebellious house a parable x and say to them: 'This is what the Sovereign LORD says:

'"Put on the cooking pot; y put it on
    and pour water into it.
4 Put into it the pieces of meat,
    all the choice pieces—the leg and the shoulder.
Fill it with the best of these bones;
5   take the pick of the flock.
Pile wood beneath it for the bones;
    bring it to a boil
    and cook the bones in it.

6 "'For this is what the Sovereign LORD says:

'"Woe to the city of bloodshed, z
    to the pot now encrusted,
    whose deposit will not go away!
Empty it piece by piece
    without casting lots for them.

7 "'For the blood she shed is in her midst:
    She poured it on the bare rock;
she did not pour it on the ground,
    where the dust would cover it. a
8 To stir up wrath and take revenge
    I put her blood on the bare rock,
    so that it would not be covered.

---

a 42 Or *drunkards*

24:1–14 Ezekiel gave this illustration in 588 B.C., three years after the first of the previous messages (see 20:1, 2). The people in Judah thought they were the choice meat because they hadn't been taken into captivity in 597 when the Babylonians last invaded the land. Ezekiel used this illustration before (chapter 11) to show that though the people thought they were safe and secure inside the cooking pot, this pot would actually be the place of their destruction. This message was given to the exiles in Babylonia the very day that the Babylonians attacked Jerusalem (24:2), beginning a siege that lasted over two years and resulted in the city's destruction. When God's punishment comes, it is relentless.

24:6–13 The city of Jerusalem was like a pot so encrusted with sin that it would not come clean. God wanted to cleanse the lives of those who lived in Jerusalem, and he wants to cleanse our lives today. Sometimes he tries to purify us through difficulties and troublesome circumstances. When you face tough times, allow the sin to be burned from your life. Look at your problems as an opportunity for your faith to grow. When these times come, unnecessary priorities and diversions are purged away. We can reexamine our lives so that we will do what really counts.

9 "Therefore this is what the Sovereign LORD says:

> "'Woe to the city of bloodshed!
> I, too, will pile the wood high.
> 10 So heap on the wood
> and kindle the fire.
> Cook the meat well,
> mixing in the spices;
> and let the bones be charred.
> 11 Then set the empty pot on the coals
> till it becomes hot and its copper glows
> so its impurities may be melted
> and its deposit burned away.[b]
> 12 It has frustrated all efforts;
> its heavy deposit has not been removed,
> not even by fire.

24:11
b Eze 22:15

13 "'Now your impurity is lewdness. Because I tried to cleanse you but you would not be cleansed from your impurity, you will not be clean again until my wrath against you has subsided.[c]

24:13
c Jer 6:28-30

14 "'I the LORD have spoken. The time has come for me to act. I will not hold back; I will not have pity, nor will I relent. You will be judged according to your conduct and your actions,[d] declares the Sovereign LORD.'"

24:14
d Eze 36:19

Ezekiel's Wife Dies

15 The word of the LORD came to me: 16 "Son of man, with one blow I am about to take away from you the delight of your eyes. Yet do not lament or weep or shed any tears.[e] 17 Groan quietly; do not mourn for the dead. Keep your turban fastened and your sandals on your feet; do not cover the lower part of your face or eat the customary food ⌊of mourners⌋."

24:16
e Jer 13:17

18 So I spoke to the people in the morning, and in the evening my wife died. The next morning I did as I had been commanded.

19 Then the people asked me, "Won't you tell us what these things have to do with us?[f]"

20 So I said to them, "The word of the LORD came to me: 21 Say to the house of Israel, 'This is what the Sovereign LORD says: I am about to desecrate my sanctuary—the stronghold in which you take pride, the delight of your eyes, the object of your affection. The sons and daughters you left behind will fall by the sword.[g] 22 And you will do as I have done. You will not cover the lower part of your face or eat the customary food ⌊of mourners⌋.[h] 23 You will keep your turbans on your heads and your sandals on your feet. You will not mourn or weep but will waste away because of[a] your sins and groan among yourselves.[i] 24 Ezekiel will be a sign[j] to you; you will do just as he has done. When this happens, you will know that I am the Sovereign LORD.'

24:19
f Eze 12:9
24:21
g Eze 23:47

24:22
h Jer 16:7
24:23
i Ps 78:64
24:24
j Eze 4:3

25 "And you, son of man, on the day I take away their stronghold, their joy and glory, the delight of their eyes, their heart's desire, and their sons and daughters as well— 26 on that day a fugitive will come to tell you the news. 27 At that time your mouth will be opened; you will speak with him and will no longer be silent. So you will be a sign to them, and they will know that I am the LORD.[k]"

24:27
k Eze 3:26

a 23 Or away in

24:15–18 God told Ezekiel that his wife would die and that he should not grieve for her. Ezekiel obeyed God fully, even as Hosea did when he was told to marry an unfaithful woman (Hosea 1:2, 3). In both cases, these unusual events were intended as symbolic acts to picture God's relationship with his people. Obeying God can carry a high cost. The only grief more excruciating than losing your spouse and not being allowed to grieve would be to miss out on eternal life because you did not turn to and obey God. Ezekiel always obeyed God wholeheartedly. We should be wholehearted in our obedience. We can begin by doing all that God commands us to do, even when we don't feel like it. Are you willing to serve God as completely as Ezekiel did?

24:20–24 Ezekiel was not allowed to mourn for his dead wife in order to show his fellow exiles that they were not to mourn over Jerusalem when it was destroyed. Any personal sorrow felt would soon be eclipsed by national sorrow over the horror of the city's total destruction. The individuals would waste away because of their sins, which caused the city's destruction.

24:27 For some time Ezekiel had not been allowed to speak except when God gave him a message to deliver to the people (3:25–27). This restriction would soon end when Jerusalem was destroyed and all Ezekiel's prophecies about Judah and Jerusalem had come true (33:21, 22).

B. MESSAGES AGAINST FOREIGN NATIONS (25:1—32:32)

These messages were given concerning seven nations which surrounded Judah. The Ammorites were judged because of their joy over the desecration of the temple, the Moabites because they scorned Judah as special people, the Edomites because of their special hatred of the Jews, and the Philistines because of their vengeance. All these nations would soon realize that God is supreme. Nations today are also under limits imposed by God.

A Prophecy Against Ammon

25:2
l Zep 2:8-9
m Jer 49:1-6
25:3
n Eze 26:2

25 The word of the LORD came to me: ²"Son of man, set your face against the Ammonites *l* and prophesy against them. *m* ³Say to them, 'Hear the word of the Sovereign LORD. This is what the Sovereign LORD says: Because you said "Aha! *n*" over my sanctuary when it was desecrated and over the land of Israel when it was laid waste and over the people of Judah when they went into exile, ⁴therefore I am going to give you to the people of the East as a possession. They will set up their camps and pitch their tents among you; they will eat your fruit and drink your milk. ⁵I will turn Rabbah *o* into a pasture for camels and Ammon into a resting place for sheep. *p* Then you will know that I am the LORD. ⁶For this is what the Sovereign LORD says: Because you have clapped your hands and stamped your feet, rejoicing with all the malice of your heart against the land of Israel, *q* ⁷therefore I will stretch out my hand against you and give you as plunder to the nations. I will cut you off from the nations and exterminate you from the countries. I will destroy you, and you will know that I am the LORD.'"

25:5
o Eze 21:20
p Isa 17:2
25:6
q Zep 2:8

A Prophecy Against Moab

25:8
r Jer 48:1; Am 2:1
25:9
s Nu 33:49
25:10
t Eze 21:32

⁸"This is what the Sovereign LORD says: 'Because Moab *r* and Seir said, "Look, the house of Judah has become like all the other nations," ⁹therefore I will expose the flank of Moab, beginning at its frontier towns—Beth Jeshimoth *s*, Baal Meon and Kiriathaim—the glory of that land. ¹⁰I will give Moab along with the Ammonites to the people of the East as a possession, so that the Ammonites will not be remembered *t* among the nations; ¹¹and I will inflict punishment on Moab. Then they will know that I am the LORD.'"

A Prophecy Against Edom

25:12
u 2Ch 28:17
25:13
v Jer 25:23

¹²"This is what the Sovereign LORD says: 'Because Edom *u* took revenge on the house of Judah and became very guilty by doing so, ¹³therefore this is what the Sovereign LORD says: I will stretch out my hand against Edom and kill its men and their animals. I will lay it waste, and from Teman to Dedan *v* they will fall by the sword. ¹⁴I will take vengeance on Edom by the hand of my people Israel, and they will deal with Edom in accordance with my anger and my wrath; they will know my vengeance, declares the Sovereign LORD.'"

A Prophecy Against Philistia

25:15
w 2Ch 28:18

¹⁵"This is what the Sovereign LORD says: 'Because the Philistines *w* acted in vengeance and took revenge with malice in their hearts, and with ancient hostility sought to destroy Judah,

---

JUDAH'S ENEMIES
Ammon, Moab, Edom, and Philistia, although once united with Judah against Babylon, had abandoned Judah and rejoiced to see its ruin. But these nations were as sinful as Judah and would also feel the sting of God's judgment.

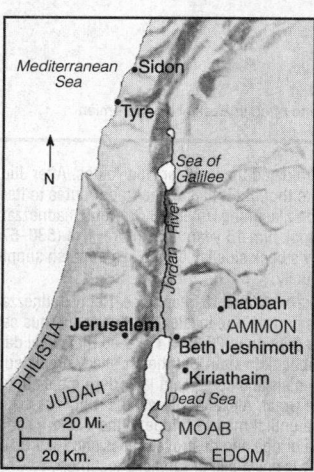

25:1ff Chapters 25—32 are God's word concerning the seven nations surrounding Judah. The judgments in these chapters are not simply the vengeful statements of Jews against their enemies; they are God's judgments on nations that failed to acknowledge the one true God and fulfill the good purposes God intended for them. The Ammonites were judged because of their joy over the desecration of the temple (25:1-7), the Moabites because they found pleasure in Judah's wickedness (25:8–11), the Edomites because of their racial hatred for the Jews (25:12–14), and the Philistines because they sought revenge against Judah for defeating them in battle (25:15–17).

25:5 Rabbah was the capital city of the Ammonites.

25:9 These towns were on the northern border of Moab.

25:12–14 The Edomites were blood brothers of the Jews, both nations having descended from Isaac (Genesis 25:19–26). Edom shared its northern border with Israel, and the two nations were always in conflict. The Edomites hated Israel so much that they rejoiced when Jerusalem, Israel's capital, was destroyed. Teman was in the northern part of Edom; Dedan was in the southern part. Thus, Ezekiel was saying that the entire country would be destroyed.

16therefore this is what the Sovereign Lord says: I am about to stretch out my hand against the Philistines, x and I will cut off the Kerethites y and destroy those remaining along the coast. 17I will carry out great vengeance on them and punish them in my wrath. Then they will know that I am the Lord, when I take vengeance on them.'"

25:16
x Jer 47:1-7
y 1Sa 30:14;
Zep 2:4-5

A Prophecy Against Tyre

26 In the eleventh year, on the first day of the month, the word of the Lord came to me: 2"Son of man, because Tyre z has said of Jerusalem, 'Aha! a The gate to the nations is broken, and its doors have swung open to me; now that she lies in ruins I will prosper,' 3therefore this is what the Sovereign Lord says: I am against you, O Tyre, and I will bring many nations against you, like the sea b casting up its waves. 4They will destroy the walls of Tyre c and pull down her towers; I will scrape away her rubble and make her a bare rock. 5Out in the sea d she will become a place to spread fishnets, for I have spoken, declares the Sovereign Lord. She will become plunder e for the nations, 6and her settlements on the mainland will be ravaged by the sword. Then they will know that I am the Lord.

26:2
z Isa 23
a Eze 25:3

26:3
b Jer 50:42

26:4
c Am 1:10

26:5
d Eze 27:32
e Eze 29:19

7"For this is what the Sovereign Lord says: From the north I am going to bring against Tyre Nebuchadnezzar a king of Babylon, king of kings, f with horses and chariots, with horsemen and a great army. 8He will ravage your settlements on the mainland with the sword; he will set up siege works against you, build a ramp g up to your walls and raise his shields against you. 9He will direct the blows of his battering rams against your walls and demolish your towers with his weapons. 10His horses will be so many that they will cover you with dust. Your walls will tremble at the noise of the war horses, wagons and chariots h when he enters your gates as men enter a city whose walls have been broken through. 11The hoofs of his horses will trample all your streets; he will kill your people with the sword, and your strong pillars i will fall to the ground. 12They will plunder your wealth and loot your merchandise; they will break down your walls and demolish your fine houses and throw your stones, timber and rubble into the sea. 13I will put an end to your noisy songs, and the music of your harps j will be heard no more. k 14I will make you a bare rock, and you will become a place to spread fishnets. You will never be rebuilt, for I the Lord have spoken, declares the Sovereign Lord.

26:7
f Ezr 7:12; Da 2:37

26:8
g Eze 21:22

26:10
h Jer 4:13

26:11
i Jer 43:13

26:13
j Isa 14:11
k Rev 18:22

15"This is what the Sovereign Lord says to Tyre: Will not the coastlands tremble l at the sound of your fall, when the wounded groan and the slaughter takes place in you? 16Then all the princes of the coast will step down from their thrones and lay aside their robes and take off their embroidered garments. Clothed with terror, they will sit on the ground, trembling every moment, appalled at you. 17Then they will take up a lament m concerning you and say to you:

26:15
l Jer 49:21

26:17
m Eze 27:32

"'How you are destroyed, O city of renown,
    peopled by men of the sea!
You were a power on the seas,
    you and your citizens;
you put your terror
    on all who lived there.
18 Now the coastlands tremble
    on the day of your fall;

a 7 Hebrew *Nebuchadrezzar*, of which *Nebuchadnezzar* is a variant; here and often in Ezekiel and Jeremiah

---

25:16 The Kerethites originated in Crete, from which they take their name. They were either a clan of the Philistines, or possibly a separate people who migrated from the Aegean to Palestine about the same time. The Kerethites and Philistines were closely intermixed once they were in Palestine and are often mentioned together.

26:1ff This message came to Ezekiel in 586 B.C. Chapters 26 and 27 are a prophecy against Tyre, the capital of Phoenicia just north of Israel. Part of the city was on the coastline, and part was on a beautiful island. Tyre rejoiced when Jerusalem fell, because Tyre and Judah always competed for the lucrative trade that came through their lands from Egypt in the south and Mesopotamia to the north. Tyre dominated the sea trading routes while Judah

dominated the land caravan routes. After Judah was defeated, Tyre thought it had all the trade routes to itself. But this gloating didn't last long. In 586 B.C., Nebuchadnezzar attacked the city. It took him 15 years to capture Tyre (586–571) because the city's back side lay on the sea so fresh supplies could be shipped in daily.

26:14 After a 15-year siege, Nebuchadnezzar could not conquer the part of Tyre located on the island; thus certain aspects of the description in 26:12, 14 exceed the actual damage done to Tyre by Nebuchadnezzar. But the prophecy predicted what would happen to the island settlement later during the conquests of Alexander the Great. Alexander threw the rubble of the mainland city into the sea until it made a bridge to the island. Then he marched across the bridge and destroyed the island (332 B.C.). Today the island city is still a pile of rubble, a testimony to God's judgment.

the islands in the sea
　　are terrified at your collapse.'

[19]"This is what the Sovereign LORD says: When I make you a desolate city, like cities no longer inhabited, and when I bring the ocean depths over you and its vast waters cover you, [20]then I will bring you down with those who go down to the pit, to the people of long ago. I will make you dwell in the earth below, as in ancient ruins, with those who go down to the pit, and you will not return or take your place[a] in the land of the living. [21]I will bring you to a horrible end and you will be no more. You will be sought, but you will never again be found, declares the Sovereign LORD."[n]

26:21
[n] Eze 27:36; 28:19

A Lament for Tyre

27 The word of the LORD came to me: [2]"Son of man, take up a lament concerning Tyre. [3]Say to Tyre, situated at the gateway to the sea, merchant of peoples on many coasts, 'This is what the Sovereign LORD says:

27:3
[o] Eze 28:2

"'You say, O Tyre,
　　"I am perfect in beauty.[o]
　[4] Your domain was on the high seas;
　　your builders brought your beauty to perfection.
　[5] They made all your timbers
　　of pine trees from Senir[b];[p]
　they took a cedar from Lebanon
　　to make a mast for you.

27:5
[p] Dt 3:9

　[6] Of oaks[q] from Bashan
　　they made your oars;
　of cypress wood[c] from the coasts of Cyprus[d]
　　they made your deck, inlaid with ivory.

27:6
[q] Zec 11:2

　[7] Fine embroidered linen from Egypt was your sail
　　and served as your banner;
　your awnings were of blue and purple
　　from the coasts of Elishah.
　[8] Men of Sidon and Arvad were your oarsmen;
　　your skilled men, O Tyre, were aboard as your seamen.[r]

27:8
[r] 1Ki 9:27

　[9] Veteran craftsmen of Gebal[e][s] were on board
　　as shipwrights to caulk your seams.
　All the ships of the sea and their sailors
　　came alongside to trade for your wares.

27:9
[s] 1Ki 5:18

[10] "'Men of Persia, Lydia and Put[t]
　　served as soldiers in your army.
　They hung their shields and helmets on your walls,
　　bringing you splendor.
[11] Men of Arvad and Helech
　　manned your walls on every side;
　men of Gammad
　　were in your towers.
　They hung their shields around your walls;
　　they brought your beauty to perfection.

27:10
[t] Eze 30:5

[12]"'Tarshish did business with you because of your great wealth of goods; they exchanged silver, iron, tin and lead for your merchandise.

[a]20 Septuagint; Hebrew *return, and I will give glory* [b]5 That is, Hermon [c]6 Targum; the Masoretic Text has a different division of the consonants. [d]6 Hebrew *Kittim* [e]9 That is, Byblos

---

27:1ff Chapter 27 is a funeral lament over Tyre's fall. It compares the city to a ship (27:1–9), mentions many of its trading partners (27:10–25), and then describes how the ship sank (27:26–36). Jesus spoke of Tyre in Matthew 11:22 as a city worthy of God's judgment.

27:3, 4 The beauty of Tyre was the source of its pride, and Tyre's pride guaranteed its judgment. Unwarranted conceit or

pride in our own accomplishments should be a danger signal to us (see James 4:13–17). God is not against our finding pleasure or satisfaction in what we do; he is against arrogant, inflated self-esteem that looks down on others. We must acknowledge God as the basis and source of our lives.

13 "'Greece, Tubal and Meshech[u] traded with you; they exchanged slaves[v] and articles of bronze for your wares.

14 "'Men of Beth Togarmah[w] exchanged work horses, war horses and mules for your merchandise.

15 "'The men of Rhodes[a][x] traded with you, and many coastlands were your customers; they paid you with ivory[y] tusks and ebony.

16 "'Aram[b] did business with you because of your many products; they exchanged turquoise,[z] purple fabric, embroidered work, fine linen, coral and rubies for your merchandise.

17 "'Judah and Israel traded with you; they exchanged wheat from Minnith[a] and confections,[c] honey, oil and balm for your wares.

18 "'Damascus,[b] because of your many products and great wealth of goods, did business with you in wine from Helbon and wool from Zahar.

19 "'Danites and Greeks from Uzal bought your merchandise; they exchanged wrought iron, cassia and calamus for your wares.

20 "'Dedan traded in saddle blankets with you.

21 "'Arabia and all the princes of Kedar[c] were your customers; they did business with you in lambs, rams and goats.

22 "'The merchants of Sheba[d] and Raamah traded with you; for your merchandise they exchanged the finest of all kinds of spices and precious stones, and gold.

23 "'Haran,[e] Canneh and Eden and merchants of Sheba, Asshur and Kilmad traded with you. 24 In your marketplace they traded with you beautiful garments, blue fabric, embroidered work and multicolored rugs with cords twisted and tightly knotted.

25 "'The ships of Tarshish[f] serve
    as carriers for your wares.
You are filled with heavy cargo
    in the heart of the sea.
26 Your oarsmen take you
    out to the high seas.
But the east wind[g] will break you to pieces
    in the heart of the sea.
27 Your wealth,[h] merchandise and wares,
    your mariners, seamen and shipwrights,
your merchants and all your soldiers,
    and everyone else on board
will sink into the heart of the sea
    on the day of your shipwreck.
28 The shorelands will quake[i]
    when your seamen cry out.
29 All who handle the oars
    will abandon their ships;
the mariners and all the seamen
    will stand on the shore.
30 They will raise their voice
    and cry bitterly over you;
they will sprinkle dust on their heads
    and roll[j] in ashes.[k]
31 They will shave their heads because of you
    and will put on sackcloth.
They will weep over you with anguish of soul
    and with bitter mourning.
32 As they wail and mourn over you,
    they will take up a lament[l] concerning you:
"Who was ever silenced like Tyre,
    surrounded by the sea?"
33 When your merchandise went out on the seas,
    you satisfied many nations;

27:13
[u] Ge 10:2
[v] Rev 18:13

27:14
[w] Eze 38:6

27:15
[x] Ge 10:7
[y] Rev 18:12

27:16
[z] Eze 28:13

27:17
[a] Jdg 11:33

27:18
[b] Eze 47:16-18

27:21
[c] Isa 60:7

27:22
[d] Ge 10:7, 28;
1Ki 10:1-2; Isa 60:6

27:23
[e] 2Ki 19:12

27:25
[f] Isa 2:16 fn

27:26
[g] Ps 48:7

27:27
[h] Pr 11:4

27:28
[i] Eze 26:15

27:30
[j] Jer 6:26
[k] Rev 18:18-19

27:32
[l] Eze 26:17

with your great wealth and your wares
>   you enriched the kings of the earth.

27:34
mZec 9:4

34 Now you are shattered by the sea
>   in the depths of the waters;
> your wares and all your company
>   have gone down with you.m

27:35
nEze 26:15

35 All who live in the coastlandsn
>   are appalled at you;
> their kings shudder with horror
>   and their faces are distorted with fear.

27:36
oJer 18:16
pEze 26:21

36 The merchants among the nations hiss at you;o
>   you have come to a horrible end
>   and will be no more.p'"

A Prophecy Against the King of Tyre

28 The word of the LORD came to me: 2"Son of man, say to the ruler of Tyre, 'This is what the Sovereign LORD says:

> "'In the pride of your heart
>   you say, "I am a god;
> I sit on the throne of a god
>   in the heart of the seas."
> But you are a man and not a god,
>   though you think you are as wise as a god.
> 3 Are you wiser than Daniela?
>   Is no secret hidden from you?
> 4 By your wisdom and understanding
>   you have gained wealth for yourself
> and amassed gold and silver
>   in your treasuries.
> 5 By your great skill in trading
>   you have increased your wealth,
> and because of your wealth
>   your heart has grown proud.

6"'Therefore this is what the Sovereign LORD says:

> "'Because you think you are wise,
>   as wise as a god,

28:7
qEze 30:11; 31:12;
32:12

> 7 I am going to bring foreigners against you,
>   the most ruthless of nations;q
> they will draw their swords against your beauty and wisdom
>   and pierce your shining splendor.
> 8 They will bring you down to the pit,
>   and you will die a violent death
>   in the heart of the seas.
> 9 Will you then say, "I am a god,"
>   in the presence of those who kill you?
> You will be but a man, not a god,
>   in the hands of those who slay you.

a3 Or Danel; the Hebrew spelling may suggest a person other than the prophet Daniel.

28:1ff Previously Ezekiel had prophesied against the city of Tyre (chapters 26; 27). Here he focused his prophecy on Tyre's leader. The chief sin of Tyre's king was pride—believing himself to be a god. But Ezekiel also may have made a broader spiritual application, speaking about the spiritual king of Tyre, Satan, whom the people were really following (see the note on 28:12–19).

28:2, 3 Daniel, an important official in Nebuchadnezzar's kingdom (14:14), was already renowned for his wisdom. Daniel proclaimed that all his wisdom came from God (Daniel 2:20–23). By contrast, the king of Tyre thought that he himself was a god. When truly wise people get closer to God, they recognize their need to depend on him for guidance.

28:6–10 The enemy army ("foreigners") that attacked Tyre was the Babylonian army under Nebuchadnezzar. This attack occurred in 573/572 B.C.

¹⁰ You will die the death of the uncircumcised[r]
    at the hands of foreigners.

I have spoken, declares the Sovereign Lord.'"

¹¹The word of the Lord came to me: ¹²"Son of man, take up a lament concerning the king
of Tyre and say to him: 'This is what the Sovereign Lord says:

"'You were the model of perfection,
    full of wisdom and perfect in beauty.[s]
¹³ You were in Eden,
    the garden of God;[t]
every precious stone adorned you:
    ruby, topaz and emerald,
    chrysolite, onyx and jasper,
    sapphire,[a] turquoise and beryl.[b]
Your settings and mountings[c] were made of gold;
    on the day you were created they were prepared.
¹⁴ You were anointed as a guardian cherub,[u]
    for so I ordained you.
You were on the holy mount of God;
    you walked among the fiery stones.
¹⁵ You were blameless in your ways
    from the day you were created
    till wickedness was found in you.
¹⁶ Through your widespread trade
    you were filled with violence,
    and you sinned.
So I drove you in disgrace from the mount of God,
    and I expelled you, O guardian cherub,
    from among the fiery stones.
¹⁷ Your heart became proud
    on account of your beauty,
and you corrupted your wisdom
    because of your splendor.
So I threw you to the earth;
    I made a spectacle of you before kings.
¹⁸ By your many sins and dishonest trade
    you have desecrated your sanctuaries.
So I made a fire come out from you,
    and it consumed you,
and I reduced you to ashes on the ground
    in the sight of all who were watching.
¹⁹ All the nations who knew you
    are appalled at you;
you have come to a horrible end
    and will be no more.[v]'"

A Prophecy Against Sidon

²⁰The word of the Lord came to me: ²¹"Son of man, set your face against[w] Sidon; prophesy against her ²²and say: 'This is what the Sovereign Lord says:

28:10
[r] Eze 31:18

28:12
[s] Eze 27:2-4

28:13
[t] Eze 31:8-9

28:14
[u] Ex 25:17-20

28:19
[v] Eze 26:21; 27:36

28:21
[w] Eze 6:2

---

[a] 13 Or *lapis lazuli* [b] 13 The precise identification of some of these precious stones is uncertain. [c] 13 The meaning of the Hebrew for this phrase is uncertain.

28:12–19 Some of the phrases in this passage describing the human king of Tyre may describe Satan. Great care must be taken to interpret these verses with discernment. It is clear that, at times, Ezekiel describes this king in terms that could not apply to a mere human. This king had been in the Garden of Eden (28:13), had been "anointed as a guardian cherub" (28:14), and had

access to the holy mountain of God (28:14), but was driven from there (28:16, 17). Ezekiel, therefore, may have been condemning not only the king of Tyre, but Satan, who had motivated the king to sin.

28:20, 21 Sidon was another famous seaport, located about 25 miles north of Tyre. God charged this city with contempt for his people. Sidon's economy was bound to Tyre's, so when Tyre fell to Nebuchadnezzar, Sidon was doomed to follow.

"'I am against you, O Sidon,
  and I will gain glory within you.
They will know that I am the Lord,
  when I inflict punishment on her
  and show myself holy within her.
  23 I will send a plague upon her
  and make blood flow in her streets.
The slain will fall within her,
  with the sword against her on every side.
Then they will know that I am the Lord. x

28:23
x Eze 38:22

24 "'No longer will the people of Israel have malicious neighbors who are painful briers and sharp thorns. y Then they will know that I am the Sovereign Lord.

28:24
y Nu 33:55;
Jos 23:13

25 "'This is what the Sovereign Lord says: When I gather the people of Israel from the nations where they have been scattered, z I will show myself holy a among them in the sight of the nations. Then they will live in their own land, which I gave to my servant Jacob. 26 They will live there in safety b and will build houses and plant vineyards; they will live in safety when I inflict punishment on all their neighbors who maligned them. Then they will know that I am the Lord their God. c'"

28:25
z Isa 11:12
a Eze 20:41

28:26
b Jer 23:6
c Am 9:14-15

A Prophecy Against Egypt

29 In the tenth year, in the tenth month on the twelfth day, the word of the Lord came to me: 2 "Son of man, set your face against Pharaoh king of Egypt and prophesy against him and against all Egypt. d 3 Speak to him and say: 'This is what the Sovereign Lord says:

29:2
d Isa 19:1-17;
Jer 46:2

29:3
e Isa 27:1; Eze 32:2

"'I am against you, Pharaoh king of Egypt,
  you great monster e lying among your streams.
You say, "The Nile is mine;
  I made it for myself."
  4 But I will put hooks in your jaws
  and make the fish of your streams stick to your scales.
I will pull you out from among your streams,
  with all the fish sticking to your scales. f
  5 I will leave you in the desert,
  you and all the fish of your streams.
You will fall on the open field
  and not be gathered or picked up.
I will give you as food
  to the beasts of the earth and the birds of the air. g

29:4
f Eze 38:4

29:5
g Jer 7:33; 34:20

6 Then all who live in Egypt will know that I am the Lord.

"'You have been a staff of reed for the house of Israel. 7 When they grasped you with their hands, you splintered and you tore open their shoulders; when they leaned on you, you broke and their backs were wrenched. a h

29:7
h Eze 17:15-17

8 "'Therefore this is what the Sovereign Lord says: I will bring a sword against you and kill your men and their animals. i 9 Egypt will become a desolate wasteland. Then they will know that I am the Lord.

29:8
i Eze 14:17

a 7 Syriac (see also Septuagint and Vulgate); Hebrew *and you caused their backs to stand*

28:24–26 This promise that God's people will live in complete safety has yet to be fulfilled. While many were allowed to return from exile under Zerubbabel, Ezra, and Nehemiah, and although the political nation is restored today, the inhabitants do not yet live in complete safety (28:26). Therefore, this promise will have its ultimate fulfillment when Christ sets up his eternal kingdom. Then all people who have been faithful to God will dwell together in harmony and complete safety.

29:1ff Chapters 29—32 contain seven prophecies, all dealing with judgment on Egypt. This is probably the first prophecy that was given by Ezekiel in 587 B.C. Hezekiah, Jehoiakim, and Zedekiah (kings of Judah) had all sought help from Egypt despite God's warnings.

This prophecy was given for three key reasons: (1) Egypt was

an ancient enemy of the Jews, having once enslaved them for 400 years; (2) Egypt worshiped many gods; (3) Egypt's wealth and power made it seem like a good ally. Egypt offered to help Judah only because of the benefits it hoped to receive from such an alliance. When the Egyptians didn't get what they hoped for, they bailed out of their agreement without regard to any promises they had made.

29:2ff Egypt had great artistic treasures, a flourishing civilization, and world-renowned military power. Unfortunately, it was also evil, egotistical, idolatrous, and it treated slaves cruelly. For those sins God condemned Egypt. At the battle of Carchemish in 605 B.C., Babylon crushed Egypt along with Assyria, its rivals for the position of world ruler.

"'Because you said, "The Nile is mine; I made it," [10] therefore I am against you and against your streams, and I will make the land of Egypt a ruin and a desolate waste from Migdol to Aswan, as far as the border of Cush.[a] [11] No foot of man or animal will pass through it; no one will live there for forty years.[i] [12] I will make the land of Egypt desolate among devastated lands, and her cities will lie desolate forty years among ruined cities. And I will disperse the Egyptians among the nations and scatter them through the countries.[k]

[13] "'Yet this is what the Sovereign LORD says: At the end of forty years I will gather the Egyptians from the nations where they were scattered. [14] I will bring them back from captivity and return them to Upper Egypt,[b] the land of their ancestry. There they will be a lowly kingdom. [15] It will be the lowliest of kingdoms and will never again exalt itself above the other nations. I will make it so weak that it will never again rule over the nations. [16] Egypt will no longer be a source of confidence[l] for the people of Israel but will be a reminder of their sin in turning to her for help. Then they will know that I am the Sovereign LORD.[m]'"

[17] In the twenty-seventh year, in the first month on the first day, the word of the LORD came to me: [18] "Son of man, Nebuchadnezzar[n] king of Babylon drove his army in a hard campaign against Tyre; every head was rubbed bare and every shoulder made raw. Yet he and his army got no reward from the campaign he led against Tyre. [19] Therefore this is what the Sovereign LORD says: I am going to give Egypt to Nebuchadnezzar king of Babylon, and he will carry off its wealth. He will loot and plunder the land as pay for his army. [20] I have given him Egypt as a reward for his efforts because he and his army did it for me, declares the Sovereign LORD.[o]

[21] "On that day I will make a horn[c] [p] grow for the house of Israel, and I will open your mouth among them. Then they will know that I am the LORD.[q]"

A Lament for Egypt

30 The word of the LORD came to me: [2] "Son of man, prophesy and say: 'This is what the Sovereign LORD says:

"'Wail[r] and say,
    "Alas for that day!"
[3] For the day is near,[s]
    the day of the LORD[t] is near—
a day of clouds,
    a time of doom for the nations.
[4] A sword will come against Egypt,
    and anguish will come upon Cush.[d]
When the slain fall in Egypt,
    her wealth will be carried away
    and her foundations torn down.[u]

[5] Cush and Put, Lydia and all Arabia, Libya[e] and the people[v] of the covenant land will fall by the sword along with Egypt.

29:11
/Eze 32:13

29:12
k Eze 30:7, 23, 26

29:16
/Isa 36:4, 6
m Isa 30:2

29:18
n Jer 27:6;
Eze 26:7-8

29:20
o Jer 25:9

29:21
p Ps 132:17
q Eze 24:27

30:2
r Isa 13:6

30:3
s Joel 2:1, 11
t Eze 7:12, 19

30:4
u Eze 29:19

30:5
v Jer 25:20

---

a 10 That is, the upper Nile region   b 14 Hebrew to Pathros   c 21 Horn here symbolizes strength.   d 4 That is, the upper Nile region; also in verses 5 and 9   e 5 Hebrew Cub

---

29:9, 10 The Nile was Egypt's pride and joy, a life-giving river cutting through the middle of the desert. Rather than thanking God, however, Egypt declared, "The Nile is mine; I made it." We do the same when we say "This house is mine; I built it," or "I have brought myself to the place where I am today," or "I have built this church, business, or reputation, from the ground up." These statements reveal our pride. Sometimes we take for granted what God has given us, thinking we have made it ourselves. Of course, we have put forth a lot of hard effort, but God supplied the resources, gave us the abilities, and provided us with the opportunities to make it happen. Instead of claiming our own greatness, as the Egyptians did, we should proclaim God's greatness and give him the credit. (Migdol is in the north of Egypt, and Aswan in the south. Thus, this meant all of Egypt.)

29:13–16 This 40-year period of desolation in Egypt is hard to pinpoint. Nebuchadnezzar attacked Egypt around 572 B.C. and carried many people off to Babylon, while others fled for safety to surrounding nations. Approximately 33 years later, Cyrus, king of the Persian empire, conquered Babylon and allowed the nations which Babylon had conquered to return to their homelands. Adding a possible seven-year regrouping and travel period, this could then make up that 40-year time period. Since that time, Egypt has never returned to its previous dominance as a world power. Upper Egypt was the region south of the Nile delta.

29:17, 18 This prophecy was given in 571 B.C. and is actually the latest prophecy in Ezekiel. Nebuchadnezzar had finally conquered Tyre after a long and costly 15-year siege (586–571 B.C.). He had not counted on such an expense, so he went south and conquered Egypt to make up for all he had lost in taking Tyre. Ezekiel placed this prophecy here to describe who would bring this punishment to Egypt. God was using Nebuchadnezzar, an evil man, as an instrument of his judgment on Tyre, Judah, and Egypt—evil nations themselves. When Babylon didn't recognize God's favor, he judged it too.

30:1–19 This is a lament for Egypt and its allies. Because of the Egyptians' pride and idolatry, they would be brought down.

6 "'This is what the Lord says:

"'The allies of Egypt will fall
    and her proud strength will fail.
From Migdol to Aswan
    they will fall by the sword within her,

                                                            declares the Sovereign Lord.

30:7
w Eze 29:12

7 "'They will be desolate
    among desolate lands,
and their cities will lie
    among ruined cities. w
8 Then they will know that I am the Lord,
    when I set fire to Egypt
    and all her helpers are crushed.

30:9
x Isa 18:1-2
y Eze 32:9-10

9 "'On that day messengers will go out from me in ships to frighten Cush x out of her complacency. Anguish will take hold of them on the day of Egypt's doom, for it is sure to come. y

30:10
z Eze 29:19

10 "'This is what the Sovereign Lord says:

"'I will put an end to the hordes of Egypt
    by the hand of Nebuchadnezzar king of Babylon. z

30:11
a Eze 28:7

11 He and his army—the most ruthless of nations a—
    will be brought in to destroy the land.
They will draw their swords against Egypt
    and fill the land with the slain.
12 I will dry up the streams of the Nile
    and sell the land to evil men;
by the hand of foreigners
    I will lay waste the land and everything in it.

I the Lord have spoken.

30:13
b Zec 10:11

13 "'This is what the Sovereign Lord says:

"'I will destroy the idols
    and put an end to the images in Memphis. a
No longer will there be a prince in Egypt, b
    and I will spread fear throughout the land.

30:14
c Eze 29:14
d Ps 78:12, 43

14 I will lay c waste Upper Egypt, b
    set fire to Zoan d
    and inflict punishment on Thebes. c
15 I will pour out my wrath on Pelusium, d
    the stronghold of Egypt,
    and cut off the hordes of Thebes.
16 I will set fire to Egypt;
    Pelusium will writhe in agony.
Thebes will be taken by storm;
    Memphis will be in constant distress.
17 The young men of Heliopolis e and Bubastis f
    will fall by the sword,
    and the cities themselves will go into captivity.
18 Dark will be the day at Tahpanhes
    when I break the yoke of Egypt;
    there her proud strength will come to an end.

a 13 Hebrew Noph; also in verse 16   b 14 Hebrew waste Pathros   c 14 Hebrew No; also in verses 15 and 16
d 15 Hebrew Sin; also in verse 16   e 17 Hebrew Awen (or On)   f 17 Hebrew Pi Beseth

30:12 Egypt's pharaohs claimed that they had made the Nile—the river on which the entire nation depended. If God dried up the Nile, the nation would be doomed.

30:13–19 The list of cities to be destroyed shows the breadth of the destruction; the drying up of the Nile (30:12) shows its depth. Egypt would be completely incapacitated. This was a clear message to Judah not to trust Egypt for help against the Babylonians.

> She will be covered with clouds,
>   and her villages will go into captivity.[e]
> 19 So I will inflict punishment on Egypt,
>   and they will know that I am the LORD.'"

20 In the eleventh year, in the first month on the seventh day, the word of the LORD came to me: 21 "Son of man, I have broken the arm of Pharaoh king of Egypt. It has not been bound up for healing[f] or put in a splint so as to become strong enough to hold a sword. 22 Therefore this is what the Sovereign LORD says: I am against Pharaoh king of Egypt. I will break both his arms, the good arm as well as the broken one, and make the sword fall from his hand. 23 I will disperse the Egyptians among the nations and scatter them through the countries.[g] 24 I will strengthen[h] the arms of the king of Babylon and put my sword[i] in his hand, but I will break the arms of Pharaoh, and he will groan before him like a mortally wounded man. 25 I will strengthen the arms of the king of Babylon, but the arms of Pharaoh will fall limp. Then they will know that I am the LORD, when I put my sword into the hand of the king of Babylon and he brandishes it against Egypt. 26 I will disperse the Egyptians among the nations and scatter them through the countries. Then they will know that I am the LORD.[j]"

A Cedar in Lebanon

31 In the eleventh year, in the third month on the first day, the word of the LORD came to me: 2 "Son of man, say to Pharaoh king of Egypt and to his hordes:

> "'Who can be compared with you in majesty?
> 3 Consider Assyria, once a cedar in Lebanon,
>   with beautiful branches overshadowing the forest;
> it towered on high,
>   its top above the thick foliage.[k]
> 4 The waters nourished it,
>   deep springs made it grow tall;
> their streams flowed
>   all around its base
> and sent their channels
>   to all the trees of the field.
> 5 So it towered higher
>   than all the trees of the field;
> its boughs increased
>   and its branches grew long,
>   spreading because of abundant waters.
> 6 All the birds of the air
>   nested in its boughs,
> all the beasts of the field
>   gave birth under its branches;
> all the great nations
>   lived in its shade.[l]
> 7 It was majestic in beauty,
>   with its spreading boughs,
> for its roots went down
>   to abundant waters.

Cross references

30:18 [e] ver 3
30:21 [f] Jer 46:11
30:23 [g] Eze 29:12
30:24 [h] Zec 10:6, 12 [i] Zep 2:12
30:26 [j] Eze 29:12
31:3 [k] Isa 10:34
31:6 [l] Eze 17:23

30:20, 21 This message came in 587 B.C. while Jerusalem was under attack from Babylon. Judah had rebelled against Babylon and made an alliance with Egypt in spite of God's warnings (Jeremiah 2:36, 37). Pharaoh Hophra made a halfhearted attempt to help Jerusalem, but when Nebuchadnezzar's army turned on him, he fled back to Egypt (Jeremiah 37:5–7). This defeat is what Ezekiel meant when he said that God had broken the arm of Pharaoh.

30:21–26 This prophecy was given to Ezekiel in 587 B.C. God destroyed Egypt's military superiority and gave it to Babylon. God allows nations to rise to power to accomplish a particular purpose, often beyond our immediate understanding. When you read about armies and wars, don't despair. Remember that God is sovereign and in charge of everything, even military might. Besides praying for your military and government leaders, pray that God's greater purposes would be carried out and that his will would be done "on earth as it is in heaven" (see Matthew 6:10).

31:1ff This message was given in 587 B.C. Ezekiel compared Egypt to Assyria, calling Assyria a great cedar tree. The Egyptians were to look at the fall of the mighty nation of Assyria (whose demise they had seen) as an example of what would happen to them. Just like Assyria, Egypt took pride in its strength and beauty; this would be its downfall. She would crash like a mighty tree and be sent to the place of the dead. There is no permanence apart from God, even for a great society with magnificent culture and military power.

31:8
m Ge 2:8-9

8 The cedars in the garden of God
could not rival it,
nor could the pine trees
equal its boughs,
nor could the plane trees
compare with its branches—
no tree in the garden of God
could match its beauty.*m*
9 I made it beautiful
with abundant branches,
the envy of all the trees of Eden
in the garden of God.

31:11
n Da 5:20
31:12
o Eze 28:7
p Eze 32:5; 35:8
31:13
q Isa 18:6; Eze 32:4

10 "'Therefore this is what the Sovereign LORD says: Because it towered on high, lifting its top above the thick foliage, and because it was proud of its height, 11 I handed it over to the ruler of the nations, for him to deal with according to its wickedness. I cast it aside,*n* 12 and the most ruthless of foreign nations*o* cut it down and left it. Its boughs fell on the mountains and in all the valleys;*p* its branches lay broken in all the ravines of the land. All the nations of the earth came out from under its shade and left it. 13 All the birds of the air settled on the fallen tree, and all the beasts of the field were among its branches. *q* 14 Therefore no other trees by the waters are ever to tower proudly on high, lifting their tops above the thick foliage. No other trees so well-watered are ever to reach such a height; they are all destined for death, for the earth below, among mortal men, with those who go down to the pit.

15 "'This is what the Sovereign LORD says: On the day it was brought down to the grave*a* I covered the deep springs with mourning for it; I held back its streams, and its abundant waters were restrained. Because of it I clothed Lebanon with gloom, and all the trees of the field withered away. 16 I made the nations tremble*r* at the sound of its fall when I brought it down to the grave with those who go down to the pit. Then all the trees*s* of Eden, the choicest and best of Lebanon, all the trees that were well-watered, were consoled*t* in the earth below. *u* 17 Those who lived in its shade, its allies among the nations, had also gone down to the grave with it, joining those killed by the sword.

31:16
r Eze 26:15
s Isa 14:8
t Eze 32:31
u Isa 14:15

31:18
v Eze 32:19, 21

18 "'Which of the trees of Eden can be compared with you in splendor and majesty? Yet you, too, will be brought down with the trees of Eden to the earth below; you will lie among the uncircumcised,*v* with those killed by the sword.

"'This is Pharaoh and all his hordes, declares the Sovereign LORD.'"

A Lament for Pharaoh

32:2
w Eze 27:2

32 In the twelfth year, in the twelfth month on the first day, the word of the LORD came to me: 2 "Son of man, take up a lament*w* concerning Pharaoh king of Egypt and say to him:

"'You are like a lion among the nations;
you are like a monster in the seas
thrashing about in your streams,
churning the water with your feet
and muddying the streams.

a 15 Hebrew *Sheol*; also in verses 16 and 17

31:9 "All the trees of Eden" may refer to all the other nations of the world who were jealous of Assyria's power and grandeur.

31:11 The "ruler of the nations" may be Nebuchadnezzar (see Daniel 2:37, 38).

32:1ff This prophecy was given in 585 B.C., two months after the news of Jerusalem's fall had reached the exiles in Babylon. Ezekiel prophesied numerous judgments upon many wicked nations. These judgments served a positive purpose: they showed that evil forces are continually being overcome and that one day God will overthrow all evil, making the world the perfect place he intended. They also serve as warnings that God alone is sover-

eign. Even the mightiest rulers, like Pharaoh, will fall before God. All are accountable to him.

32:2 Although Pharaoh thought of himself as a strong lion, in God's eyes he was nothing but a crocodile ("monster") muddying the water. God's judgment would reduce Pharaoh to his true size. Anyone who defies God will face his judgment.

3"This is what the Sovereign Lord says:

> "'With a great throng of people
>   I will cast my net over you,
>   and they will haul you up in my net.*

4 I will throw you on the land
>   and hurl you on the open field.
> I will let all the birds of the air settle on you
>   and all the beasts of the earth gorge themselves on you.

5 I will spread your flesh on the mountains
>   and fill the valleys with your remains.

6 I will drench the land with your flowing blood
>   all the way to the mountains,
>   and the ravines will be filled with your flesh.

7 When I snuff you out, I will cover the heavens
>   and darken their stars;
> I will cover the sun with a cloud,
>   and the moon will not give its light.*

8 All the shining lights in the heavens
>   I will darken over you;
> I will bring darkness over your land,

declares the Sovereign Lord.

9 I will trouble the hearts of many peoples
>   when I bring about your destruction among the nations,
>   among* lands you have not known.

10 I will cause many peoples to be appalled at you,
>   and their kings will shudder with horror because of you
>   when I brandish my sword before them.
> On the day of your downfall
>   each of them will tremble
>   every moment for his life.*

11"For this is what the Sovereign Lord says:

> "'The sword of the king of Babylon*
>   will come against you.

12 I will cause your hordes to fall
>   by the swords of mighty men—
>   the most ruthless of all nations.*
> They will shatter the pride of Egypt,
>   and all her hordes will be overthrown.

13 I will destroy all her cattle
>   from beside abundant waters
> no longer to be stirred by the foot of man
>   or muddied by the hoofs of cattle.*

14 Then I will let her waters settle
>   and make her streams flow like oil,

declares the Sovereign Lord.

15 When I make Egypt desolate
>   and strip the land of everything in it,
> when I strike down all who live there,
>   then they will know that I am the Lord.*

16"This is the lament* they will chant for her. The daughters of the nations will chant it; for Egypt and all her hordes they will chant it, declares the Sovereign Lord."

17In the twelfth year, on the fifteenth day of the month, the word of the Lord came to me: 18"Son of man, wail for the hordes of Egypt and consign to the earth below both her and

a 9 Hebrew; Septuagint bring you into captivity among the nations, / to

32:3
*Eze 12:13

32:7
*Isa 13:10;
Joel 2:2, 31; 3:15

32:10
*Eze 26:16

32:11
*Jer 46:26

32:12
*Eze 28:7

32:13
*Eze 29:8, 11

32:15
*Ex 7:5; Eze 6:7

32:16
*2Ch 35:25

32:18 The Hebrews believed in an afterlife for all people, good and bad. Ezekiel's message assumed that the evil nations had already been sent there (to the "pit") and that Egypt would share their fate. The words here are more poetic than doctrinal (see

32:18
*Eze 31:14, 16

32:19
*Eze 28:10; 31:18

32:21
*Isa 14:9

32:23
*Isa 14:15

32:24
*Jer 49:37

32:26
*Eze 27:13

32:29
*Isa 34:5-15
*Eze 25:12-14

32:30
*Eze 38:6; 39:2

32:31
*Eze 31:16

the daughters of mighty nations, with those who go down to the pit. *f* 19Say to them, 'Are you more favored than others? Go down and be laid among the uncircumcised.' *g* 20They will fall among those killed by the sword. The sword is drawn; let her be dragged off with all her hordes. 21From within the grave*a h* the mighty leaders will say of Egypt and her allies, 'They have come down and they lie with the uncircumcised, with those killed by the sword.'

22"Assyria is there with her whole army; she is surrounded by the graves of all her slain, all who have fallen by the sword. 23Their graves are in the depths of the pit*i* and her army lies around her grave. All who had spread terror in the land of the living are slain, fallen by the sword.

24"Elam is there, with all her hordes around her grave. All of them are slain, fallen by the sword.*j* All who had spread terror in the land of the living went down uncircumcised to the earth below. They bear their shame with those who go down to the pit. 25A bed is made for her among the slain, with all her hordes around her grave. All of them are uncircumcised, killed by the sword. Because their terror had spread in the land of the living, they bear their shame with those who go down to the pit; they are laid among the slain.

26"Meshech and Tubal*k* are there, with all their hordes around their graves. All of them are uncircumcised, killed by the sword because they spread their terror in the land of the living. 27Do they not lie with the other uncircumcised warriors who have fallen, who went down to the grave with their weapons of war, whose swords were placed under their heads? The punishment for their sins rested on their bones, though the terror of these warriors had stalked through the land of the living.

28"You too, O Pharaoh, will be broken and will lie among the uncircumcised, with those killed by the sword.

29"Edom*l* is there, her kings and all her princes; despite their power, they are laid with those killed by the sword. They lie with the uncircumcised, with those who go down to the pit.*m*

30"All the princes of the north*n* and all the Sidonians are there; they went down with the slain in disgrace despite the terror caused by their power. They lie uncircumcised with those killed by the sword and bear their shame with those who go down to the pit.

31"Pharaoh—he and all his army—will see them and he will be consoled *o* for all his hordes that were killed by the sword, declares the Sovereign LORD. 32Although I had him spread terror in the land of the living, Pharaoh and all his hordes will be laid among the uncircumcised, with those killed by the sword, declares the Sovereign LORD."

*a*21 Hebrew *Sheol*; also in verse 27

Job 24:19; Psalm 16:10; Isaiah 38:10, and the note on Matthew 25:46). The Egyptians had a preoccupation with the afterlife (the pyramids were built solely to ensure the pharaohs' comfort in the next life). This message should remind us that any attempt to control our afterlife and ignore God is foolish. God alone controls the future and life after death.

32:21–32 In these verses, Ezekiel conducts a guided tour of the grave—the region of the afterlife. In the grave, all of God's enemies are condemned in judgment; many of them experience the fate they so quickly imposed on others. Though Babylon is not mentioned, Ezekiel's readers would have concluded that if all the other nations would be judged for their rebellion against God, Babylon would be judged as well. These words would comfort the captives.

32:24–26 Elam was a nation of fierce warriors from the region east of Assyria. They were conquered by Nebuchadnezzar (Jeremiah 49:34–39) and eventually rebuilt themselves and became part of Persia. Meshech and Tubal were territories located in the eastern region of Asia Minor, now eastern and central Turkey. In chapters 38 and 39 they are described as allies of Gog, the chief prince of a confederacy. They are included with the evil nations who will be judged for fighting against God's people.

32:30 The princes of the north were probably the princes of the Phoenician city-states.

32:32 After reading Ezekiel's prophecies against all these foreign

nations, we may wonder if he was blindly loyal to his own nation. But Ezekiel spoke only when God gave him a message (3:27). Besides, God's prophets pronounced judgment on God's sinful people just as much as on God's enemies. But if Babylon was God's enemy, why isn't it mentioned in Ezekiel's judgments? Perhaps because (1) God wanted to foster a spirit of cooperation between the exiles and Babylon in order to preserve his people; (2) God was still using Babylon to refine his own people; (3) God wanted to use Daniel, a powerful official in Babylon, to draw the Babylonians to him.

C. MESSAGES OF HOPE (33:1—48:35)

This section begins a new direction in Ezekiel's prophecies. Ezekiel is reminded that he is the nation's watchman. Before Jerusalem's fall, he told the people of their punishment and dispersion. Now he is to proclaim the hope of restoration, but even this message does not improve the people's response. They listen to him with curiosity and then live as they please. Today we have the good news of forgiveness, but how easy it is to ignore the message and continue to live sinful lives.

1. Restoring the people of God
Ezekiel a Watchman

33 The word of the Lord came to me: 2 "Son of man, speak to your countrymen and say to them: 'When I bring the sword against a land, and the people of the land choose one of their men and make him their watchman,ᵖ 3 and he sees the sword coming against the land and blows the trumpet to warn the people, 4 then if anyone hears the trumpet but does not take warning and the sword comes and takes his life, his blood will be on his own head.�q 5 Since he heard the sound of the trumpet but did not take warning, his blood will be on his own head. If he had taken warning, he would have saved himself. 6 But if the watchman sees the sword coming and does not blow the trumpet to warn the people and the sword comes and takes the life of one of them, that man will be taken away because of his sin, but I will hold the watchman accountable for his blood.'

7 "Son of man, I have made you a watchman for the house of Israel; so hear the word I speak and give them warning from me.ʳ 8 When I say to the wicked, 'O wicked man, you will surely die,' and you do not speak out to dissuade him from his ways, that wicked man will die forᵃ his sin, and I will hold you accountable for his blood. 9 But if you do warn the wicked man to turn from his ways and he does not do so, he will die for his sin, but you will have saved yourself.

10 "Son of man, say to the house of Israel, 'This is what you are saying: "Our offenses and sins weigh us down, and we are wasting awayˢ because ofᵇ them. How then can we live?"' 11 Say to them, 'As surely as I live, declares the Sovereign Lord, I take no pleasure in the death of the wicked, but rather that they turn from their ways and live.ᵗ Turn! Turn from your evil ways! Why will you die, O house of Israel?'

12 "Therefore, son of man, say to your countrymen, 'The righteousness of the righteous man will not save him when he disobeys, and the wickedness of the wicked man will not cause him to fall when he turns from it. The righteous man, if he sins, will not be allowed to live because of his former righteousness.'ᵘ 13 If I tell the righteous man that he will surely live, but then he trusts in his righteousness and does evil, none of the righteous things he has done will be remembered; he will die for the evil he has done.ᵛ 14 And if I say to the wicked man, 'You will surely die,' but he then turns away from his sin and does what is justʷ and right— 15 if he gives back what he took in pledge for a loan, returns what he has stolen,ˣ follows the decrees that give life, and does no evil, he will surely live; he will not die.ʸ 16 None of the sins he has committed will be remembered against him. He has done what is just and right; he will surely live.ᶻ

33:2
ᵖEze 3:11

33:4
qEze 18:13;
Ac 18:6

33:7
ʳEze 3:17

33:10
ˢEze 24:23

33:11
ᵗEze 18:32; 2Pe 3:9

33:12
ᵘ2Ch 7:14;
Eze 3:20

33:13
ᵛEze 18:24

33:14
ʷEze 18:27

33:15
ˣLev 6:2-5
ʸEze 20:11

33:16
ᶻEze 18:22

ᵃ8 Or in; also in verse 9   ᵇ10 Or away in

33:1ff This chapter sets forth a new direction for Ezekiel's prophecies. Up to this point, Ezekiel has pronounced judgment upon Judah (chapters 1—24) and the surrounding evil nations (chapters 25—32) for their sins. After Jerusalem fell, he turned from messages of doom and judgment to messages of comfort, hope, and future restoration for God's people (chapters 33—48). God previously appointed Ezekiel to be a watchman warning the nation of coming judgment (see 3:17–21). Here God appointed him to be a watchman again, but this time to preach a message of hope. More warnings will come (33:23—34:10; 36:1–7), but these are part of the larger picture of hope. God will remember to bless those who are faithful to him. We must pay attention to both aspects of Ezekiel's message: warning and promise. Those who persist in rebelling against God should take warning. Those faithful to God should find encouragement and hope.

33:10–12 The exiles were discouraged by their past sins. This is an important turning point in this book—elsewhere in Ezekiel

the people had refused to face their sins. Here, they felt heavy guilt for rebelling against God for so many years. Therefore, God assured them of forgiveness if they repented. God *wants* everyone to turn to him. He looks at what we are and will become, not what we have been. God gives you the opportunity to turn to him, if you will take it. Sincerely follow God, and ask him to forgive you when you fail.

33:13 Past good deeds will not save a person who decides to turn to a life of sin. Some people think they have done enough good deeds to overshadow the sins they don't want to give up. But it's useless to try to be good in some areas so you can deliberately be bad in others. God wants wholehearted love and obedience.

33:15 While good deeds will not save us, our salvation must lead to righteous actions (see Ephesians 2:10; James 2:14–17). This includes restitution for past sins (as exemplified in the story of Zacchaeus, see Luke 19:1–10). God expects us to make restitution, whenever necessary, for the wrongs we have committed.

33:18
a Eze 18:26

17"Yet your countrymen say, 'The way of the Lord is not just.' But it is their way that is not just. 18If a righteous man turns from his righteousness and does evil, he will die for it. a 19And if a wicked man turns away from his wickedness and does what is just and right, he will live by doing so. 20Yet, O house of Israel, you say, 'The way of the Lord is not just.' But I will judge each of you according to his own ways."

Jerusalem's Fall Explained

33:21
b 2Ki 25:4, 10

33:22
c Eze 1:3
d Eze 24:27

33:24
e Isa 51:2; Ac 7:5

33:25
f Dt 12:16
g Eze 22:6, 27

21In the twelfth year of our exile, in the tenth month on the fifth day, a man who had escaped from Jerusalem came to me and said, "The city has fallen! b" 22Now the evening before the man arrived, the hand of the Lord was upon me, c and he opened my mouth before the man came to me in the morning. So my mouth was opened and I was no longer silent. d

23Then the word of the Lord came to me: 24"Son of man, the people living in those ruins in the land of Israel are saying, 'Abraham was only one man, yet he possessed the land. But we are many; surely the land has been given to us as our possession.' e 25Therefore say to them, 'This is what the Sovereign Lord says: Since you eat meat with the blood f still in it and look to your idols and shed blood, should you then possess the land? g 26You rely on your sword, you do detestable things, and each of you defiles his neighbor's wife. Should you then possess the land?'

33:27
h 1Sa 13:6

27"Say this to them: 'This is what the Sovereign Lord says: As surely as I live, those who are left in the ruins will fall by the sword, those out in the country I will give to the wild animals to be devoured, and those in strongholds and caves will die of a plague. h 28I will make the land a desolate waste, and her proud strength will come to an end, and the mountains of Israel will become desolate so that no one will cross them. 29Then they will know that I am the Lord, when I have made the land a desolate waste because of all the detestable things they have done.'

33:31
i Ps 78:36-37;
Isa 29:13

30"As for you, son of man, your countrymen are talking together about you by the walls and at the doors of the houses, saying to each other, 'Come and hear the message that has come from the Lord.' 31My people come to you, as they usually do, and sit before you to listen to your words, but they do not put them into practice. With their mouths they express devotion, but their hearts are greedy for unjust gain. i 32Indeed, to them you are nothing more than one who sings love songs with a beautiful voice and plays an instrument well, for they hear your words but do not put them into practice.

33:33
j 1Sa 3:20

33"When all this comes true—and it surely will—then they will know that a prophet has been among them. j"

Shepherds and Sheep

34 The word of the Lord came to me: 2"Son of man, prophesy against the shepherds of Israel; prophesy and say to them: 'This is what the Sovereign Lord says: Woe to the shepherds of Israel who only take care of themselves! Should not shepherds take care of the

---

33:21, 22 Near the beginning of his ministry, Ezekiel had been unable to speak except to give specific messages from God (3:26, 27). After Ezekiel's prophecies came true and the false prophets were exposed, Ezekiel was again able to talk freely. No longer needing to prove himself, he was free to offer God's message of restoration and hope.

33:30–32 The people refused to act upon Ezekiel's message. When people mock your witness for Christ or fail to act upon your advice, don't give up. You are not witnessing for them alone, but out of faithfulness to God. You cannot make them accept your message; you can only be faithful in delivering it.

33:31 In your heart, do you really love God? These people gave the appearance of following God, but they loved their money more. Many today also give the outward impression of being religious while remaining inwardly greedy. Jesus warned that we cannot love God and Money at the same time (Matthew 6:24). It's easy to say "I surrender all" when we don't have much. It's when we start gaining some money that it becomes difficult to avoid loving it.

33:32 The people were coming to listen to Ezekiel in order to be entertained. They weren't interested in hearing a message from the Lord and then putting it into practice. Many people

see church as entertainment. They enjoy the music, the people, and the activities, but they don't take the messages to heart. They don't seek to be challenged or to serve. Have you reduced church services to the level of entertainment, or does your worship truly have an impact on your life? Listen to God's words and then obey—apply his words and put them into practice in your life.

34:1ff Ezekiel called the exiles "Israel," referring to all Jews in captivity from both the northern and southern kingdoms. Ezekiel criticized Israel's leaders for taking care of themselves rather than taking care of their people. He outlined their sins (34:1–6) and pronounced judgment upon them (34:7–10). Then he promised that a true shepherd (the Messiah) would come who would take care of the people as the other leaders were supposed to do (34:11–31). This beautiful message portrays the fate of the present shepherds, the work of the new shepherd, and the future of the sheep.

flock?[k] [3]You eat the curds, clothe yourselves with the wool and slaughter the choice animals, but you do not take care of the flock.[l] [4]You have not strengthened the weak or healed the sick or bound up the injured. You have not brought back the strays or searched for the lost. You have ruled them harshly and brutally.[m] [5]So they were scattered because there was no shepherd, and when they were scattered they became food for all the wild animals. [6]My sheep wandered over all the mountains and on every high hill. They were scattered over the whole earth, and no one searched or looked for them.

[7]"'Therefore, you shepherds, hear the word of the Lord: [8]As surely as I live, declares the Sovereign Lord, because my flock lacks a shepherd and so has been plundered and has become food for all the wild animals, and because my shepherds did not search for my flock but cared for themselves rather than for my flock, [9]therefore, O shepherds, hear the word of the Lord: [10]This is what the Sovereign Lord says: I am against[n] the shepherds and will hold them accountable for my flock. I will remove them from tending the flock so that the shepherds can no longer feed themselves. I will rescue my flock from their mouths, and it will no longer be food for them.[o]

[11]"'For this is what the Sovereign Lord says: I myself will search for my sheep and look after them. [12]As a shepherd looks after his scattered flock when he is with them, so will I look after my sheep. I will rescue them from all the places where they were scattered on a day of clouds and darkness.[p] [13]I will bring them out from the nations and gather them from the countries, and I will bring them into their own land. I will pasture them on the mountains of Israel, in the ravines and in all the settlements in the land. [14]I will tend them in a good pasture, and the mountain heights of Israel will be their grazing land. There they will lie down in good grazing land, and there they will feed in a rich pasture[q] on the mountains of Israel. [15]I myself will tend my sheep and have them lie down, declares the Sovereign Lord. [16]I will search for the lost and bring back the strays. I will bind up the injured and strengthen the weak, but the sleek and the strong I will destroy. I will shepherd the flock with justice.[r]

[17]"'As for you, my flock, this is what the Sovereign Lord says: I will judge between one sheep and another, and between rams and goats.[s] [18]Is it not enough for you to feed on the good pasture? Must you also trample the rest of your pasture with your feet? Is it not enough for you to drink clear water? Must you also muddy the rest with your feet? [19]Must my flock feed on what you have trampled and drink what you have muddied with your feet?

[20]"'Therefore this is what the Sovereign Lord says to them: See, I myself will judge between the fat sheep and the lean sheep. [21]Because you shove with flank and shoulder, butting all the weak sheep with your horns[t] until you have driven them away, [22]I will save my flock, and they will no longer be plundered. I will judge between one sheep and another. [23]I will place over them one shepherd, my servant David, and he will tend[u] them; he will tend them and be their shepherd. [24]I the Lord will be their God, and my servant David will be prince among them. I the Lord have spoken.

[25]"'I will make a covenant of peace with them and rid the land of wild beasts so that they may live in the desert and sleep in the forests in safety.[v] [26]I will bless them and the places surrounding my hill.[a] I will send down showers in season; there will be showers of blessing. [27]The trees of the field will yield their fruit and the ground will yield its crops; the people will be secure in their land. They will know that I am the Lord, when I break the bars of their yoke and rescue them from the hands of those who enslaved them. [28]They will no longer be

[a]26 Or I will make them and the places surrounding my hill a blessing

**Cross references (right margin):**

34:2
[k] Jer 23:1; Jn 10:11
34:3
[l] Isa 56:11;
Eze 22:27;
Zec 11:16
34:4
[m] Zec 11:15-17
34:10
[n] Jer 21:13
[o] 1Sa 2:29-30
34:12
[p] Eze 30:3
34:14
[q] Ps 23:2
34:16
[r] Isa 10:16; Lk 5:32
34:17
[s] Mt 25:32-33
34:21
[t] Dt 33:17
34:23
[u] Isa 40:11
34:25
[v] Isa 11:6-9;
Hos 2:18

34:4–6 God would judge the religious leaders because they were selfishly caught up in their own concerns and were neglecting their service to others. Spiritual leaders must be careful not to pursue self-development at the expense of broken, scattered people. When we give too much attention to our own needs and ideas, we may push God aside and abandon those who depend on us.

34:9, 10 Those shepherds who failed their flock would be removed from office and held responsible for what happened to the people they were supposed to lead. Christian leaders must heed this warning and care for their flock, or total failure and judgment will be the result (see 1 Corinthians 9:24–27). True leadership focuses on helping others, not just on getting ahead.

34:11–16 God promises to take over as shepherd of his scattered flock. When our leaders fail us, we must not despair but remember that God is in control and that he promises to return and care for his flock. Thus we know that we can turn to God for help. He is still in control and can transform any tragic situation to produce good for his kingdom (see Genesis 50:20; Romans 8:28).

34:18–20 A bad shepherd is not only selfish but destructive. A minister who muddies the waters for others by raising unnecessary doubts, teaching false ideas, and acting sinfully is destroying his flock's spiritual nourishment.

34:23–25 In contrast to the present evil shepherds (leaders) of God's people (34:1–6), God will send a perfect shepherd, the Messiah ("my servant David"), who will take care of every need his people have and set up a kingdom of perfect peace and justice (see Psalm 23; Jeremiah 23:5, 6; John 10:11; Hebrews 13:20, 21; Revelation 21). "Peace" here means more than the absence of conflict. It is contentment, fulfillment, and security.

plundered by the nations, nor will wild animals devour them. They will live in safety, and no one will make them afraid. *w* 29 I will provide for them a land renowned for its crops, and they will no longer be victims of famine *x* in the land or bear the scorn *y* of the nations. 30 Then they will know that I, the LORD their God, am with them and that they, the house of Israel, are my people, declares the Sovereign LORD. 31 You my sheep, the sheep of my pasture, *z* are people, and I am your God, declares the Sovereign LORD.'"

A Prophecy Against Edom

35 The word of the LORD came to me: 2 "Son of man, set your face against Mount Seir; prophesy against it 3 and say: 'This is what the Sovereign LORD says: I am against you, Mount Seir, and I will stretch out my hand *a* against you and make you a desolate waste. 4 I will turn your towns into ruins and you will be desolate. Then you will know that I am the LORD.

5 "'Because you harbored an ancient hostility and delivered the Israelites over to the sword at the time of their calamity, the time their punishment reached its climax, *b* 6 therefore as surely as I live, declares the Sovereign LORD, I will give you over to bloodshed and it will pursue you. Since you did not hate bloodshed, bloodshed will pursue you. 7 I will make Mount Seir a desolate waste and cut off from it all who come and go. 8 I will fill your mountains with the slain; those killed by the sword will fall on your hills and in your valleys and in all your ravines. 9 I will make you desolate forever; your towns will not be inhabited. Then you will know that I am the LORD. *c*

10 "'Because you have said, "These two nations and countries will be ours and we will take possession of them," even though I the LORD was there, 11 therefore as surely as I live, declares the Sovereign LORD, I will treat you in accordance with the anger and jealousy you showed in your hatred of them and I will make myself known among them when I judge you. *d* 12 Then you will know that I the LORD have heard all the contemptible things you have said against the mountains of Israel. You said, "They have been laid waste and have been given over to us to devour." 13 You boasted against me and spoke against me without restraint, and I heard it. 14 This is what the Sovereign LORD says: While the whole earth rejoices, I will make you desolate. *e* 15 Because you rejoiced when the inheritance of the house of Israel became desolate, that is how I will treat you. You will be desolate, O Mount Seir, you and all of Edom. *f* Then they will know that I am the LORD.'"

A Prophecy to the Mountains of Israel

36 "Son of man, prophesy to the mountains of Israel and say, 'O mountains of Israel, hear the word of the LORD. 2 This is what the Sovereign LORD says: The enemy said of you, "Aha! *g* The ancient heights have become our possession. *h*"' 3 Therefore prophesy and say, 'This is what the Sovereign LORD says: Because they ravaged and hounded you from every side

34:28
w Jer 30:10

34:29
x Eze 36:29
y Eze 36:6

34:31
z Ps 100:3

35:3
a Jer 6:12

35:5
b Eze 21:29

35:9
c Jer 49:13

35:11
d Ps 9:16; Mt 7:2

35:14
e Jer 51:48

35:15
f Jer 50:11-13

36:2
g Eze 25:3
h Eze 35:10

BAD SHEPHERDS VERSUS GOOD SHEPHERDS	Bad Shepherds	Good Shepherds
	Take care of themselves	Take care of their flock
	Worry about their own health	Strengthen the weak and sick, search for the lost
	Rule harshly and brutally	Rule lovingly and gently
	Abandon and scatter the sheep	Gather and protect the sheep
	Keep the best for themselves	Give their best to the sheep

35:1ff Ezekiel gave another prophecy against Edom (also called Seir); his first prophecy against Edom is found in 25:12–14. In this prophecy, Ezekiel is probably using Edom to represent *all* the nations opposed to God's people. Chapter 36 says that Israel will be restored, while this chapter says that Edom (God's enemies) will be made "a desolate waste."

35:2 Edom offered to help destroy Jerusalem and rejoiced when the city fell. Edom's long-standing hostility against God's people resulted in God's judgment.

35:6-8 Ezekiel prophesied not only against the people of Edom, but also against their mountains and land. Their home territory was Mount Seir. Mountains, symbols of strength and power, represented the pride of these people who thought they could get away with evil. Edom's desire for revenge turned against them.

Edom received the punishment they were so hasty to give out. God has a way of turning our treatment of others into a boomerang. So we must be careful in our judgment of others (Matthew 7:1, 2).

36:1ff In this prophecy, Ezekiel said that Israel would be restored as a nation and would return to its own land. The mountains were symbolic of Israel's strength (see the note on 35:6–8). To the exiles in Babylon, this seemed impossible. This message again emphasizes God's sovereignty and trustworthiness. He would first judge the nations used to punish Israel (36:1–7) and then restore his people (36:8–15).

36:2 "The ancient heights" refers to the promised land—the land of Israel. Israel's enemies challenged not only their boundaries but also God's promises to Israel.

so that you became the possession of the rest of the nations and the object of people's malicious talk and slander, [4] therefore, O mountains of Israel, hear the word of the Sovereign LORD: This is what the Sovereign LORD says to the mountains and hills, to the ravines and valleys, to the desolate ruins and the deserted towns that have been plundered and ridiculed by the rest of the nations around you [i]— [5] this is what the Sovereign LORD says: In my burning zeal I have spoken against the rest of the nations, and against all Edom, for with glee and with malice in their hearts they made my land their own possession so that they might plunder its pastureland.' [j] [6] Therefore prophesy concerning the land of Israel and say to the mountains and hills, to the ravines and valleys: 'This is what the Sovereign LORD says: I speak in my jealous wrath because you have suffered the scorn of the nations. [k] [7] Therefore this is what the Sovereign LORD says: I swear with uplifted hand that the nations around you will also suffer scorn.

[8] "'But you, O mountains of Israel, will produce branches and fruit for my people Israel, for they will soon come home. [9] I am concerned for you and will look on you with favor; you will be plowed and sown, [10] and I will multiply the number of people upon you, even the whole house of Israel. The towns will be inhabited and the ruins rebuilt. [l] [11] I will increase the number of men and animals upon you, and they will be fruitful and become numerous. I will settle people on you as in the past and will make you prosper more than before. Then you will know that I am the LORD. [12] I will cause people, my people Israel, to walk upon you. They will possess you, and you will be their inheritance; you will never again deprive them of their children.

[13] "'This is what the Sovereign LORD says: Because people say to you, "You devour men [m] and deprive your nation of its children," [14] therefore you will no longer devour men or make your nation childless, declares the Sovereign LORD. [15] No longer will I make you hear the taunts of the nations, and no longer will you suffer the scorn of the peoples or cause your nation to fall, declares the Sovereign LORD. [n] '"

[16] Again the word of the LORD came to me: [17] "Son of man, when the people of Israel were living in their own land, they defiled it by their conduct and their actions. Their conduct was like a woman's monthly uncleanness in my sight. [18] So I poured out my wrath on them because they had shed blood in the land and because they had defiled it with their idols. [19] I dispersed them among the nations, and they were scattered through the countries; I judged them according to their conduct and their actions. [o] [20] And wherever they went among the nations they profaned [p] my holy name, for it was said of them, 'These are the LORD's people, and yet they had to leave his land.' [q] [21] I had concern for my holy name, which the house of Israel profaned among the nations where they had gone. [r]

[22] "Therefore say to the house of Israel, 'This is what the Sovereign LORD says: It is not for your sake, O house of Israel, that I am going to do these things, but for the sake of my holy name, which you have profaned among the nations where you have gone. [23] I will show the holiness of my great name, which has been profaned among the nations, the name you have profaned among them. Then the nations will know that I am the LORD, declares the Sovereign LORD, when I show myself holy [s] through you before their eyes.

[24] "'For I will take you out of the nations; I will gather you from all the countries and bring you back into your own land. [t] [25] I will sprinkle [u] clean water on you, and you will be clean; I will cleanse you from all your impurities and from all your idols. [v] [26] I will give you a new heart and put a new spirit in you; I will remove from you your heart of stone and give you a heart of flesh. [w] [27] And I will put my Spirit in you and move you to follow my decrees and be careful to keep my laws. [28] You will live in the land I gave your forefathers; you will be my people, and I will be your God. [x] [29] I will save you from all your uncleanness. I will call for the grain and make it plentiful and will not bring famine [y] upon you. [30] I will increase the fruit of

36:4 [i] Ps 79:4; Eze 34:28

36:5 [j] Eze 35:10, 15

36:6 [k] Ps 123:3-4; Eze 34:29

36:10 [l] ver 33

36:13 [m] Nu 13:32

36:15 [n] Eze 34:29

36:19 [o] Eze 39:24

36:20 [p] Ro 2:24 [q] Isa 52:5

36:21 [r] Ps 74:18

36:23 [s] Eze 20:41

36:24 [t] Eze 34:13; 37:21

36:25 [u] Heb 10:22 [v] Zec 13:2

36:26 [w] Eze 11:19

36:28 [x] Eze 37:14, 27

36:29 [y] Eze 34:29

36:21-23 Why did God want to protect his holy name—his reputation—among the nations of the world? God was concerned about the salvation not only of his people, but also of the whole world. To allow his people to remain in sin and be permanently destroyed by their enemies would lead other nations to conclude that their pagan gods were more powerful than Israel's God (Isaiah 48:11). Thus, to protect his holy name, God would return a remnant of his people to their land. God will not share his glory with false gods—he alone is the one true God. The people had the responsibility to represent God properly to the rest of the world.

Believers today have that same responsibility. How do you represent God to the world?

36:25-27 God promised to restore Israel not only physically, but spiritually. To accomplish this, God would give them a new heart for following him and put his Spirit within them (see 11:19, 20; Psalm 51:7-11) to transform them and empower them to do his will. Again the new covenant was promised (16:61-63; 34:23-25), ultimately to be fulfilled in Christ. No matter how impure your life is right now, God offers you a fresh start. You can have your sins washed away, receive a new heart for God, and have his Spirit within you—if you accept God's promise. Why try to patch up your old life when you can have a new one?

36:30
z Eze 34:27

36:31
a Eze 20:43

the trees and the crops of the field, so that you will no longer suffer disgrace among the nations because of famine. z 31 Then you will remember your evil ways and wicked deeds, and you will loathe yourselves for your sins and detestable practices. a 32 I want you to know that I am not doing this for your sake, declares the Sovereign Lord. Be ashamed and disgraced for your conduct, O house of Israel!

33 "This is what the Sovereign Lord says: On the day I cleanse you from all your sins, I will resettle your towns, and the ruins will be rebuilt. 34 The desolate land will be cultivated instead of lying desolate in the sight of all who pass through it. 35 They will say, "This land that

36:35
b Joel 2:3
c Isa 51:3

36:36
d Eze 22:14; 37:14

was laid waste has become like the garden of Eden;b the cities that were lying in ruins, desolate and destroyed, are now fortified and inhabited. c" 36 Then the nations around you that remain will know that I the Lord have rebuilt what was destroyed and have replanted what was desolate. I the Lord have spoken, and I will do it.' d

37 "This is what the Sovereign Lord says: Once again I will yield to the plea of the house of Israel and do this for them: I will make their people as numerous as sheep, 38 as numerous as the flocks for offerings at Jerusalem during her appointed feasts. So will the ruined cities be filled with flocks of people. Then they will know that I am the Lord."

The Valley of Dry Bones

37:1
e Eze 1:3; 8:3
f Eze 11:24

37:3
g Dt 32:39; 1Sa 2:6

37:5
h Ps 104:29-30

37:6
i Joel 2:27; 3:17

37:9
j Ps 104:30

37 The hand of the Lord was upon me,e and he brought me out by the Spiritf of the Lord and set me in the middle of a valley; it was full of bones. 2 He led me back and forth among them, and I saw a great many bones on the floor of the valley, bones that were very dry. 3 He asked me, "Son of man, can these bones live?"

I said, "O Sovereign Lord, you alone know. g"

4 Then he said to me, "Prophesy to these bones and say to them, 'Dry bones, hear the word of the Lord! 5 This is what the Sovereign Lord says to these bones: I will make breatha enter you, and you will come to life. h 6 I will attach tendons to you and make flesh come upon you and cover you with skin; I will put breath in you, and you will come to life. Then you will know that I am the Lord. i'"

7 So I prophesied as I was commanded. And as I was prophesying, there was a noise, a rattling sound, and the bones came together, bone to bone. 8 I looked, and tendons and flesh appeared on them and skin covered them, but there was no breath in them.

9 Then he said to me, "Prophesy to the breath;j prophesy, son of man, and say to it, 'This is what the Sovereign Lord says: Come from the four winds, O breath, and breathe into these

a5 The Hebrew for this word can also mean wind or spirit (see verses 6-14).

OLD AND NEW COVENANTS

Old Covenant	New Covenant
Placed upon stone	Placed upon people's hearts
Based on the law	Based on desire to love and serve God
Must be taught	Known by all
Legal relationship with God	Personal relationship with God

36:32 God said his people should be ashamed of their sins. The people had become so callous that they had lost all sensitivity to sin. First they had to "remember" (36:31) their sins, then despise them, and finally repent of them (see James 4:8, 9). As we examine our lives, we may find that we too have lost our sensitivity to certain sins. But if we measure ourselves against God's standards of right living, we will be ashamed. To regain sensitivity we must recognize our sin for what it is, feel sorry for displeasing God, and ask his forgiveness. The Holy Spirit will guide us, making us responsive and receptive to God's truth (John 14:26; 16:8, 13).

36:37, 38 God said that if the people asked, he would come to their aid. We cannot expect his mercy, however, until we have sought new hearts from him (36:26). We can be thankful that his invitation is open to all.

37:1ff This vision illustrates the promise of chapter 36—new life and a nation restored, both physically and spiritually. The dry bones are a picture of the Jews in captivity—scattered and dead. The two sticks (37:15–17) represent the reunion of the entire

nation of Israel that had divided into northern and southern kingdoms after Solomon. The scattered exiles of both Israel and Judah would be released from the "graves" of captivity and one day regathered in their homeland, with the Messiah as their leader. This vision has yet to be fulfilled. Ezekiel felt he was speaking to the dead as he preached to the exiles because they rarely responded to his message. But these bones responded! And just as God brought life to the dead bones, he would bring life again to his spiritually dead people.

37:4, 5 The dry bones represented the people's spiritually dead condition. Your church may seem like a heap of dry bones to you, spiritually dead with no hope of vitality. But just as God promised to restore his nation, he can restore any church, no matter how dry or dead it may be. Rather than give up, pray for renewal, for God can restore it to life. The hope and prayer of every church should be that God will put his Spirit into it (37:14). In fact, God is at work calling his people back to himself, bringing new life into dead churches.

slain, that they may live.'" [10]So I prophesied as he commanded me, and breath entered them; they came to life and stood up on their feet—a vast army. [k]

[11]Then he said to me: "Son of man, these bones are the whole house of Israel. They say, 'Our bones are dried up and our hope is gone; we are cut off.' [12]Therefore prophesy and say to them: 'This is what the Sovereign LORD says: O my people, I am going to open your graves and bring you up from them; I will bring you back to the land of Israel. [l] [13]Then you, my people, will know that I am the LORD, when I open your graves and bring you up from them. [14]I will put my Spirit in you and you will live, and I will settle you in your own land. Then you will know that I the LORD have spoken, and I have done it, declares the LORD. [m]'"

One Nation Under One King

[15]The word of the LORD came to me: [16]"Son of man, take a stick of wood and write on it, 'Belonging to Judah and the Israelites associated with him. [n]' Then take another stick of wood, and write on it, 'Ephraim's stick, belonging to Joseph and all the house of Israel associated with him.' [17]Join them together into one stick so that they will become one in your hand.

[18]"When your countrymen ask you, 'Won't you tell us what you mean by this?' [o] [19]say to them, 'This is what the Sovereign LORD says: I am going to take the stick of Joseph—which is in Ephraim's hand—and of the Israelite tribes associated with him, and join it to Judah's stick, making them a single stick of wood, and they will become one in my hand.' [20]Hold before their eyes the sticks you have written on [21]and say to them, 'This is what the Sovereign LORD says: I will take the Israelites out of the nations where they have gone. I will gather them from all around and bring them back into their own land. [p] [22]I will make them one nation in the land, on the mountains of Israel. There will be one king over all of them and they will never again be two nations or be divided into two kingdoms. [q] [23]They will no longer defile [r] themselves with their idols and vile images or with any of their offenses, for I will save them from all their sinful backsliding, [a] and I will cleanse them. They will be my people, and I will be their God. [s]

[24]"My servant David will be king over them, and they will all have one shepherd. [t] They will follow my laws and be careful to keep my decrees. [25]They will live in the land I gave to my servant Jacob, the land where your fathers lived. They and their children and their children's children will live there forever, and David my servant will be their prince forever. [26]I will make a covenant of peace [u] with them; it will be an everlasting covenant. I will establish them and increase their numbers, and I will put my sanctuary among them forever. [27]My dwelling place [v] will be with them; I will be their God, and they will be my people. [w] [28]Then the nations will know that I the LORD make Israel holy, [x] when my sanctuary is among them forever.'"

A Prophecy Against Gog

38

The word of the LORD came to me: [2]"Son of man, set your face against Gog, of the land of Magog, the chief prince of [b] Meshech and Tubal; [y] prophesy against him [3]and say: 'This is what the Sovereign LORD says: I am against you, O Gog, chief prince of [c] Meshech and Tubal. [4]I will turn you around, put hooks in your jaws and bring you out with your whole army—your horses, your horsemen fully armed, and a great horde with large and small shields, all of them brandishing their swords. [5]Persia, Cush [d] and Put will be with them, all with shields and helmets, [6]also Gomer [z] with all its troops, and Beth Togarmah [a] from the far north with all its troops—the many nations with you.

37:10
[k]Rev 11:11

37:12
[l]Isa 26:19;
Hos 13:14

37:14
[m]Eze 36:27-28, 36

37:16
[n]Nu 17:2-3;
2Ch 15:9

37:18
[o]Eze 24:19

37:21
[p]Eze 36:24; 39:27

37:22
[q]Jer 3:18

37:23
[r]Eze 36:25
[s]Eze 36:28

37:24
[t]Isa 40:11;
Eze 34:23

37:26
[u]Isa 55:3

37:27
[v]Jn 1:14
[w]2Co 6:16*

37:28
[x]Eze 20:12

38:2
[y]Rev 20:8

38:6
[z]Ge 10:2
[a]Eze 27:14

---

[a]23 Many Hebrew manuscripts (see also Septuagint); most Hebrew manuscripts *all their dwelling places where they sinned*   [b]2 Or *the prince of Rosh*,   [c]3 Or *Gog, prince of Rosh*,   [d]5 That is, the upper Nile region

---

37:16 The first stick was for Judah, being the leading tribe in the southern kingdom. The other was for Ephraim, the leading tribe in the northern kingdom.

37:24, 25 The Messiah was often called David because he is David's descendant. David was a good king, but the Messiah would be the perfect King (Revelation 17:14; 19:16; 21:1ff).

37:26, 27 God's promise here goes beyond the physical and geographical restoration of Israel. He promises to breathe new spiritual life into his people so that their hearts and attitudes will be right with him and united with one another. This same process is described throughout God's Word as the cleansing and renewing of our hearts by God's Spirit (Titus 3:4–6).

38:1ff In chapter 37, Ezekiel revealed how Israel (God's people)

would be restored to their land from many parts of the world. Once Israel became strong, a confederacy of nations from the north would attack, led by Gog (see also Revelation 20:8). Their purpose would be to destroy God's people. Gog's allies would come from the mountainous area southeast of the Black Sea and southwest of the Caspian Sea (central Turkey), as well as from the area that is present-day Iran, Ethiopia, Libya, and possibly the Soviet Union. Gog could be a person (he sometimes is identified with Gyges, king of Lydia in 660 B.C.), or Gog could also be a symbol of all the evil in the world. Whether symbolic or literal, Gog represents the aggregate military might of all the forces opposed to God.

Many say that the battle Ezekiel described will occur at the end of human history, but there are many differences between the events described here and those in Revelation 20. Regardless of

7"'Get ready; be prepared, you and all the hordes gathered about you, and take command of them. 8After many days you will be called to arms. In future years you will invade a land that has recovered from war, whose people were gathered from many nations to the mountains of Israel, which had long been desolate. They had been brought out from the nations, and now all of them live in safety. 9You and all your troops and the many nations with you will go up, advancing like a storm;b you will be like a cloud covering the land.

38:9
b Isa 28:2

10"'This is what the Sovereign LORD says: On that day thoughts will come into your mind and you will devise an evil scheme. 11You will say, "I will invade a land of unwalled villages; I will attack a peaceful and unsuspecting people—all of them living without walls and without gates and bars. c 12I will plunder and loot and turn my hand against the resettled ruins and the people gathered from the nations, rich in livestock and goods, living at the center of the land." 13Sheba d and Dedan and the merchants of Tarshish and all her villagesa will say to you, "Have you come to plunder? Have you gathered your hordes to loot, to carry off silver and gold, to take away livestock and goods and to seize much plunder?"'

38:11
c Jer 49:31

38:13
d Eze 27:22

14"'Therefore, son of man, prophesy and say to Gog: 'This is what the Sovereign LORD says: In that day, when my people Israel are living in safety, will you not take notice of it? 15You will come from your place in the far north, you and many nations with you, all of them riding on horses, a great horde, a mighty army. e 16You will advance against my people Israel like a cloud that covers the land. In days to come, O Gog, I will bring you against my land, so that the nations may know me when I show myself holy through you before their eyes.

38:15
e Eze 39:2

17"'This is what the Sovereign LORD says: Are you not the one I spoke of in former days by my servants the prophets of Israel? At that time they prophesied for years that I would bring you against them. 18This is what will happen in that day: When Gog attacks the land of Israel, my hot anger will be aroused, declares the Sovereign LORD. 19In my zeal and fiery wrath I declare that at that time there shall be a great earthquake in the land of Israel. f 20The fish of the sea, the birds of the air, the beasts of the field, every creature that moves along the ground, and all the people on the face of the earth will tremble at my presence. The mountains will be overturned, the cliffs will crumble and every wall will fall to the ground.g 21I will summon a sword h against Gog on all my mountains, declares the Sovereign LORD. Every man's sword will be against his brother. i 22I will execute judgmentj upon him with plague and bloodshed; I will pour down torrents of rain, hailstonesk and burning sulfur on him and on his troops and on the many nations with him. 23And so I will show my greatness and my holiness, and I will make myself known in the sight of many nations. Then they will know that I am the LORD.'

38:19
f Hag 2:6, 21
38:20
g Hos 4:3

38:21
h Eze 14:17
i 1Sa 14:20

38:22
j Isa 66:16;
Jer 25:31
k Rev 16:21

39 "Son of man, prophesy against Gog and say: 'This is what the Sovereign LORD says: I am against you, O Gog, chief prince ofb Meshech and Tubal.l 2I will turn you around and drag you along. I will bring you from the far north and send you against the mountains of Israel. 3Then I will strike your bowm from your left hand and make your arrows drop from your right hand. 4On the mountains of Israel you will fall, you and all your troops and the nations with you. I will give you as food to all kinds of carrion birds and to the wild animals.n 5You will fall in the open field, for I have spoken, declares the Sovereign LORD. 6I will send fireo on Magog and on those who live in safety in the coastlands, and they will know that I am the LORD.

39:1
l Eze 38:2, 3

39:3
m Hos 1:5
39:4
n Eze 33:27
39:6
o Am 1:4

7"'I will make known my holy name among my people Israel. I will no longer let my holy name be profaned, and the nations will know that I the LORD am the Holy One in Israel.p 8It is coming! It will surely take place, declares the Sovereign LORD. This is the day I have spoken of.

39:7
p Eze 36:16, 23

9"'Then those who live in the towns of Israel will go out and use the weapons for fuel and burn them up—the small and large shields, the bows and arrows, the war clubs and spears. For

a 13 Or her strong lions   b 1 Or Gog, prince of Rosh,

---

when this battle will occur, the message is clear: God will deliver his people—no enemy can stand before his mighty power.

38:13 Sheba and Dedan, great trading centers in Arabia, would in effect say to Gog, "Who are you to usurp our position as the world's trade leaders?" Sheba and Dedan would then join this confederacy. Tarshish was the leading trade center in the west; many believe it was in Spain.

38:21 God will directly intervene in the defense of Israel, unleashing severe natural disasters on the invaders from the north. In the end, the stricken pagan nations will turn on them-

selves in confusion and panic. All those who set themselves against God will be destroyed.

39:1ff The story of the battle continues. The defeat of the evil forces will be final and complete; they will be destroyed by divine intervention. Because of this victory, God's name will be known throughout the world. His glory will be evident, and the nations will understand that he alone is in charge of human history. God will clearly show his love for his people by restoring them to their homeland.

seven years they will use them for fuel. *q* 10 They will not need to gather wood from the fields or cut it from the forests, because they will use the weapons for fuel. And they will plunder those who plundered them and loot those who looted them, declares the Sovereign Lord. *r*

11 "'On that day I will give Gog a burial place in Israel, in the valley of those who travel east toward *a* the Sea. *b* It will block the way of travelers, because Gog and all his hordes will be buried there. So it will be called the Valley of Hamon Gog. *c*

12 "'For seven months the house of Israel will be burying them in order to cleanse the land. 13 All the people of the land will bury them, and the day I am glorified *s* will be a memorable day for them, declares the Sovereign Lord.

14 "'Men will be regularly employed to cleanse the land. Some will go throughout the land and, in addition to them, others will bury those that remain on the ground. At the end of the seven months they will begin their search. 15 As they go through the land and one of them sees a human bone, he will set up a marker beside it until the gravediggers have buried it in the Valley of Hamon Gog. 16 (Also a town called Hamonah *d* will be there.) And so they will cleanse the land.'

17 "Son of man, this is what the Sovereign Lord says: Call out to every kind of bird *t* and all the wild animals: 'Assemble and come together from all around to the sacrifice I am preparing for you, the great sacrifice on the mountains of Israel. There you will eat flesh and drink blood. 18 You will eat the flesh of mighty men and drink the blood of the princes of the earth as if they were rams and lambs, goats and bulls—all of them fattened animals from Bashan. *u* 19 At the sacrifice I am preparing for you, you will eat fat till you are glutted and drink blood till you are drunk. 20 At my table you will eat your fill of horses and riders, mighty men and soldiers of every kind,' declares the Sovereign Lord. *v*

21 "I will display my glory among the nations, and all the nations will see the punishment I inflict and the hand I lay upon them. *w* 22 From that day forward the house of Israel will know that I am the Lord their God. 23 And the nations will know that the people of Israel went into exile for their sin, because they were unfaithful to me. So I hid my face from them and handed them over to their enemies, and they all fell by the sword. *x* 24 I dealt with them according to their uncleanness and their offenses, and I hid my face from them. *y*

25 "Therefore this is what the Sovereign Lord says: I will now bring Jacob back from captivity *e z* and will have compassion *a* on all the people of Israel, and I will be zealous for my holy name. 26 They will forget their shame and all the unfaithfulness they showed toward me when they lived in safety in their land with no one to make them afraid. *b* 27 When I have brought them back from the nations and have gathered them from the countries of their enemies, I will show myself holy through them in the sight of many nations. *c* 28 Then they will know that I am the Lord their God, for though I sent them into exile among the nations, I will gather them to their own land, not leaving any behind. 29 I will no longer hide my face from them, for I will pour out my Spirit *d* on the house of Israel, declares the Sovereign Lord."

2. Restoring the worship of God
The New Temple Area

40 In the twenty-fifth year of our exile, at the beginning of the year, on the tenth of the month, in the fourteenth year after the fall of the city—on that very day the hand of

a 11 Or of   *b* 11 That is, the Dead Sea   *c* 11 Hamon Gog means hordes of Gog.   *d* 16 Hamonah means horde.
e 25 Or now restore the fortunes of Jacob

**Cross references (right margin):**

39:9 *q* Ps 46:9
39:10 *r* Isa 14:2
39:13 *s* Eze 28:22
39:17 *t* Rev 19:17
39:18 *u* Ps 22:12
39:20 *v* Rev 19:17-18
39:21 *w* Eze 38:16
39:23 *x* Isa 59:2
39:24 *y* Eze 36:19
39:25 *z* Eze 34:13; *a* Jer 30:18
39:26 *b* Isa 17:2; Eze 34:28
39:27 *c* Eze 36:23-24; 38:16
39:29 *d* Joel 2:28; Ac 2:17

39:12–16 Two themes are intertwined: God's total victory over his enemies, and the need to make it holy. After the final battle, teams will be used to give proper burial to the bodies of the dead enemies in order for the land to be cleansed. The land would have been defiled by unburied corpses. Those who would come in contact with the corpses out in the open would become ceremonially unclean (according to Numbers 19:14–16). Yet there will be so many that all kinds of birds will be called in order to help dispose of the corpses (39:17–20). This message is exciting for us: with God on our side, we are assured of ultimate victory over his foes because God will fight on our behalf (see also Zephaniah 3:14–17; Romans 8:38, 39).

39:29 Both in this prophecy and in Joel 2:28, 29, God promises to pour out his Spirit on mankind. The early church believed this began to be fulfilled at Pentecost, when God's Holy Spirit came to live in all believers (Acts 2:1–18).

40:1ff The building of the temple envisioned a time of complete restoration to the exiles, a time when God would return to his people. The temple was built in 520–515 B.C. (see Ezra 5; 6), but fell short of Ezekiel's plan (Haggai 2:3; Zechariah 4:10). This vision of the temple has been interpreted in four main ways: (1) This is the temple Zerubbabel should have built in 520–515 B.C. and is the actual blueprint Ezekiel intended. But due to disobedience (43:2–10), it was never followed. (2) This is a literal temple to be rebuilt during the millennial reign of Christ. (3) This temple is symbolic of the true worship of God by the Christian church right now. (4) This temple is symbolic of the future and eternal reign of God when his presence and blessing fill the earth.

Whether the temple is literal or symbolic, it seems clear that this is a vision of God's final perfect kingdom. This gave hope to the people of Ezekiel's time who had just seen their nation and its temple destroyed with no hope of rebuilding it in the near future.

40:1
e Eze 1:3

40:2
f Da 7:1, 7
g Rev 21:10

40:3
h Eze 1:7; Da 10:6
i Eze 47:3;
Rev 11:1; 21:15

40:4
j Eze 44:5

40:5
k Eze 42:20

40:7
l ver 36

40:17
m Rev 11:2

the Lord was upon me e and he took me there. 2 In visions f of God he took me to the land of Israel and set me on a very high mountain, g on whose south side were some buildings that looked like a city. 3 He took me there, and I saw a man whose appearance was like bronze; h he was standing in the gateway with a linen cord and a measuring rod i in his hand. 4 The man said to me, "Son of man, look with your eyes and hear with your ears and pay attention to everything I am going to show you, for that is why you have been brought here. Tell the house of Israel everything you see. j"

The East Gate to the Outer Court

5 I saw a wall completely surrounding the temple area. The length of the measuring rod in the man's hand was six long cubits, each of which was a cubit a and a handbreadth. b He measured k the wall; it was one measuring rod thick and one rod high.

6 Then he went to the gate facing east. He climbed its steps and measured the threshold of the gate; it was one rod deep. c 7 The alcoves l for the guards were one rod long and one rod wide, and the projecting walls between the alcoves were five cubits thick. And the threshold of the gate next to the portico facing the temple was one rod deep.

8 Then he measured the portico of the gateway; 9 it d was eight cubits deep and its jambs were two cubits thick. The portico of the gateway faced the temple.

10 Inside the east gate were three alcoves on each side; the three had the same measurements, and the faces of the projecting walls on each side had the same measurements. 11 Then he measured the width of the entrance to the gateway; it was ten cubits and its length was thirteen cubits. 12 In front of each alcove was a wall one cubit high, and the alcoves were six cubits square. 13 Then he measured the gateway from the top of the rear wall of one alcove to the top of the opposite one; the distance was twenty-five cubits from one parapet opening to the opposite one. 14 He measured along the faces of the projecting walls all around the inside of the gateway—sixty cubits. The measurement was up to the portico e facing the courtyard. f 15 The distance from the entrance of the gateway to the far end of its portico was fifty cubits. 16 The alcoves and the projecting walls inside the gateway were surmounted by narrow parapet openings all around, as was the portico; the openings all around faced inward. The faces of the projecting walls were decorated with palm trees.

The Outer Court

17 Then he brought me into the outer court. m There I saw some rooms and a pavement that had been constructed all around the court; there were thirty rooms along the pavement. 18 It abutted the sides of the gateways and was as wide as they were long; this was the lower pavement. 19 Then he measured the distance from the inside of the lower gateway to the outside of the inner court; it was a hundred cubits on the east side as well as on the north.

a 5 The common cubit was about 1 1/2 feet (about 0.5 meter).   b 5 That is, about 3 inches (about 8 centimeters)   c 6 Septuagint; Hebrew deep, the first threshold, one rod deep   d 8,9 Many Hebrew manuscripts, Septuagint, Vulgate and Syriac; most Hebrew manuscripts gateway facing the temple; it was one rod deep. 9 Then he measured the portico of the gateway; it   e 14 Septuagint; Hebrew projecting wall   f 14 The meaning of the Hebrew for this verse is uncertain.

The details given in this vision gave the people even more hope that what Ezekiel saw had come from God and would surely happen in the future.

40:1ff One argument against the view that Ezekiel's temple is a literal building of the future is that sacrifices are mentioned (40:38–43). If the sacrifices were to be reinstituted in the last days, then Christ's final sacrifice would not have been final. The New Testament makes it clear that Christ died once and for all (Romans 6:10; Hebrews 9:12; 10:10, 18). Our sins have been removed; no further sacrifice is needed.

In Ezekiel's day, however, the only kind of worship the people knew was the kind that revolved around the sacrifices and ceremonies described in Exodus through Deuteronomy. Ezekiel had to explain the new order of worship in terms the people would understand. The next nine chapters tell how the temple is the focal point of everything, showing that the ideal relationship with God is when all of life centers on him.

40:1ff Ezekiel explained God's dwelling place in words and images the people could understand. God wanted them to see the great splendor he had planned for those who lived faithfully. This kind of temple was never built, but it was a vision intended to typify God's

perfect plan for his people—the centrality of worship, the presence of the Lord, the blessings flowing from it, and the orderliness of worship and worship duties. Don't let the details obscure the point of this vision—one day all those who have been faithful to God will enjoy eternal life with him. Let the majesty of this vision lift you and teach you about the God you worship and serve.

40:1—43:27 This vision came to Ezekiel in 573 B.C. Chapters 40—43 give the temple's measurements and then describe how it would be filled with God's glory. Because Ezekiel was a priest, he would have been familiar with the furnishings and ceremonies of Solomon's temple. As in Revelation 11:1, 2, the command to "measure" defines the areas God has marked out for special use. As you read all these details, remember that God is sovereign over all our worship and over the timetable for restoring the faithful to himself.

40:3, 4 Who was this man? He was obviously not a human being, so he may have been the angel in 9:1–11 or one like him. Some say he may have been Christ himself because he speaks as God had been speaking to Ezekiel, calling him "Son of man."

40:5 The long cubit was about 21 inches, compared with the ordinary cubit of about 18 inches.

The North Gate

20 Then he measured the length and width of the gate facing north, leading into the outer court. 21 Its alcoves—three on each side—its projecting walls and its portico had the same measurements as those of the first gateway. It was fifty cubits long and twenty-five cubits wide. 22 Its openings, its portico n and its palm tree decorations had the same measurements as those of the gate facing east. Seven steps led up to it, with its portico opposite them. 23 There was a gate to the inner court facing the north gate, just as there was on the east. He measured from one gate to the opposite one; it was a hundred cubits.

40:22
n ver 49

The South Gate

24 Then he led me to the south side and I saw a gate facing south. He measured its jambs and its portico, and they had the same measurements as the others. 25 The gateway and its portico had narrow openings all around, like the openings of the others. It was fifty cubits long and twenty-five cubits wide. 26 Seven steps led up to it, with its portico opposite them; it had palm tree decorations on the faces of the projecting walls on each side. o 27 The inner court also had a gate facing south, and he measured from this gate to the outer gate on the south side; it was a hundred cubits.

40:26
o ver 22

Gates to the Inner Court

28 Then he brought me into the inner court through the south gate, and he measured the south gate; it had the same measurements as the others. 29 Its alcoves, its projecting walls and its portico had the same measurements as the others. The gateway and its portico had openings all around. It was fifty cubits long and twenty-five cubits wide. 30 (The porticoes p of the gateways around the inner court were twenty-five cubits wide and five cubits deep.) 31 Its portico faced the outer court; palm trees decorated its jambs, and eight steps led up to it.

40:30
p ver 21

32 Then he brought me to the inner court on the east side, and he measured the gateway; it had the same measurements as the others. 33 Its alcoves, its projecting walls and its portico had the same measurements as the others. The gateway and its portico had openings all around. It was fifty cubits long and twenty-five cubits wide. 34 Its portico faced the outer court; palm trees decorated the jambs on either side, and eight steps led up to it.

35 Then he brought me to the north gate q and measured it. It had the same measurements as the others, 36 as did its alcoves, its projecting walls and its portico, and it had openings all around. It was fifty cubits long and twenty-five cubits wide. 37 Its portico a faced the outer court; palm trees decorated the jambs on either side, and eight steps led up to it.

40:35
q Eze 44:4

The Rooms for Preparing Sacrifices

38 A room with a doorway was by the portico in each of the inner gateways, where the burnt offerings r were washed. 39 In the portico of the gateway were two tables on each side, on which the burnt offerings, sin offerings s and guilt offerings t were slaughtered. 40 By the outside wall of the portico of the gateway, near the steps at the entrance to the north gateway were two tables, and on the other side of the steps were two tables. 41 So there were four tables on one side of the gateway and four on the other—eight tables in all—on which the sacrifices were slaughtered. 42 There were also four tables of dressed stone for the burnt offerings, each a cubit and a half long, a cubit and a half wide and a cubit high. On them were placed the utensils for slaughtering the burnt offerings and the other sacrifices. 43 And double-pronged hooks, each a handbreadth long, were attached to the wall all around. The tables were for the flesh of the offerings.

40:38
r 2Ch 4:6;
Eze 42:13
40:39
s Lev 4:3, 28
t Lev 7:1

Rooms for the Priests

44 Outside the inner gate, within the inner court, were two rooms, one b at the side of the north gate and facing south, and another at the side of the south c gate and facing north. 45 He said to me, "The room facing south is for the priests who have charge of the temple, u 46 and the room facing north is for the priests who have charge of the altar. v These are the sons of Zadok, w who are the only Levites who may draw near to the LORD to minister before him. x"

40:45
u 1Ch 9:23
40:46
v Nu 18:5
w 1Ki 2:35
x Eze 43:19; 44:15

47 Then he measured the court: It was square—a hundred cubits long and a hundred cubits wide. And the altar was in front of the temple.

a 37 Septuagint (see also verses 31 and 34); Hebrew jambs   b 44 Septuagint; Hebrew were rooms for singers, which were   c 44 Septuagint; Hebrew east

40:38, 39 The washing of the sacrifices was done according to the standards of preparation established in Leviticus 1:6–9. This washing was part of the process of presenting an acceptable sacrifice to God.

The Temple

⁴⁸He brought me to the portico of the temple and measured the jambs of the portico; they were five cubits wide on either side. The width of the entrance was fourteen cubits and its projecting walls were ᵃ three cubits wide on either side. ⁴⁹The porticoʸ was twenty cubits wide, and twelveᵇ cubits from front to back. It was reached by a flight of stairs,ᶜ and there were pillars on each side of the jambs.

41 Then the man brought me to the outer sanctuary and measured the jambs; the width of the jambs was six cubitsᵈ on each side. ᵉ ²The entrance was ten cubits wide, and the projecting walls on each side of it were five cubits wide. He also measured the outer sanctuary; it was forty cubits long and twenty cubits wide. ᶻ

³Then he went into the inner sanctuary and measured the jambs of the entrance; each was two cubits wide. The entrance was six cubits wide, and the projecting walls on each side of it were seven cubits wide. ⁴And he measured the length of the inner sanctuary; it was twenty cubits, and its width was twenty cubits across the end of the outer sanctuary. ᵃ He said to me, "This is the Most Holy Place. ᵇ"

⁵Then he measured the wall of the temple; it was six cubits thick, and each side room around the temple was four cubits wide. ⁶The side rooms were on three levels, one above another, thirty on each level. There were ledges all around the wall of the temple to serve as supports for the side rooms, so that the supports were not inserted into the wall of the temple. ᶜ ⁷The side rooms all around the temple were wider at each successive level. The structure surrounding the temple was built in ascending stages, so that the rooms widened as one went upward. A stairwayᵈ went up from the lowest floor to the top floor through the middle floor.

⁸I saw that the temple had a raised base all around it, forming the foundation of the side rooms. It was the length of the rod, six long cubits. ⁹The outer wall of the side rooms was five cubits thick. The open area between the side rooms of the temple ¹⁰and the ⌐priests'⌐ rooms was twenty cubits wide all around the temple. ¹¹There were entrances to the side rooms from the open area, one on the north and another on the south; and the base adjoining the open area was five cubits wide all around.

¹²The building facing the temple courtyard on the west side was seventy cubits wide. The wall of the building was five cubits thick all around, and its length was ninety cubits.

¹³Then he measured the temple; it was a hundred cubits long, and the temple courtyard and the building with its walls were also a hundred cubits long. ¹⁴The width of the temple courtyard on the east, including the front of the temple, was a hundred cubits. ᵉ

¹⁵Then he measured the length of the building facing the courtyard at the rear of the temple, including its galleries on each side; it was a hundred cubits.

The outer sanctuary, the inner sanctuary and the portico facing the court, ¹⁶as well as the thresholds and the narrow windows and galleries around the three of them—everything beyond and including the threshold was covered with wood. The floor, the wall up to the windows, and the windows were covered. ᶠ ¹⁷In the space above the outside of the entrance to the inner sanctuary and on the walls at regular intervals all around the inner and outer sanctuary ¹⁸were carved cherubim and palm trees. ᵍ Palm trees alternated with cherubim. Each cherub had two faces: ¹⁹the face of a man toward the palm tree on one side and the face of a lion toward the palm tree on the other. They were carved all around the whole temple. ʰ ²⁰From the floor to the area above the entrance, cherubim and palm trees were carved on the wall of the outer sanctuary.

²¹The outer sanctuaryⁱ had a rectangular doorframe, and the one at the front of the Most Holy Place was similar. ²²There was a wooden altarʲ three cubits high and two cubits squareᶠ; its corners, its base ᵍ and its sides were of wood. The man said to me, "This is the table ᵏ that is before the LORD." ²³Both the outer sanctuary ˡ and the Most Holy Place had double

#### Cross references (margin)

40:49
ʸ 1Ki 6:3

41:2
ᶻ 2Ch 3:3

41:4
ᵃ 1Ki 6:20
ᵇ Heb 9:3-8

41:6
ᶜ 1Ki 6:5

41:7
ᵈ 1Ki 6:8

41:14
ᵉ Eze 40:47

41:16
ᶠ ver 25-26;
1Ki 6:15; Eze 42:3

41:18
ᵍ 1Ki 6:29; 7:36

41:19
ʰ Eze 10:14

41:21
ⁱ ver 1

41:22
ʲ Ex 30:1
ᵏ Eze 44:16;
Mal 1:7, 12

41:23
ˡ ver 1
ᵐ 1Ki 6:32

ᵃ48 Septuagint; Hebrew *entrance was* ᵇ49 Septuagint; Hebrew *eleven* ᶜ49 Hebrew; Septuagint *Ten steps led up to it* ᵈ1 The common cubit was about 1 1/2 feet (about 0.5 meter). ᵉ1 One Hebrew manuscript and Septuagint; most Hebrew manuscripts *side, the width of the tent* ᶠ22 Septuagint; Hebrew *long* ᵍ22 Septuagint; Hebrew *length*

41:4 God's holiness is a central theme throughout both the Old and New Testaments. The Most Holy Place was the innermost room in the temple (Exodus 26:33, 34). This was where the ark of the covenant was kept and where God's glory was said to dwell. This room was entered only once a year by the high priest, who performed a ceremony to atone for the nation's sins.

41:18 Cherubim are mighty angels.

41:22 The dimensions given would fit either the table of the bread of the Presence (Exodus 25:30) or the altar of incense (Exodus 30:1–3).

doors. *m* 24Each door had two leaves—two hinged leaves for each door. 25And on the doors of the outer sanctuary were carved cherubim and palm trees like those carved on the walls, and there was a wooden overhang on the front of the portico. 26On the sidewalls of the portico were narrow windows with palm trees carved on each side. The side rooms of the temple also had overhangs. *n*

41:26
*n*ver 15-16;
Eze 40:16

Rooms for the Priests

42 Then the man led me northward into the outer court and brought me to the rooms opposite the temple courtyard *o* and opposite the outer wall on the north side. 2The building whose door faced north was a hundred cubits*a* long and fifty cubits wide. 3Both in the section twenty cubits from the inner court and in the section opposite the pavement of the outer court, gallery faced gallery at the three levels. *p* 4In front of the rooms was an inner passageway ten cubits wide and a hundred cubits*b* long. Their doors were on the north. 5Now the upper rooms were narrower, for the galleries took more space from them than from the rooms on the lower and middle floors of the building. 6The rooms on the third floor had no pillars, as the courts had; so they were smaller in floor space than those on the lower and middle floors. 7There was an outer wall parallel to the rooms and the outer court; it extended in front of the rooms for fifty cubits. 8While the row of rooms on the side next to the outer court was fifty cubits long, the row on the side nearest the sanctuary was a hundred cubits long. 9The lower rooms had an entrance*q* on the east side as one enters them from the outer court.

42:1
*o*Eze 41:12-14

42:3
*p*Eze 41:16

42:9
*q*Eze 44:5; 46:19

10On the south side*c* along the length of the wall of the outer court, adjoining the temple courtyard and opposite the outer wall, were rooms 11with a passageway in front of them. These were like the rooms on the north; they had the same length and width, with similar exits and dimensions. Similar to the doorways on the north 12were the doorways of the rooms on the south. There was a doorway at the beginning of the passageway that was parallel to the corresponding wall extending eastward, by which one enters the rooms.

13Then he said to me, "The north and south rooms facing the temple courtyard are the priests' rooms, where the priests who approach the LORD will eat the most holy offerings. There they will put the most holy offerings—the grain offerings, the sin offerings *r* and the guilt offerings—for the place is holy. *s* 14Once the priests enter the holy precincts, they are not to go into the outer court until they leave behind the garments *t* in which they minister, for these are holy. They are to put on other clothes before they go near the places that are for the people. *u*"

42:13
*r*Lev 10:17
*s*Lev 6:29

42:14
*t*Eze 44:19
*u*Ex 29:9

15When he had finished measuring what was inside the temple area, he led me out by the east gate and measured the area all around: 16He measured the east side with the measuring rod; it was five hundred cubits. *d* 17He measured the north side; it was five hundred cubits*e* by the measuring rod. 18He measured the south side; it was five hundred cubits by the measuring rod. 19Then he turned to the west side and measured; it was five hundred cubits by the measuring rod. 20So he measured*v* the area on all four sides. It had a wall around it, five hundred cubits long and five hundred cubits wide, *w* to separate the holy from the common.

42:20
*v*Eze 40:5
*w*Eze 45:2

The Glory Returns to the Temple

43 Then the man brought me to the gate facing east, *x* 2and I saw the glory of the God of Israel coming from the east. His voice was like the roar of rushing waters,*y* and the land was radiant with his glory. *z* 3The vision I saw was like the vision I had seen when he*f* came to

43:1
*x*Eze 10:19; 46:1

43:2
*y*Rev 1:15
*z*Eze 11:23;
Rev 18:1

*a*2 The common cubit was about 1 1/2 feet (about 0.5 meter).   *b*4 Septuagint and Syriac; Hebrew *and one cubit*   *c*10 Septuagint; Hebrew *Eastward*   *d*16 See Septuagint of verse 17; Hebrew *rods*; also in verses 18 and 19.   *e*17 Septuagint; Hebrew *rods*   *f*3 Some Hebrew manuscripts and Vulgate; most Hebrew manuscripts *I*

42:14 Approaching our holy God must not be taken lightly. The holy garments the priests were required to wear may symbolize the importance of having a holy heart when approaching God. The priests had to wear these special clothes in order to minister in the inner rooms of the temple. Because the garments were holy, the priests had to change their clothes before going back out to the public.

42:16–20 The perfect symmetry of Ezekiel's temple may represent the order and harmony in God's future kingdom.

43:1ff This is the culmination of chapters 40—42 because God's glory returns to the temple. It reverses the negative cast of the book and serves as a fitting end for all the passages dealing with

the blessings reserved for the restored remnant. All true believers should long for that moment when God's name will finally be glorified and he will live among his people forever.

43:2 In 11:23, God's glory stopped over the Mount of Olives, to the east of Jerusalem, before leaving the city. This prophecy states that his glory would also return from the east.

43:2–4 Just as it was completely devastating when God's glory departed (11:23) from his temple, so it was overwhelming awe and joy beyond expression when Ezekiel saw God's glory return.

43:3 The Kebar River connected with the Euphrates River and was the location of a Jewish settlement of exiles in Babylonia.

43:4
a Eze 10:19

43:5
b Eze 8:3

43:7
c Lev 26:30

43:11
d Eze 44:5

43:12
e Eze 40:2

43:17
f Ex 20:26

43:18
g Lev 1:5, 11

43:19
h Eze 45:18-19
i Eze 44:15

43:21
j Ex 29:14;
Heb 13:11

43:24
k Lev 2:13

43:25
l Lev 8:33

destroy the city and like the visions I had seen by the Kebar River, and I fell facedown. 4The glory of the LORD entered the temple through the gate facing east.*a* 5Then the Spirit lifted me up*b* and brought me into the inner court, and the glory of the LORD filled the temple.

6While the man was standing beside me, I heard someone speaking to me from inside the temple. 7He said: "Son of man, this is the place of my throne and the place for the soles of my feet. This is where I will live among the Israelites forever. The house of Israel will never again defile my holy name—neither they nor their kings—by their prostitution*a* and the lifeless idols*b* of their kings at their high places.*c* 8When they placed their threshold next to my threshold and their doorposts beside my doorposts, with only a wall between me and them, they defiled my holy name by their detestable practices. So I destroyed them in my anger. 9Now let them put away from me their prostitution and the lifeless idols of their kings, and I will live among them forever.

10"Son of man, describe the temple to the people of Israel, that they may be ashamed of their sins. Let them consider the plan, 11and if they are ashamed of all they have done, make known to them the design of the temple—its arrangement, its exits and entrances—its whole design and all its regulations*c* and laws. Write these down before them so that they may be faithful to its design and follow all its regulations.*d*

12"This is the law of the temple: All the surrounding area*e* on top of the mountain will be most holy. Such is the law of the temple.

The Altar

13"These are the measurements of the altar in long cubits, that cubit being a cubit*d* and a handbreadth*e*: Its gutter is a cubit deep and a cubit wide, with a rim of one span*f* around the edge. And this is the height of the altar: 14From the gutter on the ground up to the lower ledge it is two cubits high and a cubit wide, and from the smaller ledge up to the larger ledge it is four cubits high and a cubit wide. 15The altar hearth is four cubits high, and four horns project upward from the hearth. 16The altar hearth is square, twelve cubits long and twelve cubits wide. 17The upper ledge also is square, fourteen cubits long and fourteen cubits wide, with a rim of half a cubit and a gutter of a cubit all around. The steps*f* of the altar face east."

18Then he said to me, "Son of man, this is what the Sovereign LORD says: These will be the regulations for sacrificing burnt offerings and sprinkling blood*g* upon the altar when it is built: 19You are to give a young bull*h* as a sin offering to the priests, who are Levites, of the family of Zadok,*i* who come near to minister before me, declares the Sovereign LORD. 20You are to take some of its blood and put it on the four horns of the altar and on the four corners of the upper ledge and all around the rim, and so purify the altar and make atonement for it. 21You are to take the bull for the sin offering and burn it in the designated part of the temple area outside the sanctuary.*j*

22"On the second day you are to offer a male goat without defect for a sin offering, and the altar is to be purified as it was purified with the bull. 23When you have finished purifying it, you are to offer a young bull and a ram from the flock, both without defect. 24You are to offer them before the LORD, and the priests are to sprinkle salt*k* on them and sacrifice them as a burnt offering to the LORD.

25"For seven days*l* you are to provide a male goat daily for a sin offering; you are also to provide a young bull and a ram from the flock, both without defect. 26For seven days they are to make atonement for the altar and cleanse it; thus they will dedicate it. 27At the end of these

a 7 Or *their spiritual adultery*; also in verse 9   *b 7* Or *the corpses*; also in verse 9   *c 11* Some Hebrew manuscripts and Septuagint; most Hebrew manuscripts *regulations and its whole design*   *d 13* The common cubit was about 1 1/2 feet (about 0.5 meter).   *e 13* That is, about 3 inches (about 8 centimeters)   *f 13* That is, about 9 inches (about 22 centimeters)

43:9–11 God's departure from the city had been a signal for the destruction of the city and the temple. Now for God to return, his conditions had to be met: idolatry had to be removed. Some commentators feel these verses indicate that Ezekiel was commanding the people of his day to build this temple according to the designs and regulations that the angelic architect had given. But the people never repented, the conditions were not met, so the fulfillment was postponed.

43:12 The basic law of God's temple was holiness. In all he does, God is holy, perfect, and blameless. There is no trace of evil or sin in him. Just as God is holy, so we are to be holy (Leviticus 19:1; 1 Peter 1:15, 16). People are holy when they are devoted to God

and separated from sin. If we do not understand the basic concept of holiness, we will never progress very far in our Christian growth.

43:18–27 This vision was simultaneously flashing back to Mount Sinai and forward to Mount Calvary. When the people returned from exile, they would seek forgiveness through the sacrificial system instituted in Moses' day. Today, Christ's death has made the forgiveness of our sins possible, making us acceptable to God (Hebrews 9:9–15). God stands ready to forgive those who come to him in faith.

days, from the eighth day*m* on, the priests are to present your burnt offerings and fellowship offerings*a* on the altar. Then I will accept you, declares the Sovereign LORD."

The Prince, the Levites, the Priests

44 Then the man brought me back to the outer gate of the sanctuary, the one facing east, and it was shut. ²The LORD said to me, "This gate is to remain shut. It must not be opened; no one may enter through it. *n* It is to remain shut because the LORD, the God of Israel, has entered through it. ³The prince himself is the only one who may sit inside the gateway to eat in the presence of the LORD. He is to enter by way of the portico of the gateway and go out the same way.*o*"

⁴Then the man brought me by way of the north gate to the front of the temple. I looked and saw the glory of the LORD filling the temple of the LORD, and I fell facedown.*p*

⁵The LORD said to me, "Son of man, look carefully, listen closely and give attention to everything I tell you concerning all the regulations regarding the temple of the LORD. Give attention to the entrance of the temple and all the exits of the sanctuary. *q* ⁶Say to the rebellious house*r* of Israel, 'This is what the Sovereign LORD says: Enough of your detestable practices, O house of Israel! ⁷In addition to all your other detestable practices, you brought foreigners uncircumcised in heart *s* and flesh into my sanctuary, desecrating my temple while you offered me food, fat and blood, and you broke my covenant. *t* ⁸Instead of carrying out your duty in regard to my holy things, you put others in charge of my sanctuary. ⁹This is what the Sovereign LORD says: No foreigner uncircumcised in heart and flesh is to enter my sanctuary, not even the foreigners who live among the Israelites.

¹⁰'The Levites who went far from me when Israel went astray*u* and who wandered from me after their idols must bear the consequences of their sin. ¹¹They may serve in my sanctuary, having charge of the gates of the temple and serving in it; they may slaughter the burnt offerings*v* and sacrifices for the people and stand before the people and serve them. *w* ¹²But because they served them in the presence of their idols and made the house of Israel fall into sin, therefore I have sworn with uplifted hand that they must bear the consequences of their sin, declares the Sovereign LORD. ¹³They are not to come near to serve me as priests or come near any of my holy things or my most holy offerings; they must bear the shame of their detestable practices.*x* ¹⁴Yet I will put them in charge of the duties of the temple and all the work that is to be done in it.*y*

¹⁵'But the priests, who are Levites and descendants of Zadok and who faithfully carried out the duties of my sanctuary when the Israelites went astray from me, are to come near to minister before me; they are to stand before me to offer sacrifices of fat and blood, declares the Sovereign LORD.*z* ¹⁶They alone are to enter my sanctuary; they alone are to come near my table to minister before me and perform my service.

¹⁷'When they enter the gates of the inner court, they are to wear linen clothes; they must not wear any woolen garment while ministering at the gates of the inner court or inside the temple. ¹⁸They are to wear linen turbans*a* on their heads and linen undergarments around their waists. They must not wear anything that makes them perspire. ¹⁹When they go out into the outer court where the people are, they are to take off the clothes they have been ministering in and are to leave them in the sacred rooms, and put on other clothes, so that they do not consecrate*b* the people by means of their garments. *c*

²⁰'They must not shave their heads or let their hair grow long, but they are to keep the hair

a27 Traditionally *peace offerings*

**Cross references (right margin):**

43:27
m Lev 9:1

44:2
n Eze 43:4-5

44:3
o Eze 46:2, 8

44:4
p Eze 1:28; 3:23

44:5
q Eze 40:4

44:6
r Eze 3:9

44:7
s Lev 26:41
t Lev 22:25

44:10
u 2Ki 23:8

44:11
v 2Ch 29:34
w Nu 16:9

44:13
x Nu 18:3

44:14
y Nu 18:4

44:15
z Eze 40:46

44:18
a Ex 28:39

44:19
b Eze 46:20
c Eze 42:14

44:2 Why was this east gate to remain closed? Several reasons have been suggested. (1) This was the gate through which God entered the temple, and no one else could walk where God had (43:2); (2) the closed gate indicated that God would never again leave the temple (10:19; 11:23); (3) it would prevent people from worshiping the sun as it rises in the east from within the temple grounds (8:16).

44:3 Although Christ is called a prince (37:25), this prince is probably not Christ because he offers a sacrifice to God (46:4) and he can enter only by the "portico of the gateway." He is a princely ruler of the city, but he is distinguished from other princes because he will be just and fair (see 45:8). Another view is that this picture anticipates Christ offering a sacrifice of his own life to God.

44:9 Unbelievers would not be allowed to enter the temple.

Ezekiel's vision was for a restored, purified worship where only those who prepared themselves physically and spiritually could participate. In 47:22, 23, we find that people from other nations are allowed to join in worship by accepting the standards of faith and practice declared in the law (see Leviticus 24:22; Numbers 15:29).

44:15 Zadok's descendants are mentioned because many of the priests in Zadok's line had remained faithful to God, while others had become corrupt. Zadok supported God's choice of Solomon to succeed David, and was therefore appointed high priest during his reign (1 Kings 1:32-35; 2:27, 35). Zadok's descendants were considered the true priestly line throughout the time between the Old and New Testaments.

44:20-31 These laws were originally given to God's people in the desert. They are recorded in the books of Exodus and Leviti-

44:20
ᵈLev 21:5
44:21
ᵉLev 10:9
44:22
ᶠLev 21:7
44:23
ᵍMal 2:7
44:24
ʰDt 17:8-9

of their heads trimmed. ᵈ ²¹No priest is to drink wine when he enters the inner court. ᵉ ²²They must not marry widows or divorced women; they may marry only virgins of Israelite descent or widows of priests.ᶠ ²³They are to teach my people the difference between the holy and the common and show them how to distinguish between the unclean and the clean.ᵍ

²⁴"'In any dispute, the priests are to serve as judges ʰ and decide it according to my ordinances. They are to keep my laws and my decrees for all my appointed feasts, and they are to keep my Sabbaths holy.

²⁵"'A priest must not defile himself by going near a dead person; however, if the dead person was his father or mother, son or daughter, brother or unmarried sister, then he may defile himself. ²⁶After he is cleansed, he must wait seven days. ²⁷On the day he goes into the inner court of the sanctuary to minister in the sanctuary, he is to offer a sin offering for himself, declares the Sovereign LORD.

44:28
ⁱNu 18:20
44:29
ʲLev 27:21
ᵏNu 18:9, 14

²⁸"'I am to be the only inheritance ⁱ the priests have. You are to give them no possession in Israel; I will be their possession. ²⁹They will eat the grain offerings, the sin offerings and the guilt offerings; and everything in Israel devoted ᵃ to the LORD ʲ will belong to them. ᵏ ³⁰The best of all the firstfruits and of all your special gifts will belong to the priests. You are to give them the first portion of your ground meal so that a blessing may rest on your household. ³¹The priests must not eat anything, bird or animal, found dead or torn by wild animals.

Division of the Land

45:1
ˡEze 47:21-22
ᵐEze 48:8-9, 29

45 "'When you allot the land as an inheritance,ˡ you are to present to the LORD a portion of the land as a sacred district, 25,000 cubits long and 20,000 ᵇ cubits wide; the entire area will be holy. ᵐ ²Of this, a section 500 cubits square is to be for the sanctuary, with 50 cubits around it for open land. ³In the sacred district, measure off a section 25,000 cubitsᶜ long and 10,000 cubitsᵈ wide. In it will be the sanctuary, the Most Holy Place. ⁴It will be the sacred portion of the land for the priests, who minister in the sanctuary and who draw near to minister before the LORD. It will be a place for their houses as well as a holy place for the sanctuary.ⁿ

45:4
ⁿEze 48:10-11

45:5
ᵒEze 48:13

⁵An area 25,000 cubits long and 10,000 cubits wide will belong to the Levites, who serve in the temple, as their possession for towns to live in.ᵉ ᵒ

45:6
ᵖEze 48:15-18
45:7
ᑫEze 48:21

⁶"'You are to give the city as its property an area 5,000 cubits wide and 25,000 cubits long, adjoining the sacred portion; it will belong to the whole house of Israel.ᵖ

⁷"'The prince will have the land bordering each side of the area formed by the sacred district and the property of the city. It will extend westward from the west side and eastward from the east side, running lengthwise from the western to the eastern border parallel to one of the tribal portions. ᑫ ⁸This land will be his possession in Israel. And my princes will no longer oppress my people but will allow the house of Israel to possess the land according to their tribes.ʳ

45:8
ʳEze 46:18

45:9
ˢJer 22:3
45:10
ᵗLev 19:36

⁹"'This is what the Sovereign LORD says: You have gone far enough, O princes of Israel! Give up your violence and oppression and do what is just and right.ˢ Stop dispossessing my people, declares the Sovereign LORD. ¹⁰You are to use accurate scales, an accurate ephahᶠ ᵗ and an accurate bath.ᵍ ¹¹The ephah and the bath are to be the same size, the bath containing a tenth of a homerʰ and the ephah a tenth of a homer; the homer is to be the standard measure for both. ¹²The shekelⁱ is to consist of twenty gerahs. ᵘ Twenty shekels plus twenty-five shekels plus fifteen shekels equal one mina.ʲ

45:12
ᵘEx 30:13;
Lev 27:25; Nu 3:47

Offerings and Holy Days

¹³"'This is the special gift you are to offer: a sixth of an ephah from each homer of wheat and a sixth of an ephah from each homer of barley. ¹⁴The prescribed portion of oil, measured

---

ᵃ29 The Hebrew term refers to the irrevocable giving over of things or persons to the LORD. ᵇ1 Septuagint (see also verses 3 and 5 and 48:9); Hebrew 10,000 ᶜ3 That is, about 7 miles (about 12 kilometers) ᵈ3 That is, about 3 miles (about 5 kilometers) ᵉ5 Septuagint; Hebrew temple; they will have as their possession 20 rooms ᶠ10 An ephah was a dry measure. ᵍ10 A bath was a liquid measure. ʰ11 A homer was a dry measure. ⁱ12 A shekel weighed about 2/5 ounce (about 11.5 grams). ʲ12 That is, 60 shekels; the common mina was 50 shekels.

---

cus. They reveal the importance of approaching God respectfully, and they give guidelines for the priests to live above reproach so they could carry out their responsibility to teach the people "to distinguish between the unclean and the clean" (44:23).

45:1–7 The land allotted to the temple was in the center of the nation. God is central to life. He must be our first priority.

45:9–12 Violence and oppression were two of the major social sins of the nation during this time (see Amos 5:10–13). In the

new economy there would be plenty of land for the "princes" (45:7, 8) and no longer any basis for greed. Therefore, God commanded the princes and the people to be just and right, especially in their business dealings. Consider the ways that you measure goods, money, or services. If you are paid for an hour of work, be sure you work for a full hour. If you sell a bushel of apples, make sure it is a full bushel. God is completely trustworthy, and his followers should be too.

by the bath, is a tenth of a bath from each cor (which consists of ten baths or one homer, for ten baths are equivalent to a homer). ¹⁵Also one sheep is to be taken from every flock of two hundred from the well-watered pastures of Israel. These will be used for the grain offerings, burnt offerings ᵛ and fellowship offerings ᵃ to make atonement for the people, declares the Sovereign Lᴏʀᴅ. ¹⁶All the people of the land will participate in this special gift for the use of the prince in Israel. ¹⁷It will be the duty of the prince to provide the burnt offerings, grain offerings and drink offerings at the festivals, the New Moons and the Sabbaths—at all the appointed feasts of the house of Israel. He will provide the sin offerings, grain offerings, burnt offerings and fellowship offerings to make atonement for the house of Israel.

¹⁸"This is what the Sovereign Lᴏʀᴅ says: In the first month on the first day you are to take a young bull without defect and purify the sanctuary. ¹⁹The priest is to take some of the blood of the sin offering and put it on the doorposts of the temple, on the four corners of the upper ledge of the altar ʷ and on the gateposts of the inner court. ²⁰You are to do the same on the seventh day of the month for anyone who sins unintentionally ˣ or through ignorance; so you are to make atonement for the temple.

²¹"In the first month on the fourteenth day you are to observe the Passover, ʸ a feast lasting seven days, during which you shall eat bread made without yeast. ²²On that day the prince is to provide a bull as a sin offering for himself and for all the people of the land. ᶻ ²³Every day during the seven days of the Feast he is to provide seven bulls and seven rams without defect as a burnt offering to the Lᴏʀᴅ, and a male goat for a sin offering. ᵃ ²⁴He is to provide as a grain offering an ephah for each bull and an ephah for each ram, along with a hin ᵇ of oil for each ephah.

²⁵"During the seven days of the Feast, which begins in the seventh month on the fifteenth day, he is to make the same provision for sin offerings, burnt offerings, grain offerings and oil. ᵇ

46 "This is what the Sovereign Lᴏʀᴅ says: The gate of the inner court facing east is to be shut on the six working days, but on the Sabbath day and on the day of the New Moon it is to be opened. ²The prince is to enter from the outside through the portico ᶜ of the gateway and stand by the gatepost. The priests are to sacrifice his burnt offering and his fellowship offerings. ᶜ He is to worship at the threshold of the gateway and then go out, but the gate will not be shut until evening. ᵈ ³On the Sabbaths and New Moons the people of the land are to worship in the presence of the Lᴏʀᴅ at the entrance to that gateway. ᵉ ⁴The burnt offering the prince brings to the Lᴏʀᴅ on the Sabbath day is to be six male lambs and a ram, all without defect. ⁵The grain offering given with the ram is to be an ephah, ᵈ and the grain offering with the lambs is to be as much as he pleases, along with a hin ᵉ of oil for each ephah. ᶠ ⁶On the day of the New Moon ᵍ he is to offer a young bull, six lambs and a ram, all without defect. ⁷He is to provide as a grain offering one ephah with the bull, one ephah with the ram, and with the lambs as much as he wants to give, along with a hin of oil with each ephah. ⁸When the prince enters, he is to go in through the portico ʰ of the gateway, and he is to come out the same way. ᶦ

⁹"When the people of the land come before the Lᴏʀᴅ at the appointed feasts, ʲ whoever enters by the north gate to worship is to go out the south gate; and whoever enters by the south gate is to go out the north gate. No one is to return through the gate by which he entered, but each is to go out the opposite gate. ¹⁰The prince is to be among them, going in when they go in and going out when they go out.

¹¹"At the festivals and the appointed feasts, the grain offering is to be an ephah with a bull, an ephah with a ram, and with the lambs as much as one pleases, along with a hin of oil for each ephah. ᵏ ¹²When the prince provides ᶦ a freewill offering to the Lᴏʀᴅ—whether a burnt offering or fellowship offerings—the gate facing east is to be opened for him. He

45:15	ᵛLev 1:4
45:19	ʷEze 43:20
45:20	ˣLev 4:27
45:21	ʸEx 12:11; Lev 23:5-6
45:22	ᶻLev 4:14
45:23	ᵃNu 28:16-25
45:25	ᵇLev 23:34-43; Nu 29:12-38
46:2	ᶜver 8; ᵈver 12; Eze 44:3
46:3	ᵉLk 1:10
46:5	ᶠver 11; Eze 45:24
46:6	ᵍver 1
46:8	ʰver 2; ᶦEze 44:3
46:9	ʲEx 23:14
46:11	ᵏver 5
46:12	ᶦEze 45:17

ᵃ15 Traditionally *peace offerings*; also in verse 17   ᵇ24 That is, probably about 4 quarts (about 4 liters)   ᶜ2 Traditionally *peace offerings*; also in verse 12   ᵈ5 That is, probably about 3/5 bushel (about 22 liters)   ᵉ5 That is, probably about 4 quarts (about 4 liters)

45:17 The conditions and regulations for these offerings are described in detail in Leviticus 1—7.

45:21 The Passover was an annual seven-day feast instituted by God so that his people would remember when he brought them out of slavery in Egypt. On that first Passover night, the Lord passed over the homes marked by lamb's blood; he struck only the unmarked homes (see Exodus 11; 12).

45:25 This annual feast celebrated in October is called the Feast of Tabernacles. It commemorates God's protection of his people as they traveled through the desert from Egypt to the promised land (see Leviticus 23:33–43; Deuteronomy 16:13–17).

46:1–15 Ezekiel continued to describe various aspects of daily worship. While allowing for diversity in worship, God prescribed order and continuity. This continuity gave a healthy rhythm to the spiritual life of his people.

46:12
m ver 2

46:13
n Ex 29:38;
Nu 28:3

46:15
o Ex 29:42
p Nu 28:5-6

46:17
q Lev 25:10

46:18
r Eze 45:8;
Mic 2:1-2

shall offer his burnt offering or his fellowship offerings as he does on the Sabbath day. Then he shall go out, and after he has gone out, the gate will be shut. m

13 "Every day you are to provide a year-old lamb without defect for a burnt offering to the LORD; morning by morning you shall provide it. n 14 You are also to provide with it morning by morning a grain offering, consisting of a sixth of an ephah with a third of a hin of oil to moisten the flour. The presenting of this grain offering to the LORD is a lasting ordinance. 15 So the lamb and the grain offering and the oil shall be provided morning by morning for a regular o burnt offering. p

16 "This is what the Sovereign LORD says: If the prince makes a gift from his inheritance to one of his sons, it will also belong to his descendants; it is to be their property by inheritance. 17 If, however, he makes a gift from his inheritance to one of his servants, the servant may keep it until the year of freedom; q then it will revert to the prince. His inheritance belongs to his sons only; it is theirs. 18 The prince must not take any of the inheritance r of the people, driving them off their property. He is to give his sons their inheritance out of his own property, so that none of my people will be separated from his property.'"

19 Then the man brought me through the entrance at the side of the gate to the sacred rooms facing north, which belonged to the priests, and showed me a place at the western end. 20 He said to me, "This is the place where the priests will cook the guilt offering and the sin offering and bake the grain offering, to avoid bringing them into the outer court and consecrating the people."

21 He then brought me to the outer court and led me around to its four corners, and I saw in each corner another court. 22 In the four corners of the outer court were enclosed a courts, forty cubits long and thirty cubits wide; each of the courts in the four corners was the same size. 23 Around the inside of each of the four courts was a ledge of stone, with places for fire built all around under the ledge. 24 He said to me, "These are the kitchens where those who minister at the temple will cook the sacrifices of the people."

The River From the Temple

47:1
s Joel 3:18;
Rev 22:1

47 The man brought me back to the entrance of the temple, and I saw water coming out from under the threshold of the temple toward the east (for the temple faced east). The water was coming down from under the south side of the temple, south of the altar. s 2 He then brought me out through the north gate and led me around the outside to the outer gate facing east, and the water was flowing from the south side.

47:3
t Eze 40:3

3 As the man went eastward with a measuring line t in his hand, he measured off a thousand cubits b and then led me through water that was ankle-deep. 4 He measured off another thousand cubits and led me through water that was knee-deep. He measured off another thousand and led me through water that was up to the waist. 5 He measured off another thousand, but now it was a river that I could not cross, because the water had risen and was deep enough to swim in—a river that no one could cross. 6 He asked me, "Son of man, do you see this?"

47:7
u Rev 22:2
47:8
v Dt 3:17; Jos 3:16

Then he led me back to the bank of the river. 7 When I arrived there, I saw a great number of trees on each side of the river. u 8 He said to me, "This water flows toward the eastern region and goes down into the Arabah, c v where it enters the Sea. d When it empties into the Sea, d the water there becomes fresh. 9 Swarms of living creatures will live wherever the river flows. There will be large numbers of fish, because this water flows there and makes the salt water fresh; so where the river flows everything will live. 10 Fishermen will stand along the shore;

47:10
w Eze 26:5

from En Gedi to En Eglaim there will be places for spreading nets. w The fish will be of many kinds—like the fish of the Great Sea. e 11 But the swamps and marshes will not become fresh; they will be left for salt. 12 Fruit trees of all kinds will grow on both banks of the river. x Their

47:12
x ver 7; Rev 22:2

a 22 The meaning of the Hebrew for this word is uncertain.   b 3 That is, about 1,500 feet (about 450 meters)
c 8 Or the Jordan Valley   d 8 That is, the Dead Sea   e 10 That is, the Mediterranean; also in verses 15, 19 and 20

47:1–12 This river is similar to the river mentioned in Revelation 22:1, 2. Both rivers are associated with the river in the Garden of Eden (see Genesis 2:10). The river symbolizes life from God and the blessings that flow from his throne. It is a gentle, safe, deep river, expanding as it flows.

47:8, 9 The Arabah is the geological depression in which the Dead Sea lies. The sea that will become fresh refers to the Dead Sea, a body of water so salty that nothing can live in it. The river will freshen the Dead Sea's water so it can support life. This is another picture of the life-giving nature of the water that flows

from God's temple. God's power can transform us no matter how lifeless or corrupt we may be. Even when we feel messed up and beyond hope, his power can heal us.

47:10 En Gedi and En Eglaim were on the western shore of the Dead Sea.

leaves will not wither, nor will their fruit _y_ fail. Every month they will bear, because the water from the sanctuary flows to them. Their fruit will serve for food and their leaves for healing. _z_ "

The Boundaries of the Land

13This is what the Sovereign LORD says: "These are the boundaries _a_ by which you are to divide the land for an inheritance among the twelve tribes of Israel, with two portions for Joseph. _b_ 14You are to divide it equally among them. Because I swore with uplifted hand to give it to your forefathers, this land will become your inheritance. _c_

15"This is to be the boundary of the land:

"On the north side it will run from the Great Sea by the Hethlon road _d_ past Lebo _a_ Hamath to Zedad, 16Berothah _b_ and Sibraim (which lies on the border between Damascus and Hamath), as far as Hazer Hatticon, which is on the border of Hauran. 17The boundary will extend from the sea to Hazar Enan, _c_ along the northern border of Damascus, with the border of Hamath to the north. This will be the north boundary. _e_

18 "On the east side the boundary will run between Hauran and Damascus, along the Jordan between Gilead and the land of Israel, to the eastern sea and as far as Tamar. _d_ This will be the east boundary.

19 "On the south side it will run from Tamar as far as the waters of Meribah Kadesh, _f_ then along the Wadi ∟of Egypt⌐ to the Great Sea. _g_ This will be the south boundary.

20 "On the west side, the Great Sea will be the boundary to a point opposite Lebo _e_ Hamath. This will be the west boundary.

21"You are to distribute this land among yourselves according to the tribes of Israel. 22You are to allot it as an inheritance for yourselves and for the aliens who have settled among you and who have children. You are to consider them as native-born Israelites; along with you they are to be allotted an inheritance among the tribes of Israel. _h_ 23In whatever tribe the alien settles, there you are to give him his inheritance," declares the Sovereign LORD.

The Division of the Land

48 "These are the tribes, listed by name: At the northern frontier, Dan will have one portion; it will follow the Hethlon road _i_ to Lebo _f_ Hamath; Hazar Enan and the northern border of Damascus next to Hamath will be part of its border from the east side to the west side.

2"Asher _j_ will have one portion; it will border the territory of Dan from east to west.
3"Naphtali _k_ will have one portion; it will border the territory of Asher from east to west.
4"Manasseh _l_ will have one portion; it will border the territory of Naphtali from east to west.
5"Ephraim _m_ will have one portion; it will border the territory of Manasseh from east to west.
6"Reuben _n_ will have one portion; it will border the territory of Ephraim from east to west.
7"Judah _o_ will have one portion; it will border the territory of Reuben from east to west.
8"Bordering the territory of Judah from east to west will be the portion you are to present as a special gift. It will be 25,000 cubits _g_ wide, and its length from east to west will equal one of the tribal portions; the sanctuary will be in the center of it.
9"The special portion you are to offer to the LORD will be 25,000 cubits long and 10,000 cubits _h_ wide. 10This will be the sacred portion for the priests. It will be 25,000 cubits long on the north side, 10,000 cubits wide on the west side, 10,000 cubits wide on the east side and 25,000 cubits long on the south side. In the center of it will be the sanctuary of the LORD. _p_
11This will be for the consecrated priests, the Zadokites, who were faithful in serving me and did not go astray as the Levites did when the Israelites went astray. _q_ 12It will be a special

_a 15_ Or _past the entrance to_   _b 15,16_ See Septuagint and Ezekiel 48:1; Hebrew _road to go into Zedad, 16Hamath, Berothah_   _c 17_ Hebrew _Enon,_ a variant of _Enan_   _d 18_ Septuagint and Syriac; Hebrew _Israel. You will measure to the eastern sea_   _e 20_ Or _opposite the entrance to_   _f 1_ Or _to the entrance to_   _g 8_ That is, about 7 miles (about 12 kilometers)   _h 9_ That is, about 3 miles (about 5 kilometers)

Reference column
47:12 _y_ Ps 1:3 _z_ Jer 17:8
47:13 _a_ Nu 34:2-12 _b_ Ge 48:5
47:14 _c_ Eze 20:5-6
47:15 _d_ Eze 48:1
47:17 _e_ Eze 48:1
47:19 _f_ Dt 32:51 _g_ Eze 48:28
47:22 _h_ Eph 3:6; Col 3:11
48:1 _i_ Eze 47:15-17
48:2 _j_ Jos 19:24-31
48:3 _k_ Jos 19:32-39
48:4 _l_ Jos 17:1-11
48:5 _m_ Jos 16:5-9
48:6 _n_ Jos 13:15-21
48:7 _o_ Jos 15:1-63
48:10 _p_ Eze 45:3-4
48:11 _q_ Eze 44:15

47:19 A wadi is a seasonal stream or streambed that is dry much of the year.

47:22, 23 In the restoration there will be room for foreigners ("aliens"). The regulations of Leviticus 24:22 and Numbers 15:29 provided for this. Isaiah also taught it (Isaiah 56:3–8). The children of foreigners will even inherit property like Israelites. Anyone who accepts the standards and is willing to obey may enjoy the blessings of God's rule.

48:1ff The land would be divided into 13 parallel portions (one for each tribe plus a sacred district) that would stretch from the Jordan River or Dead Sea to the Mediterranean Sea. The division of the land shows that in God's kingdom there is a place for all who believe in and obey the one true God (see John 14:1–6).

gift to them from the sacred portion of the land, a most holy portion, bordering the territory of the Levites.

¹³"Alongside the territory of the priests, the Levites will have an allotment 25,000 cubits long and 10,000 cubits wide. Its total length will be 25,000 cubits and its width 10,000 cubits. ¹⁴They must not sell or exchange any of it. This is the best of the land and must not pass into other hands, because it is holy to the Lord.ʳ

48:14
ʳ Lev 25:34; 27:10, 28

¹⁵"The remaining area, 5,000 cubits wide and 25,000 cubits long, will be for the common use of the city, for houses and for pastureland. The city will be in the center of it ¹⁶and will have these measurements: the north side 4,500 cubits, the south side 4,500 cubits, the east side 4,500 cubits, and the west side 4,500 cubits.ˢ ¹⁷The pastureland for the city will be 250 cubits on the north, 250 cubits on the south, 250 cubits on the east, and 250 cubits on the west. ¹⁸What remains of the area, bordering on the sacred portion and running the length of it, will be 10,000 cubits on the east side and 10,000 cubits on the west side. Its produce will supply food for the workers of the city. ¹⁹The workers from the city who farm it will come from all the tribes of Israel. ²⁰The entire portion will be a square, 25,000 cubits on each side. As a special gift you will set aside the sacred portion, along with the property of the city.

48:16
ˢ Rev 21:16

²¹"What remains on both sides of the area formed by the sacred portion and the city property will belong to the prince. It will extend eastward from the 25,000 cubits of the sacred portion to the eastern border, and westward from the 25,000 cubits to the western border. Both these areas running the length of the tribal portions will belong to the prince, and the sacred portion with the temple sanctuary will be in the center of them.ᵗ ²²So the property of the Levites and the property of the city will lie in the center of the area that belongs to the prince. The area belonging to the prince will lie between the border of Judah and the border of Benjamin.

48:21
ᵗ ver 8, 10; Eze 45:7

²³"As for the rest of the tribes: Benjaminᵘ will have one portion; it will extend from the east side to the west side.

48:23
ᵘ Jos 18:11-28

²⁴"Simeonᵛ will have one portion; it will border the territory of Benjamin from east to west.

48:24
ᵛ Jos 19:1-9

²⁵"Issacharʷ will have one portion; it will border the territory of Simeon from east to west.

48:25
ʷ Jos 19:17-23

²⁶"Zebulunˣ will have one portion; it will border the territory of Issachar from east to west.

48:26
ˣ Jos 19:10-16

²⁷"Gadʸ will have one portion; it will border the territory of Zebulun from east to west.

48:27
ʸ Jos 13:24-28

²⁸"The southern boundary of Gad will run south from Tamar to the waters of Meribah Kadesh, then along the Wadi ⌊of Egypt⌋ to the Great Sea.ᵃ ᶻ

48:28
ᶻ Eze 47:19

²⁹"This is the land you are to allot as an inheritance to the tribes of Israel, and these will be their portions," declares the Sovereign Lord.

The Gates of the City

³⁰"These will be the exits of the city: Beginning on the north side, which is 4,500 cubits long, ³¹the gates of the city will be named after the tribes of Israel. The three gates on the north side will be the gate of Reuben, the gate of Judah and the gate of Levi.

³²"On the east side, which is 4,500 cubits long, will be three gates: the gate of Joseph, the gate of Benjamin and the gate of Dan.

³³"On the south side, which measures 4,500 cubits, will be three gates: the gate of Simeon, the gate of Issachar and the gate of Zebulun.

³⁴"On the west side, which is 4,500 cubits long, will be three gates: the gate of Gad, the gate of Asher and the gate of Naphtali.

³⁵"The distance all around will be 18,000 cubits.

"And the name of the city from that time on will be:

48:35
ᵃ Jer 3:17; 33:16; Joel 3:21; Zec 2:10; Rev 21:3

THE LORD IS THERE.ᵃ"

ᵃ28 That is, the Mediterranean

48:28 The Great Sea is the Mediterranean.

48:35 The book of Ezekiel begins by describing the holiness of God that Israel had despised and ignored. As a result, God's presence departed from the temple, the city, and the people. The book ends with a detailed vision of the new temple, the new city, and the new people—all demonstrating God's holiness. The pressures of everyday life may persuade us to focus on the here and now

and thus forget God. That is why worship is so important; it takes our eyes off our current worries, gives us a glimpse of God's holiness, and allows us to look toward his future kingdom. God's presence makes everything glorious, and worship brings us into his presence.

DANIEL

VITAL STATISTICS

PURPOSE:
To give a historical account of the faithful Jews who lived in captivity and to show how God is in control of heaven and earth, directing the forces of nature, the destiny of nations, and the care of his people

AUTHOR:
Daniel

ORIGINAL AUDIENCE:
The other captives in Babylon

DATE WRITTEN:
Approximately 536 B.C., recording events that occurred from about 605–535 B.C.

SETTING:
Daniel had been taken captive and deported to Babylon by Nebuchadnezzar in 605 B.C. There he served in the government for about 70 years during the reigns of Nebuchadnezzar, Belshazzar, Darius, and Cyrus.

KEY VERSE:
"He [God] reveals deep and hidden things; he knows what lies in darkness, and light dwells with him" (2:22).

KEY PEOPLE:
Daniel, Nebuchadnezzar, Shadrach, Meshach, Abednego, Belshazzar, Darius

KEY PLACES:
Nebuchadnezzar's palace, the fiery furnace, Belshazzar's banquet, the den of lions

SPECIAL FEATURES:
Daniel's apocalyptic visions (chapters 7—12) give a glimpse of God's plan for the ages, including a direct prediction of the Messiah.

AN EARTHQUAKE shakes the foundation of our security; a tornado blows away a lifetime of treasures; an assassin's bullet changes national history; a drunk driver claims an innocent victim; a divorce shatters a home; terrorism frightens a nation. International and personal tragedies make our world seem a fearful place, overflowing with evil and seemingly out of control. And the litany of bombings, coups, murders, and natural disasters could cause us to think that God is absent or impotent. "Where is God?" we cry, engulfed by sorrow and despair.

Twenty-five centuries ago, Daniel could have despaired. He and thousands of his countrymen had been deported to a foreign land after Judah was conquered. Daniel found himself facing an egocentric despot and surrounded by idolaters. Instead of giving in or giving up, this courageous young man held fast to his faith in his God. Daniel knew that despite the circumstances, God was sovereign and was working out his plan for nations and individuals. The book of Daniel centers around this profound truth—the sovereignty of God.

After a brief account of Nebuchadnezzar's siege and defeat of Jerusalem, the scene quickly shifts to Daniel and his three friends, Hananiah, Mishael, and Azariah (Shadrach, Meshach, and Abednego). These men held prominent positions within the Babylonian government. Daniel, in particular, held such a position because of his ability to interpret the king's dreams that tell of God's unfolding plan (chapters 2 and 4). Sandwiched between the dreams is the fascinating account of Daniel's three friends and the furnace (chapter 3). Because they refused to bow down to an image of gold, they were condemned to a fiery death. But God intervened and spared their lives.

Belshazzar ruled Babylon after Nebuchadnezzar, and chapter 5 tells of his encounter with God's message written on a wall. Daniel, who was summoned to interpret the message, predicted Babylon's fall to the Medes and Persians. This prediction came true that very night, and Darius the Mede conquered the Babylonian kingdom.

Daniel became one of Darius's most trusted advisers. His privileged position angered other administrators, who plotted his death by convincing the king to outlaw prayer. In spite of the law, Daniel continued to pray to his sovereign Lord. As a result, he was condemned to die in a den of hungry lions. Again, God intervened, saving him, and shutting the mouths of the lions (chapter 6).

The book concludes with a series of visions that Daniel had during the reigns of Belshazzar (chapters 7—8), Darius (chapter 9), and Cyrus (chapters 10—12). These dreams dramatically outline God's future plans, beginning with Babylon and continuing to the end of the age. They give a preview of God's redemption and have been called the key to all biblical prophecy.

God is sovereign. He was in control in Babylon, and he has been moving in history, controlling the destinies of people ever since. And he is here now! Despite news reports or personal stress, we can be confident that God is in control. As you read Daniel, watch God work and find your security in his sovereignty.

THE BLUEPRINT

A. DANIEL'S LIFE
(1:1—6:28)

Daniel and his three friends chose not to eat the king's food. They did not bow down to the king's image, even under penalty of death. Daniel continued to pray even though he knew he might be noticed and sentenced to death. These men are inspiring examples for us of how to live godly lives in a sinful world. When we face trials, we can expect God to also be with us through them. May God grant us similar courage to remain faithful under pressure.

B. DANIEL'S VISIONS
(7:1—12:13)

These visions gave the captives added confidence that God is in control of history. They were to wait patiently in faith and not worship the gods of Babylon or accept society's way of life. God still rules over human activities. Evil will be overcome, so we should wait patiently and not give in to the temptations and pressures of the sinful way of life around us.

MEGATHEMES

THEME	EXPLANATION	IMPORTANCE
God Is in Control	God is all-knowing, and he is in charge of world events. God overrules and removes rebellious leaders who defy him. God will overcome evil; no one is exempt. But he will deliver the faithful who follow him.	Although nations vie for world control now, one day Christ's kingdom will replace and surpass the kingdoms of this world. Our faith is sure because our future is secure in Christ. We must have courage and put our faith in God, who controls everything.
Purpose in Life	Daniel and his three friends are examples of dedication and commitment. They determined to serve God regardless of the consequences. They did not give in to pressures from an ungodly society because they had a clear purpose in life.	It is wise to make trusting and obeying God alone our true purpose in life. This will give us direction and peace in spite of the circumstances or consequences. We should disobey anyone who asks us to disobey God. Our first allegiance must be to God.
Perseverance	Daniel served for 70 years in a foreign land that was hostile to God, yet he did not compromise his faith in God. He was truthful, persistent in prayer, and disinterested in power for personal glory.	In order to fulfill your life's purpose, you need staying power. Don't let your Christian distinctness become blurred. Be relentless in your prayers, maintain your integrity, and be content to serve God wherever he puts you.
God's Faithfulness	God was faithful in Daniel's life. He delivered him from execution, from a den of lions, and from enemies who hated him. God cares for his people and deals patiently with them.	We can trust God to be with us through any trial. Because he has been faithful to us, we should remain faithful to him.

A. DANIEL'S LIFE (1:1—6:28)

While Ezekiel was ministering to the captives in Babylon, Daniel was drafted as a counselor to King Nebuchadnezzar. With God's help, Daniel interpreted two of the king's dreams, Daniel's three friends were rescued from certain death in the fiery furnace, and Daniel was rescued from a lions' den. Daniel's life is a picture of the triumph of faith. May God grant us this type of faith so that we may also live courageously each day.

Daniel's Training in Babylon

1:1
a 2Ki 24:1
b 2Ch 36:6

1 In the third year of the reign of Jehoiakim king of Judah, Nebuchadnezzar *a* king of Babylon came to Jerusalem and besieged it. *b* 2And the Lord delivered Jehoiakim king of

---

1:1, 2 Born during the middle of Josiah's reign (2 Kings 22; 23), Daniel grew up during the king's reforms. During this time, Daniel probably heard Jeremiah, a prophet he quoted in 9:2. In 609 B.C., Josiah was killed in a battle against Egypt, and within four years, the southern kingdom of Judah had returned to its evil ways.

In 605 B.C. Nebuchadnezzar became king of Babylonia. In September of that year, he swept into Palestine and surrounded Jerusalem, making Judah his vassal state. To demonstrate his

dominance, Nebuchadnezzar took many of Jerusalem's wisest men and most beautiful women to Babylon as captives. Daniel was among this group.

1:1, 2 Nebuchadnezzar, the supreme leader of Babylonia, was feared throughout the world. When he invaded a country, defeat was certain. After a victory, the Babylonians usually took the most talented and useful people back to Babylon and left only the poor behind to take whatever land they wanted and to live peacefully

Judah into his hand, along with some of the articles from the temple of God. These he carried off to the temple of his god in Babylonia a and put in the treasure house of his god. c

3 Then the king ordered Ashpenaz, chief of his court officials, to bring in some of the Israelites from the royal family and the nobility d— 4 young men without any physical defect, handsome, showing aptitude for every kind of learning, well informed, quick to understand, and qualified to serve in the king's palace. He was to teach them the language and literature of the Babylonians. b 5 The king assigned them a daily amount of food and wine from the king's table. They were to be trained for three years, and after that they were to enter the king's service. e

6 Among these were some from Judah: Daniel, Hananiah, Mishael and Azariah. 7 The chief official gave them new names: to Daniel, the name Belteshazzar; f to Hananiah, Shadrach; to Mishael, Meshach; and to Azariah, Abednego.

8 But Daniel resolved not to defile g himself with the royal food and wine, and he asked the chief official for permission not to defile himself this way. 9 Now God had caused the official to show favor h and sympathy to Daniel, 10 but the official told Daniel, "I am afraid of my lord the king, who has assigned your c food and drink. Why should he see you looking worse than the other young men your age? The king would then have my head because of you."

11 Daniel then said to the guard whom the chief official had appointed over Daniel, Hananiah, Mishael and Azariah, 12 "Please test your servants for ten days: Give us nothing but

a 2 Hebrew Shinar   b 4 Or Chaldeans   c 10 The Hebrew for your and you in this verse is plural.

1:2 c Jer 27:19-20; Zec 5:5-11

1:3 d Isa 39:7

1:5 e ver 19

1:7 f Da 4:8; 5:12

1:8 g Eze 4:13-14

1:9 h Pr 16:7

---

there (2 Kings 24:14). This system fostered great loyalty from conquered lands and ensured a steady supply of wise and talented people for civil service.

1:2 At certain times God allows his work to suffer. In this instance, the Babylonians raided the temple of God, and took the worship articles to the temple of a god in Babylon. This god may have been Bel, also called Marduk, the chief god of the Babylonians. Those who loved the Lord must have felt disheartened and discouraged. We feel greatly disappointed when our churches suffer physical damage, split, close down for financial reasons, or are wracked by scandals. We do not know why God allows his church to experience these calamities. But like the people who witnessed the plundering of the temple by the Babylonians, we must trust that God is in control and that he is watching over all who trust in him.

1:4 The common language of Babylonia was Aramaic, while the language of scholarship included the ancient and complicated Babylonian language. The academic program would have included mathematics, astronomy, history, science, and magic. These young men demonstrated not only aptitude, but also discipline. This character trait, combined with integrity, served them well in their new culture.

1:7 Nebuchadnezzar changed the names of Daniel and his friends because he wanted to make them Babylonian—in their own eyes and in the eyes of the Babylonian people. New names would help

them assimilate into the culture. Daniel means "God is my Judge" in Hebrew; his name was changed to Belteshazzar meaning "Bel, protect his life!" (Bel, also called Marduk, was the chief Babylonian god). Hananiah means "the LORD shows grace"; his new name, Shadrach, probably means "under the command of Aku" (the moon god). Mishael means "who is like God?"; his new name, Meshach, probably means "who is like Aku?" Azariah means "the LORD helps"; his new name, Abednego, means "servant of Nego/ Nebo" (or Nabu, the god of learning and writing). This was how the king attempted to change the religious loyalty of these young men from Judah's God to Babylonia's gods.

1:8 Daniel resolved not to eat this food, either because the meat was some food forbidden by Jewish law, like pork (see Leviticus 11), or because accepting the king's food and drink was the first step toward depending on his gifts and favors. Although Daniel was in a culture that did not honor God, he still obeyed God's laws.

1:8 *Resolve* is a strong word that means to be devoted to principle and to be committed to a course of action. When Daniel resolved not to defile himself, he was being true to a lifelong determination to do what was right and not to give in to the pressures around him. We too are often assaulted by pressures to compromise our standards and live more like the world around us. Merely wanting or preferring God's will and way is not enough to stand against the onslaught of temptation. Like Daniel, we must resolve to obey God.

1:8 It is easier to resist temptation if you have thought through your convictions well before the temptation arrives. Daniel and his friends made their decision to be faithful to the laws of God before they were faced with the king's delicacies, so they did not hesitate to stick with their convictions. We will get into trouble if we have not previously decided where to draw the line. Before such situations arise, decide on your commitments. Then when temptation comes, you will be ready to say no.

1:9 God moved with an unseen hand to change the heart of this Babylonian official. The strong moral conviction of these four young men made an impact. God promises to be with his people in times of trial and temptation (Psalm 106:46; Isaiah 43:2–5; 1 Corinthians 10:13). His active intervention often comes just when we take a stand for him. Stand for God and trust him to protect you in ways you may not be able to see.

1:10 Anything short of complete obedience meant execution for the officials who served Nebuchadnezzar. Even in such a small matter as this, the official feared for his life.

1:12 The Babylonians were trying to change the *thinking* of

TAKEN TO BABYLON Daniel, as a captive of Babylonian soldiers, faced a long and difficult march to a new land. The 500-mile trek, under harsh conditions, certainly tested his faith in God.

vegetables to eat and water to drink. [13]Then compare our appearance with that of the young men who eat the royal food, and treat your servants in accordance with what you see." [14]So he agreed to this and tested them for ten days.

[15]At the end of the ten days they looked healthier and better nourished than any of the young men who ate the royal food. [16]So the guard took away their choice food and the wine they were to drink and gave them vegetables instead.

1:17
[i]Da 2:19, 30

[17]To these four young men God gave knowledge and understanding of all kinds of literature and learning. And Daniel could understand visions and dreams of all kinds. [i]

1:19
[j]Ge 41:46

[18]At the end of the time set by the king to bring them in, the chief official presented them to Nebuchadnezzar. [19]The king talked with them, and he found none equal to Daniel, Hananiah, Mishael and Azariah; so they entered the king's service. [j] [20]In every matter of wisdom and understanding about which the king questioned them, he found them ten times better than all the magicians and enchanters in his whole kingdom.

1:21
[k]Da 6:28; 10:1

[21]And Daniel remained there until the first year of King Cyrus. [k]

Nebuchadnezzar's Dream

2:1
[l]Da 4:5
[m]Ge 41:8
[n]Est 6:1

2:2
[o]Ge 41:8
[p]Ex 7:11

2 In the second year of his reign, Nebuchadnezzar had dreams; [l] his mind was troubled [m] and he could not sleep. [n] [2]So the king summoned the magicians, [o] enchanters, sorcerers[p] and astrologers[a] to tell him what he had dreamed. When they came in and stood before the king, [3]he said to them, "I have had a dream that troubles me and I want to know what it means. [b]"

[4]Then the astrologers answered the king in Aramaic, [c] "O king, live forever! Tell your servants the dream, and we will interpret it."

[a]2 Or *Chaldeans*; also in verses 4, 5 and 10   [b]3 Or *was*   [c]4 The text from here through chapter 7 is in Aramaic.

DANIEL served as a prophet to the exiles in Babylon from 605–535 B.C.	*Climate of the times*	The people of Judah were captives in a strange land, feeling hopeless.
	Main message	God is sovereign over all human history, past, present, and future.
	Importance of message	We should spend less time wondering when future events will happen and more time learning how we should live now.
	Contemporary prophets	Jeremiah (627–586 B.C.), Habakkuk (612–588 B.C.), Ezekiel (593–571 B.C.)

---

these Jews by giving them a Babylonian education, their *loyalty* by changing their names, and their *lifestyle* by changing their diet. Without compromising, Daniel found a way to live by God's standards in a culture that did not honor God. Wisely choosing to negotiate rather than to rebel, Daniel suggested an experimental ten-day diet of vegetables and water, instead of the royal foods and wine the king offered. Without compromising, Daniel quickly thought of a practical, creative solution that saved his life and the lives of his companions. As God's people, we may adjust to our culture as long as we do not compromise God's laws.

1:17 Daniel and his friends learned all they could about their new culture so they could do their work with excellence. But while they learned, they maintained steadfast allegiance to God, and God gave them skill and wisdom. Culture need not be God's enemy. If it does not violate his commands, it can aid in accomplishing his purpose. We who follow God are free to be competent leaders in our culture, but we are required to pledge our allegiance to God first.

1:20 Nebuchadnezzar put Daniel and his friends on his staff of advisers. This staff included many "magicians and enchanters." These were astrologers who claimed to be able to tell the future through occult practices. They were masters at communicating their message so that it sounded authoritative—as though it came directly from their gods. In addition to knowledge, Daniel and his three friends had wisdom and understanding, given to them by God. Thus the king was far more pleased with them than with his magicians and enchanters. As we serve others, we must

not merely pretend to have God's wisdom. Our wisdom will be genuine only when we are rightly related to God.

1:20 How did the captives survive in a foreign culture? They learned about the culture, achieved excellence in their work, served the people, prayed for God's help, and maintained their integrity. We may feel like foreigners whenever we experience change. Alien cultures come in many forms: a new job, a new school, a new neighborhood. We can use the same principles to help us adapt to our new surroundings without abandoning God.

1:21 Daniel was one of the first captives taken to Babylon, and he lived to see the first exiles return to Jerusalem in 538 B.C. Throughout this time Daniel honored God, and God honored him. While serving as an adviser to the kings of Babylon, Daniel was God's spokesman to the Babylonian empire. Babylon was a wicked nation, but it would have been much worse without Daniel's influence.

2:1–11 Dreams were considered to be messages from the gods, and the wise men were expected to interpret them. Usually the wise men could give some sort of interpretation as long as they knew what the dream was about. This time, however, Nebuchadnezzar demanded to be told the dream also. God sent a series of dreams to Nebuchadnezzar with prophetic messages that could be revealed and understood only by a servant of God. People from other time periods who received dreams from God include Jacob (Genesis 28:10–15), Joseph (Genesis 37:5–11), Pharaoh's cupbearer and his baker (Genesis 40), Pharaoh (Genesis 41), Solomon (1 Kings 3:5–15), and Joseph (Matthew 1:20–24).

5 The king replied to the astrologers, "This is what I have firmly decided: If you do not tell me what my dream was and interpret it, I will have you cut into pieces and your houses turned into piles of rubble. *q* 6 But if you tell me the dream and explain it, you will receive from me gifts and rewards and great honor.*r* So tell me the dream and interpret it for me."

7 Once more they replied, "Let the king tell his servants the dream, and we will interpret it."

8 Then the king answered, "I am certain that you are trying to gain time, because you realize that this is what I have firmly decided: 9 If you do not tell me the dream, there is just one penalty*s* for you. You have conspired to tell me misleading and wicked things, hoping the situation will change. So then, tell me the dream, and I will know that you can interpret it for me."

10 The astrologers answered the king, "There is not a man on earth who can do what the king asks! No king, however great and mighty, has ever asked such a thing of any magician or enchanter or astrologer.*t* 11 What the king asks is too difficult. No one can reveal it to the king except the gods, and they do not live among men."

12 This made the king so angry and furious that he ordered the execution of all the wise men of Babylon. 13 So the decree was issued to put the wise men to death, and men were sent to look for Daniel and his friends to put them to death. *u*

14 When Arioch, the commander of the king's guard, had gone out to put to death the wise men of Babylon, Daniel spoke to him with wisdom and tact. 15 He asked the king's officer, "Why did the king issue such a harsh decree?" Arioch then explained the matter to Daniel. 16 At this, Daniel went in to the king and asked for time, so that he might interpret the dream for him.

17 Then Daniel returned to his house and explained the matter to his friends Hananiah, Mishael and Azariah. 18 He urged them to plead for mercy *v* from the God of heaven concerning this mystery,*w* so that he and his friends might not be executed with the rest of the wise men of Babylon. 19 During the night the mystery was revealed to Daniel in a vision. *x* Then Daniel praised the God of heaven 20 and said:

> "Praise be to the name of God for ever and ever;*y*
>> wisdom and power*z* are his.
> 21 He changes times and seasons;
>> he sets up kings and deposes them.

2:5
q Ezr 6:11; Da 3:29

2:6
r Da 5:7, 16

2:9
s Est 4:11

2:10
t ver 27

2:13
u Da 1:20

2:18
v Isa 37:4
w Jer 33:3

2:19
x Job 33:15

2:20
y Ps 113:2
z Jer 32:19

2:10, 11 The astrologers told the king that "not a man on earth" could know the dreams of another person. What the king asked was humanly impossible. But Daniel could tell what the king had dreamed, and he could also give the interpretation because God was working through him. In daily life, we face many apparently impossible situations that would be hopeless if we had to handle them with our limited strength. But God specializes in working through us to achieve the impossible.

2:10, 11 The astrologers were unable to persuade the king with any amount of logic or rational argument. The king asked for something impossible and didn't want anyone to change his mind. When power goes to a leader's head, whether at work, at home, or in the church, that leader can sometimes begin demanding the impossible from subordinates. At times, this may be the challenge needed to motivate workers to achieve more than they thought they could. At other times, it may be the rantings and ravings of someone deluded with power. Just as Daniel dealt wisely in the situation, we can ask God to give us wisdom to know how to deal with unreasonable bosses.

2:11 The astrologers said that the gods "do not live among men." Of course their gods didn't—they didn't even exist! This exposed the limitations of the astrologers. They could invent interpretations of dreams but could not tell Nebuchadnezzar *what* he had dreamed. Although his request was unreasonable, Nebuchadnezzar was furious when his advisers couldn't fulfill it. It was not unusual in these times for astrologers to be in conflict with the king. They sometimes used their craft to gain political power.

2:11 By answering that the gods "do not live among men," the astrologers betrayed their concept of the gods. Theirs was a hollow religion, a religion of convenience. They believed in the gods, but that belief made no difference in their conduct. Today, many people profess to believe in God, but it is also a hollow

belief. In essence, they are practical atheists because they don't listen to him or do what he says. Do you believe in God? He *does* live among people, and he wants to change your life.

2:16–18 Daniel was at a crisis point. Imagine going to see the powerful, temperamental king who had just angrily ordered your death! Daniel did not shrink back in fear, however, but confidently believed God would tell him all the king wanted to know. When the king gave Daniel time to find the answer, Daniel found his three friends and they prayed. When you find yourself in a tight spot, share your needs with trusted friends who also believe in God's power. Prayer is more effective than panic. Panic confirms your hopelessness; prayer confirms your hope in God. Daniel's trust in God saved himself, his three friends, and all the other wise men of Babylon.

2:19–23 After Daniel asked God to reveal Nebuchadnezzar's dream to him, he saw a vision of the dream. Daniel's prayer was answered. Before rushing to Arioch with the news, Daniel took time to give God credit for all wisdom and power, thanking God for answering his request. How do you feel when your prayers are answered? Excited, surprised, relieved? There are times when we seek God in prayer and, after having been answered, dash off in our excitement, forgetting to give God credit for the answer. Match your persistence in prayer with gratitude when your requests are answered.

2:21 If you ever think that you have much to learn in life, and if you ever wish that you knew more about how to handle people, then look to God for wisdom. While educational institutions provide diplomas at great expense, God gives wisdom freely to all who ask. (See James 1:5 for more on asking God for wisdom.)

2:21 When we see evil leaders who live long and good leaders who die young, we may wonder if God controls world events. Daniel saw evil rulers with almost limitless power, but Daniel

2:21
a Jas 1:5

2:22
b Job 12:22;
Da 5:11
c Ps 139:11-12
d Isa 45:7

2:23
e Da 1:17

He gives wisdom*a* to the wise
    and knowledge to the discerning.
22 He reveals deep and hidden things;*b*
    he knows what lies in darkness,*c*
    and light*d* dwells with him.
23 I thank and praise you, O God of my fathers:
    You have given me wisdom*e* and power,
you have made known to me what we asked of you,
    you have made known to us the dream of the king."

Daniel Interprets the Dream

24 Then Daniel went to Arioch, whom the king had appointed to execute the wise men of Babylon, and said to him, "Do not execute the wise men of Babylon. Take me to the king, and I will interpret his dream for him."

2:25
f Da 1:6

25 Arioch took Daniel to the king at once and said, "I have found a man among the exiles from Judah *f* who can tell the king what his dream means."

26 The king asked Daniel (also called Belteshazzar), "Are you able to tell me what I saw in my dream and interpret it?"

2:27
g ver 10

2:28
h Ge 40:8
i Da 4:5

27 Daniel replied, "No wise man, enchanter, magician or diviner can explain to the king the mystery he has asked about,*g* 28 but there is a God in heaven who reveals mysteries.*h* He has shown King Nebuchadnezzar what will happen in days to come. Your dream and the visions that passed through your mind*i* as you lay on your bed are these:

29 "As you were lying there, O king, your mind turned to things to come, and the revealer of mysteries showed you what is going to happen. 30 As for me, this mystery has been revealed to me, not because I have greater wisdom than other living men, but so that you, O king, may know the interpretation and that you may understand what went through your mind.

2:31
j Hab 1:7

2:34
k Zec 4:6
l Da 8:25

31 "You looked, O king, and there before you stood a large statue—an enormous, dazzling statue,*j* awesome in appearance. 32 The head of the statue was made of pure gold, its chest and arms of silver, its belly and thighs of bronze, 33 its legs of iron, its feet partly of iron and partly of baked clay. 34 While you were watching, a rock was cut out, but not by human hands.*k* It struck the statue on its feet of iron and clay and smashed them.*l* 35 Then the iron, the clay, the

---

NEBUCHADNEZZAR'S DREAM FULFILLED

The large statue in Nebuchadnezzar's dream (2:24–45) represented the four kingdoms that would dominate as world powers. We recognize these as the Babylonian empire, the Medo-Persian empire, the Grecian empire, and the Roman empire. All of these will be crushed and brought to an end by the kingdom of God, which will continue forever.

Part	Material	Empire	Period of Domination
Head	Gold	Babylonian	606 B.C.–539 B.C.
Chest and Arms	Silver	Medo-Persian	539 B.C.–331 B.C.
Belly and Thighs	Bronze	Grecian	331 B.C.–146 B.C.
Legs and Feet	Iron and Clay	Roman	146 B.C.–A.D. 476

---

knew and proclaimed that God "sets up kings and deposes them," that he controls everything that happens. God governs the world according to his purposes. You may be dismayed when you see evil people prosper, but God is in control. Let this knowledge give you confidence and peace no matter what happens.

2:24 Daniel did not use his success to promote his own self-interest. He thought of others. When striving to succeed or survive, remember the needs of others.

2:27–30 Before Daniel told the king anything else, he gave credit to God, explaining that he did not know the dream through his own wisdom but only because God revealed it. How easily we take credit for what God does through us! This robs God of the honor that he alone deserves. Instead we should be like Daniel and point people to God so that we give him the glory.

2:31ff The head of gold on the statue in the dream represented Nebuchadnezzar, ruler of the Babylonian empire. The silver chest and two arms represented the Medo-Persian empire, which conquered Babylon in 539 B.C. The belly and thighs of bronze were Greece and Macedonia under Alexander the Great, who conquered the Medo-Persian empire in 334–330 B.C. The legs of iron represented Rome, which conquered the Greeks in 63 B.C. The feet of clay and iron represented the breakup of the Roman empire, when the territory Rome ruled divided into a mixture of strong and weak nations. The type of metal in each part depicted the strength of the political power it represented. The rock cut out of the mountain depicted God's kingdom, which would be ruled eternally by the Messiah, the King of kings. The dream revealed Daniel's God as the power behind all earthly kingdoms.

bronze, the silver and the gold were broken to pieces at the same time and became like chaff on a threshing floor in the summer. The wind swept them away *m* without leaving a trace. But the rock that struck the statue became a huge mountain *n* and filled the whole earth.

36"This was the dream, and now we will interpret it to the king. 37You, O king, are the king of kings. The God of heaven has given you dominion *o* and power and might and glory; 38 in your hands he has placed mankind and the beasts of the field and the birds of the air. Wherever they live, he has made you ruler over them all. *p* You are that head of gold.

39"After you, another kingdom will rise, inferior to yours. Next, a third kingdom, one of bronze, will rule over the whole earth. 40Finally, there will be a fourth kingdom, strong as iron—for iron breaks and smashes everything—and as iron breaks things to pieces, so it will crush and break all the others. *q* 41Just as you saw that the feet and toes were partly of baked clay and partly of iron, so this will be a divided kingdom; yet it will have some of the strength of iron in it, even as you saw iron mixed with clay. 42As the toes were partly iron and partly clay, so this kingdom will be partly strong and partly brittle. 43And just as you saw the iron mixed with baked clay, so the people will be a mixture and will not remain united, any more than iron mixes with clay.

44"In the time of those kings, the God of heaven will set up a kingdom that will never be destroyed, nor will it be left to another people. It will crush *r* all those kingdoms and bring them to an end, but it will itself endure forever. *s* 45This is the meaning of the vision of the rock cut out of a mountain, but not by human hands—a rock that broke the iron, the bronze, the clay, the silver and the gold to pieces.

"The great God has shown the king what will take place in the future. The dream is true and the interpretation is trustworthy."

46Then King Nebuchadnezzar fell prostrate *t* before Daniel and paid him honor and ordered that an offering *u* and incense be presented to him. 47The king said to Daniel, "Surely your God is the God of gods *v* and the Lord of kings and a revealer of mysteries, for you were able to reveal this mystery."

48Then the king placed Daniel in a high position and lavished many gifts on him. He made him ruler over the entire province of Babylon and placed him in charge of all its wise men. *w* 49Moreover, at Daniel's request the king appointed Shadrach, Meshach and Abednego administrators over the province of Babylon, while Daniel himself remained at the royal court.

The Image of Gold and the Fiery Furnace

3 King Nebuchadnezzar made an image *x* of gold, ninety feet high and nine feet *a* wide, and set it up on the plain of Dura in the province of Babylon. 2He then summoned the satraps, prefects, governors, advisers, treasurers, judges, magistrates and all the other provincial officials *y* to come to the dedication of the image he had set up. 3So the satraps, prefects, governors, advisers, treasurers, judges, magistrates and all the other provincial officials assembled for the dedication of the image that King Nebuchadnezzar had set up, and they stood before it.

a 1 Aramaic *sixty cubits high and six cubits wide* (about 27 meters high and 2.7 meters wide)

2:35
m Ps 37:10
n Isa 2:3

2:37
o Jer 27:7

2:38
p Da 4:21-22

2:40
q Da 7:7, 23

2:44
r Ps 2:9
s Da 4:34;
Mic 4:7, 13

2:46
t Ac 10:25
u Ac 14:13

2:47
v Da 11:36

2:48
w ver 6

3:1
x Isa 46:6; Hab 2:19

3:2
y ver 27

2:36 When Daniel says "we," he is referring to himself and his three friends. Just as Daniel involved them in praying for God's help, he gave them credit when he presented the interpretation. Because they helped Daniel in the prayer, he was careful to share the credit with them.

2:44 God's kingdom will never be destroyed. If you are upset by threats of war and the prosperity of evil leaders, remember that God, not world leaders, decides the outcome of history. Under God's protection, God's kingdom is indestructible. Those who believe in God are members of his kingdom and are secure in him.

2:47 Nebuchadnezzar honored Daniel and Daniel's God. If Daniel had taken the credit himself, the king would have honored only Daniel. Because Daniel gave God the credit, the king honored both of them. Part of our mission in this world is to show unbelievers what God is like. We can do that by giving God credit for what he does in our lives. Our acts of love and compassion may impress people, and if we give God credit for our actions, they will want to know more about him. Give thanks to God for what he is doing in and through you.

2:49 After being named ruler over the whole province of Babylon and placed in charge of the wise men, Daniel requested that his companions, Shadrach, Meshach, and Abednego, be appointed as his assistants. Daniel knew that he could not handle such an enormous responsibility without capable assistants, so he chose the best men he knew—his three Hebrew companions. A competent leader never does all the work alone; he or she knows how to delegate and supervise. Moses, Israel's greatest leader, shared the burden of administration with dozens of assistants. (This story is in Exodus 18:13–27.)

3:1 In Babylon's religious culture, statues were frequently worshiped. Nebuchadnezzar hoped to use this huge image (ninety feet high by nine feet wide) as a strategy to unite the nation and solidify his power by centralizing worship. This gold image may have been inspired by his dream. Instead of having only a head of gold, however, it was gold from head to toe. Nebuchadnezzar wanted his kingdom to last forever. When he made the statue, Nebuchadnezzar showed that his devotion to Daniel's God was short-lived. He neither feared nor obeyed the God who was behind the dream.

3:4
zDa 4:1; 6:25

3:5
aver 10, 15

3:6
bJer 29:22

3:9
cDa 5:10

3:10
dver 4-6

⁴Then the herald loudly proclaimed, "This is what you are commanded to do, O peoples, nations and men of every language: ᶻ ⁵As soon as you hear the sound of the horn, flute, zither, lyre, harp, pipes and all kinds of music, you must fall down and worship the image of gold that King Nebuchadnezzar has set up.ᵃ ⁶Whoever does not fall down and worship will immediately be thrown into a blazing furnace."ᵇ

⁷Therefore, as soon as they heard the sound of the horn, flute, zither, lyre, harp and all kinds of music, all the peoples, nations and men of every language fell down and worshiped the image of gold that King Nebuchadnezzar had set up.

⁸At this time some astrologersᵃ came forward and denounced the Jews. ⁹They said to King Nebuchadnezzar, "O king, live forever!ᶜ ¹⁰You have issued a decree, O king, that everyone who hears the sound of the horn, flute, zither, lyre, harp, pipes and all kinds of music must fall down and worship the image of gold,ᵈ ¹¹and that whoever does not fall down and worship will be thrown into a blazing furnace. ¹²But there are some Jews whom you have set

ᵃ8 Or *Chaldeans*

DANIEL

Daniel's early life demonstrates that there is more to being young than making mistakes. No characteristic wins the hearts of adults more quickly than wisdom in the words and actions of a young person. Daniel and his friends had been taken from their homes in Judah and exiled. Their futures were in doubt, but they all had personal traits that qualified them for jobs as servants in the king's palace. They took advantage of the opportunity without letting the opportunity take advantage of them.

Our first hint of Daniel's greatness comes in his quiet refusal to give up his convictions. He had applied God's will to his own life, and he resisted changing the good habits he had formed. Both his physical and spiritual diets were an important part of his relationship with God. He ate carefully and lived prayerfully. One of the benefits of being in training for royal service was eating food from the king's table. Daniel tactfully chose a simpler menu and proved it was a healthy choice. As with Daniel, mealtimes are obvious and regular tests of our efforts to control our appetites.

While Daniel limited his food intake, he indulged in prayer. He was able to communicate with God because he made it a habit. He put into practice his convictions, even when that meant being thrown into a den of hungry lions. His life proved he made the right choice.

Do you hold so strongly to your faith in God that whatever happens you will do what God says? Such conviction keeps you a step ahead of temptation; such conviction gives you wisdom and stability in changing circumstances. Prayerfully live out your convictions in everyday life and trust God for the results.

Strengths and accomplishments:	• Although young when deported, remained true to his faith • Served as an adviser to two Babylonian kings and two Medo-Persian kings • Was a man of prayer and a statesman with the gift of prophecy • Survived the lions' den
Lessons from his life:	• Quiet convictions often earn long-term respect • Don't wait until you are in a tough situation to learn about prayer • God can use people wherever they are
Vital statistics:	• Where: Judah and the courts of both Babylon and Persia • Occupation: A captive from Israel who became an adviser of kings • Contemporaries: Hananiah, Mishael, Azariah, Nebuchadnezzar, Belshazzar, Darius, Cyrus
Key verse:	"This man Daniel, whom the king called Belteshazzar, was found to have a keen mind and knowledge and understanding, and also the ability to interpret dreams, explain riddles and solve difficult problems. Call for Daniel, and he will tell you what the writing means" (5:12).

Daniel's story is told in the book of Daniel. He is also mentioned in Matthew 24:15.

3:2 Satraps were governors over major divisions of the empire, serving as the chief representatives of the king. Prefects were the governors over conquered cities. Governors were civil administrators over provinces.

3:6 This blazing furnace was not a small oven for cooking dinner or heating a house; it was a huge industrial furnace that could have been used for baking bricks or smelting metals. The temperatures were hot enough to assure that no one could survive. The roaring flames could be seen leaping from its top opening, and a fiery blast killed the soldiers who went up to the large opening (3:22).

3:12 We don't know if other Jews refused to fall down and

worship the image, but these three were singled out as public examples. Why didn't the three men just bow to the image and tell God that they didn't mean it? They had determined never to worship another god, and they courageously took their stand. As a result, they were condemned and led away to be executed. The men did not know whether they would be delivered from the fire; all they knew was that they would not fall down and worship an idol. Are you ready to take a stand for God no matter what? When you stand for God, you will stand out. It may be painful, and it may not always have a happy ending. Be prepared to say, "If he rescues me, or if he doesn't, I will serve only God."

over the affairs of the province of Babylon—Shadrach, Meshach and Abednego *e*—who pay no attention to you, O king. They neither serve your gods nor worship the image of gold you have set up."

3:12
e Da 2:49

13Furious *f* with rage, Nebuchadnezzar summoned Shadrach, Meshach and Abednego. So these men were brought before the king, 14and Nebuchadnezzar said to them, "Is it true, Shadrach, Meshach and Abednego, that you do not serve my gods *g* or worship the image of gold I have set up? 15Now when you hear the sound of the horn, flute, zither, lyre, harp, pipes and all kinds of music, if you are ready to fall down and worship the image I made, very good. But if you do not worship it, you will be thrown immediately into a blazing furnace. Then what god *h* will be able to rescue you from my hand?"

3:13
f Da 2:12
3:14
g Isa 46:1; Jer 50:2
3:15
h Isa 36:18-20

16Shadrach, Meshach and Abednego replied to the king, "O Nebuchadnezzar, we do not need to defend ourselves before you in this matter. 17If we are thrown into the blazing furnace, the God we serve is able to save *i* us from it, and he will rescue us from your hand, O king. 18But even if he does not, we want you to know, O king, that we will not serve your gods or worship the image of gold you have set up. *j*"

3:17
i Ps 27:1-2
3:18
j ver 28

19Then Nebuchadnezzar was furious with Shadrach, Meshach and Abednego, and his attitude toward them changed. He ordered the furnace heated seven times hotter than usual 20and commanded some of the strongest soldiers in his army to tie up Shadrach, Meshach and Abednego and throw them into the blazing furnace. 21So these men, wearing their robes, trousers, turbans and other clothes, were bound and thrown into the blazing furnace. 22The king's command was so urgent and the furnace so hot that the flames of the fire killed the soldiers who took up Shadrach, Meshach and Abednego, 23and these three men, firmly tied, fell into the blazing furnace.

24Then King Nebuchadnezzar leaped to his feet in amazement and asked his advisers, "Weren't there three men that we tied up and threw into the fire?"

They replied, "Certainly, O king."

25He said, "Look! I see four men walking around in the fire, unbound and unharmed, and the fourth looks like a son of the gods."

26Nebuchadnezzar then approached the opening of the blazing furnace and shouted, "Shadrach, Meshach and Abednego, servants of the Most High God, *k* come out! Come here!"

3:26
k Da 4:2, 34

So Shadrach, Meshach and Abednego came out of the fire, 27and the satraps, prefects, governors and royal advisers crowded around them. *l* They saw that the fire had not harmed their bodies, nor was a hair of their heads singed; their robes were not scorched, and there was no smell of fire on them.

3:27
l Heb 11:32-34

3:13 Nebuchadnezzar flew into a rage when anyone dared to disobey his commands. As the supreme ruler of Babylonia, he expected absolute obedience. But his pride had caused him to go beyond his own authority. His demands were unjust and his reactions extreme. If you find yourself angered when people don't follow your directions, ask yourself, "Why am I reacting?" Your ego may be overly involved with your authority.

3:15 The three men were given one more chance. Here are eight excuses they could have used to bow to the image and save their lives: (1) We will fall down but not actually *worship* the idol. (2) We won't become idol worshipers, but will worship this one time, and then ask God for forgiveness. (3) The king has absolute power, and we must obey him. God will understand. (4) The king appointed us—we owe this to him. (5) This is a foreign land, so God will excuse us for following the customs of the land. (6) Our ancestors set up idols in God's temple! This isn't half as bad! (7) We're not hurting anybody. (8) If we get ourselves killed and some pagans take our high positions, they won't help our people in exile!

Although all these excuses sound sensible at first, they are dangerous rationalizations. To fall down and worship the image would violate God's command in Exodus 20:3, "You shall have no other gods before me." It would also erase their testimony for God forever. Never again could they talk about the power of their God above all other gods. What excuses do you use for not standing up for him?

3:16–18 Shadrach, Meshach, and Abednego were pressured to deny God, but they chose to be faithful to him no matter what

happened! They trusted God to deliver them, but they were determined to be faithful regardless of the consequences. If God always rescued those who were true to him, Christians would not need faith. Their religion would be a great insurance policy, and there would be lines of selfish people ready to sign up. We should be faithful to serve God whether he intervenes on our behalf or not. Our eternal reward is worth any suffering we may have to endure first.

3:19 "His attitude toward them changed." When we do something that offends non-Christians, their attitude toward us often changes because they are basically selfish. Christians should be different; they should still love those who offend them.

3:25 It was obvious to those watching that this fourth person was supernatural. We cannot be certain who the fourth man was. It could have been an angel or a pre-incarnate appearance of Christ. In either case, God sent a heavenly visitor to accompany these faithful men during their time of great trial.

3:25–30 God's deliverance of Shadrach, Meshach, and Abednego was a great victory of faith for the Jews in captivity. They were protected from harm, they were comforted in trial, God was glorified, and they were rewarded. Let us determine to be true to God no matter how difficult the pressure or punishment. God's protection transcends anything we could imagine.

3:27 These young men had been completely untouched by the fire and heat. Only the rope that bound them had been burned. No human can bind us if God wants us to be free. The power available to us is the same that delivered Shadrach, Meshach, and Abednego and raised Christ from the dead (Ephesians

3:28
m Ps 34:7; Da 6:22

3:29
n Da 6:26
o Da 6:27

3:30
p Da 2:49

28 Then Nebuchadnezzar said, "Praise be to the God of Shadrach, Meshach and Abednego, who has sent his angel m and rescued his servants! They trusted in him and defied the king's command and were willing to give up their lives rather than serve or worship any god except their own God. 29 Therefore I decree n that the people of any nation or language who say anything against the God of Shadrach, Meshach and Abednego be cut into pieces and their houses be turned into piles of rubble, for no other god can save o in this way."

30 Then the king promoted Shadrach, Meshach and Abednego in the province of Babylon.p

SHADRACH/MESHACH/ABEDNEGO

Friendships make life enjoyable and difficult times bearable. Friendships are tested and strengthened by hardships. Such was the relationship between three young Jewish men deported to Babylon along with Daniel. Shadrach, Meshach, and Abednego help us think about the real meaning of friendship. As much as these friends meant to each other, they never allowed their friendship to usurp God's place in their lives—not even in the face of death.

Together they silently defied King Nebuchadnezzar's order to fall down and worship the image of gold. They shared a courageous act, while others, eager to get rid of them, told the king that the three Jews were being disloyal. While this was not true, Nebuchadnezzar could not spare them without shaming himself.

This was the moment of truth. Death was about to end their friendship. A small compromise would have allowed them to live and go on enjoying each other's friendship, serving God, and serving their people while in this foreign land. But they were wise enough to see that compromise would have poisoned the very conviction that bound them so closely—each had a higher allegiance to God. So they did not hesitate to place their lives in the hands of God. The rest was victory!

When we leave God out of our most important relationships, we tend to expect those relationships to meet needs in us that only God can meet. Friends are helpful, but they cannot meet our deepest spiritual needs. Leaving God out of our relationships indicates how unimportant he really is in our own lives. Our relationship with God should be important enough to touch our other relationships—especially our closest friendships.

Strengths and accomplishments:	• Stood with Daniel against eating food from the king's table • Shared a friendship that stood the tests of hardship, success, wealth, and possible death • Unwilling to compromise their convictions even in the face of death • Survived the fiery furnace
Lessons from their lives:	• There is great strength in real friendship • It is important to stand with others with whom we share convictions • God can be trusted even when we can't predict the outcome
Vital statistics:	• Where: Babylon • Occupations: King's servants and advisers • Contemporaries: Daniel, Nebuchadnezzar
Key verses:	"Shadrach, Meshach and Abednego replied to the king, 'O Nebuchadnezzar, we do not need to defend ourselves before you in this matter. If we are thrown into the blazing furnace, the God we serve is able to save us from it, and he will rescue us from your hand, O king. But even if he does not, we want you to know, O king, that we will not serve your gods or worship the image of gold you have set up'" (3:16–18).

The story of Shadrach (Hananiah), Meshach (Mishael), and Abednego (Azariah) is told in the book of Daniel.

1:18–20). Trust God in every situation. There are eternal reasons for temporary trials, so be thankful that your destiny is in God's hands, not in human hands.

3:28, 29 Nebuchadnezzar was not making a commitment here to serve the Hebrews' God alone. Instead, he was acknowledging that God is powerful, and he commanded his people not to speak against God. Nebuchadnezzar didn't tell the people to throw away all the other gods, but to add this one to the list.

3:30 Where was Daniel in this story? The Bible doesn't say, but there are several possibilities. (1) He may have been on official business in another part of the kingdom. (2) He may have been present, but because he was a ruler, the officials didn't accuse

him of not falling down and worshiping the image. (3) He may have been in the capital city handling the administration while Nebuchadnezzar was away. (4) He may have been considered exempt from bowing down to the image because of his reputation for interpreting dreams through his God. Whether Daniel was there or not, we can be sure that he would not have worshiped the image.

Nebuchadnezzar's Dream of a Tree

4 King Nebuchadnezzar,

To the peoples, nations and men of every language, who live in all the world:

May you prosper greatly!^q

May you prosper greatly! [q]

2 It is my pleasure to tell you about the miraculous signs and wonders that the Most High God [r] has performed for me.

> 3 How great are his signs,
>   how mighty his wonders! [s]
> His kingdom is an eternal kingdom;
>   his dominion endures [t] from generation to generation.

4 I, Nebuchadnezzar, was at home in my palace, contented and prosperous. 5 I had a dream [u] that made me afraid. As I was lying in my bed, the images and visions that passed through my mind [v] terrified me. 6 So I commanded that all the wise men of Babylon be brought before me to interpret the dream for me. 7 When the magicians, enchanters, astrologers [a] and diviners [w] came, I told them the dream, but they could not interpret it for me. 8 Finally, Daniel came into my presence and I told him the dream. (He is called Belteshazzar, [x] after the name of my god, and the spirit of the holy gods is in him.)

9 I said, "Belteshazzar, chief [y] of the magicians, I know that the spirit of the holy gods [z] is in you, and no mystery is too difficult for you. Here is my dream; interpret it for me. 10 These are the visions I saw while lying in my bed: I looked, and there before me stood a tree in the middle of the land. Its height was enormous. [a] 11 The tree grew large and strong and its top touched the sky; it was visible to the ends of the earth. 12 Its leaves were beautiful, its fruit abundant, and on it was food for all. Under it the beasts of the field found shelter, and the birds of the air lived in its branches; from it every creature was fed.

13 "In the visions I saw while lying in my bed, I looked, and there before me was a messenger, [b] a holy one, [b] coming down from heaven. 14 He called in a loud voice: 'Cut down the tree and trim off its branches; strip off its leaves and scatter its fruit. Let the animals flee from under it and the birds from its branches. [c] 15 But let the stump and its roots, bound with iron and bronze, remain in the ground, in the grass of the field.

" 'Let him be drenched with the dew of heaven, and let him live with the animals among the plants of the earth. 16 Let his mind be changed from that of a man and let him be given the mind of an animal, till seven times [c] pass by for him.

17 " 'The decision is announced by messengers, the holy ones declare the verdict, so that the living may know that the Most High [d] is sovereign [e] over the kingdoms of men and gives them to anyone he wishes and sets over them the lowliest of men.'

18 "This is the dream that I, King Nebuchadnezzar, had. Now, Belteshazzar, tell me what it means, for none of the wise men in my kingdom can interpret it for me. [f] But you can, [g] because the spirit of the holy gods is in you." [h]

Daniel Interprets the Dream

19 Then Daniel (also called Belteshazzar) was greatly perplexed for a time, and his thoughts terrified [i] him. So the king said, "Belteshazzar, do not let the dream or its meaning alarm you."

a 7 Or *Chaldeans*   b 13 Or *watchman*; also in verses 17 and 23   c 16 Or *years*; also in verses 23, 25 and 32

**Side references:**
4:1 [q] Da 6:25
4:2 [r] Da 3:26
4:3 [s] Da 6:27 [t] Da 2:44
4:5 [u] Da 2:1 [v] Da 2:28
4:7 [w] Da 2:2
4:8 [x] Da 1:7
4:9 [y] Da 2:48 [z] Da 5:11-12
4:10 [a] Eze 31:3-4
4:13 [b] ver 23
4:14 [c] Eze 31:12; Mt 3:10
4:17 [d] ver 2, 25 [e] Da 5:18-21
4:18 [f] Ge 41:8; Da 5:8, 15 [g] Ge 41:15 [h] ver 7-9
4:19 [i] Da 7:15, 28

4:2, 3 Although Nebuchadnezzar praised Daniel's God, he still did not believe in him completely or submit to him alone (4:8). Many people attend church and use spiritual language, but they really don't believe in God or obey him. Profession doesn't always mean possession. How do your beliefs match with your obedience?

4:17 One of the most difficult lessons to learn is that God is sovereign. He is above all of those who are above us. He limits the power and authority of all the government, business, and religious leaders in the world. Those who live in freedom and with a relatively high degree of autonomy find this difficult to understand. While we may feel as though we are free to do what we please, God is sovereign over all of our plans and desires.

4:19 When Daniel understood Nebuchadnezzar's dream, he was stunned, and he wondered how to break the news. He told the king he wished what the dream foreshadowed would happen to the king's enemies and not to Nebuchadnezzar. How could Daniel be so deeply grieved at the fate of Nebuchadnezzar—the king who was responsible for the destruction of Daniel's home and nation? Daniel had forgiven Nebuchadnezzar, and so God was able to use Daniel. Very often when we have been wronged by someone, we find it difficult to forget the past. We may even be glad when that

Belteshazzar answered, "My lord, if only the dream applied to your enemies and its meaning to your adversaries! 20The tree you saw, which grew large and strong, with its top touching the sky, visible to the whole earth, 21with beautiful leaves and abundant fruit, providing food for all, giving shelter to the beasts of the field, and having nesting places in its branches for the birds of the air— 22you, O king, are that tree! You have become great and strong; your greatness has grown until it reaches the sky, and your dominion extends to distant parts of the earth.*j*

23"You, O king, saw a messenger, a holy one, coming down from heaven and saying, 'Cut down the tree and destroy it, but leave the stump, bound with iron and bronze, in

4:22
j Jer 27:7

NEBUCHADNEZZAR

Nebuchadnezzar was one world leader who decided he could get more cooperation from the people he conquered by letting them keep their gods. Their lands he took, their riches he robbed, their lives he controlled, but their idols he allowed them to worship, sometimes even worshiping them himself. Nebuchadnezzar's plan worked well, with one glaring exception. When he conquered the little nation of Judah, he met a God who demanded *exclusive* worship—not just his share among many gods. In a sense, Nebuchadnezzar had always been able to rule the gods. This new God was different; this God dared to claim that he had made Nebuchadnezzar all that he was. One of the great conquerors in history was himself conquered by his Creator.

The Bible allows us to note the ways in which God worked on Nebuchadnezzar. God allowed him victories, but he was accomplishing God's purposes. God allowed him to deport the best young Jewish leaders as his palace servants, while placing close to him a young man named Daniel, who would change the king's life. God allowed Nebuchadnezzar to attempt to kill three of his servants to teach the king that he did not really have power over life and death. God warned him of the dangers in his pride, and then allowed Nebuchadnezzar to live through seven years of insanity before restoring him to the throne. God showed the king who was really in control!

These lessons are clear to us today because of our place in history. When our attention shifts to our own lives, we often find ourselves unable to see how God is working. But we do have the advantage of God's Word as our guide for today's challenges. We are commanded to obey God; we are also commanded to trust him. Trusting him covers those times when we are not sure about the outcome. God has entrusted us with this day; have we trusted him with our lives?

Strengths and accomplishments:	• Greatest of the Babylonian kings • Known as a builder of cities • Described in the Bible as one of the foreign rulers God used for his purposes
Weaknesses and mistakes:	• Thought of himself as a god and was persuaded to build an image of gold that all were to worship • Became extremely proud, which led to a bout of insanity • Tended to forget the demonstrations of God's power he had witnessed
Lessons from his life:	• History records the actions of God's willing servants and those who were his unwitting tools • A leader's greatness is affected by the quality of his advisers • Uncontrolled pride is self-destructive
Vital statistics:	• Where: Babylon • Occupation: King • Relatives: Father: Nabopolassar. Son: Evil-Merodach. Grandson: Belshazzar. • Contemporaries: Jeremiah, Ezekiel, Daniel, Jehoiakim, Jehoiachin
Key verse:	"Now I, Nebuchadnezzar, praise and exalt and glorify the King of heaven, because everything he does is right and all his ways are just. And those who walk in pride he is able to humble" (4:37).

Nebuchadnezzar's story is told in 2 Kings 24; 25; 2 Chronicles 36; Jeremiah 21—52; Daniel 1—4.

---

person suffers. Forgiveness means putting the past behind us. Can you love someone who has hurt you? Can you serve someone who mistreated you? Ask God to help you forgive, forget, and love. God may use you in an extraordinary way in that person's life!

4:23ff Although much of the world thought that Nebuchadnezzar was a mighty (even divine) king, God demonstrated that Nebuchadnezzar was an ordinary man. The king would go insane and

become like an animal for a set period of time ("seven times"). God humiliated Nebuchadnezzar to show that almighty God, not Nebuchadnezzar, was Lord of the nations. No matter how powerful a person may become, self-centered pride will push God from his or her life. Pride may be one of the most dangerous temptations you will face. Don't let your accomplishments cause you to forget God.

the grass of the field, while its roots remain in the ground. Let him be drenched with the dew of heaven; let him live like the wild animals, until seven times pass by for him.'

24"This is the interpretation, O king, and this is the decree *k* the Most High has issued against my lord the king: 25You will be driven away from people and will live with the wild animals; you will eat grass like cattle and be drenched with the dew of heaven. Seven times will pass by for you until you acknowledge that the Most High *l* is sovereign over the kingdoms of men and gives them to anyone he wishes. *m* 26The command to leave the stump of the tree with its roots means that your kingdom will be restored to you when you acknowledge that Heaven rules. 27Therefore, O king, be pleased to accept my advice: Renounce your sins by doing what is right, and your wickedness by being kind to the oppressed. *n* It may be that then your prosperity will continue. *o*"

The Dream Is Fulfilled

28All this happened to King Nebuchadnezzar. 29Twelve months later, as the king was walking on the roof of the royal palace of Babylon, 30he said, "Is not this the great Babylon I have built as the royal residence, by my mighty power and for the glory of my majesty?" *p*

31The words were still on his lips when a voice came from heaven, "This is what is decreed for you, King Nebuchadnezzar: Your royal authority has been taken from you. 32You will be driven away from people and will live with the wild animals; you will eat grass like cattle. Seven times will pass by for you until you acknowledge that the Most High is sovereign over the kingdoms of men and gives them to anyone he wishes."

33Immediately what had been said about Nebuchadnezzar was fulfilled. He was driven away from people and ate grass like cattle. His body was drenched with the dew of heaven until his hair grew like the feathers of an eagle and his nails like the claws of a bird. *q*

34At the end of that time, I, Nebuchadnezzar, raised my eyes toward heaven, and my sanity was restored. Then I praised the Most High; I honored and glorified him who lives forever. *r*

> His dominion is an eternal dominion;
>   his kingdom endures from generation to generation. *s*
> 35 All the peoples of the earth
>   are regarded as nothing. *t*
> He does as he pleases *u*
>   with the powers of heaven
>   and the peoples of the earth.
> No one can hold back his hand
>   or say to him: "What have you done?" *v*

36At the same time that my sanity was restored, my honor and splendor were returned to me for the glory of my kingdom. My advisers and nobles sought me out, and I was restored to my throne and became even greater than before. 37Now I, Nebuchadnezzar, praise and exalt and glorify the King of heaven, because everything he does is right and all his ways are just. *w* And those who walk in pride he is able to humble.

The Writing on the Wall

5 King Belshazzar gave a great banquet for a thousand of his nobles and drank wine with them. 2While Belshazzar was drinking his wine, he gave orders to bring in the gold and

4:24
k Job 40:12
4:25
l ver 17
m Jer 27:5; Da 5:21

4:27
n Isa 55:6-7
o 1Ki 21:29;
Ps 41:3; Eze 18:22

4:30
p Da 5:20

4:33
q Da 5:20-21

4:34
r Da 12:7
s Lk 1:33

4:35
t Isa 40:17
u Ps 115:3; 135:6
v Isa 45:9; Ro 9:20

4:37
w Ps 33:4-5

4:27–33 Daniel pleaded with Nebuchadnezzar to change his ways, and God gave Nebuchadnezzar 12 months to do it. Unfortunately, there was no repentance in the heart of this proud king, and so the dream was fulfilled.

4:34 Ancient kings tried to avoid mentioning their weaknesses or defeats in their monuments and official records. From Nebuchadnezzar's records, however, we can infer that for a time during his 43-year reign he did not rule. The Bible, however, explains Nebuchadnezzar's pride and punishment.

4:36 Nebuchadnezzar's pilgrimage with God is one of the themes of this book. In 2:47, he acknowledged that God revealed

mysteries to Daniel. In 3:28, 29 he praised the God who rescued the three Hebrews. Despite Nebuchadnezzar's recognition that God exists and works great miracles, in 4:30 we see that he still did not acknowledge God as his Lord. We may recognize that God exists and does wonderful miracles, but God is not going to change us until we acknowledge him as Lord.

5:1 Sixty-six years have elapsed since chapter 1, which tells of Nebuchadnezzar's second strike against Jerusalem in 605 B.C. Nebuchadnezzar died in 562 B.C. after a reign of 43 years. His son, Evil-Merodach, ruled from 562–560 B.C.; his brother-in-law Neriglissar reigned four years from 560–556 B.C.

5:2
x Jer 52:19
y Da 1:2

5:4
z Rev 9:20

5:7
a Da 4:6-7

5:10
b Da 3:9

5:11
c Da 2:47-48

5:12
d Da 1:7
e Da 6:3

5:13
f Da 6:13

5:18
g Jer 27:7;
Da 2:37-38

5:19
h Da 2:12-13

silver goblets˟ that Nebuchadnezzar his fatherᵃ had taken from the temple in Jerusalem, so that the king and his nobles, his wives and his concubines might drink from them.ʸ ³So they brought in the gold goblets that had been taken from the temple of God in Jerusalem, and the king and his nobles, his wives and his concubines drank from them. ⁴As they drank the wine, they praised the gods of gold and silver, of bronze, iron, wood and stone. ᶻ

⁵Suddenly the fingers of a human hand appeared and wrote on the plaster of the wall, near the lampstand in the royal palace. The king watched the hand as it wrote. ⁶His face turned pale and he was so frightened that his knees knocked together and his legs gave way.

⁷The king called out for the enchanters, astrologersᵇ and diviners to be brought and said to these wiseᵃ men of Babylon, "Whoever reads this writing and tells me what it means will be clothed in purple and have a gold chain placed around his neck, and he will be made the third highest ruler in the kingdom."

⁸Then all the king's wise men came in, but they could not read the writing or tell the king what it meant. ⁹So King Belshazzar became even more terrified and his face grew more pale. His nobles were baffled.

¹⁰The queen,ᶜ hearing the voices of the king and his nobles, came into the banquet hall. "O king, live forever!"ᵇ she said. "Don't be alarmed! Don't look so pale! ¹¹There is a man in your kingdom who has the spirit of the holy gods in him. In the time of your father he was found to have insight and intelligence and wisdom like that of the gods. King Nebuchadnezzar your father—your father the king, I say—appointed him chief of the magicians, enchanters, astrologers and diviners.ᶜ ¹²This man Daniel, whom the king called Belteshazzar,ᵈ was found to have a keen mind and knowledge and understanding, and also the ability to interpret dreams, explain riddles and solve difficult problems.ᵉ Call for Daniel, and he will tell you what the writing means."

¹³So Daniel was brought before the king, and the king said to him, "Are you Daniel, one of the exiles my father the king brought from Judah?ᶠ ¹⁴I have heard that the spirit of the gods is in you and that you have insight, intelligence and outstanding wisdom. ¹⁵The wise men and enchanters were brought before me to read this writing and tell me what it means, but they could not explain it. ¹⁶Now I have heard that you are able to give interpretations and to solve difficult problems. If you can read this writing and tell me what it means, you will be clothed in purple and have a gold chain placed around your neck, and you will be made the third highest ruler in the kingdom."

¹⁷Then Daniel answered the king, "You may keep your gifts for yourself and give your rewards to someone else. Nevertheless, I will read the writing for the king and tell him what it means.

¹⁸"O king, the Most High God gave your father Nebuchadnezzar sovereignty and greatness and glory and splendor.ᵍ ¹⁹Because of the high position he gave him, all the peoples and nations and men of every language dreaded and feared him. Those the king wanted to put to death, he put to death;ʰ those he wanted to spare, he spared; those he wanted to promote, he

ᵃ2 Or *ancestor*; or *predecessor*; also in verses 11, 13 and 18   ᵇ7 Or *Chaldeans*; also in verse 11
ᶜ10 Or *queen mother*

After a two-month reign by Labashi-Marduk in 556 B.C., the Babylonian empire continued from 556–539 B.C. under the command of Nabonidus. Belshazzar was the son of Nabonidus. He co-reigned with his father from 553–539 B.C. Nebuchadnezzar is called Belshazzar's "father." The term could also mean "ancestor."

5:1 Archaeologists have recently discovered Belshazzar's name on several documents. He ruled with his father, Nabonidus, staying home to administer the affairs of the kingdom while his father tried to reopen trade routes taken over by Cyrus and the Persians. Belshazzar was in charge of the city of Babylon when it was captured.

5:7 Belshazzar served as co-regent with his father Nabonidus. Thus, Nabonidus was the first ruler and his son Belshazzar, the second. The person who could read the writing would be given third place, which was the highest position and honor that Belshazzar could offer.

5:8 Although the writing on the wall contained only three words in Aramaic, a language understood by Babylonians (see 2:4), the people could not determine its prophetic significance. God

gave Daniel alone the ability to interpret the message of doom to Babylon. The wise men of the kingdom were ignorant of God's wisdom, no matter how great the reward. Daniel did not rush into the banquet hall with the others. His loyalty was to God, not money.

5:10 This queen was either Nabonidus's wife or the wife of one of his predecessors, possibly even of Nebuchadnezzar. She was not Belshazzar's wife, because his wives were with him in the banquet hall.

5:17 The king offered Daniel beautiful gifts and great power if he would explain the writing, but Daniel turned him down. Daniel was not motivated by material rewards. His entire life had been characterized by doing right. Daniel was not showing disrespect in refusing the gifts, but he was growing older himself and knew the gifts would do him little good. Besides, being third highest ruler in a kingdom Daniel knew was about to be destroyed was not exactly motivating! Daniel wanted to show that he was giving an unbiased interpretation to the king. Doing right should be our first priority, not gaining power or rewards. Do you love God enough to do what is right, even if it means giving up personal rewards?

promoted; and those he wanted to humble, he humbled. ²⁰But when his heart became arrogant and hardened with pride, *i* he was deposed from his royal throne and stripped of his glory. ²¹He was driven away from people and given the mind of an animal; he lived with the wild donkeys and ate grass like cattle; and his body was drenched with the dew of heaven, until he acknowledged that the Most High God is sovereign over the kingdoms of men and sets over them anyone he wishes.*j*

²²"But you his son,ᵃ O Belshazzar, have not humbled yourself, though you knew all this. ²³Instead, you have set yourself up against the Lord of heaven. You had the goblets from his temple brought to you, and you and your nobles, your wives and your concubines drank wine from them. You praised the gods of silver and gold, of bronze, iron, wood and stone, which cannot see or hear or understand. *k* But you did not honor the God who holds in his hand your life and all your ways. *l* ²⁴Therefore he sent the hand that wrote the inscription.

²⁵"This is the inscription that was written:

MENE, MENE, TEKEL, PARSINᵇ

²⁶"This is what these words mean:

> *Mene*ᶜ: God has numbered the days of your reign and brought it to an end. *m*
> ²⁷ *Tekel*ᵈ: You have been weighed on the scales and found wanting. *n*
> ²⁸ *Peres*ᵉ: Your kingdom is divided and given to the Medes and Persians."*o*

²⁹Then at Belshazzar's command, Daniel was clothed in purple, a gold chain was placed around his neck, and he was proclaimed the third highest ruler in the kingdom.

³⁰That very night Belshazzar, king of the Babylonians,ᶠ was slain, *p* ³¹and Darius *q* the Mede took over the kingdom, at the age of sixty-two.

Daniel in the Den of Lions

6 It pleased Darius to appoint 120 satraps to rule throughout the kingdom, ²with three administrators over them, one of whom was Daniel. *r* The satraps were made accountable to them so that the king might not suffer loss. ³Now Daniel so distinguished himself among the administrators and the satraps by his exceptional qualities that the king planned to set him over the whole kingdom. *s* ⁴At this, the administrators and the satraps tried to

**Side references:**
5:20 *i* Da 4:30
5:21 *j* Da 4:16-17, 35
5:23 *k* Ps 115:4-8; Hab 2:19 *l* Jer 10:23
5:26 *m* Isa 13:6
5:27 *n* Ps 62:9
5:28 *o* Da 6:28
5:30 *p* Jer 51:31
5:31 *q* Da 6:1; 9:1
6:2 *r* Da 2:48-49
6:3 *s* Est 10:3; Da 5:12-14

ᵃ*22 Or descendant; or successor*   ᵇ*25 Aramaic UPARSIN (that is, AND PARSIN)*   ᶜ*26 Mene can mean numbered or mina (a unit of money).*   ᵈ*27 Tekel can mean weighed or shekel.*   ᵉ*28 Peres (the singular of Parsin) can mean divided or Persia or a half mina or a half shekel.*   ᶠ*30 Or Chaldeans*

5:21-23 Belshazzar knew Babylonian history, and so he knew how God had humbled Nebuchadnezzar. Nevertheless, Belshazzar's banquet was a rebellious challenge to God's authority as he took the gold goblets from God's temple and drank from them (5:2-4). No one who understands that God is the Creator of the universe should be foolish enough to challenge him.

5:22 Often kings would kill the bearer of bad news. But Daniel was not afraid to tell the truth to the king even though it was not what he wanted to hear. We should be just as courageous in telling the truth under pressure.

5:24 Belshazzar used the goblets from the temple for his party, and God condemned him for this act. We must not use for sinful purposes what has been dedicated to God. Today this would include church buildings, financial donations, and anything else that has been set apart for serving God. Be careful how you use what is God's.

5:27 The writing on the wall was a message for all those who defy God. Although Belshazzar had power and wealth, his kingdom was totally corrupt, and he could not withstand the judgment of God. God's time of judgment comes for all people. If you have forgotten God and slipped into a sinful way of life, turn away from your sin now before he removes any opportunities to repent. Ask God to forgive you, and begin to live by his standards of justice.

5:28 The Medes and Persians joined forces to overthrow Babylon. This event was predicted in the second phase of Nebuchadnezzar's dream in chapter 2—the silver chest and arms.

5:31 Darius and his soldiers entered Babylon by diverting the river that ran through the city, then walking in on the dry riverbed.

5:31 This Darius is not to be confused with Darius I, mentioned in Ezra, Haggai, and Zechariah, or Darius II (the Persian), mentioned in Nehemiah. Darius the Mede is named only in the book of Daniel. Other records name no king between Belshazzar and Cyrus. Thus, Darius may have been (1) appointed by Cyrus to rule over Babylon as a province of Persia, (2) another name for Cyrus himself or for his son, Cambyses, or (3) a descendant of Xerxes I.

6:1-3 At this time, Daniel was over 80 years old and one of Darius's top three administrators. Daniel was working with those who did not believe in his God, but he worked more efficiently and capably than all the rest. Thus, he attracted the attention of the pagan king and earned a place of respect. One of the best ways to influence non-Christian employers is to work diligently and responsibly. How well do you represent God to your employer?

6:3, 4 Daniel made enemies at work by doing a good job. Perhaps you have had a similar experience. When you begin to excel, you will find that coworkers may look for ways to hold you back and tear you down. How should you deal with those who would cheer at your downfall and even try to hasten it? Conduct your whole life above reproach. Then you will have nothing to hide, and your enemies will have a difficult time finding legitimate charges against you. Of course, this will not always save you from attacks, and, like Daniel, you will have to rely on God for protection.

6:4, 5 The jealous officials couldn't find anything about Daniel's life to criticize, so they attacked his religion. If you face jealous critics because of your faith, be glad they're criticizing that part of your life—perhaps they had to focus on your religion as a last resort! Respond by continuing to believe and live as you should. Then remember that God is in control, fighting this battle for you.

find grounds for charges against Daniel in his conduct of government affairs, but they were unable to do so. They could find no corruption in him, because he was trustworthy and neither corrupt nor negligent. ⁵Finally these men said, "We will never find any basis for charges against this man Daniel unless it has something to do with the law of his God."

⁶So the administrators and the satraps went as a group to the king and said: "O King Darius, live forever! ᵗ ⁷The royal administrators, prefects, satraps, advisers and governors ᵘ have all agreed that the king should issue an edict and enforce the decree that anyone who prays to any god or man during the next thirty days, except to you, O king, shall be thrown into the lions' den. ᵛ ⁸Now, O king, issue the decree and put it in writing so that it cannot be altered—in accordance with the laws of the Medes and Persians, which cannot be repealed." ʷ ⁹So King Darius put the decree in writing.

¹⁰Now when Daniel learned that the decree had been published, he went home to his upstairs room where the windows opened toward Jerusalem. Three times a day he got down on his knees ˣ and prayed, giving thanks to his God, just as he had done before. ¹¹Then these men went as a group and found Daniel praying and asking God for help. ¹²So they went to the king and spoke to him about his royal decree: "Did you not publish a decree that during the next thirty days anyone who prays to any god or man except to you, O king, would be thrown into the lions' den?"

The king answered, "The decree stands—in accordance with the laws of the Medes and Persians, which cannot be repealed." ʸ

¹³Then they said to the king, "Daniel, who is one of the exiles from Judah, pays no attention ᶻ to you, O king, or to the decree you put in writing. He still prays three times a day." ¹⁴When the king heard this, he was greatly distressed; ᵃ he was determined to rescue Daniel and made every effort until sundown to save him.

¹⁵Then the men went as a group to the king and said to him, "Remember, O king, that according to the law of the Medes and Persians no decree or edict that the king issues can be changed."

¹⁶So the king gave the order, and they brought Daniel and threw him into the lions' den. The king said to Daniel, "May your God, whom you serve continually, rescue you!"

¹⁷A stone was brought and placed over the mouth of the den, and the king sealed ᵇ it with his own signet ring and with the rings of his nobles, so that Daniel's situation might not be

6:6
ᵗNe 2:3
6:7
ᵘDa 3:2
ᵛPs 59:3; Da 3:6
6:8
ʷEst 1:19

6:10
ˣPs 95:6

6:12
ʸDa 3:8-12

6:13
ᶻEst 3:8
6:14
ᵃMk 6:26

6:17
ᵇMt 27:66

KINGS DANIEL SERVED	Name	Empire	Story told in	Memorable event
	Nebuchad-nezzar	Babylonia	chapters 1—4	Shadrach, Meshach, and Abednego thrown into fiery furnace; Nebuchadnezzar went mad for 7 years
	Belshazzar	Babylonia	chapters 5, 7—8	Daniel read the writing on the wall, which signaled the end of the Babylonian empire
	Darius	Medo-Persia	chapters 6, 9	Daniel thrown into a lions' den
	Cyrus	Medo-Persia	chapters 10—12	The exiles return to their homeland in Judah and their capital city, Jerusalem

6:8, 9 In Babylon, the king's word *was* the law. In the Medo-Persian empire, however, when a law was made, even the king couldn't change it. Darius was an effective government administrator, but he had a fatal flaw—pride. By appealing to his vanity, the men talked Darius into signing a law effectively making himself a god for 30 days. This law could not be broken—not even by an important official like Daniel. Another example of the irrevocable nature of the laws of the Medes and Persians appears in Esther 8:8.

6:10 Daniel stood alone. Although he knew about the law against praying to anyone except the king, he continued to pray three times a day as he always had. Daniel had a disciplined prayer life. Our prayers are usually interrupted not by threats, but simply by the pressure of our schedules. Don't let threats or pressures cut into your prayer time. Pray regularly, no matter what, for prayer is your lifeline to God.

6:10 Daniel made no attempt to hide his daily prayer routine from his enemies in government, even though he knew he would be disobeying the new law. Hiding his daily prayers would have

been futile because surely the conspirators would have caught him at something else during the month. Also, hiding would have demonstrated that he was afraid of the other government officials. Daniel continued to pray because he could not look to the king for the guidance and strength that he needed during this difficult time. Only God could provide what he really needed.

6:16 Lions roamed the countryside and forests in Mesopotamia, and the people feared them and greatly respected their power. Some kings hunted lions for sport. The Persians captured lions, keeping them in large parks where they were fed and attended. Lions were also used for executing people. But God has ways of delivering his people (6:22) that none of us can imagine. It is always premature to give up and give in to the pressure of unbelievers, because God has power they know nothing about. God can even shut the lions' mouths.

6:16 Even unbelievers witnessed to Daniel's consistency. By his continual service, Daniel had demonstrated his faithful devotion to God. What can unbelievers determine about your life?

changed. 18Then the king returned to his palace and spent the night without eating *c* and without any entertainment being brought to him. And he could not sleep. *d*

19At the first light of dawn, the king got up and hurried to the lions' den. 20When he came near the den, he called to Daniel in an anguished voice, "Daniel, servant of the living God, has your God, whom you serve continually, been able to rescue you from the lions?" *e*

21Daniel answered, "O king, live forever! 22My God sent his angel, *f* and he shut the mouths of the lions. *g* They have not hurt me, because I was found innocent in his sight. *h* Nor have I ever done any wrong before you, O king."

23The king was overjoyed and gave orders to lift Daniel out of the den. And when Daniel was lifted from the den, no wound *i* was found on him, because he had trusted in his God.

24At the king's command, the men who had falsely accused Daniel were brought in and thrown into the lions' den, along with their wives and children. *j* And before they reached the floor of the den, the lions overpowered them and crushed all their bones.

25Then King Darius wrote to all the peoples, nations and men of every language throughout the land:

"May you prosper greatly! *k*

26"I issue a decree that in every part of my kingdom people must fear and reverence the God of Daniel. *l*

> "For he is the living God
>   and he endures forever;
> his kingdom will not be destroyed,
>   his dominion will never end. *m*
> 27 He rescues and he saves;
>   he performs signs and wonders *n*
>   in the heavens and on the earth.
> He has rescued Daniel
>   from the power of the lions."

28So Daniel prospered during the reign of Darius and the reign of Cyrus *a o* the Persian.

B. DANIEL'S VISIONS (7:1—12:13)

Daniel had many dreams and visions he did not understand. He dreamed of four beasts, which represented four kingdoms of the world, and of a ram and goat, which depicted two of those kingdoms in greater detail. Daniel's visions reveal that the Messiah will be the ruler of a spiritual kingdom that will overpower and overshadow all other earthly kingdoms. These visions help us see that we should interpret all of history in light of God's eternal kingdom.

Daniel's Dream of Four Beasts

7 In the first year of Belshazzar king of Babylon, Daniel had a dream, and visions passed through his mind *p* as he was lying on his bed. He wrote down the substance of his dream.

2Daniel said: "In my vision at night I looked, and there before me were the four winds of heaven churning up the great sea. 3Four great beasts, *q* each different from the others, came up out of the sea.

a28 Or Darius, that is, the reign of Cyrus

6:18
*c*2Sa 12:17
*d*Est 6:1

6:20
*e*Da 3:17

6:22
*f*Da 3:28
*g*Heb 11:33
*h*2Ti 4:17

6:23
*i*Da 3:27

6:24
*j*Dt 24:16; 2Ki 14:6

6:25
*k*Da 4:1

6:26
*l*Da 3:29
*m*Da 2:44

6:27
*n*Da 4:3

6:28
*o*Da 1:21

7:1
*p*Da 1:17

7:3
*q*Rev 13:1

6:21–23 The person who trusts in God and obeys his will is untouchable until God takes him or her. To trust God is to have immeasurable peace. God, who delivered Daniel, will deliver you. Do you trust him with your life?

6:24 In accordance with Persian custom, this cruel punishment was transferred to those who had conspired against the king by provoking him into an unjust action (see also Esther 7:9, 10). The king's great anger resulted in the execution of the evil officials and their families. Evil deeds often backfire on those who plan cruelty.

6:25–27 Nebuchadnezzar had come to believe that Israel's God was real because of the faithfulness of Daniel and his friends. Here Darius was also convinced of God's power because Daniel was faithful and God rescued him. Although Daniel was captive in a strange land, his devotion to God was a testimony to powerful

rulers. If you find yourself in new surroundings, take the opportunity to testify about God's power in your life. Be faithful to God so he can use you to make an impact on others.

7:1 Chronologically, this chapter takes place before chapter five. At this time, Belshazzar had just been given a position of authority (553 B.C.), and Daniel was probably in his late sixties. The first six chapters of Daniel present history; the last six chapters are visions relating mainly to the future.

7:1ff Daniel had a vision of four great beasts, each representing a world empire. This was similar to Nebuchadnezzar's dream in chapter two. Nebuchadnezzar's dream covered the political aspects of the empires; Daniel's dream depicted their moral characteristics. These nations, which would reign over Israel, were evil and cruel; but Daniel also saw God's everlasting, indestructible kingdom arrive and conquer them all.

4 "The first was like a lion, and it had the wings of an eagle. I watched until its wings were torn off and it was lifted from the ground so that it stood on two feet like a man, and the heart of a man was given to it.

7:5
r Da 2:39

5 "And there before me was a second beast, which looked like a bear. It was raised up on one of its sides, and it had three ribs in its mouth between its teeth. It was told, 'Get up and eat your fill of flesh!' r

6 "After that, I looked, and there before me was another beast, one that looked like a leopard. And on its back it had four wings like those of a bird. This beast had four heads, and it was given authority to rule.

7:7
s Da 2:40
t Rev 12:3

7 "After that, in my vision at night I looked, and there before me was a fourth beast—terrifying and frightening and very powerful. It had large iron s teeth; it crushed and devoured its victims and trampled underfoot whatever was left. It was different from all the former beasts, and it had ten horns. t

7:8
u Da 8:9
v Rev 13:5-6

8 "While I was thinking about the horns, there before me was another horn, a little u one, which came up among them; and three of the first horns were uprooted before it. This horn had eyes like the eyes of a man and a mouth that spoke boastfully. v

7:9
w Rev 1:14
x Eze 1:15

9 "As I looked,

"thrones were set in place,
    and the Ancient of Days took his seat.
His clothing was as white as snow;
    the hair of his head was white like wool. w
His throne was flaming with fire,
    and its wheels x were all ablaze.

7:10
y Ps 50:3
z Rev 5:11
a Rev 20:11-15

10 A river of fire y was flowing,
    coming out from before him. z
Thousands upon thousands attended him;
    ten thousand times ten thousand stood before him.
The court was seated,
    and the books a were opened.

7:4–8 The lion with an eagle's wings represents Babylon with her swift conquests (statues of winged lions have been recovered from Babylon's ruins). The bear that ravaged the lion is Medo-Persia. The three ribs in its mouth represent the conquests of three major enemies. The leopard is Greece. Its wings show the swiftness of Alexander the Great's campaign as he conquered much of the civilized world in four years (334–330 B.C.). The leopard's four heads are the four divisions of the Greek empire after Alexander's death.

The fourth beast points to both Rome and the end times. Many Bible scholars believe that the horns correspond to ten kings who will reign shortly before God sets up his everlasting kingdom. These ten kings had still not come to power at the time of John's vision recorded in the book of Revelation (Revelation 17:12). The little horn is a future human ruler or the antichrist (see also 2 Thessalonians 2:3, 4). God is illustrating the final end of all worldly kingdoms in contrast to his eternal kingdom.

7:7 In the book of Revelation, John also recorded a vision of a scarlet beast that had seven heads and ten horns (Revelation 17:3). The angel told John that the ten horns were ten kings (Revelation 17:12). Most likely these would be ten rulers who will rule under the antichrist. The number ten may be literal, or, more likely it symbolizes the totality of the powers on earth that will serve the antichrist and war against Christ. In John's day, Rome was the world power, but would be followed by other powers. Whoever the ten kings are, they will give their power to the Antichrist and will make war against Christ and his followers.

7:9 Here the prophecy shifts to the end times. This judgment scene is similar to one that was seen by the apostle John (Revelation 1:14, 15). The Ancient of Days is almighty God, who assigns power to kingdoms and who will himself judge those kingdoms in the end.

7:10 The book of Revelation records a similar picture of God with angels surrounding his throne. John recorded that there were "thousands upon thousands" (Revelation 5:11–12). In other words, too many angels to count surround God's throne and minister to him. Created by God, angels are spiritual beings who help carry out his work on earth.

7:10 The phrase "the books were opened" refers to judgment. Revelation refers to this final judgment where the "books were opened." Another book was opened, which is the book of life. The dead were judged according to what they had done as recorded in the books" (Revelation 20:12). The book of life is the heavenly registry of those who have accepted Christ's gift of salvation (Revelation 3:5). All believers' names are written in the book of life and they need not fear judgment. Unbelievers, however, will be judged according to their works—but their works, no matter how good, will not be able to save them.

7:10 Daniel saw God judging millions of people as they stand before him. We all must stand before almighty God and give an account of our lives. If your life were judged by God today, what would he say about it? How would he measure it against his will for us? We should live each day with the full awareness that we must appear before God to give account for how we used our lives. How will your life measure up?

¹¹"Then I continued to watch because of the boastful words the horn was speaking. I kept looking until the beast was slain and its body destroyed and thrown into the blazing fire. ᵇ ¹²(The other beasts had been stripped of their authority, but were allowed to live for a period of time.)

¹³"In my vision at night I looked, and there before me was one like a son of man, ᶜ coming with the clouds of heaven. ᵈ He approached the Ancient of Days and was led into his presence. ¹⁴He was given authority, glory and sovereign power; all peoples, nations and men of every language worshiped him. ᵉ His dominion is an everlasting dominion that will not pass away, and his kingdom is one that will never be destroyed. ᶠ

The Interpretation of the Dream

¹⁵"I, Daniel, was troubled in spirit, and the visions that passed through my mind disturbed me. ¹⁶I approached one of those standing there and asked him the true meaning of all this.

"So he told me and gave me the interpretation of these things: ¹⁷'The four great beasts are four kingdoms that will rise from the earth. ¹⁸But the saints of the Most High will receive the kingdom and will possess it forever—yes, for ever and ever.' ᵍ

¹⁹"Then I wanted to know the true meaning of the fourth beast, which was different from all the others and most terrifying, with its iron teeth and bronze claws—the beast that crushed and devoured its victims and trampled underfoot whatever was left. ²⁰I also wanted to know about the ten horns on its head and about the other horn that came up, before which three of them fell—the horn that looked more imposing than the others and that had eyes and a mouth that spoke boastfully. ²¹As I watched, this horn was waging war against the saints and defeating them, ʰ ²²until the Ancient of Days came and pronounced judgment in favor of the saints of the Most High, and the time came when they possessed the kingdom.

²³"He gave me this explanation: 'The fourth beast is a fourth kingdom that will appear on earth. It will be different from all the other kingdoms and will devour the whole earth, trampling it down and crushing it. ²⁴The ten horns ⁱ are ten kings who will come from this kingdom. After them another king will arise, different from the earlier ones; he will subdue three kings. ²⁵He will speak against the Most High and oppress his saints and try to change the set times ʲ and the laws. The saints will be handed over to him for a time, times and half a time. ᵃ

²⁶"'But the court will sit, and his power will be taken away and completely destroyed forever. ²⁷Then the sovereignty, power and greatness of the kingdoms under the whole heaven will be handed over to the saints, the people of the Most High. His kingdom will be an everlasting ᵏ kingdom, and all rulers will worship and obey him.'

²⁸"This is the end of the matter. I, Daniel, was deeply troubled by my thoughts, and my face turned pale, but I kept the matter to myself."

ᵃ25 Or for a year, two years and half a year

7:11 ᵇRev 19:20
7:13 ᶜMt 8:20*; Rev 1:13*; ᵈRev 1:7
7:14 ᵉPs 72:11; ᶠHeb 12:28
7:18 ᵍIsa 60:12-14; Rev 2:26
7:21 ʰRev 13:7
7:24 ⁱRev 17:12
7:25 ʲDa 2:21
7:27 ᵏLk 1:33; Rev 11:15

7:11, 12 The slaying of the beast represents the fall of Rome. While this beast was destroyed, the other beasts were allowed to live for a period of time. The kingdoms (or their cultures) continued to be recognizable in some form; history did not end when God intervened with his judgment.

7:13, 14 This "one like a son of man" is the Messiah. Jesus used this verse to refer to himself (Matthew 26:64; Luke 21:27; John 1:51). The clouds of heaven portray the Son of Man as divine; throughout the Bible clouds represent his majesty and awesome presence. God's glory appeared in a cloud in Exodus 16:10 and 19:9 at the giving of the law at Sinai. Revelation also records Christ coming with the clouds (Revelation 1:7).

7:18 The "saints of the Most High" are the true Israel, the people ruled by the Messiah. Jesus Christ gave the kingdom to the new Israel, his church, made up of all faithful believers. His coming ushered in the kingdom of God, and all believers are its citizens (see also 7:22, 27). Although God may allow persecution to continue for a while, the destiny of his followers is to possess the kingdom and be with him forever.

7:21, 22 This "horn" that wages war against God's people is also described in Revelation as the beast who is "given power to make war against the saints and to conquer them" (Revelation 13:7). For a while, the "horn" will defeat God's people. Yet, in reality, those who die for the faith will be the ultimate overcomers, for they will receive great rewards. In the end, however, the horn will be defeated by the Ancient of Days himself.

7:24 The ten horns, or ten kings, are also mentioned in Revelation 17:12. There were also ten toes in Nebuchadnezzar's vision (2:41, 42). While all do not agree concerning the identity of these ten kings, we are reminded in Revelation 17:12–14 that these kings will make war against Christ, but, as the King of kings, he will conquer them. The other king mentioned here in verse 24 is the future antichrist of 2 Thessalonians 2:3, 4.

7:25 The exact meaning of this "time, times and half a time" is debated. Many scholars believe that "time" means one year; "times" means two years; and "half a time" means half a year. Thus, this would refer to three and a half years. God's people will be placed under this king's control and the persecution will continue only a relatively short time. God has promised to give his kingdom to his saints.

Daniel's Vision of a Ram and a Goat

8 In the third year of King Belshazzar's reign, I, Daniel, had a vision, after the one that had already appeared to me. ²In my vision I saw myself in the citadel of Susa in the province of Elam; in the vision I was beside the Ulai Canal. ³I looked up, *l* and there before me was a ram with two horns, standing beside the canal, and the horns were long. One of the horns was longer than the other but grew up later. ⁴I watched the ram as he charged toward the west and the north and the south. No animal could stand against him, and none could rescue from his power. He did as he pleased and became great.

⁵As I was thinking about this, suddenly a goat with a prominent horn between his eyes came from the west, crossing the whole earth without touching the ground. ⁶He came toward the two-horned ram I had seen standing beside the canal and charged at him in great rage. ⁷I saw him attack the ram furiously, striking the ram and shattering his two horns. The ram was powerless to stand against him; the goat knocked him to the ground and trampled on him, and none could rescue the ram from his power. ⁸The goat became very great, but at the height of his power his large horn was broken off, *m* and in its place four prominent horns grew up toward the four winds of heaven. *n*

⁹Out of one of them came another horn, which started small but grew in power to the south and to the east and toward the Beautiful Land. *o* ¹⁰It grew until it reached the host of the heavens, and it threw some of the starry host down to the earth *p* and trampled on them. ¹¹It set itself up to be as great as the Prince of the host; *q* it took away the daily sacrifice from him, and the place of his sanctuary was brought low. *r* ¹²Because of rebellion, the host ᵢof the saints⌐ *a* and the daily sacrifice were given over to it. It prospered in everything it did, and truth was thrown to the ground.

¹³Then I heard a holy one *s* speaking, and another holy one said to him, "How long will it take for the vision to be fulfilled *t*—the vision concerning the daily sacrifice, the rebellion that causes desolation, and the surrender of the sanctuary and of the host that will be trampled underfoot?"

¹⁴He said to me, "It will take 2,300 evenings and mornings; then the sanctuary will be reconsecrated."

The Interpretation of the Vision

¹⁵While I, Daniel, was watching the vision and trying to understand it, there before me stood one who looked like a man. ¹⁶And I heard a man's voice from the Ulai calling, "Gabriel, *u* tell this man the meaning of the vision."

a 12 Or *rebellion, the armies*

8:3
l Da 10:5

8:8
m 2Ch 26:16-21
n Da 7:2

8:9
o Da 11:16

8:10
p Rev 12:4

8:11
q Da 11:36-37
r Da 11:31; 12:11

8:13
s Da 4:23
t Da 12:6

8:16
u Lk 1:19

8:1 As with chapter 7, this chapter precedes chapter 5 chronologically; the dream probably occurred in 551 B.C. when Daniel was about 70 years old. Chapters 7 and 8 correspond to the first and third years of Belshazzar and belong chronologically between chapters 4 and 5. Chapter 9 took place at approximately the same time as chapter 6. It gives us more details about the Medo-Persian and Greek empires, the two world powers that ruled after Babylonia.

8:2 Susa was one of the capitals of the Babylonian empire. Located in what is now Iran, Susa was a well-developed city. It was the winter capital of the Persian empire and a mighty fortress (citadel). In his vision, Daniel saw himself in this important location. The earliest known code of law, the Code of Hammurapi, was found there. Susa rivaled Babylon itself in cultural sophistication.

8:3 The two horns were the kings of Media and Persia (8:20). The longer horn represented the growing dominance of Persia in the Medo-Persian empire.

8:5–7 The goat represented Greece, and its large horn, Alexander the Great (8:21). This is an amazing prediction because Greece was not yet considered a world power when this prophecy was given. Alexander the Great conquered the world with great speed and military strategy, indicated by the goat's rapid movement. Shattering both horns symbolized Alexander breaking both parts of the Medo-Persian empire.

8:8 Alexander the Great died in his thirties at the height of his power. His kingdom was split into four parts under four generals:

Ptolemy I of Egypt and Palestine; Seleucus of Babylonia and Syria; Lysimachus of Asia Minor; and Antipater of Macedon and Greece.

8:9 Israel ("the Beautiful Land") was attacked by Antiochus IV Epiphanes (the small horn) in the second century B.C. He was the eighth ruler of the Seleucid empire (Babylonia and Syria). He overthrew Israel's high priest, looted the temple, and replaced worship of God with a Greek form of worship. A further fulfillment of this prophecy of a powerful horn will occur in the future with the coming of the antichrist (see 8:17, 19, 23; 11:36; 2 Thessalonians 2:4).

8:11 The "Prince of the host" here refers to a heavenly authority, perhaps an angel or even God himself. (See also Joshua 5:13–15.)

8:14 The phrase "evenings and mornings" means evening and morning sacrifices, and refers to the time from the desecration of the altar in the temple by Antiochus IV Epiphanes to the restoration of temple worship under Judas Maccabeus in 165 B.C.

8:16 Gabriel is an angel, the heavenly messenger God used to explain Daniel's visions (9:21). He also announced the birth of John the Baptist (Luke 1:11) and the Messiah (Luke 1:26).

17As he came near the place where I was standing, I was terrified and fell prostrate.v "Son of man," he said to me, "understand that the vision concerns the time of the end."

18While he was speaking to me, I was in a deep sleep, with my face to the ground.w Then he touched me and raised me to my feet.x

19He said: "I am going to tell you what will happen later in the time of wrath, because the vision concerns the appointed time of the end.a y 20The two-horned ram that you saw represents the kings of Media and Persia. 21The shaggy goat is the king of Greece, and the large horn between his eyes is the first king. 22The four horns that replaced the one that was broken off represent four kingdoms that will emerge from his nation but will not have the same power.

23"In the latter part of their reign, when rebels have become completely wicked, a stern-faced king, a master of intrigue, will arise. 24He will become very strong, but not by his own power. He will cause astounding devastation and will succeed in whatever he does. He will destroy the mighty men and the holy people.z 25He will cause deceit to prosper, and he will consider himself superior. When they feel secure, he will destroy many and take his stand against the Prince of princes. Yet he will be destroyed, but not by human power.a

26"The vision of the evenings and mornings that has been given you is true,b but seal up the vision, for it concerns the distant future."c

27I, Daniel, was exhausted and lay ill for several days. Then I got up and went about the king's business. I was appalled by the vision; it was beyond understanding.

Daniel's Prayer

9 In the first year of Darius son of Xerxesb (a Mede by descent), who was made ruler over the Babylonianc kingdom— 2in the first year of his reign, I, Daniel, understood from the Scriptures, according to the word of the Lord given to Jeremiah the prophet, that the desolation of Jerusalem would last seventyd years. 3So I turned to the Lord God and pleaded with him in prayer and petition, in fasting, and in sackcloth and ashes.e

4I prayed to the Lord my God and confessed:

"O Lord, the great and awesome God, who keeps his covenant of lovef with all who love him and obey his commands, 5we have sinned and done wrong.g We have been wicked and have rebelled; we have turned away from your commands and laws. 6We have not listened to your servants the prophets,h who spoke in your name to our kings, our princes and our fathers, and to all the people of the land.

a 19 Or because the end will be at the appointed time   b 1 Hebrew Ahasuerus   c 1 Or Chaldean

---

8:17
v Eze 1:28;
Rev 1:17

8:18
w Da 10:9
x Eze 2:2

8:19
y Hab 2:3

8:24
z Da 11:36

8:25
a Da 2:34

8:26
b Da 10:1
c Da 10:14

9:2
d 2Ch 36:21

9:3
e Jer 29:12

9:4
f Dt 7:9

9:5
g Ps 106:6

9:6
h 2Ch 36:16

8:17 The "time of the end," in this case, refers to the whole period from the end of the exile until the second coming of Christ. Many of the events that would happen under Antiochus IV Epiphanes will be repeated on a broader scale just before Christ's second coming. During these times, God deals with Israel in a radically different way, with divine discipline coming through Gentile nations. This period is sometimes referred to as the "times of the Gentiles" (Luke 21:24).

8:23 This stern-faced king describes both Antiochus IV Epiphanes and the antichrist at the end of human history (Revelation 13:1–18).

8:25 This Prince of princes is God himself. No human power could defeat the king whom Daniel saw in his vision, but God would bring him down. Antiochus IV Epiphanes reportedly went insane and died in Persia in 164 B.C. God's power and justice will prevail, so we should never give up our faith or lose hope, no matter how powerful God's enemies may seem.

9:1 The vision in chapter 9 was given to Daniel during the same time period of chapter 6. This Darius is the person mentioned in chapter 6. The Xerxes (or Ahasuerus) mentioned here is not Esther's husband. The events described in the book of Esther happened about 50 years later.

9:2, 3 Daniel pleaded with God to bring about the promised return of his people to their land. The prophet Jeremiah had written that God would not allow the captives to return to their land for 70 years (Jeremiah 25:11, 12; 29:10). Daniel knew of this prophecy and realized that this 70-year period was coming to an end.

9:3ff In Daniel's prayer for the nation he confessed his own sin, using the pronoun "we" throughout. In times of adversity, it's easy to blame others and excuse our own actions. If any Israelite was righteous, it was Daniel; and yet he confessed his sinfulness and need for God's forgiveness. Instead of looking for others to blame, first look inside and confess your own sins to God.

9:3–19 Daniel knew how to pray. As he prayed, he fasted, confessed his sins, and pleaded that God would reveal his will. He prayed with complete surrender to God and with complete openness to what God was saying to him. When you pray, do you speak openly to God? Examine your attitude. Talk to God with openness, vulnerability, and honesty, and be ready for God's reply.

9:4–6 The captives from Judah had rebelled against God. Their sins had led to their captivity. But God is merciful even to rebels, if they confess their sins and return to him. Don't let your past disobedience keep you from returning to God. He is waiting for you and wants you to return to him.

9:6 God had sent many prophets to speak to his people through the years, but their messages had been ignored. The truth had been too painful to hear. God still speaks clearly and accurately through the Bible, and he also speaks through preachers, teachers, and concerned friends. Sometimes the truth hurts, and we would rather hear words that soothe, even if they are false. If you are unwilling to accept God's message, maybe you are trying to avoid making a painful change. Don't settle for a soothing lie that will bring harsh judgment. Accepting the truth even if it is painful can only help you.

7"Lord, you are righteous, but this day we are covered with shame—the men of Judah and people of Jerusalem and all Israel, both near and far, in all the countries where you have scattered us because of our unfaithfulness to you. 8O LORD, we and our kings, our princes and our fathers are covered with shame because we have sinned against you. 9The Lord our God is merciful and forgiving, even though we have rebelled against him; *i* 10we have not obeyed the LORD our God or kept the laws he gave us through his servants the prophets. *j* 11All Israel has transgressed your law and turned away, refusing to obey you.

"Therefore the curses and sworn judgments written in the Law of Moses, the servant of God, have been poured out on us, because we have sinned *k* against you. 12You have fulfilled *l* the words spoken against us and against our rulers by bringing upon us great disaster. Under the whole heaven nothing has ever been done like what has been done to Jerusalem. *m* 13Just as it is written in the Law of Moses, all this disaster has come upon us, yet we have not sought the favor of the LORD our God by turning from our sins and giving attention to your truth. *n* 14The LORD did not hesitate to bring the disaster upon us, for the LORD our God is righteous in everything he does; yet we have not obeyed him.

15"Now, O Lord our God, who brought your people out of Egypt with a mighty hand *o* and who made for yourself a name *p* that endures to this day, we have sinned, we have done wrong. 16O Lord, in keeping with all your righteous acts, *q* turn away your anger and your wrath from Jerusalem, your city, your holy hill. Our sins and the iniquities of our fathers have made Jerusalem and your people an object of scorn to all those around us.

17"Now, our God, hear the prayers and petitions of your servant. For your sake, O Lord, look with favor *r* on your desolate sanctuary. 18Give ear, O God, and hear; open your eyes and see the desolation of the city that bears your Name. *s* We do not make requests of you because we are righteous, but because of your great mercy. 19O Lord, listen! O Lord, forgive! O Lord, hear and act! For your sake, O my God, do not delay, because your city and your people bear your Name."

The Seventy "Sevens"

20While I was speaking and praying, confessing my sin and the sin of my people Israel and making my request to the LORD my God for his holy hill— 21while I was still in prayer, Gabriel, *t* the man I had seen in the earlier vision, came to me in swift flight about the time of the evening sacrifice. 22He instructed me and said to me, "Daniel, I have now come to give you insight and understanding. 23As soon as you began to pray, an answer was given, which I have come to tell you, for you are highly esteemed. Therefore, consider the message and understand the vision: *u*

24"Seventy 'sevens' *a* are decreed for your people and your holy city to finish *b* transgression, to put an end to sin, to atone for wickedness, to bring in everlasting righteousness, to seal up vision and prophecy and to anoint the most holy. *c*

a24 Or *'weeks';* also in verses 25 and 26   *b24* Or *restrain*   *c24* Or *Most Holy Place;* or *most holy One*

9:9
*i*Ne 9:17

9:10
*j*2Ki 17:13-15

9:11
*k*Isa 1:4-6

9:12
*l*Zec 1:6
*m*Eze 5:9

9:13
*n*Isa 9:13; Jer 2:30

9:15
*o*Jer 32:21
*p*Ne 9:10

9:16
*q*Ps 31:1

9:17
*r*Nu 6:24-26
9:18
*s*Isa 37:17

9:21
*t*Da 8:16

9:23
*u*Mt 24:15

9:11–13 Daniel mentioned the curses outlined in Deuteronomy 28. God had given the people of Israel a choice: obey me and receive blessings, or disobey me and face curses. The affliction was meant to turn the people to God. When we face difficult circumstances, we should ask ourselves if God has reason to send judgment. If we think so, we must urgently seek his forgiveness. Then we can ask him to help us through our troubles.

9:14 Daniel spoke about how God continually tried to bring Israel back to himself. Yet even after disaster struck them, they refused to obey him. God still uses circumstances, other people, and, most importantly, his Word to bring his people back to him. What would it take for God to get your attention?

9:17–19 It would be a mistake to read the Bible as dry history and miss the deep personal feelings. In this section, Daniel was crying out to the Lord. He had a deep concern for his nation and his people. So often our prayers are without passion and true compassion for others. Are you willing to pray by pouring out your deep feelings to God?

9:18 Daniel begged for mercy, not for help, because he knew that his people deserved God's wrath and punishment. God sends his

help, not because we deserve it, but because he wants to show great mercy. If God would refuse to help us because of our sin, how could we complain? But when he sends mercy when we deserve punishment, how can we withhold our praise and thanksgiving?

9:23 Just as God answered Daniel's prayer, so we can have confidence that God hears and answers our prayers.

9:24, 25 Each day of these 70 weeks ("seventy 'sevens' ") may represent one year. The Bible often uses round numbers to make a point, not to give an exact count. For example, Jesus said we are to forgive others "seventy-seven" times (Matthew 18:22). He did not mean a literal 490 times, but that we should be abundantly forgiving. Similarly, some scholars see this figure of 70 weeks as a figurative time period. Others, however, interpret this time period as a literal 70 weeks or 490 years, observing that Christ's death came at the end of the 69 weeks (i.e., 483 years later). One interpretation places the 70th week as the seven years of the great tribulation, still in the future. Consequently the number would symbolize both the first and second comings of Christ.

25"Know and understand this: From the issuing of the decree a to restore and rebuild Jerusalem until the Anointed One, b the ruler, comes, there will be seven 'sevens,' and sixty-two 'sevens.' It will be rebuilt with streets and a trench, but in times of trouble. 26After the sixty-two 'sevens,' the Anointed One will be cut off v and will have nothing. c The people of the ruler who will come will destroy the city and the sanctuary. The end will come like a flood: War will continue until the end, and desolations have been decreed. 27He will confirm a covenant with many for one 'seven.' d In the middle of the 'seven' d he will put an end to sacrifice and offering. And on a wing ⌞of the temple⌟ he will set up an abomination that causes desolation, until the end that is decreed w is poured out on him. e "f

9:26
v Isa 53:8

9:27
w Isa 10:22

Daniel's Vision of a Man

10 In the third year of Cyrus king of Persia, a revelation was given to Daniel (who was called Belteshazzar). x Its message was true y and it concerned a great war. g The understanding of the message came to him in a vision.

10:1
x Da 1:7
y Da 8:26

2At that time I, Daniel, mourned for three weeks. 3I ate no choice food; no meat or wine touched my lips; and I used no lotions at all until the three weeks were over.

4On the twenty-fourth day of the first month, as I was standing on the bank of the great river, the Tigris, 5I looked up and there before me was a man dressed in linen, with a belt of the finest gold z around his waist. 6His body was like chrysolite, his face like lightning, his eyes like flaming torches, a his arms and legs like the gleam of burnished bronze, b and his voice like the sound of a multitude.

10:5
z Jer 10:9
10:6
a Rev 19:12
b Rev 1:15

7I, Daniel, was the only one who saw the vision; the men with me did not see it, but such terror overwhelmed them that they fled and hid themselves. 8So I was left alone, c gazing at this great vision; I had no strength left, my face turned deathly pale and I was helpless. 9Then I heard him speaking, and as I listened to him, I fell into a deep sleep, my face to the ground.

10:8
c Ge 32:24

10A hand touched me d and set me trembling on my hands and knees. 11He said, "Daniel, you who are highly esteemed, e consider carefully the words I am about to speak to you, and stand up, for I have now been sent to you." And when he said this to me, I stood up trembling.

10:10
d Jer 1:9
10:11
e Da 9:23

12Then he continued, "Do not be afraid, Daniel. Since the first day that you set your mind to gain understanding and to humble f yourself before your God, your words were heard, and I have come in response to them. g 13But the prince of the Persian kingdom resisted me twenty-one days. Then Michael, h one of the chief princes, came to help me, because I was detained there with the king of Persia. 14Now I have come to explain to you what will happen to your people in the future, for the vision concerns a time yet to come. i"

10:12
f Da 9:3
g Da 9:20
10:13
h ver 21; Da 12:1; Jude 1:9
10:14
i Da 2:28; 8:26

a 25 Or word   b 25 Or an anointed one; also in verse 26   c 26 Or off and will have no one; or off, but not for himself   d 27 Or 'week'   e 27 Or it   f 27 Or And one who causes desolation will come upon the pinnacle of the abominable ⌞temple⌟, until the end that is decreed is poured out on the desolated ⌞city⌟   g 1 Or true and burdensome

---

9:25 A "trench" can mean a moat or a conduit for water. This shows that Jerusalem will be rebuilt as a complete, fully functioning city.

9:26 The Messiah, the Anointed One, will be rejected and killed by his own people. His perfect eternal kingdom will come later.

9:26, 27 There has been much discussion on the numbers, times, and events in these verses, and there are three basic views: (1) the prophecy was fulfilled in the past at the desecration of the temple by Antiochus IV Epiphanes in 168–167 B.C. (see 11:31); (2) it was fulfilled in the past at the destruction of the temple by the Roman general Titus in A.D. 70 when one million Jews were killed; or (3) it is still to be fulfilled in the future under the antichrist (see Matthew 24:15).

10:1ff This is Daniel's final vision (536 B.C.). In it, he was given further insight into the great spiritual battle between God's people and those who want to destroy them. There is also more detailed information on the future, specifically the struggles between the Ptolemies (kings of the South) and the Seleucids (kings of the North).

10:1ff Prior to this vision, Cyrus allowed the Jews to return to Jerusalem, but Daniel stayed in Babylonia. Why didn't Daniel

return to Jerusalem? He may have been too old to make the long, hazardous journey (he was over 80); his government duties could have prevented him; or God may have told him to stay behind to complete the work he was called to do.

10:3 Daniel refrained from eating certain foods and using lotions because these were signs of feasting and rejoicing.

10:5, 6 The man seen by Daniel was a heavenly being. Some commentators believe that this was an appearance of Christ (see Revelation 1:13–15), while others think it was an angel (because he required Michael's help—10:13). In either case, Daniel caught a glimpse of the battle between good and evil supernatural powers.

10:6 Chrysolite is a translucent, semi-precious stone.

10:10–18 Daniel was frightened by this vision, but the messenger reassured him. Daniel lost his speech, but the messenger's touch restored it. Daniel felt weak and helpless, but the messenger's words strengthened him. God can bring us healing when we are hurt, peace when we are troubled, and strength when we are weak. Trust God to minister to you as he did to Daniel.

10:12, 13 Although God sent a messenger to Daniel, a powerful spiritual being ("prince of the Persian kingdom") detained the messenger for three weeks. Daniel faithfully continued praying and fasting, and God's messenger eventually arrived, assisted by Michael, the archangel. Answers to our prayers may be hindered

10:15
j Eze 24:27

10:16
k Jer 1:9; Da 8:15-
18

10:19
l Jdg 6:23

10:20
m Da 8:21; 11:2

10:21
n ver 13

11:1
o Da 5:31

11:3
p Da 8:4, 21

11:4
q Da 8:22

¹⁵While he was saying this to me, I bowed with my face toward the ground and was speechless.*j* ¹⁶Then one who looked like a man *a* touched my lips, and I opened my mouth and began to speak.*k* I said to the one standing before me, "I am overcome with anguish because of the vision, my lord, and I am helpless. ¹⁷How can I, your servant, talk with you, my lord? My strength is gone and I can hardly breathe."

¹⁸Again the one who looked like a man touched me and gave me strength. ¹⁹"Do not be afraid, O man highly esteemed," he said. "Peace!*l* Be strong now; be strong."

When he spoke to me, I was strengthened and said, "Speak, my lord, since you have given me strength."

²⁰So he said, "Do you know why I have come to you? Soon I will return to fight against the prince of Persia, and when I go, the prince of Greece *m* will come; ²¹but first I will tell you what is written in the Book of Truth. (No one supports me against them except Michael,*n* your prince. ¹And in the first year of Darius *o* the Mede, I took my stand to support and protect him.)

The Kings of the South and the North

²"Now then, I tell you the truth: Three more kings will appear in Persia, and then a fourth, who will be far richer than all the others. When he has gained power by his wealth, he will stir up everyone against the kingdom of Greece. ³Then a mighty king will appear, who will rule with great power and do as he pleases.*p* ⁴After he has appeared, his empire will be broken up and parceled out toward the four winds of heaven.*q* It will not go to his descendants, nor will it have the power he exercised, because his empire will be uprooted and given to others.

⁵"The king of the South will become strong, but one of his commanders will become even stronger than he and will rule his own kingdom with great power. ⁶After some years, they will become allies. The daughter of the king of the South will go to the king of the North to make an alliance, but she will not retain her power, and he and his power *b* will not last. In those days she will be handed over, together with her royal escort and her father *c* and the one who supported her.

⁷"One from her family line will arise to take her place. He will attack the forces of the king of the North and enter his fortress; he will fight against them and be victorious. ⁸He

a 16 Most manuscripts of the Masoretic Text; one manuscript of the Masoretic Text, Dead Sea Scrolls and Septuagint *Then something that looked like a man's hand*   *b 6* Or *offspring*   *c 6* Or *child* (see Vulgate and Syriac)

---

by unseen obstacles. Don't expect God's answers to come too easily or too quickly. Prayer may be challenged by evil forces, so pray fervently and pray earnestly. Then expect God to answer at the right time.

10:20, 21 The heavenly warfare was to be directed against Persia, and then Greece. Each of these nations was to have power over God's people. Both Persia and Greece were represented by evil angelic "princes," or demons. But God is in control of the past, present, and future, and he has all events recorded in his "Book of Truth."

11:2 The angelic messenger was revealing Israel's future (see 10:20, 21). Only God can reveal future events so clearly. God's work not only deals with the sweeping panorama of history, but also focuses on the intricate details of people's lives. And his plans—whether for nations or individuals—are unshakable.

11:2 The fourth Persian king may have been Xerxes I (486–465 B.C.), who launched an all-out effort against Greece in 480 (Esther 1:1).

11:2ff Babylonia was defeated by Medo-Persia. Medo-Persia was defeated by Greece under Alexander the Great, who conquered most of the Mediterranean and Middle Eastern lands. After Alexander's death, the empire was divided into four parts. The Ptolemies gained control of the southern section of Palestine, and the Seleucids took the northern part. Verses 1–20 show the conflict between the Ptolemies and Seleucids over control of Palestine in 300–200 B.C. Verses 21–35 describe the persecution of Israel under Antiochus IV Epiphanes. In verses 36–45 the prophecy shifts to the end times. Antiochus IV fades from view and the antichrist of the last days becomes the center of attention.

11:3 This mighty king of Greece was Alexander the Great, who conquered Medo-Persia and built a huge empire in only four years.

11:4, 5 Eventually Alexander the Great's empire was divided into four nations. These four weaker nations were comprised of the following regions: (1) Egypt, (2) Babylonia and Syria, (3) Asia Minor, and (4) Macedon and Greece. The king of Egypt ("the king of the South") was Ptolemy I or perhaps a reference to the Ptolemaic dynasty in general.

11:6, 7 These prophecies seem to have been fulfilled many years later in the Seleucid wars between Egypt and Syria. In 252 B.C., Ptolemy II of Egypt ("the South") gave his daughter Berenice in marriage to Antiochus II of Syria ("the North") to finalize a peace treaty between their two lands. But Berenice was murdered in Antioch by Antiochus II's former wife, Laodice. Berenice's brother, Ptolemy III, ascended the Egyptian throne and declared war against the Seleucids to avenge his sister's murder.

will also seize their gods, *r* their metal images and their valuable articles of silver and gold and carry them off to Egypt. *s* For some years he will leave the king of the North alone. ⁹Then the king of the North will invade the realm of the king of the South but will retreat to his own country. ¹⁰His sons will prepare for war and assemble a great army, which will sweep on like an irresistible flood *t* and carry the battle as far as his fortress.

¹¹"Then the king of the South will march out in a rage and fight against the king of the North, who will raise a large army, but it will be defeated. ¹²When the army is carried off, the king of the South will be filled with pride and will slaughter many thousands, yet he will not remain triumphant. ¹³For the king of the North will muster another army, larger than the first; and after several years, he will advance with a huge army fully equipped.

¹⁴"In those times many will rise against the king of the South. The violent men among your own people will rebel in fulfillment of the vision, but without success. ¹⁵Then the king of the North will come and build up siege ramps *u* and will capture a fortified city. The forces of the South will be powerless to resist; even their best troops will not have the strength to stand. ¹⁶The invader will do as he pleases; no one will be able to stand against him. *v* He will establish himself in the Beautiful Land and will have the power to destroy it. ¹⁷He will determine to come with the might of his entire kingdom and will make an alliance with the king of the South. And he will give him a daughter in marriage in order to overthrow the kingdom, but his plans*a* will not succeed or help him. ¹⁸Then he will turn his attention to the coastlands *w* and will take many of them, but a commander will put an end to his insolence and will turn his insolence back upon him. *x* ¹⁹After this, he will turn back toward the fortresses of his own country but will stumble and fall, *y* to be seen no more.

²⁰"His successor will send out a tax collector to maintain the royal splendor. *z* In a few years, however, he will be destroyed, yet not in anger or in battle.

²¹"He will be succeeded by a contemptible person who has not been given the honor of royalty. He will invade the kingdom when its people feel secure, and he will seize it through intrigue. ²²Then an overwhelming army will be swept away before him; both it and a prince of the covenant will be destroyed. *a* ²³After coming to an agreement with him, he will act deceitfully, *b* and with only a few people he will rise to power. ²⁴When the richest provinces feel secure, he will invade them and will achieve what neither his fathers nor his forefathers did. He will distribute plunder, loot and wealth among his followers. He will plot the overthrow of fortresses—but only for a time.

²⁵"With a large army he will stir up his strength and courage against the king of the South. The king of the South will wage war with a large and very powerful army, but he will not be able to stand because of the plots devised against him. ²⁶Those who eat from the king's provisions will try to destroy him; his army will be swept away, and many will fall in battle. ²⁷The two kings, with their hearts bent on evil, *c* will sit at the same table and lie to each other, but to no avail, because an end will still come at the appointed time. *d* ²⁸The king of the North will return to his own country with great wealth, but his heart will be set against the holy covenant. He will take action against it and then return to his own country.

a 17 Or *but she*

11:8
r Isa 37:19; 46:1-2
s Jer 43:12

11:10
t Isa 8:8; Jer 46:8; Da 9:26

11:15
u Eze 4:2

11:16
v Jos 1:5; Da 8:7

11:18
w Isa 66:19
x Hos 12:14

11:19
y Ps 27:2

11:20
z Isa 60:17

11:22
a Da 8:10-11

11:23
b Da 8:25

11:27
c Ps 64:6
d Hab 2:3

11:9–11 The king of Syria ("the North") was Seleucus II, and the king of Egypt ("the South") was Ptolemy IV.

11:13–16 This king of the north may have been Antiochus III (the Great). He defeated many Egyptian cities and established himself in Israel ("the Beautiful Land"). He was later defeated by the Romans at Magnesia (11:18).

11:17 The invader, Antiochus III, tried to bring peace between Egypt and Syria by having his daughter marry Ptolemy V Epiphanes of Egypt, but the plan failed.

11:20 The successor to Antiochus III was Seleucus IV. He sent Heliodorus to collect money from the temple treasury in Jerusalem.

11:21 Seleucus IV was succeeded by his brother, Antiochus IV Epiphanes, who found favor with the Romans.

11:22 The "overwhelming army" refers to the way all opposition against Antiochus IV will be broken. The prince of the covenant may be the high priest Onias III, who was assassinated by Menelaus in 170 B.C.

11:27 These two treacherous kings were probably Antiochus IV of Syria and Ptolemy VI of Egypt. Treachery and deceit are a power broker's way to position himself over someone else. When two power brokers try to gain the upper hand, it is a mutually weakening and self-destructive process. It is also futile because God ultimately holds all power in his hands.

11:30
e Ge 10:4

11:31
f Da 8:11-13;
Mt 24:15*

11:32
g Mic 5:7-9

11:33
h Mt 24:9; Jn 16:2;
Heb 11:32-38

11:34
i Mt 7:15; Ro 16:18

11:35
j Da 12:10;
Zec 13:9; Jn 15:2

11:36
k Rev 13:5-6

11:40
l Isa 5:28

11:41
m Jer 48:47

11:43
n 2Ch 12:3; Na 3:9

29 "At the appointed time he will invade the South again, but this time the outcome will be different from what it was before. 30 Ships of the western coastlands[a] [e] will oppose him, and he will lose heart. Then he will turn back and vent his fury against the holy covenant. He will return and show favor to those who forsake the holy covenant.

31 "His armed forces will rise up to desecrate the temple fortress and will abolish the daily sacrifice. Then they will set up the abomination that causes desolation. [f] 32 With flattery he will corrupt those who have violated the covenant, but the people who know their God will firmly resist [g] him.

33 "Those who are wise will instruct many, though for a time they will fall by the sword or be burned or captured or plundered. [h] 34 When they fall, they will receive a little help, and many who are not sincere [i] will join them. 35 Some of the wise will stumble, so that they may be refined, [j] purified and made spotless until the time of the end, for it will still come at the appointed time.

The King Who Exalts Himself

36 "The king will do as he pleases. He will exalt and magnify himself above every god and will say unheard-of things [k] against the God of gods. He will be successful until the time of wrath is completed, for what has been determined must take place. 37 He will show no regard for the gods of his fathers or for the one desired by women, nor will he regard any god, but will exalt himself above them all. 38 Instead of them, he will honor a god of fortresses; a god unknown to his fathers he will honor with gold and silver, with precious stones and costly gifts. 39 He will attack the mightiest fortresses with the help of a foreign god and will greatly honor those who acknowledge him. He will make them rulers over many people and will distribute the land at a price. [b]

40 "At the time of the end the king of the South will engage him in battle, and the king of the North will storm [l] out against him with chariots and cavalry and a great fleet of ships. He will invade many countries and sweep through them like a flood. 41 He will also invade the Beautiful Land. Many countries will fall, but Edom, Moab [m] and the leaders of Ammon will be delivered from his hand. 42 He will extend his power over many countries; Egypt will not escape. 43 He will gain control of the treasures of gold and silver and all the riches of Egypt, with the Libyans [n] and Nubians in submission. 44 But reports from the east and the north will alarm him, and he will set out in a great rage to destroy and annihilate many. 45 He will pitch his royal tents between the seas at [c] the beautiful holy mountain. Yet he will come to his end, and no one will help him.

a 30 Hebrew of Kittim   b 39 Or land for a reward   c 45 Or the sea and

---

11:29–31 Antiochus IV would again invade "the South," but enemy ships would cause him to retreat. On his way back, he plundered Jerusalem, desecrated the temple, and stopped the Jews' daily sacrifices. The temple was desecrated when he sacrificed pigs on an altar erected in honor of Zeus. According to Jewish law, pigs were unclean and were not to be touched or eaten. To sacrifice a pig in the temple was the worst kind of insult an enemy could level against the Jews. This happened in 168–167 B.C.

11:32 This reference to those who have violated the covenant may include Menelaus, the high priest, who was won over by Antiochus and who conspired with him against the Jews who were loyal to God. The "people who know their God" may refer to the Maccabees and their sympathizers, but a further fulfillment may lie in the future.

11:33, 34 Those who are wise will teach many, but they will also face great persecution. Difficult times remind us of our weaknesses and our inability to cope. We want answers, leadership, and clear direction. During these times, God's Word begins to interest even those who would never look at it. We should be ready to use our opportunities to share God's Word in needy times. We must also be prepared to face persecution and rejection as we teach and preach.

11:35 God's messenger described a time of trial when even wise believers may stumble. This could mean (1) falling into sin, (2) being fearful and losing faith, (3) mistakenly following wrong teaching, or (4) experiencing severe suffering and martyrdom. If

we persevere in our faith, any such experience will only refine us and make us stronger. Are you facing trials? Recognize them as opportunities to strengthen your faith. If we remain steadfast in these experiences, we will be stronger in our faith and closer to God.

11:36–39 These verses could refer to Antiochus IV Epiphanes, Titus (the Roman general), or the antichrist. Some of these events may have been fulfilled in the past, and some have yet to be fulfilled.

11:37 The "one desired by women" may refer to Tammuz, a Babylonian fertility god. Tammuz is also mentioned in Ezekiel 8:14. In other words, this person won't recognize any deity or religions at all, not even pagan ones. Instead, he will proclaim himself to be divine and the ultimate power.

11:38 The "god of fortresses" is believed by some to be Jupiter or Zeus. The implication is that this king will make *war* his god. More than all his predecessors, he will wage war and glorify its horrors.

11:40 The antichrist of the last days becomes the center of attention from this point through the rest of the book of Daniel.

11:45 "The beautiful holy mountain" is Mount Zion or the city of Jerusalem.

The End Times

12 "At that time Michael, *o* the great prince who protects your people, will arise. There will be a time of distress *p* such as has not happened from the beginning of nations until then. But at that time your people—everyone whose name is found written in the book—will be delivered. *q* 2 Multitudes who sleep in the dust of the earth will awake: some to everlasting life, others to shame and everlasting contempt. *r* 3 Those who are wise **a** *s* will shine like the brightness of the heavens, and those who lead many to righteousness, like the stars for ever and ever. 4 But you, Daniel, close up and seal the words of the scroll until the time of the end. *t* Many will go here and there to increase knowledge."

5 Then I, Daniel, looked, and there before me stood two others, one on this bank of the river and one on the opposite bank. *u* 6 One of them said to the man clothed in linen, who was above the waters of the river, "How long will it be before these astonishing things are fulfilled?"

7 The man clothed in linen, who was above the waters of the river, lifted his right hand and his left hand toward heaven, and I heard him swear by him who lives forever, saying, "It will be for a time, times and half a time. **b** *v* When the power of the holy people has been finally broken, all these things will be completed. *w*"

8 I heard, but I did not understand. So I asked, "My lord, what will the outcome of all this be?"

9 He replied, "Go your way, Daniel, because the words are closed up and sealed until the time of the end. 10 Many will be purified, made spotless and refined, but the wicked will continue to be wicked. *x* None of the wicked will understand, but those who are wise will understand.

a 3 Or *who impart wisdom*   **b** 7 Or *a year, two years and half a year*

12:1
o Da 10:13
p Rev 16:18
q Jer 30:7
12:2
r Mt 25:46
12:3
s Da 11:33
12:4
t Rev 22:10

12:5
u Da 10:4

12:7
v Da 7:25
w Lk 21:24

12:10
x Isa 32:7

12:1 Great suffering is in store for God's people throughout the years ahead. This way of describing the future is also used by Jeremiah (Jeremiah 30:7) and Jesus (Matthew 24:21ff). Yet the great suffering is tempered by a great promise of hope for true believers.

12:2 This is a clear reference to the resurrection of both the righteous and the wicked, although the eternal fates of each will be quite different. Up to this point in time, teaching about the resurrection was not common, although every Israelite believed that one day he or she would be included in the restoration of the new kingdom. This reference to a bodily resurrection of both the saved and the lost was a sharp departure from common belief. (See also Job 19:25, 26; Psalm 16:10; and Isaiah 26:19 for other Old Testament references to the resurrection.)

12:3 Many people try to be stars in the world of entertainment, only to find their stardom temporary. God tells us how we can be eternal "stars"—by being wise and leading many to God's righteousness. If we share our Lord with others, we can be true stars—radiantly beautiful in God's sight!

12:4 Closing up and sealing the words of the scroll meant that it was to be kept safe and preserved. This was to be done so that believers of all times could look back on God's work in history and find hope. Daniel did not understand the exact meaning of the times and events in his vision. We can see events as they unfold, for we are in the end times. The whole book will not be understood until the climax of earth's history.

12:7 "Time, times and half a time" may add up to 3 and a half years (see the NIV text note), and may be taken as either literal or figurative.

12:7 "The power of the holy people" seems to be crushed again and again throughout history. God's recurring purpose in this is to break the pride and self-sufficiency of his rebellious people and to bring them to accept him as their Lord.

12:10 Trials and persecutions make very little sense to us when we experience them, but they can purify us if we are willing to learn from them. After you survive a difficult time, seek to learn from it so that it can help you in the future. See Romans 5:3–5 for more on God's purpose in our sufferings.

12:11 "The abomination" set up in the temple refers to the altar of Zeus, where Antiochus IV Epiphanes sacrificed a pig. Some think it will have another fulfillment in the antichrist and one of his horrible acts of evil (Matthew 24:15). However, this and the predictions at the early part of the chapter may refer specifically to Antiochus IV Epiphanes, and the rest of the prophecy may refer to the end times.

11"From the time that the daily sacrifice is abolished and the abomination that causes desolation is set up, there will be 1,290 days. 12Blessed is the one who waits*y* for and reaches the end of the 1,335 days.

13"As for you, go your way till the end. You will rest, and then at the end of the days you will rise to receive your allotted inheritance. *z*"

12:12
y Isa 30:18

12:13
z Rev 14:13

12:11, 12 Either these are further calculations relating to the persecution of the Jews under Antiochus IV Epiphanes, or they refer to the end times. The abolishing of the daily sacrifices means the removal of worship of the true God, as well as oppression of believers. There is much speculation about these numbers in verses 11 and 12. The point is that this time of persecution has an end; God is in control of it, and he will be victorious over evil.

12:13 The promise of resurrection was reaffirmed to Daniel. He would one day see the fulfillment of his words, but he was not to spend the rest of his life wondering what his visions might mean. Instead, he was to rest in the comfort of God's sovereignty and look forward to the time when he would rise to receive and share eternal life with God. God does not reveal everything to us in this life. We must be content with the partial picture until he wants us to see more. He will tell us all we need to know.

12:13 Daniel stands tall in the gallery of God's remarkable servants. Born of royal heritage, yet taken into captivity when only a teenager, Daniel determined to remain faithful to God in the land of his captivity. Even at great personal cost, Daniel spent his entire lifetime advising his captors with unusual wisdom. God chose him as his servant to record some of the events of the captivity and some significant events concerning the future. As an old man, having been faithful to God throughout his years, Daniel was assured by God that he would rise from the dead and receive his portion in God's eternal kingdom. Faithfulness to God has a rich reward, not necessarily in this life, but most certainly in the life to come.

HOSEA

VITAL STATISTICS

PURPOSE:
To illustrate God's love for his sinful people

AUTHOR:
Hosea son of Beeri ("Hosea" means "salvation")

ORIGINAL AUDIENCE:
The people of Israel (the northern kingdom)

DATE WRITTEN:
Approximately 715 B.C., recording events from about 753–715 B.C.

SETTING:
Hosea began his ministry during the end of the prosperous but morally declining reign of Jeroboam II of Israel (the upper classes were doing well, but they were oppressing the poor). He prophesied until shortly after the fall of Samaria in 722 B.C.

KEY VERSE:
"The LORD said to me, 'Go, show your love to your wife again, though she is loved by another and is an adultress. Love her as the LORD loves the Israelites, though they turn to other gods and love the sacred raisin cakes'" (3:1).

KEY PEOPLE:
Hosea, Gomer, their children

KEY PLACES:
The northern kingdom (Israel), Samaria, Ephraim

SPECIAL FEATURES:
Hosea employs many images from daily life: God is depicted as husband, lion, leopard, bear, dew, rain, moth, and others; Israel is pictured as wife, sick person, vine, grapes, early fruit, olive tree, woman in childbirth, oven, morning mist, chaff, and smoke, to name a few.

GROOMSMEN stand at attention as the music swells and the bride begins her long walk down the aisle, arm in arm with her father. The smiling, but nervous, husband-to-be follows every step, his eyes brimming with love. Then happy tears are shed, vows stated, and families merged. A wedding is a joyous celebration of love. It is the holy mystery of two becoming one, of beginning life together, and of commitment. Marriage is ordained by God and illustrates his relationship with his people. Thus, there is perhaps no greater tragedy than the violation of those sacred vows.

God told Hosea to find a wife and revealed to him ahead of time that she would be unfaithful to him. Although she would bear many children, some of these offspring would be fathered by others. In obedience to God, Hosea married Gomer. His relationship with her, her adultery, and their children became living, prophetic examples to Israel.

The book of Hosea is a love story—real, tragic, and true. Transcending the tale of young man and wife, it tells of God's love for his people and the response of his "bride." A covenant had been made, and God had been faithful. His love was steadfast, and his commitment unbroken. But Israel, like Gomer, was adulterous and unfaithful, spurning God's love and turning instead to false gods. Then after warning of judgment, God reaffirmed his love and offered reconciliation. His love and mercy were overflowing, but justice would be served.

The book begins with God's marriage instructions to Hosea. After Hosea's marriage, children were born, and each given a name signifying a divine message (chapter 1). Then, as predicted, Gomer left Hosea to pursue her lusts (chapter 2). But Hosea (whose name means "salvation") found her, redeemed her, and brought her home again, fully reconciled (chapter 3). Images of God's love, judgment, grace, and mercy were woven into their relationship. Next, God outlined his case against the people of Israel: Their sins would ultimately cause their destruction (chapters 4; 6—7; 12) and would rouse his anger, resulting in punishment (chapters 5; 8—10; 12—13). But even in the midst of Israel's immorality, God was merciful and offered hope, expressing his infinite love for his people (chapter 11) and the fact that their repentance would bring about blessing (chapter 14).

The book of Hosea dramatically portrays our God's constant and persistent love. As you read this book, watch the prophet submit himself willingly to his Lord's direction; grieve with him over the unfaithfulness of his wife and his people; and hear the clear warning of judgment. Then reaffirm your commitment to being God's person, faithful in your love and true to your vows.

THE BLUEPRINT

A. HOSEA'S WAYWARD WIFE (1:1—3:5)

Hosea was commanded by God to marry a woman who would be unfaithful to him and would cause him many heartaches. Just as Gomer lost interest in Hosea and ran after other lovers, we, too, can easily lose appreciation for our special relationship with God and pursue dreams and goals that do not include him. When we compromise our Christian life-styles and adopt the ways of the world, we are being unfaithful.

B. GOD'S WAYWARD PEOPLE (4:1—14:9)
1. Israel's sinfulness
2. Israel's punishment
3. God's love for Israel

God wanted the people in the northern kingdom to turn from their sin and return to worshiping him alone, but they persisted in their wickedness. Throughout the book, Israel is described as ignorant of God, with no desire to please him. Israel did not understand God at all, just as Gomer did not understand Hosea. Like a loving husband or patient father, God wants people to know him and to turn to him daily.

MEGATHEMES

THEME	EXPLANATION	IMPORTANCE
The Nation's Sin	Just as Hosea's wife, Gomer, was unfaithful to him, so the nation of Israel had been unfaithful to God. Israel's idolatry was like adultery. They sought illicit relationships with Assyria and Egypt in pursuit of military might, and they mixed Baal worship with the worship of God.	Like Gomer, we can chase after other loves—love of power, pleasure, money, or recognition. The temptations in this world can be very seductive. Are we loyal to God, remaining completely faithful, or have other loves taken his rightful place?
God's Judgment	Hosea solemnly warned Judah against following Israel's example. Because Judah broke the covenant, turned away from God, and forgot her Maker, she experienced a devastating invasion and exile. Sin has terrible consequences.	Disaster surely follows ingratitude toward God and rebellion. The Lord is our only true refuge. If we harden our hearts against him, there is no safety or security anywhere else. We cannot escape God's judgment.
God's Love	Just as Hosea went after his unfaithful wife to bring her back, so the Lord pursues us with his love. His love is tender, loyal, unchanging, and undying. No matter what, God still loves us.	Have you forgotten God and become disloyal to him? Don't let prosperity diminish your love for him or let success blind you to your need for his love.
Restoration	Although God will discipline his people for sin, he encourages and restores those who have repented. True repentance opens the way to a new beginning. God forgives and restores.	There is still hope for those who turn back to God. No loyalty, achievement, or honor can be compared to loving him. Turn to the Lord while the offer is still good. No matter how far you have strayed, God is willing to forgive you

A. HOSEA'S WAYWARD WIFE (1:1—3:5)

Hosea highlights the parallels between his relationship with Gomer and God's relationship with the nation of Israel. Although the people made a covenant with the one true God, they went after false gods. In the same way, Hosea married Gomer, knowing ahead of time that she would leave him. Hosea tenderly dealt with his wife in spite of her sin. And God was merciful toward the people of Israel despite their sins. God has not changed; he is still merciful and forgiving.

1:1
a 2Ki 13:13

1 The word of the LORD that came to Hosea son of Beeri during the reigns of Uzziah, Jotham, Ahaz and Hezekiah, kings of Judah, and during the reign of Jeroboam a son of Jehoash a king of Israel:

a 1 Hebrew Joash, a variant of Jehoash

1:1 Hosea was a prophet to the northern kingdom of Israel. He served from 753 to 715 B.C. Under the reign of Jeroboam II, the northern kingdom had prospered materially but had decayed spiritually. The people were greedy and had adopted the moral behavior and idolatrous religion of the surrounding Canaanites.

Hosea's role was to show how the northern kingdom had been unfaithful to God, their "husband" and provider, and had married themselves to Baal and the gods of Canaan. He warned that unless they repented of their sin and turned back to God, they were headed for destruction. Hosea spoke of God's characteristics—

Hosea's Wife and Children

2 When the LORD began to speak through Hosea, the LORD said to him, "Go, take to your-self an adulterous[b] wife and children of unfaithfulness, because the land is guilty of the vil-est adultery[c] in departing from the LORD." 3 So he married Gomer daughter of Diblaim, and she conceived and bore him a son.

4 Then the LORD said to Hosea, "Call him Jezreel,[d] because I will soon punish the house of Jehu for the massacre at Jezreel, and I will put an end to the kingdom of Israel. 5 In that day I will break Israel's bow in the Valley of Jezreel."

6 Gomer conceived again and gave birth to a daughter. Then the LORD said to Hosea, "Call her Lo-Ruhamah,[a] for I will no longer show love to the house of Israel,[e] that I should at all forgive them. 7 Yet I will show love to the house of Judah; and I will save them—not by bow, sword or battle, or by horses and horsemen, but by the LORD their God.[f]"

8 After she had weaned Lo-Ruhamah, Gomer had another son. 9 Then the LORD said, "Call him Lo-Ammi,[b] for you are not my people, and I am not your God.

10 "Yet the Israelites will be like the sand on the seashore, which cannot be measured or counted. In the place where it was said to them, 'You are not my people,' they will be called 'sons of the living God.'[g] 11 The people of Judah and the people of Israel will be reunited,[h] and they will appoint one leader and will come up out of the land,[i] for great will be the day of Jezreel.

1:2
[b]Hos 3:1
[c]Dt 31:16; Hos 5:3

1:4
[d]2Ki 10:1-14

1:6
[e]Hos 2:4

1:7
[f]Zec 4:6

1:10
[g]Ro 9:26*

1:11
[h]Isa 11:12, 13
[i]Eze 37:15-28

a6 Lo-Ruhamah means *not loved.*   b9 Lo-Ammi means *not my people.*

---

his powerful love and fierce justice—and how their practical expe-rience of these should affect their lives and make them return to God. Unfortunately, the people had broken their covenant with God, and they would receive the punishments God had promised (Deuteronomy 27; 28).

1:2, 3 Did God really order his prophet to marry a woman who would commit adultery? Some who find it difficult to believe God could make such a request view this story as an illustration, not an historical event. Many, however, think the story is historical and give one of these explanations: (1) According to God's law, a priest could not marry a prostitute or a divorced woman (Leviti-cus 21:7). However, Hosea was not a priest. (2) It is possible that Gomer was not an adulterous woman when Hosea married her, and that God was letting Hosea know that Gomer would later turn to adultery and prostitution. In any case, Hosea knew ahead of time that his wife would be unfaithful and that their married life would become a living object lesson to the adulterous northern kingdom. Hosea's marriage to an unfaithful woman would illus-trate God's relationship to the unfaithful nation of Israel.

1:2, 3 It is difficult to imagine Hosea's feelings when God told him to marry a woman who would be unfaithful to him. He may not have wanted to do it, but he obeyed. God often required extraordi-nary obedience from his prophets who were facing extraordinary times. God may ask you to do something difficult and extraordi-nary, too. If he does, how will you respond? Will you obey him, trusting that he who knows everything has a special purpose for his request? Will you be able to accept the fact that the pain involved in obedience may benefit those you serve, and not you personally?

1:4, 5 Elijah had predicted that the family of Israel's King Ahab would be destroyed because of their wickedness (1 Kings 21: 20–22), but Jehu went too far in carrying out God's command (2 Kings 10:1–11). Therefore, Jehu's dynasty would also be punished—in the Valley of Jezreel, the very place where he carried out the massacre of Ahab's family. God's promise to put an end to Israel as an independent kingdom ("break Israel's bow") came true 25 years later when the Assyrians conquered the northern kingdom and carried the people into captivity.

1:6, 8 In 1:3, we read that Gomer "bore him [Hosea] a son." In 1:6 and 1:8, we learn that Gomer gave birth to two more children, but there is no indication that Hosea was their natural father, and some translations imply that he was not. Whether or not the chil-dren were Hosea's, the key to this part of the story is found in the names God chose for the children, showing his reaction to Israel's unfaithfulness. God's reaction to unfaithfulness is no different today. He wants our complete devotion.

1:7 Israel and Judah had been a united kingdom under David and Solomon. After Solomon's death a civil dispute had arisen, and the land was divided into a northern kingdom (Israel, whose capital was Samaria) and a southern kingdom (Judah, whose capital was Jerusalem). Although Hosea spoke mainly to the northern kingdom, his concern, like God's, was for the entire nation of Israelites including those from the kingdom of Judah. Just as Hosea prophesied, God helped Judah because Judah had a few kings who honored him. Shortly after defeating Israel, the Assyrian emperor Sennacherib invaded Judah and besieged Jeru-salem. He was driven off by an angel's powerful and dramatic intervention (Isaiah 36, 37).

1:7 God said he would personally rescue the people of Judah from their enemies with no help from their armies or weapons. Although God asks us to do our part, we should remember that he is not limited to human effort. God often chooses to work through people, but only because it is good for *them.* He can accomplish all his purposes without any help from us if he so chooses. You are very important to God, but on your own you have neither the ability to fulfill nor the power to disrupt God's plans.

1:9 Here God was in essence dissolving the covenant (Jeremiah 7:23). The name of the third child conveys the finality of God's judgment. God's warnings recorded in Deuteronomy 28:15–68 were beginning to come true: Israel was abandoning God, and in turn, he was leaving them alone and without his blessings.

1:10 The Old Testament prophetic books sometimes use the word "Israelites" to refer to the people of the united kingdom (north and south) and sometimes just to the northern kingdom. In talking about past events, Hosea usually thought of Israel as the northern kingdom with its capital in Samaria. But when Hosea spoke about future events relating to God's promises of restora-tion, it is difficult to understand his words as applying only to the northern kingdom because the exiled northerners would become hopelessly intermingled with their conquerors. Thus most schol-ars see the promises of return as either: (1) conditional—the Israelites chose not to return to God, and therefore they were not entitled to the blessings included in the promises of restoration, or (2) unconditional—God's promises of restoration have been fulfilled in Jesus Christ, and therefore the church (the new Israel) receives his blessings (Romans 9:25, 26; 1 Peter 2:10).

1:10, 11 Although Israel was unfaithful, God's commitment remained unchanged. This promise of a future reuniting reiterated the covenant made with Moses (Deuteronomy 30:1–10) and fore-shadowed the prophecies of Jeremiah (Jeremiah 29:11–14; 31:31–40) and Ezekiel (Ezekiel 11:16–21). It was a prediction of

2 "Say of your brothers, 'My people,' and of your sisters, 'My loved one.'

Israel Punished and Restored

2:2
/Isa 50:1

2 "Rebuke your mother,*/* rebuke her,
  for she is not my wife,
  and I am not her husband.
Let her remove the adulterous look from her face
  and the unfaithfulness from between her breasts.

2:3
k Eze 16:4, 22

3 Otherwise I will strip her naked
  and make her as bare as on the day she was born;*k*
I will make her like a desert,
  turn her into a parched land,
  and slay her with thirst.
4 I will not show my love to her children,
  because they are the children of adultery.

2:5
/Jer 44:17-18

5 Their mother has been unfaithful
  and has conceived them in disgrace.
She said, 'I will go after my lovers,
  who give me my food and my water,
  my wool and my linen, my oil and my drink.'*/*

2:6
m La 3:9

6 Therefore I will block her path with thornbushes;
  I will wall her in so that she cannot find her way.*m*

2:7
n Eze 16:8

7 She will chase after her lovers but not catch them;
  she will look for them but not find them.
Then she will say,
  'I will go back to my husband as at first,
  for then I was better off*n* than now.'

HOSEA
served as a
prophet to Israel
(the northern
kingdom) from
753–715 B.C.

Climate of the times . . . . . . Israel's last six kings were especially wicked; they promoted heavy taxes, oppression of the poor, idol worship, and total disregard for God. Israel was subjected to Assyria and was forced to pay tribute, which depleted its few remaining resources.

Main message . . . . The people of Israel had sinned against God, as an adulterous woman sins against her husband. Judgment was sure to come for living in total disregard for God and fellow humans. Israel fell to Assyria in 722 B.C.

Importance of message . . . . When we sin, we sever our relationship with God, breaking our commitment to him. While all must answer to God for their sins, those who seek God's forgiveness are spared eternal judgment.

Contemporary prophets . . . Jonah (793–753 B.C.), Amos (760–750 B.C.), Micah (742–687 B.C.), Isaiah (740–681 B.C.)

---

the day when all the people of God will be united under Christ. Today all believers everywhere are God's chosen people, a royal priesthood (see 1 Peter 2:9).

1:11 Just as the other children's names carried significance, so did Jezreel. In verse 4, the name depicts divine judgment; here it represents the scattering. The name means "God scatters." Here it represents the scattering a farmer does when he plants seeds. This was a sign of a new day and a new relationship between God and Israel.

2:2ff Israel's punishment and restoration are the themes of this chapter. As in a court case, the adulteress is brought to trial and found guilty. But after her punishment, she is joyfully and tenderly restored to God.

2:5–7 The Israelites were thanking false gods (specifically Baal, the god whom they believed controlled weather and thus farming) for their food, shelter, and clothing, instead of the true God who gave those blessings. Therefore, God would block Israel's "path with thornbushes" and "wall her in" by making the rewards of idol

worship so disappointing that the people would be persuaded to turn back to God. Despite Israel's unfaithfulness, God was still faithful and merciful. He would continue to hold his arms out to his people, even to the point of placing obstacles in their wayward path to turn them back to him.

2:7 Just as Gomer would return to her husband if she thought she would be better off with him, so people often return to God when they find life's struggle too difficult to handle. Returning to God out of desperation is better than rebelling against him, but it is better yet to turn to God out of gratitude for his care.

8 She has not acknowledged*o* that I was the one
    who gave her the grain, the new wine and oil,
who lavished on her the silver and gold—
    which they used for Baal.

9 "Therefore I will take away my grain*p* when it ripens,
    and my new wine*q* when it is ready.
I will take back my wool and my linen,
    intended to cover her nakedness.

10 So now I will expose her lewdness
    before the eyes of her lovers;
no one will take her out of my hands.*r*

11 I will stop all her celebrations:
    her yearly festivals, her New Moons,
    her Sabbath days—all her appointed feasts.*s*

12 I will ruin her vines and her fig trees,
    which she said were her pay from her lovers;
I will make them a thicket,*t*
    and wild animals will devour them.

13 I will punish her for the days
    she burned incense to the Baals;
she decked herself with rings and jewelry,
    and went after her lovers,
    but me she forgot,*u*"

                                                    declares the LORD.

14 "Therefore I am now going to allure her;
    I will lead her into the desert
    and speak tenderly to her.

15 There I will give her back her vineyards,
    and will make the Valley of Achor*a v* a door of hope.
There she will sing*b* as in the days of her youth,*w*
    as in the day she came up out of Egypt.

16 "In that day," declares the LORD,
    "you will call me 'my husband';
    you will no longer call me 'my master.*c*'

17 I will remove the names of the Baals from her lips;*x*
    no longer will their names be invoked.

18 In that day I will make a covenant for them
    with the beasts of the field and the birds of the air

	2:8 *o* Isa 1:3
	2:9 *p* Hos 8:7 *q* Hos 9:2
	2:10 *r* Eze 16:37
	2:11 *s* Isa 1:14; Am 8:10
	2:12 *t* Isa 5:6
	2:13 *u* Hos 4:6
	2:15 *v* Jos 7:24, 26 *w* Jer 2:2
	2:17 *x* Ex 23:13; Ps 16:4

a 15 Achor means *trouble*.   *b* 15 Or *respond*   *c* 16 Hebrew *baal*

2:8 Material possessions are success symbols in most societies. Israel was a wealthy nation at this time, and Gomer may have accumulated silver and gold. But Gomer didn't realize that Hosea had given her all she owned, just as Israel did not recognize God as the Giver of blessings. Both Gomer and Israel used their possessions irresponsibly as they ran after other lovers and other gods. How do you use your possessions? Use what God has given you to honor him.

2:12 The Israelites were so immersed in idolatry that they actually believed pagan gods gave them their vineyards and orchards ("her vines and her fig trees"). They had forgotten that the entire land was a gift from God (Deuteronomy 32:49). Today many people give credit to everything and everyone but God for their prosperity—luck, hard work, quick thinking, the right contacts. When *you* succeed, who gets the credit?

2:13 Baal was the most important of the Canaanite gods, and his name came to be used to describe all the local deities worshiped throughout the land occupied by Israel. Unfortunately, Israel did not get rid of the idols and pagan worship centers as they had been commanded. Instead, they tolerated and frequently joined Baal worshipers, often through the influence of corrupt kings.

One Israelite king especially noted for his Baal worship was Ahab. The prophet Elijah, in a dramatic showdown with Ahab's hired prophets, proved God's power far superior to Baal's (1 Kings 18).

2:14, 15 God was promising (1) to bring the people to the desert, a place free from distractions, so he could clearly communicate with them, and (2) to change what had been a time of trouble into a day of hope. The Valley of Achor ("trouble") is the site where Achan had sinned by keeping forbidden war plunder (see Joshua 7). He had brought great disaster to Joshua's troops when they were attempting to conquer the land. God uses even our negative experiences to create opportunities to turn back to him. As you face problems and trials, remember that God speaks to you in the desert, and not just in times of prosperity.

2:16 Not until Judah's exile would the entire nation begin to come to its senses, give up its idols, and turn back to God; and not until that day when God rules through Jesus the Messiah will the relationship between God and his people be restored. In that day, God will no longer be like a master to them; he will be like a husband (Isaiah 54:4–8). The relationship will be deep and personal, the kind of relationship we can know, though imperfectly, in marriage.

2:18
y Job 5:22
z Eze 34:25

and the creatures that move along the ground.y
Bow and sword and battle
    I will abolish from the land,
        so that all may lie down in safety.z
¹⁹ I will betroth you to me forever;
    I will betroth you ina righteousness and justice,
        inb love and compassion.

2:20
a Jer 31:34

²⁰ I will betroth you in faithfulness,
    and you will acknowledgea the LORD.

²¹ "In that day I will respond,"
    declares the LORD—

a 19 Or *with*; also in verse 20   b 19 Or *with*

GOMER

Gomer was a girl with a reputation. We don't know if she was already a working prostitute or was simply a promiscuous young woman by the time she met Hosea. But she was clearly a high risk for a lasting relationship. She must have been surprised and confused when, instead of propositioning her, Hosea arranged to marry her. By common cultural rule, the decisions were made by Hosea and Diblaim. Gomer may not even have been consulted. Her father was probably eager to remove an embarrassment from his life.

Hosea loved Gomer. Gomer seemed ambivalent toward her husband. Apparently, marriage simply changed the label on Gomer's behavior from promiscuity to adultery. She got pregnant three times, giving birth to two sons and a daughter. Hosea couldn't be sure if the children were his or had been fathered by other men, but he claimed them and named them as God instructed.

God's declarations about Israel overlap Hosea's struggle over Gomer's unfaithfulness. Sometime after the birth of their third child, Gomer became enslaved in prostitution. Hosea had to buy her freedom. He then insisted on her faithfulness.

What did Gomer think and feel during all this? How much did Hosea reveal to her about God's prediction that she would be unfaithful? How did she respond to Hosea's sacrificial faithfulness? We aren't told. After Hosea redeemed her, she isn't mentioned again. Her final appearance in the book leads to hopeful silence. If she responded to Hosea's love, they built a life together.

Probably the closest we come to feeling what Gomer felt are those times when we act unfaithfully toward God yet he continues to faithfully lavish his love on us. Gomer's shameful story turns out to be a thinly veiled version of our story. We know Gomer better than we might think at first, for she was what we are—sinners who are offered overwhelming grace!

Strength and accomplishment:	• May have traded a shameful past for a faithful future as a result of her husband's sacrificial love
Weaknesses and mistakes:	• Developed a persistent promiscuous lifestyle resistant even to the responsibilities of motherhood • Sold herself into sexual slavery
Lessons from her life:	• Unfaithfulness damages our integrity but does not prevent someone else from loving us in spite of our failure • God's love commits to us even though he knows our waywardness and bent toward sin
Vital statistics:	• Where: Israel • Occupation: Wife, prostitute • Relatives: Husband: Hosea. Father: Diblaim. Sons: Jezreel (God plants), Lo-Ammi (Not my people). Daughter: Lo-Ruhamah (Not loved).
Key verse:	"When the Lord began to speak through Hosea, the LORD said to him, 'Go, take to yourself an adulterous wife and children of unfaithfulness, because the land is guilty of the vilest adultery in departing from the LORD'" (Hosea 1:2).

Gomer's story is told in Hosea 1:1—3:5.

2:19, 20 The time will come when unfaithfulness will be impossible—God will bind us to himself in his perfect righteousness, justice, love, compassion, and faithfulness. Betrothal in Hosea's time was more than a simple agreement to marry. It was a binding engagement, a deep commitment between two families for a future, permanent relationship. God was promising a fresh new beginning, not just a temporary rewriting of a tired old agreement. (See Jeremiah 31:31–34.)

2:19, 20 God's wedding gift to his people, both in Hosea's day and in our own, is his compassion. Through no merit of our own, God forgives us and makes us right with him. There is no way for us by our own efforts to reach God's high standard for moral and spiritual life, but he graciously accepts us, forgives us, and draws us into a relationship with himself. In that relationship we have personal and intimate communion with him.

> "I will respond[b] to the skies,
>   and they will respond to the earth;
> 22 and the earth will respond to the grain,
>   the new wine and oil,
>   and they will respond to Jezreel.[a]
> 23 I will plant[c] her for myself in the land;
>   I will show my love to the one I called 'Not my loved one.[b][d]'
>   I will say to those called 'Not my people,[c]' 'You are my people';[e]
>   and they will say, 'You are my God.'"

2:21
[b] Zec 8:12

2:23
[c] Jer 31:27
[d] Hos 1:6
[e] Hos 1:10
[f] Ro 9:25*

Hosea's Reconciliation With His Wife

3 The LORD said to me, "Go, show your love to your wife again, though she is loved by another and is an adulteress.[g] Love her as the LORD loves the Israelites, though they turn to other gods and love the sacred raisin cakes.[h]"

3:1
[g] Hos 1:2
[h] 2Sa 6:19

2 So I bought her for fifteen shekels[d] of silver and about a homer and a letheke[e] of barley. 3 Then I told her, "You are to live with[f] me many days; you must not be a prostitute or be intimate with any man, and I will live with[f] you."

4 For the Israelites will live many days without king or prince,[i] without sacrifice[j] or sacred stones, without ephod or idol.[k] 5 Afterward the Israelites will return and seek the LORD their God and David their king. They will come trembling to the LORD and to his blessings in the last days.[l]

3:4
[i] Hos 13:11
[j] Hos 2:11
[k] Jdg 17:5-6

3:5
[l] Jer 50:4-5

B. GOD'S WAYWARD PEOPLE (4:1—14:9)

The rest of the book deals with Israel's sin and her impending judgment. Hosea points out the moral and spiritual decay of the nation. He describes the punishment awaiting the people and pleads with them to return to God. Although judgment and condemnation of sin are prevalent in the book, a strand of love and restoration runs throughout. Even in the midst of judgment, God is merciful and will restore those who repent and turn to him.

1. Israel's sinfulness

The Charge Against Israel

4 Hear the word of the LORD, you Israelites,
    because the LORD has a charge to bring
    against you who live in the land:

[a] 22 Jezreel means God plants.   [b] 23 Hebrew Lo-Ruhamah   [c] 23 Hebrew Lo-Ammi   [d] 2 That is, about 6 ounces (about 170 grams)   [e] 2 That is, probably about 10 bushels (about 330 liters)   [f] 3 Or wait for

---

3:1 This short chapter pictures the nation's exile and return. Israel would experience a time of purification in a foreign land, but God would still love the people and would be willing to accept them back. God commanded Hosea to show the same forgiving spirit to Gomer. Although Hosea had good reason to divorce Gomer, he was told to buy her back and love her.

3:1 God asked Hosea to do something almost unthinkable—to buy back his adulterous, unrepentant wife and to continue to love her! When those who knew about Gomer's adultery heard Hosea say that God loved idolatrous Israel as much as Hosea loved Gomer, they must have been amazed. The people had heard God's words many times, but they felt the impact of those words when they saw them acted out in Hosea's merciful love for his wife.

3:2 Apparently Gomer was on her own for a while. Needing to support herself, she must have either sold herself into slavery or become the mistress of another man. In either case, Hosea had to pay to get her back—although the required amount was pitifully small. Gomer was no longer worth much to anyone except Hosea, but he loved her just as God loved Israel. No matter how low we sink, God is willing to buy us back—to redeem us—and to lift us up again.

3:3 After this, Gomer is no longer mentioned by Hosea. This is explained in 3:4. Gomer's isolation showed how God would deal with the northern kingdom (5:6, 15). It is dangerous to rebel against God. If he were ever to withdraw his love and mercy, we would be without hope.

3:4 God would separate the Israelites from their treasured idolatrous practices. Sacrifices and sacred stones were elements of idol worship. Here the ephod is not the official vest of the priest, but an image used in idol worship; the idols were household gods, which were strictly forbidden for God's people.

3:4, 5 The northern kingdom had rebelled against David's dynasty and had taken Jeroboam as their king (1 Kings 12; 13). Their rebellion was both political and religious. At that time, they reverted back to the worship of golden idols. "David their king" refers to the time of Messiah's rule when all people will bow before him in humility and submission. Those who won't accept Christ's blessings now will face his power and judgment later. How much better it is to love and follow Christ now than face his angry judgment later.

4:1ff In this chapter, God brings a charge of disobedience against Israel. The religious leaders had failed to turn the people to God, and ritual prostitution had replaced right worship. The nation had declined spiritually and morally, breaking the laws that God had given them. The people found it easy to condemn Hosea's wife for her adultery. They were not so quick to see that *they* had been unfaithful to God.

4:1–3 God explained the reasons for Israel's suffering. Their lawless behavior had brought the twin judgments of increased violence and ecological crisis. There is not always a direct cause-and-effect relationship between our actions and the problems we face. Nevertheless, when we are surrounded with difficulties, we should seriously ask, "Have I done anything sinful or irrespon-

"There is no faithfulness, no love,
no acknowledgment of God in the land.

4:2
m Hos 7:1

2 There is only cursing,a lying and murder,
stealingm and adultery;
they break all bounds,
and bloodshed follows bloodshed.

4:3
n Zep 1:3

3 Because of this the land mourns,b
and all who live in it waste away;
the beasts of the field and the birds of the air
and the fish of the sea are dying.n

4:4
o Dt 17:12

4 "But let no man bring a charge,
let no man accuse another,
for your people are like those
who bring charges against a priest.o

4:5
p Hos 2:2

5 You stumble day and night,
and the prophets stumble with you.
So I will destroy your motherp—

4:6
q Hos 2:13

6 my people are destroyed from lack of knowledge.q

"Because you have rejected knowledge,
I also reject you as my priests;

a2 That is, to pronounce a curse upon   b3 Or dries up

SPIRITUAL UNFAITHFULNESS

Spiritual adultery and physical adultery are alike in many ways, and both are dangerous. God was disappointed with his people, because they had committed spiritual adultery against him, as Gomer had committed physical adultery against Hosea.

Parallels

Both spiritual and physical adultery are against God's law.

Both spiritual and physical adultery begin with disappointment and dissatisfaction— either real or imagined—with an already existing relationship.

Both spiritual and physical adultery begin with diverting affection from one object of devotion to another.

Both spiritual and physical adultery involve a process of deterioration; it is not usually an impulsive decision.

Both spiritual and physical adultery involve the creation of a fantasy about what a new object of love can do for you.

The Danger

When we break God's law in full awareness of what we're doing, our hearts become hardened to the sin, and our relationship with God is broken.

The feeling that God disappoints can lead you away from him. Feelings of disappointment and dissatisfaction are normal and, when endured, will pass.

The diverting of our affection is the first step in the blinding process that leads into sin.

The process is dangerous because you don't always realize it is happening until it is too late.

Such fantasy creates unrealistic expectations of what a new relationship can do and only leads to disappointment in all existing and future relationships.

---

sible that has caused my suffering?" If we discover that we are at fault, even partially, we must change our ways before God will help us.

4:2 This verse may allude to the assassinations of kings during Hosea's lifetime. Shallum killed Zechariah (the king, not the prophet) and took the throne. Then Menahem killed Shallum and destroyed an entire city because it refused to accept him as king (2 Kings 15:8–16). God pointed out that even murder was being taken casually in Israel.

4:4 We often blame others if we fear punishment for wrongdoing. Hosea warned the priests not to blame anyone else; the nation's sins were largely their fault. Israel's priests pointed out the people's sins, but God would not allow them to overlook their own irresponsible actions. Instead of instructing the nation in religion and morality, they had led the way toward idolatry and immorality. Their failure to lead the people in God's ways placed most of the blame for Israel's destruction on them. Knowing that God will not allow us to blame others for our sinfulness should cause us to admit our own sins. Beware of the tendency to blame others because it can keep you from feeling the need to repent.

4:4–9 Hosea leveled his charges against the religious leaders. Who were these religious leaders? When Jeroboam I rebelled against Solomon's son Rehoboam and set up a rival kingdom in the north, he also set up his own religious system (see 1 Kings 12:25–33). In violation of God's law, he made two golden calves and told the people to worship them. He also appointed his own priests, who were not descendants of Aaron. At first the residents of the northern kingdom continued to worship God, even though they were doing it in the wrong way, but very soon they also began to worship Canaanite gods. Before long they had substituted Baal for God and no longer worshiped God at all. It is not surprising that Jeroboam's false priests were unable to preserve the true worship of God.

4:6–9 God accused the religious leaders of keeping the people from knowing him ("destroyed from lack of knowledge"). They were supposed to be spiritual leaders, but they had become leaders in wrongdoing. The people may have said to one another, "It must be OK if the priests do it." Spiritual leadership is a heavy responsibility. Whether you teach a church school class, hold a church office, or lead a Bible study, don't take your leadership responsibilities lightly. Be a leader who leads others to God.

because you have ignored the law[r] of your God,
    I also will ignore your children.
7 The more the priests increased,
    the more they sinned against me;
    they exchanged[a] their[b] Glory for something disgraceful.[s]
8 They feed on the sins of my people
    and relish their wickedness.
9 And it will be: Like people, like priests.[t]
    I will punish both of them for their ways
    and repay them for their deeds.[u]

10 "They will eat but not have enough;[v]
    they will engage in prostitution but not increase,
  because they have deserted[w] the Lord
    to give themselves 11 to prostitution,
  to old wine and new,
    which take away the understanding 12 of my people.
  They consult a wooden idol[x]
    and are answered by a stick of wood.
  A spirit of prostitution leads them astray;
    they are unfaithful to their God.
13 They sacrifice on the mountaintops
    and burn offerings on the hills,
  under oak, poplar and terebinth,
    where the shade is pleasant.
  Therefore your daughters turn to prostitution
    and your daughters-in-law to adultery.[y]

14 "I will not punish your daughters
    when they turn to prostitution,
  nor your daughters-in-law
    when they commit adultery,
  because the men themselves consort with harlots
    and sacrifice with shrine prostitutes—
    a people without understanding will come to ruin!

15 "Though you commit adultery, O Israel,
    let not Judah become guilty.

  "Do not go to Gilgal;[z]
    do not go up to Beth Aven.[c]
  And do not swear, 'As surely as the Lord lives!'
16 The Israelites are stubborn,
    like a stubborn heifer.
  How then can the Lord pasture them
    like lambs in a meadow?

a 7 Syriac and an ancient Hebrew scribal tradition; Masoretic Text *I will exchange*   b 7 Masoretic Text; an ancient
Hebrew scribal tradition *my*   c 15 Beth Aven means *house of wickedness* (a name for Bethel, which means *house of God*).

4:6	[r] Hos 8:1, 12
4:7	[s] Hos 10:1, 6; 13:6
4:9	[t] Isa 24:2 [u] Jer 5:31; Hos 9:9, 15
4:10	[v] Lev 26:26; Mic 6:14 [w] Hos 7:14
4:12	[x] Jer 2:27
4:13	[y] Hos 2:13
4:15	[z] Hos 9:15; 12:11

4:8 The priests were glad when the people sinned. Every time a person brought a sin offering, the priest received a portion of it. The more the people sinned, the more the priests received. Because they couldn't eat all of the offerings themselves, they sold some and gave some to their relatives. The priests profited from the continuation of sin; it gave them power and position in the community. So instead of trying to lead the people out of sin, they encouraged sin to increase their profits.

4:10–12 The chief Canaanite gods, Baal and Asherah, represented the power of fertility and sexual reproduction. Not surprisingly, their worship included rituals with vile sexual practices. Male worshipers had sex with female temple prostitutes, or priestesses, and young women wishing to bear children had sex with male priests. But God said their efforts to increase fertility would not succeed.

4:12 The "stick of wood." or divining rod, was a way of attempting to tell the future. By divorcing themselves from God's authoritative religion centered in Jerusalem, inhabitants of the northern kingdom had effectively cut themselves off from God's word and from his way of forgiveness. The drive to be free from all restrictions can move us completely out of God's will.

4:15 God sent a warning to the southern kingdom of Judah that its priests should not become like those in Israel. Israel's priests who remained in the north had forgotten their spiritual heritage and had sold out to Baal. They were promoting idol worship and ritual prostitution. Israel would not escape punishment, but Judah could if it refused to follow Israel's example.

¹⁷ Ephraim is joined to idols;
     leave him alone!
¹⁸ Even when their drinks are gone,
     they continue their prostitution;
     their rulers dearly love shameful ways.

4:19
a Hos 12:1

¹⁹ A whirlwind*a* will sweep them away,
     and their sacrifices will bring them shame.

Judgment Against Israel

5:1
b Hos 6:9

5

"Hear this, you priests!
     Pay attention, you Israelites!
Listen, O royal house!
     This judgment is against you:
You have been a snare*b* at Mizpah,
     a net spread out on Tabor.
² The rebels are deep in slaughter.
     I will discipline all of them.
³ I know all about Ephraim;
     Israel is not hidden from me.
Ephraim, you have now turned to prostitution;
     Israel is corrupt.

5:4
c Hos 4:11

⁴ "Their deeds do not permit them
     to return to their God.
A spirit of prostitution*c* is in their heart;
     they do not acknowledge the LORD.
⁵ Israel's arrogance testifies against them;
     the Israelites, even Ephraim, stumble in their sin;
     Judah also stumbles with them.

5:6
d Mic 6:6-7

⁶ When they go with their flocks and herds
     to seek the LORD,*d*
they will not find him;
     he has withdrawn himself from them.

5:7
e Hos 6:7
f Hos 2:11-12

⁷ They are unfaithful*e* to the LORD;
     they give birth to illegitimate children.
Now their New Moon festivals
     will devour*f* them and their fields.

5:8
g Isa 10:29

⁸ "Sound the trumpet in Gibeah,
     the horn in Ramah.*g*
Raise the battle cry in Beth Aven*a*;
     lead on, O Benjamin.
⁹ Ephraim will be laid waste
     on the day of reckoning.
Among the tribes of Israel

a 8 *Beth Aven* means *house of wickedness* (a name for Bethel, which means *house of God*).

4:17 Ephraim is another name for Israel, the northern kingdom, because Ephraim was the most powerful of the ten tribes in the north. In the same way, the southern kingdom was called Judah after its most powerful tribe.

4:19 The whirlwind that would sweep Israel away referred to the Assyrian invasion that would destroy the nation about 20 years later.

5:1, 2 Mizpah and Tabor may have been sites prominent in the false worship of Baal. The leaders likely even encouraged the people to sin at these places. With both their civil and religious leaders hopelessly corrupt, the people of Israel did not have much of a chance. They looked to their leaders for guidance, and they should have found it. Today we can often choose our own leaders, but we still need to be aware of whether they are taking us toward or away from God. God held the people responsible for

what they did. Similarly, God holds us responsible for our actions and choices.

5:3 Ephraim is another name for Israel, the northern kingdom, because Ephraim was the most powerful of the ten tribes in the north. In the same way, the southern kingdom was called Judah after its most powerful tribe.

5:4 Persistent sin hardens a person's heart, making it difficult to repent. Deliberately choosing to disobey God can sear the conscience; each sin makes the next one easier to commit. Don't allow sin to groove a hard path deep within you. Steer as far away from sinful practices as possible.

5:8 Gibeah and Ramah were Israelite cities near Jerusalem. Hosea prophesied that these cities would sound the alarm of the coming judgment.

I proclaim what is certain.[h]

10 Judah's leaders are like those
    who move boundary stones.[i]
  I will pour out my wrath on them
    like a flood of water.
11 Ephraim is oppressed,
    trampled in judgment,
    intent on pursuing idols.[a][j]
12 I am like a moth to Ephraim,
    like rot to the people of Judah.

13 "When Ephraim saw his sickness,
    and Judah his sores,
  then Ephraim turned to Assyria,[k]
    and sent to the great king for help.
  But he is not able to cure you,
    not able to heal your sores.
14 For I will be like a lion to Ephraim,
    like a great lion to Judah.
  I will tear them to pieces and go away;
    I will carry them off, with no one to rescue them.[l]
15 Then I will go back to my place
    until they admit their guilt.
  And they will seek my face;
    in their misery[m] they will earnestly seek me."

2. Israel's punishment
Israel Unrepentant

6 "Come, let us return to the LORD.
  He has torn us to pieces[n]
    but he will heal us;
  he has injured us
    but he will bind up our wounds.[o]
2 After two days he will revive us;
    on the third day he will restore us,
    that we may live in his presence.
3 Let us acknowledge the LORD;
    let us press on to acknowledge him.
  As surely as the sun rises,
    he will appear;
  he will come to us like the winter rains,[p]
    like the spring rains that water the earth."

4 "What can I do with you, Ephraim?[q]
    What can I do with you, Judah?
  Your love is like the morning mist,
    like the early dew that disappears.

5:9
[h] Isa 46:10

5:10
[i] Dt 19:14

5:11
[j] Mic 6:16

5:13
[k] Hos 7:11

5:14
[l] Mic 5:8

5:15
[m] Jer 2:27

6:1
[n] Hos 5:14
[o] Dt 32:39

6:3
[p] Joel 2:23

6:4
[q] Hos 11:8

a 11 The meaning of the Hebrew for this word is uncertain.

5:10 Those who "move boundary stones" are guilty of a serious crime (Deuteronomy 27:17). Hosea was saying that the leaders of Judah were like those who cheat people by moving the boundary stones on their land (see Deuteronomy 19:14).

5:13 During the reigns of Menahem and Hoshea, Israel turned to Assyria for help (2 Kings 15:19, 20; 17:3, 4). But even the great world powers of that time could not help Israel, for God himself had determined to judge the nation. If we neglect God's call to repentance, how can we escape? (See Hebrews 2:3.)

6:1–3 This is presumption, not genuine repentance. The people did not understand the depth of their sins. They did not turn from idols, regret their sins, or pledge to make changes. They thought

that God's wrath would last only a few days; little did they know that their nation would soon be taken into exile. Israel was interested in God only for the material benefits he provided; they did not value the eternal benefits that come from worshiping him. Before judging Israel, however, consider your attitude. What do you hope to gain from your religion? Do you "repent" easily, without seriously considering what changes need to take place in your life?

6:4 God answered his people, pointing out that their profession of loyalty, like mist and dew, evaporated easily and had no substance. Many find it easy and comfortable to maintain the appearance of being committed without deep and sincere loyalty. If you profess loyalty to God, back it up with your actions.

⁵ Therefore I cut you in pieces with my prophets,
   I killed you with the words of my mouth;
   my judgments flashed like lightning upon you.
⁶ For I desire mercy, not sacrifice,^r
   and acknowledgment of God rather than burnt offerings.
⁷ Like Adam,^a they have broken the covenant—
   they were unfaithful^s to me there.
⁸ Gilead is a city of wicked men,
   stained with footprints of blood.
⁹ As marauders lie in ambush for a man,
   so do bands of priests;
   they murder on the road to Shechem,
   committing shameful crimes.
¹⁰ I have seen a horrible^t thing
   in the house of Israel.
   There Ephraim is given to prostitution
   and Israel is defiled.
¹¹ "Also for you, Judah,
   a harvest^u is appointed.

"Whenever I would restore the fortunes of my people,

7 ¹ whenever I would heal Israel,
   the sins of Ephraim are exposed
   and the crimes of Samaria revealed.^v

^a7 Or *As at Adam*; or *Like men*

6:6
^rIsa 1:11; Mt 9:13*

6:7
^sHos 5:7

6:10
^tJer 5:30

6:11
^uJoel 3:13
^vHos 6:4
^wHos 4:2

OBEDIENCE VERSUS SACRIFICES
God says many times that he doesn't want our gifts and sacrifices when we give them out of ritual or hypocrisy. God wants us first to love and obey him.

1 Samuel 15:22, 23	Obedience is far better than sacrifice.
Psalm 40:6–8	God doesn't want burnt offerings; he wants our lifelong service.
Psalm 51:16–19	God isn't interested in penance; he wants a broken and contrite heart.
Jeremiah 7:21–23	It isn't sacrifices God wants; he desires our obedience and promises that he will be our God and we will be his people.
Hosea 6:6	God doesn't want sacrifices; he wants our loving loyalty. He doesn't want offerings; he wants us to acknowledge him.
Amos 5:21–24	God hates pretense and hypocrisy; he wants to see justice roll on like a river.
Micah 6:6–8	God is not satisfied with offerings; he wants us to be fair and just and merciful, and to walk humbly with him.
Matthew 9:13	God doesn't want sacrifices; he wants us to be merciful.

6:6 Religious rituals can help people understand God and nourish their relationship with him. That is why God instituted circumcision and the sacrificial system in the Old Testament and baptism and the Lord's Supper in the New Testament. But a religious ritual is helpful only if it is carried out with an attitude of love for and obedience to God. If a person's heart is far from God, ritual will become empty mockery. God didn't want the Israelites' rituals; he wanted their hearts. Why do you worship? What is the motive behind your "offerings" and "sacrifices"?

6:7 One of Hosea's key themes is that Israel had broken the covenant God had made with them at Mount Sinai (Exodus 19; 20). God wanted to make Israel a blessing and a light to all the nations (Genesis 12:2, 3; Isaiah 49:6); and if God's chosen people obeyed him and proclaimed him to the world, he would give them special blessings. If they broke the covenant, however, they would suffer severe penalties, as they should have known (see Deuteronomy 28:15–68). Sadly, the people broke the agreement and proved themselves unfaithful to God. How about you? Have you also broken faith with God? What about your forgotten promises to serve him?

6:8, 9 Gilead was once a sacred place, but here it was corrupt. Shechem was once a city of refuge designated by Joshua (Joshua 20:1, 2, 7, 8); Gilead was a region that included Ramoth, also a city of refuge. At this time these areas were associated with murder and crime, with bands of evil priests lying in wait to murder travelers passing through the territory.

6:11 So that Judah would not become proud as they saw the northern kingdom's destruction, Hosea interjected a solemn warning about God's "harvest." God's temple was in Judah (Jerusalem), and the people thought that what happened in Israel could never happen to them. But when they had become utterly corrupt, they too were led off into captivity (see 2 Kings 25).

7:1, 2 God sees and knows everything. Like Israel, we often forget this. Thoughts like "No one will ever know," or "No one is watching" may tempt us to try to get away with sin. If you are facing difficult temptations, you will be less likely to give in if you remind yourself that God is watching. When faced with the opportunity to sin, remember that God sees everything.

They practice deceit,
   thieves break into houses,[w]
   bandits rob in the streets;
2 but they do not realize
   that I remember all their evil deeds.
Their sins engulf them;[x]
   they are always before me.

3 "They delight the king with their wickedness,
   the princes with their lies.[y]
4 They are all adulterers,[z]
   burning like an oven
whose fire the baker need not stir
   from the kneading of the dough till it rises.
5 On the day of the festival of our king
   the princes become inflamed with wine,[a]
   and he joins hands with the mockers.
6 Their hearts are like an oven;
   they approach him with intrigue.
Their passion smolders all night;
   in the morning it blazes like a flaming fire.
7 All of them are hot as an oven;
   they devour their rulers.
All their kings fall,
   and none of them calls on me.

8 "Ephraim mixes[b] with the nations;
   Ephraim is a flat cake not turned over.
9 Foreigners sap his strength,[c]
   but he does not realize it.
His hair is sprinkled with gray,
   but he does not notice.
10 Israel's arrogance testifies against him,[d]
   but despite all this
he does not return to the LORD his God
   or search[e] for him.

11 "Ephraim is like a dove,[f]
   easily deceived and senseless—
now calling to Egypt,
   now turning to Assyria.
12 When they go, I will throw my net[g] over them;
   I will pull them down like birds of the air.
When I hear them flocking together,
   I will catch them.
13 Woe to them,
   because they have strayed from me!
Destruction to them,
   because they have rebelled against me!

7:2	x Jer 2:19
7:3	y Mic 7:3
7:4	z Jer 9:2
7:5	a Isa 28:1, 7
7:8	b Ps 106:35
7:9	c Hos 8:7
7:10	d Hos 5:5 e Isa 9:13
7:11	f Hos 11:11
7:12	g Eze 12:13

7:7 "Hot as an oven" refers to the lust for power and intrigue that was burning in these leaders' hearts. Three Israelite kings were assassinated during Hosea's lifetime—Zechariah, Shallum, and Pekahiah (2 Kings 15:8–26). The kings' foreign relations and domestic lives were ruined because they ignored God and his word.

7:8 The people of Israel had intermarried with foreign people and had picked up their evil ways. When we spend a lot of time with people, we can easily pick up their attitudes and begin to imitate their actions. When you work, live, or play with unbelievers, beware of the influence they may have on you. Instead of drifting into bad habits, see if you can have a positive influence and point these people to God.

7:10 Arrogance (pride) keeps a person from returning to God because arrogance acknowledges no need of help from anyone, human or divine. Pride intensifies all our other sins because we cannot repent of any of them without first giving up our pride.

7:11 Israel's King Menahem had paid Assyria to support him in power (2 Kings 15:19, 20); King Hoshea turned against Assyria and went to Egypt for help (2 Kings 17:4). Israel's kings went back and forth, allying themselves with different nations when they should have allied themselves with God.

I long to redeem them
 but they speak lies against me.

7:14
h Jer 3:10

14 They do not cry out to me from their hearts*h*
 but wail upon their beds.
They gather together*a* for grain and new wine
 but turn away from me.

7:15
i Na 1:9, 11

15 I trained them and strengthened them,
 but they plot evil*i* against me.

7:16
j Hos 9:3

16 They do not turn to the Most High;
 they are like a faulty bow.
Their leaders will fall by the sword
 because of their insolent words.
For this they will be ridiculed
 in the land of Egypt.*j*

Israel to Reap the Whirlwind

8:1
k Jer 4:13
l Hos 4:6

8 "Put the trumpet to your lips!
 An eagle*k* is over the house of the LORD
because the people have broken my covenant
 and rebelled against my law.*l*
2 Israel cries out to me,
 'O our God, we acknowledge you!'
3 But Israel has rejected what is good;
 an enemy will pursue him.
4 They set up kings without my consent;
 they choose princes without my approval.
With their silver and gold
 they make idols for themselves
  to their own destruction.

8:5
m Jer 13:27

5 Throw out your calf-idol, O Samaria!
 My anger burns against them.
How long will they be incapable of purity?*m*
6 They are from Israel!
This calf—a craftsman has made it;
 it is not God.
It will be broken in pieces,
 that calf of Samaria.

8:7
n Pr 22:8

7 "They sow the wind
 and reap the whirlwind.*n*
The stalk has no head;
 it will produce no flour.

---

a 14 Most Hebrew manuscripts; some Hebrew manuscripts and Septuagint *They slash themselves*

7:16 A faulty bow is unreliable. Its arrows miss the target, and its owner would be quite vulnerable in battle. Life without God is as unreliable as a faulty bow. Without God's direction, our thoughts are filled with lust, cheating, selfishness, and deceit. As long as we are warped by sin, we will never reach our true potential.

7:16 People look everywhere except to God for happiness and fulfillment, pursuing possessions, activities, and relationships. In reality, only God can truly satisfy the deep longings of the soul. Look first to heaven, to the Most High God. He will meet your *spiritual* needs, not all your materialistic wants.

8:1-4 "An eagle is over the house of the LORD" referred to Assyria coming to attack Israel and take the people into captivity (2 Kings 15:28, 29). The people would call to God, but it would be too late because they had stubbornly refused to give up their idols. We, like Israel, often call on God to ease our pain without wanting him to change our behavior. And we, like Israel, may repent after it is too late to avoid the painful consequences of sin.

8:5 Samaria was the capital of the northern kingdom, and sometimes it stands for the whole kingdom of Israel. Jeroboam I had set up worship of calf-idols at Bethel and Dan and had encouraged the people to worship them (1 Kings 12:25-33). Thus the people were worshiping the image of a created animal rather than the Creator.

8:7 Crop yield is the result of good seed planted in good soil and given the proper proportions of sunlight, moisture, and fertilizer. A single seed can produce multiple fruit in good conditions. Israel, however, had sown its spiritual seed to the wind—it had invested itself in activities without substance. Like the wind that comes and goes, its idolatry and foreign alliances offered no protection. In seeking self-preservation apart from God, it had brought about its own destruction. Like a forceful whirlwind, God's judgment would come upon Israel by means of the Assyrians. When we seek security in anything except God, we expose ourselves to great danger. Without God there is no lasting security.

> Were it to yield grain,
>> foreigners would swallow it up.
> 8 Israel is swallowed up;[o]
>> now she is among the nations
>> like a worthless thing.
> 9 For they have gone up to Assyria
>> like a wild donkey wandering alone.
>> Ephraim has sold herself to lovers.
> 10 Although they have sold themselves among the nations,
>> I will now gather them together.[p]
> They will begin to waste away
>> under the oppression of the mighty king.
>
> 11 "Though Ephraim built many altars for sin offerings,
>> these have become altars for sinning.[q]
> 12 I wrote for them the many things of my law,
>> but they regarded them as something alien.
> 13 They offer sacrifices given to me
>> and they eat the meat,
>> but the Lord is not pleased with them.
> Now he will remember[r] their wickedness
>> and punish their sins:
>> They will return to Egypt.
> 14 Israel has forgotten his Maker
>> and built palaces;
>> Judah has fortified many towns.
> But I will send fire upon their cities
>> that will consume their fortresses."[s]

Punishment for Israel

9 Do not rejoice, O Israel;
>> do not be jubilant[t] like the other nations.
> For you have been unfaithful to your God;
>> you love the wages of a prostitute
>> at every threshing floor.
> 2 Threshing floors and winepresses will not feed the people;
>> the new wine[u] will fail them.
> 3 They will not remain in the Lord's land;
>> Ephraim will return to Egypt[v]
>> and eat unclean[a] food in Assyria.[w]

a3 That is, ceremonially unclean

8:8 oJer 51:34

8:10 pEze 16:37

8:11 qHos 10:1

8:13 rHos 7:2

8:14 sJer 17:27

9:1 tIsa 22:12-13

9:2 uHos 2:9

9:3 vHos 8:13
wEze 4:13

8:11 The altars that were supposed to remove sin were actually increasing sin through their misuse in worshiping Baal.

8:12 Though the laws were written for *them*, Israel considered them "alien." It is easy to listen to a sermon and think of all the people we know who should be listening, or to read the Bible and think of those who should do what the passage teaches. The Israelites did this constantly, applying God's laws to others but not to themselves. This is just another way to deflect God's will and avoid making needed changes. As you think of others who need to apply what you are hearing or reading, check to see if the same application could fit you. Apply the lessons to your own life first because often our own faults are the very first ones we see in others.

8:13 The people's sacrifices had become mere ritual, and God refused to accept them. We have rituals too—attending church, observing a regular quiet time, celebrating Christian holidays, praying before meals. Rituals give us security in a changing world. Because they are repeated often, they can drive God's lessons deep within us. But rituals can be abused. Beware if you find yourself observing a religious ritual for any of the following reasons: (1) to gain community approval, (2) to avoid the risks of doing something different, (3) to make thought unnecessary,

(4) to substitute for personal relationships, (5) to make up for bad behavior, (6) to earn God's favor. We should not reject the rituals of our worship, but we must be careful with them. Think about why you do them. Focus on God, and perform every act with sincere devotion.

8:13 In Egypt, the Israelites had been slaves (Exodus 1:11). The people would not literally return to Egypt, but they would return to slavery—this time scattered throughout the Assyrian empire.

8:14 Israel had placed its confidence in military strength, strong defenses, and economic stability, just as nations do today. But because of the people's inner moral decay, their apparent sources of strength were inadequate. There is a tendency in many nations toward removing all traces of God from daily life. But if a nation forgets its Maker, its strengths may prove worthless when put to the test.

9:1 A threshing floor was a flat area, often built on a hilltop, where harvesters beat the wheat and separated it from the chaff. Often men would stay overnight at the threshing floor to protect their grain, and prostitutes would visit there. Because of the location of threshing floors in the hilltops, they began to be used as places to sacrifice to false gods.

9:4
*x*Hag 2:13-14

4 They will not pour out wine offerings to the LORD,
    nor will their sacrifices please him.
Such sacrifices will be to them like the bread of mourners;
    all who eat them will be unclean.*x*
This food will be for themselves;
    it will not come into the temple of the LORD.

9:5
*y*Isa 10:3; Jer 5:31

5 What will you do*y* on the day of your appointed feasts,
    on the festival days of the LORD?
6 Even if they escape from destruction,
    Egypt will gather them,
    and Memphis will bury them.
Their treasures of silver will be taken over by briers,
    and thorns will overrun their tents.

9:7
*z*Isa 34:8; Jer 10:15
*a*Eze 14:9-10

7 The days of punishment*z* are coming,
    the days of reckoning are at hand.
    Let Israel know this.
Because your sins are so many
    and your hostility so great,
the prophet is considered a fool,*a*
    the inspired man a maniac.
8 The prophet, along with my God,
    is the watchman over Ephraim,*a*
yet snares await him on all his paths,
    and hostility in the house of his God.

9:9
*b*Hos 5:8

9 They have sunk deep into corruption,
    as in the days of Gibeah.*b*
God will remember their wickedness
    and punish them for their sins.

9:10
*c*Nu 25:1-5;
Ps 106:28-29

10 "When I found Israel,
    it was like finding grapes in the desert;
when I saw your fathers,
    it was like seeing the early fruit on the fig tree.
But when they came to Baal Peor,*c*
    they consecrated themselves to that shameful idol
    and became as vile as the thing they loved.

9:11
*d*Hos 4:7

11 Ephraim's glory will fly away like a bird*d*—
    no birth, no pregnancy, no conception.
12 Even if they rear children,
    I will bereave them of every one.

a8 Or *The prophet is the watchman over Ephraim, / the people of my God*

9:6 Israel's leaders vacillated between alliances with Egypt and alliances with Assyria. Hosea was saying that both were wrong. Breaking an alliance with untrustworthy Assyria and fleeing for help to the equally untrustworthy Egypt would not forestall Israel's destruction. Their only hope was to return to God.

9:7 By the time Israel began to experience the consequences of its sins, it was no longer listening to God's messengers. Refusing to hear the truth from prophets who spoke out so clearly about its sins, the nation did not hear God's warnings about what was soon to happen. We all listen and read selectively—focusing on what seems to support our present lifestyle, ignoring what demands a radical reordering of our priorities. In doing this, we are likely to miss the warnings we need most. Listen to people who think your approach is all wrong. Read articles that present viewpoints you would be unlikely to take. Ask yourself, "Is God speaking to me through these speakers and writers? Is there something I need to change?"

9:9 A couple had stopped to stay overnight in Gibeah when some wicked men gathered around the house and demanded that the man come out so they could have sex with him. Instead, the traveler gave them his concubine. They raped and abused her all night and then left her dead on the doorstep (Judges 19:14–30). That horrible act revealed the depths to which the people had sunk. Gibeah was destroyed for its evil (Judges 20:8–48), but Hosea said that the whole nation was now as evil as that city. Just as the city didn't escape punishment, neither would the nation.

9:10 Baal Peor was the god of Peor, a mountain in Moab. In Numbers 22, Balaam, a prophet, was hired by King Balak of Moab to curse the Israelites as they were coming through his land. The Moabites enticed the Israelites into sexual sin and Baal worship. Before long, the Israelites became as corrupt as the gods they worshiped. People can take on the characteristics of what or whom they love. What do you worship? Are you becoming more like God, or are you becoming more like someone or something else?

Woe to them
when I turn away from them!*e*
13 I have seen Ephraim, like Tyre,
planted in a pleasant place.
But Ephraim will bring out
their children to the slayer."

14 Give them, O LORD—
what will you give them?
Give them wombs that miscarry
and breasts that are dry.*f*

15 "Because of all their wickedness in Gilgal,
I hated them there.
Because of their sinful deeds,*g*
I will drive them out of my house.
I will no longer love them;
all their leaders are rebellious.*h*
16 Ephraim*i* is blighted,
their root is withered,
they yield no fruit.*j*
Even if they bear children,
I will slay their cherished offspring."

17 My God will reject them
because they have not obeyed*k* him;
they will be wanderers among the nations.

10 Israel was a spreading vine;
he brought forth fruit for himself.
As his fruit increased,
he built more altars;
as his land prospered,
he adorned his sacred stones.*l*
2 Their heart is deceitful,*m*
and now they must bear their guilt.*n*
The LORD will demolish their altars
and destroy their sacred stones.

3 Then they will say, "We have no king
because we did not revere the LORD.
But even if we had a king,
what could he do for us?"
4 They make many promises,
take false oaths
and make agreements;*o*
therefore lawsuits spring up
like poisonous weeds in a plowed field.

9:12
e Dt 31:17

9:14
f Lk 23:29

9:15
g Hos 7:2
h Isa 1:23

9:16
i Hos 5:11
j Hos 8:7

9:17
k Hos 4:10

10:1
l Hos 8:11

10:2
m 1Ki 18:21
n Hos 13:16

10:4
o Am 5:7

9:14 Hosea prayed this prayer when he foresaw the destruction that Israel's sins would bring (2 Kings 17:7–23). This vision of Israel's terrible fate moved him to pray that women would not get pregnant and that children would die as infants so they would not have to experience the tremendous suffering and pain that lay ahead.

9:15 At Gilgal, both the political and the religious failure of the nation began. Here idols and kings were substituted for God. Saul, the united nation's first king, was crowned at Gilgal (1 Samuel 11:15), but by Hosea's time, Baal worship flourished there (4:15; 12:11).

10:1 Israel prospered under Jeroboam II, gaining military and economic strength. But the more prosperous the nation became,

the more love it lavished on idols. It seems as though the more God gives, the more we spend. We want bigger houses, better cars, and finer clothes. But the finest things the world offers line the pathway to destruction. As you prosper, consider where your money is going. Is it being used for God's purposes, or are you consuming it all on yourself?

10:4 God was angry with the people of Israel for their insincere promises. Because the people did not keep their word, there were many lawsuits. People break their promises, but God always keeps his. Are you remaining true to your promises, both to other people and to God? If not, ask God for forgiveness and help to get back on track. Then be careful about the promises you make. Never make a promise unless you are sure you can keep it.

10:5
PHos 8:5

5 The people who live in Samaria fear
    for the calf-idol of Beth Aven.ᵃ
Its people will mourn over it,
    and so will its idolatrous priests,
those who had rejoiced over its splendor,
    because it is taken from them into exile.ᵖ

10:6
qHos 11:5
rHos 4:7

6 It will be carried to Assyriaq
    as tribute for the great king.
Ephraim will be disgraced;ʳ
    Israel will be ashamed of its wooden idols.ᵇ

10:7
sHos 13:11

7 Samaria and its king will float awayˢ
    like a twig on the surface of the waters.

10:8
t1Ki 12:28-30
uLk 23:30*;
Rev 6:16

8 The high places of wickednessᶜ ᵗ will be destroyed—
    it is the sin of Israel.
Thorns and thistles will grow up
    and cover their altars.
Then they will say to the mountains, "Cover us!"
    and to the hills, "Fall on us!"ᵘ

9 "Since the days of Gibeah, you have sinned, O Israel,
    and there you have remained.ᵈ
Did not war overtake
    the evildoers in Gibeah?

10:10
vEze 5:13

10 When I please, I will punishᵛ them;
    nations will be gathered against them
to put them in bonds for their double sin.

11 Ephraim is a trained heifer
    that loves to thresh;
so I will put a yoke
    on her fair neck.
I will drive Ephraim,
    Judah must plow,
    and Jacob must break up the ground.

10:12
wJer 4:3
xHos 12:6

12 Sow for yourselves righteousness,
    reap the fruit of unfailing love,
and break up your unplowed ground;ʷ
    for it is time to seekˣ the Lᴏʀᴅ,
until he comes
    and showers righteousness on you.

10:13
yJob 4:8; Gal 6:7-8

13 But you have planted wickedness,
    you have reaped evil,ʸ
    you have eaten the fruit of deception.
Because you have depended on your own strength
    and on your many warriors,

ᵃ5 Beth Aven means *house of wickedness* (a name for Bethel, which means *house of God*). ᵇ6 Or *its counsel*
ᶜ8 Hebrew *aven*, a reference to Beth Aven (a derogatory name for Bethel) ᵈ9 Or *there a stand was taken*

10:5 Beth Aven means "house of wickedness," and it refers to Bethel ("house of God") where false worship took place. If the Israelites' idols were really gods, they should have been able to protect the people. How ironic that the people were fearing for their gods' safety! For more information on this calf-idol, see the notes on 3:4, 5 and 8:5.

10:9, 10 For information on "the days of Gibeah," see the note on 9:9 or read Judges 19 and 20. Gibeah stands for cruelty and sensuality as in Judges, and for rebellion as in Saul's day (Gibeah was Saul's hometown; see 1 Samuel 10:5; 11:4).

10:12 Hosea repeatedly uses illustrations about fields and crops. Here he envisions a plowed field, earth that is ready to receive seeds. It is no longer stony and hard; it has been carefully prepared, and it is available. Is your life ready for God to work

in it? You can break up the unplowed ground of your heart by acknowledging your sins and receiving God's forgiveness and guidance.

10:13 The Israelites trusted in the lie that military power could keep them safe. Believers today are also capable of falling for lies. Those who want to lead others astray often follow these rules for effective lying: make it big; keep it simple; repeat it often. Believers can avoid falling for lies by asking: (1) Am I believing this because there is personal gain in it for me? (2) Am I discounting important facts? (3) Does this conflict with a direct command of Scripture? (4) Are there any Biblical parallels to the situation I'm facing that would help me know what to believe?

14 the roar of battle will rise against your people,
   so that all your fortresses will be devastated[z]—
as Shalman devastated Beth Arbel on the day of battle,
   when mothers were dashed to the ground with their children.[a]
15 Thus will it happen to you, O Bethel,
   because your wickedness is great.
When that day dawns,
   the king of Israel will be completely destroyed.

3. God's love for Israel

11   "When Israel was a child, I loved him,
   and out of Egypt I called my son.[b]
2 But the more I[a] called Israel,
   the further they went from me.[b]
They sacrificed to the Baals
   and they burned incense to images.
3 It was I who taught Ephraim to walk,
   taking them by the arms;[c]
but they did not realize
   it was I who healed them.
4 I led them with cords of human kindness,
   with ties of love;
I lifted the yoke[d] from their neck
   and bent down to feed[e] them.

5 "Will they not return to Egypt[f]
   and will not Assyria rule over them
because they refuse to repent?
6 Swords[g] will flash in their cities,
   will destroy the bars of their gates
and put an end to their plans.
7 My people are determined to turn from me.
   Even if they call to the Most High,
he will by no means exalt them.

---

a2 Some Septuagint manuscripts; Hebrew *they*   **b**2 Septuagint; Hebrew *them*

Cross-references:
10:14 [z]Isa 17:3 [a]Hos 13:16
11:1 [b]Hos 12:9, 13; Mt 2:15*
11:3 [c]Dt 1:31
11:4 [d]Lev 26:13 [e]Ps 78:25
11:5 [f]Hos 7:16
11:6 [g]Hos 13:16

10:14 Some say Shalman was Shalmaneser, king of Assyria; others say Shalman was Salmanu, a Moabite king mentioned in the inscriptions of Tiglath-Pileser. Shalman had invaded Gilead around 740 B.C. and destroyed the city of Beth Arbel, killing many people, including women and children. This kind of cruelty was not uncommon in ancient warfare. Hosea was saying such would be Israel's fate.

10:15 Because Israel had put its confidence in military might rather than in God, it would be destroyed by military power. Israel's king, who had led the people into idol worship, would be the first to fall. Divine judgment is *sometimes* swift, but it is *always* sure.

11:1ff In the final four chapters, Hosea shifts to the theme of God's intense love for Israel. God had always loved Israel as a parent loves a stubborn child, and that is why he would not release Israel from the consequences of its behavior. The Israelites were sinful, and they would be punished like a rebellious son brought by his parents before the elders (Deuteronomy 21:18–21). All through Israel's sad history, God repeatedly offered to restore the nation if it would only turn to him. By stubbornly refusing God's invitation, the northern kingdom had sealed its doom. It would be destroyed, never to rise again. Even so, Israel as a nation was not finished. A remnant of faithful Israelites would return to Jerusalem, where one day the Messiah would come, offering pardon and reconciliation to all who would faithfully follow him.

11:3 God had consistently provided for his people, but they refused to see what he had done, and they showed no interest in thanking him. Ungratefulness is a common human fault. For example, when was the last time you thanked your parents for caring for you? Your pastor for the service he gives your church? Your child's teacher for the care taken with each day's activities? Your heavenly Father for his guidance? Many of the benefits and privileges we enjoy are the result of loving actions done long ago. Look for hidden acts of nurturing, and thank those who make the world better through their love. But begin by thanking God for all his blessings.

11:4 God's discipline requires times of leading and times of feeding. Sometimes the rope is taut; sometimes it is slack. God's discipline is always loving, and its object is always the well-being of the beloved. When you are called to discipline others—children, students, employees, or church members—do not be rigid. Vary your approach according to the goals you are seeking to accomplish. In each case, ask yourself, "does this person need guidance, or does he or she need to be nurtured?"

11:5 The northern kingdom survived for only two centuries after its break with Jerusalem. Its spiritual and political leaders did not help the people learn the way to God, so as a nation they would never repent. Hosea prophesied its downfall, which happened when Shalmaneser of Assyria conquered Israel in 722 B.C. Judah also would go into captivity, but a remnant would return to their homeland.

11:8
h Ge 14:8

8 "How can I give you up, Ephraim?
How can I hand you over, Israel?
How can I treat you like Admah?
How can I make you like Zeboiim?*h*
My heart is changed within me;
all my compassion is aroused.
9 I will not carry out my fierce anger,
nor will I turn and devastate Ephraim.
For I am God, and not man—
the Holy One among you.
I will not come in wrath.*a*

11:10
i Hos 6:1-3

10 They will follow the LORD;
he will roar like a lion.
When he roars,
his children will come trembling from the west.*i*

11:11
j Eze 28:26

11 They will come trembling
like birds from Egypt,
like doves from Assyria.
I will settle them in their homes,"*j*
declares the LORD.

Israel's Sin

11:12
k Hos 4:2

12 Ephraim has surrounded me with lies,*k*
the house of Israel with deceit.
And Judah is unruly against God,
even against the faithful Holy One.

12 1 Ephraim feeds on the wind;
he pursues the east wind all day
and multiplies lies and violence.
He makes a treaty with Assyria
and sends olive oil to Egypt.

12:2
l Mic 6:2

2 The LORD has a charge*l* to bring against Judah;
he will punish Jacob*b* according to his ways
and repay him according to his deeds.

12:3
m Ge 25:26
n Ge 32:24-29

3 In the womb he grasped his brother's heel;*m*
as a man he struggled*n* with God.
4 He struggled with the angel and overcame him;
he wept and begged for his favor.
He found him at Bethel
and talked with him there—

12:5
o Ex 3:15

5 the LORD God Almighty,
the LORD is his name*o* of renown!

a 9 Or *come against any city*   *b* 2 *Jacob* means *he grasps the heel* (figuratively, *he deceives*).

11:8 Admah and Zeboiim were cities of the plain that had perished with Sodom and Gomorrah (Genesis 14:8; Deuteronomy 29:23).

11:9 "I am God, and not man." It is easy for us to define God in terms of our own expectations and behavior. In so doing, we make him just slightly larger than ourselves. In reality, God is infinitely greater than we are. We should seek to become like him rather than attempting to remake him in our image.

11:12 Unlike Israel, Judah had some fairly good kings—Asa, Jehoshaphat, Joash, Amaziah, Azariah (Uzziah), Jotham, and especially Hezekiah and Josiah. Under some of these kings, God's law was dusted off and taught to the people. The priests continued to serve in God's appointed temple in Jerusalem, and the festivals were celebrated at least some of the time. Unfortunately, the political or religious leaders were unable to completely wipe out idol worship and pagan rites (although Hezekiah and Josiah came close), which continued to fester until they eventually

erupted and infected the whole country. Still, the influence of the good kings enabled Judah to survive more than 150 years longer than Israel, and that memory of their positive influence fortified a small group—a remnant—of faithful people who would one day return and restore their land and temple.

12:2-5 Jacob, whose name was later changed to Israel, was the common ancestor of all 12 tribes of Israel (both northern and southern kingdoms). Like the nations that descended from him, Jacob practiced deceit. Unlike Israel and Judah, however, he constantly searched for God. Jacob wrestled with the angel in order to be blessed, but his descendants thought their blessings came from their own successes. Jacob purged his house of idols (Genesis 35:2), but his descendants could not quit their idol worship.

6 But you must return to your God;
maintain love and justice,
and wait for your God always.

7 The merchant uses dishonest scales;p
he loves to defraud.
8 Ephraim boasts,
"I am very rich; I have become wealthy.q
With all my wealth they will not find in me
any iniquity or sin."

9 "I am the LORD your God,
‿who brought you‿ out of a Egypt;r
I will make you live in tents again,
as in the days of your appointed feasts.
10 I spoke to the prophets,
gave them many visions
and told paraboless through them."t

11 Is Gilead wicked?
Its people are worthless!
Do they sacrifice bulls in Gilgal?
Their altars will be like piles of stones
on a plowed field.
12 Jacob fled to the country of Aramb;u
Israel served to get a wife,
and to pay for her he tended sheep.
13 The LORD used a prophet to bring Israel up from Egypt,
by a prophet he cared for him.
14 But Ephraim has bitterly provoked him to anger;
his Lord will leave upon him the guilt of his bloodshedv
and will repay him for his contempt.w

The LORD's Anger Against Israel

13 When Ephraim spoke, men trembled;
he was exalted in Israel.
But he became guilty of Baal worship and died.

a 9 Or God / ever since you were in   b 12 That is, Northwest Mesopotamia

12:7
p Am 8:5

12:8
q Rev 3:17

12:9
r Lev 23:43

12:10
s Eze 20:49
t 2Ki 17:13

12:12
u Ge 28:5

12:14
v Eze 18:13
w Da 11:18

12:6 The two principles that Hosea called his nation to live by, love and justice, are at the very foundation of God's character. They are essential to his followers, but they are not easy to keep in balance. Some people are loving to the point that they excuse wrongdoing. Others are just to the extent that they forget love. Love without justice, because it is not aiming at a higher standard, leaves people in their sins. Justice without love, because it has no heart, drives people away from God. To specialize in one at the expense of the other is to distort our witness. Today's church, just like Hosea's nation, must live by both principles.

12:7, 8 In Israel, dishonesty had become an accepted means of attaining wealth. Israelites who were financially successful could not imagine that God would consider them sinful. They thought that their wealth was a sign of God's approval, and they didn't bother to consider how they had gotten it. But God said that Israel's riches would not make up for its sin. Remember that God's measure of success is different from ours. He calls us to faithfulness, not to affluence. Character is more important to him than our pocketbooks.

12:8 Rich people and nations often claim that their material success is due to their own hard work, initiative, and intelligence. Because they have every possession they want, they don't feel the need for God. They believe that their riches are their own,

and they think that they have the right to use them any way they please. If you find yourself feeling proud of your accomplishments, remember that all your opportunities, abilities, and resources come from God, and that you hold them in sacred trust for him.

12:9 Once a year the Israelites spent a week living in tents during the Feast of Tabernacles, which commemorated God's protection as they wandered in the desert for 40 years (see Deuteronomy 1:19—2:1). Here, because of their sin, God would cause them to live in tents again—this time not as part of a festival, but in actual bondage.

12:12 Hosea was using this reference to Jacob to say, "Don't forget your humble beginnings. What you have is not a result of your own efforts, but it is yours because God has been gracious to you."

12:13 The prophet who brought Israel up from Egypt was Moses (Exodus 13:17–19).

13:1 Israel, represented here by the northern tribe of Ephraim, had been great, but by Hosea's time the people had rebelled against God and had lost their authority among the nations. Greatness in the past is no guarantee of greatness in the future. It is good to remember what God has done for you and through you, but it is equally important to keep your relationship with him vital and up-to-date. Commit yourself to God moment by moment.

2 Now they sin more and more;
>   they make idols for themselves from their silver,
>   cleverly fashioned images,
>   all of them the work of craftsmen.
>   It is said of these people,
>   "They offer human sacrifice
>   and kiss[a] the calf-idols."

13:3
x Hos 6:4
y Da 2:35

3 Therefore they will be like the morning mist,
>   like the early dew that disappears,[x]
>   like chaff swirling from a threshing floor,[y]
>   like smoke escaping through a window.

13:4
z Hos 12:9
a Isa 43:11

4 "But I am the LORD your God,
>   ⌊who brought you⌋ out of[b] Egypt.[z]
> You shall acknowledge no God but me,
>   no Savior[a] except me.

5 I cared for you in the desert,
>   in the land of burning heat.

13:6
b Dt 32:12-15;
Hos 2:13

6 When I fed them, they were satisfied;
>   when they were satisfied, they became proud;
>   then they forgot me.[b]

7 So I will come upon them like a lion,
>   like a leopard I will lurk by the path.

13:8
c 2Sa 17:8
d Ps 50:22

8 Like a bear robbed of her cubs,[c]
>   I will attack them and rip them open.
> Like a lion I will devour them;
>   a wild animal will tear them apart.[d]

9 "You are destroyed, O Israel,
>   because you are against me, against your helper.

13:10
e Hos 8:4

10 Where is your king, that he may save you?
>   Where are your rulers in all your towns,
> of whom you said,
>   'Give me a king and princes'?[e]

13:11
f 1Ki 14:10

11 So in my anger I gave you a king,
>   and in my wrath I took him away.[f]

13:12
g Dt 32:34

12 The guilt of Ephraim is stored up,
>   his sins are kept on record.[g]

a2 Or "Men who sacrifice / kiss   *b4* Or God / ever since you were in

---

**CYCLES OF
JUDGMENT/
SALVATION
IN HOSEA**

Judgment . . . . 1:2–9; 2:2–13; 4:1—5:14; 6:4—11:7; 11:12—13:16
Salvation . . . . 1:10—2:1; 2:14—3:5; 5:15—6:3; 11:8–11; 14:1–9
God promises to judge, but he also promises mercy. Here you can see the cycles of judgment and salvation in Hosea. Prophecies of judgment are consistently followed by prophecies of forgiveness.

13:4–6 When abundant possessions made Israel feel self-sufficient, it turned its back on God and forgot him. Self-sufficiency is as destructive today as it was in Hosea's time. Do you see your constant need of God's presence and help? Learn to rely on God both in good times and bad. If you are traveling along a smooth and easy path right now, beware of forgetting who gave you your good fortune. Don't depend on your gifts; depend on the Giver. See Deuteronomy 6:10–12 and 8:7–20 for God's warning.

13:11 God had warned Israel that kings would cause more problems than they would solve, and he reluctantly gave them Saul as their first king (1 Samuel 8:4–22). The second king, David, was a good king, and Solomon, David's son, had his strengths. But after the nation divided in two, the northern kingdom never had another good ruler. Evil kings led the nation deeper into idolatry and unwise political alliances. Eventually the evil kings destroyed

the nation; with Hoshea, the northern kingdom's kings were cut off (2 Kings 17:1–6).

13:12 Ephraim's (Israel's) sins were recorded for later punishment. All our sins are known and will be revealed at the day of judgment (2 Corinthians 5:10; Revelation 20:11–15). How will you live differently today knowing that everything you do will be revealed at the day of judgment?

13 Pains as of a woman in childbirth[h] come to him,
    but he is a child without wisdom;
when the time arrives,
    he does not come to the opening of the womb.

14 "I will ransom them from the power of the grave[a];[i]
    I will redeem them from death.
Where, O death, are your plagues?
    Where, O grave,[a] is your destruction?[j]

"I will have no compassion,
15   even though he thrives[k] among his brothers.
An east wind[l] from the LORD will come,
    blowing in from the desert;
his spring will fail
    and his well dry up.
His storehouse will be plundered[m]
    of all its treasures.

16 The people of Samaria must bear their guilt,[n]
    because they have rebelled against their God.
They will fall by the sword;
    their little ones will be dashed[o] to the ground,
    their pregnant women[p] ripped open."

Repentance to Bring Blessing

14 Return, O Israel, to the LORD your God.
    Your sins have been your downfall!
2 Take words with you
    and return to the LORD.
Say to him:
    "Forgive all our sins
and receive us graciously,[q]
    that we may offer the fruit of our lips.[b][r]

3 Assyria cannot save us;
    we will not mount war-horses.
We will never again say 'Our gods'[s]
    to what our own hands have made,
    for in you the fatherless[t] find compassion."

4 "I will heal their waywardness
    and love them freely,[u]
    for my anger has turned away from them.
5 I will be like the dew to Israel;
    he will blossom like a lily.
Like a cedar of Lebanon[v]
    he will send down his roots;

13:13	
[h] Mic 4:9-10	
13:14	
[i] Eze 37:12-13	
[j] 1Co 15:55*	
13:15	
[k] Hos 10:1	
[l] Eze 19:12	
[m] Jer 20:5	
13:16	
[n] Hos 10:2	
[o] Hos 10:14	
[p] 2Ki 15:16	
14:2	
[q] Mic 7:18-19	
[r] Heb 13:15	
14:3	
[s] Hos 8:6	
[t] Ps 10:14	
14:4	
[u] Zep 3:17	
14:5	
[v] Isa 35:2	

a 14 Hebrew *Sheol*   b 2 Or *offer our lips as sacrifices of bulls*

13:14 The apostle Paul used this passage to teach the resurrection of our bodies from death (1 Corinthians 15:55). For those who have trusted in Christ for deliverance from sin, death holds no threat of annihilation.

14:1ff Verses 1–3 are Hosea's call to repent. Verses 4–8 are God's promise of restoration. God had to punish Israel for its gross and repeated violations of his law, but he would do so with a heavy heart. What God really wanted to do was restore the nation and make it prosper.

14:1, 2 The people could return to God by asking him to forgive their sins. The same is true for us: we can pray Hosea's prayer and know our sins are forgiven because Christ died for them on the cross (John 3:16).
Forgiveness begins when we see the destructiveness of sin

and the futility of life without God. Then we must admit we cannot save ourselves; our only hope is in God's mercy. When we request forgiveness, we must recognize that we do not deserve it and therefore cannot demand it. Our appeal must be for God's love and mercy, not for his justice. Although we cannot demand forgiveness, we can be confident that we have received it because God is gracious and loving and wants to restore us to himself, just as he wanted to restore Israel.

14:3–8 When our will is weak, when our thinking is confused, and when our conscience is burdened with a load of guilt, we must remember that God cares for us continually; his compassion never fails. When friends and family desert us, when coworkers don't understand us, and when we are tired of being good, God's compassion never fails. When we can't see the way

14:6
wSS 4:11

6   his young shoots will grow.
        His splendor will be like an olive tree,
            his fragrance like a cedar of Lebanon.w

14:7
xPs 91:1-4
yEze 17:23

7   Men will dwell again in his shade.x
        He will flourish like the grain.
    He will blossom like a vine,
        and his fame will be like the wine from Lebanon.y
8   O Ephraim, what more have Ia to do with idols?
        I will answer him and care for him.
    I am like a green pine tree;
        your fruitfulness comes from me."

14:9
zPr 10:29; Isa 1:28
aIsa 26:7

9   Who is wise? He will realize these things.
        Who is discerning? He will understand them.z
    The ways of the LORD are right;
        the righteous walka in them,
        but the rebellious stumble in them.

a8 Or *What more has Ephraim*

---

or seem to hear God's voice, and when we lack courage to go on, God's compassion never fails. When our shortcomings and our awareness of our sins overcome us, God's compassion never fails.

14:9 Hosea closes with an appeal to listen, learn, and benefit from God's word. To those receiving the Lord's message through Hosea, this meant the difference between life and death. For you, the reader of the book of Hosea, the choice is similar: either listen to the book's message and follow God's ways, or refuse to walk along the Lord's path. But people who insist on following their own direction without God's guidance are "like deep darkness; they do not know what makes them stumble" (Proverbs 4:19).

If you are lost, you can find the way by turning from your sin and following God.

14:9 God's concern for *justice* that requires faithfulness and *love* that offers forgiveness can be seen in his dealings with Hosea. We can err by forgetting God's love and feeling that our sins are hopeless, but we can also err by forgetting his wrath against our sins and thinking he will continue to accept us no matter how we act. *Forgiveness* is a key word: when God forgives us, he judges the sin but shows mercy to the sinner. We should never be afraid to come to God for a clean slate and a renewed life.

JOEL

VITAL STATISTICS

PURPOSE:
To warn Judah of God's impending judgment because of its sins and to urge the people to turn back to God

AUTHOR:
Joel son of Pethuel

ORIGINAL AUDIENCE:
The people of Judah (the southern kingdom)

DATE WRITTEN:
Probably during the time Joel may have prophesied, from approximately 835–796 B.C.

SETTING:
The people of Judah had become prosperous and complacent. Taking God for granted, they had turned to self-centeredness, idolatry, and sin. Joel warned them that this kind of life-style would inevitably bring God's judgment.

KEY VERSES:
"'Even now,' declares the LORD, 'return to me with all your heart, with fasting and weeping and mourning.' Rend your heart and not your garments. Return to the LORD, your God, for he is gracious and compassionate, slow to anger and abounding in love, and relents from sending calamity" (2:12, 13).

KEY PEOPLE:
Joel, the people of Judah

KEY PLACE:
Jerusalem

A SINGLE bomb devastates a city, and the world is ushered into the nuclear age. A split atom—power and force such as we had never seen.

At a launch site, rockets roar and a payload is thrust into space. Discoveries dreamed of for centuries are ours as we begin to explore the edge of the universe.

Volcanos, earthquakes, tidal waves, hurricanes, and tornados unleash uncontrollable and unstoppable force. And we can only avoid them and then pick up the pieces.

Power, strength, might—we stand in awe at the natural and human-made display. But these forces cannot touch the power of omnipotent God. Creator of galaxies, atoms, and natural laws, the Sovereign Lord rules all there is and ever will be. How silly to live without him; how foolish to run and hide from him; how ridiculous to disobey him. But we do. Since Eden, we have sought independence from his control, as though we were gods and could plot our destiny. And he has allowed our rebellion. But soon *the day of the Lord* will come.

It is about this day that the prophet Joel speaks, and it is the theme of his book. On this day God will judge all unrighteousness and disobedience—all accounts will be settled and the crooked made straight.

We know very little about Joel—only that he was a prophet and the son of Pethuel. He may have lived in Jerusalem because his audience was Judah, the southern kingdom. Whoever he was, Joel speaks forthrightly and forcefully in this short and powerful book. His message is one of foreboding and warning, but it is also filled with hope. Joel states that our Creator, the omnipotent Judge, is also merciful, and he wants to bless all those who trust him.

Joel begins by describing a terrible plague of locusts that covers the land and devours the crops. The devastation wrought by these creatures is but a foretaste of the coming judgment of God, the "day of the LORD." Joel, therefore, urges the people to turn from their sin and turn back to God. Woven into this message of judgment and the need for repentance is an affirmation of God's kindness and the blessings he promises for all who follow him. In fact, "everyone who calls on the name of the LORD will be saved" (2:32).

As you read Joel, catch his vision of the power and might of God and of God's ultimate judgment of sin. Choose to follow, obey, and worship God alone as your sovereign Lord.

Jehoahaz
becomes
king of
Israel
814

Jehoash   Joel's
becomes   ministry
king of   ends
Israel   796?
798

THE BLUEPRINT

1. The day of the locusts
   (1:1—2:27)
2. The day of the LORD
   (2:28—3:21)

The locust plague was only a foretaste of the judgment to come in the day of the Lord. This is a timeless call to repentance with the promise of blessing. Just as the people faced the tragedy of their crops being destroyed, we, too, will face tragic judgment if we live in sin. But God's grace is available to us both now and in that coming day.

MEGATHEMES

THEME	EXPLANATION	IMPORTANCE
Punishment	Like a destroying army of locusts, God's punishment for sin is overwhelming, dreadful, and unavoidable. When it comes, there will be no food, no water, no protection, and no escape. The day for settling accounts with God for how we have lived is fast approaching.	God is the one with whom we all must reckon—not nature, the economy, or a foreign invader. We can't ignore or offend God forever. We must pay attention to his message now, or we will face his anger later.
Forgiveness	God stood ready to forgive and restore all those who would come to him and turn away from sin. God wanted to shower his people with his love and restore them to a proper relationship with him.	Forgiveness comes by turning from sin and turning toward God. It is not too late to receive God's forgiveness. God's greatest desire is for you to come to him.
Promise of the Holy Spirit	Joel predicts the time when God will pour out his Holy Spirit on all people. It will be the beginning of new and fresh worship of God by those who believe in him, as well as the beginning of judgment on all who reject him.	God is in control. Justice and restoration are in his hands. The Holy Spirit confirms God's love for us just as he did for the first Christians (Acts 2). We must be faithful to God and place our life under the guidance and power of his Holy Spirit.

1. The day of the locusts

1 The word of the LORD that came[a] to Joel son of Pethuel.

1:1
[a] Jer 1:2

An Invasion of Locusts

2 Hear this,[b] you elders;
   listen, all who live in the land.
Has anything like this ever happened in your days
   or in the days of your forefathers?[c]
3 Tell it to your children,
   and let your children tell it to their children,
   and their children to the next generation.
4 What the locust swarm has left
   the great locusts have eaten;

1:2
[b] Hos 5:1
[c] Joel 2:2

1:1 Joel was a prophet to the nation of Judah, also known as the southern kingdom. Although the 12 tribes of Israel had been united under David and Solomon, after Solomon's death, the kingdom had divided into two parts. Two of the tribes—Judah and Benjamin—stayed loyal to David's line and accepted Solomon's son Rehoboam as king. They became the southern kingdom, also called Judah (after the larger tribe). The other ten tribes followed Jeroboam, set up a new kingdom with a new capital at Samaria, and called themselves Israel or the northern kingdom.

The book does not mention when Joel lived, but many believe that he prophesied during the reign of King Joash (835–796 B.C.). But the date of Joel's book is not nearly so important as its timeless message: sin brings God's judgment; yet with God's justice there is also great mercy.

1:3 God urged parents to pass their history down to their children, telling over and over the important lessons they learned. One of the greatest gifts you can give younger people is your life's story to help them repeat your successes and avoid your mistakes.

what the great locusts have left
　　the young locusts have eaten;
what the young locusts have left
　　other locusts[a] have eaten.[d]

5 Wake up, you drunkards, and weep!
　　Wail, all you drinkers of wine;[e]
wail because of the new wine,
　　for it has been snatched from your lips.

6 A nation has invaded my land,
　　powerful and without number;
it has the teeth[f] of a lion,
　　the fangs of a lioness.

7 It has laid waste[g] my vines
　　and ruined my fig trees.
It has stripped off their bark
　　and thrown it away,
　　　leaving their branches white.

8 Mourn like a virgin[b] in sackcloth[h]
　　grieving for the husband[c] of her youth.

9 Grain offerings and drink offerings
　　are cut off from the house of the Lord.
The priests are in mourning,
　　those who minister before the Lord.

10 The fields are ruined,
　　the ground is dried up[d];[i]
the grain is destroyed,
　　the new wine is dried up,
　　the oil fails.

11 Despair, you farmers,
　　wail, you vine growers;
grieve for the wheat and the barley,
　　because the harvest of the field is destroyed.[j]

12 The vine is dried up
　　and the fig tree is withered;
the pomegranate, the palm and the apple tree—
　　all the trees of the field—are dried up.
Surely the joy of mankind
　　is withered away.

A Call to Repentance

13 Put on sackcloth,[k] O priests, and mourn;
　　wail, you who minister before the altar.
Come, spend the night in sackcloth,
　　you who minister before my God;
for the grain offerings and drink offerings
　　are withheld from the house of your God.

1:4
[d] Dt 28:39; Na 3:15
1:5
[e] Joel 3:3
1:6
[f] Rev 9:8
1:7
[g] Isa 5:6
1:8
[h] Isa 22:12
1:10
[i] Isa 24:4
1:11
[j] Isa 17:11
1:13
[k] Jer 4:8

---

a 4 The precise meaning of the four Hebrew words used here for locusts is uncertain.　b 8 Or young woman
c 8 Or betrothed　d 10 Or ground mourns

1:4 A locust plague can be as devastating as an invading army. Locusts gather in swarms too great to number (1:6) and fly several feet above the ground, seeming to darken the sun as they pass by (2:2). When they land, they devour almost every piece of vegetation (1:7–12), covering and entering everything in their path (2:9).

1:4 Joel's detailed description has caused many to believe that he was referring to an actual locust plague that had come or was about to come upon the land. Another view is that the locusts symbolize an invading enemy army. Both may be foreseen. The locusts represent devastation, and Joel's point was that God would punish the people because of their sin. Joel calls this judgment the "day of the Lord" (see the note on 1:15).

1:5 The people's physical and moral senses were dulled, making them oblivious to sin. Joel called them to awaken from their complacency and admit their sins before it was too late. Otherwise, everything would be destroyed, even the grapes that caused their drunkenness. Our times of peace and prosperity can lull us to sleep. We must never let material abundance hinder our spiritual readiness.

1:9 Because of the devastation, there was no grain to make fine flour for the grain offerings and no wine for the drink offerings (see Leviticus 1 and 2 for a detailed explanation of these offerings).

1:13 Sackcloth is the clothing put on by mourners at a funeral. Used here, it would be a sign of repentance.

1:14
l 2Ch 20:3

14 Declare a holy fast;*l*
　　call a sacred assembly.
　Summon the elders
　　and all who live in the land
　to the house of the LORD your God,
　　and cry out to the LORD.

1:15
m Jer 30:7
n Joel 2:1, 11, 31

15 Alas for that*m* day!
　　For the day of the LORD*n* is near;
　it will come like destruction from the Almighty.*a*

1:16
o Dt 12:7

16 Has not the food been cut off
　　before our very eyes—
　joy and gladness
　　from the house of our God?*o*

1:17
p Isa 17:10-11

17 The seeds are shriveled
　　beneath the clods.*b**p*
　The storehouses are in ruins,
　　the granaries have been broken down,
　　for the grain has dried up.

18 How the cattle moan!
　　The herds mill about
　because they have no pasture;
　　even the flocks of sheep are suffering.

1:19
q Ps 50:15
r Jer 9:10

19 To you, O LORD, I call,*q*
　　for fire has devoured the open pastures*r*
　and flames have burned up all the trees of the field.

1:20
s Ps 104:21
t 1Ki 17:7

20 Even the wild animals pant for you;*s*
　　the streams of water have dried up*t*
　and fire has devoured the open pastures.

An Army of Locusts

2 Blow the trumpet in Zion;
　　sound the alarm on my holy hill.
　Let all who live in the land tremble,

a 15 Hebrew *Shaddai*　**b** 17 The meaning of the Hebrew for this word is uncertain.

JOEL
served as a
prophet to
Judah, possibly
from 835–
796 B.C.

Climate of the times	Wicked Queen Athaliah seized power in a bloody coup but was overthrown after a few years. Joash was crowned king, but he was only seven years old and in great need of spiritual guidance. Joash followed God in his early years but then turned away from him.
Main message	A plague of locusts had come to discipline the nation. Joel called the people to turn back to God before an even greater judgment occurred.
Importance of message	God judges all people for their sins, but he is merciful to those who turn to him and offers them eternal salvation.

1:14 A fast was a period of time when no food was eaten and people approached God with humility, sorrow for sin, and urgent prayer. In the Old Testament, people often would fast during times of calamity in order to focus their attention on God and to demonstrate their change of heart and their true devotion (see, for example, Judges 20:26; 1 Kings 21:27; Ezra 8:21; Jonah 3:5). The sacred assembly was a public religious gathering called so that everyone could repent and pray to God for mercy.

1:15 The "day of the LORD" is a common phrase in the Old Testament and in the book of Joel (see 2:1, 11, 31; 3:14). It always refers to some extraordinary happening, whether a present event (like a locust plague), an event in the near future (like the destruction of Jerusalem or the defeat of enemy nations), or the final period of history when God will defeat all the forces of evil.
　Even when the day of the Lord refers to a present event, it also foreshadows the *final* day of the Lord. This final event of history has two aspects to it: (1) the last judgment on all evil and sin and (2) the final reward for faithful believers. Righteousness and truth will prevail, but not before much suffering (Zechariah 14:1–3). If you trust the Lord, looking toward this final day should give you hope, because then all who are faithful will be united forever with God.

1:15–19 Without God, destruction is sure. Those who have not personally accepted God's love and forgiveness will stand before him with no appeal. Be sure to call on God's love and mercy while you have the opportunity (2:32).

2:1ff Joel was still describing the devastating effects of the locust plague (see 2:25). The alarm showed that the crisis was at hand. However, Joel implied that the locust plague would be only the forerunner of an even greater crisis if the people didn't turn from their sins.

for the day of the LORD[u] is coming.
It is close at hand—
2   a day of darkness[v] and gloom,
     a day of clouds and blackness.
Like dawn spreading across the mountains
     a large and mighty army[w] comes,
such as never was of old
     nor ever will be in ages to come.

3 Before them fire devours,
     behind them a flame blazes.
Before them the land is like the garden of Eden,
     behind them, a desert waste[x]—
     nothing escapes them.
4 They have the appearance of horses;[y]
     they gallop along like cavalry.
5 With a noise like that of chariots[z]
     they leap over the mountaintops,
like a crackling fire consuming stubble,
     like a mighty army drawn up for battle.

6 At the sight of them, nations are in anguish;
     every face turns pale.
7 They charge like warriors;
     they scale walls like soldiers.
They all march in line,
     not swerving from their course.
8 They do not jostle each other;
     each marches straight ahead.
They plunge through defenses
     without breaking ranks.
9 They rush upon the city;
     they run along the wall.
They climb into the houses;
     like thieves they enter through the windows.[a]

10 Before them the earth shakes,[b]
     the sky trembles,
the sun and moon are darkened,
     and the stars no longer shine.
11 The LORD thunders
     at the head of his army;
his forces are beyond number,
     and mighty are those who obey his command.
The day of the LORD is great;
     it is dreadful.
     Who can endure it?

Rend Your Heart

12 "Even now," declares the LORD,
     "return[c] to me with all your heart,
     with fasting and weeping and mourning."

13 Rend your heart
     and not your garments.[d]
Return to the LORD your God,
     for he is gracious and compassionate,

Cross references
2:1 [u] Zep 1:14-16
2:2 [v] Am 5:18 [w] Joel 1:6
2:3 [x] Ps 105:34-35
2:4 [y] Rev 9:7
2:5 [z] Rev 9:9
2:9 [a] Jer 9:21
2:10 [b] Ps 18:7
2:12 [c] Hos 12:6
2:13 [d] Job 1:20

2:3 The Garden of Eden was Adam and Eve's first home (Genesis 2:8). Known for its beauty, here it is used to describe the beauty of the land prior to the devastation.
2:12, 13 God told the people to turn to him while there was still time. Destruction would soon be upon them. Time is also running out for us. Because we don't know when our lives will end, we should trust and obey God now, while we can. Don't let anything hold you back from turning to him.

2:13
e Ex 34:6

slow to anger and abounding in love,e
and he relents from sending calamity.

2:14
f Hag 2:19
g Joel 1:13

14 Who knows? He may turn and have pity
and leave behind a blessinga—
grain offerings and drink offeringsg
for the LORD your God.

2:15
h Nu 10:2

15 Blow the trumpeth in Zion,
declare a holy fast,
call a sacred assembly.
16 Gather the people,
consecrate the assembly;
bring together the elders,
gather the children,
those nursing at the breast.
Let the bridegroom leave his room
and the bride her chamber.

2:17
i Eze 8:16
j Ps 44:13
k Ps 42:3

17 Let the priests, who minister before the LORD,
weep between the temple porch and the altar.i
Let them say, "Spare your people, O LORD.
Do not make your inheritance an object of scorn,j
a byword among the nations.
Why should they say among the peoples,
'Where is their God?k'"

The LORD's Answer

2:18
l Zec 1:14

18 Then the LORD will be jealousl for his land
and take pity on his people.

2:19
m Eze 34:29

19 The LORD will replya to them:

"I am sending you grain, new wine and oil,
enough to satisfy you fully;
never again will I make you
an object of scornm to the nations.

2:20
n Jer 1:14-15
o Isa 34:3

20 "I will drive the northern armyn far from you,
pushing it into a parched and barren land,
with its front columns going into the eastern seab
and those in the rear into the western sea.c
And its stencho will go up;
its smell will rise."

Surely he has done great things.d
21 Be not afraid, O land;
be glad and rejoice.
Surely the LORD has done great things.

2:22
p Ps 65:12

22 Be not afraid, O wild animals,
for the open pastures are becoming green.p
The trees are bearing their fruit;

---

a 18,19 Or LORD was jealous . . . / and took pity . . . / 19 The LORD replied   b 20 That is, the Dead Sea   c 20 That is, the
Mediterranean   d 20 Or rise. / Surely it has done great things."

2:13 Deep remorse was often shown by tearing (rending) one's clothes. But God didn't want an outward display of penitence without true inward repentance (1 Samuel 16:7; Matthew 23:1–36). Be sure your attitude toward God is correct, not just your outward actions.

2:18 Joel reached a turning point in his prophecy, moving from prophesying about an outpouring of God's judgment to prophesying about an outpouring of God's forgiveness and blessing. But this would come only if the people began to live as God wanted them to, giving up their sins. Where there is repentance, there is hope. This section of the book feeds that hope. Without it, Joel's

prophecy could bring only despair. This promise of forgiveness should have encouraged the people to repent.

2:20 Joel foresaw the invasion from the north by the armies of Assyria and Babylon, typified by the locusts.

2:21 Joel contrasts the fear of God's judgment (2:1) with the joy of God's intervention (2:21). On the day of the Lord, sin will bring judgment, and only God's forgiveness will bring rejoicing. Unless you repent, your sin will result in punishment. Let God intervene in your life. Then you will be able to rejoice in that day because you will have nothing to fear. Before, there were fasting, plagues, and funeral dirges; then, there will be feasting, harvesting, and the fig tree and the vine yield their riches.

23 Be glad, O people of Zion,
    rejoice[q] in the LORD your God,
  for he has given you
    the autumn rains in righteousness.[a]
He sends you abundant showers,
    both autumn and spring rains, as before.
24 The threshing floors will be filled with grain;
    the vats will overflow[r] with new wine and oil.

25 "I will repay you for the years the locusts have eaten—
    the great locust and the young locust,
    the other locusts and the locust swarm[b]—
  my great army that I sent among you.
26 You will have plenty to eat, until you are full,[s]
    and you will praise the name of the LORD your God,
    who has worked wonders[t] for you;
  never again will my people be shamed.
27 Then you will know that I am in Israel,
    that I am the LORD[u] your God,
    and that there is no other;
  never again will my people be shamed.

2. The day of the LORD

28 "And afterward,
    I will pour out my Spirit[v] on all people.
Your sons and daughters will prophesy,
    your old men will dream dreams,
    your young men will see visions.
29 Even on my servants,[w] both men and women,
    I will pour out my Spirit in those days.
30 I will show wonders in the heavens[x]
    and on the earth,[y]
    blood and fire and billows of smoke.
31 The sun will be turned to darkness
    and the moon to blood
    before the coming of the great and dreadful day of the LORD.[z]
32 And everyone who calls
    on the name of the LORD will be saved;[a]
for on Mount Zion[b] and in Jerusalem
    there will be deliverance,
    as the LORD has said,
among the survivors[c]
    whom the LORD calls.

2:23 [q]Isa 41:16; Hab 3:18

2:24 [r]Mal 3:10

2:26 [s]Lev 26:5 [t]Isa 25:1

2:27 [u]Joel 3:17

2:28 [v]Eze 39:29

2:29 [w]1Co 12:13; Gal 3:28

2:30 [x]Lk 21:11 [y]Mk 13:24-25

2:31 [z]Mal 4:1, 5

2:32 [a]Ro 10:13* [b]Isa 46:13 [c]Mic 4:7; Ro 9:27

a23 Or / the teacher for righteousness: b25 The precise meaning of the four Hebrew words used here for locusts is uncertain.

---

songs of praise. When God rules, his restoration will be complete. In the meantime, we must remember that God does not promise that all his followers will be prosperous now. When God pardons, he restores our relationship with him, but this does not guarantee individual wealth. Instead, God promises to meet the deepest needs of those who love him—by loving us, forgiving us, giving us purpose in life, and giving us a caring Christian community.

2:26, 27 If the Jews would never again experience a disaster like this locust plague ("never again will my people be shamed"), how do we explain the captivity in Babylon, the Jews' slavery under the Greeks and Romans, and their persecution under Hitler? It is important not to take these verses out of context. This is still part of the "blessings" section of Joel's prophecy. Only if the people truly repented would they avoid a disaster like the one Joel had described. God's blessings are promised only to those who

sincerely and consistently follow him. God does promise that after the final day of judgment, his people will never again experience this kind of disaster (Zechariah 14:9–11; Revelation 21).

2:28–32 Peter quoted this passage (see Acts 2:16–21)—the outpouring of the Spirit predicted by Joel occurred on Pentecost. While in the past, God's Spirit seemed available to kings, prophets, and judges, Joel envisioned a time when the Spirit would be available to every believer. Ezekiel also spoke of an outpouring of the Spirit (Ezekiel 39:28, 29). God's Spirit is available now to anyone who calls on the Lord (2:32).

2:30 These "wonders" would give a hint or a picture of a coming event.

2:31, 32 The "day of the LORD" is used here as God's appointed time to judge the nations (see the note on 1:15). Judgment and mercy go hand in hand. Joel had said that if the people repented,

The Nations Judged

3
"In those days and at that time,
  when I restore the fortunes of Judah and Jerusalem,
2 I will gather all nations
  and bring them down to the Valley of Jehoshaphat.ᵃ
There I will enter into judgment*d* against them
  concerning my inheritance, my people Israel,
for they scattered my people among the nations
  and divided up my land.
3 They cast lots for my people
  and traded boys for prostitutes;
they sold girls for wine
  that they might drink.

4 "Now what have you against me, O Tyre and Sidon and all you regions of Philistia? Are you repaying me for something I have done? If you are paying me back, I will swiftly and speedily return on your own heads what you have done. 5 For you took my silver and my gold and carried off my finest treasures to your temples. *e* 6 You sold the people of Judah and Jerusalem to the Greeks, that you might send them far from their homeland.

7 "See, I am going to rouse them out of the places to which you sold them,*f* and I will return on your own heads what you have done. 8 I will sell your sons and daughters to the people of Judah, and they will sell them to the Sabeans, a nation far away." The LORD has spoken.

9 Proclaim this among the nations:
  Prepare for war!
Rouse the warriors!
Let all the fighting men draw near and attack.
10 Beat your plowshares into swords
  and your pruning hooks*g* into spears.
Let the weakling*h* say,
  "I am strong!"
11 Come quickly, all you nations from every side,
  and assemble there.

Bring down your warriors,*i* O LORD!

12 "Let the nations be roused;
  let them advance into the Valley of Jehoshaphat,
for there I will sit
  to judge*j* all the nations on every side.

ᵃ*2 Jehoshaphat* means *the LORD judges*; also in verse 12.

3:2
*d*Eze 36:5

3:5
*e*2Ch 21:16-17

3:7
*f*Isa 43:5-6;
Jer 23:8

3:10
*g*Isa 2:4; Mic 4:3
*h*Zec 12:8

3:11
*i*Isa 13:3

3:12
*j*Isa 2:4

---

the Lord would save them from judgment (2:12–14). In this day of judgment and catastrophe, therefore, some will be saved. God's intention is not to destroy but to heal and to save. However, we must accept his salvation or we will certainly perish with the unrepentant.

3:1, 2 The phrase "at that time" refers to the time when those who call on the Lord will be saved (2:32). God will not only bless believers with everything they need; he will also bless them by destroying all evil and ending the pain and suffering on earth. This prophecy had three fulfillments: immediate, ongoing, and final. Its immediate interpretation could apply to King Jehoshaphat's recent battle against several enemy nations, including Moab and Ammon (2 Chronicles 20). Its ongoing fulfillment could be the partial restoration of the people to their land after the exile to Babylon. The final fulfillment will come in the great battle that precedes the Messiah's reign over the earth (Revelation 20:7–9).

3:2 The geographic location of the Valley of Jehoshaphat is not known, and some suggest it is being used as a symbol for the place where the Lord is to judge. Some think it may be a future valley created by the splitting of the Mount of Olives when the Messiah returns (Zechariah 14:4). The most important fact for us is that the name means "the LORD judges."

3:4 Tyre and Sidon were major cities in Phoenicia to the northwest of Israel; Philistia was the nation southwest of Judah. Phoenicia and Philistia were small countries who rejoiced at the fall of Judah and Israel because they would benefit from the increased trade. God would judge them for their wrong attitude.

3:6 Jews were sold to Greeks, a pagan and unclean people. Some think this verse and 3:1 indicate that Joel lived after the captivity in Babylon (586 B.C.), when the Greek culture began to flourish. But archaeological studies have shown that the Greeks were trading with Phoenicia as early as 800 B.C. Also 3:4 mentions Tyre, Sidon, and Philistia. These places were contemporary with Judah before their captivity.

3:8 The Sabeans came from Sheba, a nation in southwestern Arabia. One of Sheba's queens had visited Solomon over a century earlier (1 Kings 10:1–13). The Sabeans controlled the eastern trade routes.

13 Swing the sickle,
        for the harvest[k] is ripe.
   Come, trample the grapes,
        for the winepress[l] is full
        and the vats overflow—
   so great is their wickedness!"

14 Multitudes, multitudes
        in the valley of decision!
   For the day of the LORD[m] is near
        in the valley of decision.
15 The sun and moon will be darkened,
        and the stars no longer shine.
16 The LORD will roar from Zion
        and thunder from Jerusalem;[n]
        the earth and the sky will tremble.
   But the LORD will be a refuge for his people,
        a stronghold for the people of Israel.

Blessings for God's People

17 "Then you will know that I, the LORD your God,
        dwell in Zion, my holy hill.
   Jerusalem will be holy;
        never again will foreigners invade her.

18 "In that day the mountains will drip new wine,
        and the hills will flow with milk;
        all the ravines of Judah will run with water.[o]
   A fountain will flow out of the LORD's house
        and will water the valley of acacias.[a]
19 But Egypt will be desolate,
        Edom a desert waste,
   because of violence done to the people of Judah,
        in whose land they shed innocent blood.
20 Judah will be inhabited forever[p]
        and Jerusalem through all generations.
21 Their bloodguilt, which I have not pardoned,
        I will pardon."

                The LORD dwells in Zion!

3:13
[k] Rev 14:15-19
[l] Rev 14:20

3:14
[m] Joel 1:15

3:16
[n] Am 1:2

3:18
[o] Isa 30:25

3:20
[p] Am 9:15

a 18 Or *Valley of Shittim*

3:14 Joel described multitudes waiting in the "valley of decision" (the valley of judgment of verses 2 and 12). Billions of people have lived on earth, and every one of them—dead, living, and yet to be born—will face judgment. Look around you. See your friends, those with whom you work and live. Have they received God's forgiveness? Have they been warned about sin's consequences? If we understand the severity of God's final judgment, we will want to take God's offer of hope to those we know.

3:17 The last word will be God's; his ultimate sovereignty will be revealed in the end. We cannot predict when that end will come, but we can have confidence in his control over the world's events. The world's history, as well as our own pilgrimage, is in God's hands. We can be secure in his love and trust him to guide our decisions.

3:18 The picture of this restored land is one of perfect beauty, similar to the Garden of Eden. The life-giving fountain flowing from the Lord's house illustrates the blessings that come from God. Those who attach themselves to him will be forever fruitful. (See also Ezekiel 47:1–12; Revelation 22:1, 2.)

3:19 Egypt and Edom were two of Israel's most persistent enemies. They represent all the nations hostile to God's people. God's promise that they would be destroyed is also a promise that all evil in the world will one day be destroyed.

3:20, 21 The word *Judah* is used here to refer to all God's people—anyone who has called on the name of the Lord. There is full assurance of victory and peace for those who trust in God (2:32).

3:21 Joel began with a prophecy about the destruction of the land and ended with a prophecy about its restoration. He began by stressing the need for repentance and ended with the promise of forgiveness that repentance brings. Joel was trying to convince the people to wake up (1:5), get rid of their complacency, and realize the danger of living apart from God. His message to us is that there is still time; anyone who calls on God's name can be saved (2:12–14, 32). Those who turn to God will enjoy the blessings mentioned in Joel's prophecy; those who refuse will face destruction.

AMOS

| Jeroboam II becomes king of Israel 793 B.C. | | Amos becomes a prophet to Israel 760 | Hosea becomes a prophet to Israel 753 | King Shallum of Israel is assassinated 752 | Amos's ministry ends 750 | Isaiah becomes a prophet to Judah 740 |

WHEN we hear, "He's a man of God," we think of some famous evangelist, a "Reverend," a missionary, or the campus minister—professionals, Christian workers, those who preach and teach the Word as a vocation.

Surely Amos was a man of God, a person whose life was devoted to serving the Lord and whose life-style reflected this devotion—but he was a layperson. Herding sheep and tending sycamore-fig trees in the Judean countryside, Amos was not the son of a prophet; he was not the son of a priest. As a humble shepherd, he could have stayed in Tekoa, doing his job, providing for his family, and worshiping his God. But God gave Amos a vision of the future (1:1) and told him to take his message to Israel, the northern kingdom (7:15). Amos obeyed and thus proved he was a man of God.

Amos's message has impacted God's people throughout the centuries, and it needs to be heard today by individuals and nations. Though divided from their southern brothers and sisters in Judah, the northern Israelites were still God's people. But they were living beneath a pious veneer of religion, worshiping idols and oppressing the poor. Amos, a fiery, fearless, and honest shepherd from the south, confronted them with their sin and warned them of the impending judgment.

The book of Amos opens with this humble shepherd watching his sheep. God then gave him a vision of what was about to happen to the nation of Israel. God condemned all the nations who had sinned against him and harmed his people. Beginning with Aram, he moved quickly through Philistia, Tyre, Edom, Ammon, and Moab. All were condemned, and we can almost hear the Israelites shouting, "Amen!" And then, even Judah, Amos's homeland, was included in God's scathing denunciation (2:4, 5). How Amos's listeners must have enjoyed hearing those words! Suddenly, however, Amos turned to the people of Israel and pronounced God's judgment on *them*. The next four chapters enumerate and describe their sins. It is no wonder that Amaziah the priest intervened and tried to stop the preaching (7:10–13). Fearlessly, Amos continued to relate the visions of future judgment that God gave to him (chapters 8—9). After all the chapters on judgment, the book concludes with a message of hope. Eventually God will restore his people and make them great again (9:8–15).

As you read Amos's book, put yourself in the place of those Israelites and listen to God's message. Have you grown complacent? Have other concerns taken God's place in your life? Do you ignore those in need or oppress the poor? Picture yourself as Amos, faithfully doing what God calls you to do. You, too, can be God's person. Listen for his clear call and do what he says, wherever it leads.

VITAL STATISTICS

PURPOSE:
To pronounce God's judgment upon Israel, the northern kingdom, for its complacency, idolatry, and oppression of the poor

AUTHOR:
Amos

ORIGINAL AUDIENCE:
The people of Israel (the northern kingdom)

DATE WRITTEN:
Probably during the reigns of Jeroboam II of Israel and Uzziah (Azariah) of Judah (approximately 760–750 B.C.)

SETTING:
The wealthy people of Israel were enjoying peace and prosperity. They were quite complacent and were oppressing the poor, even selling them into slavery. Soon, however, Israel would be conquered by Assyria, and the rich would themselves become slaves.

KEY VERSE:
"But let justice roll on like a river, righteousness like a never-failing stream!" (5:24).

KEY PEOPLE:
Amos, Amaziah, Jeroboam II

KEY PLACES:
Bethel, Samaria

SPECIAL FEATURES:
Amos uses striking metaphors from his shepherding and farming experience—a loaded cart (2:13), a roaring lion (3:8), a mutilated sheep (3:12), pampered cows (4:1), and a basket of fruit (8:1, 2).

THE BLUEPRINT

1. Announcement of judgment
   (1:1—2:16)
2. Reasons for judgment
   (3:1—6:14)
3. Visions of judgment
   (7:1—9:15)

Amos speaks with brutal frankness in denouncing sin. He collided with the false religious leaders of his day and was not intimidated by priest or king. He continued to speak his message boldly. God requires truth and goodness, justice and righteousness, from all people and nations today as well. Many of the conditions in Israel during Amos's time are evident in today's society. We need Amos's courage to ignore danger and stand against sin.

MEGATHEMES

THEME	EXPLANATION	IMPORTANCE
Everyone Answers to God	Amos pronounced judgment from God on all the surrounding nations. Then he included Judah and Israel. God is in supreme control of all the nations. Everyone is accountable to him.	All people will have to account for their sin. When those who reject God seem to get ahead, don't envy their prosperity or feel sorry for yourself. Remember that we all must answer to God for how we live.
Complacency	Everyone was optimistic, business was booming, and people were happy (except for the poor and oppressed). With all the comfort and luxury came self-sufficiency and a false sense of security. But prosperity brought corruption and destruction.	A complacent present leads to a disastrous future. Don't congratulate yourself for the blessings and benefits you now enjoy. They are from God. If you are more satisfied with yourself than with God, remember that everything is meaningless without him. A self-sufficient attitude may be your downfall.
Oppressing the Poor	The wealthy and powerful people of Samaria, the capital of Israel, had become prosperous, greedy, and unjust. Illegal and immoral slavery came as the result of over-taxation and land-grabbing. There was also cruelty and indifference toward the poor. God is weary of greed and will not tolerate injustice.	God made all people; therefore, to ignore the poor is to ignore those whom God loves and whom Christ came to save. We must go beyond feeling bad for the poor and oppressed. We must act compassionately to stop injustice and to help care for those in need.
Superficial Religion	Although many people had abandoned real faith in God, they still pretended to be religious. They were carrying on superficial religious exercises instead of having spiritual integrity and practicing heartfelt obedience toward God.	Merely participating in ceremony or ritual falls short of true religion. God wants simple trust in him, not showy external actions. Don't settle for impressing others with external rituals when God wants heartfelt obedience and commitment.

1. Announcement of judgment

1 The words of Amos, one of the shepherds of Tekoa ^a—what he saw concerning Israel two years before the earthquake,^b when Uzziah was king of Judah and Jeroboam son of Jehoash^a was king of Israel.

    ² He said:

        "The LORD roars from Zion
           and thunders from Jerusalem;^c
        the pastures of the shepherds dry up,^b
        and the top of Carmel withers."

1:1
^a2Sa 14:2
^bZec 14:5

1:2
^cJoel 3:16

^a*1* Hebrew *Joash*, a variant of *Jehoash*   ^b*2* Or *shepherds mourn*

1:1 Amos was a shepherd and fig grower from the southern kingdom (Judah), but he prophesied to the northern kingdom (Israel). Israel was politically at the height of its power with a prosperous economy, but the nation was spiritually corrupt. Idols were worshiped throughout the land, and especially at Bethel, which was supposed to be the nation's religious center. Like Hosea, Amos was sent by God to denounce this social and religious corruption. About 30 or 40 years after Amos prophesied, Assyria destroyed the capital city, Samaria, and conquered Israel (722 B.C.). Uzziah reigned in Judah from 792–740; Jeroboam II reigned in Israel from 793–753.

1:1 Tekoa, Amos's hometown, was located in the rugged sheep country of Judah, about ten miles south of Jerusalem. Long

before Amos was born, a woman of Tekoa had helped reconcile David and his rebellious son, Absalom (2 Samuel 14:1–23).

1:1 Amos raised sheep—not a particularly "spiritual" job—yet he became a channel of God's message to others. Your job may not cause you to feel spiritual or successful, but it is a vital work if you are in the place God wants you to be. God can work through you to do extraordinary things, no matter how ordinary your occupation.

1:1 The prophet Zechariah and other historical records from this period mention an earthquake that occurred at this time (Zechariah 14:5).

1:2 In the Bible, God is often pictured as a shepherd and his people as sheep. As a shepherd, God leads and protects his flock.

Judgment on Israel's Neighbors

1:3
d Isa 8:4

³ This is what the LORD says:

"For three sins of Damascus,*d*
even for four, I will not turn back ˌmy wrathˌ.
Because she threshed Gilead
with sledges having iron teeth,

1:4
e 2Ki 6:24

⁴ I will send fire upon the house of Hazael
that will consume the fortresses of Ben-Hadad.*e*

1:5
f Jer 51:30

⁵ I will break down the gate*f* of Damascus;
I will destroy the king who is in*a* the Valley of Aven*b*
and the one who holds the scepter in Beth Eden.
The people of Aram will go into exile to Kir,"

says the LORD.

1:6
g Ob 1:11

⁶ This is what the LORD says:

"For three sins of Gaza,
even for four, I will not turn back ˌmy wrathˌ.
Because she took captive whole communities
and sold them to Edom,*g*

⁷ I will send fire upon the walls of Gaza
that will consume her fortresses.

1:8
h Eze 25:16
i Zep 2:4-7

⁸ I will destroy the king*c* of Ashdod
and the one who holds the scepter in Ashkelon.
I will turn my hand against Ekron,
till the last of the Philistines*h* is dead,"

says the Sovereign LORD.*i*

a5 Or the inhabitants of   b5 Aven means wickedness.   c8 Or inhabitants

---

AMOS
served as a
prophet to Israel
(the northern
kingdom) from
760–750 B.C.

Climate of the times	Israel was enjoying peace and economic prosperity. But this blessing had caused her to become a selfish, materialistic society. Those who were well-off ignored the needs of those less fortunate. The people were self-centered and indifferent toward God.
Main message	Amos spoke against those who exploited or ignored the needy.
Importance of message	Believing in God is more than a matter of individual faith. God calls all believers to work against injustices in society and to aid those less fortunate.
Contemporary prophets	Jonah (793–753 B.C.), Hosea (753–715 B.C.)

But here God is depicted as a ferocious lion ready to devour those who are evil or unfaithful. (See also Hosea 11:10.)

1:2 Carmel means "fertile field." It was a very fertile area. A drought capable of drying up this area would have to be quite severe.

1:3 Damascus was the capital of Aram. In the past, Aram had been one of Israel's most formidable enemies. After the defeat of Aram by Assyria in 732 B.C. (2 Kings 16:9), Damascus was no longer a real threat.

1:3—2:6 Amos pronounced God's judgment on nation after nation around Israel's borders—even Judah. Perhaps the people of Israel cheered when they heard the rebukes leveled against those nations. But then Amos proclaimed God's judgment on Israel. They could not excuse their own sin just because the sins of their neighbors seemed worse. God is no respecter of persons. He judges all people fairly and impartially.

1:3—2:6 The accusation "For three sins . . . even for four" means that these nations had sinned again and again. This phrase echoes through these verses as God evaluates nation after nation. Each nation had persistently refused to follow God's commands. A sinful practice can become a way of life. Ignoring or denying

the problem will not help us. We must begin the process of correction by confessing our sins to God and asking him to forgive us. Otherwise, we have no hope but to continue our pattern of sin.

1:4 The "house of Hazael" refers to the king of Aram. Ben-Hadad was Hazael's son (2 Kings 13:24).

1:5 The Arameans had been slaves in Kir, but here they were free (9:7). Decreeing that the Arameans should go back to Kir was like saying the Israelites should go back to Egypt as slaves (Exodus 1).

1:7, 8 Gaza, Ashdod, Ashkelon, and Ekron were four of the five major cities of Philistia, an enemy who often threatened Israel. The fifth city, Gath, had probably already been destroyed. Therefore, Amos was saying that the entire nation of Philistia would be destroyed for its sins.

9 This is what the LORD says:

> "For three sins of Tyre,*j*
> even for four, I will not turn back ⌐my wrath⌐.
> Because she sold whole communities of captives to Edom,
> disregarding a treaty of brotherhood,
> 10 I will send fire upon the walls of Tyre
> that will consume her fortresses.*k*"

1:9
l Isa 23:1-18

1:10
k Zec 9:1-4

11 This is what the LORD says:

> "For three sins of Edom,*l*
> even for four, I will not turn back ⌐my wrath⌐.
> Because he pursued his brother with a sword,
> stifling all compassion,*a*
> because his anger raged continually
> and his fury flamed unchecked,
> 12 I will send fire upon Teman*m*
> that will consume the fortresses of Bozrah."

1:11
l Jer 49:7-22

1:12
m Ob 1:9-10

13 This is what the LORD says:

> "For three sins of Ammon,*n*
> even for four, I will not turn back ⌐my wrath⌐.
> Because he ripped open the pregnant women of Gilead
> in order to extend his borders,
> 14 I will set fire to the walls of Rabbah*o*
> that will consume her fortresses
> amid war cries on the day of battle,
> amid violent winds on a stormy day.
> 15 Her king*b* will go into exile,
> he and his officials together,"

1:13
n Jer 49:1-6

1:14
o Dt 3:11

> says the LORD.

2

This is what the LORD says:

> "For three sins of Moab,
> even for four, I will not turn back ⌐my wrath⌐.
> Because he burned, as if to lime,
> the bones of Edom's king,
> 2 I will send fire upon Moab
> that will consume the fortresses of Kerioth.*c*
> Moab will go down in great tumult
> amid war cries and the blast of the trumpet.
> 3 I will destroy her ruler*p*
> and kill all her officials with him,"*q*

2:3
p Ps 2:10
q Isa 40:23

> says the LORD.

a 11 Or *sword / and destroyed his allies*   *b* 15 Or / *Molech*; Hebrew *malcam*   *c* 2 Or *of her cities*

1:9 Tyre was one of two major cities in Phoenicia. Several treaties had been made with this city, which supplied the cedar used to build David's palace and God's temple (2 Samuel 5:11; 1 Kings 5).

1:11, 12 Both Edom and Israel had descended from Isaac: Edom from Isaac's son Esau, and Israel from Esau's twin brother, Jacob (Genesis 25:19–28; 27). But these two nations, like the two brothers, were always fighting. Edom had rejoiced at Israel's misfortunes. As a result, God promised to destroy Edom completely, from Teman in the south to Bozrah in the north.

1:13–15 The Ammonites had descended from an incestuous relationship between Lot and his younger daughter (Genesis 19:30–38). The Ammonites were hostile to Israel; and although Israel began to worship their idols, the Ammonites still attacked (Judges 10:6–8). After Saul had been anointed Israel's king, his first victory in battle was against the Ammonites (1 Samuel 11). Rabbah was Ammon's capital city. Amos's prophecy of Ammon's destruction was fulfilled through the Assyrian invasion.

2:1–3 The Moabites had descended from an incestuous relationship between Lot and his older daughter (Genesis 19:30–38). Balak, king of Moab, had tried to hire the prophet Balaam to curse the Israelites so they could be defeated (Numbers 22—24). Balaam spoke instead the Lord's word of blessing, but some of the Moabites had succeeded in getting Israel to worship Baal (Numbers 25:1–3). The Moabites were known for their atrocities (2 Kings 3:26, 27). An archaeological artifact, the Moabite Stone, reveals that Moab was always ready to profit from the downfall of others.

2:4
r 2Ki 17:19
s Jer 6:19

4 This is what the LORD says:

> "For three sins of Judah,r
> even for four, I will not turn back ⌐my wrath⌐.
> Because they have rejected the laws of the LORD
> and have not kept his decrees,
> because they have been led astray by false gods,a
> the godsb their ancestors followed,

2:5
t Jer 17:27;
Hos 8:14

> 5 I will send fire upon Judah
> that will consume the fortresses of Jerusalem.t"

Judgment on Israel

6 This is what the LORD says:

> "For three sins of Israel,
> even for four, I will not turn back ⌐my wrath⌐.
> They sell the righteous for silver,
> and the needy for a pair of sandals.

2:7
u Am 5:11-12

> 7 They trample on the heads of the poor
> as upon the dust of the ground
> and deny justice to the oppressed.
> Father and son use the same girl
> and so profane my holy name.u

2:8
v Ex 22:26

> 8 They lie down beside every altar
> on garments taken in pledge.v
> In the house of their god
> they drink wine taken as fines.

2:9
w Nu 21:23-26

> 9 "I destroyed the Amoritew before them,
> though he was tall as the cedars
> and strong as the oaks.
> I destroyed his fruit above
> and his roots below.

2:10
x Ex 20:2
y Dt 2:7

> 10 "I brought you up out of Egypt,x
> and I led you forty years in the deserty
> to give you the land of the Amorites.

2:11
z Jer 7:25

> 11 I also raised up prophetsz from among your sons
> and Nazirites from among your young men.
> Is this not true, people of Israel?"

> declares the LORD.

a 4 Or *by lies*   b 4 Or *lies*

2:4–6 After Solomon died, the kingdom divided, and the tribes of Judah and Benjamin became the southern kingdom (Judah) under Solomon's son, Rehoboam. The other ten tribes became the northern kingdom (Israel) and followed Jeroboam, who had rebelled against Rehoboam.

God had punished other nations harshly for their evil actions and atrocities. But God also promised to judge both Israel and Judah because they ignored the revealed law of God. The other nations were ignorant, but Judah and Israel, God's people, knew what God wanted. Still they ignored him and joined pagan nations in worshiping idols. If we know God's word and refuse to obey it, like Israel we will carry a greater guilt.

2:4–6 Amos must have won over his audience as he proclaimed God's judgment against the evil nations surrounding Israel. But then he even spoke against his own nation, Judah, before focusing on God's indictment of Israel.

2:6ff God condemned Israel for five specific sins: (1) selling the poor as slaves (see Deuteronomy 15:7–11; Amos 8:6), (2) exploiting the poor (see Exodus 23:6; Deuteronomy 16:19), (3) engaging in perverse sexual sins (see Leviticus 20:11, 12), (4) taking illegal collateral for loans (see Exodus 22:26, 27; Deuteronomy 24:6, 12, 13), and (5) worshiping false gods (see Exodus 20:3–5).

2:6, 7 Amos was speaking to the upper class. There was no middle class in the country—only the very rich and the very poor. The rich kept religious rituals. They gave extra tithes, went to places of worship, and offered sacrifices. But they were greedy and unjust, and they took advantage of the helpless. Be sure that you do not neglect the needs of the poor while you faithfully attend church and fulfill religious rituals. God expects us to live out our faith—this means responding to those in need.

2:9–11 The prophets were constantly challenging people to remember what God had done! When we read a list like this one, we are amazed at Israel's forgetfulness. But what would the prophets say about us? God's past faithfulness should have reminded the Israelites to obey him; likewise, what he has done for us should remind us to live for him.

2:11 The Nazirites took a vow of service to God. The vow included abstaining from wine and never cutting their hair. But instead of being respected for their disciplined and temperate lives, they were being urged to break their vows. If the Nazirites were corrupted, there would remain little influence for good among the Israelites.

12 "But you made the Nazirites drink wine
    and commanded the prophets not to prophesy.*a*

13 "Now then, I will crush you
    as a cart crushes when loaded with grain.

14 The swift will not escape,
    the strong will not muster their strength,
    and the warrior will not save his life.*b*

15 The archer*c* will not stand his ground,
    the fleet-footed soldier will not get away,
    and the horseman will not save his life.

16 Even the bravest warriors
    will flee naked on that day,"

                                      declares the LORD.

2. Reasons for judgment
Witnesses Summoned Against Israel

3 Hear this word the LORD has spoken against you, O people of Israel—against the whole family I brought up out of Egypt:

2 "You only have I chosen*d*
    of all the families of the earth;
  therefore I will punish you
    for all your sins.*e*"

3 Do two walk together
    unless they have agreed to do so?

4 Does a lion roar in the thicket
    when he has no prey?
  Does he growl in his den
    when he has caught nothing?

5 Does a bird fall into a trap on the ground
    where no snare has been set?
  Does a trap spring up from the earth
    when there is nothing to catch?

6 When a trumpet sounds in a city,
    do not the people tremble?
  When disaster comes to a city,
    has not the LORD caused it?*f*

7 Surely the Sovereign LORD does nothing
    without revealing his plan*g*
    to his servants the prophets.

8 The lion has roared—
    who will not fear?

2:12 *a* Isa 30:10;
Jer 11:21; Mic 2:6

2:14 *b* Ps 33:16

2:15 *c* Eze 39:3

3:2 *d* Dt 7:6
e Jer 14:10

3:6 *f* Isa 14:24-27

3:7 *g* Ge 18:17;
Jn 15:15

2:16 "That day" refers to when Assyria would attack Israel, destroy Samaria, and take the people captive (722 B.C.). This military defeat came only a few decades after this pronouncement.

2:16 Television and movies are filled with images of people who seem to have no fear. Many today have modeled their lives after these images—they want to be tough. But God is not impressed with bravado. He says that even the toughest people will run in fear when God's judgment comes. Do you know people who think they can make it through life without God? Don't be swayed by their self-assured rhetoric. Recognize that God fears no one, and one day all people will fear him.

3:2 God chose Israel to be the people through whom all other nations of the world could know him. He made this promise to Abraham, father of the Israelites (Genesis 12:1–3). Israel didn't have to do anything to be chosen; God had given them this special privilege because he wanted to, not because they

deserved special treatment (Deuteronomy 9:4–6). Pride in their privileged position, however, ruined Israel's sensitivity to the will of God and to the plight of others.

3:3–6 With a series of seven rhetorical questions, Amos shows how two events can be linked together. Once one event takes place, the second will surely follow. Amos was showing that God's revelation to him was the sure sign that judgment would follow.

3:6 This verse means that God himself would be sending disaster to Israel.

3:7 Even in anger, God is merciful: he always warned his people through prophets before punishing them. Warnings about sin and judgment apply to people today just as they did to Israel. Because we have been warned about our sin, we have no excuse when punishment comes. God had warned his people through his prophets, so they could not rationalize or complain when God punished them for refusing to repent. Do not take lightly the

The Sovereign LORD has spoken—
who can but prophesy?[h]

3:8
[h] Jer 20:9; Ac 4:20

9 Proclaim to the fortresses of Ashdod
and to the fortresses of Egypt:
"Assemble yourselves on the mountains of Samaria;[i]
see the great unrest within her
and the oppression among her people."

3:9
[i] Am 4:1

10 "They do not know how to do right," declares the LORD,
"who hoard plunder[j] and loot in their fortresses."[k]

3:10
[j] Hab 2:8
[k] Zep 1:9

11 Therefore this is what the Sovereign LORD says:

"An enemy will overrun the land;
he will pull down your strongholds
and plunder your fortresses."

12 This is what the LORD says:

3:12
[l] 1Sa 17:34

"As a shepherd saves from the lion's[l] mouth
only two leg bones or a piece of an ear,
so will the Israelites be saved,
those who sit in Samaria
on the edge of their beds
and in Damascus on their couches.[a]"

13 "Hear this and testify[m] against the house of Jacob," declares the Lord, the LORD God Almighty.

3:13
[m] Eze 2:7

14 "On the day I punish Israel for her sins,
I will destroy the altars of Bethel;
the horns of the altar will be cut off
and fall to the ground.
15 I will tear down the winter house[n]
along with the summer house;[o]
the houses adorned with ivory[p] will be destroyed
and the mansions will be demolished,"

3:15
[n] Jer 36:22
[o] Jdg 3:20
[p] 1Ki 22:39

declares the LORD.

Israel Has Not Returned to God

4:1
[q] Ps 22:12

4 Hear this word, you cows of Bashan[q] on Mount Samaria,
you women who oppress the poor and crush the needy
and say to your husbands, "Bring us some drinks!"
2 The Sovereign LORD has sworn by his holiness:
"The time will surely come
when you will be taken away[r] with hooks,
the last of you with fishhooks.

4:2
[r] Am 6:8

[a] 12 The meaning of the Hebrew for this line is uncertain.

---

warnings in God's Word about judgment. His warnings are a way of showing mercy to you.

3:9 Ashdod was a Philistine city and the site of the temple of Dagon, a pagan god. Amos pictured Philistia and Egypt summoned to witness Israel's great sins. Even Israel's most wicked and idolatrous neighbors would see God judge Israel.

3:10 Israel no longer knew how to do what was right. The more they sinned, the harder it was to remember what God wanted. The same is true for us. The longer we wait to deal with sin, the greater it holds onto us. Finally, we forget what it means to do right. Are you on the verge of forgetting?

3:11, 12 The enemy mentioned here was Assyria, who conquered Israel and did just as Amos predicted. The people were scattered to foreign lands, and foreigners were placed in the land to keep the peace. Israel's leaders had robbed their defenseless countrymen, and here they would be rendered defenseless by the

Assyrians. Amos added that even if the Israelites tried to repent, it would be too late. The destruction would be so complete that nothing of value would be left.

3:14 God's judgment against Israel's altars shows that he was rejecting Israel's entire religious system because it was so polluted. The horns of the altar stood for protection (1 Kings 1:49–53), and the false altars would soon be gone. Then the people would have no sanctuary, protection, or refuge (see 4:4) when judgment came.

4:1 Israel's wealthy women were called "cows of Bashan"— pampered, sleek, and well-fed (see Psalm 22:12). These women selfishly pushed their husbands to oppress the helpless in order to support their lavish lifestyles. Be careful not to desire material possessions so much that you are willing to oppress others and displease God to get them.

3 You will each go straight out
    through breaks in the wall,
    and you will be cast out toward Harmon,ᵃ"

                    declares the LORD.

4:4
ˢNu 28:3

4 "Go to Bethel and sin;
    go to Gilgal and sin yet more.
  Bring your sacrifices every morning,ˢ
    your tithes every three years.ᵇ

4:5
ᵗLev 7:13
ᵘLev 22:18-21

5 Burn leavened breadᵗ as a thank offering
    and brag about your freewill offeringsᵘ—
  boast about them, you Israelites,
    for this is what you love to do,"

          declares the Sovereign LORD.

4:6
ᵛJer 5:3; Hag 2:17

6 "I gave you empty stomachsᶜ in every city
  and lack of bread in every town,
    yet you have not returned to me,"

           declares the LORD.ᵛ

4:7
ʷDt 11:17

7 "I also withheld rain from you
    when the harvest was still three months away.
  I sent rain on one town,
    but withheld it from another.ʷ
  One field had rain;
    another had none and dried up.
8 People staggered from town to town for water
  but did not get enough to drink,
    yet you have not returned to me,"

           declares the LORD.

4:9
ˣDt 28:22

9 "Many times I struck your gardens and vineyards,
    I struck them with blight and mildew.ˣ
  Locusts devoured your fig and olive trees,
    yet you have not returned to me,"

           declares the LORD.

4:10
ʸEx 9:3

10 "I sent plaguesʸ among you
    as I did to Egypt.
  I killed your young men with the sword,
    along with your captured horses.
  I filled your nostrils with the stench of your camps,
    yet you have not returned to me,"

           declares the LORD.

4:11
ᶻJer 23:14

11 "I overthrew some of you
    as Iᵈ overthrew Sodom and Gomorrah.ᶻ
  You were like a burning stick snatched from the fire,
    yet you have not returned to me,"

           declares the LORD.

ᵃ3 Masoretic Text; with a different word division of the Hebrew (see Septuagint) *out, O mountain of oppression*
ᵇ4 Or *tithes on the third day* ᶜ6 Hebrew *you cleanness of teeth* ᵈ11 Hebrew *God*

4:4 Amos sarcastically invited the people to sin in Bethel and Gilgal where they worshiped idols instead of God. Bethel was where God had renewed his covenant with Abraham with Jacob (Genesis 28:10–22). At this time, Bethel was the religious center of the northern kingdom, and Jeroboam had placed an idol there to discourage the people from traveling to Jerusalem in the southern kingdom to worship (1 Kings 12:26–29). Gilgal was Israel's first campground after entering the promised land (Joshua 4:19). Here Joshua had renewed the covenant and the rite of circumcision, and the people had celebrated the Passover

(Joshua 5:2–11). Saul was crowned Israel's first king in Gilgal (1 Samuel 11:15).

4:6–13 No matter how God warned the people—through famine, drought, blight, locusts, plagues, or war—they still ignored him. Because the Israelites didn't get the message, they would have to meet God face to face in judgment. No longer would they ignore God; they would have to face the One they had rejected, the One they had refused to obey when he commanded them to care for the poor. One day each of us will meet God face to face to account for what we have done or refused to do. Are you prepared to meet him?

12 "Therefore this is what I will do to you, Israel,
        and because I will do this to you,
            prepare to meet your God, O Israel."

4:13
a Da 2:28
b Mic 1:3

13 He who forms the mountains,
        creates the wind,
        and reveals his thoughts*a* to man,
    he who turns dawn to darkness,
        and treads the high places of the earth*b*—
        the LORD God Almighty is his name.

A Lament and Call to Repentance

5 Hear this word, O house of Israel, this lament I take up concerning you:

5:2
c Am 8:14

2 "Fallen is Virgin Israel,
        never to rise again,
    deserted in her own land,
        with no one to lift her up.*c*"

3 This is what the Sovereign LORD says:

"The city that marches out a thousand strong for Israel
        will have only a hundred left;
    the town that marches out a hundred strong
        will have only ten left."

5:4
d Isa 55:3

4 This is what the LORD says to the house of Israel:

"Seek me and live;*d*
5   do not seek Bethel,
    do not go to Gilgal,*e*
        do not journey to Beersheba.*f*
    For Gilgal will surely go into exile,
        and Bethel will be reduced to nothing.*a*"
6 Seek the LORD and live,
        or he will sweep through the house of Joseph like a fire;
    it will devour,
        and Bethel will have no one to quench it.

5:5
e Am 4:4
f Am 8:14

5:7
g Am 6:12

7 You who turn justice into bitterness*g*
        and cast righteousness to the ground
8 (he who made the Pleiades and Orion,*h*
        who turns blackness into dawn
        and darkens day into night,
    who calls for the waters of the sea
        and pours them out over the face of the land—
        the LORD is his name*i*—
9 he flashes destruction on the stronghold
        and brings the fortified city to ruin),
10 you hate the one who reproves in court*j*
        and despise him who tells the truth.*k*

5:8
h Job 9:9
i Am 4:13

5:10
j Isa 29:21
k 1Ki 22:8

a 5 Or *grief*; or *wickedness*; Hebrew *aven*, a reference to Beth Aven (a derogatory name for Bethel)

5:1 Amos shocked his listeners by singing a lament or song of grief for them as though they had already been destroyed. The Israelites believed that their wealth and religious ritual made them secure, but Amos lamented their sure destruction.

5:6 There is one sure remedy for a world that is sick and dying in sin—"seek the LORD and live." Sin seeks to destroy, but hope is found in seeking God. In times of difficulty, seek God. In personal discomfort and struggle, seek God. When others are struggling, encourage them to seek God too.

5:7 The law courts should have been places of justice where the poor and oppressed could find relief. Instead, they had become places of greed and injustice.

5:8 Pleiades and Orion are star constellations. For thousands of years, navigators have staked lives and fortunes on the reliability of the stars. The constancy and orderliness of the heavens challenge us to look beyond them to their Creator.

5:10-12 "One who reproves in court" refers to an honest judge, a champion of justice. A society is in trouble when those who try to do right are hated for their commitment to justice. Any society that exploits the poor and defenseless or hates the truth is bent on destroying itself.

11 You trample on the poor
    and force him to give you grain.
Therefore, though you have built stone mansions,
    you will not live in them;
though you have planted lush vineyards,
    you will not drink their wine. *l*

12 For I know how many are your offenses
    and how great your sins.

You oppress the righteous and take bribes
    and you deprive the poor of justice in the courts. *m*

13 Therefore the prudent man keeps quiet in such times,
    for the times are evil.

14 Seek good, not evil,
    that you may live.
Then the LORD God Almighty will be with you,
    just as you say he is.

15 Hate evil, *n* love good;
    maintain justice in the courts.
Perhaps the LORD God Almighty will have mercy *o*
    on the remnant of Joseph.

16 Therefore this is what the Lord, the LORD God Almighty, says:

"There will be wailing in all the streets
    and cries of anguish in every public square.
The farmers will be summoned to weep
    and the mourners to wail.

17 There will be wailing in all the vineyards,
    for I will pass through your midst,"

says the LORD.

The Day of the LORD

18 Woe to you who long
    for the day of the LORD!
Why do you long for the day of the LORD?
    That day will be darkness, not light. *p*

19 It will be as though a man fled from a lion
    only to meet a bear,
as though he entered his house
    and rested his hand on the wall
    only to have a snake bite him. *q*

5:11
l Mic 6:15

5:12
m Am 2:6-7

5:15
n Ro 12:9
o Joel 2:14

5:18
p Isa 5:19, 30

5:19
q Jer 48:44

5:12 Why does God put so much emphasis on the way we treat the poor and needy? How we treat the rich, or those of equal standing, often reflects what we hope to get from them. But because the poor can give us nothing, how we treat them reflects our true character. Do we, like Christ, give without thought of gain? We should treat the poor as we would like God to treat us.

5:12 Here are eight common excuses for not helping the poor and needy: (1) They don't deserve help. They got themselves into poverty; let them get themselves out. (2) God's call to help the poor applies to another time. (3) We don't know any people like this. (4) I have my own needs. (5) Any money I give will be wasted, stolen, or spent. The poor will never see it. (6) I may become a victim myself. (7) I don't know where to start, and I don't have time. (8) My little bit won't make any difference.
    Instead of making lame excuses, ask what can be done to help. Does your church have programs to help the needy? Could you volunteer to work with a community group that fights poverty? As one individual, you may not be able to accomplish much, but join up with similarly motivated people and watch mountains begin to move.

5:15 If Israel were to sweep away the corrupt system of false

accusations, bribery, and corruption, and were to insist that only just decisions be given, this would show their change of heart. We dare not read this passage lightly or write it off simply as encouragement to be good. It is a command to reform our own legal and social system.

5:16 Failure to honor the dead was considered horrible in Israel, so loud weeping was common at funerals. Paid mourners, usually women, cried and mourned loudly with dirges and eulogies. Amos said there would be so many funerals that there would be a shortage of professional mourners, so farmers would be called from the fields to help. (See also Jeremiah 9:17-20.)

5:18 Here "the day of the LORD" means the imminent destruction by the Assyrian army, as well as the future day of God's judgment. For the faithful, "the day of the LORD" will be glorious, but for the unfaithful it will be a day of darkness and doom. (See Joel 1:15 for more discussion of the day of the Lord.)

5:18-24 These people were calling for the day of the Lord, thinking it would bring an end to their troubles. But God said, "You don't know what you are asking for." This "day of the LORD" would bring justice, and justice would bring the punishment the people deserved for their sins.

20 Will not the day of the LORD be darkness, not light—
    pitch-dark, without a ray of brightness?

5:21
r Lev 26:31
s Isa 1:11-16
5:22
t Mic 6:6-7
u Isa 66:3

21 "I hate, I despise your religious feasts;r
    I cannot stand your assemblies. s
22 Even though you bring me burnt offerings and grain offerings,
    I will not accept them.
Though you bring choice fellowship offerings,a
    I will have no regard for them. t, u
23 Away with the noise of your songs!
    I will not listen to the music of your harps.

5:24
v Mic 6:8

24 But let justice roll on like a river,
    righteousness like a never-failing stream!v

25 "Did you bring me sacrifices and offerings
    forty years in the desert, O house of Israel?
26 You have lifted up the shrine of your king,
    the pedestal of your idols,
    the star of your godb—
    which you made for yourselves.

5:27
w Ac 7:42-43*

27 Therefore I will send you into exile beyond Damascus,"
    says the LORD, whose name is God Almighty. w

Woe to the Complacent

6:1
x Lk 6:24
y Isa 32:9-11

6 Woe to youx who are complacent in Zion,
    and to you who feel secure on Mount Samaria,
you notable men of the foremost nation,
    to whom the people of Israel come!y
2 Go to Calneh and look at it;
    go from there to great Hamath,
    and then go down to Gath in Philistia.

a22 Traditionally *peace offerings*   b26 Or *lifted up Sakkuth your king / and Kaiwan your idols, / your star-gods*; Septuagint *lifted up the shrine of Molech / and the star of your god Rephan, / their idols*

AMOS'S VISIONS	Vision/Reference	Significance
	Swarm of locusts 7:1–3	God was preparing punishment, which he delayed only because of Amos's intervention.
	Fire 7:4–6	God was preparing to devour the land, but Amos intervened on behalf of the people.
	Wall and plumb line 7:7–9	God would see if the people were crooked, and if they were, he would punish them.
	Basket of ripe fruit 8:1ff	The people were ripe for punishment; though once beautiful, they were now rotten.
	God standing by the altar 9:1ff	Punishment was executed.

Amos had a series of visions concerning God's judgment on Israel. God was planning to judge Israel by sending a swarm of locusts or by sending fire. In spite of Amos's intercession on Israel's behalf, God would still carry out his judgment because Israel persisted in disobedience.

5:21–23 God hates false worship ("religious feasts" and "assemblies") by people who go through the motions out of pretense or for show. If we are living sinful lives and using religious ritual and traditions to make ourselves look good, God will despise our worship and will not accept what we offer. He wants sincere hearts, not the songs of hypocrites. When you worship at church, are you more concerned about your image or your attitude toward God?

5:26 In days past, Israel had turned to worshiping stars and planets, preferring nature over nature's God (2 Kings 23:4, 5). Pagan religion allowed them to indulge in sexual immorality and to become wealthy through any means possible. Because they refused to worship and obey the one true God, they would cause their own destruction.

5:27 Israel's captivity was indeed beyond Damascus—the people were taken to Assyria. God's punishment was more than defeat; it was complete exile from their homeland.

6:1–6 Amos leveled his attack at those living in complacency and luxury in both Israel and Judah. Great wealth and comfortable lifestyles may make people think they are secure, but God is not pleased if we isolate ourselves from others' needs. God wants us to care for others as he cares for us. His kingdom has no place for selfishness or indifference. We must learn to put the needs of others before our wants. Using our wealth to help others is one way to guard against pride and complacency.

6:2 Great cities to the east, north, and west had been destroyed because of their pride. What happened to them would happen to Israel because Israel's sin was just as great as theirs.

Are they better off than*z* your two kingdoms?
    Is their land larger than yours?

³ You put off the evil day
    and bring near a reign of terror.*a*
⁴ You lie on beds inlaid with ivory
    and lounge on your couches.
You dine on choice lambs
    and fattened calves.*b*
⁵ You strum away on your harps like David
    and improvise on musical instruments.
⁶ You drink wine*c* by the bowlful
    and use the finest lotions,
but you do not grieve over the ruin of Joseph.
⁷ Therefore you will be among the first to go into exile;
    your feasting and lounging will end.

The LORD Abhors the Pride of Israel

⁸The Sovereign LORD has sworn by himself—the LORD God Almighty declares:

"I abhor the pride of Jacob
    and detest his fortresses;
I will deliver up the city
    and everything in it."

⁹If ten*d* men are left in one house, they too will die. ¹⁰And if a relative who is to burn the bodies comes to carry them out of the house and asks anyone still hiding there, "Is anyone with you?" and he says, "No," then he will say, "Hush!*e* We must not mention the name of the LORD."

¹¹ For the LORD has given the command,
    and he will smash the great house*f* into pieces
    and the small house into bits.*g*

¹² Do horses run on the rocky crags?
    Does one plow there with oxen?
But you have turned justice into poison*h*
    and the fruit of righteousness into bitterness*i*—
¹³ you who rejoice in the conquest of Lo Debar*a*
    and say, "Did we not take Karnaim*b* by our own strength?"

¹⁴ For the LORD God Almighty declares,
    "I will stir up a nation*j* against you, O house of Israel,
that will oppress you all the way
    from Lebo*c* Hamath to the valley of the Arabah."

3. Visions of judgment
Locusts, Fire and a Plumb Line

7 This is what the Sovereign LORD showed me: He was preparing swarms of locusts*k* after the king's share had been harvested and just as the second crop was coming up. ²When

a 13 Lo Debar means *nothing.*   *b 13 Karnaim* means *horns;* horn here symbolizes strength.   *c 14 Or from the entrance to*

6:2 *z* Na 3:8

6:3 *a* Am 9:10

6:4 *b* Eze 34:2-3; Am 3:12

6:6 *c* Am 2:8

6:9 *d* Am 5:3

6:10 *e* Am 8:3

6:11 *f* Am 3:15
g Isa 55:11

6:12 *h* Hos 10:4
i Am 5:7

6:14 *j* Jer 5:15

7:1 *k* Joel 1:4

6:4 Ivory was an imported luxury, rare and extremely expensive. Even a small amount of ivory symbolized wealth. Something as extravagant as a bed inlaid with ivory shows the gross waste of resources that should have been used to help the poor.

6:8–11 The people had built luxurious homes to flaunt their achievements. While it is not wrong to live in comfortable houses, we must not let them become sources of inflated pride and self-glorification. God gave our homes to us, and they are to be used for service, not just for show.

6:10 Amos gives us a picture of God's fearful judgment: the people hesitate to speak God's name, even during a time of grief, for fear that they would attract his attention and be judged also.

6:13, 14 Karnaim was a city northeast of Israel, an insignificant border town compared to the nation they were about to face, Assyria. Lebo Hamath was to the north, and the valley of the Arabah to the south. The entire nation would be destroyed by Assyria (2 Kings 17).

7:1ff The following series of visions conveyed God's message to the people using images that were familiar to them—locusts, fire, and a plumb line.

7:1–6 Twice Amos was shown a vision of Israel's impending punishment, and his immediate response was to pray that God would spare Israel. Prayer is a powerful privilege. Amos's prayers should remind us to pray for our nation.

they had stripped the land clean, I cried out, "Sovereign LORD, forgive! How can Jacob survive? He is so small!'"

7:2
l Eze 11:13

³So the LORD relented. *m*

7:3
m Dt 32:36

"This will not happen," the LORD said.

⁴This is what the Sovereign LORD showed me: The Sovereign LORD was calling for judgment by fire; *n* it dried up the great deep and devoured the land. ⁵Then I cried out, "Sovereign LORD, I beg you, stop! How can Jacob survive? He is so small! *o*"

7:4
n Isa 66:16

7:5
o ver 1-2

⁶So the LORD relented.

"This will not happen either," the Sovereign LORD said.

⁷This is what he showed me: The Lord was standing by a wall that had been built true to plumb, with a plumb line in his hand. ⁸And the LORD asked me, "What do you see, Amos? *p*"

7:8
p Am 8:2
q 2Ki 21:13

"A plumb line, *q*" I replied.

Then the Lord said, "Look, I am setting a plumb line among my people Israel; I will spare them no longer.

7:9
r 2Ki 15:9; Hos 10:8

9 "The high places of Isaac will be destroyed
    and the sanctuaries of Israel will be ruined;
    with my sword I will rise against the house of Jeroboam. *r*"

Amos and Amaziah

¹⁰Then Amaziah the priest of Bethel sent a message to Jeroboam *s* king of Israel: "Amos is raising a conspiracy against you in the very heart of Israel. The land cannot bear all his words. ¹¹For this is what Amos is saying:

7:10
s 2Ki 14:23

"'Jeroboam will die by the sword,
    and Israel will surely go into exile,
    away from their native land.'"

¹²Then Amaziah said to Amos, "Get out, you seer! Go back to the land of Judah. Earn your bread there and do your prophesying there. ¹³Don't prophesy anymore at Bethel, because this is the king's sanctuary and the temple of the kingdom. *t*"

7:13
t Am 2:12

7:14
u 2Ki 2:5

7:15
v Eze 2:3-4

¹⁴Amos answered Amaziah, "I was neither a prophet *u* nor a prophet's son, but I was a shepherd, and I also took care of sycamore-fig trees. ¹⁵But the LORD took me from tending the flock and said to me, 'Go, prophesy to my people Israel.' *v* ¹⁶Now then, hear the word of the LORD. You say,

"'Do not prophesy against Israel,
    and stop preaching against the house of Isaac.'

7:17
w Hos 4:13

¹⁷"Therefore this is what the LORD says:

"'Your wife will become a prostitute *w* in the city,
    and your sons and daughters will fall by the sword.
Your land will be measured and divided up,
    and you yourself will die in a pagan *a* country.
And Israel will certainly go into exile,
    away from their native land.'"

A Basket of Ripe Fruit

8:2
x Am 7:8

8 This is what the Sovereign LORD showed me: a basket of ripe fruit. ²"What do you see, Amos? *x*" he asked.

a 17 Hebrew *an unclean*

7:7–9 A plumb line is a device used to ensure the straightness of a wall. A wall that is not straight will eventually collapse. God wants people to be right with him; he wants the sin that makes us crooked removed immediately. God's Word is the plumb line that helps us be aware of our sin. How do you measure up to God's plumb line?

7:10 Prophets like Amos were often seen as traitors and conspirators because they spoke out against the king and his advisers, questioning their authority and exposing their sin. The kings often saw the prophets as enemies rather than God's spokesmen who were really trying to help them and the nation.

7:10ff Amaziah was the chief priest in Bethel, representing Israel's official religion. He was not concerned about hearing God's message; he was only worried about his own position. Maintaining his position was more important than listening to the truth. Don't let your desire for prestige, authority, or money keep you tied to a job or position you should leave. Don't let anything come between you and obeying God.

7:14, 15 Without any special preparation, education, or upbringing, Amos obeyed God's call to "Go, prophesy to my people Israel." Obedience is the test of a faithful servant of God. Are you obeying God's call to you?

"A basket of ripe fruit," I answered.

Then the LORD said to me, "The time is ripe for my people Israel; I will spare them no longer.*y*

3"In that day," declares the Sovereign LORD, "the songs in the temple will turn to wailing.*a* Many, many bodies—flung everywhere! Silence!*z*"

4 Hear this, you who trample the needy
    and do away with the poor*a* of the land,*b*

5saying,

"When will the New Moon be over
        that we may sell grain,
    and the Sabbath be ended
        that we may market wheat?"—
    skimping the measure,
        boosting the price
        and cheating with dishonest scales,*c*
6 buying the poor with silver
    and the needy for a pair of sandals,
    selling even the sweepings with the wheat.*d*

7 The LORD has sworn by the Pride of Jacob: "I will never forget*e* anything they have done.

8 "Will not the land tremble for this,
    and all who live in it mourn?
The whole land will rise like the Nile;
    it will be stirred up and then sink
    like the river of Egypt.*f*

9"In that day," declares the Sovereign LORD,

"I will make the sun go down at noon
    and darken the earth in broad daylight.*g*
10 I will turn your religious feasts into mourning
    and all your singing into weeping.
I will make all of you wear sackcloth
    and shave your heads.
I will make that time like mourning for an only son
    and the end of it like a bitter day.*h*

11 "The days are coming," declares the Sovereign LORD,
    "when I will send a famine through the land—
not a famine of food or a thirst for water,
    but a famine of hearing the words of the LORD.*i*
12 Men will stagger from sea to sea
    and wander from north to east,
searching for the word of the LORD,
    but they will not find it.

13"In that day

"the lovely young women and strong young men
    will faint because of thirst.*j*

a3 Or "the temple singers will wail

8:2 *y* Eze 7:2-9	
8:3 *z* Am 6:10	
8:4 *a* Pr 30:14 *b* Ps 14:4	
8:5 *c* Ne 13:15-16; Mic 6:10-11	
8:6 *d* Am 2:6	
8:7 *e* Hos 8:13	
8:8 *f* Am 9:5	
8:9 *g* Job 5:14; Jer 15:9; Mic 3:6	
8:10 *h* Eze 7:18	
8:11 *i* 1Sa 3:1; 2Ch 15:3	
8:13 *j* Hos 2:3	

8:5, 6 These merchants were keeping the religious festivals, but not in spirit. They couldn't wait for the holy days and Sabbaths to be over so they could go back to making money. Their real interest was in enriching themselves, even if that meant cheating (short-changing the quantity while boosting the price, or even selling chaff as wheat). Do you take a day to rest and worship God at least once a week, or is making money more important to you than anything else? When you give time to God, is your heart in your worship? Or is your religion only a front for unethical practices?

8:11-13 The people had no appetite for God's word when prophets like Amos brought it. Because of their apathy, God said he would take away even the opportunity to hear his word. We have God's Word, the Bible. But many still look everywhere for answers to life's problems *except* in Scripture. You can help them by directing them to the Bible, showing them the parts that speak to their special needs and questions. God's Word is available to us. Let us help people know it before a time comes when they cannot find it.

8:14
k Am 5:5

14 They who swear by the shame[a] of Samaria,
    or say, 'As surely as your god lives, O Dan,'
    or, 'As surely as the god[b] of Beersheba[k] lives'—
they will fall,
    never to rise again."

Israel to Be Destroyed

9:1
l Ps 68:21

9 I saw the Lord standing by the altar, and he said:

"Strike the tops of the pillars
    so that the thresholds shake.
Bring them down on the heads[l] of all the people;
    those who are left I will kill with the sword.
Not one will get away,
    none will escape.

9:2
m Jer 51:53

2 Though they dig down to the depths of the grave,[c]
    from there my hand will take them.
Though they climb up to the heavens,[m]
    from there I will bring them down.

9:3
n Jer 16:16-17

3 Though they hide themselves on the top of Carmel,
    there I will hunt them down and seize them.
Though they hide from me at the bottom of the sea,
    there I will command the serpent to bite them.[n]

9:4
o Lev 26:33

4 Though they are driven into exile by their enemies,
    there I will command the sword[o] to slay them.
I will fix my eyes upon them
    for evil and not for good."

9:5
p Am 8:8

5 The Lord, the LORD Almighty,
    he who touches the earth and it melts,
    and all who live in it mourn—
the whole land rises like the Nile,
    then sinks like the river of Egypt[p]—

9:6
q Ps 104:1-3, 5-6,
13; Am 5:8

6 he who builds his lofty palace[d] in the heavens
    and sets its foundation[e] on the earth,
who calls for the waters of the sea
    and pours them out over the face of the land—
    the LORD is his name.[q]

9:7
r Dt 2:23

7 "Are not you Israelites
    the same to me as the Cushites[f]?"

                         declares the LORD.

"Did I not bring Israel up from Egypt,
    the Philistines from Caphtor[g][r]
    and the Arameans from Kir?

---

a 14 Or by Ashima; or by the idol   b 14 Or power   c 2 Hebrew to Sheol   d 6 The meaning of the Hebrew for this
phrase is uncertain.   e 6 The meaning of the Hebrew for this word is uncertain.   f 7 That is, people from the upper
Nile region   g 7 That is, Crete

9:1 Judgment would begin at the altar, the center of the nation's life, the place where the people expected protection and blessing. This judgment would cover all 12 tribes. Commentators disagree concerning this altar—some think it was the altar at Bethel; more likely it was the altar in the temple in Jerusalem. God would destroy their base of security in order to bring them to himself. But in 9:11 he promises to restore his renewed people and their broken world.

9:2–4 The grave was the place of the dead, and Carmel is a mountain. Both were symbols of inaccessibility. No one can escape God's judgment. This was good news for the faithful but bad news for the unfaithful. Whether we go to the mountaintops or the bottom of the sea, God will find us and judge us for our deeds. Amos pictured the judgment of the wicked as a monster

of the sea, relentlessly pursuing the condemned. For God's faithful followers, however, the judgment brings a new earth of peace and prosperity. Does God's judgment sound like good news or bad news to you?

9:7 Cush, south of Egypt, was a remote and exotic land to the Israelites. Caphtor is the island of Crete, where the Philistines lived as they migrated to Palestine. God would judge Israel no differently than he judges foreign nations. He is not the God of Israel only; he is God of the universe, and he controls all nations.

8 "Surely the eyes of the Sovereign LORD
    are on the sinful kingdom.
I will destroy it
    from the face of the earth—
yet I will not totally destroy
    the house of Jacob,"

                          declares the LORD.

9 "For I will give the command,
    and I will shake the house of Israel
    among all the nations
as grain is shaken in a sieve,s
    and not a pebble will reach the ground.
10 All the sinners among my people
    will die by the sword,
all those who say,
    'Disaster will not overtake or meet us.'t

Israel's Restoration

11 "In that day I will restore
    David's fallen tent.
I will repair its broken places,
    restore its ruins,
    and build it as it used to be,u
12 so that they may possess the remnant of Edom
    and all the nations that bear my name,a"
      declares the LORD, who will do these things. v

13"The days are coming," declares the LORD,

"when the reaper will be overtaken by the plowmanw
    and the planter by the one treading grapes.
New wine will drip from the mountains
    and flow from all the hills.x
14 I will bring back my exiledb people Israel;
    they will rebuild the ruined citiesy and live in them.
They will plant vineyards and drink their wine;
    they will make gardens and eat their fruit.
15 I will plantz Israel in their own land,
    never again to be uprooted
    from the land I have given them,"

                says the LORD your God.a

9:9 s Isa 30:28
9:10 t Am 6:3
9:11 u Ps 80:12
9:12 v Ac 15:16-17*
9:13 w Lev 26:5 x Joel 3:18
9:14 y Isa 61:4
9:15 z Isa 60:21 a Eze 34:25-28

a 12 Hebrew; Septuagint so that the remnant of men / and all the nations that bear my name may seek ⌊the Lord⌋
b 14 Or will restore the fortunes of my

9:8 Amos assured the Israelites that God would not "totally destroy" Israel—in other words, the punishment would not be permanent. God wants to redeem, not punish. But he doesn't withhold punishment. Like a loving father, God disciplines those he loves. If God disciplines you, accept it as a sign of his love.

9:8, 9 Although Assyria would destroy Israel and take the people into exile, some would be preserved. This exile had been predicted much earlier (Deuteronomy 28:63–68). Although the nation would be purified through this invasion, not one true believer would be eternally lost. Our system of justice is not perfect, but God is. Sinners will not get away, and the faithful will not be forgotten.

9:11, 12 In the punishment, the house of David was reduced to a "fallen tent." God's covenant with David stated that one of David's descendants would always sit on his throne (2 Samuel 7:12–16). The exile made this promise seem impossible. But "in that day" God would raise up and restore the kingdom to its promised glory. This was a promise to both Israel and Judah, not to be fulfilled by an earthly, political ruler, but by the Messiah, who would renew the spiritual kingdom and rule forever.

James quoted these verses (Acts 15:16, 17), finding the promise fulfilled in Christ's resurrection and in the presence of both Jews and Gentiles in the church. "Possess the remnant of Edom" envisions the Messianic kingdom, which will be universal and include Gentiles. When God brings in the Gentiles, he is restoring the ruins. After the Gentiles are called together, God will renew and restore the fortunes of the new Israel. All the land that was once under David's rule will again be part of God's nation.

9:13 This verse describes a time of such an abundance of crops that the people won't be able to harvest them all.

9:13–15 The Jews of Amos's day had lost sight of God's care and love for them. The rich were carefree and comfortable, refusing to help others in need. They observed their religious rituals in hopes of appeasing God, but they did not truly love him. Amos announced God's warnings of destruction for their evil ways.

We must not assume that going to church and being good is enough. God expects our belief in him to penetrate all areas of our conduct and to extend to all people. We should let Amos's words inspire us to live faithfully according to God's desires.

OBADIAH

WRINKLED face, tiny hands with fingernail chips, folds of new skin, and miniature eyes, nose, and mouth—she's a newborn. After months of formation, she burst forth into the world and into her family. "She has her mother's eyes." "I can sure tell who her parents are." "Now that's your nose." Relatives and friends gaze into the little face and see her mom and dad. Mother and Father rejoice in their daughter, a miracle, a new member of the family. As loving parents, they will feed, protect, nurture, guide, and discipline her. This is their duty and joy.

God, too, has children—men and women whom he has chosen as his very own. There have always been individuals marked as his, but with Abraham he promised to build a nation. Israel was to be God's country, and her people, the Jews, his very own sons and daughters. Down through the centuries, God meted out discipline and punishment, but always with love and mercy. God, the eternal Father, protected and cared for his children.

Obadiah, the shortest book in the Old Testament, is a dramatic example of God's response to anyone who would harm his children. Edom was a mountainous nation, occupying the region southeast of the Dead Sea including Petra, the spectacular city discovered by archaeologists a few decades ago. As descendants of Esau (Genesis 25:19—27:45), the Edomites were blood relatives of Israel, and like their father, they were rugged, fierce, and proud warriors with a seemingly invincible mountain home. Of all people, they should have rushed to the aid of their northern brothers. Instead, however, they gloated over Israel's problems, captured and delivered fugitives to the enemy, and even looted Israel's countryside.

Obadiah gave God's message to the Edomites. Because of their indifference to and defiance of God, their cowardice and pride, and their treachery toward their relatives in Judah, they stood condemned and would be destroyed. The book begins with the announcement that disaster was coming to Edom (verses 1–9). Despite their "impregnable" cliffs and mountains, they would not be able to escape God's judgment. Obadiah then gave the reasons for their destruction (verses 10–14)— their blatant arrogance toward God and their persecution of God's children. This concise prophecy ends with a description of the "day of the LORD," when judgment will fall on all who have harmed God's people (verses 15–21).

Today, God's holy nation is his church—all who have trusted Christ for their salvation and have given their lives to him. These men and women are God's born-again and adopted children. As you read Obadiah, catch a glimpse of what it means to be God's child, under his love and protection. See how the heavenly Father responds to all who would attack those whom he loves.

VITAL STATISTICS

PURPOSE:
To show that God judges those who have harmed his people

AUTHOR:
Obadiah. Very little is known about this man, whose name means "servant (or worshiper) of the LORD."

ORIGINAL AUDIENCE:
The Edomites and the Jews in Judah (the southern kingdom)

DATE WRITTEN:
Possibly during the reign of Jehoram in Judah, 855–841 B.C., or possibly during Jeremiah's ministry, 627–586 B.C.

SETTING:
Historically, Edom had constantly harassed the Jews. Prior to the time this book was written, they had participated in attacks against Judah. Given the dates above, this prophecy came after the division of Israel into the northern and southern kingdoms and before the conquering of Judah by Nebuchadnezzar in 586 B.C.

KEY VERSE:
"The day of the LORD is near for all nations. As you have done, it will be done to you; your evil deeds will return upon your own head" (verse 15).

KEY PEOPLE:
The Edomites

KEY PLACES:
Edom, Jerusalem

SPECIAL FEATURES:
The book of Obadiah uses vigorous poetic language and is written in the form of a dirge of doom.

THE BLUEPRINT

1. Edom's destruction (1–16)
2. Israel's restoration (17–21)

The book of Obadiah shows the outcome of the ancient feud between Edom and Israel. Edom was proud of its high position, but God would bring her down. Those who are high and powerful today should not be overconfident in themselves, whether they are a nation, a corporation, a church, or a family. Just as Edom was destroyed for its pride, so will anyone be who lives in defiance of God.

MEGATHEMES

THEME	EXPLANATION	IMPORTANCE
Justice	Obadiah predicted that God would destroy Edom as punishment for standing by when Babylon invaded Judah. Because of their treachery, Edom's land would be given to Judah in the day when God rights the wrongs against his people.	God will judge and fiercely punish all who harm his people. We can be confident in God's final victory. He is our champion, and we can trust him to bring about true justice.
Pride	Because of their seemingly invincible rock fortress, the Edomites were proud and self-confident. But God humbled them and their nation disappeared from the face of the earth.	All those who defy God will meet their doom as Edom did. Any nation who trusts in its power, wealth, technology, or wisdom more than in God will be brought low. All who are proud will one day be shocked to discover that no one is exempt from God's justice.

1. Edom's destruction

¹ The vision of Obadiah.

This is what the Sovereign LORD says about Edom ª—

> We have heard a message from the LORD:
> An envoy was sent to the nations to say,
> "Rise, and let us go against her for battle"ᵇ—

² "See, I will make you small among the nations;
   you will be utterly despised.
³ The prideᶜ of your heart has deceived you,
   you who live in the clefts of the rocksª
   and make your home on the heights,
   you who say to yourself,
   'Who can bring me down to the ground?'
⁴ Though you soar like the eagle
   and make your nest among the stars,
   from there I will bring you down,"

declares the LORD. ᵈ

1:1
ª Jer 49:7-22;
  Eze 25:12-14
ᵇ Jer 6:4-5

1:3
ᶜ Isa 16:6

1:4
ᵈ Job 20:6

ª3 Or of Sela

---

1 Obadiah was a prophet from Judah who told of God's judgment against the nation of Edom. Two commonly accepted dates for this prophecy are (1) between 853 and 841 B.C., when King Jehoram and Jerusalem were attacked by a Philistine/Arab coalition (2 Chronicles 21:16ff); (2) 586 B.C., when Jerusalem was completely destroyed by the Babylonians (2 Kings 25; 2 Chronicles 36). Edom had rejoiced over the misfortunes of both Israel and Judah, and yet the Edomites and Jews descended from two brothers—Esau and Jacob (Genesis 25:19–26). But just as these two brothers were constantly fighting, so were Israel and Edom. God pronounced judgment on Edom for their callous and malicious actions toward his people.

3 Edom was Judah's southern neighbor, sharing a common boundary. But neighbors are not always friends, and Edom liked nothing about Judah. Edom's capital at this time was Sela (perhaps the later city of Petra), a city considered impregnable because it was cut into rock cliffs and set in a canyon that could be entered only through a narrow gap. What Edom perceived as its strengths would be its downfall: (1) safety in their city (verses 3, 4)—God would send them plummeting from the heights; (2) pride in their self-sufficiency (verse 4)—God would humble them; (3) wealth (verses 5, 6)—thieves would steal all they had; (4) allies (verse 7)—God would cause them to turn against Edom; (5) wisdom (verses 8, 9)—the wise would be destroyed.

3 The Edomites felt secure, and they were proud of their self-sufficiency. But they were fooling themselves because there is no lasting security apart from God. Is your security in objects or people? Ask yourself how much lasting security they really offer. Possessions and people can disappear in a moment, but God does not change. Only he can supply true security.

4 The Edomites were proud of their city carved right into the rock. Today Sela, or Petra, is considered one of the marvels of the ancient world, but only as a tourist attraction. The Bible warns that pride is the surest route to self-destruction (Proverbs 16:18).

5 "If thieves came to you,
    if robbers in the night—
Oh, what a disaster awaits you—
    would they not steal only as much as they wanted?
If grape pickers came to you,
    would they not leave a few grapes?
6 But how Esau will be ransacked,
    his hidden treasures pillaged!
7 All your allies will force you to the border;
    your friends will deceive and overpower you;
those who eat your bread will set a trap for you,a
    but you will not detect it.

1:8
e Job 5:12;
Isa 29:14

8 "In that day," declares the LORD,
    "will I not destroye the wise men of Edom,
    men of understanding in the mountains of Esau?
9 Your warriors, O Teman, will be terrified,
    and everyone in Esau's mountains
    will be cut down in the slaughter.

1:10
f Joel 3:19
g Am 1:11-12

10 Because of the violencef against your brother Jacob,g
    you will be covered with shame;
    you will be destroyed forever.
11 On the day you stood aloof
    while strangers carried off his wealth
and foreigners entered his gates
    and cast lots for Jerusalem,
    you were like one of them.

1:12
h Eze 35:15
i Mic 4:11

12 You should not look down on your brother
    in the day of his misfortune,
nor rejoiceh over the people of Judah
    in the day of their destruction,
nor boast so much
    in the day of their trouble.i

a7 The meaning of the Hebrew for this clause is uncertain.

OBADIAH served as a prophet to Judah possibly around 853 B.C.	*Climate of the times*	Edom was a constant thorn in Judah's side. The Edomites often participated in attacks initiated by other enemies.
	Main message.	God will judge Edom for its evil actions toward God's people.
	Importance of message	Just as Edom was destroyed and disappeared as a nation, so God will destroy proud and wicked people.
	Contemporary prophets	Elijah (875–848 B.C.), Micaiah (865–853 B.C.), Jehu (853 B.C.)

Just as Petra and Edom fell, so will proud people fall. A humble person is more secure than a proud person because humility gives a more accurate perspective of oneself and the world.

4–9 Esau was named here (verse 6) because he was the father of the nation of Edom. God did not pronounce these harsh judgments against Edom out of vengeance but in order to bring about justice. God is morally perfect and demands complete justice and fairness. The Edomites were simply getting what they deserved. Because they murdered, they would be murdered. Because they robbed, they would be robbed. Because they took advantage of others, they would be used. Don't talk yourself into sin, thinking that "nobody will know" or "I won't get caught." God knows all our sins, and he will be just.

8 Edom was noted for its wise people. There is a difference, however, between human wisdom and God's wisdom. The Edomites may have been wise in the ways of the world, but they were foolish because they ignored and even mocked God.

9 Eliphaz, one of Job's three friends (Job 2:11), was from Teman, about five miles east of Petra. Teman was named after Esau's grandson (Genesis 36:11).

10, 11 The Israelites had descended from Jacob, and the Edomites from his brother, Esau (Genesis 25:19–26). Instead of helping Israel and Judah when they were in need, Edom had allowed them to be destroyed and even had plundered what was left behind. Edom, therefore, acted like an enemy and would be punished. Anyone who does not help God's people is God's enemy. If you have withheld your help from someone in a time of need, this is sin (James 4:17). Sin includes not only what we do, but also what we refuse to do. Don't ignore or refuse to help those in need.

12 Edom was glad to see Judah in trouble. Their hatred made them want the nation destroyed. For their wrong attitudes and actions, God wiped out Edom. How often do you find yourself rejoicing at the misfortunes of others? Because God alone is the judge, we must never be happy about others' misfortunes, even if we think they deserve them (see Proverbs 24:17).

13 You should not march through the gates of my people
    in the day of their disaster,
nor look down on them in their calamity
    in the day of their disaster,
nor seize their wealth
    in the day of their disaster.
14 You should not wait at the crossroads
    to cut down their fugitives,
nor hand over their survivors
    in the day of their trouble.

15 "The day of the LORD is near*j*
    for all nations.
As you have done, it will be done to you;
    your deeds*k* will return upon your own head.
16 Just as you drank on my holy hill,
    so all the nations will drink continually;
they will drink and drink
    and be as if they had never been.

1:15
j Eze 30:3
k Hab 2:8

2. Israel's restoration

17 But on Mount Zion will be deliverance;*l*
    it will be holy,
and the house of Jacob
    will possess its inheritance.
18 The house of Jacob will be a fire
    and the house of Joseph a flame;
the house of Esau will be stubble,
    and they will set it on fire and consume it.
There will be no survivors
    from the house of Esau."

1:17
l Am 9:11-15

                      The LORD has spoken.

		HISTORY OF THE CONFLICT BETWEEN ISRAEL AND EDOM
The nation of Israel descended from Jacob; the nation of Edom descended from Esau	Genesis 25:23	
Jacob and Esau struggled in their mother's womb	Genesis 25:19–26	
Esau sold his birthright and blessing to Jacob	Genesis 25:29–34	
Edom refused to let the Israelites pass through its land	Numbers 20:14–22	
Israel's kings had constant conflict with Edom.		
• Saul	1 Samuel 14:47	
• David	2 Samuel 8:13, 14	
• Solomon	1 Kings 11:14–22	
• Jehoram	2 Kings 8:20–22; 2 Chronicles 21:8ff	
• Ahaz	2 Chronicles 28:16	
Edom urged Babylon to destroy Jerusalem	Psalm 137:7	

12–14 Of all Israel and Judah's neighbors, Edom was the only one not promised any mercy from God. This was because they looted Jerusalem and rejoiced at the misfortunes of Israel and Judah. They betrayed their blood brothers in times of crisis and aided their brothers' enemies. (See also Psalm 137:7; Jeremiah 49:7–22; Ezekiel 25:12–14; Amos 1:11, 12.)

15 Why will God's judgment fall on all nations? Edom was not the only nation to rejoice at Judah's fall. All nations and individu-als will be judged for the way they have treated God's people. Some nations today treat God's people favorably, while others are hostile toward them. God will judge all people according to the way they treat others, especially believers (Revelation 20:12, 13). Jesus talked about this in Matthew 25:31–46.

17–21 The Edomites were routed by Judas Maccabeus in 164 B.C. The nation no longer existed by the first century A.D. At the time of Obadiah's prophecy, Edom may have seemed more likely to survive than Judah. Yet Edom has vanished, and Judah still exists. This demonstrates the absolute certainty of God's word and of the punishment awaiting all who have mistreated God's people.

¹⁹ People from the Negev will occupy
  the mountains of Esau,
and people from the foothills will possess
  the land of the Philistines.
They will occupy the fields of Ephraim and Samaria,
  and Benjamin will possess Gilead.

1:20
^m 1Ki 17:9-10
ⁿ Jer 33:13

²⁰ This company of Israelite exiles who are in Canaan
  will possess ˌthe landˌ as far as Zarephath;^m
the exiles from Jerusalem who are in Sepharad
  will possess the towns of the Negev.ⁿ

1:21
^o Rev 11:15

²¹ Deliverers will go up on^a Mount Zion
  to govern the mountains of Esau.
And the kingdom will be the Lord's.^o

^a21 Or *from*

---

19 The Negev was the southern part of Judah, a dry, hot region. The foothills were in the western part of Judah.

20 The boundaries of the kingdom would be extended to include the Canaanites (Phoenicians) as far south as Zarephath, located between Tyre and Sidon on the Mediterranean coast. Sepharad was most likely the city of Sardis.

21 Obadiah brought God's message of judgment on Edom. God was displeased with both their inward and their outward rebellion. People today are much the same as people in Obadiah's time, filled with arrogance, envy, and dishonesty. We may wonder where it will all end. Regardless of sin's effects, however, God is in control. Don't despair or give up hope. Know that when all is said and done, the Lord will still be King, and the confidence you place in him will not be in vain.

21 Edom is an example to all the nations that are hostile to God. Nothing can break God's promise to protect his people from complete destruction. In the book of Obadiah we see four aspects of God's message of judgment: (1) evil will certainly be punished; (2) those faithful to God have hope for a new future; (3) God is sovereign in human history; (4) God's ultimate purpose is to establish his eternal kingdom. The Edomites had been cruel to God's people. They were arrogant and proud, and they took advantage of others' misfortunes. Any nation that mistreats people who obey God will be punished, regardless of how invincible they appear. Similarly we, as individuals, cannot allow ourselves to feel so comfortable with our wealth or security that we fail to help God's people. This is sin. And because God is just, sin will be punished.

JONAH

VITAL STATISTICS

PURPOSE:
To show the extent of God's grace—the message of salvation is for *all* people

AUTHOR:
Jonah son of Amittai

ORIGINAL AUDIENCE:
All the people of Israel

DATE WRITTEN:
Approximately 785–760 B.C.

SETTING:
Jonah preceded Amos and ministered under Jeroboam II, Israel's most powerful king (793–753 B.C.; see 2 Kings 14:23–25). Assyria was Israel's great enemy; it conquered Israel in 722 B.C. Nineveh's repentance must have been short-lived, for it was destroyed in 612 B.C.

KEY VERSE:
"But Nineveh has more than a hundred and twenty thousand people who cannot tell their right hand from their left, and many cattle as well. Should I not be concerned about that great city?" (4:11).

KEY PEOPLE:
Jonah, the ship's captain and crew

KEY PLACES:
Joppa, Nineveh

SPECIAL FEATURES:
This book is different from the other prophetic books because it tells the story of the prophet and does not center on his prophecies. In fact, only one verse summarizes his message to the people of Nineveh (3:4). Jonah is a historical narrative. It is also mentioned by Jesus as a picture of his death and resurrection (Matthew 12:38–42).

SIN runs rampant in society—daily headlines and overflowing prisons bear dramatic witness to that fact. With child abuse, pornography, serial killings, terrorism, anarchy, and ruthless dictatorships, the world seems to be filled to overflowing with violence, hatred, and corruption. Reading and hearing about these tragedies—and perhaps even experiencing them—we begin to understand the necessity of God's judgment. We may even find ourselves wishing for vengeance by any means upon the violent perpetrators. Surely they are beyond redemption! But suppose that in the midst of such thoughts, God told you to take the gospel to the worst of the offenders—how would you respond?

Jonah was given such a task. Assyria—a great but evil empire—was Israel's most dreaded enemy. The Assyrians flaunted their power before God and the world through numerous acts of heartless cruelty. So when Jonah heard God tell him to go to Assyria and call the people to repentance, he ran in the opposite direction.

The book of Jonah tells the story of this prophet's flight and how God stopped him and turned him around. But it is much more than a story of a man and a great fish. Jonah's story is a profound illustration of God's mercy and grace. No one deserved God's favor less than the people of Nineveh, Assyria's capital. Jonah knew this. But he knew that God would forgive and bless them if they would turn from their sin and worship him. Jonah also knew the power of God's message, that even through his own weak preaching, they would respond and be spared God's judgment. But Jonah hated the Assyrians, and he wanted vengeance, not mercy. So he ran the other way. Eventually, Jonah obeyed and preached in the streets of Nineveh, and the people repented and were delivered from judgment. Then Jonah sulked and complained to God, "I knew that you are a gracious and compassionate God, slow to anger and abounding in love, a God who relents from sending calamity" (4:2). In the end, God confronted Jonah about his self-centered values and lack of compassion, saying, "But Nineveh has more than a hundred and twenty thousand people who cannot tell their right hand from their left, and many cattle as well. Should I not be concerned about that great city?" (4:11).

As you read Jonah, see the full picture of God's love and compassion and realize that no one is beyond redemption. The gospel is for all who will repent and believe. Begin to pray for those who seem to be farthest from the kingdom, and look for ways to tell them about God. Learn from the story of this reluctant prophet and determine to obey God, doing whatever he asks and going wherever he leads.

THE BLUEPRINT

1. Jonah forsakes his mission (1:1—2:10)
2. Jonah fulfills his mission (3:1—4:11)

Jonah was a reluctant prophet given a mission he found distasteful. He chose to run away from God rather than obey him. Like Jonah, we may have to do things in life that we don't want to do. Sometimes we find ourselves wanting to turn and run. But it is better to obey God than to defy him or run away. Often, in spite of our defiance, God in his mercy will give us another chance to serve him when we return to him.

MEGATHEMES

THEME	EXPLANATION	IMPORTANCE
God's Sovereignty	Although the prophet Jonah tried to run away from God, God was in control. By controlling the stormy seas and a great fish, God displayed his absolute, yet loving guidance.	Rather than running from God, trust him with your past, present, and future. Saying no to God quickly leads to disaster. Saying yes brings new understanding of God and his purpose in the world.
God's Message to All the World	God had given Jonah a purpose—to preach to the great Assyrian city of Nineveh. Jonah hated Nineveh, and so he responded with anger and indifference. Jonah had to learn that God loves all people. Through Jonah, God reminded Israel of its missionary purpose.	We must not limit our focus to our own people. God wants his people to proclaim his love in words and actions to the whole world. He wants us to be his missionaries wherever we are, wherever he sends us.
Repentance	When the reluctant preacher went to Nineveh, there was a great response. The people repented and turned to God. This was a powerful rebuke to the people of Israel, who thought they were better but refused to respond to God's message. God will forgive all those who turn from their sin.	God doesn't honor sham or pretense. He wants the sincere devotion of each person. It is not enough to share the privileges of Christianity; we must ask God to forgive us and to remove our sin. Refusing to repent shows that we still love our sin.
God's Compassion	God's message of love and forgiveness was not for the Jews alone. God loves all the people of the world. The Assyrians didn't deserve it, but God spared them when they repented. In his mercy, God did not reject Jonah for aborting his mission. God has great love, patience, and forgiveness.	God loves each of us, even when we fail him. But he also loves other people, including those not of our group, background, race, or denomination. When we accept his love, we must also learn to accept all those whom he loves. We will find it much easier to love others when we truly love God.

1. Jonah forsakes his mission
Jonah Flees From the LORD

1:1
a Mt 12:39-41

1 The word of the LORD came to Jonah a son of Amittai: 2 "Go to the great city of Nineveh and preach against it, because its wickedness has come up before me."

1:1, 2 Jonah is mentioned in 2 Kings 14:25. He prophesied during the reign of Jeroboam II, the king of Israel from 793–753 B.C. He may have been a member of the company of prophets mentioned in connection with Elisha's ministry (2 Kings 2:3).

God told Jonah to preach to Nineveh, the most important city in Assyria, the rising world power of Jonah's day. Within 50 years, Nineveh would become the capital of the vast Assyrian empire. Jonah doesn't say much about Nineveh's wickedness, but the prophet Nahum gives us more insight. Nahum says that Nineveh was guilty of (1) evil plots against God (Nahum 1:9); (2) exploitation of the helpless (Nahum 2:12); (3) cruelty in war

(Nahum 2:12, 13); (4) idolatry, prostitution, and witchcraft (Nahum 3:4). God told Jonah to go to Nineveh, about 500 miles northeast of Israel, to warn of judgment and to declare that the people could receive mercy and forgiveness if they repented.

³But Jonah ran *b* away from the LORD and headed for Tarshish. He went down to Joppa, where he found a ship bound for that port. After paying the fare, he went aboard and sailed for Tarshish to flee from the LORD.

⁴Then the LORD sent a great wind on the sea, and such a violent storm arose that the ship threatened to break up. *c* ⁵All the sailors were afraid and each cried out to his own god. And they threw the cargo into the sea to lighten the ship.

But Jonah had gone below deck, where he lay down and fell into a deep sleep. ⁶The captain went to him and said, "How can you sleep? Get up and call on your god! Maybe he will take notice of us, and we will not perish." *d*

⁷Then the sailors said to each other, "Come, let us cast lots to find out who is responsible for this calamity." *e* They cast lots and the lot fell on Jonah.

⁸So they asked him, "Tell us, who is responsible for making all this trouble for us? What do you do? Where do you come from? What is your country? From what people are you?"

⁹He answered, "I am a Hebrew and I worship the LORD, the God of heaven, who made the sea and the land. *f*"

¹⁰This terrified them and they asked, "What have you done?" (They knew he was running away from the LORD, because he had already told them so.)

¹¹The sea was getting rougher and rougher. So they asked him, "What should we do to you to make the sea calm down for us?"

¹²"Pick me up and throw me into the sea," he replied, "and it will become calm. I know that it is my fault that this great storm has come upon you."

1:3
b Ps 139:7

1:4
c Ps 107:23-26

1:6
d Ps 107:28

1:7
e Jos 7:10-18;
1Sa 14:42

1:9
f Ps 146:6

1:3 Nineveh was a powerful and wicked city. Jonah had grown up hating the Assyrians and fearing their atrocities. His hatred was so strong that he didn't want them to receive God's mercy. Jonah was actually afraid the people would repent (4:2, 3). Jonah's attitude is representative of Israel's reluctance to share God's love and mercy with others, even though this was their God-given mission (Genesis 12:3). They, like Jonah, did not want non-Jews (Gentiles) to obtain God's favor.

1:3 Jonah knew that God had a specific job for him, but he didn't want to do it. Tarshish could be one of any number of Phoenicia's western ports. Nineveh was toward the east. Jonah decided to go as far west as he could. When God gives us directions through his Word, sometimes we run in fear or in stubbornness, claiming that God is asking too much. It may have been fear, or anger at the wideness of God's mercy, that made Jonah run. But running got him into worse trouble. In the end, Jonah understood that it is best to do what God asks in the first place. But by then he had paid a costly price for running. It is far better to obey from the start.

1:4 Before settling in the promised land, the Israelites had been nomads, wandering from place to place, seeking good pastureland for their flocks. Although they were not a seafaring people, their location along the Mediterranean Sea and near the neighboring maritime powers of Phoenicia and Philistia allowed much contact with ships and sailors. The ship Jonah sailed on was probably a large trading vessel with a deck.

1:4 Jonah's disobedience to God endangered the lives of the ship's crew. We have a great responsibility to obey God's Word because our sin and disobedience can hurt others around us.

1:4, 5 While the storm raged, Jonah was sound asleep below deck. Even as he ran from God, Jonah's actions apparently didn't bother his conscience. But the absence of guilt isn't always a barometer of whether we are doing right. Because we can deny reality, we cannot measure obedience by our feelings. Instead, we must compare what we do with God's standards for living.

1:7 The crew cast lots to find the guilty person, relying on their superstition to give them the answer. Their system worked, but only because God intervened to let Jonah know that he couldn't run away.

1:9–12 You cannot seek God's love and run from him at the same time. Jonah soon realized that no matter where he went, he couldn't get away from God. But before Jonah could return to God, he first had to stop going in the opposite direction. What has God told you to do? If you want more of God's love and power, you must be willing to carry out the responsibilities he gives you. You cannot say that you truly believe in God if you don't do what he says (1 John 2:3–6).

1:12 Jonah knew that he had disobeyed and that the storm was his fault, but he didn't say anything until the crew cast lots and the lot fell on him (1:7). Then Jonah was willing to give his life to save the sailors, although he had refused to do the same for the people of Nineveh. Jonah's hatred for the Assyrians had affected his perspective.

JONAH'S ROUNDABOUT JOURNEY God told Jonah to go to Nineveh, the capital of the Assyrian empire. Many of Jonah's countrymen had experienced the atrocities of these fierce people. The last place Jonah wanted to go was on a missionary trip to Nineveh! So he went in the opposite direction. He boarded a ship in Joppa that was headed for Tarshish. But Jonah could not run from God.

1:15
g Lk 8:24

¹³Instead, the men did their best to row back to land. But they could not, for the sea grew even wilder than before. ¹⁴Then they cried to the LORD, "O LORD, please do not let us die for taking this man's life. Do not hold us accountable for killing an innocent man, for you, O LORD, have done as you pleased." ¹⁵Then they took Jonah and threw him overboard, and the raging sea grew calm.*g* ¹⁶At this the men greatly feared the LORD, and they offered a sacrifice to the LORD and made vows to him.

JONAH

Few Old Testament personalities can compare in transparency with the prophet Jonah. We can see right through him. And most of what we see we don't like. He reminds us too much of ourselves: fearful, selfish, spiteful, and proud.

Even when Jonah wasn't physically running away from God, he was still resisting on the inside. He was quite capable of putting on a show of obedience to cover a seething internal mutiny. When he finally arrived in Nineveh with God's message, he delivered it as a summary judgment. He offered no way of escape. Jonah flatly declared the city's destruction.

Jonah knew (as he admitted later) that God was "a merciful and compassionate God, slow to get angry and filled with unfailing love . . . eager to turn back from destroying people" (4:2). He hoped the Ninevites wouldn't listen and was offended and resentful when they did. Jonah suffered under the painful mistake of assuming that he was the center of the universe.

Some people do not even think about God until they become angry. Discouragement, disappointment and disgust seem to clear away the haziness around God and we're all too eager to blame him for our troubles. God bluntly confronted Jonah with the reality of his disobedience, the pettiness of his demand for comfort, and the sinfulness of his blatant disregard for others. The wonderful character of God that Jonah wanted to withhold from the Ninevites, he himself had been taking for granted.

Fortunately, God will be just as blunt with us. He will shatter our comfort if that will place us in the best place to meet him. As long as we are surrounded by our sense of control and importance, we will not know God as God. What has God done lately in your life to open your eyes a little wider?

Strengths and accomplishments	• Was sent (and finally went) to an enemy nation with God's message • Survived an encounter with a large fish • Was instrumental in the repentance of the population of a huge city, keeping it from destruction
Weaknesses and mistakes	• Thought he could avoid God's call in his life by running away • Thought he could avoid God's call by sacrificing himself • Thought he could avoid God's call by belligerent obedience • Thought he could nullify God's call by sulking
Lessons from his life	• God cares deeply for us as well as for people we resent and hate • God will accomplish his purposes, even through reluctant and unwilling servants • God is patient with sinners and patient with his servants
Vital statistics	• Where: Gath-hepher • Occupation: Prophet • Relatives: Father: Amittai
Key verse	"But Jonah got up and went in the opposite direction to get away from the LORD. He went down to the port of Joppa, where he found a ship leaving for Tarshish. He bought a ticket and went on board, hoping to escape from the LORD by sailing to Tarshish" (Jonah 1:3).

Jonah's story is told in the book of Jonah. He is also mentioned in 2 Kings 14:25; Matthew 12:39-41; 16:4; and Luke 11:29, 32.

1:13 By trying to save Jonah's life, the pagan sailors showed more compassion than Jonah, because Jonah did not want to warn the Ninevites of the coming judgment of God. Believers should be ashamed when unbelievers show more concern and compassion than they do. God wants us to be concerned for all of his people, lost and saved.

1:14–16 Jonah had disobeyed God. While he was running away, he stopped and submitted to God. Then the ship's crew began to worship God because they saw the storm quiet down. God is able to use even our mistakes to help others come to know him. It may be painful, but admitting our sins can be a powerful example to those who don't know God. Ironically, the pagan sailors did what the entire nation of Israel would not do—prayed to God and vowed to serve him.

¹⁷But the LORD provided a great fish to swallow Jonah,ʰ and Jonah was inside the fish three days and three nights.

1:17
ʰMt 12:40

Jonah's Prayer

2 From inside the fish Jonah prayed to the LORD his God. ²He said:

"In my distress I called to the LORD,
    and he answered me.
From the depths of the graveª I called for help,
    and you listened to my cry.
³ You hurled me into the deep,
    into the very heart of the seas,
    and the currents swirled about me;
all your waves and breakers
    swept over me.ⁱ
⁴ I said, 'I have been banished
    from your sight;ʲ
yet I will look again
    toward your holy temple.'
⁵ The engulfing waters threatened me,ᵇ
    the deep surrounded me;
    seaweed was wrapped around my head.ᵏ
⁶ To the roots of the mountains I sank down;
    the earth beneath barred me in forever.
But you brought my life up from the pit,
    O LORD my God.
⁷ "When my life was ebbing away,
    I rememberedˡ you, LORD,
and my prayer rose to you,
    to your holy temple.ᵐ

2:3
ⁱPs 42:7

2:4
ʲPs 31:22

2:5
ᵏPs 69:1-2

2:7
ˡPs 77:11-12
ᵐPs 18:6

ª2 Hebrew *Sheol* ᵇ5 Or *waters were at my throat*

Climate of the times	Nineveh was the most important city in Assyria and would soon become the capital of the huge Assyrian empire. But Nineveh was also a very wicked city.
Main message.	Jonah, who hated the powerful and wicked Assyrians, was called by God to warn the Assyrians that they would receive judgment if they did not repent.
Importance of message	Jonah didn't want to go to Nineveh, so he tried to run from God. But God has ways of teaching us to obey and follow him. When Jonah preached, the city repented and God withheld his judgment. Even the most wicked will be saved if they truly repent of their sins and turn to God.
Contemporary prophets	Joel (835–796? B.C.), Amos (760–750 B.C.)

JONAH served as a prophet to Israel and Assyria from 793–753 B.C.

1:17 Many have tried to dismiss this miraculous event as fiction, but the Bible does not describe it as a dream or a legend. We should not explain away this miracle as if we can pick and choose which of the miracles in the Bible to believe. That kind of attitude would allow us to question any part of the Bible and cause us to lose our trust in the Bible as God's true and reliable word. Jonah's experience was used by Christ himself as an illustration of Christ's death and resurrection (Matthew 12:39, 40).

1:17 Jonah was sent by God to the Assyrians, ran from the task, and was swallowed by a great fish. The Bible tells us that he "was inside the fish three days and three nights." Then he was delivered and went to Nineveh where the people responded with repentance. These events in Jonah's life were cited by Jesus. When the religious leaders demanded that Jesus give them a sign to prove his authority, Jesus said the only sign they would receive was the sign of Jonah: They would see Jesus swallowed by death and delivered after three days (Matthew 12:39–41; 16:4).

Jesus was making it very clear to the religious leaders of the day that their stubbornness to believe in him would be judged. The people of Nineveh responded to God's word spoken by Jonah, but the religious leaders refused to believe God's word spoken by his very own Son. Often people of our generation demand a sign from God, but the only sign they will receive is the sign of Jonah—the death and resurrection of Christ.

2:1ff This is a prayer of thanksgiving, not a prayer for deliverance. Jonah was simply thankful that he had not drowned. He was delivered in a most spectacular way and was overwhelmed that he had escaped certain death. Even from inside the fish, Jonah's prayer was heard by God. We can pray anywhere and at any time, and God will hear us. Your sin is never too great and your predicament is never too difficult for God.

2:1–7 Jonah said, "When my life was ebbing away, I remembered you, LORD" (2:7). Often we act the same way. When life is going well, we tend to take God for granted; but when we lose

2:9
n Ps 50:14, 23
o Ps 3:8

8 "Those who cling to worthless idols
    forfeit the grace that could be theirs.
9 But I, with a song of thanksgiving,
    will sacrifice*n* to you.
What I have vowed I will make good.
    Salvation*o* comes from the LORD."

10 And the LORD commanded the fish, and it vomited Jonah onto dry land.

2. Jonah fulfills his mission
Jonah Goes to Nineveh

3 Then the word of the LORD came to Jonah a second time: 2 "Go to the great city of Nineveh and proclaim to it the message I give you."

3 Jonah obeyed the word of the LORD and went to Nineveh. Now Nineveh was a very important city—a visit required three days. 4 On the first day, Jonah started into the city. He proclaimed: "Forty more days and Nineveh will be overturned." 5 The Ninevites believed God. They declared a fast, and all of them, from the greatest to the least, put on sackcloth.

6 When the news reached the king of Nineveh, he rose from his throne, took off his royal robes, covered himself with sackcloth and sat down in the dust. 7 Then he issued a proclamation in Nineveh:

3:7
p 2Ch 20:3

"By the decree of the king and his nobles:

3:8
q Jnh 1:6
3:9
r 2Sa 12:22
s Joel 2:14

Do not let any man or beast, herd or flock, taste anything; do not let them eat or drink.*p* 8 But let man and beast be covered with sackcloth. Let everyone call*q* urgently on God. Let them give up their evil ways and their violence. 9 Who knows?*r* God may yet relent and with compassion turn*s* from his fierce anger so that we will not perish."

**MIRACLES
IN THE BOOK
OF JONAH**

God sent a violent storm	1:4
God provided a great fish to swallow Jonah	1:17
God ordered the fish to vomit Jonah	2:10
God made a vine to shade Jonah	4:6
God arranged for a worm to eat the vine	4:7
God arranged for a scorching wind to blow on Jonah	4:8

---

hope, we cry out to him. This kind of relationship with God can result only in an inconsistent, up-and-down spiritual life. A consistent, daily commitment to God promotes a solid relationship with him. Look to God during both the good and bad times, and you will have a stronger spiritual life.

2:2 Jonah pictured his predicament in the belly of the fish as though he had been buried alive.

2:8 Those who worship worthless idols forfeit God's grace and abandon any hope for mercy from the Lord. Any object of our devotion that replaces God is a lying vanity. We deceive ourselves with something that is ultimately empty and foolish. Make sure that nothing takes God's rightful place in your life.

2:9 Obviously Jonah was not in a position to bargain with God. Instead, he simply thanked God for saving his life. Our troubles should cause us to cling tightly to God, not attempt to bargain our way out of the pain. We can thank and praise God for what he has already done for us, and for his love and mercy.

2:9 It took a miracle of deliverance to get Jonah to do as God had commanded. As a prophet, Jonah was obligated to obey God's word, but he had tried to escape his responsibilities. At this time, he pledged to fulfill his vows. Jonah's story began with a tragedy, but a greater tragedy would have happened if God had allowed him to keep running. When you know God wants you to do something, don't run. God may not stop you as he did Jonah.

3:1, 2 Jonah had run away from God, but was given a second chance to participate in God's work. You may feel as though you are disqualified from serving God because of past mistakes. But

serving God is not an earned position—no one qualifies for God's service. But God still asks us to carry out his work. You may yet have another chance.

3:1, 2 Jonah was to preach only what God told him—a message of doom to one of the most powerful cities in the world. This was not the most desirable assignment, but those who bring God's word to others should not let social pressures or fear of people dictate their words. They are called to preach God's message and his truth, no matter how unpopular it may be.

3:3 The Hebrew text makes no distinction between the city proper (the walls of which were only about eight miles in circumference, accommodating a population of about 175,000 persons) and the administrative district of Nineveh that was about 30 to 60 miles across. A "very important city," Nineveh took three days just to visit.

3:4–9 God's word is for everyone. Despite the wickedness of the Ninevite people, they were open to God's message and repented immediately. If we simply proclaim what we know about God, we may be surprised at how many people will listen.

¹⁰When God saw what they did and how they turned from their evil ways, he had compassion ᵗ and did not bring upon them the destruction ᵘ he had threatened.

3:10
ᵗAm 7:6
ᵘJer 18:8

Jonah's Anger at the LORD's Compassion

4 But Jonah was greatly displeased and became angry. ²He prayed to the LORD, "O LORD, is this not what I said when I was still at home? That is why I was so quick to flee to Tarshish. I knew that you are a gracious and compassionate God, slow to anger and abounding in love,ᵛ a God who relents from sending calamity.ʷ ³Now, O LORD, take away my life, for it is better for me to die than to live."

4:2
ᵛPs 86:5, 15
ʷJoel 2:13

⁴But the LORD replied, "Have you any right to be angry?"

⁵Jonah went out and sat down at a place east of the city. There he made himself a shelter, sat in its shade and waited to see what would happen to the city. ⁶Then the LORD God provided a vine and made it grow up over Jonah to give shade for his head to ease his discomfort, and Jonah was very happy about the vine. ⁷But at dawn the next day God provided a worm, which chewed the vine so that it withered. ⁸When the sun rose, God provided a scorching east wind, and the sun blazed on Jonah's head so that he grew faint. He wanted to die, and said, "It would be better for me to die than to live."

⁹But God said to Jonah, "Do you have a right to be angry about the vine?"

"I do," he said. "I am angry enough to die."

¹⁰But the LORD said, "You have been concerned about this vine, though you did not tend it or make it grow. It sprang up overnight and died overnight. ¹¹But Nineveh ˣ has more than a hundred and twenty thousand people who cannot tell their right hand from their left, and many cattle as well. Should I not be concerned about that great city?"

4:11
ˣJnh 1:2; 3:2

3:10 The pagan people of Nineveh believed Jonah's message and repented. What a miraculous effect God's words had on those evil people! Their repentance stood in stark contrast to Israel's stubbornness. The people of Israel had heard many messages from the prophets, but they had refused to repent. The people of Nineveh only needed to hear God's message once. Jesus said that at the judgment, the men of Nineveh will stand up to condemn the Israelites for their failure to repent (Matthew 12:39–41). It is not our hearing God's word that pleases him, but our responding obediently to it.

3:10 God responded in mercy by canceling his threatened punishment. God had said that any nation on which he had pronounced judgment would be saved if they repented (Jeremiah 18:7, 8). God forgave Nineveh, just as he had forgiven Jonah. The purpose of God's judgment is correction, not revenge. He is always ready to show compassion to anyone willing to seek him.

4:1 Why did Jonah become angry when God spared Nineveh? The Jews did not want to share God's message with Gentile nations in Jonah's day, just as they resisted that role in Paul's day (1 Thessalonians 2:14–16). They had forgotten their original purpose as a nation—to be a blessing to the rest of the world by sharing God's message with other nations (Genesis 22:18). Jonah thought that God should not freely give his salvation to a wicked pagan nation. Yet this is exactly what God does for all who come to him today in faith.

4:1, 2 Jonah revealed the reason for his reluctance to go to Nineveh (1:3). He didn't want the Ninevites forgiven; he wanted them destroyed. Jonah did not understand that the God of Israel was also the God of the whole world. Are you surprised when some unlikely person turns to God? Is it possible that your view is as narrow as Jonah's? We must not forget that, in reality, *we* do not deserve to be forgiven by God.

4:3 Jonah had run from the job of delivering God's message of destruction to Nineveh (1:2, 3); then he wanted to die because the destruction wouldn't happen. How quickly Jonah had forgotten God's mercy for him when he was in the fish (2:9, 10). Jonah was happy when God saved him, but angry when Nineveh was saved.

Jonah was learning a valuable lesson about God's mercy and forgiveness. God's forgiveness was not only for Jonah or for Israel alone; it extends to all who repent and believe.

4:3 Jonah may have been more concerned about his own reputation than God's. He knew that if the people repented, none of his warnings to Nineveh would come true. This would embarrass him, although it would give glory to God. Are you more interested in getting glory for God or for yourself?

4:5–11 God ministered tenderly to Jonah just as he had done to Nineveh and to Israel, and just as he does to us. God could have destroyed Jonah for his defiant anger, but instead he gently taught him a lesson. If we will obey God's will, he will lead us. His harsh judgment is reserved for those who persist in rebellion.

4:9 Jonah was angry at the withering of the vine, but not over what could have happened to Nineveh. Most of us have cried at the death of a pet or when an object with sentimental value is broken, but have we cried over the fact that a friend does not know God? How easy it is to be more sensitive to our own interests than to the spiritual needs of people around us.

4:10, 11 Sometimes people wish that judgment and destruction would come upon sinful people whose wickedness seems to demand immediate punishment. But God is more merciful than we can imagine. God feels compassion for the sinners we want judged, and he devises plans to bring them to himself. What is your attitude toward those who are especially wicked? Do you want them destroyed? Or do you wish that they could experience God's mercy and forgiveness?

4:11 God spared the sailors when they pleaded for mercy. God saved Jonah when he prayed from inside the fish. God saved the people of Nineveh when they responded to Jonah's preaching. God answers the prayers of those who call upon him. God will always work his will, and he desires that all come to him, trust in him, and be saved. We can be saved if we heed God's warnings to us through his Word. If we respond in obedience, God will be gracious, and we will receive his mercy, not his punishment.

MICAH

"I HATE YOU!" she screams and runs from the room. Words from a child thrown as emotional darts. Perhaps she learned the phrase from Mom and Dad, or maybe it just burst forth from that inner well of "sinful nature." Whatever the case, hate and love have become society's bywords, almost tired clichés, tossed carelessly at objects, situations, and even people.

The casual use of such words as *love* and *hate* has emptied them of their meaning. We no longer understand statements that describe a loving God who hates sin. So we picture God as gentle and kind—a cosmic pushover, and our concept of what he hates is tempered by our misconceptions and wishful thinking.

The words of the prophets stand in stark contrast to such misconceptions. God's hatred is real—burning, consuming, and destroying. He hates sin, and he stands as the righteous Judge, ready to mete out just punishment to all who defy his rule. God's love is also real. So real that he sent his Son, the Messiah, to save and accept judgment in the sinner's place. Love and hate are together—both unending, irresistible, and unfathomable.

In seven short chapters, Micah presents this true picture of God—the almighty Lord who hates sin and loves the sinner. Much of the book is devoted to describing God's judgment on Israel (the northern kingdom), on Judah (the southern kingdom), and on all the earth. This judgment will come "because of Jacob's transgression, because of the sins of the house of Israel" (1:5). And the prophet lists their despicable sins, including fraud (2:2), theft (2:8), greed (2:9), debauchery (2:11), oppression (3:3), hypocrisy (3:4), heresy (3:5), injustice (3:9), extortion and lying (6:12), murder (7:2), and other offenses. God's judgment will come.

In the midst of this overwhelming prediction of destruction, Micah gives hope and consolation because he also describes God's love. The truth is that judgment comes only after countless opportunities to repent, to turn back to true worship and obedience—"to act justly and to love mercy and to walk humbly with your God " (6:8). But even in the midst of judgment, God promises to deliver the small minority who have continued to follow him. He states, "Their king will pass through before them, the LORD at their head" (2:13). The king, of course, is Jesus; and we read in 5:2 that he will be born as a baby in Bethlehem, an obscure Judean village.

As you read Micah, catch a glimpse of God's anger in action as he judges and punishes sin. See God's love in action as he offers eternal life to all who repent and believe. And then determine to join the faithful remnant of God's people, who live according to his will.

VITAL STATISTICS

PURPOSE:
To warn God's people that judgment is coming and to offer pardon to all who repent

AUTHOR:
Micah, a native of Moresheth, near Gath, about 20 miles southwest of Jerusalem

ORIGINAL AUDIENCE:
The people of Israel (the northern kingdom) and of Judah (the southern kingdom)

DATE WRITTEN:
Possibly during the reigns of Jotham, Ahaz, and Hezekiah (742–687 B.C.)

SETTING:
The political situation is described in 2 Kings 15—20 and 2 Chronicles 26—30. Micah was a contemporary of Isaiah and Hosea.

KEY VERSE:
"He has showed you, O man, what is good. And what does the LORD require of you? To act justly and to love mercy and to walk humbly with your God" (6:8).

KEY PEOPLE:
The people of Samaria and Jerusalem

KEY PLACES:
Samaria, Jerusalem, Bethlehem

SPECIAL FEATURES:
This is a beautiful example of classical Hebrew poetry. There are three parts, each beginning with "Hear" or "Listen" (1:2; 3:1; 6:1) and closing with a promise.

THE BLUEPRINT

1. The trial of the capitals (1:1—2:13)
2. The trial of the leaders (3:1—5:15)
3. The trial of the people (6:1—7:20)

Micah emphasized the need for justice and peace. Like a lawyer, he set forth God's case against Israel and Judah, their leaders, and their people. Throughout the book are prophecies about Jesus, the Messiah, who will gather the people into one nation. He will be their king and ruler, acting mercifully toward them. Micah makes it clear that God hates unkindness, idolatry, injustice, and empty ritual—and he still hates these today. But God is very willing to pardon the sins of any who repent.

MEGATHEMES

THEME	EXPLANATION	IMPORTANCE
Perverting Faith	God will judge the false prophets, dishonest leaders, and selfish priests in Israel and Judah. While they publicly carried out religious ceremonies, they were privately seeking to gain money and influence. To mix selfish motives with an empty display of religion is to pervert faith.	Don't try to mix your own selfish desires with true faith in God. One day God will reveal how foolish it is to substitute anything for loyalty to him. Coming up with your own private blend of religion will pervert your faith.
Oppression	Micah predicted ruin for all nations and leaders who were oppressive toward others. The upper classes oppressed and exploited the poor. Yet no one was speaking against them or doing anything to stop them. God will not put up with such injustice.	We dare not ask God to help us while we ignore those who are needy and oppressed, or while we silently condone the actions of those who oppress them.
The Messiah— King of Peace	God promised to provide a new king to bring strength and peace to his people. Hundreds of years before Christ's birth, God promised that the eternal king would be born in Bethlehem. It was God's great plan to restore his people through the Messiah.	Christ our king leads us just as God promised. But until his final judgment, his leadership is only visible among those who welcome his authority. We can have God's peace now by giving up our sins and welcoming him as king.
Pleasing God	Micah preached that God's greatest desire was not the offering of sacrifices at the temple. God delights in faith that produces justice, love for others, and obedience to him.	True faith in God generates kindness, compassion, justice, and humility. We can please God by seeking these attributes in our work, our family, our church, and our neighborhood.

1. The trial of the capitals

1 The word of the LORD that came to Micah of Moresheth[a] during the reigns of Jotham, Ahaz and Hezekiah, kings of Judah—the vision he saw concerning Samaria and Jerusalem.

> [2] Hear, O peoples, all of you,[b]
>   listen, O earth and all who are in it,
> that the Sovereign LORD may witness against you,
>   the Lord from his holy temple.[c]

Judgment Against Samaria and Jerusalem

> [3] Look! The LORD is coming from his dwelling place;
>   he comes down and treads the high places of the earth.[d]
> [4] The mountains melt beneath him
>   and the valleys split apart,[e]
> like wax before the fire,
>   like water rushing down a slope.
> [5] All this is because of Jacob's transgression,
>   because of the sins of the house of Israel.
> What is Jacob's transgression?
>   Is it not Samaria?[f]

1:1 *a* Jer 26:18
1:2 *b* Ps 50:7 *c* Ps 11:4
1:3 *d* Am 4:13
1:4 *e* Na 1:5
1:5 *f* Am 8:14

1:1 Micah and Isaiah lived at the same time, about 750–680 B.C., and undoubtedly knew of each other. Micah directed his message mainly to Judah, the southern kingdom, but he also had some words for Israel, the northern kingdom. Judah was enjoying great prosperity at this time. Of the three kings mentioned, Jotham (750–732) and Hezekiah (715–686) had tried to follow God (2 Kings 15:32–38; 18—20), but Ahaz (735–715) was one of the most evil kings ever to reign in Judah (2 Kings 16). Moresheth was a Judean village, near Gath on the border with Philistia.

1:3 "High places" could simply mean "mountaintops" or may refer to the altars dedicated to various idols, usually placed in elevated areas (see also 1:5).

1:3–7 Although the 12 tribes of Israel had been united under David and Solomon, after Solomon's death, the kingdom had divided into two parts. Two of the tribes, Judah and Benjamin, stayed loyal to David's line and accepted Solomon's son as their king. They became the southern kingdom, also called Judah, with Jerusalem as their capital city. The other ten tribes became the northern kingdom, also called Israel, with Samaria as their capital city. The destruction of Samaria was literally fulfilled during Micah's lifetime, in 722 B.C. (2 Kings 17:1–18), just as he had predicted.

1:5 Two sins are identified in Micah's message—the perversion of worship (1:7; 3:5–7, 11; 5:12, 13) and injustice toward others (2:1, 2, 8, 9; 3:2, 3, 9–11; 7:2–6). Rampant in the capital cities, these sins infiltrated and infected the entire country.

> What is Judah's high place?
> Is it not Jerusalem?

1:6
g Am 5:11
h Eze 13:14

6 "Therefore I will make Samaria a heap of rubble,
>   a place for planting vineyards.
> I will pour her stones *g* into the valley
>   and lay bare her foundations. *h*

1:7
i Dt 9:21

7 All her idols will be broken to pieces;
>   all her temple gifts will be burned with fire;
>   I will destroy all her images. *i*
> Since she gathered her gifts from the wages of prostitutes,
>   as the wages of prostitutes they will again be used."

Weeping and Mourning

8 Because of this I will weep and wail;
>   I will go about barefoot and naked.
> I will howl like a jackal
>   and moan like an owl.

1:9
j 2Ki 18:13

9 For her wound is incurable;
>   it has come to Judah. *j*
> It*a* has reached the very gate of my people,
>   even to Jerusalem itself.

10 Tell it not in Gath*b*;
>   weep not at all.*c*
> In Beth Ophrah*d*
>   roll in the dust.

1:11
k Eze 23:29

11 Pass on in nakedness*k* and shame,
>   you who live in Shaphir.*e*
> Those who live in Zaanan*f*
>   will not come out.
> Beth Ezel is in mourning;
>   its protection is taken from you.

a9 Or *He*   *b10* *Gath* sounds like the Hebrew for *tell.*   *c10* Hebrew; Septuagint may suggest *not in Acco.* The Hebrew for *in Acco* sounds like the Hebrew for *weep.*   *d10* *Beth Ophrah* means *house of dust.*   *e11* *Shaphir* means *pleasant.*   *f11* *Zaanan* sounds like the Hebrew for *come out.*

MICAH
served as a
prophet to
Judah from
742–687 B.C.

Climate of the times	King Ahaz set up pagan idols in the temple and finally nailed the temple doors shut. Four different nations harassed Judah. When Hezekiah became king, the nation began a slow road to recovery and economic strength. Hezekiah probably heeded much of Micah's advice.
Main message	Prediction of the fall of both the northern kingdom of Israel and the southern kingdom of Judah. This was God's discipline upon the people, actually showing how much he cared for them. Hezekiah's good reign helped postpone Judah's punishment.
Importance of message	Choosing to live a life apart from God is making a commitment to sin. Sin leads to judgment and death. God alone shows us the way to eternal peace. His discipline often keeps us on the right path.
Contemporary prophets	Hosea (753–715 B.C.), Isaiah (740–681 B.C.)

1:9 Samaria's sins were incurable, and God's judgment on the city had already begun. This sin was not like a gash in the skin, but more like a stab wound in a vital organ, causing an injury that would soon prove fatal (Samaria was, in fact, destroyed early in Micah's ministry). Tragically, Samaria's sin had influenced Jerusalem, and judgment would come to its very gates. This probably refers to Sennacherib's siege in 701 B.C. (see 2 Kings 18, 19).

1:10–16 Micah declared God's judgment on city after city because of the people's sins. The Hebrew of 1:10–13 includes a clever wordplay (see the NIV text notes). Micah bitterly

denounced each town by using puns. *Shaphir* sounds like the Hebrew word for "pleasant"; *Zaanan* sounds like the verb meaning "come out"; *Maroth* sounds like a word for "bitter." Read 1:11 aloud, substituting the meaning for each city's name, and you will realize the effect of Micah's word choice. Not all these cities can be identified now, but Lachish was on the border with Philistia and took the brunt of the Assyrian invasion.

12 Those who live in Maroth[a] writhe in pain,
     waiting for relief,[l]
because disaster has come from the LORD,
     even to the gate of Jerusalem.
13 You who live in Lachish,[b]
     harness the team to the chariot.
You were the beginning of sin
     to the Daughter of Zion,
for the transgressions of Israel
     were found in you.
14 Therefore you will give parting gifts[m]
     to Moresheth Gath.
The town of Aczib[c][n] will prove deceptive[o]
     to the kings of Israel.
15 I will bring a conqueror against you
     who live in Mareshah.[d][p]
He who is the glory of Israel
     will come to Adullam.[q]
16 Shave your heads in mourning
     for the children in whom you delight;
make yourselves as bald as the vulture,
     for they will go from you into exile.

Man's Plans and God's

2 Woe to those who plan iniquity,
     to those who plot evil on their beds!
At morning's light they carry it out
     because it is in their power to do it.
2 They covet fields[r] and seize them,
     and houses, and take them.
They defraud a man of his home,
     a fellowman of his inheritance.

3 Therefore, the LORD says:

"I am planning disaster[s] against this people,
     from which you cannot save yourselves.
You will no longer walk proudly,[t]
     for it will be a time of calamity.
4 In that day men will ridicule you;
     they will taunt you with this mournful song:
'We are utterly ruined;
     my people's possession is divided up.
He takes it from me!
     He assigns our fields to traitors.'"

| 1:12 |
| *Jer 14:19* |

| 1:14 |
| *m*2Ki 16:8 |
| *n*Jos 15:44 |
| *o*Jer 15:18 |

| 1:15 |
| *p*Jos 15:44 |
| *q*Jos 12:15 |

| 2:2 |
| *r*Isa 5:8 |

| 2:3 |
| *s*Jer 18:11; |
| Am 3:1-2 |
| *t*Isa 2:12 |

a *12 Maroth* sounds like the Hebrew for *bitter.*   b *13 Lachish* sounds like the Hebrew for *team.*   c *14 Aczib* means
deception.   d *15 Mareshah* sounds like the Hebrew for *conqueror.*

1:13 The people of Lachish had influenced many to follow their
evil example. They were "the beginning of sin." We often do the
same when we sin. Regardless of whether you consider yourself
a leader, your daily actions and words are observed by others
who may choose to follow your example, whether you know it
or not.

1:14 Moresheth Gath was Micah's hometown (1:1).

1:15 The terrain surrounding Adullam had numerous caves.
Micah was warning that when the enemy approached, Judah's
proud princes would be forced to flee and hide in these caves.

1:16 Micah pictured the devastating sorrow of parents seeing
their children taken away to be slaves in a distant land. This
happened frequently in both Israel and Judah, most horribly

when each nation was completely conquered—Israel in 722 B.C.
and Judah in 586 B.C.

2:1, 2 Micah spoke out against those who planned evil deeds
at night and rose at dawn to do them. A person's thoughts and
plans reflect his or her character. What do you think about as you
lie down to sleep? Do your desires involve greed or stepping on
others to achieve your goals? Evil thoughts lead to evil deeds.

2:2 Micah warned against those who use their position to take
advantage of others. Less than a century earlier, King Ahab of
Israel had pouted because he couldn't get Naboth's vineyard.
So his wife, Jezebel, had Naboth killed in order to give the garden
to Ahab (1 Kings 21:1–16). This kind of injustice had spread
throughout the nation and, like a disease, was destroying the
people from the inside out.

⁵ Therefore you will have no one in the assembly of the Lord
to divide the land by lot.

False Prophets

⁶ "Do not prophesy," their prophets say.
"Do not prophesy about these things;
disgrace will not overtake us.ᵘ"

⁷ Should it be said, O house of Jacob:
"Is the Spirit of the Lord angry?
Does he do such things?"

"Do not my words do good
to him whose ways are upright?ᵛ
⁸ Lately my people have risen up
like an enemy.
You strip off the rich robe
from those who pass by without a care,
like men returning from battle.

⁹ You drive the women of my people
from their pleasant homes.ʷ
You take away my blessing
from their children forever.

¹⁰ Get up, go away!
For this is not your resting place,ˣ
because it is defiled,
it is ruined, beyond all remedy.
¹¹ If a liar and deceiver comes and says,
'I will prophesy for you plenty of wine and beer,'
he would be just the prophet for this people!

Deliverance Promised

¹² "I will surely gather all of you, O Jacob;
I will surely bring together the remnantʸ of Israel.
I will bring them together like sheep in a pen,
like a flock in its pasture;
the place will throng with people.

2:5 Those who have been oppressing others will find the tables turned. They will end up not having any share in the decisions to divide the land because they won't have any surviving relatives.

2:6, 7 If these messages seem harsh, remember that God did not want to take revenge on Israel; he wanted to get them back on the right path. The people had rejected what was true and right, and they needed stern discipline. Children may think discipline is harsh, but it helps keep them going in the right direction. If we only want God's comforting messages, we may miss what he has for us. Listen whenever God speaks, even when the message is hard to take.

2:11 The people liked the false prophets who told them only what they wanted to hear. Micah spoke against prophets who encouraged the people to feel comfortable in their sin. Preachers are popular when they don't ask too much of us and when they tell us our greed or lust might even be good for us. But a true teacher of God speaks the truth, regardless of what the listeners want to hear.

2:12, 13 Micah's prophecy telescopes two great events—Judah's return from captivity in Babylon, and the great gathering of all believers when the Messiah returns. God gave his prophets visions of various future events, but not necessarily the ability to discern when these events would happen. For example, they could not see the long period of time between the Babylonian captivity and the coming of the Messiah, but they could clearly see that the Messiah was coming. The purpose of this prophecy was not to predict exactly *how* this would occur, but *that* it would. This gave the people hope and helped them turn from sin.

13 One who breaks open the way will go up before[z] them;
    they will break through the gate and go out.
Their king will pass through before them,
    the LORD at their head."

2:13
[z] Isa 52:12

2. The trial of the leaders

Leaders and Prophets Rebuked

3

Then I said,

"Listen, you leaders[a] of Jacob,
    you rulers of the house of Israel.
Should you not know justice,

3:1
[a] Jer 5:5

2   you who hate good and love evil;
who tear the skin from my people
    and the flesh from their bones;[b]

3:2
[b] Eze 22:27

3 who eat my people's flesh,[c]
    strip off their skin
    and break their bones in pieces;[d]
who chop them up like meat for the pan,
    like flesh for the pot?"

3:3
[c] Ps 14:4
[d] Zep 3:3

4 Then they will cry out to the LORD,
    but he will not answer them.[e]
At that time he will hide his face from them
    because of the evil they have done.

3:4
[e] Ps 18:41; Isa 1:15

5 This is what the LORD says:

"As for the prophets
    who lead my people astray,[f]
if one feeds them,
    they proclaim 'peace';
if he does not,
    they prepare to wage war against him.

3:5
[f] Isa 3:12

6 Therefore night will come over you, without visions,
    and darkness, without divination.[g]
The sun will set for the prophets,
    and the day will go dark for them.

3:6
[g] Isa 8:19-22

7 The seers will be ashamed[h]
    and the diviners disgraced.
They will all cover their faces
    because there is no answer from God."

3:7
[h] Mic 7:16

8 But as for me, I am filled with power,
    with the Spirit of the LORD,
    and with justice and might,

3:1ff Micah denounced the sins of the leaders, priests, and prophets ("leaders of Jacob" and "rulers")—those responsible for teaching the people right from wrong. The leaders, who should have known the law and taught it to the people, had set the law aside and had become the worst of sinners. They were taking advantage of the very people they were supposed to serve. All sin is bad, but the sin that leads others astray is the worst of all.

3:1 The dividing line between right and wrong often seems blurred, but spiritual leaders are supposed to help others see it. The Bible is God's guidebook to show us how to distinguish right and wrong. Spiritual leaders must understand the Bible's principles, teach them clearly, and exemplify them in their lives. While leaders cannot force people to do right, they should point them in that direction.

3:2-4 The leaders had no compassion or respect for those they were supposed to serve. They were treating the people miserably in order to satisfy their own desires; then they had the gall to ask for God's help when they found themselves in trouble. We, like the leaders, should not treat God like a light switch to be turned on only as needed. Instead, we should always rely on him.

3:5-7 Micah remained true to his calling and proclaimed God's words. In contrast, the false prophets' messages were geared to the favors they received. Not all those who claim to have messages from God really do. Micah prophesied that one day the false prophets would be shamed by their actions.

3:8 Micah attributed the power of his ministry to the Spirit of the Lord. Our power comes from the same source. Jesus told his followers they would receive power to witness about him when the Holy Spirit came on them (Acts 1:8). You can't witness effectively by relying on your own strength, because fear will keep you from speaking out for God. Only by relying on the power of the Holy Spirit can you live and witness for him.

3:8
i Isa 58:1

to declare to Jacob his transgression,
  to Israel his sin. *i*
9 Hear this, you leaders of the house of Jacob,
  you rulers of the house of Israel,
who despise justice
  and distort all that is right;

3:10
j Jer 22:13
k Eze 22:27
3:11
l Isa 1:23; Jer 6:13

10 who build *j* Zion with bloodshed,
  and Jerusalem with wickedness. *k*
11 Her leaders judge for a bribe,
  her priests teach for a price,
  and her prophets tell fortunes for money. *l*
Yet they lean upon the LORD and say,
  "Is not the LORD among us?
  No disaster will come upon us."

3:12
m Jer 26:18

12 Therefore because of you,
  Zion will be plowed like a field,
Jerusalem will become a heap of rubble, *m*
  the temple hill a mound overgrown with thickets.

The Mountain of the LORD

4 In the last days

the mountain of the LORD's temple will be established
  as chief among the mountains;
it will be raised above the hills,
  and peoples will stream to it.

4:2
n Jer 31:6

2 Many nations will come and say,

"Come, let us go up to the mountain of the LORD, *n*
  to the house of the God of Jacob.
He will teach us his ways,
  so that we may walk in his paths."
The law will go out from Zion,
  the word of the LORD from Jerusalem.

4:3
o Joel 3:10
p Isa 2:4

3 He will judge between many peoples
  and will settle disputes for strong nations far and wide.
They will beat their swords into plowshares
  and their spears into pruning hooks. *o*
Nation will not take up sword against nation,
  nor will they train for war anymore. *p*

4:4
q 1Ki 4:25
r Zec 3:10

4 Every man will sit under his own vine
  and under his own fig tree, *q*
and no one will make them afraid,
  for the LORD Almighty has spoken. *r*

4:5
s 2Ki 17:29

5 All the nations may walk
  in the name of their gods; *s*

3:11 Micah warned the leaders, priests, and prophets of his day to avoid bribes. Pastors today accept bribes when they allow those who contribute much to control the church. When fear of losing money or members influences pastors to remain silent when they should speak up for what is right, their churches are in danger. We should remember that Judah was finally destroyed because of the behavior of its religious leaders. A similar warning must be directed at those who have money—*never* use your resources to influence or manipulate God's ministers—that is bribery.

3:12 Jerusalem would be destroyed just as Samaria was (1:6). This happened in 586 B.C. when Nebuchadnezzar and the Babylonian army attacked the city (2 Kings 25). Although Micah blamed the corrupt leaders, the people were not without fault.

They allowed the corruption to continue without turning to God or calling for justice.

4:1ff The phrase "in the last days" describes the days when God will reign over his perfect kingdom (see 4:1–8). The "mountain of the LORD" is Mount Zion. This will be an era of peace and blessing, a time when war will be forever ended. We cannot pinpoint its date, but God has promised that it *will* arrive (see also Isaiah 2:2; Jeremiah 16:15; Joel 3:1ff; Zechariah 14:9–11; Malachi 3:17, 18; Revelation 19—22).

Verses 9–13 predicted the Babylonian captivity in 586 B.C., even before Babylon became a powerful empire. Just as God promises a time of peace and prosperity, he also promises judgment and punishment for all who refuse to follow him. Both results are certain.

we will walk in the name of the LORD
our God for ever and ever.[t]

4:5
[t]Zec 10:12

The LORD's Plan

6 "In that day," declares the LORD,

"I will gather the lame;
I will assemble the exiles
and those I have brought to grief.[u]

4:6
[u]Eze 34:13, 16

7 I will make the lame a remnant,
those driven away a strong nation.
The LORD will rule over them in Mount Zion
from that day and forever.[v]

4:7
[v]Rev 11:15

8 As for you, O watchtower of the flock,
O stronghold[a] of the Daughter of Zion,
the former dominion will be restored to you;
kingship will come to the Daughter of Jerusalem."

9 Why do you now cry aloud—
have you no king?[w]
Has your counselor perished,
that pain seizes you like that of a woman in labor?[x]

4:9
[w]Jer 8:19
[x]Jer 30:6

10 Writhe in agony, O Daughter of Zion,
like a woman in labor,
for now you must leave the city
to camp in the open field.
You will go to Babylon;
there you will be rescued.
There the LORD will redeem you
out of the hand of your enemies.

11 But now many nations
are gathered against you.
They say, "Let her be defiled,
let our eyes gloat over Zion!"

12 But they do not know
the thoughts of the LORD;
they do not understand his plan,[y]
he who gathers them like sheaves to the threshing floor.

4:12
[y]Isa 55:8

13 "Rise and thresh, O Daughter of Zion,
for I will give you horns of iron;
I will give you hoofs of bronze
and you will break to pieces many nations."[z]

4:13
[z]Da 2:44

You will devote their ill-gotten gains to the LORD,
their wealth to the Lord of all the earth.

A Promised Ruler From Bethlehem

5 Marshal your troops, O city of troops,[b]
for a siege is laid against us.

a 8 Or *hill*   b 1 Or *Strengthen your walls, O walled city*

4:9–13 Micah predicted the end of the kings. This was a drastic statement to the people of Judah who thought that their kingdom would last forever. Micah also said that Babylon would destroy the land of Judah and carry away its king, but that after a while God would help his people return to their land. This all happened just as Micah prophesied, and these events are recorded in 2 Chronicles 36:9–23 and Ezra 1; 2.

4:12 When God reveals the future, his purpose goes beyond satisfying our curiosity. He wants us to change our present behavior because of what we know about the future. Forever begins now; and a glimpse of God's plan for his followers should motivate us to serve him, no matter what the rest of the world may do.

5:1 This ruler was probably King Zedekiah, who was reigning in Jerusalem when Nebuchadnezzar conquered the city (2 Kings 25:1, 2). Zedekiah was the last of the kings in David's line to sit on the throne in Jerusalem. Micah said that the next king in David's line would be the Messiah, who would establish a kingdom that would never end.

5:1
*a*La 3:30

They will strike Israel's ruler
    on the cheek*a* with a rod.

5:2
*b*Jn 7:42
*c*Mt 2:6*

2 "But you, Bethlehem*b* Ephrathah,
    though you are small among the clans*a* of Judah,
out of you will come for me
    one who will be ruler over Israel,
whose origins*b* are from of old,
    from ancient times.*c*"*c*

3 Therefore Israel will be abandoned
    until the time when she who is in labor gives birth
and the rest of his brothers return
    to join the Israelites.

5:4
*d*Isa 40:11;
Eze 34:11-15, 23

4 He will stand and shepherd his flock*d*
    in the strength of the LORD,
    in the majesty of the name of the LORD his God.
And they will live securely, for then his greatness
    will reach to the ends of the earth.

5:5
*e*Isa 9:6

5   And he will be their peace.*e*

Deliverance and Destruction

When the Assyrian invades our land
    and marches through our fortresses,
we will raise against him seven shepherds,
    even eight leaders of men.

5:6
*f*Ge 10:8
*g*Na 2:11-13

6 They will rule*d* the land of Assyria with the sword,
    the land of Nimrod*f* with drawn sword.*e*
He will deliver us from the Assyrian
    when he invades our land
    and marches into our borders.*g*

5:7
*h*Mic 2:12

7 The remnant*h* of Jacob will be
    in the midst of many peoples
like dew from the LORD,
    like showers on the grass,
which do not wait for man
    or linger for mankind.

5:8
*i*Mic 4:13
*j*Hos 5:14

8 The remnant of Jacob will be among the nations,
    in the midst of many peoples,
like a lion among the beasts of the forest,
    like a young lion among flocks of sheep,
which mauls and mangles*i* as it goes,
    and no one can rescue.*j*

---

a2 Or *rulers*   *b2* Hebrew *goings out*   *c2* Or *from days of eternity*   *d6* Or *crush*   *e6* Or *Nimrod in its gates*

5:1ff Jerusalem's leaders were obsessed with wealth and position, but Micah prophesied that mighty Jerusalem, with all its wealth and power, would be besieged and destroyed. Its king could not save it. In contrast, Bethlehem, a tiny town, would be the birthplace of the only king who could save his people. This deliverer, the Messiah, would be born as a baby in Bethlehem (Luke 2:4–7), and eventually would reign as the eternal King (Revelation 19—22).

5:2 Ephrathah was the district in which Bethlehem was located.

5:2 This ruler is Jesus, the Messiah. Micah accurately predicted Christ's birthplace hundreds of years before Jesus was born. The promised eternal King in David's line, who would come to live as a man, had been alive forever—"from of old, from ancient times." Although eternal, Christ entered human history as the man, Jesus of Nazareth.

5:5 This chapter provides one of the clearest Old Testament prophecies of Christ's coming. The key descriptive phrase is "and

he will be their peace." In one of Christ's final talks he said, "Peace I leave with you; my peace I give you. I do not give to you as the world gives. Do not let your hearts be troubled and do not be afraid" (John 14:27). Because of Christ's first coming, we have the opportunity to experience peace with God with no more fear of judgment and no more conflict and guilt. Christ's peace gives us assurance even though wars continue. At Christ's second coming, all wars and weapons will be destroyed (4:3–5).

5:5 Micah's prophecy of seven shepherds and eight leaders is a figurative way of saying that the Messiah will raise up many good leaders when he returns to reign. This contrasts with Micah's words in chapter three about Judah's corrupt leaders. "The Assyrian" symbolically refers to all nations in every age that oppose God's people. These good leaders will help Christ defeat all evil in the world.

5:6 The land of Nimrod is another name for Assyria, which, in this case, is a symbol of all the evil nations in the world.

9 Your hand will be lifted up[k] in triumph over your enemies,
   and all your foes will be destroyed.

10 "In that day," declares the LORD,

   "I will destroy your horses from among you
      and demolish your chariots.[l]
11 I will destroy the cities of your land
      and tear down all your strongholds.[m]
12 I will destroy your witchcraft
      and you will no longer cast spells.[n]
13 I will destroy your carved images
      and your sacred stones from among you;
   you will no longer bow down
      to the work of your hands.[o]
14 I will uproot from among you your Asherah poles[a]
      and demolish your cities.
15 I will take vengeance[p] in anger and wrath
      upon the nations that have not obeyed me."

3. The trial of the people

The LORD's Case Against Israel

6 Listen to what the LORD says:

   "Stand up, plead your case before the mountains;
      let the hills hear what you have to say.
2 Hear, O mountains, the LORD's accusation;[q]
      listen, you everlasting foundations of the earth.
   For the LORD has a case against his people;
      he is lodging a charge against Israel.

3 "My people, what have I done to you?
      How have I burdened[r] you? Answer me.
4 I brought you up out of Egypt
      and redeemed you from the land of slavery.
   I sent Moses to lead you,
      also Aaron[s] and Miriam.[t]
5 My people, remember
      what Balak[u] king of Moab counseled
      and what Balaam son of Beor answered.
   Remember ⌊your journey⌋ from Shittim[v] to Gilgal,[w]
      that you may know the righteous acts of the LORD."

a 14 That is, symbols of the goddess Asherah

Cross-references

5:9 [k] Ps 10:12
5:10 [l] Hos 14:3; Zec 9:10
5:11 [m] Am 5:9
5:12 [n] Isa 2:6
5:13 [o] Zec 13:2
5:15 [p] Isa 65:12
6:2 [q] Hos 12:2
6:3 [r] Jer 2:5
6:4 [s] Ps 77:20
6:4 [t] Ex 15:20
6:5 [u] Nu 22:5-6
6:5 [v] Nu 25:1
6:5 [w] Jos 5:9-10

5:10 When God rules in his eternal kingdom, our strength and deliverance will not be found in military might but in God's almighty power. God will destroy all the weapons that people use for security. Armies will not be needed because God will rule in the heart of every person. Instead of being overwhelmed by fear of invasion or nuclear attack, we should have confidence in God.

5:12–14 Carved images, sacred stones, and Asherah poles were all part of pagan worship.

6:1ff Here Micah pictures a courtroom. God, the judge, tells his people what he requires of them and recites all the ways they have wronged both him and others. Chapters 4 and 5 are full of hope; chapters 6 and 7 proclaim judgment and appeal to the people to repent.

6:1, 2 God called to the mountains to confirm the people's guilt. The mountains would serve as excellent witnesses, for it was in the high places that the people had built pagan altars and had sacrificed to false gods (1 Kings 14:23; Jeremiah 17:2, 3; Ezekiel 20:28).

6:3 The people would never be able to answer this question because God had done nothing wrong. In fact, God had been exceedingly patient with them, had always lovingly guided them, and had given them every opportunity to return to him. If God asked you, "What have I done to you?" how would you reply?

6:5 The story of Balak and Balaam is found in Numbers 22—24. Shittim was the Israelites' campsite east of the Jordan River just before they entered the promised land (Joshua 2:1). There the people received many of God's instructions about how to live. Gilgal, their first campsite after crossing the Jordan (Joshua 4:19), was where the people renewed their covenant with God (Joshua 5:3–9). These two places represent God's loving care for his people: his willingness both to protect them and to warn them about potential troubles. In Micah's day, the people had forgotten this covenant and its benefits and had turned away from God.

6:5 God continued to be kind to his forgetful people, but their short memory and lack of thankfulness condemned them. When people refuse to see how fortunate they are and begin to take God's gifts for granted, they become self-centered. Regularly remember God's goodness and thank him. Remembering God's past protection will help you see his present provision.

⁶ With what shall I come before the LORD
   and bow down before the exalted God?
Shall I come before him with burnt offerings,
   with calves a year old?

6:7
ˣPs 50:8-10
ʸ2Ki 16:3

⁷ Will the LORD be pleased with thousands of rams,
   with ten thousand rivers of oil?ˣ
Shall I offer my firstborn for my transgression,
   the fruit of my body for the sin of my soul?ʸ

6:8
ᶻDt 10:12-13;
Hos 6:6

⁸ He has showed you, O man, what is good.
   And what does the LORD require of you?
To act justly and to love mercy
   and to walk humbly with your God. ᶻ

Israel's Guilt and Punishment

⁹ Listen! The LORD is calling to the city—
   and to fear your name is wisdom—
"Heed the rod and the One who appointed it.ᵃ

6:10
ᵃAm 3:10

¹⁰ Am I still to forget, O wicked house,
   your ill-gotten treasures
and the short ephah,ᵇ which is accursed?ᵃ

6:11
ᵇHos 12:7

¹¹ Shall I acquit a man with dishonest scales,ᵇ
   with a bag of false weights?

6:12
ᶜJer 9:3

¹² Her rich men are violent;
   her people are liars
and their tongues speak deceitfully.ᶜ

¹³ Therefore, I have begun to destroy you,
   to ruin you because of your sins.
¹⁴ You will eat but not be satisfied;
   your stomach will still be empty.ᶜ
You will store up but save nothing,
   because what you save I will give to the sword.

6:15
ᵈAm 5:11

¹⁵ You will plant but not harvest;
   you will press olives but not use the oil on yourselves,
   you will crush grapes but not drink the wine.ᵈ

6:16
ᵉ1Ki 16:25

¹⁶ You have observed the statutes of Omriᵉ
   and all the practices of Ahab's house,
   and you have followed their traditions.
Therefore I will give you over to ruin
   and your people to derision;
   you will bear the scorn of the nations.ᵈ"

Israel's Misery

7 What misery is mine!
I am like one who gathers summer fruit
   at the gleaning of the vineyard;

ᵃ9 The meaning of the Hebrew for this line is uncertain.   ᵇ10 An ephah was a dry measure.   ᶜ14 The meaning of the Hebrew for this word is uncertain.   ᵈ16 Septuagint; Hebrew *scorn due my people*

6:6–8 Israel responded to God's request by trying to appease him with sacrifices, hoping he would then leave them alone. But sacrifices and other religious rituals aren't enough; God wants his people to be fair, just, merciful, and humble. God wants us to become *living* sacrifices (Romans 12:1, 2), not just doing religious deeds, but living rightly (Jeremiah 4:4; Hebrews 9:14). It is impossible to follow God consistently without his transforming love in our hearts.

6:8 People have tried all kinds of ways to please God (6:6, 7), but God has made his wishes clear: he wants his people to be just, merciful, and to walk humbly with him. In your efforts to please God, examine these areas on a regular basis. Are you fair in your dealings with people? Do you show mercy to those who wrong you? Are you learning humility?

6:16 Omri reigned over Israel and led the people into idol worship (1 Kings 16:21–26). Ahab, his son, was Israel's most wicked king (1 Kings 16:29–33). If the people were following the commands and practices of these kings, they were in bad shape. Such pervasive evil was ripe for punishment.

7:1ff This chapter begins in gloom (7:1–6) and ends in hope (7:8–20). Micah watched as society rotted around him. Rulers demanded gifts; judges accepted bribes; corruption was universal. But God promised to lead the people out of the darkness of sin and into his light. Then the people would praise him for his faithfulness. God alone is perfectly faithful.

7:1–4 Micah could not find an upright person anywhere in the land. Even today, uprightness (honesty, integrity) is difficult to find. Society rationalizes sin, and even Christians sometimes

there is no cluster of grapes to eat,
  none of the early figs that I crave.
2 The godly have been swept from the land;[f]
  not one upright man remains.
All men lie in wait to shed blood;
  each hunts his brother with a net.[g]
3 Both hands are skilled in doing evil;
  the ruler demands gifts,
the judge accepts bribes,
  the powerful dictate what they desire—
they all conspire together.
4 The best of them is like a brier,[h]
  the most upright worse than a thorn hedge.
The day of your watchmen has come,
  the day God visits you.
Now is the time of their confusion.[i]
5 Do not trust a neighbor;
  put no confidence in a friend.[j]
Even with her who lies in your embrace
  be careful of your words.
6 For a son dishonors his father,
  a daughter rises up against her mother,
a daughter-in-law against her mother-in-law—
  a man's enemies are the members of his own household.[k]

7 But as for me, I watch in hope for the LORD,
  I wait for God my Savior;
  my God will hear me.

Israel Will Rise

8 Do not gloat over me,[l] my enemy!
  Though I have fallen, I will rise.
Though I sit in darkness,
  the LORD will be my light.[m]
9 Because I have sinned against him,
  I will bear the LORD's wrath,[n]
until he pleads my case
  and establishes my right.
He will bring me out into the light;
  I will see his righteousness.
10 Then my enemy will see it
  and will be covered with shame,
she who said to me,
  "Where is the LORD your God?"

7:2
[f]Ps 12:1
[g]Jer 5:26

7:4
[h]Eze 2:6
[i]Hos 9:7

7:5
[j]Jer 9:4

7:6
[k]Mt 10:35-36*

7:8
[l]Pr 24:17
[m]Isa 9:2

7:9
[n]La 3:39-40

---

compromise Christian principles in order to do what they want. It is easy to convince ourselves that we deserve a few breaks, especially when "everyone else" is doing it. But the standards for honesty come from God, not society. We are to be honest because God is truth, and we are to be like him.

7:5, 6 Sin had affected the government leaders and society in general. Deceit and dishonesty had even ruined the family, the core of society. As a result, the only way left to purify the people was God's judgment. This would draw the nation back to God and restore them from the inside out.

7:7–10 Micah showed great faith in God both personally (7:7) and on Israel's behalf (7:8–10) as he proclaimed that (1) he

would wait upon God, because God hears and saves when help is needed, (2) God would bring his people through when times were tough, (3) Israel must be patient in punishment because God would bring them out of the darkness, and (4) their enemies would be punished. We, too, can have a relationship with God that can allow us to have confidence like Micah's. It doesn't take unusual talent; it simply takes faith in God and a willingness to act on that faith.

7:9 Micah understood that if the people would be patient and obedient while they were being punished, God would forgive them and show his goodness again (Lamentations 3:39–41). Punishment does not mean rejection. The people were being punished in order to bring them back to God, not to send them away from him. When you face trials because of your sin, do not be angry with God or afraid that he has rejected you. Instead, turn away from your sin, turn to God, and continue to be patient and obedient.

7:10
o Isa 51:23

My eyes will see her downfall;o
   even now she will be trampled underfoot
   like mire in the streets.

11 The day for building your walls will come,
   the day for extending your boundaries.

7:12
p Isa 19:23-25

12 In that day people will come to you
   from Assyria and the cities of Egypt,
  even from Egypt to the Euphrates
   and from sea to sea
   and from mountain to mountain.p

13 The earth will become desolate because of its inhabitants,
   as the result of their deeds.

Prayer and Praise

7:14
q Mic 5:4
r Jer 50:19

14 Shepherdq your people with your staff,
   the flock of your inheritance,
which lives by itself in a forest,
   in fertile pasturelands.a
Let them feed in Bashan and Gileadr
   as in days long ago.

7:15
s Ex 3:20

15 "As in the days when you came out of Egypt,
   I will show them my wonders.s"

7:16
t Isa 26:11

16 Nations will see and be ashamed,t
   deprived of all their power.
They will lay their hands on their mouths
   and their ears will become deaf.

7:17
u Isa 49:23

17 They will lick dust like a snake,
   like creatures that crawl on the ground.
They will come trembling out of their dens;
   they will turn in fearu to the LORD our God
   and will be afraid of you.

7:18
v Isa 43:25
w Ex 34:9

18 Who is a God like you,
   who pardons sinv and forgives the transgression
   of the remnant of his inheritance?w
You do not stay angry forever
   but delight to show mercy.

7:19
x Isa 43:25

19 You will again have compassion on us;
   you will tread our sins underfoot
   and hurl all our iniquitiesx into the depths of the sea.

7:20
y Lk 1:72

20 You will be true to Jacob,
   and show mercy to Abraham,
as you pledged on oath to our fathersy
   in days long ago.

a 14 Or *in the middle of Carmel*

7:14 Bashan and Gilead were fertile areas east of the Jordan, previously the territory of Reuben, Gad, and the half tribe of Manasseh.

7:18 God delights to show mercy! He does not forgive grudgingly, but is glad when we repent and offers forgiveness to all who come back to him. Today you can confess your sins and receive his loving forgiveness. Don't be too proud to accept God's free offer.

7:20 In an age when religion was making little difference in people's lives, Micah said that God expected his people to be just, merciful, and humble (6:8). He requires the same of Christians today. In a world that is unjust, we must act justly. In a world of tough breaks, we must be merciful. In a world of pride and self-sufficiency, we must walk humbly with God. Only when we live according to God's way will we begin to affect our homes, our society, and our world.

NAHUM

Manasseh
becomes
king of
Judah
697 B.C.

Ashurbanipal
becomes
king of
Assyria
669

The fall
of Thebes;
Nahum
becomes
a prophet
663

VITAL STATISTICS

PURPOSE:
To pronounce God's judgment on Assyria and to comfort Judah with this truth

AUTHOR:
Nahum

ORIGINAL AUDIENCE:
The people of Nineveh and of Judah (the southern kingdom)

DATE WRITTEN:
Sometime during Nahum's prophetic ministry (probably between 663 and 612 B.C.)

SETTING:
This particular prophecy took place after the fall of Thebes in 663 B.C. (see 3:8–10).

KEY VERSES:
"The LORD is good, a refuge in times of trouble. He cares for those who trust in him, but with an overwhelming flood he will make an end of ⌊Nineveh⌋; he will pursue his foes into darkness. Whatever they plot against the LORD he will bring to an end; trouble will not come a second time" (1:7–9).

KEY PLACE:
Nineveh

THE SHRILL whistle pierces the air, and all the action on the court abruptly stops. Pointing to the offending player, the referee shouts, "Foul!"

Rules, fouls, and penalties are part of any game and are regulated and enforced vigorously by referees, umpires, judges, and other officials. Every participant knows that boundaries must be set and behavior monitored, or the game will degenerate into chaos.

The world also has laws—boundaries and rules for living established by God. But men and women regularly flaunt these regulations, hiding their infractions or overpowering others and declaring that might makes right. God calls this sin—willful disobedience, rebellion against his control, or apathy. And at times it seems as though the violators succeed—no whistles blow, no fouls are called, and individual dictators rule. The truth is, however, that ultimately justice will be served in the world. God will settle all accounts.

Assyria was the most powerful nation on earth. Proud in their self-sufficiency and military might, they plundered, oppressed, and slaughtered their victims. One hundred years earlier, Jonah had preached in the streets of the great city Nineveh; the people had heard God's message and had turned from their evil. But generations later, evil was again reigning, and the prophet Nahum pronounced judgment on this wicked nation. Nineveh is called a "city of blood" (3:1), a city of cruelty (3:19), and the Assyrians are judged for their arrogance (2:13), idolatry (1:14), murder, lies, treachery, and social injustice (3:1–19). Nahum predicted that this proud and powerful nation would be utterly destroyed because of its sins. The end came within 50 years.

In this judgment of Assyria and its capital city, Nineveh, God is judging a sinful world. And the message is clear: Disobedience, rebellion, and injustice will not prevail but will be punished severely by a righteous and holy God, who rules over all the earth.

As you read Nahum, sense God's wrath as he avenges sin and brings about justice. Then decide to live under his guidance and within his rules, commands, and guidelines for life.

THE BLUEPRINT

1. Nineveh's judge
   (1:1–15)
2. Nineveh's judgment
   (2:1—3:19)

Nineveh, the capital of the Assyrian empire, is the subject of Nahum's prophecy. The news of its coming destruction was a relief for Judah, who was subject to Assyrian domination. No longer would Judah be forced to pay tribute as insurance against invasions. Judah was comforted to know that God was still in control. Nineveh is an example to all rulers and nations of the world today. God is sovereign over even those who are seemingly invincible. We can be confident that God's power and justice will one day conquer all evil.

MEGATHEMES

THEME	EXPLANATION	IMPORTANCE
God Judges	God would judge the city of Nineveh for its idolatry, arrogance, and oppression. Although Assyria was the leading military power in the world, God would completely destroy this "invincible" nation. God allows no person or power to usurp or scoff at his authority.	Anyone who remains arrogant and resists God's authority will face his anger. No ruler or nation will get away with rejecting him. No individual will be able to hide from his judgment. Yet those who keep trusting God will be kept safe forever.
God Rules	God rules over all the earth, even over those who don't acknowledge him. God is all-powerful, and no one can thwart his plans. God will overcome any who attempt to defy him. Human power is futile against God.	If you are impressed by or afraid of any weapons, armies, or powerful people, remember that God alone can truly rescue you from fear or oppression. We must place our confidence in God because he alone rules all of history, all the earth, and our life.

1. Nineveh's judge

1:1
*a*Jnh 1:2; Zep 2:13

1 An oracle concerning Nineveh. *a* The book of the vision of Nahum the Elkoshite.

The LORD's Anger Against Nineveh

1:2
*b*Ex 20:5

2 The LORD is a jealous*b* and avenging God;
    the LORD takes vengeance and is filled with wrath.
The LORD takes vengeance on his foes
    and maintains his wrath against his enemies.

1:3
*c*Ne 9:17
*d*Ps 104:3

3 The LORD is slow to anger*c* and great in power;
    the LORD will not leave the guilty unpunished.
His way is in the whirlwind and the storm,
    and clouds*d* are the dust of his feet.

1:4
*e*Isa 33:9

4 He rebukes the sea and dries it up;
    he makes all the rivers run dry.
Bashan and Carmel*e* wither
    and the blossoms of Lebanon fade.

1:5
*f*Mic 1:4

5 The mountains quake before him
    and the hills melt away.*f*
The earth trembles at his presence,
    the world and all who live in it.

1:1 Nahum, like Jonah, was a prophet to Nineveh, the capital of the Assyrian empire, and he prophesied between 663 and 612 B.C. Jonah had seen Nineveh repent a century earlier (see the book of Jonah), but the city had fallen back into wickedness. Assyria, the world power controlling the Fertile Crescent, seemed unstoppable. Its ruthless and savage warriors had already conquered Israel, the northern kingdom, and were causing great suffering in Judah. So Nahum proclaimed God's anger against Assyria's evil. Within a few decades, the mighty Assyrian empire would be toppled by Babylon.

1:1 An oracle is a message from God. Elkosh was a village thought by some to be in southwest Judah.

1:2 God alone has the right to be jealous and to carry out vengeance. Jealousy and vengeance may be surprising terms to associate with God. When humans are jealous and take vengeance, they are usually acting in a spirit of selfishness. But it is appropriate for God to insist on our complete allegiance,

and it is just for him to punish unrepentant evildoers. His jealousy and vengeance are unmixed with selfishness. Their purpose is to remove sin and restore peace to the world (Deuteronomy 4:24; 5:9).

1:3 God is slow to get angry, but when he is ready to punish, even the earth trembles. Often people avoid God because they see evildoers in the world and hypocrites in the church. They don't realize that because God is slow to anger, he gives his true followers time to share his love and truth with evildoers. But judgment *will* come; God will not allow sin to go unchecked forever. When people wonder why God doesn't punish evil immediately, help them remember that if he did, none of us would be here. We can all be thankful that God gives people time to turn to him.

1:4 Bashan and Carmel were very fertile areas.

6 Who can withstand his indignation?
   Who can endure his fierce anger?
His wrath is poured out like fire;*g*
   the rocks are shattered before him.

1:6
g Jer 10:10

7 The LORD is good,*h*
   a refuge in times of trouble.
He cares for those who trust in him,
8 but with an overwhelming flood
he will make an end of ˻Nineveh˼;
   he will pursue his foes into darkness.

1:7
h Jer 33:11

9 Whatever they plot against the LORD
   he*a* will bring to an end;
   trouble will not come a second time.
10 They will be entangled among thorns*i*
    and drunk from their wine;
    they will be consumed like dry stubble.*b* *j*
  11 From you, ˻O Nineveh,˼ has one come forth
    who plots evil against the LORD
    and counsels wickedness.

1:10
i 2Sa 23:6
j Mal 4:1

12This is what the LORD says:

"Although they have allies and are numerous,
   they will be cut off and pass away.
Although I have afflicted you, ˻O Judah,˼
   I will afflict you no more.
13 Now I will break their yoke from your neck
    and tear your shackles away."

14 The LORD has given a command concerning you, ˻Nineveh˼:
   "You will have no descendants to bear your name.
I will destroy the carved images*k* and cast idols
    that are in the temple of your gods.
I will prepare your grave,
    for you are vile."

1:14
k Mic 5:13

15 Look, there on the mountains,
    the feet of one who brings good news,*l*
    who proclaims peace!
Celebrate your festivals,*m* O Judah,
    and fulfill your vows.
No more will the wicked invade you;
    they will be completely destroyed.

1:15
l Ro 10:15
m Lev 23:2-4

a 9 Or *What do you foes plot against the LORD? / He*   *b* 10 The meaning of the Hebrew for this verse is uncertain.

1:6 No person on earth can safely defy God, the Almighty, the Creator of all the universe. God, who controls the sun, the galaxies, and the vast stretches beyond, also controls the rise and fall of nations. How could a small temporal kingdom like Assyria, no matter how powerful, challenge God's awesome power? If only Assyria could have looked ahead to see the desolate mound of rubble that it would become—yet God would still be alive and well! Don't defy God; he will be here forever with greater power than that of all armies and nations combined.

1:6–8 To people who refuse to believe, God's punishment is like an angry fire. To those who love him, his mercy is a refuge, supplying all their needs without diminishing his supply. But to God's enemies he is an overwhelming flood that will sweep them away. The relationship we have with God is up to us. What kind of relationship will you choose?

1:11 The one "who plots evil against the LORD and counsels wickedness" could have been (1) Ashurbanipal (669–627 B.C.), king of Assyria during much of Nahum's life and the one who brought Assyria to the zenith of its power; (2) Sennacherib (705–681), who openly defied God (2 Kings 18:13–35), epitomizing rebellion against God; (3) no one king in particular but the entire evil monarchy. The point is that Nineveh would be destroyed for rebelling against God.

1:12–15 The good news for Judah, whom Assyria afflicted, was that its conquerors and tormentors would be destroyed and would never rise to torment it again. Nineveh was so completely wiped out that its ruins were not identified until 1845.

2. Nineveh's judgment
Nineveh to Fall

2:1
n Jer 51:20

2 An attacker^n advances against you, ⌐Nineveh⌐.
   Guard the fortress,
   watch the road,
   brace yourselves,
   marshal all your strength!

2:2
o Eze 37:23

2 The LORD will restore^o the splendor of Jacob
   like the splendor of Israel,
   though destroyers have laid them waste
   and have ruined their vines.

2:3
p Eze 23:14-15

3 The shields of his soldiers are red;
   the warriors are clad in scarlet.^p
The metal on the chariots flashes
   on the day they are made ready;
   the spears of pine are brandished.^a

2:4
q Jer 4:13

4 The chariots^q storm through the streets,
   rushing back and forth through the squares.
They look like flaming torches;
   they dart about like lightning.

2:5
r Jer 46:12

5 He summons his picked troops,
   yet they stumble^r on their way.
They dash to the city wall;
   the protective shield is put in place.
6 The river gates are thrown open
   and the palace collapses.

2:7
s Isa 59:11

7 It is decreed^b that ⌐the city⌐
   be exiled and carried away.
Its slave girls moan^s like doves
   and beat upon their breasts.
8 Nineveh is like a pool,
   and its water is draining away.
"Stop! Stop!" they cry,
   but no one turns back.
9 Plunder the silver!
   Plunder the gold!

a 3 Hebrew; Septuagint and Syriac / *the horsemen rush to and fro*   b 7 The meaning of the Hebrew for this word is uncertain.

NAHUM
served as
a prophet
to Judah from
663–612 B.C.

Climate of the times . . . . Manasseh, one of Judah's most wicked kings, ruled the land. He openly defied God and persecuted God's people. Assyria, the world power at that time, made Judah one of its vassal states. The people of Judah wanted to be like the Assyrians, who seemed to have all the power and possessions they wanted.

Main message . . . . The mighty empire of Assyria that oppressed God's people would soon tumble.

Importance of message . . . . Those who do evil and oppress others will one day meet a bitter end.

Contemporary prophets . . . . Zephaniah (640–621 B.C.)

2:1ff This chapter predicts the events of 612 B.C., when the combined armies of the Babylonians and the Medes sacked seemingly impregnable Nineveh.

2:2 Assyria had plundered and crushed the northern kingdom (Israel) and had deported its people in 722 B.C. (2 Kings 17:3–6; 18:9–11). Assyria had also attacked the southern kingdom (here called Judah, also called Jacob) and had forced it to pay tribute. These two separate kingdoms had been formed after Solomon's reign. A civil dispute with Solomon's son had caused ten of the tribes to set up their own kingdom. They had become the northern kingdom, while the remaining two tribes (Judah and Benjamin) stayed loyal to David's line and became the southern kingdom.

2:6 This reference to the opening of river gates could refer either to the enemy flowing into Nineveh like a flood (1:8) or to an actual flood of water. Some scholars suggest that dam gates, which were found in archaeological excavations, were closed to dam up the river. When an enormous amount of water had been accumulated, the gates were opened, allowing the water to flood Nineveh.

The supply is endless,
   the wealth from all its treasures!
10 She is pillaged, plundered, stripped!
   Hearts melt, knees give way,
   bodies tremble, every face grows pale.

11 Where now is the lions' den,[t]
   the place where they fed their young,
   where the lion and lioness went,
   and the cubs, with nothing to fear?
12 The lion killed enough for his cubs
   and strangled the prey for his mate,
   filling his lairs with the kill
   and his dens with the prey.

13 "I am against[u] you,"
   declares the LORD Almighty.
"I will burn up your chariots in smoke,[v]
   and the sword will devour your young lions.
I will leave you no prey on the earth.
The voices of your messengers
   will no longer be heard."

2:11
[t] Isa 5:29

2:13
[u] Na 3:5
[v] Ps 46:9

Woe to Nineveh

3 Woe to the city of blood,
   full of lies,
full of plunder,
   never without victims!
2 The crack of whips,
   the clatter of wheels,
galloping horses
   and jolting chariots!
3 Charging cavalry,
   flashing swords
   and glittering spears!
Many casualties,
   piles of dead,
bodies without number,
   people stumbling over the corpses[w]—
4 all because of the wanton lust of a harlot,
   alluring, the mistress of sorceries,[x]
who enslaved nations by her prostitution[y]
   and peoples by her witchcraft.

5 "I am against[z] you," declares the LORD Almighty.
   "I will lift your skirts over your face.
I will show the nations your nakedness[a]
   and the kingdoms your shame.
6 I will pelt you with filth,
   I will treat you with contempt[b]

3:3
[w] Isa 34:3

3:4
[x] Isa 47:9
[y] Isa 23:17

3:5
[z] Na 2:13
[a] Isa 47:3

3:6
[b] Jer 51:37

2:12—3:1 The major source of wealth for the Assyrian economy was the plunder taken from other nations. The Assyrians had taken the food of innocent people to maintain their luxurious standard of living, depriving others to supply their excesses. Depriving innocent people to support the luxury of a few is a sin that angers God. As Christians we must stand firm against this common but evil practice.

2:13 God had given the people of Nineveh a chance to repent, which they did after hearing Jonah (see the book of Jonah). But they had returned to their sin, and its consequences were destroying them. There is a point for people, cities, and nations

after which there is no turning back; Assyria had passed that point. We must warn others to repent while there is still time.

3:4 Nineveh had used its beauty, prestige, and power to seduce other nations. Like a harlot, she had enticed them into false friendships. Then when the other nations relaxed, thinking Assyria was a friend, Assyria destroyed and plundered them. Beautiful and impressive on the outside, Nineveh was vicious and deceitful on the inside. Beneath attractive facades sometimes lie seduction and death. Don't let an institution, company, movement, or person seduce you into lowering your standards or compromising your moral principles.

3:6
c Isa 14:16

3:7
d Jer 15:5
e Isa 51:19

3:8
f Jer 46:25

3:9
g Eze 27:10

3:10
h Isa 20:4
i Isa 13:16;
Hos 13:16

3:13
j Jer 50:37

3:14
k Na 2:1

3:15
l Joel 1:4

and make you a spectacle. c

7 All who see you will flee from you and say,
  'Nineveh is in ruins—who will mourn for her?' d
  Where can I find anyone to comfort e you?"

8 Are you better than Thebes, a f
    situated on the Nile,
    with water around her?
  The river was her defense,
    the waters her wall.
9 Cush b and Egypt were her boundless strength;
    Put g and Libya were among her allies.
10 Yet she was taken captive h
    and went into exile.
  Her infants were dashed i to pieces
    at the head of every street.
  Lots were cast for her nobles,
    and all her great men were put in chains.
11 You too will become drunk;
    you will go into hiding
    and seek refuge from the enemy.

12 All your fortresses are like fig trees
    with their first ripe fruit;
  when they are shaken,
    the figs fall into the mouth of the eater.
13 Look at your troops—
    they are all women! j
  The gates of your land
    are wide open to your enemies;
    fire has consumed their bars.

14 Draw water for the siege,
    strengthen your defenses! k
  Work the clay,
    tread the mortar,
    repair the brickwork!
15 There the fire will devour you;
    the sword will cut you down
    and, like grasshoppers, consume you.
  Multiply like grasshoppers,
    multiply like locusts! l
16 You have increased the number of your merchants
    till they are more than the stars of the sky,
  but like locusts they strip the land
    and then fly away.
17 Your guards are like locusts,
    your officials like swarms of locusts
    that settle in the walls on a cold day—
  but when the sun appears they fly away,
    and no one knows where.

a 8 Hebrew No Amon   b 9 That is, the upper Nile region

3:8–10 Thebes was a city in Egypt, the previous world power, that had stood in the path of Assyria's expansion in the south. The Assyrians had conquered Thebes 51 years before this prophecy was given. To Judah, surrounded to the north and south by Assyria, the situation appeared hopeless. But God said that the same atrocities done in Thebes would happen in Nineveh.

3:8–10 No power on earth can protect us from God's judgment or be a suitable substitute for his power in our lives. Thebes and

Assyria put their trust in alliances and military power, but history would show that these were inadequate. Don't insist on learning through personal experience; instead, learn the lessons history has already taught. Put your trust in God above all else.

18 O king of Assyria, your shepherds[a] slumber;[m]
    your nobles lie down to rest.
Your people are scattered[n] on the mountains
    with no one to gather them.
19 Nothing can heal your wound;
    your injury is fatal.
Everyone who hears the news about you
    claps his hands[o] at your fall,
for who has not felt
    your endless cruelty?

3:18
mPs 76:5-6
n1Ki 22:17

3:19
oLa 2:15

a 18 Or rulers

3:19 All the nations hated to be ruled by the merciless Assyrians, but the nations wanted to be like Assyria—powerful, wealthy, prestigious—and they courted Assyria's friendship. In the same way, we don't like the idea of being ruled harshly, so we do what we can to stay on good terms with a powerful leader. And deep down, we would like to have that kind of power. The thought of being on top can be captivating. But power is seductive, so we should not scheme to get it or hold on to it. Those who lust after power will be powerfully destroyed, as was the mighty Assyrian empire.

HABAKKUK

FROM innocent childhood queries to complex university discussions, life is filled with questions. Asking how and why and when, we probe beneath the surface to find satisfying answers. But not all questions have answers wrapped and neatly tied. These unanswered interrogations create more questions and nagging, spirit-destroying doubt. Some choose to live with their doubts, ignoring them and moving on with life. Others become cynical and hardened. But many reject those options and continue to ask, looking for answers.

Habakkuk was a man who sought answers. Troubled by what he observed, he asked difficult questions. These questions were not merely intellectual exercises or bitter complaints. Habakkuk saw a dying world, and it broke his heart. Why is there evil in the world? Why do the wicked seem to be winning? He boldly and confidently took his complaints directly to God. And God answered with an avalanche of proof and prediction.

The prophet's questions and God's answers are recorded in this book. As we turn the pages, we are immediately confronted with his urgent cries, "How long, O LORD, must I call for help, but you do not listen? Or cry out to you, 'Violence!' but you do not save?" (1:2). In fact, most of the first chapter is devoted to his questions. As chapter two begins, Habakkuk declares that he will wait to hear God's answers to his complaints. Then God begins to speak, telling the prophet to write his answer plainly so that all will see and understand. It may seem, God says, as though the wicked triumph, but eventually they will be judged, and righteousness will prevail. Judgment may not come quickly, but it *will* come. God's answers fill chapter two. Then Habakkuk concludes his book with a prayer of triumph. With questions answered and a new understanding of God's power and love, Habakkuk rejoices in who God is and in what he will do. "Yet I will rejoice in the LORD, I will be joyful in God my Savior. The Sovereign LORD is my strength; he makes my feet like the feet of a deer, he enables me to go on the heights" (3:18, 19).

Listen to the profound questions that Habakkuk boldly brings to God, and realize that you can also bring your complaints and inquiries to him. Listen to God's answers and rejoice that he is at work in the world and in your life.

VITAL STATISTICS

PURPOSE:
To show that God is still in control of the world despite the apparent triumph of evil

AUTHOR:
Habakkuk

ORIGINAL AUDIENCE:
The people of Judah (the southern kingdom)

DATE WRITTEN:
Between 612 and 588 B.C.

SETTING:
Babylon was becoming the dominant world power and Judah would soon feel Babylon's destructive force.

KEY VERSE:
"LORD, I have heard of your fame; I stand in awe of your deeds, O LORD. Renew them in our day, in our time make them known; in wrath remember mercy." (3:2).

KEY PEOPLE:
Habakkuk, the Babylonians

KEY PLACE:
Judah

THE BLUEPRINT

1. Habakkuk's complaints (1:1—2:20)
2. Habakkuk's prayer (3:1–19)

When Habakkuk was troubled, he brought his concerns directly to God. After receiving God's answers, he responded with a prayer of faith. Habakkuk's example is one that should encourage us as we struggle to move from doubt to faith. We don't have to be afraid to ask questions of God. The problem is not with God and his ways but with our limited understanding of him.

MEGATHEMES

THEME	EXPLANATION	IMPORTANCE
Struggle and Doubt	Habakkuk asked God why the wicked in Judah were not being punished for their sin. He couldn't understand why a just God would allow such evil to exist. God promised to use the Babylonians to punish Judah. When Habakkuk cried out for answers in his time of struggle, God answered him with words of hope.	God wants us to come to him with our struggles and doubts. His answers may not be what we expect, however. God sustains us by revealing himself to us. Trusting him leads to quiet hope, not bitter resignation.
God's Sovereignty	Habakkuk asked God why he would use the wicked Babylonians to punish his people. God said that he would also punish the Babylonians after they had fulfilled his purpose.	God is still in control of this world in spite of the apparent triumph of evil. God doesn't overlook sin. One day he will rule the whole earth with perfect justice.
Hope	God is the Creator; he is all-powerful. He has a plan, and he will carry it out. He will punish sin. He is our strength and our place of safety. We can have confidence that he will love us and guard our relationship with him forever.	Hope means going beyond our unpleasant daily experiences to the joy of knowing God. We live by trusting in him, not by the benefits, happiness, or success we may experience in this life. Our hope comes from God

1. Habakkuk's complaints

1 The oracle *a* that Habakkuk the prophet received.

Habakkuk's Complaint

2 How long, O LORD, must I call for help,
    but you do not listen? *b*
Or cry out to you, "Violence!"
    but you do not save?
3 Why do you make me look at injustice?
    Why do you tolerate wrong?
Destruction and violence *c* are before me;
    there is strife, and conflict abounds.
4 Therefore the law *d* is paralyzed,
    and justice never prevails.
The wicked hem in the righteous,
    so that justice is perverted. *e*

The LORD's Answer

5 "Look at the nations and watch—
    and be utterly amazed.
For I am going to do something in your days
    that you would not believe,
    even if you were told. *f*

1:1 *a*Na 1:1
1:2 *b*Ps 13:1-2
1:3 *c*Jer 20:8
1:4 *d*Ps 119:126 *e*Isa 5:20
1:5 *f*Ac 13:41*

1:1 Habakkuk lived in Judah during the reign of Jehoiakim (2 Kings 23:36—24:5). He prophesied between the fall of Nineveh (the capital of Assyria) in 612 B.C. and the Babylonian invasion of Judah in 588 B.C. With Assyria in disarray, Babylon was becoming the dominant world power. This book records the prophet's dialogue with God concerning the questions, "Why does God often seem indifferent in the face of evil? Why do evil people seem to go unpunished?" While other prophetic books brought God's word to people, this brought people's questions to God. An "oracle" is a message from God.

1:2-4 Saddened by the violence and corruption he saw around him, Habakkuk poured out his heart to God. Today injustice is still rampant, but don't let your concern cause you to doubt God or rebel against him. Instead, consider the message that God gave Habakkuk and recognize God's long-range plans and purposes. Realize that God is doing right, even when you do not understand why he works as he does.

1:5 God responded to Habakkuk's questions and concerns by stating that he would do amazing acts that would astound Habakkuk. When circumstances around us become almost unbearable, we wonder if God has forgotten us. But remember, he is in control. God has a plan and will judge evildoers in his time. If we are truly humble, we will be willing to accept God's answers and await his timing.

1:5ff God told the inhabitants of Jerusalem that they would be utterly amazed at what he was about to do. The people would, in fact, see a series of unbelievable events: (1) their own independent and prosperous kingdom, Judah, would suddenly become a vassal nation; (2) Egypt, a world power for centuries, would be crushed almost overnight; (3) Nineveh, the capital of the Assyrian empire, would be so completely ransacked that people would forget where it had been; and (4) the Babylonians would rise to power. Though these words were indeed amazing, the people saw them fulfilled during their lifetime.

1:6
g 2Ki 24:2

6 I am raising up the Babylonians,a *g*
  that ruthless and impetuous people,
who sweep across the whole earth
  to seize dwelling places not their own.

1:7
h Jer 39:5-9

7 They are a feared and dreaded people;*h*
  they are a law to themselves
  and promote their own honor.
8 Their horses are swifter than leopards,
  fiercer than wolves at dusk.
Their cavalry gallops headlong;
  their horsemen come from afar.
They fly like a vulture swooping to devour;

1:9
i Hab 2:5

9 they all come bent on violence.
Their hordesᵇ advance like a desert wind
  and gather prisoners*i* like sand.

1:10
j 2Ch 36:6

10 They deride kings
  and scoff at rulers.*j*
They laugh at all fortified cities;
  they build earthen ramps and capture them.

1:11
k Jer 4:11-12

11 Then they sweep past like the wind*k* and go on—
  guilty men, whose own strength is their god."

Habakkuk's Second Complaint

1:12
l Isa 10:6

12 O LORD, are you not from everlasting?
  My God, my Holy One, we will not die.
O LORD, you have appointed*l* them to execute judgment;
  O Rock, you have ordained them to punish.
13 Your eyes are too pure to look on evil;
  you cannot tolerate wrong.
Why then do you tolerate the treacherous?
Why are you silent while the wicked
  swallow up those more righteous than themselves?

a 6 Or *Chaldeans* *b* 9 The meaning of the Hebrew for this word is uncertain.

HABAKKUK
served as a
prophet to
Judah from
612–588 B.C.

Climate of the times. . . . . . . Judah's last four kings were wicked men who rejected God
and oppressed their own people. Babylon invaded Judah twice
before finally destroying it in 586 B.C. It was a time of fear,
oppression, persecution, lawlessness, and immorality.

Main message. . . . . Habakkuk couldn't understand why God seemed to do nothing
about the wickedness in society. Then he realized that faith in
God alone would supply the answers to his questions.

Importance of message. . . . Instead of questioning the ways of God, we should realize that
he is totally just and we should have faith that he is in control
and that one day evil will be utterly destroyed.

Contemporary prophets. . . . Jeremiah (627–586 B.C.), Daniel (605–536 B.C.),
Ezekiel (593–571 B.C.)

1:6 The Babylonians, who lived northwest of the Persian Gulf,
made a rapid rise to power around 630 B.C. They began to assert
themselves against the Assyrian empire, and by 605 B.C. had
conquered Assyria and Egypt to become the strongest world
power. But they were as wicked as the Assyrians, for they loved
to collect prisoners (1:9), were proud of their warfare tactics
(1:10), and trusted in their military strength (1:11).

1:10 Armies were able to take fortified (walled) cities by building
earthen ramps—heaping mounds of earth against the walls.

1:11 Babylon was proud of its military might, strategies, armies,
and weapons. With no regard for humanity, the armies brought
home riches, plunder, prisoners, and tribute from the nations they
conquered. Such is the essence of idolatry—asking the gods we

make to help us get all we want. The essence of Christianity is
asking the God *who made us* to help us give all we can in service
to him. The goal of idolatry is self-glory; the aim of Christianity is
God's glory.

1:13 Judah's forthcoming punishment would be at the hands
of the Babylonians. Habakkuk was appalled that God would use
a nation more wicked than Judah to punish Judah. But the Babylonians did not know they were being used by God to help Judah
return to him, and Babylon's pride in its victories would be its
downfall. Evil is self-destructive, and it is never beyond God's
control. God may use whatever unusual instrument he chooses to
correct or punish us. When we deserve punishment or correction,
how can we complain about the kind of discipline God uses on us?

14 You have made men like fish in the sea,
    like sea creatures that have no ruler.
15 The wicked foe pulls all of them up with hooks,
    he catches them in his net,[m]
he gathers them up in his dragnet;
    and so he rejoices and is glad.
16 Therefore he sacrifices to his net
    and burns incense to his dragnet,
for by his net he lives in luxury
    and enjoys the choicest food.
17 Is he to keep on emptying his net,
    destroying nations without mercy?[n]

2 I will stand at my watch[o]
    and station myself on the ramparts;
I will look to see what he will say to me,
    and what answer I am to give to this complaint.[a]

The LORD's Answer

2 Then the LORD replied:

"Write[p] down the revelation
    and make it plain on tablets
so that a herald[b] may run with it.
3 For the revelation awaits an appointed time;
    it speaks of the end[q]
    and will not prove false.
Though it linger, wait for it;
    it[c] will certainly come and will not delay.[r]

4 "See, he is puffed up;
    his desires are not upright—
but the righteous will live by his faith[d] [s]—
5 indeed, wine[t] betrays him;
    he is arrogant and never at rest.
Because he is as greedy as the grave[e]
    and like death is never satisfied,
he gathers to himself all the nations
    and takes captive all the peoples.

6 "Will not all of them taunt him with ridicule and scorn, saying,

"'Woe to him who piles up stolen goods
    and makes himself wealthy by extortion!
How long must this go on?'

1:15 [m] Jer 16:16

1:17 [n] Isa 14:6

2:1 [o] Isa 21:8

2:2 [p] Rev 1:19

2:3 [q] Da 8:17
[r] Eze 12:25

2:4 [s] Ro 1:17*;
Gal 3:11*;
Heb 10:37-38*

2:5 [t] Pr 20:1

[a] 1 Or *and what to answer when I am rebuked* [b] 2 Or *so that whoever reads it* [c] 3 Or *Though he linger, wait for him; / he* [d] 4 Or *faithfulness* [e] 5 Hebrew *Sheol*

2:1 The watchman and watchtower, often used by the prophets to show an attitude of expectation (Isaiah 21:8, 11; Jeremiah 6:17; Ezekiel 3:17), are pictures of Habakkuk's attitude of patient waiting and watching for God's response. Stone watchtowers were built on city walls or ramparts so that watchmen could see people (enemies or messengers) approaching their city while still at a distance. Watchtowers were also erected in vineyards to help guard the ripening grapes (Isaiah 5:2). Habakkuk wanted to be in the best position to receive God's message.

2:2ff This chapter records God's answers to Habakkuk's questions: (1) How long would evil prevail (1:2, 3)? (2) Why was Babylon chosen to punish Judah (1:13)? God said that the judgment, though slow to come, was certain. Although God used Babylon against Judah, he knew Babylon's sins and would punish it in due time.

2:3 Evil and injustice seem to have the upper hand in the world. Like Habakkuk, Christians often feel angry and discouraged as

they see what goes on. Habakkuk complained vigorously to God about the situation. God's answer to Habakkuk is the same answer he would give us, "Be patient! I will work out my plans in my perfect timing." It isn't easy to be patient, but it helps to remember that God hates sin even more than we do. Punishment of sin will certainly come. As God told Habakkuk, "Wait for it." To trust God fully means to trust him even when we don't understand why events occur as they do.

2:4 The wicked Babylonians trusted in themselves and would fall; but the righteous will live by their faithfulness to God. This verse has inspired countless Christians. Paul quotes it in Romans 1:17 and Galatians 3:11. The writer of Hebrews quotes it in 10:38, just before the famous chapter on faith. And it is helpful to all Christians who must live through difficult times without seeing signs of hope. Christians must trust that God is directing all things according to his purposes.

2:7
u Pr 29:1

7 Will not your debtors^a suddenly arise?
    Will they not wake up and make you tremble?
    Then you will become their victim. u

2:8
v Isa 33:1

8 Because you have plundered many nations,
    the peoples who are left will plunder you. v
For you have shed man's blood;
    you have destroyed lands and cities and everyone in them.

9 "Woe to him who builds his realm by unjust gain
    to set his nest on high,
    to escape the clutches of ruin!

2:10
w Jer 26:19

10 You have plotted the ruin w of many peoples,
    shaming your own house and forfeiting your life.

2:11
x Jos 24:27;
Lk 19:40

11 The stones x of the wall will cry out,
    and the beams of the woodwork will echo it.

2:12
y Mic 3:10

12 "Woe to him who builds a city with bloodshed y
    and establishes a town by crime!

2:13
z Isa 50:11

13 Has not the LORD Almighty determined
    that the people's labor is only fuel for the fire, z
    that the nations exhaust themselves for nothing?

2:14
a Isa 11:9

14 For the earth will be filled with the knowledge of the glory of the LORD,
    as the waters cover the sea. a

15 "Woe to him who gives drink to his neighbors,
    pouring it from the wineskin till they are drunk,
    so that he can gaze on their naked bodies.

2:16
b La 4:21

16 You will be filled with shame instead of glory.
    Now it is your turn! Drink and be exposed^b! b
The cup from the LORD's right hand is coming around to you,
    and disgrace will cover your glory.

2:17
c Jer 51:35
d ver 8

17 The violence c you have done to Lebanon will overwhelm you,
    and your destruction of animals will terrify you.
For you have shed man's blood; d
    you have destroyed lands and cities and everyone in them.

2:18
e Ps 115:4-5

18 "Of what value is an idol, since a man has carved it?
    Or an image that teaches lies?
For he who makes it trusts in his own creation;
    he makes idols that cannot speak. e

2:19
f 1Ki 18:27

19 Woe to him who says to wood, 'Come to life!'
    Or to lifeless stone, 'Wake up!' f
Can it give guidance?
    It is covered with gold and silver;
    there is no breath in it.
20 But the LORD is in his holy temple;
    let all the earth be silent before him."

a 7 Or *creditors*   b 16 Masoretic Text; Dead Sea Scrolls, Aquila, Vulgate and Syriac (see also Septuagint) *and stagger*

2:9–13 Babylon's riches had come from the misfortunes of others, but these riches would only be fuel for the fire. The victims and their cities would cry out against Babylon. Money is not evil, but God condemns the love of riches and the evil means of acquiring it (1 Timothy 6:10). Be careful not to hunger for wealth so much that you lose your appetite for God. Do not allow money to take the place of family, friends, or God.

2:18 Idolatry may seem like a sin that modern people need not fear. But idolatry is not just bowing down to idols; it is trusting in what one has made, and therefore, in one's own power as creator and sustainer. If we say we worship God but put our trust in bank accounts, homes, businesses, and organizations, then we are idolaters. Do you trust God more than you trust what your hands have made?

2:20 Idols have no life, no personhood, no power; they are empty chunks of wood or stone. Temples built to idols are equally empty; no one lives there. But the Lord *is* in his temple. He is real, alive, and powerful. He is truly and fully God. Idolaters command their idols to save them, but we who worship the living God come to him in silent awe, great respect, and reverence. We acknowledge that God is in control and knows what he is doing. Idols remain silent, because they cannot answer. The living God, by contrast, speaks through his Word. Approach God reverently and wait silently to hear what he has to say.

2. Habakkuk's prayer

3 A prayer of Habakkuk the prophet. On *shigionoth*.[a]

2 LORD, I have heard of your fame;
    I stand in awe[g] of your deeds, O LORD.
  Renew them in our day,
    in our time make them known;
    in wrath remember mercy.[h]

3:2
[g]Ps 119:120
[h]Isa 54:8

3 God came from Teman,
    the Holy One from Mount Paran.   *Selah*[b]
  His glory covered the heavens
    and his praise filled the earth.[i]

3:3
[i]Ps 48:10

4 His splendor was like the sunrise;
    rays flashed from his hand,
    where his power was hidden.
5 Plague went before him;
    pestilence followed his steps.
6 He stood, and shook the earth;
    he looked, and made the nations tremble.
  The ancient mountains crumbled
    and the age-old hills collapsed.
  His ways are eternal.

7 I saw the tents of Cushan in distress,
    the dwellings of Midian[j] in anguish.[k]

3:7
[j]Jdg 7:24-25
[k]Ex 15:14

8 Were you angry with the rivers, O LORD?
    Was your wrath against the streams?
  Did you rage against the sea
    when you rode with your horses
    and your victorious chariots?[l]

3:8
[l]Ps 68:17

9 You uncovered your bow,
    you called for many arrows.   *Selah*
  You split the earth with rivers;
10   the mountains saw you and writhed.
  Torrents of water swept by;
    the deep roared
    and lifted its waves on high.

11 Sun and moon stood still in the heavens
    at the glint of your flying arrows,[m]
    at the lightning of your flashing spear.

3:11
[m]Ps 18:14

12 In wrath you strode through the earth
    and in anger you threshed[n] the nations.

3:12
[n]Isa 41:15

13 You came out to deliver your people,
    to save your anointed one.
  You crushed[o] the leader of the land of wickedness,
    you stripped him from head to foot.   *Selah*

3:13
[o]Ps 110:6

[a]1 Probably a literary or musical term [b]3 A word of uncertain meaning; possibly a musical term; also in verses 9 and 13

3:1ff Habakkuk praised God for answering his questions. Evil will not triumph forever; God is in control, and he can be completely trusted to vindicate those who are faithful to him. We must patiently wait for him to act (3:16).

3:2 Habakkuk knew that God was going to discipline the people of Judah and that it wasn't going to be a pleasant experience.

But Habakkuk accepted God's will, asking for help and mercy. Habakkuk did not ask to escape the discipline, but he accepted the truth that Judah needed to learn a lesson. God still disciplines in love to bring his children back to him (Hebrews 12:5, 6). Accept God's discipline gladly, and ask him to help you change.

3:3 The word "Selah" occurs 71 times in Psalms and three times in Habakkuk. Although its precise meaning is unknown, it most likely was a musical term. It could be a signal to lift up the hands or voice in worship, or it could be an exclamation like "Amen!" or "Hallelujah!" affirming the truth of the passage.

3:14
p Jdg 7:22

14 With his own spear you pierced his head
    when his warriors stormed out to scatter us,*p*
gloating as though about to devour
    the wretched who were in hiding.
15 You trampled the sea with your horses,
    churning the great waters.

16 I heard and my heart pounded,
    my lips quivered at the sound;
decay crept into my bones,
    and my legs trembled.
Yet I will wait patiently for the day of calamity
    to come on the nation invading us.

3:17
q Jer 5:17

17 Though the fig tree does not bud
    and there are no grapes on the vines,
though the olive crop fails
    and the fields produce no food,
though there are no sheep in the pen
    and no cattle in the stalls,*q*
18 yet I will rejoice in the LORD,
    I will be joyful in God my Savior.

3:19
r Dt 33:29
s 2Sa 22:34;
Ps 18:33

19 The Sovereign LORD is my strength;*r*
    he makes my feet like the feet of a deer,
    he enables me to go on the heights.*s*

For the director of music. On my stringed instruments.

3:17–19 Crop failure and the death of animals would devastate Judah. But Habakkuk affirmed that even in the times of starvation and loss, he would still rejoice in the Lord. Habakkuk's feelings were not controlled by the events around him but by faith in God's ability to give him strength. When nothing makes sense, and when troubles seem more than you can bear, remember that God gives strength. Take your eyes off your difficulties and look to God.

3:19 God will give his followers surefooted confidence through difficult times. They will run like deer across rough and dangerous terrain. At the proper time, God will bring about his justice and completely rid the world of evil. In the meantime, God's people need to live in the strength of his Spirit, confident in his ultimate victory over evil.

3:19 The note to the director of music was to be used when this passage was sung as a psalm in temple worship.

3:19 Habakkuk had asked God why evil people prosper while the righteous suffer. God's answer: they don't, not in the long run. Habakkuk saw his own limitations in contrast to God's unlimited control of all the world's events. God is alive and in control of the world and its events. We cannot see all that God is doing, and we cannot see all that God will do. But we can be assured that he is God and will do what is right. Knowing this can give us confidence and hope in a confusing world.

ZEPHANIAH

VITAL STATISTICS

PURPOSE:
To shake the people of Judah out of their complacency and urge them to return to God

AUTHOR:
Zephaniah

ORIGINAL AUDIENCE:
The people of Judah (the southern kingdom)

DATE WRITTEN:
Probably near the end of Zephaniah's ministry (640–621 B.C.), when King Josiah's great reforms began

SETTING:
King Josiah of Judah was attempting to reverse the evil trends set by the two previous kings of Judah—Manasseh and Amon. Josiah was able to extend his influence because no strong superpower was dominating the world at that time (Assyria was declining rapidly). Zephaniah's prophecy may have been the motivating factor in Josiah's reform. Zephaniah was a contemporary of Jeremiah.

KEY VERSE:
"Seek the LORD, all you humble of the land, you who do what he commands. Seek righteousness, seek humility; perhaps you will be sheltered on the day of the LORD'S anger" (2:3).

KEY PLACE:
Jerusalem

OVERWHELMING grief, prolonged distress, incessant abuse, continual persecution, and imminent punishment breed hopelessness and despair. "If only," we cry, as we search our mind for a way out and look to the skies for rescue. With just a glimmer of hope, we would take courage and carry on.

Hope is the silver shaft of sun breaking through the storm-darkened sky, words of comfort in the intensive care unit, the first spring bird perched on a snow-covered twig, and the finish line in sight. It is a rainbow, a song, a loving touch. Hope is knowing God and resting in his love.

As God's prophet, Zephaniah was bound to speak the truth. This he did clearly, thundering certain judgment and horrible punishment for all who would defy the Lord. God's awful wrath would sweep away everything in the land and destroy it. "'I will sweep away both men and animals; I will sweep away the birds of the air and the fish of the sea. The wicked will have only heaps of rubble when I cut off man from the face of the earth,' declares the LORD" (1:3). No living thing in the land would escape. And that terrible day was coming soon: "The great day of the LORD is near—near and coming quickly. Listen! The cry on the day of the LORD will be bitter, the shouting of the warrior there. That day will be a day of wrath, a day of distress and anguish, a day of trouble and ruin, a day of darkness and gloom, a day of clouds and blackness" (1:14, 15). We can sense the oppression and depression his listeners must have felt. They were judged guilty, and they were doomed.

But in the midst of this terrible pronouncement, there is hope. The first chapter of Zephaniah's prophecy is filled with terror. In chapter two, however, a whispered promise appears. "Seek the LORD, all you humble of the land, you who do what he commands. Seek righteousness, seek humility; perhaps you will be sheltered on the day of the LORD's anger" (2:3). And a few verses later we read of a "remnant of the house of Judah" (2:7) who will be restored.

Finally in chapter three, the quiet refrain grows to a crescendo as God's salvation and deliverance for those who are faithful to him is declared. "Sing, O Daughter of Zion; shout aloud, O Israel! Be glad and rejoice with all your heart, O Daughter of Jerusalem! The LORD has taken away your punishment, he has turned back your enemy. The LORD, the King of Israel, is with you; never again will you fear any harm" (3:14, 15). This is true hope, grounded in the knowledge of God's justice and in his love for his people.

As you read Zephaniah, listen carefully to the words of judgment. God does not take sin lightly, and it will be punished. But be encouraged by the words of hope—our God reigns, and he will rescue his own. Decide to be part of that faithful remnant of souls who humbly worship and obey the living Lord.

THE BLUEPRINT

1. The day of wrath
   (1:1—3:7)
2. The day of hope
   (3:8–20)

Zephaniah warned the people of Judah that if they refused to repent, the entire nation, including the beloved city of Jerusalem, would be lost. The people knew that God would eventually bless them, but Zephaniah made it clear that there would be judgment first, then blessing. This judgment would not be merely punishment for sin, but it would also be a means of purifying the people. Though we live in a fallen world surrounded by evil, we can hope in the perfect Kingdom of God to come, and we can allow any punishment that touches us now to purify us from sin.

MEGATHEMES

THEME	EXPLANATION	IMPORTANCE
Day of Judgment	Destruction was coming because Judah had forsaken the Lord. The people worshiped Baal, Molech, and the stars in heaven. Even the priests mixed pagan practices with faith in God. God's punishment for sin was on the way.	To escape God's judgment we must listen to him, accept his correction, trust him, and seek his guidance. If we accept him as our Lord, we can escape his condemnation.
Indifference to God	Although there had been occasional attempts at renewal, Judah had no sorrow for its sins. The people were prosperous, and they no longer cared about God. God's demands for righteous living seemed irrelevant to the people, whose security and wealth made them complacent.	Don't let material comfort be a barrier to your commitment to God. Prosperity can lead to an attitude of proud self-sufficiency. We need to admit that money won't save us and that we cannot save ourselves. Only God can save us.
Day of Cheer	The day of judgment will also be a day of cheer. God will judge all those who mistreat his people. He will purify his people, purging away all sin and evil. God will restore his people and give them hope.	When people are purged of sin, there is great relief and hope. No matter how difficult our experience now, we can look forward to the day of celebration when God will completely restore us. It will truly be a day to rejoice!

1. The day of wrath

1:1
a 2Ki 22:1

1 The word of the LORD that came to Zephaniah son of Cushi, the son of Gedaliah, the son of Amariah, the son of Hezekiah, during the reign of Josiah a son of Amon king of Judah:

Warning of Coming Destruction

2 "I will sweep away everything
   from the face of the earth,"   declares the LORD.
3 "I will sweep away both men and animals;
   I will sweep away the birds of the air
   and the fish of the sea.

1:1 Zephaniah prophesied in the days of Josiah king of Judah (640–609 B.C.). Josiah followed God, and during his reign the Book of the Law was discovered in the temple. After reading it, Josiah began a great religious revival in Judah (2 Kings 22:1—23:25). Zephaniah helped fan the flames of the revival by warning the people that judgment would come if they did not turn from their sins. Although this great revival turned the nation back to God, it did not fully eliminate idolatry and lasted only a short time. Twelve years after Josiah's death, Judah was invaded by Babylon, and a number of people were sent into exile.

1:2ff The people of Judah were clearly warned by the highest authority of all—God. They refused to listen, either because they doubted God's prophet and thus did not believe that the message was from God, or because they doubted God himself and thus did not believe that he would do what he said. If we refuse to listen to God's Word, the Bible, we are as shortsighted as the people of Judah, and like them, we will be punished.

The wicked will have only heaps of rubble[a]
when I cut off man from the face of the earth,"

declares the LORD.

Against Judah

4 "I will stretch out my hand against Judah
and against all who live in Jerusalem.
I will cut off from this place every remnant of Baal,[b]
the names of the pagan and the idolatrous priests[c]—
5 those who bow down on the roofs
to worship the starry host,
those who bow down and swear by the LORD
and who also swear by Molech,[b]
6 those who turn back from following[d] the LORD
and neither seek the LORD nor inquire[e] of him.
7 Be silent[f] before the Sovereign LORD,
for the day of the LORD is near.
The LORD has prepared a sacrifice;[g]
he has consecrated those he has invited.
8 On the day of the LORD's sacrifice
I will punish[h] the princes
and the king's sons
and all those clad
in foreign clothes.
9 On that day I will punish
all who avoid stepping on the threshold,[c]
who fill the temple of their gods
with violence and deceit.
10 "On that day," declares the LORD,
"a cry will go up from the Fish Gate,[i]
wailing from the New Quarter,
and a loud crash from the hills.
11 Wail, you who live in the market district[d];
all your merchants will be wiped out,
all who trade with[e] silver will be ruined.

1:4
[b]Mic 5:13
[c]Hos 10:5

1:6
[d]Isa 1:4
[e]Hos 7:7

1:7
[f]Hab 2:20; Zec 2:13
[g]Jer 46:10

1:8
[h]Isa 24:21

1:10
[i]2Ch 33:14

[a]3 The meaning of the Hebrew for this line is uncertain.   [b]5 Hebrew *Malcam*, that is, Milcom   [c]9 See 1 Samuel 5:5.
[d]11 Or *the Mortar*   [e]11 Or *in*

1:4 When the Israelites arrived in the promised land, God had commanded that they completely rid the land of its pagan inhabitants, who worshiped idols. But the Israelites failed to do so, and gradually they began to worship the Canaanites' gods. The Canaanites believed in many gods that represented many aspects of life, and the chief god was Baal, symbolizing strength and fertility. God was extremely angry when his people turned from him to Baal.

1:4–6 The terrain of history is littered with idols and their worship. More than just a stone statue, an idol can be anything reverenced more than God. Thus idol worship is prevalent even today as people trust in themselves, money, or power and not in God. But ultimately all idols will prove worthless, and the true God will prevail. Seek God first (Matthew 6:33), and have no other gods before him (Exodus 20:3).

1:5 The people had become polytheistic, worshiping the Lord *and* all the other gods of the land. They added the "best" of pagan worship to true faith in God. But God commands that he alone be worshiped (Exodus 20:1–5); thus the people committed a horrible sin. One of these other gods was Molech, the national god of the Ammonites. Molech worship included child sacrifice, an abominable sin. From the time of Moses, the Israelites had been warned about worshiping this false god

(Leviticus 18:21; 20:5), but they refused to take heed. Because of their sins, God would destroy them.

1:7 A day of judgment and great slaughter occurred during the lifetime of these people when Babylon invaded the land. The prophet saw these prophecies as future events, but he could not see when or in what order these events would take place. Many think that these prophecies have a double fulfillment— one for the near future (soon after the prophecy was made) and another for the distant future (possibly during the end times). Some scholars believe that these prophecies of judgment refer to events entirely in the future.

1:8, 9 Wearing "foreign" (pagan) clothes showed a desire for foreign gods and foreign ways. Leaders who should have been good examples to the people were adopting foreign practices and thus showing their contempt for the Lord by ignoring his commands against adopting pagan culture. To "avoid stepping on the threshold" was a pagan observance (see 1 Samuel 5:5).

1:12 God would search the city with lamps and punish those who deserve punishment. Because they did not search their own hearts and because they were content with the moral chaos around them ("like wine left on its dregs") and indifferent to God, God would use the Babylonians to judge them. Within 20 years, the Babylonians would enter Jerusalem, drag people

1:12
j Jer 48:11
k Eze 8:12

12 At that time I will search Jerusalem with lamps
   and punish those who are complacent,
   who are like wine left on its dregs,*j*
who think, 'The LORD will do nothing,*k*
   either good or bad.'

1:13
l Am 5:11

13 Their wealth will be plundered,
   their houses demolished.
They will build houses
   but not live in them;
they will plant vineyards
   but not drink the wine.*l*

The Great Day of the LORD

14 "The great day of the LORD is near—
   near and coming quickly.
Listen! The cry on the day of the LORD will be bitter,
   the shouting of the warrior there.

1:15
m Isa 22:5

15 That day will be a day of wrath,
   a day of distress and anguish,
a day of trouble and ruin,
   a day of darkness and gloom,
a day of clouds and blackness,*m*

1:16
n Jer 4:19

16 a day of trumpet and battle cry*n*
   against the fortified cities
   and against the corner towers.

1:17
o Ps 79:3

17 I will bring distress on the people
   and they will walk like blind men,
because they have sinned against the LORD.
Their blood will be poured out*o* like dust
   and their entrails like filth.
18 Neither their silver nor their gold
   will be able to save them
   on the day of the LORD's wrath.

ZEPHANIAH
served as a
prophet to
Judah from
640–621 B.C.

Climate of the times.	Josiah was the last good king in Judah. His bold attempts to reform the nation and turn it back to God were probably influenced by Zephaniah.
Main message.	A day will come when God, as judge, will severely punish all nations. But after judgment, he will show mercy to all who have been faithful to him.
Importance of message.	We will all be judged for our disobedience to God; but if we remain faithful to him, he will show us mercy.
Contemporary prophet.	Jeremiah (627–586 B.C.)

---

out of hiding, and take them captive or kill them. No one would
escape God's judgment; there would be no place to hide.

1:12–14 Some people think of God as an indulgent heavenly
grandfather, nice to have around, but not a real force in shaping
modern life. They don't believe in his power or his coming judgment. But God is holy, and therefore he will actively judge and
justly punish everyone who is content to live in sin, indifferent to
him, or unconcerned about justice. When people are indifferent
to God, they tend to think that he is indifferent to them and their
sin. They will be surprised to find that "the great day of the LORD
is near."

1:14–18 The great day of the Lord was near; the Babylonians
would soon come and destroy Jerusalem. The day of the Lord
is also near for us. God promises a final judgment, a day of
worldwide destruction (Revelation 20:12–15). The Babylonian
conquest occurred just as surely and horribly as Zephaniah

had predicted. And God's final day of judgment is also sure—
but so is his ability to save. To be spared from judgment,
recognize that you have sinned, that your sin will bring judgment, that you cannot save yourself, and that God alone can
save you.

1:18 Money is not evil in itself, but it is useless to save us.
In this life, money can warp our perspective, giving us feelings
of security and power. Just as the Israelites' wealth could not
save them from the Babylonian invasion, so at the final judgment, our riches will be worthless. Only Christ's redemptive
work on our behalf matters for eternity. Christ alone will ransom
us if we believe in him. Don't trust money; trust Christ.

In the fire of his jealousy
    the whole world will be consumed,ᵖ
for he will make a sudden end
    of all who live in the earth."

2 Gather together,�q gather together,
    O shameful ʳ nation,
² before the appointed time arrives
    and that day sweeps on like chaff,ˢ
before the fierce anger of the LORD comes upon you,
    before the day of the LORD's wrath comes upon you.
³ Seek ᵗ the LORD, all you humble of the land,
    you who do what he commands.
Seek righteousness, seek humility;ᵘ
    perhaps you will be sheltered
    on the day of the LORD's anger.

Against Philistia

⁴ Gaza ᵛ will be abandoned
    and Ashkelon left in ruins.
At midday Ashdod will be emptied
    and Ekron uprooted.
⁵ Woe to you who live by the sea,
    O Kerethite people;
the word of the LORD is against you,ʷ
    O Canaan, land of the Philistines.

"I will destroy you,
    and none will be left."ˣ

⁶ The land by the sea, where the Kerethitesᵃ dwell,
    will be a place for shepherds and sheep pens.
⁷ It will belong to the remnant of the house of Judah;
    there they will find pasture.
In the evening they will lie down
    in the houses of Ashkelon.
The LORD their God will care for them;
    he will restore their fortunes.ᵇ

Against Moab and Ammon

⁸ "I have heard the insults of Moab
    and the taunts of the Ammonites,

1:18
ᵖ ver 2-3; Zep 3:8

2:1
q Joel 1:14
ʳ Jer 3:3

2:2
ˢ Isa 17:13

2:3
ᵗ Am 5:6
ᵘ Am 5:14-15

2:4
ᵛ Am 1:6, 7-8;
Zec 9:5-7

2:5
ʷ Am 3:1
ˣ Isa 14:30

ᵃ6 The meaning of the Hebrew for this word is uncertain.   ᵇ7 Or *will bring back their captives*

2:1-3 There was still time for the people to avert God's judgment. They simply had to turn from their sins, humble themselves, and obey God. The Old Testament prophets announced news of destruction, but they also offered the only means of escape and protection—turning from sin and walking with God (see also Micah 6:8).

2:4 The four cities mentioned here are in Philistia, the nation southwest of Judah on the coast of the Mediterranean Sea. Age-old enemies of Israel from the days of Joshua, the Philistines were known for their cruelty. God judged these cities for their idolatry and their constant taunting of Israel. These four cities were four of the five capitals. The fifth (Gath) had probably already been destroyed.

2:5 The Kerethites were a clan of the Philistines located near southern Judah. They migrated to Palestine along with other Philistine people. Their name may have been derived from "Crete," the island where they lived before they moved to Palestine.

2:7 All the prophets, even while prophesying doom and destruction, speak of a "remnant"—a small group of God's people who remain faithful to him and whom God will restore to the land. Although God said he would destroy Judah, he also promised to save a remnant, thus keeping his original covenant to preserve Abraham's descendants (Genesis 17:4-8). Because God is holy, he cannot allow sin to continue. But God is also faithful to his promises. He cannot stay angry with Israel forever, or with you, if you are his child, because he loves his children and always seeks their good.

2:8 The Moabites and Ammonites lived to the east of Judah, and they often ridiculed and attacked Judah. These nations worshiped Chemosh and Molech (1 Kings 11:7). Moab's king once sacrificed his son on the city wall to stop an invasion (2 Kings 3:26, 27). God would judge these nations for their wickedness and for their treatment of his people.

2:8-11 Judah had been taunted and mocked by the neighboring nations, Moab and Ammon, but God reminded them that he had "heard the insults . . . and the taunts" (2:8), and that the taunters

who insulted[y] my people
   and made threats against their land.
  ⁹ Therefore, as surely as I live,"
   declares the LORD Almighty, the God of Israel,
  "surely Moab[z] will become like Sodom,[a]
   the Ammonites like Gomorrah—
a place of weeds and salt pits,
   a wasteland forever.
The remnant of my people will plunder[b] them;
   the survivors of my nation will inherit their land."

¹⁰ This is what they will get in return for their pride,
   for insulting and mocking the people of the LORD Almighty.
  ¹¹ The LORD will be awesome[c] to them
   when he destroys all the gods[d] of the land.
The nations on every shore will worship him,[e]
   every one in its own land.

Against Cush

  ¹² "You too, O Cushites,[a]
   will be slain by my sword."

Against Assyria

  ¹³ He will stretch out his hand against the north
   and destroy Assyria,
leaving Nineveh[f] utterly desolate
   and dry as the desert.
  ¹⁴ Flocks and herds will lie down there,
   creatures of every kind.
The desert owl and the screech owl
   will roost on her columns.
Their calls will echo through the windows,
   rubble will be in the doorways,
   the beams of cedar will be exposed.
  ¹⁵ This is the carefree city
   that lived in safety.[g]
She said to herself,
   "I am, and there is none besides me."
What a ruin she has become,
   a lair for wild beasts!
All who pass by her scoff
   and shake their fists.

2:8
[y] Eze 25:3

2:9
[z] Isa 15:1–16:14
[a] Dt 29:23
[b] Isa 11:14

2:11
[c] Joel 2:11
[d] Zep 1:4
[e] Zep 3:9

2:13
[f] Na 1:1

2:15
[g] Isa 47:8

---

[a] 12 That is, people from the upper Nile region

---

would be punished for their pride (2:10). At times the whole world seems to mock God and those who have faith in him. When you are ridiculed, remember that God hears and will answer. Eventually, in God's timing, justice will be carried out.

2:9 The nations of Moab and Ammon trace their roots to Lot's incest with his daughters after escaping the destruction of evil Sodom and Gomorrah (Genesis 19). Ironically, Moab and Ammon would be the same kind of perpetual wasteland that God had made those evil cities. Sodom and Gomorrah were so completely destroyed that their exact location is still unknown.

2:12 Cush, at the southern end of the Red Sea, controlled Egypt at this time. No one can escape deserved judgment. The Cushites were "slain by [God's] sword" when the Babylonians invaded Egypt in 605 B.C. (See Isaiah 18 and Ezekiel 30:9 for other prophecies concerning Cush.)

2:13 Zephaniah mentioned the large nation to the south and then moved to the nation that invaded from the north, Assyria. Though

declining, Assyria was still the strongest military power of the day, dominating the world for three centuries and destroying anyone in its path. Nineveh, the large capital city, was considered impregnable. However, just as Zephaniah predicted, Nineveh was wiped out in 612 B.C. by the Babylonians, who would become the next world power.

2:13–15 To predict the destruction of Nineveh ten years before it happened would be equivalent to predicting the destruction of London, Tokyo, Paris, or New York. Nineveh was the ancient Near Eastern center for culture, technology, and beauty. It had great libraries, buildings, and a vast irrigation system that created lush gardens in the city. The city wall was 60 miles long, 100 feet high, and over 30 feet wide and was fortified with 1,500 towers. Yet the entire city was destroyed so completely that its very existence was questioned until it was discovered, with great difficulty, by 19th century archaeologists. Nineveh had indeed become as desolate and dry as the desert.

The Future of Jerusalem

3

Woe to the city of oppressors,[h]
        rebellious and defiled!
² She obeys[i] no one,
        she accepts no correction.
She does not trust in the LORD,
        she does not draw near[j] to her God.
³ Her officials are roaring lions,
        her rulers are evening wolves,
        who leave nothing for the morning.
⁴ Her prophets are arrogant;
        they are treacherous men.
Her priests profane the sanctuary
        and do violence to the law.[k]
⁵ The LORD within her is righteous;
        he does no wrong.[l]
Morning by morning he dispenses his justice,
        and every new day he does not fail,
        yet the unrighteous know no shame.

⁶ "I have cut off nations;
        their strongholds are demolished.
I have left their streets deserted,
        with no one passing through.
Their cities are destroyed;
        no one will be left—no one at all.
⁷ I said to the city,
        'Surely you will fear me
        and accept correction!'
Then her dwelling would not be cut off,
        nor all my punishments come upon her.
But they were still eager
        to act corruptly[m] in all they did.

2. The day of hope

⁸ Therefore wait[n] for me," declares the LORD,
        "for the day I will stand up to testify.[a]
I have decided to assemble the nations,[o]
        to gather the kingdoms

---

[a]8 Septuagint and Syriac; Hebrew *will rise up to plunder*

3:1 *h* Jer 6:6

3:2 *i* Jer 22:21
j Ps 73:28

3:4 *k* Eze 22:26

3:5 *l* Dt 32:4

3:7 *m* Hos 9:9

3:8 *n* Ps 27:14
o Joel 3:2
p Zep 1:18

3:1ff After predicting the destruction of the surrounding nations, Zephaniah returned to the problem at hand—sin in Jerusalem. The city of God, and God's people themselves, had become "defiled"—as sinful as their pagan neighbors. The people pretended to worship and serve God, but in their hearts they had rejected him and continued to be complacent about their sins. They no longer cared about the consequences of turning away from God.

3:2 Do you know people who refuse to listen when someone disagrees with their opinions? Their root problem is pride—inflated self-esteem. God's people had become so proud that they would not hear or accept God's correction. Do you find it difficult to listen to the spiritual counsel of others or God's words from the Bible? Don't let pride make you unable or unwilling to let God work in your life. You will be more willing to listen when you consider how weak and sinful you really are compared to God.

3:3, 4 Leading God's people is a privilege and a responsibility. Through Zephaniah, God rebuked all types of leadership in Jerusalem—officials, rulers, prophets, and priests—because of their callous disobedience, irresponsibility, and sin. If you are a leader in the church, consider yourself in a privileged position, but be careful. God holds you responsible for the purity of your actions, the quality of your example, and the truth of your words.

3:5 Jerusalem's citizens, of all people, had no excuse for their sins. Jerusalem, where the temple was located, was the religious center of the nation. But even though the people didn't follow God, God was "within" the city, present in the midst of corruption, persecution, and unbelief. No matter how spiritually desolate the world seems, God is here, and he is at work. Ask yourself, "What is he doing now, and how can I be part of his work?"

3:7 We may wonder how the Israelites could have had such clear warnings and still not turn to God. The problem was that they had allowed sin to so harden them that they no longer cared to follow God. They refused to heed God's warnings and they refused to repent. The more God punished them, the more they sinned. In fact, they were "eager" to sin. If you disobey God now, your heart may grow hard, and you may lose your desire for God.

3:8 In the last days, God will judge all people according to what they have done (Revelation 20:12). Justice will prevail; evildoers will be punished; and the obedient will be blessed. Don't try to avenge yourself. Be patient, and God's justice will come.

and to pour out my wrath on them—
all my fierce anger.
The whole world will be consumed[p]
by the fire of my jealous anger.

3:9
q Isa 19:18

9 "Then will I purify the lips of the peoples,
that all of them may call on the name of the LORD
and serve[q] him shoulder to shoulder.

3:10
r Ps 68:31

10 From beyond the rivers of Cush[a][r]
my worshipers, my scattered people,
will bring me offerings.
11 On that day you will not be put to shame
for all the wrongs you have done to me,
because I will remove from this city
those who rejoice in their pride.
Never again will you be haughty
on my holy hill.

3:12
s Isa 14:32

12 But I will leave within you
the meek[s] and humble,
who trust in the name of the LORD.

3:13
t Mic 4:7
u Rev 14:5

13 The remnant[t] of Israel will do no wrong;
they will speak no lies,[u]
nor will deceit be found in their mouths.
They will eat and lie down
and no one will make them afraid."

14 Sing, O Daughter of Zion;
shout aloud, O Israel!
Be glad and rejoice with all your heart,
O Daughter of Jerusalem!

3:15
v Eze 37:26-28

15 The LORD has taken away your punishment,
he has turned back your enemy.
The LORD, the King of Israel, is with you;[v]
never again will you fear any harm.

3:16
w Isa 35:3-4;
Heb 12:12

16 On that day they will say to Jerusalem,
"Do not fear, O Zion;
do not let your hands hang limp.[w]

3:17
x Isa 62:4

17 The LORD your God is with you,
he is mighty to save.
He will take great delight[x] in you,
he will quiet you with his love,
he will rejoice over you with singing."

18 "The sorrows for the appointed feasts
I will remove from you;
they are a burden and a reproach to you.[b]

a 10 That is, the upper Nile region   b 18 Or *"I will gather you who mourn for the appointed feasts; / your reproach is a burden to you*

3:9 God will purify lips and unify language so that all his people from all nations will be able to worship him in unison. In the new earth, all believers will speak the same language; the confusion of languages at the tower of Babel will be reversed (Genesis 11). God will purify our hearts, so that the words coming from our lips will be pure as well.

3:10 The "scattered people" refers to Jews dispersed beyond the rivers of Cush. It symbolizes that all Jews, no matter how far they have been scattered, will return to worship God.

3:11, 12 God will remove the proud people and leave the meek and humble. God is opposed to the proud and haughty of every generation. But those who are meek and humble, both physically and spiritually, will be rewarded because they trust in God.

Self-reliance and arrogance have no place among God's people or in his kingdom.

3:14-18 The Lord himself will remove his hand of judgment, disperse Israel's enemies, and come to live among his people. He will give them gladness. We sin when we pursue happiness by cutting ourselves off from fellowship with God—the only person who can make us truly happy. Zephaniah points out that gladness results when we allow God to be with us. We do that by faithfully following him and obeying his commands. Then God rejoices over us with singing. If you want to be happy, draw close to the source of happiness by obeying God.

19 At that time I will deal
     with all who oppressed you;
   I will rescue the lame
     and gather those who have been scattered.ʸ
   I will give them praise and honor
     in every land where they were put to shame.
20 At that time I will gather you;
     at that time I will bringᶻ you home.
   I will give you honorᵃ and praise
     among all the peoples of the earth
   when I restore your fortunesᵃ
     before your very eyes,"

                                    says the LORD.

3:19
ʸEze 34:16; Mic 4:6

3:20
ᶻEze 37:12
ᵃIsa 56:5

ᵃ20 Or I bring back your captives

3:20 "Before your very eyes" does not necessarily mean that this promise would be fulfilled during Zephaniah's generation. Rather, it means that the restoration will be an obvious work of the Lord.

3:20 The message of doom in the beginning of the book becomes a message of hope by the end. There will be a new day when God will bless his people. If the leaders in the church today were to hear a message from a prophet of God, the message would probably resemble the book of Zephaniah. Under Josiah's religious reforms, the people did return to God *outwardly,* but their hearts were far from him. Zephaniah encouraged the nation to gather together and pray for salvation. We must also ask ourselves: Is our reform merely an outward show, or is it changing our hearts and lives? We need to gather together and pray, to walk humbly with God, to do what is right, and to hear the message of hope regarding the new world to come.

HAGGAI

PRESSURES, demands, expectations, and tasks push in from all sides and assault our schedules. Do this! Be there! Finish that! Call them! Everyone seems to want something from us—family, friends, employer, school, church, clubs. Soon we have little left to give as we run out of energy and time. We find ourselves rushing through life, attending to the necessary, the immediate, and the urgent. The important is all too often left in the dust. Our problem is not the volume of demands or lack of scheduling skills, but values—what is *truly* important to us.

Our values and priorities are reflected in how we use our resources—time, money, strength, and talent. Often our actions belie our words. We say God is number one, but then we relegate him to a lesser number on our "to do" lists.

Twenty-five centuries ago, a voice was heard, calling men and women to the right priorities. Haggai knew what was important and what had to be done, and he challenged God's people to respond.

In 586 B.C., the armies of Babylon had destroyed the temple in Jerusalem—God's house, the symbol of his presence. In 538 B.C. King Cyrus decreed that Jews could return to their beloved city and rebuild the temple. So they traveled to Jerusalem and began the work. But then they forgot their purpose and lost their priorities, as opposition and apathy brought the work to a standstill (Ezra 4:4, 5). Then Haggai spoke, calling them back to God's values: "Is it a time for you yourselves to be living in your paneled houses, while this house remains a ruin?" (1:4). The people were more concerned with their own needs than with doing God's will, and, as a result, they suffered. Then Haggai called them to action: "This is what the LORD Almighty says: 'Give careful thought to your ways. Go up into the mountains and bring down timber and build the house, so that I may take pleasure in it and be honored,' says the LORD" (1:7, 8). And God's message through his servant Haggai became the catalyst for finishing the work.

Although Haggai is a small book, it is filled with challenge and promise, reminding us of God's claim on our lives and our priorities. As you read Haggai, imagine him walking the streets and alleys of Jerusalem, urging the people to get back to doing God's work. And listen to Haggai speaking to you, urging you to reorder your priorities in accordance with God's will. What has God told you to do? Put all else aside and obey him.

VITAL STATISTICS

PURPOSE:
To call the people to complete the rebuilding of the temple

AUTHOR:
Haggai

ORIGINAL AUDIENCE:
The people living in Jerusalem and those who had returned from exile

DATE WRITTEN:
520 B.C.

SETTING:
The temple in Jerusalem had been destroyed in 586 B.C. Cyrus had allowed the Jews to return to their homeland and rebuild their temple in 538 B.C. They had begun the work but had been unable to complete it. Through the ministry of Haggai and Zechariah, the temple was completed (520–516 B.C.).

KEY VERSE:
"Is it a time for you yourselves to be living in your paneled houses, while this house remains a ruin?" (1:4).

KEY PEOPLE:
Haggai, Zerubbabel, Joshua

KEY PLACE:
Jerusalem

SPECIAL FEATURES:
Haggai was the first of the postexilic prophets. The other two were Zechariah and Malachi. The literary style of this book is simple and direct.

THE BLUEPRINT

1. The call to rebuild the temple (1:1–15)
2. Encouragement to complete the temple (2:1–23)

When the exiles first returned from Babylon, they set about rebuilding the temple right away. Although they began with the right attitudes, they slipped back into wrong behavior, and the work came to a standstill. We need to be on guard to keep our priorities straight. Remain active in your service to God and continue to put first things first.

MEGATHEMES

THEME	EXPLANATION	IMPORTANCE
Right Priorities	God had given the Jews the assignment to finish the temple in Jerusalem when they returned from captivity. After 15 years, they still had not completed it. They were more concerned about building their own homes than finishing God's work. Haggai told them to get their priorities straight.	It is easy to make other priorities more important than doing God's work. But God wants us to follow through and build up his kingdom. Don't stop and don't make excuses. Set your heart on what is right and do it. Get your priorities straight.
God's Encouragement	Haggai encouraged the people as they worked. He assured them of the divine presence of the Holy Spirit and of final victory, and instilled in them the hope that the Messiah would reign.	If God gives you a task, don't be afraid to get started. His resources are infinite. God will help you complete it by giving you encouragement from others along the way.

1. The call to rebuild the temple

1 In the second year of King Darius,*a* on the first day of the sixth month, the word of the LORD came through the prophet Haggai to Zerubbabel son of Shealtiel, governor*b* of Judah, and to Joshua*a* son of Jehozadak, the high priest:

1:1
a Ezr 4:24
b Ezr 5:3

² This is what the LORD Almighty says: "These people say, 'The time has not yet come for the LORD's house to be built.'"

³ Then the word of the LORD came through the prophet Haggai: ⁴ "Is it a time for you yourselves to be living in your paneled houses, while this house remains a ruin?*c*"

1:4
c ver 9

⁵ Now this is what the LORD Almighty says: "Give careful thought to your ways. ⁶ You have planted much, but have harvested little. You eat, but never have enough. You drink, but never have your fill. You put on clothes, but are not warm. You earn wages,*d* only to put them in a purse with holes in it."

1:6
d Zec 8:10

⁷ This is what the LORD Almighty says: "Give careful thought to your ways. ⁸ Go up into the mountains and bring down timber and build the house, so that I may take pleasure*e* in it and be honored," says the LORD. ⁹ "You expected much, but see, it turned out to be little. What you brought home, I blew away. Why?" declares the LORD Almighty. "Because of my house, which remains a ruin, while each of you is busy with his own house. ¹⁰ Therefore, because of you the heavens have withheld their dew and the earth its crops.*f* ¹¹ I called for a drought on the fields and the mountains, on the grain, the new wine, the oil and whatever the ground produces, on men and cattle, and on the labor of your hands.*g*"

1:8
e Ps 132:13-14

1:10
f Dt 28:23

1:11
g Hag 2:17

a 1 A variant of *Jeshua*; here and elsewhere in Haggai

1:1 Zerubbabel, governor of Judah, and Joshua, the high priest, were key leaders in rebuilding the temple. They had already reestablished the altar, but work on the temple had slowed. Haggai gave a message to these outstanding leaders and to the exiles who had returned from Babylon, encouraging them to complete the rebuilding of the temple in Jerusalem.

1:1ff The Jews who had returned from Babylon in 538 B.C. to rebuild the temple in Jerusalem were not able to finish their work because they were hindered by their enemies. After opposition put a halt to progress, no further work had been done on the temple for over 15 years. In August, 520 B.C., Haggai delivered a message to encourage the people to rebuild the temple! Haggai was probably born in captivity in Babylon and returned to Jerusalem with Zerubbabel in 538 B.C. (Ezra 1; 2). Haggai and Zechariah, two prophets who encouraged the temple rebuilding, are mentioned in Ezra 5:1.

1:2–15 Haggai encouraged the people to finish rebuilding the temple. Opposition from hostile neighbors had caused them to feel discouraged and to neglect the temple, and thus neglect God. But Haggai's message turned them around and motivated them to pick up their tools and continue the work they had begun.

1:3–6 God asked his people how they could live in luxury when his house was lying in ruins. The temple was the focal point of Judah's relationship with God, but it was still demolished. Instead of rebuilding the temple, the people put their energies into beautifying their own homes. However, the harder the people worked for themselves, the less they had, because they ignored their spiritual lives. The same happens to us. If we put God first, he will provide for our deepest needs. If we put him in any other place, all our efforts will be futile. Caring only for your physical needs while ignoring your relationship with God will lead to ruin.

1:6 Because the people had not given God first place in their lives, their work was not fruitful or productive, and their material possessions did not satisfy. While they concentrated on building and beautifying their own homes, God's blessing was withheld because they no longer put him in first place. Moses had predicted that this would be the result if the people neglected God (Deuteronomy 28:38–45).

1:9 Judah's problem was confused priorities. Like Judah, our priorities involving occupation, family, and God's work are often confused. Jobs, homes, vacations, and leisure activities may rank higher on our list of importance than God. What is most important to you? Where is God on your list of priorities?

1:11 Grain, grapes for wine, and olives for oil were Israel's major crops. The people depended on these for security while neglecting the worship of God. As a result, God would send a drought to destroy their livelihood and call them back to himself.

¹²Then Zerubbabel son of Shealtiel, Joshua son of Jehozadak, the high priest, and the whole remnant of the people obeyed the voice of the LORD their God and the message of the prophet Haggai, because the LORD their God had sent him. And the people feared the LORD.

1:13
h Ro 8:31

1:14
i Ezr 5:2

¹³Then Haggai, the LORD's messenger, gave this message of the LORD to the people: "I am with*h* you," declares the LORD. ¹⁴So the LORD stirred up the spirit of Zerubbabel*i* son of Shealtiel, governor of Judah, and the spirit of Joshua son of Jehozadak, the high priest, and the spirit of the whole remnant of the people. They came and began to work on the house of the LORD Almighty, their God, ¹⁵on the twenty-fourth day of the sixth month in the second year of King Darius.

2. Encouragement to complete the temple
The Promised Glory of the New House

2:3
j Ezr 3:12

2:4
k Zec 8:9

2 On the twenty-first day of the seventh month, the word of the LORD came through the prophet Haggai: ²"Speak to Zerubbabel son of Shealtiel, governor of Judah, to Joshua son of Jehozadak, the high priest, and to the remnant of the people. Ask them, ³'Who of you is left who saw this house*j* in its former glory? How does it look to you now? Does it not seem to you like nothing? ⁴But now be strong, O Zerubbabel,' declares the LORD. 'Be strong, *k* O Joshua son of Jehozadak, the high priest. Be strong, all you people of the land,' declares the LORD, 'and work. For I am with you,' declares the LORD Almighty. ⁵'This is what I covenanted with you when you came out of Egypt. *l* And my Spirit *m* remains among you. Do not fear.'

2:5
l Ex 29:46
m Ne 9:20;
Isa 63:11

2:6
n Heb 12:26*

⁶"This is what the LORD Almighty says: 'In a little while I will once more shake the heavens and the earth, *n* the sea and the dry land. ⁷I will shake all nations, and the desired of all

---

HAGGAI served as a prophet to Judah about 520 B.C., after the return from exile.	Climate of the times	The people of Judah had been exiled to Babylon in 586 B.C., and Jerusalem and the temple had been destroyed. Under Cyrus, king of Persia, the Jews were allowed to return to Judah and rebuild their temple.
	Main message	The people returned to Jerusalem to begin rebuilding the temple, but they hadn't finished. Haggai's message encouraged the people to finish rebuilding God's temple.
	Importance of message . . .	The temple lay half-finished while the people lived in beautiful homes. Haggai warned them against putting their possessions and jobs ahead of God. We must put God first in our lives.
	Contemporary prophet	Zechariah (520–480 B.C.)

1:14, 15 The people began rebuilding the temple just 23 days after Haggai's first message. Rarely did a prophet's message produce such a quick response. How often we hear a sermon and respond, "That was an excellent point—I ought to do that," only to leave church and forget to act. These people put their words into action. When you hear a good sermon or lesson, ask what you should *do* about it, and then make plans to put it into practice.

2:1–9 This is Haggai's second message. It was given during the Feast of Tabernacles in October, 520 B.C. The older people could remember the incredible beauty of Solomon's temple, destroyed 66 years earlier. Many were discouraged because the rebuilt temple was inferior to Solomon's. But Haggai encouraged them with God's message that the glory of this temple would surpass that of its predecessor. The most important part of the temple is God's presence. Some 500 years later, Jesus Christ would walk in the temple courts.

2:4 "Be strong . . . and work. For I am with you." Judah's people had returned to worshiping God, and God had promised to bless their efforts. But it was time for them to *work*. We must be people of prayer, Bible study, and worship—but eventually we must get out and *do* what God has in mind for us. He wants to change the world through us. God has given you a job to do in the church, at your place of employment, and at home. The time has come to be strong and work because God is with you!

2:5 The Israelites had been led from captivity in Egypt to their promised land. They were God's chosen people, guided and cared for by his Holy Spirit. Although God had punished them for their

sins, he kept his promise and never left them (Exodus 29:45, 46). No matter what difficulties we face or how frustrating our work may be, God's Spirit is with us.

2:6–9 The focus shifts from the local temple being rebuilt in Jerusalem to the worldwide reign of the Messiah on earth. The words "in a little while" are not limited to the immediate historical context; they refer to God's control of history—he can act any time he chooses. God will act *in his time* (see also Hebrews 12:26, 27).

2:7 When God promised to shake all the nations with his judgment, he was speaking of both his present judgment on evil nations and future judgment during the last days.

2:7–9 The "desired of all nations" has two possible meanings: (1) It could refer to the Messiah, Jesus, who, some 500 years later, would enter the temple and fill it with his glory and his peace (Luke 2:27, 32). (2) It could also refer to the riches that would flow into the temple, given as offerings to God's people.

nations will come, and I will fill this house^o with glory,' says the LORD Almighty. ^{8}'The silver is mine and the gold is mine,' declares the LORD Almighty. ^{9}'The glory of this present house will be greater than the glory of the former house,' says the LORD Almighty. 'And in this place I will grant peace,' declares the LORD Almighty."

2:7
^{o}Isa 60:7

Blessings for a Defiled People

^{10}On the twenty-fourth day of the ninth month, in the second year of Darius, the word of the LORD came to the prophet Haggai: ^{11}"This is what the LORD Almighty says: 'Ask the priests^p what the law says: ^{12}If a person carries consecrated meat in the fold of his garment, and that fold touches some bread or stew, some wine, oil or other food, does it become consecrated?$^{q'}$"

2:11
^{p}Lev 10:10-11
2:12
^{q}Mt 23:19

The priests answered, "No."

^{13}Then Haggai said, "If a person defiled by contact with a dead body touches one of these things, does it become defiled?"

"Yes," the priests replied, "it becomes defiled."

^{14}Then Haggai said, "'So it is with this people and this nation in my sight,' declares the LORD. 'Whatever they do and whatever they offer there is defiled.

^{15}"'Now give careful thought^r to this from this day on^a—consider how things were before one stone was laid on another in the LORD's temple.^{s} ^{16}When anyone came to a heap of twenty measures, there were only ten. When anyone went to a wine vat to draw fifty measures, there were only twenty.^{t} ^{17}I struck all the work of your hands with blight,^{u} mildew and hail, yet you did not turn to me,' declares the LORD. ^{18}'From this day on, from this twenty-fourth day of the ninth month, give careful thought to the day when the foundation^v of the LORD's temple was laid. Give careful thought: ^{19}Is there yet any seed left in the barn? Until now, the vine and the fig tree, the pomegranate and the olive tree have not borne fruit.

"'From this day on I will bless you.'"

2:15
^{r}Hag 1:5
^{s}Ezr 4:24
2:16
^{t}Hag 1:6
2:17
^{u}Dt 28:22
2:18
^{v}Zec 8:9

Zerubbabel the LORD's Signet Ring

^{20}The word of the LORD came to Haggai a second time on the twenty-fourth day of the month: ^{21}"Tell Zerubbabel governor of Judah that I will shake the heavens and the earth. ^{22}I will overturn royal thrones and shatter the power of the foreign kingdoms.^{w} I will overthrow chariots^x and their drivers; horses and their riders will fall, each by the sword of his brother.

2:22
^{w}Da 2:44
^{x}Mic 5:10

^{23}"'On that day,' declares the LORD Almighty, 'I will take you, my servant Zerubbabel son of Shealtiel,' declares the LORD, 'and I will make you like my signet ring, for I have chosen you,' declares the LORD Almighty."

^{a}15 Or to the days past

2:8, 9 God wanted the temple to be rebuilt, and he had the gold and silver to do it, but he needed willing hands. God has chosen to do his work through people. He provides the resources, but willing hands must do the work. Are your hands available for God's work in the world?

2:10–19 The example given in this message (delivered in December, 520 B.C.) makes it clear that holiness will not rub off on others, but contamination will. ("Consecrated meat" is meat made holy for the sacrifice.) As the people began to obey God, God promised to encourage and prosper them. But they needed to understand that activities in the temple would not clean up their sin; only repentance and obedience could do that. If we insist on harboring wrong attitudes and sins or on maintaining close relationships with sinful people, we will be defiled. Holy living will come only when we are empowered by God's Holy Spirit.

2:14 When a child eats spaghetti sauce, very soon his or her face, hands, and clothes become red. Sin and selfish attitudes produce the same result: they stain everything they touch. Even good deeds done for God can be tainted by sinful attitudes. The only remedy is God's cleansing.

2:16 A "heap" refers to a stack of grain at the harvest. For many years, the grain had only given 50 percent of the expected yield, and wine had done even worse.

2:18, 19 The people relaid the temple foundation, and immediately God blessed them. He did not wait for the project to be completed. God often sends his encouragement and approval with our first few obedient steps. He is eager to bless us!

2:20–23 Haggai's final message acknowledged that he was merely the messenger who brings the word of the Lord. It is addressed to Zerubbabel, the governor of Judah.

2:23 A signet ring was used to guarantee the authority and authenticity of a letter. It served as a signature when pressed in soft wax on a written document. God was reaffirming and guaranteeing his promise of a Messiah through David's line (Matthew 1:12).

2:23 God closed his message to Zerubbabel with this tremendous affirmation: "I have chosen you." Such a proclamation is ours as well—each of us has been chosen by God (Ephesians 1:4). This truth should make us see our value in God's eyes and motivate us to work for him. When you feel down, remind yourself, "God has chosen me!"

2:23 Haggai's message to the people sought to get their priorities straight, help them quit worrying, and motivate them to rebuild the temple. Like them, we often place a higher priority on our personal comfort than on God's work and true worship. But God is pleased and promises strength and guidance when we give him first place in our lives.

ZECHARIAH

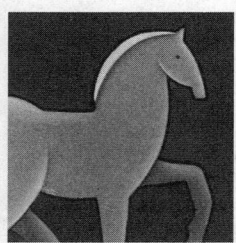

THE FUTURE—that vast uncharted sea of the unknown, holding joy or terror, comfort or pain, love or loneliness. Some people fear the days to come, wondering what evils lurk in the shadows; others consult seers and future-telling charlatans, trying desperately to discover its secrets. But tomorrow's story is known only to God and to those special messengers called prophets, to whom God has revealed a chapter or two.

A prophet's primary task was to proclaim the word of the Lord, pointing out sin, explaining its consequences, and calling men and women to repentance and obedience. Elijah, Elisha, Isaiah, Jeremiah, Ezekiel, Hosea, and Amos stand with scores of others who faithfully delivered God's message despite rejection, ridicule, and persecution. And at times they were given prophetic visions foretelling coming events.

Nestled near the end of the Old Testament, among what are known as "minor prophets," is the book of Zechariah. As one of three postexilic prophets, along with Haggai and Malachi, Zechariah ministered to the small remnant of Jews who had returned to Judah to rebuild the temple and their nation. Like Haggai, he encouraged the people to finish rebuilding the temple, but his message went far beyond those physical walls and contemporary issues. With spectacular apocalyptic imagery and graphic detail, Zechariah told of the Messiah, the one whom God would send to rescue his people and to reign over all the earth. Zechariah is one of our most important prophetic books, giving detailed Messianic references that were clearly fulfilled in the life of Jesus Christ. The rebuilding of the temple, he says, was just the first act in the drama of the end times and the ushering in of the Messianic age. Zechariah proclaimed a stirring message of hope to these ex-captives and exiles—their King was coming!

Jesus is Messiah, the promised "great deliverer" of Israel. Unlike Zechariah's listeners, we can look back at Christ's ministry and mission. As you study Zechariah's prophecy, you will see details of Christ's life that were written 500 years before their fulfillment. Read and stand in awe of our God, who keeps his promises. But there is also a future message that has not yet been fulfilled—the return of Christ at the end of the age. As you read Zechariah, think through the implications of this promised event. *Your King is coming,* and he will reign forever and ever.

God knows and controls the future. We may never see more than a moment ahead, but we can be secure if we trust in him. Read Zechariah and strengthen your faith in God—he alone is your hope and security.

VITAL STATISTICS

PURPOSE:
To give hope to God's people by revealing God's future deliverance through the Messiah

AUTHOR:
Zechariah

ORIGINAL AUDIENCE:
The Jews in Jerusalem who had returned from their captivity in Babylon

DATE WRITTEN:
Chapters 1—8 were written approximately 520–518 B.C. Chapters 9—14 were written around 480 B.C.

SETTING:
The exiles had returned from Babylon to rebuild the temple, but the work had been thwarted and stalled. Haggai and Zechariah confronted the people with their task and encouraged them to complete it.

KEY VERSES:
"Rejoice greatly, O Daughter of Zion! Shout, Daughter of Jerusalem! See, your king comes to you, righteous and having salvation, gentle and riding on a donkey, on a colt, the foal of a donkey. I will take away the chariots from Ephraim and the war-horses from Jerusalem, and the battle bow will be broken. He will proclaim peace to the nations. His rule will extend from sea to sea and from the River to the ends of the earth" (9:9, 10).

KEY PEOPLE:
Zerubbabel, Joshua

KEY PLACE:
Jerusalem

SPECIAL FEATURES:
This book is the most apocalyptic and Messianic of all the minor prophets.

THE BLUEPRINT

A. MESSAGES WHILE REBUILDING THE TEMPLE (1:1—8:23)
  1. Zechariah's night visions
  2. Zechariah's words of encouragement

Zechariah encouraged the people to put away the sin in their lives and to continue rebuilding the temple. His visions described the judgment of Israel's enemies, the blessings to Jerusalem, and the need for God's people to remain pure—avoiding hypocrisy, superficiality, and sin. Zechariah's visions provided hope for the people. We also need to carefully follow the instruction to remain pure until Christ returns.

B. MESSAGES AFTER
    COMPLETING THE TEMPLE
    (9:1—14:21)

Besides encouragement and hope, Zechariah's messages were also a warning that God's Messianic kingdom would not begin as soon as the temple was complete. Israel's enemies would be judged and the King would come, but God's people would themselves face many difficult circumstances before experiencing the blessing of the Messianic kingdom. We, too, may face much sorrow, disappointment, and distress before coming into Christ's eternal kingdom.

MEGATHEMES

THEME	EXPLANATION	IMPORTANCE
God's Jealousy	God was angry at his people for ignoring his prophets through the years, and he was concerned that they not follow the careless and false leaders who exploited them. Disobedience was the root of their problems and the cause of their misery. God was jealous for their devotion to him.	God is jealous for our devotion. To avoid Israel's ruin, don't walk in their steps. Don't reject God, follow false teachers, or lead others astray. Turn to God, faithfully obey his commands, and make sure you are leading others correctly.
Rebuild the Temple	The Jews were discouraged. They were free from exile, yet the temple was not completed. Zechariah encouraged them to rebuild it. God would both protect his workmen and empower them by his Holy Spirit to carry out his work.	More than the rebuilding of the Temple was at stake—the people were staging the first act in God's wonderful drama of the end times. Those of us who love God must complete his work. To do so we must have the Holy Spirit's help. God will empower us with his Spirit.
The King Is Coming	The Messiah will come both to rescue people from sin and to reign as king. He will establish his kingdom, conquer all his enemies, and rule over all the earth. Everything will one day be under his loving and powerful control.	The Messiah came as a servant to die for us. He will return as a victorious king. At that time, he will usher in peace throughout the world. Submit to his leadership now to be ready for the King's triumphant return.
God's Protection	There was opposition to God's plan in Zechariah's day, and he prophesied future times of trouble. But God's Word endures. God remembers the covenants he makes with his people. He cares for his people and will deliver them from all the world powers that oppress them.	Although evil is still present, God's infinite love and personal care have been demonstrated through the centuries. God keeps his promises. Although our bodies may be destroyed, we need never fear our ultimate destiny if we love and obey him.

A. MESSAGES WHILE REBUILDING THE TEMPLE (1:1—8:23)

Zechariah begins by describing eight visions that came to him at night. Then he gives a collection of messages about the crowning of Joshua, answers to questions of feasting and fasting, and encouragement to continue rebuilding the temple. We, too, can be inspired to continue following God in faithfulness throughout our life.

1. Zechariah's night visions

A Call to Return to the LORD

1 In the eighth month of the second year of Darius,[a] the word of the LORD came to the prophet Zechariah son of Berekiah, the son of Iddo:[b] ² "The LORD was very angry with your forefathers. ³ Therefore tell the people: This is what the LORD Almighty says: 'Return to me,' declares the LORD Almighty, 'and I will return to you,'[c] says the LORD Almighty. ⁴ Do not be like your forefathers,[d] to whom the earlier prophets proclaimed: This is what the LORD Almighty says: 'Turn from your evil ways and your evil practices.' But they would not listen or pay attention to me, [e] declares the LORD.

1:1
[a] Ezr 4:24
[b] Ne 12:4

1:3
[c] Mal 3:7; Jas 4:8

1:4
[d] 2Ch 36:15
[e] Jer 6:17

1:1 Born in Babylon during the exile, Zechariah was a fairly young man when he returned to Jerusalem in 538 B.C. King Cyrus of Persia had defeated Babylon in 539 and had decreed that captives in exile could return to their homelands. Zechariah and Haggai were among the first to leave. Zechariah, a prophet and a priest, began ministering at the same time as the prophet Haggai (520–518 B.C.). His first prophecy was delivered two months after Haggai's first prophecy.

Like Haggai, Zechariah encouraged the people to continue rebuilding the temple, whose reconstruction had been halted for nearly 15 years. Zechariah combated the people's spiritual apathy, despair over pressures from their enemies, and discouragement about the smaller scale of the new temple foundation. Neglect of our spiritual priorities can be just as devastating today to fulfilling God's purpose.

1:2–6 The familiar phrase "Like father, like son," implies that children turn out like their parents. But here, God warned Israel *not* to be like their forefathers, who disobeyed him and reaped the consequences—his punishment. We are responsible before God for our actions. We aren't trapped by our heredity or environment, and we can't use these as excuses for our sins. We are free to choose, and individually we must return to God and follow him.

1:6
*f*La 2:17

⁵Where are your forefathers now? And the prophets, do they live forever? ⁶But did not my words and my decrees, which I commanded my servants the prophets, overtake your forefathers?

"Then they repented and said, 'The Lᴏʀᴅ Almighty has done to us what our ways and practices deserve,*f* just as he determined to do.'"

The Man Among the Myrtle Trees

⁷On the twenty-fourth day of the eleventh month, the month of Shebat, in the second year of Darius, the word of the Lᴏʀᴅ came to the prophet Zechariah son of Berekiah, the son of Iddo.

1:8
*g*Rev 6:4
*h*Zec 6:2-7

⁸During the night I had a vision—and there before me was a man riding a red*g* horse! He was standing among the myrtle trees in a ravine. Behind him were red, brown and white horses.*h*

⁹I asked, "What are these, my lord?"

The angel who was talking with me answered, "I will show you what they are."

¹⁰Then the man standing among the myrtle trees explained, "They are the ones the Lᴏʀᴅ has sent to go throughout the earth."

1:11
*i*Isa 14:7

¹¹And they reported to the angel of the Lᴏʀᴅ, who was standing among the myrtle trees, "We have gone throughout the earth and found the whole world at rest and in peace."*i*

1:13
*j*Zec 4:1

¹²Then the angel of the Lᴏʀᴅ said, "Lᴏʀᴅ Almighty, how long will you withhold mercy from Jerusalem and from the towns of Judah, which you have been angry with these seventy years?" ¹³So the Lᴏʀᴅ spoke kind and comforting words to the angel who talked with me.*j*

1:14
*k*Zec 8:2

¹⁴Then the angel who was speaking to me said, "Proclaim this word: This is what the Lᴏʀᴅ Almighty says: 'I am very jealous*k* for Jerusalem and Zion, ¹⁵but I am very angry with the nations that feel secure. I was only a little angry, but they added to the calamity.'*l*

1:15
*l*Am 1:11

1:16
*m*Zec 2:1-2

¹⁶"Therefore, this is what the Lᴏʀᴅ says: 'I will return to Jerusalem with mercy, and there my house will be rebuilt. And the measuring line*m* will be stretched out over Jerusalem,' declares the Lᴏʀᴅ Almighty.

1:17
*n*Isa 51:3
*o*Zec 2:12

¹⁷"Proclaim further: This is what the Lᴏʀᴅ Almighty says: 'My towns will again overflow with prosperity, and the Lᴏʀᴅ will again comfort*n* Zion and choose Jerusalem.'"*o*

ZECHARIAH served as a prophet to Judah about 520 B.C., after the return from exile.

Climate of the times.	The exiles had returned from captivity to rebuild their temple. But work on the temple had stalled, and the people were ignoring their service to God.
Main message.	Zechariah, like Haggai, encouraged the people to finish rebuilding the temple. His visions gave the people hope. He told the people of a future king who would one day establish an eternal kingdom.
Importance of message.	Even in times of discouragement and despair, God is working out his plan. God protects and guides us; we must trust and follow him.
Contemporary prophet.	Haggai (approximately 520 B.C.)

1:5, 6 The words God had spoken through his prophets a century earlier, before the captivity, also applied to Zechariah's generation, and they are still relevant for us. Because God's Word endures, we must read, study, and apply what is preserved for us in Scripture. Learn the lessons of God's Word so you will not have to repeat the mistakes of others.

1:7–17 The man among the myrtle trees was the angel of the Lord (1:11). The horses and their colors were symbols of God's involvement in world governments. The full meaning of the colors is unknown, although the red horse is often associated with war and the white horse with final victory.

1:11 The angel of the Lord saw that all the nations were secure and at peace while Israel was still oppressed and despised. But God was planning a change. He had released his people, and he would allow them to return and rebuild his temple.

1:12 Seventy years was the time that God had decreed for Israel to remain in captivity (Jeremiah 25:11; 29:10). This time was over, and the angel asked God to act swiftly to complete the promised return of his people to Jerusalem.

1:13 God's people had lived under his judgment for 70 years during their captivity in Babylon. But here God spoke words of comfort and assurance. God promises that when we return to him, he will heal us (Hosea 6:1). If you feel wounded and torn by the events of your life, turn to God so he can heal and comfort you.

1:15 Although the pagan nations afflicted God's people beyond his intentions, God was not powerless to stop them. God used these nations to punish his sinful people. When the nations went beyond his plans by trying to destroy Israel as a nation, he intervened.

Four Horns and Four Craftsmen

¹⁸Then I looked up—and there before me were four horns! ¹⁹I asked the angel who was speaking to me, "What are these?"

He answered me, "These are the horns that scattered Judah, Israel and Jerusalem."

²⁰Then the LORD showed me four craftsmen. ²¹I asked, "What are these coming to do?" He answered, "These are the horns that scattered Judah so that no one could raise his head, but the craftsmen have come to terrify them and throw down these horns of the nations who lifted up their horns against the land of Judah to scatter its people."ᵖ

1:21
ᵖPs 75:10

A Man With a Measuring Line

2 Then I looked up—and there before me was a man with a measuring line in his hand! ²I asked, "Where are you going?"

He answered me, "To measure Jerusalem, to find out how wide and how long it is."�q

³Then the angel who was speaking to me left, and another angel came to meet him ⁴and said to him: "Run, tell that young man, 'Jerusalem will be a city without walls' because of the great number of men and livestock in it. ⁵And I myself will be a wall ˢ of fire around it,' declares the LORD, 'and I will be its glory within.'

⁶"Come! Come! Flee from the land of the north," declares the LORD, "for I have scattered you to the four winds of heaven,"ᵗ declares the LORD.

⁷"Come, O Zion! Escape, you who live in the Daughter of Babylon!" ⁸For this is what the LORD Almighty says: "After he has honored me and has sent me against the nations that have plundered you—for whoever touches you touches the apple of his eyeᵘ— ⁹I will surely raise my hand against them so that their slaves will plunder them.ᵃ Then you will know that the LORD Almighty has sent me. ᵛ

¹⁰"Shout and be glad, O Daughter of Zion. For I am coming, and I will live among you," declares the LORD. ¹¹"Many nations will be joined with the LORD in that day and will become my people. I will live among you and you will know that the LORD Almighty has sent me to you. ¹²The LORD will inherit Judah as his portion in the holy land and will again choose ʷ Jerusalem. ¹³Be stillˣ before the LORD, all mankind, because he has roused himself from his holy dwelling."

2:2
qRev 21:15

2:4
ʳEze 38:11
2:5
ˢIsa 26:1

2:6
ᵗEze 17:21
2:8
ᵘDt 32:10

2:9
ᵛZec 4:9

2:12
ʷZec 1:17
2:13
ˣHab 2:20

Clean Garments for the High Priest

3 Then he showed me Joshuaᵇ the high priest standing before the angel of the LORD, and Satanᶜ ʸ standing at his right side to accuse him. ²The LORD said to Satan, "The LORD rebuke you,ᶻ Satan! The LORD, who has chosen Jerusalem, rebuke you! Is not this man a burning stick snatched from the fire?"ᵃ

3:1
ʸPs 109:6
3:2
ᶻJude 1:9
ᵃJude 1:23

ᵃ8,9 Or *says after . . . eye:* ⁹"I . . . plunder them."   ᵇ1 A variant of *Jeshua;* here and elsewhere in Zechariah
ᶜ1 *Satan* means *accuser.*

1:18–21 The horns were the four world powers that oppressed Israel—Egypt, Assyria, Babylon, and Medo-Persia. The four craftsmen (1:20) were the nations used to overthrow Israel's enemies. God raised them up to judge the oppressors of his people.

2:1 The man with the measuring line symbolizes the hope of a rebuilt Jerusalem and a restored people. The man would be measuring to mark out the boundaries for a foundation (see 1:16; and Jeremiah 31:38–40).

2:6, 7 Many of the captive Israelites did not return to Jerusalem because they preferred to stay with the security and wealth they had experienced in Babylon. But Zechariah instructed them to leave Babylon quickly. This was an urgent request because Babylon would be destroyed and because its decadent culture would cause God's people to forget their spiritual priorities. A vast majority of the Israelites rejected these warnings and remained in Babylon.

2:8 Believers are precious to God (Psalm 116:15); they are his very own children (Psalm 103:13). Treating any believer unkindly is the same as treating God that way. As Jesus told his disciples, when we help others we are helping him; when we neglect or abuse them, we are neglecting or abusing him (Matthew 25:34–46). Be careful, therefore, how you treat fellow believers—that is the way you are treating God.

2:9–12 *Me* (2:9) may refer to the Messiah who, in the end, will judge all who have oppressed God's people. God promises to live

among his people, and he says that many nations will come to know him (John 1:14; Revelation 21:3).

2:11, 12 God did not forget his words to Abraham, "All peoples on earth will be blessed through you" (Genesis 12:3). Abraham, the father of the nation of Israel, was promised that his descendants would bless the whole world. Since the coming of Jesus, the Messiah, this promise is being fulfilled—people from all nations are coming to God through him.

3:1 Joshua was Israel's high priest when the remnant returned to Jerusalem and began rebuilding the walls (Haggai 1:1, 12; 2:4).

3:1–3 Satan accused Joshua, who here represents the nation of Israel. The accusations were accurate—Joshua stood in "filthy clothes" (sins). Yet God revealed his mercy, stating that he chose to save his people in spite of their sin. Satan is always accusing people of their sins before God (Job 1:6). But he greatly misunderstands the breadth of God's mercy and forgiveness toward those who believe in him. Satan the accuser will ultimately be destroyed (Revelation 12:10), while everyone who is a believer will be saved (John 3:16). To be prepared, we can ask God to remove our clothing of sin and dress us with his goodness.

3:2 God punished Judah through the fire of great trials, but he rescued the nation before it was completely destroyed, like "a burning stick snatched from the fire."

3 Now Joshua was dressed in filthy clothes as he stood before the angel. 4 The angel said to those who were standing before him, "Take off his filthy clothes."

Then he said to Joshua, "See, I have taken away your sin, and I will put rich garments on you."

5 Then I said, "Put a clean turban on his head." So they put a clean turban on his head and clothed him, while the angel of the LORD stood by.

ZECHARIAH'S VISIONS	Vision	Reference	Significance
	Zechariah sees messengers reporting to God that the surrounding nations that have oppressed Judah are living in careless and sinful ease.	1:7–17	Israel was asking, "Why isn't God punishing the wicked?" Wicked nations may prosper, but not forever. God will bring upon them the judgment they deserve.
	Zechariah sees four horns, representing the four world powers that oppressed and scattered the people of Judah and Israel. Then he sees four craftsmen who will throw down the horns.	1:18–21	God will do what he promised. After the evil nations have carried out his will in punishing his people, God will destroy these nations for their sin.
	Zechariah sees a man measuring the city of Jerusalem. The city will one day be full of people, and God himself will be a wall around the city.	2:1–13	The city will be restored in God's future kingdom. God will keep his promise to protect his people.
	Zechariah sees Joshua the high priest standing before God. Joshua's filthy clothes are exchanged for clean garments; Satan's accusations against him are rejected by God.	3:1–10	The story of Joshua the high priest pictures how the filthy clothes of sin are replaced with the pure linen of God's righteousness. Christ has taken our clothes of sin and replaced them with God's righteousness. (See Ephesians 4:24; 1 John 1:9.)
	Zechariah sees a lampstand that is continually kept burning by an unlimited reservoir of oil. This picture reminds the people that it is only through God's Spirit that they will succeed, not by their own might and resources.	4:1–14	The Spirit of God is given without measure. Human effort does not make a difference. The work of God is not accomplished in human strength.
	Zechariah sees a flying scroll, which represents God's curse.	5:1–4	By God's word and Spirit, every person will be judged. The individual's sin is the focus here, not the sins of the nation. God's curse is a symbol of destruction; all sin will be judged and removed.
	Zechariah sees a vision of a woman in a basket. She represents the wickedness of the nations. The angel packed the woman back into the basket and sent her back to Babylon.	5:5–11	Sins of the individual were judged in the last vision (5:1–4); now sin is being removed from society. Sin has to be eradicated in order to clean up the nation and the individual.
	Zechariah sees a vision of four horses and chariots. The horses represent God's judgment on the world—one is sent north, the direction from which most of Judah's enemies came. The other horses are patrolling the world, ready to execute judgment at God's command.	6:1–8	Judgment will come upon those who oppress God's people—it will come in God's time and at his command.

3:2–4 Zechariah's vision graphically portrays how we receive God's mercy. We do nothing ourselves. God removes our filthy clothes (sins), then provides us with new, clean, rich garments (the righteousness and holiness of God—2 Corinthians 5:21; Ephesians 4:24; Revelation 19:8). All we need to do is repent and ask God to forgive us. When Satan tries to make you feel dirty and unworthy, remember that the clean clothes of Christ's righteousness make you worthy to draw near to God.

3:5–7 The Greek name for Joshua is Jesus, meaning "the LORD saves." This Joshua should not be confused with the warrior of the book of Joshua. Both the warrior Joshua and the high priest Joshua, however, have been seen as symbols of Jesus, the Messiah.

6 The angel of the LORD gave this charge to Joshua: 7 "This is what the LORD Almighty says: 'If you will walk in my ways and keep my requirements, then you will govern my house *b* and have charge of my courts, and I will give you a place among these standing here.

8 "'Listen, O high priest Joshua and your associates seated before you, who are men symbolic *c* of things to come: I am going to bring my servant, the Branch. 9 See, the stone I have set in front of Joshua! There are seven eyes *a* on that one stone, *d* and I will engrave an inscription on it,' says the LORD Almighty, 'and I will remove the sin of this land in a single day.

10 "'In that day each of you will invite his neighbor to sit under his vine and fig tree,*e*' declares the LORD Almighty."

The Gold Lampstand and the Two Olive Trees

4 Then the angel who talked with me returned and wakened *f* me, as a man is wakened from his sleep. 2 He asked me, "What do you see?"

I answered, "I see a solid gold lampstand with a bowl at the top and seven lights *g* on it, with seven channels to the lights. 3 Also there are two olive trees *h* by it, one on the right of the bowl and the other on its left."

4 I asked the angel who talked with me, "What are these, my lord?"

5 He answered, "Do you not know what these are?"

"No, my lord," I replied.

6 So he said to me, "This is the word of the LORD to Zerubbabel: 'Not by might nor by power, but by my Spirit,'*i* says the LORD Almighty.

7 "What *b* are you, O mighty mountain? Before Zerubbabel you will become level ground.*j* Then he will bring out the capstone *k* to shouts of 'God bless it! God bless it!'"

8 Then the word of the LORD came to me: 9 "The hands of Zerubbabel have laid the foundation *l* of this temple; his hands will also complete it.*m* Then you will know that the LORD Almighty has sent me *n* to you.

10 "Who despises the day of small things?*o* Men will rejoice when they see the plumb line in the hand of Zerubbabel.

"(These seven are the eyes of the LORD, which range throughout the earth.)"

11 Then I asked the angel, "What are these two olive trees*p* on the right and the left of the lampstand?"

12 Again I asked him, "What are these two olive branches beside the two gold pipes that pour out golden oil?"

*a*9 Or *facets*   *b*7 Or *Who*

3:7
b Dt 17:8-11;
Eze 44:15-16

3:8
c Eze 12:11
3:9
d Isa 28:16

3:10
e Mic 4:4

4:1
f Da 8:18
4:2
g Rev 4:5
4:3
h Rev 11:4

4:6
i Hos 1:7

4:7
j Jer 51:25
k Ps 118:22
4:9
l Ezr 3:11
m Ezr 6:15
n Zec 2:9

4:10
o Hag 2:3

4:11
p ver 3

3:7-10 There was no priesthood during the exile, so it had to be reinstated upon the return to the land. In this vision, Joshua is installed as high priest. One of the high priest's duties was to offer a sacrifice on the Day of Atonement to make amends for all the sins of the people. The priest was the mediator between God and the nation. Thus, he represented the coming Messiah (Isaiah 11:1), who would change the entire order of God's dealing with people's sin (Hebrews 10:8-14 explains this in detail). Jesus, the Messiah, was the High Priest who offered, once for all, the sacrifice of himself to take away our sins. In the new order, every Christian is a priest offering a holy, cleansed life to God (1 Peter 2:9; Revelation 5:10).

3:8, 9 The "Branch" refers to the Messiah. The meaning of the stone with seven eyes is unclear. It could mean (1) the Branch himself as the foundation stone of the Temple, (2) the rock struck by Moses that produced water for the Israelites (Numbers 20:7-11), or (3) the renewed spiritual priesthood of the church (1 Peter 2:5). These verses were fulfilled hundreds of years later by Jesus Christ. God said, "I will remove the sin of this land in a single day," and this was fulfilled in Christ who "died for sins once for all, the righteous for the unrighteous, to bring you to God" (1 Peter 3:18). You cannot remove your sins by your own effort. You must allow God to remove them through Christ.

3:10 God promises that each person will have his or her own place of security during Christ's reign (see also Micah 4:4). Sitting under the vine and fig tree was a symbol of peace and prosperity.

4:1 The gold lampstand with a bowl and seven lights on it represents a steady supply of oil, signifying that God's power would be reflected in the light. Oil was obtained from crushed olives and used in bowls with wicks to produce light. The two olive trees stood for the priestly and royal offices.

4:6 Zerubbabel was given the responsibility of rebuilding the temple in Jerusalem (Ezra 3:2, 8; Haggai 1:1; 2:23). While the prophets Haggai and Zechariah gave the moral and spiritual encouragement to resume work on the temple, Zerubbabel saw that the task was carried out. As the work was being completed, the prophets encouraged Zerubbabel and told him of a time when spiritual apathy and foreign oppression would forever be abolished.

4:6 Many people believe that to survive in this world a person must be tough, strong, unbending, and harsh. But God says, "Not by might nor by power, but by my Spirit." The key words are "by my Spirit." It is *only* through God's Spirit that anything of lasting value is accomplished. The returned exiles were indeed weak—harassed by their enemies, tired, discouraged, and poor. But actually they had God on their side! As you live for God, determine not to trust in your own strength or abilities. Instead, depend on God and work in the power of his Spirit! (See also Hosea 1:7.)

4:9 The temple was completed in 516 B.C. (Ezra 6:14, 15).

4:10 Many of the older Jews were disheartened when they realized this new temple would not match the size and splendor of the previous temple built during King Solomon's reign. But bigger and more beautiful is not always better. What you do for God may seem small and insignificant at the time, but God rejoices in what is right, not necessarily in what is big. Be faithful in the small opportunities. Begin where you are and do what you can, and leave the results to God.

[13]He replied, "Do you not know what these are?"

"No, my lord," I said.

[14]So he said, "These are the two who are anointed to[a] serve the Lord of all the earth."

The Flying Scroll

5 I looked again—and there before me was a flying scroll! [2]He asked me, "What do you see?"

I answered, "I see a flying scroll, thirty feet long and fifteen feet wide.[b]"

[3]And he said to me, "This is the curse[q] that is going out over the whole land; for according to what it says on one side, every thief will be banished, and according to what it says on the other, everyone who swears falsely will be banished. [4]The LORD Almighty declares, 'I will send it out, and it will enter the house of the thief and the house of him who swears falsely by my name. It will remain in his house and destroy it, both its timbers and its stones.[r]'"

The Woman in a Basket

[5]Then the angel who was speaking to me came forward and said to me, "Look up and see what this is that is appearing."

[6]I asked, "What is it?"

He replied, "It is a measuring basket.[c]" And he added, "This is the iniquity[d] of the people throughout the land."

[7]Then the cover of lead was raised, and there in the basket sat a woman! [8]He said, "This is wickedness," and he pushed her back into the basket and pushed the lead cover down over its mouth.[s]

[9]Then I looked up—and there before me were two women, with the wind in their wings! They had wings like those of a stork, and they lifted up the basket between heaven and earth.

[10]"Where are they taking the basket?" I asked the angel who was speaking to me.

[11]He replied, "To the country of Babylonia[e][t] to build a house[u] for it. When it is ready, the basket will be set there in its place."

Four Chariots

6 I looked up again—and there before me were four chariots coming out from between two mountains—mountains of bronze! [2]The first chariot had red horses, the second black,[v] [3]the third white, and the fourth dappled—all of them powerful. [4]I asked the angel who was speaking to me, "What are these, my lord?"

[5]The angel answered me, "These are the four spirits[f][w] of heaven, going out from standing in the presence of the Lord of the whole world. [6]The one with the black horses is going toward the north country, the one with the white horses toward the west,[g] and the one with the dappled horses toward the south."

[7]When the powerful horses went out, they were straining to go throughout the earth. And he said, "Go throughout the earth!" So they went throughout the earth.

[8]Then he called to me, "Look, those going toward the north country have given my Spirit[h] rest in the land of the north."

a 14 Or two who bring oil and   b 2 Hebrew twenty cubits long and ten cubits wide (about 9 meters long and 4.5 meters wide)   c 6 Hebrew an ephah; also in verses 7-11   d 6 Or appearance   e 11 Hebrew Shinar   f 5 Or winds   g 6 Or horses after them   h 8 Or spirit

5:3
q Mal 3:9

5:4
r Lev 14:34-45;
Mal 3:5

5:8
s Mic 6:11

5:11
t Ge 10:10
u Jer 29:5, 28

6:2
v Rev 6:5

6:5
w Eze 37:9;
Mt 24:31; Rev 7:1

4:14 The two anointed ones may be Joshua and Zerubbabel, dedicated for this special task. Also note that in Revelation 11:3, two witnesses arise to prophesy to the nations during the time of tribulation. These witnesses will be killed but will rise again.

5:1–9 The judgment of the flying scroll was leveled against those who violated God's law, specifically by stealing and lying (5:1–4). The woman in a basket personified wickedness, and so this vision showed that wickedness would be not only severely punished (the vision of the flying scroll), but also banished (the vision of the woman in a basket, 5:6–9).

5:9–11 The woman in a basket was carried away "to the country of Babylonia," which had become a symbol for the center of world idolatry and wickedness. This woman was a picture to Zechariah that wickedness and sin would be taken away from Israel, and one day sin would be removed from the entire earth. When Christ died,

he removed sin's power and penalty. When we trust Christ to forgive us, he removes the penalty of sin and gives us the power to overcome sin in our lives. When Christ returns, he will remove all sin from the earth, allowing people to live in eternal safety and security.

6:1–8 The four chariots were similar to the four horsemen in the first vision. These chariots represent the four angels of God's judgment on the earth.

6:8 The black horse that went north executed God's judgment in the north country. God is angry with sin and with the wicked (Psalm 7:11), and his anger is expressed in judgment. As much as we like to concentrate on God's love and mercy, anger and judgment are also part of his righteous character. If you have unconfessed or habitual sin in your life, confess it and turn away from it. Confession releases God's mercy, but refusing to repent invites his judgment.

2. Zechariah's words of encouragement
A Crown for Joshua

9 The word of the LORD came to me: 10 "Take ⌊silver and gold⌋ from the exiles Heldai, Tobijah and Jedaiah, who have arrived from Babylon.ˣ Go the same day to the house of Josiah son of Zephaniah. 11 Take the silver and gold and make a crown, and set it on the head of the high priest, Joshua son of Jehozadak.ʸ 12 Tell him this is what the LORD Almighty says: 'Here is the man whose name is the Branch,ᶻ and he will branch out from his place and build the temple of the LORD.ᵃ 13 It is he who will build the temple of the LORD, and he will be clothed with majesty and will sit and rule on his throne. And he will be a priestᵇ on his throne. And there will be harmony between the two.' 14 The crown will be given to Heldai,ᵃ Tobijah, Jedaiah and Henᵇ son of Zephaniah as a memorial in the temple of the LORD. 15 Those who are far away will come and help to build the temple of the LORD,ᶜ and you will know that the LORD Almighty has sent me to you. This will happen if you diligently obeyᵈ the LORD your God."

6:10
ˣ Jer 28:6

6:11
ʸ Ezr 3:2

6:12
ᶻ Zec 3:8
ᵃ Zec 4:6-9

6:13
ᵇ Ps 110:4

6:15
ᶜ Isa 60:10
ᵈ Zec 3:7

Justice and Mercy, Not Fasting

7 In the fourth year of King Darius, the word of the LORD came to Zechariah on the fourth day of the ninth month, the month of Kislev.ᵉ 2 The people of Bethel had sent Sharezer and Regem-Melech, together with their men, to entreat the LORD 3 by asking the priests of the house of the LORD Almighty and the prophets, "Should I mourn and fast in the fifthᶠ month, as I have done for so many years?"

4 Then the word of the LORD Almighty came to me: 5 "Ask all the people of the land and the priests, 'When you fastedᵍ and mourned in the fifth and seventh months for the past seventy years, was it really for me that you fasted? 6 And when you were eating and drinking, were you not just feasting for yourselves? 7 Are these not the words the LORD proclaimed through the earlier prophets when Jerusalem and its surrounding towns were at restʰ and prosperous, and the Negev and the western foothills were settled?'"

8 And the word of the LORD came again to Zechariah: 9 "This is what the LORD Almighty says: 'Administer true justice;ⁱ show mercy and compassion to one another. 10 Do not oppress the widow or the fatherless, the alien or the poor. In your hearts do not think evil of each other.'

11 "But they refused to pay attention; stubbornly they turned their backs and stopped up their ears.ʲ 12 They made their hearts as hard as flint and would not listen to the law or to the words that the LORD Almighty had sent by his Spirit through the earlier prophets.ᵏ So the LORD Almighty was very angry.

13 "'When I called, they did not listen; so when they called, I would not listen,'ˡ says the LORD Almighty. 14 'I scattered them with a whirlwind among all the nations, where they were strangers. The land was left so desolate behind them that no one could come or go. This is how they made the pleasant land desolate.ᵐ'"

7:1
ᵉ Ne 1:1

7:3
ᶠ Zec 8:19

7:5
ᵍ Isa 58:5

7:7
ʰ Jer 22:21

7:9
ⁱ Zec 8:16

7:11
ʲ Jer 11:10

7:12
ᵏ Ne 9:29

7:13
ˡ Isa 1:15

7:14
ᵐ Jer 44:6

ᵃ 14 Syriac; Hebrew *Helem*   ᵇ 14 Or *and the gracious one, the*

6:9–15 This vision is about the Messiah, the King-Priest. In the days of the kings and after the exile, Judah's government was to be ruled by two distinct persons—the king, ruling the nation's political life, and the high priest, ruling its religious life. Kings and priests had often been corrupt. God was telling Zechariah that someone worthy of the crown would come to rule as both king ("rule on his throne") and priest ("a priest on his throne"). This was an unlikely combination for that day.

6:15 Some of God's promises are conditional—we must obey him to receive them. The rebuilding of the temple required careful obedience. God would protect the people as long as they obeyed. Casual or occasional obedience, the result of a halfhearted or divided commitment, would not lead to blessing. Many of God's blessings come to us as a result of diligent obedience. Inconsistent obedience can't produce consistent blessing.

7:1ff The fourth year of King Darius's reign was 518 B.C. For the previous 70 years, the people had been holding a fast in August to remember the destruction of Jerusalem. Because Jerusalem was being rebuilt, they came to the temple to ask if they had to continue this annual fast. God did not answer their question

directly. Instead, he told them that their acts of justice and mercy were more important than their fasting. What he wanted from his people was true justice in their dealings and mercy and compassion for the weak.

7:5–7 The Israelites had lost their sincere desire for a loving relationship with God. Zechariah told them that they had been fasting without a proper attitude of repentance or worship. They fasted and mourned during their exile with no thought of God or their sins that had caused the exile in the first place. When you go to church, pray, or have fellowship with other believers, are you doing these from habit or for what you get out of it? God says that an attitude of worship without a sincere desire to know and love him will lead to ruin.

7:7 The Negev was the southern part of Judah.

7:11, 12 Zechariah explained to the people that their ancestors brought God's great wrath on themselves by hardening their hearts. Any sin seems more natural the second time—each repetition is easier. Ignoring or refusing God's warning hardens you each time you do wrong. Read God's Word and apply it to your life. Sensitivity and submission to God's Word can soften your heart and allow you to live as you should.

The LORD Promises to Bless Jerusalem

8 Again the word of the LORD Almighty came to me. 2 This is what the LORD Almighty says: "I am very jealous for Zion; I am burning with jealousy for her."

3 This is what the LORD says: "I will return to Zion and dwell in Jerusalem. Then Jerusalem will be called the City of Truth, and the mountain of the LORD Almighty will be called the Holy Mountain."

4 This is what the LORD Almighty says: "Once again men and women of ripe old age will sit in the streets of Jerusalem,ⁿ each with cane in hand because of his age. 5 The city streets will be filled with boys and girls playing there. ᵒ"

6 This is what the LORD Almighty says: "It may seem marvelous to the remnant of this people at that time,ᵖ but will it seem marvelous to me?" declares the LORD Almighty.

7 This is what the LORD Almighty says: "I will save my people from the countries of the east and the west. �q 8 I will bring them back to live in Jerusalem; they will be my people,ʳ and I will be faithful and righteous to them as their God."

9 This is what the LORD Almighty says: "You who now hear these words spoken by the prophetsˢ who were there when the foundation was laid for the house of the LORD Almighty, let your hands be strongᵗ so that the temple may be built. 10 Before that time there were no wages for man or beast. No one could go about his business safely because of his enemy, for I had turned every man against his neighbor. 11 But now I will not deal with the remnant of this people as I did in the past," declares the LORD Almighty.

12 "The seed will grow well, the vine will yield its fruit,ᵘ the ground will produce its crops, and the heavens will drop their dew. I will give all these things as an inheritance to the remnant of this people. 13 As you have been an object of cursingᵛ among the nations, O Judah and Israel, so will I save you, and you will be a blessing. Do not be afraid, but let your hands be strong."

14 This is what the LORD Almighty says: "Just as I had determined to bring disaster upon you and showed no pity when your fathers angered me," says the LORD Almighty, 15 "so now I have determined to do goodʷ again to Jerusalem and Judah. Do not be afraid. 16 These are the things you are to do: Speak the truthˣ to each other, and render true and sound judgment in your courts;ʸ 17 do not plot evilᶻ against your neighbor, and do not love to swear falsely. I hate all this," declares the LORD.

18 Again the word of the LORD Almighty came to me. 19 This is what the LORD Almighty says: "The fasts of the fourth, fifth, seventh and tenthᵃ months will become joyful and glad occasions and happy festivals for Judah. Therefore love truthᵇ and peace."

20 This is what the LORD Almighty says: "Many peoples and the inhabitants of many cities will yet come, 21 and the inhabitants of one city will go to another and say, 'Let us go at once to entreat the LORD and seek the LORD Almighty. I myself am going.' 22 And many peoples and powerful nations will come to Jerusalem to seek the LORD Almighty and to entreat him."

8:4
ⁿ Isa 65:20

8:5
ᵒ Jer 30:20

8:6
ᵖ Ps 118:23

8:7
q Isa 11:11

8:8
ʳ Zec 2:11

8:9
ˢ Ezr 5:1
ᵗ Hag 2:4

8:12
ᵘ Joel 2:22

8:13
ᵛ Jer 42:18

8:15
ʷ Jer 29:11

8:16
ˣ Eph 4:25
ʸ Zec 7:9

8:17
ᶻ Pr 3:29

8:19
ᵃ Jer 52:4
ᵇ ver 16

8:3 One day Christ will reign in his kingdom on earth. There all his people will live with him. This truth should encourage us to look forward to the Messiah's reign.

8:4, 5 In troubled times, the very old and very young are the first to suffer and die. But both groups are plentiful in this vision, filling the streets with their normal everyday activities. This is a sign of the complete peace and prosperity of God's new earth.

8:6 The remnant was the small group of exiles who had returned from Babylon to rebuild Jerusalem and the temple. Struggling to survive in the land, they became discouraged over the opposition they often faced from hostile neighbors. It was hard to believe that one day God himself would reign from this city and that their land would enjoy great peace and prosperity. Our God is all-powerful; he can do anything! When confronting seemingly impossible tasks or situations, remember that "with God all things are possible" (Matthew 19:26).

8:8 The covenant relationship will be renewed, and the whole community will be filled with the presence of God. This promise of forgiveness and restoration extends to all God's people wherever they may be found. (For other references to this promise, see Exodus 6:6, 7; 19:5, 6; 29:45; Leviticus 26:12; Deuteronomy 7:6; Jeremiah 31:1, 33.)

8:9 God had to give the temple workers a little push to get them moving. They had heard the prophets' words of encouragement;

at this time they needed to stop just listening and get to work. We need to listen to what God says, but after he has made our course of action plain, we need to "be strong" and do what he wants.

8:13–15 For more than 15 years, God and his prophets had been urging the people to finish building the temple. Here again, God encouraged them with visions of the future. We may be tempted to slow down for many reasons: people aren't responding; we feel physically or emotionally drained; the workers are uncooperative; the work is distasteful, too difficult, or not worth the effort. God's promises about the future should encourage us *now*. He knows what the results of our labors will be, and thus he can give us a perspective that will help us continue in our work for him.

8:14–17 God promised to give his people rich rewards, reassuring them that despite the punishments they had endured, he would not change his mind to bless them. But he also said they had a job to do—"These are the things you are to do." God will be faithful, but we also have responsibilities: to tell the truth, exercise justice, and live peacefully. If you expect God to do his part, be sure to do yours.

8:19–22 There will come a time when fasting for sins will be replaced by feasting and joy. People from all nations will "seek the LORD Almighty." This was also promised in 2:11.

23 This is what the Lord Almighty says: "In those days ten men from all languages and nations will take firm hold of one Jew by the hem of his robe and say, 'Let us go with you, because we have heard that God is with you.'" [c]

8:23
[c] 1Co 14:25

B. MESSAGES AFTER COMPLETING THE TEMPLE (9:1—14:21)

After the temple was completed, Zechariah gave several prophecies about Israel's future, which describe the first and second comings of Jesus Christ. This book contains more about the person, work, and glory of Christ than the other minor prophets combined. Israel's King would come, but he would be rejected by his people. They would later repent and be restored to God. The King who is coming is our king. May we be found faithful and pure in his sight when we meet him face to face.

Judgment on Israel's Enemies

An Oracle

9

The word of the Lord is against the land of Hadrach
  and will rest upon Damascus—
for the eyes of men and all the tribes of Israel
  are on the Lord—[a]
2 and upon Hamath[d] too, which borders on it,
  and upon Tyre[e] and Sidon, though they are very skillful.
3 Tyre has built herself a stronghold;
  she has heaped up silver like dust,
  and gold like the dirt of the streets.
4 But the Lord will take away her possessions
  and destroy her power on the sea,
  and she will be consumed by fire.[f]
5 Ashkelon will see it and fear;
  Gaza will writhe in agony,
  and Ekron too, for her hope will wither.
Gaza will lose her king
  and Ashkelon will be deserted.
6 Foreigners will occupy Ashdod,
  and I will cut off the pride of the Philistines.
7 I will take the blood from their mouths,
  the forbidden food from between their teeth.
Those who are left will belong to our God
  and become leaders in Judah,
  and Ekron will be like the Jebusites.
8 But I will defend my house
  against marauding forces.
Never again will an oppressor overrun my people,
  for now I am keeping watch.

9:2
[d] Jer 49:23
[e] Eze 28:1-19

9:4
[f] Isa 23:1

[a] 1 Or *Damascus. / For the eye of the Lord is on all mankind, / as well as on the tribes of Israel,*

8:23 In the past, Jerusalem had often borne the brunt of cruel jokes from other nations (8:13). The city was not respected; its citizens had sinned so much that God let them be kicked around by their enemies. But eventually, says Zechariah, Jerusalem will be a holy place—respected highly throughout the world because its people will have a change of heart toward God. People from other nations will see how God has rewarded his people for their faithfulness and will want to be included in their great blessings.

9:1–17 An oracle is a message from God. Hadrach was probably a city in northern Aram. The last six chapters of the book are two messages delivered late in Zechariah's life. These messages point to the Messiah and his second coming. Some of these prophecies were fulfilled before the Messiah came, perhaps by

Alexander the Great; others were fulfilled during the Messiah's time on earth; and others will be fulfilled when he returns. Those who oppressed Jerusalem—Aram, Philistia, Phoenicia—would be crushed. Zion's promised King would come—first as a servant on a donkey's colt, later as a powerful ruler and judge.

9:5–7 Zechariah mentions four key cities in Philistia: Ashkelon, Gaza, and Ekron would be destroyed, and Ashdod would be overtaken by foreigners. This would happen because of their great evil and idolatry. But those left in the land would be adopted into Israel as a new clan, as the Jebusites were (when David conquered Jerusalem, he did not wipe out the Jebusites, but absorbed them into Judah).

9:8 Several centuries after Zechariah's day, Antiochus IV Epiphanes would invade Israel; and in A.D. 70, Titus, a Roman general, would completely destroy the temple. This promise, therefore, may have been conditional upon the people's obedience. The day will come, however, when God's people will never again have to worry about invading enemies (Joel 3:17).

The Coming of Zion's King

9:9
g Isa 9:6-7;
Zep 3:14-15
h Mt 21:5*;
Jn 12:15*

9 Rejoice greatly, O Daughter of Zion!
   Shout, Daughter of Jerusalem!
See, your king*a* comes to you,
   righteous and having salvation,*g*
   gentle and riding on a donkey,
   on a colt, the foal of a donkey.*h*

9:10
i Hos 1:7

10 I will take away the chariots from Ephraim
   and the war-horses from Jerusalem,
   and the battle bow will be broken.*i*
He will proclaim peace to the nations.
   His rule will extend from sea to sea
   and from the River*b* to the ends of the earth.*c*

9:11
j Ex 24:8

11 As for you, because of the blood of my covenant*j* with you,
   I will free your prisoners from the waterless pit.
12 Return to your fortress, O prisoners of hope;
   even now I announce that I will restore twice as much to you.

9:13
k Joel 3:6

13 I will bend Judah as I bend my bow
   and fill it with Ephraim.
I will rouse your sons, O Zion,
   against your sons, O Greece,*k*
   and make you like a warrior's sword.

The LORD Will Appear

9:14
l Ps 18:14
m Isa 21:1

14 Then the LORD will appear over them;
   his arrow will flash like lightning.*l*
The Sovereign LORD will sound the trumpet;
   he will march in the storms*m* of the south,

9:15
n Isa 37:35
o Ex 27:2

15   and the LORD Almighty will shield*n* them.
They will destroy
   and overcome with slingstones.
They will drink and roar as with wine;
   they will be full like a bowl
   used for sprinkling*d* the corners*o* of the altar.

9:16
p Jer 31:11

16 The LORD their God will save them on that day
   as the flock of his people.
They will sparkle in his land
   like jewels in a crown.*p*
17 How attractive and beautiful they will be!
   Grain will make the young men thrive,
   and new wine the young women.

a 9 Or *King*   *b* 10 That is, the Euphrates   *c* 10 Or *the end of the land*   *d* 15 Or *bowl, / like*

9:9 The Triumphal Entry of Jesus riding into Jerusalem (Matthew 21:1–11) was predicted here more than 500 years before it happened. Just as this prophecy was fulfilled when Jesus came to earth, so the prophecies of his second coming are just as certain to come true. We are to be ready for his return, for he is coming!

9:10 When we view two distant mountains, they appear to be close together, perhaps even to touch each other. But as we approach them, we can see that they are in fact far apart, even separated by a huge valley. This is the situation with many Old Testament prophecies. Verse 9 was clearly fulfilled in Christ's first coming, but verse 10 can now be seen to refer to his second coming. At that time all nations will be subject to Christ, and his rule will extend over the whole earth. In Philippians 2:9, 10, we are told that at that time every knee will bow to Christ and every tongue will confess him as Lord.

9:11 Covenants in Old Testament times were sealed or confirmed with blood, much as we would sign our name

to a contract. The old covenant was sealed by the blood of sacrifices, pointing ahead to the blood Christ would shed at Calvary, his "signature" that confirmed God's new covenant with his people. Because God had made a covenant with these people, he delivered them from the "waterless pit," the cistern-like prison of exile.

9:14–17 After Solomon's reign, the kingdom was divided into the northern kingdom (called Israel or Ephraim) and the southern kingdom (called Judah). This prophecy says that all Israel, north and south, will someday be reunited. The first part of this chapter tells how God will help his people avoid war; here God explains that he will appear to help his people when war is inevitable. Verses 14–16 explain how the Jews will win over the Greeks, but it is also a figurative picture of the ultimate future victory over evil by God's people.

The LORD Will Care for Judah

10 Ask the LORD for rain in the springtime;
　　　it is the LORD who makes the storm clouds.
　　He gives showers of rain to men,
　　　and plants of the field to everyone.

2 The idols*q* speak deceit,
　　　diviners see visions that lie;
　　they tell dreams that are false,
　　　they give comfort in vain.
　　Therefore the people wander like sheep
　　　oppressed for lack of a shepherd.*r*

3 "My anger burns against the shepherds,
　　　and I will punish the leaders;*s*
　　for the LORD Almighty will care
　　　for his flock, the house of Judah,
　　　and make them like a proud horse in battle.

4 From Judah will come the cornerstone,
　　　from him the tent peg,
　　　from him the battle bow,
　　　from him every ruler.

5 Together they*a* will be like mighty men
　　　trampling the muddy streets in battle.*t*
　　Because the LORD is with them,
　　　they will fight and overthrow the horsemen.*u*

6 "I will strengthen the house of Judah
　　　and save the house of Joseph.
　　I will restore them
　　　because I have compassion on them.
　　They will be as though
　　　I had not rejected them,
　　for I am the LORD their God
　　　and I will answer*v* them.

7 The Ephraimites will become like mighty men,
　　　and their hearts will be glad as with wine.
　　Their children will see it and be joyful;
　　　their hearts will rejoice in the LORD.

8 I will signal*w* for them
　　　and gather them in.
　　Surely I will redeem them;
　　　they will be as numerous*x* as before.

9 Though I scatter them among the peoples,
　　　yet in distant lands they will remember me.
　　They and their children will survive,
　　　and they will return.

a 4,5 Or *ruler, all of them together.* / *s* *They*

10:2
q Eze 21:21
r Eze 34:5; Hos 3:4

10:3
s Jer 25:34

10:5
t 2Sa 22:43
u Hag 2:22

10:6
v Zec 13:9

10:8
w Isa 5:26
x Eze 36:11

10:2 We often create idols of money, power, fame, or success, and then we expect them to give us happiness and security. But these idols can't supply what we need any more than a stone image can make it rain. How foolish it is to trust in idols. Instead, trust God's promises for your future.

10:4 Zechariah's prophecy, more than 500 years before Christ's first coming, called Christ a "cornerstone" (see also Isaiah 28:16), a "tent peg" (Isaiah 22:23), a "bow" that wins the battle, and a "ruler" who was a man of action (see also Genesis 49:10; Micah 5:2). This Messiah would be strong, stable, victorious, and trustworthy—all in all, the answer to Israel's problems. Only in the Messiah will all the promises to God's people be fulfilled.

10:6 The "house of Judah" refers to the southern kingdom, and the "house of Joseph" refers to the northern kingdom. Ephraim, the leading tribe of the northern kingdom, was the son of Joseph. One day God will unite all his people. This verse tells about God's reuniting of the Jews (see also Jeremiah 31:10). This was a startling idea: the people of the northern kingdom of Israel were so completely absorbed into other cultures after their captivity in 722 B.C. that a regathering could not be done by human means, but only by God.

10:6, 12 God promises to strengthen his people. When we stay closely connected to God, his Spirit will enable us to do his will, despite the obstacles. When we stray away from God, we will be cut off from our power source.

10:10
y Isa 11:11

¹⁰ I will bring them back from Egypt
    and gather them from Assyria.*y*
I will bring them to Gilead and Lebanon,
    and there will not be room enough for them.

10:11
z Isa 19:5-7
a Eze 30:13

¹¹ They will pass through the sea of trouble;
    the surging sea will be subdued
    and all the depths of the Nile will dry up.*z*
Assyria's pride will be brought down
    and Egypt's scepter*a* will pass away.

10:12
b Mic 4:5

¹² I will strengthen them in the LORD
    and in his name they will walk,*b*"

                           declares the LORD.

11:1
c Eze 31:3

11:2
d Isa 32:19

11

Open your doors, O Lebanon,*c*
    so that fire may devour your cedars!
² Wail, O pine tree, for the cedar has fallen;
    the stately trees are ruined!
Wail, oaks of Bashan;
    the dense forest*d* has been cut down!
³ Listen to the wail of the shepherds;
    their rich pastures are destroyed!
Listen to the roar of the lions;
    the lush thicket of the Jordan is ruined!

Two Shepherds

11:5
e Jer 50:7

11:6
f Mic 5:8

⁴ This is what the LORD my God says: "Pasture the flock marked for slaughter. ⁵ Their buyers slaughter them and go unpunished. Those who sell them say, 'Praise the LORD, I am rich!' Their own shepherds do not spare them.*e* ⁶ For I will no longer have pity on the people of the land," declares the LORD. "I will hand everyone over to his neighbor and his king. They will oppress the land, and I will not rescue them from their hands."*f*

⁷ So I pastured the flock marked for slaughter, particularly the oppressed of the flock. Then I took two staffs and called one Favor and the other Union, and I pastured the flock. ⁸ In one month I got rid of the three shepherds.

11:9
g Jer 15:2

The flock detested me, and I grew weary of them ⁹ and said, "I will not be your shepherd. Let the dying die, and the perishing perish.*g* Let those who are left eat one another's flesh."

11:10
h Jer 14:21

¹⁰ Then I took my staff called Favor and broke it, revoking*h* the covenant I had made with all the nations. ¹¹ It was revoked on that day, and so the afflicted of the flock who were watching me knew it was the word of the LORD.

11:12
i Ex 21:32; Mt 26:15

¹² I told them, "If you think it best, give me my pay; but if not, keep it." So they paid me thirty pieces of silver.*i*

10:10 This pictured return from Egypt and Assyria was a symbolic way of saying that the people would be returned from all the countries where they had been dispersed. Egypt and Assyria evoked memories of slavery and separation.

10:11 The "sea of trouble" refers to the Red Sea, through which the Israelites were miraculously delivered from Egypt. Just as the Israelites returned once again from Egypt and other lands, they would continue to be protected by God's miraculous power.

11:4–17 In this message, God told Zechariah to act out the roles of two different kinds of shepherds. The first type of shepherd demonstrated how God would reject his people (the sheep) because they rejected him (11:4–14). The second type of shepherd demonstrated how God would give over his people to evil shepherds (11:15–17). (See Ezekiel 34 for a detailed portrayal of the evil shepherds of Israel.)

11:4 God told Zechariah to take a job as shepherd of a flock of sheep being fattened for slaughter. The Messiah would shepherd God's people during a time of spiritual and political confusion. The flock represented the people feeding on their own greed and evil desires until they were ripe for God's judgment.

11:7 Zechariah took two shepherd's staffs and named them "Favor" and "Union." He broke the first one ("Favor") to show that God's gracious covenant with his people was broken. He broke the second one ("Union") to show that "the brotherhood between Judah and Israel" was broken (11:14).

11:8 The identity of the three evil shepherds is not known. But God knew they were unfit to shepherd his people, and so he removed them.

11:12 To pay this shepherd 30 pieces of silver was an insult—this was the price paid to an owner for a slave gored by an ox (Exodus 21:32). This is also the amount Judas received for betraying Jesus (Matthew 27:3–10). The priceless Messiah was sold for the price of a slave.

13And the LORD said to me, "Throw it to the potter"—the handsome price at which they priced me! So I took the thirty pieces of silver and threw them into the house of the LORD to the potter.*j*

11:13
*l*Mt 27:9-10*

14Then I broke my second staff called Union, breaking the brotherhood between Judah and Israel.

15Then the LORD said to me, "Take again the equipment of a foolish shepherd. 16For I am going to raise up a shepherd over the land who will not care for the lost, or seek the young, or heal the injured, or feed the healthy, but will eat the meat of the choice sheep, tearing off their hoofs.

> 17 "Woe to the worthless shepherd,
>   who deserts the flock!
> May the sword strike his arm and his right eye!
>   May his arm be completely withered,
>   his right eye totally blinded!"*k*

11:17
*k*Jer 23:1

Jerusalem's Enemies to Be Destroyed

An Oracle

12 This is the word of the LORD concerning Israel. The LORD, who stretches out the heavens, who lays the foundation of the earth, and who forms the spirit of man *l* within him, declares: 2"I am going to make Jerusalem a cup that sends all the surrounding peoples reeling. *m* Judah *n* will be besieged as well as Jerusalem. 3On that day, when all the nations *o* of the earth are gathered against her, I will make Jerusalem an immovable rock for all the nations. All who try to move it will injure themselves. 4On that day I will strike every horse with panic and its rider with madness," declares the LORD. "I will keep a watchful eye over the house of Judah, but I will blind all the horses of the nations. 5Then the leaders of Judah will say in their hearts, 'The people of Jerusalem are strong, because the LORD Almighty is their God.'

6"On that day I will make the leaders of Judah like a firepot in a woodpile, like a flaming torch among sheaves. They will consume*p* right and left all the surrounding peoples, but Jerusalem will remain intact in her place.

7"The LORD will save the dwellings of Judah first, so that the honor of the house of David and of Jerusalem's inhabitants may not be greater than that of Judah. 8On that day the LORD will shield *q* those who live in Jerusalem, so that the feeblest among them will be like David, and the house of David will be like God, like the Angel of the LORD going before them. 9On that day I will set out to destroy all the nations that attack Jerusalem.

12:1
*l*Isa 57:16

12:2
*m*Isa 51:23
*n*Zec 14:14

12:3
*o*Zec 14:2

12:6
*p*Ob 1:18

12:8
*q*Zec 9:15

11:13 Potters were in the lowest social class. The "handsome price" (a sarcastic comment) was so little that it could be thrown to the potter. It is significant that the 30 pieces of silver paid to Judas for betraying Jesus were returned to the temple and used to buy a potter's field (Matthew 27:3–10).

11:14 Because the people had rejected the Messiah, God would reject them—symbolized by Zechariah breaking the staff called "Union." Not long after Zechariah's time, the Jews began to divide into numerous factions—Pharisees, Sadducees, Essenes, Herodians, and Zealots. The discord among these groups was a key factor leading to the destruction of Jerusalem in A.D. 70.

11:15–17 Israel would not only reject the true shepherd; it would accept instead a worthless shepherd. This shepherd would serve his own concerns rather than the concerns of his flock and would destroy rather than defend them. Condemnation is his rightful fate because he trusted his arm (military might) and his eye (intellect). God would destroy both areas.

11:17 It is a great tragedy for God's people when their leaders fail to care for them adequately. God holds leaders particularly accountable for the condition of his people. The New Testament tells church leaders, "Not many of you should presume to be teachers, . . . because you know that we who teach will be judged more strictly" (James 3:1). If God puts you in a position of leadership, remember that it is also a place of great responsibility.

12:1–14 This chapter pictures the final siege against the people of Jerusalem.

12:3, 4 This speaks of a great future battle against Jerusalem. Some say it is Armageddon, the last great battle on earth. Those who oppose God's people will not prevail forever. Eventually, evil, pain, and oppression will be abolished once and for all.

12:7 As water flows downhill, so a city's influence usually flows to its surrounding countryside. But this time, the countryside of Judah (the "dwellings") would have priority over Jerusalem so that the people of Jerusalem would not become proud. Don't think you have to witness first to the "important" people—professional athletes, movie stars, and prominent businessmen. Christ came to seek and save the lost (Luke 19:10), even the "down-and-out" lost. We must be careful to avoid spiritual pride or we, like Jerusalem, may be the last to know what God is doing.

Mourning for the One They Pierced

12:10
r Isa 44:3;
Eze 39:29;
Joel 2:28-29
s Jn 19:34, 37*;
Rev 1:7

12:11
t 2Ki 23:29

10 "And I will pour out on the house of David and the inhabitants of Jerusalem a spirit*a* of grace and supplication. *r* They will look on*b* me, the one they have pierced, *s* and they will mourn for him as one mourns for an only child, and grieve bitterly for him as one grieves for a firstborn son. 11 On that day the weeping in Jerusalem will be great, like the weeping of Hadad Rimmon in the plain of Megiddo. *t* 12 The land will mourn, each clan by itself, with their wives by themselves: the clan of the house of David and their wives, the clan of the house of Nathan and their wives, 13 the clan of the house of Levi and their wives, the clan of Shimei and their wives, 14 and all the rest of the clans and their wives.

Cleansing From Sin

13:1
u Ps 51:2

13 "On that day a fountain will be opened to the house of David and the inhabitants of Jerusalem, to cleanse*u* them from sin and impurity.

13:2
v Jer 23:14-15

2 "On that day, I will banish the names of the idols from the land, and they will be remembered no more," declares the LORD Almighty. "I will remove both the prophets *v* and the spirit of impurity from the land. 3 And if anyone still prophesies, his father and mother, to whom he was born, will say to him, 'You must die, because you have told lies in the LORD's name.' When he prophesies, his own parents will stab him. *w*

13:3
w Dt 18:20

13:4
x Mt 3:4

4 "On that day every prophet will be ashamed of his prophetic vision. He will not put on a prophet's garment *x* of hair in order to deceive. 5 He will say, 'I am not a prophet. I am a farmer; the land has been my livelihood since my youth.*c* ' *y* 6 If someone asks him, 'What are these wounds on your body*d* ?' he will answer, 'The wounds I was given at the house of my friends.'

13:5
y Am 7:14

The Shepherd Struck, the Sheep Scattered

13:7
z Jer 47:6
a Isa 40:11
b Mt 26:31*

7 "Awake, O sword,*z* against my shepherd,*a*
     against the man who is close to me!"
     declares the LORD Almighty.
"Strike the shepherd,
     and the sheep will be scattered,*b*
     and I will turn my hand against the little ones.
8 In the whole land," declares the LORD,
     "two-thirds will be struck down and perish;
     yet one-third will be left in it.

13:9
c 1Pe 1:6-7

9 This third I will bring into the fire;
     I will refine them like silver*c*
     and test them like gold.

a 10 Or *the Spirit*   *b* 10 Or *to*   *c* 5 Or *farmer; a man sold me in my youth*   *d* 6 Or *wounds between your hands*

12:10 The Holy Spirit was poured out at Pentecost, 50 days after Christ's resurrection (see Acts 2). Zechariah calls the Spirit "a spirit of grace and supplication." It is this Spirit who convicts us of sin, reveals to us God's righteousness and judgment, and helps us as we pray. "In the same way, the Spirit helps us in our weakness. We do not know what we ought to pray for, but the Spirit himself intercedes for us with groans that words cannot express" (Romans 8:26). Ask God to fill you with his Spirit.

12:10-14 Eventually *all* people will realize that Jesus, the man who was pierced and killed, is indeed the Messiah. There will be an awakening, with sorrow for sin and genuine revival. The crucified Messiah will be clearly revealed (Philippians 2:10; Revelation 5:13).

12:11 Hadad Rimmon could refer to the place near the plain of Megiddo where King Josiah was killed. Josiah's death was greatly mourned by his people (see 2 Chronicles 35:22–25).

12:12-14 These verses are saying that all Israel will mourn—king, prophet, priest, and people. Each family will go into private mourning, husbands and wives by themselves, to face their sorrow.

13:1ff There will be a never-ending supply of God's mercy, forgiveness, and cleansing power. This picture of a fountain is similar to the never-ending stream flowing out from the temple (Ezekiel 47:1). The fountain is used in Scripture to symbolize God's forgiveness. In John 4, Jesus tells of his "living water" that

satisfies completely. Are you spiritually thirsty? Do you need to experience God's forgiveness? Drink from the fountain—ask Jesus to forgive you and give you his salvation.

13:2-6 This chapter pictures the final days of the earth as we know it. For God's new era to begin, there must be a cleansing—all evil must be abolished. Therefore, idols will be banished, and false prophets will be ashamed of themselves and will no longer try to deceive God's people.

13:7 Just before his arrest, Jesus quoted from this verse, referring to himself and his disciples (Matthew 26:31, 32). He knew beforehand that his disciples would scatter when he was arrested. The Roman "sword" was the military power that put Christ to death.

13:9 This "third" was a remnant, a small part of the whole. Throughout the history of Israel, whenever the whole nation seemed to turn against God, God said that a righteous remnant still trusted and followed him. These believers were refined like silver and gold through the fire of their difficult circumstances. Determine to be part of God's remnant, that small part of the whole that is obedient to him. Obey God no matter what the rest of the world does. This may mean trials and troubles at times; but as fire purifies gold and silver, you will be purified and made more like Christ.

They will call on my name
  and I will answer them;
I will say, 'They are my people,'d
  and they will say, 'The LORD is our God.'"

The LORD Comes and Reigns

14 A day of the LORD e is coming when your plunder will be divided among you. 2I will gather all the nations to Jerusalem to fight against it; the city will be captured, the houses ransacked, and the women raped. Half of the city will go into exile, but the rest of the people will not be taken from the city.

3Then the LORD will go out and fight against those nations, as he fights in the day of battle. 4On that day his feet will stand on the Mount of Olives, f east of Jerusalem, and the Mount of Olives will be split in two from east to west, forming a great valley, with half of the mountain moving north and half moving south. 5You will flee by my mountain valley, for it will extend to Azel. You will flee as you fled from the earthquakea g in the days of Uzziah king of Judah. Then the LORD my God will come, and all the holy ones with him.

6On that day there will be no light, no cold or frost. 7It will be a unique day, without daytime or nighttime—a day known to the LORD. When evening comes, there will be light. h

8On that day living water i will flow out from Jerusalem, half to the eastern seab and half to the western sea,c in summer and in winter.

9The LORD will be king over the whole earth. j On that day there will be one LORD, and his name the only name.

10The whole land, from Geba to Rimmon, south of Jerusalem, will become like the Arabah. But Jerusalem will be raised upk and remain in its place, l from the Benjamin Gate to the site of the First Gate, to the Corner Gate, and from the Tower of Hananel to the royal winepresses. 11It will be inhabited; never again will it be destroyed. Jerusalem will be secure.

12This is the plague with which the LORD will strike all the nations that fought against Jerusalem: Their flesh will rot while they are still standing on their feet, their eyes will rot in their sockets, and their tongues will rot in their mouths. m 13On that day men will be stricken by the LORD with great panic. Each man will seize the hand of another, and they will attack each other. n 14Judah too will fight at Jerusalem. The wealth of all the surrounding nations will be collected—great quantities of gold and silver and clothing. 15A similar plague o will strike the horses and mules, the camels and donkeys, and all the animals in those camps.

16Then the survivors from all the nations that have attacked Jerusalem will go up year after year to worship the King, the LORD Almighty, and to celebrate the Feast of Tabernacles. p 17If any of the peoples of the earth do not go up to Jerusalem to worship the King, the LORD Almighty, they will have no rain. q 18If the Egyptian people do not go up and take part, they will have no rain. The LORDd will bring on them the plague he inflicts on the nations that do not go up to celebrate the Feast of Tabernacles. r 19This will be the punishment of Egypt and the punishment of all the nations that do not go up to celebrate the Feast of Tabernacles.

a5 Or 5My mountain valley will be blocked and will extend to Azel. It will be blocked as it was blocked because of the earthquake   b8 That is, the Dead Sea   c8 That is, the Mediterranean   d18 Or part, then the LORD

13:9
d Jer 30:22

14:1
e Mal 4:1

14:4
f Eze 11:23

14:5
g Am 1:1

14:7
h Isa 30:26

14:8
i Eze 47:1-12;
Rev 22:1-2

14:9
j Rev 11:15

14:10
k Am 9:11
l Zec 12:6

14:12
m Dt 28:22

14:13
n Zec 11:6

14:15
o ver 12

14:16
p Isa 60:6-9

14:17
q Am 4:7

14:18
r ver 12

14:1 Many times in the Bible we are encouraged to watch for the day of the Lord. What if you knew exactly when this would happen? Would you live differently? Christ could return at any moment. Be ready for him by studying the Scriptures carefully and by making sure that you live as he intends—in obedience and spiritual readiness.

14:1–21 This chapter portrays the eventual triumph of the Messiah over all the earth and his reign over God's people. But the chronological order of these future events is not clear. They show that God has various ways of dealing with his people. Now we are to watch as the events unfold and God provides an escape for his people.

14:4 On the Mount of Olives, Jesus spoke with his disciples about the end times (Matthew 24). Near this mountain, an angel

promised that Jesus would return in the same manner as he had left (Acts 1:11; see also Ezekiel 11:23).

14:5 Only God's people will escape God's punishment (Matthew 24:16–20). In this time of confusion, God will clearly know who his people are. (See the fourth note on Amos 1:1 concerning the earthquake in King Uzziah's day.)

14:8 The eastern sea and the western sea refer to the Dead Sea and the Mediterranean Sea respectively.

14:10 Jerusalem is honored as the city of God and the focal point of all the world's worship. Jerusalem's elevation is a dramatic way of showing God's supremacy.

14:16 This Feast of Tabernacles is the only feast still appropriate during the Messiah's reign. The Passover was fulfilled in Christ's death; the Day of Atonement, in acceptance of Christ's salvation; the Feast of First Fruits, in his resurrection; and Pentecost, with the arrival of the Holy Spirit. But the Feast of Tabernacles, a festival of thanksgiving, celebrates the harvest of human souls for the Lord. Jesus may have alluded to it in John 4:35.

14:21
s 1Co 10:31
t Ne 8:10

²⁰On that day HOLY TO THE LORD will be inscribed on the bells of the horses, and the cooking pots in the LORD's house will be like the sacred bowls in front of the altar. ²¹Every pot in Jerusalem and Judah will be holy s to the LORD Almighty, and all who come to sacrifice will take some of the pots and cook in them. And on that day t there will no longer be a Canaanite a in the house of the LORD Almighty.

a 21 Or *merchant*

14:20, 21 In the future, even such common objects as horses' bells and cooking pots will be holy. This vision of a restored, holy Jerusalem stands in contrast to its broken walls and unpleasant living conditions. One day God would fulfill the people's dreams for Jerusalem beyond what they could imagine. God still wants to do much more for us than we can imagine (Ephesians 3:20). When we walk with him, we will discover this more deeply each day.

14:21 Zechariah was speaking to a people who were enduring hardships—they were being harassed by neighbors; they were discouraged over their small numbers and seemingly inadequate temple; and their worship was apathetic. But God said, "I am very jealous for Jerusalem" (1:14). He promised to restore their land, their city, and their temple. Like other prophets, Zechariah blended prophecies of the present, near future, and final days into one sweeping panorama. Through his message we learn that our hope is found in God and his Messiah, who are in complete control of the world.

MALACHI

VITAL STATISTICS

PURPOSE:
To confront the people with their sins and to restore their relationship with God

AUTHOR:
Malachi

ORIGINAL AUDIENCE:
The people in Jerusalem

DATE WRITTEN:
Approximately 430 B.C.

SETTING:
Malachi, Haggai, and Zechariah were postexilic prophets to Judah (the southern kingdom). Haggai and Zechariah rebuked the people for their failure to rebuild the Temple. Malachi confronted them with their neglect of the Temple and their false and profane worship.

KEY VERSES:
"Surely the day is coming; it will burn like a furnace. . . But for you who revere my name, the sun of righteousness will rise with healing in its wings. And you will go out and leap like calves released from the stall" (4:1, 2).

KEY PEOPLE:
Malachi, the priests

KEY PLACES:
Jerusalem, the Temple

SPECIAL FEATURES:
Malachi's literary style employs a dramatic use of questions asked by God and his people (for example, see 3:7, 8).

A VASE shatters, brushed by a careless elbow; a toy breaks, handled roughly by young fingers; fabric rips, pulled by strong and angry hands. Spills and rips take time to clean up, effort to repair, and money to replace, but far more costly are shattered relationships. Unfaithfulness, untruths, hateful words, and forsaken vows tear delicate personal bonds and inflict wounds not easily healed. Most tragic, however, is a broken relationship with God.

God loves perfectly and completely. And his love is a love of action—giving, guiding, and guarding. He is altogether faithful, true to his promises to his chosen people. But consistently they spurn their loving God, breaking the covenant, following other gods, and living for themselves. So their relationship with him is shattered.

But the breach is not irreparable; all hope is not lost. God can heal and mend and reweave the fabric. Forgiveness is available. And that is grace.

This is the message of Malachi, God's prophet in Jerusalem. His words reminded the Jews, God's chosen nation, of their willful disobedience, beginning with the priests (1:1—2:9) and then including every person (2:10—3:15). They had shown contempt for God's name (1:6), offered false worship (1:7–14), led others into sin (2:7–9), broken God's laws (2:11–16), called evil "good" (2:17), kept God's tithes and offerings for themselves (3:8, 9), and become arrogant (3:13–15). The relationship was broken, and judgment and punishment would be theirs. In the midst of this wickedness, however, a faithful few—the remnant—still loved and honored God. God would shower his blessings upon these men and women (3:16–18).

Malachi paints a stunning picture of Israel's unfaithfulness that clearly shows the people to be worthy of punishment, but woven throughout this message is hope—the possibility of forgiveness. This is beautifully expressed in 4:2—"But for you who revere my name, the sun of righteousness will rise with healing in its wings. And you will go out and leap like calves released from the stall."

Malachi concludes with a promise of the coming of "the prophet Elijah," who will offer God's forgiveness to all people through repentance and faith (4:5, 6).

The book of Malachi forms a bridge between the Old Testament and the New Testament. As you read Malachi, see yourself as the recipient of this word of God to his people. Evaluate the depth of your commitment, the sincerity of your worship, and the direction of your life. Then allow God to restore your relationship with him through his love and forgiveness.

THE BLUEPRINT

1. The sinful priests (1:1—2:9)
2. The sinful people (2:10—3:15)
3. The faithful few (3:16—4:6)

Malachi rebuked the people and the priests for neglecting the worship of God and failing to live according to his will. The priests were corrupt; how could they lead the people? They had become stumbling blocks instead of spiritual leaders. The men were divorcing their wives and marrying pagan women; how could they have godly children? Their relationship to God had become inconsequential. If our relationship with God is unimportant, we need to take stock of ourselves by setting aside our sinful habits, putting the Lord first, and giving God our best each day.

MEGATHEMES

THEME	EXPLANATION	IMPORTANCE
God's Love	God loves his people even when they ignore or disobey him. He has great blessings to bestow on those who are faithful to him. His love never ends.	Because God loves us so much, he hates hypocrisy and careless living. This kind of living denies him the relationship he wants to have with us. What we give and how we live reflects the sincerity of our love for God.
The Sin of the Priests	Malachi singled out the priests for condemnation. They knew what God required, yet their sacrifices were unworthy and their service was insincere; they were lazy, arrogant, and insensitive. They had a casual attitude toward the worship of God and observance of God's standards.	If religious leaders go wrong, how will the people be led? We are all leaders in some capacity. Don't neglect your responsibilities or be ruled by what is convenient. Neglect and insensitivity are acts of disobedience. God wants leaders who are faithful and sincere.
The Sin of the People	The people had not learned the lesson of the Exile, nor had they listened to the prophets. Men were callously divorcing their faithful wives to marry younger pagan women. This was against God's law because it disobeyed his commands about marriage and threatened the religious training of the children. But pride had hardened the hearts of the people.	God deserves our very best honor, respect, and faithfulness. But sin hardens our heart to our true condition. Pride is unwarranted self-esteem; it is setting your own judgment above God's and looking down on others. Don't let pride keep you from giving God your devotion, money, marriage, and family.
The Lord's Coming	God's love for his faithful people is demonstrated by the Messiah's coming. The Messiah will lead the people to the realization of all their fondest hopes. The day of the Lord's coming will be a day of comfort and healing for a faithful few, and a day of judgment for those who reject him.	At Christ's first coming, he refined and purified all those who believed in him. Upon his return, he will expose and condemn those who are proud, insensitive, or unprepared. Yet God is able to heal and forgive. Forgiveness is available to all who come to him.

1. The sinful priests

1:1
a Na 1:1

1 An oracle: *a* The word of the LORD to Israel through Malachi. *a*

Jacob Loved, Esau Hated

1:2
b Ro 9:13*

² "I have loved you," says the LORD.

"But you ask, 'How have you loved us?'

"Was not Esau Jacob's brother?" the LORD says. "Yet I have loved Jacob, *b* ³ but Esau I have hated, and I have turned his mountains into a wasteland and left his inheritance to the desert jackals."

a 1 Malachi means *my messenger*.

1:1 An oracle is a message from God. Malachi, the last Old Testament prophet, preached after Haggai, Zechariah, and Nehemiah—about 430 B.C. The temple had been rebuilt for almost a century, and the people were losing their enthusiasm for worship. Apathy and disillusionment had set in because the exciting Messianic prophecies of Isaiah, Jeremiah, and Micah had not been fulfilled. Many of the sins that had brought the downfall of Jerusalem in 586 B.C. were still being practiced in Judah. Malachi confronted the hypocrites with their sin by portraying a graphic dialogue between a righteous God and his hardened people.

1:2 God's first message through Malachi was "I have loved you." Although this message applied specifically to Israel, it is a message of hope for all people in all times. Unfortunately, many people are cynical about God's love, using political and economic progress as a measure of success. Because the government was

corrupt and the economy poor, the Israelites assumed that God didn't love them. They were wrong. God loves all people because he made them; however, his *eternal* rewards go only to those who are faithful to him.

1:2-5 The phrase "Esau I have hated" does not refer to Esau's eternal destiny. It simply means that God chose Jacob, not his brother Esau, to be the one through whom the nation of Israel and the Messiah would come (see Romans 9:10–13). God allowed Esau to father a nation, but this nation, Edom, later became one of Israel's chief enemies. The story of Jacob and Esau is found in Genesis 25:19–26. Because God chose Jacob and his descendants as the nation through whom the world would be blessed, God cared for them in a special way. Ironically, they rejected God after he chose them.

⁴Edom may say, "Though we have been crushed, we will rebuild the ruins."

But this is what the Lord Almighty says: "They may build, but I will demolish. They will be called the Wicked Land, a people always under the wrath of the Lord. ⁵You will see it with your own eyes and say, 'Great ᶜ is the Lord—even beyond the borders of Israel!'

1:5
ᶜPs 35:27

Blemished Sacrifices

⁶"A son honors his father, and a servant his master. If I am a father, where is the honor due me? If I am a master, where is the respect due me?" says the Lord Almighty. "It is you, O priests, who show contempt for my name.

"But you ask, 'How have we shown contempt for your name?'

⁷"You place defiled food ᵈ on my altar.

"But you ask, 'How have we defiled you?'

1:7
ᵈver 12; Lev 21:6

"By saying that the Lord's table is contemptible. ⁸When you bring blind animals for sacrifice, is that not wrong? When you sacrifice crippled or diseased animals, ᵉ is that not wrong? Try offering them to your governor! Would he be pleased with you? Would he accept you?" says the Lord Almighty.

1:8
ᵉLev 22:22

⁹"Now implore God to be gracious to us. With such offerings from your hands, will he accept you?"—says the Lord Almighty.

¹⁰"Oh, that one of you would shut the temple doors, so that you would not light useless fires on my altar! I am not pleased ᶠ with you," says the Lord Almighty, "and I will accept no offering ᵍ from your hands. ¹¹My name will be great among the nations, from the rising to the setting of the sun. In every place incense ʰ and pure offerings will be brought to my name, because my name will be great among the nations," says the Lord Almighty.

1:10
ᶠHos 5:6
ᵍIsa 1:11-14;
Jer 14:12
1:11
ʰIsa 60:6-7;
Rev 8:3

¹²"But you profane it by saying of the Lord's table, 'It is defiled,' and of its food, ⁱ 'It is contemptible.' ¹³And you say, 'What a burden!' ʲ and you sniff at it contemptuously," says the Lord Almighty.

1:12
ⁱver 7
1:13
ʲIsa 43:22-24

"When you bring injured, crippled or diseased animals and offer them as sacrifices, should I accept them from your hands?" says the Lord. ¹⁴"Cursed is the cheat who has an acceptable male in his flock and vows to give it, but then sacrifices a blemished animal ᵏ to the Lord. For I am a great king," says the Lord Almighty, "and my name is to be feared among the nations.

1:14
ᵏLev 22:18-21

1:6ff God charged the priests with failing to honor him (to the point of showing contempt for his name) and failing to be good spiritual examples to the people. The temple had been rebuilt in 516 B.C., and worship was being conducted there, but the priests did not worship God properly—they were not following his laws for the sacrifices. Ezra, the priest, had sparked a great revival around 458 B.C. However, by Malachi's time, the nation's leaders had once again fallen away from God, and the people right along with them. The worship of God was no longer from heartfelt adoration; instead it was simply a burdensome job for the priests.

1:6–8 God's law required that only perfect animals be offered to God (see for example, Leviticus 1:3). But these priests were allowing the people to offer blind, crippled, and diseased animals to God. God accused them of dishonoring him by offering imperfect sacrifices, and he was greatly displeased. The New Testament says that our lives should be living sacrifices to God (Romans 12:1). If we give God only our leftover time, money, and energy, we repeat the same sin as these worshipers who didn't want to bring anything valuable to God. What we give God reflects our true attitude toward him.

1:7, 8 The people sacrificed to God wrongly through (1) expedience—being as cheap as possible, (2) neglect—not caring how they offered the sacrifice, and (3) outright disobedience—sacrificing their own way and not as God had commanded. Their methods of giving showed their real attitudes toward God. How about your attitude? Do expedience, neglect, or disobedience characterize your giving?

1:10 As intermediaries between God and the people, priests were responsible for reflecting God's attitudes and character. By accepting imperfect sacrifices, they were leading the people to believe that God accepted those sacrifices as well. But God says, "I am not pleased with you." As Christians, we are often in the same position as these priests because we reflect God to our friends and family. What image of God's character and attitudes do they see in you? If you casually accept sin, you are like these priests in Malachi's day, and God will not be pleased with you.

1:11 A theme that can be heard throughout the Old Testament is affirmed in this book—"my name will be great among the nations." God had a chosen people, the Jews, through whom he planned to save and bless the entire world. Today God still wants to save and bless the world through all who believe in him—Jews and Gentiles. Christians are now his chosen people, and our pure offering to the Lord is our new life in Christ. Are you available to God to be used in making his name honored by the nations? This mission begins in our homes and in our neighborhoods, but it doesn't stop there. We must work and pray for God's worldwide mission.

1:13 Worship was a "burden" to these priests. Too many think that following God is supposed to make life easy and more comfortable. They are looking for a God of convenience. The truth is that it often takes hard work to live by God's high standards. He may call us to face poverty or suffering. But if serving God is more important to us than anything else, what we must give up is of little importance compared to what we gain—eternal life with God.

Admonition for the Priests

2 "And now this admonition is for you, O priests. 2 If you do not listen, and if you do not set your heart to honor my name," says the LORD Almighty, "I will send a curse upon you, and I will curse your blessings. Yes, I have already cursed them, because you have not set your heart to honor me.

3 "Because of you I will rebuke[a] your descendants[b]; I will spread on your faces the offal[l] from your festival sacrifices, and you will be carried off with it. 4 And you will know that I have sent you this admonition so that my covenant with Levi may continue," says the LORD Almighty. 5 "My covenant was with him, a covenant of life and peace,[m] and I gave them to him; this called for reverence and he revered me and stood in awe of my name. 6 True instruction was in his mouth and nothing false was found on his lips. He walked with me in peace and uprightness, and turned many from sin.[n]

7 "For the lips of a priest ought to preserve knowledge, and from his mouth men should seek instruction—because he is the messenger of the LORD Almighty. 8 But you have turned from the way and by your teaching have caused many to stumble;[o] you have violated the covenant with Levi," says the LORD Almighty. 9 "So I have caused you to be despised and humiliated before all the people, because you have not followed my ways but have shown partiality in matters of the law."

2. The sinful people
Judah Unfaithful

10 Have we not all one Father[c]?[p] Did not one God create us? Why do we profane the covenant[q] of our fathers by breaking faith with one another?

a3 Or *cut off* (see Septuagint)   b3 Or *will blight your grain*   c10 Or *father*

**Cross references (margin):**
2:3 *l* Ex 29:14
2:5 *m* Nu 25:12
2:6 *n* Jer 23:22
2:8 *o* Jer 18:15
2:10 *p* 1Co 8:6 *q* Ex 19:5

MALACHI served as a prophet to Judah about 430 B.C. He was the last of the Old Testament prophets.

Climate of the times	The city of Jerusalem and the temple had been rebuilt for almost a century, but the people had become complacent in their worship of God.
Main message	The people's relationship with God was broken because of their sin, and they would soon be punished. But the few who repented would receive God's blessing, highlighted in his promise to send a Messiah.
Importance of message	Hypocrisy, neglecting God, and careless living have devastating consequences. Serving and worshiping God must be the primary focus of our life, both now and in eternity.
Contemporary prophets	None

2:1, 2 God warned the priests that if they did not honor his name, he would punish them. Like these priests, we too are called to honor God's name—to worship him. This means acknowledging God for who he is—the almighty Creator of the universe who alone is perfect and who reaches down to sinful mankind with perfect love. According to this definition, are you honoring God's name?

2:1, 2 The priests didn't take seriously (set their hearts to) God's priority, even though he had reminded them through his word many times. How do you find out what is most important to God? Begin by loving him with all your heart, soul, and strength (Deuteronomy 6:5). This means listening to what God says in his Word and then setting your heart, mind, and will on doing what he says. When we love God, his Word becomes a shining light that guides our daily activities. The priests in Malachi's day had stopped loving God, and thus they did not know nor care what he wanted.

2:4–6 The Levites "walked with [God] . . . and turned many from sin" (2:6). Levi was the ancestor of the tribe of Levites, the tribe set apart for service to God (Numbers 1:47–54). The Levites became God's ministers, first in the tabernacle, then in the temple. In these verses, God was addressing the priests who were from this tribe, saying that they should listen to the laws he gave their ancestor Levi, and follow his example.

2:7, 8 Malachi was angry at the priests because, though they were to be God's messengers, they did not know God's will. And this lack of knowledge caused them to lead God's people astray. Their ignorance was willful and inexcusable. Pastors and leaders of God's people *must* know God's Word—what it says, what it means, and how it applies to daily life. How much time do you spend in God's Word?

2:9 The priests had allowed influential and favored people to break the law. The priests were so dependent on these people for support that they could not afford to confront them when they did wrong. In your church, are certain people allowed to do wrong without criticism? There should be no double standard based on wealth or position. Let your standards be those presented in God's Word. Playing favorites is contemptible in God's sight (see James 2:1–9).

2:10–16 The people were being unfaithful. Though not openly saying they rejected God, they were living as if he did not exist. Men were marrying pagan women who worshiped idols. Divorce was common, occurring for no reason other than a desire for change. People acted as if they could do anything without being punished. And they wondered why God refused to accept their offerings and bless them (2:13)! We cannot successfully separate our dealings with God from the rest of our lives. He must be Lord of all.

¹¹Judah has broken faith. A detestable thing has been committed in Israel and in Jerusalem: Judah has desecrated the sanctuary the LORD loves, by marrying the daughter of a foreign god. ¹²As for the man who does this, whoever he may be, may the LORD cut him off from the tents of Jacob ᵃ—even though he brings offerings ʳ to the LORD Almighty.

¹³Another thing you do: You flood the LORD's altar with tears. You weep and wail because he no longer pays attention to your offerings or accepts them with pleasure from your hands. ¹⁴You ask, "Why?" It is because the LORD is acting as the witness between you and the wife of your youth, ˢ because you have broken faith with her, though she is your partner, the wife of your marriage covenant.

¹⁵Has not ⌊the LORD⌋ made them one? ᵗ In flesh and spirit they are his. And why one? Because he was seeking godly offspring. ᵇ So guard yourself in your spirit, and do not break faith with the wife of your youth.

¹⁶"I hate divorce, ᵘ" says the LORD God of Israel, "and I hate a man's covering himself ᶜ with violence as well as with his garment," says the LORD Almighty.

So guard yourself in your spirit, and do not break faith.

The Day of Judgment

¹⁷You have wearied ᵛ the LORD with your words.

"How have we wearied him?" you ask.

By saying, "All who do evil are good in the eyes of the LORD, and he is pleased with them" or "Where is the God of justice?"

3 "See, I will send my messenger, who will prepare the way before me. ʷ Then suddenly the Lord you are seeking will come to his temple; the messenger of the covenant, whom you desire, will come," says the LORD Almighty.

²But who can endure ˣ the day of his coming? Who can stand when he appears? For he will be like a refiner's fire ʸ or a launderer's soap. ³He will sit as a refiner and purifier of silver; he will purify ᶻ the Levites and refine them like gold and silver. Then the LORD will have men who will bring offerings in righteousness, ⁴and the offerings ᵃ of Judah and Jerusalem will be acceptable to the LORD, as in days gone by, as in former years.

⁵"So I will come near to you for judgment. I will be quick to testify against sorcerers, adulterers and perjurers, against those who defraud laborers of their wages, ᵇ who oppress the widows and the fatherless, and deprive aliens of justice, but do not fear me," says the LORD Almighty.

ᵃ 12 Or ¹²May the LORD cut off from the tents of Jacob anyone who gives testimony in behalf of the man who does this
ᵇ 15 Or ¹⁵But the one [who is our father] did not do this, not as long as life remained in him. And what was he seeking? An offspring from God   ᶜ 16 Or his wife

2:12 ʳMal 1:10

2:14 ˢPr 5:18

2:15 ᵗMt 19:4-6

2:16 ᵘDt 24:1; Mt 5:31-32

2:17 ᵛIsa 43:24

3:1 ʷMt 11:10*; Mk 1:2*; Lk 7:27*

3:2 ˣRev 6:17 ʸMt 3:10-12

3:3 ᶻIsa 1:25

3:4 ᵃMal 1:11

3:5 ᵇLev 19:13

2:11, 12 After the temple had been rebuilt and the walls completed, the people were excited to see past prophecies coming true. But as time passed, the prophecies about the destruction of God's enemies and a coming Messiah were not immediately fulfilled. The people became discouraged, and they grew complacent about obeying all of God's laws. This complacency gradually led to blatant sin, such as marriage to those who worshiped idols. Ezra and Nehemiah also had confronted this problem years earlier (Ezra 9; 10; Nehemiah 13:23–31).

2:14 The people were complaining about their adverse circumstances when they had only themselves to blame. People often try to avoid guilt feelings by shifting the blame. But this doesn't solve the problem. When you face problems, look first at yourself. If you changed your attitude or behavior, would the problem be solved?

2:14, 15 Divorce in these times was practiced exclusively by men. They broke faith with their wives and ignored the bonding between a husband and a wife that God instills (the two become one person), as well as his purpose for them (raising children who love the Lord, "godly offspring"). Not only were men breaking faith with their wives, they also were ignoring the bonding relationship and spiritual purpose of being united with God.

2:15, 16 "Guard yourself in your spirit, and do not break faith" means to have the same commitment to marriage that God has to his promises with his people. We need passion in the marriage relationship to keep the commitment and intimacy satisfying, but this passion should be focused exclusively on our spouse.

2:17—3:6 God was tired of the way the people had cynically twisted his truths. He would punish those who insisted that because God was silent, he approved of their actions or at least would never punish them. God would also punish those who professed a counterfeit faith while acting sinfully (see 3:5).

3:1 There are two messengers in this verse. The first is usually understood to be John the Baptist (Matthew 11:10; Luke 7:27). The second messenger is Jesus, the Messiah, for whom both Malachi and John the Baptist prepared the way.

3:2, 3 In the process of refining metals, the raw metal is heated with fire until it melts. The impurities separate from it and rise to the surface. They are skimmed off, leaving the pure metal. Without this heating and melting, there could be no purifying. As the impurities are skimmed off the top, the reflection of the worker appears in the smooth, pure surface. As we are purified by God, his reflection in our lives will become more and more clear to those around us. God says that leaders (here the Levites) should be especially open to his purification process in their lives. Launderer's soap was alkali used to whiten cloth. It is also used here as a symbol of the purifying process.

Robbing God

3:6
c Nu 23:19; Jas 1:17

3:7
d Ac 7:51
e Zec 1:3

3:8
f Ne 13:10-12

3:12
g Isa 61:9
h Isa 62:4

3:13
i Mal 2:17

3:14
j Isa 58:3

3:15
k Jer 7:10

⁶"I the LORD do not change.ᶜ So you, O descendants of Jacob, are not destroyed. ⁷Ever since the time of your forefathers you have turned awayᵈ from my decrees and have not kept them. Return to me, and I will return to you,"ᵉ says the LORD Almighty.

"But you ask, 'How are we to return?'

⁸"Will a man rob God? Yet you rob me.

"But you ask, 'How do we rob you?'

"In tithesᶠ and offerings. ⁹You are under a curse—the whole nation of you—because you are robbing me. ¹⁰Bring the whole tithe into the storehouse, that there may be food in my house. Test me in this," says the LORD Almighty, "and see if I will not throw open the floodgates of heaven and pour out so much blessing that you will not have room enough for it. ¹¹I will prevent pests from devouring your crops, and the vines in your fields will not cast their fruit," says the LORD Almighty. ¹²"Then all the nations will call you blessed,ᵍ for yours will be a delightful land,"ʰ says the LORD Almighty.

¹³"You have said harsh thingsⁱ against me," says the LORD.

"Yet you ask, 'What have we said against you?'

¹⁴"You have said, 'It is futile to serve God. What did we gain by carrying out his requirements and going about like mournersʲ before the LORD Almighty? ¹⁵But now we call the arrogant blessed. Certainly the evildoersᵏ prosper, and even those who challenge God escape.'"

GIVING A TENTH

Many ancient peoples observed the practice of tithing—that is, giving a tenth of their earnings (or produce, harvest, etc.) back to a leader or a god. Malachi reminded the people of God's command to tithe. The first instance is Abraham's tithe to Melchizedek.

The Israelites were required to tithe of their crops, fruit, and herds.	Leviticus 27:30–32
The tithe was received by the Levites to support them.	Numbers 18:21, 24
The Levites, in turn, gave "a tithe of the tithe" to support the priests.	Numbers 18:26–29; Nehemiah 10:39
The Israelites were to bring their tithes to Jerusalem, and offering them came in the form of a ritual meal in which Levites were invited to share. If Jerusalem was too far for a person to transport the tithe, he could take the tithe there in the form of money. Every third year the tithe could be offered in one's local area, but the person was still to go to Jerusalem to worship.	Deuteronomy 12:5–7, 11–19; 14:22–29; 26:12–15
God promises blessings for those who faithfully tithe, and he says that refusing to tithe is like robbing him.	Malachi 3:8–12
Tithing, without love for or obedience to God, amounts to nothing more than a meaningless ritual.	Matthew 23:23; Luke 11:42

3:7 God's patience seems endless! Throughout history, his people have disobeyed, even scorned, his laws, but he has always been willing to accept them back. Here, however, the people have the nerve to imply that they never disobeyed ("How are we to return?")! Many people have turned their backs on forgiveness and restoration because they have refused to admit their sin. Don't follow their example. God is ready to return to us if we are willing to return to him.

3:8–12 Malachi urged the people to stop holding back their tithes, to stop keeping from God what he deserved. The tithing system began during the time of Moses (Leviticus 27:30–34; Deuteronomy 14:22). The Levites received some of the tithe because they could not possess land of their own (Numbers 18:20, 21). During Malachi's day, the people were not giving tithes, so the Levites went to work to earn a living, thereby neglecting their God-given responsibilities to care for the temple and for the service of worship. Everything we have is from God; so when we refuse to return to him a part of what he has given, we rob him. Do you selfishly want to keep 100 percent of what God gives, or are you willing to return at least 10 percent for helping to advance God's kingdom?

3:8–12 The people of Malachi's day ignored God's command to give a tithe of their income to his temple. They may have feared

losing what they had worked so hard to get, but in this they misjudged God. "Give, and it will be given to you," he says (Luke 6:38). When we give, we must remember that the blessings God promises are not always material and may not be experienced completely here on earth, but we will certainly receive them in our future life with him.

3:10 The "storehouse" was a place in the temple for storing grain and other food given as tithes. The priests lived off these gifts.

3:13–15 These verses describe the people's arrogant attitude toward God. When we ask, "What good does it do to serve God?" we are really asking, "What good does it do for *me?*" Our focus is selfish. Our real question should be, "What good does it do for God?" We must serve God just because he is God and deserves to be served.

3:16 The "scroll of remembrance" may or may not be an actual book. The point is that God will remember those who remain faithful to him, and who love, fear, honor, and respect him.

3. The faithful few

16 Then those who feared the LORD talked with each other, and the LORD listened and heard. *l* A scroll *m* of remembrance was written in his presence concerning those who feared the LORD and honored his name.

17 "They will be mine," says the LORD Almighty, "in the day when I make up my treasured possession.**a** *n* I will spare *o* them, just as in compassion a man spares his son who serves him. 18 And you will again see the distinction between the righteous *p* and the wicked, between those who serve God and those who do not.

The Day of the LORD

4 "Surely the day is coming; *q* it will burn like a furnace. All the arrogant and every evildoer will be stubble, and that day that is coming will set them on fire," says the LORD Almighty. "Not a root or a branch will be left to them. 2 But for you who revere my name, the sun of righteousness *r* will rise with healing in its wings. And you will go out and leap like calves released from the stall. 3 Then you will trample down the wicked; they will be ashes under the soles of your feet on the day when I do these things," says the LORD Almighty.

4 "Remember the law of my servant Moses, the decrees and laws I gave him at Horeb for all Israel.

5 "See, I will send you the prophet Elijah *s* before that great and dreadful day of the LORD comes. 6 He will turn the hearts of the fathers to their children, and the hearts of the children to their fathers; or else I will come and strike the land with a curse."

a 17 Or Almighty, "my treasured possession, in the day when I act

3:16
l Ps 34:15
m Ps 56:8

3:17
n Dt 7:6
o Ps 103:13

3:18
p Ge 18:25

4:1
q Joel 2:31

4:2
r Lk 1:78; Eph 5:14

4:5
s Mt 11:14; Lk 1:17

3:17 God's treasured possession are those faithful to him. This fulfills the promise he made in the covenant to his people (Exodus 19:5). According to 1 Peter 2:9, believers are God's treasured possession. Have you committed your life to God for safekeeping?

4:2 In the day of the Lord, God's wrath toward the wicked will burn like a furnace (4:1). But he will be like the healing warmth of the sun to those who love and obey him. John the Baptist prophesied that with the coming of Jesus, the dawn was about to break with light for those in sin's darkness (Luke 1:76–79). In Isaiah 60:20 and Revelation 21:23, 24 we learn that no light will be needed in God's holy city, because God himself will be the light.

4:2ff These last verses of the Old Testament are filled with hope. Regardless of how life looks now, God controls the future, and everything will be made right. We who have loved and served God look forward to a joyful celebration. This hope for the future becomes ours when we trust God with our lives.

4:4 These laws, given to Moses at Horeb (Mount Sinai), were the foundation of the nation's civil, moral, and ceremonial life (Exodus 20; Deuteronomy 4:5, 6). We still must obey the moral laws because they apply to all generations.

4:5, 6 Elijah was one of the greatest prophets who ever lived (his story is recorded in 1 Kings 17—2 Kings 2). With Malachi's death, the voice of God's prophets would be silent for 400 years.

Then a prophet would come, like Elijah, to herald Christ's coming (Matthew 17:10–13; Luke 1:17). This prophet was John the Baptist. John prepared people's hearts for Jesus by urging people to repent of their sins. Christ's coming would bring unity and peace, but also judgment on those who refused to turn from their sins.

4:6 Malachi gives us practical guidelines about commitment to God. God deserves the best we have to offer (1:7–10). We must be willing to change our wrong ways of living (2:1, 2). We should make family a lifelong priority (2:13–16). We should welcome God's refining process in our lives (3:3). We should tithe our income (3:8–12). There is no room for pride (3:13–15).

Malachi closes his messages by pointing to that great final day of judgment. For those who are committed to God, judgment day will be a day of joy because it will usher in eternity in God's presence. Those who have ignored God will be "stubble," to be burned up (4:1). To help the people prepare for that day of judgment, God would send a prophet like Elijah (John the Baptist), who would prepare the way for Jesus, the Messiah. The New Testament begins with this prophet calling the people to turn from their sins and to turn toward God. Such a commitment to God demands great sacrifice on our part, but we can be sure it will be worth it all in the end.

THE TIME BETWEEN THE OLD & NEW TESTAMENTS

THE INTERLUDE in our English Bible is scarcely noticeable. A simple turn of the page and you leave behind the Old Testament to enter the New Testament. If you are reading the Bible chronologically, like a story, you find that the first chapter of Matthew re-acquaints you with characters you've already come to know and admire: Abraham, Isaac, Jacob, David, and more. Yet a new character—indeed, a person who will claim to be the main character of the entire Bible—is now introduced: Jesus Christ.

You'll also soon notice that the world in which Jesus travels bears little resemblance to the one left behind in Malachi. The Eastern empires of the Israelites' captivity—Babylon, Assyria, and Persia—no longer dominate the region. Instead, a new power has risen in the West: the empire of Rome. Its boundaries extend from the Mediterranean to North Africa and even Europe. Its ruler in Palestine, a cruel and self-serving king named Herod, sits enthroned over the Jews.

You will recall that the northern kingdom of Israel had been taken into captivity by Assyria, and then the southern kingdom of Judah later went into captivity in Babylon. All of this occurred because the people had sinned and refused to remain faithful to God. The prophets had warned the people over and over, but they refused to believe. In Malachi, the Israelites had recently returned to Judah and their capital city from Babylonian captivity and rebuilt the temple, their center of worship. Under the guidance of priests and prophets, the community's leaders since ancient times, they had sought to repopulate the land, drive out their enemies, and learn again how to worship God in the way he desired. In Matthew, however, the Jews are settled and secure under the *Pax Romana,* the peace of Rome. They no longer worship in the temple alone but also in dozens of synagogues scattered throughout the country's towns and villages. Priests continue to provide leadership, but the people now look to a new array of religious authorities as well, including Pharisees, Sadducees, and teachers of the law (also known as scribes). Over all of these authorities sits a governing body called the Sanhedrin, which functions something like a religious Supreme Court.

Most noticeable, perhaps, is the lack of prophets. Whereas Malachi had followed a succession of prophets going back hundreds of years, not a single divine spokesperson appeared before the nation during the years between the Old and New Testaments. Anyone who claimed to be a prophet was proven to be an imposter. For more than 400 years, the heavens seemed closed to the nation of Israel. They heard nothing from God.

Nothing but silence.

Then, one ordinary night in the tiny village of Bethlehem, Jesus was born. With his first cries, God's voice once again graced the land. For Jews with ears to hear and eyes to see, it became clear throughout Jesus' life that he was the Son of God, the Savior for whom they had been waiting. God had used the years of silence to prepare the perfect time and place for Jesus' arrival. During the years between the Testaments—years of war and upheaval, flawed heroes and unfulfilled hopes—God had set the stage for the final era of salvation history, an era of Good News for Jews and Gentiles alike.

In the very first year of his reign, Cyrus the king of Persia had freed the Israelites from their captivity and encouraged them to return to their homeland (Ezra 1). His successor, King Darius, continued Persia's pro-Israel policy, even threatening with capital punishment those who hindered the Israelites from rebuilding their temple and resettling their land (Ezra 6). The Jews dwelt in relative peace.

THE PERSIAN PERIOD (539–336 B.C.)

However, several key developments began to reshape their practice of religion. Likely as a result of their many years in exile, the Jews began to worship in local synagogues spread throughout the Persian empire. They continued this new practice in their own land, even after the temple was rebuilt. Although priests served in the temple and performed the required sacrifices, worship in the synagogues centered on the study of the Law, and teachers of the law became the influential preservers and interpreters of the law. People with questions about God became more likely to turn to a teacher of the law than a priest.

During this time, the Israelites also came into religious conflict with the Samaritans. Descendants of Israelites who had been left behind during the Babylonian exile, the Samaritans had intermarried with Babylonians, Syrians, and others. As a result, their worship grew syncretistic, incorporating elements of pagan religions with worship of Yahweh, the God of Israel. While the Jews rebuilt the temple in Jerusalem, the Samaritans built a rival temple in the north. The ensuing religious and ethnic strife between Jews and Samaritans proved to be long lasting, which made it all the more amazing when Jesus later took the time to speak to an adulterous Samaritan woman (John 4).

With the fall of Persia to Alexander the Great, the age of the great Eastern empires ended. Western might came to dominate the Mediterranean and Middle East. Indeed, the Greek empire became the largest the world had ever seen, extending even into western India. Although Alexander the Great died young amidst suspicious circumstances, his empire continued under the rule of his generals, who split it into four sections. Ptolemy Soter claimed both Egypt and Israel.

THE HELLENISTIC PERIOD (336–165 B.C.)

Politically, little changed for the Jews under Greek and Ptolemaic rule. They continued to live and worship under the authority of a distant and foreign ruler, much as they had for generations. Culturally, however, they became more and more influenced by Greek (Hellenistic) civilization. Alexander's strategy for preserving his empire had been to unite the diverse, subjugated peoples around a common culture. The Ptolemaic dynasty carried out this policy with vigor, promoting Greek language and thought by all possible means. Thousands of Jews were forcibly resettled in Alexandria. Although Jews both at home and abroad resisted adapting to Greek religion, they couldn't escape all aspects of Hellenistic influence. They soon began to speak Greek, the trade language of the empire. Their worship came to reflect a Greek preference for aesthetics over content. More significantly, a group of Jewish scholars during this time translated the Old Testament from its original Hebrew into Greek. Called the Septuagint, this Greek translation came to be widely used by Jews everywhere. Jesus himself later quoted from the Septuagint, as did many New Testament authors.

In 198 B.C., the Syrian section of the empire overthrew the Egyptian section. For the first time, Israel came under the rule of a leader who tried to stamp out Judaism completely. Antiochus Epiphanes desecrated the temple, forbade sacrifices to Yahweh, outlawed circumcision, forced Jews to eat pork, and canceled Sabbaths and feast days. Some Jews attempted to conciliate Antiochus and cooperate with his demands; others resisted. These two groups were known as the Hellenists and the Hasidim (pious ones), forerunners of the Pharisees. Also, a group loyal to the high priest emerged, the precursors of the Sadducees.

The conflict in Israel finally reached a boiling point when an elderly priest named Mattathias refused to offer a required pagan sacrifice. Mattathias killed a Syrian officer and a reprobate Jew, fled to the hills, and called faithful Jews everywhere to join him in rebellion. During the ensuing guerrilla war, Mattathias's son, Judas Maccabeus, eventually overcame the Syrians and achieved independence for Israel—its last period of self-rule until the emergence of the modern state of Israel in 1948.

THE MACCABEAN PERIOD (165–63 B.C.)

However, independence proved to be both short-lived and disastrous. As the political dynasty of the Maccabees, also called the Hasmoneans, assumed both the throne and the office of high priest, the nation became beset by infighting. The Sadducees supported Hasmonean rulers as both kings and priests, whereas the Pharisees insisted that a true king could only be a descendant of David and a priest could only be a descendant of Aaron. The founder of the Essenes (the community which preserved for posterity the Dead Sea Scrolls) may have also founded his Qumran community around this time, in reaction against the Hasmoneans. As successive rulers became more and more unpopular (for example, Alexander Janneas was pelted by Jews at a festival when he attempted to perform his priestly duties—he responded by massacring 6,000 of them) the country became increasingly unstable.

Israelite factions turned to mercenaries and outside nations for support. By the time the growing Roman empire turned its attention toward Israel, the nation was able to offer little resistance. In 63 B.C., Pompey sacked Jerusalem. Soon the Jews were once again under the command of a foreign ruler, in this case an Idumean named Antipater who had been installed by Rome. Antipater's son, Herod the Great, followed him as king of the Jews, and it was under his rule that Jesus was born—and that all the babies in Bethlehem were killed.

THE ROMAN PERIOD (63 B.C.– A.D. 135)

Finally, God's silence ended. As Matthew opens his Gospel, the Jews are now unwilling subjects of the Roman empire. They are allowed freedom of worship and limited authority in overseeing their own affairs. But they long for more. They read the prophecies of the Old Testament and watch expectantly for the promised Messiah. They dream about the day that Israel will once again be the powerful nation it was under King David. They worship under the guidance of the high priest, dispute religious matters in the Sanhedrin, struggle to survive under Rome, and all the while await the coming Savior. Yet they expect a warrior, and not the baby lying in a manger that God's angels announce.

And Jesus will never live up to their expectations. Both of the main religious factions will disapprove of him. The Pharisees are the legalists of the day. They devote themselves to the law of Moses and apply it strictly to everyday life. They believe in the supernatural, angels, and the resurrection. They take their religious traditions seriously, so they cannot accept Jesus' disregard for their rules and his claim to forgive sins. The Sadducees are the rationalists of the day. They are skeptical toward religion. Although they believe in a literal interpretation of Moses' law, they do not allow it to have much impact on their everyday lives. They deny the supernatural and the resurrection; they focus on temporal, political concerns. They see Jesus primarily as a threat, a rabble-rouser who might catch the attention of Rome and thus imperil the nation.

In the end, these factions come to agree on one point, at least—that Jesus must be killed. They work together in the high council to sentence him. They stir up crowds and pressure the Roman authorities to have Jesus crucified. They succeed. Yet in the end, it was God's plan that ultimately succeeded. His suffering Servant lived and died as the payment for sin, and he rose again as the hope of the world.

Looking back on the years between the Old and New Testaments, it is clear that God brought about the perfect political and religious setting for the work of his Son. Instigated by the Jewish religious factions the Romans put Jesus to death. The power and highway system of Rome allowed the message of his resurrection to spread. And through the writing of the New Testament, the Greek language proclaimed the gospel in a tongue nearly everyone could understand. As Paul wrote in Galatians 4:4: "When the time had fully come, God sent his Son."

Turn the page. The New Testament tells the story.

new TESTAMENT

MATTHEW

VITAL STATISTICS

PURPOSE:
To prove that Jesus is the Messiah, the eternal King

AUTHOR:
Matthew (Levi)

ORIGINAL AUDIENCE:
Matthew wrote especially to the Jews.

DATE WRITTEN:
Approximately A.D. 60–65

SETTING:
Matthew was a Jewish tax collector who became one of Jesus' disciples. This Gospel forms the connecting link between the Old and New Testaments because of its emphasis on the fulfillment of prophecy.

KEY VERSE:
"Do not think that I have come to abolish the Law or the Prophets; I have not come to abolish them but to fulfill them" (5:17).

KEY PEOPLE:
Jesus, Mary, Joseph, John the Baptist, the disciples, the religious leaders, Caiaphas, Pilate, Mary Magdalene

KEY PLACES:
Bethlehem, Jerusalem, Capernaum, Galilee, Judea

SPECIAL FEATURES:
Matthew is filled with messianic language ("Son of David" is used throughout) and Old Testament references (53 quotes and 76 other references). This Gospel was not written as a chronological account; its purpose was to present the clear evidence that Jesus is the Messiah, the Savior.

AS the motorcade slowly winds through the city, thousands pack the sidewalks hoping to catch a glimpse. Marching bands with great fanfare announce the arrival, and protective agents scan the crowd and run alongside the limousine. Pomp, ceremony, protocol—modern symbols of position and evidences of importance—herald the arrival of a head of state. Whether they are leaders by birth or election, we honor and respect them.

The Jews waited for a leader who had been promised centuries before by prophets. They believed that this leader—the Messiah ("anointed one")—would rescue them from their Roman oppressors and establish a new kingdom. As their king, he would rule the world with justice. Many Jews, however, overlooked prophecies that also spoke of this king as a suffering servant who would be rejected and killed. It is no wonder, then, that few recognized Jesus as the Messiah. How could this humble carpenter's son from Nazareth be their king? But Jesus was and is the King of all the earth!

Matthew (Levi) was one of Jesus' 12 disciples. Once he was a despised tax collector, but his life was changed by this man from Galilee. Matthew wrote this Gospel to his fellow Jews to prove that Jesus is the Messiah and to explain God's kingdom.

Matthew begins his account by giving Jesus' genealogy. He then tells of Jesus' birth and early years, including the family's escape to Egypt from the murderous Herod and their return to Nazareth. Following Jesus' baptism by John (3:16, 17) and his defeat of Satan in the desert, Jesus began his public ministry by calling his first disciples and giving the Sermon on the Mount (chapters 5—7). Matthew shows Christ's authority by reporting his miracles of healing the sick and the demon-possessed, and even raising the dead.

Despite opposition from the Pharisees and others in the religious establishment (chapters 12—15), Jesus continued to teach concerning the kingdom of heaven (chapters 16—20). During this time, Jesus spoke with his disciples about his imminent death and resurrection (16:21) and revealed his true identity to Peter, James, and John (17:1–5). Near the end of his ministry, Jesus entered Jerusalem in a triumphant procession (21:1–11). But soon opposition mounted, and Jesus knew that his death was near. So he taught his disciples about the future—what they could expect before his return (chapter 24) and how to live until then (chapter 25).

In Matthew's finale (chapters 26—28), he focuses on Jesus' final days on earth—the Last Supper, his prayer in Gethsemane, the betrayal by Judas, the flight of the disciples, Peter's denial, the trials before Caiaphas and Pilate, Jesus' final words on the cross, and his burial in a borrowed tomb. But the story does not end there, for the Messiah rose from the dead—conquering death and then telling his followers to continue his work by making disciples in all nations.

As you read this Gospel, listen to Matthew's clear message: Jesus is the Christ, the King of kings and Lord of lords. Celebrate his victory over evil and death, and make Jesus the Lord of your life.

THE BLUEPRINT

A. BIRTH AND PREPARATION OF JESUS, THE KING (1:1—4:11)

The people of Israel were waiting for the Messiah, their king. Matthew begins his book by showing how Jesus Christ was a descendant of David. But Matthew goes on to show that God did not send Jesus to be an earthly king but a heavenly king. His kingdom would be much greater than David's because it would never end. Even at Jesus' birth, many recognized him as a king. Herod, the ruler, as well as Satan, was afraid of Jesus' kingship and tried to stop him, but others worshiped him and brought royal gifts. We must be willing to recognize Jesus for who he really is and worship him as king of our lives.

B. MESSAGE AND MINISTRY OF JESUS, THE KING (4:12—25:46)
1. Jesus begins his ministry
2. Jesus gives the Sermon on the Mount
3. Jesus performs many miracles
4. Jesus teaches about the kingdom
5. Jesus encounters differing reactions to his ministry
6. Jesus faces conflict with the religious leaders
7. Jesus teaches on the Mount of Olives

Jesus gave the Sermon on the Mount, directions for living in his kingdom. He also told many parables about the difference between his kingdom and the kingdoms of earth. Forgiveness, peace, and putting others first are some of the characteristics that make one great in the kingdom of God. And to be great in God's kingdom, we must live by God's standards right now. Jesus came to show us how to live as faithful subjects in his kingdom.

C. DEATH AND RESURRECTION OF JESUS, THE KING (26:1—28:20)

Jesus was formally presented to the nation of Israel but was rejected. How strange for the king to be accused, arrested, and crucified. But Jesus demonstrated his power, even over death, through his resurrection and gained access for us into his kingdom. With all this evidence that Jesus is God's Son, we, too, should accept him as our Lord.

MEGATHEMES

THEME	EXPLANATION	IMPORTANCE
Jesus Christ, the King	Jesus is revealed as the King of kings. His miraculous birth, his life and teaching, his miracles, and his triumph over death show his true identity.	Jesus cannot be equated with any person or power. He is the supreme ruler of time and eternity, heaven and earth, humans and angels. We should give him his rightful place as king of our lives.
The Messiah	Jesus was the Messiah, the one for whom the Jews had waited to deliver them from Roman oppression. Yet, tragically, they didn't recognize him when he came because his kingship was not what they expected. The true purpose of God's anointed deliverer was to die for all people to free them from sin's oppression.	Because Jesus was sent by God, we can trust him with our lives. It is worth everything we have to acknowledge him and give ourselves to him, because he came to be our Messiah, our Savior.
Kingdom of God	Jesus came to earth to begin his kingdom. His full kingdom will be realized at his return and will be made up of anyone who has faithfully followed him.	The way to enter God's kingdom is by faith—believing in Christ to save us from sin and change our lives. We must do the work of his kingdom now to be prepared for his return.

Teachings	Jesus taught the people through sermons, illustrations, and parables. Through his teachings, he showed the true ingredients of faith and how to guard against a fruitless and hypocritical life.	Jesus' teachings show us how to prepare for life in his eternal kingdom by living properly right now. He lived what he taught, and we, too, must practice what we preach.
Resurrection	When Jesus rose from the dead, he rose in power as the true king. In his victory over death, he established his credentials as king and his power and authority over evil.	The Resurrection shows Jesus' all-powerful life for us—not even death could stop his plan of offering eternal life. Those who believe in Jesus can hope for a resurrection like his. Our role is to tell his story to all the earth so that everyone may share in his victory.

KEY PLACES IN MATTHEW

Jesus' earthly story begins in the town of Bethlehem in the Roman province of Judea (2:1). A threat to kill the infant king led Joseph to take his family to Egypt (2:14). When they returned, God led them to settle in Nazareth in Galilee (2:22, 23). At about age 30, Jesus was baptized in the Jordan River and was tempted by Satan in the Judean desert (3:13; 4:1). Jesus set up his base of operations in Capernaum (4:12, 13) and from there ministered throughout Israel, telling parables, teaching about the kingdom, and healing the sick. He traveled to the region of the Gadarenes around Gadara and healed two demon-possessed men (8:28ff); fed over 5,000 people with five loaves and two fish on the shores of Galilee near Bethsaida (14:15ff); healed the sick in Gennesaret (14:34ff); ministered to the Gentiles in Tyre and Sidon (15:21ff); visited Caesarea Philippi, where Peter declared him to be the Messiah (16:13ff); and taught in Perea, east of the Jordan (19:1). As he set out on his last visit to Jerusalem, he told the disciples what would happen to him there (20:17ff). He spent some time in Jericho (20:29) and then stayed in Bethany at night as he went back and forth to Jerusalem during his last week (21:17ff). In Jerusalem he would be crucified, but he would rise again.

The broken lines (–·–·–) indicate modern boundaries.

A. BIRTH AND PREPARATION OF JESUS, THE KING (1:1—4:11)

Matthew opens his Gospel with a genealogy to prove that Jesus is a descendant of both King David and Abraham, just as the Old Testament had predicted. Jesus' birth didn't go unnoticed, for both shepherds and Magi came to worship him. The Jewish people were waiting for the Messiah to appear. However, after he was born, the Jews didn't recognize him because they were looking for a different kind of king.

The Record of Jesus' Ancestors (3/Luke 3:23—28)

1:1
a Isa 11:1; Ro 1:3
b Ge 22:18

1 A record of the genealogy of Jesus Christ the son of David,*a* the son of Abraham:*b*

1:2
c Ge 25:26
d Ge 29:35

2 Abraham was the father of Isaac,
Isaac the father of Jacob,*c*
Jacob the father of Judah and his brothers,*d*

1:3
e Ge 38:27-30

3 Judah the father of Perez and Zerah, whose mother was Tamar,*e*
Perez the father of Hezron,
Hezron the father of Ram,
4 Ram the father of Amminadab,
Amminadab the father of Nahshon,
Nahshon the father of Salmon,
5 Salmon the father of Boaz, whose mother was Rahab,
Boaz the father of Obed, whose mother was Ruth,
Obed the father of Jesse,

1:6
f 1Sa 16:1
g 2Sa 12:24

6 and Jesse the father of King David.*f*

David was the father of Solomon, whose mother had been Uriah's wife,*g*
7 Solomon the father of Rehoboam,
Rehoboam the father of Abijah,
Abijah the father of Asa,
8 Asa the father of Jehoshaphat,
Jehoshaphat the father of Jehoram,
Jehoram the father of Uzziah,
9 Uzziah the father of Jotham,
Jotham the father of Ahaz,
Ahaz the father of Hezekiah,

1:10
h 2Ki 20:21

10 Hezekiah the father of Manasseh,*h*
Manasseh the father of Amon,
Amon the father of Josiah,

1:1 Presenting this record of ancestors (called a genealogy) was one of the most interesting ways that Matthew could begin a book for a Jewish audience. Because a person's family line proved his or her standing as one of God's chosen people, Matthew began by showing that Jesus was a descendant of Abraham, the father of all Jews, and a direct descendant of David, fulfilling Old Testament prophecies about the Messiah's line. The facts of this ancestry were carefully preserved. This is the first of many proofs recorded by Matthew to show that Jesus is the true Messiah.

1:1ff More than 400 years had passed since the last Old Testament prophecies, and faithful Jews all over the world were still waiting for the Messiah (Luke 3:15). Matthew wrote this book to Jews to present Jesus as King and Messiah, the promised descendant of David who would reign forever (Isaiah 11:1–5). The Gospel of Matthew links the Old and New Testaments and contains many references that show how Jesus fulfilled Old Testament prophecy.

1:1ff Jesus entered human history when the land of Palestine was controlled by Rome and considered an insignificant outpost of the vast and mighty Roman empire. The presence of Roman soldiers in Israel gave the Jews military peace, but at the price of oppression, slavery, injustice, and immorality. Into this kind of world came the promised Messiah.

1:1–17 In the first 17 verses we meet 46 people whose lifetimes span 2,000 years. All were ancestors of Jesus, but they varied considerably in personality, spirituality, and experience.

Some were heroes of faith—like Abraham, Isaac, Ruth, and David. Some had shady reputations—like Rahab and Tamar. Many were very ordinary—like Hezron, Ram, Nahshon, and Akim. And others were evil—like Manasseh and Abijah. God's work in history is not limited by human failures or sins, and he works through ordinary people. Just as God used all kinds of people to bring his Son into the world, he uses all kinds today to accomplish his will. And God wants to use you.

1:3–6 Matthew's inclusion of four particular women (Tamar, Rahab, Ruth, and Bathsheba—here called "Uriah's wife") reveals his concern to do more than relay historical data. These women raise both ethnic and ethical questions. At least two of them were not Israelites by birth and all four of them had reputations that could have made them unmentionable in an ancestral tree. Yet this was the line into which God's Son was born. Jesus' genealogy makes it clear, not that there were a few disreputable people in his family, but that all of them were sinners. God sent his Son as Savior of *all* people—Jews, Gentiles, men, and women. No matter what the sins of the people, God's plan was never thwarted. It continues to unfold. That plan includes you.

11 and Josiah the father of Jeconiah [a] and his brothers at the time of the exile to
   Babylon. [i]

12 After the exile to Babylon:
   Jeconiah was the father of Shealtiel, [j]
   Shealtiel the father of Zerubbabel,
13 Zerubbabel the father of Abiud,
   Abiud the father of Eliakim,
   Eliakim the father of Azor,
14 Azor the father of Zadok,
   Zadok the father of Akim,
   Akim the father of Eliud,
15 Eliud the father of Eleazar,
   Eleazar the father of Matthan,
   Matthan the father of Jacob,
16 and Jacob the father of Joseph, the husband of Mary, of whom was born Jesus,
   who is called Christ.

17 Thus there were fourteen generations in all from Abraham to David, fourteen from
David to the exile to Babylon, and fourteen from the exile to the Christ. [b]

An Angel Appears to Joseph (8)

18 This is how the birth of Jesus Christ came about: His mother Mary was pledged to be
married to Joseph, but before they came together, she was found to be with child through
the Holy Spirit. [k] 19 Because Joseph her husband was a righteous man and did not want to expose her to public disgrace, he had in mind to divorce [l] her quietly.
   20 But after he had considered this, an angel of the Lord appeared to him in a dream and
said, "Joseph son of David, do not be afraid to take Mary home as your wife, because what is
conceived in her is from the Holy Spirit. 21 She will give birth to a son, and you are to give him
the name Jesus, [c] [m] because he will save his people from their sins." [n]

1:11 /2Ki 24:14-16;
Jer 27:20;
Da 1:1, 2
1:12 /1Ch 3:17

1:18 [k] Lk 1:35

1:19 [l] Dt 24:1

1:21 [m] Lk 1:31
[n] Lk 2:11;
Ac 13:23, 28

a 11 That is, Jehoiachin; also in verse 12   b 17 Or *Messiah*. "The Christ" (Greek) and "the Messiah" (Hebrew) both
mean "the Anointed One."   c 21 *Jesus* is the Greek form of *Joshua*, which means *the LORD saves.*

1:11 The exile to Babylon occurred in 586 B.C. when Nebuchadnezzar, king of Babylonia, conquered Judah, destroyed Jerusalem, and took thousands of people captive.

1:16 Because Mary was a virgin when she became pregnant,
Matthew lists Joseph only as the husband of Mary, not the
father of Jesus. Matthew's genealogy gives Jesus' legal (or
royal) lineage through Joseph. Mary's ancestral line is recorded
in Luke 3:23–38. Both Mary and Joseph were direct descendants of David.

Matthew traced the genealogy back to Abraham, while Luke
traced it back to Adam. Matthew wrote to the Jews, so Jesus was
shown as a descendant of their father, Abraham. Luke wrote to
the Gentiles, so he emphasized Jesus as the Savior of all people.

1:17 Matthew breaks Israel's history into three sets of 14 generations, but there were probably more generations than those
listed here. Genealogies often compressed history, meaning that
not every generation of ancestors was specifically listed. Thus the
phrase "the father of" can also be translated "the ancestor of."

1:18 A Jewish marriage involved three basic steps. First, the two
families agreed to the union. Second, a public announcement was
made. At this point, the couple was "pledged." This was similar to
engagement today except that their relationship could be broken
only through death or divorce (even though sexual relations were
not yet permitted). Third, the couple was married and began living
together. Because Mary and Joseph were engaged, Mary's apparent unfaithfulness carried a severe social stigma. According to
Jewish civil law, Joseph had a right to divorce her, and the Jewish
authorities could have had her stoned to death (Deuteronomy
22:23, 24).

1:18 Why is the virgin birth important to the Christian faith?
Jesus Christ, God's Son, had to be free from the sinful nature
passed on to all other human beings by Adam. Because Jesus

was born of a woman, he was a human being; but as the Son of
God, Jesus was born without any trace of human sin. Jesus is
both fully human and fully divine.

Because Jesus lived as a man, we know that he fully understands our experiences and struggles (Hebrews 4:15, 16).
Because he is God, he has the power and authority to deliver us
from sin (Colossians 2:13–15). We can tell Jesus all our
thoughts, feelings, and needs. He has been where we are now,
and he has the ability to help.

1:19 Joseph was faced with a difficult choice after discovering
that Mary was pregnant. Perhaps Joseph thought he had only two
options: divorce Mary quietly, or have her stoned. But God had a
third option—marry her (1:20–23). In view of the circumstances,
this had not occurred to Joseph. But God often shows us that
there are more options available than we think. Although Joseph
seemed to be doing the right thing by breaking the engagement,
only God's guidance helped him make the best decision. But that
did not make it an easy decision. Consenting to marry Mary
surely cast doubt on his own innocence regarding the pregnancy,
as well as leaving them both with a social stigma they would carry
for the rest of their lives. Yet Joseph chose to obey the angel's
command (1:24). When our decisions affect the lives of others,
we must always seek God's wisdom and then be willing to follow
through no matter how difficult it may be.

1:20 The conception and birth of Jesus Christ are supernatural
events beyond human logic or reasoning. Because of this, God
sent angels to help certain people understand the significance of
what was happening (see 2:13, 19; Luke 1:11, 26; 2:9).

Angels are spiritual beings created by God who help carry
out his work on earth. They bring God's messages to people
(Luke 1:26), protect God's people (Daniel 6:22), offer encouragement (Genesis 16:7ff), give guidance (Exodus 14:19), carry

1:23
°Isa 7:14

²²All this took place to fulfill what the Lord had said through the prophet: ²³"The virgin will be with child and will give birth to a son, and they will call him Immanuel"ᵃ °—which means, "God with us."

ᵃ23 Isaiah 7:14

JOSEPH

The strength of what we believe is measured by how much we are willing to suffer for those beliefs. Joseph was a man with strong beliefs. He was prepared to do what was right, despite the pain he knew it would cause. But Joseph had another trait: He not only tried to do what was right, he also tried to do it in the right way.

When Mary told Joseph about her pregnancy, Joseph knew the child was not his. His respect for Mary's character and the explanation she gave him, as well as her attitude toward the expected child, must have made it hard to think his bride had done something wrong. Still, someone else was the child's father—and it was mind-boggling to accept that the "someone else" was God.

Joseph decided he had to break the engagement, but he was determined to do it in a way that would not cause public shame to Mary. He intended to act with justice and love.

At this point, God sent a messenger to Joseph to confirm Mary's story and open another way of obedience for Joseph—to take Mary as his wife. Joseph obeyed God, married Mary, and honored her virginity until the baby was born.

We do not know how long Joseph lived his role as Jesus' earthly father—he is last mentioned when Jesus was 12 years old. But Joseph trained his son in the trade of carpentry, made sure he had good spiritual training in Nazareth, and took the whole family on the yearly trip to Jerusalem for the Passover, which Jesus continued to observe during his adult years.

Joseph knew Jesus was someone special from the moment he heard the angel's words. His strong belief in that fact, and his willingness to follow God's leading, empowered him to be Jesus' chosen earthly father.

Strengths and accomplishments:	• A man of integrity • A descendant of King David • Jesus' legal and earthly father • A person sensitive to God's guidance and willing to do God's will no matter what the consequence
Lessons from his life:	• God honors integrity • Social position is of little importance when God chooses to use us • Being obedient to the guidance we have from God leads to more guidance from him • Feelings are not accurate measures of the rightness or wrongness of an action
Vital statistics:	• Where: Nazareth, Bethlehem • Occupation: Carpenter • Relatives: Wife: Mary. Children: Jesus, James, Joses, Judas, Simon, and daughters. • Contemporaries: Herod the Great, John the Baptist, Simeon, Anna
Key verses:	"Because Joseph her husband was a righteous man and did not want to expose her to public disgrace, he had in mind to divorce her quietly. But after he had considered this, an angel of the Lord appeared to him in a dream and said, 'Joseph son of David, do not be afraid to take Mary home as your wife, because what is conceived in her is from the Holy Spirit'" (Matthew 1:19, 20).

Joseph's story is told in Matthew 1:16—2:23; Luke 1:26—2:52.

out punishment (2 Samuel 24:16), patrol the earth (Zechariah 1:9–14), and fight the forces of evil (2 Kings 6:16–18; Revelation 20:1, 2). There are both good and bad angels (Revelation 12:7), but because bad angels are allied with the devil, or Satan, they have considerably less power and authority than good angels. Eventually the main role of angels will be to offer continuous praise to God (Revelation 7:11, 12).

1:20–23 The angel declared to Joseph that Mary's child was conceived by the Holy Spirit and would be a son. This reveals an important truth about Jesus—he is both God and human. The infinite, unlimited God took on the limitations of humanity so he could live and die for the salvation of all who would believe in him.

Jesus means "the LORD saves." Jesus came to earth to save

us because we can't save ourselves from sin and its consequences. No matter how good we are, we can't eliminate the sinful nature present in all of us. Only Jesus can do that. Jesus didn't come to help people save themselves; he came to be their Savior from the power and penalty of sin. Thank Christ for his death on the cross for your sin, and then ask him to take control of your life. Your new life begins at that moment.

Jesus would fulfill the prophecy of Isaiah, for he would be *Immanuel* ("God with us," see Isaiah 7:14). Jesus was God in the flesh; thus God was literally among us, "with us." Through the Holy Spirit, Christ is present today in the life of every believer. Perhaps not even Isaiah understood how far-reaching the meaning of "Immanuel" would be.

²⁴When Joseph woke up, he did what the angel of the Lord had commanded him and took Mary home as his wife. ²⁵But he had no union with her until she gave birth to a son. And he gave him the name Jesus.

Visitors Arrive from Eastern Lands (12)

2 After Jesus was born in Bethlehem in Judea,ᵖ during the time of King Herod, Magi ᵃ from the east came to Jerusalem ²and asked, "Where is the one who has been born king of the Jews?ᑫ We saw his starʳ in the eastᵇ and have come to worship him."

³When King Herod heard this he was disturbed, and all Jerusalem with him. ⁴When he had called together all the people's chief priests and teachers of the law, he asked them where the Christᶜ was to be born. ⁵"In Bethlehemˢ in Judea," they replied, "for this is what the prophet has written:

2:1
ᵖLk 2:4-7

2:2
ᑫJer 23:5; Jn 1:49
ʳNu 24:17

2:5
ˢJn 7:42

ᵃ*1* Traditionally *Wise Men*   ᵇ*2* Or *star when it rose*   ᶜ*4* Or *Messiah*

1:24 Joseph changed his plans quickly after learning that Mary had not been unfaithful to him (1:19). He obeyed God and proceeded with the marriage plans. Although others may have disapproved of his decision, Joseph went ahead with what he knew was right. Sometimes we avoid doing what is right because of what others might think. Like Joseph, we must choose to obey God rather than seek the approval of others.

2:1 Bethlehem is a small town five miles south of Jerusalem. It sits on a high ridge over 2,000 feet above sea level. It is mentioned in more detail in the Gospel of Luke. Luke also explains why Joseph and Mary were in Bethlehem when Jesus was born, rather than in Nazareth, their hometown.

2:1 The land of Israel was divided into four political districts and several lesser territories. Judea was to the south, Samaria in the middle, Galilee to the north, and Idumea to the southeast. Bethlehem of Judea (also called Judah, 2:6) had been prophesied as the Messiah's birthplace (Micah 5:2). Jerusalem was also in Judea and was the seat of government for Herod the Great, king over all four political districts. After Herod's death, the districts were divided among three separate rulers (see the note on 2:19–22). Although he was a ruthless, evil man who murdered many in his own family, Herod the Great supervised the renovation of the temple, making it much larger and more beautiful. This made him popular with many Jews. Jesus would visit Jerusalem many times because the great Jewish festivals were held there.

2:1, 2 Not much is known about these Magi (traditionally called wise men). We don't know where they came from or how many there were. Tradition says they were men of high position from Parthia, near the site of ancient Babylon. How did they know that the star represented the Messiah? (1) They could have been Jews

THE FLIGHT TO EGYPT
Herod planned to kill the baby Jesus, whom he perceived to be a future threat to his position. Warned of this treachery in a dream, Joseph took his family to Egypt until Herod's death, which occurred a year or two later. They then planned to return to Judea, but God led them instead to Nazareth in Galilee.

who remained in Babylon after the exile and knew the Old Testament predictions of the Messiah's coming. (2) They may have been eastern astrologers who studied ancient manuscripts from around the world. Because of the Jewish exile centuries earlier, they would have had copies of the Old Testament in their land. (3) They may have had a special message from God directing them to the Messiah. Some scholars say these Magi were each from a different land, representing the entire world bowing before Jesus. These men from faraway lands recognized Jesus as the Messiah when most of God's chosen people in Israel did not. Matthew pictures Jesus as King over the whole world, not just Judea.

2:1, 2 The Magi traveled thousands of miles to see the king of the Jews. When they finally found him, they responded with joy, worship, and gifts. This is so different from the approach people often take today. We expect God to come looking for us, to explain himself, prove who he is, and give *us* gifts. But those who are wise still seek and worship Jesus today, not for what they can get, but for who he is.

2:2 The Magi said they saw Jesus' star. Balaam referred to a coming "star . . . out of Jacob" (Numbers 24:17). Some say this star may have been a conjunction of Jupiter, Saturn, and Mars in 6 B.C., and others offer other explanations. But couldn't God, who created the heavens, have created a special star to signal the arrival of his Son? Whatever the nature of the star, these Magi traveled thousands of miles searching for a king, and they found him.

2:3 Herod the Great was quite disturbed when the Magi asked about a newborn king of the Jews because: (1) Herod was not the rightful heir to the throne of David; therefore many Jews hated him as a usurper. If Jesus really was an heir, trouble would arise. (2) Herod was ruthless and, because of his many enemies, he was suspicious that someone would try to overthrow him. (3) Herod didn't want the Jews, a religious people, to unite around a religious figure. (4) If these Magi were of Jewish descent and from Parthia (the most powerful region next to Rome), they would have welcomed a Jewish king who could swing the balance of power away from Rome. The land of Israel, far from Rome, would have been easy prey for a nation trying to gain more control.

The text tells us that not only was Herod disturbed, but so was everyone in Jerusalem. When Jesus was born into the world, people immediately began to react. His presence did not soothe and comfort most people; instead, it startled and disturbed them. In some he awakened spiritual longings; in others, fear and insecurity. Things have not changed that much. Jesus still disturbs people. If it is true that God entered our world when Jesus was born, we dare not sit idly by ignoring and rationalizing our inaction. We must acknowledge Jesus as the rightful King of our lives.

2:4–6 The chief priests and teachers of the law were aware of Micah 5:2 and other prophecies about the Messiah. Matthew repeatedly highlighted their knowledge and unbelief. The Magi's news troubled Herod because he knew that the Jewish people expected the Messiah to come soon (Luke 3:15). Most Jews

6 "'But you, Bethlehem, in the land of Judah,
are by no means least among the rulers of Judah;
for out of you will come a ruler
who will be the shepherd of my people Israel.'a"

7 Then Herod called the Magi secretly and found out from them the exact time the star had appeared. 8 He sent them to Bethlehem and said, "Go and make a careful search for the child. As soon as you find him, report to me, so that I too may go and worship him."

9 After they had heard the king, they went on their way, and the star they had seen in the east b went ahead of them until it stopped over the place where the child was. 10 When they saw the star, they were overjoyed. 11 On coming to the house, they saw the child with his mother Mary, and they bowed down and worshiped him. t Then they opened their treasures and presented him with gifts u of gold and of incense and of myrrh. 12 And having been warned v in a dream not to go back to Herod, they returned to their country by another route.

2:11
t Isa 60:3
u Ps 72:10
2:12
v Heb 11:7

The Escape to Egypt (13)

13 When they had gone, an angel of the Lord appeared to Joseph in a dream. "Get up," he said, "take the child and his mother and escape to Egypt. Stay there until I tell you, for Herod is going to search for the child to kill him."

a6 Micah 5:2   b9 Or seen when it rose

GOSPEL ACCOUNTS FOUND ONLY IN MATTHEW	Passage	Subject
	1:20–24	Joseph's dream*
	2:1–12	The visit of the Magi
	2:13–15	Escape to Egypt*
	2:16–18	Slaughter of the male children*
	27:3–10	The death of Judas*
	27:19	The dream of Pilate's wife
	27:52	The other resurrections
	28:11–15	The bribery of the guards
	28:19, 20	The baptism emphasis in the Great Commission*

Matthew records nine special events that are not mentioned in any of the other Gospels. In each case, the most apparent reason for Matthew's choice has to do with his purpose in communicating the gospel to Jewish people. Five cases are fulfillments of Old Testament prophecies (marked with asterisks above). The other four would have been of particular interest to the Jews of Matthew's day.

expected the Messiah to be a great military and political deliverer, like Alexander the Great. Herod's counselors would have told Herod this. No wonder this ruthless man took no chances and ordered all the baby boys in Bethlehem killed (2:16)!

2:6 Most religious leaders believed in a literal fulfillment of all Old Testament prophecy; therefore, they believed the Messiah would be born in Bethlehem as foreseen by the prophet Micah seven centuries earlier (Micah 5:2). Ironically, when Jesus was born, these same religious leaders became his greatest enemies. When the Messiah for whom they had been waiting finally came, they didn't recognize him.

2:8 Herod did not want to worship Christ—he was lying. This was a trick to get the Magi to return to him and reveal the whereabouts of the newborn king. Herod's plan was to kill Jesus.

2:11 Jesus was probably one or two years old when the Magi found him. By this time, Mary and Joseph were married, living in a house, and intending to stay in Bethlehem for a while. For more on why Joseph and Mary stayed, see the note on Luke 2:39.

2:11 The Magi gave these expensive gifts as worthy acknowledgement for a future king. Bible students have seen in the gifts symbols of Christ's identity and what he would accomplish. Gold was a gift for royalty; incense, a gift for deity; myrrh, a spice for a person who was going to die. These gifts may have provided the financial resources for the trip to Egypt and back.

2:11 The Magi brought gifts and worshiped Jesus for who he was. This is the essence of true worship—honoring Christ for who he is and being willing to give him what is valuable to you. Worship God because he is the perfect, just, and almighty Creator of the universe, worthy of the best you have to give.

2:12 After finding Jesus and worshiping him, the Magi were warned by God not to return through Jerusalem as they had intended. Finding Jesus may mean that your life must take a different direction, one that is responsive and obedient to God's Word. In what ways has Jesus affected the direction of your life?

2:13 This was the second dream or vision that Joseph received from God. Joseph's first dream revealed Jesus as Mary's child would be the Messiah (1:20, 21). His second dream told him how to protect the child's life. Although Joseph was not Jesus' natural father, he was Jesus' legal father and was responsible for his safety and well-being. Divine guidance comes only to prepared hearts. Joseph remained receptive to God's guidance.

14So he got up, took the child and his mother during the night and left for Egypt, 15where he stayed until the death of Herod. And so was fulfilled what the Lord had said through the prophet: "Out of Egypt I called my son."a w

16When Herod realized that he had been outwitted by the Magi, he was furious, and he gave orders to kill all the boys in Bethlehem and its vicinity who were two years old and under, in accordance with the time he had learned from the Magi. 17Then what was said through the prophet Jeremiah was fulfilled:

> 18 "A voice is heard in Ramah,
>   weeping and great mourning,
>   Rachel weeping for her children
>   and refusing to be comforted,
>   because they are no more."b x

The Return to Nazareth (14)

19After Herod died, an angel of the Lord appeared in a dream to Joseph in Egypt 20and said, "Get up, take the child and his mother and go to the land of Israel, for those who were trying to take the child's life are dead."

21So he got up, took the child and his mother and went to the land of Israel. 22But when he heard that Archelaus was reigning in Judea in place of his father Herod, he was afraid to go there. Having been warned in a dream,y he withdrew to the district of Galilee,z 23and he went and lived in a town called Nazareth. a So was fulfilled what was said through the prophets: "He will be called a Nazarene."b

John the Baptist Prepares the Way for Jesus (16/Mark 1:1–8; Luke 3:1–17)

3 In those days John the Baptistc came, preaching in the Desert of Judea 2and saying, "Repent, for the kingdom of heavend is near." 3This is he who was spoken of through the prophet Isaiah:

a 15 Hosea 11:1   b 18 Jer. 31:15

2:15 w Ex 4:22, 23; Hos 11:1

2:18 x Jer 31:15

2:22 y ver 12, 13, 19 z Lk 2:39

2:23 a Lk 1:26 b Mk 1:24

3:1 c Lk 3:2-19

3:2 d Da 2:44; Mt 4:17

2:14, 15 Going to Egypt was not unusual because there were colonies of Jews in several major Egyptian cities. These colonies had developed during the time of the great captivity (see Jeremiah 43; 44). There is an interesting parallel between this flight to Egypt and Israel's history. As an infant nation, Israel went to Egypt, just as Jesus did as a child. God led Israel out (Hosea 11:1); God brought Jesus back. Both events show God working to save his people.

2:16 Herod, the king of the Jews, killed all the boys under two years of age in an obsessive attempt to kill Jesus, the newborn King. He stained his hands with blood, but he did not harm Jesus. Herod was king by a human appointment; Jesus was King by a divine appointment. No one can thwart God's plans.

2:16 Herod was afraid that this newborn king would one day take his throne. He completely misunderstood the reason for Christ's coming. Jesus didn't want Herod's throne; he wanted to be king of Herod's life. Jesus wanted to give Herod eternal life, not take away his present life. Today people are often afraid that Christ wants to take things away when, in reality, he wants to give them real freedom, peace, and joy. Don't fear Christ—give him the throne of your life.

2:17, 18 Rachel had been the favored wife of Jacob, one of the great men of God in the Old Testament. As such, she was considered the mother of a nation. From Jacob's 12 sons had come the 12 tribes of Israel. Rachel was buried near Bethlehem (Genesis 35:19). For more about the significance of this verse, see the note on Jeremiah 31:15, from which this verse was quoted.

2:19–22 Herod the Great died in 4 B.C. of an incurable disease. Rome trusted him but didn't trust his sons. Herod knew that Rome wouldn't give his successor as much power, so he divided his kingdom into three parts, one for each son. Archelaus received Judea, Samaria, and Idumea; Herod Antipas received Galilee and Perea; Herod Philip II received Traconitis. Archelaus, a violent man, began his reign by slaughtering 3,000 influential people. Nine years later, he was banished. God didn't want Joseph's family to go into the region of this evil ruler.

2:23 Nazareth sat in the hilly area of southern Galilee near the crossroads of great caravan trade routes. The town itself was rather small. The Roman garrison in charge of Galilee was housed there. The people of Nazareth had constant contact with people from all over the world, so world news reached them quickly. The people of Nazareth had an attitude of independence that many of the Jews despised. This may have been why Nathanael commented, "Nazareth! Can anything good come from there?" (see John 1:46).

2:23 The Old Testament does not record this specific statement, "He will be called a Nazarene." Many scholars believe, however, that Matthew is referring to Isaiah 11:1 where the Hebrew word for "branch" is similar to the word for Nazarene. Or he may be referring to a prophecy unrecorded in the Bible. In any case, Matthew paints the picture of Jesus as the true Messiah announced by God through the prophets; and he makes the point that Jesus, the Messiah, had unexpectedly humble beginnings, just as the Old Testament had predicted (see Micah 5:2).

3:1, 2 Almost 30 years had passed since the events of chapter 2. Here John the Baptist burst onto the scene. His theme was "Repent!" Repentance means doing an about-face—a 180-degree turn—from the kind of self-centeredness that leads to wrong actions such as lying, cheating, stealing, gossiping, taking revenge, abusing, and indulging in sexual immorality. A person who repents stops rebelling and begins following God's way of living prescribed in his Word. The first step in turning to God is to admit your sin, as John urged. Then God will receive you and help you live the way he wants. Remember that only God can get rid of sin. He doesn't expect us to clean up our lives *before* we come to him.

3:1, 2 John the Baptist's Profile is found in John 1, p. 1737.

3:2 The kingdom of heaven began when God himself entered human history as a man. Today Jesus Christ reigns in the hearts of believers, but the kingdom of heaven will not be fully realized until all evil in the world is judged and removed. Christ came to earth first as a suffering servant; he will come again as King and Judge to rule victoriously over all the earth.

3:3 The prophet quoted is Isaiah (40:3), one of the greatest prophets of the Old Testament and one of the most quoted in the New.

3:3
e Isa 40:3; Lk 1:76;
Jn 1:23

"A voice of one calling in the desert,
'Prepare the way for the Lord,
make straight paths for him.'"ᵃ ᵉ

3:4
f 2Ki 1:8
g Lev 11:22

⁴John's clothes were made of camel's hair, and he had a leather belt around his waist.ᶠ His food was locusts ᵍ and wild honey. ⁵People went out to him from Jerusalem and all Judea

ᵃ*3* Isaiah 40:3

The Bible records history. It has proven itself an accurate and reliable record of people, events, and places. Independent historical accounts verify the Bible's descriptions and details of many famous lives. One of these was the father of the Herodian family, Herod the Great.

Herod is remembered as a builder of cities and the lavish rebuilder of the temple in Jerusalem. But he also destroyed people. He showed little greatness in either his personal actions or his character. He was ruthless in ruling his territory. His suspicions and jealousy led to the murder of several of his children and the death of his wife Mariamne.

Herod's title, king of the Jews, was granted by Rome but never accepted by the Jewish people. He was not part of the Davidic family line, and he was only partly Jewish. Although Israel benefited from Herod's lavish efforts to repair the temple in Jerusalem, he won little admiration because he also rebuilt various pagan temples. Herod's costly attempt to gain the loyalty of the people failed because it was superficial. His only loyalty was to himself.

Because his royal title was not genuine, Herod was constantly worried about losing his position. His actions when hearing from the Magi about their search for the new king are consistent with all that we know about Herod. He planned to locate and kill the child before he could become a threat. The murder of innocent children that followed is a tragic lesson in what can happen when actions are motivated by selfishness. Herod's suspicions did not spare even his own family. His life was self-destructive.

Strengths and accomplishments:	• Was given the title king of the Jews by the Romans • Held on to his power for more than 30 years • Was an effective, though ruthless, ruler • Sponsored a great variety of large building projects
Weaknesses and mistakes:	• Tended to treat those around him with fear, suspicion, and jealousy • Had several of his own children and at least one wife killed • Ordered the killing of the infants in Bethlehem • Although claiming to be a God-worshiper, he was still involved in many forms of pagan religion
Lessons from his life:	• Great power brings neither peace nor security • No one can prevent God's plans from being carried out • Superficial loyalty does not impress people or God
Vital statistics:	• Occupation: King of Judea from 37 to 4 B.C. • Relatives: Father: Antipater. Sons: Archelaus, Antipater, Antipas, Philip, and others. Wives: Doris, Mariamne, and others. • Contemporaries: Zechariah, Elizabeth, Mary, Joseph, Mark Antony, Augustus
Key verse:	"When Herod realized that he had been outwitted by the Magi, he was furious, and he gave orders to kill all the boys in Bethlehem and its vicinity who were two years old and under" (Matthew 2:16).

Herod the Great is mentioned in Matthew 2:1–22 and Luke 1:5.

Like Isaiah, John was a prophet who urged the people to confess their sins and live for God. Both prophets taught that the message of repentance is good news to those who listen and seek the healing forgiveness of God's love, but terrible news to those who refuse to listen and thus cut off their only hope.

3:3 John the Baptist *prepared* the way for Jesus by preparing others to welcome him. People who do not know Jesus need to be prepared to meet him. We can prepare them by explaining their need for forgiveness, demonstrating Christ's teachings by our conduct, and telling them how Christ can give their lives meaning. We can "make straight paths for him" by correcting misconceptions that might be hindering people from approaching Christ. Someone you know may be open to a relationship with Christ. How are you helping those around you to welcome Jesus?

3:4 John was markedly different from other religious leaders of his day. While many were greedy, selfish, and preoccupied with winning the praise of the people, John was concerned only with the praise of God. Having separated himself from the evil and hypocrisy of his

day, John lived differently from other people to show that his message was new. John not only preached God's law, he *lived* it. Do you practice what you preach? Could people discover what you believe by observing the way you live?

3:4–6 John must have presented a strange image! Many people came to hear this preacher who wore odd clothes and ate unusual food. Some probably came simply out of curiosity and ended up repenting of their sins as they listened to his powerful message. People may be curious about your Christian lifestyle and values. You can use their simple curiosity as an opener to share how Christ makes a difference in you.

3:5 Why did John attract so many people? He was the first true prophet in 400 years. He publicly blasted both Herod and the religious leaders, daring words that fascinated the common people. But John also had a strong message for his audience—they too were sinners and needed to repent. His words were powerful and true. The people were expecting a prophet like Elijah (Malachi 4:5; Luke 1:17), and John seemed to be the one!

and the whole region of the Jordan. 6 Confessing their sins, they were baptized by him in the Jordan River.

7 But when he saw many of the Pharisees and Sadducees coming to where he was baptizing, he said to them: "You brood of vipers! h Who warned you to flee from the coming wrath? i 8 Produce fruit in keeping with repentance. j 9 And do not think you can say to yourselves, 'We have Abraham as our father.' I tell you that out of these stones God can raise up children for Abraham. 10 The ax is already at the root of the trees, and every tree that does not produce good fruit will be cut down and thrown into the fire. k

11 "I baptize you with a water for repentance. But after me will come one who is more powerful than I, whose sandals I am not fit to carry. He will baptize you with the Holy Spirit and with fire. l 12 His winnowing fork is in his hand, and he will clear his threshing floor, gathering his wheat into the barn and burning up the chaff with unquenchable fire." m

a 11 Or in

3:7
h Mt 12:34; 23:33
i Ro 1:18; 1Th 1:10

3:8
j Ac 26:20

3:10
k Mt 7:19

3:11
l Isa 4:4

3:12
m Mt 13:30

3:6 When you wash dirty hands, the results are immediately visible. But repentance happens inside with a cleansing that isn't seen right away. So John used a symbolic action that people could see: baptism. The Jews used baptism to initiate converts, so John's audience was familiar with the rite. Here, baptism was used as a sign of repentance and forgiveness. *Repent* means "to turn," implying a change in behavior. It is turning from sin toward God. Have you repented of sin in your life? Can others see the difference it makes in you? A changed life with new and different behavior makes your repentance real and visible.

3:6 The Jordan River is about 70 miles long, its main section stretching between the Sea of Galilee and the Dead Sea. Jerusalem lies about 20 miles west of the Jordan. This river was Israel's eastern border, and many significant events in the nation's history took place there. It was by the Jordan River that the Israelites renewed their covenant with God before entering the promised land (Joshua 1; 2). Here John the Baptist calls them to renew their covenant with God again, this time through baptism.

3:7 The Jewish religious leaders were divided into several groups. Two of the most prominent groups were the Pharisees and the Sadducees. The Pharisees separated themselves from

anything non-Jewish and carefully followed both the Old Testament laws and the oral traditions handed down through the centuries. The Sadducees believed the Pentateuch alone (Genesis—Deuteronomy) to be God's Word. They were descended mainly from priestly nobility, while the Pharisees came from all classes of people. The two groups disliked each other greatly, and both opposed Jesus. John the Baptist criticized the Pharisees for being legalistic and hypocritical, following the letter of the law while ignoring its true intent. He criticized the Sadducees for using religion to advance their political position. For more information on these two groups, see the chart in Mark 2, p. 1609.

3:8 John the Baptist called people to more than words or ritual; he told them to change their behavior. "Produce fruit in keeping with repentance" means that God looks beyond our words and religious activities to see if our conduct backs up what we say, and he judges our words by the actions that accompany them. Do your actions match your words?

3:9, 10 Just as a fruit tree is expected to bear fruit, God's people should produce a crop of good deeds. God has no use for people who call themselves Christians but do nothing about it. Like many people in John's day who were God's people in name only, we are of no value if we are Christians in name only. If others can't see our faith in the way we treat them, we may not be God's people at all.

3:10 God's message hasn't changed since the Old Testament—people will be judged for their unproductive lives. God calls us to be *active* in our obedience. John compared people who claim they believe God but don't live for God to unproductive trees that will be cut down. To be productive for God, we must obey his teachings, resist temptation, actively serve and help others, and share our faith. How productive are you for God?

3:11 John baptized people as a sign that they had asked God to forgive their sins and had decided to live as he wanted them to live. Baptism was an *outward* sign of commitment. To be effective, it had to be accompanied by an *inward* change of attitude leading to a changed life—the work of the Holy Spirit. John said that Jesus would baptize with the Holy Spirit and fire. This looked ahead to Pentecost (Acts 2), when the Holy Spirit would be sent by Jesus in the form of tongues of fire, empowering his followers to preach the gospel. John's statement also symbolizes the work of the Holy Spirit in bringing God's judgment on those who refuse to repent. Everyone will one day be baptized—either now by God's Holy Spirit, or later by the fire of his judgment.

3:12 A winnowing fork is a pitchfork used to toss wheat in the air to separate the wheat from chaff. The wheat is the part of the plant that is useful; chaff is the worthless outer shell. Because it is useless, chaff is burned; wheat, however, is gathered. "Winnowing" is often used as a picture of God's judgment. Unrepentant people will be judged and discarded because they are worthless in doing God's work; those who repent and believe will be saved and used by God.

JESUS BEGINS HIS MINISTRY
From his childhood home, Nazareth, Jesus set out to begin his earthly ministry. He was baptized by John the Baptist in the Jordan River, tempted by Satan in the desert, and then returned to Galilee. Between the temptation and his move to Capernaum (4:12, 13), he ministered in Judea, Samaria, and Galilee (see John 1—4).

John Baptizes Jesus (17/Mark 1:9–11; Luke 3:21–22)

13Then Jesus came from Galilee to the Jordan to be baptized by John. 14But John tried to deter him, saying, "I need to be baptized by you, and do you come to me?"

15Jesus replied, "Let it be so now; it is proper for us to do this to fulfill all righteousness." Then John consented.

3:16
n Isa 11:2

3:17
o Ps 2:7
p Mt 12:18; Lk 9:35

16As soon as Jesus was baptized, he went up out of the water. At that moment heaven was opened, and he saw the Spirit of God n descending like a dove and lighting on him. 17And a voice from heaven said, "This is my Son, o whom I love; with him I am well pleased."p

---

THE PHARISEES AND SADDUCEES	Name	Positive Characteristics	Negative Characteristics
The Pharisees and Sadducees were the two major religious groups in Israel at the time of Christ. The Pharisees were more religiously minded, while the Sadducees were more politically minded. Although the groups disliked and distrusted each other, they became allies in their common hatred for Jesus.	PHARISEES	• Were committed to obeying all of God's commands • Were admired by the common people for their apparent piety • Believed in a bodily resurrection and eternal life • Believed in angels and demons	• Behaved as though their own religious rules were just as important as God's rules for living • Their piety was often hypocritical, and their efforts often forced others to try to live up to standards they themselves could not live up to • Believed that salvation came from perfect obedience to the law and was not based on forgiveness of sins • Became so obsessed with obeying their legal interpretations in every detail that they completely ignored God's message of mercy and grace • Were more concerned with appearing to be good than obeying God
	SADDUCEES	• Believed strongly in the law of Moses and in Levitical purity • Were more practically minded than the Pharisees	• Relied on logic while placing little importance on faith • Did not believe all the Old Testament was God's Word • Did not believe in a bodily resurrection or eternal life • Did not believe in angels or demons • Were often willing to compromise their values with the Romans and others in order to maintain their status and influential positions

---

3:13–15 John had been explaining that Jesus' baptism would be much greater than his, when suddenly Jesus came to him and asked to be baptized! John felt unqualified. He wanted Jesus to baptize *him.* Why did Jesus ask to be baptized? It was not for repentance for sin because Jesus never sinned. "To fulfill all righteousness" means to accomplish God's mission. Jesus saw his baptism as advancing God's work. Jesus was baptized because (1) he was confessing sin on behalf of the nation, as Nehemiah, Ezra, Moses, and Daniel had done; (2) he was showing support for what John was doing; (3) he was inaugurating his public ministry; (4) he was identifying with the penitent people of God, not with the critical Pharisees who were only watching. Jesus, the perfect man, didn't need baptism for sin, but he accepted baptism in obedient service to the Father, and God showed his approval.

3:15 Put yourself in John's shoes. Your work is going well, people are taking notice, everything is growing. But you know that the purpose of your work is to prepare the people for Jesus (John 1:35–37). Then Jesus arrives, and his coming tests your integrity. Will you be able to turn your followers over to him? John passed the test by publicly baptizing Jesus. Soon he would say, "He must become greater; I must become less" (John 3:30). Can we, like John, put our egos and profitable work aside in order to point others to Jesus? Are we willing to lose some of our status so that everyone will benefit?

3:16, 17 The doctrine of the Trinity, which appeared later in church history, teaches that God is three persons and yet one in essence. In this passage, all three persons of the Trinity are present and active. God the Father speaks; God the Son is baptized; God the Holy Spirit descends on Jesus. God is one, yet in three persons at the same time. This is one of God's incomprehensible mysteries. Other Bible references that speak of the Father, Son, and Holy Spirit are Matthew 28:19; John 15:26; 1 Corinthians 12:4–13; 2 Corinthians 13:14; Ephesians 2:18; 1 Thessalonians 1:2–5; and 1 Peter 1:2.

Satan Tempts Jesus in the Desert (*18*/Mark 1:12–13; Luke 4:1–13)

4 Then Jesus was led by the Spirit into the desert to be tempted by the devil. ²After fasting forty days and forty nights,�q he was hungry. ³The tempterʳ came to him and said, "If you are the Son of God, tell these stones to become bread."

⁴Jesus answered, "It is written: 'Man does not live on bread alone, but on every word that comes from the mouth of God.'ᵃ"ˢ

⁵Then the devil took him to the holy cityᵗ and had him stand on the highest point of the temple. ⁶"If you are the Son of God," he said, "throw yourself down. For it is written:

"'He will command his angels concerning you,
    and they will lift you up in their hands,
    so that you will not strike your foot against a stone.'ᵇ"ᵘ

⁷Jesus answered him, "It is also written: 'Do not put the Lord your God to the test.'ᶜ"ᵛ

⁸Again, the devil took him to a very high mountain and showed him all the kingdoms of the world and their splendor. ⁹"All this I will give you," he said, "if you will bow down and worship me."

a*4* Deut. 8:3   b*6* Psalm 91:11,12   c*7* Deut. 6:16

4:2
q1Ki 19:8

4:3
r1Th 3:5

4:4
sDt 8:3

4:5
tNe 11:1; Mt 27:53

4:6
uPs 91:11, 12

4:7
vDt 6:16

4:1 This time of testing showed that Jesus really was the Son of God, able to overcome the devil and his temptations. A person has not shown true obedience if he or she has never had an opportunity to disobey. We read in Deuteronomy 8:2 that God led Israel into the desert to humble and test them. God wanted to see whether or not his people would really obey him. We too will be tested. Because we know that testing will come, we should be alert and ready for it. Remember, your convictions are only strong if they hold up under pressure!

4:1 The devil, also called Satan, tempted Eve in the Garden of Eden, and here he tempted Jesus in the desert. Satan is a fallen angel. He is *real*, not symbolic, and is constantly fighting against those who follow and obey God. Satan's temptations are real, and he is always trying to get us to live his way or our way rather than God's way. Jesus will one day reign over all creation, but Satan tried to force his hand and get him to declare his kingship prematurely. If Jesus had given in, his mission on earth—to die for our sins and give us the opportunity to have eternal life—would have been lost. When temptations seem especially strong, or when you think you can rationalize giving in, consider whether Satan may be trying to block God's purposes for your life or for someone else's life.

4:1ff This temptation by the devil shows us that Jesus was human, and it gave Jesus the opportunity to reaffirm God's plan for his ministry. It also gives us an example to follow when we are tempted. Jesus' temptation was an important demonstration of his sinlessness. He would face temptation and not give in.

Although we may feel dirty after being tempted, we should remember that temptation itself is not sin. We sin when we give in and disobey God. Remembering this will help us turn away from the temptation.

4:1ff Jesus wasn't tempted inside the temple or at his baptism but in the desert where he was tired, alone, and hungry, and thus most vulnerable. The devil often tempts us when we are vulnerable—when we are under physical or emotional stress (for example, lonely, tired, weighing big decisions, or faced with uncertainty). But he also likes to tempt us through our strengths, where we are most susceptible to pride (see the note on Luke 4:3ff). We must guard at all times against his attacks.

4:1–10 The devil's temptations focused on three crucial areas: (1) physical needs and desires, (2) possessions and power, and (3) pride (see 1 John 2:15, 16 for a similar list). But Jesus did not give in. Hebrews 4:15 says that Jesus "has been tempted in every way, just as we are—yet was without sin." He knows firsthand what we are experiencing, and he is willing and able to help us in our struggles. When you are tempted, turn to him for strength.

4:3, 4 Jesus was hungry and weak after fasting for 40 days, but he chose not to use his divine power to satisfy his natural desire for

food. Food, hunger, and eating are good, but the timing was wrong. Jesus was in the desert to fast, not to eat. And because Jesus had given up the unlimited, independent use of his divine power in order to experience humanity fully, he wouldn't use his power to change the stones to bread. We also may be tempted to satisfy a perfectly normal desire in a wrong way or at the wrong time. If we indulge in sex before marriage or if we steal to get food, we are trying to satisfy God-given desires in wrong ways. Remember, many of your desires are normal and good, but God wants you to satisfy them in the right way and at the right time.

4:3, 4 Jesus was able to resist all of the devil's temptations because he not only knew Scripture, but he also obeyed it. Ephesians 6:17 says that God's Word is a sword to use in spiritual combat. Knowing Bible verses is an important step in helping us resist the devil's attacks, but we must also obey the Bible. Note that Satan had memorized Scripture, but he failed to obey it. Knowing and obeying the Bible helps us follow God's desires rather than the devil's.

4:5 The temple was the religious center of the Jewish nation and the place where the people expected the Messiah to arrive (Malachi 3:1). Herod the Great had renovated the temple in hopes of gaining the Jews' confidence. The temple was the tallest building in the area, and this "highest point" was probably the corner wall that jutted out of the hillside, overlooking the valley below. From this spot, Jesus could see all of Jerusalem behind him and the country for miles in front of him.

4:5–7 God is not our magician in the sky ready to perform on request. In response to Satan's temptations, Jesus said not to put God to a test (Deuteronomy 6:16). You may want to ask God to do something to prove his existence or his love for you. Jesus once taught through a parable that people who don't believe what is written in the Bible won't believe even if someone were to come back from the dead to warn them (Luke 16:31)! God wants us to live by faith, not by magic. Don't try to manipulate God by asking for signs.

4:6 The devil used Scripture to try to convince Jesus to sin! Sometimes friends or associates will present attractive and convincing reasons why you should try something you know is wrong. They may even find Bible verses that *seem* to support their viewpoint. Study the Bible carefully, especially the broader contexts of specific verses, so that you understand God's principles for living and what he wants for your life. Only if you really understand what the *whole* Bible says will you be able to recognize errors of interpretation when people take verses out of context and twist them to say what they want them to say.

4:8, 9 Did the devil have the power to give Jesus the kingdoms of the world? Didn't God, the Creator of the world, have control

4:10
wDt 6:13

[10]Jesus said to him, "Away from me, Satan! For it is written: 'Worship the Lord your God, and serve him only.'[a]"[w]

4:11
xLk 22:43

[11]Then the devil left him, and angels came and attended him.[x]

B. MESSAGE AND MINISTRY OF JESUS, THE KING (4:12—25:46)

Matthew features Jesus' sermons. The record of Jesus' actions is interspersed with great passages of his teaching. This section of Matthew is topical rather than chronological. Matthew records for us the Sermon on the Mount, the parables of the kingdom, Jesus' teachings on forgiveness, and parables about the end of the age.

1. Jesus begins his ministry

Jesus Preaches in Galilee (30/Mark 1:14–15; Luke 4:14–15; John 4:43–45)

[12]When Jesus heard that John had been put in prison, he returned to Galilee. [13]Leaving Nazareth, he went and lived in Capernaum, which was by the lake in the area of Zebulun and Naphtali— [14]to fulfill what was said through the prophet Isaiah:

> [15] "Land of Zebulun and land of Naphtali,
> the way to the sea, along the Jordan,
> Galilee of the Gentiles—

a10 Deut. 6:13

THE TEMPTATIONS	Temptation	Real needs used as basis for temptation	Possible doubts that made the temptations real	Potential weaknesses Satan sought to exploit	Jesus' answer
	Make bread	Physical need: Hunger	Would God provide food?	Hunger, impatience, need to "prove his Sonship"	Deuteronomy 8:3 "Depend on God" Focus: God's purpose
	Dare God to rescue you (based on misapplied Scripture, Psalm 91:11, 12)	Emotional need: Security	Would God protect?	Pride, insecurity, need to test God	Deuteronomy 6:16 "Don't test God" Focus: God's plan
	Worship me! (Satan)	Psychological need: significance, power, achievement	Would God rule?	Desire for quick power, easy solutions, need to prove equality with God	Deuteronomy 6:13 "No compromise with evil" Focus: God's person

As if going through a final test of preparation, Jesus was tempted by Satan in the wilderness. Three specific parts of the temptation are listed by Matthew. They are familiar because we face the same kinds of temptations. As the chart shows, temptation is often the combination of a real need and a possible doubt that creates an inappropriate desire. Jesus demonstrates both the importance and effectiveness of knowing and applying Scripture to combat temptation.

---

over these kingdoms? The devil may have been lying about his implied power, or he may have based his offer on his temporary control and free rein over the earth because of humanity's sinfulness. Jesus' temptation was to take the world as a political ruler right then, without carrying out his plan to save the world from sin. Satan was trying to distort Jesus' perspective by making him focus on worldly power and not on God's plans.

4:8-10 The devil offered the whole world to Jesus if Jesus would only bow down and worship him. Today the devil offers us the world by trying to entice us with materialism and power. We can resist temptations the same way Jesus did. If you find yourself craving something that the world offers, quote Jesus' words to the devil: "Worship the Lord your God, and serve him only."

4:11 Angels, like these who waited on Jesus, have a significant role as God's messengers. These spiritual beings were involved in Jesus' life on earth by (1) announcing Jesus' birth to Mary, (2) reassuring Joseph, (3) naming Jesus, (4) announcing Jesus' birth to the shepherds, (5) protecting Jesus by sending his family

to Egypt, (6) ministering to Jesus in Gethsemane. For more on angels, see the note on 1:20.

4:12, 13 Jesus moved from Nazareth, his hometown, to Capernaum, about 20 miles farther north. Capernaum became Jesus' home base during his ministry in Galilee. Jesus probably moved (1) to get away from intense opposition in Nazareth, (2) to have an impact on the greatest number of people (Capernaum was a busy city and Jesus' message could reach more people and spread more quickly), and (3) to utilize extra resources and support for his ministry.

Jesus' move fulfilled the prophecy of Isaiah 9:1, 2, which states that the Messiah will be a light to the land of Zebulun and Naphtali, the region of Galilee where Capernaum was located. Zebulun and Naphtali were two of the original 12 tribes of Israel.

4:14-16 By quoting from the book of Isaiah, Matthew continues to tie Jesus' ministry to the Old Testament. This was helpful for his Jewish readers, who were familiar with these Scriptures. In addition, it shows the unity of God's purposes as he works with his people throughout all ages.

¹⁶ the people living in darkness
　　　have seen a great light;
　　on those living in the land of the shadow of death
　　　a light has dawned."ᵃ ʸ

4:16
ʸIsa 9:1, 2

¹⁷From that time on Jesus began to preach, "Repent, for the kingdom of heavenᶻ is near."

4:17
ᶻMt 3:2

Four Fishermen Follow Jesus (33/Mark 1:16–20)

¹⁸As Jesus was walking beside the Sea of Galilee, he saw two brothers, Simon called Peter and his brother Andrew. They were casting a net into the lake, for they were fishermen. ¹⁹"Come, follow me," ᵃ Jesus said, "and I will make you fishers of men." ²⁰At once they left their nets and followed him.

4:19
ᵃMk 10:21, 28, 52

²¹Going on from there, he saw two other brothers, James son of Zebedee and his brother John. They were in a boat with their father Zebedee, preparing their nets. Jesus called them, ²²and immediately they left the boat and their father and followed him.

Jesus Preaches throughout Galilee (36/Mark 1:35–39; Luke 4:42–44)

²³Jesus went throughout Galilee, ᵇ teaching in their synagogues, ᶜ preaching the good news ᵈ of the kingdom, and healing every disease and sickness among the people. ²⁴News about him spread all over Syria,ᵉ and people brought to him all who were ill with various diseases, those suffering severe pain, the demon-possessed, ᶠ those having seizures, and the paralyzed, and he healed them. ²⁵Large crowds from Galilee, the Decapolis,ᵇ Jerusalem, Judea and the region across the Jordan followed him. ᵍ

4:23
ᵇMk 1:39;
Lk 4:15, 44
ᶜMt 9:35; Mk 1:21
ᵈMk 1:14
4:24
ᵉLk 2:2
ᶠMk 1:32
4:25
ᵍMk 3:7, 8

2. Jesus gives the Sermon on the Mount
Jesus Gives the Beatitudes (49/Luke 6:17–26)

5 Now when he saw the crowds, he went up on a mountainside and sat down. His disciples came to him, ²and he began to teach them, saying:

ᵃ16 Isaiah 9:1,2　　ᵇ25 That is, the Ten Cities

4:17 The "kingdom of heaven" has the same meaning as the "kingdom of God" in Mark and Luke. Matthew uses this phrase because the Jews, out of their intense reverence and respect, did not pronounce God's name. The kingdom of heaven is still near because it has arrived in our hearts. See the note on 3:2 for more on the kingdom of heaven.

4:17 Jesus started his ministry with the very word people had heard John the Baptist say: "Repent." The message is the same today as when Jesus and John gave it. Becoming a follower of Christ means turning away from our self-centeredness and "self" control and turning our lives over to Christ's direction and control.

4:18 The Sea of Galilee is really a large lake. About 30 fishing towns surrounded it during Jesus' day, and Capernaum was the largest.

4:18–20 These men already knew Jesus. He had talked to Peter and Andrew previously (John 1:35–42) and had been preaching in the area. When Jesus called them, they knew what kind of man he was and were willing to follow him. Jesus told Peter and Andrew to leave their fishing business and become "fishers of men," to help others find God. Jesus was calling them away from their productive trades to be productive spiritually. We all need to fish for souls. If we practice Christ's teachings and share the gospel with others, we will be able to draw those around us to Christ like a fisherman who pulls fish into his boat with nets.

4:21, 22 James and his brother, John, along with Peter and Andrew, were the first disciples that Jesus called to work with him. Jesus' call motivated these men to get up and leave their jobs—immediately. They didn't make excuses about why it wasn't a good time. They left at once and followed. Jesus calls each of us to follow him. When Jesus asks us to serve him, we must be like the disciples and do it at once.

4:23 Jesus was teaching, preaching, and healing. These were the three main aspects of his ministry. *Teaching* shows Jesus' concern for understanding; *preaching* shows his concern for commitment; and *healing* shows his concern for wholeness. His

miracles of healing authenticated his teaching and preaching, proving that he truly was from God.

4:23 Jesus soon developed a powerful preaching ministry and often spoke in the synagogues. Most towns that had ten or more Jewish families had a synagogue. The building served as a religious gathering place on the Sabbath and as a school during the week. The leader of the synagogue was not a preacher as much as an administrator. His job was to find and invite rabbis to teach and preach. It was customary to invite visiting rabbis like Jesus to speak.

4:23, 24 Jesus preached the gospel—the Good News—to everyone who wanted to hear it. The gospel is that the kingdom of heaven has come, that God is with us, and that he cares for us. Christ can heal us, not just of physical sickness, but of spiritual sickness as well. There's no sin or problem too great or too small for him to handle. Jesus' words were good news because they offered freedom, hope, peace of heart, and eternal life with God.

4:25 Decapolis was a league of ten Gentile cities east of the Sea of Galilee, joined together for better trade and mutual defense. The word about Jesus was out, and Jews and Gentiles were coming long distances to hear him.

5:1ff Matthew 5—7 is called the Sermon on the Mount because Jesus gave it on a hillside near Capernaum. This "sermon" probably covered several days of preaching. In it, Jesus proclaimed his attitude toward the law. Position, authority, and money are not important in his kingdom—what matters is faithful obedience from the heart. The Sermon on the Mount challenged the proud and legalistic religious leaders of the day. It called them back to the messages of the Old Testament prophets who, like Jesus, taught that heartfelt obedience is more important than legalistic observance.

5:1, 2 Enormous crowds were following Jesus—he was the talk of the town, and everyone wanted to see him. The disciples, who were the closest associates of this popular man, were certainly tempted to feel important, proud, and possessive. Being with

3 "Blessed are the poor in spirit,
for theirs is the kingdom of heaven.

5:4
h Isa 61:2, 3

4 Blessed are those who mourn,
for they will be comforted. *h*

5:5
i Ps 37:11

5 Blessed are the meek,
for they will inherit the earth. *i*

5:6
j Isa 55:1, 2

6 Blessed are those who hunger and thirst for righteousness,
for they will be filled. *j*

7 Blessed are the merciful,
for they will be shown mercy.

KEY LESSONS FROM THE SERMON ON THE MOUNT

Beatitude	Old Testament anticipation	Clashing worldly values	God's reward	How to develop this attitude
Poor in spirit (5:3)	Isaiah 57:15	Pride and personal independence	Kingdom of Heaven	James 4:7–10
Mourning (5:4)	Isaiah 61:1, 2	Happiness at any cost	Comfort (2 Corinthians 1:4)	Psalm 51 James 4:7–10
Meekness (5:5)	Psalm 37:5–11	Power	Inherit the earth	Matthew 11:27–30
Righteousness (5:6)	Isaiah 11:4, 5; 42:1–4	Pursuing personal needs	Filled (satisfied)	John 16:5–11 Philippians 3:7–11
Mercy (5:7)	Psalm 41:1	Strength without feeling	Be shown mercy	Ephesians 5:1, 2
Pure in heart (5:8)	Psalms 24:3, 4; 51:10	Deception is acceptable	See God	1 John 3:1–3
Peacemaker (5:9)	Isaiah 57:18, 19; 60:17	Personal peace is pursued without concern for the world's chaos	Be called sons of God	Romans 12:9–21 Hebrews 12:10, 11
Persecuted (5:10)	Isaiah 52:13; 53:12	Weak commitments	Inherit the kingdom of Heaven	2 Timothy 3:12

In his longest recorded sermon, Jesus began by describing the traits he was looking for in his followers. He said that God blesses those who live out those traits. Each beatitude is an almost direct contradiction of society's typical way of life. In the last beatitude, Jesus even points out that a serious effort to develop these traits is bound to create opposition. The best example of each trait is found in Jesus himself. If our goal is to become like him, applying the beatitudes will challenge the way we live each day.

Jesus gave them not only prestige, but also opportunity for receiving money and power.

The crowds were gathering once again. But before speaking to them, Jesus pulled his disciples aside and warned them about the temptations they would face as his associates. Don't expect fame and fortune, Jesus was saying, but mourning, hunger, and persecution. Nevertheless, Jesus assured his disciples, they would be rewarded—but perhaps not in this life. There may be times when following Jesus will bring us great popularity. If we don't live by Jesus' words in this sermon, we will find ourselves using God's message only to promote our personal interests.

5:3-5 Jesus began his sermon with words that seem to contradict each other. But God's way of living usually contradicts the world's. If you want to live for God you must be ready to say and do what seems strange to the world. You must be willing to give when others take, to love when others hate, to help when others abuse. By giving up your own rights in order to serve others, you will one day receive everything God has in store for you.

5:3-12 The Beatitudes can be understood in at least four ways: (1) They are a code of ethics for the disciples and a standard of conduct for all believers. (2) They contrast kingdom values (what is eternal) with worldly values (what is temporary). (3) They contrast the superficial "faith" of the Pharisees with the real faith

Christ wants. (4) They show how the Old Testament expectations will be fulfilled in the new kingdom. These beatitudes are not multiple choice—pick what you like and leave the rest. They must be taken as a whole. They describe what we should be like as Christ's followers.

5:3-12 Each beatitude tells how to be *blessed*. "Blessed" means more than happiness. It implies the fortunate or enviable state of those who are in God's kingdom. The Beatitudes don't promise laughter, pleasure, or earthly prosperity. To Jesus, "blessed" means the experience of hope and joy, independent of outward circumstances. To find hope and joy, the deepest form of happiness, follow Jesus no matter what the cost.

5:3-12 With Jesus' announcement that the kingdom was near (4:17), people were naturally asking, "How do I qualify to be in God's kingdom?" Jesus said that God's kingdom is organized differently from worldly kingdoms. In the kingdom of heaven, wealth and power and authority are unimportant. Kingdom people seek different blessings and benefits, and they have different attitudes. Are your attitudes a carbon copy of the world's selfishness, pride, and lust for power, or do they reflect the humility and self-sacrifice of Jesus, your King?

8 Blessed are the pure in heart,
     for they will see God. *k*

9 Blessed are the peacemakers,
     for they will be called sons of God. *l*

10 Blessed are those who are persecuted because of righteousness, *m*
     for theirs is the kingdom of heaven.

5:8
kHeb 12:14

5:9
lRo 8:14

5:10
m1Pe 3:14

11 "Blessed are you when people insult you, *n* persecute you and falsely say all kinds of evil against you because of me. 12 Rejoice and be glad, because great is your reward in heaven, for in the same way they persecuted the prophets who were before you. *o*

5:11
n1Pe 4:14

5:12
oAc 7:52

Jesus Teaches about Salt and Light (50)

13 "You are the salt of the earth. But if the salt loses its saltiness, how can it be made salty again? It is no longer good for anything, except to be thrown out and trampled by men. *p* 14 "You are the light of the world. A city on a hill cannot be hidden. 15 Neither do people light a lamp and put it under a bowl. Instead they put it on its stand, and it gives light to everyone in the house. *q* 16 In the same way, let your light shine before men, that they may see your good deeds and praise your Father in heaven.

5:13
pMk 9:50;
Lk 14:34, 35

5:15
qMk 4:21; Lk 8:16

Jesus Teaches about the Law (51)

17 "Do not think that I have come to abolish the Law or the Prophets; I have not come to abolish them but to fulfill them. 18 I tell you the truth, until heaven and earth disappear, not the smallest letter, not the least stroke of a pen, will by any means disappear from the Law until everything is accomplished. *r* 19 Anyone who breaks one of the least of these commandments *s* and teaches others to do the same will be called least in the kingdom of heaven, but whoever practices and teaches these commands will be called great in the kingdom of heaven. 20 For I tell you that unless your righteousness surpasses that of the Pharisees and the teachers of the law, you will certainly not enter the kingdom of heaven.

5:18
rLk 16:17

5:19
sJas 2:10

5:11, 12 Jesus said to rejoice when we're persecuted. Persecution can be good because (1) it takes our eyes off earthly rewards, (2) it strips away superficial belief, (3) it strengthens the faith of those who endure, and (4) our attitude through it serves as an example to others who follow. We can be comforted to know that God's greatest prophets were persecuted (Elijah, Jeremiah, Daniel). The fact that we are being persecuted proves that we have been faithful; faithless people would be unnoticed. In the future God will reward the faithful by receiving them into his eternal kingdom where there is no more persecution.

5:13 If a seasoning has no flavor, it has no value. If Christians make no effort to affect the world around them, they are of little value to God. If we are too much like the world, we are worthless. Christians should not blend in with everyone else. Instead, we should affect others positively, just as seasoning brings out the best flavor in food.

5:14–16 Can you hide a city that is sitting on top of a hill? Its light at night can be seen for miles. If we live for Christ, we will glow like lights, showing others what Christ is like. We hide our light by (1) being quiet when we should speak, (2) going along with the crowd, (3) denying the light, (4) letting sin dim our light, (5) not explaining our light to others, or (6) ignoring the needs of others. Be a beacon of truth—don't shut your light off from the rest of the world.

5:17 God's moral and ceremonial laws were given to help people love God with all their hearts and minds. Throughout Israel's history, however, these laws had been often misquoted and misapplied. By Jesus' time, religious leaders had turned the laws into a confusing mass of rules. When Jesus talked about a new way to understand God's law, he was actually trying to bring people back to its *original* purpose. Jesus did not speak against the law itself, but against the abuses and excesses to which it had been subjected. (See John 1:17.)

5:17–20 If Jesus did not come to abolish the law, does that mean all the Old Testament laws still apply to us today? In the Old Testament, there were three categories of law: ceremonial, civil, and moral.

(1) The *ceremonial law* related specifically to Israel's worship (see Leviticus 1:2, 3, for example). Its primary purpose was to point forward to Jesus Christ; these laws, therefore, were no longer necessary after Jesus' death and resurrection. While we are no longer bound by ceremonial laws, the principles behind them—to worship and love a holy God—still apply. Jesus was often accused by the Pharisees of violating ceremonial law.

(2) The *civil law* applied to daily living in Israel (see Deuteronomy 24:10, 11, for example). Because modern society and culture are so radically different from that time and setting, all of these guidelines cannot be followed specifically. But the principles behind the commands are timeless and should guide our conduct. Jesus demonstrated these principles by example.

(3) The *moral law* (such as the Ten Commandments) is the direct command of God, and it requires strict obedience (see Exodus 20:13, for example). The moral law reveals the nature and will of God, and it still applies today. Jesus obeyed the moral law completely.

5:19 Some of those in the crowd were experts at telling others what to do, but they missed the central point of God's laws themselves. Jesus made it clear, however, that obeying God's law is more important than explaining it. It's much easier to study God's laws and tell others to obey them than to put them into practice. How are you doing at obeying God *yourself*?

5:20 The Pharisees were exacting and scrupulous in their attempts to follow their laws. So how could Jesus reasonably call us to a greater righteousness than theirs? The Pharisees' weakness was that they were content to obey the laws outwardly without allowing God to change their hearts (or attitudes). They looked pious, but they were far from the kingdom of God. God judges our hearts as well as our deeds, for it is in the heart that our real allegiance lies.

Jesus was saying that his listeners needed a different kind of righteousness altogether (love and obedience), not just a more intense version of the Pharisees' righteousness (legal compli-

Jesus Teaches about Anger (52)

5:21
*Ex 20:13
5:22
*1Jn 3:15

21 "You have heard that it was said to the people long ago, 'Do not murder,[a][t] and anyone who murders will be subject to judgment.' 22 But I tell you that anyone who is angry with his brother[b] will be subject to judgment.[u] Again, anyone who says to his brother, 'Raca,[c]' is answerable to the Sanhedrin. But anyone who says, 'You fool!' will be in danger of the fire of hell.

23 "Therefore, if you are offering your gift at the altar and there remember that your brother has something against you, 24 leave your gift there in front of the altar. First go and be reconciled to your brother; then come and offer your gift.

25 "Settle matters quickly with your adversary who is taking you to court. Do it while you are still with him on the way, or he may hand you over to the judge, and the judge may hand you over to the officer, and you may be thrown into prison. 26 I tell you the truth, you will not get out until you have paid the last penny.[d]

*a21 Exodus 20:13 *b22 Some manuscripts *brother without cause* *c22 An Aramaic term of contempt
*d26 Greek *kodrantes*

	Reference	Example	It's not enough to	We must also
SIX WAYS TO THINK LIKE CHRIST	5:21, 22	Murder	Avoid killing	Avoid anger and hatred
	5:23–26	Offerings	Offer regular gifts	Have right relationships with God and others
	5:27–30	Adultery	Avoid adultery	Keep our hearts from lusting and be faithful
	5:31, 32	Divorce	Be legally married	Live out our marriage commitments
	5:33–37	Oaths	Make an oath	Avoid casual and irresponsible commitments to God
	5:38–47	Revenge	Seek justice for ourselves	Show mercy and love to others

We, more often than not, avoid the extreme sins but regularly commit the types of sins with which Jesus was most concerned. In these six examples, our real struggle with sin is exposed. Jesus pointed out what kind of lives would be required of his followers. Are you living as Jesus taught?

ance). Our righteousness must (1) come from what God does in us, not what we can do by ourselves, (2) be God-centered, not self-centered, (3) be based on reverence for God, not approval from people, and (4) go beyond keeping the law to living by the principles behind the law. We should be just as concerned about our attitudes that people don't see as about our actions that are seen by all.

5:21, 22 When Jesus said, "But I tell you," he was not doing away with the law or adding his own beliefs. Rather, he was giving a fuller understanding of why God made that law in the first place. For example, Moses said, "You shall not murder" (Exodus 20:13); Jesus taught that we should not even become angry enough to murder, for then we have already committed murder in our heart. The Pharisees read this law and, not having literally murdered anyone, felt righteous. Yet they were angry enough with Jesus that they would soon plot his death, though they would not do the dirty work themselves. We miss the intent of God's Word when we read his rules for living without trying to understand why he made them. When do you keep God's rules but close your eyes to his intent?

5:21, 22 Killing is a terrible sin, but *anger* is a great sin too because it also violates God's command to love. Anger in this case refers to a seething, brooding bitterness against someone. It is a dangerous emotion that always threatens to leap out of control, leading to violence, emotional hurt, increased mental stress, and spiritual damage. Anger keeps us from developing a spirit pleasing to God. Have you ever been proud that you didn't strike out and say what was really on your mind? Self-control is good, but Christ wants us to practice thought-

control as well. Jesus said that we will be held accountable even for our attitudes.

5:23, 24 Broken relationships can hinder our relationship with God. If we have a problem or grievance with a friend, we should resolve the problem as soon as possible. We are hypocrites if we claim to love God while we hate others. Our attitudes toward others reflect our relationship with God (1 John 4:20).

5:25, 26 In Jesus' day, someone who couldn't pay a debt was thrown into prison until the debt was paid. Unless someone came to pay the debt for the prisoner, he or she would probably die there. It is practical advice to resolve our differences with our enemies before their anger causes more trouble (Proverbs 25:8–10). You may not get into a disagreement that takes you to court, but even small conflicts mend more easily if you try to make peace right away. In a broader sense, these verses advise us to get things right with our brothers and sisters before we have to stand before God.

Jesus Teaches about Lust (53)

27"You have heard that it was said, 'Do not commit adultery.'*a v* 28But I tell you that anyone who looks at a woman lustfully has already committed adultery with her in his heart.*w*
29If your right eye causes you to sin,*x* gouge it out and throw it away. It is better for you to
lose one part of your body than for your whole body to be thrown into hell. 30And if your
right hand causes you to sin, cut it off and throw it away. It is better for you to lose one part
of your body than for your whole body to go into hell.

5:27
vEx 20:14; Dt 5:18
5:28
wPr 6:25
5:29
xMk 9:42-47

Jesus Teaches about Divorce (54)

31"It has been said, 'Anyone who divorces his wife must give her a certificate of
divorce.'*b y* 32But I tell you that anyone who divorces his wife, except for marital unfaithfulness, causes her to become an adulteress, and anyone who marries the divorced
woman commits adultery. *z*

5:31
yDt 24:1-4
5:32
zLk 16:18

Jesus Teaches about Vows (55)

33"Again, you have heard that it was said to the people long ago, 'Do not break your oath,*a*
but keep the oaths you have made to the Lord.'*b* 34But I tell you, Do not swear at all:*c* either
by heaven, for it is God's throne;*d* 35or by the earth, for it is his footstool; or by Jerusalem, for
it is the city of the Great King. *e* 36And do not swear by your head, for you cannot make even
one hair white or black. 37Simply let your 'Yes' be 'Yes,' and your 'No,' 'No'; anything beyond
this comes from the evil one.

5:33
aLev 19:12
bNu 30:2;
Mt 23:16-22
5:34
cJas 5:12
dIsa 66:1
5:35
ePs 48:2

Jesus Teaches about Revenge (56)

38"You have heard that it was said, 'Eye for eye, and tooth for tooth.'*c f* 39But I tell you, Do
not resist an evil person. If someone strikes you on the right cheek, turn to him the other
also. *g* 40And if someone wants to sue you and take your tunic, let him have your cloak as
well. 41If someone forces you to go one mile, go with him two miles. 42Give to the one who
asks you, and do not turn away from the one who wants to borrow from you. *h*

5:38
fEx 21:24;
Lev 24:20; Dt 19:21
5:39
gLk 6:29; 1Co 6:7
5:42
hLk 6:30

a27 Exodus 20:14   *b31* Deut. 24:1   *c38* Exodus 21:24; Lev. 24:20; Deut. 19:21

5:27, 28 The Old Testament law said that it is wrong for a person to have sex with someone other than his or her spouse
(Exodus 20:14). But Jesus said that the *desire* to have sex with
someone other than your spouse is mental adultery and thus sin.
Jesus emphasized that if the *act* is wrong, then so is the *intention.*
To be faithful to your spouse with your body but not your mind
is to break the trust so vital to a strong marriage. Jesus is not
condemning natural interest in the opposite sex or even healthy
sexual desire, but the deliberate and repeated filling of one's mind
with fantasies that would be evil if acted out.

5:27, 28 Some think that if lustful thoughts are sin, why shouldn't
a person go ahead and do the lustful actions too? Acting out sinful
desires is harmful in several ways: (1) it causes people to excuse
sin rather than to stop sinning; (2) it destroys marriages; (3) it is
deliberate rebellion against God's Word; (4) it always hurts someone else in addition to the sinner. Sinful action is more dangerous
than sinful desire, and that is why desires should not be acted out.
Nevertheless, sinful desire is just as damaging to righteousness.
Left unchecked, wrong desires will result in wrong actions and turn
people away from God.

5:29, 30 When Jesus said to get rid of your hand or your eye, he
was speaking figuratively. He didn't mean literally to gouge out your
eye, because even a blind person can lust. But if that were the only
choice, it would be better to go into heaven with one eye or hand
than to go to hell with two. We sometimes tolerate sins in our lives
that, left unchecked, could eventually destroy us. It is better to
experience the pain of removal (getting rid of a bad habit or something we treasure, for instance) than to allow the sin to bring judgment and condemnation. Examine your life for anything that causes
you to sin, and take every necessary action to remove it.

5:31, 32 Divorce is as hurtful and destructive today as in Jesus'
day. God intends marriage to be a lifetime commitment (Genesis
2:24). When entering into marriage, people should never consider
divorce an option for solving problems or a way out of a rela-

ship that seems dead. In these verses, Jesus is also attacking
those who purposefully abuse the marriage contract, using
divorce to satisfy their lustful desire to marry someone else. Are
your actions today helping your marriage grow stronger, or are
you tearing it apart?

5:32 Jesus said that divorce is not permissible except for unfaithfulness. This does not mean that divorce should automatically
occur when a spouse commits adultery. The word translated
"unfaithfulness" implies a sexually immoral lifestyle, not a confessed and repented act of adultery. Those who discover that their
partner has been unfaithful should first make every effort to forgive, reconcile, and restore their relationship. We are always to
look for reasons to restore the marriage relationship rather than
for excuses to leave it.

5:33ff Here, Jesus was emphasizing the importance of telling the
truth. People were breaking promises and using sacred language
casually and carelessly. Keeping oaths and promises is important;
it builds trust and makes committed human relationships possible.
The Bible condemns making vows or taking oaths casually, giving
your word while knowing that you won't keep it, or swearing
falsely in God's name (Exodus 20:7; Leviticus 19:12; Numbers
30:1, 2; Deuteronomy 19:16–20). Oaths are needed in certain situations only because we live in a sinful society that breeds distrust.

5:33–37 Oaths, or vows, were common, but Jesus told his
followers not to use them—their word alone should be enough
(see James 5:12). Are you known as a person of your word?
Truthfulness seems so rare that we feel we must end our statements with "I promise." If we tell the truth all the time, we will
have less pressure to back up our words with an oath or promise.

5:38 God's purpose behind this law was an expression of mercy.
The law was given to judges and said, in effect, "Make the punish-
ment fit the crime." It was not a guide for personal revenge
(Exodus 21:23–25; Leviticus 24:19, 20; Deuteronomy 19:21).
These laws were given to *limit* vengeance and help the court

Jesus Teaches about Loving Enemies (57/Luke 6:27–36)

5:43
/Lev 19:18
/Dt 23:6

5:44
kLk 6:27, 28;
Ac 7:60

5:48
/Lev 19:2

43"You have heard that it was said, 'Love your neighbor a/and hate your enemy.'/ 44But I tell you: Love your enemiesb and pray for those who persecute you,k 45that you may be sons of your Father in heaven. He causes his sun to rise on the evil and the good, and sends rain on the righteous and the unrighteous. 46If you love those who love you, what reward will you get? Are not even the tax collectors doing that? 47And if you greet only your brothers, what are you doing more than others? Do not even pagans do that? 48Be perfect, therefore, as your heavenly Father is perfect./

Jesus Teaches about Giving to the Needy (58)

6 "Be careful not to do your 'acts of righteousness' before men, to be seen by them. If you do, you will have no reward from your Father in heaven.

2"So when you give to the needy, do not announce it with trumpets, as the hypocrites do in the synagogues and on the streets, to be honored by men. I tell you the truth, they have

a43 Lev. 19:18   b44 Some late manuscripts *enemies, bless those who curse you, do good to those who hate you*

JESUS AND THE OLD TESTAMENT LAW

Reference	Examples of Old Testament mercy in justice:
Leviticus 19:18	"Do not seek revenge or bear a grudge against one of your people, but love your neighbor as yourself. I am the LORD."
Proverbs 24:28, 29	"Do not testify against your neighbor without cause, or use your lips to deceive. Do not say, 'I'll do to him as he has done to me; I'll pay that man back for what he did.'"
Proverbs 25:21, 22	"If your enemy is hungry, give him food to eat; if he is thirsty, give him water to drink. In doing this, you will heap burning coals on his head, and the LORD will reward you."
Lamentations 3:30, 31	"Let him offer his cheek to one who would strike him, and let him be filled with disgrace. For men are not cast off by the LORD forever."

What seems to be a case of Jesus contradicting the laws of the Old Testament deserves a careful look. It is too easy to overlook how much mercy was written into the Old Testament laws. Above are several examples. What God designed as a system of justice with mercy had been distorted over the years into a license for revenge. It was this misapplication of the law that Jesus attacked.

---

administer punishment that was neither too strict nor too lenient. Some people, however, were using this phrase to justify their vendettas against others. People still try to excuse their acts of revenge by saying, "I was just doing to him what he did to me."

5:38–42 When we are wronged, often our first reaction is to get even. Instead Jesus said we should do *good* to those who wrong us! Our desire should not be to keep score, but to love and forgive. This is not natural—it is supernatural. Only God can give us the strength to love as he does. Instead of planning vengeance, pray for those who hurt you.

5:39–44 To many Jews of Jesus' day, these statements were offensive. Any Messiah who would turn the other cheek was not the military leader they wanted to lead a revolt against Rome. Since they were under Roman oppression, they wanted retaliation against their enemies, whom they hated. But Jesus suggested a new, radical response to injustice: instead of demanding rights, give them up freely! According to Jesus, it is more important to *give* justice and mercy than to receive it.

5:43, 44 By telling us not to retaliate, Jesus keeps us from taking the law into our own hands. By loving and praying for our enemies, we can overcome evil with good.

The Pharisees interpreted Leviticus 19:18 as teaching that they should love only those who love in return, and Psalm 139:19–22 and 140:9–11 as meaning that they should hate their enemies. But Jesus says we are to love our enemies. If you love your enemies and treat them well, you will truly show that Jesus is Lord of your life. This is possible only for those who give themselves fully to God, because only he can deliver people

from natural selfishness. We must trust the Holy Spirit to help us *show* love to those for whom we may not *feel* love.

5:48 How can we be perfect? (1) *In character.* In this life we cannot be flawless, but we can aspire to be as much like Christ as possible. (2) *In holiness.* Like the Pharisees, we are to separate ourselves from the world's sinful values. But unlike the Pharisees, we are to be devoted to God's desires rather than our own, and carry his love and mercy into the world. (3) *In maturity.* We can't achieve Christlike character and holy living all at once, but we must grow toward maturity and wholeness. Just as we expect different behavior from a baby, a child, a teenager, and an adult, so God expects different behavior from us, depending on our stage of spiritual development. (4) *In love.* We can seek to love others as completely as God loves us.

We can be perfect if our behavior is appropriate for our maturity level—perfect, yet with much room to grow. Our tendency to sin must never deter us from striving to be more like Christ. Christ calls all of his disciples to excel, to rise above mediocrity, and to mature in every area, becoming like him. Those who strive to become perfect will one day be perfect, even as Christ is perfect (1 John 3:2, 3).

6:2 The term *hypocrites,* as used here, describes people who do good acts for appearances only—not out of compassion or other good motives. Their actions may be good, but their motives are hollow. These empty acts are their only reward, but God will reward those who are sincere in their faith.

received their reward in full. ³But when you give to the needy, do not let your left hand know what your right hand is doing, ⁴so that your giving may be in secret. Then your Father, who sees what is done in secret, will reward you.

Jesus Teaches about Prayer (59)

⁵"And when you pray, do not be like the hypocrites, for they love to pray standing*m* in the synagogues and on the street corners to be seen by men. I tell you the truth, they have received their reward in full. ⁶But when you pray, go into your room, close the door and pray to your Father,*n* who is unseen. Then your Father, who sees what is done in secret, will reward you. ⁷And when you pray, do not keep on babbling like pagans, for they think they will be heard because of their many words.*o* ⁸Do not be like them, for your Father knows what you need before you ask him.

⁹"This, then, is how you should pray:

> "'Our Father in heaven,
> hallowed be your name,
> 10 your kingdom come,
> your will be done*p*
> on earth as it is in heaven.
> 11 Give us today our daily bread.*q*
> 12 Forgive us our debts,
> as we also have forgiven our debtors.*r*
> 13 And lead us not into temptation,
> but deliver us from the evil one.*a*'

a 13 Or *from evil*; some late manuscripts *one, / for yours is the kingdom and the power and the glory forever. Amen.*

6:5
*m*Mk 11:25

6:6
*n*2Ki 4:33

6:7
*o*1Ki 18:26-29

6:10
*p*Mt 26:39

6:11
*q*Pr 30:8

6:12
*r*Mt 18:21-35

6:3 When Jesus says not to let your left hand know what your right hand is doing, he is teaching that our motives for giving to God and to others must be pure. It is easy to give with mixed motives, to do something for someone if it will benefit us in return. But believers should avoid all scheming and give for the pleasure of giving and as a response to God's love. Why do *you* give?

6:3, 4 It's easier to do what's right when we gain recognition and praise. To be sure our motives are not selfish, we should do our good deeds quietly or in secret, with no thought of reward. Jesus says we should check our motives in three areas: generosity (6:4), prayer (6:6), and fasting (6:18). Those acts should not be self-centered, but God-centered, done not to make us look good but to make God look good. The reward God promises is not material, and it is never given to those who seek it. Doing something only for ourselves is not a loving sacrifice. With your next good deed, ask, "Would I still do this if no one would ever know I did it?"

6:5, 6 Some people, especially the religious leaders, wanted to be seen as "holy," and public prayer was one way to get attention. Jesus saw through their self-righteous acts, however, and taught that the essence of prayer is not public style but private communication with God. There is a place for public prayer, but to pray only where others will notice you indicates that your real audience is not God.

6:6 Some have concluded that Jesus' directions about private prayer call into question all public prayer. Jesus' own practice indicates this wasn't his intention. The Gospels record Jesus at prayer both privately (14:23) and publicly (14:18, 19). Again, Jesus was drawing attention to the motives behind actions. The point really wasn't a choice between public and private prayer but between heartfelt and hypocritical prayer. When asked to pray in public, focus on addressing God, not on how you're coming across to others.

6:7, 8 Repeating the same words over and over like a magic incantation is no way to ensure that God will hear your prayer. It's not wrong to come to God many times with the same requests— Jesus encourages *persistent* prayer. But he condemns the shallow repetition of words that are not offered with a sincere heart. We can never pray too much if our prayers are honest and sincere. Before you start to pray, make sure you mean what you say.

6:9 This is often called the Lord's Prayer because Jesus gave it to the disciples as a model for them (and us) to keep in mind as we pray. Jesus provided a pattern to be imitated as well as duplicated. We should praise God, pray for his work in the world, pray for our daily needs, and pray for help in our daily struggles. To what extent do you use the items in the Lord's Prayer to guide your own prayer times?

6:9 The phrase "Our Father in heaven" indicates that God is not only majestic and holy, but also personal and loving. The first line of this model prayer is a statement of praise and a commitment to hallow, or honor, God's holy name. We can honor God's name by being careful to use it respectfully. If we use God's name lightly, we aren't remembering God's holiness.

6:10 The phrase "Your kingdom come" is a reference to God's spiritual reign, not Israel's freedom from Rome. God's kingdom was announced in the covenant with Abraham (8:11; Luke 13:28), is present in Christ's reign in believers' hearts (Luke 17:21), and will be complete when all evil is destroyed and God establishes the new heaven and earth (Revelation 21:1).

6:10 When we pray "Your will be done," we are not resigning ourselves to fate, but praying that God's perfect purpose will be accomplished in this world as well as in the next. And how does God accomplish his will on earth? He does it largely through people willing to obey him. This part of the prayer allows us to offer ourselves as doers of God's will, asking him to guide, lead, and give us the means to accomplish his purposes.

6:11 When we pray "Give us today our daily bread," we are acknowledging that God is our sustainer and provider. It is a misconception to think that we provide for our needs ourselves. We must trust God *daily* to provide what he knows we need.

6:13 God doesn't lead us into temptations, but sometimes he allows us to be tested by them. As disciples, we should pray to be delivered from these trying times and for deliverance from Satan ("the evil one") and his deceit. All Christians struggle with temptation. Sometimes it is so subtle that we don't even realize what is happening to us. God has promised that he won't allow us to be tempted beyond what we can bear (1 Corinthians 10:13). Ask God to help you recognize temptation and to give

6:14
s Mk 11:25, 26;
Col 3:13

6:15
t Mt 18:35

6:16
u Isa 58:5

6:18
v ver 4, 6

6:19
w Heb 13:5

6:20
x Mt 19:21;
Lk 12:33; 1Ti 6:19

6:24
y Lk 16:13

¹⁴For if you forgive men when they sin against you, your heavenly Father will also forgive you. s ¹⁵But if you do not forgive men their sins, your Father will not forgive your sins. t

Jesus Teaches about Fasting (60)

¹⁶"When you fast, do not look somber u as the hypocrites do, for they disfigure their faces to show men they are fasting. I tell you the truth, they have received their reward in full. ¹⁷But when you fast, put oil on your head and wash your face, ¹⁸so that it will not be obvious to men that you are fasting, but only to your Father, who is unseen; and your Father, who sees what is done in secret, will reward you. v

Jesus Teaches about Money (61)

¹⁹"Do not store up for yourselves treasures on earth, w where moth and rust destroy, and where thieves break in and steal. ²⁰But store up for yourselves treasures in heaven, x where moth and rust do not destroy, and where thieves do not break in and steal. ²¹For where your treasure is, there your heart will be also.

²²"The eye is the lamp of the body. If your eyes are good, your whole body will be full of light. ²³But if your eyes are bad, your whole body will be full of darkness. If then the light within you is darkness, how great is that darkness!

²⁴"No one can serve two masters. Either he will hate the one and love the other, or he will be devoted to the one and despise the other. You cannot serve both God and Money. y

---

SEVEN REASONS NOT TO WORRY		
6:25	. . . .	The same God who created life in you can be trusted with the details of your life.
6:26	. . . .	Worrying about the future hampers your efforts for today.
6:27	. . . .	Worrying is more harmful than helpful.
6:28–30	. . . .	God does not ignore those who depend on him.
6:31, 32	. . . .	Worrying shows a lack of faith in and understanding of God.
6:33	. . . .	Worrying keeps us from real challenges God wants us to pursue.
6:34	. . . .	Living one day at a time keeps us from being consumed with worry.

---

you strength to overcome it and choose God's way instead. For more on temptation, see the notes on 4:1.

6:14, 15 Jesus gives a startling warning about forgiveness: if we refuse to forgive others, God will also refuse to forgive us. Why? Because when we don't forgive others, we are denying our common ground as sinners in need of God's forgiveness. God's forgiveness of sin is not the direct result of our forgiving others, but it is based on our realizing what forgiveness means (see Ephesians 4:32). It is easy to ask God for forgiveness, but difficult to grant it to others. Whenever we ask God to forgive us for sin, we should ask ourselves, "Have I forgiven the people who have wronged me?"

6:16 Fasting—going without food in order to spend time in prayer—is noble *and* difficult. It gives us time to pray, teaches self-discipline, reminds us that we can live with a lot less, and helps us appreciate God's gifts. Jesus was not condemning fasting, but hypocrisy—fasting in order to gain public approval. Fasting was mandatory for the Jewish people once a year, on the Day of Atonement (Leviticus 23:32). The Pharisees voluntarily fasted twice a week to impress the people with their "holiness." Jesus commended acts of self-sacrifice done quietly and sincerely. He wanted people to adopt spiritual disciplines for the right reasons, not from a selfish desire for praise.

6:20 Storing up treasures in heaven is not limited to tithing but is accomplished by all acts of obedience to God. There is a sense in which giving our money to God's work is like investing in heaven. But our intention should be to seek the fulfillment of God's purposes in all we do, not merely what we do with our money.

6:21 Jesus made it clear that having the wrong treasures leads to our hearts being in the wrong place. What we treasure the

most controls us, whether we admit it or not. If possessions or money become too important to us, we must re-establish control or get rid of items. Jesus calls for a decision that allows us to live contentedly with whatever we have because we have chosen eternal values over temporary, earthly treasures.

6:22, 23 Spiritual vision is our capacity to see clearly what God wants us to do and to see the world from his point of view. But this spiritual insight can be easily clouded. Self-serving desires, interests, and goals block that vision. Serving God is the best way to restore it. A "good" eye is one that is fixed on God.

6:24 Jesus says we can have only one master. We live in a materialistic society where many people serve money. They spend all their lives collecting and storing it, only to die and leave it behind. Their desire for money and what it can buy far outweighs their commitment to God and spiritual matters. Whatever you store up, you will spend much of your time and energy thinking about. Don't fall into the materialistic trap, because "the love of money is a root of all kinds of evil" (1 Timothy 6:10). Can you honestly say that God, and not money, is your master? One test is to ask which one occupies more of your thoughts, time, and efforts.

6:24 Jesus contrasted heavenly values with earthly values when he explained that our first loyalty should be to those things that do not fade, cannot be stolen or used up, and never wear out. We should not be fascinated with our possessions, lest *they* possess *us*. God alone deserves to be our master. Either we store our treasures with God (6:20, 21), focus our "eyes" on him (6:22, 23), and serve him alone—or else we do not serve him at all. Where does your ultimate allegiance lie?

Jesus Teaches about Worry (62)

25 "Therefore I tell you, do not worry[z] about your life, what you will eat or drink; or about your body, what you will wear. Is not life more important than food, and the body more important than clothes? 26 Look at the birds of the air; they do not sow or reap or store away in barns, and yet your heavenly Father feeds them. [a] Are you not much more valuable than they? 27 Who of you by worrying can add a single hour to his life[a]?[b]

28 "And why do you worry about clothes? See how the lilies of the field grow. They do not labor or spin. 29 Yet I tell you that not even Solomon in all his splendor[c] was dressed like one of these. 30 If that is how God clothes the grass of the field, which is here today and tomorrow is thrown into the fire, will he not much more clothe you, O you of little faith?[d] 31 So do not worry, saying, 'What shall we eat?' or 'What shall we drink?' or 'What shall we wear?' 32 For the pagans run after all these things, and your heavenly Father knows that you need them. 33 But seek first his kingdom and his righteousness, and all these things will be given to you as well. [e] 34 Therefore do not worry about tomorrow, for tomorrow will worry about itself. Each day has enough trouble of its own.

Jesus Teaches about Judging Others (63/Luke 6:37–42)

7 "Do not judge, or you too will be judged.[f] 2 For in the same way you judge others, you will be judged, and with the measure you use, it will be measured to you.[g]

3 "Why do you look at the speck of sawdust in your brother's eye and pay no attention to the plank in your own eye? 4 How can you say to your brother, 'Let me take the speck out of your eye,' when all the time there is a plank in your own eye? 5 You hypocrite, first take the plank out of your own eye, and then you will see clearly to remove the speck from your brother's eye.

6 "Do not give dogs what is sacred; do not throw your pearls to pigs. If you do, they may trample them under their feet, and then turn and tear you to pieces.

Jesus Teaches about Asking, Looking, Knocking (64)

7 "Ask and it will be given to you;[h] seek and you will find; knock and the door will be opened to you. 8 For everyone who asks receives; he who seeks finds;[i] and to him who knocks, the door will be opened.

[a]27 Or *single cubit to his height*

6:25 z Lk 12:11, 22; Php 4:6; 1Pe 5:7
6:26 a Ps 147:9
6:27 b Ps 39:5
6:29 c 1Ki 10:4-7
6:30 d Mt 8:26
6:33 e Mt 19:29; Mk 10:29-30
7:1 f 1Co 4:5
7:2 g Mk 4:24
7:7 h Mk 11:24; Jn 15:7, 16; 16:23, 24; 1Jn 3:22; 5:14, 15
7:8 i Jer 29:12, 13

6:25 Because of the ill effects of worry, Jesus tells us not to worry about those needs that God promises to supply. Worry may (1) damage your health, (2) cause the object of your worry to consume your thoughts, (3) disrupt your productivity, (4) negatively affect the way you treat others, and (5) reduce your ability to trust in God. How many ill effects of worry are you experiencing? Here is the difference between worry and genuine concern—worry immobilizes, but concern moves you to action.

6:33 To "seek first his kingdom and his righteousness" means to turn to God first for help, to fill your thoughts with his desires, to take his character for your pattern, and to serve and obey him in everything. What is really important to you? People, objects, goals, and other desires all compete for priority. Any of these can quickly become most important to you if you don't actively choose to give God first place in *every* area of your life.

6:34 Planning for tomorrow is time well spent; worrying about tomorrow is time wasted. Sometimes it's difficult to tell the difference. Careful planning is thinking ahead about goals, steps, and schedules, and trusting in God's guidance. When done well, planning can help alleviate worry. Worriers, by contrast, are consumed by fear and find it difficult to trust God. They let their plans interfere with their relationship with God. Don't let worries about tomorrow affect your relationship with God today.

7:1, 2 Jesus tells us to examine our own motives and conduct instead of judging others. The traits that bother us in others are often the habits we dislike in ourselves. Our untamed bad habits and behavior patterns are the very ones that we most

want to change in others. Do you find it easy to magnify others' faults while excusing your own? If you are ready to criticize someone, check to see if you deserve the same criticism. Judge yourself first, and then lovingly forgive and help your neighbor.

7:1–5 Jesus' statement, "Do not judge," is against the kind of hypocritical, judgmental attitude that tears others down in order to build oneself up. It is not a blanket statement against all critical thinking, but a call to be *discerning* rather than negative. Jesus said to expose false teachers (7:15–23), and Paul taught that we should exercise church discipline (1 Corinthians 5:1, 2) and trust God to be the final Judge (1 Corinthians 4:3–5).

7:6 Pigs were unclean animals according to God's law (Deuteronomy 14:8). Anyone who touched an unclean animal became "ceremonially unclean" and could not go to the temple to worship until the uncleanness was removed. Jesus says that we should not entrust holy teachings to unholy or unclean people. It is futile to try to teach holy concepts to people who don't want to listen and will only tear apart what we say. We should not stop giving God's Word to unbelievers, but we should be wise and discerning in what we teach to whom, so that we will not be wasting our time.

7:7, 8 Jesus tells us to persist in pursuing God. People often give up after a few halfhearted efforts and conclude that God cannot be found. But knowing God takes faith, focus, and follow-through, and Jesus assures us that we will be rewarded. Don't give up in your efforts to seek God. Continue to ask him for more knowledge, patience, wisdom, love, and understanding. He will give them to you.

9"Which of you, if his son asks for bread, will give him a stone? 10Or if he asks for a fish, will give him a snake? 11If you, then, though you are evil, know how to give good gifts to your children, how much more will your Father in heaven give good gifts to those who ask him! 12So in everything, do to others what you would have them do to you,ʲ for this sums up the Law and the Prophets.ᵏ

7:12
ʲLk 6:31
ᵏRo 13:8-10;
Gal 5:14

Jesus Teaches about the Way to Heaven (65)

13"Enter through the narrow gate.ˡ For wide is the gate and broad is the road that leads to destruction, and many enter through it. 14But small is the gate and narrow the road that leads to life, and only a few find it.

7:13
ˡLk 13:24

Jesus Teaches about Fruit in People's Lives (66/Luke 6:43–45)

15"Watch out for false prophets.ᵐ They come to you in sheep's clothing, but inwardly they are ferocious wolves.ⁿ 16By their fruit you will recognize them.ᵒ Do people pick grapes from thornbushes, or figs from thistles? 17Likewise every good tree bears good fruit, but a bad tree bears bad fruit. 18A good tree cannot bear bad fruit, and a bad tree cannot bear good fruit. 19Every tree that does not bear good fruit is cut down and thrown into the fire. 20Thus, by their fruit you will recognize them.

7:15
ᵐMk 13:22;
2Pe 2:1; 1Jn 4:1
ⁿAc 20:29
7:16
ᵒLk 6:44

Jesus Teaches about Building on a Solid Foundation (67/Luke 6:46–49)

21"Not everyone who says to me, 'Lord, Lord,'ᵖ will enter the kingdom of heaven, but only he who does the will of my Father who is in heaven.�q 22Many will say to me on that day, 'Lord, Lord, did we not prophesy in your name, and in your name drive out demons and perform many miracles?' 23Then I will tell them plainly, 'I never knew you. Away from me, you evildoers!'ʳ

7:21
ᵖMt 25:11
qJas 1:22

7:23
ʳPs 6:8;
Lk 13:25-27

7:9, 10 The child in Jesus' example asked his father for bread and fish—good and necessary items. If the child had asked for a poisonous snake, would the wise father have granted his request? Sometimes God knows we are praying for "snakes" and does not give us what we ask for, even though we persist in our prayers. Nor will God give us "stones" or "snakes" instead of what we need. As we learn to know God better as a loving Father, we learn to ask for what is good for us, and then he grants it.

7:11 Christ is showing us the heart of God the Father. God is not selfish, begrudging, or stingy, and we don't have to beg or grovel as we come with our requests. He is a loving Father who understands, cares, and comforts. If humans can be kind, imagine how kind God, the Creator of kindness, can be.

7:11 Jesus used the expression "If you, then, though you are evil" to contrast sinful and fallible human beings with the holy and perfect God.

7:12 This is commonly known as the Golden Rule. In many religions it is stated negatively: "Don't do to others what you don't want done to you." By stating it positively, Jesus made it more significant. It is not very hard to refrain from harming others; it is much more difficult to take the initiative in doing something good for them. The Golden Rule as Jesus formulated it is the foundation of active goodness and mercy—the kind of love God shows to us every day. Think of a good and merciful action you can take today.

7:13, 14 The gate that leads to eternal life (John 10:7–9) is called "narrow." This does not mean that it is difficult to become a Christian, but that there is only one way to live eternally with God and only a few that decide to walk that road. Believing in Jesus is the only way to heaven, because he alone died for our sins and made us right before God. Living his way may not be popular, but it is true and right. Thank God there is one way!

7:15 False prophets were common in Old Testament times. They prophesied only what the king and the people wanted to hear, claiming it was God's message. Jesus indicates that false prophets were just as prevalent in his time. False teachers are just as common today. Jesus says to beware of those

whose words sound religious but who are motivated by money, fame, or power. You can tell who they are because in their teaching they minimize Christ and glorify themselves.

7:20 We should evaluate teachers' words by examining their lives. Just as trees are consistent in the kind of fruit they produce, good teachers consistently exhibit good behavior and high moral character as they attempt to live out the truths of Scripture. This does not mean we should have witch hunts, throwing out church school teachers, pastors, and others who are less than perfect. Every one of us is subject to sin, and we must show the same mercy to others that we need for ourselves. When Jesus talks about bad trees, he means teachers who deliberately teach false doctrine. We must examine the teachers' motives, the direction they are taking, and the results they are seeking.

7:21 Some self-professed athletes can "talk" a great game, but that tells you nothing about their athletic skills. And not everyone who talks about heaven belongs to God's kingdom. Jesus is more concerned about our walk than our talk. He wants us to do right, not just say the right words. What you do cannot be separated from what you believe.

7:21–23 Jesus exposed those people who sounded religious but had no personal relationship with him. On "that day" (the day of judgment), only our relationship with Christ—our acceptance of him as Savior and our obedience to him—will matter. Many people think that if they are "good" people and say religious things, they will be rewarded with eternal life. In reality, faith in Christ is what will count at the judgment.

7:22 "That day" is the final day of reckoning when God will settle all accounts, judging sin and rewarding faith.

24"Therefore everyone who hears these words of mine and puts them into practice is like a wise man who built his house on the rock. 25The rain came down, the streams rose, and the winds blew and beat against that house; yet it did not fall, because it had its foundation on the rock. 26But everyone who hears these words of mine and does not put them into practice is like a foolish man who built his house on sand. 27The rain came down, the streams rose, and the winds blew and beat against that house, and it fell with a great crash."

28When Jesus had finished saying these things, s the crowds were amazed at his teaching, t 29because he taught as one who had authority, and not as their teachers of the law.

7:28
sMt 13:53
tMk 1:22; 6:2;
Lk 4:32

3. Jesus performs many miracles
Jesus Heals a Man with Leprosy (38/Mark 1:40–45; Luke 5:12–16)

8 When he came down from the mountainside, large crowds followed him. 2A man with leprosya came and knelt before him and said, "Lord, if you are willing, you can make me clean."

3Jesus reached out his hand and touched the man. "I am willing," he said. "Be clean!" Immediately he was curedb of his leprosy. 4Then Jesus said to him, "See that you don't tell anyone.u But go, show yourself to the priest and offer the gift Moses commanded,v as a testimony to them."

8:4
uMk 5:43
vLev 14:2-32

A Roman Officer Demonstrates Faith (68/Luke 7:1–10)

5When Jesus had entered Capernaum, a centurion came to him, asking for help. 6"Lord," he said, "my servant lies at home paralyzed and in terrible suffering." 7Jesus said to him, "I will go and heal him."

a2 The Greek word was used for various diseases affecting the skin—not necessarily leprosy.   b3 Greek *made clean*

7:24 To build "on the rock" means to be a hearing, responding disciple, not a phony, superficial one. Practicing obedience becomes the solid foundation to weather the storms of life. See James 1:22–27 for more on putting into practice what we hear.

7:24–27 The two lives Jesus compares at the end of the Sermon on the Mount have several points in common: they both build, they both hear Jesus' teaching, and they both experience the same set of circumstances in life. The difference between them isn't caused by ignorance but by one ignoring what Jesus said. Externally, their lives may look similar; but the lasting, structural differences will be revealed by the storms of life. The immediate differences in your life when you follow Jesus may not be obvious, but eventually they will turn out to affect even

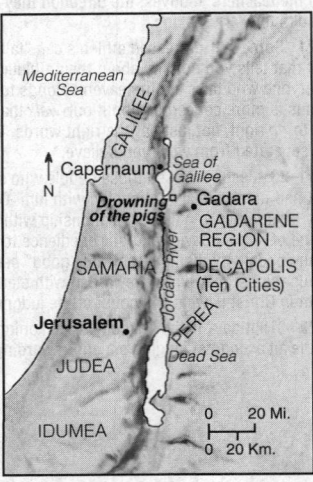

**JESUS'
MIRACULOUS
POWER
DISPLAYED**
Jesus finished the sermon he had given on a hillside near Galilee and returned to Capernaum. As he and his disciples crossed the Sea of Galilee, Jesus calmed a fierce storm. Then, in the Gentile Gadarene region, Jesus commanded demons to come out of two men.

your eternal destiny. To what degree does your life reflect the directions Jesus gave in this sermon?

7:26, 27 Like a house of cards, the fool's life crumbles. Most people do not deliberately seek to build on a false or inferior foundation; instead, they just don't think about their life's purpose. Many people are headed for destruction, not out of stubbornness but out of thoughtlessness. Part of our responsibility as believers is to help others stop and think about where their lives are headed and to point out the consequences of ignoring Christ's message.

7:29 The teachers of the law (religious scholars) often cited traditions and quoted authorities to support their arguments and interpretations. But Jesus spoke with a new authority— his own. He didn't need to quote anyone because he was the original Word (John 1:1).

8:2, 3 Leprosy, like AIDS today, was a terrifying disease because there was no known cure. In Jesus' day, the Greek word for *leprosy* was used for a variety of similar diseases, and some forms were contagious. If a person contracted the contagious type, a priest declared him a leper and banished him from his home and city. The leper was sent to live in a community with other lepers until he either got better or died. Yet when the leper begged Jesus to heal him, Jesus reached out and touched him, even though his skin was covered with the dread disease.

Sin is also an incurable disease—and we all have it. Only Christ's healing touch can miraculously take away our sins and restore us to real living. But first, just like the leper, we must realize our inability to cure ourselves and ask for Christ's saving help.

8:4 The law required a healed leper to be examined by the priest (Leviticus 14). Jesus wanted this man to give his story firsthand to the priest to prove that his leprosy was completely gone so that he could be restored to his community.

8:5, 6 The centurion could have let many obstacles stand between him and Jesus—pride, doubt, money, language, distance, time, self-sufficiency, power, race. But he didn't. If he did not let these barriers block his approach to Jesus, we don't need to either. What keeps you from Christ?

⁸The centurion replied, "Lord, I do not deserve to have you come under my roof. But just say the word, and my servant will be healed. ⁹For I myself am a man under authority, with soldiers under me. I tell this one, 'Go,' and he goes; and that one, 'Come,' and he comes. I say to my servant, 'Do this,' and he does it."

¹⁰When Jesus heard this, he was astonished and said to those following him, "I tell you the truth, I have not found anyone in Israel with such great faith. ¹¹I say to you that many will come from the east and the west,ʷ and will take their places at the feast with Abraham, Isaac and Jacob in the kingdom of heaven.ˣ ¹²But the subjects of the kingdom will be thrown outside, into the darkness, where there will be weeping and gnashing of teeth."ʸ

¹³Then Jesus said to the centurion, "Go! It will be done just as you believed it would." And his servant was healed at that very hour.

Jesus Heals Peter's Mother-in-Law and Many Others (35/Mark 1:29–34; Luke 4:38–41)

¹⁴When Jesus came into Peter's house, he saw Peter's mother-in-law lying in bed with a fever. ¹⁵He touched her hand and the fever left her, and she got up and began to wait on him.

¹⁶When evening came, many who were demon-possessed were brought to him, and he drove out the spirits with a word and healed all the sick. ¹⁷This was to fulfill what was spoken through the prophet Isaiah:

> "He took up our infirmities
> and carried our diseases."ᵃᶻ

Jesus Teaches about the Cost of Following Him (122/Luke 9:51–62)

¹⁸When Jesus saw the crowd around him, he gave orders to cross to the other side of the lake.ᵃ ¹⁹Then a teacher of the law came to him and said, "Teacher, I will follow you wherever you go."

²⁰Jesus replied, "Foxes have holes and birds of the air have nests, but the Son of Man has no place to lay his head."

ᵃ *17* Isaiah 53:4

8:11
ʷIsa 49:12; 59:19;
Mal 1:11
ˣLk 13:29

8:12
ʸMt 13:42, 50;
22:13; 24:51;
25:30; Lk 13:28

8:17
ᶻIsa 53:4

8:18
ᵃMk 4:35

8:8–12 A centurion was a career military officer in the Roman army with control over 100 soldiers. Roman soldiers, of all people, were hated by the Jews for their oppression, control, and ridicule. Yet this man's genuine faith amazed Jesus! This hated Gentile's faith put to shame the stagnant piety of many of the Jewish religious leaders.

8:10–12 Jesus told the crowd that many religious Jews who should be in the kingdom would be excluded because of their lack of faith. Entrenched in their religious traditions, they could not accept Christ and his new message. We must be careful not to become so set in our religious habits that we expect God to work only in specified ways. Don't limit God by your mind-set and lack of faith.

8:11, 12 "The east and the west" stands for the four corners of the earth. All the faithful people of God will be gathered to feast with the Messiah (Isaiah 6; 55). The Jews should have known that when the Messiah came, his blessings would be for Gentiles too (see Isaiah 66:12, 19). But this message came as a shock because they were too wrapped up in their own affairs and destiny. In claiming God's promises, we must not apply them so personally or culturally that we forget to see what God wants to do to reach *all* the people he loves.

8:11, 12 Matthew emphasizes this universal theme—Jesus' message is for everyone. The Old Testament prophets knew this (see Isaiah 56:3, 6–8; 66:12, 19; Malachi 1:11), but many New Testament Jewish leaders chose to ignore it. Each individual has to choose to accept or reject the gospel, and no one can become part of God's kingdom on the basis of heritage or connections. Having a Christian family is a wonderful blessing, but it won't guarantee you eternal life. *You* must believe in and follow Christ.

8:14, 15 Peter's mother-in-law gives us a beautiful example to follow. Her response to Jesus' touch was to wait on Jesus and his disciples—immediately. Has God ever helped you through a dangerous or difficult situation? If so, you should ask, "How can I express my gratitude to him?" Because God has promised us all the rewards of his kingdom, we should look for ways to serve him and his followers now.

8:16, 17 Matthew continues to show Jesus' kingly nature. Through a single touch, Jesus healed (8:3, 15); when he spoke a single word, evil spirits fled his presence (8:16). Jesus has authority over all evil powers and all earthly disease. He also has power and authority to conquer sin. Sickness and evil are consequences of living in a fallen world. But in the future, when God removes all sin, there will be no more sickness and death. Jesus' healing miracles were a taste of what the whole world will one day experience in God's kingdom.

8:19, 20 Following Jesus is not always easy or comfortable. Often it means great cost and sacrifice, with no earthly rewards or security. Jesus didn't have a place to call home. You may find that following Christ costs you popularity, friendships, leisure time, or treasured habits. But while the cost of following Christ is high, the value of being Christ's disciple is even higher. Discipleship is an investment that lasts for eternity and yields incredible rewards.

21Another disciple said to him, "Lord, first let me go and bury my father."
22But Jesus told him, "Follow me, and let the dead bury their own dead."

Jesus Calms the Storm (87/Mark 4:35–41; Luke 8:22–25)

23Then he got into the boat and his disciples followed him. 24Without warning, a furious storm came up on the lake, so that the waves swept over the boat. But Jesus was sleeping. 25The disciples went and woke him, saying, "Lord, save us! We're going to drown!"

26He replied, "You of little faith, why are you so afraid?" Then he got up and rebuked the winds and the waves, and it was completely calm.*b*

27The men were amazed and asked, "What kind of man is this? Even the winds and the waves obey him!"

Jesus Sends Demons into a Herd of Pigs (88/Mark 5:1–20; Luke 8:26–29)

28When he arrived at the other side in the region of the Gadarenes,*a* two demon-possessed men coming from the tombs met him. They were so violent that no one could pass that way. 29"What do you want with us,*c* Son of God?" they shouted. "Have you come here to torture us before the appointed time?"

30Some distance from them a large herd of pigs was feeding. 31The demons begged Jesus, "If you drive us out, send us into the herd of pigs."

32He said to them, "Go!" So they came out and went into the pigs, and the whole herd rushed down the steep bank into the lake and died in the water. 33Those tending the pigs ran off, went into the town and reported all this, including what had happened to the demon-possessed men. 34Then the whole town went out to meet Jesus. And when they saw him, they pleaded with him to leave their region.*d*

a28 Some manuscripts Gergesenes; others Gerasenes

8:26
b Ps 65:7; 89:9;
107:29

8:29
c Jdg 11:12;
2Sa 16:10;
Mk 1:24; Jn 2:4

8:34
d Lk 5:8; Ac 16:39

8:21, 22 It is possible that this disciple was not asking permission to go to his father's funeral, but rather to put off following Jesus until his elderly father died. Perhaps he was the firstborn son and wanted to be sure to claim his inheritance. Perhaps he didn't want to face his father's wrath if he left the family business to follow an itinerant preacher. Whether his concern was financial security, family approval, or something else, he did not want to commit himself to Jesus just yet. Jesus, however, would not accept his excuse.

Jesus was always direct with those who wanted to follow him. He made sure they counted the cost and set aside any conditions they might have for following him. As God's Son, Jesus did not hesitate to demand complete loyalty. Even family loyalty was not to take priority over the demands of obedience. His direct challenge forces us to ask ourselves about our own priorities in following him. The decision to follow Jesus should not be put off, even though other loyalties compete for our attention. Nothing should be placed above a total commitment to living for him.

8:23 The boat used here was probably the kind familiar to many of Jesus' disciples who were fishermen. Josephus, an ancient historian, wrote that there were usually more than 300 fishing boats on the Sea of Galilee at one time. This boat was large enough to hold Jesus and his 12 disciples and was powered both by oars and sails. During a storm, however, the sails were taken down to keep them from ripping and to make the boat easier to control.

8:24 The Sea of Galilee is an unusual body of water. It is relatively small (13 miles long, 7 miles wide), but it is 150 feet deep, and the shoreline is 680 feet below sea level. Sudden storms can appear over the surrounding mountains with little warning, stirring the water into violent 20-foot waves. The disciples had not foolishly set out in a storm. They had been caught without warning, and their danger was great.

8:25 Although the disciples had witnessed many miracles, they panicked in this storm. As experienced sailors, they knew its danger; what they did not know was that Christ could control the forces of nature. There is often a stormy area of our human nature where we feel God can't or won't work. When we truly understand who God is, however, we will realize that he controls both the storms of nature and the storms of the troubled heart. Jesus' power that calmed this storm can also help us deal with

the problems we face. Jesus is willing to help if we only ask him. We should never discount his power even in terrible trials.

8:28 The region of the Gadarenes is located southeast of the Sea of Galilee, near the town of Gadara, one of the most important cities of the region (see map). Gadara was a member of the Decapolis (see the note on Mark 5:20). These ten cities with independent governments were largely inhabited by Gentiles, which explains the herd of pigs (8:30). The Jews did not raise pigs because pigs were considered unclean and thus unfit to eat.

8:28 Demon-possessed people are under the control of one or more demons. Demons are fallen angels who joined Satan in his rebellion against God and are now evil spirits under Satan's control. They help Satan tempt people to sin and have great destructive powers. But whenever they are confronted by Jesus, they lose their power. These demons recognized Jesus as God's Son (8:29), but they didn't think they had to obey him. Just believing is not enough (see James 2:19 for a discussion of belief and devils). Faith is more than belief. By faith, you accept what Jesus has done for you, receive him as the only one who can save you from sin, and live out your faith by obeying his commands.

8:28 Matthew says there were two demon-possessed men, while Mark and Luke refer only to one. Apparently Mark and Luke mention only the man who did the talking.

8:28 According to Jewish ceremonial laws, the men Jesus encountered were unclean in three ways: they were Gentiles (non-Jews), they were demon-possessed, and they lived in a graveyard. Jesus helped them anyway. We should not turn our backs on people who are "unclean" or repulsive to us, or who violate our moral standards and religious beliefs. Instead, we must realize that every human individual is a unique creation of God, needing to be touched by his love.

8:29 The Bible tells us that at the end of the world the devil and his angels will be thrown into the lake of burning sulfur (Revelation 20:10). When the demons asked if Jesus had come to torment them "before the appointed time," they showed they knew their ultimate fate.

8:32 When the demons entered the pigs, they drove the animals into the sea. The demons' action proves their destructive intent—if they could not destroy the men, they would destroy the pigs.

Jesus Heals a Paralyzed Man (39/Mark 2:1–12; Luke 5:17–26)

9:1
e Mt 4:13

9 Jesus stepped into a boat, crossed over and came to his own town. *e* 2 Some men brought to him a paralytic, lying on a mat. When Jesus saw their faith, he said to the paralytic, "Take heart, son; your sins are forgiven."

MATTHEW

More than any other disciple, Matthew had a clear idea of how much it would cost to follow Jesus, yet he did not hesitate a moment. When he left his tax-collecting booth, he guaranteed himself unemployment. For several of the other disciples, there was always fishing to return to, but for Matthew, there was no turning back.

Two changes happened to Matthew when he decided to follow Jesus. First, Jesus gave him a new life. He not only belonged to a new group; he belonged to the Son of God. He was not just accepting a different way of life; he was now an accepted person. For a despised tax collector, that change must have been wonderful! Second, Jesus gave Matthew a new purpose for his skills. When he followed Jesus, the only tool from his past job that he carried with him was his pen. From the beginning, God had made him a record-keeper. Jesus' call eventually allowed him to put his skills to their finest work. Matthew was a keen observer, and he undoubtedly recorded what he saw going on around him. The Gospel that bears his name came as a result.

Matthew's experience points out that each of us, from the beginning, is one of God's works in progress. Much of what God has for us he gives long before we are able to consciously respond to him. He trusts us with skills and abilities ahead of schedule. He has made each of us capable of being his servant. When we trust him with what he has given us, we begin a life of real adventure. Matthew couldn't have known that God would use the very skills he had sharpened as a tax collector to record the greatest story ever lived. And God has no less meaningful a purpose for each one of us. Have you recognized Jesus saying to you, "Follow me"? What has been your response?

Strengths and accomplishments:	• Was one of Jesus' 12 disciples • Responded immediately to Jesus' call • Invited many friends to his home to meet Jesus • Compiled the Gospel of Matthew • Clarified for his Jewish audience Jesus' fulfillment of Old Testament prophecies
Lessons from his life:	• Jesus consistently accepted people from every level of society • Matthew was given a new life, and his God-given skills of record keeping and attention to detail were given new purpose • Having been accepted by Jesus, Matthew immediately tried to bring others into contact with Jesus
Vital statistics:	• Where: Capernaum • Occupations: Tax collector, disciple of Jesus • Relative: Father: Alphaeus • Contemporaries: Jesus, Pilate, Herod Antipas, other disciples
Key verse:	"As he walked along, he saw Levi son of Alphaeus sitting at the tax collector's booth. 'Follow me,' Jesus told him, and Levi got up and followed him" (Mark 2:14).

Matthew's story is told in the Gospels. He is also mentioned in Acts 1:13.

Jesus' action, by contrast, shows the value he places on each human life.

8:34 Why did the people ask Jesus to leave? Unlike their own pagan gods, Jesus could not be contained, controlled, or appeased. They feared Jesus' supernatural power, a power that they had never before witnessed. And they were upset about losing a herd of pigs more than they were glad about the deliverance of the demon-possessed men. Are you more concerned about property and programs than people? Human beings are created in God's image and have eternal value. How foolish and yet how easy it is to value possessions, investments, and even animals above human life. Would you rather have Jesus leave you than finish his work in you?

9:1 "His own town" was Capernaum, a good choice for Jesus' base of operations. It was a wealthy city due to fishing and trade. Situated on the Sea of Galilee in a densely populated area, Capernaum housed the Roman garrison that kept peace in the region. The city was a cultural melting pot, greatly influenced by Greek and Roman manners, dress, architecture, and politics.

9:2 Among the first words Jesus said to the paralyzed man were "Your sins are forgiven." Then he healed the man. We must be careful not to concentrate on God's power to heal physical sickness more than on his power to forgive spiritual sickness in the form of sin. Jesus saw that even more than physical health, this man needed spiritual health. Spiritual health comes only from Jesus' healing touch.

9:2 Both the man's body and his spirit were paralyzed—he could not walk, and he did not know Jesus. But the man's spiritual state was Jesus' first concern. If God does not heal us or someone we love, we need to remember that physical healing is not Christ's only concern. We will all be completely healed in Christ's coming kingdom; but first we have to come to know Jesus.

3At this, some of the teachers of the law said to themselves, "This fellow is blaspheming!"

4Knowing their thoughts,[f] Jesus said, "Why do you entertain evil thoughts in your hearts? 5Which is easier: to say, 'Your sins are forgiven,' or to say, 'Get up and walk'? 6But so that you may know that the Son of Man has authority on earth to forgive sins. . ." Then he said to the paralytic, "Get up, take your mat and go home." 7And the man got up and went home. 8When the crowd saw this, they were filled with awe; and they praised God,[g] who had given such authority to men.

Jesus Eats with Sinners at Matthew's House (40/Mark 2:13–17; Luke 5:27–32)

9As Jesus went on from there, he saw a man named Matthew sitting at the tax collector's booth. **"Follow me,"** he told him, and Matthew got up and followed him.

10While Jesus was having dinner at Matthew's house, many tax collectors and "sinners" came and ate with him and his disciples. 11When the Pharisees saw this, they asked his disciples, "Why does your teacher eat with tax collectors and 'sinners'?"[h]

12On hearing this, Jesus said, "It is not the healthy who need a doctor, but the sick. 13But go and learn what this means: 'I desire mercy, not sacrifice.'[a][i] For I have not come to call the righteous, but sinners."[j]

Religious Leaders Ask Jesus about Fasting (41/Mark 2:18–22; Luke 5:33–39)

14Then John's disciples came and asked him, "How is it that we and the Pharisees fast,[k] but your disciples do not fast?"

15Jesus answered, "How can the guests of the bridegroom mourn while he is with them?[l] The time will come when the bridegroom will be taken from them; then they will fast.[m]

16"No one sews a patch of unshrunk cloth on an old garment, for the patch will pull away from the garment, making the tear worse. 17Neither do men pour new wine into old wineskins. If they do, the skins will burst, the wine will run out and the wineskins will be ruined. No, they pour new wine into new wineskins, and both are preserved."

a 13 Hosea 6:6

9:4 /Mt 12:25; Lk 6:8; 9:47; 11:17

9:8 gMt 5:16; Ac 4:21

9:11 hMt 11:19

9:13 iHos 6:6; Mt 12:7 /1Ti 1:15

9:14 kLk 18:12

9:15 /Jn 3:29 mAc 13:2, 3

9:3 Blaspheming is claiming to be God and applying his characteristics to yourself. The religious leaders rightly saw that Jesus was claiming to be God. What they did not understand was that he *is* God and thus has the authority to heal and to forgive sins.

9:5, 6 It's easy to tell someone his sins are forgiven; it's a lot more difficult to reverse a case of paralysis! Jesus backed up his words by healing the man's legs. Jesus' action showed that his words were true; he had the power to forgive as well as to heal. Talk is cheap, but our words lack meaning if our actions do not back them up. We can say we love God or others, but if we are not taking practical steps to demonstrate that love, our words are empty and meaningless. How well do your actions back up what you say?

9:9 Matthew was a Jew who was appointed by the Romans to be the area's tax collector. He collected taxes from the citizens as well as from merchants passing through town. Tax collectors were expected to take a commission on the taxes they collected, but most of them overcharged and kept the profits. Thus, tax collectors were hated by the Jews because of their reputation for cheating and because of their support of Rome.

9:9 When Jesus called Matthew to be one of his disciples, Matthew got up and followed, leaving a lucrative career. When God calls you to follow or obey him, do you do it with as much abandon as Matthew? Sometimes the decision to follow Christ requires difficult or painful choices. Like Matthew, we must decide to leave behind those things that would keep us from following Christ.

9:10–13 When he visited Matthew, Jesus hurt his own reputation among the religious elites in order to reach out to those who were lost. Matthew's reputation hadn't yet caught up with his new life as a disciple, but he became a bridge for Jesus' message to Matthew's past associates. We should not be afraid to reach out to people who are living in sin. God's message changes people—and their friends, too!

9:11, 12 The Pharisees constantly tried to trap Jesus, and they thought his association with these "lowlifes" was the perfect opportunity. They were more concerned with their own appearance of holiness than with helping people, with criticism than encouragement, with outward respectability than practical help. But God is concerned for all people, including the sinful and hurting ones. The Christian life is not a popularity contest! Following Jesus' example, we should share the gospel with the poor, immoral, lonely, and outcast, not just the rich, moral, popular, and powerful.

9:13 Those who are sure that they are righteous can't be saved because the first step in following Jesus is acknowledging our need and admitting that we don't have all the answers. For more on "I desire mercy, not sacrifice," see the chart in Hosea 7, p. 1403.

9:14 John's disciples fasted (went without food) as a sign of mourning for sin and to prepare for the Messiah's coming. Jesus' disciples did not need to fast because he is the Messiah and was with them! Jesus did not condemn fasting—he himself fasted (4:2). He emphasized that fasting must be done for the right reasons.

9:14 John the Baptist's message was harsh, and it focused on law. When people look at God's law and compare themselves to it, they realize how far they fall short and how badly they need to repent. Jesus' message focused on life, the result of turning from sin and turning to him. John's disciples had the right start, but they needed to take the next step and trust in Jesus. Where is your focus—on law or on Christ?

9:15 The arrival of the kingdom of heaven was like a wedding feast with Jesus as the bridegroom. His disciples, therefore, were filled with joy. It would not be right to mourn or fast when the bridegroom was present.

9:17 In Bible times, wine was not kept in glass bottles but in goatskins sewn around the edges to form watertight bags. New wine expanded as it fermented, stretching its wineskin. After the wine had aged, the stretched skin would burst if more new wine was poured into it. New wine, therefore, was always put into new wineskins.

Jesus used this description to explain that he had not come

Jesus Heals a Bleeding Woman and Restores a Girl to Life
(89/Mark 5:21–43; Luke 8:40–56)

9:20
n Mt 14:36

18While he was saying this, a ruler came and knelt before him and said, "My daughter has just died. But come and put your hand on her, and she will live." 19Jesus got up and went with him, and so did his disciples.

9:22
o Lk 7:50; 17:19; 18:42
p Mt 15:28

20Just then a woman who had been subject to bleeding for twelve years came up behind him and touched the edge of his cloak.*n* 21She said to herself, "If I only touch his cloak, I will be healed."

22Jesus turned and saw her. "Take heart, daughter," he said, "your faith has healed you."*o* And the woman was healed from that moment.*p*

9:23
q 2Ch 35:25

9:24
r Ac 20:10
s Jn 11:11-14

23When Jesus entered the ruler's house and saw the flute players and the noisy crowd,*q* 24he said, "Go away. The girl is not dead*r* but asleep."*s* But they laughed at him. 25After the crowd had been put outside, he went in and took the girl by the hand, and she got up. 26News of this spread through all that region.

Jesus Heals the Blind and Mute (90)

9:27
t Mt 15:22; Mk 10:47

27As Jesus went on from there, two blind men followed him, calling out, "Have mercy on us, Son of David!"*t*

28When he had gone indoors, the blind men came to him, and he asked them, "Do you believe that I am able to do this?"

"Yes, Lord," they replied.

9:30
u Mt 8:4

9:31
v Mk 7:36

29Then he touched their eyes and said, "According to your faith will it be done to you"; 30and their sight was restored. Jesus warned them sternly, "See that no one knows about this."*u* 31But they went out and spread the news about him all over that region.*v*

---

to patch up the old religious system of Judaism with its rules and traditions. His purpose was to bring in something new, though it had been prophesied for centuries. This new message, the gospel, said that Jesus Christ, God's Son, came to earth to offer all people forgiveness of sins and reconciliation with God. The gospel did not fit into the old rigid legalistic system of religion. It needed a fresh start. The message will always remain "new" because it must be accepted and applied in every generation. When we follow Christ, we must be prepared for new ways to live, new ways to look at people, and new ways to serve.

9:18 Mark and Luke say this man's name was Jairus (Mark 5:22; Luke 8:41). As ruler of the synagogue, Jairus was responsible for administration—looking after the building, supervising worship, running the school on weekdays, and finding rabbis to teach on the Sabbath. For more information on synagogues, read the note on Mark 1:21, 22.

9:20–22 This woman had suffered for 12 years with bleeding (perhaps a menstrual disorder). In our times of desperation, we don't have to worry about the correct way to reach out to God. Like this woman, we can simply reach out in faith. He will respond.

9:22 God changed a situation that had been a problem for years. Like the leper and the demon-possessed men (see the notes on 8:2, 3 and the second note on 8:28), this diseased woman was considered unclean. For 12 years, she too had been one of the "untouchables" and had not been able to lead a normal life. But Jesus changed that and restored her. Sometimes we are tempted to give up on people or situations that have not changed for many years. God can change what seems unchangeable, giving new purpose and hope.

9:23–26 The synagogue ruler didn't come to Jesus until his daughter was dead—it was too late for anyone else to help. But Jesus simply went to the girl and raised her! In our lives, Christ can make a difference when it seems too late for anyone else to help. He can bring healing to broken relationships, release from addicting habits, and forgiveness and healing to emotional scars. If your situation looks hopeless, remember that Christ can do the impossible.

9:27 "Son of David" was a popular way of addressing Jesus as the Messiah because it was known that the Messiah would be a descendant of David (Isaiah 9:7). This is the first time the title is used in Matthew. Jesus' ability to give sight to the blind was prophesied in Isaiah 29:18; 35:5; 42:7.

9:27–30 Jesus didn't respond immediately to the blind men's pleas. He waited to see if they had faith. Not everyone who says he wants help really believes God can help him. Jesus may have waited and questioned these men to emphasize and increase their faith. When you think that God is too slow in answering your prayers, consider that he might be testing you as he did the blind men. Do you believe that God can help you? Do you *really* want his help?

9:28 These blind men were persistent. They went right into the house where Jesus was staying. They knew Jesus could heal them, and they would let nothing stop them from finding him. That's real faith in action. If you believe Jesus is the answer to your every need, don't let anyone or anything stop you from reaching him.

9:30 Jesus told the people to keep quiet about his healings because he did not want to be known only as a miracle worker. He healed because he had compassion on people, but he also wanted to bring *spiritual* healing to a sin-sick world.

32 While they were going out, a man who was demon-possessed and could not talk^w was brought to Jesus. 33 And when the demon was driven out, the man who had been mute spoke. The crowd was amazed and said, "Nothing like this has ever been seen in Israel."

34 But the Pharisees said, "It is by the prince of demons that he drives out demons."^x

9:32
w Mt 12:22-24

9:34
x Mt 12:24; Lk 11:15

Jesus Urges the Disciples to Pray for Workers (92)

35 Jesus went through all the towns and villages, teaching in their synagogues, preaching the good news of the kingdom and healing every disease and sickness. 36 When he saw the crowds, he had compassion on them, because they were harassed and helpless, like sheep without a shepherd. 37 Then he said to his disciples, "The harvest is plentiful but the workers are few.^y 38 Ask the Lord of the harvest, therefore, to send out workers into his harvest field."

9:37
y Lk 10:2

Jesus Sends Out the Twelve Disciples (93/Mark 6:7–13; Luke 9:1–6)

10 He called his twelve disciples to him and gave them authority to drive out evil^a spirits^z and to heal every disease and sickness.

2 These are the names of the twelve apostles: first, Simon (who is called Peter) and his brother Andrew; James son of Zebedee, and his brother John; 3 Philip and Bartholomew; Thomas and Matthew the tax collector; James son of Alphaeus, and Thaddaeus; 4 Simon the Zealot and Judas Iscariot, who betrayed him.^a

5 These twelve Jesus sent out with the following instructions: "Do not go among the Gentiles or enter any town of the Samaritans.^b 6 Go rather to the lost sheep of Israel.^c 7 As you go, preach this message: 'The kingdom of heaven^d is near.' 8 Heal the sick, raise the dead, cleanse those who have leprosy,^b drive out demons. Freely you have received, freely give. 9 Do not take along any gold or silver or copper in your belts; 10 take no bag for the journey, or extra tunic, or sandals or a staff; for the worker is worth his keep.^e

10:1
z Mk 3:13-15

10:4
a Jn 13:2, 26, 27

10:5
b Lk 9:52

10:6
c Mt 15:24

10:7
d Mt 3:2

10:10
e 1 Ti 5:18

^a1 Greek *unclean*   ^b8 The Greek word was used for various diseases affecting the skin—not necessarily leprosy.

9:32 While Jesus was on earth, demonic forces were especially active. Although we cannot always be sure why or how demon-possession occurs, it causes both physical and mental problems. In this case, the demon made the man unable to talk. For more on demons and demon-possession, read the notes on 8:28 and Mark 1:23.

9:34 In chapter 9, the Pharisees accuse Jesus of four different sins: blasphemy, befriending outcasts, impiety, and serving Satan. Matthew shows how Jesus was maligned by those who should have received him most gladly. Why did the Pharisees do this? (1) Jesus bypassed their religious authority. (2) He weakened their control over the people. (3) He challenged their cherished beliefs. (4) He exposed their insincere motives.

While the Pharisees questioned, debated, and dissected Jesus, people were being healed and lives changed right in front of them. Their skepticism was based not on insufficient evidence but on jealousy of Jesus' popularity.

9:36 Jesus was overwhelmed with compassionate pity for the people. His response echoes the deep inner mercy of God, often described in the Old Testament. Ezekiel also compared Israel to sheep without a shepherd (Ezekiel 34:5, 6). Jesus came to be the Shepherd, the One who could show people how to avoid life's pitfalls (see John 10:14).

9:37, 38 Jesus looked at the crowds following him and referred to them as a field ripe for harvest. Many people are ready to give their lives to Christ if someone would show them how. Jesus commands us to pray that people will respond to this need for workers. Often, when we pray for something, God answers our prayers by using *us*. Be prepared for God to use you to show another person the way to him.

10:1 Jesus *called* his 12 disciples. He didn't draft them, force them, or ask them to volunteer; he chose them to serve him in a special way. Christ calls us today. He doesn't twist our arms and make us do something we don't want to do. We can choose to join him or remain behind. When Christ calls you to follow him, how do you respond?

10:2–4 The list of Jesus' 12 disciples doesn't give us many details—probably because there weren't many impressive details

to tell. Jesus called people from all walks of life—fishermen, political activists, tax collectors. He called common people and uncommon leaders; rich and poor; educated and uneducated. Today, many people think only certain people are fit to follow Christ, but this was not the attitude of the Master himself. God can use anyone, no matter how insignificant he or she appears. When you feel small and useless, remember that God uses ordinary people to do his extraordinary work.

10:3 Bartholomew is probably another name for Nathanael, whom we meet in John 1:45–51. Thaddaeus is also known as Judas son of James. The disciples are also listed in Mark 3:16–19; Luke 6:14–16; and Acts 1:13.

10:4 Simon the Zealot may have been a member of the Zealots, a radical political party working for the violent overthrow of Roman rule in Israel.

10:5, 6 Why didn't Jesus send the disciples to the Gentiles or the Samaritans? A Gentile is anyone who is not a Jew. The Samaritans were a race that resulted from intermarriage between Jews and Gentiles after the Old Testament captivities (see 2 Kings 17:24). Jesus asked his disciples to go only to the Jews because he came *first* to the Jews (Romans 1:16). God chose them to tell the rest of the world about him. Jewish disciples and apostles preached the gospel of the risen Christ all around the Roman empire, and soon Gentiles were pouring into the church. The Bible clearly teaches that God's message of salvation is for *all* people, regardless of race, sex, or national origin (Genesis 12:3; Isaiah 25:6; 56:3–7; Malachi 1:11; Acts 10:34, 35; Romans 3:29, 30; Galatians 3:28).

10:7 The Jews were waiting for the Messiah to usher in his kingdom. They hoped for a political and military kingdom that would free them from Roman rule and bring back the days of glory under David and Solomon. But Jesus was talking about a spiritual kingdom. The gospel today is that the kingdom is still *near*. Jesus, the Messiah, has already begun his kingdom on earth in the hearts of his followers. One day the kingdom will be fully realized. Then evil will be destroyed and all people will live in peace with one another.

10:8 Jesus gave the disciples a principle to guide their actions as

11 "Whatever town or village you enter, search for some worthy person there and stay at his house until you leave. 12 As you enter the home, give it your greeting. 13 If the home is deserving, let your peace rest on it; if it is not, let your peace return to you. 14 If anyone will not welcome you or listen to your words, shake the dust off your feet*f* when you leave that home or town. 15 I tell you the truth, it will be more bearable for Sodom and Gomorrah on the day of judgment than for that town.*g* 16 I am sending you out like sheep among wolves.*h* Therefore be as shrewd as snakes and as innocent as doves.*i*

10:14
*f*Ac 13:51

10:15
*g*Mt 11:22, 24

10:16
*h*Lk 10:3
*i*Ro 16:19

Jesus Prepares the Disciples for Persecution (94)

17 "Be on your guard against men; they will hand you over to the local councils and flog you in their synagogues.*j* 18 On my account you will be brought before governors and kings as witnesses to them and to the Gentiles. 19 But when they arrest you, do not worry about what to say or how to say it. At that time you will be given what to say, 20 for it will not be you speaking, but the Spirit of your Father speaking through you.

10:17
*j*Mk 13:9

21 "Brother will betray brother to death, and a father his child; children will rebel against their parents*k* and have them put to death. 22 All men will hate you because of me, but he who stands firm to the end will be saved. 23 When you are persecuted in one place, flee to another. I tell you the truth, you will not finish going through the cities of Israel before the Son of Man comes.

10:21
*k*Mic 7:6

COUNTING THE COST OF FOLLOWING CHRIST	Who may oppose us?	Natural response	Possible pressures	Needed truth
	GOVERNMENT 10:18–19		Threats 10:26	→ The truth will be revealed (10:26)
			Physical harm 10:28	→ Our soul cannot be harmed (10:28)
	RELIGIOUS PEOPLE 10:17	Fear and worry	Public ridicule 10:22	→ God himself will acknowledge us if we acknowledge him (10:32)
	FAMILY 10:21		Rejection by loved ones 10:34–37	→ God's love can sustain us (10:31)

Jesus helped his disciples prepare for the rejection many of them would experience by being Christians. Being God's person will usually create reactions from others who are resisting him.

they ministered to others: "Freely you have received, freely give." Because God has showered us with his blessings, we should give generously to others of our time, love, and possessions.

10:10 Jesus said that those who minister are to be cared for. The disciples could expect food and shelter in return for the spiritual service they provided. Who ministers to you? Make sure you take care of the pastors, missionaries, and teachers who serve God by serving you (see 1 Corinthians 9:9, 10; 1 Timothy 5:17).

10:10 Mark's account (6:8) says to take a staff (walking stick), and Matthew and Luke (9:3) say not to. Jesus may have meant that they were not to take an *extra* pair of sandals, staff, and bag. In any case, the principle was that they were to go out ready for duty and travel, unencumbered by excess material goods.

10:14 Why did Jesus tell his disciples to shake the dust off their feet if a city or home didn't welcome them? When leaving Gentile cities, pious Jews often shook the dust from their feet to show their separation from Gentile practices. If the disciples shook the dust of a *Jewish* town from their feet, it would show their separation from Jews who rejected their Messiah. This gesture was to show the people that they were making a wrong choice—that the opportunity to choose Christ might not present itself again. Are you receptive to teaching from God? If you ignore the Spirit's prompting, you may not get another chance.

10:15 The cities of Sodom and Gomorrah were destroyed by fire from heaven because of their wickedness (Genesis 19:24, 25). Those who reject the gospel when they hear it will be worse off than the wicked people of these destroyed cities, who never heard the gospel at all.

10:16 The opposition of the Pharisees would be like ravaging wolves. The disciples' only hope would be to look to their Shepherd for protection. We may face similar hostility. Like the disciples, we are not to be sheeplike in our attitude but sensible and prudent. We are not to be gullible pawns but neither are we to be deceitful connivers. We must find a balance between wisdom and vulnerability to accomplish God's work.

10:17, 18 Later the disciples experienced these hardships (Acts 5:40; 12:1–3), not only from without (governments, courts), but also from within (friends, family; 10:21). Living for God often brings on persecution, but with it comes the opportunity to tell the good news of salvation. In times of persecution, we can be confident because Jesus has "overcome the world" (John 16:33). And those who stand firm to the end will be saved (10:22).

10:19, 20 Jesus told the disciples that when arrested for preaching the gospel, they should not worry about what to say in their defense—God's Spirit would speak through them. This promise was fulfilled in Acts 4:8–14 and elsewhere. Some mistakenly think this means we don't have to prepare to present the gospel because God will take care of everything. Scripture teaches, however, that we are to make carefully prepared, thoughtful statements (Colossians 4:6). Jesus is not telling us to stop preparing but to stop worrying.

10:22 Standing firm to the end is not a way to be saved but the evidence that a person is really committed to Jesus. Persistence is not a means to earn salvation; it is the by-product of a truly devoted life.

24"A student is not above his teacher, nor a servant above his master. [l] 25 It is enough for the student to be like his teacher, and the servant like his master. If the head of the house has been called Beelzebub,[a][m] how much more the members of his household!

26"So do not be afraid of them. There is nothing concealed that will not be disclosed, or hidden that will not be made known. [n] 27 What I tell you in the dark, speak in the daylight; what is whispered in your ear, proclaim from the roofs. 28 Do not be afraid of those who kill the body but cannot kill the soul. Rather, be afraid of the One [o] who can destroy both soul and body in hell. 29 Are not two sparrows sold for a penny[b]? Yet not one of them will fall to the ground apart from the will of your Father. 30 And even the very hairs of your head are all numbered. [p] 31 So don't be afraid; you are worth more than many sparrows.

32"Whoever acknowledges me before men, [q] I will also acknowledge him before my Father in heaven. 33 But whoever disowns me before men, I will disown him before my Father in heaven.

34"Do not suppose that I have come to bring peace to the earth. I did not come to bring peace, but a sword. 35 For I have come to turn

> "'a man against his father,
>   a daughter against her mother,
>   a daughter-in-law against her mother-in-law—
> 36   a man's enemies will be the members of his own household.'[c][r]

37"Anyone who loves his father or mother more than me is not worthy of me; anyone who loves his son or daughter more than me is not worthy of me; [s] 38 and anyone who does not take his cross and follow me is not worthy of me. 39 Whoever finds his life will lose it, and whoever loses his life for my sake will find it. [t]

40"He who receives you receives me, [u] and he who receives me receives the one who sent me. [v] 41 Anyone who receives a prophet because he is a prophet will receive a prophet's reward, and anyone who receives a righteous man because he is a righteous man will receive a righteous man's reward. 42 And if anyone gives even a cup of cold water to one of these little ones because he is my disciple, I tell you the truth, he will certainly not lose his reward." [w]

a25 Greek Beezeboul or Beelzeboul   b29 Greek an assarion   c36 Micah 7:6

10:24
[l]Lk 6:40; Jn 13:16; 15:20

10:25
[m]Mk 3:22

10:26
[n]Mk 4:22; Lk 8:17

10:28
[o]Heb 10:31

10:30
[p]Lk 21:18; Ac 27:34

10:32
[q]Ro 10:9

10:36
[r]Mic 7:6

10:37
[s]Lk 14:26

10:39
[t]Jn 12:25

10:40
[u]Gal 4:14
[v]Lk 9:48; Jn 12:44

10:42
[w]Mt 25:40; Heb 6:10

10:25 Beelzebub was also known as the lord of flies and the prince of demons. The Pharisees accused Jesus of using Beelzebub's power to drive out demons (see 12:24). Good is sometimes labeled evil. If Jesus, who is perfect, was called evil, his followers should expect that similar accusations will be directed at them. But those who stand firm will be vindicated (10:22).

10:29-31 Jesus said that God is aware of everything that happens even to sparrows, and you are far more valuable to him than they are. You are so valuable that God sent his only Son to die for you (John 3:16). Because God places such value on you, you need never fear personal threats or difficult trials. These can't shake God's love or dislodge his Spirit from within you.

This doesn't mean, however, that God will take away all your troubles (see 10:16). The real test of value is how well something holds up under the wear, tear, and abuse of everyday life. Those who stand up for Christ in spite of their troubles truly have lasting value and will receive great rewards (see 5:11, 12).

10:32 Anyone who acknowledges Jesus Christ (that is, publicly confesses faith in or declares allegiance to him) will be acknowledged by Christ before his Father in heaven. Jesus' followers would face earthly courts of law where they would have to publicly claim to belong to Jesus Christ, usually at their peril (10:17-25). Genuine discipleship always involves acknowledging Jesus Christ, whether or not we face pressure and persecution.

10:34 Jesus did not come to bring the kind of peace that glosses over deep differences just for the sake of superficial harmony. Conflict and disagreement will arise between those who choose to follow Christ and those who don't. Yet we can look forward to the day when all conflict will be resolved. For more on Jesus as peacemaker, see Isaiah 9:6; Matthew 5:9; John 14:27.

10:34-39 Christian commitment may separate friends and loved ones. In saying this, Jesus was not encouraging disobedience to parents or conflict at home. Rather, he was showing that his presence demands a decision. Because some will follow Christ and some won't, conflict will inevitably arise. As we take our cross and follow him, our different values, morals, goals, and purposes will set us apart from others. Christ calls us to a higher mission than to find comfort and tranquility in this life. Love of family is a law of God, but even this love can be self-serving and used as an excuse not to serve God or do his work. Don't neglect your family, but remember that your commitment to God is even more important. God should be your first priority.

10:38 To take our cross and follow Jesus means to be willing to publicly identify with him, to experience almost certain opposition, and to be committed to face even suffering and death for his sake.

10:39 This verse is a positive and negative statement of the same truth: clinging to this life may cause us to forfeit the best from Christ in this world *and* in the next. The more we love this life's rewards (leisure, power, popularity, financial security), the more we will discover how empty they really are. The best way to enjoy life, therefore, is to loosen our greedy grasp on earthly rewards so that we can be free to follow Christ. In doing so, we will inherit eternal life and begin at once to experience the benefits of following Christ.

10:42 How much we love God can be measured by how well we treat others. Jesus' example of giving a cup of cold water to a thirsty child is a good model of unselfish service. A child usually can't or won't return a favor. God notices every good deed we do or don't do as if he were the one receiving it. Is there something unselfish you can do for someone else today? Although no one else may see you, God will notice.

4. Jesus teaches about the kingdom
Jesus Eases John's Doubt (70/Luke 7:18–35)

11

After Jesus had finished instructing his twelve disciples, he went on from there to teach and preach in the towns of Galilee.[a]

11:2
ˣMt 14:3

2 When John heard in prison[x] what Christ was doing, he sent his disciples 3 to ask him, "Are you the one who was to come, or should we expect someone else?"

11:5
ʸIsa 35:4-6; 61:1;
Lk 4:18, 19

4 Jesus replied, "Go back and report to John what you hear and see: 5 The blind receive sight, the lame walk, those who have leprosy[b] are cured, the deaf hear, the dead are raised, and the good news is preached to the poor.[y] 6 Blessed is the man who does not fall away on account of me."

11:7
ᶻMt 3:1

7 As John's[z] disciples were leaving, Jesus began to speak to the crowd about John: "What did you go out into the desert to see? A reed swayed by the wind? 8 If not, what did you go out to see? A man dressed in fine clothes? No, those who wear fine clothes are in kings' palaces.

11:9
ᵃLk 1:76

9 Then what did you go out to see? A prophet?[a] Yes, I tell you, and more than a prophet. 10 This is the one about whom it is written:

11:10
ᵇMal 3:1; Mk 1:2

> "'I will send my messenger ahead of you,
> who will prepare your way before you.'[cb]

11 I tell you the truth: Among those born of women there has not risen anyone greater than John the Baptist; yet he who is least in the kingdom of heaven is greater than he. 12 From the days of John the Baptist until now, the kingdom of heaven has been forcefully advancing, and forceful men lay hold of it. 13 For all the Prophets and the Law prophesied until John.

11:14
ᶜMal 4:5; Lk 1:17

14 And if you are willing to accept it, he is the Elijah who was to come.[c] 15 He who has ears, let him hear.[d]

11:15
ᵈMt 13:9, 43

16 "To what can I compare this generation? They are like children sitting in the market-places and calling out to others:

> 17 "'We played the flute for you,
> and you did not dance;
> we sang a dirge,
> and you did not mourn.'

11:19
ᵉMt 9:11

18 For John came neither eating nor drinking, and they say, 'He has a demon.' 19 The Son of Man came eating and drinking, and they say, 'Here is a glutton and a drunkard, a friend of tax collectors and "sinners."'[e] But wisdom is proved right by her actions."

a 1 Greek *in their towns*   b 5 The Greek word was used for various diseases affecting the skin—not necessarily leprosy.   c 10 Mal. 3:1

11:2, 3 John had been put in prison by Herod. Herod had married his own sister-in-law, and John publicly rebuked Herod's flagrant sin (14:3–5). John's Profile is found in John 1, p. 1737. Herod's Profile is found in Mark 6, p. 1621.

11:4–6 As John sat in prison, he began to have some doubts about whether Jesus really was the Messiah. If John's purpose was to prepare people for the coming Messiah (3:3), and if Jesus really was that Messiah, then why was John in prison when he could have been preaching to the crowds, preparing their hearts?

Jesus answered John's doubts by pointing to the acts of healing the blind, lame, and deaf, curing the lepers, raising the dead, and preaching the good news to the poor. With so much evidence, Jesus' identity was obvious. If you sometimes doubt your salvation, the forgiveness of your sins, or God's work in your life, look at the evidence in Scripture and the changes in your life. When you doubt, don't turn away from Christ; turn *to* him.

11:11 No man ever fulfilled his God-given purpose better than John. Yet in God's coming kingdom all members will have a greater spiritual heritage than John because they will have seen and known Christ and his finished work on the cross.

11:12 There are three common views about the meaning of this verse. (1) Jesus may have been referring to a vast movement toward God, the momentum that began with John's preaching. (2) He may have been reflecting the Jewish activists' expecta-

tion that God's kingdom would come through a violent overthrow of Rome. (3) Or he may have meant that entering God's kingdom takes courage, unwavering faith, determination, and endurance because of the growing opposition leveled at Jesus' followers. In any case, Jesus was pointing out that John's ministry had ushered in the kingdom of heaven.

11:14 John was not a resurrected Elijah, but he took on Elijah's prophetic role—boldly confronting sin and pointing people to God (Malachi 3:1). See Elijah's Profile in 1 Kings 18, p. 527.

11:16–19 Jesus condemned the attitude of his generation. No matter what he said or did, they took the opposite view. They were cynical and skeptical because he challenged their comfortable, secure, and self-centered lives. Too often we justify our inconsistencies because listening to God may require us to change the way we live.

Jesus Promises Rest for the Soul (71)

20Then Jesus began to denounce the cities in which most of his miracles had been performed, because they did not repent. 21"Woe to you, Korazin! Woe to you, Bethsaida! If the miracles that were performed in you had been performed in Tyre and Sidon, they would have repented long ago in sackcloth and ashes.f 22But I tell you, it will be more bearable for Tyre and Sidon on the day of judgment than for you.g 23And you, Capernaum, will you be lifted up to the skies? No, you will go down to the depths.a h If the miracles that were performed in you had been performed in Sodom, it would have remained to this day. 24But I tell you that it will be more bearable for Sodom on the day of judgment than for you."i

25At that time Jesus said,"I praise you, Father, Lord of heaven and earth, because you have hidden these things from the wise and learned, and revealed them to little children. 26Yes, Father, for this was your good pleasure.

27"All things have been committed to mej by my Father.k No one knows the Son except the Father, and no one knows the Father except the Son and those to whom the Son chooses to reveal him.

28"Come to me,l all you who are weary and burdened, and I will give you rest. 29Take my yoke upon you and learn from me,m for I am gentle and humble in heart, and you will find rest for your souls.n 30For my yoke is easy and my burden is light."

The Disciples Pick Wheat on the Sabbath (45/Mark 2:23–28; Luke 6:1–5)

12 At that time Jesus went through the grainfields on the Sabbath. His disciples were hungry and began to pick some heads of graino and eat them. 2When the Pharisees saw this, they said to him,"Look! Your disciples are doing what is unlawful on the Sabbath."p

3He answered,"Haven't you read what David did when he and his companions were hungry? q 4He entered the house of God, and he and his companions ate the consecrated bread—which was not lawful for them to do, but only for the priests. 5Or haven't you read in

a23 Greek Hades

11:21
f Jnh 3:5-9
11:22
g ver 24; Mt 10:15
11:23
h Isa 14:13-15
11:24
i Mt 10:15

11:27
j Mt 28:18
k Jn 3:35
11:28
l Jn 7:37
11:29
m Jn 13:15; Php 2:5; 1Pe 2:21; 1Jn 2:6
n Jer 6:16

12:1
o Dt 23:25
12:2
p ver 10; Lk 13:14; 14:3; Jn 5:10; 9:16
12:3
q 1Sa 21:6

11:21–24 Tyre, Sidon, and Sodom were ancient cities with a long-standing reputation for wickedness (Genesis 18; 19; Ezekiel 27; 28). Each was destroyed by God for its evil. The people of Bethsaida, Korazin, and Capernaum saw Jesus firsthand, and yet they stubbornly refused to repent of their sins and believe in him. Jesus said that if some of the wickedest cities in the world had seen him, they would have repented. Because Bethsaida, Korazin, and Capernaum saw Jesus and didn't believe, they would suffer even greater punishment than that of the wicked cities who didn't see Jesus. Similarly, nations and cities with churches on every corner and Bibles in every home will have no excuse on judgment day if they do not repent and believe.

11:25 Jesus mentioned two kinds of people in his prayer: the "wise"—arrogant in their own knowledge—and the "little children"—humbly open to receive the truth of God's Word. Are you wise in your own eyes, or do you seek the truth in childlike faith, realizing that only God holds all the answers?

11:27 In the Old Testament, "know" means more than knowledge. It implies an intimate relationship. The communion between God the Father and God the Son is the core of their relationship. For anyone else to know God, God must reveal himself to that person, by the Son's choice. How fortunate we are that Jesus has clearly revealed to us God, his truth, and how we can know him.

11:28–30 A yoke is a heavy wooden harness that fits over the shoulders of an ox or oxen. It is attached to a piece of equipment the oxen are to pull. A person may be carrying heavy burdens of (1) sin, (2) excessive demands of religious leaders (23:4; Acts 15:10), (3) oppression and persecution, or (4) weariness in the search for God.

Jesus frees people from all these burdens. The rest that Jesus promises is love, healing, and peace with God, not the end of all labor. A relationship with God changes meaningless, wearisome toil into spiritual productivity and purpose.

11:30 In what sense was Jesus' yoke easy? The yoke emphasizes the challenges, work, and difficulties of partnering with Christ in life. Responsibilities weigh us down, even the effort of

staying true to God. But Jesus' yoke remains easy compared to the crushing alternative.

Jesus doesn't offer a life of luxurious ease—the yoke is still an oxen's tool for working hard. But it's a shared yoke, with weight falling on bigger shoulders than yours. Someone with more pulling power is up front helping. Suddenly you are participating in life's responsibilities with a great Partner—and now that frown can turn into a smile, and that gripe into a song.

12:1, 2 The Pharisees had established 39 categories of actions forbidden on the Sabbath, based on interpretations of God's law and on Jewish custom. Harvesting was one of those forbidden actions. By picking wheat and rubbing it in their hands, the disciples were technically harvesting, according to the religious leaders. Jesus and the disciples were picking grain because they were hungry, not because they wanted to harvest the grain for a profit. They were not working on the Sabbath. The Pharisees, however, could not (and did not want to) see beyond their law's technicalities. They had no room for compassion, and they were determined to accuse Jesus of wrongdoing.

12:4 This story is recorded in 1 Samuel 21:1–6. The bread of the Presence was replaced every week, and the old loaves were eaten by the priests. The loaves given to David were the old loaves that had just been replaced with fresh ones. Although the priests were the only ones allowed to eat this bread, God did not punish David because his need for food was more important than the priestly regulations. Jesus was saying, "If you condemn me, you must also condemn David," something the religious leaders could never do without causing a great uproar among the people. Jesus was not condoning disobedience to God's laws. Instead he was emphasizing discernment and compassion in enforcing the laws.

12:5 The Ten Commandments prohibit work on the Sabbath (Exodus 20:8–11). That was the *letter* of the law. But because the *purpose* of the Sabbath is to rest and to worship God, the priests were allowed to work by performing sacrifices and conducting worship services. This "Sabbath work" was serving and worship-

12:5
ʳNu 28:9, 10
12:7
ˢHos 6:6

the Law that on the Sabbath the priests in the temple desecrate the dayʳ and yet are innocent? ⁶I tell you that oneᵃ greater than the temple is here. ⁷If you had known what these words mean, 'I desire mercy, not sacrifice,'ᵇˢ you would not have condemned the innocent. ⁸For the Son of Man is Lord of the Sabbath."

Jesus Heals a Man's Hand on the Sabbath (46/Mark 3:1–6; Luke 6:6–11)

12:10
ᵗLk 13:14

⁹Going on from that place, he went into their synagogue, ¹⁰and a man with a shriveled hand was there. Looking for a reason to accuse Jesus, they asked him, "Is it lawful to heal on the Sabbath?"ᵗ

¹¹He said to them, "If any of you has a sheep and it falls into a pit on the Sabbath, will you not take hold of it and lift it out? ¹²How much more valuable is a man than a sheep! Therefore it is lawful to do good on the Sabbath."

12:14
ᵘMk 3:6; Jn 11:53

¹³Then he said to the man, "Stretch out your hand." So he stretched it out and it was completely restored, just as sound as the other. ¹⁴But the Pharisees went out and plotted how they might kill Jesus. ᵘ

Large Crowds Follow Jesus (47/Mark 3:7–12)

12:18
ᵛMt 3:17

¹⁵Aware of this, Jesus withdrew from that place. Many followed him, and he healed all their sick, ¹⁶warning them not to tell who he was. ¹⁷This was to fulfill what was spoken through the prophet Isaiah:

¹⁸ "Here is my servant whom I have chosen,
　　the one I love, in whom I delight;ᵛ
I will put my Spirit on him,
　　and he will proclaim justice to the nations.
¹⁹ He will not quarrel or cry out;
　　no one will hear his voice in the streets.

ᵃ6 Or *something*; also in verses 41 and 42　ᵇ7 Hosea 6:6

---

ing God. Jesus always emphasized the intent of the law, the meaning behind the letter. The Pharisees had lost the spirit of the law and were rigidly demanding that the letter (and their interpretation of it) be obeyed.

12:6 The Pharisees were so concerned about religious rituals that they missed the whole purpose of the temple—to bring people to God. And because Jesus Christ is even greater than the temple, how much better can he bring people to God. God is far more important than the created instruments of worship. If we become more concerned with the means of worship than with the One we worship, we will miss God even as we think we are worshiping him.

12:7 Jesus repeated to the Pharisees words the Jewish people had heard time and again throughout their history (1 Samuel 15:22, 23; Psalm 40:6–8; Isaiah 1:11–17; Jeremiah 7:21–23; Hosea 6:6). Our heart attitude toward God comes first. Only then can we properly obey and observe religious regulations and rituals.

12:8 When Jesus said he was Lord of the Sabbath, he claimed to be greater than the law and above the law. To the Pharisees, this was heresy. They did not realize that Jesus, the divine Son of God, had created the Sabbath. The Creator is always greater than the creation; thus Jesus had the authority to overrule their traditions and regulations.

12:10 As they pointed to the man with the shriveled hand, the Pharisees tried to trick Jesus by asking him if it was legal to heal on the Sabbath. Their Sabbath rules said that people could be helped on the Sabbath only if their lives were in danger. Jesus healed on the Sabbath several times, and none of those healings were in response to emergencies. If Jesus had waited until another day, he would have been submitting to the Pharisees' authority, showing that their petty rules were equal to God's law. If he healed the man on the Sabbath, the Pharisees could claim that because Jesus broke their rules, his power was not from God. But Jesus made it clear how ridiculous and petty their rules were. God is a God of people, not rules. The best time to reach out to someone is when he or she needs help.

12:10–12 The Pharisees placed their laws above human need. They were so concerned about Jesus breaking one of their rules that they did not care about the man's shriveled hand. What is your attitude toward others? If your convictions don't allow you to help certain people, your convictions may not be in tune with God's Word. Don't allow rule keeping to blind you to human need.

12:14 The Pharisees plotted Jesus' death because they were proud, fearful, and outraged. Jesus had overruled their authority (Luke 6:11) and had exposed their evil attitudes in front of the entire crowd in the synagogue. Jesus had showed that the Pharisees were more loyal to their religious system than to God.

12:15 Up to this point, Jesus had been aggressively confronting the Pharisees' hypocrisy. Here he decided to withdraw from the synagogue before a major confrontation developed because it was not time for him to die. Jesus had many lessons still to teach his disciples and the people.

12:16 Jesus did not want those he healed to tell others about his miracles because he didn't want the people coming to him for the wrong reasons. That would hinder his teaching ministry and arouse false hopes about an earthly kingdom. But the news of Jesus' miracles spread, and many came to see for themselves (see Mark 3:7, 8).

12:17–21 The people expected the Messiah to be a king. This quotation from Isaiah's prophecy (Isaiah 42:1–4) showed that the Messiah was indeed a king, but it illustrated what *kind* of king—a gentle ruler who brings justice to the nations. Like the crowd in Jesus' day, we may want Christ to rule as a king and bring great and visible victories in our lives. But often Christ's work is quiet, and it happens according to *his* perfect timing, not ours.

20 A bruised reed he will not break,
   and a smoldering wick he will not snuff out,
     till he leads justice to victory.
21   In his name the nations will put their hope."a

Religious Leaders Accuse Jesus of Getting His Power from Satan (74/Mark 3:20–30)

22 Then they brought him a demon-possessed man who was blind and mute, and Jesus healed him, so that he could both talk and see. w 23 All the people were astonished and said, "Could this be the Son of David?"

24 But when the Pharisees heard this, they said, "It is only by Beelzebub,b the prince of demons, that this fellow drives out demons." x

25 Jesus knew their thoughtsy and said to them, "Every kingdom divided against itself will be ruined, and every city or household divided against itself will not stand. 26 If Satan drives out Satan, he is divided against himself. How then can his kingdom stand? 27 And if I drive out demons by Beelzebub, by whom do your peoplez drive them out? So then, they will be your judges. 28 But if I drive out demons by the Spirit of God, then the kingdom of God has come upon you.

29 "Or again, how can anyone enter a strong man's house and carry off his possessions unless he first ties up the strong man? Then he can rob his house.

30 "He who is not with me is against me, and he who does not gather with me scatters. 31 And so I tell you, every sin and blasphemy will be forgiven men, but the blasphemy against the Spirit will not be forgiven. a 32 Anyone who speaks a word against the Son of Man will be forgiven, but anyone who speaks against the Holy Spirit will not be forgiven, either in this age or in the age to come.

33 "Make a tree good and its fruit will be good, or make a tree bad and its fruit will be bad, for a tree is recognized by its fruit. b 34 You brood of vipers,c how can you who are evil say anything good? For out of the overflow of the heart the mouth speaks. d 35 The good man brings good things out of the good stored up in him, and the evil man brings evil things out of the evil stored up in him. 36 But I tell you that men will have to give account on the day of judgment for every careless word they have spoken. 37 For by your words you will be acquitted, and by your words you will be condemned."

Religious Leaders Ask Jesus for a Miraculous Sign (75)

38 Then some of the Pharisees and teachers of the law said to him, "Teacher, we want to see a miraculous sign from you." e

a 21 Isaiah 42:1-4   b 24 Greek Beezeboul or Beelzeboul; also in verse 27

12:22 w Mt 9:32-33
12:24 x Mt 9:34
12:25 y Mt 9:4
12:27 z Ac 19:13
12:31 a Lk 12:10
12:33 b Mt 7:16, 17
12:34 c Mt 3:7; 23:33 d Lk 6:45
12:38 e Mt 16:1; Mk 8:11, 12; Jn 2:18; 1Co 1:22

12:24 The Pharisees had already accused Jesus of being in league with the prince of demons (9:34). They were trying to discredit him by using an emotional argument. Refusing to believe that Jesus came from God, they said he was in league with Satan. Jesus easily exposed the foolishness of their argument.

12:25 In the incarnation, Jesus gave up the complete and unlimited use of his supernatural abilities. But he still had profound insight into human nature. His discernment stopped the religious leaders' attempts to trick him. The resurrected Christ knows all our thoughts. This can be comforting because he knows what we really mean when we speak to him. It can be threatening because we cannot hide from him, and he knows any selfish motives.

12:29 At Jesus' birth, Satan's power and control were disrupted. In the desert Jesus overcame the devil's temptations, and at the resurrection he defeated Satan's ultimate weapon, death. Eventually Satan will be constrained forever (Revelation 20:10), and evil will no longer pervade the earth. Jesus has complete power and authority over Satan and all his forces.

12:30 It is impossible to be neutral about Christ. Anyone who is not actively following him has chosen to reject him. Any person who tries to remain neutral in the struggle of good against evil is choosing to be separated from God, who alone is good. To refuse to follow Christ is to choose to be on Satan's team.

12:31, 32 The Pharisees had blasphemed against the Spirit by attributing the power by which Christ did miracles to Satan (12:24) instead of the Holy Spirit. The unpardonable sin is the deliberate refusal to acknowledge God's power in Christ. It indicates a deliberate and irreversible hardness of heart. Sometimes believers worry that they have accidentally committed this unforgivable sin. But only those who have turned their backs on God and rejected all faith have any need to worry. Jesus said they can't be forgiven—not because their sin is worse than any other, but because they will never ask for forgiveness. Whoever rejects the prompting of the Holy Spirit removes himself or herself from the only force that can lead him or her to repentance and restoration to God.

12:34–36 Jesus reminds us that what we say reveals what is in our hearts. What kinds of words come from your mouth? That is an indication of what your heart is really like. You can't solve your heart problem, however, just by cleaning up your speech. You must allow the Holy Spirit to fill you with new attitudes and motives; then your speech will be cleansed at its source.

12:38–40 The Pharisees were asking for another miraculous sign, but they were not sincerely seeking to know Jesus. Jesus knew they had already seen enough miraculous proof to convince them that he was the Messiah if they would just open their hearts. But they had already decided not to believe in him, and more miracles would not change that.

Many people have said, "If I could just see a real miracle, then

12:39
f Mt 16:4

12:40
g Jnh 1:17

12:41
h Jnh 3:5

12:42
i 1Ki 10:1; 2Ch 9:1

39 He answered, "A wicked and adulterous generation asks for a miraculous sign! But none will be given it except the sign of the prophet Jonah. *f* 40 For as Jonah was three days and three nights in the belly of a huge fish, *g* so the Son of Man will be three days and three nights in the heart of the earth. 41 The men of Nineveh will stand up at the judgment with this generation and condemn it; for they repented at the preaching of Jonah, *h* and now one *a* greater than Jonah is here. 42 The Queen of the South will rise at the judgment with this generation and condemn it; for she came *i* from the ends of the earth to listen to Solomon's wisdom, and now one greater than Solomon is here.

12:45
j 2Pe 2:20

43 "When an evil *b* spirit comes out of a man, it goes through arid places seeking rest and does not find it. 44 Then it says, 'I will return to the house I left.' When it arrives, it finds the house unoccupied, swept clean and put in order. 45 Then it goes and takes with it seven other spirits more wicked than itself, and they go in and live there. And the final condition of that man is worse than the first. *j* That is how it will be with this wicked generation."

Jesus Describes His True Family (76/Mark 3:31–35; Luke 8:19–21)

12:46
k Mt 13:55; Jn 2:12; 7:3, 5; Ac 1:14; 1Co 9:5; Gal 1:19

46 While Jesus was still talking to the crowd, his mother and brothers *k* stood outside, wanting to speak to him. 47 Someone told him, "Your mother and brothers are standing outside, wanting to speak to you." *c*

48 He replied to him, "Who is my mother, and who are my brothers?" 49 Pointing to his disciples, he said, "Here are my mother and my brothers. 50 For whoever does the will of my Father in heaven is my brother and sister and mother."

Jesus Tells the Parable of the Four Soils (77/Mark 4:1–9; Luke 8:4–8)

13:2
l Lk 5:3

13 That same day Jesus went out of the house and sat by the lake. 2 Such large crowds gathered around him that he got into a boat *l* and sat in it, while all the people stood on the shore. 3 Then he told them many things in parables, saying: "A farmer went out to sow his seed. 4 As he was scattering the seed, some fell along the path, and the birds came and ate it up. 5 Some fell on rocky places, where it did not have much soil. It sprang up quickly, because the soil was shallow. 6 But when the sun came up, the plants were scorched, and they withered because they had no root. 7 Other seed fell among thorns, which grew up and

a 41 Or *something*; also in verse 42   *b* 43 Greek *unclean*   *c* 47 Some manuscripts do not have verse 47.

I could really believe in God." But Jesus' response to the Pharisees applies to us. We have plenty of evidence—Jesus' birth, death, resurrection, and ascension, and centuries of his work in believers around the world. Instead of looking for additional evidence or miracles, accept what God has already given and move forward. He may use your life as evidence to reach another person.

12:39–41 Jonah was a prophet sent to the Assyrian city of Nineveh (see the book of Jonah). Because Assyria was such a cruel and warlike nation, Jonah tried to run from his assignment and ended up spending three days in the belly of a huge fish. When Jonah got out, he grudgingly went to Nineveh, preached God's message, and saw the city repent. By contrast, when Jesus came to his people, they refused to repent. Here Jesus is clearly saying that his resurrection will prove he is the Messiah. Three days after his death Jesus will come back to life, just as Jonah was given a new chance at life after three days in the fish.

12:41, 42 In Jonah's day, Nineveh was the capital of the Assyrian empire, and it was as powerful as it was evil (Jonah 1:2). But the entire city repented at Jonah's preaching. The Queen of the South traveled far to see Solomon, king of Israel, and learn about his great wisdom (1 Kings 10:1–10; also see the note on Luke 11:31, 32 for more on the Queen of Sheba). These Gentiles recognized the truth about God when it was presented to them, unlike the religious leaders who ignored the truth even though it stared them in the face. How have you responded to the evidence and truth that you have?

12:43–45 Jesus was describing the attitude of the nation of Israel and the religious leaders in particular. Just cleaning up one's life without filling it with God leaves plenty of room for

Satan to enter. The book of Ezra records how the people rid themselves of idolatry, but failed to replace it with love for God and obedience to him. Ridding our lives of sin is the first step. We must also take the second step: filling our lives with God's Word and the Holy Spirit. Unfilled and complacent people are easy targets for Satan.

12:46–50 Jesus was not denying his responsibility to his earthly family. On the contrary, he criticized the religious leaders for not following the Old Testament command to honor their parents (15:1–9). He provided for his mother's security as he hung on the cross (John 19:25–27). His mother and brothers were present in the upper room at Pentecost (Acts 1:14). Instead Jesus was pointing out that spiritual relationships are as binding as physical ones, and he was paving the way for a new community of believers (the universal church), our spiritual family.

13:2, 3 Jesus used many illustrations, or *parables*, when speaking to the crowds. A parable compares something familiar to something unfamiliar. It helps us understand spiritual truth by using everyday objects and relationships. Parables compel listeners to discover truth, while at the same time concealing the truth from those too lazy or too stubborn to see it. To those who are honestly searching, the truth becomes clear. We must be careful not to read too much into parables, forcing them to say what they don't mean. Each parable has a central meaning unless otherwise specified by Jesus.

choked the plants. [8]Still other seed fell on good soil, where it produced a crop—a hundred,[m] sixty or thirty times what was sown. [9]He who has ears, let him hear."[n]

13:8 [m]Ge 26:12

Jesus Explains the Parable of the Four Soils (78/Mark 4:10–25; Luke 8:9–18)

[10]The disciples came to him and asked, "Why do you speak to the people in parables?" [11]He replied, "The knowledge of the secrets of the kingdom of heaven has been given to you,[o] but not to them. [12]Whoever has will be given more, and he will have an abundance. Whoever does not have, even what he has will be taken from him.[p] [13]This is why I speak to them in parables:

13:9 [n]Mt 11:15
13:11 [o]1Co 2:10, 14; 1Jn 2:20, 27
13:12 [p]Mt 25:29; Lk 19:26

"Though seeing, they do not see;
   though hearing, they do not hear or understand.

[14]In them is fulfilled the prophecy of Isaiah:

"'You will be ever hearing but never understanding;
   you will be ever seeing but never perceiving.
[15] For this people's heart has become calloused;
   they hardly hear with their ears,
   and they have closed their eyes.
Otherwise they might see with their eyes,
   hear with their ears,
   understand with their hearts
and turn, and I would heal them.'[a][q]

13:15 [q]Isa 6:9, 10; Jn 12:40; Ac 28:26, 27

[16]But blessed are your eyes because they see, and your ears because they hear.[r] [17]For I tell you the truth, many prophets and righteous men longed to see what you see[s] but did not see it, and to hear what you hear but did not hear it.

[18]"Listen then to what the parable of the sower means: [19]When anyone hears the message about the kingdom[t] and does not understand it, the evil one comes and snatches away what was sown in his heart. This is the seed sown along the path. [20]The one who received the seed that fell on rocky places is the man who hears the word and at once receives it with joy. [21]But since he has no root, he lasts only a short time. When trouble or persecution comes because of the word, he quickly falls away.[u] [22]The one who received the seed that fell among the thorns is the man who hears the word, but the worries of this life and the deceitfulness of wealth[v] choke it, making it unfruitful. [23]But the one who received the seed that fell on good soil is the man who hears the word and understands it. He produces a crop, yielding a hundred, sixty or thirty times what was sown."

13:16 [r]Mt 16:17
13:17 [s]Heb 11:13; 1Pe 1:10-12
13:19 [t]Mt 4:23
13:21 [u]Mt 11:6
13:22 [v]Mt 19:23; 1Ti 6:9, 10, 17

Jesus Tells the Parable of the Weeds (80)

[24]Jesus told them another parable: "The kingdom of heaven is like a man who sowed good seed in his field. [25]But while everyone was sleeping, his enemy came and sowed weeds among the wheat, and went away. [26]When the wheat sprouted and formed heads, then the weeds also appeared.

[a]15 Isaiah 6:9,10

13:8 This parable should encourage spiritual "sowers"—those who teach, preach, and lead others. The farmer sowed good seed, but not all the seed sprouted, and even the plants that grew had varying yields. Don't be discouraged if you do not always see results as you faithfully teach the Word. Belief cannot be forced to follow a mathematical formula (i.e., a 4:1 ratio of seeds planted to seeds sprouted). Rather, it is a miracle of God's Holy Spirit as he uses your words to lead others to him.

13:9, 10 Human ears hear many sounds, but there is a deeper kind of listening that results in spiritual understanding. When speaking in parables, Jesus was not hiding truth from sincere seekers, because those who were receptive to spiritual truth understood the illustrations. To others they were only stories without meaning.

13:12 This phrase means that we are responsible to use well what we have. When people reject Jesus, their hardness of

heart drives away or renders useless even the little understanding they had.

13:22 How easy it is to agree with Christ with no intention of obeying. It is easy to denounce worries of this life and the deceitfulness of wealth, and still do nothing to change our ways. In light of eternal life with God, are your present worries justified? If you had everything you could want but forfeited eternal life with God, would those things be so desirable?

13:23 The four types of soil represent different responses to God's message. People respond differently because they are in different states of readiness. Some are hardened, others are shallow, others are contaminated by distracting worries, and some are receptive. How has God's Word taken root in your life? What kind of soil are you?

13:24ff Jesus gives the meaning of this parable in verses 36–43. All the parables in this chapter teach us about God and his kingdom. They explain what the kingdom is really like as

27"The owner's servants came to him and said, 'Sir, didn't you sow good seed in your field? Where then did the weeds come from?'

28"'An enemy did this,' he replied.

"The servants asked him, 'Do you want us to go and pull them up?'

29"'No,' he answered, 'because while you are pulling the weeds, you may root up the wheat with them. 30 Let both grow together until the harvest. At that time I will tell the harvesters: First collect the weeds and tie them in bundles to be burned; then gather the wheat and bring it into my barn.'" w

13:30
w Mt 3:12

Jesus Tells the Parable of the Mustard Seed (81/Mark 4:30–34)

31 He told them another parable: "The kingdom of heaven is like a mustard seed, which a man took and planted in his field. 32 Though it is the smallest of all your seeds, yet when it grows, it is the largest of garden plants and becomes a tree, so that the birds of the air come and perch in its branches." x

13:32
x Ps 104:12;
Eze 17:23; Da 4:12

Jesus Tells the Parable of the Yeast (82)

33 He told them still another parable: "The kingdom of heaven is like yeast that a woman took and mixed into a large amount a of flour y until it worked all through the dough."

34 Jesus spoke all these things to the crowd in parables; he did not say anything to them without using a parable. z 35 So was fulfilled what was spoken through the prophet:

"I will open my mouth in parables,
    I will utter things hidden since the creation of the world." b a

13:33
y Ge 18:6

13:34
z Mk 4:33

13:35
a Ps 78:2; 1Co 2:7

Jesus Explains the Parable of the Weeds (83)

36 Then he left the crowd and went into the house. His disciples came to him and said, "Explain to us the parable of the weeds in the field."

37 He answered, "The one who sowed the good seed is the Son of Man. 38 The field is the world, and the good seed stands for the sons of the kingdom. The weeds are the sons of the evil one, b 39 and the enemy who sows them is the devil. The harvest is the end of the age, c and the harvesters are angels.

40 "As the weeds are pulled up and burned in the fire, so it will be at the end of the age. 41 The Son of Man will send out his angels, and they will weed out of his kingdom everything that causes sin and all who do evil. 42 They will throw them into the fiery furnace, where there will be weeping and gnashing of teeth. d 43 Then the righteous will shine like the sun e in the kingdom of their Father. He who has ears, let him hear.

13:38
b Jn 8:44, 45

13:39
c Mt 24:3

13:42
d ver 50; Mt 8:12

13:43
e Da 12:3

a 33 Greek three satas (probably about 1/2 bushel or 22 liters)   b 35 Psalm 78:2

---

opposed to our expectations of it. The kingdom of heaven is not a geographic location, but a spiritual realm where God rules and where we share in his eternal life. We join that kingdom when we trust in Christ as Savior.

13:30 The young weeds and the young blades of wheat look the same and can't be distinguished until they are grown and ready for harvest. Weeds (unbelievers) and wheat (believers) must live side by side in this world. God allows unbelievers to remain for a while, just as a farmer allows weeds to remain in his field so the surrounding wheat isn't uprooted with them. At the harvest, however, the weeds will be uprooted and thrown away. God's harvest (judgment) of all people is coming. We are to make ourselves ready by making sure that our faith is sincere.

13:31, 32 The mustard seed was the smallest seed a farmer used. Jesus used this parable to show that the kingdom has small beginnings but will grow and produce great results.

13:33 In other Bible passages, yeast is used as a symbol of evil or uncleanness. Here it is a positive symbol of growth. Although yeast looks like a minor ingredient, it permeates the whole loaf. Although the kingdom began small and was nearly invisible, it would soon grow and have a great impact on the world.

13:40–43 At the end of the world, angels will separate the evil from the good. There are true and false believers in churches

today, but we should be cautious in our judgments because only Christ is qualified to make the final separation. If you start judging, you may damage some of the good "plants." It's more important to judge our own response to God than to analyze others' responses.

13:42 Jesus often uses these terms to refer to the coming judgment. The weeping indicates sorrow or remorse, and gnashing of teeth shows extreme anxiety or pain. Those who say they don't care what happens to them after they die don't realize what they are saying. They will be punished for living in selfishness and indifference to God.

13:43 Those who receive God's favor stand in bright contrast to those who receive his judgment. A similiar illustration is used in Daniel 12:3.

Jesus Tells the Parable of the Hidden Treasure (84)

44 "The kingdom of heaven is like treasure hidden in a field. When a man found it, he hid it again, and then in his joy went and sold all he had and bought that field. *f*

13:44
f Isa 55:1;
Php 3:7, 8

Jesus Tells the Parable of the Pearl Merchant (85)

45 "Again, the kingdom of heaven is like a merchant looking for fine pearls. 46 When he found one of great value, he went away and sold everything he had and bought it.

Jesus Tells the Parable of the Fishing Net (86)

47 "Once again, the kingdom of heaven is like a net that was let down into the lake and caught all kinds *g* of fish. 48 When it was full, the fishermen pulled it up on the shore. Then they sat down and collected the good fish in baskets, but threw the bad away. 49 This is how it will be at the end of the age. The angels will come and separate the wicked from the righteous *h* 50 and throw them into the fiery furnace, where there will be weeping and gnashing of teeth.

13:47
g Mt 22:10

13:49
h Mt 25:32

51 "Have you understood all these things?" Jesus asked.

"Yes," they replied.

52 He said to them, "Therefore every teacher of the law who has been instructed about the kingdom of heaven is like the owner of a house who brings out of his storeroom new treasures as well as old."

5. Jesus encounters differing reactions to his ministry
The People of Nazareth Refuse to Believe (91/Mark 6:1–6)

53 When Jesus had finished these parables, *i* he moved on from there. 54 Coming to his hometown, he began teaching the people in their synagogue, *j* and they were amazed. *k* "Where did this man get this wisdom and these miraculous powers?" they asked. 55 "Isn't this the carpenter's son? *l* Isn't his mother's *m* name Mary, and aren't his brothers James, Joseph, Simon and Judas? 56 Aren't all his sisters with us? Where then did this man get all these things?" 57 And they took offense at him.

13:53
i Mt 7:28

13:54
j Mt 4:23
k Mt 7:28

13:55
l Jn 6:42
m Mt 12:46

13:44 The kingdom of heaven is more valuable than anything else we can have, and a person must be willing to give up everything to obtain it. The man who discovered the treasure hidden in the field stumbled upon it by accident but knew its value when he found it. Although the transaction cost the man everything, he paid nothing for the priceless treasure itself. It came free, with the field. Nothing is more precious than the kingdom of heaven; yet God gives it to us as a gift.

13:45, 46 In this parable, the kingdom of heaven is not the precious pearl, but the merchant. In contrast to the previous picture, Jesus is now displaying another aspect of the kingdom. The contrast becomes vivid in the transaction—the kingdom pays the ultimate price to possess the pearl, the price God was willing to pay to redeem us.

13:47–49 The parable of the fishing net has the same meaning as the parable of the wheat and weeds. We are to obey God and tell others about his grace and goodness, but we cannot dictate who is part of the kingdom of heaven and who is not. This sorting will be done at the last judgment by those infinitely more qualified than we.

13:52 Anyone who understands God's real purpose in the law as revealed in the Old Testament has a real treasure. The Old Testament points the way to Jesus, the Messiah. Jesus always upheld its authority and relevance. But there is a double benefit to those who understand Jesus' teaching about the kingdom of heaven. This was a new treasure that Jesus was revealing. Both the old and new teaching give practical guidelines for faith and for living in the world. The religious leaders, however, were trapped in the old and blind to the new. They were looking for a future kingdom *preceded* by judgment. Jesus, however, taught that the kingdom was *now* and the judgment was future. The religious leaders were looking for a physical and temporal kingdom (via military rebellion and physical rule), but they were blind to the spiritual significance of the kingdom that Christ brought.

NAZARETH REJECTS JESUS
Chronologically, this return to Nazareth occurred after Jesus was in the Gadarene region and healed the demon-possessed men (8:28–34), then recrossed the sea to Capernaum. From there he traveled to Nazareth, where he had grown up, only to discover that the people refused to believe he was the Christ.

13:55 The residents of Jesus' hometown had known Jesus since he was a young child and were acquainted with his family; they could not bring themselves to believe in his message. They were too close to the situation. Jesus had come to them as a prophet, one who challenged them to respond to unpopular spiritual truth. They did not listen to the timeless message because they could not see beyond the man.

13:57 Jesus was not the first prophet to be rejected in his own country. Jeremiah experienced rejection in his hometown, even by members of his own family (Jeremiah 12:5, 6).

13:57
n Jn 4:44

But Jesus said to them, "Only in his hometown and in his own house is a prophet without honor." n

58 And he did not do many miracles there because of their lack of faith.

Herod Kills John the Baptist (95/Mark 6:14–29; Luke 9:7–9)

14:1
o Mk 8:15; Ac 4:27
p Lk 9:7-9

14 At that time Herod o the tetrarch heard the reports about Jesus, p 2 and he said to his attendants, "This is John the Baptist; he has risen from the dead! That is why miraculous powers are at work in him."

14:3
q Lk 3:19, 20

3 Now Herod had arrested John and bound him and put him in prison because of Herodias, his brother Philip's wife, q 4 for John had been saying to him: "It is not lawful for you to

14:4
r Lev 18:16; 20:21

have her." r 5 Herod wanted to kill John, but he was afraid of the people, because they considered him a prophet.

6 On Herod's birthday the daughter of Herodias danced for them and pleased Herod so much 7 that he promised with an oath to give her whatever she asked. 8 Prompted by her mother, she said, "Give me here on a platter the head of John the Baptist." 9 The king was distressed, but because of his oaths and his dinner guests, he ordered that her request be granted 10 and had John beheaded in the prison. 11 His head was brought in on a platter and given to the girl, who carried it to her mother. 12 John's disciples came and took his body and buried it. Then they went and told Jesus.

Jesus Feeds Five Thousand (96/Mark 6:30–44; Luke 9:10–17; John 6:1–15)

13 When Jesus heard what had happened, he withdrew by boat privately to a solitary place. Hearing of this, the crowds followed him on foot from the towns. 14 When Jesus landed and

14:14
s Mt 9:36

saw a large crowd, he had compassion on them s and healed their sick.

15 As evening approached, the disciples came to him and said, "This is a remote place, and it's already getting late. Send the crowds away, so they can go to the villages and buy themselves some food."

16 Jesus replied, "They do not need to go away. You give them something to eat."

14:17
t Mt 16:9

17 "We have here only five loaves t of bread and two fish," they answered.

14:19
u 1 Sa 9:13;
Lk 24:30

18 "Bring them here to me," he said. 19 And he directed the people to sit down on the grass. Taking the five loaves and the two fish and looking up to heaven, he gave thanks and broke the loaves. u Then he gave them to the disciples, and the disciples gave them to the people. 20 They all ate and were satisfied, and the disciples picked up twelve basketfuls of broken pieces that were left over. 21 The number of those who ate was about five thousand men, besides women and children.

13:58 Jesus did few miracles in his hometown "because of their lack of faith." Lack of faith blinds people to the truth and robs them of hope. These people missed the Messiah. How does your faith measure up? If you can't see God's work, perhaps it is because of your unbelief. Believe, ask God for a mighty work in your life, and expect him to act. Look with the eyes of faith.

14:1 Herod was a tetrarch—one of four rulers over the four districts of Palestine. His territory included the regions of Galilee and Perea. He was the son of Herod the Great, who ordered the killing of the babies in Bethlehem (2:16). Also known as Herod Antipas, he heard Jesus' case before Jesus' crucifixion (Luke 23:6–12). His Profile is found in Mark 6, p. 1621.

14:2 For more information on John the Baptist, see his Profile in John 1, p. 1737.

14:3 Philip, Herod's half brother, was another of Palestine's four rulers. His territories were Iturea and Traconitis, northeast of the Sea of Galilee (Luke 3:1). Philip's wife, Herodias, left Philip to live with Herod Antipas. John the Baptist condemned the two for living immorally (see Mark 6:17, 18).

14:9 Herod did not want to kill John the Baptist, but he gave the order so that he wouldn't be embarrassed in front of his guests. How easy it is to give in to the crowd and to let ourselves be pressured into doing wrong. Don't get in a situation where it will be too embarrassing to do what is right. Determine to do what is right, no matter how embarrassing or painful it may be.

14:13, 14 Jesus sought solitude after the news of John's death. Sometimes we may need to deal with our grief alone. Jesus did not dwell on his grief, but returned to the ministry he came to do.

14:14 Jesus performed some miracles as signs of his identity. He used other miracles to teach important truths. But here we read that he healed people because he "had compassion on them." Jesus was, and is, a loving, caring, and feeling person. When you are suffering, remember that Jesus hurts with you. He has compassion on you.

14:19–21 Jesus multiplied five loaves and two fish to feed over 5,000 people. What he was originally given seemed insufficient, but in his hands it became more than enough. We often feel that our contribution to Jesus is meager, but he can use and multiply whatever we give him, whether it is talent, time, or treasure. It is when we give them to Jesus that our resources are multiplied.

14:21 The text states that there were 5,000 men present, *besides* women and children. Therefore, the total number of people Jesus fed could have been 10 to 15 thousand. The number of men is listed separately because in the Jewish culture of the day, men and women usually ate separately when in public. The children ate with the women.

Jesus Walks on Water (97/Mark 6:45–52; John 6:16–21)

22 Immediately Jesus made the disciples get into the boat and go on ahead of him to the other side, while he dismissed the crowd. 23 After he had dismissed them, he went up on a mountainside by himself to pray. When evening came, he was there alone, 24 but the boat was already a considerable distance[a] from land, buffeted by the waves because the wind was against it.

25 During the fourth watch of the night Jesus went out to them, walking on the lake. 26 When the disciples saw him walking on the lake, they were terrified. "It's a ghost,"[v] they said, and cried out in fear.

27 But Jesus immediately said to them: "Take courage![w] It is I. Don't be afraid."[x]

28 "Lord, if it's you," Peter replied, "tell me to come to you on the water."

29 "Come," he said.

Then Peter got down out of the boat, walked on the water and came toward Jesus. 30 But when he saw the wind, he was afraid and, beginning to sink, cried out, "Lord, save me!"

31 Immediately Jesus reached out his hand and caught him. "You of little faith,"[y] he said, "why did you doubt?"

32 And when they climbed into the boat, the wind died down. 33 Then those who were in the boat worshiped him, saying, "Truly you are the Son of God."[z]

Jesus Heals All Who Touch Him (98/Mark 6:53–56)

34 When they had crossed over, they landed at Gennesaret. 35 And when the men of that place recognized Jesus, they sent word to all the surrounding country. People brought all their sick to him 36 and begged him to let the sick just touch the edge of his cloak,[a] and all who touched him were healed.

[a] 24 Greek *many stadia*

14:26
v Lk 24:37

14:27
w Mt 9:2
x Mt 17:7; 28:10;
Rev 1:17

14:31
y Mt 6:30

14:33
z Ps 2:7

14:36
a Mt 9:20

14:23 Seeking solitude was an important priority for Jesus (see also 14:13). He made room in his busy schedule to be alone with the Father. Spending time with God in prayer nurtures a vital relationship and equips us to meet life's challenges and struggles. Develop the discipline of spending time alone with God—it will help you grow spiritually and become more and more like Christ.

14:28 Peter was not putting Jesus to the test, something we are told not to do (4:7). Instead he was the only one in the boat to react in faith. His impulsive request led him to experience a

JESUS WALKS ON THE SEA
The miraculous feeding of the 5,000 occurred on the shores of the Sea of Galilee near Bethsaida. Jesus then sent his disciples across the lake. Several hours later they encountered a storm, and Jesus came to them—walking on the water. The boat then landed at Gennesaret.

rather unusual demonstration of God's power. Peter started to sink because he took his eyes off Jesus and focused on the high waves around him. His faith wavered when he realized what he was doing. We may not walk on water, but we do walk through tough situations. If we focus on the waves of difficult circumstances around us without looking to Jesus for help, we too may despair and sink. To maintain your faith when situations are difficult, keep your eyes on Jesus' power rather than on your inadequacies.

14:30, 31 Although we start out with good intentions, sometimes our faith falters. This doesn't necessarily mean we have failed. When Peter's faith faltered, he reached out to Christ, the only one who could help. He was afraid, but he still looked to Christ. When you are apprehensive about the troubles around you and doubt Christ's presence or ability to help, you must remember that he is the *only* one who can really help.

14:34 Gennesaret was located on the west side of the Sea of Galilee in a fertile, well-watered area.

14:35, 36 The people recognized Jesus as a great healer, but how many understood who he truly was? They came to Jesus for physical healing, but did they come for spiritual healing? They came to prolong their lives on earth, but did they come to secure their eternal lives? People may seek Jesus to learn valuable lessons from his life or in hopes of finding relief from pain. But we miss Jesus' whole message if we seek him only to heal our bodies but not our souls, if we look to him for help only in this life, rather than for his eternal plan for us. Only when we understand the real Jesus Christ can we appreciate how he can truly change our lives.

14:36 Jewish men wore tassels on the lower edges of their robes according to God's command (Deuteronomy 22:12). By Jesus' day, elaborate versions of these tassels were seen as signs of holiness (23:5). There is no indication that the tassels on the edge of Jesus' robe were anything more than typical. It was natural that people seeking healing should reach out and touch the edge of his cloak. But as one sick woman learned, healing came from faith and not from Jesus' cloak (9:19–22).

Jesus Teaches about Inner Purity (102/Mark 7:1–23)

15 Then some Pharisees and teachers of the law came to Jesus from Jerusalem and asked, 2"Why do your disciples break the tradition of the elders? They don't wash their hands before they eat!"*b*

3Jesus replied, "And why do you break the command of God for the sake of your tradition? 4For God said, 'Honor your father and mother'*ac* and 'Anyone who curses his father or mother must be put to death.'*b d* 5But you say that if a man says to his father or mother, 'Whatever help you might otherwise have received from me is a gift devoted to God,' 6he is not to 'honor his father*c*' with it. Thus you nullify the word of God for the sake of your tradition. 7You hypocrites! Isaiah was right when he prophesied about you:

8 "'These people honor me with their lips,
    but their hearts are far from me.
9 They worship me in vain;
    their teachings are but rules taught by men.'*e'd f*"

10Jesus called the crowd to him and said, "Listen and understand. 11What goes into a man's mouth does not make him 'unclean,'*g* but what comes out of his mouth, that is what makes him 'unclean.'"

12Then the disciples came to him and asked, "Do you know that the Pharisees were offended when they heard this?"

13He replied, "Every plant that my heavenly Father has not planted *h* will be pulled up by the roots. 14Leave them; they are blind guides.*e i* If a blind man leads a blind man, both will fall into a pit."*j*

15Peter said, "Explain the parable to us."*k*

*a*4 Exodus 20:12; Deut. 5:16   *b*4 Exodus 21:17; Lev. 20:9   *c*6 Some manuscripts *father or his mother*
*d*9 Isaiah 29:13   *e*14 Some manuscripts *guides of the blind*

15:2
*b*Lk 11:38

15:4
*c*Ex 20:12; Dt 5:16
*d*Lev 20:9

15:9
*e*Col 2:20-22
*f*Isa 29:13

15:11
*g*Ac 10:14, 15

15:13
*h*Isa 60:21
15:14
*i*Mt 23:16, 24
*j*Lk 6:39
15:15
*k*Mt 13:36

15:1, 2 The Pharisees and teachers of the law came from Jerusalem, the center of Jewish authority, to scrutinize Jesus' activities. Over the centuries since the Jews' return from Babylonian captivity, hundreds of religious traditions had been added to God's laws. The Pharisees and teachers of the law considered them all equally important. Many traditions are not bad in themselves. Certain religious traditions can add richness and meaning to life. But we must not assume that because our traditions have been practiced for years they should be elevated to a sacred standing. God's principles never change, and his law doesn't need additions. Traditions should help us understand God's laws better, not become laws themselves.

15:5, 6 This was the practice of *Corban* (literally, "offering"; see Mark 7:11). Anyone who made a Corban vow was required to dedicate money to God's temple that otherwise would have gone to support his parents. Corban had become a religiously acceptable way to neglect parents, circumventing the child's responsibility to them. Although the action—giving money to God—seemed worthy and no doubt conferred prestige on the giver, many people who took the Corban vow were disregarding God's command to care for needy parents. These religious leaders were ignoring God's clear command to honor their parents.

15:8, 9 The prophet Isaiah also criticized hypocrites (Isaiah 29:13), and Jesus applied Isaiah's words to these religious leaders. The Pharisees knew a lot about God, but they didn't know God. When we claim to honor God while our hearts are far from him, our worship means nothing. It is not enough to study about religion or even to study the Bible; it is not enough to act religious. Our actions and our attitudes must be sincere. If they are not, Isaiah's words also describe us.

15:11 Jesus was referring to the Jewish regulations concerning food and drink. This verse could be paraphrased: "You aren't made unclean by eating nonkosher food! It is what you *say* and *think* that makes you unclean!" This statement offended the Pharisees who were very concerned about what people ate and drank.

15:13, 14 Jesus told his disciples to leave the Pharisees alone because the Pharisees were blind to God's truth. Anyone who listened to their teaching would risk spiritual blindness as well. Not all religious leaders clearly see God's truth. Make sure that those you listen to and learn from are those with good spiritual eyesight—they teach and follow the principles of Scripture.

15:15 Later Peter would be faced with the issue of clean and unclean food (see the notes on 15:11 and Acts 10:12). Then he would learn that nothing should be a barrier to proclaiming the gospel to the Gentiles (non-Jews).

MINISTRY IN PHOENICIA

After preaching again in Capernaum, Jesus left Galilee for Phoenicia, where he preached in Tyre and Sidon. On his return, he traveled through the region of the Decapolis (Ten Cities), fed the 4,000 beside the sea, then crossed to Magadan.

16"Are you still so dull?" *l* Jesus asked them. 17"Don't you see that whatever enters the mouth goes into the stomach and then out of the body? 18But the things that come out of the mouth come from the heart, *m* and these make a man 'unclean.' 19For out of the heart come evil thoughts, murder, adultery, sexual immorality, theft, false testimony, slander. *n* 20These are what make a man 'unclean'; but eating with unwashed hands does not make him 'unclean.'"

Jesus Sends a Demon Out of a Girl (*103*/Mark 7:24–30)

21Leaving that place, Jesus withdrew to the region of Tyre and Sidon. 22A Canaanite woman from that vicinity came to him, crying out, "Lord, Son of David,*o* have mercy on me! My daughter is suffering terribly from demon-possession."*p*

23Jesus did not answer a word. So his disciples came to him and urged him, "Send her away, for she keeps crying out after us."

24He answered, "I was sent only to the lost sheep of Israel."*q*

25The woman came and knelt before him. *r* "Lord, help me!" she said.

26He replied, "It is not right to take the children's bread and toss it to their dogs."

27"Yes, Lord," she said, "but even the dogs eat the crumbs that fall from their masters' table."

28Then Jesus answered, "Woman, you have great faith! *s* Your request is granted." And her daughter was healed from that very hour.

Jesus Heals Many People (*104*/Mark 7:31–37)

29Jesus left there and went along the Sea of Galilee. Then he went up on a mountainside and sat down. 30Great crowds came to him, bringing the lame, the blind, the crippled, the mute and many others, and laid them at his feet; and he healed them. *t* 31The people were amazed when they saw the mute speaking, the crippled made well, the lame walking and the blind seeing. And they praised the God of Israel. *u*

Jesus Feeds Four Thousand (*105*/Mark 8:1–10)

32Jesus called his disciples to him and said, "I have compassion for these people;*v* they have already been with me three days and have nothing to eat. I do not want to send them away hungry, or they may collapse on the way."

33His disciples answered, "Where could we get enough bread in this remote place to feed such a crowd?"

15:16
l Mt 16:9

15:18
m Mt 12:34; Jas 3:6

15:19
n Gal 5:19-21

15:22
o Mt 9:27
p Mt 4:24

15:24
q Mt 10:6, 23

15:25
r Mt 8:2

15:28
s Mt 9:22

15:30
t Mt 4:23

15:31
u Mt 9:8

15:32
v Mt 9:36

15:16-20 We work hard to keep our outward appearance attractive, but what is in our hearts is even more important. The way we are deep down (where others can't see) matters much to God. What are you like inside? When people become Christians, God makes them different on the inside. He will continue the process of change inside them if they only ask. God wants us to seek healthy thoughts and motives, not just healthy food and exercise.

15:23 Puzzled by Jesus' silence, the disciples asked him to get rid of the woman because she was bothering them with her nagging persistence. They showed no compassion for her or sensitivity to her needs. It is possible to become so occupied with spiritual matters that we miss real needs right around us. This is especially likely if we are prejudiced against needy people or if they cause us inconvenience. Instead of being bothered, be aware of the opportunities that surround you. Be open to the beauty of God's message for *all* people, and make an effort not to shut out those who are different from you.

15:24 Jesus' words do not contradict the truth that God's message is for all people (Psalm 22:27; Isaiah 56:7; Matthew 28:19; Romans 15:9–12). After all, when Jesus said these words, he was in Gentile territory on a mission to Gentile people. He ministered to Gentiles on many other occasions also. Jesus was simply telling the woman that Jews were to have the first opportunity to accept him as the Messiah because God wanted them to present the message of salvation to the rest of the world (see Genesis 12:3). Jesus was not rejecting the Canaanite woman. He may have wanted to test her faith, or he may have wanted to use the situation as another opportunity to teach that faith is available to all people.

15:26-28 *Dog* was a term the Jews commonly applied to Gentiles because the Jews considered these pagan people no more likely than dogs to receive God's blessing. Jesus was not degrading the woman by using this term, he was reflecting the Jews' attitude so as to contrast it with his own. The woman did not argue. Instead, using Jesus' choice of words, she agreed to be considered a dog as long as she could receive God's blessing for her daughter. Ironically, many Jews would lose God's blessing and salvation because they rejected Jesus, and many Gentiles would find salvation because they recognized and accepted him.

15:29-31 A great crowd was brought to Jesus to be healed, and he healed them all. Jesus is still able to heal broken lives, and we can be the ones who bring suffering people to him. Who do you know that needs Christ's healing touch? You can bring them to Jesus through prayer or through explaining to them the reason for the hope that you have (1 Peter 3:15). Then let Christ do the healing.

15:32ff This feeding of 4,000 is a separate event from the feeding of the 5,000 (14:13–21), confirmed by Mark 8:19, 20. This was the beginning of Jesus' expanded ministry to the Gentiles.

15:33 Jesus had already fed more than 5,000 people with five loaves and two fish. Here, in a similar situation, the disciples were again perplexed. How easily we throw up our hands in despair when faced with difficult situations. Like the disciples, we often forget that if God has cared for us in the past, he will do the same now. When facing a difficult situation, remember how God cared for you and trust him to work faithfully again.

34 "How many loaves do you have?" Jesus asked.

"Seven," they replied, "and a few small fish."

35 He told the crowd to sit down on the ground. 36 Then he took the seven loaves and the fish, and when he had given thanks, he broke them w and gave them to the disciples, and they in turn to the people. 37 They all ate and were satisfied. Afterward the disciples picked up seven basketfuls of broken pieces that were left over. x 38 The number of those who ate was four thousand, besides women and children. 39 After Jesus had sent the crowd away, he got into the boat and went to the vicinity of Magadan.

15:36
w Mt 14:19

15:37
x Mt 16:10

Leaders Demand a Miraculous Sign (106/Mark 8:11–13)

16 The Pharisees and Sadducees came to Jesus and tested him by asking him to show them a sign from heaven. y

2 He replied, a "When evening comes, you say, 'It will be fair weather, for the sky is red,' 3 and in the morning, 'Today it will be stormy, for the sky is red and overcast.' You know how to interpret the appearance of the sky, but you cannot interpret the signs of the times. z 4 A wicked and adulterous generation looks for a miraculous sign, but none will be given it except the sign of Jonah." a Jesus then left them and went away.

16:1
y Mt 12:38

16:3
z Lk 12:54-56

16:4
a Mt 12:39

Jesus Warns against Wrong Teaching (107/Mark 8:14–21)

5 When they went across the lake, the disciples forgot to take bread. 6 "Be careful," Jesus said to them. "Be on your guard against the yeast of the Pharisees and Sadducees." b

7 They discussed this among themselves and said, "It is because we didn't bring any bread."

8 Aware of their discussion, Jesus asked, "You of little faith, c why are you talking among yourselves about having no bread? 9 Do you still not understand? Don't you remember the five loaves for the five thousand, and how many basketfuls you gathered? d 10 Or the seven loaves for the four thousand, and how many basketfuls you gathered? e 11 How is it you don't understand that I was not talking to you about bread? But be on your guard against the yeast of the Pharisees and Sadducees." 12 Then they understood that he was not telling them to guard against the yeast used in bread, but against the teaching of the Pharisees and Sadducees.

16:6
b Lk 12:1

16:8
c Mt 6:30

16:9
d Mt 14:17-21

16:10
e Mt 15:34-38

a 2 Some early manuscripts do not have the rest of verse 2 and all of verse 3.

16:1 The Pharisees and Sadducees were Jewish religious leaders of two different parties, and their views were diametrically opposed on many issues. The Pharisees carefully followed their religious rules and traditions, believing that this was the way to God. They also believed in the authority of all Scripture and in the resurrection of the dead. The Sadducees accepted only the books of Moses as Scripture and did not believe in life after death. In Jesus, however, these two groups had a common enemy, and they joined forces to try to kill him. For more information on the Pharisees and Sadducees, see the charts in chapter 3, p. 1533 and Mark 2, p. 1609.

16:1 The Pharisees and Sadducees demanded a sign *from heaven.* They tried to explain away Jesus' other miracles as sleight of hand, coincidence, or use of evil power, but they believed that only God could do a sign in the sky. This, they were sure, would be a feat beyond Jesus' power. Although Jesus could have easily impressed them, he refused. He knew that even a miracle in the sky would not convince them he was the Messiah because they had already decided not to believe in him.

16:4 By using the sign of Jonah, who was inside a great fish for three days, Jesus was predicting his death and resurrection (see also 12:38–42).

16:4 Many people, like these Jewish leaders, say they want to see a miracle so that they can believe. But Jesus knew that miracles never convince the skeptical. Jesus had been healing, raising people from the dead, and feeding thousands, and still people wanted him to prove himself. Do you doubt Christ because you haven't *seen* a miracle? Do you expect God to prove himself to you personally before you believe? Jesus says,

"Blessed are those who have not seen and yet have believed" (John 20:29). We have all the miracles recorded in the Old and New Testaments, 2,000 years of church history, and the witness of thousands. With all this evidence, those who won't believe are either too proud or too stubborn. If you simply step forward in faith and believe, then you will begin to see the miracles that God can do with your life!

16:12 Yeast is put into bread to make it rise, and it takes only a little to affect a whole batch of dough. Jesus used yeast as an example of how a small amount of evil can affect a large group of people. The wrong teachings of the Pharisees and Sadducees were leading many people astray. Beware of the tendency to say, "How can this little wrong possibly affect anyone?"

Peter Says Jesus Is the Messiah (109/Mark 8:27–30; Luke 9:18–20)

13When Jesus came to the region of Caesarea Philippi, he asked his disciples, "Who do people say the Son of Man is?"

14They replied, "Some say John the Baptist;f others say Elijah; and still others, Jeremiah or one of the prophets."g

15"But what about you?" he asked. "Who do you say I am?"

16Simon Peter answered, "You are the Christ,a the Son of the living God."h

17Jesus replied, "Blessed are you, Simon son of Jonah, for this was not revealed to you by man,i but by my Father in heaven. 18And I tell you that you are Peter,bi and on this rock I will build my church, and the gates of Hadesc will not overcome it. d 19I will give you the keys of the kingdom of heaven; whatever you bind on earth will bee bound in heaven, and whatever you loose on earth will bee loosed in heaven." k 20Then he warned his disciples not to tell anyone that he was the Christ.

Jesus Predicts His Death the First Time (110/Mark 8:31—9:1; Luke 9:21–27)

21From that time on Jesus began to explain to his disciples that he must go to Jerusalem and suffer many thingsl at the hands of the elders, chief priests and teachers of the law, and that he must be killed and on the third day be raised to life. m

a16 Or *Messiah*; also in verse 20   b18 Peter means *rock*.   c18 Or *hell*   d18 Or *not prove stronger than it*   e19 Or *have been*

16:14
fMt 14:2
gMk 6:15; Jn 1:21

16:16
hJn 11:27

16:17
i1Co 15:50;
Gal 1:16

16:18
jJn 1:42

16:19
kMt 18:18; Jn 20:23

16:21
lLk 17:25
mMk 9:31

16:13 Caesarea Philippi was located several miles north of the Sea of Galilee, in the territory ruled by Philip. The influence of Greek and Roman culture was everywhere, and pagan temples and idols abounded. When Philip became ruler, he rebuilt and renamed the city after the emperor (Caesar) and himself. The city was originally called Caesarea, the same name as the capital city of Philip's brother Herod's territory.

16:13–17 The disciples answered Jesus' question with the common view—that Jesus was one of the great prophets come back to life. This belief may have stemmed from Deuteronomy 18:18, where God said he would raise up a prophet from among the people. (John the Baptist's Profile is in John 1, p. 1737; Elijah's Profile is in 1 Kings 18, p. 527; and Jeremiah's Profile is in Jeremiah 2, p. 1183.) Peter, however, confessed Jesus as divine and as the promised and long-awaited Messiah. If Jesus were to ask you this question, how would you answer? Is he your Lord and Messiah?

16:18 The rock on which Jesus would build his church has been identified as: (1) Jesus himself (his work of salvation by dying for us on the cross); (2) Peter (the first great leader in the church at

Jerusalem); (3) the confession of faith that Peter gave and that all subsequent true believers would give. It seems most likely that the rock refers to Peter as the leader of the church. Just as Peter had revealed the true identity of Christ, so Jesus revealed Peter's identity and role.

Later, Peter reminds Christians that they are the church built on the foundation of the apostles and prophets, with Jesus Christ as the cornerstone (1 Peter 2:4–6). All believers are joined into this church by faith in Jesus Christ as Savior, the same faith that Peter expressed here (see also Ephesians 2:20, 21). Jesus praised Peter for his confession of faith. It is faith like Peter's that is the foundation of Christ's kingdom.

16:19 The meaning of this verse has been a subject of debate for centuries. Some say the "keys" represent the authority to carry out church discipline, legislation, and administration (18:15–18), while others say the keys give the authority to announce the forgiveness of sins (John 20:23). Still others say the keys may be the opportunity to bring people to the kingdom of heaven by presenting them with the message of salvation found in God's Word (Acts 15:7–9). The religious leaders thought they held the keys of the kingdom, and they tried to shut some people out. We cannot decide to open or close the kingdom of heaven for others, but God uses us to help others find the way inside. To all who believe in Christ and obey his words, the kingdom doors are swung wide open.

16:20 Jesus warned the disciples not to publicize Peter's confession because they did not yet fully understand the kind of Messiah he had come to be—not a military commander but a suffering servant. They needed to come to a full understanding of Jesus and their mission as disciples before they could proclaim it to others in a way that would not cause a rebellion. They would have a difficult time understanding what Jesus came to do until his earthly mission was complete.

16:21 The phrase "From that time on" marks a turning point. In 4:17 it signaled Jesus' announcement of the kingdom of heaven. Here it points to his new emphasis on his death and resurrection. The disciples still didn't grasp Jesus' true purpose because of their preconceived notions about what the Messiah should be. This is the first of three times that Jesus predicted his death (see 17:22, 23; 20:18 for others).

16:21–28 This passage corresponds to Daniel's prophecies: the Messiah would be cut off (Daniel 9:26); there would be a period of trouble (9:27); and the king would come in glory (7:13, 14). The disciples would endure the same suffering as their King and, like him, would be rewarded in the end.

JOURNEY TO CAESAREA PHILIPPI

Jesus left Magadan, crossed the lake, and landed in Bethsaida. There he healed a man who had been born blind. From there, he and his disciples went to Caesarea Philippi, where Peter confessed Jesus as the Messiah and Son of God.

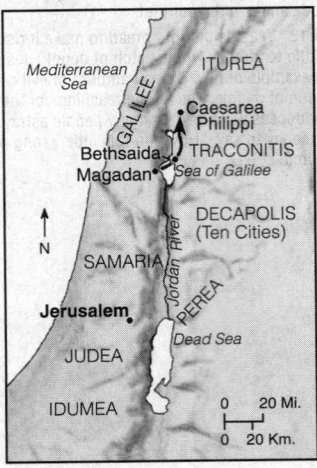

²²Peter took him aside and began to rebuke him. "Never, Lord!" he said. "This shall never happen to you!"

²³Jesus turned and said to Peter, "Get behind me, Satan! You are a stumbling block to me; you do not have in mind the things of God, but the things of men."

16:24
ⁿ Mt 10:38; Lk 14:27

²⁴Then Jesus said to his disciples, "If anyone would come after me, he must deny himself and take up his cross and follow me. *ⁿ* ²⁵For whoever wants to save his life ᵃ will lose it, but whoever loses his life for me will find it. ²⁶What good will it be for a man if he gains the whole world, yet forfeits his soul? Or what can a man give in exchange for his soul? ²⁷For the Son of Man is going to come in his Father's glory with his angels, and then he will reward each person according to what he has done. *ᵒ* ²⁸I tell you the truth, some who are standing here will not taste death before they see the Son of Man coming in his kingdom."

16:27
ᵒ Ro 2:6; 2Co 5:10; Rev 22:12

Jesus Is Transfigured on the Mountain (111/Mark 9:2–13; Luke 9:28–36)

17 After six days Jesus took with him Peter, James and John the brother of James, and led them up a high mountain by themselves. ²There he was transfigured before them. His face shone like the sun, and his clothes became as white as the light. ³Just then there appeared before them Moses and Elijah, talking with Jesus.

⁴Peter said to Jesus, "Lord, it is good for us to be here. If you wish, I will put up three shelters—one for you, one for Moses and one for Elijah."

ᵃ25 The Greek word means either *life* or *soul*; also in verse 26.

16:22 Peter, Jesus' friend and devoted follower who had just eloquently proclaimed Jesus' true identity, sought to protect him from the suffering he prophesied. But if Jesus hadn't suffered and died, Peter (and we) would have died in his sins. Great temptations can come from those who love us and seek to protect us. Be cautious of advice from a friend who says, "Surely God doesn't want you to face this." Often our most difficult temptations come from those who are only trying to protect us from discomfort.

16:23 In his desert temptations, Jesus heard the message that he could achieve greatness without dying (4:6). Here he heard the same message from Peter. Peter had just recognized Jesus as Messiah; here, however, he forsook God's perspective and evaluated the situation from a human one. Satan is always trying to get us to leave God out of the picture. Jesus rebuked Peter for this attitude.

16:24 When Jesus used this picture of his followers taking up their crosses to follow him, the disciples knew what he meant. Crucifixion was a common Roman method of execution, and condemned criminals had to carry their crosses through the streets to the execution site. Following Jesus, therefore, meant a true commitment, the risk of death, and no turning back (see 10:39).

16:25 The possibility of losing their lives was very real for the disciples as well as for Jesus. Real discipleship implies real commitment—pledging our whole existence to his service. If we try to save our physical life from death, pain, or discomfort, we may risk losing our true eternal life. If we protect ourselves from pain, we begin to die spiritually and emotionally. Our lives turn inward, and we lose our intended purpose. When we give our lives in service to Christ, however, we discover the real purpose of living.

16:26 When we don't know Christ, we make choices as though this life were all we have. In reality, this life is just the introduction to eternity. How we live this brief span, however, determines our eternal state. What we accumulate on earth has no value in purchasing eternal life. Even the highest social or civic honors cannot earn us entrance into heaven. Evaluate all that happens from an eternal perspective, and you will find your values and decisions changing.

16:27 Jesus Christ has been given the authority to judge all the earth (Romans 14:9–11; Philippians 2:9–11). Although his judgment is already working in our lives, there is a future, final judgment when Christ returns (25:31–46) and everyone's life is reviewed and evaluated. This will not be confined to unbelievers;

Christians too will face a judgment. Their eternal destiny is secure, but Jesus will look at how they handled gifts, opportunities, and responsibilities in order to determine their heavenly rewards. At the time of judgment, God will deliver the righteous and condemn the wicked. We should not judge others' salvation; that is God's work.

16:28 Because all the disciples died *before* Christ's return, many believe that Jesus' words were fulfilled at the transfiguration when Peter, James, and John saw his glory (17:1–3). Others say this statement refers to the resurrection (Matthew 28; Mark 16; Luke 24; John 20) and ascension of Jesus (Acts 1). Still others believe that Pentecost (Acts 2) and the beginning of Christ's church fulfilled Jesus' words. In any case, certain disciples were eyewitnesses to the power and glory of Christ's kingdom.

17:1ff The transfiguration was a vision, a brief glimpse of the true glory of the King (16:27, 28). This was a special revelation of Jesus' divinity to three of the disciples, and it was God's divine affirmation of everything Jesus had done and was about to do.

17:3 The transfiguration was a foretaste of heaven; the participants were doing something worth noting—talking together. In God's world, interactions count highly. People are individuals, with minds, hearts, and opinions. People are also part of a wider whole, connected by relationships built on sharing between whole persons. Friendship is the key. Make time and opportunities to talk with others. Good conversations act as training for eternity.

17:3–5 Moses and Elijah were the two greatest prophets in the Old Testament. Moses represents the law, or the old covenant. He wrote the Pentateuch, and he predicted the coming of a great prophet (Deuteronomy 18:15–19). Elijah represents the prophets who foretold the coming of the Messiah (Malachi 4:5, 6). Moses' and Elijah's presence with Jesus confirmed Jesus' Messianic mission—to fulfill God's law and the words of God's prophets. Just as God's voice in the cloud over Mount Sinai gave authority to his law (Exodus 19:9), God's voice at the transfiguration gave authority to Jesus' words.

17:4 Peter wanted to build three shelters for these three great men. He had the right idea about Christ, but his timing was wrong. Peter wanted to act, but this was a time for worship and adoration. He wanted to capture the moment, but he was supposed to learn and move on.

5 While he was still speaking, a bright cloud enveloped them, and a voice from the cloud said, "This is my Son, whom I love; with him I am well pleased. p Listen to him!" q

6 When the disciples heard this, they fell facedown to the ground, terrified. 7 But Jesus came and touched them. "Get up," he said. "Don't be afraid." r 8 When they looked up, they saw no one except Jesus.

9 As they were coming down the mountain, Jesus instructed them, "Don't tell anyone what you have seen, until the Son of Man has been raised from the dead." s

10 The disciples asked him, "Why then do the teachers of the law say that Elijah must come first?"

11 Jesus replied, "To be sure, Elijah comes and will restore all things. t 12 But I tell you, Elijah has already come, u and they did not recognize him, but have done to him everything they wished. v In the same way the Son of Man is going to suffer w at their hands." 13 Then the disciples understood that he was talking to them about John the Baptist.

Jesus Heals a Demon-Possessed Boy (112/Mark 9:14–29; Luke 9:37–43)

14 When they came to the crowd, a man approached Jesus and knelt before him. 15 "Lord, have mercy on my son," he said. "He has seizures and is suffering greatly. He often falls into the fire or into the water. 16 I brought him to your disciples, but they could not heal him."

17 "O unbelieving and perverse generation," Jesus replied, "how long shall I stay with you? How long shall I put up with you? Bring the boy here to me." 18 Jesus rebuked the demon, and it came out of the boy, and he was healed from that moment.

19 Then the disciples came to Jesus in private and asked, "Why couldn't we drive it out?"

20 He replied, "Because you have so little faith. I tell you the truth, if you have faith x as small as a mustard seed, y you can say to this mountain, 'Move from here to there' and it will move. z Nothing will be impossible for you. a "

Jesus Again Predicts His Death the Second Time (113/Mark 9:30–32; Luke 9:44–45)

22 When they came together in Galilee, he said to them, "The Son of Man is going to be betrayed into the hands of men. 23 They will kill him, and on the third day he will be raised to life." And the disciples were filled with grief.

a 20 Some manuscripts you. 21 But this kind does not go out except by prayer and fasting.

17:5 Mt 3:17; 2Pe 1:17
q Ac 3:22, 23

17:7 r Mt 14:27

17:9 s Mt 16:21

17:11 t Mal 4:6; Lk 1:16, 17

17:12 u Mt 11:14
v Mt 14:3, 10
w Mt 16:21

17:20 x Mt 21:21
y Mk 11:23; Lk 17:6
z 1Co 13:2

17:5 Jesus is more than just a great leader, a good example, a good influence, or a great prophet. He is the Son of God. When you understand this profound truth, the only adequate response is worship. When you have a correct understanding of Christ, you will obey him.

17:9 Jesus told Peter, James, and John not to tell anyone what they had seen until after his resurrection because Jesus knew that they didn't fully understand it and could not explain what they didn't understand. Their question (17:10ff) revealed their misunderstandings. They knew that Jesus was the Messiah, but they had much more to learn about the significance of his death and resurrection.

17:10–12 Based on Malachi 4:5, 6, the teachers of the Old Testament law believed that Elijah must appear before the Messiah would appear. Jesus referred to John the Baptist, not to the Old Testament prophet Elijah. John the Baptist took on Elijah's prophetic role—boldly confronting sin and pointing people to God. Malachi had prophesied that a prophet like Elijah would come (Malachi 4:5).

17:17 The disciples had been given the authority to do the healing, but they had not yet learned how to appropriate the power of God. Jesus' frustration is with the unbelieving and unresponsive generation. His disciples were merely a reflection of that attitude in this instance. Jesus' purpose was not to criticize the disciples, but to encourage them to greater faith.

17:17-20 The disciples had been unable to drive out this demon, and they asked Jesus why. He pointed to their lack of faith. It is the power of God, not our faith, that moves mountains, but faith must be present to do so. The mustard seed was the smallest particle imaginable. Even small or undeveloped faith would have been sufficient. Perhaps the disciples had tried to drive out the demon with their own ability rather than God's. There is great potential in even a little faith when God is with us. If we feel weak or powerless as Christians, we should examine our faith, making sure we are trusting not in our own abilities to produce results, but in God's.

17:20 Jesus wasn't condemning the disciples for substandard faith; he was trying to show how important faith would be in their future ministry. If you are facing a problem that seems as big and immovable as a mountain, turn your eyes from the mountain and look to Christ for more faith. Only then will your work for him become useful and vibrant.

17:22, 23 Once again Jesus predicted his death (see also 16:21); but more important, he told of his resurrection. Unfortunately, the disciples heard only the first part of Jesus' words and became discouraged. They couldn't understand why Jesus wanted to go back to Jerusalem where he would walk right into trouble.

The disciples didn't fully comprehend the purpose of Jesus' death and resurrection until Pentecost (Acts 2). They didn't know that Jesus' death and resurrection would make his kingdom possible. We shouldn't get upset at ourselves for being slow to understand everything about Jesus. After all, the disciples were with him, saw his miracles, heard his words, and still had difficulty understanding. Despite their questions and doubts, however, they believed. We should do no less.

Peter Finds the Coin in the Fish's Mouth (114)

17:24
a Ex 30:13

24After Jesus and his disciples arrived in Capernaum, the collectors of the two-drachma tax*a* came to Peter and asked, "Doesn't your teacher pay the temple tax*a*?"

17:25
b Mt 22:17-21;
Ro 13:7

25"Yes, he does," he replied.

When Peter came into the house, Jesus was the first to speak. "What do you think, Simon?" he asked. "From whom do the kings of the earth collect duty and taxes*b*—from their own sons or from others?"

26"From others," Peter answered.

17:27
c Jn 6:61

"Then the sons are exempt," Jesus said to him. 27"But so that we may not offend*c* them, go to the lake and throw out your line. Take the first fish you catch; open its mouth and you will find a four-drachma coin. Take it and give it to them for my tax and yours."

The Disciples Argue about Who Would Be the Greatest (115/Mark 9:33–37; Luke 9:46–48)

18 At that time the disciples came to Jesus and asked, "Who is the greatest in the kingdom of heaven?"

18:3
d Mt 19:14; 1Pe 2:2

2He called a little child and had him stand among them. 3And he said: "I tell you the truth, unless you change and become like little children,*d* you will never enter the kingdom of heaven. 4Therefore, whoever humbles himself like this child is the greatest in the kingdom of heaven.

18:6
e Lk 17:2

5"And whoever welcomes a little child like this in my name welcomes me. 6But if anyone causes one of these little ones who believe in me to sin, it would be better for him to have a large millstone hung around his neck and to be drowned in the depths of the sea.*e*

Jesus Warns against Temptation (117/Mark 9:42–50)

18:7
f Lk 17:1
18:8
g Mt 5:29;
Mk 9:43, 45
18:9
h Mt 5:29

7"Woe to the world because of the things that cause people to sin! Such things must come, but woe to the man through whom they come!*f* 8If your hand or your foot causes you to sin,*g* cut it off and throw it away. It is better for you to enter life maimed or crippled than to have two hands or two feet and be thrown into eternal fire. 9And if your eye causes you to sin,*h* gouge it out and throw it away. It is better for you to enter life with one eye than to have two eyes and be thrown into the fire of hell.

a 24 Greek *the two drachmas*

17:24 All Jewish males had to pay a temple tax to support temple upkeep (Exodus 30:11–16). Tax collectors set up booths to collect these taxes. Only Matthew records this incident—perhaps because he had been a tax collector himself.

17:24–27 Peter answered a question without really knowing the answer, putting Jesus and the disciples in an awkward position. Jesus used this situation, however, to emphasize his kingly role. Just as kings pay no taxes and collect none from their family, Jesus, the King, owed no taxes. But Jesus supplied the tax payment for both himself and Peter rather than offend those who didn't understand his kingship. Although Jesus supplied the tax money, Peter had to go and get it. Ultimately all that we have comes to us from God's supply, but he may want us to be active in the process.

17:24–27 As God's people, we are foreigners on earth because our loyalty is always to our real King—Jesus. Still we have to cooperate with the authorities and be responsible citizens. An ambassador to another country keeps the local laws in order to represent well the one who sent him. We are Christ's ambassadors (2 Corinthians 5:20). Are you being a good foreign ambassador for him to this world?

18:1 From Mark's Gospel we learn that Jesus precipitated this conversation by asking the disciples what they had been discussing among themselves earlier (Mark 9:33, 34).

18:1–4 Jesus used a child to help his self-centered disciples get the point. We are not to be *childish* (like the disciples, arguing over petty issues), but rather *childlike*, with humble and sincere hearts. In what areas of your life do you tend to struggle with childishness? In what ways are you making progress with child-likeness?

18:3, 4 The disciples had become so preoccupied with the organization of Jesus' earthly kingdom that they had lost sight of its divine purpose. Instead of seeking a place of service, they sought positions of advantage. It is easy to lose our eternal perspective and compete for promotions or status in the church. It is difficult, but healthy, to identify with "children"—weak and dependent people with no status or influence.

18:6 Children are trusting by nature. They trust adults, and through that trust their capacity to trust God grows. God holds parents and other adults who influence young children accountable for how they affect these little ones' ability to trust. Jesus warned that anyone who turns little children away from faith will receive severe punishment.

18:7ff Jesus warned the disciples about two ways to cause "little ones" to sin: tempting them (18:7–9) and neglecting or demeaning them (18:10–14). As leaders, we are to help young people or new believers avoid anything or anyone that could cause them to stumble in their faith and lead them to sin. We must never take lightly the spiritual education and protection of those young in age or young in the faith.

18:8, 9 We must remove stumbling blocks that cause us to sin. This does not mean to cut off a part of the body; it means that any person, program, or teaching in the church that threatens the spiritual growth of the body must be removed. For the individual, any relationship, practice, or activity that leads to sin should be stopped. Jesus says it would be better to go to heaven with one hand than to hell with both. Sin, of course, affects more than our hands; it affects our minds and hearts.

Jesus Warns against Looking Down on Others (118)

10"See that you do not look down on one of these little ones. For I tell you that their an- *18:10*
gels*i* in heaven always see the face of my Father in heaven. *a*   *iPs 34:7*

12"What do you think? If a man owns a hundred sheep, and one of them wanders away,
will he not leave the ninety-nine on the hills and go to look for the one that wandered off?
13And if he finds it, I tell you the truth, he is happier about that one sheep than about the
ninety-nine that did not wander off. 14In the same way your Father in heaven is not willing
that any of these little ones should be lost.

Jesus Teaches How to Treat a Believer Who Sins (119)

15"If your brother sins against you,*b* go and show him his fault,*j* just between the two of   *18:15*
you. If he listens to you, you have won your brother over. 16But if he will not listen, take one   *jLev 19:17; Lk 17:3;*
or two others along, so that 'every matter may be established by the testimony of two or   *Jas 5:19, 20*
three witnesses.'*ck* 17If he refuses to listen to them, tell it to the church; and if he refuses to   *18:16*
listen even to the church, treat him as you would a pagan or a tax collector.   *kDt 19:15; Jn 8:17;*
                                                                                2Co 13:1;
                                                                                Heb 10:28
18"I tell you the truth, whatever you bind on earth will be*d* bound in heaven, and whatever   *18:18*
you loose on earth will be*d* loosed in heaven.*l*   *lMt 16:19; Jn 20:23*

19"Again, I tell you that if two of you on earth agree about anything you ask for, it will be
done for you by my Father in heaven. 20For where two or three come together in my name,
there am I with them."

Jesus Tells the Parable of the Unforgiving Debtor (120)

21Then Peter came to Jesus and asked, "Lord, how many times shall I forgive my brother   *18:21*
when he sins against me? Up to seven times?"*m*   *mLk 17:4*

22Jesus answered, "I tell you, not seven times, but seventy-seven times.*en*   *18:22*
                                                                                nGe 4:24
23"Therefore, the kingdom of heaven is like a king who wanted to settle accounts*o* with   *18:23*
his servants. 24As he began the settlement, a man who owed him ten thousand talents*f* was   *oMt 25:19*
brought to him. 25Since he was not able to pay,*p* the master ordered that he and his wife and   *18:25*
his children and all that he had be sold*q* to repay the debt.   *pLk 7:42*
                                                                                q2Ki 4:1; Ne 5:5, 8
26"The servant fell on his knees before him.*r* 'Be patient with me,' he begged, 'and I will   *18:26*
pay back everything.' 27The servant's master took pity on him, canceled the debt and let   *rMt 8:2*
him go.

*a 10 Some manuscripts heaven. 11 The Son of Man came to save what was lost. b 15 Some manuscripts do not
have against you. c 16 Deut. 19:15 d 18 Or have been e 22 Or seventy times seven f 24 That is, millions
of dollars*

18:10 Our concern for children must match God's treatment of
them. Certain angels are assigned to watch over children, and
they have direct access to God. These words ring out sharply in
cultures where children are taken lightly, ignored, or aborted. If
their angels have constant access to God, the least we can do is
to allow children to approach us easily in spite of our far too busy
schedules.

18:14 Just as a shepherd is concerned enough about one lost
sheep to go search the hills for it, so God is concerned about
every human being he has created (he is "not wanting anyone to
perish," 2 Peter 3:9). You come in contact with children who need
Christ at home, at school, in church, and in the neighborhood.
Steer them toward Christ by your example, your words, and your
acts of kindness.

18:15–17 These are Jesus' guidelines for dealing with those
who sin against us. They were meant for (1) Christians, not
unbelievers, (2) sins committed against *you* and not others,
and (3) conflict resolution in the context of the church, not the
community at large. Jesus' words are not a license for a frontal
attack on every person who hurts or slights us. They are not a
license to start a destructive gossip campaign or to call for a
church trial. They are designed to reconcile those who disagree
so that all Christians can live in harmony.

When someone wrongs us, we often do the opposite of what
Jesus recommends. We turn away in hatred or resentment, seek

revenge, or engage in gossip. By contrast, we should go to that
person *first*, as difficult as that may be. Then we should forgive
that person as often as he or she needs it (18:21, 22). This will
create a much better chance of restoring the relationship.

18:18 This *binding* and *loosing* refers to the decisions of the
church in conflicts. Among believers, there should need to be
no court of appeals beyond the church. Ideally, the church's
decisions should be God-guided and based on discernment
of his Word. Believers have the responsibility, therefore, to
bring their problems to the church, and the church has the
responsibility to use God's guidance in seeking to resolve conflicts. Handling problems God's way will have an impact now and
for eternity.

18:19, 20 Jesus looked ahead to a new day when he would be
present with his followers not in body, but through his Holy
Spirit. In the body of believers (the church), the sincere agreement of two people is more powerful than the superficial agreement of thousands, because Christ's Holy Spirit is with them.
Two or more believers, *filled with the Holy Spirit,* will pray
according to God's will, not their own; thus their requests will
be granted.

18:22 The rabbis taught that people should forgive those who
offend them—but only three times. Peter, trying to be especially
generous, asked Jesus if seven (the "perfect" number) was
enough times to forgive someone. But Jesus answered, "Seventy-
seven times," meaning that we shouldn't even keep track of how
many times we forgive someone. We should always forgive those
who are truly repentant, no matter how many times they ask.

28"But when that servant went out, he found one of his fellow servants who owed him a hundred denarii.ᵃ He grabbed him and began to choke him. 'Pay back what you owe me!' he demanded.

29"His fellow servant fell to his knees and begged him, 'Be patient with me, and I will pay you back.'

30"But he refused. Instead, he went off and had the man thrown into prison until he could pay the debt. 31 When the other servants saw what had happened, they were greatly distressed and went and told their master everything that had happened.

32"Then the master called the servant in. 'You wicked servant,' he said, 'I canceled all that debt of yours because you begged me to. 33 Shouldn't you have had mercy on your fellow servant just as I had on you?' 34 In anger his master turned him over to the jailers to be tortured, until he should pay back all he owed.

18:35
ˢ Mt 6:14

35"This is how my heavenly Father will treat each of you unless you forgive your brother from your heart."ˢ

6. Jesus faces conflict with the religious leaders
Jesus Teaches about Marriage and Divorce (173/Mark 10:1–12)

19:2
ᵗ Mt 4:23

19
When Jesus had finished saying these things, he left Galilee and went into the region of Judea to the other side of the Jordan. 2 Large crowds followed him, and he healed them ᵗ there.

19:3
ᵘ Mt 5:31

3 Some Pharisees came to him to test him. They asked, "Is it lawful for a man to divorce his wife ᵘ for any and every reason?"

19:4
ᵛ Ge 1:27; 5:2

19:5
ʷ Ge 2:24;
1Co 6:16; Eph 5:31

4 "Haven't you read," he replied, "that at the beginning the Creator 'made them male and female,'ᵇ ᵛ 5 and said, 'For this reason a man will leave his father and mother and be united to his wife, and the two will become one flesh'ᶜ? ʷ 6 So they are no longer two, but one. Therefore what God has joined together, let man not separate."

ᵃ28 That is, a few dollars   ᵇ4 Gen. 1:27   ᶜ5 Gen. 2:24

JESUS AND FORGIVENESS

Jesus forgave . . .

	Reference
the paralyzed man lowered on a mat through the roof	Matthew 9:2–8
the woman caught in adultery	John 8:3–11
the woman who anointed his feet with oil	Luke 7:44–50
Peter, for denying he knew Jesus	John 18:15–18, 25–27; 21:15–19
the criminal on the cross	Luke 23:39–43
the people who crucified him	Luke 23:34

Jesus not only taught frequently about forgiveness, he also demonstrated his own willingness to forgive. Here are several examples that should be an encouragement to recognize his willingness to forgive us also.

18:30 In Bible times, serious consequences awaited those who could not pay their debts. A person lending money could seize the borrower who couldn't pay and force him or his family to work until the debt was paid. The debtor could also be thrown into prison, or his family could be sold into slavery to help pay off the debt. It was hoped that the debtor, while in prison, would sell off his landholdings or that relatives would pay the debt. If not, the debtor could remain in prison for life.

18:35 Because God has forgiven all our sins, we should not withhold forgiveness from others. Realizing how completely Christ has forgiven us should produce a free and generous attitude of forgiveness toward others. When we don't forgive others, we are setting ourselves outside and above Christ's law of love.

19:3–12 John had been put in prison and killed, at least in part, for his public opinions on marriage and divorce, so the Pharisees hoped to trap Jesus too. They were trying to trick Jesus by having him choose sides in a theological controversy. Two schools of thought represented two opposing views of divorce. One group supported divorce for almost any reason. The other believed that divorce could be allowed only for marital unfaithfulness. This

conflict hinged on how each group interpreted Deuteronomy 24:1–4. In his answer, however, Jesus focused on marriage rather than divorce. He pointed out that God intended marriage to be permanent and gave four reasons for the importance of marriage (19:4–6).

19:4–6 Today, many homosexuals want to commit to "marry" with the blessing of the church. Reasons for homosexual feelings and desires are complex and serious. Christians should not trivialize the situation or flippantly condemn the homosexual person. But Jesus made God's ideal very plain: At creation he approved one kind of marriage bond, man to woman. These become one flesh—one before God. See Romans 1:24–27 for further discussion.

Where does that leave homosexual marriage? At best, it is a human invention without any biblical precedent. God created man and woman. Heterosexual monogamy is God's plan for marriage—the best plan, the only one.

7"Why then," they asked, "did Moses command that a man give his wife a certificate of divorce and send her away?"ˣ

19:7
ˣDt 24:1-4

8Jesus replied, "Moses permitted you to divorce your wives because your hearts were hard. But it was not this way from the beginning. 9I tell you that anyone who divorces his wife, except for marital unfaithfulness, and marries another woman commits adultery."ʸ

19:9
ʸMt 5:32; Lk 16:18

10The disciples said to him, "If this is the situation between a husband and wife, it is better not to marry."

11Jesus replied, "Not everyone can accept this word, but only those to whom it has been given. ᶻ 12For some are eunuchs because they were born that way; others were made that way by men; and others have renounced marriageᵃ because of the kingdom of heaven. The one who can accept this should accept it."

19:11
ᶻMt 13:11;
1Co 7:7-9, 17

Jesus Blesses the Children (*174/Mark 10:13–16; Luke 18:15–17*)

13Then little children were brought to Jesus for him to place his hands on them and pray for them. But the disciples rebuked those who brought them.

14Jesus said, "Let the little children come to me, and do not hinder them, for the kingdom of heaven belongs to such as these."ᵃ 15When he had placed his hands on them, he went on from there.

19:14
ᵃMt 18:3; 1Pe 2:2

Jesus Speaks to the Rich Young Man (*175/Mark 10:17–31; Luke 18:18–30*)

16Now a man came up to Jesus and asked, "Teacher, what good thing must I do to get eternal life ᵇ?" ᶜ

19:16
ᵇMt 25:46
ᶜLk 10:25

17"Why do you ask me about what is good?" Jesus replied. "There is only One who is good. If you want to enter life, obey the commandments."

ᵃ12 Or *have made themselves eunuchs*

19:7, 8 This law is found in Deuteronomy 24:1–4. In Moses' day, as well as in Jesus' day, the practice of marriage fell far short of God's intention. The same is true today. Jesus said that Moses gave this law only because of the people's hard hearts—permanent marriage was God's intention. But because sinful human nature made divorce inevitable, Moses instituted some laws to help its victims. These were civil laws designed especially to protect the women who, in that culture, were quite vulnerable when living alone. Because of Moses' law, a man could no longer just throw his wife out—he had to write a formal letter of dismissal. This was a radical step toward civil rights, for it made men think twice about divorce. God designed marriage to be indissoluble. Instead of looking for reasons to leave each other, married couples should concentrate on how to stay together (19:3–9).

19:10–12 Although divorce was relatively easy in Old Testament times (19:7), it is not what God originally intended. Couples should decide against divorce from the start and build their marriage on mutual commitment. There are also many good reasons for not marrying, one being to have more time to work for God's kingdom. Don't assume that God wants everyone to marry. For many it may be better if they don't. Be sure that you prayerfully seek God's will before you make the lifelong commitment of marriage.

19:12 A "eunuch" is an emasculated male—a man with no testicles. Jesus' point here is that some people have physical limitations that prevent their marrying, while others choose not to marry because, in their particular situation, they can serve God better as single people. Jesus was not teaching us to avoid marriage because it is inconvenient or takes away our freedom. That would be selfishness. A good reason to remain single is to use the time and freedom to serve God. Paul elaborates on this in 1 Corinthians 7.

19:13–15 The disciples must have forgotten what Jesus had said about children (18:4–6). Jesus wanted little children to come because he loves them and because they have the kind of attitude needed to approach God. All people need childlike faith in God. The receptiveness of little children was a great contrast to the stubbornness of the religious leaders who let their education and sophistication stand in the way of the simple faith needed to believe in Jesus.

19:16 To this man seeking assurance of eternal life, Jesus pointed out that salvation does not come from good deeds unaccompanied by love for God. The man needed a whole new starting point. Instead of adding another commandment to keep or good deed to perform, the young man needed to submit humbly to the lordship of Christ.

19:17ff In response to the young man's question about what good deed he needed to do in order to be assured of eternal life, Jesus told him to keep God's Ten Commandments. Jesus then listed six of them, all referring to relationships with others. When the young man replied that he had kept the commandments, Jesus told him that he must do something more—sell everything and give the money to the poor. Jesus' statement exposed the man's weakness. In reality, his wealth was his god, his idol, and he would not give it up. Thus he violated the first and greatest commandment (Exodus 20:3; Matthew 22:36–40).

JESUS TRAVELS TOWARD JERUSALEM
Jesus left Galilee for the last time—heading toward Jerusalem and death. He again crossed the Jordan, spending some time in Perea before going on to Jericho.

Mediterranean Sea
GALILEE
Capernaum
Sea of Galilee
N
SAMARIA
Jordan River
Jericho
Jerusalem
PEREA
Dead Sea
JUDEA
IDUMEA
0   20 Mi.
0   20 Km.

19:18
d Jas 2:11

19:19
e Lev 19:18

19:21
f Lk 12:33; Ac 2:45;
4:34-35
g Mt 6:20

19:23
h Mt 13:22

19:26
i Ge 18:14;
Job 42:2; Jer 32:17;
Zec 8:6

19:28
j Lk 22:28-30;
Rev 3:21

19:30
k Mt 20:16; Lk 13:30

20:1
l Mt 13:24

¹⁸"Which ones?" the man inquired.

Jesus replied, " 'Do not murder, do not commit adultery,*d* do not steal, do not give false testimony, ¹⁹honor your father and mother,'*a* and 'love your neighbor as yourself.'*b* "*e*

²⁰"All these I have kept," the young man said. "What do I still lack?"

²¹Jesus answered, "If you want to be perfect, go, sell your possessions and give to the poor,*f* and you will have treasure in heaven.*g* Then come, follow me."

²²When the young man heard this, he went away sad, because he had great wealth.

²³Then Jesus said to his disciples, "I tell you the truth, it is hard for a rich man*h* to enter the kingdom of heaven. ²⁴Again I tell you, it is easier for a camel to go through the eye of a needle than for a rich man to enter the kingdom of God."

²⁵When the disciples heard this, they were greatly astonished and asked, "Who then can be saved?"

²⁶Jesus looked at them and said, "With man this is impossible, but with God all things are possible."*i*

²⁷Peter answered him, "We have left everything to follow you! What then will there be for us?"

²⁸Jesus said to them, "I tell you the truth, at the renewal of all things, when the Son of Man sits on his glorious throne, you who have followed me will also sit on twelve thrones, judging the twelve tribes of Israel.*j* ²⁹And everyone who has left houses or brothers or sisters or father or mother*c* or children or fields for my sake will receive a hundred times as much and will inherit eternal life. ³⁰But many who are first will be last, and many who are last will be first.*k*

Jesus Tells the Parable of the Vineyard Workers (176)

20 "For the kingdom of heaven is like*l* a landowner who went out early in the morning to hire men to work in his vineyard. ²He agreed to pay them a denarius for the day and sent them into his vineyard.

³"About the third hour he went out and saw others standing in the marketplace doing nothing. ⁴He told them, 'You also go and work in my vineyard, and I will pay you whatever is right.' ⁵So they went.

"He went out again about the sixth hour and the ninth hour and did the same thing. ⁶About the eleventh hour he went out and found still others standing around. He asked them, 'Why have you been standing here all day long doing nothing?'

a 19 Exodus 20:12-16; Deut. 5:16-20   *b 19* Lev. 19:18   *c 29* Some manuscripts *mother or wife*

19:21 When Jesus told this young man that he would "be perfect" if he gave everything he had to the poor, Jesus wasn't speaking in the temporal, human sense. He was explaining how to be justified and made whole or complete in God's sight.

19:21 Should all believers sell everything they own? No. We are responsible to care for our own needs and the needs of our families so as not to be a burden on others. We should, however, be willing to give up anything if God asks us to do so. This kind of attitude allows nothing to come between us and God and keeps us from using our God-given wealth selfishly. If you are relieved by the fact that Christ did not tell all his followers to sell all their possessions, then you may be too attached to what you have.

19:22 We cannot love God with all our hearts and yet keep our money to ourselves. Loving him totally means using our money in ways that please him.

19:24–26 Because it is impossible for a camel to go through the eye of a needle, it appears impossible for a rich person to get into the kingdom of God. The disciples were astounded. They thought that if anyone could be saved, it would be the rich, whom their culture considered especially blessed by God. Jesus explained, however, that "with God all things are possible" (19:26). Even rich people can enter the kingdom if God brings them in. Faith in Christ, not in self or riches, is what counts. On what are you counting for salvation?

19:27 In the Bible, God gives rewards to his people according to his justice. In the Old Testament, obedience often brought reward in this life (Deuteronomy 28), but obedience and immediate

reward are not always linked. If they were, good people would always be rich, and suffering would always be a sign of sin. As believers, our true reward is God's presence and power through the Holy Spirit. Later, in eternity, we will be rewarded for our faith and service. If material rewards in this life came to us for every faithful deed, we would be tempted to boast about our achievements and act out of wrong motivations.

19:29 Jesus assured the disciples that anyone who gives up something valuable for his sake will be repaid many times over in this life, although not necessarily in the same form. For example, a person may be rejected by his or her family for accepting Christ, but he or she will gain the larger family of believers.

19:30 Jesus turned the world's values upside down. Consider the most powerful or well-known people in our world—how many got where they are by being humble, self-effacing, and gentle? Not many! But in the life to come, the last will be first—if they got in last place by choosing to follow Jesus. Don't forfeit eternal rewards for temporary benefits. Be willing to make sacrifices now for greater rewards later. Be willing to accept human disapproval, while knowing that you have God's approval.

20:1ff Jesus further clarified the membership rules of the kingdom of heaven—entrance is by God's grace alone. In this parable, God is the landowner, and believers are the workers. This parable speaks especially to those who feel superior because of heritage or favored position, to those who feel superior because they have spent so much time with Christ, and to new believers as reassurance of God's grace.

7 "'Because no one has hired us,' they answered.

"He said to them, 'You also go and work in my vineyard.'

8 "When evening came,*m* the owner of the vineyard said to his foreman, 'Call the workers and pay them their wages, beginning with the last ones hired and going on to the first.'

9 "The workers who were hired about the eleventh hour came and each received a denarius. 10 So when those came who were hired first, they expected to receive more. But each one of them also received a denarius. 11 When they received it, they began to grumble against the landowner. 12 'These men who were hired last worked only one hour,' they said, 'and you have made them equal to us who have borne the burden of the work and the heat*n* of the day.'

13 "But he answered one of them, 'Friend, I am not being unfair to you. Didn't you agree to work for a denarius? 14 Take your pay and go. I want to give the man who was hired last the same as I gave you. 15 Don't I have the right to do what I want with my own money? Or are you envious because I am generous?'*o*

16 "So the last will be first, and the first will be last."*p*

Jesus Predicts His Death the Third Time (*177*/Mark 10:32–34; Luke 18:31–34)

17 Now as Jesus was going up to Jerusalem, he took the twelve disciples aside and said to them, 18 "We are going up to Jerusalem, and the Son of Man will be betrayed to the chief priests and the teachers of the law. *q* They will condemn him to death 19 and will turn him over to the Gentiles to be mocked and flogged*r* and crucified.*s* On the third day he will be raised to life!"

Jesus Teaches about Serving Others (*178*/Mark 10:35–45)

20 Then the mother of Zebedee's sons*t* came to Jesus with her sons and, kneeling down, asked a favor of him.

21 "What is it you want?" he asked.

She said, "Grant that one of these two sons of mine may sit at your right and the other at your left in your kingdom."*u*

22 "You don't know what you are asking," Jesus said to them. "Can you drink the cup*v* I am going to drink?"

"We can," they answered.

23 Jesus said to them, "You will indeed drink from my cup,*w* but to sit at my right or left is not for me to grant. These places belong to those for whom they have been prepared by my Father."

20:8
m Lev 19:13

20:12
n Jnh 4:8; Jas 1:11

20:15
o Dt 15:9; Mk 7:22

20:16
p Mt 19:30

20:18
q Mt 16:21

20:19
r Mt 16:21
s Ac 2:23

20:20
t Mt 4:21

20:21
u Mt 19:28

20:22
v Mt 26:39, 42;
Lk 22:42; Jn 18:11

20:23
w Ac 12:2; Rev 1:9

20:15 This parable is not about rewards but about salvation. It is a strong teaching about *grace,* God's generosity. We shouldn't begrudge those who turn to God in the last moments of life, because, in reality, *no one* deserves eternal life.

Many people we don't expect to see in the kingdom will be there. The criminal who repented as he was dying (Luke 23:40–43) will be there along with people who have believed and served God for many years. Do you resent God's gracious acceptance of the despised, the outcast, and the sinners who have turned to him for forgiveness? Are you ever jealous of what God has given to another person? Instead, focus on God's gracious benefits to you, and be thankful for what you have.

20:17–19 Jesus predicted his death and resurrection for the third time (see 16:21 and 17:22, 23 for the first two times). But the disciples still didn't accept and believe what he meant. They continued to argue over their positions in Christ's kingdom (20:20–28).

20:20 The mother of James and John came to Jesus and "kneeling down, asked a favor of him." She gave Jesus worship, but her real motive was to get something from him. Too often this happens in our churches and in our lives. We play religious games, expecting God to give us something in return. True worship, however, adores and praises Christ for who he is and for what he has done.

20:20 The mother of James and John asked Jesus to give her sons special positions in his kingdom. Parents naturally want to see their children promoted and honored, but this desire is dangerous if it causes them to lose sight of God's specific will for their children. God may have different work in mind—not as glamorous, but just as important. Thus parents' desires for their children's advancement must be held in check as they pray that God's will be done in their children's lives.

20:20 According to 27:56, the mother of James and John was at the cross when Jesus was crucified. Some have suggested that she was the sister of Mary, the mother of Jesus. A close family relationship may have prompted her to make this request for her sons.

20:22 James, John, and their mother failed to grasp Jesus' previous teachings on rewards (19:16–30) and eternal life (20:1–16). They failed to understand the suffering they must face before living in the glory of God's kingdom. The "cup" was the suffering and crucifixion that Christ faced. Both James and John would also face great suffering. James would be put to death for his faith, and John would be exiled.

20:23 Jesus was showing that he was under the authority of the Father, who alone makes the decisions about leadership in heaven. Such rewards are not granted as favors. They are for those who have maintained their commitment to Jesus in spite of severe trials.

20:26
x Mt 23:11; Mk 9:35

20:28
y Jn 13:13-16;
Php 2:7
z Mt 26:28; 1Ti 2:6;
Tit 2:14; Heb 9:28

²⁴When the ten heard about this, they were indignant with the two brothers. ²⁵Jesus called them together and said, "You know that the rulers of the Gentiles lord it over them, and their high officials exercise authority over them. ²⁶Not so with you. Instead, whoever wants to become great among you must be your servant,ˣ ²⁷and whoever wants to be first must be your slave— ²⁸just as the Son of Man did not come to be served, but to serve,ʸ and to give his life as a ransomᶻ for many."

Jesus Heals Two Blind Beggars (*179*/Mark 10:46–52; Luke 18:35–43)

20:30
a Mt 9:27

²⁹As Jesus and his disciples were leaving Jericho, a large crowd followed him. ³⁰Two blind men were sitting by the roadside, and when they heard that Jesus was going by, they shouted, "Lord, Son of David,ᵃ have mercy on us!"

³¹The crowd rebuked them and told them to be quiet, but they shouted all the louder, "Lord, Son of David, have mercy on us!"

³²Jesus stopped and called them. "What do you want me to do for you?" he asked.

³³"Lord," they answered, "we want our sight."

³⁴Jesus had compassion on them and touched their eyes. Immediately they received their sight and followed him.

Jesus Rides into Jerusalem on a Donkey
(*183*/Mark 11:1–11; Luke 19:28–44; John 12:12–19)

21 As they approached Jerusalem and came to Bethphage on the Mount of Olives, Jesus sent two disciples, ²saying to them, "Go to the village ahead of you, and at once you will find a donkey tied there, with her colt by her. Untie them and bring them to me. ³If anyone says anything to you, tell him that the Lord needs them, and he will send them right away."

⁴This took place to fulfill what was spoken through the prophet:

5 "Say to the Daughter of Zion,
  'See, your king comes to you,

20:24 The other disciples were upset with James and John for trying to grab the top positions. *All* the disciples wanted to be the greatest (18:1), but Jesus taught them that the greatest person in God's kingdom is the servant of all. Authority is given not for self-importance, ambition, or respect, but for useful service to God and his creation.

20:27 Jesus described leadership from a new perspective. Instead of using people, we are to serve them. Jesus' mission was to serve others and to give his life away. A real leader has a servant's heart. Servant leaders appreciate others' worth and realize that they're not above any job. If you see something that needs to be done, don't wait to be asked. Take the initiative and do it like a faithful servant.

20:28 A ransom was the price paid to release a slave from bondage. Jesus often told his disciples that he must die, but here he told them why—to redeem all people from the bondage of sin and death. The disciples thought that as long as Jesus was alive, he could save them. But Jesus revealed that only his death would save them and the world.

20:29-34 Matthew records that there were two blind men, while Mark and Luke mention only one. This is probably the same event, but Mark and Luke singled out the more vocal of the two men.

20:30 The blind men called Jesus "Son of David" because the Jews knew that the Messiah would be a descendant of David (see Isaiah 9:6, 7; 11:1; Jeremiah 23:5, 6). These blind beggars could *see* that Jesus was the long-awaited Messiah, while the religious leaders who witnessed Jesus' miracles were blind to his identity, refusing to open their eyes to the truth. Seeing with your eyes doesn't guarantee seeing with your heart.

20:32, 33 Although Jesus was concerned about the coming events in Jerusalem, he demonstrated what he had just told the disciples about service (20:28) by stopping to care for the blind men.

21:2-5 Matthew mentions a donkey and a colt, while the other Gospels mention only the colt. This was the same event, but Matthew focuses on the prophecy in Zechariah 9:9, where a donkey and a colt are mentioned. He shows how Jesus' actions fulfilled the prophet's words, thus giving another indication that Jesus was indeed the Messiah. When Jesus entered Jerusalem on a donkey's colt, he affirmed his Messianic royalty as well as his humility. On the practical side, what better way to lead an unbroken colt for its first ride down a crowded road than to have its mother with it?

PREPARATION FOR THE TRIUMPHAL ENTRY
On their way from Jericho, Jesus and the disciples neared Bethphage, on the slope of the Mount of Olives, just outside Jerusalem. Two disciples went into the village, as Jesus told them, to bring back a donkey and its colt. Jesus rode into Jerusalem on the colt, an unmistakable sign of his kingship.

gentle and riding on a donkey,
    on a colt, the foal of a donkey.'"a b

21:5
bIsa 62:11; Zec 9:9

6 The disciples went and did as Jesus had instructed them. 7 They brought the donkey and the colt, placed their cloaks on them, and Jesus sat on them. 8 A very large crowd spread their cloaks on the road, while others cut branches from the trees and spread them on the road. 9 The crowds that went ahead of him and those that followed shouted,

21:9
cPs 118:26

"Hosanna b to the Son of David!"

"Blessed is he who comes in the name of the Lord!"c c

"Hosanna b in the highest!"

10 When Jesus entered Jerusalem, the whole city was stirred and asked, "Who is this?" 11 The crowds answered, "This is Jesus, the prophet d from Nazareth in Galilee."

21:11
dJn 6:14; 7:40

Jesus Clears the Temple Again (184/Mark 11:12–19; Luke 19:45–48)

12 Jesus entered the temple area and drove out all who were buying and selling there. He overturned the tables of the money changers and the benches of those selling doves. 13 "It is written," he said to them, "'My house will be called a house of prayer,'d e but you are making it a 'den of robbers.'e "f

21:13
eIsa 56:7
fJer 7:11

14 The blind and the lame came to him at the temple, and he healed them. 15 But when the chief priests and the teachers of the law saw the wonderful things he did and the children shouting in the temple area, "Hosanna to the Son of David," they were indignant.

16 "Do you hear what these children are saying?" they asked him.

21:16
gPs 8:2

"Yes," replied Jesus, "have you never read,

"'From the lips of children and infants
    you have ordained praise'f?"g

17 And he left them and went out of the city to Bethany, where he spent the night.

Jesus Says the Disciples Can Pray for Anything (188/Mark 11:20–26)

18 Early in the morning, as he was on his way back to the city, he was hungry. 19 Seeing a fig tree by the road, he went up to it but found nothing on it except leaves. Then he said to it, "May you never bear fruit again!" Immediately the tree withered.

20 When the disciples saw this, they were amazed. "How did the fig tree wither so quickly?" they asked.

21 Jesus replied, "I tell you the truth, if you have faith and do not doubt,h not only can you do what was done to the fig tree, but also you can say to this mountain, 'Go, throw yourself into the sea,' and it will be done. 22 If you believe, you will receive whatever you ask for i in prayer."

21:21
hMt 17:20; Lk 17:6;
Jas 1:6
21:22
iMt 7:7

a5 Zech. 9:9   b9 A Hebrew expression meaning "Save!" which became an exclamation of praise; also in verse 15
c9 Psalm 118:26   d13 Isaiah 56:7   e13 Jer. 7:11   f16 Psalm 8:2

21:8 This verse is one of the few places where the Gospels record that Jesus' glory is recognized on earth. Jesus boldly rode as the King of peace, and the crowd gladly joined him. But these same people would bow to political pressure and desert him in just a few days. Today we celebrate this event on Palm Sunday. That day should remind us to guard against superficial acclaim for Christ.

21:12 This is the second time Jesus cleared the temple (see John 2:13–17). Merchants and money changers set up their booths in the court of the Gentiles in the temple, crowding out the Gentiles who had come from all over the civilized world to worship God. The merchants sold sacrificial animals at high prices, taking advantage of those who had come long distances. The money changers exchanged all international currency for the special temple coins—the only money the merchants would accept. They often deceived foreigners who didn't know the exchange rates. Their commercialism in God's house frustrated people's attempts

at worship. This, of course, greatly angered Jesus. Any practice that interferes with worshiping God should be stopped.

21:19 Why did Jesus curse the fig tree? This was not a thoughtless, angry act, but an acted-out parable. Jesus was showing his anger at religion without substance. Just as the fig tree looked good from a distance but was fruitless on close examination, so the temple looked impressive at first glance, but its sacrifices and other activities were hollow because they were not done to worship God sincerely (see 21:43). If you only appear to have faith without putting it to work in your life, you are like the fig tree that withered and died because it bore no fruit. Genuine faith means bearing fruit for God's kingdom. For more information about the fig tree, see the note on Mark 11:13–26.

21:21 Many have wondered about Jesus' statement that if we have faith and don't doubt, we can move mountains. Jesus, of course, was not suggesting that his followers use prayer as "magic" and perform capricious "mountain-moving" acts. Instead, he was making a strong point about the disciples' (and our) lack of faith. What kinds of mountains do you face? Have you talked to God about them? How strong is your faith?

Religious Leaders Challenge Jesus' Authority (**189**/Mark 11:27–33; Luke 20:1–8)

21:23
j Ac 4:7

23 Jesus entered the temple courts, and, while he was teaching, the chief priests and the elders of the people came to him. "By what authority *j* are you doing these things?" they asked. "And who gave you this authority?"

24 Jesus replied, "I will also ask you one question. If you answer me, I will tell you by what authority I am doing these things. 25 John's baptism—where did it come from? Was it from heaven, or from men?"

21:26
k Mk 6:20

They discussed it among themselves and said, "If we say, 'From heaven,' he will ask, 'Then why didn't you believe him?' 26 But if we say, 'From men'—we are afraid of the people, for they all hold that John was a prophet." *k*

27 So they answered Jesus, "We don't know."

Then he said, "Neither will I tell you by what authority I am doing these things.

Jesus Tells the Parable of the Two Sons (**190**)

21:28
l ver 33

28 "What do you think? There was a man who had two sons. He went to the first and said, 'Son, go and work today in the vineyard.' *l*

29 "'I will not,' he answered, but later he changed his mind and went.

30 "Then the father went to the other son and said the same thing. He answered, 'I will, sir,' but he did not go.

21:31
m Lk 7:29
n Lk 7:50

31 "Which of the two did what his father wanted?"

"The first," they answered.

Jesus said to them, "I tell you the truth, the tax collectors *m* and the prostitutes *n* are entering the kingdom of God ahead of you. 32 For John came to you to show you the way of righteousness, *o* and you did not believe him, but the tax collectors *p* and the prostitutes did. And even after you saw this, you did not repent and believe him.

21:32
o Mt 3:1-12
p Lk 3:12, 13

Jesus Tells the Parable of the Evil Farmers (**191**/Mark 12:1–12; Luke 20:9–19)

21:33
q Ps 80:8
r Isa 5:1-7
s Mt 25:14, 15

33 "Listen to another parable: There was a landowner who planted *q* a vineyard. He put a wall around it, dug a winepress in it and built a watchtower. *r* Then he rented the vineyard to some farmers and went away on a journey. *s* 34 When the harvest time approached, he sent his servants to the tenants to collect his fruit.

21:35
t 2Ch 24:21;
Mt 23:34, 37;
Heb 11:36, 37

35 "The tenants seized his servants; they beat one, killed another, and stoned a third. *t* 36 Then he sent other servants to them, more than the first time, and the tenants treated them the same way. 37 Last of all, he sent his son to them. 'They will respect my son,' he said.

21:38
u Heb 1:2
v Ps 2:8

38 "But when the tenants saw the son, they said to each other, 'This is the heir. *u* Come, let's kill him and take his inheritance.' *v* 39 So they took him and threw him out of the vineyard and killed him.

21:22 This verse is not a guarantee that we can get *anything* we want simply by asking Jesus and believing. God does not grant requests that would hurt us or others or that would violate his own nature or will. Jesus' statement is not a blank check. To be fulfilled, our requests must be in harmony with the principles of God's kingdom. The stronger our belief, the more likely our prayers will be in line with God's will, and then God will be happy to grant them.

21:23-27 The Pharisees demanded to know where Jesus got his authority. If Jesus said his authority came from God, they would accuse him of blasphemy. If he said that he was acting on his own authority, the crowds would be convinced that the Pharisees had the greater authority. But Jesus answered them with a seemingly unrelated question that exposed their real motives. They didn't really want an answer to their question; they only wanted to trap him. Jesus showed that the Pharisees wanted the truth only if it supported their own views and causes.

21:25 For more information on John the Baptist, see Matthew 3 and his Profile in John 1, p. 1737.

21:30 The son who said he would obey and then didn't represented many of the people of Israel in Jesus' day, particularly the religious leaders. They said they wanted to do God's will, but they constantly disobeyed. They were phony, just going through the motions. It is dangerous to pretend to obey God when our hearts

are far from him because God knows our true intentions. Our actions must match our words.

21:33ff The main elements in this parable are (1) the landowner—God, (2) the vineyard—Israel, (3) the tenants—the Jewish religious leaders, (4) the landowner's servants—the prophets and priests who remained faithful to God and preached to Israel, (5) the son—Jesus (21:38), and (6) the other tenants—the Gentiles. Jesus was exposing the religious leaders' murderous plot (21:45).

21:37 In trying to reach us with his love, God finally sent his own Son. Jesus' perfect life, his words of truth, and his sacrifice of love are meant to cause us to listen to him and to follow him as Lord. If we ignore God's gracious gift of his Son, we reject God himself.

⁴⁰"Therefore, when the owner of the vineyard comes, what will he do to those tenants?"

⁴¹"He will bring those wretches to a wretched end," they replied, "and he will rent the vineyard to other tenants,ʷ who will give him his share of the crop at harvest time."

⁴²Jesus said to them, "Have you never read in the Scriptures:

"'The stone the builders rejected
   has become the capstoneᵃ;
the Lord has done this,
   and it is marvelous in our eyes'ᵇ?ˣ

⁴³"Therefore I tell you that the kingdom of God will be taken away from youʸ and given to a people who will produce its fruit. ⁴⁴He who falls on this stone will be broken to pieces, but he on whom it falls will be crushed."ᶜ

⁴⁵When the chief priests and the Pharisees heard Jesus' parables, they knew he was talking about them. ⁴⁶They looked for a way to arrest him, but they were afraid of the crowd because the people held that he was a prophet.ᶻ

Jesus Tells the Parable of the Wedding Feast (192)

22 Jesus spoke to them again in parables, saying: ²"The kingdom of heaven is likeᵃ a king who prepared a wedding banquet for his son. ³He sent his servantsᵇ to those who had been invited to the banquet to tell them to come, but they refused to come.

⁴"Then he sent some more servantsᶜ and said, 'Tell those who have been invited that I have prepared my dinner: My oxen and fattened cattle have been butchered, and everything is ready. Come to the wedding banquet.'

⁵"But they paid no attention and went off—one to his field, another to his business. ⁶The rest seized his servants, mistreated them and killed them. ⁷The king was enraged. He sent his army and destroyed those murderersᵈ and burned their city.

⁸"Then he said to his servants, 'The wedding banquet is ready, but those I invited did not deserve to come. ⁹Go to the street corners and invite to the banquet anyone you find.' ¹⁰So the servants went out into the streets and gathered all the people they could find, both good and bad, and the wedding hall was filled with guests.

¹¹"But when the king came in to see the guests, he noticed a man there who was not wearing wedding clothes. ¹²'Friend,'ᵉ he asked, 'how did you get in here without wedding clothes?' The man was speechless.

¹³"Then the king told the attendants, 'Tie him hand and foot, and throw him outside, into the darkness, where there will be weeping and gnashing of teeth.'ᶠ

¹⁴"For many are invited, but few are chosen."

Religious Leaders Question Jesus about Paying Taxes
(193/Mark 12:13–17; Luke 20:20–26)

¹⁵Then the Pharisees went out and laid plans to trap him in his words. ¹⁶They sent their disciples to him along with the Herodians.ᵍ "Teacher," they said, "we know you are a man of

ᵃ42 Or *cornerstone* ᵇ42 Psalm 118:22,23 ᶜ44 Some manuscripts do not have verse 44.

Cross-references

21:41
ʷAc 13:46; 18:6; 28:28

21:42
ˣPs 118:22, 23; Ac 4:11

21:43
ʸMt 8:12

21:46
ᶻver 11, 26

22:2
ᵃMt 13:24

22:3
ᵇMt 21:34

22:4
ᶜMt 21:36

22:7
ᵈLk 19:27

22:12
ᵉMt 20:13; 26:50

22:13
ᶠMt 8:12

22:16
ᵍMk 3:6

21:42 Jesus refers to himself as "the stone the builders rejected." Although Jesus was rejected by many of his people, he will become the capstone, or cornerstone, of his new building, the church (see Acts 4:11; 1 Peter 2:7).

21:44 Jesus used this metaphor to show that one truth can affect people different ways, depending on how they relate to it (see Isaiah 8:14, 15; 28:16; Daniel 2:34, 44, 45). Ideally they will build on it; many, however, will trip over it. And at the last judgment God's enemies will be crushed by it. In the end, Christ, the "building block," will become the "crushing stone." He offers mercy and forgiveness *now* and promises judgment later. We should choose him now!

22:1–14 In this culture, two invitations were expected when banquets were given. The first asked the guests to attend; the second announced that all was ready. In this story the king invited his guests three times—and each time they rejected

his invitation. God wants us to join him at his banquet, which will last for eternity. That's why he sends us invitations again and again. Have you accepted his invitation?

22:11, 12 It was customary for wedding guests to be given garments to wear to the banquet. It was unthinkable to refuse to wear these garments. That would insult the host, who could only assume that the guest was arrogant and thought he didn't need these garments, or that he did not want to take part in the wedding celebration. The wedding clothes picture the righteousness needed to enter God's kingdom—the total acceptance in God's eyes that Christ gives every believer. Christ has provided this garment of righteousness for everyone, but each person must choose to put it on in order to enter the King's banquet (eternal life). There is an open invitation, but we must be ready. For more on the imagery of clothes of righteousness and salvation, see Psalm 132:16; Isaiah 61:10; Zechariah 3:3–5; Revelation 3:4, 5; 19:7, 8.

22:15–17 The Pharisees, a religious group, opposed the Roman occupation of Palestine. The Herodians, a political party,

22:17
h Mt 17:25

integrity and that you teach the way of God in accordance with the truth. You aren't swayed by men, because you pay no attention to who they are. ¹⁷Tell us then, what is your opinion? Is it right to pay taxes *h* to Caesar or not?"

¹⁸But Jesus, knowing their evil intent, said, "You hypocrites, why are you trying to trap me? ¹⁹Show me the coin used for paying the tax." They brought him a denarius, ²⁰and he asked them, "Whose portrait is this? And whose inscription?"

22:21
i Ro 13:7

²¹"Caesar's," they replied.

Then he said to them, "Give to Caesar what is Caesar's, *i* and to God what is God's."
²²When they heard this, they were amazed. So they left him and went away.

Religious Leaders Question Jesus about the Resurrection
(194/Mark 12:18–27; Luke 20:27–40)

22:23
j Ac 23:8
22:24
k Dt 25:5, 6

²³That same day the Sadducees, who say there is no resurrection, *j* came to him with a question. ²⁴"Teacher," they said, "Moses told us that if a man dies without having children, his brother must marry the widow and have children for him. *k* ²⁵Now there were seven brothers among us. The first one married and died, and since he had no children, he left his wife to his brother. ²⁶The same thing happened to the second and third brother, right on down to the seventh. ²⁷Finally, the woman died. ²⁸Now then, at the resurrection, whose wife will she be of the seven, since all of them were married to her?"

22:29
l Jn 20:9

²⁹Jesus replied, "You are in error because you do not know the Scriptures *l* or the power of God. ³⁰At the resurrection people will neither marry nor be given in marriage; they will be like the angels in heaven. ³¹But about the resurrection of the dead—have you not read what God said to you, ³²'I am the God of Abraham, the God of Isaac, and the God of Jacob'*a*?*m* He is not the God of the dead but of the living."

22:32
m Ex 3:6; Ac 7:32
22:33
n Mt 7:28

³³When the crowds heard this, they were astonished at his teaching. *n*

Religious Leaders Question Jesus about the Greatest Commandment
(195/Mark 12:28–34)

22:35
o Lk 7:30; 10:25;
11:45

³⁴Hearing that Jesus had silenced the Sadducees, the Pharisees got together. ³⁵One of them, an expert in the law, *o* tested him with this question: ³⁶"Teacher, which is the greatest commandment in the Law?"

a 32 Exodus 3:6

---

supported Herod Antipas and the policies instituted by Rome. Normally these two groups were bitter enemies, but here they united against Jesus. Thinking they had a foolproof plan to corner him, together their representatives asked Jesus about paying Roman taxes. If Jesus agreed that it was right to pay taxes to Caesar, the Pharisees would say he was opposed to God, the only King they recognized. If Jesus said the taxes should not be paid, the Herodians would hand him over to Herod on the charge of rebellion. In this case the Pharisees were not motivated by love for God's laws, and the Herodians were not motivated by love for Roman justice. Jesus' answer exposed their evil motives and embarrassed them both.

22:17 The Jews were required to pay taxes to support the Roman government. They hated this taxation because the money went directly into Caesar's treasury, where some of it went to support the pagan temples and decadent lifestyle of the Roman aristocracy. Caesar's image on the coins was a constant reminder of Israel's subjection to Rome.

22:21 Jesus avoided this trap by showing that we have dual citizenship (1 Peter 2:17). Our citizenship in the nation requires that we pay money for the services and benefits we receive. Our citizenship in the kingdom of heaven requires that we pledge to God our ultimate obedience and commitment.

22:23ff After the Pharisees and Herodians had failed to trap Jesus, the Sadducees smugly stepped in to try. They did not believe in the resurrection because the Pentateuch (Genesis— Deuteronomy) has no direct teaching on it. The Pharisees had never been able to come up with a convincing argument from the Pentateuch for the resurrection, and the Sadducees thought they had trapped Jesus for sure. But Jesus was about to show them otherwise (see 22:31, 32 for Jesus' answer).

22:24 The law said that when a woman's husband died without having a son, the man's brother had a responsibility to marry and care for the widow (Deuteronomy 25:5, 6). This law protected women who were left alone, because in that culture they usually had no other means to support themselves.

22:29, 30 The Sadducees asked Jesus what marriage would be like in heaven. Jesus said it was more important to understand God's power than know what heaven will be like. In every generation and culture, ideas of eternal life tend to be based on images and experiences of present life. Jesus answered that these faulty ideas are caused by ignorance of God's Word. We must not make up our own ideas about eternity and heaven by thinking of it and God in human terms. We should concentrate more on our relationship with God than about what heaven will look like. Eventually we will find out, and it will be far beyond our greatest expectations.

22:31, 32 Because the Sadducees accepted only the Pentateuch as God's divine Word, Jesus answered them from the book of Exodus (3:6). God would not have said, "I am the God of Abraham, the God of Isaac, and the God of Jacob" if God thought of Abraham, Isaac, and Jacob as dead. From God's perspective, they are alive. Jesus' use of the present tense pointed to the resurrection and the eternal life that all believers enjoy in him.

22:34 We might think the Pharisees would have been glad to see the Sadducees silenced. The question that the Sadducees had always used to trap them was finally answered by Jesus. But the Pharisees were too proud to be impressed. Jesus' answer gave them a theological victory over the Sadducees, but they were more interested in defeating Jesus than in learning the truth.

37 Jesus replied: "'Love the Lord your God with all your heart and with all your soul and with all your mind.'a p 38 This is the first and greatest commandment. 39 And the second is like it: 'Love your neighbor as yourself.'b q 40 All the Law and the Prophets hang on these two commandments."r

22:37
p Dt 6:5
22:39
q Lev 19:18;
Mt 19:19
22:40
r Mt 7:12

Religious Leaders Cannot Answer Jesus' Question
(196/Mark 12:35–37; Luke 20:41–44)

41 While the Pharisees were gathered together, Jesus asked them, 42 "What do you think about the Christc? Whose son is he?"

"The son of David," they replied.

43 He said to them, "How is it then that David, speaking by the Spirit, calls him 'Lord'? For he says,

44   "'The Lord said to my Lord:
        "Sit at my right hand
        until I put your enemies
        under your feet."'d s

22:44
s Ps 110:1; Ac 2:34,
35; Heb 1:13; 10:13

45 If then David calls him 'Lord,' how can he be his son?" 46 No one could say a word in reply, and from that day on no one dared to ask him any more questions.t

22:46
t Mk 12:34

Jesus Warns against the Religious Leaders (197/Mark 12:38–40; Luke 20:45–47)

23 Then Jesus said to the crowds and to his disciples: 2 "The teachers of the law and the Pharisees sit in Moses' seat. 3 So you must obey them and do everything they tell you. But do not do what they do, for they do not practice what they preach. 4 They tie up heavy loads and put them on men's shoulders, but they themselves are not willing to lift a finger to move them. u

5 "Everything they do is done for men to see: v They make their phylacteriese w wide and the tassels on their garments long; 6 they love the place of honor at banquets and the most important seats in the synagogues;x 7 they love to be greeted in the marketplaces and to have men call them 'Rabbi.'

8 "But you are not to be called 'Rabbi,' for you have only one Master and you are all brothers. 9 And do not call anyone on earth 'father,' for you have one Father, and he is in heaven.

23:4
u Lk 11:46

23:5
v Mt 6:1, 2, 5, 16
w Dt 6:8

23:6
x Lk 11:43

a 37 Deut. 6:5   b 39 Lev. 19:18   c 42 Or *Messiah*   d 44 Psalm 110:1   e 5 That is, boxes containing Scripture verses, worn on forehead and arm

---

22:35–40 The Pharisees, who had classified over 600 laws, often tried to distinguish the more important from the less important. So one of them, an "expert in the law," asked Jesus to identify the most important law. Jesus quoted from Deuteronomy 6:5 and Leviticus 19:18. By fulfilling these two commands, a person keeps all the others. They summarize the Ten Commandments and the other Old Testament moral laws.

22:37–40 Jesus says that if we truly love God and our neighbor, we will naturally keep the commandments. This is looking at God's law positively. Rather than worrying about all we should *not* do, we should concentrate on all we *can* do to show our love for God and others.

22:41–45 The Pharisees, Herodians, and Sadducees had asked their questions. Then Jesus turned the tables and asked them a penetrating question—who they thought the Messiah was. The Pharisees knew that the Messiah would be a descendant of David, but they did not understand that he would be God himself. Jesus quoted from Psalm 110:1 to show that the Messiah would be greater than David. (Hebrews 1:13 uses the same text as proof of Christ's deity.) The most important question we will ever answer

is what we believe about Christ. Other theological questions are irrelevant until we believe that Jesus is who he said he is.

23:2, 3 The Pharisees' traditions and their interpretations and applications of the laws had become as important to them as God's law itself. Their laws were not all bad—some were beneficial. The problem arose when the religious leaders (1) took manmade rules as seriously as God's laws, (2) told the people to obey these rules but did not do so themselves, or (3) obeyed the rules not to honor God but to make themselves look good. Usually Jesus did not condemn what the Pharisees taught, but what they *were*—hypocrites.

23:5 Phylacteries were little leather boxes containing Scripture verses. Very religious people wore these boxes on their forehead and arms in order to obey Deuteronomy 6:8 and Exodus 13:9, 16. But the phylacteries had become more important for the status they gave than for the truth they contained.

23:5–7 Jesus again exposed the hypocritical attitudes of the religious leaders. They knew the Scriptures but did not live by them. They didn't care about *being* holy—just *looking* holy in order to receive the people's admiration and praise. Today, like the Pharisees, many people who know the Bible do not let it change their lives. They say they follow Jesus, but they don't live by his standards of love. People who live this way are hypocrites. We must make sure that our actions match our beliefs.

23:5–7 People desire positions of leadership not only in business but also in the church. It is dangerous when love for the position grows stronger than loyalty to God. This is what happened to the Pharisees and teachers of the law. Jesus condemned leaders who serve themselves rather than others.

23:11
y Mt 20:26

23:12
z Lk 14:11

10 Nor are you to be called 'teacher,' for you have one Teacher, the Christ. a 11 The greatest among you will be your servant. y 12 For whoever exalts himself will be humbled, and whoever humbles himself will be exalted. z

Jesus Condemns the Religious Leaders (198)

23:13
a Lk 11:52

13 "Woe to you, teachers of the law and Pharisees, you hypocrites! You shut the kingdom of heaven in men's faces. You yourselves do not enter, nor will you let those enter who are trying to. b a

15 "Woe to you, teachers of the law and Pharisees, you hypocrites! You travel over land and sea to win a single convert, and when he becomes one, you make him twice as much a son of hell as you are.

23:16
b ver 24
c Mt 5:33-35

23:17
d Ex 30:29

23:19
e Ex 29:37

23:22
f Mt 5:34

23:23
g Lk 11:42

16 "Woe to you, blind guides! b You say, 'If anyone swears by the temple, it means nothing; but if anyone swears by the gold of the temple, he is bound by his oath.' c 17 You blind fools! Which is greater: the gold, or the temple that makes the gold sacred? d 18 You also say, 'If anyone swears by the altar, it means nothing; but if anyone swears by the gift on it, he is bound by his oath.' 19 You blind men! Which is greater: the gift, or the altar that makes the gift sacred? e 20 Therefore, he who swears by the altar swears by it and by everything on it. 21 And he who swears by the temple swears by it and by the one who dwells in it. 22 And he who swears by heaven swears by God's throne and by the one who sits on it. f

23 "Woe to you, teachers of the law and Pharisees, you hypocrites! You give a tenth of your spices—mint, dill and cummin. But you have neglected the more important matters of the law—justice, mercy and faithfulness. g You should have practiced the latter, without neglecting the former. 24 You blind guides! You strain out a gnat but swallow a camel.

a 10 Or Messiah   b 13 Some manuscripts to. 14 Woe to you, teachers of the law and Pharisees, you hypocrites! You devour widows' houses and for a show make lengthy prayers. Therefore you will be punished more severely.

THE SEVEN WOES

23:13	Not letting others enter the kingdom of heaven and not entering yourselves
23:15	Converting people away from God to be like yourselves
23:16–22	Blindly leading God's people to follow man-made traditions instead of God's Word
23:23, 24	Involving yourself in every last detail and ignoring what is really important: justice, mercy, and faith
23:25, 26	Keeping up appearances while your private world is corrupt
23:27, 28	Acting spiritual to cover up sin
23:29–36	Pretending to have learned from past history, but your present behavior shows you have learned nothing

Jesus mentioned seven ways to guarantee God's anger, when he told the religious leaders about the "seven woes." These seven statements were strong and unforgettable. They are still applicable anytime we become so involved in perfecting the practice of religion that we forget that God is also concerned with mercy, real love, and forgiveness.

23:11, 12 Jesus challenged society's norms. To him, greatness comes from serving—giving of yourself to help God and others. Service keeps us aware of others' needs, and it stops us from focusing only on ourselves. Jesus came as a servant. What kind of greatness do you seek?

23:13, 14 Being a religious leader in Jerusalem was very different from being a pastor in a secular society today. Israel's history, culture, and daily life centered around its relationship with God. The religious leaders were the best known, most powerful, and most respected of all leaders. Jesus made these stinging accusations because the leaders' hunger for more power, money, and status had made them lose sight of God, and their blindness was spreading to the whole nation.

23:15 The Pharisees' converts were attracted to religion, not to God. By getting caught up in the details of their additional laws and regulations, they completely missed God, to whom the laws pointed. A religion of works puts pressure on people to surpass others in what they know and do. Thus, a hypocritical teacher was likely to have students who were even more hypocritical. We must make sure we are not creating

Pharisees by emphasizing outward obedience at the expense of inner renewal.

23:23, 24 It's possible to obey the details of the laws but still be disobedient in our general behavior. For example, we could be very precise and faithful about giving 10 percent of our money to God, but refuse to give one minute of our time in helping others. Tithing is important, but giving a tithe does not exempt us from fulfilling God's other directives.

23:24 The Pharisees strained their water so they wouldn't accidentally swallow a gnat—an unclean insect according to the law. Meticulous about the details of ceremonial cleanliness, they nevertheless had lost their perspective on inner purity—in essence, they would then swallow a camel and not even notice. Ceremonially clean on the outside, they had corrupt hearts.

25"Woe to you, teachers of the law and Pharisees, you hypocrites! You clean the outside of the cup and dish,[h] but inside they are full of greed and self-indulgence.[i] 26Blind Pharisee! First clean the inside of the cup and dish, and then the outside also will be clean.

27"Woe to you, teachers of the law and Pharisees, you hypocrites! You are like whitewashed tombs,[j] which look beautiful on the outside but on the inside are full of dead men's bones and everything unclean. 28In the same way, on the outside you appear to people as righteous but on the inside you are full of hypocrisy and wickedness.

29"Woe to you, teachers of the law and Pharisees, you hypocrites! You build tombs for the prophets[k] and decorate the graves of the righteous. 30And you say, 'If we had lived in the days of our forefathers, we would not have taken part with them in shedding the blood of the prophets.' 31So you testify against yourselves that you are the descendants of those who murdered the prophets.[l] 32Fill up, then, the measure of the sin of your forefathers!

33"You snakes! You brood of vipers![m] How will you escape being condemned to hell? 34Therefore I am sending you prophets and wise men and teachers. Some of them you will kill and crucify;[n] others you will flog in your synagogues[o] and pursue from town to town. 35And so upon you will come all the righteous blood that has been shed on earth, from the blood of righteous Abel[p] to the blood of Zechariah son of Berekiah, whom you murdered between the temple and the altar.[q] 36I tell you the truth, all this will come upon this generation.

Jesus Grieves over Jerusalem Again (199)

37"O Jerusalem, Jerusalem, you who kill the prophets and stone those sent to you,[r] how often I have longed to gather your children together, as a hen gathers her chicks under her wings, but you were not willing. 38Look, your house is left to you desolate. 39For I tell you, you will not see me again until you say, 'Blessed is he who comes in the name of the Lord.'[a]"[s]

7. Jesus teaches on the Mount of Olives
Jesus Tells about the Future (201/Mark 13:1–23; Luke 21:5–24)

24 Jesus left the temple and was walking away when his disciples came up to him to call his attention to its buildings. 2"Do you see all these things?" he asked. "I tell you the truth, not one stone here will be left on another;[t] every one will be thrown down."

3As Jesus was sitting on the Mount of Olives, the disciples came to him privately. "Tell us," they said, "when will this happen, and what will be the sign of your coming and of the end of the age?"

a39 Psalm 118:26

23:25	
h Mk 7:4	
i Lk 11:39	
23:27	
j Lk 11:44	
23:29	
k Lk 11:47, 48	
23:31	
l Ac 7:51-52	
23:33	
m Mt 3:7	
23:34	
n Lk 11:49	
o Mt 10:17	
23:35	
p Ge 4:8	
q 2Ch 24:21	
23:37	
r 2Ch 24:21	
23:39	
s Ps 118:26; Mt 21:9	
24:2	
t Lk 19:44	

23:25-28 Jesus condemned the Pharisees and religious leaders for outwardly appearing saintly and holy but inwardly remaining full of corruption and greed. Living our Christianity merely as a show for others is like washing a cup on the outside only. When we are clean on the inside, our cleanliness on the outside won't be a sham.

23:34-36 These prophets, wise men, and teachers were probably leaders in the early church who were persecuted, scourged, and killed, as Jesus predicted. The people of Jesus' generation said they would not act as their fathers did in killing the prophets whom God had sent to them (23:30), but they were about to kill the Messiah himself and his faithful followers. Thus they would become guilty of all the righteous blood shed through the centuries.

23:35 Jesus summarized the history of Old Testament martyrdom. Abel was the first martyr (Genesis 4); Zechariah was the last mentioned in the Hebrew Bible, which ended with 2 Chronicles. Zechariah is a classic example of a man of God who was killed by those who claimed to be God's people (see 2 Chronicles 24:20, 21).

23:37 Jesus wanted to gather his people together as a hen protects her chicks under her wings, but they wouldn't let him. Jesus also wants to protect us if we will just come to him. Many times we hurt and don't know where to turn. We reject Christ's help because we don't think he can give us what we need. But who knows our needs better than our Creator? Those who turn to Jesus will find that he helps and comforts as no one else can.

23:37 Jerusalem was the capital city of God's chosen people, the ancestral home of David, Israel's greatest king, and the location of the temple, the earthly dwelling place of God. It was intended to be the center of worship of the true God and a symbol of justice to all people. But Jerusalem had become blind to God and insensitive to human need. Here we see the depth of Jesus' feelings for lost people and for his beloved city, which would soon be destroyed.

24:1, 2 Although no one knows exactly what this temple looked like, it must have been beautiful. Herod had helped the Jews remodel and beautify it, no doubt to stay on friendly terms with his subjects. Next to the inner temple, where the sacred objects were kept and the sacrifices offered, there was a large area called the court of the Gentiles (this was where the money changers and merchants had their booths). Outside these courts were long porches. Solomon's porch was 1,562 feet long; the royal portico was decorated with 160 columns stretching along its 921-foot length. Gazing at this glorious and massive structure, the disciples found Jesus' words about its destruction difficult to believe. But the temple was indeed destroyed only 40 years later when the Romans sacked Jerusalem in A.D. 70.

24:3ff Jesus was sitting on the Mount of Olives, the very place where the prophet Zechariah had predicted that the Messiah would stand when he came to establish his kingdom (Zechariah

24:5
u ver 11, 23, 24

4 Jesus answered: "Watch out that no one deceives you. 5 For many will come in my name, claiming, 'I am the Christ,ᵃ' and will deceive many. u 6 You will hear of wars and rumors of wars, but see to it that you are not alarmed. Such things must happen, but the end is still to come. 7 Nation will rise against nation, and kingdom against kingdom. v There will be famines and earthquakes in various places. 8 All these are the beginning of birth pains.

24:7
v Isa 19:2

24:9
w Mt 10:17
x Jn 16:2

24:13
y Mt 10:22

24:14
z Ro 10:18; Col 1:6, 23; Rev 3:10; 16:14

9 "Then you will be handed over to be persecuted w and put to death, x and you will be hated by all nations because of me. 10 At that time many will turn away from the faith and will betray and hate each other, 11 and many false prophets will appear and deceive many people. 12 Because of the increase of wickedness, the love of most will grow cold, 13 but he who stands firm to the end will be saved. y 14 And this gospel of the kingdom will be preached in the whole worldᶻ as a testimony to all nations, and then the end will come.

24:15
a Da 9:27; 12:11

24:19
b Lk 23:29

24:21
c Joel 2:2

15 "So when you see standing in the holy place 'the abomination that causes desolation,'ᵇᵃ spoken of through the prophet Daniel—let the reader understand— 16 then let those who are in Judea flee to the mountains. 17 Let no one on the roof of his house go down to take anything out of the house. 18 Let no one in the field go back to get his cloak. 19 How dreadful it will be in those days for pregnant women and nursing mothers! b 20 Pray that your flight will not take place in winter or on the Sabbath. 21 For then there will be great distress, unequaled from the beginning of the world until now—and never to be equaled again. c 22 If those days had not been cut short, no one would survive, but for the sake of the elect those days will be shortened. 23 At that time if anyone says to you, 'Look, here is the Christ!' or, 'There he is!' do not believe it. d 24 For false Christs and false prophets will appear and perform great signs and miraclesᵉ to deceive even the elect—if that were possible. 25 See, I have told you ahead of time.

24:23
d Lk 17:23; 21:8

24:24
e 2Th 2:9-11

a 5 Or *Messiah*; also in verse 23   b 15 Daniel 9:27; 11:31; 12:11

14:4). It was a fitting place for the disciples to ask Jesus when he would come in power and what they could expect then. Jesus' reply emphasized the events that would take place before the end of the age. He pointed out that his disciples should be less concerned with knowing the exact date and more concerned with being prepared—living God's way consistently so that no matter when Jesus came in glory, he would claim them as his own.

24:4 The disciples asked Jesus for the sign of his coming and of the end of the age. Jesus' first response was "Watch out that no one deceives you." The fact is that whenever we look for signs, we become very susceptible to being deceived. There are many "false prophets" (24:11, 24) around with counterfeit signs of spiritual power and authority. The only sure way to keep from being deceived is to focus on Christ and his words. Don't look for special signs, and don't spend time looking at other people. Look at Christ.

24:9–13 You may not be facing intense persecution now, but Christians in other parts of the world are. As you hear about Christians suffering for their faith, remember that they are your brothers and sisters in Christ. Pray for them. Ask God what you can do to help them in their troubles. When one part suffers, the *whole* body suffers. But when all the parts join together to ease the suffering, the whole body benefits (1 Corinthians 12:26).

24:11 The Old Testament frequently mentions false prophets (see 2 Kings 3:13; Isaiah 44:25; Jeremiah 23:16; Ezekiel 13:2, 3; Micah 3:5; Zechariah 13:2). False prophets claimed to receive messages from God, but they preached a "health and wealth" message. They said what the people wanted to hear, even when the nation was not following God as it should. There were false prophets in Jesus' day, and we have them today. They are the popular leaders who tell people what they want to hear—such as "God wants you to be rich," "Do whatever your desires tell you," or "There is no such thing as sin or hell." Jesus said false teachers would come, and he warned his disciples, as he warns us, not to listen to their dangerous words.

24:12 With false teaching and loose morals comes a particularly destructive disease—the loss of true love for God and others. Sin cools your love for God and others by turning your focus on yourself. You cannot truly love if you think only of yourself.

24:14 Jesus said that before he returns, the gospel of the kingdom (the message of salvation) would be preached throughout the world. This was the disciples' mission—and it is ours today. Jesus talked about the end times and final judgment to show his followers the urgency of spreading the good news of salvation to everyone.

24:15, 16 What was this "abomination that causes desolation" mentioned by both Daniel and Jesus? Rather than one specific object, event, or person, it could be seen as any deliberate attempt to mock and deny the reality of God's presence. Daniel's prediction came true in 168 B.C. when Antiochus Epiphanes sacrificed a pig to Zeus on the sacred temple altar (Daniel 9:27; 11:30, 31). Jesus' words were remembered in A.D. 70 when Titus placed an idol on the site of the burned temple after destroying Jerusalem. In the end times the antichrist will set up an image of himself and order everyone to worship it (2 Thessalonians 2:4; Revelation 13:14, 15). These are all "abominations" that mock God.

24:21, 22 Jesus, talking about the end times, telescoped near future and far future events, as did the Old Testament prophets. Many of these persecutions have already occurred; more are yet to come. But God is in control of even the length of persecutions. He will not forget his people. This is all we need to know about the future to motivate us to live rightly now.

24:23, 24 Jesus' warnings about false teachers still hold true. Upon close examination it becomes clear that many nice-sounding messages don't agree with God's message in the Bible. Only a solid foundation in God's Word can equip us to perceive the errors and distortions in false teaching.

24:24–28 In times of persecution even strong believers will find it difficult to be loyal. To keep from being deceived by false messiahs, we must understand that Jesus' return will be unmistakable (Mark 13:26); no one will doubt that it is he. If you have to be told that the Messiah has come, then he hasn't (24:27). Christ's coming will be obvious to everyone.

Jesus Tells about His Return (*202*/Mark 13:24–31; Luke 21:25–33)

26 "So if anyone tells you, 'There he is, out in the desert,' do not go out; or, 'Here he is, in the inner rooms,' do not believe it. 27 For as lightning *f* that comes from the east is visible even in the west, so will be the coming of the Son of Man. 28 Wherever there is a carcass, there the vultures will gather. *g*

29 "Immediately after the distress of those days

> "'the sun will be darkened,
>> and the moon will not give its light;
>> the stars will fall from the sky,
>> and the heavenly bodies will be shaken.' *a h*

30 "At that time the sign of the Son of Man will appear in the sky, and all the nations of the earth will mourn. They will see the Son of Man coming on the clouds of the sky, *i* with power and great glory. 31 And he will send his angels with a loud trumpet call, *j* and they will gather his elect from the four winds, from one end of the heavens to the other.

32 "Now learn this lesson from the fig tree: As soon as its twigs get tender and its leaves come out, you know that summer is near. 33 Even so, when you see all these things, you know that it *b* is near, right at the door. *k* 34 I tell you the truth, this generation *c* will certainly not pass away until all these things have happened. *l* 35 Heaven and earth will pass away, but my words will never pass away.

Jesus Tells about Remaining Watchful (*203*/Mark 13:32–37; Luke 21:34–38)

36 "No one knows about that day or hour, not even the angels in heaven, nor the Son, *d* but only the Father. *m* 37 As it was in the days of Noah, *n* so it will be at the coming of the Son of Man. 38 For in the days before the flood, people were eating and drinking, marrying and giving in marriage, up to the day Noah entered the ark; 39 and they knew nothing about what would happen until the flood came and took them all away. That is how it will be at the coming of the Son of Man. 40 Two men will be in the field; one will be taken and the other left. *o* 41 Two women will be grinding with a hand mill; one will be taken and the other left.

42 "Therefore keep watch, because you do not know on what day your Lord will come. *p* 43 But understand this: If the owner of the house had known at what time of night the thief was coming, *q* he would have kept watch and would not have let his house be broken into. 44 So you also must be ready, because the Son of Man will come at an hour when you do not expect him.

45 "Who then is the faithful and wise servant, *r* whom the master has put in charge of the servants in his household to give them their food at the proper time? 46 It will be good for that servant whose master finds him doing so when he returns. *s* 47 I tell you the truth, he will put him in charge of all his possessions. *t* 48 But suppose that servant is wicked and says to himself, 'My master is staying away a long time,' 49 and he then begins to beat his fellow servants and to eat and drink with drunkards. 50 The master of that servant will come on a day when he does not expect him and at an hour he is not aware of. 51 He will cut him to pieces and assign him a place with the hypocrites, where there will be weeping and gnashing of teeth. *u*

a29 Isaiah 13:10; 34:4   *b33* Or he   *c34* Or race   *d36* Some manuscripts do not have *nor the Son.*

24:27 *f* Lk 17:24
24:28 *g* Lk 17:37
24:29 *h* Eze 32:7; Joel 2:10, 31
24:30 *i* Da 7:13; Rev 1:7
24:31 *j* Isa 27:13; 1Co 15:52
24:33 *k* Jas 5:9
24:34 *l* Mt 16:28
24:36 *m* Ac 1:7
24:37 *n* Ge 6:5
24:40 *o* Lk 17:34
24:42 *p* Mt 25:13
24:43 *q* Lk 12:39
24:45 *r* Mt 25:21, 23
24:46 *s* Rev 16:15
24:47 *t* Mt 25:21, 23
24:51 *u* Mt 8:12

24:30 The nations of the earth will mourn because unbelievers will suddenly realize they have chosen the wrong side. Everything they have scoffed about will be happening, and it will be too late for them.

24:36 It is good that we don't know exactly when Christ will return. If we knew the precise date, we might be tempted to be lazy in our work for Christ. Worse yet, we might plan to keep sinning and then turn to God right at the end. Heaven is not our only goal; we have work to do here. And we must keep on doing it until death or until we see the unmistakable return of our Savior.

24:40–42 Christ's second coming will be swift and sudden. There will be no opportunity for last-minute repentance or bargaining. The choice we have already made will determine our eternal destiny.

24:44 Jesus' purpose in telling about his return is not to stimulate predictions and calculations about the date, but to warn us to be prepared. Will you be ready? The only safe choice is to obey him *today* (24:46).

24:45–47 Jesus asks us to spend the time of waiting taking care of his people and doing his work here on earth, both within the church and outside it. This is the best way to prepare for Christ's return.

24:51 "Weeping and gnashing of teeth" is a phrase used to describe despair. God's coming judgment is as certain as Jesus' return to earth.

Jesus Tells the Parable of the Ten Bridesmaids (204)

25:1
v Mt 13:24
w Rev 19:7

25:5
x 1Th 5:6

25 "At that time the kingdom of heaven will be like ᵛ ten virgins who took their lamps and went out to meet the bridegroom. ʷ ²Five of them were foolish and five were wise. ³The foolish ones took their lamps but did not take any oil with them. ⁴The wise, however, took oil in jars along with their lamps. ⁵The bridegroom was a long time in coming, and they all became drowsy and fell asleep. ˣ

⁶"At midnight the cry rang out: 'Here's the bridegroom! Come out to meet him!'

⁷"Then all the virgins woke up and trimmed their lamps. ⁸The foolish ones said to the wise, 'Give us some of your oil; our lamps are going out.'

⁹"'No,' they replied, 'there may not be enough for both us and you. Instead, go to those who sell oil and buy some for yourselves.'

¹⁰"But while they were on their way to buy the oil, the bridegroom arrived. The virgins who were ready went in with him to the wedding banquet. And the door was shut.

¹¹"Later the others also came. 'Sir! Sir!' they said. 'Open the door for us!'

25:13
y Mt 24:42, 44

¹²"But he replied, 'I tell you the truth, I don't know you.'

¹³"Therefore keep watch, because you do not know the day or the hour. ʸ

Jesus Tells the Parable of the Loaned Money (205)

25:14
z Mt 21:33; Lk 19:12
25:15
a Mt 18:24, 25

¹⁴"Again, it will be like a man going on a journey, ᶻ who called his servants and entrusted his property to them. ¹⁵To one he gave five talentsᵃ of money, to another two talents, and to another one talent, each according to his ability. ᵃ Then he went on his journey. ¹⁶The man who had received the five talents went at once and put his money to work and gained five more. ¹⁷So also, the one with the two talents gained two more. ¹⁸But the man who had received the one talent went off, dug a hole in the ground and hid his master's money.

25:19
b Mt 18:23

¹⁹"After a long time the master of those servants returned and settled accounts with them. ᵇ ²⁰The man who had received the five talents brought the other five. 'Master,' he said, 'you entrusted me with five talents. See, I have gained five more.'

25:21
c Mt 24:45, 47

²¹"His master replied, 'Well done, good and faithful servant! You have been faithful with a few things; I will put you in charge of many things. ᶜ Come and share your master's happiness!'

²²"The man with the two talents also came. 'Master,' he said, 'you entrusted me with two talents; see, I have gained two more.'

25:23
d ver 21

²³"His master replied, 'Well done, good and faithful servant! You have been faithful with a few things; I will put you in charge of many things. ᵈ Come and share your master's happiness!'

---

a 15 A talent was worth more than a thousand dollars.

25:1ff Jesus told the following parables to clarify further what it means to be ready for his return and how to live until he comes. In the story of the ten virgins (25:1–13), we are taught that every person is responsible for his or her own spiritual condition. The story of the talents (25:14–30) shows the necessity of using well what God has entrusted to us. The parable of the sheep and goats (25:31–46) stresses the importance of serving others in need. No parable by itself *completely* describes our preparation. Instead, each paints one part of the whole picture.

25:1ff This parable is about a wedding. On the wedding day the bridegroom went to the bride's house for the ceremony; then the bride and groom, along with a great procession, returned to the groom's house where a feast took place, often lasting a full week.

These ten virgins were waiting to join the procession, and they hoped to take part in the wedding banquet. But when the groom didn't come at the expected time, five of them were out of lamp oil. By the time they had purchased extra oil, it was too late to join the feast.

When Jesus returns to take his people to heaven, we must be ready. Spiritual preparation cannot be bought or borrowed at the last minute. Our relationship with God must be our own.

25:15 The master divided the money (talents) among his servants according to their abilities. No one received more or less

than he could handle. If he failed in his assignment, his excuse could not be that he was overwhelmed. Failure could come only from laziness or hatred toward the master. The talents represent any kind of resource we are given. God gives us time, gifts, and other resources according to our abilities, and he expects us to invest them wisely until he returns. We are responsible to use well what God has given us. The issue is not how much we have, but how well we use what we have.

25:21 Jesus is coming back—we know this is true. Does this mean we must quit our jobs in order to serve God? No, it means we are to use our time, talents, and treasures diligently in order to serve God completely in whatever we do. For a few people, this may mean changing professions. For most of us, it means doing our daily work out of love for God.

24 "Then the man who had received the one talent came. 'Master,' he said, 'I knew that you are a hard man, harvesting where you have not sown and gathering where you have not scattered seed. 25 So I was afraid and went out and hid your talent in the ground. See, here is what belongs to you.'

26 "His master replied, 'You wicked, lazy servant! So you knew that I harvest where I have not sown and gather where I have not scattered seed? 27 Well then, you should have put my money on deposit with the bankers, so that when I returned I would have received it back with interest.

28 "'Take the talent from him and give it to the one who has the ten talents. 29 For everyone who has will be given more, and he will have an abundance. Whoever does not have, even what he has will be taken from him. e 30 And throw that worthless servant outside, into the darkness, where there will be weeping and gnashing of teeth.' f

25:29
e Mt 13:12

25:30
f Mt 8:12

Jesus Tells about the Final Judgment (206)

31 "When the Son of Man comes g in his glory, and all the angels with him, he will sit on his throne h in heavenly glory. 32 All the nations will be gathered before him, and he will separate the people one from another as a shepherd separates the sheep from the goats. i 33 He will put the sheep on his right and the goats on his left.

34 "Then the King will say to those on his right, 'Come, you who are blessed by my Father; take your inheritance, the kingdom j prepared for you since the creation of the world. k 35 For I was hungry and you gave me something to eat, I was thirsty and you gave me something to drink, I was a stranger and you invited me in, l 36 I needed clothes and you clothed me, m I was sick and you looked after me, I was in prison and you came to visit me.' n

37 "Then the righteous will answer him, 'Lord, when did we see you hungry and feed you, or thirsty and give you something to drink? 38 When did we see you a stranger and invite you in, or needing clothes and clothe you? 39 When did we see you sick or in prison and go to visit you?'

40 "The King will reply, 'I tell you the truth, whatever you did for one of the least of these brothers of mine, you did for me.' o

41 "Then he will say to those on his left, 'Depart from me, p you who are cursed, into the eternal fire q prepared for the devil and his angels. r 42 For I was hungry and you gave me nothing to eat, I was thirsty and you gave me nothing to drink, 43 I was a stranger and you did not invite me in, I needed clothes and you did not clothe me, I was sick and in prison and you did not look after me.'

44 "They also will answer, 'Lord, when did we see you hungry or thirsty or a stranger or needing clothes or sick or in prison, and did not help you?'

25:31
g Mt 16:27
h Mt 19:28

25:32
i Eze 34:17, 20

25:34
j 1Co 15:50
k Rev 13:8

25:35
l Isa 58:7; Eze 18:7;
Heb 13:2

25:36
m Jas 2:15, 16
n 2Ti 1:16

25:40
o Pr 19:17;
Mt 10:40, 42

25:41
p Mt 7:23
q Mk 9:43, 48;
Jude 7
r 2Pe 2:4

25:24-30 This last man was thinking only of himself. He hoped to play it safe and protect himself from his hard master, but he was judged for his self-centeredness. We must not make excuses to avoid doing what God calls us to do. If God truly is our Master, we must obey willingly. Our time, abilities, and money aren't ours in the first place—we are caretakers, not owners. When we ignore, squander, or abuse what we are given, we are rebellious and deserve to be punished.

25:29, 30 This parable describes the consequences of two attitudes to Christ's return. The person who diligently prepares for it by investing his or her time and talent to serve God will be rewarded. The person who has no heart for the work of the kingdom will be punished. God rewards faithfulness. Those who bear no fruit for God's kingdom cannot expect to be treated the same as those who are faithful.

25:31-46 God will separate his obedient followers from pretenders and unbelievers. The real evidence of our belief is the way we

act. To treat all persons we encounter as if they are Jesus is no easy task. What we do for others demonstrates what we really think about Jesus' words to us—feed the hungry, give the homeless a place to stay, look after the sick. How well do your actions separate you from pretenders and unbelievers?

25:32 Jesus used sheep and goats to picture the division between believers and unbelievers. Sheep and goats often grazed together but were separated when it came time to shear the sheep. Ezekiel 34:17-24 also refers to the separation of sheep and goats.

25:34-40 This parable describes acts of mercy we all can do every day. These acts do not depend on wealth, ability, or intelligence; they are simple acts freely given and freely received. We have no excuse to neglect those who have deep needs, and we cannot hand over this responsibility to the church or government. Jesus demands our personal involvement in caring for others' needs (Isaiah 58:7).

25:40 There has been much discussion about the identity of the "brothers." Some have said they are the Jews; others say they are all Christians; still others say they are suffering people everywhere. Such a debate is much like the lawyer's earlier question to Jesus, "Who is my neighbor?" (Luke 10:29). The point of this parable is not the *who*, but the *what*—the importance of serving where service is needed. The focus of this parable is that we should love every person and serve anyone we can. Such love for others glorifies God by reflecting our love for him.

25:45
s Pr 14:31

25:46
t Da 12:2; Jn 5:29

45 "He will reply, 'I tell you the truth, whatever you did not do for one of the least of these, you did not do for me.' s

46 "Then they will go away to eternal punishment, but the righteous to eternal life." t

C. DEATH AND RESURRECTION OF JESUS, THE KING (26:1—28:20)

After facing much opposition for his teaching, Jesus is betrayed by Judas, denied by the disciples, crucified, and he dies. Three days later he rises from the dead and appears to the disciples, confirming that he is indeed King over life and death. The long-awaited King has brought in his Kingdom, but it is different than expected, for he reigns in our heart until the day he comes again to establish a new and perfect world.

Religious Leaders Plot to Kill Jesus (207/Mark 14:1–2; Luke 22:1–2)

26:1
u Mt 7:28

26:2
v Jn 13:1

26:3
w Ps 2:2
x Jn 11:47-53

26 When Jesus had finished saying all these things, u he said to his disciples, 2 "As you know, the Passover v is two days away—and the Son of Man will be handed over to be crucified."

3 Then the chief priests and the elders of the people assembled w in the palace of the high priest, whose name was Caiaphas, x 4 and they plotted to arrest Jesus in some sly way and kill him. 5 "But not during the Feast," they said, "or there may be a riot among the people."

A Woman Anoints Jesus with Perfume (182/Mark 14:3–9; John 12:1–11)

26:6
y Mt 21:17

6 While Jesus was in Bethany y in the home of a man known as Simon the Leper, 7 a woman came to him with an alabaster jar of very expensive perfume, which she poured on his head as he was reclining at the table.

8 When the disciples saw this, they were indignant. "Why this waste?" they asked. 9 "This perfume could have been sold at a high price and the money given to the poor."

25:46 Eternal punishment takes place in hell (the lake of fire, or Gehenna), the place of punishment after death for all those who refuse to repent. In the Bible, three words are used in connection with eternal punishment.

(1) *Sheol*, or "the grave," is used in the Old Testament to mean the place of the dead, generally thought to be under the earth. (See Job 24:19; Psalm 16:10; Isaiah 38:10.)

(2) *Hades* is the Greek word for the underworld, the realm of the dead. It is the word used in the New Testament for Sheol. (See Matthew 16:18; Revelation 1:18; 20:13, 14.)

(3) *Gehenna*, or hell, was named after the Valley of Hinnom near Jerusalem where children were sacrificed by fire to the pagan gods (see 2 Kings 23:10; 2 Chronicles 28:3). This is the place of eternal fire (Matthew 5:22; 10:28; Mark 9:43; Luke 12:5; James 3:6; Revelation 19:20) prepared for the devil, his angels, and all those who do not believe in God (25:46; Revelation 20:9, 10). This is the final and eternal state of the wicked after the resurrection and the last judgment.

When Jesus warns against unbelief, he is trying to save us from agonizing, eternal punishment.

26:3 Caiaphas was the ruling high priest during Jesus' ministry. He was the son-in-law of Annas, the previous high priest. The Roman government had taken over the process of appointing all political and religious leaders. Caiaphas served for 18 years, longer than most high priests, suggesting that he was gifted at cooperating with the Romans. He was the first to recommend Jesus' death in order to "save" the nation (John 11:49, 50).

26:3–5 This was a deliberate plot to kill Jesus. Without this plot, there would have been no groundswell of popular opinion against him. In fact, because of Jesus' popularity, the religious leaders were afraid to arrest him during the Passover. They did not want their actions to incite a riot.

26:6–13 Matthew and Mark put this event just before the Last Supper, while John has it just before the Triumphal Entry. Of the three, John places this event in the most likely chronological order. We must remember that the main purpose of the Gospel writers was to give an accurate record of Jesus' message, not to present an exact chronological account of his life. Matthew and Mark may have chosen to place this event here to contrast the

complete devotion of Mary with the betrayal of Judas, the next event they record in their Gospels.

26:7 This woman was Mary, the sister of Martha and Lazarus, who lived in Bethany (John 12:1–3). Alabaster jars were carved from a translucent gypsum. These jars were used to hold perfumed oil.

26:8 All the disciples were indignant, but John's Gospel singles out Judas Iscariot as especially so (John 12:4).

Mediterranean Sea · GALILEE · Sea of Galilee · N · Jordan River · SAMARIA · Jericho · PEREA · **Jerusalem** · Bethphage · Bethany · Dead Sea · JUDEA · IDUMEA · 0   20 Mi. · 0   20 Km.

VISIT IN BETHANY Chronologically, the events of Matthew 26:6–13 precede the events of 21:1ff. In 20:29, Jesus left Jericho, heading toward Jerusalem. Then he arrived in Bethany, where a woman anointed him. From there he went toward Bethphage, where two of his disciples got the donkey that he would ride into Jerusalem.

¹⁰Aware of this, Jesus said to them, "Why are you bothering this woman? She has done a beautiful thing to me. ¹¹The poor you will always have with you,ᶻ but you will not always have me. ¹²When she poured this perfume on my body, she did it to prepare me for burial. ¹³I tell you the truth, wherever this gospel is preached throughout the world, what she has done will also be told, in memory of her."

Judas Agrees to Betray Jesus (208/Mark 14:10–11; Luke 22:3–6)

¹⁴Then one of the Twelve—the one called Judas Iscariot—went to the chief priests ¹⁵and asked, "What are you willing to give me if I hand him over to you?" So they counted out for him thirty silver coins.ᵃ ¹⁶From then on Judas watched for an opportunity to hand him over.

Disciples Prepare for the Passover (209/Mark 14:12–16; Luke 22:7–13)

¹⁷On the first day of the Feast of Unleavened Bread,ᵇ the disciples came to Jesus and asked, "Where do you want us to make preparations for you to eat the Passover?"

¹⁸He replied, "Go into the city to a certain man and tell him, 'The Teacher says: My appointed time is near. I am going to celebrate the Passover with my disciples at your house.'" ¹⁹So the disciples did as Jesus had directed them and prepared the Passover.

Jesus and the Disciples Share the Last Supper
(211/Mark 14:17–25; Luke 22:14–30; John 13:21–30)

²⁰When evening came, Jesus was reclining at the table with the Twelve. ²¹And while they were eating, he said, "I tell you the truth, one of you will betray me."

²²They were very sad and began to say to him one after the other, "Surely not I, Lord?"

²³Jesus replied, "The one who has dipped his hand into the bowl with me will betray me.ᶜ ²⁴The Son of Man will go just as it is written about him.ᵈ But woe to that man who betrays the Son of Man! It would be better for him if he had not been born."

²⁵Then Judas, the one who would betray him, said, "Surely not I, Rabbi?"

26:11
ᶻDt 15:11

26:15
ᵃZec 11:12

26:17
ᵇEx 12:18-20

26:23
ᶜJn 13:18

26:24
ᵈIsa 53; Mk 9:12;
Lk 24:25-27, 46;
Ac 17:2, 3

THE PASSOVER MEAL AND GETHSEMANE Jesus, who would soon be the final Passover Lamb, ate the traditional Passover meal with his disciples in the upper room of a house in Jerusalem. During the meal they partook of the bread and wine, which would be the elements of future communion celebrations, and then went out to the Garden of Gethsemane on the Mount of Olives.

26:11 Here Jesus brought back to mind Deuteronomy 15:11: "There will always be poor people in the land." This statement does not justify ignoring the needs of the poor. Scripture continually calls us to care for the needy. The passage in Deuteronomy continues: "Therefore I command you to be openhanded toward your brothers and toward the poor and needy in your land." Rather, by saying this, Jesus highlighted the special sacrifice Mary made for him.

26:14, 15 Why would Judas want to betray Jesus? Judas, like the other disciples, expected Jesus to start a political rebellion and overthrow Rome. As treasurer, Judas certainly assumed (as did the other disciples—see Mark 10:35–37) that he would be given an important position in Jesus' new government. But when Jesus praised Mary for pouring out perfume worth a year's salary, Judas may have realized that Jesus' kingdom was not physical or political, but spiritual. Judas's greedy desire for money and status could not be realized if he followed Jesus, so he betrayed Jesus in exchange for money and favor from the religious leaders.

26:15 Matthew alone records the exact amount of money Judas accepted to betray Jesus—30 silver coins, the price of a slave (Exodus 21:32). The religious leaders had planned to wait until after the Passover to take Jesus, but with Judas's unexpected offer, they accelerated their plans.

26:17 The Passover took place on one night and at one meal, but the Feast of Unleavened Bread, which was celebrated with it, continued for a week. The people removed all yeast from their homes in commemoration of their ancestors' exodus from Egypt, when they did not have time to let the bread dough rise. Thousands of people poured into Jerusalem from all over the Roman empire for this feast. For more information on how the Passover was celebrated, see the notes on Mark 14:1 and in Exodus 12.

26:23 In Jesus' time, some food was eaten from a common bowl into which everyone dipped their hand.

26:26
e 1Co 10:16

26:28
f Heb 9:20
g Mt 20:28

26:30
h Mk 14:26

Jesus answered, "Yes, it is you." a

26 While they were eating, Jesus took bread, gave thanks and broke it, e and gave it to his disciples, saying, "Take and eat; this is my body."

27 Then he took the cup, gave thanks and offered it to them, saying, "Drink from it, all of you. 28 This is my blood of the b covenant, f which is poured out for many for the forgiveness of sins. g 29 I tell you, I will not drink of this fruit of the vine from now on until that day when I drink it anew with you in my Father's kingdom."

30 When they had sung a hymn, they went out to the Mount of Olives. h

a 25 Or *"You yourself have said it"*   b 28 Some manuscripts *the new*

MARY

LAZARUS'S SISTER

Hospitality is an art. Making sure a guest is welcomed, warmed, and well fed requires creativity, organization, and teamwork. Their ability to accomplish these goals makes Mary and her sister, Martha, one of the best hospitality teams in the Bible. Their frequent guest was Jesus Christ.

For Mary, hospitality meant giving more attention to the guest himself than to the needs he might have. She would rather talk than cook. She was more interested in her guest's words than in the cleanliness of her home or the timeliness of her meals. She let her older sister, Martha, take care of those details. Mary's approach to events shows her to be mainly a "responder." She did little preparation—her role was participation. Unlike her sister, who had to learn to stop and listen, Mary needed to learn that action is often appropriate and necessary.

We first meet Mary during a visit Jesus paid to her home. She simply sat at his feet and listened. When Martha became irritated at her sister's lack of help, Jesus stated that Mary's choice to enjoy his company was the most appropriate response at the time. Our last glimpse of Mary shows her to have become a woman of thoughtful and worshipful action. Again she was at Jesus' feet, washing them with perfume and wiping them with her hair. She seemed to understand, better even than the disciples, why Jesus was going to die. Jesus said her act of worship would be told everywhere, along with the gospel, as an example of costly service.

What kind of hospitality does Jesus receive from your life? Are you so busy planning and running your life that you neglect precious time with him? Or do you respond to him by listening to his Word, then finding ways to worship him with your life? It is that kind of hospitality he longs for from each of us.

Strengths and accomplishments:
- Perhaps the only person who understood and accepted Jesus' coming death, taking time to anoint his body while he was still living
- Learned when to listen and when to act

Lessons from her life:
- The busyness of serving God can become a barrier to knowing him personally
- Small acts of obedience and service have widespread effects

Vital statistics:
- Where: Bethany
- Relatives: Sister: Martha. Brother: Lazarus.

Key verses:
"When she poured this perfume on my body, she did it to prepare me for burial. I tell you the truth, wherever this gospel is preached throughout the world, what she has done will also be told, in memory of her" (Matthew 26:12, 13).

Mary's story is told in Matthew 26:6–13; Mark 14:3–9; Luke 10:38–42; John 11:17–45; 12:1–11.

26:26 Each name we use for this sacrament brings out a different dimension to it. It is the *Lord's Supper* because it commemorates the Passover meal Jesus ate with his disciples; it is the *Eucharist* (thanksgiving) because in it we thank God for Christ's work for us; it is *Communion* because through it we commune with God and with other believers. As we eat the bread and drink the wine, we should be quietly reflective as we recall Jesus' death and his promise to come again, grateful for God's wonderful gift to us, and joyful as we meet with Christ and the body of believers.

26:28 How does Jesus' blood relate to the new covenant? People under the old covenant (those who lived before Jesus) could approach God only through a priest and an animal sacrifice. Now all people can come directly to God through faith because Jesus' death has made us acceptable in God's eyes (Romans 3:21–24).

The old covenant was a shadow of the new (Jeremiah 31:31;

Hebrews 8:1ff), pointing forward to the day when Jesus himself would be the final and ultimate sacrifice for sin. Rather than an unblemished lamb slain on the altar, the perfect Lamb of God was slain on the cross, a sinless sacrifice so that our sins could be forgiven once and for all. All those who believe in Christ receive that forgiveness.

26:29 Again Jesus assured his disciples of victory over death and of their future with him. The next few hours would bring apparent defeat, but soon they would experience the power of the Holy Spirit and witness the great spread of the gospel message. And one day, they would all be together again in God's new kingdom.

26:30 It is possible that the hymn the disciples sang was from Psalms 115—118, the traditional psalms sung as part of the Passover meal.

Jesus Again Predicts Peter's Denial (222/Mark 14:26–31)

31 Then Jesus told them, "This very night you will all fall away on account of me, for it is written:

> "'I will strike the shepherd,
>   and the sheep of the flock will be scattered.'a*i*

32 But after I have risen, I will go ahead of you into Galilee."*j*
33 Peter replied, "Even if all fall away on account of you, I never will."
34 "I tell you the truth," Jesus answered, "this very night, before the rooster crows, you will disown me three times."*k*
35 But Peter declared, "Even if I have to die with you,*l* I will never disown you." And all the other disciples said the same.

26:31
i Zec 13:7; Jn 16:32

26:32
j Mt 28:7, 10, 16

26:34
k Jn 13:38

26:35
l Jn 13:37

Jesus Agonizes in the Garden (223/Mark 14:32–42; Luke 22:39–46)

36 Then Jesus went with his disciples to a place called Gethsemane, and he said to them, "Sit here while I go over there and pray." 37 He took Peter and the two sons of Zebedee*m* along with him, and he began to be sorrowful and troubled. 38 Then he said to them, "My soul is overwhelmed with sorrow*n* to the point of death. Stay here and keep watch with me."
39 Going a little farther, he fell with his face to the ground and prayed, "My Father, if it is possible, may this cup*o* be taken from me. Yet not as I will, but as you will."*p*
40 Then he returned to his disciples and found them sleeping. "Could you men not keep watch with me*q* for one hour?" he asked Peter. 41 "Watch and pray so that you will not fall into temptation. The spirit is willing, but the body is weak."
a*31* Zech. 13:7

26:37
m Mt 4:21

26:38
n Jn 12:27

26:39
o Mt 20:22
p Jn 6:38

26:40
q ver 38

Antonia Fortress
(later Praetorium?)

Mount of
Olives
Garden of
Gethsemane

Temple

Hasmonean
Palace

Herod's
Royal
Palace

Herod's
Lower
Palace

UPPER CITY

Caiaphas's
House?

JERUSALEM

Traditional
Upper
Room?

LOWER CITY

N

0   .1 Mi.

0   .1 Km.

JESUS' TRIAL After Judas singled Jesus out for arrest, the mob took Jesus first to Caiaphas, the high priest. This trial, a mockery of justice, ended at daybreak with their decision to kill him; but the Jews needed Rome's permission for the death sentence. Jesus was taken to Pilate (who was probably in the Praetorium), then to Herod (Luke 23:5–12), and back to Pilate, who sentenced him to die.

26:35 All the disciples declared that they would die before disowning Jesus. A few hours later, however, they all scattered. Talk is cheap. It is easy to say we are devoted to Christ, but our claims are meaningful only when they are tested in the crucible of persecution. How strong is your faith? Is it strong enough to stand up under intense trial?

26:37, 38 Jesus was in great anguish over his approaching physical pain, separation from the Father, and death for the sins of the world. The divine course was set, but he, in his human nature, still struggled (Hebrews 5:7–9). Because of the anguish Jesus experienced, he can relate to our suffering. Jesus' strength to obey came from his relationship with God the Father, who is also the source of our strength (John 17:11, 15, 16, 21, 26).

26:39 Jesus was not rebelling against his Father's will when he asked that the cup of suffering and separation be taken away. In fact, he reaffirmed his desire to do God's will by saying, "Yet not as I will, but as you will." His prayer reveals to us his terrible suffering. His agony was worse than death because he paid for *all* sin by being separated from God. The sinless Son of God took our sins upon himself to save us from suffering and separation.

26:39 In times of suffering people sometimes wish they knew the future, or they wish they could understand the reason for their anguish. Jesus knew what lay ahead of him, and he knew the reason. Even so, his struggle was intense—more wrenching than any struggle we will ever have to face. What does it take to be able to say "as you will"? It takes firm trust in God's plans; it takes prayer and obedience each step of the way.

26:40, 41 Jesus used Peter's drowsiness to warn him about the kinds of temptation he would soon face. The way to overcome temptation is to keep watch and pray. Watching means being aware of the possibilities of temptation, sensitive to the subtleties, and spiritually equipped to fight it. Because temptation strikes where we are most vulnerable, we can't resist it alone. Prayer is essential because God's strength can shore up our defenses and defeat Satan's power.

⁴²He went away a second time and prayed, "My Father, if it is not possible for this cup to be taken away unless I drink it, may your will be done."

⁴³When he came back, he again found them sleeping, because their eyes were heavy. ⁴⁴So he left them and went away once more and prayed the third time, saying the same thing.

⁴⁵Then he returned to the disciples and said to them, "Are you still sleeping and resting? Look, the hour is near, and the Son of Man is betrayed into the hands of sinners. ⁴⁶Rise, let us go! Here comes my betrayer!"

Jesus Is Betrayed and Arrested
(224/Mark 14:43–52; Luke 22:47–53; John 18:1–11)

⁴⁷While he was still speaking, Judas, one of the Twelve, arrived. With him was a large crowd armed with swords and clubs, sent from the chief priests and the elders of the people. ⁴⁸Now the betrayer had arranged a signal with them: "The one I kiss is the man; arrest him." ⁴⁹Going at once to Jesus, Judas said, "Greetings, Rabbi!"ʳ and kissed him.

⁵⁰Jesus replied, "Friend,ˢ do what you came for."ᵃ

Then the men stepped forward, seized Jesus and arrested him. ⁵¹With that, one of Jesus' companions reached for his sword, drew it out and struck the servant of the high priest, cutting off his ear.ᵗ

⁵²"Put your sword back in its place," Jesus said to him, "for all who draw the sword will die by the sword.ᵘ ⁵³Do you think I cannot call on my Father, and he will at once put at my disposal more than twelve legions of angels?ᵛ ⁵⁴But how then would the Scriptures be fulfilledʷ that say it must happen in this way?"

⁵⁵At that time Jesus said to the crowd, "Am I leading a rebellion, that you have come out with swords and clubs to capture me? Every day I sat in the temple courts teaching, and you did not arrest me. ⁵⁶But this has all taken place that the writings of the prophets might be fulfilled." Then all the disciples deserted him and fled.

Caiaphas Questions Jesus *(226/Mark 14:53–65)*

⁵⁷Those who had arrested Jesus took him to Caiaphas, the high priest, where the teachers of the law and the elders had assembled. ⁵⁸But Peter followed him at a distance, right up to the courtyard of the high priest.ˣ He entered and sat down with the guards to see the outcome.

ᵃ50 Or *"Friend, why have you come?"*

26:49
ʳver 25
26:50
ˢMt 20:13; 22:12
26:51
ᵗJn 18:10
26:52
ᵘGe 9:6; Rev 13:10
26:53
ᵛ2Ki 6:17; Da 7:10
26:54
ʷver 24

26:58
ˣJn 18:15

BETRAYED!		
Delilah betrayed Samson to the Philistines		Judges 16:16–21
Absalom betrayed David, his father		2 Samuel 15:10–16
Jehu betrayed Joram and killed him		2 Kings 9:14–27
Officials betrayed Joash and killed him		2 Kings 12:20, 21
Judas betrayed Jesus		Matthew 26:46–56

Scripture records a number of occasions on which a person or group was betrayed. The tragedies caused by these violations of trust are a strong lesson about the importance of keeping our commitments.

26:48 Judas had told the crowd to arrest the man he kissed. This was not an arrest by Roman soldiers under Roman law, but an arrest by the religious leaders. Judas pointed Jesus out not because Jesus was hard to recognize, but because Judas had agreed to be the formal accuser in case a trial was called. Judas was able to lead the group to one of Jesus' retreats where no onlookers would interfere with the arrest.

26:51–53 The man who cut off the servant's ear was Peter (John 18:10). Peter was trying to prevent what he saw as *defeat*. He didn't realize that Jesus had to die in order to gain *victory*. But Jesus demonstrated perfect commitment to his Father's will. His kingdom would not be advanced with swords, but with faith and obedience. Luke 22:51 records that Jesus then touched the servant's ear and healed him.

26:55 Although the religious leaders could have arrested Jesus at any time, they came at night because they were afraid of the crowds that followed him each day (see 26:5).

26:56 A few hours earlier, this band of men had said they would rather die than desert their Lord (see the note on 26:35).

26:57 Earlier in the evening, Jesus had been questioned by Annas (the former high priest and father-in-law of Caiaphas). Annas then sent Jesus to Caiaphas's home to be questioned (John 18:12–24). Because of their haste to complete the trial and see Jesus die before the Sabbath, less than 24 hours away, the religious leaders met in Caiaphas's home at night instead of waiting for daylight and meeting in the temple.

59 The chief priests and the whole Sanhedrin were looking for false evidence against Jesus so that they could put him to death. 60 But they did not find any, though many false witnesses *y* came forward.

Finally two *z* came forward 61 and declared, "This fellow said, 'I am able to destroy the temple of God and rebuild it in three days.'"

62 Then the high priest stood up and said to Jesus, "Are you not going to answer? What is this testimony that these men are bringing against you?" 63 But Jesus remained silent. *a*

The high priest said to him, "I charge you under oath *b* by the living God: Tell us if you are the Christ, *a* the Son of God."

64 "Yes, it is as you say," Jesus replied. "But I say to all of you: In the future you will see the Son of Man sitting at the right hand of the Mighty One *c* and coming on the clouds of heaven." *d*

65 Then the high priest tore his clothes and said, "He has spoken blasphemy! Why do we need any more witnesses? Look, now you have heard the blasphemy. 66 What do you think?"

"He is worthy of death," *e* they answered.

67 Then they spit in his face and struck him with their fists. *f* Others slapped him 68 and said, "Prophesy to us, Christ. Who hit you?" *g*

Peter Denies Knowing Jesus (227/Mark 14:66–72; Luke 22:54–65; John 18:25–27)

69 Now Peter was sitting out in the courtyard, and a servant girl came to him. "You also were with Jesus of Galilee," she said.

70 But he denied it before them all. "I don't know what you're talking about," he said.

71 Then he went out to the gateway, where another girl saw him and said to the people there, "This fellow was with Jesus of Nazareth."

72 He denied it again, with an oath: "I don't know the man!"

73 After a little while, those standing there went up to Peter and said, "Surely you are one of them, for your accent gives you away."

74 Then he began to call down curses on himself and he swore to them, "I don't know the man!"

Immediately a rooster crowed. 75 Then Peter remembered the word Jesus had spoken: "Before the rooster crows, you will disown me three times." *h* And he went outside and wept bitterly.

a 63 Or Messiah; also in verse 68

26:60
y Ps 27:12; 35:11;
Ac 6:13
z Dt 19:15

26:63
a Mt 27:12, 14
b Lev 5:1

26:64
c Ps 110:1
d Da 7:13

26:66
e Lev 24:16; Jn 19:7

26:67
f Mt 27:30

26:68
g Lk 22:63-65

26:75
h ver 34; Jn 13:38

26:59 The Sanhedrin was the most powerful religious and political body of the Jewish people. Although the Romans controlled Israel's government, they gave the people power to handle religious disputes and some civil disputes, so the Sanhedrin made many of the local decisions affecting daily life. But a death sentence had to be approved by the Romans (John 18:31).

26:60, 61 The Sanhedrin tried to find witnesses who would distort some of Jesus' teachings. Finally they found two witnesses who distorted Jesus' words about the temple (see John 2:19). They claimed that Jesus had said he could destroy the temple—a blasphemous boast. Actually Jesus had said, "Destroy this temple, and I will raise it again in three days" (John 2:19). Jesus, of course, had been talking about his body, not the building. Ironically, the religious leaders were about to destroy Jesus' body just as he had said, and three days later he would rise from the dead.

26:64 Jesus declared his royalty in no uncertain terms. In calling himself the Son of Man, Jesus was claiming to be the Messiah, as his listeners well knew. He knew this declaration would be his undoing, but he did not panic. He was calm, courageous, and determined.

26:65, 66 The high priest accused Jesus of blasphemy—calling himself God. To the Jews, this was a great crime, punishable by death (Leviticus 24:16). The religious leaders refused even to consider that Jesus' words might be true. They had decided against Jesus, and in so doing, they sealed their own fate as well as his. Like the members of the Sanhedrin, you must decide whether Jesus' words are blasphemy or truth. Your decision has eternal implications.

26:69ff There were three stages to Peter's denial. First he acted confused and tried to divert attention from himself by changing the subject. Second, using an oath he denied that he knew Jesus. Third, he began to curse and swear. Believers who deny Christ often begin doing so subtly by pretending not to know him. When opportunities to discuss religious issues come up, they walk away or pretend they don't know the answers. With only a little more pressure, they can be induced to deny flatly their relationship with Christ. If you find yourself subtly diverting conversation so you don't have to talk about Christ, watch out. You may be on the road to disowning him.

26:72–74 That Peter denied that he knew Jesus, using an oath and calling down curses, does not mean he used foul language. This was the kind of swearing that a person does in a court of law. Peter was swearing that he did not know Jesus and was invoking a curse on himself if his words were untrue. In effect he was saying, "May God strike me dead if I am lying."

The Council of Religious Leaders Condemns Jesus
(228/Mark 15:1; Luke 22:66–71)

27:1
*Mk 15:1; Lk 22:66

27:2
*Mt 20:19
*Ac 3:13

27 Early in the morning, all the chief priests and the elders of the people came to the decision to put Jesus to death. *2* They bound him, led him away and handed him over* to Pilate, the governor. *

Judas Hangs Himself (229)

27:3
*Mt 26:14, 15

3 When Judas, who had betrayed him, saw that Jesus was condemned, he was seized with remorse and returned the thirty silver coins* to the chief priests and the elders. *4* "I have sinned," he said, "for I have betrayed innocent blood."

PETER

Jesus' first words to Simon Peter were "Come, follow me" (Mark 1:17). His last words to him were "You must follow me" (John 21:22). Every step of the way between those two challenges, Peter never failed to follow—even though he often stumbled.

When Jesus entered Peter's life, this plain fisherman became a new person with new goals and new priorities. He did not become a perfect person, however, and he never stopped being Simon Peter. We may wonder what Jesus saw in Simon that made him greet this potential disciple with a new name: Peter—the "rock." Impulsive Peter certainly didn't act like a rock much of the time. But when Jesus chose his followers, he wasn't looking for models; he was looking for real people. He chose people who could be changed by his love, and then he sent them out to communicate that his acceptance was available to anyone—even to those who often fail.

We may wonder what Jesus sees in us when he calls us to follow him. But we know Jesus accepted Peter, and, in spite of his failures, Peter went on to do great things for God. Are you willing to keep following Jesus, even when you fail?

Strengths and accomplishments:	• Became the recognized leader among Jesus' disciples—one of the inner group of three • Was the first great voice of the gospel during and after Pentecost • Probably knew Mark and gave him information for the Gospel of Mark • Wrote 1 and 2 Peter
Weaknesses and mistakes:	• Often spoke without thinking; was brash and impulsive • During Jesus' trial, denied three times that he even knew Jesus • Later found it hard to treat Gentile Christians as equals
Lessons from his life:	• Enthusiasm has to be backed up by faith and understanding, or it fails • God's faithfulness can compensate for our greatest unfaithfulness • It is better to be a follower who sometimes fails than one who fails to follow
Vital statistics:	• Occupations: Fisherman, disciple • Relatives: Father: John. Brother: Andrew. • Contemporaries: Jesus, Pilate, Herod Antipas
Key verse:	"And I tell you that you are Peter, and on this rock I will build my church, and the gates of Hades will not overcome it" (Matthew 16:18).

Peter's story is told in the Gospels and the book of Acts. He is mentioned in Galatians 1:18 and 2:7–14; and he wrote the books of 1 and 2 Peter.

27:1, 2 The religious leaders had to persuade the Roman government to sentence Jesus to death because they did not have the authority to do it themselves. The Romans had taken away the religious leaders' authority to inflict capital punishment. Politically, it looked better for the religious leaders anyway if someone else was responsible for killing Jesus. They wanted the death to appear Roman-sponsored so the crowds couldn't blame them. The Jewish leaders had arrested Jesus on theological grounds—blasphemy. Because this charge would be thrown out of a Roman court, however, they had to come up with a political reason for Jesus' death. Their strategy was to show Jesus as a rebel who claimed to be a king and thus a threat to Caesar.

27:2 Pilate was the Roman governor for the regions of Samaria and Judea from A.D. 26–36. Jerusalem was located in Judea. Pilate took special pleasure in demonstrating his authority over the Jews; for example, he impounded money from the temple treasuries to build an aqueduct. Pilate was not popular, but the religious leaders had no other way to get rid of Jesus than to go

to him. Ironically, when Jesus, a Jew, came before him for trial, Pilate found him innocent. He could not find a single fault in Jesus, nor could he contrive one.

27:3, 4 Jesus' formal accuser (see 26:48 note) wanted to drop his charges, but the religious leaders refused to halt the trial. When he betrayed Jesus, perhaps Judas was trying to force Jesus' hand to get him to lead a revolt against Rome. This did not work, of course. Whatever his reason, Judas changed his mind, but it was too late. Many of the plans we set into motion cannot be reversed. It is best to think of the potential consequences before we launch into an action we may later regret.

27:4 The priests' job was to teach people about God and act as intercessors for them, helping administer the sacrifices to cover their sins. Judas returned to the priests, exclaiming that he had sinned. Rather than helping him find forgiveness, however, the priests said, "That's your responsibility." Not only had they rejected the Messiah, they had rejected their role as priests.

"What is that to us?" they replied. "That's your responsibility." m

5 So Judas threw the money into the temple and left. Then he went away and hanged himself. n

6 The chief priests picked up the coins and said, "It is against the law to put this into the treasury, since it is blood money." 7 So they decided to use the money to buy the potter's field as a burial place for foreigners. 8 That is why it has been called the Field of Blood o to this day. 9 Then what was spoken by Jeremiah the prophet was fulfilled: "They took the thirty silver coins, the price set on him by the people of Israel, 10 and they used them to buy the potter's field, as the Lord commanded me." a

Jesus Stands Trial before Pilate
(230/Mark 15:2–5; Luke 23:1–5; John 18:28–38)

11 Meanwhile Jesus stood before the governor, and the governor asked him, "Are you the king of the Jews?"

"Yes, it is as you say," Jesus replied.

12 When he was accused by the chief priests and the elders, he gave no answer. p 13 Then Pilate asked him, "Don't you hear the testimony they are bringing against you?" q 14 But Jesus made no reply, not even to a single charge—to the great amazement of the governor.

Pilate Hands Jesus Over to Be Crucified
(232/Mark 15:6–15; Luke 23:13–25; John 18:39—19:16)

15 Now it was the governor's custom at the Feast to release a prisoner r chosen by the crowd. 16 At that time they had a notorious prisoner, called Barabbas. 17 So when the crowd had gathered, Pilate asked them, "Which one do you want me to release to you: Barabbas, or Jesus who is called Christ?" 18 For he knew it was out of envy that they had handed Jesus over to him.

a 10 See Zech. 11:12,13; Jer. 19:1-13; 32:6-9.

27:4
m ver 24
27:5
n Ac 1:18

27:8
o Ac 1:19

27:12
p Mt 26:63; Jn 19:9
27:13
q Mt 26:62

27:15
r Jn 18:39

Golgotha (other possible site) □

Antonia Fortress (later Praetorium?)

Traditional Golgotha □

Temple

Hasmonean Palace

Herod's Royal Palace

Herod's Lower Palace

UPPER CITY

Caiaphas's House?

JERUSALEM

Traditional Upper Room?

LOWER CITY

N

0   .1 Mi.

0   .1 Km.

THE WAY OF THE CROSS The Roman soldiers took Jesus into their headquarters at the Praetorium and mocked him, dressing him in a scarlet robe and a crown of thorns. They then led him to the crucifixion site outside the city. He was so weakened by his beatings that he could not carry his cross, and a man from Cyrene was forced to carry it to Golgotha.

27:5 According to Matthew, Judas hanged himself. Acts 1:18, however, says that he fell and burst open. The best explanation is that the limb from which he was hanging broke, and the resulting fall split open his body.

27:6 These chief priests felt no guilt in giving Judas money to betray an innocent man, but when Judas returned the money, the priests couldn't accept it because it was wrong to accept blood money—payment for murder! Their hatred for Jesus had caused them to lose all sense of right and wrong.

27:9, 10 This prophecy is found specifically in Zechariah 11:12, 13, but may also have been taken from Jeremiah 17:2, 3; 18:1–4; 19:1–11; or 32:6–15. In Old Testament times, Jeremiah was considered the collector of some of the prophets' writings, so perhaps his name is cited rather than Zechariah.

27:12 Standing before Pilate, the religious leaders accused Jesus of a different crime than the ones for which they had arrested him. They arrested him for blasphemy (claiming to be God), but that charge would mean nothing to the Romans. So the religious leaders had to accuse Jesus of crimes that would have concerned the Roman government, such as encouraging the people not to pay taxes, claiming to be a king, and causing riots. These accusations were not true, but the religious leaders were determined to kill Jesus, and they broke several commandments in order to do so.

27:14 Jesus' silence fulfilled the words of the prophet (Isaiah 53:7). Pilate was amazed that Jesus didn't try to defend himself. He recognized the obvious plot against Jesus and wanted to let him go, but Pilate was already under pressure from Rome to keep peace in his territory. The last thing he needed was a rebellion over this quiet and seemingly insignificant man.

27:15, 16 Barabbas had taken part in a rebellion against the Roman government (Mark 15:7). Although an enemy to Rome, he may have been a hero to the Jews. Ironically, Barabbas was guilty of the crime for which Jesus was accused.

27:19
�day 24

19While Pilate was sitting on the judge's seat, his wife sent him this message: "Don't have anything to do with that innocentˢ man, for I have suffered a great deal today in a dream because of him."

27:20
ᵗAc 3:14

20But the chief priests and the elders persuaded the crowd to ask for Barabbas and to have Jesus executed.ᵗ

21"Which of the two do you want me to release to you?" asked the governor.

"Barabbas," they answered.

22"What shall I do, then, with Jesus who is called Christ?" Pilate asked.

They all answered, "Crucify him!"

23"Why? What crime has he committed?" asked Pilate.

But they shouted all the louder, "Crucify him!"

27:24
ᵘMt 26:5
ᵛDt 21:6-8

24When Pilate saw that he was getting nowhere, but that instead an uproarᵘ was starting, he took water and washed his hands in front of the crowd. "I am innocent of this man's blood,"ᵛ he said. "It is your responsibility!"

27:25
ʷJos 2:19; Ac 5:28

25All the people answered, "Let his blood be on us and on our children!"ʷ

27:26
ˣIsa 53:5

26Then he released Barabbas to them. But he had Jesus flogged,ˣ and handed him over to be crucified.

Roman Soldiers Mock Jesus (233/Mark 15:16–20)

27:29
ʸIsa 53:3

27Then the governor's soldiers took Jesus into the Praetorium and gathered the whole company of soldiers around him. 28They stripped him and put a scarlet robe on him, 29and then twisted together a crown of thorns and set it on his head. They put a staff in his right hand and knelt in front of him and mocked him. "Hail, king of the Jews!" they said.ʸ 30They spit on him, and took the staff and struck him on the head again and again.ᶻ 31After they had mocked him, they took off the robe and put his own clothes on him. Then they led him away to crucify him.ᵃ

27:30
ᶻMt 26:67

27:31
ᵃIsa 53:7

**THE SEVEN
LAST WORDS
OF JESUS ON
THE CROSS**

"Father, forgive them, for they do not know what
they are doing.".. Luke 23:34

"I tell you the truth, today you will be with me in paradise." ..... Luke 23:43

Speaking to Mary and John: "Dear woman, here is your
son. . . . Here is your mother." .... John 19:26, 27

"My God, my God, why have you forsaken me?" .... Matthew 27:46; Mark 15:34

"I am thirsty.".. John 19:28

"It is finished." .... John 19:30

"Father, into your hands I commit my spirit." .... Luke 23:46

The statements that Jesus made from the cross have been treasured by all who have followed him as Lord. They demonstrate both his humanity and his divinity. They also capture the last moments of all that Jesus went through to gain our forgiveness.

27:19 For a leader who was supposed to administer justice, Pilate proved to be more concerned about political expediency than about doing what was right. He had several opportunities to make the right decision. His conscience told him Jesus was innocent; Roman law said an innocent man should not be put to death; and his wife had a troubling dream that caused her to encourage her husband to let Jesus go. Pilate had no good excuse to condemn Jesus, but he was afraid of the crowd.

27:21 Crowds are fickle. They loved Jesus on Sunday because they thought he was going to inaugurate his kingdom. Then they hated him on Friday when his power appeared broken. In the face of the mass uprising against Jesus, his friends were afraid to speak up.

27:24 At first Pilate hesitated to give the religious leaders permission to crucify Jesus. He perceived that they were simply jealous of a teacher who was more popular with the people than they were. But when the Jews threatened to report Pilate to Caesar (John 19:12), Pilate became afraid. Historical records indicate that the Jews had already threatened to lodge a formal complaint against Pilate for his stubborn flouting of their tradi-

tions—and such a complaint would most likely have led to his recall by Rome. His job was in jeopardy. The Roman government could not afford to put large numbers of troops in all the regions under their control, so one of Pilate's main duties was to do whatever was necessary to maintain peace.

27:24 In making no decision, Pilate made the decision to let the crowds crucify Jesus. Although he washed his hands, the guilt remained. Washing your hands of a tough situation doesn't cancel your guilt. It merely gives you a false sense of peace. Don't make excuses—take responsibility for the decisions you make.

27:27 A company of soldiers was a division of the Roman legion, containing about 200 men.

Jesus Is Led Away to Be Crucified
(234/Mark 15:21–24; Luke 23:26–31; John 19:17)
Jesus Is Placed on the Cross
(235/Mark 15:25–32; Luke 23:32–43; John 19:18–27)

32 As they were going out,[b] they met a man from Cyrene, named Simon, and they forced him to carry the cross.[c] 33 They came to a place called Golgotha (which means The Place of the Skull).[d] 34 There they offered Jesus wine to drink, mixed with gall;[e] but after tasting it, he refused to drink it. 35 When they had crucified him, they divided up his clothes by casting lots.[a][f] 36 And sitting down, they kept watch[g] over him there. 37 Above his head they placed the written charge against him: THIS IS JESUS, THE KING OF THE JEWS. 38 Two robbers were crucified with him, one on his right and one on his left. 39 Those who passed by hurled insults at him, shaking their heads[h] 40 and saying, "You who are going to destroy the temple and build it in three days,[i] save yourself! Come down from the cross, if you are the Son of God!"

41 In the same way the chief priests, the teachers of the law and the elders mocked him. 42 "He saved others," they said, "but he can't save himself! He's the King of Israel![j] Let him come down now from the cross, and we will believe in him. 43 He trusts in God. Let God rescue him[k] now if he wants him, for he said, 'I am the Son of God.'" 44 In the same way the robbers who were crucified with him also heaped insults on him.

Jesus Dies on the Cross (236/Mark 15:33–41; Luke 23:44–49; John 19:28–37)

45 From the sixth hour until the ninth hour darkness came over all the land. 46 About the ninth hour Jesus cried out in a loud voice, *"Eloi, Eloi,[b] lama sabachthani?"*—which means, "My God, my God, why have you forsaken me?"[c][l]

47 When some of those standing there heard this, they said, "He's calling Elijah." 48 Immediately one of them ran and got a sponge. He filled it with wine vinegar,[m] put it on a stick, and offered it to Jesus to drink. 49 The rest said, "Now leave him alone. Let's see if Elijah comes to save him."

50 And when Jesus had cried out again in a loud voice, he gave up his spirit.

51 At that moment the curtain of the temple[n] was torn in two from top to bottom. The earth shook and the rocks split. 52 The tombs broke open and the bodies of many holy people who had died were raised to life. 53 They came out of the tombs, and after Jesus' resurrection they went into the holy city and appeared to many people.

[a] 35 A few late manuscripts *lots that the word spoken by the prophet might be fulfilled: "They divided my garments among themselves and cast lots for my clothing"* (Psalm 22:18)   [b] 46 Some manuscripts *Eli, Eli*   [c] 46 Psalm 22:1

27:32 [b] Heb 13:12 [c] Mk 15:21
27:33 [d] Jn 19:17
27:34 [e] Ps 69:21
27:35 [f] Ps 22:18
27:36 [g] ver 54
27:39 [h] Ps 22:7; 109:25
27:40 [i] Mt 26:61; Jn 2:19
27:42 [j] Jn 1:49
27:43 [k] Ps 22:8
27:46 [l] Ps 22:1
27:48 [m] Ps 69:21
27:51 [n] Ex 26:31-33

27:32 Condemned prisoners had to carry their own crosses to the execution site. Jesus, weakened from the beatings he had received, was physically unable to carry his cross any farther. Thus a bystander, Simon, was forced to do so. Simon was from Cyrene, in northern Africa, and was probably one of the thousands of Jews visiting Jerusalem for the Passover.

27:33 Some scholars say Golgotha ("skull") derives its name from its appearance. Golgotha may have been a regular place of execution in a prominent public place outside the city. Executions held there would serve as a deterrent to criminals.

27:34 Wine mixed with gall was offered to Jesus to help reduce his pain, but Jesus refused to drink it. Gall is generally understood to be a narcotic that was used to deaden pain. Jesus would suffer fully conscious and with a clear mind.

27:35 The soldiers customarily took the clothing of those they crucified. These soldiers cast lots and divided Jesus' clothing among themselves, fulfilling the prophecy made by David. Much of Psalm 22 parallels Jesus' crucifixion.

27:40 This accusation was used against Jesus in his trial by the Sanhedrin (26:61). It is ironic that Jesus was in the very process of fulfilling his own prophecy. Because Jesus is the Son of God, who always obeys the will of the Father, he did not come down from the cross.

27:44 Later one of these robbers repented. Jesus promised that the repentant robber would join him in paradise (Luke 23:39–43).

27:45 We do not know how this darkness occurred, but it is clear that God caused it. Nature testified to the gravity of Jesus'

death, while Jesus' friends and enemies alike fell silent in the encircling gloom. The darkness on that Friday afternoon was both physical and spiritual.

27:46 Jesus was not questioning God; he was quoting the first line of Psalm 22—a deep expression of the anguish he felt when he took on the sins of the world, which caused him to be separated from his Father. *This* was what Jesus dreaded as he prayed to God in the garden to take the cup from him (26:39). The physical agony was horrible, but even worse was the period of spiritual separation from God. Jesus suffered this double death so that we would never have to experience eternal separation from God.

27:47 The bystanders misinterpreted Jesus' words and thought he was calling for Elijah. Because Elijah ascended into heaven without dying (2 Kings 2:11), they thought he would return again to rescue them from great trouble (Malachi 4:5). At their annual Passover feast, each family set an extra place for Elijah in expectation of his return.

27:51 The temple had three main parts—the courts, the Holy Place (where only the priests could enter), and the Most Holy Place (where only the high priest could enter, and only once a year, to atone for the sins of the nation—Leviticus 16:1–35). The curtain separating the Holy Place from the Most Holy Place was torn in two at Christ's death, symbolizing that the barrier between God and humanity was removed. Now all people are free to approach God because of Christ's sacrifice for our sins (see Hebrews 9:1–14; 10:19–22).

27:52, 53 Christ's death was accompanied by at least four miraculous events: darkness, the tearing in two of the curtain in

27:54
o ver 36

27:55
p Lk 8:2, 3

27:60
q Mk 16:4

27:63
r Mt 16:21

27:66
s Da 6:17

54 When the centurion and those with him who were guarding*o* Jesus saw the earthquake and all that had happened, they were terrified, and exclaimed, "Surely he was the Son*a* of God!"

55 Many women were there, watching from a distance. They had followed Jesus from Galilee to care for his needs.*p* 56 Among them were Mary Magdalene, Mary the mother of James and Joses, and the mother of Zebedee's sons.

Jesus Is Laid in the Tomb (237/Mark 15:42–47; Luke 23:50–56; John 19:38–42)

57 As evening approached, there came a rich man from Arimathea, named Joseph, who had himself become a disciple of Jesus. 58 Going to Pilate, he asked for Jesus' body, and Pilate ordered that it be given to him. 59 Joseph took the body, wrapped it in a clean linen cloth, 60 and placed it in his own new tomb*q* that he had cut out of the rock. He rolled a big stone in front of the entrance to the tomb and went away. 61 Mary Magdalene and the other Mary were sitting there opposite the tomb.

Guards Are Posted at the Tomb (238)

62 The next day, the one after Preparation Day, the chief priests and the Pharisees went to Pilate. 63 "Sir," they said, "we remember that while he was still alive that deceiver said, 'After three days I will rise again.'*r* 64 So give the order for the tomb to be made secure until the third day. Otherwise, his disciples may come and steal the body and tell the people that he has been raised from the dead. This last deception will be worse than the first."

65 "Take a guard," Pilate answered. "Go, make the tomb as secure as you know how." 66 So they went and made the tomb secure by putting a seal*s* on the stone and posting the guard.

a 54 Or *a son*

HOW JESUS' TRIAL WAS ILLEGAL

1. Even before the trial began, it had been determined that Jesus must die (Mark 14:1; John 11:50). There was no "innocent until proven guilty" approach.
2. False witnesses were sought to testify against Jesus (Matthew 26:59). Usually the religious leaders went through an elaborate system of screening witnesses to ensure justice.
3. No defense for Jesus was sought or allowed (Luke 22:67–71).
4. The trial was conducted at night (Mark 14:53–65; 15:1), which was illegal according to the religious leaders' own laws.
5. The high priest put Jesus under oath, but then incriminated him for what he said (Matthew 26:63–66).
6. Cases involving such serious charges were to be tried only in the Sanhedrin's regular meeting place, not in the high priest's palace (Mark 14:53–65).

The religious leaders were not interested in giving Jesus a fair trial. In their minds, Jesus had to die. This blind obsession led them to pervert the justice they were appointed to protect. Above are many examples of the actions taken by the religious leaders that were illegal according to their own laws.

---

the temple, an earthquake, and dead people rising from their tombs. Jesus' death, therefore, could not have gone unnoticed. Everyone knew something significant had happened.

27:57, 58 Joseph of Arimathea was a secret disciple of Jesus. He was a religious leader, an honored member of the Sanhedrin (Mark 15:43). Joseph courageously asked to take Jesus' body from the cross and to bury it. The disciples who publicly followed Jesus had fled, but this Jewish leader, who followed Jesus in secret, came forward and did what was right.

27:60 The tomb where Jesus was laid was probably a manmade cave cut out of one of the many limestone hills in the area. These caves were often large enough to walk into.

27:64-66 The religious leaders took Jesus' resurrection claims more seriously than the disciples did. The disciples didn't remember Jesus' teaching about his resurrection (20:17–19); but the religious leaders remembered and took steps they thought would prevent it (or at least a fabrication of it). Because of his claims, they were almost as afraid of Jesus after his death as when he was alive. They tried to take every precaution that his body would

remain in the tomb. Because the tomb was hewn out of rock in the side of a hill, there was only one entrance. The tomb was sealed by stringing a cord across the stone that was rolled over the entrance. The cord was sealed at each end with clay. But the religious leaders took a further precaution, asking that guards be placed at the tomb's entrance. The Pharisees failed to understand that no rock, seal, guard, or army could prevent the Son of God from rising again.

Jesus Rises from the Dead (*239*/Mark 16:1–8; Luke 24:1–12; John 20:1–10)

28 After the Sabbath, at dawn on the first day of the week, Mary Magdalene and the other Mary *t* went to look at the tomb.

²There was a violent earthquake, for an angel of the Lord came down from heaven and, going to the tomb, rolled back the stone and sat on it. ³His appearance was like lightning, and his clothes were white as snow. *u* ⁴The guards were so afraid of him that they shook and became like dead men.

⁵The angel said to the women, "Do not be afraid, for I know that you are looking for Jesus, who was crucified. ⁶He is not here; he has risen, just as he said. *v* Come and see the place where he lay. ⁷Then go quickly and tell his disciples: 'He has risen from the dead and is going ahead of you into Galilee. *w* There you will see him.' Now I have told you."

28:1
*t*Mt 27:56

28:3
*u*Da 10:6

28:6
*v*Mt 16:21
28:7
*w*Mt 26:32

Jesus Appears to the Women (*241*)

⁸So the women hurried away from the tomb, afraid yet filled with joy, and ran to tell his disciples. ⁹Suddenly Jesus met them. "Greetings," he said. They came to him, clasped his feet and worshiped him. ¹⁰Then Jesus said to them, "Do not be afraid. Go and tell my brothers *x* to go to Galilee; there they will see me."

28:10
*x*Ro 8:29;
Heb 2:11-13, 17

Religious Leaders Bribe the Guards (*242*)

¹¹While the women were on their way, some of the guards went into the city and reported to the chief priests everything that had happened. ¹²When the chief priests had met with the elders and devised a plan, they gave the soldiers a large sum of money, ¹³telling them, "You are to say, 'His disciples came during the night and stole him away while we were asleep.' ¹⁴If this report gets to the governor, we will satisfy him and keep you out of trouble." ¹⁵So the soldiers took the money and did as they were instructed. And this story has been widely circulated among the Jews to this very day.

28:1 The other Mary was not Jesus' mother. She could have been the wife of Clopas (John 19:25). Or, if she was the mother of James and John (Matthew 27:56), she may have been Jesus' aunt.

28:2 The stone was not rolled aside so Jesus could get out, but so others could get in and see that Jesus had indeed risen from the dead, just as he had promised.

28:5–7 The angel who announced the good news of the resurrection to the women gave them four messages: (1) *Do not be afraid.* The reality of the resurrection brings joy, not fear. When you are afraid, remember the empty tomb. (2) *He is not here.* Jesus is not dead and is not to be looked for among the dead. He is alive, with his people. (3) *Come and see.* The women could check the evidence themselves. The tomb was empty then, and it is empty today. The resurrection is a historical fact. (4) *Go quickly and tell.* They were to spread the joy of the resurrection. We too are to spread the great news about Jesus' resurrection.

28:6 Jesus' resurrection is the key to the Christian faith. Why? (1) Just as he promised, Jesus rose from the dead. We can be confident, therefore, that he will accomplish all he has promised. (2) Jesus' bodily resurrection shows us that the living Christ is ruler of God's eternal kingdom, not a false prophet or imposter. (3) We can be certain of our resurrection because he was resurrected. Death is not the end—there is future life. (4) The power that brought Jesus back to life is available to us to bring our spiritually dead selves back to life. (5) The resurrection is the basis for the church's witness to the world. Jesus is more than just a human leader; he is the Son of God.

28:10 By "brothers," Jesus probably meant his disciples. This showed that he had forgiven them, even after they had disowned and deserted him. Jesus told the women to pass a message on to the disciples—that he would meet them in Galilee, as he had previously told them (Mark 14:28). But the disciples, afraid of the religious leaders, stayed hidden behind locked doors in Jerusalem (John 20:19). So Jesus met them first there (Luke 24:36) and then later in Galilee (John 21).

28:11–15 Jesus' resurrection was already causing a great stir in Jerusalem. A group of women were moving quickly through the streets, looking for the disciples to tell them the amazing news that Jesus was alive. At the same time, a group of religious leaders was plotting how to cover up the resurrection.

Today there is still a great stir over the resurrection, and there are still only two choices—to believe that Jesus rose from the dead, or to be closed to the truth—denying it, ignoring it, or trying to explain it away.

Jesus Gives the Great Commission (*248*/Mark 16:15–18)

28:16
y ver 7, 10; Mt 26:32

28:18
z Da 7:13, 14;
Php 2:9, 10

28:19
a Mk 16:15, 16

28:20
b Ac 2:42

¹⁶Then the eleven disciples went to Galilee, to the mountain where Jesus had told them to go. *y* ¹⁷When they saw him, they worshiped him; but some doubted. ¹⁸Then Jesus came to them and said, "All authority in heaven and on earth has been given to me. *z* ¹⁹Therefore go and make disciples of all nations, *a* baptizing them in *a* the name of the Father and of the Son and of the Holy Spirit, ²⁰and teaching *b* them to obey everything I have commanded you. And surely I am with you always, to the very end of the age."

a 19 Or *into*; see Acts 8:16; 19:5; Romans 6:3; 1 Cor. 1:13; 10:2 and Gal. 3:27.

28:18 God gave Jesus authority over heaven and earth. On the basis of that authority, Jesus told his disciples to make more disciples as they preached, baptized, and taught. With this same authority, Jesus still commands us to tell others the Good News and make them disciples for the kingdom.

28:18–20 When someone is dying or leaving us, his or her last words are very important. Jesus left the disciples with these last words of instruction: they were under his authority; they were to make more disciples; they were to baptize and teach these new disciples to obey Christ; Christ would be with them always. Whereas in previous missions Jesus had sent his disciples only to the Jews (10:5, 6), their mission from now on would be worldwide. Jesus is Lord of the earth, and he died for the sins of people from all nations.

We are to go—whether it is next door or to another country—and make disciples. It is not an option, but a command to all who call Jesus "Lord." We are not all evangelists in the formal sense, but we have all received gifts that we can use to help fulfill the Great Commission. As we obey, we have comfort in the knowledge that Jesus is always with us.

28:19 Jesus' words affirm the reality of the Trinity. Some people accuse theologians of making up the concept of the Trinity and reading it into Scripture. As we see here, the concept comes directly from Jesus himself. He did not say baptize them into the *names*, but into the *name* of the Father, Son, and Holy Spirit. The word *Trinity* does not occur in Scripture, but it well describes the three-in-one nature of the Father, Son, and Holy Spirit.

28:19 The disciples were to baptize people because baptism unites a believer with Jesus Christ in his or her death to sin and resurrection to new life. Baptism symbolizes submission to Christ, a willingness to live God's way, and identification with God's covenant people.

28:20 How is Jesus *with* us? Jesus was with the disciples physically until he ascended into heaven, and then spiritually through the Holy Spirit (Acts 1:4). The Holy Spirit would be Jesus' presence that would never leave them (John 14:26). Jesus continues to be with us today through his Spirit.

28:20 The Old Testament prophecies and genealogies in the book of Matthew present Jesus' credentials for being King of the world—not a military or political leader, as the disciples had originally hoped, but a spiritual King who can overcome all evil and rule in the heart of every person. If we refuse to serve the King faithfully, we are disloyal subjects, fit only to be banished from the kingdom. We must make Jesus King of our lives and worship him as our Savior, King, and Lord.

MARK

Herod the Great begins to rule 37 B.C.	Jesus is born 6/5 B.C.	Escape to Egypt 5/4 B.C.	Herod the Great dies 4 B.C.	Return to Nazareth 4/3 B.C.	Jesus visits temple as a boy A.D. 6/7

VITAL STATISTICS

PURPOSE:
To present the person, work, and teachings of Jesus

AUTHOR:
John Mark. He was not one of the 12 disciples, but he accompanied Paul on his first missionary journey (Acts 13:13).

ORIGINAL AUDIENCE:
The Christians in Rome, where the Gospel was written

DATE WRITTEN:
Between A.D. 55 and 65

SETTING:
The Roman empire under Tiberius Caesar. The empire, with its common language and excellent transportation and communication systems, was ripe to hear Jesus' message, which spread quickly from nation to nation.

KEY VERSE:
"For even the Son of Man did not come to be served, but to serve, and to give his life as a ransom for many" (10:45).

KEY PEOPLE:
Jesus, the 12 disciples, Pilate, the Jewish religious leaders

KEY PLACES:
Capernaum, Nazareth, Caesarea Philippi, Jericho, Bethany, Mount of Olives, Jerusalem, Golgotha

SPECIAL FEATURES:
Mark was probably the first Gospel written. The other Gospels quote all but 31 verses of Mark. Mark records more miracles than does any other Gospel.

WE'RE number one! . . . The greatest, strongest, prettiest . . . champions! Daily such proclamations boldly assert claims of supremacy. Everyone wants to be associated with a winner. Losers are those who finish less than first. In direct contrast are the words of Jesus: "And whoever wants to be first must be slave of all. For even the Son of Man did not come to be served, but to serve, and to give his life as a ransom for many" (10:44, 45). Jesus *is* the greatest—God incarnate, our Messiah—but he entered history as a servant.

This is the message of Mark. Written to encourage Roman Christians and to prove beyond a doubt that Jesus is the Messiah, Mark presents a rapid succession of vivid pictures of Jesus in action—his true identity revealed by what he does, not necessarily by what he says. It is Jesus on the move.

Omitting the birth of Jesus, Mark begins with John the Baptist's preaching. Then, moving quickly past Jesus' baptism, temptation in the desert, and call of the disciples, Mark takes us directly into Jesus' public ministry. We see Jesus confronting a demon, healing a man with leprosy, and forgiving and healing the paralyzed man lowered into Jesus' presence by friends.

Next, Jesus calls Matthew (Levi) and has dinner with him and his questionable associates. This initiates the conflict with the Pharisees and other religious leaders, who condemn Jesus for eating with sinners and breaking the Sabbath.

In chapter 4, Mark pauses to give a sample of Jesus' teaching—the parable of the sower and the illustration of the mustard seed—and then plunges back into the action. Jesus calms the waves, drives out demons, and raises Jairus's daughter from the dead.

After returning to Nazareth for a few days and experiencing rejection in his hometown, Jesus commissions the disciples to spread the Good News everywhere. Opposition from Herod and the Pharisees increases, and John the Baptist is beheaded. But Jesus continues to move, feeding 5,000, reaching out to the Syrophoenician, healing the deaf man, and feeding 4,000.

Finally, it is time to reveal his true identity to the disciples. Do they really know who Jesus is? Peter proclaims him Messiah but then promptly shows that he does not understand Jesus' mission. After the transfiguration, Jesus continues to teach and heal, confronting the Pharisees about divorce and the rich young man about eternal life. Blind Bartimaeus is healed.

Events move rapidly toward a climax. The Last Supper, the betrayal, the crucifixion, and the resurrection are dramatically portrayed, along with more examples of Jesus' teachings. Mark shows us Jesus—moving, serving, sacrificing, and saving! As you read Mark, be ready for action, be open for God's move in your life, and be challenged to move into your world to serve.

THE BLUEPRINT

A. BIRTH AND PREPARATION OF JESUS, THE SERVANT (1:1–13)

Jesus did not arrive unannounced or unexpected. The Old Testament prophets had clearly predicted the coming of a great one, sent by God himself, who would offer salvation and eternal peace to Israel and the entire world. Then came John the Baptist, who announced that the long-awaited Messiah had finally come and would soon be among the people. In God's work in the world today, Jesus does not come unannounced or unexpected. Yet many still reject him. We have the witness of the Bible, but some choose to ignore it, just as many ignored John the Baptist in his day.

B. MESSAGE AND MINISTRY OF JESUS, THE SERVANT (1:14—13:37)
1. Jesus' ministry in Galilee
2. Jesus' ministry beyond Galilee
3. Jesus' ministry in Jerusalem

Jesus had all the power of God: He raised the dead, gave sight to the blind, restored deformed bodies, and quieted stormy seas. But with all this power, Jesus came to humanity as a servant. We can use his life as a pattern for how to live today. As Jesus served God and others, so should we.

C. DEATH AND RESURRECTION OF JESUS, THE SERVANT (14:1—16:20)

Jesus came as a servant, so many did not recognize or acknowledge him as the Messiah. We must be careful that we also don't reject God or his will because he doesn't quite fit our image of what God should be.

MEGATHEMES

THEME	EXPLANATION	IMPORTANCE
Jesus Christ	Jesus Christ alone is the Son of God. In Mark, Jesus demonstrates his divinity by overcoming disease, demons, and death. Although he had the power to be king of the earth, Jesus chose to obey the Father and die for us.	When Jesus rose from the dead, he proved that he was God, that he could forgive sin, and that he has the power to change our lives. By trusting in him for forgiveness, we can begin a new life with him as our guide.
Servant	As the Messiah, Jesus fulfilled the prophecies of the Old Testament by coming to earth. He did not come as a conquering king; he came as a servant. He helped people by telling them about God and healing them. Even more, by giving his life as a sacrifice for sin, he performed the ultimate act of service.	Because of Jesus' example, we should be willing to serve God and others. Real greatness in Christ's kingdom is shown by service and sacrifice. Ambition or love of power or position should not be our motive; instead, we should do God's work because we love him.
Miracles	Mark records more of Jesus' miracles than sermons. Jesus is clearly a man of power and action, not just words. Jesus did miracles to convince the people who he was and to confirm to the disciples his true identity—God.	The more convinced we become that Jesus is God, the more we will see his power and his love. His mighty works show us he is able to save anyone regardless of his or her past. His miracles of forgiveness bring healing, wholeness, and changed lives to those who trust him.
Spreading the Gospel	Jesus directed his public ministry to the Jews first. When the Jewish leaders opposed him, Jesus also went to the non-Jewish world, healing and preaching. Roman soldiers, Syrians, and other Gentiles heard the Good News. Many believed and followed him. Jesus' final message to his disciples challenged them to go into all the world and preach the gospel of salvation.	Jesus crossed national, racial, and economic barriers to spread his Good News. Jesus' message of faith and forgiveness is for the whole world—not just our church, neighborhood, or nation. We must reach out beyond our own people and needs to fulfill the worldwide vision of Jesus Christ so that people everywhere may hear this great message and be saved from sin and death.

A. BIRTH AND PREPARATION OF JESUS, THE SERVANT (1:1–13)

Mark, the shortest of the four Gospels, opens with Jesus' baptism and temptation. Moving right into action, Mark quickly prepares us for Christ's ministry. The Gospel of Mark is concise, straightforward, and chronological.

John the Baptist Prepares the Way for Jesus (16/Matthew 3:1–12; Luke 3:1–18)

1 The beginning of the gospel about Jesus Christ, the Son of God.ᵃ

2 It is written in Isaiah the prophet:

> "I will send my messenger ahead of you,
> who will prepare your way"ᵇ ᵃ—
> 3 "a voice of one calling in the desert,
> 'Prepare the way for the Lord,
> make straight paths for him.'"ᶜ ᵇ

4 And so John came, baptizing in the desert region and preaching a baptism of repentance for the forgiveness of sins. 5 The whole Judean countryside and all the people of Jerusalem went out to him. Confessing their sins, they were baptized by him in the Jordan River. 6 John wore clothing made of camel's hair, with a leather belt around his waist, and he ate locusts and wild honey. 7 And this was his message: "After me will come one more powerful than I,

a 1 Some manuscripts do not have *the Son of God.*   b 2 Mal. 3:1   c 3 Isaiah 40:3

1:2
a Mal 3:1; Mt 11:10; Lk 7:27

1:3
b Isa 40:3

1:1 When you experience the excitement of a big event, you naturally want to tell someone. Telling the story can bring back that original thrill as you relive the experience. Reading Mark's first words, you can sense his excitement. Picture yourself in the crowd as Jesus heals and teaches. Imagine yourself as one of the disciples. Respond to his words of love and encouragement. And remember that Jesus came for us who live today as well as for those who lived 2,000 years ago.

1:1 Mark was not one of the 12 disciples of Jesus, but he probably knew Jesus personally. Mark wrote his Gospel in the form of a fast-paced story, like a popular novel. The book portrays Jesus as a man who backed up his words with action that constantly proved who he is—the Son of God. Because Mark wrote the Gospel for Christians in Rome, where many gods were worshiped, he wanted his readers to know that Jesus is *the one true* Son of God.

Without God's revelation, our finite minds cannot comprehend the infinite. But because of what we know about Jesus (thanks to writers like Mark), we can understand what God is like. Mark gave the "punch line" of his Gospel in the very first verse, but both Jesus' enemies and his disciples would not get it until Jesus' resurrection. For us who read Mark today, the message is clear that we must not ignore or reject Jesus Christ.

1:2 Jesus came at a time in history when the entire civilized world was relatively peaceful under Roman rule, travel was easy, and there was a common language. The news about Jesus' life, death, and resurrection could spread quickly throughout the vast Roman empire.

In Israel, common men and women were ready for Jesus too. There had been no God-sent prophets for 400 years, since the days of Malachi (who wrote the last book of the Old Testament). There was growing anticipation that a great prophet, or the Messiah mentioned in the Old Testament, would soon come (see Luke 3:15).

1:2, 3 Isaiah was one of the greatest prophets of the Old Testament. The second half of the book of Isaiah is devoted to the promise of salvation. Isaiah wrote about the coming of the Messiah, Jesus Christ, and the man who would announce his coming, John the Baptist. John's call to "make straight paths for him" meant that people should give up their selfish way of living, renounce their sins, seek God's forgiveness, and establish a relationship with the almighty God by believing and obeying his words as found in Scripture (Isaiah 1:18–20; 57:15).

1:2, 3 Mark 1:2, 3 is a composite quotation, taken first from Malachi 3:1 and then from Isaiah 40:3.

1:2–4 Hundreds of years earlier, the prophet Isaiah had predicted that John the Baptist and Jesus would come. Isaiah's words comforted many people as they looked forward to the Messiah, and knowing that God keeps his promises can comfort you too. As you read the book of Mark, realize that it is more than just a story; it is part of God's Word. In it God is revealing to you his plans for human history—and offering the Good News of his salvation to you.

1:3 John the Baptist prepared the way for Jesus. People who do not know Jesus need to be prepared to meet him. We can "prepare the way" by explaining their need for forgiveness, demonstrating Christ's teaching by our conduct, and telling them how Christ can give their lives meaning. We can "make straight paths for him" by correcting misconceptions that might be hindering people from approaching Christ. Someone you know may be open to a relationship with Christ. What can you do to prepare the way for this person?

1:4 Why does the Gospel of Mark begin with the story of John the Baptist and not mention the story of Jesus' birth? Important Roman officials of this day were always preceded by an announcer or herald. When the herald arrived in town, the people knew that someone of prominence would soon arrive. Because Mark's audience was primarily Roman Christians, he began his book with John the Baptist, whose mission it was to announce the coming of Jesus, the most important man who ever lived. Roman Christians would have been less interested in Jesus' birth than in this messenger who prepared the way.

1:4 In John's ministry, baptism was a visible sign that a person had decided to change his or her life, giving up a sinful and selfish way of living and turning to God. John took a known custom and gave it new meaning. The Jews often baptized non-Jews who had converted to Judaism. But to baptize a Jew as a sign of repentance was a radical departure from Jewish custom. The early church took baptism a step further, associating it with Jesus' death and resurrection (see, for example, Romans 6:3, 4; 1 Peter 3:21).

1:5 Jesus came at a time in history when the entire civilized world was relatively peaceful under Roman rule, travel was easy, and there was a common language. The news about Jesus' life, death, and resurrection could spread quickly throughout the vast Roman empire.

In Israel, people were ready for Jesus, too, and they flocked to hear this desert preacher. There had been no God-sent prophets for 400 years, since the days of Malachi (who wrote the last book of the Old Testament). Anticipation was growing that a great

KEY PLACES IN MARK

The broken lines (—·—·—·) indicate modern boundaries.

Of the four Gospels, Mark's narrative is the most chronological—that is, most of the stories are positioned in the order they actually occurred. Though the shortest of the four, the Gospel of Mark contains the most events; it is action-packed. Most of this action centers in Galilee, where Jesus began his ministry. Capernaum served as his base of operation (1:21; 2:1; 9:33), from which he would go out to cities like Bethsaida, where he healed a blind man (8:22ff); Gennesaret, where he performed many healings (6:53ff); Tyre and Sidon (to the far north), where he healed many, drove out demons, and met the Syrophoenician woman (3:8; 7:24ff); and Caesarea Philippi, where Peter declared him to be the Messiah (8:27ff). After his ministry in Galilee and the surrounding regions, Jesus headed for Jerusalem (10:1). Before going there, Jesus told his disciples three times that he would be crucified there and then come back to life (8:31; 9:31; 10:33, 34).

---

prophet, or the Messiah prophesied in the Old Testament, would soon come (see Luke 3:15).

1:5 The purpose of John's preaching was to prepare people to accept Jesus as God's Son. When John challenged the people to confess sin individually, he signaled the start of a new way to relate to God.

Is change needed in your life before you can hear and understand Jesus' message? You have to admit that you need forgiveness before you can accept it. To prepare to receive Christ, repent. Turn away from the world's dead-end attractions, sinful temptations, and harmful attitudes, and turn to God. He can give you a new start.

1:6 John dressed much like the prophet Elijah (2 Kings 1:8) in order to distinguish himself from the religious leaders, whose flowing robes reflected their great pride in their position (12:38). John's striking appearance reinforced his striking message.

1:7, 8 Although John was the first genuine prophet in 400 years, Jesus the Messiah would be infinitely greater than he. John was pointing out how insignificant he was compared to the one who was coming. John was not even worthy of doing the most menial tasks for him, like untying his sandals. What John began, Jesus finished. What John prepared, Jesus fulfilled.

the thongs of whose sandals I am not worthy to stoop down and untie. *c* 8 I baptize you with*a* water, but he will baptize you with the Holy Spirit." *d*

1:7
c Ac 13:25
1:8
d Isa 44:3

The Baptism of Jesus (17/Matthew 3:13–17; Luke 3:21–22)

9At that time Jesus came from Nazareth in Galilee and was baptized by John in the Jordan. 10As Jesus was coming up out of the water, he saw heaven being torn open and the Spirit descending on him like a dove. *e* 11And a voice came from heaven: "You are my Son, *f* whom I love; with you I am well pleased."

1:10
e Jn 1:32
1:11
f Mt 3:17

Satan Tempts Jesus in the Wilderness (18/Matthew 4:1–11; Luke 4:1–13)

12At once the Spirit sent him out into the desert, 13and he was in the desert forty days, being tempted by Satan. He was with the wild animals, and angels attended him.

B. MESSAGE AND MINISTRY OF JESUS, THE SERVANT (1:14—13:37)

Mark tells us dramatic, action-packed stories. He gives us the most vivid account of Christ's activities. He features facts and actions, rather than teachings. The way Jesus lived his life is the perfect example of how we should live our lives today.

1. Jesus' ministry in Galilee

Jesus Preaches in Galilee (30/Matthew 4:12–17; Luke 4:14–15; John 4:43–45)

14After John was put in prison, Jesus went into Galilee, proclaiming the good news of God. *g* 15"The time has come," *h* he said. "The kingdom of God is near. Repent and believe the good news!" *i*

1:14
g Mt 4:23
1:15
h Gal 4:4; Eph 1:10
i Ac 20:21

a 8 Or *in*

1:8 John said Jesus would baptize them with the Holy Spirit, sending the Holy Spirit to live within each believer. John's baptism with water prepared a person to receive Christ's message. This baptism demonstrated repentance, humility, and willingness to turn from sin. This was the *beginning* of the spiritual process. When Jesus baptizes with the Holy Spirit, the entire person is transformed by the Spirit's power. Jesus offers to us both forgiveness of sin and the power to live for him.

1:9 Jesus grew up in Nazareth, where he had lived since he was a young boy (Matthew 2:22, 23). Nazareth was a small town in Galilee, located about halfway between the Sea of Galilee and the Mediterranean Sea. The city was despised and avoided by many Jews (John 1:46). Nazareth was a crossroads for trade routes and had contact with many cultures.

1:9 If John's baptism was for repentance from sin, why was Jesus baptized? While even the greatest prophets (Isaiah, Jeremiah, Ezekiel) had to confess their sinfulness and need for repentance, Jesus didn't need to admit sin—he was sinless. Although

Jesus didn't need forgiveness, he was baptized for the following reasons: (1) to begin his mission to bring the message of salvation to all people; (2) to show support for John's ministry; (3) to identify with our humanness and (4) to give us an example to follow. We know that John's baptism was different from Christian baptism in the church because Paul had John's followers baptized again (see Acts 19:2–5).

1:10, 11 The Spirit descended like a dove on Jesus, and the voice from heaven proclaimed the Father's approval of Jesus as his divine Son. Here we see all three members of the Trinity together—God the Father, God the Son, and God the Holy Spirit. (See also Matthew 28:19; Luke 1:35; John 15:26; 1 Corinthians 12:4–13; 2 Corinthians 13:14; Ephesians 2:18; 1 Thessalonians 1:2–5; 1 Peter 1:2.)

1:11 The dove and the voice from heaven were signs that Jesus was the Messiah. Many people want something tangible, visible, and "real" before they will believe. So Jesus did healings and other miracles, and God raised him from the dead. Still people doubt.

Will visible signs convince anyone? The "sign" that really brings us to faith is the power of God's message to answer the cry of the heart. To the confused, God offers a mind enlightened by faith. To the depressed, God offers a reason for joy. To the lonely, God offers eternal companionship. Don't look for a spectacular visible sign; instead, seek a cleansed and renewed life as evidence of his presence.

1:12, 13 Satan is an angel who rebelled against God. He is real, not symbolic, and is constantly working against God and those who obey him. Satan tempted Eve in the garden and persuaded her to sin; he tempted Jesus in the desert and did not persuade him to fall. To be tempted is not a sin. Tempting others or giving in to temptation *is* sin. For a more detailed account of Jesus' temptation, read Matthew 4:1–11.

1:12, 13 To identify fully with human beings, Jesus had to endure Satan's temptations. Although Jesus is God, he is also man. And as fully human, he was not exempt from Satan's attacks. Because Jesus faced temptations and overcame them, he can assist us in two important ways: (1) as an example of how to face temptation without sinning, and (2) as a helper who knows just what we need because he went through the same experience. (See Hebrews 4:15.)

JESUS BEGINS HIS MINISTRY
When Jesus came from his home in Nazareth to begin his ministry, he first took two steps in preparation—baptism by John in the Jordan River and temptation by Satan in the rough Judean desert. After the temptations, Jesus returned to Galilee and later set up his home base in Capernaum.

Four Fishermen Follow Jesus (33/Matthew 4:18–22)

¹⁶As Jesus walked beside the Sea of Galilee, he saw Simon and his brother Andrew casting a net into the lake, for they were fishermen. ¹⁷"Come, follow me," Jesus said, "and I will make you fishers of men." ¹⁸At once they left their nets and followed him.

¹⁹When he had gone a little farther, he saw James son of Zebedee and his brother John in a boat, preparing their nets. ²⁰Without delay he called them, and they left their father Zebedee in the boat with the hired men and followed him.

Jesus Teaches with Authority (34/Luke 4:31–37)

²¹They went to Capernaum, and when the Sabbath came, Jesus went into the synagogue and began to teach. ²²The people were amazed at his teaching, because he taught them as one who had authority, not as the teachers of the law.ʲ ²³Just then a man in their synagogue who was possessed by an evilᵃ spirit cried out, ²⁴"What do you want with us,ᵏ Jesus of Nazareth? Have you come to destroy us? I know who you are—the Holy One of God!"

²⁵"Be quiet!" said Jesus sternly. "Come out of him!" ²⁶The evil spirit shook the man violently and came out of him with a shriek.

²⁷The people were all so amazedˡ that they asked each other, "What is this? A new teaching—and with authority! He even gives orders to evil spirits and they obey him." ²⁸News about him spread quickly over the whole region of Galilee.

Jesus Heals Peter's Mother-in-Law and Many Others (35/Matthew 8:14–17; Luke 4:38–41)

²⁹As soon as they left the synagogue,ᵐ they went with James and John to the home of Simon and Andrew. ³⁰Simon's mother-in-law was in bed with a fever, and they told Jesus about her. ³¹So he went to her, took her hand and helped her up. The fever left her and she began to wait on them.

ᵃ23 Greek *unclean*; also in verses 26 and 27

1:22
ʲMt 7:28, 29

1:24
ᵏMt 8:29

1:27
ˡMk 10:24, 32

1:29
ᵐver 21, 23

1:16–20 We often assume that Jesus' disciples were great men of faith from the first time they met Jesus. But they had to grow in their faith just as all believers do (14:48–50, 66–72; John 14:1–9; 20:26–29). This is apparently not the only time Jesus called Peter (Simon), James, and John to follow him (see Luke 5:1–11 and John 1:35–42 for two other times). Although it took time for Jesus' call and his message to get through, the disciples *followed*. In the same way, we may question and falter, but we must never stop following Jesus.

1:17 Fishing was a major industry around the Sea of Galilee. Fishing with nets was the most common method. Jesus called the disciples to fish for people with the same energy they had used to fish for food. The gospel would be like a net, lifting people from dark waters into the light of day and transforming their lives. How can God use you to fish for people's souls? How can you train new converts to find new seas and cast new nets where waters have never been fished before? The gospel makes missionaries of all God's people. Where are you casting your net?

1:21 Jesus had recently moved to Capernaum from Nazareth (Matthew 4:12, 13). Capernaum was a thriving town with great wealth as well as great sin and decadence. Because it was the headquarters for many Roman troops, pagan influences from all over the Roman empire were pervasive. This was an ideal place for Jesus to challenge both Jews and non-Jews with the gospel of God's kingdom.

1:21 Because the temple in Jerusalem was too far for many Jews to travel to regularly for worship, many towns had synagogues serving both as places of worship and as schools. Beginning in the days of Ezra, about 450 B.C., a group of ten Jewish families could start a synagogue. There, during the week, Jewish boys were taught the Old Testament law and Jewish religion. Girls could not attend. Each Saturday, the Sabbath, the Jewish men would gather to listen to a rabbi teach from the Scriptures. Because there was no permanent rabbi or teacher, it was customary for the synagogue leader to ask visiting teachers to speak. This is why Jesus often taught in the synagogues in the towns he

visited. While the Jewish teachers often quoted from well-known rabbis to give their words more authority, Jesus didn't have that need. Because Jesus is God, he knew exactly what the Scriptures said and meant. He was the ultimate authority.

1:23 Evil spirits, or demons, are ruled by Satan. They work to tempt people to sin. They were not created by Satan because God is the Creator of all. Rather they are fallen angels who joined Satan in his rebellion. Though not all disease comes from Satan, demons can cause a person to become mute, deaf, blind, or insane. But in every case where demons confronted Jesus, they lost their power. Thus God limits what evil spirits can do; they can do nothing without his permission. During Jesus' life on earth, demons were allowed to be very active to demonstrate once and for all Christ's power and authority over them.

1:23ff Some people dismiss all accounts of demon-possession as a primitive way to describe mental illness. Although throughout history mental illness has often been wrongly diagnosed as demon-possession, clearly a hostile outside force controlled the man described here. Mark emphasized Jesus' conflict with evil powers to show his superiority over them, so he recorded many stories about Jesus driving out evil spirits. Jesus didn't have to conduct an elaborate exorcism ritual. His word was enough to send out the demons.

1:23, 24 The evil spirit knew at once that Jesus was the Holy One of God. By including this event in his Gospel, Mark was establishing Jesus' credentials, showing that even the spiritual underworld recognized Jesus as the Messiah.

1:29–31 Each Gospel writer had a slightly different perspective as he wrote; thus the comparable stories in the Gospels often highlight different details. In Matthew, Jesus touched the woman's hand. In Mark, he helped her up. In Luke, he spoke to the fever, and it left her. The accounts do not conflict. Just as four people might witness the same event and all recount different details, so each Gospel writer simply emphasized different details of this story.

32 That evening after sunset the people brought to Jesus all the sick and demon-possessed. n 33 The whole town gathered at the door, 34 and Jesus healed many who had various
diseases. o He also drove out many demons, but he would not let the demons speak because
they knew who he was. p

1:32
n Mt 4:24
1:34
o Mt 4:23
p Mk 3:12;
Ac 16:17, 18

Jesus Preaches throughout Galilee (36/Matthew 4:23–25; Luke 4:42–44)

35 Very early in the morning, while it was still dark, Jesus got up, left the house and went
off to a solitary place, where he prayed. 36 Simon and his companions went to look for him,
37 and when they found him, they exclaimed: "Everyone is looking for you!"

38 Jesus replied, "Let us go somewhere else—to the nearby villages—so I can preach there
also. That is why I have come." q 39 So he traveled throughout Galilee, preaching in their synagogues r and driving out demons. s

1:38
q Isa 61:1
1:39
r Mt 4:23
s Mt 4:24

Jesus Heals a Man with Leprosy (38/Matthew 8:1–4; Luke 5:12–16)

40 A man with leprosy a came to him and begged him on his knees, t "If you are willing, you
can make me clean."

1:40
t Mk 10:17

41 Filled with compassion, Jesus reached out his hand and touched the man. "I am willing," he said. "Be clean!" 42 Immediately the leprosy left him and he was cured.

43 Jesus sent him away at once with a strong warning: 44 "See that you don't tell this to anyone. u But go, show yourself to the priest v and offer the sacrifices that Moses commanded
for your cleansing, w as a testimony to them." 45 Instead he went out and began to talk freely,
spreading the news. As a result, Jesus could no longer enter a town openly but stayed outside
in lonely places. x Yet the people still came to him from everywhere. y

1:44
u Mt 8:4
v Lev 13:49
w Lev 14:1-32
1:45
x Lk 5:15, 16
y Mk 2:13; Lk 5:17;
Jn 6:2

Jesus Heals a Paralyzed Man (39/Matthew 9:1–8; Luke 5:17–26)

2 A few days later, when Jesus again entered Capernaum, the people heard that he had
come home. 2 So many z gathered that there was no room left, not even outside the door,
and he preached the word to them. 3 Some men came, bringing to him a paralytic, a carried
by four of them. 4 Since they could not get him to Jesus because of the crowd, they made an

2:2
z ver 13; Mk 1:45
2:3
a Mt 4:24

a 40 The Greek word was used for various diseases affecting the skin—not necessarily leprosy.

1:32, 33 The people came to Jesus in the evening after sunset.
That day had been the Sabbath (1:21), their day of rest, lasting
from sunset Friday to sunset Saturday. The Jewish leaders had
proclaimed that it was against the law to be healed on the Sabbath
(Matthew 12:10; Luke 13:14). The people didn't want to break this
law or the Jewish law that prohibited traveling on the Sabbath,
so they waited until sunset. After the sun went down on Saturday,
the crowds were free to find Jesus so he could heal them.

1:34 Why didn't Jesus want the demons to reveal who he was?
(1) By commanding the demons to remain silent, Jesus proved his
authority and power over them. (2) Jesus wanted the people to
believe he was the Messiah because of what he said and did, not
because of the demons' words. (3) Jesus wanted to reveal his identity as the Messiah according to his timetable, not according to
Satan's timetable. Satan wanted the people to follow Jesus around
for what they could get out of him, not because he was the Son of
God who could truly set them free from sin's guilt and power.

1:35–37 Were the disciples impatient that Jesus prayed in solitude while so much ministry waited to be done? How would you
have responded if you had been the one to find Jesus in prayer?
It's easy to be so caught up with ministry that you neglect times
of solitude, individual worship, and prayer. Perhaps you need to
redesign your schedule to find time for earnest prayer. It is vitally
important to: (1) seek the Lord before your busy schedule takes
over your thoughts; (2) withdraw from noise and demands so you
can focus on God; (3) take Jesus' attitude of regular communion
with the Father; (4) reflect on the priorities Jesus had for his life;
(5) determine to pray on a more regular basis, not just in times of
crisis. If prayer was important for Jesus, then it must be important
for his followers. Pray—even if you have to get up very early in the
morning to do it!

1:39 The Romans divided the land of Israel into three separate
regions: Galilee, Samaria, and Judea. Galilee was the northernmost

region, an area about 60 miles long and 30 miles wide. Jesus did
much of his ministry in this area, an ideal place for him to teach
because there were over 250 towns concentrated there, with many
synagogues.

1:40, 41 In keeping with the law in Leviticus 13 and 14, Jewish
leaders declared people with leprosy unclean. This meant that
lepers were unfit to participate in any religious or social activity.
Because the law said that contact with any unclean person made
a person unclean too, some people even threw rocks at lepers to
keep them at a safe distance. Even the mention of the name of this
disabling disease terrified people. How astounding it was, then,
when Jesus reached out and touched this man who had leprosy.

The real value of a person is inside, not outside. Although a
person's body may be diseased or deformed, the person inside is
no less valuable to God. In a sense, we are all people with leprosy
because we have all been deformed by the ugliness of sin. But God,
by sending his Son Jesus, has touched us, giving us the opportunity to be healed.

1:43, 44 Although leprosy was incurable, many different types
of skin diseases were classified together as "leprosy." According
to the Old Testament laws about leprosy (Leviticus 13; 14), when
a leper was cured, he or she had to go to a priest to be examined.
Then the leper was to give a thank offering at the temple. Jesus
adhered to these laws by sending the man to the priest, demonstrating Jesus' complete regard for God's law. Sending a healed
leper to a priest was also a way to verify Jesus' great miracle to
the community.

2:3 The paralytic's need moved his friends to action, and they
brought him to Jesus. When you recognize someone's need, do
you act? Many people have physical and spiritual needs you can
meet, either by yourself or with others who are also concerned.
Human need moved these four men; let it also move you to
compassionate action.

opening in the roof above Jesus and, after digging through it, lowered the mat the paralyzed man was lying on. [5]When Jesus saw their faith, he said to the paralytic, "Son, your sins are forgiven."

2:7
[b] Isa 43:25

[6]Now some teachers of the law were sitting there, thinking to themselves, [7]"Why does this fellow talk like that? He's blaspheming! Who can forgive sins but God alone?" [b]

PROMINENT JEWISH RELIGIOUS AND POLITICAL GROUPS	Name and Selected References	Description	Agreement with Jesus	Disagreement with Jesus
	PHARISEES Matthew 5:20 Matthew 23:1–36 Luke 6:2 Luke 7:36–47	Strict group of religious Jews who advocated obedience to the most minute portions of the Jewish law and traditions. Very influential in the synagogues.	Respect for the law, belief in the resurrection of the dead, committed to obeying God's will.	Rejected Jesus' claim to be Messiah because he did not follow all their traditions and associated with notoriously wicked people.
	SADDUCEES Matthew 3:7 Matthew 16:11, 12 Mark 12:18	Wealthy, upper class, Jewish priestly party. Rejected the authority of the Bible beyond the five books of Moses. Profited from business in the temple. They, along with the Pharisees, were one of the two major parties of the Jewish Sanhedrin.	Showed great respect for the five books of Moses, as well as the sanctity of the temple.	Denied the resurrection of the dead. Thought the temple could also be used as a place to transact business.
	TEACHERS OF THE LAW Matthew 7:29 Mark 2:6 Mark 2:16	Professional interpreters of the law—who especially emphasized the traditions. Many teachers of the law were Pharisees.	Respect for the law. Committed to obeying God.	Denied Jesus' authority to reinterpret the law. Rejected Jesus as Messiah because he did not obey all of their traditions.
	HERODIANS Matthew 22:16 Mark 3:6 Mark 12:13	A Jewish political party of King Herod's supporters.	Unknown. In the Gospels they tried to trap Jesus with questions and plotted to kill him.	Afraid of Jesus causing political instability. They saw Jesus as a threat to their political future at a time when they were trying to regain from Rome some of their lost political power.
	ZEALOTS Luke 6:15 Acts 1:14	A fiercely dedicated group of Jewish patriots determined to end Roman rule in Israel.	Concerned about the future of Israel. Believed in the Messiah but did not recognize Jesus as the one sent by God.	Believed that the Messiah must be a political leader who would deliver Israel from Roman occupation.
	ESSENES none	Jewish monastic group practicing ritual purity and personal holiness.	Emphasized justice, honesty, commitment.	Believed ceremonial rituals made them righteous.

2:4 The crowd that had gathered made it impossible to bring the paralyzed man close to Jesus. Successful churches or busy Christians can be oblivious to needy people who want to see Jesus. In some churches, if the crowd is too thick and too disinterested, a needy person will simply wander away. How sad when the people in a church are so preoccupied with their own relationships and agendas that they don't even see those who are trying to get in. That should never happen. Where Jesus is present, may the faces of the faithful reflect his love, may their hands extend to greet all newcomers and seekers as friends, and may they open a way for others to come in.

2:4 Houses in Bible times were built of stone. They had flat roofs made of mud mixed with straw. Outside stairways led to the roofs. These friends may have carried the lame man up the outside stairs

to the roof. They then could easily have taken apart the mud and straw mixture to make a hole through which to lower their friend to Jesus.

2:6, 7 The teachers of religious law were in a perfect position, sitting where they could observe and criticize. Some sitting Christians follow their example. Is the music at church too fast or too loud? Is the sermon too long or too short? Do people aggravate you by sitting in your pew or dressing too casually? How much time do you spend worshiping in church and how much time do you spend complaining and criticizing? How about trying a little healthy activism—the kind that gets involved to work with fellow believers toward real progress on common goals, such as sharing the Good News, helping the needy, and building strong and caring disciples of Christ. Are you criticizing the church or changing the world?

8 Immediately Jesus knew in his spirit that this was what they were thinking in their hearts, and he said to them, "Why are you thinking these things? 9 Which is easier: to say to the paralytic, 'Your sins are forgiven,' or to say, 'Get up, take your mat and walk'? 10 But that you may know that the Son of Man has authority on earth to forgive sins. . ." He said to the paralytic, 11 "I tell you, get up, take your mat and go home." 12 He got up, took his mat and walked out in full view of them all. This amazed everyone and they praised God, c saying, "We have never seen anything like this!" d

2:12
c Mt 9:8
d Mt 9:33

Jesus Eats with Sinners at Matthew's House (40/Matthew 9:9–13; Luke 5:27–32)

13 Once again Jesus went out beside the lake. A large crowd came to him, e and he began to teach them. 14 As he walked along, he saw Levi son of Alphaeus sitting at the tax collector's booth. "Follow me," Jesus told him, and Levi got up and followed him.

2:13
e Mk 1:45

15 While Jesus was having dinner at Levi's house, many tax collectors and "sinners" were eating with him and his disciples, for there were many who followed him. 16 When the teachers of the law who were Pharisees f saw him eating with the "sinners" and tax collectors, they asked his disciples: "Why does he eat with tax collectors and 'sinners'?" g

2:16
f Ac 23:9
g Mt 9:11

17 On hearing this, Jesus said to them, "It is not the healthy who need a doctor, but the sick. I have not come to call the righteous, but sinners." h

2:17
h Lk 19:10; 1Ti 1:15

Religious Leaders Ask Jesus about Fasting (41/Matthew 9:14–17; Luke 5:33–39)

18 Now John's disciples and the Pharisees were fasting. Some people came and asked Jesus, "How is it that John's disciples and the disciples of the Pharisees are fasting, but yours are not?"

19 Jesus answered, "How can the guests of the bridegroom fast while he is with them? They cannot, so long as they have him with them. 20 But the time will come when the bridegroom will be taken from them, i and on that day they will fast.

2:20
i Lk 17:22

21 "No one sews a patch of unshrunk cloth on an old garment. If he does, the new piece will pull away from the old, making the tear worse. 22 And no one pours new wine into old wineskins. If he does, the wine will burst the skins, and both the wine and the wineskins will be ruined. No, he pours new wine into new wineskins."

2:8–11 Before saying to the paralytic, "Get up," Jesus said, "Son, your sins are forgiven." To the Jewish leaders this statement was blasphemous—claiming to do something only God could do. According to the law, the punishment for this sin was death (Leviticus 24:15, 16). The religious leaders understood correctly that Jesus was claiming divine prerogatives, but their judgment was wrong. Jesus was not blaspheming; his claim was true. Jesus is God, and he proved his claim by healing the paralytic (2:9–12).

2:10 This is the first time in Mark that Jesus is referred to as the "Son of Man," a title emphasizing that Jesus is fully human. The title, Son of God (see, for example, John 20:31) emphasizes that he is fully God. As God's Son, Jesus has the authority to forgive sin. As a man, he can identify with our deepest needs and sufferings and help us overcome sin (see also the note on 8:31).

2:14 Levi is another name for Matthew, the disciple who wrote the Gospel of Matthew. See Matthew's Profile in Matthew 9, p. 1549 for more information.

2:14 Capernaum (2:1) was a key military center for Roman troops, as well as a thriving business community. Several major highways intersected in Capernaum, with merchants passing through from as far away as Egypt to the south and Mesopotamia to the north. Levi (Matthew), a Jew, worked for the Romans as the area's tax collector, collecting taxes from citizens as well as from merchants passing through town. Tax collectors were expected to take a commission on the taxes they collected. Most of them overcharged and vastly enriched themselves. Tax collectors were despised by the Jews because of their reputation for cheating and their support of Rome.

2:16, 17 The self-righteous Pharisees were indignant that Jesus would eat a meal with such sinners. But Jesus gladly associated with sinners because he loved them and because he knew that they needed to hear what he had to say. Jesus spent time with whoever needed or wanted to hear his message—poor, rich, bad,

good. We, too, must befriend those who need Christ, even if they do not seem to be ideal companions. Are there people you have been neglecting because of their reputation? They may be the ones who most need to see and hear the message of Christ's love in and from you.

2:18ff John the Baptist had two goals: to lead people to repent of their sin, and to prepare them for Christ's coming. John's message was sobering, so he and his followers fasted. Fasting is both an outward sign of humility and regret for sin, and an inner discipline that clears the mind and keeps the spirit alert. Fasting empties the body of food; repentance empties the life of sin. Jesus' disciples did not need to fast to prepare for his coming because he was with them. Jesus did not condemn fasting, however. He himself fasted for 40 days (Matthew 4:2). Nevertheless, Jesus emphasized fasting with the right motives. The Pharisees fasted twice a week to show others how holy they were. Jesus explained that if people fast only to impress others, they will be twisting the purpose of fasting.

2:19 Jesus compared himself to a bridegroom. In the Bible, the image of a bride is often used for God's people, and the image of a bridegroom for the God who loves them (Isaiah 62:5; Matthew 25:1–14; Revelation 21:2).

2:21 Jesus did not come to patch up the old religious system of Judaism with its rules and traditions. His purpose was to fulfill it and start something new (though this "new" thing had been prophesied for centuries). Jesus Christ, God's Son, came to earth to offer all people forgiveness of sins and reconciliation with God. This new Good News did not fit into the old rigid legalistic system of religion. It needed a fresh start. The message will always remain "new" because it must be accepted and applied in every generation. When you follow Christ, be prepared for new ways to live, new ways to look at people, and new ways to serve.

2:22 A wineskin was a goatskin sewed together at the edges to form a watertight bag. New wine, expanding as it aged, stretched

The Disciples Pick Wheat on the Sabbath (45/Matthew 12:1–8; Luke 6:1–5)

2:23
j Dt 23:25

2:24
k Mt 12:2

23 One Sabbath Jesus was going through the grainfields, and as his disciples walked along, they began to pick some heads of grain. *j* 24 The Pharisees said to him, "Look, why are they doing what is unlawful on the Sabbath?" *k*

2:26
l 2Sa 8:17
m Lev 24:5-9
n 1Sa 21:1-6

25 He answered, "Have you never read what David did when he and his companions were hungry and in need? 26 In the days of Abiathar the high priest, *l* he entered the house of God and ate the consecrated bread, which is lawful only for priests to eat. *m* And he also gave some to his companions." *n*

2:27
o Ex 23:12; Dt 5:14
p Col 2:16

27 Then he said to them, "The Sabbath was made for man, *o* not man for the Sabbath. *p* 28 So the Son of Man is Lord even of the Sabbath."

Jesus Heals a Man's Hand on the Sabbath (46/Matthew 12:9–14; Luke 6:6–11)

3:1
q Mk 1:21

3:2
r Mt 12:10
s Lk 14:1

3 Another time he went into the synagogue, *q* and a man with a shriveled hand was there. 2 Some of them were looking for a reason to accuse Jesus, so they watched him closely *r* to see if he would heal him on the Sabbath. *s* 3 Jesus said to the man with the shriveled hand, "Stand up in front of everyone."

4 Then Jesus asked them, "Which is lawful on the Sabbath: to do good or to do evil, to save life or to kill?" But they remained silent.

3:6
t Mt 22:16; Mk 12:13
u Mt 12:14

5 He looked around at them in anger and, deeply distressed at their stubborn hearts, said to the man, "Stretch out your hand." He stretched it out, and his hand was completely restored. 6 Then the Pharisees went out and began to plot with the Herodians *t* how they might kill Jesus. *u*

---

the wineskin. New wine, therefore, could not be put into a wineskin that had already been stretched, or the taut skin would burst.

The Pharisees had become rigid like old wineskins. They could not accept faith in Jesus that would not be contained or limited by man-made ideas or rules. Your heart, like a wineskin, can become rigid and prevent you from accepting the new life that Christ offers. Keep your heart pliable and open to accepting the life-changing truths of Christ.

2:23 Jesus and his disciples were not stealing when they picked the grain. Leviticus 19:9, 10 and Deuteronomy 23:25 say that farmers were to leave the edges of their fields unharvested so that some of their crops could be picked by travelers and by the poor. Just as walking on a sidewalk is not trespassing on private property, picking heads of grain at the edge of a field was not stealing.

2:24 God's law said that crops should not be harvested on the Sabbath (Exodus 34:21). This law prevented farmers from becoming greedy and ignoring God on the Sabbath. It also protected laborers from being overworked.

The Pharisees interpreted the action of Jesus and his disciples—picking the grain and eating it as they walked through the fields—as harvesting; and so they judged Jesus a lawbreaker. But Jesus and the disciples clearly were not harvesting the grain for personal gain; they were simply looking for something to eat. The Pharisees were so focused on the words of the rule that they missed its intent.

2:25–28 Jesus used the example of David to point out how ridiculous the Pharisees' accusations were (this incident occurred in 1 Samuel 21:1–6). God created the Sabbath for our benefit; we are restored both physically and spiritually when we take time to rest and to focus on God. For the Pharisees, Sabbath rules had become more important than Sabbath rest. Both David and Jesus understood that the intent of God's law is to promote love for God and others.

The Christian faith involves many rules that are meant to be governed by love. That makes love the highest rule, but it also moves Christians toward personal sacrifice, discipline, and responsibility—scarce resources in today's world. When confronted with rules of your own or others' making, ask: (1) Does the rule serve God's purposes? (2) Does the rule reveal God's character? (3) Does the rule help people get into God's family, or keep them out? (4) Does the rule have biblical roots that can be supported in the context of all of Scripture? Good rules pass all four tests.

2:26 The "consecrated bread" was set before God on a table in the Holy Place in the tabernacle (and later in the temple). Every Sabbath, 12 freshly-baked loaves of bread were set out, and the priests ate the old loaves. See Exodus 25:30 and Leviticus 24:5–9 for more about the consecrated bread, also called the bread of the Presence.

3:2 Already many of the religious leaders had turned against Jesus and become his "enemies.". They were jealous of his popularity, his miracles, and the authority in his teaching and actions. They valued their status in the community and their opportunity for personal gain so much that they lost sight of their goal as religious leaders—to point people toward God. Of all people, the Pharisees should have recognized the Messiah, but they refused to acknowledge him because they were not willing to give up their treasured position and power. When Jesus exposed their attitudes, he became their enemy instead of their Messiah, and they began looking for ways to turn the people against him.

3:5 Jesus was angry about the Pharisees' uncaring attitudes. Anger itself is not wrong. It depends on what makes us angry and what we do with our anger. Too often we express our anger in selfish and harmful ways. By contrast, Jesus expressed his anger by correcting a problem—healing the man's hand. Use your anger to find constructive solutions rather than to tear people down.

3:6 The Pharisees were a Jewish religious group that zealously followed the Old Testament laws, as well as their own religious traditions. They were highly respected in the community, but they hated Jesus because he challenged their proud attitudes and dishonorable motives.

The Herodians were a Jewish political party that hoped to restore Herod the Great's line to the throne. Jesus was a threat to them as well because he challenged their political ambitions. These two groups were normally at odds, but they joined forces against Jesus.

3:6 The Pharisees had accused Jesus of breaking their law that said medical attention could be given to no one on the Sabbath except in matters of life and death. Ironically, the Pharisees themselves were breaking God's law by plotting murder.

THE TWELVE

Name	Occupation	Outstanding Characteristics	Major Events in His Life
SIMON PETER (son of John)	Fisherman	Impulsive; later— bold in preaching about Jesus	One of three in core group of disciples; recognized Jesus as the Messiah; denied Christ and repented; preached Pentecost sermon; a leader of the Jerusalem church; baptized Gentiles; wrote 1 and 2 Peter.
JAMES (son of Zebedee), he and his brother, John, were called the "Sons of Thunder"	Fisherman	Ambitious, short-tempered, judgmental, deeply committed to Jesus	Also in core group; he and his brother, John, asked Jesus for places of honor in his kingdom; wanted to call fire down to destroy a Samaritan village; first disciple to be martyred.
JOHN (son of Zebedee), James's brother, and "the disciple whom Jesus loved"	Fisherman	Ambitious, judgmental, later—very loving	Third disciple in core group; asked Jesus for a place of honor in his kingdom; wanted to call down fire on a Samaritan village; a leader of the Jerusalem church; wrote the Gospel of John, 1, 2, 3 John, and Revelation.
ANDREW (Peter's brother)	Fisherman	Eager to bring others to Jesus	Accepted John the Baptist's testimony about Jesus; told Peter about Jesus; he and Philip told Jesus that Greeks wanted to see him.
PHILIP	Fisherman	Questioning attitude	Told Nathanael about Jesus; wondered how Jesus could feed the 5,000; asked Jesus to show his followers God the Father; he and Andrew told Jesus that Greeks wanted to see him.
BARTHOLOMEW (Nathanael)	Unknown	Honest and straight-forward	Initially rejected Jesus because Jesus was from Nazareth but acknowledged him as the "Son of God" and "King of Israel" when they met.
MATTHEW (Levi)	Tax collector	Despised outcast because of his dishonest career	Abandoned his corrupt (and financially profitable) way of life to follow Jesus; invited Jesus to a party with his notorious friends; wrote the Gospel of Matthew.
THOMAS (the Twin)	Unknown	Courage and doubt	Suggested the disciples go with Jesus to Bethany—even if it meant death; asked Jesus about where he was going; refused to believe Jesus was risen until he could see Jesus alive and touch his wounds.
JAMES (son of Alphaeus)	Unknown	Unknown	Became one of Jesus' disciples.
THADDAEUS (Judas son of James)	Unknown	Unknown	Asked Jesus why he would reveal himself to his followers and not to the world.
SIMON THE ZEALOT	Unknown	Fierce patriotism	Became a disciple of Jesus.
JUDAS ISCARIOT	Unknown	Treacherous and greedy	Became one of Jesus' disciples; betrayed Jesus; committed suicide.

Jesus' faithful disciples were ordinary men who became extraordinary because of Jesus Christ. Despite their confusion and lack of understanding during his lifetime, they became powerful witnesses to his resurrection. Their lives were transformed by God's power. The story of Jesus' disciples does not end with the Gospels. It continues in the book of Acts and many of the letters.

DISCIPLES

What Jesus Said about Him	A Key Lesson from His Life	Selected References
Named him Peter, "rock"; called him "Satan" when he urged Jesus to reject the cross; said he would become a fisher of men; he received revelation from God; he would deny Jesus; he would later be crucified for his faith.	Christians falter at times, but when they return to Jesus, he forgives them and strengthens their faith	Matthew 4:18–20 Mark 8:29–33 Luke 22:31–34 John 21:15–19 Acts 2:14–41 Acts 10:1—11:18
Called James and John "Sons of Thunder"; said he would become a fisher of men; would drink the cup Jesus drank.	Christians must be willing to die for Jesus.	Mark 3:17 Mark 10:35–40 Luke 9:52–56 Acts 12:1, 2
Called John and James "Sons of Thunder"; said he would become a fisher of men; would drink the cup Jesus drank; would take care of Jesus' mother after Jesus' death.	The transforming power of the love of Christ is available to all.	Mark 1:19 Mark 10:35–40 Luke 9:52–56 John 19:26, 27 John 21:20–24
Said he would become a fisher of men.	Christians are to tell other people about Jesus.	Matthew 4:18–20 John 1:35–42; 6:8, 9 John 12:20–24
Asked if Philip realized that to know and see him was to know and see the Father.	God uses our questions to teach us.	Matthew 10:3 John 1:43–46; 6:2–7 John 12:20–22 John 14:8–11
Called him "a true Israelite" and "a man in whom there is nothing false."	Jesus respects honesty in people—even if they challenge him because of it.	Mark 3:18 John 1:45–51 John 21:1–13
Called him to be a disciple.	Christianity is not for people who think they're already good; it is for people who know they've failed and want help.	Matthew 9:9–13 Mark 2:15–17 Luke 5:27–32
Said Thomas believed because he actually saw Jesus after the resurrection.	Even when Christians experience serious doubts, Jesus reaches out to them to restore their faith.	Matthew 10:3 John 14:5; 20:24–29 John 21:1–13
Unknown	Unknown	Matthew 10:3 Mark 3:18 Luke 6:15
Unknown	Christians follow Jesus because they believe in him; they do not always understand the details of God's plan.	Matthew 10:3 Mark 3:18 John 14:22
Unknown	If we are willing to give up our plans for the future, we can participate in Jesus' plans.	Matthew 10:4 Mark 3:18 Luke 6:15
Called him "a devil"; said Judas would betray Jesus.	It is not enough to be familiar with Jesus' teachings. Jesus' true followers love and obey him.	Matthew 26:20–25 Luke 22:47, 48 John 12:4–8

Large Crowds Follow Jesus (47/Matthew 12:15–21)

7 Jesus withdrew with his disciples to the lake, and a large crowd from Galilee followed. ᵛ 8 When they heard all he was doing, many people came to him from Judea, Jerusalem, Idumea, and the regions across the Jordan and around Tyre and Sidon. 9 Because of the crowd he told his disciples to have a small boat ready for him, to keep the people from crowding him. 10 For he had healed many,ʷ so that those with diseases were pushing forward to touch him. ˣ 11 Whenever the evilᵃ spirits saw him, they fell down before him and cried out, "You are the Son of God."ʸ 12 But he gave them strict orders not to tell who he was. ᶻ

3:7
ᵛMt 4:25

3:10
ʷMt 4:23
ˣMt 9:20

3:11
ʸMk 1:23, 24

3:12
ᶻMk 1:24, 25, 34

Jesus Chooses the Twelve Disciples (48/Luke 6:12–16)

13 Jesus went up on a mountainside and called to him those he wanted, and they came to him. ᵃ 14 He appointed twelve—designating them apostles ᵇ—that they might be with him and that he might send them out to preach 15 and to have authority to drive out demons. 16 These are the twelve he appointed: Simon (to whom he gave the name Peter);ᵇ 17 James son of Zebedee and his brother John (to them he gave the name Boanerges, which means Sons of Thunder); 18 Andrew, Philip, Bartholomew, Matthew, Thomas, James son of Alphaeus, Thaddaeus, Simon the Zealot 19 and Judas Iscariot, who betrayed him.

3:13
ᵃMt 5:1

3:16
ᵇJn 1:42

Religious Leaders Accuse Jesus of Getting His Power from Satan (74/Matthew 12:22–37)

20 Then Jesus entered a house, and again a crowd gathered, so that he and his disciples were not even able to eat. ᶜ 21 When his family heard about this, they went to take charge of him, for they said, "He is out of his mind."ᵈ

22 And the teachers of the law who came down from Jerusalem said, "He is possessed by Beelzebubᶜ!ᵉ By the prince of demons he is driving out demons."ᶠ

3:20
ᶜMk 6:31

3:21
ᵈJn 10:20; Ac 26:24

3:22
ᵉMt 10:25; Jn 7:20;
8:48, 52; 10:20
ᶠMt 9:34

ᵃ11 Greek *unclean*; also in verse 30   ᵇ14 Some manuscripts do not have *designating them apostles.*   ᶜ22 Greek *Beezeboul* or *Beelzeboul*

3:7-11 The evil spirits knew that Jesus was the Son of God, but they had no intention of following him. Many people followed Jesus but didn't understand his true purpose for coming. Some people came for miracles, some came to hear his teaching, but they didn't understand the way of the cross. Knowing about Jesus, or even believing that he is God's Son, does not guarantee salvation. You must also follow and obey him (see James 2:17).

3:12 Jesus warned the evil spirits not to reveal his identity because he did not want them to reinforce a popular misconception. The huge crowds were looking for a political and military leader who would free them from Rome's control, and they thought that the Messiah predicted by the Old Testament prophets would be this kind of man. Jesus wanted to teach the people about the kind of Messiah he really was—one who was far different from their expectations. Christ's kingdom is spiritual. It begins not with the overthrow of governments, but with the overthrow of sin in people's hearts.

3:13 What does it mean to hear the "call" of God? First, God calls you to faith in Jesus. You will know this call by the growing desire in your heart to settle the matter of peace with God speedily. Respond to him—answer with a grateful, "Yes, Lord, I need you!"

Second, God calls you to serᴠice in Jesus' name. Wherever you are (and sometimes you need to move), whatever you're doing (and sometimes you need to upgrade your skills), God has a place of service for you. Jesus calls you and he wants you. Answer this call thoughtfully, seriously, in consultation with other Christians, saying, "Yes, Lord, I love you and will follow you!"

3:14 From the hundreds of people who followed him from place to place, Jesus chose 12 to be his *apostles. Apostle* means messenger or authorized representative. Why did Jesus choose 12 disciples? The number 12 corresponds to the 12 tribes of Israel (Matthew 19:28), showing the continuity between the old religious system and the new one based on Jesus' message. Many people followed Jesus, but these 12 received the most intense training.

Jesus did not choose these 12 to be his associates and companions because of their faith; their faith often faltered. He didn't

choose them because of their talent and ability; no one stood out with unusual ability. The disciples represented a wide range of backgrounds and life experiences, but apparently they had no more leadership potential than those who were not chosen. The one characteristic they all shared was their willingness to obey Jesus. After Jesus' ascension, they were filled with the Holy Spirit and empowered to carry out special roles in the growth of the early church. We should not disqualify ourselves from service to Christ because we do not have the expected credentials. Being a good disciple is simply a matter of following Jesus with a willing heart.

3:21 With the crowds pressing in on him, Jesus didn't even take time to eat. Because of this, his friends and family came to take charge of him (3:31, 32), thinking he had gone "over the edge" as a religious fanatic. They were concerned for him, but they missed the point of his ministry. Even those who were closest to Jesus were slow to understand who he was and what he had come to do.

3:21 The family may be the most difficult place to be a witness for Jesus. To be the first or only Christian may go against the grain. Your faith may be misinterpreted as criticism. Your zeal may be misunderstood. You may be accused of being a hypocrite because other areas of your life still fall short of Christ's ideals. Uncommitted people may view your new commitment to the Bible as unreasonable bigotry.

Family members require the most patience. They see you at your worst when your guard is down. Remember that Christ's family rejected and ridiculed him. Jesus knows what you face by trying to be a witness for him in your own family. Stay true to your faith. Don't respond negatively to the attacks that may come. Over time, your love for your family will have a positive effect.

3:22-27 These teachers of the law brought a nonsensical accusation against Jesus. They tried to say that Jesus was driving out demons by the power of the prince of demons—in other words, that Jesus' power came from Satan, not God. They wanted the people to believe that Jesus himself was possessed (3:30). This would disprove his claim as the Messiah and place him instead in league with the devil.

3:23
g Mk 4:2

3:27
h Isa 49:24, 25

23 So Jesus called them and spoke to them in parables: *g* "How can Satan drive out Satan? 24 If a kingdom is divided against itself, that kingdom cannot stand. 25 If a house is divided against itself, that house cannot stand. 26 And if Satan opposes himself and is divided, he cannot stand; his end has come. 27 In fact, no one can enter a strong man's house and carry off his possessions unless he first ties up the strong man. Then he can rob his house. *h* 28 I tell you the truth, all the sins and blasphemies of men will be forgiven them. 29 But whoever blasphemes against the Holy Spirit will never be forgiven; he is guilty of an eternal sin."

30 He said this because they were saying, "He has an evil spirit."

Jesus Describes His True Family (76/Matthew 12:46–50; Luke 8:19–21)

31 Then Jesus' mother and brothers arrived. Standing outside, they sent someone in to call him. 32 A crowd was sitting around him, and they told him, "Your mother and brothers are outside looking for you."

33 "Who are my mother and my brothers?" he asked.

34 Then he looked at those seated in a circle around him and said, "Here are my mother and my brothers! 35 Whoever does God's will is my brother and sister and mother."

Jesus Tells the Parable of the Four Soils (77/Matthew 13:1–9; Luke 8:4–8)

4:1
i Mk 2:13; 3:7

4:2
j Mk 3:23

4 Again Jesus began to teach by the lake. *i* The crowd that gathered around him was so large that he got into a boat and sat in it out on the lake, while all the people were along the shore at the water's edge. 2 He taught them many things by parables, *j* and in his teaching said: 3 "Listen! A farmer went out to sow his seed. 4 As he was scattering the seed, some fell along the path, and the birds came and ate it up. 5 Some fell on rocky places, where it did not have much soil. It sprang up quickly, because the soil was shallow. 6 But when the sun came up, the plants were scorched, and they withered because they had no root. 7 Other seed fell among thorns, which grew up and choked the plants, so that they did not bear grain. 8 Still other seed fell on good soil. It came up, grew and produced a crop, multiplying thirty, sixty, or even a hundred times." *k*

4:8
k Jn 15:5; Col 1:6

4:9
l Mt 11:15

9 Then Jesus said, "He who has ears to hear, let him hear." *l*

The more effective you are in your Christian life, the more extreme will be the attacks of the enemy. Even the most ridiculous accusation will convince some when it's cleverly packaged to sound sincere and concerned. Stand firm for the truth, even when clever attacks come.

3:27 Although God permits Satan to work in our world, God is still in control. Jesus, because he is God, has power over Satan; Jesus is able to drive out demons and end their terrible work in people's lives. One day Satan will be bound forever (Revelation 20:10).

3:28, 29 Christians sometimes wonder if they have committed this sin of blaspheming the Holy Spirit. Christians need not worry about this sin because this sin is attributing to the devil what is the work of the Holy Spirit. It reveals a heart-attitude of unbelief and unrepentance. Deliberate, ongoing rejection of the work of the Holy Spirit is blasphemy because it is rejecting God himself. The religious leaders accused Jesus of blasphemy, but ironically they were the guilty ones when they looked Jesus in the face and accused him of being possessed by Satan.

3:31–35 Jesus' mother was Mary (Luke 1:30, 31), and his brothers were probably the other children Mary and Joseph had after Jesus (see also 6:3). Some Christians believe the ancient tradition that Jesus was Mary's only child. If this is true, the "brothers" were possibly cousins (cousins were often called brothers in those days). Some have offered yet another suggestion: when Joseph married Mary, he was a widower, and these were his children by his first marriage. Most likely, however, these were Jesus' half brothers (see Mark 6:3, 4).

Jesus' family did not yet fully understand his ministry, as can be seen in verse 21. Jesus explained that in our spiritual family, the relationships are ultimately more important and longer lasting than those formed in our physical families.

3:33–35 God's family is accepting and doesn't exclude anyone. Although Jesus cared for his mother and brothers, he also cared

for all those who loved him. Jesus did not show partiality; he allowed everyone the privilege of obeying God and becoming part of his family. In our increasingly computerized, impersonal world, warm relationships among members of God's family take on major importance. The church should give the loving, personalized care that many people find nowhere else.

4:2 Jesus taught the people by telling parables, short stories using familiar scenes to explain spiritual truth. This method of teaching compels the listener to think. It conceals the truth from those who are too stubborn or prejudiced to hear what is being taught. Most parables have one main point, so we must be careful not to go beyond what Jesus intended to teach.

4:3 Seed was sown by hand. As the farmer walked across the field, he threw handfuls of seed onto the ground from a large bag slung across his shoulders. The plants did not grow in neat rows as accomplished by today's machine planting. No matter how skillful, no farmer could keep some of his seed from falling by the wayside, from being scattered among rocks and thorns, or from being carried off by the wind. So the farmer would throw the seed liberally, and enough would fall on good ground to ensure the harvest.

4:9 The hearing Jesus wants from us is not the kind we use when we listen to background music or when someone starts to recount a long story we've already heard. To truly "hear" Jesus' words is to believe them, to use them immediately in decisions and attitudes, and to base life on them—your recreation and work, family plans and money matters, praying and singing. To hear Jesus' words is to make Jesus your true Lord. What is Jesus saying to you?

Jesus Explains the Parable of the Four Soils (*78*/Matthew 13:10–23; Luke 8:9–18)

¹⁰ When he was alone, the Twelve and the others around him asked him about the parables. ¹¹ He told them, "The secret of the kingdom of God has been given to you. But to those on the outside *m* everything is said in parables ¹² so that,

> "'they may be ever seeing but never perceiving,
> and ever hearing but never understanding;
> otherwise they might turn and be forgiven!'*a* " *n*

¹³ Then Jesus said to them, "Don't you understand this parable? How then will you understand any parable? ¹⁴ The farmer sows the word. ¹⁵ Some people are like seed along the path, where the word is sown. As soon as they hear it, Satan comes and takes away the word that was sown in them. ¹⁶ Others, like seed sown on rocky places, hear the word and at once receive it with joy. ¹⁷ But since they have no root, they last only a short time. When trouble or persecution comes because of the word, they quickly fall away. ¹⁸ Still others, like seed sown among thorns, hear the word; ¹⁹ but the worries of this life, the deceitfulness of wealth and the desires for other things come in and choke the word, making it unfruitful. ²⁰ Others, like seed sown on good soil, hear the word, accept it, and produce a crop—thirty, sixty or even a hundred times what was sown."

²¹ He said to them, "Do you bring in a lamp to put it under a bowl or a bed? Instead, don't you put it on its stand? *o* ²² For whatever is hidden is meant to be disclosed, and whatever is concealed is meant to be brought out into the open. *p* ²³ If anyone has ears to hear, let him hear." *q*

²⁴ "Consider carefully what you hear," he continued. "With the measure you use, it will be measured to you—and even more. *r* ²⁵ Whoever has will be given more; whoever does not have, even what he has will be taken from him." *s*

Jesus Tells the Parable of the Growing Seed (*79*)

²⁶ He also said, "This is what the kingdom of God is like. *t* A man scatters seed on the ground. ²⁷ Night and day, whether he sleeps or gets up, the seed sprouts and grows, though he does not know how. ²⁸ All by itself the soil produces grain—first the stalk, then the head, then the full kernel in the head. ²⁹ As soon as the grain is ripe, he puts the sickle to it, because the harvest has come." *u*

a 12 Isaiah 6:9,10

4:11
m 1Co 5:12, 13;
Col 4:5; 1Th 4:12;
1Ti 3:7
4:12
n Isa 6:9, 10

4:21
o Mt 5:15
4:22
p Mt 10:26; Lk 8:17
4:23
q Mt 11:15
4:24
r Mt 7:2; Lk 6:38
4:25
s Mt 13:12; 25:29

4:26
t Mt 13:24

4:29
u Rev 14:15

4:14-20 This parable should encourage spiritual "farmers"—those who teach, preach, and lead others. The farmer sowed good seed, but not all the seed sprouted, and even the plants that grew had varying yields. Don't be discouraged if you do not always see results as you faithfully teach the Word. Some people do not understand God's truth because they are not ready for it. God reveals truth to people who will act on it, who will make it visible in their lives. When you talk with people about God, be aware that they will not understand if they are not yet ready. Be patient, taking every chance to tell them more of the truth about God, and praying that the Holy Spirit will open their minds and hearts to receive the truth and act on it. Productivity is in God's hands.

4:14-20 The four soils represent four different ways people respond to God's message. Usually we think that Jesus was talking about four different kinds of people. But he may also have been talking about (1) different times or phases in a person's life, or (2) how we willingly receive God's message in some areas of our lives and resist it in others. For example, you may be open to God about your future, but closed concerning how you spend your money. You may respond like good soil to God's demand for worship, but like rocky soil to his demand to give to people in need. We must strive to be like good soil in every area of our lives at all times.

4:19 Worries of this life, the false sense of security brought on by prosperity, and the desire for things plagued first-century disciples just as they do us today. How easy it is for our daily routines to become overcrowded. A life packed with materialistic pursuits crowds out God's Word and leaves us unfruitful for him. Stay free so you can hear God when he speaks.

4:21 Many Christians today are hidden from sight, reluctant to be identified as Christians. Such a Christian is like a brand-new light that never leaves the carton it came in. If a lamp doesn't help people see, it isn't worth much. Does your life show other people how to find God and how to live for him? If not, ask what "baskets" have hidden your light. Complacency, resentment, embarrassment, stubbornness of heart, or disobedience could keep you from shining. What do you need to do to let your light shine?

4:24, 25 The light of Jesus' truth is revealed to us, not hidden. But we may not be able to see or to use all of that truth right now. Only as we put God's teachings into practice will we understand and see more of the truth. The truth is clear, but our ability to understand is imperfect. As we obey, we will sharpen our vision and increase our understanding (see James 1:22–25).

4:25 Jesus' words may have been directed to the Jews who had no understanding of Jesus and would lose even what they had—their privileged status as God's people. Or Jesus might have meant that when people reject him, their hardness of heart drives away or renders useless even the little understanding they had; thus, any opportunity to share in God's kingdom will eventually be taken away completely. To understand Jesus' message, people must listen and respond. Those who listen casually, for whatever reason, will miss the point.

4:26-29 God promises that his harvest will be magnificent and prolific—the best fruit ever grown. Your witness may be weak and your efforts may seem to influence so few, but the Word of God is a powerful growth agent. Keep your eyes on the great harvest to come and don't let bad soil or weeds discourage you from faithful service and witness.

Jesus Tells the Parable of the Mustard Seed (*81*/Matthew 13:31–32)

4:30
v Mt 13:24

30 Again he said, "What shall we say the kingdom of God is like,ᵛ or what parable shall we use to describe it? 31 It is like a mustard seed, which is the smallest seed you plant in the ground. 32 Yet when planted, it grows and becomes the largest of all garden plants, with such big branches that the birds of the air can perch in its shade."

4:33
w Jn 16:12
4:34
x Jn 16:25

33 With many similar parables Jesus spoke the word to them, as much as they could understand. ʷ 34 He did not say anything to them without using a parable. ˣ But when he was alone with his own disciples, he explained everything.

Jesus Calms the Storm (*87*/Matthew 8:23–27; Luke 8:22–25)

4:36
y ver 1; Mk 3:9;
5:2, 21; 6:32, 45

35 That day when evening came, he said to his disciples, "Let us go over to the other side." 36 Leaving the crowd behind, they took him along, just as he was, in the boat.ʸ There were also other boats with him. 37 A furious squall came up, and the waves broke over the boat, so that it was nearly swamped. 38 Jesus was in the stern, sleeping on a cushion. The disciples woke him and said to him, "Teacher, don't you care if we drown?"

39 He got up, rebuked the wind and said to the waves, "Quiet! Be still!" Then the wind died down and it was completely calm.

4:40
z Mt 14:31;
Mk 16:14

40 He said to his disciples, "Why are you so afraid? Do you still have no faith?"ᶻ 41 They were terrified and asked each other, "Who is this? Even the wind and the waves obey him!"

Jesus Sends Demons into a Herd of Pigs (*88*/Matthew 8:28–34; Luke 8:26–39)

5:2
a Mk 4:1
b Mk 1:23

5 They went across the lake to the region of the Gerasenes.ᵃ 2 When Jesus got out of the boat,ᵃ a man with an evilᵇ spiritᵇ came from the tombs to meet him. 3 This man lived in the tombs, and no one could bind him any more, not even with a chain. 4 For he had often been chained hand and foot, but he tore the chains apart and broke the irons on his feet. No one was strong enough to subdue him. 5 Night and day among the tombs and in the hills he would cry out and cut himself with stones.

5:7
c Mt 8:29
d Mt 4:3; Ac 16:17;
Heb 7:1

6 When he saw Jesus from a distance, he ran and fell on his knees in front of him. 7 He shouted at the top of his voice, "What do you want with me,ᶜ Jesus, Son of the Most High God? ᵈ Swear to God that you won't torture me!" 8 For Jesus had said to him, "Come out of this man, you evil spirit!"

9 Then Jesus asked him, "What is your name?"

ᵃ 1 Some manuscripts *Gadarenes*; other manuscripts *Gergesenes*   ᵇ 2 Greek *unclean*; also in verses 8 and 13

4:30–32 Jesus used this parable to explain that although Christianity had very small beginnings, it would grow into a worldwide community of believers. When you feel alone in your stand for Christ, realize that God is building a worldwide kingdom. He has faithful followers in every part of the world. Your faith, no matter how small, can join with that of others to accomplish great things.

4:37 Problems occur in every area of life. The disciples needed rest, but they encountered a terrible storm. The Christian life may have more stormy weather than calm seas. As Christ's follower, be prepared for the storms that will surely come. Do not surrender to the stress, but remain resilient and recover from setbacks. With faith in Christ, you can pray, trust, and move ahead. When a squall approaches, lean into the wind and trust God.

4:37, 38 The Sea of Galilee is 680 feet below sea level and is surrounded by hills. Winds blowing across the land intensify close to the sea, often causing violent and unexpected storms. The disciples were seasoned fishermen who had spent their lives fishing on this huge lake, but during this squall they panicked.

4:41 The disciples lived with Jesus, but they underestimated him. They did not see that his power applied to their very own situation. Jesus has been with his people for 20 centuries, and yet we, like the disciples, underestimate his power to handle crises in our lives. The disciples did not yet know enough about Jesus. We cannot make the same excuse.

5:1, 2 Although we cannot be sure why demon-possession occurs, we know that evil spirits can use the human body to distort and destroy man's relationship with God and likeness to him. Even today, demons are dangerous, powerful, and destructive. While it is important to recognize their evil activity, we should avoid any curiosity about or involvement with demonic forces or the occult (Deuteronomy 18:10–12). If we resist the devil and his influences, he will flee from us (James 4:7).

5:7 The demon screamed at Jesus, "What do you want with me?" It was a shriek of fear, defense, and rebellion against God. No one today would like to admit to being demon possessed, but most of our society, like the demon, is screaming at God, the church, and Christian values, "What do you want with me? Get out of my life!" When people reject Jesus Christ and his authority, they put themselves on the side of the demons and are heading in the same direction. Every person must ask: Will I choose autonomy and self-will leading to destruction, or will I choose Christ's loving leadership over my life, giving me forgiveness, healing from sin, cleansing, and true freedom? The answer has eternal implications.

5:9 The evil spirit said its name was Legion. A legion was the largest unit of the Roman army, consisting of 3,000 to 6,000 soldiers. This man was possessed by many demons.

"My name is Legion," e he replied, "for we are many." 10And he begged Jesus again and again not to send them out of the area.

11A large herd of pigs was feeding on the nearby hillside. 12The demons begged Jesus, "Send us among the pigs; allow us to go into them." 13He gave them permission, and the evil spirits came out and went into the pigs. The herd, about two thousand in number, rushed down the steep bank into the lake and were drowned.

14Those tending the pigs ran off and reported this in the town and countryside, and the people went out to see what had happened. 15When they came to Jesus, they saw the man who had been possessed by the legion f of demons, g sitting there, dressed and in his right mind; and they were afraid. 16Those who had seen it told the people what had happened to the demon-possessed man—and told about the pigs as well. 17Then the people began to plead with Jesus to leave their region.

18As Jesus was getting into the boat, the man who had been demon-possessed begged to go with him. 19Jesus did not let him, but said, "Go home to your family and tell them how much the Lord has done for you, and how he has had mercy on you." 20So the man went away and began to tell in the Decapolis a h how much Jesus had done for him. And all the people were amazed.

Jesus Heals a Bleeding Woman and Restores a Girl to Life
(89/Matthew 9:18–26; Luke 8:40–56)

21When Jesus had again crossed over by boat to the other side of the lake,i a large crowd gathered around him while he was by the lake. 22Then one of the synagogue rulers,j named Jairus, came there. Seeing Jesus, he fell at his feet 23and pleaded earnestly with him, "My little daughter is dying. Please come and put your hands on k her so that she will be healed and live." 24So Jesus went with him.

a20 That is, the Ten Cities

5:9
e ver 15

5:15
f ver 9
g ver 16, 18; Mt 4:24

5:20
h Mt 4:25; Mk 7:31

5:21
i Mt 9:1

5:22
j Lk 13:14; Ac 13:15; 18:8, 17

5:23
k Mk 6:5; 7:32; 8:23

5:10 Mark often highlights the supernatural struggle between Jesus and Satan. The demons' goal was to control the humans they inhabited; Jesus' goal was to give people freedom from sin and Satan's control. The demons knew they had no power over Jesus, so they simply begged not to be sent out of the area ("into the Abyss" in Luke 8:31). Jesus granted their request to enter into the herd of pigs (5:13), but ended their destructive work in people. Perhaps Jesus let the demons destroy the pigs to demonstrate his own superiority over a very powerful yet destructive force. He could have sent them to hell, but he did not, because the time for judgment had not yet come. In the end, the devil and all his angels will be sent into eternal fire (Matthew 25:41).

5:11 According to Old Testament law (Leviticus 11:7), pigs were "unclean" animals. This meant that they could not be eaten or even touched by a Jew. This incident took place southeast of the

HEALING A DEMON-POSSESSED MAN
From Capernaum, Jesus and his disciples crossed the Sea of Galilee. A storm blew up unexpectedly, but Jesus calmed it. Landing in the region of the Gerasenes, Jesus sent demons out of a man and into a herd of pigs that plunged over the steep bank into the lake.

Mediterranean Sea
GALILEE
N
Capernaum
Sea of Galilee
Drowning of the pigs
Gadara
GERASENE REGION
Jordan River
Jerusalem
Dead Sea
0   20 Mi.
0   20 Km.

Sea of Galilee in the region of the Gerasenes, a Gentile region, which explains how a herd of pigs could be involved.

5:17 After such a wonderful miracle of saving a man's life, why did the people want Jesus to leave? They were undoubtedly afraid of his supernatural power. They may have also feared that Jesus would continue destroying their pigs—their livelihood. They would rather give up Jesus than lose their source of income and security.

5:19 Jesus told this man to tell his friends about the miraculous healing. Most of the time, Jesus urged those he healed to keep quiet. Why the difference? (1) The demon-possessed man had been alone and unable to speak. Telling others what Jesus did for him would prove that he was healed. (2) This was mainly a Gentile and pagan area, so Jesus was not expecting great crowds to follow him or religious leaders to hinder him. (3) By sending the man away with this good news, Jesus was expanding his ministry to people who were not Jews.

5:19, 20 This man had been demon-possessed but became a living example of Jesus' power. He wanted to go with Jesus, but Jesus told him to go home and share his story with his friends. If you have experienced Jesus' power, you too are a living example. Are you, like this man, enthusiastic about sharing the Good News with those around you? Just as we would tell others about a doctor who cured a physical disease, we should tell about Christ who cures our sin.

5:20 Decapolis, or the Ten Cities, was located southeast of the Sea of Galilee. Ten cities, each with its own independent government, formed an alliance for protection and for increased trade opportunities. These cities had been settled several centuries earlier by Greek traders and immigrants. Although Jews also lived in the area, they were not in the majority. Many people from the Decapolis followed Jesus (Matthew 4:25).

5:22 Jesus went back across the Sea of Galilee, probably landing at Capernaum. Jairus was the elected ruler of the local synagogue, responsible for supervising worship, running the weekly school, and caring for the building. Many synagogue rulers had close ties to the Pharisees. It is likely, therefore, that some synagogue rulers had been pressured not to support Jesus. For Jairus to bow before

5:25
l Lev 15:25-30

A large crowd followed and pressed around him. 25And a woman was there who had been subject to bleeding*l* for twelve years. 26She had suffered a great deal under the care of many doctors and had spent all she had, yet instead of getting better she grew worse. 27When she heard about Jesus, she came up behind him in the crowd and touched his cloak, 28because she thought, "If I just touch his clothes, I will be healed." 29Immediately her bleeding stopped and she felt in her body that she was freed from her suffering.*m*

5:29
m ver 34

5:30
n Lk 5:17

30At once Jesus realized that power *n* had gone out from him. He turned around in the crowd and asked, "Who touched my clothes?"

31"You see the people crowding against you," his disciples answered, "and yet you can ask, 'Who touched me?'"

32But Jesus kept looking around to see who had done it. 33Then the woman, knowing what had happened to her, came and fell at his feet and, trembling with fear, told him the whole truth. 34He said to her, "Daughter, your faith has healed you. *o* Go in peace and be freed from your suffering."

5:34
o Mt 9:22

THE TOUCH OF JESUS

What kind of people did Jesus associate with? Whom did he consider important enough to touch? Here we see many of the people Jesus came to know. Some reached out to him; he reached out to them all. Regardless of how great or unknown, rich or poor, young or old, sinner or saint—Jesus cares equally for all. No person is beyond the loving touch of Jesus.

Jesus talked with . . .	Reference
A despised tax collector.	Matthew 9:9
An insane hermit.	Mark 5:1–15
The Roman governor	Mark 15:1–15
A young boy	Mark 9:17–27
A prominent religious leader.	John 3:1–21
A homemaker.	Luke 10:38–42
An expert in the law	Matthew 22:35
A criminal	Luke 23:40–43
A synagogue ruler.	Mark 5:22
Fishermen.	Matthew 4:18–20
A king.	Luke 23:7–11
A poor widow.	Luke 7:11–17; 21:1–4
A Roman centurion.	Luke 7:1–10
A group of children.	Mark 10:13–16
A prophet.	Matthew 3
An adulterous woman.	John 8:1–11
The Jewish high council.	Luke 22:66–71
A sick woman.	Mark 5:25–34
A rich man.	Mark 10:17–23
A blind beggar.	Mark 10:46
Jewish political leaders.	Mark 12:13
A group of women.	Luke 8:2, 3
The high priest.	Matthew 26:62–68
An outcast with leprosy.	Luke 17:11–19
A royal official.	John 4:46–53
A young girl.	Mark 5:41, 42
A traitor.	John 13:1–3, 27
A helpless and paralyzed man.	Mark 2:1–12
An angry mob of soldiers and police.	John 18:3–9
A woman from a foreign land.	Mark 7:25–30
A doubting follower.	John 20:24–29
An enemy who hated him.	Acts 9:1–9
A Samaritan woman.	John 4:1–26

Jesus was a significant and perhaps daring act of respect and worship.

5:25–34 This woman had a seemingly incurable condition causing her to bleed constantly. This may have been a menstrual or uterine disorder that would have made her ritually unclean (Leviticus 15:25–27) and excluded her from most social contact. She desperately wanted Jesus to heal her, but she knew that her bleeding would cause Jesus to be unclean under Jewish law if she touched him. Sometimes we feel that our problems will keep us from God. But he is always ready to help, no matter how impossible the problem seems to us. We should never allow our fear to keep us from approaching him.

5:31 It was virtually impossible to get close to Jesus, but one woman fought her way desperately through the crowd in order to touch him. As soon as she did, she was healed. What a difference between the crowds who are curious about Jesus and the few who reach out and touch him! Today, many people are vaguely familiar with Jesus, but nothing in their lives is changed or bettered by this passing acquaintance. It is only faith that releases God's healing power. Move beyond curiosity. Reach out to Christ in faith. That touch will change your life forever.

35 While Jesus was still speaking, some men came from the house of Jairus, the synagogue ruler.ᵖ "Your daughter is dead," they said. "Why bother the teacher any more?"

36 Ignoring what they said, Jesus told the synagogue ruler, "Don't be afraid; just believe."

37 He did not let anyone follow him except Peter, James and John the brother of James. 38 When they came to the home of the synagogue ruler, Jesus saw a commotion, with people crying and wailing loudly. 39 He went in and said to them, "Why all this commotion and wailing? The child is not dead but asleep." 40 But they laughed at him.

After he put them all out, he took the child's father and mother and the disciples who were with him, and went in where the child was. 41 He took her by the hand and said to her, *"Talitha koum!"* (which means, "Little girl, I say to you, get up!"). �q 42 Immediately the girl stood up and walked around (she was twelve years old). At this they were completely astonished. 43 He gave strict orders not to let anyone know about this,ʳ and told them to give her something to eat.

The People of Nazareth Refuse to Believe (91/Matthew 13:53–58)

6 Jesus left there and went to his hometown, accompanied by his disciples. 2 When the Sabbath came, he began to teach in the synagogue, ˢ and many who heard him were amazed.

"Where did this man get these things?" they asked. "What's this wisdom that has been given him, that he even does miracles? 3 Isn't this the carpenter? Isn't this Mary's son and the brother of James, Joseph,ᵃ Judas and Simon?ᵗ Aren't his sisters here with us?" And they took offense at him. ᵘ

4 Jesus said to them, "Only in his hometown, among his relatives and in his own house is a prophet without honor."ᵛ 5 He could not do any miracles there, except lay his hands onʷ a few sick people and heal them. 6 And he was amazed at their lack of faith.

ᵃ3 Greek *Joses*, a variant of *Joseph*

5:35
ᵖ ver 22

5:41
�q Ac 9:40

5:43
ʳ Mt 8:4

6:2
ˢ Mt 4:23

6:3
ᵗ Mt 12:46
ᵘ Mt 11:6

6:4
ᵛ Jn 4:44

6:5
ʷ Mk 5:23

6:6
ˣ Mt 9:35; Lk 13:22

5:35, 36 Jairus's crisis made him feel confused, afraid, and without hope. Jesus' words to Jairus in the midst of crisis speak to us as well: "Don't be afraid; just believe." In Jesus there is both hope and promise. The next time you feel hopeless and afraid, look at your problem from Jesus' point of view. Then don't be afraid; just have faith.

5:38 Loud weeping and wailing was customary at a person's death. Lack of it was the ultimate disgrace and disrespect. Some people, usually women, made mourning a profession and were paid by the dead person's family to weep over the body. On the day of death, the body was carried through the streets, followed by mourners, family members, and friends.

**PREACHING
IN GALILEE**
After returning to his hometown, Nazareth, from Capernaum, Jesus preached in the villages of Galilee and sent his disciples out to preach as well. After meeting back in Capernaum, they left by boat to rest, only to be met by the crowds who followed the boat along the shore.

5:39, 40 The mourners laughed at Jesus when he said, "The child is not dead but asleep." The girl was dead, but Jesus used the image of sleep to indicate that her condition was temporary and that she would be restored.

Jesus tolerated the crowd's abuse in order to teach an important lesson about maintaining hope and trust in him. Today, most of the world laughs at Christ's claims. When you are belittled for expressing faith in Jesus and hope for eternal life, remember that unbelievers don't see from God's perspective. For a clear statement about life after death, see 1 Thessalonians 4:13, 14.

5:41 *Talitha koum* is Aramaic, one of the original languages of Palestine. Jesus' disciples spoke not only Aramaic, but probably Greek and Hebrew also.

5:41, 42 Jesus not only demonstrated great power; he also showed tremendous compassion. Jesus' power over nature, evil spirits, and death was motivated by compassion—for a demon-possessed man who lived among tombs, a diseased woman, and the family of a dead girl. The rabbis of the day considered such people unclean. Polite society avoided them. But Jesus reached out and helped.

5:43 Jesus told the girl's parents not to spread the news of the miracle. He wanted the facts to speak for themselves, and the time was not yet right for a major confrontation with the religious leaders. Jesus still had much to accomplish, and he didn't want people following him just to see his miracles.

6:4 Jesus said that a prophet (in other words, a worker for God) is never honored in his hometown. But that doesn't make his work any less important. A person doesn't need to be respected or honored to be useful to God. If friends, neighbors, or family don't respect your Christian work, don't let their rejection keep you from serving God.

6:5 Jesus could have done greater miracles in Nazareth, but he chose not to because of the people's pride and unbelief. The miracles he did had little effect on the people because they did not accept his message or believe that he was from God. Therefore, Jesus looked elsewhere, seeking those who would respond to his miracles and message.

Jesus Sends Out the Twelve Disciples (*93*/Matthew 10:1–15; Luke 9:1–6)

6:7
y Mk 3:13
z Mt 10:1

Then Jesus went around teaching from village to village.*x* 7 Calling the Twelve to him,*y* he sent them out two by two and gave them authority over evil*a* spirits.*z*

8 These were his instructions: "Take nothing for the journey except a staff—no bread, no bag, no money in your belts. 9 Wear sandals but not an extra tunic. 10 Whenever you enter a

a 7 Greek *unclean*

HEROD ANTIPAS

Most people dislike having their sins pointed out, especially in public. The shame of being exposed is often stronger than the guilt brought on by the wrongdoing. Herod Antipas was a man experiencing both guilt and shame.

Herod's ruthless ambition was public knowledge, as was his illegal marriage to his brother's wife, Herodias. One man made Herod's sin a public issue. That man was John the Baptist. John had been preaching in the desert, and thousands flocked to hear him. Apparently it was no secret that John had rebuked Herod for his adulterous marriage. Herodias was particularly anxious to have John silenced. As a solution, Herod imprisoned John.

Herod liked John. John was probably one of the few people he met who spoke only the truth to him. But the truth about his sin was a bitter pill to swallow, and Herod wavered at the point of conflict: he couldn't afford to have John constantly reminding the people of their leader's sinfulness, but he was afraid to have John killed. He put off the choice. Eventually Herodias forced his hand, and John was executed. Of course, this only served to increase Herod's guilt.

Upon hearing about Jesus, Herod immediately identified him with John. He couldn't decide what to do about Jesus. He didn't want to repeat the mistake he had made with John, so he tried to threaten Jesus just before Jesus' final journey to Jerusalem. When the two met briefly during Jesus' trial, Jesus would not speak to Herod. Herod had proved himself a poor listener to John, and Jesus had nothing to add to John's words. Herod responded with spite and mocking. Having rejected the messenger, he found it easy to reject the Messiah.

For each person, God chooses the best possible ways to reveal himself. He uses his Word, various circumstances, our minds, or other people to get our attention. He is persuasive and persistent, but never forces himself on us. To miss or resist God's message, as did Herod, is tragedy. How aware are you of God's attempts to enter your life? Have you welcomed him?

Strengths and accomplishments:	• Built the city of Tiberias and oversaw other architectural projects • Ruled the region of Galilee for the Romans
Weaknesses and mistakes:	• Consumed with his quest for power • Put off decisions or made wrong ones under pressure • Divorced his wife to marry the wife of his half brother, Philip • Imprisoned John the Baptist and later ordered his execution • Had a minor part in the execution of Jesus
Lessons from his life:	• A life motivated by ambition is usually characterized by self-destruction • Opportunities to do good usually come to us in the form of choices to be made
Vital statistics:	• Where: Jerusalem • Occupation: Roman tetrarch of the region of Galilee and Perea • Relatives: Father: Herod the Great. Mother: Malthace. First wife: daughter of Aretas IV. Second wife: Herodias. • Contemporaries: John the Baptist, Jesus, Pilate
Key verse:	"When Herod heard John, he was greatly puzzled; yet he liked to listen to him" (Mark 6:20).

Herod Antipas's story is told in the Gospels. He is also mentioned in Acts 4:27; 13:1.

6:7 The disciples were sent out in pairs. Individually they could have reached more areas of the country, but this was not Christ's plan. The advantages in going out by twos include: (1) They could strengthen and encourage each other. (2) They could provide comfort in rejection. (3) They could give each other discernment, and fewer mistakes would be made. (4) They could stir each other to action as a counter to idleness or indifference. Our strength comes from God, but he meets many of our needs through our teamwork with others. As you serve Christ, don't try to go it alone.

6:8, 9 Mark records that the disciples were instructed to take nothing with them *except* staffs, while in the Matthew and Luke

accounts Jesus told them *not* to take staffs. One explanation is that Matthew and Luke were referring to a club used for protection, whereas Mark was talking about a shepherd's crook. In any case, the point in all three accounts is the same—the disciples were to leave at once, without extensive preparation, trusting in God's care rather than in their own resources.

house, stay there until you leave that town. ¹¹And if any place will not welcome you or listen to you, shake the dust off your feet*a* when you leave, as a testimony against them."

¹²They went out and preached that people should repent. *b* ¹³They drove out many demons and anointed many sick people with oil *c* and healed them.

Herod Kills John the Baptist (95/Matthew 14:1–12; Luke 9:7–9)

¹⁴King Herod heard about this, for Jesus' name had become well known. Some were saying,*a* "John the Baptist has been raised from the dead, and that is why miraculous powers are at work in him."

¹⁵Others said, "He is Elijah."

And still others claimed, "He is a prophet, *d* like one of the prophets of long ago." *e*

¹⁶But when Herod heard this, he said, "John, the man I beheaded, has been raised from the dead!"

¹⁷For Herod himself had given orders to have John arrested, and he had him bound and put in prison. He did this because of Herodias, his brother Philip's wife, whom he had married. ¹⁸For John had been saying to Herod, "It is not lawful for you to have your brother's wife." *f* ¹⁹So Herodias nursed a grudge against John and wanted to kill him. But she was not able to, ²⁰because Herod feared John and protected him, knowing him to be a righteous and holy man.*g* When Herod heard John, he was greatly puzzled*b*; yet he liked to listen to him.

²¹Finally the opportune time came. On his birthday Herod gave a banquet *h* for his high officials and military commanders and the leading men of Galilee. *i* ²²When the daughter of Herodias came in and danced, she pleased Herod and his dinner guests.

The king said to the girl, "Ask me for anything you want, and I'll give it to you." ²³And he promised her with an oath, "Whatever you ask I will give you, up to half my kingdom." *j*

a 14 Some early manuscripts He was saying   *b 20 Some early manuscripts he did many things*

6:11	*a Mt 10:14
6:12	*b Lk 9:6
6:13	*c Jas 5:14
6:15	*d Mt 21:11 *e Mt 16:14; Mk 8:28
6:18	*f Lev 18:16; 20:21
6:20	*g Mt 21:26
6:21	*h Est 1:3; 2:18 *i Lk 3:1
6:23	*j Est 5:3, 6; 7:2

6:11 Pious Jews shook the dust from their feet after passing through Gentile cities or territory to show their separation from Gentile influences and practices. When the disciples shook the dust from their feet after leaving a *Jewish* town, it was a vivid sign that they wished to remain separate from people who had rejected Jesus and his message. Jesus made it clear that the listeners were responsible for what they did with the gospel. The disciples were not to blame if the message was rejected, as long as they had faithfully and carefully presented it. We are not responsible when others reject Christ's message of salvation, but we do have the responsibility to share the gospel clearly and faithfully.

6:14, 15 Herod, along with many others, wondered who Jesus really was. Unable to accept Jesus' claim to be God's Son, many people made up their own explanations for his power and authority. Herod thought that Jesus was John the Baptist come back to life, while those who were familiar with the Old Testament thought he was Elijah (Malachi 4:5). Still others believed that Jesus was a teaching prophet in the tradition of Moses, Isaiah, or Jeremiah. Today people still have to make up their minds about Jesus. Some think that if they can name what he is—prophet, teacher, good man—they can weaken the power of his claim on their lives. But what they *think* does not change who Jesus *is*.

6:17–19 Palestine was divided into four territories, each with a different ruler. Herod Antipas, called Herod in the Gospels, was ruler over Galilee; his brother Philip ruled over Traconitis and Iturea. Philip's wife was Herodias, but she had left him to marry Herod Antipas. When John confronted the two for committing adultery, Herodias formulated a plot to kill him. Instead of trying to get rid of her sin, Herodias tried to get rid of the one who brought it to public attention. This is also exactly what the religious leaders were trying to do to Jesus.

6:18 Christians today face a world of moral compromise. Secular power sets standards that correspond to majority vote; Christian standards, however, begin and end with God's Word. To be faithful to God's Word, we must stand up against what is morally wrong. Responsible Christians must choose their battles. Start with prayers for wisdom, then prayers for courage. Once your battle is chosen, speak and act as a faithful follower of the living God. Witness with strength; move mountains by faith; overcome in love. Show the compromised world a little of John's stubbornness, fortitude, and faith.

6:20 Herod arrested John the Baptist under pressure from his wife and advisers. Though Herod respected John's integrity, in the end Herod had John killed because of pressure from his peers and family. What you do under pressure often shows what you are really like.

6:22, 23 As a ruler under Roman authority, Herod had no kingdom to give. The offer of half his kingdom was Herod's way to say that he would give Herodias's daughter almost anything she wanted. When Herodias asked for John's head, Herod would have been greatly embarrassed in front of his guests if he had denied her request. Words are powerful. Because they can lead to great sin, we should use them with great care.

JESUS WALKS ON THE WATER
After feeding the people who had followed to hear him at Bethsaida, Jesus sent the people home, sent his disciples by boat toward Bethsaida, and went to pray. The disciples encountered a storm, and Jesus walked to them on the water. They landed at Gennesaret.

Mediterranean Sea
N
Sea of Galilee
Bethsaida
Gennesaret
Jordan River
Jerusalem
Dead Sea

0   20 Mi.
0   20 Km.

24 She went out and said to her mother, "What shall I ask for?"

"The head of John the Baptist," she answered.

25 At once the girl hurried in to the king with the request: "I want you to give me right now the head of John the Baptist on a platter."

26 The king was greatly distressed, but because of his oaths and his dinner guests, he did not want to refuse her. 27 So he immediately sent an executioner with orders to bring John's head. The man went, beheaded John in the prison, 28 and brought back his head on a platter. He presented it to the girl, and she gave it to her mother. 29 On hearing of this, John's disciples came and took his body and laid it in a tomb.

Jesus Feeds Five Thousand (96/Matthew 14:13–21; Luke 9:10–17; John 6:1–15)

6:30
k Lk 9:10; Ac 1:2, 26
l Lk 9:10

30 The apostles k gathered around Jesus and reported to him all they had done and taught. l 31 Then, because so many people were coming and going that they did not even have a chance to eat,m he said to them, "Come with me by yourselves to a quiet place and get some rest."

6:31
m Mk 3:20

6:32
n ver 45; Mk 4:36

32 So they went away by themselves in a boat n to a solitary place. 33 But many who saw them leaving recognized them and ran on foot from all the towns and got there ahead of them. 34 When Jesus landed and saw a large crowd, he had compassion on them, because they were like sheep without a shepherd. o So he began teaching them many things.

6:34
o Mt 9:36

35 By this time it was late in the day, so his disciples came to him. "This is a remote place," they said, "and it's already very late. 36 Send the people away so they can go to the surrounding countryside and villages and buy themselves something to eat."

6:37
p 2Ki 4:42-44

37 But he answered, "You give them something to eat."p

They said to him, "That would take eight months of a man's wages a ! Are we to go and spend that much on bread and give it to them to eat?"

6:38
q Mt 15:34; Mk 8:5

38 "How many loaves do you have?" he asked. "Go and see."

When they found out, they said, "Five—and two fish."q

6:41
r Mt 14:19

39 Then Jesus directed them to have all the people sit down in groups on the green grass. 40 So they sat down in groups of hundreds and fifties. 41 Taking the five loaves and the two fish and looking up to heaven, he gave thanks and broke the loaves. r Then he gave them to

a 37 Greek take two hundred denarii

REAL LEADERSHIP
Mark gives us some of the best insights into Jesus' character.

Herod as a leader	Jesus as a leader
Selfish	Compassionate
Murderer	Healer
Immoral	Just and good
Political opportunist	Servant
King over small territory	King over all creation

6:30 Mark uses the word *apostles* here and in 3:14. *Apostle* means "one sent" as messenger, authorized agent, or missionary. The word became an official title for Jesus' 12 disciples after his death and resurrection (Acts 1:25, 26; Ephesians 2:20).

6:31 When the disciples had returned from their mission, Jesus took them away to rest. Doing God's work is very important, but Jesus recognized that to do it effectively we need periodic rest and renewal. Jesus and his disciples, however, did not always find it easy to get the rest they needed!

6:34 This crowd was as pitiful as a flock of sheep without a shepherd. Sheep are easily scattered; without a shepherd they are in grave danger. Jesus was the Shepherd who could teach them what they needed to know and keep them from straying from God. See Psalm 23; Isaiah 40:11; and Ezekiel 34:5ff for descriptions of the Good Shepherd.

6:37–42 When Jesus asked the disciples to provide food for over 5,000 people, they asked in astonishment if they should go and spend eight months' wages on bread. How do you react when you are given an impossible task? A situation that seems impossible with human resources is simply an opportunity for God. The disciples did everything they could by gathering the available food and organizing the people into groups. Then, in answer to prayer, God did the impossible. When facing a seemingly impossible task, do what you can and ask God to do the rest. He may see fit to make the impossible happen.

6:37–42 Why did Jesus bother to feed these people? He could just as easily have sent them on their way. Jesus does not ignore needs, however. He is concerned with every aspect of our lives— the physical as well as the spiritual.

We might well ask why the church has taken so lightly the command, "You give them something to eat." Jesus' compassion for these hungry people is recorded in all four Gospels. For people who are desperately hungry, there is no better way for us to show God's love to them than to help to provide for their physical needs. As we work to bring wholeness to people's lives, we must never ignore the fact that all of us have both physical and spiritual needs. It is impossible to minister effectively to the spiritual need without considering the physical need. (See also James 2:14–17.)

his disciples to set before the people. He also divided the two fish among them all. 42 They all ate and were satisfied, 43 and the disciples picked up twelve basketfuls of broken pieces of bread and fish. 44 The number of the men who had eaten was five thousand.

Jesus Walks on Water (97/Matthew 14:22–23; John 6:16–21)

45 Immediately Jesus made his disciples get into the boat s and go on ahead of him to Bethsaida, t while he dismissed the crowd. 46 After leaving them, he went up on a mountainside to pray.

47 When evening came, the boat was in the middle of the lake, and he was alone on land. 48 He saw the disciples straining at the oars, because the wind was against them. About the fourth watch of the night he went out to them, walking on the lake. He was about to pass by them, 49 but when they saw him walking on the lake, they thought he was a ghost. They cried out, 50 because they all saw him and were terrified.

Immediately he spoke to them and said, "Take courage! It is I. Don't be afraid." u 51 Then he climbed into the boat v with them, and the wind died down. They were completely amazed, 52 for they had not understood about the loaves; their hearts were hardened. w

Jesus Heals All Who Touch Him (98/Matthew 14:34–36)

53 When they had crossed over, they landed at Gennesaret and anchored there. x 54 As soon as they got out of the boat, people recognized Jesus. 55 They ran throughout that whole region and carried the sick on mats to wherever they heard he was. 56 And wherever he went—into villages, towns or countryside—they placed the sick in the marketplaces. They begged him to let them touch even the edge of his cloak, y and all who touched him were healed.

Jesus Teaches about Inner Purity (102/Matthew 15:1–20)

7 The Pharisees and some of the teachers of the law who had come from Jerusalem gathered around Jesus and 2 saw some of his disciples eating food with hands that were "unclean," z that is, unwashed. 3 (The Pharisees and all the Jews do not eat unless they give their hands a ceremonial washing, holding to the tradition of the elders. a 4 When they come from the marketplace they do not eat unless they wash. And they observe many other traditions, such as the washing of cups, pitchers and kettles. a) b

5 So the Pharisees and teachers of the law asked Jesus, "Why don't your disciples live according to the tradition of the elders c instead of eating their food with 'unclean' hands?"

6 He replied, "Isaiah was right when he prophesied about you hypocrites; as it is written:

a4 Some early manuscripts *pitchers, kettles and dining couches*

6:45
s ver 32
t Mt 11:21

6:50
u Mt 14:27
6:51
v ver 32
6:52
w Mk 8:17-21

6:53
x Jn 6:24, 25

6:56
y Mt 9:20

7:2
z Ac 10:14, 28
7:3
a ver 5, 8, 9, 13
7:4
b Mt 23:25
7:5
c ver 3; Gal 1:14

6:49, 50 The disciples were afraid, but Jesus' presence calmed their fears. When you experience fear, do you try to deal with it yourself, or do you let Jesus deal with it? In times of fear and uncertainty, it is calming to know that Christ is always with you (Matthew 28:20). To recognize Christ's presence is the antidote for fear.

6:52 The disciples didn't want to believe, perhaps because (1) they couldn't accept the fact that this human named Jesus was really the Son of God; (2) they dared not believe that the Messiah would choose them as his followers; (3) they still did not understand the real purpose for Jesus' coming to earth. Their disbelief took the form of misunderstanding. Even after watching Jesus miraculously feed 5,000 people, they still could not take the final step of faith and believe that he was God's Son. If they had, they would not have been amazed that Jesus could walk on water.

Is your heart hardened against Jesus? Even Christians can be hard-hearted to Jesus' words. We can be informed about what his Word says, and we can be amazed at how he has worked in other people's lives, but we can refuse to believe he will come to our aid in our time of trouble. Such a reaction is not unbelief, but willful, hard-hearted rejection of Christ's ability to help. Instead, "take courage," and trust that he is there for you.

6:53 Gennesaret was a small fertile plain located on the west side of the Sea of Galilee. Capernaum, Jesus' home, sat at the northern edge of this plain.

7:1ff The religious leaders sent some investigators from their headquarters in Jerusalem to check up on Jesus. The delegation didn't like what they found, however, because Jesus scolded them for keeping the law and the traditions in order to look holy instead of to honor God. The prophet Isaiah accused the religious leaders of his day of doing the same thing (Isaiah 29:13). Jesus used Isaiah's words to accuse these men.

7:3, 4 Mark explained these Jewish rituals because he was writing to a non-Jewish audience. Before each meal, devout Jews performed a short ceremony, washing their hands and arms in a specific way. The disciples did not have dirty hands, but they were simply not carrying out this traditional cleansing. The Pharisees thought this ceremony cleansed them from any contact they might have had with anything considered unclean. Jesus said they were wrong in thinking they were acceptable to God just because they were clean on the outside.

7:4 Christians become like Pharisees when they worry that contact with unbelievers may leave them tainted—avoiding "worldly" places where sinners hang out or rejecting books or speakers whose ideas do not conform to theirs. Some Christians and some Pharisees have a lot in common: both would try to stop Jesus from working certain places or talking to certain people. Jesus wants us to go out into the world and make contact. Jesus didn't intend for us to withdraw, purify ourselves, and never reach out.

7:6, 7 Hypocrisy is pretending to be something you are not and have no intention of being. Jesus called the Pharisees hypocrites

7:7
d Isa 29:13

"'These people honor me with their lips,
but their hearts are far from me.
⁷ They worship me in vain;
their teachings are but rules taught by men.'*a d*

⁸You have let go of the commands of God and are holding on to the traditions of men."

7:10
e Ex 20:12; Dt 5:16
f Ex 21:17; Lev 20:9

7:11
g Mt 23:16, 18

⁹And he said to them: "You have a fine way of setting aside the commands of God in order to observe*b* your own traditions! ¹⁰For Moses said, 'Honor your father and your mother,'*c e* and, 'Anyone who curses his father or mother must be put to death.'*d f* ¹¹But you say*g* that if a man says to his father or mother: 'Whatever help you might otherwise have received from me is Corban' (that is, a gift devoted to God), ¹²then you no longer let him do anything for his father or mother. ¹³Thus you nullify the word of God by your tradition that you have handed down. And you do many things like that."

¹⁴Again Jesus called the crowd to him and said, "Listen to me, everyone, and understand this. ¹⁵Nothing outside a man can make him 'unclean' by going into him. Rather, it is what comes out of a man that makes him 'unclean.'*e* "

7:17
h Mk 9:28

7:19
i Ro 14:1-12;
Col 2:16
j Ac 10:15

¹⁷After he had left the crowd and entered the house, his disciples asked him*h* about this parable. ¹⁸"Are you so dull?" he asked. "Don't you see that nothing that enters a man from the outside can make him 'unclean'? ¹⁹For it doesn't go into his heart but into his stomach, and then out of his body." (In saying this, Jesus declared all foods*i* "clean.")*j*

7:22
k Mt 20:15

²⁰He went on: "What comes out of a man is what makes him 'unclean.' ²¹For from within, out of men's hearts, come evil thoughts, sexual immorality, theft, murder, adultery, ²²greed,*k* malice, deceit, lewdness, envy, slander, arrogance and folly. ²³All these evils come from inside and make a man 'unclean.'"

a6,7 Isaiah 29:13   *b9* Some manuscripts *set up*   *c 10* Exodus 20:12; Deut. 5:16   *d 10* Exodus 21:17; Lev. 20:9
e 15 Some early manuscripts *'unclean.'*   *16*If anyone has ears to hear, let him hear.

GOSPEL ACCOUNTS FOUND ONLY IN MARK	Section	Topic	Significance
	4:26–29	Story of the growing seed	We must share the Good News of Jesus with other people, but only God makes it grow in their lives.
	7:31–37	Jesus heals a deaf man who could hardly talk	Jesus cares about our physical as well as spiritual needs.
	8:22–26	Jesus heals the blind man at Bethsaida	Jesus is considerate because he makes sure this man's sight is fully restored.

---

because they worshiped God for the wrong reasons. Their worship was not motivated by love, but by a desire to attain profit, to appear holy, and to increase their status. We become hypocrites when we (1) pay more attention to reputation than to character, (2) carefully follow certain religious practices while allowing our hearts to remain distant from God, and (3) emphasize our virtues but others' sins.

7:8, 9 The Pharisees had added hundreds of their own rules and regulations to God's holy laws, and then they tried to force people to follow these rules. These men claimed to know God's will in every detail of life. There are still religious leaders today who add rules and regulations to God's Word, causing much confusion among believers. It is idolatry to claim that your interpretation of God's Word is as important as God's Word itself. It is especially dangerous to set up unbiblical standards for *others* to follow. Instead, look to Christ for guidance about your own behavior, and let him lead others in the details of their lives.

7:8, 9 Jesus wasn't against all tradition, but he was against those who made their traditions as important, if not more important, than God's Word. Good traditions shine a spotlight on God's Word, move us to obedient service, and help our hearts sing. They explain and reinforce the teachings of God. God's Word should always be the focus, and tradition a means of bringing that Word alive. Celebrate your traditions with the prayer that Christ would be exalted. Change your traditions if they become more important than God's Word.

7:10, 11 The Pharisees used God as an excuse to avoid helping their families. They thought it was more important to put money in the temple treasury than to help their needy parents, although God's law specifically says to honor fathers and mothers (Exodus 20:12) and to care for those in need (Leviticus 25:35–43). (For an explanation of *Corban,* see the note on Matthew 15:5, 6.) We should give money and time to God, but we must never use God as an excuse to neglect our responsibilities. Helping those in need is one of the most important ways to honor God.

7:18, 19 As they interpreted the dietary laws (Leviticus 11), the Jews believed they could be clean before God because of what they refused to eat. Jesus pointed out that sin begins in the attitudes and intentions of the inner person. Jesus did not degrade the law, but he paved the way for the change made clear in Acts 10:9–29 when God removed the cultural restrictions regarding food. While being concerned about what we put into our bodies is a good, healthy practice, very few people are as stringent about what they put into their minds through reading or watching television. Jesus was more concerned about mind-set and thought processes than about food laws. Do you worry about what foods you eat, but put "junk food" in your mind?

7:20–23 An evil action begins with a single thought. Allowing our minds to dwell on lust, envy, hatred, or revenge will lead to sin. Don't defile yourself by focusing on evil. Instead, follow Paul's advice in Philippians 4:8 and think about what is true, noble, right, pure, lovely, and admirable.

2. Jesus' ministry beyond Galilee

Jesus Sends a Demon Out of a Girl (103/Matthew 15:21–28)

24 Jesus left that place and went to the vicinity of Tyre.[a] / He entered a house and did not want anyone to know it; yet he could not keep his presence secret. 25 In fact, as soon as she heard about him, a woman whose little daughter was possessed by an evil[b] spirit came and fell at his feet. 26 The woman was a Greek, born in Syrian Phoenicia. She begged Jesus to drive the demon out of her daughter.

27 "First let the children eat all they want," he told her, "for it is not right to take the children's bread and toss it to their dogs."

28 "Yes, Lord," she replied, "but even the dogs under the table eat the children's crumbs."

29 Then he told her, "For such a reply, you may go; the demon has left your daughter."

30 She went home and found her child lying on the bed, and the demon gone.

7:24
/ Mt 11:21

Jesus Heals Many People (104/Matthew 15:29–31)

31 Then Jesus left the vicinity of Tyre[m] and went through Sidon, down to the Sea of Galilee[n] and into the region of the Decapolis.[c] [o] 32 There some people brought to him a man who was deaf and could hardly talk,[p] and they begged him to place his hand on[q] the man.

33 After he took him aside, away from the crowd, Jesus put his fingers into the man's ears. Then he spit[r] and touched the man's tongue. 34 He looked up to heaven[s] and with a deep sigh[t] said to him, "Ephphatha!" (which means, "Be opened!"). 35 At this, the man's ears were opened, his tongue was loosened and he began to speak plainly.[u]

36 Jesus commanded them not to tell anyone.[v] But the more he did so, the more they kept talking about it. 37 People were overwhelmed with amazement. "He has done everything well," they said. "He even makes the deaf hear and the mute speak."

7:31
m ver 24; Mt 11:21
n Mt 4:18
o Mt 4:25; Mk 5:20
7:32
p Mt 9:32; Lk 11:14
q Mk 5:23
7:33
r Mk 8:23
7:34
s Mk 6:41; Jn 11:41
t Mk 8:12
7:35
u Isa 35:5, 6
7:36
v Mt 8:4

Jesus Feeds Four Thousand (105/Matthew 15:32–39)

8 During those days another large crowd gathered. Since they had nothing to eat, Jesus called his disciples to him and said, 2 "I have compassion for these people;[w] they have already been with me three days and have nothing to eat. 3 If I send them home hungry, they will collapse on the way, because some of them have come a long distance."

8:2
w Mt 9:36

a 24 Many early manuscripts Tyre and Sidon   b 25 Greek unclean   c 31 That is, the Ten Cities

---

7:24 Jesus traveled about 30 miles to Tyre and then went to Sidon. These were port cities on the Mediterranean Sea north of Israel. Both cities had flourishing trade and were very wealthy. They were proud, historic Canaanite cities.

In David's day, Tyre was on friendly terms with Israel (2 Samuel 5:11), but soon afterward the city became known for its wickedness. Its king even claimed to be God (Ezekiel 28:1ff). Tyre rejoiced when Jerusalem was destroyed in 586 B.C., because without Israel's competition, Tyre's trade and profits would increase. It was into this evil and materialistic culture that Jesus brought his

MINISTRY IN PHOENICIA
Jesus' ministry was to all people—first to Jews but also to Gentiles. Jesus took his disciples from Galilee to Tyre and Sidon, large cities in Phoenicia, where he healed a Gentile woman's daughter.

message. It is interesting that Jesus stressed the importance of inner purity just before visiting Tyre.

7:26 This woman is called a Greek, born in Syrian Phoenicia, in Mark and a Canaanite in Matthew. Mark's designation refers to her political background. His Roman audience would easily identify her by the part of the empire that was her home. Matthew's description was designed for his Jewish audience, who remembered the Canaanites as bitter enemies when Israel was settling the promised land.

7:27, 28 On the surface, Jesus' words may seem harsh and unsympathetic, but the woman recognized them as a wide-open door to God's throne. Jesus did not use the negative term for dogs that referred to scavengers (the word sometimes used by Jews to refer to Gentiles); instead, he used the term for a household pet. The woman did not try to argue. Using Jesus' choice of imagery, she pointed out that she was willing to be considered an interruption as long as she could receive God's healing for her daughter. Ironically, many Jews would lose God's spiritual healing because they rejected Jesus, while many Gentiles, whom the Jews rejected, would find salvation because they recognized Jesus.

7:29 This miracle shows that Jesus' power over demons is so great that he doesn't need to be present physically in order to free someone. His power transcends any distance.

7:36 Jesus asked the people not to talk about this healing, because he didn't want to be seen simply as a miracle worker. He didn't want the people to miss his real message. We must not be so concerned about what Jesus can do for us that we forget to listen to his message.

8:1ff This is a different miracle from the feeding of the 5,000 described in chapter 6. At that time, those fed were mostly Jews. This time Jesus was ministering to a non-Jewish crowd in the Gentile region of the Decapolis. Jesus' actions and message were

4 His disciples answered, "But where in this remote place can anyone get enough bread to feed them?"

5 "How many loaves do you have?" Jesus asked.

"Seven," they replied.

6 He told the crowd to sit down on the ground. When he had taken the seven loaves and given thanks, he broke them and gave them to his disciples to set before the people, and they did so. 7 They had a few small fish as well; he gave thanks for them also and told the disciples to distribute them. *x* 8 The people ate and were satisfied. Afterward the disciples picked up seven basketfuls of broken pieces that were left over. *y* 9 About four thousand men were present. And having sent them away, 10 he got into the boat with his disciples and went to the region of Dalmanutha.

Leaders Demand a Miraculous Sign (106/Matthew 16:1–4)

11 The Pharisees came and began to question Jesus. To test him, they asked him for a sign from heaven. *z* 12 He sighed deeply *a* and said, "Why does this generation ask for a miraculous sign? I tell you the truth, no sign will be given to it." 13 Then he left them, got back into the boat and crossed to the other side.

Jesus Warns against Wrong Teaching (107/Matthew 16:5–12)

14 The disciples had forgotten to bring bread, except for one loaf they had with them in the boat. 15 "Be careful," Jesus warned them. "Watch out for the yeast of the Pharisees *b* and that of Herod." *c*

16 They discussed this with one another and said, "It is because we have no bread."

17 Aware of their discussion, Jesus asked them: "Why are you talking about having no bread? Do you still not see or understand? Are your hearts hardened? *d* 18 Do you have eyes but fail to see, and ears but fail to hear? And don't you remember? 19 When I broke the five loaves for the five thousand, how many basketfuls of pieces did you pick up?"

"Twelve," *e* they replied.

20 "And when I broke the seven loaves for the four thousand, how many basketfuls of pieces did you pick up?"

They answered, "Seven." *f*

21 He said to them, "Do you still not understand?" *g*

8:7
x Mt 14:19
8:8
y ver 20

8:11
z Mt 12:38
8:12
a Mk 7:34

8:15
b Lk 12:1
c Mt 14:1; Mk 12:13

8:17
d Mk 6:52

8:19
e Mt 14:20; Mk 6:41-44; Lk 9:17; Jn 6:13
8:20
f ver 6-9; Mt 15:37
8:21
g Mk 6:52

---

beginning to have an impact on large numbers of Gentiles. That Jesus would compassionately minister to non-Jews was very reassuring to Mark's primarily Roman audience.

8:1–3 Do you ever feel that God is so busy with important concerns that he can't possibly be aware of your needs? Just as Jesus was concerned about these people's need for food, he is concerned about our daily needs. At another time Jesus said, "So do not worry, saying, 'What shall we eat?' or 'What shall we drink?' or 'What shall we wear?' . . . your heavenly Father knows that you need them" (Matthew 6:31, 32). Do you have concerns that you think would not interest God? There is nothing too large for him to handle and no need too small to escape his interest.

8:11 The Pharisees had tried to explain away Jesus' previous miracles by claiming they were done by luck, coincidence, or evil power. Here they demanded a sign from heaven—something only God could do. Jesus refused their demand because he knew that even this kind of miracle would not convince them. They had already decided not to believe. Hearts can become so hard that even the most convincing facts and demonstrations will not change them.

8:15 Mark mentions the yeast of the Pharisees and Herod, while Matthew talks about the yeast of the Pharisees and Sadducees. Mark's audience, mostly non-Jews, would have known about Herod, but not necessarily about the Jewish religious sect of the Sadducees. Thus Mark quoted the part of Jesus' statement that his readers would understand. This reference to Herod may mean the Herodians, a group of Jews who supported the king. Many Herodians were also Sadducees. Yeast in this passage symbolizes evil. Just as only a small amount of yeast is needed to make a batch of bread rise, so the hardheartedness of the religious and political leaders could permeate and contaminate the entire society and make it rise up against Jesus.

8:17, 18 Jesus rebuked the disciples for their hard hearts. Today the Hardhearts believe: (1) that poverty is always caused by laziness; helping the poor only enables them; (2) that worship is best conducted in one way—our way—which has worked very well for forty years, thank you, and need not be changed; (3) that evangelism doesn't apply; people will never change anyway, so we don't need to do it. Joining the Hardhearts requires only one pledge: You must refuse to listen to Jesus' questions. Don't be a Hardheart. Be open to Christ's truth. Let him soften your heart.

CONTINUED MINISTRY
After taking a roundabout way back to Galilee through Decapolis (the Ten Cities), Jesus returned to Dalmanutha where Jewish leaders questioned his authority. From there he went to Bethsaida and on to Caesarea Philippi. Here he talked with his disciples about his authority and coming events.

Jesus Restores Sight to a Blind Man (108)

22 They came to Bethsaida,^h and some people brought a blind man and begged Jesus to touch him. 23 He took the blind man by the hand and led him outside the village. When he had spitⁱ on the man's eyes and put his hands on^j him, Jesus asked, "Do you see anything?"

24 He looked up and said, "I see people; they look like trees walking around."

25 Once more Jesus put his hands on the man's eyes. Then his eyes were opened, his sight was restored, and he saw everything clearly. 26 Jesus sent him home, saying, "Don't go into the village.^a"

8:22
h Mt 11:21

8:23
i Mk 7:33
j Mk 5:23

Peter Says Jesus Is the Messiah (109/Matthew 16:13–20; Luke 9:18–20)

27 Jesus and his disciples went on to the villages around Caesarea Philippi. On the way he asked them, "Who do people say I am?"

28 They replied, "Some say John the Baptist; others say Elijah; and still others, one of the prophets."

29 "But what about you?" he asked. "Who do you say I am?"

Peter answered, "You are the Christ.^b"^k

30 Jesus warned them not to tell anyone about him.

8:29
k Jn 6:69; 11:27

Jesus Predicts His Death the First Time (110/Matthew 16:21–28; Luke 9:21–27)

31 He then began to teach them that the Son of Man must suffer many things^l and be rejected by the elders, chief priests and teachers of the law, and that he must be killed and after three days rise again. 32 He spoke plainly^m about this, and Peter took him aside and began to rebuke him.

33 But when Jesus turned and looked at his disciples, he rebuked Peter. "Get behind me, Satan!"ⁿ he said. "You do not have in mind the things of God, but the things of men."

34 Then he called the crowd to him along with his disciples and said: "If anyone would

8:31
l Mt 16:21

8:32
m Jn 18:20

8:33
n Mt 4:10

a26 Some manuscripts Don't go and tell anyone in the village   b29 Or Messiah. "The Christ" (Greek) and "the Messiah" (Hebrew) both mean "the Anointed One."

8:25 Why did Jesus touch the man a second time before he could see? This miracle was not too difficult for Jesus, but he chose to do it in stages, possibly to show the disciples that some healing would be gradual rather than instantaneous or to demonstrate that spiritual truth is not always perceived clearly at first. Before Jesus left, however, the man was healed completely.

8:27 Caesarea Philippi was an especially pagan city known for its worship of Greek gods and its temples devoted to the ancient god Pan. The ruler Philip, referred to in 6:17, changed the city's name from Caesarea to Caesarea Philippi so that it would not be confused with the coastal city of Caesarea (Acts 8:40), the capital of the territory ruled by his brother Herod Antipas. This pagan city where many gods were recognized was a fitting place for Jesus to ask the disciples to recognize him as the Son of God.

8:28 For the story of John the Baptist, see Mark 1:1–11 and 6:14–29. For the story of Elijah, see 1 Kings 17—20 and 2 Kings 1—2.

8:29 Jesus asked the disciples who other people thought he was; then he asked them the same question. It is not enough to know what others say about Jesus: you must know, understand, and accept for yourself that he is the Messiah. You must move from curiosity to commitment, from admiration to adoration.

8:29–31 The name for Jesus, *Son of Man*, is Jesus' most common title for himself. It comes from Daniel 7:13, where the Son of Man is a heavenly figure who, in the end times, has authority and power. The name refers to Jesus as the Messiah, the representative man, the human agent of God who is vindicated by God. In this passage, *Son of Man* is linked closely with Peter's confession of Jesus as the Christ and confirms its Messianic significance.

From this point on, Jesus spoke plainly and directly to his disciples about his death and resurrection. He began to prepare them for what was going to happen to him by telling them three times that he would soon die (8:31; 9:31; 10:33, 34).

8:30 Why did Jesus warn his own disciples not to tell anyone

the truth about him? Jesus knew they needed more instruction about the work he would accomplish through his death and resurrection. Without more teaching, the disciples would have only half the picture. When they confessed Jesus as the Christ, they still didn't know all that it meant.

8:32, 33 In this moment, Peter was not considering God's purposes, but only his own natural human desires and feelings. Peter wanted Christ to be king, but not the suffering servant prophesied in Isaiah 53. He was ready to receive the glory of following the Messiah, but not the persecution.

The Christian life is not a paved road to wealth and ease. It often involves hard work, persecution, deprivation, and deep suffering. Peter saw only part of the picture. Don't repeat his mistake. Instead, focus on the good that God can bring out of apparent evil, and the resurrection that follows crucifixion.

8:33 Peter was often the spokesman for all the disciples. In singling him out, Jesus may have been addressing all of them indirectly. Unknowingly, the disciples were trying to prevent Jesus from going to the cross and thus fulfilling his mission on earth. Satan also tempted Jesus to avoid the way of the cross (Matthew 4). Whereas Satan's motives were evil, the disciples were motivated by love and admiration for Jesus. Nevertheless, the disciples' job was not to guide and protect Jesus, but to follow him. Only after Jesus' death and resurrection would they fully understand why he had to die.

8:34 The Romans, Mark's original audience, knew what taking up the cross meant. Death on a cross was a form of execution used by Rome for dangerous criminals. A prisoner carried his own cross to the place of execution, signifying submission to Rome's control.

Jesus used the image of carrying a cross to illustrate the ultimate submission required of his followers. He is not against pleasure, nor is he saying that we should seek pain needlessly. Jesus was talking about the heroic effort needed to follow him moment by moment, to do his will even when the work is difficult and the future looks bleak.

8:34
*o*Mt 10:38; Lk 14:27

8:35
*p*Jn 12:25

8:38
*q*Mt 8:20
*r*Mt 10:33; Lk 12:9

9:1
*s*Mt 24:30

9:3
*t*Mt 28:3

9:5
*u*Mt 23:7

9:9
*v*Mk 8:30

come after me, he must deny himself and take up his cross and follow me. *o* 35 For whoever wants to save his life *a* will lose it, but whoever loses his life for me and for the gospel will save it. *p* 36 What good is it for a man to gain the whole world, yet forfeit his soul? 37 Or what can a man give in exchange for his soul? 38 If anyone is ashamed of me and my words in this adulterous and sinful generation, the Son of Man *q* will be ashamed of him *r* when he comes in his Father's glory with the holy angels."

9 And he said to them, "I tell you the truth, some who are standing here will not taste death before they see the kingdom of God come with power." *s*

Jesus is Transfigured on the Mountain (111/Matthew 17:1–13; Luke 9:28–36)

2 After six days Jesus took Peter, James and John with him and led them up a high mountain, where they were all alone. There he was transfigured before them. 3 His clothes became dazzling white, *t* whiter than anyone in the world could bleach them. 4 And there appeared before them Elijah and Moses, who were talking with Jesus.

5 Peter said to Jesus, "Rabbi, *u* it is good for us to be here. Let us put up three shelters—one for you, one for Moses and one for Elijah." 6 (He did not know what to say, they were so frightened.)

7 Then a cloud appeared and enveloped them, and a voice came from the cloud: "This is my Son, whom I love. Listen to him!"

8 Suddenly, when they looked around, they no longer saw anyone with them except Jesus.

9 As they were coming down the mountain, Jesus gave them orders not to tell anyone *v* what they had seen until the Son of Man had risen from the dead. 10 They kept the matter to themselves, discussing what "rising from the dead" meant.

11 And they asked him, "Why do the teachers of the law say that Elijah must come first?"

a 35 The Greek word means either *life* or *soul*; also in verse 36.

8:35 We should be willing to lose our lives for the sake of the gospel, not because our lives are useless but because nothing—not even life itself—can compare to what we gain with Christ. Jesus wants us to *choose* to follow him rather than to lead a life of sin and self-satisfaction. He wants us to stop trying to control our own destiny and to let him direct us. This makes good sense because, as the Creator, Christ knows better than we do what real life is about. He asks for submission, not self-hatred; he asks us only to lose our self-centered determination to be in charge.

8:36, 37 Many people spend all their energy seeking pleasure. Jesus said, however, that a world of pleasure centered on possessions, position, or power is ultimately worthless. Whatever you have on earth is only temporary; it cannot be exchanged for your soul. If you work hard at getting what you want, you might eventually have a "pleasurable" life, but in the end you will find it hollow and empty. Are you willing to make the pursuit of God more important than the selfish pursuit of pleasure? Follow Jesus, and you will know what it means to live abundantly now and to have eternal life as well.

8:38 Jesus constantly turns the world's perspective upside down with talk of first and last, saving and losing. Here he gives us a choice. We can reject Jesus now and be rejected by him at his second coming, or we can accept him now and be accepted by him then. Rejecting Christ may help us escape shame for the time being, but it will guarantee an eternity of shame later.

9:1 What did Jesus mean when he said that some of the disciples would see the kingdom of God come with power? There are several possibilities. He could have been foretelling his transfiguration, resurrection and ascension, the coming of the Holy Spirit at Pentecost, or his second coming. The transfiguration is a strong possibility because Mark immediately tells that story. In the transfiguration (9:2–8), Peter, James and John saw Jesus' glory, identity, and power as the Son of God (2 Peter 1:16).

9:2 We don't know why Jesus singled out Peter, James, and John for this special revelation of his glory and purity. Perhaps they were the ones most ready to understand and accept this

great truth. These three disciples were the inner circle of the group of 12. They were among the first to hear Jesus' call (1:16–19). They headed the Gospel lists of disciples (3:16). And they were present at certain healings where others were excluded (Luke 8:51).

9:2 Jesus took the disciples to either Mount Hermon or Mount Tabor. A mountain was often associated with closeness to God and readiness to receive his words. God had appeared to both Moses (Exodus 24:12–18) and Elijah (1 Kings 19:8–18) on mountains.

9:3ff The transfiguration revealed Christ's divine nature. God's voice exalted Jesus above Moses and Elijah as the long-awaited Messiah with full divine authority. Moses represented the law, and Elijah, the prophets. Their appearance showed Jesus as the fulfillment of both the Old Testament law and the prophetic promises.

Jesus was not a reincarnation of Elijah or Moses. He was not merely one of the prophets. As God's only Son, he far surpasses them in authority and power. Many voices try to tell us how to live and how to know God personally. Some of these are helpful; many are not. We must first listen to the Bible, and then evaluate all other authorities in light of God's revelation.

9:9, 10 Jesus told Peter, James, and John not to speak about what they had seen because they would not fully understand it until Jesus had risen from the dead. Then they would realize that only through dying could Jesus show his power over death and his authority to be King of all. The disciples could not be powerful witnesses for God until they had grasped this truth.

It was natural for the disciples to be confused about Jesus' death and resurrection because they could not see into the future. We, on the other hand, have God's revealed Word, the Bible, to give us the full meaning of Jesus' death and resurrection. We have no excuse for our unbelief.

9:11–13 When Jesus said that Elijah had indeed come, he was speaking of John the Baptist (Matthew 17:11–13), who had fulfilled the role prophesied for Elijah.

12Jesus replied, "To be sure, Elijah does come first, and restores all things. Why then is it written that the Son of Man must suffer much[w] and be rejected?[x] 13But I tell you, Elijah has come,[y] and they have done to him everything they wished, just as it is written about him."

9:12
wMt 16:21
xLk 23:11
9:13
yMt 11:14

Jesus Heals a Demon–Possessed Boy (112/Matthew 17:14–21; Luke 9:37–43)

14When they came to the other disciples, they saw a large crowd around them and the teachers of the law arguing with them. 15As soon as all the people saw Jesus, they were overwhelmed with wonder and ran to greet him.

16"What are you arguing with them about?" he asked.

17A man in the crowd answered, "Teacher, I brought you my son, who is possessed by a spirit that has robbed him of speech. 18Whenever it seizes him, it throws him to the ground. He foams at the mouth, gnashes his teeth and becomes rigid. I asked your disciples to drive out the spirit, but they could not."

19"O unbelieving generation," Jesus replied, "how long shall I stay with you? How long shall I put up with you? Bring the boy to me."

20So they brought him. When the spirit saw Jesus, it immediately threw the boy into a convulsion. He fell to the ground and rolled around, foaming at the mouth.[z]

9:20
zMk 1:26

21Jesus asked the boy's father, "How long has he been like this?"

"From childhood," he answered. 22"It has often thrown him into fire or water to kill him. But if you can do anything, take pity on us and help us."

23"'If you can'?" said Jesus. "Everything is possible for him who believes."[a]

9:23
aMk 11:23;
Jn 11:40

24Immediately the boy's father exclaimed, "I do believe; help me overcome my unbelief!"

25When Jesus saw that a crowd was running to the scene,[b] he rebuked the evil[a] spirit. "You deaf and mute spirit," he said, "I command you, come out of him and never enter him again."

9:25
bver 15

26The spirit shrieked, convulsed him violently and came out. The boy looked so much like a corpse that many said, "He's dead." 27But Jesus took him by the hand and lifted him to his feet, and he stood up.

28After Jesus had gone indoors, his disciples asked him privately,[c] "Why couldn't we drive it out?"

9:28
cMk 7:17

29He replied, "This kind can come out only by prayer.[b]"

Jesus Predicts His Death the Second Time (113/Matthew 17:22–23; Luke 9:44–45)

30They left that place and passed through Galilee. Jesus did not want anyone to know where they were, 31because he was teaching his disciples. He said to them, "The Son of Man is going to be betrayed into the hands of men. They will kill him,[d] and after three days[e] he will rise." 32But they did not understand what he meant[f] and were afraid to ask him about it.

9:31
dver 12
eMt 16:21
9:32
fLk 2:50; 9:45;
18:34; Jn 12:16

a25 Greek unclean   b29 Some manuscripts prayer and fasting

9:12, 13 It was difficult for the disciples to grasp the idea that their Messiah would have to suffer. The Jews who studied the Old Testament prophecies expected the Messiah to be a great king like David, who would overthrow the enemy, Rome. Their vision was limited to their own time and experience. They did not understand that the values of God's eternal kingdom were different from the values of the world. They wanted relief from their present problems, but deliverance from sin is far more important than deliverance from physical suffering or political oppression. Our understanding of and appreciation for Jesus must go beyond what he can do for us here and now.

9:18 As the three disciples came down from the mountain with Jesus, they passed from a reassuring experience of God's presence to a frightening experience of evil. The beauty they had just seen must have made the ugliness seem even uglier. As our spiritual vision improves and allows us to see and understand God better, we will also be able to see and understand evil better. We would be overcome by its horror if we did not have Jesus with us to take us through it safely. Don't be afraid to confront evil and suffering, no matter how ugly or horrible. Jesus goes with you.

9:18 Why couldn't the disciples drive out the evil spirit? In 6:13 we read that they drove out demons while on their mission to the villages. Perhaps they had special authority only for that trip, or perhaps their faith was faltering. Mark tells this story to show that the battle with Satan is a difficult, ongoing struggle. Victory over sin and temptation comes through faith in Jesus Christ, not through our own efforts.

9:23 Jesus' words do not mean that we can automatically obtain anything we want if we just think positively. Jesus meant that anything is *possible* if we believe, because nothing is too difficult for God. We cannot have everything we pray for as if by magic; but with faith, we can have everything we need to serve him.

9:24 The attitude of trust and confidence that the Bible calls *belief* or *faith* (Hebrews 11:1, 6) is not something we can obtain without help. Faith is a gift from God (Ephesians 2:8, 9). No matter how much faith we have, we never reach the point of being self-sufficient. Faith is not stored away like money in the bank. Growing in faith is a constant process of daily renewing our trust in Jesus.

9:29 The disciples would often face difficult situations that could be resolved only through prayer. Prayer is the key that unlocks faith in our lives. Effective prayer needs both the attitude of complete dependence and the action of asking. Prayer demonstrates our reliance on God as we humbly invite him to fill us with faith and power. There is no substitute for prayer, especially in circumstances that seem impossible.

9:30, 31 Leaving Caesarea Philippi, Jesus began his last tour through the region of Galilee.

The Disciples Argue about Who Would Be the Greatest
(115/Matthew 18:1–6; Luke 9:46–48)

9:34
g Lk 22:24

33 They came to Capernaum. When he was in the house, he asked them, "What were you arguing about on the road?" 34 But they kept quiet because on the way they had argued about who was the greatest. *g*

9:35
h Mt 20:26;
Mk 10:43; Lk 22:26

35 Sitting down, Jesus called the Twelve and said, "If anyone wants to be first, he must be the very last, and the servant of all." *h*

9:36
i Mk 10:16

9:37
j Mt 10:40

36 He took a little child and had him stand among them. Taking him in his arms, *i* he said to them, 37 "Whoever welcomes one of these little children in my name welcomes me; and whoever welcomes me does not welcome me but the one who sent me." *j*

The Disciples Forbid Another to Use Jesus' Name (116/Luke 9:49–50)

9:38
k Nu 11:27-29

38 "Teacher," said John, "we saw a man driving out demons in your name and we told him to stop, because he was not one of us." *k*

9:40
l Mt 12:30

9:41
m Mt 10:42

39 "Do not stop him," Jesus said. "No one who does a miracle in my name can in the next moment say anything bad about me, 40 for whoever is not against us is for us. *l* 41 I tell you the truth, anyone who gives you a cup of water in my name because you belong to Christ will certainly not lose his reward. *m*

Jesus Warns against Temptation (117/Matthew 18:7–9)

9:42
n Lk 17:2

9:43
o Mt 5:29
p Mt 5:30

9:47
q Mt 5:29

9:48
r Isa 66:24

42 "And if anyone causes one of these little ones who believe in me to sin, it would be better for him to be thrown into the sea with a large millstone tied around his neck. *n* 43 If your hand causes you to sin, *o* cut it off. It is better for you to enter life maimed than with two hands to go into hell, *p* where the fire never goes out. *a* 45 And if your foot causes you to sin, cut it off. It is better for you to enter life crippled than to have two feet and be thrown into hell. *b* 47 And if your eye causes you to sin, *q* pluck it out. It is better for you to enter the kingdom of God with one eye than to have two eyes and be thrown into hell, 48 where

"'their worm does not die,
and the fire is not quenched.' *c r*

a 43 Some manuscripts *out, 44 where / "'their worm does not die, / and the fire is not quenched.'* *b* 45 Some manuscripts *hell, 46 where / "'their worm does not die, / and the fire is not quenched.'* *c* 48 Isaiah 66:24

9:34 The disciples, caught up in their constant struggle for personal success, were embarrassed to answer Jesus' question. It is always painful to compare our motives with Christ's. It is not wrong for believers to be industrious or ambitious, but when ambition pushes aside obedience and service, it becomes sin. We are all like the disciples and even like the Pharisees in this regard. Pride or insecurity can cause us to overvalue position and prestige. In God's kingdom, such motives are destructive. The only safe ambition is directed toward Christ's kingdom, not our own advancement. We must renounce pride and status seeking. They are Satan's tools, not Christ's.

9:35 Serving others is real leadership. Jesus described leadership from a new perspective. Instead of *using* people, we are to *serve* them. Jesus' mission was to serve others and to give his life away. A real leader has a servant's heart. Servant leaders appreciate others' worth and realize that they're not above any job. If you see something that needs to be done, don't wait to be asked; take the initiative and do it like a faithful servant. Don't approach life expecting high positions, honors, and special privileges. Look instead for ways to help others.

9:36, 37 Jesus taught the disciples to welcome children. This was a new approach in a society where children were usually treated as second-class citizens. It is important not only to treat children well, but also to teach them about Jesus. Children's ministries should never be regarded as less important than those for adults.

9:38-40 Jesus was not saying that being indifferent or neutral toward him is as good as being committed. As he explained in Matthew 12:30, "He who is not with me is against me." In both cases, Jesus was pointing out that neutrality toward him is not possible. Nevertheless, his followers will not all resemble each

other or belong to the same groups. People who are on Jesus' side have the same goal of building up the kingdom of God, and they should not let their differences interfere with this goal. Those who share a common faith in Christ should cooperate. People don't have to be just like us to be following Jesus with us.

9:41, 42 Luke 9:48 states, "He who is least among you all—he is the greatest." In Jesus' eyes, whoever welcomes a child welcomes Jesus; giving a cup of cold water to a person in need is the same as giving an offering to God. By contrast, harming others or failing to care for them is a sin, even if they are unimportant people in the world's eyes. It is possible for thoughtless, selfish people to gain a measure of worldly greatness, but lasting greatness is measured by God's standards. What do you use as your measure—personal achievement or unselfish service?

9:42 This caution against harming little ones in the faith applies both to what we do individually as teachers and examples and to what we allow to fester in our Christian fellowship. Our thoughts and actions must be motivated by love (1 Corinthians 13), and we must be careful about judging others (Matthew 7:1–5; Romans 14:1—15:4). However, we also have a responsibility to confront flagrant sin within the church (1 Corinthians 5:12, 13).

9:43ff This startling language is not meant to promote self-mutilation, but instead stresses the importance of cutting sin out of our lives. Painful discipline is required of his true followers. Giving up a relationship, job, or habit that is against God's will may seem just as painful as cutting off a hand, but Christ is worth any possible loss or discomfort. Nothing should stand in the way of faith. We must be ruthless in removing sins from our lives now in order to avoid being stuck with them for eternity. Make your choices from an eternal perspective.

49 Everyone will be salted s with fire.

50 "Salt is good, but if it loses its saltiness, how can you make it salty again? t Have salt in yourselves, u and be at peace with each other." v

Jesus Teaches about Marriage and Divorce (173/Matthew 19:1–12)

10 Jesus then left that place and went into the region of Judea and across the Jordan. w Again crowds of people came to him, and as was his custom, he taught them.

2 Some Pharisees came and tested him by asking, "Is it lawful for a man to divorce his wife?"

3 "What did Moses command you?" he replied.

4 They said, "Moses permitted a man to write a certificate of divorce and send her away." x

5 "It was because your hearts were hard that Moses wrote you this law," Jesus replied. 6 "But at the beginning of creation God 'made them male and female.' a y 7 'For this reason a man will leave his father and mother and be united to his wife, b 8 and the two will become one flesh.' c z So they are no longer two, but one. 9 Therefore what God has joined together, let man not separate."

10 When they were in the house again, the disciples asked Jesus about this. 11 He answered, "Anyone who divorces his wife and marries another woman commits adultery against her. a 12 And if she divorces her husband and marries another man, she commits adultery."

Jesus Blesses the Children (174/Matthew 19:13–15; Luke 18:15–17)

13 People were bringing little children to Jesus to have him touch them, but the disciples rebuked them. 14 When Jesus saw this, he was indignant. He said to them, "Let the little children

a 6 Gen. 1:27   b 7 Some early manuscripts do not have *and be united to his wife*.   c 8 Gen. 2:24

9:49 s Lev 2:13
9:50 t Mt 5:13; Lk 14:34, 35   u Col 4:6   v Ro 12:18; 2Co 13:11
10:1 w Jn 10:40
10:4 x Dt 24:1-4
10:6 y Ge 1:27; 5:2
10:8 z Ge 2:24
10:11 a Mt 5:32; Lk 16:18

9:50 Jesus used salt to illustrate three qualities that should be found in his people: (1) *We should remember God's faithfulness*, just as salt when used with a sacrifice recalled God's covenant with his people (Leviticus 2:13). (2) *We should make a difference in the "flavor" of the world we live in*, just as salt changes meat's flavor (see Matthew 5:13). (3) *We should counteract the moral decay in society*, just as salt preserves food from decay. When we lose this desire to "salt" the earth with the love and message of God, we become useless to him.

10:2 The Pharisees were trying to trap Jesus with their question. If he supported divorce, he would be upholding the Pharisees' procedures, and they doubted that he would do that. If Jesus spoke against divorce, however, some members of the crowd would dislike his position—some may have used the law to their advantage to divorce their wives. More important, he might incur the wrath of Herod, who had already killed John the Baptist for speaking out against divorce and adultery (6:17–28). This is what the Pharisees wanted.

The Pharisees saw divorce as a legal issue rather than a spiritual one. Jesus used this test as an opportunity to review God's intended purpose for marriage and to expose the Pharisees' selfish motives. They were not thinking about what God intended for marriage and were quoting Moses unfairly and out of context. Jesus showed these legal experts how superficial their knowledge really was.

10:5–9 God allowed divorce as a concession to people's sinfulness. Unfortunately, the Pharisees used Deuteronomy 24:1 as a proof text for the sanctioning of divorce. Jesus explained that divorce was not God's ideal; instead, God wants married people to consider their marriage permanent. Don't enter marriage with the option of getting out. Your marriage is more likely to be happy if from the outset you are committed to permanence. Don't be hard-hearted like these Pharisees, but be hardheaded in your determination, with God's help, to stay together.

That said, we know that in our world, divorce is sometimes necessary (for physical survival, for well-being of children, etc.). Jesus clearly gave God's ideal for marriage in Genesis priority over Moses' permission for divorce. Jesus did not cancel Moses' teaching, however. For possible exceptions, see Matthew 5:32 and 19:9, where Jesus permitted divorce when the spouse had been unfaithful; and 1 Corinthians 7:15, where Paul recognized divorce when the unbelieving partner leaves the marriage. Divorce is wrong; it severs a holy union. But divorce is permitted. Jesus did not elaborate on the permissible reasons, but his high view of marriage surely requires that divorce be a last resort to avoid greater disaster.

10:6–9 Women were often treated as property. Marriage and divorce were regarded as transactions similar to buying and selling land. But Jesus condemned this attitude, clarifying God's original intention—that marriage bring oneness (Genesis 2:24). Jesus held up God's ideal for marriage and told his followers to live by that ideal.

10:13–16 Jesus was often criticized for spending too much time with the wrong people—children, tax collectors, and sinners (Matthew 9:11; Luke 15:1, 2; 19:7). Some, including the disciples, thought Jesus should be spending more time with important leaders and the devout because this was the way to improve his position and avoid criticism. But Jesus didn't need to improve his position. He was God, and he wanted to speak to those who needed him most.

10:14 Adults are not as trusting as little children. To feel secure, all children need is a loving look and gentle touch from someone who cares. Complete intellectual understanding is not one of their requirements. They believe us if they trust us. Jesus said that

FINAL TRIP TO JUDEA
Jesus quietly left Capernaum, heading toward the borders of Judea before crossing the Jordan River. He preached there before going to Jericho. This trip from Galilee was his last; he would not return before his death.

Mediterranean Sea

GALILEE

Capernaum

Sea of Galilee

N

Jordan River

SAMARIA

Jerusalem

Jericho

Dead Sea

JUDEA

0   20 Mi.

0   20 Km.

10:15
b Mt 18:3

come to me, and do not hinder them, for the kingdom of God belongs to such as these. 15 I tell you the truth, anyone who will not receive the kingdom of God like a little child will never enter it." b 16 And he took the children in his arms, put his hands on them and blessed them.

Jesus Speaks to the Rich Young Man (175/Matthew 19:16–30; Luke 18:18–30)

10:17
c Mk 1:40
d Lk 10:25

17 As Jesus started on his way, a man ran up to him and fell on his knees c before him. "Good teacher," he asked, "what must I do to inherit eternal life?" d

10:19
e Ex 20:12-16

18 "Why do you call me good?" Jesus answered. "No one is good—except God alone. 19 You know the commandments: 'Do not murder, do not commit adultery, do not steal, do not give false testimony, do not defraud, honor your father and mother.' a " e

20 "Teacher," he declared, "all these I have kept since I was a boy."

10:21
f Mt 6:20; Lk 12:33

21 Jesus looked at him and loved him. "One thing you lack," he said. "Go, sell everything you have and give to the poor, and you will have treasure in heaven. f Then come, follow me."

22 At this the man's face fell. He went away sad, because he had great wealth.

23 Jesus looked around and said to his disciples, "How hard it is for the rich to enter the kingdom of God!"

24 The disciples were amazed at his words. But Jesus said again, "Children, how hard it is b to enter the kingdom of God! 25 It is easier for a camel to go through the eye of a needle than for a rich man to enter the kingdom of God."

26 The disciples were even more amazed, and said to each other, "Who then can be saved?"

10:27
g Mt 19:26

27 Jesus looked at them and said, "With man this is impossible, but not with God; all things are possible with God." g

28 Peter said to him, "We have left everything to follow you!"

29 "I tell you the truth," Jesus replied, "no one who has left home or brothers or sisters or

a 19 Exodus 20:12-16; Deut. 5:16-20   b 24 Some manuscripts *is for those who trust in riches*

---

people should believe in him with this kind of childlike faith. We should not have to understand all the mysteries of the universe; it should be enough to know that God loves us and provides forgiveness for our sin.

10:15 How can you "receive the kingdom of God like a little child"? Adults considering the Christian faith for the first time will have life experiences that take them way past the ability to be as innocent as children. Jesus does not ask us to put aside our experiences, but he does require a change of attitude: adult self-sufficiency must recognize its need for the sovereign God; adult moral defensiveness must humble itself before the holy God; and adult skeptical toughness must soften before the loving God. Children do not feel supremely powerful, perfectly righteous, or totally autonomous. These are adult fantasies. Coming to Jesus means to accept his goodness on your behalf, confess your need, and commit your life to his tender guidance.

10:17-23 This young man wanted to be sure he would get eternal life, so he asked what he could *do*. He said he'd never once broken any of the laws Jesus mentioned (10:19), and perhaps he had even kept the Pharisees' additional regulations as well. But Jesus lovingly broke through the young man's pride with a challenge that brought out his true motives: "Go, sell everything you have and give to the poor." This challenge exposed the barrier that could keep this young man out of the kingdom: his love of money. Money represented his pride of accomplishment and self-effort. Ironically, his attitude made him unable to keep the first commandment, to let nothing be more important than God (Exodus 20:3). He could not meet the one requirement Jesus gave—to turn his whole heart and life over to God. The man came to Jesus wondering what he could do; he left seeing what he was unable to do. What barriers are keeping you from turning your life over to Christ?

10:18 When Jesus asked this question, he was saying, "Do you really know the One to whom you are talking?" Because only God is truly good, the man was calling Jesus "God," whether or not he realized it.

10:21 What does your money mean to you? Although Jesus wanted this man to sell everything and give his money to the poor, this does not mean that all believers should sell all their possessions. Most of his followers did not sell everything, although they used their possessions to serve others. Instead, this story shows us that we must not let anything we have or desire keep us from following Jesus. We must remove all barriers to serving him fully. If Jesus asked, could you give up your house? your car? your level of income? your position on the ladder of promotion? Your reaction may show your attitude toward money—whether it is your servant or your master.

10:21 Jesus showed genuine love for this man, even though he knew that the man might not follow him. Love is able to give tough advice; it doesn't hedge around the truth. Christ loved us enough to die for us, and he also loves us enough to talk straight to us. If his love were superficial, he would give us only his approval; but because his love is complete, he gives us life-changing challenges.

10:23 Jesus said it was very difficult for the rich to enter the kingdom of God. This is true because the rich, with most of their basic physical needs met, often become self-reliant. When they feel empty, they can buy something new to dull the pain that was meant to drive them toward God. Their abundance and self-sufficiency become their deficiency. The person who has everything on earth can still lack what is most important—eternal life.

10:26 The disciples were amazed. Was not wealth a blessing from God, a reward for being good? This misconception is still common today. Although many believers enjoy material prosperity, many others live in hardship. Wealth is not a sign of faith or of partiality on God's part.

10:29, 30 Jesus assured the disciples that anyone who gives up something valuable for his sake will be repaid a hundred times over in this life, although not necessarily in the same form. For example, someone may be rejected by his family for accepting Christ, but he or she will gain the larger family of believers. Along with these rewards, however, we experience persecution because the world hates God. Jesus emphasized persecution to make sure that people do not selfishly follow him only for the rewards.

mother or father or children or fields for me and the gospel [30]will fail to receive a hundred times as much[h] in this present age (homes, brothers, sisters, mothers, children and fields— and with them, persecutions) and in the age to come, eternal life. [31]But many who are first will be last, and the last first."[i]

10:30
[h]Mt 6:33

10:31
[i]Mt 19:30

Jesus Predicts His Death the Third Time (177/Matthew 20:17–19; Luke 18:31–34)

[32]They were on their way up to Jerusalem, with Jesus leading the way, and the disciples were astonished, while those who followed were afraid. Again he took the Twelve aside and told them what was going to happen to him. [33]"We are going up to Jerusalem," he said, "and the Son of Man will be betrayed to the chief priests and teachers of the law. They will condemn him to death and will hand him over to the Gentiles, [34]who will mock him and spit on him, flog him[j] and kill him. Three days later he will rise."

10:34
[j]Mt 16:21

Jesus Teaches about Serving Others (178/Matthew 20:20–28)

[35]Then James and John, the sons of Zebedee, came to him. "Teacher," they said, "we want you to do for us whatever we ask."

[36]"What do you want me to do for you?" he asked.

[37]They replied, "Let one of us sit at your right and the other at your left in your glory."[k]

[38]"You don't know what you are asking," Jesus said. "Can you drink the cup[l] I drink or be baptized with the baptism I am baptized with?"[m]

10:37
[k]Mt 19:28

10:38
[l]Mt 20:22
[m]Lk 12:50

[39]"We can," they answered.

Jesus said to them, "You will drink the cup I drink and be baptized with the baptism I am baptized with,[n] [40]but to sit at my right or left is not for me to grant. These places belong to those for whom they have been prepared."

10:39
[n]Ac 12:2; Rev 1:9

[41]When the ten heard about this, they became indignant with James and John. [42]Jesus called them together and said, "You know that those who are regarded as rulers of the Gentiles lord it over them, and their high officials exercise authority over them. [43]Not so with you. Instead, whoever wants to become great among you must be your servant,[o] [44]and whoever wants to be first must be slave of all. [45]For even the Son of Man did not come to be served, but to serve,[p] and to give his life as a ransom for many."

10:43
[o]Mk 9:35

10:45
[p]Mt 20:28

Jesus Heals a Blind Beggar (179/Matthew 20:29–34; Luke 18:35–43)

[46]Then they came to Jericho. As Jesus and his disciples, together with a large crowd, were leaving the city, a blind man, Bartimaeus (that is, the Son of Timaeus), was sitting by the

---

10:31 Jesus explained that in the world to come, the values of this world will be reversed. Those who seek status and importance here will have none in heaven. Those who are humble here will be great in heaven. The corrupt condition of our society encourages confusion in values. We are bombarded by messages that tell us how to be important and how to feel good, and Jesus' teaching about service to others seems alien. But those who have humbly served others are most qualified to be great in heaven.

10:33, 34 Jesus' death and resurrection should have come as no surprise to the disciples. Here he clearly explained to them what would happen to him. Unfortunately, they didn't really hear what he was saying. Jesus said he was the Messiah, but they thought the Messiah would be a conquering king. He spoke to them of resurrection, but they heard only his words about death. Because Jesus often spoke in parables, the disciples may have thought that his words on death and resurrection were another parable they weren't astute enough to understand. The Gospels include Jesus' predictions of his death and resurrection to show that these events were God's plan from the beginning and not accidents.

10:35 Mark records that John and James went to Jesus with their request; in Matthew, their mother also made the request. Apparently mother and sons were in agreement in requesting honored places in Christ's kingdom.

10:37 The disciples, like most Jews of that day, had the wrong idea of the Messiah's kingdom as predicted by the Old Testament prophets. They thought Jesus would establish an earthly kingdom that would free Israel from Rome's oppression. James and John wanted honored places in it. But Jesus' kingdom is not of this world; it is not centered in palaces and thrones, but in the hearts and lives of his followers. The disciples did not understand this until after Jesus' resurrection.

10:38, 39 James and John said they were willing to face any trial for Christ. Both did suffer: James died as a martyr (Acts 12:2), and John was forced to live in exile (Revelation 1:9). It is easy to say we will endure anything for Christ, and yet most of us complain over the most minor problems. If we say we are willing to suffer on a large scale for Christ, we must also be willing to suffer the irritations that come with serving others.

10:42–45 James and John wanted the highest positions in Jesus' kingdom. But Jesus told them that true greatness comes in serving others. Peter, one of the disciples who had heard this message, expands the thought in 1 Peter 5:1–4.

Most businesses, organizations, and institutions measure greatness by high personal achievement. In Christ's kingdom, however, service is the way to get ahead. The desire to be on top will hinder, not help. Rather than seeking to have your needs met, look for ways that you can minister to the needs of others.

10:45 This verse reveals not only the motive for Jesus' ministry, but also the basis for our salvation. A ransom was the price paid to release a slave. Jesus paid a ransom for us because we could not pay it ourselves. His death released all of us from our slavery to sin. The disciples thought Jesus' life and power would save them from Rome; Jesus said his *death* would save them from sin, an even greater slavery than Rome's. More about the ransom Jesus paid for us is found in 1 Peter 1:18, 19.

10:46 Jericho was a popular resort city rebuilt by Herod the Great in the Judean desert, not far from the Jordan River cross-roadside begging. ⁴⁷When he heard that it was Jesus of Nazareth,*q* he began to shout, "Jesus, Son of David,*r* have mercy on me!"

⁴⁸Many rebuked him and told him to be quiet, but he shouted all the more, "Son of David, have mercy on me!"

⁴⁹Jesus stopped and said, "Call him."

So they called to the blind man, "Cheer up! On your feet! He's calling you." ⁵⁰Throwing his cloak aside, he jumped to his feet and came to Jesus.

⁵¹"What do you want me to do for you?" Jesus asked him.

The blind man said, "Rabbi,*s* I want to see."

⁵²"Go," said Jesus, "your faith has healed you."*t* Immediately he received his sight and followed Jesus along the road.

3. Jesus' ministry in Jerusalem
Jesus Rides into Jerusalem on a Young Donkey
(183/Matthew 21:1–11; Luke 19:28–44; John 12:12–19)

11 As they approached Jerusalem and came to Bethphage and Bethany*u* at the Mount of Olives,*v* Jesus sent two of his disciples, ²saying to them, "Go to the village ahead of you, and just as you enter it, you will find a colt tied there, which no one has ever ridden. Untie it and bring it here. ³If anyone asks you, 'Why are you doing this?' tell him, 'The Lord needs it and will send it back here shortly.'"

⁴They went and found a colt outside in the street, tied at a doorway. *w* As they untied it, ⁵some people standing there asked, "What are you doing, untying that colt?" ⁶They answered as Jesus had told them to, and the people let them go. ⁷When they brought the colt to Jesus and threw their cloaks over it, he sat on it. ⁸Many people spread their cloaks on the road, while others spread branches they had cut in the fields. ⁹Those who went ahead and those who followed shouted,

---

ing. Jesus was on his way to Jerusalem (10:32), and, after crossing over from Perea, he would naturally enter Jericho.

10:46 Beggars were a common sight in most towns. Because most occupations of that day required physical labor, anyone with a crippling disease or disability was at a severe disadvantage and was usually forced to beg, even though God's laws commanded care for such needy people (Leviticus 25:35–38). Blindness was considered a curse from God for sin (John 9:2), but Jesus refuted this idea when he reached out to heal the blind.

10:47 "Son of David" was a popular way of addressing Jesus as the Messiah, because it was known that the Messiah would be a descendant of King David (Isaiah 9:7). The fact that Bartimaeus called Jesus the Son of David shows that he recognized Jesus as the Messiah. His faith in Jesus as the Messiah brought about his healing.

10:47 We do not know how long Bartimaeus had been blind, but it only took a moment for him to decide to call on Jesus for help. Jesus met many spiritually blind people—religious leaders, family members, people in the crowd. Though their eyes were fine, they could not see the truth about Jesus. But blind Bartimaeus heard the report that Jesus was coming and boldly cried out.

In coming to Jesus, we need Bartimaeus's boldness. We must overcome our reticence and doubts and take the step to call on him. Bartimaeus had not seen Jesus' miracles, but he responded in faith to what he had heard. We have heard Jesus described in the Gospels. May we be like those of whom Peter wrote, "Though you have not seen him, you love him; and even though you do not see him now, you believe in him and are filled with an inexpressible and glorious joy" (1 Peter 1:8).

11:1, 2 This was Sunday of the week that Jesus would be crucified, and the great Passover festival was about to begin. Jews came to Jerusalem from all over the Roman world during this week-long celebration to remember the great exodus from Egypt (see Exodus 12:37–51). Many in the crowds had heard of or seen Jesus and were hoping he would come to the temple (John 11:55–57).

Jesus did come, not as a warring king on a horse or in a chariot, but as a gentle and peaceable king on a donkey's colt, just as

Zechariah 9:9 had predicted. Jesus knew that those who would hear him teach at the temple would return to their homes throughout the world and announce the coming of the Messiah.

11:9, 10 The people exclaimed "Hosanna" (meaning, "Save!"), because they recognized that Jesus was fulfilling the prophecy in Zechariah 9:9. (See also Psalm 24:7–10; 118:26.) They spoke of David's kingdom because of God's words to David in 2 Samuel 7:12–14. The crowd correctly saw Jesus as the fulfillment of these prophecies, but they did not understand where Jesus' kingship would lead him. This same crowd cried out "Crucify him!" when Jesus stood on trial only a few days later.

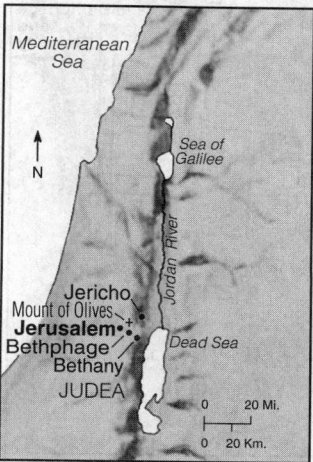

JESUS NEARS JERUSALEM
Leaving Jericho, Jesus headed toward acclaim, then crucifixion, in Jerusalem. During his last week, he stayed outside the city in Bethany, a village on the eastern slope of the Mount of Olives, entering Jerusalem to teach, eat the Passover, and finally be crucified.

"Hosanna!ᵃ"

"Blessed is he who comes in the name of the Lord!"ᵇˣ

10 "Blessed is the coming kingdom of our father David!"

"Hosanna in the highest!"

11Jesus entered Jerusalem and went to the temple. He looked around at everything, but since it was already late, he went out to Bethany with the Twelve.ʸ

Jesus Clears the Temple Again (184/Matthew 21:12–17; Luke 19:45–48)

12The next day as they were leaving Bethany, Jesus was hungry. 13Seeing in the distance a fig tree in leaf, he went to find out if it had any fruit. When he reached it, he found nothing but leaves, because it was not the season for figs. 14Then he said to the tree, "May no one ever eat fruit from you again." And his disciples heard him say it.

15On reaching Jerusalem, Jesus entered the temple area and began driving out those who were buying and selling there. He overturned the tables of the money changers and the benches of those selling doves, 16and would not allow anyone to carry merchandise through the temple courts. 17And as he taught them, he said, "Is it not written:

"'My house will be called
    a house of prayer for all nations'ᶜ?ᶻ

But you have made it 'a den of robbers.'ᵈ"ᵃ

18The chief priests and the teachers of the law heard this and began looking for a way to kill him, for they feared him,ᵇ because the whole crowd was amazed at his teaching.ᶜ

19When evening came, theyᵉ went out of the city.ᵈ

ᵃ9 A Hebrew expression meaning "Save!" which became an exclamation of praise; also in verse 10
ᵇ9 Psalm 118:25,26   ᶜ17 Isaiah 56:7   ᵈ17 Jer. 7:11   ᵉ19 Some early manuscripts he

11:9
ˣPs 118:25, 26;
Mt 23:39

11:11
ʸMt 21:12, 17

11:17
ᶻIsa 56:7
ᵃJer 7:11

11:18
ᵇMt 21:46;
Mk 12:12; Lk 20:19
ᶜMt 7:28

11:19
ᵈLk 21:37

11:10 Like those who witnessed Jesus' victory parade into Jerusalem, we have expectations for what we think God should do to make life better, safer, and more enjoyable. Like excited spectators, we can't wait to see suffering stopped, injustice corrected, and prosperity begun. Like the people on the road to Jerusalem that day, we have much to learn about Jesus' death and resurrection.

CLEARING THE TEMPLE On Monday morning of his last week, Jesus left Bethany, entered Jerusalem, and cleared the temple of money changers and merchants.

We must not let our personal desires catch us up in the celebration and shouting lest we miss the meaning of true discipleship. In our excitement and celebration, we must remember that following Christ involves hardships. It may include suffering, even death.

11:11–21 In this passage, two unusual incidents are related: the cursing of the fig tree and the clearing of the temple. The cursing of the fig tree was an acted-out parable related to the clearing of the temple. The temple was supposed to be a place of worship, but true worship had disappeared. The fig tree showed promise of fruit, but it produced none. Jesus was showing his anger at religious life without substance. If you claim to have faith without putting it to work in your life, you are like the barren fig tree. Genuine faith has great potential; ask God to help you bear fruit for his kingdom.

11:13–26 Fig trees, a popular source of inexpensive food in Israel, require three years from the time they are planted until they can bear fruit. Each tree yields a great amount of fruit twice a year, in late spring and in early autumn. This incident occurred early in the spring fig season when the leaves were beginning to bud. The figs normally grow as the leaves fill out, but this tree, though full of leaves, had no figs. The tree looked promising but offered no fruit. Jesus' harsh words to the fig tree could be applied to the nation of Israel. Fruitful in appearance only, Israel was spiritually barren.

11:15–17 Jesus became angry, but he did not sin. There is a place for righteous indignation. Christians are right to be upset about sin and injustice and should take a stand against them. Unfortunately, believers are often passive about these important issues and instead get angry over personal insults and petty irritations. Make sure your anger is directed toward the right issues.

11:15–17 Money changers and merchants did big business during Passover. Those who came from foreign countries had to have their money changed into temple currency because this was the only money accepted for the temple tax and for the purchase of sacrificial animals. Often the inflated exchange rate enriched the money changers, and the exorbitant prices of animals made the merchants wealthy. Their stalls were set up in the temple's

Jesus Says the Disciples Can Pray for Anything (*188*/Matthew 21:18–22)

11:21
e Mt 23:7

11:23
f Mt 21:21

11:24
g Mt 7:7

11:25
h Mt 6:14

²⁰In the morning, as they went along, they saw the fig tree withered from the roots. ²¹Peter remembered and said to Jesus, "Rabbi, e look! The fig tree you cursed has withered!"

²²"Have a faith in God," Jesus answered. ²³"I tell you the truth, if anyone says to this mountain, 'Go, throw yourself into the sea,' and does not doubt in his heart but believes that what he says will happen, it will be done for him. f ²⁴Therefore I tell you, whatever you ask for in prayer, believe that you have received it, and it will be yours. g ²⁵And when you stand praying, if you hold anything against anyone, forgive him, so that your Father in heaven may forgive you your sins. b " h

Religious Leaders Challenge Jesus' Authority (189/Matthew 21:23–27; Luke 20:1–8)

²⁷They arrived again in Jerusalem, and while Jesus was walking in the temple courts, the chief priests, the teachers of the law and the elders came to him. ²⁸"By what authority are you doing these things?" they asked. "And who gave you authority to do this?"

²⁹Jesus replied, "I will ask you one question. Answer me, and I will tell you by what authority I am doing these things. ³⁰John's baptism—was it from heaven, or from men? Tell me!"

a22 Some early manuscripts *If you have*   b25 Some manuscripts *sins. 26But if you do not forgive, neither will your Father who is in heaven forgive your sins.*

KEY CHARACTERISTICS OF CHRIST IN THE GOSPELS	Characteristic	Reference
	Jesus is the Son of God	Matthew 16:15, 16; Mark 1:1; Luke 22:70, 71; John 8:24
	Jesus is God who became human	John 1:1, 2, 14; 20:28
	Jesus is the Christ, the Messiah.	Matthew 26:63, 64; Mark 14:61, 62; Luke 9:20; John 4:25, 26
	Jesus came to help sinners	Matthew 9:13; Luke 5:32
	Jesus has power to forgive sins	Mark 2:9–12; Luke 24:47
	Jesus has authority over death	Matthew 28:5, 6; Mark 5:22–24, 35–42; Luke 24:5, 6; John 11:1–44
	Jesus has power to give eternal life	John 10:28; 17:2
	Jesus healed the sick	Matthew 8:5–13; Mark 1:32–34; Luke 5:12–15; John 9:1–7
	Jesus taught with authority	Matthew 7:29; Mark 1:21, 22
	Jesus was compassionate	Matthew 9:36; Mark 1:41; 8:2
	Jesus experienced sorrow	Matthew 26:38; John 11:35
	Jesus never disobeyed God.	Matthew 3:15; John 8:46

court of the Gentiles, making it all but impossible for non-Jews to spend any time in worship (Isaiah 56:6, 7). Jesus became angry because God's house of worship had become a place of extortion and a barrier to Gentiles who wanted to worship.

11:22, 23 The kind of prayer that moves mountains is prayer for the fruitfulness of God's kingdom. It would seem impossible to move a mountain into the sea, so Jesus used that picture to say that God can do anything. God will answer your prayers, but not as a result of your positive mental attitude. Other conditions must be met: (1) you must be a believer; (2) you must not hold a grudge against another person; (3) you must not pray with selfish motives; (4) your request must be for the good of God's kingdom. To pray effectively, you need faith in God, not faith in the object of your request. If you focus only on your request, you will be left with nothing if your request is refused.

11:24 Jesus, our example for prayer, prayed, "Everything is possible for you . . . Yet not what I will, but what you will" (14:36). Our prayers are often motivated by our own interests and desires. We like to hear that we can have anything. But Jesus prayed with *God's* interests in mind. When we pray, we should express our desires, but want his will above ours. Check yourself to see if your prayers focus on your interests or God's.

11:25 Forgiving others is tough work—so much so that many people would rather do something totally distasteful than offer forgiveness to someone who has wronged them. For a person to pray while bearing a grudge, however, is like a tree sprouting leaves and bearing no fruit (11:13). True faith changes the heart. Real prayer dismantles pride and vengeance, filling the holes with love. Real faith seeks peace. For our churches to have prayer power, there must be harmony and forgiveness evident in the body of believers. Let go of hurts, abandon grudges, and forgive others.

11:27–33 The religious leaders were in a quandary. They had wanted to trap Jesus with a question that would show him to be either a blasphemer or a weird fanatic. Instead, Jesus had countered their question with a question about John the Baptist. Now they would have to try to save face. They had not stood up for John or tried to get him released—John had irritated them just as Jesus was doing (see Matthew 3:7–10). Always cloaked in self-interest, these religious leaders were only concerned about position and reputation; they weren't looking for the truth. In John 3:19, Jesus summed up this attitude: "Men loved darkness instead of light because their deeds were evil." People who reject Jesus' claims have a greater problem than intellectual doubt; they are rebelling against Christ's control of their lives. They try to ask tricky questions, but don't really want an answer. Sincere seekers, however, will find the truth (Matthew 7:7, 8).

³¹They discussed it among themselves and said, "If we say, 'From heaven,' he will ask, 'Then why didn't you believe him?' ³²But if we say, 'From men'..." (They feared the people, for everyone held that John really was a prophet.)

³³So they answered Jesus, "We don't know."

Jesus said, "Neither will I tell you by what authority I am doing these things."

Jesus Tells the Parable of the Evil Farmers (*191/Matthew 21:33–46; Luke 20:9–19*)

12 He then began to speak to them in parables: "A man planted a vineyard.ⁱ He put a wall around it, dug a pit for the winepress and built a watchtower. Then he rented the vineyard to some farmers and went away on a journey. ²At harvest time he sent a servant to the tenants to collect from them some of the fruit of the vineyard. ³But they seized him, beat him and sent him away empty-handed. ⁴Then he sent another servant to them; they struck this man on the head and treated him shamefully. ⁵He sent still another, and that one they killed. He sent many others; some of them they beat, others they killed.

⁶"He had one left to send, a son, whom he loved. He sent him last of all,ʲ saying, 'They will respect my son.'

⁷"But the tenants said to one another, 'This is the heir. Come, let's kill him, and the inheritance will be ours.' ⁸So they took him and killed him, and threw him out of the vineyard.

⁹"What then will the owner of the vineyard do? He will come and kill those tenants and give the vineyard to others. ¹⁰Haven't you read this scripture:

"'The stone the builders rejected
has become the capstoneᵃ;ᵏ
¹¹ the Lord has done this,
and it is marvelous in our eyes'ᵇ?"ˡ

¹²Then they looked for a way to arrest him because they knew he had spoken the parable against them. But they were afraid of the crowd;ᵐ so they left him and went away.ⁿ

Religious Leaders Question Jesus about Paying Taxes (*193/Matthew 22:15–22; Luke 20:20–26*)

¹³Later they sent some of the Pharisees and Herodians ᵒ to Jesus to catch him in his words. ¹⁴They came to him and said, "Teacher, we know you are a man of integrity. You aren't swayed by men, because you pay no attention to who they are; but you teach the way of God in accordance with the truth. Is it right to pay taxes to Caesar or not? ¹⁵Should we pay or shouldn't we?"

But Jesus knew their hypocrisy. "Why are you trying to trap me?" he asked. "Bring me a denarius and let me look at it." ¹⁶They brought the coin, and he asked them, "Whose portrait is this? And whose inscription?"

"Caesar's," they replied.

¹⁷Then Jesus said to them, "Give to Caesar what is Caesar's and to God what is God's."ᵖ

And they were amazed at him.

ᵃ*10* Or *cornerstone*   ᵇ*11* Psalm 118:22,23

12:1
ⁱIsa 5:1-7

12:6
ʲHeb 1:1-3

12:10
ᵏAc 4:11

12:11
ˡPs 118:22, 23

12:12
ᵐMk 11:18
ⁿMt 22:22

12:13
ᵒMt 22:16; Mk 3:6

12:17
ᵖRo 13:7

11:30 For more information, see John the Baptist's Profile in John 1, p. 1737.

12:1ff In this parable, the man who planted the vineyard is God; the vineyard is the nation Israel; the tenants are Israel's religious leaders; the servants are the prophets and priests who remained faithful to God; the son is Jesus; and the others are the Gentiles. The religious leaders not only frustrated their nation's purpose but also killed those who were trying to fulfill it. They were so jealous and possessive that they ignored the welfare of the very people they were supposed to be bringing to God. By telling this story, Jesus exposed the religious leaders' plot to kill him and warned that their sins would be punished.

12:10, 11 Jesus referred to himself as the stone rejected by the builders. Although he would be rejected by most of the Jewish leaders, he would become the cornerstone of a new "building," the church (Acts 4:11, 12). The cornerstone was used as a base to make sure the other stones of the building were straight and level. Likewise, Jesus' life and teaching would be the church's foundation.

12:13 The Pharisees were primarily a religious group concerned for ritual purity; the Herodians were a Jewish political group that approved of Herod's compromises with Rome. The Pharisees did not like Jesus because he exposed their hypocrisy. The Herodians also saw Jesus as a threat. Supporters of the dynasty of Herod the Great, they had lost political control when, as a result of reported unrest, Rome deposed Archelaus (Herod's son with authority over Judea), and replaced him with a Roman governor. The Herodians feared that Jesus would cause still more instability in Judea, and that Rome might react by never allowing the Roman leaders to step down and be replaced by a descendant of Herod.

12:14 Anyone who avoided paying taxes faced harsh penalties. The Jews hated to pay taxes to Rome because the money supported their oppressors and symbolized their subjection. Much of the tax money also went to maintain the pagan temples and luxurious life-styles of Rome's upper class. The Pharisees and Herodians hoped to trap Jesus with this tax question. A yes would mean he supported Rome, which would turn the people against him. A no would bring accusations of treason and rebellion against Rome and could lead to civil penalties.

12:17 Jesus avoided the trick question by showing that believers have dual citizenship (1 Peter 2:17). Our citizenship in the nation

Religious Leaders Question Jesus about the Resurrection (*194*/Matthew 22:23–33; Luke 20:27–40)

12:18
q Ac 23:8
12:19
r Dt 25:5

18Then the Sadducees, who say there is no resurrection, q came to him with a question. 19"Teacher," they said, "Moses wrote for us that if a man's brother dies and leaves a wife but no children, the man must marry the widow and have children for his brother. r 20Now there were seven brothers. The first one married and died without leaving any children. 21The second one married the widow, but he also died, leaving no child. It was the same with the third. 22In fact, none of the seven left any children. Last of all, the woman died too. 23At the resurrection a whose wife will she be, since the seven were married to her?"

24Jesus replied, "Are you not in error because you do not know the Scriptures or the power

a23 Some manuscripts *resurrection, when men rise from the dead,*

WHAT JESUS SAID ABOUT LOVE

In Mark 12:28 a teacher of the law asked Jesus which of all the commandments was the most important to follow. Jesus mentioned two commandments, one from Deuteronomy 6:5, the other from Leviticus 19:18. Both had to do with love. Why is love so important? Jesus said that all of the comandments were given for two simple reasons: to help us love God and love others as we should.

What else did Jesus say about love?	Reference
God loves us.	John 3:16
We are to love God.	Matthew 22:37
Because God loves us, he cares for us	Matthew 6:25–34
God wants everyone to know how much he loves them.	John 17:23
God loves even those who hate him; we are to do the same.	Matthew 5:43–47; Luke 6:35
God seeks out even those most alienated from him.	Luke 15
God must be our first love.	Matthew 6:24; 10:37
We love God when we obey him	John 14:21; 15:10
God loves Jesus, his Son.	John 5:20; 10:17
Jesus loves God.	John 14:31
Those who refuse Jesus don't have God's love	John 5:41–44
Jesus loves us just as God loves Jesus.	John 15:9
Jesus proved his love for us by dying on the cross so that we could live eternally with him.	John 3:14, 15; 15:13, 14
The love between God and Jesus is the perfect example of how we are to love others	John 17:21–26
We are to love one another (John 13:34, 35) and demonstrate that love.	Matthew 5:40–42; 10:42
We are *not* to love the praise of men (John 12:43), selfish recognition (Matthew 23:6), earthly belongings (Luke 6:19–31), or anything more than God.	Luke 16:13
Jesus' love extends to each individual	Mark 10:21; John 10:11–15
Jesus wants us to love him through the good and through the difficult times	Matthew 26:31–35
Jesus wants our love to be genuine.	John 21:15–17

---

requires that we pay money for the services and benefits we receive. Our citizenship in the kingdom of heaven requires that we pledge to God our primary obedience and commitment. (See Acts 4:18, 19 and 5:29 for discussions on obeying God rather than people.) As God's followers, we have legitimate obligations to both God and the government. But it is important to keep our priorities straight. When the two authorities conflict, our duty to God always must come before our duty to the government. The coin bearing the emperor's image should be given to the emperor; our lives, bearing God's image, belong to God. Are you giving to God what is rightfully his?

12:18–23 After the Pharisees and Herodians failed to trap Jesus with their tax question, the Sadducees stepped in with a question they were sure would stump him. This was a question that they had successfully used against the Pharisees, who could not come up with an answer. The Sadducees did not believe in life after death because the Pentateuch (Genesis—Deuteronomy) had no direct teaching about it, and the writings of Moses were the only Scriptures they followed. But Jesus was about to point out that Moses' books support the idea of eternal life (12:26).

12:19 According to Old Testament law, when a man died without a son, his brother had to marry the widow and produce children to care for her and allow the family line to continue. The first son of this marriage was considered the heir of the dead man (Deuteronomy 25:5, 6).

12:24 What life will be like after the resurrection is far beyond our ability to understand or imagine (Isaiah 64:4; 1 Corinthians 2:9). We need not be afraid of eternal life because of the unknowns, however. Instead of wondering what God's coming kingdom will be like, we should concentrate on our relationship with Christ right now because in the new kingdom, we will be with him. If we learn to love and trust Christ *now*, we will not be afraid of what he has in store for us then.

of God? 25 When the dead rise, they will neither marry nor be given in marriage; they will be like the angels in heaven. ˢ 26 Now about the dead rising—have you not read in the book of Moses, in the account of the bush, how God said to him, 'I am the God of Abraham, the God of Isaac, and the God of Jacob'ᵃ?ᵗ 27 He is not the God of the dead, but of the living. You are badly mistaken!"

Religious Leaders Question Jesus about the Greatest Commandment (195/Matthew 22:34–40)

28 One of the teachers of the lawᵘ came and heard them debating. Noticing that Jesus had given them a good answer, he asked him, "Of all the commandments, which is the most important?"

29 "The most important one," answered Jesus, "is this: 'Hear, O Israel, the Lord our God, the Lord is one.ᵇ 30 Love the Lord your God with all your heart and with all your soul and with all your mind and with all your strength.'ᶜ ᵛ 31 The second is this: 'Love your neighbor as yourself.'ᵈ ʷ There is no commandment greater than these."

32 "Well said, teacher," the man replied. "You are right in saying that God is one and there is no other but him.ˣ 33 To love him with all your heart, with all your understanding and with all your strength, and to love your neighbor as yourself is more important than all burnt offerings and sacrifices."ʸ

34 When Jesus saw that he had answered wisely, he said to him, "You are not far from the kingdom of God." And from then on no one dared ask him any more questions. ᶻ

Religious Leaders Cannot Answer Jesus' Question (196/Matthew 22:41–46; Luke 20:41–44)

35 While Jesus was teaching in the temple courts,ᵃ he asked, "How is it that the teachers of the law say that the Christᵉ is the son of David?ᵇ 36 David himself, speaking by the Holy Spirit, declared:

> "'The Lord said to my Lord:
> "Sit at my right hand
> until I put your enemies
> under your feet."'ᶠᶜ

37 David himself calls him 'Lord.' How then can he be his son?"

The large crowdᵈ listened to him with delight.

ᵃ26 Exodus 3:6   ᵇ29 Or the Lord our God is one Lord   ᶜ30 Deut. 6:4,5   ᵈ31 Lev. 19:18   ᵉ35 Or Messiah
ᶠ36 Psalm 110:1

**Cross references (right margin):**

12:25 ˢ1Co 15:42, 49, 52
12:26 ᵗEx 3:6
12:28 ᵘLk 10:25-28; 20:39
12:30 ᵛDt 6:4, 5
12:31 ʷLev 19:18
12:32 ˣDt 4:35, 39; Isa 45:6, 14; 46:9
12:33 ʸ1Sa 15:22; Hos 6:6; Mic 6:6-8
12:34 ᶻMt 22:46
12:35 ᵃMt 26:55 ᵇMt 9:27
12:36 ᶜPs 110:1
12:37 ᵈJn 12:9

12:25-27 Jesus' statement does not mean that people won't recognize their spouses in the coming kingdom. It simply means that God's new order will not be an extension of this life and that the same physical and natural rules won't apply. Jesus' comment in verse 25 was not intended to be the final word on marriage in heaven; instead, this response was Jesus' refusal to answer the Sadducees' riddle and fall into their trap. Sidestepping their question about the much-married woman, he gave a definitive answer to their real question about the doctrine of resurrection. Because the Sadducees believed only in the Pentateuch (Genesis through Deuteronomy), Jesus quoted from Exodus 3:6 to prove that there is life after death. God spoke of Abraham, Isaac, and Jacob years after their deaths as if they *still lived*. God's covenant with all people exists beyond death.

12:28 By Jesus' time, the Jews had accumulated hundreds of laws—613 by one historian's count. Some religious leaders tried to distinguish between major and minor laws, and some taught that all laws were equally binding and that it was dangerous to make any distinctions. This teacher's question could have provoked controversy among these groups, but Jesus' answer summarized all of God's laws.

12:29-31 God's laws are not burdensome. They can be reduced to two simple principles: love God and love others. These commands are from the Old Testament (Deuteronomy 6:5; Leviticus 19:18). When you love God completely and care for others as you care for yourself, then you have fulfilled the intent of the Ten Commandments and the other Old Testament laws. According to Jesus, these two commandments summarize all God's laws. Let them rule your thoughts, decisions, and actions. When you are uncertain about what to do, ask yourself which course of action best demonstrates love for God and love for others.

12:32-34 This Pharisee had caught the intent of God's law—that true obedience comes from the heart. Because all the Old Testament commands lead to Christ, his next step was faith in Jesus himself. This, however, was the most difficult step to take. We do not know if this Pharisee ever became a true believer, but we must remember that being "close" to being a Christian is infinitely far away if a person never commits to Christ. Salvation cannot rest on intellectual knowledge alone. You must repent, follow Christ, and be made a new person by his Holy Spirit. Don't be content with being close; take the step and make the commitment.

12:35-37 Jesus quoted Psalm 110:1 to show that David considered the Messiah to be his Lord, not just his descendant. The religious leaders did not understand that the Messiah would be far more than a human descendant of David; he would be God himself in human form.

Jesus Warns against the Religious Leaders (*197*/Matthew 23:1–12; Luke 20:45–47)

12:39
e Lk 11:43

[38] As he taught, Jesus said, "Watch out for the teachers of the law. They like to walk around in flowing robes and be greeted in the marketplaces, [39] and have the most important seats in the synagogues and the places of honor at banquets. *e* [40] They devour widows' houses and for a show make lengthy prayers. Such men will be punished most severely."

A Poor Widow Gives All She Has (*200*/Luke 21:1–4)

12:41
f 2Ki 12:9; Jn 8:20

[41] Jesus sat down opposite the place where the offerings were put *f* and watched the crowd putting their money into the temple treasury. Many rich people threw in large amounts. [42] But a poor widow came and put in two very small copper coins, *a* worth only a fraction of a penny. *b*

12:44
g 2Co 8:12

[43] Calling his disciples to him, Jesus said, "I tell you the truth, this poor widow has put more into the treasury than all the others. [44] They all gave out of their wealth; but she, out of her poverty, put in everything—all she had to live on." *g*

Jesus Tells about the Future (*201*/Matthew 24:1–25; Luke 21:5–24)

13 As he was leaving the temple, one of his disciples said to him, "Look, Teacher! What massive stones! What magnificent buildings!"

13:2
h Lk 19:44

[2] "Do you see all these great buildings?" replied Jesus. "Not one stone here will be left on another; every one will be thrown down." *h*

a 42 Greek *two lepta*   *b* 42 Greek *kodrantes*

JESUS' PROPHECIES IN THE OLIVET DISCOURSE	Type of Prophecy	Old Testament References	Other New Testament References
	The Last Days		
	Mark 13:1–23	Daniel 9:26, 27	John 15:21
	Matthew 24:1–28	Daniel 11:31	Revelation 11:2
	Luke 21:5–24	Joel 2:2	1 Timothy 4:1, 2
	The Second Coming of Christ		
	Mark 13:24–27	Isaiah 13:6–10	Revelation 6:12
	Luke 21:25–28	Ezekiel 32:7	Mark 14:62
	Matthew 24:29–31	Daniel 7:13, 14	1 Thessalonians 4:16

In Mark 13, often called the Olivet Discourse, Jesus talked a lot about two things: the end times and his second coming. Jesus was not trying to encourage his disciples to speculate about exactly when he would return by sharing these prophecies with them. Instead, he urges all his followers to be watchful and prepared for his coming. If we serve Jesus faithfully now, we will be ready when he returns.

12:38–40 Jesus again exposed the religious leaders' impure motives. The teachers of the law received no pay, so they depended on the hospitality extended by devout Jews. Some of them used this custom to exploit people, cheating the poor out of everything they had and taking advantage of the rich. Through their pious actions they hoped to gain status, recognition, and respect.

12:38–40 Jesus warned against trying to make a good impression. These teachers of the law were religious hypocrites who had no love for God. True followers of Christ are not distinguished by showy spirituality. Reading the Bible, praying in public, or following church rituals can be phony if the motive for doing them is to be noticed or honored. Let your actions be consistent with your beliefs. Live for Christ, even when no one is looking.

12:41 There were several boxes in the temple where money could be placed. Some were for collecting the temple tax from Jewish males; the others were for freewill offerings. This particular collection box was probably in the court of the women.

12:41–44 This widow gave all she had to live on, in contrast to the way most people handle their money. When we consider giving a certain percentage of our income a great accomplishment, we resemble those who gave "out of their wealth." Here,

Jesus was admiring generous and sacrificial giving. As believers, we should consider increasing our giving—whether of money, time, or talents—to a point beyond convenience or calculation.

13:1, 2 About 15 years before Jesus was born (20 B.C.), Herod the Great began to remodel and rebuild the temple, which had stood for nearly 500 years since the days of Ezra (Ezra 6:14, 15). Herod made the temple one of the most beautiful buildings in Jerusalem—not to honor God, but to appease the Jews whom he ruled. The magnificent building project was not completely finished until A.D. 64. Jesus' prophecy that not one stone would be left on another was fulfilled in A.D. 70, when the Romans completely destroyed the temple and the entire city of Jerusalem.

³As Jesus was sitting on the Mount of Olives opposite the temple, Peter, James, John and Andrew asked him privately, ⁴"Tell us, when will these things happen? And what will be the sign that they are all about to be fulfilled?"

⁵Jesus said to them: "Watch out that no one deceives you. *ⁱ* ⁶Many will come in my name, claiming, 'I am he,' and will deceive many. ⁷When you hear of wars and rumors of wars, do not be alarmed. Such things must happen, but the end is still to come. ⁸Nation will rise against nation, and kingdom against kingdom. There will be earthquakes in various places, and famines. These are the beginning of birth pains.

⁹"You must be on your guard. You will be handed over to the local councils and flogged in the synagogues. *ʲ* On account of me you will stand before governors and kings as witnesses to them. ¹⁰And the gospel must first be preached to all nations. ¹¹Whenever you are arrested and brought to trial, do not worry beforehand about what to say. Just say whatever is given you at the time, for it is not you speaking, but the Holy Spirit. *ᵏ*

¹²"Brother will betray brother to death, and a father his child. Children will rebel against their parents and have them put to death. *ˡ* ¹³All men will hate you because of me, *ᵐ* but he who stands firm to the end will be saved. *ⁿ*

¹⁴"When you see 'the abomination that causes desolation'*ᵃᵒ* standing where it*ᵇ* does not belong—let the reader understand—then let those who are in Judea flee to the mountains. ¹⁵Let no one on the roof of his house go down or enter the house to take anything out. ¹⁶Let no one in the field go back to get his cloak. ¹⁷How dreadful it will be in those days for pregnant women and nursing mothers! ¹⁸Pray that this will not take place in winter, ¹⁹because those will be days of distress unequaled from the beginning, when God created the world, until now—and never to be equaled again. *ᵖ* ²⁰If the Lord had not cut short those days, no one would survive. But for the sake of the elect, whom he has chosen, he has shortened them. ²¹At that time if anyone says to you, 'Look, here is the Christ*ᶜ*!' or, 'Look, there he is!' do not believe it. *q* ²²For false Christs and false prophets*ʳ* will appear and perform signs and miracles*ˢ* to deceive the elect—if that were possible. ²³So be on your guard; *ᵗ* I have told you everything ahead of time.

a*14* Daniel 9:27; 11:31; 12:11   b*14* Or *he*; also in verse 29   c*21* Or *Messiah*

13:5
*ⁱ*Eph 5:6

13:9
*ʲ*Mt 10:17

13:11
*ᵏ*Mt 10:19, 20; Lk 12:11, 12

13:12
*ˡ*Mic 7:6; Mt 10:21

13:13
*ᵐ*Jn 15:21
*ⁿ*Mt 10:22

13:14
*ᵒ*Da 9:27; 11:31; 12:11

13:19
*ᵖ*Da 9:26

13:21
*q*Lk 17:23

13:22
*ʳ*Mt 7:15
*ˢ*Jn 4:48

13:23
*ᵗ*2Pe 3:17

13:3ff The disciples wanted to know when the temple would be destroyed. Jesus gave them a prophetic picture of that time, including events leading up to it. He also talked about future events connected with his return to earth to judge all people. Jesus predicted both near and distant events without putting them in chronological order. Some of the disciples lived to see the destruction of Jerusalem in A.D. 70. This event would assure them that everything else Jesus predicted would also happen.

Jesus warned his followers about the future so that they could learn how to live in the present. Many predictions Jesus made in this passage have not yet been fulfilled. He did not make them so that we would guess when they might be fulfilled, but to help us remain spiritually alert and prepared at all times as we wait for his return.

13:3, 4 The Mount of Olives rises above Jerusalem to the east. From its slopes a person can look down into the city and see the temple. Zechariah 14:1–4 predicts that the Messiah will stand on this very mountain when he returns to set up his eternal kingdom.

13:5–7 What are the signs of the end times? There have been people in every generation since Christ's resurrection claiming to know exactly when Jesus would return. No one has been right yet, however, because Christ will return on God's timetable, not ours. Jesus predicted that before his return, many believers would be misled by false teachers claiming to have revelations from God.

According to Scripture, the one clear sign of Christ's return will be his unmistakable appearance in the clouds, which will be seen by all people (13:26; Revelation 1:7). In other words, you do not have to wonder whether a certain person is the Messiah or whether these are the "end times." When Jesus returns, *you will know* beyond a doubt, because it will be evident to all true believers. Beware of groups who claim special knowledge of the last days, because no one knows when that time will be (13:32). Be cautious about saying, "This is it!" but be bold in your total commitment to have your heart and life ready for Christ's return.

13:9–11 As the early church began to grow, most of the disciples experienced the kind of persecution Jesus was talking about. Since the time of Christ, Christians have been persecuted in their own lands and on foreign mission fields. Though you may be safe from persecution now, your vision of God's kingdom must not be limited by what happens only to you. A glance at a newspaper will reveal that many Christians in other parts of the world daily face hardships and persecution. Persecutions are an opportunity for Christians to witness for Christ to those opposed to him. These persecutions serve God's desire that the gospel be proclaimed to everyone.

13:11 Jesus was teaching the kind of attitude we should have when we must take a stand for the gospel. We don't have to be fearful or defensive about our faith because the Holy Spirit will be present to give us the right words to say.

13:13 To believe in Jesus and stand "firm to the end" will take perseverance because our faith will be challenged and opposed. Severe trials will sift true Christians from fair-weather believers. Enduring to the end does not earn salvation for us, but marks us as already saved. The assurance of our salvation will keep us going through the times of persecution.

13:14 The "abomination that causes desolation" is the desecration of the temple by God's enemies. This happened repeatedly in Israel's history: in 597 B.C. when Nebuchadnezzar looted the temple and took Judean captives to Babylon (2 Chronicles 36); in 168 B.C. when Antiochus Epiphanes sacrificed a pig to Zeus on the sacred temple altar (Daniel 9:27; 11:30, 31); in A.D. 70 when the Roman general Titus placed an idol on the site of the burned-out temple after the destruction of Jerusalem. Just a few years after Jesus gave this warning, in A.D. 38, the emperor Caligula made plans to put his own statue in the temple, but he died before this could be carried out.

13:17 Some Christian couples who are contemplating pregnancy have been discouraged by this verse. They wonder if kids

Jesus Tells about His Return (*202*/Matthew 24:26–35; Luke 21:25–33)

24"But in those days, following that distress,

> "'the sun will be darkened,
> and the moon will not give its light;
> 25 the stars will fall from the sky,
> and the heavenly bodies will be shaken.'*a u*

13:25
u Isa 34:4

13:26
v Da 7:13; Mt 16:27;
Rev 1:7

13:27
w Zec 2:6

26"At that time men will see the Son of Man coming in clouds*v* with great power and glory. 27 And he will send his angels and gather his elect from the four winds, from the ends of the earth to the ends of the heavens.*w*

28"Now learn this lesson from the fig tree: As soon as its twigs get tender and its leaves come out, you know that summer is near. 29 Even so, when you see these things happening, you know that it is near, right at the door. 30 I tell you the truth, this generation*b* will certainly not pass away until all these things have happened.*x* 31 Heaven and earth will pass away, but my words will never pass away.*y*

13:30
x Mk 9:1

13:31
y Mt 5:18

Jesus Tells about Remaining Watchful (*203*/Matthew 24:36–51; Luke 21:34–38)

13:32
z Ac 1:7

13:33
a 1 Th 5:6

13:34
b Mt 25:14

32"No one knows about that day or hour, not even the angels in heaven, nor the Son, but only the Father.*z* 33 Be on guard! Be alert*c* !*a* You do not know when that time will come. 34 It's like a man going away: He leaves his house and puts his servants*b* in charge, each with his assigned task, and tells the one at the door to keep watch.

35"Therefore keep watch because you do not know when the owner of the house will come back—whether in the evening, or at midnight, or when the rooster crows, or at dawn. 36 If he comes suddenly, do not let him find you sleeping. 37 What I say to you, I say to everyone: 'Watch!'"

*a*25 Isaiah 13:10; 34:4   *b*30 Or *race*   *c*33 Some manuscripts *alert and pray*

---

should be brought into a world filled with sin, evil, and terror. Jesus was not making a general warning against pregnancy, however. Many times in history have had risks and drawbacks; no place or time is perfect. We must remember that God will look out for the welfare of our children as he has looked out for us.

13:20 The "elect" are God's chosen people, those who are saved. See Romans 8:29, 30 and Ephesians 1:4, 5 for more on God's choice.

13:22, 23 Is it possible for Christians to be deceived? Yes. So convincing will be the arguments and proofs from deceivers in the end times that it will be difficult *not* to fall away from Christ. If we are prepared, Jesus says, we can remain faithful. But if we are not prepared, we will turn away. To penetrate the disguises of false teachers we can ask: (1) Have their predictions come true, or do they have to revise them to fit what's already happened? (2) Does any teaching utilize a small section of the Bible to the neglect of the whole? (3) Does the teaching contradict what the Bible says about God? (4) Are the practices meant to glorify the teacher or Christ? (5) Do the teachings promote hostility toward other Christians?

13:31 The truth that heaven and earth will disappear is all that much more believable in our age of nuclear power and terrorism. Jesus tells us, however, that even though the earth will pass away, the truth of his words will never be changed or abolished. God and his Word provide the only stability in our unstable world. How shortsighted people are who spend their time learning about this temporary world and accumulating its possessions, while neglecting the Bible and its eternal truths!

13:32 When Jesus said that even he did not know the time of the end, he was affirming his humanity. Of course God the Father knows the time, and Jesus and the Father are one. But when Jesus became a man, he voluntarily gave up the unlimited use of his divine attributes.

The emphasis of this verse is not on Jesus' lack of knowledge, but rather on the fact that no one knows. It is God the Father's

secret to be revealed when he wills. No one can predict by Scripture or science the exact day of Jesus' return. Jesus is teaching that preparation, not calculation, is needed.

13:33, 34 Months of planning go into a wedding, the birth of a baby, a career change, a speaking engagement, the purchase of a home. Do you place the same importance on preparing for Christ's return, the most important event in your life? Its results will last for eternity. You dare not postpone your preparations because you do not know when his return will occur. The way to prepare is to study God's Word and live by its instructions each day. Only then will you be ready.

13:35–37 Mark 13 tells us how to live while we wait for Christ's return: (1) We are not to be misled by confusing claims or speculative interpretations of what will happen (13:5, 6). (2) We should not be afraid to tell people about Christ, despite what they might say or do to us (13:9–11). (3) We must stand firm by faith and not be surprised by persecutions (13:13). (4) We must be morally alert, obedient to the commands for living found in God's Word. This chapter was not given to promote discussions on prophetic timetables, but to stimulate right living for God in a world where he is largely ignored.

C. DEATH AND RESURRECTION OF JESUS, THE SERVANT (14:1—16:20)

Mark tells us about Jesus' ultimate deed of servanthood—dying for us on the cross. Jesus
died for our sin so we wouldn't have to. Now we can have eternal fellowship with God instead
of eternal suffering and death. When first written in Rome, this Gospel was encouraging to
Roman Christians during times of persecution. Christ's victory through suffering can encourage us during difficult times, too.

Religious Leaders Plot to Kill Jesus (*207/Matthew 26:1–5; Luke 22:1–2*)

14 Now the Passover *c* and the Feast of Unleavened Bread were only two days away, and
the chief priests and the teachers of the law were looking for some sly way to arrest
Jesus and kill him. *d* 2"But not during the Feast," they said, "or the people may riot."

14:1
c Jn 11:55; 13:1
d Mt 12:14

A Woman Anoints Jesus with Perfume (*182/Matthew 26:6–13; John 12:1–11*)

3While he was in Bethany, *e* reclining at the table in the home of a man known as Simon
the Leper, a woman came with an alabaster jar of very expensive perfume, made of pure
nard. She broke the jar and poured the perfume on his head. *f*

4Some of those present were saying indignantly to one another, "Why this waste of perfume? 5It could have been sold for more than a year's wages *a* and the money given to the
poor." And they rebuked her harshly.

6"Leave her alone," said Jesus. "Why are you bothering her? She has done a beautiful
thing to me. 7The poor you will always have with you, and you can help them any time you
want. *g* But you will not always have me. 8She did what she could. She poured perfume on
my body beforehand to prepare for my burial. *h* 9I tell you the truth, wherever the gospel is
preached throughout the world, what she has done will also be told, in memory of her."

14:3
e Mt 21:17
f Lk 7:37-39

14:7
g Dt 15:11

14:8
h Jn 19:40

Judas Agrees to Betray Jesus (*208/Matthew 26:14–16; Luke 22:3–6*)

10Then Judas Iscariot, one of the Twelve, went to the chief priests to betray Jesus to them.
11They were delighted to hear this and promised to give him money. So he watched for an
opportunity to hand him over.

Disciples Prepare for the Passover (*209/Matthew 26:17–19; Luke 22:7–13*)

12On the first day of the Feast of Unleavened Bread, when it was customary to sacrifice
the Passover lamb, *i* Jesus' disciples asked him, "Where do you want us to go and make preparations for you to eat the Passover?"

14:12
i Ex 12:1-11;
1Co 5:7

a 5 Greek *than three hundred denarii*

14:1 The Passover commemorated the night the Israelites were
freed from Egypt (Exodus 12), when God "passed over" homes
marked by the blood of a lamb while killing firstborn sons in
unmarked homes. The day of Passover was followed by a seven-
day festival called the Feast of Unleavened Bread. This, too,
recalled the Israelites' quick escape from Egypt when they didn't
have time to let their bread rise, so they baked it without yeast
(leaven). On this holiday, Jewish families still gather for a special
meal that includes lamb, wine, bitter herbs, and unleavened bread.

14:2 The Jews were preparing to observe Passover, a time of
remembrance for families to celebrate when the blood of lambs
had saved their ancestors. But some of the religious leaders had
another agenda. Jesus had disrupted their security, revealed their
sham, and opposed their authority. Now they would put him
away. But the world is controlled by our all-wise God, not puny
politicians. God would turn the religious leaders' murder plot into
the greatest blessing that mankind would ever know. Another
Lamb would be slain, and his blood would save all people. When
grief or disaster seem to be dominating, remember that your life
is in God's hands and remember what Jesus did for you.

14:3 Bethany is located on the eastern slope of the Mount of
Olives (Jerusalem is on the western side). This town was the home
of Jesus' friends Lazarus, Mary, and Martha, who were also present at this dinner (John 11:2). The woman who anointed Jesus'
feet was Mary, Lazarus's and Martha's sister (John 12:1–3). An
alabaster jar was a beautiful and expensive carved vase. Nard was
expensive perfume.

14:3–9 Matthew and Mark placed this event just before the Last
Supper, while John placed it a week earlier, just before the Trium-

phal Entry. It must be remembered that the main purpose of the
Gospel writers was not to present an exact chronological account
of Christ's life, but to give an accurate record of his message.
Matthew and Mark may have chosen to place this event here to
contrast the complete devotion of Mary with the betrayal of
Judas, the next event in both Gospels.

14:4, 5 Where Mark says "some of those present," John specifically mentions Judas (John 12:4, 5). Judas's indignation over
Mary's act of worship was based not on concern for the poor
but on greed. Because Judas was the treasurer of Jesus' ministry
and had embezzled funds (John 12:6), he no doubt wanted the
perfume sold so that the proceeds could be put into his care.

14:6, 7 Jesus was not saying that we should neglect the poor,
nor was he justifying indifference to them. (For Jesus' teaching
about the poor, see Matthew 6:2–4; Luke 6:20, 21; 14:13, 21;
18:22.) Jesus was praising Mary for her unselfish act of worship.
The essence of worshiping Christ is to regard him with utmost
love, respect, and devotion and to be willing to sacrifice to him
what is most precious.

14:10 Why would Judas want to betray Jesus? Very likely, Judas
expected Jesus to start a political rebellion and overthrow Rome.
As treasurer, Judas certainly assumed (as did the other disciples,
see 10:35–37) that he would be given an important position in
Jesus' new government. But when Jesus praised Mary for pouring out the perfume, thought to be worth a year's salary, Judas
finally began to realize that Jesus' kingdom was not physical or
political. Judas's greedy desire for money and status could not
be fulfilled if he followed Jesus, so he betrayed him in exchange
for money and favor from the religious leaders.

¹³So he sent two of his disciples, telling them, "Go into the city, and a man carrying a jar of water will meet you. Follow him. ¹⁴Say to the owner of the house he enters, 'The Teacher asks: Where is my guest room, where I may eat the Passover with my disciples?' ¹⁵He will show you a large upper room, furnished and ready. Make preparations for us there."

¹⁶The disciples left, went into the city and found things just as Jesus had told them. So they prepared the Passover.

Jesus and the Disciples Share the Last Supper
(211/Matthew 26:20–30; Luke 22:14–30; John 13:21–30)

¹⁷When evening came, Jesus arrived with the Twelve. ¹⁸While they were reclining at the table eating, he said, "I tell you the truth, one of you will betray me—one who is eating with me."

¹⁹They were saddened, and one by one they said to him, "Surely not I?"

²⁰"It is one of the Twelve," he replied, "one who dips bread into the bowl with me. ²¹The Son of Man will go just as it is written about him. But woe to that man who betrays the Son of Man! It would be better for him if he had not been born."

14:22
/Mt 14:19
²²While they were eating, Jesus took bread, gave thanks and broke it,ʲ and gave it to his disciples, saying, "Take it; this is my body."

14:23
ᵏ1Co 10:16
²³Then he took the cup, gave thanks and offered it to them, and they all drank from it. ᵏ
²⁴"This is my blood of theᵃ covenant, which is poured out for many," he said to them. ²⁵"I

ᵃ24 Some manuscripts *the new*

14:13 The two men Jesus sent were Peter and John (Luke 22:8).

14:14, 15 Many homes had large upstairs rooms, sometimes with stairways both inside and outside the house. The preparations for the Passover would have included setting the table and buying and preparing the Passover lamb, unleavened bread, sauces, and other ceremonial food and drink.

14:19 Judas, the very man who would betray Jesus, was at the table with the others. Judas had already determined to betray Jesus, but in cold-blooded hypocrisy he shared the fellowship of this meal. It is easy to become enraged or shocked by what Judas did; yet professing commitment to Christ and then denying him with one's life is also betraying him. It is denying Christ's love to disobey him; it is denying his truth to distrust him; it is denying his deity to reject his authority. Do your words and actions match?

14:20 It was often the practice to eat from a common bowl. Meat or bread was dipped into a bowl filled with sauce often made from fruit.

14:22–25 Mark records the origin of the Last Supper, which is still celebrated in worship services today. Jesus and his disciples ate a meal, sang psalms, read Scripture, and prayed. Then Jesus took two traditional parts of the Passover meal, the passing of bread and the drinking of wine, and gave them new meaning as representations of his body and blood. He used the bread and wine to explain the significance of what he was about to do on the cross. For more on the significance of the Last Supper, see 1 Corinthians 11:23–29.

The Last Supper is remembered by different terms. Each name believers use for this sacrament brings out a different dimension to it. It is the "Lord's Supper" because it commemorates the Passover meal that Jesus ate with his disciples; it is the "Eucharist" (thanksgiving) because in it we thank God for Christ's work for us; it is "Communion" because through it we commune with God and with other believers. As we eat the bread and drink the wine, we should be quietly reflective as we recall Jesus' death and his promise to come again, grateful for God's wonderful gift to us, and joyful as we meet with Christ and the body of believers.

14:23 Whatever name your church uses for this event (Communion, Lord's Supper, or Eucharist) and on whatever schedule you celebrate it, the importance is that through celebrating Communion together believers experience the presence of Christ. The celebration of Communion: (1) humbles us before God. We confess our sin and restate our need for Christ to guide us. (2) reminds us that we are forgiven. We remember that his shed blood paid the price. (3) expresses our oneness in Christ. We are unified in our faith.

(4) encourages us to recommit. We are reminded to pledge ourselves to serve him who died for us.

14:24 Jesus' death for us on the cross seals a new covenant between God and people. The old covenant involved forgiveness of sins through the blood of an animal sacrifice (Exodus 24:6–8). But instead of a spotless lamb on the altar, Jesus offered himself, the spotless Lamb of God, as a sacrifice that would forgive sin once and for all. Jesus was the final sacrifice for sins, and his blood sealed the new agreement between God and us. Now all of us can come to God through Jesus, in full confidence that God will hear us and save us from our sins.

UPPER ROOM AND GETHSEMANE Jesus and the disciples ate the traditional Passover meal in an upper room in the city and then went to the Mount of Olives into a garden called Gethsemane. In the cool of the evening, Jesus prayed for strength to face the trial and suffering ahead.

tell you the truth, I will not drink again of the fruit of the vine until that day when I drink it anew in the kingdom of God."

26 When they had sung a hymn, they went out to the Mount of Olives. *l*

14:26
l Mt 21:1

Jesus Again Predicts Peter's Denial (222/Matthew 26:31–35)

27 "You will all fall away," Jesus told them, "for it is written:

14:27
m Zec 13:7

"'I will strike the shepherd,
and the sheep will be scattered.' *a m*

28 But after I have risen, I will go ahead of you into Galilee." *n*

29 Peter declared, "Even if all fall away, I will not."

30 "I tell you the truth," Jesus answered, "today—yes, tonight—before the rooster crows twice *b* you yourself will disown me three times." *o*

14:28
n Mk 16:7
14:30
o ver 66-72;
Lk 22:34; Jn 13:38

31 But Peter insisted emphatically, "Even if I have to die with you, I will never disown you." And all the others said the same.

Jesus Agonizes in the Garden (223/Matthew 26:36–46; Luke 22:39–46)

32 They went to a place called Gethsemane, and Jesus said to his disciples, "Sit here while I pray." 33 He took Peter, James and John along with him, and he began to be deeply distressed and troubled. 34 "My soul is overwhelmed with sorrow to the point of death," *p* he said to them. "Stay here and keep watch."

14:34
p Jn 12:27

35 Going a little farther, he fell to the ground and prayed that if possible the hour *q* might pass from him. 36 "*Abba,* *c* Father," *r* he said, "everything is possible for you. Take this cup from me. Yet not what I will, but what you will." *s*

14:35
q ver 41
14:36
r Ro 8:15; Gal 4:6
s Mt 26:39

37 Then he returned to his disciples and found them sleeping. "Simon," he said to Peter, "are you asleep? Could you not keep watch for one hour? 38 Watch and pray so that you will not fall into temptation. *t* The spirit is willing, but the body is weak." *u*

14:38
t Mt 6:13
u Ro 7:22, 23

39 Once more he went away and prayed the same thing. 40 When he came back, he again found them sleeping, because their eyes were heavy. They did not know what to say to him.

41 Returning the third time, he said to them, "Are you still sleeping and resting? Enough! The hour *v* has come. Look, the Son of Man is betrayed into the hands of sinners. 42 Rise! Let us go! Here comes my betrayer!"

14:41
v ver 35

Jesus Is Betrayed and Arrested
(224/Matthew 26:47–56; Luke 22:47–53; John 18:1–11)

43 Just as he was speaking, Judas, one of the Twelve, appeared. With him was a crowd armed with swords and clubs, sent from the chief priests, the teachers of the law, and the elders.

44 Now the betrayer had arranged a signal with them: "The one I kiss is the man; arrest

a 27 Zech. 13:7 *b 30* Some early manuscripts do not have *twice.* *c 36* Aramaic for *Father*

14:26 The hymn they sang was most likely taken from Psalms 115—118, traditionally sung at the Passover meal.

14:27–31 This was the second time in the same evening that Jesus predicted the disciples' denial and desertion, which probably explains their strong reaction (14:31). For Jesus' earlier prediction, see Luke 22:31–34 and John 13:36–38.

14:31 Peter was so emphatic. It is easy to say we are devoted to Christ, but our claims are meaningful only when they are tested in the crucible of persecution. How strong is your faith? Is it strong enough to stand up under intense trial? We need the Holy Spirit, not boastfulness and human resolve. We must never discount our vulnerability to pride, greed, or even indifference.

14:35, 36 Was Jesus trying to get out of his task? Jesus expressed his true feelings, but he did not deny or rebel against God's will. He reaffirmed his desire to do what God wanted. Jesus' prayer highlights the terrible suffering he had to endure—an agony so much more magnified because he had to take on the sins of the whole world. This "cup" was the agony of alienation from God, his Father, at the cross (Hebrews 5:7–9). The sinless Son of God took on our sins and was separated for a while from God so that we could be eternally saved.

14:36 While praying, Jesus was aware of what doing the

Father's will would cost him. He understood the suffering he was about to encounter, and he did not want to have to endure the horrible experience. But Jesus prayed, "Not what I will, but what you will." Anything worth having costs something. What does your commitment to God cost you? Be willing to pay any price to gain eternal life.

14:38 You may not face execution for your faith, but you probably face many problems that wear you down. You deal with irritating people whom you must love and serve; you face the burden of unfinished tasks or lack of obvious results; when one is weak, others are strong. (4) *Focus on the purpose God has given you* (14:36)—this is how you do God's will and not your own.

14:43–45 Judas was given a contingent of police and soldiers (John 18:3) in order to seize Jesus and bring him before the religious court for trial. The religious leaders had issued the warrant for Jesus' arrest, and Judas was acting as Jesus' official accuser.

14:45
w Mt 23:7

him and lead him away under guard." ⁴⁵Going at once to Jesus, Judas said, "Rabbi!" *w* and kissed him. ⁴⁶The men seized Jesus and arrested him. ⁴⁷Then one of those standing near drew his sword and struck the servant of the high priest, cutting off his ear.

14:49
x Isa 53:7-12

⁴⁸"Am I leading a rebellion," said Jesus, "that you have come out with swords and clubs to capture me? ⁴⁹Every day I was with you, teaching in the temple courts, and you did not arrest me. But the Scriptures must be fulfilled." *x* ⁵⁰Then everyone deserted him and fled. *y*

14:50
y ver 27

JUDAS ISCARIOT

It is easy to overlook the fact that Jesus chose Judas to be his disciple. We may also forget that while Judas betrayed Jesus, *all* the disciples abandoned him. With the other disciples, Judas shared a persistent misunderstanding of Jesus' mission. They all expected Jesus to make the right political moves. When he kept talking about dying, they all felt varying degrees of anger, fear, and disappointment. They didn't understand why they had been chosen if Jesus' mission was doomed to fail.

The exact motivation behind Judas's betrayal is unclear. What is clear is that Judas allowed his desires to place him in a position where Satan could manipulate him. Judas accepted payment to set Jesus up for the religious leaders. He identified Jesus for the guards in the dimly lit Garden of Gethsemane. It is possible that he was trying to force Jesus' hand: would Jesus now rebel against Rome and set up a new political government?

Whatever his plan, though, at some point Judas realized he didn't like the way things were turning out. He tried to undo the evil he had done by returning the money to the priests, but it was too late. The wheels of God's sovereign plan had been set into motion. How sad that Judas ended his life in despair without ever experiencing the gift of reconciliation God could give even to him through Jesus Christ.

Human feelings toward Judas have always been mixed. Some have fervently hated him for his betrayal. Others have pitied him for not realizing what he was doing. A few have tried to make him a hero for his part in ending Jesus' earthly mission. Some have questioned God's fairness in allowing one man to bear such guilt. While there are many feelings about Judas, there are some facts to consider as well. He, by his own choice, betrayed God's Son into the hands of soldiers (Luke 22:48). He was a thief (John 12:6). Jesus knew that Judas's life of evil would not change (John 6:70). Judas's betrayal of Jesus was part of God's sovereign plan (Psalm 41:9; Zechariah 11:12, 13; Matthew 20:18; 26:20–25; Acts 1:16, 20).

In betraying Jesus, Judas made the greatest mistake in history. But the fact that Jesus knew Judas would betray him doesn't mean that Judas was a puppet of God's will. Judas made the choice. God knew what that choice would be and confirmed it. Judas didn't lose his relationship with Jesus; rather, he never found Jesus in the first place. He is called "doomed to destruction" (John 17:12) because he was never saved.

Judas does us a favor if he makes us think a second time about our commitment to God and the presence of God's Spirit within us. Are we true disciples and followers, or uncommitted pretenders? We can choose despair and death, or we can choose repentance, forgiveness, hope, and eternal life. Judas's betrayal sent Jesus to the cross to guarantee that second choice, our only chance. Will we accept Jesus' free gift, or, like Judas, betray him?

Strengths and accomplishments:	• He was chosen as one of the 12 disciples; the only non-Galilean • He was in charge of the disciples' funds • He was able to recognize the evil in his betrayal of Jesus
Weaknesses and mistakes:	• He was greedy (John 12:6) • He betrayed Jesus • He committed suicide instead of seeking forgiveness
Lessons from his life:	• Evil plans and motives leave us open to being used by Satan for even greater evil • The consequences of evil are so devastating that even small lies and little wrongdoings have serious results • God's plan and his purposes are worked out even in the worst possible events
Vital statistics:	• Where: Possibly from the town of Kerioth • Occupation: Disciple of Jesus • Relative: Father: Simon • Contemporaries: Jesus, Pilate, Herod Antipas, the other 11 disciples
Key verses:	"Then Satan entered Judas, called Iscariot, one of the Twelve. And Judas went to the chief priests and the officers of the temple guard and discussed with them how he might betray Jesus" (Luke 22:3, 4).

Judas's story is told in the Gospels. He is also mentioned in Acts 1:18, 19.

14:47 According to John 18:10, the person who pulled the sword was Peter. Luke 22:51 records that Jesus immediately healed the man's ear and prevented any further bloodshed.

14:50 Just hours earlier, these disciples had vowed never to desert Jesus (14:31).

51A young man, wearing nothing but a linen garment, was following Jesus. When they seized him, 52 he fled naked, leaving his garment behind.

Caiaphas Questions Jesus (226/Matthew 26:57–68)

53 They took Jesus to the high priest, and all the chief priests, elders and teachers of the law came together. 54 Peter followed him at a distance, right into the courtyard of the high priest. *z* There he sat with the guards and warmed himself at the fire. *a*

55 The chief priests and the whole Sanhedrin *b* were looking for evidence against Jesus so that they could put him to death, but they did not find any. 56 Many testified falsely against him, but their statements did not agree.

57 Then some stood up and gave this false testimony against him: 58 "We heard him say, 'I will destroy this man-made temple and in three days will build another, *c* not made by man.'" 59 Yet even then their testimony did not agree.

60 Then the high priest stood up before them and asked Jesus, "Are you not going to answer? What is this testimony that these men are bringing against you?" 61 But Jesus remained silent and gave no answer. *d*

Again the high priest asked him, "Are you the Christ,*a* the Son of the Blessed One?"

62 "I am," said Jesus. "And you will see the Son of Man sitting at the right hand of the Mighty One and coming on the clouds of heaven."

63 The high priest tore his clothes. *e* "Why do we need any more witnesses?" he asked. 64 "You have heard the blasphemy. What do you think?"

They all condemned him as worthy of death. *f* 65 Then some began to spit at him; they blindfolded him, struck him with their fists, and said, "Prophesy!" And the guards took him and beat him.

Peter Denies Knowing Jesus (227/Matthew 26:69–75; Luke 22:54–65; John 18:25–27)

66 While Peter was below in the courtyard, *g* one of the servant girls of the high priest came by. 67 When she saw Peter warming himself, *h* she looked closely at him.

"You also were with that Nazarene, Jesus," *i* she said.

a 61 Or Messiah

14:54
z Mt 26:3
a Jn 18:18

14:55
b Mt 5:22

14:58
c Mk 15:29; Jn 2:19

14:61
d Isa 53:7

14:63
e Nu 14:6; Ac 14:14
14:64
f Lev 24:16

14:66
g ver 54
14:67
h ver 54
i Mk 1:24

JESUS' TRIAL From Gethsemane, Jesus' trial began at the home of Caiaphas, the high priest. Jesus was then taken to Pilate, the Roman governor. Luke records that Pilate sent him to Herod, who was in Jerusalem—presumably in one of his two palaces (Luke 23:5–12). Herod sent him back to Pilate, who handed Jesus over to be crucified.

14:51, 52 Tradition says that this young man may have been John Mark, the writer of this Gospel. The incident is not mentioned in any of the other accounts.

14:53ff This trial by the Sanhedrin had two phases. A small group met at night (John 18:12–24), and then the full Sanhedrin met at daybreak (Luke 22:66–71). They tried Jesus for religious offenses such as calling himself the Son of God, which, according to law, was blasphemy. The trial was fixed: these religious leaders had already decided to kill Jesus (Luke 22:2).

14:55 The Romans controlled Israel, but the Jews were given some authority over religious and minor civil disputes. The Jewish ruling body, the Sanhedrin, was made up of 71 of Israel's religious leaders. It was assumed that these men would be just. Instead, they showed great injustice in the trial of Jesus, even to the point of making up lies to use against him (14:57).

14:58 The statement that the false witnesses finally agreed to use as an accusation twisted Jesus' actual words. Jesus did not say, "I will destroy this man-made temple;" he said, "Destroy this temple, and I will raise it again in three days" (John 2:19). Jesus was not talking about Herod's temple, but about his own body.

14:60–64 To the first question, Jesus made no reply because it was based on confusing and erroneous evidence. Not answering was wiser than trying to clarify the fabricated accusations. But if Jesus had refused to answer the second question, it could have been taken as a denial of his mission. Instead, his answer predicted a powerful role reversal. Sitting on the right hand of power, he would come to judge his accusers, and they would have to answer *his* questions (Psalm 110:1; Revelation 20:11–13).

14:66, 67 Caiaphas's home, where Jesus was tried (14:53), was part of a huge palace with several courtyards. John was apparently acquainted with the high priest, and he was let into the courtyard along with Peter (John 18:15, 16).

68 But he denied it. "I don't know or understand what you're talking about," he said, and went out into the entryway. a

69 When the servant girl saw him there, she said again to those standing around, "This fellow is one of them." 70 Again he denied it. j

After a little while, those standing near said to Peter, "Surely you are one of them, for you are a Galilean." k

71 He began to call down curses on himself, and he swore to them, "I don't know this man you're talking about."

72 Immediately the rooster crowed the second time. b Then Peter remembered the word Jesus had spoken to him: "Before the rooster crows twice c you will disown me three times." l And he broke down and wept.

The Council of Religious Leaders Condemns Jesus
(228/Matthew 27:1–2; Luke 22:66–71)

15 Very early in the morning, the chief priests, with the elders, the teachers of the law m and the whole Sanhedrin, n reached a decision. They bound Jesus, led him away and handed him over to Pilate.

14:70
/ver 30, 68, 72
k Ac 2:7

14:72
/ver 30, 68

15:1
m Mt 27:1; Lk 22:66
n Mt 5:22

a 68 Some early manuscripts *entryway and the rooster crowed*   b 72 Some early manuscripts do not have *the second time.*   c 72 Some early manuscripts do not have *twice.*

MAJOR EVENTS OF PASSION WEEK	Day	Event	References
Sunday through Wednesday Jesus spent each night in Bethany, just two miles east of Jerusalem on the opposite slope of the Mount of Olives. He probably stayed at the home of Mary, Martha, and Lazarus. Jesus spent Thursday night praying in the Garden of Gethsemane. Friday and Saturday nights Jesus' body lay in the garden tomb.	Sunday	Triumphal Entry into Jerusalem	Matthew 21:1–11; Mark 11:1–10; Luke 19:29–40; John 12:12–19
	Monday	Jesus clears the temple	Matthew 21:12, 13; Mark 11:15–17; Luke 19:45, 46
	Tuesday	Jesus' authority challenged in the temple	Matthew 21:23–27; Mark 11:27–33; Luke 20:1–8
		Jesus teaches in stories and confronts the Jewish leaders	Matthew 21:28—23:36; Mark 12:1–40; Luke 20:9–47
		Greeks ask to see Jesus	John 12:20–26
		The Olivet Discourse	Matthew 24; Mark 13; Luke 21:5–38
		Judas agrees to betray Jesus	Matthew 26:14–16; Mark 14:10, 11; Luke 22:3–6
	Wednesday	The Bible does not say what Jesus did on this day; he probably remained in Bethany with his disciples	
	Thursday	The Last Supper	Matthew 26:26–29; Mark 14:22–25; Luke 22:14–20
		Jesus speaks to the disciples in the upper room	John 13—17
		Jesus struggles in Gethsemane	Matthew 26:36–46; Mark 14:32–42; Luke 22:39–46; John 18:1
		Jesus is betrayed and arrested	Matthew 26:47–56; Mark 14:43–52; Luke 22:47–53; John 18:2–12
	Friday	Jesus is tried by Jewish and Roman authorities and is denied by Peter	Matthew 26:57—27:2, 11–31; Mark 14:53—15:20; Luke 22:54—23:25; John 18:13—19:16
		Jesus is crucified	Matthew 27:31–56; Mark 15:20–41; Luke 23:26–49; John 19:17–30
	Sunday	The resurrection	Matthew 28:1–10; Mark 16:1–11; Luke 24:1–12; John 20:1–18

14:71 It is easy to get angry at the Sanhedrin and the Roman governor for their injustice in condemning Jesus, but Peter and the rest of the disciples also contributed to Jesus' pain by deserting him (14:50). While most of us may not be like the Jewish and Roman leaders, we are like the disciples because all of us have been guilty of denying Christ as Lord in vital areas of our lives. We may pride ourselves that we have not committed certain sins, but we are all guilty of sin. Don't try to excuse yourself by pointing at others whose sins seem worse than yours.

15:1 Why did the Jewish leaders send Jesus to Pilate, the Roman governor? The Romans had taken away the Jews' right to inflict capital punishment; so in order for Jesus to be condemned to death, he had to be sentenced by a Roman leader. The Jewish leaders wanted Jesus executed on a cross, a method of death that they believed brought a curse from God (see Deuteronomy 21:23). They hoped to persuade the people that Jesus was cursed, not blessed, by God.

Jesus Stands Trial before Pilate (*230*/Matthew 27:11–14; Luke 23:1–5; John 18:28–37)

2"Are you the king of the Jews?" asked Pilate.

"Yes, it is as you say," Jesus replied.

3The chief priests accused him of many things. 4So again Pilate asked him, "Aren't you going to answer? See how many things they are accusing you of."

5But Jesus still made no reply, and Pilate was amazed.

Pilate Hands Jesus Over to Be Crucified (*232*/Matthew 27:15–26; Luke 23:13–25; John 18:38—19:16)

6Now it was the custom at the Feast to release a prisoner whom the people requested. 7A man called Barabbas was in prison with the insurrectionists who had committed murder in the uprising. 8The crowd came up and asked Pilate to do for them what he usually did.

9"Do you want me to release to you the king of the Jews?" asked Pilate, 10knowing it was out of envy that the chief priests had handed Jesus over to him. 11But the chief priests stirred up the crowd to have Pilate release Barabbas° instead.

15:11
°Ac 3:14

12"What shall I do, then, with the one you call the king of the Jews?" Pilate asked them.

13"Crucify him!" they shouted.

14"Why? What crime has he committed?" asked Pilate.

But they shouted all the louder, "Crucify him!"

15Wanting to satisfy the crowd, Pilate released Barabbas to them. He had Jesus flogged, and handed him over to be crucified.

Roman Soldiers Mock Jesus (*233*/Matthew 27:27–31)

16The soldiers led Jesus away into the palace (that is, the Praetorium) and called together the whole company of soldiers. 17They put a purple robe on him, then twisted together a crown of thorns and set it on him. 18And they began to call out to him, "Hail, king of the Jews!" 19Again and again they struck him on the head with a staff and spit on him. Falling on their knees, they paid homage to him. 20And when they had mocked him, they took off the purple robe and put his own clothes on him. Then they led him out to crucify him.

15:3, 4 The Jewish leaders had to fabricate new accusations against Jesus when they brought him before Pilate. The charge of blasphemy would mean nothing to the Roman governor, so they accused Jesus of three other crimes: (1) encouraging the people not to pay their taxes to Rome, (2) claiming he was a king—"the king of the Jews," and (3) causing riots all over the countryside. Tax evasion, treason, and terrorism—all these would be cause for Pilate's concern (see also Luke 23:2).

15:5 Why didn't Jesus answer Pilate's questions? It would have been futile to answer, and the time had come to give his life to save the world. Jesus had no reason to try to prolong the trial or save himself. His was the ultimate example of self-assurance and peace, which no ordinary criminal could imitate. Nothing would stop him from completing the work he had come to earth to do (Isaiah 53:7).

15:7 Barabbas was arrested for his part in a rebellion against the Roman government, and, although he had committed a murder, he may have been a hero among the Jews. The fiercely independent Jews hated to be ruled by pagan Romans. They hated paying taxes to support the despised government and its gods. Most of the Roman authorities who had to settle Jewish disputes hated the Jews in return. The time was ripe for rebellion.

15:8 This crowd was most likely a group of people loyal to the Jewish leaders. But where were the disciples and the crowds who days earlier had shouted, "Hosanna in the highest" (11:10)? Jesus' sympathizers were afraid of the Jewish leaders, so they went into hiding. Another possibility is that the multitude included many people who were in the Palm Sunday parade, but who turned against Jesus when they saw that he was not going to be an earthly conqueror and their deliverer from Rome.

15:10 The Jews hated Pilate, but they went to him for the favor of condemning Jesus to crucifixion. Pilate could see that this was a frame-up. Why else would these people, who hated him and the Roman empire he represented, ask him to convict one of their fellow Jews of treason and give him the death penalty?

15:13 Crucifixion was the Roman penalty for rebellion. Only slaves or those who were not Roman citizens could be crucified. If Jesus died by crucifixion, he would die the death of a rebel and slave, not of the king he claimed to be. This is just what the Jewish religious leaders wanted, and the reason they whipped the mob into a frenzy. In addition, crucifixion would put the responsibility for killing Jesus on the Romans.

15:15 The region of Judea where Pilate ruled as governor was little more than a hot and dusty outpost of the Roman empire. Because Judea was so far from Rome, Pilate was given just a small army. His primary job was to keep peace. We know from historical records that Pilate had already been warned about other uprisings in his region. Although he may have seen no guilt in Jesus and no reason to condemn him to death, Pilate wavered when the Jews in the crowd threatened to report him to Caesar (John 19:12). Such a report, accompanied by a riot, could cost him his position and hopes for advancement.

Although Jesus was innocent according to Roman law, Pilate caved in to political pressure. He abandoned what he knew was right. Trying to second-guess the Jewish leaders, Pilate gave a decision that would please everyone while keeping himself safe. When we lay aside God's clear statements of right and wrong and make decisions based on the preferences of our audience, we fall into compromise and lawlessness. God promises to honor those who do right, not those who make everyone happy.

15:19 The brutal guards, the power-hungry governor, and the conniving religious leaders had the upper hand. But they did not know the true power and authority of this man they were torturing and had condemned to death. Worldly powers and philosophies that mock Jesus' lordship will not be so arrogant when Jesus returns in judgment (see Philippians 2:10, 11). When you feel that unjust people who have control and viewpoints hostile to Christianity are carrying the day, rest assured that Jesus holds the highest place and will return in glory.

placed it in a tomb cut out of rock. Then he rolled a stone against the entrance of the tomb. ⁴⁷Mary Magdalene and Mary the mother of Joses saw where he was laid.

Jesus Rises from the Dead (*239*/Matthew 28:1–7; Luke 24:1–12; John 20:1–10)

16:1
ᶠLk 23:56;
Jn 19:39, 40

16 When the Sabbath was over, Mary Magdalene, Mary the mother of James, and Salome bought spicesᶠ so that they might go to anoint Jesus' body. ²Very early on the first day

PILATE

In Jesus' day, any death sentence had to be approved by the Roman official in charge of the administrative district. Pontius Pilate was governor of the province of Judea, where Jerusalem was located. When the Jewish leaders had Jesus in their power and wanted to kill him, they had to obtain Pilate's permission. So it happened that early one morning Pilate found a crowd at his door demanding a man's death.

Pilate's relationship with the Jews had always been stormy. His Roman toughness and fairness had been weakened by cynicism, compromises, and mistakes. On several occasions his actions had deeply offended the religious leaders. The resulting riots and chaos must have made Pilate wonder what he had gotten himself into. He was trying to control people who treated their Roman conquerors without respect. Jesus' trial was another episode in Pilate's ongoing problems.

For Pilate, there was never a doubt about Jesus' innocence. Three separate times he declared Jesus not guilty. He couldn't understand why these people wanted to kill Jesus, but his fear of the Jews' political pressure made him decide to allow Jesus' crucifixion. Because of the people's threat to inform the emperor that Pilate hadn't eliminated a rebel against Rome, Pilate went against what he knew was right. In desperation, he chose to do wrong.

We share a common humanity with Pilate. At times we know what is right but choose what is wrong. He had his moment in history, and now we have ours. What have we done with our opportunities and responsibilities? What judgment have we passed on Jesus?

Strength and accomplishment:
• Roman governor of Judea

Weaknesses and mistakes:
• He failed in his attempt to rule a people who were defeated militarily but never dominated by Rome
• His constant political struggles made him a cynical and uncaring compromiser, susceptible to pressure
• Although he realized Jesus was innocent, he bowed to the public demand for his execution

Lessons from his life:
• Great evil can happen when truth is at the mercy of political pressures
• Resisting the truth leaves a person without purpose or direction

Vital statistics:
• Where: Judea
• Occupation: Roman governor of Judea
• Relative: Wife: unnamed
• Contemporaries: Jesus, Caiaphas, Herod Antipas

Key verses:
"'What is truth?' Pilate asked. With this he went out again to the Jews and said, 'I find no basis for a charge against him. But it is your custom for me to release to you one prisoner at the time of the Passover. Do you want me to release "the king of the Jews"?'" (John 18:38, 39).

Pilate's story is told in the Gospels. He is also mentioned in Acts 3:13; 4:27; 13:28; 1 Timothy 6:13.

stationed guards by the tomb and sealed the stone to make sure that no one would steal Jesus' body and claim he had risen from the dead (Matthew 27:62–66).

15:47 These women could do very little. They couldn't speak before the Sanhedrin in Jesus' defense; they couldn't appeal to Pilate; they couldn't stand against the crowds; they couldn't overpower the Roman guards. But they did what they could. They stayed at the cross when the disciples had fled, they followed Jesus' body to its tomb, and they prepared spices for his body. Because these women used the opportunities they had, they were the first to witness the resurrection. God blessed their devotion and diligence. As believers, we should take advantage of the opportunities we have and do what we *can* for Christ, instead of worrying about what we *cannot* do.

16:1, 2 The women purchased the spices on Saturday evening after the Sabbath had ended so they could go to the tomb early the next morning and anoint Jesus' body as a sign of love, devotion, and respect. Bringing spices to the tomb was like bringing flowers to a grave today. But these women faced two overwhelming problems as they set out to honor Jesus' body—the Roman guards and the huge rock in the tomb's doorway. Impossible obstacles. So what did these women expect to accomplish that early Sunday morning? Urged on by love and gratitude, they walked on—even as they wondered the same questions aloud.

The church's mission—to send the gospel to all the world—is fraught with overwhelming obstacles. Any one of them appears devastating. Against human stubbornness, disease, danger, terrorism, loneliness, sin, greed, and even church strife and corruption, what can a few missionaries hope to accomplish? Yet like these solitary women, we go out with love and gratitude for Jesus and leave the big obstacles to God.

of the week, just after sunrise, they were on their way to the tomb ³and they asked each other, "Who will roll the stone away from the entrance of the tomb?" *g*

⁴But when they looked up, they saw that the stone, which was very large, had been rolled away. ⁵As they entered the tomb, they saw a young man dressed in a white robe *h* sitting on the right side, and they were alarmed.

⁶"Don't be alarmed," he said. "You are looking for Jesus the Nazarene, *i* who was crucified. He has risen! He is not here. See the place where they laid him. ⁷But go, tell his disciples and Peter, 'He is going ahead of you into Galilee. There you will see him, just as he told you.'" *j*

⁸Trembling and bewildered, the women went out and fled from the tomb. They said nothing to anyone, because they were afraid.

16:3
g Mk 15:46

16:5
h Jn 20:12

16:6
i Mk 1:24
16:7
j Mk 14:28

[The earliest manuscripts and some other ancient witnesses do not have Mark 16:9–20.]

Jesus Appears to Mary Magdalene (*240*/John 20:11–18)

⁹When Jesus rose early on the first day of the week, he appeared first to Mary Magdalene, *k* out of whom he had driven seven demons. ¹⁰She went and told those who had been with him and who were mourning and weeping. ¹¹When they heard that Jesus was alive and that she had seen him, they did not believe it. *l*

16:9
k Jn 20:11-18
16:11
l Lk 24:11

Jesus Appears to Two Believers Traveling on the Road (*243*/Luke 24:13–34)

¹²Afterward Jesus appeared in a different form to two of them while they were walking in the country. *m* ¹³These returned and reported it to the rest; but they did not believe them either.

16:12
m Lk 24:13-32

Jesus Appears to the Disciples Including Thomas (*245*/John 20:24–31)

¹⁴Later Jesus appeared to the Eleven as they were eating; he rebuked them for their lack of faith and their stubborn refusal to believe those who had seen him after he had risen. *n*

16:14
n Lk 24:36-43

Jesus Gives the Great Commission (*248*/Matthew 28:16–20)

¹⁵He said to them, "Go into all the world and preach the good news to all creation. *o* ¹⁶Whoever believes and is baptized will be saved, but whoever does not believe will be condemned. *p* ¹⁷And these signs will accompany those who believe: In my name they will drive out demons; *q* they will speak in new tongues; *r* ¹⁸they will pick up snakes with their hands; and when they drink deadly poison, it will not hurt them at all; they will place their hands on sick people, and they will get well."

16:15
o Mt 28:18-20
16:16
p Ac 16:31
16:17
q Lk 10:17
r Ac 2:4

16:5 Mark says that one angel met the women at the tomb, while Luke mentions two angels. Each Gospel writer chose to highlight different details as he explained the same story, just as eyewitnesses to a news story each may highlight a different aspect of that event. Mark probably emphasized only the angel who spoke. The unique emphasis of each Gospel shows that the four accounts were written independently. This should give us confidence that all four are true and reliable.

16:6 The resurrection is vitally important for many reasons: (1) Jesus kept his promise to rise from the dead, so we can believe he will keep all his other promises. (2) The resurrection ensures that the ruler of God's eternal kingdom will be the living Christ, not just an idea, hope, or dream. (3) Christ's resurrection gives us the assurance that we also will be resurrected. (4) The power of God that brought Christ's body back from the dead is available to us to bring our morally and spiritually dead selves back to life so that we can change and grow (1 Corinthians 15:12–19). (5) The resurrection provides the substance of the church's witness to the world. We do not merely tell lessons from the life of a good teacher; we proclaim the reality of the resurrection of Jesus Christ.

16:7 The angel made special mention of Peter to show that, in spite of Peter's denials, Jesus had not disowned and deserted him. Jesus had great responsibilities for Peter to fulfill in the church that was not yet born.

16:7 The angel told the disciples to meet Jesus in Galilee "as he told you" (see 14:28). This is where Jesus had called most of

them and had said they would become "fishers of men" (Matthew 4:19), and it would be where this mission would be restated (John 21). But the disciples, filled with fear, remained behind locked doors in Jerusalem (John 20:19). Jesus met them first in Jerusalem (Luke 24:36) and later in Galilee (John 21). Then he returned to Jerusalem where he ascended into heaven from the Mount of Olives (Acts 1:12).

16:15 Jesus told his disciples to go into all the world, telling everyone that he had paid the penalty for sin and that those who believe in him can be forgiven and live eternally with God. Christian disciples today in all parts of the world are preaching this gospel to people who haven't heard about Christ. The driving power that carries missionaries around the world and sets Christ's church in motion is the faith that comes from the resurrection. Do you ever feel as though you don't have the skill or determination to be a witness for Christ? You must personally realize that Jesus rose from the dead and lives for you today. As you grow in your relationship with Christ, he will give you both the opportunities and the inner strength to tell his message.

16:16 It is not the water of baptism that saves, but God's grace accepted through faith in Christ. Because of Jesus' response to the criminal on the cross who died with him, we know it is possible to be saved without being baptized (Luke 23:43). Baptism alone, without faith, does not automatically bring a person to heaven. Those who refuse to believe will be condemned, regardless of whether or not they have been baptized.

16:18 There are times when God intervenes miraculously to

Jesus Ascends into Heaven (250/Luke 24:50–53)

16:19
s Lk 24:50, 51
t Ps 110:1

¹⁹After the Lord Jesus had spoken to them, he was taken up into heaven s and he sat at the right hand of God. t ²⁰Then the disciples went out and preached everywhere, and the Lord worked with them and confirmed his word by the signs that accompanied it.

EVIDENCE THAT JESUS ACTUALLY DIED AND AROSE	Proposed Explanations for Empty Tomb	Evidence against These Explanations	References
This evidence demonstrates Jesus' uniqueness in history and proves that he is God's Son. No one else was able to predict his own resurrection and then accomplish it.	Jesus was only unconscious and later revived.	A Roman soldier told Pilate that Jesus was dead.	Mark 15:44, 45
		The Roman soldiers did not break Jesus' legs because he had already died, and one of them pierced Jesus' side with a spear.	John 19:32–34
		Joseph of Arimathea and Nicodemus wrapped Jesus' body and placed it in the tomb.	John 19:38–40
	The women made a mistake and went to the wrong tomb.	Mary Magdalene and Mary the mother of Joseph saw Jesus placed in the tomb.	Matthew 27:59–61 Mark 15:47 Luke 23:55
	Unknown thieves stole Jesus' body.	On Sunday morning Peter and John also went to the same tomb.	John 20:3–9
	The disciples stole Jesus' body.	The tomb was sealed and guarded by Roman soldiers.	Matthew 27:65, 66
		The disciples were ready to die for their faith. Stealing Jesus' body would have been admitting that their faith was meaningless.	Acts 12:2
	The religious leaders stole Jesus' body to produce it later.	If the religious leaders had taken Jesus' body, they would have produced it to stop the rumors of his resurrection.	None

protect his followers. Occasionally he gives them special powers. Paul handled a snake safely (Acts 28:5), and the disciples healed the sick (Matthew 10:1; Acts 3:7, 8). This does not mean, however, that we should test God by putting ourselves in dangerous situations or try to tempt the laws of nature. No one should build a religion on a portion of Scripture. God calls us to live as new citizens in the eternal kingdom and to witness by word and service to God's love and power. Our witness should center on Jesus, not on superhero-type stunts.

16:19 When Jesus ascended into heaven, his physical presence left the disciples (Acts 1:9). Jesus' sitting at God's right hand signifies the completion of his work, his authority as God, and his coronation as King.

16:20 Mark's Gospel emphasizes Christ's power as well as his servanthood. Jesus' life and teaching turn the world upside down. The world sees power as a way to gain control over others. But Jesus, with all authority and power in heaven and earth, chose to serve others. He held children in his arms, healed the sick, washed the disciples' feet, and died for the sins of the world. Following Jesus means receiving this same power to serve. As believers, we are called to be servants of Christ. As Christ served, so we are to serve.

LUKE

VITAL STATISTICS

PURPOSE:
To present an accurate account of the life of Christ and to present Christ as the perfect human and Savior

AUTHOR:
Luke—a doctor (Colossians 4:14), a Greek, and Gentile Christian. He is the only known Gentile author in the New Testament. Luke was a close friend and companion of Paul. He also wrote Acts, and the two books go together.

ORIGINAL AUDIENCE:
Theophilus ("one who loves God"), Gentiles

DATE WRITTEN:
About A.D. 60

SETTING:
Luke wrote from Rome or possibly from Caesarea.

KEY VERSES:
"Jesus said to him, 'Today salvation has come to this house, because this man, too, is a son of Abraham. For the Son of Man came to seek and to save what was lost.'" (19:9, 10).

KEY PEOPLE:
Jesus, Elizabeth, Zechariah, John the Baptist, Mary, the disciples, Herod the Great, Pilate, Mary Magdalene

KEY PLACES:
Bethlehem, Galilee, Judea, Jerusalem

SPECIAL FEATURES:
This is the most comprehensive of the Gospels. The general vocabulary and diction show that the author was educated. He makes frequent references to illnesses and diagnoses. Luke stresses Jesus' relationships with people; emphasizes prayer, miracles, and angels; records inspired hymns of praise; gives a prominent place to women. Most of 9:51—18:35 is not found in any other Gospel.

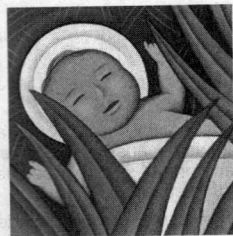

EVERY birth is a miracle, and every child is a gift from God. But nearly 20 centuries ago, the miracle of miracles occurred. A baby was born, but he was the Son of God. The Gospels tell of this birth, but Dr. Luke, as though he were the attending physician, provides most of the details surrounding this awesome occasion. With a divine Father and a human mother, Jesus entered history—God in the flesh.

Luke affirms Jesus' divinity, but the real emphasis of his book is on Jesus' humanity—Jesus, the Son of God, is also the Son of Man. As a doctor, Luke was a man of science, and as a Greek, he was a man of detail. It is not surprising, then, that he begins by outlining his extensive research and explaining that he is reporting the facts (1:1–4). Luke also was a close friend and traveling companion of Paul, so he could interview the other disciples, had access to other historical accounts, and was an eyewitness to the birth and growth of the early church. His Gospel and book of Acts are reliable, historical documents.

Luke's story begins with angels appearing to Zechariah and then to Mary, telling them of the upcoming births of their sons. From Zechariah and Elizabeth would come John the Baptist, who would prepare the way for Christ. And Mary would conceive a child by the Holy Spirit and bear Jesus, the Son of God. Soon after John's birth, Caesar Augustus declared a census, and so Mary and Joseph traveled to Bethlehem, the town of David, their ancient ancestor. There the child was born. Angels announced the joyous event to shepherds, who rushed to the manger. When the shepherds left, they went praising God and spreading the news. Eight days later, Jesus was circumcised and then dedicated to God in the temple, where Simeon and Anna confirmed Jesus' identity as the Savior, their Messiah.

Luke gives us a glimpse of Jesus at age 12—discussing theology with the Jewish teachers of the law at the temple (2:41–52). Eighteen years later Jesus went out in the desert to be baptized by John the Baptist before beginning his public ministry (3:1–23). At this point, Luke traces Jesus' genealogy on his stepfather Joseph's side, through David and Abraham back to Adam, underscoring Jesus' identity as the Son of Man (3:23–38).

After the temptation (4:1–13), Jesus returned to Galilee to preach, teach, and heal (4:14ff). During this time, he began gathering his group of 12 disciples (5:1–11, 27–29). Later Jesus commissioned the disciples and sent them out to proclaim the kingdom of God. When they returned, Jesus revealed to them his mission, his true identity, and what it meant to be his disciple (9:18–62). His mission would take him to Jerusalem (9:51–53), where he would be rejected, tried, and crucified.

While Jesus carried his own cross to Golgotha, some women in Jerusalem wept for him, but Jesus told them to weep for themselves and for their children (23:28). Luke's Gospel does not end in sadness, however. It concludes with the thrilling account of Jesus' resurrection from the dead, his appearances to the disciples, and his promise to send the Holy Spirit (24:1–53). Read Luke's beautifully written and accurate account of the life of Jesus, Son of Man and Son of God. Then praise God for sending the Savior—our risen and triumphant Lord—for all people.

Tiberius Caesar becomes emperor 14		John's ministry begins 26	Jesus begins his ministry 26/27	Jesus chooses twelve disciples 28	Jesus feeds 5,000 29	Jesus is crucified, rises again, and ascends 30

THE BLUEPRINT

A. **BIRTH AND PREPARATION OF JESUS, THE SAVIOR (1:1—4:13)**

From an infant who could do nothing on his own, Jesus grew to become completely able to fulfill his mission on earth. He was fully human, developing in all ways like us. Yet he remained fully God. He took no shortcuts and was not isolated from the pressures and temptations of life. There are no shortcuts for us either as we prepare for lives of service to God.

B. **MESSAGE AND MINISTRY OF JESUS, THE SAVIOR (4:14—21:38)**
   1. Jesus' ministry in Galilee
   2. Jesus' ministry on the way to Jerusalem
   3. Jesus' ministry in Jerusalem

Jesus taught great crowds of people, especially through parables, which are stories that illustrate great truths. But only those with ears to hear will understand. We should pray that God's Spirit would help us understand the implications of these truths for our lives so we can become more and more like Jesus.

C. **DEATH AND RESURRECTION OF JESUS, THE SAVIOR (22:1—24:53)**

The Savior of the world was arrested and executed. But death could not destroy him, and Jesus came back to life and ascended to heaven. In Luke's careful, historical account, we receive the facts about Jesus' resurrection. We must not only believe that these facts are true, but we must also trust Christ as our Savior. It is shortsighted to neglect the facts, but how sad it is to accept the facts and neglect the forgiveness that Jesus offers to each of us.

MEGATHEMES

THEME	EXPLANATION	IMPORTANCE
Jesus Christ, the Savior	Luke describes how God's Son entered human history. Jesus lived as the perfect example of a human. After a perfect ministry, he provided a perfect sacrifice for our sin so we could be saved.	Jesus is our perfect leader and Savior. He offers forgiveness to all who will accept him as Lord of their lives and believe that what he says is true.
History	Luke was a medical doctor and historian. He put great emphasis on dates and details, connecting Jesus to events and people in history.	Luke gives details so we can believe in the reliability of the history of Jesus' life. Even more important, we can believe with certainty that Jesus is God.
People	Jesus was deeply interested in people and relationships. He showed warm concern for his followers and friends—men, women, and children.	Jesus' love for people is good news for everyone. His message is for all people in every nation. Each one of us has an opportunity to respond to him in faith.
Compassion	As a perfect human, Jesus showed tender sympathy to the poor, the despised, the hurt, and the sinful. No one was rejected or ignored by him.	Jesus is more than a good teacher—he cares for you. Because of his deep love for you, he can satisfy your needs.
Holy Spirit	The Holy Spirit was present at Jesus' birth, baptism, ministry, and resurrection. As a perfect example for us, Jesus lived in dependence on the Holy Spirit.	The Holy Spirit was sent by God as confirmation of Jesus' authority. The Holy Spirit is given to enable people to live for Christ. By faith we can have the indwelling Holy Spirit's presence and power to witness and to serve.

A. BIRTH AND PREPARATION OF JESUS, THE SAVIOR (1:1—4:13)
Luke gives us the most detailed account of Jesus' birth. In describing Jesus' birth, childhood, and development, Luke lifts up the humanity of Jesus. Our Savior was the ideal human. Fully prepared, the ideal human was now ready to live the perfect life.

Luke's Purpose in Writing (1)

1 Many have undertaken to draw up an account of the things that have been fulfilled[a] among us, 2 just as they were handed down to us by those who from the first[a] were eyewitnesses[b] and servants of the word. 3 Therefore, since I myself have carefully investigated everything from the beginning, it seemed good also to me to write an orderly account[c] for you, most excellent Theophilus,[d] 4 so that you may know the certainty of the things you have been taught.

1:2
a Jn 15:27
b Heb 2:3; 2Pe 1:16
1:3
c Ac 11:4
d Ac 1:1

An Angel Promises the Birth of John to Zechariah (4)

5 In the time of Herod king of Judea[e] there was a priest named Zechariah, who belonged to the priestly division of Abijah;[f] his wife Elizabeth was also a descendant of Aaron. 6 Both of them were upright in the sight of God, observing all the Lord's commandments and regulations blamelessly. g 7 But they had no children, because Elizabeth was barren; and they were both well along in years.

8 Once when Zechariah's division was on duty and he was serving as priest before God,[h] 9 he was chosen by lot, according to the custom of the priesthood, to go into the temple of the Lord and burn incense.[i] 10 And when the time for the burning of incense came, all the assembled worshipers were praying outside.[j]

11 Then an angel of the Lord appeared to him, standing at the right side of the altar of incense. 12 When Zechariah saw him, he was startled and was gripped with fear. 13 But the angel said to him: "Do not be afraid, Zechariah; your prayer has been heard. Your wife Elizabeth will bear you a son, and you are to give him the name John. k 14 He will be a joy and

1:5
e Mt 2:1
f 1Ch 24:10
1:6
g Ge 7:1
1:8
h 1Ch 24:19;
2Ch 8:14
1:9
i Ex 30:7, 8
1:10
j Lev 16:17
1:13
k ver 60, 63

a 1 Or been surely believed

1:1, 2 Luke tells Jesus' story from Luke's unique perspective of a Gentile, a physician, and the first historian of the early church. Though not an eyewitness of Jesus' ministry, Luke nevertheless was concerned that eyewitness accounts be preserved accurately and that the foundations of Christian belief be transmitted intact to the next generation. In Luke's Gospel are many of Jesus' parables. In addition, more than any other Gospel, it gives specific instances of Jesus' concern for women.

1:1–4 There was a lot of interest in Jesus, and many people had written firsthand accounts about him. Luke may have used these accounts and all other available resources as material for an accurate and complete account of Jesus' life, teachings, and ministry. Because truth was important to Luke, he relied heavily on eyewitness accounts. Christianity doesn't say, "Close your eyes and believe," but rather, "Check it out for yourself." The Bible encourages you to investigate its claims thoroughly (John 1:46; 21:24; Acts 17:11, 12) because your conclusion about Jesus is a life-and-death matter.

1:3 *Theophilus* means "one who loves God." The book of Acts, also written by Luke, is likewise addressed to Theophilus. This preface may be a general dedication to all Christian readers. Theophilus may have been Luke's patron who helped to finance the book's writing. More likely, Theophilus was a Roman acquaintance of Luke's with a strong interest in the new Christian religion.

1:3, 4 As a medical doctor, Luke knew the importance of being thorough. He used his skills in observation and analysis to thoroughly investigate the stories about Jesus. His diagnosis? The gospel of Jesus Christ is true! You can read Luke's account of Jesus' life with confidence that it was written by a clear thinker and a thoughtful researcher. Because the gospel is founded on historical truth, our spiritual growth must involve careful, disciplined, and thorough investigation of God's Word so that we can understand how God has acted in history. If this kind of study is not part of your life, find a pastor, teacher, or even a book to help you get started and to guide you in this important part of Christian growth.

1:5 This was Herod the Great, confirmed by the Roman Senate as king of the Jews. Only half Jewish himself and eager to please his Roman superiors, Herod expanded and beautified the Jerusalem temple—but he placed a Roman eagle over the entrance. When he helped the Jews, it was for political purposes and not because he cared about their God. Later, Herod the Great would order a massacre of infants in a futile attempt to kill the infant Jesus, whom some were calling the new "king of the Jews" (Matthew 2:2).

1:5 A Jewish priest was a minister of God who worked at the temple managing its upkeep, teaching the people the Scriptures, and directing the worship services. At this time there were about 20,000 priests throughout the country—far too many to minister in the temple at one time. Therefore the priests were divided into 24 separate groups of about 1,000 each, according to David's instructions (1 Chronicles 24:3–19).

Zechariah was a member of the Abijah division, on duty this particular week. Each morning a priest was to enter the Holy Place in the temple and burn incense. The priests would cast lots to decide who would enter the sacred room, and one day the lot fell to Zechariah. But it was not by chance that Zechariah was on duty and that he was chosen that day to enter the Holy Place— perhaps a once-in-a-lifetime opportunity. God was guiding the events of history to prepare the way for Jesus to come to earth.

1:6 Zechariah and Elizabeth didn't merely go through the motions in following God's laws; they backed up their outward compliance with inward obedience. Unlike the religious leaders whom Jesus called hypocrites, Zechariah and Elizabeth did not stop with the letter of the law. Their obedience was from the heart, and that is why they are called "upright in the sight of God."

1:7 God answers prayer in his own way and in his own time. He worked in an "impossible" situation—Elizabeth's age and barrenness—to bring about the fulfillment of all the prophecies concerning the Messiah. If you want to have your prayers answered, you must be open to what God can do in impossible situations. And you must wait for God to work in his way and in his time.

KEY PLACES IN LUKE

The broken lines (— · —) indicate modern boundaries.

Luke begins his account in the temple in Jerusalem, giving us the background for the birth of John the Baptist, then moves on to the town of Nazareth and the story of Mary, chosen to be Jesus' mother (1:26ff). As a result of Caesar's call for a census, Mary and Joseph had to travel to Bethlehem, where Jesus was born in fulfillment of prophecy (2:1ff). Jesus grew up in Nazareth and began his earthly ministry by being baptized by John (3:21, 22) and tempted by Satan (4:1ff). Much of his ministry focused on Galilee: He set up his "home" in Capernaum (4:31ff), and from there he taught throughout the region (8:1ff). Later he visited the Gerasene region (also called Gadara), where he healed a demon-possessed man (8:36ff). He fed more than 5,000 people with one lunch on the shores of the Sea of Galilee near Bethsaida (9:10ff). Jesus always traveled to Jerusalem for the major festivals, and he enjoyed visiting friends in nearby Bethany (10:38ff). He healed 10 men with leprosy on the border between Galilee and Samaria (17:11) and helped a dishonest tax collector in Jericho turn his life around (19:1ff). The little villages of Bethphage and Bethany on the Mount of Olives were Jesus' resting places during his last days on earth. He was crucified outside Jerusalem's walls, but he would rise again. Two of Jesus' followers walking on the road leading to Emmaus were among the first to see the resurrected Christ (24:13ff).

1:9 Incense was burned in the temple twice daily (Exodus 30:7–10). When the people saw the smoke from the burning incense, they prayed. The smoke drifting heavenward symbolized their prayers ascending to God's throne.

1:11, 12 Angels are spirit beings who live in God's presence and do his will. Only two angels are mentioned by name in Scripture—Michael and Gabriel—but there are many who act as God's messengers. Here, Gabriel (1:19) delivered a special message to Zechariah. This was not a dream or a vision. The angel appeared in visible form and spoke audible words to the priest.

1:13 While burning incense on the altar, Zechariah was also praying, most likely for the coming of the Messiah to his people.

How odd it must have seemed that the angel would say that his prayer was answered and Zechariah would soon have a son. Yet the greatest desire of Zechariah's heart—to have a son—would come true. At the same time, the answer to the nation's prayer for the Messiah would also come true. Zechariah's son would grow up to prepare the way for the Messiah.

1:13 *John* means "the LORD is gracious," and *Jesus* means "the LORD saves." Both names were prescribed by God, not chosen by human parents. Throughout the Gospels, God acts graciously and saves his people. He will not withhold salvation from anyone who sincerely comes to him.

delight to you, and many will rejoice because of his birth, 15for he will be great in the sight of the Lord. He is never to take wine or other fermented drink,¹ and he will be filled with the Holy Spirit even from birth.ᵃ ᵐ 16Many of the people of Israel will he bring back to the Lord their God. 17And he will go on before the Lord, in the spirit and power of Elijah,ⁿ to turn the hearts of the fathers to their children and the disobedient to the wisdom of the righteous— to make ready a people prepared for the Lord."

18Zechariah asked the angel, "How can I be sure of this? I am an old man and my wife is well along in years."ᵒ

19The angel answered, "I am Gabriel.ᵖ I stand in the presence of God, and I have been sent to speak to you and to tell you this good news. 20And now you will be silent and not able to speak until the day this happens, because you did not believe my words, which will come true at their proper time."

21Meanwhile, the people were waiting for Zechariah and wondering why he stayed so long in the temple. 22When he came out, he could not speak to them. They realized he had seen a vision in the temple, for he kept making signsᵈ to them but remained unable to speak.

23When his time of service was completed, he returned home. 24After this his wife Elizabeth became pregnant and for five months remained in seclusion. 25"The Lord has done this for me," she said. "In these days he has shown his favor and taken away my disgraceʳ among the people."

An Angel Promises the Birth of Jesus to Mary (5)

26In the sixth month, God sent the angel Gabriel to Nazareth, a town in Galilee, 27to a virgin pledged to be married to a man named Joseph,ˢ a descendant of David. The virgin's name was Mary. 28The angel went to her and said, "Greetings, you who are highly favored! The Lord is with you."

29Mary was greatly troubled at his words and wondered what kind of greeting this might be. 30But the angel said to her, "Do not be afraid, Mary, you have found favor with God.

ᵃ 15 Or *from his mother's womb*

1:15
¹Nu 6:3; Jdg 13:4;
Lk 7:33
ᵐJer 1:5

1:17
ⁿMt 11:14

1:18
ᵒGe 17:17

1:19
ᵖDa 8:16; 9:21

1:22
ᵈver 62

1:25
ʳGe 30:23; Isa 4:1

1:27
ˢMt 1:16, 18, 20

1:15 John was set apart for special service to God. He may have been forbidden to drink wine as part of the Nazirite vow, an ancient vow of consecration to God (see Numbers 6:1–8). Samson (Judges 13) was under the Nazirite vow, and Samuel may have been also (1 Samuel 1:11).

1:15 This is Luke's first mention of the Holy Spirit, the third person of the Trinity; Luke refers to the Holy Spirit more than any other Gospel writer. Because Luke also wrote the book of Acts, we know he was thoroughly informed about the work of the Holy Spirit. Luke recognized and emphasized the Holy Spirit's work in directing the founding of Christianity and in guiding the early church. The presence of the Spirit is God's gift to the entire church at Pentecost. Prior to that, God's Spirit was given to the faithful for special tasks. We need the Holy Spirit's help to do God's work effectively.

1:17 John's role was to be almost identical to that of an Old Testament prophet—to encourage people to turn away from sin and back to God. John is often compared to the great prophet Elijah, who was known for standing up to evil rulers (Malachi 4:5; Matthew 11:14; 17:10–13). See Elijah's Profile in 1 Kings 18, p. 527.

1:18–20 When told he would have a son, Zechariah doubted the angel's word. From Zechariah's human perspective, his doubts were understandable—but with God, anything is possible. What God promises, he delivers. And God delivers *on time!* You can have complete confidence that God will keep his promises. Their fulfillment may not be the next day, but they will be "at their proper time." If you are waiting for God to answer some request or to fill some need, remain patient. No matter how impossible God's promises may seem, what he has said in his Word will come true at the right time.

1:21 The people were waiting outside for Zechariah to come out and pronounce the customary blessing upon them as found in Numbers 6:24–26.

1:25 Zechariah and Elizabeth were both faithful people, yet they

were suffering. Some Jews at that time did not believe in a bodily resurrection, so their hope of immortality was in their children. In addition, children cared for their parents in their old age and added to the family's financial security and social status. Children were considered a blessing, and childlessness was seen as a curse. Zechariah and Elizabeth had been childless for many years, and at this time they were too old to expect any change in their situation. They felt humiliated and hopeless. But God was waiting for the right time to encourage them and take away their disgrace.

1:26 Gabriel appeared not only to Zechariah and to Mary but also to the prophet Daniel more than 500 years earlier (Daniel 8:15–17; 9:21). Each time Gabriel appeared, he brought important messages from God.

1:26 Nazareth, Joseph's and Mary's hometown, was a long way from Jerusalem, the center of Jewish life and worship. Located on a major trade route, Nazareth was frequently visited by Gentile merchants and Roman soldiers. It was known for its independent and aloof attitude. Jesus was born in Bethlehem but grew up in Nazareth. Nevertheless, the people of Nazareth would reject him as the Messiah (4:22–30).

1:27, 28 Mary was young, poor, female—all characteristics that, to the people of her day, would make her seem unusable by God for any major task. But God chose Mary for one of the most important acts of obedience he has ever demanded of anyone. You may feel that your ability, experience, or education makes you an unlikely candidate for God's service. Don't limit God's choices. He can use you if you trust him.

1:30, 31 God's favor does not automatically bring instant success or fame. His blessing on Mary, the honor of being the mother of the Messiah, would lead to much pain: her peers would ridicule her; her fiancé would come close to leaving her; her son would be rejected and murdered. But through her son would come the world's only hope, and this is why Mary has been praised by countless generations as the young girl who "found favor with God." Her submission was part of God's plan to bring about our

1:31
t Lk 2:21

1:32
u Mk 5:7

1:33
v Da 2:44; 7:14, 27

1:35
w ver 32, 76
x Mt 4:3

1:37
y Mt 19:26

31 You will be with child and give birth to a son, and you are to give him the name Jesus. *t* 32 He will be great and will be called the Son of the Most High. *u* The Lord God will give him the throne of his father David, 33 and he will reign over the house of Jacob forever; his kingdom will never end." *v*

34 "How will this be," Mary asked the angel, "since I am a virgin?"

35 The angel answered, "The Holy Spirit will come upon you, and the power of the Most High *w* will overshadow you. So the holy one to be born will be called *a* the Son of God. *x* 36 Even Elizabeth your relative is going to have a child in her old age, and she who was said to be barren is in her sixth month. 37 For nothing is impossible with God." *y*

a 35 Or *So the child to be born will be called holy,*

ZECHARIAH

Zechariah, a Jewish priest, was told before anyone else that God was setting in motion his own visit to earth. Zechariah and his wife, Elizabeth, were known for their personal holiness. They were well suited to doing a special work for God. But they shared the pain of not having children, and in Jewish culture this was considered not having God's blessing. Zechariah and Elizabeth were old, and they had stopped even asking for children.

One day while on duty at the temple in Jerusalem, Zechariah received an unexpected blessing. He was chosen to be the priest who would enter the Holy Place to offer incense to God for the people. Suddenly, much to his surprise and terror, he found himself face to face with an angel. The angel's message was too good to be true! But the news of the coming Savior was eclipsed by doubts about his own ability to father the child the angel promised him. His age spoke more loudly than God's promise. As a result, God prevented Zechariah from speaking until the promise became reality.

The record of the prayer in Luke 1 is our last glimpse of Zechariah. Like so many of God's most faithful servants, he passed quietly from the scene once his part was done. He becomes our hero for those times when we doubt God and yet are willing to obey. We gain hope from Zechariah's story that God can do great things through anyone who is available to him.

Strengths and accomplishments:	• Known as a righteous man • Was a priest before God • One of the few people to be directly addressed by an angel • Fathered John the Baptist
Weakness and mistake:	• Momentarily doubted the angel's promise of a son because of his own old age
Lessons from his life:	• Physical limitations do not limit God • God accomplishes his will, sometimes in unexpected ways
Vital statistics:	• Occupation: Priest • Relatives: Wife: Elizabeth. Son: John the Baptist.
Key verses:	"Both of them were upright in the sight of God, observing all the Lord's commandments and regulations blamelessly. But they had no children, because Elizabeth was barren; and they were both well along in years" (Luke 1:6, 7).

Zechariah's story is told in Luke 1.

---

salvation. If sorrow weighs you down and dims your hope, think of Mary and wait patiently for God to finish working out his plan.

1:31 *Jesus,* a Greek form of the Hebrew name *Joshua,* was a common name meaning "the LORD saves." Just as Joshua had led Israel into the promised land (see Joshua 1:1, 2), so Jesus would lead his people into eternal life. The symbolism of his name was not lost on the people of his day, who took names seriously and saw them as a source of power. In Jesus' name people were healed, demons were banished, and sins were forgiven.

1:32, 33 Centuries earlier, God had promised David that David's kingdom would last forever (2 Samuel 7:16). This promise was fulfilled in the coming of Jesus, a direct descendant of David, whose kingdom will never end.

1:34 The birth of Jesus to a virgin is a miracle that many people find hard to believe. These three facts can aid our faith: (1) Luke was a medical doctor, and he knew perfectly well how babies are made. It would have been just as hard for him to believe in a virgin birth as it is for us, yet he reports it as fact. (2) Luke was a painstaking researcher who based his Gospel on eyewitness accounts. Tradition holds that he talked with Mary about the

events he recorded in the first two chapters. This is Mary's story, not a fictional invention. (3) Christians and Jews, who worship God as the Creator of the universe, should believe that God has the power to create a child in a virgin's womb.

1:35 Why is the Virgin Birth important to the Christian faith? Jesus was born without the sin that entered the world through Adam. He was born holy, just as Adam was created sinless. In contrast to Adam, who disobeyed God, Jesus obeyed God and was thus able to face sin's consequences in our place and make us acceptable to God (Romans 5:14–19). Jesus Christ, God's Son, had to be free from the sinful nature passed on to all other human beings by Adam. Because Jesus was born of a woman, he was a human being; but as the Son of God, Jesus was born without any trace of human sin. Jesus is both fully human and fully divine. Because Jesus lived as a man, human beings know that he fully understands their experiences and struggles (Hebrews 4:15–16). Because he is God, he has the power and authority to deliver people from sin (Colossians 2:13–15). People can tell Jesus all their thoughts, feelings, and needs. He has been where they are, and he has the ability to help.

38 "I am the Lord's servant," Mary answered. "May it be to me as you have said." Then the angel left her.

Mary Visits Elizabeth (6)

39 At that time Mary got ready and hurried to a town in the hill country of Judea,z 40 where she entered Zechariah's home and greeted Elizabeth. 41 When Elizabeth heard Mary's greeting, the baby leaped in her womb, and Elizabeth was filled with the Holy Spirit. 42 In a loud voice she exclaimed: "Blessed are you among women,a and blessed is the child you will bear! 43 But why am I so favored, that the mother of my Lord should come to me? 44 As soon as the sound of your greeting reached my ears, the baby in my womb leaped for joy. 45 Blessed is she who has believed that what the Lord has said to her will be accomplished!"

The Magnificat: Mary's Song of Praise

46 And Mary said:

"My soul glorifies the Lordb
47 　and my spirit rejoices in God my Savior,
48 for he has been mindful
　　of the humble state of his servant.c
From now on all generations will call me blessed,d
49 　for the Mighty One has done great thingse for me—
　　holy is his name.
50 His mercy extends to those who fear him,
　　from generation to generation.f
51 　He has performed mighty deeds with his arm;g
　　he has scattered those who are proud in their inmost thoughts.
52 He has brought down rulers from their thrones
　　but has lifted up the humble.
53 He has filled the hungry with good things
　　but has sent the rich away empty.
54 He has helped his servant Israel,
　　remembering to be mercifulh
55 to Abraham and his descendantsi forever,
　　even as he said to our fathers."

56 Mary stayed with Elizabeth for about three months and then returned home.

1:39 z ver 65
1:42 a Jdg 5:24
1:46 b Ps 34:2, 3
1:48 c Ps 138:6
d Lk 11:27
1:49 e Ps 71:19
1:50 f Ps 103:17
1:51 g Ps 98:1
1:54 h Ps 98:3
1:55 i Ge 17:19;
Ps 132:11; Gal 3:16

1:38 A young unmarried girl who became pregnant risked disaster. Unless the father of the child agreed to marry her, she would probably remain unmarried for life. If her own father rejected her, she could be forced into begging or prostitution in order to earn her living. And Mary, with her story about being made pregnant by the Holy Spirit, risked being considered crazy as well. Still Mary said, despite the possible risks, "May it be to me as you have said." When Mary said that, she didn't know about the tremendous opportunity she would have. She only knew that God was asking her to serve him, and she willingly obeyed. Don't wait to see the bottom line before offering your life to God. Offer yourself willingly, even when the outcome seems disastrous.

1:38 God's announcement of a child to be born was met with various responses throughout Scripture. Sarah, Abraham's wife, laughed (Genesis 18:9–15). Zechariah doubted (Luke 1:18). By contrast, Mary submitted. She believed the angel's words and agreed to bear the child, even under humanly impossible circumstances. God is able to do the impossible. Our response to his demands should not be laughter, or doubt, but willing acceptance.

1:41–43 Apparently the Holy Spirit told Elizabeth that Mary's child was the Messiah because Elizabeth called her young relative "the mother of my Lord" as she greeted her. As Mary rushed off to visit her relative, she must have been wondering if the events of the last few days had been real. Elizabeth's greeting must have strengthened her faith. Mary's pregnancy may have seemed impossible, but her wise relative believed in the Lord's faithfulness and rejoiced in Mary's blessed condition.

1:42, 43 Even though she herself was pregnant with a long-awaited son, Elizabeth could have envied Mary, whose son would be even greater than her own. Instead she was filled with joy that the mother of her Lord would visit her. Have you ever envied people whom God has apparently singled out for special blessing? A cure for jealousy is to rejoice with those individuals, realizing that God uses his people in ways best suited to his purpose.

1:46–55 This song is often called the *Magnificat*, the first word in the Latin translation of this passage. Mary's song has often been used as the basis for choral music and hymns. Like Hannah, the mother of Samuel (1 Samuel 2:1–10), Mary glorified God in song for what he was going to do for the world through her. Notice that in both songs, God is pictured as a champion of the poor, the oppressed, and the despised.

1:48 When Mary said, "From now on all generations will call me blessed," was she being proud? No, she was recognizing and accepting the gift God had given her. Pride is refusing to accept God's gifts or taking credit for what God has done; humility is accepting the gifts and using them to praise and serve God. Don't deny, belittle, or ignore your gifts. Thank God for them and use them to his glory.

1:54, 55 God kept his promise to Abraham to be merciful to God's people forever (Genesis 22:16–18). Christ's birth fulfilled the promise, and Mary understood this. She was not surprised when her special son eventually announced that he was the Messiah. She had known Jesus' mission from before his birth. Some of God's promises to Israel are found in 2 Samuel 22:50, 51; Psalms 89:2–4; 103:17, 18; Micah 7:18–20.

1:56 Because travel was difficult, long visits were customary.

John the Baptist Is Born (7)

57 When it was time for Elizabeth to have her baby, she gave birth to a son. 58 Her neighbors and relatives heard that the Lord had shown her great mercy, and they shared her joy.

1:59
j Ge 17:12; Lev 12:3

59 On the eighth day they came to circumcise*j* the child, and they were going to name him after his father Zechariah, 60 but his mother spoke up and said, "No! He is to be called John."

61 They said to her, "There is no one among your relatives who has that name."

1:62
k ver 22

62 Then they made signs*k* to his father, to find out what he would like to name the child. 63 He asked for a writing tablet, and to everyone's astonishment he wrote, "His name is John." 64 Immediately his mouth was opened and his tongue was loosed, and he began to speak, praising God. 65 The neighbors were all filled with awe, and throughout the hill

1:66
l Ge 39:2; Ac 11:21

country of Judea people were talking about all these things. 66 Everyone who heard this wondered about it, asking, "What then is this child going to be?" For the Lord's hand was with him. *l*

Zechariah's Prophecy

1:67
m Joel 2:28

67 His father Zechariah was filled with the Holy Spirit and prophesied: *m*

1:68
n Ps 111:9; Lk 7:16

68 "Praise be to the Lord, the God of Israel,
because he has come and has redeemed his people. *n*

1:69
o Ps 18:2; 132:17

69 He has raised up a horn*a o* of salvation for us
in the house of his servant David

1:70
p Jer 23:5

70 (as he said through his holy prophets of long ago),*p*
71 salvation from our enemies
and from the hand of all who hate us—
72 to show mercy to our fathers
and to remember his holy covenant,
73 the oath he swore to our father Abraham:

a 69 *Horn* here symbolizes strength.

GOD'S UNUSUAL METHODS OF COMMUNICATING	Person/Group	Method	Reference
One of the best ways to understand God's willingness to communicate to people is to note the various methods, some of them quite unexpected, that he has used to give his message.	Jacob, Zechariah, Mary, shepherds	Angels	Genesis 32:22–32; Luke 1:13, 30; 2:10
	Jacob, Joseph, a baker, a cup/bearer, Pharaoh, Isaiah, Joseph, the Magi	Dreams	Genesis 28:10–22; 37:5–10; 40:5; 41:7, 8; Isaiah 1:1; Matthew 1:20; 2:12, 13
	Belshazzar	Writing on the wall	Daniel 5:5–9
	Balaam	Talking donkey	Numbers 22:21–35
	People of Israel	Pillar of cloud and fire	Exodus 13:21, 22
	Jonah	Being swallowed by a fish	Jonah 2
	Abraham, Moses, Jesus at his baptism, Paul	Verbally	Genesis 12:1–4; Exodus 7:8; Matthew 3:13–17; Acts 18:9
	Moses	Fire	Exodus 3:2
	Us	God's Son	Hebrews 1:1, 2

Mary must have been a great help to Elizabeth, who was experiencing the discomforts of a first pregnancy in old age.

1:59 The circumcision ceremony was an important event to the family of a Jewish baby boy. God commanded circumcision when he was beginning to form his holy nation (Genesis 17:4–14), and he had reaffirmed it through Moses (Leviticus 12:1–3). This ceremony was a time of joy when friends and family members would celebrate the baby's becoming part of God's covenant nation.

1:59 Family lines and family names were important to the Jews. The people naturally assumed the child would receive Zechariah's name or at least a family name. They were surprised, therefore, that both Elizabeth and Zechariah wanted to name the boy John. This was the name the angel had given them (see 1:13).

1:62 Zechariah's relatives talked to him by gestures, because he

was apparently deaf as well as speechless and had not heard what his wife had said.

1:67–79 Zechariah praised God with his first words after months of silence. In a song that is often called the *Benedictus* after the first words in the Latin translation of this passage, Zechariah prophesied the coming of a Savior who would redeem his people and predicted that his son John would prepare the Messiah's way. All the Old Testament prophecies were coming true—no wonder Zechariah praised God! The Messiah would come in Zechariah's lifetime, and his son had been chosen to pave the way.

1:72, 73 This was God's promise to Abraham to bless all peoples through him (see Genesis 12:3). It would be fulfilled through the Messiah, Abraham's descendant.

74 to rescue us from the hand of our enemies,
    and to enable us to serve him*q* without fear
75 in holiness and righteousness*r* before him all our days.

76 And you, my child, will be called a prophet*s* of the Most High;
    for you will go on before the Lord to prepare the way for him,*t*
77 to give his people the knowledge of salvation
    through the forgiveness of their sins,*u*
78 because of the tender mercy of our God,
    by which the rising sun will come to us from heaven
79 to shine on those living in darkness
    and in the shadow of death,*v*
    to guide our feet into the path of peace."

80 And the child grew and became strong in spirit;*w* and he lived in the desert until he appeared publicly to Israel.

1:74 *q*Heb 9:14
1:75 *r*Eph 4:24
1:76 *s*Mt 11:9 *t*Mal 3:1
1:77 *u*Mk 1:4
1:79 *v*Isa 9:2; Mt 4:16
1:80 *w*Lk 2:40, 52

Jesus Is Born in Bethlehem (9)

2 In those days Caesar Augustus*x* issued a decree that a census should be taken of the entire Roman world. 2(This was the first census that took place while Quirinius was governor of Syria.) 3And everyone went to his own town to register.

4 So Joseph also went up from the town of Nazareth in Galilee to Judea, to Bethlehem the town of David, because he belonged to the house and line of David. 5He went there to register with Mary, who was pledged to be married to him and was expecting a child. 6While they were there, the time came for the baby to be born, 7and she gave birth to her firstborn, a son.

2:1 *x*Lk 3:1

1:76 Zechariah had just recalled hundreds of years of God's sovereign work in history, beginning with Abraham and going on into eternity. Then, in tender contrast, he personalized the story. His son had been chosen for a key role in the drama of the ages. Although God has unlimited power, he chooses to work through frail humans who begin as helpless babies. Don't minimize what God can do through those who are faithful to him.

1:80 Why did John live out in the desert? Prophets used the isolation of the uninhabited desert to enhance their spiritual growth and to focus their message on God. By being in the desert, John remained separate from the economic and political powers so that he could aim his message against them. He also remained separate from the hypocritical religious leaders of his day. His message was different from theirs, and his life proved it.

2:1 Luke is the only Gospel writer who related the events he recorded to world history. His account was addressed to a predominantly Greek audience that would have been interested in and familiar with the political situation. Palestine was under the rule of the Roman empire with Emperor Caesar Augustus, the first Roman emperor, in charge. The Roman rulers, considered to be like gods, stood in contrast to the tiny baby in a manger who was truly God in the flesh.

2:1 A Roman census (registration) was taken to aid military conscription or tax collection. The Jews weren't required to serve in the Roman army, but they could not avoid paying taxes. Augustus's decree went out in God's perfect timing and according to God's perfect plan to bring his Son into the world.

2:1-6 The Romans ruled the civilized world at this time. By contrast, Joseph controlled very little. Against his better judgment and political convictions, he complied with the Roman order to make a long trip just to pay his taxes. His fiancée, who had to go with him, was about to give birth.

    The Romans were in control insofar as human authority can get its way by exerting human power. But the Romans did not recognize their limitations. In reality, God controls the world. In all times and places, he works his will. By the decree of Emperor Augustus, Jesus was born in the very town prophesied for his birth (Micah 5:2), even though his parents did not live there. Joseph and Mary were both descendants of David. The Old Testament is filled with prophecies that the Messiah would be born in David's royal line (see, for example, Isaiah 11:1; Jeremiah 33:15; Ezekiel 37:24; Hosea 3:5). Rome made the decree, just as God intended.

2:4, 5 Sometimes we think to ourselves, "I'm being obedient, so why aren't things going better?" We face discomfort or inconvenience and immediately think either that we have misread God's will or that God has made a mistake. But watch this quiet couple as they head toward Bethlehem. God did not soften Joseph's bumpy road, but strengthened him. God did not provide a luxurious inn for Joseph and Mary, but brought his Son into the world in humble surroundings. When we do God's will, we are not guaranteed comfort and convenience. But we are promised that everything, even discomfort and inconvenience, has meaning in God's plan. He will guide you and provide all you need. Like Joseph, live each day by faith, trusting that God is in charge.

2:7 Bands of cloth were used to keep a baby warm and give it a sense of security. These cloths were believed to protect its inter-

THE JOURNEY TO BETHLEHEM Caesar's decree for a census of the entire Roman empire made it necessary for Joseph and Mary to leave their hometown, Nazareth, and journey the 70 miles to the Judean village of Bethlehem.

Mediterranean Sea
GALILEE
N
Sea of Galilee
Nazareth
SAMARIA
Jordan River
Jerusalem
Bethlehem
PEREA
JUDEA
Dead Sea
IDUMEA
0   20 Mi.
0   20 Km.

She wrapped him in cloths and placed him in a manger, because there was no room for them in the inn.

Shepherds Visit Jesus (10)

8And there were shepherds living out in the fields nearby, keeping watch over their flocks at night. 9An angel*y* of the Lord appeared to them, and the glory of the Lord shone around them, and they were terrified. 10But the angel said to them, "Do not be afraid. *z* I bring you good news of great joy that will be for all the people. 11Today in the town of David a Savior has been born to you; he is Christ*a a* the Lord. 12This will be a sign*b* to you: You will find a baby wrapped in cloths and lying in a manger."

13Suddenly a great company of the heavenly host appeared with the angel, praising God and saying,

> 14 "Glory to God in the highest,
> and on earth peace*c* to men on whom his favor rests."

15When the angels had left them and gone into heaven, the shepherds said to one another, "Let's go to Bethlehem and see this thing that has happened, which the Lord has told us about."

a 11 Or *Messiah.* "The Christ" (Greek) and "the Messiah" (Hebrew) both mean "the Anointed One"; also in verse 26.

2:9
y Lk 1:11; Ac 5:19

2:10
z Mt 14:27

2:11
a Mt 1:16; 16:16, 20; Ac 2:36

2:12
b 1Sa 2:34

2:14
c Ro 5:1

DOUBTERS IN THE BIBLE

Doubter	Doubtful Moment	Reference
Abraham	When told he would be a father in old age	Genesis 17:17
Sarah	When she heard she would be a mother in old age	Genesis 18:12
Moses	When told to return to Egypt to lead the people	Exodus 3:10–15
Israelites	Whenever they faced difficulties in the desert	Exodus 16:1–3
Gideon	When told he would be a judge and leader	Judges 6:14–23
Zechariah	When told he would be a father in old age	Luke 1:18
Thomas	When told Jesus had risen from the dead	John 20:24, 25

Many of the people God used to accomplish great things started out as real doubters. With all of them, God showed great patience. Honest doubt was not a bad starting point as long as they didn't stay there. How great a part does doubt have in your willingness to trust God?

---

nal organs. The custom of wrapping infants this way is still practiced in many Mid-eastern countries.

2:7 This mention of the manger is the basis for the traditional belief that Jesus was born in a stable. Stables were often caves with feeding troughs (mangers) carved into the rock walls. Despite popular Christmas card pictures, the surroundings were dark and dirty. This was not the atmosphere the Jews expected as the birthplace of the Messiah King. They thought their promised Messiah would be born in royal surroundings. We should not limit God by our expectations. He is at work wherever he is needed in our sin-darkened and dirty world.

2:7 Although our first picture of Jesus is as a baby in a manger, it must not be our last. The Christ-child in the manger is the subject of a beautiful Christmas scene, but we must not leave him there. This tiny, helpless baby lived an amazing life, died for us, ascended to heaven, and will return to earth as King of kings. Christ will rule the world and judge all people according to their decisions about him. Do you still picture Jesus as a baby in a manger—or is he your Lord? Make sure you don't underestimate Jesus. Let him grow up in your life.

2:8 God continued to reveal the news about his Son, but not to those we might expect. Luke records that Jesus' birth was announced to shepherds in the fields. These may have been the shepherds who supplied the lambs for the temple sacrifices that were performed for the forgiveness of sin. Here the angels invited these shepherds to greet the Lamb of God (John 1:36), who would take away the sins of the world forever.

2:8–15 What a birth announcement! The shepherds were terrified, but their fear turned to joy as the angels announced the Messiah's birth. First the shepherds ran to see the baby; then they spread the word. Jesus is *your* Messiah, *your* Savior. Do you look forward to meeting him in prayer and in his Word each day? Have you discovered a Lord so wonderful that you can't help sharing your joy with your friends?

2:9, 10 The greatest event in history had just happened! The Messiah had been born! For ages the Jews had waited for this, and when it finally occurred, the announcement came to humble shepherds. The good news about Jesus is that he comes to all, including the plain and the ordinary. He comes to anyone with a heart humble enough to accept him. Whoever you are, whatever you do, you can have Jesus in your life. Don't think you need extraordinary qualifications—he accepts you as you are.

2:11–14 Some of the Jews were waiting for a savior to deliver them from Roman rule; others hoped the Christ (Messiah) would deliver them from physical ailments. But Jesus, while healing their illnesses and establishing a spiritual kingdom, delivered them from sin. His work is more far-reaching than anyone could imagine. Christ paid the price for sin and opened the way to peace with God. He offers us more than temporary political or physical changes—he offers us new hearts that will last for eternity.

2:14 The story of Jesus' birth resounds with music that has inspired composers for 2,000 years. The angels' song is an all-time favorite. Often called the *Gloria* after its first word in the Latin translation, it is the basis of modern choral works, traditional Christmas carols, and ancient liturgical chants.

[16]So they hurried off and found Mary and Joseph, and the baby, who was lying in the manger. [17]When they had seen him, they spread the word concerning what had been told them about this child, [18]and all who heard it were amazed at what the shepherds said to them. [19]But Mary treasured up all these things and pondered them in her heart. [d] [20]The shepherds returned, glorifying and praising God for all the things they had heard and seen, which were just as they had been told.

2:19
[d] ver 51

Mary and Joseph Bring Jesus to the Temple (11)

[21]On the eighth day, when it was time to circumcise him,[e] he was named Jesus, the name the angel had given him before he had been conceived.[f]

2:21
[e] Lk 1:59
[f] Lk 1:31

[22]When the time of their purification according to the Law of Moses had been completed, Joseph and Mary took him to Jerusalem to present him to the Lord [23](as it is written in the Law of the Lord, "Every firstborn male is to be consecrated to the Lord"[a]),[g] [24]and to offer a sacrifice in keeping with what is said in the Law of the Lord: "a pair of doves or two young pigeons."[b]

2:23
[g] Ex 13:2, 12, 15

The Prophecy of Simeon

[25]Now there was a man in Jerusalem called Simeon, who was righteous and devout. He was waiting for the consolation of Israel,[h] and the Holy Spirit was upon him. [26]It had been revealed to him by the Holy Spirit that he would not die before he had seen the Lord's Christ. [27]Moved by the Spirit, he went into the temple courts. When the parents brought in the child Jesus to do for him what the custom of the Law required, [28]Simeon took him in his arms and praised God, saying:

2:25
[h] ver 38

[29] "Sovereign Lord, as you have promised,[i]
    you now dismiss[c] your servant in peace.

2:29
[i] ver 26

[30] For my eyes have seen your salvation,[j]
[31]   which you have prepared in the sight of all people,

2:30
[j] Isa 52:10

[32] a light for revelation to the Gentiles
    and for glory to your people Israel."[k]

2:32
[k] Isa 42:6; 49:6;
Ac 13:47

[33]The child's father and mother marveled at what was said about him. [34]Then Simeon blessed them and said to Mary, his mother: "This child is destined to cause the falling[l] and rising of many in Israel, and to be a sign that will be spoken against, [35]so that the thoughts of many hearts will be revealed. And a sword will pierce your own soul too."

2:34
[l] Mt 21:44;
1Co 1:23; 2Co 2:16;
1Pe 2:7, 8

[a]23 Exodus 13:2,12   [b]24 Lev. 12:8   [c]29 Or promised, / now dismiss

---

2:21-24 Jewish families went through several ceremonies soon after a baby's birth: (1) *Circumcision.* Every boy was circumcised and named on the eighth day after birth (Leviticus 12:3; Luke 1:59, 60). Circumcision symbolized the Jews' separation from Gentiles and their unique relationship with God (see the note on 1:59). (2) *Redemption of the firstborn.* A firstborn son was presented to God one month after birth (Exodus 13:2, 11–16; Numbers 18:15, 16). The ceremony included buying back— "redeeming"—the child from God through an offering. This way, the parents acknowledged that the child belonged to God, who alone has the power to give life. (3) *Purification of the mother.* For 40 days after the birth of a son and 80 days after the birth of a daughter, the mother was ceremonially unclean and could not enter the temple. At the end of her time of separation, the parents were to bring a lamb for a burnt offering and a dove or pigeon for a sin offering. The priest would sacrifice these animals and declare her to be clean. If a lamb was too expensive, the parents could bring a second dove or pigeon instead. This is what Mary and Joseph did.

Jesus was God's Son, but his family carried out these ceremonies according to God's law. Jesus was not born above the law; instead, he fulfilled it perfectly.

2:28-32 When Mary and Joseph brought Jesus to the temple to be consecrated to God, they met an old man who told them what their child would become. Simeon's song is often called the *Nunc Dimittis,* from the first words of its Latin translation. Simeon could die in peace because he had seen the Messiah.

2:32 The Jews were well acquainted with the Old Testament prophecies that spoke of the Messiah's blessings to their nation. They did not always give equal attention to the prophecies stating that he would bring salvation to the entire world, not just the Jews (see, for example, Isaiah 49:6). Many thought that Christ had come to save only his own people. Luke made sure his Greek audience understood that Christ had come to save *all* who believe, Gentiles as well as Jews.

2:33 Joseph and Mary "marveled" (were amazed) when this old man took their son into his arms and spoke such stunning words. Simeon said that Jesus was a gift from God, and he recognized Jesus as the Messiah who would be a light to the entire world. This was at least the second time that Mary had been greeted with a prophecy about her son; the first time was when Elizabeth had welcomed her as the mother of her Lord (1:42–45).

2:34, 35 Simeon prophesied that Jesus would have a paradoxical effect on Israel. Some would fall because of him (see Isaiah 8:14, 15), while others would rise (see Malachi 4:2). With Jesus, there would be no neutral ground: people would either joyfully accept him or totally reject him. As Jesus' mother, Mary would be grieved by the widespread rejection he would face. This is the first note of sorrow in Luke's Gospel.

The Prophecy of Anna

2:37
m 1 Ti 5:5

2:38
n ver 25

2:40
o ver 52; Lk 1:80

2:41
p Ex 23:15;
Dt 16:1-8

36 There was also a prophetess, Anna, the daughter of Phanuel, of the tribe of Asher. She was very old; she had lived with her husband seven years after her marriage, 37 and then was a widow until she was eighty-four.a She never left the temple but worshiped night and day, fasting and praying. m 38 Coming up to them at that very moment, she gave thanks to God and spoke about the child to all who were looking forward to the redemption of Jerusalem.n

39 When Joseph and Mary had done everything required by the Law of the Lord, they returned to Galilee to their own town of Nazareth. 40 And the child grew and became strong; he was filled with wisdom, and the grace of God was upon him. o

Jesus Speaks with the Religious Teachers (15)

41 Every year his parents went to Jerusalem for the Feast of the Passover.p 42 When he was twelve years old, they went up to the Feast, according to the custom. 43 After the Feast was over, while his parents were returning home, the boy Jesus stayed behind in Jerusalem, but they were unaware of it. 44 Thinking he was in their company, they traveled on for a day. Then they began looking for him among their relatives and friends. 45 When they did not find him, they went back to Jerusalem to look for him. 46 After three days they found him in the temple courts, sitting among the teachers, listening to them and asking them questions.

a 37 Or widow for eighty-four years

TO FEAR OR NOT TO FEAR	Person	Reference	Person	Reference
	Abraham	Genesis 15:1	Zechariah	Luke 1:13
	Moses	Numbers 21:34	Mary	Luke 1:30
		Deuteronomy 3:2	Shepherds	Luke 2:10
	Joshua	Joshua 8:1	Peter	Luke 5:10
	Jeremiah	Lamentations 3:57	Paul	Acts 27:23, 24
	Daniel	Daniel 10:12, 19	John	Revelation 1:17, 18

People in the Bible who were confronted by God or his angels all had one consistent response—fear. To each of them, God's response was always the same—don't be afraid. As soon as they sensed that God accepted them and wanted to communicate with them, their fear subsided. He had given them freedom to be his friends. He has given you the same freedom.

2:36 Although Simeon and Anna were very old, they had never lost their hope that they would see the Messiah. Led by the Holy Spirit, they were among the first to bear witness to Jesus. In the Jewish culture, elders were respected; thus, because of Simeon's and Anna's ages, their prophecies carried extra weight. In contrast, our society values youthfulness over wisdom, and potential contributions by the elderly are often ignored. As Christians, we should reverse those values wherever we can. Encourage older people to share their wisdom and experience. Listen carefully when they speak. Offer them your friendship and help them find ways to continue to serve God.

2:36, 37 Anna was called a prophetess, indicating that she was unusually close to God. Prophets did not necessarily predict the future. Their main role was to speak for God, proclaiming his truth.

2:39 Did Mary and Joseph return immediately to Nazareth, or did they remain in Bethlehem for a time (as implied in Matthew 2)? Apparently there is a gap of several years between verses 38 and 39—ample time for them to find a place to live in Bethlehem, flee to Egypt to escape Herod's wrath, and return to Nazareth when it was safe to do so.

2:41, 42 According to God's law, every male was required to go to Jerusalem three times a year for the great festivals (Deuteronomy 16:16). In the spring, the Passover was celebrated, followed immediately by the week-long Feast of Unleavened Bread. Passover commemorated the night of the Jews' escape from Egypt when God had killed the Egyptian firstborn but had passed over Israelite homes (see Exodus 12:21–36). Passover was the most important of the three annual festivals.

2:43–45 At age 12, Jesus was considered almost an adult, so he probably didn't spend a lot of time with his parents during the feast. Those who attended these feasts often traveled in caravans for protection from robbers along the Palestine roads. The women and children usually would travel at the front of the caravan, with the men bringing up the rear. A 12-year-old boy conceivably could have been in either group, so both Mary and Joseph probably assumed that Jesus was with the other one. But when the caravan left Jerusalem, Jesus stayed behind, absorbed in his discussion with the religious leaders.

2:46, 47 The temple courts were famous throughout Judea as a place of learning. The apostle Paul studied in Jerusalem, perhaps in the temple courts, under Gamaliel, one of its foremost teachers (Acts 22:3). At the time of the Passover, the greatest rabbis of the land would assemble to teach and to discuss great truths among themselves. The coming Messiah would no doubt have been a popular discussion topic, for everyone was expecting him soon. Jesus would have been eager to listen and to ask probing questions. It was not his youth, but the depth of his wisdom, that astounded these teachers.

47Everyone who heard him was amazed at his understanding and his answers. 48When his parents saw him, they were astonished. His mother said to him, "Son, why have you treated us like this? Your father and I have been anxiously searching for you."

49"Why were you searching for me?" he asked. "Didn't you know I had to be in my Father's house?" q 50But they did not understand what he was saying to them.

51Then he went down to Nazareth with them and was obedient to them. But his mother treasured all these things in her heart. r 52And Jesus grew in wisdom and stature, and in favor with God and men. s

2:49
q Jn 2:16

2:51
r ver 19

2:52
s ver 40

John the Baptist Prepares the Way for Jesus (16/Matthew 3:1–12; Mark 1:1–8)

3 In the fifteenth year of the reign of Tiberius Caesar—when Pontius Pilate was governor of Judea, Herod tetrarch of Galilee, his brother Philip tetrarch of Iturea and Traconitis, and Lysanias tetrarch of Abilene— 2during the high priesthood of Annas and Caiaphas, t the word of God came to John son of Zechariah in the desert. 3He went into all the country around the Jordan, preaching a baptism of repentance for the forgiveness of sins. 4As is written in the book of the words of Isaiah the prophet:

3:2
t Jn 18:13; Ac 4:6

"A voice of one calling in the desert,
'Prepare the way for the Lord,
　make straight paths for him.
5 Every valley shall be filled in,
　every mountain and hill made low.

2:48 Mary had to let go of her child and let him become a man, God's Son, the Messiah. Fearful that she hadn't been careful enough with this God-given child, she searched frantically for him. But she was looking for a boy, not the young man who was in the temple astounding the religious leaders with his questions. Letting go of people or projects we have nurtured can be very difficult. It is both sweet and painful to see our children as adults, our students as teachers, our subordinates as managers, our inspirations as institutions. But when the time comes to step back and let go, we must do so in spite of the hurt. Then our protégés can exercise their wings, take flight, and soar to the heights God intended for them.

2:49, 50 This is the first mention of Jesus' awareness that he was God's Son. But even though he knew his real Father, Jesus did not reject his earthly parents. He went back to Nazareth with them and lived under their authority for another 18 years. God's people do not despise human relationships or family responsibilities. If the Son of God obeyed his human parents, how much more should we honor our family members! Don't use commitment to God's work to justify neglecting your family.

2:50 Jesus' parents didn't understand what he meant about his Father's house. They didn't realize he was making a distinction between his earthly father and his heavenly Father. Jesus knew that he had a unique relationship with God. Although Mary and Joseph knew he was God's Son, they didn't understand what his mission would involve. Besides, they had to raise him, along with his brothers and sisters (Matthew 13:55, 56), as a normal child. They knew he was unique, but they did not know what was going on in his mind.

2:52 The Bible does not record any events of the next 18 years of Jesus' life, but Jesus undoubtedly was learning and maturing. As the oldest in a large family, he undoubtedly assisted Joseph in his carpentry work. Joseph may have died during this time, leaving Jesus to provide for the family. The normal routines of daily life gave Jesus a solid understanding of the Judean people.

2:52 The second chapter of Luke shows us that although Jesus was unique, he had a normal childhood and adolescence. In terms of development, he went through the same progression we do. He grew physically and mentally, he related to other people, and he was loved by God. A full human life is balanced. Thus, it was important to Jesus—and it should be important to all believers— to develop fully and harmoniously in each of these key areas: physical, mental, social, and spiritual.

3:1 Tiberius, the Roman emperor, ruled from A.D. 14 to 37. Pilate was the Roman governor responsible for the province of Judea; Herod (Antipas) and Philip were half brothers and sons of the cruel Herod the Great, who had been dead more than 20 years. Antipas, Philip, Pilate, and Lysanias apparently had equal powers in governing their separate territories. All were subject to Rome and responsible for keeping peace in their respective lands.

3:2 Jewish law provided for only one high priest. He was appointed from Aaron's line, and he held his position for life. By this time, however, the religious system had been corrupted, and the Roman government was appointing its own religious leaders to maintain greater control over the Jews. Apparently the Roman authorities had deposed the Jewish-appointed Annas and had replaced him with Annas's son-in-law, Caiaphas. Nevertheless, Annas retained his title (see Acts 4:6) and probably also much of the power it carried. Because the Jews believed the high priest's position to be for life, they would have continued to call Annas their high priest.

3:2 This is John the Baptist, whose birth story is told in chapter 1. See his Profile in John 1, p. 1737.

3:2 Pilate, Herod, and Caiaphas were the most powerful leaders in Palestine, but they were upstaged by a desert prophet from rural Judea. God chose to speak through the loner John the Baptist, who has gone down in history as greater than any of the rulers of his day. How often people judge others by the superficial standards of power, wealth, and beauty, and miss the truly great people through whom God works! Greatness is not measured by what you have, but by your faith in God. Like John, give yourself entirely to God so God's power can work through you.

3:3 Repentance has two sides—turning away from sins and turning toward God. To be truly repentant, we must do both. We can't just say we believe and then live any way we choose (see 3:7, 8); neither can we simply live a morally correct life without a personal relationship with God because that cannot bring forgiveness from sin. Determine to rid your life of any sins God points out, and then determine to live in a way that pleases him.

3:4, 5 In John's day, before a king would take a trip, messengers would tell those he was planning to visit to prepare the roads for him. Similarly John told his listeners to make their lives ready so the Lord could come to them. This does not mean that you must get rid of all your sin or wrongdoing before you can accept Christ; rather, when you accept him, he takes care of all your sinfulness. To "prepare the way" means clearing aside the baggage of the past

The crooked roads shall become straight,
the rough ways smooth.
6 And all mankind will see God's salvation.'"a u

3:6
u Ps 98:2; Isa 52:10;
Lk 2:30

3:8
v Jn 8:33, 39

7 John said to the crowds coming out to be baptized by him, "You brood of vipers! Who warned you to flee from the coming wrath? 8 Produce fruit in keeping with repentance. And do not begin to say to yourselves, 'We have Abraham as our father.' v For I tell you that out of these stones God can raise up children for Abraham. 9 The ax is already at the root of the trees, and every tree that does not produce good fruit will be cut down and thrown into the fire."

a 6 Isaiah 40:3-5

ELIZABETH

In societies like Israel, in which a woman's value was largely measured by her ability to bear children, to be without children often led to personal hardship and public shame. For Elizabeth, a childless old age was a painful and lonely time, but she still remained faithful to God.

Both Elizabeth and Zechariah came from priestly families. For two weeks each year, Zechariah had to go to the temple in Jerusalem to attend to his priestly duties. After one of those trips, Zechariah returned home excited but speechless. He had to write down his good news, because he couldn't give it any other way. And what a wonderful surprise he had for his wife: their faded dream would become an exciting reality! Soon Elizabeth became pregnant, and she knew her child was a long-hoped-for gift from God.

News traveled fast among the family. Seventy miles to the north, in Nazareth, Elizabeth's relative Mary also unexpectedly became pregnant. Within days after the angel's message that she would bear the Messiah, Mary went to visit Elizabeth. They were instantly bound together by the unique gifts God had given them. Elizabeth knew that Mary's son would be even greater than her own, for John would be the messenger for Mary's son.

When her baby was born, Elizabeth insisted on his God-given name: John. Zechariah's written agreement freed his tongue, and everyone in town wondered what would become of this obviously special child.

Elizabeth whispered her praise as she cared for God's gift. Knowing about Mary must have made her marvel at God's timing. Things had worked out even better than she could have planned. We too need to remember that God is in control of every situation. When did you last pause to recognize God's timing in the events of your life?

Strengths and accomplishments:	• Known as a deeply spiritual woman • Showed no doubts about God's ability to fulfill his promise • Mother of John the Baptist • The first woman besides Mary to hear of the coming Savior
Lessons from her life:	• God does not forget those who have been faithful to him • God's timetable and methods do not have to conform to what we expect
Vital statistics:	• Occupation: Homemaker • Relatives: Husband: Zechariah. Son: John the Baptist. Relative: Mary. • Contemporaries: Joseph, Herod the Great
Key verses:	"But why am I so favored, that the mother of my Lord should come to me? As soon as the sound of your greeting reached my ears, the baby in my womb leaped for joy. Blessed is she who has believed that what the Lord has said to her will be accomplished!" (Luke 1:43–45).

Elizabeth's story is told in Luke 1:5–80.

---

and the doubts of the present in order to let the King come into your life. He'll take it from there.

3:6 This book was written to a non-Jewish audience. Luke quoted from Isaiah to show that salvation is for all people, not just the Jews (Isaiah 40:3–5; 52:10). John the Baptist called "all mankind" to prepare to meet Jesus. That includes you, no matter what your nationality, social standing, religious affiliation, or political position. God is calling to all people. Don't let feelings of being an outsider cause you to hold back. No one who wants to follow Jesus is an outsider in God's kingdom.

3:7–9 Some people wanted to be baptized by John so they could escape eternal punishment, but they were not really repenting from sin nor were they willing to change the way they lived. John had harsh words for such people. He knew that God values reformation above ritual. Confession of sins and a changed life are

inseparable. Faith without deeds is dead (James 2:14–26). Jesus also spoke harsh words to the respectable religious leaders who lacked the willingness to repent. They wanted to be known as religious authorities and they wanted eternal life, but they didn't want to repent of their sins. Thus, their lives were unproductive. Turning from sin must be tied to action. Following Jesus means more than saying the right words; it means acting on what he says.

3:8 Many of John's hearers were shocked when he said that being Abraham's descendants was not enough to ensure salvation. The religious leaders relied more on their family lines than on their faith for their standing with God. For them, religion was inherited. But a personal relationship with God cannot be handed down from parents to children. Everyone has to commit to it on his or her own. Don't rely on someone else's faith for your salvation. Have you made that personal decision to trust Christ?

10"What should we do then?"w the crowd asked.

11John answered, "The man with two tunics should share with him who has none, and the one who has food should do the same."

12Tax collectors also came to be baptized.x "Teacher," they asked, "what should we do?"

13"Don't collect any more than you are required to,"y he told them.

14Then some soldiers asked him, "And what should we do?"

He replied, "Don't extort money and don't accuse people falsely z—be content with your pay."

15The people were waiting expectantly and were all wondering in their hearts if John might possibly be the Christ.a 16John answered them all, "I baptize you withb water. But one more powerful than I will come, the thongs of whose sandals I am not worthy to untie. He will baptize you with the Holy Spirit and with fire. 17His winnowing forka is in his hand to clear his threshing floor and to gather the wheat into his barn, but he will burn up the chaff with unquenchable fire." b 18And with many other words John exhorted the people and preached the good news to them.

Herod Puts John in Prison (26)

19But when John rebuked Herod the tetrarch because of Herodias, his brother's wife, and all the other evil things he had done, 20Herod added this to them all: He locked John up in prison. c

The Baptism of Jesus (17/Matthew 3:13–17; Mark 1:9–11)

21When all the people were being baptized, Jesus was baptized too. And as he was praying,d heaven was opened 22 and the Holy Spirit descended on hime in bodily form like a dove. And a voice came from heaven: "You are my Son, whom I love; with you I am well pleased."

a 15 Or Messiah   b 16 Or in

3:10
w Ac 2:37

3:12
x Lk 7:29

3:13
y Lk 19:8

3:14
z Ex 23:1; Lev 19:11

3:17
a Isa 30:24
b Mt 13:30

3:20
c Mt 14:3, 4;
Mk 6:17-18

3:21
d Mt 14:23; Lk 5:16;
9:18, 28

3:22
e Ac 10:38

3:11–14 John's message demanded at least three specific responses: (1) share what you have with those who need it, (2) whatever your job is, do it well and with fairness, and (3) be content with what you're earning. John had no time to address comforting messages to those who lived careless or selfish lives—he was calling the people to right living as he prepared the way for their Messiah. What changes can you make in sharing what you have, doing your work honestly and well, and being content?

3:12 Tax collectors were notorious for their dishonesty. Romans gathered funds for their government by farming out the collection privilege. Tax collectors earned their own living by adding a sizable sum—whatever they could get away with—to the total and keeping this money for themselves. Unless the people revolted and risked Roman retaliation, they had to pay whatever was demanded. Obviously the people hated the tax collectors, who were generally corrupt and greedy. Yet, said John, God would accept even these men; God desires to pour out mercy on those who confess, and then to give strength to live changed lives.

3:12–14 John's message took root in unexpected places—among the poor, the dishonest, and even the hated occupation army. These people were painfully aware of their needs and they were honestly seeking to know what to do to change their lives. Did anyone follow John's advice? Surely some did, and their softened hearts became ready to receive the message of the One who was to come.

3:14 These soldiers were the Roman troops sent to keep peace in this distant province. Many of them oppressed the poor and used their power to take advantage of all the people. John called them to repent and change their ways.

3:15 Israel had not seen a prophet for more than 400 years. It was widely believed that when the Messiah would come, prophecy would reappear (Joel 2:28, 29; Malachi 3:1; 4:5). When John burst onto the scene, the people were excited. He was obviously a great prophet, and they were sure that the eagerly awaited age of the Messiah had come. Some, in fact, thought John himself was the Messiah. John spoke like the prophets of old, saying that the people must turn from their sin to avoid punishment and turn to

God to experience his mercy and approval. This is a message for all times and places, but John spoke it with particular urgency—he was preparing the people for the coming Messiah.

3:16 John's baptism with water symbolized the washing away of sins. His baptism coordinated with his message of repentance and reformation. Jesus' baptism with fire includes the power needed to do God's will. The baptism with the Holy Spirit was fulfilled at Pentecost (Acts 2) when the Holy Spirit came upon believers in the form of tongues of fire, empowering them to proclaim Jesus' resurrection in many languages. The baptism with fire also symbolizes the work of the Holy Spirit in bringing God's judgment on those who refuse to repent.

3:17 John warned of impending judgment by comparing those who refuse to live for God to chaff, the useless outer husk of the grain. By contrast, John compared those who repent and reform their lives to the nourishing wheat itself. The winnowing fork was a pitchfork used to toss wheat so that the kernels would separate from the blades. Those who refuse to be used by God will be discarded because they have no value in furthering God's work. Those who repent and believe, however, hold great value in God's eyes because they are beginning a new life of productive service for him.

3:19, 20 In these two verses Luke flashes forward to continue his explanation about John the Baptist. (See the Harmony of the Gospels for the chronological order of events.) This is Herod Antipas (see Mark 6, p. 1621 for his Profile). Herodias was Herod's niece and also his brother's wife. She would treacherously plot John the Baptist's death (Matthew 14:1–12). The Herods were a murderous and deceitful family. Rebuking a tyrannical Roman official who could imprison and execute him was extremely dangerous, yet that is what John did. Herod seemingly would have the last word, but the story is not finished. At the last judgment, Herod, not John, will face God's punishment—for eternity.

3:21 Luke emphasizes Jesus' human nature. Jesus was born to humble parents, a birth unannounced except to shepherds and foreigners. This baptism recorded here was the first public declaration of Jesus' ministry. Instead of going to Jerusalem and identifying with the established religious leaders, Jesus went to a river and

The Record of Jesus' Ancestors (3/Matthew 1:1–17)

3:23
Mt 4:17; Ac 1:1

²³ Now Jesus himself was about thirty years old when he began his ministry. *f* He was the son, so it was thought, of Joseph,

---

SIMEON & ANNA

When Joseph and Mary took the eight-day-old Jesus to the temple for his circumcision, they had two unexpected but delightful encounters. Well-worn examples of patient waiting met them—Simeon and Anna. Both of these godly saints recognized Jesus' identity as the Messiah. Simeon and Anna give us a picture of godly expectation in an environment ripe with expectations.

Simeon was certain he would see the Messiah before he died. We don't know how surprised he was to discover the Savior as a baby in Mary's arms. We do know that he recognized Jesus and gave God praise for his faithfulness. When Simeon saw the baby, he considered his life complete.

Simeon's exuberance caught Anna's attention. She was another regular in the temple. Anna's brief marriage ended in widowhood and she spent the remainder of her eighty-four plus years serving as a prophetess. Anna overheard Simeon's prophecy about Jesus and immediately added her own excited words of praise for the Savior.

Anna discovered that God can make every passage of life meaningful and useful. The long years of widowhood were also effective years of worship and service. Both she and Simeon dedicated their lives to God and were rewarded in ways we can only fully appreciate if we are willing to live the same way.

As you interact with people at various stages of life today, think about the development of your relationship with God. When talking to a younger person, ask yourself: "How was God involved in my life at that age?" When noticing someone older ask: "How do I want my relationship with God to mature by that point in my life?"

Strengths and accomplishments:	• Exercised faithful anticipation regarding God's promised Messiah • Did not hesitate to give praise to God for his work in the world • Both spoke from the powerful authority of their faith and age
Lessons from their lives:	• God does give to some of his faithful followers a deeper insight and clarity about his plans • There were those in Israel who did recognize Jesus • Advancing age does not invalidate a person's usefulness in God's purposes
Vital statistics:	• Where: Jerusalem • Contemporaries: Joseph, Mary, Herod the Great
Key verses:	"Now there was a man in Jerusalem called Simeon, who was righteous and devout. He was waiting for the consolation of Israel, and the Holy Spirit was upon him. It had been revealed to him by the Holy Spirit that he would not die before he had seen the Lord's Christ. . . . [Anna] never left the temple but worshiped night and day, fasting and praying" (Luke 2:25, 26, 37).

Simeon and Anna's stories are told in Luke 2:21–38.

---

identified with those who were repenting of sin. When Jesus, at age 12, had visited the temple, he had understood his mission (2:49). Eighteen years later, at his baptism, he began carrying it out. And as Jesus prayed, God spoke and confirmed his decision to act. God was breaking into human history through Jesus the Christ.

3:21, 22 Theologians have long been troubled by Jesus allowing himself to be baptized by John. After all, this baptism was for sinners. Why, then, did Jesus do it? He did it because he is both God and human—he underwent baptism and even death as only a human could; he lived a sinless life and rose from the dead as only God could. This baptism by John in the Jordan River was another step in his identification with us sinful people; and the arrival of the dove signifies God's approval. Now Jesus would officially begin his ministry as God's beloved Son walking the dusty roads of Israel. When you are hurting, depressed, broken, remember: You have a Savior who understands your humanity. When you sin, remember: He has paid the price for your disobedience.

3:21, 22 This is one of several places in Scripture where all the members of the Trinity are mentioned—Father, Son, and Holy Spirit. In the traditional words of the church, the one God exists in three persons but one substance, coeternal and coequal. No explanation can adequately portray the power and intricacy of

this unique relationship. There are no perfect analogies in nature because there is no other relationship like the Trinity.

3:23 Imagine the Savior of the world working in a small-town carpenter's shop until he was 30 years old! It seems incredible that Jesus would have been content to remain in Nazareth all that time, but he patiently trusted the Father's timing for his life and ministry. Thirty was the prescribed age for priests to begin their ministry (Numbers 4:3). Joseph was 30 years old when he began serving the king of Egypt (Genesis 41:46), and David was 30 years old when he began to reign over Judah (2 Samuel 5:4). Age 30, then, was a good time to begin an important task in the Jewish culture. Like Jesus, we need to resist the temptation to jump ahead before receiving the Spirit's direction. Are you waiting and wondering what your next step should be? Don't jump ahead—trust God's timing.

3:23–38 Matthew's genealogy goes back to Abraham and shows that Jesus was related to all Jews (Matthew 1). Luke's genealogy goes back to Adam, showing that Jesus is related to all human beings. This is consistent with Luke's picture of Jesus as the Savior of the whole world.

the son of Heli, 24 the son of Matthat,
the son of Levi, the son of Melki,
the son of Jannai, the son of Joseph,
25 the son of Mattathias, the son of Amos,
the son of Nahum, the son of Esli,
the son of Naggai, 26 the son of Maath,
the son of Mattathias, the son of Semein,
the son of Josech, the son of Joda,
27 the son of Joanan, the son of Rhesa,
the son of Zerubbabel,g the son of Shealtiel,
the son of Neri, 28 the son of Melki,
the son of Addi, the son of Cosam,
the son of Elmadam, the son of Er,
29 the son of Joshua, the son of Eliezer,
the son of Jorim, the son of Matthat,
the son of Levi, 30 the son of Simeon,
the son of Judah, the son of Joseph,
the son of Jonam, the son of Eliakim,
31 the son of Melea, the son of Menna,
the son of Mattatha, the son of Nathan,h
the son of David, 32 the son of Jesse,
the son of Obed, the son of Boaz,
the son of Salmon,a the son of Nahshon,
33 the son of Amminadab, the son of Ram,b
the son of Hezron, the son of Perez,i
the son of Judah, 34 the son of Jacob,
the son of Isaac, the son of Abraham,
the son of Terah, the son of Nahor,j
35 the son of Serug, the son of Reu,
the son of Peleg, the son of Eber,
the son of Shelah, 36 the son of Cainan,
the son of Arphaxad,k the son of Shem,
the son of Noah, the son of Lamech,
37 the son of Methuselah, the son of Enoch,
the son of Jared, the son of Mahalalel,
the son of Kenan, 38 the son of Enosh,
the son of Seth, the son of Adam,
the son of God.

3:27
g Mt 1:12

3:31
h 2Sa 5:14; 1Ch 3:5

3:33
i Ru 4:18-22;
1Ch 2:10-12

3:34
j Ge 11:24, 26

3:36
k Ge 11:12

Satan Tempts Jesus in the Wilderness (18/Matthew 4:1–11; Mark 1:12–13)

4 Jesus, full of the Holy Spirit,l returned from the Jordan and was led by the Spiritm in the desert, 2 where for forty daysn he was tempted by the devil. He ate nothing during those days, and at the end of them he was hungry.

4:1
l ver 14, 18
m Lk 2:27

4:2
n Ex 34:28

a 32 Some early manuscripts *Sala*   b 33 Some manuscripts *Amminadab, the son of Admin, the son of Arni*; other
manuscripts vary widely.

4:1 Sometimes we feel that if the Holy Spirit leads us, it will always be "beside quiet waters" (Psalm 23:2). But that is not necessarily true. He led Jesus into the desert for a long and difficult time of testing, and he may also lead us into difficult situations. When facing trials, first make sure you haven't brought them on yourself through sin or unwise choices. If you find no sin to confess or unwise behavior to change, then ask God to strengthen you for your test. Finally, be careful to follow faithfully wherever the Holy Spirit leads.

4:1, 2 The devil, who tempted Adam and Eve in the garden, also tempted Jesus in the desert. Satan is a real being, a created but rebellious fallen angel, and not a symbol or an idea. He constantly fights against God and those who follow and obey God. Jesus was a prime target for the devil's temptations. Satan had succeeded with Adam and Eve, and he hoped to succeed with Jesus as well.

4:1–13 Knowing and obeying God's Word is an effective weapon against temptation, the only *offensive* weapon provided in the Christian's "armor" (Ephesians 6:17). Jesus used Scripture to counter Satan's attacks, and so should we. But to use it effectively, we must have faith in God's promises, because Satan also knows Scripture and is adept at twisting it to suit his purpose. Obeying the Scriptures is more important than simply having a verse to quote, so read them daily and apply them to your life. Then your "sword" will always be sharp.

4:2 Why was it necessary for Jesus to be tempted? First, temptation is part of the human experience. For Jesus to be fully human, for him to understand us completely, he had to face temptation (see Hebrews 4:15). Second, Jesus had to undo Adam's work. Adam, though created perfect, gave in to temptation and passed sin on to the whole human race.

4:4
o Dt 8:3

³ The devil said to him, "If you are the Son of God, tell this stone to become bread."

⁴ Jesus answered, "It is written: 'Man does not live on bread alone.' ª " *o*

⁵ The devil led him up to a high place and showed him in an instant all the kingdoms of the

ª*4* Deut. 8:3

MARY

Motherhood is a painful privilege. Young Mary of Nazareth had the unique privilege of being mother to the very Son of God. Yet the pains and pleasures of her motherhood can be understood by mothers everywhere. Mary was the only human present at Jesus' birth who also witnessed his death. She saw him arrive as her baby son, and she watched him die as her Savior.

Until Gabriel's unexpected visit, Mary's life was quite satisfactory. She had recently become engaged to a carpenter, Joseph, and was anticipating married life. But her life was about to change forever.

Angels don't usually make appointments before visiting. Feeling as if she were being congratulated for winning the grand prize in a contest she had never entered, Mary found the angel's greeting puzzling and his presence frightening. What she heard next was the news almost every woman in Israel hoped to hear—that her child would be the Messiah, God's promised Savior. Mary did not doubt the message, but rather asked how pregnancy would be possible. Gabriel told her the baby would be God's Son. Her answer was the one God waits in vain to hear from so many other people: "I am the Lord's servant. . . . May it be to me as you have said" (Luke 1:38). Later, her song of joy shows us how well she knew God, for her thoughts were filled with his words from the Old Testament.

When he was eight days old Jesus was taken to the temple to be dedicated to God. There Joseph and Mary were met by two devout people, Simeon and Anna, who recognized the child as the Messiah and praised God. Simeon directed some words to Mary that must have come to her mind many times in the years that followed: "A sword will pierce your own soul" (Luke 2:35). A big part of her painful privilege of motherhood would be to see her son rejected and crucified by the people he came to save.

We can imagine that even if she had known all she would suffer as Jesus' mother, Mary would still have given the same response. Are you, like Mary, available to be used by God?

Strengths and accomplishments:	• The mother of Jesus, the Messiah • The one human who was with Jesus from birth to death • Willing to be available to God • Knew and applied Old Testament Scriptures
Lessons from her life:	• God's best servants are often ordinary people who make themselves available to him • God's plans involve extraordinary events in ordinary people's lives • A person's character is revealed by his or her response to the unexpected
Vital statistics:	• Where: Nazareth, Bethlehem • Occupation: Homemaker • Relatives: Husband: Joseph. Relatives: Zechariah and Elizabeth. Children: Jesus, James, Joseph, Judas, Simon, and daughters.
Key verse:	"'I am the Lord's servant,' Mary answered. 'May it be to me as you have said.' Then the angel left her" (Luke 1:38).

Mary's story is told throughout the Gospels. She is also mentioned in Acts 1:14.

Jesus, by contrast, resisted Satan. His victory offers salvation to all of Adam's descendants (see Romans 5:12–19).

4:3 Satan may tempt us to doubt Christ's true identity. He knows that once we begin to question whether or not Jesus is God, it's far easier to get us to do what he wants. Times of questioning can help us sort out our beliefs and strengthen our faith, but those times can also be dangerous. If you are dealing with doubt, realize that you are especially vulnerable to temptation. Even as you search for answers, protect yourself by meditating on the unshakable truths of God's Word.

4:3 Sometimes what we are tempted to do isn't wrong in itself. Turning stones into bread wasn't necessarily bad. The sin was not in the act but in the reason behind it. The devil was trying to get Jesus to take a shortcut, to solve Jesus' immediate problem at the expense of his long-range goals, to seek comfort at the sacrifice of his discipline. Satan often works that way—persuading us to take action, even right action, for the wrong reason or at the

wrong time. The fact that something is not wrong in itself does not mean that it is good for you at a given time. Many people sin by attempting to fulfill legitimate desires outside of God's will or ahead of his timetable. First ask, "Is the Holy Spirit leading me to do this? Or is Satan trying to get me off the track?"

4:3ff Often we are tempted not through our weaknesses, but through our strengths. The devil tempted Jesus where he was strong. Jesus had power over stones, the kingdoms of the world, and even angels, and Satan wanted him to use that power without regard to his mission. When we give in to the devil and wrongly use our strengths, we become proud and self-reliant. Trusting in our own powers, we feel little need of God. To avoid this trap, we must realize that all our strengths are God's gifts to us, and we must dedicate those strengths to his service.

world. 6And he said to him, "I will give you all their authority and splendor, for it has been given to me,p and I can give it to anyone I want to. 7So if you worship me, it will all be yours."

8Jesus answered, "It is written: 'Worship the Lord your God and serve him only.'a "q

9The devil led him to Jerusalem and had him stand on the highest point of the temple. "If you are the Son of God," he said, "throw yourself down from here. 10For it is written:

> "'He will command his angels concerning you
>   to guard you carefully;
> 11 they will lift you up in their hands,
>   so that you will not strike your foot against a stone.'b "r

12Jesus answered, "It says: 'Do not put the Lord your God to the test.'c "s

13When the devil had finished all this tempting,t he left him until an opportune time.

B. MESSAGE AND MINISTRY OF JESUS, THE SAVIOR (4:14—21:38)

Luke accurately records the actions and teachings of Christ, helping us understand the way of salvation. There is much unique material in Luke, especially the parables of Jesus. Jesus came to teach us how to live and how to find salvation. How carefully, then, we should study the words and life of our Savior.

1. Jesus' ministry in Galilee
Jesus Preaches in Galilee (30/Matthew 4:12–17; Mark 1:14–15; John 4:43–45)

14Jesus returned to Galilee u in the power of the Spirit, and news about him spread through the whole countryside. 15He taught in their synagogues, and everyone praised him.

Jesus Is Rejected at Nazareth (32)

16He went to Nazareth, where he had been brought up, and on the Sabbath day he went into the synagogue,v as was his custom. And he stood up to read. 17The scroll of the prophet Isaiah was handed to him. Unrolling it, he found the place where it is written:

a8 Deut. 6:13   b11 Psalm 91:11,12   c12 Deut. 6:16

4:6
p Jn 12:31
4:8
q Dt 6:13

4:11
r Ps 91:11, 12
4:12
s Dt 6:16
4:13
t Heb 4:15

4:14
u Mt 4:12

4:16
v Mt 13:54

4:6, 7 The devil arrogantly hoped to succeed in his rebellion against God by diverting Jesus from his mission and winning his worship. "This world is mine, not God's," he was saying, "and if you hope to do anything worthwhile here, you'd better recognize that fact." Jesus didn't argue with Satan about who owns the world, but Jesus refused to validate Satan's claim by worshiping him. Jesus knew that he would redeem the world through giving up his life on the cross, not through making an alliance with a corrupt angel.

4:9–11 Here the devil misinterpreted Scripture. The intention of Psalm 91 is to show God's protection of his people, not to incite them to use God's power for sensational or foolish displays.

**JESUS'
TEMPTATION
AND RETURN
TO GALILEE**
Jesus was tempted by Satan in the rough Desert of Judea before returning to his boyhood home, Nazareth. John's Gospel tells of Jesus' journeys in Galilee, Samaria, and Judea (see John 1–4) before he moved to Capernaum to set up his base of operations (see Matthew 4:12, 13).

4:13 Christ's defeat of the devil in the desert was decisive but not final. Throughout his ministry, Jesus would confront Satan in many forms. Too often we see temptation as once and for all. In reality, we need to be constantly on guard against the devil's ongoing attacks. Where are you most susceptible to temptation right now? How are you preparing to withstand it?

4:13 What would it take for you to "sell out"? What is there in life that would cause you to compromise your faith? Whatever it is— sexual temptation, financial inducement, fear of alienating or offending someone—it will be placed in your path at some point. The enemy wants to destroy believers or at least neutralize them through sin, shame, and guilt. When that temptation rears its seductive head, do what Jesus did: rely on the Word of God and stand fast in your commitment to worship God alone, above all else. No matter the cost or the sacrifice, no matter how appealing the come-on, believers must follow Jesus' example and stand strong.

4:15, 16 Synagogues were very important in Jewish religious life. During the exile when the Jews no longer had their temple, synagogues were established as places of worship on the Sabbath and as schools for young boys during the week. Synagogues continued to exist even after the temple was rebuilt. A synagogue could be set up in any town with at least ten Jewish families. It was administered by one leader and an assistant. At the synagogue, the leader often would invite a visiting rabbi to read from the Scriptures and to teach. Itinerant rabbis, like Jesus, were always welcome to speak to those gathered each Sabbath in the synagogues. The apostle Paul also took advantage of this practice (see Acts 13:5; 14:1).

4:16 Jesus went to the synagogue "as was his custom." Even though he was the perfect Son of God, and his local synagogue undoubtedly left much to be desired, Jesus attended services every week. His example makes our excuses for not attending church sound weak and self-serving. Make regular worship a part of your life.

4:17–21 Jesus was quoting from Isaiah 61:1, 2. Isaiah pictures the deliverance of Israel from exile in Babylon as a Year of Jubilee

18 "The Spirit of the Lord is on me,
    because he has anointed me
    to preach good news to the poor.
He has sent me to proclaim freedom for the prisoners
    and recovery of sight for the blind,
    to release the oppressed,
19   to proclaim the year of the Lord's favor."a w

4:19
w Isa 61:1, 2

4:20
x ver 17

20 Then he rolled up the scroll, gave it back to the attendant and sat down.x The eyes of everyone in the synagogue were fastened on him, 21 and he began by saying to them, "Today this scripture is fulfilled in your hearing."

4:22
y Mt 13:54, 55;
Jn 6:42

22 All spoke well of him and were amazed at the gracious words that came from his lips. "Isn't this Joseph's son?" they asked.y

23 Jesus said to them, "Surely you will quote this proverb to me: 'Physician, heal yourself! Do here in your hometown what we have heard that you did in Capernaum.'"

4:24
z Mt 13:57; Jn 4:44

4:25
a 1Ki 18:1; Jas 5:17, 18

24 "I tell you the truth," he continued, "no prophet is accepted in his hometown.z 25 I assure you that there were many widows in Israel in Elijah's time, when the sky was shut for three and a half years and there was a severe famine throughout the land.a 26 Yet Elijah was not sent to any of them, but to a widow in Zarephath in the region of Sidon.b 27 And there were many in Israel with leprosyb in the time of Elisha the prophet, yet not one of them was cleansed—only Naaman the Syrian."c

4:26
b 1Ki 17:8-16

4:27
c 2Ki 5:1-14

4:29
d Nu 15:35; Ac 7:58

4:30
e Jn 8:59; 10:39

28 All the people in the synagogue were furious when they heard this. 29 They got up, drove him out of the town,d and took him to the brow of the hill on which the town was built, in order to throw him down the cliff. 30 But he walked right through the crowd and went on his way.e

Jesus Teaches with Authority (34/Mark 1:21–28)

4:31
f Mt 4:13

4:32
g Mt 7:28

31 Then he went down to Capernaum,f a town in Galilee, and on the Sabbath began to teach the people. 32 They were amazed at his teaching,g because his message had authority.

4:34
h ver 41

33 In the synagogue there was a man possessed by a demon, an evilc spirit. He cried out at the top of his voice, 34 "Ha! What do you want with us, Jesus of Nazareth? Have you come to destroy us? I know who you are—the Holy One of God!"h

4:35
i ver 39, 41; Mt 8:26

35 "Be quiet!" Jesus said sternly.i "Come out of him!" Then the demon threw the man down before them all and came out without injuring him.

4:36
j ver 32

36 All the people were amazed and said to each other, "What is this teaching? With authorityj and power he gives orders to evil spirits and they come out!" 37 And the news about him spread throughout the surrounding area.k

4:37
k ver 14

a 19 Isaiah 61:1,2   b 27 The Greek word was used for various diseases affecting the skin—not necessarily leprosy.
c 33 Greek *unclean*; also in verse 36

---

when all debts are cancelled, all slaves are freed, and all property is returned to original owners (Leviticus 25). But the release from Babylonian exile had not brought the expected fulfillment; they were still a conquered and oppressed people. So Isaiah must have been referring to a future Messianic age. Jesus boldly announced, "Today this scripture is fulfilled in your hearing." Jesus was proclaiming himself as the One who would bring this good news to pass, but he would do so in a way that the people were not yet able to grasp.

4:24 Even Jesus himself was not accepted as a prophet in his hometown. Many people have a similar attitude. Don't be surprised if your Christian life and faith are not easily understood or accepted by those who know you well. Because they know your background, your failures, and your foibles, they may not see past those to the new person you have become. Let God work in your life, pray to be a positive witness for him, and be patient.

4:28 Jesus' remarks filled the people of Nazareth with rage because he was saying that God sometimes chose to reach Gentiles rather than Jews. Jesus implied that his hearers were as unbelieving as the citizens of the northern kingdom of Israel in the days of Elijah and Elisha, a time notorious for its great wickedness.

4:31 Jesus had recently moved to Capernaum from Nazareth (Matthew 4:13). Capernaum was a thriving city with great wealth

as well as great decadence. Because it was the headquarters for many Roman troops, word about Jesus could spread all over the Roman empire from there.

4:33 A man possessed by a demon was in the synagogue where Jesus was teaching. This man made his way into the place of worship and verbally abused Jesus. It is naive to think that we will be sheltered from evil in the church. Satan is happy to invade our presence wherever and whenever he can. But Jesus' authority is much greater than Satan's, and where Jesus is present, demons cannot stay for long.

4:34-36 The people were amazed at Jesus' authority to drive out demons—evil spirits ruled by Satan and sent to harass people, tempt them to sin, and ultimately destroy them. Demons are fallen angels who have joined Satan in rebellion against God. Jesus faced many demons during his time on earth, and he always exerted authority over them. Not only did the evil spirit leave this man; Luke records that the man was not even injured.

While we may not often see cases of demon possession today, it does still exist. However, we would not doubt that evil permeates our world. We need not be fearful, however. Jesus' power is far greater than Satan's. The first step toward conquering fear of evil is to recognize Jesus' authority and power. He has overcome all evil, including Satan himself.

Jesus Heals Peter's Mother-in-Law and Many Others
(35/Matthew 8:14–17; Mark 1:29–34)

38 Jesus left the synagogue and went to the home of Simon. Now Simon's mother-in-law was suffering from a high fever, and they asked Jesus to help her. 39 So he bent over her and rebuked *l* the fever, and it left her. She got up at once and began to wait on them.

40 When the sun was setting, the people brought to Jesus all who had various kinds of sickness, and laying his hands on each one, *m* he healed them. *n* 41 Moreover, demons came out of many people, shouting, "You are the Son of God!" *o* But he rebuked them and would not allow them to speak, *p* because they knew he was the Christ. *a*

4:39
l ver 35, 41

4:40
m Mk 5:23
n Mt 4:23

4:41
o Mt 4:3
p Mt 8:4

Jesus Preaches throughout Galilee (36/Matthew 4:23–25; Mark 1:35–39)

42 At daybreak Jesus went out to a solitary place. The people were looking for him and when they came to where he was, they tried to keep him from leaving them. 43 But he said, "I must preach the good news of the kingdom of God to the other towns also, because that is why I was sent." 44 And he kept on preaching in the synagogues of Judea. *b*

Jesus Provides a Miraculous Catch of Fish (37)

5 One day as Jesus was standing by the Lake of Gennesaret, *c* with the people crowding around him and listening to the word of God, 2 he saw at the water's edge two boats, left there by the fishermen, who were washing their nets. 3 He got into one of the boats, the one belonging to Simon, and asked him to put out a little from shore. Then he sat down and taught the people from the boat. *q*

4 When he had finished speaking, he said to Simon, "Put out into deep water, and let down *d* the nets for a catch." *r*

5 Simon answered, "Master, *s* we've worked hard all night and haven't caught anything. But because you say so, I will let down the nets."

6 When they had done so, they caught such a large number of fish that their nets began to break. 7 So they signaled their partners in the other boat to come and help them, and they came and filled both boats so full that they began to sink.

8 When Simon Peter saw this, he fell at Jesus' knees and said, "Go away from me, Lord;

5:3
q Mt 13:2

5:4
r Jn 21:6

5:5
s Lk 8:24, 45;
9:33, 49; 17:13

a 41 Or *Messiah*   *b* 44 Or *the land of the Jews*; some manuscripts *Galilee*   *c* 1 That is, Sea of Galilee   *d* 4 The Greek verb is plural.

4:39 Jesus healed Simon's (Peter's) mother-in-law so completely that not only did the fever leave, but her strength was restored, and immediately she got up and took care of others' needs. What a beautiful attitude of service she showed! God gives us health so that we may serve others.

4:40 The people came to Jesus when the sun was setting because this was the Sabbath (4:31), their day of rest. Sabbath lasted from sunset on Friday to sunset on Saturday. The people didn't want to break the law that prohibited travel on the Sabbath, so they waited until the sun set on the Sabbath before coming to Jesus. Then, as Luke the physician notes, they came with all kinds of diseases, and Jesus healed each one.

4:40 When you've faced a particularly difficult time, what helped you most? While some may have said kind words, most likely it was the presence of a friend and his or her touch. A hug, an arm around your shoulder, or even just a hand laid gently on top of yours—these simple wordless gestures mean so much to those in pain. In healing the sick and the demon possessed, Jesus had already demonstrated that he could heal with just a word (4:39). Yet here in Capernaum, Luke records that the touch of Jesus' hand healed the sick. Why not just speak a word and heal the whole crowd at once? Why go to all the trouble of treating each person individually, face-to-face? Because human touch is so very important. Does someone need a touch from you today?

4:41 Why didn't Jesus want the demons to reveal who he was? (1) Jesus commanded them to remain silent to show his authority over them. (2) Jesus wanted his listeners to believe he was the Messiah because of his words, not because of the demons' words. (3) Jesus was going to reveal his identity according to God's timetable, and he would not be pushed by Satan's evil plans. The demons called Jesus "Son of God" or "the Holy One

of God" (4:34) because they knew he was the Christ. But Jesus was going to show himself to be the suffering servant before he became the great King. To reveal his identity as King too soon would stir up the crowds with the wrong expectations of what he had come to do.

4:42 Jesus had to get up very early just to get some time alone. If Jesus needed solitude for prayer and refreshment, how much more is this true for us? Don't become so busy that life turns into a flurry of activity leaving no room for quiet fellowship alone with God. No matter how much you have to do, you should always have time for prayer.

4:43 The kingdom of God is good news! It was good news to the Jews because they had been awaiting the coming of the promised Messiah ever since the Babylonian captivity. It is good news for us also because it means freedom from slavery to sin and selfishness. The kingdom of God is here and now because the Holy Spirit lives in the hearts of believers. Yet it is also in the future because Jesus will return to reign over a perfect kingdom where sin and evil will no longer exist.

5:1 The Lake of Gennesaret was also known as the Sea of Galilee or the Sea of Tiberias.

5:2 Fishermen on the Sea of Galilee used nets, often bell-shaped ones with lead weights around the edges. A net would be thrown flat onto the water, and the lead weights would cause it to sink around the fish. Then the fishermen would pull on a cord, drawing the net around the fish. Nets had to be kept in good condition, so they would be washed to remove weeds and then mended.

5:8 Simon (Peter) was awestruck at this miracle, and his first response was to realize his own insignificance in comparison to this man's greatness. Peter knew that Jesus had healed the sick

5:10
t Mt 14:27

5:11
u ver 28

5:12
v Mt 8:2

5:14
w Lev 14:2-32

5:15
x Mt 9:26

5:16
y Mt 14:23; Lk 3:21

5:17
z Mt 15:1; Lk 2:46
a Mk 5:30; Lk 6:19

5:20
b Lk 7:48, 49

5:21
c Isa 43:25

I am a sinful man!" 9 For he and all his companions were astonished at the catch of fish they had taken, 10 and so were James and John, the sons of Zebedee, Simon's partners.

Then Jesus said to Simon, "Don't be afraid;*t* from now on you will catch men." 11 So they pulled their boats up on shore, left everything and followed him. *u*

Jesus Heals a Man with Leprosy (38/Matthew 8:1–4; Mark 1:40–45)

12 While Jesus was in one of the towns, a man came along who was covered with leprosy.*a* *v* When he saw Jesus, he fell with his face to the ground and begged him, "Lord, if you are willing, you can make me clean."

13 Jesus reached out his hand and touched the man. "I am willing," he said. "Be clean!" And immediately the leprosy left him.

14 Then Jesus ordered him, "Don't tell anyone, but go, show yourself to the priest and offer the sacrifices that Moses commanded *w* for your cleansing, as a testimony to them."

15 Yet the news about him spread all the more,*x* so that crowds of people came to hear him and to be healed of their sicknesses. 16 But Jesus often withdrew to lonely places and prayed.*y*

Jesus Heals a Paralyzed Man (39/Matthew 9:1–8; Mark 2:1–12)

17 One day as he was teaching, Pharisees and teachers of the law,*z* who had come from every village of Galilee and from Judea and Jerusalem, were sitting there. And the power of the Lord was present for him to heal the sick.*a* 18 Some men came carrying a paralytic on a mat and tried to take him into the house to lay him before Jesus. 19 When they could not find a way to do this because of the crowd, they went up on the roof and lowered him on his mat through the tiles into the middle of the crowd, right in front of Jesus.

20 When Jesus saw their faith, he said, "Friend, your sins are forgiven."*b*

21 The Pharisees and the teachers of the law began thinking to themselves, "Who is this fellow who speaks blasphemy? Who can forgive sins but God alone?"*c*

a 12 The Greek word was used for various diseases affecting the skin—not necessarily leprosy.

---

and driven out demons, but he was amazed that Jesus cared about his day-to-day routine and understood his needs. God is interested not only in saving us, but also in helping us in our daily activities.

5:11 God has two requirements for coming to him. Like Peter, we must recognize our own sinfulness. Then, like these fishermen, we must realize that we can't save ourselves. If we know that we need help, and if we know that Jesus is the only one who can help us, we will be ready to leave everything and follow him.

5:11 This was the disciples' second call. After the first call (Matthew 4:18–22; Mark 1:16–20), Peter, Andrew, James, and John had gone back to fishing. They continued to watch Jesus, however, as he established his authority in the synagogue, healed the sick, and drove out demons. Here he also established his authority in their lives—he met them on their level and helped them in their work. From this point on, they left their nets and remained with Jesus. For us, following Jesus means more than just acknowledging him as Savior. We must leave our past behind and commit our future to him.

5:12 Leprosy was a feared disease because there was no known cure for it, and some forms of it were highly contagious. Leprosy had a similar emotional impact and terror associated with it as AIDS does today. (Sometimes called Hansen's disease, leprosy still exists in a less contagious form that can be treated.) The priests monitored the disease, banishing lepers who were in a contagious stage to prevent the spread of infection and readmitting lepers whose disease was in remission. Because leprosy destroys the nerve endings, lepers often would unknowingly damage their fingers, toes, and noses. This man with leprosy had an advanced case, so he undoubtedly had lost much bodily tissue. Still, he believed that Jesus could heal every trace of the disease. And Jesus did just that, reaching out to touch this untouchable, contagious man in order to restore him. For more on the power of touch, see the second note on 4:40.

5:16 People were flocking to hear Jesus preach and to have their diseases healed, but Jesus made sure he often withdrew to quiet, solitary places to pray. Many things clamor for our attention, and

we often run ourselves ragged attending to them. Like Jesus, however, we should take time to withdraw to a quiet and deserted place to pray. Strength comes from God, and we can only be strengthened by spending time with him.

5:17 The religious leaders spent much time defining and discussing the huge body of religious tradition that had been accumulating for more than 400 years since the Jews' return from exile. They were so concerned with these man-made traditions, in fact, that they often lost sight of Scripture. Here these leaders felt threatened because Jesus challenged their sincerity and because the people were flocking to him.

5:18, 19 In Bible times, houses were built of stone and had flat roofs made of mud mixed with straw. Outside stairways led to the roof. These men carried their friend up the stairs to the roof where they took apart as much of the mud and straw mixture as was necessary to lower him in front of Jesus.

5:18–20 It wasn't the paralytic's faith that impressed Jesus, but the faith of his friends. Jesus responded to their faith and healed the man. For better or worse, our faith affects others. We cannot make another person a Christian, but we can do much through our words, actions, and love to give him or her a chance to respond. Look for opportunities to bring your friends to the living Christ.

5:21 When Jesus told the paralytic his sins were forgiven, the Jewish leaders accused Jesus of blasphemy—claiming to be God or to do what only God can do. In Jewish law, blasphemy was punishable by death (Leviticus 24:16). In labeling Jesus' claim to forgive sins blasphemous, the religious leaders showed they did not understand that Jesus *is* God, and that he has God's power to heal both the body and the soul. Forgiveness of sins was a sign that the Messianic age had come (Isaiah 40:2; Joel 2:32; Micah 7:18, 19; Zechariah 13:1).

22 Jesus knew what they were thinking and asked, "Why are you thinking these things in your hearts? 23 Which is easier: to say, 'Your sins are forgiven,' or to say, 'Get up and walk'? 24 But that you may know that the Son of Man has authority on earth to forgive sins. . ." He said to the paralyzed man, "I tell you, get up, take your mat and go home." 25 Immediately he stood up in front of them, took what he had been lying on and went home praising God. 26 Everyone was amazed and gave praise to God. They were filled with awe and said, "We have seen remarkable things today."

Jesus Eats with Sinners at Matthew's House (40/Matthew 9:9–13; Mark 2:13–17)

27 After this, Jesus went out and saw a tax collector by the name of Levi sitting at his tax booth. "Follow me," Jesus said to him, 28 and Levi got up, left everything and followed him. [d]

29 Then Levi held a great banquet for Jesus at his house, and a large crowd of tax collectors [e] and others were eating with them. 30 But the Pharisees and the teachers of the law who belonged to their sect [f] complained to his disciples, "Why do you eat and drink with tax collectors and 'sinners'?"

31 Jesus answered them, "It is not the healthy who need a doctor, but the sick. 32 I have not come to call the righteous, but sinners to repentance."

Religious Leaders Ask Jesus about Fasting (41/Matthew 9:14–17; Mark 2:18–22)

33 They said to him, "John's disciples [g] often fast and pray, and so do the disciples of the Pharisees, but yours go on eating and drinking."

34 Jesus answered, "Can you make the guests of the bridegroom fast while he is with them? 35 But the time will come when the bridegroom will be taken from them; [h] in those days they will fast."

36 He told them this parable: "No one tears a patch from a new garment and sews it on an old one. If he does, he will have torn the new garment, and the patch from the new will not match the old. 37 And no one pours new wine into old wineskins. If he does, the new wine will burst the skins, the wine will run out and the wineskins will be ruined. 38 No, new wine must be poured into new wineskins. 39 And no one after drinking old wine wants the new, for he says, 'The old is better.'"

The Disciples Pick Wheat on the Sabbath (45/Matthew 12:1–8; Mark 2:23–28)

6 One Sabbath Jesus was going through the grainfields, and his disciples began to pick some heads of grain, rub them in their hands and eat the kernels. [i] 2 Some of the Pharisees asked, "Why are you doing what is unlawful on the Sabbath?"

5:28
[d] ver 11
5:29
[e] Lk 15:1
5:30
[f] Ac 23:9

5:33
[g] Lk 7:18

5:35
[h] Lk 17:22

6:1
[i] Dt 23:25

5:24 God offers the same forgiveness given to the paralytic to all who believe. The Greek word *aphiemi*, translated "forgiven," means to leave or let go, to give up a debt, to send away from oneself. Forgiveness means that a relationship has been renewed despite a wrong that has been done. But the act cannot be erased or changed. The notion of *aphiemi*, however, goes far beyond human forgiveness, for it includes the "putting away" of sin in two ways: (1) The law and justice are satisfied because Jesus paid the penalty that sin deserved; thus, sins can no longer be held against a believer. (2) The guilt caused by sin is removed and replaced with Christ's righteousness. Believers are so forgiven that, in God's eyes, it is as if they had never sinned. Do you carry a heavy burden for sins you have committed? Confess all to Christ and receive *aphiemi*—ultimate forgiveness.

5:27 For more about Levi (who was also named Matthew), the disciple and author of the Gospel of Matthew, see his Profile in Matthew 9, p. 1546.

5:28, 29 Levi responded as Jesus would want all his followers to do—he followed his Lord immediately, and he called his friends together to meet him too. Levi left a lucrative, though probably dishonest, tax-collecting business to follow Jesus. Then he held a banquet for his fellow tax collectors and other notorious "sinners" so they could meet Jesus too. Levi, who left behind a material fortune in order to gain a spiritual fortune, was proud to be associated with Jesus.

5:30–32 The Pharisees wrapped their sin in respectability. They made themselves appear good by publicly doing good deeds and pointing at the sins of others. Jesus chose to spend time not with these proud, self-righteous religious leaders, but with people who sensed their own sin and knew that they were not good enough for God. In order to come to God, we must repent; in order to renounce our sin, we must recognize it for what it is.

5:35 Jesus knew his death was coming. After that time, fasting would be in order. Although he was fully human, Jesus knew he was God and knew why he had come—to die for the sins of the world.

5:36–39 "Wineskins" were goatskins sewed together at the edges to form watertight bags. Because new wine expands as it ages, it had to be put in new, pliable wineskins. A used skin, having become more rigid, would burst and spill the wine. Like old wineskins, the Pharisees were too rigid to accept Jesus, who could not be contained in their traditions or rules. Christianity required new approaches, new traditions, new structures. Our church programs and ministries should not be so structured that they have no room for a fresh touch of the Spirit, a new method, or a new idea. We, too, must be careful that our hearts do not become so rigid that they prevent us from accepting the new way of thinking that Christ brings. We need to keep our hearts pliable so we can accept Jesus' life-changing message.

6:1, 2 Jewish legal tradition had 39 categories of activities forbidden on the Sabbath—and harvesting was one of them. The teachers of the law even went so far as to describe different methods of harvesting. One method was to rub the heads of grain between the hands, as the disciples were doing here. God's law

6:3
/1Sa 21:6

6:4
kLev 24:5, 9

³Jesus answered them, "Have you never read what David did when he and his companions were hungry?/ ⁴He entered the house of God, and taking the consecrated bread, he ate what is lawful only for priests to eat. k And he also gave some to his companions." ⁵Then Jesus said to them, "The Son of Man is Lord of the Sabbath."

Jesus Heals a Man's Hand on the Sabbath (46/Matthew 12:9–14; Mark 3:1–6)

6:6
/ver 1

⁶On another Sabbath/ he went into the synagogue and was teaching, and a man was there whose right hand was shriveled. ⁷The Pharisees and the teachers of the law were looking for a reason to accuse Jesus, so they watched him closely to see if he would heal on the Sabbath.

6:8
mMt 9:4

⁸But Jesus knew what they were thinking m and said to the man with the shriveled hand, "Get up and stand in front of everyone." So he got up and stood there.

⁹Then Jesus said to them, "I ask you, which is lawful on the Sabbath: to do good or to do evil, to save life or to destroy it?"

¹⁰He looked around at them all, and then said to the man, "Stretch out your hand." He did so, and his hand was completely restored. ¹¹But they were furious and began to discuss with one another what they might do to Jesus.

Jesus Chooses the Twelve Disciples (48/Mark 3:13–19)

6:13
nMk 6:30

¹²One of those days Jesus went out to a mountainside to pray, and spent the night praying to God. ¹³When morning came, he called his disciples to him and chose twelve of them, whom he also designated apostles: n ¹⁴Simon (whom he named Peter), his brother Andrew, James, John, Philip, Bartholomew, ¹⁵Matthew, Thomas, James son of Alphaeus, Simon who was called the Zealot, ¹⁶Judas son of James, and Judas Iscariot, who became a traitor.

Jesus Gives the Beatitudes (49/Matthew 5:1–12)

6:17
oMt 4:25; Mk 3:7, 8

¹⁷He went down with them and stood on a level place. A large crowd of his disciples was there and a great number of people from all over Judea, from Jerusalem, and from the coast of Tyre and Sidon,o ¹⁸who had come to hear him and to be healed of their diseases. Those

---

said farmers were to leave the edges of their fields unplowed so travelers and the poor could eat from this bounty (Deuteronomy 23:25); thus, the disciples were not guilty of stealing grain. Neither were they breaking the Sabbath by doing their daily work on it. In fact, though they may have been violating the Pharisees' rules, they were not breaking any divine law.

6:3–5 Each week 12 consecrated loaves of bread, representing the 12 tribes of Israel, would be placed on a table in the temple. This bread was called the bread of the Presence. After its use in the temple, it was to be eaten only by priests. Jesus, accused of Sabbath-breaking, referred to a well-known story about David (1 Samuel 21:1–6). On one occasion, when fleeing from Saul, David and his men had eaten this consecrated bread. Their need had been more important than ceremonial regulations. Jesus was appealing to the same principle: human need is more important than human regulations and rules. By comparing himself and his disciples with David and his men, Jesus was saying, "If you condemn me, you must also condemn David."

6:5 When Jesus said he was "Lord of the Sabbath," he meant that he had the authority to overrule the Pharisees' traditions and regulations because he had created the Sabbath. The Creator is always greater than the creation.

6:6, 7 According to the tradition of the religious leaders, no healing could be done on the Sabbath. Healing, they said, was practicing medicine, and a person could not practice his or her profession on the Sabbath. The religious leaders were more concerned about protecting their laws than freeing a person from painful suffering. The religious leaders were more concerned with negatives: what rules should *not* be broken, what activities should *not* be done. Jesus was positive: doing good and helping those in need.

Which would an objective observer say is more characteristic of your Christianity—the positives or the negatives? Are you more concerned about what people shouldn't be doing than you are about advancing God's kingdom? Is your way of being a Christian the only way? And what about your church? The Pharisees thought their religious system had all the answers. They

could not accept Jesus because he did not fit into their system. Beware of thinking that you or your church has all the answers. No religious system is big enough to contain Christ completely or to fulfill perfectly all his desires for the world. Christianity is the most positive force to ever hit this planet. Make sure you don't let it degenerate into a bunch of negatives.

6:11 Jesus' enemies were furious. Not only had he read their minds; he also had flouted their laws and exposed the hatred in their hearts. Ironically, their hatred, combined with their zeal for the law, drove them to plot murder—an act that was clearly against their law.

6:12 The Gospel writers note that before every important event in Jesus' life, he would take time to go off by himself and pray. This time Jesus was preparing to choose his inner circle, the 12 disciples. Make sure that all your important decisions are grounded in prayer.

6:13 Jesus had many *disciples* (learners), but he chose only 12 *apostles* (messengers). The apostles were his inner circle, to whom he gave special training and whom he sent out with his own authority. These were the men who started the Christian church. In the Gospels these 12 men are usually called the disciples, but in the book of Acts they are called apostles.

6:13–16 Jesus selected "ordinary" men with a mixture of backgrounds and personalities to be his disciples. Today, God calls "ordinary" people together to build his church, teach salvation's message, and serve others out of love. Alone we may feel unqualified to serve Christ effectively, but together we make up a group strong enough to serve God in any way. Ask for patience to accept the diversity of people in your church, and build on the variety of strengths represented in your group.

6:14–16 The disciples are not always listed by the same names. For example, Peter is sometimes called Simon or Cephas. Matthew is also known as Levi. Bartholomew is thought to be the same person as Nathanael (John 1:45). Judas the son of James is also called Thaddaeus.

troubled by evil[a] spirits were cured, [19]and the people all tried to touch him, because power was coming from him and healing them all.[p]

6:19
p Mt 14:36; Lk 5:17

[20]Looking at his disciples, he said:

> "Blessed are you who are poor,
>   for yours is the kingdom of God.
> [21] Blessed are you who hunger now,
>   for you will be satisfied.
> Blessed are you who weep now,
>   for you will laugh.[q]
> [22] Blessed are you when men hate you,
>   when they exclude you[r] and insult you
>   and reject your name as evil,
>   because of the Son of Man.

6:21
q Isa 61:2, 3

6:22
r Jn 9:22; 16:2

[23]"Rejoice in that day and leap for joy, because great is your reward in heaven. For that is how their fathers treated the prophets.

> [24] "But woe to you who are rich,[s]
>   for you have already received your comfort.[t]
> [25] Woe to you who are well fed now,
>   for you will go hungry.[u]
> Woe to you who laugh now,
>   for you will mourn and weep.[v]
> [26] Woe to you when all men speak well of you,
>   for that is how their fathers treated the false prophets.

6:24
s Jas 5:1
t Lk 16:25

6:25
u Isa 65:13
v Pr 14:13

Jesus Teaches about Loving Enemies (57/Matthew 5:43–48)

[27]"But I tell you who hear me: Love your enemies, do good to those who hate you,[w] [28]bless those who curse you, pray for those who mistreat you. [29]If someone strikes you on one cheek, turn to him the other also. If someone takes your cloak, do not stop him from taking your tunic. [30]Give to everyone who asks you, and if anyone takes what belongs to you, do not demand it back.[x] [31]Do to others as you would have them do to you.[y]

[32]"If you love those who love you, what credit is that to you?[z] Even 'sinners' love those who love them. [33]And if you do good to those who are good to you, what credit is that to you? Even 'sinners' do that. [34]And if you lend to those from whom you expect repayment, what credit is that to you?[a] Even 'sinners' lend to 'sinners,' expecting to be repaid in full. [35]But

6:27
w ver 35; Mt 5:44;
Ro 12:20

6:30
x Dt 15:7, 8, 10;
Pr 21:26

6:31
y Mt 7:12

6:32
z Mt 5:46

6:34
a Mt 5:42

a 18 Greek unclean

6:19 Once word of Jesus' healing power spread, crowds gathered just to touch him. For many, he had become a symbol of good fortune, a lucky charm, or a magician. Instead of desiring God's pardon and love, they only wanted physical healing or a chance to see spectacular events. Some people still see God as a cosmic magician and consider prayer as a way to get God to do his tricks. But God is not a magician—he is the Master. Prayer is not a way for us to control God; it is a way for us to put ourselves under his control.

6:20ff This may be Luke's account of the sermon that Matthew records in Matthew 5—7, or it may be that Jesus gave similar sermons on several different occasions. Some believe that this was not one sermon, but a composite based on Jesus' customary teachings.

6:20–23 These verses are called the *Beatitudes,* from the Latin word meaning "blessing." They describe what it means to be Christ's follower, give standards of conduct, and contrast kingdom values with worldly values, showing what Christ's followers can expect from the world and what God will give them. In addition, they contrast fake piety with true humility. They also show how Old Testament expectations are fulfilled in God's kingdom.

6:21 Some believe that the hunger about which Jesus spoke is a hunger for righteousness (Matthew 5:6). Others say this is physical hunger. In any case, in a nation where riches were seen as a sign of God's favor, Jesus startled his hearers by pronouncing

blessings on the hungry. In doing so, however, he was in line with an ancient tradition. The Old Testament is filled with texts proclaiming God's concern for the poor and needy. See, for example, 1 Samuel 2:5; Psalm 146:7; Isaiah 58:6, 7; and Jesus' own mother's prayer in Luke 1:53.

6:24 If you are trying to find fulfillment only through riches, wealth may be the only reward you will ever get—and it does not last. We should not seek comfort now at the expense of eternal life.

6:26 Many false prophets lived during Old Testament times. They were praised by kings and crowds because their predictions—prosperity and victory in war—were exactly what the people wanted to hear. But popularity is no guarantee of truth, and human flattery does not bring God's approval. Sadness lies ahead for those who chase after the crowd's praise rather than God's truth.

6:27 The Jews despised the Romans because they oppressed God's people, but Jesus told the people to love these enemies. Such words turned many away from Christ. Jesus wasn't talking about having affection for enemies; he was talking about an act of the will. You can't "fall into" this kind of love—it takes conscious effort. Loving our enemies means acting in their best interests. We can pray for them, and we can think of ways to help them. Jesus loves the whole world, even though the world is in rebellion against God. Jesus asks us to follow his example by loving our enemies. Grant your enemies the same respect and rights as you desire for yourself.

love your enemies, do good to them, and lend to them without expecting to get anything back. Then your reward will be great, and you will be sons of the Most High, because he is kind to the ungrateful and wicked. 36 Be merciful, just as your Father is merciful.

Jesus Teaches about Judging Others (63/Matthew 7:1–6)

6:37
b Mt 7:1

6:38
c Mk 4:24

37 "Do not judge, and you will not be judged. *b* Do not condemn, and you will not be condemned. Forgive, and you will be forgiven. 38 Give, and it will be given to you. A good measure, pressed down, shaken together and running over, will be poured into your lap. For with the measure you use, it will be measured to you." *c*

6:39
d Mt 15:14

6:40
e Mt 10:24; Jn 13:16

39 He also told them this parable: "Can a blind man lead a blind man? Will they not both fall into a pit? *d* 40 A student is not above his teacher, but everyone who is fully trained will be like his teacher. *e*

41 "Why do you look at the speck of sawdust in your brother's eye and pay no attention to the plank in your own eye? 42 How can you say to your brother, 'Brother, let me take the speck out of your eye,' when you yourself fail to see the plank in your own eye? You hypocrite, first take the plank out of your eye, and then you will see clearly to remove the speck from your brother's eye.

Jesus Teaches about Fruit in People's Lives (66/Matthew 7:15–20)

6:44
f Mt 12:33

6:45
g Mt 12:34, 35; Mk 7:20

43 "No good tree bears bad fruit, nor does a bad tree bear good fruit. 44 Each tree is recognized by its own fruit. *f* People do not pick figs from thornbushes, or grapes from briers. 45 The good man brings good things out of the good stored up in his heart, and the evil man brings evil things out of the evil stored up in his heart. For out of the overflow of his heart his mouth speaks. *g*

Jesus Teaches about Building on a Solid Foundation (67/Matthew 7:21–29)

6:46
h Mal 1:6; Mt 7:21

6:47
i Jas 1:22-25

46 "Why do you call me, 'Lord, Lord,' and do not do what I say? *h* 47 I will show you what he is like who comes to me and hears my words and puts them into practice. *i* 48 He is like a man building a house, who dug down deep and laid the foundation on rock. When a flood came, the torrent struck that house but could not shake it, because it was well built. 49 But the one who hears my words and does not put them into practice is like a man who built a house on the ground without a foundation. The moment the torrent struck that house, it collapsed and its destruction was complete."

6:37, 38 A forgiving spirit demonstrates that a person has received God's forgiveness. Jesus used the picture of measuring grain in a basket to ensure the full amount. If we are critical rather than compassionate, we will also receive criticism. If we treat others generously, graciously, and compassionately, however, these qualities will come back to us in full measure. We are to love others, not judge them.

6:39, 40 Make sure you're following the right teachers and leaders, because you will go no farther than they do. Look for leaders who will show you more about faith and whose guidance you can trust.

6:41 Jesus doesn't mean we should ignore wrongdoing, but we should not be so worried about others' sins that we overlook our own. We often rationalize our sins by pointing out the same mistakes in others. What kinds of specks in others' eyes are the easiest for you to criticize? Remember your own "planks" when you feel like criticizing, and you may find that you have less to say.

6:42 We should not be so afraid of the label *hypocrite* that we stand still in our Christian life, hiding our faith and making no attempts to grow. A person who tries to do right but often fails is not a hypocrite. Neither are those who fulfill their duty even when they don't feel like doing it. Often it is necessary and good to set aside our desires in order to do what needs to be done. It is not hypocrisy to be weak in faith. A hypocrite is a person who only puts on religious behavior in order to gain attention, approval, acceptance, or admiration from others.

6:45 Jesus reminds us that our speech and actions reveal our true underlying beliefs, attitudes, and motivations. The good impressions we try to make cannot last if we are being deceptive. What is in your heart will come out in your speech and behavior.

6:46–49 Why would people build a house without a foundation? Perhaps to save time and avoid the hard work of preparing the stone. Possibly because the waterfront scenery is more attractive or because beach houses have higher social status than cliff houses. Perhaps because they want to join their friends who have already settled in sandy areas. Maybe because they haven't heard about the violent storms coming, because they have discounted the reports, or because they think disaster can't happen to them. Whatever their reason, those with no foundation are shortsighted, and they will be sorry. Obeying God is like building a house on a strong, solid foundation that stands firm when storms come. When life is calm, our foundations don't seem to matter. But when crises come, our foundations are tested. Be sure your life is built on the solid foundation of knowing and trusting Jesus Christ.

A Roman Officer Demonstrates Faith (68/Matthew 8:5–13)

7 When Jesus had finished saying all this / in the hearing of the people, he entered Capernaum. ²There a centurion's servant, whom his master valued highly, was sick and about to die. ³The centurion heard of Jesus and sent some elders of the Jews to him, asking him to come and heal his servant. ⁴When they came to Jesus, they pleaded earnestly with him, "This man deserves to have you do this, ⁵because he loves our nation and has built our synagogue." ⁶So Jesus went with them.

He was not far from the house when the centurion sent friends to say to him: "Lord, don't trouble yourself, for I do not deserve to have you come under my roof. ⁷That is why I did not even consider myself worthy to come to you. But say the word, and my servant will be healed. ⁸For I myself am a man under authority, with soldiers under me. I tell this one, 'Go,' and he goes; and that one, 'Come,' and he comes. I say to my servant, 'Do this,' and he does it."

⁹When Jesus heard this, he was amazed at him, and turning to the crowd following him, he said, "I tell you, I have not found such great faith even in Israel." ¹⁰Then the men who had been sent returned to the house and found the servant well.

Jesus Raises a Widow's Son from the Dead (69)

¹¹Soon afterward, Jesus went to a town called Nain, and his disciples and a large crowd went along with him. ¹²As he approached the town gate, a dead person was being carried out—the only son of his mother, and she was a widow. And a large crowd from the town was with her. ¹³When the Lord ᵏ saw her, his heart went out to her and he said, "Don't cry."

¹⁴Then he went up and touched the coffin, and those carrying it stood still. He said, "Young man, I say to you, get up!" / ¹⁵The dead man sat up and began to talk, and Jesus gave him back to his mother.

¹⁶They were all filled with awe ᵐ and praised God. ⁿ "A great prophet ᵒ has appeared among us," they said. "God has come to help his people." ᵖ ¹⁷This news about Jesus spread throughout Judea ᵃ and the surrounding country. �q

ᵃ 17 Or *the land of the Jews*

7:1
/Mt 7:28

7:13
ᵏver 19; Lk 10:1;
13:15; 17:5; 22:61;
24:34; Jn 11:2

7:14
/Lk 8:54; Jn 11:43;
Ac 9:40

7:16
ᵐLk 1:65
ⁿMt 9:8
ᵒMt 21:11
ᵖLk 1:68

7:17
qMt 9:26

7:1ff This passage marks a turning point in Luke's account of Jesus' ministry. Up to this point, Jesus has dealt exclusively with the Jews; here he begins to include the Gentiles. Notice who the main characters are in this short drama: the Jewish elders, a Roman centurion, and the centurion's servant—very different racial and religious backgrounds, and vastly different standings on the social ladder. Jesus broke through all those barriers, all the way to the sick man's need. The gospel travels well across ethnic, racial, national, and religious barriers. Are you willing to work through them as well? Jesus was no respecter of artificial divisions, and we should follow his example. Reach out to those whom Jesus came to save.

7:2 A *centurion* was a Roman army officer in charge of 100 men. The officer heard about Jesus, so obviously he also heard about Jesus' healing power. He sent a request through some of the Jewish elders on behalf of his servant. He may have heard about the healing of the Roman official's son (which probably occurred earlier, see John 4:46–54). He knew Jesus had the power to heal his servant.

7:3 Matthew 8:5 says the Roman centurion visited Jesus himself, while Luke 7:3 says he sent Jewish elders to present his request to Jesus. In those days, dealing with a person's messengers was considered the same as dealing with the one who had sent them. Thus, in dealing with the messengers, Jesus was dealing with the centurion. For his Jewish audience, Matthew emphasized the Roman officer's faith. For his Gentile audience, Luke highlighted the good relationship between the Jewish elders and the Roman. This centurion daily delegated work and sent groups on missions, so this was how he chose to get his message to Jesus.

7:9 The Roman centurion didn't come to Jesus, and he didn't expect Jesus to come to him. Just as this officer did not need to be present to have his orders carried out, so Jesus didn't need to be present to heal. The centurion's faith was especially

amazing because he was a Gentile who had not been brought up to know a loving God. Hence Jesus' comment.

7:11–15 The widow's situation was serious. She had lost her husband, and now her only son had died—her last means of support. The crowd of mourners would go home, and she would be left penniless and alone. The widow was probably past the age of childbearing and would not marry again. Unless a relative came to her aid, her future was bleak. She would be an easy prey for swindlers, and she would likely be reduced to begging for food. In fact, as Luke repeatedly emphasizes, this woman was just the kind of person Jesus had come to help—and help her he did. Jesus has great compassion on your pain, and he has the power to bring hope out of any tragedy.

7:11–17 This story illustrates salvation. The whole world was dead in sin (Ephesians 2:1), just as the widow's son was dead. Being dead, we could do nothing to help ourselves—we couldn't even ask for help. But God had compassion on us, and he sent Jesus to raise us to life with him (Ephesians 2:4–7). The dead man did not earn his second chance at life, and we cannot earn our new life in Christ. But we can accept God's gift of life, praise God for it, and use our lives to do his will.

7:12 Honoring the dead was important in Jewish tradition. A funeral procession—the relatives of the dead person following the body that was wrapped and carried on a kind of stretcher—would make its way through town, and bystanders would be expected to join the procession. In addition, hired mourners would cry aloud and draw attention to the procession. The family's mourning would continue for 30 days.

7:16 The people thought of Jesus as a prophet because, like the Old Testament prophets, he boldly proclaimed God's message and sometimes raised the dead. Both Elijah and Elisha raised children from the dead (1 Kings 17:17–24; 2 Kings 4:18–37). The people were correct in thinking that Jesus was a prophet, but he was much more—he was God himself.

Jesus Eases John's Doubt (70/Matthew 11:1–19)

¹⁸John's disciples told him about all these things. Calling two of them, ¹⁹he sent them to the Lord to ask, "Are you the one who was to come, or should we expect someone else?"

²⁰When the men came to Jesus, they said, "John the Baptist sent us to you to ask, 'Are you the one who was to come, or should we expect someone else?'"

²¹At that very time Jesus cured many who had diseases, sicknesses ʳ and evil spirits, and gave sight to many who were blind. ²²So he replied to the messengers, "Go back and report to John what you have seen and heard: The blind receive sight, the lame walk, those who have leprosyᵃ are cured, the deaf hear, the dead are raised, and the good news is preached to the poor. ˢ ²³Blessed is the man who does not fall away on account of me."

²⁴After John's messengers left, Jesus began to speak to the crowd about John: "What did you go out into the desert to see? A reed swayed by the wind? ²⁵If not, what did you go out to see? A man dressed in fine clothes? No, those who wear expensive clothes and indulge in luxury are in palaces. ²⁶But what did you go out to see? A prophet? Yes, I tell you, and more than a prophet. ²⁷This is the one about whom it is written:

"'I will send my messenger ahead of you,
who will prepare your way before you.'ᵇᵗ

²⁸I tell you, among those born of women there is no one greater than John; yet the one who is least in the kingdom of God is greater than he."

²⁹(All the people, even the tax collectors, when they heard Jesus' words, acknowledged that God's way was right, because they had been baptized by John. ᵘ ³⁰But the Pharisees and experts in the law ᵛ rejected God's purpose for themselves, because they had not been baptized by John.)

³¹"To what, then, can I compare the people of this generation? What are they like? ³²They are like children sitting in the marketplace and calling out to each other:

"'We played the flute for you,
and you did not dance;

**Margin references:**

7:21 ʳMt 4:23
7:22 ˢIsa 29:18, 19; 35:5, 6; 61:1, 2; Lk 4:18
7:27 ᵗMal 3:1; Mt 11:10; Mk 1:2
7:29 ᵘMt 21:32; Lk 3:12
7:30 ᵛMt 22:35

ᵃ22 The Greek word was used for various diseases affecting the skin—not necessarily leprosy.　ᵇ27 Mal. 3:1

7:18–23 John was confused because the reports he received about Jesus were unexpected and incomplete. John's doubts were natural, and Jesus didn't rebuke him for them. Instead, he responded in a way that John would understand: Jesus explained that he had accomplished what the Messiah was supposed to accomplish. God can handle our doubts, and he welcomes our questions. Do you have questions about Jesus—about who he is or what he expects of you? Admit them to yourself and to God, and begin looking for answers. Only as you face your doubts honestly can you begin to resolve them.

7:20–22 The proofs listed here for Jesus' being the Messiah are significant. They consist of observable deeds, not theories—actions that Jesus' contemporaries saw and reported for us to read today. The prophets had said that the Messiah would do these very acts (see Isaiah 35:5, 6; 61:1). These physical proofs helped John—and will help all of us—to recognize who Jesus is.

7:28 Of all people, no one fulfilled his God-given purpose better than John. Yet in God's kingdom, all who come after John have a greater spiritual heritage because they have clearer knowledge of the purpose of Jesus' death and resurrection. John was the last to function like the Old Testament prophets, the last to prepare the people for the coming Messianic age. Jesus was not contrasting the man John with individual Christians; he was contrasting life before Christ with life in the fullness of Christ's kingdom.

7:29, 30 The common people, including the tax collectors (who embodied evil in most people's minds) heard John's message and repented. In contrast, the Pharisees and experts in the law—religious leaders—rejected his words. Wanting to live their own way, they justified their own point of view and refused to listen to other ideas. They "rejected God's purpose." They were so close to Jesus, and yet so far away. The truth stood before them, and they rejected it. What have you done with the truth you read in God's Word?

7:31–35 The religious leaders hated both John and Jesus, but they did not bother to be consistent in their faultfinding. They criticized John the Baptist because he fasted and drank no wine; they criticized Jesus because he ate heartily and drank wine with tax collectors and sinners. Their real objection to both men, of course, had nothing to do with dietary habits. What the Pharisees and experts in the law couldn't stand was being exposed for their hypocrisy.

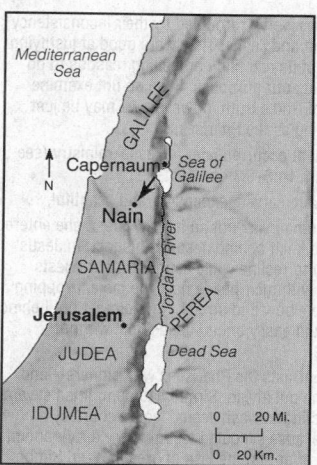

JESUS RAISES A WIDOW'S SON FROM THE DEAD Jesus traveled to Nain and met a funeral procession leaving the village. A widow's only son had died, but Jesus brought the young man back to life. This miracle, recorded only in Luke, reveals Jesus' compassion for people's needs.

Mediterranean Sea
GALILEE
Capernaum — *Sea of Galilee*
Nain
SAMARIA
Jordan River
Jerusalem
PEREA
JUDEA
Dead Sea
IDUMEA
0　　20 Mi.
0　　20 Km.

> we sang a dirge,
> and you did not cry.'

33 For John the Baptist came neither eating bread nor drinking wine,ʷ and you say, 'He has a demon.' 34 The Son of Man came eating and drinking, and you say, 'Here is a glutton and a drunkard, a friend of tax collectors and "sinners."'ˣ 35 But wisdom is proved right by all her children."

7:33
ʷLk 1:15

7:34
ˣLk 5:29, 30;
15:1, 2

A Sinful Woman Anoints Jesus' Feet (72)

36 Now one of the Pharisees invited Jesus to have dinner with him, so he went to the Pharisee's house and reclined at the table. 37 When a woman who had lived a sinful life in that town learned that Jesus was eating at the Pharisee's house, she brought an alabaster jar of perfume, 38 and as she stood behind him at his feet weeping, she began to wet his feet with her tears. Then she wiped them with her hair, kissed them and poured perfume on them.

39 When the Pharisee who had invited him saw this, he said to himself, "If this man were a prophet,ʸ he would know who is touching him and what kind of woman she is—that she is a sinner."

7:39
ʸver 16

40 Jesus answered him, "Simon, I have something to tell you."

"Tell me, teacher," he said.

41 "Two men owed money to a certain moneylender. One owed him five hundred denarii,ᵃ and the other fifty. 42 Neither of them had the money to pay him back, so he canceled the debts of both. Now which of them will love him more?"

43 Simon replied, "I suppose the one who had the bigger debt canceled."

"You have judged correctly," Jesus said.

44 Then he turned toward the woman and said to Simon, "Do you see this woman? I came into your house. You did not give me any water for my feet,ᶻ but she wet my feet with her tears and wiped them with her hair. 45 You did not give me a kiss, but this woman, from the time I entered, has not stopped kissing my feet. 46 You did not put oil on my head,ᵃ but she has poured perfume on my feet. 47 Therefore, I tell you, her many sins have been forgiven—for she loved much. But he who has been forgiven little loves little."

7:44
ᶻGe 18:4; 19:2;
43:24; Jdg 19:21;
1Ti 5:10

7:46
ᵃPs 23:5; Ecc 9:8

48 Then Jesus said to her, "Your sins are forgiven."ᵇ

7:48
ᵇMt 9:2

49 The other guests began to say among themselves, "Who is this who even forgives sins?"

50 Jesus said to the woman, "Your faith has saved you;ᶜ go in peace."

7:50
ᶜMt 9:22; Mk 5:34;
Lk 8:48

Women Accompany Jesus and the Disciples (73)

8 After this, Jesus traveled about from one town and village to another, proclaiming the good news of the kingdom of God.ᵈ The Twelve were with him, 2 and also some women

8:1
ᵈMt 4:23

ᵃ41 A denarius was a coin worth about a day's wages.

7:33, 34 The Pharisees weren't troubled by their inconsistency toward John the Baptist and Jesus. They were good at justifying their "wisdom." Most of us can find compelling reasons to do or believe whatever suits our purposes. If we do not examine our ideas in the light of God's truth, however, we may be just as obviously self-serving as the Pharisees.

7:36ff A similar incident occurred later in Jesus' ministry (see Matthew 26:6–13; Mark 14:3–9; John 12:1–11).

7:37 Alabaster jars were carved, expensive, and beautiful.

7:38 Although the woman was not an invited guest, she entered the house anyway and knelt behind Jesus at his feet. In Jesus' day, it was customary to recline while eating. Dinner guests would lie on couches with their heads near the table, propping themselves up on one elbow and stretching their feet out behind them. The woman could easily anoint Jesus' feet without approaching the table.

7:44ff Again Luke contrasts the Pharisees with sinners—and again the sinners come out ahead. Simon had committed several social errors in neglecting to wash Jesus' feet (a courtesy extended to guests because sandaled feet got very dirty), anoint his head with oil, and offer him the kiss of greeting. Did Simon perhaps feel that he was too good for Jesus? Was he trying to give Jesus a subtle put-down? Whatever the case, the contrast is vivid. The sinful woman lavished tears, expensive perfume, and

kisses on her Savior. In this story it is the grateful prostitute, and not the religious leader, whose sins were forgiven. Although God's grace through faith is what saves us, and not acts of love or generosity, this woman's act demonstrated her true faith, and Jesus honored her.

7:47 Overflowing love is the natural response to forgiveness and the appropriate consequence of faith. But only those who realize the depth of their sin can appreciate the complete forgiveness that God offers them. Jesus has rescued all of his followers, whether they were once extremely wicked or conventionally good, from eternal death. Do you appreciate the wideness of God's mercy? Are you grateful for his forgiveness?

7:49, 50 The Pharisees believed that only God could forgive sins, so they wondered why this man, Jesus, was saying that the woman's sins were forgiven. They did not grasp the fact that Jesus was indeed God. (See also 5:17–26 and notes there.)

8:2, 3 Jesus lifted women up from degradation and servitude to the joy of fellowship and service. In Jewish culture, women were not supposed to learn from rabbis. By allowing these women to travel with him, Jesus was showing that all people are equal under God. These women supported Jesus' ministry with their own money. They owed a great debt to him because he had driven demons out of some and had healed others.

8:2, 3 Here we catch a glimpse of a few of the people behind the

8:2
e Mt 27:55, 56

8:3
f Mt 14:1

who had been cured of evil spirits and diseases: Mary (called Magdalene) *e* from whom seven demons had come out; 3 Joanna the wife of Cuza, the manager of Herod's *f* household; Susanna; and many others. These women were helping to support them out of their own means.

Jesus Tells the Parable of the Four Soils (*77*/Matthew 13:1–9; Mark 4:1–9)

8:8
g Mt 11:15

4 While a large crowd was gathering and people were coming to Jesus from town after town, he told this parable: 5 "A farmer went out to sow his seed. As he was scattering the seed, some fell along the path; it was trampled on, and the birds of the air ate it up. 6 Some fell on rock, and when it came up, the plants withered because they had no moisture. 7 Other seed fell among thorns, which grew up with it and choked the plants. 8 Still other seed fell on good soil. It came up and yielded a crop, a hundred times more than was sown."

When he said this, he called out, "He who has ears to hear, let him hear." *g*

Jesus Explains the Parable of the Four Soils (*78*/Matthew 13:10–23; Mark 4:10–25)

8:10
h Isa 6:9;
Mt 13:13, 14

9 His disciples asked him what this parable meant. 10 He said, "The knowledge of the secrets of the kingdom of God has been given to you, but to others I speak in parables, so that,

"'though seeing, they may not see;
though hearing, they may not understand.' *a h*

11 "This is the meaning of the parable: The seed is the word of God. 12 Those along the path are the ones who hear, and then the devil comes and takes away the word from their hearts, so that they may not believe and be saved. 13 Those on the rock are the ones who receive the word with joy when they hear it, but they have no root. They believe for a while, but in the time of testing they fall away. 14 The seed that fell among thorns stands for those who hear, but as they go on their way they are choked by life's worries, riches and pleasures, and they do not mature. 15 But the seed on good soil stands for those with a noble and good heart, who hear the word, retain it, and by persevering produce a crop.

8:16
i Mt 5:15; Mk 4:21;
Lk 11:33

8:17
j Mt 10:26; Mk 4:22;
Lk 12:2

8:18
k Mt 13:12; 25:29;
Lk 19:26

16 "No one lights a lamp and hides it in a jar or puts it under a bed. Instead, he puts it on a stand, so that those who come in can see the light. *i* 17 For there is nothing hidden that will not be disclosed, and nothing concealed that will not be known or brought out into the open. *j* 18 Therefore consider carefully how you listen. Whoever has will be given more; whoever does not have, even what he thinks he has will be taken from him." *k*

a 10 Isaiah 6:9

---

scenes in Jesus' ministry. The ministry of those in the foreground is often supported by those whose work is less visible but just as essential. Offer your resources to God, whether or not you will be on center stage.

8:4 Jesus often communicated spiritual truth through *parables*—short stories or descriptions that take a familiar object or situation and give it a startling new twist. By linking the known with the hidden and forcing listeners to think, parables can point to spiritual truths. A parable compels listeners to discover the truth for themselves, and it conceals the truth from those too lazy or dull to understand it. In reading Jesus' parables, we must be careful not to read too much into them. Most have only one point and one meaning.

8:5 Why would a farmer allow precious seed to land on the path, on rocks, or among thorns? This is not an irresponsible farmer scattering seeds at random. He is using the acceptable method of hand-seeding a large field—tossing it by handfuls as he walks through the field. His goal is to get as much seed as possible to take root in good soil, but waste is inevitable as some falls or is blown into less productive areas. That some of the seed produces no crop is not the fault of the faithful farmer or of the seed. The yield depends on the condition of the soil where the seed falls. It is our responsibility to spread the seed (God's message), but we should not give up when some of our efforts fail. Remember, not every seed falls on good soil.

8:10 Why didn't the crowds understand Jesus' words? Perhaps they were looking for a military leader or a political Messiah and could not fit his gentle teaching style into their preconceived

idea. Perhaps they were afraid of pressure from religious leaders and did not want to look too deeply into Jesus' words. God told Isaiah that people would hear without understanding and see without learning anything (Isaiah 6:9), and that kind of reaction confronted Jesus. The parable of the farmer was an accurate picture of the people's reaction to the rest of his parables.

8:11-15 "Path" people, like many of the religious leaders, refuse to believe God's message. "Rock" people, like many in the crowds who followed Jesus, believe his message but never get around to doing anything about it. "Thorn patch" people, overcome by worries and the lure of materialism, leave no room in their lives for God. "Good soil" people, in contrast to all the other groups, follow Jesus no matter what the cost. Which type of soil are you?

8:16, 17 When the light of the truth about Jesus illuminates us, we have the duty to shine that light to help others. Our witness for Christ should be public, not hidden. We should not keep the benefits for ourselves alone but pass them on to others. In order to be helpful, we need to be well placed. Seek opportunities to shine your light when unbelievers need help to see.

8:18 Applying God's Word helps us grow. This is a principle of growth in physical, mental, and spiritual life. For example, a muscle, when exercised, will grow stronger, but an unused muscle will grow weak and flabby. If you are not growing stronger, you are growing weaker; it is impossible for you to stand still. How are you using what God has taught you?

Jesus Describes His True Family (*76*/Matthew 12:46–50; Mark 3:31–35)

19Now Jesus' mother and brothers came to see him, but they were not able to get near him because of the crowd. 20Someone told him, "Your mother and brothers are standing outside, wanting to see you."

21He replied, "My mother and brothers are those who hear God's word and put it into practice."*l*

Jesus Calms the Storm (*87*/Matthew 8:23–27; Mark 4:35–41)

22One day Jesus said to his disciples, "Let's go over to the other side of the lake." So they got into a boat and set out. 23As they sailed, he fell asleep. A squall came down on the lake, so that the boat was being swamped, and they were in great danger.

24The disciples went and woke him, saying, "Master, Master,*m* we're going to drown!"

He got up and rebuked*n* the wind and the raging waters; the storm subsided, and all was calm. 25"Where is your faith?" he asked his disciples.

In fear and amazement they asked one another, "Who is this? He commands even the winds and the water, and they obey him."

Jesus Sends Demons into a Herd of Pigs (*88*/Matthew 8:28–34; Mark 5:1–20)

26They sailed to the region of the Gerasenes,*a* which is across the lake from Galilee. 27When Jesus stepped ashore, he was met by a demon-possessed man from the town. For a long time this man had not worn clothes or lived in a house, but had lived in the tombs. 28When he saw Jesus, he cried out and fell at his feet, shouting at the top of his voice, "What do you want with me,*o* Jesus, Son of the Most High God?*p* I beg you, don't torture me!" 29For Jesus had commanded the evil*b* spirit to come out of the man. Many times it had seized him, and though he was chained hand and foot and kept under guard, he had broken his chains and had been driven by the demon into solitary places.

30Jesus asked him, "What is your name?"

"Legion," he replied, because many demons had gone into him. 31And they begged him repeatedly not to order them to go into the Abyss.*q*

*a*26 Some manuscripts *Gadarenes*; other manuscripts *Gergesenes*; also in verse 37   *b*29 Greek *unclean*

8:21 Jesus' true family are those who hear *and* obey his words. Hearing without obeying is not enough. As Jesus loved his mother (see John 19:25–27), so he loves us. Christ offers us an intimate family relationship with him (Romans 8:14–16).

8:23 The Sea of Galilee (actually a large lake) is even today the scene of fierce storms, sometimes with waves as high as 20 feet. Jesus' disciples were not frightened without cause. Even though several of them were expert fishermen and knew how to handle a boat, their peril was real.

8:23–25 When caught in the storms of life, it is easy to think that God has lost control and that we're at the mercy of the winds of fate. In reality, God is sovereign. He controls the history of the world as well as our personal destinies. Just as Jesus calmed the waves, he can calm whatever storms you may face.

8:26 The region of the Gerasenes was a Gentile region southeast of the Sea of Galilee, location of the Decapolis, or the Ten Cities. These were Greek cities that belonged to no country and were self-governing. Although Jews would not have raised pigs because the Jewish religion labeled them unclean, the Gentiles had no such aversion.

8:27, 28 These demons recognized Jesus and his authority immediately. They knew who Jesus was and what his great power could do to them. Demons, Satan's messengers, are powerful and destructive. Still active today, they attempt to distort and destroy people's relationship with God. Demons and demon-possession are real. It is vital that believers recognize the power of Satan and his demons, but we shouldn't let curiosity lead us to get involved with demonic forces (Deuteronomy 18:10–12). Demons are powerless against those who trust in Jesus. If we resist the devil, he will leave us alone (James 4:7).

8:29–31 The demons begged Jesus to spare them from the Abyss, which is also mentioned in Revelation 9:1 and 20:1–3 as the place of confinement for Satan and his messengers. The demons, of course, knew all about this place of confinement, and they didn't want to go there.

8:30 The demon's name was Legion. A legion was the largest unit in the Roman army, having between 3,000 and 6,000 soldiers. The man was possessed by not one, but many demons.

HEALING A DEMON-POSSESSED MAN
As he traveled through Galilee, Jesus told many parables and met many people, as recorded in Matthew and Mark. Later, from Capernaum, Jesus and the disciples set out in a boat, only to encounter a fierce storm. Jesus calmed the storm and, when they landed, exorcised a "legion" of demons.

8:33
ʳver 22, 23

³²A large herd of pigs was feeding there on the hillside. The demons begged Jesus to let them go into them, and he gave them permission. ³³When the demons came out of the man, they went into the pigs, and the herd rushed down the steep bank into the lake ʳ and was drowned.

8:35
ˢLk 10:39

8:36
ᵗMt 4:24

8:37
ᵘAc 16:39

³⁴When those tending the pigs saw what had happened, they ran off and reported this in the town and countryside, ³⁵and the people went out to see what had happened. When they came to Jesus, they found the man from whom the demons had gone out, sitting at Jesus' feet,ˢ dressed and in his right mind; and they were afraid. ³⁶Those who had seen it told the people how the demon-possessedᵗ man had been cured. ³⁷Then all the people of the region of the Gerasenes asked Jesus to leave them,ᵘ because they were overcome with fear. So he got into the boat and left.

³⁸The man from whom the demons had gone out begged to go with him, but Jesus sent him away, saying, ³⁹"Return home and tell how much God has done for you." So the man went away and told all over town how much Jesus had done for him.

Jesus Heals a Bleeding Woman and Restores a Girl to Life
(89/Matthew 9:18–26; Mark 5:21–43)

8:41
ᵛver 49; Mk 5:22

⁴⁰Now when Jesus returned, a crowd welcomed him, for they were all expecting him. ⁴¹Then a man named Jairus, a ruler of the synagogue,ᵛ came and fell at Jesus' feet, pleading with him to come to his house ⁴²because his only daughter, a girl of about twelve, was dying.

JESUS AND WOMEN

Jesus talks to a Samaritan woman at the well	John 4:1–26
Jesus raises a widow's son from the dead	Luke 7:11–17
A sinful woman anoints Jesus' feet	Luke 7:36–50
Jesus forgives an adulterous woman	John 8:1–11
A group of women travels with Jesus	Luke 8:1–3
Jesus visits Mary and Martha	Luke 10:38–42
Jesus heals a crippled woman	Luke 13:10–17
Jesus heals the daughter of a Gentile woman	Mark 7:24–30
Weeping women follow Jesus on his way to the cross	Luke 23:27–31
Jesus' mother and other women gather at the cross	John 19:25–27
Jesus appears to Mary Magdalene	Mark 16:9–11
Jesus appears to other women after his resurrection	Matthew 28:8–10

As a non-Jew recording the words and works of Jesus' life, Luke demonstrates a special sensitivity to other "outsiders" with whom Jesus came into contact. For instance, Luke records five events involving women that are not mentioned in the other Gospels. In first-century Jewish culture, women were usually treated as second-class citizens with few of the rights men had. But Jesus crossed those barriers, and Luke showed the special care Jesus had for women. Jesus treated all people with equal respect. The above passages tell of his encounters with women.

8:33 Why didn't Jesus just destroy these demons—or send them to the Abyss? Because the time for such work had not yet come. He healed many people of the destructive effects of demon-possession, but he did not yet destroy demons. The same question could be asked today—why doesn't Jesus stop all the evil in the world? His time for that has not yet come. But it will come. The book of Revelation portrays the future victory of Jesus over Satan, his demons, and all evil.

8:33-37 A man had been freed from the devil's power, but the people in the town thought only about their livestock. People have always tended to value financial gain above needy people. Much injustice and oppression, both at home and abroad, is the direct result of some individual's or company's urge to get rich. People are continually being sacrificed to the god of money. Don't think more highly of "pigs" than of people.

8:38, 39 Often Jesus would ask those he healed to be quiet about the healing, but he urged this man to return to his family and tell them what God had done for him. Why? (1) Jesus knew the man would be an effective witness to those who knew his previous condition and could attest to the miraculous healing. (2) Jesus wanted to expand his ministry by introducing his message into this Gentile area. (3) Jesus knew that the Gentiles, since they were not expecting a Messiah, would not divert his ministry by trying to crown him king. (In fact, the people in this region had asked him to go away.) When God touches your life, don't be afraid to share the wonderful events with your family and friends.

8:41 The synagogue was the local center of worship. The synagogue ruler was responsible for administration, building maintenance, and worship supervision. It would have been quite unusual for a respected synagogue ruler to fall at the feet of an itinerant preacher and beg him to heal his daughter. Jesus honored this man's humble faith (8:50, 54–56).

As Jesus was on his way, the crowds almost crushed him. 43And a woman was there who had been subject to bleeding for twelve years,a but no one could heal her. 44She came up behind him and touched the edge of his cloak, and immediately her bleeding stopped.

45"Who touched me?" Jesus asked.

When they all denied it, Peter said, "Master, w the people are crowding and pressing against you."

46But Jesus said, "Someone touched me; I know that power has gone out from me."x

47Then the woman, seeing that she could not go unnoticed, came trembling and fell at his feet. In the presence of all the people, she told why she had touched him and how she had been instantly healed. 48Then he said to her, "Daughter, your faith has healed you.y Go in peace."

49While Jesus was still speaking, someone came from the house of Jairus, the synagogue ruler. z "Your daughter is dead," he said. "Don't bother the teacher any more."

50Hearing this, Jesus said to Jairus, "Don't be afraid; just believe, and she will be healed."

51When he arrived at the house of Jairus, he did not let anyone go in with him except Peter, John and James, and the child's father and mother. 52Meanwhile, all the people were wailing and mourninga for her. "Stop wailing," Jesus said. "She is not dead but asleep."b

53They laughed at him, knowing that she was dead. 54But he took her by the hand and said, "My child, get up!" c 55Her spirit returned, and at once she stood up. Then Jesus told them to give her something to eat. 56Her parents were astonished, but he ordered them not to tell anyone what had happened. d

Jesus Sends Out the Twelve Disciples (93/Matthew 10:1–15; Mark 6:7–13)

9 When Jesus had called the Twelve together, he gave them power and authority to drive out all demonse and to cure diseases, 2and he sent them out to preach the kingdom of God and to heal the sick. 3He told them: "Take nothing for the journey—no staff, no bag, no

a43 Many manuscripts years, and she had spent all she had on doctors

8:45
wLk 5:5

8:46
xLk 5:17; 6:19

8:48
yMt 9:22

8:49
zver 41

8:52
aLk 23:27
bJn 11:11, 13

8:54
cLk 7:14

8:56
dMt 8:4

9:1
eMt 10:1

8:43–48 Many people surrounded Jesus as he made his way toward Jairus's house. It was virtually impossible to get through the multitude, but one woman fought her way desperately through the crowd in order to touch Jesus. As soon as she did so, she was healed. What a difference there is between the crowds that are curious about Jesus and the few who reach out and touch him! Today, many people are vaguely familiar with Jesus, but nothing in their lives is changed or bettered by this passing acquaintance. It is only faith that releases God's healing power. Are you just curious about God, or do you reach out to him in faith, knowing that his mercy will bring healing to your body, soul, and spirit?

8:45, 46 Certainly Jesus knew who had touched him—he knew that someone had intentionally touched him in order to receive some sort of healing. Jesus wanted the woman to step forward and identify herself. To let her slip away would have meant a lost opportunity for Jesus to teach her that his cloak did not have magical properties, it had been her faith in him that had healed her. He may also have wanted to teach the crowds a lesson. According to Jewish law, a man who touched a menstruating woman became ceremonially unclean (Leviticus 15:19–28). This was true whether her bleeding was normal or, as in this woman's case, the result of illness. To protect themselves from such defilement, Jewish men carefully avoided touching, speaking to, or even looking at women. By contrast, Jesus proclaimed to hundreds of people that this "unclean" woman had touched him—and then he healed her. In Jesus' mind, this suffering woman was not to be overlooked. As God's creation, she deserved attention and respect.

8:50 Anyone with a child can readily put himself or herself emotionally in Jairus's place. His daughter had died while they were on the way home. Luke did not record it, but the poor man probably cried out in grief. Jesus surely felt the father's very human grief. Jesus said, "Don't be afraid; just believe." Again, Luke didn't record Jairus's reaction to these words, but Jairus must have had at least some flicker of hope because he did complete his mission in bringing Jesus to his house. When you experience intense grief over the loss of a loved one, breakup of a marriage, loss of a job, or rejection of a close friend, don't

abandon hope. Don't turn away from the one Person who can help you. Do what Jairus did: Don't be afraid; just believe. Your hope is found in the resurrected Lord, the one with power over life and death.

8:56 Jesus told the parents not to talk about their daughter's healing because he knew the facts would speak for themselves. Jesus was concerned for his ministry. He did not want to be known as just a miracle-worker; he wanted people to listen to his words that would heal their broken spiritual lives.

9:1–10 Note Jesus' methods of leadership. He empowered his disciples (9:1), gave them specific instructions so they knew what to do (9:3, 4), told them how to deal with tough times (9:5), and held them accountable (9:10). As you lead others, study the Master Leader's pattern. Which of these elements do you need to incorporate into your leadership?

9:2 Jesus announced his kingdom by both preaching and healing, and he sent his disciples out to do the same. If he had limited himself to preaching, people might have seen his kingdom as spiritual only. If he had healed without preaching, people might not have realized the spiritual importance of his mission. Most of his listeners expected a Messiah who would bring wealth and power to their nation; they preferred material benefits to spiritual discernment. The truth about Jesus is that he is both God and man, both spiritual and physical; and the salvation that he offers is both for the soul and the body. Any group or teaching that emphasizes soul at the expense of body, or body at the expense of soul, is in danger of distorting Jesus' Good News.

9:3, 4 Why were the disciples instructed to depend on others while they went from town to town preaching the gospel? Their purpose was to blanket Judea with Jesus' message, and by traveling light they could move quickly. Their dependence on others had other good effects as well: (1) It clearly showed that the Messiah had not come to offer wealth to his followers. (2) It forced the disciples to rely on God's power and not on their own provision. (3) It involved the villagers and made them more eager to hear the message. This was an excellent approach for the disciples' short-term mission; it was not intended, however, to be a permanent way of life for them.

9:3
f Lk 10:4; 22:35

9:5
g Mt 10:14

9:7
h Mt 14:1
i ver 19

bread, no money, no extra tunic. *f* 4Whatever house you enter, stay there until you leave that town. 5If people do not welcome you, shake the dust off your feet when you leave their town, as a testimony against them." *g* 6So they set out and went from village to village, preaching the gospel and healing people everywhere.

Herod Kills John the Baptist (95/Matthew 14:1–12; Mark 6:14–29)

7Now Herod *h* the tetrarch heard about all that was going on. And he was perplexed, because some were saying that John had been raised from the dead, *i* 8others that Elijah had

JAMES

Jesus singled out three of his 12 disciples for special training. James, his brother John, and Peter made up this inner circle. Each eventually played a key role in the early church. Peter became a great speaker, John became a major writer, and James was the first of the 12 disciples to die for his faith.

The fact that his name is always mentioned before John's indicates that James was the older brother. Zebedee, their father, owned a fishing business in which they worked alongside Peter and Andrew. When Peter, Andrew, and John left Galilee to see John the Baptist, James stayed back with the boats and fishing nets. Later, when Jesus called them, James was as eager as his partners to follow.

James enjoyed being in the inner circle of Jesus' disciples, but he misunderstood Jesus' purpose. He and his brother even tried to secure their role in Jesus' kingdom by asking Jesus to promise them each a special position. Like the other disciples, James had a limited view of what Jesus was doing on earth, picturing only an earthly kingdom that would overthrow Rome and restore Israel's former glory. But above all, James wanted to be with Jesus. He had found the right leader, even though he was still on the wrong timetable. It took Jesus' death and resurrection to correct his view.

James was the first of the 12 disciples to die for the gospel. He was willing to die because he knew Jesus had conquered death, the doorway to eternal life. Our expectations about life will be limited if this life is all we can see. Jesus promised eternal life to those willing to trust him. If we believe this promise, he will give us the courage to stand for him even during dangerous times.

Strengths and accomplishments:	• One of the 12 disciples • One of a special inner circle of three with Peter and John • First of the 12 disciples to be killed for his faith
Weaknesses and mistakes:	• Two outbursts from James indicate struggles with temper (Luke 9:54) and selfishness (Mark 10:37). Both times, he and his brother, John, spoke as one
Lesson from his life:	• Loss of life is not too heavy a price to pay for following Jesus
Vital statistics:	• Where: Galilee • Occupations: Fisherman, disciple • Relatives: Father: Zebedee. Mother: Salome. Brother: John. • Contemporaries: Jesus, Pilate, Herod Agrippa
Key verses:	"Then James and John, the sons of Zebedee, came to him. 'Teacher,' they said, 'we want you to do for us whatever we ask.' 'What do you want me to do for you?' he asked. They replied, 'Let one of us sit at your right and the other at your left in your glory'" (Mark 10:35–37).

James's story is told in the Gospels. He is also mentioned in Acts 1:13 and 12:2.

9:4 The disciples were told to stay in only one home in each town because they were not to offend their hosts by moving to a home that was more comfortable or socially prominent. To remain in one home was not a burden for the homeowner, because the disciples' stay in each community was short. (See also 10:7.)

9:5 Shaking the dust of certain towns from their feet had deep cultural implications. Pious Jews would do this after passing through Gentile cities to show their separation from Gentile practices. If the disciples were to shake the dust of a *Jewish* town from their feet, it would show their separation from Jews who rejected their Messiah. This action also would show that the disciples were not responsible for how the people responded to their message. Neither are we responsible if we have carefully and truthfully presented Christ, but our message is rejected. Like the disciples, we must move on to others whom God desires to reach.

9:7 For more information on Herod, also known as Herod Antipas, see his Profile in Mark 6, p. 1621.

9:7, 8 People found accepting Jesus as the Son of God so difficult that they tried to come up with other solutions—most of which sound quite unbelievable to us. Many thought that Jesus must be someone who had come back to life, perhaps John the Baptist or another prophet. Some suggested that he was Elijah, the great prophet who had not died but had been taken to heaven in a chariot of fire (2 Kings 2:1–11). Very few found the correct answer, as Peter did (9:20). Many people today still have difficulty accepting Jesus as the fully human yet fully divine Son of God. People are still trying to find alternate explanations—a great prophet, a radical political leader, a self-deceived rabble-rouser. None of these explanations can account for Jesus' miracles or, especially, his glorious resurrection. In the end, the attempts to explain away Jesus are far more difficult to believe than the truth.

appeared, and still others that one of the prophets of long ago had come back to life. [9] But
Herod said, "I beheaded John. Who, then, is this I hear such things about?" And he tried to
see him. [j]

9:9
/ Lk 23:8

Jesus Feeds Five Thousand (96/Matthew 14:13–21; Mark 6:30–44; John 6:1–15)

[10] When the apostles [k] returned, they reported to Jesus what they had done. Then he took
them with him and they withdrew by themselves to a town called Bethsaida, [l] [11] but the
crowds learned about it and followed him. He welcomed them and spoke to them about the
kingdom of God, and healed those who needed healing.

9:10
k Mk 6:30
l Mt 11:21

[12] Late in the afternoon the Twelve came to him and said, "Send the crowd away so they
can go to the surrounding villages and countryside and find food and lodging, because we
are in a remote place here."

[13] He replied, "You give them something to eat."

They answered, "We have only five loaves of bread and two fish—unless we go and buy
food for all this crowd." [14] (About five thousand men were there.)

But he said to his disciples, "Have them sit down in groups of about fifty each." [15] The disciples did so, and everybody sat down. [16] Taking the five loaves and the two fish and looking
up to heaven, he gave thanks and broke them. Then he gave them to the disciples to set before the people. [17] They all ate and were satisfied, and the disciples picked up twelve basketfuls of broken pieces that were left over.

Peter Says Jesus Is the Messiah (109/Matthew 16:13–20; Mark 8:27–30)

[18] Once when Jesus was praying in private and his disciples were with him, he asked them,
"Who do the crowds say I am?"

[19] They replied, "Some say John the Baptist; others say Elijah; and still others, that one of
the prophets of long ago has come back to life." [m]

9:19
m ver 7, 8
9:20
n Jn 6:66-69

[20] "But what about you?" he asked. "Who do you say I am?"

Peter answered, "The Christ [a] of God." [n]

Jesus Predicts His Death the First Time (110/Matthew 16:21–28; Mark 8:31—9:1)

[21] Jesus strictly warned them not to tell this to anyone. [o] [22] And he said, "The Son of Man
must suffer many things [p] and be rejected by the elders, chief priests and teachers of the
law, and he must be killed and on the third day be raised to life."

9:21
o Mt 16:20; Mk 8:30
9:22
p Mt 16:21

a 20 Or Messiah

9:9 For the story of how Herod had John beheaded, see Mark 6:14–29.

9:10, 11 Jesus had tried to slip quietly away from the crowds, but they found out where he was going and followed him. Instead of showing impatience at this interruption, Jesus welcomed the people and ministered to their needs. How do you see people who interrupt your schedule—as nuisances, or as the reason for your life and ministry?

9:11 The kingdom of God was a focal point of Jesus' teaching. He explained that it was not just a future kingdom; it was among them, embodied in him, the Messiah. Even though the kingdom will not be complete until Jesus comes again in glory, we do not have to wait to experience it. The kingdom of God begins in the hearts of those who believe in Jesus (17:21). It is as present with us today as it was with the Judeans over 2,000 years ago.

9:13, 14 When the disciples expressed concern about where the crowd of thousands would eat, Jesus offered a surprising solution—"You give them something to eat." The disciples protested, focusing their attention on what they didn't have (food and money). Do you think God would ask you to do something that you and he together couldn't handle? Don't let your lack of resources blind you to seeing God's power.

9:16, 17 Why did Jesus bother to feed these people? He could just as easily have sent them on their way, but Jesus does not ignore needs. He is concerned with every aspect of our lives—the physical as well as the spiritual. As we work to bring wholeness to people's lives, we must never ignore the fact that all of us have both physical and spiritual needs. It is impossible to minister effectively to one type of need without considering the other.

9:18–20 The Christian faith goes beyond knowing what others believe. It requires us to hold beliefs for ourselves. When Jesus asks, "Who do you say I am?" he wants us to take a stand. Who do *you* say Jesus is?

9:21 Jesus told his disciples not to tell anyone that he was the Christ because at this point they didn't fully understand the significance of that confession—nor would anyone else. Everyone still expected the Messiah to come as a conquering king. But even though Jesus was the Messiah, he still had to suffer, be rejected by the leaders, be killed, and rise from the dead. When the disciples saw all this happen to Jesus, they would understand what the Messiah had come to do. Only then would they be equipped to share the gospel that the Messiah had come and brought his kingdom to people's hearts.

9:22 This was the turning point in Jesus' instruction to his disciples. From then on he began teaching clearly and specifically what they could expect, so that they would not be surprised when it happened. He explained that he would not *now* be the conquering Messiah because he first had to suffer, die, and rise again. But one day he would return in great glory to set up his eternal kingdom.

9:23
qMt 10:38; Lk 14:27

23 Then he said to them all: "If anyone would come after me, he must deny himself and take up his cross daily and follow me. q 24 For whoever wants to save his life will lose it, but whoever loses his life for me will save it. 25 What good is it for a man to gain the whole world, and yet lose or forfeit his very self? 26 If anyone is ashamed of me and my words, the Son of Man will be ashamed of him r when he comes in his glory and in the glory of the Father and of the holy angels. 27 I tell you the truth, some who are standing here will not taste death before they see the kingdom of God."

9:26
rMt 10:33; Lk 12:9;
2Ti 2:12

Jesus Is Transfigured on the Mountain (111/Matthew 17:1–13; Mark 9:2–13)

9:28
sLk 3:21

9:31
t2Pe 1:15

9:32
uMt 26:43

9:33
vLk 5:5

28 About eight days after Jesus said this, he took Peter, John and James with him and went up onto a mountain to pray. s 29 As he was praying, the appearance of his face changed, and his clothes became as bright as a flash of lightning. 30 Two men, Moses and Elijah, 31 appeared in glorious splendor, talking with Jesus. They spoke about his departure, t which he was about to bring to fulfillment at Jerusalem. 32 Peter and his companions were very sleepy, u but when they became fully awake, they saw his glory and the two men standing with him. 33 As the men were leaving Jesus, Peter said to him, "Master, v it is good for us to be here. Let us put up three shelters—one for you, one for Moses and one for Elijah." (He did not know what he was saying.)

9:35
wMt 3:17

9:36
xMt 17:9

34 While he was speaking, a cloud appeared and enveloped them, and they were afraid as they entered the cloud. 35 A voice came from the cloud, saying, "This is my Son, whom I have chosen; listen to him." w 36 When the voice had spoken, they found that Jesus was alone. The disciples kept this to themselves, and told no one at that time what they had seen. x

Jesus Heals a Demon-Possessed Boy (112/Matthew 17:14–21; Mark 9:14–29)

37 The next day, when they came down from the mountain, a large crowd met him. 38 A man in the crowd called out, "Teacher, I beg you to look at my son, for he is my only child.

9:23 To take up the cross meant to carry one's own cross to the place of crucifixion. Many Galileans had been killed that way by the Romans—and Jesus would face it as well. With this word picture, Christ presented a clear and challenging description of the Christian life. Being his disciple means putting aside selfish desires, shouldering one's "cross" every day, and following him. It is simple and yet so demanding. For the original Twelve, this meant literal suffering and death. For believers today, it means understanding that we belong to him and that we live to serve his purposes. Consider this: Do you think of your relationship with God primarily in terms of what's in it for you (which is considerable) or in terms of what you can do for him? Are you willing to deny yourself, take up your cross daily, and follow him? Anything less is not discipleship; it is merely superficial lip service. (See also the note on 14:27.)

9:24, 25 If this present life is most important to you, you will do everything you can to protect it. You will not want to do anything that might endanger your safety, health, or comfort. By contrast, if following Jesus is most important, you may find yourself in unsafe, unhealthy, and uncomfortable places. You will risk death, but you will not fear it because you know that Jesus will raise you to eternal life. Nothing material can compensate for the loss of eternal life. Jesus' disciples are not to use their lives on earth merely to please themselves; they should spend their lives serving God and people.

9:26 Luke's Greek audience may have had difficulty understanding a God who could die, just as Jesus' Jewish audience would have been perplexed by a Messiah who would let himself be captured and killed. Both would be ashamed of Jesus if they did not look past his death to his glorious resurrection and second coming. Then they would see Jesus not as a loser but as the Lord of the universe, who through his death brought salvation to those who believe.

9:27 When Jesus said some would not die without seeing the kingdom, he may have been referring to: (1) Peter, James, and John, who would witness the transfiguration eight days later; (2) all who would witness the resurrection and ascension; (3) all who would take part in the spread of the church after Pentecost. Jesus'

listeners would not have to wait for another, future Messiah—the kingdom was among them, and would soon come in power.

9:29, 30 Jesus took Peter, James, and John to the top of a mountain to show them who he really was—not merely a great prophet, but God's own Son. Moses, representing the law, and Elijah, representing the prophets, appeared with Jesus. Then God's voice singled out Jesus as the long-awaited Messiah who possessed divine authority. Jesus would fulfill both the Law and the Prophets (Matthew 5:17).

9:33 When Peter suggested making three shelters, he may have been thinking of the Feast of Tabernacles, where shelters were set up to commemorate the exodus, God's deliverance from slavery in Egypt. Peter wanted to keep Moses and Elijah with them, but this was not what God wanted. Peter's desire to build shelters for Jesus, Moses, and Elijah may also show his understanding that real faith is built on three cornerstones: the law, the prophets, and Jesus. But Peter grew in his understanding, and eventually he would write of Jesus as the "chosen and precious cornerstone" of the church (1 Peter 2:6).

9:35 As God's Son, Jesus has God's power and authority; thus his words should be our final authority. If a person's teaching is true, it will agree with Jesus' teachings. Don't be hasty to seek advice and guidance from merely human sources and thereby neglect Christ's message. Test everything you hear against Jesus' words and you will not be led astray. If we believe he is God's Son, then we surely will want to do what he says.

9:37–39 Peter, James, and John experienced a wonderful moment on the mountain, and they probably didn't want to leave. Sometimes we too have such an inspiring experience that we want to stay where we are—away from the reality and problems of our daily life. Knowing that struggles await us in the valley encourages us to linger on the mountaintop. Yet staying on top of a mountain prohibits our ministering to others. Instead of becoming spiritual giants, we would soon become dwarfed by our self-centeredness. We need times of retreat and renewal but only so we can return to minister to the world. Our faith must make sense off the mountain as well as on it.

39A spirit seizes him and he suddenly screams; it throws him into convulsions so that he foams at the mouth. It scarcely ever leaves him and is destroying him. 40 I begged your disciples to drive it out, but they could not."

41"O unbelieving and perverse generation," Jesus replied, "how long shall I stay with you and put up with you? Bring your son here."

42 Even while the boy was coming, the demon threw him to the ground in a convulsion. But Jesus rebuked the evila spirit, healed the boy and gave him back to his father. 43And they were all amazed at the greatness of God.

Jesus Predicts His Death the Second Time (113/Matthew 17:22–23; Mark 9:30–32)

While everyone was marveling at all that Jesus did, he said to his disciples, 44"Listen carefully to what I am about to tell you: The Son of Man is going to be betrayed into the hands of men." y 45 But they did not understand what this meant. It was hidden from them, so that they did not grasp it,z and they were afraid to ask him about it.

9:44
yver 22
9:45
zMk 9:32

The Disciples Argue about Who Would Be the Greatest (115/Matthew 18:1–6; Mark 9:33–37)

46An argument started among the disciples as to which of them would be the greatest. 47 Jesus, knowing their thoughts,a took a little child and had him stand beside him. 48 Then he said to them, "Whoever welcomes this little child in my name welcomes me; and whoever welcomes me welcomes the one who sent me. b For he who is least among you all—he is the greatest."

9:47
aMt 9:4
9:48
bMt 10:40

The Disciples Forbid Another to Use Jesus' Name (116/Mark 9:38–41)

49"Master," said John, "we saw a man driving out demons in your name and we tried to stop him, because he is not one of us."

50"Do not stop him," Jesus said, "for whoever is not against you is for you." c

9:50
cMt 12:30; Lk 11:23

2. Jesus' ministry on the way to Jerusalem
Jesus Teaches about the Cost of Following Him (122/Matthew 8:18–22)

51As the time approached for him to be taken up to heaven, d Jesus resolutely set out for Jerusalem. e 52And he sent messengers on ahead, who went into a Samaritan f village to get things ready for him; 53 but the people there did not welcome him, because he was heading for Jerusalem. 54 When the disciples James and John saw this, they asked, "Lord, do you want us to call fire down from heaven to destroy themb?"g 55 But Jesus turned and rebuked them, 56 andc they went to another village.

9:51
dMk 16:19
eLk 13:22; 17:11;
18:31; 19:28
9:52
fMt 10:5
9:54
g2Ki 1:10, 12

a42 Greek unclean   b54 Some manuscripts them, even as Elijah did   c55,56 Some manuscripts them. And he said, "You do not know what kind of spirit you are of, for the Son of Man did not come to destroy men's lives, but to save them." 56And

---

9:40 Why couldn't the disciples drive out the evil spirit? For a possible answer, see the note on Mark 9:18.

9:45, 46 The disciples didn't understand Jesus' words about his death. They still thought of Jesus as only an earthly king, and they were concerned about their places in the kingdom he would set up. So they ignored Jesus' words about his death and began arguing about who would be the greatest.

9:48 Our care for others is a measure of our greatness. How much concern do you show to others? This is a vital question that can accurately measure your greatness in God's eyes. How have you expressed your care for others lately, especially the helpless, the needy, the poor—those who can't return your love and concern? Your honest answer to that question will give you a good idea of your real greatness.

9:49, 50 The disciples were jealous. Nine of them together had been unable to drive out a single evil spirit (9:40), but when they saw a man who was not one of their group driving out demons, they told him to stop. Our pride is hurt when someone else succeeds where we have failed, but Jesus says there is no room for such jealousy in the spiritual warfare of his kingdom. Share Jesus' open-arms attitude to Christian workers outside your group. Rejoice when they are able to bring people to Christ.

9:51 Although Jesus knew he would face persecution and death in Jerusalem, he was determined to go there. That kind of resolve should characterize our lives as well. When God gives us a course of action, we must move steadily toward our destination, regardless of the potential hazards that await us there.

9:53 After Assyria invaded Israel, the northern kingdom, and resettled it with its own people (2 Kings 17:24–41), the mixed race that developed became known as the Samaritans. "Pure-bred" Jews hated these "half-breeds," and the Samaritans in turn hated the Jews. So many tensions arose between the two peoples that Jewish travelers between Galilee and southern Judea often would walk around rather than through Samaritan territory, even though this would lengthen their trip considerably. Jesus held no such prejudices, and he sent messengers ahead to get things ready in a Samaritan village. But the village refused to welcome these Jewish travelers who were headed for Jerusalem.

9:54 When the Samaritan village did not welcome Jesus and his disciples, James and John didn't want to stop at shaking the dust from their feet (9:5). They wanted to retaliate by calling down fire from heaven on the people, as Elijah had done on the servants of a wicked king of Israel (2 Kings 1). When others reject or scorn us, we too may feel like retaliating. We must remember that judgment belongs to God, and we must not expect him to use his power to carry out personal vendettas.

9:57
h ver 51

9:58
i Mt 8:20

57 As they were walking along the road,*h* a man said to him, "I will follow you wherever you go."

58 Jesus replied, "Foxes have holes and birds of the air have nests, but the Son of Man*i* has no place to lay his head."

59 He said to another man, "Follow me."

But the man replied, "Lord, first let me go and bury my father."

60 Jesus said to him, "Let the dead bury their own dead, but you go and proclaim the kingdom of God."

9:61
j 1Ki 19:20

61 Still another said, "I will follow you, Lord; but first let me go back and say good-by to my family."*j*

62 Jesus replied, "No one who puts his hand to the plow and looks back is fit for service in the kingdom of God."

Jesus Sends Out Seventy-Two Messengers (130)

10:1
k Lk 7:13
l Lk 9:1, 2, 51, 52
m Mk 6:7
n Mt 10:1

10:2
o Mt 9:37, 38;
Jn 4:35

10:3
p Mt 10:16

10 After this the Lord *k* appointed seventy-two *a* others *l* and sent them two by two *m* ahead of him to every town and place where he was about to go.*n* 2 He told them, "The harvest is plentiful, but the workers are few. Ask the Lord of the harvest, therefore, to send out workers into his harvest field. *o* 3 Go! I am sending you out like lambs among wolves. *p* 4 Do not take a purse or bag or sandals; and do not greet anyone on the road.

5 "When you enter a house, first say, 'Peace to this house.' 6 If a man of peace is there, your

a 1 Some manuscripts *seventy*; also in verse 17

A COLLECTION OF ATTITUDES ABOUT OTHERS' NEEDS

To the expert in the law	the wounded man was a subject to discuss.
To the robbers	the wounded man was someone to use and exploit.
To the religious men	the wounded man was a problem to be avoided.
To the innkeeper	the wounded man was a customer to serve for a fee.
To the Samaritan	the wounded man was a human being worth being cared for and loved.
To Jesus	all of them and all of us were worth dying for.

Confronting the needs of others brings out various attitudes in us. Jesus used the story of the good but despised Samaritan to make clear what attitude was acceptable to him. If we are honest, we often will find ourselves in the place of the expert in religious law, needing to learn again who our neighbor is. Note these different attitudes toward the wounded man.

9:59 Luke does not say whether the father is already dead or terminally ill. It seems likely that if the father were dead, the son would have been fulfilling the burial duties. Jesus was proclaiming that true discipleship requires instant action. Jesus did not teach people to forsake responsibilities to family, but he often gave commands to people in light of their real motives. Perhaps this man wanted to delay following Christ and was using his father as an excuse. Following Jesus has a cost, and each of us must be ready to serve, even when it requires sacrifice.

9:62 What does Jesus want from us? Total dedication, not halfhearted commitment. We can't pick and choose among Jesus' ideas and follow him selectively; we have to accept the cross along with the crown. We must count the cost and be willing to abandon everything else that has given us security—without looking back. With our focus on Jesus, we should allow nothing to distract us from following him.

10:1, 2 Far more than 12 people had been following Jesus. Here Jesus designated a group of 72 to prepare a number of towns for his later visit. These disciples were not unique in their qualifications. They were not better educated, more capable, or of higher status than Jesus' other followers. What equipped them for this mission was their awareness of Jesus' power and a vision to reach all the people. It is important to dedicate our skills to God's kingdom, but we

must also be equipped with his power and have a clear vision of what he wants us to do.

10:2 Christian service has no unemployment. God has work enough for everyone. Jesus encouraged the disciples not just to do the work but also to pray for workers. Part of every missionary's job is to pray for new workers and to help newcomers learn the ropes. Whatever your role in God's work, pray today for more helpers. Believers are not always to work alone. God wants them to pray, recruit, and equip others to join them as they explore opportunities to serve Jesus. Some people, as soon as they understand the gospel, want to go to convert people immediately. Jesus gave a different approach: begin by mobilizing people to pray. And before praying for unsaved people, pray that other concerned disciples will join you in reaching out to them. God will lead you to an important responsibility, but prayer comes first.

10:3 Jesus said he was sending his disciples out "like lambs among wolves." They would have to be careful because they would surely meet with opposition. We too are sent into the world like lambs among wolves. Be alert, and remember to face your enemies not with aggression but with love and gentleness. A dangerous mission requires sincere commitment.

peace will rest on him; if not, it will return to you. [7]Stay in that house, eating and drinking whatever they give you, for the worker deserves his wages. [q] Do not move around from house to house.

[8]"When you enter a town and are welcomed, eat what is set before you. [9]Heal the sick who are there and tell them, 'The kingdom of God[r] is near you.' [10]But when you enter a town and are not welcomed, go into its streets and say, [11]'Even the dust of your town that sticks to our feet we wipe off against you.[s] Yet be sure of this: The kingdom of God is near.' [12]I tell you, it will be more bearable on that day for Sodom[t] than for that town.

[13]"Woe to you, Korazin! Woe to you, Bethsaida! For if the miracles that were performed in you had been performed in Tyre and Sidon, they would have repented long ago, sitting in sackcloth and ashes. [14]But it will be more bearable for Tyre and Sidon at the judgment than for you. [15]And you, Capernaum, will you be lifted up to the skies? No, you will go down to the depths.[a]

[16]"He who listens to you listens to me; he who rejects you rejects me; but he who rejects me rejects him who sent me."[u]

The Seventy-Two Messengers Return (131)

[17]The seventy-two returned with joy and said, "Lord, even the demons submit to us in your name."

[18]He replied, "I saw Satan fall like lightning from heaven.[v] [19]I have given you authority to trample on snakes[w] and scorpions and to overcome all the power of the enemy; nothing will harm you. [20]However, do not rejoice that the spirits submit to you, but rejoice that your names are written in heaven."[x]

[21]At that time Jesus, full of joy through the Holy Spirit, said, "I praise you, Father, Lord of heaven and earth, because you have hidden these things from the wise and learned, and revealed them to little children. Yes, Father, for this was your good pleasure.

a 15 Greek *Hades*

10:7
[q]Mt 10:10;
1Co 9:14; 1Ti 5:18

10:9
[r]Mt 3:2; 10:7

10:11
[s]Mt 10:14; Mk 6:11

10:12
[t]Mt 10:15

10:16
[u]Mt 10:40; Jn 13:20

10:18
[v]Rev 9:1

10:19
[w]Mk 16:18

10:20
[x]Ex 32:32;
Ps 69:28; Da 12:1;
Php 4:3; Heb 12:23;
Rev 13:8; 20:12;
21:27

10:7 Jesus' direction to stay in one house avoided certain problems. Shifting from house to house could offend the families who first took them in. Some families might begin to compete for the disciples' presence, and some might think they weren't good enough to hear their message. If the disciples appeared not to appreciate the hospitality offered them, the town might not accept Jesus when he followed them there. In addition, by staying in one place, the disciples would not have to worry continually about getting good accommodations. They could settle down and focus on their appointed task. (See also 9:4.)

10:7 Jesus told his disciples to accept hospitality graciously because their work entitled them to it. Ministers of the gospel deserve to be supported, and our responsibility is to make sure they have what they need. There are several ways to encourage those who serve God in his church. First, see that they have an adequate salary. Second, see that they are supported emotionally; plan a time to express appreciation for something they have done. Third, lift their spirits with special surprises from time to time. Our ministers deserve to know we are giving to them cheerfully and generously.

10:8, 9 Jesus gave two rules for the disciples to follow as they traveled. They were to eat what was set before them—that is, they were to accept hospitality without being picky—and they were to heal the sick. Because of the healings, people would be willing to listen to the gospel.

10:12 Sodom was an evil city that God had destroyed because of its great sinfulness (Genesis 19). The city's name is often used to symbolize wickedness and immorality. Sodom will suffer at judgment day, but cities who saw the Messiah and rejected him will suffer even more.

10:13 Korazin was a city near the Sea of Galilee, probably about two miles north of Capernaum. Tyre and Sidon were cities destroyed by God as punishment for their wickedness (see Ezekiel 26—28).

10:15 Capernaum was Jesus' base for his Galilean ministry. The city was located at an important crossroads used by traders and the Roman army, so a message proclaimed in Capernaum was likely to go far. Many people of Capernaum did not understand Jesus' miracles or believe his teaching, however, and the city was included among those who would be judged for rejecting him.

10:17-20 The disciples had seen tremendous results as they ministered in Jesus' name and with his authority. They were elated by the victories they had witnessed, and Jesus shared their enthusiasm. He helped them get their priorities right, however, by reminding them of their most important victory—that their names were written in heaven. This honor was more important than any of their accomplishments. As we see God's wonders at work in and through us, we should not lose sight of the greatest wonder of all—our heavenly citizenship.

10:18, 19 Jesus may have been looking ahead to his victory over Satan at the cross. John 12:31, 32 indicates that Satan would be judged and driven out at the time of Jesus' death. On the other hand, Jesus may have been warning his disciples against pride. Perhaps he was referring to Isaiah 14:12-17, which begins, "How you have fallen from heaven, O morning star, son of the dawn!" Some interpreters identify this verse with Satan and explain that Satan's pride led to all the evil we see on earth today. To Jesus' disciples, who were thrilled with their power over evil spirits ("snakes and scorpions"), he may have been giving this stern warning: "Yours is the kind of pride that led to Satan's downfall. Be careful!"

10:21 Jesus thanked God that spiritual truth was for everyone, and not just for the elite. Many of life's rewards seem to go to the intelligent, the rich, the good-looking, or the powerful, but the kingdom of God is equally available to all, regardless of position or abilities. We come to Jesus not through strength or brains, but through childlike trust. Jesus is not opposed to engaging in scholarly pursuits; he is opposed to spiritual pride (being wise in one's own eyes). Join Jesus in thanking God that we all have equal access to him. Trust in God's grace, not in your personal qualifications, for your citizenship in the kingdom.

22"All things have been committed to me by my Father. No one knows who the Son is except the Father, and no one knows who the Father is except the Son and those to whom the Son chooses to reveal him."

23Then he turned to his disciples and said privately, "Blessed are the eyes that see what you see. 24For I tell you that many prophets and kings wanted to see what you see but did not see it, and to hear what you hear but did not hear it."

Jesus Tells the Parable of the Good Samaritan (132)

25On one occasion an expert in the law stood up to test Jesus. "Teacher," he asked, "what must I do to inherit eternal life?" y

26"What is written in the Law?" he replied. "How do you read it?"

27He answered: "'Love the Lord your God with all your heart and with all your soul and with all your strength and with all your mind'a; z and, 'Love your neighbor as yourself.'b " a

28"You have answered correctly," Jesus replied. "Do this and you will live." b

29But he wanted to justify himself, c so he asked Jesus, "And who is my neighbor?"

30In reply Jesus said: "A man was going down from Jerusalem to Jericho, when he fell into the hands of robbers. They stripped him of his clothes, beat him and went away, leaving him half dead. 31A priest happened to be going down the same road, and when he saw the man, he passed by on the other side. 32So too, a Levite, when he came to the place and saw him, passed by on the other side. 33But a Samaritan, as he traveled, came where the man was; and when he saw him, he took pity on him. 34He went to him and bandaged his wounds, pouring on oil and wine. Then he put the man on his own donkey, took him to an inn and took care of him. 35The next day he took out two silver coinsc and gave them to the innkeeper. 'Look after him,' he said, 'and when I return, I will reimburse you for any extra expense you may have.'

36"Which of these three do you think was a neighbor to the man who fell into the hands of robbers?"

37The expert in the law replied, "The one who had mercy on him."

Jesus told him, "Go and do likewise."

Jesus Visits Martha and Mary (133)

38As Jesus and his disciples were on their way, he came to a village where a woman named Martha opened her home to him. 39She had a sister called Mary, who sat at the Lord's feet d listening to what he said. 40But Martha was distracted by all the preparations that had to be made. She came to him and asked, "Lord, don't you care that my sister has left me to do the work by myself? Tell her to help me!"

a27 Deut. 6:5   b27 Lev. 19:18   c35 Greek two denarii

**Cross references (margin):**

10:25 yMt 19:16

10:27 zDt 6:5   aLev 19:18

10:28 bLev 18:5

10:29 cLk 16:15

10:39 dLk 8:35

10:22 Christ's mission was to reveal God the Father to people. His words brought difficult ideas down to earth. He explained God's love through parables, teachings, and, most of all, his life. By examining Jesus' actions, principles, and attitudes, we can understand God more clearly.

10:23, 24 Old Testament men of God, such as David and Isaiah, made many God-inspired predictions that Jesus fulfilled. As Peter later wrote, these prophets wondered what their words meant and when they would be fulfilled (1 Peter 1:10–13). The disciples had the fantastic opportunity of being eyewitnesses to the fulfillment of those prophecies. For many months, however, they took Jesus for granted, not really listening to him or obeying him. We also have a privileged position, with knowledge of 2,000 years of church history, availability of the Bible in hundreds of languages and translations, and access to many excellent pastors and speakers. Yet often we take these for granted. Remember, with privilege comes responsibility. Because we are privileged to know so much about Christ, we must be careful to follow him.

10:27 This expert in the law was quoting Deuteronomy 6:5 and Leviticus 19:18. He correctly understood that the law demanded total devotion to God and love for one's neighbor. Jesus talked more about these laws elsewhere (see Matthew 19:16–22 and Mark 10:17–22).

10:27–37 The law expert treated the wounded man as a topic for discussion; the robbers, as an object to exploit; the priest, as a problem to avoid; and the Levite, as an object of curiosity. Only

the Samaritan treated him as a person to love. From the parable we learn three principles about loving our neighbor: (1) lack of love is often easy to justify, even though it is never right; (2) our neighbor is anyone of any race, creed, or social background who is in need; (3) love means acting to meet the person's need. Wherever you live, needy people are close by. There is no good reason for refusing to help.

10:33–37 A deep hatred existed between Jews and Samaritans. The Jews saw themselves as pure descendants of Abraham, while the Samaritans were a mixed race produced when Jews from the northern kingdom intermarried with other peoples after Israel's exile (see also the note on 9:53). To this law expert, the person least likely to act correctly would be the Samaritan. In fact, he did not even say the word "Samaritan" in answer to Jesus' question. This "expert's" attitude betrayed his lack of the very thing that he had earlier said the law commanded—love.

10:38–42 Mary and Martha both loved Jesus. On this occasion they were both serving him. But Martha thought Mary's style of serving was inferior to hers. She didn't realize that in her desire to serve, she was actually neglecting her guest. Are you so busy doing things *for* Jesus that you're not spending any time *with* him? Don't let your service become self-serving. Jesus did not blame Martha for being concerned about household chores. He was only asking her to set priorities. Service to Christ can degenerate into mere busywork that is no longer full of devotion to God.

⁴¹"Martha, Martha," the Lord answered, "you are worried ᵉ and upset about many things, ⁴²but only one thing is needed. ᵃ ᶠ Mary has chosen what is better, and it will not be taken away from her."

10:41
ᵉMt 6:25-34
10:42
ᶠPs 27:4

Jesus Teaches His Disciples about Prayer (134)

11 One day Jesus was praying ᵍ in a certain place. When he finished, one of his disciples said to him, "Lord, teach us to pray, just as John taught his disciples."

11:1
ᵍLk 3:21

²He said to them, "When you pray, say:

"'Father, ᵇ
hallowed be your name,
your kingdom come. ᶜ
³ Give us each day our daily bread.
⁴ Forgive us our sins,
for we also forgive everyone who sins against us. ᵈ ʰ
And lead us not into temptation. ᵉ'"

11:4
ʰMt 18:35;
Mk 11:25

⁵Then he said to them, "Suppose one of you has a friend, and he goes to him at midnight and says, 'Friend, lend me three loaves of bread, ⁶because a friend of mine on a journey has come to me, and I have nothing to set before him.'

⁷"Then the one inside answers, 'Don't bother me. The door is already locked, and my children are with me in bed. I can't get up and give you anything.' ⁸I tell you, though he will not get up and give him the bread because he is his friend, yet because of the man's boldness ᶠ he will get up and give him as much as he needs. ⁱ

11:8
ⁱLk 18:1-6

⁹"So I say to you: Ask and it will be given to you; ʲ seek and you will find; knock and the door will be opened to you. ¹⁰For everyone who asks receives; he who seeks finds; and to him who knocks, the door will be opened.

11:9
ʲMt 7:7

¹¹"Which of you fathers, if your son asks for ᵍ a fish, will give him a snake instead? ¹²Or if he asks for an egg, will give him a scorpion? ¹³If you then, though you are evil, know how to give good gifts to your children, how much more will your Father in heaven give the Holy Spirit to those who ask him!"

ᵃ42 Some manuscripts *but few things are needed—or only one*   ᵇ2 Some manuscripts *Our Father in heaven*
ᶜ2 Some manuscripts *come. May your will be done on earth as it is in heaven.*   ᵈ4 Greek *everyone who is indebted to us*   ᵉ4 Some manuscripts *temptation but deliver us from the evil one*   ᶠ8 Or *persistence*   ᵍ11 Some manuscripts *for bread, will give him a stone; or if he asks for*

11:2-13 Notice the order in this prayer. First Jesus praised God; then he made his requests. Praising God first puts us in the right frame of mind to tell him about our needs. Too often our prayers are more like shopping lists than conversations. These verses focus on three aspects of prayer: its content (11:2-4), our persistence (11:5-10), and God's faithfulness (11:11-13).

11:3 God's provision is daily, not all at once. We cannot store it up and then cut off communication with God. And we dare not be self-satisfied. If you are running low on strength, ask yourself—how long have I been away from the Source?

11:4 When Jesus taught his disciples to pray, he made forgiveness the cornerstone of their relationship with God. God has forgiven our sins; we must now forgive those who have wronged us. To remain unforgiving shows we have not understood that we ourselves deeply need to be forgiven. Think of some people who have wronged you. Have you forgiven them? How will God deal with you if he treats you as you treat others?

11:8 Persistence, or boldness, in prayer overcomes *our* insensitivity, not God's. To practice persistence does more to change our hearts and minds than his, and it helps us understand and express the intensity of our need. Persistence in prayer helps us recognize God's work.

11:13 Even though good fathers make mistakes, they treat their children well. How much better our perfect heavenly Father treats his children! The most important gift he could ever give us is the Holy Spirit (Acts 2:1-4), whom he promised to give all believers after his death, resurrection, and return to heaven (John 15:26).

11:14-23 A similar and possibly separate event is reported in Matthew 12:22-45 and Mark 3:20-30. The event described by Luke happened in Judea while the other took place in Galilee. According to Luke, Jesus spoke to the crowds; in Matthew and Mark, he accused the Pharisees.

JESUS VISITS MARY AND MARTHA
After teaching throughout Galilee, Jesus returned to Jerusalem for the Feast of Tabernacles (John 7:2ff). He spoke in Jerusalem and then visited his friends Mary and Martha in Bethany, a tiny village on the eastern slope of the Mount of Olives.

Jesus Answers Hostile Accusations (135)

11:14
ᵏMt 9:32, 33

11:15
ˡMt 9:34

11:16
ᵐMt 12:38

11:18
ⁿMt 4:10

¹⁴Jesus was driving out a demon that was mute. When the demon left, the man who had been mute spoke, and the crowd was amazed.ᵏ ¹⁵But some of them said, "By Beelzebub,ᵃ the prince of demons, he is driving out demons."ˡ ¹⁶Others tested him by asking for a sign from heaven.ᵐ

¹⁷Jesus knew their thoughts and said to them: "Any kingdom divided against itself will be ruined, and a house divided against itself will fall. ¹⁸If Satan ⁿ is divided against himself,

ᵃ 15 Greek *Beezeboul* or *Beelzeboul*; also in verses 18 and 19

MARTHA

Many older brothers and sisters have an irritating tendency to take charge, a habit developed while growing up. We can easily see this pattern in Martha, the older sister of Mary and Lazarus. She was used to being in control.

The fact that Martha, Mary, and Lazarus are remembered for their hospitality takes on added significance when we note that hospitality was a social requirement in their culture. It was considered shameful to turn anyone away from your door. Apparently Martha's family met this requirement very well.

Martha worried about details. She wished to please, to serve, to do the right thing—but she often succeeded in making everyone around her uncomfortable. Perhaps as the oldest she feared shame if her home did not measure up to expectations. She tried to do everything she could to make sure that wouldn't happen. As a result, she found it hard to relax and enjoy her guests and even harder to accept Mary's lack of cooperation in all the preparations. Martha's frustration was so intense that she finally asked Jesus to settle the matter. He gently corrected her attitude and showed her that her priorities, though good, were not the best. The personal attention she gave her guests should be more important than the comforts she tried to provide for them.

Later, following her brother Lazarus's death, Martha could hardly help being herself. When she heard Jesus was finally coming, she rushed out to meet him and expressed her inner conflict of disappointment and hope. Jesus pointed out that her hope was too limited. He was not only Lord beyond death, he was Lord over death—the resurrection and the life! Moments later, Martha again spoke without thinking, pointing out that four-day-old corpses are well on their way to decomposition. Her awareness of details sometimes kept her from seeing the whole picture, but Jesus was consistently patient with her.

In our last picture of Martha, she is once again serving a meal to Jesus and his disciples. She has not stopped serving. But the Bible records her silence this time. She has begun to learn what her younger sister already knew—that worship begins with silence and listening.

Strengths and accomplishments:	• Known as a hospitable homemaker • Believed in Jesus with growing faith • Had a strong desire to do everything exactly right
Weaknesses and mistakes:	• Expected others to agree with her priorities • Was overly concerned with details • Tended to feel sorry for herself when her efforts were not recognized • Limited Jesus' power to this life
Lessons from her life:	• Getting caught up in details can make us forget the main reasons for our actions • There is a proper time to listen to Jesus and a proper time to work for him
Vital statistics:	• Where: Bethany • Relatives: Sister: Mary. Brother: Lazarus.
Key verse:	"But Martha was distracted by all the preparations that had to be made. She came to him and asked, 'Lord, don't you care that my sister has left me to do the work by myself? Tell her to help me!'" (Luke 10:40).

Martha's story is told in Luke 10:38–42 and John 11:17–45.

11:15-20 Some of the Pharisees' followers also were exorcists— that is, they drove out demons. The Pharisees' accusations were becoming more desperate. To accuse Jesus of being empowered by Beelzebub, the prince of demons (or Satan himself), because Jesus was driving out demons was also to say that the Pharisees' own exorcists were doing Satan's work. Jesus turned the religious leaders' accusation against them. Jesus first dismissed their claim as absurd (Why would the devil drive out his own demons?). Then he engaged in a little irony ("By whom do your followers drive them out?"). Finally he concluded that his work of driving out demons proves that the kingdom of God has arrived.

Satan, who had controlled the kingdom of this world for thousands of years, was now being controlled and overpowered by Jesus and the kingdom of heaven. Jesus' kingdom began to come into power at Jesus' birth, grew as he resisted the desert temptations, established itself through his teachings and healings, blossomed in victory at his resurrection and at Pentecost, and will become permanent and universal at his second coming.

how can his kingdom stand? I say this because you claim that I drive out demons by Beelze-bub. ¹⁹Now if I drive out demons by Beelzebub, by whom do your followers drive them out? So then, they will be your judges. ²⁰But if I drive out demons by the finger of God,^o then the kingdom of God^p has come to you.

²¹"When a strong man, fully armed, guards his own house, his possessions are safe. ²²But when someone stronger attacks and overpowers him, he takes away the armor in which the man trusted and divides up the spoils.

²³"He who is not with me is against me, and he who does not gather with me, scatters. ^q

²⁴"When an evil^a spirit comes out of a man, it goes through arid places seeking rest and does not find it. Then it says, 'I will return to the house I left.' ²⁵When it arrives, it finds the house swept clean and put in order. ²⁶Then it goes and takes seven other spirits more wicked than itself, and they go in and live there. And the final condition of that man is worse than the first."^r

²⁷As Jesus was saying these things, a woman in the crowd called out, "Blessed is the mother who gave you birth and nursed you."^s

²⁸He replied, "Blessed rather are those who hear the word of God and obey it."^t

Jesus Warns against Unbelief (136)

²⁹As the crowds increased, Jesus said, "This is a wicked generation. It asks for a miraculous sign,^u but none will be given it except the sign of Jonah. ³⁰For as Jonah was a sign to the Nine-vites, so also will the Son of Man be to this generation. ³¹The Queen of the South will rise at the judgment with the men of this generation and condemn them; for she came from the ends of the earth to listen to Solomon's wisdom,^v and now one^b greater than Solomon is here. ³²The men of Nineveh will stand up at the judgment with this generation and condemn it; for they repented at the preaching of Jonah,^w and now one greater than Jonah is here.

Jesus Teaches about the Light Within (137)

³³"No one lights a lamp and puts it in a place where it will be hidden, or under a bowl. In-stead he puts it on its stand, so that those who come in may see the light.^x ³⁴Your eye is the lamp of your body. When your eyes are good, your whole body also is full of light. But when they are bad, your body also is full of darkness. ³⁵See to it, then, that the light within you is not darkness. ³⁶Therefore, if your whole body is full of light, and no part of it dark, it will be completely lighted, as when the light of a lamp shines on you."

^a24 Greek *unclean*   ^b31 Or *something*; also in verse 32

11:20
^oEx 8:19
^pMt 3:2

11:23
^qMt 12:30; Lk 9:50

11:26
^r2Pe 2:20

11:27
^sLk 23:29
11:28
^tLk 8:21

11:29
^uMt 12:38

11:31
^v1Ki 10:1

11:32
^wJnh 3:5

11:33
^xMt 5:15; Mk 4:21; Lk 8:16

11:21, 22 Jesus may have been referring to Isaiah 49:24–26. Regardless of how great Satan's power is, Jesus is stronger still. He will bind Satan and dispose of him for eternity (see Revelation 20:2, 10).

11:23 How does this verse relate to 9:50: "Whoever is not against you is for you"? In the earlier passage, Jesus was talking about a person who was driving out demons in Jesus' name. Those who fight evil, he was saying, are on the same side as one driving out demons in Jesus' name. Here, by contrast, he was talking about the conflict between God and the devil. In this battle, if a person is not on God's side, he or she is on Satan's. There is no neutral ground. Because God has already won the battle, why be on the losing side? If you aren't actively for Christ, you are against him.

11:24–26 Jesus was illustrating an unfortunate human tendency—our desire to reform often does not last long. In Israel's history, almost as soon as a good king would pull down idols, a bad king would set them up again. It is not enough to be emptied of evil; we must then be filled with the power of the Holy Spirit to accomplish God's new purpose in our lives (see also Matthew 12:43–45; Galatians 5:22).

11:27, 28 Jesus was speaking to people who put extremely high value on family ties. Their genealogies were important guarantees that they were part of God's chosen people. A man's value came from his ancestors, and a woman's value came from the sons she bore. Jesus' response to the woman meant that a person's obedi-ence to God is more important than his or her place on the family tree. The patient work of consistent obedience is even more important than the honor of bearing a respected son.

11:29, 30 What was the sign of Jonah? God had asked Jonah to preach repentance to the Gentiles (non-Jews). Jesus was affirm-ing Jonah's message. Salvation is not only for Jews, but for all people. Matthew 12:40 adds another explanation: Jesus would die and rise after three days, just as the prophet Jonah was rescued after three days in the belly of the great fish.

11:29–32 The cruel, warlike men of Nineveh, capital of Assyria, repented when Jonah preached to them—and Jonah did not even care about them. The pagan Queen of the South (Sheba) praised the God of Israel when she heard Solomon's wisdom, and Solo-mon was full of faults. By contrast, Jesus, the perfect Son of God, came to people that he loved dearly—but they rejected him. Thus God's chosen people made themselves more liable to judgment than either a notoriously wicked nation or a powerful pagan queen. Compare 10:12–15 where Jesus says the evil cities of Sodom, Tyre, and Sidon will be judged less harshly than the cities in Judea and Galilee that rejected Jesus' message.

11:31, 32 The Ninevites and the Queen of the South had turned to God with far less evidence than Jesus was giving his listeners—and far less than we have today. We have eyewitness reports of the risen Jesus, the continuing power of the Holy Spirit unleashed at Pentecost, easy access to the Bible, and knowledge of 2,000 years of Christ's acts through his church. With the knowledge and insight available to us, our response to Christ ought to be even more complete and wholehearted.

11:33–36 The lamp is Christ; the eye represents spiritual under-standing and insight. Evil desires make the eye less sensitive and blot out the light of Christ's presence. If you have a hard time

Jesus Criticizes the Religious Leaders (138)

11:38
yMk 7:3, 4

37 When Jesus had finished speaking, a Pharisee invited him to eat with him; so he went in and reclined at the table. 38 But the Pharisee, noticing that Jesus did not first wash before the meal,y was surprised.

11:39
zMt 23:25, 26
11:41
aLk 12:33

39 Then the Lord said to him, "Now then, you Pharisees clean the outside of the cup and dish, but inside you are full of greed and wickedness. z 40 You foolish people! Did not the one who made the outside make the inside also? 41 But give what is inside ˌthe dish, a to the poor,a and everything will be clean for you.

11:42
bLk 18:12
cMt 23:23

42 "Woe to you Pharisees, because you give God a tenth b of your mint, rue and all other kinds of garden herbs, but you neglect justice and the love of God. You should have practiced the latter without leaving the former undone. c

11:43
dMt 23:6, 7;
Mk 12:38-39
11:44
eMt 23:27

43 "Woe to you Pharisees, because you love the most important seats in the synagogues and greetings in the marketplaces. d

44 "Woe to you, because you are like unmarked graves, e which men walk over without knowing it."

45 One of the experts in the law answered him, "Teacher, when you say these things, you insult us also."

11:46
fMt 23:4

46 Jesus replied, "And you experts in the law, woe to you, because you load people down with burdens they can hardly carry, and you yourselves will not lift one finger to help them. f

47 "Woe to you, because you build tombs for the prophets, and it was your forefathers who killed them. 48 So you testify that you approve of what your forefathers did; they killed the prophets, and you build their tombs. 49 Because of this, God in his wisdom g said, 'I will send them prophets and apostles, some of whom they will kill and others they will persecute.' h 50 Therefore this generation will be held responsible for the blood of all the prophets that has been shed since the beginning of the world, 51 from the blood of Abel i to the blood of Zechariah,j who was killed between the altar and the sanctuary. Yes, I tell you, this generation will be held responsible for it all.

11:49
g1Co 1:24, 30
hMt 23:34
11:51
iGe 4:8
j2Ch 24:20, 21
11:52
kMt 23:13

52 "Woe to you experts in the law, because you have taken away the key to knowledge. You yourselves have not entered, and you have hindered those who were entering." k

a41 Or what you have

---

seeing God at work in the world and in your life, check your vision. Are any sinful desires blinding you to Christ?

11:37–39 This washing was done not for health reasons, but as a symbol of washing away any contamination from touching anything unclean. Not only did the Pharisees make a public show of their washing, but they also commanded everyone else to follow a practice originally intended only for the priests.

11:41 The Pharisees loved to think of themselves as "clean," but their stinginess toward God and the poor proved that they were not as clean as they thought. How do you use the resources God has entrusted to you? Are you generous in meeting the needs around you? Your generosity reveals much about the purity of your heart.

11:42 It is easy to rationalize not helping others because we have already given to the church, but a person who follows Jesus should share with needy neighbors. While tithing is important to the life of the church, our compassion must not stop there. Where we can help, we should help.

11:42–52 Jesus criticized the Pharisees and the experts in the law harshly because they (1) washed their outsides but not their insides, (2) remembered to give a tenth of even their garden herbs, but neglected justice, (3) loved praise and attention, (4) loaded people down with burdensome religious demands, (5) would not accept the truth about Jesus, and (6) prevented others from believing the truth as well. They went wrong by focusing on outward appearances and ignoring the inner condition of their hearts. People do the same when their service comes from a desire to be seen rather than from a pure heart and out of a love for others. People may sometimes be fooled, but God isn't. Don't be a Christian on the outside only. Bring your inner life under God's control and your outer life will naturally reflect him.

11:44 The Old Testament laws said a person who touched a

grave was unclean (Numbers 19:16). Jesus accused the Pharisees of making others unclean by their spiritual rottenness. Like unmarked graves hidden in a field, the Pharisees corrupted everyone who came in contact with them.

11:46 These "burdens" were the details the Pharisees had added to God's law. To the commandment, "Remember the Sabbath day by keeping it holy" (Exodus 20:8), for example, they had added instructions regarding how far a person could walk on the Sabbath, which kinds of knots could be tied, and how much weight could be carried. Healing a person was considered unlawful work on the Sabbath although rescuing a trapped animal was permitted (14:5). No wonder Jesus condemned their additions to the law.

11:49 God's prophets have been persecuted and murdered throughout history. But this generation was rejecting more than a human prophet—they were rejecting God himself. This quotation is not from the Old Testament. Jesus, the greatest Prophet of all, was directly giving them God's message.

11:51 Abel's death is recorded in Genesis 4:8. For more about him, see his Profile in Genesis 6, p. 15. Zechariah's death is recorded in 2 Chronicles 24:20–22 (the last book in the Hebrew canon). Why would all these sins come upon this particular generation? Because they were rejecting the Messiah himself, the One to whom all their history and prophecy were pointing.

11:52 How did the law experts take away the "key to knowledge"? Through their erroneous interpretations of Scripture and their added man-made rules, they made God's truth hard to understand and practice. On top of that, these men were bad examples, arguing their way out of the demanding rules they placed on others. Caught up in a religion of their own making, they could no longer lead the people to God. They had closed the door of God's love to the people and had thrown away the key.

53 When Jesus left there, the Pharisees and the teachers of the law began to oppose him fiercely and to besiege him with questions, 54 waiting to catch him in something he might say. *l*

Jesus Speaks against Hypocrisy (139)

12 Meanwhile, when a crowd of many thousands had gathered, so that they were trampling on one another, Jesus began to speak first to his disciples, saying: "Be on your guard against the yeast of the Pharisees, which is hypocrisy. *m* 2 There is nothing concealed that will not be disclosed, or hidden that will not be made known. *n* 3 What you have said in the dark will be heard in the daylight, and what you have whispered in the ear in the inner rooms will be proclaimed from the roofs.

4 "I tell you, my friends, *o* do not be afraid of those who kill the body and after that can do no more. 5 But I will show you whom you should fear: Fear him who, after the killing of the body, has power to throw you into hell. Yes, I tell you, fear him. *p* 6 Are not five sparrows sold for two pennies a ? Yet not one of them is forgotten by God. 7 Indeed, the very hairs of your head are all numbered. *q* Don't be afraid; you are worth more than many sparrows. *r*

8 "I tell you, whoever acknowledges me before men, the Son of Man will also acknowledge him before the angels of God. 9 But he who disowns me before men will be disowned before the angels of God. 10 And everyone who speaks a word against the Son of Man will be forgiven, but anyone who blasphemes against the Holy Spirit will not be forgiven. *s*

11 "When you are brought before synagogues, rulers and authorities, do not worry about how you will defend yourselves or what you will say, *t* 12 for the Holy Spirit will teach you at that time what you should say." *u*

a 6 Greek *two assaria*

11:54 *l* Mk 12:13

12:1 *m* Mt 16:6, 11, 12; Mk 8:15

12:2 *n* Mk 4:22; Lk 8:17

12:4 *o* Jn 15:14, 15

12:5 *p* Heb 10:31

12:7 *q* Mt 10:30 *r* Mt 12:12

12:10 *s* Mt 12:31, 32; Mk 3:28-29; 1 Jn 5:16

12:11 *t* Mt 10:17, 19; Mk 13:11

12:12 *u* Mt 10:20

11:53, 54 The teachers of the law and the Pharisees hoped to arrest Jesus for blasphemy, heresy, and lawbreaking. They were enraged by Jesus' words about them, but they couldn't arrest him for merely speaking words. They had to find a legal way to get rid of Jesus.

12:1, 2 As Jesus watched the huge crowds waiting to hear him, he warned his disciples against hypocrisy—trying to appear good when one's heart is far from God. The Pharisees could not keep their attitudes hidden forever. Their selfishness would act like yeast, and soon they would expose themselves for what they really were—power-hungry impostors, not devoted religious leaders. It is easy to be angry at the blatant hypocrisy of the Pharisees, but each of us must resist the temptation to settle for the appearance of respectability when our hearts are far from God.

12:1, 2 What are the signs of hypocrisy? (1) Hypocrisy is knowing the truth but not obeying it. People can say they follow Jesus, but not be obedient to his Word. (2) Hypocrisy is living a self-serving life. People may desire leadership only because they love position and control, not because they want to serve others. (3) Hypocrisy reduces faith to rigid rules. People can end up worshiping their own rules and regulations about what they think God wants instead of worshiping God himself. (4) Hypocrisy is outward conformity without inner reality. People can obey the details but still be disobedient in general behavior. For example, a person may carefully tithe his income, but be rude and obnoxious to his coworkers.

Many non-Christians use the supposed (or real) hypocrisy of Christians as an excuse to stay away from God and the church. Look carefully at your life. You are not perfect; therefore, at times an action or behavior might provide the ammunition for someone to label you a hypocrite. However, you must discern your own heart. Consider the signs of hypocrisy noted above and make sure you are not guilty. Then ask God to help you live rightly.

12:4, 5 Fear of opposition or ridicule can weaken our witness for Christ. Often we cling to peace and comfort, even at the cost of our walk with God. Jesus reminds us here that we should fear God, who controls eternal, not merely temporal, consequences. Don't allow fear of a person or group to keep you from standing up for Christ.

12:7 Our true value is God's estimate of our worth, not our peers' estimate. Other people evaluate and categorize us according to how we perform, what we achieve, and how we look. But God cares for us, as he does for all of his creatures, because we belong to him. Thus, we can face life without fear; we are very valuable to God.

12:8, 9 We disown Jesus when we (1) hope no one will think we are Christians, (2) decide *not* to speak up for what is right, (3) are silent about our relationship with God, (4) blend into society, (5) accept our culture's non-Christian values. By contrast, we acknowledge him when we (1) live moral, upright, Christ-honoring lives, (2) look for opportunities to share our faith with others, (3) help others in need, (4) take a stand for justice, (5) love others, (6) acknowledge our loyalty to Christ, (7) use our lives and resources to carry out his desires rather than our own.

12:10 Jesus said that blasphemy against the Holy Spirit is unforgivable. This has worried many sincere Christians, but it does not need to. The unforgivable sin means attributing to Satan the work that the Holy Spirit accomplishes (see the notes on Matthew 12:31, 32; Mark 3:28, 29). Thus it is deliberate and ongoing rejection of the Holy Spirit's work and even of God himself. A person who has committed this sin has shut himself or herself off from God so thoroughly that he or she is unaware of any sin at all. A person who fears having committed it shows, by his or her very concern, that he or she has not sinned in this way.

12:11, 12 The disciples knew they could never dominate a religious dispute with the well-educated Jewish leaders. Nevertheless, they would not be left unprepared. Jesus promised that the Holy Spirit would supply the needed words. The disciples' testimony might not make them look impressive, but it would still point out God's work in the world through Jesus' life. We need to pray for opportunities to speak for God, and then trust him to help us with our words. This promise of the Spirit's help, however, does not compensate for lack of preparation. Remember that these disciples had three years of personal instruction and practical application. We too must study God's Word. Then God will bring his truths to mind when we most need them, helping us present them in the most effective way.

Jesus Tells the Parable of the Rich Fool (140)

¹³Someone in the crowd said to him, "Teacher, tell my brother to divide the inheritance with me."

¹⁴Jesus replied, "Man, who appointed me a judge or an arbiter between you?" ¹⁵Then he said to them, "Watch out! Be on your guard against all kinds of greed; a man's life does not consist in the abundance of his possessions."

¹⁶And he told them this parable: "The ground of a certain rich man produced a good crop. ¹⁷He thought to himself, 'What shall I do? I have no place to store my crops.'

¹⁸"Then he said, 'This is what I'll do. I will tear down my barns and build bigger ones, and there I will store all my grain and my goods. ¹⁹And I'll say to myself, "You have plenty of good things laid up for many years. Take life easy; eat, drink and be merry."'

²⁰"But God said to him, 'You fool! ᵛ This very night your life will be demanded from you. ʷ Then who will get what you have prepared for yourself?' ˣ

²¹"This is how it will be with anyone who stores up things for himself but is not rich toward God." ʸ

Jesus Warns about Worry (141)

²²Then Jesus said to his disciples: "Therefore I tell you, do not worry about your life, what you will eat; or about your body, what you will wear. ²³Life is more than food, and the body more than clothes. ²⁴Consider the ravens: They do not sow or reap, they have no storeroom or barn; yet God feeds them. ᶻ And how much more valuable you are than birds! ²⁵Who of you by worrying can add a single hour to his life ᵃ? ²⁶Since you cannot do this very little thing, why do you worry about the rest?

²⁷"Consider how the lilies grow. They do not labor or spin. Yet I tell you, not even Solomon in all his splendorᵃ was dressed like one of these. ²⁸If that is how God clothes the grass of the field, which is here today, and tomorrow is thrown into the fire, how much more will he clothe you, O you of little faith! ᵇ ²⁹And do not set your heart on what you will eat or drink; do not worry about it. ³⁰For the pagan world runs after all such things, and your Father knows that you need them. ᶜ ³¹But seek his kingdom, and these things will be given to you as well.

³²"Do not be afraid, ᵈ little flock, for your Father has been pleased to give you the kingdom. ³³Sell your possessions and give to the poor. ᵉ Provide purses for yourselves that will

12:20
ᵛ Jer 17:11
ʷ Job 27:8
ˣ Ps 39:6
12:21
ʸ ver 33

12:24
ᶻ Job 38:41

12:27
ᵃ 1Ki 10:4-7
12:28
ᵇ Mt 6:30

12:30
ᶜ Mt 6:8
12:32
ᵈ Mt 14:27
12:33
ᵉ Mt 19:21

ᵃ25 Or *single cubit to his height*

12:13ff Problems like this were often brought to rabbis for them to settle. Jesus' response, though not directly to the topic, is not a change of subject. Rather, Jesus is pointing to a higher issue—a correct attitude toward the accumulation of wealth. Life is more than material goods; far more important is our relationship with God. Jesus put his finger on this questioner's heart. When we bring problems to God in prayer, he often does the same—showing us how we need to change and grow in our attitude toward the problem. This answer is often not the one we were looking for, but it is more effective in helping us trace God's hand in our lives.

12:15 Jesus says that the good life has nothing to do with being wealthy, so be on guard against greed (desire for what we don't have). This is the exact opposite of what society usually says. Advertisers spend millions of dollars to entice us to think that if we buy more and more of their products, we will be happier, more fulfilled, more comfortable. How do you respond to the constant pressure to buy? Learn to tune out expensive enticements and concentrate instead on the truly good life—living in a relationship with God and doing his work.

12:16–21 The rich man in Jesus' story died before he could begin to use what was stored in his big barns. Planning for retirement—preparing for life *before* death—is wise, but neglecting life *after* death is disastrous. If you accumulate wealth only to enrich yourself, with no concern for helping others, you will enter eternity empty-handed.

12:18–20 Why do you save money? To retire? To buy more expensive cars or toys? To be secure? Jesus challenges us to think beyond earthbound goals and to use what we have been given for God's kingdom. Faith, service, and obedience are the way to become rich toward God.

12:22–34 Jesus commands us not to worry. But how can we avoid it? Only faith can free us from the anxiety caused by greed and covetousness. Working and planning responsibly are good; dwelling on all the ways our planning could go wrong is bad. Worry is pointless because it can't fill any of our needs; worry is foolish because the Creator of the universe loves us and knows what we need. He promises to meet all our real needs, but not necessarily all our desires.

Overcoming worry requires: (1) Simple trust in God, your heavenly Father. This trust is expressed by praying to him rather than worrying. (2) Perspective on your problems. This can be gained by developing a strategy for addressing and correcting your problems. (3) A support team to help. Find some believers who will pray for you to find wisdom and strength to deal with your worries.

12:31 Seeking the kingdom of God above all else means making Jesus the Lord and King of your life. He must control every area—your work, play, plans, relationships. Is the kingdom only one of your many concerns, or is it central to all you do? Are you holding back any areas of your life from God's control? As Lord and Creator, he wants to help provide what you need as well as guide how you use what he provides.

12:33 Money seen as an end in itself quickly traps us and cuts us off from both God and the needy. The key to using money wisely is to see how much we can use for God's purposes, not how much we can accumulate for ourselves. Does God's love touch your wallet? Does your money free you to help others? If so, you are storing up lasting treasures in heaven. If your financial goals and possessions hinder you from giving generously, loving others, or serving God, sell what you must to bring your life into line with his purposes.

not wear out, a treasure in heaven *f* that will not be exhausted, where no thief comes near and no moth destroys. 34 For where your treasure is, there your heart will be also. *g*

Jesus Warns about Preparing for His Coming (142)

35 "Be dressed ready for service and keep your lamps burning, 36 like men waiting for their master to return from a wedding banquet, so that when he comes and knocks they can immediately open the door for him. 37 It will be good for those servants whose master finds them watching when he comes. *h* I tell you the truth, he will dress himself to serve, will have them recline at the table and will come and wait on them. 38 It will be good for those servants whose master finds them ready, even if he comes in the second or third watch of the night. 39 But understand this: If the owner of the house had known at what hour the thief *i* was coming, he would not have let his house be broken into. 40 You also must be ready, *j* because the Son of Man will come at an hour when you do not expect him."

41 Peter asked, "Lord, are you telling this parable to us, or to everyone?"

42 The Lord *k* answered, "Who then is the faithful and wise manager, whom the master puts in charge of his servants to give them their food allowance at the proper time? 43 It will be good for that servant whom the master finds doing so when he returns. 44 I tell you the truth, he will put him in charge of all his possessions. 45 But suppose the servant says to himself, 'My master is taking a long time in coming,' and he then begins to beat the menservants and maidservants and to eat and drink and get drunk. 46 The master of that servant will come on a day when he does not expect him and at an hour he is not aware of. He will cut him to pieces and assign him a place with the unbelievers.

47 "That servant who knows his master's will and does not get ready or does not do what his master wants will be beaten with many blows. *l* 48 But the one who does not know and does things deserving punishment will be beaten with few blows. *m* From everyone who has been given much, much will be demanded; and from the one who has been entrusted with much, much more will be asked.

Jesus Warns about Coming Division (143)

49 "I have come to bring fire on the earth, and how I wish it were already kindled! 50 But I have a baptism *n* to undergo, and how distressed I am until it is completed! 51 Do you think I came to bring peace on earth? No, I tell you, but division. 52 From now on there will be five in one family divided against each other, three against two and two against three. 53 They will be divided, father against son and son against father, mother against daughter and daughter against mother, mother-in-law against daughter-in-law and daughter-in-law against mother-in-law." *o*

12:33
f Mt 6:20
12:34
g Mt 6:21

12:37
h Mt 24:42, 46

12:39
i Mt 6:19; 1Th 5:2; 2Pe 3:10; Rev 3:3; 16:15
12:40
j Mk 13:33; Lk 21:36

12:42
k Lk 7:13

12:47
l Dt 25:2
12:48
m Lev 5:17; Nu 15:27-30

12:50
n Mk 10:38

12:53
o Mic 7:6; Mt 10:21

12:34 If you concentrate your money in your business, your thoughts will center on making the business profitable. If you direct it toward other people, you will become concerned with their welfare. Where do you put your time, money, and energy? What do you think about most? How should you change the way you use your resources in order to reflect kingdom values more accurately?

12:35–40 Jesus repeatedly said that he would leave this world but would return at some future time (see Matthew 24; 25; John 14:1–3). He also said that a kingdom was being prepared for his followers. Many Greeks envisioned this as a heavenly, idealized, spiritual kingdom. Jews—like Isaiah and John, the writer of Revelation—saw it as a restored earthly kingdom.

12:40 Christ's return at an unexpected time is not a trap, a trick by which God hopes to catch us off guard. In fact, God is delaying his return so more people will have the opportunity to follow him (see 2 Peter 3:9). Before Christ's return, we have time to live out our beliefs and to reflect Jesus' love as we relate to others.

People who are ready for their Lord's return are (1) not hypocritical, but sincere (12:1), (2) not fearful, but ready to witness (12:4–9), (3) not worried, but trusting (12:25, 26), (4) not greedy, but generous (12:34), (5) not lazy, but diligent (12:37). May your life be more like Christ's so that when he comes, you will be ready to greet him joyfully.

12:42–44 Jesus promises a reward for those who have been faithful to the Master. While we sometimes experience immediate

and material rewards for our obedience to God, this is not always the case. If so, we would be tempted to boast about our achievements and do good only for what we get. Jesus said that if we look for rewards now, we will lose them later (see Mark 8:36). Our heavenly rewards will be the most accurate reflection of what we have done on earth, and they will be far greater than we can imagine.

12:48 Jesus has told us how to live until he comes: we must watch for him, work diligently, and obey his commands. Such attitudes are especially necessary for leaders. Watchful and faithful leaders will be given increased opportunities and responsibilities. The more resources, talents, and understanding we have, the more we are responsible to use them effectively. God will not hold us responsible for gifts he has not given us, but all of us have enough gifts and duties to keep us busy until Jesus returns.

12:50 The "baptism" to which Jesus referred was his coming crucifixion. Jesus was dreading the physical pain, of course, but even worse would be the spiritual pain of complete separation from God that would accompany his death for the sins of the world.

12:51–53 In these strange and unsettling words, Jesus revealed that his coming often results in conflict. He demands a response, so intimate groups may be torn apart when some choose to follow him and others refuse to do so. Jesus allows no middle ground. Loyalties must be declared and commitments made, sometimes to the point of severing other relationships. Are you willing to risk your family's approval in order to follow the Lord?

Jesus Warns about the Future Crisis (144)

12:54
p Mt 16:2

⁵⁴He said to the crowd:"When you see a cloud rising in the west, immediately you say, 'It's going to rain,' and it does. *p* ⁵⁵And when the south wind blows, you say, 'It's going to be hot,' and it is. ⁵⁶Hypocrites! You know how to interpret the appearance of the earth and the sky. How is it that you don't know how to interpret this present time? *q*

12:56
q Mt 16:3

12:58
r Mt 5:25

⁵⁷"Why don't you judge for yourselves what is right? ⁵⁸As you are going with your adversary to the magistrate, try hard to be reconciled to him on the way, or he may drag you off to the judge, and the judge turn you over to the officer, and the officer throw you into prison. *r*

12:59
s Mk 12:42

⁵⁹I tell you, you will not get out until you have paid the last penny. *a* *s*

Jesus Calls the People to Repent (145)

13:1
t Mt 27:2

13:2
u Jn 9:2, 3

13:4
v Jn 9:7, 11

13 Now there were some present at that time who told Jesus about the Galileans whose blood Pilate *t* had mixed with their sacrifices. ²Jesus answered, "Do you think that these Galileans were worse sinners than all the other Galileans because they suffered this way? *u* ³I tell you, no! But unless you repent, you too will all perish. ⁴Or those eighteen who died when the tower in Siloam *v* fell on them—do you think they were more guilty than all the others living in Jerusalem? ⁵I tell you, no! But unless you repent, you too will all perish."

13:6
w Isa 5:2; Mt 21:19

13:7
x Mt 3:10

⁶Then he told this parable:"A man had a fig tree, planted in his vineyard, and he went to look for fruit on it, but did not find any. *w* ⁷So he said to the man who took care of the vineyard, 'For three years now I've been coming to look for fruit on this fig tree and haven't found any. Cut it down! *x* Why should it use up the soil?'

⁸"'Sir,' the man replied, 'leave it alone for one more year, and I'll dig around it and fertilize it. ⁹If it bears fruit next year, fine! If not, then cut it down.'"

a 59 Greek *lepton*

**SEVEN
SABBATH
MIRACLES**

Jesus sends a demon out of a man . . . . Mark 1:21–28

Jesus heals Peter's mother-in-law . . . . Mark 1:29–31

Jesus heals a lame man by the Pool Bethesda . . . . John 5:1–18

Jesus heals a man with a shriveled hand . . . . Mark 3:1–6

Jesus restores a crippled woman . . . . Luke 13:10–17

Jesus heals a man with dropsy . . . . Luke 14:1–6

Jesus heals a man born blind . . . . John 9:1–16

Over the centuries, the Jewish religious leaders had added rule after rule to God's law. For example, God's law said the Sabbath is a day of rest (Exodus 20:10, 11). But the religious leaders added to that law, creating one that said, "You cannot heal on the Sabbath" because that is "work." Seven times Jesus healed people on the Sabbath. In doing this, he was challenging these religious leaders to look beyond their rules to their true purpose—to honor God by helping those in need. Would God have been pleased if Jesus had ignored these people?

12:54–57 For most of recorded history, the world's principal occupation was farming. The farmer depended directly on the weather for his livelihood. He needed just the right amounts of sun and rain—not too much, not too little—to make his living, and he grew skilled at interpreting natural signs. Jesus was announcing an earthshaking event that would be much more important than the year's crops—the coming of God's kingdom. Like a rainstorm or a sunny day, there were signs that the kingdom would soon arrive. But Jesus' hearers, though skilled at interpreting weather signs, were intentionally ignoring the signs of the times.

13:1–5 Pilate may have killed the Galileans because he thought they were rebelling against Rome; those killed by the tower of Siloam may have been working for the Romans on an aqueduct there. The Pharisees, who were opposed to using force to deal with Rome, would have said that the Galileans killed by Pilate deserved to die for rebelling. The Zealots, a group of anti-Roman terrorists, would have said the aqueduct workers deserved to die for cooperating. Jesus dismissed the idea that accidents or human cruelties were God's judgment on especially bad sinners.

Neither the Galileans nor the workers should be blamed for their calamities. Whether a person is killed in a tragic accident or miraculously survives is not a measure of righteousness. Everyone has to die. Jesus did not explain why some live and some die tragically; instead he pointed to everyone's need for repentance. No matter how or when it occurs, death is not the end. Jesus promises that those who believe in him will not perish but have eternal life (John 3:16).

13:6–9 In the Old Testament, a fruitful tree was often used as a symbol of godly living (see, for example, Psalm 1:3 and Jeremiah 17:7, 8). Jesus pointed out what would happen to the other kind of tree—the kind that took valuable time and space and still produced nothing for the patient gardener. This was one way Jesus warned his listeners that God would not tolerate forever their lack of productivity. (Luke 3:9 records John the Baptist's version of the same message.) Have you been enjoying God's special treatment without giving anything in return? If so, respond to the Gardener's patient care, and begin to bear the fruit God has created you to produce.

Jesus Heals the Crippled Woman (146)

10 On a Sabbath Jesus was teaching in one of the synagogues,ʸ 11 and a woman was there who had been crippled by a spirit for eighteen years. ᶻ She was bent over and could not straighten up at all. 12 When Jesus saw her, he called her forward and said to her, "Woman, you are set free from your infirmity." 13 Then he put his hands on her,ᵃ and immediately she straightened up and praised God.

14 Indignant because Jesus had healed on the Sabbath,ᵇ the synagogue rulerᶜ said to the people, "There are six days for work. ᵈ So come and be healed on those days, not on the Sabbath."

15 The Lord answered him, "You hypocrites! Doesn't each of you on the Sabbath untie his ox or donkey from the stall and lead it out to give it water?ᵉ 16 Then should not this woman, a daughter of Abraham,ᶠ whom Satanᵍ has kept bound for eighteen long years, be set free on the Sabbath day from what bound her?"

17 When he said this, all his opponents were humiliated, but the people were delighted with all the wonderful things he was doing.

Jesus Teaches about the Kingdom of God (147)

18 Then Jesus asked, "What is the kingdom of God like? What shall I compare it to? 19 It is like a mustard seed, which a man took and planted in his garden. It grew and became a tree, and the birds of the air perched in its branches."

20 Again he asked, "What shall I compare the kingdom of God to? 21 It is like yeast that a woman took and mixed into a large amountᵃ of flour until it worked all through the dough."

Jesus Teaches about Entering the Kingdom (153)

22 Then Jesus went through the towns and villages, teaching as he made his way to Jerusalem. ʰ 23 Someone asked him, "Lord, are only a few people going to be saved?"

He said to them, 24 "Make every effort to enter through the narrow door,ⁱ because many, I tell you, will try to enter and will not be able to. 25 Once the owner of the house gets up and closes the door, you will stand outside knocking and pleading, 'Sir, open the door for us.'

"But he will answer, 'I don't know you or where you come from.'ʲ

26 "Then you will say, 'We ate and drank with you, and you taught in our streets.'

27 "But he will reply, 'I don't know you or where you come from. Away from me, all you evildoers!'ᵏ

28 "There will be weeping there, and gnashing of teeth,ˡ when you see Abraham, Isaac and Jacob and all the prophets in the kingdom of God, but you yourselves thrown out. 29 People

a21 Greek three satas (probably about 1/2 bushel or 22 liters)

13:10	ʸMt 4:23
13:11	ᶻver 16
13:13	ᵃMk 5:23
13:14	ᵇLk 14:3 ᶜMk 5:22 ᵈEx 20:9
13:15	ᵉLk 14:5
13:16	ᶠLk 19:9 ᵍMt 4:10
13:22	ʰLk 9:51
13:24	ⁱMt 7:13
13:25	ʲMt 7:23; 25:10-12
13:27	ᵏMt 7:23; 25:41
13:28	ˡMt 8:12

13:10-17 Why was healing considered work? The religious leaders saw healing as part of a doctor's profession, and practicing one's profession on the Sabbath was prohibited. The synagogue ruler could not see beyond the law to Jesus' compassion in healing this crippled woman. Jesus shamed him and the other leaders by pointing out their hypocrisy. They would untie their animals and care for them, but they refused to rejoice when a human being was freed from Satan's bondage.

13:16 In our fallen world, disease and disability are common. Their causes are many and often multiple—inadequate nutrition, contact with a source of infection, lowered defenses, and even direct attack by Satan. Whatever the immediate cause of our illness, we can trace its original source to Satan, the author of all the evil in our world. The good news is that Jesus is more powerful than any devil or any disease. He often brings physical healing in this life; and when he returns, he will put an end to all disease and disability.

13:18-21 The general expectation among Jesus' hearers was that the Messiah would come as a great king and leader, freeing the nation from Rome and restoring Israel's former glory. But Jesus said his kingdom was beginning quietly. Like the tiny mustard seed that grows into an enormous tree, or the spoonful of yeast that makes the bread dough double in size, the kingdom of God would eventually push outward until the whole world was changed.

13:22 This is the second time Luke reminds us that Jesus was

intentionally going to Jerusalem (the other time is in 9:51). Jesus knew he was on his way to die, but he continued preaching to large crowds. The prospect of death did not deter Jesus from his mission.

13:24, 25 Finding salvation requires more concentrated effort than most people are willing to put forth. Obviously we cannot save ourselves—there is no way we can work ourselves into God's favor. The effort we must put out "to enter through the narrow door" is earnestly desiring to know Jesus and diligently striving to follow him whatever the cost. We dare not put off making this decision because the door will not stay open forever.

13:26, 27 The people were eager to know who would be in God's kingdom. Jesus explained that although many people know something about God, only a few have acknowledged their sins and accepted his forgiveness. We may not necessarily see the people we expect to find in the kingdom of God. Some perfectly respectable religious leaders claiming allegiance to Jesus will not be there because they were not true followers and secretly were morally corrupt. Just listening to Jesus' words or admiring his miracles is not enough—we must turn from sin and trust in God to save us.

13:29 God's kingdom will include people from every part of the world. Israel's rejection of Jesus as Messiah would not stop God's plan. True Israel includes all people who believe in Christ. This was an important fact for Luke to stress as he was directing his Gospel to a Gentile audience (see also Romans 4:16-25; Galatians 3:6-9).

13:29
m Mt 8:11
13:30
n Mt 19:30

will come from east and west *m* and north and south, and will take their places at the feast in the kingdom of God. 30 Indeed there are those who are last who will be first, and first who will be last." *n*

Jesus Grieves over Jerusalem (154)

31 At that time some Pharisees came to Jesus and said to him, "Leave this place and go somewhere else. Herod wants to kill you."

13:32
o Heb 2:10
13:33
p Mt 21:11
13:34
q Mt 23:37
13:35
r Ps 118:26;
Mt 21:9; Lk 19:38

32 He replied, "Go tell that fox, 'I will drive out demons and heal people today and tomorrow, and on the third day I will reach my goal.' *o* 33 In any case, I must keep going today and tomorrow and the next day—for surely no prophet *p* can die outside Jerusalem!

34 "O Jerusalem, Jerusalem, you who kill the prophets and stone those sent to you, how often I have longed to gather your children together, as a hen gathers her chicks under her wings, *q* but you were not willing! 35 Look, your house is left to you desolate. I tell you, you will not see me again until you say, 'Blessed is he who comes in the name of the Lord.' *a* " *r*

Jesus Heals a Man with Swollen Limbs (155)

14:3
s Mt 22:35
t Mt 12:2
14:5
u Lk 13:15

14 One Sabbath, when Jesus went to eat in the house of a prominent Pharisee, he was being carefully watched. 2 There in front of him was a man suffering from dropsy. 3 Jesus asked the Pharisees and experts in the law, *s* "Is it lawful to heal on the Sabbath or not?" *t* 4 But they remained silent. So taking hold of the man, he healed him and sent him away.

5 Then he asked them, "If one of you has a son *b* or an ox that falls into a well on the Sabbath day, will you not immediately pull him out?" *u* 6 And they had nothing to say.

Jesus Teaches about Seeking Humility (156)

7 When he noticed how the guests picked the places of honor at the table, he told them this parable: 8 "When someone invites you to a wedding feast, do not take the place of honor, for a person more distinguished than you may have been invited. 9 If so, the host who invited both of you will come and say to you, 'Give this man your seat.' Then, humiliated, you will have to take the least important place. 10 But when you are invited, take the lowest place, so that when your host comes, he will say to you, 'Friend, move up to a better place.' Then you will be honored in the presence of all your fellow guests. 11 For everyone who exalts himself will be humbled, and he who humbles himself will be exalted." *v*

14:11
v Mt 23:12; Lk 18:14

a 35 Psalm 118:26   *b* 5 Some manuscripts *donkey*

13:30 God's kingdom will have many surprises. Some who are despised now will be greatly honored then; some influential people here will be left outside the gates. Many "great" people on this earth (in God's eyes) are virtually ignored by the rest of the world. What matters to God is not a person's earthly popularity, status, wealth, heritage, or power, but his or her commitment to Christ. How do your values match what the Bible tells you to value? Put God in first place, and you will join people from all over the world who will take their places at the feast in the kingdom of heaven.

13:31–33 The Pharisees weren't interested in protecting Jesus from danger; they were trying to trap him themselves. The Pharisees urged Jesus to leave because they wanted to stop him from going to Jerusalem, not because they feared Herod. But Jesus' life, work, and death would not be determined by Herod or the Pharisees. His life was planned and directed by God himself, and his mission would unfold in God's time and according to God's plan.

13:33 Why was Jesus focusing on Jerusalem? Jerusalem, the city of God, symbolized the entire nation. It was Israel's largest city and the nation's spiritual and political capital, and Jews from around the world frequently visited it. But Jerusalem had a history of rejecting God's prophets (1 Kings 19:10; 2 Chronicles 24:19; Jeremiah 2:30; 26:20–23). It would reject the Messiah just as it had rejected his forerunners.

14:1–6 Earlier Jesus had been invited to a Pharisee's home for discussion (7:36). This time a prominent Pharisee invited Jesus to his home specifically to trap him into saying or doing something for which he could be arrested. It may be surprising to see Jesus on the Pharisees' turf after he had denounced them so many times. But he was not afraid to face them, even though he knew that their purpose was to trick him into breaking their laws.

14:2 Luke, the physician, identifies this man's disease—he was suffering from *dropsy*, an abnormal accumulation of fluid in bodily tissues and cavities.

14:7–11 Jesus advised people not to rush for the best places at a feast. People today are just as eager to raise their social status, whether by being with the right people, dressing for success, or driving the right car. Whom do you try to impress? Rather than aiming for prestige, look for a place where you can serve. If God wants you to serve on a wider scale, he will invite you to take a higher place.

14:7–14 Jesus taught two lessons here. First, he spoke to the guests, telling them not to seek places of honor. Service is more important in God's kingdom than status. Second, he told the host not to be exclusive about whom he invites. God opens his kingdom to everyone.

14:11 How can we humble ourselves? Some people try to give the appearance of humility in order to manipulate others. Others think that humility means putting themselves down. Truly humble people compare themselves only with Christ, realize their sinfulness, and understand their limitations. On the other hand, they also recognize their gifts and strengths and are willing to use them as Christ directs. Humility is not self-degradation; it is realistic assessment and commitment to serve.

12Then Jesus said to his host, "When you give a luncheon or dinner, do not invite your friends, your brothers or relatives, or your rich neighbors; if you do, they may invite you back and so you will be repaid. 13But when you give a banquet, invite the poor, the crippled, the lame, the blind, w 14and you will be blessed. Although they cannot repay you, you will be repaid at the resurrection of the righteous." x

14:13
wver 21

14:14
xAc 24:15

Jesus Tells the Parable of the Great Feast (157)

15When one of those at the table with him heard this, he said to Jesus, "Blessed is the man who will eat at the feast y in the kingdom of God."

14:15
yRev 19:9

16Jesus replied: "A certain man was preparing a great banquet and invited many guests. 17At the time of the banquet he sent his servant to tell those who had been invited, 'Come, for everything is now ready.'

18"But they all alike began to make excuses. The first said, 'I have just bought a field, and I must go and see it. Please excuse me.'

19"Another said, 'I have just bought five yoke of oxen, and I'm on my way to try them out. Please excuse me.'

20"Still another said, 'I just got married, so I can't come.'

21"The servant came back and reported this to his master. Then the owner of the house became angry and ordered his servant, 'Go out quickly into the streets and alleys of the town and bring in the poor, the crippled, the blind and the lame.' z

14:21
zver 13

22"'Sir,' the servant said, 'what you ordered has been done, but there is still room.'

23"Then the master told his servant, 'Go out to the roads and country lanes and make them come in, so that my house will be full. 24I tell you, not one of those men who were invited will get a taste of my banquet.'" a

14:24
aMt 21:43;
Ac 13:46

Jesus Teaches about the Cost of Being a Disciple (158)

25Large crowds were traveling with Jesus, and turning to them he said: 26"If anyone comes to me and does not hate his father and mother, his wife and children, his brothers and sisters—yes, even his own life—he cannot be my disciple. b 27And anyone who does not carry his cross and follow me cannot be my disciple. c

14:26
bMt 10:37

14:27
cMt 10:38; Lk 9:23

28"Suppose one of you wants to build a tower. Will he not first sit down and estimate the cost to see if he has enough money to complete it? 29For if he lays the foundation and is not able to finish it, everyone who sees it will ridicule him, 30saying, 'This fellow began to build and was not able to finish.'

31"Or suppose a king is about to go to war against another king. Will he not first sit down and consider whether he is able with ten thousand men to oppose the one coming against

---

14:15-24 The man sitting at the table with Jesus envisioned the glory of God's kingdom, but he did not yet understand how to have a share in it. In Jesus' story, many people turned down the invitation to the banquet because the timing was inconvenient. We too can resist or delay responding to God's invitation, and our excuses may sound reasonable—work duties, family responsibilities, financial needs, or other reasons. Nevertheless, God's invitation is the most important event in our lives, no matter how inconveniently it may be timed. Are you making excuses to avoid responding to God's call? Jesus reminds us that the time will come when God will pull his invitation and offer it to others—then it will be too late to get into the banquet.

14:16ff The custom was to send two invitations to a party—the first to announce the event and the second to tell the guests that everything was ready. The guests in Jesus' story insulted the host by making excuses when he issued the second invitation. In Israel's history, God's first invitation came from Moses and the prophets; the second came from his Son. The religious leaders accepted the first invitation. They believed that God had called them to be his people, but they insulted God by refusing to accept his Son. Thus, as the master in the story sent his servant into the streets to invite the needy to his banquet, so God sent his Son to the whole world of needy people to tell them that God's kingdom had arrived and was ready for them.

14:16ff In this chapter we read Jesus' words against seeking status, and in favor of hard work and even suffering. Let us not

lose sight of the end result of all our humility and self-sacrifice—a joyous banquet with our Lord! God never asks us to suffer for the sake of suffering. He never asks us to give up something good unless he plans to replace it with something even better. Jesus is not calling us to join him in a labor camp but in a feast—the wedding supper of the Lamb (Revelation 19:6-9), when God and his beloved church will be joined forever.

14:27 Jesus' audience was well aware of what it meant to carry one's own cross. When the Romans led a criminal to his execution site, he was forced to carry the cross on which he would die. This showed his submission to Rome and warned observers that they had better submit too. Jesus made this statement to get the crowds to think through their enthusiasm for him. He encouraged those who were superficial either to go deeper or to turn back. Following Christ means total submission to him—perhaps even to the point of death. (See also the note on 9:23.)

14:28-30 When a builder doesn't count the cost or estimates it inaccurately, the building may be left uncompleted. Will you abandon the Christian life after a little while because you did not count the cost of commitment to Jesus? What are those costs? Christians may face loss of social status or wealth. They have to give up control over their money, their time, or their career. They may be hated, separated from their family, and even put to death. Following Christ does not mean a trouble-free life. We must carefully count the cost of becoming Christ's disciples so that we will know what we are getting into and won't be tempted later to turn back.

14:33
d Php 3:7, 8
14:34
e Mk 9:50
14:35
f Mt 5:13
g Mt 11:15

him with twenty thousand? 32 If he is not able, he will send a delegation while the other is still a long way off and will ask for terms of peace. 33 In the same way, any of you who does not give up everything he has cannot be my disciple. *d*

34 "Salt is good, but if it loses its saltiness, how can it be made salty again? *e* 35 It is fit neither for the soil nor for the manure pile; it is thrown out. *f*

"He who has ears to hear, let him hear." *g*

Jesus Tells the Parable of the Lost Sheep (*159*)

15:1
h Lk 5:29
15:2
i Mt 9:11

15 Now the tax collectors *h* and "sinners" were all gathering around to hear him. 2 But the Pharisees and the teachers of the law muttered, "This man welcomes sinners and eats with them." *i*

15:7
j ver 10

3 Then Jesus told them this parable: 4 "Suppose one of you has a hundred sheep and loses one of them. Does he not leave the ninety-nine in the open country and go after the lost sheep until he finds it? 5 And when he finds it, he joyfully puts it on his shoulders 6 and goes home. Then he calls his friends and neighbors together and says, 'Rejoice with me; I have found my lost sheep.' 7 I tell you that in the same way there will be more rejoicing in heaven over one sinner who repents than over ninety-nine righteous persons who do not need to repent. *j*

Jesus Tells the Parable of the Lost Coin (*160*)

15:10
k ver 7

8 "Or suppose a woman has ten silver coins *a* and loses one. Does she not light a lamp, sweep the house and search carefully until she finds it? 9 And when she finds it, she calls her friends and neighbors together and says, 'Rejoice with me; I have found my lost coin.' 10 In the same way, I tell you, there is rejoicing in the presence of the angels of God over one sinner who repents." *k*

Jesus Tells the Parable of the Lost Son (*161*)

15:11
l Mt 21:28
15:12
m Dt 21:17
n ver 30

11 Jesus continued: "There was a man who had two sons. *l* 12 The younger one said to his father, 'Father, give me my share of the estate.' *m* So he divided his property *n* between them.

13 "Not long after that, the younger son got together all he had, set off for a distant country and there squandered his wealth in wild living. 14 After he had spent everything, there was a

a 8 Greek *ten drachmas*, each worth about a day's wages

14:34 Salt can lose its flavor. When it gets wet and then dries, nothing is left but a tasteless residue. Many Christians blend into the world and avoid the cost of standing up for Christ. But Jesus says if Christians lose their distinctive saltiness, they become worthless. Just as salt flavors and preserves food, we are to preserve the good in the world, help keep it from spoiling, and bring new flavor to life. This requires careful planning, willing sacrifice, and unswerving commitment to Christ's kingdom. Being "salty" is not easy, but if a Christian fails in this function, he or she fails to represent Christ in the world. How salty are you?

15:2 Why were the Pharisees and teachers of the law bothered that Jesus associated with these people? The religious leaders were always careful to stay "clean" according to Old Testament law. In fact, they went well beyond the law in their avoidance of certain people and situations and in their ritual washings. By contrast, Jesus took their concept of "cleanness" lightly. He risked defilement by touching those who had leprosy and by neglecting to wash in the Pharisees' prescribed manner, and he showed complete disregard for their sanctions against associating with certain classes of people. He came to offer salvation to sinners, to show that God loves them. Jesus didn't worry about the accusations. Instead he continued going to those who needed him, regardless of the effect these rejected people might have on his reputation. How are you following Jesus' example?

15:3–6 It may seem foolish for the shepherd to leave 99 sheep to go search for just one. But the shepherd knew that the 99 would be safe in the sheepfold, whereas the lost sheep was in danger. Because each sheep was of high value, the shepherd knew that it was worthwhile to search diligently for the lost one. God's love for the individual is so great that he seeks each one out and rejoices when he or she is found. Jesus associated with

sinners because he wanted to bring the lost sheep—people considered beyond hope—the gospel of God's kingdom. Before you were a believer, God sought you; and he is still seeking those who are yet lost.

15:4, 5 We may be able to understand a God who would forgive sinners who come to him for mercy. But a God who tenderly searches for sinners and then joyfully forgives them must possess an extraordinary love! This is the kind of love that prompted Jesus to come to earth to search for lost people and save them. This is the kind of extraordinary love that God has for you.

15:8–10 Palestinian women received ten silver coins as a wedding gift. Besides their monetary value, these coins held sentimental value like that of a wedding ring, and to lose one would be extremely distressing. Just as a woman would rejoice at finding her lost coin, so the angels would rejoice over a repentant sinner. Each individual is precious to God. He grieves over every loss and rejoices whenever one of his children is found and brought into the kingdom. Perhaps we would have more joy in our churches if we shared Jesus' love and concern for the lost, diligently seeking them, and rejoicing when they come to the Savior.

15:12 The younger son's share of the estate would have been one-third, with the older son receiving two-thirds (Deuteronomy 21:17). In most cases he would have received this at his father's death, although fathers sometimes chose to divide up their inheritance early and retire from managing their estates. What is unusual here is that the younger one initiated the division of the estate. This showed arrogant disregard for his father's authority as head of the family.

severe famine in that whole country, and he began to be in need. ¹⁵So he went and hired himself out to a citizen of that country, who sent him to his fields to feed pigs. ¹⁶He longed to fill his stomach with the pods that the pigs were eating, but no one gave him anything.

¹⁷"When he came to his senses, he said, 'How many of my father's hired men have food to spare, and here I am starving to death! ¹⁸I will set out and go back to my father and say to him: Father, I have sinned against heaven and against you. ¹⁹I am no longer worthy to be called your son; make me like one of your hired men.' ²⁰So he got up and went to his father.

"But while he was still a long way off, his father saw him and was filled with compassion for him; he ran to his son, threw his arms around him and kissed him. *o*

²¹"The son said to him, 'Father, I have sinned against heaven and against you. *p* I am no longer worthy to be called your son. *a* '

²²"But the father said to his servants, 'Quick! Bring the best robe *q* and put it on him. Put a ring on his finger *r* and sandals on his feet. ²³Bring the fattened calf and kill it. Let's have a feast and celebrate. ²⁴For this son of mine was dead and is alive again; *s* he was lost and is found.' So they began to celebrate. *t*

²⁵"Meanwhile, the older son was in the field. When he came near the house, he heard music and dancing. ²⁶So he called one of the servants and asked him what was going on. ²⁷'Your brother has come,' he replied, 'and your father has killed the fattened calf because he has him back safe and sound.'

²⁸"The older brother became angry and refused to go in. So his father went out and pleaded with him. ²⁹But he answered his father, 'Look! All these years I've been slaving for you and never disobeyed your orders. Yet you never gave me even a young goat so I could celebrate with my friends. ³⁰But when this son of yours who has squandered your property *u* with prostitutes *v* comes home, you kill the fattened calf for him!'

³¹"'My son,' the father said, 'you are always with me, and everything I have is yours. ³²But we had to celebrate and be glad, because this brother of yours was dead and is alive again; he was lost and is found.'" *w*

Jesus Tells the Parable of the Shrewd Manager (162)

16 Jesus told his disciples: "There was a rich man whose manager was accused of wasting his possessions. *x* ²So he called him in and asked him, 'What is this I hear about you? Give an account of your management, because you cannot be manager any longer.'

a21 Some early manuscripts son. Make me like one of your hired men.

15:20 *o*Ge 45:14, 15; 46:29; Ac 20:37

15:21 *p*Ps 51:4

15:22 *q*Zec 3:4; Rev 6:11 *r*Ge 41:42

15:24 *s*Eph 2:1, 5; 5:14; 1Ti 5:6 *t*ver 32

15:30 *u*ver 12, 13 *v*Pr 29:3

15:32 *w*ver 24

16:1 *x*Lk 15:13, 30

15:15, 16 According to Moses' law, pigs were unclean animals (Leviticus 11:2–8; Deuteronomy 14:8). This meant that pigs could not be eaten or used for sacrifices. To protect themselves from defilement, Jews would not even touch pigs. For a Jew to stoop to feeding pigs was a great humiliation, and for this young man to eat food that the pigs had touched was to be degraded beyond belief. The younger son had truly sunk to the depths.

15:17 The younger son, like many who are rebellious and immature, wanted to be free to live as he pleased, and he had to hit bottom before he came to his senses. It often takes great sorrow and tragedy to cause people to look to the only One who can help them. Are you trying to live life your own way, selfishly pushing aside any responsibility or commitment that gets in your way? Stop and look before you hit bottom. You will save yourself and your family much grief.

15:20 In the two preceding stories, the seeker actively looked for the coin and the sheep, which could not return by themselves. In this story, the father watched and waited. He was dealing with a human being with a will of his own, but he was ready to greet his son if he returned. In the same way, God's love is constant and patient and welcoming. He will search for us and give us opportunities to respond, but he will not force us to come to him. Like the father in this story, God waits patiently for us to come to our senses.

15:24 The sheep was lost because it foolishly wandered away (15:4); the coin was lost through no fault of its own (15:8); and the son left out of selfishness (15:12). God's great love reaches out and finds sinners no matter why or how they got lost.

15:25–31 The older brother found great difficulty in accepting his younger brother when he returned, and it is just as difficult to accept "younger brothers" today. People who repent after leading notoriously sinful lives are often held in suspicion; churches are sometimes unwilling to admit them to membership. Instead, we should rejoice like the angels in heaven when an unbeliever repents and turns to God. Like the father, accept repentant sinners wholeheartedly and give them the support and encouragement that they need to grow in Christ.

15:30 In the story of the lost son, the father's response is contrasted with the older brother's. The father forgave because he was filled with love. The son refused to forgive because he was bitter. His resentment rendered him just as lost to the father's love as his younger brother had been. Don't let anything keep you from forgiving others. If you are refusing to forgive people, you are missing a wonderful opportunity to experience joy and share it with others. Make your joy grow: forgive somebody who has hurt you.

15:32 In Jesus' story, the older brother represents the Pharisees, who were angry and resentful that sinners were being welcomed into God's kingdom. After all, the Pharisees must have thought, we have sacrificed and done *so much* for God. How easy it is to resent God's gracious forgiveness of others whom we consider to be far worse sinners than ourselves. But when our self-righteousness gets in the way of rejoicing when others come to Jesus, we are no better than the Pharisees.

16:1–8 Our use of money is a good test of the lordship of Christ. (1) Money belongs to God, not us; let us use our resources wisely. (2) Money can be used for good or evil; let us use ours for good. (3) Money has a lot of power; let us use it carefully and thoughtfully. We must use our material goods in a way that will foster faith and obedience (see 12:33, 34).

3"The manager said to himself, 'What shall I do now? My master is taking away my job. I'm not strong enough to dig, and I'm ashamed to beg— 4I know what I'll do so that, when I lose my job here, people will welcome me into their houses.'

5"So he called in each one of his master's debtors. He asked the first, 'How much do you owe my master?'

6"'Eight hundred gallonsª of olive oil,' he replied.

"The manager told him, 'Take your bill, sit down quickly, and make it four hundred.'

7"Then he asked the second, 'And how much do you owe?'

"'A thousand bushelsᵇ of wheat,' he replied.

"He told him, 'Take your bill and make it eight hundred.'

8"The master commended the dishonest manager because he had acted shrewdly. For the people of this world are more shrewd in dealing with their own kind than are the people of the light. *y* 9I tell you, use worldly wealth to gain friends for yourselves, so that when it is gone, you will be welcomed into eternal dwellings. *z*

10"Whoever can be trusted with very little can also be trusted with much,ª and whoever is dishonest with very little will also be dishonest with much. 11So if you have not been trustworthy in handling worldly wealth, who will trust you with true riches? 12And if you have not been trustworthy with someone else's property, who will give you property of your own?

13"No servant can serve two masters. Either he will hate the one and love the other, or he will be devoted to the one and despise the other. You cannot serve both God and Money."ᵇ

14The Pharisees, who loved money, heard all this and were sneering at Jesus. *c* 15He said to them, "You are the ones who justify yourselves *d* in the eyes of men, but God knows your hearts. *e* What is highly valued among men is detestable in God's sight.

16"The Law and the Prophets were proclaimed until John. *f* Since that time, the good news of the kingdom of God is being preached, *g* and everyone is forcing his way into it. 17It is easier for heaven and earth to disappear than for the least stroke of a pen to drop out of the Law. *h*

18"Anyone who divorces his wife and marries another woman commits adultery, and the man who marries a divorced woman commits adultery. *i*

ª6 Greek *one hundred batous* (probably about 3 kiloliters)   ᵇ7 Greek *one hundred korous* (probably about 35 kiloliters)

16:8
y Jn 12:36; Eph 5:8; 1Th 5:5

16:9
z Mt 19:21

16:10
a Mt 25:21, 23

16:13
b Mt 6:24

16:14
c Lk 23:35

16:15
d Lk 10:29
e 1Sa 16:7

16:16
f Mt 11:12, 13
g Mt 4:23

16:17
h Mt 5:18

16:18
i Mt 5:31, 32; Mk 10:11; 1Co 7:10, 11

16:9 We are to make wise use of the financial opportunities we have, not to earn heaven, but so that heaven ("eternal dwellings") will be a welcome experience for those we help. If we use our money to help those in need or to help others find Christ, our earthly investment will bring eternal benefit. When we obey God's will, the unselfish use of possessions will follow.

16:10, 11 Our integrity often meets its match in money matters. God calls us to be honest even in small details we could easily rationalize away. Heaven's riches are far more valuable than earthly wealth. But if we are not trustworthy with our money here (no matter how much or little we have), we will be unfit to handle the vast riches of God's kingdom. Don't let your integrity slip in small matters, and it will not fail you in crucial decisions either.

16:13 Money can easily take God's place in your life. It can become your master. How can you tell if you are a slave to money? Ask yourself: Do I think and worry about it frequently? Do I give up doing what I should do or would like to do in order to make more money? Do I spend a great deal of my time caring for my possessions? Is it hard for me to give money away? Am I in debt?

Money is a hard and deceptive master. Wealth promises power and control, but often it cannot deliver. Great fortunes can be made—and lost—overnight, and no amount of money can provide health, happiness, or eternal life. How much better it is to let God be your Master. His servants have peace of mind and security, both now and forever.

16:14 Because the Pharisees loved money, they took exception to Jesus' teaching. We live in an age that measures people's worth by how much money they make. Do you laugh at Jesus' warnings against serving money? Do you try to explain them

away? Do you apply them to someone else? Unless we take Jesus' statements seriously, we may be acting like Pharisees ourselves.

16:15 The Pharisees acted piously to get praise from others, but God knew what was in their hearts. They considered their wealth to be a sign of God's approval. God detested their wealth because it caused them to abandon true spirituality. Though prosperity may earn people's praise, it must never substitute for devotion and service to God.

16:16, 17 John the Baptist's ministry was the dividing line between the Old and New Testaments (John 1:15–18). With the arrival of Jesus came the realization of all the prophets' hopes. Jesus emphasized that his kingdom fulfilled the law (the Old Testament); it did not cancel it (Matthew 5:17). His was not a new system but the culmination of the old. The same God who worked through Moses was working through Jesus.

16:18 Most religious leaders of Jesus' day permitted a man to divorce his wife for nearly any reason. Jesus' teaching about divorce went beyond Moses' (Deuteronomy 24:1–4). Stricter than any of the then-current schools of thought, Jesus' teachings shocked his hearers (see Matthew 19:10) just as they shake today's readers. Jesus says in no uncertain terms that marriage is a lifetime commitment. To leave your spouse for another person may be legal, but it is adultery in God's eyes. As you think about marriage, remember that God intends it to be a permanent commitment.

Jesus Tells about the Rich Man and the Beggar (163)

19"There was a rich man who was dressed in purple and fine linen and lived in luxury every day. 20At his gate was laid a beggar[i] named Lazarus, covered with sores 21and longing to eat what fell from the rich man's table. Even the dogs came and licked his sores.

22"The time came when the beggar died and the angels carried him to Abraham's side. The rich man also died and was buried. 23In hell,[a] where he was in torment, he looked up and saw Abraham far away, with Lazarus by his side. 24So he called to him, 'Father Abraham, have pity on me and send Lazarus to dip the tip of his finger in water and cool my tongue, because I am in agony in this fire.'

25"But Abraham replied, 'Son, remember that in your lifetime you received your good things, while Lazarus received bad things, but now he is comforted here and you are in agony.[k] 26And besides all this, between us and you a great chasm has been fixed, so that those who want to go from here to you cannot, nor can anyone cross over from there to us.'

27"He answered, 'Then I beg you, father, send Lazarus to my father's house, 28for I have five brothers. Let him warn them, so that they will not also come to this place of torment.'

29"Abraham replied, 'They have Moses[l] and the Prophets;[m] let them listen to them.'

30"'No, father Abraham,' he said, 'but if someone from the dead goes to them, they will repent.'

31"He said to him, 'If they do not listen to Moses and the Prophets, they will not be convinced even if someone rises from the dead.'"

Jesus Tells about Forgiveness and Faith (164)

17 Jesus said to his disciples: "Things that cause people to sin are bound to come, but woe to that person through whom they come.[n] 2It would be better for him to be thrown into the sea with a millstone tied around his neck than for him to cause one of these little ones to sin. 3So watch yourselves.

"If your brother sins, rebuke him,[o] and if he repents, forgive him. 4If he sins against you seven times in a day, and seven times comes back to you and says, 'I repent,' forgive him."[p]

5The apostles[q] said to the Lord, "Increase our faith!"

6He replied, "If you have faith as small as a mustard seed,[r] you can say to this mulberry tree, 'Be uprooted and planted in the sea,' and it will obey you.

a23 Greek *Hades*

16:20
iAc 3:2

16:25
kLk 6:21, 24, 25

16:29
lJn 5:45-47;
Ac 15:21
mLk 4:17

17:1
nMt 18:7

17:3
oMt 18:15

17:4
pMt 18:21, 22

17:5
qMk 6:30

17:6
rMt 17:20

16:19–31 The Pharisees considered wealth to be a proof of a person's righteousness. Jesus startled them with this story where a diseased beggar is rewarded and a rich man is punished. The rich man did not go to hell because of his wealth but because he was selfish, refusing to feed Lazarus, take him in, or care for him. The rich man was hardhearted in spite of his great blessings. The amount of money we have is not as important as the way we use it. What is your attitude toward your money and possessions? Do you hoard them selfishly, or do you use them to help others?

16:20 This Lazarus is merely a character in a story and should not be confused with the Lazarus whom Jesus raised from the dead in John 11.

16:29–31 The rich man thought that his five brothers would surely believe a messenger who had been raised from the dead. But Jesus said that if they did not believe Moses and the prophets, who spoke constantly of the duty to care for the poor, not even a resurrection would convince them. Notice the irony in Jesus' statement; on his way to Jerusalem to die, he was fully aware that even when he had risen from the dead, most of the religious leaders would not accept him. They were set in their ways, and neither Scripture nor God's Son himself would shake them loose.

17:1–3 Jesus warned about God's wrath for those who offend, abuse, or lead astray the little ones. Jesus warns off any predators who would hurt children in any way. How appropriate such a warning is in this day when corruption enters our homes every day in many television programs or on the Internet. While Christians must guard against physical abuse, they also must be aware of and work against the mental and spiritual corruption that unfiltered television and unsupervised Internet surfing can bring.

Jesus' warning envisions an additional group, however. The "little ones" can be new disciples. Indifference to the training and treatment of new Christians can leave them theologically vulnerable. Make the follow-through care of recent converts and new members a high priority in your church.

17:3, 4 To rebuke does not mean to point out every sin we see; it means to bring sin to a person's attention with the purpose of restoring him or her to God and to fellow humans. When you feel you must rebuke another Christian for a sin, check your attitudes before you speak. Do you love the person? Are you willing to forgive? Unless rebuke is tied to forgiveness, it will not help the sinning person.

17:5, 6 The disciples' request was genuine; they wanted the faith necessary for such radical forgiveness. But Jesus didn't directly answer their question because the amount of faith is not as important as its genuineness. What is faith? It is total dependence on God and a willingness to do his will. Faith is not something we use to put on a show for others. It is complete and humble obedience to God's will, readiness to do whatever he calls us to do. The amount of faith isn't as important as the right kind of faith—faith in our all-powerful God.

17:6 A mustard seed is small, but it is alive and growing. Like a tiny seed, a small amount of genuine faith in God will take root and grow. Almost invisible at first, the seed will begin to spread, first under the ground and then visibly. Although each change will be gradual and imperceptible, soon this faith will have produced major results that will uproot and destroy competing loyalties. We don't need more faith; a tiny seed of faith is enough, if it is alive and growing.

17:8
sLk 12:37

7"Suppose one of you had a servant plowing or looking after the sheep. Would he say to the servant when he comes in from the field, 'Come along now and sit down to eat'? 8 Would he not rather say, 'Prepare my supper, get yourself ready and wait on me s while I eat and drink; after that you may eat and drink'? 9 Would he thank the servant because he did what he was told to do? 10 So you also, when you have done everything you were told to do, should say, 'We are unworthy servants; we have only done our duty.'"

Jesus Heals Ten Men with Leprosy (169)

17:11
tLk 9:51
uJn 4:3, 4

17:12
vLev 13:45, 46

17:14
wMt 8:4

17:15
xMt 9:8

17:16
yMt 10:5

17:19
zMt 9:22

11Now on his way to Jerusalem, t Jesus traveled along the border between Samaria and Galilee. u 12As he was going into a village, ten men who had leprosya met him. They stood at a distance v 13and called out in a loud voice, "Jesus, Master, have pity on us!"

14When he saw them, he said, "Go, show yourselves to the priests." w And as they went, they were cleansed.

15One of them, when he saw he was healed, came back, praising God x in a loud voice. 16He threw himself at Jesus' feet and thanked him—and he was a Samaritan. y

17Jesus asked, "Were not all ten cleansed? Where are the other nine? 18 Was no one found to return and give praise to God except this foreigner?" 19Then he said to him, "Rise and go; your faith has made you well." z

Jesus Teaches about the Coming of the Kingdom of God (170)

17:21
aver 23

17:22
bMt 9:15

20Once, having been asked by the Pharisees when the kingdom of God would come, Jesus replied, "The kingdom of God does not come with your careful observation, 21 nor will people say, 'Here it is,' or 'There it is,' a because the kingdom of God is within b you."

22Then he said to his disciples, "The time is coming when you will long to see one of the days of the Son of Man, but you will not see it. b 23 Men will tell you, 'There he is!' or 'Here he

a 12 The Greek word was used for various diseases affecting the skin—not necessarily leprosy.   b 21 Or among

---

17:7-10 If we have obeyed God, we have only done our duty and we should regard it as a privilege. Do you sometimes feel that you deserve extra credit for serving God? Remember, obedience is not something extra we do; it is our duty. Jesus is not rendering our service as meaningless or useless, nor is he doing away with rewards. He is attacking unwarranted self-esteem and spiritual pride.

17:11-14 Because leprosy was contagious, people who had leprosy were required to try to stay away from other people and to announce their presence if they had to come near. Sometimes leprosy would go into remission. If a leper thought his leprosy had gone away, he was supposed to present himself to a priest who could declare him clean (Leviticus 14). Jesus sent the ten lepers to the priest *before* they were healed—and they went! They responded in faith, and Jesus healed them on the way. Is your trust in God so strong that you act on what he says even before you see evidence that it will work?

17:16 Jesus healed all ten lepers, but only one returned to thank him. It is possible to receive God's great gifts with an ungrateful spirit—nine of the ten men did so. Only the thankful man, however, learned that his faith had played a role in his healing; and only grateful Christians grow in understanding God's grace. God does not demand that we thank him, but he is pleased when we do so. And he uses our responsiveness to teach us more about himself.

17:16 Not only was this man a leper, he was also a Samaritan—a race despised by the Jews as idolatrous half-breeds (see the note on 10:33). Once again Luke is pointing out that God's grace is for everybody.

17:20, 21 The Pharisees asked when God's kingdom would come, not knowing that it had already arrived. The kingdom of God is not like an earthly kingdom with geographical boundaries. Instead, it begins with the work of God's Spirit in people's lives and in relationships. Still today we must resist looking to institutions or programs for evidence of the progress of God's kingdom. Instead, we should look for what God is doing in people's hearts.

17:23, 24 Many will claim to be the Messiah and many will claim that Jesus has returned—and people will believe them. Jesus

warns us never to take such reports seriously, no matter how convincing they may sound. When Jesus returns, his power and presence will be evident to everyone. No one will need to spread the message because all will see for themselves.

17:23-36 Life will be going on as usual on the day Christ returns. No warning will sound. Most people will be going about their everyday tasks, indifferent to the demands of God. They will be as surprised by Christ's return as the people in Noah's day were by the flood (Genesis 6—8) or the people in Lot's day by the destruction of Sodom (Genesis 19). We don't know the time of Christ's return, but we do know that he is coming. He may come today, tomorrow, or centuries in the future. Whenever Christ comes, we must be morally and spiritually ready. Live as if Jesus were returning today.

LAST TRIP FROM GALILEE
Jesus left Galilee for the last time—he would not return before his death. He passed through Samaria, met and healed 10 men who had leprosy, and continued to Jerusalem. He spent some time east of the Jordan (Mark 10:1) before going to Jericho (Luke 19:1).

is!' Do not go running off after them. c 24 For the Son of Man in his daya will be like the lightning,d which flashes and lights up the sky from one end to the other. 25 But first he must suffer many things and be rejected e by this generation.

26 "Just as it was in the days of Noah,f so also will it be in the days of the Son of Man. 27 People were eating, drinking, marrying and being given in marriage up to the day Noah entered the ark. Then the flood came and destroyed them all.

28 "It was the same in the days of Lot. People were eating and drinking, buying and selling, planting and building. 29 But the day Lot left Sodom, fire and sulfur rained down from heaven and destroyed them all.

30 "It will be just like this on the day the Son of Man is revealed.g 31 On that day no one who is on the roof of his house, with his goods inside, should go down to get them. Likewise, no one in the field should go back for anything. h 32 Remember Lot's wife!i 33 Whoever tries to keep his life will lose it, and whoever loses his life will preserve it. 34 I tell you, on that night two people will be in one bed; one will be taken and the other left. 35 Two women will be grinding grain together; one will be taken and the other left.b "j

37 "Where, Lord?" they asked.

He replied, "Where there is a dead body, there the vultures will gather."k

Jesus Tells the Parable of the Persistent Widow (171)

18 Then Jesus told his disciples a parable to show them that they should always pray and not give up. l 2 He said: "In a certain town there was a judge who neither feared God nor cared about men. 3 And there was a widow in that town who kept coming to him with the plea, 'Grant me justice against my adversary.'

4 "For some time he refused. But finally he said to himself, 'Even though I don't fear God or care about men, 5 yet because this widow keeps bothering me, I will see that she gets justice, so that she won't eventually wear me out with her coming!'"m

6 And the Lord said, "Listen to what the unjust judge says. 7 And will not God bring about justice for his chosen ones, who cry outn to him day and night? Will he keep putting them off? 8 I tell you, he will see that they get justice, and quickly. However, when the Son of Man comes, will he find faith on the earth?"

Jesus Tells the Parable of Two Men Who Prayed (172)

9 To some who were confident of their own righteousnesso and looked down on everybody else, Jesus told this parable: 10 "Two men went up to the temple to pray, one a Pharisee and the other a tax collector. 11 The Pharisee stood upp and prayed aboutc himself: 'God, I thank you that I am not like other men—robbers, evildoers, adulterers—or even like this tax collector. 12 I fastq twice a week and give a tenthr of all I get.'

Cross references:

17:23
c Mt 24:23;
Mk 13:21; Lk 21:8

17:24
d Mt 24:27

17:25
e Lk 9:22

17:26
f Ge 7:6-24

17:30
g 2Th 1:7

17:31
h Mt 24:17, 18;
Mk 13:15-16

17:32
i Ge 19:26

17:35
j Mt 24:41

17:37
k Mt 24:28

18:1
l Lk 11:5-8

18:5
m Lk 11:8

18:7
n Rev 6:10

18:9
o Lk 16:15

18:11
p Mk 11:25

18:12
q Mt 9:14
r Lk 11:42

a24 Some manuscripts do not have *in his day*.   b35 Some manuscripts *left. 36Two men will be in the field; one will be taken and the other left*.   c11 Or *to*

17:26–35 Jesus warned against false security. We are to abandon the values and attachments of this world in order to be ready for Christ's return. His return will happen suddenly, and when he comes, there will be no second chances. Some will be taken to be with him; the rest will be left behind.

17:33 Those clinging to this life are those seeking to escape physical persecution. Those who live for themselves display these common attitudes: (1) *Materialism*—I want it and work hard to get it. All that I see is real. Unseen things are merely ideas and dreams.(2) *Individualism*—I work hard for me, and you work hard for you. I may make it; you may not. That's your problem, not mine.(3) *Skepticism*—Anything I'm not convinced about can't be important. Everything important to know I can figure out.

Those who have these attitudes may protect themselves, but they will lose the spiritual dimension to their lives. Keep your commitment to Christ at full strength. Then you'll be ready when he returns.

17:37 To answer the disciples' question, Jesus quoted a familiar proverb. One vulture circling overhead does not mean much, but a gathering of vultures means that a carcass is nearby. Likewise, one sign of the end may not be significant, but when many signs occur, the second coming is near.

18:1 To persist in prayer and not give up does not mean endless repetition or painfully long prayer sessions. Always praying means keeping our requests constantly before God as we live for him day by day, believing he will answer. When we live by faith, we are not to give up. God may delay answering, but his delays always have good reasons. As we persist in prayer we grow in character, faith, and hope.

18:3 Widows and orphans were among the most vulnerable of all God's people, and both Old Testament prophets and New Testament apostles insisted that these needy people be properly cared for. See, for example, Exodus 22:22–24; Isaiah 1:17; 1 Timothy 5:3; James 1:27.

18:6, 7 If unjust judges respond to constant pressure, how much more will a great and loving God respond to us? If we know he loves us, we can believe he will hear our cries for help.

18:10 The people who lived near Jerusalem often would go to the temple to pray. The temple was the center of their worship.

18:11–14 The Pharisee did not go to the temple to pray to God but to announce to all within earshot how good he was. The tax collector went recognizing his sin and begging for mercy. Self-righteousness is dangerous. It leads to pride, causes a person to despise others, and prevents him or her

18:13
s Lk 23:48

13 "But the tax collector stood at a distance. He would not even look up to heaven, but beat his breast s and said, 'God, have mercy on me, a sinner.'

18:14
t Mt 23:12; Lk 14:11

14 "I tell you that this man, rather than the other, went home justified before God. For everyone who exalts himself will be humbled, and he who humbles himself will be exalted." t

Jesus Blesses the Children (174/Matthew 19:13–15; Mark 10:13–16)

15 People were also bringing babies to Jesus to have him touch them. When the disciples saw this, they rebuked them. 16 But Jesus called the children to him and said, "Let the little children come to me, and do not hinder them, for the kingdom of God belongs to such as these. 17 I tell you the truth, anyone who will not receive the kingdom of God like a little child u will never enter it."

18:17
u Mt 18:3

Jesus Speaks to the Rich Young Man (175/Matthew 19:16–30; Mark 10:17–31)

18:18
v Lk 10:25

18 A certain ruler asked him, "Good teacher, what must I do to inherit eternal life?" v

18:20
w Ex 20:12-16;
Dt 5:16-20; Ro 13:9

19 "Why do you call me good?" Jesus answered. "No one is good—except God alone. 20 You know the commandments: 'Do not commit adultery, do not murder, do not steal, do not give false testimony, honor your father and mother.'a " w

21 "All these I have kept since I was a boy," he said.

18:22
x Mt 6:20

22 When Jesus heard this, he said to him, "You still lack one thing. Sell everything you have and give to the poor, and you will have treasure in heaven. x Then come, follow me."

18:24
y Pr 11:28

23 When he heard this, he became very sad, because he was a man of great wealth. 24 Jesus looked at him and said, "How hard it is for the rich to enter the kingdom of God! y 25 Indeed, it is easier for a camel to go through the eye of a needle than for a rich man to enter the kingdom of God."

26 Those who heard this asked, "Who then can be saved?"

18:27
z Mt 19:26

27 Jesus replied, "What is impossible with men is possible with God." z

28 Peter said to him, "We have left all we had to follow you!"

18:30
a Mt 12:32

29 "I tell you the truth," Jesus said to them, "no one who has left home or wife or brothers or parents or children for the sake of the kingdom of God 30 will fail to receive many times as much in this age and, in the age to come, a eternal life."

a 20 Exodus 20:12-16; Deut. 5:16-20

---

from learning anything from God. The tax collector's prayer should be our prayer because we all need God's mercy everyday. Don't let pride in your achievements cut you off from God.

18:15, 16 It was customary for a mother to bring her children to a rabbi for a blessing, and that is why these mothers gathered around Jesus. The disciples, however, thought the children were unworthy of the Master's time—less important than whatever else he was doing. But Jesus welcomed them, because little children have the kind of faith and trust needed to enter God's kingdom. It is important that we introduce our children to Jesus.

18:17 How does someone "receive the kingdom of God like a little child"? It means having the simple, trusting attitude that children show to adults on whom they depend. Jesus wants his people to enjoy prayer by delighting in his company, find ways in a busy day to read the Bible enthusiastically, seek God's help in any problem, rely on him for guidance, and trust him explicitly. Children do all that with adults who love them. How much more should believers have that attitude toward Jesus, who loves them.

18:18ff This ruler sought reassurance, some way of knowing for sure that he had eternal life. He wanted Jesus to measure and grade his qualifications, or to give him some task he could do to assure his own immortality. So Jesus gave him a task—the one thing the rich ruler knew he could not do. "Who then can be saved?" the bystanders asked. "No one can, by his or her own achievements," Jesus' answer implied. "What is impossible with men is possible with God." Salvation cannot be earned—it is God's gift (see Ephesians 2:8–10).

18:18, 19 Jesus' question to the ruler who came and called him "Good teacher" was, in essence, "Do you know who I am?" Undoubtedly the man did not catch the implications of Jesus' reply—that the man was right in calling him good because Jesus truly is God.

18:22, 23 This man's wealth made his life comfortable and gave him power and prestige. By telling him to sell everything he owned, Jesus was touching the very basis of his security and identity. The man did not understand that he would be even more secure if he followed Jesus than he was with all his wealth. Jesus does not ask all believers to sell everything they have, although this may be his will for some. He does ask us all, however, to get rid of anything that has become more important than God. If your basis for security has shifted from God to what you own, it would be better for you to get rid of those possessions.

18:26–30 Peter and the other disciples had paid a high price—leaving their homes and jobs—to follow Jesus. But Jesus reminded Peter that following him has its benefits as well as its sacrifices. Any believer who has had to give up something to follow Christ will be repaid in this life as well as in the next. For example, if you must give up a secure job, you will find that God offers a secure relationship with himself now and forever. If you must give up your family's approval, you will gain the love of the family of God. The disciples had begun to pay the price of following Jesus, and Jesus said they would be rewarded. Don't dwell on what you have given up; think about what you have gained and give thanks for it. You can never outgive God.

Jesus Predicts His Death the Third Time (177/Matthew 20:17–19; Mark 10:32–34)

31 Jesus took the Twelve aside and told them, "We are going up to Jerusalem,[b] and everything that is written by the prophets[c] about the Son of Man will be fulfilled. 32 He will be handed over to the Gentiles.[d] They will mock him, insult him, spit on him, flog him[e] and kill him. 33 On the third day he will rise again."

34 The disciples did not understand any of this. Its meaning was hidden from them, and they did not know what he was talking about.[f]

Jesus Heals a Blind Beggar (179/Matthew 20:29–34; Mark 10:46–52)

35 As Jesus approached Jericho, a blind man was sitting by the roadside begging. 36 When he heard the crowd going by, he asked what was happening. 37 They told him, "Jesus of Nazareth is passing by."

38 He called out, "Jesus, Son of David,[g] have mercy on me!"

39 Those who led the way rebuked him and told him to be quiet, but he shouted all the more, "Son of David, have mercy on me!"

40 Jesus stopped and ordered the man to be brought to him. When he came near, Jesus asked him, 41 "What do you want me to do for you?"

"Lord, I want to see," he replied.

42 Jesus said to him, "Receive your sight; your faith has healed you."[h] 43 Immediately he received his sight and followed Jesus, praising God. When all the people saw it, they also praised God.[i]

Jesus Brings Salvation to Zacchaeus's Home (180)

19 Jesus entered Jericho[j] and was passing through. 2 A man was there by the name of Zacchaeus; he was a chief tax collector and was wealthy. 3 He wanted to see who Jesus was, but being a short man he could not, because of the crowd. 4 So he ran ahead and climbed a sycamore-fig[k] tree to see him, since Jesus was coming that way.

5 When Jesus reached the spot, he looked up and said to him, "Zacchaeus, come down immediately. I must stay at your house today." 6 So he came down at once and welcomed him gladly.

7 All the people saw this and began to mutter, "He has gone to be the guest of a 'sinner.'"[l]

8 But Zacchaeus stood up and said to the Lord,[m] "Look, Lord! Here and now I give half of my possessions to the poor, and if I have cheated anybody out of anything, I will pay back four times the amount."[n]

9 Jesus said to him, "Today salvation has come to this house, because this man, too, is a son of Abraham.[o] 10 For the Son of Man came to seek and to save what was lost."

18:31
[b] Lk 9:51
[c] Ps 22

18:32
[d] Lk 23:1
[e] Mt 16:21

18:34
[f] Mk 9:32; Lk 9:45

18:38
[g] Mt 9:27

18:42
[h] Mt 9:22

18:43
[i] Mt 9:8

19:1
[j] Lk 18:35

19:4
[k] 1Ki 10:27; 1Ch 27:28

19:7
[l] Mt 9:11

19:8
[m] Lk 7:13
[n] Ex 22:1; Lev 6:4, 5; Nu 5:7; 2Sa 12:6

19:9
[o] Lk 3:8; 13:16; Ro 4:16; Gal 3:7

18:31-34 Some predictions about what would happen to Jesus are found in Psalm 41:9 (betrayal); Psalm 22:16–18 and Isaiah 53:4–7 (crucifixion); Psalm 16:10 (resurrection). The disciples didn't understand Jesus, apparently because they were focusing on what he had said about his death and were ignoring what he had said about his resurrection. Even though Jesus had spoken plainly, they would not grasp the significance of his words until they saw the risen Christ face to face.

18:35 Beggars often would wait along the roads near cities because that was where they could contact the most people. Usually disabled in some way, beggars were unable to earn a living. Medical help was not available for their problems, and people tended to ignore their obligation to care for the needy (Leviticus 25:35–38). Thus beggars had little hope of escaping their degrading way of life. But this blind beggar took hope in the Messiah. He shamelessly cried out for Jesus' attention, and Jesus said that his faith allowed him to see. No matter how desperate your situation may seem, if you call out to Jesus in faith, he will help you.

18:38 The blind man called Jesus "Son of David," a title for the Messiah (Isaiah 11:1–3). This means that he understood Jesus to be the long-awaited Messiah. A poor and blind beggar could *see* that Jesus was the Messiah, while the religious leaders who saw his miracles were blinded to his identity and refused to recognize him as the Messiah.

19:1-10 To finance their great world empire, the Romans levied heavy taxes on all nations under their control. The Jews opposed these taxes because they supported a secular government and its pagan gods, but they were still forced to pay. Tax collectors were among the most unpopular people in Israel. Jews by birth, they chose to work for Rome and were considered traitors. Besides, it was common knowledge that tax collectors were making themselves rich by gouging their fellow Jews. No wonder the people muttered when Jesus went home with the tax collector Zacchaeus. But despite the fact that Zacchaeus was both a cheater and a turncoat, Jesus loved him; and in response, the little tax collector was converted. In every society, certain groups of people are considered "untouchable" because of their political views, their immoral behavior, or their lifestyle. We should not give in to social pressure to avoid these people. Jesus loves them, and they need to hear his Good News.

19:8 Judging from the crowd's reaction to him, Zacchaeus must have been a very crooked tax collector. After he met Jesus, however, he realized that his life needed straightening out. By giving to the poor and making restitution—with generous interest—to those he had cheated, Zacchaeus demonstrated inward change by outward action. Following Jesus in your head or heart alone is not enough. You must show your faith by changed behavior. Has your faith resulted in action? What changes do you need to make?

19:9, 10 When Jesus said Zacchaeus was a son of Abraham and yet was lost, he must have shocked his hearers in at least two

Jesus Tells the Parable of the King's Ten Servants (181)

19:11
P Ac 1:6

[11] While they were listening to this, he went on to tell them a parable, because he was near Jerusalem and the people thought that the kingdom of God was going to appear at once. *P* [12] He said: "A man of noble birth went to a distant country to have himself appointed king and then to return. [13] So he called ten of his servants and gave them ten minas. *a* 'Put this money to work,' he said, 'until I come back.'

[14] "But his subjects hated him and sent a delegation after him to say, 'We don't want this man to be our king.'

[15] "He was made king, however, and returned home. Then he sent for the servants to whom he had given the money, in order to find out what they had gained with it.

[16] "The first one came and said, 'Sir, your mina has earned ten more.'

19:17
q Lk 16:10

[17] "'Well done, my good servant!' his master replied. 'Because you have been trustworthy in a very small matter, take charge of ten cities.' *q*

[18] "The second came and said, 'Sir, your mina has earned five more.'

[19] "His master answered, 'You take charge of five cities.'

19:21
r Mt 25:24

[20] "Then another servant came and said, 'Sir, here is your mina; I have kept it laid away in a piece of cloth. [21] I was afraid of you, because you are a hard man. You take out what you did not put in and reap what you did not sow.' *r*

19:22
s 2Sa 1:16; Job 15:6
t Mt 25:26

[22] "His master replied, 'I will judge you by your own words, *s* you wicked servant! You knew, did you, that I am a hard man, taking out what I did not put in, and reaping what I did not sow? *t* [23] Why then didn't you put my money on deposit, so that when I came back, I could have collected it with interest?'

[24] "Then he said to those standing by, 'Take his mina away from him and give it to the one who has ten minas.'

[25] "'Sir,' they said, 'he already has ten!'

a 13 A mina was about three months' wages.

---

ways. They would not have liked to acknowledge that this unpopular tax collector was a fellow son of Abraham, and they would not have wished to admit that sons of Abraham could be lost. But a person is not saved by a good heritage or condemned by a bad one; faith is more important than genealogy. Jesus still loves to bring the lost into his kingdom, regardless of their background or previous way of life. Through faith, the lost can be forgiven and made new.

19:11ff The people still hoped for a political leader who would set up an earthly kingdom and get rid of Roman domination. Jesus' parable showed that his kingdom would not take this form right away. First he would go away for a while, and his followers would need to be faithful and productive during his absence. Upon his return, Jesus would inaugurate a kingdom more powerful and just than anything they could expect or imagine.

19:11ff This story showed Jesus' followers what they were to do during the time between Jesus' departure and his second coming. Because we live in that time period, it applies directly to us. We have been given excellent resources to build and expand God's kingdom. Jesus expects us to use these talents so that they multiply and the kingdom grows. He asks each of us to account for what we do with his gifts. While awaiting the coming of the kingdom of God in glory, we must do Christ's work.

19:20–27 Why was the king so hard on this man who had not increased the money? He punished the man because (1) he didn't share his master's interest in the kingdom; (2) he didn't trust his master's intentions; (3) his only concern was for himself, and (4) he did nothing to use the money. Like the king in this story, God has given you gifts to use for the benefit of his kingdom. Do you want the kingdom to grow? Do you trust God to govern it fairly? Are you as concerned for others' welfare as you are for your own? Are you willing to use faithfully what he has entrusted to you?

26"He replied, 'I tell you that to everyone who has, more will be given, but as for the one who has nothing, even what he has will be taken away.*u* 27But those enemies of mine who did not want me to be king over them—bring them here and kill them in front of me.'"

19:26
*u*Mt 13:12; 25:29;
Lk 8:18

3. Jesus' ministry in Jerusalem
Jesus Rides into Jerusalem on a Young Donkey
(183/Matthew 21:1–11; Mark 11:1–11; John 12:12–19)

28After Jesus had said this, he went on ahead, going up to Jerusalem.*v* 29As he approached Bethphage and Bethany at the hill called the Mount of Olives,*w* he sent two of his disciples, saying to them, 30"Go to the village ahead of you, and as you enter it, you will find a colt tied there, which no one has ever ridden. Untie it and bring it here. 31If anyone asks you, 'Why are you untying it?' tell him, 'The Lord needs it.'"

19:28
*v*Mk 10:32
19:29
*w*Mt 21:1

32Those who were sent ahead went and found it just as he had told them. 33As they were untying the colt, its owners asked them, "Why are you untying the colt?"

34They replied, "The Lord needs it."

35They brought it to Jesus, threw their cloaks on the colt and put Jesus on it. 36As he went along, people spread their cloaks*x* on the road.

19:36
*x*2Ki 9:13

37When he came near the place where the road goes down the Mount of Olives, the whole crowd of disciples began joyfully to praise God in loud voices for all the miracles they had seen:

38 "Blessed is the king who comes in the name of the Lord!"*a**y*

"Peace in heaven and glory in the highest!"*z*

19:38
*y*Ps 118:26;
Lk 13:35
*z*Lk 2:14

39Some of the Pharisees in the crowd said to Jesus, "Teacher, rebuke your disciples!"*a*

40"I tell you," he replied, "if they keep quiet, the stones will cry out."*b*

41As he approached Jerusalem and saw the city, he wept over it*c* 42and said, "If you, even you, had only known on this day what would bring you peace—but now it is hidden from your eyes. 43The days will come upon you when your enemies will build an embankment

19:39
*a*Mt 21:15, 16
19:40
*b*Hab 2:11
19:41
*c*Lk 13:34, 35

a38 Psalm 118:26

19:30–35 By this time Jesus was extremely well known. Everyone coming to Jerusalem for the Passover feast had heard of him, and, for a time, the popular mood was favorable toward him. "The Lord needs it" was all the disciples had to say, and the colt's owners gladly turned their animal over to them.

19:35–38 Christians celebrate this event on Palm Sunday. The people lined the road, praising God, waving palm branches, and throwing their cloaks in front of the colt as it passed before them. "Long live the King" was the meaning behind their joyful shouts, because they knew that Jesus was intentionally fulfilling the prophecy in Zechariah 9:9: "See, your king comes to you, righ-

LAST WEEK IN JERUSALEM
As they approached Jerusalem from Jericho (19:1), Jesus and the disciples came to the villages of Bethany and Bethphage, nestled on the eastern slope of the Mount of Olives, only a few miles outside Jerusalem. Jesus stayed in Bethany during the nights of that last week, entering Jerusalem during the day.

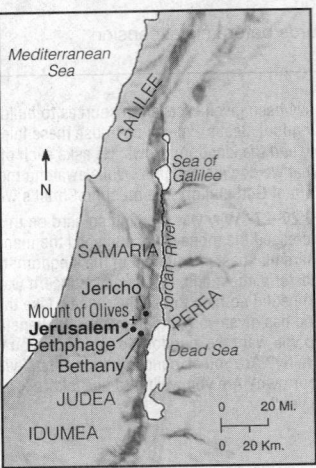

teous and having salvation, gentle and riding on a donkey, on a colt, the foal of a donkey." To announce that he was indeed the Messiah, Jesus chose a *time* when all Israel would be gathered at Jerusalem, a *place* where huge crowds could see him, and a *way* of proclaiming his mission that was unmistakable. The people went wild. They were sure their liberation was at hand.

19:38 The people who were praising God for giving them a king had the wrong idea about Jesus. They expected him to be a national leader who would restore their nation to its former glory; thus, they were deaf to the words of their prophets and blind to Jesus' real mission. When it became apparent that Jesus was not going to fulfill their hopes, many people would turn against him.

19:39, 40 The Pharisees thought the crowd's words were sacrilegious and blasphemous. They didn't want someone challenging their power and authority, and they didn't want a revolt that would bring the Roman army down on them. So they asked Jesus to keep his people quiet. But Jesus said that if the people were quiet, the stones would immediately cry out. Why? Not because Jesus was setting up a powerful political kingdom, but because he was establishing God's eternal kingdom, a reason for the greatest celebration of all.

19:41–44 The Jewish leaders had rejected their King (19:47). They had gone too far. They had refused God's offer of salvation in Jesus Christ when they were visited by God himself ("the time of God's coming"), and soon their nation would suffer. God did not turn away from the Jewish people who obeyed him, however. He continues to offer salvation to the people he loves, both Jews and Gentiles. Eternal life is within your reach—accept it while the opportunity is still offered.

19:43, 44 About 40 years after Jesus said these words, they came true. In A.D. 66, the Jews revolted against Roman control. Three years later Titus, son of the Emperor Vespasian, was sent to crush the rebellion. Roman soldiers attacked Jerusalem and broke through the northern wall but still couldn't take the city.

against you and encircle you and hem you in on every side. *d* 44 They will dash you to the ground, you and the children within your walls. They will not leave one stone on another, *e* because you did not recognize the time of God's coming *f* to you."

Jesus Clears the Temple Again (*184*/Matthew 21:12–17; Mark 11:12–19)

45 Then he entered the temple area and began driving out those who were selling. 46 "It is written," he said to them, "'My house will be a house of prayer' *a*; *g* but you have made it 'a den of robbers.' *b* " *h*

47 Every day he was teaching at the temple. *i* But the chief priests, the teachers of the law and the leaders among the people were trying to kill him. *j* 48 Yet they could not find any way to do it, because all the people hung on his words.

Religious Leaders Challenge Jesus' Authority (*189*/Matthew 21:23–27; Mark 11:27–33)

20 One day as he was teaching the people in the temple courts *k* and preaching the gospel, *l* the chief priests and the teachers of the law, together with the elders, came up to him. 2 "Tell us by what authority you are doing these things," they said. "Who gave you this authority?" *m*

3 He replied, "I will also ask you a question. Tell me, 4 John's baptism—was it from heaven, or from men?"

5 They discussed it among themselves and said, "If we say, 'From heaven,' he will ask, 'Why didn't you believe him?' 6 But if we say, 'From men,' all the people will stone us, because they are persuaded that John was a prophet."

7 So they answered, "We don't know where it was from."

8 Jesus said, "Neither will I tell you by what authority I am doing these things."

Jesus Tells the Parable of the Evil Farmers (*191*/Matthew 21:33–46; Mark 12:1–12)

9 He went on to tell the people this parable: "A man planted a vineyard, rented it to some farmers and went away for a long time. 10 At harvest time he sent a servant to the tenants so they would give him some of the fruit of the vineyard. But the tenants beat him and sent him away empty-handed. 11 He sent another servant, but that one also they beat and treated shamefully and sent away empty-handed. 12 He sent still a third, and they wounded him and threw him out.

13 "Then the owner of the vineyard said, 'What shall I do? I will send my son, whom I love; perhaps they will respect him.'

14 "But when the tenants saw him, they talked the matter over. 'This is the heir,' they said. 'Let's kill him, and the inheritance will be ours.' 15 So they threw him out of the vineyard and killed him.

"What then will the owner of the vineyard do to them? 16 He will come and kill those tenants *n* and give the vineyard to others."

When the people heard this, they said, "May this never be!"

17 Jesus looked directly at them and asked, "Then what is the meaning of that which is written:

a46 Isaiah 56:7   *b46* Jer. 7:11

**Marginal references:**

19:43
d Isa 29:3; Jer 6:6; Eze 4:2; Lk 21:20

19:44
e Mt 24:2; Mk 13:2; Lk 21:6
f 1Pe 2:12

19:46
g Isa 56:7
h Jer 7:11

19:47
i Mt 26:55
j Mk 11:18

20:1
k Mt 26:55
l Lk 8:1

20:2
m Ac 4:7; 7:27

20:16
n Lk 19:27

Finally they laid siege to it, and in A.D. 70 they were able to enter the severely weakened city and burn it. Six hundred thousand Jews were killed during Titus's onslaught.

19:47 Who were the "leaders among the people"? This group probably included wealthy leaders in politics, commerce, and law. They had several reasons for wanting to get rid of Jesus. He had damaged business in the temple by driving the merchants out. In addition, he was preaching against injustice, and his teachings often favored the poor over the rich. Further, his great popularity was in danger of attracting Rome's attention, and the leaders of Israel wanted as little as possible to do with Rome.

20:1–8 This group of leaders wanted to get rid of Jesus, so they tried to trap him with their question. If Jesus would answer that his authority came from God—if he stated openly that he was the Messiah and the Son of God—they would accuse him of blasphemy and bring him to trial. Jesus did not let himself be caught.

Instead, he turned the question on them. Thus he exposed their motives and avoided their trap.

20:9–16 The characters in this story are easily identified. Even the religious leaders understood it. The owner of the vineyard is God; the vineyard is Israel; the tenants are the religious leaders; the servants are the prophets and priests God sent to Israel; the son is the Messiah, Jesus; and the others are the Gentiles. Jesus' parable indirectly answered the religious leaders' question about his authority; it also showed them that he knew about their plan to kill him.

20:17–19 Quoting Psalm 118:22, Jesus showed the unbelieving leaders that even their rejection of the Messiah had been prophesied in Scripture. Ignoring the capstone, or cornerstone, was dangerous. A person could be tripped or crushed (judged and punished). Jesus' comments were veiled, but the religious leaders had no trouble interpreting them. They immediately wanted to arrest him.

> "'The stone the builders rejected
> has become the capstone[a] '[b]?[o]

20:17
oPs 118:22

18 Everyone who falls on that stone will be broken to pieces, but he on whom it falls will be crushed."

19 The teachers of the law and the chief priests looked for a way to arrest him[p] immediately, because they knew he had spoken this parable against them. But they were afraid of the people.

20:19
pLk 19:47

Religious Leaders Question Jesus about Paying Taxes
(*193*/Matthew 22:15–22; Mark 12:13–17)

20 Keeping a close watch on him, they sent spies, who pretended to be honest. They hoped to catch Jesus in something he said[q] so that they might hand him over to the power and authority of the governor.[r] 21 So the spies questioned him: "Teacher, we know that you speak and teach what is right, and that you do not show partiality but teach the way of God in accordance with the truth.[s] 22 Is it right for us to pay taxes to Caesar or not?"

20:20
qMt 12:10
rMt 27:2
20:21
sJn 3:2

23 He saw through their duplicity and said to them, 24 "Show me a denarius. Whose portrait and inscription are on it?"

25 "Caesar's," they replied.

He said to them, "Then give to Caesar what is Caesar's,[t] and to God what is God's."

20:25
tLk 23:2; Ro 13:7

26 They were unable to trap him in what he had said there in public. And astonished by his answer, they became silent.

Religious Leaders Question Jesus about the Resurrection
(*194*/Matthew 22:23–33; Mark 12:18–27)

27 Some of the Sadducees, who say there is no resurrection,[u] came to Jesus with a question. 28 "Teacher," they said, "Moses wrote for us that if a man's brother dies and leaves a wife but no children, the man must marry the widow and have children for his brother.[v] 29 Now there were seven brothers. The first one married a woman and died childless. 30 The second 31 and then the third married her, and in the same way the seven died, leaving no children. 32 Finally, the woman died too. 33 Now then, at the resurrection whose wife will she be, since the seven were married to her?"

20:27
uAc 23:8
20:28
vDt 25:5

34 Jesus replied, "The people of this age marry and are given in marriage. 35 But those who are considered worthy of taking part in that age[w] and in the resurrection from the dead will neither marry nor be given in marriage, 36 and they can no longer die; for they are like the angels. They are God's children,[x] since they are children of the resurrection. 37 But in the account of the bush, even Moses showed that the dead rise, for he calls the Lord 'the God of Abraham, and the God of Isaac, and the God of Jacob.'[c][y] 38 He is not the God of the dead, but of the living, for to him all are alive."

20:35
wMt 12:32
20:36
xJn 1:12; 1Jn 3:1-2
20:37
yEx 3:6

a 17 Or *cornerstone*   b 17 Psalm 118:22   c 37 Exodus 3:6

20:18 The word "broken" conjures up uniformly negative images: broken bones, broken hearts, broken toys. You don't want something you value to be broken. Conversely, in God's dictionary, brokenness is not only good but also essential. He uses only people whose hearts, volition, and pride have been broken. Jesus gives a double warning: those who stumble over that stone—himself—"will be broken to pieces," while it will crush anyone it falls on. God offers a choice of "brokennesses." Those who cast themselves on Jesus, submitting their wills and all that they are to him, will be broken by him of arrogance, hardheartedness, and self-centeredness. It is not a pleasant process but an absolutely necessary one.

20:20-26 Jesus turned his enemies' attempt to trap him into a powerful lesson: As God's followers, we have legitimate obligations to both God and the government. But it is important to keep our priorities straight. When the two authorities conflict, our duty to God always must come before our duty to the government.

20:22 This was a loaded question. The Jews were enraged at having to pay taxes to Rome, thus supporting the pagan government and its gods. They hated the system that allowed tax collectors to charge exorbitant rates and keep the extra for themselves. If Jesus said they should pay taxes, they would call him a traitor

to their nation and their religion. But if he said they should not, they could report him to Rome as a rebel. Jesus' questioners thought they had him this time, but he outwitted them again.

20:24 The denarius was the usual pay for one day's work.

20:27-38 The Sadducees, a group of conservative religious leaders, honored only the Pentateuch—Genesis through Deuteronomy—as Scripture. They also did not believe in a resurrection of the dead because they could find no mention of it in those books. The Sadducees decided to try their hand at tricking Jesus, so they brought him a question that they probably had used successfully to stump the Pharisees. After addressing their question about marriage, Jesus answered the *real* question about resurrection. Basing his answer on the writings of Moses—an authority they respected—he upheld belief in resurrection.

20:34, 35 Jesus' statement does not mean that people will not recognize their spouses in heaven. It simply means that we must not think of heaven as an extension of life as we now know it. Our relationships in this life are limited by time, death, and sin. We don't know everything about our resurrection life, but Jesus affirms that relationships will be different from what we are used to here and now.

20:37, 38 Jesus answered the Sadducees' question, then he

20:40
z Mt 22:46;
Mk 12:34

39 Some of the teachers of the law responded, "Well said, teacher!" 40 And no one dared to ask him any more questions. z

Religious Leaders Cannot Answer Jesus' Question (*196*/Matthew 22:41–46; Mark 12:35–37)

41 Then Jesus said to them, "How is it that they say the Christ[a] is the Son of David? 42 David himself declares in the Book of Psalms:

> "'The Lord said to my Lord:
> "Sit at my right hand
> 43 until I make your enemies
> a footstool for your feet."'[b][a]

20:43
a Ps 110:1

44 David calls him 'Lord.' How then can he be his son?"

Jesus Warns against the Religious Leaders (*197*/Matthew 23:1–12; Mark 12:38–40)

20:46
b Lk 11:43

45 While all the people were listening, Jesus said to his disciples, 46 "Beware of the teachers of the law. They like to walk around in flowing robes and love to be greeted in the marketplaces and have the most important seats in the synagogues and the places of honor at banquets. b 47 They devour widows' houses and for a show make lengthy prayers. Such men will be punished most severely."

A Poor Widow Gives All She Has (*200*/Mark 12:41–44)

21:1
c Mt 27:6
21:4
d 2Co 8:12

21 As he looked up, Jesus saw the rich putting their gifts into the temple treasury. c 2 He also saw a poor widow put in two very small copper coins. c 3 "I tell you the truth," he said, "this poor widow has put in more than all the others. 4 All these people gave their gifts out of their wealth; but she out of her poverty put in all she had to live on."d

Jesus Tells about the Future (*201*/Matthew 24:1–25; Mark 13:1–23)

21:6
e Lk 19:44

5 Some of his disciples were remarking about how the temple was adorned with beautiful stones and with gifts dedicated to God. But Jesus said, 6 "As for what you see here, the time will come when not one stone will be left on another;e every one of them will be thrown down."

a 41 Or *Messiah*   b 43 Psalm 110:1   c 2 Greek *two lepta*

---

went beyond it to the real issue. When people ask you tough religious questions—"How can a loving God allow people to starve?" "If God knows what I'm going to do, do I have any free choice?"—follow Jesus' example. First answer the question to the best of your ability; then look for the real issue—hurt over a personal tragedy, for example, or difficulty in making a decision. Often the spoken question is only a test, not of your ability to answer hard questions, but of your willingness to listen and care.

20:41-44 The Pharisees and Sadducees had asked their questions. Then Jesus turned the tables and asked them a question that went right to the heart of the matter—what they thought about the Messiah's identity. The Pharisees knew that the Messiah would be a descendant of David, but they did not understand that he would be more than a human descendant—he was God in the flesh. Jesus quoted from Psalm 110:1 to show that David knew that the Messiah would be both human and divine. The Pharisees expected only a human ruler to restore Israel's greatness as in the days of David and Solomon.

The central issue of life is what we believe about Jesus. Other spiritual questions are irrelevant unless we first decide to believe that Jesus is who he said he is. The Pharisees and Sadducees could not do this. They remained confused over Jesus' identity.

20:45-47 The teachers of the law loved the benefits associated with their position, and they sometimes cheated the poor in order to get even more benefits. Every job has its rewards, but gaining rewards should never become more important than doing the job faithfully. God will punish people who use their position of responsibility to cheat others. Whatever resources you have been given, use them to help others and not just yourself.

20:47 How strange to think that the teachers of the law would receive the worst punishment. But behind their appearance of holiness and respectability, they were arrogant, crafty, selfish, and uncaring. Jesus exposed their evil hearts. He showed that despite their pious words, they were neglecting God's laws and doing as they pleased. Religious deeds do not cancel sin. Jesus said that God's most severe judgment awaited these teachers because they should have been living examples of mercy and justice.

21:1, 2 Jesus was in the area of the temple called the court of women. The treasury was located there or in an adjoining walkway. In this area were seven boxes in which worshipers could deposit their temple tax and six boxes for freewill offerings like the one this woman gave. Not only was she poor; as a widow she had few resources for making money. Her small gift was a sacrifice, but she gave it willingly.

21:1-4 This widow gave all she had to live on, in contrast to the way most of us handle our money. When we consider giving a certain percentage of our income a great accomplishment, we resemble those who gave "out of their wealth." Here, Jesus was admiring generous and sacrificial giving. As believers, we should consider increasing our giving—whether of money, time, or talents—to a point beyond convenience or comfort.

21:5, 6 The temple the disciples were admiring was not Solomon's temple—that had been destroyed by the Babylonians in the seventh century B.C. This temple had been built by Ezra after the return from exile in the sixth century B.C., desecrated by the Seleucids in the second century B.C., reconsecrated by the Maccabees soon afterward, and enormously expanded by Herod the Great over a 46-year period. It was a beautiful, imposing structure with a significant history, but Jesus said that it would be completely destroyed. This happened in A.D. 70 when the Roman army burned Jerusalem.

7"Teacher," they asked, "when will these things happen? And what will be the sign that they are about to take place?"

8 He replied: "Watch out that you are not deceived. For many will come in my name, claiming, 'I am he,' and, 'The time is near.' Do not follow them.*f* 9 When you hear of wars and revolutions, do not be frightened. These things must happen first, but the end will not come right away."

10 Then he said to them: "Nation will rise against nation, and kingdom against kingdom.*g* 11 There will be great earthquakes, famines and pestilences in various places, and fearful events and great signs from heaven.

12 "But before all this, they will lay hands on you and persecute you. They will deliver you to synagogues and prisons, and you will be brought before kings and governors, and all on account of my name. 13 This will result in your being witnesses to them.*h* 14 But make up your mind not to worry beforehand how you will defend yourselves.*i* 15 For I will give you*j* words and wisdom that none of your adversaries will be able to resist or contradict. 16 You will be betrayed even by parents, brothers, relatives and friends,*k* and they will put some of you to death. 17 All men will hate you because of me. 18 But not a hair of your head will perish.*l* 19 By standing firm you will gain life.

20 "When you see Jerusalem being surrounded by armies,*m* you will know that its desolation is near. 21 Then let those who are in Judea flee to the mountains, let those in the city get out, and let those in the country not enter the city.*n* 22 For this is the time of punishment*o* in fulfillment of all that has been written. 23 How dreadful it will be in those days for pregnant women and nursing mothers! There will be great distress in the land and wrath against this people. 24 They will fall by the sword and will be taken as prisoners to all the nations. Jerusalem will be trampled*p* on by the Gentiles until the times of the Gentiles are fulfilled.

Jesus Tells about His Return (202/Matthew 24:26–35; Mark 16:24–31)

25 "There will be signs in the sun, moon and stars. On the earth, nations will be in anguish and perplexity at the roaring and tossing of the sea.*q* 26 Men will faint from terror, apprehensive of what is coming on the world, for the heavenly bodies will be shaken. 27 At that time they will see the Son of Man coming in a cloud*r* with power and great glory. 28 When these things begin to take place, stand up and lift up your heads, because your redemption is drawing near."*s*

29 He told them this parable: "Look at the fig tree and all the trees. 30 When they sprout leaves, you can see for yourselves and know that summer is near. 31 Even so, when you see these things happening, you know that the kingdom of God*t* is near.

32 "I tell you the truth, this generation*a* will certainly not pass away until all these things have happened. 33 Heaven and earth will pass away, but my words will never pass away.

*a*32 Or race

21:8
*f*Lk 17:23

21:10
*g*2Ch 15:6

21:13
*h*Php 1:12

21:14
*i*Lk 12:11

21:15
*j*Lk 12:12

21:16
*k*Lk 12:52, 53

21:18
*l*Mt 10:30

21:20
*m*Lk 19:43

21:21
*n*Lk 17:31

21:22
*o*Isa 63:4;
Da 9:24-27

21:24
*p*Isa 63:18;
Da 8:13; Rev 11:2

21:25
*q*2Pe 3:10, 12

21:27
*r*Rev 1:7

21:28
*s*Lk 18:7

21:31
*t*Mt 3:2

21:7ff Jesus did not leave his disciples unprepared for the difficult years ahead. He warned them about false messiahs, natural disasters, and persecutions; however, he assured the disciples that he would be with them to protect them and make his kingdom known through them. In the end, Jesus promised that he would return in power and glory to save them. Jesus' warnings and promises to his disciples also apply to us as we look forward to his return.

21:12, 13 These persecutions soon began. Luke recorded many of them in the book of Acts. Paul wrote from prison that he suffered gladly because it helped him know Christ better and do Christ's work for the church (Philippians 3:10; Colossians 1:24). The early church thrived despite intense persecution. In fact, late in the second century the church father Tertullian wrote, "The blood of Christians is seed," because opposition helped spread Christianity.

21:14–19 Jesus warned that in the coming persecutions his followers would be betrayed by their family members and friends. Christians of every age have had to face this possibility. It is reassuring to know that even when we feel completely abandoned, the Holy Spirit will stay with us. He will comfort us, protect us, and give us the words we need. This assurance can give us the courage and hope to stand firm for Christ no matter how difficult the situation.

21:18 Jesus was *not* saying that believers would be exempt from physical harm or death during the persecutions. Remember that most of the disciples were martyred. Rather he was saying that none of his followers would suffer spiritual or eternal loss. On earth, everyone will die, but believers in Jesus will be saved for eternal life.

21:24 The "times of the Gentiles" began with Babylon's destruction of Jerusalem in 586 B.C. and the exile of the Jewish people. Israel was no longer an independent nation but was under the control of Gentile rulers. In Jesus' day, Israel was governed by the Roman empire, and a Roman general would destroy the city in A.D. 70. Jesus was saying that the domination of God's people by his enemies would continue until God decided to end it. The "times of the Gentiles" refers not just to the repeated destructions of Jerusalem, but also to the continuing and mounting persecution of God's people until the end.

21:28 The picture of the coming persecutions and natural disasters is gloomy, but ultimately it is a cause not for worry but for great joy. When believers see these events happening, they will know that the return of their Messiah is near, and they can look forward to his reign of justice and peace. Rather than being terrified by what is happening in our world, we should confidently await Christ's return to bring justice and restoration to his people.

Jesus Tells about Remaining Watchful (203/Matthew 24:36–51; Mark 13:32–37)

21:34
uMk 4:19
v1Th 5:2-7

34"Be careful, or your hearts will be weighed down with dissipation, drunkenness and the anxieties of life,u and that day will close on you unexpectedlyv like a trap. 35For it will come upon all those who live on the face of the whole earth. 36Be always on the watch, and pray that you may be able to escape all that is about to happen, and that you may be able to stand before the Son of Man."

21:37
wMk 11:19

37Each day Jesus was teaching at the temple, and each evening he went outw to spend the night on the hill called the Mount of Olives, 38and all the people came early in the morning to hear him at the temple.

C. DEATH AND RESURRECTION OF JESUS, THE SAVIOR (22:1—24:53)

The perfect man was a high ideal in Greek culture. Written with Greeks in mind, Luke's Gospel shows how Jesus was the perfect man given as the perfect sacrifice for the sin of all people. Christ is the ideal human—the perfect model for us to follow. We must stand in awe of his character, which met humanity's highest ideals as well as God's demand for an atonement for sin. He is, at one and the same time, our model and our Savior.

Religious Leaders Plot to Kill Jesus (207/Matthew 26:1–5; Mark 14:1–2)
Judas Agrees to Betray Jesus (208/Matthew 26:14–16; Mark 14:10–11)

22:2
xMt 12:14

22:3
yJn 13:2

22:5
zZec 11:12

22 Now the Feast of Unleavened Bread, called the Passover, was approaching, 2and the chief priests and the teachers of the law were looking for some way to get rid of Jesus,x for they were afraid of the people. 3Then Satany entered Judas, called Iscariot, one of the Twelve. 4And Judas went to the chief priests and the officers of the temple guard and discussed with them how he might betray Jesus. 5They were delighted and agreed to give him money. z 6He consented, and watched for an opportunity to hand Jesus over to them when no crowd was present.

21:34–36 Jesus told the disciples to keep a constant watch for his return. Although nearly 2,000 years have passed since he spoke these words, their truth remains: Christ is coming again, and we need to watch and be spiritually fit. This means working faithfully at the tasks God has given us. Don't let your mind and spirit be dulled by careless living, drinking, or foolishly pursuing pleasure. Don't let life's anxieties overburden you, so that you will be ready to move at God's command.

21:36 Only days after telling the disciples to pray that they might escape persecution, Jesus himself asked God to spare him the agonies of the cross, if that was God's will (22:41, 42). It is abnormal to *want* to suffer, but as Jesus' followers we are willing to suffer if by doing so we can help build God's kingdom. We have two wonderful promises to help us as we suffer: God will always be with us (Matthew 28:20), and he will one day rescue us and give us eternal life (Revelation 21:1–4).

22:1 All Jewish males over the age of 12 were required to go to Jerusalem for the Passover festival, followed by a seven-day festival called the Feast of Unleavened Bread. For these feasts, Jews from all over the Roman empire would converge on Jerusalem to celebrate one of the most important events in their history. To learn more about the Passover and the Feast of Unleavened Bread, see the first note on Mark 14:1.

22:3 Satan's part in the betrayal of Jesus does not remove any of the responsibility from Judas. Disillusioned because Jesus was talking about dying rather than about setting up his kingdom, Judas may have been trying to force Jesus' hand and make him use his power to prove he was the Messiah. Or perhaps Judas, not understanding Jesus' mission, no longer believed that Jesus was God's chosen one. (For more information on Judas, see his Profile in Mark 14, p. 1647.) Whatever Judas thought, Satan assumed that Jesus' death would end Jesus' mission and thwart God's plan. Like Judas, he did not know that Jesus' death and resurrection were the most important parts of God's plan all along.

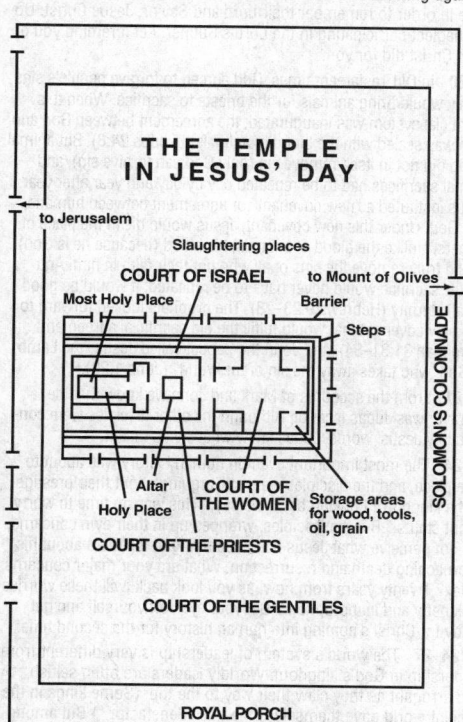

THE TEMPLE IN JESUS' DAY

Disciples Prepare for the Passover (209/Matthew 26:17–19; Mark 14:12–16)

7 Then came the day of Unleavened Bread on which the Passover lamb had to be sacrificed. 8 Jesus sent Peter and John, [a] saying, "Go and make preparations for us to eat the Passover." 9 "Where do you want us to prepare for it?" they asked.

10 He replied, "As you enter the city, a man carrying a jar of water will meet you. Follow him to the house that he enters, 11 and say to the owner of the house, 'The Teacher asks: Where is the guest room, where I may eat the Passover with my disciples?' 12 He will show you a large upper room, all furnished. Make preparations there."

13 They left and found things just as Jesus had told them. So they prepared the Passover.

Jesus and the Disciples Share the Last Supper (211/Matthew 26:20–30; Mark 14:17–26; John 13:21–30)

14 When the hour came, Jesus and his apostles reclined at the table. [b] 15 And he said to them, "I have eagerly desired to eat this Passover with you before I suffer. 16 For I tell you, I will not eat it again until it finds fulfillment in the kingdom of God." [c]

17 After taking the cup, he gave thanks and said, "Take this and divide it among you. 18 For I tell you I will not drink again of the fruit of the vine until the kingdom of God comes."

19 And he took bread, gave thanks and broke it, and gave it to them, saying, "This is my body given for you; do this in remembrance of me."

20 In the same way, after the supper he took the cup, saying, "This cup is the new covenant in my blood, which is poured out for you. 21 But the hand of him who is going to betray me is with mine on the table. 22 The Son of Man will go as it has been decreed, [d] but woe to that man who betrays him." 23 They began to question among themselves which of them it might be who would do this.

24 Also a dispute arose among them as to which of them was considered to be greatest. [e] 25 Jesus said to them, "The kings of the Gentiles lord it over them; and those who exercise authority over them call themselves Benefactors. 26 But you are not to be like that. Instead, the

22:8
[a] Ac 3:1, 11

22:14
[b] Mt 26:20; Mk 14:17, 18

22:16
[c] Lk 14:15; Rev 19:9

22:22
[d] Ac 2:23; 4:28

22:24
[e] Mk 9:34; Lk 9:46

22:7, 8 The Passover meal included the sacrifice of a lamb because of the association with the Jews' exodus from Egypt. When the Jews were getting ready to leave, God told them to kill a lamb and paint its blood on the doorframes of their houses. They then were to prepare the meat for food. Peter and John had to buy and prepare the lamb as well as the unleavened bread, herbs, wine, and other ceremonial food.

22:10 Ordinarily women, not men, would go to the well and bring home the water. So this man with the jar of water would have stood out in the crowd.

22:14-18 The Passover commemorated Israel's escape from Egypt when the blood of a lamb painted on their doorframes had saved their firstborn sons from death. This event foreshadowed Jesus' work on the cross. As the spotless Lamb of God, his blood would be spilled in order to save his people from the penalty of death brought by sin.

22:17, 20 Luke mentions two cups of wine, while Matthew and Mark mention only one. In the traditional Passover meal, wine is served four times. Christ spoke the words about his body and his blood when he offered the fourth and last cup.

22:17-20 Christians differ in their interpretation of the meaning of the commemoration of the Lord's Supper. There are three main views: (1) the bread and wine actually become Christ's body and blood; (2) the bread and wine remain unchanged, yet Christ is spiritually present by faith in and through them; (3) the bread and wine, which remain unchanged, are lasting memorials of Christ's sacrifice. No matter which view they favor, all Christians agree that the Lord's Supper commemorates Christ's death on the cross for our sins and points to the coming of his kingdom in glory. When we partake of it, we show our deep gratitude for Christ's work on our behalf, and our faith is strengthened.

22:19 Jesus asked the disciples to eat the broken bread "in remembrance of me." He wanted them to remember his sacrifice, the basis for forgiveness of sins, and also his friendship that they could continue to enjoy through the work of the Holy Spirit. Although the exact meaning of Communion has been strongly

debated throughout church history, Christians still take bread and wine in order to remember their Lord and Savior, Jesus Christ. Do not neglect participating in the Lord's Supper. Let it remind you of what Christ did for you.

22:20 In Old Testament times, God agreed to forgive people's sins if they would bring animals for the priests to sacrifice. When this sacrificial system was inaugurated, the agreement between God and man was sealed with the blood of animals (Exodus 24:8). But animal blood did not in itself remove sin (only God can forgive sin), and animal sacrifices had to be repeated day by day and year after year. Jesus instituted a "new covenant" or agreement between humans and God. Under this new covenant, Jesus would die in the place of sinners. Unlike the blood of animals, his blood (because he is God) would truly remove the sins of all who put their faith in him. And Jesus' sacrifice would never have to be repeated; it would be good for all eternity (Hebrews 9:23–28). The prophets looked forward to this new covenant that would fulfill the old sacrificial agreement (Jeremiah 31:31–34), and John the Baptist called Jesus "the Lamb of God, who takes away the sin of the world" (John 1:29).

22:21 From the accounts of Mark and John we know that the betrayer was Judas Iscariot. Although the other disciples were confused by Jesus' words, Judas knew what Jesus meant.

22:24 The most important event in human history was about to take place, and the disciples were still arguing about their prestige in the kingdom! Looking back, we say, "This was no time to worry about status." But the disciples, wrapped up in their own concerns, did not perceive what Jesus had been trying to tell them about his approaching death and resurrection. What are your major concerns today? Twenty years from now, as you look back, will these worries look petty and inappropriate? Get your eyes off yourself and get ready for Christ's coming into human history for the second time.

22:24-27 The world's system of leadership is very different from leadership in God's kingdom. Worldly leaders are often selfish and arrogant as they claw their way to the top. (Some kings in the ancient world gave themselves the title "Benefactor.") But among Christians, the leader is to be the one who *serves* best. There are

22:26
f 1Pe 5:5
g Lk 9:48

22:27
h Mt 20:28; Lk 12:37

22:29
i 2Ti 2:12

22:30
j Mt 19:28

22:31
k Am 9:9

22:32
l Jn 17:9, 15
m Jn 21:15-17

22:35
n Mt 10:9, 10;
Lk 9:3; 10:4

22:37
o Isa 53:12

greatest among you should be like the youngest, *f* and the one who rules like the one who serves. *g* 27 For who is greater, the one who is at the table or the one who serves? Is it not the one who is at the table? But I am among you as one who serves. *h* 28 You are those who have stood by me in my trials. 29 And I confer on you a kingdom, *i* just as my Father conferred one on me, 30 so that you may eat and drink at my table in my kingdom and sit on thrones, judging the twelve tribes of Israel. *j*

Jesus Predicts Peter's Denial (212/John 13:31–38)

31 "Simon, Simon, Satan has asked to sift you a as wheat. *k* 32 But I have prayed for you, *l* Simon, that your faith may not fail. And when you have turned back, strengthen your brothers." *m*

33 But he replied, "Lord, I am ready to go with you to prison and to death."

34 Jesus answered, "I tell you, Peter, before the rooster crows today, you will deny three times that you know me."

35 Then Jesus asked them, "When I sent you without purse, bag or sandals, *n* did you lack anything?"

"Nothing," they answered.

36 He said to them, "But now if you have a purse, take it, and also a bag; and if you don't have a sword, sell your cloak and buy one. 37 It is written: 'And he was numbered with the transgressors' *b*; *o* and I tell you that this must be fulfilled in me. Yes, what is written about me is reaching its fulfillment."

a 31 The Greek is plural.   *b* 37 Isaiah 53:12

JESUS' TRIAL	Event	Probable Reasons	References
	Trial before Annas (powerful ex-high priest)	Although no longer the high priest, he may have still wielded much power	John 18:13–23
	Trial before Caiaphas (the ruling high priest)	To gather evidence for the full Sanhedrin hearing to follow	Matthew 26:57–68 Mark 14:53–65 Luke 22:54, 63–65 John 18:24
	Trial before the Sanhedrin	Formal religious trial and condemnation to death	Matthew 27:1 Mark 15:1 Luke 22:66–71
	Trial before Pilate (highest Roman authority)	All death sentences needed Roman approval	Matthew 27:2, 11–14 Mark 15:1–5 Luke 23:1–6 John 18:28–38
	Trial before Herod (ruler of Galilee)	A courteous and guilt-sharing act by Pilate because Jesus was from Galilee, Herod's district	Luke 23:7–12
	Trial before Pilate	Pilate's last effort to avoid condemning an obviously innocent man	Matthew 27:15–26 Mark 15:6–15 Luke 23:13–25 John 18:39—19:16

Jesus' trial was actually a series of hearings, carefully controlled to accomplish the death of Jesus. The verdict was predecided, but certain "legal" procedures were necessary. A lot of effort went into condemning and crucifying an innocent man. Jesus went through an unfair trial in our place so that we would not have to face a fair trial and receive the well-deserved punishment for our sins.

---

different styles of leadership—some lead through public speaking, some through administering, some through relationships—but every Christian leader needs a servant's heart. Ask the people you lead how you can serve them better.

22:31, 32 Satan wanted to crush Simon Peter and the other disciples like grains of wheat. He hoped to find only chaff and blow it away. But Jesus assured Peter that his faith, although it would falter, would not be destroyed. It would be renewed, and Peter would become a powerful leader.

22:33, 34 Jesus predicted that Judas would betray him, and he said that calamity awaited the traitor (22:22). Jesus then pre-

dicted that Peter would deny that he knew Jesus. Later, however, Peter would repent and receive a commission to feed Jesus' lambs (John 21:15). Betraying and denying—one is just about as bad as the other. But Judas and Peter had entirely different fates because one repented.

22:35–38 Here Jesus reversed his earlier advice regarding how to travel (9:3). The disciples were to bring bags, money, and swords. They would be facing hatred and persecution and would need to be prepared. When Jesus said "That is enough," he may have meant it was not time to think of using swords. In either case, mention of a sword vividly communicated the trials they would soon face.

38 The disciples said, "See, Lord, here are two swords."

"That is enough," he replied.

Jesus Agonizes in the Garden (*223*/Matthew 26:36–46; Mark 14:32–42)

39 Jesus went out as usual p to the Mount of Olives, and his disciples followed him. 40 On reaching the place, he said to them, "Pray that you will not fall into temptation." q 41 He withdrew about a stone's throw beyond them, knelt down and prayed, 42 "Father, if you are willing, take this cup from me; yet not my will, but yours be done." 43 An angel from heaven appeared to him and strengthened him. r 44 And being in anguish, he prayed more earnestly, and his sweat was like drops of blood falling to the ground. a

45 When he rose from prayer and went back to the disciples, he found them asleep, exhausted from sorrow. 46 "Why are you sleeping?" he asked them. "Get up and pray so that you will not fall into temptation." s

Jesus Is Betrayed and Arrested
(*224*/Matthew 26:47–56; Mark 14:43–52; John 18:1–11)

47 While he was still speaking a crowd came up, and the man who was called Judas, one of the Twelve, was leading them. He approached Jesus to kiss him, 48 but Jesus asked him, "Judas, are you betraying the Son of Man with a kiss?"

49 When Jesus' followers saw what was going to happen, they said, "Lord, should we strike with our swords?" t 50 And one of them struck the servant of the high priest, cutting off his right ear.

51 But Jesus answered, "No more of this!" And he touched the man's ear and healed him.

52 Then Jesus said to the chief priests, the officers of the temple guard, u and the elders, who had come for him, "Am I leading a rebellion, that you have come with swords and clubs? 53 Every day I was with you in the temple courts, and you did not lay a hand on me. But this is your hour v—when darkness reigns."

a 44 Some early manuscripts do not have verses 43 and 44.

22:39
p Lk 21:37
22:40
q Mt 6:13
22:43
r Mt 4:11

22:46
s ver 40

22:49
t ver 38

22:52
u ver 4
22:53
v Jn 12:27

JESUS' TRIAL Taken from Gethsemane, Jesus first appeared before the Jewish council, which had convened at daybreak at Caiaphas's house. From there he went to Pilate, the Roman governor; then to Herod, tetrarch of Galilee, who was visiting in Jerusalem; and back to Pilate, who, in desperation, sentenced Jesus to die.

22:39 The Mount of Olives was located just to the east of Jerusalem. Jesus went up the southwestern slope to an olive grove called Gethsemane, which means "oil press."

22:40 Jesus asked the disciples to pray that they would not fall into temptation because he knew that he would soon be leaving them. Jesus also knew that they would need extra strength to face the temptations ahead—temptations to run away or to deny their relationship with him. They were about to see Jesus die. Would they still think he was the Messiah? The disciples' strongest temptation would undoubtedly be to think that they had been deceived.

22:41, 42 Was Jesus trying to get out of his mission? It is never wrong to express our true feelings to God. Jesus exposed his dread of the coming trials, but he also reaffirmed his commitment to do what God wanted. The cup he spoke of meant the terrible agony he knew he would endure—not only the horror of the crucifixion but, even worse, the total separation from God that he would have to experience in order to die for the world's sins.

22:44 Only Luke tells us that Jesus' sweat resembled drops of blood. Jesus was in extreme agony, but he did not give up or give in. He went ahead with the mission for which he had come.

22:46 These disciples were asleep. How tragic it is that many Christians act as though they are sound asleep when it comes to devotion to Christ and service for him. Don't be found insensitive to or unprepared for Christ's work.

22:47 A kiss was and still is the traditional greeting among men in certain parts of the world. In this case, it was also the agreed-upon signal to point out Jesus (Matthew 26:48). It is ironic that a gesture of greeting would be the means of betrayal. It was a hollow gesture because of Judas's treachery. Have any of your religious practices become empty gestures? We still betray Christ when our acts of service or giving are insincere or carried out merely for show.

22:50 We learn from the Gospel of John that the man who cut off the servant's ear was Peter (John 18:10).

22:53 The religious leaders had not arrested Jesus in the

Peter Denies Knowing Jesus
(227/Matthew 26:69–75; Mark 14:66–72; John 18:25–27)

22:54
w Mt 26:57;
Mk 14:53
x Mt 26:58;
Mk 14:54; Jn 18:15

54 Then seizing him, they led him away and took him into the house of the high priest. *w* Peter followed at a distance. *x* 55 But when they had kindled a fire in the middle of the courtyard and had sat down together, Peter sat down with them. 56 A servant girl saw him seated there in the firelight. She looked closely at him and said, "This man was with him."

57 But he denied it. "Woman, I don't know him," he said.

58 A little later someone else saw him and said, "You also are one of them."

"Man, I am not!" Peter replied.

59 About an hour later another asserted, "Certainly this fellow was with him, for he is a Galilean."

22:61
y Lk 7:13
z ver 34

60 Peter replied, "Man, I don't know what you're talking about!" Just as he was speaking, the rooster crowed. 61 The Lord *y* turned and looked straight at Peter. Then Peter remembered the word the Lord had spoken to him: "Before the rooster crows today, you will disown me three times." *z* 62 And he went outside and wept bitterly.

63 The men who were guarding Jesus began mocking and beating him. 64 They blindfolded him and demanded, "Prophesy! Who hit you?" 65 And they said many other insulting things to him.

The Council of Religious Leaders Condemns Jesus
(228/Matthew 27:1–2; Mark 15:1)

22:66
a Mt 27:1; Mk 15:1

66 At daybreak the council of the elders of the people, both the chief priests and teachers of the law, met together, *a* and Jesus was led before them. 67 "If you are the Christ, *a* " they said, "tell us."

Jesus answered, "If I tell you, you will not believe me, 68 and if I asked you, you would not answer. 69 But from now on, the Son of Man will be seated at the right hand of the mighty God."

22:70
b Mt 27:11; Lk 23:3

70 They all asked, "Are you then the Son of God?"

He replied, "You are right in saying I am." *b*

71 Then they said, "Why do we need any more testimony? We have heard it from his own lips."

a 67 Or Messiah

---

temple for fear of a riot. Instead, they came secretly at night, under the influence of the prince of darkness, Satan himself. Although it looked as if Satan was getting the upper hand, everything was proceeding according to God's plan. It was time for Jesus to die.

22:54 Jesus was immediately taken to the high priest's house, even though this was the middle of the night. The Jewish leaders were in a hurry—they wanted to complete the execution before the Sabbath and get on with the Passover celebration. This residence was a palace with outer walls enclosing a courtyard where servants and soldiers warmed themselves around a fire.

22:55 Peter's experiences in the next few hours would change his life. He would change from a halfhearted follower to a repentant disciple, and finally to the kind of person Christ could use to build his church. For more information on Peter, see his Profile in Matthew 27, p. 1595.

22:60 Sin, like cancer, has a way of growing if unchecked. Notice the progression of how Peter disowned Jesus: In 22:57, he denied knowing Jesus; in 22:58, he denied being one of his followers; in 22:60, he denied even knowing what they were talking about. Sin has a way of spreading. As it does, the cover-up gets bigger as well. The time to get a grip on sin and its cancerous effects is in the very beginning, before it has time to multiply its poisons in your life. Better yet, kill it before it even begins. Confess your sins or your desire to sin to the Lord, and ask his help to avoid Peter's mistakes.

22:62 Peter wept bitterly, not only because he realized that he had denied his Lord, the Messiah, but also because he had turned away from a very dear friend, a person who had loved

and taught him for three years. Peter had said that he would *never* disown Christ, despite Jesus' prediction (Mark 14:29–31; Luke 22:33, 34). But when frightened, he went against all he had boldly promised. Unable to stand up for his Lord for even 12 hours, he had failed as a disciple and as a friend. We need to be aware of our own breaking points and not become overconfident or self-sufficient. If we fail him, we must remember that Christ can use those who recognize their failure. From this humiliating experience Peter learned much that would help him later when he assumed leadership of the young church.

22:70 Jesus in effect agreed that he was the Son of God when he simply turned the high priest's question around by saying, "You are right in saying I am." And Jesus identified himself with God by using a familiar title for God found in the Old Testament: "I am" (Exodus 3:14). The high priest recognized Jesus' claim and accused him of blasphemy. For any other human this claim would have been blasphemy, but in this case it was true. Blasphemy, the sin of claiming to be God or of attacking God's authority and majesty in any way, was punishable by death. The Jewish leaders had the evidence they wanted.

Jesus Stands Trial before Pilate
(230/Matthew 27:11–14; Mark 15:2–5; John 18:28–37)

23 Then the whole assembly rose and led him off to Pilate. c 2And they began to accuse him, saying, "We have found this man subverting our nation. He opposes payment of taxes to Caesar d and claims to be Christ,a a king." e

3So Pilate asked Jesus, "Are you the king of the Jews?"

"Yes, it is as you say," Jesus replied.

4Then Pilate announced to the chief priests and the crowd, "I find no basis for a charge against this man."

5But they insisted, "He stirs up the people all over Judeab by his teaching. He started in Galilee and has come all the way here."

Jesus Stands Trial before Herod (231)

6On hearing this, Pilate asked if the man was a Galilean. 7When he learned that Jesus was under Herod's jurisdiction, he sent him to Herod,f who was also in Jerusalem at that time.

8When Herod saw Jesus, he was greatly pleased, because for a long time he had been wanting to see him. g From what he had heard about him, he hoped to see him perform some miracle. 9He plied him with many questions, but Jesus gave him no answer. 10The chief priests and the teachers of the law were standing there, vehemently accusing him. 11Then Herod and his soldiers ridiculed and mocked him. Dressing him in an elegant robe,h they sent him back to Pilate. 12That day Herod and Pilate became friendsi—before this they had been enemies.

Pilate Hands Jesus Over to Be Crucified
(232/Matthew 27:15–26; Mark 15:6–15; John 18:39—19:16)

13Pilate called together the chief priests, the rulers and the people, 14and said to them, "You brought me this man as one who was inciting the people to rebellion. I have examined him in your presence and have found no basis for your charges against him.j 15Neither has Herod, for he sent him back to us; as you can see, he has done nothing to deserve death. 16Therefore, I will punish himk and then release him.c "

a2 Or Messiah; also in verses 35 and 39   b5 Or over the land of the Jews   c16 Some manuscripts him." 17Now he was obliged to release one man to them at the Feast.

23:1	cMt 27:2; Mk 15:1; Jn 18:28
23:2	dLk 20:22
	eJn 19:12
23:7	fMt 14:1; Lk 3:1
23:8	gLk 9:9
23:11	hMk 15:17-19; Jn 19:2, 3
23:12	iAc 4:27
23:14	jver 4
23:16	kMt 27:26; Jn 19:1

23:1 Pilate was the Roman governor of Judea, where Jerusalem was located. He had a reputation for seeming to take special pleasure in harassing the Jews. For example, Pilate had taken money from the temple treasury and had used it to build an aqueduct. And he had insulted the Jewish religion by bringing imperial images into the city. As Pilate well knew, such acts could backfire. If the people were to lodge a formal complaint against his administration, Rome might remove him from his post. Pilate was already beginning to feel insecure in his position when the Jewish leaders brought Jesus to trial. Would he continue to badger the Jews and risk his political future, or would he give in to their demands and condemn a man who, he was quite sure, was innocent? That was the question facing Pilate that springtime Friday morning nearly 2,000 years ago. For more about Pilate, see his Profile in Mark 15, p. 1653.

23:7 Herod, also called Herod Antipas, was in Jerusalem that weekend for the Passover celebration. (This was the Herod who had killed John the Baptist.) Pilate hoped to pass Jesus off on Herod because he knew that Jesus had lived and worked in Galilee. But Herod was not much help. He was curious about Jesus and enjoyed making fun of him. But when Herod sent Jesus back to Pilate, it was with the verdict of "not guilty." For more about Herod Antipas, see his Profile in Mark 6, p. 1621.

23:12 Herod was the part-Jewish ruler of Galilee and Perea. Pilate was the Roman governor of Judea and Samaria. Those four provinces, together with several others, had been united under Herod the Great. But when Herod died in 4 B.C., the kingdom was divided among his sons, each of whom was called "tetrarch" (meaning "ruler of a fourth part of a region"). Archelaus, the son who had received Judea and Samaria, was removed from office within ten years, and his provinces were then ruled by a succession of Roman governors, of whom Pilate was the fifth.

Herod Antipas had two advantages over Pilate: he came from a hereditary part-Jewish monarchy and he had held his position much longer. But Pilate had two advantages over Herod: he was a Roman citizen and an envoy of the emperor, and his position was created to replace that of Herod's ineffective half brother. It is not surprising that the two men were uneasy around each other. Jesus' trial, however, brought them together. Because Pilate recognized Herod's authority over Galilee, Herod stopped feeling threatened by the Roman politician. And because neither man knew what to do in this predicament, their common problem united them.

23:13–25 Pilate wanted to release Jesus, but the crowd loudly demanded his death; so Pilate sentenced Jesus to die. No doubt Pilate did not want to risk losing his position, which may already have been shaky, by allowing a riot to occur in his province. As a career politician, he knew the importance of compromise, and he saw Jesus more as a political threat than as a human being with rights and dignity.

When the stakes are high, it is difficult to stand up for what is right, and it is easy to see our opponents as problems to be solved rather than as people to be respected. Had Pilate been a man of real courage, he would have released Jesus no matter what the consequences. But the crowd roared, and Pilate buckled. We are like Pilate when we know what is right, but decide not to do it. When you have a difficult decision to make, don't discount the effects of peer pressure. Realize beforehand that the right decision could have unpleasant consequences: social rejection, career derailment, public ridicule. Then think of Pilate and resolve to stand up for what is right no matter what other people pressure you to do.

23:15 Jesus was tried six times, by both Jewish and Roman authorities, but he was never convicted of a crime deserving death. Today, no one can find fault in Jesus. But just like Pilate, Herod, and the religious leaders, many still refuse to acknowledge him as Lord.

23:18
l Ac 3:13, 14

18With one voice they cried out, "Away with this man! Release Barabbas to us!"*l* 19(Barabbas had been thrown into prison for an insurrection in the city, and for murder.)

20Wanting to release Jesus, Pilate appealed to them again. 21But they kept shouting, "Crucify him! Crucify him!"

22For the third time he spoke to them: "Why? What crime has this man committed? I have found in him no grounds for the death penalty. Therefore I will have him punished and then release him."

23But with loud shouts they insistently demanded that he be crucified, and their shouts prevailed. 24So Pilate decided to grant their demand. 25He released the man who had been thrown into prison for insurrection and murder, the one they asked for, and surrendered Jesus to their will.

Jesus Is Led Away to Be Crucified
(234/Matthew 27:32–34; Mark 15:21–24; John 19:17)

23:26
m Mt 27:32
n Jn 19:17
23:27
o Lk 8:52
23:29
p Mt 24:19
23:30
q Isa 2:19;
Hos 10:8; Rev 6:16

26As they led him away, they seized Simon from Cyrene,*m* who was on his way in from the country, and put the cross on him and made him carry it behind Jesus.*n* 27A large number of people followed him, including women who mourned and wailed*o* for him. 28Jesus turned and said to them, "Daughters of Jerusalem, do not weep for me; weep for yourselves and for your children. 29For the time will come when you will say, 'Blessed are the barren women, the wombs that never bore and the breasts that never nursed!'*p* 30Then

> "'they will say to the mountains, "Fall on us!"
> and to the hills, "Cover us!"'*a q*

23:31
r Eze 20:47

31For if men do these things when the tree is green, what will happen when it is dry?"*r*

a 30 Hosea 10:8

23:18, 19 Barabbas had been part of a rebellion against the Roman government (Mark 15:7). As a political insurgent, he was no doubt a hero among some of the Jews. How ironic it is that Barabbas, who was released, was guilty of the very crime Jesus was accused of (23:14).

23:18, 19 Who was Barabbas? Jewish men had names that identified them with their fathers. Simon Peter, for example, is called Simon son of Jonah (Matthew 16:17). Barabbas is never identified by his given name, and this name is not much help either—*bar-abbas* means "son of *Abba*" (or "son of daddy"). He could have been anybody's son—and that's just the point. Barabbas, son of an unnamed father, committed a crime. Because Jesus died in his place, this man was set free. We too are sinners and criminals who have broken God's holy law. Like Barabbas, we deserve to die. But Jesus has died in our place, for our sins, and we have been set free. We don't have to be "very important people" to accept our freedom in Christ. In fact, thanks to Jesus, God adopts us all as his own sons and daughters and gives us the right to call him *Abba*—"daddy" (see Galatians 4:4–6).

23:22 When Pilate said he would have Jesus "punished," he was referring to a punishment that could have killed Jesus. The usual procedure was to bare the upper half of the victim's body and tie his hands to a pillar before whipping him with a three-pronged whip. The number of lashes was determined by the severity of the crime; up to 40 were permitted under Jewish law. After being flogged, Jesus also endured other agonies as recorded in Matthew and Mark. He was slapped, struck with fists, and mocked. A crown of thorns was placed on his head, and he was beaten with a stick and stripped before being hung on the cross.

23:23, 24 Pilate did not want to give Jesus the death sentence. He thought the Jewish leaders were simply jealous men who wanted to get rid of a rival. When they threatened to report Pilate to Caesar (John 19:12), however, Pilate became frightened. Historical records indicate that Pilate had already been warned by Roman authorities about tensions in this region. The last thing he needed was a riot in Jerusalem at Passover time, when the city was crowded with Jews from all over the empire. So Pilate turned Jesus over to the mob to do with as they pleased.

23:27–29 Luke alone mentions the tears of the Jewish women while Jesus was being led through the streets to his execution. Jesus told them not to weep for him but for themselves. He knew that in only about 40 years, Jerusalem and the temple would be destroyed by the Romans.

JESUS LED AWAY TO DIE As Jesus was led away through the streets of Jerusalem, he could no longer carry his cross, and Simon of Cyrene was given the burden. Jesus was crucified, along with common criminals, on a hill outside Jerusalem.

Jesus Is Placed on the Cross
(235/Matthew 27:35–44; Mark 15:25–32; John 19:18–27)

32 Two other men, both criminals, were also led out with him to be executed. s 33 When they came to the place called the Skull, there they crucified him, along with the criminals— one on his right, the other on his left. 34 Jesus said, "Father, forgive them, for they do not know what they are doing." a And they divided up his clothes by casting lots. t

35 The people stood watching, and the rulers even sneered at him. u They said, "He saved others; let him save himself if he is the Christ of God, the Chosen One."

36 The soldiers also came up and mocked him. They offered him wine vinegar v 37 and said, "If you are the king of the Jews, save yourself."

38 There was a written notice above him, which read: THIS IS THE KING OF THE JEWS.

39 One of the criminals who hung there hurled insults at him: "Aren't you the Christ? Save yourself and us!" w

40 But the other criminal rebuked him. "Don't you fear God," he said, "since you are under the same sentence? 41 We are punished justly, for we are getting what our deeds deserve. But this man has done nothing wrong."

42 Then he said, "Jesus, remember me when you come into your kingdom. b "

43 Jesus answered him, "I tell you the truth, today you will be with me in paradise." x

Jesus Dies on the Cross (236/Matthew 27:45–56; Mark 15:33–41; John 19:28–37)

44 It was now about the sixth hour, and darkness came over the whole land until the ninth hour, 45 for the sun stopped shining. And the curtain of the temple was torn in two. 46 Jesus called out with a loud voice, y "Father, into your hands I commit my spirit." z When he had said this, he breathed his last. a

47 The centurion, seeing what had happened, praised God and said, "Surely this was a righteous man." 48 When all the people who had gathered to witness this sight saw what took place, they beat their breasts and went away. 49 But all those who knew him, including the women who had followed him from Galilee, b stood at a distance, c watching these things.

a 34 Some early manuscripts do not have this sentence.   b 42 Some manuscripts come with your kingly power

23:32
s Mt 27:38
23:34
t Ps 22:18
23:35
u Ps 22:17
23:36
v Mt 27:48
23:39
w ver 35, 37
23:43
x 2Co 12:3, 4;
Rev 2:7
23:46
y Mt 27:50
z Ps 31:5; 1Pe 2:23
a Jn 19:30
23:49
b Lk 8:2
c Ps 38:11

23:31 This proverb is difficult to interpret. Some feel it means: if the innocent Jesus (green tree) suffered at the hands of the Romans, what would happen to the guilty Jews (dry tree)?

23:32, 33 The place called the Skull, or Golgotha, was probably a hill outside Jerusalem along a main road. The Romans executed people publicly as examples to the people.

23:32, 33 When James and John asked Jesus for the places of honor next to him in his kingdom, he told them they didn't know what they were asking (Mark 10:35–39). Here, as Jesus was preparing to inaugurate his kingdom through his death, the places on his right and on his left were taken by dying men—criminals. As Jesus explained to his two position-conscious disciples, a person who wants to be close to Jesus must be prepared to suffer and die. The way to the kingdom is the way of the cross.

23:34 Jesus asked God to forgive the people who were putting him to death—Jewish leaders, Roman politicians and soldiers, bystanders—and God answered that prayer by opening up the way of salvation even to Jesus' murderers. Jesus was suffering the most horrible, painful death ever devised by sinful man, and he looked at the people responsible for his suffering and prayed for their forgiveness. The Roman centurion and soldiers who witnessed the crucifixion said, "Surely he was the Son of God" (Matthew 27:54). Soon many priests were converted to the Christian faith (Acts 6:7). Because we are all sinners, we all played a part in putting Jesus to death. The gospel—the Good News— is that God is gracious. He will forgive us and give us new life through his Son.

23:34 Roman soldiers customarily divided up the clothing of executed criminals among themselves. When they cast lots for Jesus' clothes, they fulfilled the prophecy in Psalm 22:18.

23:38 This sign was meant to be ironic. A king, stripped and executed in public view, had obviously lost his kingdom forever. But Jesus, who turns the world's wisdom upside down, was just

coming into his kingdom. His death and resurrection would strike the deathblow to Satan's rule and would establish Christ's eternal authority over the earth. Few people reading the sign that bleak afternoon understood its real meaning, but the sign was absolutely true. All was not lost. Jesus is King of the Jews—and the Gentiles, and the whole universe.

23:39–43 As this man was about to die, he turned to Christ for forgiveness, and Christ accepted him. This shows that our deeds don't save us—our faith in Christ does. It is never too late to turn to God. Even in his misery, Jesus had mercy on this criminal who decided to believe in him. Our lives will be much more useful and fulfilling if we turn to God early, but even those who repent at the very last moment will be with God in paradise.

23:42, 43 The dying criminal had more faith than the rest of Jesus' followers put together. Although the disciples continued to love Jesus, their hopes for the kingdom were shattered. Most of them had gone into hiding. As one of his followers sadly said two days later, "We had hoped that he was the one who was going to redeem Israel" (24:21). By contrast, the criminal looked at the man who was dying next to him and said, "Jesus, remember me when you come into your kingdom." By all appearances, the kingdom was finished. How awe-inspiring is the faith of this man who alone saw beyond the present shame to the coming glory!

23:44 Darkness covered the entire land for about three hours in the middle of the day. All nature seemed to mourn over the stark tragedy of the death of God's Son.

23:45 This significant event symbolized Christ's work on the cross. The temple had three parts: the courts for all the people; the Holy Place, where only priests could enter; and the Most Holy Place, where the high priest alone could enter once a year to atone for the sins of the people. It was in the Most Holy Place that the ark of the covenant, and God's presence with it, rested. The curtain that was torn was the one that closed off the Most Holy Place from view. At Christ's death, the barrier between God and

Jesus Is Laid in the Tomb
(237/Matthew 27:57–61; Mark 15:42–47; John 19:38–42)

23:51
*d*Lk 2:25, 38

⁵⁰Now there was a man named Joseph, a member of the Council, a good and upright man, ⁵¹who had not consented to their decision and action. He came from the Judean town of Arimathea and he was waiting for the kingdom of God. *d* ⁵²Going to Pilate, he asked for Jesus' body. ⁵³Then he took it down, wrapped it in linen cloth and placed it in a tomb cut in the rock, one in which no one had yet been laid. ⁵⁴It was Preparation Day,*e* and the Sabbath was about to begin.

23:54
*e*Mt 27:62

23:56
*f*Mk 16:1
*g*Ex 20:10

⁵⁵The women who had come with Jesus from Galilee followed Joseph and saw the tomb and how his body was laid in it. ⁵⁶Then they went home and prepared spices and perfumes.*f* But they rested on the Sabbath in obedience to the commandment. *g*

Jesus Rises from the Dead *(239/Matthew 28:1–7; Mark 16:1–8; John 20:1–10)*

24:1
*h*Lk 23:56

24 On the first day of the week, very early in the morning, the women took the spices they had prepared *h* and went to the tomb. ²They found the stone rolled away from the tomb, ³but when they entered, they did not find the body of the Lord Jesus. ⁴While they were wondering about this, suddenly two men in clothes that gleamed like lightning*i* stood beside them. ⁵In their fright the women bowed down with their faces to the ground, but the men said to them, "Why do you look for the living among the dead? ⁶He is not here; he has risen! Remember how he told you, while he was still with you in Galilee:*j* ⁷'The Son of Man must be delivered into the hands of sinful men, be crucified and on the third day be raised again.'" ⁸Then they remembered his words. *k*

24:4
*i*Jn 20:12

24:6
*j*Mt 17:22, 23;
Mk 9:30-31

24:8
*k*Jn 2:22

⁹When they came back from the tomb, they told all these things to the Eleven and to all the others. ¹⁰It was Mary Magdalene, Joanna, Mary the mother of James, and the others

---

man was split in two. Now all people can approach God directly through Christ (Hebrews 9:1–14; 10:19–22).

23:50–52 Joseph of Arimathea was a wealthy and honored member of the Jewish Council. He was also a secret disciple of Jesus (John 19:38). The disciples who had publicly followed Jesus fled, but Joseph boldly took a stand that could cost him dearly. He cared enough about Jesus to ask for his body so he could give it a proper burial.

23:53 The tomb was likely a man-made cave cut out of one of the many limestone hills in the area around Jerusalem. Such a tomb was large enough to walk into. After burial, a large stone would have been rolled across the entrance (John 20:1).

23:55 The Galilean women followed Joseph to the tomb, so they knew exactly where to find Jesus' body when they returned after the Sabbath with their spices and perfumes. These women could not do "great" things for Jesus—they were not permitted to stand up before the Jewish council or the Roman governor and testify on his behalf—but they did what they could. They stayed at the cross when most of the disciples had fled, and they got ready to anoint their Lord's body. Because of their devotion, they were the first to know about the resurrection. As believers, we may feel we can't do much for Jesus. But we are called to take advantage of the opportunities given us, doing what we *can* do and not worrying about what we cannot do.

24:1 The women brought spices to the tomb as we would bring flowers—as a sign of love and respect. The women went home and kept the Sabbath as the law required, from sundown Friday to sundown Saturday, before gathering up their spices and perfumes and returning to the tomb.

24:1–9 The two angels (appearing as "men in clothes that gleamed like lightning") asked the women why they were looking in a tomb for someone who was alive. Often we run into people who are looking for God among the dead. They study the Bible as a mere historical document and go to church as if going to a memorial service. But Jesus is not among the dead—he lives! He reigns in the hearts of Christians, and he is the head of his church. Do you look for Jesus among the living? Do you expect him to be active in the world and in the church? Look for signs of his power—they are all around you.

24:6, 7 The angels reminded the women that Jesus had accurately predicted all that had happened to him (9:22, 44; 18:31–33).

24:6, 7 The resurrection of Jesus from the dead is the central fact of Christian history. On it, the church is built; without it, there would be no Christian church today. Jesus' resurrection is unique. Other religions have strong ethical systems, concepts about paradise and afterlife, and various holy scriptures. Only Christianity has a God who became human, literally died for his people, and was raised again in power and glory to rule his church forever.

Why is the resurrection so important? (1) Because Christ was raised from the dead, we know that the kingdom of heaven has broken into earth's history. Our world is now headed for redemption, not disaster. God's mighty power is at work destroying sin, creating new lives, and preparing us for Jesus' second coming. (2) Because of the resurrection, we know that death has been conquered, and we too will be raised from the dead to live forever with Christ. (3) The resurrection gives authority to the church's witness in the world. Look at the early evangelistic sermons in the book of Acts: the apostles' most important message was the proclamation that Jesus Christ had been raised from the dead! (4) The resurrection gives meaning to the church's regular feast, the Lord's Supper. Like the disciples on the Emmaus Road, we break bread with our risen Lord, who comes in power to save us. (5) The resurrection helps us find meaning even in great tragedy. No matter what happens to us as we walk with the Lord, the resurrection gives us hope for the future. (6) The resurrection assures us that Christ is alive and ruling his kingdom. He is not legend; he is alive and real. (7) God's power that brought Jesus back from the dead is available to us so that we can live for him in an evil world.

Christians can look very different from one another, and they can hold widely varying beliefs about politics, lifestyle, and even theology. But one central belief unites and inspires all true Christians—Jesus Christ rose from the dead! (For more on the importance of the resurrection, see 1 Corinthians 15:12–58.)

with them / who told this to the apostles. ¹¹But they did not believe the women, because their words seemed to them like nonsense. ¹²Peter, however, got up and ran to the tomb. Bending over, he saw the strips of linen lying by themselves,ᵐ and he went away, wondering to himself what had happened.

Jesus Appears to Two Believers Traveling on the Road (243/Mark 16:12–13)

¹³Now that same day two of them were going to a village called Emmaus, about seven miles ᵃ from Jerusalem. ⁿ ¹⁴They were talking with each other about everything that had happened. ¹⁵As they talked and discussed these things with each other, Jesus himself came up and walked along with them; ¹⁶but they were kept from recognizing him. ᵒ

¹⁷He asked them, "What are you discussing together as you walk along?"

They stood still, their faces downcast. ¹⁸One of them, named Cleopas,ᵖ asked him, "Are you only a visitor to Jerusalem and do not know the things that have happened there in these days?"

¹⁹"What things?" he asked.

"About Jesus of Nazareth," they replied. "He was a prophet,�q powerful in word and deed before God and all the people. ²⁰The chief priests and our rulers handed him over to be sentenced to death, and they crucified him; ²¹but we had hoped that he was the one who was going to redeem Israel.ʳ And what is more, it is the third day since all this took place. ²²In addition, some of our women amazed us. They went to the tomb early this morning ²³but didn't find his body. They came and told us that they had seen a vision of angels, who said he was alive. ²⁴Then some of our companions went to the tomb and found it just as the women had said, but him they did not see."

²⁵He said to them, "How foolish you are, and how slow of heart to believe all that the

ᵃ13 Greek *sixty stadia* (about 11 kilometers)

24:10
ⁱLk 8:1-3
24:12
ᵐJn 20:3-7

24:13
ⁿMk 16:12

24:16
ᵒJn 20:14; 21:4
24:18
ᵖJn 19:25

24:19
qMt 21:11

24:21
ʳLk 1:68

24:11, 12 People who hear about the resurrection for the first time may need time before they can comprehend this amazing story. Like the disciples, they may pass through four stages of belief. (1) At first, they may think it is a fairy tale, impossible to believe. (2) Like Peter, they may check out the facts but still be puzzled about what happened. (3) Only when they encounter Jesus personally will they be able to accept the fact of the resurrection. (4) Then, as they commit themselves to Jesus and devote their lives to serving him, they will begin fully to understand the reality of his presence with them.

24:12 From John 20:3, 4, we learn that another disciple ran to the tomb with Peter. That other disciple was almost certainly John, the author of the fourth Gospel.

24:13ff The two disciples returning to Emmaus at first missed the significance of history's greatest event because they were

ON THE ROAD TO EMMAUS

After Jesus' death, two of his followers were walking from Jerusalem back toward Emmaus when a stranger joined them. During dinner in Emmaus, Jesus revealed himself to them and then disappeared. They immediately returned to Jerusalem to tell the disciples the good news that Jesus was alive!

too focused on their disappointments and problems. In fact, they didn't recognize Jesus when he was walking beside them. To compound the problem, they were walking in the wrong direction— away from the fellowship of believers in Jerusalem. We are likely to miss Jesus and withdraw from the strength found in other believers when we become preoccupied with our dashed hopes and frustrated plans. Only when we are looking for Jesus in our midst will we experience the power and help he can bring.

24:18 The news about Jesus' crucifixion had spread throughout Jerusalem. Because this was Passover week, Jews visiting the city from all over the Roman empire now knew about his death. This was not a small, insignificant event, affecting only the disciples—the whole nation was interested.

24:21 The disciples from Emmaus had been counting on Jesus to redeem Israel—that is, to rescue the nation from its enemies. Most Jews believed that the Old Testament prophecies pointed to a military and political Messiah; they didn't realize that the Messiah had come to redeem people from slavery to sin. When Jesus died, therefore, they lost all hope. They didn't understand that Jesus' death offered the greatest hope possible.

24:24 These disciples knew that the tomb was empty but didn't understand that Jesus had risen, and they were filled with sadness. Despite the women's witness, which was verified by other disciples, and despite the Biblical prophecies of this very event, they still didn't believe. Today the resurrection still catches people by surprise. In spite of 2,000 years of evidence and witness, many people refuse to believe. What more will it take? For these disciples it took the living, breathing Jesus in their midst. For many people today, it takes the presence of living, breathing Christians.

24:25 Even though these Jewish men knew the Biblical prophecies well, they failed to understand that Christ's suffering was his path to glory. They could not understand why God had not intervened to save Jesus from the cross. They were so caught up in the world's admiration of political power and military might that they were unprepared for the reversal of values in God's kingdom—that the last will be first, and that life grows out of death. The world has not changed its values: a suffering servant is no more popular today than 2,000 years ago. But we have not only the witness of the Old Testament prophets; we have also the

24:26
s 1Pe 1:11

24:27
t Ge 3:15; Nu 21:9;
Dt 18:15
u Isa 7:14; 9:6;
Eze 34:23

24:30
v Mt 14:19

24:34
w 1Co 15:5

24:36
x Jn 20:19, 21, 26

24:37
y Mk 6:49

24:43
z Ac 10:41

24:44
a Mt 16:21;
Lk 18:31-33
24:47
b Ac 5:31; 13:38
c Mt 28:19
24:48
d Ac 1:8
24:49
e Ac 1:4

prophets have spoken! 26 Did not the Christ a have to suffer these things and then enter his glory?" s 27 And beginning with Moses t and all the Prophets, u he explained to them what was said in all the Scriptures concerning himself.

28 As they approached the village to which they were going, Jesus acted as if he were going farther. 29 But they urged him strongly, "Stay with us, for it is nearly evening; the day is almost over." So he went in to stay with them.

30 When he was at the table with them, he took bread, gave thanks, broke it v and began to give it to them. 31 Then their eyes were opened and they recognized him, and he disappeared from their sight. 32 They asked each other, "Were not our hearts burning within us while he talked with us on the road and opened the Scriptures to us?"

33 They got up and returned at once to Jerusalem. There they found the Eleven and those with them, assembled together 34 and saying, "It is true! The Lord has risen and has appeared to Simon." w 35 Then the two told what had happened on the way, and how Jesus was recognized by them when he broke the bread.

Jesus Appears to His Disciples (244/John 20:19–23)

36 While they were still talking about this, Jesus himself stood among them and said to them, "Peace be with you." x

37 They were startled and frightened, thinking they saw a ghost. y 38 He said to them, "Why are you troubled, and why do doubts rise in your minds? 39 Look at my hands and my feet. It is I myself! Touch me and see; a ghost does not have flesh and bones, as you see I have."

40 When he had said this, he showed them his hands and feet. 41 And while they still did not believe it because of joy and amazement, he asked them, "Do you have anything here to eat?" 42 They gave him a piece of broiled fish, 43 and he took it and ate it in their presence. z

Jesus Appears to the Disciples in Jerusalem (249)

44 He said to them, "This is what I told you while I was still with you: Everything must be fulfilled a that is written about me in the Law of Moses, the Prophets and the Psalms."

45 Then he opened their minds so they could understand the Scriptures. 46 He told them, "This is what is written: The Christ will suffer and rise from the dead on the third day, 47 and repentance and forgiveness of sins will be preached in his name b to all nations, c beginning at Jerusalem. 48 You are witnesses d of these things. 49 I am going to send you what my Father has promised; e but stay in the city until you have been clothed with power from on high."

a 26 Or Messiah; also in verse 46

---

witness of the New Testament apostles and the history of the Christian church all pointing to Jesus' victory over death. Will we step outside the values of our culture and put our faith in Jesus? Or will we foolishly continue to be baffled by his Good News?

24:25–27 After the two disciples had explained their sadness and confusion, Jesus responded by going to Scripture and applying it to his ministry. When we are puzzled by questions or problems, we too can go to Scripture and find authoritative help. If we, like these two disciples, do not understand what the Bible means, we can turn to other believers who know the Bible and have the wisdom to apply it to our situation.

24:27 Beginning with the promised offspring in Genesis (Genesis 3:15) and going through the suffering servant in Isaiah (Isaiah 53), the pierced one in Zechariah (Zechariah 12:10), and the messenger of the covenant in Malachi (Malachi 3:1), Jesus reintroduced these disciples to the Old Testament. Christ is the thread woven through all the Scriptures, the central theme that binds them together. Following are several key passages Jesus may have mentioned on this walk to Emmaus: Genesis 3; 12; Psalms 22; 69; 110; Isaiah 53; Jeremiah 31; Zechariah 9; 13; Malachi 3.

24:33, 34 Paul also mentions that Jesus appeared to Peter alone (1 Corinthians 15:5). This appearance is not further described in the Gospels. Jesus showed individual concern for Peter because Peter felt completely unworthy after disowning his Lord. But Peter repented, and Jesus approached him and forgave him. Soon God would use Peter in building Christ's church (see the first half of the book of Acts).

24:36–43 Jesus' body wasn't a figment of the imagination or the appearance of a ghost—the disciples touched him, and he ate food. On the other hand, his body wasn't a restored human body like Lazarus's (John 11)—he was able to appear and disappear. Jesus' resurrected body was immortal. This is the kind of body we will be given at the resurrection of the dead (see 1 Corinthians 15:42–50).

24:44 Many days may have elapsed between verses 43 and 44 because Jesus and his followers traveled to Galilee and back before he returned to heaven (Matthew 28:16; John 21). In his second book, Acts, Luke makes it clear that Jesus spent 40 days with his disciples between his resurrection and ascension.

24:44–46 The Law of Moses, the Prophets, and the Psalms is a way to describe the entire Old Testament. In other words, the entire Old Testament points to the Messiah. For example, his role as prophet was foretold in Deuteronomy 18:15–20; his sufferings were prophesied in Psalm 22 and Isaiah 53; his resurrection was predicted in Psalm 16:9–11 and Isaiah 53:10, 11.

24:45 Jesus opened these people's minds to understand the Scriptures. The Holy Spirit does this in our lives today when we study the Bible. Have you ever wondered how to understand a difficult Bible passage? Besides reading surrounding passages, asking other people, and consulting reference works, pray that the Holy Spirit will open your mind to understand, giving you the needed insight to put God's Word into action in your life.

24:47 Luke wrote to the Greek-speaking world. He wanted them to know that Christ's message of God's love and forgiveness should go to all the world. We must never ignore the worldwide scope of Christ's gospel. God wants all the world to hear the Good News of salvation.

Jesus Ascends into Heaven (*250*/Mark 16:19–20)

⁵⁰When he had led them out to the vicinity of Bethany, he lifted up his hands and blessed them. ⁵¹While he was blessing them, he left them and was taken up into heaven. ⁵²Then they worshiped him and returned to Jerusalem with great joy. ⁵³And they stayed continually at the temple,ᶠ praising God.

24:53
ᶠAc 2:46

24:50–53 As the disciples stood and watched, Jesus began rising into the air, and soon he disappeared into heaven. Seeing Jesus leave must have been frightening, but the disciples knew that Jesus would keep his promise to be with them through the Holy Spirit. This same Jesus, who lived with the disciples, who died and was buried, and who rose from the dead, loves us and promises to be with us always. We can get to know him better through studying the Scriptures, praying, and allowing the Holy Spirit to make us more like Jesus.

24:51 Jesus' physical presence left the disciples when he returned to heaven (Acts 1:9), but the Holy Spirit soon came to comfort them and empower them to spread the gospel of salvation (Acts 2:1–4). Today Jesus' work of salvation is completed, and he is sitting at God's right hand, where he has authority over heaven and earth.

24:53 Luke's Gospel portrays Jesus as the perfect example of a life lived according to God's plan—as a child living in obedience to his parents and yet amazing the religious leaders in the temple, as an adult serving God and others through preaching

and healing, and finally as a condemned man suffering without complaint. This emphasis was well suited to Luke's Greek audience, who placed high value on being an example and improving oneself, and who often discussed the meaning of perfection. The Greeks, however, had a difficult time understanding the spiritual importance of the physical world. To them, the spiritual was always more important than the physical. To help them understand the God-man who united the spiritual and the physical, Luke emphasized that Jesus was not a phantom human but a real human being who healed people and fed them because he was concerned with their physical health as well as the state of their souls.

As believers living according to God's plan, we too should obey our Lord in every detail as we seek to restore people's bodies and souls to the health and salvation God has in store for them. If we want to know how to live a perfect life, we can look to Jesus as our example.

KEY PLACES IN JOHN

The broken lines (—·—·—) indicate modern boundaries.

John's story begins as John the Baptist ministers near Bethany east of the Jordan (1:28ff). Jesus also begins his ministry, talking to some of the men who would later become his 12 disciples. Jesus' ministry in Galilee began with a visit to a wedding in Cana (2:1ff). Then he went to Capernaum, which became his new home (2:12). He journeyed to Jerusalem for the special feasts (2:13) and there met with Nicodemus, a religious leader (3:1ff). When Jesus left Judea, he traveled through Samaria and ministered to the Samaritans (4:1ff). Jesus did miracles in Galilee (4:46ff) and in Judea and Jerusalem (5:1ff). We follow him as he fed 5,000 near Bethsaida beside the Sea of Galilee (Sea of Tiberias) (6:1ff), walked on the water to his frightened disciples (6:16ff), preached through Galilee (7:1), returned to Jerusalem (7:2ff), preached beyond the Jordan in Perea (10:40), raised Lazarus from the dead in Bethany (11:1ff), and finally entered Jerusalem for the last time to celebrate the Passover with his disciples and give them key teachings about what was to come and how they should act. His last hours before his crucifixion were spent in the city (13:1ff), in a grove of olive trees (the Garden of Gethsemane) (18:1ff), and finally in various buildings in Jerusalem during his trial (18:12ff). He would be crucified, but he would rise again as he had promised.

JOHN

VITAL STATISTICS

PURPOSE:
To prove conclusively that Jesus is the Son of God and that all who believe in him will have eternal life

AUTHOR:
John the apostle, son of Zebedee, brother of James, called a "Son of Thunder"

ORIGINAL AUDIENCE:
New Christians and searching non-Christians

DATE WRITTEN:
Probably A.D. 85–90

SETTING:
Written after the destruction of Jerusalem in A.D. 70 and before John's exile to the island of Patmos

KEY VERSES:
"Jesus did many other miraculous signs in the presence of his disciples, which are not recorded in this book. But these are written that you may believe that Jesus is the Christ, the Son of God, and that by believing you may have life in his name" (20:30, 31).

KEY PEOPLE:
Jesus, John the Baptist, the disciples, Mary, Martha, Lazarus, Jesus' mother, Pilate, Mary Magdalene

KEY PLACES:
Judean countryside, Samaria, Galilee, Bethany, Jerusalem

SPECIAL FEATURES:
Of the eight miracles recorded, six are unique (among the Gospels) to John, as is the "Upper Room Discourse" (chapters 14—17). Over 90 percent of John is unique to his Gospel—John does not contain a genealogy or any record of Jesus' birth, childhood, temptation, transfiguration, appointment of the disciples, nor any account of Jesus' parables, ascension, or Great Commission.

HE SPOKE, and galaxies whirled into place, stars burned the heavens, and planets began orbiting their suns—words of awesome, unlimited, unleashed power. He spoke again, and the waters and lands were filled with plants and creatures, running, swimming, growing, and multiplying—words of animating, breathing, pulsing life. Again he spoke, and man and woman were formed, thinking, speaking, and loving—words of personal and creative glory. Eternal, infinite, unlimited—he was, is, and always will be the Maker and Lord of all that exists.

And then he came in the flesh to a speck in the universe called planet Earth. The mighty Creator became a part of the creation, limited by time and space and susceptible to aging, sickness, and death. But love propelled him, and so he came to rescue and save those who were lost and to give them the gift of eternity. He is *the Word*; he is Jesus, the Christ.

It is this truth that the apostle John brings to us in this book. John's Gospel is not a life of Christ; it is a powerful argument for the incarnation, a conclusive demonstration that Jesus was, and is, the very heaven-sent Son of God and the only source of eternal life.

John discloses Jesus' identity with his very first words, "In the beginning was the Word, and the Word was with God, and the Word was God. He was with God in the beginning" (1:1, 2); and the rest of the book continues the theme. John, the eyewitness, chose eight of Jesus' miracles (or signs, as he calls them) to reveal his divine/human nature and his life-giving mission. These signs are (1) turning water to wine (2:1–11), (2) healing the official's son (4:46–54), (3) healing the invalid at Bethesda (5:1–9), (4) feeding the 5,000 with just a few loaves and fish (6:1–14), (5) walking on the water (6:15–21), (6) restoring sight to the blind man (9:1–41), (7) raising Lazarus from the dead (11:1–44), and, after the resurrection, (8) giving the disciples an overwhelming catch of fish (21:1–14).

In every chapter Jesus' deity is revealed. And Jesus' true identity is underscored through the titles he is given—the Word, the One and Only, Lamb of God, Son of God, true bread, life, resurrection, vine. And the formula is "I am." When Jesus uses this phrase, he affirms his preexistence and eternal deity. Jesus says, *I am* the bread of life (6:35); *I am* the light of the world (8:12; 9:5); *I am* the gate (10:7); *I am* the good shepherd (10:11, 14); *I am* the resurrection and the life (11:25); *I am* the way, and the truth and the life (14:6); and *I am* the true vine (15:1).

The greatest sign, of course, is the resurrection, and John provides a stirring eyewitness account of finding the empty tomb. Then he records various post-Resurrection appearances by Jesus.

John, the devoted follower of Christ, has given us a personal and powerful look at Jesus Christ, the eternal Son of God. As you read his story, commit yourself to believe in and follow him.

THE BLUEPRINT

A. BIRTH AND PREPARATION OF JESUS, THE SON OF GOD
   (1:1—2:11)

John makes it clear that Jesus is not just a man; he is the eternal Son of God. He is the light of the world because he offers this gift of eternal life to all people. How blind and foolish to call Jesus nothing more than an unusually good man or moral teacher. Yet we sometimes act as if this were true when we casually toss around his words and go about living our own way. If Jesus is the eternal Son of God, we should pay attention to his divine identity and life-giving message.

B. MESSAGE AND MINISTRY OF JESUS, THE SON OF GOD (2:12—12:50)
   1. Jesus encounters belief and unbelief from the people
   2. Jesus encounters conflict with the religious leaders
   3. Jesus encounters crucial events in Jerusalem

Jesus meets with individuals, preaches to great crowds, trains his disciples, and debates with the religious leaders. The message that he is the Son of God receives a mixed reaction. Some worship him, some are puzzled, some shrink back, and some move to silence him. We see the same varied reactions today. Times have changed, but people's hearts remain hard. May we see ourselves in these encounters Jesus had with people, and may our response be to worship and follow him.

C. DEATH AND RESURRECTION OF JESUS, THE SON OF GOD
   (13:1—21:25)
   1. Jesus teaches his disciples
   2. Jesus completes his mission

Jesus carefully instructed the disciples how to continue to believe even after his death, yet they could not take it in. After he died and the first reports came back that Jesus was alive, the disciples could not believe it. Thomas is especially remembered as one who refused to believe even when he heard the eyewitness accounts from other disciples. May we not be like Thomas, demanding a physical face-to-face encounter, but may we accept the eyewitness testimony of the disciples that John has recorded in this Gospel.

MEGATHEMES

THEME	EXPLANATION	IMPORTANCE
Jesus Christ, Son of God	John shows us that Jesus is unique as God's special Son, yet he is fully God. Because he is fully God, Jesus is able to reveal God to us clearly and accurately.	Because Jesus is God's Son, we can perfectly trust what he says. By trusting him, we can gain an open mind to understand God's message and fulfill his purpose in our lives.
Eternal Life	Because Jesus is God, he lives forever. Before the world began, he lived with God, and he will reign forever with him. In John we see Jesus revealed in power and magnificence even before his resurrection.	Jesus offers eternal life to us. We are invited to begin living in a personal, eternal relationship with him now. Although we must grow old and die, by trusting him we can have a new life that lasts forever.
Belief	John records eight specific signs, or miracles, that show the nature of Jesus' power and love. We see his power over everything created, and we see his love of all people. These signs encourage us to believe in him.	Believing is active, living, and continuous trust in Jesus as God. When we believe in his life, his words, his death, and his resurrection, we are cleansed from sin and receive power to follow him. But we must respond to him by believing.
Holy Spirit	Jesus taught his disciples that the Holy Spirit would come after he ascended from earth. The Holy Spirit would then indwell, guide, counsel, and comfort those who follow Jesus. Through the Holy Spirit, Christ's presence and power are multiplied in all who believe.	Through God's Holy Spirit, we are drawn to him in faith. We must know the Holy Spirit to understand all Jesus taught. We can experience Jesus' love and guidance as we allow the Holy Spirit to do his work in us.
Resurrection	On the third day after he died, Jesus rose from the dead. This was verified by his disciples and many eyewitnesses. This reality changed the disciples from frightened deserters to dynamic leaders in the new church. This fact is the foundation of the Christian faith.	We can be changed as the disciples were and have confidence that our bodies will one day be raised to live with Christ forever. The same power that raised Christ to life can give us the ability to follow Christ each day.

A. BIRTH AND PREPARATION OF JESUS, THE SON OF GOD (1:1—2:11)

In this Gospel, John provides clear evidence that Jesus is the Son of God and that by believing in him we may have eternal life. John also provides unique material about Jesus' birth. He did not come into being when he was born, because he is eternal.

God Became a Human (2)

1 In the beginning was the Word, and the Word was with God, *a* and the Word was God. ² He was with God in the beginning.

³ Through him all things were made; without him nothing was made that has been made. *b* ⁴ In him was life, *c* and that life was the light of men. ⁵ The light shines in the darkness, but the darkness has not understood *a* it. *d*

⁶ There came a man who was sent from God; his name was John. *e* ⁷ He came as a witness to testify concerning that light, so that through him all men might believe. ⁸ He himself was not the light; he came only as a witness to the light. ⁹ The true light *f* that gives light to every man *g* was coming into the world. *b*

¹⁰ He was in the world, and though the world was made through him, *h* the world did not recognize him. ¹¹ He came to that which was his own, but his own did not receive him. ¹² Yet to all who received him, to those who believed in his name, he gave the right to become children of God *i*— ¹³ children born not of natural descent, *c* nor of human decision or a husband's will, but born of God. *j*

¹⁴ The Word became flesh *k* and made his dwelling among us. We have seen his glory, the glory of the One and Only, *d* who came from the Father, full of grace and truth.

a5 Or darkness, and the darkness has not overcome *b9 Or This was the true light that gives light to every man who comes into the world* *c13 Greek of bloods* *d14 Or the Only Begotten*

1:1	*a* 1Jn 1:2
1:3	*b* Col 1:16
1:4	*c* Jn 5:26
1:5	*d* Jn 3:19
1:6	*e* Mt 3:1
1:9	*f* 1Jn 2:8 *g* Isa 49:6
1:10	*h* Heb 1:2
1:12	*i* Gal 3:26
1:13	*j* Jn 3:6; 1Pe 1:23
1:14	*k* Gal 4:4; 1Ti 3:16

1:1 What Jesus taught and what he did are tied inseparably to who he is. John shows Jesus as fully human and fully God. Although Jesus took upon himself full humanity and lived as a man, he never ceased to be the eternal God who has always existed, the Creator and Sustainer of all things, and the source of eternal life. This is the truth about Jesus, and the foundation of all truth. If we cannot or do not believe this basic truth, we will not have enough faith to trust our eternal destiny to him. That is why John wrote this Gospel—to build faith and confidence in Jesus Christ so that we may believe that he truly was and is the Son of God (20:30, 31).

1:1 John wrote to believers everywhere, both Jews and non-Jews (Gentiles). As one of Jesus' 12 disciples, John writes with credibility and the details of an eyewitness. His book is not a biography (like the book of Luke); it is a thematic presentation of Jesus' life. Many in John's original audience had a Greek background. Greek culture encouraged worship of many mythological gods, whose supernatural characteristics were as important to Greeks as genealogies were to Jews. John shows that Jesus is not only different from but superior to these gods of mythology.

1:1ff What does John mean by "the Word"? *The Word* was a term used by theologians and philosophers, both Jews and Greeks, in many different ways. In Hebrew Scripture, *the Word* was an agent of creation (Psalm 33:6), the source of God's message to his people through the prophets (Hosea 1:2), and God's law, his standard of holiness (Psalm 119:11). In Greek philosophy, *the Word* was the principle of reason that governed the world, or the thought still in the mind, while in Hebrew thought, *the Word* was another expression for God. John's description shows clearly that he is speaking of Jesus (see especially 1:14)—a human being he knew and loved, but at the same time the Creator of the universe, the ultimate revelation of God, the living picture of God's holiness, the One in whom "all things hold together" (Colossians 1:17). To Jewish readers, "the Word was God" was blasphemous. To Greek readers, "the Word became flesh" (1:14) was unthinkable. To John, this new understanding of the Word was gospel, the Good News of Jesus Christ.

1:3 When God created, he made something from nothing. Because we are created beings, we have no basis for pride. Remember that you exist only because God made you, and you have special gifts only because God gave them to you. With God you are something valuable and unique; apart from God you are

nothing, and if you try to live without him, you will be abandoning the purpose for which you were made.

1:3–5 Do you ever feel that your life is too complex for God to understand? Remember, God created the entire universe, and nothing is too difficult for him. God created you; he is alive today, and his love is bigger than any problem you may face.

1:4, 5 "The darkness has not understood it" means the darkness of evil never has and never will overcome or extinguish God's light. Jesus Christ is the Creator of life, and his life brings light to mankind. In his light, we see ourselves as we really are (sinners in need of a Savior). When we follow Jesus, the true Light, we can avoid walking blindly and falling into sin. He lights the path ahead of us so we can see how to live. He removes the darkness of sin from our lives. In what ways have you allowed the light of Christ to shine into your life? Let Christ guide your life, and you'll never need to stumble in darkness.

1:6–8 In this book, the name *John* refers to John the Baptist. For more information on John the Baptist, see his Profile in this chapter, p. 1737.

1:8 We, like John the Baptist, are not the source of God's light; we merely reflect that light. Jesus Christ is the true Light; he helps us see our way to God and shows us how to walk along that way. But Christ has chosen to reflect his light through his followers to an unbelieving world, perhaps because unbelievers are not able to bear the full blazing glory of his light firsthand. The word *witness* indicates our role as reflectors of Christ's light. We are never to present ourselves as the light to others, but are always to point them to Christ, the Light.

1:10, 11 Although Christ created the world, the people he created didn't recognize him (1:10). Even the people chosen by God to prepare the rest of the world for the Messiah rejected him (1:11), although the entire Old Testament pointed to his coming.

1:12, 13 All who welcome Jesus Christ as Lord of their lives are reborn spiritually, receiving new life from God. Through faith in Christ, this new birth changes us from the inside out—rearranging our attitudes, desires, and motives. Being born makes you physically alive and places you in your parents' family (1:13). Being born of God makes you spiritually alive and puts you in God's family (1:12). Have you asked Christ to make you a new person? This fresh start in life is available to all who believe in Christ.

1:14 "The Word became flesh" means becoming human. By

1:15
l Mt 3:11

1:16
m Col 1:19

¹⁵John testifies concerning him. He cries out, saying, "This was he of whom I said, 'He who comes after me has surpassed me because he was before me.'"*l* ¹⁶From the fullness*m* of his grace we have all received one blessing after another. ¹⁷For the law was given through

---

JOHN THE BAPTIST

There's no getting around it—John the Baptist was unique. He wore odd clothes and ate strange food and preached an unusual message to the Judeans who went out to the wastelands to see him.

But John did not aim at uniqueness for its own sake. Instead, he aimed at obedience. He knew he had a specific role to play in the world—announcing the coming of the Savior—and he put all his energies into this task. Luke tells us that John was in the desert when God's word of direction came to him. John was ready and waiting. The angel who had announced John's birth to Zechariah had made it clear this child was to be a Nazirite—one set apart for God's service. John remained faithful to that calling.

This wild-looking man had no power or position in the Jewish political system, but he spoke with almost irresistible authority. People were moved by his words because he spoke the truth, challenging them to turn from their sins and baptizing them as a symbol of their repentance. They responded by the hundreds. But even as people crowded to him, he pointed beyond himself, never forgetting that his main role was to announce the coming of the Savior.

The words of truth that moved many to repentance goaded others to resistance and resentment. John even challenged Herod to admit his sin. Herodias, the woman Herod had married illegally, decided to get rid of this desert preacher. Although she was able to have him killed, she was not able to stop his message. The One John had announced was already on the move. John had accomplished his mission.

God has given each of us a purpose for living, and we can trust him to guide us. John did not have the complete Bible as we know it today, but he focused his life on the truth he knew from the available Old Testament Scriptures. Likewise we can discover in God's Word the truths he wants us to know. And as these truths work in us, others will be drawn to him. God can use you in a way he can use no one else. Let him know your willingness to follow him today.

Strengths and accomplishments:	• The God-appointed messenger to announce the arrival of Jesus • A preacher whose theme was repentance • A fearless confronter • Known for his remarkable lifestyle • Uncompromising
Lessons from his life:	• God does not guarantee an easy or safe life to those who serve him • Doing what God desires is the greatest possible life investment • Standing for the truth is more important than life itself
Vital statistics:	• Where: Judea • Occupation: Prophet • Relatives: Father: Zechariah. Mother: Elizabeth. Distant relative: Jesus. • Contemporaries: Herod Anitpas, Herodias
Key verse:	"I tell you the truth: Among those born of women there has not risen anyone greater than John the Baptist; yet he who is least in the kingdom of heaven is greater than he" (Matthew 11:11).

John's story is told in all four Gospels. His coming was predicted in Isaiah 40:3 and Malachi 4:5; and he is mentioned in Acts 1:5, 22; 10:37; 11:16; 13:24, 25; 18:25; 19:3, 4.

---

doing so, Christ became (1) *the perfect teacher*—in Jesus' life we see how God thinks and therefore how we should think (Philippians 2:5–11); (2) *the perfect example*—as a model of what we are to become, he shows us how to live and gives us the power to live that way (1 Peter 2:21); (3) *the perfect sacrifice*—Jesus came as a sacrifice for all sins, and his death satisfied God's requirements for the removal of sin (Colossians 1:15–23).

1:14 "The One and Only, who came from the Father" means Jesus is God's only and unique Son. The emphasis is on *unique*. Jesus is one of a kind and enjoys a relationship with God unlike all believers who are called "children" and said to be "born of God."

1:14 When Christ was born, God became a man. He was not part man and part God; he was completely human and completely divine (Colossians 2:9). Before Christ came, people could know God partially. After Christ came, people could know

God fully because he became visible and tangible in Christ. Christ is the perfect expression of God in human form. The two most common errors people make about Jesus are to minimize his humanity or to minimize his divinity. Jesus is both God and man.

1:17 Law and grace are both aspects of God's nature that he uses in dealing with us. Moses emphasized God's law and justice, while Jesus Christ came to highlight God's mercy, love, and forgiveness. Moses could only be the giver of the law, while Christ came to fulfill the law (Matthew 5:17). The nature and will of God were revealed in the law; now the nature and will of God are revealed in Jesus Christ. Rather than coming through cold stone tablets, God's revelation (truth) now comes through a person's life. As we get to know Christ better, our understanding of God will increase.

Moses; grace and truth came through Jesus Christ. [18]No one has ever seen God,[n] but God the One and Only,[a, b] [o] who is at the Father's side, has made him known.

[n]Ex 33:20; Jn 6:46
[o]1Jn 4:9

John the Baptist Declares His Mission (19)

[19]Now this was John's testimony when the Jews of Jerusalem sent priests and Levites to ask him who he was. [20]He did not fail to confess, but confessed freely, "I am not the Christ.[c] "[p]

1:20
[p]Lk 3:15, 16

[21]They asked him, "Then who are you? Are you Elijah?"[q]

He said, "I am not."

"Are you the Prophet?"[r]

He answered, "No."

1:21
[q]Mt 11:14
[r]Dt 18:15

[22]Finally they said, "Who are you? Give us an answer to take back to those who sent us. What do you say about yourself?"

[23]John replied in the words of Isaiah the prophet, "I am the voice of one calling in the desert, 'Make straight the way for the Lord.'"[d] [s]

1:23
[s]Isa 40:3

[24]Now some Pharisees who had been sent [25]questioned him, "Why then do you baptize if you are not the Christ, nor Elijah, nor the Prophet?"

[26]"I baptize with[e] water," John replied, "but among you stands one you do not know. [27]He is the one who comes after me, the thongs of whose sandals I am not worthy to untie." [28]This all happened at Bethany on the other side of the Jordan,[t] where John was baptizing.

1:28
[t]Jn 3:26

John the Baptist Proclaims Jesus as the Messiah (20)

[29]The next day John saw Jesus coming toward him and said, "Look, the Lamb of God,[u] who takes away the sin of the world! [30]This is the one I meant when I said, 'A man who comes after me has surpassed me because he was before me.'[v] [31]I myself did not know him, but the reason I came baptizing with water was that he might be revealed to Israel."

1:29
[u]Isa 53:7; 1Pe 1:19
1:30
[v]ver 15, 27

[a]18 Or the Only Begotten   [b]18 Some manuscripts but the only (or only begotten) Son   [c]20 Or Messiah. "The Christ" (Greek) and "the Messiah" (Hebrew) both mean "the Anointed One"; also in verse 25.   [d]23 Isaiah 40:3   [e]26 Or in; also in verses 31 and 33

1:18 God communicated through various people in the Old Testament, usually prophets who were told to give specific messages. But no one ever *saw* God. "God the One and Only" is a title showing that Jesus is both God and the Father's unique Son. In Christ, God revealed his nature and essence in a way that could be seen and touched. In Christ, God became a man who lived on earth.

1:19 The priests and Levites were respected religious leaders in Jerusalem. Priests served in the temple, and Levites assisted them. The leaders that came to see John were Pharisees (1:24), a group that both John the Baptist and Jesus often denounced. Many of them outwardly obeyed God's laws to look pious, while inwardly their hearts were filled with pride and greed. The Pharisees believed that their own oral traditions were just as important as God's inspired Word. For more information on the Pharisees, see the charts in Matthew 3, p. 1533 and Mark 2, p. 1609.

These leaders came to see John the Baptist for several reasons: (1) Their duty as guardians of the faith included investigating any new teaching or movement (Deuteronomy 13:1–5; 18:20–22). (2) They wanted to find out if John had the credentials of a prophet. (3) John had quite a following, and it was growing. They were probably jealous and wanted to see why this man was so popular.

1:21–23 In the Pharisees' minds, there were four options regarding John the Baptist's identity: he was (1) the prophet foretold by Moses (Deuteronomy 18:15), (2) Elijah (Malachi 4:5), (3) the Messiah, or (4) a false prophet. John denied being the first three personages. Instead he called himself, in the words of the Old Testament prophet Isaiah, "A voice of one calling: 'In the desert prepare the way for the LORD'" (Isaiah 40:3). The leaders kept pressing John to say who he was because people were expecting the Messiah to come (Luke 3:15). But John emphasized only *why* he had come—to prepare the way for the Messiah. The Pharisees missed the point. They wanted to know who John was, but John wanted to prepare them to recognize who Jesus was.

1:25, 26 John was baptizing Jews. The Essenes (a strict, monastic sect of Judaism) practiced baptism for purification, but

normally only non-Jews (Gentiles) were baptized when they converted to Judaism. When the Pharisees questioned John's authority to baptize, they were asking who gave John the right to treat God's chosen people like Gentiles. John said, "I baptize with water"—he was merely helping the people perform a symbolic act of repentance. But soon one would come who would truly *forgive* sins, something only the Son of God—the Messiah—could do.

1:27 John the Baptist said he was not even worthy to be Christ's slave, to perform the humble task of unfastening his shoes. But according to Luke 7:28, Jesus said that John was the greatest of all prophets. If such a great person felt inadequate even to be Christ's slave, how much more should we lay aside our pride to serve Christ! When we truly understand who Christ is, our pride and self-importance melt away.

1:29 Every morning and evening, a lamb was sacrificed in the temple for the sins of the people (Exodus 29:38–42). Isaiah 53:7 prophesied that the Messiah, God's servant, would be led to the slaughter like a lamb. To pay the penalty for sin, a life had to be given—and God chose to provide the sacrifice himself. The sins of the world were removed when Jesus died as the perfect sacrifice. This is the way our sins are forgiven (1 Corinthians 5:7). The "sin of the world" means everyone's sin, the sin of each individual. Jesus paid the price of *your* sin by his death. You can receive forgiveness by confessing your sin to him and asking for his forgiveness.

1:30 Although John the Baptist was a well-known preacher who attracted large crowds, he was content for Jesus to take the higher place. This is true humility, the basis for greatness in preaching, teaching, or any other work we do for Christ. When you are content to do what God wants you to do and let Jesus Christ be honored for it, God will do great things through you.

1:31–34 At Jesus' baptism, John the Baptist had declared Jesus to be the Messiah. At that time God had given John a sign to show him that Jesus truly had been sent from God (1:33). John and Jesus were related (see Luke 1:36), so John probably knew who he was. But it wasn't until Jesus' baptism that John understood

1:32
ʷMt 3:16; Mk 1:10
1:33
ˣMt 3:11
1:34
ʸver 49

³²Then John gave this testimony: "I saw the Spirit come down from heaven as a dove and remain on him. ʷ ³³I would not have known him, except that the one who sent me to baptize with water told me, 'The man on whom you see the Spirit come down and remain is he who will baptize with the Holy Spirit.' ˣ ³⁴I have seen and I testify that this is the Son of God." ʸ

The First Disciples Follow Jesus (21)

1:36
ᶻver 29

³⁵The next day John was there again with two of his disciples. ³⁶When he saw Jesus passing by, he said, "Look, the Lamb of God!" ᶻ

³⁷When the two disciples heard him say this, they followed Jesus. ³⁸Turning around, Jesus saw them following and asked, "What do you want?"

They said, "Rabbi" (which means Teacher), "where are you staying?"

³⁹"Come," he replied, "and you will see."

So they went and saw where he was staying, and spent that day with him. It was about the tenth hour.

1:41
ªJn 4:25
1:42
ᵇMt 16:18

⁴⁰Andrew, Simon Peter's brother, was one of the two who heard what John had said and who had followed Jesus. ⁴¹The first thing Andrew did was to find his brother Simon and tell him, "We have found the Messiah" (that is, the Christ). ª ⁴²And he brought him to Jesus.

Jesus looked at him and said, "You are Simon son of John. You will be called Cephas" (which, when translated, is Peterª). ᵇ

1:43
ᶜMt 10:3; Jn 14:8, 9
1:44
ᵈJn 12:21
1:45
ᵉJn 21:2
ᶠLk 24:27
ᵍMt 2:23

⁴³The next day Jesus decided to leave for Galilee. Finding Philip,ᶜ he said to him, "Follow me."

⁴⁴Philip, like Andrew and Peter, was from the town of Bethsaida. ᵈ ⁴⁵Philip found Nathanaelᵉ and told him, "We have found the one Moses wrote about in the Law,ᶠ and about whom the prophets also wrote—Jesus of Nazareth,ᵍ the son of Joseph."

ª42 Both *Cephas* (Aramaic) and *Peter* (Greek) mean *rock*.

---

that Jesus was the Messiah. Jesus' baptism is described in Matthew 3:13–17; Mark 1:9–11; and Luke 3:21, 22.

1:33 John the Baptist's baptism with water was preparatory, because it was for repentance and symbolized the washing away of sins. Jesus, by contrast, would baptize with the Holy Spirit. He would send the Holy Spirit upon all believers, empowering them to live and to teach the message of salvation. This outpouring of the Spirit came after Jesus had risen from the dead and ascended into heaven (see 20:22; Acts 2).

1:34 John the Baptist's job was to point people to Jesus, their long-awaited Messiah. Today people are looking for someone to give them security in an insecure world. Our job is to point them to Christ and to show that he is the one whom they seek.

1:35ff These new disciples used several names for Jesus: Lamb of God (1:36), Rabbi (1:38), Messiah (1:41), Son of God (1:49), and King of Israel (1:49). As they got to know Jesus, their appreciation for him grew. The more time we spend getting to know Christ, the more we will understand and appreciate who he is. We may be drawn to him for his teaching, but we will come to know him as the Son of God. Although these disciples made this verbal shift in a few days, they would not fully understand Jesus until three years later (Acts 2). What they so easily professed had to be worked out in experience. We may find that words of faith come easily, but deep appreciation for Christ comes with living by faith.

1:37 One of the two disciples was Andrew (1:40). The other was probably John, the writer of this book. Why did these disciples leave John the Baptist? Because that's what John wanted them to do—he was pointing the way to Jesus, the one John had prepared them to follow. These were Jesus' first disciples, along with Simon Peter (1:42) and Nathanael (1:45).

1:38 When the two disciples began to follow Jesus, he asked them, "What do you want?" Following Christ is not enough; we must follow him for the right reasons. To follow Christ for our own purposes would be asking Christ to follow us—to align with us to support and advance our cause, not his. We must examine our motives for following him. Are we seeking his glory or ours?

1:40–42 Andrew accepted John the Baptist's testimony about Jesus and immediately went to tell his brother, Simon, about him.

There was no question in Andrew's mind that Jesus was the Messiah. Not only did he tell his brother, he was also eager to introduce others to Jesus (see 6:8, 9; 12:22). How many people in your life have heard you talk about your relationship with Jesus?

1:42 Jesus saw not only who Simon was, but who he would become. That is why he gave him a new name—*Cephas* in Aramaic, *Peter* in Greek (the name means "a rock"). Peter is not presented as rock-solid throughout the Gospels, but he became a solid rock in the days of the early church, as we learn in the book of Acts. By giving Simon a new name, Jesus introduced a change in character. For more on Simon Peter, see his Profile in Matthew 27, p. 1595.

JESUS' FIRST TRAVELS
After his baptism by John in the Jordan River and the temptation by Satan in the desert (see the map in Mark 1, p. 1605), Jesus returned to Galilee. He visited Nazareth, Cana, and Capernaum, and then returned to Jerusalem for the Passover.

46"Nazareth! Can anything good come from there?" [h] Nathanael asked.

"Come and see," said Philip.

47When Jesus saw Nathanael approaching, he said of him, "Here is a true Israelite, [i] in whom there is nothing false."

48"How do you know me?" Nathanael asked.

Jesus answered, "I saw you while you were still under the fig tree before Philip called you."

49Then Nathanael declared, "Rabbi, you are the Son of God; you are the King of Israel." [j]

50Jesus said, "You believe[a] because I told you I saw you under the fig tree. You shall see greater things than that." 51He then added, "I tell you[b] the truth, you[b] shall see heaven open, and the angels of God ascending and descending[k] on the Son of Man."

Jesus Turns Water into Wine (22)

2 On the third day a wedding took place at Cana in Galilee.[l] Jesus' mother was there, 2and Jesus and his disciples had also been invited to the wedding. 3When the wine was gone, Jesus' mother said to him, "They have no more wine."

4"Dear woman,[m] why do you involve me?" Jesus replied. "My time[n] has not yet come."

5His mother said to the servants, "Do whatever he tells you."

6Nearby stood six stone water jars, the kind used by the Jews for ceremonial washing,[o] each holding from twenty to thirty gallons.[c]

7Jesus said to the servants, "Fill the jars with water"; so they filled them to the brim.

8Then he told them, "Now draw some out and take it to the master of the banquet."

They did so, 9and the master of the banquet tasted the water that had been turned into wine.[p] He did not realize where it had come from, though the servants who had drawn the water knew. Then he called the bridegroom aside 10and said, "Everyone brings out the choice wine first and then the cheaper wine after the guests have had too much to drink; but you have saved the best till now."

a50 Or *Do you believe . . . ?*   b51 The Greek is plural.   c6 Greek *two to three metretes* (probably about 75 to 115 liters).

1:46 [h] Jn 7:41, 42, 52

1:47 [i] Ro 9:4, 6

1:49 [j] Jn 12:13

1:51 [k] Ge 28:12

2:1 [l] Jn 4:46

2:4 [m] Jn 19:26 [n] Jn 7:6

2:6 [o] Mk 7:3, 4; Jn 3:25

2:9 [p] Jn 4:46

1:46 Nazareth was despised by the Jews because a Roman army garrison was located there. Some have speculated that an aloof attitude or a poor reputation in morals and religion on the part of the people of Nazareth led to Nathanael's harsh comment. Nathanael's hometown was Cana, about four miles from Nazareth.

1:46 When Nathanael heard that the Messiah was from Nazareth, he was surprised. Philip responded, "Come and see." Fortunately for Nathanael, he went to meet Jesus and became a disciple. If he had stuck to his prejudice without investigating further, he would have missed the Messiah! Don't let people's stereotypes about Christ cause them to miss his power and love. Invite them to come and see who Jesus really is.

1:47–49 Jesus knew about Nathanael before the two ever met. Jesus also knows what we are really like. An honest person will feel comfortable with the thought that Jesus knows him or her through and through. A dishonest person will feel uncomfortable. You can't pretend to be something you're not. God knows the real you and wants *you* to follow him.

1:51 This is a reference to Jacob's dream recorded in Genesis 28:12. As the unique God-man, Jesus would be the ladder between heaven and earth. Jesus is not saying that this would be a physical experience (that they would see the ladder with their eyes) like the transfiguration, but that they would have spiritual insight into Jesus' true nature and purpose for coming.

2:1, 2 Jesus was on a mission to save the world, the greatest mission in the history of mankind. Yet he took time to attend a wedding and take part in its festivities. We may be tempted to think we should not take time out from our "important" work for social occasions. But maybe these social occasions are part of our mission. Jesus valued these wedding festivities because they involved people, and Jesus came to be with people. Our mission can often be accomplished in joyous times of celebration with others. Bring balance to your life by bringing Jesus into times of pleasure as well as times of work.

2:1–3 Weddings in Jesus' day were weeklong festivals. Banquets would be prepared for many guests, and the week would be spent celebrating the new life of the married couple. Often the whole town was invited, and everybody would come—it was considered an insult to refuse an invitation to a wedding. To accommodate many people, careful planning was needed. To run out of wine was more than embarrassing; it broke the strong unwritten laws of hospitality. Jesus was about to respond to a heartfelt need.

2:4 Mary was probably not asking Jesus to do a miracle; she was simply hoping that her son would help solve this major problem and find some wine. Tradition says that Joseph, Mary's husband, was dead, so she probably was used to asking for her son's help in certain situations. Jesus' answer to Mary is difficult to understand, but maybe that is the point. Although Mary did not understand what Jesus was going to do, she trusted him to do what was right. Those who believe in Jesus but run into situations they cannot understand must continue to trust that he will work in the best way.

2:5 Mary submitted to Jesus' way of doing things. She recognized that Jesus was more than her human son—he was the Son of God. When we bring our problems to Christ, we may think we know how he should take care of them. But he may have a completely different plan. Like Mary, we should submit and allow him to deal with the problem as he sees best.

2:6 The six stone water jars were normally used for ceremonial washing. When full, the pots would hold 20 to 30 gallons. According to the Jews' ceremonial law, people became symbolically unclean by touching objects of everyday life. Before eating, the Jews would pour water over their hands to cleanse themselves of any bad influences associated with what they had touched.

2:10 People look everywhere but to God for excitement and meaning. For some reason, they expect God to be dull and lifeless. Just as the wine Jesus made was the best, so life in him is better than life on our own. Why wait until everything else runs out before trying God? Why save the best until last?

2:11
q Jn 1:14

¹¹This, the first of his miraculous signs, Jesus performed at Cana in Galilee. He thus revealed his glory,q and his disciples put their faith in him.

B. MESSAGE AND MINISTRY OF JESUS, THE SON OF GOD (2:12—12:50)

John stresses the deity of Christ. He gives us eight miracles that serve as signs that Jesus is the Messiah. In this section he records Jesus describing himself as the bread of life, the water of life, the light of the world, the door, and the good shepherd. John provides teachings of Jesus found nowhere else. This is the most theological of the four Gospels.

1. Jesus encounters belief and unbelief from the people
Jesus Clears the Temple (23)

2:12
r Mt 12:46

¹²After this he went down to Capernaum with his mother and brothersr and his disciples. There they stayed for a few days.

NICODEMUS

God specializes in finding and changing people we consider out of reach. It took a while for Nicodemus to come out of the dark, but God was patient with this "undercover" believer.

Afraid of being discovered, Nicodemus made an appointment to see Jesus at night. Daylight conversations between Pharisees and Jesus tended to be antagonistic, but Nicodemus really wanted to learn. He probably got a lot more than he expected—a challenge to a new life! We know very little about Nicodemus, but we know that he left that evening's encounter a changed man. He came away with a whole new understanding of both God and himself.

Nicodemus next appears as part of the Jewish council. As the group discussed ways to eliminate Jesus, Nicodemus raised the question of justice. Although his objection was overruled, he had spoken up. He had begun to change.

Our last picture of Nicodemus shows him joining Joseph of Arimathea in asking for Jesus' body in order to provide for its burial. Realizing what he was risking, Nicodemus was making a bold move. He was continuing to grow.

God looks for steady growth, not instant perfection. How well does your present level of spiritual growth match up with how long you have known Jesus?

Strengths and accomplishments:	• One of the few religious leaders who believed in Jesus • A member of the powerful Jewish council • A Pharisee who was attracted by Jesus' character and miracles • Joined with Joseph of Arimathea in burying Jesus
Weakness and mistake:	• Limited by his fear of being publicly exposed as Jesus' follower
Lessons from his life:	• Unless we are born again, we can never be part of the kingdom of God • God is able to change those we might consider unreachable • God is patient, but persistent • If we are available, God can use us
Vital statistics:	• Where: Jerusalem • Occupation: Religious leader • Contemporaries: Jesus, Annas, Caiaphas, Pilate, Joseph of Arimathea
Key verse:	"'How can a man be born when he is old?' Nicodemus asked. 'Surely he cannot enter a second time into his mother's womb to be born!'" (John 3:4).

Nicodemus's story is told in John 3:1–21; 7:50–52; and 19:39, 40.

2:11 When the disciples saw Jesus' miracle, they believed. The miracle showed his power over nature and revealed the way he would go about his ministry—helping others, speaking with authority, and being in personal touch with people.

Miracles are not merely superhuman events, but events that demonstrate God's power. Almost every miracle Jesus did was a renewal of fallen creation—restoring sight, making the lame walk, even restoring life to the dead. Believe in Christ not because he is a superman but because he is the God who continues his creation, even in those of us who are poor, weak, crippled, orphaned, blind, deaf, or with some other desperate need.

2:12 Capernaum became Jesus' home base during his ministry in Galilee. Located on a major trade route, it was an important city in the region, with a Roman garrison and a customs station. At Capernaum, Matthew was called to be a disciple (Matthew 9:9). The city was also the home of several other disciples (Matthew 4:13–19) and a high-ranking government official (4:46). It had at least one major synagogue. Although Jesus made this city his base of operations in Galilee, he condemned it for the people's unbelief (Matthew 11:23; Luke 10:15).

13When it was almost time for the Jewish Passover, Jesus went up to Jerusalem. s 14In the
temple courts he found men selling cattle, sheep and doves, and others sitting at tables exchanging money. 15So he made a whip out of cords, and drove all from the temple area, both
sheep and cattle; he scattered the coins of the money changers and overturned their tables.
16To those who sold doves he said, "Get these out of here! How dare you turn my Father's
house t into a market!"

17His disciples remembered that it is written: "Zeal for your house will consume me."a u

18Then the Jews demanded of him, "What miraculous sign can you show us to prove your
authority to do all this?" v

19Jesus answered them, "Destroy this temple, and I will raise it again in three days." w

20The Jews replied, "It has taken forty-six years to build this temple, and you are going to
raise it in three days?" 21But the temple he had spoken of was his body. x 22After he was
raised from the dead, his disciples recalled what he had said.y Then they believed the Scripture and the words that Jesus had spoken.

23Now while he was in Jerusalem at the Passover Feast, many people saw the miraculous
signs he was doing and believed in his name. b 24But Jesus would not entrust himself to
them, for he knew all men. 25He did not need man's testimony about man, for he knew what
was in a man.z

a 17 Psalm 69:9   b 23 Or and believed in him

2:13 sDt 16:1-6

2:16 tLk 2:49

2:17 uPs 69:9

2:18 vMt 12:38

2:19 wMt 26:61; 27:40; Mk 14:58

2:21 x1Co 6:19

2:22 yLk 24:5-8

2:25 zJn 6:61, 64

2:13 The Passover celebration took place yearly at the temple in Jerusalem. Every Jewish male was expected to make a pilgrimage to Jerusalem during this time (Deuteronomy 16:16). This was a weeklong festival—the Passover was one day, and the Feast of Unleavened Bread lasted the rest of the week. The entire week commemorated the freeing of the Jews from slavery in Egypt (Exodus 12:1–13).

2:13 Jerusalem was both the religious and the political seat of Palestine, and the place where the Messiah was expected to arrive. The temple was located there, and many Jewish families from all over the world would travel to Jerusalem during the key feasts. The temple was on an imposing site, a hill overlooking the city. Solomon had built the first temple on this same site almost 1,000 years earlier (959 B.C.), but his temple had been destroyed by the Babylonians (2 Kings 25). The temple was rebuilt in 515 B.C., and Herod the Great had enlarged and remodeled it.

2:14 The temple area was always crowded during Passover with thousands of out-of-town visitors. The religious leaders crowded it even further by allowing money changers and merchants to set up booths in the court of the Gentiles. They rationalized this prac-tice as a convenience for the worshipers and as a way to make money for temple upkeep. But the religious leaders did not seem to care that the court of the Gentiles was so full of merchants that foreigners found it difficult to worship. And worship was the main purpose for visiting the temple. No wonder Jesus was angry!

2:14 The temple tax had to be paid in local currency, so foreign-ers had to have their money changed. But the money changers often charged exorbitant exchange rates. The people also were required to make sacrifices for sins. Because of the long journey, many could not bring their own animals. Some who brought animals had them rejected for imperfections. So animal mer-chants conducted a flourishing business in the temple courtyard. The price of sacrificial animals was much higher in the temple area than elsewhere. Jesus was angry at the dishonest, greedy practices of the money changers and merchants, and he particu-larly disliked their presence on the temple grounds. They were making a mockery of God's house of worship.

2:14ff John records this first clearing, or cleansing, of the temple. A second clearing occurred at the end of Jesus' ministry, about three years later, and that event is recorded in Matthew 21:12–17; Mark 11:12–19; Luke 19:45–48.

2:14–16 God's temple was being misused by people who had turned it into a marketplace. They had forgotten, or didn't care, that God's house is a place of worship, not a place for making a profit. Our attitude toward the church is wrong if we see it as

a place for personal contacts or business advantage. Make sure you attend church to worship God.

2:15, 16 Jesus was obviously angry at the merchants who exploited those who had come to God's house to worship. There is a difference between uncontrolled rage and righteous indignation—yet both are called anger. We must be very careful how we use the powerful emotion of anger. It is right to be angry about injustice and sin; it is wrong to be angry over trivial personal offenses.

2:15, 16 Jesus made a whip and chased out the money chang-ers. Does his example permit us to use violence against wrong-doers? Certain authority is granted to some, but not to all. For example, the authority to use weapons and restrain people is granted to police officers, but not to the general public. The authority to imprison people is granted to judges, but not to individual citizens. Jesus had God's authority, something we cannot have. While we want to live like Christ, we should never try to claim his authority where it has not been given to us.

2:17 Jesus took the evil acts in the temple as an insult against God, and thus he did not deal with them halfheartedly. He was consumed with righteous anger against such flagrant disrespect for God.

2:19, 20 The Jews understood Jesus to mean the temple out of which he had just driven the merchants and money changers. This was the temple Zerubbabel had built over 500 years earlier, but Herod the Great had begun remodeling it, making it much larger and far more beautiful. It had been 46 years since this remodeling had started (20 B.C.), and it still wasn't completely finished. They understood Jesus' words to mean that this impos-ing building could be torn down and rebuilt in three days, and they were startled.

2:21, 22 Jesus was not talking about the temple made of stones, but about his body. His listeners didn't realize it, but Jesus was greater than the temple (Matthew 12:6). His words would take on meaning for his disciples after his resurrection. That Christ so perfectly fulfilled this prediction became the strongest proof for his claims to be God.

2:23–25 The Son of God knows all about human nature. Jesus was well aware of the truth of Jeremiah 17:9, which states, "The heart is deceitful above all things and beyond cure. Who can understand it?" Jesus was discerning, and he knew that the faith of some followers was superficial. Some of the same people claiming to believe in Jesus at this time would later yell "Crucify him!" It's easy to believe when it is exciting and everyone else believes the same way. But keep your faith firm even when it isn't popular to follow Christ.

Nicodemus Visits Jesus at Night (24)

3:2
a Jn 9:16, 33
b Ac 2:22; 10:38

3 Now there was a man of the Pharisees named Nicodemus, a member of the Jewish ruling council. ²He came to Jesus at night and said, "Rabbi, we know you are a teacher who has come from God. For no one could perform the miraculous signs a you are doing if God were not with him." b

³In reply Jesus declared, "I tell you the truth, no one can see the kingdom of God unless he is born again. a "

⁴"How can a man be born when he is old?" Nicodemus asked. "Surely he cannot enter a second time into his mother's womb to be born!"

⁵Jesus answered, "I tell you the truth, no one can enter the kingdom of God unless he is born of water and the Spirit. ⁶Flesh gives birth to flesh, but the Spirit b gives birth to spirit. ⁷You should not be surprised at my saying, 'You c must be born again.' ⁸The wind blows wherever it pleases. You hear its sound, but you cannot tell where it comes from or where it is going. So it is with everyone born of the Spirit."

⁹"How can this be?" Nicodemus asked.

3:11
c Jn 7:16, 17

¹⁰"You are Israel's teacher," said Jesus, "and do you not understand these things? ¹¹I tell you the truth, we speak of what we know, c and we testify to what we have seen, but still you people do not accept our testimony. ¹²I have spoken to you of earthly things and you do not believe; how then will you believe if I speak of heavenly things? ¹³No one has ever gone into

a3 Or *born from above*; also in verse 7   b6 Or *but spirit*   c7 The Greek is plural.

3:1 Nicodemus was a Pharisee and a member of the ruling council (called the high council, or the Sanhedrin). The Pharisees were a group of religious leaders whom Jesus and John the Baptist often criticized for being hypocrites (see the note on Matthew 3:7 for more on the Pharisees). Most Pharisees were intensely jealous of Jesus because he undermined their authority and challenged their views. But Nicodemus was searching, and he believed that Jesus had some answers. A learned teacher himself, he came to Jesus to be taught. No matter how intelligent and well educated you are, you must come to Jesus with an open mind and heart so he can teach you the truth about God.

3:1ff Nicodemus came to Jesus personally, although he could have sent one of his assistants. He wanted to examine Jesus for himself to separate fact from rumor. Perhaps Nicodemus was afraid of what his peers, the Pharisees, would say about his visit, so he came after dark. Later, when he understood that Jesus was truly the Messiah, he spoke up boldly in his defense (7:50, 51). Like Nicodemus, we must examine Jesus for ourselves—others cannot do it for us. Then, if we believe he is who he says, we will want to speak up for him.

3:3 What did Nicodemus know about the kingdom? From the Bible he knew it would be ruled by God, it would be restored on earth, and it would incorporate God's people. Jesus revealed to this devout Pharisee that the kingdom would come to the whole world (3:16), not just the Jews, and that Nicodemus wouldn't be a part of it unless he was personally born again (3:5). This was a revolutionary concept: the kingdom is personal, not national or ethnic, and its entrance requirements are repentance and spiritual rebirth. Jesus later taught that God's kingdom has *already begun* in the hearts of believers (Luke 17:21). It will be fully realized when Jesus returns again to judge the world and abolish evil forever (Revelation 21; 22).

3:5, 6 "Born of water and the Spirit" could refer to (1) the contrast between physical birth (water) and spiritual birth (Spirit), or (2) being regenerated by the Spirit and signifying that rebirth by Christian baptism. The water may also represent the cleansing action of God's Holy Spirit (Titus 3:5). Nicodemus undoubtedly would have been familiar with God's promise in Ezekiel 36:25, 26. Jesus was explaining the importance of a spiritual rebirth, saying that people don't enter the kingdom by living a better life, but by being spiritually reborn.

3:6 Who is the Holy Spirit? God is three persons in one—the Father, the Son, and the Holy Spirit. God became a man in Jesus so that Jesus could die for our sins. Jesus rose from the dead to

offer salvation to all people through spiritual renewal and rebirth. When Jesus ascended into heaven, his physical presence left the earth, but he promised to send the Holy Spirit so that his spiritual presence would still be among mankind (see Luke 24:49). The Holy Spirit first became available to all believers at Pentecost (Acts 2). Whereas in Old Testament days the Holy Spirit empowered specific individuals for specific purposes, now all believers have the power of the Holy Spirit available to them. For more on the Holy Spirit, read 14:16–28; Romans 8:9; 1 Corinthians 12:13; and 2 Corinthians 1:22.

3:8 Jesus explained that we cannot control the work of the Holy Spirit. He works in ways we cannot predict or understand. Just as you did not control your physical birth, so you cannot control your spiritual birth. It is a gift from God through the Holy Spirit (Romans 8:16; 1 Corinthians 2:10–12; 1 Thessalonians 1:5, 6).

3:10, 11 This Jewish teacher of the Bible knew the Old Testament thoroughly, but he didn't understand what it said about the Messiah. Knowledge is not salvation. You should know the Bible, but even more important, you should understand the God whom the Bible reveals and the salvation that God offers.

Mediterranean Sea
GALILEE
N
Cana • Capernaum
Sea of Galilee
Nazareth •
Mount Ebal
SAMARIA
Mount Gerizim
Sychar
Jerusalem •
Jordan River
PEREA
JUDEA
Dead Sea
IDUMEA
0   20 Mi.
0   20 Km.

THE VISIT IN SAMARIA
Jesus went to Jerusalem for the Passover, cleared the temple, and talked with Nicodemus, a religious leader, about eternal life. He then left Jerusalem and traveled in Judea. On his way to Galilee, he visited Sychar and other villages in Samaria. Unlike most Jews of the day, he did not try to avoid the region of Samaria.

heaven *d* except the one who came from heaven *e* —the Son of Man. *a* 14 Just as Moses lifted up the snake in the desert, *f* so the Son of Man must be lifted up, *g* 15 that everyone who believes in him may have eternal life. *b*

16 "For God so loved *h* the world that he gave his one and only Son, *c* that whoever believes in him shall not perish but have eternal life. 17 For God did not send his Son into the world to condemn the world, but to save the world through him. *i* 18 Whoever believes in him is not condemned, *j* but whoever does not believe stands condemned already because he has not believed in the name of God's one and only Son. *d* 19 This is the verdict: Light *k* has come into the world, but men loved darkness instead of light because their deeds were evil. 20 Everyone who does evil hates the light, and will not come into the light for fear that his deeds will be exposed. *l* 21 But whoever lives by the truth comes into the light, so that it may be seen plainly that what he has done has been done through God." *e*

John the Baptist Tells More about Jesus (25)

22 After this, Jesus and his disciples went out into the Judean countryside, where he spent some time with them, and baptized. *m* 23 Now John also was baptizing at Aenon near Salim, because there was plenty of water, and people were constantly coming to be baptized. 24 (This was before John was put in prison.) 25 An argument developed between some of John's disciples and a certain Jew *f* over the matter of ceremonial washing. 26 They came to John and said to him, "Rabbi, that man who was with you on the other side of the Jordan— the one you testified *n* about—well, he is baptizing, and everyone is going to him."

27 To this John replied, "A man can receive only what is given him from heaven. 28 You yourselves can testify that I said, 'I am not the Christ *g* but am sent ahead of him.' *o* 29 The bride belongs to the bridegroom. The friend who attends the bridegroom waits and listens for him, and is full of joy when he hears the bridegroom's voice. That joy is mine, and it is now complete. *p* 30 He must become greater; I must become less.

a 13 Some manuscripts *Man, who is in heaven*   *b* 15 Or *believes may have eternal life in him*   *c* 16 Or *his only begotten Son*   *d* 18 Or *God's only begotten Son*   *e* 21 Some interpreters end the quotation after verse 15. *f* 25 Some manuscripts *and certain Jews*   *g* 28 Or *Messiah*

Cross references

3:13   *d* Pr 30:4; Ac 2:34; Eph 4:8-10; *e* Jn 6:38, 42

3:14   *f* Nu 21:8, 9; *g* Jn 8:28

3:16   *h* Ro 5:8; 1Jn 4:9, 10

3:17   *i* Jn 12:47; 1Jn 4:14

3:18   *j* Jn 5:24

3:19   *k* Jn 1:4

3:20   *l* Eph 5:11, 13

3:22   *m* Jn 4:2

3:26   *n* Jn 1:7

3:28   *o* Jn 1:20, 23

3:29   *p* Jn 16:24

3:14, 15 When the Israelites were wandering in the desert, God sent a plague of snakes to punish the people for their rebellious attitudes. Those doomed to die from snakebite could be healed by obeying God's command to look up at the elevated bronze snake and by believing that God would heal them if they did (see Numbers 21:8, 9). Similarly, our salvation happens when we look up to Jesus, believing he will save us. God has provided this way for us to be healed of sin's deadly bite.

3:16 The entire gospel comes to a focus in this verse. God's love is not static or self-centered; it reaches out and draws others in. Here God sets the pattern of true love, the basis for all love relationships—when you love someone dearly, you are willing to give freely to the point of self-sacrifice. God paid dearly with the life of his Son, the highest price he could pay. Jesus accepted our punishment, paid the price for our sins, and then offered us the new life that he had bought for us. When we share the gospel with others, our love must be like Jesus'—willingly giving up our own comfort and security so that others might join us in receiving God's love.

3:16 Some people are repulsed by the idea of eternal life because their lives are miserable. But eternal life is not an extension of a person's miserable, mortal life; eternal life is God's life embodied in Christ given to all believers now as a guarantee that they will live forever. In eternal life there is no death, sickness, enemy, evil, or sin. When we don't know Christ, we make choices as though this life is all we have. In reality, this life is just the introduction to eternity. Receive this new life by faith and begin to evaluate all that happens from an eternal perspective.

3:16 To "believe" is more than intellectual agreement that Jesus is God. It means to put our trust and confidence in him that he alone can save us. It is to put Christ in charge of our present plans and eternal destiny. Believing is both trusting his words as reliable, and relying on him for the power to change. If you have never trusted Christ, let this promise of everlasting life be yours—and believe.

3:18 People often try to protect themselves from their fears by putting their faith in something they do or have: good deeds, skill or intelligence, money or possessions. But only God can save us from the one thing that we really need to fear—eternal condemnation. We believe in God by recognizing the insufficiency of our own efforts to find salvation and by asking him to do his work in us. When Jesus talks about unbelievers, he means those who reject or ignore him completely, not those who have momentary doubts.

3:19-21 Many people don't want their lives exposed to God's light because they are afraid of what will be revealed. They don't want to be changed. Don't be surprised when these same people are threatened by your desire to obey God and do what is right, because they are afraid that the light in you may expose some of the darkness in their lives. Rather than giving in to discouragement, keep praying that they will come to see how much better it is to live in light than in darkness.

3:25ff Some people look for points of disagreement so they can sow seeds of discord, discontent, and doubt. John the Baptist ended this theological argument by focusing on his devotion to Christ. It is divisive to try to force others to believe our way. Instead, let's witness about what Christ has done for us. How can anyone argue with us about that?

3:26 John the Baptist's disciples were disturbed because people were following Jesus instead of John. It is easy to grow jealous of the popularity of another person's ministry. But we must remember that our true mission is to influence people to follow Christ, not us.

3:27 Why did John the Baptist continue to baptize after Jesus came onto the scene? Why didn't he become a disciple, too? John explained that because God had given him his work, he had to continue it until God called him to do something else. John's main purpose was to point people to Christ. Even with Jesus beginning his own ministry, John could still turn people to Jesus.

3:30 John's willingness to decrease in importance shows unusual humility. Pastors and other Christian leaders can be tempted to focus more on the success of their ministries than on Christ. Beware of those who put more emphasis on their own achievements than on God's kingdom.

3:31
q Jn 8:23

3:32
r ver 11

3:35
s Mt 28:18;
Jn 5:20, 22; 17:2

³¹"The one who comes from above is above all; the one who is from the earth belongs to the earth, and speaks as one from the earth. q The one who comes from heaven is above all. ³²He testifies to what he has seen and heard, but no one accepts his testimony. r ³³The man who has accepted it has certified that God is truthful. ³⁴For the one whom God has sent speaks the words of God, for Godᵃ gives the Spirit without limit. ³⁵The Father loves the Son and has placed everything in his hands. s ³⁶Whoever believes in the Son has eternal life, but whoever rejects the Son will not see life, for God's wrath remains on him."ᵇ

Jesus Talks to a Woman at the Well (27)

4:1
t Jn 3:22, 26

4:3
u Jn 3:22

4:5
v Ge 33:19; 48:22;
Jos 24:32

4:8
w ver 5, 39

4:9
x Lk 9:52, 53

4:10
y Isa 44:3

4 The Pharisees heard that Jesus was gaining and baptizing more disciples than John,ᵗ ²although in fact it was not Jesus who baptized, but his disciples. ³When the Lord learned of this, he left Judeaᵘ and went back once more to Galilee.

⁴Now he had to go through Samaria. ⁵So he came to a town in Samaria called Sychar, near the plot of ground Jacob had given to his son Joseph. v ⁶Jacob's well was there, and Jesus, tired as he was from the journey, sat down by the well. It was about the sixth hour.

⁷When a Samaritan woman came to draw water, Jesus said to her, "Will you give me a drink?" ⁸(His disciples had gone into the townʷ to buy food.)

⁹The Samaritan woman said to him, "You are a Jew and I am a Samaritanˣ woman. How can you ask me for a drink?" (For Jews do not associate with Samaritans.ᶜ)

¹⁰Jesus answered her, "If you knew the gift of God and who it is that asks you for a drink, you would have asked him and he would have given you living water."ʸ

¹¹"Sir," the woman said, "you have nothing to draw with and the well is deep. Where can you get this living water? ¹²Are you greater than our father Jacob, who gave us the well and drank from it himself, as did also his sons and his flocks and herds?"

ᵃ34 Greek *he*   ᵇ36 Some interpreters end the quotation after verse 30.   ᶜ9 Or *do not use dishes Samaritans have used*

3:31–35 Jesus' testimony was trustworthy because he had come from heaven and was speaking of what he had seen there. His words were the very words of God. Your whole spiritual life depends on your answer to one question: Who is Jesus Christ? If you accept Jesus as only a prophet or teacher, you have to reject his teaching, for he claimed to be God's Son, even God himself. The heartbeat of John's Gospel is the dynamic truth that Jesus Christ is God's Son, the Messiah, the Savior, who was from the beginning and will continue to live forever. This same Jesus has invited us to accept him and live with him eternally. When we understand who Jesus is, we are compelled to believe what he said.

3:34 God's Spirit was upon Jesus without limit or measure. Thus Jesus was the highest revelation of God to humanity (Hebrews 1:2).

3:36 Jesus says that those who believe in him *have* (not *will* have) everlasting life. To receive eternal life is to join in God's life, which by nature is eternal. Thus, eternal life begins at the moment of spiritual rebirth.

3:36 John, the author of this Gospel, has been demonstrating that Jesus is the true Son of God. Jesus sets before us the greatest choice in life. We are responsible to decide today whom we will obey (Joshua 24:15), and God wants us to choose him and life (Deuteronomy 30:15–20). God's angry judgment refers to his final rejection of those who reject him. To put off the choice is to choose not to follow Christ. Indecision is a fatal decision.

4:1–3 Already opposition was rising against Jesus, especially from the Pharisees. They resented Jesus' popularity as well as his message, which challenged much of their teachings. Because Jesus was just beginning his ministry, it wasn't yet time to confront these leaders openly; so he left Jerusalem and traveled north toward Galilee.

4:4 To go from the territory of Judea to Galilee meant passing through a central territory called Samaria. Most Jews did everything they could to avoid traveling through Samaria. The reason goes way back into their history.

After the northern kingdom, with its capital at Samaria, fell to the Assyrians, many Jews were deported to Assyria, and foreign-ers were brought in to settle the land and help keep the peace (2 Kings 17:24). The intermarriage between those foreigners and the remaining Jews resulted in a mixed race, impure in the opinion of Jews who lived in the southern kingdom. Thus the pure Jews hated this mixed race, called Samaritans, because they felt that their fellow Jews who had intermarried had betrayed their people and nation. The Samaritans had set up an alternate center for worship on Mount Gerizim (4:20) to parallel the temple at Jerusalem, but it had been destroyed 150 years earlier. While there was long-standing prejudice between Jews and Samaritans, Jesus did not live by such restrictions. The route through Samaria was shorter, and that was the route he took.

4:5–7 Jacob's well was on the property originally owned by Jacob (Genesis 33:18, 19). It was not a spring-fed well, but a well into which water seeped from rain and dew, collecting at the bottom. Wells were almost always located outside the city along the main road. Twice each day, morning and evening, women came to draw water. This woman came at noon, however, probably to avoid meeting people who knew her reputation. Jesus gave this woman an extraordinary message about fresh and pure water that would quench her spiritual thirst forever.

4:7–9 This woman (1) was a Samaritan, a member of the hated mixed race, (2) was known to be living in sin, and (3) was in a public place. No respectable Jewish man would talk to a woman under such circumstances. But Jesus did. The gospel is for every person, no matter what his or her race, social position, or past sins. We must be prepared to share this gospel at any time and in any place. Jesus crossed all barriers to share the gospel, and we who follow him must do no less.

4:10 What did Jesus mean by "living water"? In the Old Testament, many verses speak of thirsting after God as one thirsts for water (Psalm 42:1; Isaiah 55:1; Jeremiah 2:13; Zechariah 13:1). God is called the fountain of life (Psalm 36:9) and the spring of living water (Jeremiah 17:13). In saying he would bring living water that could forever quench a person's thirst for God, Jesus was claiming to be the Messiah. Only the Messiah could give this gift that satisfies the soul's desire.

13Jesus answered, "Everyone who drinks this water will be thirsty again, 14but whoever drinks the water I give him will never thirst. *z* Indeed, the water I give him will become in him a spring of water *a* welling up to eternal life."

15The woman said to him, "Sir, give me this water so that I won't get thirsty *b* and have to keep coming here to draw water."

16He told her, "Go, call your husband and come back."

17"I have no husband," she replied.

Jesus said to her, "You are right when you say you have no husband. 18The fact is, you have had five husbands, and the man you now have is not your husband. What you have just said is quite true."

19"Sir," the woman said, "I can see that you are a prophet. 20Our fathers worshiped on this mountain, but you Jews claim that the place where we must worship is in Jerusalem."

21Jesus declared, "Believe me, woman, a time is coming when you will worship the Father neither on this mountain nor in Jerusalem. *c* 22You Samaritans worship what you do not know; *d* we worship what we do know, for salvation is from the Jews. *e* 23Yet a time is coming and has now come *f* when the true worshipers will worship the Father in spirit *g* and truth, for they are the kind of worshipers the Father seeks. 24God is spirit, *h* and his worshipers must worship in spirit and in truth."

25The woman said, "I know that Messiah" (called Christ) *i* "is coming. When he comes, he will explain everything to us."

26Then Jesus declared, "I who speak to you am he." *j*

Jesus Tells about the Spiritual Harvest (28)

27Just then his disciples returned *k* and were surprised to find him talking with a woman. But no one asked, "What do you want?" or "Why are you talking with her?"

28Then, leaving her water jar, the woman went back to the town and said to the people, 29"Come, see a man who told me everything I ever did. *l* Could this be the Christ *a* ?" *m* 30They came out of the town and made their way toward him.

31Meanwhile his disciples urged him, "Rabbi, eat something."

32But he said to them, "I have food to eat that you know nothing about."

33Then his disciples said to each other, "Could someone have brought him food?"

34"My food," said Jesus, "is to do the will *n* of him who sent me and to finish his work. 35Do you not say, 'Four months more and then the harvest'? I tell you, open your eyes and

a29 Or Messiah

Cross references

4:14
z Jn 6:35
a Jn 7:38

4:15
b Jn 6:34

4:21
c Mal 1:11; 1Ti 2:8

4:22
d 2Ki 17:28-41
e Isa 2:3; Ro 9:4, 5

4:23
f Jn 5:25
g Php 3:3

4:24
h Php 3:3

4:25
i Mt 1:16

4:26
j Jn 8:24

4:27
k ver 8

4:29
l ver 17, 18
m Jn 7:26, 31

4:34
n Jn 6:38; 17:4; 19:30

4:13-15 Many spiritual functions parallel physical functions. As our bodies hunger and thirst, so do our souls. But our souls need *spiritual* food and water. The woman confused the two kinds of water, perhaps because no one had ever talked with her about her spiritual hunger and thirst before. We would not think of depriving our bodies of food and water when they hunger or thirst. Why then should we deprive our souls? The living Word, Jesus Christ, and the written Word, the Bible, can satisfy our hungry and thirsty souls.

4:15 The woman mistakenly believed that if she received the water Jesus offered, she would not have to return to the well each day. She was interested in Jesus' message because she thought it could make her life easier. But if that were always the case, people would accept Christ's message for the wrong reasons. Christ did not come to take away challenges, but to change us on the inside and to empower us to deal with problems from God's perspective.

4:16-20 When this woman discovered that Jesus knew all about her private life, she quickly changed the subject. Often people become uncomfortable when the conversation is too close to home, and they try to talk about something else. As we witness, we should gently guide the conversation back to Christ. His presence exposes sin and makes people squirm, but only Christ can forgive sins and give new life.

4:20-24 The woman brought up a popular theological issue—the correct place to worship. But her question was a smoke screen to keep Jesus away from her deepest need. Jesus directed the conversation to a much more important point: the *location* of worship is not nearly as important as the *attitude* of the worshipers.

4:22 When Jesus said, "Salvation is from the Jews," he meant that only through the Jewish Messiah would the whole world find salvation. God had promised that through the Jewish race the whole earth would be blessed (Genesis 12:3). The Old Testament prophets had called the Jews to be a light to the other nations of the world, bringing them to a knowledge of God; and they had predicted the Messiah's coming. The woman at the well may have known of these passages and was expecting the Messiah, but she didn't realize that she was talking to him!

4:24 "God is spirit" means he is not a physical being limited to one place. He is present everywhere, and he can be worshiped anywhere, at any time. It is not where we worship that counts, but how we worship. Is your worship genuine and true? Do you have the Holy Spirit's help? How does the Holy Spirit help us worship? The Holy Spirit prays for us (Romans 8:26), teaches us the words of Christ (14:26), and tells us we are loved (Romans 5:5).

4:34 The "food" about which Jesus was speaking was his spiritual nourishment. It includes more than Bible study, prayer, and attending church. Spiritual nourishment also comes from doing God's will and helping to bring his work of salvation to completion. We are nourished not only by what we take in, but also by what we give out for God. In 17:4, Jesus refers to completing God's work on earth.

4:35 Sometimes Christians excuse themselves from witnessing by saying that their family or friends aren't ready to believe. Jesus, however, makes it clear that around us a continual harvest waits to be reaped. Don't let Jesus find you making excuses. Look around. You will find people ready to hear God's Word.

4:35
o Mt 9:37; Lk 10:2

4:36
p Ro 1:13

4:37
q Job 31:8

look at the fields! They are ripe for harvest. *o* 36 Even now the reaper draws his wages, even now he harvests *p* the crop for eternal life, so that the sower and the reaper may be glad together. 37 Thus the saying 'One sows and another reaps' *q* is true. 38 I sent you to reap what you have not worked for. Others have done the hard work, and you have reaped the benefits of their labor."

Many Samaritans Believe in Jesus (29)

4:39
r ver 29

39 Many of the Samaritans from that town believed in him because of the woman's testimony, "He told me everything I ever did." *r* 40 So when the Samaritans came to him, they urged him to stay with them, and he stayed two days. 41 And because of his words many more became believers.

4:42
s 1Jn 4:14

42 They said to the woman, "We no longer believe just because of what you said; now we have heard for ourselves, and we know that this man really is the Savior of the world." *s*

Jesus Preaches in Galilee (30/Matthew 4:12–17; Mark 1:14–15; Luke 4:14–15)

4:44
t Mt 13:57

4:45
u Jn 2:23

43 After the two days he left for Galilee. 44 (Now Jesus himself had pointed out that a prophet has no honor in his own country.) *t* 45 When he arrived in Galilee, the Galileans welcomed him. They had seen all that he had done in Jerusalem at the Passover Feast, *u* for they also had been there.

Jesus Heals a Government Official's Son (31)

4:46
v Jn 2:1-11

4:47
w ver 3, 54

4:48
x Da 4:2, 3

46 Once more he visited Cana in Galilee, where he had turned the water into wine. *v* And there was a certain royal official whose son lay sick at Capernaum. 47 When this man heard that Jesus had arrived in Galilee from Judea, *w* he went to him and begged him to come and heal his son, who was close to death.

48 "Unless you people see miraculous signs and wonders," *x* Jesus told him, "you will never believe."

49 The royal official said, "Sir, come down before my child dies."

50 Jesus replied, "You may go. Your son will live."

The man took Jesus at his word and departed. 51 While he was still on the way, his servants met him with the news that his boy was living. 52 When he inquired as to the time when his son got better, they said to him, "The fever left him yesterday at the seventh hour."

4:36–38 The wages Jesus offers are the joy of working for him and seeing the harvest of believers. These wages come to sower and reaper alike because both find joy in seeing new believers come into Christ's kingdom. The phrase "others have done the hard work" (4:38) may refer to the Old Testament prophets and to John the Baptist, who paved the way for the gospel.

4:39 The Samaritan woman immediately shared her experience with others. Despite her reputation, many took her invitation and came out to meet Jesus. Perhaps there are sins in our past of which we're ashamed. But Christ changes us. As people see these changes, they become curious. Use these opportunities to introduce them to Christ.

4:46–49 This royal official was probably an officer in Herod's service. He had walked 20 miles to see Jesus and addressed him as "Sir," putting himself under Jesus even though he had legal authority over Jesus.

4:48 This miracle was more than a favor to one official; it was a sign to all the people. John's Gospel was written to all mankind to urge faith in Christ. Here a government official had faith that Jesus could do what he claimed. The official believed; *then* he saw a miraculous sign.

4:50 This government official not only believed Jesus could heal; he also obeyed Jesus by returning home, thus demonstrating his faith. It isn't enough for us to say we believe that Jesus can take care of our problems. We need to act as if he can. When you pray about a need or problem, live as though you believe Jesus can do what he says.

4:51 Jesus' miracles were not mere illusions. Although the official's son was 20 miles away, he was healed when Jesus spoke the word. Distance was no problem because Christ has mastery over space. We can never put so much space between ourselves and Christ that he can no longer help us.

JESUS RETURNS TO GALILEE
Jesus stayed in Sychar for two days, then went on to Galilee. He visited Nazareth and various towns in Galilee before arriving in Cana. From there he spoke the word of healing, and a government official's son in Capernaum was healed. The Gospel of Matthew tells us Jesus then settled in Capernaum (Matthew 4:12, 13).

53 Then the father realized that this was the exact time at which Jesus had said to him, "Your son will live." So he and all his household [y] believed.

4:53
y Ac 11:14

54 This was the second miraculous sign that Jesus performed, having come from Judea to Galilee.

Jesus Heals a Lame Man by a Pool (42)

5 Some time later, Jesus went up to Jerusalem for a feast of the Jews. 2 Now there is in Jerusalem near the Sheep Gate [z] a pool, which in Aramaic is called Bethesda [a] and which is surrounded by five covered colonnades. 3 Here a great number of disabled people used to lie—the blind, the lame, the paralyzed. [b] 5 One who was there had been an invalid for thirty-eight years. 6 When Jesus saw him lying there and learned that he had been in this condition for a long time, he asked him, "Do you want to get well?"

5:2
z Ne 3:1; 12:39

7 "Sir," the invalid replied, "I have no one to help me into the pool when the water is stirred. While I am trying to get in, someone else goes down ahead of me."

8 Then Jesus said to him, "Get up! Pick up your mat and walk." [a] 9 At once the man was cured; he picked up his mat and walked.

5:8
a Mt 9:5, 6; Mk 2:11; Lk 5:24

The day on which this took place was a Sabbath, [b] 10 and so the Jews said to the man who had been healed, "It is the Sabbath; the law forbids you to carry your mat." [c]

5:9
b Jn 9:14

11 But he replied, "The man who made me well said to me, 'Pick up your mat and walk.'"

12 So they asked him, "Who is this fellow who told you to pick it up and walk?"

5:10
c Ne 13:15-22; Jer 17:21; Mt 12:2

13 The man who was healed had no idea who it was, for Jesus had slipped away into the crowd that was there.

14 Later Jesus found him at the temple and said to him, "See, you are well again. Stop sinning [d] or something worse may happen to you." 15 The man went away and told the Jews that it was Jesus who had made him well.

5:14
d Jn 8:11

Jesus Claims to Be the Son of God (43)

16 So, because Jesus was doing these things on the Sabbath, the Jews persecuted him. 17 Jesus said to them, "My Father is always at his work to this very day, and I, too, am working."

---

a 2 Some manuscripts *Bethzatha*; other manuscripts *Bethsaida*   b 3 Some less important manuscripts *paralyzed—and they waited for the moving of the waters.* 4 *From time to time an angel of the Lord would come down and stir up the waters. The first one into the pool after each such disturbance would be cured of whatever disease he had.*

4:53 Notice how the official's faith grew. First, he believed enough to ask Jesus to help his son. Second, he believed Jesus' assurance that his son would live, and he acted on it. Third, he and his whole house believed in Jesus. Faith is a gift that grows as we use it.

5:1 Three feasts required all Jewish males to come to Jerusalem: (1) the Feast of Passover and Unleavened Bread, (2) the Feast of Weeks (also called Pentecost), and (3) the Feast of Tabernacles.

5:6 After 38 years, this man's problem had become a way of life. No one had ever helped him. He had no hope of ever being healed.

JESUS TEACHES IN JERUSALEM
Between chapters 4 and 5 of John, Jesus ministered throughout Galilee, especially in Capernaum. He had been calling certain men to follow him, but it wasn't until after this trip to Jerusalem (5:1) that he chose his 12 disciples from among them.

The man's situation looked hopeless. But no matter how trapped you feel in your infirmities, God can minister to your deepest needs. Don't let a problem or hardship cause you to lose hope. God may have special work for you to do in spite of your condition, or even because of it. Many have ministered effectively to hurting people because they have triumphed over their own hurts.

5:10 According to the Pharisees, carrying a mat on the Sabbath was work and was therefore unlawful. It did not break an Old Testament law, but the Pharisees' *interpretation* of God's command to "remember the Sabbath day by keeping it holy" (Exodus 20:8). This was just one of hundreds of rules they had added to the Old Testament law.

5:10 A man who hadn't walked for 38 years had been healed, but the Pharisees were more concerned about their petty rules than the life and health of a human being. The Jewish leaders saw both a mighty miracle of healing and a broken rule. They threw the miracle aside as they focused their attention on the broken rule, because the rule was more important to them than the miracle. It is easy to get so caught up in our man-made structures and rules that we forget the people involved. Are your guidelines for living God-made or man-made? Are they helping people, or have they become needless stumbling blocks?

5:14 This man had been lame, or paralyzed, and suddenly he could walk. This was a great miracle. But he needed an even greater miracle—to have his sins forgiven. The man was delighted to be physically healed, but he had to turn from his sins and seek God's forgiveness to be spiritually healed. God's forgiveness is the greatest gift you will ever receive. Don't neglect his gracious offer.

5:17 If God stopped every kind of work on the Sabbath, nature would fall into chaos, and sin would overrun the world. Genesis 2:2 says that God rested on the seventh day, but this can't mean

5:18
e Jn 7:1
f Jn 10:30, 33

5:19
g Jn 8:28

5:20
h Jn 3:35

5:21
i Jn 11:25

5:22
j Ac 10:42; 17:31

5:23
k 1Jn 2:23

5:24
l Jn 3:18
m 1Jn 3:14

5:27
n ver 22

18For this reason the Jews tried all the harder to kill him;*e* not only was he breaking the Sabbath, but he was even calling God his own Father, making himself equal with God.*f*

19Jesus gave them this answer: "I tell you the truth, the Son can do nothing by himself;*g* he can do only what he sees his Father doing, because whatever the Father does the Son also does. 20For the Father loves the Son*h* and shows him all he does. Yes, to your amazement he will show him even greater things than these. 21For just as the Father raises the dead and gives them life, even so the Son gives life*i* to whom he is pleased to give it. 22Moreover, the Father judges no one, but has entrusted all judgment to the Son,*j* 23that all may honor the Son just as they honor the Father. He who does not honor the Son does not honor the Father, who sent him.*k*

24"I tell you the truth, whoever hears my word and believes him who sent me has eternal life and will not be condemned;*l* he has crossed over from death to life.*m* 25I tell you the truth, a time is coming and has now come when the dead will hear the voice of the Son of God and those who hear will live. 26For as the Father has life in himself, so he has granted the Son to have life in himself. 27And he has given him authority to judge*n* because he is the Son of Man.

THE CLAIMS OF CHRIST

Those who read the life of Christ are faced with one unavoidable question—was Jesus God? Part of any reasonable conclusion has to include the fact that he did claim to be God. We have no other choice but to agree or disagree with his claim. Eternal life is at stake in the choice.

Jesus claimed to be:	Matthew	Mark	Luke	John
the fulfillment of Old Testament prophecies	5:17; 14:33; 16:16, 17; 26:31, 53–56; 27:43	14:21, 61, 62	4:16–21; 7:18–23; 18:31; 22:37; 24:44	2:22; 5:45–47; 6:45; 7:40; 10:34–36; 13:18; 15:25; 20:9
the Son of Man	8:20; 12:8; 16:27; 19:28; 20:18, 19; 24:27, 44; 25:31; 26:2, 45, 64	8:31, 38; 9:9; 10:45; 14:41	6:22; 7:33, 34; 12:8; 17:22; 18:8, 31; 19:10; 21:36	1:51; 3:13, 14; 6:27, 53; 12:23, 34
the Son of God	11:27; 14:33; 16:16, 17; 27:43	3:11, 12; 14:61, 62	8:28; 10:22	1:18; 3:35, 36; 5:18–26; 6:40; 10:36; 11:4; 17:1; 19:7
the Messiah/ the Christ	23:9, 10; 26:63, 64	8:29, 30	4:41; 23:1, 2; 24:25–27	4:25, 26; 10:24, 25; 11:27
Teacher/Master	26:18			13:13, 14
One with authority to forgive		2:1–12	7:48, 49	
Lord		5:19		13:13, 14; 20:28, 29
Savior			19:10	3:17; 10:9

that he stopped doing good. Jesus wanted to teach that when the opportunity to do good presents itself, it should not be ignored, even on the Sabbath.

5:17ff Jesus was identifying himself with God, his Father. There could be no doubt as to his claim to be God. Jesus does not leave us the option to believe in God while ignoring God's Son (5:23). The Pharisees also called God their Father, but they realized Jesus was claiming a unique relationship with him. In response to Jesus' claim, the Pharisees had two choices: to believe him, or to accuse him of blasphemy. They chose the second.

5:19–23 Because of his unity with God, Jesus lived as God wanted him to live. Because of our identification with Jesus, we must honor him and live as he wants us to live. The questions "What would Jesus do?" may help us make the right choices.

5:24 "Eternal life"—living forever with God—begins when you accept Jesus Christ as Savior. At that moment, new life begins in you (2 Corinthians 5:17). It is a completed transaction. You still will face physical death, but when Christ returns again, your body will be resurrected to live forever (1 Corinthians 15).

5:25 In saying that the dead will hear his voice, Jesus was talking about the spiritually dead who hear, understand, and accept him. Those who accept Jesus, the Word, will have eternal life. Jesus was also talking about the physically dead. He raised several dead people while he was on earth, and at his second coming all the "dead in Christ" will rise to meet him (1 Thessalonians 4:16).

5:26 God is the source and Creator of life, for there is no life apart from God, here or hereafter. The life in us is a gift from him (see Deuteronomy 30:20; Psalm 36:9). Because Jesus is eternally existent with God, the Creator, he too is "the life" (14:6) through whom we may live eternally (see 1 John 5:11).

5:27 The Old Testament mentioned three signs of the coming Messiah. In this chapter, John shows that Jesus has fulfilled all three signs. All power and authority are given to him as the Son of Man (cf. 5:27 with Daniel 7:13, 14). The lame and sick are healed (cf. 5:20, 21 with Isaiah 35:6; Jeremiah 31:8, 9). The dead are raised to life (cf. 5:21, 28 with Deuteronomy 32:39; 1 Samuel 2:6; 2 Kings 5:7).

²⁸"Do not be amazed at this, for a time is coming when all who are in their graves will hear his voice ²⁹and come out—those who have done good will rise to live, and those who have done evil will rise to be condemned. ⁰ ³⁰By myself I can do nothing; I judge only as I hear, and my judgment is just, for I seek not to please myself but him who sent me.

Jesus Supports His Claim (44)

³¹"If I testify about myself, my testimony is not valid. ᵖ ³²There is another who testifies in my favor, and I know that his testimony about me is valid.

³³"You have sent to John and he has testified to the truth. ³⁴Not that I accept human testimony; but I mention it that you may be saved. ³⁵John was a lamp that burned and gave light, and you chose for a time to enjoy his light.

³⁶"I have testimony weightier than that of John. For the very work that the Father has given me to finish, and which I am doing, testifies that the Father has sent me. ⁹ ³⁷And the Father who sent me has himself testified concerning me. ʳ You have never heard his voice nor seen his form, ³⁸nor does his word dwell in you, for you do not believe the one he sent. ³⁹You diligently study ᵃ the Scriptures because you think that by them you possess eternal life. These are the Scriptures that testify about me, ˢ ⁴⁰yet you refuse to come to me to have life.

⁴¹"I do not accept praise from men, ⁴²but I know you. I know that you do not have the love of God in your hearts. ⁴³I have come in my Father's name, and you do not accept me; but if someone else comes in his own name, you will accept him. ⁴⁴How can you believe if you accept praise from one another, yet make no effort to obtain the praise that comes from the only God ᵇ? ᵗ

⁴⁵"But do not think I will accuse you before the Father. Your accuser is Moses, ᵘ on whom your hopes are set. ᵛ ⁴⁶If you believed Moses, you would believe me, for he wrote about me. ʷ ⁴⁷But since you do not believe what he wrote, how are you going to believe what I say?" ˣ

Jesus Feeds Five Thousand (96/Matthew 14:13–21; Mark 6:30–44; Luke 9:10–17)

6 Some time after this, Jesus crossed to the far shore of the Sea of Galilee (that is, the Sea of Tiberias), ²and a great crowd of people followed him because they saw the miraculous signs ʸ he had performed on the sick. ³Then Jesus went up on a mountainside and sat down with his disciples. ⁴The Jewish Passover Feast ᶻ was near.

⁵When Jesus looked up and saw a great crowd coming toward him, he said to Philip, ᵃ "Where shall we buy bread for these people to eat?" ⁶He asked this only to test him, for he already had in mind what he was going to do.

⁷Philip answered him, "Eight months' wages ᶜ would not buy enough bread for each one to have a bite!"

ᵃ39 Or *Study diligently* (the imperative) ᵇ44 Some early manuscripts *the Only One* ᶜ7 Greek *two hundred denarii*

Cross-references:

5:29 ⁰Da 12:2; Mt 25:46

5:31 ᵖJn 8:14

5:36 ⁹Jn 10:25

5:37 ʳJn 8:18

5:39 ˢLk 24:27, 44

5:44 ᵗRo 2:29

5:45 ᵘJn 9:28 ᵛRo 2:17

5:46 ʷLk 24:27, 44

5:47 ˣLk 16:29, 31

6:2 ʸJn 2:11

6:4 ᶻJn 2:13

6:5 ᵃJn 1:43

5:29 Those who have rebelled against Christ will be resurrected, too, but to hear God's judgment against them and to be sentenced to eternity apart from him. There are those who wish to live well on earth, ignore God, and then see death as final rest. Jesus does not allow unbelieving people to see death as the end of it all. There is a judgment to face.

5:31ff Jesus claimed to be equal with God (5:18), to give eternal life (5:24), to be the source of life (5:26), and to judge sin (5:27). These statements make it clear that Jesus was claiming to be divine—an almost unbelievable claim, but one that was supported by another witness, John the Baptist.

5:39, 40 The religious leaders knew what the Bible said but failed to apply its words to their lives. They knew the teachings of the Scriptures but failed to see the Messiah to whom the Scriptures pointed. They knew the rules but missed the Savior. Entrenched in their own religious system, they refused to let the Son of God change their lives. Don't become so involved in "religion" that you miss Christ.

5:41 Whose praise do you seek? The religious leaders enjoyed great prestige in Israel, but their stamp of approval meant nothing to Jesus. He was concerned about God's approval. This is a good

principle for us. If even the highest officials in the world approve of our actions and God does not, we should be concerned. But if God approves, even though others don't, we should be content.

5:45 The Pharisees prided themselves on being the true followers of their ancestor Moses. They were trying to follow every one of his laws to the letter, and they even added some of their own. Jesus' warning that Moses would accuse them stung them to fury. Moses wrote about Jesus (Genesis 3:15; Numbers 21:9; 24:17; Deuteronomy 18:15), yet the religious leaders refused to believe Jesus when he came.

6:5 If anyone knew where to get food, it would have been Philip because he was from Bethsaida, a town about nine miles away (1:44). Jesus was testing Philip to strengthen his faith. By asking for a human solution (knowing that there was none), Jesus highlighted the powerful and miraculous act that he was about to perform.

6:5–7 When Jesus asked Philip where they could buy a great amount of bread, Philip started assessing the probable cost. Jesus wanted to teach him that financial resources are not the most important ones. We can limit what God does in us by assuming what is and is not possible. Is there some impossible task that you believe God wants you to do? Don't let your estimate of what can't be done keep you from taking on the task. God can do the miraculous; trust him to provide the resources.

6:8
b Jn 1:40
6:9
c 2Ki 4:43

8 Another of his disciples, Andrew, Simon Peter's brother,b spoke up, 9 "Here is a boy with five small barley loaves and two small fish, but how far will they go among so many?"c

10 Jesus said, "Have the people sit down." There was plenty of grass in that place, and the men sat down, about five thousand of them. 11 Jesus then took the loaves, gave thanks, and distributed to those who were seated as much as they wanted. He did the same with the fish.

12 When they had all had enough to eat, he said to his disciples, "Gather the pieces that are left over. Let nothing be wasted." 13 So they gathered them and filled twelve baskets with the pieces of the five barley loaves left over by those who had eaten.

6:14
d Dt 18:15, 18;
Mt 11:3
6:15
e Jn 18:36
f Mt 14:23

14 After the people saw the miraculous sign that Jesus did, they began to say, "Surely this is the Prophet who is to come into the world." d 15 Jesus, knowing that they intended to come and make him king e by force, withdrew again to a mountain by himself. f

Jesus Walks on Water (97/Matthew 14:22–33; Mark 6:45–52)

16 When evening came, his disciples went down to the lake, 17 where they got into a boat and set off across the lake for Capernaum. By now it was dark, and Jesus had not yet joined them. 18 A strong wind was blowing and the waters grew rough. 19 When they had rowed three or three and a half miles,a they saw Jesus approaching the boat, walking on the water; and they were terrified. 20 But he said to them, "It is I; don't be afraid." 21 Then they were willing to take him into the boat, and immediately the boat reached the shore where they were heading.

Jesus Is the True Bread from Heaven (99)

6:22
g ver 2
6:23
h ver 11

22 The next day the crowd that had stayed on the opposite shore of the lakeg realized that only one boat had been there, and that Jesus had not entered it with his disciples, but that they had gone away alone. 23 Then some boats from Tiberias landed near the place where the people had eaten the bread after the Lord had given thanks. h 24 Once the crowd realized that neither Jesus nor his disciples were there, they got into the boats and went to Capernaum in search of Jesus.

25 When they found him on the other side of the lake, they asked him, "Rabbi, when did you get here?"

a 19 Greek rowed twenty-five or thirty stadia (about 5 or 6 kilometers)

6:8, 9 The disciples are contrasted with the youngster who brought what he had. They certainly had more resources than the boy, but they knew they didn't have enough, so they didn't give anything at all. The boy gave what little he had, and it made all the difference. If we offer nothing to God, he will have nothing to use. But he can take what little we have and turn it into something great.

6:8, 9 In performing his miracles, Jesus usually preferred to work through people. Here he took what a young child offered and used it to accomplish one of the most spectacular miracles recorded in the Gospels. Age is no barrier to Christ. Never think you are too young or old to be of service to him.

6:13 There is a lesson in the leftovers. God gives in abundance. He takes whatever we can offer him in time, ability, or resources and multiplies its effectiveness beyond our wildest expectations. If you take the first step in making yourself available to God, he will show you how greatly you can be used to advance the work of his kingdom.

6:14 "The Prophet" is the one prophesied by Moses (Deuteronomy 18:15).

6:18 The Sea of Galilee is 650 feet below sea level, 150 feet deep, and surrounded by hills. These physical features make it subject to sudden windstorms that would cause extremely high waves. Such storms were expected on this lake, but they were nevertheless frightening. When Jesus came to the disciples during a storm, walking on the water (three and a half miles from shore), he told them not to be afraid. We often face spiritual and emotional storms and feel tossed about like a small boat on a big lake. In spite of terrifying circumstances, if we trust our lives to Christ for his safekeeping, he will give us peace in any storm.

6:18, 19 The disciples, terrified, probably thought they were seeing a ghost (Mark 6:49). But if they had thought about all they had already seen Jesus do, they could have accepted this miracle. They were frightened—they didn't expect Jesus to come, and they weren't prepared for his help. Faith is a mind-set that expects God to act. When we act on this expectation, we can overcome our fears.

JESUS WALKS ON THE WATER Jesus fed the 5,000 on a hill near the Sea of Galilee at Bethsaida. The disciples set out across the sea toward Capernaum. But they encountered a storm—and Jesus came walking to them on the water! The boat landed at Gennesaret (Mark 6:53); from there they went back to Capernaum.

26 Jesus answered, "I tell you the truth, you are looking for me,[i] not because you saw miraculous signs but because you ate the loaves and had your fill. 27 Do not work for food that spoils, but for food that endures[j] to eternal life,[k] which the Son of Man will give you. On him God the Father has placed his seal of approval."

28 Then they asked him, "What must we do to do the works God requires?"

29 Jesus answered, "The work of God is this: to believe[l] in the one he has sent."

30 So they asked him, "What miraculous sign then will you give that we may see it and believe you?[m] What will you do? 31 Our forefathers ate the manna[n] in the desert; as it is written: 'He gave them bread from heaven to eat.'[a][o]

32 Jesus said to them, "I tell you the truth, it is not Moses who has given you the bread from heaven, but it is my Father who gives you the true bread from heaven. 33 For the bread of God is he who comes down from heaven and gives life to the world."

34 "Sir," they said, "from now on give us this bread."[p]

35 Then Jesus declared, "I am the bread of life.[q] He who comes to me will never go hungry, and he who believes in me will never be thirsty. 36 But as I told you, you have seen me and still you do not believe. 37 All that the Father gives me will come to me, and whoever comes to me I will never drive away. 38 For I have come down from heaven not to do my will but to do the will of him who sent me. 39 And this is the will of him who sent me, that I shall lose none of all that he has given me,[r] but raise them up at the last day. 40 For my Father's will is that everyone who looks to the Son and believes in him shall have eternal life, and I will raise him up at the last day."

The People Disagree that Jesus Is from Heaven (100)

41 At this the Jews began to grumble about him because he said, "I am the bread that came down from heaven." 42 They said, "Is this not Jesus, the son of Joseph,[s] whose father and mother we know? How can he now say, 'I came down from heaven'?"

43 "Stop grumbling among yourselves," Jesus answered. 44 "No one can come to me unless the Father who sent me draws him, and I will raise him up at the last day. 45 It is written in the Prophets: 'They will all be taught by God.'[b][t] Everyone who listens to the Father and learns from him comes to me. 46 No one has seen the Father except the one who is from God;[u] only

[a]31 Exodus 16:4; Neh. 9:15; Psalm 78:24,25   [b]45 Isaiah 54:13

Cross references:
- 6:26 [i]ver 24
- 6:27 [j]Isa 55:2; [k]Jn 4:14
- 6:29 [l]1Jn 3:23
- 6:30 [m]Mt 12:38
- 6:31 [n]Nu 11:7-9; [o]Ex 16:4, 15; Ne 9:15; Ps 78:24
- 6:34 [p]Jn 4:15
- 6:35 [q]ver 48, 51
- 6:39 [r]Jn 10:28; 17:12; 18:9
- 6:42 [s]Lk 4:22
- 6:45 [t]Isa 54:13; Jer 31:33, 34; Heb 8:10, 11
- 6:46 [u]Jn 1:18

6:26 Jesus criticized the people who followed him only for the physical and temporal benefits and not for the satisfying of their spiritual hunger. Many people use religion to gain prestige, comfort, or even political votes. But those are self-centered motives. True believers follow Jesus simply because they know he has the truth and his way is the way to live.

6:28, 29 Many sincere seekers for God are puzzled about what he wants them to do. The religions of the world are people's attempts to answer this question. But Jesus' reply is brief and simple: we must believe on him whom God has sent. Satisfying God does not come from the work we *do*, but from whom we *believe*. The first step involves accepting that Jesus is who he claims to be. All spiritual development is built on this affirmation. Declare to Jesus, "You are the Christ, the Son of the living God" (Matthew 16:16), and embark on a life of belief that is satisfying to your Creator.

6:35 People eat bread to satisfy physical hunger and to sustain physical life. We can satisfy spiritual hunger and sustain spiritual life only by a right relationship with Jesus Christ. No wonder he called himself the bread of life. But bread must be eaten to sustain life, and Christ must be invited into our daily walk to sustain spiritual life.

6:37, 38 Jesus did not work independently of God the Father, but in union with him. This should give us even more assurance of being welcomed into God's presence and being protected by him. Jesus' purpose was to do the will of God, not to satisfy Jesus' human desires. When we follow Jesus, we should have the same purpose.

6:39 Jesus said he would not lose even one person whom the Father had given him. Thus anyone who makes a sincere commitment to believe in Jesus Christ as Savior is secure in God's promise of eternal life. Christ will not let his people be overcome by Satan and lose their salvation (see also 17:12; Philippians 1:6).

6:40 Those who put their faith in Christ will be resurrected from physical death to eternal life with God when Christ comes again (see 1 Corinthians 15:52; 1 Thessalonians 4:16).

6:41 When John says "Jews," he is referring to the Jewish leaders who were hostile to Jesus, not to Jews in general. John himself was a Jew, and so was Jesus.

6:41 Some of the people grumbled in disagreement because they could not accept Jesus' claim of divinity. They saw him only as a carpenter from Nazareth. They refused to believe that Jesus was God's divine Son, and they could not tolerate his message. Many people reject Christ because they say they cannot believe he is the Son of God. In reality, the demands that Christ makes for their loyalty and obedience are what they can't accept. So to protect themselves from the message, they reject the messenger.

6:44 God, not man, plays the most active role in salvation. When someone chooses to believe in Jesus Christ as Savior, he or she does so only in response to the urging of God's Holy Spirit. God does the urging; then we decide whether or not to believe. Thus no one can believe in Jesus without God's help.

6:45 Jesus was alluding to an Old Testament view of the Messianic kingdom in which all people are taught directly by God (Isaiah 54:13; Jeremiah 31:31–34). He was stressing the importance of not merely hearing, but learning. We are taught by God through the Bible, our experiences, the thoughts the Holy Spirit brings, and relationships with other Christians. Are you open to God's teaching?

6:48
v ver 35, 51
6:49
w ver 31, 58

6:52
x Jn 9:16; 10:19

6:56
y 1Jn 3:24; 4:15

6:58
z ver 49-51

6:60
a ver 66

6:62
b Jn 3:13
6:63
c 2Co 3:6
6:64
d Jn 2:25

6:66
e ver 60

6:70
f Jn 13:27

he has seen the Father. 47 I tell you the truth, he who believes has everlasting life. 48 I am the bread of life. v 49 Your forefathers ate the manna in the desert, yet they died. w 50 But here is the bread that comes down from heaven, which a man may eat and not die. 51 I am the living bread that came down from heaven. If anyone eats of this bread, he will live forever. This bread is my flesh, which I will give for the life of the world."

52 Then the Jews began to argue sharply among themselves, x "How can this man give us his flesh to eat?"

53 Jesus said to them, "I tell you the truth, unless you eat the flesh of the Son of Man and drink his blood, you have no life in you. 54 Whoever eats my flesh and drinks my blood has eternal life, and I will raise him up at the last day. 55 For my flesh is real food and my blood is real drink. 56 Whoever eats my flesh and drinks my blood remains in me, and I in him. y 57 Just as the living Father sent me and I live because of the Father, so the one who feeds on me will live because of me. 58 This is the bread that came down from heaven. Your forefathers ate manna and died, but he who feeds on this bread will live forever." z 59 He said this while teaching in the synagogue in Capernaum.

Many Disciples Desert Jesus (101)

60 On hearing it, many of his disciples a said, "This is a hard teaching. Who can accept it?"

61 Aware that his disciples were grumbling about this, Jesus said to them, "Does this offend you? 62 What if you see the Son of Man ascend to where he was before! b 63 The Spirit gives life; c the flesh counts for nothing. The words I have spoken to you are spirit a and they are life. 64 Yet there are some of you who do not believe." For Jesus had known d from the beginning which of them did not believe and who would betray him. 65 He went on to say, "This is why I told you that no one can come to me unless the Father has enabled him."

66 From this time many of his disciples e turned back and no longer followed him.

67 "You do not want to leave too, do you?" Jesus asked the Twelve.

68 Simon Peter answered him, "Lord, to whom shall we go? You have the words of eternal life. 69 We believe and know that you are the Holy One of God."

70 Then Jesus replied, "Have I not chosen you, the Twelve? Yet one of you is a devil!" f 71 (He meant Judas, the son of Simon Iscariot, who, though one of the Twelve, was later to betray him.)

a 63 Or Spirit

6:47 As used here, *believes* means "continues to believe." We do not believe merely once; we keep on believing in and trusting Jesus.

6:47ff The religious leaders frequently asked Jesus to prove to them why he was better than the prophets they already had. Jesus here referred to the manna that Moses had given their ancestors in the desert (see Exodus 16). This bread was physical and temporal. The people ate it, and it sustained them for a day. But they had to get more bread every day, and this bread could not keep them from dying. Jesus, who is much greater than Moses, offers himself as the spiritual bread from heaven that satisfies completely and leads to eternal life.

6:51 How can Jesus give us his flesh as bread to eat? To eat living bread means to accept Christ into our lives and become united with him. We are united with Christ in two ways: (1) by believing in his death (the sacrifice of his flesh) and resurrection and (2) by devoting ourselves to living as he requires, depending on his teaching for guidance, and trusting in the Holy Spirit for power.

6:56 This was a shocking message—to eat flesh and drink blood sounded cannibalistic. The idea of drinking any blood, let alone human blood, was repugnant to the religious leaders because the law forbade it (Leviticus 17:10, 11). Jesus was not talking about literal blood, of course. He was saying that his life had to become their own, but they could not accept this concept. The Gospel writers, as well as the apostle Paul, used the body and blood imagery in talking about communion (see 1 Corinthians 11:23–26).

6:63, 65 The Holy Spirit gives spiritual life; without the work of the Holy Spirit we cannot even see our need for new life (14:17). All spiritual renewal begins and ends with God. He reveals truth to us, lives within us, and then enables us to respond to that truth.

6:66 Why did Jesus' words cause many of his followers to desert him? (1) They may have realized that he wasn't going to be the conquering Messiah-King they expected. (2) He refused to give in to their self-centered requests. (3) He emphasized faith, not deeds. (4) His teachings were difficult to understand, and some of his words were offensive. As we grow in our faith, we may be tempted to turn away because Jesus' lessons are difficult. Will your response be to give up, ignore certain teachings, or reject Christ? Instead, ask God to show you what the teachings mean and how they apply to your life. Then have the courage to act on God's truth.

6:67 There is no middle ground with Jesus. When he asked the disciples if they would also leave, he was showing that they could either accept or reject him. Jesus was not trying to repel people with his teachings. He was simply telling the truth. The more the people heard Jesus' real message, the more they divided into two camps—the honest seekers who wanted to understand more, and those who rejected Jesus because they didn't like what they had heard.

6:67, 68 After many of Jesus' followers had deserted him, he asked the 12 disciples if they were also going to leave. Peter replied, "To whom shall we go?" In his straightforward way, Peter answered for all of us—there is no other way. Though there are many philosophies and self-styled authorities, Jesus alone has the words of eternal life. People look everywhere for eternal life and miss Christ, the only source. Stay with him, especially when you are confused or feel alone.

6:70 In response to Jesus' message, some people left; others stayed and truly believed; and some, like Judas, stayed but tried to use Jesus for personal gain. Many people today turn away from Christ. Others pretend to follow, going to church for status, approval of family and friends, or business contacts. But there are only two real responses to Jesus—you either accept him or reject him. How have you responded to Christ?

6:71 For more information on Judas, see his Profile in Mark 14, p. 1647.

2. Jesus encounters conflict with the religious leaders
Jesus' Brothers Ridicule Him (121)

7 After this, Jesus went around in Galilee, purposely staying away from Judea because the Jews there were waiting to take his life. *g* 2 But when the Jewish Feast of Tabernacles *h* was near, 3 Jesus' brothers *i* said to him, "You ought to leave here and go to Judea, so that your disciples may see the miracles you do. 4 No one who wants to become a public figure acts in secret. Since you are doing these things, show yourself to the world." 5 For even his own brothers did not believe in him. *j*

6 Therefore Jesus told them, "The right time for me has not yet come; for you any time is right. 7 The world cannot hate you, but it hates me because I testify that what it does is evil. *k* 8 You go to the Feast. I am not yet *a* going up to this Feast, because for me the right time has not yet come." 9 Having said this, he stayed in Galilee.

Jesus Teaches Openly at the Temple (123)

10 However, after his brothers had left for the Feast, he went also, not publicly, but in secret. 11 Now at the Feast the Jews were watching for him *l* and asking, "Where is that man?"

12 Among the crowds there was widespread whispering about him. Some said, "He is a good man."

Others replied, "No, he deceives the people." *m* 13 But no one would say anything publicly about him for fear of the Jews. *n*

14 Not until halfway through the Feast did Jesus go up to the temple courts and begin to teach. 15 The Jews were amazed and asked, "How did this man get such learning without having studied?"

16 Jesus answered, "My teaching is not my own. It comes from him who sent me. 17 If anyone chooses to do God's will, he will find out whether my teaching comes from God or whether I speak on my own. 18 He who speaks on his own does so to gain honor for himself, *o* but he who works for the honor of the one who sent him is a man of truth; there is nothing false about him. 19 Has not Moses given you the law? *p* Yet not one of you keeps the law. Why are you trying to kill me?"

20 "You are demon-possessed," *q* the crowd answered. "Who is trying to kill you?"

a 8 Some early manuscripts do not have yet.

7:1 *g* Jn 5:18
7:2 *h* Lev 23:34
7:3 *i* Mt 12:46
7:5 *j* Mk 3:21
7:7 *k* Jn 3:19, 20
7:11 *l* Jn 11:56
7:12 *m* ver 40, 43
7:13 *n* Jn 9:22; 12:42; 19:38
7:18 *o* Jn 5:41; 8:50, 54
7:19 *p* Jn 1:17
7:20 *q* Jn 8:48; 10:20

7:2 The Feast of Tabernacles is described in Leviticus 23:33ff. This event occurred in October, about six months after the Passover celebration mentioned in John 6:2–5. The feast commemorated the days when the Israelites wandered in the desert and lived in booths (Leviticus 23:43).

7:3–5 Jesus' brothers had a difficult time believing in him. Some of these brothers would eventually become leaders in the church (James, for example), but for several years they were embarrassed by Jesus. After Jesus died and rose again, they finally believed. We today have every reason to believe because we have the full record of Jesus' miracles, death, and resurrection. We also have the evidence of what the gospel has done in people's lives through the centuries. Don't miss this opportunity to believe in God's Son.

7:7 Because the world hated Jesus, we who follow him can expect that many people will hate us as well. If circumstances are going too well, ask if you are following Christ as you should. We can be grateful when life goes well, but we must make sure it is not at the cost of following Jesus halfheartedly or not at all.

7:10 Jesus came with the greatest gift ever offered, so why did he often act secretly? The religious leaders hated him, and many would refuse his gift of salvation, no matter what he said or did. The more Jesus taught and worked publicly, the more these leaders would cause trouble for him and his followers. So it was necessary for Jesus to teach and work as quietly as possible. Many people today have the privilege of teaching, preaching, and worshiping publicly with little persecution. These believers should be grateful and make the most of their opportunities to proclaim the gospel.

7:13 The Jewish religious leaders had a great deal of power over the common people. Apparently these leaders couldn't do much

to Jesus at this time, but they threatened anyone who might publicly support him. Excommunication from the synagogue was one of the reprisals for believing in Jesus (9:22). To a Jew, this was a severe punishment.

7:13 Everyone was talking about Jesus! But when it came time to speak up for him in public, no one said a word. All were afraid. Fear can stifle our witness. Although many people talk about Christ in church, when it comes to making a public statement about their faith, they are often embarrassed. Jesus says that he will acknowledge us before God if we acknowledge him before others (Matthew 10:32). Be courageous! Speak up for Christ!

7:16–18 Those who attempt to know God's will and do it will know intuitively that Jesus was telling the truth about himself. Have you ever listened to religious speakers and wondered if they were telling the truth? Test them: (1) their words should agree with, not contradict, the Bible; (2) their words should point to God and his will, not to themselves.

7:19 The Pharisees spent their days trying to achieve holiness by keeping the meticulous rules that they had added to God's laws. Jesus' accusation that they didn't keep Moses' laws stung them deeply. In spite of their pompous pride in themselves and their rules, they did not even fulfill a legalistic religion, for they were living far below what the law of Moses required. Murder was certainly against the law. Jesus' followers should do *more* than the moral law requires, not by adding to its requirements, but by going beyond and beneath the mere do's and don'ts of the law to worship the spirit of the law.

7:20 Most of the people were probably not aware of the plot to kill Jesus (5:18). There was a small group looking for the right opportunity to kill him, but most were still trying to decide what they believed about him.

7:22
r Ge 17:10-14

21 Jesus said to them, "I did one miracle, and you are all astonished. 22 Yet, because Moses gave you circumcision (though actually it did not come from Moses, but from the patriarchs),*r* you circumcise a child on the Sabbath. 23 Now if a child can be circumcised on the Sabbath so that the law of Moses may not be broken, why are you angry with me for healing the whole man on the Sabbath? 24 Stop judging by mere appearances, and make a right judgment."*s*

7:24
s Jn 8:15

25 At that point some of the people of Jerusalem began to ask, "Isn't this the man they are trying to kill? 26 Here he is, speaking publicly, and they are not saying a word to him. Have the authorities really concluded that he is the Christ *a* ? 27 But we know where this man is from;*t* when the Christ comes, no one will know where he is from."

7:27
t Mt 13:55

28 Then Jesus, still teaching in the temple courts, cried out, "Yes, you know me, and you know where I am from. I am not here on my own, but he who sent me is true. You do not know him, 29 but I know him *u* because I am from him and he sent me."

7:29
u Mt 11:27

7:31
v Jn 8:30

30 At this they tried to seize him, but no one laid a hand on him, because his time had not yet come. 31 Still, many in the crowd put their faith in him. *v* They said, "When the Christ comes, will he do more miraculous signs than this man?"

Religious Leaders Attempt to Arrest Jesus (124)

32 The Pharisees heard the crowd whispering such things about him. Then the chief priests and the Pharisees sent temple guards to arrest him.

7:33
w Jn 13:33; 16:16

33 Jesus said, "I am with you for only a short time,*w* and then I go to the one who sent me. 34 You will look for me, but you will not find me; and where I am, you cannot come."*x*

7:34
x Jn 8:21; 13:33

7:35
y Jas 1:1

35 The Jews said to one another, "Where does this man intend to go that we cannot find him? Will he go where our people live scattered*y* among the Greeks, and teach the Greeks? 36 What did he mean when he said, 'You will look for me, but you will not find me,' and 'Where I am, you cannot come'?"

7:37
z Isa 55:1

37 On the last and greatest day of the Feast, Jesus stood and said in a loud voice, "If anyone is thirsty, let him come to me and drink. *z* 38 Whoever believes in me, as *b* the Scripture has said, streams of living water will flow from within him." 39 By this he meant the Spirit, *a* whom those who believed in him were later to receive. Up to that time the Spirit had not been given, since Jesus had not yet been glorified. *b*

7:39
a Joel 2:28
b Jn 12:23

40 On hearing his words, some of the people said, "Surely this man is the Prophet."

7:41
c Jn 1:46

41 Others said, "He is the Christ."

7:42
d Mic 5:2; Mt 2:5, 6;
Lk 2:4

Still others asked, "How can the Christ come from Galilee? *c* 42 Does not the Scripture say that the Christ will come from David's family*c* and from Bethlehem,*d* the town where David

a 26 Or *Messiah*; also in verses 27, 31, 41 and 42   *b 37,38* Or */ If anyone is thirsty, let him come to me. / And let him drink,* *38* *who believes in me. / As*   *c 42* Greek *seed*

7:21–23 According to Moses' law, circumcision was to be performed eight days after a baby's birth (Genesis 17:9–14; Leviticus 12:3). This rite was carried out on all Jewish males to demonstrate their identity as part of God's covenant people. If the eighth day after birth was a Sabbath, the circumcision would still be performed (even though it was considered work). While the religious leaders allowed certain exceptions to Sabbath laws, they allowed none to Jesus, who was simply showing mercy to those who needed healing.

7:26 This chapter shows the many reactions people had toward Jesus. They called him a good man (7:12), a deceiver (7:12), demon possessed (7:20), the Christ (7:26), and the Prophet (7:40). We must make up our own minds about who Jesus is, knowing that whatever we decide will have eternal consequences.

7:27 There was a popular tradition that the Messiah would simply appear. But those who believed this tradition were ignoring the Scriptures that clearly predicted the Messiah's birthplace (Micah 5:2).

7:37 Jesus' words, "come to me and drink," alluded to the theme of many Bible passages that talk about the Messiah's life-giving blessings (Isaiah 12:2, 3; 44:3, 4; 58:11). In promising to give the Holy Spirit to all who believed, Jesus was claiming to be the Messiah, for that was something only the Messiah could do.

7:38 Jesus used the term *living water* in 4:10 to indicate eternal life. Here he uses the term to refer to the Holy Spirit. The two go together: Wherever the Holy Spirit is accepted, he brings eternal life. Jesus teaches more about the Holy Spirit in chapters 14—16. The Holy Spirit empowered Jesus' followers at Pentecost (Acts 2) and has since been available to all who believe in Jesus as Savior.

7:40–44 The crowd was asking questions about Jesus. Some believed, others were hostile, and others disqualified Jesus as the Messiah because he was from Nazareth, not Bethlehem (Micah 5:2). But he *was* born in Bethlehem (Luke 2:1–7), although he grew up in Nazareth. He may have had a pronounced Galilean accent. If they had looked more carefully, they would not have jumped to the wrong conclusions. When you search for God's truth, make sure you look carefully and thoughtfully at the Bible with an open heart and mind. Don't jump to conclusions before knowing more of what the Bible says.

lived?" [43] Thus the people were divided[e] because of Jesus. [44] Some wanted to seize him, but no one laid a hand on him.[f]

[45] Finally the temple guards went back to the chief priests and Pharisees, who asked them, "Why didn't you bring him in?"

[46] "No one ever spoke the way this man does," the guards declared.

[47] "You mean he has deceived you also?" the Pharisees retorted. [48] "Has any of the rulers or of the Pharisees believed in him?[g] [49] No! But this mob that knows nothing of the law—there is a curse on them."

[50] Nicodemus, who had gone to Jesus earlier and who was one of their own number, asked, [51] "Does our law condemn anyone without first hearing him to find out what he is doing?"

[52] They replied, "Are you from Galilee, too? Look into it, and you will find that a prophet[a] does not come out of Galilee."

7:43
e Jn 9:16; 10:19
7:44
f ver 30

7:48
g Jn 12:42

[The earliest manuscripts and many other ancient witnesses
do not have John 7:53—8:11.]

[53] Then each went to his own home.

Jesus Forgives an Adulterous Woman (125)

8 But Jesus went to the Mount of Olives. [2] At dawn he appeared again in the temple courts, where all the people gathered around him, and he sat down to teach them. [3] The teachers of the law and the Pharisees brought in a woman caught in adultery. They made her stand before the group [4] and said to Jesus, "Teacher, this woman was caught in the act of adultery. [5] In the Law Moses commanded us to stone such women.[h] Now what do you say?" [6] They were using this question as a trap, in order to have a basis for accusing him.

But Jesus bent down and started to write on the ground with his finger. [7] When they kept on questioning him, he straightened up and said to them, "If any one of you is without sin, let him be the first to throw a stone[i] at her."[j] [8] Again he stooped down and wrote on the ground.

[9] At this, those who heard began to go away one at a time, the older ones first, until only Jesus was left, with the woman still standing there. [10] Jesus straightened up and asked her, "Woman, where are they? Has no one condemned you?"

8:5
h Lev 20:10;
Dt 22:22

8:7
i Dt 17:7
j Ro 2:1, 22

a52 Two early manuscripts *the Prophet*

7:44–46 Although the Romans ruled Palestine, they gave the Jewish religious leaders authority over minor civil and religious affairs. The religious leaders supervised their own temple guards and gave the officers power to arrest anyone causing a disturbance or breaking any of their ceremonial laws. Because these leaders had developed hundreds of trivial laws, it was almost impossible for anyone, even the leaders themselves, not to break, neglect, or ignore at least a few of them some of the time. But these temple guards couldn't find one reason to arrest Jesus. And as they listened to Jesus to try to find evidence, they couldn't help hearing the wonderful words he said.

7:46–49 The Jewish leaders saw themselves as an elite group that alone had the truth, and they resisted the truth about Christ because it wasn't *theirs* to begin with. It is easy to think that we have the truth and that those who disagree with us do not have any truth at all. But God's truth is available to everyone. Don't copy the Pharisees' self-centered and narrow attitude.

7:50–52 This passage offers additional insight into Nicodemus, the Pharisee who visited Jesus at night (chapter 3). Apparently Nicodemus had become a secret believer. Since most of the Pharisees hated Jesus and wanted to kill him, Nicodemus risked his reputation and high position even though he only spoke up indirectly for Jesus. His statement was bold, and the Pharisees immediately became suspicious. After Jesus' death, Nicodemus brought spices for his body (19:39). That is the last time he is mentioned in Scripture.

7:51 Nicodemus confronted the Pharisees with their failure to keep their own laws. The Pharisees were losing ground—the temple guards came back impressed by Jesus (7:46), and one of the Pharisees' own, Nicodemus, was defending him. With their hypocritical motives being exposed and their prestige slowly eroding, they began to move to protect themselves. Pride would interfere with their ability to reason, and soon they would become obsessed with getting rid of Jesus just to save face. What was good and right no longer mattered.

8:3–6 The Jewish leaders had already disregarded the law by arresting the woman without the man. The law required that both parties to adultery be stoned (Leviticus 20:10; Deuteronomy 22:22). The leaders were using the woman as a trap so they could trick Jesus. If Jesus said the woman should not be stoned, they would accuse him of violating Moses' law. If he urged them to execute her, they would report him to the Romans, who did not permit the Jews to carry out their own executions (18:31).

8:7 This is a significant statement about judging others. Because Jesus upheld the legal penalty for adultery, stoning, he could not be accused of being against the law. But by saying that only a sinless person could throw the first stone, he highlighted the importance of compassion and forgiveness. When others are caught in sin, are you quick to pass judgment? To do so is to act as though you have never sinned. It is God's role to judge, not ours. Our role is to show forgiveness and compassion.

8:9 When Jesus said that only someone who had not sinned

8:11
k Jn 3:17
l Jn 5:14

11"No one, sir," she said.

"Then neither do I condemn you,"k Jesus declared. "Go now and leave your life of sin."l

---

Jesus Is the Light of the World (126)

8:12
m Jn 1:4

12When Jesus spoke again to the people, he said, "I am the light of the world. m Whoever follows me will never walk in darkness, but will have the light of life."

8:13
n Jn 5:31

13The Pharisees challenged him, "Here you are, appearing as your own witness; your testimony is not valid."n

8:14
o Jn 7:28; 9:29

14Jesus answered, "Even if I testify on my own behalf, my testimony is valid, for I know where I came from and where I am going. But you have no idea where I come from o or

8:15
p Jn 7:24
q Jn 3:17

where I am going. 15You judge by human standards; p I pass judgment on no one. q 16But if I do judge, my decisions are right, because I am not alone. I stand with the Father, who sent

8:17
r Mt 18:16

me. 17In your own Law it is written that the testimony of two men is valid. r 18I am one who

8:18
s Jn 5:37

testifies for myself; my other witness is the Father, who sent me."s

8:19
t Jn 16:3

19Then they asked him, "Where is your father?"

"You do not know me or my Father,"t Jesus replied. "If you knew me, you would know my

8:20
u Mk 12:41

Father also." 20He spoke these words while teaching in the temple area near the place where the offerings were put. u Yet no one seized him, because his time had not yet come.

Jesus Warns of Coming Judgment (127)

8:21
v Jn 7:34

21Once more Jesus said to them, "I am going away, and you will look for me, and you will die in your sin. Where I go, you cannot come."v

22This made the Jews ask, "Will he kill himself? Is that why he says, 'Where I go, you cannot come'?"

8:23
w Jn 3:31

23But he continued, "You are from below; I am from above. You are of this world; I am not of this world. w 24I told you that you would die in your sins; if you do not believe that I am the one I claim to be,a you will indeed die in your sins."

25"Who are you?" they asked.

8:26
x Jn 7:28
y Jn 3:32; 15:15

"Just what I have been claiming all along," Jesus replied. 26"I have much to say in judgment of you. But he who sent me is reliable, x and what I have heard from him I tell the world."y

a24 Or I am he; also in verse 28

---

should throw the first stone, the leaders slipped quietly away, from oldest to youngest. Evidently the older men were more aware of their sins than the younger. Age and experience often temper youthful self-righteousness. But whatever your age, take an honest look at your life. Recognize your sinful nature, and look for ways to help others rather than hurt them.

8:11 Jesus didn't condemn the woman accused of adultery, but neither did he ignore or condone her sin. He told her to leave her life of sin. Jesus stands ready to forgive any sin in your life, but confession and repentance mean a change of heart. With God's help we can accept Christ's forgiveness and stop our wrongdoing.

8:12 To understand what Jesus meant by "the light of the world," see the notes on 1:4, 5.

8:12 Jesus was speaking in the treasury—the part of the temple where the offerings were put (8:20) and where candles burned to symbolize the pillar of fire that led the people of Israel through the desert (Exodus 13:21, 22). In this context, Jesus called himself the light of the world. The pillar of fire represented God's presence, protection, and guidance. Likewise, Jesus brings God's presence, protection, and guidance. Is he the light of *your* world?

8:12 What does it mean to follow Christ? As a soldier follows his captain, so we should follow Christ, our commander. As a slave follows his master, so we should follow Christ, our Lord. As we follow the advice of a trusted counselor, so we should follow Jesus' commands to us in Scripture. As we follow the laws of our nation, so we should follow the laws of the kingdom of heaven.

8:13, 14 The Pharisees thought Jesus was either a lunatic or a liar. Jesus provided them with a third alternative: he was telling the truth. Because most of the Pharisees refused to consider the third alternative, they never recognized him as Messiah and Lord. If you are seeking to know who Jesus is, do not close any door before looking through it honestly. Only with an open mind will you know the truth that he is Messiah and Lord.

8:13-18 The Pharisees argued that Jesus' claim was legally invalid because he had no other witnesses. Jesus responded that his confirming witness was God himself. Jesus and the Father made two witnesses, the number required by the law (Deuteronomy 19:15).

8:20 The temple treasury was located in the court of women. In this area, 13 collection boxes were set up to receive money offerings. Seven of the boxes were for the temple tax; the other six were for freewill offerings. On another occasion, a widow placed her money in one of these boxes, and Jesus taught a profound lesson from her action (Luke 21:1–4).

8:24 People will die in their sins if they reject Christ, because they are rejecting the only way to be rescued from sin. Sadly, many are so taken up with the values of this world that they are blind to the priceless gift Christ offers. Where are you looking? Don't focus on this world's values and miss what is most valuable—eternal life with God.

27 They did not understand that he was telling them about his Father. 28 So Jesus said, "When you have lifted up the Son of Man,z then you will know that I am ⌞the one I claim to be⌟ and that I do nothing on my own but speak just what the Father has taught me. 29 The one who sent me is with me; he has not left me alone, for I always do what pleases him." a 30 Even as he spoke, many put their faith in him. b

8:28
z Jn 12:32

8:29
a Jn 4:34

8:30
b Jn 7:31

Jesus Speaks about God's True Children (128)

31 To the Jews who had believed him, Jesus said, "If you hold to my teaching, you are really my disciples. 32 Then you will know the truth, and the truth will set you free."

33 They answered him, "We are Abraham's descendantsa c and have never been slaves of anyone. How can you say that we shall be set free?"

8:33
c Mt 3:9

8:34
d Ro 6:16; 2Pe 2:19

34 Jesus replied, "I tell you the truth, everyone who sins is a slave to sin. d 35 Now a slave has no permanent place in the family, but a son belongs to it forever. e 36 So if the Son sets you free, you will be free indeed. 37 I know you are Abraham's descendants. Yet you are ready to kill me, because you have no room for my word. 38 I am telling you what I have seen in the Father's presence, f and you do what you have heard from your father. b "

8:35
e Gal 4:30

8:38
f Jn 5:19, 30

39 "Abraham is our father," they answered.

"If you were Abraham's children," g said Jesus, "then you wouldc do the things Abraham did. 40 As it is, you are determined to kill me, a man who has told you the truth that I heard from God. h Abraham did not do such things. 41 You are doing the things your own father does."

"We are not illegitimate children," they protested. "The only Father we have is God himself." i

8:39
g Ro 9:7; Gal 3:7

8:40
h ver 26

8:41
i Isa 63:16; 64:8

42 Jesus said to them, "If God were your Father, you would love me,j for I came from God and now am here. I have not come on my own;k but he sent me. 43 Why is my language not clear to you? Because you are unable to hear what I say. 44 You belong to your father, the devil,l and you want to carry out your father's desire. He was a murderer from the beginning, not holding to the truth, for there is no truth in him. When he lies, he speaks his native language, for he is a liar and the father of lies. 45 Yet because I tell the truth, you do not believe me! 46 Can any of you prove me guilty of sin? If I am telling the truth, why don't you believe me? 47 He who belongs to God hears what God says. The reason you do not hear is that you do not belong to God."

8:42
j 1Jn 5:1
k Jn 7:28

8:44
l 1Jn 3:8

Jesus States He Is Eternal (129)

48 The Jews answered him, "Aren't we right in saying that you are a Samaritan and demon-possessed?" m

8:48
m Jn 7:20

49 "I am not possessed by a demon," said Jesus, "but I honor my Father and you dishonor me. 50 I am not seeking glory for myself;n but there is one who seeks it, and he is the judge. 51 I tell you the truth, if anyone keeps my word, he will never see death."

8:50
n Jn 5:41

a 33 Greek seed; also in verse 37   b 38 Or presence. Therefore do what you have heard from the Father.
c 39 Some early manuscripts "If you are Abraham's children," said Jesus, "then

---

8:32 Jesus himself is the truth that sets us free (8:36). He is the source of truth, the perfect standard of what is right. He frees us from continued slavery to sin, from self-deception, and from deception by Satan. He shows us clearly the way to eternal life with God. Thus Jesus does not give us freedom to do what we want, but freedom to follow God. As we seek to serve God, Jesus' perfect truth frees us to be all that God meant us to be.

8:34, 35 Sin has a way of enslaving us, controlling us, dominating us, and dictating our actions. Jesus can free you from this slavery that keeps you from becoming the person God created you to be. If sin is restraining, mastering, or enslaving you, Jesus can break its power over your life.

8:41 Jesus made a distinction between illegitimate children and true children. The religious leaders were descendants of Abraham (founder of the Jewish nation) and therefore claimed to be children of God. But their actions showed them to be true children of Satan, for they lived under Satan's guidance. True children of Abraham (faithful followers of God) would not act as they did. Your church membership and family connections will not make you a true child of God. Your true father is the one you imitate and obey.

8:43 The religious leaders were unable to understand because they refused to listen. Satan used their stubbornness, pride, and prejudices to keep them from believing in Jesus.

8:44, 45 The attitudes and actions of these leaders clearly identified them as followers of Satan. They may not have been conscious of this, but their hatred of truth, their lies, and their murderous intentions indicated how much control the devil had over them. They were his tools in carrying out his plans; they spoke the very same language of lies. Satan still uses people to obstruct God's work (Genesis 4:8; Romans 5:12; 1 John 3:12).

8:46, 47 In a number of places Jesus intentionally challenged his listeners to test him. He welcomed those who wanted to question his claims and character as long as they were willing to follow through on what they discovered. Jesus' challenge clarifies the two most frequent reasons that people miss when encountering him: (1) they never accept his challenge to test him, or (2) they test him but are not willing to believe what they discover. Have you made either of those mistakes?

8:51 To keep Jesus' word means to hear his words and obey them. When Jesus says those who obey won't die, he is talking

⁵²At this the Jews exclaimed, "Now we know that you are demon-possessed! Abraham died and so did the prophets, yet you say that if anyone keeps your word, he will never taste death. ⁵³Are you greater than our father Abraham? He died, and so did the prophets. Who do you think you are?"

⁵⁴Jesus replied, "If I glorify myself, my glory means nothing. My Father, whom you claim as your God, is the one who glorifies me. ⁵⁵Though you do not know him, I know him. ᵒ If I said I did not, I would be a liar like you, but I do know him and keep his word. ⁵⁶Your father Abraham rejoiced at the thought of seeing my day; he saw it ᵖ and was glad."

⁵⁷"You are not yet fifty years old," the Jews said to him, "and you have seen Abraham!"

⁵⁸"I tell you the truth," Jesus answered, "before Abraham was born,�q I am!" ⁵⁹At this, they picked up stones to stone him, ʳ but Jesus hid himself, slipping away from the temple grounds.

Jesus Heals the Man Who Was Born Blind (148)

9 As he went along, he saw a man blind from birth. ²His disciples asked him, "Rabbi, who sinned,ˢ this man or his parents, that he was born blind?"

³"Neither this man nor his parents sinned," said Jesus, "but this happened so that the work of God might be displayed in his life.ᵗ ⁴As long as it is day,ᵘ we must do the work of him who sent me. Night is coming, when no one can work. ⁵While I am in the world, I am the light of the world."ᵛ

⁶Having said this, he spit ʷ on the ground, made some mud with the saliva, and put it on the man's eyes. ⁷"Go," he told him, "wash in the Pool of Siloam" (this word means Sent). So the man went and washed, and came home seeing.

⁸His neighbors and those who had formerly seen him begging asked, "Isn't this the same man who used to sit and beg?" ⁹Some claimed that he was.

Others said, "No, he only looks like him."

But he himself insisted, "I am the man."

¹⁰"How then were your eyes opened?" they demanded.

¹¹He replied, "The man they call Jesus made some mud and put it on my eyes. He told me to go to Siloam and wash. So I went and washed, and then I could see."ˣ

¹²"Where is this man?" they asked him.

"I don't know," he said.

8:55
ᵒ Jn 7:28, 29
8:56
ᵖ Heb 11:13
8:58
q Jn 17:5, 24
8:59
ʳ Jn 10:31; 11:8

9:2
ˢ ver 34

9:3
ᵗ Jn 11:4
9:4
ᵘ Jn 11:9; 12:35
9:5
ᵛ Jn 8:12; 12:46
9:6
ʷ Mk 7:33; 8:23

9:11
ˣ ver 7

---

about spiritual death, not physical death. Even physical death, however, will eventually be overcome. Those who follow Christ will be raised to live eternally with him.

8:56 God told Abraham, the father of the Jewish nation, that through him all nations would be blessed (Genesis 12:1–7; 15:1–21). Abraham had been able to see this through the eyes of faith. Jesus, a descendant of Abraham, blessed all people through his death, resurrection, and offer of salvation.

8:58 This is one of the most powerful statements uttered by Jesus. When he said that he existed before Abraham was born, he undeniably proclaimed his divinity. Not only did Jesus say that he existed before Abraham; he also applied God's holy name (*I Am*—Exodus 3:14) to himself. This claim demands a response. It cannot be ignored. The Jewish leaders tried to stone Jesus for blasphemy because he claimed equality with God. But Jesus *is* God. How have you responded to Jesus, the Son of God?

8:59 In accordance with the law in Leviticus 24:16, the religious leaders were ready to stone Jesus for claiming to be God. They well understood what Jesus was claiming, and because they didn't believe him, they charged him with blasphemy. It is ironic that *they* were really the blasphemers, cursing and attacking the very God they claimed to serve!

9:1ff In chapter 9, we see four different reactions to Jesus. The neighbors revealed surprise and skepticism; the Pharisees showed disbelief and prejudice; the parents believed but kept quiet for fear of excommunication; and the healed man showed consistent, growing faith. Each reaction to Jesus allowed the man to reach a clearer understanding of the one who had healed him.

9:2, 3 A common belief in Jewish culture was that calamity or suffering was the result of some great sin. But Christ used this man's suffering to teach about faith and to glorify God. We live in a fallen world where good behavior is not always rewarded and bad behavior not always punished. Therefore, innocent people sometimes suffer. If God took suffering away whenever we asked, we would follow him for comfort and convenience, not out of love and devotion. Regardless of the reasons for our suffering, Jesus has the power to help us deal with it. When you suffer from a disease, tragedy, or disability, try not to ask, "Why did this happen to me?" or "What did I do wrong?" Instead, ask God to give you strength for the trial and a clearer perspective on what is happening.

9:6 When Jesus spit on the ground and made mud in order to repair the man's eyes, he was working with original materials. Genesis 2:7 states that God formed Adam's body from the dust of the ground. Jesus was demonstrating a creator's awareness of the materials he first used to shape the human body.

9:7 The pool of Siloam was built by Hezekiah. His workers constructed an underground tunnel from a spring outside the city walls to carry water into the city. Thus the people could always get water without fear of being attacked. This was especially important during times of siege (see 2 Kings 20:20; 2 Chronicles 32:30).

Religious Leaders Question the Blind Man (149)

¹³They brought to the Pharisees the man who had been blind. ¹⁴Now the day on which Jesus had made the mud and opened the man's eyes was a Sabbath.ʸ ¹⁵Therefore the Pharisees also asked him how he had received his sight. "He put mud on my eyes," the man replied, "and I washed, and now I see."

¹⁶Some of the Pharisees said, "This man is not from God, for he does not keep the Sabbath."

But others asked, "How can a sinner do such miraculous signs?" So they were divided. ᶻ

¹⁷Finally they turned again to the blind man, "What have you to say about him? It was your eyes he opened."

The man replied, "He is a prophet."ᵃ

¹⁸The Jews still did not believe that he had been blind and had received his sight until they sent for the man's parents. ¹⁹"Is this your son?" they asked. "Is this the one you say was born blind? How is it that now he can see?"

²⁰"We know he is our son," the parents answered, "and we know he was born blind. ²¹But how he can see now, or who opened his eyes, we don't know. Ask him. He is of age; he will speak for himself." ²²His parents said this because they were afraid of the Jews,ᵇ for already the Jews had decided that anyone who acknowledged that Jesus was the Christ ᵃ would be put out of the synagogue. ᶜ ²³That was why his parents said, "He is of age; ask him."

²⁴A second time they summoned the man who had been blind. "Give glory to God,ᵇ "ᵈ they said. "We know this man is a sinner."ᵉ

²⁵He replied, "Whether he is a sinner or not, I don't know. One thing I do know. I was blind but now I see!"

²⁶Then they asked him, "What did he do to you? How did he open your eyes?"

²⁷He answered, "I have told you already and you did not listen. Why do you want to hear it again? Do you want to become his disciples, too?"

²⁸Then they hurled insults at him and said, "You are this fellow's disciple! We are disciples of Moses! ᶠ ²⁹We know that God spoke to Moses, but as for this fellow, we don't even know where he comes from."

³⁰The man answered, "Now that is remarkable! You don't know where he comes from, yet he opened my eyes. ³¹We know that God does not listen to sinners. He listens to the godly man who does his will.ᵍ ³²Nobody has ever heard of opening the eyes of a man born blind. ³³If this man were not from God,ʰ he could do nothing."

³⁴To this they replied, "You were steeped in sin at birth;ⁱ how dare you lecture us!" And they threw him out.

Jesus Teaches about Spiritual Blindness (150)

³⁵Jesus heard that they had thrown him out, and when he found him, he said, "Do you believe in the Son of Man?"

³⁶"Who is he, sir?" the man asked. "Tell me so that I may believe in him."

³⁷Jesus said, "You have now seen him; in fact, he is the one speaking with you."ʲ

³⁸Then the man said, "Lord, I believe," and he worshiped him.

ᵃ22 Or *Messiah* ᵇ24 A solemn charge to tell the truth (see Joshua 7:19)

9:14
ʸJn 5:9

9:16
ᶻJn 7:43; 10:19

9:17
ᵃMt 21:11

9:22
ᵇJn 7:13
ᶜJn 12:42

9:24
ᵈJos 7:19
ᵉver 16

9:28
ᶠJn 5:45

9:31
ᵍPs 34:15, 16; 66:18; Pr 15:29; Isa 1:15

9:33
ʰver 16

9:34
ⁱver 2

9:37
ʲJn 4:26

9:13–17 While the Pharisees conducted investigations and debated about Jesus, people were being healed and lives were being changed. The Pharisees' skepticism was based not on insufficient evidence, but on jealousy of Jesus' popularity and his influence on the people.

9:14–16 The Jewish Sabbath, Saturday, was the weekly holy day of rest. The Pharisees had made a long list of specific do's and don'ts regarding the Sabbath. Kneading the clay and healing the man were considered work and therefore were forbidden. Jesus may have purposely made the clay in order to emphasize his teaching about the Sabbath—that it is right to care for others' needs even if it involves working on a day of rest.

9:25 By now the man who had been blind had heard the same questions over and over. He did not know how or why he was

healed, but he knew that his life had been miraculously changed, and he was not afraid to tell the truth. You don't need to know all the answers in order to share Christ with others. It is important to tell them how he has changed your life. Then trust that God will use your words to help others believe in him too.

9:28, 34 The man's new faith was severely tested by some of the authorities. He was cursed and evicted from the synagogue. Persecution may come when you follow Jesus. You may lose friends; you may even lose your life. But no one can ever take away the eternal life that Jesus gives you.

9:38 This man gained not only physical sight but also spiritual sight as he recognized Jesus first as a prophet (9:17), then as his Lord. When you turn to Christ, you begin to see him differently. The longer you walk with him, the better you will understand who he is. Peter tells us to "grow in the grace and knowledge of our Lord and Savior Jesus Christ" (2 Peter 3:18). If you want to know more about Jesus, keep trusting him in every area of life.

9:39
k Jn 5:22
l Mt 13:13

9:40
m Ro 2:19

9:41
n Jn 15:22, 24

39 Jesus said, "For judgment k I have come into this world, so that the blind will see and those who see will become blind." l

40 Some Pharisees who were with him heard him say this and asked, "What? Are we blind too?" m

41 Jesus said, "If you were blind, you would not be guilty of sin; but now that you claim you can see, your guilt remains. n

Jesus Is the Good Shepherd (151)

10 "I tell you the truth, the man who does not enter the sheep pen by the gate, but climbs in by some other way, is a thief and a robber. 2 The man who enters by the gate is the shepherd of his sheep. 3 The watchman opens the gate for him, and the sheep listen to his voice. He calls his own sheep by name and leads them out. 4 When he has brought out all his own, he goes on ahead of them, and his sheep follow him because they know his voice. 5 But they will never follow a stranger; in fact, they will run away from him because they do not recognize a stranger's voice." 6 Jesus used this figure of speech, but they did not understand what he was telling them.

7 Therefore Jesus said again, "I tell you the truth, I am the gate for the sheep. 8 All who ever came before me were thieves and robbers, but the sheep did not listen to them. 9 I am the gate; whoever enters through me will be saved. a He will come in and go out, and find pasture. 10 The thief comes only to steal and kill and destroy; I have come that they may have life, and have it to the full.

10:11
o Isa 40:11;
Eze 34:11-16, 23;
Heb 13:20; 1 Pe 5:4

11 "I am the good shepherd. o The good shepherd lays down his life for the sheep. 12 The hired hand is not the shepherd who owns the sheep. So when he sees the wolf coming, he abandons the sheep and runs away. Then the wolf attacks the flock and scatters it. 13 The man runs away because he is a hired hand and cares nothing for the sheep.

10:15
p Mt 11:27

10:16
q Isa 56:8
r Eph 2:11-19

14 "I am the good shepherd; I know my sheep and my sheep know me— 15 just as the Father knows me and I know the Father p —and I lay down my life for the sheep. 16 I have other sheep q that are not of this sheep pen. I must bring them also. They too will listen to my voice, and there shall be one flock r and one shepherd. 17 The reason my Father loves me is that I lay down my life—only to take it up again. 18 No one takes it from me, but I lay it down of my own accord. I have authority to lay it down and authority to take it up again. This command I received from my Father." s

10:18
s Jn 15:10

10:19
t Jn 7:43

19 At these words the Jews were again divided. t 20 Many of them said, "He is demon-possessed and raving mad. Why listen to him?"

a 9 Or kept safe

9:40, 41 The Pharisees were shocked that Jesus thought they were spiritually blind. Jesus countered by saying that it was only blindness (stubbornness and stupidity) that could excuse their behavior. To those who remained open and recognized how sin had truly blinded them from knowing the truth, he gave spiritual understanding and insight. But he rejected those who had become complacent, self-satisfied, and blind.

10:1 At night, sheep were often gathered into a sheep pen to protect them from thieves, weather, or wild animals. The sheep pens were caves, sheds, or open areas surrounded by walls made of stones or branches. The shepherd often slept across the doorway of the pen to protect the sheep. Just as a shepherd cares for his sheep, Jesus, the good shepherd, cares for his flock (those who follow him). The prophet Ezekiel, in predicting the coming of the Messiah, called him a shepherd (Ezekiel 34:23).

10:7 In the sheep pen, the shepherd functioned as a gate, letting the sheep in and protecting them. Jesus is the gate to God's salvation for us. He offers access to safety and security. Christ is our protector. Some people resent that Jesus is the gate, the only way of access to God. But Jesus is God's Son—why should we seek any other way or want to customize a different approach to God? (See also the note on 14:6.)

10:10 In contrast to the thief who takes life, Jesus gives life. The life he gives right now is abundantly richer and fuller. It is eternal, yet it begins immediately. Life in Christ is lived on a higher plane because of his overflowing forgiveness, love, and guidance. Have you taken Christ's offer of life?

10:11, 12 A hired hand tends the sheep for money, while the shepherd does it for love. The shepherd owns the sheep and is committed to them. Jesus is not merely doing a job; he is committed to love us and even lay down his life for us. False teachers and false prophets do not have this commitment.

10:16 The "other sheep" were non-Jews. Jesus came to save Gentiles as well as Jews. This is an insight into his worldwide mission—to die for the sins of the world. People tend to want to restrict God's blessings to their own group, but Jesus refuses to be limited by the fences we build.

10:17, 18 Jesus' death and resurrection, as part of God's plan for the salvation of the world, were under God's full control. No one could kill Jesus without his consent.

10:19, 20 If Jesus had been merely a man, his claims to be God would have proven him insane. But his miracles proved his words true—he really was God. The Jewish leaders could not see beyond their own prejudices, and they looked at Jesus only from a human perspective—Jesus confined in a human box. But Jesus was not limited by their restricted vision.

21 But others said, "These are not the sayings of a man possessed by a demon. Can a demon open the eyes of the blind?" *u*

Religious Leaders Surround Jesus at the Temple (152)

22 Then came the Feast of Dedication*a* at Jerusalem. It was winter, 23 and Jesus was in the temple area walking in Solomon's Colonnade. *v* 24 The Jews gathered around him, saying, "How long will you keep us in suspense? If you are the Christ,*b* tell us plainly."

25 Jesus answered, "I did tell you, but you do not believe. The miracles I do in my Father's name speak for me,*w* 26 but you do not believe because you are not my sheep. *x* 27 My sheep listen to my voice; I know them,*y* and they follow me. *z* 28 I give them eternal life, and they shall never perish; no one can snatch them out of my hand. 29 My Father, who has given them to me, is greater than all*c*; no one can snatch them out of my Father's hand. 30 I and the Father are one." *a*

31 Again the Jews picked up stones to stone him,*b* 32 but Jesus said to them, "I have shown you many great miracles from the Father. For which of these do you stone me?"

33 "We are not stoning you for any of these," replied the Jews, "but for blasphemy, because you, a mere man, claim to be God." *c*

34 Jesus answered them, "Is it not written in your Law, 'I have said you are gods'*d*? *d* 35 If he called them 'gods,' to whom the word of God came—and the Scripture cannot be broken— 36 what about the one whom the Father set apart as his very own and sent into the world? *e* Why then do you accuse me of blasphemy because I said, 'I am God's Son'? *f* 37 Do not believe me unless I do what my Father does. *g* 38 But if I do it, even though you do not believe me, believe the miracles, that you may know and understand that the Father is in me, and I in the Father." *h* 39 Again they tried to seize him,*i* but he escaped their grasp. *j*

40 Then Jesus went back across the Jordan*k* to the place where John had been baptizing in the early days. Here he stayed 41 and many people came to him. They said, "Though John never performed a miraculous sign, all that John said about this man was true." 42 And in that place many believed in Jesus.

*a*22 That is, Hanukkah   *b*24 Or *Messiah*   *c*29 Many early manuscripts *What my Father has given me is greater than all*   *d*34 Psalm 82:6

10:21 *u*Ex 4:11; Jn 9:32, 33

10:23 *v*Ac 3:11; 5:12

10:25 *w*Jn 5:36

10:26 *x*Jn 8:47

10:27 *y*ver 14   *z*ver 4

10:30 *a*Jn 17:21-23

10:31 *b*Jn 8:59

10:33 *c*Jn 5:18

10:34 *d*Ps 82:6

10:36 *e*Jn 3:17   *f*Jn 5:17, 18

10:37 *g*Jn 15:24

10:38 *h*Jn 14:10, 11, 20; 17:21

10:39 *i*Jn 7:30   *j*Jn 8:59

10:40 *k*Jn 1:28

10:22, 23 The Feast of Dedication commemorated the cleansing of the temple under Judas Maccabeus in 164 B.C. after Antiochus Epiphanes had defiled it by sacrificing a pig on the altar of burnt offering. The feast was celebrated toward the end of December. This is also the present-day Feast of Lights called Hanukkah.

10:23 Solomon's Colonnade was a roofed walkway supported by large stone columns, just inside the walls of the temple courtyard.

10:24 Many people asking for proof do so for the wrong reasons. Most of these questioners didn't want to follow Jesus

in the way that required them to submit to his leadership. They hoped that Jesus would declare himself Messiah for perverted reasons. They, along with the disciples and everyone else in the Jewish nation, would have been delighted to have him drive out the Romans. Many of them didn't think he was going to do that, however. These doubters hoped he would identify himself so they could accuse him of telling lies (as the Pharisees did in 8:13).

10:28, 29 Just as a shepherd protects his sheep, Jesus protects his people from eternal harm. While believers can expect to suffer on earth, Satan cannot harm their souls or take away their eternal life with God. There are many reasons to be afraid here on earth because this is the devil's domain (1 Peter 5:8). But if you choose to follow Jesus, he will give you everlasting safety.

10:30 This is the clearest statement of Jesus' divinity he ever made. Jesus and his Father are not the same person, but they are one in essence and nature. Thus Jesus is not merely a good teacher—he is God. His claim to be God was unmistakable. The religious leaders wanted to kill him because their laws said that anyone claiming to be God should die. Nothing could persuade them that Jesus' claim was true.

10:31 The Jewish leaders attempted to carry out the directive found in Leviticus 24:16 regarding those who blaspheme (claim to be God). They intended to stone Jesus.

10:34-36 Jesus referred to Psalm 82:6, where the Israelite rulers and judges are called "gods" (see also Exodus 4:16; 7:1). If God called the Israelite leaders gods because they were agents of God's revelation and will, how could it be blasphemy for Jesus to call himself the Son of God? Jesus was rebuking the religious leaders, because he is the Son of God in a unique, unparalleled relationship of oneness with the Father.

10:35 "The Scripture cannot be broken" is a clear statement of the truth of the Bible. If we accept Christ as Lord, we also must accept his testimony to the Bible as God's Word.

MINISTRY EAST OF THE JORDAN Jesus had been in Jerusalem for the Feast of Tabernacles (7:2); then he preached in various towns, probably in Judea, before returning to Jerusalem for the Feast of Dedication. He again angered the religious leaders, who tried to arrest him, but he left the city and went to the region east of the Jordan to preach.

3. Jesus encounters crucial events in Jerusalem
Lazarus Becomes Sick and Dies (165)

11:1
l Lk 10:38
11:2
m Jn 12:3

11 Now a man named Lazarus was sick. He was from Bethany, the village of Mary and her sister Martha.*l* 2 This Mary, whose brother Lazarus now lay sick, was the same one who poured perfume on the Lord and wiped his feet with her hair.*m* 3 So the sisters sent word to Jesus, "Lord, the one you love is sick."

11:4
n ver 40; Jn 9:3

4 When he heard this, Jesus said, "This sickness will not end in death. No, it is for God's glory*n* so that God's Son may be glorified through it." 5 Jesus loved Martha and her sister and Lazarus. 6 Yet when he heard that Lazarus was sick, he stayed where he was two more days.

7 Then he said to his disciples, "Let us go back to Judea."

11:8
o Jn 10:31
11:9
p Jn 9:4

8 "But Rabbi," they said, "a short while ago the Jews tried to stone you,*o* and yet you are going back there?"

9 Jesus answered, "Are there not twelve hours of daylight? A man who walks by day will not stumble, for he sees by this world's light.*p* 10 It is when he walks by night that he stumbles, for he has no light."

11:11
q Ac 7:60
11:13
r Mt 9:24

11 After he had said this, he went on to tell them, "Our friend Lazarus has fallen asleep;*q* but I am going there to wake him up."

12 His disciples replied, "Lord, if he sleeps, he will get better." 13 Jesus had been speaking of his death, but his disciples thought he meant natural sleep.*r*

THE NAMES OF JESUS
In different settings, Jesus gave himself names that pointed to special roles he was ready to fulfill for people. Some of these refer back to the Old Testament promises of the Messiah. Others were ways to help people understand him.

Reference	Name	Significance
6:27	Son of Man	Jesus' favorite reference to himself. It emphasized his humanity—but the way he used it, it was a claim to divinity.
6:35	Bread of life	Refers to his life-giving role—that he is the only source of eternal life.
8:12	Light of the world	Light is a symbol of spiritual truth. Jesus is the universal answer for people's need of spiritual truth.
10:7	Gate for the sheep	Jesus is the only way into God's kingdom.
10:11	Good shepherd	Jesus appropriated the prophetic images of the Messiah pictured in the Old Testament. This is a claim to divinity, focusing on Jesus' love and guidance.
11:25	The resurrection and the life	Not only is Jesus the source of life; he is the power over death.
14:6	The way, the truth, and the life	Jesus is the method, the message, and the meaning for all people. With this title, he summarized his purpose in coming to earth.
15:1	The vine	This title has an important second part, "you are the branches." As in so many of his other names, Jesus reminds us that just as branches gain life from the vine and cannot live apart from it, so we are completely dependent on Christ for spiritual life.

11:1 The village of Bethany was located about two miles east of Jerusalem on the road to Jericho. It was near enough to Jerusalem for Jesus and the disciples to be in danger, but far enough away so as not to attract attention prematurely.

11:3 As their brother grew very sick, Mary and Martha turned to Jesus for help. They believed in his ability to help because they had seen his miracles. We too know of Jesus' miracles, both from Scripture and through changed lives we have seen. When we need extraordinary help, Jesus offers extraordinary resources. We should not hesitate to ask him for assistance.

11:4 Any trial a believer faces can ultimately bring glory to God, because God can bring good out of any bad situation (Genesis 50:20; Romans 8:28). When trouble comes, do you grumble, complain, and blame God, or do you see your problems as opportunities to honor him?

11:5–7 Jesus loved this family and often stayed with them. He knew their pain but did not respond immediately. His delay had

a specific purpose. God's timing, especially his delays, may make us think he is not answering or is not answering the way we want. But he will meet all our needs according to his perfect schedule and purpose (Philippians 4:19). Patiently await his timing.

11:9, 10 *Day* symbolizes the knowledge of God's will and reliance on his guidance, and *night* the absence of this knowledge combined with self-reliance. When we move ahead in darkness, we will be likely to stumble.

14So then he told them plainly, "Lazarus is dead, 15and for your sake I am glad I was not there, so that you may believe. But let us go to him."

16Then Thomas (called Didymus) said to the rest of the disciples, "Let us also go, that we may die with him."

Jesus Comforts Mary and Martha (166)

17On his arrival, Jesus found that Lazarus had already been in the tomb for four days. 18Bethany was less than two miles a from Jerusalem, 19and many Jews had come to Martha and Mary to comfort them in the loss of their brother. s 20When Martha heard that Jesus was coming, she went out to meet him, but Mary stayed at home.

21"Lord," Martha said to Jesus, "if you had been here, my brother would not have died. 22But I know that even now God will give you whatever you ask." t

23Jesus said to her, "Your brother will rise again."

24Martha answered, "I know he will rise again in the resurrection u at the last day."

25Jesus said to her, "I am the resurrection and the life. v He who believes in me will live, even though he dies; 26and whoever lives and believes in me will never die. Do you believe this?"

27"Yes, Lord," she told him, "I believe that you are the Christ,b the Son of God,w who was to come into the world." x

28And after she had said this, she went back and called her sister Mary aside. "The Teacher y is here," she said, "and is asking for you." 29When Mary heard this, she got up quickly and went to him. 30Now Jesus had not yet entered the village, but was still at the place where Martha had met him. 31When the Jews who had been with Mary in the house, comforting her,z noticed how quickly she got up and went out, they followed her, supposing she was going to the tomb to mourn there.

32When Mary reached the place where Jesus was and saw him, she fell at his feet and said, "Lord, if you had been here, my brother would not have died." a

33When Jesus saw her weeping, and the Jews who had come along with her also weeping, he was deeply moved in spirit and troubled. b 34"Where have you laid him?" he asked.

a 18 Greek *fifteen stadia* (about 3 kilometers)   b 27 Or *Messiah*

11:19
s Job 2:11

11:22
t Jn 9:31

11:24
u Jn 5:28, 29

11:25
v Jn 1:4

11:27
w Mt 16:16
x Jn 6:14

11:28
y Mt 26:18; Jn 13:13

11:31
z ver 19

11:32
a ver 21

11:33
b Jn 12:27

11:14, 15 If Jesus had been with Lazarus during the final moments of Lazarus's sickness, he might have healed him rather than let him die. But Lazarus died so that Jesus' power over death could be shown to his disciples and others. The raising of Lazarus was an essential display of his power, and the resurrection from the dead is a crucial belief of Christian faith. Jesus not only raised himself from the dead (10:18), but he has the power to raise others.

11:16 We often remember Thomas as "the doubter," because he doubted Jesus' resurrection (John 20:25). But here he

JESUS RAISES LAZARUS
Jesus had been preaching in the villages beyond the Jordan, probably in Perea, when he received the news of Lazarus's sickness. Jesus did not leave immediately, but waited two days before returning to Judea. He knew Lazarus would be dead when he arrived in Bethany, but he was going to do a great miracle.

demonstrated love and courage. The disciples knew the dangers of going with Jesus to Jerusalem, and they tried to talk him out of it. Thomas merely expressed what all of them felt. When their objections failed, they were willing to go, even though it appeared they might have to die with Jesus. They may not have understood why Jesus would be killed, but they were loyal. There are unknown dangers in doing God's work. It is wise to consider the high cost of being Jesus' disciple.

11:25, 26 Jesus has power over life and death as well as power to forgive sins. This is because he is the Creator of life (see John 14:6). He who *is* life can surely restore life. Whoever believes in Christ has a spiritual life that death cannot conquer or diminish in any way. When we realize his power and how wonderful his offer to us really is, how can we help but commit our lives to him! To those of us who believe, what wonderful assurance and certainty we have: "Because I live, you also will live" (14:19).

11:27 Martha is best known for being too busy to sit down and talk with Jesus (Luke 10:38–42). But here we see her as a woman of deep faith. Her statement of faith is exactly the response that Jesus wants from us.

11:33–37 John stresses that we have a God who cares. When Jesus saw the weeping and wailing, he too wept openly. Perhaps he empathized with their grief, or perhaps he was troubled at their unbelief. In either case, Jesus showed that he cares enough for us to weep with us in our sorrow. This portrait contrasts with the Greek concept of God that was popular in that day—a God with no emotions and no messy involvement with humans. Here we see many of Jesus' emotions—compassion, indignation, sorrow, even frustration. He often expressed deep emotion, and we must never be afraid to reveal our true feelings to him. He understands them, for he experienced them. Be honest, and don't try to hide anything from your Savior. He cares.

11:35
c Lk 19:41

11:37
d Jn 9:6, 7

"Come and see, Lord," they replied.

35 Jesus wept. *c*

36 Then the Jews said, "See how he loved him!"

37 But some of them said, "Could not he who opened the eyes of the blind man *d* have kept this man from dying?"

Jesus Raises Lazarus from the Dead (167)

11:38
e Mt 27:60

38 Jesus, once more deeply moved, came to the tomb. It was a cave with a stone laid across the entrance. *e* 39 "Take away the stone," he said.

"But, Lord," said Martha, the sister of the dead man, "by this time there is a bad odor, for he has been there four days."

11:40
f ver 23-25
g ver 4

40 Then Jesus said, "Did I not tell you that if you believed, *f* you would see the glory of God?" *g*

11:42
h Jn 12:30

41 So they took away the stone. Then Jesus looked up and said, "Father, I thank you that you have heard me. 42 I knew that you always hear me, but I said this for the benefit of the people standing here, *h* that they may believe that you sent me."

11:44
i Jn 19:40
j Jn 20:7

43 When he had said this, Jesus called in a loud voice, "Lazarus, come out!" 44 The dead man came out, his hands and feet wrapped with strips of linen, *i* and a cloth around his face. *j*

Jesus said to them, "Take off the grave clothes and let him go."

LAZARUS

The details surrounding death may vary, but the reality is universal. Scenes like Lazarus's funeral in Bethany are repeated many times around the world each day. A grieving family gathers at a graveside. Friends agonize over what to say. Their helpless silence, downcast eyes, and shuffling feet provide more distraction than comfort. When death is unexpected, the whys hang in the air like choking smog.

Drawn by grief and duty, people came from Jerusalem and the surrounding area to pay their last respects to a citizen of Bethany. Jesus' friend Lazarus was dead. His brief sickness proved stronger than any available medicine. Jesus had been sent for, but had failed to arrive in time. Death didn't wait. Following the wisdom of hot countries, the body was soon wrapped and buried. Four days later, Jesus arrived.

Lazarus's sisters, Mary and Martha, reacted in shock. Grief-stricken, they struggled to understand why Jesus had delayed in coming. We have no idea how Lazarus reacted to his own death. In fact, we don't have a record of a single word he said. We do know that he listened to Jesus. Even when the curtain of death was between them, Lazarus responded to Jesus' voice. He came hobbling out of his cave-tomb, still wrapped with strips of linen. Jesus raised him from the dead!

When all is said and done, only what God accomplished through us will really matter. We will take little credit. Jesus worked in and around Lazarus just as he does with us. We have Christ's invitation to participate in his work, but we must not forget that he will do much more than we will know. Meanwhile, we delight in what Christ does with the little we have to offer him.

Lazarus's resurrection poses an important question: When you die, do you fully expect that your next conscious experience will be hearing the voice of Jesus call you by name?

Strengths and accomplishments:	• Regularly hosted Jesus in his home • Raised from the dead by Jesus after four days in the grave
Lessons from his life:	• Once we have given God ownership of our lives, we can't predict what he will do with them • Jesus' circle of relationships went beyond the 12 disciples • Jesus declared that the events surrounding Lazarus's sickness and death would glorify God
Vital statistics:	• Where: Bethany • Relatives: Sisters: Mary and Martha
Key verse:	"This sickness will not end in death. No, it is for God's glory so that God's Son may be glorified through it" (John 11:4).

Lazarus's role as an "active spectator" is recorded in John 11:1–12:11.

11:38 Tombs at this time were usually caves carved in the limestone rock of a hillside. A tomb was often large enough for people to walk inside. Several bodies would be placed in one tomb. After burial, a large stone was rolled across the entrance to the tomb.

11:44 Jesus raised others from the dead, including Jairus's daughter (Matthew 9:18–26; Mark 5:41, 42; Luke 8:40–56) and a widow's son (Luke 7:11–15).

Religious Leaders Plot to Kill Jesus (168)

45 Therefore many of the Jews who had come to visit Mary, and had seen what Jesus did,*k* put their faith in him. 46 But some of them went to the Pharisees and told them what Jesus had done. 47 Then the chief priests and the Pharisees called a meeting *l* of the Sanhedrin.

"What are we accomplishing?" they asked. "Here is this man performing many miraculous signs. 48 If we let him go on like this, everyone will believe in him, and then the Romans will come and take away both our place*a* and our nation."

49 Then one of them, named Caiaphas,*m* who was high priest that year,*n* spoke up, "You know nothing at all! 50 You do not realize that it is better for you that one man die for the people than that the whole nation perish."*o*

51 He did not say this on his own, but as high priest that year he prophesied that Jesus would die for the Jewish nation, 52 and not only for that nation but also for the scattered children of God, to bring them together and make them one.*p* 53 So from that day on they plotted to take his life.

54 Therefore Jesus no longer moved about publicly among the Jews.*q* Instead he withdrew to a region near the desert, to a village called Ephraim, where he stayed with his disciples.

55 When it was almost time for the Jewish Passover,*r* many went up from the country to Jerusalem for their ceremonial cleansing*s* before the Passover. 56 They kept looking for Jesus,*t* and as they stood in the temple area they asked one another, "What do you think? Isn't he coming to the Feast at all?" 57 But the chief priests and Pharisees had given orders that if anyone found out where Jesus was, he should report it so that they might arrest him.

A Woman Anoints Jesus with Perfume (182/Matthew 26:6–13; Mark 14:3–9)

12 Six days before the Passover,*u* Jesus arrived at Bethany, where Lazarus lived, whom Jesus had raised from the dead. 2 Here a dinner was given in Jesus' honor. Martha served,*v* while Lazarus was among those reclining at the table with him. 3 Then Mary took about a pint*b* of pure nard, an expensive perfume; she poured it on Jesus' feet and wiped his feet with her hair.*w* And the house was filled with the fragrance of the perfume.

4 But one of his disciples, Judas Iscariot, who was later to betray him, objected, 5 "Why wasn't this perfume sold and the money given to the poor? It was worth a year's wages. *c* " 6 He did not say this because he cared about the poor but because he was a thief; as keeper of the money bag,*x* he used to help himself to what was put into it.

a 48 Or *temple* *b 3* Greek *a litra (probably about 0.5 liter)* *c 5* Greek *three hundred denarii*

11:45
k Jn 2:23

11:47
l Mt 26:3

11:49
m Mt 26:3
n Jn 18:13, 14

11:50
o Jn 18:14

11:52
p Isa 49:6; Jn 10:16

11:54
q Jn 7:1

11:55
r Mk 14:1
s 2Ch 30:17, 18

11:56
t Jn 7:11

12:1
u Jn 11:55

12:2
v Lk 10:38-42

12:3
w Jn 11:2

12:6
x Jn 13:29

11:45–53 Even when confronted point-blank with the power of Jesus' deity, some refused to believe. These eyewitnesses not only rejected Jesus; they plotted his murder. They were so hardened that they preferred to reject God's Son rather than admit that they were wrong. They preferred "closure" instead of being open to God's marvelous power. Beware of pride. If we allow it to grow, it can lead us into enormous sin.

11:48 The Jewish leaders knew that if they didn't stop Jesus, the Romans would lash out against all of them. Rome gave partial freedom to the Jews as long as they were quiet and obedient. Jesus' miracles often caused a disturbance. The leaders feared that Rome's displeasure would bring additional hardship to their nation.

11:51 John regarded Caiaphas's statement as a prophecy. As high priest, Caiaphas was used by God to explain Jesus' death even though Caiaphas didn't realize what he was doing.

12:3 Pure nard was a fragrant ointment imported from the mountains of India. Thus it was very expensive. The amount Mary used was worth a year's wages.

12:4–6 Judas often dipped into the disciples' money bag for his own use. Jesus knew what Judas was doing (2:24, 25; 6:64), but never did or said anything about it. Similarly, when we choose the way of sin, God may not immediately do anything to stop us, but this does not mean he approves of our actions. What we deserve will come.

12:5, 6 Judas used a pious phrase to hide his true motives. But Jesus knew what was in his heart. Judas's life had become a lie, and the devil was gaining more and more control over him (13:27). Satan is the father of lies, and a lying character opens the door to his influence. Jesus' knowledge of us should make us want to keep our actions consistent with our words. Because we have nothing to fear with him, we should have nothing to hide.

TIME WITH THE DISCIPLES
Lazarus's return to life became the last straw for the religious leaders, who were bent on killing Jesus. So Jesus stopped his public ministry and took his disciples away from Jerusalem to Ephraim. From there they returned to Galilee for a while (see the map in Luke 17, p. 1711).

Mediterranean Sea
GALILEE
N
Sea of Galilee
SAMARIA
Jordan River
Ephraim
Jerusalem
PEREA
Dead Sea
JUDEA
IDUMEA
0   20 Mi.
0   20 Km.

12:7
y Jn 19:40

7 "Leave her alone," Jesus replied. " ⌊It was intended⌋ that she should save this perfume for the day of my burial. y 8 You will always have the poor among you, but you will not always have me."

12:9
z Jn 11:43, 44

9 Meanwhile a large crowd of Jews found out that Jesus was there and came, not only because of him but also to see Lazarus, whom he had raised from the dead. z 10 So the chief priests made plans to kill Lazarus as well, 11 for on account of him a many of the Jews were going over to Jesus and putting their faith in him.

12:11
a ver 17, 18;
Jn 11:45

CAIAPHAS

Caiaphas was the leader of the religious group called the Sadducees. Educated and wealthy, they were politically influential in the nation. As the elite group, they were on fairly good terms with Rome. They hated Jesus because he endangered their secure lifestyles and taught a message they could not accept. A kingdom in which leaders *served* had no appeal to them.

Caiaphas's usual policy was to remove any threats to his power by whatever means necessary. For Caiaphas, whether Jesus should die was not in question; the only point to be settled was *when* his death should take place. Not only did Jesus have to be captured and tried; the Jewish council also needed Roman approval before they could carry out the death sentence. Caiaphas's plans were unexpectedly helped by Judas's offer to betray Christ.

Caiaphas did not realize that his schemes were actually part of a wonderful plan God was carrying out. Caiaphas's willingness to sacrifice another man to preserve his own security was clearly selfish. By contrast, Jesus' willingness to die for us was a clear example of loving self-sacrifice. Caiaphas thought he had won the battle as Jesus hung on the cross, but he did not count on the resurrection!

Caiaphas's mind was closed. He couldn't accept the resurrection even when the evidence was overwhelming, and he attempted to silence those whose lives had been forever changed by the risen Christ (Matthew 28:12, 13). Caiaphas represents those people who will not believe because they think it will cost them too much to accept Jesus as Lord. They choose the fleeting power, prestige, and pleasures of this life instead of the eternal life God offers those who receive his Son. What is your choice?

Strength and accomplishment:	• High priest for 18 years
Weaknesses and mistakes:	• One of those most directly responsible for Jesus' death • Used his office as a means to power and personal security • Planned Jesus' capture, carried out his illegal trial, pressured Pilate to approve the crucifixion, attempted to prevent the resurrection, and later tried to cover up the fact of the resurrection • Kept up religious appearances while compromising with Rome • Involved in the later persecution of Christians
Lessons from his life:	• God uses even the twisted motives and actions of his enemies to bring about his will • When we cover selfish motives with spiritual objectives and words, God still sees our intentions
Vital statistics:	• Where: Jerusalem • Occupation: High priest • Relative: Father-in-law: Annas • Contemporaries: Jesus, Pilate, Herod Antipas
Key verses:	"Caiaphas, who was high priest that year, spoke up, 'You know nothing at all! You do not realize that it is better for you that one man die for the people than that the whole nation perish'" (John 11:49, 50).

Caiaphas is mentioned in Matthew 26:57; Luke 3:2; John 11; 18; and in Acts 4:6.

12:7, 8 This act and Jesus' response to it do not teach us to ignore the poor so we can spend money extravagantly for Christ. This was a unique act for a specific occasion—an anointing that anticipated Jesus' burial and a public declaration of faith in him as Messiah. Jesus' words should have taught Judas a valuable lesson about the worth of money. Unfortunately, Judas did not take heed; soon he would sell his Master's life for 30 pieces of silver.

12:10, 11 The chief priests' blindness and hardness of heart caused them to sink ever deeper into sin. They rejected the Messiah and planned to kill him, and then plotted to murder Lazarus as well. One sin leads to another. From the Jewish leaders' point of view, they could accuse Jesus of blasphemy because he claimed equality with God. But Lazarus had done nothing of the kind. They wanted Lazarus dead simply because he was a living witness to Jesus' power. This is a warning to us to avoid sin. Sin leads to more sin, a downward spiral that can be stopped only by repentance and the power of the Holy Spirit to change our behavior.

Jesus Rides into Jerusalem on a Young Donkey
(183/Matthew 21:1–11; Mark 11:1–11; Luke 19:28–44)

12The next day the great crowd that had come for the Feast heard that Jesus was on his way to Jerusalem. 13They took palm branches and went out to meet him, shouting,

> "Hosanna!a"
>
> "Blessed is he who comes in the name of the Lord!"b b
>
> "Blessed is the King of Israel!"

14Jesus found a young donkey and sat upon it, as it is written,

> 15 "Do not be afraid, O Daughter of Zion;
>   see, your king is coming,
>   seated on a donkey's colt."c c

16At first his disciples did not understand all this. Only after Jesus was glorifiedd did they realize that these things had been written about him and that they had done these things to him.

17Now the crowd that was with him when he called Lazarus from the tomb and raised him from the dead continued to spread the word. 18Many people, because they had heard that he had given this miraculous sign,e went out to meet him. 19So the Pharisees said to one another, "See, this is getting us nowhere. Look how the whole world has gone after him!"

Jesus Explains Why He Must Die (185)

20Now there were some Greeks among those who went up to worship at the Feast. 21They came to Philip, who was from Bethsaida in Galilee, with a request. "Sir," they said, "we would like to see Jesus." 22Philip went to tell Andrew; Andrew and Philip in turn told Jesus.

23Jesus replied, "The hour has come for the Son of Man to be glorified.f 24I tell you the truth, unless a kernel of wheat falls to the ground and dies,g it remains only a single seed. But if it dies, it produces many seeds. 25The man who loves his life will lose it, while the man who hates his life in this world will keep ith for eternal life. 26Whoever serves me must follow me; and where I am, my servant also will be.i My Father will honor the one who serves me.

27"Now my heart is troubled,j and what shall I say? 'Father, save me from this hour'? No, it was for this very reason I came to this hour. 28Father, glorify your name!"

a 13 A Hebrew expression meaning "Save!" which became an exclamation of praise   b 13 Psalm 118:25,26
c 15 Zech. 9:9

**Cross references (margin):**
12:13 bPs 118:25, 26
12:15 cZec 9:9
12:16 dJn 7:39
12:18 ever 11
12:23 fJn 13:32
12:24 g1Co 15:36
12:25 hMt 10:39
12:26 iJn 14:3
12:27 jMt 26:38, 39

12:13 Jesus began his last week on earth by riding into Jerusalem on a donkey under a canopy of palm branches, with crowds hailing him as their king. To announce that he was indeed the Messiah, Jesus chose a *time* when all Israel was gathered at Jerusalem, a *place* where huge crowds could see him, and a *way* of proclaiming his mission that was unmistakable. On Palm Sunday we celebrate Jesus' Triumphal Entry into Jerusalem as Lord of lords and King of Peace.

12:13 The people who were praising God for giving them a king had the wrong idea about Jesus. They were sure he would be a national leader who would restore their nation to its former glory, and thus they were deaf to the words of their prophets and blind to Jesus' real mission. When it became apparent that Jesus was not going to fulfill their hopes, many people turned against him.

12:16 After Jesus' resurrection, the disciples understood for the first time many of the prophecies that they had missed along the way. Jesus' words and actions took on new meaning and made more sense. In retrospect, the disciples saw how Jesus had led them into a deeper and better understanding of his truth. Stop now and think about the events in your life leading up to where you are now. How has God led you to this point? As you grow older, you will look back and see God's involvement more clearly than you do now.

12:18 The people flocked to Jesus because they had heard about his great miracle in raising Lazarus from the dead. Their adoration was short-lived and their commitment shallow, for in a few days they would do nothing to stop his crucifixion. Devotion based only on curiosity or popularity fades quickly.

12:20, 21 These Greeks probably were converts to the Jewish faith. They may have gone to Philip because, though he was a Jew, he had a Greek name.

12:23–25 This is a beautiful picture of the necessary sacrifice of Jesus. Unless a kernel of wheat is buried in the ground, it will not become a blade of wheat producing many more seeds. Jesus had to die to pay the penalty for our sin, but also to show his power over death. His resurrection proves he has eternal life. Because Jesus is God, Jesus can give this same eternal life to all who believe in him.

12:25 We must be so committed to living for Christ that we "hate" our lives by comparison. This does not mean that we long to die or that we are careless or destructive with the life God has given, but that we are willing to die if doing so will glorify Christ. We must disown the tyrannical rule of our own self-centeredness. By laying aside our striving for advantage, security, and pleasure, we can serve God lovingly and freely. Releasing control of our lives and transferring control to Christ bring eternal life and genuine joy.

12:26 Many believed that Jesus came for the Jews only. But when Jesus said, "Whoever serves me must follow me," he was talking to these Greeks as well. No matter who the sincere seekers are, Jesus welcomes them. His message is for everyone. Don't allow social or racial differences to become barriers to the gospel. Take the Good News to all people.

12:27 Jesus knew his crucifixion lay ahead, and because he was human he dreaded it. He knew he would have to take the sins of the world on himself, and he knew this would separate him from his Father. He wanted to be delivered from this horrible death, but

12:28
k Mt 3:17

12:30
l Jn 11:42

12:31
m Jn 16:11
n Jn 14:30; Eph 2:2

12:32
o Jn 3:14

12:33
p Jn 18:32

12:34
q Ps 110:4;
Eze 37:25

12:35
r Eph 5:8

12:36
s Lk 16:8
t Jn 8:59

Then a voice came from heaven, *k* "I have glorified it, and will glorify it again." 29 The crowd that was there and heard it said it had thundered; others said an angel had spoken to him.

30 Jesus said, "This voice was for your benefit, *l* not mine. 31 Now is the time for judgment on this world; *m* now the prince of this world *n* will be driven out. 32 But I, when I am lifted up from the earth, *o* will draw all men to myself." 33 He said this to show the kind of death he was going to die. *p*

34 The crowd spoke up, "We have heard from the Law that the Christ *a* will remain forever, *q* so how can you say, 'The Son of Man must be lifted up'? Who is this 'Son of Man'?"

35 Then Jesus told them, "You are going to have the light just a little while longer. Walk while you have the light, *r* before darkness overtakes you. The man who walks in the dark does not know where he is going. 36 Put your trust in the light while you have it, so that you may become sons of light." *s* When he had finished speaking, Jesus left and hid himself from them. *t*

a 34 Or Messiah

GREAT EXPECTATIONS:
Jesus Does the Unexpected
Wherever he went, Jesus exceeded people's expectations.

What was expected	What Jesus did	Reference
A man looked for healing.	Jesus also forgave his sins.	Mark 2:1–12
The disciples were expecting an ordinary day of fishing.	They found the Savior.	Luke 5:1–11
A widow was resigned to bury her dead son.	Jesus restored her son to life.	Luke 7:11–17
The religious leaders wanted a miracle.	Jesus offered them the Creator of miracles.	Matthew 12:38–45
A woman who wanted to be healed touched Jesus.	Jesus helped her see it was her faith that had healed her.	Mark 5:25–34
The disciples thought the crowd should be sent home because there was no food.	Jesus used a small meal to feed thousands, and there were leftovers!	John 6:1–15
The crowds looked for a political leader to set up a new kingdom to overthrow Rome's control.	Jesus offered them an eternal, spiritual kingdom to overthrow sin's control.	A theme throughout the Gospels
The disciples wanted to eat the Passover meal with Jesus, their Master.	Jesus washed their feet, showing that he was also their servant.	John 13:1–20
The religious leaders wanted Jesus killed and got their wish.	But Jesus rose from the dead!	John 11:53; 19:30; 20:1–29

---

he knew that God sent him into the world to die for our sins, in our place. Jesus said no to his human desires in order to obey his Father and glorify him. Although we will never have to face such a difficult and awesome task, we are still called to obedience. Whatever the Father asks, we should do his will and bring glory to his name.

12:31 The prince of this world is Satan, an angel who rebelled against God. Satan is real, not symbolic, and is constantly working against God and those who obey him. Satan tempted Eve in the garden and persuaded her to sin; he tempted Jesus in the desert and did not persuade him to fall (Matthew 4:1–11). Satan has great power, but people can be delivered from his reign of spiritual darkness because of Christ's victory on the cross. Satan is powerful, but Jesus is much more powerful. Jesus' resurrection shattered Satan's deathly power (Colossians 1:13, 14). To overcome Satan we need faithful allegiance to God's Word, determination to stay away from sin, and the support of other believers.

12:32–34 The crowd could not believe what Jesus was saying about the Messiah. They were waving palm branches for a victorious Messiah who would set up a political, earthly kingdom that would never end. From their reading of certain Scriptures, they thought the Messiah would never die (Psalms 89:35, 36; 110:4;

Isaiah 9:7). Other passages, however, showed that he would (Isaiah 53:5–9). Jesus' words did not mesh with their concept of the Messiah. First he had to suffer and die—then he would one day set up his eternal kingdom. What kind of Messiah, or Savior, are you seeking? Beware of trying to force Jesus into your own mold—he won't fit.

12:35, 36 Jesus said he would be with them in person for only a short time, and they should take advantage of his presence while they had it. Like a light shining in a dark place, he would point out the way they should walk. If they walked in his light, they would become "sons of light," revealing the truth and pointing people to God. As Christians, we are to be Christ's light bearers, letting his light shine through us. How brightly is your light shining? Can others see Christ in your actions?

Most of the People Do Not Believe in Jesus (186)

37 Even after Jesus had done all these miraculous signs in their presence, they still would not believe in him. 38 This was to fulfill the word of Isaiah the prophet:

> "Lord, who has believed our message
> and to whom has the arm of the Lord been revealed?"[a][u]

39 For this reason they could not believe, because, as Isaiah says elsewhere:

> 40 "He has blinded their eyes
> and deadened their hearts,
> so they can neither see with their eyes,
> nor understand with their hearts,
> nor turn—and I would heal them."[b][v]

41 Isaiah said this because he saw Jesus' glory[w] and spoke about him.

42 Yet at the same time many even among the leaders believed in him. But because of the Pharisees[x] they would not confess their faith for fear they would be put out of the synagogue;[y] 43 for they loved praise from men more than praise from God.[z]

Jesus Summarizes His Message (187)

44 Then Jesus cried out, "When a man believes in me, he does not believe in me only, but in the one who sent me.[a] 45 When he looks at me, he sees the one who sent me.[b] 46 I have come into the world as a light,[c] so that no one who believes in me should stay in darkness.

47 "As for the person who hears my words but does not keep them, I do not judge him. For I did not come to judge the world, but to save it.[d] 48 There is a judge for the one who rejects me and does not accept my words; that very word which I spoke will condemn him at the last day. 49 For I did not speak of my own accord, but the Father who sent me commanded me[e] what to say and how to say it. 50 I know that his command leads to eternal life. So whatever I say is just what the Father has told me to say."

12:38
u Isa 53:1

12:40
v Isa 6:10;
Mt 13:13, 15

12:41
w Isa 6:1-4

12:42
x Jn 7:13
y Jn 9:22

12:43
z Jn 5:44

12:44
a Mt 10:40

12:45
b Jn 14:9

12:46
c Jn 3:19

12:47
d Jn 3:17

12:49
e Jn 14:31

C. DEATH AND RESURRECTION OF JESUS, THE SON OF GOD (13:1—21:25)

John begins his Gospel with eternity and ends with Jesus coming to earth again. He features Jesus teaching his disciples privately just before his arrest and death. We see, clearly, the deep love Jesus has for the believer and the peace that comes from faith. Knowing the love Jesus has for believers, we, too, should believe and allow Jesus to forgive our sins. Only then will we experience peace in a world filled with turmoil.

1. Jesus teaches his disciples

Jesus Washes the Disciples' Feet (210)

13 It was just before the Passover Feast. Jesus knew that the time had come for him to leave this world and go to the Father.[f] Having loved his own who were in the world, he now showed them the full extent of his love.[c]

13:1
f Jn 16:28

a 38 Isaiah 53:1   b 40 Isaiah 6:10   c 1 Or he loved them to the last

---

12:37, 38 Jesus had performed many miracles, but most people still didn't believe in him. Likewise, many today won't believe despite all God does. Don't be discouraged if your witness for Christ doesn't turn as many to him as you'd like. Your job is to continue as a faithful witness. You are responsible to reach out to others, but they are responsible for their own decisions.

12:39–41 People in Jesus' time, like those in the time of Isaiah, would not believe despite the evidence (12:37). As a result, God hardened their hearts. Does that mean God intentionally prevented these people from believing in him? No, he simply confirmed their own choices. After a lifetime of resisting God, they had become so set in their ways that they wouldn't even try to understand Jesus' message. For such people, it is virtually impossible to come to God—their hearts have been permanently hardened. Other instances of hardened hearts because of constant stubbornness are recorded in Exodus 9:12, Romans 1:24–28, and 2 Thessalonians 2:8–12.

12:42, 43 Along with those who refused to believe, many believed but refused to admit it. This is just as bad, and Jesus had strong words for such people (see Matthew 10:32, 33). People who will not take a stand for Jesus are afraid of rejection or ridicule. Many

Jewish leaders wouldn't admit to faith in Jesus because they feared excommunication from the synagogue (which was their livelihood) and loss of their prestigious place in the community. But the praise of others is fickle and short-lived. We should be much more concerned about God's eternal acceptance than about the temporary approval of other people.

12:45 We often wonder what God is like. How can we know the Creator when he doesn't make himself visible? Jesus said plainly that those who see him see God, because he is God. If you want to know what God is like, study the person and words of Jesus Christ.

12:48 The purpose of Jesus' first mission on earth was not to judge people, but to show them the way to find salvation and eternal life. When he comes again, one of his main purposes will be to judge people for how they lived on earth. Christ's words that we would not accept and obey will condemn us. On the day of judgment, those who accepted Jesus and lived his way will be raised to eternal life (1 Corinthians 15:51–57; 1 Thessalonians 4:15–18; Revelation 21:1–8), and those who rejected Jesus and lived any way they pleased will face eternal punishment (Revelation 20:11–15). Decide now which side you'll be on, for the consequences of your decision last forever.

² The evening meal was being served, and the devil had already prompted Judas Iscariot, son of Simon, to betray Jesus. ³ Jesus knew that the Father had put all things under his power, and that he had come from God *g* and was returning to God; ⁴ so he got up from the meal, took off his outer clothing, and wrapped a towel around his waist. ⁵ After that, he poured water into a basin and began to wash his disciples' feet, drying them with the towel that was wrapped around him.

⁶ He came to Simon Peter, who said to him, "Lord, are you going to wash my feet?"

13:3
g Jn 8:42

JOHN

Being loved is the most powerful motivation in the world! Our ability to love is often shaped by our experience of love. We usually love others as we have been loved.

Some of the greatest statements about God's loving nature were written by a man who experienced God's love in a unique way. John, Jesus' disciple, expressed his relationship to the Son of God by calling himself "the disciple whom Jesus loved" (John 21:20). Although Jesus' love is clearly communicated in all the Gospels, in John's Gospel it is a central theme. Because his own experience of Jesus' love was so strong and personal, John was sensitive to those words and actions of Jesus that illustrated how the One who *is* love loved others.

Jesus knew John fully and loved him fully. He gave John and his brother James the nickname "Sons of Thunder" (Mark 3:17), perhaps from an occasion when the brothers asked Jesus for permission to "call fire down from heaven" (Luke 9:54) on a village that had refused to welcome Jesus and the disciples. In John's Gospel and letters, we see the great God of love, while the thunder of God's justice bursts from the pages of Revelation.

Jesus confronts each of us as he confronted John. We cannot know the depth of Jesus' love unless we are willing to face the fact that he knows us completely. Otherwise we are fooled into believing he must love the people we pretend to be, not the sinners we actually are. John and all the disciples convince us that God is able and willing to accept us as we are. Being aware of God's love is a great motivator for change. His love is not given in exchange for our efforts; his love frees us to really live. Have you accepted that love?

Strengths and accomplishments:	• One of John the Baptist's disciples before following Jesus • One of the 12 disciples and, with Peter and James, one of the inner three that were closest to Jesus • Wrote five New Testament books: the Gospel of John; 1, 2, and 3 John; and Revelation
Weaknesses and mistakes:	• Along with James, shared a tendency to outbursts of selfishness and anger • Asked for a special position in Jesus' kingdom
Lessons from his life:	• Those who realize how much they are loved are able to love much • When God changes a life, he does not take away personality characteristics, but puts them to effective use in his service
Vital statistics:	• Occupations: Fisherman, disciple • Relatives: Father: Zebedee. Mother: Salome. Brother: James. • Contemporaries: Jesus, Pilate, Herod Antipas
Key verses:	"Dear friends, I am not writing you a new command but an old one, which you have had since the beginning. This old command is the message you have heard. Yet I am writing you a new command; its truth is seen in him and you, because the darkness is passing and the true light is already shining" (1 John 2:7, 8).

John's story is told throughout the Gospels, Acts, and Revelation.

13:1 Jesus knew he would be betrayed by one of his disciples, disowned by another, and deserted by all of them for a time. Still "he now showed them the full extent of his love." God knows us completely, as Jesus knew his disciples (2:24, 25; 6:64). He knows the sins we have committed and the ones we will yet commit. Still, he loves us. How do you respond to that kind of love?

13:1ff Chapters 13—17 tell us what Jesus said to his disciples on the night before his death. These words were all spoken in one evening when, with only the disciples as his audience, he gave final instructions to prepare them for his death and resurrection, events that would change their lives forever.

13:1–3 For more information on Judas Iscariot, see his Profile in Mark 14, p. 1647.

13:1–17 Jesus was the model servant, and he showed his servant attitude to his disciples. Washing guests' feet was a job for a household servant to carry out when guests arrived. But Jesus wrapped a towel around his waist, as the lowliest slave would do, and washed and dried his disciples' feet. If even he, God in the flesh, is willing to serve, we his followers must also be servants, willing to serve in any way that glorifies God. Are you willing to follow Christ's example of serving? Whom can you serve today? There is a special blessing for those who not only agree that humble service is Christ's way, but who also follow through and do it (13:17).

13:6, 7 Imagine being Peter and watching Jesus wash the others' feet, all the while moving closer to you. Seeing his Master behave like a slave must have confused Peter. He still did not understand Jesus' teaching that to be a leader, a person must be a servant. This is not a comfortable passage for leaders who find it hard to serve those beneath them. How do you treat those who work under you (whether children, employees, or volunteers)?

7 Jesus replied, "You do not realize now what I am doing, but later you will understand."

8 "No," said Peter, "you shall never wash my feet."

Jesus answered, "Unless I wash you, you have no part with me."

9 "Then, Lord," Simon Peter replied, "not just my feet but my hands and my head as well!"

10 Jesus answered, "A person who has had a bath needs only to wash his feet; his whole body is clean. And you are clean,*h* though not every one of you." 11 For he knew who was going to betray him, and that was why he said not every one was clean.

12 When he had finished washing their feet, he put on his clothes and returned to his place. "Do you understand what I have done for you?" he asked them. 13 "You call me 'Teacher' and 'Lord,'*i* and rightly so, for that is what I am. 14 Now that I, your Lord and Teacher, have washed your feet, you also should wash one another's feet. 15 I have set you an example that you should do as I have done for you. 16 I tell you the truth, no servant is greater than his master,*j* nor is a messenger greater than the one who sent him. 17 Now that you know these things, you will be blessed if you do them.*k*

18 "I am not referring to all of you; I know those I have chosen. But this is to fulfill the scripture: 'He who shares my bread has lifted up his heel against me.'*a l*

19 "I am telling you now before it happens, so that when it does happen you will believe*m* that I am He. 20 I tell you the truth, whoever accepts anyone I send accepts me; and whoever accepts me accepts the one who sent me."*n*

Jesus and the Disciples Share the Last Supper
(211/Matthew 26:20–30; Mark 14:17–26; Luke 22:14–30)

21 After he had said this, Jesus was troubled in spirit and testified, "I tell you the truth, one of you is going to betray me."

22 His disciples stared at one another, at a loss to know which of them he meant. 23 One of them, the disciple whom Jesus loved,*o* was reclining next to him. 24 Simon Peter motioned to this disciple and said, "Ask him which one he means."

25 Leaning back against Jesus, he asked him, "Lord, who is it?"

26 Jesus answered, "It is the one to whom I will give this piece of bread when I have dipped it in the dish." Then, dipping the piece of bread, he gave it to Judas Iscariot, son of Simon. 27 As soon as Judas took the bread, Satan entered into him.*p*

"What you are about to do, do quickly," Jesus told him, 28 but no one at the meal understood why Jesus said this to him. 29 Since Judas had charge of the money,*q* some thought Jesus was telling him to buy what was needed for the Feast, or to give something to the poor. 30 As soon as Judas had taken the bread, he went out. And it was night.

Jesus Predicts Peter's Denial (212/Luke 22:31–38)

31 When he was gone, Jesus said, "Now is the Son of Man glorified and God is glorified in him.*r* 32 If God is glorified in him,*b* God will glorify the Son in himself, and will glorify him at once.

a *18* Psalm 41:9   b *32* Many early manuscripts do not have *If God is glorified in him.*

**Cross-references (right margin):**

13:10 *h* Jn 15:3

13:13 *i* Php 2:11

13:16 *j* Mt 10:24

13:17 *k* Jas 1:25

13:18 *l* Ps 41:9

13:19 *m* Jn 14:29; 16:4

13:20 *n* Mt 10:40; Lk 10:16

13:23 *o* Jn 19:26; 20:2; 21:7, 20

13:27 *p* Lk 22:3

13:29 *q* Jn 12:6

13:31 *r* Jn 14:13; 1Pe 4:11

13:8, 9 When Jesus responded: "Unless I wash you, you have no part with me," he may have meant (1) that unless he washed away Peter's sins by his death on the cross, then Peter could have no relationship with him, or (2) that unless Peter submitted to him and allowed Jesus to minister in this way, Peter would never learn the lesson of humility. Either way, Peter seemed to grasp the significance of Jesus' words, for he then wanted to be bathed completely: "Not just my feet but my hands and my head as well!"

13:12ff Jesus did not wash his disciples' feet just to get them to be nice to each other. His far greater goal was to extend his mission on earth after he was gone. These men were to move into the world serving God, serving each other, and serving all people to whom they took the message of salvation.

13:22 Judas was not the obvious betrayer. After all, he was the one the disciples trusted to keep the money (12:6; 13:29).

13:26 The honored guest at a meal was often singled out in this way.

13:27 Satan's part in the betrayal of Jesus does not remove any of the responsibility from Judas. Disillusioned because Jesus was talking about dying rather than setting up his kingdom, Judas may have been trying to force Jesus' hand and make him use his power to prove he was the Messiah. Or perhaps Judas, not understanding Jesus' mission, no longer believed Jesus was God's chosen one. Whatever Judas thought, Satan assumed that Jesus' death would end his mission and thwart God's plan. Like Judas, Satan did not know that Jesus' death was the most important part of God's plan all along.

13:27–38 John describes these few moments in clear detail. We can see that Jesus knew exactly what was going to happen. He knew about Judas and about Peter, but he did not change the situation, nor did he stop loving them. In the same way, Jesus knows exactly what you will do to hurt him. Yet he still loves you unconditionally and will forgive you whenever you ask for it. Judas couldn't understand this, and his life ended tragically. Peter understood, and despite his shortcomings, his life ended triumphantly because he never let go of his faith in the One who loved him.

33 "My children, I will be with you only a little longer. You will look for me, and just as I told the Jews, so I tell you now: Where I am going, you cannot come.

34 "A new command s I give you: Love one another. t As I have loved you, so you must love one another. 35 By this all men will know that you are my disciples, if you love one another." u

36 Simon Peter asked him, "Lord, where are you going?"

Jesus replied, "Where I am going, you cannot follow now, but you will follow later." v

37 Peter asked, "Lord, why can't I follow you now? I will lay down my life for you."

38 Then Jesus answered, "Will you really lay down your life for me? I tell you the truth, before the rooster crows, you will disown me three times!

Jesus Is the Way to the Father (213)

14 "Do not let your hearts be troubled. Trust in God a; trust also in me. 2 In my Father's house are many rooms; if it were not so, I would have told you. I am going there w to prepare a place for you. 3 And if I go and prepare a place for you, I will come back and take you to be with me that you also may be where I am. x 4 You know the way to the place where I am going."

5 Thomas said to him, "Lord, we don't know where you are going, so how can we know the way?"

6 Jesus answered, "I am the way y and the truth and the life. No one comes to the Father except through me. 7 If you really knew me, you would know b my Father as well. From now on, you do know him and have seen him."

8 Philip said, "Lord, show us the Father and that will be enough for us."

9 Jesus answered: "Don't you know me, Philip, even after I have been among you such a long time? Anyone who has seen me has seen the Father. z How can you say, 'Show us the Father'? 10 Don't you believe that I am in the Father, and that the Father is in me? a The words I say to you are not just my own. Rather, it is the Father, living in me, who is doing his work. 11 Believe me when I say that I am in the Father and the Father is in me; or at least believe on the evidence of the miracles themselves. b 12 I tell you the truth, anyone who has faith in me will do what I have been doing. He will do even greater things than these, because I am going

a1 Or You trust in God   b7 Some early manuscripts If you really have known me, you will know

**Cross references (left margin):**
13:34 s1Jn 2:7-11 tLev 19:18; 1Pe 1:22
13:35 u1Jn 4:20
13:36 vJn 21:18, 19; 2Pe 1:14
14:2 wJn 13:33, 36
14:3 xJn 12:26
14:6 yJn 10:9
14:9 zJn 12:45
14:10 aJn 10:38
14:11 bJn 10:38

13:34 To love others was not a new commandment (see Leviticus 19:18), but to love others as much as Christ loved others was revolutionary. Now we are to love others based on Jesus' sacrificial love for us. Such love will not only bring unbelievers to Christ; it will also keep believers strong and united in a world hostile to God. Jesus was a living example of God's love, as we are to be living examples of Jesus' love.

13:34, 35 Jesus says that our Christlike love will show we are his disciples. Do people see petty bickering, jealousy, and division in your church? Or do they know you are Jesus' followers by your love for one another?

Love is more than simply warm feelings; it is an attitude that reveals itself in action. How can we love others as Jesus loves us? By helping when it's not convenient, by giving when it hurts, by devoting energy to others' welfare rather than our own, by absorbing hurts from others without complaining or fighting back. This kind of loving is hard to do. That is why people notice when you do it and know you are empowered by a supernatural source. The Bible has another beautiful description of love in 1 Corinthians 13.

13:37, 38 Peter proudly told Jesus that he was ready to die for him. But Jesus corrected him. He knew Peter would deny that he knew Jesus that very night to protect himself (18:25–27). In our enthusiasm, it is easy to make promises, but God knows the extent of our commitment. Paul tells us not to think of ourselves more highly than we ought (Romans 12:3). Instead of bragging, demonstrate your commitment step-by-step as you grow in your knowledge of God's Word and in your faith.

14:1–3 Jesus' words show that the way to eternal life, though unseen, is secure—as secure as your trust in Jesus. He has already prepared the way to eternal life. The only issue that may still be unsettled is your willingness to believe.

14:2, 3 There are few verses in Scripture that describe eternal

life, but these few verses are rich with promises. Here Jesus says, "I am going there to prepare a place for you," and "I will come back." We can look forward to eternal life because Jesus has promised it to all who believe in him. Although the details of eternity are unknown, we need not fear because Jesus is preparing for us and will spend eternity with us.

14:5, 6 This is one of the most basic and important passages in Scripture. How can we know the way to God? Only through Jesus. Jesus is the way because he is both God and man. By uniting our lives with his, we are united with God. Trust Jesus to take you to the Father, and all the benefits of being God's child will be yours.

14:6 Jesus says he is the *only* way to God the Father. Some people may argue that this way is too narrow. In reality, it is wide enough for the whole world, if the world chooses to accept it. Instead of worrying about how limited it sounds to have only one way, we should be saying, "Thank you, God, for providing a sure way to get to you!"

14:6 As the *way*, Jesus is our path to the Father. As the *truth*, he is the reality of all God's promises. As the *life*, he joins his divine life to ours, both now and eternally. Jesus is, in truth, the only living way to the Father.

14:9 Jesus is the visible, tangible image of the invisible God. He is the complete revelation of what God is like. Jesus explained to Philip, who wanted to see the Father, that to know Jesus is to know God. The search for God, for truth and reality, ends in Christ. (See also Colossians 1:15; Hebrews 1:1–4.)

14:12, 13 Jesus is not saying that his disciples would do more amazing miracles—after all, raising the dead is about as amazing as you can get. Rather, the disciples, working in the power of the Holy Spirit, would carry the gospel of God's kingdom out of Palestine and into the whole world.

to the Father. 13 And I will do whatever you ask in my name, so that the Son may bring glory to the Father. 14 You may ask me for anything in my name, and I will do it.

Jesus Promises the Holy Spirit (214)

15 "If you love me, you will obey what I command. *c* 16 And I will ask the Father, and he will give you another Counselor *d* to be with you forever— 17 the Spirit of truth. *e* The world cannot accept him, *f* because it neither sees him nor knows him. But you know him, for he lives with you and will be*a* in you. 18 I will not leave you as orphans; I will come to you. *g* 19 Before long, the world will not see me anymore, but you will see me. *h* Because I live, you also will live. 20 On that day you will realize that I am in my Father, *i* and you are in me, and I am in you. 21 Whoever has my commands and obeys them, he is the one who loves me. He who loves me will be loved by my Father, and I too will love him and show myself to him."

22 Then Judas (not Judas Iscariot) said, "But, Lord, why do you intend to show yourself to us and not to the world?"

23 Jesus replied, "If anyone loves me, he will obey my teaching. My Father will love him, and we will come to him and make our home with him. 24 He who does not love me will not obey my teaching. These words you hear are not my own; they belong to the Father who sent me.

25 "All this I have spoken while still with you. 26 But the Counselor, *j* the Holy Spirit, whom the Father will send in my name, will teach you all things*k* and will remind you of everything I have said to you. 27 Peace I leave with you; my peace I give you. *l* I do not give to you as the world gives. Do not let your hearts be troubled and do not be afraid.

28 "You heard me say, 'I am going away and I am coming back to you.' *m* If you loved me, you would be glad that I am going to the Father, for the Father is greater than I. 29 I have told

a 17 Some early manuscripts *and is*

14:15
c Jn 15:10; 1Jn 5:3
14:16
d Jn 15:26
14:17
e Jn 16:13; 1Jn 4:6
f 1Co 2:14
14:18
g ver 3, 28
14:19
h Jn 16:16
14:20
i Jn 10:38
14:26
j Jn 15:26
k 1Jn 2:20, 27
14:27
l Php 4:7; Col 3:15
14:28
m ver 2-4, 18

14:14 When Jesus says we can ask for anything, we must remember that our asking must be in his name—that is, according to God's character and will. God will not grant requests contrary to his nature or his will, and we cannot use his name as a magic formula to fulfill our selfish desires. If we are sincerely following God and seeking to do his will, then our requests will be in line with what he wants, and he will grant them. (See also 15:16; 16:23.)

14:15, 16 Jesus was soon going to leave the disciples, but he would remain with them. How could this be? The Counselor—the Spirit of God himself—would come after Jesus was gone to care for and guide the disciples. The regenerating power of the Spirit came on the disciples just before Jesus' ascension (20:22), and the Spirit was poured out on all the believers at Pentecost (Acts 2), shortly after Jesus ascended to heaven. The Holy Spirit is the very presence of God within us and all believers, helping us live as God wants and building Christ's church on earth. By faith we can appropriate the Spirit's power each day.

14:16 The word translated *Counselor* combines the ideas of comfort and counsel. The word could also be translated Comforter, Encourager, or Advocate. The Holy Spirit is a powerful person on our side, working for and with us.

14:17ff The following chapters teach these truths about the Holy Spirit: he will be with us forever (14:16); the world at large cannot accept him (14:17); he lives with us and in us (14:17); he teaches us (14:26); he reminds us of Jesus' words (14:26; 15:26); he convicts us of sin, shows us God's righteousness, and announces God's judgment on evil (16:8); he guides into truth and gives insight into future events (16:13); he brings glory to Christ (16:14). The Holy Spirit has been active among people from the beginning of time, but after Pentecost (Acts 2) he came to live in all believers. Many people are unaware of the Holy Spirit's activities, but to those who hear Christ's words and understand the Spirit's power, the Spirit gives a whole new way to look at life.

14:18 When Jesus said, "I will come to you," he meant it. Although Jesus ascended to heaven, he sent the Holy Spirit to live in believers, and to have the Holy Spirit is to have Jesus himself.

14:19–21 Sometimes people wish they knew the future so they could prepare for it. God has chosen not to give us this knowledge. He alone knows what will happen, but he tells us all we need

to know to *prepare* for the future. When we live by his standards, he will not leave us; he will come to us, he will be in us, and he will show himself to us. God knows what will happen and, because he will be with us through it all, we need not fear. We don't have to know the future to have faith in God; we have to have faith in God to be secure about the future.

14:21 Jesus said that his followers show their love for him by obeying him. Love is more than lovely words; it is commitment and conduct. If you love Christ, then prove it by obeying what he says in his Word.

14:22, 23 Because the disciples were still expecting Jesus to establish an earthly kingdom and overthrow Rome, they found it hard to understand why he did not tell the world at large that he was the Messiah. Not everyone, however, could understand Jesus' message. Ever since Pentecost, the gospel of the kingdom has been proclaimed in the whole world, and yet not everyone is receptive to it. Jesus saves the deepest revelations of himself for those who love and obey him.

14:26 Jesus promised the disciples that the Holy Spirit would help them remember what he had been teaching them. This promise ensures the validity of the New Testament. The disciples were eyewitnesses of Jesus' life and teachings, and the Holy Spirit helped them remember without taking away their individual perspectives. We can be confident that the Gospels are accurate records of what Jesus taught and did (see 1 Corinthians 2:10–14). The Holy Spirit can help us in the same way. As we study the Bible, we can trust him to plant truth in our mind, convince us of God's will, and remind us when we stray from it.

14:27 The end result of the Holy Spirit's work in our lives is deep and lasting peace. Unlike worldly peace, which is usually defined as the absence of conflict, this peace is confident assurance in any circumstance; with Christ's peace, we have no need to fear the present or the future. Sin, fear, uncertainty, doubt, and numerous other forces are at war within us. The peace of God moves into our hearts and lives to restrain these hostile forces and offer comfort in place of conflict. Jesus says he will give us that peace if we are willing to accept it from him. If your life is full of stress, allow the Holy Spirit to fill you with Christ's peace (see Philippians 4:6, 7 for more on experiencing God's peace).

14:28 As God the Son, Jesus willingly submits to God the

14:29
n Jn 13:19

14:30
o Jn 12:31

14:31
p Jn 10:18

you now before it happens, so that when it does happen you will believe. *n* 30 I will not speak with you much longer, for the prince of this world *o* is coming. He has no hold on me, 31 but the world must learn that I love the Father and that I do exactly what my Father has commanded me. *p*

"Come now; let us leave."

Jesus Teaches about the Vine and the Branches (215)

15:1
q Isa 5:1-7

15:3
r Jn 13:10;
Eph 5:26

15 "I am the true vine, *q* and my Father is the gardener. 2 He cuts off every branch in me that bears no fruit, while every branch that does bear fruit he prunes *a* so that it will be even more fruitful. 3 You are already clean because of the word I have spoken to you. *r* 4 Remain in me, and I will remain in you. No branch can bear fruit by itself; it must remain in the vine. Neither can you bear fruit unless you remain in me.

5 "I am the vine; you are the branches. If a man remains in me and I in him, he will bear much fruit; apart from me you can do nothing. 6 If anyone does not remain in me, he is like a branch that is thrown away and withers; such branches are picked up, thrown into the fire and burned. 7 If you remain in me and my words remain in you, ask whatever you wish, and it

15:8
s Jn 8:31

15:10
t Jn 14:15

15:12
u Jn 13:34

15:13
v Jn 10:11;
Ro 5:7, 8

15:14
w Mt 12:50

will be given you. 8 This is to my Father's glory, that you bear much fruit, showing yourselves to be my disciples. *s*

9 "As the Father has loved me, so have I loved you. Now remain in my love. 10 If you obey my commands, *t* you will remain in my love, just as I have obeyed my Father's commands and remain in his love. 11 I have told you this so that my joy may be in you and that your joy may be complete. 12 My command is this: Love each other as I have loved you. *u* 13 Greater love has no one than this, that he lay down his life for his friends. *v* 14 You are my friends if you do what I command. *w* 15 I no longer call you servants, because a servant does not know his master's

a 2 The Greek for *prunes* also means *cleans.*

Father. On earth, Jesus also submitted to many of the physical limitations of his humanity (Philippians 2:6).

14:30, 31 Although Satan, the prince of this world, was unable to overpower Jesus (Matthew 4), he still had the arrogance to try. Satan's power exists only because God allows him to act. But because Jesus is sinless, Satan has no power over him. If we obey Jesus and align ourselves closely with God's purposes, Satan can have no power over us.

14:31 "Come now; let us leave" suggests that chapters 15—17 may have been spoken en route to the Garden of Gethsemane. Another view is that Jesus was asking the disciples to get ready to leave the upper room, but they did not actually do so until 18:1.

15:1 The grapevine is a prolific plant; a single vine supports numerous branches and bears many grapes. In the Old Testament, grapes symbolized Israel's fruitfulness in doing God's work on the earth (Psalm 80:8; Isaiah 5:1–7; Ezekiel 19:10–14). In the Passover meal, the fruit of the vine symbolized God's goodness to his people.

15:1ff Christ is the vine, and God is the gardener who cares for the branches to make them fruitful. The branches are all those who claim to be followers of Christ. The fruitful branches are true believers who by their living union with Christ produce much fruit. But those who become unproductive—those who turn back from following Christ after making a superficial commitment—will be separated from the vine. Unproductive followers are as good as dead and will be cut off and tossed aside.

15:2, 3 Jesus makes a distinction between two kinds of pruning: (1) separating and (2) cutting back branches. Fruitful branches are cut back to promote growth. In other words, God must sometimes discipline us to strengthen our character and faith. But branches that don't bear fruit are cut off at the trunk because not only are they worthless, but they often infect the rest of the tree. People who won't bear fruit for God or who try to block the efforts of God's followers will be cut off from his life-giving power.

15:5 "Fruit" is not limited to soul winning. In this chapter, answered prayer, joy, and love are mentioned as fruit (15:7, 11, 12). Galatians 5:22–24 and 2 Peter 1:5–8 describe additional fruit: qualities of Christian character.

15:5, 6 Remaining in Christ means (1) believing that he is God's Son (1 John 4:15), (2) receiving him as Savior and Lord (John 1:12), (3) doing what God says (1 John 3:24), (4) continuing to believe the gospel (1 John 2:24), and (5) relating in love to the community of believers, Christ's body (John 15:12).

15:5–8 Many people try to be good, honest people who do what is right. But Jesus says that the only way to live a truly good life is to stay close to him, like a branch attached to the vine. Apart from Christ our efforts are unfruitful. Are you receiving the nourishment and life offered by Christ, the vine? If not, you are missing a special gift he has for you.

15:8 When a vine bears "much fruit," God is glorified, for daily he sent the sunshine and rain to make the crops grow, and constantly he nurtured each tiny plant and prepared it to blossom. What a moment of glory for the Lord of the harvest when the harvest is brought into the barns, mature and ready for use! He made it all happen. This farming analogy shows how God is glorified when people come into a right relationship with him and begin to "bear much fruit" in their lives.

15:11 When things are going well, we feel elated. When hardships come, we sink into depression. But true joy transcends the rolling waves of circumstance. Joy comes from a consistent relationship with Jesus Christ. When our lives are intertwined with his, he will help us walk through adversity without sinking into debilitating lows and manage prosperity without moving into deceptive highs. The joy of living with Jesus Christ daily will keep us levelheaded, no matter how high or low our circumstances.

15:12, 13 We are to love each other as Jesus loved us, and he loved us enough to give his life for us. We may not have to die for someone, but there are other ways to practice sacrificial love: listening, helping, encouraging, giving. Think of someone in particular who needs this kind of love today. Give all the love you can, and then try to give a little more.

15:15 Because Jesus Christ is Lord and Master, he should call us servants; instead he calls us friends. How comforting and reassuring to be chosen as Christ's friends. Because he is Lord and Master, we owe him our unqualified obedience, but most of all, Jesus asks us to obey him because we love him.

business. Instead, I have called you friends, for everything that I learned from my Father I have made known to you. 16 You did not choose me, but I chose you and appointed you[x] to go and bear fruit—fruit that will last. Then the Father will give you whatever you ask in my name. 17 This is my command: Love each other.

15:16
x Jn 13:18

Jesus Warns about the World's Hatred (216)

18 "If the world hates you,[y] keep in mind that it hated me first. 19 If you belonged to the world, it would love you as its own. As it is, you do not belong to the world, but I have chosen you out of the world. That is why the world hates you.[z] 20 Remember the words I spoke to you: 'No servant is greater than his master.'[a] If they persecuted me, they will persecute you also. If they obeyed my teaching, they will obey yours also. 21 They will treat you this way because of my name, for they do not know the One who sent me. 22 If I had not come and spoken to them, they would not be guilty of sin. Now, however, they have no excuse for their sin.[a] 23 He who hates me hates my Father as well. 24 If I had not done among them what no one else did, they would not be guilty of sin. But now they have seen these miracles, and yet they have hated both me and my Father. 25 But this is to fulfill what is written in their Law: 'They hated me without reason.'[b][b]

26 "When the Counselor comes, whom I will send to you from the Father, the Spirit of truth[c] who goes out from the Father, he will testify about me.[d] 27 And you also must testify,[e] for you have been with me from the beginning.

15:18
y 1Jn 3:13
15:19
z Jn 17:14

15:22
a Jn 9:41

15:25
b Ps 35:19; 69:4
15:26
c Jn 14:17
d 1Jn 5:7
15:27
e Lk 24:48

16 "All this I have told you so that you will not go astray.[f] 2 They will put you out of the synagogue;[g] in fact, a time is coming when anyone who kills you will think he is offering a service to God.[h] 3 They will do such things because they have not known the Father or me.[i] 4 I have told you this, so that when the time comes you will remember[j] that I warned you. I did not tell you this at first because I was with you.

16:1
f Mt 11:6

16:2
g Jn 9:22
h Ac 26:9, 10

16:3
i Jn 15:21

16:4
j Jn 13:19

Jesus Teaches about the Holy Spirit (217)

5 "Now I am going to him who sent me,[k] yet none of you asks me, 'Where are you going?' 6 Because I have said these things, you are filled with grief. 7 But I tell you the truth: It is for your good that I am going away. Unless I go away, the Counselor[l] will not come to you; but if I go, I will send him to you. 8 When he comes, he will convict the world of guilt[c] in regard to sin and righteousness and judgment: 9 in regard to sin, because men do not believe in me; 10 in regard to righteousness,[m] because I am going to the Father, where you can see me no longer; 11 and in regard to judgment, because the prince of this world now stands condemned.

16:5
k Jn 7:33
16:7
l Jn 14:16, 26

16:10
m Ac 3:14

a20 John 13:16   b25 Psalms 35:19; 69:4   c8 Or *will expose the guilt of the world*

15:16 Jesus made the first choice—to love and to die for us, to invite us to live with him forever. We make the next choice—to accept or reject his offer. Without *his* choice, we would have no choice to make.

15:17 Christians will get plenty of hatred from the world; from each other we need love and support. Do you allow small problems to get in the way of loving other believers? Jesus commands that you love them, and he will give you the strength to do it.

15:26 Once again Jesus offers hope. The Holy Spirit gives strength to endure the unreasonable hatred and evil in our world and the hostility many have toward Christ. This is especially comforting for those facing persecution.

15:26 Jesus uses two names for the Holy Spirit—*Counselor* and *Spirit of truth*. The word *Counselor* conveys the helping, encouraging, and strengthening work of the Spirit. *Spirit of truth* points to the teaching, illuminating, and reminding work of the Spirit. The Holy Spirit ministers to both the head and the heart, and both dimensions are important.

16:1–16 In his last moments with his disciples, Jesus (1) warned them about further persecution, (2) told them where, when, and why he was going, and (3) assured them that they would not be left alone, but that the Spirit would come. Jesus knew what lay ahead, and he did not want the disciples' faith shaken or destroyed. God wants you to know you are not alone. You have the Holy Spirit to comfort you, teach you truth, and help you.

16:2 Saul (who later became Paul), under the authority of the high priest, went through the land hunting down and persecuting Christians, convinced that he was doing the right thing (Acts 9:1, 2; 26:9–11).

16:5 Although the disciples had asked Jesus about his death (13:36; 14:5), they had never wondered about its meaning. They were mostly concerned about themselves. If Jesus went away, what would become of them?

16:7 Unless Jesus did what he came to do, there would be no gospel. If he did not die, he could not remove our sins; he could not rise again and defeat death. If he did not go back to the Father, the Holy Spirit would not come. Christ's presence on earth was limited to one place at a time. His leaving meant he could be present to the whole world through the Holy Spirit.

16:8–11 Three important tasks of the Holy Spirit are (1) convicting the world of its sin and calling it to repentance, (2) revealing the standard of God's righteousness to anyone who believes, because Christ would no longer be physically present on earth, and (3) demonstrating Christ's judgment over Satan.

16:9 According to Jesus, not believing in him is *sin*.

16:10, 11 Christ's death on the cross made a personal relationship with God available to us. When we confess our sin, God declares us righteous and delivers us from judgment for our sins.

16:13
n Jn 14:17
o Jn 14:26

16:16
p Jn 14:18-24

¹²"I have much more to say to you, more than you can now bear. ¹³But when he, the Spirit of truth,*n* comes, he will guide you into all truth.*o* He will not speak on his own; he will speak only what he hears, and he will tell you what is yet to come. ¹⁴He will bring glory to me by taking from what is mine and making it known to you. ¹⁵All that belongs to the Father is mine. That is why I said the Spirit will take from what is mine and make it known to you.

¹⁶"In a little while you will see me no more, and then after a little while you will see me."*p*

Jesus Teaches about Using His Name in Prayer (218)

¹⁷Some of his disciples said to one another, "What does he mean by saying, 'In a little while you will see me no more, and then after a little while you will see me,' and 'Because I am going to the Father'?" ¹⁸They kept asking, "What does he mean by 'a little while'? We don't understand what he is saying."

16:20
q Jn 20:20

16:21
r 1Th 5:3

16:23
s Mt 7:7; Jn 15:16

16:24
t Jn 15:11

16:25
u Mt 13:34; Jn 10:6

16:27
v Jn 14:21, 23

16:28
w Jn 13:3

¹⁹Jesus saw that they wanted to ask him about this, so he said to them, "Are you asking one another what I meant when I said, 'In a little while you will see me no more, and then after a little while you will see me'? ²⁰I tell you the truth, you will weep and mourn while the world rejoices. You will grieve, but your grief will turn to joy.*q* ²¹A woman giving birth to a child has pain*r* because her time has come; but when her baby is born she forgets the anguish because of her joy that a child is born into the world. ²²So with you: Now is your time of grief, but I will see you again and you will rejoice, and no one will take away your joy. ²³In that day you will no longer ask me anything. I tell you the truth, my Father will give you whatever you ask in my name.*s* ²⁴Until now you have not asked for anything in my name. Ask and you will receive, and your joy will be complete.*t*

²⁵"Though I have been speaking figuratively,*u* a time is coming when I will no longer use this kind of language but will tell you plainly about my Father. ²⁶In that day you will ask in my name. I am not saying that I will ask the Father on your behalf. ²⁷No, the Father himself loves you because you have loved me*v* and have believed that I came from God. ²⁸I came from the Father and entered the world; now I am leaving the world and going back to the Father."*w*

²⁹Then Jesus' disciples said, "Now you are speaking clearly and without figures of speech. ³⁰Now we can see that you know all things and that you do not even need to have anyone ask you questions. This makes us believe that you came from God."

16:32
x Mt 26:31

³¹"You believe at last!"*a* Jesus answered. ³²"But a time is coming, and has come, when you will be scattered,*x* each to his own home. You will leave me all alone. Yet I am not alone, for my Father is with me.

16:33
y Jn 14:27
z Ro 8:37

³³"I have told you these things, so that in me you may have peace.*y* In this world you will have trouble. But take heart! I have overcome*z* the world."

a31 Or *"Do you now believe?"*

16:13 The truth into which the Holy Spirit guides us is the truth about Christ. The Spirit also helps us, through patient practice, to discern right from wrong.

16:13 Jesus said the Holy Spirit would tell them "what is yet to come"—the nature of their mission, the opposition they would face, and the final outcome of their efforts. They didn't fully understand these promises until the Holy Spirit came after Jesus' death and resurrection. Then the Holy Spirit revealed truths to the disciples that they wrote down in the books that now form the New Testament.

16:16 Jesus was referring to his death, now only a few hours away, and his resurrection three days later.

16:20 What a contrast between the disciples and the world! The world rejoiced as the disciples wept, but the disciples would see him again (in three days) and rejoice. The world's values are often the opposite of God's values. This can cause Christians to feel like misfits. But even if life is difficult now, one day we will rejoice. Keep your eye on the future and on God's promises!

16:23–27 Jesus is talking about a new relationship between the believer and God. Previously, people approached God through priests. After Jesus' resurrection, any believer could approach God directly. A new day has dawned and now all believers are priests, talking with God personally and directly (see Hebrews 10:19–23). We approach God, not because of our own merit, but because Jesus, our great high priest, has made us acceptable to God.

16:30 The disciples believed Jesus' words because they were convinced that he knew everything. But their belief was only a first step toward the great faith they would receive when the Holy Spirit came to live in them.

16:31–33 As Christians, we should expect continuing tension with an unbelieving world that is "out of sync" with Christ, his gospel, and his people. At the same time, we can expect our relationship with Christ to produce peace and comfort because we are "in sync" with him.

16:32 The disciples scattered after Jesus was arrested (see Mark 14:50). Jesus accepted their statement of faith even though he knew their weakness. He knew they would have to grow into people whose words and lives matched even to the point of death. He takes us through the same process. How well are you living out what you say you believe about Jesus?

16:33 Jesus summed up all he had told them this night, tying together themes from 14:27–29; 16:1–4; and 16:9–11. With these words he told his disciples to take courage. In spite of the inevitable struggles they would face, they would not be alone. Jesus does not abandon us to our struggles either. If we remember that the ultimate victory has already been won, we can claim the peace of Christ in the most troublesome times.

Jesus Prays for Himself (219)

17 After Jesus said this, he looked toward heaven and prayed:

"Father, the time has come. Glorify your Son, that your Son may glorify you. *a* 2For you granted him authority over all people that he might give eternal life to all those you have given him. *b* 3Now this is eternal life: that they may know you, the only true God, and Jesus Christ, whom you have sent. 4I have brought you glory*c* on earth by completing the work you gave me to do. *d* 5And now, Father, glorify me in your presence with the glory I had with you*e* before the world began.

Jesus Prays for His Disciples (220)

6"I have revealed you*a* to those whom you gave me*f* out of the world. They were yours; you gave them to me and they have obeyed your word. 7Now they know that everything you have given me comes from you. 8For I gave them the words you gave me and they accepted them. They knew with certainty that I came from you,*g* and they believed that you sent me. 9I pray for them. I am not praying for the world, but for those you have given me, for they are yours. 10All I have is yours, and all you have is mine.*h* And glory has come to me through them. 11I will remain in the world no longer, but they are still in the world,*i* and I am coming to you.*j* Holy Father, protect them by the power of your name— the name you gave me—so that they may be one as we are one. 12While I was with them, I protected them and kept them safe by that name you gave me. None has been lost except the one doomed to destruction*k* so that Scripture would be fulfilled.

13"I am coming to you now, but I say these things while I am still in the world, so that they may have the full measure of my joy within them. 14I have given them your word and the world has hated them, for they are not of the world any more than I am of the world. *l* 15My prayer is not that you take them out of the world but that you protect them from the evil one. 16They are not of the world, even as I am not of it. 17Sanctify*b* them by the truth; your word is truth. 18As you sent me into the world, I have sent them into the world. *m* 19For them I sanctify myself, that they too may be truly sanctified.

Jesus Prays for Future Believers (221)

20"My prayer is not for them alone. I pray also for those who will believe in me through their message, 21that all of them may be one, Father, just as you are in me and I am in you. *n* May they also be in us so that the world may believe that you have sent

*a*6 Greek *your name*; also in verse 26 *b*17 Greek *hagiazo (set apart for sacred use* or *make holy)*; also in verse 19

17:1	*a* Jn 12:23
17:2	*b* Da 7:14
17:4	*c* Jn 13:31
	d Jn 4:34
17:5	*e* Php 2:6
17:6	*f* Jn 6:37, 39
17:8	*g* Jn 16:27
17:10	*h* Jn 16:15
17:11	*i* Jn 13:1
	j Jn 7:33
17:12	*k* Jn 6:70
17:14	*l* Jn 8:23
17:18	*m* Jn 20:21
17:21	*n* Jn 10:38

17:1ff This entire chapter is Jesus' prayer. From it, we learn that the world is a tremendous battleground where the forces under Satan's power and those under God's authority are at war. Satan and his forces are motivated by bitter hatred for Christ and his forces. Jesus prayed for his disciples, including those of us who follow him today. He prayed that God would keep his chosen believers safe from Satan's power, setting them apart and making them pure and holy, uniting them through his truth.

17:3 How do we get eternal life? Jesus tells us clearly here— by knowing God the Father himself through his Son, Jesus Christ. Eternal life requires entering into a personal relationship with God in Jesus Christ. When we admit our sin and turn away from it, Christ's love lives in us by the Holy Spirit.

17:5 Before Jesus came to earth, he was one with God. At this point, when his mission on earth was almost finished, Jesus was asking his Father to restore him to his original place of honor and authority. Jesus' resurrection and ascension—and Stephen's dying exclamation (Acts 7:56)—attest that Jesus did return to his exalted position at the right hand of God.

17:10 What did Jesus mean when he said "glory has come to me through them"? God's glory is the revelation of his character and presence. The lives of Jesus' disciples reveal his character, and he is present to the world through them. Does your life reveal Jesus' character and presence?

17:11 Jesus was asking that the disciples be united in harmony and love as the Father, Son, and Holy Spirit are united—the strongest of all unions. (See the note on 17:21–23.)

17:12 Judas was the "one doomed to destruction," who was lost because he betrayed Jesus (see Psalm 41:9).

17:13 Joy is a common theme in Christ's teachings—he wants us to be joyful (see 15:11; 16:24, 33). The key to immeasurable joy is living in intimate contact with Christ, the source of all joy. When we do, we will experience God's special care and protection and see the victory God brings even when defeat seems certain.

17:14 The world hates Christians because Christians' values differ from the world's. Because Christ's followers don't cooperate with the world by joining in their sin, they are living accusations against the world's immorality. The world follows Satan's agenda, and Satan is the avowed enemy of Jesus and his people.

17:17 A follower of Christ becomes sanctified (set apart for sacred use, cleansed, and made holy) through believing and obeying the Word of God (Hebrews 4:12). He or she has already accepted forgiveness through Christ's sacrificial death (Hebrews 7:26, 27). But daily application of God's Word has a purifying effect on our minds and hearts. Scripture points out sin, motivates us to confess, renews our relationship with Christ, and guides us back to the right path.

17:18 Jesus didn't ask God to take believers *out* of the world but instead to use them *in* the world. Because Jesus sends us into the world, we should not try to escape from the world, nor should we avoid all relationships with non-Christians. We are called to be salt and light (Matthew 5:13–16), and we are to do the work that God sent us to do.

17:20 Jesus prayed for all who would follow him, including you and others you know. He prayed for unity (17:11), protection from

17:22
o Jn 14:20

17:24
p Jn 12:26
q ver 5

17:25
r Jn 15:21
s Jn 7:29; 16:27

17:26
t ver 6
u Jn 15:9

18:1
v 2Sa 15:23

18:2
w Lk 21:37; 22:39

18:3
x Ac 1:16

18:7
y ver 4

18:9
z Jn 17:12

me. ²¹I have given them the glory that you gave me, that they may be one as we are one:ᵒ ²³I in them and you in me. May they be brought to complete unity to let the world know that you sent me and have loved them even as you have loved me.

²⁴"Father, I want those you have given me to be with me where I am,ᵖ and to see my glory, the glory you have given me because you loved me before the creation of the world. q

²⁵"Righteous Father, though the world does not know you,ʳ I know you, and they know that you have sent me. ˢ ²⁶I have made you known to them,ᵗ and will continue to make you known in order that the love you have for me may be in themᵘ and that I myself may be in them."

2. Jesus completes his mission
Jesus Is Betrayed and Arrested
(224/Matthew 26:47–56; Mark 14:43–52; Luke 22:47–53)

18 When he had finished praying, Jesus left with his disciples and crossed the Kidron Valley. ᵛ On the other side there was an olive grove, and he and his disciples went into it.

²Now Judas, who betrayed him, knew the place, because Jesus had often met there with his disciples. ʷ ³So Judas came to the grove, guidingˣ a detachment of soldiers and some officials from the chief priests and Pharisees. They were carrying torches, lanterns and weapons.

⁴Jesus, knowing all that was going to happen to him, went out and asked them, "Who is it you want?"

⁵"Jesus of Nazareth," they replied.

"I am he," Jesus said. (And Judas the traitor was standing there with them.) ⁶When Jesus said, "I am he," they drew back and fell to the ground.

⁷Again he asked them, "Who is it you want?"ʸ

And they said, "Jesus of Nazareth."

⁸"I told you that I am he," Jesus answered. "If you are looking for me, then let these men go." ⁹This happened so that the words he had spoken would be fulfilled: "I have not lost one of those you gave me."ᵃ ᶻ

ᵃ9 John 6:39

---

the evil one (17:15), and sanctity (holiness) (17:17). Knowing that Jesus prayed for us should give us confidence as we work for his kingdom.

17:21-23 Jesus' great desire for his disciples was that they would become one. He wanted them unified as a powerful witness to the reality of God's love. Are you helping to unify the body of Christ, the church? You can pray for other Christians, avoid gossip, build others up, work together in humility, give your time and money, exalt Christ, and refuse to get sidetracked arguing over divisive matters.

17:21-23 Jesus prayed for unity among the believers based on the believers' unity with him and the Father. Christians can know unity among themselves if they are living in union with God. For example, each branch living in union with the vine is united with all other branches doing the same.

18:3 The officials from the chief priests and Pharisees were probably members of the temple guard; they were Jews given authority by the religious leaders to make arrests for minor infractions. The soldiers may have been a small contingent of Roman soldiers who did not participate in the arrest but accompanied the temple guard to make sure matters didn't get out of control.

18:4, 5 John does not record Judas's kiss of greeting (Matthew 26:49; Mark 14:45; Luke 22:47, 48), but Judas's kiss marked a turning point for the disciples. With Jesus' arrest, each one's life would be radically different. For the first time, Judas openly betrayed Jesus before the other disciples. For the first time, Jesus' loyal disciples ran away from him (Matthew 26:56). The band of disciples would undergo severe testing before they were transformed from hesitant followers to dynamic leaders.

18:6 The men may have been startled by the boldness of Jesus' question, or by the words "I am he," a declaration of his divinity (Exodus 3:14). Or perhaps they were overcome by his obvious power and authority.

BETRAYAL IN THE GARDEN After eating the Passover meal in the upper room, Jesus and his disciples went to Gethsemane, where Judas led the temple guard to arrest Jesus. Jesus was then taken to Caiaphas's house for his first of many trials.

10Then Simon Peter, who had a sword, drew it and struck the high priest's servant, cutting off his right ear. (The servant's name was Malchus.)

11Jesus commanded Peter, "Put your sword away! Shall I not drink the cup *a* the Father has given me?"

18:11
a Mt 20:22

Annas Questions Jesus (225)

12Then the detachment of soldiers with its commander and the Jewish officials arrested Jesus. They bound him 13and brought him first to Annas, who was the father-in-law of Caiaphas, the high priest that year. 14Caiaphas was the one who had advised the Jews that it would be good if one man died for the people. *b*

18:14
b Jn 11:49-51

15Simon Peter and another disciple were following Jesus. Because this disciple was known to the high priest, he went with Jesus into the high priest's courtyard, *c* 16but Peter had to wait outside at the door. The other disciple, who was known to the high priest, came back, spoke to the girl on duty there and brought Peter in.

18:15
c Mt 26:58;
Mk 14:54; Lk 22:54

17"You are not one of his disciples, are you?" the girl at the door asked Peter.

He replied, "I am not."

18It was cold, and the servants and officials stood around a fire *d* they had made to keep warm. Peter also was standing with them, warming himself. *e*

18:18
d Jn 21:9
e Mk 14:54, 67

19Meanwhile, the high priest questioned Jesus about his disciples and his teaching.

20"I have spoken openly to the world," Jesus replied. "I always taught in synagogues or at the temple, *f* where all the Jews come together. I said nothing in secret. *g* 21Why question me? Ask those who heard me. Surely they know what I said."

18:20
f Mt 26:55
g Jn 7:26

22When Jesus said this, one of the officials nearby struck him in the face. *h* "Is this the way you answer the high priest?" he demanded.

18:22
h Jn 19:3

23"If I said something wrong," Jesus replied, "testify as to what is wrong. But if I spoke the truth, why did you strike me?" *i* 24Then Annas sent him, still bound, to Caiaphas the high priest. *a*

18:23
i Ac 23:2-5

Peter Denies Knowing Jesus (227/Matthew 26:69–75; Mark 14:66–72; Luke 22:54–65)

25As Simon Peter stood warming himself, *j* he was asked, "You are not one of his disciples, are you?"

18:25
j ver 18

a 24 Or (Now Annas had sent him, still bound, to Caiaphas the high priest.)

18:10, 11 Trying to protect Jesus, Peter pulled a sword and wounded the high priest's servant. But Jesus told Peter to put away his sword and allow God's plan to unfold. At times it is tempting to take matters into our own hands, to force the issue. Most often such moves lead to sin. Instead we must trust God to work out his plan. Think of it—if Peter had had his way, Jesus would not have gone to the cross, and God's plan of redemption would have been thwarted. Luke records that Jesus touched the man's ear and healed him (Luke 22:51).

18:11 The cup means the suffering, isolation, and death that Jesus would have to endure in order to atone for the sins of the world.

18:12, 13 Jesus was immediately taken to the high priest's residence, even though this was the middle of the night. The religious leaders were in a hurry—they wanted to complete the execution before the Sabbath and get on with the Passover celebration. This residence was a palace whose outer walls enclosed a courtyard where servants and soldiers would warm themselves around a fire.

18:13 Both Annas and Caiaphas had been high priests. Annas was Israel's high priest from A.D. 6 to 15, when he was deposed by Roman rulers. Caiaphas, Annas's son-in-law, was appointed high priest from A.D. 18 to 36/37. According to Jewish law, the office of high priest was held for life. Many Jews therefore still considered Annas the high priest and still called him by that title. But although Annas retained much authority among the Jews, Caiaphas made the final decisions.

Both Caiaphas and Annas cared more about their political ambitions than about their responsibility to lead the people to God. Though religious leaders, they had become evil. As the nation's spiritual leaders, they should have been sensitive to God's revelation. They should have known that Jesus was the Messiah about

whom the Scriptures spoke, and they should have pointed the people to him. But when deceitful men and women pursue evil, they want to eliminate all opposition. Instead of honestly evaluating Jesus' claims based on their knowledge of Scripture, these religious leaders sought to further their own selfish ambitions and were even willing to kill God's Son, if that's what it took, to do it.

18:15, 16 The other disciple is probably John, the author of this Gospel. He knew the high priest and identified himself to the girl at the door. Because of his connections, John got himself and Peter into the courtyard. But Peter refused to identify himself as Jesus' follower. Peter's experiences in the next few hours would change his life. For more information about Peter, see his Profile in Matthew 26, p. 1595.

18:19ff During the night, Jesus had a pretrial hearing before Annas prior to being taken to Caiaphas and the entire Sanhedrin (Mark 14:53–65). The religious leaders knew they had no grounds for charging Jesus, so they tried to build evidence against him by using false witnesses (Mark 14:55–59).

18:22–27 We can easily blame the Sanhedrin for their injustice in condemning Jesus, but we must remember that Peter and the rest of the disciples also contributed to Jesus' pain by deserting and disowning him (Matthew 26:56, 75). While most of us are not like the religious leaders, we are all like the disciples, for all of us have been guilty of denying that Christ is Lord in vital areas of our lives or of keeping secret our identity as believers in times of pressure. Don't excuse yourself by pointing at others whose sins seem worse than yours. Instead, come to Jesus for forgiveness and healing.

18:25 The other three Gospels say that Peter's three denials happened near a fire in the courtyard outside Caiaphas's palace. John places the first denial outside Annas's home and the other two denials outside Caiaphas's home. This was very likely the same

He denied it, saying, "I am not."

26 One of the high priest's servants, a relative of the man whose ear Peter had cut off, challenged him, "Didn't I see you with him in the olive grove?" 27 Again Peter denied it, and at that moment a rooster began to crow. k

18:27
k Jn 13:38

Jesus Stands Trial before Pilate (*230*/Matthew 27:11–14; Mark 15:2–5; Luke 23:1–5)

18:28
l Mt 27:2; Mk 15:1;
Lk 23:1
m Jn 11:55

28 Then the Jews led Jesus from Caiaphas to the palace of the Roman governor. l By now it was early morning, and to avoid ceremonial uncleanness the Jews did not enter the palace; they wanted to be able to eat the Passover. m 29 So Pilate came out to them and asked, "What charges are you bringing against this man?"

30 "If he were not a criminal," they replied, "we would not have handed him over to you."

THE SIX STAGES OF JESUS' TRIAL Although Jesus' trial lasted less than 18 hours, he was taken to six different hearings.	Before Jewish Authorities	Preliminary Hearing before Annas (John 18:12–24)	Because the office of high priest was for life, Annas was still the "official" high priest in the eyes of the Jews, even though the Romans had appointed another. Thus, Annas still carried much weight among the Sanhedrin.
		Hearing before Caiaphas (Matthew 26:57–68)	Like the hearing before Annas, this hearing was conducted at night in secrecy. It was full of illegalities that made a mockery of justice (see the chart in Matthew, p. 1599).
		Trial before the Sanhedrin (Matthew 27:1, 2)	Just after daybreak, 70 members of the Sanhedrin met to rubber-stamp their approval of the previous hearings to make them appear legal. The purpose of this trial was not to determine justice, but to justify their own preconceptions of Jesus' guilt.
	Before Roman Authorities	First Hearing before Pilate (Luke 23:1–5)	The religious leaders had condemned Jesus to death on religious grounds, but only the Roman government could grant the death penalty. Thus, they took Jesus to Pilate, the Roman governor, and accused him of treason and rebellion, crimes for which the Roman government gave the death penalty. Pilate saw at once that Jesus was innocent, but he was afraid about the uproar being caused by the religious leaders.
		Hearing before Herod (Luke 23:6–12)	Because Jesus' home was in the region of Galilee, Pilate sent Jesus to Herod Antipas, the ruler of Galilee, who was in Jerusalem for the Passover celebration. Herod was eager to see Jesus do a miracle, but when Jesus remained silent, Herod wanted nothing to do with him and sent him back to Pilate.
		Last Hearing before Pilate (Luke 23:13–25)	Pilate didn't like the religious leaders. He wasn't interested in condemning Jesus because he knew Jesus was innocent. However, he knew that another uprising in his district might cost him his job. First he tried to compromise with the religious leaders by having Jesus beaten, an illegal action in itself. But finally he gave in and handed Jesus over to be executed. Pilate's self-interest was stronger than his sense of justice.

---

courtyard. The high priest's compound was large, and Annas and Caiaphas undoubtedly lived near each other.

18:25–27 Imagine standing outside while Jesus, your Lord and Master, is questioned. Imagine watching this man, whom you have come to believe is the long-awaited Messiah, being abused and beaten. Naturally Peter was confused and afraid. It is a serious sin to disown Christ, but Jesus forgave Peter (21:15–17). No sin is too great for Jesus to forgive if you are truly repentant. He will forgive even your worst sin if you turn from it and ask his pardon.

18:27 This fulfilled Jesus' words to Peter after he promised he would never disown him (Mark 14:31; John 13:38).

18:28 By Jewish law, entering the house of a Gentile would cause a Jewish person to be ceremonially defiled. As a result, he could not take part in worship at the temple or celebrate the feasts until he was restored to a state of "cleanness." Afraid of being defiled,

these men stayed outside the house where they had taken Jesus for trial. They kept the ceremonial requirements of their religion while harboring murder and treachery in their hearts.

18:29 This Roman governor, Pilate, was in charge of Judea (the region where Jerusalem was located) from A.D. 26 to 36. Pilate was unpopular with the Jews because he had raided the temple treasuries for money to build an aqueduct. He did not like the Jews, but when Jesus, the King of the Jews, stood before him, Pilate found him innocent.

18:30 Pilate knew what was going on; he knew that the religious leaders hated Jesus, and he did not want to act as their executioner. They could not sentence him to death themselves—permission had to come from a Roman leader. But Pilate initially refused to sentence Jesus without sufficient evidence. Jesus' life became a pawn in a political power struggle.

31 Pilate said, "Take him yourselves and judge him by your own law."

"But we have no right to execute anyone," the Jews objected. 32 This happened so that the words Jesus had spoken indicating the kind of death he was going to die *n* would be fulfilled.

18:32
n Mt 20:19; Jn 12:32, 33

33 Pilate then went back inside the palace, *o* summoned Jesus and asked him, "Are you the king of the Jews?" *p*

18:33
o Jn 19:9
p Lk 23:3

34 "Is that your own idea," Jesus asked, "or did others talk to you about me?"

35 "Am I a Jew?" Pilate replied. "It was your people and your chief priests who handed you over to me. What is it you have done?"

36 Jesus said, "My kingdom is not of this world. If it were, my servants would fight to prevent my arrest by the Jews. *q* But now my kingdom is from another place." *r*

18:36
q Mt 26:53
r Jn 6:15

37 "You are a king, then!" said Pilate.

18:37
s Jn 8:47; 1Jn 4:6

Jesus answered, "You are right in saying I am a king. In fact, for this reason I was born, and for this I came into the world, to testify to the truth. Everyone on the side of truth listens to me." *s*

Pilate Hands Jesus Over to Be Crucified
(232/Matthew 27:15–26; Mark 15:6–15; Luke 23:13–25)

38 "What is truth?" Pilate asked. With this he went out again to the Jews and said, "I find no basis for a charge against him. *t* 39 But it is your custom for me to release to you one prisoner at the time of the Passover. Do you want me to release 'the king of the Jews'?"

18:38
t Lk 23:4; Jn 19:4, 6

40 They shouted back, "No, not him! Give us Barabbas!" Now Barabbas had taken part in a rebellion. *u*

18:40
u Ac 3:14

JESUS' TRIAL AND CRUCIFIXION Jesus was taken from trial before the Jewish Sanhedrin to trial before the Roman governor, Pilate, in Pilate's palace. Pilate sent him to Herod (Luke 23:5–12), but Herod just returned Jesus to Pilate. Responding to threats from the mob, Pilate finally turned Jesus over to be crucified.

18:31ff Pilate made four attempts to deal with Jesus: (1) he tried to put the responsibility on someone else (18:31); (2) he tried to find a way of escape so he could release Jesus (18:39); (3) he tried to compromise having Jesus flogged rather than handing him over to die (19:1–3); and (4) he tried a direct appeal to the sympathy of the accusers (19:15). Everyone has to decide what to do with Jesus. Pilate tried to let everyone else decide for him—and in the end, he lost.

18:32 This prediction is recorded in Matthew 20:19. Crucifixion was a common method of execution for criminals who were not Roman citizens.

18:34 If Pilate was asking this question in his role as the Roman governor, he would have been inquiring whether Jesus was setting up a rebel government. But the Jews were using the word *king* to mean their religious ruler, the Messiah. Israel was a captive nation, under the authority of the Roman empire. A rival king might have threatened Rome; a Messiah could have been a purely religious leader.

18:36, 37 Pilate asked Jesus a straightforward question, and Jesus answered clearly. Jesus is a king, but one whose kingdom is not of this world. There seems to have been no question in Pilate's mind that Jesus spoke the truth and was innocent of any crime. It also seems apparent that while recognizing the truth, Pilate chose to reject it. It is a tragedy when we fail to recognize the truth. It is a greater tragedy when we recognize the truth but fail to heed it.

18:38 Pilate was cynical; he thought that all truth was relative. To many government officials, truth was whatever the majority of people agreed with or whatever helped advance their own personal power and political goals. When there is no standard or acknowledgement of truth, there is no basis for moral right and wrong. Justice becomes whatever works or whatever helps those in power. In Jesus and his Word we have a standard for truth and for our moral behavior.

18:40 Barabbas was a rebel against Rome and, although he had committed murder, he was probably a hero among the Jews. The Jews hated being governed by Rome and paying taxes to the despised government. Barabbas, who had led a rebellion and failed, was released instead of Jesus, the only One who could truly help Israel. For more on Barabbas, see the note on Luke 23:17–19.

19:1
ᵛMt 27:26

19 Then Pilate took Jesus and had him flogged. ᵛ ²The soldiers twisted together a crown of thorns and put it on his head. They clothed him in a purple robe ³and went up to him again and again, saying, "Hail, king of the Jews!" And they struck him in the face.

19:4
ʷJn 18:38
ˣver 6

⁴Once more Pilate came out and said to the Jews, "Look, I am bringing him out ʷ to you to let you know that I find no basis for a charge against him." ˣ ⁵When Jesus came out wearing the crown of thorns and the purple robe, Pilate said to them, "Here is the man!"

19:6
ʸAc 3:13

⁶As soon as the chief priests and their officials saw him, they shouted, "Crucify! Crucify!"

But Pilate answered, "You take him and crucify him. ʸ As for me, I find no basis for a charge against him."

19:7
ᶻLev 24:16
ᵃMt 26:63-66;
Jn 5:18; 10:33

⁷The Jews insisted, "We have a law, and according to that law he must die,ᶻ because he claimed to be the Son of God."ᵃ

⁸When Pilate heard this, he was even more afraid, ⁹and he went back inside the palace. "Where do you come from?" he asked Jesus, but Jesus gave him no answer. ¹⁰"Do you refuse to speak to me?" Pilate said. "Don't you realize I have power either to free you or to crucify you?"

19:11
ᵇJn 18:28-30

¹¹Jesus answered, "You would have no power over me if it were not given to you from above. Therefore the one who handed me over to youᵇ is guilty of a greater sin."

19:12
ᶜLk 23:2

¹²From then on, Pilate tried to set Jesus free, but the Jews kept shouting, "If you let this man go, you are no friend of Caesar. Anyone who claims to be a king ᶜ opposes Caesar."

¹³When Pilate heard this, he brought Jesus out and sat down on the judge's seat at a place known as the Stone Pavement (which in Aramaic is Gabbatha). ¹⁴It was the day of

19:14
ᵈMt 27:62
ᵉMk 15:25
ᶠver 19, 21

Preparationᵈ of Passover Week, about the sixth hour. ᵉ

"Here is your king,"ᶠ Pilate said to the Jews.

¹⁵But they shouted, "Take him away! Take him away! Crucify him!"

"Shall I crucify your king?" Pilate asked.

"We have no king but Caesar," the chief priests answered.

19:16
ᵍMt 27:26;
Mk 15:15; Lk 23:25

¹⁶Finally Pilate handed him over to them to be crucified. ᵍ

19:1ff To grasp the full picture of Jesus' crucifixion, read John's perspective along with the other three accounts in Matthew 27, Mark 15, and Luke 23. Each writer adds meaningful details, but each has the same message—Jesus died on the cross, in fulfillment of Old Testament prophecy, so that we could be saved from our sins and given eternal life.

19:1-3 Flogging could have killed Jesus. The usual procedure was to bare the upper half of the victim's body and tie his hands to a pillar before whipping him with a three-pronged whip. The number of lashes was determined by the severity of the crime; up to 40 were permitted under Jewish law (Deuteronomy 25:3). After being flogged, Jesus also endured other agonies recorded here and in the other Gospels.

19:2-5 The soldiers went beyond their orders to whip Jesus— they also mocked his claim to royalty by placing a crown on his head and a royal robe on his shoulders.

19:7 The truth finally came out—the religious leaders had not brought Jesus to Pilate because he was causing rebellion against Rome, but because they thought he had broken their religious laws. Blasphemy, one of the most serious crimes in Jewish law, deserved the death penalty. Accusing Jesus of blasphemy would give credibility to their case in the eyes of the Jews; accusing Jesus of treason would give credibility to their case in the eyes of the Romans. They didn't care which accusation Pilate listened to, as long as he would cooperate with them in killing Jesus.

19:10 Throughout the trial we see that Jesus was in control, not Pilate or the religious leaders. Pilate vacillated, the Jewish leaders reacted out of hatred and anger, but Jesus remained composed. He knew the truth, he knew God's plan, and he knew the reason for his trial. Despite the pressure and persecution, Jesus remained unmoved. It was really Pilate and the religious leaders who were on trial, not Jesus. When you are questioned or ridiculed because of your faith, remember that while you may be on trial before your accusers, they are on trial before God.

19:11 When Jesus said the man who delivered him to Pilate was guiltier than Pilate, he was not excusing Pilate for reacting to the political pressure placed on him. Pilate was responsible for his decision about Jesus. Caiaphas and the other religious leaders were guilty of a greater sin because they premeditated Jesus' murder.

19:12, 13 This veiled threat by the Jewish leaders pressured Pilate into allowing Jesus to be crucified. As Roman governor of the area, Pilate was expected to keep the peace. Because Rome could not afford to keep large numbers of troops in the outlying regions, they maintained control by crushing rebellions immediately with brute force. Pilate was afraid that reports to Caesar of insurrection in his region would cost Pilate his job and perhaps even his life. When we face a tough decision, we can take the easy way out, or we can stand for what is right regardless of the cost. If we know the good we ought to do and don't do it, we sin (James 4:17).

19:13 The Stone Pavement was part of the Tower of Antonia bordering the northwest corner of the temple complex.

19:15 The Jewish leaders were so desperate to get rid of Jesus that, despite their intense hatred for Rome, they shouted, "We have no king but Caesar." How ironic that they feigned allegiance to Rome while rejecting their own Messiah! Their own words condemned them, for God was to be their only true King, and they had abandoned every trace of loyalty to him. The priests had truly lost their reasons for existence—instead of turning people to God, they claimed allegiance to Rome in order to kill their Messiah.

Jesus Is Led Away to Be Crucified
(234/Matthew 27:32–37; Mark 15:21–24; Luke 23:26–31)

Jesus Is Placed on the Cross
(235/Matthew 27:35–44; Mark 15:25–32; Luke 23:32–43)

So the soldiers took charge of Jesus. [17]Carrying his own cross,[h] he went out to the place of the Skull[i] (which in Aramaic is called Golgotha). [18]Here they crucified him, and with him two others—one on each side and Jesus in the middle.

[19]Pilate had a notice prepared and fastened to the cross. It read: JESUS OF NAZARETH, THE KING OF THE JEWS. [20]Many of the Jews read this sign, for the place where Jesus was crucified was near the city, and the sign was written in Aramaic, Latin and Greek. [21]The chief priests of the Jews protested to Pilate, "Do not write 'The King of the Jews,' but that this man claimed to be king of the Jews."[j]

[22]Pilate answered, "What I have written, I have written."

[23]When the soldiers crucified Jesus, they took his clothes, dividing them into four shares, one for each of them, with the undergarment remaining. This garment was seamless, woven in one piece from top to bottom.

[24]"Let's not tear it," they said to one another. "Let's decide by lot who will get it."

This happened that the scripture might be fulfilled which said,

"They divided my garments among them
     and cast lots for my clothing."[a][k]

So this is what the soldiers did.

[25]Near the cross[l] of Jesus stood his mother, his mother's sister, Mary the wife of Clopas, and Mary Magdalene. [m] [26]When Jesus saw his mother there, and the disciple whom he loved[n] standing nearby, he said to his mother, "Dear woman, here is your son," [27]and to the disciple, "Here is your mother." From that time on, this disciple took her into his home.

Jesus Dies on the Cross (236/Matthew 27:45–56; Mark 15:33–41; Luke 23:44–49)

[28]Later, knowing that all was now completed,[o] and so that the Scripture would be fulfilled, Jesus said, "I am thirsty." [29]A jar of wine vinegar[p] was there, so they soaked a sponge in it, put the sponge on a stalk of the hyssop plant, and lifted it to Jesus' lips. [30]When he had received the drink, Jesus said, "It is finished."[q] With that, he bowed his head and gave up his spirit.

[a]24 Psalm 22:18

19:17 [h]Lk 23:26
[i]Lk 23:33

19:21 [j]ver 14

19:24 [k]Ps 22:18

19:25 [l]Mt 27:55, 56; Mk 15:40, 41; Lk 23:49
[m]Lk 24:18
19:26 [n]Jn 13:23

19:28 [o]Jn 13:1
19:29 [p]Ps 69:21
19:30 [q]Jn 17:4

19:17 This place called *Golgotha*, "the skull," was probably a hill outside Jerusalem along a main road. Many executions took place here so the Romans could use them as an example to the people.

19:18 Crucifixion was a Roman form of execution. The condemned man was forced to carry his cross along a main road to the execution site, as a warning to the people. Types of crosses and methods of crucifixion varied. Jesus was nailed to his cross; some people were tied with ropes. Death came by suffocation because the weight of the body made breathing difficult as the victim lost strength. Crucifixion was a hideously slow and painful death.

19:19 This sign was meant to be ironic. A king, stripped nearly naked and executed in public view, had obviously lost his kingdom forever. But Jesus, who turns the world's wisdom upside down, was just coming into his kingdom. His death and resurrection would strike the deathblow to Satan's rule and would establish Jesus' eternal authority over the earth. Few people reading the sign that bleak afternoon understood its real meaning, but the sign was absolutely true. All was not lost. Jesus was King of the Jews—and the Gentiles, and the whole universe.

19:20 The placard was written in three languages: Aramaic for the native Jews, Latin for the Roman occupation forces, and Greek for foreigners and Jews visiting from other lands. In a double irony, the multilingual sign declared that Jesus was Lord of all.

19:23, 24 Roman soldiers in charge of crucifixions customarily took for themselves the clothes of the condemned men. They divided Jesus' clothing, casting lots to determine who would get his seamless garment, the most valuable piece of clothing. This fulfilled the prophecy in Psalm 22:18.

19:25–27 Even while dying on the cross, Jesus was concerned about his family. He instructed John to care for Mary, Jesus' mother. Our families are precious gifts from God, and we should value and care for them under all circumstances. Neither Christian work nor key responsibilities in any job or position excuse us from caring for our families. What can you do today to show your love to your family?

19:27 Jesus asked his close friend John, the writer of this Gospel, to care for Jesus' mother, Mary, whose husband, Joseph, must have been dead by this time. Why didn't Jesus assign this task to his brothers? As the oldest son, Jesus entrusted his mother to a person who stayed with him at the cross—and that was John.

19:29 This vinegar was a cheap wine that the Roman soldiers drank while waiting for those crucified to die.

19:30 Until this time, a complicated system of sacrifices had atoned for sins. Sin separates people from God, and only through the sacrifice of an animal, a substitute, could people be forgiven and become clean before God. But people sin continually, so frequent sacrifices were required. Jesus, however, became the final and ultimate sacrifice for sin. The word *finished* is the same as "paid in full." Jesus came to *finish* God's work of salvation (4:34; 17:4), to pay the full penalty for our sins. With his death, the complex sacrificial system ended because Jesus took all sin upon himself. Now we can freely approach God because of what Jesus did for us. Those who believe in Jesus' death and resurrection can live eternally with God and escape the penalty that comes from sin.

19:31
r Dt 21:23

31 Now it was the day of Preparation, and the next day was to be a special Sabbath. Because the Jews did not want the bodies left on the crosses r during the Sabbath, they asked Pilate to have the legs broken and the bodies taken down. 32 The soldiers therefore came and broke the legs of the first man who had been crucified with Jesus, and then those of the other.

19:34
s 1Jn 5:6, 8
19:35
t Jn 15:27

33 But when they came to Jesus and found that he was already dead, they did not break his legs. 34 Instead, one of the soldiers pierced Jesus' side with a spear, bringing a sudden flow of blood and water. s 35 The man who saw it has given testimony, and his testimony is true. t He knows that he tells the truth, and he testifies so that you also may believe. 36 These things happened so that the scripture would be fulfilled: "Not one of his bones will be broken," a u

19:36
u Ex 12:46; Nu 9:12;
Ps 34:20
19:37
v Zec 12:10

37 and, as another scripture says, "They will look on the one they have pierced." b v

a36 Exodus 12:46; Num. 9:12; Psalm 34:20   b37 Zech. 12:10

MARY MAGDALENE

The absence of women among the 12 disciples has bothered a few people. But it is clear that there were many women among Jesus' followers. It is also clear that Jesus did not treat women as others in his culture did; he treated them with dignity, as people with worth.

Mary of Magdala was an early follower of Jesus who certainly deserves to be called a disciple. An energetic, impulsive, caring woman, she not only traveled with Jesus, but also contributed to the needs of the group. She was present at the crucifixion and was on her way to anoint Jesus' body on Sunday morning when she discovered the empty tomb. Mary was the first to see Jesus after his resurrection.

Mary Magdalene is a heartwarming example of thankful living. Her life was miraculously freed by Jesus when he drove seven demons out of her. In every glimpse we have of her, she was acting out her appreciation for the freedom Christ had given her. That freedom allowed her to stand under Christ's cross when all the disciples except John were hiding in fear. After Jesus' death, she intended to give his body every respect. Like the rest of Jesus' followers, she never expected his bodily resurrection—but she was overjoyed to discover it.

Mary's faith was not complicated, but it was direct and genuine. She was more eager to believe and obey than to understand everything. Jesus honored her childlike faith by appearing to her first and by entrusting her with the first message of his resurrection.

Strengths and accomplishments:	• Contributed to the needs of Jesus and his disciples • One of the few faithful followers present at Jesus' death on the cross • First to see the risen Christ
Weakness and mistake:	• Jesus had to drive seven demons out of her
Lessons from her life:	• Those who are obedient grow in understanding • Women are vital to Jesus' ministry • Jesus relates to women as he created them—as equal reflectors of God's image
Vital statistics:	• Where: Magdala, Jerusalem • Occupation: We are not told, but she seems to have been wealthy • Contemporaries: Jesus, the 12 disciples, Mary, Martha, Lazarus, Jesus' mother Mary
Key verse:	"When Jesus rose early on the first day of the week, he appeared first to Mary Magdalene, out of whom he had driven seven demons" (Mark 16:9).

Mary Magdalene's story is told in Matthew 27, 28; Mark 15, 16; Luke 23, 24; and John 19, 20. She is also mentioned in Luke 8:2.

19:31 It was against God's law to leave the body of a dead person exposed overnight (Deuteronomy 21:23), and it was also against the law to work after sundown on Friday, when the Sabbath began. This is why the religious leaders urgently wanted to get Jesus' body off the cross and buried by sundown.

19:31-35 These Romans were experienced soldiers. They knew from many previous crucifixions whether a man was dead or alive. There was no question that Jesus was dead when they checked him, so they decided not to break his legs as they had done to the other victims. Piercing his side and seeing the sudden flow of blood and water (indicating that the sac surrounding the heart and the heart itself had been pierced) was further proof of his death. Some people say Jesus didn't really die, that he only passed out—and that's how he came back to life. But we have the

witness of an impartial party, the Roman soldiers, that Jesus died on the cross (see Mark 15:44, 45).

19:32 The Roman soldiers would break victims' legs to hasten the death process. When a person hung on a cross, death came by suffocation, but the victim could push against the cross with his legs to hold up his body and keep breathing. With broken legs, he would suffocate almost immediately.

19:34, 35 The graphic details of Jesus' death are especially important in John's record because he was an eyewitness.

19:36, 37 Jesus died as the lambs for the Passover meal were being slain. Not a bone was to be broken in these sacrificial lambs (Exodus 12:46; Numbers 9:12). Jesus, the Lamb of God, was the perfect sacrifice for the sins of the world (1 Corinthians 5:7).

Jesus Is Laid in the Tomb (*237/Matthew 27:56–61; Mark 15:42–47; Luke 23:50–56*)

38 Later, Joseph of Arimathea asked Pilate for the body of Jesus. Now Joseph was a disciple of Jesus, but secretly because he feared the Jews. With Pilate's permission, he came and took the body away. 39 He was accompanied by Nicodemus, *w* the man who earlier had visited Jesus at night. Nicodemus brought a mixture of myrrh and aloes, about seventy-five pounds. a 40 Taking Jesus' body, the two of them wrapped it, with the spices, in strips of linen. *x* This was in accordance with Jewish burial customs. *y* 41 At the place where Jesus was crucified, there was a garden, and in the garden a new tomb, in which no one had ever been laid. 42 Because it was the Jewish day of Preparation *z* and since the tomb was nearby, they laid Jesus there.

19:39
w Jn 3:1

19:40
x Lk 24:12
y Mt 26:12

19:42
z ver 14, 31

Jesus Rises from the Dead (*239/Matthew 28:1–7; Mark 16:1–8; Luke 24:1–12*)

20 Early on the first day of the week, while it was still dark, Mary Magdalene went to the tomb and saw that the stone had been removed from the entrance. a 2 So she came running to Simon Peter and the other disciple, the one Jesus loved, *b* and said, "They have taken the Lord out of the tomb, and we don't know where they have put him!"

3 So Peter and the other disciple started for the tomb. *c* 4 Both were running, but the other disciple outran Peter and reached the tomb first. 5 He bent over and looked in at the strips of linen *d* lying there but did not go in. 6 Then Simon Peter, who was behind him, arrived and went into the tomb. He saw the strips of linen lying there, 7 as well as the burial cloth that had been around Jesus' head. The cloth was folded up by itself, separate from the linen. 8 Finally the other disciple, who had reached the tomb first, also went inside. He saw and believed. 9 (They still did not understand from Scripture that Jesus had to rise from the dead.)

20:1
a Mt 27:60, 66

20:2
b Jn 13:23

20:3
c Lk 24:12

20:5
d Jn 19:40

Jesus Appears to Mary Magdalene (*240/Mark 16:9–11*)

10 Then the disciples went back to their homes, 11 but Mary stood outside the tomb crying. As she wept, she bent over to look into the tomb 12 and saw two angels in white, *e* seated where Jesus' body had been, one at the head and the other at the foot.

13 They asked her, "Woman, why are you crying?"

20:12
e Mk 16:5

a *39* Greek *a hundred litrai* (about 34 kilograms)

19:38, 39 Four people were changed in the process of Jesus' death. The criminal, dying on the cross beside Jesus, asked Jesus to include him in his kingdom (Luke 23:39–43). The Roman centurion proclaimed that surely Jesus was the Son of God (Mark 15:39). Joseph and Nicodemus, members of the Jewish council and secret followers of Jesus (7:50–52), came out of hiding. These men were changed more by Jesus' death than by his life. They realized who Jesus was, and that realization brought out their belief, proclamation, and action. When confronted with Jesus and his death, we should be changed—to believe, proclaim, and act.

19:38–42 Joseph of Arimathea and Nicodemus were secret followers of Jesus. They were afraid to make this allegiance known because of their positions in the Jewish community. Joseph was a leader and honored member of the Jewish council. Nicodemus, also a member of the council, had come to Jesus by night (3:1) and later tried to defend him before the other religious leaders (7:50–52). Yet they risked their reputations to provide for Jesus' burial. Are you a secret believer? Do you hide your faith from your friends and fellow workers? This is an appropriate time to step out of hiding and let others know whom you follow.

19:42 As they buried Jesus, Nicodemus and Joseph had to hurry to avoid working on the Sabbath, which began Friday evening at sundown. This tomb was probably a cave carved out of the stone hillside. It was large enough for a person to walk into, so Joseph and Nicodemus carried Jesus' body into it. A large stone was rolled in front of the entrance.

20:1 Other women came to the tomb along with Mary Magdalene. The other Gospel accounts give their names. For more information on Mary Magdalene, see her Profile in this chapter, p. 1785.

20:1 The stone was not rolled away from the entrance to the tomb so Jesus could get out. He could have left easily without

moving the stone. It was rolled away so others could get *in* and see that Jesus was gone.

20:1ff People who hear about the resurrection for the first time may need time before they can comprehend this amazing story. Like Mary and the disciples, they may pass through four stages of belief. (1) At first, they may think the story is a fabrication, impossible to believe (20:2). (2) Like Peter, they may check out the facts and still be puzzled about what happened (20:6). (3) Only when they encounter Jesus personally are they able to accept the fact of the resurrection (20:16). (4) Then, as they commit themselves to the risen Lord and devote their lives to serving him, they begin to understand fully the reality of his presence with them (20:28).

20:6, 7 The grave clothes were left as if Jesus' body had simply vacated them. The headpiece was rolled up in the shape of a head, and it was at about the right distance from the wrappings that had enveloped Jesus' body. A grave robber couldn't possibly have made off with Jesus' body and left the linens as if they were still shaped around it.

20:9 As further proof that the disciples did not fabricate this story, we find that Peter and John were surprised that Jesus was not in the tomb. When John saw the grave clothes looking like an empty cocoon from which Jesus had emerged, he believed that Jesus had risen. It wasn't until after they had seen the empty tomb that they remembered what the Scriptures and Jesus had said—he would die, but he would also rise again!

20:9 Jesus' resurrection is the key to the Christian faith. Why? (1) Just as he said, Jesus rose from the dead. We can be confident, therefore, that he will accomplish all he has promised. (2) Jesus' bodily resurrection shows us that the living Christ, not a false prophet or imposter, is ruler of God's eternal kingdom. (3) We can be certain of our own resurrection because Jesus was

"They have taken my Lord away," she said, "and I don't know where they have put him." ¹⁴At this, she turned around and saw Jesus standing there,^f but she did not realize that it was Jesus.^g

20:14
^fMk 16:9
^gJn 21:4

¹⁵"Woman," he said, "why are you crying? Who is it you are looking for?"

Thinking he was the gardener, she said, "Sir, if you have carried him away, tell me where you have put him, and I will get him."

¹⁶Jesus said to her, "Mary."

She turned toward him and cried out in Aramaic, "Rabboni!" (which means Teacher).

20:17
^hMt 28:10
ⁱJn 7:33

¹⁷Jesus said, "Do not hold on to me, for I have not yet returned to the Father. Go instead to my brothers^h and tell them, 'I am returning to my Fatherⁱ and your Father, to my God and your God.'"

20:18
^jLk 24:10, 22, 23

¹⁸Mary Magdalene went to the disciples^j with the news: "I have seen the Lord!" And she told them that he had said these things to her.

THOMAS

Thomas, so often remembered as "Doubting Thomas," deserves to be respected for his faith. He was a doubter, but his doubts had a purpose—he wanted to know the truth. Thomas did not idolize his doubts; he gladly believed when given reasons to do so. He expressed his doubts fully and had them answered completely. Doubting was only his way of responding, not his way of life.

Although our glimpses of Thomas are brief, his character comes through with consistency. He struggled to be faithful to what he knew, despite what he felt. At one point, when it was plain to everyone that Jesus' life was in danger, only Thomas put into words what most were feeling, "Let us also go, that we may die with him" (John 11:16). He didn't hesitate to follow Jesus.

We don't know why Thomas was absent the first time Jesus appeared to the disciples after the resurrection, but he was reluctant to believe their witness to Christ's resurrection. Not even ten friends could change his mind!

We can doubt without having to live a doubting way of life. Doubt encourages rethinking. Its purpose is more to sharpen the mind than to change it. Doubt can be used to pose the question, get an answer, and push for a decision. But doubt was never meant to be a permanent condition. Doubt is one foot lifted, poised to step forward or backward. There is no motion until the foot comes down.

When you experience doubt, take encouragement from Thomas. He didn't stay in his doubt, but allowed Jesus to bring him to belief. Take encouragement also from the fact that countless other followers of Christ have struggled with doubts. The answers God gave them may help you too. Don't settle into doubts, but move on from them to decision and belief. Find another believer with whom you can share your doubts. Silent doubts rarely find answers.

Strengths and accomplishments:	• One of Jesus' 12 disciples • Intense both in doubt and belief • A loyal and honest man
Weaknesses and mistakes:	• Along with the others, abandoned Jesus at his arrest • Refused to believe the others' claims to have seen Christ and demanded proof • Struggled with a pessimistic outlook
Lessons from his life:	• Jesus does not reject doubts that are honest and directed toward belief • Better to doubt out loud than to disbelieve in silence
Vital statistics:	• Where: Galilee, Judea, Samaria • Occupation: Disciple of Jesus • Contemporaries: Jesus, other disciples, Herod Antipas, Pilate
Key verses:	"Then he said to Thomas, 'Put your finger here; see my hands. Reach out your hand and put it into my side. Stop doubting and believe.' Thomas said to him, 'My Lord and my God!'" (John 20:27, 28).

Thomas's story is told in the Gospels. He is also mentioned in Acts 1:13.

---

resurrected. Death is not the end—there is future life. (4) The divine power that brought Jesus back to life is now available to us to bring our spiritually dead selves back to life. (5) The resurrection is the basis for the church's witness to the world.

20:17 Mary did not want to lose Jesus again. She had not yet understood the resurrection. Perhaps she thought this was his promised second coming (14:3). But Jesus did not want to be detained at the tomb. If he did not ascend to heaven, the Holy

Spirit could not come. Both he and Mary had important work to do.

20:18 Mary didn't recognize Jesus at first. Her grief had blinded her; she couldn't see him because she didn't expect to see him. Then he spoke her name, and immediately she recognized him. Imagine the love that flooded her heart when she heard her Savior saying her name. Jesus is near you, and he is calling your name. Can you, like Mary, regard him as your Lord?

Jesus Appears to His Disciples (244/Luke 24:36–43)

19On the evening of that first day of the week, when the disciples were together, with the doors locked for fear of the Jews, Jesus came and stood among them and said, "Peace be with you!"k 20After he said this, he showed them his hands and side. The disciples were overjoyed l when they saw the Lord.

21Again Jesus said, "Peace be with you! As the Father has sent me, I am sending you." m 22And with that he breathed on them and said, "Receive the Holy Spirit. 23If you forgive anyone his sins, they are forgiven; if you do not forgive them, they are not forgiven." n

Jesus Appears to the Disciples Including Thomas (245/Mark 16:14)

24Now Thomas o (called Didymus), one of the Twelve, was not with the disciples when Jesus came. 25So the other disciples told him, "We have seen the Lord!"

But he said to them, "Unless I see the nail marks in his hands and put my finger where the nails were, and put my hand into his side,p I will not believe it."

26A week later his disciples were in the house again, and Thomas was with them. Though the doors were locked, Jesus came and stood among them and said, "Peace be with you!" 27Then he said to Thomas, "Put your finger here; see my hands. Reach out your hand and put it into my side. Stop doubting and believe." q

28Thomas said to him, "My Lord and my God!"

29Then Jesus told him, "Because you have seen me, you have believed; blessed are those who have not seen and yet have believed." r

30Jesus did many other miraculous signs in the presence of his disciples, which are not recorded in this book. s 31But these are written that you may a believe t that Jesus is the Christ, the Son of God, and that by believing you may have life in his name.

a31 Some manuscripts may continue to

20:19 k Lk 24:36-39
20:20 l Jn 16:20, 22
20:21 m Mt 28:19; Jn 17:18
20:23 n Mt 16:19; 18:18
20:24 o Jn 11:16
20:25 p ver 20
20:27 q Lk 24:40
20:29 r 1Pe 1:8
20:30 s Jn 21:25
20:31 t Jn 3:15

20:18 Mary did not meet the risen Christ until she had discovered the empty tomb. She responded with joy and obedience by going to tell the disciples. We cannot meet Christ until we discover that he is indeed alive, that his tomb is empty. Are you filled with joy by this good news, and do you share it with others?

20:21 Jesus again identified himself with his Father. He told the disciples by whose authority he did his work. Then he passed the job to his disciples of spreading the gospel of salvation around the world. Whatever God has asked you to do, remember: (1) your authority comes from God, and (2) Jesus has demonstrated by words and actions how to accomplish the job he has given you. As the Father sent Jesus, Jesus sends his followers . . . and you.

20:22 This may have been a special filling of the Holy Spirit for the disciples, a foretaste of what all believers would experience from the time of Pentecost (Acts 2) and forever after. To do God's work, we need the guidance and power of the Holy Spirit. We must avoid trying to do his work in our own strength.

20:22 There is life in the breath of God. Man was created but did not come alive until God breathed into him the breath of life (Genesis 2:7). God's first breath made man different from all other forms of creation. Now, through the breath of Jesus, God imparted eternal, spiritual life. With this inbreathing came the power to do God's will on earth.

20:23 Jesus was giving the disciples their Spirit-powered and Spirit-guided mission—to preach the Good News about Jesus so people's sins might be forgiven. The disciples did not have the power to forgive sins (only God can forgive sins), but Jesus gave them the privilege of telling new believers that their sins have been forgiven because they have accepted Jesus' message (see the notes on Matthew 16:19 and 18:18). All believers have this same privilege. We can announce the forgiveness of sin with certainty when we ourselves find repentance and faith.

20:24-29 Have you ever wished you could actually see Jesus, touch him, and hear his words? Are there times you want to sit down with him and get his advice? Thomas wanted Jesus' physical presence. But God's plan is wiser. He has not limited himself to one physical body; he wants to be present with you at all times. Even now he is with you in the form of the Holy Spirit. You can talk to him, and you can find his words to you in the pages of the Bible. He can be as real to you as he was to Thomas.

20:25-28 Jesus wasn't hard on Thomas for his doubts. Despite his skepticism, Thomas was still loyal to the believers and to Jesus himself. Some people need to doubt before they believe. If doubt leads to questions, questions lead to answers, and the answers are accepted, then doubt has done good work. It is when doubt becomes stubbornness and stubbornness becomes a prideful lifestyle that doubt harms faith. When you doubt, don't stop there. Let your doubt deepen your faith as you continue to search for the answer.

20:27 Jesus' resurrected body was unique. It was not the same kind of flesh and blood Lazarus had when he came back to life. Jesus' body was no longer subject to the same laws of nature as before his death. He could appear in a locked room; yet he was not a ghost or apparition because he could be touched and could eat. Jesus' resurrection was literal and physical—he was not a disembodied spirit.

20:29 Some people think they would believe in Jesus if they could see a definite sign or miracle. But Jesus says we are blessed if we can believe without seeing. We have all the proof we need in the words of the Bible and the testimony of believers. A physical appearance would not make Jesus any more real to us than he is now.

20:30, 31 To understand the life and mission of Jesus more fully, all we need to do is study the Gospels. John tells us that his Gospel records only a few of the many events in Jesus' life on earth. But the gospel includes everything we need to know to believe that Jesus is the Christ, the Son of God, through whom we receive eternal life.

Jesus Appears to Seven Disciples (246)

21:1
u Jn 20:19, 26
v Jn 6:1
21:2
w Jn 1:45
x Mt 4:21
21:3
y Lk 5:5
21:4
z Jn 20:14

21:6
a Lk 5:4-7

21:7
b Jn 13:23

21:14
c Jn 20:19, 26

21 Afterward Jesus appeared again to his disciples, *u* by the Sea of Tiberias. *a v* It happened this way: [2]Simon Peter, Thomas (called Didymus), Nathanael *w* from Cana in Galilee, the sons of Zebedee, *x* and two other disciples were together. [3]"I'm going out to fish," Simon Peter told them, and they said, "We'll go with you." So they went out and got into the boat, but that night they caught nothing. *y*

[4]Early in the morning, Jesus stood on the shore, but the disciples did not realize that it was Jesus. *z*

[5]He called out to them, "Friends, haven't you any fish?"

"No," they answered.

[6]He said, "Throw your net on the right side of the boat and you will find some." When they did, they were unable to haul the net in because of the large number of fish. *a*

[7]Then the disciple whom Jesus loved *b* said to Peter, "It is the Lord!" As soon as Simon Peter heard him say, "It is the Lord," he wrapped his outer garment around him (for he had taken it off) and jumped into the water. [8]The other disciples followed in the boat, towing the net full of fish, for they were not far from shore, about a hundred yards. *b* [9]When they landed, they saw a fire of burning coals there with fish on it, and some bread.

[10]Jesus said to them, "Bring some of the fish you have just caught."

[11]Simon Peter climbed aboard and dragged the net ashore. It was full of large fish, 153, but even with so many the net was not torn. [12]Jesus said to them, "Come and have breakfast." None of the disciples dared ask him, "Who are you?" They knew it was the Lord. [13]Jesus came, took the bread and gave it to them, and did the same with the fish. [14]This was now the third time Jesus appeared to his disciples *c* after he was raised from the dead.

Jesus Challenges Peter (247)

[15]When they had finished eating, Jesus said to Simon Peter, "Simon son of John, do you truly love me more than these?"

a 1 That is, Sea of Galilee *b* 8 Greek *about two hundred cubits* (about 90 meters)

JESUS' APPEARANCES AFTER HIS RESURRECTION		
Mary Magdalene	Mark 16:9–11; John 20:11–18	
The other women at the tomb	Matthew 28:8–10	
Peter in Jerusalem	Luke 24:34; 1 Corinthians 15:5	
The two travelers on the road	Mark 16:12, 13	
Ten disciples behind closed doors	Mark 16:14; Luke 24:36–43; John 20:19–25	
All the disciples, with Thomas (excluding Judas Iscariot)	John 20:26–31; 1 Corinthians 15:5	
Seven disciples while fishing	John 21:1–14	
Eleven disciples on the mountain	Matthew 28:16–20	
A crowd of 500	1 Corinthians 15:6	
Jesus' brother James	1 Corinthians 15:7	
Those who watched Jesus ascend into heaven	Luke 24:44–49; Acts 1:3–8	

The truth of Christianity rests heavily on the resurrection. If Jesus rose from the grave, who saw him? How trustworthy were the witnesses? Those who claimed to have seen the risen Jesus went on to turn the world upside down. Most of them also died for being followers of Christ. People rarely die for halfhearted belief. These are the people who saw Jesus risen from the grave.

21:1ff This chapter tells how Jesus commissioned Peter. Perhaps Peter needed special encouragement after his denial—he may have felt completely worthless. Verses 1–14 set the scene for Jesus' conversation with Peter.

21:7 Only John ("the disciple whom Jesus loved") recognized Jesus in the dim morning light, undoubtedly because Jesus had performed a similar miracle earlier (Luke 5:1–11).

21:15–17 In this beach scene, Jesus led Peter through an experience that would remove the cloud of his denial. Peter had disowned Jesus three times. Three times Jesus asked Peter if he loved him. When Peter answered yes, Jesus told him to feed his sheep. It is one thing to say you love Jesus, but the real test is willingness to serve him. Peter had repented, and here Jesus was asking him to commit his life. Peter's life changed when he finally realized who Jesus was. His occupation changed from fisherman to evangelist; his identity changed from impetuous to "rock"; and his relationship to Jesus changed—he was forgiven, and he finally understood the significance of Jesus' words about his death and resurrection.

"Yes, Lord," he said, "you know that I love you."[d]
Jesus said, "Feed my lambs."

16Again Jesus said, "Simon son of John, do you truly love me?"
He answered, "Yes, Lord, you know that I love you."
Jesus said, "Take care of my sheep."[e]

17The third time he said to him, "Simon son of John, do you love me?"
Peter was hurt because Jesus asked him the third time, "Do you love me?" He said, "Lord, you know all things;[f] you know that I love you."

Jesus said, "Feed my sheep. 18I tell you the truth, when you were younger you dressed yourself and went where you wanted; but when you are old you will stretch out your hands, and someone else will dress you and lead you where you do not want to go." 19Jesus said this to indicate the kind of death by which Peter would glorify God.[g] Then he said to him, "Follow me!"

20Peter turned and saw that the disciple whom Jesus loved was following them. (This was the one who had leaned back against Jesus at the supper and had said, "Lord, who is going to betray you?")[h] 21When Peter saw him, he asked, "Lord, what about him?"

22Jesus answered, "If I want him to remain alive until I return,[i] what is that to you? You must follow me." 23Because of this, the rumor spread among the brothers[j] that this disciple would not die. But Jesus did not say that he would not die; he only said, "If I want him to remain alive until I return, what is that to you?"

24This is the disciple who testifies to these things and who wrote them down. We know that his testimony is true.[k]

25Jesus did many other things as well.[l] If every one of them were written down, I suppose that even the whole world would not have room for the books that would be written.

21:15
[d]Mt 26:33, 35

21:16
[e]Ac 20:28;
1Pe 5:2, 3

21:17
[f]Jn 16:30

21:19
[g]2Pe 1:14

21:20
[h]Jn 13:25

21:22
[i]Mt 16:27

21:23
[j]Ac 1:16

21:24
[k]Jn 19:35

21:25
[l]Jn 20:30

21:15–17 Jesus asked Peter three times if he loved him. The first time Jesus said, "Do you truly love (Greek *agape*: volitional, self-sacrificial love) me more than these?" The second time, Jesus focused on Peter alone and still used the word translated into Greek, *agape*. The third time, Jesus used the word translated into Greek, *phileo* (signifying affection, affinity, or brotherly love) and asked, in effect, "Are you even my friend?" Each time Peter responded with the word translated into Greek as *phileo*. Jesus doesn't settle for quick, superficial answers. He has a way of getting to the heart of the matter. Peter had to face his true feelings and motives when Jesus confronted him. How would you respond if Jesus asked you, "Do you truly love me? Do you really love me? Are you even my friend?"

21:18, 19 This was a prediction of Peter's death by crucifixion. Tradition indicates that Peter was crucified for his faith—upside down because he did not feel worthy of dying as his Lord did. Despite what Peter's future held, Jesus told him to follow him. We may be uncertain and fearful about our future. But if we know God is in control, we can confidently follow Christ.

21:21, 22 Peter asked Jesus how John would die. Jesus replied that Peter should not concern himself with that. We tend to compare our lives to others, whether to rationalize our own level of devotion to Christ or to question God's justice. Jesus responds to us as he did to Peter: "What is that to you? You must follow me."

21:23 Early church history reports that after John spent several years as an exile on the island of Patmos, he returned to Ephesus where he died as an old man, near the end of the first century.

21:25 John's stated purpose for writing his Gospel was to show that Jesus was the Son of God. He clearly and systematically presented the evidence for Jesus' claims. When evidence is presented in the courtroom, those who hear it must make a choice. Those who read the Gospel of John must also make a choice—is Jesus the Son of God, or isn't he? You are the jury. The evidence has been clearly presented. You must decide. Read John's Gospel and believe!

250 EVENTS IN THE LIFE OF CHRIST/ A HARMONY OF THE GOSPELS

All four books in the Bible that tell the story of Jesus Christ—Matthew, Mark, Luke, and John—stand alone, emphasizing a unique aspect of Jesus' life. But when these are blended into one complete account, or harmonized, we gain new insights about the life of Christ.

This harmony combines the four Gospels into a single chronological account of Christ's life on earth. It includes every chapter and verse of each Gospel, leaving nothing out.

The harmony is divided into 250 events. The title of each event is identical to the title found in the corresponding Gospel. Parallel passages found in more than one Gospel have identical titles, helping you to identify them quickly.

Each of the 250 events in the harmony is numbered. The number of the event corresponds to the number next to the title in the Bible text. When reading one of the Gospel accounts, you will notice, at times, that some numbers are missing or out of sequence. The easiest way to locate these events is to refer to the harmony.

In addition, if you are looking for a particular event in the life of Christ, the harmony can help you locate it more rapidly than paging through all four Gospels. Each of the 250 events has a distinctive title keyed to the main emphasis of the passage to help you locate and remember the events.

This harmony will help you to better visualize the travels of Jesus, study the four Gospels comparatively, and appreciate the unity of their message.

I. BIRTH AND PREPARATION OF JESUS CHRIST

	Matthew	Mark	Luke	John
1. Luke's purpose in writing			1:1–4	
2. God became a human being				1:1–18
3. The ancestors of Jesus	1:1–17		3:23–38	
4. An angel promises the birth of John to Zechariah			1:5–25	
5. An angel promises the birth of Jesus to Mary			1:26–38	
6. Mary visits Elizabeth			1:39–56	
7. John the Baptist is born			1:57–80	
8. An angel appears to Joseph	1:18–25			
9. Jesus is born in Bethlehem			2:1–7	
10. Shepherds visit Jesus			2:8–20	
11. Mary and Joseph bring Jesus to the temple			2:21–40	
12. Visitors arrive from eastern lands	2:1–12			
13. The escape to Egypt	2:13–18			
14. The return to Nazareth	2:19–23			
15. Jesus speaks with the religious teachers			2:41–52	
16. John the Baptist prepares the way for Jesus	3:1–12	1:1–8	3:1–18	
17. John baptizes Jesus	3:13–17	1:9–11	3:21, 22	
18. Satan tempts Jesus in the desert	4:1–11	1:12, 13	4:1–13	
19. John the Baptist declares his mission				1:19–28
20. John the Baptist proclaims Jesus as the Messiah				1:29–34
21. The first disciples follow Jesus				1:35–51
22. Jesus turns water into wine				2:1–12

II. MESSAGE AND MINISTRY OF JESUS CHRIST

	Matthew	Mark	Luke	John
23. Jesus clears the temple	2:12–25			
24. Nicodemus visits Jesus at night				3:1–21
25. John the Baptist tells more about Jesus				3:22–36
26. Herod puts John in prison			3:19, 20	
27. Jesus talks to a woman at the well				4:1–26
28. Jesus tells about the spiritual harvest				4:27–38
29. Many Samaritans believe in Jesus				4:39–42
30. Jesus preaches in Galilee	4:12–17	1:14, 15	4:14, 15	4:43–45
31. Jesus heals a government official's son				4:46–54
32. Jesus is rejected at Nazareth			4:16–30	
33. Four fishermen follow Jesus	4:18–22	1:16–20		
34. Jesus teaches with great authority		1:21–28	4:31–37	
35. Jesus heals Peter's mother–in–law and many others	8:14–17	1:29–34	4:38–41	
36. Jesus preaches throughout Galilee	4:23–25	1:35–39	4:42–44	
37. Jesus provides a miraculous catch of fish			5:1–11	
38. Jesus heals a man with leprosy	8:1–4	1:40–45	5:12–16	
39. Jesus heals a paralyzed man	9:1–8	2:1–12	5:17–26	
40. Jesus eats with sinners at Matthew's house	9:9–13	2:13–17	5:27–32	
41. Religious leaders ask Jesus about fasting	9:14–17	2:18–22	5:33–39	
42. Jesus heals a lame man by the pool				5:1–18
43. Jesus claims to be God's Son				5:19–30
44. Jesus supports his claim				5:31–47
45. The disciples pick wheat on the Sabbath	12:1–8	2:23–28	6:1–5	
46. Jesus heals a man's hand on the Sabbath	12:9–14	3:1–6	6:6–11	
47. Large crowds follow Jesus	12:15–21	3:7–12		
48. Jesus selects the twelve disciples		3:13–19	6:12–16	
49. Jesus gives the Beatitudes	5:1–12		6:17–26	
50. Jesus teaches about salt and light	5:13–16			
51. Jesus teaches about the law	5:17–20			
52. Jesus teaches about anger	5:21–26			
53. Jesus teaches about lust	5:27–30			
54. Jesus teaches about divorce	5:31, 32			
55. Jesus teaches about vows	5:33–37			
56. Jesus teaches about retaliation	5:38–42			
57. Jesus teaches about loving enemies	5:43–48		6:27–36	
58. Jesus teaches about giving to the needy	6:1–4			
59. Jesus teaches about prayer	6:5–15			
60. Jesus teaches about fasting	6:16–18			
61. Jesus teaches about money	6:19–24			
62. Jesus teaches about worry	6:25–34			
63. Jesus teaches about criticizing others	7:1–6		6:37–42	
64. Jesus teaches about asking, seeking, knocking	7:7–12			
65. Jesus teaches about the way to heaven	7:13, 14			
66. Jesus teaches about fruit in people's lives	7:15–20		6:43–45	
67. Jesus teaches about those who build houses on rock and sand	7:21–29		6:46–49	
68. A Roman centurion demonstrates faith	8:5–13		7:1–10	
69. Jesus raises a widow's son from the dead			7:11–17	
70. Jesus eases John's doubt	11:1–19		7:18–35	
71. Jesus promises rest for the soul	11:20–30			
72. A sinful woman anoints Jesus' feet			7:36–50	
73. Women accompany Jesus and the disciples			8:1–3	
74. Religious leaders accuse Jesus of being under Satan's power	12:22–37	3:20–30		
75. Religious leaders ask Jesus for a miracle	12:38–45			
76. Jesus describes his true family	12:46–50	3:31–35	8:19–21	
77. Jesus tells the parable of the four soils	13:1–9	4:1–9	8:4–8	
78. Jesus explains the parable of the four soils	13:10–23	4:10–25	8:9–18	
79. Jesus tells the parable of the growing seed		4:26–29		
80. Jesus tells the parable of the weeds	13:24–30			
81. Jesus tells the parable of the mustard seed	13:31, 32	4:30–34		
82. Jesus tells the parable of the yeast	13:33–35			
83. Jesus explains the parable of the weeds	13:36–43			
84. Jesus tells the parable of hidden treasure	13:44			

	Matthew	Mark	Luke	John
85. Jesus tells the parable of the pearl merchant	13:45, 46			
86. Jesus tells the parable of the fishing net	13:47–52			
87. Jesus calms the storm	8:23–27	4:35–41	8:22–25	
88. Jesus sends the demons into a herd of pigs	8:28–34	5:1–20	8:26–39	
89. Jesus heals a bleeding woman and restores a girl to life	9:18–26	5:21–43	8:40–56	
90. Jesus heals the blind and mute	9:27–34			
91. The people of Nazareth refuse to believe	13:53–58	6:1–6		
92. Jesus urges the disciples to pray for workers	9:35–38			
93. Jesus sends out the twelve disciples	10:1–16	6:7–13	9:1–6	
94. Jesus prepares the disciples for persecution	10:17–42			
95. Herod kills John the Baptist	14:1–12	6:14–29	9:7–9	
96. Jesus feeds five thousand	14:13–21	6:30–44	9:10–17	6:1–15
97. Jesus walks on water	14:22–33	6:45–52		6:16–21
98. Jesus heals all who touch him	14:34–36	6:53–56		
99. Jesus is the true bread from heaven				6:22–40
100. The Jews disagree that Jesus is from heaven				6:41–59
101. Many disciples desert Jesus				6:60–71
102. Jesus teaches about inner purity	15:1–20	7:1–23		
103. Jesus sends a demon out of a girl	15:21–28	7:24–30		
104. The crowd marvels at Jesus' healings	15:29–31	7:31–37		
105. Jesus feeds four thousand	15:32–39	8:1–10		
106. Religious leaders ask for a sign in the sky	16:1–4	8:11–13		
107. Jesus warns against wrong teaching	16:5–12	8:14–21		
108. Jesus restores sight to a blind man		8:22–26		
109. Peter says Jesus is the Messiah	16:13–20	8:27–30	9:18–20	
110. Jesus predicts his death the first time	16:21–28	8:31—9:1	9:21–27	
111. Jesus is transfigured on the mountain	17:1–13	9:2–13	9:28–36	
112. Jesus heals a demon–possessed boy	17:14–21	9:14–29	9:37–43	
113. Jesus predicts his death the second time	17:22, 23	9:30–32	9:44, 45	
114. Peter finds the coin in the fish's mouth	17:24–27			
115. The disciples argue about who would be the greatest	18:1–6	9:33–37	9:46–48	
116. The disciples forbid another to use Jesus' name		9:38–41	9:49, 50	
117. Jesus warns against temptation	18:7–9	9:42–50		
118. Jesus warns against looking down on others	18:10–14			
119. Jesus teaches how to treat a believer who sins	18:15–20			
120. Jesus tells the parable of the unforgiving debtor	18:21–35			
121. Jesus' brothers ridicule him				7:1–9
122. Jesus teaches about the cost of following him	8:18–22		9:51–62	
123. Jesus teaches openly at the temple				7:10–31
124. Religious leaders attempt to arrest Jesus				7:32–52
125. Jesus forgives an adulterous woman				7:53—8:11
126. Jesus is the light of the world				8:12–20
127. Jesus warns of coming judgment				8:21–30
128. Jesus speaks about God's true children				8:31–47
129. Jesus states he is eternal				8:48–59
130. Jesus sends out seventy–two messengers			10:1–16	
131. The seventy–two messengers return			10:17–24	
132. Jesus tells the parable of the Good Samaritan			10:25–37	
133. Jesus visits Mary and Martha			10:38–42	
134. Jesus teaches his disciples about prayer			11:1–13	
135. Jesus answers hostile accusations			11:14–28	
136. Jesus warns against unbelief			11:29–32	
137. Jesus teaches about the light within			11:33–36	
138. Jesus criticizes the religious leaders			11:37–54	
139. Jesus speaks against hypocrisy			12:1–12	
140. Jesus tells the parable of the rich fool			12:13–21	
141. Jesus warns about worry			12:22–34	
142. Jesus warns about preparing for his coming			12:35–48	
143. Jesus warns about coming division			12:49–53	
144. Jesus warns about the future crisis			12:54–59	
145. Jesus calls the people to repent			13:1–9	
146. Jesus heals the crippled woman			13:10–17	
147. Jesus teaches about the kingdom of God			13:18–21	
148. Jesus heals the man who was born blind				9:1–12
149. Religious leaders question the blind man				9:13–34

	Matthew	Mark	Luke	John
150. Jesus teaches about spiritual blindness				9:35–41
151. Jesus is the Good Shepherd				10:1–21
152. Religious leaders surround Jesus at the temple				10:22–42
153. Jesus teaches about entering the kingdom			13:22–30	
154. Jesus grieves over Jerusalem			13:31–35	
155. Jesus heals a man with dropsy			14:1–6	
156. Jesus teaches about seeking honor			14:7–14	
157. Jesus tells the parable of the great feast			14:15–24	
158. Jesus teaches about the cost of being a disciple			14:25–35	
159. Jesus tells the parable of the lost sheep			15:1–7	
160. Jesus tells the parable of the lost coin			15:8–10	
161. Jesus tells the parable of the lost son			15:11–32	
162. Jesus tells the parable of the shrewd manager			16:1–18	
163. Jesus tells about the rich man and the beggar			16:19–31	
164. Jesus tells about forgiveness and faith			17:1–10	
165. Lazarus becomes ill and dies				11:1–16
166. Jesus comforts Mary and Martha				11:17–37
167. Jesus raises Lazarus from the dead				11:38–44
168. Religious leaders plot to kill Jesus				11:45–57
169. Jesus heals ten men with leprosy			17:11–19	
170. Jesus teaches about the coming of the kingdom of God			17:20–37	
171. Jesus tells the parable of the persistent widow			18:1–8	
172. Jesus tells the parable of two men who prayed			18:9–14	
173. Jesus teaches about marriage and divorce	19:1–12	10:1–12		
174. Jesus blesses little children	19:13–15	10:13–16	18:15–17	
175. Jesus speaks to the rich young man	19:16–30	10:17–31	18:18–30	
176. Jesus tells the parable of the workers paid equally	20:1–16			
177. Jesus predicts his death the third time	20:17–19	10:32–34	18:31–34	
178. Jesus teaches about serving others	20:20–28	10:35–45		
179. Jesus heals a blind beggar	20:29–34	10:46–52	18:35–43	
180. Jesus brings salvation to Zacchaeus's home			19:1–10	
181. Jesus tells the parable of the king's ten servants			19:11–27	
182. A woman anoints Jesus with perfume	26:6–13	14:3–9		12:1–11
183. Jesus rides into Jerusalem on a donkey	21:1–11	11:1–11	19:28–44	12:12–19
184. Jesus clears the temple again	21:12–17	11:12–19	19:45–48	
185. Jesus explains why he must die				12:20–36
186. Most of the people do not believe in Jesus				12:37–43
187. Jesus summarizes his message				12:44–50
188. Jesus says the disciples can pray for anything	21:18–22	11:20–26		
189. Religious leaders challenge Jesus' authority	21:23–27	11:27–33	20:1–8	
190. Jesus tells the parable of the two sons	21:28–32			
191. Jesus tells the parable of the wicked tenants	21:33–46	12:1–12	20:9–19	
192. Jesus tells the parable of the wedding feast	22:1–14			
193. Religious leaders question Jesus about paying taxes	22:15–22	12:13–17	20:20–26	
194. Religious leaders question Jesus about the resurrection	22:23–33	12:18–27	20:27–40	
195. Religious leaders question Jesus about the greatest commandment	22:34–40	12:28–34		
196. Religious leaders cannot answer Jesus' question	22:41–46	12:35–37	20:41–44	
197. Jesus warns against the religious leaders	23:1–12	12:38–40	20:45–47	
198. Jesus condemns the religious leaders	23:13–36			
199. Jesus grieves over Jerusalem again	23:37–39			
200. A poor widow gives all she has			12:41–44	21:1–4
201. Jesus tells about the future	24:1–25	13:1–23	21:5–24	
202. Jesus tells about his return	24:26–35	13:24–31	21:25–33	
203. Jesus tells about remaining watchful	24:36–51	13:32–37	21:34–38	
204. Jesus tells the parable of the ten bridesmaids	25:1–13			
205. Jesus tells the parable of the loaned money	25:14–30			
206. Jesus tells about the final judgment	25:31–46			

III. DEATH AND RESURRECTION OF JESUS CHRIST

	Matthew	Mark	Luke	John
207. Religious leaders plot to kill Jesus	26:1–5	14:1, 2	22:1, 2	
208. Judas agrees to betray Jesus	26:14–16	14:10, 11	22:3–6	

	Matthew	Mark	Luke	John
209. Disciples prepare for the Passover	26:17–19	14:12–16	22:7–13	
210. Jesus washes the disciples' feet				13:1–20
211. Jesus and the disciples have the Last Supper	26:20–30	14:17–26	22:14–30	13:21–30
212. Jesus predicts Peter's denial			22:31–38	13:31–38
213. Jesus is the way to the Father				14:1–14
214. Jesus promises the Holy Spirit				14:15–31
215. Jesus teaches about the vine and the branches				15:1–17
216. Jesus warns about the world's hatred				15:18—16:4
217. Jesus teaches about the Holy Spirit				16:5–15
218. Jesus teaches about using his name in prayer				16:16–33
219. Jesus prays for himself				17:1–5
220. Jesus prays for his disciples				17:6–19
221. Jesus prays for future believers				17:20–26
222. Jesus again predicts Peter's denial	26:31–35	14:27–31		
223. Jesus agonizes in the garden	26:36–46	14:32–42	22:39–46	
224. Jesus is betrayed and arrested	26:47–56	14:43–52	22:47–53	18:1–11
225. Annas questions Jesus				18:12–24
226. Caiaphas questions Jesus	26:57–68	14:53–65		
227. Peter denies knowing Jesus	26:69–75	14:66–72	22:54–65	18:25–27
228. The council of religious leaders condemns Jesus	27:1, 2	15:1	22:66–71	
229. Judas kills himself	27:3–10			
230. Jesus stands trial before Pilate	27:11–14	15:2–5	23:1–5	18:28–37
231. Jesus stands trial before Herod			23:6–12	
232. Pilate hands Jesus over to be crucified	27:15–26	15:6–15	23:13–25	18:38—19:16
233. Roman soldiers mock Jesus	27:27–31	15:16–20		
234. Jesus is led away to be crucified	27:32–34	15:21–24	23:26–31	19:17
235. Jesus is placed on the cross	27:35–44	15:25–32	23:32–43	19:18–27
236. Jesus dies on the cross	27:45–56	15:33–41	23:44–49	19:28–37
237. Jesus is laid in the tomb	27:57–61	15:42–47	23:50–56	19:38–42
238. Guards are posted at the tomb	27:62–66			
239. Jesus rises from the dead	28:1–7	16:1–8	24:1–12	20:1–9
240. Jesus appears to Mary Magdalene		16:9–11		20:10–18
241. Jesus appears to the women	28:8–10			
242. Religious leaders bribe the guards	28:11–15			
243. Jesus appears to two believers traveling on the road		16:12, 13	24:13–35	
244. Jesus appears to the disciples behind locked doors			24:36–43	20:19–23
245. Jesus appears to the disciples including Thomas		16:14		20:24–31
246. Jesus appears to the disciples while fishing				21:1–14
247. Jesus talks with Peter				21:15–25
248. Jesus gives the Great Commission	28:16–20	16:15–18		
249. Jesus appears to the disciples in Jerusalem			24:44–49	
250. Jesus ascends into heaven		16:19, 20	24:50–53	

COMPARISON OF THE FOUR GOSPELS		Matthew	Mark	Luke	John
All four Gospels present the life and teachings of Jesus. Each book, however, focuses on a unique facet of Jesus and his character. To understand more about the specific characteristics of Jesus, read any one of the four Gospels.	Jesus is . . .	The promised King	The Servant of God	The Son of Man	The Son of God
	The original readers were . . .	Jews	Gentiles, Romans	Greeks	Christians throughout the world
	Significant themes . . .	Jesus is the Messiah because he fulfilled Old Testament prophecy	Jesus backed up his words with action	Jesus was God but also fully human	Belief in Jesus is required for salvation
	Character of the writer . . .	Teacher	Storyteller	Historian	Theologian
	Greatest emphasis is on . . .	Jesus' sermons and words	Jesus' miracles and actions	Jesus' humanity	The principles of Jesus' teaching

I. Teaching Parables
  A. About the Kingdom of God
    1. The Soils (Matthew 13:3–8; Mark 4:4–8; Luke 8:5–8)
    2. The Weeds (Matthew 13:24–30)
    3. The Mustard Seed (Matthew 13:31, 32; Mark 4:30–32; Luke 13:18, 19)
    4. The Yeast (Matthew 13:33; Luke 13:20, 21)
    5. The Treasure (Matthew 13:44)
    6. The Pearl (Matthew 13:45, 46)
    7. The Fishing Net (Matthew 13:47–50)
    8. The Growing Wheat (Mark 4:26–29)
  B. About Service and Obedience
    1. The Workers in the Harvest (Matthew 20:1–16)
    2. The Loaned Money (Matthew 25:14–30)
    3. The Nobleman's Servants (Luke 19:11–27)
    4. The Servant's Role (Luke 17:7–10)
  C. About Prayer
    1. The Friend at Midnight (Luke 11:5–8)
    2. The Unjust Judge (Luke 18:1–8)
  D. About Neighbors
    1. The Good Samaritan (Luke 10:30–37)
  E. About Humility
    1. The Wedding Feast (Luke 14:7–11)
    2. The Proud Pharisee and the Corrupt Tax Collector (Luke 18:9–14)
  F. About Wealth
    1. The Rich Fool (Luke 12:16–21)
    2. The Great Feast (Luke 14:16–24)
    3. The Shrewd Manager (Luke 16:1–9)
II. Gospel Parables
  A. About God's Love
    1. The Lost Sheep (Matthew 18:12–14; Luke 15:3–7)
    2. The Lost Coin (Luke 15:8–10)
    3. The Lost Son (Luke 15:11–32)
  B. About Thankfulness
    1. The Forgiven Debts (Luke 7:41–43)
III. Parables of Judgment and the Future
  A. About Christ's Return
    1. The Ten Virgins (Matthew 25:1–13)
    2. The Wise and Faithful Servants (Matthew 24:45–51; Luke 12:42–48)
    3. The Traveling Owner of the House (Mark 13:34–37)
  B. About God's Values
    1. The Two Sons (Matthew 21:28–32)
    2. The Wicked Tenants (Matthew 21:33, 34; Mark 12:1–9; Luke 20:9–16)
    3. The Unproductive Fig Tree (Luke 13:6–9)
    4. The Marriage Feast (Matthew 22:1–14)
    5. The Unforgiving Servant (Matthew 18:23–35)

JESUS' MIRACLES

John and the other Gospel writers were able to record only a fraction of the people who were touched and healed by Jesus. But enough of Jesus' words and works have been saved so that we also might be able to know him and be his disciples in this day. There follows a listing of the miracles that are included in the Gospels. They were supernatural events that pointed people to God, and they were acts of love by one who is love.

	Matthew	Mark	Luke	John
Five thousand people are fed	14:15–21	6:35–44	9:12–17	6:5–14
Calming the storm	8:23–27	4:35–41	8:22–25	
Demons sent into the pigs	8:28–34	5:1–20	8:26–39	
Jairus's daughter raised	9:18–26	5:22–24, 35–43	8:41, 42, 49–56	
A sick woman is healed	9:20–22	5:25–34	8:43–48	
Jesus heals a paralytic	9:1–8	2:1–12	5:17–26	
A leper is healed at Gennesaret	8:1–4	1:40–45	5:12–15	
Peter's mother–in–law healed	8:14–17	1:29–31	4:38, 39	
A shriveled hand is restored	12:9–13	3:1–5	6:6–11	
A boy with an evil spirit is healed	17:14–21	9:14–29	9:37–42	
Jesus walks on the water	14:22–33	6:45–52		6:17–21
Blind Bartimaeus receives sight	20:29–34	10:46–52	18:35–43	
A girl is freed from a demon	15:21–28	7:24–30		
Four thousand are fed	15:32–38	8:1–9		
Cursing the fig tree	21:18–22	11:12–14, 20–24		
A centurion's servant is healed	8:5–13		7:1–10	
An evil spirit is sent out of a man		1:23–27	4:33–36	
A mute demoniac is healed	12:22		11:14	
Two blind men find sight	9:27–31			
Jesus heals the mute man	9:32, 33			
A coin in a fish's mouth	17:24–27			
A deaf and mute man is healed		7:31–37		
A blind man sees at Bethsaida		8:22–26		
The first miraculous catch of fish			5:1–11	
A widow's son is raised			7:11–16	
A crippled woman is healed			13:10–17	
Jesus heals a sick man			14:1–6	
Ten lepers are healed			17:11–19	
Jesus restores a man's ear			22:49–51	
Jesus turns water into wine				2:1–11
An official's son is healed at Cana				4:46–54
A lame man is healed				5:1–16
Jesus heals a man born blind				9:1–7
Lazarus is raised from the dead				11:1–45
The second miraculous catch of fish				21:1–14

	Old Testament Prophecies	New Testament Fulfillments
1. Messiah was to be born in Bethlehem	Micah 5:2	Matthew 2:1–6 Luke 2:1–20
2. Messiah was to be born of a virgin	Isaiah 7:14	Matthew 1:18–25 Luke 1:26–38
3. Messiah was to be a prophet like Moses	Deuteronomy 18:15, 18, 19	John 7:40
4. Messiah was to enter Jerusalem in triumph	Zechariah 9:9	Matthew 21:1–9 John 12:12–16
5. Messiah was to be rejected by his own people	Isaiah 53:1, 3 Psalm 118:22	Matthew 26:3, 4 John 12:37–43 Acts 4:1–12
6. Messiah was to be betrayed by one of his followers	Psalm 41:9	Matthew 26:14–16, 47–50 Luke 22:19–23
7. Messiah was to be tried and condemned	Isaiah 53:8	Luke 23:1–25 Matthew 27:1, 2
8. Messiah was to be silent before his accusers	Isaiah 53:7	Matthew 27:12–14 Mark 15:3, 4 Luke 23:8–10
9. Messiah was to be struck and spat on by his enemies	Isaiah 50:6	Matthew 26:67; 27:30 Mark 14:65
10. Messiah was to be mocked and insulted	Psalm 22:7, 8	Matthew 27:39–44 Luke 23:11, 35
11. Messiah was to die by crucifixion	Psalm 22:14, 16, 17	Matthew 27:31 Mark 15:20, 25
12. Messiah was to suffer with criminals and pray for his enemies	Isaiah 53:12	Matthew 27:38 Mark 15:27, 28 Luke 23:32–34
13. Messiah was to be given vinegar and gall	Psalm 69:21	Matthew 27:34 John 19:28–30
14. Others were to cast lots for Messiah's garments	Psalm 22:18	Matthew 27:35 John 19:23, 24
15. Messiah's bones were not to be broken	Exodus 12:46	John 19:31–36
16. Messiah was to die as a sacrifice for sin	Isaiah 53:5, 6, 8, 10, 11, 12	John 1:29; 11:49–52 Acts 10:43; 13:38, 39
17. Messiah was to be raised from the dead	Psalm 16:10	Acts 2:22–32 Matthew 28:1–10
18. Messiah is now at God's right hand	Psalm 110:1	Mark 16:19 Luke 24:50, 51

MESSIANIC PROPHECIES AND FULFILL-MENTS

For the Gospel writers, one of the main reasons for believing in Jesus was the way his life fulfilled the Old Testament prophecies about the Messiah. Following is a list of some of the main prophecies.

KEY PLACES IN ACTS

Modern names and boundaries are shown in gray.

The apostle Paul, whose missionary journeys fill much of this book, traveled tremendous distances as he tirelessly spread the gospel across much of the Roman empire. His combined trips, by land and sea, equal more than 13,000 air miles.

1 Judea Jesus ascended to heaven from the Mount of Olives, outside Jerusalem, and his followers returned to the city to await the infilling of the Holy Spirit, which occurred at Pentecost. Peter gave a powerful sermon that was heard by Jews from across the empire. The Jerusalem church grew, but Stephen was martyred for his faith by Jewish leaders who did not believe in Jesus (1:1—7:60).

2 Samaria After Stephen's death, persecution of Christians intensified, but it caused the believers to leave Jerusalem and spread the gospel to other cities in the empire. Philip took the gospel into Samaria, and even to a man from Ethiopia (8:1-40).

3 Syria Paul (Saul) began his story as a persecutor of Christians, only to be met by Jesus himself on the road to Damascus. He became a believer, but his new faith caused opposition, so he returned to Tarsus, his home, for safety. Barnabas sought out Paul in Tarsus and brought him to the church in Antioch in Syria, where they worked together. Meanwhile, Peter had received a vision that led him to Caesarea, where he presented the gospel to a Gentile family, who became believers (9:1—12:25).

4 Cyprus and Galatia Paul and Barnabas were dedicated by the church in Antioch in Syria for God's work of spreading the gospel to other cities. They set off on their first missionary journey through Cyprus and Galatia (13:1—14:28).

5 Jerusalem Controversy between Jewish Christians and Gentile Christians over the matter of keeping the law led to a special council, with delegates from the churches in Antioch and Jerusalem meeting in Jerusalem. Together, they resolved the conflict and the news was taken back to Antioch (15:1-35).

6 Macedonia Barnabas traveled to Cyprus while Paul took a second missionary journey. He revisited the churches in Galatia and headed toward Ephesus, but the Holy Spirit said no. So he turned north toward Bithynia and Pontus but again was told not to go. He then received the "Macedonian call," and followed the Spirit's direction into the cities of Macedonia (15:36—17:14).

7 Achaia Paul traveled from Macedonia to Athens and Corinth in Achaia, then traveled by ship to Ephesus before returning to Caesarea, Jerusalem, and finally back to Antioch (17:15—18:22).

8 Ephesus Paul's third missionary journey took him back through Cilicia and Galatia, this time straight to Ephesus in Asia. He visited other cities in Asia before going back to Macedonia and Achaia. He returned to Jerusalem by ship, despite his knowledge that arrest awaited him there (18:23—23:30).

9 Caesarea Paul was arrested in Jerusalem and taken to Antipatris, then on to Caesarea under Roman guard. Paul always took advantage of any opportunity to share the gospel, and he did so before many Gentile leaders. Because Paul appealed his case to Caesar, he began the long journey to Rome (23:31—26:32).

10 Rome After storms, layovers in Crete, and shipwreck on the island of Malta, Paul arrived in Sicily and finally in Italy, where he traveled by land, under guard, to his long-awaited destination: Rome, the capital of the empire (27:1—28:31).

ACTS

VITAL STATISTICS

PURPOSE:
To give an accurate account of the birth and growth of the Christian church

AUTHOR:
Luke (a Gentile physician)

ORIGINAL AUDIENCE:
Theophilus

DATE WRITTEN:
Between A.D. 63 and 70

SETTING:
Acts is the connecting link between Christ's life and the life of the church, between the Gospels and the Letters.

KEY VERSE:
"But you will receive power when the Holy Spirit comes on you; and you will be my witnesses in Jerusalem, and in all Judea, and Samaria, and to the ends of the earth" (1:8).

KEY PEOPLE:
Peter, John, James, Stephen, Philip, Paul, Barnabas, Cornelius, James (Jesus' brother), Timothy, Lydia, Silas, Titus, Apollos, Agabus, Ananias, Felix, Festus, Agrippa, Luke

KEY PLACES:
Jerusalem, Samaria, Lydda, Joppa, Antioch, Cyprus, Pisidian Antioch, Iconium, Lystra, Derbe, Philippi, Thessalonica, Berea, Athens, Corinth, Ephesus, Caesarea, Malta, Rome

SPECIAL FEATURES:
Acts is a sequel to the Gospel of Luke. Because Acts ends so abruptly, Luke may have planned to write a third book, continuing the story.

WITH a flick of a match, friction occurs and a spark leaps from match to tinder. A small flame burns the edges and grows, fueled by wood and air. Heat builds, and soon the kindling is licked by reddish orange tongues. Higher and wider it spreads, consuming the wood. The flame has become a fire.

Nearly 2,000 years ago, a match was struck in Palestine. At first, just a few in that corner of the world were touched and warmed, but the fire spread beyond Jerusalem and Judea out to the world and to all people. Acts provides an eyewitness account of the flame and fire—the birth and spread of the church. Beginning in Jerusalem with a small group of disciples, the message traveled across the Roman empire. Empowered by the Holy Spirit, this courageous band preached, taught, healed, and demonstrated love in synagogues, schools, homes, marketplaces, and courtrooms, and on streets, hills, ships, and desert roads—wherever God sent them, lives and history were changed.

Written by Luke as a sequel to his Gospel, Acts is an accurate historical record of the early church. But Acts is also a theological book, with lessons and living examples of the work of the Holy Spirit, church relationships and organization, the implications of grace, and the law of love. And Acts is an apologetic work, building a strong case for the validity of Christ's claims and promises.

The book of Acts begins with the outpouring of the promised Holy Spirit and the commencement of the proclamation of the gospel of Jesus Christ. This Spirit-inspired evangelism began in Jerusalem and eventually spread to Rome, covering most of the Roman empire. The gospel first went to the Jews, but they, as a nation, rejected it. A remnant of Jews, of course, gladly received the Good News. But the continual rejection of the gospel by the vast majority of the Jews led to the ever-increasing proclamation of the gospel to the Gentiles. This was according to Jesus' plan: The gospel was to go from Jerusalem, to Judea, to Samaria, and to the ends of the earth (1:8). This, in fact, is the pattern that the Acts narrative follows. The glorious proclamation began in Jerusalem (chapters 1—7), went to Judea and Samaria (chapters 8 and following), and to the countries beyond Judea (11:19; 13:4 and on to the end of Acts). The second half of Acts is focused primarily on Paul's missionary journeys to many countries north of the Mediterranean Sea. He, with his companions, took the gospel first to the Jews and then to the Gentiles. Some of the Jews believed, and many of the Gentiles received the Good News with joy. New churches were started, and new believers began to grow in the Christian life.

As you read Acts, put yourself in the place of the disciples: Identify with them as they are filled with the Holy Spirit, and experience the thrill of seeing thousands respond to the gospel message. Sense their commitment as they give every ounce of talent and treasure to Christ. And as you read, watch the Spirit-led boldness of these first-century believers, who through suffering and in the face of death take every opportunity to tell of their crucified and risen Lord. Then decide to be a twenty-first-century version of those men and women of God.

THE BLUEPRINT

A. PETER'S MINISTRY
(1:1—12:25)
1. Establishment of the church
2. Expansion of the church

After the resurrection of Jesus Christ, Peter preached boldly and performed many miracles. Peter's actions demonstrate vividly the source and effects of Christian power. Because of the Holy Spirit, God's people were empowered so they could accomplish their tasks. The Holy Spirit is still available to empower believers today. We should turn to the Holy Spirit to give us the strength, courage, and insight to accomplish our work for God.

B. PAUL'S MINISTRY
(13:1—28:31)
1. First missionary journey
2. The council at Jerusalem
3. Second missionary journey
4. Third missionary journey
5. Paul on trial

Paul's missionary adventures show us the progress of Christianity. The gospel could not be confined to one corner of the world. This was a faith that offered hope to all humanity. We, too, should venture forth and share in this heroic task to witness for Christ in all the world.

MEGATHEMES

THEME	EXPLANATION	IMPORTANCE
Church Beginnings	Acts is the history of how Christianity was founded and organized and solved its problems. The community of believers began by faith in the risen Christ and in the power of the Holy Spirit, who enabled them to witness, to love, and to serve.	New churches are continually being founded. By faith in Jesus Christ and through the power of the Holy Spirit, the church can be a vibrant agent for change. As we face new problems, Acts gives important remedies for solving them.
Holy Spirit	The church did not start or grow by its own power or enthusiasm. The disciples were empowered by God's Holy Spirit. He was the promised Counselor and Guide sent when Jesus went to heaven.	The Holy Spirit's work demonstrated that Christianity was supernatural. Thus, the church became more Holy Spirit-conscious than problem-conscious. By faith, any believer can claim the Holy Spirit's power to do Christ's work.
Church Growth	Acts presents the history of a dynamic, growing community of believers from Jerusalem to Syria, Africa, Asia, and Europe. In the first century, Christianity spread from believing Jews to non-Jews in 39 cities and 30 countries, islands, or provinces.	When the Holy Spirit works, there is movement, excitement, and growth. He gives us the motivation, energy, and ability to get the gospel to the whole world. How are you fitting into God's plan for spreading Christianity? What is your place in this movement?
Witnessing	Peter, John, Philip, Paul, Barnabas, and thousands more witnessed to their new faith in Christ. By personal testimony, preaching, or defense before authorities, they told the story with boldness and courage to groups of all sizes.	We are God's people, chosen to be part of his plan to reach the world. In love and by faith, we can have the Holy Spirit's help as we witness or preach. Witnessing is also beneficial to us because it strengthens our faith as we confront those who challenge it.
Opposition	Through imprisonment, beatings, plots, and riots, Christians were persecuted by both Jews and Gentiles. But the opposition became a catalyst for the spread of Christianity. Growth during times of oppression showed that Christianity was not the work of humans, but of God.	God can work through any opposition. When persecution from hostile unbelievers comes, realize that it has come because you have been a faithful witness and you have looked for the opportunity to present the Good News about Christ. Seize the opportunities that opposition brings.

A. PETER'S MINISTRY (1:1—12:25)

The book of Acts begins where the Gospels leave off, reporting the actions of the apostles and the work of the Holy Spirit. Beginning in Jerusalem, the church is established and grows rapidly, then faces intense persecution, which drives the believers out into the surrounding areas. Through this dispersion, Samaritans and Gentiles hear the Good News and believe.

1. Establishment of the church

Jesus Taken Up Into Heaven

1 In my former book,[a] Theophilus, I wrote about all that Jesus began to do and to teach [2]until the day he was taken up to heaven, after giving instructions [b] through the Holy Spirit to the apostles he had chosen. [3]After his suffering, he showed himself to these men and gave many convincing proofs that he was alive. He appeared to them[c] over a period of forty days and spoke about the kingdom of God. [4]On one occasion, while he was eating with them, he gave them this command:"Do not leave Jerusalem, but wait for the gift my Father promised, which you have heard me speak about.[d] [5]For John baptized with[a] water, but in a few days you will be baptized with the Holy Spirit."

[6]So when they met together, they asked him, "Lord, are you at this time going to restore the kingdom to Israel?"

[a]5 Or *in*

1:1
[a]Lk 1:1-4
1:2
[b]Mt 28:19, 20
1:3
[c]Mt 28:17
1:4
[d]Lk 24:49; Jn 14:16

1:1 In the book of Acts, Luke continues the story he began in his Gospel, covering the 30 years after Jesus was taken up into heaven. During that short time the church was established, and the gospel of salvation was spread throughout the world, even to the capital of the Roman empire. Those preaching the gospel, though ordinary people with human frailties and limitations, were empowered by the Holy Spirit to take the Good News "all over the world" (17:6). In the book of Acts we learn about the nature of the church and how we, like these early believers, can turn our world upside down.

1:1 Luke's former book was the Gospel of Luke; that book was also addressed to Theophilus, whose name means "one who loves God." (See note on Luke 1:3.)

1:1ff Verses 1–11 are the bridge between the events recorded in the Gospels and the events marking the beginning of the church. Jesus spent 40 days teaching his disciples, and they were changed drastically. Before the resurrection, they had argued with each other and had deserted their Lord. One of them (Peter) even lied about knowing Jesus. Here, in a series of meetings with the living, resurrected Christ, the disciples had many questions answered. They became convinced about the resurrection, learned about the kingdom of God, and discovered their power source—the Holy Spirit. By reading the Bible, we can sit with the resurrected Christ in his school of discipleship. By believing in him, we can receive his power through the Holy Spirit to be new people. By joining with other Christians in Christ's church, we can take part in doing his work on earth.

1:1–3 Luke says that the disciples were eyewitnesses to all that had happened to Jesus Christ—his life before his crucifixion ("suffering"), and the 40 days after his resurrection as he taught them more about the kingdom of God. Today people still doubt Jesus' resurrection. But Jesus appeared to the disciples on many occasions after his resurrection, proving that he was alive. Consider the change the resurrection made in the disciples' lives. At Jesus' death, they had scattered, were disillusioned, and feared for their lives. After seeing the resurrected Christ, they became fearless and risked everything to spread the Good News about him around the world. They faced imprisonment, beatings, rejection, and martyrdom, yet they never compromised their mission. These men would not have risked—and in some cases, given—their lives for something they knew was a fraud. They knew Jesus was alive, and the early church was fired with their enthusiasm to tell others. We need to know this so we can have confidence in their testimony. Twenty centuries later we can still be confident that our faith is based on fact.

1:3 Jesus explained that his coming inaugurated the kingdom of God. When he returned to heaven, God's kingdom would remain in the hearts of all believers through the presence of the Holy Spirit. But the kingdom of God will not be fully realized until Jesus Christ returns to judge all people and remove all evil from the world. Before that time, believers are to work to spread God's kingdom across the world. The book of Acts records how this work was begun. What the early church started, we must continue.

1:4, 5 The *Trinity* is a description of the unique relationship of God the Father, the Son, and the Holy Spirit. If Jesus had stayed on earth, his physical presence would have limited the spread of the gospel, because physically he could be in only one place at a time. After Christ was taken up into heaven, he would be spiritually present everywhere through the Holy Spirit. The Holy Spirit was sent so that God would be with and within his followers after Christ returned to heaven. The Spirit would comfort them, guide them to know his truth, remind them of Jesus' words, give them the right words to say, and fill them with power (see John 14—16).

1:5 At Pentecost (2:1–4) the Holy Spirit was made available to all who believed in Jesus. We receive the Holy Spirit (are baptized with him) when we receive Jesus Christ. The baptism of the Holy Spirit must be understood in the light of his total work in Christians.

(1) The Spirit marks the beginning of the Christian experience. We cannot belong to Christ without his Spirit (Romans 8:9); we cannot be united to Christ without his Spirit (1 Corinthians 6:17); we cannot be adopted as his children without his Spirit (Romans 8:14–17; Galatians 4:6, 7); we cannot be in the body of Christ except by baptism in the Spirit (1 Corinthians 12:13).

(2) The Spirit is the power of our new lives. He begins a lifelong process of change making us more like Christ (Galatians 3:3; Philippians 1:6). When we receive Christ by faith, we begin an immediate personal relationship with God. The Holy Spirit works in us to help us become like Christ.

(3) The Spirit unites the Christian community in Christ (Ephesians 2:19–22). The Holy Spirit can be experienced by all, and he works through all (1 Corinthians 12:11; Ephesians 4:4).

1:6 During the years of Jesus' ministry on earth, the disciples continually wondered about his kingdom. When would it come? What would be their role? In the traditional view, the Messiah would be an earthly conqueror who would free Israel from Rome. But the kingdom Jesus spoke about was, first of all, a *spiritual* kingdom established in the hearts and lives of believers (Luke 17:21). God's presence and power dwell in believers in the person of the Holy Spirit.

1:6, 7 Like other Jews, the disciples chafed under their Roman rulers. They wanted Jesus to free Israel from Roman power and then become their king. Jesus replied that God the Father sets the timetable for all events—worldwide, national, and personal. If you

1:7
e Mt 24:36

1:8
f Ac 2:1-4
g Lk 24:48

1:9
h ver 2

1:10
i Jn 20:12

7 He said to them:"It is not for you to know the times or dates the Father has set by his own authority. *e* 8 But you will receive power when the Holy Spirit comes on you; *f* and you will be my witnesses *g* in Jerusalem, and in all Judea and Samaria, and to the ends of the earth."

9 After he said this, he was taken up *h* before their very eyes, and a cloud hid him from their sight.

10 They were looking intently up into the sky as he was going, when suddenly two men dressed in white *i* stood beside them. 11 "Men of Galilee," they said, "why do you stand here looking into the sky? This same Jesus, who has been taken from you into heaven, will come back in the same way you have seen him go into heaven."

Matthias Chosen to Replace Judas

1:13
j Ac 9:37; 20:8
k Lk 6:14-16

1:14
l Lk 23:49, 55

12 Then they returned to Jerusalem from the hill called the Mount of Olives, a Sabbath day's walk *a* from the city. 13 When they arrived, they went upstairs to the room *j* where they were staying. Those present were Peter, John, James and Andrew; Philip and Thomas, Bartholomew and Matthew; James son of Alphaeus and Simon the Zealot, and Judas son of James. *k* 14 They all joined together constantly in prayer, along with the women *l* and Mary the mother of Jesus, and with his brothers.

1:17
m Jn 6:70, 71
n ver 25

1:18
o Mt 26:14, 15
p Mt 27:3-10

15 In those days Peter stood up among the believers *b* (a group numbering about a hundred and twenty) 16 and said, "Brothers, the Scripture had to be fulfilled which the Holy Spirit spoke long ago through the mouth of David concerning Judas, who served as guide for those who arrested Jesus— 17 he was one of our number *m* and shared in this ministry." *n* 18 (With the reward *o* he got for his wickedness, Judas bought a field; *p* there he fell headlong, his body burst open and all his intestines spilled out. 19 Everyone in Jerusalem heard about this, so they called that field in their language Akeldama, that is, Field of Blood.)

a 12 That is, about 3/4 mile (about 1,100 meters)   *b 15* Greek *brothers*

---

want changes that God isn't making immediately, don't become impatient. Instead, trust God's timetable.

1:8 The "power" believers receive from the Holy Spirit includes courage, boldness, confidence, insight, ability, and authority. The disciples would need all these gifts to fulfill their mission. If you believe in Jesus Christ, you can experience the power of the Holy Spirit in your life.

1:8 Jesus had instructed his disciples to witness to people of all nations about him (Matthew 28:19, 20). But they were told to wait first for the Holy Spirit (Luke 24:49). God has important work for you to do for him, but you must do it by the power of the Holy Spirit. We often like to get on with the job, even if it means running ahead of God. But waiting is sometimes part of God's plan. Are you waiting and listening for God's complete instructions, or are you running ahead of his plans? We need God's timing and power to be truly effective.

1:8 This verse describes a series of ever-widening circles. The gospel was to spread, geographically, from Jerusalem, into Judea and Samaria, and finally to the ends of the earth. It would begin with the devout Jews in Jerusalem and Samaria, spread to the mixed race in Samaria, and, finally, be offered to Gentiles all over the world. God's gospel has not reached its final destination if someone in your family, your workplace, your school, or your community hasn't heard the Good News about Jesus Christ. Make sure that you are contributing in some way to the ever-widening circle of God's loving message.

1:9–11 After 40 days with his disciples (1:3), Jesus returned to heaven. It was important for the disciples to see Jesus taken up into heaven; they knew without a doubt that he was God and that his home was in heaven. The two men dressed in white were angels who proclaimed to the disciples that one day Jesus would return in the same way he had gone—bodily and visibly. History is not haphazard or cyclical; it is moving toward a specific point— the return of Jesus to judge and rule over the earth. We should be ready for his sudden return (1 Thessalonians 5:2), not by standing around "looking into the sky," but by working hard to share the gospel so that others will be able to share in God's great blessings.

1:12, 13 After Christ was taken up into heaven, the disciples immediately returned to Jerusalem and had a prayer meeting. Jesus had said they would be baptized with the Holy Spirit in a few days, so they waited and prayed. When you face a difficult task, an important decision, or a baffling dilemma, don't rush into the work and just hope it comes out the way it should. Instead, make your first step prayer for the Holy Spirit's power and guidance.

1:13 A "Zealot" could mean anyone zealous for the Jewish law. The Zealots may have been a radical political party working for the violent overthrow of Roman rule in Israel.

1:14 At this time, Jesus' brothers were with the disciples. During Jesus' lifetime, they had not believed he was the Messiah (John 7:5), but his resurrection must have convinced them. Jesus' special appearance to James, one of his brothers, may have been an especially significant event in their conversion (see 1 Corinthians 15:7).

1:15–26 This was the first church business meeting. The small group of 11 had already grown to more than 120. The main order of business was to appoint a new disciple, or apostle, as the 12 were now called. While the apostles waited, they were doing what they could—praying, seeking God's guidance, and getting organized. Waiting for God to work does not mean sitting around doing nothing. We must do what we can, while we can, as long as we don't run ahead of God.

1:16, 17 How could someone who had been with Jesus daily betray him? Judas had received the same calling and teaching as everyone else. But he had chosen to reject Christ. Judas hardened his heart and joined in the plot with Jesus' enemies to put him to death. Judas remained unrepentant to the end, and he finally committed suicide. Although Jesus predicted this would happen, it was Judas's choice. Those privileged to be *close* to the truth are not necessarily *committed* to the truth. See Judas's Profile in Mark 14, p. 1647 for more information on his life.

1:18 Matthew says that Judas hanged himself (Matthew 27:5); Acts says that he fell. The traditional explanation is that when Judas hanged himself, the rope or branch broke, Judas fell, and his body burst open.

20"For," said Peter, "it is written in the book of Psalms,

"'May his place be deserted;
    let there be no one to dwell in it,'a q

and,

"'May another take his place of leadership.'b r

21Therefore it is necessary to choose one of the men who have been with us the whole time the Lord Jesus went in and out among us, 22beginning from John's baptism to the time when Jesus was taken up from us. For one of these must become a witness with us of his resurrection."

23So they proposed two men: Joseph called Barsabbas (also known as Justus) and Matthias. 24Then they prayed, "Lord, you know everyone's heart.s Show us which of these two you have chosen 25to take over this apostolic ministry, which Judas left to go where he belongs." 26Then they cast lots, and the lot fell to Matthias; so he was added to the eleven apostles.

The Holy Spirit Comes at Pentecost

2 When the day of Pentecost t came, they were all together in one place. 2Suddenly a sound like the blowing of a violent wind came from heaven and filled the whole house where they were sitting. u 3They saw what seemed to be tongues of fire that separated and came to rest on each of them. 4All of them were filled with the Holy Spirit and began to speak in other tonguesc v as the Spirit enabled them.

5Now there were staying in Jerusalem God-fearing Jews from every nation under heaven. 6When they heard this sound, a crowd came together in bewilderment, because each one heard them speaking in his own language. 7Utterly amazed, they asked: "Are not all these men who are speaking Galileans?w 8Then how is it that each of us hears them in his own native language? 9Parthians, Medes and Elamites; residents of Mesopotamia, Judea and Cappadocia, Pontus and Asia,x 10Phrygia and Pamphylia, Egypt and the parts of Libya near Cyrene; visitors from Rome 11(both Jews and converts to Judaism); Cretans and

a20 Psalm 69:25   b20 Psalm 109:8   c4 Or languages; also in verse 11

Cross references:
1:20 qPs 69:25; rPs 109:8
1:24 s1Sa 16:7; Jer 17:10; Rev 2:23
2:1 tLev 23:15, 16
2:2 uAc 4:31
2:4 vMk 16:17; 1Co 12:10
2:7 wAc 1:11
2:9 xAc 16:6

1:21, 22 Many consistently followed Jesus throughout his ministry on earth. The 12 disciples were his inner circle, but others shared the disciples' deep love for and commitment to Jesus.

1:21–25 The apostles had to choose a replacement for Judas Iscariot. They outlined specific criteria for making the choice. After finalists were chosen, the apostles prayed, asking God to guide the selection process. This gives us a good example of how to proceed when we are making important decisions. Set up criteria consistent with the Bible, examine the alternatives, and pray for wisdom and guidance to reach a wise decision.

1:26 The disciples became *apostles. Disciple* means follower or learner, and *apostle* means messenger or missionary. These men now had the special assignment of spreading the Good News of Jesus' death and resurrection.

2:1 Held 50 days after Passover, Pentecost was also called the Feast of Weeks. It was one of three major annual feasts (Deuteronomy 16:16), a festival of thanksgiving for the harvested crops. Jesus was crucified at Passover time, and he ascended 40 days after his resurrection. The Holy Spirit came 50 days after the resurrection, ten days after the ascension. Jews of many nations had gathered in Jerusalem for this festival. Thus Peter's speech (2:14ff) was given to an international audience, and it resulted in a worldwide harvest of new believers—the first converts to Christianity.

2:3, 4 This was a fulfillment of John the Baptist's words about the Holy Spirit's baptizing with fire (Luke 3:16), and of the prophet Joel's words about the outpouring of the Holy Spirit (Joel 2:28, 29).

Why tongues of fire? Tongues symbolize speech and the communication of the gospel. Fire symbolizes God's purifying presence, which burns away the undesirable elements of our lives and sets our hearts aflame to ignite the lives of others. On Mount Sinai, God confirmed the validity of the Old Testament law with fire from heaven (Exodus 19:16–18). At Pentecost, God confirmed the validity of the Holy Spirit's ministry by sending fire. At Mount Sinai, fire had come down on one place; at Pentecost, fire came down on many believers, symbolizing that God's presence is now available to all who believe in him.

2:3, 4 God made his presence known to this group of believers in a spectacular way—violent wind, fire, and his Holy Spirit. Would you like God to reveal himself to you in such recognizable ways? He may do so, but be wary of forcing your expectations on God. In 1 Kings 19:10–13, Elijah also needed a message from God. First came a great wind, then an earthquake, and finally a fire. But God's message came in a "gentle whisper." God may use dramatic methods to work in your life—or he may speak in gentle whispers. Wait patiently and always listen.

2:4–11 These people literally spoke in other languages—a miraculous attention-getter for the international crowd gathered in town for the feast. All the nationalities represented recognized their own languages being spoken. More than miraculous speaking drew people's attention, however; they saw the presence and power of the Holy Spirit. The apostles continued to minister in the Holy Spirit's power wherever they went.

2:7, 8 Christianity is not limited to any race or group of people. Christ offers salvation to all people without regard to nationality. Visitors in Jerusalem were surprised to hear the apostles and other believers speaking in languages other than their own, but they need not have been. God works all kinds of miracles to spread the gospel, using many languages as he calls all kinds

A JOURNEY THROUGH THE BOOK OF ACTS

Beginning with a brief summary of Jesus' last days on earth with his disciples, his ascension, and the selection of a replacement for Judas Iscariot, Luke moves quickly to his subject— the spread of the gospel and the growth of the church. Pentecost, highlighted by the filling of the Holy Spirit (2:1–13) and Peter's powerful sermon (2:14–42), was the beginning. Then the Jerusalem church grew daily through the bold witness of Peter and John and the love of the believers (2:43—4:37). The infant church was not without problems, however, with external opposition (resulting in imprisonment, beatings, and death) and internal deceit and complaining. Greek-speaking Jewish believers were appointed to help with the administration of the church to free the apostles to preach. Stephen and Philip were among the first deacons, and Stephen became the church's first martyr (5:1—8:3).

Instead of stopping Christianity, opposition and persecution served as catalysts for its spread because the believers took the message with them wherever they fled (8:4). Soon there were converts throughout **Samaria** and even in **Ethiopia** (8:5–40).

At this point, Luke introduces us to a bright young Jew, zealous for the law and intent on ridding Judaism of the Jesus heresy. But on the way to **Damascus** to capture believers, Saul was converted when he was confronted in person by the risen Christ (9:1–9). Through the ministry of Ananias and the sponsorship of Barnabas, Saul (Paul) was welcomed into the fellowship and then sent to **Tarsus** for safety (9:10–30).

Meanwhile, the church continued to thrive throughout **Judea, Galilee,** and **Samaria**. Luke recounts Peter's preaching and how Peter healed Aeneas in **Lydda** and Dorcas in **Joppa** (9:31–43). While in **Joppa,** Peter learned through a vision that he could take the gospel to the "unclean" Gentiles. Peter understood, and he faithfully shared the truth with Cornelius, whose entire household became believers (chapter 10). This was startling news to the **Jerusalem** church; but when Peter told his story, they praised God for his plan for *all* people to hear the Good News (11:1–18). This pushed the church into even wider circles as the message was preached to Greeks in **Antioch,** where Barnabas went to encourage the believers. Then he went on to **Tarsus** to find Saul (11:20–26).

To please the Jewish leaders, Herod joined in the persecution of the **Jerusalem** church, killing James (John's brother) and imprisoning Peter. But God freed Peter, and Peter walked from prison to a prayer meeting on his behalf at John Mark's house (chapter 12).

Here Luke shifts the focus to Paul's ministry. Commissioned by the **Antioch** church for a missionary tour (13:1–3), Paul and Barnabas took the gospel to **Cyprus** and south **Galatia** with great success (13:4—14:28). But the Jewish-Gentile controversy still smoldered, and with so many Gentiles responding to Christ, the controversy threatened to divide the church. So a council met in **Jerusalem** to rule on the relationship of Gentile Christians to the Old Testament laws. After hearing both sides, James (Jesus' brother and the leader of the Jerusalem church) resolved the issue and sent messengers to the churches with the decision (15:1–31).

After the council, Paul and Silas preached in **Antioch.** Then they left for **Syria** and **Cilicia** as Barnabas and Mark sailed for **Cyprus** (15:35–41). On this second missionary journey, Paul and Silas traveled throughout **Macedonia** and **Achaia,** establishing churches in **Philippi, Thessalonica, Berea, Corinth,** and **Ephesus** before returning to **Antioch** (16:1—18:22). Luke also tells of the ministry of Apollos (18:24–28).

On Paul's third missionary trip, he traveled through **Galatia, Phrygia, Macedonia,** and **Achaia,** encouraging and teaching the believers (19:1—21:9). During this time, he felt compelled to go to **Jerusalem;** and although he was warned by Agabus and others of impending imprisonment (21:10–12), he continued his journey in that direction.

While in **Jerusalem,** Paul was accosted in the temple by an angry mob and taken into protective custody by the Roman commander (21:17—22:29). Now we see Paul as a prisoner and on trial before the Jewish Sanhedrin (23:1–9), Governor Felix (23:23—24:27), and Festus and Agrippa (25:1—26:32). In each case, Paul gave a strong and clear witness for his Lord.

Because Paul appealed to Caesar, however, he was sent to **Rome** for the final hearing of his case. But on the way, the ship was destroyed in a storm, and the sailors and prisoners had to swim ashore. Even in this circumstance Paul shared his faith (27:1—28:10). Eventually the journey continued and Paul arrived in Rome, where he was held under house arrest while awaiting trial (28:11–31).

Luke ends Acts abruptly with the encouraging word that Paul had freedom in his captivity as he talked to visitors and guards, "boldly and without hindreance he preached the Kingdom of God and taught about the Lord Jesus Christ." (28:31).

---

of people to become his followers. No matter what your race, color, nationality, or language, God speaks to you. Are you listening?

2:9–11 Why are all these places mentioned? This is a list of many lands from which Jews had come to the festivals in Jerusalem. These Jews were not living in Palestine because they had been dispersed throughout the world through captivities and persecutions. Very likely, some of the Jews who responded to Peter's message returned to their homelands with God's

Good News of salvation. Thus God prepared the way for the spread of the gospel. As you read Acts, you will see how the way was often prepared for Paul and other messengers by people who had become believers at Pentecost. The church at Rome, for example, was probably begun by such Jewish believers.

Arabs—we hear them declaring the wonders of God in our own tongues!" 12Amazed and perplexed, they asked one another, "What does this mean?"

13Some, however, made fun of them and said, "They have had too much wine.ᵃ"

Peter Addresses the Crowd

14Then Peter stood up with the Eleven, raised his voice and addressed the crowd: "Fellow Jews and all of you who live in Jerusalem, let me explain this to you; listen carefully to what I say. 15These men are not drunk, as you suppose. It's only nine in the morning!ʸ 16No, this is what was spoken by the prophet Joel:

17 "'In the last days, God says,
    I will pour out my Spirit on all people.
Your sons and daughters will prophesy,
    your young men will see visions,
    your old men will dream dreams.
18 Even on my servants, both men and women,
    I will pour out my Spirit in those days,
    and they will prophesy.ᶻ
19 I will show wonders in the heaven above
    and signs on the earth below,
    blood and fire and billows of smoke.
20 The sun will be turned to darkness
    and the moon to bloodᵃ
    before the coming of the great and glorious day of the Lord.
21 And everyone who calls
    on the name of the Lord will be saved.'ᵇ ᵇ

22"Men of Israel, listen to this: Jesus of Nazareth was a man accredited by God to you by miracles, wonders and signs,ᶜ which God did among you through him,ᵈ as you yourselves know. 23This man was handed over to you by God's set purpose and foreknowledge;ᵉ and you, with the help of wicked men,ᶜ put him to death by nailing him to the cross. 24But God raised him from the dead,ᶠ freeing him from the agony of death, because it was impossible for death to keep its hold on him. 25David said about him:

2:15
ʸ1Th 5:7

2:18
ᶻAc 21:9-12

2:20
ᵃMt 24:29

2:21
ᵇRo 10:13

2:22
ᶜJn 4:48; Ac 10:38
ᵈJn 3:2

2:23
ᵉLk 22:22; Ac 3:18

2:24
ᶠ2Co 4:14;
Eph 1:20; Col 2:12;
Heb 13:20

ᵃ13 Or *sweet wine*   ᵇ21 Joel 2:28-32   ᶜ23 Or *of those not having the law* (that is, Gentiles)

2:12 When the gathered crowd recognized that something super-natural was taking place, they naturally wanted an explanation. At this point, Peter stepped forward and explained the truth about God. This should be the pattern in our lives as well. Hopefully we are living in such a way that people will see Christ in us. If we *do* shine and sparkle (Matthew 5:14; Philippians 2:15) and if we are "salty" (Matthew 5:13), we will get the attention of others. They will surely want to know what is so attractive and different about us. Then we can explain our "hope" (1 Peter 3:15). What is different about your life? What supernatural evidence would cause someone to stop you and say, "What does this mean?"

2:14 Peter had been an unstable leader during Jesus' ministry, letting his bravado be his downfall, even denying that he knew Jesus (John 18:15–18, 25–27). But Christ had forgiven and restored him (John 21). This was a new Peter, humble but bold. His confidence came from the Holy Spirit, who made him a power-ful and dynamic speaker. Have you ever felt as if you've made such bad mistakes that God could never forgive and use you? No matter what sins you have committed, God promises to forgive you and make you useful for his kingdom. Allow him to forgive you and use you effectively to serve him.

2:14ff Peter tells the people that they should listen to the testi-mony of the believers: because the Old Testament prophecies had been entirely fulfilled in Jesus (2:14–21), because Jesus is the Messiah (2:25–36), and because the risen Christ could change their lives (2:37–40).

2:16–21 Not everything mentioned in Joel 2:28, 29 was happen-ing that particular morning. The "last days" include all the days between Christ's first and second comings, and is another way of saying "from now on." "The great and glorious day of the Lord"

(2:20) denotes the whole Christian age. Even Moses yearned for the Lord to put his spirit on everyone (Numbers 11:29). At Pente-cost the Holy Spirit was released throughout the entire world—to men, women, slaves, Jews, Gentiles. Now *everyone* can receive the Spirit. This was a revolutionary thought for first-century Jews.

2:23 Everything that happened to Jesus was under God's control. His plans were never disrupted by the Roman government or the Jewish officials. This was especially comforting to those facing oppression during the time of the early Christian church.

2:24 Peter spoke forthrightly about the resurrection. As Peter preached, the events of Christ's death and resurrection were still hot news, less than two months old. Christ's execution had been carried out in public before many witnesses. His empty tomb was available for inspection just a short distance away. If Christ had not truly died, Peter's message would have been laughed at or ignored. If Christ had not been resurrected, authorities could have produced his body and put an end to this new faith. But Peter and the apostles had witnessed the risen Christ. Changed men, they announced the news with great passion and conviction.

Our faith and our credibility also rest on the truth of the empty tomb. Why? For a number of important reasons. According to the apostle Paul in 1 Corinthians 15, the resurrection of Christ means that he is the Son of God and that his word can be trusted. It means that his sacrifice for sin was acceptable to God, so we can be completely forgiven. It means that our Savior is alive and active, able to help us in times of need. It also means that one day we, too, will conquer death. The Christian faith rests on the basic fact of the empty tomb. Don't neglect this essential part of the gospel when you share your faith with others.

2:25–32 Peter quoted from Psalm 16:8–11—a psalm written by

> "'I saw the Lord always before me.
>   Because he is at my right hand,
>   I will not be shaken.
> 26 Therefore my heart is glad and my tongue rejoices;
>   my body also will live in hope,
> 27 because you will not abandon me to the grave,
>   nor will you let your Holy One see decay.
> 28 You have made known to me the paths of life;
>   you will fill me with joy in your presence.'a

2:29
g Ac 13:36

2:30
h 2Sa 7:12;
Ps 132:11

2:32
i ver 24
j Ac 1:8

2:33
k Ac 10:45

29 "Brothers, I can tell you confidently that the patriarch David died and was buried,g and his tomb is here to this day. 30 But he was a prophet and knew that God had promised him on oath that he would place one of his descendants on his throne. h 31 Seeing what was ahead, he spoke of the resurrection of the Christ,b that he was not abandoned to the grave, nor did his body see decay. 32 God has raised this Jesus to life,i and we are all witnessesj of the fact. 33 Exalted to the right hand of God, he has received from the Father the promised Holy Spirit and has poured outk what you now see and hear. 34 For David did not ascend to heaven, and yet he said,

2:35
l Ps 110:1

> "'The Lord said to my Lord:
>   "Sit at my right hand
> 35 until I make your enemies
>   a footstool for your feet."'c l

36 "Therefore let all Israel be assured of this: God has made this Jesus, whom you crucified, both Lord and Christ."

2:37
m Lk 3:10, 12, 14

2:38
n Lk 24:47; Ac 3:19

2:39
o Eph 2:13

37 When the people heard this, they were cut to the heart and said to Peter and the other apostles, "Brothers, what shall we do?" m

38 Peter replied, "Repent and be baptized, every one of you, in the name of Jesus Christ for the forgiveness of your sins. n And you will receive the gift of the Holy Spirit. 39 The promise is for you and your children and for all who are far offo—for all whom the Lord our God will call."

40 With many other words he warned them; and he pleaded with them, "Save yourselves from this corrupt generation." 41 Those who accepted his message were baptized, and about three thousand were added to their number that day.

The Fellowship of the Believers

42 They devoted themselves to the apostles' teaching and to the fellowship, to the breaking of bread and to prayer. 43 Everyone was filled with awe, and many wonders and miraculous signs were done by the apostles. 44 All the believers were together and had everything in

a 28 Psalm 16:8-11   b 31 Or *Messiah*. "The Christ" (Greek) and "the Messiah" (Hebrew) both mean "the Anointed One"; also in verse 36.   c 35 Psalm 110:1

David. He explained that David was not writing about himself, because David died and was buried (2:29). Instead, he was writing as a prophet (2:30) who spoke of the Messiah who would be resurrected. The audience understood "decay" (2:27) to mean the grave. The emphasis here is that Jesus' body was *not* left to decay but was in fact resurrected and glorified.

2:33 He "has poured out what you now see and hear" could be paraphrased, "gave Jesus the authority to send the Holy Spirit, with the results you are seeing and hearing today."

2:37 After Peter's powerful, Spirit-filled message, the people were deeply moved and asked, "What shall we do?" This is the basic question we must ask. It is not enough to be sorry for our sins—we must let God forgive them, and then we must live like forgiven people. Has God spoken to you through his Word or through the words of another believer? Like Peter's audience, ask God what you should do, and then obey.

2:38, 39 If you want to follow Christ, you must "repent and be baptized." To repent means to *turn from* sin, changing the direction of your life from selfishness and rebellion against God's laws. At the same time, you must *turn to* Christ, depending on him for forgiveness, mercy, guidance, and purpose. We cannot save

ourselves—only God can save us. Baptism identifies us with Christ and with the community of believers. It is a condition of discipleship and a sign of faith.

2:40–43 About 3,000 people became new believers when Peter preached the Good News about Christ. These new Christians were united with the other believers, taught by the apostles, and included in the prayer meetings and fellowship. New believers in Christ need to be in groups where they can learn God's Word, pray, and mature in the faith. If you have just begun a relationship with Christ, seek out other believers for fellowship, prayer, and teaching. This is the way to grow.

2:44 Recognizing the other believers as brothers and sisters in the family of God, the Christians in Jerusalem shared all they had so that all could benefit from God's gifts. It is tempting—especially if we have material wealth—to cut ourselves off from one another, each taking care of his or her own interests, each providing for and enjoying his or her own little piece of the world. But as part of God's spiritual family, it is our responsibility to help one another in every way possible. God's family works best when its members work together.

common. p 45 Selling their possessions and goods, they gave to anyone as he had need. 46 Every day they continued to meet together in the temple courts. They broke bread q in their homes and ate together with glad and sincere hearts, 47 praising God and enjoying the favor of all the people. And the Lord added to their number r daily those who were being saved.

Peter Heals the Crippled Beggar

3 One day Peter and John were going up to the temple at the time of prayer—at three in the afternoon. s 2 Now a man crippled from birth t was being carried to the temple gate called Beautiful, where he was put every day to beg from those going into the temple courts. 3 When he saw Peter and John about to enter, he asked them for money. 4 Peter looked straight at him, as did John. Then Peter said, "Look at us!" 5 So the man gave them his attention, expecting to get something from them.

6 Then Peter said, "Silver or gold I do not have, but what I have I give you. In the name of Jesus Christ of Nazareth, u walk." 7 Taking him by the right hand, he helped him up, and instantly the man's feet and ankles became strong. 8 He jumped to his feet and began to walk. Then he went with them into the temple courts, walking and jumping, and praising God. 9 When all the people v saw him walking and praising God, 10 they recognized him as the same man who used to sit begging at the temple gate called Beautiful, and they were filled with wonder and amazement at what had happened to him.

Peter Speaks to the Onlookers

11 While the beggar held on to Peter and John, all the people were astonished and came running to them in the place called Solomon's Colonnade. w 12 When Peter saw this, he said to them: "Men of Israel, why does this surprise you? Why do you stare at us as if by our own power or godliness we had made this man walk? 13 The God of Abraham, Isaac and Jacob, the God of our fathers, x has glorified his servant Jesus. You handed him over to be killed, and you disowned him before Pilate, y though he had decided to let him go. 14 You disowned the Holy z and Righteous One a and asked that a murderer be released to you. 15 You killed the

2:44
p Ac 4:32
2:46
q Ac 20:7
2:47
r Ac 5:14

3:1
s Ps 55:17
3:2
t Ac 14:8

3:6
u Ac 4:10

3:9
v Ac 4:16, 21

3:11
w Jn 10:23; Ac 5:12

3:13
x Ac 5:30
y Mt 27:2

3:14
z Mk 1:24; Ac 4:27
a Ac 7:52

2:46 A common misconception about the first Christians (who were Jews) was that they rejected the Jewish religion. But these believers saw Jesus' message and resurrection as the fulfillment of everything they knew and believed from the Old Testament. The Jewish believers at first did not separate from the rest of the Jewish community. They still went to the temple and synagogues for worship and instruction in the Scriptures. But their belief in Jesus created great friction with Jews who didn't believe that Jesus was the Messiah. Thus, believing Jews were forced to meet in private homes for communion, prayer, and teaching about Christ. By the end of the first century, many of these Jewish believers were excommunicated from their synagogues.

2:47 A healthy Christian community attracts people to Christ. The Jerusalem church's zeal for worship and brotherly love was contagious. A healthy, loving church will grow in numbers. What are you doing to make your church the kind of place that will attract others to Christ?

3:1 The Jews observed three times of prayer—morning (9:00 a.m.), afternoon (3:00 p.m.), and evening (sunset). At these times devout Jews and Gentiles who believed in God often would go to the temple to pray. Peter and John were going to the temple at 3:00 p.m.

3:2 The gate called Beautiful was an entrance to the temple, not to the city. It was one of the favored entrances, and many people passed through it on their way to worship. Giving money to beggars was considered praiseworthy in the Jewish religion. So the beggar wisely placed himself where he would be seen by the most people who were on their way to worship at the temple.

3:5, 6 The crippled man asked for money, but Peter gave him something much better—the use of his legs. We often ask God to solve a small problem, but he wants to give us a whole new life and help for *all* our problems. When we ask God for help, he may say, "I've got something even better for you." Ask God for what you want, but don't be surprised when he gives you what you really *need*.

3:6 "In the name of Jesus Christ" means "by the authority of Jesus Christ." The apostles were doing this healing through the Holy Spirit's power, not their own.

3:7–10 In his excitement, the formerly crippled man began to jump and walk around. He also praised God! Then others were awed by God's power. Don't forget to thank people who help you, but also remember to praise God for his care and protection.

3:11 Solomon's Colonnade was part of the temple complex built by King Herod the Great in an attempt to strengthen his relationship with the Jews. A colonnade is an entrance or porch supported by columns. Jesus taught and performed miracles in the temple many times. When the apostles went to the temple, they were undoubtedly in close proximity to the same religious leaders who had conspired to put Jesus to death.

3:11ff Peter had an audience, and he capitalized on the opportunity to share Jesus Christ. He clearly presented his message by telling (1) who Jesus is, (2) how the Jews had rejected him, (3) why their rejection was fatal, and (4) what they needed to do to change the situation. Peter told the crowd that they still had a choice; God still offered them the opportunity to believe and receive Jesus as their Messiah and as their Lord. Displays of God's mercy and grace, such as the healing of this crippled man, often create teachable moments. Pray to have courage like Peter to see these opportunities and to use them to speak up for Christ.

3:13, 14 Pilate had decided to release Jesus, but the people had clamored to have Barabbas, a murderer, released instead (see Luke 23:13–25). When Peter said "You handed him over to be killed," he meant it literally. Jesus' trial and death had occurred right there in Jerusalem only weeks earlier. It wasn't an event of the distant past—most of these people had heard about it, and some may very well have taken part in condemning Jesus.

3:15 The religious leaders thought they had put an end to Jesus when they crucified him. But their confidence was shaken when Peter told them that Jesus was alive again and that this time they could not harm him. Peter's message emphasized that (1) the

3:15
b Ac 2:24

3:17
c Lk 23:34
d Ac 13:27

3:18
e Ac 26:22, 23

3:19
f Ac 2:38

3:21
g Ac 1:11
h Mt 17:11
i Lk 1:70

3:22
j Dt 18:15, 18;
Ac 7:37

3:25
k Ac 2:39
l Ro 9:4, 5

3:26
m Ac 13:46

4:1
n Lk 22:4

author of life, but God raised him from the dead.*b* We are witnesses of this. 16By faith in the name of Jesus, this man whom you see and know was made strong. It is Jesus' name and the faith that comes through him that has given this complete healing to him, as you can all see.

17"Now, brothers, I know that you acted in ignorance,*c* as did your leaders.*d* 18But this is how God fulfilled what he had foretold through all the prophets, saying that his Christ *a* would suffer.*e* 19Repent, then, and turn to God, so that your sins may be wiped out,*f* that times of refreshing may come from the Lord, 20and that he may send the Christ, who has been appointed for you—even Jesus. 21He must remain in heaven*g* until the time comes for God to restore everything,*h* as he promised long ago through his holy prophets.*i* 22For Moses said, 'The Lord your God will raise up for you a prophet like me from among your own people; you must listen to everything he tells you.*j* 23Anyone who does not listen to him will be completely cut off from among his people.'*b*

24"Indeed, all the prophets from Samuel on, as many as have spoken, have foretold these days. 25And you are heirs*k* of the prophets and of the covenant*l* God made with your fathers. He said to Abraham, 'Through your offspring all peoples on earth will be blessed.'*c* 26When God raised up his servant, he sent him first*m* to you to bless you by turning each of you from your wicked ways."

Peter and John Before the Sanhedrin

4 The priests and the captain of the temple guard*n* and the Sadducees came up to Peter and John while they were speaking to the people. 2They were greatly disturbed because the apostles were teaching the people and proclaiming in Jesus the resurrection of the dead.

a 18 Or Messiah; also in verse 20   *b 23 Deut. 18:15,18,19   *c 25 Gen. 22:18; 26:4

---

people and their religious leaders had killed Jesus (3:17), (2) God had brought him back to life, and (3) the apostles had been witnesses to this fact. After pointing out the sin and injustice of these leaders, Peter showed the significance of the resurrection, God's triumph and power over death.

3:16 Jesus, not the apostles, received the glory for the healing of the crippled man. In those days a man's name represented his character; it stood for his authority and power. By using Jesus' name, Peter showed who gave him the authority and power to heal. The apostles did not emphasize what *they* could do, but what God could do through them. Jesus' name is not to be used as magic—it must be used in faith. When we pray in Jesus' name, we must remember that it is Christ himself, not merely the sound of his name, who gives our prayers their power.

3:18 Some of these prophecies are in Psalm 22 and Isaiah 50:6 and Isaiah 53. Peter was explaining the kind of Messiah God had sent to earth. The Jews had expected a great ruler, not a suffering servant.

3:19 John the Baptist had prepared the way for Jesus by preaching repentance. The apostles' message of salvation also included the call to repentance—acknowledging personal sin and turning away from it. Many people want the benefits of being identified with Christ without admitting their own disobedience and turning from sin. The key to forgiveness is confessing your sin and turning from it (see 2:38).

3:19, 20 When we repent, God promises not only to wipe out our sins, but to bring spiritual refreshment. Repentance may at first seem painful because it is hard to give up certain sins. But God will give you a better way. As Hosea promised, "Let us acknowledge the Lord; let us press on to acknowledge him. As surely as the sun rises, he will appear; he will come to us like the winter rains, like the spring rains that water the earth" (Hosea 6:3). Do you feel a need to be refreshed?

3:21 The time when God will "restore everything" refers to the second coming, the Last Judgment, and the removal of sin from the world.

3:21, 22 Most Jews thought that Joshua was this prophet predicted by Moses (Deuteronomy 18:15). Peter was saying that the prophet was Jesus Christ. Peter wanted to show that their long-awaited Messiah had come! He and all the apostles were calling

the Jewish nation to realize what they had done to their Messiah, to repent, and to believe. From this point on in Acts, we see many Jews rejecting the gospel. So the message went also to the Gentiles, many of whom were open to receive Jesus.

3:24 The prophet Samuel had lived during the transition between the judges and the kings of Israel, and he had been seen as the first in a succession of prophets. Samuel anointed David king, founding David's royal line, from which the Messiah eventually came. All the prophets pointed to a future Messiah. For more on Samuel, see his Profile in 1 Samuel 8, p. 403.

3:25 God had promised Abraham that he would bless the world through Abraham's descendants, the Jewish race (Genesis 12:3), from which the Messiah would come. God intended the Jewish nation to be a separate and holy nation that would teach the world about God, introduce the Messiah, and then carry on his work in the world. After the days of Solomon, the nation gave up its mission to tell the world about God. Here too, in apostolic times as well as in the time Jesus spent on earth, the Jews rejected their Messiah.

4:1 These priests may have been chief priests, who had special influence and were often close relatives of the high priests. The captain of the temple guard was the leader of the guards who were set around the temple to ensure order. The Sadducees were members of a small but powerful Jewish religious sect that did not believe in the resurrection of the dead. They were the religious leaders who stood to gain financially by cooperating with the Romans. Most of those who planned and carried out Jesus' arrest and crucifixion were from these three groups.

4:2, 3 Peter and John spoke to the people during the afternoon prayer time. The Sadducees moved in quickly to investigate. Because they did not believe in the resurrection, they were understandably disturbed with what the apostles were saying. Peter and John were refuting one of their fundamental beliefs and thus threatening their authority as religious teachers. Even though the nation was under Roman rule, the Sadducees had almost unlimited power over the temple grounds. Thus they were able to arrest Peter and John for no other reason than teaching something that contradicted their beliefs.

3 They seized Peter and John, and because it was evening, they put them in jail⁰ until the next day. 4 But many who heard the message believed, and the number of men grew to about five thousand.

5 The next day the rulers, elders and teachers of the law met in Jerusalem. 6 Annas the high priest was there, and so were Caiaphas, ᴾ John, Alexander and the other men of the high priest's family. 7 They had Peter and John brought before them and began to question them: "By what power or what name did you do this?"

8 Then Peter, filled with the Holy Spirit, said to them: "Rulers and elders of the people! �q 9 If we are being called to account today for an act of kindness shown to a cripple and are asked how he was healed, 10 then know this, you and all the people of Israel: It is by the name of Jesus Christ of Nazareth, whom you crucified but whom God raised from the dead, that this man stands before you healed. 11 He is

> "'the stone you builders rejected,
> which has become the capstone.ᵃ'ᵇ ʳ

12 Salvation is found in no one else, for there is no other name under heaven given to men by which we must be saved." ˢ

13 When they saw the courage of Peter and John and realized that they were unschooled, ordinary men, ᵗ they were astonished and they took note that these men had been with Jesus. 14 But since they could see the man who had been healed standing there with them, there was nothing they could say. 15 So they ordered them to withdraw from the Sanhedrin and then conferred together. 16 "What are we going to do with these men?" ᵘ they asked. "Everybody living in Jerusalem knows they have done an outstanding miracle, ᵛ and we cannot deny it. 17 But to stop this thing from spreading any further among the people, we must warn these men to speak no longer to anyone in this name."

18 Then they called them in again and commanded them not to speak or teach at all in the name of Jesus. ʷ 19 But Peter and John replied, "Judge for yourselves whether it is right in God's sight to obey you rather than God. ˣ 20 For we cannot help speaking about what we have seen and heard."

ᵃ 11 Or *cornerstone*   ᵇ 11 Psalm 118:22

**Cross references (right margin):**

4:3 ⁰ Ac 5:18

4:6 ᴾ Mt 26:3; Lk 3:2

4:8 q Lk 23:13

4:11 ʳ Ps 118:22; Mt 21:42

4:12 ˢ Mt 1:21; Ac 10:43; 1Ti 2:5

4:13 ᵗ Mt 11:25

4:16 ᵘ Jn 11:47; ᵛ Ac 3:6-10

4:18 ʷ Ac 5:40

4:19 ˣ Ac 5:29

4:3 Seldom will sharing the gospel send us to jail as it did Peter and John. Still, we run risks in trying to win others to Christ. We might be willing to face a night in jail if it would bring 5,000 people to Christ, but shouldn't we also be willing to suffer for the sake of even one? What do you risk in witnessing—rejection, persecution? Whatever the risks, realize that nothing done for God is ever wasted.

4:5, 6 The rulers, elders, and teachers of the law made up the Jewish council—the same council that had condemned Jesus to death (Luke 22:66). It had 70 members plus the current high priest, who presided over the group. The Sadducees held a majority in this ruling group. These were the wealthy, intellectual, and powerful men of Jerusalem. Jesus' followers stood before the same council that Jesus had.

4:6 Annas had been deposed as high priest by the Romans, who then had appointed Caiaphas, Annas's son-in-law, in his place. Because the Jews considered the office of high priest a lifetime position, however, they still called Annas by that title and gave him respect and authority within the council. Annas and Caiaphas had played significant roles in Jesus' trial (John 18:24, 28). They were not pleased that the man they thought they had sacrificed for the good of the nation (John 11:49–51) had followers who were just as persistent and who promised to be just as troublesome as he had been.

4:7 The council asked Peter and John by what power they had healed the man (3:6, 7) and by what authority they preached (3:12–26). The actions and words of Peter and John threatened these religious leaders who, for the most part, were more interested in their reputations and positions than in God. Through the help of the Holy Spirit (Mark 13:11), Peter spoke boldly before the council, actually putting the council on trial by showing them that the One they had crucified had risen again. Instead of being

defensive, the apostles went on the offensive, boldly speaking out for God and presenting the gospel to these leaders.

4:11 The capstone unites the two sides of an arch and holds it together. Peter said that the Jews rejected Christ, but now Christ has become the capstone of the church (Psalm 118:22; Mark 12:10; 1 Peter 2:7). Without him there would be no church, because it wouldn't be able to stand.

4:12 Many people react negatively to the fact that there is no other name than that of Jesus to call on for salvation. Yet this is not something the church decided; it is the specific teaching of Jesus himself (John 14:6). If God designated Jesus to be the Savior of the world, no one else can be his equal. Christians are to be open-minded on many issues, but not on how we are saved from sin. No other religious teacher could die for our sins; no other religious teacher came to earth as God's only Son; no other religious teacher rose from the dead. Our focus should be on Jesus, whom God offered as the way to have an eternal relationship with himself. There is no other name or way!

4:13 Knowing that Peter and John were untrained, the council was amazed at what being with Jesus had done for them. A changed life convinces people of Christ's power. One of your greatest testimonies is the difference others see in your life and attitudes since you have believed in Christ.

4:13–18 Although the evidence was overwhelming and irrefutable (changed lives and a healed man), the religious leaders refused to believe in Christ and continued to try to suppress the truth. Don't be surprised if some people reject you and your positive witness for Christ. When minds are closed, even the clearest presentation of the facts can't open them. But don't give up either. Pray for those people and continue to spread the gospel.

4:20 We sometimes may be afraid to share our faith in Christ because people might feel uncomfortable and might reject us. But

4:21
y Ac 5:26

21After further threats they let them go. They could not decide how to punish them, because all the people y were praising God for what had happened. 22 For the man who was miraculously healed was over forty years old.

The Believers' Prayer

23 On their release, Peter and John went back to their own people and reported all that the chief priests and elders had said to them. 24 When they heard this, they raised their voices together in prayer to God. "Sovereign Lord," they said, "you made the heaven and the earth and the sea, and everything in them. 25 You spoke by the Holy Spirit through the mouth of your servant, our father David:

4:26
z Ps 2:1, 2

"'Why do the nations rage
 and the peoples plot in vain?
26 The kings of the earth take their stand
 and the rulers gather together
against the Lord
 and against his Anointed One.ª 'b z

4:28
ª Ac 2:23

4:29
b ver 13, 31

4:30
c ver 27

4:31
d Ac 2:2

27 Indeed Herod and Pontius Pilate met together with the Gentiles and the people c of Israel in this city to conspire against your holy servant Jesus, whom you anointed. 28 They did what your power and will had decided beforehand should happen. ª 29 Now, Lord, consider their threats and enable your servants to speak your word with great boldness. b 30 Stretch out your hand to heal and perform miraculous signs and wonders through the name of your holy servant Jesus." c

31After they prayed, the place where they were meeting was shaken. d And they were all filled with the Holy Spirit and spoke the word of God boldly.

The Believers Share Their Possessions

4:32
e Ac 2:44

4:34
f Ac 2:45

4:35
g ver 37; Ac 5:2
h Ac 2:45

32All the believers were one in heart and mind. No one claimed that any of his possessions was his own, but they shared everything they had. e 33 With great power the apostles continued to testify to the resurrection of the Lord Jesus, and much grace was upon them all. 34 There were no needy persons among them. For from time to time those who owned lands or houses sold them, f brought the money from the sales 35 and put it at the apostles' feet, g and it was distributed to anyone as he had need. h

ª26 That is, Christ or Messiah   b26 Psalm 2:1,2   c27 The Greek is plural.

Peter and John's zeal for the Lord was so strong that they could not keep quiet, even when threatened. If your courage to witness for God has weakened, pray that your boldness may increase. Remember Jesus' promise, "Whoever acknowledges me before men, I will also acknowledge him before my Father in heaven" (Matthew 10:32).

4:24–30 Notice how the believers prayed. First they praised God; then they told God their specific problem and asked for his help. They did not ask God to remove the problem, but to help them deal with it. We can follow this model when we pray. We may ask God to remove our problems, and he may choose to do so. But we must recognize that often he will leave the problem in place and give us the strength and courage to deal with it.

4:27 This Herod was Herod Antipas, appointed by the Romans to rule over the territory of Galilee. For more information on Herod, see his Profile in Mark 6, p. 1621. Pontius Pilate was the Roman governor over Judea. He bowed to pressure from the crowd and sentenced Jesus to death. For more information on Pilate, see his Profile in Mark 15, p. 1653.

4:28 God is the sovereign Lord of all events who rules history to fulfill his purposes. What his will determines, his power carries out. No leader, army, government, or council can stand in God's way.

4:29–31 Boldness is not reckless impulsiveness. Boldness requires courage to press on through our fears and do what we know is right. How can we be more bold? Like the disciples, we need to pray with others. To gain boldness, you can (1) pray for the power of the Holy Spirit to give you courage, (2) look for

opportunities in your family and neighborhood to talk about Christ, (3) realize that rejection, social discomfort, and embarrassment are not necessarily persecution, and (4) start where you are by being bolder in small ways.

4:32 Differences of opinion are inevitable among human personalities and can actually be helpful, if handled well. But spiritual unity is essential—loyalty, commitment, and love for God and his Word. Without spiritual unity, the church could not survive. Paul wrote the letter of 1 Corinthians to urge the church in Corinth toward greater unity.

4:32 None of these Christians felt that what they had was their own, so they were able to give and share, eliminating poverty among them. They would not let a brother or sister suffer when others had plenty. How do you feel about your possessions? We should adopt the attitude that everything we have comes from God, and we are only sharing what is already his.

4:32–35 The early church was able to share possessions and property as a result of the unity brought by the Holy Spirit working in and through the believers' lives. This way of living is different from communism because (1) the sharing was voluntary; (2) it didn't involve *all* private property, but only as much as was needed; (3) it was not a membership requirement in order to be a part of the church. The spiritual unity and generosity of these early believers attracted others to them. This organizational structure is not a Biblical command, but it offers vital principles for us to follow.

36 Joseph, a Levite from Cyprus, whom the apostles called Barnabas (which means Son of Encouragement), 37 sold a field he owned and brought the money and put it at the apostles' feet. *i*

4:37
i ver 35; Ac 5:2

Ananias and Sapphira

5 Now a man named Ananias, together with his wife Sapphira, also sold a piece of property. 2 With his wife's full knowledge he kept back part of the money for himself, but brought the rest and put it at the apostles' feet.

3 Then Peter said, "Ananias, how is it that Satan has so filled your heart that you have lied to the Holy Spirit *j* and have kept for yourself some of the money you received for the land? 4 Didn't it belong to you before it was sold? And after it was sold, wasn't the money at your disposal? What made you think of doing such a thing? You have not lied to men but to God."

5:3
j ver 9

5 When Ananias heard this, he fell down and died. *k* And great fear *l* seized all who heard what had happened. 6 Then the young men came forward, wrapped up his body, *m* and carried him out and buried him.

5:5
k ver 10
l ver 11

7 About three hours later his wife came in, not knowing what had happened. 8 Peter asked her, "Tell me, is this the price you and Ananias got for the land?"

5:6
m Jn 19:40

"Yes," she said, "that is the price."

9 Peter said to her, "How could you agree to test the Spirit of the Lord? *n* Look! The feet of the men who buried your husband are at the door, and they will carry you out also."

5:9
n ver 3

10 At that moment she fell down at his feet and died. *o* Then the young men came in and, finding her dead, carried her out and buried her beside her husband. 11 Great fear *p* seized the whole church and all who heard about these events.

5:10
o ver 5
5:11
p ver 5

The Apostles Heal Many

12 The apostles performed many miraculous signs and wonders among the people. And all the believers used to meet together in Solomon's Colonnade. *q* 13 No one else dared join them, even though they were highly regarded by the people. *r* 14 Nevertheless, more and more men and women believed in the Lord and were added to their number. 15 As a result, people brought the sick into the streets and laid them on beds and mats so that at least Peter's shadow might fall on some of them as he passed by. *s* 16 Crowds gathered also from the towns around Jerusalem, bringing their sick and those tormented by evil *a* spirits, and all of them were healed.

5:12
q Ac 3:11
5:13
r Ac 2:47; 4:21
5:15
s Ac 19:12

a 16 Greek *unclean*

4:36 Barnabas (Joseph) was a respected leader of the church. He was a Levite by birth, a member of the Jewish tribe that carried out temple duties. But his family had moved to Cyprus, so Barnabas didn't serve in the temple. He traveled with Paul on Paul's first missionary journey (13:1ff). For more information on Barnabas, see his Profile in chapter 13, p. 1837.

5:1ff In Acts 5:1—8:3 we see both internal and external problems facing the early church. Inside, the church had dishonesty (5:1–11) and administrative headaches (6:1–7). Outside, the church was being pressured by persecution. While church leaders were careful and sensitive in dealing with the internal problems, they could not do much to prevent the external pressures. Through it all, the leaders kept their focus on what was most important—spreading the gospel of Jesus Christ.

5:3 Even after the Holy Spirit had come, the believers were not immune to Satan's temptations. Although Satan was defeated by Christ at the cross, he was still actively trying to make the believers stumble—as he does today (Ephesians 6:12; 1 Peter 5:8). Satan's overthrow is inevitable, but it will not occur until the last days, when Christ returns to judge the world (Revelation 20:10).

5:3ff The sin Ananias and Sapphira committed was not stinginess or holding back part of the money—it was their choice whether or not to sell the land and how much to give. Their sin was lying to God and God's people—saying they gave the whole amount but holding back some for themselves and trying to make themselves appear more generous than they really were. This act was judged harshly because dishonesty, greed, and covetousness are destructive in a church, preventing the Holy Spirit from work-

ing effectively. All lying is bad, but when we lie to try to deceive God and his people about our relationship with him, we destroy our testimony about Christ.

5:11 Some read the account of Ananias and Sapphira being struck down and accuse God of being harsh. "I thought God was supposed to be loving and forgiving. I thought all that wrath stuff was for Old Testament times." With an emphasis on grace and mercy, it's easy to overlook the equally important truth of God's holiness. We must remember that God has not changed (Malachi 3:6). He still hates sin as much as he ever did. God's judgment on Ananias and Sapphira produced shock and fear among the believers, making them realize how seriously God regards sin in the church.

5:14 What makes Christianity attractive? It is easy to be drawn to churches because of programs, good speakers, size, beautiful facilities, or fellowship. People were attracted to the early church, however, by expressions of God's power at work, the generosity, sincerity, honesty, and unity of the members, and the character of the leaders. Have our standards slipped? God wants to add believers to his *church*, not just newer and better programs or larger and fancier facilities.

5:15, 16 People who passed within Peter's shadow were healed, not by Peter's shadow, but by God's power working through Peter. What did these miraculous healings do for the early church? (1) They attracted new believers. (2) They confirmed the truth of the apostles' teaching. (3) They demonstrated that the power of the Messiah who had been crucified and risen was now with his followers.

The Apostles Persecuted

5:17
t Ac 4:1

17Then the high priest and all his associates, who were members of the party of the Sadducees,*t* were filled with jealousy. **18**They arrested the apostles and put them in the public jail. **19**But during the night an angel of the Lord opened the doors of the jail and brought them out. **20**"Go, stand in the temple courts," he said, "and tell the people the full message of this new life."*u*

5:20
u Jn 6:63, 68

5:21
v Ac 4:5, 6

21At daybreak they entered the temple courts, as they had been told, and began to teach the people.

When the high priest and his associates *v* arrived, they called together the Sanhedrin—the full assembly of the elders of Israel—and sent to the jail for the apostles. **22**But on arriving at the jail, the officers did not find them there. So they went back and reported, **23**"We found the jail securely locked, with the guards standing at the doors; but when we opened them, we found no one inside." **24**On hearing this report, the captain of the temple guard and the chief priests *w* were puzzled, wondering what would come of this.

5:24
w Ac 4:1

25Then someone came and said, "Look! The men you put in jail are standing in the temple courts teaching the people." **26**At that, the captain went with his officers and brought the apostles. They did not use force, because they feared that the people would stone them.

27Having brought the apostles, they made them appear before the Sanhedrin to be questioned by the high priest. **28**"We gave you strict orders not to teach in this name,"*x* he said. "Yet you have filled Jerusalem with your teaching and are determined to make us guilty of this man's blood."*y*

5:28
x Ac 4:18
y Mt 23:35; Ac 2:23, 36; 3:14, 15; 7:52

5:29
z Ac 4:19

29Peter and the other apostles replied: "We must obey God rather than men!*z* **30**The God of our fathers*a* raised Jesus from the dead—whom you had killed by hanging him on a tree.*b* **31**God exalted him to his own right hand as Prince and Savior that he might give repentance and forgiveness of sins to Israel. **32**We are witnesses of these things, and so is the Holy Spirit,*c* whom God has given to those who obey him."

5:30
a Ac 3:13
b Ac 10:39; Gal 3:13

5:32
c Jn 15:26

5:33
d Ac 2:37; 7:54

33When they heard this, they were furious *d* and wanted to put them to death. **34**But a Pharisee named Gamaliel, a teacher of the law, who was honored by all the people, stood up in the Sanhedrin and ordered that the men be put outside for a little while. **35**Then he addressed them: "Men of Israel, consider carefully what you intend to do to these men. **36**Some time ago Theudas appeared, claiming to be somebody, and about four hundred men rallied to him. He was killed, all his followers were dispersed, and it all came to nothing. **37**After him, Judas the Galilean appeared in the days of the census and led a band of people in revolt. He too was killed, and all his followers were scattered. **38**Therefore, in the present case I advise

---

5:17, 18 The apostles experienced power to do miracles, great boldness in preaching, and God's presence in their lives, yet they were not free from hatred and persecution. They were arrested, put in jail, beaten, and slandered by community leaders. Faith in God does not make troubles disappear; it makes troubles appear less frightening because it puts them in the right perspective. Don't expect everyone to react favorably when you share something as dynamic as your faith in Christ. Some will be jealous, afraid, or threatened. Expect some negative reactions, and remember that you must be more concerned about serving God than about the reactions of people (see 5:29).

5:19 The angel of the Lord gave the apostles a command that, when followed, would lead to a brutal flogging (5:40). If that strikes you as odd, it is probably because of the prevailing idea among many believers that obedience inevitably leads to blessing (defined as "a problem-free, blissful existence"). Serious students of the Bible know, however, that obeying God often results in pain and suffering. They also recognize that being persecuted for Christ is a deeper kind of blessing. What biblical commands, if obeyed, might result in discomfort for you today? Will you commit to live them out anyway?

5:21 The temple at daybreak was a busy place. Many people stopped at the temple to pray and worship at sunrise. The apostles were already there, ready to tell them the good news of new life in Jesus Christ. Also at daybreak, the "full assembly of the elders of Israel" (also called the Sanhedrin) was gathering, preparing to question the apostles. This was going to be no small trial. The religious leaders would do anything to stop these apos-

tles from challenging their authority, threatening their secure position, and exposing their hypocritical motives to the people.

5:29 The apostles knew their priorities. While we should try to live at peace with everyone (Romans 12:18), conflict with the world and its authorities is sometimes inevitable for a Christian (John 15:18). There will be situations where you cannot obey both God and man. Then you must obey God and trust his Word. Let Jesus' words in Luke 6:22 encourage you: "Blessed are you when men hate you, when they exclude you and insult you and reject your name as evil, because of the Son of Man."

5:34 The Pharisees were the other major party in the Jewish council with the Sadducees (5:17). The Pharisees were the strict keepers of the law—not only God's law, but hundreds of other rules they had added to God's law. They were careful about outward purity, but many had hearts full of impure motives. Jesus confronted the Pharisees often during his ministry on earth. Oddly enough, a Pharisee named Gamaliel became an unexpected ally for the apostles, although he probably did not support their teachings. He was a distinguished member of the council and a teacher. While Gamaliel may have saved the apostles' lives, his real intentions probably were to prevent a division in the council and to avoid arousing the Romans. The apostles were popular among the people, and killing them might start a riot. Gamaliel's advice to the council gave the apostles some breathing room to continue their work. The council decided to wait, hoping that this would all fade away harmlessly. They couldn't have been more wrong. Ironically, Paul, later one of the greatest apostles, was one of Gamaliel's students (22:3).

you: Leave these men alone! Let them go! For if their purpose or activity is of human origin, it will fail. ³⁹ But if it is from God, you will not be able to stop these men; you will only find yourselves fighting against God."

⁴⁰ His speech persuaded them. They called the apostles in and had them flogged. ͤ Then they ordered them not to speak in the name of Jesus, and let them go.

⁴¹ The apostles left the Sanhedrin, rejoicing because they had been counted worthy of suffering disgrace for the Name. ⁴² Day after day, in the temple courts ͫ and from house to house, they never stopped teaching and proclaiming the good news that Jesus is the Christ.ᵃ

5:40
ᵉ Mt 10:17

5:42
ᶠ Ac 2:46

The Choosing of the Seven

6 In those days when the number of disciples was increasing, the Grecian Jews ᵍ among them complained against the Hebraic Jews because their widows were being overlooked in the daily distribution of food. ͪ ² So the Twelve gathered all the disciples together and said, "It would not be right for us to neglect the ministry of the word of God in order to wait on tables. ³ Brothers, choose seven men from among you who are known to be full of the Spirit and wisdom. We will turn this responsibility over to them ⁴ and will give our attention to prayer and the ministry of the word."

⁵ This proposal pleased the whole group. They chose Stephen, a man full of faith and of the Holy Spirit; also Philip, ͥ Procorus, Nicanor, Timon, Parmenas, and Nicolas from Antioch, a convert to Judaism. ⁶ They presented these men to the apostles, who prayed ͩ and laid their hands on them. ᵏ

⁷ So the word of God spread. ͭ The number of disciples in Jerusalem increased rapidly, and a large number of priests became obedient to the faith.

6:1
ᵍ Ac 9:29
ͪ Ac 4:35

6:5
ͥ Ac 8:5-40; 21:8

6:6
ͩ Ac 1:24
ᵏ Ac 9:17; 1 Ti 4:14

6:7
ͭ Ac 12:24; 19:20

ᵃ42 Or *Messiah*

5:39 Gamaliel presented some sound advice about reacting to religious movements. Unless disciples in these groups endorse obviously dangerous doctrines or practices, it is often wiser to be tolerant rather than repressive. Sometimes only time will tell if they are presenting merely human ideas or if God is trying to say something through them. The next time a group promotes differing religious ideas, consider Gamaliel's advice, just in case you "find yourselves fighting against God."

5:40–42 Peter and John had been warned repeatedly not to preach, but they continued in spite of the threats. We, too, should live as Christ has asked us to, sharing our faith no matter what the cost. We may not be beaten or thrown in jail, but we may be ridiculed, ostracized, or slandered. To what extent are you willing to suffer for the sake of sharing the gospel with others?

5:41 Have you ever thought of persecution as a blessing, as something worth rejoicing about? This beating suffered by Peter and John was the first time any of the apostles had been physically abused for their faith. These men knew how Jesus had suffered, and they praised God that he had allowed them to be persecuted like their Lord. If you are mocked or persecuted for your faith, it isn't because you're doing something wrong, but because God has counted you "worthy of suffering disgrace for the Name."

5:42 Home Bible studies are not new. As the believers needed to grow in their new faith, home Bible studies met their needs, as well as serving as a means to introduce new people to the Christian faith. During later times of persecution, meeting in homes became the primary method of passing on Bible knowledge. Christians throughout the world still use this approach when under persecution and as a way to build up believers.

6:1 When we read the descriptions of the early church—the miracles, the sharing and generosity, the fellowship—we may wish we could have been a part of this "perfect" church. In reality, the early church had problems just as we do today. No church has ever been or will ever be perfect until Christ and his followers are united at his second coming. All churches have problems. If your church's shortcomings distress you, ask yourself: "Would a perfect church allow me to be a member?" Then do what you can to make your church better. A church does not have to be perfect to be faithful.

6:1ff Another internal problem developed in the early church

between the Hebrew-speaking Christians (probably local Jews who had been converted) and the Greek-speaking Christians (probably Jews from other lands who had been converted at Pentecost). The Greek-speaking Christians complained that their widows were being unfairly treated. This favoritism was probably not intentional, but was more likely caused by the language barrier. To correct the situation, the apostles put seven respected Greek-speaking men in charge of the food distribution program. This solved the problem and allowed the apostles to keep their focus on teaching and preaching the Good News about Jesus.

6:2 "The Twelve" are the 11 original disciples plus Matthias, who had been chosen to replace Judas Iscariot (1:26).

6:2–4 As the early church increased in size, so did its needs. One great need was to organize the distribution of food to the poor. The apostles needed to focus on preaching, so they chose others to administer the food program. Each person has a vital part to play in the life of the church (see 1 Corinthians 12). If you are in a position of leadership and find yourself overwhelmed by responsibilities, determine *your* God-given abilities and priorities and then find others to help. If you are not in leadership, you have gifts that can be used by God in various areas of the church's ministry. Offer these gifts in service to him.

6:3 This administrative task was not taken lightly. Notice the requirements for the men who were to handle the food program: full of the Holy Spirit and wisdom. People who carry heavy responsibilities and work closely with others should have these qualities. We must look for spiritually mature and wise men and women to lead our churches.

6:4 The apostles' priorities were correct. The ministry of the Word should never be neglected because of administrative burdens. Pastors should not try, or be expected to try, to do everything. Instead, the work of the church should be spread out among its members.

6:6 Spiritual leadership is serious business and must not be taken lightly by the church or its leaders. In the early church, the chosen men were ordained or commissioned (by prayer and laying on of hands) by the apostles. Laying hands on someone, an ancient Jewish practice, was a way to set a person apart for special service (see Numbers 27:23; Deuteronomy 34:9).

6:7 Jesus had told the apostles that they were to witness first in

Stephen Seized

8 Now Stephen, a man full of God's grace and power, did great wonders and miraculous signs among the people. 9 Opposition arose, however, from members of the Synagogue of the Freedmen (as it was called)—Jews of Cyrene and Alexandria as well as the provinces of Cilicia and Asia. These men began to argue with Stephen, 10 but they could not stand up against his wisdom or the Spirit by whom he spoke.

11 Then they secretly persuaded some men to say, "We have heard Stephen speak words of blasphemy against Moses and against God."

12 So they stirred up the people and the elders and the teachers of the law. They seized Stephen and brought him before the Sanhedrin. 13 They produced false witnesses, who testified, "This fellow never stops speaking against this holy place and against the law. 14 For we have heard him say that this Jesus of Nazareth will destroy this place and change the customs Moses handed down to us."

15 All who were sitting in the Sanhedrin looked intently at Stephen, and they saw that his face was like the face of an angel.

Stephen's Speech to the Sanhedrin

7 Then the high priest asked him, "Are these charges true?"

7:2
m Ac 22:1

2 To this he replied: "Brothers and fathers, *m* listen to me! The God of glory appeared to our father Abraham while he was still in Mesopotamia, before he lived in Haran. 3 'Leave

7:3
n Ge 12:1

your country and your people,' God said, 'and go to the land I will show you.' *a n*

7:4
o Ge 12:5

4 "So he left the land of the Chaldeans and settled in Haran. After the death of his father, God sent him to this land where you are now living. *o* 5 He gave him no inheritance here, not

7:5
p Ge 12:7

even a foot of ground. But God promised him that he and his descendants after him would possess the land, *p* even though at that time Abraham had no child. 6 God spoke to him in this way: 'Your descendants will be strangers in a country not their own, and they will be enslaved

7:7
q Ex 3:12

and mistreated four hundred years. 7 But I will punish the nation they serve as slaves,' God said, 'and afterward they will come out of that country and worship me in this place.' *b q* 8 Then

a 3 Gen. 12:1   *b 7* Gen. 15:13,14

Jerusalem (1:8). In a short time, their message had infiltrated the entire city and all levels of society. Even some Jewish priests were being converted, an obvious violation of the wishes of the council that would endanger their position.

6:7 The word of God spread like ripples on a pond where, from a single center, each wave touches the next, spreading wider and farther. The gospel still spreads this way today. You don't have to change the world single-handedly—it is enough just to be part of the wave, touching those around you, who in turn will touch others until all have felt the movement. Don't ever feel that your part is insignificant or unimportant.

6:9 The Freedmen was a group of Jewish slaves who had been freed by Rome and had formed their own synagogue in Jerusalem.

6:11 These men lied about Stephen, causing him to be arrested and brought before the Jewish council. The Sadducees, the dominant party in the council, accepted and studied only the writings of Moses (Genesis through Deuteronomy). In their view, to speak blasphemy against Moses was a crime. But from Stephen's speech (chapter 7), we learn that this accusation was false. Stephen based his review of Israel's history on Moses' writings.

6:14 When Stephen was brought before the Sanhedrin (the council of religious leaders), the accusation against him was the same that the religious leaders had used against Jesus (Matthew 26:59–61). The group falsely accused Stephen of wanting to change Moses' customs, because they knew that the Sadducees, who controlled the council, believed *only* in Moses' laws.

7:1 This high priest was probably Caiaphas, the same man who had earlier questioned and condemned Jesus (John 18:24).

7:2ff Stephen launched into a long speech about Israel's relationship with God. From Old Testament history he showed that the Jews had constantly rejected God's message and his prophets, and that this council had rejected the Messiah, God's Son. He made three main points: (1) Israel's history is the history of God's acts

in the world; (2) people worshiped God long before there was a temple, because God does not live in a temple; (3) Jesus' death was just one more example of Israel's rebellion against and rejection of God.

7:2ff Stephen didn't really defend himself. Instead, he took the offensive, seizing the opportunity to summarize his teaching about Jesus. Stephen was accusing these religious leaders of failing to obey God's laws—the laws they prided themselves in following so meticulously. This was the same accusation that Jesus had leveled against them. When we witness for Christ, we don't need to be on the defensive. Instead we can simply share our faith.

7:8 Circumcision was a sign of the promise or covenant made between God, Abraham, and the entire nation of Israel (Genesis 17:9–13). Because Stephen's speech summarized Israel's history, he summarized how this covenant fared during that time. Stephen pointed out that God always had kept his side of the promise, but Israel had failed again and again to uphold its end. Although the Jews in Stephen's day still circumcised their baby boys, they failed to obey God. The people's hearts were far from God. Their lack of faith and lack of obedience meant that they had failed to keep their part of the covenant.

7:8 The Jewish rite of circumcision, like Israel's regular sacrifices and annual feasts, was intended to be a very meaningful event. As with all religious rituals, circumcision was designed to serve as an outer symbol of an inner reality. Those who participated thoughtfully would be reminded of profound spiritual truths. But we know from our own experiences of repeating the church creeds, saying the Lord's Prayer, or celebrating ordinances like baptism and the Lord's Supper, that it is difficult to avoid merely going through the motions. We are often guilty of participating passively and mindlessly in religious exercises. Make it your goal to give God your full attention (body, soul, and spirit) the next time you pray, take Communion, or take part in a church ceremony.

he gave Abraham the covenant of circumcision.[r] And Abraham became the father of Isaac and circumcised him eight days after his birth.[s] Later Isaac became the father of Jacob,[t] and Jacob became the father of the twelve patriarchs.[u]

9 "Because the patriarchs were jealous of Joseph,[v] they sold him as a slave into Egypt.[w] But God was with him[x] 10 and rescued him from all his troubles. He gave Joseph wisdom and enabled him to gain the goodwill of Pharaoh king of Egypt; so he made him ruler over Egypt and all his palace.

11 "Then a famine struck all Egypt and Canaan, bringing great suffering, and our fathers could not find food.[y] 12 When Jacob heard that there was grain in Egypt, he sent our fathers on their first visit.[z] 13 On their second visit, Joseph told his brothers who he was,[a] and Pharaoh learned about Joseph's family. 14 After this, Joseph sent for his father Jacob and his whole family,[b] seventy-five in all.[c] 15 Then Jacob went down to Egypt, where he and our fathers died.[d] 16 Their bodies were brought back to Shechem and placed in the tomb that Abraham had bought from the sons of Hamor at Shechem for a certain sum of money.[e]

17 "As the time drew near for God to fulfill his promise to Abraham, the number of our people in Egypt greatly increased.[f] 18 Then another king, who knew nothing about Joseph, became ruler of Egypt. 19 He dealt treacherously with our people and oppressed our forefathers by forcing them to throw out their newborn babies so that they would die.[g]

20 "At that time Moses was born, and he was no ordinary child.[a] For three months he was cared for in his father's house. 21 When he was placed outside, Pharaoh's daughter took him and brought him up as her own son. 22 Moses was educated in all the wisdom of the Egyptians and was powerful in speech and action.

23 "When Moses was forty years old, he decided to visit his fellow Israelites. 24 He saw one of them being mistreated by an Egyptian, so he went to his defense and avenged him by killing the Egyptian. 25 Moses thought that his own people would realize that God was using him to rescue them, but they did not. 26 The next day Moses came upon two Israelites who were fighting. He tried to reconcile them by saying, 'Men, you are brothers; why do you want to hurt each other?'

27 "But the man who was mistreating the other pushed Moses aside and said, 'Who made you ruler and judge over us? 28 Do you want to kill me as you killed the Egyptian yesterday?'[b] 29 When Moses heard this, he fled to Midian, where he settled as a foreigner and had two sons.[h]

30 "After forty years had passed, an angel appeared to Moses in the flames of a burning bush in the desert near Mount Sinai. 31 When he saw this, he was amazed at the sight. As he went over to look more closely, he heard the Lord's voice: 32 'I am the God of your fathers, the God of Abraham, Isaac and Jacob.'[c] Moses trembled with fear and did not dare to look.

33 "Then the Lord said to him, 'Take off your sandals; the place where you are standing is holy ground.[i] 34 I have indeed seen the oppression of my people in Egypt. I have heard their groaning and have come down to set them free. Now come, I will send you back to Egypt.'[d][j]

35 "This is the same Moses whom they had rejected with the words, 'Who made you ruler and judge?' He was sent to be their ruler and deliverer by God himself, through the angel who appeared to him in the bush. 36 He led them out of Egypt[k] and did wonders and miraculous signs in Egypt, at the Red Sea[e] and for forty years in the desert.

37 "This is that Moses who told the Israelites, 'God will send you a prophet like me from your own people.'[f][l] 38 He was in the assembly in the desert, with the angel who spoke to him on Mount Sinai, and with our fathers; and he received living words to pass on to us.[m]

7:8
[r]Ge 17:9-14
[s]Ge 21:2-4
[t]Ge 25:26
[u]Ge 29:31-35

7:9
[v]Ge 37:4, 11
[w]Ge 37:28
[x]Ge 39:2, 21, 23

7:11
[y]Ge 41:54

7:12
[z]Ge 42:1, 2

7:13
[a]Ge 45:1-4

7:14
[b]Ge 45:9, 10
[c]Ge 46:26, 27; Dt 10:22

7:15
[d]Ge 46:5-7; Ex 1:6

7:16
[e]Ge 23:16-20; 33:18, 19; Jos 24:32

7:17
[f]Ex 1:7

7:19
[g]Ex 1:10-22

7:29
[h]Ex 2:11-15

7:33
[i]Ex 3:5

7:34
[j]Ex 3:7-10

7:36
[k]Ex 12:41

7:37
[l]Dt 18:15, 18

7:38
[m]Ro 3:2

[a]20 Or was fair in the sight of God   [b]28 Exodus 2:14   [c]32 Exodus 3:6   [d]34 Exodus 3:5,7,8,10   [e]36 That is, Sea of Reeds   [f]37 Deut. 18:15

7:17 Stephen's review of Jewish history gives a clear testimony of God's faithfulness and sovereignty. Despite the continued failures of his chosen people and the swirling world events, God was working out his plan. When faced by a confusing array of circumstances, remember that: (1) God is in control—nothing surprises him; (2) this world is not all there is—it will pass away, but God is eternal; (3) God is just, and he will make things right—punishing the wicked and rewarding the faithful; (4) God wants to use you (like Joseph, Moses, and Stephen) to make a difference in the world.

7:37 The Jews originally thought this "prophet" was Joshua. But Moses was prophesying about the coming Messiah (Deuteronomy 18:15). Peter also quoted this verse in referring to the Messiah (3:22).

7:38 Stephen used the word "ekklesia" (translated "assembly") to describe the congregation or people of God in the desert. This word means "called out ones" and was used by the first-century Christians to describe their own community or "assembly." Stephen's point was that the giving of the law through Moses to the Jews was the sign of the covenant. By obedience, then, would they continue to be God's covenant people. But because they disobeyed (7:39), they broke the covenant and forfeited their right to be the chosen people.

7:38 From Galatians 3:19 and Hebrews 2:2, it appears that God had given the law to Moses through angels. Exodus 31:18 says God wrote the Ten Commandments himself ("inscribed by the

7:40
ⁿ Ex 32:1, 23
7:41
ᵒ Ex 32:4-6

³⁹"But our fathers refused to obey him. Instead, they rejected him and in their hearts turned back to Egypt. ⁴⁰They told Aaron, 'Make us gods who will go before us. As for this fellow Moses who led us out of Egypt—we don't know what has happened to him!'ᵃ ⁿ ⁴¹That was the time they made an idol in the form of a calf. They brought sacrifices to it and held a celebration in honor of what their hands had made. ᵒ ⁴²But God turned away and gave them over to the worship of the heavenly bodies. This agrees with what is written in the book of the prophets:

"'Did you bring me sacrifices and offerings
   forty years in the desert, O house of Israel?

7:43
ᵖ Am 5:25-27

⁴³ You have lifted up the shrine of Molech
    and the star of your god Rephan,
    the idols you made to worship.
Therefore I will send you into exile'ᵇ ᵖ beyond Babylon.

ᵃ*40* Exodus 32:1   ᵇ*43* Amos 5:25-27

STEPHEN

Around the world, the gospel has most often taken root in places prepared by the blood of martyrs. Before people can *give* their lives for the gospel, however, they must first *live* their lives for the gospel. One way God trains his servants is to place them in insignificant positions. Their desire to serve Christ is translated into the reality of serving others. Stephen was an effective administrator and messenger before becoming a martyr.

Long before violent persecution broke out against Christians, there was already social ostracism. Jews who accepted Jesus as Messiah were usually cut off from their families. As a result, the believers depended on each other for support. The sharing of homes, food, and resources was both a practical and necessary mark of the early church. Eventually, the number of believers made it necessary to organize the sharing. People were being overlooked. There were complaints. Seven men were chosen to oversee the distribution of food in the early church. They were chosen for their integrity, wisdom, and sensitivity to God. Stephen was one of them.

Besides being a good administrator, Stephen was also a powerful speaker. When confronted in the temple by various antagonistic groups, Stephen's logic in responding was convincing. This is clear from the defense he made before the Sanhedrin. He presented a summary of the Jews' own history and made powerful applications that stung his listeners. During his defense Stephen must have known he was speaking his own death sentence. Members of the council could not stand to have their evil motives exposed. They stoned him to death while he prayed for their forgiveness. His final words show how much like Jesus he had become in a short time. His death had a lasting impact on young Saul (Paul) of Tarsus, who would move from being a violent persecutor of Christians to being one of the greatest champions of the gospel the church has known.

Stephen's life is a continual challenge to all Christians. Because he was the first to die for the faith, his sacrifice raises questions: How many risks do we take in being Jesus' followers? Would we be willing to die for him? Are we really willing to live for him?

Strengths and accomplishments:	• One of seven leaders chosen to supervise food distribution to the needy in the early church • Known for his spiritual qualities of faith, wisdom, grace, and power; also known for the Spirit's presence in his life • Outstanding leader, teacher, and debater • First to give his life for the gospel
Lessons from his life:	• Striving for excellence in small assignments prepares one for greater responsibilities • Real understanding of God always leads to practical and compassionate actions toward people
Vital statistics:	• Occupation: Organizer of food distribution • Contemporaries: Paul, Caiaphas, Gamaliel, the apostles
Key verses:	"While they were stoning him, Stephen prayed, 'Lord Jesus, receive my spirit.' Then he fell on his knees and cried out, 'Lord, do not hold this sin against them.' When he had said this, he fell asleep" (Acts 7:59, 60).

Stephen's story is told in Acts 6:3—8:2. He is also mentioned in Acts 11:19; 22:20.

---

finger of God"). Apparently God used angelic messengers as mediators to deliver his law to Moses.

7:42 The *heavenly bodies* refers to their practice of worshiping deities associated with stars and planets.

7:43 Here Stephen gave more details of the idolatry referred

to in 7:40. These were idols worshiped by Israel during their desert wanderings (Exodus 32:4). Molech was the god associated with child sacrifice, and Rephan was an Egyptian god. Amos also names Assyrian deities worshiped by Israel (Amos 5:25—27).

44"Our forefathers had the tabernacle of the Testimony with them in the desert. It had been made as God directed Moses, according to the pattern he had seen. *q* 45 Having received the tabernacle, our fathers under Joshua brought it with them when they took the land from the nations God drove out before them. *r* It remained in the land until the time of David, 46 who enjoyed God's favor and asked that he might provide a dwelling place for the God of Jacob. *a s* 47 But it was Solomon who built the house for him.

48"However, the Most High does not live in houses made by men. *t* As the prophet says:

49 "'Heaven is my throne,
    and the earth is my footstool. *u*
What kind of house will you build for me?

                                                        says the Lord.

    Or where will my resting place be?
50 Has not my hand made all these things?' *b v*

51"You stiff-necked people, with uncircumcised hearts *w* and ears! You are just like your fathers: You always resist the Holy Spirit! 52 Was there ever a prophet your fathers did not persecute? *x* They even killed those who predicted the coming of the Righteous One. And now you have betrayed and murdered him *y*— 53 you who have received the law that was put into effect through angels *z* but have not obeyed it."

The Stoning of Stephen

54 When they heard this, they were furious *a* and gnashed their teeth at him. 55 But Stephen, full of the Holy Spirit, looked up to heaven and saw the glory of God, and Jesus standing at the right hand of God. 56 "Look," he said, "I see heaven open *b* and the Son of Man standing at the right hand of God."

57 At this they covered their ears and, yelling at the top of their voices, they all rushed at him, 58 dragged him out of the city *c* and began to stone him. *d* Meanwhile, the witnesses laid their clothes at the feet of a young man named Saul.

59 While they were stoning him, Stephen prayed, "Lord Jesus, receive my spirit." 60 Then he fell on his knees *e* and cried out, "Lord, do not hold this sin against them." When he had said this, he fell asleep.

a 46 Some early manuscripts *the house of Jacob*   *b 50* Isaiah 66:1,2

Reference	
7:44	*q* Ex 25:8, 9, 40
7:45	*r* Jos 3:14-17; Ps 44:2
7:46	*s* 2Sa 7:8-16
7:48	*t* 1Ki 8:27
7:49	*u* Mt 5:34, 35
7:50	*v* Isa 66:1, 2
7:51	*w* Lev 26:41
7:52	*x* 2Ch 36:16 *y* Ac 3:14
7:53	*z* Gal 3:19
7:54	*a* Ac 5:33
7:56	*b* Mt 3:16
7:58	*c* Lk 4:29 *d* Lev 24:14, 16; Dt 13:9
7:60	*e* Ac 9:40

7:44–50 Stephen had been accused of speaking against the temple (6:13). Although he recognized the importance of the temple, he knew that it was not more important than God. God is not limited; he doesn't live only in a house of worship, but wherever hearts of faith are open to receive him (Isaiah 66:1, 2). Solomon knew this when he prayed at the dedication of the temple (2 Chronicles 6:18). God wants to live in us. Is living in you?

7:52 Indeed many prophets were persecuted and killed: Uriah (Jeremiah 26:20–23); Jeremiah (Jeremiah 38:1–6); Isaiah (tradition says he was killed by King Manasseh; see 2 Kings 21:16); Amos (Amos 7:10–13); Zechariah (not the author of the Bible book, but the son of Jehoiada the priest, 2 Chronicles 24:20–22); Elijah (1 Kings 19:1, 2). Jesus also told a parable about how the Jews had constantly rejected God's messages and persecuted his messengers (Luke 20:9–19). The Righteous One refers to the Messiah.

7:55–58 Stephen saw the glory of God and Jesus the Messiah standing at God's right hand. Stephen's words are similar to Jesus' words spoken before the council (Matthew 26:64; Mark 14:62; Luke 22:69). Stephen's vision supported Jesus' claim and angered the Jewish leaders who had condemned Jesus to death for blasphemy. They would not tolerate Stephen's words, so they dragged him out and killed him. People may not kill us for witnessing about Christ, but they will let us know they don't want to hear the truth and will often try to silence us. Keep honoring God in your conduct and words; though many may turn against you and your message, some will follow Christ. Remember, Stephen's death made a profound impact on Paul, who later became the world's greatest missionary. Even those who oppose you now may later turn to Christ.

7:58 Saul is also called Paul (see 13:9), the great missionary who wrote many of the letters in the New Testament. Saul was his Hebrew name; Paul, his Greek name, was used as he began his ministry to the Gentiles. When Luke introduces him, Paul was hating and persecuting Jesus' followers. This is a great contrast to the Paul about whom Luke will write for most of the rest of the book of Acts—a devoted follower of Christ and a gifted gospel preacher. Paul was uniquely qualified to talk to the Jews about Jesus because he had once persecuted those who believed in Jesus, and he understood how the opposition felt. Paul is a powerful example of how no one is impossible for God to reach and change.

7:59 The penalty for blasphemy, speaking irreverently about God, was death by stoning (Leviticus 24:14). The religious leaders, who were furious, had Stephen stoned without a trial. They did not understand that Stephen's words were true, because they were not seeking the truth. They only wanted support for their own views.

7:60 As Stephen died, he spoke words very similar to Jesus' words on the cross (Luke 23:34). For telling others the good news of Jesus' death, burial, and resurrection the members of the early church were persecuted. Sometimes, as in the case of Stephen, they were even put to death. Christ had promised his followers that living for him would lead to trouble (see Luke 21:12–19). This is still true. If we boldly live out our faith, the light of our lives will expose the sinfulness of others. Our words of truth will pierce their souls. Some will be convicted and yield to the leading of the Spirit. Others will become angry and hardened in their hatred of the truth. As Jesus said, "They will treat you this way because of my name, for they do not know the One who sent me" (John 15:21). We shouldn't be surprised or abandon our faith when we are persecuted.

8:1
f Ac 7:58
g Ac 11:19

8 And Saul f was there, giving approval to his death.

2. Expansion of the church
The Church Persecuted and Scattered

On that day a great persecution broke out against the church at Jerusalem, and all except the apostles were scattered g throughout Judea and Samaria. 2 Godly men buried Stephen and mourned deeply for him. 3 But Saul h began to destroy the church. i Going from house to house, he dragged off men and women and put them in prison.

8:3
h Ac 7:58
i 1Co 15:9;
Gal 1:13, 23;
Php 3:6; 1Ti 1:13

Philip in Samaria

4 Those who had been scattered preached the word wherever they went. 5 Philip j went down to a city in Samaria and proclaimed the Christ a there. 6 When the crowds heard Philip and saw the miraculous signs he did, they all paid close attention to what he said. 7 With shrieks, evil b spirits came out of many, and many paralytics and cripples were healed. 8 So there was great joy in that city.

8:5
j Ac 6:5

Simon the Sorcerer

9 Now for some time a man named Simon had practiced sorcery k in the city and amazed all the people of Samaria. He boasted that he was someone great, l 10 and all the people, both high and low, gave him their attention and exclaimed, "This man is the divine power known as the Great Power." 11 They followed him because he had amazed them for a long time with his magic. 12 But when they believed Philip as he preached the good news of the kingdom of God m and the name of Jesus Christ, they were baptized, both men and women. 13 Simon himself believed and was baptized. And he followed Philip everywhere, astonished by the great signs and miracles n he saw.

8:9
k Ac 13:6
l Ac 5:36

8:12
m Ac 1:3

8:13
n Ac 19:11

a 5 Or Messiah   b 7 Greek unclean

THE EFFECTS OF STEPHEN'S DEATH

Stephen's death was not in vain. Below are some of the events that were by-products (either directly or indirectly) of the persecution that began with Stephen's martyrdom.

1. Philip's evangelistic tour (Acts 8:4–40)
2. Paul's (Saul's) conversion (Acts 9:1–30)
3. Peter's missionary tour (Acts 9:32—11:18)
4. The church in Antioch in Syria founded (Acts 11:19ff)

8:1–4 Persecution pushed the Christians beyond Jerusalem and into Judea and Samaria—thus fulfilling the second part of Jesus' command (see 1:8). The persecution helped spread the gospel. God would bring great results from the believers' suffering.

8:4 Persecution forced the believers out of their homes in Jerusalem, and along with them went the gospel. Sometimes we have to become uncomfortable before we'll move. We may not want to experience it, but discomfort may be best for us because God may be working through our hurts. When you are tempted to complain about uncomfortable or painful circumstances, stop and ask if God might be preparing you for a special task.

8:5 This is not the apostle Philip (see John 1:43, 44), but a Greek-speaking Jew, "full of the Spirit and wisdom" (6:3), who was one of the seven deacons chosen to help with the food distribution program in the church (6:5).

8:5 Israel had been divided into three main regions—Galilee in the north, Samaria in the middle, and Judea in the south. The city of Samaria (in the region of Samaria) had been the capital of the northern kingdom of Israel in the days of the divided kingdom, before it was conquered by Assyria in 722 B.C. During that war, the Assyrian king had taken many captives, leaving only the poorest people in the land and resettling it with foreigners. These foreigners had intermarried with the Jews who were left, and the mixed race became known as Samaritans. The Samaritans were

considered half-breeds by the "pure" Jews in the southern kingdom of Judah, and the two groups hated each other intensely. But Jesus himself went into Samaria (John 4), and he commanded his followers to spread the gospel there (1:8).

8:7 Jesus encountered and drove out many demons during his ministry on earth. Demons, or evil spirits, are ruled by Satan. Most scholars believe that demons are fallen angels who joined Satan in his rebellion against God, and who can cause a person to be mute, deaf, blind, or insane. Demons also tempt people to sin. Although they can be powerful, they are not able to read our minds and cannot be everywhere at once. Demons are real and active, but Jesus has authority over them; and he gave this authority to his followers. Although Satan is allowed to work in our world, God is in complete control. He can drive demons out and end their destructive work in people's lives. Eventually Satan and his demons will be thrown into the lake of fire, forever ending their evil work in the world (Revelation 20:10).

8:9–11 In the days of the early church, sorcerers and magicians were numerous and influential. They worked wonders, performed healings and exorcisms, and practiced astrology. Their wonders may simply have been magic tricks, or the sorcerers may have been empowered by Satan (Matthew 24:24; 2 Thessalonians 2:9). Simon had done so many wonders that some even thought that he was the Messiah; but his powers did not come from God (see 8:18–24).

14When the apostles in Jerusalem heard that Samaria had accepted the word of God, they sent Peter and John to them. 15When they arrived, they prayed for them that they might receive the Holy Spirit,ᵒ 16because the Holy Spirit had not yet come upon any of them;ᵖ they had simply been baptized intoᵃ the name of the Lord Jesus.�q 17Then Peter and John placed their hands on them,ʳ and they received the Holy Spirit.

18When Simon saw that the Spirit was given at the laying on of the apostles' hands, he offered them money 19and said, "Give me also this ability so that everyone on whom I lay my hands may receive the Holy Spirit."

20Peter answered: "May your money perish with you, because you thought you could buy the gift of God with money!ˢ 21You have no part or share in this ministry, because your heart is not right before God. 22Repent of this wickedness and pray to the Lord. Perhaps he will forgive you for having such a thought in your heart. 23For I see that you are full of bitterness and captive to sin."

24Then Simon answered, "Pray to the Lord for me so that nothing you have said may happen to me."

25When they had testified and proclaimed the word of the Lord, Peter and John returned to Jerusalem, preaching the gospel in many Samaritan villages.

Philip and the Ethiopian

26Now an angelᵗ of the Lord said to Philip, "Go south to the road—the desert road—that goes down from Jerusalem to Gaza." 27So he started out, and on his way he met an Ethiopianᵇ eunuch, an important official in charge of all the treasury of Candace, queen of the Ethiopians. This man had gone to Jerusalem to worship,ᵘ 28and on his way home was sitting

a 16 Or in   b 27 That is, from the upper Nile region

8:15
ᵒAc 2:38
8:16
ᵖAc 19:2
qMt 28:19
8:17
ʳAc 6:6

8:20
ˢ2Ki 5:16; Mt 10:8;
Ac 2:38

8:26
ᵗAc 5:19
8:27
ᵘJn 12:20

8:14 Peter and John were sent to Samaria to find out whether or not the Samaritans were truly becoming believers. The Jewish Christians, even the apostles, were still unsure whether Gentiles (non-Jews) and half-Jews could receive the Holy Spirit. It wasn't until Peter's experience with Cornelius (chapter 10) that the apostles became fully convinced that the Holy Spirit was for all people. John had asked Jesus if they should call fire down from heaven to burn up a Samaritan village that refused to welcome them (Luke 9:51–55). Here he and Peter went to the Samaritans to pray with them.

8:15–17 This was a crucial moment for the spread of the gospel and for the growth of the church. Peter and John had to go to Samaria to help keep this new group of believers from becoming separated from other believers. When Peter and John saw the Lord working in these people, they were assured that the Holy Spirit worked through *all* believers—Gentiles and mixed races as well as "pure" Jews.

PHILIP'S MINISTRY
To escape persecution in Jerusalem, Philip fled to Samaria, where he continued preaching the gospel. While he was there, an angel commanded him to meet an Ethiopian official on the road between Jerusalem and Gaza. The man became a believer before continuing on to Ethiopia. Philip then went from Azotus to Caesarea.

8:15–17 Many scholars believe that God chose to give this dramatic filling of his Spirit as a sign at this special moment in history—the spread of the gospel into Samaria through the powerful, effective preaching of believers. Normally, the Holy Spirit enters a person's life at conversion. This was a special event. The pouring out of the Spirit would happen again with Cornelius and his family (10:44–47), a sign that the uncircumcised Gentiles could receive the gospel.

8:18–23 "Everything has a price" seems to be true in our world of bribes, wealth, and materialism. Simon thought he could buy the Holy Spirit's power, but Peter harshly rebuked him. Why? The only way to receive God's power is to do what Peter told Simon to do—repent, ask God for forgiveness, and be filled with his Spirit. No amount of money can buy salvation, forgiveness of sin, or God's power. These are only gained by repentance and belief in Christ as Savior. In addition, Simon apparently wanted that ability for selfish reasons: to have power, to make money, or to gain prestige. God doesn't give us abilities to enhance our own lives. He grants us gifts so that we may bring him glory by building up others. When you find yourself wishing for an ability that would put you into the limelight or somehow enrich you personally, check your motives. Instead of sitting around wishing for talents you don't have, spend your time serving God and others with the gifts you *do* possess.

8:24 The last time a parent or friend rebuked you, were you hurt, angry, or defensive? Learn a lesson from Simon and his reaction to what Peter told him. He exclaimed, "Pray to the Lord for me." If you are rebuked for a serious mistake, it is for your good. Admit your error, repent quickly, and ask for prayer.

8:26 Philip was having a successful preaching ministry to great crowds in Samaria (8:5–8), but he obediently left that ministry to travel on a desert road. Because Philip went where God sent him, Ethiopia was opened up to the gospel. Follow God's leading, even if it seems like a demotion. At first you may not understand his plans, but the results will prove that God's way is right.

8:27 Ethiopia was located in Africa south of Egypt. The eunuch was obviously very dedicated to God because he had traveled such a long distance to worship in Jerusalem. The Jews had contact with Ethiopia (known as Cush) in ancient days (Psalm 68:31; Jeremiah 38:7), so this man may have been a Gentile convert to Judaism. Because he was in charge of the treasury of Ethiopia, this man's in his chariot reading the book of Isaiah the prophet. 29 The Spirit told Philip, "Go to that chariot and stay near it."

30 Then Philip ran up to the chariot and heard the man reading Isaiah the prophet. "Do you understand what you are reading?" Philip asked.

31 "How can I," he said, "unless someone explains it to me?" So he invited Philip to come up and sit with him.

32 The eunuch was reading this passage of Scripture:

"He was led like a sheep to the slaughter,
    and as a lamb before the shearer is silent,
        so he did not open his mouth.
    33 In his humiliation he was deprived of justice.
    Who can speak of his descendants?
    For his life was taken from the earth."a v

34 The eunuch asked Philip, "Tell me, please, who is the prophet talking about, himself or someone else?" 35 Then Philip began with that very passage of Scripture w and told him the good news about Jesus.

36 As they traveled along the road, they came to some water and the eunuch said, "Look, here is water. Why shouldn't I be baptized?"b x 38 And he gave orders to stop the chariot. Then both Philip and the eunuch went down into the water and Philip baptized him.

a 33 Isaiah 53:7,8   b 36 Some late manuscripts baptized?" 37 Philip said, "If you believe with all your heart, you may." The eunuch answered, "I believe that Jesus Christ is the Son of God."

8:33
v Isa 53:7, 8

8:35
w Lk 24:27;
Ac 18:28

8:36
x Ac 10:47

MISSIONARIES OF THE NEW TESTAMENT AND THEIR JOURNEYS	Name	Journey's Purpose	Scripture Reference in Acts
	Philip	One of the first to preach the gospel outside Jerusalem	8:4–40
	Peter and John	Visited new Samaritan believers to encourage them	8:14–25
	Paul (journey to Damascus)	Set out to capture Christians but was captured by Christ	9:1–25
	Peter	Led by God to one of the first Gentile families to become Christians—Cornelius's family	9:32—10:48
	Barnabas	Went to Antioch as an encourager; traveled on to Tarsus to bring Paul back to Antioch; took famine relief to Jerusalem	11:25–30
	Barnabas, Paul, John Mark	Left Antioch for Cyprus, Pamphylia, and Galatia on the first missionary journey	13:1—14:28
	Barnabas and John Mark	Left Antioch for Cyprus after a disagreement with Paul	15:36–41
	Paul, Silas, Timothy, Luke	Left Antioch to revisit churches in Galatia; then traveled on to Asia, Macedonia, and Achaia on the second missionary journey	15:36—18:22
	Apollos	Left Alexandria for Ephesus; learned the complete gospel story from Priscilla and Aquila; preached in Athens and Corinth	18:24–28
	Paul, Timothy, Erastus	Revisited churches in Galatia, Asia, Macedonia, and Achaia on the third major missionary journey	18:23; 19:1—21:14

conversion brought Christianity into the power structures of another government. This is the beginning of the witness "to the ends of the earth" (1:8). See the prophecy in Isaiah 56:3–5 for words about foreigners and eunuchs.

8:29–35 Philip found the Ethiopian man reading Scripture. Taking advantage of this opportunity to explain the gospel, Philip asked the man if he understood what he was reading. Philip (1) followed the Spirit's leading, (2) began the discussion from where the man was (immersed in the prophecies of Isaiah), and (3) explained how Jesus Christ fulfilled Isaiah's prophecies. When we share the gospel, we should start where the other person's concerns are focused. Then we can show how God's Word applies to those concerns.

8:35 Some think that the Old Testament is not relevant today, but Philip led this man to faith in Jesus Christ by using the Old Testament. Jesus Christ is found in the pages of both the Old and New Testaments. God's entire Word is applicable to all people in all ages. Don't avoid or neglect to use the Old Testament. It too is God's Word.

8:38 Baptism was a sign of identification with Christ and with the Christian community. Although Philip was the only witness, it was still important for the eunuch to take this step.

39 When they came up out of the water, the Spirit of the Lord suddenly took Philip away,y and the eunuch did not see him again, but went on his way rejoicing. 40 Philip, however, appeared at Azotus and traveled about, preaching the gospel in all the towns until he reached Caesarea.

8:39
y 1Ki 18:12;
2Ki 2:16;
Eze 3:12, 14

Saul's Conversion

9 Meanwhile, Saul was still breathing out murderous threats against the Lord's disciples.z He went to the high priest 2 and asked him for letters to the synagogues in Damascus, so that if he found any there who belonged to the Way,a whether men or women, he might take them as prisoners to Jerusalem. 3 As he neared Damascus on his journey, suddenly a light from heaven flashed around him.b 4 He fell to the ground and heard a voice say to him, "Saul, Saul, why do you persecute me?"

5 "Who are you, Lord?" Saul asked.

"I am Jesus, whom you are persecuting," he replied. 6 "Now get up and go into the city, and you will be told what you must do."

7 The men traveling with Saul stood there speechless; they heard the sound but did not see anyone. 8 Saul got up from the ground, but when he opened his eyes he could see nothing. So they led him by the hand into Damascus. 9 For three days he was blind, and did not eat or drink anything.

10 In Damascus there was a disciple named Ananias. The Lord called to him in a vision, "Ananias!"

"Yes, Lord," he answered.

11 The Lord told him, "Go to the house of Judas on Straight Street and ask for a man from Tarsusc named Saul, for he is praying. 12 In a vision he has seen a man named Ananias come and place his hands on him to restore his sight."

13 "Lord," Ananias answered, "I have heard many reports about this man and all the harm he has done to your saints in Jerusalem. 14 And he has come here with authority from the chief priestsd to arrest all who call on your name."

9:1
z Ac 8:3

9:2
a Ac 19:9, 23

9:3
b 1Co 15:8

9:11
c Ac 21:39; 22:3

9:14
d ver 2, 21

8:39, 40 Why was Philip suddenly transported to a different city? This miraculous sign showed the urgency of bringing the Gentiles to belief in Christ. Azotus is Ashdod, one of the ancient Philistine capitals. Philip probably lived in Caesarea for the next 20 years (21:8).

9:2 Saul (later called Paul) was so zealous for his Jewish beliefs that he began a persecution campaign against anyone who believed in Christ ("who belonged to the Way"). Why would the Jews in Jerusalem want to persecute Christians as far away as Damascus? There are several possibilities: (1) to seize the Christians who had fled, (2) to prevent the spread of Christianity to other major cities, (3) to keep the Christians from causing any

trouble with Rome, (4) to advance Saul's career and build his reputation as a true Pharisee, zealous for the law, (5) to unify the factions of Judaism by giving them a common enemy.

9:2–5 As Saul traveled to Damascus, pursuing Christians, he was confronted by the risen Christ and brought face to face with the truth of the gospel. Sometimes God breaks into a life in a spectacular manner, and sometimes conversion is a quiet experience. Beware of people who insist that you must have a particular type of conversion experience. The right way to come to faith in Jesus is whatever way God brings *you*.

9:3 Damascus, a key commercial city, was located about 175 miles northeast of Jerusalem in the Roman province of Syria. Several trade routes linked Damascus to other cities throughout the Roman world. Saul may have thought that by stamping out Christianity in Damascus, he could prevent its spread to other areas.

9:3–5 Paul refers to this experience as the start of his new life in Christ (1 Corinthians 9:1; 15:8; Galatians 1:15, 16). At the center of this wonderful experience was Jesus Christ. Paul did not see a vision; he saw the risen Christ himself (9:17). Paul acknowledged Jesus as Lord, confessed his own sin, surrendered his life to Christ, and resolved to obey him. True conversion comes from a personal encounter with Jesus Christ and leads to a new life in relationship with him.

9:5 Saul thought he was pursuing heretics, but he was persecuting Jesus himself. Anyone who persecutes believers today is also guilty of persecuting Jesus (see Matthew 25:40, 45), because believers are the body of Christ on earth.

9:13, 14 "Not him, Lord; that's impossible. He could never become a Christian!" In essence, that's what Ananias said when God told him of Saul's conversion. After all, Saul had pursued believers to their death. Despite these understandable feelings, Ananias obeyed God and ministered to Saul. We must not limit God—he can do anything. We must obey and follow God's leading, even when he leads us to difficult people and places.

SAUL TRAVELS TO DAMASCUS
Many Christians fled Jerusalem when persecution began after Stephen's death, seeking refuge in other cities and countries. Saul tracked them down, even traveling 150 miles to Damascus in Syria to bring Christians back in chains to Jerusalem. But as he neared the ancient city, he discovered that God had other plans for him (9:15).

Mediterranean Sea
SYRIA   To Arabia
Damascus
Sea of Galilee
N
Jordan River
Jerusalem
Dead Sea
JUDEA
0   20 Mi.
0   20 Km.

9:15
e Ac 13:2; Ro 1:1
f Ro 11:13;
Gal 2:7, 8
g Ac 25:22, 23;
26:1
9:16
h Ac 20:23; 21:11;
2Co 11:23-27

¹⁵But the Lord said to Ananias, "Go! This man is my chosen instrument*e* to carry my name before the Gentiles*f* and their kings*g* and before the people of Israel. ¹⁶I will show him how much he must suffer for my name."*h*

¹⁷Then Ananias went to the house and entered it. Placing his hands on Saul, he said, "Brother Saul, the Lord—Jesus, who appeared to you on the road as you were coming here—has sent me so that you may see again and be filled with the Holy Spirit." ¹⁸Immediately, something like scales fell from Saul's eyes, and he could see again. He got up and was baptized, ¹⁹and after taking some food, he regained his strength.

PHILIP

Jesus' last words to his followers were a command to take the gospel everywhere, but they seemed reluctant to leave Jerusalem. It took intense persecution to scatter the believers from Jerusalem and into Judea and Samaria, where Jesus had instructed them to go. Philip, one of the men in charge of food distribution, left Jerusalem and, like most Jewish Christians, spread the gospel wherever he went; but unlike most of them, he did not limit his audience to other Jews. He went directly to Samaria, the last place many Jews would go due to age-old prejudice.

The Samaritans responded in large numbers. When word got back to Jerusalem, Peter and John were sent to evaluate Philip's ministry. They quickly became involved themselves, seeing firsthand God's acceptance of those who previously were considered unacceptable.

In the middle of all this success and excitement, God directed Philip out to the desert for an appointment with an Ethiopian eunuch, another foreigner, who had been in Jerusalem. Philip went immediately. His effectiveness in sharing the gospel with this man placed a Christian in a significant position in a distant country, and may well have had an effect on an entire nation.

Philip ended up in Caesarea, where events allowed him to be Paul's host many years later. Paul, who as the leading persecutor of the Christians had been instrumental in pushing Philip and others out of Jerusalem, had himself become an effective believer. Philip began the conversion of the Gentiles, which Paul continued across the entire Roman empire.

Whether or not you are a follower of Christ, Philip's life presents a challenge. To those still outside the gospel, he is a reminder that the gospel is for you also. To those who have accepted Christ, he is a reminder that we are not free to disqualify anyone from hearing about Jesus. How much like Philip would your neighbors say you are?

Strengths and accomplishments:	• One of the seven organizers of food distribution in the early church • Became an evangelist, one of the first traveling missionaries • One of the first to obey Jesus' command to take the gospel to all people • A careful student of the Bible who could explain its meaning clearly
Lessons from his life:	• God finds great and various uses for those willing to obey wholeheartedly • The gospel is universal Good News • The whole Bible, not just the New Testament, helps us understand more about Jesus • Both mass response (the Samaritans) and individual response (the man from Ethiopia) to the gospel are valuable
Vital statistics:	• Occupations: Organizer of food distribution, evangelist • Relatives: Four daughters • Contemporaries: Paul, Stephen, the apostles
Key verse:	"Then Philip began with that very passage of Scripture and told him the good news about Jesus" (Acts 8:35).

Philip's story is told in Acts 6:1–7; 8:5–40; 21:8–10.

9:15, 16 Faith in Christ brings great blessings but often great suffering too. Paul would suffer for his faith (see 2 Corinthians 11:23–27). God calls us to commitment, not to comfort. He promises to be with us *through* suffering and hardship, not to spare us from them.

9:17 Ananias found Saul, as he had been instructed, and greeted him as "Brother Saul." Ananias feared this meeting because Saul had come to Damascus to capture the believers and take them as prisoners to Jerusalem (9:2). In obedience to the Holy Spirit, however, Ananias greeted Saul lovingly. It is not always easy to love others, especially when we are afraid of them or doubt their motives. Nevertheless, we must follow Jesus' command (John 13:34) and Ananias's example, showing loving acceptance to other believers.

9:17, 18 Although Acts makes no mention of a special filling of the Holy Spirit for Saul, his changed life and subsequent accomplishments bear strong witness to the Holy Spirit's presence and power in him. Evidently, the Holy Spirit had filled Saul when he received his sight and was baptized. See the second note on 8:15–17 for more on the filling of the Holy Spirit.

Saul in Damascus and Jerusalem

Saul spent several days with the disciples in Damascus. *i* 20At once he began to preach in the synagogues that Jesus is the Son of God. 21All those who heard him were astonished and asked, "Isn't he the man who raised havoc in Jerusalem among those who call on this name?*i* And hasn't he come here to take them as prisoners to the chief priests?" 22Yet Saul grew more and more powerful and baffled the Jews living in Damascus by proving that Jesus is the Christ.ª *k*

23After many days had gone by, the Jews conspired to kill him, 24but Saul learned of their plan. Day and night they kept close watch on the city gates in order to kill him. 25But his followers took him by night and lowered him in a basket through an opening in the wall.

26When he came to Jerusalem,*l* he tried to join the disciples, but they were all afraid of him, not believing that he really was a disciple. 27But Barnabas*m* took him and brought him to the apostles. He told them how Saul on his journey had seen the Lord and that the Lord had spoken to him, and how in Damascus he had preached fearlessly in the name of Jesus.*n* 28So Saul stayed with them and moved about freely in Jerusalem, speaking boldly in the name of the Lord. 29He talked and debated with the Grecian Jews,*o* but they tried to kill him. 30When the brothers learned of this, they took him down to Caesarea and sent him off to Tarsus.

31Then the church throughout Judea, Galilee and Samaria*p* enjoyed a time of peace. It was strengthened; and encouraged by the Holy Spirit, it grew in numbers, living in the fear of the Lord.

Aeneas and Dorcas

32As Peter traveled about the country, he went to visit the saints in Lydda. 33There he found a man named Aeneas, a paralytic who had been bedridden for eight years. 34"Aeneas," Peter said to him, "Jesus Christ heals you.*q* Get up and take care of your mat." Immediately Aeneas got up. 35All those who lived in Lydda and Sharon*r* saw him and turned to the Lord.*s*

9:19
i Ac 26:20
9:21
j Ac 8:3
9:22
k Ac 18:5, 28

9:26
l Ac 22:17
9:27
m Ac 4:36
n ver 20, 22

9:29
o Ac 6:1

9:31
p Ac 8:1

9:34
q Ac 3:6, 16
9:35
r 1Ch 5:16
s Ac 11:21

ª22 Or *Messiah*

9:20 Immediately after receiving his sight and spending some time with the believers in Damascus, Saul went to the synagogue to tell the Jews about Jesus Christ. Some Christians counsel new believers to wait until they are thoroughly grounded in their faith before attempting to share the gospel. Saul took time alone to learn about Jesus before beginning his worldwide ministry, but he did not wait to witness. Although we should not rush into a ministry unprepared, we do not need to wait before telling others what has happened to us.

9:21, 22 Saul's arguments were powerful because he was a brilliant scholar. Even more convincing, however, was his changed life. People knew that what Saul taught was real because they could see the evidence in the way he lived. It is important to know what the Bible teaches and how to defend the faith, but your life should back up your words.

9:23 According to Galatians 1:17, 18, Paul left Damascus and traveled to Arabia, the desert region just southeast of Damascus, where he lived for three years. It is unclear whether his three-year stay occurred between verses 22 and 23, or between verses 25 and 26. Some commentators say that "many days" could mean a long period of time. They suggest that when Paul returned to Damascus, the governor under Aretas ordered his arrest (2 Corinthians 11:32), in an effort to keep peace with influential Jews.

The other possibility is that Paul's night escape occurred during his first stay in Damascus, just after his conversion, when the Pharisees were especially upset over his defection from their ranks. He would have fled to Arabia to spend time alone with God and to let the Jewish religious leaders cool down. Regardless of which theory is correct, there was a period of at least three years between Paul's conversion (9:3–6) and his trip to Jerusalem (9:26).

9:26, 27 It is difficult to change your reputation, and Saul had a terrible reputation with the Christians. But Barnabas, a Jewish convert (mentioned in 4:36), became the bridge between Saul and the apostles. New Christians (especially those with tarnished reputations) need sponsors, people who will come alongside, encourage, teach, and introduce them to other believers. In what ways can you become a Barnabas to new believers?

9:27 Galatians 1:18, 19 explains that Paul was in Jerusalem only 15 days and that he met only with Peter and James.

SAUL'S RETURN TO TARSUS
At least three years elapsed between Acts 9:22 and 9:26. After time alone in Arabia (see Galatians 1:16–18), Saul (Paul) returned to Damascus and then to Jerusalem. The apostles were reluctant to believe that this former persecutor could have become one of them.He escaped to Caesarea, where he caught a ship and returned to Tarsus.

PAUL

No person, apart from Jesus himself, shaped the history of Christianity like the apostle Paul. Even before he was a believer, his actions were significant. His frenzied persecution of Christians following Stephen's death got the church started in obeying Christ's final command to take the gospel worldwide. Paul's personal encounter with Jesus changed his life. He never lost his fierce intensity, but from then on it was channeled for the gospel.

Paul was very religious. His training under Gamaliel was the finest available. His intentions and efforts were sincere. He was a good Pharisee who knew the Bible and sincerely believed that this Christian movement was dangerous to Judaism. Thus, Paul hated the Christian faith and persecuted Christians without mercy.

Paul got permission to travel to Damascus to capture Christians and bring them back to Jerusalem. But God stopped him in his hurried tracks on the Damascus road. Paul personally met Jesus Christ, and his life was never the same.

Until Paul's conversion, little had been done about carrying the gospel to non-Jews. Philip had preached in Samaria and to an Ethiopian man; Cornelius, a Gentile, was converted under Peter; and in Antioch in Syria, some Greeks had joined the believers. When Barnabas was sent from Jerusalem to check on this situation, he went to Tarsus to find Paul and bring him to Antioch, and together they worked among the believers there. They were then sent on a missionary journey, the first of three Paul would take that would carry the gospel across the Roman empire.

The thorny issue of whether Gentile believers had to obey Jewish laws before they could become Christians caused many problems in the early church. Paul worked hard to convince the Jews that Gentiles were acceptable to God, but he spent even more time convincing the Gentiles that they were acceptable to God. The lives Paul touched were changed and challenged by meeting Christ through him.

God did not waste any part of Paul—his background, his training, his citizenship, his mind, or even his weaknesses. Are you willing to let God do the same for you? You will never know all he can do with you until you allow him to have all that you are!

Strengths and accomplishments:	• Transformed by God from a persecutor of Christians to a preacher for Christ
	• Preached for Christ throughout the Roman empire on three missionary journeys
	• Wrote letters to various churches, which became part of the New Testament
	• Was never afraid to face an issue head-on and deal with it
	• Was sensitive to God's leading and, despite his strong personality, always did as God directed
	• Is often called the apostle to the Gentiles
Weaknesses and mistakes:	• Witnessed and approved of Stephen's stoning
	• Set out to destroy Christianity by persecuting Christians
Lessons from his life:	• The Good News is that forgiveness and eternal life are gifts of God's grace through faith in Christ and are available to all people
	• Obedience results from a relationship with God, but obedience will never create or earn that relationship
	• Real freedom doesn't come until we no longer have to prove our freedom
	• God does not waste our time; he will use our past and present so we may serve him with our future
Vital statistics:	• Where: Born in Tarsus but became a world traveler for Christ
	• Occupations: Trained as a Pharisee, learned the tentmaking trade, served as a missionary
	• Contemporaries: Gamaliel, Stephen, the apostles, Luke, Barnabas, Timothy
Key verses:	"For to me, to live is Christ and to die is gain. If I am to go on living in the body, this will mean fruitful labor for me. Yet what shall I choose? I do not know! I am torn between the two: I desire to depart and be with Christ, which is better by far; but it is more necessary for you that I remain in the body" (Philippians 1:21–24).

Paul's story is told in Acts 7:58—28:31 and throughout his New Testament letters.

9:29, 30 In these short sentences we can see two characteristics of Paul, even as a new believer in Christ: He was bold, and he stirred up controversy. These would characterize Paul's ministry the rest of his life. The Grecian Jews were Greek-speaking Jews.

9:30 Saul's visit to Tarsus helped quiet conflicts with the Jews and allowed him time to prove his commitment. After

Saul, the most zealous persecutor, was converted, the church enjoyed a brief time of peace. "Brothers" refers to fellow Christians, members of God's family.

36 In Joppa there was a disciple named Tabitha (which, when translated, is Dorcas[a]), who was always doing good[t] and helping the poor. 37 About that time she became sick and died, and her body was washed and placed in an upstairs room. [u] 38 Lydda was near Joppa; so when the disciples[v] heard that Peter was in Lydda, they sent two men to him and urged him, "Please come at once!"

39 Peter went with them, and when he arrived he was taken upstairs to the room. All the widows[w] stood around him, crying and showing him the robes and other clothing that Dorcas had made while she was still with them.

40 Peter sent them all out of the room;[x] then he got down on his knees[y] and prayed. Turning toward the dead woman, he said, "Tabitha, get up." She opened her eyes, and seeing Peter she sat up. 41 He took her by the hand and helped her to her feet. Then he called the believers and the widows and presented her to them alive. 42 This became known all over Joppa, and many people believed in the Lord. 43 Peter stayed in Joppa for some time with a tanner named Simon.[z]

Cornelius Calls for Peter

10 At Caesarea there was a man named Cornelius, a centurion in what was known as the Italian Regiment. 2 He and all his family were devout and God-fearing;[a] he gave generously to those in need and prayed to God regularly. 3 One day at about three in the afternoon[b] he had a vision. He distinctly saw an angel of God, who came to him and said, "Cornelius!"

4 Cornelius stared at him in fear. "What is it, Lord?" he asked.

The angel answered, "Your prayers and gifts to the poor have come up as a memorial offering before God. [c] 5 Now send men to Joppa to bring back a man named Simon who is called Peter. 6 He is staying with Simon the tanner,[d] whose house is by the sea."

a36 Both *Tabitha* (Aramaic) and *Dorcas* (Greek) mean *gazelle.*

9:36 l 1 Ti 2:10
9:37 u Ac 1:13
9:38 v Ac 11:26
9:39 w Ac 6:1
9:40 x Mt 9:25 y Ac 7:60
9:43 z Ac 10:6
10:2 a ver 22, 35
10:3 b Ac 3:1
10:4 c Rev 8:4
10:6 d Ac 9:43

9:36 The important harbor city of Joppa sits 125 feet above sea level overlooking the Mediterranean Sea. Joppa was the town into which the cedars of Lebanon had been floated to be shipped to Jerusalem and used in the temple construction (2 Chronicles 2:16; Ezra 3:7). The prophet Jonah had left the port of Joppa on his ill-fated trip (Jonah 1:3).

9:36–42 Dorcas made an enormous impact on her community by "always doing good and helping the poor," by making robes and other clothing (9:39). When she died, the room was filled with mourners, very likely many of the people she had helped. And when she was brought back to life, the news raced through the town. God uses great preachers like Peter and Paul, but he also uses those who have gifts of kindness like Dorcas. Rather than wishing you had other gifts, make good use of the gifts God has given you.

9:43 In Joppa, Peter stayed at the home of Simon, a tanner. Tanners made animal hides into leather. It is significant that Peter was at Simon's house, because tanning involved contact with dead animals, and Jewish law considered it an "unclean" occupation. Peter was already beginning to break down his prejudice against people who were not of his kind and customs that did not adhere to Jewish religious traditions.

10:1 This Caesarea, sometimes called Palestinian Caesarea, was located on the coast of the Mediterranean Sea, 32 miles north of Joppa. The largest and most important port city on the Mediterranean in Palestine, Caesarea served as the capital of the Roman province of Judea. This was the first city to have Gentile Christians and a non-Jewish church.

10:1 This Roman officer was a *centurion,* a commander of 100 soldiers. Although stationed in Caesarea, Cornelius would probably return soon to Rome. Thus his conversion was a major stepping-stone for spreading the gospel to the empire's capital city.

10:2 "What will happen to the heathen who have never heard about Christ?" This question is often asked about God's justice. Cornelius wasn't a believer in Christ, but he was seeking God, and he was reverent and generous. Therefore God sent Peter to tell Cornelius about Christ. Cornelius is an example that God "rewards those who earnestly seek him" (Hebrews 11:6). Cornelius's story demonstrates God's willingness to use extraordinary means to reach those who desire to know him. Those who sincerely seek God will find him! God made Cornelius's knowledge complete.

10:3 Cornelius had a vision featuring a heavenly messenger. God spoke to other Bible characters through a variety of means—the burning bush of Moses (Exodus 3:1–4); the talking donkey of Balaam (Numbers 22:21–30); the gentle whisper heard by Elijah (1 Kings 19:11–14); the strange object lessons of Jeremiah (Jeremiah 13:1–11). Simply put, God speaks to his people in remarkably different ways—through the written Scriptures, through the words of others, through circumstances and events. It is up to us to listen, to be perceptive, to be alert. What is God trying to say to you today?

PETER'S MINISTRY
Peter traveled to the ancient crossroads town of Lydda, where he healed crippled Aeneas. The believers in Joppa, an old port city, sent for him after a wonderful woman died. Peter went and brought her back to life. While in Joppa, Peter had a vision that led him to take the gospel to Cornelius, a Gentile, in Caesarea.

7When the angel who spoke to him had gone, Cornelius called two of his servants and a devout soldier who was one of his attendants. 8He told them everything that had happened and sent them to Joppa.

Peter's Vision

9About noon the following day as they were on their journey and approaching the city, Peter went up on the roof to pray. 10He became hungry and wanted something to eat, and while the meal was being prepared, he fell into a trance. 11He saw heaven opened and something like a large sheet being let down to earth by its four corners. 12It contained all kinds of

GREAT ESCAPES IN THE BIBLE

Who escaped	Reference	What happened	What the escape accomplished	Application
Jacob	Genesis 31:1–55	Fled from his father-in-law, Laban, after almost 20 years of service	Allowed Jacob to return home for Isaac's death and for reconciliation with Esau, his brother	A time away from home often puts the really important things into perspective
Moses	Exodus 2:11–15	Fled Egypt after killing an Egyptian in defense of a fellow Israelite	Saved his own life and began another part of God's training	God fits even our mistakes into his plan
Israelites	Exodus 12:28–42	Escaped Egypt after 430 years, most of that time in slavery	God confirmed his choice of Abraham's descendants	God will not forget his promises
Spies	Joshua 2:1–24	Escaped searchers in Jericho by hiding in Rahab's house	Prepared the destruction of Jericho and preserved Rehab, who would become one of David's ancestors—as well as an ancestor of Jesus	God's plan weaves lives together in a pattern beyond our understanding
Ehud	Judges 3:15–30	Escaped undetected after assassinating the Moabite king Eglon	Broke the control of Moab over Israel and began 80 years of peace	Punishments by God are often swift and deadly
Samson	Judges 16:1–3	Escaped a locked city by ripping the gates from their hinges	Merely postponed Samson's self-destruction because of his lack of self-control	Without dependence on God and his guidance, even great ability is wasted
Elijah	1 Kings 19:1–18	Fled into the desert out of fear of Queen Jezebel	Preserved Elijah's life but also displayed his human weakness	Even at moments of real success, our personal weaknesses are our greatest challenges
Saul (Paul)	Acts 9:23–25	Lowered over the wall in a basket to get out of Damascus	Saved this new Christian for great service to God	God has a purpose for every life, which leads to a real adventure for those willing to cooperate
Peter	Acts 12:1–11	Freed from prison by an angel	Saved Peter for God's further plans for his life	God can use extraordinary means to carry out his plan—often when we least expect it
Paul and Silas	Acts 16:22–40	Chains loosened and doors opened by an earthquake, but they chose not to leave the prison	Pointed out the powerlessness of humans before God	When our dependence and attention are focused on God rather than our problems, he is able to offer help in unexpected ways

10:12 According to Jewish law, certain foods were forbidden to be eaten (see Leviticus 11). The food laws made it difficult for Jews to eat with Gentiles without risking defilement. In fact, the Gentiles themselves were often seen as "unclean." Peter's vision meant that he should not look upon the Gentiles as inferior people whom God would not redeem. Before having the vision, Peter would have thought that a Gentile Roman officer could not become a follower of Christ. Afterward, he understood that it was his responsibility to go with the messengers into a Gentile home and tell Cornelius the Good News of salvation in Jesus Christ.

four-footed animals, as well as reptiles of the earth and birds of the air. [13]Then a voice told him, "Get up, Peter. Kill and eat."

[14]"Surely not, Lord!" Peter replied. "I have never eaten anything impure or unclean."[e]

[15]The voice spoke to him a second time, "Do not call anything impure that God has made clean."[f]

[16]This happened three times, and immediately the sheet was taken back to heaven.

[17]While Peter was wondering about the meaning of the vision, the men sent by Cornelius found out where Simon's house was and stopped at the gate. [18]They called out, asking if Simon who was known as Peter was staying there.

[19]While Peter was still thinking about the vision, the Spirit said to him, "Simon, three[a] men are looking for you. [20]So get up and go downstairs. Do not hesitate to go with them, for I have sent them."[g]

[21]Peter went down and said to the men, "I'm the one you're looking for. Why have you come?"

[22]The men replied, "We have come from Cornelius the centurion. He is a righteous and God-fearing man, who is respected by all the Jewish people. A holy angel told him to have you come to his house so that he could hear what you have to say." [23]Then Peter invited the men into the house to be his guests.

Peter at Cornelius's House

The next day Peter started out with them, and some of the brothers from Joppa went along.[h] [24]The following day he arrived in Caesarea. Cornelius was expecting them and had called together his relatives and close friends. [25]As Peter entered the house, Cornelius met him and fell at his feet in reverence. [26]But Peter made him get up. "Stand up," he said, "I am only a man myself."[i]

[27]Talking with him, Peter went inside and found a large gathering of people. [28]He said to them: "You are well aware that it is against our law for a Jew to associate with a Gentile or visit him.[j] But God has shown me that I should not call any man impure or unclean.[k] [29]So when I was sent for, I came without raising any objection. May I ask why you sent for me?"

[30]Cornelius answered: "Four days ago I was in my house praying at this hour, at three in the afternoon. Suddenly a man in shining clothes stood before me [31]and said, 'Cornelius, God has heard your prayer and remembered your gifts to the poor. [32]Send to Joppa for Simon who is called Peter. He is a guest in the home of Simon the tanner, who lives by the sea.' [33]So I sent for you immediately, and it was good of you to come. Now we are all here in the presence of God to listen to everything the Lord has commanded you to tell us."

[34]Then Peter began to speak: "I now realize how true it is that God does not show favoritism[l] [35]but accepts men from every nation who fear him and do what is right.[m] [36]You know the message God sent to the people of Israel, telling the good news of peace through Jesus Christ, who is Lord of all.[n] [37]You know what has happened throughout Judea, beginning in Galilee after the baptism that John preached— [38]how God anointed Jesus of Nazareth with the Holy Spirit and power, and how he went around doing good and healing all who were under the power of the devil, because God was with him.[o]

[a] 19 One early manuscript *two*; other manuscripts do not have the number.

10:14
[e] Dt 14:3-20;
Eze 4:14
10:15
[f] Mt 15:11;
Ro 14:14, 17, 20;
1Co 10:25; 1Ti 4:3,
4; Tit 1:15

10:20
[g] Ac 15:7-9

10:23
[h] Ac 11:12

10:26
[i] Rev 19:10

10:28
[j] Jn 4:9; 18:28;
Ac 11:3
[k] Ac 15:8, 9

10:34
[l] Dt 10:17; Ro 2:11;
Eph 6:9; Col 3:25;
1Pe 1:17
10:35
[m] Ac 15:9
10:36
[n] Mt 28:18
10:38
[o] Jn 3:2

10:15, 16 Steeped in Jewish tradition and filled with certain biases, Peter was convinced his views on the Gentiles were correct. It took a three-part heavenly vision for God to change Peter's mind. One of the most basic and practical lessons from this encounter is that when God speaks, we must not challenge what he says. Doubting God is the rebellion of Eden. When God says something is so, we must not debate with him. The right response is humble submission to his revealed truth. Are you trying to argue with God over some point that he has already made clear?

10:21, 22 Cornelius was religious, devoted, generous, respected, and sincere (10:1, 2). However, he was still spiritually separated from God. Because he needed to understand the gospel, God sent Peter to present to him the truth about salvation. Be careful not to equate earnestness with righteousness before God. We are brought into right standing with God by faith in Christ alone. Have you trusted in Jesus? Are you sharing with others—even those who seem religious— the truth that Christ is the only way to God?

10:34, 35 Perhaps the greatest barrier to the spread of the

gospel in the first century was the Jewish-Gentile conflict. Most of the early believers were Jewish, and they thought it scandalous even to think of associating with Gentiles. But God told Peter to take the gospel to a Roman, and Peter obeyed despite his background and personal feelings. (Later Peter struggled with this again—see Galatians 2:11–14.) God was making it clear that the Good News of Christ is for everyone! We should not allow any barrier—language, culture, race, geography, economic level, or educational level—to keep us from telling others about Christ.

10:35 Every nation has people who are restless for God, ready to receive the gospel—but someone must take it to them. Seeking God is not enough—people must find him. How then shall seekers find God without someone to point the way? Is God asking you to show someone the way to him? (See Romans 10:14, 15.)

10:37–43 Peter's brief and powerful sermon contains a concise statement of the gospel: Jesus' perfect life of servanthood; his death on the cross; his resurrection, personally witnessed and experienced by Peter; Jesus' fulfillment of the Scriptures; the

10:39
p Ac 5:30

10:40
q Ac 2:24

10:41
r Jn 14:17, 22

10:42
s Jn 5:22; 1Pe 4:5

10:43
t Isa 53:11

10:45
u ver 23

39 "We are witnesses of everything he did in the country of the Jews and in Jerusalem. They killed him by hanging him on a tree,p 40 but God raised him from the dead q on the third day and caused him to be seen. 41 He was not seen by all the people,r but by witnesses whom God had already chosen—by us who ate and drank with him after he rose from the dead. 42 He commanded us to preach to the people and to testify that he is the one whom God appointed as judge of the living and the dead. s 43 All the prophets testify about him t that everyone who believes in him receives forgiveness of sins through his name."

44 While Peter was still speaking these words, the Holy Spirit came on all who heard the message. 45 The circumcised believers who had come with Peter u were astonished that the gift of the Holy Spirit had been poured out even on the Gentiles. 46 For they heard them speaking in tongues a and praising God.

a 46 Or other languages

CORNELIUS

The early days of Christianity were exciting as God's Spirit moved and people's lives were changed. Converts were pouring in from surprising backgrounds. Even the dreaded Saul (Paul) became a Christian, and non-Jews were responding to the Good News about Jesus. Among the first of these was the Roman centurion, Cornelius.

Because of frequent outbreaks of violence, Roman soldiers had to be stationed throughout Israel to keep the peace. But most Romans, hated as conquerors, did not get along well in the nation. As an army officer, Cornelius was in a difficult position. He represented Rome, but his home was in Caesarea. During his years in Israel, he himself had been conquered by the God of Israel. He had a reputation as a godly man who put his faith into action, and he was respected by the Jews.

Four significant aspects of Cornelius's character are noted in Acts. (1) He actively sought God, (2) he revered God, (3) he was generous in meeting other people's needs, and (4) he prayed. God told him to send for Peter, because Peter would give him more knowledge about the God he was already seeking to please.

When Peter entered Cornelius's home, Peter broke a whole list of Jewish rules. Peter confessed he wasn't comfortable, but here was an eager audience and he couldn't hold back his message. He had no sooner started sharing the gospel when God gave overwhelming approval by filling that Roman family with his Holy Spirit. Peter saw he had no choice but to baptize them and welcome them as equals in the growing Christian church. Another step had been taken in carrying the gospel to the whole world.

Cornelius is a welcome example of God's willingness to use extraordinary means to reach those who desire to know him. He does not play favorites, and he does not hide from those who want to find him. God sent his Son because he loves the whole world—and that includes Peter, Cornelius, and you.

Strengths and accomplishments:	• A godly and generous Roman • Well-respected by the Jews even though he was an officer in the occupying army • He responded to God and encouraged his family to do the same • His conversion helped the young church realize that the Good News was for all people, both Jews and Gentiles
Lessons from his life:	• God reaches those who want to know him • The gospel is for all people • There are people everywhere eager to believe • When we are willing to seek the truth and be obedient to the light God gives us, God will reward us richly
Vital statistics:	• Where: Caesarea • Occupation: Roman centurion • Contemporaries: Peter, Philip, the apostles
Key verse:	"He and all his family were devout and God-fearing; he gave generously to those in need and prayed to God regularly" (Acts 10:2).

Cornelius's story is told in Acts 10:1—11:18.

necessity of personal faith in him. A sermon or witness for Christ does not need to be long to be effective. It should be Spirit-led and should center on Christ, the way and the truth and the life.

10:43 Two examples of prophets testifying about Jesus and his forgiveness of sins are Isaiah 52:13—53:12 and Ezekiel 36:25, 26.

10:45 Cornelius and Peter were very different people. Cornelius was wealthy, a Gentile, and a military man. Peter was a Jewish fisherman turned preacher. But God's plan included both of them. In Cornelius's house that day, a new chapter in Christian history

was written as a Jewish Christian leader and a Gentile Christian convert each discovered something significant about God at work in the other person. Cornelius needed Peter and his gospel to know the way to salvation. Peter needed Cornelius and his salvation experience to know that Gentiles were included in God's plan. You and another believer may also need each other to understand how God works!

10:45 "The circumcised believers" could be translated, "the Jewish believers" (see also 11:2).

Then Peter said, [47]"Can anyone keep these people from being baptized with water? [v] They have received the Holy Spirit just as we have."[w] [48]So he ordered that they be baptized in the name of Jesus Christ.[x] Then they asked Peter to stay with them for a few days.

Peter Explains His Actions

11 The apostles and the brothers throughout Judea heard that the Gentiles also had received the word of God. [2]So when Peter went up to Jerusalem, the circumcised believers[y] criticized him [3]and said, "You went into the house of uncircumcised men and ate with them."[z]

[4]Peter began and explained everything to them precisely as it had happened: [5]"I was in the city of Joppa praying, and in a trance I saw a vision.[a] I saw something like a large sheet being let down from heaven by its four corners, and it came down to where I was. [6]I looked into it and saw four-footed animals of the earth, wild beasts, reptiles, and birds of the air. [7]Then I heard a voice telling me, 'Get up, Peter. Kill and eat.'

[8]"I replied, 'Surely not, Lord! Nothing impure or unclean has ever entered my mouth.'

[9]"The voice spoke from heaven a second time, 'Do not call anything impure that God has made clean.' [10]This happened three times, and then it was all pulled up to heaven again.

[11]"Right then three men who had been sent to me from Caesarea stopped at the house where I was staying. [12]The Spirit told[b] me to have no hesitation about going with them.[c] These six brothers also went with me, and we entered the man's house. [13]He told us how he had seen an angel appear in his house and say, 'Send to Joppa for Simon who is called Peter. [14]He will bring you a message through which you and all your household will be saved.'

[15]"As I began to speak, the Holy Spirit came on them as he had come on us at the beginning.[d] [16]Then I remembered what the Lord had said: 'John baptized with[a] water, but you will be baptized with the Holy Spirit.'[e] [17]So if God gave them the same gift as he gave us,[f] who believed in the Lord Jesus Christ, who was I to think that I could oppose God?"

[18]When they heard this, they had no further objections and praised God, saying, "So then, God has granted even the Gentiles repentance unto life."

The Church in Antioch

[19]Now those who had been scattered by the persecution in connection with Stephen[g] traveled as far as Phoenicia, Cyprus and Antioch, telling the message only to Jews. [20]Some of

ª16 Or in

**Cross references (right margin):**
10:47
v Ac 8:36
w Ac 11:17
10:48
x Ac 2:38
11:2
y Ac 10:45
11:3
z Ac 10:25, 28; Gal 2:12
11:5
a Ac 10:9-32
11:12
b Ac 8:29
c Ac 15:9
11:15
d Ac 2:4
11:16
e Mk 1:8; Ac 1:5
11:17
f Ac 10:45, 47
11:19
g Ac 8:1, 4

10:47, 48 In this case, the people were baptized *after* they received the Holy Spirit, publicly declaring their allegiance to Christ and identification with the Christian community.

10:48 Cornelius wanted Peter to stay with him for several days. He was a new believer and realized his need for teaching and fellowship. Are you as eager to learn more about Christ? Recognize your need to be with more mature Christians, and strive to learn from them.

11:1–3 A Gentile was anyone who was not a Jew; the Jewish believers are sometimes referred to as "the circumcised believers" (11:2). Most Jewish believers thought that God offered salvation only to the Jews because God had given his law to them (Exodus 19; 20). A group in Jerusalem believed that Gentiles could be saved, but only if they followed all the Jewish laws and traditions—in essence, if they first became Jews before becoming Christians. Both groups were mistaken. God chose the Jews and taught them his laws so they could bring the message of salvation to *all* people (see Genesis 12:3; Psalm 22:27; Isaiah 42:4; 49:6; 56:3–7; 60:1–3; Jeremiah 16:19–21; Zechariah 2:11; Malachi 1:11; Romans 15:9–12).

11:2–18 When Peter brought the news of Cornelius's conversion back to Jerusalem, the believers were shocked that Peter had eaten with Gentiles. After they heard the whole story, however, they praised God (11:18). Their reactions teach us how to handle disagreements with other Christians. Before judging the behavior of fellow believers, it is important to hear them out. The Holy Spirit may have something important to teach us through them.

11:8 God had promised throughout Scripture that he would reach the nations. This began with his general promise to Abraham

(Genesis 12:3; 18:18) and became very specific in Malachi's statement: "My name will be great among the nations, from the rising to the setting of the sun" (Malachi 1:11). But this was an extremely difficult truth for Jews, even Jewish believers, to accept. The Jewish believers understood how certain prophecies were fulfilled in Christ, but they overlooked other Old Testament teachings. Too often we are inclined to accept only the parts of God's Word that appeal to us and support our own agendas, ignoring the teachings we don't like. We must accept all of God's Word as absolute truth.

11:12ff Peter's defense for eating with Gentiles was a simple restatement of what happened. He brought six witnesses with him to back him up, and then he quoted Jesus' promise about the coming of the Holy Spirit (11:16). These Gentiles' lives had been changed, and that was all the evidence Peter and the other believers needed. Changed lives are an equally powerful evidence today.

11:16 Jesus had also demonstrated clearly that he and his message were for all people. He had preached in Samaria (John 4:1–42); in the region of the Gerasenes, populated by Greeks (Mark 5:1–20); and he had even reached out to Romans (Luke 7:1–10). The apostles shouldn't have been surprised that they were called to do the same.

11:18 The intellectual questions ended and the theological discussion stopped with the report that God had given the Holy Spirit to the Gentiles. This was a turning point for the early church. They had to accept those whom God had chosen, even if they were Gentiles. But joy over the conversion of Gentiles was not unanimous. This continued to be a struggle for some Jewish Christians throughout the first century.

11:20, 21 In Antioch, Christianity was launched on its world-

11:20
h Ac 4:36

11:21
i Lk 1:66
j Ac 2:47

11:23
k Ac 13:43

11:24
l ver 21; Ac 5:14

11:25
m Ac 9:11

11:27
n 1Co 12:28, 29

11:28
o Ac 21:10

11:29
p Ro 15:26

11:30
q Ac 12:25

them, however, men from Cyprus *h* and Cyrene, went to Antioch and began to speak to Greeks also, telling them the good news about the Lord Jesus. ²¹The Lord's hand was with them, *i* and a great number of people believed and turned to the Lord. *j*

²²News of this reached the ears of the church at Jerusalem, and they sent Barnabas to Antioch. ²³When he arrived and saw the evidence of the grace of God, *k* he was glad and encouraged them all to remain true to the Lord with all their hearts. ²⁴He was a good man, full of the Holy Spirit and faith, and a great number of people were brought to the Lord. *l*

²⁵Then Barnabas went to Tarsus *m* to look for Saul, ²⁶and when he found him, he brought him to Antioch. So for a whole year Barnabas and Saul met with the church and taught great numbers of people. The disciples were called Christians first at Antioch.

²⁷During this time some prophets *n* came down from Jerusalem to Antioch. ²⁸One of them, named Agabus, *o* stood up and through the Spirit predicted that a severe famine would spread over the entire Roman world. (This happened during the reign of Claudius.) ²⁹The disciples, each according to his ability, decided to provide help *p* for the brothers living in Judea. ³⁰This they did, sending their gift to the elders by Barnabas and Saul. *q*

---

wide mission and there the believers aggressively preached to the Gentiles (non-Jews who did not worship God). Philip had preached in Samaria, but the Samaritans were part Jewish (8:5); Peter had preached to Cornelius, but he already worshiped God (10:2). Believers who were scattered after the outbreak of persecution in Jerusalem spread the gospel to other Jews in the lands they fled to (11:19). The seeds of this missionary work had been sown after Stephen's death. At this time, the believers began actively sharing the Good News with Gentiles.

11:22 With the exception of Jerusalem, Antioch of Syria played a more important role in the early church than any other city. After Rome and Alexandria, Antioch was the largest city in the Roman world. In Antioch, the first Gentile church was founded, and there the believers were first called Christians (11:26). Paul used the city as his home base during his missionary journeys. Antioch was the center of worship for several pagan cults that promoted much sexual immorality and other forms of evil common to pagan religions. It was also a vital commercial center—the gateway to the eastern world. Antioch was a key city both to Rome and to the early church.

11:22–26 Barnabas presents a wonderful example of how to help new Christians. He demonstrated strong faith; he ministered joyfully with kindness and encouragement; he taught new believers further lessons about God (see 9:26–30). Remember Barnabas when you see new believers, and think of ways to help them grow in their faith.

11:25 Saul had been sent to his home in Tarsus for protection after his conversion had caused an uproar among the Jewish leaders in Jerusalem (9:26–30). He stayed there for several years before Barnabas brought him to help the church at Antioch.

11:26 The young church at Antioch was a curious mixture of Jews (who spoke Greek or Aramaic) and Gentiles. It is significant that this is the first place where the believers were called Christians (or "Christ-ones"), because all they had in common was Christ—not race, culture, or even language. Christ can cross all boundaries and unify all people.

11:26 Barnabas and Saul stayed at Antioch for a full year, teaching the new believers. They could have left for other cities, but they saw the importance of follow-through and training. Have you helped someone believe in Christ? Spend time teaching and encouraging that person. Are you a new believer? Remember, you are just beginning your Christian life. Your faith needs to grow and mature through consistent Bible study and teaching.

11:27, 28 Prophets were found not only in the Old Testament, but also in the early church. Their role was to present God's will

to the people and to instruct them in God's Word. Sometimes, like Agabus, they also had the gift of predicting the future.

11:28, 29 Serious food shortages occurred during the reign of the Roman emperor Claudius (A.D. 41–54) because of a drought that had extended across much of the Roman empire for many years. It is significant that the church in Antioch assisted the church in Jerusalem. The daughter church had grown enough to be able to help the established church.

11:29 The people of Antioch were motivated to give generously because they cared about the needs of others. This is the cheerful giving that the Bible commends (2 Corinthians 9:7). Reluctant giving reflects a lack of concern for people. Focus your concern on the needy, and you will be motivated to give.

BARNABAS AND SAUL IN ANTIOCH Persecution scattered the believers into Phoenicia, Cyprus, and Antioch, and the gospel went with them. Most spoke only to Jews, but in Antioch, some Gentiles were converted. The church sent Barnabas to investigate, and he was pleased with what he found. Barnabas went to Tarsus to bring Saul (Paul) back to Antioch.

Peter's Miraculous Escape From Prison

12 It was about this time that King Herod arrested some who belonged to the church, intending to persecute them. 2 He had James, the brother of John,[r] put to death with the sword. 3 When he saw that this pleased the Jews, he proceeded to seize Peter also. This happened during the Feast of Unleavened Bread.[s] 4 After arresting him, he put him in prison, handing him over to be guarded by four squads of four soldiers each. Herod intended to bring him out for public trial after the Passover.

5 So Peter was kept in prison, but the church was earnestly praying to God for him.

6 The night before Herod was to bring him to trial, Peter was sleeping between two soldiers, bound with two chains, and sentries stood guard at the entrance. 7 Suddenly an angel[t] of the Lord appeared and a light shone in the cell. He struck Peter on the side and woke him up. "Quick, get up!" he said, and the chains fell off Peter's wrists.

8 Then the angel said to him, "Put on your clothes and sandals." And Peter did so. "Wrap your cloak around you and follow me," the angel told him. 9 Peter followed him out of the prison, but he had no idea that what the angel was doing was really happening; he thought he was seeing a vision. 10 They passed the first and second guards and came to the iron gate leading to the city. It opened for them by itself,[u] and they went through it. When they had walked the length of one street, suddenly the angel left him.

11 Then Peter came to himself and said, "Now I know without a doubt that the Lord sent his angel and rescued me[v] from Herod's clutches and from everything the Jewish people were anticipating."

12 When this had dawned on him, he went to the house of Mary the mother of John, also called Mark,[w] where many people had gathered and were praying.[x] 13 Peter knocked at the outer entrance, and a servant girl named Rhoda came to answer the door. 14 When she recognized Peter's voice, she was so overjoyed she ran back without opening it and exclaimed, "Peter is at the door!"

15 "You're out of your mind," they told her. When she kept insisting that it was so, they said, "It must be his angel."[y]

16 But Peter kept on knocking, and when they opened the door and saw him, they were astonished. 17 Peter motioned with his hand[z] for them to be quiet and described how the Lord had brought him out of prison. "Tell James and the brothers about this," he said, and then he left for another place.

18 In the morning, there was no small commotion among the soldiers as to what had become of Peter. 19 After Herod had a thorough search made for him and did not find him, he cross-examined the guards and ordered that they be executed.[a]

12:2
[r] Mt 4:21

12:3
[s] Ex 12:15; 23:15

12:7
[t] Ac 5:19

12:10
[u] Ac 16:26

12:11
[v] Da 3:28; 6:22

12:12
[w] Ac 15:37, 39
[x] ver 5

12:15
[y] Mt 18:10

12:17
[z] Ac 13:16; 19:33; 21:40

12:19
[a] Ac 16:27

12:1 This King Herod was Herod Agrippa I, the son of Aristobulus and grandson of Herod the Great. His sister was Herodias, who had been responsible for the death of John the Baptist (see Mark 6:17–28). Herod Agrippa I was partly Jewish. The Romans had appointed him to rule over most of Palestine, including the territories of Galilee, Perea, Judea, and Samaria. He persecuted the Christians in order to please the Jewish leaders who opposed them, hoping that would solidify his position. Agrippa I died suddenly in A.D. 44 (see 12:20–23). His death was also recorded by the historian Josephus.

12:2 James and John were two of Jesus' original 12 disciples. They had asked Jesus for special recognition in his kingdom (Mark 10:35–40). Jesus had said that to be a part of his kingdom would mean suffering with Jesus (drink from the same cup—Mark 10:38, 39). James and John did indeed suffer—Herod executed James, and later John was exiled (see Revelation 1:9).

12:2–11 Why did God allow James to die and yet miraculously save Peter? Life is full of difficult questions like this. Why is one child physically disabled and another child athletically gifted? Why do people die seemingly before realizing their potential? Questions like these we cannot possibly answer in this life because we do not see all that God sees. He has chosen to allow evil in this world for a time. But we can trust God's leading because he has promised to destroy all evil eventually. In the meantime, we know that God will help us use our suffering to strengthen us and glorify him. For more on this question, see the notes on Job 1:1ff; 2:10; 3:23–26.

12:3–5 Herod had Peter arrested during the Passover celebration.

This was a strategic move, since more Jews were in the city than usual, and Herod could impress the most people. Herod's plan undoubtedly was to execute Peter, but the believers were praying for Peter's safety. The earnest prayer of the church significantly affected the outcome of these events. Prayer changes things, so pray often and with confidence.

12:7 God sent an angel to rescue Peter. Angels are God's messengers. They are divinely created beings with supernatural powers, and they sometimes take on human appearance in order to talk to people. Angels should not be worshiped, because they are not divine. They are God's servants, just as we are.

12:12 John Mark wrote the Gospel of Mark. His mother's house was large enough to accommodate a meeting of many believers. An upstairs room in this house may have been the location of Jesus' last supper with his disciples (Luke 22:8ff).

12:13–15 The prayers of the group of believers were answered, even as they prayed. But when the answer arrived at the door, they didn't believe it. We should be people of faith who believe that God answers the prayers of those who seek his will. When you pray, believe you'll get an answer. And when the answer comes, don't be surprised; be thankful!

12:17 This James was Jesus' brother, who became a leader in the Jerusalem church (15:13; Galatians 1:19). The James who was killed (12:2) was John's brother and one of the original 12 disciples.

12:19 Under Roman law, guards who allowed a prisoner to

Herod's Death

12:20
b 1Ki 5:9, 11;
Eze 27:17

Then Herod went from Judea to Caesarea and stayed there a while. ²⁰He had been quarreling with the people of Tyre and Sidon; they now joined together and sought an audience with him. Having secured the support of Blastus, a trusted personal servant of the king, they asked for peace, because they depended on the king's country for their food supply. *b*

12:23
c 2Sa 24:16, 17

²¹On the appointed day Herod, wearing his royal robes, sat on his throne and delivered a public address to the people. ²²They shouted, "This is the voice of a god, not of a man." ²³Immediately, because Herod did not give praise to God, an angel of the Lord struck him down, *c* and he was eaten by worms and died.

HEROD AGRIPPA I

For good or evil, families have lasting and powerful influence on their children. Traits and qualities are passed on to the next generation, and often with the mistakes and sins of the parents being repeated by the children. Four generations of the Herod family are mentioned in the Bible. Each leader left his evil mark: Herod the Great murdered the baby boys in Bethlehem; Herod Antipas was involved in Jesus' trial and John the Baptist's execution; Herod Agrippa I murdered the apostle James; and Herod Agrippa II was one of Paul's judges.

Herod Agrippa I related fairly well to his Jewish subjects. He had a Jewish grandmother of royal blood (Mariamne), which allowed the people to accept him—though grudgingly. As a youth he had been temporarily imprisoned by the emperor Tiberias, but he was now trusted by Rome and got along well with the emperors Caligula and Claudius.

An unexpected opportunity for Herod to gain new favor with the Jews was created by the Christian movement. Gentiles began to be accepted into the church in large numbers. Many Jews had been tolerating this new movement as a sect within Judaism, but its rapid growth alarmed them. Persecution of Christians was revived, and even the apostles were not spared. James was killed, and Peter was thrown into prison.

But soon Herod made a fatal error. During a visit to Caesarea, the people called him a god, and he accepted their praise. Herod was immediately struck with a painful disease, and he died within a week.

Like his grandfather and uncle before him, and his son after him, Herod Agrippa I came close to the truth but missed it. Because religion was important only as an aspect of politics, he had no reverence and no qualms about taking praise that only God should receive. His mistake is a common one. Whenever we become proud of our own abilities and accomplishments, not recognizing them as gifts from God, we repeat Herod's sin.

Strengths and accomplishments:	• Capable administrator and negotiator • Managed to maintain good relations with the Jews in his region and with Rome
Weaknesses and mistakes:	• Arranged the murder of the apostle James • Imprisoned Peter with plans to execute him • Allowed the people to praise him as a god
Lessons from his life:	• Those who set themselves against God are doomed to ultimate failure • There is great danger in accepting praise that only God deserves • Family traits can influence children toward great good or great evil
Vital statistics:	• Where: Jerusalem • Occupation: Roman-appointed king of the Jews • Relatives: Grandfather: Herod the Great. Father: Aristobulus. Uncle: Herod Antipas. Sister: Herodias. Wife: Cypros. Son: Herod Agrippa II. Daughters: Bernice, Mariamne, Drusilla. • Contemporaries: Emperors Tiberias, Caligula, and Claudius. James, Peter, the apostles.
Key verse:	"Immediately, because Herod did not give praise to God, an angel of the Lord struck him down, and he was eaten by worms and died" (Acts 12:23).

Herod Agrippa I's story is told in Acts 12:1–23.

---

escape were subject to the same punishment the prisoner was to receive. Thus these 16 guards were sentenced to death.

12:19 The Jews considered Jerusalem their capital, but the Romans made Caesarea their headquarters in Palestine. That is where Herod Agrippa I lived.

12:20 These coastal cities, Tyre and Sidon, were free and self-governing but economically dependent on Judea (see the map in the introduction to Acts for their location). We don't know why

Herod had quarreled with them, but now representatives from those cities were trying to appease him through his personal servant.

12:23 Herod died a horrible death accompanied by intense pain; he was literally eaten alive, from the inside out, by worms. Pride is a serious sin, and in this case, God chose to punish it immediately. God does not immediately punish all sin, but he *will* judge everyone (Hebrews 9:27). Accept Christ's offer of forgiveness today. No one can afford to wait.

24 But the word of God continued to increase and spread. *d*

25 When Barnabas and Saul had finished their mission, *e* they returned from *a* Jerusalem, taking with them John, also called Mark.

12:24
d Ac 6:7; 19:20
12:25
e Ac 11:30

B. PAUL'S MINISTRY (13:1—28:31)

The book focuses now on the ministry to the Gentiles and the spread of the church around the world, and Paul replaces Peter as the central figure in the book. Paul completes three missionary journeys and ends up being imprisoned in Jerusalem and transported to Rome. The book of Acts ends abruptly, showing that the history of the church is not yet complete. We are to be a part of the sequel.

1. First missionary journey

Barnabas and Saul Sent Off

13 In the church at Antioch there were prophets and teachers: Barnabas, *f* Simeon called Niger, Lucius of Cyrene, Manaen (who had been brought up with Herod the tetrarch) and Saul. 2 While they were worshiping the Lord and fasting, the Holy Spirit said, "Set apart for me Barnabas and Saul for the work *g* to which I have called them." 3 So after they had fasted and prayed, they placed their hands on them *h* and sent them off.

13:1
f Ac 11:22-26
13:2
g Ac 14:26
13:3
h Ac 6:6

On Cyprus

4 The two of them, sent on their way by the Holy Spirit, went down to Seleucia and sailed from there to Cyprus. *i* 5 When they arrived at Salamis, they proclaimed the word of God in the Jewish synagogues. John was with them as their helper.

6 They traveled through the whole island until they came to Paphos. There they met a Jewish sorcerer *j* and false prophet named Bar-Jesus, 7 who was an attendant of the proconsul, Sergius Paulus. The proconsul, an intelligent man, sent for Barnabas and Saul because he

13:4
i Ac 4:36
13:6
j Ac 8:9

a 25 Some manuscripts *to*

12:25 John Mark was Barnabas's cousin (Colossians 4:10). His mother, Mary, often would open her home to the apostles (12:12), so John Mark would have been exposed to most of the great men and teachings of the early church. Later, John Mark joined Paul and Barnabas on their first missionary journey, but for unknown reasons, he left them in the middle of the trip. John Mark was criticized by Paul for abandoning the mission (15:37–39), but he wrote the Gospel of Mark and was later acclaimed by Paul as a vital help in the growth of the early church (2 Timothy 4:11).

MINISTRY IN CYPRUS

The leaders of the church in Antioch chose Paul and Barnabas to take the gospel westward. Along with John Mark, they boarded ship at Seleucia and set out across the Mediterranean for Cyprus. They preached in Salamis, the largest city, and went across the island to Paphos.

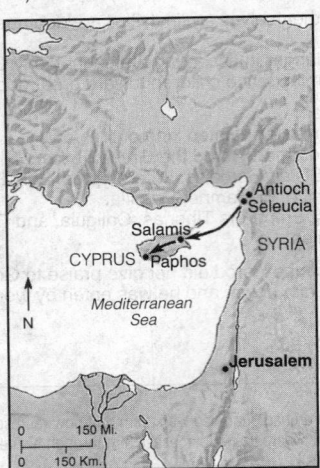

13:1 What variety there is in the church! The common thread among these five men was their deep faith in Christ. We must never exclude anyone whom Christ has called to follow him. Like the early church, if believers today do their part to reach out to all who are lost, church congregations will eventually be comprised of people from different racial and cultural backgrounds. When this happens, we most often see our propensity to label and categorize. We are most comfortable with those who are just like us. Clearly, at the root of these tendencies is the ugly sin of prejudice. The more we understand the gospel and embrace God's version of the body of Christ, however, the more we will begin to transcend these differences. More than merely getting along, we will be able to honestly and authentically say from our hearts that we love each other.

13:2, 3 The church set apart Barnabas and Saul to the work God had for them. To *set apart* means to dedicate for a special purpose. We too should dedicate our pastors, missionaries, and Christian workers for their tasks. We can also dedicate ourselves to use our time, money, and talents for God's work. Ask God what he wants you to set apart for him.

13:2, 3 This was the beginning of Paul's first missionary journey. The church was involved in sending Paul and Barnabas, but it was God's plan. Why did Paul and Barnabas go where they did? (1) The Holy Spirit led them. (2) They followed the communication routes of the Roman empire—this made travel easier. (3) They visited key population and cultural centers to reach as many people as possible. (4) They went to cities with synagogues, speaking first to the Jews in hopes that they would see Jesus as the Messiah and help spread the Good News to everyone.

13:4 Located in the Mediterranean Sea, the island of Cyprus, with a large Jewish population, was Barnabas's home. Their first stop was in familiar territory.

13:6, 7 A proconsul was a high Roman official. Here he functioned as the governor of the island. Such leaders often kept private sorcerers. Bar-Jesus realized that if Sergius Paulus believed in Jesus, he would soon be out of a job.

13:8
k Ac 8:9
l Ac 6:7

13:9
m Ac 4:8

13:10
n Mt 13:38

13:11
o 1Sa 5:6, 7

wanted to hear the word of God. ⁸ But Elymas the sorcerer*k* (for that is what his name means) opposed them and tried to turn the proconsul from the faith. *l* ⁹ Then Saul, who was also called Paul, filled with the Holy Spirit, *m* looked straight at Elymas and said, ¹⁰"You are a child of the devil*n* and an enemy of everything that is right! You are full of all kinds of deceit and trickery. Will you never stop perverting the right ways of the Lord? ¹¹Now the hand of the Lord is against you. *o* You are going to be blind, and for a time you will be unable to see the light of the sun."

Immediately mist and darkness came over him, and he groped about, seeking someone to lead him by the hand. ¹²When the proconsul saw what had happened, he believed, for he was amazed at the teaching about the Lord.

JOHN MARK

Mistakes are effective teachers. Their consequences have a way of making lessons painfully clear. But those who learn from their mistakes are wise. John Mark was a good learner who just needed some time and encouragement.

Mark was eager to do the right thing, but he had trouble staying with a task. In his Gospel, Mark mentions a young man (probably referring to himself) who fled in such fear during Jesus' arrest that he left his clothes behind. This tendency to run showed up later when Paul and Barnabas took him as their assistant on their first missionary journey. At their second stop, Mark left them and returned to Jerusalem. It was a decision Paul did not easily accept. In preparing for their second journey two years later, Barnabas again suggested Mark as a traveling companion, but Paul flatly refused. As a result, the team was divided. Barnabas took Mark with him, and Paul chose Silas. Barnabas was patient with Mark, and the young man repaid his investment. Paul and Mark were later reunited, and the older apostle became a close friend of the young disciple.

Mark was a valuable companion to three early Christian leaders: Barnabas, Paul, and Peter. The material in Mark's Gospel seems to have come mostly from Peter. Mark's role as a serving assistant allowed him to be an observer. He heard Peter's accounts of the years with Jesus over and over, and he was one of the first to put Jesus' life in writing.

Barnabas played a key role in Mark's life. He stood beside the young man despite his failure, giving him patient encouragement. Mark challenges us to learn from our mistakes and appreciate the patience of others. Is there a Barnabas in your life you need to thank for his or her encouragement to you?

Strengths and accomplishments:	• Wrote the Gospel of Mark • Provided his family's home as one of the main meeting places for the Christians in Jerusalem • Persisted beyond his youthful mistakes • Was an assistant and traveling companion to three of the greatest early missionaries
Weaknesses and mistakes:	• Probably the nameless young man described in the Gospel of Mark who fled in panic when Jesus was arrested • Left Paul and Barnabas for unknown reasons during the first missionary journey
Lessons from his life:	• Personal maturity usually comes from a combination of time and mistakes • Mistakes are not usually as important as what can be learned from them • Effective living is not measured as much by what we accomplish as by what we overcome in order to accomplish it • Encouragement can change a person's life
Vital statistics:	• Where: Jerusalem • Occupations: Missionary-in-training, Gospel writer, traveling companion • Relatives: Mother: Mary. Cousin: Barnabas. • Contemporaries: Paul, Peter, Timothy, Luke, Silas
Key verse:	"Only Luke is with me. Get Mark and bring him with you, because he is helpful to me in my ministry" (Paul writing in 2 Timothy 4:11).

John Mark's story is told in Acts 12:23—13:13 and 15:36–39. He is also mentioned in Colossians 4:10; 2 Timothy 4:11; Philemon 24; 1 Peter 5:13.

13:9, 10 Here is where Saul is first called Paul.
13:10 The Holy Spirit led Paul to confront Bar-Jesus with his sin. There is a time to be nice and a time to confront. Ask

God to show you the difference and to give you the courage to do what is right.

In Pisidian Antioch

13From Paphos, Paul and his companions sailed to Perga in Pamphylia, where John left them to return to Jerusalem. 14From Perga they went on to Pisidian Antioch.P On the Sabbath q they entered the synagogue and sat down. 15After the reading from the Law and the Prophets, the synagogue rulers sent word to them, saying, "Brothers, if you have a message of encouragement for the people, please speak."

16Standing up, Paul motioned with his hand and said: "Men of Israel and you Gentiles who worship God, listen to me! 17The God of the people of Israel chose our fathers; he made the people prosper during their stay in Egypt, with mighty power he led them out of that country,r 18he endured their conducta s for about forty years in the desert, 19he overthrew seven nations in Canaan and gave their land to his people t as their inheritance. 20All this took about 450 years.

"After this, God gave them judges u until the time of Samuel the prophet. v 21Then the people asked for a king,w and he gave them Saul son of Kish, of the tribe of Benjamin, who ruled forty years. 22After removing Saul,x he made David their king.y He testified concerning him: 'I have found David son of Jesse a man after my own heart;z he will do everything I want him to do.'

23"From this man's descendants God has brought to Israel the Savior Jesus,a as he promised. 24Before the coming of Jesus, John preached repentance and baptism to all the people of Israel. 25As John was completing his work, he said: 'Who do you think I am? I am not that one. No, but he is coming after me, whose sandals I am not worthy to untie.'b

26"Brothers, children of Abraham, and you God-fearing Gentiles, it is to us that this message of salvation has been sent. 27The people of Jerusalem and their rulers did not recognize

a 18 Some manuscripts *and cared for them*

13:14
P Ac 14:19, 21
q Ac 16:13

13:17
r Dt 7:6-8

13:18
s Dt 1:31

13:19
t Jos 19:51

13:20
u Jdg 2:16
v 1Sa 3:19, 20

13:21
w 1Sa 8:5, 19

13:22
x 1Sa 15:23, 26
y Ps 89:20
z 1Sa 13:14

13:23
a Mt 1:21

13:25
b Mt 3:11

13:13 No reason is given why John Mark left Paul and Barnabas. Some suggestions are: (1) he was homesick; (2) he resented the change in leadership from Barnabas (his cousin) to Paul; (3) he became ill (an illness that may have affected all of them—see Galatians 4:13); (4) he was unable to withstand the rigors and dangers of the missionary journey; (5) he may have planned to go only that far but had not communicated this to Paul and Barnabas. Paul implicitly accused John Mark of lacking courage and commitment, refusing to take him along on another journey (see 15:37, 38). It is clear from Paul's later letters, however, that he grew to respect Mark (Colossians 4:10), and that he needed Mark in his work (2 Timothy 4:11).

13:14 Pisidian Antioch was a different city from Antioch of Syria where there was already a flourishing church (11:26). This Antioch, in the region of Pisidia, was a hub of good roads and trade, with a large Jewish population.

MINISTRY IN PAMPHYLIA AND GALATIA Paul, Barnabas, and John Mark left Paphos and landed at Perga in the humid region of Pamphylia, a narrow strip of land between the sea and the Taurus Mountains. John Mark left them in Perga, but Paul and Barnabas traveled up the steep road into the higher elevation of Pisidia in Galatia. When the Jews rejected his message, Paul preached to Gentiles, and the Jews drove Paul and Barnabas out of the Pisidian city of Antioch.

13:14 When they went to a new city to witness for Christ, Paul and Barnabas would go first to the synagogue. The Jews who were there believed in God and diligently studied the Scriptures. Tragically, however, many could not accept Jesus as the promised Messiah because they had the wrong idea of what the Messiah should be. He was not, as they desired, a military king who would overthrow Rome's control, but a servant king who would defeat sin in people's hearts. (Only later, when Christ returns, will he judge the nations of the world.) Paul and Barnabas did not separate themselves from the synagogues but tried to show clearly that the very Scriptures the Jews studied pointed to Jesus.

13:14, 15 What happened in a synagogue service? First the *Shema* was recited (this is Deuteronomy 6:4, which Jews repeated several times daily). Certain prayers were spoken; then there was a reading from the law (the books of Genesis through Deuteronomy), a reading from the prophets intending to illustrate the law, and a sermon. The synagogue leader decided who would lead the service and give the sermon. A different person was chosen to lead each week. Since it was customary for the synagogue leader to invite visiting rabbis to speak, Paul and Barnabas usually had an open door when they first went to a synagogue. But as soon as they spoke about Jesus as Messiah, the door would often slam shut. They were usually not invited back by the religious leaders, and sometimes they would be thrown out of town!

13:16ff Paul's message to the Jews in the synagogue in Antioch began with an emphasis on God's covenant with Israel. This was a point of agreement, because all Jews were proud to be God's chosen people. Then Paul explained how the gospel fulfilled the covenant. Some Jews found this message hard to swallow.

13:23-31 Paul began where his listeners were and then introduced them to Christ. Because Paul was speaking to devout Jews, he began with the covenant, Abraham, David, and other familiar themes. Later, when speaking to the Greek philosophers in Athens (17:22–32), he would begin by talking about what he had observed in their city. In both cases, however, he centered the sermon around Christ and emphasized the resurrection. When you share the Good News, begin where your audience is—then tell them about Christ.

13:27
c Ac 3:17

13:28
d Mt 27:20-25

13:29
e Lk 18:31

13:31
f Mt 28:16

13:32
g Ro 4:13

Jesus, c yet in condemning him they fulfilled the words of the prophets that are read every Sabbath. 28 Though they found no proper ground for a death sentence, they asked Pilate to have him executed. d 29 When they had carried out all that was written about him, e they took him down from the tree and laid him in a tomb. 30 But God raised him from the dead, 31 and for many days he was seen by those who had traveled with him from Galilee to Jerusalem. f They are now his witnesses to our people.

32 "We tell you the good news: What God promised our fathers g 33 he has fulfilled for us, their children, by raising up Jesus. As it is written in the second Psalm:

> "'You are my Son;
> today I have become your Father. a 'b

a 33 Or have begotten you   b 33 Psalm 2:7

BARNABAS

Every group needs an "encourager" because everyone needs encouragement at one time or another. However, the value of encouragement is often missed because it tends to be private rather than public. In fact, people most need encouragement when they feel most alone. A man named Joseph was such an encourager that he earned the nickname "Son of Encouragement," or Barnabas, from the Jerusalem Christians.

Barnabas was drawn to people he could encourage, and he was a great help to those around him. It is delightful that wherever Barnabas encouraged Christians, non-Christians flocked to become believers!

Barnabas's actions were crucial to the early church. In a way, we can thank him for most of the New Testament. God used his relationship with Paul at one point and with Mark at another to keep these two men going when either might have failed. Barnabas did wonders with encouragement!

When Paul arrived in Jerusalem for the first time following his conversion, the local Christians were understandably reluctant to welcome him. They thought his story was a trick to capture more Christians. But Barnabas proved willing to risk his life to meet with Paul and then convince the others that their former enemy was now a vibrant believer in Jesus. We can only wonder what might have happened to Paul without Barnabas.

It was Barnabas who encouraged Mark to go with him and Paul to Antioch. Mark joined them on their first missionary journey, but decided during the trip to return home. Later, Barnabas wanted to invite Mark to join them for another journey, but Paul would not agree. As a result, the partners went separate ways, Barnabas with Mark and Paul with Silas. This actually doubled the missionary effort. Barnabas's patient encouragement was a huge boost for the effectiveness of Mark's eventual ministry. Paul and Mark were later reunited in missionary efforts.

As Barnabas's life shows, we are rarely in a situation where there isn't someone we can encourage. Our tendency, however, is to criticize instead. It may be important at times to point out someone's shortcomings, but before we have the right to do this, we must build that person's trust through encouragement. Are you prepared to encourage those with whom you come in contact today?

Strengths and accomplishments:	• One of the first to sell possessions to help the Christians in Jerusalem • First to travel with Paul as a missionary team • Was an encourager, as his nickname shows, and thus one of the most quietly influential people in the early days of Christianity • Called an apostle, although not one of the original 12
Weakness and mistake:	• Like Peter, temporarily stayed aloof from Gentile believers until Paul corrected him
Lessons from his life:	• Encouragement is one of the most effective ways to help • Sooner or later, true obedience to God will involve risk • There is always someone who needs encouragement
Vital statistics:	• Where: Cyprus, Jerusalem, Antioch • Occupations: Missionary, teacher • Relatives: Aunt: Mary. Cousin: John Mark. • Contemporaries: Peter, Silas, Paul, Herod Agrippa I
Key verses:	"When he arrived and saw the evidence of the grace of God, he was glad and encouraged them all to remain true to the Lord with all their hearts. He was a good man, full of the Holy Spirit and faith, and a great number of people were brought to the Lord" (Acts 11:23, 24).

Barnabas's story is told in Acts 4:36, 37; 9:27—15:39. He is also mentioned in 1 Corinthians 9:6; Galatians 2:1, 9, 13; Colossians 4:10.

34 The fact that God raised him from the dead, never to decay, is stated in these words:

"'I will give you the holy and sure blessings promised to David.'ᵃ ʰ

13:34
ʰ Isa 55:3

35 So it is stated elsewhere:

"'You will not let your Holy One see decay.'ᵇ ⁱ

13:35
ⁱ Ps 16:10

36 "For when David had served God's purpose in his own generation, he fell asleep; he was buried with his fathers ʲ and his body decayed. 37 But the one whom God raised from the dead did not see decay.

13:36
ʲ Ac 2:29

38 "Therefore, my brothers, I want you to know that through Jesus the forgiveness of sins is proclaimed to you. ᵏ 39 Through him everyone who believes is justified from everything you could not be justified from by the law of Moses. ˡ 40 Take care that what the prophets have said does not happen to you:

13:38
ᵏ Lk 24:47
13:39
ˡ Ro 3:28

41 "'Look, you scoffers,
    wonder and perish,
for I am going to do something in your days
    that you would never believe,
    even if someone told you.'ᶜ "ᵐ

13:41
ᵐ Hab 1:5

42 As Paul and Barnabas were leaving the synagogue, the people invited them to speak further about these things on the next Sabbath. 43 When the congregation was dismissed, many of the Jews and devout converts to Judaism followed Paul and Barnabas, who talked with them and urged them to continue in the grace of God. ⁿ

13:43
ⁿ Ac 11:23

44 On the next Sabbath almost the whole city gathered to hear the word of the Lord. 45 When the Jews saw the crowds, they were filled with jealousy and talked abusively against what Paul was saying.

46 Then Paul and Barnabas answered them boldly: "We had to speak the word of God to you first. ᵒ Since you reject it and do not consider yourselves worthy of eternal life, we now turn to the Gentiles. ᵖ 47 For this is what the Lord has commanded us:

13:46
ᵒ Ac 3:26
ᵖ Ac 18:6; 28:28
13:47
ᵍ Lk 2:32
ʳ Isa 49:6

"'I have made youᵈ a light for the Gentiles,ᵍ
    that youᵈ may bring salvation to the ends of the earth.'ᵉ "ʳ

48 When the Gentiles heard this, they were glad and honored the word of the Lord; and all who were appointed for eternal life believed.

ᵃ34 Isaiah 55:3   ᵇ35 Psalm 16:10   ᶜ41 Hab. 1:5   ᵈ47 The Greek is singular.   ᵉ47 Isaiah 49:6

CONTINUED MINISTRY IN GALATIA Paul and Barnabas, thrown out of Antioch in Pisidia, descended the mountains, going east into Lycaonia. They went first to Iconium, a commercial center on the road between Asia and Syria. After preaching there, they had to flee to Lystra, 25 miles south. Paul was stoned in Lystra, but he and Barnabas traveled the 50 miles to Derbe, a border town. The pair then boldly retraced their steps.

13:38, 39 This is the Good News of the gospel: that forgiveness of sins and freedom from guilt are available through faith in Christ to all people—including *you*. Have you received this forgiveness? Are you refreshed by it each day?

13:42–45 The Jewish leaders undoubtedly brought theological arguments against Paul and Barnabas, but Luke tells us that the real reason for their hostility was that "they were filled with jealousy." When we see others succeeding where we haven't, or receiving the affirmation we crave, it is hard to rejoice with them. Jealousy is a natural reaction. But how tragic it is when our jealous feelings make us try to stop God's work. If a work is God's work, rejoice in it—no matter who is doing it.

13:46 Why was it necessary for the gospel to go first to the Jews? God planned that through the Jewish nation *all* the world would know of God (Genesis 12:3). Paul, a Jew himself, loved his people (Romans 9:1–5) and wanted to give them every opportunity to join him in proclaiming God's salvation. Unfortunately, many Jews did not recognize Jesus as Messiah, and they did not understand that God was offering salvation to anyone, Jew or Gentile, who comes to him through faith in Christ.

13:47 God had planned for Israel to be this light (Isaiah 49:6). Through Israel came Jesus, the light of the nations (Luke 2:32). This light would spread out and enlighten the Gentiles.

49 The word of the Lord spread through the whole region. 50 But the Jews incited the God-fearing women of high standing and the leading men of the city. They stirred up persecution against Paul and Barnabas, and expelled them from their region. 51 So they shook the dust from their feet*s* in protest against them and went to Iconium. 52 And the disciples were filled with joy and with the Holy Spirit.

In Iconium

14 At Iconium Paul and Barnabas went as usual into the Jewish synagogue. There they spoke so effectively that a great number of Jews and Gentiles believed. 2 But the Jews who refused to believe stirred up the Gentiles and poisoned their minds against the brothers. 3 So Paul and Barnabas spent considerable time there, speaking boldly for the Lord, who confirmed the message of his grace by enabling them to do miraculous signs and wonders.*t* 4 The people of the city were divided; some sided with the Jews, others with the apostles. 5 There was a plot afoot among the Gentiles and Jews, together with their leaders, to mistreat them and stone them. 6 But they found out about it and fled to the Lycaonian cities of Lystra and Derbe and to the surrounding country, 7 where they continued to preach the good news.

In Lystra and Derbe

8 In Lystra there sat a man crippled in his feet, who was lame from birth and had never walked. 9 He listened to Paul as he was speaking. Paul looked directly at him, saw that he had faith to be healed 10 and called out, "Stand up on your feet!" At that, the man jumped up and began to walk.

11 When the crowd saw what Paul had done, they shouted in the Lycaonian language, "The gods have come down to us in human form!"*u* 12 Barnabas they called Zeus, and Paul they called Hermes because he was the chief speaker. 13 The priest of Zeus, whose temple was just outside the city, brought bulls and wreaths to the city gates because he and the crowd wanted to offer sacrifices to them.

14 But when the apostles Barnabas and Paul heard of this, they tore their clothes and rushed out into the crowd, shouting: 15 "Men, why are you doing this? We too are only men,*v* human like you. We are bringing you good news, telling you to turn from these worthless things*w* to the living God, who made heaven and earth and sea and everything in them.*x* 16 In the past, he let*y* all nations go their own way.*z* 17 Yet he has not left himself without testimony:*a* He has shown kindness by giving you rain from heaven and crops in their seasons;*b*

13:51
s Mt 10:14; Ac 18:6

14:3
t Jn 4:48; Heb 2:4

14:11
u Ac 8:10; 28:6

14:15
v Ac 10:26; Jas 5:17
w 1Sa 12:21
x Ps 146:6;
Rev 14:7

14:16
y Ac 17:30
z Ps 81:12

14:17
a Ro 1:20
b Dt 11:14;
Job 5:10; Ps 65:10

13:50 Instead of accepting the truth, the Jewish leaders stirred up opposition and ran Paul and Barnabas out of town. When confronted by a disturbing truth, people often turn away and refuse to listen. When God's Spirit points out needed changes in our lives, we must listen to him. Otherwise we may be pushing the truth so far away that it no longer affects us.

13:51 Often Jews would shake the dust off their feet when leaving a Gentile town, on the way back to their own land. This symbolized cleansing themselves from the contamination of those who did not worship God. For Paul and Barnabas to do this to Jews demonstrated that Jews who reject the gospel are not truly part of Israel and are no better than pagans.

13:51 Jesus had told his disciples to shake from their feet the dust of any town that would not accept or listen to them (Mark 6:11). The disciples were not to blame if the message was rejected, as long as they had faithfully presented it. When we share Christ carefully and sensitively, God does not hold us responsible for the other person's decision.

14:3, 4 We may wish we could perform a miraculous act that would convince everyone once and for all that Jesus is the Lord. But we see here that even if we could perform a miracle, it wouldn't convince everyone. God gave these men power to do great wonders as confirmation of the message of grace, but people were still divided. Don't spend your time and energy wishing for miracles. Sow your seeds of Good News on the best ground you can find in the best way you can, and leave the convincing to the Holy Spirit.

14:6 Iconium (14:1), Lystra, and Derbe were three cities Paul visited in the southern part of the region of Galatia. Paul probably

wrote a letter to these churches—the letter to the Galatians—because many Jewish Christians were claiming that non-Jewish Christians couldn't be saved unless they followed Jewish laws and customs. Paul's letter refuted this and brought the believers back to a right understanding of faith in Jesus (see Galatians 3:3, 5). Paul may have written his letter soon after leaving the region (see the note on 14:28).

14:11 "The Lycaonian language" refers to their local dialect.

14:11, 12 Zeus and Hermes (also known as Jupiter and Mercury) were two popular gods in the Roman world. People from Lystra claimed that these gods had once visited their city. According to legend, no one offered them hospitality except an old couple, so Zeus and Hermes killed the rest of the people and rewarded the old couple. When the citizens of Lystra saw the miracles of Paul and Barnabas, they assumed that the gods were revisiting them. Remembering the story of what had happened to the previous citizens, they immediately honored Paul and Barnabas and showered them with gifts.

14:15–18 Responding to the people of Lystra, Paul and Barnabas reminded them that God never leaves himself "without testimony." Rain and crops, for example, are evidence of his goodness. Later Paul wrote that this evidence in nature leaves people without an excuse for unbelief (Romans 1:20). When in doubt about God, look around and you will see abundant evidence that he is at work in the world.

he provides you with plenty of food and fills your hearts with joy." 18Even with these words, they had difficulty keeping the crowd from sacrificing to them.

19Then some Jews *c* came from Antioch and Iconium and won the crowd over. They stoned Paul *d* and dragged him outside the city, thinking he was dead. 20But after the disciples had gathered around him, he got up and went back into the city. The next day he and Barnabas left for Derbe.

The Return to Antioch in Syria

21They preached the good news in that city and won a large number of disciples. Then they returned to Lystra, Iconium and Antioch, 22strengthening the disciples and encouraging them to remain true to the faith. "We must go through many hardships *e* to enter the kingdom of God," they said. 23Paul and Barnabas appointed elders *a* for them in each church and, with prayer and fasting, committed them to the Lord, in whom they had put their trust. 24After going through Pisidia, they came into Pamphylia, 25and when they had preached the word in Perga, they went down to Attalia.

26From Attalia they sailed back to Antioch, where they had been committed to the grace of God for the work they had now completed. *f* 27On arriving there, they gathered the church together and reported all that God had done through them *g* and how he had opened the door *h* of faith to the Gentiles. 28And they stayed there a long time with the disciples.

2. The council at Jerusalem

15 Some men *i* came down from Judea to Antioch and were teaching the brothers: "Unless you are circumcised, *j* according to the custom taught by Moses, you cannot be

a23 Or Barnabas ordained elders; or Barnabas had elders elected

14:19
c Ac 13:45
d 2Co 11:25;
2Ti 3:11

14:22
e 2Ti 3:12

14:26
f Ac 13:1, 3

14:27
g Ac 15:4, 12; 21:19
h 1Co 16:9;
2Co 2:12; Col 4:3

15:1
i Gal 2:12
j ver 5; Gal 5:2, 3

14:18, 19 Only days after the people in Lystra had thought that Paul and Barnabas were gods and wanted to offer sacrifices to them, they stoned Paul and left him for dead. That's human nature. Jesus understood how fickle crowds can be (John 2:24, 25). When many people approve of us, we feel good, but that should never cloud our thinking or affect our decisions. We should not live to please the crowd—especially in our spiritual lives. Be like Jesus. Know the nature of the crowd and don't put your trust in it. Put your trust in God alone.

14:18–20 Paul and Barnabas were persistent in their preaching of the Good News, considering the cost to themselves to be nothing in comparison with obedience to Christ. They had just narrowly escaped being stoned in Iconium (14:1–7), but Jews from Antioch and Iconium tracked Paul down, stoned him, and left him for dead. But Paul got up and went back into the city to preach the Good News. That's commitment! Being a disciple of Christ calls for total commitment. As Christians, we no longer belong to ourselves but to our Lord, for whom we are called to suffer.

THE END OF THE FIRST JOURNEY From Antioch in Pisidia, Paul and Barnabas went down the mountains back to Pamphylia on the coast. Stopping first in Perga, where they had landed, they went west to Attalia, the main port that sent goods from Asia to Syria and Egypt. There they found a ship bound for Seleucia, the port of Antioch in Syria. This ended their first missionary journey.

14:21, 22 Paul and Barnabas returned to visit the believers in all the cities where they had recently been threatened and physically attacked. These men knew the dangers they faced, yet they believed that they had a responsibility to encourage the new believers. No matter how inconvenient or uncomfortable the task may seem, we must always support new believers who need our help and encouragement. It was not convenient or comfortable for Jesus to go to the cross for us!

14:23 Part of the reason that Paul and Barnabas risked their lives to return to these cities was to organize the churches' leadership. They were not just following up on a loosely knit group; they were helping the believers get organized with spiritual leaders who could help them grow. Churches grow under Spirit-led leaders, both laypersons and pastors. Pray for your church leaders and support them; and if God puts his finger on you, humbly accept the responsibility of a leadership role in your church.

14:28 Paul probably wrote his letter to the Galatians while he was staying in Antioch (A.D. 48 or 49) after completing his first missionary journey. There are several theories as to what part of Galatia Paul was addressing, but most agree that Iconium, Lystra, and Derbe were part of that region for whom the letter is intended. Galatians was probably written before the Jerusalem council (Acts 15), because in the letter the question of whether Gentile believers should be required to follow Jewish law was not yet resolved. The council met to solve that problem.

15:1 The delegates to the council at Jerusalem came from the churches in Jerusalem and Antioch. The conversion of Gentiles was raising an urgent question for the early church: The real problem for the Jewish Christians was not whether Gentiles could be saved, but whether Gentile believers had to adhere to the laws of Moses and other Jewish traditions. The test of following these laws was circumcision. One group of Jewish Christians insisted that following the law, including submitting to the rite of circumcision, was necessary for salvation. The Gentiles, however, did not think they needed to become Jewish first in order to become Christians. The Jewish Christians also were worried because soon Gentile Christians would outnumber Jewish Christians. And they were afraid of weakening moral standards among believers if they did not follow Jewish laws. So Paul and Barnabas discussed this problem with the leaders of the church. Paul, Barnabas, and the other church

15:2
ᵏGal 2:2

15:3
ˡAc 14:27

15:4
ᵐver 12; Ac 14:27

15:8
ⁿAc 10:44, 47

15:9
ᵒAc 10:28, 34

15:10
ᵖMt 23:4; Gal 5:1

15:11
�q Ro 3:24;
Eph 2:5-8

15:12
ʳAc 14:27

15:13
ˢAc 12:17

saved." 2 This brought Paul and Barnabas into sharp dispute and debate with them. So Paul and Barnabas were appointed, along with some other believers, to go up to Jerusalem ᵏ to see the apostles and elders about this question. 3 The church sent them on their way, and as they traveled through Phoenicia and Samaria, they told how the Gentiles had been converted. ˡ This news made all the brothers very glad. 4 When they came to Jerusalem, they were welcomed by the church and the apostles and elders, to whom they reported everything God had done through them. ᵐ

5 Then some of the believers who belonged to the party of the Pharisees stood up and said, "The Gentiles must be circumcised and required to obey the law of Moses."

6 The apostles and elders met to consider this question. 7 After much discussion, Peter got up and addressed them: "Brothers, you know that some time ago God made a choice among you that the Gentiles might hear from my lips the message of the gospel and believe. 8 God, who knows the heart, showed that he accepted them by giving the Holy Spirit to them, ⁿ just as he did to us. 9 He made no distinction between us and them, ᵒ for he purified their hearts by faith. 10 Now then, why do you try to test God by putting on the necks of the disciples a yoke ᵖ that neither we nor our fathers have been able to bear? 11 No! We believe it is through the grace q of our Lord Jesus that we are saved, just as they are."

12 The whole assembly became silent as they listened to Barnabas and Paul telling about the miraculous signs and wonders God had done among the Gentiles through them. ʳ 13 When they finished, James ˢ spoke up: "Brothers, listen to me. 14 Simon ᵃ has described to us how God at first showed his concern by taking from the Gentiles a people for himself. 15 The words of the prophets are in agreement with this, as it is written:

16 "'After this I will return
     and rebuild David's fallen tent.

ᵃ14 Greek *Simeon*, a variant of *Simon*; that is, Peter

---

leaders believed that the Old Testament law was very important but was not a prerequisite to salvation. The law cannot save; only by grace through faith in Jesus Christ can a person be saved. The council upheld the convictions expressed by Paul and Barnabas that following the Jewish laws, including being circumcised, was not essential for salvation.

15:2 The question of whether the Gentile believers should obey the law of Moses to be saved was extremely critical at this point in Christianity's history and could have potentially split the early church if not handled carefully. The controversy had intensified largely due to the success of the new Gentile churches. The conservatives in the Jerusalem church were led by converted Pharisees (15:5) who preferred a legalistic religion to one based on faith alone. If the conservatives had won, the Gentiles would have been required to be circumcised and converted to Judaism. This would have seriously confined Christianity to simply being another sect within Judaism. There is something of a "Pharisee" in each one of us. We may unwittingly mistake upholding tradition, structure, and legal requirements for obeying God. Make sure the gospel brings freedom and life to those you are trying to reach.

15:2ff It is helpful to see how the churches in Antioch and Jerusalem resolved their conflict: (1) the church in Antioch sent a delegation to help seek a solution; (2) the delegates met with the church leaders to give their reports and set another date to continue the discussion; (3) Paul and Barnabas gave their report; (4) James summarized the reports and drew up the decision; (5) everyone agreed to abide by the decision; (6) the council sent a letter with delegates back to Antioch to report the decision.

This is a wise way to handle conflicts within the church. Problems must be confronted, and all sides of the argument must be given a fair hearing. The discussion should be held in the presence of leaders who are spiritually mature and trustworthy to make wise decisions. Everyone should then abide by the decisions.

15:10 If the law was a yoke that the Jews could not bear, how did having the law help them throughout their history? Paul wrote that the law was a guide that pointed out their sins so they could repent and return to God and right living (see Galatians 3:24, 25). It was, and still is, impossible to obey the law completely.

15:13 This James is Jesus' brother. He became the leader of the church in Jerusalem and wrote the book of James.

15:14 Simon is another name for Peter.

15:16-18 Despite the compelling experiences of Peter, Barnabas, and Paul, James turned to God's Word as the ultimate test of truth. This should be the way we evaluate events. We all have beliefs (some of them fervent); we all have experiences, and our tendency is to want to measure others by our yardstick. It is common for believers to think that their experiences, their convictions, are true and should be the norm. Different ideas are thought to be inferior or invalid. Ultimately, however, what matters is what God's Word says. The more we know God's Word, the more we read it, study it, memorize it, and meditate on it, the better we will be able to discern what is right and best in times of controversy or doctrinal disagreement.

THE JERUSALEM COUNCIL
A dispute arose when some Jewish believers taught that Gentile believers had to be circumcised to be saved. Paul and Barnabas went to Jerusalem to discuss this situation with the leaders there. After the Jerusalem council made its decision, Paul and Barnabas returned to Antioch with the news.

PAUL'S FIRST MISSIONARY JOURNEY (ACTS 13:1—14:28)

PAUL'S SECOND MISSIONARY JOURNEY (ACTS 15:36—18:22)

PAUL'S THIRD MISSIONARY JOURNEY (ACTS 18:23 – 21:16)

PAUL'S JOURNEY TO ROME (ACTS 21:17 – 28:31)

> Its ruins I will rebuild,
>> and I will restore it,
> 17 that the remnant of men may seek the Lord,
>> and all the Gentiles who bear my name,
> says the Lord, who does these things'ᵃ ᵗ
> 18   that have been known for ages.ᵇ

15:17
ᵗAm 9:11, 12

19"It is my judgment, therefore, that we should not make it difficult for the Gentiles who are turning to God. 20Instead we should write to them, telling them to abstain from food polluted by idols, ᵘ from sexual immorality, from the meat of strangled animals and from blood. ᵛ 21For Moses has been preached in every city from the earliest times and is read in the synagogues on every Sabbath."

15:20
ᵘ1Co 10:14-28
ᵛGe 9:4

The Council's Letter to Gentile Believers

22Then the apostles and elders, with the whole church, decided to choose some of their own men and send them to Antioch with Paul and Barnabas. They chose Judas (called Barsabbas) and Silas, two men who were leaders among the brothers. 23With them they sent the following letter:

The apostles and elders, your brothers,

To the Gentile believers in Antioch, Syria and Cilicia:

Greetings.

24We have heard that some went out from us without our authorization and disturbed you, troubling your minds by what they said. ʷ 25So we all agreed to choose some men and send them to you with our dear friends Barnabas and Paul— 26men who have risked their livesˣ for the name of our Lord Jesus Christ. 27Therefore we are sending Judas and Silas to confirm by word of mouth what we are writing. 28It seemed good to the Holy Spirit and to us not to burden you with anything beyond the following requirements: 29You are to abstain from food sacrificed to idols, from blood, from the meat of strangled animals and from sexual immorality.ʸ You will do well to avoid these things.

15:24
ʷver 1

15:26
ˣAc 14:19

15:29
ʸver 20; Ac 21:25

Farewell.

30The men were sent off and went down to Antioch, where they gathered the church together and delivered the letter. 31The people read it and were glad for its encouraging

ᵃ17 Amos 9:11,12   ᵇ17,18 Some manuscripts things'— / ¹⁸known to the Lord for ages is his work

---

15:19–21 James' judgment was that Gentile believers did not have to be circumcised, but they should stay away from food polluted by idols, from sexual immorality (a common part of idol worship), and from eating meat of strangled animals and from consuming blood (reflecting the Biblical teaching that the life is in the blood—Leviticus 17:14). If Gentile Christians would abstain from these practices, they would please God and get along better with their Jewish brothers and sisters in Christ. Of course, other actions were inappropriate for believers, but the Jews were especially concerned about these four. This compromise helped the church grow unhindered by the cultural differences of Jews and Gentiles. When we share our message across cultural and economic boundaries, we must be sure that the requirements for faith we set up are God's, not people's.

15:19–21 The early church experienced the difficulty of bringing together diverse peoples. Jews and Gentiles had so little in common! Different histories, traditions, practices, customs, cultures, languages. How do you possibly take such dissimilar groups and make them one? One solution is to decide not to, to decide that it is impossible. So you segregate, isolate, and study each other with suspicion. This response profoundly affects Christianity's effectiveness and attractiveness. When there is snobbery or a judgmental atmosphere, the church betrays the teachings of Christ and loses all appeal.

The other solution is to submit our prejudices and presuppositions to the greater purposes of God. When we imitate him (Ephesians 5:1), we become tolerant, understanding, and accepting. However, such tolerance is not meant to include sinful lifestyles. James mentioned a few laws that the Gentile believers should keep, with an understanding that basic morality and living for God would cover the rest. When believers of different races, ethnic backgrounds, and social strata come together in love and worship of the Savior, nothing gives greater glory to God or provides a more compelling witness.

15:22 Later Silas accompanied Paul on Paul's second missionary journey in place of Barnabas, who visited different cities with John Mark.

15:23–29 This letter answered their questions and brought great joy to the Gentile Christians in Antioch (15:31). Beautifully written, it appeals to the Holy Spirit's guidance and explains what is to be done as though the readers already knew it. Believers should be careful not only in what they say, but also in how they say it. We may be correct in our content, but we can lose our audience by our tone of voice or by our attitude.

15:31 The debate over circumcision could have split the church, but Paul, Barnabas, and the Jews in Antioch made the right decision—they sought counsel from the church leaders

15:33
z 1Co 16:11

message. 32Judas and Silas, who themselves were prophets, said much to encourage and strengthen the brothers. 33After spending some time there, they were sent off by the brothers with the blessing of peace z to return to those who had sent them. a 35But Paul and Barnabas remained in Antioch, where they and many others taught and preached the word of the Lord.

3. Second missionary journey
Disagreement Between Paul and Barnabas

15:36
a Ac 13:4, 13, 14,
51; 14:1, 6, 24, 25

15:37
b Ac 12:12

15:38
c Ac 13:13

36Some time later Paul said to Barnabas, "Let us go back and visit the brothers in all the towns a where we preached the word of the Lord and see how they are doing." 37Barnabas wanted to take John, also called Mark, b with them, 38but Paul did not think it wise to take him, because he had deserted them c in Pamphylia and had not continued with them in the work. 39They had such a sharp disagreement that they parted company. Barnabas took Mark

a33 Some manuscripts *them,* 34*but Silas decided to remain there*.

THE FIRST CHURCH CONFERENCE	Group	Position	Reasons
	Judaizers (some Jewish Christians)	Gentiles must become Jewish first to be eligible for salvation	1. They were devout, practicing Jews who found it difficult to set aside a tradition of gaining merit with God by keeping the law.
			2. They thought grace was too easy for the Gentiles.
			3. They were afraid of seeming too non-Jewish in the practice of their new faith—which could lead to death.
			4. The demands on the Gentiles were a way of maintaining control and authority in the movement.
	Gentile Christians	Faith in Christ as Savior is the only requirement for salvation	1. To submit to Jewish demands would be to doubt what God had already done for them by grace alone.
			2. They resisted exchanging their pagan rituals for a system of Jewish rituals—neither of which had power to save.
			3. They sought to obey Christ by baptism (rather than by circumcision) as a sign of their new faith.
	Peter and James	Faith is the only requirement, but there must be evidence of change by rejecting the old life-style	1. They tried to distinguish between what was true from God's Word versus what was just human tradition.
			2. They had Christ's command to preach to all the world.
			3. They wanted to preserve unity.
			4. They saw that Christianity could never survive as just a sect within Judaism.

As long as most of the first Christians were Jewish, there was little difficulty in welcoming new believers; however, Gentiles (non-Jews) began to accept Jesus' offer of salvation. The evidence in their lives and the presence of God's Spirit in them showed that God was accepting them. Some of the early Christians believed that non-Jewish Christians needed to meet certain conditions before they could be worthy to accept Christ. The issue could have destroyed the church, so a conference was called in Jerusalem, and the issue was formally settled there, although it continued to be a problem for many years following. Above is an outline of the three points of view at the conference.

and from God's Word. Our differences should be settled the same way, by seeking wise counsel and abiding by the decisions. Don't let disagreements divide you from other believers. Third-party assistance is a sound method for resolving problems and preserving unity.

15:36–39 Paul and Barnabas disagreed sharply over Mark. Paul didn't want to take him along because he had left them earlier (13:13). This disagreement caused the two great preachers to form two teams, opening up two missionary endeavors instead

of one. God works even through conflict and disagreements. Later, Mark became vital to Paul's ministry (Colossians 4:10). Christians do not always agree, but problems can be solved by agreeing to disagree and letting God work his will.

and sailed for Cyprus, 40but Paul chose Silas and left, commended by the brothers to the grace of the Lord. 41He went through Syria and Cilicia, strengthening the churches. *d*

15:41
*d*Ac 16:5

Timothy Joins Paul and Silas

16 He came to Derbe and then to Lystra,*e* where a disciple named Timothy*f* lived, whose mother was a Jewess and a believer, but whose father was a Greek. 2The brothers at Lystra and Iconium spoke well of him. 3Paul wanted to take him along on the journey, so he circumcised him because of the Jews who lived in that area, for they all knew that his father was a Greek. *g* 4As they traveled from town to town, they delivered the decisions reached by the apostles and elders *h* in Jerusalem for the people to obey. *i* 5So the churches were strengthened in the faith and grew daily in numbers.

16:1
*e*Ac 14:6
*f*Ac 19:22;
Ro 16:21; 1Co 4:17;
2Ti 1:2, 5, 6

16:3
*g*Gal 2:3

16:4
*h*Ac 11:30
*i*Ac 15:28, 29

Paul's Vision of the Man of Macedonia

6Paul and his companions traveled throughout the region of Phrygia*j* and Galatia, having been kept by the Holy Spirit from preaching the word in the province of Asia. 7When they came to the border of Mysia, they tried to enter Bithynia, but the Spirit of Jesus would not allow them to. 8So they passed by Mysia and went down to Troas.*k* 9During the night Paul had a vision*l* of a man of Macedonia standing and begging him, "Come over to Macedonia and help us." 10After Paul had seen the vision, we got ready at once to leave for Macedonia, concluding that God had called us to preach the gospel to them.

16:6
*j*Ac 18:23

16:8
*k*2Co 2:12; 2Ti 4:13

16:9
*l*Ac 9:10

Lydia's Conversion in Philippi

11From Troas we put out to sea and sailed straight for Samothrace, and the next day on to Neapolis. 12From there we traveled to Philippi,*m* a Roman colony and the leading city of that district of Macedonia. And we stayed there several days.

16:12
*m*Php 1:1

15:40 Paul's second missionary journey, this time with Silas as his coworker, began approximately three years after his first one ended. The two visited many of the cities covered on Paul's first journey, plus others. This journey laid the groundwork for the church in Greece.

15:40 Silas had been involved in the Jerusalem council and had been one of the two men chosen to represent the Jerusalem church by taking the letter and decision back to Antioch (15:22). Paul, from the Antioch church, chose Silas, from the Jerusalem church, and they traveled together to many cities to spread the Good News. This teamwork demonstrated the church's unity after the decision at the Jerusalem council.

16:1 Timothy is the first second-generation Christian mentioned in the New Testament. His mother, Eunice, and grandmother, Lois (2 Timothy 1:5), had become believers and had faithfully influenced him for the Lord. Although Timothy's father apparently

was not a Christian, the faithfulness of his mother and grandmother prevailed. Never underestimate the far-reaching consequences of raising one small child to love the Lord.

16:2, 3 Timothy and his mother, Eunice, were from Lystra. Eunice had probably heard Paul's preaching when he was there during his first missionary journey (14:6–18). Timothy was the son of a Jewish mother and Greek father—to the Jews, a half-breed like a Samaritan. So Paul asked Timothy to be circumcised to remove some of the stigma he may have had with Jewish believers. Timothy was not required to be circumcised (the Jerusalem council had decided that—chapter 15), but he voluntarily did this to overcome any barriers to his witness for Christ. Sometimes we need to go beyond the minimum requirements in order to help our audience receive our testimony.

16:6 We don't know how the Holy Spirit told Paul that he and his companions should not go into Asia. It may have been through a prophet, a vision, an inner conviction, or some other circumstance. To know God's will does not mean we must hear his voice. He leads in different ways. When seeking God's will, (1) make sure your plan is in harmony with God's Word; (2) ask mature Christians for their advice; (3) check your own motives to see if you are seeking to do what you want or what you think God wants; (4) pray for God to open and close the doors as he desires.

16:7–9 The "Spirit of Jesus" is another name for the Holy Spirit. The Holy Spirit had closed the door twice for Paul, so Paul must have wondered which geographical direction to take in spreading the gospel. Then, in a vision (16:9), Paul was given definite direction, and he and his companions obediently traveled into Macedonia. The Holy Spirit guides us to the right places, but he also guides us away from the wrong places. As we seek God's will, we need to know what God wants us to do and where he wants us to go, but we also need to know what God does not want us to do and where he does not want us to go.

16:10 The use of the pronoun *we* indicates that Luke, the author of the Gospel of Luke and of this book, joined Paul, Silas, and Timothy on their journey. He was an eyewitness to most of the remaining incidents recorded in this book.

16:12 Philippi was the key city in the region of Macedonia (northern Greece today). Paul founded a church during this visit

THE SECOND JOURNEY BEGINS Paul and Silas set out on a second missionary journey to visit the cities Paul had preached in earlier. This time they set out by land rather than sea, traveling the Roman road through Cilicia and the Cilician Gates—a gorge through the Taurus Mountains—then northwest toward Derbe, Lystra, and Iconium. The Spirit told them not to go into Asia, so they turned northward toward Bithynia. Again the Spirit said no, so they turned west through Mysia to the harbor city of Troas.

16:13
n Ac 13:14

[13]On the Sabbath *n* we went outside the city gate to the river, where we expected to find a place of prayer. We sat down and began to speak to the women who had gathered there.

SILAS

The lives of the first Christian missionaries can be described with many words, but *boring* is not one of them. There were days of great excitement as men and women who had never heard of Jesus responded to the gospel. There were dangerous journeys over land and sea. Health risks and hunger were part of the daily routine. And there was open and hostile resistance to Christianity in many cities. Silas was one of the first missionaries, and he found out that serving Jesus Christ was certainly not boring!

Silas's name appears in Acts at the end of the first church council on the Jewish/Gentile problem. The majority of early Christians were Jews who realized that Jesus was the fulfillment of God's Old Testament promises to his people; however, the universal application of those promises had been overlooked. Thus, many felt that becoming Jewish was a prerequisite to becoming a Christian. The idea that God could accept a Gentile pagan was too incredible. But Gentiles began to accept Christ as Savior, and the transformation of their lives and the presence of God's Spirit confirmed their conversions. Some Jews were still reluctant, however, and insisted these new Christians take on various Jewish customs. The issue came to a boiling point at the Jerusalem council, but was peacefully resolved. Silas was one of the representatives from Jerusalem sent with Paul and Barnabas back to Antioch with an official letter of welcome and acceptance to the Gentile Christians. Having fulfilled this mission, Silas returned to Jerusalem. Within a short time, however, he was back in Antioch at Paul's request to join him on his second missionary journey.

Paul, Silas, and Timothy began a far-ranging ministry that included some exciting adventures. Paul and Silas spent a night singing in a Philippian jail after being severely beaten. An earthquake, the loosing of their chains, and the resulting panic led to the conversion of their jailer and his family. Later, they narrowly missed another beating in Thessalonica, prevented by an evening escape. In Berea there was more trouble, but Silas and Timothy stayed to teach the young believers, while Paul traveled on to Athens. The team was finally reunited in Corinth. In each place they visited, they left behind a small group of Christians.

Silas leaves the story as suddenly as he entered it. Peter mentions him as the co-author of 1 Peter, but we do not know when he joined Peter. He was an effective believer before leaving Jerusalem, and he doubtless continued to minister after his work with Paul was completed. He took advantage of opportunities to serve God and was not discouraged by the setbacks and opposition he met along the way. Silas, though not the most famous of the early missionaries, was certainly a hero worth imitating.

Strengths and accomplishments:	• A leader in the Jerusalem church • Represented the church in carrying the "acceptance letter" prepared by the Jerusalem council to the Gentile believers in Antioch • Was closely associated with Paul from the second missionary journey on • Sang songs of praise to God while in jail with Paul in Philippi • Worked as a writing secretary for both Paul and Peter
Lessons from his life:	• Partnership is a significant part of effective ministry • God never guarantees that his servants will not suffer • Obedience to God will often mean giving up what makes us feel secure
Vital statistics:	• Where: Roman citizen living in Jerusalem • Occupation: One of the first career missionaries • Contemporaries: Paul, Timothy, Peter, Mark, Barnabas
Key verses:	"So we all agreed to choose some men and send them to you with our dear friends Barnabas and Paul—men who have risked their lives for the name of our Lord Jesus Christ. Therefore we are sending Judas and Silas to confirm by word of mouth what we are writing" (Acts 15:25–27).

Silas's story is told in Acts 15:22—19:10. He is also mentioned in 2 Corinthians 1:19; 1 Thessalonians 1:1; 2 Thessalonians 1:1; 1 Peter 5:12.

(A.D. 50–51). Later Paul wrote a letter to the church, the book of Philippians, probably from a prison in Rome (A.D. 61). The letter was personal and tender, showing Paul's deep love for and friendship with the believers there. In it he thanked them for a gift they had sent, alerted them to a coming visit by Timothy and Epaphroditus, urged the church to clear up any disunity, and encouraged the believers not to give in to persecution.

16:13 Inscribed on the arches outside the city of Philippi was a prohibition against bringing an unrecognized religion into the city; therefore, this prayer meeting was held outside the city, beside the river.

16:13, 14 After following the Holy Spirit's leading into Macedonia, Paul made his first evangelistic contact with a small group of women. Paul never allowed gender or cultural boundaries to keep him from preaching the gospel. He preached to these women, and Lydia, an influential merchant, believed. This opened the way for ministry in that region. God often worked in and through women in the early church.

14One of those listening was a woman named Lydia, a dealer in purple cloth from the city of Thyatira, who was a worshiper of God. The Lord opened her heart *o* to respond to Paul's message. 15When she and the members of her household were baptized, she invited us to her home. "If you consider me a believer in the Lord," she said, "come and stay at my house." And she persuaded us.

16:14
o Lk 24:45

Paul and Silas in Prison

16Once when we were going to the place of prayer, we were met by a slave girl who had a spirit *p* by which she predicted the future. She earned a great deal of money for her owners by fortune-telling. 17This girl followed Paul and the rest of us, shouting, "These men are servants of the Most High God, *q* who are telling you the way to be saved." 18She kept this up for many days. Finally Paul became so troubled that he turned around and said to the spirit, "In the name of Jesus Christ I command you to come out of her!" At that moment the spirit left her.

16:16
p 1Sa 28:3, 7

16:17
q Mk 5:7

19When the owners of the slave girl realized that their hope of making money *r* was gone, they seized Paul and Silas and dragged *s* them into the marketplace to face the authorities. 20They brought them before the magistrates and said, "These men are Jews, and are throwing our city into an uproar *t* 21by advocating customs unlawful for us Romans to accept or practice."

16:19
r Ac 19:25, 26
s Jas 2:6

16:20
t Ac 17:6

22The crowd joined in the attack against Paul and Silas, and the magistrates ordered them to be stripped and beaten. *u* 23After they had been severely flogged, they were thrown into prison, and the jailer was commanded to guard them carefully. 24Upon receiving such orders, he put them in the inner cell and fastened their feet in the stocks. *v*

16:22
u 2Co 11:25;
1Th 2:2

16:24
v Jer 20:2, 3

16:14 Lydia was a dealer in purple cloth, so she was probably wealthy. Purple cloth was valuable and expensive. It was often worn as a sign of nobility or royalty.

16:14ff Luke highlights the stories of three individuals who became believers through Paul's ministry in Philippi: Lydia, the influential businesswoman (16:14), the demon-possessed slave girl (16:16–18), and the jailer (16:27–30). The gospel was affecting all strata of society, just as it does today.

16:15 Why was Lydia's household baptized after Lydia responded in faith to the gospel? Baptism was a public sign of identification with Christ and the Christian community. Although all members of her household may not have chosen to follow Christ (we don't know), it was now a Christian home.

16:15 Lydia practically begged for the opportunity to host Paul and Silas in her home. Rather than seeing the men as a burden and their presence as a disruption of her family and business routine, Lydia laid out the welcome mat. The notion of hospitality is related to the word "hospital." In other words, we practice

hospitality when we generously and cordially throw open the doors of our homes to care for others. In hospitality, we nurture, strengthen, and serve. The result is that others find physical, spiritual, and emotional help. When they leave us, they are healthier and more whole than when they came. Is this your practice? Is your home a "hospital" for hurting or needy souls?

16:16 This girl's fortune-telling ability came from evil spirits. Fortune-telling was a common practice in Greek and Roman culture. There were many superstitious methods by which people thought they could foretell future events, from interpreting omens in nature to communicating with the spirits of the dead. This young slave girl had an evil spirit, and she made her master rich by interpreting signs and telling people their fortunes. The master was exploiting her unfortunate condition for personal gain.

16:17, 18 What the slave girl said was true, although the source of her knowledge was a demon. Why did a demon announce the truth about Paul, and why did this annoy Paul? If Paul accepted the demon's words, he would appear to be linking the gospel with demon-related activities. This would damage his message about Christ. Truth and evil do not mix.

16:19 Faced with the loss of their slave girl's fortune-telling ability, the Philippian entrepreneurs were furious. Never mind that Paul and Silas were speaking eternal truths, never mind that the poor slave girl had been delivered from an awful existence; these men could only bemoan their economic loss! The gospel would also later hurt Ephesian idol makers financially (chapter 19), resulting in a citywide riot. When people care more about their own economic well being than the glory of God and the salvation of lost souls, it is a clear sign of idolatry, greed, and worldliness.

16:22–25 Paul and Silas were stripped, beaten, and placed in stocks in the inner cell. Stocks were made of two boards joined with iron clamps, leaving holes just big enough for the ankles. The prisoner's legs were placed across the lower board, and then the upper board was closed over them. Sometimes both wrists and ankles were placed in stocks. Paul and Silas, who had committed no crime and who were peaceful men, were put in stocks designed for holding the most dangerous prisoners in absolute security. Despite this dismal situation, they praised God, praying and singing as the other prisoners listened. No matter what our circumstances, we should praise God. Others may come to Christ because of our example.

PAUL TRAVELS TO MACEDONIA At Troas, Paul received the Macedonian call (16:9), and he, Silas, Timothy, and Luke boarded a ship. They sailed to the island of Samothrace, then on to Neapolis, the port for the city of Philippi. Philippi sat on the Egnatian Way, a main transportation artery connecting the eastern provinces with Italy.

16:25
w Eph 5:19

16:26
x Ac 4:31
y Ac 12:10
z Ac 12:7

25 About midnight Paul and Silas were praying and singing hymns w to God, and the other prisoners were listening to them. 26 Suddenly there was such a violent earthquake that the foundations of the prison were shaken.x At once all the prison doors flew open,y and everybody's chains came loose.z 27 The jailer woke up, and when he saw the prison doors open, he drew his sword and was about to kill himself because he thought the prisoners had escaped. 28 But Paul shouted, "Don't harm yourself! We are all here!"

16:30
a Ac 2:37

29 The jailer called for lights, rushed in and fell trembling before Paul and Silas. 30 He then brought them out and asked, "Sirs, what must I do to be saved?" a

16:33
b ver 25

31 They replied, "Believe in the Lord Jesus, and you will be saved—you and your household." 32 Then they spoke the word of the Lord to him and to all the others in his house. 33 At that hour of the night b the jailer took them and washed their wounds; then immediately he and all his family were baptized. 34 The jailer brought them into his house and set a meal before them; he was filled with joy because he had come to believe in God—he and his whole family.

LYDIA

Almost everywhere Paul and Silas traveled, they found people open to the gospel message. When they arrived in Philippi they met just such a disciple-in-the-making. Her name was Lydia.

Lydia's business as a dealer in fine purple cloth and dye probably means she was wealthy. No husband is mentioned, but she was responsible for a household. Lydia was also a spiritual searcher. She was among the Gentile women who gathered outside Philippi on each Sabbath to pray to the God of the Jews. One eventful day, Paul and Silas visited the group.

Lydia's attendance at the prayer gathering demonstrated her willingness to respond to as much about God as she knew. God responded to her quest by providing her with more truth. When she heard the gospel message about Jesus Christ, she listened and believed. She is remembered as Paul's first European convert.

Luke described with swift strokes the first two steps in Lydia's life as a disciple: (1) She was baptized, (2) she brought the rest of the members of her household to Paul and they apparently believed as well, because they were baptized as well. Lydia's response was both inward and outward. She immediately understood that her new faith created all kinds of opportunities for practical application. Then, as now, the gospel had life-changing effects. The first actions of new believers often indicate how deeply they have understood and received the gift of salvation. The Christian life is a gift we continue to receive by sharing it with others.

Thinking of Lydia, how would you describe the initial effects of the gospel in your life? When you accepted Christ, what changes did others notice in you? How did Christ's presence affect your behavior? To what degree has your life continued to display that gratefulness you felt when you first believed?

Strengths and accomplishments:	• Successful businesswoman • The first convert to Christianity in Philippi, and therefore, Europe • Brought her entire household to hear about Jesus, and all were baptized as a result • Provided housing in Philippi for Paul and Silas
Lessons from her life:	• God rewards those who honestly seek him • One of the marks of conversion is care for others—physically and spiritually
Vital statistics:	• Where: From Thyatira, living in Philippi • Occupation: Merchant specializing in costly purple cloth • Relatives: A household that was baptized with her
Key verse	"One of those listening was a woman named Lydia, a dealer in purple cloth from the city of Thyatira, who was a worshiper of God. The Lord opened her heart to respond to Paul's message" (Acts 16:14).

The events surrounding Lydia's conversion are found in Acts 16:11–40.

16:27 The jailer drew his sword to kill himself because jailers were responsible for their prisoners and would be held accountable for their escape.

16:30, 31 Paul and Silas's reputation in Philippi was well known. When the jailer realized his own condition and need, he risked everything to find the answer. The Christian Good News of salvation is simply expressed: Believe in the Lord Jesus, and you will be saved (see Romans 10:9; 1 Corinthians 12:3; Ephesians 2:8, 9; Philippians 2:11). When we recognize Jesus as Lord and trust in him with our entire life, salvation is assured to us. If you have

never trusted in Jesus to save you, do so quickly. Your life can be filled with joy, just as the jailer's was (16:34).

16:31–34 Paul and Silas took the family unit seriously. So the offer of salvation was made to the jailer's entire household—family and servants. Yet it was not the jailer's faith that saved them; they all needed to come to Jesus in faith and believe in him in the same way the jailer had. Yet his entire family did believe and all were saved. Pray that God will use you to introduce Jesus to your family and that they will come to believe in him.

35 When it was daylight, the magistrates sent their officers to the jailer with the order: "Release those men." 36 The jailer*c* told Paul, "The magistrates have ordered that you and Silas be released. Now you can leave. Go in peace."

37 But Paul said to the officers: "They beat us publicly without a trial, even though we are Roman citizens, *d* and threw us into prison. And now do they want to get rid of us quietly? No! Let them come themselves and escort us out."

38 The officers reported this to the magistrates, and when they heard that Paul and Silas were Roman citizens, they were alarmed. 39 They came to appease them and escorted them from the prison, requesting them to leave the city. *e* 40 After Paul and Silas came out of the prison, they went to Lydia's house,*f* where they met with the brothers and encouraged them. Then they left.

16:36	*c* ver 23, 27
16:37	*d* Ac 22:25-29
16:39	*e* Mt 8:34
16:40	*f* ver 14

In Thessalonica

17 When they had passed through Amphipolis and Apollonia, they came to Thessalonica,*g* where there was a Jewish synagogue. 2 As his custom was, Paul went into the synagogue,*h* and on three Sabbath*i* days he reasoned with them from the Scriptures, 3 explaining and proving that the Christ*a* had to suffer*j* and rise from the dead. "This Jesus I am proclaiming to you is the Christ,*a* "*k* he said. 4 Some of the Jews were persuaded and joined Paul and Silas,*l* as did a large number of God-fearing Greeks and not a few prominent women.

5 But the Jews were jealous; so they rounded up some bad characters from the marketplace, formed a mob and started a riot in the city. They rushed to Jason's*m* house in search of Paul and Silas in order to bring them out to the crowd. *b* 6 But when they did not find them, they dragged*n* Jason and some other brothers before the city officials, shouting: "These men who have caused trouble all over the world have now come here,*o* 7 and Jason has welcomed

17:1	*g* 1Th 1:1
17:2	*h* Ac 9:20 ; *i* Ac 13:14
17:3	*j* Lk 24:26 ; *k* Ac 18:28
17:4	*l* Ac 15:22
17:5	*m* Ro 16:21
17:6	*n* Ac 16:19 ; *o* Ac 16:20

a 3 Or *Messiah*   *b* 5 Or *the assembly of the people*

16:37, 38 Paul refused to take his freedom and run. He wanted to teach the rulers in Philippi a lesson and to protect the other believers from the treatment he and Silas had received. The word would spread that Paul and Silas had been found innocent and freed by the leaders, expressing the truth that believers should not be persecuted—especially if they were Roman citizens. Roman citizenship carried with it certain privileges. These Philippian authorities were alarmed because it was illegal to whip a Roman citizen. In addition, every citizen had the right to a fair trial—which Paul and Silas had not been given.

17:1 Thessalonica was one of the wealthiest and most influential cities in Macedonia. This is the first city Paul visited where his teachings attracted a large group of socially prominent citizens. The church he planted grew quickly, but in A.D. 50–51, Paul was forced out of the city by a mob (17:5, 6, 10). He later sent Timothy back to Thessalonica to see how the Christians were doing. Soon

MINISTRY IN MACEDONIA

Luke stayed in Philippi while Paul, Silas, and Timothy continued on the Egnatian Way to Amphipolis, Apollonia, and Thessalonica. But trouble arose in Thessalonica, and they fled to Berea. When their enemies from Thessalonica pursued them, Paul set out by sea to Athens, leaving Silas and Timothy to encourage the believers.

afterward, Paul wrote two letters to the Thessalonian believers (1 and 2 Thessalonians), encouraging them to remain faithful and to refuse to listen to false teachers who tried to refute their beliefs.

17:1, 2 A synagogue, a group of Jews who gathered for teaching and prayer, could be established wherever ten Jewish males lived. Paul's regular practice was to preach in synagogues as long as the Jews allowed it. Often those who weren't Jews would come to these services and hear Paul's preaching. For a description of a synagogue service, see the note on 13:14, 15.

17:2, 3 When Paul spoke in the synagogues, he wisely began by talking about Old Testament writings and explaining how the Messiah fulfilled them, moving from the known to the unknown. This is a good strategy for us. When we witness for Christ, we should begin where people are, affirming the truth they do know, and then we can present Christ, the One who is truth.

17:5 The Jewish leaders didn't try to refute the theology of Paul and Silas, but they were jealous of the popularity of these itinerant preachers. Their motives for causing the riot were rooted in personal jealousy, not doctrinal purity.

17:6 We don't know much about Jason except that he evidently was the local host and sponsor of Paul and Silas; thus he took the heat for all the problems. Jason is just one of many "unsung heroes" who faithfully played their part to help spread the gospel. Because of Jason's courage, Paul and Silas were able to minister more effectively. You may not receive much attention (in fact you may receive only grief) for your service for Christ. But God wants to use you. Lives will be changed because of your courage and faithfulness.

17:6 What a reputation these early Christians had! The power of the gospel revolutionized lives, broke down all social barriers, threw open prison doors, caused people to care deeply for one another, and stirred them to worship God. Our world needs to be turned upside down, to be transformed. The gospel doesn't merely improve programs and encourage good conduct; it dynamically transforms lives. Take courage and ask God how you can help spread his Good News throughout *your* world.

17:7 The Jewish leaders had difficulty manufacturing an accusation that would be heard by the city government. The Romans did

17:7
pLk 23:2

them into his house. They are all defying Caesar's decrees, saying that there is another king, one called Jesus."p 8 When they heard this, the crowd and the city officials were thrown into turmoil. 9 Then they made Jason and the others post bond and let them go.

In Berea

17:10
qAc 20:4

17:11
rLk 16:29; Jn 5:39

10 As soon as it was night, the brothers sent Paul and Silas away to Berea. q On arriving there, they went to the Jewish synagogue. 11 Now the Bereans were of more noble character than the Thessalonians, for they received the message with great eagerness and examined the Scriptures r every day to see if what Paul said was true. 12 Many of the Jews believed, as did also a number of prominent Greek women and many Greek men.

17:14
sAc 16:1

17:15
tver 16, 21, 22
uAc 18:5

13 When the Jews in Thessalonica learned that Paul was preaching the word of God at Berea, they went there too, agitating the crowds and stirring them up. 14 The brothers immediately sent Paul to the coast, but Silas and Timothys stayed at Berea. 15 The men who escorted Paul brought him to Athens t and then left with instructions for Silas and Timothy to join him as soon as possible. u

In Athens

17:18
vAc 4:2

16 While Paul was waiting for them in Athens, he was greatly distressed to see that the city was full of idols. 17 So he reasoned in the synagogue with the Jews and the God-fearing Greeks, as well as in the marketplace day by day with those who happened to be there. 18 A group of Epicurean and Stoic philosophers began to dispute with him. Some of them asked, "What is this babbler trying to say?" Others remarked, "He seems to be advocating foreign gods." They said this because Paul was preaching the good news about Jesus and the resurrection. v 19 Then they took him and brought him to a meeting of the Areopagus, where they said to him, "May we know what this new teaching is that you are presenting? 20 You are bringing some strange ideas to our ears, and we want to know what they mean." 21 (All the Athenians and the foreigners who lived there spent their time doing nothing but talking about and listening to the latest ideas.)

THE BOOKS OF THE NEW TESTAMENT: WHEN WERE THEY WRITTEN?
Dates are approximate.

Galatians	A.D. 49	Philemon	60	Acts	66/68
James	49	Philippians	61	2 Peter	66/68
1, 2 Thessalonians	51/52	Matthew	61/64	2 Timothy	66/67
1, 2 Corinthians	55	Luke	61/64	Hebrews	68/70
Romans	57	1 Timothy	64	John	85
Mark	58/60	Titus	64	1, 2, 3 John	85/90
Ephesians	60	1 Peter	64/65	Revelation	95
Colossians	60	Jude	65		

---

not care about theological disagreements between the Jews and these preachers. Treason, however, was a serious offense in the Roman empire. Paul and Silas were not advocating rebellion against Roman law, but their loyalty to another king sounded suspicious.

17:8, 9 Jason posted bond—putting up cash for freedom. By doing so, he promised that the trouble would cease or his own property and possibly his own life would be taken.

17:11 How do you evaluate sermons and teachings? The people in Berea opened the Scriptures for themselves and searched for truths to verify or disprove the message they heard. Always compare what you hear with what the Bible says. A preacher or teacher who gives God's true message will never contradict or explain away anything that is found in God's Word.

17:16 Athens, with its magnificent buildings and many gods, was a center for Greek culture, philosophy, and education. Philosophers and educated men were always ready to hear something new, so they invited Paul to speak to them at the meeting of the Areopagus (17:18, 19).

17:16 Paul was "greatly distressed to see that the city was full of idols." The word translated "distressed" is the Greek word "paroxysm," meaning "sudden, violent emotion." Paul was filled

with a combination of anger and grief. Seeing people spiritually lost, blinded by Satan, and trapped in a pagan culture caused Paul to be in a state of emotional upheaval. Though highly educated, the Athenians were ignorant of the one true God. It's interesting to note that Paul turned his internal turmoil into positive action: he looked for opportunities to share the truth about Jesus. Does the lostness of people move you to action? And if so, do you seek opportunities to share the gospel?

17:18 The Epicureans and Stoics were the dominant philosophers in Greek culture. The Epicureans believed that seeking happiness or pleasure was the primary goal of life. By contrast, the Stoics placed thinking above feeling and tried to live in harmony with nature and reason, suppressing their desire for pleasure. Thus they were very disciplined.

17:19 For a time the Council or Court (here called the Areopagus) met on a low hill in Athens near the Acropolis. As Paul stood there and spoke about the one true God, his audience could look down on the city and see the many idols representing gods that Paul knew were worthless.

22 Paul then stood up in the meeting of the Areopagus and said: "Men of Athens! I see that in every way you are very religious. 23 For as I walked around and looked carefully at your objects of worship, I even found an altar with this inscription: TO AN UNKNOWN GOD. Now what you worship as something unknown I am going to proclaim to you.

24 "The God who made the world and everything in it w is the Lord of heaven and earth x and does not live in temples built by hands. y 25 And he is not served by human hands, as if he needed anything, because he himself gives all men life and breath and everything else. z 26 From one man he made every nation of men, that they should inhabit the whole earth; and he determined the times set for them and the exact places where they should live. a 27 God did this so that men would seek him and perhaps reach out for him and find him, though he is not far from each one of us. b 28 'For in him we live and move and have our being.' As some of your own poets have said, 'We are his offspring.'

29 "Therefore since we are God's offspring, we should not think that the divine being is like gold or silver or stone—an image made by man's design and skill. c 30 In the past God overlooked d such ignorance, but now he commands all people everywhere to repent. e 31 For he has set a day when he will judge the world with justice by the man he has appointed. f He has given proof of this to all men by raising him from the dead." g

32 When they heard about the resurrection of the dead, some of them sneered, but others said, "We want to hear you again on this subject." 33 At that, Paul left the Council. 34 A few men became followers of Paul and believed. Among them was Dionysius, a member of the Areopagus, h also a woman named Damaris, and a number of others.

In Corinth

18 After this, Paul left Athens i and went to Corinth. 2 There he met a Jew named Aquila, a native of Pontus, who had recently come from Italy with his wife Priscilla, j because Claudius had ordered all the Jews to leave Rome. Paul went to see them, 3 and because he was a tentmaker as they were, he stayed and worked with them. k 4 Every Sabbath he reasoned in the synagogue, trying to persuade Jews and Greeks.

17:24
w Ac 14:15
x Mt 11:25
y Ac 7:48
17:25
z Isa 42:5
17:26
a Dt 32:8
17:27
b Ac 14:17
17:29
c Isa 40:18-20
17:30
d Ac 14:16; Ro 3:25
e Lk 24:47;
Tit 2:11, 12
17:31
f Ac 10:42
g Ac 2:24
17:34
h ver 19, 22
18:1
i Ac 17:15
18:2
j Ro 16:3;
1Co 16:19; 2Ti 4:19
18:3
k Ac 20:34;
1Co 4:12

17:22 Paul was well prepared to speak to this group. He came from Tarsus, an educational center, and had the training and knowledge to present his beliefs clearly and persuasively. Paul was a rabbi, taught by the finest scholar of his day, Gamaliel, and he had spent much of his life thinking and reasoning through the Scriptures.

It is not enough to teach or preach with conviction. Like Paul, we must be prepared. The more we know about the Bible, what it means, and how to apply it to life, the more convincing our words will be. This does not mean that we should avoid presenting the gospel until we feel adequately prepared. We should work with what we know, but always want to know more in order to reach more people and answer their questions and arguments more effectively.

17:22ff Paul's address is a good example of how to communicate the gospel. Paul did not begin by reciting Jewish history, as he usually did, for this would have been meaningless to his Greek audience. He began by building a case for the one true God, using examples they understood (17:22, 23). The Athenians had built an idol to the unknown god for fear of missing blessings or receiving punishment. Paul's opening statement to the men of Athens was about their unknown god. Paul was not endorsing this god but using the inscription as a point of entry for his witness to the one true God. Then he established common ground by emphasizing what they agreed on about God (17:24–29). Finally he moved his message to the person of Christ, centering on the resurrection (17:30, 31). When you witness to others, you can follow Paul's approach: Use examples, establish common ground, and then move people toward a decision about Jesus Christ.

17:23 Paul explained the one true God to these educated men of Athens; although these men were, in general, very religious, they did not know God. Today we have a "Christian" society, but to most people, God is still unknown. We need to proclaim who he is and make it clear what he did for all mankind through his Son Jesus Christ. We cannot assume that even religious people around us truly know Jesus or understand the importance of faith in him.

17:27, 28 God is in his creation and close to every one of us. But he is not trapped in his creation—he is transcendent. God is the Creator, not the creation. This means that God is sovereign and in control, while at the same time he is close and personal. Let the Creator of the universe rule your life.

17:30, 31 Paul did not leave his message unfinished. He confronted his listeners with Jesus' resurrection and its meaning to all people—either blessing or punishment. The Greeks had no concept of judgment. Most of them preferred worshiping many gods instead of just one, and the concept of resurrection was unbelievable and offensive to them. Paul did not hold back the truth, however, no matter what they might think of it. Paul often changed his approach to fit his audience, but he never changed his basic message.

17:32–34 Paul's speech received a mixed reaction: some sneered, some kept searching for more information, and a few believed. Don't hesitate to tell others about Christ because you fear that some will not believe you. Don't expect a unanimously positive response to your witnessing. Even if only a few believe, it's worth the effort.

18:1 Corinth was the political and commercial center of Greece, surpassing Athens in importance. It had a reputation for great wickedness and immorality. A temple to Aphrodite—goddess of love and war—had been built on the large hill behind the city. In this popular religion, people worshiped the goddess by giving money to the temple and taking part in sexual acts with male and female temple prostitutes. Paul found Corinth a challenge and a great ministry opportunity. Later, he would write a series of letters to the Corinthians dealing in part with the problems of immorality. First and Second Corinthians are two of those letters.

18:2, 3 Each Jewish boy learned a trade and tried to earn his living with it. Paul and Aquila had been trained in tentmaking, cutting and sewing the woven cloth of goats' hair into tents. Tents were used to house soldiers, so these tents may have been sold to the Roman army. As a tentmaker, Paul was able to go wherever

18:5
l Ac 17:14, 15
m ver 28; Ac 17:3

18:6
n 2Sa 1:16
o Ac 20:26
p Ac 13:46

18:8
q 1Co 1:14

⁵ When Silas and Timothy came from Macedonia,*l* Paul devoted himself exclusively to preaching, testifying to the Jews that Jesus was the Christ.*a* *m* ⁶ But when the Jews opposed Paul and became abusive, he shook out his clothes in protest and said to them, "Your blood be on your own heads!*n* I am clear of my responsibility. *o* From now on I will go to the Gentiles."*p*

⁷ Then Paul left the synagogue and went next door to the house of Titius Justus, a worshiper of God. ⁸ Crispus, *q* the synagogue ruler, and his entire household believed in the Lord; and many of the Corinthians who heard him believed and were baptized.

⁹ One night the Lord spoke to Paul in a vision: "Do not be afraid; keep on speaking, do not be silent. ¹⁰ For I am with you, and no one is going to attack and harm you, because I

a 5 Or Messiah; also in verse 28

One of the essential qualities of a good doctor is compassion. People need to know that their doctor cares. Even if he or she doesn't know what is wrong or isn't sure what to do, real concern is always a doctor's good medicine. Doctor Luke was a person of compassion.

Although we know few facts of his life, Luke has left us a strong impression of himself by what he wrote. In his Gospel, he emphasizes Jesus Christ's compassion. He vividly recorded both the power demonstrated by Christ's life and the care with which Christ treated people. Luke highlighted the relationships Jesus had with women. His writing in Acts is full of sharp verbal pictures of real people caught up in the greatest events of history.

Luke was also a doctor. He had a traveling medical practice as Paul's companion. Since the gospel was often welcomed with whips and stones, the doctor was undoubtedly seldom without patients. It is even possible that Paul's "thorn in the flesh" was some kind of physical ailment that needed Luke's regular attention (see 2 Corinthians 12:7). Paul deeply appreciated Luke's skills and faithfulness.

God also made special use of Luke as the historian of the early church. Repeatedly, the details of Luke's descriptions have been proven accurate. The first words in his Gospel indicate his interest in the truth.

Luke's compassion reflected his Lord's. Luke's skill as a doctor helped Paul. His passion for the facts as he recorded the life of Christ, the spread of the early church, and the lives of Christianity's missionaries gives us dependable sources for the basis of our faith. He accomplished all this while staying out of the spotlight. Perhaps his greatest example is the challenge to greatness even when we are not the center of attention.

Strengths and accomplishments:	• A humble, faithful, and useful companion of Paul • A well-educated and trained physician • A careful and exact historian • Writer of both the Gospel of Luke and the book of Acts
Lessons from his life:	• The words we leave behind will be a lasting picture of who we are • Even the most successful person needs the personal care of others • Excellence is shown by how we work when no one is noticing
Vital statistics:	• Where: Probably met Paul in Troas • Occupations: Doctor, historian, traveling companion • Contemporaries: Paul, Timothy, Silas, Peter
Key verses:	"Many have undertaken to draw up an account of the things that have been fulfilled among us, just as they were handed down to us by those who from the first were eyewitnesses and servants of the word. Therefore, since I myself have carefully investigated everything from the beginning, it seemed good also to me to write an orderly account for you, most excellent Theophilus, so that you may know the certainty of the things you have been taught" (Luke 1:1–4).

Luke includes himself in the *we* sections of Acts 16—28. He is also mentioned in Luke 1:3; Acts 1:1; Colossians 4:14; 2 Timothy 4:11; Philemon 24.

God led him, carrying his livelihood with him. The word "tentmaker" in Greek was also used to describe a leather worker.

18:6 Paul told the Jews he had done all he could for them. Because they had rejected Jesus as their Messiah, he would go to the Gentiles, who would be more receptive.

18:10 In a vision, Christ told Paul that he had many people in Corinth. Sometimes we can feel alone or isolated, especially when we see wickedness all around us and when we are persecuted for our faith. Usually, however, there are others in the neighborhood or community who also follow Christ. Ask God to lead you to them.

18:10, 11 Others who became Christians in Corinth were Phoebe (Romans 16:1—Cenchrea was the port city of Corinth), Tertius (Romans 16:22), Erastus (Romans 16:23), Quartus (Romans 16:23), Chloe (1 Corinthians 1:11), Gaius (1 Corinthians 1:14), Stephanas and his household (1 Corinthians 16:15), Fortunatus (1 Corinthians 16:17), and Achaicus (1 Corinthians 16:17).

have many people in this city." ¹¹So Paul stayed for a year and a half, teaching them the word of God.

¹²While Gallio was proconsul of Achaia, the Jews made a united attack on Paul and brought him into court. ¹³"This man," they charged, "is persuading the people to worship God in ways contrary to the law."

¹⁴Just as Paul was about to speak, Gallio said to the Jews, "If you Jews were making a complaint about some misdemeanor or serious crime, it would be reasonable for me to listen to you. ¹⁵But since it involves questions about words and names and your own law—settle the matter yourselves. I will not be a judge of such things." ¹⁶So he had them ejected from the court. ¹⁷Then they all turned on Sosthenes' the synagogue ruler and beat him in front of the court. But Gallio showed no concern whatever.

18:17
ʳ1Co 1:1

Priscilla, Aquila and Apollos

¹⁸Paul stayed on in Corinth for some time. Then he left the brothers and sailed for Syria, accompanied by Priscilla and Aquila. Before he sailed, he had his hair cut off at Cenchrea ˢ because of a vow he had taken.ᵗ ¹⁹They arrived at Ephesus, where Paul left Priscilla and Aquila. He himself went into the synagogue and reasoned with the Jews. ²⁰When they asked

18:18
ˢRo 16:1
ᵗNu 6:2, 5, 18;
Ac 21:24

MINISTRY IN CORINTH AND EPHESUS
Paul left Athens and traveled on to Corinth, one of the greatest commercial centers of the empire, located on a narrow neck of land offering direct passage between the Aegean and Adriatic seas. When Paul left from the port of Corinth at Cenchrea, he visited Ephesus. He then traveled to Caesarea, from where he went on to Jerusalem to report on his trip before returning to Antioch.

18:11 During the year and a half that Paul stayed in Corinth, he established a church and wrote two letters to the believers in Thessalonica (the books of 1 and 2 Thessalonians). Although Paul had been in Thessalonica for only a short time (17:1–15), he commended the believers there for their loving deeds, strong faith, and endurance inspired by hope. While encouraging them to stay away from immorality, he dealt with the themes of salvation, suffering, and the second coming of Jesus Christ. Paul told them to continue to work hard while they awaited Christ's return.

18:12 Gallio was proconsul of Achaia (modern Greece) and the brother of Seneca the philosopher. He came to power in A.D. 51–52.

18:13 Paul was charged with promoting a religion not approved by Roman law. This charge amounted to treason. Paul was not encouraging obedience to a human king other than Caesar (see 17:7), nor was he speaking against the Roman empire. Instead he was speaking about Christ's eternal kingdom.

18:14–16 This was an important judicial decision for the spread of the gospel in the Roman empire. Judaism was a recognized

religion under Roman law. As long as Christians were seen as part of Judaism, the court refused to hear cases brought against them. If they had claimed to be a new religion, they could easily have been outlawed by the government. In effect Gallio was saying, "I don't understand all your terminology and finer points of theology. Handle the matter yourself and don't bother me."

18:17 Crispus had been the ruler of the synagogue, but he and his family were converted and joined the Christians (18:8). Sosthenes had been chosen to take his place. The mob could have been Greeks venting their feelings against the Jews for causing turmoil, or the crowd may have included some Jews. In any case, they beat Sosthenes for losing the case and leaving the synagogue worse off than before. A person named Sosthenes is mentioned in 1 Corinthians 1:1, and many believe this was the same man who, in time, became a convert and a companion of Paul.

18:18 This vow Paul took was probably a temporary Nazirite vow that ended with shaving of the head and offering the hair as a sacrifice (Numbers 6:18).

18:21
u 1Co 4:19

18:22
v Ac 11:19

him to spend more time with them, he declined. ²¹But as he left, he promised, "I will come back if it is God's will." *u* Then he set sail from Ephesus. ²²When he landed at Caesarea, he went up and greeted the church and then went down to Antioch. *v*

4. Third missionary journey

²³After spending some time in Antioch, Paul set out from there and traveled from place to place throughout the region of Galatia and Phrygia, strengthening all the disciples.

18:24
w 1Co 1:12;
3:5, 6, 22; 4:6;
Tit 3:13

18:25
x Ac 19:3

²⁴Meanwhile a Jew named Apollos, *w* a native of Alexandria, came to Ephesus. He was a learned man, with a thorough knowledge of the Scriptures. ²⁵He had been instructed in the way of the Lord, and he spoke with great fervor *a* and taught about Jesus accurately, though he knew only the baptism of John. *x* ²⁶He began to speak boldly in the synagogue. When Priscilla and Aquila heard him, they invited him to their home and explained to him the way of God more adequately.

a 25 Or with fervor in the Spirit

AQUILA, PRISCILLA

Some couples know how to make the most of life. They complement each other, capitalize on each other's strengths, and form an effective team. Their united efforts affect those around them. Aquila and Priscilla were such a couple. They are never mentioned separately in the Bible. In marriage and ministry, they operated as one.

Priscilla and Aquila met Paul in Corinth during his second missionary journey. They had just been expelled from Rome by Emperor Claudius's decree against Jews. Their home was as movable as the tents they made to support themselves. They opened their home to Paul, and he joined them in tentmaking. He shared with them his wealth of spiritual wisdom.

Priscilla and Aquila made the most of their spiritual education. They listened carefully to sermons and evaluated what they heard. When they heard Apollos speak, they were impressed by his ability but realized that his information was not complete. Instead of open confrontation, the couple quietly took Apollos home and shared with him what he needed to know. Until then, Apollos had only been aware of John the Baptist's message about Christ. Priscilla and Aquila told him about Jesus' life, death, and resurrection, and the reality of God's indwelling Spirit. He continued to preach powerfully—but now with the full story.

As for Priscilla and Aquila, they went on using their home as a warm place for training and worship. Back in Rome years later, they hosted one of the house churches that developed.

In an age when the focus is mostly on what happens *between* husband and wife, Aquila and Priscilla are an example of what can happen *through* husband and wife. Their effectiveness together is the result of their good relationship with each other. Their hospitality opened the doorway of salvation to many. The Christian home is still one of the best tools for spreading the gospel. Do guests find Christ in your home?

Strengths and accomplishments:	• Outstanding husband/wife team who ministered in the early church • Supported themselves by tentmaking while serving Christ • Close friends of Paul • Explained to Apollos the full message of Christ
Lessons from their lives:	• Couples can have an effective ministry together • The home is a valuable tool for evangelism • Every believer needs to be well educated in the faith, whatever his or her role in the church
Vital statistics:	• Where: Originally from Rome, moved to Corinth, then Ephesus • Occupation: Tentmakers • Contemporaries: Emperor Claudius, Paul, Timothy, Apollos
Key verses:	"Greet Priscilla and Aquila, my fellow workers in Christ Jesus. They risked their lives for me. Not only I but all the churches of the Gentiles are grateful to them" (Romans 16:3, 4).

Their story is told in Acts 18. They are also mentioned in Romans 16:3–5; 1 Corinthians 16:19; 2 Timothy 4:19.

18:22 This verse marks the end of Paul's second missionary journey and the beginning of the third, which lasted from A.D. 53–57. Leaving the church at Antioch (his home base), Paul headed toward Ephesus, but along the way he revisited the churches in Galatia and Phrygia (18:23). The heart of this trip was a lengthy stay (two to three years) in Ephesus. Before returning to Jerusalem, he also visited believers in Macedonia and Greece.

18:24-26 Apollos had heard only what John the Baptist had said about Jesus (see Luke 3:1–18), so his message was not the complete story. John focused on repentance from sin, the first step. But the whole message is to repent from sin and then believe in Christ. Apollos did not know about Jesus' life, crucifixion, and resurrection. Nor did he know about the coming of the Holy Spirit. Priscilla and Aquila explained the way of salvation to him.

27 When Apollos wanted to go to Achaia, the brothers encouraged him and wrote to the disciples there to welcome him. On arriving, he was a great help to those who by grace had believed. 28 For he vigorously refuted the Jews in public debate, proving from the Scriptures that Jesus was the Christ. y

18:28
y ver 5

Paul in Ephesus

19 While Apollos was at Corinth, Paul took the road through the interior and arrived at Ephesus. There he found some disciples 2 and asked them, "Did you receive the Holy Spirit when a you believed?"

They answered, "No, we have not even heard that there is a Holy Spirit."

3 So Paul asked, "Then what baptism did you receive?"

"John's baptism," they replied.

4 Paul said, "John's baptism was a baptism of repentance. He told the people to believe in the one coming after him, that is, in Jesus." 5 On hearing this, they were baptized into b the name of the Lord Jesus. 6 When Paul placed his hands on them, z the Holy Spirit came on them, a and they spoke in tongues c b and prophesied. 7 There were about twelve men in all.

8 Paul entered the synagogue and spoke boldly there for three months, arguing persuasively about the kingdom of God. c 9 But some of them became obstinate; they refused to

19:6
z Ac 6:6; 8:17
a Ac 2:4
b Ac 10:46

19:8
c Ac 1:3; 28:23

a 2 Or after   b 5 Or in   c 6 Or other languages

18:27, 28 Apollos was from Alexandria in Egypt, the second most important city in the Roman empire, and the home of a great university. Alexandria had a thriving Jewish population. Apollos was a scholar, orator, and debater; and after his knowledge about Christ was made more complete, God greatly used these gifts to strengthen and encourage the church. Reason is a powerful tool in the right hands and in the right situation. Apollos used the gift of reason to convince many in Greece of the truth of the gospel.

As often happens however, abilities sometimes cause division because of jealousy, pride, or other problems. Apollos's abilities eventually created a problem. Some of the Corinthians became more enamored with Apollos than with his message. There is no evidence to suggest that Apollos encouraged this behavior, and Paul never blamed Apollos for this development. Still, Paul eventually had to confront the Corinthians about their divisiveness (see 1 Corinthians 1:12, 13). Be glad for God's gifts but always remember that they are given to bring honor to him. *He* is the point! *His* glory is the issue! Use the gift, but more than that, praise the Giver of the gifts and use them to his glory.

18:27, 28 Not all the work of a minister or missionary is drudgery, setback, or suffering. Chapter 18 is triumphant, showing victories in key cities and the addition of exciting new leaders such as Priscilla, Aquila, and Apollos to the church. Rejoice in the victories Christ brings, and don't let the hazards create a negative mind-set.

PAUL TAKES A THIRD JOURNEY What prompted Paul's third journey may have been the need to correct any misunderstandings in the churches Paul had planted. So he hurried north, then west, returning to many of the cities he had previously visited. This time, however, he stayed on a more direct westward route toward Ephesus.

19:1 Ephesus was the capital and leading business center of the Roman province of Asia (part of present-day Turkey). A hub of sea and land transportation, it ranked with Antioch in Syria and Alexandria in Egypt as one of the great cities on the Mediterranean Sea. Paul stayed in Ephesus for a little over two years. There he wrote his first letter to the Corinthians to counter several problems the church in Corinth was facing. Later, while imprisoned in Rome, Paul wrote a letter to the Ephesian church (the book of Ephesians).

19:2–4 John's baptism was a sign of repentance from sin only, not a sign of new life in Christ. Like Apollos (18:24–26), these Ephesian believers needed further instruction on the message and ministry of Jesus Christ. They believed in Jesus as the Messiah, but they did not understand the significance of his death and resurrection or the work of the Holy Spirit. Becoming a Christian involves turning from sin (repentance) and turning to Christ (faith). These believers were incomplete.

In the book of Acts, believers received the Holy Spirit in a variety of ways. Usually the Holy Spirit would fill a person as soon as he or she professed faith in Christ. Here that filling happened later because these disciples' knowledge was incomplete. God was confirming to these believers, who did not initially know about the Holy Spirit, that they were a part of the church. The Holy Spirit's filling endorsed them as believers.

Pentecost was the formal outpouring of the Holy Spirit on the church. The other outpourings in the book of Acts were God's way of uniting new believers to the church. The mark of the true church is not merely right doctrine, but right actions, the true evidence of the Holy Spirit's work.

19:6 When Paul laid his hands on these disciples, they received the Holy Spirit, just as the disciples had at Pentecost, resulting in outward, visible signs of the Holy Spirit's presence. This also had happened when the Holy Spirit had come on Gentiles (non-Jews, see 10:45–47). Much has been made about this passage and others in Acts that depict believers speaking in tongues. Some have uncomfortably downplayed or dismissed these historical events. Others have tried to duplicate them. Few issues have prompted more argument and confusion or split more churches. We should remember that tongues-speaking is not the central theme of the book of Acts. The point of Luke's history is the faithful communication of the gospel to the ends of the earth. If we want to be doers of the Word (James 1:22), we will faithfully be involved in the same process of evangelism. Seek to share your faith in the power of the Holy Spirit (1:8) and leave it up to God to give you whatever experiences he thinks you need.

19:9 Paul spoke in a lecture hall at this school. Such halls were used in the morning for teaching philosophy, but they were empty

19:9
d Ac 9:2

19:10
e Ac 20:31

19:12
f Ac 5:15

19:13
g Mt 12:27

believe and publicly maligned the Way. *d* So Paul left them. He took the disciples with him and had discussions daily in the lecture hall of Tyrannus. ¹⁰This went on for two years, *e* so that all the Jews and Greeks who lived in the province of Asia heard the word of the Lord.

¹¹God did extraordinary miracles through Paul, ¹²so that even handkerchiefs and aprons that had touched him were taken to the sick, and their illnesses were cured *f* and the evil spirits left them.

¹³Some Jews who went around driving out evil spirits*g* tried to invoke the name of the Lord Jesus over those who were demon-possessed. They would say, "In the name of Jesus, whom

APOLLOS

Some people have an amazing natural talent for public speaking. Some even have a great message to go along with it. When Apollos arrived in Ephesus shortly after Paul's departure, he made an immediate impact. He spoke boldly in public, interpreting and applying the Old Testament Scriptures effectively. He debated opponents of Christianity forcefully and effectively. It didn't take long for him to be noticed by Priscilla and Aquila.

The couple quickly realized that Apollos did not have the whole story. His preaching was based on the Old Testament and John the Baptist's message. He was probably urging people to repent and prepare for the coming Messiah. Priscilla and Aquila took him home with them and brought him up to date on all that had happened. As they told him of the life of Jesus, his death, and his resurrection, and the coming of the Holy Spirit, Apollos must have seen Scripture after Scripture become clear. He was filled with new energy and boldness now that he knew the complete gospel.

Apollos next decided to travel to Achaia. His friends in Ephesus were able to send along a glowing letter of introduction. He quickly became the verbal champion of the Christians in Corinth, debating the opponents of the gospel in public. As often happens, Apollos's abilities eventually created a problem. Some of the Corinthians began to follow Apollos rather than his message. Paul had to confront the Corinthians about their divisiveness. They had been forming little groups named after their favorite preacher. Apollos left Corinth and hesitated to return. Paul wrote warmly of Apollos as a fellow minister who had "watered" the seeds of the gospel that Paul had planted in Corinth. Paul last mentions Apollos briefly to Titus. Apollos was still a traveling representative of the gospel who deserved Titus's help.

Although his natural abilities could have made him proud, Apollos proved himself willing to learn. God used Priscilla and Aquila, fresh from months of learning from Paul, to give Apollos the complete gospel. Because Apollos did not hesitate to be a student, he became an even better teacher. How much does your willingness to learn affect God's efforts to help you become all he wants you to be?

Strengths and accomplishments:	• A gifted and persuasive preacher and apologist in the early church • Willing to be taught • One of the possible candidates for the unknown author of Hebrews
Lessons from his life:	• Effective communication of the gospel includes an accurate message delivered with God's power • A clear verbal defense of the gospel can be a real encouragement to believers, while convincing non-believers of its truth
Vital statistics:	• Where: From Alexandria in Egypt • Occupations: Traveling preacher, apologist • Contemporaries: Priscilla, Aquila, Paul
Key verses:	"He had been instructed in the way of the Lord, and he spoke with great fervor and taught about Jesus accurately, though he knew only the baptism of John. He began to speak boldly in the synagogue. When Priscilla and Aquila heard him, they invited him to their home and explained to him the way of God more adequately" (Acts 18:25, 26).

Apollos's story is told in Acts 18:24—19:1. He is also mentioned in 1 Corinthians 1:12; 3:4–6, 22; 4:1, 6; 16:12; Titus 3:13.

during the hot part of the day (about 11 a.m. to 4 p.m.). Because many people did not work during those hours, they would come to hear Paul's preaching.

19:10 "The province of Asia" refers to Asia Minor or modern-day Turkey. During this time, Paul and his coworkers spread the gospel throughout the land.

19:13 These Jews traveled from town to town making a living by claiming to heal and drive out demons. Often they would recite a whole list of names in their incantation to be sure of including the right deity. Here they were trying to use Jesus' name in an effort to match Paul's power.

19:13–16 Some Ephesians engaged in exorcism and occult practices for profit (see 19:18, 19). The sons of Sceva were impressed by Paul's work, whose power to drive out demons came from God's Holy Spirit, not from witchcraft, and was obviously more powerful than theirs. They discovered, however, that no one can control or duplicate God's power. These men were calling on the name of Jesus without knowing the person. The power to change people comes from Christ. It cannot be tapped by reciting his name like a magic charm. God works his power only through those he chooses.

Paul preaches, I command you to come out." [14]Seven sons of Sceva, a Jewish chief priest, were doing this. [15]⌜One day⌟ the evil spirit answered them, "Jesus I know, and I know about Paul, but who are you?" [16]Then the man who had the evil spirit jumped on them and overpowered them all. He gave them such a beating that they ran out of the house naked and bleeding.

[17]When this became known to the Jews and Greeks living in Ephesus, they were all seized with fear,[h] and the name of the Lord Jesus was held in high honor. [18]Many of those who believed now came and openly confessed their evil deeds. [19]A number who had practiced sorcery brought their scrolls together and burned them publicly. When they calculated the value of the scrolls, the total came to fifty thousand drachmas.[a] [20]In this way the word of the Lord spread widely and grew in power.[i]

[21]After all this had happened, Paul decided to go to Jerusalem,[j] passing through Macedonia and Achaia. "After I have been there," he said, "I must visit Rome also."[k] [22]He sent two of his helpers,[l] Timothy and Erastus,[m] to Macedonia, while he stayed in the province of Asia a little longer.

The Riot in Ephesus

[23]About that time there arose a great disturbance about the Way. [24]A silversmith named Demetrius, who made silver shrines of Artemis, brought in no little business for the craftsmen. [25]He called them together, along with the workmen in related trades, and said: "Men, you know we receive a good income from this business. [26]And you see and hear how this fellow Paul has convinced and led astray large numbers of people here in Ephesus and in practically the whole province of Asia. He says that man-made gods are no gods at all.[n] [27]There is danger not only that our trade will lose its good name, but also that the temple of the great goddess Artemis will be discredited, and the goddess herself, who is worshiped throughout the province of Asia and the world, will be robbed of her divine majesty."

[28]When they heard this, they were furious and began shouting: "Great is Artemis of the Ephesians!" [29]Soon the whole city was in an uproar. The people seized Gaius and Aristarchus,[o] Paul's traveling companions from Macedonia, and rushed as one man into the theater. [30]Paul wanted to appear before the crowd, but the disciples would not let him. [31]Even some of the officials of the province, friends of Paul, sent him a message begging him not to venture into the theater.

[32]The assembly was in confusion: Some were shouting one thing, some another. Most of the people did not even know why they were there. [33]The Jews pushed Alexander to the

a 19 A drachma was a silver coin worth about a day's wages.

19:17
h Ac 5:5, 11

19:20
i Ac 6:7; 12:24

19:21
j Ro 15:25
k Ro 15:24, 28

19:22
l Ac 13:5
m Ro 16:23;
2Ti 4:20

19:26
n Ps 115:4;
Isa 44:10-20;
Jer 10:3-5

19:29
o Ac 20:4; 27:2;
Col 4:10; Phm 24

19:18, 19 Ephesus was a center for black magic and other occult practices. The people cooked up magical formulas to give them wealth, happiness, and success in marriage. Superstition and sorcery were commonplace. God clearly forbids such practices (Deuteronomy 18:9–13). You cannot be a believer and hold on to the occult, black magic, or sorcery. Once you begin to dabble in these areas, you may become obsessed by them because Satan is very powerful. But God's power is even greater (1 John 4:4; Revelation 20:10). If you are mixed up in the occult, learn a lesson from the Ephesians and get rid of anything that could trap you in such practices.

19:21 Why did Paul say he had to go to Rome? Wherever he went, he could see Rome's influence. Paul wanted to take the message of Christ to the world's center of influence and power.

19:22 Paul mentions Timothy in more detail in the books of 1 and 2 Timothy. Erastus was a committed follower of Christ who was not only Paul's helpful assistant, but also Corinth's director of public works (see Romans 16:23).

19:23 "The Way" refers to those who followed the way of Christ—the Christians.

19:24 Artemis was a goddess of fertility. She was represented by a carved female figure with many breasts. A large statue of Artemis (which was said to have come from heaven, 19:35) was in the great temple at Ephesus. That temple was one of the wonders of the ancient world. The festival of Artemis involved wild orgies and carousing. Obviously the religious and commercial life of Ephesus reflected the city's worship of this pagan deity.

19:25–27 When Paul preached in Ephesus, Demetrius and his fellow craftsmen did not quarrel with his doctrine. Their anger boiled because his preaching threatened their profits. They made silver statues of the Ephesian goddess Artemis. The craftsmen knew that if people started believing in God and discarding the idols, their livelihood would suffer.

19:27 Demetrius's strategy for stirring up a riot was to appeal to his fellow workmen's love of money and then to encourage them to hide their greed behind the mask of patriotism and religious loyalty. The rioters couldn't see the selfish motives for their rioting—instead they saw themselves as heroes for the sake of their land and beliefs.

19:29–31 Paul often sought others to help him in his work. On this occasion, his traveling companions were Aristarchus (who would accompany him on other journeys; see 20:3, 4 and 27:1, 2), and Gaius (probably not the same Gaius mentioned in Romans 16:23 or 1 Corinthians 1:14). Paul wanted to go to the theater to speak up and defend his companions, but the other believers wouldn't let him go, fearing for his safety. The officials who begged him not to risk his life were government officials, responsible for the religious and political order of the region. Paul's message had reached all levels of society, crossing all social barriers and giving Paul friends in high places.

19:33, 34 The mob had become anti-Jewish as well as anti-Christian. This Alexander may have been pushed forward by the Jews as a spokesman to explain that the Jews had no part in the Christian community, and thus were not involved in the economic problem of the silversmiths.

19:33
p Ac 12:17

19:37
q Ro 2:22

20:3
r Ac 9:23, 24

20:4
s Ac 19:29
t Ac 16:1
u Eph 6:21; Col 4:7;
Tit 3:12
v Ac 21:29; 2Ti 4:20

20:6
w Ac 16:8

20:7
x 1Co 16:2;
Rev 1:10

20:8
y Ac 1:13

front, and some of the crowd shouted instructions to him. He motioned p for silence in order to make a defense before the people. 34 But when they realized he was a Jew, they all shouted in unison for about two hours: "Great is Artemis of the Ephesians!"

35 The city clerk quieted the crowd and said: "Men of Ephesus, doesn't all the world know that the city of Ephesus is the guardian of the temple of the great Artemis and of her image, which fell from heaven? 36 Therefore, since these facts are undeniable, you ought to be quiet and not do anything rash. 37 You have brought these men here, though they have neither robbed temples q nor blasphemed our goddess. 38 If, then, Demetrius and his fellow craftsmen have a grievance against anybody, the courts are open and there are proconsuls. They can press charges. 39 If there is anything further you want to bring up, it must be settled in a legal assembly. 40 As it is, we are in danger of being charged with rioting because of today's events. In that case we would not be able to account for this commotion, since there is no reason for it." 41 After he had said this, he dismissed the assembly.

Through Macedonia and Greece

20 When the uproar had ended, Paul sent for the disciples and, after encouraging them, said good-by and set out for Macedonia. 2 He traveled through that area, speaking many words of encouragement to the people, and finally arrived in Greece, 3 where he stayed three months. Because the Jews made a plot against him r just as he was about to sail for Syria, he decided to go back through Macedonia. 4 He was accompanied by Sopater son of Pyrrhus from Berea, Aristarchus s and Secundus from Thessalonica, Gaius from Derbe, Timothy t also, and Tychicus u and Trophimus v from the province of Asia. 5 These men went on ahead and waited for us at Troas. 6 But we sailed from Philippi after the Feast of Unleavened Bread, and five days later joined the others at Troas, w where we stayed seven days.

Eutychus Raised From the Dead at Troas

7 On the first day of the week x we came together to break bread. Paul spoke to the people and, because he intended to leave the next day, kept on talking until midnight. 8 There were many lamps in the upstairs room y where we were meeting. 9 Seated in a window was a young man named Eutychus, who was sinking into a deep sleep as Paul talked on and on.

19:38 A proconsul served as a civil magistrate or governor of a Roman province.

19:40 The city of Ephesus was under the domination of the Roman empire. The main responsibility of the local city leaders was simply to maintain peace and order. If they failed to control the people, Rome would remove the appointed officials from office. The entire town could also be put under martial law, taking away many civic freedoms.

19:41 The riot in Ephesus convinced Paul that it was time to move on. But it also showed that the law still provided some protection for Christians as they challenged the worship of the goddess Artemis and the most idolatrous religion in Asia.

20:1–3 While in Greece, Paul spent much of his time in Corinth. From there he wrote the letter to the Romans. Although Paul had not yet been to Rome, believers had already started a church there (2:10; 18:2). Paul wrote to tell the church that he planned to visit the Roman believers. The letter to the Romans is a theological essay on the meaning of faith and salvation, an explanation of the relation between Jews and Gentiles in Christ, and a list of practical guidelines for the church.

20:4 These men who were traveling with Paul represented churches that Paul had started in Asia. Each man was carrying an offering from his home church to be given to the believers in Jerusalem. Having each man deliver the gift gave the gifts a personal touch and strengthened the unity of the believers. This was also an effective way to teach the church about giving, because the men were able to report back to their churches the way God was working through their giving. Paul discussed this gift in one of his letters to the Corinthian church (see 2 Corinthians 8:1–21).

20:5, 6 The use of *us* and *we* shows that this is where Luke again joined the group. The last *we* occurred in chapter 16.

20:6 Jewish believers celebrated the Passover (which was

immediately followed by the Feast of Unleavened Bread) according to Moses' instructions (see Exodus 12:43–51) even if they couldn't be at Jerusalem for the occasion.

20:8, 9 The many lamps were candles in lanterns. The combination of the heat from the candles and the gathered number of people in an upstairs room probably made the room very warm. This no doubt helped Eutychus fall asleep, as well as the fact that Paul spoke for a long time. Eutychus was probably somewhere in the range of 8–14 years old (the age of a "young man").

THROUGH MACEDONIA AND ACHAIA
A riot in Ephesus sent Paul to Troas, then through Macedonia to the region of Achaia. In Achaia he went to Corinth to deal with problems there. Paul had planned to sail from Corinth straight to Antioch in Syria, but a plot against his life was discovered. So he retraced his steps through Macedonia.

When he was sound asleep, he fell to the ground from the third story and was picked up dead. ¹⁰Paul went down, threw himself on the young man *z* and put his arms around him. "Don't be alarmed," he said. "He's alive!" *a* ¹¹Then he went upstairs again and broke bread and ate. After talking until daylight, he left. ¹²The people took the young man home alive and were greatly comforted.

20:10
z 1Ki 17:21
a Mt 9:23, 24

Paul's Farewell to the Ephesian Elders

¹³We went on ahead to the ship and sailed for Assos, where we were going to take Paul aboard. He had made this arrangement because he was going there on foot. ¹⁴When he met us at Assos, we took him aboard and went on to Mitylene. ¹⁵The next day we set sail from there and arrived off Kios. The day after that we crossed over to Samos, and on the following day arrived at Miletus. ¹⁶Paul had decided to sail past Ephesus to avoid spending time in the province of Asia, for he was in a hurry to reach Jerusalem, *b* if possible, by the day of Pentecost. *c*

20:16
b Ac 19:21
c Ac 2:1

¹⁷From Miletus, Paul sent to Ephesus for the elders of the church. ¹⁸When they arrived, he said to them: "You know how I lived the whole time I was with you, *d* from the first day I came into the province of Asia. ¹⁹I served the Lord with great humility and with tears, although I was severely tested by the plots of the Jews. ²⁰You know that I have not hesitated to preach anything *e* that would be helpful to you but have taught you publicly and from house to house. ²¹I have declared to both Jews *f* and Greeks that they must turn to God in repentance *g* and have faith in our Lord Jesus.

20:18
d Ac 18:19-21;
19:1-41

20:20
e ver 27

20:21
f Ac 18:5
g Ac 2:38

²²"And now, compelled by the Spirit, I am going to Jerusalem, not knowing what will happen to me there. ²³I only know that in every city the Holy Spirit warns me that prison and hardships are facing me. ²⁴However, I consider my life worth nothing to me, *h* if only I may finish the race and complete the task the Lord Jesus has given me *i*—the task of testifying to the gospel of God's grace.

20:24
h Ac 21:13
i Gal 1:1

²⁵"Now I know that none of you among whom I have gone about preaching the kingdom will ever see me again. ²⁶Therefore, I declare to you today that I am innocent of the blood of all men. *j* ²⁷For I have not hesitated to proclaim to you the whole will of God. *k* ²⁸Keep watch over yourselves and all the flock of which the Holy Spirit has made you overseers. *a l* Be

20:26
j Ac 18:6

20:27
k ver 20

20:28
l 1Pe 5:2

a 28 Traditionally *bishops*

20:16 Paul had missed attending the Passover in Jerusalem, so he was especially interested in arriving on time for Pentecost, which was 50 days after Passover. He was carrying with him gifts for the Jerusalem believers from churches in Asia and Greece (see Romans 15:25, 26; 1 Corinthians 16:1ff; 2 Corinthians 8, 9). The Jerusalem church was experiencing difficult times. Paul may have been anxious to deliver this gift to the believers at Pentecost because it was a day of celebration and thanksgiving to God for his provision.

PAUL TRAVELS FROM TROAS TO MILETUS
From Troas, Paul traveled overland to Assos, then boarded a ship to Mitylene and Samos on its way to Miletus. He summoned the elders of the Ephesian church to say farewell to them, because he knew he would probably not see them again.

20:18-21 The way of the believer is not an easy road; being a Christian does not solve or remove all problems. Paul served humbly and "with tears," but he never quit, never gave up. The message of salvation was so important that he never missed an opportunity to share it. And although he preached his message in different ways to fit different audiences, the message remained the same—turning away from sin and turning to Christ by faith. The Christian life will have its rough times, tears, and sorrows, as well as joys, but we should always be ready to tell others what good things God has done for us. His blessings far outweigh life's difficulties.

20:22 "Compelled by the Spirit" could be paraphrased, "drawn irresistably by the Holy Spirit."

20:23 The Holy Spirit showed Paul that he would be imprisoned and experience suffering. Even knowing this, Paul did not shrink from fulfilling his mission. His strong character was a good example to the Ephesian elders, some of whom would also suffer for Christ.

20:24 We often feel that life is a failure unless we're getting a lot out of it: recognition, fun, money, success. But Paul considered life worth *nothing* unless he used it for God's work. What he put *into* life was far more important than what he got out. Which is more important to you—what you get out of life, or what you put into it?

20:24 Single-mindedness is a quality needed by anyone who wishes to do God's work. Paul was a single-minded person, and the most important goal of his life was to tell others about Christ (Philippians 3:7-13). It is no wonder that Paul was the greatest missionary who ever lived. God is looking for more men and women who focus on that one great task God has given them to do.

20:31
m Ac 19:10

20:32
n Col 1:12; 3:24;
1Pe 1:4
o Ac 26:18

20:33
p 1Co 9:12;
2Co 12:14-17

20:34
q Ac 18:3

20:36
r Ac 21:5

20:38
s ver 25

shepherds of the church of God,a which he bought with his own blood. 29 I know that after I leave, savage wolves will come in among you and will not spare the flock. 30 Even from your own number men will arise and distort the truth in order to draw away disciples after them. 31 So be on your guard! Remember that for three years m I never stopped warning each of you night and day with tears.

32 "Now I commit you to God and to the word of his grace, which can build you up and give you an inheritance n among all those who are sanctified. o 33 I have not coveted anyone's silver or gold or clothing. p 34 You yourselves know that these hands of mine have supplied my own needs and the needs of my companions. q 35 In everything I did, I showed you that by this kind of hard work we must help the weak, remembering the words the Lord Jesus himself said: 'It is more blessed to give than to receive.'"

36 When he had said this, he knelt down with all of them and prayed. r 37 They all wept as they embraced him and kissed him. 38 What grieved them most was his statement that they would never see his face again. s Then they accompanied him to the ship.

On to Jerusalem

21 After we had torn ourselves away from them, we put out to sea and sailed straight to Cos. The next day we went to Rhodes and from there to Patara. 2 We found a ship crossing over to Phoenicia, went on board and set sail. 3 After sighting Cyprus and passing to the south of it, we sailed on to Syria. We landed at Tyre, where our ship was to unload its

a 28 Many manuscripts *of the Lord*

PAUL RETURNS TO JERUSALEM
The ship sailed from Miletus to Cos, Rhodes, and Patara. Paul and his companions then boarded a cargo ship bound for Phoenicia. They passed Cyprus and landed at Tyre, then Ptolemais, and finally Caesarea, where Paul disembarked and returned by land to Jerusalem.

20:31, 36–38 Paul's relationship with these believers is a beautiful example of Christian fellowship. He had cared for them and loved them, even cried over their needs. They responded with love and care for him and sorrow over his leaving. They had prayed together and comforted one another. Like Paul, you can build strong relationships with other Christians by sharing, caring, sorrowing, rejoicing, and praying with them. You will gather others around you only by giving yourself away to them.

20:33 Paul was satisfied with whatever he had, wherever he was, as long as he could do God's work. Examine your attitudes toward wealth and comfort. If you focus more on what you don't have than on what you do have, it's time to reexamine your priorities and put God's work back in first place.

20:34 Paul was a tentmaker, and he supported himself with this trade. Paul worked not in order to become rich, but to be free from being dependent on anyone. He supported himself and others who traveled with him (he also mentions this in some of his letters; see Philippians 4:11–13; 1 Thessalonians 2:9).

20:35 These words of Jesus are not recorded in the Gospels. Obviously, not all of Jesus' words were written down (John 21:25); this saying may have been passed on orally through the apostles.

cargo. 4Finding the disciples there, we stayed with them seven days. Through the Spirit *t* they urged Paul not to go on to Jerusalem. 5But when our time was up, we left and continued on our way. All the disciples and their wives and children accompanied us out of the city, and there on the beach we knelt to pray. *u* 6After saying good-by to each other, we went aboard the ship, and they returned home.

7We continued our voyage from Tyre and landed at Ptolemais, where we greeted the brothers and stayed with them for a day. 8Leaving the next day, we reached Caesarea and stayed at the house of Philip *v* the evangelist, *w* one of the Seven. 9He had four unmarried daughters who prophesied.

10After we had been there a number of days, a prophet named Agabus *x* came down from Judea. 11Coming over to us, he took Paul's belt, tied his own hands and feet with it and said, "The Holy Spirit says, 'In this way the Jews of Jerusalem will bind the owner of this belt and will hand him over to the Gentiles.'"

12When we heard this, we and the people there pleaded with Paul not to go up to Jerusalem. 13Then Paul answered, "Why are you weeping and breaking my heart? I am ready not only to be bound, but also to die *y* in Jerusalem for the name of the Lord Jesus." 14When he would not be dissuaded, we gave up and said, "The Lord's will be done."

15After this, we got ready and went up to Jerusalem. 16Some of the disciples from Caesarea accompanied us and brought us to the home of Mnason, where we were to stay. He was a man from Cyprus and one of the early disciples.

5. Paul on trial
Paul's Arrival at Jerusalem

17When we arrived at Jerusalem, the brothers received us warmly. *z* 18The next day Paul and the rest of us went to see James, and all the elders were present. 19Paul greeted them and reported in detail what God had done among the Gentiles through his ministry. *a*

20When they heard this, they praised God. Then they said to Paul: "You see, brother, how many thousands of Jews have believed, and all of them are zealous *b* for the law. 21They have been informed that you teach all the Jews who live among the Gentiles to turn away from Moses, telling them not to circumcise their children *c* or live according to our customs. 22What shall we do? They will certainly hear that you have come, 23so do what we tell you. There are four men with us who have made a vow. *d* 24Take these men, join in their purification rites and pay their expenses, so that they can have their heads shaved. Then everybody will know there is no truth in these reports about you, but that you yourself are living in obedience to the law. 25As for the Gentile believers, we have written to them our decision that

Marginal cross-references

21:4
t Ac 20:23

21:5
u Ac 20:36

21:8
v Ac 6:5
w Eph 4:11; 2Ti 4:5

21:10
x Ac 11:28

21:13
y Ac 20:24

21:17
z Ac 15:4

21:19
a Ac 1:17

21:20
b Ac 22:3; Ro 10:2; Gal 1:14

21:21
c 1Co 7:18, 19

21:23
d Ac 18:18

21:4 Did Paul disobey the Holy Spirit by going to Jerusalem? No. More likely, the Holy Spirit warned these believers about the suffering that Paul would face in Jerusalem. They drew the conclusion that he should not go there because of that danger. This is supported by 21:10–12 where the local believers, after hearing that Paul would be turned over to the Romans, begged him to turn back.

21:8 This is the Philip mentioned in 6:5 and 8:26–40.

21:9 Obviously the gift of prophecy was given to both men and women. Women actively participated in God's work (2:17; Philippians 4:3). Other women who prophesied include Miriam (Exodus 15:20), Deborah (Judges 4:4), Huldah (2 Kings 22:14), Noadiah (Nehemiah 6:14), Isaiah's wife (Isaiah 8:3), and Anna (Luke 2:36–38).

21:10 Fifteen years earlier, Agabus had predicted the famine in Jerusalem (11:27–29).

21:13, 14 Paul knew he would be imprisoned in Jerusalem. Although his friends pleaded with him to not go there, he knew that he had to because God wanted him to. No one enjoys pain, but a faithful disciple wants above all else to please God. Our desire to please God should overshadow our desire to avoid hardship and suffering. When we really want to do God's will, we must accept all that comes with it—even the pain. Then we can say with Paul, "The Lord's will be done."

21:18 James, Jesus' brother, was the leader of the Jerusalem church (15:13–21; Galatians 1:19; 2:9). He was called an apostle even though he wasn't one of the original 12 who followed Jesus.

21:21 The Jerusalem council (Acts 15) had settled the issue of circumcision of Gentile believers. Evidently rumor said that Paul had gone far beyond their decision, even forbidding Jews to circumcise their children. This, of course, was not true, so Paul willingly submitted to Jewish custom to show that he was not working against the council's decision and that he was still Jewish in his lifestyle. Sometimes we must go the second mile to avoid offending others, especially when doing so would hinder God's work.

21:23, 24 Evidently these four men had made a religious vow. Because Paul was going to participate with them in the vow (apparently he had been asked to pay for some of the required expenses), he would need to take part in the purification ceremony for entering the temple (Numbers 6:9–20). Paul submitted himself to this Jewish custom to keep peace in the Jerusalem church. Although Paul was a man of strong convictions, he was willing to compromise on non-essential points, becoming all things to all people so that he might save some (1 Corinthians 9:19–23). Often churches split over disagreements about minor issues or traditions. Like Paul, we should remain firm on Christian essentials but flexible on non-essentials. Of course, no one should violate his or her true convictions, but sometimes we need to exercise the gift of mutual submission for the sake of the gospel.

21:23, 24 The Jewish laws can be thought of in two ways. Paul rejected one way and accepted the other. (1) Paul rejected the idea that the Old Testament laws bring salvation to those who keep them. Salvation is freely given by God's gracious act. We receive salvation through faith. The laws are of no value for salvation

21:25
e Ac 15:20, 29

they should abstain from food sacrificed to idols, from blood, from the meat of strangled animals and from sexual immorality." e

21:26
f Nu 6:13-20

26 The next day Paul took the men and purified himself along with them. Then he went to the temple to give notice of the date when the days of purification would end and the offering would be made for each of them. f

Paul Arrested

21:27
g Ac 24:18

21:28
h Ac 24:5, 6

21:29
i Ac 20:4

27 When the seven days were nearly over, some Jews from the province of Asia saw Paul at the temple. They stirred up the whole crowd and seized him, g 28 shouting, "Men of Israel, help us! This is the man who teaches all men everywhere against our people and our law and this place. And besides, he has brought Greeks into the temple area and defiled this holy place." h 29 (They had previously seen Trophimus i the Ephesian in the city with Paul and assumed that Paul had brought him into the temple area.)

21:30
j Ac 26:21

21:32
k Ac 23:27

30 The whole city was aroused, and the people came running from all directions. Seizing Paul, j they dragged him from the temple, and immediately the gates were shut. 31 While they were trying to kill him, news reached the commander of the Roman troops that the whole city of Jerusalem was in an uproar. 32 He at once took some officers and soldiers and ran down to the crowd. When the rioters saw the commander and his soldiers, they stopped beating Paul. k

21:33
l ver 11
m Ac 20:23

33 The commander came up and arrested him and ordered him to be bound l with two chains. m Then he asked who he was and what he had done. 34 Some in the crowd shouted one thing and some another, and since the commander could not get at the truth because of the uproar, he ordered that Paul be taken into the barracks. 35 When Paul reached the steps, the violence of the mob was so great he had to be carried by the soldiers. 36 The crowd that followed kept shouting, "Away with him!" n

21:36
n Lk 23:18; Ac 22:22

Paul Speaks to the Crowd

37 As the soldiers were about to take Paul into the barracks, he asked the commander, "May I say something to you?"

21:38
o Ac 5:36

"Do you speak Greek?" he replied. 38 "Aren't you the Egyptian who started a revolt and led four thousand terrorists out into the desert some time ago?" o

21:39
p Ac 9:11

39 Paul answered, "I am a Jew, from Tarsus p in Cilicia, a citizen of no ordinary city. Please let me speak to the people."

21:40
q Ac 12:17

22:1
r Ac 7:2

22:3
s Ac 21:39

40 Having received the commander's permission, Paul stood on the steps and motioned q **22** to the crowd. When they were all silent, he said to them in Aramaic a: 1 "Brothers and fathers, listen now to my defense."

2 When they heard him speak to them in Aramaic, they became very quiet.

Then Paul said: 3 "I am a Jew, s born in Tarsus of Cilicia, but brought up in this city. Under

a 40 Or possibly *Hebrew*; also in 22:2

---

except to show us our sin. (2) Paul accepted the view that the Old Testament laws prepare for and teach about the coming of Jesus Christ. Christ fulfilled the law and released us from its burden of guilt. But the law still teaches many valuable principles and provides guidelines for grateful living. Paul was not observing the laws in order to be saved. He was simply keeping the laws as custom to avoid offending those he wished to reach with the gospel (see Romans 3:21-31; 7:4-6; 13:9, 10). For more on the law, see Galatians 3:23-29; 4:21-31, and the chart in Galatians 4, p. 1971.

21:31 Because Jerusalem was under Roman control, an uproar in the city would be investigated by Roman authorities. The commander of the troops at this time was Claudius Lysias (23:26). This commander was head of a cohort (a special group, part of a legion) of Roman soldiers. He was the senior Roman official in Jerusalem.

21:37, 38 By speaking in Greek, Paul showed that he was a cultured, educated man and not just a common rebel starting riots in the streets. The language grabbed the commander's attention and gave Paul protection and the opportunity to give his defense.

21:38 The historian Josephus wrote of an Egyptian who had led a revolt of 4,000 people in Jerusalem in A.D. 54 and then had disappeared. The commander assumed that Paul was this rebel.

21:40—22:2 Paul was speaking in Aramaic, the common language among Palestinian Jews. He used Aramaic not only to communicate in the language of his listeners, but also to show that he was a devout Jew and had respect for the Jewish laws and customs. Paul spoke Greek to the Roman officials and Aramaic to the Jews.

22:3 Gamaliel was the most honored rabbi of the first century. He was well known and respected as an expert on religious law and as a voice for moderation (5:34). Paul was showing his credentials as a well-educated man trained under the most respected Jewish rabbi.

22:3 By saying that at one time he was as zealous for God as any of his listeners, Paul was acknowledging their sincere motives behind their desire to kill him and recognizing that he would have done the same to Christian leaders a few years earlier. Paul always tried to establish a common point of contact with his audience before launching into a full-scale defense of Christianity. When you witness for Christ, first identify yourself with your audience. They will be much more likely to listen if they feel a common bond with you.

Gamaliel I was thoroughly trained in the law of our fathers[t] and was just as zealous[u] for God as any of you are today. [4]I persecuted[v] the followers of this Way to their death, arresting both men and women and throwing them into prison, [5]as also the high priest and all the Council[w] can testify. I even obtained letters from them to their brothers in Damascus,[x] and went there to bring these people as prisoners to Jerusalem to be punished.

[6]"About noon as I came near Damascus, suddenly a bright light from heaven flashed around me. [7]I fell to the ground and heard a voice say to me, 'Saul! Saul! Why do you persecute me?'

[8]"'Who are you, Lord?' I asked.

"'I am Jesus of Nazareth, whom you are persecuting,' he replied. [9]My companions saw the light, but they did not understand the voice[y] of him who was speaking to me.

[10]"'What shall I do, Lord?' I asked.

"'Get up,' the Lord said, 'and go into Damascus. There you will be told all that you have been assigned to do.' [11]My companions led me by the hand into Damascus, because the brilliance of the light had blinded me.

[12]"A man named Ananias came to see me. [z] He was a devout observer of the law and highly respected by all the Jews living there. [13]He stood beside me and said, 'Brother Saul, receive your sight!' And at that very moment I was able to see him.

[14]"Then he said: 'The God of our fathers[a] has chosen you to know his will and to see the Righteous One and to hear words from his mouth. [15]You will be his witness to all men of what you have seen and heard. [16]And now what are you waiting for? Get up, be baptized[b] and wash your sins away,[c] calling on his name.'

[17]"When I returned to Jerusalem and was praying at the temple, I fell into a trance[d] [18]and saw the Lord speaking. 'Quick!' he said to me. 'Leave Jerusalem immediately, because they will not accept your testimony about me.'

[19]"'Lord,' I replied, 'these men know that I went from one synagogue to another to imprison[e] and beat[f] those who believe in you. [20]And when the blood of your martyr[a] Stephen was shed, I stood there giving my approval and guarding the clothes of those who were killing him.'[g]

[21]"Then the Lord said to me, 'Go; I will send you far away to the Gentiles.' "[h]

Paul the Roman Citizen

[22]The crowd listened to Paul until he said this. Then they raised their voices and shouted, "Rid the earth of him![i] He's not fit to live!"[j]

[23]As they were shouting and throwing off their cloaks and flinging dust into the air, [k] [24]the commander ordered Paul to be taken into the barracks. He directed that he be flogged and questioned in order to find out why the people were shouting at him like this. [25]As they stretched him out to flog him, Paul said to the centurion standing there, "Is it legal for you to flog a Roman citizen who hasn't even been found guilty?"[l]

a[20] Or witness

22:3 [t]Ac 26:5 [u]Ac 21:20
22:4 [v]Ac 8:3
22:5 [w]Lk 22:66 [x]Ac 9:2
22:9 [y]Ac 9:7
22:12 [z]Ac 9:17
22:14 [a]Ac 3:13
22:16 [b]Ac 2:38 [c]Heb 10:22
22:17 [d]Ac 10:10
22:19 [e]ver 4; Ac 8:3 [f]Mt 10:17
22:20 [g]Ac 8:1
22:21 [h]Ac 9:15
22:22 [i]Ac 21:36 [j]Ac 25:24
22:23 [k]2Sa 16:13
22:25 [l]Ac 16:37

22:6ff After gaining a hearing and establishing common ground with his audience, Paul gave his testimony. He shared how he had come to faith in Christ. Sound reasoning is good, but it is also important to simply share what Christ has done in our lives. No matter how we present the message, however, not everyone will accept it, as Paul knew. We must faithfully and responsibly present the gospel, and leave the results to God.

22:21, 22 These people listened intently to Paul, but the word *Gentile* brought out all their anger and exposed their pride. They were supposed to be a light to the Gentiles, telling them about the one true God. But they had renounced that mission by becoming separatist and exclusive. God's plan, however, would not be thwarted; the Gentiles were hearing the Good News through Jewish Christians such as Paul and Peter.

22:25–28 Paul's question stopped the centurion because, by law, a Roman citizen could not be punished until he had been proven guilty of a crime. Paul had been born a Roman citizen, whereas the commander had purchased his citizenship. Buying citizenship was a common practice and a good source of income for the Roman government. Bought citizenship was considered inferior to citizenship by birth.

IMPRISONMENT IN CAESAREA
Paul brought news of his third journey to the elders of the Jerusalem church, who rejoiced at his ministry. But Paul's presence soon stirred up the Jews, who persuaded the Romans to arrest him. A plot to kill Paul was uncovered, so Paul was taken by night to Antipatris and then transferred to the provincial prison in Caesarea.

26 When the centurion heard this, he went to the commander and reported it. "What are you going to do?" he asked. "This man is a Roman citizen."

27 The commander went to Paul and asked, "Tell me, are you a Roman citizen?"

"Yes, I am," he answered.

28 Then the commander said, "I had to pay a big price for my citizenship."

"But I was born a citizen," Paul replied.

29 Those who were about to question him withdrew immediately. The commander himself was alarmed when he realized that he had put Paul, a Roman citizen, in chains.

Before the Sanhedrin

30 The next day, since the commander wanted to find out exactly why Paul was being accused by the Jews, *m* he released him and ordered the chief priests and all the Sanhedrin to assemble. Then he brought Paul and had him stand before them.

23 Paul looked straight at the Sanhedrin *n* and said, "My brothers, I have fulfilled my duty to God in all good conscience *o* to this day." 2 At this the high priest Ananias ordered those standing near Paul to strike him on the mouth. *p* 3 Then Paul said to him, "God will strike you, you whitewashed wall! You sit there to judge me according to the law, yet you yourself violate the law by commanding that I be struck!" *q*

4 Those who were standing near Paul said, "You dare to insult God's high priest?"

5 Paul replied, "Brothers, I did not realize that he was the high priest; for it is written: 'Do not speak evil about the ruler of your people.' **a** " *r*

a *5* Exodus 22:28

22:30
m Ac 23:28

23:1
n Ac 22:30
o Ac 24:16;
2Co 1:12; 2Ti 1:3

23:2
p Jn 18:22

23:3
q Dt 25:1, 2; Jn 7:51

23:5
r Ex 22:28

UNSUNG HEROES IN ACTS	Hero	Reference	Heroic Action
When we think of the success of the early church, we often think of the work of the apostles. But the church could have died if it hadn't been for the unsung heroes, the men and women who through some small but committed act moved the church forward.	Crippled man	3:9–12	After his healing, he praised God. As the crowds gathered to see what happened, Peter used the opportunity to tell many about Jesus.
	Five deacons	6:2–5	Everyone has heard of Stephen, and many know of Philip, but there were five other men chosen to be deacons. They not only laid the foundation for service in the church, but their hard work also gave the apostles the time they needed to preach the gospel.
	Ananias	9:10–19	He had the responsibility of being the first to demonstrate Christ's love to Saul (Paul) after his conversion.
	Cornelius	10:30–35	His example showed Peter that the gospel was for *all* people, Jews and Gentiles.
	Rhoda	12:13–15	Her persistence brought Peter inside Mary's home, where he would be safe.
	James	15:13–21	He took command of the Jerusalem council and had the courage and discernment to help form a decision that would affect literally millions of Christians over many generations.
	Lydia	16:13–15	She opened her home to Paul, from which he led many to Christ and founded a church in Philippi.
	Jason	17:5–9	He risked his life for the gospel by allowing Paul to stay in his home. He stood up for what was true and right, even though he faced persecution for it.
	Paul's nephew	23:16–24	He saved Paul's life by telling officials of a murder plot.
	Julius	27:1, 43	He spared Paul when the other soldiers wanted to kill him.

22:30 Paul used his times of persecution as an opportunity for him to witness. Even his enemies were creating a platform for him to address the entire Sanhedrin (Jewish council). If we are sensitive to the Holy Spirit's leading, we will see increased opportunities to share our faith, even in the face of opposition.

23:2–5 Josephus, a respected first-century historian, described Ananias as profane, greedy, and hot-tempered. Paul's outburst came as a result of the illegal command that Ananias had given. Ananias had violated Jewish law by assuming that Paul was guilty without a trial and ordering his punishment (see Deuteronomy 19:15). Paul didn't recognize Ananias as the high priest, probably

because Ananias's command broke the law he was pledged to represent. As Christians, we are to represent Christ. When those around us say, "I didn't know you were a Christian," we have failed to represent him as we should. We are not merely Christ's followers; we are his representatives to others.

6 Then Paul, knowing that some of them were Sadducees and the others Pharisees, called out in the Sanhedrin, "My brothers,^{s} I am a Pharisee,^{t} the son of a Pharisee. I stand on trial because of my hope in the resurrection of the dead." 7 When he said this, a dispute broke out between the Pharisees and the Sadducees, and the assembly was divided. 8 (The Sadducees say that there is no resurrection,^{u} and that there are neither angels nor spirits, but the Pharisees acknowledge them all.)

9 There was a great uproar, and some of the teachers of the law who were Pharisees stood up and argued vigorously. "We find nothing wrong with this man," they said. "What if a spirit or an angel has spoken to him?"^{v} 10 The dispute became so violent that the commander was afraid Paul would be torn to pieces by them. He ordered the troops to go down and take him away from them by force and bring him into the barracks.

11 The following night the Lord stood near Paul and said, "Take courage!^{w} As you have testified about me in Jerusalem, so you must also testify in Rome."^{x}

The Plot to Kill Paul

12 The next morning the Jews formed a conspiracy and bound themselves with an oath not to eat or drink until they had killed Paul. 13 More than forty men were involved in this plot. 14 They went to the chief priests and elders and said, "We have taken a solemn oath not to eat anything until we have killed Paul. 15 Now then, you and the Sanhedrin^y petition the commander to bring him before you on the pretext of wanting more accurate information about his case. We are ready to kill him before he gets here."

16 But when the son of Paul's sister heard of this plot, he went into the barracks and told Paul.

17 Then Paul called one of the centurions and said, "Take this young man to the commander; he has something to tell him." 18 So he took him to the commander.

The centurion said, "Paul, the prisoner, sent for me and asked me to bring this young man to you because he has something to tell you."

19 The commander took the young man by the hand, drew him aside and asked, "What is it you want to tell me?"

20 He said: "The Jews have agreed to ask you to bring Paul before the Sanhedrin tomorrow on the pretext of wanting more accurate information about him.^{z} 21 Don't give in to them, because more than forty of them are waiting in ambush for him. They have taken an oath not to eat or drink until they have killed him. They are ready now, waiting for your consent to their request."

22 The commander dismissed the young man and cautioned him, "Don't tell anyone that you have reported this to me."

Paul Transferred to Caesarea

23 Then he called two of his centurions and ordered them, "Get ready a detachment of two hundred soldiers, seventy horsemen and two hundred spearmen^a to go to Caesarea at nine tonight.^{a} 24 Provide mounts for Paul so that he may be taken safely to Governor Felix."^{b}

^{a}23 The meaning of the Greek for this word is uncertain.

23:6	^{s}Ac 22:5
	^{t}Ac 26:5; Php 3:5
23:8	^{u}Mt 22:23
23:9	^{v}Ac 22:7, 17, 18
23:11	^{w}Ac 18:9
	^{x}Ac 19:21
23:15	^{y}Ac 22:30
23:20	^{z}ver 14, 15
23:23	^{a}ver 33
23:24	^{b}Ac 24:1-3, 10

23:6-8 The Sadducees and Pharisees were two groups of religious leaders, but with strikingly different beliefs. The Pharisees believed in a bodily resurrection, but the Sadducees did not. The Sadducees adhered only to Genesis through Deuteronomy, which contain no explicit teaching on resurrection. Paul's words moved the debate away from himself and toward their festering controversy about the resurrection. The Jewish council was split.

23:6-8 Paul's sudden insight that the council was a mixture of Sadducees and Pharisees is an example of the power that Jesus promised to believers (Mark 13:9-11). God will help us when we are under fire for our faith. Like Paul, we should always be ready to present our testimony. The Holy Spirit will give us power to speak boldly.

23:14, 15 When the Pharisee/Sadducee controversy died down, the religious leaders refocused their attention on Paul. To these leaders, politics and position had become more important than God. They were ready to plan another murder, just as they had done with Jesus. But as always, God was in control.

23:16 This is the only Biblical reference to Paul's family. Some scholars believe that Paul's family had disowned Paul when he became a Christian. Paul wrote of having suffered the loss of everything for Christ (Philippians 3:8). Paul's nephew was able to see Paul, even though Paul was in protective custody, because Roman prisoners were accessible to their relatives and friends who could bring them food and other amenities.

23:16-22 It is easy to overlook children, assuming that they aren't old enough to do much for the Lord. But a young man played an important part in protecting Paul's life. God can use anyone, of any age, who is willing to yield to him. Jesus made it clear that children are important (Matthew 18:2-6). Give children the importance God gives them.

23:23, 24 The Roman commander ordered Paul sent to Caesarea. Jerusalem was the seat of Jewish government, but Caesarea was the Roman headquarters for the area. God works in amazing and amusing ways. God could have used any number of ways to get Paul to Caesarea, but he chose to use the Roman army to deliver Paul from his enemies. God's ways are not our ways. Ours are limited; his are not. Don't limit God by asking him to respond your

²⁵He wrote a letter as follows:

²⁶Claudius Lysias,

To His Excellency,ᶜ Governor Felix:

Greetings.ᵈ

23:26
ᶜAc 24:3
ᵈAc 15:23

²⁷This man was seized by the Jews and they were about to kill him, but I came with my troops and rescued him,ᵉ for I had learned that he is a Roman citizen. ²⁸I wanted to know why they were accusing him, so I brought him to their Sanhedrin.ᶠ ²⁹I found that the accusation had to do with questions about their law,ᵍ but there was no charge against himʰ that deserved death or imprisonment. ³⁰When I was informedⁱ of a plot to be carried out against the man, I sent him to you at once. I also ordered his accusersʲ to present to you their case against him.

23:27
ᵉAc 21:33
23:28
ᶠAc 22:30
23:29
ᵍAc 18:15; 25:19
ʰAc 26:31
23:30
ⁱver 20, 21
ʲAc 24:19

³¹So the soldiers, carrying out their orders, took Paul with them during the night and brought him as far as Antipatris. ³²The next day they let the cavalry go on with him, while they returned to the barracks. ³³When the cavalryᵏ arrived in Caesarea, they delivered the letter to the governor ˡ and handed Paul over to him. ³⁴The governor read the letter and asked what province he was from. Learning that he was from Cilicia,ᵐ ³⁵he said, "I will hear your case when your accusersⁿ get here." Then he ordered that Paul be kept under guardᵒ in Herod's palace.

23:33
ᵏver 23, 24
ˡver 26
23:34
ᵐAc 21:39
23:35
ⁿAc 25:16
ᵒAc 24:27

The Trial Before Felix

24:1
ᵖAc 23:2
�q Ac 23:30, 35

24 Five days later the high priest Ananiasᵖ went down to Caesarea with some of the elders and a lawyer named Tertullus, and they brought their charges�q against Paul before the governor. ²When Paul was called in, Tertullus presented his case before Felix: "We have enjoyed a long period of peace under you, and your foresight has brought about reforms in this nation. ³Everywhere and in every way, most excellent ʳ Felix, we acknowledge this with profound gratitude. ⁴But in order not to weary you further, I would request that you be kind enough to hear us briefly.

24:3
ʳAc 23:26

⁵"We have found this man to be a troublemaker, stirring up riotsˢ among the Jews all over the world. He is a ringleader of the Nazarene sect ⁶and even tried to desecrate the temple;ᵗ so we seized him. ⁸Byᵃ examining him yourself you will be able to learn the truth about all these charges we are bringing against him."

24:5
ˢAc 16:20; 17:6
24:6
ᵗAc 21:28

⁹The Jews joined in the accusation, asserting that these things were true.

24:10
ᵘAc 23:24

¹⁰When the governorᵘ motioned for him to speak, Paul replied: "I know that for a number of years you have been a judge over this nation; so I gladly make my defense. ¹¹You can

ᵃ6-8 Some manuscripts *him and wanted to judge him according to our law.* ⁷*But the commander, Lysias, came and with the use of much force snatched him from our hands* ⁸*and ordered his accusers to come before you. By*

---

way. When God intervenes, anything can happen, so much more and so much better than you could ever anticipate.

23:26 Felix was the Roman governor or procurator of Judea from A.D. 52 to 59. This was the same position Pontius Pilate had held. While the Jews were given much freedom to govern themselves, the governor ran the army, kept the peace, and gathered the taxes.

23:26 How did Luke know what was written in the letter from Claudius Lysias? In his concern for historical accuracy, Luke used many sources to make sure that his writings were correct (see Luke 1:1–4). This letter was probably read aloud in court when Paul came before Felix to answer the Jews' accusations. Also, because Paul was a Roman citizen, a copy may have been given to him as a courtesy.

24:1 The accusers arrived—Ananias, the high priest; Tertullus, the lawyer; and certain Jewish leaders. They traveled 60 miles to Caesarea, the Roman center of government, to bring their false accusations against Paul. Their murder plot had failed (23:12–15), but they persisted in trying to kill him. This attempt at murder was both premeditated and persistent.

24:2ff Tertullus was a special orator called to present the reli-

gious leaders' case before the Roman governor. He made three accusations against Paul: (1) he was a troublemaker, stirring up riots among the Jews around the world; (2) he was the ringleader of an unrecognized religious cult, which was against Roman law; (3) he had tried to desecrate the temple. The religious leaders hoped that these accusations would persuade Felix to execute Paul in order to keep the peace in Palestine.

24:5 While the charge that Paul was a troublemaker was insulting to Paul, it was too vague to be a substantial legal charge. The Nazarene sect refers to the Christians—named here after Jesus' hometown of Nazareth.

24:10ff Tertullus and the religious leaders seemed to have a strong argument against Paul, but Paul refuted their accusations point by point. Paul was also able to present the gospel message through his defense. Paul's accusers were unable to present specific evidence to support their general accusations. For example, Paul was accused of starting trouble among the Jews in the province of Asia (24:18, 19), but the Jews in the province of Asia (western Turkey) were not present to confirm this. This is another example of Paul using every opportunity to witness for Christ (see 24:14, 24).

easily verify that no more than twelve days v ago I went up to Jerusalem to worship. 12My accusers did not find me arguing with anyone at the temple, w or stirring up a crowd in the synagogues or anywhere else in the city. 13And they cannot prove to you the charges they are now making against me. 14However, I admit that I worship the God of our fathers as a follower of the Way, x which they call a sect. I believe everything that agrees with the Law and that is written in the Prophets, y 15and I have the same hope in God as these men, that there will be a resurrection of both the righteous and the wicked. 16So I strive always to keep my conscience clear z before God and man.

17"After an absence of several years, I came to Jerusalem to bring my people gifts for the poor a and to present offerings. 18I was ceremonially clean b when they found me in the temple courts doing this. There was no crowd with me, nor was I involved in any disturbance. 19But there are some Jews from the province of Asia, who ought to be here before you and bring charges if they have anything against me. c 20Or these who are here should state what crime they found in me when I stood before the Sanhedrin— 21unless it was this one thing I shouted as I stood in their presence: 'It is concerning the resurrection of the dead that I am on trial before you today.'" d

22Then Felix, who was well acquainted with the Way, adjourned the proceedings. "When Lysias the commander comes," he said, "I will decide your case." 23He ordered the centurion to keep Paul under guard but to give him some freedom e and permit his friends to take care of his needs. f

24Several days later Felix came with his wife Drusilla, who was a Jewess. He sent for Paul and listened to him as he spoke about faith in Christ Jesus. 25As Paul discoursed on righteousness, self-control and the judgment to come, Felix was afraid and said, "That's enough for now! You may leave. When I find it convenient, I will send for you." 26At the same time he was hoping that Paul would offer him a bribe, so he sent for him frequently and talked with him.

27When two years had passed, Felix was succeeded by Porcius Festus, but because Felix wanted to grant a favor to the Jews, g he left Paul in prison.

The Trial Before Festus

25 Three days after arriving in the province, Festus went up from Caesarea to Jerusalem, 2where the chief priests and Jewish leaders appeared before him and presented the charges against Paul. h 3They urgently requested Festus, as a favor to them, to have Paul transferred to Jerusalem, for they were preparing an ambush to kill him along the way. 4Festus answered, "Paul is being held at Caesarea, and I myself am going there soon. 5Let some of your leaders come with me and press charges against the man there, if he has done anything wrong."

6After spending eight or ten days with them, he went down to Caesarea, and the next day he convened the court and ordered that Paul be brought before him. 7When Paul appeared, the Jews who had come down from Jerusalem stood around him, bringing many serious charges against him, i which they could not prove. j

24:11
v Ac 21:27
24:12
w Ac 25:8
24:14
x Ac 9:2
y Ac 26:6, 22
24:16
z Ac 23:1
24:17
a Ac 11:29, 30;
2Co 8:1-4; Gal 2:10
24:18
b Ac 21:26
24:19
c Ac 23:30
24:21
d Ac 23:6
24:23
e Ac 28:16
f Ac 27:3
24:27
g Ac 12:3
25:2
h ver 15; Ac 24:1
25:7
i Ac 24:5, 6
j Ac 24:13

24:22 Felix had been governor for six years and would have known about the Christians ("the Way"), a topic of conversation among the Romans leaders. The Christians' peaceful lifestyles had already proven to the Romans that Christians didn't go around starting riots.

24:25 Paul's talk with Felix became so personal that Felix grew frightened. Felix, like Herod Antipas (Mark 6:17, 18), had taken another man's wife. Paul's words were interesting until they focused on "righteousness, self-control, and the judgment to come." Many people will be glad to discuss the gospel with you as long as it doesn't touch their lives too personally. When it does, some will resist or run. But this is what the gospel is all about—God's power to change lives. The gospel is not effective until it moves from principles and doctrine into a life-changing dynamic. When someone resists or runs from your witness, you have undoubtedly succeeded in making the gospel personal.

24:27 The Jews were in the majority, and the Roman political leaders wanted to defer to them to help keep the peace. Paul seemed to incite problems among the Jews everywhere he went. By keeping him in prison, Felix left office on good terms with the

Jews. Felix lost his job as governor and was called back to Rome. Porcius Festus took over as governor in late 59 or early 60. He was more just than Felix, who had kept Paul in prison for two years, in hopes that perhaps Paul would bribe him, and that by detaining Paul, the Jews would be kept happy. When Festus came into office, he immediately ordered Paul's trial to resume.

24:27 Though God had promised that Paul would preach the gospel in Rome (23:11), the great apostle had to endure more than two years of Felix's refusal to decide his fate. In addition to this custody, Paul was subjected to other long stretches of time during which he could do little but trust God and wait for him to act. What do you do when it comes to the issue of waiting on God? Do you become anxious? angry? discouraged? Few things test our patience and faith like being forced to wait—which perhaps explains why our sovereign God often puts us in situations where we have no other choice.

25:1–9 Although two years had passed, the Jewish leaders still were looking for a way to kill Paul. They told Festus about Paul and tried to convince him to hold the trial in Jerusalem (so they could prepare an ambush). But God and Paul thwarted their schemes again.

25:8
k Ac 6:13; 28:17

25:9
l Ac 24:27
m ver 20

25:11
n Ac 26:32; 28:19

25:14
o Ac 24:27

25:15
p ver 2

25:16
q ver 4, 5

25:17
r ver 6, 10

25:19
s Ac 18:15; 23:29

25:21
t ver 11, 12

25:22
u Ac 9:15

25:24
v ver 2, 3, 7
w Ac 22:22

25:25
x Ac 23:9

[8] Then Paul made his defense: "I have done nothing wrong against the law of the Jews or against the temple [k] or against Caesar."

[9] Festus, wishing to do the Jews a favor,[l] said to Paul, "Are you willing to go up to Jerusalem and stand trial before me there on these charges?"[m]

[10] Paul answered: "I am now standing before Caesar's court, where I ought to be tried. I have not done any wrong to the Jews, as you yourself know very well. [11] If, however, I am guilty of doing anything deserving death, I do not refuse to die. But if the charges brought against me by these Jews are not true, no one has the right to hand me over to them. I appeal to Caesar!"[n]

[12] After Festus had conferred with his council, he declared: "You have appealed to Caesar. To Caesar you will go!"

Festus Consults King Agrippa

[13] A few days later King Agrippa and Bernice arrived at Caesarea to pay their respects to Festus. [14] Since they were spending many days there, Festus discussed Paul's case with the king. He said: "There is a man here whom Felix left as a prisoner.[o] [15] When I went to Jerusalem, the chief priests and elders of the Jews brought charges against him[p] and asked that he be condemned.

[16] "I told them that it is not the Roman custom to hand over any man before he has faced his accusers and has had an opportunity to defend himself against their charges.[q] [17] When they came here with me, I did not delay the case, but convened the court the next day and ordered the man to be brought in.[r] [18] When his accusers got up to speak, they did not charge him with any of the crimes I had expected. [19] Instead, they had some points of dispute[s] with him about their own religion and about a dead man named Jesus who Paul claimed was alive. [20] I was at a loss how to investigate such matters; so I asked if he would be willing to go to Jerusalem and stand trial there on these charges. [21] When Paul made his appeal to be held over for the Emperor's decision, I ordered him held until I could send him to Caesar."[t]

[22] Then Agrippa said to Festus, "I would like to hear this man myself."

He replied, "Tomorrow you will hear him."[u]

Paul Before Agrippa

[23] The next day Agrippa and Bernice came with great pomp and entered the audience room with the high ranking officers and the leading men of the city. At the command of Festus, Paul was brought in. [24] Festus said: "King Agrippa, and all who are present with us, you see this man! The whole Jewish community[v] has petitioned me about him in Jerusalem and here in Caesarea, shouting that he ought not to live any longer.[w] [25] I found he had done nothing deserving of death,[x] but because he made his appeal to the Emperor I decided to send him to Rome. [26] But I have nothing definite to write to His Majesty about him. Therefore I have brought him before all of you, and especially before you, King Agrippa, so that as a result of this investigation I may have something to write. [27] For I think it is unreasonable to send on a prisoner without specifying the charges against him."

25:10, 11 Paul knew that he was innocent of the charges against him and could appeal to Caesar's judgment. He knew his rights as a Roman citizen and as an innocent person. Paul had met his responsibilities as a Roman, and so he had the opportunity to claim Rome's protection. Every Roman citizen had the right to appeal to Caesar. This didn't mean that Caesar himself would hear the case, but that the citizen's case would be tried by the highest courts in the empire. Festus saw Paul's appeal as a way to send him out of the country and thus pacify the Jews. Paul wanted to go to Rome to preach the gospel (Romans 1:10), and he knew that his appeal would give him the opportunity. To go to Rome as a prisoner was better than not to go there at all.

25:13 This was Herod Agrippa II, son of Herod Agrippa I, and a descendant of Herod the Great. He had power over the temple, controlled the temple treasury, and could appoint and remove the high priest. Bernice was the sister of Herod Agrippa II. She had married her uncle, Herod Chalcis, had become mistress to her brother Agrippa II, and then had become mistress to the emperor Vespasian's son, Titus. Here Agrippa and Bernice were

making an official visit to Festus. Agrippa, of Jewish descent, could help clarify Paul's case for the Roman governor. Agrippa and Festus were anxious to cooperate in governing their neighboring territories.

25:19 Even though Festus knew little about Christianity, he somehow sensed that the resurrection was central to Christian belief.

25:23ff Paul was in prison, but that didn't stop him from making the most of his situation. Military officers and prominent city leaders met in the palace room with Agrippa to hear this case. Paul saw this new audience as yet another opportunity to present the gospel. Rather than complain about your present situation, look for ways to use every opportunity to serve God and share him with others. Your problems may be opportunities in disguise.

26 Then Agrippa said to Paul, "You have permission to speak for yourself." *y* So Paul motioned with his hand and began his defense: 2"King Agrippa, I consider myself fortunate to stand before you today as I make my defense against all the accusations of the Jews, 3 and especially so because you are well acquainted with all the Jewish customs and controversies. Therefore, I beg you to listen to me patiently.

4"The Jews all know the way I have lived ever since I was a child, *z* from the beginning of my life in my own country, and also in Jerusalem. 5 They have known me for a long time *a* and can testify, if they are willing, that according to the strictest sect of our religion, I lived as a Pharisee. *b* 6 And now it is because of my hope *c* in what God has promised our fathers *d* that I am on trial today. 7 This is the promise our twelve tribes *e* are hoping to see fulfilled as they earnestly serve God day and night. *f* O king, it is because of this hope that the Jews are accusing me. 8 Why should any of you consider it incredible that God raises the dead?

9"I too was convinced *g* that I ought to do all that was possible to oppose *h* the name of Jesus of Nazareth. 10 And that is just what I did in Jerusalem. On the authority of the chief priests I put many of the saints in prison, *i* and when they were put to death, I cast my vote against them. 11 Many a time I went from one synagogue to another to have them punished, and I tried to force them to blaspheme. In my obsession against them, I even went to foreign cities to persecute them.

12"On one of these journeys I was going to Damascus with the authority and commission of the chief priests. 13 About noon, O king, as I was on the road, I saw a light from heaven, brighter than the sun, blazing around me and my companions. 14 We all fell to the ground, and I heard a voice saying to me in Aramaic, *a* 'Saul, Saul, why do you persecute me? It is hard for you to kick against the goads.'

15"Then I asked, 'Who are you, Lord?'

"'I am Jesus, whom you are persecuting,' the Lord replied. 16'Now get up and stand on your feet. *j* I have appeared to you to appoint you as a servant and as a witness of what you have seen of me and what I will show you. *k* 17 I will rescue you from your own people and from the Gentiles. I am sending you to them 18 to open their eyes *l* and turn them from darkness to light, *m* and from the power of Satan to God, so that they may receive forgiveness of sins and a place among those who are sanctified by faith in me.'

19"So then, King Agrippa, I was not disobedient to the vision from heaven. 20 First to those in Damascus, *n* then to those in Jerusalem *o* and in all Judea, and to the Gentiles also, I preached that they should repent and turn to God and prove their repentance by their deeds. *p* 21 That is why the Jews seized me *q* in the temple courts and tried to kill me. 22 But I have had God's help to this very day, and so I stand here and testify to small and great alike. I am saying nothing beyond what the prophets and Moses said would happen *r*— 23 that the Christ *b* would suffer and, as the first to rise from the dead, *s* would proclaim light to his own people and to the Gentiles." *t*

24 At this point Festus interrupted Paul's defense. "You are out of your mind, *u* Paul!" he shouted. "Your great learning is driving you insane."

25"I am not insane, most excellent *v* Festus," Paul replied. "What I am saying is true and reasonable. 26 The king is familiar with these things, and I can speak freely to him. I am convinced that none of this has escaped his notice, because it was not done in a corner. 27 King Agrippa, do you believe the prophets? I know you do."

a 14 Or Hebrew   b 23 Or Messiah

26:1
y Ac 9:15

26:4
z Gal 1:13, 14

26:5
a Ac 22:3
b Ac 23:6

26:6
c Ac 23:6
d Ac 13:32

26:7
e Jas 1:1
f 1Th 3:10; 1Ti 5:5

26:9
g 1Ti 1:13
h Jn 16:2

26:10
i Ac 8:3

26:16
j Eze 2:1
k Ac 22:14, 15

26:18
l Isa 35:5
m Isa 42:7, 16;
Eph 5:8; Col 1:13;
1Pe 2:9

26:20
n Ac 9:19-25
o Ac 9:26-29
p Mt 3:8

26:21
q Ac 21:27, 30

26:22
r Lk 24:27, 44;
Ac 24:14

26:23
s 1Co 15:20, 23;
Col 1:18; Rev 1:5
t Lk 2:32

26:24
u Jn 10:20

26:25
v Ac 23:26

26:3ff This speech is a good example of Paul's powerful oratory. Beginning with a compliment to Agrippa, he told his story, including the resurrection of Christ, and the royal audience was spellbound.

26:14 An oxgoad was a sharp stick used to prod cattle. "It is hard for you to kick against the goads" (oxgoads) means, "You are only hurting yourself."

26:17, 18 Paul took every opportunity to remind his audience that the Gentiles have an equal share in God's inheritance. This inheritance is the promise and blessing of the covenant that God had made with Abraham (see Ephesians 2:19; 1 Peter 1:3, 4). Paul's mission was to preach the Good News to the Gentiles.

26:24 Paul was risking his life for a message that was offensive to the Jews and unbelievable to the Gentiles. Jesus received the

same response to his message (Mark 3:21; John 10:20). To a worldly, materialistic mind, it seems insane to risk so much to gain what seems to be so little. But as you follow Christ, you soon discover that temporary possessions look so small next to even the smallest eternal reward.

26:26 Paul was appealing to the *facts*—people were still alive who had heard Jesus and seen his miracles; the empty tomb could still be seen; and the Christian message was turning the world upside down (17:6). The history of Jesus' life and the early church are facts that are still open for us to examine. We still have eyewitness accounts of Jesus' life recorded in the Bible as well as historical and archaeological records of the early church to study. Examine the events and facts as verified by many witnesses. Strengthen your faith with the truth of these accounts.

28 Then Agrippa said to Paul, "Do you think that in such a short time you can persuade me to be a Christian?"

29 Paul replied, "Short time or long—I pray God that not only you but all who are listening to me today may become what I am, except for these chains."

26:30
w Ac 25:23

26:32
x Ac 25:11

27:1
y Ac 25:12, 25

27:2
z Ac 19:29

30 The king rose, and with him the governor and Bernice w and those sitting with them. 31 They left the room, and while talking with one another, they said, "This man is not doing anything that deserves death or imprisonment."

32 Agrippa said to Festus, "This man could have been set free if he had not appealed to Caesar." x

Paul Sails for Rome

27 When it was decided that we would sail for Italy,y Paul and some other prisoners were handed over to a centurion named Julius, who belonged to the Imperial Regiment. 2 We boarded a ship from Adramyttium about to sail for ports along the coast of the province of Asia, and we put out to sea. Aristarchus, z a Macedonian from Thessalonica, was with us.

Like great-grandfather, like grandfather, like father, like son—this tells the story of Herod Agrippa II. He inherited the character flaws of generations of powerful men with flawed personalities. Each son followed his father in weaknesses, mistakes, and missed opportunities. Each generation had a confrontation with God but failed to realize the importance of the decision. Herod Agrippa II's great-uncle, Herod Antipas, actually met Jesus during his trial, but failed to see Jesus for who he was. Agrippa II heard the gospel from Paul but considered the message mild entertainment. He found it humorous that Paul actually tried to convince him to become a Christian.

Like so many before and after, Agrippa II stopped within hearing distance of the kingdom of God. He left himself without excuse. He heard the gospel but decided it wasn't worth responding to personally. Sadly, his mistake is not uncommon. Many who read his story also will not believe. Their problem, like his, is not really that the gospel isn't convincing or that they don't need to know God personally; it is that they choose not to respond.

What has been your response to the gospel? Has it turned your life around and given you the hope of eternal life, or has it been a message to resist or reject? Perhaps it has just been entertainment. It may seem like too great a price to give God control of your life, but the price is minimal compared to living eternally apart from him because you have chosen not to be his child.

HEROD AGRIPPA II

Strengths and accomplishments:	• Last of the Herod dynasty that ruled parts of Palestine from 40 B.C. to A.D. 100 • Continued his father's success in mediating between Rome and Palestine • Continued the family tradition of building and improving cities
Weaknesses and mistakes:	• Was not convinced by the gospel and consciously rejected it • Carried on an incestuous relationship with his sister Bernice
Lessons from his life:	• Families pass on both positive and negative influences to children • There are no guarantees of multiple opportunities to respond to God
Vital statistics:	• Occupation: Ruler of northern and eastern Palestine • Relatives: Great-grandfather: Herod the Great. Father: Herod Agrippa I. Great-uncle: Herod Antipas. Sisters: Bernice, Drusilla. • Contemporaries: Paul, Felix, Festus, Peter, Luke
Key verse:	"Then Agrippa said to Paul, 'Do you think that in such a short time you can persuade me to be a Christian?'" (Acts 26:28).

Herod Agrippa II's story is told in Acts 25:13—26:32.

26:28, 29 Agrippa responded to Paul's presentation with a sarcastic remark. Paul didn't react to the brush-off, but made a personal appeal to which he hoped all his listeners would respond. Paul's response is a good example for us as we tell others about God's plan of salvation. A sincere personal appeal or personal testimony can show the depth of our concern and break through hardened hearts.

26:28, 29 Paul's heart is revealed here in his words: he was more concerned for the salvation of these strangers than for the removal of his own chains. Ask God to give you a burning desire to see others come to Christ—a desire so strong that it overshadows your problems.

27:1, 2 Use of the pronoun we indicates that Luke accompanied Paul on this journey. Aristarchus is the man who had been dragged into the theater at the beginning of the riot in Ephesus (19:29; 20:4; Philemon 24).

27:1–3 Julius, a Roman centurion, was assigned to guard Paul. Obviously he had to remain close to Paul at all times. Through this contact, Julius developed a respect for Paul. He gave Paul a certain amount of freedom (27:3) and later spared his life (27:43). How would your character look, up close and personal?

3 The next day we landed at Sidon; and Julius, in kindness to Paul, allowed him to go to his friends so they might provide for his needs. *a* 4 From there we put out to sea again and passed to the lee of Cyprus because the winds were against us. 5 When we had sailed across the open sea off the coast of Cilicia and Pamphylia, we landed at Myra in Lycia. 6 There the centurion found an Alexandrian ship*b* sailing for Italy and put us on board. 7 We made slow headway for many days and had difficulty arriving off Cnidus. When the wind did not allow us to hold our course, we sailed to the lee of Crete, opposite Salmone. 8 We moved along the coast with difficulty and came to a place called Fair Havens, near the town of Lasea.

9 Much time had been lost, and sailing had already become dangerous because by now it was after the Fast. *a c* So Paul warned them, 10 "Men, I can see that our voyage is going to be disastrous and bring great loss to ship and cargo, and to our own lives also." 11 But the centurion, instead of listening to what Paul said, followed the advice of the pilot and of the owner of the ship. 12 Since the harbor was unsuitable to winter in, the majority decided that we should sail on, hoping to reach Phoenix and winter there. This was a harbor in Crete, facing both southwest and northwest.

The Storm

13 When a gentle south wind began to blow, they thought they had obtained what they wanted; so they weighed anchor and sailed along the shore of Crete. 14 Before very long, a wind of hurricane force,*d* called the "northeaster," swept down from the island. 15 The ship was caught by the storm and could not head into the wind; so we gave way to it and were driven along. 16 As we passed to the lee of a small island called Cauda, we were hardly able to make the lifeboat secure. 17 When the men had hoisted it aboard, they passed ropes under the ship itself to hold it together. Fearing that they would run aground on the sandbars of Syrtis, they lowered the sea anchor and let the ship be driven along. 18 We took such a violent battering from the storm that the next day they began to throw the cargo overboard. *e* 19 On the third day, they threw the ship's tackle overboard with their own hands. 20 When neither sun nor stars appeared for many days and the storm continued raging, we finally gave up all hope of being saved.

21 After the men had gone a long time without food, Paul stood up before them and said: "Men, you should have taken my advice*f* not to sail from Crete;*g* then you would have spared yourselves this damage and loss. 22 But now I urge you to keep up your courage,*h* because not one of you will be lost; only the ship will be destroyed. 23 Last night an angel*i* of the God whose I am and whom I serve*j* stood beside me*k* 24 and said, 'Do not be afraid, Paul. You must stand trial before Caesar;*l* and God has graciously given you the lives of all who sail with you.'*m* 25 So keep up your courage,*n* men, for I have faith in God that it will happen just as he told me. *o* 26 Nevertheless, we must run aground on some island."*p*

The Shipwreck

27 On the fourteenth night we were still being driven across the Adriatic *b* Sea, when about midnight the sailors sensed they were approaching land. 28 They took soundings and found that the water was a hundred and twenty feet *c* deep. A short time later they took soundings again and found it was ninety feet *d* deep. 29 Fearing that we would be dashed

27:3	*a* Ac 24:23
27:6	*b* Ac 28:11
27:9	*c* Lev 23:27-29
27:14	*d* Mk 4:37
27:18	*e* Jnh 1:5
27:21	*f* ver 10
	g ver 7
27:22	*h* ver 25, 36
27:23	*i* Ac 5:19
	j Ro 1:9
	k Ac 23:11
27:24	*l* Ac 23:11
	m ver 44
27:25	*n* ver 22, 36
	o Ro 4:20, 21
27:26	*p* Ac 28:1

a 9 That is, the Day of Atonement (Yom Kippur)   *b 27* In ancient times the name referred to an area extending well south of Italy.   *c 28* Greek *twenty orguias* (about 37 meters)   *d 28* Greek *fifteen orguias* (about 27 meters)

27:9 The "Fast" was the Day of Atonement. Ships in ancient times had no compasses, so they navigated by the stars. Overcast weather made sailing almost impossible and very dangerous. Sailing was doubtful in September and impossible by November. This event occurred in October (A.D. 59).

27:12 Although this was not the best time to sail, the pilot and the owner of the ship didn't want to spend the winter in Lasea, or Fair Havens, so the pilot took a chance. At first the winds and weather were favorable, but then the deadly storm arose.

27:17 The measures they took to survive included passing ropes under the ship to hold it together. Syrtis was on the northern coast of Africa.

27:21 Why would Paul talk to the crew this way? Paul was not taunting them with an "I told you so," but was reminding them that, with God's guidance, he had predicted this very problem

(27:10). In the future, they listened to him (27:30–32) and their lives were spared because of it.

27:27 The Adriatic Sea referred to the central part of the Mediterranean Sea between Italy, Crete, and the northern coast of Africa.

27:28 Soundings were made by throwing a weighted, marked line into the water. When the lead hit the bottom, sailors could tell the depth of the water from the marks on the rope.

27:29 In the middle of a midnight squall, the passengers and crew (led by Paul) did all they could possibly do—they dropped some anchors to try to stop the runaway ship. Then they prayed. Of course, Paul alone was praying to the one God who could do anything about their situation. This is a good reminder for us. We must never rely solely on our own wisdom or skills. But it is equally wrong to sit and do nothing when there are still actions

27:30
q ver 16

against the rocks, they dropped four anchors from the stern and prayed for daylight. ³⁰In an attempt to escape from the ship, the sailors let the lifeboat q down into the sea, pretending they were going to lower some anchors from the bow. ³¹Then Paul said to the centurion and the soldiers, "Unless these men stay with the ship, you cannot be saved." ³²So the soldiers cut the ropes that held the lifeboat and let it fall away.

27:34
r Mt 10:30

³³Just before dawn Paul urged them all to eat. "For the last fourteen days," he said, "you have been in constant suspense and have gone without food—you haven't eaten anything. ³⁴Now I urge you to take some food. You need it to survive. Not one of you will lose a single hair from his head." r ³⁵After he said this, he took some bread and gave thanks to God in front of them all. Then he broke it and began to eat. ³⁶They were all encouraged s and ate some food themselves. ³⁷Altogether there were 276 of us on board. ³⁸When they had eaten as much as they wanted, they lightened the ship by throwing the grain into the sea. t

27:36
s ver 22, 25
27:38
t ver 18
27:39
u Ac 28:1
27:40
v ver 29
27:41
w 2Co 11:25

³⁹When daylight came, they did not recognize the land, but they saw a bay with a sandy beach, u where they decided to run the ship aground if they could. ⁴⁰Cutting loose the anchors, v they left them in the sea and at the same time untied the ropes that held the rudders. Then they hoisted the foresail to the wind and made for the beach. ⁴¹But the ship struck a sandbar and ran aground. The bow stuck fast and would not move, and the stern was broken to pieces by the pounding of the surf. w

27:43
x ver 3
27:44
y ver 22, 31

⁴²The soldiers planned to kill the prisoners to prevent any of them from swimming away and escaping. ⁴³But the centurion wanted to spare Paul's life x and kept them from carrying out their plan. He ordered those who could swim to jump overboard first and get to land. ⁴⁴The rest were to get there on planks or on pieces of the ship. In this way everyone reached land in safety. y

Ashore on Malta

28:1
z Ac 27:26, 39

28 Once safely on shore, we found out that the island z was called Malta. ²The islanders showed us unusual kindness. They built a fire and welcomed us all because it was

THE TRIP TOWARD ROME
Paul began his 2,000-mile trip to Rome at Caesarea. To avoid the open seas, the ship followed the coastline. At Myra, Paul was put on a vessel bound for Italy. It arrived with difficulty at Cnidus, then went to Crete, landing at the port of Fair Havens. The next stop was Phoenix, but the ship was blown south around the island of Cauda, then drifted for two weeks until it was shipwrecked on the island of Malta.

we can take to overcome certain problems. Do all that you can to fix the problem. Then trust God to do his part.

27:42, 43 The soldiers would pay with their own lives if any of their prisoners escaped. Their instinctive reaction was to kill the prisoners so they wouldn't get away. Julius, the centurion, was impressed with Paul and wanted to save his life. Julius was the highest ranking official; therefore, he could make this decision. This act preserved Paul for his later ministry in Rome and fulfilled Paul's prediction that all the people on the ship would be saved (27:22).

28:1, 2 The island of Malta is 60 miles south of Sicily. It had excellent harbors and was ideally located for trade. The islanders on Malta were of Phoenician ancestry.

raining and cold. ³Paul gathered a pile of brushwood and, as he put it on the fire, a viper, driven out by the heat, fastened itself on his hand. ⁴When the islanders saw the snake hanging from his hand, they said to each other, "This man must be a murderer; for though he escaped from the sea, Justice has not allowed him to live."*a* ⁵But Paul shook the snake off into the fire and suffered no ill effects.*b* ⁶The people expected him to swell up or suddenly fall dead, but after waiting a long time and seeing nothing unusual happen to him, they changed their minds and said he was a god.*c*

⁷There was an estate nearby that belonged to Publius, the chief official of the island. He welcomed us to his home and for three days entertained us hospitably. ⁸His father was sick in bed, suffering from fever and dysentery. Paul went in to see him and, after prayer,*d* placed his hands on him and healed him. ⁹When this had happened, the rest of the sick on the island came and were cured. ¹⁰They honored us in many ways and when we were ready to sail, they furnished us with the supplies we needed.

28:4
a Lk 13:2, 4
28:5
b Lk 10:19
28:6
c Ac 14:11

28:8
d Jas 5:14, 15

Arrival at Rome

¹¹After three months we put out to sea in a ship that had wintered in the island. It was an Alexandrian ship*e* with the figurehead of the twin gods Castor and Pollux. ¹²We put in at Syracuse and stayed there three days. ¹³From there we set sail and arrived at Rhegium. The next day the south wind came up, and on the following day we reached Puteoli. ¹⁴There we found some brothers*f* who invited us to spend a week with them. And so we came to Rome. ¹⁵The brothers there had heard that we were coming, and they traveled as far as the Forum of Appius and the Three Taverns to meet us. At the sight of these men Paul thanked God and was encouraged. ¹⁶When we got to Rome, Paul was allowed to live by himself, with a soldier to guard him.*g*

28:11
e Ac 27:6

28:14
f Ac 1:16

28:16
g Ac 24:23; 27:3

Paul Preaches at Rome Under Guard

¹⁷Three days later he called together the leaders of the Jews. When they had assembled, Paul said to them: "My brothers, although I have done nothing against our people *h* or against the customs of our ancestors,*i* I was arrested in Jerusalem and handed over to the Romans. ¹⁸They examined me*j* and wanted to release me, because I was not guilty of any crime deserving death. ¹⁹But when the Jews objected, I was compelled to appeal to Caesar *k*—not that I had any charge to bring against my own people. ²⁰For this reason I have asked to see you and talk with you. It is because of the hope of Israel*l* that I am bound with this chain."

28:17
h Ac 25:8
i Ac 6:14
28:18
j Ac 22:24
28:19
k Ac 25:11
28:20
l Ac 26:6, 7

28:3 God had promised safe passage to Paul (27:23–25), and he would let nothing stop his servant. The poisonous viper that bit Paul was unable to harm him. Our lives are in God's hands, to continue on or to come to an end in his good timing. God still had work for Paul to do.

PAUL ARRIVES IN ROME
The shipwreck occurred on Malta, where the ship's company spent three months. Finally, another ship gave them passage for the 100 miles to Syracuse, capital of Sicily, then sailed on to Rhegium, finally dropping anchor at Puteoli. Paul was taken to the Forum of Appias and to the Three Taverns before arriving in Rome.

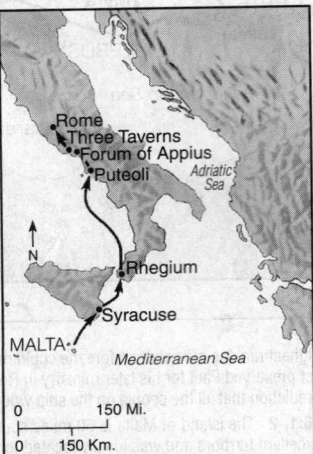

28:6 These people were very superstitious and believed in many gods. When they saw that Paul was unhurt by the poisonous viper, they thought he was a god. A similar assessment is reported in 14:11–18.

28:7, 8 Paul continued to minister to others, even as a shipwrecked prisoner. On this trip alone, his centurion, the chief official of Malta, and many others were affected. It is no wonder that the gospel spread like wildfire.

28:15 Where did the Roman believers come from? The gospel message had spread to Rome by various methods. Many Jews who lived in Rome would visit Jerusalem for religious festivals. Some had been present at Pentecost (2:10), had believed in Jesus, and had brought the message back to Rome. Also, Paul had written his letter to the Romans before this time.

28:15 The Forum of Appius was a town about 43 miles south of Rome; Three Taverns was located about 35 miles south of Rome. A *tavern* was a shop, or a place that provided food and lodging for travelers. The Christians openly went to meet Paul and encourage him.

28:17 The decree of Claudius expelling Jews from Rome (18:2) must have been temporary, because Jewish leaders were back in Rome.

28:17–20 Paul wanted to preach the gospel in Rome, and he eventually got there—in chains, through shipwreck, and after many trials. Although he may have wished for an easier passage, he knew that God had blessed him greatly in allowing him to meet the believers in Rome and preach the message to both Jews and Gentiles in that great city. In all things, God worked for Paul's

28:22
m Ac 24:5, 14

28:23
n Ac 19:8
o Ac 17:3

28:24
p Ac 14:4

21 They replied, "We have not received any letters from Judea concerning you, and none of the brothers who have come from there has reported or said anything bad about you. 22 But we want to hear what your views are, for we know that people everywhere are talking against this sect." *m*

23 They arranged to meet Paul on a certain day, and came in even larger numbers to the place where he was staying. From morning till evening he explained and declared to them the kingdom of God *n* and tried to convince them about Jesus *o* from the Law of Moses and from the Prophets. 24 Some were convinced by what he said, but others would not believe. *p* 25 They disagreed among themselves and began to leave after Paul had made this final statement: "The Holy Spirit spoke the truth to your forefathers when he said through Isaiah the prophet:

26 "'Go to this people and say,
   "You will be ever hearing but never understanding;
      you will be ever seeing but never perceiving."
27 For this people's heart has become calloused;
      they hardly hear with their ears,
      and they have closed their eyes.

PAUL'S JOURNEY TO ROME	Reference	What Happened
	21:30–34	When Paul arrived in Jerusalem, a riot broke out. Seeing the riot, Roman soldiers put Paul into protective custody. Paul asked for a chance to defend himself to the people. His speech was interrupted by the crowd when he told about what God was doing in the lives of Gentiles.
	22:24, 25	A Roman commander ordered a beating to get a confession from Paul. Paul claimed Roman citizenship and escaped the whip.
	22:30	Paul was brought before the Jewish Sanhedrin. Because of his Roman citizenship, he was rescued from the religious leaders who wanted to kill him.
	23:10	The Roman commander put Paul back under protective custody.
	23:21–24	Due to a plot to kill Paul, the commander transferred him to Caesarea, which was under Governor Felix's control.
	23:35	Paul was in prison until the Jews arrived to accuse him. Paul defended himself before Felix.
	24:25, 26	Paul was in prison for two years, speaking occasionally to Felix and Drusilla.
	24:27	Felix was replaced by Festus.
	25:1, 10	New accusations were brought against Paul—Jews wanted him back in Jerusalem for a trial. Paul claimed his right to a hearing before Caesar.
	25:12	Festus promised to send him to Rome.
	25:13, 14	Festus discussed Paul's case with Herod Agrippa II.
	26:1	Agrippa and Festus heard Paul speak. Paul again told his story.
	26:24–28	Agrippa interrupted with a sarcastic rejection of the gospel.
	26:30–32	Group consensus was that Paul was guilty of nothing and could have been released if he had not appealed to Rome.
	27:1, 2	Paul left for Rome, courtesy of the Roman empire.

One of Paul's most important journeys was to Rome, but he didn't get there the way he expected. It turned out to be more of a legal journey than a missionary journey. Through a series of legal trials and transactions, Paul was delivered to Rome, where his presentation of the gospel would even penetrate the walls of the emperor's palace. Sometimes when our plans don't work out as we want them to, they work out even better than we expected.

good (Romans 8:28). You can trust God to do the same for you. God may not make you comfortable or secure, but he will provide the opportunity to do his work.

28:22 Christians were denounced everywhere by the Romans because they were seen as a threat to the Roman establishment. They believed in one God, whereas the Romans had many gods,

including Caesar. The Christians were committed to an authority higher than Caesar.

28:23 Paul used the Old Testament to teach the Jews that Jesus was the Messiah, the fulfillment of God's promises. The book of Romans, written ten years earlier, reveals Paul's ongoing dialogue with the Jews in Rome.

> Otherwise they might see with their eyes,
> hear with their ears,
> understand with their hearts
> and turn, and I would heal them.'ª q

28 "Therefore I want you to know that God's salvation has been sent to the Gentiles,ʳ and they will listen!"ᵇ

30 For two whole years Paul stayed there in his own rented house and welcomed all who came to see him. 31 Boldly and without hindrance he preached the kingdom of God and taught about the Lord Jesus Christ.

ª27 Isaiah 6:9,10   ᵇ28 Some manuscripts *listen!" 29After he said this, the Jews left, arguing vigorously among themselves.*

28:27
q Isa 6:9, 10

28:28
r Ac 13:46

28:30 Paul remained in Rome under guard (28:16) in a rented house for two years (28:30). There sat the greatest apostle and spokesman for Christianity—unable to move freely and minister as he desired. However, Paul didn't complain or despair. He simply did what he could. Able to receive visitors, he taught, preached, and counseled even while he was confined to quarters. He wrote letters, commonly called his Prison Letters, to the Ephesians, Colossians, and Philippians—letters that have impacted millions of believers down through the centuries. He also wrote personal letters, such as the one to Philemon. Luke was with Paul in Rome (2 Timothy 4:11). Timothy often visited him (Philippians 1:1; Colossians 1:1; Philemon 1), as did Tychicus (Ephesians 6:21), Epaphroditus (Philippians 4:18), and Mark (Colossians 4:10). Paul witnessed to the whole Roman guard (Philippians 1:13) and was involved with the Roman believers. If you find yourself in a "negative" or unpleasant situation, look for ways to redeem the circumstances. There is never a time or place in which you can't glorify and serve God.

28:30 Tradition says that Paul was released after two years of house arrest in Rome and that he then left on a fourth missionary journey. Some reasons for this tradition are as follows: (1) Luke does not give us an account of Paul's trial before Caesar, and Luke was a detailed chronicler; (2) the prosecution had two years to bring the case to trial, and time may have run out; (3) in his letter to the Philippians, written during his imprisonment in Rome, Paul implied that he would soon be released and would do further traveling; (4) Paul mentions several places where he intended to take the gospel, but he never visited those places in his first three journeys; (5) early Christian literature talks plainly about other travels by Paul.

During his time of freedom, Paul may have continued to travel extensively, even going to Spain (see Romans 15:24, 28) and back to the churches in Greece. The books of 1 Timothy and Titus were written during this time. Later, Paul was imprisoned again, probably in Rome, where he wrote his last letter (2 Timothy).

28:31 Why does the book of Acts end here and so abruptly? The book is not about the life of Paul, but about the spread of the gospel, and that has been clearly presented. God apparently thought it was not necessary for someone to write an additional book describing the continuing history of the early church. Now that the gospel had been preached and established at the center of trade and government, it would spread across the world.

28:31 The book of Acts deals with the history of the Christian church and its expansion in ever-widening circles touching Jerusalem, Antioch, Ephesus, and Rome—the most influential cities in the western world. Acts also shows the mighty miracles and testimonies of the heroes and martyrs of the early church—Peter, Stephen, James, Paul. All the ministry was prompted and held together by the Holy Spirit working in the lives of ordinary people—merchants, travelers, slaves, jailers, church leaders, males, females, Gentiles, Jews, rich, poor. Many unsung heroes of the faith continued the work, through the Holy Spirit, in succeeding generations, changing the world with a changeless message—that Jesus Christ is Savior and Lord for all who call on him. Today we can be the unsung heroes in the continuing story of the spread of the gospel. It is that same message that we Christians are to take to our world so that many more may hear and believe.

ROMANS

KNOWLEDGEABLE and experienced, the district attorney makes his case. Calling key witnesses to the stand, he presents the evidence. After discrediting the testimonies of witnesses for the defense by skillfully cross-examining them, he concludes with an airtight summary and stirring challenge for the jury. The announced verdict is no surprise. "Guilty" states the foreman, and justice is served.

The apostle Paul was intelligent, articulate, and committed to his calling. Like a skilled lawyer, he presented the case for the gospel clearly and forthrightly in his letter to the believers in Rome.

Paul had heard of the church at Rome, but he had not yet been there, nor had any of the other apostles. Evidently the church had been started by Jews who had come to faith during Pentecost (Acts 2). They had spread the gospel on their return to Rome, and the church had grown.

Although many barriers separated them, Paul felt a bond with these believers in Rome. They were his brothers and sisters in Christ, and he longed to see them face to face. He had never met most of the believers there, yet he loved them. He sent this letter to introduce himself and to make a clear declaration of the faith.

After a brief introduction, Paul presents the facts of the gospel (1:3) and declares his allegiance to it (1:16, 17). He continues by building an airtight case for the lostness of humanity and the necessity for God's intervention (1:18—3:20).

Then Paul presents the Good News: Salvation is available to all, regardless of a person's identity, sin, or heritage. We are saved by *grace* (unearned, undeserved favor from God) through *faith* (complete trust) in Christ and his finished work. Through him we can stand before God justified, "not guilty" (3:21—5:21). With this foundation Paul moves directly into a discussion of the freedom that comes from being saved—freedom from the power of sin (6:1–23), freedom from the domination of the law (7:1–25), freedom to become like Christ and discover God's limitless love (8:1–39).

Speaking directly to his Jewish brothers and sisters, Paul shares his concern for them and explains how they fit into God's plan (9:1—11:12). God has made the way for Jews and Gentiles to be united in the body of Christ; both groups can praise God for his wisdom and love (11:13–36).

Paul explains what it means to live in complete submission to Christ: Use spiritual gifts to serve others (12:3–8), genuinely love others (12:9–21), and be good citizens (13:1–14). Freedom must be guided by love as we build each other up in the faith, being sensitive and helpful to those who are weak (14:1—15:4). Paul stresses unity, especially between Gentiles and Jews (15:5–13). He concludes by reviewing his reasons for writing, outlining his personal plans (15:22–33), greeting his friends, and giving a few final thoughts and greetings from his traveling companions (16:1–27).

As you read Romans, reexamine your commitment to Christ, and reconfirm your relationships with other believers in Christ's body.

VITAL STATISTICS

PURPOSE:
To introduce Paul to the Romans and to give a sample of his message before he arrives in Rome

AUTHOR:
Paul

ORIGINAL AUDIENCE:
The Christians in Rome

DATE WRITTEN:
About A.D. 57, from Corinth, as Paul was preparing for his visit to Jerusalem.

SETTING:
Apparently Paul had finished his work in the east, and he planned to visit Rome on his way to Spain after first bringing a collection to Jerusalem for the poor Christians there (15:23–28). The Roman church was mostly Jewish but also contained a great number of Gentiles.

KEY VERSE:
"Therefore, since we have been justified through faith, we have peace with God through our Lord Jesus Christ" (5:1).

KEY PEOPLE:
Paul, Phoebe

KEY PLACE:
Rome

SPECIAL FEATURES:
Paul wrote Romans as an organized and carefully presented statement of his faith—it does not have the form of a typical letter. He does, however, spend considerable time greeting people in Rome at the end of the letter.

THE BLUEPRINT

A. WHAT TO BELIEVE
   (1:1—11:36)
   1. Sinfulness of humanity
   2. Forgiveness of sin through Christ
   3. Freedom from sin's grasp
   4. Israel's past, present, and future

B. HOW TO BEHAVE
   (12:1—16:27)
   1. Personal responsibility
   2. Personal notes

Paul clearly sets forth the foundations of the Christian faith. All people are sinful; Christ died to forgive sin; we are made right with God through faith; this begins a new life with a new relationship with God. Like a sports team that constantly reviews the basics, we will be greatly helped in our faith by keeping close to these foundations. If we study Romans carefully, we will never be at a loss to know what to believe.

Paul gives clear, practical guidelines for the believers in Rome. The Christian life is not abstract theology unconnected with life, but it has practical implications that will affect how we choose to behave each day. It is not enough merely to know the gospel; we must let it transform our lives and let God impact every aspect of our lives.

MEGATHEMES

THEME	EXPLANATION	IMPORTANCE
Sin	Sin means refusing to do God's will and failing to do all that God wants. Since Adam's rebellion against God, our nature is to disobey him. Our sin cuts us off from God. Sin causes us to want to live our own way rather than God's way. Because God is morally perfect, just, and fair, he is right to condemn sin.	Each person has sinned, either by rebelling against God or by ignoring his will. No matter what our background or how hard we try to live good and moral lives, we cannot earn salvation or remove our sin. Only Christ can save us.
Salvation	Our sin points out our need to be forgiven and cleansed. Although we don't deserve it, God, in his kindness, reached out to love and forgive us. He provides the way for us to be saved. Christ's death paid the penalty for our sin.	It is good news that God saves us from our sin. But in order to enter into a wonderful new relationship with God, we must believe that Jesus died for us and that he forgives all our sin.
Growth	By God's power, believers are sanctified—made holy. This means we are set apart from sin, enabled to obey and to become more like Christ. When we are growing in our relationship with Christ, the Holy Spirit frees us from the demands of the law and from fear of judgment.	Because we are free from sin's control, the law's demands, and fear of God's punishment, we can grow in our relationship with Christ. By trusting in the Holy Spirit and allowing him to help us, we can overcome sin and temptation.
Sovereignty	God oversees and cares about his people—past, present, and future. God's ways of dealing with people are always fair. Because God is in charge of all creation, he can save whomever he wills.	Because of God's mercy, both Jews and Gentiles can be saved. We all must respond to his mercy and accept his gracious offer of forgiveness. Because he is sovereign, let him reign in your heart.
Service	When our purpose is to give credit to God for his love, power, and perfection in all we do, we can serve him properly. Serving him unifies all believers and enables them to show love and sensitivity to others.	None of us can be fully Christlike by ourselves—it takes the entire body of Christ to fully express Christ. By actively and vigorously building up other believers, Christians can be a symphony of service to God.

A. WHAT TO BELIEVE (1:1—11:36)

Paul begins his message to the Romans by vividly portraying the sinfulness of all people, explaining how forgiveness is available through faith in Christ, and showing what believers experience in life through their new faith. In this section, we learn of the centrality of faith to becoming a Christian and to living the Christian life. Apart from faith, we have no hope in life.

1. Sinfulness of humanity

1 Paul, a servant of Christ Jesus, called to be an apostle and set apart *a* for the gospel of God— 2 the gospel he promised beforehand through his prophets in the Holy Scriptures *b* 3 regarding his Son, who as to his human nature was a descendant of David, 4 and who through

1:1
a Ac 9:15
1:2
b Gal 3:8

1:1 Paul wrote this letter to the church in Rome. Neither he nor the other church leaders, James and Peter, had yet been to Rome. Most likely, the Roman church had been established by believers who had been at Jerusalem for Pentecost (Acts 2:10) and travelers who had heard the Good News in other places and had brought it back to Rome (for example, Priscilla and Aquila, Acts 18:2; Romans 16:3–5). Paul wrote the letter to the Romans during his ministry in Corinth (at the end of his third missionary journey just before returning to Jerusalem—Acts 20:3; Romans 15:25) to encourage the believers and to express his desire to visit them someday (within three years he would). The Roman church had no New Testament because the Gospels were not yet being circulated in their final written form. Thus, this letter may well have been the first piece of Christian literature the

1:5
c Ac 9:15
d Ac 6:7

the Spirit a of holiness was declared with power to be the Son of God b by his resurrection from the dead: Jesus Christ our Lord. 5 Through him and for his name's sake, we received grace and apostleship to call people from among all the Gentiles c to the obedience that comes from faith. d 6 And you also are among those who are called to belong to Jesus Christ.

a 4 Or who as to his spirit   b 4 Or was appointed to be the Son of God with power

**THE GOSPEL
GOES
TO ROME**
When Paul wrote
his letter to the
church in Rome,
he had not yet
been there, but
he had taken
the gospel "from
Jerusalem all the
way around to
Illyricum" (15:19).
He planned to visit
and preach in
Rome one day and
hoped to continue
to take the gospel
farther west—
even to Spain.

Roman believers had seen. Written to both Jewish and Gentile Christians, the letter to the Romans is a systematic presentation of the Christian faith.

1:1 When Paul, a devout Jew who had at first persecuted the Christians, became a believer, God used him to spread the gospel throughout the world. Although it was as a prisoner, Paul did eventually preach in Rome (Acts 28), perhaps even to Caesar himself. Paul's Profile is found in Acts 9, p. 1825.

1:1 Paul humbly calls himself a servant of Jesus Christ and an apostle ("one who is sent"). For a Roman citizen—which Paul was—to choose to be a servant was unthinkable. But Paul chose to be completely dependent on and obedient to his beloved Master. What is your attitude toward Christ, your Master? Our willingness to serve and obey Jesus Christ enables us to be useful and usable servants to do work for him—work that really matters. Obedience begins as we renounce other masters, identify ourselves with Jesus, discover his will and live according to it, and consciously turn away from conflicting interests, even if these interests have been important to us in the past.

1:2 Some of the prophecies predicting the Good News regarding Jesus Christ are found in Genesis 12:3; Psalms 16:10; 40:6–10; 118:22; Isaiah 11:1ff; Zechariah 9:9–11; 12:10; Malachi 4:1–6.

1:3, 4 Paul states that Jesus is the Son of God, the promised Messiah, and the resurrected Lord. Paul calls Jesus a descendant of King David to emphasize that Jesus truly had fulfilled the Old Testament Scriptures predicting that the Messiah would come from David's line. With this statement of faith, Paul declares his agreement with the teaching of all Scripture and of the apostles.

1:3–5 Here Paul summarizes the Good News about Jesus Christ, who (1) came as a human by natural descent, (2) was part of the Jewish royal line through David, (3) died and was raised from the dead, and (4) opened the door for God's grace and kindness to be poured out on us. The book of Romans is an expansion of these themes.

1:5 Christians have both a privilege and a great responsibility. Paul and the apostles received forgiveness ("grace") as an undeserved privilege. But they also received the responsibility to share the message of God's forgiveness with others. God also graciously forgives our sins when we believe in him as Lord. In doing this, we are committing ourselves to begin a new life. Paul's new life also involved a God-given responsibility—to witness about God's Good News to the world as a missionary. God may or may not call you to be an overseas missionary, but he does call you (and all believers) to witness to and be an example of the changed life that Jesus Christ has begun in you.

1:6, 7 Paul says that those who become Christians are invited by Jesus Christ to (1) become part of God's family, and (2) be holy people ("to be saints," set apart, dedicated for his service). What a wonderful expression of what it means to be a Christian! In being reborn into God's family we have the greatest experience of love and the greatest inheritance. Because of all that God has done for us, we strive to be his holy people.

7 To all in Rome who are loved by God and called to be saints:

Grace and peace to you from God our Father and from the Lord Jesus Christ. *e*

1:7
e 1Co 1:3

Paul's Longing to Visit Rome

8 First, I thank my God through Jesus Christ for all of you, because your faith is being reported all over the world. 9 God, whom I serve with my whole heart in preaching the gospel of his Son, is my witness how constantly I remember you 10 in my prayers at all times; and I pray that now at last by God's will the way may be opened for me to come to you. *f*

1:10
f Ro 15:32

11 I long to see you so that I may impart to you some spiritual gift to make you strong— 12 that is, that you and I may be mutually encouraged by each other's faith. 13 I do not want you to be unaware, brothers, that I planned many times to come to you (but have been prevented from doing so until now) in order that I might have a harvest among you, just as I have had among the other Gentiles.

14 I am obligated both to Greeks and non-Greeks, both to the wise and the foolish. 15 That is why I am so eager to preach the gospel also to you who are at Rome.

16 I am not ashamed of the gospel, because it is the power of God *g* for the salvation of everyone who believes: first for the Jew, then for the Gentile. 17 For in the gospel a righteousness from God is revealed, *h* a righteousness that is by faith from first to last, *a* just as it is written: "The righteous will live by faith." *b i*

1:16
g 1Co 1:18
1:17
h Ro 3:21
i Gal 3:11

a 17 Or is from faith to faith   *b 17 Hab. 2:4*

1:7 Rome was the capital of the Roman empire that had spread over most of Europe, North Africa, and the Near East. In New Testament times, Rome was experiencing a golden age. The city was wealthy, literary, and artistic. It was a cultural center, but it was also morally decadent. The Romans worshiped many pagan gods, and even some of the emperors were worshiped. In stark contrast to the Romans, the followers of Christ believed in only one God and lived by his high moral standards.

Christianity was also at odds with the Romans' dependence on military strength. Many Romans were naively pragmatic, believing that any means to accomplish the intended task was good. And for them, nothing worked better than physical might. The Romans trusted in their strong military power to protect them against all enemies. Christians in every age need to be reminded that God is the only permanent source of our security and salvation, and at the same time he is "our Father"!

1:8 Paul uses the phrase "I thank my God through Jesus Christ" to emphasize the point that Christ is the one and only mediator between God and humans. Through Christ, God sends his love and forgiveness to us; through Christ, we send our thanks to God (see 1 Timothy 2:5).

1:8 The Roman Christians, at the Western world's political power center, were highly visible. Fortunately, their reputation was excellent; their strong faith was making itself known around the world. When people talk about your congregation or your denomination, what do they say? Are their comments accurate? Would you rather they noticed other features? What is the best way to get the public to recognize your faith?

1:9, 10 When you pray continually about a concern, don't be surprised at how God answers. Paul prayed to visit Rome so he could teach the Christians there. When he finally arrived in Rome, it was as a prisoner (see Acts 28:16). Paul prayed for a safe trip, and he did arrive safely—after getting arrested, slapped in the face, shipwrecked, and bitten by a poisonous snake. When you sincerely pray, God will answer—although sometimes with timing and in ways you do not expect.

1:11–13 A reading of the first few verses of Romans relates Paul's ardent desire to visit Rome and the sovereign hand of God that had prevented him from getting there for quite some time. The combination of these two factors—Paul's impassioned desire to go to Rome and God's sovereign "no"—resulted in his sitting down to write this letter to the Romans. This letter is a powerful exposition of the Christian faith and has helped countless millions of believers across the centuries since Paul first penned it to the

group of believers in Rome. Perhaps there are some "no's" in our lives that God is planning to use greatly if we would just faithfully do what lies directly ahead of us instead of worrying about why we didn't get our way.

1:13 By the end of his third missionary journey, Paul had traveled through Syria, Galatia, Asia, Macedonia, and Achaia. The churches in these areas were made up mostly of Gentile believers.

1:14 By "Greeks and non-Greeks," Paul was referring to those of the Greek culture and those not of the Greek culture. "The wise and the foolish" refers to educated and uneducated people. What was Paul's obligation? After his experience with Christ on the road to Damascus (Acts 9), his whole life was consumed with spreading the Good News of salvation. His obligation was to Christ for being his Savior, and he was obligated to the entire world. He met his obligation by proclaiming Christ's salvation to *all* people—both Jews and Gentiles, across all cultural, social, racial, and economic lines. We also are obligated to Christ because he took on the punishment we deserve for our sin. Although we cannot repay Christ for all he has done, we can demonstrate our gratitude by showing his love to others.

1:15 Paul was eager to preach the gospel. Is our Christian service done in a spirit of eagerness? Or do we serve out of habit, a feeling of obligation, or perhaps even with a feeling of reluctant duty (much like a child who has to take a bath)? When we fully understand what Christ has done for us and what he offers to others, we will be motivated to share the Good News. Ask God to rekindle that fresh eager attitude that wants to obey him and to tell others about Christ.

1:16 Paul was not ashamed because his message was the gospel of Christ, the Good News. It was a message of salvation, it had life-changing power, and it was for everyone. When you are tempted to be ashamed, remember what the Good News is all about. If you focus on God and on what God is doing in the world rather than on your own inadequacy, you won't be ashamed or embarrassed.

1:16 Why did the message go to the Jews first? They had been God's special people for more than 2,000 years, ever since God chose Abraham and promised great blessings to his descendants (Genesis 12:1–3). God did not choose the Jews because they deserved to be chosen (Deuteronomy 7:7, 8; 9:4–6), but because he wanted to show his love and mercy to them, teach them, and prepare them to welcome his Messiah into the world. God chose them, not to play favorites, but so that they would tell the world about his plan of salvation.

God's Wrath Against Mankind

1:18
/Eph 5:6

1:19
kAc 14:17

18The wrath of God/ is being revealed from heaven against all the godlessness and wickedness of men who suppress the truth by their wickedness, 19since what may be known about God is plain to them, because God has made it plain to them. k 20For since the creation

---

WHAT IS FAITH?

Faith is a word with many meanings. It can mean faithfulness (Matthew 24:45). It can mean absolute trust, as shown by some of the people who came to Jesus for healing (Luke 7:2–10). It can mean confident hope (Hebrews 11:1). Or, as James points out, it can even mean a barren belief that does not result in good deeds (James 2:14–26). What does Paul mean when, in Romans, he speaks of "saving faith"?

We must be very careful to understand faith as Paul uses the word because he ties faith so closely to salvation. It is *not* something we must do in order to earn salvation—if that were true, then faith would be just one more deed, and Paul clearly states that human deeds can never save us (Galatians 2:16). Instead, faith is a gift God gives us *because* he is saving us (Ephesians 2:8). It is God's grace, not our faith, that saves us. In his mercy, however, when he saves us, he gives us faith—a relationship with his Son that helps us become like him. Through the faith he gives us, he carries us from death into life (John 5:24).

Even in Old Testament times, grace, not deeds, was the basis of salvation. As Hebrews points out, "it is impossible for the blood of bulls and goats to take away sins" (10:4). God intended for his people to look beyond the animal sacrifices to him, but all too often they instead put their confidence in fulfilling the requirements of the law—that is, performing the required sacrifices. When Jesus triumphed over death, he canceled the charges against us and opened the way to the Father (Colossians 2:12–15). Because he is merciful, he offers us faith. How tragic if we turn faith into a deed and try to develop it on our own! We can never come to God through our own faith any more than his Old Testament people could come through their own sacrifices. Instead, we must accept his gracious offer with thanksgiving and allow him to plant the seed of faith within us.

For centuries the Jews had been learning about God by obeying his laws, keeping his feasts, and living according to his moral principles. Often they would forget God's promises and requirements; often they would have to be disciplined; but still they had a precious heritage of belief in the one true God. Of all the people on earth, the Jews should have been the most ready to welcome the Messiah and to understand his mission and message—and some of them were (see Luke 2:25, 36–38). Of course, the disciples and the great apostle Paul were faithful Jews who recognized in Jesus God's most precious gift to the human race.

1:16 Jews and Christians alike stood against the idolatrous Roman religions, and Roman officials often confused the two groups. This was especially easy to do since the Christian church in Rome could have been originally composed of Jewish converts who had attended the Feast of Pentecost (see Acts 2:1ff). By the time Paul wrote this letter to the Romans, however, many Gentiles had joined the church. The Jews and the Gentiles needed to know the relationship between Judaism and Christianity.

1:17 The gospel shows us both how righteous God is in his plan for us to be saved, and also how we may be made fit for eternal life. By trusting Christ, our relationship with God is made right. "From first to last" God declares us to be righteous because of faith and faith alone. Paul then quotes from Habakkuk 2:4 to show that as we trust God, we are saved; we have life both now and forever.

1:18 Why is God angry at sinful people? Because they have substituted the truth about him with a lie (1:25). They have stifled the truth God naturally reveals to all people in order to believe anything that supports their own self-centered lifestyles. God cannot tolerate sin because his nature is morally perfect. He cannot ignore or condone such willful rebellion. God wants to remove the sin and restore the sinner—and he is able to, as long as the sinner does not stubbornly distort or reject the truth. But his anger erupts against those who persist in sinning. Make sure you are not pursuing a lie rather than the true God. Don't suppress the truth about him merely to protect your own lifestyle.

1:18ff Romans 1:18—3:20 develops Paul's argument that no one can claim by his or her own efforts or merit to be good in God's sight—not the masses, not the Romans, not even the Jews. All people everywhere deserve God's condemnation for their sin.

1:18–20 In these verses, Paul answers a common objection to belief in God: How could a loving God send anyone to hell, especially someone who has never heard about Christ? In fact, says Paul, God has revealed himself plainly in the creation to *all* people. And yet people reject even this basic knowledge of God. Also, everyone has an inner sense of what God requires, but they choose not to live up to it. Put another way, people's moral standards are always better than their behavior. If people suppress God's truth in order to live their own way, they have no excuse. They know the truth, and they will have to endure the consequences of ignoring it.

1:18–20 Some people wonder why we need missionaries if people can know about God through nature (the creation). The answer: (1) Although people know that God exists, they suppress that truth by their wickedness and thus refuse a relationship with him. Missionaries sensitively expose their error and point them to a new beginning. (2) Although people may believe there is a God, they refuse to commit themselves to him. Missionaries help persuade them, both through loving words and caring actions. (3) Missionaries convince people who reject God of the dangerous consequences of their actions. (4) Missionaries help the church obey the Great Commission of our Lord (Matthew 28:19, 20). (5) Most important, though nature reveals God, people need to be told about Jesus and how, through him, they can have a personal relationship with God.

Knowing that God exists is not enough. People must learn that God is loving. They must understand what he did to demonstrate his love for us (5:8). They must be shown how to accept God's forgiveness of their sins. (See also 10:14, 15.)

1:19 Does anyone have an excuse for not believing in God? The Bible answers an emphatic *no*. God has revealed what he is like in and through his creation. Every person, therefore, either accepts or rejects God. Don't be fooled. When the day comes for God to judge your response to him, no excuses will be accepted. Begin today to give your devotion and worship to him.

1:20 What kind of God does nature reveal? Nature shows us a God of might, intelligence, and intricate detail; a God of order and beauty; a God who controls powerful forces. That is *general* revelation. Through *special* revelation (the Bible and the coming of Jesus), we learn about God's love and forgiveness, and the of the world God's invisible qualities—his eternal power and divine nature—have been clearly seen, being understood from what has been made,^{l} so that men are without excuse.

^{21}For although they knew God, they neither glorified him as God nor gave thanks to him, but their thinking became futile and their foolish hearts were darkened. ^{m} ^{22}Although they claimed to be wise, they became fools ^{23}and exchanged the glory of the immortal God for images ^{n} made to look like mortal man and birds and animals and reptiles.

^{24}Therefore God gave them over ^{o} in the sinful desires of their hearts to sexual impurity for the degrading of their bodies with one another. ^{25}They exchanged the truth of God for a lie, ^{p} and worshiped and served created things ^{q} rather than the Creator—who is forever praised. Amen.

^{26}Because of this, God gave them over to shameful lusts. Even their women exchanged natural relations for unnatural ones. ^{r} ^{27}In the same way the men also abandoned natural relations with women and were inflamed with lust for one another. Men committed indecent acts with other men, and received in themselves the due penalty for their perversion. ^{s}

^{28}Furthermore, since they did not think it worthwhile to retain the knowledge of God, he gave them over to a depraved mind, to do what ought not to be done. ^{29}They have become filled with every kind of wickedness, evil, greed and depravity. They are full of envy, murder, strife, deceit and malice. They are gossips, ^{30}slanderers, God-haters, insolent, arrogant and boastful; they invent ways of doing evil; they disobey their parents; ^{t} ^{31}they are senseless,

1:20
^{l} Ps 19:1-6

1:21
^{m} Jer 2:5;
Eph 4:17, 18

1:23
^{n} Ps 106:20

1:24
^{o} Eph 4:19

1:25
^{p} Isa 44:20
^{q} Jer 10:14

1:26
^{r} Lev 18:22, 23

1:27
^{s} Lev 18:22

1:30
^{t} 2Ti 3:2

---

promise of eternal life. God has graciously given us both sources that we might fully believe in him.

1:20 God reveals his divine nature and personal qualities through creation, even though creation's testimony has been distorted by the fall. Adam's sin resulted in a divine curse upon the whole natural order (Genesis 3:17–19); thorns and thistles were an immediate result, and natural disasters have been common from Adam's day to ours. In Romans 8:19–21, Paul says that nature itself is eagerly awaiting its own redemption from the effects of sin (see Revelation 22:3).

1:21–23 How could intelligent people turn to idolatry? Idolatry begins when people reject what they know about God. Instead of looking to him as the Creator and sustainer of life, they see themselves as the center of the universe. They soon invent "gods" that are convenient projections of their own selfish plans and decrees. These gods may be wooden figures, but they may also be goals or things we pursue such as money, power, or comfort. They may even be misrepresentations of God himself—making God in our image, instead of the reverse. The common denominator is this— idolaters worship the things God made rather than God himself. Is there anything you feel you can't live without? Is there any priority greater than God? Do you have a dream you would sacrifice everything to realize? Does God take first place? Do you worship God or idols of your own making?

1:21–32 Paul clearly portrays the inevitable downward spiral into sin. First, people reject God; next, they make up their own ideas of what a god should be and do; then they fall into sin— sexual sin, greed, hatred, envy, murder, strife, deceit, malice, gossip. Finally, they grow to hate God and encourage others to do so. God does not cause this steady progression toward evil. Rather, when people reject him, he allows them to live as they choose. God gives them over or permits them to experience the natural consequences of their sin. Once caught in the downward spiral, no one can pull himself or herself out. Sinners must trust Christ alone to put them on the path of escape.

1:23 When Paul says that men exchanged the glory of the immortal God for images of birds, animals, and reptiles, he seems to deliberately state man's wickedness in the terms used in the Genesis narrative of Adam's fall (see Genesis 1:20–26). When we worship the creature instead of the Creator, we lose sight of our own identity as those who are higher than the animals—made in the image of God.

1:24–32 These people chose to reject God, and God allowed them to do it. God does not usually stop us from making choices that are against his will. He lets us declare our supposed independence from him, even though he knows that in time we will become

slaves to our own rebellious choices—we will lose our freedom not to sin. Does life without God look like freedom to you? Look more closely. There is no worse slavery than slavery to sin.

1:25 People tend to believe lies that reinforce their own selfish, personal beliefs. Today, more than ever, we need to be careful about the input we allow to form our beliefs. With TV, music, movies, and the rest of the media often presenting sinful lifestyles and unwholesome values, we find ourselves constantly bombarded by attitudes and beliefs that are totally opposed to the Bible. Be careful about what you allow to form your opinions. The Bible is the only standard of truth. Evaluate all other opinions in light of its teachings.

1:26, 27 God's plan for natural sexual relationships is his ideal for his creation. Unfortunately, sin distorts the natural use of God's gifts. Sin often means not only denying God, but also denying the way we are made. When people say that any sex act is acceptable as long as nobody gets hurt, they are fooling themselves. In the long run (and often in the short run), sin hurts people—individuals, families, whole societies. Because sex is such a powerful and essential part of what it means to be human, it must be treated with great respect. Sexual desires are of such importance that the Bible gives them special attention and counsels more careful restraint and self-control than with any other desire. One of the clearest indicators of a society or person in rebellion against God is the rejection of God's guidelines for the use of sex.

1:26, 27 Homosexuality (to exchange or abandon natural relations of sex) was as widespread in Paul's day as it is in ours. Many pagan practices encouraged it. God is willing to receive anyone who comes to him in faith, and Christians should love and accept others no matter what their background. Yet, homosexuality is strictly forbidden in Scripture (Leviticus 18:22). Homosexuality is considered an acceptable practice by many in our world today— even by some churches. But society does not set the standard for God's law. Many homosexuals believe that their desires are normal and that they have a right to express them. But God does not obligate nor encourage us to fulfill all our desires (even normal ones). Those desires that violate his laws must be controlled.

If you have these desires, you can and must resist acting upon them. Consciously avoid places or activities you know will kindle temptations of this kind. Don't underestimate the power of Satan to tempt you, nor the potential for serious harm if you yield to these temptations. Remember, God can and will forgive sexual sins just as he forgives other sins. Surrender yourself to the grace and mercy of God, asking him to show you the way out of sin and into the light of his freedom and his love. Prayer, Bible study, and strong support in a Christian church can help you to gain strength

1:32
u Ro 6:23

faithless, heartless, ruthless. [32]Although they know God's righteous decree that those who do such things deserve death, [u] they not only continue to do these very things but also approve of those who practice them.

God's Righteous Judgment

2:1
v Ro 1:20
w 2Sa 12:5-7;
Mt 7:1, 2

2 You, therefore, have no excuse, [v] you who pass judgment on someone else, for at whatever point you judge the other, you are condemning yourself, because you who pass judgment do the same things. [w] [2]Now we know that God's judgment against those who do such things is based on truth. [3]So when you, a mere man, pass judgment on them and yet do the same things, do you think you will escape God's judgment? [4]Or do you show contempt for the riches [x] of his kindness, tolerance [y] and patience, [z] not realizing that God's kindness leads you toward repentance? [a]

2:4
x Eph 1:7, 18
y Ro 3:25
z Ex 34:6
a 2Pe 3:9

[5]But because of your stubbornness and your unrepentant heart, you are storing up wrath against yourself for the day of God's wrath, when his righteous judgment will be revealed. [6]God "will give to each person according to what he has done." [a] [b] [7]To those who by persistence in doing good seek glory, honor and immortality, he will give eternal life. [8]But for those who are self-seeking and who reject the truth and follow evil, [c] there will be wrath and anger. [9]There will be trouble and distress for every human being who does evil: first for the Jew, then for the Gentile; [10]but glory, honor and peace for everyone who does good: first for the Jew, then for the Gentile. [d] [11]For God does not show favoritism. [e]

2:6
b Ps 62:12

2:8
c 2Th 2:12

2:10
d ver 9

2:11
e Ac 10:34

a 6 Psalm 62:12; Prov. 24:12

SALVATION'S FREEWAY
Verses in Romans that describe the way to salvation.

Romans 3:23	. . . .	Everyone has sinned.
Romans 6:23	. . . .	The penalty for our sin is death.
Romans 5:8	. . . .	Jesus Christ died for sin.
Romans 10:8–10	. . . .	To be forgiven for our sin, we must believe and confess that Jesus is Lord. Salvation comes through Jesus Christ.

---

to resist these powerful temptations. If you are already deeply involved in homosexual behavior, seek help from a trustworthy, professional, pastoral counselor.

1:32 How were these people aware of God's death penalty? Human beings, created in God's image, have a basic moral nature and a conscience. This truth is understood beyond religious circles. Psychologists, for example, say that the rare person who has no conscience has a serious personality disorder that is extremely difficult to treat. Most people instinctively know when they do wrong—but they may not care. Some people will even risk an early death for the freedom to indulge their desires now. "I know it's wrong, but I really want it," they say; or, "I know it's dangerous, but it's worth the risk." For such people, part of the "fun" is going against God's law, the community's moral standards, common sense, or their own sense of right and wrong. But deep down inside they know that sin deserves the punishment of death (6:23).

2:1 Whenever we find ourselves feeling justifiably angry about someone's sin, we should be careful. We need to speak out against sin, but we must do so in a spirit of humility. Often the sins we notice most clearly in others are the ones that have taken root in us. If we look closely at ourselves, we may find that we are committing the same sins in more socially acceptable forms. For example, a person who gossips may be very critical of others who gossip about him or her.

2:1ff When Paul's letter was read in the Roman church, no doubt many heads nodded as he condemned idol worshipers, homosexual practices, and violent people. But what surprise his listeners must have felt when he turned on them and said in effect, "You have no excuse. You are just as bad!" Paul was emphatically stressing that *nobody* is good enough to save himself or herself. If we want to avoid punishment and live eternally with Christ, all of us, whether we have been murderers and molesters or whether we have been honest, hardworking, solid citizens, must depend totally on God's grace. Paul is not discussing whether some sins are worse than others. Any sin is enough to lead us to depend on Jesus Christ for salvation and eternal life. We have all sinned repeatedly, and there is no way apart from Christ to be saved from sin's consequences.

2:4 In his kindness, God holds back his judgment, giving people time to repent. It is easy to mistake God's patience for approval of the wrong way we are living. Self-evaluation is difficult, and it is even more difficult to expose our conduct to God and let him tell us where we need to change. But as Christians we must pray constantly that God will point out our sins, so that he can heal them. Unfortunately, we are more likely to be amazed at God's patience with others than humbled at his patience with us.

2:5–11 Although God does not usually punish us immediately for sin, his eventual judgment is certain. We don't know exactly when it will happen, but we know that no one will escape that final encounter with the Creator. For more on judgment, see John 12:48 and Revelation 20:11–15.

2:7 Paul says that those who patiently and persistently *do* God's will find eternal life. He is not contradicting his previous statement that salvation comes by faith alone (1:16, 17). We are not saved by good deeds, but when we commit our lives fully to God, we want to please him and do his will. As such, our good deeds are a grateful *response* to what God has done, not a prerequisite to earning his grace.

¹²All who sin apart from the law will also perish apart from the law, and all who sin under the law*f* will be judged by the law. ¹³For it is not those who hear the law who are righteous in God's sight, but it is those who obey *g* the law who will be declared righteous. ¹⁴(Indeed, when Gentiles, who do not have the law, do by nature things required by the law, they are a law for themselves, even though they do not have the law, ¹⁵since they show that the requirements of the law are written on their hearts, their consciences also bearing witness, and their thoughts now accusing, now even defending them.) ¹⁶This will take place on the day when God will judge men's secrets through Jesus Christ,*h* as my gospel declares.

The Jews and the Law

¹⁷Now you, if you call yourself a Jew; if you rely on the law and brag about your relationship to God; *i* ¹⁸if you know his will and approve of what is superior because you are instructed by the law; ¹⁹if you are convinced that you are a guide for the blind, a light for those who are in the dark, ²⁰an instructor of the foolish, a teacher of infants, because you have in the law the embodiment of knowledge and truth— ²¹you, then, who teach others, do you not teach yourself? You who preach against stealing, do you steal? *j* ²²You who say that people should not commit adultery, do you commit adultery? You who abhor idols, do you rob temples? ²³You who brag about the law,*k* do you dishonor God by breaking the law? ²⁴As it is written: "God's name is blasphemed among the Gentiles because of you."*a l*

²⁵Circumcision has value if you observe the law,*m* but if you break the law, you have become as though you had not been circumcised. ²⁶If those who are not circumcised keep the law's requirements,*n* will they not be regarded as though they were circumcised? ²⁷The one who is not circumcised physically and yet obeys the law will condemn you *o* who, even though you have the*b* written code and circumcision, are a lawbreaker.

²⁸A man is not a Jew if he is only one outwardly,*p* nor is circumcision merely outward and physical.*q* ²⁹No, a man is a Jew if he is one inwardly; and circumcision is circumcision of the heart, by the Spirit, not by the written code. Such a man's praise is not from men, but from God.*r*

a24 Isaiah 52:5; Ezek. 36:22   *b27* Or *who, by means of a*

2:12
f 1Co 9:20, 21
2:13
g Jas 1:22, 23, 25

2:16
h Ac 10:42

2:17
i Mic 3:11

2:21
j Mt 23:3, 4

2:23
k ver 17
2:24
l Isa 52:5
2:25
m Gal 5:3
2:26
n Ro 8:4
2:27
o Mt 12:41, 42
2:28
p Jn 8:39
q Gal 6:15
2:29
r 2Co 10:18

2:12-15 People are condemned not for what they don't know, but for what they do with what they know. Those who know God's written Word and his law will be judged by them. Those who have never seen a Bible still know right from wrong, and they will be judged because they did not keep even those standards that their own consciences dictated. Our modern-day sense of fair play and the rights of the individual often balks at God's judgment. But keep in mind that people violate the very standards they create for themselves.

2:12-15 If you traveled around the world, you would find evidence in every society and culture of God's moral law. For example, all cultures prohibit murder, and yet in all societies that law has been broken. We belong to a stubborn race. We know what's right, but we insist on doing what's wrong. It is not enough to know what's right; we must also do it. Admit to yourself and to God that you fit the human pattern and frequently fail to live up to your own standards (much more to God's standards). That's the first step to forgiveness and healing.

2:17ff Paul continues to argue that all stand guilty before God. After describing the fate of the unbelieving, pagan Gentiles, he moves to that of the religiously privileged. Despite their knowledge of God's will, they are guilty because they too have refused to live by their beliefs. Those of us who have grown up in Christian families are the religiously privileged of today. Paul's condemnation applies to us if we do not live up to what we know.

2:21, 22 Paul explained to the Jews that they needed to teach *themselves*, not others, by their law. They knew the law so well that they had learned how to excuse their own actions while criticizing others. But the law is more than legalistic minimum requirements—it is a guideline for living according to God's will. It is also a reminder that we cannot please God without a proper relationship to him. As Jesus pointed out, even withholding what rightfully belongs to someone else is stealing (Mark 7:9-13), and

looking on another person with lustful, adulterous intent is adultery (Matthew 5:27, 28). Before we accuse others, we must look at ourselves and see if that sin, in any form, exists within us.

2:21-27 These verses are a scathing criticism of hypocrisy. It is much easier to tell others how to behave than to behave properly ourselves. It is easier to say the right words than to allow them to take root in our lives. Do you ever advise others to do something you are unwilling to do yourself? Make sure that your actions match your words.

2:24 If you claim to be one of God's people, your life should reflect what God is like. When you disobey God, you dishonor his name. People may even blaspheme or profane God's name because of you. What do people think about God from watching your life?

2:25-29 *Circumcision* refers to the sign of God's special covenant with his people. Submitting to this rite was required for all Jewish males (Genesis 17:9-14). According to Paul, being a Jew (being circumcised) meant nothing if the person didn't obey God's laws. On the other hand, the Gentiles (the uncircumcised) would receive God's love and approval if they kept the law's requirements. Paul goes on to explain that a real Jew (one who pleases God) is not someone who has been circumcised (a Jew "outwardly") but someone whose heart is right with God and obeys him (a Jew "inwardly").

2:28, 29 To be a Jew meant you were in God's family, an heir to all his promises. Yet Paul made it clear that membership in God's family is based on internal, not external, qualities. All whose hearts are right with God are real Jews—that is, part of God's family (see also Galatians 3:7). Attending church or being baptized, confirmed, or accepted for membership is not enough, just as submitting to circumcision was not enough for the Jews. God desires our heartfelt devotion and obedience. (See also Deuteronomy 10:16; Jeremiah 4:4 for more on "circumcision of the heart.")

God's Faithfulness

3:2
sDt 4:8; Ps 147:19

3:3
tHeb 4:2

3:4
uPs 51:4

3 What advantage, then, is there in being a Jew, or what value is there in circumcision? ²Much in every way! First of all, they have been entrusted with the very words of God.s ³What if some did not have faith?t Will their lack of faith nullify God's faithfulness? ⁴Not at all! Let God be true, and every man a liar. As it is written:

> "So that you may be proved right when you speak
> and prevail when you judge."a u

3:5
vGal 3:15

3:6
wGe 18:25

⁵But if our unrighteousness brings out God's righteousness more clearly, what shall we say? That God is unjust in bringing his wrath on us? (I am using a human argument.)v ⁶Certainly not! If that were so, how could God judge the world?w ⁷Someone might argue, "If my falsehood enhances God's truthfulness and so increases his glory, why am I still condemned as a sinner?" ⁸Why not say—as we are being slanderously reported as saying and as some claim that we say—"Let us do evil that good may result"? Their condemnation is deserved.

No One Is Righteous

3:9
xGal 3:22

⁹What shall we conclude then? Are we any betterb? Not at all! We have already made the charge that Jews and Gentiles alike are all under sin.x ¹⁰As it is written:

a4 Psalm 51:4   b9 Or *worse*

CRUCIAL CONCEPTS IN ROMANS		
	ELECTION............. Romans 9:10–13	God's choice of an individual or group for a specific purpose or destiny.
	JUSTIFICATION.......... Romans 4:25; 5:18	God's act of declaring us "not guilty" for our sins, making us "right" with him.
	PROPITIATION........... Romans 3:25	The removal of God's punishment for sin through the perfect sacrifice of Jesus Christ.
	REDEMPTION............ Romans 3:24; 8:23	Jesus Christ has paid the price so we can go free. The price of sin is death; Jesus paid the price.
	SANCTIFICATION........ Romans 5:2; 15:16	Becoming more and more like Jesus Christ through the work of the Holy Spirit.
	GLORIFICATION.......... Romans 8:18, 19, 30	The ultimate state of the believer after death when he or she becomes like Christ (1 John 3:2).

3:1ff In this chapter Paul contends that everyone stands guilty before God. Paul has dismantled the common excuses of people who refuse to admit they are sinners: (1) "There is no God" or "I follow my conscience"—1:18–32; (2) "I'm not as bad as other people"—2:1–16; (3) "I'm a church member" or "I'm a religious person"—2:17–29. No one will be exempt from God's judgment on sin. Every person must accept that he or she is sinful and condemned before God. Only then can we understand and receive God's wonderful gift of salvation.

3:1ff What a depressing picture Paul is painting! All of us—pagan Gentiles, humanitarians, and religious people—are condemned by our own actions. The law, which God gave to show the way to live, holds up our evil deeds to public view. Is there any hope for us? Yes, says Paul. The law condemns us, it is true, but the law is not the basis of our hope. God himself is. He, in his righteousness and wonderful love, offers us eternal life. We receive our salvation not through law but through faith in Jesus Christ. We do not—cannot—earn it; we accept it as a gift from our loving heavenly Father.

3:2 The Jewish nation had many advantages. (1) They were entrusted with God's laws ("the very words of God," Exodus 19, 20; Deuteronomy 4:8). (2) They were the race through whom the Messiah came to earth (Isaiah 11:1–10; Matthew 1:1–17). (3) They were the beneficiaries of covenants with God himself (Genesis 17:1–16; Exodus 19:3–6). But these privileges did not make them better than anyone else (see 3:9). In fact, because of them the Jews were even more responsible to live up to God's requirements.

3:5–8 Some may think they don't have to worry about sin because (1) it's God's job to forgive; (2) God is so loving that he won't judge us; (3) sin isn't so bad—it teaches us valuable lessons, or (4) we need to stay in touch with the culture around us. It is far too easy to take God's grace for granted. But God cannot overlook sin. Sinners, no matter how many excuses they make, will have to answer to God for their sin.

3:10–12 Paul is referring to Psalm 14:1–3. "There is no one righteous" means "no one is innocent." Every person is valuable in God's eyes because God created us in his image and he loves us. But no one is righteous (that is, no one can earn right standing with God). Though valuable, we have fallen into sin. But God, through Jesus his Son, has redeemed us and offers to forgive us if we return to him in faith.

3:10–18 Paul uses these Old Testament references to show that humanity in general, in its present sinful condition, is unacceptable before God. Have you ever thought to yourself, "Well, I'm not too bad. I'm a pretty good person"? Look at these verses and see if any of them apply to you. Have you ever lied? Have you ever hurt someone's feelings by your words or tone of voice? Are you bitter toward anyone? Do you become angry with those who strongly disagree with you? In thought, word, and deed, you, like everyone else in the world, stand guilty before God. We must remember who we are in his sight—alienated sinners. Don't deny that you are a sinner. Instead, allow your desperate need to point you toward Christ.

> "There is no one righteous, not even one;
> 11　　there is no one who understands,
> 　　　　no one who seeks God.
> 12　All have turned away,
> 　　　　they have together become worthless;
> 　　there is no one who does good,
> 　　　　not even one."^a
> 13　"Their throats are open graves;
> 　　　　their tongues practice deceit."^{b y}
> 　　"The poison of vipers is on their lips."^c
> 14　　"Their mouths are full of cursing and bitterness."^{d z}
> 15　"Their feet are swift to shed blood;
> 16　　ruin and misery mark their ways,
> 17　and the way of peace they do not know."^e
> 18　　"There is no fear of God before their eyes."^{f a}

¹⁹Now we know that whatever the law says,^b it says to those who are under the law, so that every mouth may be silenced and the whole world held accountable to God. ²⁰Therefore no one will be declared righteous in his sight by observing the law;^c rather, through the law we become conscious of sin.^d

3:13
^yPs 5:9

3:14
^zPs 10:7

3:18
^aPs 36:1

3:19
^bJn 10:34

3:20
^cAc 13:39; Gal 2:16
^dRo 7:7

2. Forgiveness of sin through Christ

Righteousness Through Faith

²¹But now a righteousness from God,^e apart from law, has been made known, to which the Law and the Prophets testify. ²²This righteousness from God comes through faith in Jesus Christ to all who believe. There is no difference,^f ²³for all have sinned and fall short of the glory of God, ²⁴and are justified freely by his grace^g through the redemption that came by Christ Jesus. ²⁵God presented him as a sacrifice of atonement, ^g through faith in his blood.^h He did this to demonstrate his justice, because in his forbearance he had left the sins committed beforehand unpunished— ²⁶he did it to demonstrate his justice at the present time, so as to be just and the one who justifies those who have faith in Jesus.

3:21
^eRo 1:17

3:22
^fRo 10:12; Gal 3:28

3:24
^gRo 4:16

3:25
^hHeb 9:12, 14

^a*12* Psalms 14:1-3; 53:1-3; Eccles. 7:20 　^b*13* Psalm 5:9 　^c*13* Psalm 140:3 　^d*14* Psalm 10:7 　^e*17* Isaiah 59:7,8
^f*18* Psalm 36:1 　^g*25* Or *as the one who would turn aside his wrath, taking away sin*

3:19 The last time someone accused you of wrongdoing, what was your reaction? Denial, argument, and defensiveness? The Bible tells us the world stands silent and accountable before Almighty God. No excuses or arguments are left. Have you reached the point with God where you are ready to hang up your defenses and await his decision? If you haven't, stop now and admit your sin to him. If you have, the following verses are truly good news for you!

3:20, 31 In these verses we see two functions of God's law. First, it shows us where we go wrong. Because of the law, we know that we are helpless sinners and that we must come to Jesus Christ for mercy. Second, the moral code revealed in the law can serve to guide our actions by holding up God's moral standards. We do not earn salvation by keeping the law (no one except Christ ever kept or could keep God's law perfectly), but we do please God when our lives conform to his revealed will for us.

3:21–29 After all this bad news about our sinfulness and God's condemnation, Paul gives the wonderful news. There is a way to be declared not guilty—by trusting Jesus Christ to take away our sins. Trusting means putting our confidence in Christ to forgive our sins, to make us right with God, and to empower us to live the way he taught us. God's solution is available to all of us regardless of our background or past behavior.

3:23 Some sins seem bigger than others because their obvious consequences are much more serious. Murder, for example, seems to us to be worse than hatred, and adultery seems worse than lust. But this does not mean that because we do lesser sins we deserve eternal life. All sin makes us sinners, and all sin cuts us off from our holy God. All sin, therefore, leads to death (because it disqualifies us from living with God), regardless of how great or small it

seems. Don't minimize "little" sins or overrate "big" sins. They all separate us from God, but they all can be forgiven.

3:24 *Justified* means to be declared not guilty. When a judge in a court of law declares the defendant not guilty, all the charges are removed from his record. Legally, it is as if the person had never been accused. When God forgives our sins, our record is wiped clean. From his perspective, it is as though we had never sinned.

3:24 Redemption refers to Christ setting sinners free from slavery to sin. In Old Testament times, a person's debts could result in his being sold as a slave. The next of kin could redeem him—buy his freedom. Christ purchased our freedom and the price was his life.

3:25 Christ is our sacrifice of atonement. In other words, he died in our place, for our sins. God is justifiably angry at sinners. They have rebelled against him and cut themselves off from his life-giving power. But God declares Christ's death to be the appropriate, designated sacrifice for our sin. Christ then stands in our place, having paid the penalty of death for our sin, and he completely satisfies God's demands. His sacrifice brings pardon, deliverance, and freedom.

3:25 What happened to people who lived before Christ came and died for sin? If God condemned them, was he being unfair? If he saved them, was Christ's sacrifice unnecessary? Paul shows that God forgave all human sin at the cross of Jesus. Old Testament believers looked forward in faith to Christ's coming and were saved, even though they did not know Jesus' name or the details of his earthly life. Unlike the Old Testament believers, you know about the God who loved the world so much that he gave his own Son (John 3:16). Have you put your trust in him?

3:27
i Ro 2:17, 23;
1Co 1:29-31

3:30
j Gal 3:8

4:3
k Ge 15:6; Gal 3:6;
Jas 2:23

4:4
l Ro 11:6

27 Where, then, is boasting? *i* It is excluded. On what principle? On that of observing the law? No, but on that of faith. 28 For we maintain that a man is justified by faith apart from observing the law. 29 Is God the God of Jews only? Is he not the God of Gentiles too? Yes, of Gentiles too, 30 since there is only one God, who will justify the circumcised by faith and the uncircumcised through that same faith. *j* 31 Do we, then, nullify the law by this faith? Not at all! Rather, we uphold the law.

Abraham Justified by Faith

4 What then shall we say that Abraham, our forefather, discovered in this matter? 2 If, in fact, Abraham was justified by works, he had something to boast about—but not before God. 3 What does the Scripture say? "Abraham believed God, and it was credited to him as righteousness." *a* *k*

4 Now when a man works, his wages are not credited to him as a gift, *l* but as an obligation. 5 However, to the man who does not work but trusts God who justifies the wicked, his faith is credited as righteousness. 6 David says the same thing when he speaks of the blessedness of the man to whom God credits righteousness apart from works:

7 "Blessed are they
  whose transgressions are forgiven,
  whose sins are covered.
8 Blessed is the man
  whose sin the Lord will never count against him." *b*

9 Is this blessedness only for the circumcised, or also for the uncircumcised? We have been saying that Abraham's faith was credited to him as righteousness. 10 Under what

a 3 Gen. 15:6; also in verse 22 *b* 8 Psalm 32:1,2

3:27, 28 Most religions prescribe specific duties that must be performed to make a person acceptable to a god. Christianity is unique in teaching that the good deeds we do will not make us right with God. No amount of human achievement or progress in personal development will close the gap between God's moral perfection and our imperfect daily performance. Good deeds are important, but they will not earn us eternal life. We are saved only by trusting in what God has done for us (see Ephesians 2:8–10).

3:28 Why does God save us by faith alone? (1) Faith eliminates the pride of human effort, because faith is not a deed that we do. (2) Faith exalts what God has done, not what people do. (3) Faith admits that we can't keep the law or measure up to God's standards—we need help. (4) Faith is based on our relationship with God, not our performance for God.

3:31 There were some misunderstandings between the Jewish and Gentile Christians in Rome. Worried Jewish Christians were asking Paul, "Does faith wipe out everything Judaism stands for? Does it cancel our Scriptures, put an end to our customs, declare that God is no longer working through us?" (This is essentially the question used to open chapter 3.) "Absolutely not!" says Paul. When we understand the way of salvation through faith, we understand the Jewish religion better. We know why Abraham was chosen, why the law was given, why God worked patiently with Israel for centuries. Faith does not wipe out the Old Testament. Rather, it makes God's dealings with the Jewish people understandable. In chapter 4, Paul will expand on this theme (see 5:20, 21; 8:3, 4; 13:9, 10; Galatians 3:24–29; and 1 Timothy 1:8 for more on this concept).

4:1–3 The Jews were proud to be called children of Abraham. Paul uses Abraham as a good example of someone who was saved by faith. By emphasizing faith, Paul is not saying that God's laws are unimportant (4:13) but that it is impossible to be saved simply by obeying them. For more about Abraham, see his Profile in Genesis 18.

4:4 This verse means that if a person could earn right standing with God by being good, the granting of that gift wouldn't be a free act; it would be an obligation. Our self-reliance is futile; all we can do is cast ourselves on God's mercy and grace.

4:5 When some people learn that they are saved by God through faith, they start to worry. "Do I have enough faith?" they wonder, "Is my faith strong enough to save me?" These people miss the point. It is Jesus Christ who saves us, not *our* feelings or actions, and he is strong enough to save us no matter how weak our faith is. Jesus offers us salvation as a gift because he loves us, not because we have earned it through our powerful faith. What, then, is the role of faith? Faith is believing and trusting in Jesus Christ, and reaching out to accept his wonderful gift of salvation.

4:6–8 What can we do to get rid of guilt? King David was guilty of terrible sins—adultery, murder, lying—and yet he experienced the joy of forgiveness. We too can have this joy when we (1) quit denying our guilt and recognize that we have sinned, (2) admit our guilt to God and ask for his forgiveness, and (3) let go of our guilt and believe that God has forgiven us. This can be difficult when a sin has taken root and grown over many years, when it is very serious, or when it involves others. We must remember that Jesus is willing and able to forgive every sin. In view of the tremendous price he paid on the cross, it is arrogant to think that any of our sins are too great for him to cover. Even though our faith is weak, our conscience is sensitive, and our memory haunts us, God's Word declares that sins confessed are sins forgiven (1 John 1:9).

4:10 Circumcision was a sign to others and a personal seal or certification for the Jews that they were God's special people. Circumcision of all Jewish boys set the Jewish people apart from the nations who worshiped other gods; thus it was a very important ceremony. God gave the blessing and the command for this ceremony to Abraham (Genesis 17:9–14).

4:10–12 Rituals did not earn any reward for Abraham; he had been blessed long before the circumcision ceremony was introduced. Abraham found favor with God by faith alone, before he was circumcised. Genesis 12:1–4 tells of God's call to Abraham when he was 75 years old; the circumcision ceremony was introduced when he was 99 (Genesis 17:1–14). Ceremonies and rituals serve as reminders of our faith, and they instruct new and younger believers. But we should not think that they give us any special merit before God. They are outward signs and seals that demonstrate inward belief and trust. The focus of our faith should be on Christ and his saving actions, not on our own actions.

circumstances was it credited? Was it after he was circumcised, or before? It was not after, but before! [11]And he received the sign of circumcision, a seal of the righteousness that he had by faith while he was still uncircumcised. *m* So then, he is the father *n* of all who believe but have not been circumcised, in order that righteousness might be credited to them. [12]And he is also the father of the circumcised who not only are circumcised but who also walk in the footsteps of the faith that our father Abraham had before he was circumcised.

[13]It was not through law that Abraham and his offspring received the promise that he would be heir of the world, *o* but through the righteousness that comes by faith. [14]For if those who live by law are heirs, faith has no value and the promise is worthless,*p* [15]because law brings wrath. *q* And where there is no law there is no transgression. *r*

[16]Therefore, the promise comes by faith, so that it may be by grace *s* and may be guaranteed to all Abraham's offspring—not only to those who are of the law but also to those who are of the faith of Abraham. He is the father of us all. [17]As it is written: "I have made you a father of many nations."*a t* He is our father in the sight of God, in whom he believed—the God who gives life to the dead and calls things that are not *u* as though they were.

[18]Against all hope, Abraham in hope believed and so became the father of many nations, just as it had been said to him, "So shall your offspring be."*b v* [19]Without weakening in his faith, he faced the fact that his body was as good as dead *w*—since he was about a hundred years old *x*—and that Sarah's womb was also dead. [20]Yet he did not waver through unbelief regarding the promise of God, but was strengthened in his faith and gave glory to God, [21]being fully persuaded that God had power to do what he had promised. *y* [22]This is why "it was credited to him as righteousness." [23]The words "it was credited to him" were written not for him alone, [24]but also for us,*z* to whom God will credit righteousness—for us who believe in him who raised Jesus our Lord from the dead. *a* [25]He was delivered over to death for our sins and was raised to life for our justification.

Peace and Joy

5 Therefore, since we have been justified through faith, we*c* have peace with God through our Lord Jesus Christ, [2]through whom we have gained access *b* by faith into this grace in which we now stand. *c* And we*c* rejoice in the hope of the glory of God. [3]Not only so, but we*c*

a 17 Gen. 17:5   *b 18* Gen. 15:5   *c 1,2,3* Or *let us*

**Cross references (right margin):**

4:11
m Ge 17:10, 11
n Lk 19:9

4:13
o Ge 17:4-6

4:14
p Gal 3:18

4:15
q Gal 3:10
r Ro 3:20

4:16
s Ro 3:24

4:17
t Ge 17:5
u 1Co 1:28

4:18
v Ge 15:5

4:19
w Heb 11:11, 12
x Ge 17:17

4:21
y Heb 11:19

4:24
z Ro 15:4
a Ac 2:24

5:2
b Eph 2:18
c 1Co 15:1

4:16 Paul explains that Abraham had pleased God through Abraham's faith alone, before he had ever heard about the rituals that would become so important to the Jewish people. We too are saved by faith plus nothing. It is not by loving God and doing good that we are saved; neither is it by faith plus love or by faith plus good deeds. We are saved only through faith in Christ, trusting him to forgive all our sins. For more on Abraham, see his Profile in Genesis 17.

4:17 The promise (or covenant) God gave Abraham stated that Abraham would be the father of many nations (Genesis 17:2–4) and that the entire world would be blessed through him (Genesis 12:3). This promise was fulfilled in Jesus Christ. Jesus was from Abraham's line, and truly the whole world was blessed through him.

4:21 Abraham never doubted that God would fulfill his promise. Abraham's life was marked by mistakes, sins, and failures as well as by wisdom and goodness, but he consistently trusted God. His faith was strengthened by the obstacles he faced, and his life was an example of faith in action. If he had looked only at his own resources for subduing Canaan and founding a nation, he would have given up in despair. But Abraham looked to God, obeyed him, and waited for God to fulfill his word.

4:25 When we believe, an exchange takes place. We give Christ our sins, and he gives us his righteousness and forgiveness (see 2 Corinthians 5:21). There is nothing we can do to earn this. Only through Christ can we receive God's righteousness. What an incredible bargain this is for us! But sadly, many still choose to pass up this gift to continue "enjoying" their sin.

5:1 We are now at peace *with God*, which may differ from peaceful feelings such as calmness and tranquility. Peace with God means that we have been reconciled with him. There is no more

hostility between us, no sin blocking our relationship with him. Peace with God is possible only because Jesus paid the price for our sins through his death on the cross.

5:1-5 These verses introduce a section that contains some difficult concepts. To understand the next four chapters, it helps to keep in mind the two-sided reality of the Christian life. On the one hand, we are complete in Christ (our acceptance with him is secure). On the other hand, we are growing in Christ (we are becoming more and more like him). At one and the same time we have the status of kings and the duties of slaves. We feel both the presence of Christ and the pressure of sin. We enjoy the peace that comes from being made right with God, but we still face daily problems that often help us grow. If we remember these two sides of the Christian life, we will not grow discouraged as we face temptations and problems. Instead, we will learn to depend on the power available to us from Christ, who lives in us by the Holy Spirit.

5:2 Paul states that, as believers, we now stand in a place of highest privilege ("this grace in which we now stand"). Not only has God declared us not guilty; he has drawn us close to himself. Instead of being enemies, we have become his friends—in fact, his own children (John 15:15; Galatians 4:5).

5:2-5 As Paul states clearly in 1 Corinthians 13:13, faith, hope, and love are at the heart of the Christian life. Our relationship with God begins with *faith*, which helps us realize that we are delivered from our past by Christ's death. *Hope* grows as we learn all that God has in mind for us; it gives us the promise of the future. And God's *love* fills our lives and gives us the ability to reach out to others.

5:3, 4 For first-century Christians, suffering was the rule rather than the exception. Paul tells us that in the future we will *become*,

5:3
d Jas 1:2, 3

also rejoice in our sufferings, because we know that suffering produces perseverance; *d* ⁴perseverance, character; and character, hope. ⁵And hope does not disappoint us, because God has poured out his love into our hearts by the Holy Spirit, whom he has given us.

5:6
e Ro 4:25

5:8
f Jn 15:13

⁶You see, at just the right time, when we were still powerless, Christ died for the ungodly. *e* ⁷Very rarely will anyone die for a righteous man, though for a good man someone might possibly dare to die. ⁸But God demonstrates his own love for us in this: While we were still sinners, Christ died for us. *f*

5:9
g Ro 3:25

5:10
h Ro 11:28
i 2Co 5:18, 19

⁹Since we have now been justified by his blood, *g* how much more shall we be saved from God's wrath through him! ¹⁰For if, when we were God's enemies, *h* we were reconciled *i* to him through the death of his Son, how much more, having been reconciled, shall we be saved through his life! ¹¹Not only is this so, but we also rejoice in God through our Lord Jesus Christ, through whom we have now received reconciliation.

Death Through Adam, Life Through Christ

5:12
j 1Co 15:21, 22
k Ge 2:17

5:13
l Ro 4:15

5:14
m 1Co 15:22, 45

¹²Therefore, just as sin entered the world through one man, *j* and death through sin, *k* and in this way death came to all men, because all sinned— ¹³for before the law was given, sin was in the world. But sin is not taken into account when there is no law. *l* ¹⁴Nevertheless, death reigned from the time of Adam to the time of Moses, even over those who did not sin by breaking a command, as did Adam, who was a pattern of the one to come. *m*

WHAT WE HAVE AS GOD'S CHILDREN

What we have as Adam's children	What we have as God's children
Ruin 5:9	Rescue 5:8
Sin 5:12, 15, 21	Righteousness 5:18
Death 5:12, 16, 21	Eternal life 5:17, 21
Separation from God 5:18	Relationship with God 5:11, 19
Disobedience 5:12, 19	Obedience 5:19
Judgment 5:18	Deliverance 5:10, 11
Law 5:20	Grace 5:20

---

but until then we must *overcome.* This means we will experience difficulties that help us grow. We rejoice in suffering not because we like pain or deny its tragedy, but because we know God is using life's difficulties and Satan's attacks to build our character. The problems that we run into will develop our perseverance— which in turn will strengthen our character, deepen our trust in God, and give us greater confidence about the future. You probably find your patience tested in some way every day. Thank God for those opportunities to grow, and deal with them in his strength (see also James 1:2–4; 1 Peter 1:6, 7).

5:5, 6 All three members of the Trinity are involved in salvation. The Father loved us so much that he sent his Son to bridge the gap between us (John 3:16). The Father and the Son send the Holy Spirit to fill our lives with love and to enable us to live by his power (Acts 1:8). With all this loving care, how can we do less than serve him completely!

5:6 We were weak and helpless because we could do nothing on our own to save ourselves. Someone had to come and rescue us. Not only did Christ come at a good time in history; he came at exactly the right time—according to God's own schedule. God controls all history, and he controlled the timing, methods, and results of Jesus' death.

5:8 "While we were still sinners"—these are amazing words. God sent Jesus Christ to die for us, not because we were good enough, but because he loved us. Whenever you feel uncertain about God's love for you, remember that he loved you even before you turned to him. If God loved you when you were a rebel, he can surely strengthen you, now that you love him in return.

5:9, 10 The love that caused Christ to die is the same love that sends the Holy Spirit to live in us and guide us every day. The power that raised Christ from the dead is the same power that saved you and is available to you in your daily life. Be assured

that, having begun a life with Christ, you have a reserve of power and love to call on each day, for help to meet every challenge or trial. You can pray for God's power and love as you need it.

5:11 God is holy, and he will not be associated with sin. All people are sinful and so they are separated from God. In addition, all sin deserves punishment. Instead of punishing us with the death we deserve, however, Christ took our sins upon himself and took our punishment by dying on the cross. Now we can "rejoice in God." Through faith in *Christ's* work, we become close to God (reconciled) rather than being enemies and outcasts.

5:12 How can we be declared guilty for something Adam did thousands of years ago? Many feel it isn't right for God to judge us because of Adam's sin. Yet each of us confirms our solidarity with Adam by our own sins each day. We are made of the same stuff and are prone to rebel, and we are judged for the sins *we* commit. Because we are sinners, it isn't fairness we need—it's mercy.

5:13, 14 Paul has shown that keeping the law does not bring salvation. Here he adds that breaking the law is not what brings death. Death is the result of Adam's sin and of the sins we all commit, even if they don't resemble Adam's. Paul reminds his readers that for thousands of years the law had not yet been explicitly given, and yet people died. The law was added, he explains in 5:20, to help people see their sinfulness, to show them the seriousness of their offenses, and to drive them to God for mercy and pardon. This was true in Moses' day, and it is still true today. Sin is a deep discrepancy between who we are and who we were created to be. The law points out our sin and places the responsibility for it squarely on our shoulders. But the law offers no remedy. When we are convicted of sin, we must turn to Jesus Christ for healing.

5:14 Adam is a *pattern;* he is the counterpart of Christ. Just as Adam was a representative of created humanity, so is Christ the representative of a new spiritual humanity.

15But the gift is not like the trespass. For if the many died by the trespass of the one man, how much more did God's grace and the gift that came by the grace of the one man, Jesus Christ,n overflow to the many! 16Again, the gift of God is not like the result of the one man's sin: The judgment followed one sin and brought condemnation, but the gift followed many trespasses and brought justification. 17For if, by the trespass of the one man, death reigned through that one man, how much more will those who receive God's abundant provision of grace and of the gift of righteousness reign in life through the one man, Jesus Christ.

18Consequently, just as the result of one trespass was condemnation for all men, so also the result of one act of righteousness was justification o that brings life for all men. 19For just as through the disobedience of the one man the many were made sinners, so also through the obedience of the one man the many will be made righteous.

20The law was added so that the trespass might increase.p But where sin increased, grace increased all the more, q 21so that, just as sin reigned in death, so also grace might reign through righteousness to bring eternal life through Jesus Christ our Lord.

3. Freedom from sin's grasp
Dead to Sin, Alive in Christ

6 What shall we say, then? Shall we go on sinning so that grace may increase?r 2By no means! We died to sin;s how can we live in it any longer? 3Or don't you know that all of us who were baptized into Christ Jesus were baptized into his death? 4We were therefore buried with him through baptism into death in order that, just as Christ was raised from the dead t through the glory of the Father, we too may live a new life. u

5If we have been united with him like this in his death, we will certainly also be united with him in his resurrection. 6For we know that our old self was crucified with him v so that the body of sin w might be done away with,a that we should no longer be slaves to sin— 7because anyone who has died has been freed from sin.

a6 Or *be rendered powerless*

5:15
nAc 15:11

5:18
oRo 4:25

5:20
pGal 3:19
q1Ti 1:13, 14

6:1
rRo 3:5, 8

6:2
sCol 3:3, 5;
1Pe 2:24

6:4
tCol 2:12
uGal 6:15; Col 3:10

6:6
vGal 2:20
wRo 7:24

5:15–19 We were all born into Adam's physical family—the family line that leads to certain death. All of us have reaped the results of Adam's sin. We have inherited his guilt, a sinful nature (the tendency to sin), and God's punishment. Because of Jesus, however, we can trade judgment for forgiveness. We can trade our sin for Jesus' righteousness. Christ offers us the opportunity to be born into his spiritual family—the family line that begins with forgiveness and leads to eternal life. If we do nothing, we have death through Adam; but if we come to God by faith, we have life through Christ. Which family line do you now belong to?

5:20 As a sinner, separated from God, you see his law from below, as a ladder to be climbed to get to God. Perhaps you have repeatedly tried to climb it, only to fall to the ground every time you have advanced one or two rungs. Or perhaps the sheer height of the ladder seems so overwhelming that you have never even started up. In either case, what relief you should feel to see Jesus offering with open arms to lift you above the ladder of the law, to take you directly to God! Once Jesus lifts you into God's presence, you are free to obey—out of love, not necessity, and through God's power, not your own. You know that if you stumble, you will not fall back to the ground. Instead, you will be caught and held in Christ's loving arms.

6:1—8:39 This section deals with *sanctification*—the change God makes in our lives as we grow in the faith. Chapter 6 explains that believers are free from sin's control. Chapter 7 discusses the continuing struggle believers have with sin. Chapter 8 describes how we can have victory over sin.

6:1, 2 If God loves to forgive, why not give him more to forgive? If forgiveness is guaranteed, do we have the freedom to sin as much as we want? Paul's forceful answer is *By no means!* Such an attitude—deciding ahead of time to take advantage of God—shows that a person does not understand the seriousness of sin. God's forgiveness does not make sin less serious; his Son's death for sin shows us the dreadful serious-

ness of sin. Jesus paid with his life so we could be forgiven. The availability of God's mercy must not become an excuse for careless living and moral laxness.

6:1–4 In the church of Paul's day, immersion was the usual form of baptism—that is, new Christians were completely "buried" in water. They understood this form of baptism to symbolize the death and burial of the old way of life. Coming up out of the water symbolized resurrection to new life with Christ. If we think of our old, sinful life as dead and buried, we have a powerful motive to resist sin. We can consciously choose to treat the desires and temptations of the old nature as if they were dead. Then we can continue to enjoy our wonderful new life with Jesus (see Galatians 3:27 and Colossians 2:12 and 3:1–4 for more on this concept).

6:5ff We can enjoy our new life in Christ because we are united with him in his death and resurrection. Our evil desires, our bondage to sin, and our love of sin died with him. Now, united by faith with him in his resurrection life, we have unbroken fellowship with God and freedom from sin's hold on us. For more on the difference between our new life in Christ and our old sinful nature, read Ephesians 4:21–24 and Colossians 3:3–15.

6:6 The power and penalty of sin died with Christ on the cross. Our "old self," our sinful nature, died once and for all, so we are freed from its power. The "body of sin" is not the human body, but our rebellious sin-loving nature inherited from Adam. Though our body willingly cooperates with our sinful nature, we must not regard the body as evil. It is the sin in us that is evil. And it is this power of sin at work in our body that is defeated. Paul has already stated that through faith in Christ we stand acquitted, "not guilty" before God. Here Paul emphasizes that we need no longer live under sin's power. God does not take us out of the world or make us robots—we will still feel like sinning, and sometimes we will sin. The difference is that before we were saved we were slaves to our sinful nature, but now we can choose to live for Christ (see Galatians 2:20).

6:9
x Rev 1:18

⁸ Now if we died with Christ, we believe that we will also live with him. ⁹ For we know that since Christ was raised from the dead, he cannot die again; death no longer has mastery over him. x ¹⁰ The death he died, he died to sin once for all; but the life he lives, he lives to God.

¹¹ In the same way, count yourselves dead to sin but alive to God in Christ Jesus. ¹² Therefore do not let sin reign in your mortal body so that you obey its evil desires. ¹³ Do not offer the parts of your body to sin, as instruments of wickedness, y but rather offer yourselves to God, as those who have been brought from death to life; and offer the parts of your body to him as instruments of righteousness. z ¹⁴ For sin shall not be your master, because you are not under law, a but under grace. b

6:13
y Ro 7:5
z Ro 12:1
6:14
a Gal 5:18
b Ro 3:24

Slaves to Righteousness

¹⁵ What then? Shall we sin because we are not under law but under grace? By no means! ¹⁶ Don't you know that when you offer yourselves to someone to obey him as slaves, you are slaves to the one whom you obey—whether you are slaves to sin, c which leads to death, or to obedience, which leads to righteousness? ¹⁷ But thanks be to God that, though you used to be slaves to sin, you wholeheartedly obeyed the form of teaching d to which you were entrusted. ¹⁸ You have been set free from sin e and have become slaves to righteousness.

6:16
c Jn 8:34; 2Pe 2:19
6:17
d 2Ti 1:13
6:18
e Ro 8:2

WHAT HAS GOD DONE ABOUT SIN?	He has given us		Principle	Importance
	New life	6:2, 3	Sin's power is broken.	We can be certain that sin's power is broken.
		6:4	Sin-loving nature is buried.	
		6:6	You are no longer under sin's control.	
	New nature	6:5	Now you share his new life.	We can see ourselves as unresponsive to the old power and alive to the new.
		6:11	Look upon your old self as dead; instead, be alive to God.	
	New freedom	6:12	Do not let sin control you.	We can commit ourselves to obey Christ in perfect freedom.
		6:13	Give yourselves completely to God.	
		6:14	You are free.	
		6:16	You can choose your own master.	

6:8 Because of Christ's death and resurrection, his followers need never fear death. That assurance frees us to enjoy fellowship with him and to do his will. This will affect all our activities—work and worship, play, Bible study, quiet times, and times of caring for others. When you know that you don't have to fear death, you will experience a new vigor in life.

6:11 "Count yourselves dead to sin" means that we should regard our old sinful nature as dead and unresponsive to sin. Because of our union and identification with Christ, we are no longer obligated to carry out those old motives, desires, and goals. So let us consider ourselves to be what God has in fact made us. We have a new start, and the Holy Spirit will help us become in our daily experience what Christ has declared us to be.

6:12 How can we keep this command to not let sin reign over us, to not give in to its desires? We can take the following steps: (1) Identify our personal weaknesses, (2) recognize the things that tempt us, (3) stay away from sources of temptation, (4) practice self-restraint, (5) consciously invest our time in good habits and service, and (5) lean on God's strength and grace.

6:13 The phrase "instruments of wickedness" referred to a tool or a weapon. Our skills, capabilities, and bodies can serve many purposes, good or bad. In sin, every part of our bodies are vulnerable. In Christ, every part can be an instrument for service. It is the one to whom we offer our service that makes the difference. We are like lasers that can burn destructive holes in steel places or do delicate cataract surgery. Will you give yourself completely to God, asking him to put you to good use for his glory?

6:14, 15 If we're no longer under the law but under grace, are we now free to sin and disregard the Ten Commandments? Paul says, "By no means." When we were under the law, sin was our master—the law does not justify us or help us overcome sin. But now that we are bound to Christ, he is our Master, and he gives us power to do good rather than evil.

6:16–18 In certain skilled crafts, an apprentice works under a master, who trains, shapes, and molds his apprentice in the finer points of his craft. All people choose a master and pattern themselves after him. Without Jesus, we would have no choice—we would have to apprentice ourselves to sin, and the results would be guilt, suffering, and separation from God. Thanks to Jesus, however, we can now choose God as our Master. Following him, we can enjoy new life and learn how to work for him. Are you still serving your first master, sin? Or have you apprenticed yourself to God?

6:17 To obey wholeheartedly means to give yourself fully to God, to love him "with all your heart and with all your soul and with all your mind" (Matthew 22:37). And yet so often our efforts to know and obey God's commands can best be described as "halfhearted." How do you rate your heart's obedience? God wants to give you the power to obey him with all your heart.

6:17 The "form of teaching" they were to obey refers to the Good News that Jesus died for their sins and was raised to give them new life. Many believe that this refers to the early church's statement of faith found in 1 Corinthians 15:1–11.

¹⁹I put this in human terms ᶠ because you are weak in your natural selves. Just as you used to offer the parts of your body in slavery to impurity and to ever-increasing wickedness, so now offer them in slavery to righteousness leading to holiness. ²⁰When you were slaves to sin, you were free from the control of righteousness. ²¹What benefit did you reap at that time from the things you are now ashamed of? Those things result in death! ᵍ ²² But now that you have been set free from sin and have become slaves to God, the benefit you reap leads to holiness, and the result is eternal life. ²³For the wages of sin is death, ʰ but the gift of God is eternal life in ᵃ Christ Jesus our Lord.

6:19
ᶠRo 3:5

6:21
ᵍver 23

6:23
ʰRo 5:12;
Gal 6:7, 8

An Illustration From Marriage

7 Do you not know, brothers—for I am speaking to men who know the law—that the law has authority over a man only as long as he lives? ²For example, by law a married woman is bound to her husband as long as he is alive, but if her husband dies, she is released from the law of marriage. ʲ ³So then, if she marries another man while her husband is still alive, she is called an adulteress. But if her husband dies, she is released from that law and is not an adulteress, even though she marries another man.

7:2
ʲ1Co 7:39

⁴So, my brothers, you also died to the law ʲ through the body of Christ, ᵏ that you might belong to another, to him who was raised from the dead, in order that we might bear fruit to God. ⁵For when we were controlled by the sinful nature, ᵇ the sinful passions aroused by the law were at work in our bodies, ˡ so that we bore fruit for death. ⁶But now, by dying to what once bound us, we have been released from the law so that we serve in the new way of the Spirit, and not in the old way of the written code. ᵐ

7:4
ʲGal 2:19
ᵏCol 1:22

7:5
ˡRo 6:13

7:6
ᵐRo 2:29

Struggling With Sin

⁷What shall we say, then? Is the law sin? Certainly not! Indeed I would not have known what sin was except through the law. ⁿ For I would not have known what coveting really was if the law had not said, "Do not covet." ᶜ ᵒ ⁸But sin, seizing the opportunity afforded by the commandment, produced in me every kind of covetous desire. For apart from law, sin is dead. ᵖ ⁹Once I was alive apart from law; but when the commandment came, sin sprang to

7:7
ⁿRo 3:20
ᵒEx 20:17; Dt 5:21

7:8
ᵖRo 4:15;
1Co 15:56

ᵃ23 Or *through*   ᵇ5 Or *the flesh*; also in verse 25   ᶜ7 Exodus 20:17; Deut. 5:21

6:19–22 It is impossible to be neutral. Every person has a master—either God or sin. A Christian is not someone who cannot sin, but someone who is no longer a slave to sin. He or she belongs to God.

6:23 You are free to choose between two masters, but you are not free to adjust the consequences of your choice. Each of the two masters pays with his own kind of currency. The currency of sin is eternal death. That is all you can expect or hope for in life without God. Christ's currency is eternal life—new life with God that begins on earth and continues forever with God. What choice have you made?

6:23 Eternal life is a free gift from God. If it is a gift, then it is not something that we earn, nor something that must be paid back. Consider the foolishness of someone who receives a gift given out of love and then offers to pay for it. A gift cannot be purchased by the recipient. A more appropriate response to a loved one who offers a gift is graceful acceptance with gratitude. Our salvation is a gift of God, not something of our own doing (Ephesians 2:8, 9). He saved us because of his mercy, not because of any righteous things that we have done (Titus 3:5). How much more we should accept with thanksgiving the gift that God has freely given to us.

7:1ff Paul shows that the law is powerless to save the sinner (7:7–14), the lawkeeper (7:15–22), and even the person with a new nature (7:23–25). The sinner is condemned by the law; the lawkeeper can't live up to it; and the person with the new nature finds his or her obedience to the law sabotaged by the effects of the old nature. Once again, Paul declares that salvation cannot be found by obeying the law. No matter who we are, only Jesus Christ can set us free.

7:2–6 Paul uses marriage to illustrate our relationship to the law. When a spouse dies, the law of marriage no longer applies. Because we have died with Christ, the law can no longer condemn us. We rose again when Christ was resurrected and, as new people,

we "belong" to Christ. His Spirit enables us to produce good fruit for God. We now serve not by obeying a set of rules, but out of renewed hearts and minds that overflow with love for God.

7:4 When a person dies to the old life and belongs to Christ, a new life begins. An unbeliever's mind-set is centered on his or her own personal gratification. Those who don't follow Christ have only their own self-determination as their source of power. By contrast, God is at the center of a Christian's life. God supplies the power for the Christian's daily living. Believers find that their whole way of looking at the world changes when they come to Christ.

7:6 Some people try to earn their way to God by keeping a set of rules (obeying the Ten Commandments, attending church faithfully, or doing good deeds), but all they earn for their efforts is frustration and discouragement. However, because of Christ's sacrifice, the way to God is already open, and we can become his children simply by putting our faith in him. No longer trying to reach God by keeping rules, we can become more and more like Jesus as we live with him day by day. Let the Holy Spirit turn your eyes away from your own performance and toward Jesus. He will free you to serve him out of love and gratitude. This is living "in the new way of the Spirit."

7:6 Keeping the rules, laws, and customs of Christianity doesn't save us. Even if we could keep our actions pure, we would still be doomed because our hearts and minds are perverse and rebellious. Like Paul, we can find no relief in the synagogue or church until we look to Jesus Christ himself for our salvation—which he gives us freely. When we do come to Jesus, we are flooded with relief and gratitude. Will we keep the rules any better? Most likely, but we will be motivated by love and gratitude, not by the desire to get God's approval. We will not be merely submitting to an external code, but willingly and lovingly seeking to do God's will.

7:9–11 Where there is no law, there is no sin, because people cannot know that their actions are sinful unless a law forbids those

7:10
qLev 18:5

7:12
r1Ti 1:8

7:14
s2Ki 17:17

7:15
tGal 5:17

7:22
uEph 3:16
vPs 1:2

7:23
wGal 5:17

7:24
xRo 6:6

8:2
y1Co 15:45
zRo 6:18

life and I died. [10]I found that the very commandment that was intended to bring life q actually brought death. [11]For sin, seizing the opportunity afforded by the commandment, deceived me, and through the commandment put me to death. [12]So then, the law is holy, and the commandment is holy, righteous and good. r

[13]Did that which is good, then, become death to me? By no means! But in order that sin might be recognized as sin, it produced death in me through what was good, so that through the commandment sin might become utterly sinful.

[14]We know that the law is spiritual; but I am unspiritual, sold s as a slave to sin. [15]I do not understand what I do. For what I want to do I do not do, but what I hate I do. t [16]And if I do what I do not want to do, I agree that the law is good. [17]As it is, it is no longer I myself who do it, but it is sin living in me. [18]I know that nothing good lives in me, that is, in my sinful nature. a For I have the desire to do what is good, but I cannot carry it out. [19]For what I do is not the good I want to do; no, the evil I do not want to do—this I keep on doing. [20]Now if I do what I do not want to do, it is no longer I who do it, but it is sin living in me that does it.

[21]So I find this law at work: When I want to do good, evil is right there with me. [22]For in my inner being u I delight in God's law; v [23]but I see another law at work in the members of my body, waging war w against the law of my mind and making me a prisoner of the law of sin at work within my members. [24]What a wretched man I am! Who will rescue me from this body of death? x [25]Thanks be to God—through Jesus Christ our Lord!

So then, I myself in my mind am a slave to God's law, but in the sinful nature a slave to the law of sin.

Life Through the Spirit

8 Therefore, there is now no condemnation for those who are in Christ Jesus, b [2]because through Christ Jesus the law of the Spirit of life y set me free z from the law of sin and

a 18 Or my flesh　b 1 Some later manuscripts Jesus, who do not live according to the sinful nature but according to the Spirit,

---

actions. God's law makes people realize that they are sinners doomed to die, yet it offers no help. Sin is real, and it is dangerous. Imagine a sunny day at the beach. You plunge into the surf; then you notice a sign on the pier: "No swimming. Sharks in water." Your day is ruined. Is it the sign's fault? Are you angry with the people who put it up? The law is like the sign. It is essential, and we are grateful for it—but it doesn't get rid of the sharks.

7:11, 12 Sin deceives people by misusing the law. The law was holy, expressing God's nature and will for people. In the Garden of Eden (Genesis 3), the serpent deceived Eve by taking her focus off the freedom she had and putting it on the one restriction God had made. Ever since then, we have all been rebels. Sin looks good to us precisely because God has said it is wrong. When we are tempted to rebel, we need to look at the law from a wider perspective—in the light of God's grace and mercy. If we focus on his great love for us, we will understand that he only restricts us from actions and attitudes that ultimately will harm us.

7:15 Paul shares three lessons that he learned in trying to deal with his sinful desires. (1) Knowledge of the rules is not the answer (7:9). Paul felt fine as long as he did not understand what the law demanded. When he learned the truth, he knew he was doomed. (2) Self-determination (struggling in one's own strength) doesn't succeed (7:15). Paul found himself sinning in ways that weren't even attractive to him. (3) Becoming a Christian does not stamp out all sin and temptation from a person's life (7:22–25).

Being born again takes a moment of faith, but becoming like Christ is a lifelong process. Paul compares Christian growth to a strenuous race or fight (1 Corinthians 9:24–27; 2 Timothy 4:7). Thus, as Paul has been emphasizing since the beginning of this letter, no one in the world is innocent; no one deserves to be saved—not the pagan who doesn't know God's laws, not the person who knows them and tries to keep them. All of us must depend totally on the work of Christ for our salvation. We cannot earn it by our good behavior.

7:15 This is more than the cry of one desperate man—it describes the experience of any Christian struggling against sin or trying to please God by keeping rules and laws without the

Spirit's help. We must never underestimate the power of sin. We must never attempt to fight it in our own strength. Satan is a crafty tempter, and we have an amazing ability to make excuses. Instead of trying to overcome sin with human willpower, we must take hold of the tremendous power of Christ that is available to us. This is God's provision for victory over sin—he sends the Holy Spirit to live in us and give us power. And when we fall, he lovingly reaches out to help us up.

7:23–25 The "law at work in the members of my body" is the sin deep within us. This is our vulnerability to sin; it refers to everything within us that is more loyal to our old way of selfish living than to God.

7:23–25 There is great tension in daily Christian experience. The conflict is that we agree with God's commands but cannot do them. As a result, we are painfully aware of our sin. This inward struggle with sin was as real for Paul as it is for us. From Paul we learn what to do about it. Whenever he felt overwhelmed by the spiritual battle, he would return to the beginnings of his spiritual life, remembering how he had been freed from sin by Jesus Christ. When we feel confused and overwhelmed by sin's appeal, let us claim the freedom Christ gave us. His power can lift us to victory.

8:1 "Not guilty; let him go free"—what would those words mean to you if you were on death row? The fact is that the whole human race is on death row, justly condemned for repeatedly breaking God's holy law. Without Jesus we would have no hope at all. But thank God! He has declared us not guilty and has offered us freedom from sin and power to do his will.

8:2 This Spirit of life is the Holy Spirit. He was present at the creation of the world (Genesis 1:2), and he is the power behind the rebirth of every Christian. He gives us the power we need to live the Christian life. For more about the Holy Spirit, read the notes on John 3:6; Acts 1:3; 1:4, 5; 1:5.

death. ³For what the law was powerless*ᵃ* to do in that it was weakened by the sinful nature,*ᵃ* God did by sending his own Son in the likeness of sinful man to be a sin offering.*ᵇ* And so he condemned sin in sinful man,*ᶜ* ⁴in order that the righteous requirements of the law might be fully met in us, who do not live according to the sinful nature but according to the Spirit.

⁵Those who live according to the sinful nature have their minds set on what that nature desires; but those who live in accordance with the Spirit have their minds set on what the Spirit desires.*ᵇ* ⁶The mind of sinful man*ᵈ* is death, but the mind controlled by the Spirit is life*ᶜ* and peace; ⁷the sinful mind*ᵉ* is hostile to God.*ᵈ* It does not submit to God's law, nor can it do so. ⁸Those controlled by the sinful nature cannot please God.

⁹You, however, are controlled not by the sinful nature but by the Spirit, if the Spirit of God lives in you. *ᵉ* And if anyone does not have the Spirit of Christ, he does not belong to Christ. ¹⁰But if Christ is in you, your body is dead because of sin, yet your spirit is alive because of righteousness. ¹¹And if the Spirit of him who raised Jesus from the dead*ᶠ* is living in you, he who raised Christ from the dead will also give life to your mortal bodies through his Spirit, who lives in you.

¹²Therefore, brothers, we have an obligation—but it is not to the sinful nature, to live according to it. ¹³For if you live according to the sinful nature, you will die; but if by the Spirit you put to death the misdeeds of the body, you will live,*ᵍ* ¹⁴because those who are led by the Spirit of God*ʰ* are sons of God. ¹⁵For you did not receive a spirit that makes you a slave again to fear,*ⁱ* but you received the Spirit of sonship.*ᶠ* And by him we cry, "*Abba*,*ᵍ* Father." ¹⁶The Spirit himself testifies with our spirit that we are God's children. ¹⁷Now if we are children, then we are heirs—heirs of God and co-heirs with Christ, if indeed we share in his sufferings in order that we may also share in his glory.

8:3	*ᵃ*Ac 13:39; Heb 7:18
8:5	*ᵇ*Gal 5:22-25
8:6	*ᶜ*Gal 6:8
8:7	*ᵈ*Jas 4:4
8:9	*ᵉ*1Co 6:19; Gal 4:6
8:11	*ᶠ*Ac 2:24
8:13	*ᵍ*Gal 6:8
8:14	*ʰ*Gal 5:18
8:15	*ⁱ*2Ti 1:7; Heb 2:15

ᵃ3 Or the flesh; also in verses 4, 5, 8, 9, 12 and 13 ᵇ3 Or man, for sin ᶜ3 Or in the flesh ᵈ6 Or mind set on the flesh ᵉ7 Or The mind set on the flesh ᶠ15 Or adoption ᵍ15 Aramaic for Father

---

8:3 Jesus gave himself as a *sacrifice* ("sin offering") for our sins. In Old Testament times, animal sacrifices were continually offered at the temple. The sacrifices showed the Israelites the seriousness of sin: blood had to be shed before sins could be pardoned (see Leviticus 17:11). But animal blood could not really remove sins (Hebrews 10:4). The sacrifices could only point to Jesus' sacrifice, which paid the penalty for all sins.

8:5, 6 Paul divides people into two categories—those who are dominated by their sinful nature, and those who are controlled by the Holy Spirit. All of us would be in the first category if Jesus hadn't offered us a way out. Once we have said yes to Jesus, we will want to continue following him, because his way brings life and peace. Daily we must consciously choose to center our lives on God. Use the Bible to discover God's guidelines, and then follow them. In every perplexing situation ask yourself, "What would Jesus want me to do?" When the Holy Spirit points out what is right, do it eagerly. For more on our sinful natures versus our new life in Christ, see 6:6–8, Ephesians 4:22–24; Colossians 3:3–15.

8:9 Have you ever worried about whether or not you really are a Christian? A Christian is anyone who has the Spirit of God living in him or her. If you have sincerely trusted Christ for your salvation and acknowledged him as Lord, then the Holy Spirit has come into your life, and you are a Christian. You won't know that the Holy Spirit has come if you are waiting for a certain feeling; you will know he has come because Jesus promised he would. When the Holy Spirit is working within you, you will believe that Jesus Christ is God's Son and that eternal life comes through him (1 John 5:5); you will begin to act as Christ directs (Romans 8:5; Galatians 5:22, 23); you will find help in your daily problems and in your praying (Romans 8:26, 27); you will be empowered to serve God and do his will (Acts 1:8; Romans 12:6ff); and you will become part of God's plan to build up his church (Ephesians 4:12, 13).

8:11 The Holy Spirit is God's promise or guarantee of eternal life for those who believe in him. The Spirit is in us now by faith, and by faith we are certain to live with Christ forever. See Romans 8:23; 1 Corinthians 6:14; 2 Corinthians 4:14; 1 Thessalonians 4:14.

8:13 "Put to death the misdeeds of the body" means to regard as dead the power of sin in your body (see 6:11; Galatians 5:24). When we regard sin's appeal as dead and lifeless, we can ignore temptation when it comes.

8:14–17 Paul uses adoption or "sonship" to illustrate the believer's new relationship with God. In Roman culture, the adopted person lost all rights in his old family and gained all the rights of a legitimate child in his new family. He became a full heir to his new father's estate. Likewise, when a person becomes a Christian, he or she gains all the privileges and responsibilities of a child in God's family. One of these outstanding privileges is being led by the Spirit (see Galatians 4:5, 6). We may not always feel as though we belong to God, but the Holy Spirit is our witness. His inward presence reminds us of who we are and encourages us with God's love (5:5).

8:14–17 We are no longer cringing and fearful slaves; instead, we are the Master's children. What a privilege! Because we are God's children, we share in great treasures as coheirs. God has already given us his best gifts: his Son, his Holy Spirit, forgiveness, and eternal life; and he encourages us to ask him for whatever we need.

8:17 There is a price for being identified with Jesus. Along with being "heirs of God," Paul also mentions the suffering that Christians must face. What kinds of suffering are we to endure? For first-century believers, there was economic and social persecution, and some even faced death. We too must pay a price for following Jesus. In many parts of today's world, Christians face pressures just as severe as those faced by Christ's first followers. Even in countries where Christianity is tolerated or encouraged, Christians must not become complacent. To live as Jesus did—serving others, giving up one's own rights, resisting pressures to conform to the world—always exacts a price. Nothing we suffer, however, can compare to the great price that Jesus paid to save us.

Future Glory

8:18
j 2Co 4:17

8:20
k Ge 3:17-19

8:21
l Ac 3:21

18I consider that our present sufferings are not worth comparing with the glory that will be revealed in us.*j* 19The creation waits in eager expectation for the sons of God to be revealed. 20For the creation was subjected to frustration, not by its own choice, but by the will of the one who subjected it,*k* in hope 21that a the creation itself will be liberated from its bondage to decay*l* and brought into the glorious freedom of the children of God.

8:23
m 2Co 5:2, 4

22We know that the whole creation has been groaning as in the pains of childbirth right up to the present time. 23Not only so, but we ourselves, who have the firstfruits of the Spirit, groan*m* inwardly as we wait eagerly for our adoption as sons, the redemption of our bodies. 24For in this hope we were saved. But hope that is seen is no hope at all. Who hopes for what he already has? 25But if we hope for what we do not yet have, we wait for it patiently.

8:27
n Rev 2:23

26In the same way, the Spirit helps us in our weakness. We do not know what we ought to pray for, but the Spirit himself intercedes for us with groans that words cannot express. 27And he who searches our hearts *n* knows the mind of the Spirit, because the Spirit intercedes for the saints in accordance with God's will.

More Than Conquerors

8:29
o Php 3:21

8:30
p Eph 1:5, 11
q 1Co 6:11

28And we know that in all things God works for the good of those who love him,*b* who*c* have been called according to his purpose. 29For those God foreknew he also predestined to be conformed to the likeness of his Son,*o* that he might be the firstborn among many brothers. 30And those he predestined,*p* he also called; those he called, he also justified;*q* those he justified, he also glorified.

a 20,21 Or *subjected it in hope.* 21For   b 28 Some manuscripts *And we know that all things work together for good to those who love God*   c 28 Or *works together with those who love him to bring about what is good—with those who*

8:19-22 Sin has caused all creation to fall from the perfect state in which God created it. So the world is subject to frustration and bondage to decay so that it cannot fulfill its intended purpose. One day all creation will be liberated and transformed. Until that time it waits in eager expectation for the resurrection of God's children.

8:19-22 Christians see the world as it is—physically decaying and spiritually infected with sin. But Christians do not need to be pessimistic, because they have hope for future glory. They look forward to the new heaven and new earth that God has promised, and they wait for God's new order that will free the world of sin, sickness, and evil. In the meantime, Christians go with Christ into the world where they heal people's bodies and souls and fight the evil effects of sin in the world.

8:23 We will be resurrected with glorified bodies like the body Christ now has in heaven (see 1 Corinthians 15:25-58). We have the "firstfruits," the first installment or down payment of the Holy Spirit as a guarantee of our resurrection life (see 2 Corinthians 1:22; 5:5; Ephesians 1:14).

8:24, 25 It is natural for children to trust their parents, even though parents sometimes fail to keep their promises. Our heavenly Father, however, never makes promises he won't keep. Nevertheless, his plan may take more time than we expect. What are we waiting for? New bodies, a new heaven and new earth, rest and rewards, our eternal family and home, the absence of sin and suffering, and being face to face with Jesus! Rather than acting like impatient children as we wait for God's will to unfold, we should place our confidence in God's goodness and wisdom.

8:24, 25 In Romans, Paul presents the idea that salvation is past, present, and future. It is past because we *were* saved the moment we believed in Jesus Christ as Savior (3:21-26; 5:1-11; 6:1-11, 22, 23); our new life (eternal life) begins at that moment. And it is present because we *are being* saved; this is the process of sanctification (see the note on 6:1—8:39). But at the same time, we have not fully received all the benefits and blessings of salvation that will be ours when Christ's new kingdom is completely established. That's our future salvation. While we can be confident of our salvation, we still look ahead with hope and trust toward that complete change of body and personality that lies beyond this life, when we will be like Christ (1 John 3:2).

8:26, 27 As a believer, you are not left to your own resources to cope with problems. Even when you don't know the right words to pray, the Holy Spirit prays with and for you, and God answers. With God helping you pray, you don't need to be afraid to come before him. Ask the Holy Spirit to intercede for you "in accordance with God's will." Then, when you bring your requests to God, trust that he will always do what is best.

8:28 God works in "all things"—not just isolated incidents—for our good. This does not mean that all that happens to us is good. Evil is prevalent in our fallen world, but God is able to turn every circumstance around for our long-range good. Note that God is not working to make us happy, but to fulfill his purpose. Note also that this promise is not for everybody. It can be claimed only by those who love God and are called according to his purpose. Those who are "called" are those the Holy Spirit convinces and enables to receive Christ. Such people have a new perspective, a new mind-set on life. They trust in God, not life's treasures; they look for their security in heaven, not on earth; they learn to accept, not resent, pain and persecution because God is with them.

8:29 God's ultimate goal for us is to make us like Christ (1 John 3:2). As we become more and more like him, we discover our true selves, the persons we were created to be. How can we be conformed to Christ's likeness? By reading and heeding the Word, by studying his life on earth through the Gospels, by being filled with his Spirit, and by doing his work in the world.

8:29, 30 Some believe these verses mean that before the beginning of the world, God chose certain people to receive his gift of salvation. They point to verses like Ephesians 1:11 that says we are "predestined according to the plan of him who works out everything in conformity with the purpose of his will." Others believe that God *foreknew* those who would respond to him and upon those he set his mark (predestined). What is clear is that God's *purpose* for people was not an afterthought; it was settled before the foundation of the world. People are to serve and honor God. If you have believed in Christ, you can rejoice in the fact that God's love has always known you. God's love is eternal. His wisdom and power are supreme. He will guide and protect you until you one day stand in his presence.

8:30 *Called* means summoned or invited. For more on justification and glorification, see the chart in chapter 3, p. 1885.

31 What, then, shall we say in response to this? If God is for us, who can be against us? *r* 32 He who did not spare his own Son, *s* but gave him up for us all—how will he not also, along with him, graciously give us all things? 33 Who will bring any charge *t* against those whom God has chosen? It is God who justifies. 34 Who is he that condemns? Christ Jesus, who died—more than that, who was raised to life—is at the right hand of God and is also interceding for us. *u* 35 Who shall separate us from the love of Christ? Shall trouble or hardship or persecution or famine or nakedness or danger or sword? 36 As it is written:

> "For your sake we face death all day long;
>   we are considered as sheep to be slaughtered."*a v*

37 No, in all these things we are more than conquerors *w* through him who loved us. 38 For I am convinced that neither death nor life, neither angels nor demons, *b* neither the present nor the future, nor any powers, *x* 39 neither height nor depth, nor anything else in all creation, will be able to separate us from the love of God that is in Christ Jesus our Lord.

4. Israel's past, present, and future
God's Sovereign Choice

9 I speak the truth in Christ—I am not lying, *y* my conscience confirms it in the Holy Spirit— 2 I have great sorrow and unceasing anguish in my heart. 3 For I could wish that I myself *z* were cursed and cut off from Christ for the sake of my brothers, those of my own race, 4 the people of Israel. Theirs is the adoption as sons; theirs the divine glory, the covenants, *a* the receiving of the law, *b* the temple worship *c* and the promises. 5 Theirs are the patriarchs, and from them is traced the human ancestry of Christ, who is God over all, *d* forever praised! *c* Amen.

6 It is not as though God's word had failed. For not all who are descended from Israel are Israel. *e* 7 Nor because they are his descendants are they all Abraham's children. On the contrary, "It is through Isaac that your offspring will be reckoned." *d* 8 In other words, it is not the natural children who are God's children, but it is the children of the promise who are regarded as Abraham's offspring. 9 For this was how the promise was stated: "At the appointed time I will return, and Sarah will have a son." *e f*

10 Not only that, but Rebekah's children had one and the same father, our father Isaac. *g* 11 Yet, before the twins were born or had done anything good or bad—in order that God's

a *36* Psalm 44:22 **b** *38* Or *nor heavenly rulers* **c** *5* Or *Christ, who is over all. God be forever praised!* Or *Christ. God who is over all be forever praised!* **d** *7* Gen. 21:12 **e** *9* Gen. 18:10,14

8:31 *r* Ps 118:6
8:32 *s* Jn 3:16; Ro 4:25; 5:8
8:33 *t* Isa 50:8, 9
8:34 *u* Heb 7:25; 9:24; 1Jn 2:1
8:36 *v* Ps 44:22; 2Co 4:11
8:37 *w* 1Co 15:57
8:38 *x* Eph 1:21
9:1 *y* 1Ti 2:7
9:3 *z* Ex 32:32
9:4 *a* Ac 3:25 *b* Ps 147:19 *c* Heb 9:1
9:5 *d* Jn 1:1
9:6 *e* Gal 6:16
9:9 *f* Ge 18:10, 14
9:10 *g* Ge 25:21

8:31-34 Do you ever think that because you aren't good enough for God, he will not save you? Do you ever feel as if salvation is for everyone else but you? Then these verses are especially for you. If God gave his Son for you, he isn't going to hold back the gift of salvation! If Christ gave his life for you, he isn't going to turn around and condemn you! He will not withhold anything you need to live for him. The book of Romans is more than a theological explanation of God's redeeming grace—it is a letter of comfort and confidence addressed to you.

8:34 Paul says that Jesus is interceding for us in heaven. God has acquitted us and has removed our sin and guilt, so it is Satan, not God, who accuses us. When he does, Jesus, the advocate for our defense, stands at God's right hand to present our case. For more on the concept of Christ as our advocate, see the notes on Hebrews 4:14; 4:15.

8:35, 36 These words were written to a church that would soon undergo terrible persecution. In just a few years, Paul's hypothetical situations would turn into painful realities. This passage reaffirms God's profound love for his people. No matter what happens to us, no matter where we are, we can never be lost to his love. Suffering should not drive us away from God, but help us to identify with him further and allow his love to reach us and heal us.

8:35-39 These verses contain one of the most comforting promises in all Scripture. Believers have always had to face hardships in many forms: persecution, illness, imprisonment, even death. These could cause them to fear that they have been abandoned by Christ. But Paul exclaims that it is *impossible* to be separated from Christ. His death for us is proof of his unconquerable love.

Nothing can stop Christ's constant presence with us. God tells us how great his love is so that we will feel totally secure in him. If we believe these overwhelming assurances, we will not be afraid.

8:38 *Powers* are unseen forces of evil in the universe, forces like Satan and his fallen angels (see Ephesians 6:12). In Christ we are super-conquerors, and his love will protect us from any such forces.

9:1-3 Paul expressed concern for his Jewish "brothers" by saying that he would willingly take their punishment if that could save them. While the only one who can save us is Christ, Paul showed a rare depth of love. Like Jesus, he was willing to sacrifice for others. How concerned are you for those who don't know Christ? Are you willing to sacrifice your time, money, energy, comfort, and safety to see them come to faith in Jesus?

9:4 The Jews viewed God's choosing of Israel in the Old Testament as being like adoption. They were undeserving and without rights as natural children. Yet God adopted them and granted them the status of his sons and daughters.

9:6 God's word in the form of beautiful covenant promises came to Abraham. Covenant people, the true children of Abraham, are not just his biological descendants. They are all those who trust in God and in what Jesus Christ has done for them. (See also 2:29; Galatians 3:7.)

9:11 The Jews were proud of the fact that their lineage came from Isaac, whose mother was Sarah (Abraham's legitimate wife), rather than Ishmael, whose mother was Hagar (Sarah's maidservant). Paul asserts that no one can claim to be chosen by God because of his or her heritage or good deeds. God freely chooses

9:12
h Ge 25:23

9:13
i Mal 1:2, 3

9:15
j Ex 33:19

9:17
k Ex 9:16

9:20
l Isa 29:16

9:23
m Ro 8:30

9:24
n Ro 3:29

purpose in election might stand: [12]not by works but by him who calls—she was told, "The older will serve the younger."*a h* [13]Just as it is written: "Jacob I loved, but Esau I hated."*b i*

[14]What then shall we say? Is God unjust? Not at all! [15]For he says to Moses,

"I will have mercy on whom I have mercy,
and I will have compassion on whom I have compassion."*c j*

[16]It does not, therefore, depend on man's desire or effort, but on God's mercy. [17]For the Scripture says to Pharaoh: "I raised you up for this very purpose, that I might display my power in you and that my name might be proclaimed in all the earth."*d k* [18]Therefore God has mercy on whom he wants to have mercy, and he hardens whom he wants to harden.

[19]One of you will say to me: "Then why does God still blame us? For who resists his will?" [20]But who are you, O man, to talk back to God? "Shall what is formed say to him who formed it, 'Why did you make me like this?' "*e l* [21]Does not the potter have the right to make out of the same lump of clay some pottery for noble purposes and some for common use?

[22]What if God, choosing to show his wrath and make his power known, bore with great patience the objects of his wrath—prepared for destruction? [23]What if he did this to make the riches of his glory known to the objects of his mercy, whom he prepared in advance for glory*m*— [24]even us, whom he also called, not only from the Jews but also from the Gentiles?*n* [25]As he says in Hosea:

a 12 Gen. 25:23   *b* 13 Mal. 1:2,3   *c* 15 Exodus 33:19   *d* 17 Exodus 9:16   *e* 20 Isaiah 29:16; 45:9

WARNING SIGNS OF DEVELOPING HARDNESS

Hardening is like a callus or like the tough bone fibers that bridge a fracture. Spiritual hardening begins with self-sufficiency, security in one's self, and self-satisfaction. The real danger is that at some point, repeated resistance to God will yield an actual inability to respond, which the Bible describes as a hardened heart. Insensitivity indicates advanced hardening. Here are some of the warning signs:

Warning Sign	Reference
Disobeying—Pharaoh's willful disobedience led to his hardened heart.	Exodus 4:21
Having wealth and prosperity—Taking God's blessings for granted can cause us to feel as if they were owed to us.	Deuteronomy 8:6–14
Rebelling and being discontented—Suffering or discomfort can create an attitude that blames God.	Psalm 95:8
Rejecting a deserved rebuke—Rejecting God's gift makes our neck stiff and our heart hard.	Proverbs 29:1
Refusing to listen—Refusing to listen leads to a loss of spiritual hearing.	Zechariah 7:11–13
Failing to respond—Listening to God with no intention of obeying produces an inability to obey.	Matthew 13:11–15

---

to save whomever he wills. The doctrine of election teaches that it is God's sovereign choice to save us by his goodness and mercy, and not by our own merit.

9:12–14 Was it right for God to choose Jacob, the younger, to be over Esau? In Malachi 1:2, 3, the statement "Jacob I loved, but Esau I hated" refers to the nations of Israel and Edom rather than to the individual brothers. God chose Jacob to continue the family line of the faithful because he knew his heart was for God. But he did not exclude Esau from knowing and loving him. Keep in mind the kind of God we worship: he is sovereign; he is not arbitrary; in all things he works for our good; he is trustworthy; he will save all who believe in him. When we understand these qualities of God, we know that his choices are good even if we don't understand all his reasons.

9:16 The fallacy of gaining salvation by human effort remains as strong as ever—people still think good intentions are the key to unlock the door to eternal life. By the time they get to try the lock, the will find that their key does not fit. Others imagine that their efforts are building an invisible ladder to heaven made up of service, family, position, reputation, good work, and desire, although none of these rungs will support a feather. People are

so busy trying to reach God that they completely miss the truth that God has already reached down to them. We cannot earn God's mercy—if we could, it would not be mercy.

9:17, 18 Paul quotes from Exodus 9:16, where God foretold how Pharaoh would be used to declare God's power. Paul uses this argument to show that salvation was God's proper work, not man's. God's judgment on Pharaoh's choice to resist God was to confirm that sin and harden his heart. The consequences of Pharaoh's rebellion would be his own punishment.

9:21 With this illustration, Paul is not saying that some of us are worth more than others, but simply that the Creator has control over the created object. The created object, therefore, has no right to demand anything from its Creator—its very existence depends on him. Keeping this perspective removes any temptation to have pride in personal achievement.

9:25, 26 About seven hundred years before Jesus' birth, Hosea told of God's intention to restore his people. Paul applies Hosea's message to God's intention to bring Gentiles into his family after the Jews rejected his plan. Verse 25 is a quotation from Hosea 2:23 and verse 26 is from Hosea 1:10.

"I will call them 'my people' who are not my people;
   and I will call her 'my loved one' who is not my loved one,"[a o]

9:25
o Hos 2:23

26 and,

"It will happen that in the very place where it was said to them,
   'You are not my people,'
they will be called 'sons of the living God.'"[b p]

9:26
p Hos 1:10

27 Isaiah cries out concerning Israel:

"Though the number of the Israelites be like the sand by the sea,
   only the remnant will be saved.[q]
   28 For the Lord will carry out
      his sentence on earth with speed and finality."[c r]

9:27
q Ro 11:5

9:28
r Isa 10:22, 23

29 It is just as Isaiah said previously:

"Unless the Lord Almighty
   had left us descendants,
we would have become like Sodom,
   we would have been like Gomorrah."[d s]

9:29
s Isa 13:19

Israel's Unbelief

30 What then shall we say? That the Gentiles, who did not pursue righteousness, have obtained it, a righteousness that is by faith; 31 but Israel, who pursued a law of righteousness,[t] has not attained it. [u] 32 Why not? Because they pursued it not by faith but as if it were by works. They stumbled over the "stumbling stone." 33 As it is written:

9:31
t Ro 10:2, 3
u Gal 5:4

9:33
v Isa 28:16

"See, I lay in Zion a stone that causes men to stumble
   and a rock that makes them fall,
   and the one who trusts in him will never be put to shame."[e v]

10 Brothers, my heart's desire and prayer to God for the Israelites is that they may be saved. 2 For I can testify about them that they are zealous[w] for God, but their zeal is not based on knowledge. 3 Since they did not know the righteousness that comes from God and sought to establish their own, they did not submit to God's righteousness. [x] 4 Christ is the end of the law[y] so that there may be righteousness for everyone who believes.

10:2
w Ac 21:20

10:3
x Ro 1:17

10:4
y Gal 3:24

[a]*25* Hosea 2:23   [b]*26* Hosea 1:10   [c]*28* Isaiah 10:22,23   [d]*29* Isaiah 1:9   [e]*33* Isaiah 28:16

9:27–29 Isaiah prophesied that only a small number—a remnant—of God's original people, the Jews, would be saved. Paul saw this happening in every city where he preached. Even though he went to the Jews first, relatively few ever accepted the message. Verses 27 and 28 are based on Isaiah 10:22, 23; and 9:29 is from Isaiah 1:9.

9:31–33 Sometimes we are like these people, trying to get right with God by keeping his laws. We may think that attending church, doing church work, giving offerings, and being nice will be enough. After all, we've played by the rules, haven't we? But Paul's words sting—this approach never succeeds. Paul explains that God's plan is not for those who try to earn his favor by being good; it is for those who realize that they can never be good enough and so must depend on Christ. We can be saved only by putting our faith in what Jesus Christ has done. If we do that, we will never be "put to shame" or be disappointed.

9:32 The Jews had a worthy goal—to honor God. But they tried to achieve it the wrong way—by rigid and painstaking obedience to the law. Thus some of them became more dedicated to the law than to God. They thought that if they kept the law, God would have to accept them as his people. But God cannot be controlled. The Jews did not see that their Scriptures, the Old Testament, taught salvation by faith, and not by human effort (see Genesis 15:6).

9:32 The "stumbling stone" was Jesus. The Jews did not believe in him, because he didn't meet their expectations for the Messiah. Some people still stumble over Christ because salvation by faith doesn't make sense to them. They would rather try to earn their

way to God, or else they expect God simply to overlook their sins. Others stumble over Christ because his values are the opposite of the world's. He asks for humility, and many are unwilling to humble themselves before him. He requires obedience, and many refuse to put their wills at his disposal. Have you stumbled over this rock, or have you chosen to build your life on it?

10:1 What will happen to the Jewish people who believe in God but not in Christ? Since they believe in the same God, won't they be saved? If that were true, Paul would not have worked so hard and sacrificed so much to teach them about Christ. Because Jesus is the most complete revelation of God, we cannot fully know God apart from Christ; and because God appointed Jesus to bring God and man together, we cannot come to God by another path. The Jews, like everyone else, can find salvation only through Jesus Christ (John 14:6; Acts 4:12). Like Paul, we should wish that all Jews might be saved. We should pray for them and lovingly share the Good News with them.

10:3–5 Rather than living by faith in God, the Jews established customs and traditions (in addition to God's law) to try to make themselves acceptable in God's sight. But human effort, no matter how sincere, can never substitute for the righteousness God offers us by faith. The only way to *earn* salvation is to be perfect—and that is impossible. We can only hold out our empty hands and receive salvation as a gift.

10:4 Christ is the "end of the law" in two ways. He fulfills the purpose and goal of the law (Matthew 5:17) in that he perfectly exemplified God's desires on earth. But he is also the termination

10:5
z Ne 9:29

5 Moses describes in this way the righteousness that is by the law: "The man who does these things will live by them." a z 6 But the righteousness that is by faith says: "Do not say in your heart, 'Who will ascend into heaven?' b " (that is, to bring Christ down) 7 "or 'Who will descend into the deep?' c " (that is, to bring Christ up from the dead). 8 But what does it say?

10:8
a Dt 30:14

10:9
b Mt 10:32

"The word is near you; it is in your mouth and in your heart," d a that is, the word of faith we are proclaiming: 9 That if you confess b with your mouth, "Jesus is Lord," and believe in your heart that God raised him from the dead, you will be saved. 10 For it is with your heart that you believe and are justified, and it is with your mouth that you confess and are saved. 11 As

10:11
c Isa 28:16

10:12
d Ro 3:22, 29

the Scripture says, "Anyone who trusts in him will never be put to shame." e c 12 For there is no difference between Jew and Gentile d—the same Lord is Lord of all and richly blesses all who call on him, 13 for, "Everyone who calls on the name of the Lord e will be saved." f f

10:13
e Ac 2:21
f Joel 2:32

14 How, then, can they call on the one they have not believed in? And how can they believe in the one of whom they have not heard? And how can they hear without someone preaching to them? 15 And how can they preach unless they are sent? As it is written, "How beautiful are the feet of those who bring good news!" g g

10:15
g Isa 52:7

10:16
h Isa 53:1

16 But not all the Israelites accepted the good news. For Isaiah says, "Lord, who has believed our message?" h h 17 Consequently, faith comes from hearing the message, and the message is heard through the word of Christ. 18 But I ask: Did they not hear? Of course they did:

10:18
i Ps 19:4

"Their voice has gone out into all the earth,
     their words to the ends of the world." i i

10:19
j Ro 11:11, 14

19 Again I ask: Did Israel not understand? First, Moses says,

"I will make you envious j by those who are not a nation;
     I will make you angry by a nation that has no understanding." j

10:20
k Isa 65:1

20 And Isaiah boldly says,

"I was found by those who did not seek me;
     I revealed myself to those who did not ask for me." k k

10:21
l Isa 65:2

21 But concerning Israel he says,

"All day long I have held out my hands
     to a disobedient and obstinate people." l l

a 5 Lev. 18:5   b 6 Deut. 30:12   c 7 Deut. 30:13   d 8 Deut. 30:14   e 11 Isaiah 28:16   f 13 Joel 2:32   g 15 Isaiah 52:7   h 16 Isaiah 53:1   i 18 Psalm 19:4   j 19 Deut. 32:21   k 20 Isaiah 65:1   l 21 Isaiah 65:2

---

of the law because in comparison to Christ, the law is powerless to save.

10:5 In order to be saved by the law, a person would have to live a perfect life, not sinning once. Then why did God give the law since he knew people couldn't keep it? According to Paul, one reason the law was given was to show people how guilty they are (Galatians 3:19). The law was a shadow of Christ—that is, the sacrificial system educated the people so that when the true sacrifice came, they would be able to understand his work (Hebrews 10:1–4). The system of ceremonial laws was to last until the coming of Christ. The law points to our need for a Savior.

10:6–8 Paul adapts Moses' farewell challenge from Deuteronomy 30:11–14 to apply to Christ. Christ has provided our salvation through his incarnation (coming to earth) and resurrection (coming back from the dead). God's salvation is right in front of us. He will come to us wherever we are. All we need to do is to respond and accept his gift of salvation. The *deep* as used here refers to the grave or Hades, the place of the dead.

10:8–12 Have you ever been asked, "How do I become a Christian?" These verses give you the beautiful answer—salvation is as close as your own mouth and heart. People think it must be a complicated process, but it is not. If we believe in our hearts and say with our mouths that Christ is the risen Lord, we will be saved.

10:14 In telling others about Christ, an effective witness must include more than being a good example. Eventually, we will have

to explain the content, the *what* and the *how* of the gospel. Modeling the Christian life is important, but we will need to connect the mind of the unbeliever and the message of the gospel. There should never be a debate between those who favor lifestyle evangelism (one's living proclaims the gospel) and confrontational evangelism (declaring the message). Both should be used together in promoting the gospel.

10:15 We must take God's great message of salvation to others so that they can respond to the Good News. How will your loved ones and neighbors hear it unless someone tells them? Is God calling you to take a part in making his message known in your community? Think of one person who needs to hear the Good News, and think of something you can do to help him or her hear it. Then take that step as soon as possible.

10:18–20 Many Jews who looked for the Messiah refused to believe in him when he came. God offered his salvation to the Gentiles ("those who are not a nation" and "a nation that has no understanding"); thus many Gentiles who didn't even know about a Messiah found and believed in him. Some religious people are spiritually blind, while those who have never been in a church are sometimes the most responsive to God's message. Because appearances are deceiving, and we can't see into people's hearts, beware of judging beforehand who will respond to the gospel and who will not.

The Remnant of Israel

11 I ask then: Did God reject his people? By no means! *m* I am an Israelite myself, a descendant of Abraham, *n* from the tribe of Benjamin. *o* 2 God did not reject his people, whom he foreknew. *p* Don't you know what the Scripture says in the passage about Elijah—how he appealed to God against Israel: 3 "Lord, they have killed your prophets and torn down your altars; I am the only one left, and they are trying to kill me"*a* ? *q* 4 And what was God's answer to him? "I have reserved for myself seven thousand who have not bowed the knee to Baal."*b* *r* 5 So too, at the present time there is a remnant *s* chosen by grace. 6 And if by grace, then it is no longer by works; *t* if it were, grace would no longer be grace.*c*

7 What then? What Israel sought so earnestly it did not obtain, *u* but the elect did. The others were hardened, *v* 8 as it is written:

"God gave them a spirit of stupor,
    eyes so that they could not see
    and ears so that they could not hear,
to this very day."*d w*

9 And David says:

"May their table become a snare and a trap,
    a stumbling block and a retribution for them.
10 May their eyes be darkened so they cannot see,
    and their backs be bent forever."*e x*

Ingrafted Branches

11 Again I ask: Did they stumble so as to fall beyond recovery? Not at all! Rather, because of their transgression, salvation has come to the Gentiles *y* to make Israel envious. 12 But if their transgression means riches for the world, and their loss means riches for the Gentiles, how much greater riches will their fullness bring!

13 I am talking to you Gentiles. Inasmuch as I am the apostle to the Gentiles, *z* I make much of my ministry 14 in the hope that I may somehow arouse my own people to envy and save some of them. 15 For if their rejection is the reconciliation of the world, what will their

11:1	*m* 1Sa 12:22
	n 2Co 11:22
	o Php 3:5
11:2	*p* Ro 8:29
11:3	*q* 1Ki 19:10, 14
11:4	*r* 1Ki 19:18
11:5	*s* Ro 9:27
11:6	*t* Ro 4:4
11:7	*u* Ro 9:31
	v Ro 9:18
11:8	*w* Dt 29:4; Isa 29:10
11:10	*x* Ps 69:22, 23
11:11	*y* Ac 13:46
11:13	*z* Ac 9:15
11:15	*a* Lk 15:24, 32

a 3 1 Kings 19:10,14   *b 4* 1 Kings 19:18   *c 6* Some manuscripts *be grace. But if by works, then it is no longer grace; if it were, work would no longer be work.*   *d 8* Deut. 29:4; Isaiah 29:10   *e 10* Psalm 69:22,23

11:1ff In this chapter Paul points out that not *all* Jews have rejected God's message of salvation. There is still a faithful remnant (11:5). Paul himself, after all, was a Jew, and so were Jesus' disciples and nearly all of the early Christian missionaries.

11:2 Elijah was a great reforming prophet who challenged the northern kingdom of Israel to repent. See his Profile in 1 Kings 18, p. 527 for more information.

11:2 God chose the Jews ("his people, whom he foreknew") to be the people through whom the rest of the world could find salvation. But this did not mean the entire Jewish nation would be saved; only those who were faithful to God (the remnant) were considered true Jews (11:5). We are saved through faith in Christ, not because we are part of a nation, religion, or family. On whom or on what are you depending for salvation?

11:6 Do you think it's easier for God to love you when you're good? Do you secretly suspect that God chose you because you deserved it? Do you think some people's behavior is so bad that God couldn't possibly save them? If you ever think this way, you don't entirely understand that salvation is by grace, a free gift. It cannot be earned, in whole or in part; it can only be accepted with thankfulness and praise.

11:7 "The others were hardened" was God's punishment for their sin. It was a confirmation of their own stubbornness. In judging them, God removed their ability to see and hear, and to repent; thus they would experience the consequences of their rebellion. Resisting God is like saying to him, "Leave me alone!" But because God is always and everywhere present, his answer to that prayer might be to agree and make that person less sensitive, more hardened to him. The very possibility of that happening

ought to keep us asking God specifically for ears that really hear and eyes that really see—openness and responsiveness to him.

11:8-10 These verses describe the punishment for hardened hearts predicted by the prophet Isaiah (Isaiah 6:9-13). If people refuse to hear God's Good News, they eventually will be unable to understand it. Paul saw this happening in the Jewish congregations he visited on his missionary journeys. (Verse 8 is based on Deuteronomy 29:4 and Isaiah 29:10. Verses 9 and 10 are from Psalm 69:22, 23.)

11:11ff Paul had a vision of a church where all Jewish and Gentile believers would be united in their love of God and in obedience to Christ. While respecting God's law, this ideal church would look to Christ alone for salvation. A person's ethnic background and social status would be irrelevant (see Galatians 3:28)—what mattered would be his or her faith in Christ.

But Paul's vision has not yet been realized. Many Jewish people rejected the gospel. They depended on their heritage for salvation, and they did not have the heart of obedience that was so important to the Old Testament prophets and to Paul. Once Gentiles became dominant in many of the Christian churches, they began rejecting Jews and even persecuting them. Unfortunately, this practice has recurred through the centuries.

True Christians should not persecute others. Both Gentiles and Jews have done so much to damage the cause of the God they claim to serve that Paul's vision often seems impossible to fulfill. Yet God chose the Jews, just as he chose the Gentiles, and he is still working to unite Jew and Gentile in a new Israel, a new Jerusalem, ruled by his Son (see Ephesians 2:11-22).

11:13-15 Paul was appointed as a missionary to the Gentiles. He reminded his Jewish brothers of this fact, hoping that they too acceptance be but life from the dead?ᵃ ¹⁶If the part of the dough offered as firstfruits is holy, then the whole batch is holy; if the root is holy, so are the branches.

11:17
b Jer 11:16
c Eph 2:11-13

¹⁷If some of the branches have been broken off,ᵇ and you, though a wild olive shoot, have been grafted in among the othersᶜ and now share in the nourishing sap from the olive root, ¹⁸do not boast over those branches. If you do, consider this: You do not support the root, but the root supports you. ¹⁹You will say then, "Branches were broken off so that I could be grafted in." ²⁰Granted. But they were broken off because of unbelief, and you stand by faith.ᵈ Do not be arrogant,ᵉ but be afraid. ²¹For if God did not spare the natural branches, he will not spare you either.

11:20
d 1Co 10:12
e Ro 12:16

²²Consider therefore the kindness and sternness of God: sternness to those who fell, but kindness to you, provided that you continueᶠ in his kindness. Otherwise, you also will be cut off.ᵍ ²³And if they do not persist in unbelief, they will be grafted in, for God is able to graft them in again.ʰ ²⁴After all, if you were cut out of an olive tree that is wild by nature, and contrary to nature were grafted into a cultivated olive tree, how much more readily will these, the natural branches, be grafted into their own olive tree!

11:22
f 1Co 15:2; Heb 3:6
g Jn 15:2
11:23
h 2Co 3:16

All Israel Will Be Saved

11:25
i Lk 21:24

²⁵I do not want you to be ignorant of this mystery, brothers, so that you may not be conceited: Israel has experienced a hardening in part until the full number of the Gentiles has come in.ⁱ ²⁶And so all Israel will be saved, as it is written:

"The deliverer will come from Zion;
he will turn godlessness away from Jacob.

11:27
j Isa 27:9

²⁷ And this isᵃ my covenant with them
when I take away their sins."ᵇ ʲ

11:28
k Dt 7:8

²⁸As far as the gospel is concerned, they are enemies on your account; but as far as election is concerned, they are loved on account of the patriarchs,ᵏ ²⁹for God's gifts and his call are irrevocable. ³⁰Just as you who were at one time disobedient to God have now received mercy as a result of their disobedience, ³¹so they too have now become disobedient in order that they too may nowᶜ receive mercy as a result of God's mercy to you. ³²For God has bound all men over to disobedienceˡ so that he may have mercy on them all.

11:32
l Ro 3:9

Doxology

11:33
m Ps 92:5

³³ Oh, the depth of the riches of the wisdom andᵈ knowledge of God!ᵐ
How unsearchable his judgments,
and his paths beyond tracing out!

ᵃ27 Or *will be* ᵇ27 Isaiah 59:20,21; 27:9; Jer. 31:33,34 ᶜ31 Some manuscripts do not have *now*. ᵈ33 Or *riches and the wisdom and the*

---

would want to be saved. The Jews had been rejected, and thus Gentiles were being offered salvation. But when a Jew comes to Christ, there is great rejoicing, as if a dead person has come back to life.

11:17-24 Speaking to Gentile Christians, Paul warns them not to feel superior because God rejected some Jews. Abraham's faith is like the root of a productive tree, and the Jewish people are the tree's natural branches. Because of faithlessness, the Jews were the broken branches. Gentile believers have been grafted into the tree like a wild olive shoot. Both Jews and Gentiles share the tree's nourishment based on faith in God; neither can rest on heritage or culture for salvation.

11:22 "Continue in his kindness" refers to steadfast perseverance in faith. Steadfastness is a proof of the reality of faith and a by-product of salvation, not a means to it.

11:26 Some say the phrase "And so all Israel will be saved" means that the majority of Jews in the final generation before Christ's return will turn to Christ for salvation. Others say that Paul is using the term *Israel* for the "spiritual" nation of Israel made up of everyone—Jew and Gentile—who has received salvation through faith in Christ. Thus *all Israel* (or all believers) will receive God's promised gift of salvation. Still others say that *all Israel* means Israel as a whole will have a role in Christ's kingdom. Their identity as a people won't be discarded. God chose the nation of Israel, and he has never rejected it. He also chose the church,

through Jesus Christ, and he will never reject it either. This does not mean, of course, that all Jews or all church members will be saved. It is possible to belong to a nation or to an organization without ever responding in faith. But just because some people have rejected Christ does not mean that God stops working with either Israel or the church. He continues to offer salvation freely to all. Still others say that the phrase "and so" means "in this way" or "this is how," referring to the necessity of faith in Christ.

11:28-32 In this passage Paul shows how the Jews and the Gentiles benefit each other. Whenever God shows mercy to one group, the other shares the blessing. In God's original plan, the Jews would be the source of God's blessing to the Gentiles (see Genesis 12:3). When the Jews neglected this mission, God blessed the Gentiles anyway through the Jewish Messiah. He still maintained his love for the Jews because of his promises to Abraham, Isaac, and Jacob ("on account of the patriarchs"). The privileges and invitation of God given to Israel will never be withdrawn. But someday the faithful Jews will share in God's mercy. God's plans will not be thwarted: he will "have mercy on them all." For a beautiful picture of Jews and Gentiles experiencing rich blessings, see Isaiah 60.

11:33 This doxology is a prayer of praise to God for the wisdom of his plan. Although God's method and means are beyond our comprehension, God himself is not arbitrary. He governs the universe and our lives in perfect wisdom, justice, and love.

34 "Who has known the mind of the Lord?
     Or who has been his counselor?"ᵃ ⁿ
35 "Who has ever given to God,
     that God should repay him?"ᵇ
36 For from him and through him and to him are all things.ᵒ
     To him be the glory forever! Amen.

11:34
ⁿ Isa 40:13, 14;
Job 36:22

11:36
ᵒ 1Co 8:6; Col 1:16

B. HOW TO BEHAVE (12:1—16:27)

Moving from the theological to the practical, Paul gives guidelines for living as a redeemed
people in a fallen world. We are to give ourselves to Christ as living sacrifices, obey the
government, love our neighbors, and take special care of those who are weak in the faith. He
closes with personal remarks. Throughout this section, we learn how to live our faith each day.

1. Personal responsibility
Living Sacrifices

12 Therefore, I urge you, brothers, in view of God's mercy, to offer your bodies as living
sacrifices,ᵖ holy and pleasing to God—this is your spiritualᶜ act of worship. ²Do not
conform �q any longer to the pattern of this world, but be transformed by the renewing of
your mind.ʳ Then you will be able to test and approve what God's will is—his good, pleasing
and perfect will.

³For by the grace given meˢ I say to every one of you: Do not think of yourself more highly
than you ought, but rather think of yourself with sober judgment, in accordance with the
measure of faith God has given you. ⁴Just as each of us has one body with many members,
and these members do not all have the same function,ᵗ ⁵so in Christ we who are many form
one body, and each member belongs to all the others. ⁶We have different gifts,ᵘ according
to the grace given us. If a man's gift is prophesying, let him use it in proportion to hisᵈ faith.
⁷If it is serving, let him serve; if it is teaching, let him teach; ⁸if it is encouraging, let him encourage;ᵛ if it is contributing to the needs of others, let him give generously;ʷ if it is leadership, let him govern diligently; if it is showing mercy, let him do it cheerfully.

12:1
ᵖ Ro 6:13, 16, 19

12:2
q 1Pe 1:14
ʳ Eph 4:23

12:3
ˢ Ro 15:15; Eph 4:7

12:4
ᵗ 1Co 12:12-14;
Eph 4:16

12:6
ᵘ 1Co 12:4, 8-10

12:8
ᵛ Ac 15:32
ʷ 2Co 9:5-13

ᵃ34 Isaiah 40:13   ᵇ35 Job 41:11   ᶜ1 Or *reasonable*   ᵈ6 Or *in agreement with the*

11:34–36 The implication of these questions is that no one has
fully understood the mind of the Lord. No one has been his counselor. And God owes nothing to any one of us. Isaiah and Jeremiah asked similar questions to show that we are unable to give
advice to God or criticize his ways (Isaiah 40:13; Jeremiah 23:18).
God alone is the possessor of absolute power and absolute
wisdom. In the final analysis, all of us are absolutely dependent
on God. He is the source of all things, including ourselves. He is
the power that sustains and rules the world that we live in. And
God works out all things to bring glory to himself. The all-powerful God deserves our praise.

12:1 When sacrificing an animal according to God's law, a priest
would kill the animal, cut it in pieces, and place it on the altar.
Sacrifice was important, but even in the Old Testament God made
it clear that obedience from the heart was much more important
(see 1 Samuel 15:22; Psalm 40:6; Amos 5:21–24). God wants us
to offer ourselves, not animals, as *living* sacrifices—daily laying
aside our own desires to follow him, putting all our energy and
resources at his disposal and trusting him to guide us. We do this
out of gratitude that our sins have been forgiven.

12:1, 2 God has good, pleasing, and perfect plans for his children.
He wants us to be transformed people with renewed minds, living
to honor and obey him. Because he wants only what is best for us,
and because he gave his Son to make our new lives possible, we
should joyfully give ourselves as living sacrifices for his service.

12:2 Christians are called to "not conform any longer to the
pattern of this world," with its behavior and customs that are
usually selfish and often corrupting. Many Christians wisely
decide that much worldly behavior is off limits for them. Our
refusal to conform to this world's values, however, must go even
deeper than the level of behavior and customs—it must be firmly
planted in our minds—"be transformed by the renewing of your
mind." It is possible to avoid most worldly customs and still be
proud, covetous, selfish, stubborn, and arrogant. Only when the

Holy Spirit renews, reeducates, and redirects our minds are we
truly transformed (see 8:5).

12:3 Healthy self-esteem is important because some of us think
too little of ourselves; on the other hand, some of us overestimate
ourselves. The key to an honest and accurate evaluation is knowing the basis of our self-worth—our identity in Christ. Apart from
him, we aren't capable of very much by eternal standards; in him,
we are valuable and capable of worthy service. Evaluating yourself
by the worldly standards of success and achievement can cause
you to think too much about your worth in the eyes of others and
thus miss your true value in God's eyes.

12:4, 5 Paul uses the concept of the human body to teach how
Christians should live and work together. Just as the parts of the
body function under the direction of the brain, so Christians are to
work together under the command and authority of Jesus Christ
(see 1 Corinthians 12:12–31; Ephesians 4:1–16).

12:6 God gives us gifts so we can build up his church. To use
them effectively, we must (1) realize that all gifts and abilities
come from God; (2) understand that not everyone has the same
gifts; (3) know who we are and what we do best; (4) dedicate our
gifts to God's service and not to our personal success; (5) be willing to utilize our gifts wholeheartedly, not holding back anything
from God's service. God's gifts differ in nature, power, and effectiveness according to his wisdom and graciousness, not according to our faith. Our role is to be faithful and to seek ways to serve
others with what Christ has given us.

12:6 *Prophesying* in Scripture is not always predicting the
future. Often it means preaching God's messages (1 Corinthians
14:1–3).

12:6–8 Look at this list of gifts and imagine the kinds of people
who would have each gift. Prophets are often bold and articulate.
Servers (those in ministry) are faithful and loyal. Teachers are
clear thinkers. Encouragers know how to motivate others. Givers

Love

12:10
×Php 2:3

12:12
yHeb 10:32, 36

12:14
zMt 5:44

12:16
aRo 15:5

12:17
b2Co 8:21

12:20
cMt 5:44

⁹Love must be sincere. Hate what is evil; cling to what is good. ¹⁰Be devoted to one another in brotherly love. Honor one another above yourselves. × ¹¹Never be lacking in zeal, but keep your spiritual fervor, serving the Lord. ¹²Be joyful in hope, patient in affliction, y faithful in prayer. ¹³Share with God's people who are in need. Practice hospitality.

¹⁴Bless those who persecute you; z bless and do not curse. ¹⁵Rejoice with those who rejoice; mourn with those who mourn. ¹⁶Live in harmony with one another. a Do not be proud, but be willing to associate with people of low position. a Do not be conceited.

¹⁷Do not repay anyone evil for evil. Be careful to do what is right in the eyes of everybody. b ¹⁸If it is possible, as far as it depends on you, live at peace with everyone. ¹⁹Do not take revenge, my friends, but leave room for God's wrath, for it is written: "It is mine to avenge; I will repay," b says the Lord. ²⁰On the contrary:

> "If your enemy is hungry, feed him;
>   if he is thirsty, give him something to drink.
> In doing this, you will heap burning coals on his head." c c

²¹Do not be overcome by evil, but overcome evil with good.

a *16* Or *willing to do menial work*   b *19* Deut. 32:35   c*20* Prov. 25:21,22

---

are generous and trusting. Leaders are good organizers and managers. Those who show mercy are caring people who are happy to give their time to others. It would be difficult for one person to embody all these gifts. An assertive prophet would not usually make a good counselor, and a generous giver might fail as a leader. When you identify your own gifts (and this list is far from complete), ask how you can use them to build up God's family. At the same time, realize that your gifts can't do the work of the church all alone. Be thankful for people whose gifts are completely different from yours. Let your strengths balance their weaknesses, and be grateful that their abilities make up for your deficiencies. Together you can build Christ's church.

12:9–10 Most of us have learned how to pretend to love others—how to speak kindly, avoid hurting their feelings, and appear to take an interest in them. We may even be skilled in pretending to feel moved with compassion when we hear of others' needs, or to become indignant when we learn of injustice. But God calls us to real and sincere love that goes far beyond pretense and politeness. Sincere love requires concentration and effort. It means helping others become better people. It demands our time, money, and personal involvement. No individual has the capacity to express love to a whole community, but the body of Christ in your town does. Look for people who need your love, and look for ways you and your fellow believers can love your community for Christ.

12:10 We can honor others in one of two ways. One involves ulterior motives. We honor our bosses so they will reward us, our employees so they will work harder, the wealthy so they will contribute to our cause, the powerful so they will use their power for us and not against us. God's other way involves love. As Christians, we honor people because they have been created in God's image, because they are our brothers and sisters in Christ, and because they have a unique contribution to make to Christ's church. Does God's way of honoring others sound too difficult for your competitive nature? Why not try to outdo one another in showing honor? Put others first!

12:13 Christian hospitality differs from social entertaining. Entertaining focuses on the host—the home must be spotless; the food must be well prepared and abundant; the host must appear relaxed and good-natured. Hospitality, by contrast, focuses on the guests. Their needs—whether for a place to stay, nourishing food, a listening ear, or acceptance—are the primary concern. Hospitality can happen in a messy home. It can happen around a dinner table where the main dish is canned soup. It can even happen while the host and the guest are doing chores together. Don't hesitate to offer hospitality just because you are too tired, too busy, or not wealthy enough to entertain.

12:16 Many people use their contacts and relationships for selfish ambition. They select those people who will help them climb the social ladder. Christ demonstrated and taught that we should treat all people with respect—those of a different race, the handicapped, the poor, young and old, male and female. We must never consider others as being beneath us. Paul says we need to live in harmony with others and not be too proud to enjoy the company of ordinary people. Are you able to do humble tasks with others? Do you welcome conversation with unattractive, non-prestigious people? Are you willing to befriend newcomers and entry-level people? Or do you relate only to those who will help you get ahead?

12:17–21 These verses summarize the core of Christian living. If we love someone the way Christ loves us, we will be willing to forgive. If we have experienced God's grace, we will want to pass it on to others. And remember, grace is *undeserved* favor. By giving an enemy a drink, we're not excusing his misdeeds. We're recognizing him, forgiving him, and loving him in spite of his sins—just as Christ did for us.

12:19–21 In this day of constant lawsuits and incessant demands for legal rights, Paul's command sounds almost impossible. When someone hurts you deeply, instead of giving him what he deserves, Paul says to befriend him. Why does Paul tell us to forgive our enemies? (1) Forgiveness may break a cycle of retaliation and lead to mutual reconciliation. (2) It may make the enemy feel ashamed and change his or her ways. (3) By contrast, repaying evil for evil hurts you just as much as it hurts your enemy. Even if your enemy never repents, forgiving him or her will free you of a heavy load of bitterness.

12:19–21 Forgiveness involves both attitudes and actions. If you find it difficult to *feel* forgiving toward someone who has hurt you, try responding with kind actions. If appropriate, tell this person that you would like to heal your relationship. Lend a helping hand. Send him or her a gift. Smile at him or her. Many times you will discover that right actions lead to right feelings.

12:20 What does it mean to "heap burning coals" on someone's head? This may refer to an Egyptian tradition of carrying a pan of burning charcoal on one's head as a public act of repentance. By referring to this proverb, Paul was saying that we should treat our enemies with kindness so that they will become ashamed and turn from their sins. The best way to get rid of enemies is to turn them into friends.

Submission to the Authorities

13 Everyone must submit himself to the governing authorities,*d* for there is no authority except that which God has established. *e* The authorities that exist have been established by God. 2 Consequently, he who rebels against the authority is rebelling against what God has instituted, and those who do so will bring judgment on themselves. 3 For rulers hold no terror for those who do right, but for those who do wrong. Do you want to be free from fear of the one in authority? Then do what is right and he will commend you. *f* 4 For he is God's servant to do you good. But if you do wrong, be afraid, for he does not bear the sword for nothing. He is God's servant, an agent of wrath to bring punishment on the wrongdoer.*g* 5 Therefore, it is necessary to submit to the authorities, not only because of possible punishment but also because of conscience.

6 This is also why you pay taxes, for the authorities are God's servants, who give their full time to governing. 7 Give everyone what you owe him: If you owe taxes, pay taxes;*h* if revenue, then revenue; if respect, then respect; if honor, then honor.

Love, for the Day Is Near

8 Let no debt remain outstanding, except the continuing debt to love one another, for he who loves his fellowman has fulfilled the law. 9 The commandments, "Do not commit adultery," "Do not murder," "Do not steal," "Do not covet,"*a i* and whatever other commandment there may be, are summed up in this one rule: "Love your neighbor as yourself." *b* 10 Love does no harm to its neighbor. Therefore love is the fulfillment of the law.

11 And do this, understanding the present time. The hour has come *j* for you to wake up from your slumber, because our salvation is nearer now than when we first believed. 12 The night is nearly over; the day is almost here. So let us put aside the deeds of darkness*k* and put

a 9 Exodus 20:13-15,17; Deut. 5:17-19,21   *b 9* Lev. 19:18

13:1   *d* 1Pe 2:13, 14   *e* Da 2:21

13:3   *f* 1Pe 2:14

13:4   *g* 1Th 4:6

13:7   *h* Mt 22:17, 21

13:9   *i* Ex 20:13-15, 17

13:11   *j* 1Co 7:29-31

13:12   *k* Eph 5:11

13:1 Are there times when we should not submit to the government? We should never allow government to force us to disobey God. Jesus and his apostles never disobeyed the government for personal reasons; when they disobeyed, it was in order to follow their higher loyalty to God. Their disobedience was not cheap: they were threatened, beaten, thrown into jail, tortured, or executed for their convictions. Like them, if we are compelled to disobey, we must be ready to accept the consequences.

13:1ff Christians understand Romans 13 in different ways. All Christians agree that we are to live at peace with the state as long as the state allows us to live by our religious convictions. For hundreds of years, however, there have been at least three interpretations of how we are to do this.

(1) Some Christians believe that the state is so corrupt that Christians should have as little to do with it as possible. Although they should be good citizens as long as they can do so without compromising their beliefs, they should not work for the government, vote in elections, or serve in the military.

(2) Others believe that God has given the state authority in certain areas and the church authority in others. Christians can be loyal to both and can work for either. They should not, however, confuse the two. In this view, church and state are concerned with two totally different spheres—the spiritual and the physical—and thus complement each other but do not work together.

(3) Still others believe that Christians have a responsibility to make the state better. They can do this politically, by electing Christian or other high-principled leaders. They can also do this morally, by serving as an influence for good in society. In this view, church and state ideally work together for the good of all.

None of these views advocate rebelling against or refusing to obey the government's laws or regulations unless those laws clearly require you to violate the moral standards revealed by God. Wherever we find ourselves, we must be responsible citizens, as well as responsible Christians.

13:3, 4 Willingly or unwittingly, people in authority are God's servants. They are allowed their positions in order to do good. When authorities are unjust, however, upright people are afraid. When authorities are just, people who are doing right have nothing to fear. This provides our principal motivation to pray for our leaders. Praying for those in authority over us will also mean that we will watch them closely. If we pray diligently for our leaders, we will be functioning as God's sentinels.

13:8 Why is love for others called a debt? We are permanently in debt to Christ for the lavish love he has poured out on us. The only way we can even begin to repay this debt is by fulfilling our obligation to love others in turn. Because Christ's love will always be infinitely greater than ours, we will always have the obligation to love our neighbors.

13:9 Somehow many of us have gotten the idea that self-love is wrong. But if this were the case, it would be pointless to love our neighbors as ourselves. But Paul explains what he means by self-love. Even if you have low self-esteem, you probably don't willingly let yourself go hungry. You clothe yourself reasonably well. You make sure there's a roof over your head if you can. You try not to let yourself be cheated or injured. And you get angry if someone tries to ruin your marriage. This is the kind of love we need to have for our neighbors. Do we see that others are fed, clothed, and housed as well as they can be? Are we concerned about issues of social justice? Loving others as ourselves means to be actively working to see that their needs are met. Interestingly, people who focus on others rather than on themselves rarely suffer from low self-esteem.

13:10 Christians must obey the law of love, which supersedes both religious and civil laws. How easy it is to excuse our indifference to others merely because we have no legal obligation to help them, and even to justify harming them if our actions are technically legal! But Jesus does not leave loopholes in the law of love. Whenever love demands it, we are to go beyond human legal requirements and imitate the God of love. See James 2:8, 9; 4:11 and 1 Peter 2:16, 17 for more about this law of love.

13:12–14 The *night* refers to the present evil time. The *day* refers to the time of Christ's return. Some people are surprised that Paul lists dissension and jealousy with the gross and obvious sins of orgies, drunkenness, and sexual immorality. Like Jesus in his Sermon on the Mount (Matthew 5—7), Paul considers attitudes as important as actions. Just as hatred leads to murder, so jealousy leads to strife and lust to adultery. When Christ returns, he wants to find his people clean on the inside as well as on the outside.

on the armor of light. [13]Let us behave decently, as in the daytime, not in orgies and drunkenness, not in sexual immorality and debauchery, not in dissension and jealousy. [14]Rather,
clothe yourselves with the Lord Jesus Christ,[l] and do not think about how to gratify the desires of the sinful nature.[a]

13:14
[l]Gal 3:27; Eph 4:24

The Weak and the Strong

14 Accept him whose faith is weak, without passing judgment on disputable matters.
[2]One man's faith allows him to eat everything, but another man, whose faith is weak,
eats only vegetables. [3]The man who eats everything must not look down on him who does
not, and the man who does not eat everything must not condemn the man who does, for God
has accepted him. [4]Who are you to judge someone else's servant? To his own master he
stands or falls. And he will stand, for the Lord is able to make him stand.

[5]One man considers one day more sacred than another;[m] another man considers every
day alike. Each one should be fully convinced in his own mind. [6]He who regards one day as
special, does so to the Lord. He who eats meat, eats to the Lord, for he gives thanks to God;[n]
and he who abstains, does so to the Lord and gives thanks to God. [7]For none of us lives to
himself alone[o] and none of us dies to himself alone. [8]If we live, we live to the Lord; and if we
die, we die to the Lord. So, whether we live or die, we belong to the Lord.[p]

[9]For this very reason, Christ died and returned to life so that he might be the Lord of both
the dead and the living.[q] [10]You, then, why do you judge your brother? Or why do you look
down on your brother? For we will all stand before God's judgment seat.[r] [11]It is written:

14:5
[m]Gal 4:10

14:6
[n]1Co 10:30, 31;
1Ti 4:3, 4

14:7
[o]Gal 2:20

14:8
[p]Php 1:20

14:9
[q]2Co 5:15

14:10
[r]2Co 5:10

[a]14 Or *the flesh*

13:14 How do we clothe ourselves with the Lord Jesus Christ?
First we identify with Christ by being baptized (Galatians 3:27).
This shows our solidarity with other Christians and with the
death, burial, and resurrection of Jesus Christ. Second, we exemplify the qualities Jesus showed while he was here on earth (love,
humility, truth, service). In a sense, we role-play what Jesus
would do in our situation (see Ephesians 4:24–32; Colossians
3:10–17). We also must not give our desires any opportunity to
lead us into sin. Avoid those situations that open the door to gratifying sinful desires.

14:1 Who is weak in faith and who is strong? We are all weak
in some areas and strong in others. Our faith is strong in an area
if we can survive contact with sinners without falling into their
patterns. It is weak in an area if we must avoid certain activities,
people, or places in order to protect our spiritual life. It is important to take a self-inventory in order to find out our strengths and
weaknesses. Whenever in doubt, we should ask, "Can I do that
without sinning? Can I influence others for good, rather than
being influenced by them?"

In areas of strength, we should not fear being defiled by the
world; rather we should go and serve God. In areas of weakness,
we need to be cautious. If we have a strong faith but shelter it, we
are not doing Christ's work in the world. If we have a weak faith
but expose it, we are being extremely foolish.

14:1 This verse assumes there will be differences of opinion in
the church (disputable matters). Paul says we are not to quarrel
about issues that are matters of opinion. Differences should not
be feared or avoided, but accepted and handled with love. Don't
expect everyone, even in the best possible church, to agree on
every subject. Through sharing ideas we can come to a fuller
understanding of what the Bible teaches. Accept, listen to, and
respect others. Differences of opinion need not cause division.
They can be a source of learning and richness in our relationships.

14:1ff What is weak faith? Paul is speaking about immature faith
that has not yet developed the muscle it needs to stand against
external pressures. For example, if a person who once worshiped
idols were to become a Christian, he might understand perfectly
well that Christ saved him through faith and that idols have no
real power. Still, because of his past associations, he might be
badly shaken if he knowingly ate meat that had been used in idol
worship as part of a pagan ritual. If a person who once worshiped
God on the required Jewish holy days were to become a Christian, he might well know that Christ saved him through faith, not

through his keeping of the law. Still, when the feast days came,
he might feel empty and unfaithful if he didn't dedicate those days
to God.

Paul responds to both weak brothers in love. Both are acting
according to their consciences, but their honest scruples do not
need to be made into rules for the church. Certainly some issues
are central to the faith and worth fighting for—but many are
based on individual differences and should not be legislated. Our
principle should be: In essentials, unity; in nonessentials, liberty;
in everything, love.

14:2 Eating "everything" may refer to freedom from dietary
restrictions, or it may refer to eating meat offered to idols, while
the person weaker in the faith eats only vegetables and refuses to
eat meat that has been offered to idols. But how would Christians
end up eating meat that had been offered to idols? The ancient
system of sacrifice was at the center of the religious, social, and
domestic life of the Roman world. After a sacrifice was presented
to a god in a pagan temple, only part of it was burned. The remainder was often sent to the market to be sold. Thus a Christian might
easily—even unknowingly—buy such meat in the marketplace
or eat it at the home of a friend. Should a Christian question the
source of his meat? Some thought there was nothing wrong with
eating meat that had been offered to idols because idols were
worthless and phony. Others carefully checked the source of their
meat or gave up meat altogether, in order to avoid a guilty conscience. The problem was especially acute for Christians who had
once been idol worshipers. For them, such a strong reminder of
their pagan days might weaken their newfound faith. Paul also
deals with this problem in 1 Corinthians 8.

14:10–12 Each person is accountable to Christ, not to others.
While the church must be uncompromising in its stand against
activities that are expressly forbidden by Scripture (adultery,
homosexuality, murder, theft), it should not create additional
rules and regulations and give them equal standing with God's
law. Many times Christians base their moral judgments on opinion, personal dislikes, or cultural bias rather than on the Word of
God. When they do this, they show that their own faith is weak—
they do not think that God is powerful enough to guide his children. When we stand before God's court of justice ("judgment
seat"), we won't be worried about what our Christian neighbor
has done (see 2 Corinthians 5:10).

"'As surely as I live,' says the Lord,
'every knee will bow before me;
every tongue will confess to God.'"ᵃˢ

¹²So then, each of us will give an account of himself to God. ᵗ

¹³Therefore let us stop passing judgment on one another. Instead, make up your mind not to put any stumbling block or obstacle in your brother's way. ¹⁴As one who is in the Lord Jesus, I am fully convinced that no food ᵇ is unclean in itself. But if anyone regards something as unclean, then for him it is unclean. ᵘ ¹⁵If your brother is distressed because of what you eat, you are no longer acting in love. Do not by your eating destroy your brother for whom Christ died. ᵛ ¹⁶Do not allow what you consider good to be spoken of as evil. ¹⁷For the kingdom of God is not a matter of eating and drinking,ʷ but of righteousness, peace and joy in the Holy Spirit,ˣ ¹⁸because anyone who serves Christ in this way is pleasing to God and approved by men.ʸ

¹⁹Let us therefore make every effort to do what leads to peaceᶻ and to mutual edification. ²⁰Do not destroy the work of God for the sake of food.ᵃ All food is clean, but it is wrong for a man to eat anything that causes someone else to stumble. ᵇ ²¹It is better not to eat meat or drink wine or to do anything else that will cause your brother to fall.

²²So whatever you believe about these things keep between yourself and God. Blessed is the man who does not condemn ᶜ himself by what he approves. ²³But the man who has doubts is condemned if he eats, because his eating is not from faith; and everything that does not come from faith is sin.

15 We who are strong ought to bear with the failings of the weakᵈ and not to please ourselves. ²Each of us should please his neighbor for his good,ᵉ to build him up. ᶠ ³For even Christ did not please himself but, as it is written: "The insults of those who insult you have fallen on me."ᶜ ᵍ ⁴For everything that was written in the past was written to teach us, so that through endurance and the encouragement of the Scriptures we might have hope.

⁵May the God who gives endurance and encouragement give you a spirit of unity among yourselves as you follow Christ Jesus, ⁶so that with one heart and mouth you may glorify the God and Father of our Lord Jesus Christ.

ᵃ11 Isaiah 45:23   ᵇ14 Or *that nothing*   ᶜ3 Psalm 69:9

14:11
ˢIsa 45:23

14:12
ᵗMt 12:36; 1Pe 4:5

14:14
ᵘ1Co 8:7

14:15
ᵛ1Co 8:11

14:17
ʷ1Co 8:8
ˣRo 15:13

14:18
ʸ2Co 8:21

14:19
ᶻRo 12:18

14:20
ᵃver 15
ᵇ1Co 8:9-12

14:22
ᶜ1Jn 3:21

15:1
ᵈRo 14:1;
Gal 6:1, 2

15:2
ᵉ1Co 10:33
ᶠRo 14:19

15:3
ᵍPs 69:9

14:13 Both strong and weak Christians can cause their brothers and sisters to stumble. The strong but insensitive Christian may flaunt his or her freedom and intentionally offend others' consciences. The scrupulous but weak Christian may try to fence others in with petty rules and regulations, thus causing dissension. Paul wants his readers to be both strong in the faith and sensitive to others' needs. Because we are all strong in some areas and weak in others, we need constantly to monitor the effects of our behavior on others.

14:13ff Some Christians use an invisible weaker brother to support their own opinions, prejudices, or standards. "You must live by these standards," they say, "or you will be offending the weaker brother." In truth, the person would often be offending no one but the speaker. While Paul urges us to be sensitive to those whose faith may be harmed by our actions, we should not sacrifice our liberty in Christ just to satisfy the selfish motives of those who are trying to force their opinions on us. Neither fear them nor criticize them, but follow Christ as closely as you can.

14:14 At the Jerusalem council (Acts 15), the Jewish church in Jerusalem asked the Gentile church in Antioch not to eat meat that had been sacrificed to idols. Paul was at the Jerusalem council, and he accepted this request not because he felt that eating such meat was wrong in itself, but because this practice would deeply offend many Jewish believers. Paul did not think the issue was worth dividing the church over; his desire was to promote unity. So he concludes, "if anyone regards something as unclean, then for him it is unclean." Paul's practice was to honor, as far as possible, the convictions of others.

Believers are called to accept one another without judging our varied opinions. However, when the situation has to be faced, how should we deal with those who disagree with us? Paul's response is that all believers should act in love so as to maintain peace in the church.

14:20, 21 Sin is not just a private matter. Everything we do affects others, and we have to think of them constantly. God created us to be interdependent, not independent. We who are strong in our faith must, without pride or condescension, treat others with love, patience, and self-restraint.

14:23 We try to steer clear of actions forbidden by Scripture, of course, but sometimes Scripture is silent. Then we should follow our consciences. "Everything that does not come from faith is sin" means that to go against a conviction will leave a person with a guilty or uneasy conscience. When God shows us that something is wrong for us, we should avoid it. But we should not look down on other Christians who exercise their freedom in those areas.

15:4 The knowledge of the Scriptures affects our attitude toward the present and the future. The more we know about what God has done in years past, the greater the confidence we have about what he will do in the days ahead. We should read our Bibles diligently to increase our trust that God's will is best for us.

15:5–7 The Roman church was a diverse community. It was made up of Jews and Gentiles, slaves and free people, rich and poor, strong and weak. So it was difficult for them to accept one another. Accepting means taking people into our homes as well as into our hearts, sharing meals and activities, and avoiding racial and economic discrimination. We must go out of our way to avoid favoritism. Consciously spend time greeting those you don't normally talk to, minimize differences, and seek common ground for fellowship. In this way you are accepting others as Christ has accepted you, and God is given glory.

15:7
h Ro 14:1

15:8
i Mt 15:24;
Ac 3:25, 26
j 2Co 1:20

15:9
k Ps 18:49

15:10
l Dt 32:43

15:11
m Ps 117:1

15:12
n Rev 5:5

15:16
o Ac 9:15

15:18
p Ac 21:19; Ro 1:5

15:19
q Ac 19:11

15:20
r 2Co 10:15, 16

15:21
s Isa 52:15

15:22
t Ro 1:13

7Accept one another,h then, just as Christ accepted you, in order to bring praise to God. 8For I tell you that Christ has become a servant of the Jewsa i on behalf of God's truth, to confirm the promisesj made to the patriarchs 9so that the Gentiles may glorify God for his mercy, as it is written:

"Therefore I will praise you among the Gentiles;
I will sing hymns to your name."b k

10Again, it says,

"Rejoice, O Gentiles, with his people."c l

11And again,

"Praise the Lord, all you Gentiles,
and sing praises to him, all you peoples."d m

12And again, Isaiah says,

"The Root of Jessen will spring up,
one who will arise to rule over the nations;
the Gentiles will hope in him."e

13May the God of hope fill you with all joy and peace as you trust in him, so that you may overflow with hope by the power of the Holy Spirit.

2. Personal notes
Paul the Minister to the Gentiles

14I myself am convinced, my brothers, that you yourselves are full of goodness, complete in knowledge and competent to instruct one another. 15I have written you quite boldly on some points, as if to remind you of them again, because of the grace God gave me 16to be a minister of Christ Jesus to the Gentileso with the priestly duty of proclaiming the gospel of God, so that the Gentiles might become an offering acceptable to God, sanctified by the Holy Spirit.

17Therefore I glory in Christ Jesus in my service to God. 18I will not venture to speak of anything except what Christ has accomplished through me in leading the Gentilesp to obey God by what I have said and done— 19by the power of signs and miracles,q through the power of the Spirit. So from Jerusalem all the way around to Illyricum, I have fully proclaimed the gospel of Christ. 20It has always been my ambition to preach the gospel where Christ was not known, so that I would not be building on someone else's foundation. r 21Rather, as it is written:

"Those who were not told about him will see,
and those who have not heard will understand."f s

22This is why I have often been hindered from coming to you. t

a8 Greek circumcision   b9 2 Samuel 22:50; Psalm 18:49   c10 Deut. 32:43   d11 Psalm 117:1   e12 Isaiah 11:10
f21 Isaiah 52:15

15:8 This verse means that Jesus came to bring the truth to the Jews and to show that God is true to his promises.

15:12 The "Root of Jesse" refers to Christ as the heir from the family line of Jesse, David's father (1 Samuel 16:1).

15:19 Illyricum was a Roman territory on the Adriatic Sea between present-day Italy and Greece. It covered much the same territory as present-day Yugoslavia. See the map in chapter 1, p. 1879.

15:20 Paul says that he has "ambition." Ambition can be a difficult topic for Christians because we see so many bad examples of ambitious people who claw their way to the top. But certainly that isn't the kind of ambition one sees in Paul. Instead of looking out for himself and working hard for personal advancement, he was ambitious to serve God—for Paul that meant to "preach the gospel where Christ was not known." Are you ambitious for God? Do you want, more than anything else, to please him and to do his will? Ask God for "holy ambition."

15:22 Paul wanted to visit the church at Rome, but he had delayed his visit because he had heard many good reports about the believers there and he knew they were doing well on their own. It was more important for him to preach in areas that had not yet heard the Good News.

Paul's Plan to Visit Rome

23 But now that there is no more place for me to work in these regions, and since I have been longing for many years to see you, u 24 I plan to do so when I go to Spain. I hope to visit you while passing through and to have you assist me on my journey there, after I have enjoyed your company for a while. 25 Now, however, I am on my way to Jerusalem v in the service w of the saints there. 26 For Macedonia and Achaia were pleased to make a contribution for the poor among the saints in Jerusalem. 27 They were pleased to do it, and indeed they owe it to them. For if the Gentiles have shared in the Jews' spiritual blessings, they owe it to the Jews to share with them their material blessings. x 28 So after I have completed this task and have made sure that they have received this fruit, I will go to Spain and visit you on the way. 29 I know that when I come to you, I will come in the full measure of the blessing of Christ.

30 I urge you, brothers, by our Lord Jesus Christ and by the love of the Spirit, to join me in my struggle by praying to God for me. y 31 Pray that I may be rescued from the unbelievers in Judea and that my service in Jerusalem may be acceptable to the saints there, 32 so that by God's will z I may come to you a with joy and together with you be refreshed. 33 The God of peace b be with you all. Amen.

Personal Greetings

16 I commend to you our sister Phoebe, a servant a of the church in Cenchrea. c 2 I ask you to receive her in the Lord d in a way worthy of the saints and to give her any help she may need from you, for she has been a great help to many people, including me.

3 Greet Priscilla b and Aquila, e my fellow workers in Christ Jesus. 4 They risked their lives for me. Not only I but all the churches of the Gentiles are grateful to them.
5 Greet also the church that meets at their house. f
Greet my dear friend Epenetus, who was the first convert g to Christ in the province of Asia.
6 Greet Mary, who worked very hard for you.

a 1 Or *deaconess*   b 3 Greek *Prisca*, a variant of *Priscilla*

15:23
u Ac 19:21;
Ro 1:10, 11

15:25
v Ac 19:21
w Ac 24:17

15:27
x 1Co 9:11

15:30
y 2Co 1:11; Col 4:12

15:32
z Ac 18:21
a Ro 1:10, 13

15:33
b Ro 16:20;
2Co 13:11; Php 4:9

16:1
c Ac 18:18

16:2
d Php 2:29

16:3
e Ac 18:2

16:5
f 1Co 16:19;
Col 4:15
g 1Co 16:15

15:23, 24 Paul was referring to the completion of his work in Corinth, the city from which he most likely wrote this letter. Most of Paul's three-month stay in Achaia (see Acts 20:3) was probably spent in Corinth. He believed that he had accomplished what God wanted him to do there, and he was looking forward to taking the gospel to new lands west of Rome. When Paul eventually went to Rome, however, it was as a prisoner (see Acts 28). Tradition says that Paul was released for a time, and that he used this opportunity to go to Spain to preach the Good News. This journey is not mentioned in the book of Acts.

15:27 If the Gentiles had received the gospel ("spiritual blessings") originally from Jerusalem, surely they would want to offer financial help ("material blessings").

15:28 Paul's future plan was to go to Spain because Spain was at the very western end of the civilized world. He wanted to extend Christianity there. Also, Spain had many great minds and influential leaders in the Roman world (Lucan, Martial, Hadrian), and perhaps Paul thought Christianity would advance greatly in such an atmosphere.

15:30 Too often we see prayer as a time for comfort, reflection, or making requests to God. But here Paul urges believers to join in his *struggle* by means of prayer. Prayer is a weapon that all believers should use in interceding for others. Many of us know believers who are living in difficult places in order to communicate the gospel. Sending them funds is part of joining them in their struggles, but prayer is also a crucial way of being with them. Missionaries strongly desire the prayers of those who have sent them out. Do your prayers reflect that struggle on their behalf?

15:33 This phrase sounds like it should signal the end of the book, and it does pronounce the end of Paul's teaching. He concludes his letter, then, with personal greetings and remarks.

16:1, 2 Phoebe was known as a servant (the Greek word used here is often translated "deaconess") and a helper. Apparently she was a wealthy person who helped support Paul's ministry. Phoebe was highly regarded in the church, and she may have delivered this letter from Corinth to Rome. This provides evidence that women had important roles in the early church. Cenchrea, the town where Phoebe lived, was the eastern port of Corinth, six miles from the city center.

16:3 Priscilla and Aquila were a married couple who had become Paul's close friends. They, along with all other Jews, had been expelled from Rome by the emperor (Acts 18:2, 3) and had moved to Corinth. There they met Paul and invited him to live with them. They were Christians before they met Paul, and probably told him much about the Roman church. Like Paul, Priscilla and Aquila were missionaries. They helped believers in Ephesus (Acts 18:18–28), in Rome when they were allowed to return, and again at Ephesus (2 Timothy 4:19).

16:3 Priscilla and Aquila ministered effectively behind the scenes. Their tools were hospitality, friendship, and person-to-person teaching. They were not public speakers, but private evangelists. For some of the Romans, their home was used for church meetings (16:5). Priscilla and Aquila challenge us with what a couple can do together to serve Christ. Do we regard our families and homes as gifts through which God can accomplish his work? How might God want to use your home and family to serve him?

16:5ff Paul's personal greetings went to Romans and Greeks, Jews and Gentiles, men and women, prisoners and prominent citizens. The church's base was broad: it crossed cultural, social, and economic lines. From this list we learn that the Christian community was mobile. Though Paul had not yet been to Rome, he had met these people in other places on his journeys.

7 Greet Andronicus and Junias, my relatives who have been in prison with me. They are outstanding among the apostles, and they were in Christ before I was.

8 Greet Ampliatus, whom I love in the Lord.

9 Greet Urbanus, our fellow worker in Christ, and my dear friend Stachys.

10 Greet Apelles, tested and approved in Christ.

Greet those who belong to the household of Aristobulus.

11 Greet Herodion, my relative.

Greet those in the household of Narcissus who are in the Lord.

12 Greet Tryphena and Tryphosa, those women who work hard in the Lord.

Greet my dear friend Persis, another woman who has worked very hard in the Lord.

13 Greet Rufus, chosen in the Lord, and his mother, who has been a mother to me, too.

14 Greet Asyncritus, Phlegon, Hermes, Patrobas, Hermas and the brothers with them.

15 Greet Philologus, Julia, Nereus and his sister, and Olympas and all the saints with them.

16:16
h 1Co 16:20;
2Co 13:12

16 Greet one another with a holy kiss. *h*

All the churches of Christ send greetings.

16:17
i 2Th 3:6, 14

16:18
j Php 3:19
k Col 2:4

16:19
l Ro 1:8
m Mt 10:16

17 I urge you, brothers, to watch out for those who cause divisions and put obstacles in your way that are contrary to the teaching you have learned. Keep away from them. *i* 18 For such people are not serving our Lord Christ, but their own appetites. *j* By smooth talk and flattery they deceive *k* the minds of naive people. 19 Everyone has heard *l* about your obedience, so I am full of joy over you; but I want you to be wise about what is good, and innocent about what is evil. *m*

16:20
n Ro 15:33

20 The God of peace *n* will soon crush Satan under your feet.

The grace of our Lord Jesus be with you.

16:21
o Ac 16:1
p Ac 13:1
q Ac 17:5

21 Timothy, *o* my fellow worker, sends his greetings to you, as do Lucius, *p* Jason *q* and Sosipater, my relatives.

22 I, Tertius, who wrote down this letter, greet you in the Lord.

23 Gaius, whose hospitality I and the whole church here enjoy, sends you his greetings.

Erastus, who is the city's director of public works, and our brother Quartus send you their greetings. *a*

25 Now to him who is able to establish you by my gospel and the proclamation of Jesus Christ, according to the revelation of the mystery hidden for long ages past, 26 but now revealed and made known through the prophetic writings by the command of the eternal God, so that all nations might believe and obey him— 27 to the only wise God be glory forever through Jesus Christ! Amen.

a 23 Some manuscripts their greetings. 24 May the grace of our Lord Jesus Christ be with all of you. Amen.

16:7 The fact that Andronicus and Junias were "outstanding among the apostles" could mean they had distinguished themselves as apostles. They may have been a husband and wife team. Paul notes that they were "relatives" (fellow Jews) who at one time had been in prison with him.

16:17–20 When we read books or listen to sermons, we should check the content of what is written or said and not be fooled by smooth style. Christians who study God's Word will not be fooled, even though superficial listeners may easily be taken in. For an example of believers who carefully checked God's Word, see Acts 17:10–12.

16:21 Timothy was a key person in the growth of the early church, traveling with Paul on his second missionary journey (Acts 16:1–3). Later Paul wrote two letters to him as he worked to strengthen the churches in Ephesus—1 and 2 Timothy. See his Profile in the book of 1 Timothy, p. 2037.

16:25–27 Paul exclaims that it is wonderful to be alive when the mystery, God's secret—his way of saving the Gentiles—

is becoming known throughout the world! All the Old Testament prophecies were coming true, and God was using Paul as his instrument to tell this Good News.

16:25–27 As Jerusalem was the center of Jewish life, Rome was the world's political, religious, social, and economic center. There the major governmental decisions were made, and from there the gospel spread to the ends of the earth. The church in Rome was a cosmopolitan mixture of Jews, Gentiles, slaves, free people, men, women, Roman citizens, and world travelers; therefore, it had potential for both great influence and great conflict.

Paul had not yet been to Rome to meet all the Christians there, and, of course, he has not yet met us. We too live in a cosmopolitan setting with the entire world open to us. We also have the potential for both widespread influence and wrenching conflict. We should listen carefully to and apply Paul's teaching about unity, service, and love.

1 CORINTHIANS

VITAL STATISTICS

PURPOSE:
To identify problems in the Corinthian church, to offer solutions, and to teach the believers how to live for Christ in a corrupt society

AUTHOR:
Paul

ORIGINAL AUDIENCE:
The church in Corinth

DATE WRITTEN:
Approximately A.D. 55, near the end of Paul's three-year ministry in Ephesus, during his third missionary journey

SETTING:
Corinth was a major cosmopolitan city, a seaport and major trade center—the most important city in Achaia. It was also filled with idolatry and immorality. The church was largely made up of Gentiles. Paul had established this church on his second missionary journey.

KEY VERSE:
"I appeal to you, brothers, in the name of our Lord Jesus Christ, that all of you agree with one another so that there may be no divisions among you and that you may be perfectly united in mind and thought" (1:10).

KEY PEOPLE:
Paul, Timothy, members of Chloe's household

KEY PLACES:
Worship meetings in Corinth

SPECIAL FEATURES:
This is a strong, straight-forward letter.

ON A bed of grass, a chameleon's skin turns green. On the earth, it becomes brown. The animal changes to match the environment. Many creatures blend into nature with God-given camouflage suits to aid their survival. It's natural to fit in and adapt to the environment. But followers of Christ are *new creations,* born from above and changed from within, with values and life-styles that confront the world and clash with accepted morals. True believers don't blend in very well.

The Christians in Corinth were struggling with their environment. Surrounded by corruption and every conceivable sin, they felt the pressure to adapt. They knew they were free in Christ, but what did this freedom mean? How should they view idols or sexuality? What should they do about marriage, women in the church, and the gifts of the Spirit? These were more than theoretical questions—the church was being undermined by immorality and spiritual immaturity. The believers' faith was being tried in the crucible of immoral Corinth, and some of them were failing the test.

Paul heard of their struggles and wrote this letter to address their problems, heal their divisions, and answer their questions. Paul confronted them with their sin and their need for corrective action and clear commitment to Christ.

After a brief introduction (1:1–9), Paul immediately turns to the question of unity (1:10—4:21). He emphasizes the clear and simple gospel message around which all believers should rally, he explains the role of church leaders, and he urges them to grow up in their faith.

Paul then deals with the immorality of certain church members and the issue of lawsuits among Christians (5:1—6:8). He tells the believers to exercise church discipline and to settle their internal matters themselves. Because so many of the problems in the Corinthian church involved sex, Paul denounces sexual sin in the strongest possible terms (6:9–20).

Next, Paul answers some of the Corinthians' questions. Because prostitution and immorality were pervasive, marriages in Corinth were in shambles, and Christians weren't sure how to react. Paul gives pointed and practical answers (7:1–40). Concerning the question of meat sacrificed to idols, Paul suggests that they show complete commitment to Christ and sensitivity to other believers, especially weaker brothers and sisters (8:1—11:1).

Paul goes on to talk about worship, and he carefully explains the role of women, the Lord's Supper, and spiritual gifts (11:2—14:40). Sandwiched in the middle of this section is his magnificent description of the greatest gift—love (chapter 13). Then Paul concludes with a discussion of the resurrection (15:1–58), some final thoughts, greetings, and a benediction (16:1–24).

This letter confronts the Corinthians about their sins and shortcomings. And 1 Corinthians calls all Christians to be careful not to blend in with the world and accept its values and life-styles. We must live Christ-centered, blameless, loving lives that make a difference for God. As you read 1 Corinthians, examine your values in light of complete commitment to Christ.

THE BLUEPRINT

A. PAUL ADDRESSES CHURCH
   PROBLEMS
   (1:1—6:20)
   1. Divisions in the church
   2. Disorder in the church

B. PAUL ANSWERS CHURCH
   QUESTIONS
   (7:1—16:24)
   1. Instruction on Christian marriage
   2. Instruction on Christian freedom
   3. Instruction on public worship
   4. Instruction on resurrection

Without Paul's presence, the Corinthian church had fallen into divisiveness and disorder. This resulted in many problems, which Paul addressed squarely. We must be concerned for unity and order in our local churches, but we should not mistake inactivity for order and cordiality for unity. We, too, must squarely address problems in our churches.

The Corinthians had sent Paul a list of questions, and he answered them in a way meant to correct abuses in the church and to show how important it is that they live what they believe. Paul gives us a Christian approach to problem solving. He analyzed the problem thoroughly to uncover the underlying issue and then highlighted the biblical values that should guide our actions.

MEGATHEMES

THEME	EXPLANATION	IMPORTANCE
Loyalties	The Corinthians were rallying around various church leaders and teachers—Peter, Paul, and Apollos. These loyalties led to intellectual pride and created a spirit of division in the church.	Our loyalty to human leaders or human wisdom must never divide Christians into camps. We must care for our fellow believers, not fight with them. Your allegiance must be to Christ. Let him lead you.
Immorality	Paul received a report of uncorrected sexual sin in the church at Corinth. The people had grown indifferent to immorality. Others had misconceptions about marriage. We are to live morally, keeping our bodies for God's service at all times.	Christians must never compromise with sinful ideas and practices. We should not blend in with people around us. You must live up to God's standard of morality and not condone immoral behavior, even if society accepts it.
Freedom	Paul taught freedom of choice on practices not expressly forbidden in Scripture. Some believers felt certain actions—like eating the meat of animals used in pagan rituals—were corrupt by association. Others felt free to participate in such actions without feeling that they had sinned.	We are free in Christ, yet we must not abuse our Christian freedom by being inconsiderate and insensitive to others. We must never encourage others to do something they feel is wrong just because we have done it. Let love guide your behavior.
Worship	Paul addressed disorder in worship. People were taking the Lord's Supper without first confessing sin. There was misuse of spiritual gifts and confusion over women's roles in the church.	Worship must be carried out properly and in an orderly manner. Everything we do to worship God should be done in a manner worthy of his high honor. Make sure that worship is harmonious, useful, and edifying to all believers.
Resurrection	Some people denied that Christ rose from the dead. Others felt that people would not physically be resurrected. Christ's resurrection assures us that we will have new, living bodies after we die. The hope of the resurrection forms the secret of Christian confidence.	Since we will be raised again to life after we die, our life is not in vain. We must stay faithful to God in our morality and our service. We are to live today knowing we will spend eternity with Christ.

A. PAUL ADDRESSES CHURCH PROBLEMS (1:1—6:20)

Through various sources, Paul had received reports of problems in the Corinthian church, including jealousy, divisiveness, sexual immorality, and failure to discipline members. Churches today must also address the problems they face. We can learn a great deal by observing how Paul handled these delicate situations.

1 Paul, called to be an apostle *a* of Christ Jesus by the will of God, *b* and our brother Sosthenes,

1:1
a Ro 1:1
b 2Co 1:1

2 To the church of God in Corinth, to those sanctified in Christ Jesus and called *c* to be holy, together with all those everywhere who call on the name of our Lord Jesus Christ—their Lord and ours:

1:2
c Ro 1:7

3 Grace and peace to you from God our Father and the Lord Jesus Christ. *d*

1:3
d Ro 1:7

Thanksgiving

4 I always thank God for you *e* because of his grace given you in Christ Jesus. **5** For in him you have been enriched in every way—in all your speaking and in all your knowledge— **6** because our testimony *f* about Christ was confirmed in you. **7** Therefore you do not lack any spiritual gift as you eagerly wait for our Lord Jesus Christ to be revealed. *g* **8** He will keep you strong to the end, so that you will be blameless on the day of our Lord Jesus Christ. **9** God, who has called you into fellowship with his Son Jesus Christ our Lord, is faithful. *h*

1:4
e Ro 1:8
1:6
f Rev 1:2
1:7
g Php 3:20;
2Pe 3:12
1:9
h Isa 49:7

1:1 Paul wrote this letter to the church in Corinth while he was visiting Ephesus during his third missionary journey (Acts 19:1—20:1). Corinth and Ephesus faced each other across the Aegean Sea. Paul knew the Corinthian church well because he had spent 18 months in Corinth during his second missionary journey (Acts 18:1–18). While in Ephesus, he had heard about problems in Corinth (1:11). About the same time, a delegation from the Corinthian church had visited Paul to ask his advice about their conflicts (16:17). Paul's purpose for writing was to correct those problems and to answer questions church members had asked in a previous letter (7:1).

1:1 Paul was given a special calling from God to preach about Jesus Christ. Each Christian has a job to do, a role to take, or a contribution to make. One assignment may seem more spectacular than another, but all are necessary to carry out God's greater plans for his church and for his world (12:12–27). Be available to God by placing your gifts at his service. Then as you discover what he calls you to do, be ready to do it.

1:1 Sosthenes may have been Paul's secretary who wrote down this letter as Paul dictated it. He was probably the Jewish synagogue leader in Corinth (Acts 18:17) who had been beaten during an attack on Paul, and then later became a believer. Sosthenes was well known to the members of the Corinthian church, and so Paul included his familiar name in the opening of the letter.

1:2 Corinth, a giant cultural melting pot with a great diversity of wealth, religions, and moral standards, had a reputation for being fiercely independent and as decadent as any city in the world. The Romans had destroyed Corinth in 146 B.C. after a rebellion. But in 46 B.C., the Roman Emperor Julius Caesar rebuilt it because of its strategic seaport. By Paul's day (A.D. 50), the Romans had made Corinth the capital of Achaia (present-day Greece). It was a large city, offering Rome great profits through trade as well as the military protection of its ports. But the city's prosperity made it ripe for all sorts of corruption. Idolatry flourished, and there were more than a dozen pagan temples employing at least a thousand prostitutes. Corinth's reputation was such that prostitutes in other cities began to be called "Corinthian girls."

1:2 A personal invitation makes a person feel wanted and welcome. We are "called to be holy." God personally invites us to be citizens of his eternal kingdom. But Jesus Christ, God's Son, is the only one who can bring us into this glorious kingdom because he is the only one who removes our sins.

Sanctified means that we are chosen or set apart by Christ for his service. We accept God's invitation by accepting his Son, Jesus Christ, and by trusting in the work he did on the cross to forgive our sins.

1:2 By including a salutation to "all those everywhere who call on the name of our Lord Jesus Christ," Paul is making it clear that this is not a private letter. Although it deals with specific issues facing the church at Corinth, all believers can learn from it. The Corinthian church included a great cross section of believers—wealthy merchants, common laborers, former temple prostitutes, and middle-class families. Because of the wide diversity of people and backgrounds, Paul takes great pains to stress the need for both spiritual unity and Christlike character.

1:3 Grace is God's free gift of salvation given to us in Christ. Receiving it brings us peace (see Romans 5:1). In a world of noise, confusion, and relentless pressures, people long for peace. Many give up the search, thinking it impossible to find, but true peace of heart and mind is available to us through faith in Jesus Christ.

1:4–6 Paul thanked God for the Corinthian believers. During the Thanksgiving holiday, we focus on our blessings and express our gratitude to God for them. But thanks should be expressed every day. We can never say thank you enough to parents, friends, leaders, and especially to God. When thanksgiving becomes an integral part of your life, you will find that your attitude toward life will change. You will become more positive, gracious, loving, and humble. Whom do you need to thank today?

1:7 The Corinthian church members had all the spiritual gifts they needed to live the Christian life, to witness for Christ, and to stand against the paganism and immorality of Corinth. But instead of using what God had given them, they were arguing over which gifts were more important. Paul addresses this issue in depth in chapters 12—14.

1:7–9 Before tackling the problems, Paul described his hope for the Corinthians. He guaranteed these believers that God would consider them "blameless" when Christ returns (see also Ephesians 1:7–10). This guarantee was not because of their great gifts or their shining performance, but because of what Jesus Christ accomplished for them through his death and resurrection. *All* who believe in the Lord Jesus will be considered blameless when Jesus Christ returns (see also 1 Thessalonians 3:13; Hebrews 9:28). Today's struggles, difficulties, and failures don't tell the whole story. Keep the big picture in mind. If you have faith in Christ, even if it is weak, you *are* and *will be* saved.

1. Divisions in the church

¹⁰I appeal to you, brothers, in the name of our Lord Jesus Christ, that all of you agree with one another so that there may be no divisions among you and that you may be perfectly united in mind and thought. ¹¹My brothers, some from Chloe's household have informed me that there are quarrels among you. ¹²What I mean is this: One of you says, "I follow Paul"; another, "I follow Apollos"; another, "I follow Cephas ᵃ"; still another, "I follow Christ."

¹³Is Christ divided? Was Paul crucified for you? Were you baptized into ᵇ the name of Paul? ¹⁴I am thankful that I did not baptize any of you except Crispus ᶦ and Gaius, ʲ ¹⁵so no one can say that you were baptized into my name. ¹⁶(Yes, I also baptized the household of

1:14
ᶦ Ac 18:8; Ro 16:23
ʲ Ac 19:29

ᵃ 12 That is, Peter   ᵇ 13 Or in; also in verse 15

CORINTH AND EPHESUS
Paul wrote this letter to Corinth during his three-year visit in Ephesus on his third missionary journey. The two cities sat across from each other on the Aegean Sea—both were busy and important ports. Titus may have carried this letter from Ephesus to Corinth (2 Corinthians 12:18).

1:10 Paul founded the church in Corinth on his second missionary journey. Eighteen months after he left, arguments and divisions arose, and some church members slipped back into an immoral lifestyle. Paul wrote this letter to address the problems, to clear up confusion about right and wrong, and to remove the immorality among them. The Corinthian people had a reputation for jumping from fad to fad; Paul wanted to keep Christianity from degenerating into just another fad.

1:10 By saying "brothers," Paul is emphasizing that all Christians are part of God's family. Believers share a unity that runs even deeper than that of blood brothers and sisters.

1:10, 11 Like a frustrated coach watching his team bicker on the court, Paul called for a time-out. He saw the danger of divisions and arguments. The Corinthian believers' lack of unity was obvious. They may have been playing in the same "uniform," but they were doing as much as the opposition to bring about their own defeat. The problems weren't so much differences of opinion as divided allegiances. They were arguing over which position on the team was most important in a way that made them ineffective as a unit. They were on the field, but out of the game.

Divisions between Christians work like brick walls and barbed-wire fences to undermine the effectiveness of the message that believers are to proclaim. Focus on your coach, Jesus Christ, and the purpose he has for you. Strive for harmony. Keep arguments about allegiances off the team.

1:12ff In this large and diverse Corinthian church, the believers favored different preachers. Because there was as yet no written New Testament, the believers depended heavily on preaching and teaching for spiritual insight into the meaning of the Old Testament. Some followed Paul, who had founded their church; some who had heard Peter (Cephas) in Jerusalem followed him; while others listened only to Apollos, an eloquent and popular preacher who had had a dynamic ministry in Corinth (Acts 18:24; 19:1). Although these three preachers were united in their message, their personalities attracted different people. At this time the church was in danger of dividing. By mentioning Jesus Christ ten times in the first ten verses, Paul makes it clear who it is all preachers and teachers should emphasize. God's message is much more important than any human messenger.

1:12, 13 Paul wondered whether the Corinthians' quarrels had "divided" Christ. This is a graphic picture of what happens when the church (the body of Christ) is divided into factions. With the many churches and styles of worship available today, we could get caught up in the same game of "my preacher is better than yours!" To do so would divide Christ again. But Christ is not divided, and his true followers should not allow anything to divide them. Don't let your appreciation for any teacher, preacher, or author lead you into intellectual pride. Our allegiance must be to Christ and to the unity that he desires.

Stephanas;*k* beyond that, I don't remember if I baptized anyone else.) ¹⁷For Christ did not send me to baptize, but to preach the gospel—not with words of human wisdom, lest the cross of Christ be emptied of its power.

1:16
k 1Co 16:15

Christ the Wisdom and Power of God

¹⁸For the message of the cross is foolishness to those who are perishing, but to us who are being saved it is the power of God. *l* ¹⁹For it is written:

> "I will destroy the wisdom of the wise;
>   the intelligence of the intelligent I will frustrate."*a m*

1:18
l Ro 1:16

1:19
m Isa 29:14

²⁰Where is the wise man? Where is the scholar? Where is the philosopher of this age? Has not God made foolish*n* the wisdom of the world? ²¹For since in the wisdom of God the world through its wisdom did not know him, God was pleased through the foolishness of what was preached to save those who believe. ²²Jews demand miraculous signs*o* and Greeks look for wisdom, ²³but we preach Christ crucified: a stumbling block*p* to Jews and foolishness*q* to Gentiles, ²⁴but to those whom God has called, both Jews and Greeks, Christ the power of God and the wisdom of God.*r* ²⁵For the foolishness of God is wiser than man's wisdom, and the weakness of God is stronger than man's strength.

1:20
n Ro 1:22

1:22
o Mt 12:38

1:23
p Gal 5:11
q 1Co 2:14

1:24
r Col 2:3

²⁶Brothers, think of what you were when you were called. Not many of you were wise by human standards; not many were influential; not many were of noble birth. ²⁷But God chose*s* the foolish things of the world to shame the wise; God chose the weak things of the world to shame the strong. ²⁸He chose the lowly things of this world and the despised things—and the things that are not—to nullify the things that are, ²⁹so that no one may boast before him.*t* ³⁰It is because of him that you are in Christ Jesus, who has become for us wisdom from God—that is, our righteousness, holiness and redemption. *u* ³¹Therefore, as it is written: "Let him who boasts boast in the Lord."*b v*

1:27
s Jas 2:5

1:29
t Eph 2:9

1:30
u Eph 1:7, 14

1:31
v Jer 9:23, 24

a 19 Isaiah 29:14   *b 31* Jer. 9:24

1:17 When Paul said that Christ didn't send him to baptize, he wasn't minimizing the importance of baptism. Baptism was commanded by Jesus himself (Matthew 28:19) and practiced by the early church (Acts 2:41). Paul was emphasizing that no one person should do everything. Paul's gift was preaching, and that's what he did. Christian ministry should be a team effort; no preacher or teacher is a complete link between God and people, and no individual can do all that the apostles did. We must be content with the contribution God has given us to make, and carry it out wholeheartedly. (For more on different gifts, see chapters 12 and 13.)

1:17 Some speakers use impressive words, but they are weak on content. Paul stressed solid content and practical help for his listeners. He wanted them to be impressed with his *message*, not just his style (see 2:1–5). You don't need to be a great speaker with a large vocabulary to share the gospel effectively. The persuasive power is in the story, not the storyteller. Paul was not against those who carefully prepare what they say (see 2:6), but against those who try to impress others only with their own knowledge or speaking ability.

1:19 Paul summarizes Isaiah 29:14 to emphasize a point Jesus often made: God's way of thinking is not like the world's way (normal human wisdom). And God offers eternal life, which the world can never give. We can spend a lifetime accumulating human wisdom and yet never learn how to have a personal relationship with God. We must come to the crucified and risen Christ to receive eternal life and the joy of a personal relationship with our Savior.

1:22–24 Many Jews considered the Good News of Jesus Christ to be foolish, because they thought the Messiah would be a conquering king accompanied by signs and miracles. Jesus had not restored David's throne as they expected. Besides, he was executed as a criminal, and how could a criminal be a savior? Greeks, too, considered the gospel foolish: they did not believe in a bodily resurrection; they did not see in Jesus the powerful characteristics of their mythological gods; and they thought no reputable person would be crucified. To them, death was defeat, not victory.

The Good News of Jesus Christ still sounds foolish to many. Our society worships power, influence, and wealth. Jesus came as a humble, poor servant, and he offers his kingdom to those who have faith, not to those who do all kinds of good deeds to try to earn his gifts. This looks foolish to the world, but Christ is our power, the only way we can be saved. Knowing Christ personally is the greatest wisdom anyone could have.

1:25 The message of Christ's death for sins sounds foolish to those who don't believe. Death seems to be the end of the road, the ultimate weakness. But Jesus did not stay dead. His resurrection demonstrated his power even over death. And he will save us from eternal death and give us everlasting life if we trust him as Savior and Lord. This sounds so simple that many people won't accept it. They try other ways to obtain eternal life (being good, being wise, etc.). But all their attempts will not work. The "foolish" people who simply accept Christ's offer are actually the wisest of all, because they alone will live eternally with God.

1:27 Is Christianity against rational thinking? Christians clearly do believe in using their minds to weigh the evidence and make wise choices. Paul is declaring that no amount of human knowledge can replace or bypass Christ's work on the cross. If it could, Christ would be accessible only to the intellectually gifted and well educated, and not to ordinary people or to children.

1:28–31 Paul continues to emphasize that the way to receive salvation is so simple that *any* person who wants to can understand it. Skill and wisdom do not get a person into God's kingdom—simple faith does—so no one can boast that his or her achievements helped him or her secure eternal life. Salvation is totally from God through Jesus' death. There is *nothing* we can do to earn our salvation; we need only accept what Jesus has already done for us.

1:30 God is the source of and the reason for our personal and living relationship with Christ. Our union and identification with Christ results in our having God's wisdom and knowledge (Colossians 2:3), possessing right standing with God (*righteousness*, 2 Corinthians 5:21), being holy (1 Thessalonians 4:3–7),

2:1
ʷ1Co 1:17

2:2
ˣGal 6:14

2:4
ʸRo 15:19

2:5
ᶻ2Co 4:7

2 When I came to you, brothers, I did not come with eloquence or superior wisdom ʷ as I proclaimed to you the testimony about God. ᵃ ²For I resolved to know nothing while I was with you except Jesus Christ and him crucified. ˣ ³I came to you in weakness and fear, and with much trembling. ⁴My message and my preaching were not with wise and persuasive words, but with a demonstration of the Spirit's power, ʸ ⁵so that your faith might not rest on men's wisdom, but on God's power. ᶻ

Wisdom From the Spirit

2:6
ᵃ1Co 1:20

⁶We do, however, speak a message of wisdom among the mature, but not the wisdom of this age ᵃ or of the rulers of this age, who are coming to nothing. ⁷No, we speak of God's secret wisdom, a wisdom that has been hidden and that God destined for our glory before time began. ⁸None of the rulers of this age understood it, for if they had, they would not have crucified the Lord of glory. ⁹However, as it is written:

2:9
ᵇIsa 64:4

"No eye has seen,
    no ear has heard,
    no mind has conceived
        what God has prepared for those who love him" ᵇ ᵇ—

2:11
ᶜPr 20:27

2:12
ᵈRo 8:15

¹⁰but God has revealed it to us by his Spirit.

The Spirit searches all things, even the deep things of God. ¹¹For who among men knows the thoughts of a man except the man's spirit ᶜ within him? In the same way no one knows the thoughts of God except the Spirit of God. ¹²We have not received the spirit ᵈ of the world

ᵃ1 Some manuscripts *as I proclaimed to you God's mystery*   ᵇ9 Isaiah 64:4

HIGHLIGHTS OF 1 CORINTHIANS	The Meaning of the Cross 1:18—2:16	Be considerate of one another because of what Christ has done for us. There is no place for pride or a know-it-all attitude. We are to have the mind of Christ.
	The Story of the Last Supper 11:23–29	The Last Supper is a time of reflection on Christ's final words to his disciples before he died on the cross; we must celebrate this in an orderly and correct manner.
	The Poem of Love 13:1–13	Love is to guide all we do. We have different gifts, abilities, likes, dislikes—but we are called, without exception, to love.
	The Christian's Destiny 15:42–58	We are promised by Christ, who died for us, that as he came back to life after death, so our perishable bodies will be exchanged for heavenly bodies. Then we will live and reign with Christ.

---

and having the penalty for our sins paid by Jesus (*redemption*, Mark 10:45).

2:1 Paul was referring to his first visit to Corinth during his second missionary journey (A.D. 51), when he founded the church (Acts 18:1ff).

2:1–5 A brilliant scholar, Paul could have overwhelmed his listeners with intellectual arguments. Instead he shared the simple message of Jesus Christ by allowing the Holy Spirit to guide his words. In sharing the gospel with others, we should follow Paul's example and keep our message simple and basic. The Holy Spirit will give power to our words and use them to bring glory to Jesus.

2:4 Paul's confidence was not in his keen intellect or speaking ability but in his knowledge that the Holy Spirit was helping and guiding him. Paul is not denying the importance of study and preparation for preaching—he had a thorough education in the Scriptures. Effective preaching must combine studious preparation with reliance on the work of the Holy Spirit. Don't use Paul's statement as an excuse for not studying or preparing.

2:7 God's "secret wisdom . . . that has been hidden" was his offer of salvation to all people. Originally unknown to humanity, this plan became crystal clear when Jesus rose from the dead. His resurrection proved that he had power over sin and death and could offer us this power as well (see also 1 Peter 1:10–12 and the first note on Romans 16:25–27). God's plan, however, is still

hidden to unbelievers because they either refuse to accept it, choose to ignore it, or simply haven't heard about it.

2:8 Jesus was misunderstood and rejected by those whom the world considered wise and great. He was put to death by the rulers in Palestine—the high priest, King Herod, Pilate, and the Pharisees and Sadducees. Jesus' rejection by these rulers had been predicted in Isaiah 53:3 and Zechariah 12:10, 11.

2:9 We cannot imagine all that God has in store for us, both in this life and for eternity. He will create a new heaven and a new earth (Isaiah 65:17; Revelation 21:1), and we will live with him forever. Until then, his Holy Spirit comforts and guides us. Knowing the wonderful and eternal future that awaits us gives us hope and courage to press on in this life, to endure hardship, and to avoid giving in to temptation. This world is not all there is. The best is yet to come.

2:10 The "deep things of God" refers to God's unfathomable nature and his wonderful plan—Jesus' death and resurrection—and to the promise of salvation, revealed only to those who believe that what God says is true. Those who believe in Christ's death and resurrection and put their faith in him will know all they need to know to be saved. This knowledge, however, can't be grasped by even the wisest people unless they accept God's message. All who reject God's message are foolish, no matter how wise the world thinks they are.

but the Spirit who is from God, that we may understand what God has freely given us. ¹³This is what we speak, not in words taught us by human wisdom but in words taught by the Spirit, expressing spiritual truths in spiritual words.ᵃ ¹⁴The man without the Spirit does not accept the things that come from the Spirit of God, for they are foolishnessᵉ to him, and he cannot understand them, because they are spiritually discerned. ¹⁵The spiritual man makes judgments about all things, but he himself is not subject to any man's judgment:

> ¹⁶ "For who has known the mind of the Lord
>   that he may instruct him?"ᵇ

But we have the mind of Christ.ᶠ

On Divisions in the Church

3 Brothers, I could not address you as spiritualᵍ but as worldlyʰ—mere infantsⁱ in Christ. ²I gave you milk, not solid food,ʲ for you were not yet ready for it. Indeed, you are still not ready. ³You are still worldly. For since there is jealousy and quarrelingᵏ among you, are you not worldly? Are you not acting like mere men? ⁴For when one says, "I follow Paul," and another, "I follow Apollos," are you not mere men?

⁵What, after all, is Apollos? And what is Paul? Only servants, through whom you came to believe—as the Lord has assigned to each his task. ⁶I planted the seed,ˡ Apollos watered it, but God made it grow. ⁷So neither he who plants nor he who waters is anything, but only God, who makes things grow. ⁸The man who plants and the man who waters have one purpose, and each will be rewarded according to his own labor. ⁹For we are God's fellow workers;ᵐ you are God's field, God's building.ⁿ

¹⁰By the grace God has given me,ᵒ I laid a foundation as an expert builder, and someone else is building on it. But each one should be careful how he builds. ¹¹For no one can lay any

ᵃ *13* Or *Spirit, interpreting spiritual truths to spiritual men*   ᵇ *16* Isaiah 40:13

2:14
ᵉ 1Co 1:18

2:16
ᶠ Jn 15:15

3:1
ᵍ 1Co 2:15
ʰ 1Co 2:14
ⁱ Heb 5:13

3:2
ʲ Heb 5:12-14;
1Pe 2:2

3:3
ᵏ Gal 5:20

3:6
ˡ Ac 18:4-11

3:9
ᵐ 2Co 6:1
ⁿ Eph 2:20-22

3:10
ᵒ Ro 12:3

2:13 Everyone wants to be wise. Yet Paul taught the Corinthians that true wisdom or discernment requires the believer to be guided by the Holy Spirit. Because Satan's greatest impact on us occurs when he deceives us, we need the Holy Spirit's help. Spiritual discernment enables us to draw conclusions based on God's perspective, make wise decisions in difficult circumstances, recognize the activities of God's Spirit, distinguish the correct and incorrect use of Scripture, and identify and expose false teachers. Ask God to give you his discernment as you serve him. Let that discernment guide you in your daily walk.

2:14, 15 Non-Christians cannot understand God, and they cannot grasp the concept that God's Spirit lives in believers. Don't expect most people to approve of or understand your decision to follow Christ. It all seems so silly to them. Just as a tone-deaf person cannot appreciate fine music, the person who rejects God cannot understand God's beautiful message. With the lines of communication broken, he or she won't be able to hear what God is saying to him or her.

We must not remain silent, however, using others' difficulty in understanding as an excuse. We are still one of God's communication channels. We must be alert to opportunities. Another person's question may be evidence that God's Spirit is drawing him or her to the point of decision. How would you respond today if someone asked you about your faith?

2:15, 16 No one can comprehend God (Romans 11:34), but through the guidance of the Holy Spirit, believers have insight into some of God's plans, thoughts, and actions—they, in fact, have the "mind of Christ." Through the Holy Spirit we can begin to know God's thoughts, talk with him, and expect his answers to our prayers. Are you spending enough time with Christ to have his very mind in you? An intimate relationship with Christ comes only from spending time consistently in his presence and in his Word. Read Philippians 2:5ff for more on the mind of Christ.

3:1-3 Paul called the Corinthians infants in the Christian life because they were not yet spiritually healthy and mature. The proof was that they quarreled like children, allowing divisions to distract them. Immature Christians are "worldly," controlled by

their own desires; mature believers are in tune with God's desires. How much influence do your desires have on your life? Your goal should be to let God's desires be yours. Being controlled by your own desires will stunt your growth.

3:6 Paul planted the seed of the gospel message in people's hearts. He was a missionary pioneer; he brought the message of salvation. Apollos's role was to water—to help the believers grow stronger in the faith. Paul founded the church in Corinth, and Apollos built on that foundation. Tragically, the believers in Corinth had split into factions, pledging loyalty to different teachers (see 1:11–13). After the preachers' work is completed, God keeps on making Christians grow. Our leaders should certainly be respected, but we should never place them on pedestals that create barriers between people or set them up as a substitute for Christ.

3:7–9 God's work involves many different individuals with a variety of gifts and abilities. There are no superstars in this task, only team members performing their own special roles. We can become useful members of God's team by setting aside our desires to receive glory for what we do. Don't seek the praise that comes from people—it is comparatively worthless. Instead, seek approval from God.

3:10, 11 The foundation of the church—of all believers—is Jesus Christ. Nothing and no one else will do, wrote Paul. A building with no foundation, or one poorly constructed, will not last. The finest materials used to construct a home quickly rot and fall apart if they are resting on the ground. And a building is only as solid as its foundation. The foundation of our life is Jesus Christ; he is our base, our reason for being. Everything we are and do must fit into the pattern provided by him. Are you building your life on the only real and lasting foundation, or are you building on a faulty foundation, such as wealth, security, success, or fame? Be careful how you build.

3:10–17 While some have applied these verses to personal spiritual growth, Paul's teaching has to do with ministry to others. What do we do to build others up? Do we build on Christ as foundation? Do we build with perishable materials? The Corinthians could construct their church with lasting, eternal teaching or with the changing, temporary wisdom of the day.

3:11
p Eph 2:20

3:13
q 2Th 1:7-10

3:15
r Jude 23

3:16
s 2Co 6:16

3:19
t Job 5:13

3:20
u Ps 94:11

3:21
v Ro 8:32

3:23
w 2Co 10:7;
Gal 3:29

4:4
x Ro 2:13

4:5
y Ro 2:1
z Ro 2:29

foundation other than the one already laid, which is Jesus Christ. p 12If any man builds on this foundation using gold, silver, costly stones, wood, hay or straw, 13his work will be shown for what it is, because the Day q will bring it to light. It will be revealed with fire, and the fire will test the quality of each man's work. 14If what he has built survives, he will receive his reward. 15If it is burned up, he will suffer loss; he himself will be saved, but only as one escaping through the flames. r

16Don't you know that you yourselves are God's temple s and that God's Spirit lives in you? 17If anyone destroys God's temple, God will destroy him; for God's temple is sacred, and you are that temple.

18Do not deceive yourselves. If any one of you thinks he is wise by the standards of this age, he should become a "fool" so that he may become wise. 19For the wisdom of this world is foolishness in God's sight. As it is written: "He catches the wise in their craftiness" a ; t 20and again, "The Lord knows that the thoughts of the wise are futile." b u 21So then, no more boasting about men! All things are yours, v 22whether Paul or Apollos or Cephas c or the world or life or death or the present or the future—all are yours, 23and you are of Christ, w and Christ is of God.

Apostles of Christ

4 So then, men ought to regard us as servants of Christ and as those entrusted with the secret things of God. 2Now it is required that those who have been given a trust must prove faithful. 3I care very little if I am judged by you or by any human court; indeed, I do not even judge myself. 4My conscience is clear, but that does not make me innocent. x It is the Lord who judges me. 5Therefore judge nothing y before the appointed time; wait till the Lord comes. He will bring to light what is hidden in darkness and will expose the motives of men's hearts. At that time each will receive his praise from God. z

6Now, brothers, I have applied these things to myself and Apollos for your benefit, so that

a 19 Job 5:13   b 20 Psalm 94:11   c 22 That is, Peter

Paul's words challenge our methods of discipleship. Do we attach others to ourselves as the foundation, or to Christ? Do we use our abilities and spiritual gifts to build up others in the church or keep them tied to us? Do we use Bible-based teaching or merely adaptations of worldly wisdom?

3:13–15 Two sure ways to destroy a building are to tamper with the foundation and to build with inferior materials. The church must be built on Christ, not on any other person or principle. Christ will evaluate each person's contribution to the life of the church, and the day of judgment ("the Day") will reveal the sincerity of each person's work. God will determine whether or not they have been faithful to Jesus' instructions. Good work will be rewarded; unfaithful or inferior work will be discounted. The builder "will be saved, but only as one escaping through the flames" means that unfaithful workers will be saved, but like people escaping from a burning building. All their possessions (accomplishments) will be lost.

3:16, 17 Paul wanted the Corinthians to understand that they were a unified assembly ("you yourselves are God's temple" and "God's Spirit lives in you"). They were not to see themselves as a collection of competing interests or independent individuals. Paul was emphasizing the intent of Jesus' prayer in John 17:21–23 that believers be unified in God. What actions could you take this week to strengthen your ties to fellow Christians in the church of Jesus Christ?

3:18–21 Paul was not telling the Corinthian believers to neglect the pursuit of knowledge. He was warning them that if worldly wisdom holds them back from God, it is not wisdom at all. God's way of thinking is far more valuable, even though it may seem foolish to the world (1:27). The Corinthians were using so-called worldly wisdom to evaluate their leaders and teachers. Their pride made them value the presentation of the message more than its content.

3:22 Paul says that both life and death are ours. While nonbelievers are victims of life, swept along by its current and wondering if there is meaning to it, believers can use life well because

they understand its true purpose. Nonbelievers can only fear death. For believers, however, death holds no terrors because Christ has conquered all fears (see 1 John 4:18). Death is only the beginning of eternal life with God.

4:1, 2 Paul urged the Corinthians to think of him, Peter (Cephas), and Apollos not as leaders of factions, but as servants of Christ entrusted with the secret things of God (see the note on 2:7). A servant does what his master tells him to do. We must do what God tells us to do in the Bible and through his Holy Spirit. Each day God presents us with needs and opportunities that challenge us to do what we know is right.

4:5 It is tempting to judge fellow Christians, evaluating whether or not they are good followers of Christ. But only God knows a person's heart, and he is the only one with the right to judge. Paul's warning to the Corinthians should also warn us. We are to confront those who are sinning (see 5:12, 13), but we must not judge who is a better servant for Christ. When you judge someone, you invariably consider yourself better—and that is arrogant.

4:6, 7 How easy it is for us to become attached to a spiritual leader. When someone has helped us, it's natural to feel loyalty. But Paul warns against having such pride in our favorite leaders that we cause divisions in the church. Any true spiritual leader is a representative of Christ and has nothing to offer that God hasn't given him or her. Don't let your loyalty cause strife, slander, or broken relationships. Make sure that your deepest loyalties are to Christ and not to his human agents. Those who spend more time debating church leadership than declaring Christ's message don't have Christ as their top priority.

4:6–13 The Corinthians had split into various cliques, each following its favorite preacher (Paul, Apollos, Peter, etc.). Each clique really believed it was the only one to have the whole truth, and thus felt spiritually proud. But Paul told the groups not to boast about being tied to a particular preacher because each preacher was simply a humble servant who had suffered for the same message of salvation in Jesus Christ. No preacher of God has more status than another.

you may learn from us the meaning of the saying, "Do not go beyond what is written." Then you will not take pride in one man over against another. *a* 7For who makes you different from anyone else? What do you have that you did not receive? And if you did receive it, why do you boast as though you did not?

8Already you have all you want! Already you have become rich!*b* You have become kings—and that without us! How I wish that you really had become kings so that we might be kings with you! 9For it seems to me that God has put us apostles on display at the end of the procession, like men condemned to die in the arena. We have been made a spectacle *c* to the whole universe, to angels as well as to men. 10We are fools for Christ,*d* but you are so wise in Christ! We are weak, but you are strong! You are honored, we are dishonored! 11To this very hour we go hungry and thirsty, we are in rags, we are brutally treated, we are homeless. *e* 12We work hard with our own hands. *f* When we are cursed, we bless; when we are persecuted, we endure it; 13when we are slandered, we answer kindly. Up to this moment we have become the scum of the earth, the refuse of the world.

14I am not writing this to shame you, but to warn you, as my dear children.*g* 15Even though you have ten thousand guardians in Christ, you do not have many fathers, for in Christ Jesus I became your father through the gospel. 16Therefore I urge you to imitate me. *h* 17For this reason I am sending to you Timothy, my son whom I love, who is faithful in the Lord. He will remind you of my way of life in Christ Jesus, which agrees with what I teach everywhere in every church. *i*

18Some of you have become arrogant, as if I were not coming to you. 19But I will come to you very soon,*j* if the Lord is willing, and then I will find out not only how these arrogant people are talking, but what power they have. 20For the kingdom of God is not a matter of talk but of power. 21What do you prefer? Shall I come to you with a whip,*k* or in love and with a gentle spirit?

2. Disorder in the church
Expel the Immoral Brother!

5 It is actually reported that there is sexual immorality among you, and of a kind that does not occur even among pagans: A man has his father's wife. *l* 2And you are proud! Shouldn't you rather have been filled with grief *m* and have put out of your fellowship the man who did this? 3Even though I am not physically present, I am with you in spirit. *n* And I have already passed judgment on the one who did this, just as if I were present. 4When you are assembled in the name of our Lord Jesus and I am with you in spirit, and the power of our Lord Jesus is present, 5hand this man over *o* to Satan, so that the sinful nature*a* may be destroyed and his spirit saved on the day of the Lord.

a5 Or that his body; or *that the flesh*

4:6
*a*1Co 1:12

4:8
*b*Rev 3:17, 18

4:9
*c*Heb 10:33

4:10
*d*Ac 17:18

4:11
*e*Ro 8:35

4:12
*f*Ac 18:3

4:14
*g*1Th 2:11

4:16
*h*1Th 1:6

4:17
*i*1Co 7:17

4:19
*j*2Co 1:15, 16

4:21
*k*2Co 1:23; 13:2, 10

5:1
*l*Lev 18:8

5:2
*m*2Co 7:7-11

5:3
*n*Col 2:5

5:5
*o*1Ti 1:20

4:15 In Paul's day, a guardian was a slave who was assigned as a special tutor and caretaker of a child. Paul was portraying his special affection for the Corinthians (greater than a slave) and his special role (more than a caretaker). In an attempt to unify the church, Paul appealed to his relationship with them. By *father*, he meant he was the church's founder. Because he started the church, he could be trusted to have its best interests at heart. Paul's tough words were motivated by love—like the love a good father has for his children (see also 1 Thessalonians 2:11).

4:16 Paul told the Corinthians to imitate him. He was able to make this statement because he walked close to God, spent time in God's Word and in prayer, and was aware of God's presence in his life at all times. God was Paul's example; therefore, Paul's life could be an example to other Christians. Paul wasn't expecting others to imitate everything he did, but they should imitate those aspects of his beliefs and conduct that were modeling Christ's way of living.

4:17 Timothy had traveled with Paul on Paul's second missionary journey (see Acts 16:1–3) and was a key person in the growth of the early church. Timothy may have delivered this letter to Corinth, but more likely he arrived there shortly after the letter came (see 16:10). Timothy's role was to see that Paul's advice was received, read, and implemented. Then he was to return to Paul and report on the church's progress.

4:18–20 Some people talk a lot about faith, but that's all it is—

talk. They may know all the right words to say, but their lives don't reflect God's power. Paul says that the kingdom of God is to be *lived*, not just discussed. There is a big difference between knowing the right words and living them out. Don't be content to have the right answers about Christ. Let your life show that God's power is really working in you.

4:19 It is not known whether Paul ever returned to Corinth, but it is likely. In 2 Corinthians 2:1, he writes that he decided not to make "another painful visit," implying that he had had a previous painful confrontation with the Corinthian believers (see 2 Corinthians 12:14; 13:1; and the note on 2 Corinthians 2:1).

5:1ff The church must discipline flagrant sin among its members—such sins, left unchecked, can polarize and paralyze a church. The correction, however, should never be vengeful. Instead, it should be given to help bring about a cure. There was a specific sin in the church, but the Corinthian believers had refused to deal with it. In this case, a man was having an affair with his mother (or stepmother), and the church members were trying to ignore the situation. Paul was telling the church that it had a responsibility to maintain the standards of morality found in God's commandments. God tells us not to judge others. But he also tells us not to tolerate flagrant sin because leaving that sin undisciplined will have a dangerous influence on other believers (5:6).

5:5 To "hand this man over to Satan" means to exclude him from

5:6
PGal 5:9

5:7
q1Pe 1:19

5:8
rDt 16:3

5:9
sEph 5:11

5:10
t1Co 10:27

5:12
uMk 4:11
v1Co 6:1-4

5:13
wDt 13:5

⁶Your boasting is not good. Don't you know that a little yeast works through the whole batch of dough?ᴾ ⁷Get rid of the old yeast that you may be a new batch without yeast—as you really are. For Christ, our Passover lamb, has been sacrificed. q ⁸Therefore let us keep the Festival, not with the old yeast, the yeast of malice and wickedness, but with bread without yeast,ʳ the bread of sincerity and truth.

⁹I have written you in my letter not to associate ˢ with sexually immoral people— ¹⁰not at all meaning the people of this worldᵗ who are immoral, or the greedy and swindlers, or idolaters. In that case you would have to leave this world. ¹¹But now I am writing you that you must not associate with anyone who calls himself a brother but is sexually immoral or greedy, an idolater or a slanderer, a drunkard or a swindler. With such a man do not even eat.

¹²What business is it of mine to judge those outside ᵘ the church? Are you not to judge those inside?ᵛ ¹³God will judge those outside. "Expel the wicked man from among you."ᵃ ʷ

ᵃ 13 Deut. 17:7; 19:19; 21:21; 22:21,24; 24:7

SET AN EXAMPLE FOR OTHERS
Throughout Scripture, setting an example is stressed as an important element of discipleship.

- *Matthew 11:29—"Take my yoke upon you."*
  Jesus told his followers to learn from his example of gentleness and humility.

- *Philippians 3:17—"Join with others in following my example."*
  Paul urged believers to follow his example of enthusiasm, perseverance, and maturity.

- *1 Thessalonians 1:6–7—"You became imitators of us and of the Lord. . . . You became a model to all the believers."*
  The new Christians at Thessalonica received training in discipleship from Paul, and even in suffering they expressed what they had learned.

- *1 Timothy 1:16—"I was shown mercy so that in me, the worst of sinners, Christ Jesus might display his unlimited patience as an example for those who would believe on him and receive eternal life."*
  Paul used his unworthiness to receive Christ as an example of grace so that no one would hold back from coming to Christ.

- *1 Peter 5:2, 3—"Be . . . eager to serve; not lording it over those entrusted to you, but being examples to the flock."*
  Peter taught Christian leaders to lead by example, not by commands.

Paul told the Corinthian believers to imitate him (4:16). As the body of Christ, believers must show Christ to the world by being examples. Nonbelievers should be able to see Christ in believers and be so drawn to what they see that they seek Christ and his salvation. What kind of example are you?

---

the fellowship of believers. Without the spiritual support of Christians, this man would be left alone with his sin and Satan, and perhaps this emptiness would drive him to repentance. "That the sinful nature may be destroyed" states the hope that the experience would bring him to God to destroy his sinful nature through repentance. *Sinful nature* could mean his body or flesh (see the NIV text note). This alternative translation would imply that Satan would afflict him physically and thus bring him to God. Putting someone out of the church should be a last resort in disciplinary action. It should not be done out of vengeance, but out of love, just as parents punish children to correct and restore them. The church's role should be to help, not hurt, offenders, motivating them to repent of their sins and to return to the fellowship of the church.

5:6 Paul was writing to those who wanted to ignore this church problem. They didn't realize that allowing public sin to exist in the church affects all its members. Paul does not expect anyone to be sinless—all believers struggle with sin daily. Instead, he is speaking against those who deliberately sin, feel no guilt, and refuse to repent. This kind of sin cannot be tolerated in the church because it affects others. We have a responsibility to other believers. Yeast makes bread dough rise. A little bit affects the whole batch. Blatant sins, left uncorrected, confuse and divide the congregation. While believers should encourage, pray for, and build up one another, they must also be intolerant of sin that jeopardizes the spiritual health of the church.

5:7, 8 As the Hebrews prepared for their exodus from slavery in Egypt, they were commanded to prepare bread without yeast

because they didn't have time to wait for it to rise. And because yeast also was a symbol of sin, they were commanded to sweep all of it out of the house (Exodus 12:15; 13:7). Christ is our Passover lamb, the perfect sacrifice for our sin. Because he has delivered us from the slavery of sin, we should have nothing to do with the sins of the past ("old yeast").

5:9 Paul is referring to an earlier letter to the Corinthian church, often called the lost letter because it has not been preserved.

5:10, 11 Paul makes it clear that we should not disassociate ourselves from unbelievers—otherwise, we could not carry out Christ's command to tell them about salvation (Matthew 28:18–20). But we are to distance ourselves from the person who claims to be a Christian, yet indulges in sins explicitly forbidden in Scripture and then rationalizes his or her actions. By rationalizing sin, a person harms others for whom Christ died and dims the image of God in himself or herself. A church that includes such people is hardly fit to be the light of the world. To do so would distort the picture of Christ it presents to the world. Church leaders must be ready to correct, in love, for the sake of spiritual unity.

5:12 The Bible consistently tells us not to criticize people by gossiping or making rash judgments. At the same time, however, we are to judge and deal with sin that can hurt others. Paul's instructions should not be used to handle trivial matters or to take revenge; nor should they be applied to individual problems between believers. These verses are instructions for dealing with open sin in the church, with a person who claims to be a Christian and yet who sins without remorse. The church is to confront and discipline such a person in love. Also see the notes on 4:5 and 5:1ff.

Lawsuits Among Believers

6 If any of you has a dispute with another, dare he take it before the ungodly for judgment instead of before the saints? 2 Do you not know that the saints will judge the world? *x* And if you are to judge the world, are you not competent to judge trivial cases? 3 Do you not know that we will judge angels? How much more the things of this life! 4 Therefore, if you have disputes about such matters, appoint as judges even men of little account in the church!*a* 5 I say this to shame you. Is it possible that there is nobody among you wise enough to judge a dispute between believers? 6 But instead, one brother goes to law against another—and this in front of unbelievers!

7 The very fact that you have lawsuits among you means you have been completely defeated already. Why not rather be wronged? Why not rather be cheated? *y* 8 Instead, you yourselves cheat and do wrong, and you do this to your brothers. *z*

9 Do you not know that the wicked will not inherit the kingdom of God? *a* Do not be deceived: Neither the sexually immoral nor idolaters nor adulterers nor male prostitutes nor homosexual offenders 10 nor thieves nor the greedy nor drunkards nor slanderers nor swindlers will inherit the kingdom of God. 11 And that is what some of you were. But you were washed, you were sanctified, you were justified in the name of the Lord Jesus Christ and by the Spirit of our God.

Sexual Immorality

12 "Everything is permissible for me"—but not everything is beneficial. *b* "Everything is permissible for me"—but I will not be mastered by anything. 13 "Food for the stomach and

6:2
x Mt 19:28

6:7
y Mt 5:39, 40
6:8
z 1Th 4:6
6:9
a Gal 5:21

6:12
b 1Co 10:23

a 4 Or *matters, do you appoint as judges men of little account in the church?*

6:1–6 In chapter 5, Paul explained what to do with open immorality in the congregation. In chapter 6, he teaches how the congregation should handle smaller problems between believers. Society has set up a legal system where disagreements can be resolved in courts. But Paul declares that disagreeing Christians should not have to go to a secular court to resolve their differences. As Christians, we have the Holy Spirit and the mind of Christ, so why should we turn to those who lack God's wisdom? Because of all that we have been given as believers, and because of the authority that we will have in the future to judge the world and the angels, we should be able to deal with disputes among ourselves. The *saints* are believers. See John 5:22 and Revelation 3:21 for more on judging the world. Judging angels is mentioned in 2 Peter 2:4 and Jude 6.

6:6–8 Why did Paul say that Christians should not take their disagreements to unbelievers in secular courts? (1) If the judge and jury are not Christians, they are not likely to be sensitive to Christian values. (2) The basis for going to court is often revenge; this should never be a Christian's motive. (3) Lawsuits make the church look bad, causing unbelievers to focus on its problems rather than on its purpose.

6:9 "Male prostitutes" refers to those who practice homosexuality. The temple of Apollo employed men whose job it was to fulfill the sexual desires of male and female worshipers.

Some attempt to legitimize homosexuality as an acceptable alternative lifestyle. Even some Christians say that people have a right to choose their sexual preference. But the Bible specifically calls homosexual behavior sin (see Leviticus 18:22–29; Romans 1:18–32; 1 Timothy 1:9–11). Christians must be careful, however, to condemn only the practice, not the people. Those who commit homosexual acts are not to be feared, ridiculed, or hated. They can be forgiven, and their lives can be transformed. The church should be a haven of forgiveness and healing for repentant homosexuals without compromising its stance against homosexual behavior.

6:9–11 Paul is describing characteristics of unbelievers. He doesn't mean that idolaters, adulterers, male prostitutes, homosexuals, thieves, greedy people, drunkards, slanderers or swindlers are automatically and irrevocably excluded from heaven. Christians come out of all kinds of different backgrounds, including these. They may still struggle with evil

desires, but they should not continue in these practices. In 6:11, Paul clearly states that even those who sin in these ways can have their lives changed by Christ. However, those who say that they are Christians but persist in these practices with no sign of remorse will not inherit the kingdom of God. Such people need to reevaluate their lives to see if they truly believe in Christ.

6:9–11 In a permissive society it is easy for Christians to overlook or tolerate some immoral behaviors (greed, drunkenness, etc.) while remaining outraged at others (homosexuality, thievery). We must not participate in sin or condone it in any way, nor may we be selective about what we condemn or excuse. Staying away from more "acceptable" forms of sin is difficult, but it is no harder for us than it was for the Corinthians. God expects his followers in any age to have high standards.

6:11 Paul emphasizes God's action in making believers new people. The three aspects of God's work are all part of our salvation: our sins were washed away, we were set apart for special use ("sanctified"), and we were pronounced not guilty ("justified") for our sins.

6:12 Apparently the church had been quoting and misapplying the words "everything is permissible for me." Some Christians in Corinth were excusing their sins by saying that (1) Christ had taken away all sin, and so they had complete freedom to live as they pleased, or (2) what they were doing was not strictly forbidden by Scripture. Paul answered both these excuses. (1) While Christ has taken away our sin, this does not give us freedom to go on doing what we know is wrong. The New Testament specifically forbids many sins (see 6:9, 10) that were originally prohibited in the Old Testament (see Romans 12:9–21; 13:8–10). (2) Some actions are not sinful in themselves, but they are not appropriate because they can control our lives and lead us away from God. (3) Some actions may hurt others. Anything we do that hurts rather than helps others is not right.

6:12, 13 Many of the world's religions teach that the soul or spirit is important but the body is not; and Christianity has sometimes been influenced by these ideas. In truth, however, Christianity takes very seriously the realm of the physical. We worship a God who created a physical world and pronounced

6:15
c Ro 12:5

6:16
d Ge 2:24; Mt 19:5;
Eph 5:31

6:17
e Jn 17:21-23

6:18
f Heb 13:4
g Ro 6:12

6:19
h Ro 14:7, 8

6:20
i 1Pe 1:18, 19;
Rev 5:9

the stomach for food"—but God will destroy them both. The body is not meant for sexual immorality, but for the Lord, and the Lord for the body. 14By his power God raised the Lord from the dead, and he will raise us also. 15Do you not know that your bodies are members of Christ himself? c Shall I then take the members of Christ and unite them with a prostitute? Never! 16Do you not know that he who unites himself with a prostitute is one with her in body? For it is said, "The two will become one flesh." a d 17But he who unites himself with the Lord is one with him in spirit. e

18Flee from sexual immorality. f All other sins a man commits are outside his body, but he who sins sexually sins against his own body. g 19Do you not know that your body is a temple of the Holy Spirit, who is in you, whom you have received from God? You are not your own; h 20you were bought at a price. i Therefore honor God with your body.

a 16 Gen. 2:24

CHURCH DISCIPLINE

The church, at times, must exercise discipline toward members who have sinned. But church discipline must be handled carefully, straightforwardly, and lovingly.

Situations	Steps (Matthew 18:15–17)
Unintentional error and/or private sin	1. Go to the brother or sister; show the fault to him or her in private.
Public sin and/or those done flagrantly and arrogantly	2. If he/she does not listen, go with one or two witnesses.
	3. If he/she refuses to listen, take the matter before the church.

After these steps have been carried out, the next steps are

1. Remove the one in error from the fellowship (1 Corinthians 5:2–13).

2. The church gives united disapproval, but forgiveness and comfort are in order if he/she chooses to repent (2 Corinthians 2:5–8).

3. Do not associate with the disobedient person; and if you must, speak to him/her as one who needs a warning (2 Thessalonians 3:14, 15).

4. After two warnings, reject the person from the fellowship (Titus 3:10).

---

it good. He promises us a new earth where real people have transformed physical lives—not a pink cloud where disembodied souls listen to harp music. At the heart of Christianity is the story of God himself taking on flesh and blood and coming to live with us, offering both physical healing and spiritual restoration.

We humans, like Adam, are a combination of dust and spirit. Just as our spirits affect our bodies, so our physical bodies affect our spirits. We cannot commit sin with our bodies without damaging our souls because our bodies and souls are inseparably joined. In the new earth we will have resurrection bodies that are not corrupted by sin. Then we will enjoy the fullness of our salvation.

6:12, 13 Freedom is a mark of the Christian faith—freedom from sin and guilt, and freedom to use and enjoy anything that comes from God. But Christians should not abuse this freedom and hurt themselves or others. Drinking too much leads to alcoholism, gluttony leads to obesity. Be careful that what God has allowed you to enjoy doesn't grow into a bad habit that controls you. For more about Christian freedom and everyday behavior, read chapter 8.

6:13 Sexual immorality is a temptation that is always before us. In movies and on television, sex outside marriage is treated as a normal, even desirable, part of life, while marriage is often shown as confining and joyless. We can even be looked down on by others if we are suspected of being pure. But God does not forbid sexual sin just to be difficult. He knows its power to destroy us physically and spiritually. No one should underestimate the power of sexual immorality. It has devastated countless lives and destroyed families, churches, communities, and even nations. God wants to protect us from damaging ourselves and others, and so he offers to fill us—our loneliness, our desires—with himself.

6:15–17 This teaching about sexual immorality and prostitutes was especially important for the Corinthian church because the temple of the love goddess Aphrodite was in Corinth. This temple employed more than a thousand prostitutes as priestesses, and sex was part of the worship ritual. Paul clearly stated that Christians are to have no part in sexual immorality, even if it is acceptable and popular in our culture.

6:18 Christians are free to be all they can be for God, but they are not free *from* God. God created sex to be a beautiful and essential ingredient of marriage, but sexual sin—sex outside the marriage relationship—*always* hurts someone. It hurts God because it shows that we prefer following our own desires instead of the leading of the Holy Spirit. It hurts others because it violates the commitment so necessary to a relationship. It often brings disease to our bodies. And it deeply affects our personalities, which respond in anguish when we harm ourselves physically and spiritually.

6:19, 20 What did Paul mean when he said that our bodies belong to God? Many people say they have the right to do whatever they want with their own bodies. Although they think that this is freedom, they are really enslaved to their own desires. When we become Christians, the Holy Spirit fills and lives in us. Therefore, we no longer own our bodies. "Bought at a price" refers to slaves purchased at auction. Christ's death freed us from sin, but also obligates us to his service. If you live in a building owned by someone else, you try not to violate the building's rules. Because your body belongs to God, you must not violate his standards for living.

B. PAUL ANSWERS CHURCH QUESTIONS (7:1—16:24)

After discussing disorder in the church, Paul moves to the list of questions that the Corinthians had sent him, including subjects of marriage, singleness, eating meat offered to idols, propriety in worship, orderliness in the Lord's Supper, spiritual gifts, and the resurrection. Questions that plague churches today are remarkably similar to these, so we can receive specific guidance in these areas from this letter.

1. Instruction on Christian marriage

7 Now for the matters you wrote about: It is good for a man not to marry. a / 2 But since there is so much immorality, each man should have his own wife, and each woman her own husband. 3 The husband should fulfill his marital duty to his wife, and likewise the wife to her husband. 4 The wife's body does not belong to her alone but also to her husband. In the same way, the husband's body does not belong to him alone but also to his wife. 5 Do not deprive each other except by mutual consent and for a time, k so that you may devote yourselves to prayer. Then come together again so that Satan will not tempt you because of your lack of self-control. 6 I say this as a concession, not as a command. l 7 I wish that all men were as I am. m But each man has his own gift from God; one has this gift, another has that. n

8 Now to the unmarried and the widows I say: It is good for them to stay unmarried, as I am. o 9 But if they cannot control themselves, they should marry, p for it is better to marry than to burn with passion.

10 To the married I give this command (not I, but the Lord): A wife must not separate from her husband. q 11 But if she does, she must remain unmarried or else be reconciled to her husband. And a husband must not divorce his wife.

12 To the rest I say this (I, not the Lord): If any brother has a wife who is not a believer and she is willing to live with him, he must not divorce her. 13 And if a woman has a husband who is not a believer and he is willing to live with her, she must not divorce him. 14 For the unbelieving husband has been sanctified through his wife, and the unbelieving wife has been

a 1 Or *"It is good for a man not to have sexual relations with a woman."*

7:1 /ver 8, 26

7:5 k Ex 19:15; 1Sa 21:4, 5

7:6 l 2Co 8:8

7:7 m 1Co 9:5 n 1Co 12:4, 11

7:8 o ver 1, 26

7:9 p 1Ti 5:14

7:10 q Mal 2:14-16; Mt 5:32; 19:3-9; Mk 10:11; Lk 16:18

7:1 The Corinthians had written to Paul, asking him several questions relating to the Christian life and problems in the church. The first question was whether it was good to be married. Paul answers this and other questions in the remainder of this letter.

7:1ff Christians in Corinth were surrounded by sexual temptation. The city had a reputation even among pagans for sexual immorality and religious prostitution. It was to this kind of society that Paul delivered these instructions on sex and marriage. The Corinthians needed special, specific instructions because of their culture's immoral standards. For more on Paul's teaching about marriage, see Ephesians 5.

7:3–5 Sexual temptations are difficult to withstand because they appeal to the normal and natural desires that God has given us. Marriage provides God's way to satisfy these natural sexual desires and to strengthen the partners against temptation. Married couples have the responsibility to care for each other; therefore, husbands and wives should not withhold themselves sexually from one another, but should fulfill each other's needs and desires. (See also the note on 10:13.)

7:3–11 The Corinthian church was in turmoil because of the immorality of the culture around them. Some Greeks, in rejecting immorality, rejected sex and marriage altogether. The Corinthian Christians wondered if this was what they should do also, so they asked Paul several questions: "Because sex is perverted, shouldn't we also abstain in marriage?" "If my spouse is unsaved, should I seek a divorce?" "Should unmarried people and widows remain unmarried?" Paul answered many of these questions by saying, "For now, stay put. Be content in the situation where God has placed you. If you're married, don't seek to be single. If you're single, don't seek to be married. Live God's way, one day at a time, and he will show you what to do."

7:4 Spiritually, our bodies belong to God when we become Christians because Jesus Christ bought us by paying the price to release us from sin (see 6:19, 20). Physically, our bodies belong to our spouses because God designed marriage so that, through the union of husband and wife, the two become one (Genesis

2:24). Paul stressed complete equality in sexual relationships. Neither male nor female should seek dominance or autonomy.

7:7 Both marriage and singleness are gifts from God. One is not morally better than the other, and both are valuable to accomplishing God's purposes. It is important for us, therefore, to accept our present situation. When Paul said he wished that all people were like him (i.e., unmarried), he was expressing his desire that more people would devote themselves *completely* to the ministry without the added concerns of spouse and family, as he had done. He was not criticizing marriage—after all, it is God's created way of providing companionship and populating the earth.

7:9 Sexual pressure is not the best motive for getting married, but it is better to marry the right person than to "burn with passion." Many new believers in Corinth thought that all sex was wrong, and so engaged couples were deciding not to get married. In this passage, Paul was telling couples who wanted to marry that they should not frustrate their normal sexual drives by avoiding marriage. This does not mean, however, that people who have trouble controlling themselves should marry the first person who comes along. It is better to deal with the pressure of desire than to deal with an unhappy marriage.

7:12 Paul's *command* about the permanence of marriage (7:10) comes from the Old Testament (Genesis 2:24) and from Jesus (Mark 10:2–12). His *suggestion* in this verse is based on God's command, and Paul applies it to the situation the Corinthians were facing. Paul ranked the command above the suggestion because one is an eternal principle while the other is a specific application. Nevertheless, for people in similar situations, Paul's suggestion is the best advice they will get. Paul was a man of God, an apostle, and he had the mind of Christ.

7:12–14 Because of their desire to serve Christ, some people in the Corinthian church thought they ought to divorce their pagan spouses and marry Christians. But Paul affirmed the marriage commitment. God's ideal is for marriages to stay together—even when one spouse is not a believer. The Christian spouse should try to win the other to Christ. It would be easy to rationalize leaving; however, Paul makes a strong case for staying with the unbelieving

7:14
r Mal 2:15

7:15
s Ro 14:19

7:16
t 1Pe 3:1

7:17
u 1Co 4:17

7:18
v Ac 15:1, 2

7:19
w Gal 5:6

7:22
x Jn 8:32, 36
y Eph 6:6

7:23
z 1Co 6:20

7:25
a 1Ti 1:13, 16

7:26
b ver 1, 8

7:29
c Ro 13:11, 12

sanctified through her believing husband. Otherwise your children would be unclean, but as it is, they are holy. *r*

15But if the unbeliever leaves, let him do so. A believing man or woman is not bound in such circumstances; God has called us to live in peace. *s* 16How do you know, wife, whether you will save your husband? *t* Or, how do you know, husband, whether you will save your wife?

17Nevertheless, each one should retain the place in life that the Lord assigned to him and to which God has called him. This is the rule I lay down in all the churches. *u* 18Was a man already circumcised when he was called? He should not become uncircumcised. Was a man uncircumcised when he was called? He should not be circumcised. *v* 19Circumcision is nothing and uncircumcision is nothing. *w* Keeping God's commands is what counts. 20Each one should remain in the situation which he was in when God called him. 21Were you a slave when you were called? Don't let it trouble you—although if you can gain your freedom, do so. 22For he who was a slave when he was called by the Lord is the Lord's freedman; *x* similarly, he who was a free man when he was called is Christ's slave. *y* 23You were bought at a price; *z* do not become slaves of men. 24Brothers, each man, as responsible to God, should remain in the situation God called him to.

25Now about virgins: I have no command from the Lord, but I give a judgment as one who by the Lord's mercy *a* is trustworthy. 26Because of the present crisis, I think that it is good for you to remain as you are. *b* 27Are you married? Do not seek a divorce. Are you unmarried? Do not look for a wife. 28But if you do marry, you have not sinned; and if a virgin marries, she has not sinned. But those who marry will face many troubles in this life, and I want to spare you this.

29What I mean, brothers, is that the time is short. *c* From now on those who have wives

---

spouse and being a positive influence on the marriage. Paul, like Jesus, believed that marriage is permanent (see Mark 10:1–9).

7:14 The blessings that flow to believers don't stop there, but extend to others. God regards the marriage as "sanctified" (set apart for his use) by the presence of one Christian spouse. The other does not receive salvation automatically, but is helped by this relationship. The children of such a marriage are to be regarded as "holy" (because of God's blessing on the family unit) until they are old enough to decide for themselves.

7:15, 16 This verse is misused by some as a loophole to get out of marriage. But Paul's statements were given to encourage the Christian spouse to try to get along with the unbeliever and make the marriage work. If, however, the unbelieving spouse insisted on leaving, Paul said to let him or her go. The only alternative would be for the Christian to deny his or her faith to preserve the marriage, and that would be worse than dissolving the marriage. Paul's chief purpose in writing this was to urge the married couples to seek unity, not separation (see 7:17; 1 Peter 3:1, 2).

7:17 Apparently the Corinthians were ready to make wholesale changes without thinking through the ramifications. Paul was writing to say that people should be Christians where they are. You can do God's work and demonstrate your faith *anywhere*. If you became a Christian after marriage, and your spouse is not a believer, remember that you don't have to be married to a Christian to live for Christ. Don't assume that you are in the wrong place, or stuck with the wrong person. You may be just where God wants you (see 7:20).

7:18, 19 The ceremony of circumcision was an important part of the Jews' relationship with God. In fact, before Christ came, circumcision was commanded by God for those who claimed to follow him (Genesis 17:9–14). But after Christ's death, circumcision was no longer necessary (Acts 15; Romans 4:9–11; Galatians 5:2–4; Colossians 2:11). Pleasing God and obeying him is more important than observing traditional ceremonies.

7:20 Often we are so concerned about what we *could* be doing for God somewhere else that we miss great opportunities right where we are. Paul says that when someone becomes a Christian, he or she should usually continue with the work he or she has previously been doing—provided it isn't immoral or unethical. Every job can become Christian work when you realize that the purpose of your life is to honor, serve, and speak out for Christ.

Because God has placed you where you are, look carefully for opportunities to serve him there.

7:23 Slavery was common throughout the Roman empire. Some Christians in the Corinthian church were undoubtedly slaves. Paul said that although the Christian slaves were slaves to other human beings, they were free from the power of sin in their lives. People today are slaves to sin until they commit their lives to Christ, who alone can conquer sin's power. Sin, pride, and fear no longer have any claim over us, just as a slave owner no longer has power over the slaves he has sold. The Bible says we become Christ's slaves when we become Christians (Romans 6:18), but this actually means we gain our freedom, because sin no longer controls us.

7:26 Paul probably foresaw the impending persecution that the Roman government would soon bring upon Christians. He gave this practical advice because being unmarried would mean less suffering and more freedom to throw one's life into the cause of Christ (7:29), even to the point of fearlessly dying for him. Paul's advice reveals his single-minded devotion to spreading the Good News.

7:28 Many people naively think that marriage will solve all their problems. Here are some problems marriage won't solve: (1) loneliness, (2) sexual temptation, (3) satisfaction of one's deepest emotional needs, (4) elimination of life's difficulties. Marriage alone does not hold two people together, but commitment does— commitment to Christ and to each other despite conflicts and problems. As wonderful as it is, marriage does not automatically solve every problem. Whether married or single, we must be content with our situation and focus on Christ, not on loved ones, to help address our problems.

7:29 Paul urges all believers to make the most of their time before Christ's return. Every person in every generation should have this sense of urgency about telling the Good News to others. Life is short—there's not much time!

7:29–31 Paul urges believers not to regard marriage, home, or financial security as the ultimate goals of life. As much as possible, we should live unhindered by the cares of this world, not getting involved with burdensome mortgages, budgets, investments, or debts that might keep us from doing God's work. A married man or woman, as Paul points out (7:33, 34), must take care of earthly responsibilities—but they should make every effort to keep them modest and manageable.

should live as if they had none; ³⁰ those who mourn, as if they did not; those who are happy, as if they were not; those who buy something, as if it were not theirs to keep; ³¹ those who use the things of the world, as if not engrossed in them. For this world in its present form is passing away.ᵈ

³² I would like you to be free from concern. An unmarried man is concerned about the Lord's affairsᵉ—how he can please the Lord. ³³ But a married man is concerned about the affairs of this world—how he can please his wife— ³⁴ and his interests are divided. An unmarried woman or virgin is concerned about the Lord's affairs: Her aim is to be devoted to the Lord in both body and spirit. But a married woman is concerned about the affairs of this world—how she can please her husband. ³⁵ I am saying this for your own good, not to restrict you, but that you may live in a right way in undivided devotion to the Lord.

³⁶ If anyone thinks he is acting improperly toward the virgin he is engaged to, and if she is getting along in years and he feels he ought to marry, he should do as he wants. He is not sinning. They should get married. ³⁷ But the man who has settled the matter in his own mind, who is under no compulsion but has control over his own will, and who has made up his mind not to marry the virgin—this man also does the right thing. ³⁸ So then, he who marries the virgin does right, but he who does not marry her does even better.ᵃ

³⁹ A woman is bound to her husband as long as he lives.ᶠ But if her husband dies, she is free to marry anyone she wishes, but he must belong to the Lord.ᵍ ⁴⁰ In my judgment, she is happier if she stays as she is—and I think that I too have the Spirit of God.

2. Instruction on Christian freedom
Food Sacrificed to Idols

8 Now about food sacrificed to idols:ʰ We know that we all possess knowledge.ᵇ Knowledge puffs up, but love builds up. ² The man who thinks he knows something does not yet know as he ought to know.ⁱ ³ But the man who loves God is known by God.ʲ

⁴ So then, about eating food sacrificed to idols: We know that an idol is nothing at all in the world and that there is no God but one.ᵏ ⁵ For even if there are so-called gods, whether in heaven or on earth (as indeed there are many "gods" and many "lords"), ⁶ yet for us there is but one God, the Father,ˡ from whom all things cameᵐ and for whom we live; and there is but one Lord, Jesus Christ, through whom all things came and through whom we live.

⁷ But not everyone knows this. Some people are still so accustomed to idols that when they eat such food they think of it as having been sacrificed to an idol, and since their conscience is weak,ⁿ it is defiled. ⁸ But food does not bring us near to God;ᵒ we are no worse if we do not eat, and no better if we do.

⁹ Be careful, however, that the exercise of your freedom does not become a stumbling blockᵖ to the weak. ¹⁰ For if anyone with a weak conscience sees you who have this

ª 36-38 Or ³⁶ If anyone thinks he is not treating his daughter properly, and if she is getting along in years, and he feels she ought to marry, he should do as he wants. He is not sinning. He should let her get married. ³⁷ But the man who has settled the matter in his own mind, who is under no compulsion but has control over his own will, and who has made up his mind to keep the virgin unmarried—this man also does the right thing. ³⁸ So then, he who gives his virgin in marriage does right, but he who does not give her in marriage does even better.   ᵇ 1 Or "We all possess knowledge," as you say

7:31
ᵈ 1Jn 2:17

7:32
ᵉ 1Ti 5:5

7:39
ᶠ Ro 7:2, 3
ᵍ 2Co 6:14

8:1
ʰ Ac 15:20

8:2
ⁱ 1Co 13:8, 9, 12;
1Ti 6:4

8:3
ʲ Gal 4:9

8:4
ᵏ Dt 6:4

8:6
ˡ Mal 2:10
ᵐ Ro 11:36

8:7
ⁿ Ro 14:14

8:8
ᵒ Ro 14:17

8:9
ᵖ Gal 5:13

7:32–34 Some single people feel tremendous pressure to be married. They think their lives can be complete only with a spouse. But Paul underlines one advantage of being single—the potential of a greater focus on Christ and his work. If you are unmarried, use your special opportunity to serve Christ wholeheartedly.

7:38 When Paul says the unmarried person does even better, he is talking about the potential time available for service to God. The single person does not have the responsibility of caring for a spouse and raising a family. Singleness, however, does not ensure service to God—involvement in service depends on the commitment of the individual.

7:40 Paul's advice comes from the Holy Spirit, who guides and equips both single and married people to fulfill their roles.

8:1 Meat bought in the marketplace was likely to have been symbolically offered to an idol in one of the many pagan temples. Animals were brought to a temple, killed before an idol as part of a pagan religious ceremony, and eaten at a feast in the idol's temple or taken to butchers who sold the meat in the marketplace. The believers wondered if by eating such meat, they were somehow participating in the worship of pagan idols.

8:1–3 Love is more important than knowledge. Knowledge can make us look good and feel important, but we can all too easily develop an arrogant, know-it-all attitude. Many people with strong opinions are unwilling to listen to and learn from God and others. We can obtain God's knowledge only by loving him (see James 3:17, 18). And we can know and be known by God only when we model him by showing love (1 John 4:7, 8).

8:4–9 Paul addressed these words to believers who weren't bothered by eating meat that had been sacrificed to idols. Although idols were phony, and the pagan ritual of sacrificing to them was meaningless, eating such meat offended Christians with more sensitive consciences. Paul said, therefore, that if a weaker or less mature believer misunderstood their actions, they should, out of consideration, avoid eating meat offered to idols.

8:10–13 Christian freedom does not mean that anything goes. It means that our salvation is not determined by good deeds or legalistic rules, but by the free gift of God (Ephesians 2:8, 9). Christian freedom, then, is inseparably tied to Christian responsibility. New believers are often very sensitive to what is right or wrong, what they should or shouldn't do. Some actions may be

8:11
q Ro 14:15, 20

8:13
r Ro 14:21

9:1
s 2Co 12:12
t 1Co 3:6

9:7
u Dt 20:6
9:9
v Dt 25:4; 1Ti 5:18

9:11
w Ro 15:27
9:12
x 2Co 11:7-12

knowledge eating in an idol's temple, won't he be emboldened to eat what has been sacrificed to idols? ¹¹So this weak brother, for whom Christ died, is destroyed q by your knowledge. ¹²When you sin against your brothers in this way and wound their weak conscience, you sin against Christ. ¹³Therefore, if what I eat causes my brother to fall into sin, I will never eat meat again, so that I will not cause him to fall. r

The Rights of an Apostle

9 Am I not free? Am I not an apostle? s Have I not seen Jesus our Lord? Are you not the result of my work in the Lord? t ²Even though I may not be an apostle to others, surely I am to you! For you are the seal of my apostleship in the Lord.

³This is my defense to those who sit in judgment on me. ⁴Don't we have the right to food and drink? ⁵Don't we have the right to take a believing wife along with us, as do the other apostles and the Lord's brothers and Cephas a? ⁶Or is it only I and Barnabas who must work for a living?

⁷Who serves as a soldier at his own expense? Who plants a vineyard u and does not eat of its grapes? Who tends a flock and does not drink of the milk? ⁸Do I say this merely from a human point of view? Doesn't the Law say the same thing? ⁹For it is written in the Law of Moses: "Do not muzzle an ox while it is treading out the grain." b v Is it about oxen that God is concerned? ¹⁰Surely he says this for us, doesn't he? Yes, this was written for us, because when the plowman plows and the thresher threshes, they ought to do so in the hope of sharing in the harvest. ¹¹If we have sown spiritual seed among you, is it too much if we reap a material harvest from you? w ¹²If others have this right of support from you, shouldn't we have it all the more?

But we did not use this right. On the contrary, we put up with anything rather than hinder x

a 5 That is, Peter   b 9 Deut. 25:4

STRONGER, WEAKER BELIEVERS

Advice to

Stronger believers . . . . Don't be proud of your maturity; don't flaunt your freedom. Act in love so you do not cause a weaker believer to stumble.

Pastors and leaders . . . . . . Although you may not feel the same freedom in some areas as in others, take your time, pray to God, but do not force others to adhere to your stipulations. You would hinder other believers by making up rules and standards for how everyone ought to behave. Make sure your convictions are based on God's Word and are not simply an expression of your opinions.

Weaker believers. . . . . Teach correctly from God's Word, helping Christians to understand what is right and wrong in God's eyes and to see that they can have varied opinions on other issues and still be unified. Don't allow potential problems to get out of hand, causing splits and divisions.

Paul advises those who are more mature in the faith about how they must care about their brothers and sisters in Christ who have more tender consciences; those "weaker" brothers and sisters are advised concerning their growth; and pastors and leaders are instructed on how to deal with the conflicts that easily could arise between these groups.

---

perfectly all right for us to do, but may harm a Christian brother or sister who is still young in the faith and learning what the Christian life is all about. We must be careful not to offend a sensitive or younger Christian or, by our example, to cause him or her to sin. When we love others, our freedom should be less important to us than strengthening the faith of a brother or sister in Christ.

9:1 Some Corinthians were questioning Paul's authority and rights as an apostle, so Paul gave his credentials—he actually had seen and talked with the resurrected Christ, who had called him to be an apostle (see Acts 9:3–18). Such credentials make the advice he gives in this letter more persuasive. In 2 Corinthians 10—13, Paul defends his apostleship in greater detail.

9:1 Changed lives were the evidence that God was using Paul. Does your faith have an impact on others? You can be a life-changer, helping others grow spiritually, if you dedicate yourself to being used by God and letting him make you effective.

9:4ff Paul uses himself as an illustration of giving up personal rights. Paul had the right to hospitality, to be married, and to be paid for his work. But he willingly gave up these rights to win people to Christ. When your focus is on living for Christ, your rights become comparatively unimportant.

9:4–10 Jesus said that workers deserve their wages (Luke 10:7). Paul echoes this thought and urges the church to be sure to pay their Christian workers. We have the responsibility to care for our pastors, teachers, and other spiritual leaders. It is our duty to see that those who serve us in the ministry are fairly and adequately compensated. When the annual budget of your church comes up for review, support a proper salary for your ministers and staff.

9:5 The brothers of Jesus attained leadership status in the church at Jerusalem. James (one of the "Lord's brothers"), for example, led the way to an agreement at the Jerusalem council in Acts 15, and wrote the book of James.

the gospel of Christ. ¹³Don't you know that those who work in the temple get their food from the temple, and those who serve at the altar share in what is offered on the altar?*ʸ* ¹⁴In the same way, the Lord has commanded that those who preach the gospel should receive their living from the gospel.

¹⁵But I have not used any of these rights.*ᶻ* And I am not writing this in the hope that you will do such things for me. I would rather die than have anyone deprive me of this boast.*ᵃ* ¹⁶Yet when I preach the gospel, I cannot boast, for I am compelled to preach.*ᵇ* Woe to me if I do not preach the gospel! ¹⁷If I preach voluntarily, I have a reward;*ᶜ* if not voluntarily, I am simply discharging the trust committed to me.*ᵈ* ¹⁸What then is my reward? Just this: that in preaching the gospel I may offer it free of charge, and so not make use of my rights in preaching it.

¹⁹Though I am free and belong to no man, I make myself a slave to everyone,*ᵉ* to win as many as possible.*ᶠ* ²⁰To the Jews I became like a Jew, to win the Jews.*ᵍ* To those under the law I became like one under the law (though I myself am not under the law), so as to win those under the law. ²¹To those not having the law I became like one not having the law*ʰ* (though I am not free from God's law but am under Christ's law), so as to win those not having the law. ²²To the weak I became weak, to win the weak. I have become all things to all men so that by all possible means I might save some. ²³I do all this for the sake of the gospel, that I may share in its blessings.

²⁴Do you not know that in a race all the runners run, but only one gets the prize? Run*ⁱ* in such a way as to get the prize. ²⁵Everyone who competes in the games goes into strict training. They do it to get a crown that will not last; but we do it to get a crown that will last forever. ²⁶Therefore I do not run like a man running aimlessly; I do not fight like a man beating the air. ²⁷No, I beat my body*ʲ* and make it my slave so that after I have preached to others, I myself will not be disqualified for the prize.

Warnings From Israel's History

10 For I do not want you to be ignorant of the fact, brothers, that our forefathers were all under the cloud*ᵏ* and that they all passed through the sea.*ˡ* ²They were all baptized into Moses in the cloud and in the sea. ³They all ate the same spiritual food ⁴and drank the

**Cross-references (right margin):**

9:13
ʸ Lev 6:16, 26
9:15
ᶻ Ac 18:3
ᵃ 2Co 11:9, 10
9:16
ᵇ Ro 1:14
9:17
ᶜ 1Co 3:8, 14
ᵈ Gal 2:7; Col 1:25
9:19
ᵉ Gal 5:13
ᶠ Mt 18:15
9:20
ᵍ Ac 16:3
9:21
ʰ Ro 2:12, 14
9:24
ⁱ 2Ti 4:7
9:27
ʲ Ro 8:13
10:1
ᵏ Ex 13:21
ˡ Ex 14:22, 29

9:13–15 As part of their pay, priests in the temple would receive a portion of the offerings as their food (see Numbers 18:8–24). These verses concerning Paul's rights and the church's responsibility have a two-part challenge for the church today. First, the church must support its workers in a fair and equitable way. That is the church's responsibility. It can research pay scales, examine the standard of living in its community, and do what is right and fair. Second, Christian workers must not let their attitude about pay and benefits hinder the gospel. It is too easy for desire for more pay to enter into a person's mind and distract from serving. Ministers need Paul's attitude: a willingness not to demand their rights if to do so would hinder the gospel.

9:16 Preaching the gospel was Paul's gift and calling, and he said he couldn't stop preaching even if he wanted to. Paul was driven by the desire to do what God wanted, using his gifts for God's glory. What special gifts has God given you? Are you motivated, like Paul, to honor God with your gifts?

9:19–27 In 9:19–22 Paul asserts that he has freedom to do anything; in 9:24–27 he emphasizes a life of strict discipline. The Christian life involves both freedom and discipline. The goals of Paul's life were to glorify God and bring people to Christ. Thus he stayed free of any philosophical position or material entanglement that might sidetrack him, while he strictly disciplined himself to carry out his goal. For Paul, both freedom and discipline were important tools to be used in God's service.

9:22, 23 Paul gives several important principles for ministry: (1) find common ground with those you contact; (2) avoid a know-it-all attitude; (3) make others feel accepted; (4) be sensitive to their needs and concerns; and (5) look for opportunities to tell them about Christ. These principles are just as valid for us as they were for Paul.

9:24–27 Winning a race requires purpose and discipline. Paul uses this illustration to explain that the Christian life takes hard work, self-denial, and grueling preparation. As Christians, we are running toward our heavenly reward. The essential disciplines of prayer, Bible study, and worship equip us to run with vigor and stamina. Don't merely observe from the grandstand; don't just turn out to jog a couple of laps each morning. Train diligently—your spiritual progress depends upon it.

9:25 Whatever happened to self-discipline? Many books and speakers guide wandering souls to self-fulfillment, self-satisfaction, and self-awareness. Not many tackle self-discipline.

Self-discipline requires an honest look at your strengths and weaknesses, with emphasis on the latter. It means building the will to say no when a powerful appetite inside you screams yes. For example, when you have self-discipline, you can (1) say no to friends or situations that will lead you away from Christ, (2) say no to casual sex, saving intimacy for marriage, and (3) say no to laziness in favor of "can do" and "will do." Self-discipline is a long, steady course in learning attitudes that do not come naturally, and channeling natural appetites toward God's purposes. Where are your weak points? Pray with a friend for God's help to redirect weakness into strength.

9:27 When Paul says he might be disqualified, he does not mean that he could lose his salvation, but rather that he could lose his privilege of telling others about Christ. It is easy to tell others how to live and then not to take our own advice. We must be careful to practice what we preach.

10:1ff In chapter 9, Paul used himself as an example of a mature Christian who disciplines himself to better serve God. In chapter 10, he uses Israel as an example of spiritual immaturity, shown in their overconfidence and lack of self-discipline.

10:1–5 The cloud and the sea mentioned here refer to Israel's escape from slavery in Egypt when God led them by a cloud and brought them safely through the Red Sea (Exodus 14). The spiritual food and drink are the miraculous provisions God gave as they traveled through the desert (Exodus 15; 16).

10:2 "Baptized into Moses" means that just as we are united in

10:4
m Ex 17:6

10:5
n Nu 14:29

10:9
o Nu 21:5, 6

10:10
p Ex 12:23

10:12
q Ro 11:20

10:13
r 2Pe 2:9

same spiritual drink; for they drank from the spiritual rock *m* that accompanied them, and that rock was Christ. 5 Nevertheless, God was not pleased with most of them; their bodies were scattered over the desert. *n*

6 Now these things occurred as examples *a* to keep us from setting our hearts on evil things as they did. 7 Do not be idolaters, as some of them were; as it is written: "The people sat down to eat and drink and got up to indulge in pagan revelry." *b* 8 We should not commit sexual immorality, as some of them did—and in one day twenty-three thousand of them died. 9 We should not test the Lord, as some of them did—and were killed by snakes. *o* 10 And do not grumble, as some of them did—and were killed by the destroying angel. *p*

11 These things happened to them as examples and were written down as warnings for us, on whom the fulfillment of the ages has come. 12 So, if you think you are standing firm, *q* be careful that you don't fall! 13 No temptation has seized you except what is common to man. And God is faithful; he will not let you be tempted beyond what you can bear. *r* But when you are tempted, he will also provide a way out so that you can stand up under it.

a 6 Or *types*; also in verse 11   *b* 7 Exodus 32:6

WHY WE DON'T GIVE UP

Perseverance, persistence, the prize!! The Christian life was never promised as an easy way to live; instead, Paul constantly reminds us that we must have a purpose and a plan because times will be difficult and Satan will attack. But we never persevere without the promise of a prize— a promise God will keep.

Reference	The Purpose	The Plan	The Prize
1 Corinthians 9:24–27	• Run to get the prize • Run straight to the goal	• Discipline your body, training it	• A crown that will last forever
Galatians 6:7–10	• Don't become weary in doing good • Don't give up • Do good to everyone	• Sow to please the Spirit	• Reap eternal life
Ephesians 6:10–20	• Put on the full armor of God • Pray on all occasions	• Use all the pieces of God's armor to resist the enemy	• Taking your stand against the devil's schemes
Philippians 3:12–14	• Press on toward the day when you will be all God wants you to be	• Forget the past; strain toward what is ahead	• The heavenly prize for which God calls you heavenward
2 Timothy 2:1–13	• Entrust these great truths to people who are able to pass them on to others • Be strong in Christ's grace, even when your faith is faltering	• Endure hardship like a soldier, and don't get involved in worldly affairs • Follow the Lord's rules, as an athlete must do in order to win • Work hard, like a farmer who tends his crops for the harvest	• You will live with Christ; you will reign with him • He remains faithful

---

Christ by baptism, so the Israelites were united under Moses' leadership in the events of the exodus.

10:7-10 The incident referred to in 10:7 took place when the Israelites made a golden calf and worshiped it in the desert (Exodus 32). The incident in 10:8 is recorded in Numbers 25:1–9 when the Israelites worshiped Baal of Peor and engaged in sexual immorality with Moabite women. The reference in 10:9 is to the Israelites' complaint about their food (Numbers 21:5, 6). They put the Lord to the test by seeing how far they could go. In 10:10, Paul refers to when the people complained against Moses and Aaron, and the plague that resulted (Numbers 14:2, 36; 16:41–50). The destroying angel is referred to in Exodus 12:23.

10:10 Paul warned the Corinthian believers not to grumble. We start to grumble when our attention shifts from what we have to what we don't have. The people of Israel didn't seem to notice what God was doing for them—setting them free, making them a nation, giving them a new land—because they were so wrapped up in what God wasn't doing for them. They could think of nothing but the delicious Egyptian food they had left behind (Numbers 11:5).

Before we judge the Israelites too harshly, it's helpful to think about what occupies our attention most of the time. Are we grateful for what God has given us, or are we always thinking about

what we would like to have? Don't allow your unfulfilled desires to cause you to forget God's gifts of life, family, friends, food, health, and work.

10:11 Today's pressures make it easy to ignore or forget the lessons of the past. But Paul cautions us to remember the lessons the Israelites learned about God so we can avoid repeating their errors. The key to remembering is to study the Bible regularly so that these lessons remind us of how God wants us to live. We need not repeat their mistakes!

10:13 In a culture filled with moral depravity and sin-inducing pressures, Paul gave strong encouragement to the Corinthians about temptation. He said: (1) wrong desires and temptations happen to everyone, so don't feel you've been singled out; (2) others have resisted temptation, and so can you; (3) any temptation can be resisted because God will help you resist it. God helps you resist temptation by helping you (1) recognize those people and situations that give you trouble, (2) run from anything you know is wrong, (3) choose to do only what is right, (4) pray for God's help, and (5) seek friends who love God and can offer help when you are tempted. Running from a tempting situation is your first step on the way to victory (see 2 Timothy 2:22).

Idol Feasts and the Lord's Supper

¹⁴Therefore, my dear friends, flee from idolatry. ¹⁵I speak to sensible people; judge for yourselves what I say. ¹⁶Is not the cup of thanksgiving for which we give thanks a participation in the blood of Christ? And is not the bread that we break a participation in the body of Christ?ˢ ¹⁷Because there is one loaf, we, who are many, are one body,ᵗ for we all partake of the one loaf.

¹⁸Consider the people of Israel: Do not those who eat the sacrifices participate in the altar? ¹⁹Do I mean then that a sacrifice offered to an idol is anything, or that an idol is anything? ²⁰No, but the sacrifices of pagans are offered to demons,ᵘ not to God, and I do not want you to be participants with demons. ²¹You cannot drink the cup of the Lord and the cup of demons too; you cannot have a part in both the Lord's table and the table of demons.ᵛ ²²Are we trying to arouse the Lord's jealousy?ʷ Are we stronger than he?

The Believer's Freedom

²³"Everything is permissible"—but not everything is beneficial.ˣ "Everything is permissible"—but not everything is constructive. ²⁴Nobody should seek his own good, but the good of others.ʸ

²⁵Eat anything sold in the meat market without raising questions of conscience, ²⁶for, "The earth is the Lord's, and everything in it."ᵃ ᶻ

²⁷If some unbeliever invites you to a meal and you want to go, eat whatever is put before youᵃ without raising questions of conscience. ²⁸But if anyone says to you, "This has been offered in sacrifice," then do not eat it, both for the sake of the man who told you and for conscience' sake ᵇ— ²⁹the other man's conscience, I mean, not yours. For why should my freedomᵇ be judged by another's conscience? ³⁰If I take part in the meal with thankfulness, why am I denounced because of something I thank God for?ᶜ

ᵃ26 Psalm 24:1   ᵇ28 Some manuscripts *conscience' sake, for "the earth is the Lord's and everything in it"*

10:16	ˢMt 26:26-28
10:17	ᵗ1Co 12:27
10:20	ᵘDt 32:17; Ps 106:37
10:21	ᵛ2Co 6:15, 16
10:22	ʷDt 32:16, 21
10:23	ˣ1Co 6:12
10:24	ʸRo 15:1, 2
10:26	ᶻPs 24:1
10:27	ᵃLk 10:7
10:29	ᵇRo 14:16
10:30	ᶜRo 14:6

10:14 Idol worship was the major expression of religion in Corinth. There were several pagan temples in the city, and they were very popular. The statues of wood or stone were not evil in themselves, but people gave them credit for what only God could do, such as provide good weather, crops, and children. Idolatry is still a serious problem today, but it takes a different form. We don't put our trust in statues of wood and stone, but in paper money and plastic cards. Trusting anything for what God alone provides is idolatry. Our modern idols are those symbols of power, pleasure, or prestige that we so highly regard. When we understand contemporary parallels to idolatry, Paul's words to "flee from idolatry" become much more meaningful.

10:16-21 The idea of unity and fellowship with God through eating a sacrifice was strong in Judaism and Christianity as well as in paganism. In Old Testament days, when a Jew offered a sacrifice, he ate a part of that sacrifice as a way of restoring his unity with God, against whom he had sinned (Deuteronomy 12:17, 18). Similarly, Christians participate in Christ's once-for-all sacrifice when they eat the bread and drink the wine symbolizing his body and blood. Recent converts from paganism could not help being affected if they knowingly ate with pagans in their feasts the meat offered to idols.

10:21 As followers of Christ we must give him our total allegiance. We cannot, as Paul explains, have a part in "both the Lord's table and the table of demons." Eating at the Lord's table means communing with Christ and identifying with his death. Eating at the demons' table means identifying with Satan by worshiping or promoting pagan (or evil) activities. Are you trying to lead two lives, following the desires of both Christ and the crowd? The Bible says that you can't do both at the same time.

10:23, 24 Sometimes it's hard to know when to defer to weaker believers. Paul gives a simple rule of thumb to help in making the decision—we should be sensitive and gracious. The goal here is not a general hypersensitivity that worries about what others might possibly think. Rather, it is a genuine awareness of others and a willingness to limit what we do when there is a real possibility of misunderstanding and offense. Some actions may not be wrong, but they may not be in the best interest of others. We have freedom in Christ, but we shouldn't exercise our freedom at the cost of hurting a Christian brother or sister. We are not to consider only ourselves, but we must also consider the needs and perspectives of others. For more on the proper attitude toward a weaker believer, see the notes on 8:10–13 and Romans 14.

10:25-27 Paul gave one answer to the dilemma—to buy whatever meat is sold at the market without asking whether it was offered to idols. It doesn't matter anyway, and no one's conscience would be troubled. When we become too worried about our every action, we become legalistic and cannot enjoy life. Everything belongs to God, and he has given us all things to enjoy. If we know something is a problem, then we can deal with it, but we don't need to go looking for problems.

10:28-33 Why should we be limited by another person's conscience? Simply because we are to do all things for God's glory, even our eating and drinking. Nothing we do should cause another believer to stumble. We do what is best for others, so that they might be saved. We should also be sensitive to the meaning of our actions to new Christians who are sorting out how to renounce sinful ways from the past and live for Christ.

However, Christians should not make a career out of being the offended people with oversensitive consciences. Believers must not project their standards onto others. Many believers who have been Christians for years are still oversensitive and judgmental of others. Instead of being the offended weaker brothers and sisters, they are no more than offended "Pharisees."

Christian leaders and teachers should carefully teach about the freedom Christians have in matters not expressly forbidden by Scripture. New or weak Christians should not remain in a weak or sensitive state but should grow into maturity and discernment lest they prove to be an unnecessary burden on others' freedom in Christ.

10:31
*d*Col 3:17; 1Pe 4:11

10:32
*e*Ac 20:28

10:33
*f*Ro 15:2

31 So whether you eat or drink or whatever you do, do it all for the glory of God. *d* 32 Do not cause anyone to stumble, whether Jews, Greeks or the church of God *e* — 33 even as I try to please everybody in every way. *f* For I am not seeking my own good but the good of many, so

11 that they may be saved. 1 Follow my example, as I follow the example of Christ.

3. Instruction on public worship
Propriety in Worship

11:2
*g*1Co 4:17

2 I praise you for remembering me in everything *g* and for holding to the teachings, *a* just as I passed them on to you.

*a*2 Or *traditions*

MAKING CHOICES ON SENSITIVE ISSUES

All of us make hundreds of choices every day. Most choices have no right or wrong attached to them—like what you wear or what you eat. But we always face decisions that carry a little more weight. We don't want to do wrong, and we don't want to cause others to do wrong, so how can we make such decisions?

If I choose one course of action:

. . . does it help my witness for Christ? (9:19–22)

. . . am I motivated by a desire to help others know Christ? (9:23; 10:33)

. . . does it help me do my best? (9:25)

. . . is it against a specific command in Scripture and would thus cause me to sin? (10:12)

. . . is it the best and most beneficial course of action? (10:23, 33)

. . . am I thinking only of myself, or do I truly care about the other person? (10:24)

. . . am I acting lovingly or selfishly? (10:28–31)

. . . does it glorify God? (10:31)

. . . will it cause someone else to sin? (10:32)

10:31 God's love must so permeate our motives that all we do will be for his glory. Keep this as a guiding principle by asking, "Is this action glorifying God?" or "How can I honor God through this action?"

10:33 Paul's criterion for all his actions was not what he liked best, but what was best for those around him. The opposite attitude would be: (1) being insensitive and doing what we want, no matter who is hurt by it; (2) being oversensitive and doing nothing, for fear that someone may be displeased; (3) being a "yes person" by going along with everything, trying to gain approval from people rather than from God. In this age of "me first" and "looking out for number one," Paul's startling statement is a good standard. If we make the good of others one of our primary goals, we will develop a serving attitude that pleases God.

11:1 Why did Paul say, "Follow my example"? Paul wasn't being arrogant—he did not think of himself as sinless. At this time, however, the Corinthian believers did not know much about the life and ministry of Christ. Paul could not tell them to imitate Jesus, because the Gospels had not yet been written, so they did not know what Jesus was like. The best way to point these new Christians to Christ was to point them to a Christian whom they trusted (see also Galatians 4:12; Philippians 3:17; 1 Thessalonians 1:6; 2:14; 2 Thessalonians 3:7, 9). Paul had been in Corinth almost two years and had built a relationship of trust with many of these new believers.

11:2ff In this section Paul's main concern is irreverence in worship. We need to read it in the context of the situation in Corinth. The matter of wearing hats or head coverings, although seemingly insignificant, had become a big problem because two cultural backgrounds were colliding. Jewish women always covered their heads in worship. For a woman to uncover her head in public was a sign of loose morals. On the other hand, Greek women may have been used to worshiping without head coverings.

In this letter Paul had already spoken about divisions and disorder in the church. Both are involved in this issue. Paul's solution comes from his desire for unity among church members and for appropriateness in the worship service. He accepted God's sovereignty in creating the rules for relationships.

11:2–16 This section focuses primarily on proper attitudes and conduct in worship, not on the marriage relationship or on the role of women in the church. While Paul's specific instructions may be cultural (women covering their heads in worship), the principles behind his specific instructions are timeless, principles like respect for spouse, reverence and appropriateness in worship, and focus of all of life on God. If anything you do can easily offend members and divide the church, then change your ways to promote church unity. Thus Paul told the women who were not wearing head coverings to wear them, not because it was a Scriptural command, but because it kept the congregation from dividing over a petty issue that served only to take people's minds off Christ.

3Now I want you to realize that the head of every man is Christ, and the head of the woman is man,[h] and the head of Christ is God. 4Every man who prays or prophesies with his head covered dishonors his head. 5And every woman who prays or prophesies[i] with her head uncovered dishonors her head—it is just as though her head were shaved.[j] 6If a woman does not cover her head, she should have her hair cut off; and if it is a disgrace for a woman to have her hair cut or shaved off, she should cover her head. 7A man ought not to cover his head,[a] since he is the image[k] and glory of God; but the woman is the glory of man. 8For man did not come from woman, but woman from man;[l] 9neither was man created for woman, but woman for man. [m] 10For this reason, and because of the angels, the woman ought to have a sign of authority on her head.

11In the Lord, however, woman is not independent of man, nor is man independent of woman. 12For as woman came from man, so also man is born of woman. But everything comes from God. 13Judge for yourselves: Is it proper for a woman to pray to God with her head uncovered? 14Does not the very nature of things teach you that if a man has long hair, it is a disgrace to him, 15but that if a woman has long hair, it is her glory? For long hair is given to her as a covering. 16If anyone wants to be contentious about this, we have no other practice—nor do the churches of God.[n]

The Lord's Supper

17In the following directives I have no praise for you,[o] for your meetings do more harm than good. 18In the first place, I hear that when you come together as a church, there are divisions[p] among you, and to some extent I believe it. 19No doubt there have to be differences among you to show which of you have God's approval.[q] 20When you come together, it is not the Lord's Supper you eat, 21for as you eat, each of you goes ahead without waiting

a4-7 Or 4Every man who prays or prophesies with long hair dishonors his head. 5And every woman who prays or prophesies with no covering [of hair] on her head dishonors her head—she is just like one of the "shorn women." 6If a woman has no covering, let her be for now with short hair, but since it is a disgrace for a woman to have her hair shorn or shaved, she should grow it again. 7A man ought not to have long hair

11:3
hEph 5:23

11:5
iAc 21:9
jDt 21:12

11:7
kGe 1:26

11:8
lGe 2:21-23

11:9
mGe 2:18

11:16
n1Co 7:17

11:17
over 2, 22

11:18
p1Co 1:10-12

11:19
q1Jn 2:19

11:3 The phrase, "the head of every man is Christ," could mean that: (1) because Christ was present at Creation, he is the Creator of every man; and (2) Christ is every believer's source of life in the new creation.

In the phrase, "the head of the woman is man," *head* is not used to indicate control or supremacy, but rather, "the source of." Because man was created first, the woman derives her existence from man, as man does from Christ and Christ from God. Evidently Paul was correcting some excesses in worship in which the emancipated Corinthian women were engaging.

The phrase, "the head of Christ is God," does not mean that Christ was inferior to God in any way. Paul was referring to the incarnation of Christ. Through Christ's coming to earth, believers receive forgiveness and are united with God and with one another. From this theological base, then, Paul began to address the issue of head coverings.

11:3 Submission is a key element in the smooth functioning of any business, government, or family. God ordained submission in certain relationships to prevent chaos. It is essential to understand that submission is not surrender, withdrawal, or apathy. It does not mean inferiority, because God created all people in his image and because all have equal value. Submission is mutual commitment and cooperation.

Thus God calls for submission among *equals*. He did not make the man superior; he made a way for the man and woman to work together. Jesus Christ, although equal with God the Father, submitted to him to carry out the plan for salvation. Likewise, although equal to man under God, the wife should submit to her husband for the sake of their marriage and family. Submission between equals is submission by choice, not by force. We serve God in these relationships by willingly submitting to others in our church, to our spouses, and to our government leaders.

11:9–11 God created lines of authority in order for his created world to function smoothly. Although there must be lines of authority, even in marriage, there should *not* be lines of superiority. God created men and women with unique and complementary characteristics. One sex is not better than the other. We must not

let the issue of authority and submission become a wedge to destroy oneness in marriage. Instead, we should use our unique gifts to strengthen our marriages and to glorify God.

11:10 "Because of the angels, the woman ought to have a sign of authority on her head" may mean that the woman should wear a covering on her head as a sign that she is under the man's authority. This is a fact even the angels understand as they observe Christians in worship. See the note on 11:2ff for an explanation of head coverings.

11:14, 15 In talking about head coverings and length of hair, Paul is saying that believers should look and behave in ways that are honorable within their own culture. In many cultures long hair on men is considered appropriate and masculine. In Corinth, it was thought to be a sign of male prostitution in the pagan temples. And women with short hair were labeled prostitutes. Paul was saying that in the Corinthian culture, Christian women should keep their hair long. If short hair on women was a sign of prostitution, then a Christian woman with short hair would find it even more difficult to be a believable witness for Jesus Christ. Paul wasn't saying we should adopt all the practices of our culture, but that we should avoid appearances and behavior that detract from our ultimate goal of being believable witnesses for Jesus Christ while demonstrating our Christian faith.

11:17–34 The Lord's Supper (11:20) is a visible representation of the Good News of the death of Christ for our sins. It reminds us of Christ's death and the glorious hope of his return. Our participation in it strengthens our faith through fellowship with Christ and with other believers.

11:19 Paul allows that there might be differences among church members. When they develop into self-willed divisions, they are destructive to the congregation. Those who cause division only serve to highlight those who are genuine believers.

11:21, 22 When the Lord's Supper was celebrated in the early church, it included a feast or fellowship meal followed by the celebration of Communion. In the church in Corinth, the fellowship meal had become a time when some ate and drank excessively

11:21
r Jude 12

11:22
s 1Co 10:32
t Jas 2:6

11:23
u 1Co 15:3

11:25
v Lk 22:20

for anybody else. r One remains hungry, another gets drunk. 22 Don't you have homes to eat and drink in? Or do you despise the church of God s and humiliate those who have nothing? t What shall I say to you? Shall I praise you for this? Certainly not!

23 For I received from the Lord what I also passed on to you: u The Lord Jesus, on the night he was betrayed, took bread, 24 and when he had given thanks, he broke it and said, "This is my body, which is for you; do this in remembrance of me." 25 In the same way, after supper he took the cup, saying, "This cup is the new covenant v in my blood; do this, whenever you drink it, in remembrance of me." 26 For whenever you eat this bread and drink this cup, you proclaim the Lord's death until he comes.

11:28
w 2Co 13:5

27 Therefore, whoever eats the bread or drinks the cup of the Lord in an unworthy manner will be guilty of sinning against the body and blood of the Lord. 28 A man ought to examine himself w before he eats of the bread and drinks of the cup. 29 For anyone who eats and drinks without recognizing the body of the Lord eats and drinks judgment on himself. 30 That is why many among you are weak and sick, and a number of you have fallen asleep.

11:32
x Ps 94:12

31 But if we judged ourselves, we would not come under judgment. 32 When we are judged by the Lord, we are being disciplined x so that we will not be condemned with the world.

11:34
y 1Co 4:19

33 So then, my brothers, when you come together to eat, wait for each other. 34 If anyone is hungry, he should eat at home, so that when you meet together it may not result in judgment.

And when I come y I will give further directions.

---

while others went hungry. There was little sharing and caring. This certainly did not demonstrate the unity and love that should characterize the church, nor was it a preparation for Communion. Paul condemned these actions and reminded the church of the real purpose of the Lord's Supper.

11:24, 25 What does the Lord's Supper mean? The early church remembered that Jesus instituted the Lord's Supper on the night of the Passover meal (Luke 22:13–20). Just as Passover celebrated deliverance from slavery in Egypt, so the Lord's Supper celebrates deliverance from sin by Christ's death.

Christians pose several different possibilities for what Christ meant when he said, "This is my body." (1) Some believe that the wine and bread actually become Christ's physical blood and body. (2) Others believe that the bread and wine remain unchanged, but Christ is spiritually present with the bread and wine. (3) Still others believe that the bread and wine symbolize Christ's body and blood. Christians generally agree, however, that participating in the Lord's Supper is an important element in the Christian faith and that Christ's presence, however we understand it, strengthens us spiritually.

11:25 What is this new covenant? In the old covenant, people could approach God only through the priests and the sacrificial system. Jesus' death on the cross ushered in the new covenant or agreement between God and us. Now all people can personally approach God and communicate with him. The people of Israel first entered into this agreement after their exodus from Egypt (Exodus 24), and it was designed to point to the day when Jesus Christ would come. The new covenant completes, rather than replaces, the old covenant, fulfilling everything the old covenant looked forward to (see Jeremiah 31:31–34). Eating the bread and drinking the cup shows that we are remembering Christ's death for us and renewing our commitment to serve him.

11:25 Jesus said, "Do this, whenever you drink it, in remembrance of me." How do we remember Christ in the Lord's Supper? By thinking about what he did and why he did it. Further, the remembering has both a backward and forward look. We remember Christ's death, and we remember that he is coming! If the Lord's Supper becomes just a ritual or a pious habit, it loses its significance. But when we appreciate what Christ has done and anticipate what he will do when he returns, the Lord's Supper takes on a profound sense of purpose. Take time to prepare yourself spiritually for Communion. Gratefully recall Christ's loving sacrifice for you. Let the reality that your sins are forgiven motivate you to love and serve him better.

11:27ff Paul gives specific instructions on how the Lord's Supper should be observed. (1) We should take the Lord's Supper thoughtfully because we are proclaiming that Christ died for our sins (11:26). (2) We should take it worthily, with due reverence and respect (11:27). (3) We should examine ourselves for any unconfessed sin or resentful attitude (11:28). We are to be properly prepared, based on our belief in and love for Christ. (4) We should be considerate of others (11:33), waiting until everyone is there and then eating in an orderly and unified manner.

11:27–34 When Paul said that no one should take the Lord's Supper in an unworthy manner, he was speaking to the church members who were rushing into it without thinking of its meaning. To not honor the "body of Christ" means not understanding what the Lord's Supper means and not distinguishing it from a normal meal. Those who did so were "guilty of sinning against the body and blood of the Lord." Instead of honoring his sacrifice, they were sharing in the guilt of those who crucified Christ. In reality, *no one* is worthy to take the Lord's Supper. We are all sinners saved by grace. This is why we should prepare ourselves for Communion through healthy introspection, confession of sin, and resolution of differences with others. These actions remove the barriers that affect our relationship with Christ and with other believers. Awareness of your sin should not keep you away from Communion but should drive you to participate in it.

11:30 "Fallen asleep" is another way of describing death. That some of the people had died may have been a special supernatural judgment on the Corinthian church. This type of disciplinary judgment highlights the seriousness of the Communion service. The Lord's Supper is not to be taken lightly; this new covenant cost Jesus his life. It is not a meaningless ritual, but a sacrament given by Christ to help strengthen our faith.

11:34 People should come to this meal desiring to fellowship with other believers and prepare for the Lord's Supper to follow, not to fill up on a big dinner. "If anyone is hungry, he should eat at home" means that they should eat dinner beforehand, so as to come to the fellowship meal in the right frame of mind.

Spiritual Gifts

12 Now about spiritual gifts,*z* brothers, I do not want you to be ignorant. ²You know that when you were pagans,*a* somehow or other you were influenced and led astray to mute idols. *b* ³Therefore I tell you that no one who is speaking by the Spirit of God says, "Jesus be cursed," and no one can say, "Jesus is Lord," except by the Holy Spirit. *c*

⁴There are different kinds of gifts, but the same Spirit. *d* ⁵There are different kinds of service, but the same Lord. ⁶There are different kinds of working, but the same God works all of them in all men.

⁷Now to each one the manifestation of the Spirit is given for the common good. ⁸To one there is given through the Spirit the message of wisdom,*e* to another the message of knowledge *f* by means of the same Spirit, ⁹to another faith by the same Spirit, to another gifts of healing by that one Spirit, ¹⁰to another miraculous powers,*g* to another prophecy, to another distinguishing between spirits,*h* to another speaking in different kinds of tongues,*a* and to still another the interpretation of tongues. *a* ¹¹All these are the work of one and the same Spirit, and he gives them to each one, just as he determines.

One Body, Many Parts

¹²The body is a unit, though it is made up of many parts; and though all its parts are many, they form one body. So it is with Christ. ¹³For we were all baptized by *b* one Spirit into one body—whether Jews or Greeks, slave or free *i*—and we were all given the one Spirit to drink.

a 10 Or *languages*; also in verse 28   *b 13* Or *with*; or *in*

12:1
z Ro 1:11;
1Co 14:1, 37

12:2
a Eph 2:11, 12
b Ps 115:5; 1Th 1:9

12:3
c 1Jn 4:2, 3

12:4
d Ro 12:4-8

12:8
e 1Co 2:6
f 2Co 8:7

12:10
g Gal 3:5
h 1Jn 4:1

12:13
i Gal 3:28; Col 3:11

12:1ff The spiritual gifts given to each person by the Holy Spirit are special abilities that are to be used to minister to the needs of the body of believers. This chapter is not an exhaustive list of spiritual gifts (see Romans 12; Ephesians 4; 1 Peter 4:10, 11 for more examples). There are many gifts, people have different gifts, some people have more than one gift, and one gift is not superior to another. All spiritual gifts come from the Holy Spirit, and their purpose is to build up Christ's body, the church.

12:1ff Instead of building up and unifying the Corinthian church, the issue of spiritual gifts was splitting it. Spiritual gifts had become symbols of spiritual power, causing rivalries because some people thought they were more "spiritual" than others because of their gifts. This was a terrible misuse of spiritual gifts because their purpose is always to help the church function more effectively, not to divide it. We can be divisive if we insist on using our gift our own way without being sensitive to others. We must never use gifts as a means of manipulating others or serving our own self-interest.

12:3 Anyone can claim to speak for God, and the world is full of false teachers. Paul gives us a test to help us discern whether or not a messenger is really from God: does he or she confess Christ as Lord? Don't naively accept the words of all who claim to speak for God; test their credentials by finding out what they teach about Christ.

12:6 God is completely involved in the giving, using, and empowering of gifts. Specific gifts, places of service, and activities vary, but they all have their best effects when they build up the body of Christ—the church. God creates a unique place in the body for every believer. Gifts and ministries may overlap, but each believer has a specialized, God-designed role. Part of the exciting adventure of following Christ involves discovering one's service contribution and then making it available to God. Make serving God and his people your motive as you utilize your gifts.

12:9 All Christians have faith. Some, however, have the spiritual gift of faith, which is an unusual measure of trust in the Holy Spirit's power.

12:10 "Prophecy" does not just refer to predicting the future; it can also mean giving a message received from God to the community of believers: "Everyone who prophesies speaks to men for their strengthening, encouragement and comfort" (14:3). The prophet Joel had written the words of the Lord, "I will pour out my Spirit on all people. Your sons and daughters will prophesy" (Joel 2:28). As with the gift of faith, the ability to share one's faith with

power is available to everyone (see 14:1–5), but to some the Spirit gives a special measure of this gift. Paul wrote in Romans, "We have different gifts, according to the grace given us. If a man's gift is prophesying, let him use it in proportion to his faith" (Romans 12:6). Some have interpreted "prophecy" to be fulfilled in various sermons throughout church history. Others, however, say that prophecy is not a sermon, but a spontaneous, Spirit-inspired message that is orally delivered in the congregation for the edification and encouragement of the body of Christ.

12:10 Opinions differ over exactly what Paul meant by "tongues." Some believe that this refers to speaking in earthly languages that a person did not know before (the same as the gift described in Acts 2:4–8). Other scholars say that this refers to an "ecstatic" language, a "heavenly" language. Most likely the second view is correct. Probably the only time that the word "tongues" refers to other earthly languages is when describing Pentecost. The rest of the time in the New Testament, the word refers to ecstatic languages unknown to anyone—languages of angels (13:1).

Speaking in tongues *is* a legitimate gift of the Spirit. The exercise of the gift demands some guidelines (as noted in chapter 14) so that the *purpose* of the gift—to help the body of Christ—is not lost. Those who speak in tongues should follow the guidelines; those who do not speak in tongues ought *not* seek the gift as a sign of salvation or of special closeness with God, for it is neither. It is a gift of God, given only to whomever God chooses. If a person has not experienced the gift of tongues, he or she ought not seek it but seek what gifts God *has* given. For more, see the notes in chapter 14.

12:11 No matter what gift(s) a person has, all spiritual gifts are distributed by the Holy Spirit. The Holy Spirit decides which gifts each believer should have. We are responsible to use and sharpen our gifts, but we can take no credit for what God has freely given us.

Note that discussions about spiritual gifts usually create difficulties when two central points are overlooked: (1) Properly used, spiritual gifts are not self-serving but serve the whole body of Christ (12:7); (2) each gift becomes practically useless when used without love (chapter 13). As you seek to identify and utilize the gifts God has given you, make loving God and loving fellow Christians your highest motives.

12:12 Paul compares the body of Christ to a human body. Each part has a specific function that is necessary to the body as a whole. The parts are different for a purpose, and in their differences they must work together. Christians must avoid two common errors: (1) being too proud of their abilities, or (2) think-

¹⁴Now the body is not made up of one part but of many. ¹⁵If the foot should say, "Because I am not a hand, I do not belong to the body," it would not for that reason cease to be part of the body. ¹⁶And if the ear should say, "Because I am not an eye, I do not belong to the body," it would not for that reason cease to be part of the body. ¹⁷If the whole body were an eye, where would the sense of hearing be? If the whole body were an ear, where would the sense of smell be? ¹⁸But in fact God has arranged*j* the parts in the body, every one of them, just as he wanted them to be. ¹⁹If they were all one part, where would the body be? ²⁰As it is, there are many parts, but one body.

²¹The eye cannot say to the hand, "I don't need you!" And the head cannot say to the feet, "I don't need you!" ²²On the contrary, those parts of the body that seem to be weaker are indispensable, ²³and the parts that we think are less honorable we treat with special honor. And the parts that are unpresentable are treated with special modesty, ²⁴while our presentable parts need no special treatment. But God has combined the members of the body and has given greater honor to the parts that lacked it, ²⁵so that there should be no division in the body, but that its parts should have equal concern for each other. ²⁶If one part suffers, every part suffers with it; if one part is honored, every part rejoices with it.

²⁷Now you are the body of Christ,*k* and each one of you is a part of it.*l* ²⁸And in the church God has appointed first of all apostles,*m* second prophets, third teachers, then workers of miracles, also those having gifts of healing,*n* those able to help others, those with gifts of administration,*o* and those speaking in different kinds of tongues.*p* ²⁹Are all apostles? Are all prophets? Are all teachers? Do all work miracles? ³⁰Do all have gifts of healing? Do all speak in tongues*a*? Do all interpret? ³¹But eagerly desire*b q* the greater gifts.

Love

And now I will show you the most excellent way.

13
If I speak in the tongues*c* of men and of angels, but have not love, I am only a resounding gong or a clanging cymbal. ²If I have the gift of prophecy and can fathom all mysteries*r* and all knowledge, and if I have a faith that can move mountains, but have not love, I am nothing. ³If I give all I possess to the poor*s* and surrender my body to the flames,*d* but have not love, I gain nothing.

*a*30 Or *other languages*   *b*31 Or *But you are eagerly desiring*   *c*1 Or *languages*   *d*3 Some early manuscripts *body that I may boast*

12:18
*j*ver 28

12:27
*k*Eph 1:23; 4:12; Col 1:18, 24
*l*Ro 12:5

12:28
*m*Eph 4:11
*n*ver 9
*o*Ro 12:6-8
*p*ver 10

12:31
*q*1Co 14:1, 39

13:2
*r*1Co 14:2

13:3
*s*Mt 6:2

---

ing they have nothing to give to the body of believers. Instead of comparing ourselves to one another, we should use our different gifts, together, to spread the Good News of salvation.

12:13 The church is composed of many types of people from a variety of backgrounds with a multitude of gifts and abilities. It is easy for these differences to divide people, as was the case in Corinth. But despite the differences, all believers have one thing in common—faith in Christ. On this essential truth the church finds unity. All believers are baptized by one Holy Spirit into one body of believers, the church. We don't lose our individual identities, but we have an overriding oneness in Christ. When a person becomes a Christian, the Holy Spirit takes up residence, and he or she is born into God's family. "We were all given the one Spirit to drink" means that the same Holy Spirit completely fills our innermost beings. As members of God's family, we may have different interests and gifts, but we have a common goal.

12:23, 24 Paul argued for diversity of gifts and acceptance of the full range of gifts that God gives to his people. No one should feel superior about his or her gift; instead, all should use their gifts to willingly serve. Too often the "up-front" gifts, like speaking or teaching, are more highly regarded than the "behind-the-scenes" gifts, like helping and serving. No one should discount the contribution of another person, no matter how insignificant it may seem. We should not be dissatisfied with the gift God has given us but be eager to serve. Nor should we envy those who seem to have more gifts than we do. In love, treat everyone's gift, yours included, as valuable to God.

12:25, 26 What is your response when a fellow Christian is honored? How do you respond when someone is suffering? We are called to rejoice with those who rejoice and weep with those

who weep (Romans 12:15). Too often, unfortunately, we are jealous of those who rejoice and apathetic toward those who weep. Believers are in the world together—there is no such thing as private or individualistic Christianity. We shouldn't stop with enjoying only our own relationship with God; we need to get involved in the lives of others.

12:30 Paul discusses the subject of speaking in and interpreting tongues in more detail in chapter 14. See also the second note at 12:10.

12:31 The greater gifts are those that are more beneficial to the body of Christ. Paul has already made it clear that one gift is not superior to another, but he urges the believers to discover how they can serve Christ's body with the gifts God has given them. Your spiritual gifts are not for your own self-advancement. They were given to you for serving God and enhancing the spiritual growth of the body of believers.

13:1ff In chapter 12, Paul gave evidence of the Corinthians' lack of love in the utilization of spiritual gifts; chapter 13 defines real love; and chapter 14 shows how love works. Love is more important than all the spiritual gifts exercised in the church body. Great faith, acts of dedication or sacrifice, and miracle-working power produce very little without love. Love makes our actions and gifts useful. Although people have different gifts, love is available to everyone.

⁴Love is patient, love is kind. It does not envy, it does not boast, it is not proud. ⁵It is not rude, it is not self-seeking,ᵗ it is not easily angered, it keeps no record of wrongs. ⁶Love does not delight in evil but rejoices with the truth. ᵘ ⁷It always protects, always trusts, always hopes, always perseveres.

⁸Love never fails. But where there are prophecies, they will cease; where there are tongues, they will be stilled; where there is knowledge, it will pass away. ⁹For we know in partᵛ and we prophesy in part, ¹⁰but when perfection comes, ʷ the imperfect disappears. ¹¹When I was a child, I talked like a child, I thought like a child, I reasoned like a child. When I became a man, I put childish ways behind me. ¹²Now we see but a poor reflection as in a mirror; then we shall see face to face.ˣ Now I know in part; then I shall know fully, even as I am fully known.ʸ

¹³And now these three remain: faith, hope and love. But the greatest of these is love.

Gifts of Prophecy and Tongues

14 Follow the way of love and eagerly desire ᶻ spiritual gifts, especially the gift of prophecy. ²For anyone who speaks in a tongueᵃ does not speak to men but to God. Indeed, no one understands him; he utters mysteriesᵃ with his spirit.ᵇ ³But everyone who prophesies speaks to men for their strengthening, encouragement and comfort. ⁴He who speaks in a tongue edifies himself, but he who prophesies edifies the church. ⁵I would like every one of you to speak in tongues,ᶜ but I would rather have you prophesy.ᵇ He who prophesies is greater than one who speaks in tongues,ᶜ unless he interprets, so that the church may be edified.

⁶Now, brothers, if I come to you and speak in tongues, what good will I be to you, unless I bring you some revelationᶜ or knowledge or prophecy or word of instruction? ⁷Even in the

13:5
ᵗ1Co 10:24
13:6
ᵘ2Jn 4

13:9
ᵛ1Co 8:2
13:10
ʷPhp 3:12
13:12
ˣ2Co 5:7; 1Jn 3:2
ʸ1Co 8:3

14:1
ᶻ1Co 12:31
14:2
ᵃ1Co 13:2

14:5
ᵇNu 11:29

14:6
ᶜver 26

ᵃ2 Or *another language*; also in verses 4, 13, 14, 19, 26 and 27   ᵇ2 Or *by the Spirit*   ᶜ5 Or *other languages*; also in verses 6, 18, 22, 23 and 39

13:4 Paul says that love "is patient." Sometimes we're irritated or angered by others, and we don't know why. Not all irritability stems from sinful or selfish motives, although the irritable treatment of others surely is wrong. Much irritability comes from a love of perfection, a deep desire that programs, meetings, and structures be run perfectly. A desire to run things perfectly can erupt into anger at events or people who get in the way or ruin that desire. Those who are easily irritated need to remember that perfection exists only in God. We need to love him and our fellow Christians, not the visions we have for perfection here on earth.

13:4–7 Our society confuses love and lust. Unlike lust, God's kind of love is directed outward toward others, not inward toward ourselves. It is utterly unselfish. This kind of love goes against our natural inclinations. It is possible to practice this love only if God helps us set aside our own desires and instincts, so that we can give love while expecting nothing in return. Thus the more we become like Christ, the more love we will show to others.

13:10–12 When Paul wrote of knowing "fully," he was referring to when we must see Christ face to face. God gives believers spiritual gifts for their lives on earth in order to build up, serve, and strengthen fellow Christians. The spiritual gifts are for the church. In eternity, we will be made perfect and complete and will be in the very presence of God. We will no longer need the spiritual gifts, so they will come to an end. Then, we will have a full understanding and appreciation for one another as unique expressions of God's infinite creativity. We will use our differences as a reason to praise God! Based on that perspective, let us treat each other with the same love and unity that we will one day share.

13:13 Paul wrote that love endures forever. In morally corrupt Corinth, love had become a mixed-up term with little meaning. Today, people are still confused about love. Love is the greatest of all human qualities and is an attribute of God himself (1 John 4:8). Love involves unselfish service to others. *Faith* is the foundation and content of God's message; *hope* is the attitude and focus; *love* is action. When faith and hope are in line, you are free to love completely because you understand how God loves. Does your faith fully express itself in loving others?

14:1 Prophecy may involve predicting future events, but its main purpose is to communicate God's message to people, providing insight, warning, correction, and encouragement. See also the first note on 12:10.

14:2 The gift of speaking in a tongue was a concern of the Corinthian church because the use of the gift had caused disorder in worship. Speaking in tongues is a legitimate gift of the Holy Spirit, but the Corinthian believers were using it as a sign of spiritual superiority rather than as a means to spiritual unity. Spiritual gifts are beneficial only when they are properly used to help everyone in the church. We should not exercise them only to make *ourselves* feel good. See also the second note at 12:10.

14:2–5 Paul's words to the Corinthians about tongues and prophecy have much to say to our generation. Many Christians struggle with the discussion of tongues. Paul would clearly say that no one should put down those Christians who speak in tongues, and those who speak in tongues should not disparage those who do not. Paul makes several points about speaking in tongues: (1) It is a spiritual gift from God (14:2); (2) it is a desirable gift even though it isn't a requirement of faith (12:28–31); (3) it is less important than prophecy and teaching (14:4). Believers need unity and love. The enemy is not each other but the sinful world, Satan, and our selfish, sinful desires. But Paul would have another word for today: "I would like every one of you to speak in tongues." Although Paul himself spoke in tongues, he stresses prophecy (preaching) because it benefits the whole church, while speaking in tongues primarily benefits the speaker. Paul would encourage us to be so in tune with the Spirit that his messages of comfort, encouragement, and edification would be heard in our congregations today. Make sure your actions are encouraging and edifying.

14:7–12 As musical instruments must play each note in order for the music to be clear, so Paul says words preached in the hearers' language are more clear and helpful. There are many languages in the world (14:10), and people who speak different languages can rarely understand each other. It is the same with speaking in tongues. Although this gift is helpful to many people in private worship, and helpful in public worship with interpretation, Paul says he would rather speak five words that his hearers can understand than 10,000 that they cannot (14:19).

14:8
d Nu 10:9

case of lifeless things that make sounds, such as the flute or harp, how will anyone know what tune is being played unless there is a distinction in the notes? 8Again, if the trumpet does not sound a clear call, who will get ready for battle? d 9So it is with you. Unless you speak intelligible words with your tongue, how will anyone know what you are saying? You will just be speaking into the air. 10Undoubtedly there are all sorts of languages in the world, yet none of them is without meaning. 11If then I do not grasp the meaning of what someone is saying, I am a foreigner to the speaker, and he is a foreigner to me. 12So it is with you. Since you are eager to have spiritual gifts, try to excel in gifts that build up the church.

14:15
e Eph 5:19; Col 3:16
14:16
f 1Ch 16:36
g 1Co 11:24

13For this reason anyone who speaks in a tongue should pray that he may interpret what he says. 14For if I pray in a tongue, my spirit prays, but my mind is unfruitful. 15So what shall I do? I will pray with my spirit, but I will also pray with my mind; I will sing e with my spirit, but I will also sing with my mind. 16If you are praising God with your spirit, how can one who finds himself among those who do not understand a say "Amen" f to your thanksgiving, g since he does not know what you are saying? 17You may be giving thanks well enough, but the other man is not edified.

18I thank God that I speak in tongues more than all of you. 19But in the church I would rather speak five intelligible words to instruct others than ten thousand words in a tongue.

14:20
h Eph 4:14;
Heb 5:12, 13;
1Pe 2:2
i Ro 16:19
14:21
j Jn 10:34
k Isa 28:11, 12

20Brothers, stop thinking like children. h In regard to evil be infants, i but in your thinking be adults. 21In the Law j it is written:

"Through men of strange tongues
    and through the lips of foreigners
I will speak to this people,
    but even then they will not listen to me," b k

says the Lord.

14:23
l Ac 2:13

22Tongues, then, are a sign, not for believers but for unbelievers; prophecy, however, is for believers, not for unbelievers. 23So if the whole church comes together and everyone speaks in tongues, and some who do not understand c or some unbelievers come in, will they not say that you are out of your mind? l 24But if an unbeliever or someone who does not understand d comes in while everybody is prophesying, he will be convinced by all that he is a sinner and will be judged by all, 25and the secrets of his heart will be laid bare. So he will fall down and worship God, exclaiming, "God is really among you!" m

14:25
m Isa 45:14;
Zec 8:23

Orderly Worship

14:26
n 1Co 12:7-10

26What then shall we say, brothers? When you come together, everyone n has a hymn, or a word of instruction, a revelation, a tongue or an interpretation. All of these must be done for the strengthening of the church. 27If anyone speaks in a tongue, two—or at the most three— should speak, one at a time, and someone must interpret. 28If there is no interpreter, the speaker should keep quiet in the church and speak to himself and God.

a 16 Or among the inquirers   b 21 Isaiah 28:11,12   c 23 Or some inquirers   d 24 Or or some inquirer

---

14:9 Paul confronted the self-oriented use of the gift of tongues. Spiritual people must be careful not to pursue self-development at the expense of broken, lost people. When we give too much attention to our own needs, ideas, and spiritual expression, we may push aside the Spirit's true desire and abandon those who need encouragement. Follow Paul's advice and make encouraging and edifying others the highest goal.

14:13-20 Up to this point, Paul has been explaining that the gift of speaking in tongues was of no value to the congregation as a whole, only to the person who speaks to God in the unknown language. But if the person also has the gift of interpretation, the tongue could be used in public worship if the one praying (or someone else with the gift of interpretation) would then interpret what has been said. That way, the entire church would be edified by this gift.

14:15 There is a proper place for the intellect in Christianity. In praying and singing, both the mind and the spirit are to be fully engaged. When we sing, we should also think about the meaning of the words. When we pour out our feelings to God in prayer, we should not turn off our capacity to think. True Christianity is neither barren intellectualism nor thoughtless

emotionalism. See also Ephesians 1:17, 18; Philippians 1:9–11; Colossians 1:9.

14:22–25 The way the Corinthians were speaking in tongues was helping no one because believers did not understand what was being said, and unbelievers thought that the people speaking in tongues were crazy. Speaking in tongues was supposed to be a *sign* to unbelievers (as it was in Acts 2). After speaking in tongues, believers were supposed to explain what was said and give the credit to God. The unsaved people would then be convinced of a spiritual reality and motivated to look further into the Christian faith. While this is one way to reach unbelievers, Paul says that clear preaching is usually better (14:5).

14:26ff Everything done in worship services must be beneficial to the worshipers. Every worshiper ought to consider himself or herself a contributor. These principles touch every aspect—singing, preaching, and the exercise of spiritual gifts. Contributions to the service (by singing, speaking, reading, praying, playing instruments, giving) must have love as their chief motivation. As you prepare to lead or participate in worship, seek to strengthen the faith of other believers.

29 Two or three prophets should speak, and the others should weigh carefully what is said. o 30 And if a revelation comes to someone who is sitting down, the first speaker should stop. 31 For you can all prophesy in turn so that everyone may be instructed and encouraged. 32 The spirits of prophets are subject to the control of prophets. 33 For God is not a God of disorder but of peace.

As in all the congregations of the saints, 34 women should remain silent in the churches. They are not allowed to speak, but must be in submission, p as the Law says. 35 If they want to inquire about something, they should ask their own husbands at home; for it is disgraceful for a woman to speak in the church.

36 Did the word of God originate with you? Or are you the only people it has reached? 37 If anybody thinks he is a prophet q or spiritually gifted, let him acknowledge that what I am writing to you is the Lord's command. r 38 If he ignores this, he himself will be ignored. a

39 Therefore, my brothers, be eager s to prophesy, and do not forbid speaking in tongues. 40 But everything should be done in a fitting and orderly t way.

4. Instruction on resurrection
The Resurrection of Christ

15 Now, brothers, I want to remind you of the gospel I preached to you, which you received and on which you have taken your stand. 2 By this gospel you are saved, if you hold firmly to the word I preached to you. Otherwise, you have believed in vain.

3 For what I received I passed on to you as of first importance b: that Christ died for our sins u according to the Scriptures, v 4 that he was buried, that he was raised on the third day according to the Scriptures, w 5 and that he appeared to Peter, c x and then to the Twelve. 6 After that, he appeared to more than five hundred of the brothers at the same time, most of whom are still living, though some have fallen asleep. 7 Then he appeared to James, then to all the apostles, y 8 and last of all he appeared to me also, z as to one abnormally born.

a 38 Some manuscripts *If he is ignorant of this, let him be ignorant*   b 3 Or *you at the first*   c 5 Greek *Cephas*

14:29
o 1Co 12:10

14:34
p 1Ti 2:11, 12

14:37
q 2Co 10:7
r 1Jn 4:6

14:39
s 1Co 12:31

14:40
t ver 33

15:3
u Isa 53:5; 1Pe 2:24
v Lk 24:27;
Ac 26:22, 23

15:4
w Ac 2:25, 30, 31

15:5
x Lk 24:34

15:7
y Ac 1:3, 4

15:8
z Ac 9:3-6, 17

14:34, 35 Does this mean that women should not speak in church services today? It is clear from 11:5 that women prayed and prophesied in public worship. It is also clear in chapters 12—14 that women are given spiritual gifts and are encouraged to exercise them in the body of Christ. Women have much to contribute and can participate in worship services.

In the Corinthian culture, women were not allowed to confront men in public. Apparently some of the women who had become Christians thought that their Christian freedom gave them the right to question the men in public worship. This was causing division in the church. In addition, women of that day did not receive formal religious education as did the men. Women may have been raising questions in the worship services that could have been answered at home without disrupting the services. Paul was asking the women not to flaunt their Christian freedom during worship. The purpose of Paul's words was to promote unity, not to teach about women's role in the church.

14:40 Paul stated that God is not a God of disorder but of peace (14:33). Note that the preferred alternative to disorder is "peace." Too often, in resisting disorder, Christians have opted for rigid, predictable, and unvarying forms of worship in which God's presence is as difficult to find as in disorderly gatherings. When there is chaos, the church is not allowing God to work among believers as he would like. Worship that is "done in a fitting and orderly way" should not, however, rule out God's creativity, joy, and unpredictability. Do your part to have worship be a joyful, peaceful, winsome experience that draws people into it.

15:2 Most churches contain people who do not yet believe. Some are moving in the direction of belief, and others are simply pretending. Imposters, however, are not to be removed (see Matthew 13:28, 29), for that is the Lord's work alone. The Good News about Jesus Christ will save us *if* we continue to believe it and faithfully follow it.

15:3, 4 The central theme of the gospel is given in these verses, a key text for the defense of Christianity. The three most important points are:
(1) *Christ died for our sins according to the Scriptures.* With-

out the truth of this message, Christ's death was worthless, and those who believe in him are still in their sins and without hope. However, Christ as the sinless Son of God took the punishment of sin so that those who believe can have their sins removed. "The Scriptures" refers to Old Testament prophecies such as Psalm 16:8–11 and Isaiah 53:5, 6. Christ's death on the cross was no accident or afterthought. It had been part of God's plan from all eternity in order to bring about the salvation of all who believe.

(2) *He was buried.* The fact of Christ's death is revealed in the fact of his burial. Many have tried to discount the actual death of Christ, but Jesus did in fact die and was buried in a tomb.

(3) *He was raised on the third day according to the Scriptures.* Christ was raised permanently, forever; his Father raised him from the dead "on the third day" as noted in the Gospels (Friday afternoon to Sunday morning—three days in Jewish reckoning of time). This also occurred "according to the Scriptures." Jesus quoted the prophet Jonah in Matthew 12:40 (see Jonah 1:17) to show the connection to "three days" as prophesied in the Old Testament. Psalm 16:8–11 and Psalm 110 also foretell the resurrection of the Messiah.

15:5–8 There will always be people who say that Jesus didn't rise from the dead. Paul assures us that many people saw Jesus after his resurrection: Peter; the disciples (the Twelve); more than 500 Christian believers (most of whom were still alive when Paul wrote this, although some had died); James (Jesus' brother); all the apostles; and finally Paul himself. The resurrection is an historical fact. Don't be discouraged by doubters who deny the resurrection. Be filled with hope because of the knowledge that one day you, and they, will see the living proof when Christ returns. (For more evidence on the resurrection, see the chart in Mark 16, p. 1655.)

15:7 This James is Jesus' brother, who at first did not believe that Jesus was the Messiah (John 7:5). After seeing the resurrected Christ, he became a believer and ultimately a leader of the church in Jerusalem (Acts 15:13). James wrote the New Testament book of James.

15:8, 9 Paul's most important credential to be an apostle was

15:9
a Eph 3:8
b Ac 8:3

15:10
c 2Co 11:23
d Php 2:13

⁹For I am the least of the apostles *a* and do not even deserve to be called an apostle, because I persecuted *b* the church of God. ¹⁰But by the grace of God I am what I am, and his grace to me was not without effect. No, I worked harder than all of them *c*—yet not I, but the grace of God that was with me. *d* ¹¹Whether, then, it was I or they, this is what we preach, and this is what you believed.

The Resurrection of the Dead

15:15
e Ac 2:24

¹²But if it is preached that Christ has been raised from the dead, how can some of you say that there is no resurrection of the dead? ¹³If there is no resurrection of the dead, then not even Christ has been raised. ¹⁴And if Christ has not been raised, our preaching is useless and so is your faith. ¹⁵More than that, we are then found to be false witnesses about God, for we have testified about God that he raised Christ from the dead. *e* But he did not raise him if in fact the dead are not raised. ¹⁶For if the dead are not raised, then Christ has not been raised either. ¹⁷And if Christ has not been raised, your faith is futile; you are still in your sins. ¹⁸Then those also who have fallen asleep in Christ are lost. ¹⁹If only for this life we have hope in Christ, we are to be pitied more than all men.

15:20
f 1Pe 1:3
g Ac 26:23

15:21
h Ro 5:12

²⁰But Christ has indeed been raised from the dead, *f* the firstfruits *g* of those who have fallen asleep. ²¹For since death came through a man, *h* the resurrection of the dead comes

---

PHYSICAL AND RESURRECTION BODIES

Physical Bodies	Resurrection Bodies
Perishable	Imperishable
Sown in dishonor	Raised in glory
Sown in weakness	Raised in power
Natural	Spiritual
From the dust	From heaven

We all have a body—each looks different; each has different strengths and weaknesses. But as physical, earthly bodies, they are all alike. All believers are promised life after death and a body like Christ's (15:49), a resurrection body.

---

that he was an eyewitness of the risen Christ (see Acts 9:3–6). "Abnormally born" means that his was a special case. The other apostles saw Christ in the flesh. Paul was in the next generation of believers—yet Christ appeared to him.

15:9, 10 As a zealous Pharisee, Paul had been an enemy of the Christian church—even to the point of capturing and persecuting believers (see Acts 9:1–3). Thus he felt unworthy to be called an apostle of Christ. Though undoubtedly the most influential of the apostles, Paul was deeply humble. He knew that he had worked hard and accomplished much, but only because God had poured kindness and grace upon him. True humility is not convincing yourself that you are worthless, but recognizing God's work in you. It is having God's perspective on who you are and acknowledging his grace in developing your abilities.

15:10 Paul wrote of working harder than the other apostles. This was not an arrogant boast because he knew that his power came from God and that it really didn't matter who worked hardest. Because of his prominent position as a Pharisee, Paul's conversion made him the object of even greater persecution than the other apostles; thus he had to work harder to preach the same message.

15:12ff Most Greeks did not believe that people's bodies would be resurrected after death. They saw the afterlife as something that happened only to the soul. According to Greek philosophers, the soul was the real person, imprisoned in a physical body, and at death the soul was released. There was no immortality for the body, but the soul entered an eternal state. Christianity, by contrast, affirms that the body and soul will be united after resurrection. The church at Corinth was in the heart of Greek culture. Thus many believers had a difficult time believing in a bodily resurrection. Paul wrote this part of his letter to clear up this confusion about the resurrection.

15:13–18 The bodily resurrection of Christ is the center of the Christian faith. Because Christ rose from the dead, as he promised, we know that what he said is true and that he is God. The resurrection affirms the truthfulness of Jesus' life and words. The resurrection confirms Jesus' unique authority to say, "I am the resurrection and the life" (John 11:25). Because he rose, we have certainty that our sins are forgiven. Because he rose, he lives and represents us before God. Because he rose and defeated death, we know we also will be raised. Christ's resurrection guaranteed both his promise to us and his authority to make that promise. We must take him at his word and believe.

15:19 Why does Paul say believers should be pitied if there were only earthly value to Christianity? In Paul's day, Christianity often brought a person persecution, ostracism from family, and, in many cases, poverty. There were few tangible benefits from being a Christian in that society. It was certainly not a step up the social or career ladder. Even more important, however, is the fact that if Christ had not been resurrected from death, Christians could not be forgiven for their sins and would have no hope of eternal life. If what Christians believe is a lie, we would be pitiful because we would be going through such suffering for no purpose. Fortunately, that is not the case!

15:20 Firstfruits were the first part of the harvest that faithful Jews brought to the temple as an offering (Leviticus 23:10ff). Although Christ was not the first to rise from the dead (he raised Lazarus and others), he was the first to never die again. He is the forerunner for us, the proof of our eventual resurrection to eternal life.

15:21 Death came into the world as a result of Adam and Eve's sin. In Romans 5:12–21, Paul explained why Adam's sin brought sin to all people, how death and sin spread to all humans because of this first sin, and the parallel between Adam's death and Christ's death.

also through a man. 22 For as in Adam all die, so in Christ all will be made alive. 23 But each in his own turn: Christ, the firstfruits; then, when he comes, those who belong to him. 24 Then the end will come, when he hands over the kingdom *i* to God the Father after he has destroyed all dominion, authority and power. 25 For he must reign until he has put all his enemies under his feet. 26 The last enemy to be destroyed is death. *j* 27 For he "has put everything under his feet." *a k* Now when it says that "everything" has been put under him, it is clear that this does not include God himself, who put everything under Christ. 28 When he has done this, then the Son himself will be made subject to him who put everything under him, *l* so that God may be all in all. *m*

29 Now if there is no resurrection, what will those do who are baptized for the dead? If the dead are not raised at all, why are people baptized for them? 30 And as for us, why do we endanger ourselves every hour? *n* 31 I die every day—I mean that, brothers—just as surely as I glory over you in Christ Jesus our Lord. 32 If I fought wild beasts *o* in Ephesus for merely human reasons, what have I gained? If the dead are not raised,

> "Let us eat and drink,
> for tomorrow we die." *b p*

33 Do not be misled: "Bad company corrupts good character." 34 Come back to your senses as you ought, and stop sinning; for there are some who are ignorant of God—I say this to your shame.

The Resurrection Body

35 But someone may ask, "How are the dead raised? With what kind of body will they come?" *q* 36 How foolish! What you sow does not come to life unless it dies. *r* 37 When you sow, you do not plant the body that will be, but just a seed, perhaps of wheat or of something else. 38 But God gives it a body as he has determined, and to each kind of seed he gives its own body. 39 All flesh is not the same: Men have one kind of flesh, animals have another, birds another and fish another. 40 There are also heavenly bodies and there are earthly bodies; but the splendor of the heavenly bodies is one kind, and the splendor of the earthly bodies is another. 41 The sun has one kind of splendor, the moon another and the stars another; and star differs from star in splendor.

42 So will it be *s* with the resurrection of the dead. The body that is sown is perishable, it is raised imperishable; 43 it is sown in dishonor, it is raised in glory; *t* it is sown in weakness, it is raised in power; 44 it is sown a natural body, it is raised a spiritual body.

a 27 Psalm 8:6   *b 32* Isaiah 22:13

15:24
i Da 7:14, 27

15:26
j Rev 20:14

15:27
k Ps 8:6

15:28
l Php 3:21
m 1Co 3:23

15:30
n 2Co 11:26

15:32
o 2Co 1:8
p Lk 12:19

15:35
q Eze 37:3

15:36
r Jn 12:24

15:42
s Mt 13:43

15:43
t Php 3:21

15:24–28 This is not a chronological sequence of events, and no specific time for these events is given. Paul's point is that the resurrected Christ will conquer all evil, including death. See Revelation 20:14 for words about the final destruction of death.

15:25–28 Although God the Father and God the Son are equal, each has a special work to do and an area of sovereign control (15:28). Christ is not inferior to the Father, but his work is to defeat all evil on earth. First he defeated sin and death on the cross, and in the final days, he will defeat Satan and all evil. World events may seem out of control and justice may seem scarce. But God is in control, allowing evil to remain for a time until he sends Jesus to earth again. Then Christ will present to God a perfect new world.

15:29 Some believers were baptized on behalf of others who had died unbaptized. Nothing more is known about this practice, but it obviously affirms a belief in resurrection. Paul is not promoting baptism for the dead; he is illustrating his argument that the resurrection is a reality.

15:30–34 If death ends it all, enjoying the moment would be all that matters. But Christians know that life continues beyond the grave and that our life on earth is only a preparation for our life that will never end. What you do today matters for eternity. In light of eternity, sin is a foolish gamble. Your belief in the resurrection will affect your view of the future. It also ought to affect how you live today.

15:31, 32 "I die every day" refers to Paul's daily exposure to danger. There is no evidence that Paul actually "fought wild beasts

in Ephesus," but rather he was referring to the savage opposition he had faced.

15:33 Keeping company with those who deny the resurrection could corrupt good Christian character. Don't let your relationships with unbelievers lead you away from Christ or cause your faith to waver.

15:35ff Paul launches into a discussion about what our resurrected bodies will be like. If you could select your own body, what kind would you choose—strong, athletic, beautiful? Paul explains that we will be recognized in our resurrected bodies, yet they will be better than we can imagine, for they will be made to live forever. We will still have our own personalities and individualities, but these will be perfected through Christ's work. The Bible does not reveal everything that our resurrected bodies will be able to do, but we know they will be perfect, without sickness or disease (see Philippians 3:21).

15:35ff Paul compares the resurrection of our bodies with the growth in a garden. Seeds placed in the ground don't grow unless they "die" first. The plant that grows looks very different from the seed because God gives it a new "body." There are different kinds of bodies—people, animals, fish, birds. Even the angels in heaven have bodies that are different in beauty and glory. Our resurrected bodies will be very different in some ways, but not all, from our earthly bodies.

15:42–44 Our present bodies are perishable and prone to decay. Our resurrection bodies will be transformed. These spiritual bodies

15:45
u Ge 2:7
v Ro 5:14

15:47
w Ge 3:19

15:49
x Ge 5:3
y Ro 8:29

15:52
z Mt 24:31

15:53
a 2Co 5:2, 4

15:54
b Isa 25:8

15:55
c Hos 13:14

15:56
d Ro 4:15

16:1
e Ac 24:17
f Ac 9:13

16:2
g Ac 20:7

If there is a natural body, there is also a spiritual body. 45 So it is written: "The first man Adam became a living being" a; u the last Adam, v a life-giving spirit. 46 The spiritual did not come first, but the natural, and after that the spiritual. 47 The first man was of the dust of the earth, w the second man from heaven. 48 As was the earthly man, so are those who are of the earth; and as is the man from heaven, so also are those who are of heaven. 49 And just as we have borne the likeness of the earthly man, x so shall we b bear the likeness of the man from heaven. y

50 I declare to you, brothers, that flesh and blood cannot inherit the kingdom of God, nor does the perishable inherit the imperishable. 51 Listen, I tell you a mystery: We will not all sleep, but we will all be changed— 52 in a flash, in the twinkling of an eye, at the last trumpet. For the trumpet will sound, z the dead will be raised imperishable, and we will be changed. 53 For the perishable must clothe itself with the imperishable, a and the mortal with immortality. 54 When the perishable has been clothed with the imperishable, and the mortal with immortality, then the saying that is written will come true: "Death has been swallowed up in victory." c b

55 "Where, O death, is your victory?
Where, O death, is your sting?" d c

56 The sting of death is sin, and the power of sin is the law. d 57 But thanks be to God! He gives us the victory through our Lord Jesus Christ.

58 Therefore, my dear brothers, stand firm. Let nothing move you. Always give yourselves fully to the work of the Lord, because you know that your labor in the Lord is not in vain.

The Collection for God's People

16 Now about the collection e for God's people: f Do what I told the Galatian churches to do. 2 On the first day of every week, g each one of you should set aside a sum of money in keeping with his income, saving it up, so that when I come no collections will have to be made. 3 Then, when I arrive, I will give letters of introduction to the men you approve and send them with your gift to Jerusalem. 4 If it seems advisable for me to go also, they will accompany me.

Personal Requests

5 After I go through Macedonia, I will come to you—for I will be going through Macedonia. 6 Perhaps I will stay with you awhile, or even spend the winter, so that you can help me

a 45 Gen. 2:7   b 49 Some early manuscripts *so let us*   c 54 Isaiah 25:8   d 55 Hosea 13:14

---

will not be limited by the laws of nature. This does not necessarily mean we'll be superpeople, but our bodies will be different from and more capable than our present earthly bodies. Our spiritual bodies will not be weak, will never get sick, and will never die.

15:45 The "last Adam" refers to Christ. Because Christ rose from the dead, he is a life-giving spirit. This means that he entered into a new form of existence (see the note on 2 Corinthians 3:17). He is the source of the spiritual life that will result in our resurrection. Christ's new glorified human body now suits his new glorified life—just as Adam's human body was suitable to his natural life. When we are resurrected, God will give us a transformed, eternal body suited to our new eternal life.

15:50–53 We all face limitations. Those who have physical, mental, or emotional disabilities are especially aware of this. Some may be blind, but they can see a new way to live. Some may be deaf, but they can hear God's Good News. Some may be lame, but they can walk in God's love. In addition, they have the encouragement that those disabilities are only temporary. Paul tells us that we all will be given new bodies when Christ returns and that these bodies will be without disabilities, never to die or become sick. This can give us hope in our suffering.

15:51, 52 "We will not all sleep" means that Christians alive at that day will not have to die but will be transformed immediately. A trumpet blast will usher in the new heaven and earth. The Jews would understand the significance of this because trumpets were always blown to signal the start of great festivals and other extraordinary events (Numbers 10:10).

15:54–56 Satan seemed to be victorious in the Garden of Eden (Genesis 3) and at the cross of Jesus. But God turned Satan's apparent victory into defeat when Jesus Christ rose from the dead (Colossians 2:15; Hebrews 2:14, 15). Thus death is no longer a source of dread or fear. Christ overcame it, and one day we will also. The law will no longer make sinners out of us who cannot keep it. Death has been defeated, and we have hope beyond the grave.

15:58 Paul says that because of the resurrection, nothing we do is in vain. Sometimes we hesitate to do good because we don't see any results. But if we can maintain a heavenly perspective, we will understand that we often will not see the good that results from our efforts. If we truly believe that Christ has won the ultimate victory, that fact must affect the way we live right now. Don't let discouragement over an apparent lack of results keep you from working. Do the good that you have opportunity to do, knowing that your work will have eternal results.

16:1ff Paul had just said that no good deed is ever in vain (15:58). In this chapter he mentions some practical deeds that have value for all Christians.

16:1–4 The Christians in Jerusalem were suffering from poverty and famine, so Paul was collecting money for them (Romans 15:25–31; 2 Corinthians 8:4; 9:1ff). He suggested that believers set aside a certain amount each week and give it to the church until he arrived to take it on to Jerusalem. Paul had planned to go straight to Corinth from Ephesus, but he changed his mind (2 Corinthians 1; 2). When he finally arrived, he took the gift and delivered it to the Jerusalem church (Acts 21:18; 24:17).

on my journey, wherever I go. [7] I do not want to see you now and make only a passing visit; I hope to spend some time with you, if the Lord permits. [h] [8] But I will stay on at Ephesus until Pentecost, [9] because a great door for effective work has opened to me, and there are many who oppose me.

[10] If Timothy[i] comes, see to it that he has nothing to fear while he is with you, for he is carrying on the work of the Lord,[j] just as I am. [11] No one, then, should refuse to accept him. [k] Send him on his way in peace[l] so that he may return to me. I am expecting him along with the brothers.

[12] Now about our brother Apollos: I strongly urged him to go to you with the brothers. He was quite unwilling to go now, but he will go when he has the opportunity.

[13] Be on your guard; stand firm[m] in the faith; be men of courage; be strong. [n] [14] Do everything in love.

[15] You know that the household of Stephanas were the first converts in Achaia, and they have devoted themselves to the service of the saints. I urge you, brothers, [16] to submit to such as these and to everyone who joins in the work, and labors at it. [17] I was glad when Stephanas, Fortunatus and Achaicus arrived, because they have supplied what was lacking from you. [o] [18] For they refreshed my spirit and yours also. Such men deserve recognition.[p]

Final Greetings

[19] The churches in the province of Asia send you greetings. Aquila and Priscilla[a] greet you warmly in the Lord, and so does the church that meets at their house. [q] [20] All the brothers here send you greetings. Greet one another with a holy kiss.

[21] I, Paul, write this greeting in my own hand.

[22] If anyone does not love the Lord[r]—a curse be on him. Come, O Lord[b] !

[23] The grace of the Lord Jesus be with you. [s]

[24] My love to all of you in Christ Jesus. Amen. [c]

a 19 Greek *Prisca*, a variant of *Priscilla*   **b** 22 In Aramaic the expression *Come, O Lord* is *Marana tha*.   **c** 24 Some manuscripts do not have *Amen*.

16:7	h Ac 18:21
16:10	i Ac 16:1 / 1Co 15:58
16:11	k 1Ti 4:12 / Ac 15:33
16:13	m Php 1:27 / n Eph 6:10
16:17	o 2Co 11:9
16:18	p Php 2:29
16:19	q Ro 16:5
16:22	r Eph 6:24
16:23	s Ro 16:20

16:10, 11 Paul was sending Timothy ahead to Corinth. Paul respected Timothy and had worked closely with him (Philippians 2:22; 1 Timothy 1:2). Although Timothy was young, Paul encouraged the Corinthian church to welcome him because he was doing the Lord's work. God's work is not limited by age. Paul wrote two personal letters to Timothy that have been preserved in the Bible (1 and 2 Timothy).

16:12 Apollos, who had preached in Corinth, was doing evangelistic work in Greece (see Acts 18:24–28; 1 Corinthians 3:3ff). Apollos didn't go to Corinth right away, partly because he knew of the factions there and didn't want to cause any more divisions.

16:13, 14 As the Corinthians awaited Paul's next visit, they were directed to (1) *be on their guard*—they were to be constantly watchful or alert for spiritual enemies that might slip in and threaten to destroy them whether it be divisions, pride, sin, disorder, or erroneous theology; (2) *stand firm* in what they believed—that is, the gospel that they had been taught in the beginning, the gospel that had brought them salvation; (3) *be men of courage* so that they could stand against false teachers, deal with sin in the congregation, and straighten out other problems; (4) *be strong*, with the strength given by the Holy Spirit; and (5) *do everything in love* because without love, they would be no more than prideful noisemakers. Today, as we wait for the return of Christ, we should follow the same instructions.

16:19 Aquila and Priscilla were tentmakers (or leather workers) whom Paul had met in Corinth (Acts 18:1–3). They followed Paul to Ephesus and lived there with him, helping to teach others about Jesus (Romans 16:3–5). Many in the Corinthian church

would have known this Christian couple. They are also mentioned in Acts 18:18, 26; Romans 16:3; 2 Timothy 4:19.

16:20 Kissing was a normal way of greeting each other in Paul's day. Paul encouraged the "holy kiss" as a way to greet Christians, and a way to help break down the divisions in this church.

16:21 Paul had a helper, or secretary, who wrote down this letter while he dictated. Paul wrote the final words, however, in his own handwriting. This is similar to adding a handwritten postscript (P.S.) to a typewritten letter. It also served to verify that this was a genuine letter from the apostle, and not a forgery.

16:22 The Lord Jesus Christ is coming back to earth again. To Paul, this was a glad hope, the very best he could look forward to. He was not afraid of seeing Christ—he could hardly wait! Do you share Paul's eager anticipation? Those who love Christ are looking forward to that wonderful time of his return (Titus 2:13). To those who did not love the Lord, however, Paul says, let them be cursed.

16:24 The church at Corinth was a church in trouble. Paul lovingly and forcefully confronted their problems and pointed them back to Christ. He dealt with divisions and conflicts, selfishness, inconsiderate use of freedom, disorder in worship, misuse of spiritual gifts, and wrong attitudes about the resurrection.

In every church, there are enough problems to create tensions and divisions. We should not ignore or gloss over problems in our churches or in our lives. Instead, like Paul, we should deal with problems head on as they arise. The lesson for us in 1 Corinthians is that unity and love in a church are far more important than leaders and labels.

WHAT THE BIBLE TEACHES ABOUT WORSHIP

Worship is first and foremost an encounter with the living and holy God.

"'Do not come any closer,' the LORD warned. 'Take off your sandals, for you are standing on holy ground'" (Exodus 3:5).

God is our friend, but he is also our sovereign Lord. To approach him frivolously shows a lack of respect and sincerity. When you come to God in worship, do you approach him casually, or do you come as though you were an invited guest before a king?

Worship is only as real as the involvement of those participating.

"The LORD gave these instructions to Moses on Mount Sinai when he commanded the Israelites to present their offerings to the LORD in the wilderness of Sinai" (Leviticus 7:38).

All the rituals in Leviticus were meant to teach the people valuable lessons. But over time, the people became indifferent. When your church appears to be conducting dry, meaningless rituals, try rediscovering the meaning and purpose behind them. Your worship will be revitalized.

A true worship experience is often a direct result of preparation for worship.

"The LORD said to Moses, 'Give these instructions to the people of Israel: The offerings you present as special gifts are a pleasing aroma to me; they are my food. See to it that they are brought at the appointed times and offered according to my instructions'" (Numbers 28:1-2).

Following these rituals took time, and this gave the people the opportunity to prepare their hearts for worship. Unless your heart is ready, worship is meaningless. God is delighted when you are prepared to come before him in a spirit of thankfulness.

Believers should take advantage of every opportunity and praise God.

"Sing praises to God, our strength. Sing to the God of Jacob. Sing! Beat the tambourine. Play the sweet lyre and the harp. Blow the ram's horn at new moon, and again at full moon to call a festival!" (Psalm 81:1-3).

Israel's holidays reminded the nation of God's great miracles. Remember the spiritual origin of the holidays you celebrate, and use them as opportunities to worship God for his goodness to you, your family, and your nation.

Worship and music go hand in hand.

"David and the army commanders then appointed men from the families of Asaph, Heman, and Jeduthun to proclaim God's messages to the accompaniment of lyres, harps and cymbals" (1 Chronicles 25:1).

David instituted music for the temple worship services. Worship should involve the whole person, and music helps lift a person's thoughts and emotions to God. Through music you can celebrate God's greatness.

Worship is bringing the best believers have to Christ.

"They entered the house and saw the child with his mother, Mary, and they bowed down and worshiped him. Then they opened their treasure chests and gave him gifts of gold, frankincense, and myrrh" (Matthew 2:11).

The wise men brought gifts and worshiped Jesus for who he was. This is the essence of true worship—honoring Christ for who he is and being willing to give to him what is valuable to you. Worship God because he is worthy of the best you have to give.

Genuine worship results in submission and obedience to Jesus.

"Since you are so eager to have the special abilities the Spirit gives, seek those that will strengthen the whole church" (1 Corinthians 14:12).

Jesus is more than just a great leader. He is the Son of God. When you understand this profound truth, the only adequate response is worship. When you have a correct understanding of Christ, you will obey him.

Everything done in corporate worship must be beneficial to the worshipers.

"But even as he spoke, a bright cloud came over them, and a voice from the cloud said, 'This is my dearly loved Son, who brings me great joy. Listen to him'"(Matthew 17:5).

This principle touches every aspect of worship. Those contributing to a worship service must speak useful words or participate in a way that will strengthen the faith of other believers.

In worship, everything must be done in harmony and with order.

"Be sure that everything is done properly and in order" (1 Corinthians 14:40).

Even when the gifts of the Holy Spirit are being exercised, there is no excuse for disorder. When there is chaos, the church is not allowing God to work among believers as he would like. Make sure that what you bring to worship is appropriate, but also make sure that you participate.

2 CORINTHIANS

VITAL STATISTICS

PURPOSE:
To affirm Paul's ministry, defend his authority as an apostle, and refute the false teachers in Corinth

AUTHOR:
Paul

ORIGINAL AUDIENCE:
The church in Corinth

DATE WRITTEN:
Approximately A.D. 55–57, from Macedonia

SETTING:
Paul had already written three letters to the Corinthians (two are now lost). In 1 Corinthians (the second of these letters), he used strong words to correct and teach. Most of the church had responded in the right spirit; there were, however, those who were denying Paul's authority and questioning his motives.

KEY VERSE:
"We are therefore Christ's ambassadors, as though God were making his appeal through us. We implore you on Christ's behalf: Be reconciled to God" (5:20)

KEY PEOPLE:
Paul, Timothy, Titus, false teachers

KEY PLACES:
Corinth, Jerusalem

SPECIAL FEATURES:
This is an intensely personal and autobiographical letter.

SLITHERING through the centuries, the serpent whispers his smooth-tongued promises, beguiling, deceiving, and tempting—urging men and women to reject God and to follow Satan. Satan's emissaries have been many—false prophets contradicting God's ancient spokesmen, "pious" leaders hurling blasphemous accusations, and heretical teachers infiltrating churches. And the deception continues. Our world is filled with cults, "isms," and ideologies, all claiming to provide the way to God.

Paul constantly struggled with those who would mislead God's people, and he poured his life into spreading the Good News to the uttermost parts of the world. During three missionary trips and other travels, he proclaimed Christ, made converts, and established churches. But often young believers were easy prey for false teachers, who were a constant threat to the gospel and the early church. So Paul had to spend much time warning and correcting these new Christians.

The church at Corinth was weak. Surrounded by idolatry and immorality, they struggled with their Christian faith and lifestyle. Through personal visits and letters, Paul tried to instruct them in the faith, resolve their conflicts, and solve some of their problems. First Corinthians was sent to deal with specific moral issues in the church and to answer questions about sex, marriage, and tender consciences. That letter confronted the issues directly and was well received by most. But there were false teachers who denied Paul's authority and slandered him. Paul then wrote 2 Corinthians to defend his position and to denounce those who were twisting the truth.

Second Corinthians must have been a difficult letter for Paul to write because he had to list his credentials as an apostle. Paul was reluctant to do so as a humble servant of Christ, but he knew it was necessary. Paul also knew that most of the believers in Corinth had taken his previous words to heart and were beginning to mature in their faith. He affirmed their commitment to Christ.

Second Corinthians begins with Paul reminding his readers of (1) his relationship to them—Paul had always been honest and straightforward with them (1:12–14), (2) his itinerary—he was planning to visit them again (1:15—2:2), and (3) his previous letter (2:3–11). Paul then moves directly to the subject of false teachers (2:17), and he reviews his ministry among the Corinthians to demonstrate the validity of his message and to urge them not to turn away from the truth (3:1—7:16).

Paul next turns to the issue of collecting money for the poor Christians in Jerusalem. He tells them how others have given, and he urges them to show their love in a tangible way as well (8:1—9:15). Paul then gives a strong defense of his authority as a genuine apostle while pointing out the deceptive influence of the false apostles (10:1—13:10).

As you read this intensely personal letter, listen to Paul's words of love and exhortation, and be committed to the truth of God's Word and prepared to reject all false teaching.

THE BLUEPRINT

1. Paul explains his actions (1:1—2:11)
2. Paul defends his ministry (2:12—7:16)
3. Paul defends the collection (8:1—9:15)
4. Paul defends his authority (10:1—13:14)

In responding to the attacks on his character and authority, Paul explains the nature of Christian ministry and, as an example, openly shares about his ministry. This is an important letter for all who wish to be involved in any kind of Christian ministry, because it has much to teach us about how we should handle our ministries today. Like Paul, those involved in ministry should be blameless, sincere, confident, caring, open, and willing to suffer for the sake of Christ.

MEGATHEMES

THEME	EXPLANATION	IMPORTANCE
Trials	Paul experienced great suffering, persecution, and opposition in his ministry. He even struggled with a personal weakness—a "thorn" in the flesh. Through it all, Paul affirmed God's faithfulness.	God is faithful. His strength is sufficient for any trial. When trials come, they keep us from pride and teach us dependence on God. He comforts us so we can comfort others.
Church Discipline	Paul defends his role in church discipline. Neither immorality nor false teaching could be ignored. The church was to be neither too lax nor too severe in administering discipline. The church was to restore the corrected person when he or she repented.	The goal of all discipline in the church should be correction, not vengeance. For churches to be effective, they must confront and solve problems, not ignore them. In everything, we must act in love.
Hope	To encourage the Corinthians as they faced trials, Paul reminded them that they would receive new bodies in heaven. This would be a great victory in contrast to their present suffering.	To know we will receive new bodies offers us hope. No matter what adversity we face, we can keep going. Our faithful service will result in triumph.
Giving	Paul organized a collection of funds for the poor in the Jerusalem church. Many of the Asian churches gave money. Paul explains and defends his beliefs about giving, and he urges the Corinthians to follow through on their previous commitment.	Like the Corinthians, we should follow through on our financial commitments. Our giving must be generous, sacrificial, well planned, and based on need. Our generosity not only helps those in need but enables them to thank God.
Sound Doctrine	False teachers were challenging Paul's ministry and authority as an apostle. Paul asserts his authority in order to preserve correct Christian doctrine. His sincerity, his love for Christ, and his concern for the people were his defense.	We should share Paul's concern for correct teaching in our churches. But in so doing, we must share his motivation—love for Christ and people—and his sincerity.

1. Paul explains his actions

1 Paul, an apostle of Christ Jesus by the will of God,*a* and Timothy our brother,

1:1
a Col 1:1

To the church of God in Corinth, together with all the saints throughout Achaia:

² Grace and peace to you from God our Father and the Lord Jesus Christ. *b*

1:2
b Ro 1:7

The God of All Comfort

³ Praise be to the God and Father of our Lord Jesus Christ,*c* the Father of compassion and the God of all comfort, ⁴ who comforts us in all our troubles, so that we can comfort those in any trouble with the comfort we ourselves have received from God. ⁵ For just as the sufferings of Christ flow over into our lives,*d* so also through Christ our comfort overflows. ⁶ If we are distressed, it is for your comfort and salvation;*e* if we are comforted, it is for your comfort, which produces in you patient endurance of the same sufferings we suffer. ⁷ And our hope for you is firm, because we know that just as you share in our sufferings, so also you share in our comfort.

1:3
c Eph 1:3; 1Pe 1:3

1:5
d 2Co 4:10

1:6
e 2Co 4:15

⁸ We do not want you to be uninformed, brothers, about the hardships we suffered*f* in the province of Asia. We were under great pressure, far beyond our ability to endure, so that we despaired even of life. ⁹ Indeed, in our hearts we felt the sentence of death. But this happened that we might not rely on ourselves but on God, who raises the dead. ¹⁰ He has delivered us from such a deadly peril, and he will deliver us. On him we have set our hope that he will continue to deliver us, ¹¹ as you help us by your prayers.*g* Then many will give thanks*h* on our*a* behalf for the gracious favor granted us in answer to the prayers of many.

1:8
f 1Co 15:32

1:11
g Ro 15:30; Php 1:19
h 2Co 4:15

a 11 Many manuscripts *your*

1:1 Paul visited Corinth on his second missionary journey and founded a church there (Acts 18:1ff). He later wrote several letters to the believers in Corinth, two of which are included in the Bible. Paul's first letter to the Corinthians is lost (1 Corinthians 5:9–11), his second letter to them is our book of 1 Corinthians, his third letter is lost (2:6–9; 7:12), and his fourth letter is our book of 2 Corinthians. Second Corinthians was written less than a year after 1 Corinthians.

Paul wrote 1 Corinthians to deal with divisions in the church. When his advice was not taken and their problems weren't solved, Paul visited Corinth a second time. That visit was painful both for Paul and for the church (2:1). He then planned a third visit, but delayed it and wrote 2 Corinthians instead. After writing 2 Corinthians, Paul visited Corinth once more (Acts 20:2, 3).

1:1 Paul had great respect for Timothy (see also Philippians 2:19, 20; 1 Timothy 1:2), one of his traveling companions (Acts 16:1–3). Timothy had accompanied Paul to Corinth on his second missionary journey, and Paul had recently sent him there to minister (1 Corinthians 4:17; 16:10). Timothy's report to Paul about the crisis in the Corinthian church prompted Paul to make an unplanned visit to the church to deal with the problem in person (see 2:1). For more information on Timothy, see his Profile in 1 Timothy, p. 2037.

1:1 The Romans had made Corinth the capital of Achaia (the southern half of present-day Greece). The city was a flourishing trade center because of its seaport. With the thousands of merchants and sailors who disembarked there each year, it had developed a reputation as one of the most immoral cities in the ancient world; its many pagan temples encouraged the practice of sexual immorality along with idol worship. In fact, the Greek word "to Corinthianize" came to mean "to practice sexual immorality." A Christian church in the city would face many pressures and conflicts. For more information on Corinth, see the first note on 1 Corinthians 1:2.

1:3–5 Many think that when God comforts us, our troubles should go away. But if that were always so, people would turn to God only out of a desire to be relieved of pain and not out of love for him. We must understand that being *comforted* can also mean receiving strength, encouragement, and hope to deal with our troubles. The more we suffer, the more comfort God gives us. If you are feeling overwhelmed, allow God to comfort you. Remem-

ber that every trial you endure will help you comfort other people who are suffering similar troubles.

1:5 The "sufferings of Christ" are those afflictions we experience as we do Christ's ministry. At the same time, Christ suffers with his people, since they are united with him. In Acts 9:4, 5, Christ asked Paul why he was persecuting him. This implies that Christ suffered with the early Christians when they were persecuted.

1:6, 7 Paul had a radically different view of suffering. Suffering—especially trials and discomfort associated with the advancement of Christ's kingdom—is God's way of allowing Christians to become more like Jesus, to suffer for the gospel just as Jesus suffered for it (Philippians 1:29; 3:10). Peter agreed with Paul: Christians should rejoice when they suffer, for in their own suffering they will in some small way experience what it meant for Jesus to suffer for their sins (1 Peter 4:12, 13).

In addition to drawing people closer to Christ, suffering can also help them grow in their faith. God uses suffering to improve his people and shape them into better Christians. In fact, suffering should be thought of as the necessary pain that accompanies spiritual growth. In Romans, Paul noted that suffering produces perseverance, which, in turn produces Christian character (Romans 5:3, 4; see also James 1:3, 4; 2 Peter 1:6; Revelation 2:2, 19). This passage highlights another benefit to suffering: It teaches the sufferer how to encourage others who are also suffering.

1:8–10 Paul does not give details about their hardships in Asia, although his accounts of all three missionary journeys record many difficult trials he faced (Acts 13:2—14:28; Acts 15:40—21:17). He does write that they felt that they were going to die, and realized that they could do nothing to help themselves—they simply had to rely on God.

1:8–10 We often depend on our own skills and abilities when life seems easy, but we turn to God when we feel unable to help ourselves. Depending on God is a realization of our own powerlessness without him and our need for his constant touch in our lives. God is our source of power, and we receive his help by keeping in touch with him. With this attitude of dependence, problems will drive us to God rather than away from him. Learn how to rely on God daily.

1:11 Paul requested prayer for himself and his companions as they traveled to spread God's message. Pray for pastors, teach-

Paul's Change of Plans

12Now this is our boast: Our conscience testifies that we have conducted ourselves in the world, and especially in our relations with you, in the holiness and sincerity that are from God. We have done so not according to worldly wisdom but according to God's grace. 13For we do not write you anything you cannot read or understand. And I hope that, 14as you have understood us in part, you will come to understand fully that you can boast of us just as we will boast of you in the day of the Lord Jesus.

15Because I was confident of this, I planned to visit you first so that you might benefit twice. *i* 16I planned to visit you on my way *j* to Macedonia and to come back to you from Macedonia, and then to have you send me on my way to Judea. 17When I planned this, did I do it lightly? Or do I make my plans in a worldly manner *k* so that in the same breath I say, "Yes, yes" and "No, no"?

18But as surely as God is faithful, our message to you is not "Yes" and "No." 19For the Son of God, Jesus Christ, who was preached among you by me and Silas*a* and Timothy, was not "Yes" and "No," but in him it has always *l* been "Yes." 20For no matter how many promises *m* God has made, they are "Yes" in Christ. And so through him the "Amen" is spoken by us to the glory of God. 21Now it is God who makes both us and you stand firm in Christ. He anointed *n* us, 22set his seal of ownership on us, and put his Spirit in our hearts as a deposit, guaranteeing what is to come.

a 19 Greek Silvanus, a variant of Silas

1:15
i Ro 1:11, 13
1:16
j 1Co 16:5-7
1:17
k 2Co 10:2, 3
1:19
l Heb 13:8
1:20
m Ro 15:8
1:21
n 1Jn 2:20, 27

DIFFERENCES BETWEEN 1 AND 2 CORINTHIANS

The two letters to the Corinthian church that we find in the Bible are very different, with different tones and focuses.

1 Corinthians/Practical	*2 Corinthians*/Personal
Focuses on the character of the Corinthian church	Focuses on Paul as he bares his soul and tells of his love for the Corinthian church
Deals with questions on marriage, freedom, spiritual gifts, and order in the church	Deals with the problem of false teachers, whereby Paul defends his authority and the truth of his message
Paul instructs in matters concerning the church's well-being	Paul gives his testimony because he knows that acceptance of his advice is vital to the church's well-being
Contains advice to help the church combat the pagan influences in the wicked city of Corinth	Contains testimony to help the church combat the havoc caused by false teachers

---

ers, missionaries, and others who are spreading the gospel. Satan will challenge anyone making a real difference for God.

1:12–14 Paul knew the importance of holiness and sincerity in word and action, especially in a situation as in Corinth, where constructive criticism was necessary. So Paul did not come with impressive human knowledge (worldly wisdom). God wants us to be real and transparent in all our relationships. If we aren't, we may end up lowering ourselves to spreading rumors, gossiping, and second-guessing.

1:15–17 Paul had recently made a brief, unscheduled visit to Corinth that was very painful for him and the church (see 2:1). After that visit, he told the church when he would return. But Paul changed his original travel plans. Instead of sailing from Ephesus to Corinth before going to Macedonia, he traveled from Ephesus directly to Macedonia, where he wrote a letter to the Corinthians that caused him much anguish and them much sorrow (7:8, 9). He had made his original plans thinking that the church would have solved its problems. When the time came for Paul's scheduled trip to Corinth, however, the crisis had not been fully resolved (although progress was being made in some areas; 7:11–16). So he wrote a letter instead (2:3, 4; 7:8) because another visit may have only made matters worse. Thus Paul stayed away from Corinth because he was concerned over the church's unity, not because he was fickle.

1:17–20 Paul's change of plans caused some of his accusers to say that he couldn't be trusted, hoping to undermine his authority. Paul said that he was not the type of person to say "yes" when he

meant "no." Paul explained that it was not indecision but concern for their feelings that forced him to change his plans. The reason for his trip—to bring joy (1:24)—could not be accomplished with the present crisis. Paul didn't want to visit them only to rebuke them severely (1:23). Just as the Corinthians could trust God to keep his promises, they could trust Paul as God's representative to keep his. He would still visit them, but at a better time.

1:19, 20 Instead of defending himself, Paul reminded the Corinthians of God's faithfulness. There was no duplicity in God. His promises would be fulfilled. There would be no wavering between "yes" and "no." In Jesus Christ, all of God's promises have been fulfilled. Jesus is the embodiment of God's faithfulness. Because Jesus Christ is faithful, Paul (a messenger appointed by Jesus) would also be faithful in his ministry.

1:21, 22 Paul mentions two gifts God gives when we become believers: (1) a *seal of ownership* to show who our Master is, and (2) the Holy Spirit, who guarantees that we belong to him and will receive all his benefits (Ephesians 1:13, 14). The Holy Spirit guarantees that salvation is ours now, and that we will receive so much more when Christ returns. The great comfort and power the Holy Spirit gives in this life is a foretaste or down payment ("deposit") of the benefits of our eternal life in God's presence. With the privilege of belonging to God comes the responsibility of identifying ourselves as his faithful servants. Don't be ashamed to let others know that you are his.

23 I call God as my witness that it was in order to spare you ᵒ that I did not return to Corinth. 24 Not that we lord it over ᵖ your faith, but we work with you for your joy, because it is by

2 faith you stand firm. ᑫ 1 So I made up my mind that I would not make another painful visit to you. 2 For if I grieve you, who is left to make me glad but you whom I have grieved? 3 I wrote as I did so that when I came I should not be distressed ʳ by those who ought to make me rejoice. I had confidence in all of you, that you would all share my joy. 4 For I wrote you ˢ out of great distress and anguish of heart and with many tears, not to grieve you but to let you know the depth of my love for you.

Forgiveness for the Sinner

5 If anyone has caused grief, ᵗ he has not so much grieved me as he has grieved all of you, to some extent—not to put it too severely. 6 The punishment ᵘ inflicted on him by the majority is sufficient for him. 7 Now instead, you ought to forgive and comfort him, ᵛ so that he will not be overwhelmed by excessive sorrow. 8 I urge you, therefore, to reaffirm your love for him. 9 The reason I wrote you was to see if you would stand the test and be obedient in everything. ʷ 10 If you forgive anyone, I also forgive him. And what I have forgiven—if there was anything to forgive—I have forgiven in the sight of Christ for your sake, 11 in order that Satan might not outwit us. For we are not unaware of his schemes.

2. Paul defends his ministry
Ministers of the New Covenant

12 Now when I went to Troas ˣ to preach the gospel of Christ and found that the Lord had opened a door for me, 13 I still had no peace of mind, ʸ because I did not find my brother Titus ᶻ there. So I said good-by to them and went on to Macedonia.

1:23
ᵒ1Co 4:21;
2Co 2:1, 3
1:24
ᵖ1Pe 5:3
ᑫRo 11:20;
1Co 15:1
2:3
ʳ2Co 12:21
2:4
ˢ2Co 7:8, 12

2:5
ᵗ1Co 5:1, 2
2:6
ᵘ1Co 5:4, 5
2:7
ᵛGal 6:1
2:9
ʷ2Co 10:6

2:12
ˣAc 16:8
2:13
ʸ2Co 7:5
ᶻ2Co 7:6, 13

1:23 The Corinthian church had written to Paul with questions about their faith (see 1 Corinthians 7:1). In response, Paul had written 1 Corinthians. But the church did not follow his instructions.

Paul had planned to visit them again, but instead he wrote a letter that caused sorrow (7:8, 9) but also caused them to change their ways. He had not wanted to visit and repeat the same advice for the same problems. He wrote the emotional letter to encourage them to follow the advice that he had already given in previous letters and visits.

1:24 Standing firm is not a way to be saved but the evidence that a person is really committed to Jesus. Endurance is not a means to earn salvation; it is the by-product of a truly devoted life. Endurance grows out of commitment to Jesus Christ. In Matthew 10:22, Jesus predicted that his followers would be severely persecuted by those who hated what he stood for. In the midst of terrible persecutions, however, they could have hope, knowing that salvation was theirs. Times of trial serve to sift true Christians from false or fair-weather Christians. When you are pressured to give up and turn your back on Christ, don't do it. Remember the benefits of standing firm and continue to live for Christ.

2:1 Paul's phrase, "another painful visit," indicates that he had already made one difficult trip to Corinth (see the notes on 1:1; 1:15–17) since founding the church. Paul had gone there to deal with those in the church who had been attacking and undermining his authority as an apostle of Jesus Christ, thus confusing other believers.

2:3 Paul's last letter, referred to here, was not the book of 1 Corinthians, but a letter written between 1 and 2 Corinthians, just after his unplanned, painful visit (2:1). Paul refers to this letter again in 7:8.

2:4 Paul did not enjoy reprimanding his friends and fellow believers, but he cared enough about the Corinthians to confront them with their wrongdoing. Proverbs 27:6 says: "Wounds from a friend can be trusted, but an enemy multiplies kisses." Sometimes our friends make choices that we know are wrong. If we ignore their behavior and let them continue in it, we won't be showing love to them. We show love by honestly sharing our concerns in order to help these friends do and be their very best for God. When we don't make any move to help, we show that we are more concerned about being well liked than about what will happen to them.

2:5–11 Paul explained that it was time to forgive the man who had been punished by the church and had subsequently repented. He needed forgiveness, acceptance, and comfort. Satan would gain an advantage if they permanently separated this man from the congregation rather than forgiving and restoring him. This may have been the man who had required the disciplinary action described in 1 Corinthians 5, or he may have been the chief opponent of Paul who had caused Paul the anguish described in 2:1–11. The sorrowful letter had finally brought about the repentance of the Corinthians (7:8–14), and their discipline of the man had led to his repentance. Church discipline should seek restoration. Two mistakes in church discipline should be avoided—being too lenient and not correcting mistakes, or being too harsh and not forgiving the sinner. There is a time to confront and a time to comfort.

2:11 We use church discipline to help keep the church pure and to help wayward people repent. But Satan tries to harm the church by tempting it to use discipline in an unforgiving way. This causes those exercising discipline to become proud of their purity, and it causes the person who is being disciplined to become bitter and perhaps leave the church entirely. We must remember that our purpose in discipline is to *restore* a person to the fellowship, not to destroy him or her. We must be cautious that personal anger is not vented under the guise of church discipline.

2:13 Titus was a Greek convert whom Paul greatly loved and trusted (the book of Titus is a letter that Paul wrote to him). Titus was one of the men responsible for collecting the money for the poverty-stricken Jerusalem church (8:6). Paul may also have sent Titus with the sorrowful letter. On his way to Macedonia, Paul was supposed to meet Titus in Troas. When Paul didn't find him there, he was worried for Titus's safety and left Troas to search for him in Macedonia. There Paul found him (7:6), and the good news that Paul received (7:8–16) led to this letter. Paul would send Titus back to Corinth with this letter (8:16, 17).

¹⁴But thanks be to God, who always leads us in triumphal procession in Christ and through us spreads everywhere the fragrance of the knowledge of him. ¹⁵For we are to God the aroma of Christ among those who are being saved and those who are perishing. ¹⁶To the one we are the smell of death;^a to the other, the fragrance of life. And who is equal to such a task? ¹⁷Unlike so many, we do not peddle the word of God for profit. On the contrary, in Christ we speak before God with sincerity, like men sent from God. ^b

3 Are we beginning to commend ourselves^c again? Or do we need, like some people, letters of recommendation^d to you or from you? ²You yourselves are our letter, written on our hearts, known and read by everybody. ^e ³You show that you are a letter from Christ, the result of our ministry, written not with ink but with the Spirit of the living God, not on tablets of stone but on tablets of human hearts. ^f

2:16
^aLk 2:34

2:17
^b2Co 1:12

3:1
^c2Co 5:12
^dAc 18:27

3:2
^e1Co 9:2

3:3
^fEze 11:19

PAUL SEARCHES FOR TITUS
Paul had searched for Titus, hoping to meet him in Troas and receive news about the Corinthian church. When he did not find Titus in Troas, he went on to Macedonia (2:13), most likely to Philippi, where he found Titus.

2:14ff In the middle of discussing his unscheduled trip to Macedonia, Paul thanked God for his ministry, his relationship with the Corinthian believers, and the way God had used him to help others wherever he went, despite difficulties (2:14—7:4). In 7:5, Paul resumed his story of his trip to Macedonia.

2:14–16 In a Roman triumphal procession, the Roman general would display his treasures and captives amidst a cloud of incense burned for the gods. To the victors, the aroma was sweet; to the captives in the parade, it was the smell of slavery and death. When Christians preach the gospel, it is good news to some and repulsive news to others. Believers recognize the life-giving fragrance of the message. To nonbelievers, however, it smells foul, like death—their own.

2:16, 17 Paul asks "who is equal" to the task of representing Christ? Our adequacy is always from God (1 Corinthians 15:10; 2 Corinthians 3:5). He has already commissioned and sent us (see Matthew 28:18–20). He has given us the Holy Spirit to enable us to speak with Christ's power. He keeps his eye on us, protecting us as we work for him. So, if we realize that God makes us competent and useful, we can overcome our feelings of inadequacy. Serving Christ, therefore, requires that we focus on what he can do through us, not on what we can't do by ourselves.

2:17 Some preachers in Paul's day were "peddlers" of God's word, preaching without understanding God's message or caring

about what happened to their listeners. They weren't concerned about furthering God's kingdom—they just wanted money. Today there are still religious teachers who care only about money, and not about truth. Those who truly speak for God should have sincerity and integrity, and should never preach for selfish reasons (1 Timothy 6:5–10).

3:1–3 Some false teachers had started carrying forged letters of recommendation to authenticate their authority. In no uncertain terms, Paul stated that he needed no such letters. The believers to whom Paul and his companions had preached were enough of a recommendation. Paul did use letters of introduction, however, many times. He wrote them on behalf of Phoebe (Romans 16:1, 2) and Timothy (1 Corinthians 16:10, 11). These letters helped Paul's trusted companions and friends find a welcome in various churches.

3:3 Paul uses powerful imagery from famous Old Testament passages predicting the promised day of new hearts and new beginnings for God's people (see Jeremiah 31:33; Ezekiel 11:19; 36:26). No human minister can take credit for this process of conversion. It is the work of God's Spirit. We do not become believers by following some manual or using some technique. Our conversion is a result of God's implanting his Spirit in our hearts, giving us new power to live for him.

4 Such confidence as this is ours through Christ before God. 5 Not that we are competent in ourselves to claim anything for ourselves, but our competence comes from God. g 6 He has made us competent as ministers of a new covenant—not of the letter but of the Spirit; for the letter kills, but the Spirit gives life. h

3:5
g 1Co 15:10

3:6
h Jn 6:63

The Glory of the New Covenant

7 Now if the ministry that brought death, which was engraved in letters on stone, came with glory, so that the Israelites could not look steadily at the face of Moses because of its glory, i fading though it was, 8 will not the ministry of the Spirit be even more glorious? 9 If the ministry that condemns men is glorious, how much more glorious is the ministry that brings righteousness! j 10 For what was glorious has no glory now in comparison with the surpassing glory. 11 And if what was fading away came with glory, how much greater is the glory of that which lasts!

3:7
i Ex 34:29-35

3:9
j Ro 1:17

12 Therefore, since we have such a hope, we are very bold. 13 We are not like Moses, who would put a veil over his face to keep the Israelites from gazing at it while the radiance was fading away. 14 But their minds were made dull, for to this day the same veil remains when the old covenant is read. It has not been removed, because only in Christ is it taken away. 15 Even to this day when Moses is read, a veil covers their hearts. 16 But whenever anyone turns to the Lord, k the veil is taken away. 17 Now the Lord is the Spirit, and where the Spirit of the Lord is, there is freedom. 18 And we, who with unveiled faces all reflect a l the Lord's glory, m are being transformed into his likeness n with ever-increasing glory, which comes from the Lord, who is the Spirit.

3:16
k Ro 11:23

3:18
l 1Co 13:12
m 2Co 4:4, 6
n Ro 8:29

Treasures in Jars of Clay

4 Therefore, since through God's mercy o we have this ministry, we do not lose heart. 2 Rather, we have renounced secret and shameful ways; we do not use deception, nor do we distort the word of God. p On the contrary, by setting forth the truth plainly we commend

4:1
o 1Co 7:25

4:2
p 2Co 2:17

a 18 Or *contemplate*

3:4, 5 Paul was not boasting; he gave God the credit for all his accomplishments. While the false teachers boasted of their own power and prestige, Paul expressed his humility before God. No one can claim to be adequate without God's help. No one is competent to carry out the responsibilities of God's calling in his or her own strength. Without the Holy Spirit's enabling, our natural talent can carry us only so far. As Christ's witnesses, we need the character and special strength that only God gives.

3:6 "The letter kills, but the Spirit gives life" means that trying to be saved by keeping the Old Testament laws will end in death. Only by believing in the Lord Jesus Christ can a person receive eternal life through the Holy Spirit. No one but Jesus has ever fulfilled the law perfectly, and thus the whole world is condemned to death. The law makes people realize their sin, but it cannot give life. Under the new covenant, which means promise or agreement, eternal life comes from the Holy Spirit. The Spirit gives new life to all who believe in Christ. The moral law (Ten Commandments) still points out sin and shows us how to obey God, but forgiveness comes only through the grace and mercy of Christ (see Romans 7:10—8:2).

3:7–11 Paul recalled the stone tablets on which God had written the old covenant—calling it "the ministry that brought death." He identified the law, although leading to death, as nonetheless glorious because it was God's provision and proof of his intervention in the life of his people. But that which was summarized on stone is nowhere near as glorious as what came with "the ministry that brings righteousness"—life in the Holy Spirit. The Holy Spirit was present at the creation of the world as one of the agents in the origin of life itself (Genesis 1:2). He is the power behind the rebirth of every Christian and the one who helps us live the Christian life. By his power, we will be transformed into Christ's perfect likeness when he returns. Thank God for the fact that the best is yet to be.

3:13–18 When Moses came down Mount Sinai with the Ten Commandments, his face glowed from being in God's presence (Exodus 34:29–35). Moses had to put on a veil to keep the people

from being terrified by the brightness of his face. Paul adds that this veil kept them from seeing the radiance fade away. Moses and his veil illustrate the fading of the old system and the veiling of the people's minds and understanding by their pride, hardness of heart, and refusal to repent. The veil kept them from understanding the references to Christ in the Scriptures. When anyone becomes a Christian, Christ removes the veil (3:16), giving eternal life and freedom from trying to be saved by keeping laws. And without the veil, we can be like mirrors reflecting God's glory.

3:17 Those who were trying to be saved by keeping the Old Testament law were soon tied up in rules and ceremonies. But now, through the Holy Spirit, God provides freedom from sin and condemnation (Romans 8:1). When we trust Christ to save us, he removes our heavy burden of trying to please him and our guilt for failing to do so. By trusting Christ we are loved, accepted, forgiven, and freed to live for him. "Where the Spirit of the Lord is, there is freedom."

3:18 The glory that the Spirit imparts to the believer is more excellent and lasts longer than the glory that Moses experienced. By gazing at the nature of God with unveiled minds, we can be more like him. In the gospel, we see the truth about Christ, and it transforms us morally as we understand and apply it. Through learning about Christ's life, we can understand how wonderful God is and what he is really like. As our knowledge deepens, the Holy Spirit helps us to change. Becoming Christlike is a progressive experience (see Romans 8:29; Galatians 4:19; Philippians 3:21; 1 John 3:2). The more closely we follow Christ, the more we will be like him.

4:2 Paul condemned those who twist God's Word. Preachers, teachers, and anyone else who talks about Jesus Christ must remember that they stand in God's presence—he hears every word. Many Christian ministers and leaders twist Scripture in their attempt to motivate audiences. Others take Scripture out of context to promise their own views. When you tell people about Christ, be careful not to distort the message to please your audience. Proclaim the truth of God's Word.

4:3
q 1Co 1:18

ourselves to every man's conscience in the sight of God. ³And even if our gospel is veiled, it is veiled to those who are perishing. *q* ⁴The god of this age has blinded the minds of unbelievers, so that they cannot see the light of the gospel of the glory of Christ, who is the image of God. ⁵For we do not preach ourselves, but Jesus Christ as Lord, and ourselves as your servants for Jesus' sake. ⁶For God, who said, "Let light shine out of darkness," *a* *r* made his light shine in our hearts *s* to give us the light of the knowledge of the glory of God in the face of Christ.

4:6
r Ge 1:3
s 2Pe 1:19

4:7
t 1Co 2:5

⁷But we have this treasure in jars of clay to show that this all-surpassing power is from God *t* and not from us. ⁸We are hard pressed on every side, *u* but not crushed; perplexed, but not in despair; ⁹persecuted, but not abandoned; struck down, but not destroyed. *v* ¹⁰We always carry around in our body the death of Jesus, so that the life of Jesus may also be revealed in our body. ¹¹For we who are alive are always being given over to death for Jesus' sake, so that his life may be revealed in our mortal body. ¹²So then, death is at work in us, but life is at work in you.

4:8
u 2Co 7:5

4:9
v Ps 37:24

4:13
w Ps 116:10

¹³It is written: "I believed; therefore I have spoken." *b* *w* With that same spirit of faith we also believe and therefore speak, ¹⁴because we know that the one who raised the Lord Jesus from the dead will also raise us with Jesus and present us with you in his presence. ¹⁵All this is for your benefit, so that the grace that is reaching more and more people may cause thanksgiving to overflow to the glory of God.

4:16
x Ro 7:22
y Col 3:10

¹⁶Therefore we do not lose heart. Though outwardly we are wasting away, yet inwardly *x* we are being renewed *y* day by day. ¹⁷For our light and momentary troubles are achieving for us an eternal glory that far outweighs them all. *z* ¹⁸So we fix our eyes not on what is seen, but on what is unseen. *a* For what is seen is temporary, but what is unseen is eternal.

4:17
z Ro 8:18

4:18
a Ro 8:24; Heb 11:1

a 6 Gen. 1:3   *b* 13 Psalm 116:10

4:3, 4 The gospel is open and revealed to everyone, except to those who refuse to believe. Satan is "the god of this age." His work is to deceive, and he has blinded those who don't believe in Christ (see 11:14, 15). The allure of money, power, and pleasure blinds people to the light of Christ's gospel. Those who reject Christ and prefer their own pursuits have unknowingly made Satan their god.

4:5 The focus of Paul's preaching was Christ and not himself. When you witness, tell people about what Christ has done, and not about your abilities and accomplishments. People must be introduced to Christ, not to you. And if you hear someone preaching himself or his own ideas rather than Christ, beware—he is a false teacher.

4:5 Paul willingly served the Corinthian church even though the people must have deeply disappointed him. Serving people requires a sacrifice of time and personal desires. Being Christ's follower means serving others, even when they do not measure up to our expectations.

4:7 The supremely valuable message of salvation in Jesus Christ has been entrusted by God to frail and fallible human beings ("jars of clay"). Paul's focus, however, was not on the perishable container but on its priceless contents—God's power dwelling in us. Though we are weak, God uses us to spread his Good News, and he gives us power to do his work. Knowing that the power is his, not ours, should keep us from pride and motivate us to keep daily contact with God, our power source. Our responsibility is to let people see God through us.

4:8–12 Paul reminds us that though we may think we are at the end of our rope, we are never at the end of our hope. Our perishable bodies are subject to sin and suffering, but God never abandons us. Because Christ has won the victory over death, we have eternal life. All our risks, humiliations, and trials are opportunities for Christ to demonstrate his power and presence in and through us. We must ask ourselves, "Could I handle the suffering and opposition that Paul did?" The success syndrome is a great enemy of effective ministry. From an earthly perspective, Paul was not very successful. Like Paul, we must carry out our ministry, looking to God for strength. When opposition, slander, or disappointment threaten to rob you of the victory, remember that no one can destroy what God has accomplished through you.

4:15–18 Paul had faced sufferings, trials, and distress as he preached the Good News. But he knew that they would one day be over, and he would obtain God's rest and rewards. As we face great troubles, it's easy to focus on the pain rather than on our ultimate goal. Just as athletes concentrate on the finish line and ignore their discomfort, we too must focus on the reward for our faith and the joy that lasts forever. No matter what happens to us in this life, we have the assurance of eternal life, when all suffering will end and all sorrow will flee away (Isaiah 35:10).

4:16 It is easy to lose heart and quit. We all have faced problems in our relationships or in our work that have caused us to want to think about laying down the tools and walking away. Rather than giving up when persecution wore him down, Paul concentrated on experiencing the inner strength from the Holy Spirit (Ephesians 3:16). Don't let fatigue, pain, or criticism force you off the job. Renew your commitment to serving Christ. Don't forsake your eternal reward because of the intensity of today's pain. Your very weakness allows the resurrection power of Christ to strengthen you moment by moment.

4:17 Our troubles should not diminish our faith or disillusion us. We should realize that there is a purpose in our suffering. Problems and human limitations have several benefits: (1) they remind us of Christ's suffering for us; (2) they keep us from pride; (3) they cause us to look beyond this brief life; (4) they prove our faith to others; and (5) they give God the opportunity to demonstrate his power. See your troubles as opportunities!

4:18 Our ultimate hope when we are experiencing terrible illness, persecution, or pain is the realization that this life is not all there is—there is life after death! Knowing that we will live forever with God in a place without sin and suffering can help us live above the pain that we face in this life.

Our Heavenly Dwelling

5 Now we know that if the earthly tent we live in is destroyed, we have a building from God, an eternal house in heaven, not built by human hands. ²Meanwhile we groan, *b* longing to be clothed with our heavenly dwelling, ³because when we are clothed, we will not be found naked. ⁴For while we are in this tent, we groan and are burdened, because we do not wish to be unclothed but to be clothed with our heavenly dwelling, *c* so that what is mortal may be swallowed up by life. ⁵Now it is God who has made us for this very purpose and has given us the Spirit as a deposit, guaranteeing what is to come. *d*

⁶Therefore we are always confident and know that as long as we are at home in the body we are away from the Lord. ⁷We live by faith, not by sight. ⁸We are confident, I say, and would prefer to be away from the body and at home with the Lord. ⁹So we make it our goal to please him, whether we are at home in the body or away from it. ¹⁰For we must all appear before the judgment seat of Christ, that each one may receive what is due him *e* for the things done while in the body, whether good or bad.

The Ministry of Reconciliation

¹¹Since, then, we know what it is to fear the Lord, *f* we try to persuade men. What we are is plain to God, and I hope it is also plain to your conscience. *g* ¹²We are not trying to commend ourselves to you again, *h* but are giving you an opportunity to take pride in us, *i* so that you can answer those who take pride in what is seen rather than in what is in the heart. ¹³If we are out of our mind, *j* it is for the sake of God; if we are in our right mind, it is for you. ¹⁴For Christ's love compels us, because we are convinced that one died for all, and therefore all died. ¹⁵And he died for all, that those who live should no longer live for themselves but for him who died for them and was raised again.

5:2
b Ro 8:23

5:4
c 1Co 15:53, 54

5:5
d Ro 8:23

5:10
e Ro 14:10; Eph 6:8

5:11
f Heb 10:31
g 2Co 4:2

5:12
h 2Co 3:1
i 2Co 1:14

5:13
j 2Co 11:1, 16, 17

5:1–10 Paul contrasts our earthly bodies ("earthly tent") and our future resurrection bodies ("a building from God, an eternal house in heaven, not built by human hands"). Paul clearly states that our present bodies make us groan, but when we die we will not be spirits without bodies ("be found naked"). We will have new bodies that will be perfect for our everlasting life.

Paul wrote as he did because the church at Corinth was in the heart of Greek culture, and many believers had difficulty with the concept of bodily resurrection. Greeks did not believe in a bodily resurrection. Most saw the afterlife as something that happened only to the soul, with the real person imprisoned in a physical body. They believed that at death the soul is released—there is no immortality for the body, and the soul enters an eternal state. But the Bible teaches that the body and soul are not permanently separated.

Paul describes our resurrected bodies in more detail in 1 Corinthians 15:46–58. We will still have personalities and recognizable characteristics in our resurrected bodies, but through Christ's work, our bodies will be better than we can imagine. The Bible does not tell us everything about our resurrected bodies, but we know they will be perfect, without sickness, disease, or pain (see Philippians 3:21; Revelation 21:4).

5:4 Paul's knowledge that his dying body would be swallowed up by eternal life, is a universal hope. According to the writer of Ecclesiastes, God "has also set eternity in the hearts of men" (Ecclesiastes 3:11). Human beings have a natural sense of transcendence and longing for ultimate reality experienced only in the eternal presence of God. This spiritual desire is addressed by every world religion and cult and (at least secretly) desired by every person. What occurrences in daily life can provide you an opportunity to witness God's solution to this universal spiritual search? A baby's birth, a parent's death, or the death of a dream all can be springboards for sharing the hope you have in Christ.

5:5 The Holy Spirit is God's guarantee of what will come. His work in our lives today assures us that the healing process will be thoroughly completed in Christ's presence. Each time the Holy Spirit reminds you of Scripture, convicts you of sin, restrains you from selfish behavior, or prompts you to love, you have evidence that he is present. You have the Spirit within you beginning the transformation process. Whether you deal with aches and pains

or even disabling limitations, trust God that his total renovation of your body and soul is in process.

5:6–8 Paul was not afraid to die, because he was confident of spending eternity with Christ. Of course, facing the unknown may cause us anxiety, and leaving loved ones hurts deeply, but if we believe in Jesus Christ, we can share Paul's hope and confidence of eternal life with Christ. Death is only a prelude to eternal life with God. We will continue to live. Let this hope give you confidence and inspire you to faithful service.

5:9, 10 While eternal life is a free gift given on the basis of God's grace (Ephesians 2:8, 9), each of us will still be judged by Christ. This judgment will reward us for how we have lived. God's gracious gift of salvation does not free us from the requirement for faithful obedience. All Christians must give account for how they have lived (see Matthew 16:27; Romans 14:10–12; 1 Corinthians 3:10–15).

5:11 To "fear the Lord" does not mean that believers become paralyzed. On the contrary, knowing God's perfection and that he will judge everyone's actions (5:10) should spur Christians to good deeds, to what pleases our God. The fear of the Lord also frees believers from all of life's anxieties and worries. Knowing that God is "for us" (Romans 8:31) can keep believers unafraid of earthly powers—people, governments, or the forces of nature (Proverbs 3:25, 26). God takes care of his own. The fear of God gives us uncommon courage in the face of life's troubles.

5:12 Those who "take pride in what is seen rather than in what is in the heart" are the false preachers (see 2:17) who were concerned only about getting ahead in this world. They were preaching the gospel for money and popularity, while Paul and his companions were preaching out of concern for eternity. You can identify false preachers by finding out what really motivates them. If they are more concerned about themselves than about Christ, avoid them and their message.

5:13–15 Everything that Paul and his companions did was to honor God. Not only did fear of God motivate them (5:11), but Christ's love compelled their actions. The word for "compels" means "to hold fast." In other words, the love of Christ was constraining them to certain courses of action. They knew that Jesus, out of his great love, had given up his life for their sakes. He

5:17
k Rev 21:4, 5

5:18
l Ro 5:10

5:20
m 2Co 6:1; Eph 6:20

5:21
n 1Pe 2:22, 24;
1Jn 3:5

6:1
o 1Co 3:9; 2Co 5:20

6:2
p Isa 49:8

6:3
q 1Co 9:12

6:5
r 2Co 11:23-25

6:7
s 2Co 10:4;
Eph 6:10-18

[16]So from now on we regard no one from a worldly point of view. Though we once regarded Christ in this way, we do so no longer. [17]Therefore, if anyone is in Christ, he is a new creation; the old has gone, the new has come! k [18]All this is from God, who reconciled us to himself through Christ l and gave us the ministry of reconciliation: [19]that God was reconciling the world to himself in Christ, not counting men's sins against them. And he has committed to us the message of reconciliation. [20]We are therefore Christ's ambassadors, m as though God were making his appeal through us. We implore you on Christ's behalf: Be reconciled to God. [21]God made him who had no sin n to be sin[a] for us, so that in him we might become the righteousness of God.

6 As God's fellow workers o we urge you not to receive God's grace in vain. [2]For he says,

> "In the time of my favor I heard you,
>   and in the day of salvation I helped you."[b] p

I tell you, now is the time of God's favor, now is the day of salvation.

Paul's Hardships

[3]We put no stumbling block in anyone's path, q so that our ministry will not be discredited. [4]Rather, as servants of God we commend ourselves in every way: in great endurance; in troubles, hardships and distresses; [5]in beatings, imprisonments r and riots; in hard work, sleepless nights and hunger; [6]in purity, understanding, patience and kindness; in the Holy Spirit and in sincere love; [7]in truthful speech and in the power of God; with weapons of righteousness s in the right hand and in the left; [8]through glory and dishonor, bad report

[a]21 Or be a sin offering   [b]2 Isaiah 49:8

---

had not acted out of his own self-interest, selfishly holding on to the glory of heaven that he already possessed (Philippians 2:6). Instead, Jesus had willingly "died for all." Because Christ died for us, we also are dead to our old lives. Like Paul, we should no longer live to please ourselves; we should spend our lives pleasing Christ.

5:17 Christians are brand-new people on the *inside*. The Holy Spirit gives them new life, and they are not the same anymore. We are not reformed, rehabilitated, or reeducated—we are re-created (new creations), living in vital union with Christ (Colossians 2:6, 7). At conversion we are not merely turning over a new leaf; we are beginning a new life under a new Master.

While this newness is true individually, Paul is saying much more. Not only are believers changed from within, but a whole new order of creative energy began with Christ. There is a new covenant, a new perspective, a new body, a new church. All of creation is being renewed. So take notice. This is not a superficial change that will be quickly superseded by another novelty. This is an entirely new order of all creation under Christ's authority. It requires a new way of looking at all people and all of creation. Does your life reflect this new perspective?

5:18, 19 God brings us back to himself (reconciles us) by blotting out our sins (see also Ephesians 2:13–18) and making us righteous. We are no longer God's enemies, or strangers or foreigners to him, when we trust in Christ. Because we have been reconciled to God, we have the privilege of encouraging others to do the same, and thus we are those who have the "ministry of reconciliation."

5:20 An ambassador is an official representative on behalf of one country to another. As believers, we are Christ's ambassadors, sent with his message of reconciliation to the world. An ambassador of reconciliation has an important responsibility. We dare not take this responsibility lightly. How well are you fulfilling your commission as Christ's ambassador?

5:21 When we trust in Christ, we make an exchange—our sin for his righteousness. Our sin was poured into Christ at his crucifixion. His righteousness is poured into us at our conversion. This is what Christians mean by Christ's atonement for sin. In the world, bartering works only when two people exchange goods of relatively equal value. But God offers to trade his righteousness for our sin—something of immeasurable worth for something completely worthless. How grateful we should be for his kindness to us.

6:1 How could the Corinthian believers ignore God's message ("receive God's grace in vain")? Perhaps they were doubting Paul and his words, confused by the false teachers who taught a different message. The people heard God's message, but did not let it affect what they said and did. How often does God's message reach you in vain?

6:2 God offers salvation to all people. Many people put off a decision for Christ, thinking that there will be a better time—but they could easily miss their opportunity altogether. There is no time like the present to receive God's forgiveness. Don't let anything hold you back from coming to Christ. The right time is now!

6:3 In everything he did, Paul always considered what his actions communicated about Jesus Christ. If you are a believer, you are a minister for God. In the course of each day, non-Christians observe you. Don't let your careless or undisciplined actions be another person's excuse for rejecting Christ.

6:5 Being put in jail would cause many people to become bitter or to give up, but Paul saw jail time as one more opportunity to spread the gospel of Christ. Paul realized that his current circumstances weren't as important as what he did with them. Turning a bad situation into a good one, he reached out to the Roman soldiers who made up the palace guard and encouraged Christians who were afraid of persecution. We may not be in prison, but we still have plenty of opportunities to be discouraged—times of indecision, financial burdens, family conflict, church conflict, or the loss of our jobs. How we act in such situations will reflect what we believe. Like Paul, look for ways to demonstrate your faith even in bad situations. Whether or not the situation improves, your faith will grow stronger.

6:7 See Romans 13:2; 2 Corinthians 10:3–5; and Ephesians 6:10–18 for more about the weapons of righteousness. Weapons for the right hand are offensive weapons; those for the left hand are defensive. No soldier is fully prepared for battle without both.

6:8–10 What a difference it makes to know Jesus! He cares for us in spite of what the world thinks. Christians don't have to give in to public opinion and pressure. Paul stood faithful to God whether people praised him or condemned him. He remained active, joyous, and content in the most difficult hardships. Don't let circumstances or people's expectations control you. Be firm as you stand true to God, and refuse to compromise his standards for living.

and good report; genuine, yet regarded as impostors; 9 known, yet regarded as unknown; dying, and yet we live on;*t* beaten, and yet not killed; 10 sorrowful, yet always rejoicing; poor, yet making many rich; having nothing, and yet possessing everything.

11 We have spoken freely to you, Corinthians, and opened wide our hearts to you. *u* 12 We are not withholding our affection from you, but you are withholding yours from us. 13 As a fair exchange—I speak as to my children—open wide your hearts also.

Do Not Be Yoked With Unbelievers

14 Do not be yoked together *v* with unbelievers. For what do righteousness and wickedness have in common? Or what fellowship can light have with darkness? *w* 15 What harmony is there between Christ and Belial *a*? What does a believer have in common with an unbeliever? 16 What agreement is there between the temple of God and idols? For we are the temple *x* of the living God. As God has said: "I will live with them and walk among them, and I will be their God, and they will be my people." *b*

> 17 "Therefore come out from them *y*
>   and be separate,
>   says the Lord.
> Touch no unclean thing,
>   and I will receive you." *c z*
> 18 "I will be a Father to you,
>   and you will be my sons and daughters,
>   says the Lord Almighty." *d*

7 Since we have these promises, dear friends, let us purify ourselves from everything that contaminates body and spirit, perfecting holiness out of reverence for God.

Paul's Joy

2 Make room for us in your hearts. We have wronged no one, we have corrupted no one, we have exploited no one. 3 I do not say this to condemn you; I have said before that you have

a 15 Greek *Beliar*, a variant of *Belial*   *b 16* Lev. 26:12; Jer. 32:38; Ezek. 37:27   *c 17* Isaiah 52:11; Ezek. 20:34,41
d 18 2 Samuel 7:14; 7:8

6:9
t 2Co 1:8-10;
4:10, 11

6:11
u 2Co 7:3

6:14
v 1Co 5:9, 10
w Eph 5:7, 11

6:16
x 1Co 3:16

6:17
y Rev 18:4
z Isa 52:11

6:11–13 "Opened wide our hearts to you" and "not withholding our affection from you" mean that Paul had told the Corinthian believers his true feelings for them, clearly revealing how much he loved them. The Corinthians were reacting coldly to Paul's words, but Paul explained that his harsh words came from his love for them. It is easy to react against those whom God has placed over us in leadership, rather than to accept their exhortations as a sign of their love for us. We need an open rather than a closed heart toward God's messengers.

6:14–18 Paul urges believers not to form binding relationships with nonbelievers, because this might weaken their Christian commitment, integrity, or standards. It would be a mismatch. Earlier, Paul had explained that this did not mean isolating oneself from nonbelievers (see 1 Corinthians 5:9, 10). Paul even tells Christians to stay with their nonbelieving spouses (1 Corinthians 7:12, 13). Paul wants believers to be active in their witness for Christ to nonbelievers, but they should not lock themselves into personal or business relationships that could cause them to compromise the faith. Believers should do everything in their power to avoid situations that could force them to divide their loyalties.

These verses also have strong application to marriage. Paul did not want single believers to enter into marriage with unbelievers. Such marriages cannot have unity in the most important issue in life—commitment and obedience to God. Because marriage involves two people becoming one, faith may become an issue, and one spouse may have to compromise beliefs for the sake of unity. Many people discount this problem only to regret it later. Don't allow emotion or passion to bind you with someone who will not be your spiritual partner. For those who have discovered God's light, there can be no fellowship or compromise with the darkness (1 Corinthians 10:20, 21).

6:15 Belial is a name that Paul uses for Satan.

6:16 Quoting from the prophet Isaiah, Paul asserted that the church is the temple of the living God. Corinth had an abundance of temples of pagan deities, so the recipients of his letter were able to visualize the contrast the apostle intended. Those who follow Christ are not known by a building; they are known as those in whom the Spirit of God lives. The church is not where believers go, it is who they are. God is not waiting for his people in some stained-glass setting. He is always with them. That is a sobering and yet a comforting thought. How does your behavior reflect on the God you represent?

6:17 Separation from the world involves more than keeping our distance from sinful practices; it means staying close to God (see 7:1, 2). It involves more than avoiding entertainment that leads to sin; it extends into how we spend our time and money. There is no way to separate ourselves totally from all sinful influences. Nevertheless, we are to resist the sin around us, without either giving up or giving in. When you know what God wants you to do, make a clean break with sinful practices.

7:1 Purifying ourselves is a twofold action: turning *away* from sin, and turning *toward* God. "Perfecting holiness" means that the Corinthians were to have nothing to do with paganism; they were to make a clean break with their past and give themselves to God alone. Paul wasn't suggesting that the Corinthians could become sinless in this life. Instead, he was prodding them to work at maturing in their faith. God had provided them with all the resources they needed, and Christ's Spirit would empower them to become Christlike (Romans 8:2).

7:2 Paul insisted that the Corinthians should open their hearts for him. He knew how much those in the church need one another. If fellowship was necessary in Paul's day, it is all the more crucial today, when time is more valuable than money. Each day holds barely enough time to care for personal and family needs, let alone

7:3
*a*2Co 6:11, 12

7:5
*b*2Co 2:13
*c*2Co 4:8
*d*Dt 32:25

7:6
*e*2Co 2:13

7:8
*f*2Co 2:2, 4

7:12
*g*ver 8

7:13
*h*ver 6

7:15
*i*2Co 2:9
*j*Php 2:12

8:1
*k*Ac 16:9

8:3
*l*1Co 16:2

8:4
*m*Ac 24:17

8:6
*n*ver 17; 2Co 12:18

such a place in our hearts *a* that we would live or die with you. 4 I have great confidence in you; I take great pride in you. I am greatly encouraged; in all our troubles my joy knows no bounds.

5 For when we came into Macedonia, *b* this body of ours had no rest, but we were harassed at every turn *c*—conflicts on the outside, fears within. *d* 6 But God, who comforts the downcast, comforted us by the coming of Titus, *e* 7 and not only by his coming but also by the comfort you had given him. He told us about your longing for me, your deep sorrow, your ardent concern for me, so that my joy was greater than ever.

8 Even if I caused you sorrow by my letter, *f* I do not regret it. Though I did regret it—I see that my letter hurt you, but only for a little while— 9 yet now I am happy, not because you were made sorry, but because your sorrow led you to repentance. For you became sorrowful as God intended and so were not harmed in any way by us. 10 Godly sorrow brings repentance that leads to salvation and leaves no regret, but worldly sorrow brings death. 11 See what this godly sorrow has produced in you: what earnestness, what eagerness to clear yourselves, what indignation, what alarm, what longing, what concern, what readiness to see justice done. At every point you have proved yourselves to be innocent in this matter. 12 So even though I wrote to you, *g* it was not on account of the one who did the wrong or of the injured party, but rather that before God you could see for yourselves how devoted to us you are. 13 By all this we are encouraged.

In addition to our own encouragement, we were especially delighted to see how happy Titus *h* was, because his spirit has been refreshed by all of you. 14 I had boasted to him about you, and you have not embarrassed me. But just as everything we said to you was true, so our boasting about you to Titus has proved to be true as well. 15 And his affection for you is all the greater when he remembers that you were all obedient, *i* receiving him with fear and trembling. *j* 16 I am glad I can have complete confidence in you.

3. Paul defends the collection
Generosity Encouraged

8 And now, brothers, we want you to know about the grace that God has given the Macedonian *k* churches. 2 Out of the most severe trial, their overflowing joy and their extreme poverty welled up in rich generosity. 3 For I testify that they gave as much as they were able, *l* and even beyond their ability. Entirely on their own, 4 they urgently pleaded with us for the privilege of sharing in this service *m* to the saints. 5 And they did not do as we expected, but they gave themselves first to the Lord and then to us in keeping with God's will. 6 So we urged *n* Titus, since he had earlier made a beginning, to bring also to completion this act of grace on

---

to meet the needs of others. Yet the activities that occupy our time are not as important as the community described in these verses. Paul's intention is not "coffee and donuts between church" fellowship. Believers need accountability that comes from lives intertwined by the cords of commitment and love. If you are not in a small group Bible study, take the first steps. Offer hospitality to fellow believers; when others extend the hand of fellowship to you, grasp it enthusiastically.

7:5 Here Paul resumed the story that he left in 2:13, where he said he went to Macedonia to look for Titus. Though Paul still had many problems and hardships to face, he still found comfort and joy in the progress of the ministry.

7:8ff "My letter" refers to the third letter (now lost) that Paul had written to the Corinthians. Apparently it had caused the people to begin to change. For an explanation of the chronology of Paul's letters to Corinth, see the first note on 1:1.

7:10 "Godly sorrow brings repentance that leads to salvation" refers to the sorrow for our sins that results in changed behavior. Many people are sorry only for the effects of their sins or for being caught ("worldly sorrow"). Compare Peter's remorse and repentance with Judas's bitterness and act of suicide. Both disowned Christ. One repented and was restored to faith and service; the other took his own life.

7:11 Paul affirmed the Corinthians for their right response to the correction he had given them. It's difficult to accept criticism, correction, or rebuke with poise and grace. It is much more natu-

ral to be defensive and then counterattack. We can accept criticism with self-pity, thinking we don't really deserve it. We can be angry and resentful. But a mature Christian should graciously accept constructive criticism, sincerely evaluate it, and grow from it.

8:1ff Paul, writing from Macedonia, hoped that news of the generosity of these churches would encourage the Corinthian believers and motivate them to solve their problems and unite in fellowship.

8:2–5 During his third missionary journey, Paul had collected money for the impoverished believers in Jerusalem. The churches in Macedonia—Philippi, Thessalonica, and Berea—had given money even though they were poor, and they had given more than Paul expected. This was sacrificial giving—they were poor themselves, but they wanted to help. The point of giving is not so much the amount we give, but why and how we give. God does not want gifts given grudgingly. Instead, he wants us to give as these churches did—out of dedication to Christ, love for fellow believers, the joy of helping those in need, as well as the fact that it was simply the good and right thing to do. How well does your giving measure up to the standards set by the Macedonian churches?

8:3–6 The kingdom of God spreads through believers' concern and eagerness to help others. Here we see several churches joining to help others beyond their own circle of friends and their own city. Explore ways that you might link up with a ministry outside your city, either through your church or through a Christian organization. By joining with other believers to do God's work, you increase Christian unity and help the kingdom grow.

your part. 7But just as you excel in everything º—in faith, in speech, in knowledge,ᵖ in complete earnestness and in your love for usª—see that you also excel in this grace of giving.

8I am not commanding you,�q but I want to test the sincerity of your love by comparing it with the earnestness of others. 9For you know the grace of our Lord Jesus Christ,ʳ that though he was rich, yet for your sakes he became poor,ˢ so that you through his poverty might become rich.

10And here is my adviceᵗ about what is best for you in this matter: Last year you were the first not only to give but also to have the desire to do so.ᵘ 11Now finish the work, so that your eager willingness to do it may be matched by your completion of it, according to your means. 12For if the willingness is there, the gift is acceptable according to what one has,ᵛ not according to what he does not have.

13Our desire is not that others might be relieved while you are hard pressed, but that there might be equality. 14At the present time your plenty will supply what they need, so that in turn their plenty will supply what you need. Then there will be equality, 15as it is written: "He who gathered much did not have too much, and he who gathered little did not have too little."ᵇ ʷ

Titus Sent to Corinth

16I thank God, who put into the heart of Titus the same concern I have for you. 17For Titus not only welcomed our appeal, but he is coming to you with much enthusiasm and on his own initiative.ˣ 18And we are sending along with him the brotherʸ who is praised by all the churches for his service to the gospel. 19What is more, he was chosen by the churches to accompany usᶻ as we carry the offering, which we administer in order to honor the Lord himself and to show our eagerness to help. 20We want to avoid any criticism of the way we administer this liberal gift. 21For we are taking pains to do what is right, not only in the eyes of the Lord but also in the eyes of men. ª

ª7 Some manuscripts *in our love for you*   ᵇ15 Exodus 16:18

8:7
º2Co 9:8
ᵖ1Co 1:5

8:8
q1Co 7:6

8:9
ʳ2Co 13:14
ˢPhp 2:6-8

8:10
ᵗ1Co 7:25, 40
ᵘ2Co 9:2

8:12
ᵛMk 12:43, 44

8:15
ʷEx 16:18

8:17
ˣver 6

8:18
ʸ2Co 12:18

8:19
ᶻ1Co 16:3, 4

8:21
ªRo 12:17

8:7, 8 The Corinthian believers excelled in everything—they had faith, good preaching (speech), much knowledge, much earnestness, much love. Paul encouraged them to also excel in the grace of giving. Too often, stewardship of money is given a different status than other aspects of discipleship. Most believers would not want growth in faith, knowledge, or love to stop at a certain level. Yet many decide a fixed percentage of their money to give and stay there for life. True discipleship includes growing in the mature use of all resources, so giving should expand as well. God can give you the desire and enable you to increase your capacity to give. Don't miss this opportunity for growth.

8:9 There is no evidence that Jesus was any poorer than most first-century Palestinians; rather, Jesus became poor by giving up his rights as God and becoming human. In his incarnation God voluntarily became man—the wholly human person, Jesus of Nazareth. As a man, Jesus was subject to place, time, and other human limitations. He did not give up his eternal power when he became human, but he did set aside his glory and his rights (see the note on Philippians 2:5–7). In response to the Father's will, he limited his power and knowledge. Christ became "poor" when he became human, because he set aside so much. Yet by doing so, he made us "rich" because we received salvation and eternal life.

What made Jesus' humanity unique was his freedom from sin. In his full humanity, we can see everything about God's character that can be conveyed in human terms. The incarnation is explained further in these Bible passages: John 1:1–14; Romans 1:2–5; Philippians 2:6–11; 1 Timothy 3:16; Hebrews 2:14; 1 John 1:1–3.

8:10–15 The Corinthian church had money, and apparently they had planned to collect money for the Jerusalem churches a year previously (see also 9:2). Paul challenges them to act on their plans. Four principles of giving emerge here: (1) your willingness to give cheerfully is more important than the amount you give; (2) you should strive to fulfill your financial commitments; (3) if you give to others in need, they will, in turn, help you when you are in need; (4) you should give as a response to Christ, not for anything you can get out of it. How you give reflects your devotion to Christ.

8:12 How do you decide how much to give? What about differences in the financial resources Christians have? Paul gives the Corinthian church several principles to follow: (1) each person should follow through on previous promises (8:10, 11; 9:3); (2) each person should give as much as he or she is able (8:12; 9:6); (3) each person must make up his or her own mind how much to give (9:7); and (4) each person should give in proportion to what God has given him or her (9:10). God gives to us so that we can give to others.

8:12 Paul says that we should give of what we have, not what we don't have. Sacrificial giving must be responsible. Paul wants believers to give generously, but not to the extent that those who depend on the givers (their families, for example) must go without having their basic needs met. Give until it hurts, but don't give so that it hurts your family and/or relatives who need your financial support.

8:18–21 Another "brother" was traveling with Paul and Titus, a man who was elected by the churches to also take the large financial gift to Jerusalem. Paul explained that by traveling together there could be no suspicion and people would know that the gift was being handled honestly. The church did not need to worry that the bearers of the collection would misuse the money.

Paul used every safeguard to maintain integrity in the collection of money for the Jerusalem church. Those outside the church can view skeptically the way believers handle money in the church. Financial scandals among high-profile ministries have alerted the non-believing world to the unethical gimmicks that some Christians use. It is possible to avoid mismanagement of God's resources. Does your church or organization have a system of checks and balances that prevent wrongful behavior? Are there financial practices in your ministry that need to be reviewed? Christians must have the highest standard of financial responsibility.

8:23
b Php 2:25

8:24
c 2Co 9:2

9:2
d 2Co 8:10

9:3
e 1Co 16:2

9:5
f Php 4:17

9:7
g 2Co 8:12
h Ro 12:8

9:9
i Ps 112:9

22 In addition, we are sending with them our brother who has often proved to us in many ways that he is zealous, and now even more so because of his great confidence in you. 23 As for Titus, he is my partner and fellow worker *b* among you; as for our brothers, they are representatives of the churches and an honor to Christ. 24 Therefore show these men the proof of your love and the reason for our pride in you, *c* so that the churches can see it.

9 There is no need for me to write to you about this service to the saints. 2 For I know your eagerness to help, and I have been boasting about it to the Macedonians, telling them that since last year *d* you in Achaia were ready to give; and your enthusiasm has stirred most of them to action. 3 But I am sending the brothers in order that our boasting about you in this matter should not prove hollow, but that you may be ready, as I said you would be. *e* 4 For if any Macedonians come with me and find you unprepared, we—not to say anything about you—would be ashamed of having been so confident. 5 So I thought it necessary to urge the brothers to visit you in advance and finish the arrangements for the generous gift you had promised. Then it will be ready as a generous gift, *f* not as one grudgingly given.

Sowing Generously

6 Remember this: Whoever sows sparingly will also reap sparingly, and whoever sows generously will also reap generously. 7 Each man should give what he has decided in his heart to give, *g* not reluctantly or under compulsion, for God loves a cheerful giver. *h* 8 And God is able to make all grace abound to you, so that in all things at all times, having all that you need, you will abound in every good work. 9 As it is written:

> "He has scattered abroad his gifts to the poor;
> his righteousness endures forever." *a i*

a 9 Psalm 112:9

PRINCIPLES OF CONFRONTATION IN 2 CORINTHIANS	Method	Reference
	Be firm and bold	7:9; 10:2
	Affirm all you see that is good	7:4
	Be accurate and honest	7:14; 8:21
	Know the facts	11:22–27
	Follow up after the confrontation	7:13; 12:14
	Be gentle after being firm	7:15; 13:11–13
	Speak words that reflect Christ's message, not your own ideas	10:3; 10:12, 13; 12:19
	Use discipline only when all else fails	13:2

Sometimes rebuke is necessary, but it must be used with caution. The purpose of any rebuke, confrontation, or discipline is to help people, not hurt them.

9:1, 2 By describing how their own "enthusiasm" had incited the Macedonians to give, Paul was, in effect, prodding the Corinthians to rekindle their initial enthusiasm for giving. Paul wasn't naive about human behavior. The start and end of a marathon are much more thrilling than the miles in between. It takes stubborn determination to keep going. Paul also knew that it took a community to persevere. Just as teammates will cheer their runner on in a race, so Paul was sending Titus and two other believers to the Corinthians to cheer them on.

9:3–5 Paul reminded the Corinthians to fulfill the commitment that they had already made (see also 8:10–12). They had said that they would collect a financial gift to send to the church in Jerusalem. Paul was sending a few men ahead of him to make sure their gift was ready, so it would be a real gift and not look like people had to give under pressure at the last minute ("ready as a generous gift, not as one grudgingly given"). He was holding them accountable to keep their promise, so that neither Paul nor the Corinthians would be embarrassed.

9:6–8 People may hesitate to give generously to God if they worry about having enough money left over to meet their own needs. Paul assured the Corinthians that God was able to meet their needs. The person who gives only a little will receive only a little in return. Don't let a lack of faith keep you from giving freely and generously.

9:7 A giving attitude is more important than the amount given. The person who can give only a small gift shouldn't be embarrassed. God is concerned about *how* a person gives from his or her resources (see Mark 12:41–44). According to that standard, the giving of the Macedonian churches would be difficult to match (8:3). God himself is a cheerful giver. Consider all he has done for us. He is pleased when we who are created in his image give generously and joyfully. Do you have a difficult time letting go of your money? It may reflect ungratefulness to God.

9:10 God gives us resources to use and invest for him. Paul uses the illustration of seed to explain that the resources God gives us are not to be hidden, foolishly devoured, or thrown away. Instead, they should be cultivated in order to produce more crops. When we invest what God has given us in his service, he will provide us with even more to give in his service.

10 Now he who supplies seed to the sower and bread for food *j* will also supply and increase your store of seed and will enlarge the harvest of your righteousness. *k* 11 You will be made rich in every way so that you can be generous on every occasion, and through us your generosity will result in thanksgiving to God.

12 This service that you perform is not only supplying the needs *l* of God's people but is also overflowing in many expressions of thanks to God. 13 Because of the service by which you have proved yourselves, men will praise God *m* for the obedience that accompanies your confession of the gospel of Christ, and for your generosity in sharing with them and with everyone else. 14 And in their prayers for you their hearts will go out to you, because of the surpassing grace God has given you. 15 Thanks be to God for his indescribable gift! *n*

4. Paul defends his authority

10 By the meekness and gentleness of Christ, I appeal to you—I, Paul, *o* who am "timid" when face to face with you, but "bold" when away! 2 I beg you that when I come I may not have to be as bold *p* as I expect to be toward some people who think that we live by the standards of this world. 3 For though we live in the world, we do not wage war as the world does. 4 The weapons we fight with are not the weapons of the world. On the contrary, they have divine power *q* to demolish strongholds. *r* 5 We demolish arguments and every pretension that sets itself up against the knowledge of God, and we take captive every thought to make it obedient to Christ. 6 And we will be ready to punish every act of disobedience, once your obedience is complete.

7 You are looking only on the surface of things. *a s* If anyone is confident that he belongs to Christ, *t* he should consider again that we belong to Christ just as much as he. 8 For even if I boast somewhat freely about the authority the Lord gave us for building you up rather than pulling you down, *u* I will not be ashamed of it. 9 I do not want to seem to be trying to frighten you with my letters. 10 For some say, "His letters are weighty and forceful, but in person he is unimpressive *v* and his speaking amounts to nothing." *w* 11 Such people should realize that what we are in our letters when we are absent, we will be in our actions when we are present.

12 We do not dare to classify or compare ourselves with some who commend themselves. When they measure themselves by themselves and compare themselves with themselves,

a 7 Or Look at the obvious facts

Cross-references

9:10 *j* Isa 55:10 *k* Hos 10:12

9:12 *l* 2Co 8:14

9:13 *m* Mt 9:8

9:15 *n* Ro 5:15, 16

10:1 *o* Gal 5:2

10:2 *p* 1Co 4:21; 2Co 13:2, 10

10:4 *q* 1Co 2:5 *r* Jer 1:10

10:7 *s* Jn 7:24 *t* 1Co 14:37

10:8 *u* 2Co 13:10

10:10 *v* 1Co 2:3; Gal 4:13, 14 *w* 1Co 1:17

9:13 Paul wanted his readers to be generous on every occasion. As he appealed to the Corinthians to give sacrificially to aid the Jerusalem congregation, he reminded them that God is the source of everything good (9:10). Believers are called to be generous because of the example of the Lord of life. A stingy Christian should be an extinct species. Generosity proves that a person's heart has been cleansed of self-interest and filled with the servant spirit of Jesus himself. That is why acts of generosity result in God being praised. Do neighbors see generosity in your actions?

10:1, 2 Paul's opponents questioned his authority. From 7:8–16 we know that the majority of Corinthian believers sided with Paul. However, a minority continued to slander him, saying that he was bold in his letters but had no authority in person. Chapters 10—13 are Paul's response to this charge.

10:3–6 We, like Paul, are merely weak humans, but we don't need to use human plans and methods to win our battles. God's mighty weapons are available to us as we fight against Satan's "strongholds." The Christian must choose whose methods to use, God's or the world's. Paul assures us that God's mighty weapons—prayer, faith, hope, love, God's Word, the Holy Spirit—are powerful and effective (see Ephesians 6:13–18)! These weapons can break down the proud human arguments against God and the walls that Satan builds to keep people from finding God. When dealing with the pride that keeps people from a relationship with Christ, we may be tempted to use our own methods. But nothing can break down these barriers like God's weapons.

10:5 Paul uses military terminology to describe this warfare against sin and Satan. God must be the commander in chief—even our thoughts must be submitted to his control as we live for him. Spirit-empowered believers must capture every thought and

yield it to Christ. When exposed to ideas or opportunities that might lead to wrong desires, you have a choice. You can recognize the danger and turn away, or you can allow unhealthy thoughts to take you captive. You capture your fantasies and desires when you honestly admit them to the Lord and ask him to redirect your thinking. Ask God to give you the spirit of discernment to keep your thoughts focused on his truth.

10:7–9 Those who opposed Paul portrayed him as weak and powerless, but Paul reminded the Corinthians that he claimed the power and authority of Christ. False teachers were encouraging the believers to ignore Paul, but Paul explained that the words in his letters were to be taken seriously. Paul had authority because he and his companions had been the first to bring the Good News to Corinth (10:14). On the basis of this authority over them, Paul wrote to them to help them grow.

10:10 Some said that Paul's speaking amounted to nothing. Greece was known for its eloquent and persuasive orators. Evidently, some were judging Paul by comparing him to other speakers they had heard, and Paul was perhaps not the most powerful preacher (although he was an excellent debater). But Paul responded obediently to God's call and thus introduced Christianity to the Roman empire. Moses and Jeremiah also had problems with speaking (see Exodus 4:10–12; Jeremiah 1:6). Preaching ability is not the first prerequisite of a great leader!

10:12, 13 Paul criticized the false teachers who were trying to prove their goodness by comparing themselves with others rather than with God's standards. When we compare ourselves with others, we may feel pride because we think we're better. But when we measure ourselves against God's standards, it becomes obvious that we have no basis for pride. Don't worry about other people's accomplishments. Instead, continually ask:

10:13
x ver 15, 16

10:15
y Ro 15:20

10:17
z Jer 9:24; 1Co 1:31

10:18
a Ro 2:29

they are not wise. ¹³We, however, will not boast beyond proper limits, but will confine our boasting to the field God has assigned to us,ˣ a field that reaches even to you. ¹⁴We are not going too far in our boasting, as would be the case if we had not come to you, for we did get as far as you with the gospel of Christ. ¹⁵Neither do we go beyond our limits by boasting of work done by others.ᵃ ʸ Our hope is that, as your faith continues to grow, our area of activity among you will greatly expand, ¹⁶so that we can preach the gospel in the regions beyond you. For we do not want to boast about work already done in another man's territory. ¹⁷But, "Let him who boasts boast in the Lord."ᵇ ᶻ ¹⁸For it is not the one who commends himself who is approved, but the one whom the Lord commends.ᵃ

Paul and the False Apostles

11:1
b 2Co 5:13

11:2
c Hos 2:19

11:3
d Ge 3:1-6, 13

11:4
e Gal 1:6-9

11:6
f 1Co 1:17
g Eph 3:4

11 I hope you will put up with a little of my foolishness;ᵇ but you are already doing that. ²I am jealous for you with a godly jealousy. I promised you to one husband,ᶜ to Christ, so that I might present you as a pure virgin to him. ³But I am afraid that just as Eve was deceived by the serpent's cunning,ᵈ your minds may somehow be led astray from your sincere and pure devotion to Christ. ⁴For if someone comes to you and preaches a Jesus other than the Jesus we preached, or if you receive a different spirit from the one you received, or a different gospelᵉ from the one you accepted, you put up with it easily enough. ⁵But I do not think I am in the least inferior to those "super-apostles." ⁶I may not be a trained speaker,ᶠ but I do have knowledge.ᵍ We have made this perfectly clear to you in every way.

ᵃ 13-15 Or ¹³We, however, will not boast about things that cannot be measured, but we will boast according to the standard of measurement that the God of measure has assigned us—a measurement that relates even to you. ¹⁴ . . . ¹⁵Neither do we boast about things that cannot be measured in regard to the work done by others.
ᵇ 17 Jer. 9:24

RAISING FUNDS HONORABLY

Be dedicated to God	8:5	Be accountable.	9:3
Provide information	8:4	Let people give willingly	9:7
Show definite purpose and goal	8:4	Be generous yourselves	8:7
Be enthusiastic.	8:7, 8, 11	Have someone to keep it moving	8:18–22
Reveal honesty and integrity	8:21	Be persistent, trusting God to provide	8:2ff

The topic of fund-raising is not one to be avoided or one that should embarrass us, but all fund-raising efforts should be planned and conducted responsibly.

How does my life measure up to what God wants? How does my life compare to Jesus Christ?

10:17, 18 When we do something well, we want to tell others and be recognized. But recognition is dangerous—it can lead to inflated pride. How much better it is to seek the praise of God rather than the praise of people. Then, when we receive praise, we will be free to give God the credit. What should you change about the way you live in order to receive God's commendation?

11:1 Paul asked the Corinthian believers to bear with him as he talked a little "foolishness." In other words, Paul felt foolish rehearsing his credentials as a preacher of the gospel (11:16–21). But he thought that he had to do this in order to silence the false teachers (11:13).

11:2 Paul was anxious that the church's love should be for Christ alone, just as a pure virgin saves her love for one man alone. By "virgin" he meant one who was unaffected by false doctrine.

11:3 The Corinthians' sincere and pure devotion to Christ was being threatened by false teaching. Paul did not want the believers to lose their single-minded love for Christ. Keeping Christ first in your life can be very difficult when you have so many distractions threatening to sidetrack your faith. Just as Eve lost her focus by listening to the serpent, you, too, can lose your focus by letting your life become overcrowded and confused. Is there anything that weakens your commitment to keep Christ first in your life? How can you minimize the distractions that threaten your devotion to him?

11:4 The Corinthian believers were falling for smooth talk and messages that sounded good and seemed to make sense. Today there are many false teachings that seem to make sense. Don't

believe someone simply because he or she sounds like an authority or says words you like to hear. Search the Bible and check his or her teachings against God's Word. The Bible should be your authoritative guide. The false teachers distorted the truth about Jesus and ended up preaching a different Jesus, a different spirit than the Holy Spirit, and a different gospel than God's way of salvation. Because the Bible is God's infallible Word, those who teach anything different from what it says are both mistaken and misleading.

11:5 Paul was saying that these marvelous teachers ("super-apostles") were no better than he was. They may have been more eloquent speakers, but they spoke lies and were servants of Satan.

11:6 Paul, a brilliant thinker, was not a trained, spellbinding speaker. Although his ministry was effective (see Acts 17), he had not been trained in the Greek schools of oratory and speech-making, as many of the false teachers probably had been. Paul believed in a simple presentation of the gospel (see 1 Corinthians 1:17), and some people thought this showed simple-mindedness. Thus Paul's speaking performance was often used against him by false teachers.

Content is far more important than the presentation. A simple, clear presentation that helps listeners understand will be of great value. God's Word stands on its own merit and is not dependent on imperfect human beings to create its own hearing. Many people feel that if they can't sing, speak, teach, or preach as well as their idolized heroes, they are insecure about saying or doing anything. Don't apologize for your inadequacies. Accept your limitations with the same humility that you accept the strengths God has given you.

7 Was it a sin for me to lower myself in order to elevate you by preaching the gospel of God to you free of charge? 8 I robbed other churches by receiving support from them so as to serve you. 9 And when I was with you and needed something, I was not a burden to anyone, for the brothers who came from Macedonia supplied what I needed. I have kept myself from being a burden to you in any way, and will continue to do so. 10 As surely as the truth of Christ is in me,*h* nobody in the regions of Achaia will stop this boasting*i* of mine. 11 Why? Because I do not love you? God knows I do! 12 And I will keep on doing what I am doing in order to cut the ground from under those who want an opportunity to be considered equal with us in the things they boast about.

13 For such men are false apostles,*j* deceitful workmen, masquerading as apostles of Christ.*k* 14 And no wonder, for Satan himself masquerades as an angel of light. 15 It is not surprising, then, if his servants masquerade as servants of righteousness. Their end will be what their actions deserve.*l*

Paul Boasts About His Sufferings

16 I repeat: Let no one take me for a fool. But if you do, then receive me just as you would a fool, so that I may do a little boasting. 17 In this self-confident boasting I am not talking as the Lord would,*m* but as a fool. 18 Since many are boasting in the way the world does, I too will boast. 19 You gladly put up with fools since you are so wise!*n* 20 In fact, you even put up with anyone who enslaves you or exploits you or takes advantage of you or pushes himself forward or slaps you in the face. 21 To my shame I admit that we were too weak for that!

What anyone else dares to boast about—I am speaking as a fool—I also dare to boast about. 22 Are they Hebrews? So am I. Are they Israelites? So am I.*o* Are they Abraham's descendants? So am I. 23 Are they servants of Christ? (I am out of my mind to talk like this.) I am more. I have worked much harder,*p* been in prison more frequently, been flogged more severely, and been exposed to death again and again. 24 Five times I received from the Jews the forty lashes*q* minus one. 25 Three times I was beaten with rods,*r* once I was stoned,*s* three

11:10
h Ro 9:1
i 1Co 9:15

11:13
j 2Pe 2:1
k Rev 2:2

11:15
l Php 3:19

11:17
m 1Co 7:12, 25

11:19
n 1Co 4:10

11:22
o Ro 9:4

11:23
p 1Co 15:10

11:24
q Dt 25:3

11:25
r Ac 16:22
s Ac 14:19

11:7 The Corinthians may have thought that preachers could be judged by how much money they demand. A good speaker would charge a large sum, a fair speaker would be a little cheaper, and a poor speaker would speak for free. The false teachers may have argued that because Paul asked no fee for his preaching, he must have been an amateur, with little authority or competence. Believers today must be careful not to assume that every speaker who is well known and demands a large honorarium necessarily teaches the truth.

11:7-12 Paul could have asked the Corinthian church for financial support. Jesus himself taught that those who minister for God should be supported by the people to whom they minister (Matthew 10:10). But Paul thought that asking for support in Corinth might be misunderstood. There were many false teachers who hoped to make a good profit from preaching (2:17), and Paul might look like one of them. Paul separated himself completely from those false teachers in order to silence those who only claimed to do God's work.

11:14, 15 One Jewish writing (the Apocalypse of Moses) says that the story of Eve's temptation includes Satan masquerading as an angel. Paul may have been thinking of this story, or he could have been referring to Satan's typical devices. In either case, nothing could be more deceitful than Satan, the prince of darkness (Ephesians 6:12; Colossians 1:13), disguising himself as an angel of light. In the same way, when the false teachers were claiming to represent Christ as servants of righteousness, they were lying shamelessly.

11:14, 15 Satan and his servants can deceive us by appearing to be attractive, good, and moral. Many unsuspecting people follow smooth-talking, Bible-quoting leaders into cults that alienate them from their families and lead them into the practice of immorality and deceit. Don't be fooled by external appearances. Our impressions alone are not an accurate indicator of who is or isn't a true follower of Christ; so it helps to ask these questions: (1) Do the teachings confirm Scripture (Acts 17:11)? (2) Does the teacher

affirm and proclaim that Jesus Christ is God who came into the world as a man to save people from their sins (1 John 4:1–3)? (3) Is the teacher's lifestyle consistent with Biblical morality (Matthew 12:33–37)?

11:15 Paul reminds the Corinthians that for the false teachers and hypocritical leaders, "their end will be what their actions deserve." The principle of judgment applies to all who speak on God's behalf. The apostle James said that teachers will be judged by the Lord with closer scrutiny than will those who sit under their teaching (James 3:1). It if is not already your practice, each time you sit down with the Scriptures to prepare a lesson or a sermon, spend some quiet moments in prayer asking the Holy Spirit to guide your preparation.

11:22, 23 Paul presented his credentials to counteract the charges that the false teachers were making against him. He felt foolish boasting like this, but his list of credentials would silence any doubts about his authority. Paul wanted to keep the Corinthians from slipping under the spell of the false teachers and turning away from the gospel. Paul also gave a list of his credentials in his letter to the Philippians (see Philippians 3:4–8).

11:23–29 Paul was angry that the false teachers had impressed and deceived the Corinthians (11:13–15). Therefore, he had to reestablish his credibility and authority by listing the trials he had endured in his service for Christ. Some of these trials are recorded in the book of Acts (Acts 14:19; 16:22–24). Because Paul wrote this letter during his third missionary journey (Acts 18:23—21:17), his trials weren't over. He would experience yet further difficulties and humiliations for the cause of Christ (see Acts 21:30–33; 22:24–30). Paul was sacrificing his life for the gospel, something the false teachers would never do. The trials and hurts we experience for Christ's sake build our character, demonstrate our faith, and prepare us for further service to the Lord.

11:25 Sea travel was not as safe as it is today. Paul had been shipwrecked three times, and he would face another accident on his voyage to Rome (see Acts 27). By this time, Paul had probably made at least eight or nine voyages.

11:26
t Ac 21:31

11:27
u 1Co 4:11, 12

times I was shipwrecked, I spent a night and a day in the open sea. 26 I have been constantly on the move. I have been in danger from rivers, in danger from bandits, in danger from my own countrymen, in danger from Gentiles; in danger in the city,*t* in danger in the country, in danger at sea; and in danger from false brothers. 27 I have labored and toiled and have often gone without sleep; I have known hunger and thirst and have often gone without food;*u* I have been cold and naked. 28 Besides everything else, I face daily the pressure of my concern for all the churches. 29 Who is weak, and I do not feel weak? Who is led into sin, and I do not inwardly burn?

PAUL'S CREDENTIALS

One of Paul's biggest problems with the church in Corinth was his concern that they viewed him as no more than a blustering preacher; thus, they were not taking seriously his advice in his letters and on his visits. Paul addressed this attitude in the letter of 2 Corinthians, pointing out his credentials as an apostle of Christ and why the Corinthians should take his advice.

1:1, 21; 4:1	Commissioned by God
1:12	Acted in holiness, sincerity, and dependence on God alone in his dealings with them
1:13, 14	Was straightforward and sincere in his letters
1:18; 4:2	Spoke truthfully
1:22	Had God's Holy Spirit
2:4; 6:11; 11:11	Loved the Corinthian believers
2:17	Spoke with sincerity and Christ's authority
3:2, 3	Worked among them and changed their lives
4:1, 16	Did not give up
4:2	Taught the Bible with integrity
4:5	Had Christ as the center of his message
4:8-12; 6:4, 5, 9, 10	Endured persecution as he taught the Good News
5:18-20	Was Christ's ambassador, called to tell the Good News
6:3, 4	Tried to live an exemplary life so others would not be kept from God
6:6	Led a pure life, understood the gospel, and displayed patience with the Corinthians
6:7	Was truthful and filled with God's power
6:8	Stood true to God first and always
7:2; 11:7-9	Never led anyone astray or took advantage of anyone
8:20, 21	Handled their offering for the Jerusalem believers in a responsible, blameless manner
10:1-6	Used God's weapons, not his own, for God's work
10:7, 8	Was confident that he belonged to Christ
10:12, 13	Would boast not in himself but in the Lord
10:14, 15	Had authority because he taught them the Good News
11:23-33	Endured pain and danger as he fulfilled his calling
12:2-4	Was blessed with an astounding vision
12:6	Lived as an example to the believers
12:7-10	Was constantly humbled by a "thorn" in the flesh that God refused to take away
12:12	Did miracles among them
12:19	Was always motivated to strengthen others spiritually
13:4	Was filled with God's power
13:5, 6	Passed the test
13:9	Was always concerned that his spiritual children become mature believers

---

11:28, 29 Not only did Paul face beatings and dangers, he also carried the daily concern for the young churches, worrying that they were staying true to the gospel and free from false teachings and inner strife. Paul was concerned for individuals in the churches he served. If God has placed you in a position of leadership and authority, treat people with Paul's kind of empathy and concern.

11:32 King Aretas, king of the Nabateans (Edomites) from 9 B.C. to A.D. 40, had appointed a governor to oversee the Nabatean segment of the population in Damascus. Somehow the Jews in Damascus had been able to enlist this governor to help them try to capture Paul (see Acts 9:22–25). Paul gave a

"for instance" here, describing his escape from Damascus in a basket lowered from a window in the city wall. Paul recounted this incident to show what he had endured for Christ. The false teachers couldn't make such claims.

30 If I must boast, I will boast of the things that show my weakness. *v* 31 The God and Father of the Lord Jesus, who is to be praised forever, knows that I am not lying. 32 In Damascus the governor under King Aretas had the city of the Damascenes guarded in order to arrest me. *w* 33 But I was lowered in a basket from a window in the wall and slipped through his hands.

11:30
v 1Co 2:3
11:32
w Ac 9:24

Paul's Vision and His Thorn

12 I must go on boasting. Although there is nothing to be gained, I will go on to visions and revelations from the Lord. 2 I know a man in Christ who fourteen years ago was caught up to the third heaven. *x* Whether it was in the body or out of the body I do not know—God knows. 3 And I know that this man—whether in the body or apart from the body I do not know, but God knows— 4 was caught up to paradise. *y* He heard inexpressible things, things that man is not permitted to tell. 5 I will boast about a man like that, but I will not boast about myself, except about my weaknesses. 6 Even if I should choose to boast, I would not be a fool, *z* because I would be speaking the truth. But I refrain, so no one will think more of me than is warranted by what I do or say.

12:2
x Eph 4:10

12:4
y Lk 23:43; Rev 2:7

12:6
z 2Co 11:16

7 To keep me from becoming conceited because of these surpassingly great revelations, there was given me a thorn in my flesh, a messenger of Satan, to torment me. 8 Three times I pleaded with the Lord to take it away from me. *a* 9 But he said to me, "My grace is sufficient for you, for my power *b* is made perfect in weakness." Therefore I will boast all the more gladly about my weaknesses, so that Christ's power may rest on me. 10 That is why, for Christ's sake, I delight in weaknesses, in insults, in hardships, *c* in persecutions, in difficulties. For when I am weak, then I am strong.

12:8
a Mt 26:39, 44
12:9
b Php 4:13
12:10
c 2Co 6:4

Paul's Concern for the Corinthians

11 I have made a fool of myself, but you drove me to it. I ought to have been commended by you, for I am not in the least inferior to the "super-apostles," *d* even though I am nothing. 12 The things that mark an apostle—signs, wonders and miracles—were done among you with great perseverance. 13 How were you inferior to the other churches, except that I was never a burden to you? *e* Forgive me this wrong! *f*

12:11
d 2Co 11:5

12:13
e 1Co 9:12, 18
f 2Co 11:7

12:2, 3 Paul continued his "boasting" by telling about visions and revelations he had received from the Lord. "I know a man in Christ" means that he was speaking about himself. He explained that he didn't know if he was taken up in his body or in his spirit, but he was in paradise ("the third heaven," perhaps referring to the highest part of the heavens, beyond the atmosphere and the stars, where God himself lives). This incident cannot be positively identified with a recorded event in Paul's career, although some think this may have been when he was stoned and left for dead (Acts 14:19, 20). Paul told about this incident to show that he had been uniquely touched by God.

12:7, 8 We don't know what Paul's thorn in the flesh was, because he doesn't tell us. Some have suggested that it was malaria, epilepsy, or a disease of the eyes (see Galatians 4:13–15). Whatever the case, it was a chronic and debilitating problem, which at times kept him from working. This thorn was a hindrance to his ministry, and he prayed for its removal; but God refused. Paul was a very self-sufficient person, so this thorn must have been difficult for him.

Three times Paul prayed for healing and did not receive it. He received, however, things far greater because he received greater grace from God, a stronger character, humility, and an ability to empathize with others. In addition, it benefited those around him as they saw God at work in his life. God, according to his sovereign plan, doesn't heal some believers of their physical ailments. We don't know why some are spared and others aren't. God chooses according to his divine purposes. Our task is to pray, to believe, and to trust. Paul is living proof that holy living and courageous faith do not ensure instant physical healing. When we pray for healing, we must trust our bodies to God's care. We must recognize that nothing separates us from his love (Romans

8:35–39) and that our spiritual condition is always more important than our physical condition.

12:9 Although God did not remove Paul's physical affliction, he promised to demonstrate his power in Paul. The fact that God's power is displayed in weak people should give us courage. Though we recognize our limitations, we will not congratulate ourselves and rest at that. Instead, we will turn to God to seek pathways for effectiveness. We must rely on God for our effectiveness rather than simply on our own energy, effort, or talent. Our weakness not only helps develop Christian character; it also deepens our worship, because in admitting our weakness, we affirm God's strength.

12:10 When we are strong in abilities or resources, we are tempted to do God's work on our own, and that can lead to pride. When we are weak, allowing God to fill us with *his* power, then we are stronger than we could ever be on our own. God does not intend for us to seek to be weak, passive, or ineffective—life provides enough hindrances and setbacks without us creating them. When those obstacles come, we must depend on God. Only his power will make us effective for him and will help us do work that has lasting value.

12:11-15 Paul was not merely revealing his feelings; he was defending his authority as an apostle of Jesus Christ. Paul was hurt that the church in Corinth doubted and questioned him, so he defended himself for the cause of the gospel, not to satisfy his ego. When you are "put on trial," do you think only about saving your reputation or are you more concerned about what people will think about Christ?

12:13 Paul explained that the only thing he did for the other churches that he didn't do in Corinth was to become a burden—to ask the believers to feed and house him. When he said, "Forgive me this wrong," he was clearly being sarcastic. He actually did more for the Corinthians than for any other church, but still they misunderstood him.

12:14
9 2Co 13:1
h 1Co 4:14, 15
12:15
i Php 2:17

14 Now I am ready to visit you for the third time, 9 and I will not be a burden to you, because what I want is not your possessions but you. After all, children should not have to save up for their parents, h but parents for their children. 15 So I will very gladly spend for you everything I have and expend myself as well. i If I love you more, will you love me less? 16 Be that as it may, I have not been a burden to you. Yet, crafty fellow that I am, I caught you by trickery!

12:18
j 2Co 8:6, 16
k 2Co 8:18

17 Did I exploit you through any of the men I sent you? 18 I urged j Titus to go to you and I sent our brother k with him. Titus did not exploit you, did he? Did we not act in the same spirit and follow the same course?

12:19
l Ro 9:1

19 Have you been thinking all along that we have been defending ourselves to you? We have been speaking in the sight of God l as those in Christ; and everything we do, dear friends, is for your strengthening. 20 For I am afraid that when I come I may not find you as I want you to be, and you may not find me as you want me to be. I fear that there may be quarreling, m jealousy, outbursts of anger, factions, slander, gossip, arrogance and disorder. 21 I am afraid that when I come again my God will humble me before you, and I will be grieved over many who have sinned earlier n and have not repented of the impurity, sexual sin and debauchery in which they have indulged.

12:20
m 1Co 1:11
12:21
n 2Co 13:2

Final Warnings

13:1
o 2Co 12:14
p Mt 18:16
13:2
q 2Co 1:23
13:3
r Mt 10:20; 1Co 5:4
13:4
s Php 2:7, 8;
1Pe 3:18
t Ro 1:4; 6:4
13:5
u 1Co 11:28

13 This will be my third visit to you. o "Every matter must be established by the testimony of two or three witnesses." a p 2 I already gave you a warning when I was with you the second time. I now repeat it while absent: On my return I will not spare q those who sinned earlier or any of the others, 3 since you are demanding proof that Christ is speaking through me. r He is not weak in dealing with you, but is powerful among you. 4 For to be sure, he was crucified in weakness, s yet he lives by God's power. t Likewise, we are weak in him, yet by God's power we will live with him to serve you.

5 Examine yourselves u to see whether you are in the faith; test yourselves. Do you not realize that Christ Jesus is in you—unless, of course, you fail the test? 6 And I trust that you will discover that we have not failed the test. 7 Now we pray to God that you will not do anything wrong. Not that people will see that we have stood the test but that you will do what is right even though we may seem to have failed. 8 For we cannot do anything against the truth, but only for the truth. 9 We are glad whenever we are weak but you are strong; and our prayer is for your perfection. 10 This is why I write these things when I am absent, that when I come I may not have to be harsh in my use of authority—the authority the Lord gave me for building you up, not for tearing you down. v

13:10
v 2Co 10:8

a 1 Deut. 19:15

12:14 Paul had founded the church in Corinth on his first visit there (Acts 18:1). He subsequently made a second visit (2:1). He was planning what would be his third visit (see also 13:1). Paul explained that, as before, he didn't want to be paid, fed, or housed; he only wanted the believers to be nourished with the spiritual food he would feed them.

12:16–19 Although Paul asked nothing of the Corinthian believers, some doubters were still saying that Paul must have been crafty and made money from them somehow. But Paul again explained that everything he did for the believers was for their edification, not to enrich himself.

12:20, 21 After reading this catalog of sins, it is hard to believe that these are the people that Paul said possessed great gifts and excelled as leaders (8:7). Paul feared that the practices of wicked Corinth had invaded the congregation. He wrote sternly, hoping that they would straighten out their lives before he arrived. We must live differently than unbelievers, not letting secular society dictate how we are to treat others. Don't let culture invade your practices at church.

13:2 When Paul arrived the third time in Corinth, he would not be lenient toward unrepentant sinners. His actions could include (1) confronting and publicly denouncing their behavior; (2) exercising church discipline by calling them before the church leaders; or (3) excommunicating them from the church.

13:5 The Corinthians were called to examine and test themselves to see if they really were Christians. Just as we get physical check-ups, Paul urges us to give ourselves spiritual checkups.

We should look for a growing awareness of Christ's presence and power in our lives. Only then will we know if we are true Christians or merely imposters. If we're not taking active steps to grow closer to God, we are drawing further away from him.

13:8, 9 Just as parents want their children to grow into mature adults, so Paul wanted the Corinthians to grow into mature believers. As we share the gospel, our goal should be not merely to see others profess faith or begin attending church, but to see them become mature in their faith. Don't set your sights too low.

13:10 The authority Paul had received from the Lord was to strengthen the believers, not to tear them down. Paul gives good advice for our day. Fellow believers are the temple of the Holy Spirit. There is no room in the household of faith for the deprecation of a fellow worker. Before the week is over, write a note of encouragement to several people in your sphere of influence who probably aren't being built up by others in the church. Remind them how much their presence and abilities are needed in your congregation. Express how much you appreciate them.

Final Greetings

11Finally, brothers, good-by. Aim for perfection, listen to my appeal, be of one mind, live in peace. And the God of love and peace *w* will be with you.

12Greet one another with a holy kiss. *x* 13All the saints send their greetings. *y*

14May the grace of the Lord Jesus Christ, and the love of God, and the fellowship of the Holy Spirit *z* be with you all.

13:11
w Ro 15:33;
Eph 6:23

13:12
x Ro 16:16

13:13
y Php 4:22

13:14
z Php 2:1

13:11 Paul's closing words—what he wanted the Corinthians to remember about the needs facing their church—are still fitting for the church today. When these qualities are not present, there are problems that must be dealt with. These traits do not come to a church by glossing over problems, conflicts, and difficulties. They are not produced by neglect, denial, withdrawal, or bitterness. They are the by-products of the extremely hard work of solving problems. Just as Paul and the Corinthians had to hammer out difficulties to bring peace, so we must *apply* the principles of God's Word and not just hear them.

13:14 Paul's farewell blessing invokes all three members of the Trinity—Father (God), Son (Lord Jesus Christ), and Holy Spirit. Although the term *Trinity* is not explicitly used in Scripture, verses such as this one show that it was believed and experienced through knowing God's grace, love, and fellowship. See Luke 1:35—the angel Gabriel's announcement of Jesus' birth to Mary; Matthew 3:17—the Father's voice heard at the baptism of Jesus; and Matthew 28:19—Jesus' commission to the disciples.

13:14 Paul was dealing with an ongoing problem in the Corinthian church. He could have refused to communicate until they cleared up their situation, but he loved them and reached out to them again with the love of Christ. Love, however, means that sometimes we must confront those we care about. Both authority and personal concern are needed in dealing with people who are ruining their lives with sin. But there are several wrong approaches in confronting others, and these can further break relationships rather than heal them. We can be legalistic and blast people away with the laws they should be obeying. We can turn away from them because we don't want to face the situation. We can isolate them by gossiping about their problem and turning others against them as well. Or, like Paul, we can seek to build relationships by taking a better approach—sharing, communicating, and caring. This is a difficult approach that can drain us emotionally, but it is the best way for the other person, and it is the only Christlike way to deal with others' sin.

GALATIANS

A FAMILY, executing their carefully planned escape at midnight, dashing for the border . . . a man standing outside prison walls, gulping fresh air, awash in the new sun . . . a young woman with every trace of the ravaging drug gone from her system . . . they are FREE! With fresh anticipation, they can begin life anew.

Whether fleeing oppression, stepping out of prison, or breaking a strangling habit, freedom means life. There is nothing so exhilarating as knowing that the past is forgotten and that new options await. People yearn to be free.

The book of Galatians is the charter of Christian freedom. In this profound letter, Paul proclaims the reality of our liberty in Christ—freedom from the law and the power of sin, and freedom to serve our living Lord.

Most of the first converts and early leaders in the church were Jewish Christians who proclaimed Jesus as their Messiah. As Jewish Christians, they struggled with a dual identity: Their Jewishness constrained them to be strict followers of the law; their newfound faith in Christ invited them to celebrate a holy liberty. They wondered how Gentiles (non-Jews) could be part of the kingdom of heaven.

This controversy tore the early church. Judaizers—an extremist Jewish faction within the church—taught that Gentile Christians had to submit to Jewish laws and traditions *in addition to* believing in Christ. As a missionary to the Gentiles, Paul had to confront this issue many times.

Galatians was written, therefore, to refute the Judaizers and to call believers back to the pure gospel. The Good News is for all people—Jews and Gentiles alike. Salvation is by God's grace through faith in Christ Jesus *and nothing else.* Faith in Christ means true freedom.

After a brief introduction (1:1–5), Paul addresses those who were accepting the Judaizers' perverted gospel (1:6–9). He summarizes the controversy, including his personal confrontation with Peter and other church leaders (1:10—2:16). He then demonstrates that salvation is by faith alone by alluding to his conversion (2:17–21), appealing to his readers' own experience of the gospel (3:1–5), and showing how the Old Testament teaches about grace (3:6–20). Next, he explains the purpose of God's laws and the relationship between law, God's promises, and Christ (3:21—4:31).

Having laid the foundation, Paul builds his case for Christian liberty. We are saved by faith, not by keeping the law (5:1–12); our freedom means that we are free to love and serve one another, not to do wrong (5:13–26); and Christians should carry each other's burdens and be kind to each other (6:1–10). In 6:11–18, Paul takes the pen into his own hand and shares his final thoughts.

As you read Galatians, try to understand this first-century conflict between grace and law, or faith and deeds, but also be aware of modern parallels. Like Paul, defend the truth of the gospel and reject all those who would add to or twist this truth. You are *free* in Christ—step into the light and celebrate!

VITAL STATISTICS

PURPOSE:
To refute the Judaizers (who taught that Gentile believers must obey the Jewish law in order to be saved), and to call Christians to faith and freedom in Christ

AUTHOR:
Paul

ORIGINAL AUDIENCE:
The churches in southern Galatia, founded on Paul's first missionary journey (including Iconium, Lystra, Derbe)

DATE WRITTEN:
Approximately A.D. 49, from Antioch, prior to the Jerusalem council (A.D. 50)

SETTING:
The most pressing controversy in the early church was the relationship of new believers, particularly Gentiles, to the Jewish laws. This was especially a problem for the converts and for the young churches that Paul had founded on his first missionary journey. Paul wrote to correct this problem. Later, at the council in Jerusalem, the conflict was officially resolved by the church leaders.

KEY VERSE:
"It is for freedom that Christ has set us free. Stand firm, then, and do not let yourselves be burdened again by a yoke of slavery" (5:1).

KEY PEOPLE:
Paul, Peter, Barnabas, Titus, Abraham, false teachers

KEY PLACES:
Galatia, Jerusalem

SPECIAL FEATURES:
This letter is not addressed to any specific body of believers and was probably circulated to several churches in Galatia.

THE BLUEPRINT

1. Authenticity of the gospel
   (1:1—2:21)
2. Superiority of the gospel
   (3:1—4:31)
3. Freedom of the gospel
   (5:1—6:18)

In response to attacks from false teachers, Paul wrote to defend his apostleship and the authority of the gospel. The Galatians were beginning to turn from faith to legalism. The struggle between the gospel and legalism is still a relevant issue. Many today would have us return to trying to earn God's favor through following rituals or obeying a set of rules. As Christians, we are not boxed in but set free. To preserve our freedom, we must stay close to Christ and resist any who promote subtle ways for us to earn our salvation.

MEGATHEMES

THEME	EXPLANATION	IMPORTANCE
Law	A group of Jewish teachers insisted that non-Jewish believers must obey Jewish law and traditional rules. They believed a person was saved by following the law of Moses (with emphasis on circumcision, the sign of the covenant), in addition to faith in Christ. Paul opposed them by showing that the law can't save anyone.	We can't be saved by keeping the Old Testament law, even the Ten Commandments. The law served as a guide to point out our need to be forgiven. Christ fulfilled the obligations of the law for us. We must turn to him to be saved. He alone can make us right with God.
Faith	We are saved from God's judgment and penalty for sin by God's gracious gift to us. We receive salvation by faith—trusting in him—not in anything else. Becoming a Christian is in no way based on our initiative, wise choice, or good character. We can be right with God only by believing in him.	Your acceptance with God comes by believing in Christ alone. You must never add to or twist this truth. We are saved by faith, not by the good that we do. Have you placed your whole trust and confidence in Christ? He alone can forgive you and bring you into a relationship with God.
Freedom	Galatians is our charter of Christian freedom. We are not under the jurisdiction of Jewish laws and traditions nor under the authority of Jerusalem. Faith in Christ brings true freedom from sin and from the futile attempt to be right with God by keeping the law.	We are free in Christ, and yet freedom is a privilege. We are not free to disobey Christ or practice immorality, but we are free to serve the risen Christ. Let us use our freedom to love and to serve, not to do wrong.
Holy Spirit	We become Christians through the work of the Holy Spirit. He brings new life; even our faith to believe is a gift from him. The Holy Spirit instructs, guides, leads, and gives us power. He ends our bondage to evil desires, and he creates in us love, joy, peace, and many other wonderful changes.	When the Holy Spirit leads us, he produces his fruit in us. Just as we are saved by faith, not deeds, we also grow by faith. By believing, we can have the Holy Spirit within us, helping us live for Christ. Obey Christ by following the Holy Spirit's leading.

1. Authenticity of the gospel

1 Paul, an apostle—sent not from men nor by man, but by Jesus Christ and God the Father, who raised him from the dead *a*— ²and all the brothers with me,*b*

To the churches in Galatia:*c*

1:1
a Ac 2:24

1:2
b Php 4:21
c 1Co 16:1

1:1 Paul and Barnabas had just completed their first missionary journey (Acts 13:2—14:28). They had visited Iconium, Lystra, and Derbe, cities in the Roman province of Galatia (present-day Turkey). Upon returning to Antioch, Paul was accused by some Jewish Christians of diluting Christianity to make it more appealing to Gentiles. These Jewish Christians disagreed with Paul's statements that Gentiles did not have to follow many of the religious laws that the Jews had obeyed for centuries. Some of Paul's accusers had even followed him to those Galatian cities and had told the Gentile converts they had to be circumcised and follow all the Jewish laws and customs in order to be saved. According to these men, Gentiles had to first become Jews in order to become Christians.

In response to this threat, Paul wrote this letter to the Galatian churches. In it, he explains that following the Old Testament laws or the Jewish laws will not bring salvation. A person is saved by grace through faith. Paul wrote this letter about A.D. 49, shortly

before the meeting of the Jerusalem council, which settled the law-versus-grace controversy (Acts 15).

1:1 Paul explained his apostleship in these words, not to separate himself from the original Twelve, but to show that his apostleship rested on the same basis as theirs. If the believers in Galatia questioned Paul's apostleship, then they also should question the apostleship of Peter, John, James, and all the others—and such questioning would be absurd. All the apostles were called by Jesus Christ and God the Father, and they answered to God as their final authority.

1:1 For more information about Paul's life, see his Profile in Acts 9, p. 1825. Paul had been a Christian for about 15 years at this time.

1:2 In Paul's time, *Galatia* was the Roman province located in the center section of present-day Turkey. Much of the region rests on a large and fertile plateau, and large numbers of people had moved to the region because of its favorable agriculture. One of Paul's goals during his missionary journeys was to visit

1:4
d Mt 20:28; Ro 4:25

³Grace and peace to you from God our Father and the Lord Jesus Christ, ⁴who gave himself for our sins *d* to rescue us from the present evil age, according to the will of our God and Father, ⁵to whom be glory for ever and ever. Amen.

No Other Gospel

⁶I am astonished that you are so quickly deserting the one who called you by the grace of Christ and are turning to a different gospel— ⁷which is really no gospel at all. Evidently

CITIES IN GALATIA

Paul visited several cities in Galatia on each of his three missionary journeys. On his first journey he went through Antioch in Pisidia, Iconium, Lystra, and Derbe, and then retraced his steps; on his second journey he went by land from Antioch in Syria through the four cities in Galatia; on his third journey he also went through those cities on the main route to Ephesus.

1:3–5 God's plan all along was to save us by Jesus' death. We have been rescued from the power of this present evil age—a world ruled by Satan and full of cruelty, tragedy, temptation, and deception. Being rescued from this evil age doesn't mean that we are taken out of it, but that we are no longer enslaved to it. You were saved to live for God. Does your life reflect your gratitude for being rescued? Have you transferred your loyalty from this world to Christ?

1:6 Some people were preaching "a different gospel." They were teaching that to be saved, Gentile believers had to follow Jewish laws and customs, especially the rite of circumcision. Faith in Christ was not enough. This message undermined the truth of the good news that salvation is a gift, not a reward for certain deeds. Jesus Christ has made this gift available to all people, not just to Jews. Beware of people who say that we need more than simple faith in Christ to be saved. When people set up additional requirements for salvation, they deny the power of Christ's death on the cross (see 3:1–5).

1:7 There is only one way given to us by God to be forgiven of sin—through believing in Jesus Christ as Savior and Lord. No other person, method, or ritual can give eternal life. Attempting to be open-minded and tolerant, some people assert that all religions are equally valid paths to God. In a free society, people have the right to their religious opinions, but this doesn't guarantee that their ideas are right. God does not accept man-made religion as a substitute for faith in Jesus Christ. He has provided just one way—Jesus Christ (John 14:6).

1:7 Those who had confused the Galatian believers and perverted the gospel were zealous Jewish Christians who believed that the Old Testament practices, such as circumcision and dietary restrictions, were required of all believers. Because these teachers wanted to turn the Gentile Christians into Jews, they were called *Judaizers*.

Most of the Galatian Christians were Greeks who were unfamiliar with Jewish laws and customs. The Judaizers were an extreme faction of Jewish Christians. Both groups believed in Christ, but their lifestyles differed considerably. We do not know why the Judaizers may have traveled no small distance to teach their mistaken notions to the new Gentile converts. They may have been motivated by (1) a sincere wish to integrate Judaism with the new Christian faith, (2) a sincere love for their Jewish heritage, or (3) a jealous desire to destroy Paul's authority. Whether or not these Judaizers were sincere, their teaching threatened these new churches and had to be countered. When Paul called their teaching a perversion of the gospel, he was not rejecting everything Jewish. He himself was a Jew who worshiped in the temple and attended the religious festivals. But he was concerned that *nothing* get in the way of the simple truth of his message—that salvation, for Jews and Gentiles alike, is through faith in Jesus Christ alone. Some time after the letter to the Galatians was sent, Paul met with the apostles in Jerusalem to discuss this matter further (see Acts 15).

1:7 A twisting of the truth is more difficult to spot than an outright lie. The Judaizers were twisting the truth about Christ. They claimed to follow him, but they denied that Jesus' work on the cross was sufficient for salvation. There will always be people who pervert the Good News. Either they do not understand what the Bible teaches, some people are throwing you into confusion e and are trying to pervert the gospel of Christ. **1:7** e Ac 15:24

8 But even if we or an angel from heaven should preach a gospel other than the one we preached to you, let him be eternally condemned! f 9 As we have already said, so now I say again: If anybody is preaching to you a gospel other than what you accepted, let him be eternally condemned!

1:8 f Ro 9:3

10 Am I now trying to win the approval of men, or of God? Or am I trying to please men? g If I were still trying to please men, I would not be a servant of Christ.

1:10 g Ro 2:29; 1Th 2:4

Paul Called by God

11 I want you to know, brothers, h that the gospel I preached is not something that man made up. 12 I did not receive it from any man, nor was I taught it; rather, I received it by revelation from Jesus Christ.

1:11 h 1Co 15:1

13 For you have heard of my previous way of life in Judaism, how intensely I persecuted the church of God and tried to destroy it. i 14 I was advancing in Judaism beyond many Jews of my own age and was extremely zealous for the traditions of my fathers. j 15 But when God, who set me apart from birth a k and called me by his grace, was pleased 16 to reveal his Son in me so that I might preach him among the Gentiles, I did not consult any man, l 17 nor did I go up to Jerusalem to see those who were apostles before I was, but I went immediately into Arabia and later returned to Damascus.

1:13 i Ac 8:3

1:14 j Mt 15:2

1:15 k Isa 49:1, 5

1:16 l Mt 16:17

18 Then after three years, I went up to Jerusalem m to get acquainted with Peter b and stayed with him fifteen days. 19 I saw none of the other apostles—only James, the Lord's

1:18 m Ac 9:26, 27

a 15 Or *from my mother's womb*   b 18 Greek *Cephas*

---

or they are uncomfortable with the truth as it stands. How can we tell when people are twisting the truth? Before accepting the teachings of any group, find out what the group teaches about Jesus Christ. If their teaching does not match the truth in God's Word, then it is not true.

1:8, 9 Paul strongly denounced the Judaizers' perversion of the gospel of Christ. He said that even if an angel from heaven comes preaching another message, that angel should be "eternally condemned." If an angel came preaching another message, he would not be from heaven, no matter how he looked. In 2 Corinthians 11:14, 15, Paul warned that Satan masquerades as an angel of light. Here he invoked a curse on any angel who spreads a false gospel—a fitting response to an emissary of hell. Paul extended that curse to include himself if he should pervert the gospel. His message must never change, for the truth of the gospel never changes. Paul used strong language because he was dealing with a life-and-death issue.

1:10 Do you spend your life trying to please everybody? Paul had to speak harshly to the Christians in Galatia because they were in serious danger. He did not apologize for his straightforward words, knowing that he could not serve Christ faithfully if he allowed the Galatian Christians to remain on the wrong track. Whose approval are you seeking—others' or God's? Pray for the courage to seek God's approval above anyone else's.

1:11ff Why should the Galatians have listened to Paul instead of the Judaizers? Paul answered this implicit question by furnishing his credentials: his message was received directly from Christ (1:12); he had been an exemplary Jew (1:13, 14); he had had a special conversion experience (1:15, 16; see also Acts 9:1–9); he had been confirmed and accepted in his ministry by the other apostles (1:18, 19; 2:1–9). Paul also presented his credentials to the Corinthian and Philippian churches (2 Corinthians 11; 12; Philippians 3:4–9).

1:12 There are two possible meanings consistent with the grammar of the phrase, "revelation from Jesus Christ." (1) This was a revelation by Christ to Paul that spelled out the gospel message, or (2) it was a personal revelation by Christ of his true identity that suddenly confirmed the gospel message against which Paul had been in bitter conflict. Within each meaning the fact remains that God provided the revelation and its content was the gospel.

1:13, 14 Paul had been one of the most religious Jews of his day, scrupulously keeping the law and relentlessly persecuting Christians (see Acts 9:1, 2). Before his conversion Paul had been even more zealous for the law than the Judaizers. He had surpassed his contemporaries in religious knowledge and practice. Paul had been sincere in his zeal—but wrong. When he met Jesus Christ, his life changed. He then directed all his energies toward building up the Christian church.

1:14 The word *Judaism* refers not only to nationality but also to religion. To be fully Jewish, a person must have descended from Abraham. In addition, a faithful Jew adhered to the Jewish laws. *Gentiles* (1:16) are non-Jews, whether in nationality or religion. In Paul's day, Jews thought of all Gentiles as pagans. Jews avoided Gentiles, believing that contact with Gentiles brought spiritual corruption. Although Gentiles could become Jews in religion by undergoing circumcision and by following Jewish laws and customs, they were never fully accepted.

Many Jews had difficulty understanding that God's message is for Jews and Gentiles alike. Some Jews thought that Gentiles had to become Jews before they could become Christians. But God planned to save both Jews and Gentiles. He had revealed this plan through Old Testament prophets (see, for example, Genesis 12:3; Isaiah 42:6; 66:19), and he had fulfilled it through Jesus Christ; he was proclaiming it to the Gentiles through Paul.

1:15, 16 Because God was guiding his ministry, Paul wasn't doing anything that God hadn't already planned and given him power to do. Similarly, God told Jeremiah that God had called him, even before he was born, to do special work for God (Jeremiah 1:5). God knows you intimately as well, and he chose you to be his even before you were born (see Psalm 139). He wants you to draw close to him and to fulfill the purpose he has for your life.

1:15–24 Paul tells of his conversion to show that his message came directly from God. God commissioned him to preach the Good News to the Gentiles. After his call, Paul did not consult with anyone; instead he spent three years in Arabia. Then he spoke with Peter and James, but he had no other contact with Jewish Christians for several more years. During those years, Paul preached to the Gentiles the message God had given him. His Good News did not come from human insight; it came from God.

1:18 This was Paul's first visit to Jerusalem as a Christian, as recorded in Acts 9:26–30.

brother. 20I assure you before God that what I am writing you is no lie. n 21Later I went to Syria and Cilicia. 22I was personally unknown to the churches of Judea o that are in Christ. 23They only heard the report: "The man who formerly persecuted us is now preaching the faith he once tried to destroy." 24And they praised God because of me.

Paul Accepted by the Apostles

2 Fourteen years later I went up again to Jerusalem, p this time with Barnabas. I took Titus along also. 2I went in response to a revelation and set before them the gospel that I preach among the Gentiles. But I did this privately to those who seemed to be leaders, for fear

THE MARKS OF THE TRUE GOSPEL AND OF FALSE GOSPELS	Marks of a false gospel	Marks of the true gospel
	2:21 . . . . Treats Christ's death as meaningless	1:11, 12 . . . . Teaches that the source of the gospel is God
	3:12 . . . . Says people must obey the law in order to be saved	2:20 . . . . Knows that life is obtained through death; we trust in the Son of God who loved us and died for us so that we might die to sin and live for him
	4:10 . . . . Tries to find favor with God by observing certain rituals	3:14 . . . . Explains that all believers have the Holy Spirit through faith
	5:4 . . . . Counts on keeping laws to be right with God	3:21, 22 . . . . Declares that we cannot be saved by keeping laws; the only way of salvation is through faith in Christ, which is available to all
		3:26–28 . . . . Says that all believers are one in Christ, so there is no basis for discrimination of any kind
		5:24, 25 . . . . Proclaims that we are free from the grip of sin and that the Holy Spirit's power fills and guides us

1:21 Because of opposition in Jerusalem (see Acts 9:29, 30), Paul had gone to Syria and Cilicia. In those remote areas, he had no opportunity to receive instruction from the apostles.

1:23 Paul was making the point that his authority and ministry were recognized by people who had never even seen him; yet the Galatians had met him, listened to him, and believed his message, only to turn around and doubt him! The Judean Christians only knew what people were saying: that the one who had persecuted believers was now preaching the faith he had tried to destroy. Instead of doubting Paul's credibility, the churches in Judea had believed and glorified God.

1:24 Paul's changed life had brought praise from those who saw him or heard about him. His new life had astonished them. They had praised God because only God could have turned this zealous persecutor of Christians into a Christian himself. We may not have had as dramatic a change as Paul, but still our new lives should honor God in every way. When people look at you, do they recognize that God has made changes in you? If not, perhaps you are not living as you should.

2:1 Paul was converted around A.D. 35. The 14 years he mentions are probably calculated from the time of his conversion. Therefore, this trip to Jerusalem was not his first. Most likely, he made his first trip to Jerusalem around A.D. 38 (see Acts 9:26–30), and other trips to Jerusalem in approximately A.D. 44 (Acts 11:29, 30; Galatians 2:1–10), A.D. 49/50 (Acts 15), A.D. 52 (Acts 18:22, where *the church* refers to the church in Jerusalem), and A.D. 57 (Acts 21:15ff). Paul probably visited Jerusalem on several other occasions as well.

2:1 Barnabas and Titus were two of Paul's close friends. Barnabas and Paul visited Galatia together on their first missionary journey. Paul wrote a personal letter to Titus, a faithful believer and church leader serving on the island of Crete (see the book of Titus). For more information on Barnabas, see his Profile in

Acts 13, p. 1837. For more information on Titus, see the letter Paul wrote to him in the New Testament.

2:1 After his conversion, Paul spent many years preparing for the ministry to which God had called him. This preparation period included time alone with God (1:16, 17), as well as time conferring with other Christians. Often new Christians, in their zeal, want to begin a full-time ministry without investing the necessary time studying the Bible and learning from qualified teachers. We need not wait to share Christ with our friends, but we may need more preparation before embarking on a special ministry, whether volunteer or paid. While we wait for God's timing, we should continue to study, learn, and grow.

2:2 God told Paul, through a revelation, to confer with the church leaders in Jerusalem about the message he was preaching to the Gentiles, so they would understand and approve of what he was doing. The essence of Paul's message to both Jews and Gentiles was that God's salvation is offered to all people regardless of race, sex, nationality, wealth, social standing, educational level, or anything else. Anyone can be forgiven by trusting in Christ (see Romans 10:8–13).

2:2, 3 Even though God had specifically sent him to the Gentiles (Acts 9:15, 16), Paul needed to discuss his gospel message with the leaders of the Jerusalem church (Acts 15). This meeting prevented a major split in the church, and it formally acknowledged the apostles' approval of Paul's preaching. Sometimes we avoid conferring with others because we fear that problems or arguments may develop. Instead, we should openly discuss our plans and actions with friends, counselors, and advisers. Good communication helps everyone understand the situation better, it reduces gossip, and it builds unity in the church.

that I was running or had run my race q in vain. 3 Yet not even Titus, who was with me, was
compelled to be circumcised, even though he was a Greek. r 4 This matter arose, because
some false brothers s had infiltrated our ranks to spy on the freedom t we have in Christ Jesus
and to make us slaves. 5 We did not give in to them for a moment, so that the truth of the gospel u might remain with you.

6 As for those who seemed to be important v—whatever they were makes no difference to
me; God does not judge by external appearance w—those men added nothing to my message. 7 On the contrary, they saw that I had been entrusted with the task x of preaching the
gospel to the Gentiles, a just as Peter had been to the Jews. b 8 For God, who was at work in the
ministry of Peter as an apostle to the Jews, was also at work in my ministry as an apostle to
the Gentiles. 9 James, Peter c and John, those reputed to be pillars, gave me and Barnabas the
right hand of fellowship when they recognized the grace given to me. y They agreed that we
should go to the Gentiles, and they to the Jews. 10 All they asked was that we should continue
to remember the poor, z the very thing I was eager to do.

Paul Opposes Peter

11 When Peter came to Antioch, I opposed him to his face, because he was clearly in the
wrong. 12 Before certain men came from James, he used to eat with the Gentiles. a But when
they arrived, he began to draw back and separate himself from the Gentiles because he was
afraid of those who belonged to the circumcision group. 13 The other Jews joined him in his
hypocrisy, so that by their hypocrisy even Barnabas was led astray.

14 When I saw that they were not acting in line with the truth of the gospel, b I said to Peter
in front of them all, "You are a Jew, yet you live like a Gentile and not like a Jew. How is it, then,
that you force Gentiles to follow Jewish customs?

a 7 Greek uncircumcised   b 7 Greek circumcised ; also in verses 8 and 9   c 9 Greek Cephas; also in verses 11 and 14

2:2
q Php 2:16

2:3
r Ac 16:3

2:4
s 2Co 11:26
t Ac 15:1

2:5
u ver 14

2:6
v Gal 6:3
w Ac 10:34

2:7
x 1Th 2:4

2:9
y Ro 12:3

2:10
z Ac 24:17

2:12
a Ac 11:3

2:14
b ver 5

2:3–5 When Paul took Titus, a Greek Christian, to Jerusalem, the
Judaizers (false brothers) said that Titus should be circumcised.
Paul adamantly refused to give in to their demands. The apostles
agreed that circumcision was an unnecessary rite for Gentile
converts. Several years later, Paul circumcised Timothy, another
Greek Christian (Acts 16:3). Unlike Titus, however, Timothy was
half Jewish. Paul did not deny Jews the right to be circumcised;
he was simply saying that Gentiles should not be asked to
become Jews before becoming Christians.

2:4 These false brothers were most likely from the party of the
Pharisees (Acts 15:5). These were the strictest religious leaders
of Judaism, some of whom had been converted. We don't know
if these were representatives of well-meaning converts or of
those trying to pervert Christianity. Most commentators agree
that neither Peter nor James had any part in this conspiracy.

2:5 We normally think of taking a stand against those who might
lead us into immoral behavior, but Paul had to take a hard line
against the most moral of people. We must not give in to those
who make the keeping of man-made standards a condition for
salvation, even when such people are morally upright or in
respected positions.

2:6 It's easy to rate people on the basis of their official status
and to be intimidated by powerful people. But Paul was not intimidated by "those who seemed to be important" because all believers are equal in Christ. We should show respect for our spiritual
leaders, but our ultimate allegiance must be to Christ. We are to
serve him with our whole being. God doesn't rate us according to
our status; he looks at the attitude of our hearts (1 Samuel 16:7).
We should encourage leaders who show humility and a heartfelt
desire to please God.

2:7–9 The church leaders ("pillars")—James (the half brother
of Jesus, not the apostle), Peter, and John—realized that God
was using Paul to reach the Gentiles, just as Peter was being
used so greatly to reach the Jews. After hearing Paul's message,
they gave Paul and Barnabas their approval ("the right hand of
fellowship") to continue working among the Gentiles.

2:10 The apostles were referring to the poor of Jerusalem. While
many Gentile converts were financially comfortable, the Jerusalem church had suffered from the effects of a severe famine in

Palestine (see Acts 11:28–30) and was struggling. So on his journeys, Paul had gathered funds for the Jewish Christians (Acts
24:17; Romans 15:25–29; 1 Corinthians 16:1–4; 2 Corinthians 8).
The need for believers to care for the poor is a constant theme
in Scripture. But often we do nothing, caught up in meeting our
own needs and desires. Perhaps we don't see enough poverty
to remember the needs of the poor. The world is filled with poor
people, here and in other countries. What can you do to help?

2:11 This was Antioch in Syria (distinguished from Antioch in
Pisidia), a major trade center in the ancient world. Heavily popu-
lated by Greeks, it eventually became a strong Christian center.
In Antioch the believers were first called Christians (Acts 11:26).
Antioch in Syria became the headquarters for the Gentile church
and was Paul's base of operations.

2:11ff The Judaizers accused Paul of watering down the gospel
to make it easier for Gentiles to accept, while Paul accused the
Judaizers of nullifying the truth of the gospel by adding conditions to it. The basis of salvation was the issue—is salvation
through Christ alone, or does it come through Christ and adherence to the law? The argument came to a climax when Peter,
Paul, the Judaizers, and some Gentile Christians all gathered
together in Antioch to share a meal. Peter probably thought that
by staying away from the Gentiles, he was promoting harmony—
he did not want to offend James and the Jewish Christians.
James had a very prominent position and presided over the Jerusalem council (Acts 15). But Paul charged that Peter's action
violated the gospel. By joining the Judaizers, Peter implicitly was
supporting their claim that Christ was not sufficient for salvation.
Compromise is an important element in getting along with others,
but we should never compromise the truth of God's Word. If we
feel we have to change our Christian beliefs to match those of our
companions, we are on dangerous ground.

2:11, 12 Although Peter was a leader of the church, he was
acting like a hypocrite. He knew better, yet he was driven by fear
of what James and the others would think. Proverbs 29:25 says,
"Fear of man will prove to be a snare." Paul knew that he had to
confront Peter before his actions damaged the church. So, Paul
publicly opposed Peter. Note, however, that Paul did not go to the
other leaders, nor did he write letters to the churches telling them

2:16
c Ac 13:39; Ro 9:30

15"We who are Jews by birth and not 'Gentile sinners' 16know that a man is not justified by observing the law, but by faith in Jesus Christ. c So we, too, have put our faith in Christ Jesus that we may be justified by faith in Christ and not by observing the law, because by observing the law no one will be justified.

17"If, while we seek to be justified in Christ, it becomes evident that we ourselves are sinners, does that mean that Christ promotes sin? Absolutely not! 18If I rebuild what I destroyed, I prove that I am a lawbreaker. 19For through the law I died to the law so that I might live for God. d 20I have been crucified with Christ and I no longer live, but Christ lives in me. The life I live in the body, I live by faith in the Son of God, who loved me and gave himself for me. 21I do not set aside the grace of God, for if righteousness could be gained through the law, Christ died for nothing!"a

2:19
d 2Co 5:15

a21 Some interpreters end the quotation after verse 14.

JUDAIZERS VERSUS PAUL

What the Judaizers said about Paul	Paul's defense
They said he was perverting the truth.	He received his message from Christ himself (1:11, 12).
They said he was a traitor to the Jewish faith.	Paul had been one of the most dedicated Jews of his time. Yet, in the midst of one of his most zealous acts, God transformed him through a revelation of the Good News about Jesus (1:13–16; Acts 9:1–30).
They said he compromised and watered down his message for the Gentiles.	The other apostles declared that the message Paul preached was the true gospel (2:1–10).
They said he was disregarding the law of Moses.	Far from degrading the law, Paul puts the law in its proper place. He says it shows people where they have sinned, and it points them to Christ (3:19–29).

As the debate raged between the Gentile Christians and the Judaizers, Paul found it necessary to write to the churches in Galatia. The Judaizers were trying to undermine Paul's authority, and they taught a false gospel. In reply, Paul defended his authority as an apostle and the truth of his message. The debate over Jewish laws and Gentile Christians was officially resolved at the Jerusalem council (Acts 15), yet it continued to be a point of contention after that time.

---

not to follow Peter's example. Instead, he opposed Peter face-to-face. Sometimes sincere Christians, even Christian leaders, make mistakes. And it may take other sincere Christians to get them back on track. If you are convinced that someone is doing harm to himself/herself or the church, try the direct approach. There is no place for backstabbing in the body of Christ.

2:15, 16 If observing the Jewish laws cannot justify us, why should we still obey the Ten Commandments and other Old Testament laws? We know that Paul was not saying the law is bad, because in another letter he wrote, "the Law is holy" (Romans 7:12). Instead, he is saying that the law can never make us acceptable to God. The law still has an important role to play in the life of a Christian. The law (1) guards us from sin by giving us standards for behavior; (2) convicts us of sin, leaving us the opportunity to ask for God's forgiveness; (3) drives us to trust in the sufficiency of Christ, because we can never keep the Ten Commandments perfectly. The law cannot possibly save us. But after we have become Christians, it can guide us to live as God requires.

2:17–19 Through studying the Old Testament Scriptures, Paul realized that he could not be saved by obeying God's laws. The prophets knew that God's plan of salvation did not rest on keeping the law (see the chart in chapter 4, p. 1971 for references). Because we have all been infected by sin, we cannot keep God's laws perfectly. Fortunately, God has provided a way of salvation that depends on Jesus Christ, not on our own efforts. Even though we know this truth, we must guard against the temptation of using service, good deeds, charitable giving, or any other effort as a substitute for faith.

2:20 How have our old selves been crucified with Christ? Legally, God looks at us as if we had died with Christ. Because

our sins died with him, we are no longer condemned (Colossians 2:13–15). Relationally, we have become one with Christ, and his experiences are ours. Our Christian life began when, in unity with him, we died to our old life (see Romans 6:5–11). In our daily life, we must regularly crucify sinful desires that keep us from following Christ. This too is a kind of dying with him (Luke 9:23–25).

And yet the focus of Christianity is not dying, but living. Because we have been crucified with Christ, we have also been raised with him (Romans 6:5). Legally, we have been reconciled with God (2 Corinthians 5:19) and are free to grow into Christ's likeness (Romans 8:29). And in our daily life, we have Christ's resurrection power as we continue to fight sin (Ephesians 1:19, 20). We are no longer alone, for Christ lives in us—he is our power for living and our hope for the future (Colossians 1:27).

2:21 Believers today may still be in danger of acting as if there was no need for Christ to die. How? By replacing Jewish legalism with their own brand of Christian legalism, they are giving people extra laws to obey. By believing they can earn God's favor by what they do, they are not trusting completely in Christ's work on the cross. By struggling to appropriate God's power to change them (sanctification), they are not resting in God's power to save them (justification). If we could be saved by being good, then Christ did not have to die. But the cross is the only way to salvation.

2. Superiority of the gospel

Faith or Observance of the Law

3 You foolish Galatians! Who has bewitched you?*e* Before your very eyes Jesus Christ was clearly portrayed as crucified. ²I would like to learn just one thing from you: Did you receive the Spirit by observing the law, or by believing what you heard?*f* ³Are you so foolish? After beginning with the Spirit, are you now trying to attain your goal by human effort? ⁴Have you suffered so much for nothing—if it really was for nothing? ⁵Does God give you his Spirit and work miracles among you because you observe the law, or because you believe what you heard?

⁶Consider Abraham: "He believed God, and it was credited to him as righteousness."*a g* ⁷Understand, then, that those who believe are children of Abraham. ⁸The Scripture foresaw that God would justify the Gentiles by faith, and announced the gospel in advance to Abraham: "All nations will be blessed through you."*b h* ⁹So those who have faith are blessed along with Abraham, the man of faith.

¹⁰All who rely on observing the law are under a curse, for it is written: "Cursed is everyone who does not continue to do everything written in the Book of the Law."*c i* ¹¹Clearly no one is justified before God by the law, because, "The righteous will live by faith."*d j* ¹²The law is not based on faith; on the contrary, "The man who does these things will live by them."*e k* ¹³Christ redeemed us from the curse of the law by becoming a curse for us, for it is written: "Cursed is everyone who is hung on a tree."*f l* ¹⁴He redeemed us in order that the blessing given to Abraham might come to the Gentiles through Christ Jesus,*m* so that by faith we might receive the promise of the Spirit.*n*

The Law and the Promise

¹⁵Brothers, let me take an example from everyday life. Just as no one can set aside or add to a human covenant that has been duly established, so it is in this case. ¹⁶The promises were spoken to Abraham and to his seed. The Scripture does not say "and to seeds," meaning many people, but "and to your seed,"*g* meaning one person, who is Christ. ¹⁷What I mean is

a 6 Gen. 15:6   *b 8* Gen. 12:3; 18:18; 22:18   *c 10* Deut. 27:26   *d 11* Hab. 2:4   *e 12* Lev. 18:5   *f 13* Deut. 21:23
g 16 Gen. 12:7; 13:15; 24:7

3:1 *e* Gal 5:7

3:2 *f* Ro 10:17

3:6 *g* Ge 15:6; Ro 4:3

3:8 *h* Ge 12:3

3:10 *i* Dt 27:26

3:11 *j* Hab 2:4; Gal 2:16; Heb 10:38

3:12 *k* Lev 18:5; Ro 10:5

3:13 *l* Dt 21:23

3:14 *m* Ro 4:9, 16 *n* Ac 2:33

3:1 The Galatian believers had become fascinated by the false teachers' arguments, almost as though they had been bewitched. Magic was common in Paul's day (Acts 8:9–11; 13:6, 7). Magicians used both optical illusions and Satan's power to perform miracles, and people were drawn into the magician's mysterious rites without recognizing their dangerous source.

3:2, 3 The believers in Galatia, some of whom may have been in Jerusalem at Pentecost and received the Holy Spirit there, knew that they hadn't received God's Spirit by obeying the Jewish laws. Paul stressed that just as they began their Christian lives in the power of the Spirit, so they should grow by the Spirit's power. The Galatians had taken a step backward when they had decided to insist on keeping the Jewish laws. We must realize that we grow spiritually because of God's work in us by his Spirit, not by following special rules.

3:5 The Galatians knew that they had received the Holy Spirit when they believed, not when they obeyed the law. People still feel insecure in their faith, because faith alone seems too easy. People still try to get closer to God by following rules. While certain disciplines (Bible study, prayer) and service may help us grow, they must not take the place of the Holy Spirit in us or become ends in themselves. By asking these questions, Paul hoped to get the Galatians to focus again on Christ as the foundation of their faith.

3:5 The Holy Spirit gives Christians great power to live for God. Some Christians want more than this. They want to live in a state of perpetual excitement. The tedium of everyday living leads them to conclude that something is wrong spiritually. Often the Holy Spirit's greatest work is teaching us to persist, to keep on doing what is right even when it no longer seems interesting or exciting. The Galatians quickly turned from Paul's Good News to the teachings of the newest teachers in town; what they needed was the Holy Spirit's gift of persistence. If the Christian life seems ordi-

nary, you may need the Spirit to stir you up. Every day offers a challenge to live for Christ.

3:6–9 The main argument of the Judaizers was that Gentiles had to become Jews in order to become Christians. Paul exposed the flaw in this argument by showing that real children of Abraham are those who have faith, not those who keep the law. Abraham himself was saved by his faith (Genesis 15:6). All believers in every age and from every nation share Abraham's blessing. This is a comforting promise to us, a great heritage for us, and a solid foundation for living.

3:10 Paul quoted Deuteronomy 27:26 to prove that, contrary to what the Judaizers claimed, the law cannot justify and save— it can only condemn. Breaking even one commandment brings a person under condemnation. And because everyone has broken the commandments, everyone stands condemned. The law can do nothing to reverse the condemnation (Romans 3:20–24). But Christ took the curse of the law upon himself when he hung on the cross. He did this so we wouldn't have to bear our own punishment. The only condition is that we accept Christ's death on our behalf as the means to be saved (Colossians 1:20–23).

3:11 Trying to be right with God ("justified") by our own effort doesn't work. Good intentions such as "I'll do better next time" or "I'll never do that again" usually end in failure. Paul points to Habakkuk's declaration (Habakkuk 2:4) that by trusting God— believing in his provision for our sins and living each day in his power—we can break this cycle of failure.

3:17 In the same way that we claim Jesus' death as God's provision for our salvation, Abraham believed in God and his promises, although they would not be made fully evident until centuries later on the cross. God promised, and Abraham answered in faith, even during the trial of God asking him to sacrifice his son. This is the heart of Christian faith. God promises to save us when we trust in Christ and take him at his word, just as Abraham did. We

3:17
o Ex 12:40

3:18
p Ro 4:14

3:19
q Ac 7:53

3:20
r Heb 8:6

3:22
s Ro 11:32

this: The law, introduced 430 years *o* later, does not set aside the covenant previously established by God and thus do away with the promise. 18For if the inheritance depends on the law, then it no longer depends on a promise; *p* but God in his grace gave it to Abraham through a promise.

19What, then, was the purpose of the law? It was added because of transgressions until the Seed to whom the promise referred had come. The law was put into effect through angels *q* by a mediator. 20A mediator, *r* however, does not represent just one party; but God is one.

21Is the law, therefore, opposed to the promises of God? Absolutely not! For if a law had been given that could impart life, then righteousness would certainly have come by the law. 22But the Scripture declares that the whole world is a prisoner of sin, *s* so that what was promised, being given through faith in Jesus Christ, might be given to those who believe.

23Before this faith came, we were held prisoners by the law, locked up until faith should be revealed. 24So the law was put in charge to lead us to Christ *a* that we might be justified by faith. 25Now that faith has come, we are no longer under the supervision of the law.

a24 Or charge until Christ came

DO WE STILL HAVE TO OBEY THE OLD TESTAMENT LAWS?	When Paul says that non-Jews (Gentiles) are no longer bound by these laws, he is not saying that the Old Testament laws do not apply to us today. He is saying certain types of laws may not apply to us. In the Old Testament there were three categories of laws:
Ceremonial law	This kind of law relates specifically to Israel's worship (see, for example, Leviticus 1:1–13). Its primary purpose was to point forward to Jesus Christ. Therefore, these laws were no longer necessary after Jesus' death and resurrection. While we are no longer bound by ceremonial laws, the principles behind them—to worship and love a holy God—still apply. The Jewish Christians often accused the Gentile Christians of violating the ceremonial law.
Civil law	This type of law dictated Israel's daily living (see Deuteronomy 24:10, 11, for example). Because modern society and culture are so radically different, some of these guidelines cannot be followed specifically. But the principles behind the commands should guide our conduct. At times, Paul asked Gentile Christians to follow some of these laws, not because they had to, but in order to promote unity.
Moral law	This sort of law is the direct command of God—for example, the Ten Commandments (Exodus 20:1–17). It requires strict obedience. It reveals the nature and will of God, and it still applies to us today. We are to obey this moral law, not to obtain salvation, but to live in ways pleasing to God.

---

know in greater detail how God worked out his plan of grace in Christ. We have much less excuse for our unbelief!

3:18, 19 The law has two functions. On the positive side, it reveals the nature and will of God and shows people how to live. On the negative side, it points out people's sins and shows them that it is impossible to please God by trying to obey all his laws completely. God's promise to Abraham dealt with Abraham's faith; the law focuses on actions. The covenant with Abraham shows that faith is the only way to be saved; the law shows how to obey God in grateful response. Faith does not annul the law; but the more we know God, the more we see how sinful we are. Then we are driven to depend on our faith in Christ alone for our salvation.

3:19, 20 When God gave his promise to Abraham, he did it by himself alone, without angels or Moses as mediators. Although it is not mentioned in Exodus, Jews believed that the Ten Commandments had been given to Moses by angels (Stephen referred to this in his speech, see Acts 7:38, 53). Paul was showing the superiority of salvation and growth by faith over trying to be saved by keeping the Jewish laws. Christ is the best and only way given by God for us to come to him (1 Timothy 2:5).

3:21, 22 Before faith in Christ delivered us, we were imprisoned by sin, beaten down by past mistakes, and choked by desires that

we knew were wrong. God knew we were sin's prisoners, but he provided a way of escape—faith in Jesus Christ. Without Christ, everyone is held in sin's grasp, and only those who place their faith in Christ ever get out of it. Look to Christ—he is reaching out to set you free.

3:24, 25 "The supervision of the law" is like the supervision given by a tutor to a young child. We no longer need that kind of supervision. The law teaches us the *need* for salvation; God's grace *gives* us that salvation. The Old Testament still applies today. In it, God reveals his nature, his will for humanity, his moral laws, and his guidelines for living. But we cannot be saved by keeping that law; we must trust in Christ.

Sons of God

26 You are all sons of God[t] through faith in Christ Jesus, 27 for all of you who were baptized into Christ[u] have clothed yourselves with Christ. [v] 28 There is neither Jew nor Greek, slave nor free, male nor female, for you are all one in Christ Jesus. [w] 29 If you belong to Christ, then you are Abraham's seed, and heirs according to the promise.

4 What I am saying is that as long as the heir is a child, he is no different from a slave, although he owns the whole estate. 2 He is subject to guardians and trustees until the time set by his father. 3 So also, when we were children, we were in slavery under the basic principles of the world. [x] 4 But when the time had fully come, God sent his Son, born of a woman, born under law, [y] 5 to redeem those under law, that we might receive the full rights[z] of sons. 6 Because you are sons, God sent the Spirit of his Son into our hearts, [a] the Spirit who calls out, "Abba, [a] Father." 7 So you are no longer a slave, but a son; and since you are a son, God has made you also an heir. [b]

Paul's Concern for the Galatians

8 Formerly, when you did not know God, [c] you were slaves to those who by nature are not gods. 9 But now that you know God—or rather are known by God[d]—how is it that you are turning back to those weak and miserable principles? Do you wish to be enslaved by them all over again? [e] 10 You are observing special days and months and seasons and years! [f] 11 I fear for you, that somehow I have wasted my efforts on you. [g]

12 I plead with you, brothers, become like me, for I became like you. You have done me no wrong. 13 As you know, it was because of an illness[h] that I first preached the gospel to you. 14 Even though my illness was a trial to you, you did not treat me with contempt or scorn. Instead, you welcomed me as if I were an angel of God, as if I were Christ Jesus himself. 15 What

[a] 6 Aramaic for *Father*

3:26	[t] Ro 8:14
3:27	[u] Ro 6:3
	[v] Ro 13:14
3:28	[w] Eph 2:14, 15
4:3	[x] Col 2:8, 20
4:4	[y] Lk 2:27
4:5	[z] Jn 1:12
4:6	[a] Ro 5:5
4:7	[b] Ro 8:17
4:8	[c] Eph 2:12; 1Th 4:5
4:9	[d] 1Co 8:3
	[e] Col 2:20
4:10	[f] Ro 14:5
4:11	[g] 1Th 3:5
4:13	[h] 1Co 2:3

3:26, 27 In Roman society, a youth coming of age laid aside the robe of childhood and put on a new toga. This represented his move into adult citizenship with full rights and responsibilities. Paul combined this cultural understanding with the concept of baptism. By becoming Christians and being baptized, the Galatian believers were becoming spiritually grown up and ready to take on the privileges and responsibilities of the more mature. Paul was saying that they had laid aside the old clothes of the law, and were putting on Christ's new robe of righteousness (see 2 Corinthians 5:21; Ephesians 4:23, 24).

3:28 Some Jewish males greeted each new day by praying, "Lord, I thank you that I am not a Gentile, a slave, or a woman." The role of women was enhanced by Christianity. Faith in Christ transcends these differences and makes all believers one in Christ. Make sure you do not impose distinctions that Christ has removed. Because all believers are his heirs, no one is more privileged than or superior to anyone else.

3:28 It's our natural inclination to feel uncomfortable around people who are different from us and to gravitate toward those who are similar to us. But when we allow our differences to separate us from our fellow believers, we are disregarding clear Biblical teaching. Make a point to seek out and appreciate people who are not just like you and your friends. You may find that you have a lot in common with them.

3:29 The original promise to Abraham was intended for the whole world, not just for Abraham's physical descendants (see Genesis 12:3). All believers participate in this promise and are blessed as children of Abraham.

4:3–7 The "basic principles of the world" are the elementary stages of religious practice, whether in the Jewish or pagan religion. Paul uses the illustration of slavery to show that before Christ came and died for sins, people were in bondage to the law. Thinking they could be saved by it, they became enslaved to trying—and failing—to keep it. But we who were once slaves are now God's very own children who have an intimate relationship with him. Because of Christ, there is no reason to be afraid of God. We can come boldly into his presence, knowing that he will welcome us as his family members.

4:4 "When the time had fully come," God sent Jesus to earth to die for our sins. For centuries the Jews had been wondering when their Messiah would come—but God's timing was perfect. We may sometimes wonder if God will ever respond to our prayers. But we must never doubt him or give up hope. At the right time he will respond. Are you waiting for God's timing? Trust his judgment and trust that he has your best interests in mind.

4:4, 5 Jesus was born of a woman—he was human. He was born as a Jew—he was subject to God's law and fulfilled it perfectly. Thus Jesus was the perfect sacrifice because, although he was fully human, he never sinned. His death bought freedom for us who were enslaved to sin so that we could be adopted into God's family.

4:5–7 Under Roman law, an adopted child was guaranteed all legal rights to his father's property, even if he was formerly a slave. He was not a second-class son; he was equal to all other sons, biological or adopted, in his father's family. *Abba* is an Aramaic word for father. It was used by Christ in his prayer in Mark 14:36. As adopted children of God, we share with Jesus all rights to God's resources. As God's heirs, we can claim what he has provided for us—our full identity as his children (see Romans 8:15–17).

4:13, 14 Paul's illness was a sickness that he was enduring while he visited the Galatian churches. The world is often callous to people's pain and misery. Paul commended the Galatians for not scorning him, even though his condition was a trial to them (he didn't explain what was wrong with him). Such caring was what Jesus meant when he called us to serve the homeless, hungry, sick, and imprisoned as if they were Jesus himself (Matthew 25:34–40). Do you avoid those in pain or those facing difficulty—or are you willing to care for them as if they were Jesus Christ himself?

4:15 Have you lost your joy? Paul sensed that the Galatians had lost the joy of their salvation because of legalism. Legalism can take away joy because (1) it makes people feel guilty rather than loved; (2) it produces self-hatred rather than humility; (3) it stresses performance over relationship; (4) it points out how far short we fall rather than how far we've come because of what has happened to all your joy? I can testify that, if you could have done so, you would have torn out your eyes and given them to me. ¹⁶Have I now become your enemy by telling you the truth?

¹⁷Those people are zealous to win you over, but for no good. What they want is to alienate you ⌊from us⌋, so that you may be zealous for them. ¹⁸It is fine to be zealous, provided the

THREE DISTORTIONS OF CHRISTIANITY	Group	Their definition of a Christian	Their genuine concern	The danger	Application question
Almost from the beginning there were forces at work within Christianity that would have destroyed or sidetracked the movement. Of these, three created many problems then and have continued to reappear in other forms even today. The three aberrations are contrasted to true Christianity.	Judaized Christianity	Christians are Jews who have recognized Jesus as the promised Savior. Therefore, any Gentile desiring to become a Christian must first become a Jew.	Having a high regard for the Scriptures and God's choice of Jews as his people, they did not want to see God's commands overlooked or broken.	Tends to add human traditions and standards to God's law. Also subtracts from the Scriptures God's clear concern for all nations.	Do you appreciate God's choice of a unique people through whom he offered forgiveness and eternal life to all peoples?
	Legalized Christianity	Christians are those who live by a long list of "don'ts." God's favor is earned by good behavior.	Recognized that real change brought about by God should lead to changes in behavior.	Tends to make God's love something to earn rather than to accept freely. Would reduce Christianity to a set of impossible rules and transform the Good News into bad news.	As important as change in action is, can you see that God may be desiring different changes in you than in others?
	Lawless Christianity	Christians live above the law. They need no guidelines. God's Word is not as important as our personal sense of God's guidance.	Recognized that forgiveness from God cannot be based on our ability to live up to his perfect standards. It must be received by faith as a gift made possible by Christ's death on the cross.	Forgets that Christians are still human and fail consistently when trying to live only by what they "feel" God wants.	Do you recognize the ongoing need for God's expressed commands as you live out your gratitude for his great salvation?
	True Christianity	Christians are those who believe inwardly and outwardly that Jesus' death has allowed God to offer them forgiveness and eternal life as a gift. They have accepted that gift through faith and are seeking to live a life of obedient gratitude for what God has done for them.	Christianity is both private and public, with heart-belief and mouth-confession. Our relationship to God and the power he provides result in obedience. Having received forgiveness and eternal life, we are now daily challenged to live that life with his help.	Avoids the above dangers.	How would those closest to you describe your Christianity? Do they think you live so that God will accept you, or do they know that you live because God has accepted you in Christ?

Christ did for us. If you feel guilty and inadequate, check your focus. Are you living by faith in Christ or by trying to live up to the demands and expectations of others?

4:16 Paul did not gain great popularity when he rebuked the Galatians for turning away from their first faith in Christ. Human nature hasn't changed much—we still get angry when we're scolded. But don't write off someone who challenges you. There may be truth in what he or she says. Receive his or her words with humility; carefully think them over. If you discover that you need to change an attitude or action, take steps to do it.

4:17 "Those people" refers to false teachers who claimed to be religious authorities and experts in Judaism and Christianity. Appealing to the believers' desire to do what was right, they drew quite a following. Paul said, however, that they were wrong and that their motives were selfish. False teachers are often respectable and persuasive. That is why all teachings should be checked against the Bible.

purpose is good, and to be so always and not just when I am with you. 19My dear children,[i] for whom I am again in the pains of childbirth until Christ is formed in you,[j] 20how I wish I could be with you now and change my tone, because I am perplexed about you!

Hagar and Sarah

21Tell me, you who want to be under the law, are you not aware of what the law says? 22For it is written that Abraham had two sons, one by the slave woman and the other by the free woman.[k] 23His son by the slave woman was born in the ordinary way;[l] but his son by the free woman was born as the result of a promise.[m]

24These things may be taken figuratively, for the women represent two covenants. One covenant is from Mount Sinai and bears children who are to be slaves: This is Hagar. 25Now Hagar stands for Mount Sinai in Arabia and corresponds to the present city of Jerusalem, because she is in slavery with her children. 26But the Jerusalem that is above[n] is free, and she is our mother. 27For it is written:

> "Be glad, O barren woman,
>   who bears no children;
> break forth and cry aloud,
>   you who have no labor pains;
> because more are the children of the desolate woman
>   than of her who has a husband."[a][o]

28Now you, brothers, like Isaac, are children of promise. 29At that time the son born in the ordinary way persecuted the son born by the power of the Spirit.[p] It is the same now. 30But what does the Scripture say? "Get rid of the slave woman and her son, for the slave woman's son will never share in the inheritance with the free woman's son."[b][q] 31Therefore, brothers, we are not children of the slave woman, but of the free woman.

3. Freedom of the gospel
Freedom in Christ

5 It is for freedom that Christ has set us free. Stand firm, then, and do not let yourselves be burdened again by a yoke of slavery.

2Mark my words! I, Paul, tell you that if you let yourselves be circumcised,[r] Christ will be of no value to you at all. 3Again I declare to every man who lets himself be circumcised that he is obligated to obey the whole law.[s] 4You who are trying to be justified by law have been alienated from Christ; you have fallen away from grace.[t] 5But by faith we eagerly await through the Spirit the righteousness for which we hope.[u] 6For in Christ Jesus neither circumcision nor uncircumcision has any value. The only thing that counts is faith expressing itself through love.

a27 Isaiah 54:1   b30 Gen. 21:10

4:19 [i]1Co 4:15 [j]Eph 4:13

4:22 [k]Ge 21:2

4:23 [l]Ro 9:7, 8 [m]Heb 11:11

4:26 [n]Heb 12:22

4:27 [o]Isa 54:1

4:29 [p]Ge 21:9

4:30 [q]Ge 21:10

5:2 [r]Ac 15:1

5:3 [s]Gal 3:10

5:4 [t]Heb 12:15

5:5 [u]Ro 8:23, 24

4:19 Paul led many people to Christ and helped them mature spiritually. Perhaps one reason for his success as a spiritual father was the deep concern he felt for his spiritual children; he compared his pain over their faithlessness to the pain of childbirth. We should have the same intense care for those to whom we are spiritual parents. When you lead people to Christ, remember to stand by them to help them grow.

4:21ff People are saved because of their faith in Christ, not because of what they do. Paul contrasted those who are enslaved to the law (represented by Hagar, the slave woman) with those who are free from the law (represented by Sarah, the free woman). Hagar's abuse of Sarah (Genesis 16:4) was like the persecution that the Gentile Christians were getting from the Judaizers who insisted on keeping the law in order to be saved. Eventually Sarah triumphed because God kept his promise to give her a son, just as those who worship Christ in faith will also triumph.

4:24 Paul explained that what happened to Sarah and Hagar is an allegory or picture of the relationship between God and mankind. Paul was using a type of argument that was common in his day and that was probably being used against him by his opponents.

5:1 Christ died to set us free from sin and from a long list of laws and regulations. Christ came to set us free—not free to do

whatever we want because that would lead us back into slavery to our selfish desires. Rather, thanks to Christ, we are now free and able to do what was impossible before—to live unselfishly. Those who appeal to their freedom so that they can have their own way or indulge their own desires are falling back into sin. But it is also wrong to put a burden of law keeping on Christians. We must stand against those who would enslave us with rules, methods, or special conditions for being saved or growing in Christ.

5:2–4 Trying to be saved by keeping the law and being saved by grace are two entirely different approaches. "Christ will be of no value to you at all" means that Christ's provision for our salvation will not help us if we are trying to save ourselves. Obeying the law does not make it any easier for God to save us. All we can do is accept his gracious gift through faith. Our deeds of service must never be used to try to earn God's love or favor.

5:3, 4 Circumcision was a symbol of having the right background and doing everything required by religion. No amount of work, discipline, or moral behavior can save us. If a person were counting on finding favor with God by being circumcised, he would also have to obey the rest of God's law completely. Trying to save ourselves by keeping all God's laws only separates us from God.

5:6 We are saved by faith, not by deeds. But love for others

5:9
v 1Co 5:6

5:10
w 2Co 2:3
x Gal 1:7

5:11
y Gal 6:12

5:13
z 1Co 8:9; 1Pe 2:16
a 1Co 9:19

7 You were running a good race. Who cut in on you and kept you from obeying the truth? 8 That kind of persuasion does not come from the one who calls you. 9 "A little yeast works through the whole batch of dough." v 10 I am confident w in the Lord that you will take no other view. The one who is throwing you into confusion x will pay the penalty, whoever he may be. 11 Brothers, if I am still preaching circumcision, why am I still being persecuted? y In that case the offense of the cross has been abolished. 12 As for those agitators, I wish they would go the whole way and emasculate themselves!

13 You, my brothers, were called to be free. But do not use your freedom to indulge the sinful nature a; z rather, serve one another a in love. 14 The entire law is summed up in a single command: "Love your neighbor as yourself." b 15 If you keep on biting and devouring each other, watch out or you will be destroyed by each other.

a 13 Or *the flesh*; also in verses 16, 17, 19 and 24   b 14 Lev. 19:18

VICES AND VIRTUES

The Bible mentions many specific actions and attitudes that are either right or wrong. Look at the list included here. Are there a number of characteristics from the wrong column that are influencing you?

VICES (Neglecting God and others)	VIRTUES (The by-products of living for God)
Sexual immorality *(Galatians 5:19)*	Love *(Galatians 5:22)*
Impurity *(Galatians 5:19)*	Joy *(Galatians 5:22)*
Lust *(Colossians 3:5)*	Peace *(Galatians 5:22)*
Hatred *(Galatians 5:20)*	Patience *(Galatians 5:22)*
Discord *(Galatians 5:20)*	Kindness *(Galatians 5:22)*
Jealousy *(Galatians 5:20)*	Goodness *(Galatians 5:22)*
Anger *(Galatians 5:20)*	Faithfulness *(Galatians 5:22)*
Selfish ambition *(Galatians 5:20)*	Gentleness *(Galatians 5:23)*
Dissension *(Galatians 5:20)*	Self-control *(Galatians 5:23)*
Arrogance *(2 Corinthians 12:20)*	
Envy *(Galatians 5:21)*	
Murder *(Revelation 22:12–16)*	
Idolatry *(Galatians 5:20; Ephesians 5:5)*	
Witchcraft *(Galatians 5:20)*	
Drunkenness *(Galatians 5:21)*	
Wild living *(Luke 15:13; Galatians 5:21)*	
Cheating *(1 Corinthians 6:8)*	
Adultery *(1 Corinthians 6:9, 10)*	
Homosexuality *(1 Corinthians 6:9, 10)*	
Greed *(1 Corinthians 6:9, 10; Ephesians 5:5)*	
Stealing *(1 Corinthians 6:9, 10)*	
Lying *(Revelation 22:12–16)*	

---

and for God is the response of those whom God has forgiven. God's forgiveness is complete, and Jesus said that those who are forgiven much love much (Luke 7:47). Because faith expresses itself through love, you can check your love for others as a way to monitor your faith.

5:9 A little yeast causes a whole lump of dough to rise. It only takes one wrong person to infect all the others.

5:11 Persecution proved that Paul was preaching the true gospel. If he had taught what the false teachers were teaching, no one would be offended. But because he was teaching the truth, he was persecuted by both Jews and Judaizers. Have friends or loved ones rejected you because you have taken a stand for Christ? Jesus said not to be surprised if the world hates you, because it hated him (John 15:18, 19). Just as Paul continued to faithfully proclaim the message about Christ, you should continue doing the ministry God has given you—in spite of the obstacles others may put in your way.

5:13 Paul distinguishes between freedom to sin and freedom to serve. Freedom or license to sin is no freedom at all, because it enslaves you to Satan, others, or your own sinful nature. Christians, by contrast, should not be slaves to sin, because they are free to do right and to glorify God through loving service to others.

5:14, 15 When we believers lose the motivation of love, we become critical of others. We stop looking for good in them and see only their faults. Soon we lose our unity. Have you focused on others' shortcomings instead of their strengths? Remind yourself of Jesus' command to love others as you love yourself (Matthew 22:39). When you begin to feel critical of someone, make a list of that person's positive qualities. When problems need to be addressed, confront in love rather than gossip.

Life by the Spirit

¹⁶So I say, live by the Spirit, and you will not gratify the desires of the sinful nature. ¹⁷For the sinful nature desires what is contrary to the Spirit, and the Spirit what is contrary to the sinful nature. They are in conflict with each other, so that you do not do what you want. *b* ¹⁸But if you are led by the Spirit, you are not under law.

¹⁹The acts of the sinful nature are obvious: sexual immorality, impurity and debauchery; ²⁰idolatry and witchcraft; hatred, discord, jealousy, fits of rage, selfish ambition, dissensions, factions ²¹and envy; drunkenness, orgies, and the like. I warn you, as I did before, that those who live like this will not inherit the kingdom of God.

²²But the fruit*c* of the Spirit is love,*d* joy, peace, patience, kindness, goodness, faithfulness, ²³gentleness and self-control. Against such things there is no law. ²⁴Those who belong to Christ Jesus have crucified the sinful nature*e* with its passions and desires. ²⁵Since we live by the Spirit, let us keep in step with the Spirit. ²⁶Let us not become conceited,*f* provoking and envying each other.

Doing Good to All

6 Brothers, if someone is caught in a sin, you who are spiritual*g* should restore him gently. But watch yourself, or you also may be tempted. ²Carry each other's burdens, and in this way you will fulfill the law of Christ. ³If anyone thinks he is something*h* when he is nothing, he deceives himself. ⁴Each one should test his own actions. Then he can take pride in himself, without comparing himself to somebody else, ⁵for each one should carry his own load.

⁶Anyone who receives instruction in the word must share all good things with his instructor.*i*

5:17
b Ro 7:15-23

5:22
c Eph 5:9
d Col 3:12-15

5:24
e Ro 6:6

5:26
f Php 2:3

6:1
g 1Co 2:15

6:3
h Ro 12:3

6:6
i 1Co 9:11, 14

5:16–18 If your desire is to have the qualities listed in 5:22, 23, then you know that the Holy Spirit is leading you. At the same time, be careful not to confuse your subjective feelings with the Spirit's leading. Being led by the Holy Spirit involves the desire to hear, the readiness to obey God's Word, and the sensitivity to discern between your feelings and his promptings. Live each day controlled and guided by the Holy Spirit. Then the words of Christ will be in your mind, the love of Christ will be behind your actions, and the power of Christ will help you control your selfish desires.

5:17 Paul describes the two forces conflicting within us—the Holy Spirit and the sinful nature (our evil desires or inclinations that stem from our bodies; see also 5:16, 19, 24). Paul is not saying that these forces are equal—the Holy Spirit is infinitely stronger. But if we rely on our own wisdom, we will make wrong choices. If we try to follow the Spirit by our own human effort, we will fail. Our only way to freedom from our evil desires is through the empowering of the Holy Spirit (see Romans 8:9; Ephesians 4:23, 24; Colossians 3:3–8).

5:19–21 We all have evil desires, and we can't ignore them. In order for us to follow the Holy Spirit's guidance, we must deal with them decisively (crucify them—5:24). These desires include obvious sins such as sexual immorality and witchcraft. They also include less obvious sins such as selfish ambition, hatred, and jealousy. Those who ignore such sins or refuse to deal with them reveal that they have not received the gift of the Spirit that leads to a transformed life.

5:22, 23 The fruit of the Spirit is the spontaneous work of the Holy Spirit in us. The Spirit produces these character traits that are found in the nature of Christ. They are the by-products of Christ's control—we can't obtain them by *trying* to get them without his help. If we want the fruit of the Spirit to grow in us, we must join our lives to his (see John 15:4, 5). We must know him, love him, remember him, and imitate him. As a result, we will fulfill the intended purpose of the law—to love God and our neighbors. Which of these qualities do you want the Spirit to produce in you?

5:23 Because the God who sent the law also sent the Spirit, the by-products of the Spirit-filled life are in perfect harmony with the intent of God's law. A person who exhibits the fruit of the Spirit fulfills the law far better than a person who observes the rituals but has little love in his or her heart.

5:24 In order to accept Christ as Savior, we need to turn from our sins and willingly nail our sinful nature to the cross. This doesn't mean, however, that we will never see traces of its evil desires again. As Christians we still have the capacity to sin, but we have been set free from sin's power over us and no longer have to give in to it. We must daily commit our sinful tendencies to God's control, daily crucify them, and moment by moment draw on the Spirit's power to overcome them (see 2:20; 6:14).

5:25 God is interested in every part of our lives, not just the spiritual part. As we live by the Holy Spirit's power, we need to submit every aspect of our lives to God—emotional, physical, social, intellectual, vocational. Paul says that because we're saved, we should live like it! The Holy Spirit is the source of your new life, so keep in step with his leading. Don't let anything or anyone else determine your values and standards in any area of your life.

5:26 Everyone needs a certain amount of approval from others. But those who go out of their way to secure honors or to win popularity become conceited and show they are not following the Holy Spirit's leading. Those who look to God for approval won't need to envy others. Because we are God's sons and daughters, we have his Holy Spirit as the loving guarantee of his approval. Seek to please God, and the approval of others won't seem so important.

6:1–3 No Christian should ever think that he or she is totally independent and doesn't need help from others, and no one should feel excused from the task of helping others. The body of Christ—the church—functions only when the members work together for the common good. Do you know someone who needs help? Is there a Christian brother or sister who needs correction or encouragement? Humbly and gently reach out to that person, offering to lift his or her load (John 13:34, 35).

6:4 When you do your very best, you feel good about the results. There is no need to compare yourself with others. People make comparisons for many reasons. Some point out others' flaws in order to feel better about themselves. Others simply want reassurance that they are doing well. When you are tempted to compare, look at Jesus Christ. His example will inspire you to do your very best, and his loving acceptance will comfort you when you fall short of your expectations.

6:6 Paul says that students should take care of the material needs of their teachers (1 Corinthians 9:7–12). It is easy to receive the benefit of good Bible teaching and then to take our

6:7
j 1Co 6:9

6:8
k Job 4:8

6:9
l 1Co 15:58

6:10
m Eph 2:19

7 Do not be deceived:*j* God cannot be mocked. A man reaps what he sows. 8 The one who sows to please his sinful nature, from that nature*a* will reap destruction;*k* the one who sows to please the Spirit, from the Spirit will reap eternal life. 9 Let us not become weary in doing good,*l* for at the proper time we will reap a harvest if we do not give up. 10 Therefore, as we have opportunity, let us do good to all people, especially to those who belong to the family*m* of believers.

Not Circumcision but a New Creation

11 See what large letters I use as I write to you with my own hand!

6:12
n Gal 5:11

12 Those who want to make a good impression outwardly are trying to compel you to be circumcised. The only reason they do this is to avoid being persecuted *n* for the cross of Christ. 13 Not even those who are circumcised obey the law, yet they want you to be circumcised that they may boast about your flesh. 14 May I never boast except in the cross of our Lord Jesus Christ, through which*b* the world has been crucified to me, and I to the world. *o*

6:14
o Ro 6:2, 6

6:15
p 2Co 5:17

15 Neither circumcision nor uncircumcision means anything; what counts is a new creation.*p* 16 Peace and mercy to all who follow this rule, even to the Israel of God.

17 Finally, let no one cause me trouble, for I bear on my body the marks of Jesus.

18 The grace of our Lord Jesus Christ be with your spirit, brothers. Amen.

a 8 Or *his flesh, from the flesh*   *b* 14 Or *whom*

OUR WRONG DESIRES VERSUS THE FRUIT OF THE SPIRIT
The will of the Holy Spirit is in constant opposition to our sinful desires. The two are on opposite sides of the spiritual battle.

Our wrong desires are	The fruit of the Spirit is
Evil	Good
Destructive	Productive
Easy to ignite	Difficult to ignite
Difficult to stifle	Easy to stifle
Self-centered	Self-giving
Oppressive and possessive	Liberating and nurturing
Decadent	Uplifting
Sinful	Holy
Deadly	Abundant life

---

spiritual leaders for granted, ignoring their financial and physical needs. We should care for our teachers, not grudgingly or reluctantly, but with a generous spirit, showing honor and appreciation for all they have done (1 Timothy 5:17, 18).

6:7, 8 It would certainly be a surprise if you planted corn and pumpkins came up. It's a natural law to reap what we sow. It's true in other areas too. If you gossip about your friends, you will lose their friendship. Every action has results. If you plant to please your own desires, you'll reap a crop of sorrow and evil. If you plant to please God, you'll reap joy and everlasting life. What kind of seeds are you sowing?

6:9, 10 It is discouraging to continue to do right and receive no word of thanks or see no tangible results. But Paul challenged the Galatians and he challenges us to keep on doing good and to trust God for the results. In due time, we will reap a harvest of blessing.

6:11 Up to this point, Paul had probably dictated the letter to a scribe. Here he takes the pen into his own hand to write his final, personal greetings. Paul did this in other letters as well, to add emphasis to his words and to validate that the letter was genuine.

6:13 Some of the Judaizers were emphasizing circumcision as proof of holiness, but were ignoring the other Jewish laws. People often choose a certain principle or prohibition and make it the measure of faith. Some may condemn drunkenness but ignore gluttony. Others may despise promiscuity but tolerate prejudice. Some who are adamant against homosexuality ignore child abuse. The Bible in its entirety is our rule of faith and practice. We cannot pick and choose the mandates we will follow.

6:14 The world is full of enticements. Daily we are confronted with subtle cultural pressures and overt propaganda. The only way to escape these destructive influences is to ask God to help crucify our interest in them, just as Paul did. How much do the interests of this world matter to you? (See 2:20 and 5:24 for more on this concept.)

6:15 It is easy to get caught up with the externals. Beware of those who emphasize actions that we should or shouldn't do, with no concern for the inward condition of the heart. Living a good life without an inward change leads to a shallow or empty spiritual walk. What matters to God is that we be completely changed from the inside out (2 Corinthians 5:17).

6:18 Paul's letter to the Galatians boldly declares the freedom of the Christian. Doubtless these early Christians in Galatia wanted to grow in the Christian life, but they were being misled by those who said this could be done only by keeping certain Jewish laws.

How strange it would be for a prisoner who had been set free to walk back into his or her cell and refuse to leave! How strange for an animal, released from a trap, to go back inside it! How sad for a believer to be freed from the bondage of sin, only to return to rigid conformity to a set of rules and regulations!

If you believe in Jesus Christ, you have been set free. Instead of going back into some form of slavery, whether to legalism or to sin, use your freedom to live for Christ and serve him as he desires.

EPHESIANS

VITAL STATISTICS

PURPOSE:
To strengthen the believers in Ephesus in their Christian faith by explaining the nature and purpose of the church, the body of Christ

AUTHOR:
Paul

ORIGINAL AUDIENCE:
The church at Ephesus, then circulated to neighboring local churches

DATE WRITTEN:
Approximately A.D. 60, from Rome, during Paul's imprisonment there

SETTING:
The letter was not written to confront any heresy or problem in the churches. It was sent with Tychicus to strengthen and encourage the churches in the area. Paul had spent over three years with the Ephesian church. As a result, he was very close to them. Paul met with the elders of the Ephesian church at Miletus (Acts 20:17–38)—a meeting that was filled with great sadness because he was leaving them for what he thought would be the last time. Because the letter contains no specific references to people or problems in the Ephesian church and because the words "at Ephesus" (1:1) are not present in some early manuscripts, Paul may have intended this to be a circular letter to be read to all the churches in the area.

KEY VERSES:
"There is one body and one Spirit—just as you were called to one hope when you were called—one Lord, one faith, one baptism; one God and Father of all, who is over all and through all and in all" (4:4–6).

KEY PEOPLE:
Paul, Tychicus

OUR churches come in all styles and shapes—secret meetings in homes; wide-open gatherings in amphitheaters; worship services packing thousands into a sanctuary while an overflow crowd watches on closed-circuit television; handfuls who kneel in urban storefronts. Buildings will vary, but the church is not confined to four walls. The church of Jesus Christ is *people,* his people, of every race and nation, who love Christ and are committed to serving him.

The "church age" began at Pentecost (Acts 2). Born in Jerusalem, the church spread rapidly through the ministry of the apostles and the early believers. Fanned by persecution, the gospel flame then spread to other cities and nations. On three courageous journeys, Paul and his associates established local assemblies in scores of Gentile cities.

One of the most prominent of those churches was at Ephesus. It was established in A.D. 53 on Paul's homeward journey to Jerusalem. But Paul returned a year later, on his third missionary trip, and stayed there for three years, preaching and teaching with great effectiveness (Acts 19:1–20). At another time, Paul met with the Ephesian elders, and he sent Timothy to serve as their leader (1 Timothy 1:3). Just a few years later, Paul was sent as a prisoner to Rome. While there, he was visited by messengers from various churches, including Tychicus of Ephesus. Paul wrote this letter to the church and sent it with Tychicus. Not written to counteract heresy or to confront any specific problem, Ephesians is a letter of encouragement. In it Paul describes the nature and appearance of the church, and he challenges believers to function as the living body of Christ on earth.

After a warm greeting (1:1, 2), Paul affirms the nature of the church—the glorious fact that believers in Christ have been showered with God's kindness (1:3–8), chosen for greatness (1:9–12), marked with the Holy Spirit (1:13, 14), filled with the Spirit's power (1:15–23), freed from sin's curse and bondage (2:1–10), and brought near to God (2:11–18). As part of God's "household," we stand with the prophets, apostles, Jews, Gentiles, and Christ himself (2:19—3:13). Then, as though overcome with emotion by remembering all that God has done, Paul challenges the Ephesians to live close to Christ, and he breaks into spontaneous praise (3:14–21).

Paul then turns his attention to the implications of being in the body of Christ, the church. Believers should have unity in their commitment to Christ and their use of spiritual gifts (4:1–16). They should have the highest moral standards (4:17—6:9). For the individual, this means rejecting pagan practices (4:17—5:20), and for the family, this means mutual submission and love (5:21—6:9).

Paul then reminds believers that the church is in a constant battle with the forces of darkness and that they should use every spiritual weapon at their disposal (6:10–17). He concludes by asking for their prayers, commissioning Tychicus, and giving a benediction (6:18–24).

As you read this masterful description of the church, thank God for the diversity and unity in his family, pray for your brothers and sisters across the world, and draw close to those in your local church.

THE BLUEPRINT

1. Unity in Christ
   (1:1—3:21)
2. Unity in the body of Christ
   (4:1—6:24)

In this letter, Paul explains the wonderful things that we have received through Christ and refers to the church as a body to illustrate unity of purpose and show how each individual member is a part that must work together with all the other parts. In our own life, we should work to eradicate all backbiting, gossip, criticism, jealousy, anger, and bitterness, because these are barriers to unity in the church.

MEGATHEMES

THEME	EXPLANATION	IMPORTANCE
God's Purpose	According to God's eternal, loving plan, he directs, carries out, and sustains our salvation.	When we respond to Christ's love by trusting in him, his purpose becomes our mission. Have you committed yourself to fulfilling God's purpose?
Christ the Center	Christ is exalted as the center of the universe and the focus of history. He is the head of the body, the church. He is the Creator and Sustainer of all creation.	Because Christ is central to everything, his power must be central in us. Begin by placing all your priorities under his control.
Living Church	Paul describes the nature of the church. The church, under Christ's control, is a living body, a family, a dwelling. God gives believers special abilities by his Holy Spirit to build the church.	We are part of Christ's body, and we must live in vital union with him. Our conduct must be consistent with this living relationship. Use your God-given abilities to equip believers for service. Fulfill your role in the living church.
New Family	Because God through Christ paid our penalty for sin and forgave us, we have been reconciled—brought near to him. We are a new society, a new family. Being united with Christ means we are to treat one another as family members.	We are one family in Christ, so there should be no barriers, no divisions, no basis for discrimination. We all belong to him, so we should live in harmony with one another.
Christian Conduct	Paul encourages all Christians to wise, dynamic Christian living, for with privileges goes family responsibility. As a new community, we are to live by Christ's new standards.	God provides his Holy Spirit to enable us to live his way. To utilize the Spirit's power, we must lay aside our evil desires and draw on the power of his new life. Submit your will to Christ, and seek to love others.

1. Unity in Christ

1:1
a 2Co 1:1

1 Paul, an apostle of Christ Jesus by the will of God,a

To the saints in Ephesus,a the faithfulb in Christ Jesus:

2 Grace and peace to you from God our Father and the Lord Jesus Christ.

a 1 Some early manuscripts do not have *in Ephesus*. b 1 Or *believers who are*

1:1 Paul wrote this letter to the Ephesian believers and all other believers to give them in-depth teaching about how to nurture and maintain the unity of the church. He wanted to put this important information in written form because he was in prison for preaching the gospel and could not visit the churches himself. The words "in Ephesus" are not present in some early manuscripts (see the NIV text note). Therefore, this was very likely a circular letter—it was first sent to Ephesus and then circulated to neighboring local churches. Paul mentions no particular problems or local situations, and he offers no personal greetings.

1:1 Paul had been a Christian for nearly 30 years. He had taken three missionary trips and established churches all around the Mediterranean Sea. When he wrote Ephesians, Paul was under house arrest in Rome (see Acts 28:16ff). Though a prisoner, he

was free to have visitors and write letters. For more information on Paul, see his Profile in Acts 9, p. 1825.

1:1 Ephesus was one of the five major cities in the Roman empire, along with Rome, Corinth, Antioch, and Alexandria. Paul first visited Ephesus on his second missionary journey (Acts 18:19–21). During his third missionary journey, he stayed there for almost three years (Acts 19). Paul later met again with the elders of the Ephesian church at Miletus (Acts 20:16–38). Ephesus was a commercial, political, and religious center for all of Asia Minor. The temple to the Greek goddess Artemis (Diana is her Roman equivalent) was located there.

1:1 "Faithful in Christ Jesus"—what an excellent reputation! Such a label would be an honor for any believer. What would it take for others to characterize you as faithful to Christ Jesus? Hold fast to

Spiritual Blessings in Christ

³Praise be to the God and Father of our Lord Jesus Christ,ᵇ who has blessed us in the heavenly realms with every spiritual blessing in Christ. ⁴For he chose us in him before the creation of the world to be holy and blameless in his sight. In love ⁵heᵃ predestinedᶜ us to be adopted as his sons through Jesus Christ, in accordance with his pleasure and will— ⁶to the praise of his glorious grace, which he has freely given us in the One he loves. ᵈ ⁷In him we have redemption through his blood, the forgiveness of sins, in accordance with the riches of God's grace ⁸that he lavished on us with all wisdom and understanding. ⁹And heᵇ made known to us the mysteryᵉ of his will according to his good pleasure, which he purposed in Christ, ¹⁰to be put into effect when the times will have reached their fulfillment—to bring all things in heaven and on earth together under one head, even Christ.

¹¹In him we were also chosen,ᶜ having been predestined according to the plan of him who works out everything in conformity with the purposeᶠ of his will, ¹²in order that we, who were the first to hope in Christ, might be for the praise of his glory. ¹³And you also were included in Christ when you heard the word of truth, the gospel of your salvation. Having believed, you were marked in him with a seal,ᵍ the promised Holy Spirit, ¹⁴who is a deposit guaranteeing our inheritance until the redemption of those who are God's possession—to the praise of his glory.

Thanksgiving and Prayer

¹⁵For this reason, ever since I heard about your faith in the Lord Jesus and your love for all the saints,ʰ ¹⁶I have not stopped giving thanks for you, remembering you in my prayers. ¹⁷I

1:3
ᵇ2Co 1:3

1:5
ᶜRo 8:29, 30

1:6
ᵈMt 3:17

1:9
ᵉRo 16:25

1:11
ᶠEph 3:11

1:13
ᵍEph 4:30

1:15
ʰCol 1:4

ᵃ4,5 Or *sight in love.* ⁵*He* ᵇ8,9 Or *us. With all wisdom and understanding,* ⁹*he* ᶜ11 Or *were made heirs*

---

your faith, one day at a time; faithfully obey God, even in the details of life. Then, like the Ephesians, you will be known as a person who is faithful to the Lord.

1:3 "Who has blessed us in the heavenly realms with every spiritual blessing" means that in Christ we have all the benefits of knowing God—being chosen for salvation, being adopted as his children, forgiveness, insight, the gifts of the Spirit, power to do God's will, the hope of living forever with Christ. Because we have an intimate relationship with Christ, we can enjoy these blessings now. The *heavenly realms* means that these blessings are eternal, not temporal. The blessings come from Christ's spiritual realm, not the earthly realm of the goddess Artemis. Other references to the heavenly realms in this letter include 1:20; 2:6; 3:10. Such passages reveal Christ in his victorious, exalted role as ruler of all.

1:4 Paul says that God "chose us in him" to emphasize that salvation depends totally on God. We are not saved because we deserve it, but because God is gracious and freely gives salvation. We did not influence God's decision to save us; he saved us according to his plan. Thus there is no way to take credit for our salvation or to allow room for pride. The mystery of salvation originated in the timeless mind of God long before we existed. It is hard to understand how God could accept us. But because of Christ, we are holy and blameless in his sight. God chose us, and when we belong to him through Jesus Christ, God looks at us as if we had never sinned. All we can do is express our thanks for his wonderful love.

1:5 "Predestined" means marked out beforehand. This is another way of saying that salvation is God's work and not our own doing. In his infinite love, God has adopted us as his own children. Through Jesus' sacrifice, he has brought us into his family and made us heirs along with Jesus (Romans 8:17). In Roman law, adopted children had the same rights and privileges as biological children, even if they had been slaves. Paul uses this term to show how strong our relationship to God is. Have you entered into this loving relationship with God? For more on the meaning of adoption, see Galatians 4:5–7.

1:6 "Freely given us in the One he loves" means that God graciously accepts us (though we don't deserve it) now that we belong to his dearly loved Son.

1:7 To speak of Jesus' blood was an important first-century way of speaking of Christ's death. His death points to two wonderful

truths—redemption and forgiveness. *Redemption* was the price paid to gain freedom for a slave (Leviticus 25:47–54). Through his death, Jesus paid the price to release us from slavery to sin. *Forgiveness* was granted in Old Testament times on the basis of the shedding of animals' blood (Leviticus 17:11). Now we are forgiven on the basis of the shedding of Jesus' blood—he died as the perfect and final sacrifice. (See also Romans 5:9; Ephesians 2:13; Colossians 1:20; Hebrews 9:22; 1 Peter 1:19.)

1:7, 8 Grace is God's voluntary and loving favor given to those he saves. We can't earn salvation, nor do we deserve it. No religious, intellectual, or moral effort can gain it, because it comes only from God's mercy and love. Without God's grace, no person can be saved. To receive it, we must acknowledge that we cannot save ourselves, that only God can save us, and that our only way to receive this loving favor is through faith in Christ.

1:9, 10 God was not intentionally keeping his plan a secret ("the mystery of his will"), but his plan for the world could not be fully understood until Christ rose from the dead. His purpose for sending Christ was to unite Jews and Gentiles in one body with Christ as the head. Many people still do not understand God's plan; but when the time is right ("when the times will have reached their fulfillment"), he will bring us together to be with him forever. Then everyone will understand. On that day, all people will bow to Jesus as Lord, either because they love him or because they fear his power (see Philippians 2:10, 11).

1:11 God's purpose is to offer salvation to the world, just as he planned to do long ago. God is sovereign; he is in charge. When your life seems chaotic, rest in this truth: Jesus is Lord, and God is in control. God's purpose to save you cannot be thwarted, no matter what evil Satan may bring.

1:13, 14 The Holy Spirit is God's seal that we belong to him and his deposit guaranteeing that he will do what he has promised. The Holy Spirit is like a down payment, a deposit, a validating signature on the contract. The presence of the Holy Spirit in us demonstrates the genuineness of our faith, proves that we are God's children, and secures eternal life for us. His power works in us to transform us now, and what we experience now is a taste of the total change we will experience in eternity.

1:16, 17 Paul prayed for the believers to know God better. How do you get to know someone? By reading biographical information or historical data about him? That will help you know a lot

1:17
/Jn 20:17
/Col 1:9

1:20
k Ac 2:24

1:21
/Php 2:9, 10
1:22
m Eph 4:15

keep asking that the God of our Lord Jesus Christ, the glorious Father, / may give you the Spirit a of wisdom / and revelation, so that you may know him better. 18I pray also that the eyes of your heart may be enlightened in order that you may know the hope to which he has called you, the riches of his glorious inheritance in the saints, 19and his incomparably great power for us who believe. That power is like the working of his mighty strength, 20which he exerted in Christ when he raised him from the dead k and seated him at his right hand in the heavenly realms, 21far above all rule and authority, power and dominion, and every title / that can be given, not only in the present age but also in the one to come. 22And God placed all things under his feet and appointed him to be head m over everything for the church, 23which is his body, the fullness of him who fills everything in every way.

a 17 Or *a spirit*

LOCATION OF EPHESUS
Ephesus was a strategic city, ranking in importance with Alexandria in Egypt and Antioch in Syria as a port. It lay on the most western edge of Asia Minor (modern-day Turkey), the most important port on the Aegean Sea on the main route from Rome to the east.

about that person, but it won't enable you to actually *know* him. If you want to get to know someone, you have to spend time with that person; there is no shortcut. The same holds true with God. Reading the Bible, great works of theology, and devotional material is wonderful, but there is no substitute for knowing God personally. What about you? Do you really *know* God, or do you just know *about* him? The difference is in spending time with him. Study Jesus' life in the Gospels to see what he was like on earth two thousand years ago, and get to know him in prayer now. Personal knowledge of Christ will change your life.

1:18 The hope we have is not a vague feeling that the future will be positive, but it is complete assurance of certain victory through God. This complete certainty comes to us through the Holy Spirit who is working in us. For more on hope, see Romans 8:23, 24; Ephesians 4:4; Colossians 1:5; 1 Thessalonians 1:3; 1 Peter 3:15.

1:19, 20 The world fears the power of the atom, yet we belong to the God of the universe who not only created that atomic power but also raised Jesus Christ from the dead. God's incomparably great power is available to help you. There is nothing too difficult for him.

1:20–22 Having been raised from the dead, Christ is now the head of the church, the ultimate authority over the world. Jesus

is the Messiah, God's Anointed One, the One Israel longed for, the One who would set their broken world right. As Christians we can be confident that God has won the final victory and is in control of everything. We need not fear any dictator or nation, or even death or Satan himself. The contract has been signed and sealed; we are waiting just a short while for delivery. Paul says, in Romans 8:37–39, that nothing can separate us from God and his love.

1:22, 23 *Fullness* refers to Christ filling the church with gifts and blessings. The church should be the full expression of Christ, who himself fills everything (see 3:19). When reading Ephesians, it is important to remember that it was written primarily to the entire church, not merely to an individual. Christ is the head and we are the body of his church (Paul uses this metaphor in Romans 12:4, 5; 1 Corinthians 12:12–27; and Colossians 3:15 as well as throughout the book of Ephesians). The image of the body shows the church's unity. Each member is involved with all the others as they go about doing Christ's work on earth. We should not attempt to work, serve, or worship merely on our own. We need the entire body.

Made Alive in Christ

2 As for you, you were dead in your transgressions and sins, *n* 2 in which you used to live when you followed the ways of this world and of the ruler of the kingdom of the air, *o* the spirit who is now at work in those who are disobedient. *p* 3 All of us also lived among them at one time, gratifying the cravings of our sinful nature *a* *q* and following its desires and thoughts. Like the rest, we were by nature objects of wrath. 4 But because of his great love for us, God, who is rich in mercy, 5 made us alive with Christ even when we were dead in transgressions *r*—it is by grace you have been saved. 6 And God raised us up with Christ and seated us with him *s* in the heavenly realms in Christ Jesus, 7 in order that in the coming ages he might show the incomparable riches of his grace, expressed in his kindness *t* to us in Christ Jesus. 8 For it is by grace you have been saved, through faith—and this not from yourselves, it is the gift of God— 9 not by works, so that no one can boast. 10 For we are God's workmanship, created in Christ Jesus to do good works, which God prepared in advance for us to do.

2:1
n Col 2:13
2:2
o Eph 6:12
p Eph 5:6
2:3
q Gal 5:16
2:5
r ver 1
2:6
s Eph 1:20
2:7
t Tit 3:4

One in Christ

11 Therefore, remember that formerly you who are Gentiles by birth and called "uncircumcised" by those who call themselves "the circumcision" (that done in the body by the hands of men) *u*— 12 remember that at that time you were separate from Christ, excluded from citizenship in Israel and foreigners to the covenants of the promise, without hope and without God in the world. 13 But now in Christ Jesus you who once were far away have been brought near *v* through the blood of Christ.

2:11
u Col 2:11

2:13
v Ac 2:39

a 3 Or *our flesh*

2:1, 2 Immediately after his prayer, Paul reminds the Ephesians of the reality of personal sin. Like them, we must never forget our past, the condition from which Jesus saved us. Those memories are the best fuel for our gratitude to Christ for all he has done in our behalf.

2:2 Paul describes Satan, the devil, as "the ruler of the kingdom of the air." Paul's readers believed that Satan and the evil spiritual forces inhabited the region between earth and sky. Satan is thus pictured as ruling an evil spiritual kingdom—the demons and those who are against Christ. In the resurrection, Christ was victorious over Satan and his power. Therefore, Jesus Christ is the permanent ruler of the whole world; Satan is only the temporary ruler of the part of the world that chooses to follow him.

2:3 The fact that all people, without exception, commit sin proves that without Christ we have a sinful nature. We are lost in sin and cannot save ourselves. Does this mean only Christians do good? Of course not—many people do good to others. On a relative scale, many are moral, kind, and law-abiding. Comparing these people to criminals, we would say that they are very good indeed. But on God's absolute scale, *no one* is good enough to earn salvation ("you were dead in your transgressions and sins," 2:1). Only through being united with Christ's perfect life can we become good in God's sight. "Objects of wrath" refers to those who are to receive God's wrath because of their rejection of Christ.

2:4, 5 In the previous verses Paul wrote about our old sinful nature (2:1–3). Here Paul emphasizes that we do not need to live any longer under sin's power. The penalty of sin and its power over us were miraculously destroyed by Christ on the cross. Through faith in Christ we stand acquitted, or not guilty, before God (Romans 3:21, 22). God does not take us out of the world or make us robots—we will still feel like sinning, and sometimes we will sin. The difference is that before we became Christians, we were dead in sin and were slaves to our sinful nature. But now we are alive with Christ (see also Galatians 2:20).

2:6 Because of Christ's resurrection, we know that our bodies will also be raised from the dead (1 Corinthians 15:2–23) and that we have been given the power to live as Christians now (1:19). These ideas are combined in Paul's image of sitting with Christ in "the heavenly realms" (see the note on 1:3). Our eternal life with Christ is certain because we are united in his powerful victory.

2:8, 9 When someone gives you a gift, do you say, "That's very nice—now how much do I owe you?" No, the appropriate response to a gift is "Thank you." Yet how often Christians, even after they have been given the gift of salvation, feel obligated to try to work their way to God. Because our salvation and even our faith are gifts, we should respond with gratitude, praise, and joy.

2:8–10 We become Christians through God's unmerited grace, not as the result of any effort, ability, intelligent choice, or act of service on our part. However, out of gratitude for this free gift, we will seek to help and serve others with kindness, love, and gentleness, and not merely to please ourselves. While no action or work we do can help us obtain salvation, God's intention is that our salvation will result in acts of service. We are not saved merely for our own benefit but to serve Christ and build up the church (4:12).

2:10 We are God's workmanship (work of art, masterpiece). Our salvation is something only God can do. It is his powerful, creative work in us. If God considers us his works of art, we dare not treat ourselves or others with disrespect or as inferior work.

2:11–13 Pious Jews ("the circumcision") considered all non-Jews (the "uncircumcised") ceremonially unclean. They thought of themselves as pure and clean because of their national heritage and religious ceremonies. Paul pointed out that Jews and Gentiles alike were unclean before God and needed to be cleansed by Christ. In order to realize how great a gift salvation is, we need to remember our former natural, unclean condition. Have you ever felt separate, excluded, hopeless? These verses are for you. No one is alienated from Christ's love or from the body of believers.

2:11–13 Jews and Gentiles alike could be guilty of spiritual pride—Jews for thinking their faith and traditions elevated them above everyone else, Gentiles for trusting in their achievements, power, or position. Spiritual pride blinds us to our own faults and magnifies the faults of others. Be careful not to become proud of your salvation. Instead, humbly thank God for what he has done, and encourage others who might be struggling in their faith.

2:11–16 Before Christ's coming, Gentiles and Jews kept apart from one another. Jews considered Gentiles beyond God's saving power and therefore without hope. Gentiles resented Jewish claims. Christ revealed the total sinfulness of both Jews and Gentiles, and then he offered his salvation to both. Only Christ breaks down the walls of prejudice, reconciles all believers to God, and unifies us in one body.

2:15
w Col 1:21, 22

2:17
x Isa 57:19

2:18
y 1Co 12:13

2:19
z Php 3:20
a Gal 6:10

2:20
b Mt 16:18

¹⁴For he himself is our peace, who has made the two one and has destroyed the barrier, the dividing wall of hostility, ¹⁵by abolishing in his flesh w the law with its commandments and regulations. His purpose was to create in himself one new man out of the two, thus making peace, ¹⁶and in this one body to reconcile both of them to God through the cross, by which he put to death their hostility. ¹⁷He came and preached peace to you who were far away and peace to those who were near. x ¹⁸For through him we both have access to the Father by one Spirit. y

¹⁹Consequently, you are no longer foreigners and aliens, but fellow citizens z with God's people and members of God's household, a ²⁰built on the foundation b of the apostles and

---

OUR TRUE IDENTITY IN CHRIST

Romans 3:24	We are justified (declared "not guilty" of sin).
Romans 8:1	No condemnation awaits us.
Romans 8:2	We are set free from the law of sin that leads to death.
1 Corinthians 1:2	We are sanctified (made holy) and made acceptable in Jesus Christ.
1 Corinthians 1:30	We are righteous and holy in Christ.
1 Corinthians 15:22	We will be made alive at the resurrection.
2 Corinthians 5:17	We are new creations.
2 Corinthians 5:21	We receive God's righteousness.
Galatians 3:28	We are one in Christ with all other believers.
Ephesians 1:3	We are blessed with every spiritual blessing in Christ.
Ephesians 1:4	We are holy and blameless.
Ephesians 1:5, 6	We are adopted as God's children.
Ephesians 1:7	Our sins are taken away, and we are forgiven.
Ephesians 1:10, 11	We will be brought under Christ's authority.
Ephesians 1:13	We are identified as belonging to God by the Holy Spirit.
Ephesians 2:6	We have been raised up to sit with Christ in glory.
Ephesians 2:10	We are God's work of art.
Ephesians 2:13	We have been brought near to God.
Ephesians 3:6	We share in the promise of blessings through Christ.
Ephesians 3:12	We can come with freedom and confidence into God's presence.
Ephesians 5:29, 30	We are members of Christ's body, the church.
Colossians 2:10	We are made complete in Christ.
Colossians 2:11	We are set free from our sinful nature.
2 Timothy 2:10	We will have eternal glory.

2:14ff Christ has destroyed the barriers people build between themselves. Because these walls have been removed, we can have real unity with people who are not like us. This is true reconciliation. Because of Christ's death, we are all one (2:14); our hostility against each other has been put to death (2:16); we can all have access to the Father by the Holy Spirit (2:18); we are no longer foreigners or aliens to God (2:19); and we are all being built into a holy temple with Christ as our chief cornerstone (2:20, 21).

2:14–22 There are many barriers that can divide us from other Christians: age, appearance, intelligence, political persuasion, economic status, race, theological perspective. One of the best ways to stifle Christ's love is to be friendly with only those people that we like. Fortunately, Christ has knocked down the barriers and has unified all believers in one family. His cross should be the focus of our unity. The Holy Spirit helps us look beyond the barriers to the unity we are called to enjoy.

2:15 By his death, Christ ended the angry resentment between Jews and Gentiles, caused by the Jewish laws that favored the Jews and excluded the Gentiles. Christ died to abolish that whole system of Jewish laws. Then he took the two groups that had been opposed to each other and made them parts of himself. "One new man" means that Christ made a single entity or person

out of the two. Thus he fused all believers together to become one in himself.

2:17, 18 The Jews were near to God because they already knew of him through the Scriptures and worshiped him in their religious ceremonies. The Gentiles were far away because they knew little or nothing about God. Because neither group could be saved by good deeds, knowledge, or sincerity, both needed to hear about the salvation available through Jesus Christ. Both Jews and Gentiles are now free to come to God through Christ. You have been brought near to him (2:13).

2:19–22 A church building is sometimes called God's house. In reality, God's household is not a building, but a group of people. He lives in us and shows himself to a watching world through us. People can see that God is love and that Christ is Lord as we live in harmony with each other and in accordance with what God says in his Word. We are citizens of God's kingdom and members of his household.

2:20 What does it mean to be built on the foundation of the apostles and prophets? It means that the church is not built on modern ideas, but rather on the spiritual heritage given to us by the early apostles and prophets of the Christian church.

prophets, with Christ Jesus himself as the chief cornerstone. 21 In him the whole building is
joined together and rises to become a holy temple*c* in the Lord. 22 And in him you too are being built together to become a dwelling in which God lives by his Spirit.

2:21
c 1Co 3:16, 17

Paul the Preacher to the Gentiles

3 For this reason I, Paul, the prisoner*d* of Christ Jesus for the sake of you Gentiles—
2 Surely you have heard about the administration of God's grace that was given to me for
you, 3 that is, the mystery*e* made known to me by revelation,*f* as I have already written
briefly. 4 In reading this, then, you will be able to understand my insight into the mystery of
Christ, 5 which was not made known to men in other generations as it has now been revealed
by the Spirit to God's holy apostles and prophets.*g* 6 This mystery is that through the gospel
the Gentiles are heirs*h* together with Israel, members together of one body, and sharers together in the promise in Christ Jesus.

3:1
d Ac 23:18
3:3
e Ro 16:25
f 1Co 2:10
3:5
g Ro 16:26
3:6
h Gal 3:29

7 I became a servant of this gospel by the gift of God's grace given me through the working
of his power. 8 Although I am less than the least of all God's people,*i* this grace was given me:
to preach to the Gentiles the unsearchable riches of Christ, 9 and to make plain to everyone
the administration of this mystery, which for ages past was kept hidden in God, who created
all things. 10 His intent was that now, through the church, the manifold wisdom of God*j*
should be made known*k* to the rulers and authorities in the heavenly realms, 11 according to
his eternal purpose which he accomplished in Christ Jesus our Lord. 12 In him and through
faith in him we may approach God*l* with freedom and confidence.*m* 13 I ask you, therefore,
not to be discouraged because of my sufferings for you, which are your glory.

3:8
i 1Co 15:9
3:10
j 1Co 2:7
k 1Pe 1:12
3:12
l Eph 2:18
m Heb 4:16

A Prayer for the Ephesians

14 For this reason I kneel*n* before the Father, 15 from whom his whole family*a* in heaven
and on earth derives its name. 16 I pray that out of his glorious riches he may strengthen you

3:14
n Php 2:10

a 15 Or *whom all fatherhood*

3:1 Paul was under house arrest in Rome for preaching about
Christ. The religious leaders in Jerusalem, who felt threatened by
Christ's teachings and didn't believe he was the Messiah, pressured the Romans to arrest Paul and bring him to trial for treason
and for causing rebellion among the Jews. Paul had appealed for
his case to be heard by the emperor, and he was awaiting trial
(see Acts 28:16–31). Even though he was under arrest, Paul maintained his firm belief that God was in control of all that happened
to him. Do circumstances make you wonder if God has lost control of this world? Like Paul, remember that no matter what
happens, God directs the world's affairs.

3:2, 3 "The administration of God's grace" means the special
stewardship, trust, or commitment that Paul had been given. He
had been assigned the special work of preaching the Good News
to the Gentiles, God's great plan shown to Paul in a revelation.
"As I have already written briefly" may refer to a previous letter
that was not preserved by the church, or it may refer to an earlier
part of this letter (especially 1:9ff; 2:11ff).

3:5, 6 God's plan was hidden from previous generations, not
because God wanted to keep something from his people, but
because he would reveal it to everyone in his perfect timing.
God planned to have Jews and Gentiles comprise one body,
the church. It was known in the Old Testament that the Gentiles
would receive salvation (Isaiah 49:6); but it was never revealed
in the Old Testament that all Gentile and Jewish believers would
become equal in the body of Christ. Yet this equality was accomplished when Jesus destroyed the "dividing wall" and created
the "one new man" (2:14, 15).

3:7 When Paul became a servant of the gospel, God gave him
the ability to share the gospel of Christ effectively. You are not an
apostle, and you may not be an evangelist, but God will give you
opportunities to tell others about Christ. And with the opportunities he will provide the ability, courage, and power. Make yourself
available to God as his servant whenever an opportunity presents
itself. As you focus on the other person and his or her needs, God
will communicate your caring attitude. Your words will be natural,
loving, and compelling.

3:8 When Paul describes himself as "less than the least of all
God's people," he means that without God's help, he would
never be able to do God's work. Yet God chose him to share the
gospel with the Gentiles and gave him the power to do it. If we
feel that our role is minor, we may be right—except that we have
forgotten what a difference God makes. How does God want to
use you? Draw on his power, do your part, and faithfully perform
the special role God has called you to play in his plan.

3:9 "The administration of this mystery" refers to the way God's
great plan is carried out through the church and to Paul's work to
demonstrate and teach God's great purpose in Christ (see 3:2).

3:10 The "rulers and authorities in the heavenly realms" are
either angels who are witnesses to these events (see 1 Peter
1:12), or hostile spiritual forces opposed to God (2:2; 6:12).

3:12 It is an awesome privilege to be able to approach God with
freedom and confidence. Most of us would be apprehensive in
the presence of a powerful ruler. But thanks to Christ, by faith we
can enter directly into God's presence through prayer. We know
we'll be welcomed with open arms because we are God's children
through our union with Christ. Don't be afraid of God. Talk with
him about everything. He is waiting to hear from you.

3:13 Why should Paul's suffering make the Ephesians feel
honored ("which are your glory")? If Paul had not preached the
gospel, he would not be in jail—but then the Ephesians would
not have heard the Good News and been converted either. Just
as a mother endures the pain of childbirth in order to bring new
life into the world, Paul endured the pain of persecution in order
to bring new believers to Christ. Obeying Christ is never easy. He
calls you to take up your cross and follow him (Matthew 16:24)—
that is, to be willing to endure pain so that God's message of
salvation can reach the entire world. We should feel honored that
others have suffered and sacrificed for us so that we might reap
the benefit.

3:14, 15 The family of God includes all who have believed in
him in the past, all who believe in the present, and all who will
believe in the future. We are all a family because we have the
same Father. He is the source of all creation, the rightful owner

3:16
o Col 1:11
p Ro 7:22

3:19
q Eph 1:23

3:20
r Ro 16:25

3:21
s Ro 11:36

4:1
t Col 1:10

4:2
u Eph 1:4

4:3
v Col 3:14

4:6
w Ro 11:36

with power *o* through his Spirit in your inner being, *p* ¹⁷so that Christ may dwell in your hearts through faith. And I pray that you, being rooted and established in love, ¹⁸may have power, together with all the saints, to grasp how wide and long and high and deep is the love of Christ, ¹⁹and to know this love that surpasses knowledge—that you may be filled to the measure of all the fullness of God. *q*

²⁰Now to him who is able *r* to do immeasurably more than all we ask or imagine, according to his power that is at work within us, ²¹to him be glory in the church and in Christ Jesus throughout all generations, for ever and ever! Amen. *s*

2. Unity in the body of Christ

4 As a prisoner for the Lord, then, I urge you to live a life worthy *t* of the calling you have received. ²Be completely humble and gentle; be patient, bearing with one another in love. *u* ³Make every effort to keep the unity *v* of the Spirit through the bond of peace. ⁴There is one body and one Spirit—just as you were called to one hope when you were called— ⁵one Lord, one faith, one baptism; ⁶one God and Father of all, who is over all and through all and in all. *w*

OUR LIVES BEFORE AND AFTER CHRIST

Before	After
Dead in transgressions	Made alive with Christ
Objects of wrath	Shown God's mercy and given salvation
Followed the ways of the world	Stand for Christ and truth
God's enemies	God's children
Enslaved to Satan	Free in Christ to love, serve, and sit with him
Followed our evil thoughts and desires	Raised up with Christ to glory

---

of everything. God promises his love and power to his family, the church (3:16–21). If we want to receive God's blessings, it is important that we stay in contact with other believers in the body of Christ. Those who isolate themselves from God's family and try to go it alone cut themselves off from God's power.

3:17–19 God's love is total, says Paul. It reaches every corner of our experience. It is *wide*—it covers the breadth of our own experience, and it reaches out to the whole world. God's love is *long*—it continues the length of our lives. It is *high*—it rises to the heights of our celebration and elation. His love is *deep*—it reaches to the depths of discouragement, despair, and even death. When you feel shut out or isolated, remember that you can never be lost to God's love. For another prayer about God's immeasurable and inexhaustible love, see Paul's words in Romans 8:38, 39.

3:19 "The fullness of God" is expressed only in Christ (Colossians 2:9, 10). In union with Christ and through his empowering Spirit, we are complete. We have all the fullness of God available to us. But we must appropriate that fullness through faith and through prayer as we daily live for him. Paul's prayer for the Ephesians is also for you. You can ask the Holy Spirit to fill every aspect of your life to the fullest.

3:20, 21 This *doxology*—prayer of praise to God—ends Part One of Ephesians. In the first section, Paul described the timeless role of the church. In Part Two (chapters 4—6), he will explain how church members should live in order to bring about the unity God wants. As in most of his books, Paul first lays a doctrinal foundation and then makes practical applications of the truths he has presented.

4:1, 2 God has chosen us to be Christ's representatives on earth. In light of this truth, Paul challenges us to live lives worthy of the calling we have received—the awesome privilege of being called Christ's very own. This includes being humble, gentle, patient, understanding, and peaceful. People are watching your life. Can they see Christ in you? How well are you doing as his representative?

4:1–6 "There is one body," says Paul. Unity does not just happen; we have to work at it. Often differences among people can lead to division, but this should not be true in the church. Instead of concentrating on what divides us, we should remember what unites us: *one* body, *one* Spirit, *one* hope, *one* Lord, *one* faith, *one* baptism, *one* God! Have you learned to appreciate people who are different from you? Can you see how their differing gifts and viewpoints can help the church as it does God's work? Learn to enjoy the way we members of Christ's body complement one another. (See 1 Corinthians 12:12, 13 for more on this thought.)

4:2 No one is ever going to be perfect here on earth, so we must accept and love other Christians in spite of their faults. When we see faults in fellow believers, we should be patient and gentle. Is there someone whose actions or personality really annoys you? Rather than dwelling on that person's weaknesses or looking for faults, pray for him or her. Then do even more—spend time together and see if you can learn to like him or her.

4:3 To build unity is one of the Holy Spirit's important roles. He leads, but we have to be willing to be led and to do our part to keep the peace. We do that by focusing on God, not on ourselves. For more about who the Holy Spirit is and what he does, see the notes on John 3:6; Acts 1:5; and Ephesians 1:13, 14.

4:4–7 All believers in Christ belong to one body; all are united under one head, Christ himself (see 1 Corinthians 12:12–26). Each believer has God-given abilities that can strengthen the whole body. Your special ability may seem small or large, but it is yours to use in God's service. Ask God to use your unique gifts to contribute to the strength and health of the body of believers.

4:6 God is *over all*—this shows his overruling care (transcendence). He is *through all and in all*—this shows his active presence in the world and in the lives of believers (immanence). Any view of God that violates either his transcendence or his immanence does not paint a true picture of God.

7 But to each one of us grace has been given as Christ apportioned it. 8 This is why it[a] says:

> "When he ascended on high,
> he led captives in his train
> and gave gifts to men."[b][x]

4:8
[x]Ps 68:18

9 (What does "he ascended" mean except that he also descended to the lower, earthly regions[c]? 10 He who descended is the very one who ascended higher than all the heavens, in order to fill the whole universe.) 11 It was he who gave some to be apostles,[y] some to be prophets, and some to be evangelists, and some to be pastors and teachers, 12 to prepare God's people for works of service, so that the body of Christ[z] may be built up 13 until we all reach unity in the faith and in the knowledge of the Son of God and become mature, attaining to the whole measure of the fullness of Christ.

4:11
[y]1Co 12:28

4:12
[z]1Co 12:27

14 Then we will no longer be infants,[a] tossed back and forth by the waves, and blown here and there by every wind of teaching and by the cunning and craftiness of men in their deceitful scheming. 15 Instead, speaking the truth in love, we will in all things grow up into him who is the Head,[b] that is, Christ. 16 From him the whole body, joined and held together by every supporting ligament, grows and builds itself up in love, as each part does its work.

4:14
[a]1Co 14:20

4:15
[b]Eph 1:22

Living as Children of Light

17 So I tell you this, and insist on it in the Lord, that you must no longer live as the Gentiles do, in the futility of their thinking.[c] 18 They are darkened in their understanding and separated from the life of God because of the ignorance that is in them due to the hardening of their hearts. 19 Having lost all sensitivity,[d] they have given themselves over to sensuality so as to indulge in every kind of impurity, with a continual lust for more.

4:17
[c]Ro 1:21

4:19
[d]1Ti 4:2

[a]8 Or *God*   [b]8 Psalm 68:18   [c]9 Or *the depths of the earth*

4:8 In Psalm 68:18, God is pictured as a conqueror marching to the gates and taking tribute from the fallen city. Paul uses that picture to teach that Christ, in his crucifixion and resurrection, was victorious over Satan. When Christ ascended to heaven, he gave gifts to the church, some of which Paul discusses in 4:11–13.

4:9 The "lower, earthly regions" may be (1) the earth itself (lowly by comparison to heaven), (2) the grave, or (3) Hades (many believe Hades is the resting place of souls between death and resurrection). However we understand it, Christ is Lord of the whole universe, past, present, and future. Nothing or no one is hidden from him. The Lord of all came to earth and faced death to rescue all people. No one is beyond his reach.

4:11, 12 Our oneness in Christ does not destroy our individuality. The Holy Spirit has given each Christian special gifts for building up the church. Now that we have these gifts, it is crucial to use them. Are you spiritually mature, exercising the gifts God has given you? If you know what your gifts are, look for opportunities to serve. If you don't know, ask God to show you, perhaps with the help of your minister or Christian friends. Then, as you begin to recognize your special area of service, use your gifts to strengthen and encourage the church.

4:12, 13 God has given his church an enormous responsibility—to make disciples in every nation (Matthew 28:18–20). This involves preaching, teaching, healing, nurturing, giving, administering, building, and many other tasks. If we had to fulfill this command as individuals, we might as well give up without trying—it would be impossible. But God calls us as members of his body. Some of us can do one task; some can do another. Together we can obey God more fully than any of us could alone. It is a human tendency to overestimate what we can do by ourselves and to underestimate what we can do as a group. But as the body of Christ, we can accomplish more together than we would dream possible working by ourselves. Working together, the church can express the fullness of Christ (see the note on 3:19).

4:14–16 Christ is the truth (John 14:6), and the Holy Spirit who guides the church is the Spirit of truth (John 16:13). Satan, by contrast, is the father of lies (John 8:44). As followers of Christ, we must be committed to the truth. This means both that our words should be honest and that our actions should reflect

Christ's integrity. Speaking the truth in love is not always easy, convenient, or pleasant, but it is necessary if the church is going to do Christ's work in the world.

4:15 In describing the mature Christian, Paul says that one of the marks is "speaking the truth in love." This sounds so simple, but it seems so hard for us to do. Some of us are fairly good at speaking the truth, but we forget to be loving. Some of us are good at being loving, but we don't have it in us to level with others if the truth is painful. The instruction here is to do both: Speak the truth, but do it in a loving manner. Think of the trouble we would spare ourselves if we followed this practice, especially in the church! When you have a problem with another believer, don't go to someone else with it. Go directly to that person, and speak the truth in love.

4:15, 16 Some Christians fear that any mistake will destroy their witness for the Lord. They see their own weaknesses, and they know that many non-Christians seem to have stronger character than they do. How can we grow up into Christ? The answer is that Christ forms us into a body—into a group of individuals who are united in their purpose and in their love for one another and for the Lord. If an individual stumbles, the rest of the group is there to pick him or her up and help him or her walk with God again. If an individual sins, he or she can find restoration through the church (Galatians 6:1) even as the rest of the body continues to witness to God's truth. As part of Christ's body, do you reflect part of Christ's character and carry out your special role in his work?

4:17 Living "in the futility of their thinking" refers to the natural tendency of human beings to think their way away from God. Intellectual pride, rationalizations, and excuses all keep people from God. Don't be surprised if people can't grasp the gospel. The gospel will seem foolish to those who forsake faith and rely on their own understanding.

4:17–24 People should be able to see a difference between Christians and non-Christians because of the way Christians live. We are to live as children of light (5:8). Paul told the Ephesians to leave behind the old life of sin, since they were followers of Christ. Living the Christian life is a process. Although we have a new nature, we don't automatically think all good thoughts and express all right attitudes when we become new people in Christ. But if we keep listening to God, we will be changing all the time.

20You, however, did not come to know Christ that way. 21Surely you heard of him and were taught in him in accordance with the truth that is in Jesus. 22You were taught, with regard to your former way of life, to put off your old self, which is being corrupted by its deceitful desires; 23to be made new in the attitude of your minds;e 24and to put on the new self,f created to be like God in true righteousness and holiness.

25Therefore each of you must put off falsehood and speak truthfullyg to his neighbor, for we are all members of one body.h 26"In your anger do not sin"a: Do not let the sun go down while you are still angry, 27and do not give the devil a foothold. 28He who has been stealing must steal no longer, but must work,i doing something useful with his own hands, that he may have something to share with those in need.j

29Do not let any unwholesome talk come out of your mouths, but only what is helpful for building others up according to their needs, that it may benefit those who listen. 30And do not grieve the Holy Spirit of God,k with whom you were sealed for the day of redemption. 31Get rid of all bitterness, rage and anger, brawling and slander, along with every form of malice.l 32Be kind and compassionate to one another, forgiving each other, just as in Christ God forgave you.

5 Be imitators of God,m therefore, as dearly loved children 2and live a life of love, just as Christ loved us and gave himself up for us as a fragrant offering and sacrifice to God.n

3But among you there must not be even a hint of sexual immorality, or of any kind of impurity, or of greed, because these are improper for God's holy people. 4Nor should there

a26 Psalm 4:4

4:23 eCol 3:10
4:24 fRo 6:4
4:25 gZec 8:16 hRo 12:5
4:28 iAc 20:35 jLk 3:11
4:30 k1Th 5:19
4:31 lCol 3:8
5:1 mLk 6:36
5:2 n2Co 2:15

THE ONENESS OF ALL BELIEVERS

Believers are one in	Our unity is experienced in
Body	The fellowship of believers—the church
Spirit	The Holy Spirit, who activates the fellowship
Hope	That glorious future to which we are all called
Lord	Christ, to whom we all belong
Faith	Our singular commitment to Christ
Baptism	Baptism—the sign of entry into the church
God	God, who is our Father who keeps us for eternity

Too often believers are separated because of minor differences in doctrine. But Paul here shows those areas where Christians must agree to attain true unity. When believers have this unity of spirit, petty differences should never be allowed to dissolve that unity.

As you look back over last year, do you see a process of change for the better in your thoughts, attitudes, and actions? Although change may be slow, it comes as you trust God to change you. For more about our new nature as believers, see Romans 6:6; 8:9; Galatians 5:16–26; Colossians 3:3–8.

4:22-24 Our old way of life before we believed in Christ is completely in the past. We should put it behind us like old clothes to be thrown away. This is both a once-for-all decision when we decide to accept Christ's gift of salvation (2:8–10) and also a daily conscious commitment. We are not to be driven by desire and impulse. We must put on the new role, head in the new direction, and have the new way of thinking that the Holy Spirit gives.

4:25 Lying to each other disrupts unity by creating conflicts and destroying trust. It tears down relationships and leads to open warfare in a church.

4:26, 27 The Bible doesn't tell us that we shouldn't feel angry, but it points out that it is important to handle our anger properly. If vented thoughtlessly, anger can hurt others and destroy relationships. If bottled up inside, it can cause us to become bitter and destroy us from within. Paul tells us to deal with our anger immediately in a way that builds relationships rather than destroys them. If we nurse our anger, we will give Satan an opportunity to divide us. Are you angry with someone right now? What can you do to resolve your differences? Don't let the day end before you begin to work on mending your relationship.

4:28-32 We can grieve the Holy Spirit by the way we live. Paul warns us against unwholesome language, bitterness, improper use of anger, brawling, slander, and bad attitudes toward others. Instead of acting that way, we should be forgiving, just as God has forgiven us. Are you grieving or pleasing God with your attitudes and actions? Act in love toward your brothers and sisters in Christ, just as God acted in love by sending his Son to die for your sins.

4:30 The Holy Spirit within us is a seal or guarantee that we belong to God. For more on this thought, see the note on 1:13, 14.

4:32 This is Christ's law of forgiveness as taught in the Gospels (Matthew 6:14, 15; 18:35; Mark 11:25). We also see it in the Lord's Prayer—"Forgive us our debts, as we also have forgiven our debtors" (Luke 11:4). God does not forgive us *because* we forgive others, but solely because of his great mercy. As we come to understand his mercy, however, we will want to be like him. Having received forgiveness, we will pass it on to others. Those who are unwilling to forgive have not become one with Christ, who was willing to forgive even those who crucified him (Luke 23:34).

5:1, 2 Just as children imitate their parents, we should imitate Christ. His great love for us led him to sacrifice himself so that we might live. Our love for others should be of the same kind—a love that goes beyond affection to self-sacrificing service.

5:4 Obscenity and coarse joking are so common that we begin to take them for granted. Paul cautions, however, that improper language should have no place in the Christian's conversation because it does not reflect God's gracious presence in us. How can we praise God and remind others of his goodness when we are speaking coarsely?

be obscenity, foolish talk or coarse joking, which are out of place, but rather thanksgiving. ⁵For of this you can be sure: No immoral, impure or greedy person—such a man is an idolater°—has any inheritance in the kingdom of Christ and of God.ᵃᵖ ⁶Let no one deceive you with empty words, for because of such things God's wrathᑫ comes on those who are disobedient. ⁷Therefore do not be partners with them.

⁸For you were once darkness, but now you are light in the Lord. Live as children of lightʳ ⁹(for the fruitˢ of the light consists in all goodness, righteousness and truth) ¹⁰and find out what pleases the Lord. ¹¹Have nothing to do with the fruitless deeds of darkness, but rather expose them. ¹²For it is shameful even to mention what the disobedient do in secret. ¹³But everything exposed by the light becomes visible, ¹⁴for it is light that makes everything visible. This is why it is said:

> "Wake up, O sleeper,
>   rise from the dead,
> and Christ will shine on you."ᵗ

¹⁵Be very careful, then, how you live—not as unwise but as wise, ¹⁶making the most of every opportunity,ᵘ because the days are evil. ¹⁷Therefore do not be foolish, but understand what the Lord's will is.ᵛ ¹⁸Do not get drunk on wine,ʷ which leads to debauchery. Instead, be filled with the Spirit. ¹⁹Speak to one another with psalms, hymns and spiritual songs.ˣ Sing and make music in your heart to the Lord, ²⁰always giving thanks to God the Father for everything, in the name of our Lord Jesus Christ.

²¹Submit to one another out of reverence for Christ.

ᵃ5 Or kingdom of the Christ and God

5:5
°Col 3:5
ᵖ1Co 6:9
5:6
ᑫRo 1:18
5:8
ʳLk 16:8
5:9
ˢGal 5:22
5:14
ᵗIsa 60:1
5:16
ᵘCol 4:5
5:17
ᵛRo 12:2; 1Th 4:3
5:18
ʷPr 20:1
5:19
ˣAc 16:25

5:5-7 Paul does not forbid all contact with unbelievers. Jesus taught his followers to befriend sinners and lead them to him (Luke 5:30–32). Instead, Paul writes against the lifestyle of people who make excuses for bad behavior and recommend its practice to others—whether they are in the church or outside of it. Such people quickly pollute the church and endanger its unity and purpose. We must befriend unbelievers if we are to lead them to Christ, but we must be wary of those who are viciously evil, immoral, or opposed to all that Christianity stands for. Such people are more likely to influence us for evil than we are to influence them for good.

5:8 As people who have light from the Lord, your actions should reflect your faith. You should live above reproach morally so that you will reflect God's goodness to others. Jesus stressed this truth in the Sermon on the Mount (Matthew 5:15, 16).

5:10-14 It is important to avoid the "fruitless deeds of darkness" (any pleasure or activity that results in sin), but we must go even further. Paul instructs us to expose these deeds, because our silence may be interpreted as approval. God needs people who will take a stand for what is right. Christians must lovingly speak out for what is true and right.

5:14 This is not a direct quote from Scripture but was probably taken from a hymn well known to the Ephesians. The hymn seems to have been based on Isaiah 26:19; 51:17; 52:1; 60:1; and Malachi 4:2. Paul was appealing to the Ephesians to wake up and realize the dangerous condition into which some of them had been slipping.

5:15, 16 By saying, "the days are evil," Paul was communicating his sense of urgency because of evil's pervasiveness. We need the same sense of urgency because our days are also difficult. We must keep our standards high, act wisely, and do good whenever we can.

5:18 Paul contrasts getting drunk with wine, which produces a temporary "high," to being filled with the Spirit, which produces lasting joy. Getting drunk with wine is associated with the old way of life and its selfish desires. In Christ, we have a better joy, higher and longer lasting, to cure our depression, monotony, or tension. We should not be concerned with how much of the Holy Spirit we have, but how much of us the Holy Spirit has. Submit yourself daily to his leading and draw constantly on his power.

5:18, 19 The effects of alcohol are obvious, but what happens when we are under the influence of the Holy Spirit? In these verses, Paul lists three by-products of the Spirit's influence in our lives: singing, making music, and giving thanks. Paul did not intend to suggest that believers only discuss religious matters, but that whatever we do or say should be permeated with an attitude of joy, thankfulness to God, and encouragement of others. Instead of whining and complaining—which our culture has raised to an art form—we are to focus on the goodness of God and his mercies toward us. How would others characterize your words and attitudes?

5:20 When you feel down, you may find it difficult to give thanks. Take heart—in all things God works for our good if we love him and are called according to his purpose (Romans 8:28). Thank God, not for your problems, but for the strength he is building in you through the difficult experiences of your life. You can be sure that God's perfect love will see you through.

5:21, 22 Submitting to another person is an often misunderstood concept. It does not mean becoming a doormat. Christ—at whose name "every knee should bow, in heaven and on earth and under the earth" (Philippians 2:10)—submitted his will to the Father, and we honor Christ by following his example. When we submit to God, we become more willing to obey his command to submit to others, that is, to subordinate our rights to theirs. In a marriage relationship, both husband and wife are called to submit. For the wife, this means willingly following her husband's leadership in Christ. For the husband, it means putting aside his own interests in order to care for his wife. Submission is rarely a problem in homes where both partners have a strong relationship with Christ and where each is concerned for the happiness of the other.

Wives and Husbands

5:22
y Eph 6:5

5:23
z 1Co 11:3

5:25
a Col 3:19

5:27
b Col 1:22

5:31
c Mt 19:5

22 Wives, submit to your husbands as to the Lord. *y* 23 For the husband is the head of the wife as Christ is the head of the church, *z* his body, of which he is the Savior. 24 Now as the church submits to Christ, so also wives should submit to their husbands in everything.

25 Husbands, love your wives, *a* just as Christ loved the church and gave himself up for her 26 to make her holy, cleansing *a* her by the washing with water through the word, 27 and to present her to himself as a radiant church, without stain or wrinkle or any other blemish, but holy and blameless. *b* 28 In this same way, husbands ought to love their wives as their own bodies. He who loves his wife loves himself. 29 After all, no one ever hated his own body, but he feeds and cares for it, just as Christ does the church— 30 for we are members of his body. 31 "For this reason a man will leave his father and mother and be united to his wife, and the two will become one flesh." *b c* 32 This is a profound mystery—but I am talking about Christ and the church. 33 However, each one of you also must love his wife as he loves himself, and the wife must respect her husband.

Children and Parents

6:1
d Col 3:20

6 Children, obey your parents in the Lord, for this is right. *d* 2 "Honor your father and mother"—which is the first commandment with a promise— 3 "that it may go well with you and that you may enjoy long life on the earth." *c*

a 26 Or *having cleansed* *b* 31 Gen. 2:24 *c* 3 Deut. 5:16

5:22–24 In Paul's day, women, children, and slaves were to submit to the head of the family—slaves would submit until they were freed, male children until they grew up, and women and girls their whole lives. Paul emphasized the equality of all believers in Christ (Galatians 3:28), but he did not suggest overthrowing Roman society to achieve it. Instead, he counseled all believers to submit to one another by choice—wives to husbands and also husbands to wives; slaves to masters and also masters to slaves; children to parents and also parents to children. This kind of mutual submission preserves order and harmony in the family while it increases love and respect among family members.

5:22–24 Although some people have distorted Paul's teaching on submission by giving unlimited authority to husbands, we cannot get around it—Paul told wives to submit to their husbands. The fact that a teaching is not popular is no reason to discard it. One way to disarm the antagonism that the external culture may inject into the marriage relationship is to remember that the wife gets to submit and the husband gets to die. According to the Bible, the man is the spiritual head of the family, and his wife should acknowledge his leadership. But real spiritual leadership involves loving service (a form of dying). Just as Christ served the disciples, even to the point of washing their feet, so the husband is to serve his wife. A wise and Christ-honoring husband will not take advantage of his leadership role, and a wise and Christ-honoring wife will not try to undermine her husband's leadership. Either approach causes disunity and friction in marriage.

5:22–28 Why did Paul tell wives to submit and husbands to love? Perhaps Christian women, newly freed in Christ, found submission difficult; perhaps Christian men, used to the Roman custom of giving unlimited power to the head of the family, were not used to treating their wives with respect and love. Of course both husbands and wives should submit to each other (5:21), just as both should love each other.

5:25ff Some Christians have thought that Paul was negative about marriage because of the counsel he gave in 1 Corinthians 7:32–38. These verses in Ephesians, however, show a high view of marriage. Here marriage is not a practical necessity or a cure for lust, but a picture of the relationship between Christ and his church! Why the apparent difference? Paul's counsel in 1 Corinthians was designed for a state of emergency during a time of persecution and crisis. Paul's counsel to the Ephesians is more the Biblical ideal for marriage. Marriage, for Paul, is a holy union, a living symbol, a precious relationship that needs tender, self-sacrificing care.

5:25–30 Paul devotes twice as many words to telling husbands to love their wives as to telling wives to submit to their husbands. How should a man love his wife? (1) He should be willing to sacrifice everything for her. (2) He should make her well-being of primary importance. (3) He should care for her as he cares for his own body. No wife needs to fear submitting to a man who treats her in this way.

5:26, 27 Christ's death sanctifies and cleanses the church. He cleanses us from the old ways of sin and sets us apart for his special sacred service (Hebrews 10:29; 13:12). Christ cleansed the church by the "washing" of baptism. Through baptism we are prepared for entrance into the church just as ancient Near Eastern brides were prepared for marriage by a ceremonial bath. It is God's Word that cleanses us (John 17:17; Titus 3:5).

5:31–33 The union of husband and wife merges two persons in such a way that little can affect one without also affecting the other. Oneness in marriage does not mean losing your personality in the personality of the other. Instead, it means caring for your spouse as you care for yourself, learning to anticipate his or her needs, helping the other person become all he or she can be. The creation story tells of God's plan that husband and wife should be one (Genesis 2:24), and Jesus also referred to this plan (Matthew 19:4–6).

6:1, 2 There is a difference between obeying and honoring. To obey means to do as one is told; to honor means to respect and love. Children are not commanded to disobey God in obeying their parents. Adult children are not asked to be subservient to domineering parents. Children are to obey while under their parents' care, but the responsibility to honor parents is for life.

6:1–4 If our faith in Christ is real, it will usually prove itself at home, in our relationships with those who know us best. Children and parents have a responsibility to each other. Children should honor their parents even if the parents are demanding and unfair. Parents should care gently for their children, even if the children are disobedient and unpleasant. Ideally, of course, Christian parents and Christian children will relate to each other with thoughtfulness and love. This will happen if both parents and children put the others' interests above their own—that is, if they submit to one another.

6:3 Some societies honor their elders. They respect their wisdom, defer to their authority, and pay attention to their comfort and happiness. This is how Christians should act. Where elders are respected, long life is a blessing, not a burden to them.

4 Fathers, do not exasperate your children;*e* instead, bring them up in the training and instruction of the Lord.*f*

Slaves and Masters

5 Slaves, obey your earthly masters with respect*g* and fear, and with sincerity of heart,*h* just as you would obey Christ. 6 Obey them not only to win their favor when their eye is on you, but like slaves of Christ, doing the will of God from your heart. 7 Serve wholeheartedly, as if you were serving the Lord, not men, 8 because you know that the Lord will reward everyone for whatever good he does, whether he is slave or free.

9 And masters, treat your slaves in the same way. Do not threaten them, since you know that he who is both their Master and yours is in heaven, and there is no favoritism with him.

The Armor of God

10 Finally, be strong in the Lord and in his mighty power. 11 Put on the full armor of God so that you can take your stand against the devil's schemes. 12 For our struggle is not against flesh and blood, but against the rulers, against the authorities, against the powers*i* of this dark world and against the spiritual forces of evil in the heavenly realms. 13 Therefore put on the full armor of God, so that when the day of evil comes, you may be able to stand your ground, and after you have done everything, to stand. 14 Stand firm then, with the belt of truth buckled around your waist,*j* with the breastplate of righteousness in place,*k* 15 and with your feet fitted with the readiness that comes from the gospel of peace.*l* 16 In addition to all this, take up the shield of faith, with which you can extinguish all the flaming arrows of the evil one. 17 Take the helmet of salvation and the sword of the Spirit, which is the word of God.*m* 18 And pray in the Spirit on all occasions*n* with all kinds of prayers and requests. With this in mind, be alert and always keep on praying for all the saints.

19 Pray also for me, that whenever I open my mouth, words may be given me so that I will fearlessly*o* make known the mystery of the gospel, 20 for which I am an ambassador*p* in chains. Pray that I may declare it fearlessly, as I should.

6:4 *e* Col 3:21
f Ge 18:19

6:5 *g* 1Ti 6:1
h Col 3:22

6:12 *i* Ro 8:38

6:14 *j* Isa 11:5
k Isa 59:17

6:15 *l* Isa 52:7

6:17 *m* Heb 4:12

6:18 *n* Lk 18:1

6:19 *o* 2Co 3:12

6:20 *p* 2Co 5:20

6:4 The purpose of parental discipline is to help children grow, not to exasperate and provoke them to anger or discouragement (see also Colossians 3:21). Parenting is not easy—it takes lots of patience to raise children in a loving, Christ-honoring manner. But frustration and anger should not be causes for discipline. Instead, parents should act in love, treating their children as Jesus treats the people he loves. This is vital to children's development and to their understanding of what Christ is like.

6:5 Slaves played a significant part in this society. There were several million of them in the Roman empire at this time. Because many slaves and owners had become Christians, the early church had to deal straightforwardly with the question of master/slave relations. Paul's statement neither condemns nor condones slavery. Instead, it tells masters and slaves how to live together in Christian households. In Paul's day, women, children, and slaves had few rights. In the church, however, they had freedoms that society denied them. Paul tells husbands, parents, and masters to be caring.

6:6–8 Paul's instructions encourage responsibility and integrity on the job. Christian employees should do their jobs as if Jesus Christ were their supervisor. And Christian employers should treat their employees fairly and with respect. Can you be trusted to do your best, even when the boss is not around? Do you work hard and with enthusiasm? Do you treat your employees as people, not machines? Remember that no matter whom you work for, and no matter who works for you, the One you ultimately should want to please is your Father in heaven.

6:9 Although Christians may be at different levels in earthly society, we are all equal before God. He does not play favorites; no one is more important than anyone else. Paul's letter to Philemon stresses the same point: Philemon, the master, and Onesimus, his slave, were brothers in Christ.

6:10–17 In the Christian life we battle against rulers and authorities (the powerful evil forces of fallen angels headed by Satan, who is a vicious fighter, see 1 Peter 5:8). To withstand their attacks, we must depend on God's strength and use every piece of his armor. Paul is not only giving this counsel to the church, the body of Christ, but to all individuals within the church. The whole body needs to be armed. As you do battle against "the powers of this dark world," fight in the strength of the church, whose power comes from the Holy Spirit.

6:12 These who are not "flesh and blood" are demons over whom Satan has control. They are not mere fantasies—they are very real. We face a powerful army whose goal is to defeat Christ's church. When we believe in Christ, these beings become our enemies, and they try every device to turn us away from him and back to sin. Although we are assured of victory, we must engage in the struggle until Christ returns, because Satan is constantly battling against all who are on the Lord's side. We need supernatural power to defeat Satan, and God has provided this by giving us his Holy Spirit within us and his armor surrounding us. If you feel discouraged, remember Jesus' words to Peter: "On this rock I will build my church, and the gates of Hades will not overcome it" (Matthew 16:18).

6:18 How can anyone pray on all occasions? One way is to make quick, brief prayers your habitual response to every situation you meet throughout the day. Another way is to order your life around God's desires and teachings so that your very life becomes a prayer. You don't have to isolate yourself from other people and from daily work in order to pray constantly. You can make prayer your life and your life a prayer while living in a world that needs God's powerful influence. "Praying for all the saints" means praying for all believers in Christ; so pray for the Christians you know and for the church around the world.

6:19, 20 Undiscouraged and undefeated, Paul wrote powerful letters of encouragement from prison. Paul did not ask the Ephesians to pray that his chains would be removed, but that he would continue to speak fearlessly for Christ in spite of them. God can use us in any circumstance to do his will. Even as we pray for a change in our circumstances, we should also pray that God will

Final Greetings

6:21
q Ac 20:4

21 Tychicus, q the dear brother and faithful servant in the Lord, will tell you everything, so that you also may know how I am and what I am doing. 22 I am sending him to you for this very purpose, that you may know how we are, and that he may encourage you.

6:23
r 1 Pe 5:14

23 Peace r to the brothers, and love with faith from God the Father and the Lord Jesus Christ. 24 Grace to all who love our Lord Jesus Christ with an undying love.

GOD'S ARMOR FOR US	Piece of Armor	Use	Application
We are engaged in a spiritual battle—all believers find themselves subject to the devil's attacks because they are no longer on the devil's side. Thus, Paul tells us to use *every piece* of God's armor to resist the devil's attacks and to stand true to God in the midst of those attacks.	Belt	Truth	Satan fights with lies, and sometimes his lies *sound* like truth; but only believers have God's truth, which can defeat Satan's lies.
	Breastplate	Righteousness	The devil often attacks our heart—the seat of our emotions, self-worth, and trust. God's righteousness is the breastplate that protects our heart and ensures his approval. He approves of us because he loves us and sent his Son to die for us.
	Footgear	Readiness to spread the Good News	Satan wants us to think that telling others the Good News is a worthless and hopeless task—the size of the task is too big and the negative responses are too much to handle. But the footgear God gives us is the motivation to continue to proclaim the true peace that is available in God—news everyone needs to hear.
	Shield	Faith	What *we* see are Satan's attacks in the form of insults, setbacks, and temptations. But the shield of faith protects us from Satan's flaming arrows. With God's perspective, we can see beyond our circumstances and know that ultimate victory is ours.
	Helmet	Salvation	Satan wants to make us doubt God, Jesus, and our salvation. The helmet protects our mind from doubting God's saving work for us.
	Sword	Word of God	The sword is the only weapon of *offense* in this list of armor. There are times when we need to take the offensive against Satan. When we are tempted, we need to trust in the truth of God's Word.

accomplish his plan through us right where we are. Knowing God's eternal purpose for us will help us through the difficult times.

6:21 Tychicus is also mentioned in Acts 20:4, Colossians 4:7, 2 Timothy 4:12, and Titus 3:12.

6:24 This letter was written to the church at Ephesus, but it was also meant for circulation among other churches. In this letter, Paul highlights the supremacy of Christ, gives information on both the nature of the church and on how church members

should live, and stresses the unity of all believers—male, female, parent, child, master, slave—regardless of sex, nationality, or social rank. The home and the church are difficult places to live the Christian life, because our real self comes through to those who know us well. Close relationships between imperfect people can lead to trouble—or to increased faith and deepened dependence on God. We can build unity in our churches through willing submission to Christ's leadership and humble service to one another.

PHILIPPIANS

VITAL STATISTICS

PURPOSE:
To thank the Philippians for the gift they had sent Paul and to strengthen these believers by showing them that true joy comes from Jesus Christ alone

AUTHOR:
Paul

ORIGINAL AUDIENCE:
The Christians at Philippi

DATE WRITTEN:
Approximately A.D. 61, from Rome during Paul's imprisonment there

SETTING:
Paul and his companions began the church at Philippi on his second missionary journey (Acts 16:11–40). This was the first church established on the European continent. The Philippian church had sent a gift with Epaphroditus (one of their members) to be delivered to Paul (4:18). Paul was in a Roman prison at the time. He wrote this letter to thank them for their gift and to encourage them in their faith.

KEY VERSE:
"Rejoice in the Lord always, I will say it again: Rejoice!" (4:4)

KEY PEOPLE:
Paul, Timothy, Epaphroditus, Euodia, and Syntyche

KEY PLACE:
Philippi

THE WORD *happiness* evokes visions of unwrapping gifts on Christmas morning, strolling hand in hand with the one you love, being surprised on your birthday, responding with unbridled laughter to a comedian, or vacationing in an exotic locale. Everyone wants to be happy; we make chasing this elusive ideal a lifelong pursuit: spending money, collecting things, and searching for new experiences. But if happiness depends on our circumstances, what happens when the toys rust, loved ones die, health deteriorates, money is stolen, and the party's over? Often happiness flees and despair sets in.

In contrast to *happiness* stands *joy*. Running deeper and stronger, joy is the quiet, confident assurance of God's love and work in our lives—that he will be there no matter what! Happiness depends on happenings, but joy depends on Christ.

Philippians is Paul's joy letter. The church in that Macedonian city had been a great encouragement to Paul. The Philippian believers had enjoyed a very special relationship with him, so he wrote them a personal expression of his love and affection. They had brought him great joy (4:1). Philippians is also a joyful book because it emphasizes the real joy of the Christian life. The concept of *rejoicing* or *joy* appears sixteen times in four chapters, and the pages radiate this positive message, culminating in the exhortation to "Rejoice in the Lord always, I will say it again: Rejoice!" (4:4).

In a life dedicated to serving Christ, Paul had faced excruciating poverty, abundant wealth, and everything in between. He even wrote this joyful letter from prison. Whatever the circumstances, Paul had learned to be content (4:11, 12), finding real joy as he focused all of his attention and energy on knowing Christ (3:8) and obeying him (3:12, 13).

Paul's desire to know Christ above all else is wonderfully expressed in the following words: "What is more, I consider everything a loss compared to the surpassing greatness of knowing Christ Jesus my Lord, for whose sake I have lost all things. I consider them rubbish, that I may gain Christ and be found in him. . . . I want to know Christ and the power of his resurrection and the fellowship of sharing in his sufferings, becoming like him in his death" (3:8–10). May we share Paul's aspiration and seek to know Jesus Christ more and more. Rejoice with Paul in Philippians, and rededicate yourself to finding joy in Christ.

THE BLUEPRINT

1. Joy in suffering (1:1–30)
2. Joy in serving (2:1–30)
3. Joy in believing (3:1—4:1)
4. Joy in giving (4:2–23)

Although Paul was writing from prison, joy is a dominant theme in this letter. The secret of his joy is grounded in his relationship with Christ. People today desperately want to be happy but are tossed and turned by daily successes, failures, and inconveniences. Christians are to be joyful in every circumstance, even when things are going badly, even when we feel like complaining, even when no one else is joyful. Christ still reigns, and we still know him, so we can rejoice at all times.

MEGATHEMES

THEME	EXPLANATION	IMPORTANCE
Humility	Christ showed true humility when he laid aside his rights and privileges as God to become human. He poured out his life to pay the penalty we deserve. Laying aside self-interest is essential to all our relationships.	We are to take Christ's attitude in serving others. We must renounce personal recognition and merit. When we give up our self-interest, we can serve with joy, love, and kindness.
Self-Sacrifice	Christ suffered and died so we might have eternal life. With courage and faithfulness, Paul sacrificed himself for the ministry. He preached the gospel even while he was in prison.	Christ gives us power to lay aside our personal needs and concerns. To utilize his power, we must imitate those leaders who show self-denying concern for others. We dare not be self-centered.
Unity	In every church, in every generation, there are divisive influences (issues, loyalties, and conflicts). In the midst of hardships, it is easy to turn on one another. Paul encouraged the Philippians to agree with one another, stop complaining, and work together.	As believers, we should not contend with one another but unite against a mutual enemy. When we are unified in love, Christ's strength is most abundant. Keep before you the ideals of teamwork, consideration of others, and unselfishness.
Christian Living	Paul shows us how to live successful Christian lives. We can become mature by being so identified with Christ that his attitude of humility and self-sacrifice becomes ours. Christ is both our source of power and our guide.	Developing our character begins with God's work in us. But growth also requires self-discipline, obedience to God's Word, and concentration on our part.
Joy	Believers can have profound contentment, serenity, and peace no matter what happens. This joy comes from knowing Christ personally and from depending on his strength rather than our own.	We can have joy, even in hardship. Joy does not come from outward circumstances but from inward strength. As Christians, we must not rely on what we have or what we experience to give us joy but on Christ within us.

1. Joy in suffering

1:1
a Ac 16:1

1 Paul and Timothy,*a* servants of Christ Jesus,

To all the saints in Christ Jesus at Philippi, together with the overseers*a* and deacons:

²Grace and peace to you from God our Father and the Lord Jesus Christ.

a 1 Traditionally bishops

1:1 This is a personal letter to the Philippians, not intended for general circulation to all the churches as was the letter to the Ephesians. Paul wanted to thank the believers for helping him when he had a need. He also wanted to tell them why he could be full of joy despite his imprisonment and upcoming trial. In this uplifting letter, Paul counseled the Philippians about humility and unity and warned them about potential problems.

1:1 On Paul's first missionary journey, he visited towns close to his headquarters in Antioch of Syria. On his second and third journeys, he traveled farther away. Because of the great distance between the congregations that Paul had founded, he could no longer personally oversee them all. Thus he was compelled to write letters to teach and encourage the believers. Fortunately, Paul had a staff of volunteers (including Timothy, Mark, and Epaphras) who personally delivered these letters and often remained with the congregations for a while to teach and encourage them.

1:1 For more information on Paul, see his Profile in Acts 9, p. XXX. Timothy's Profile is found in 1 Timothy 6, p. XXX.

1:1 The Roman colony of Philippi was located in northern Greece (called Macedonia in Paul's day). Philip II of Macedon (the father of Alexander the Great) took the town from ancient Thrace in about 357 B.C., enlarged and strengthened it, and gave it his name. This thriving commercial center sat at the crossroads between Europe and Asia. In about A.D. 50, Paul, Silas, Timothy, and Luke crossed the Aegean Sea from Asia Minor and landed at Philippi (Acts 16:11–40). The church in Philippi consisted mostly of Gentile (non-Jewish) believers. Because they were not familiar with the Old Testament, Paul did not specifically quote any Old Testament passages in this letter.

1:1 Overseers (bishops or pastors) and deacons led the early Christian churches. The qualifications and duties of the overseers are explained in detail in 1 Timothy 3:1–7 and Titus 1:5–9. The qualifications and duties of deacons are spelled out in 1 Timothy 3:8–13. The saints are all those who believe in Christ.

1:2 We get upset at children who fail to appreciate small gifts, yet we undervalue God's immeasurable gifts of grace and peace. Instead, we seek the possessions and shallow experiences the world offers. Compared to the big and bright "packages" of our

Thanksgiving and Prayer

3 I thank my God every time I remember you. 4 In all my prayers for all of you, I always pray *b* with joy 5 because of your partnership *c* in the gospel from the first day *d* until now, 6 being confident of this, that he who began a good work in you will carry it on to completion until the day of Christ Jesus.

7 It is right *e* for me to feel this way about all of you, since I have you in my heart; for whether I am in chains or defending and confirming the gospel, all of you share in God's grace with me. 8 God can testify *f* how I long for all of you with the affection of Christ Jesus.

1:4
b Ro 1:10

1:5
c Ac 2:42
d Ac 16:12-40

1:7
e 2Pe 1:13

1:8
f Ro 1:9

LOCATION OF PHILIPPI
Philippi sat on the Egnatian Way, the main transportation route in Macedonia, an extension of the Appian Way, which joined the eastern empire with Italy.

culture, grace and peace appear insignificant. But when we unwrap them, we discover God's wonderful personal dealings with us. Inside the tiny package marked "grace and peace," we find an inexhaustible treasure of God's daily presence in our lives. Using these two words in his greetings to all the churches to whom he wrote, Paul wasn't offering something new. He was reminding his readers of what they already possessed in Christ. Thank God for his grace, and live in his peace.

1:4 This is the first of many times Paul used the word *joy* in this letter. The Philippians were remembered with joy and thanksgiving whenever Paul prayed. By helping Paul, they were helping Christ's cause. The Philippians were willing to be used by God for whatever he wanted them to do. When others think about you, what comes to their minds? Are you remembered with joy by them? Do your acts of kindness lift up others?

1:4, 5 The Philippians first heard the gospel about ten years earlier when Paul and his companions visited Philippi (during Paul's second missionary journey) and founded the church there.

1:5 When Paul said that the Philippians were partners in spreading the gospel, he was remembering how they contributed through their practical help when Paul was in Philippi, and through their financial support when he was in prison. As we help our ministers, missionaries, and evangelists through prayer, hospitality, and financial donations, we become partners with them in spreading the gospel message.

1:6 The God who began a good work in us continues it throughout our lifetime and will finish it when we meet him face-to-face. God's work *for* us began when Christ died on the cross in our

place. His work *in* us began when we first believed. Now the Holy Spirit lives in us, enabling us to be more like Christ every day. Paul is describing the process of Christian growth and maturity that began when we accepted Jesus and continues until Christ returns.

1:6 Do you sometimes feel as though you aren't making progress in your spiritual life? When God starts a project, he completes it! As with the Philippians, God will help you grow in grace until he has completed his work in your life. When you are discouraged, remember that God won't give up on you. He promises to finish the work he has begun. When you feel incomplete, unfinished, or distressed by your shortcomings, remember God's promise and provision. Don't let your present condition rob you of the joy of knowing Christ or keep you from growing closer to him.

1:7 When he said, "in chains," Paul was probably referring to his imprisonment in Philippi, recorded in Acts 16:22–36. In verses 13 and 14, Paul speaks of his Roman imprisonment. Wherever Paul was, even in prison, he faithfully preached the Good News. Remember Paul's inspiring example when hindrances, small or large, slow down your work for God.

1:7, 8 Have you ever longed to see a friend with whom you share fond memories? Paul had such a longing to see the Christians at Philippi. His love and affection for them was based not merely on past experiences, but also on the unity that comes when believers draw upon Christ's love. All Christians are part of God's family and thus share equally in the transforming power of his love. Do you feel a deep love for fellow Christians, friends and strangers alike? Let Christ's love motivate you to love other Christians and to express that love in your actions toward them.

1:9
g 1Th 3:12

1:10
h 1Co 1:8

⁹And this is my prayer: that your love *g* may abound more and more in knowledge and depth of insight, ¹⁰so that you may be able to discern what is best and may be pure and blameless until the day of Christ, *h* ¹¹filled with the fruit of righteousness that comes through Jesus Christ—to the glory and praise of God.

Paul's Chains Advance the Gospel

¹²Now I want you to know, brothers, that what has happened to me has really served to advance the gospel. ¹³As a result, it has become clear throughout the whole palace guard *a* and to everyone else that I am in chains for Christ. ¹⁴Because of my chains, most of the brothers in the Lord have been encouraged to speak the word of God more courageously and fearlessly.

1:17
i Php 2:3

¹⁵It is true that some preach Christ out of envy and rivalry, but others out of goodwill. ¹⁶The latter do so in love, knowing that I am put here for the defense of the gospel. ¹⁷The former preach Christ out of selfish ambition, *i* not sincerely, supposing that they can stir up trouble for me while I am in chains. *b* ¹⁸But what does it matter? The important thing is that in every way, whether from false motives or true, Christ is preached. And because of this I rejoice.

1:19
j 2Co 1:11

Yes, and I will continue to rejoice, ¹⁹for I know that through your prayers *j* and the help

a 13 Or *whole palace*   *b* 16,17 Some late manuscripts have verses 16 and 17 in reverse order.

1:9 Often the best way to influence someone is to pray for him or her. Paul's prayer for the Philippians was that they would be unified in love. Their love was to result in greater knowledge of Christ and deeper insight (moral discernment). Their love was not based on feelings but on what Christ had done for them. As you grow in Christ's love, your heart and mind must grow together. Is your love and insight growing?

1:10 Paul prayed that the Philippian believers would "discern what is best"—in other words, that they would have the ability to differentiate between right and wrong, good and bad, vital and trivial. We ought to pray for moral discernment so we can maintain our Christian morals and values. Hebrews 5:14 emphasizes the need for discernment.

1:10 The "day of Christ" refers to the time when God will judge the world through Jesus Christ. We should live each day as though he could return at any moment.

1:11 The "fruit of righteousness" includes all of the character traits flowing from a right relationship with God. There is no other way for us to gain this fruit of righteousness than through Christ. See Galatians 5:22, 23 for the "fruit of the Spirit."

1:12 In the past, missionaries—those who spread the gospel—boarded ships to go to foreign lands and did not expect to see their homeland shores again. Their good-byes were final, in terms of earth time. There was no turning back. While air travel, e-mail, and other technologies have made worldwide separation much easier, pioneering with the gospel still requires a high sacrifice. Paul's passion was for others to discover the Good News of eternal life through Jesus Christ, no matter what the cost would be. Pressing through frontiers of spiritual darkness still requires pioneers today—people who will reach neglected people or new people groups. Pray for missionaries, support them, join them.

1:12–14 Being imprisoned would cause many people to become bitter or to give up, but Paul saw it as one more opportunity to spread the Good News of Christ. Paul realized that his current circumstances weren't as important as what he did with them. Turning a bad situation into a good one, he reached out to the Roman soldiers who made up the palace guard and encouraged those Christians who were afraid of persecution. We may not be in prison, but we still have plenty of opportunities to be discouraged—times of indecision, financial burdens, family conflict, church conflict, or the loss of our jobs. How we act in such situations will reflect what we believe. Like Paul, look for ways to demonstrate your faith even in bad situations. Whether or not the situation improves, your faith will grow stronger.

1:13 How did Paul end up in chains in a Roman prison? While he was visiting Jerusalem, some Jews had him arrested for preaching the gospel, but he appealed to Caesar to hear his case

(Acts 21:15—25:12). He was then escorted by soldiers to Rome, where he was placed under house arrest while awaiting trial—not a trial for breaking civil law, but for proclaiming the Good News of Christ. At that time, the Roman authorities did not consider this to be a serious charge. A few years later, however, Rome would take a different view of Christianity and make every effort to stamp it out of existence. Paul's house arrest allowed him some degree of freedom. He could have visitors, continue to preach, and write letters such as this one. A brief record of Paul's time in Rome is found in Acts 28:11–31. The "whole palace guard" refers to the Praetorian guard, the elite troops housed in the emperor's palace.

1:14 When we speak fearlessly for Christ, or live faithfully for him during difficult situations, we encourage others to do the same. Be an encouragement by the way that you live.

1:15–18 Paul had an amazingly selfless attitude. He knew that some were preaching to build their own reputations, taking advantage of Paul's imprisonment to try to make a name for themselves. Regardless of the motives of these preachers, Paul rejoiced that the gospel was being preached. Some Christians serve for the wrong reasons. Paul wouldn't condone, nor does God excuse, their motives, but we should be glad if God uses their message, regardless of their motives.

1:16 Paul could have become depressed, discouraged, or disillusioned. He could have wallowed in self-pity and despair. Instead, he regarded his imprisonment as being appointed by God. In fact, God had used Paul's imprisonment in Rome to bring the gospel to the center of the empire, as well as to give Paul lots of time to write letters that would one day end up in the New Testament and give us much teaching and encouragement. Do you have difficulty accepting your station in life? Do you resent where God has placed you? Although education and focused effort may enable us to take a new role or get a new job, often God puts us in a place to serve. Whether it is an actual prison or a place that feels like one, God wants you to serve him faithfully and joyfully.

1:19–21 This was not Paul's final imprisonment in Rome. But he didn't know that. Awaiting trial, he knew he could either be released or executed. However, he trusted Christ to work it out for his deliverance. Paul's prayer was that when he stood trial, he would speak courageously for Christ and not be timid or ashamed. Whether he lived or died, he wanted to exalt Christ. As it turned out, he was released from this imprisonment but arrested again two or three years later. Only faith in Christ could sustain Paul in such adversity.

given by the Spirit of Jesus Christ, what has happened to me will turn out for my deliverance.[a] [20]I eagerly expect[k] and hope that I will in no way be ashamed, but will have sufficient courage so that now as always Christ will be exalted in my body, whether by life or by death. [21]For to me, to live is Christ and to die is gain. [22]If I am to go on living in the body, this will mean fruitful labor for me. Yet what shall I choose? I do not know! [23]I am torn between the two: I desire to depart[l] and be with Christ,[m] which is better by far; [24]but it is more necessary for you that I remain in the body. [25]Convinced of this, I know that I will remain, and I will continue with all of you for your progress and joy in the faith, [26]so that through my being with you again your joy in Christ Jesus will overflow on account of me.

[27]Whatever happens, conduct yourselves in a manner worthy[n] of the gospel of Christ. Then, whether I come and see you or only hear about you in my absence, I will know that you stand firm in one spirit, contending as one man for the faith of the gospel [28]without being frightened in any way by those who oppose you. This is a sign to them that they will be destroyed, but that you will be saved—and that by God. [29]For it has been granted to you[o] on behalf of Christ not only to believe on him, but also to suffer for him, [30]since you are going through the same struggle[p] you saw[q] I had, and now hear that I still have.

2. Joy in serving
Imitating Christ's Humility

2 If you have any encouragement from being united with Christ, if any comfort from his love, if any fellowship with the Spirit,[r] if any tenderness and compassion,[s] [2]then make my joy complete[t] by being like-minded, having the same love, being one in spirit and purpose. [3]Do nothing out of selfish ambition or vain conceit,[u] but in humility consider others better than yourselves.[v] [4]Each of you should look not only to your own interests, but also to the interests of others.

[a] *19* Or *salvation*

1:20
[k] Ro 8:19

1:23
[l] 2Ti 4:6
[m] 2Co 5:8

1:27
[n] Eph 4:1

1:29
[o] Mt 5:11, 12

1:30
[p] 1Th 2:2
[q] Ac 16:19-40

2:1
[r] 2Co 13:14
[s] Col 3:12

2:2
[t] Jn 3:29

2:3
[u] Gal 5:26
[v] Ro 12:10

1:20, 21 To those who don't believe in God, life on earth is all there is, and so it is natural for them to strive for this world's values—money, popularity, power, pleasure, and prestige. For Paul, however, to live meant to develop eternal values and to tell others about Christ, who alone could help them see life from an eternal perspective. Paul's whole purpose in life was to speak out boldly for Christ and to become more like him. Thus Paul could confidently say that dying would be even better than living, because in death he would be removed from worldly troubles, and he would see Christ face-to-face (1 John 3:2, 3). If you're not ready to die, then you're not ready to live. Make certain of your eternal destiny; then you will be free to serve—devoting your life to what really counts, without fear of death.

1:24 Paul had a purpose for living when he served the Philippians and others. We also need a purpose for living that goes beyond providing for our own physical needs. Whom can you serve or help? What is your purpose for living?

1:27 Paul encourages the believers to be unified, as they "stand firm in one spirit, contending as one man for the faith." How sad that much time and effort is lost in some churches by fighting against one another instead of uniting against the real opposition! It takes a courageous church to resist in-fighting and to maintain the common purpose of serving Christ.

1:29 Paul considered it a privilege to suffer for Christ. We do not by nature consider suffering a privilege. Yet when we suffer, if we faithfully represent Christ, our message and example affect us and others for good (see Acts 5:41). Suffering has these additional benefits: (1) it takes our eyes off of earthly comforts; (2) it weeds out superficial believers; (3) it strengthens the faith of those who endure; (4) it serves as an example to others who may follow us. When we suffer for our faith, it doesn't mean that we have done something wrong. In fact, the opposite is often true—it verifies that we have been faithful. Use suffering to build your character. Don't resent it or let it tear you down.

1:30 Throughout his life Paul suffered for spreading the gospel. Like the Philippians, we are in conflict with anyone who would discredit the saving message of Christ. All true believers are in this fight together, uniting against the same enemy for a common cause.

Paul never urges Christians to seek suffering, as if there were virtue in pain. But we should not forget those who suffer. If your cupboard is full, share your food. If you control the wheels of power, work for justice and mercy. If you are wealthy, give generously to the poor. When life is comfortable, willingly take a share of someone else's pain, and so tell the world that the gospel is true.

2:1–5 Many people—even Christians—live only to make a good impression on others or to please themselves. But "selfish ambition or vain conceit" brings discord. Paul therefore stressed spiritual unity, asking the Philippians to love one another and to be one in spirit and purpose. When we work together, caring for the problems of others as if they were our problems, we demonstrate Christ's example of putting others first, and we experience unity. Don't be so concerned about making a good impression or meeting your own needs that you strain relationships in God's family.

2:3 Selfish ambition can ruin a church, but genuine humility can build it. Being humble involves having a true perspective about ourselves (see Romans 12:3). It does not mean that we should put ourselves down. Before God, we are sinners, saved only by God's grace, but we *are* saved and therefore have great worth in God's kingdom. We are to lay aside selfishness and treat others with respect and common courtesy. Considering others' interests as more important than our own links us with Christ, who was a true example of humility.

2:4 Philippi was a cosmopolitan city. The composition of the church reflected great diversity, with people from a variety of backgrounds and walks of life. Acts 16 gives us some indication of the diverse makeup of this church. The church included Lydia, a Jewish convert from Asia and a wealthy businesswoman (Acts 16:14); the slave girl (Acts 16:16, 17), probably a native Greek; and the jailer serving this colony of the empire, probably a Roman (Acts 16:25–36). With so many different backgrounds among the members, unity must have been difficult to maintain. Although there is no evidence of division in the church, its unity had to be safeguarded (3:2; 4:2). Paul encourages us to guard against any selfishness, prejudice, or jealousy that might lead to dissension. Showing genuine interest in others is a positive step forward in maintaining unity among believers.

2:5
w Mt 11:29

⁵ Your attitude should be the same as that of Christ Jesus: *w*

6 Who, being in very nature*a* God,
    did not consider equality with God something to be grasped,

2:7
x Jn 1:14

7 but made himself nothing,
    taking the very nature*b* of a servant,
    being made in human likeness. *x*

2:8
y Mt 26:39 Heb 5:8

8 And being found in appearance as a man,
    he humbled himself
    and became obedient to death*y*—
        even death on a cross!

2:9
z Ac 2:33; Heb 2:9
a Eph 1:20, 21

9 Therefore God exalted him*z* to the highest place
    and gave him the name that is above every name,*a*

10 that at the name of Jesus every knee should bow,
    in heaven and on earth and under the earth,

2:11
b Jn 13:13

11 and every tongue confess that Jesus Christ is Lord,*b*
    to the glory of God the Father.

Shining as Stars

12 Therefore, my dear friends, as you have always obeyed—not only in my presence, but now much more in my absence—continue to work out your salvation with fear and trembling, 13 for it is God who works in you to will and to act according to his good purpose.

a 6 Or *in the form of*   *b* 7 Or *the form*

2:5 Jesus Christ was humble, willing to give up his rights in order to obey God and serve people. Like Christ, we should have a servant's attitude, serving out of love for God and for others, not out of guilt or fear. Remember, you can choose your attitude. You can approach life expecting to be served, or you can look for opportunities to serve others. See Mark 10:45 for more on Christ's attitude of servanthood.

2:5-7 The *incarnation* was the act of the preexistent Son of God voluntarily assuming a human body and human nature. Without ceasing to be God, he became a human being, the man called Jesus. He did not give up his deity to become human, but he set aside the right to his glory and power. In submission to the Father's will, Christ limited his power and knowledge. Jesus of Nazareth was subject to place, time, and many other human limitations. What made his humanity unique was his freedom from sin. In his full humanity, Jesus showed us everything about God's character that can be conveyed in human terms. The incarnation is explained further in these passages: John 1:1-14; Romans 1:2-5; 2 Corinthians 8:9; 1 Timothy 3:16; Hebrews 2:14; and 1 John 1:1-3.

2:5-11 These verses are probably from a hymn sung by the early Christian church. The passage holds many parallels to the prophecy of the suffering servant in Isaiah 53. As a hymn, it was not meant to be a complete statement about the nature and work of Christ. Several key characteristics of Jesus Christ, however, are praised in this passage: (1) Christ has always existed with God; (2) Christ is equal to God because he *is* God (John 1:1ff; Colossians 1:15-19); (3) though Christ is God, he became a man in order to fulfill God's plan of salvation for all people; (4) Christ did not just have the appearance of being a man—he actually became human to identify with our sins; (5) Christ voluntarily laid aside his divine rights and privileges out of love for his Father; (6) Christ died on the cross for our sins so we wouldn't have to face eternal death; (7) God glorified Christ because of his obedience; (8) God raised Christ to his original position at the Father's right hand, where he will reign forever as our Lord and Judge. How can we do anything less than praise Christ as our Lord and dedicate ourselves to his service!

2:5-11 Often people excuse selfishness, pride, or evil by claiming their rights. They think, "I can cheat on this test; after all, I deserve to pass this class," or "I can spend all this money on myself—I worked hard for it," or "I can get an abortion; I have a right to control my own body." But as believers, we should have a different attitude, one that enables us to lay aside our rights in order to

serve others. If we say we follow Christ, we must also say we want to live as he lived. We should develop his attitude of humility as we serve, even when we are not likely to get recognition for our efforts. Are you selfishly clinging to your rights, or are you willing to serve?

2:8 Death on a cross (crucifixion) was the form of capital punishment that Romans used for notorious criminals. It was excruciatingly painful and humiliating. Prisoners were nailed or tied to a cross and left to die. Death might not come for several days, and it usually came by suffocation when the weight of the weakened body made breathing more and more difficult. Jesus died as one who was cursed (Galatians 3:13). How amazing that the perfect man should die this most shameful death so that we would not have to face eternal punishment!

2:9-11 At the last judgment even those who are condemned will recognize Jesus' authority and right to rule. People can choose to regard Jesus as Lord now as a step of willing and loving commitment, or be forced to acknowledge him as Lord when he returns. Christ may return at any moment. Are you prepared to meet him?

2:12 "Therefore" ties this verse to the previous section. "Work out your salvation," in light of the preceding exhortation to unity, may mean that the entire church was to work together to rid themselves of divisions and discord. The Philippian Christians needed to be especially careful to obey Christ, now that Paul wasn't there to continually remind them about what was right. We too must be careful about what we believe and how we live, especially when we are on our own. In the absence of cherished Christian leaders, we must focus our attention and devotion even more on Christ so that we won't be sidetracked.

2:13 What do we do when we don't feel like obeying? God has not left us alone in our struggles to do his will. He wants to come alongside us and be within us to help. God gives us the *desire* and the *power* to do what pleases him. The secret to a changed life is to submit to God's control and let him work. Next time, ask God to help you *want* to do his will.

2:13 To be like Christ, we must train ourselves to think like Christ. To change our desires to be more like Christ's, we need the power of the indwelling Spirit (1:19), the influence of faithful Christians, obedience to God's Word (not just exposure to it), and sacrificial service. Often it is in *doing* God's will that we gain the *desire* to do it (see 4:8, 9). Do what he wants and trust him to change your desires.

¹⁴Do everything without complaining or arguing, ¹⁵so that you may become blameless and pure, children of God *c* without fault in a crooked and depraved generation, in which you shine like stars in the universe ¹⁶as you hold out *a* the word of life—in order that I may boast on the day of Christ that I did not run or labor for nothing. ¹⁷But even if I am being poured out like a drink offering *d* on the sacrifice *e* and service coming from your faith, I am glad and rejoice with all of you. ¹⁸So you too should be glad and rejoice with me.

Timothy and Epaphroditus

¹⁹I hope in the Lord Jesus to send Timothy to you soon, that I also may be cheered when I receive news about you. ²⁰I have no one else like him, who takes a genuine interest in your welfare. ²¹For everyone looks out for his own interests, *f* not those of Jesus Christ. ²²But you know that Timothy has proved himself, because as a son with his father he has served with me in the work of the gospel. ²³I hope, therefore, to send him as soon as I see how things go with me. ²⁴And I am confident *g* in the Lord that I myself will come soon.

²⁵But I think it is necessary to send back to you Epaphroditus, my brother, fellow worker and fellow soldier, *h* who is also your messenger, whom you sent to take care of my needs. *i* ²⁶For he longs for all of you and is distressed because you heard he was ill. ²⁷Indeed he was ill, and almost died. But God had mercy on him, and not on him only but also on me, to spare me sorrow upon sorrow. ²⁸Therefore I am all the more eager to send him, so that when you see him again you may be glad and I may have less anxiety. ²⁹Welcome him in the Lord with great joy, and honor men like him, *j* ³⁰because he almost died for the work of Christ, risking his life to make up for the help you could not give me. *k*

3. Joy in believing
No Confidence in the Flesh

3 Finally, my brothers, rejoice in the Lord! It is no trouble for me to write the same things to you again, and it is a safeguard for you.

a 16 Or *hold on to*

2:15
c Mt 5:45, 48;
Eph 5:1

2:17
d 2Ti 4:6
e Ro 15:16

2:21
f 1Co 10:24

2:24
g Php 1:25
2:25
h Phm 2
i Php 4:18

2:29
j 1Co 16:18
2:30
k 1Co 16:17

2:14–16 Why are complaining and arguing so harmful? If all that people know about a church is that its members constantly argue, complain, and gossip, they get a false impression of Christ and the gospel. Belief in Christ should unite those who trust him. If your church is always complaining and arguing, it lacks the unifying power of Jesus Christ. Stop arguing with other Christians or complaining about people and conditions within the church; instead, let the world see Christ.

2:14–16 Our lives should be characterized by moral purity, patience, and peacefulness, so that we will "shine like stars" in a dark and depraved world. A transformed life is an effective witness to the power of God's Word. Are you shining brightly, or are you clouded by complaining and arguing? Don't let dissensions snuff out your light. Shine out for God. Your role is to shine until Jesus returns and bathes the world in his radiant glory.

2:17 The drink offering was an important part of the sacrificial system of the Jews (for an explanation, see Numbers 28:7). Because this church had little Jewish background, the drink offering may refer to the wine poured out to pagan deities prior to important public events. Paul regarded his life as a sacrifice.

2:17 Even if he had to die, Paul was content, knowing that he had helped the Philippians live for Christ. When you're totally committed to serving Christ, sacrificing to build the faith of others brings a joyous reward.

2:19, 22 When Paul wrote these words, most vocational training was done by fathers, and sons stayed loyal to the family business. Timothy displayed that same loyalty in his spiritual apprenticeship with Paul. Timothy was with Paul in Rome when Paul wrote this letter. He traveled with Paul on his second missionary journey when the church at Philippi was begun. (For more information on Timothy, see his Profile in 1 Timothy, p. 2037.)

Just as a skilled workman trains an apprentice, Paul was preparing Timothy to carry on the ministry in his absence. Paul encouraged younger Christians to learn, to observe, to help, and then to lead. Paul expected older Christians to teach, to model, to mentor, and then to turn over leadership. The benefits of such a process are new enthusiasm and vision, new methods and energy. Are you a teacher? Whom are you apprenticing for God's work? Are you a learner? How are you showing your eagerness to fulfill the call God has on your life?

2:21 Paul observed that most believers are too preoccupied with their own needs to spend time working for Christ. Don't let your schedule and concerns crowd out your Christian service to and love for others.

2:23 Paul was in prison (either awaiting his trial or its verdict) for preaching about Christ. He was telling the Philippians that when he learned of the court's decision, he would send Timothy to them with the news. Paul wanted them to know that he was ready to accept whatever came (1:21–26).

2:25 Epaphroditus delivered money from the Philippians to Paul; then he returned with this thank-you letter to Philippi. Epaphroditus may have been an elder in Philippi (2:25–30; 4:18) who, while staying with Paul, became ill (2:27, 30). After Epaphroditus recovered, he returned home. He is mentioned only in Philippians.

2:29, 30 The world honors those who are intelligent, beautiful, rich, and powerful. What kind of people should the church honor? Paul indicates that we should honor those who give their lives for the sake of Christ, going where we cannot go ourselves. Our missionaries do that for us today by providing ministry where we are not able to go.

3:1 As a safeguard, Paul reviewed the basics with these believers. The Bible is our safeguard both morally and theologically. When we read it individually and publicly in church, it alerts us to corrections we need to make in our thoughts, attitudes, and actions.

3:3
l Gal 6:15

2 Watch out for those dogs, those men who do evil, those mutilators of the flesh. 3 For it is we who are the circumcision,*l* we who worship by the Spirit of God, who glory in Christ Jesus, and who put no confidence in the flesh— 4 though I myself have reasons for such confidence.

3:5
m 2Co 11:22
n Ro 11:1

If anyone else thinks he has reasons to put confidence in the flesh, I have more: 5 circumcised on the eighth day, of the people of Israel,*m* of the tribe of Benjamin,*n* a Hebrew of Hebrews; in regard to the law, a Pharisee; 6 as for zeal, persecuting the church; as for legalistic righteousness, faultless.

THREE STAGES OF PERFECTION	*1. Perfect Relationship*	We are perfect because of our eternal union with the infinitely perfect Christ. When we become his children, we are declared "not guilty" and thus righteous because of what Christ, God's beloved Son, has done for us. This perfection is absolute and unchangeable, and it is this perfect relationship that guarantees that we will one day be "completely perfect" (below). See Colossians 2:8–10; Hebrews 10:8–14.
	2. Perfect Progress	We can grow and mature spiritually as we continue to trust Christ, learn more about him, draw closer to him, and obey him. Our progress is changeable (in contrast to our relationship, above) because it depends on our daily walk—at times in life we mature more than at other times. But we are growing toward perfection if we "press on" (Philippians 3:12). These good deeds do not perfect us; rather, as God perfects us, we do good deeds for him. See Philippians 3:1–15.
	3. Completely Perfect	When Christ returns to take us into his eternal kingdom, we will be glorified and made completely perfect. See Philippians 3:20, 21.
		All phases of perfection are grounded in faith in Christ and what he has done, not what we can do for him. We cannot perfect ourselves; only God can work in and through us to "carry it on to completion until the day of Christ Jesus" (1:6).

3:2, 3 These "dogs" and "men who do evil" were very likely *Judaizers*—Jewish Christians who wrongly believed that it was essential for Gentiles to follow all the Old Testament Jewish laws, especially submission to the rite of circumcision, in order to receive salvation. Many Judaizers were motivated by spiritual pride. Because they had invested so much time and effort in keeping their laws, they couldn't accept the fact that all their efforts couldn't bring them a step closer to salvation.

Paul criticized the Judaizers because they looked at Christianity backwards—thinking that what they *did* (*circumcision*—cutting or mutilating the flesh) made them believers rather than the free gift of grace given by Christ. What believers do is a *result* of faith, not a *prerequisite* to faith. This had been confirmed by the early church leaders at the Jerusalem council 11 years earlier (Acts 15). Who are the Judaizers of our day? They are those who say that people must add something else to simple faith. No person should add anything to Christ's offer of salvation by grace through faith.

3:2, 3 It is easy to place more emphasis on religious effort ("confidence in the flesh") than on internal faith, but God values the attitude of our hearts above all else. Don't judge people's spirituality by their fulfillment of duties or by their level of human activity. And don't think that you will satisfy God by feverishly doing his work. God notices all you do for him and will reward you for it, but only if it comes as a loving response to his free gift of salvation.

3:4–6 At first glance, it looks like Paul is boasting about his achievements. But he is actually doing the opposite, showing that human achievements, no matter how impressive, cannot earn a person salvation and eternal life with God. Paul had impressive credentials: upbringing, nationality, family background, inheritance, orthodoxy, activity, and morality (see 2 Corinthians 11; Galatians 1:13–24, for more of his credentials). However, his conversion to faith in Christ (Acts 9) wasn't based on what he had done, but on God's grace. Paul did not depend on his deeds to please God because even the most impressive credentials fall short of God's holy standards. Are you depending on Christian parents, church affiliation, or just being good to make you right with God? Credentials, accomplishments, or reputation cannot earn salvation. Salvation comes only through faith in Christ.

3:5 Paul belonged to the tribe of Benjamin, a heritage greatly esteemed among the Jews. From this tribe had come Israel's first king, Saul (1 Samuel 10:20–24). The tribes of Benjamin and Judah were the only two tribes to return to Israel after the exile (Ezra 4:1). Paul was also a Pharisee, a member of a very devout Jewish sect that scrupulously kept its own numerous rules in addition to the laws of Moses. Paul explains for these mostly-Gentile believers that his Jewish credentials were impeccable.

3:6 Why had Paul, a devout Jewish leader, persecuted the church? Agreeing with the leaders of the religious establishment, Paul had thought that Christianity was heretical and blasphemous. Because Jesus did not meet his expectations of what the Messiah would be like, Paul had assumed that Jesus' claims were false—and therefore wicked. In addition, he had seen Christianity as a political menace because it threatened to disrupt the fragile harmony between the Jews and the Roman government.

[7]But whatever was to my profit I now consider loss *o* for the sake of Christ. [8]What is more, I consider everything a loss compared to the surpassing greatness of knowing *p* Christ Jesus my Lord, for whose sake I have lost all things. I consider them rubbish, that I may gain Christ [9]and be found in him, not having a righteousness of my own that comes from the law, but that which is through faith in Christ—the righteousness that comes from God and is by faith. [10]I want to know Christ and the power of his resurrection and the fellowship of sharing in his sufferings, *q* becoming like him in his death, *r* [11]and so, somehow, to attain to the resurrection from the dead.

Pressing on Toward the Goal

[12]Not that I have already obtained all this, or have already been made perfect, but I press on to take hold *s* of that for which Christ Jesus took hold of me. [13]Brothers, I do not consider myself yet to have taken hold of it. But one thing I do: Forgetting what is behind *t* and straining toward what is ahead, [14]I press on *u* toward the goal to win the prize for which God has called me heavenward in Christ Jesus.

[15]All of us who are mature *v* should take such a view of things. *w* And if on some point you think differently, that too God will make clear to you. [16]Only let us live up to what we have already attained.

3:7
o Mt 13:44
3:8
p Eph 4:13

3:10
q Ro 8:17
r Ro 6:3-5

3:12
s 1Ti 6:12
3:13
t Lk 9:62
3:14
u Heb 6:1
3:15
v 1Co 2:6
w Gal 5:10

3:7 When Paul spoke of his "profit," he was referring to his credentials, credits, and successes. After showing that he could beat the Judaizers at their own game (being proud of who they were and what they had done), Paul showed that it was the wrong game. Be careful of considering past achievements so important that they get in the way of your relationship with Christ.

3:8 After Paul considered everything he had accomplished in his life, he decided to write it all off as "rubbish" when compared with the greatness of knowing Christ. We should value our relationship with Christ as more important than anything else. To know Christ should be our ultimate goal. Yet how do we know him better? (1) Study the life of Christ in the Gospels. See how Christ lived and responded to people (Matthew 11:29). (2) Study all the New Testament references to Christ (Colossians 1:15—2:15). (3) As you worship and pray, let the Holy Spirit remind you of Christ's words (John 14:26). (4) Take up Christ's mission to preach the gospel and learn from his sufferings (Matthew 28:19; Philippians 3:10).

To do these things, however, may mean that you must make major changes in your thinking and in your lifestyle. Are you willing to change your values in order to know Christ better? Will you fix or rearrange your crowded schedule in order to set aside a few minutes each day for prayer and Bible study? Will you change some of your plans, goals, and desires in order to conform with what you learn about Christ? Whatever you must change or give up, having Christ and becoming one with him will be more than worth the sacrifice.

3:9 No amount of law keeping, self-improvement, discipline, or religious effort can make us right with God. Righteousness comes only from God, and we are made righteous (receive right standing with him) by trusting in Christ. He exchanges our sin and shortcomings for his complete righteousness. See 2 Corinthians 5:21 for more on Christ's gift of righteousness.

3:9, 10 Paul gave up everything—family, friendship, and freedom—in order to know Christ and his resurrection power. We too have access to this knowledge and this power, but we may have to make sacrifices to enjoy it fully. What are you willing to give up in order to know Christ? A crowded schedule in order to set aside a few minutes each day for prayer and Bible study? Your friend's approval? Some of your plans or pleasures? Whatever it is, knowing Christ is more than worth the sacrifice.

3:10 When we are united with Christ by trusting in him, we experience the power that raised him from the dead. That same mighty power will help us live morally renewed and regenerated lives. But before we can walk in newness of life, we must also die to sin. Just as the resurrection gives us Christ's power to

live for him, his crucifixion marks the death of our old sinful nature. We can't know the victory of the resurrection without personally applying the crucifixion.

3:11 When Paul wrote, "somehow, to attain to the resurrection" he was not implying uncertainty or doubt. He was unsure of the way that he would meet God, whether by execution or by natural death. He did not doubt that he would be raised, but attainment of it was within God's power and not his own.

3:11 Just as Christ was exalted after his resurrection, so we will one day share Christ's glory (Revelation 22:1–7). Paul knew that he might die soon, but he had faith that he would be raised to life again.

3:12–14 Paul says that his goal is to know Christ, to be like Christ, and to be all Christ has in mind for him. This goal absorbs all Paul's energy. This is a helpful example for us. We should not let anything take our eyes off our goal—knowing Christ. With the single-mindedness of an athlete in training, we must lay aside everything harmful and forsake anything that may distract us from being effective Christians. What is holding you back?

3:13, 14 Paul had reason to forget what was behind—he had held the coats of those who had stoned Stephen, the first Christian martyr (Acts 7:57, 58, Paul is called Saul here). We have all done things for which we are ashamed, and we live in the tension of what we have been and what we want to be. Because our hope is in Christ, however, we can let go of past guilt and look forward to what God will help us become. Don't dwell on your past. Instead, grow in the knowledge of God by concentrating on your relationship with him *now*. Realize that you are forgiven, and then move on to a life of faith and obedience. Look forward to a fuller and more meaningful life because of your hope in Christ.

3:15, 16 Sometimes trying to live a perfect Christian life can be so difficult that it leaves us drained and discouraged. We may feel so far removed that we can never please God with our lives. Paul used *perfect* (3:12) to mean mature or complete, not flawless in every detail. Those who are mature should press on in the Holy Spirit's power, knowing that Christ will reveal and fill in any discrepancy between what we are and what we should be. Christ's provision is no excuse for lagging devotion, but it provides relief and assurance for those who feel driven.

3:16 Christian maturity involves acting on the guidance that you have already received. We can always make excuses that we still have so much to learn. The instruction for us is to live up to what we already know and live out what we have already learned. We do not have to be sidetracked by an unending search for truth.

3:17
x 1Pe 5:3

3:19
y Ro 8:5, 6

3:20
z Col 3:1
a 1Co 1:7

3:21
b Eph 1:19
c 1Co 15:43-53

4:1
d Php 1:8

[17]Join with others in following my example,*x* brothers, and take note of those who live according to the pattern we gave you. [18]For, as I have often told you before and now say again even with tears, many live as enemies of the cross of Christ. [19]Their destiny is destruction, their god is their stomach, and their glory is in their shame. Their mind is on earthly things.*y* [20]But our citizenship is in heaven.*z* And we eagerly await a Savior from there, the Lord Jesus Christ,*a* [21]who, by the power *b* that enables him to bring everything under his control, will transform our lowly bodies *c* so that they will be like his glorious body.

4 Therefore, my brothers, you whom I love and long for,*d* my joy and crown, that is how you should stand firm in the Lord, dear friends!

TRAINING FOR THE CHRISTIAN LIFE

As a great amount of training is needed for athletic activities, so we must train diligently for the Christian life. Such training takes time, dedication, energy, continued practice, and vision. We must all commit ourselves to the Christian life, but we must first know the rules as prescribed in God's Word (2 Timothy 2:5).

Reference	Metaphors	Training	Our Goal as Believers
1 Corinthians 9:24–27	Race	Go into strict training in order to get the prize.	We train ourselves to run the race of life. So we keep our eyes on Christ—the goal—and don't get sidetracked or slowed down. When we do this, we will win a reward in Christ's kingdom.
Philippians 3:13, 14	Race	Focus all your energies toward winning the race.	Living the Christian life demands all of our energies. We can forget the past and strain to reach the goal because we know Christ promises eternity with him at the race's end.
1 Timothy 4:7–10	Exercise	Spiritual exercise will help you grow in faith and character.	As we must repeat exercises to tone our bodies, so we must steadily repeat spiritual exercises to be spiritually fit: when we do this, we become better Christians, living in accordance with God's will. Such a life will attract others to Christ and pay dividends in both this life and the next.
2 Timothy 4:7, 8	Fight Race	Fighting the good fight and persevering to the end.	The Christian life is a fight against evil forces from without and temptation from within. If we stay true to God through it all, he promises an end, a rest, and a crown.

3:17 Paul challenged the Philippians to pursue Christlikeness by following Paul's own pattern or example. This did not mean, of course, that they should copy everything he did; he had just stated that he was not perfect (3:12). But as he focused his life on being like Christ, so should they. The Gospels may not yet have been in circulation, so Paul could not tell them to read the Bible to see what Christ was like. Therefore he urged them to imitate him. That Paul could tell people to follow his example is a testimony to his character. Can you do the same? What kind of follower would a new Christian become if he or she imitated you?

3:17-21 Paul criticized not only the Judaizers (see the first note on 3:2, 3), but also the self-indulgent Christians, people who claim to be Christians but don't live up to Christ's model of servanthood and self-sacrifice. These people satisfy their own desires before even thinking about the needs of others. Freedom in Christ does not mean freedom to be selfish. It means taking every opportunity to serve and to become the best person you can be.

3:19 Paul gets tough with people who live to appease their appetites, who believe so strongly in their greatness that they become slaves to pride. What horrible people these must be—so concerned with earthly trivia that during worship their minds wander; so consumed with work that worship is inconvenient; so busy planning the next party that there is no time for prayer. Paul says they are headed for destruction because all they can think about is this life here on earth.

But then we must ask ourselves: Is too much of our time spent on efforts that will not endure in eternity, seeking earthly pleasures, or satisfying our physical desires? We must set our minds on knowing Christ, not on the pursuits of this world.

3:20 Citizens of a Roman colony were expected to promote the interests of Rome and maintain the dignity of the city. In the same way, citizens of heaven ought to promote heaven's interests on earth and lead lives worthy of heavenly citizenship. Too many Christians have failed to transfer their citizenship to heaven. They still seek earthly pleasures and treasures instead of heavenly ones. Paul told the Philippians to remember that they are citizens of heaven, where the Lord Jesus Christ lives. Have you transferred your citizenship? How are you promoting heaven's interests?

3:21 The phrase "lowly bodies" does not imply any negative attitude toward the human body. However, the bodies we will receive when we are raised from the dead will be glorious, like Christ's resurrected body. Those who struggle with pain, physical limitations, or disabilities can have wonderful hope in the resurrection. For a more detailed discussion of our new bodies, see 1 Corinthians 15:35ff and 2 Corinthians 5:1–10.

4:1 How do we "stand firm in the Lord"? This refers to what Paul has just taught in 3:20, 21. The way to stand firm is to keep our eyes on Christ, to remember that this world is not our home, and to focus on the fact that Christ will bring everything under his control. Standing firm means steadfastly resisting the negative influences of temptation, false teaching, or persecution. It requires perseverance when we are challenged or opposed. Don't lose heart or give up. God promises to give us strength of character. With the Holy Spirit's help and with the help of fellow believers, you can stay true to the Lord.

4. Joy in giving

Exhortations

2 I plead with Euodia and I plead with Syntyche to agree with each other *e* in the Lord. 3 Yes, and I ask you, loyal yokefellow,a help these women who have contended at my side in the cause of the gospel, along with Clement and the rest of my fellow workers, whose names are in the book of life.

4 Rejoice in the Lord always. I will say it again: Rejoice! 5 Let your gentleness be evident to all. The Lord is near. 6 Do not be anxious about anything,*f* but in everything, by prayer and petition, with thanksgiving, present your requests to God. 7 And the peace of God,*g* which transcends all understanding, will guard your hearts and your minds in Christ Jesus.

8 Finally, brothers, whatever is true, whatever is noble, whatever is right, whatever is pure, whatever is lovely, whatever is admirable—if anything is excellent or praiseworthy—think about such things. 9 Whatever you have learned or received or heard from me, or seen in me—put it into practice. And the God of peace *h* will be with you.

Thanks for Their Gifts

10 I rejoice greatly in the Lord that at last you have renewed your concern for me. Indeed, you have been concerned, but you had no opportunity to show it. 11 I am not saying this because I am in need, for I have learned to be content *i* whatever the circumstances. 12 I know what it is to be in need, and I know what it is to have plenty. I have learned the secret of being content in any and every situation, whether well fed or hungry,*j* whether living in plenty or in want. 13 I can do everything through him who gives me strength.

a 3 Or loyal Syzygus

4:2
e Php 2:2

4:6
f Mt 6:25-34

4:7
g Jn 14:27 Col 3:15

4:9
h Ro 15:33

4:11
i 1Ti 6:6, 8

4:12
j 1Co 4:11

4:2, 3 Paul did not warn the Philippian church of doctrinal errors, but he did address some relational problems. These two women had been workers for Christ in the church. Their broken relationship was no small matter, because many had become believers through their efforts. It is possible to believe in Christ, work hard for his kingdom, and yet have broken relationships with others who are committed to the same cause. But there is no excuse for remaining unreconciled. Do you need to be reconciled to someone today? If you're facing a conflict you can't resolve, don't let the tension build into an explosion. Don't withdraw or resort to cruel power plays. Don't stand idly by and wait for the dispute to resolve itself. Instead, seek the help of those known for peacemaking.

4:3 The identity of this "loyal yokefellow" remains a mystery. It could be Epaphroditus, the bearer of this letter, or a comrade of Paul in prison. It could also be someone named Syzygus, another way to understand the word for yokefellow.

4:3 Those "whose names are in the book of life" are all who are marked for salvation through their faith in Christ (see also Luke 10:17–20; Revelation 20:11–15).

4:4 It seems strange that a man in prison would be telling a church to rejoice. But Paul's attitude teaches us an important lesson: Our inner attitudes do not have to reflect our outward circumstances. Paul was full of joy because he knew that no matter what happened to him, Jesus Christ was with him. Several times in this letter, Paul urged the Philippians to be joyful, probably because they needed to hear this. It's easy to get discouraged about unpleasant circumstances or to take unimportant events too seriously. If you haven't been joyful lately, you may not be looking at life from the right perspective.

4:4, 5 Ultimate joy comes from Christ dwelling within us. Christ is near, and at his second coming we will fully realize this ultimate joy. He who lives within us will fulfill his final purposes for us.

4:5 We are to be gentle (reasonable, fair minded, and charitable) to those outside the church, and not just to fellow believers. This means we are not to seek revenge against those who treat us unfairly, nor are we to be overly vocal about our personal rights.

4:6, 7 Imagine never being "anxious about anything"! It seems like an impossibility—we all have worries on the job, in our homes, at school. But Paul's advice is to turn our worries into prayers. Do you want to worry less? Then pray more! Whenever you start to worry, stop and pray.

4:7 God's peace is different from the world's peace (see John 14:27). True peace is not found in positive thinking, in absence of conflict, or in good feelings. It comes from knowing that God is in control. Our citizenship in Christ's kingdom is sure, our destiny is set, and we can have victory over sin. Let God's peace guard your heart against anxiety.

4:8 What we put into our minds determines what comes out in our words and actions. Paul tells us to program our minds with thoughts that are true, noble, right, pure, lovely, admirable, excellent, and praiseworthy. Do you have problems with impure thoughts and daydreams? Examine what you are putting into your mind through television, Internet, books, conversations, movies, and magazines. Replace harmful input with wholesome material. Above all, read God's Word and pray. Ask God to help you focus your mind on what is good and pure. It takes practice, but it can be done.

4:9 It's not enough to hear or read the Word of God, or even to know it well. We must also put it into practice. How easy it is to listen to a sermon and forget what the preacher said. How easy it is to read the Bible and not think about how to live differently. How easy it is to debate what a passage means and not live out that meaning. Exposure to God's Word is not enough. It must lead to obedience.

4:10 In 1 Corinthians 9:11–18, Paul wrote that he didn't accept gifts from the Corinthian church because he didn't want to be accused of preaching only to get money. But Paul maintained that it was a church's responsibility to support God's ministers (1 Corinthians 9:14). He accepted the Philippians' gift because they gave it willingly and because he was in need.

4:10–14 Are you content in any circumstances you face? Paul knew how to be content whether he had plenty or whether he was in need. The secret was drawing on Christ's power for strength. Do you have great needs, or are you discontented because you don't have what you want? Learn to rely on God's promises and Christ's power to help you be content. If you always want more, ask God to remove that desire and teach you contentment in every circumstance. He will supply all your needs, but in a way that he knows is best for you (see the note on 4:19 for more on God supplying our needs).

4:15
k 2Co 11:8, 9

14 Yet it was good of you to share in my troubles. 15 Moreover, as you Philippians know, in the early days of your acquaintance with the gospel, when I set out from Macedonia, not one church shared with me in the matter of giving and receiving, except you only; k 16 for even when I was in Thessalonica, you sent me aid again and again when I was in need. 17 Not that I am looking for a gift, but I am looking for what may be credited to your account. 18 I have received full payment and even more; I am amply supplied, now that I have received from Epaphroditus l the gifts you sent. They are a fragrant offering, an acceptable sacrifice, pleasing to God. 19 And my God will meet all your needs m according to his glorious riches in Christ Jesus.

4:18
l Php 2:25

4:19
m Ps 23:1

4:20
n Gal 1:4

20 To our God and Father n be glory for ever and ever. Amen.

Final Greetings

4:21
o Gal 1:2

21 Greet all the saints in Christ Jesus. The brothers who are with me o send greetings. 22 All the saints send you greetings, especially those who belong to Caesar's household. 23 The grace of the Lord Jesus Christ be with your spirit. Amen. a

a 23 Some manuscripts do not have *Amen*.

4:12, 13 Paul was content because he could see life from God's point of view. He focused on what he was supposed to *do*, not what he felt he should *have*. Paul had his priorities straight, and he was grateful for everything God had given him. Paul had detached himself from the nonessentials so that he could concentrate on the eternal. Often the desire for more or better possessions is really a longing to fill an empty place in a person's life. To what are you drawn when you feel empty inside? How can you find true contentment? The answer lies in your perspective, your priorities, and your source of power.

4:13 Can we really do everything? The power we receive in union with Christ is sufficient to do his will and to face the challenges that arise from our commitment to doing it. He does not grant us superhuman ability to accomplish anything we can imagine without regard to his interests. As we contend for the faith we will face troubles, pressures, and trials. As they come, ask Christ to strengthen you.

4:14 The Philippians shared in Paul's financial support while he was in prison.

4:15 What makes money so magnetic and giving it away so stressful? Money measures our energy; it represents our day-to-day security. Giving money away puts our work and our futures at risk. Not every charity deserves your attention, and you're wise to scrutinize missionary appeals as well. But once you've determined that a project honors the Lord, don't hold back—give generously and joyfully. Like the Philippians, you'll be establishing an eternal partnership.

4:17 When we give to those in need, there is not only benefit to the receiver, but we are benefited as well. It was not the Philippians' gift, but their spirit of love and devotion that Paul appreciated most.

4:18 Paul was not referring to a sin offering but to a thank offering, "a fragrant offering, an acceptable sacrifice, pleasing to God" (Leviticus 7:12–15 contains the instructions for thank offerings). Although the Greek and Roman Christians were not Jews, and they had not offered sacrifices according to the Old Testament laws, they were well acquainted with the pagan rituals of offering sacrifices.

4:19 We can trust that God will always meet our needs. Whatever we need on earth he will always supply, even if it is the courage to face death as Paul did. Whatever we need in heaven he will supply. We must remember, however, the difference between our wants and our needs. Most people want to feel good and avoid discomfort or pain. We may not get all that we want. By trusting in Christ, our attitudes and appetites can change from wanting everything to accepting his provision and power to live for him.

4:22 There were many Christians in Rome; some were even in Caesar's household. Perhaps Paul, while awaiting trial, was making converts of the Roman civil service! Paul sent greetings from these Roman Christians to the believers at Philippi. The gospel had spread to all strata of society, linking people who had no other bond but Christ. The Roman Christians and the Philippian Christians were brothers and sisters because of their unity in Christ. Believers today are also linked to others across cultural, economic, and social barriers. Because all believers are brothers and sisters in Christ, let us live like God's true family.

4:23 In many ways the Philippian church was a model congregation. It was made up of many different kinds of people who were learning to work together. But Paul recognized that problems could arise, so in his thank-you letter he prepared the Philippians for difficulties that could crop up within a body of believers. Though a prisoner in Rome, Paul had learned the true secret of joy and peace—imitating Christ and serving others. By focusing our minds on Christ we will learn unity, humility, joy, and peace. We will also be motivated to live for him. We can live confidently for him because we have "the grace of the Lord Jesus Christ" with us.

COLOSSIANS

REMOVE the head coach, and the team flounders; break the fuel line, and the car won't run; unplug the electrical appliance, and it has no power. Whether for leadership, power, or life, connections are vital!

Colossians is a book of connections. Writing from prison in Rome, Paul combatted false teachings, which had infiltrated the Colossian church. The problem was "syncretism," combining ideas from other philosophies and religions (such as paganism, strains of Judaism, and Greek thought) with Christian truth. The resulting heresy later became known as "Gnosticism," emphasizing special knowledge (*gnosis* in Greek) and denying Christ as God and Savior. To combat this devious error, Paul stressed Christ's deity—his connection with the Father—and his sacrificial death on the cross for sin. Only by being connected with Christ through faith can anyone have eternal life, and only through a continuing connection with him can anyone have power for living. Christ is God incarnate and the *only* way to forgiveness and peace with God the Father. Paul also emphasized believers' connections with each other as Christ's body on earth.

Paul's introduction to the Colossians includes a greeting, a note of thanksgiving, and a prayer for spiritual wisdom and strength for these brothers and sisters in Christ (1:1–12). He then moves into a doctrinal discussion of the person and work of Christ (1:13–23), stating that Christ is the "image of the invisible God" (1:15), the Creator (1:16), the "head of the body, the church" (1:18), and the "beginning and the firstborn from among the dead" (1:18). His death on the cross makes it possible for us to stand in the presence of God (1:22).

Paul then explains how the world's teachings are totally empty when compared with God's plan, and he challenges the Colossians to reject shallow answers and to live in union with Christ (1:24—2:23).

Against this theological backdrop, Paul turns to practical considerations—what the divinity, death, and resurrection of Jesus should mean to all believers (3:1—4:6). Because our eternal destiny is sure, heaven should fill our thoughts (3:1–4), sexual impurity and other worldly lusts should not be named among us (3:5–8), and truth, love, and peace should mark our lives (3:9–15). Our love for Christ should also translate into love for others—friends, fellow believers, spouses, children, parents, slaves, and masters (3:16—4:1). We should constantly communicate with God through prayer (4:2–4), and we should take every opportunity to tell others the Good News (4:5, 6). In Christ we have everything we need for salvation and for living the Christian life.

Paul had probably never visited Colosse, so he concludes this letter with personal comments about their common Christian associations, providing a living lesson of the connectedness of the body of Christ.

Read Colossians as a book for an embattled church in the first century, but read it also for its timeless truths. Gain a fresh appreciation for Christ as the *fullness* of God and the *only* source for living the Christian life. Know that he is your leader, head, and power source, and make sure of your connection to him.

THE BLUEPRINT

1. What Christ has done
   (1:1—2:23)
2. What Christians should do
   (3:1—4:18)

In this letter Paul clearly teaches that Christ has paid for sin, that Christ has reconciled us to God, and that Christ gives us the pattern and the power to grow spiritually. Because Christ is the exact likeness of God, when we learn what he is like, we see what we need to become. Since Christ is Lord over all creation, we should crown him Lord over our lives. Since Christ is the head of the body, his church, we should nurture our vital connection to him.

MEGATHEMES

THEME	EXPLANATION	IMPORTANCE
Christ Is God	Jesus Christ is God in the flesh, Lord of all creation, and Lord of the new creation. He is the expressed reflection of the invisible God. He is eternal, pre-existent, omnipotent, equal with the Father. He is supreme and complete.	Because Christ is supreme, our lives must be Christ-centered. To recognize him as God means to regard our relationship with him as most vital and to make his interests our top priority.
Christ Is Head of the Church	Because Christ is God, he is the head of the church, his true believers. Christ is the founder, the leader, and the highest authority on earth. He requires first place in all our thoughts and activities.	To acknowledge Christ as our head, we must welcome his leadership in all we do or think. No person, group, or church can regard any loyalty as more critical than that of loyalty to Christ.
Union with Christ	Because our sin has been forgiven and we have been reconciled to God, we have a union with Christ that can never be broken. In our faith connection with him, we identify with his death, burial, and resurrection.	We should live in constant contact and communication with God. When we do, we all will be unified with Christ and with one another.
Man-made Religion	False teachers were promoting a man-made religion that stressed self-made rules (legalism). They also sought spiritual growth by discipline of the body (asceticism) and visions (mysticism). This search created pride in their self-centered efforts.	We must not cling to our own ideas and try to blend them into Christianity. Nor should we let our hunger for a more fulfilling Christian experience cause us to trust in a teacher, a group, or a system of thought more than in Christ himself. Christ is our hope and our true source of wisdom.

1. What Christ has done

1 Paul, an apostle of Christ Jesus by the will of God, and Timothy our brother,

2 To the holy and faithful[a] brothers in Christ at Colosse:

Grace and peace to you from God our Father.[b] [a]

1:2
[a] Ro 1:7

[a]2 Or *believing*   [b]2 Some manuscripts *Father and the Lord Jesus Christ*

1:1 Colossians, along with Philippians, Ephesians, and Philemon, is called a *Prison Letter* because Paul wrote it from prison in Rome. This prison was actually a house where Paul was kept under close guard at all times (probably chained to a soldier) but given certain freedoms not offered to most prisoners. He was allowed to write letters and to see any visitors he wanted to see.

1:1 Paul was an apostle "by the will of God." Paul often would establish his credentials as chosen and sent by God because he had not been one of the original 12 disciples. *Apostle* means chosen and sent by God as a missionary or ambassador. *By the will of God* means that he was appointed; this was not just a matter of his own personal aspirations.

1:1 Paul mentions Timothy in other New Testament letters as well: 2 Corinthians, Philippians, 1 and 2 Thessalonians, and Philemon. Paul also wrote two letters to Timothy (1 and 2 Timothy). For more information on these men, two of the greatest missionaries of the early church, see Paul's Profile in Acts 9, p. 1825 and Timothy's Profile in 1 Timothy, p. 2037.

1:2 The city of Colosse was 100 miles east of Ephesus on the Lycus River. It was not as influential as the nearby city of Laodicea, but as a trading center it was a crossroads for ideas and religions. Colosse had a large Jewish population—many Jews had fled there when they were forced out of Jerusalem under the persecutions of Antiochus III and IV, almost 200 years before Christ. The church in

Thanksgiving and Prayer

³We always thank God, the Father of our Lord Jesus Christ, when we pray for you, ⁴because we have heard of your faith in Christ Jesus and of the love you have for all the saints ᵇ— ⁵the faith and love that spring from the hope ᶜ that is stored up for you in heaven ᵈ and that you have already heard about in the word of truth, the gospel ⁶that has come to you. All over the world this gospel is bearing fruit and growing, just as it has been doing among you since the day you heard it and understood God's grace in all its truth. ⁷You learned it from Epaphras,ᵉ our dear fellow servant, who is a faithful minister of Christ on our ᵃ behalf, ⁸and who also told us of your love in the Spirit. ᶠ

ᵃ7 Some manuscripts *your*

1:4
ᵇEph 1:15

1:5
ᶜ1Th 5:8
ᵈ1Pe 1:4

1:7
ᵉPhm 23

1:8
ᶠRo 15:30

LOCATION OF COLOSSE

Paul had no doubt been through Laodicea on his third missionary journey, as it lay on the main route to Ephesus, but he had never been to Colosse. Though a large city with a significant population, Colosse was smaller and less important than the nearby cities of Laodicea and Hierapolis.

Colosse had been founded by Epaphras (1:7), one of Paul's converts. Paul had not yet visited this church. His purpose in writing was to refute heretical teachings about Christ that had been causing confusion among the Christians there.

1:2, 3 Letters in Paul's day frequently would begin with identifying the writer and the readers, followed by a greeting of peace. Paul usually would add Christian elements to his greetings, reminding his readers of his call by God to spread the gospel, emphasizing that the authority for his words came from God, and giving thanks for God's blessings.

1:4, 5 Throughout this letter Paul combats a heresy similar to *Gnosticism* (see the notes on 1:9–14; 1:15–23; 2:4ff). Gnostics believed that it took special knowledge to be accepted by God; for them, even for those who claimed to be Christians, Christ alone was not the way of salvation (1:20). In his introductory comments, therefore, Paul commended the Colossians for their faith, love, and hope—three main emphases of Christianity (1 Corinthians 13:13). He deliberately omitted the word *knowledge* because of the "special knowledge" aspect of the heresy. It is not *what* we know that brings salvation, but *whom* we know. Knowing Christ is knowing God.

1:5 We can hope in what God has for us in heaven because we know that our future destination and salvation are sure (1 Peter 1:3, 4). We are free to live for Christ and love others. When you

find yourself doubting or wavering in your faith or love, remember your destination—heaven.

1:6 Wherever Paul went, he preached the gospel—to Gentile audiences, to hostile Jewish leaders, and even to his Roman guards. Whenever people believed in the message that Paul spoke, they were changed. God's Word is not just for our information, it is for our transformation! Becoming a Christian means beginning a whole new relationship with God, not just turning over a new leaf or determining to do right. New believers have a changed purpose, direction, attitude, and behavior. They are no longer seeking to serve themselves, but they are bearing fruit for God. How is the gospel reaching others through your life?

1:7 Epaphras had founded the church at Colosse while Paul was living in Ephesus (Acts 19:10). Epaphras may have been converted in Ephesus, and then he returned to Colosse, his hometown. For some reason, he visited Rome and, while there, told Paul about the problem with the Colossian heresy. This prompted Paul to write this letter. Epaphras is also mentioned in Philemon 23 (the Colossian church met in Philemon's house).

1:8 Because of their love for one another, Christians can have an impact that goes far beyond their neighborhoods and communities. Christian love comes from the Holy Spirit (see Galatians 5:22). The Bible speaks of it as an action and attitude, not just an emotion. Love is a by-product of our new life in Christ (see

1:9
g Eph 1:15
1:10
h Eph 4:1
1:11
i Eph 3:16
j Eph 4:2
1:12
k Eph 5:20
1:13
l Eph 6:12; 2Pe 1:11
1:14
m Eph 1:7

9 For this reason, since the day we heard about you, g we have not stopped praying for you and asking God to fill you with the knowledge of his will through all spiritual wisdom and understanding. 10 And we pray this in order that you may live a life worthy h of the Lord and may please him in every way: bearing fruit in every good work, growing in the knowledge of God, 11 being strengthened with all power i according to his glorious might so that you may have great endurance and patience, j and joyfully 12 giving thanks to the Father, k who has qualified you a to share in the inheritance of the saints in the kingdom of light. 13 For he has rescued us from the dominion of darkness and brought us into the kingdom l of the Son he loves, 14 in whom we have redemption, b the forgiveness of sins. m

a 12 Some manuscripts us   b 14 A few late manuscripts redemption through his blood

---

THE COLOSSIAN HERESY

Paul answered the various tenets of the Colossian heresy that threatened itself the church. This heresy was a "mixed bag," containing elements from several different heresies, some of which contradicted each other (as the chart shows).

The Heresy	Reference	Paul's Answer
Spirit is good; matter is evil.	1:15–20	God created heaven and earth for his glory.
One must follow ceremonies, rituals, and restrictions in order to be saved or perfected.	2:11, 16–23; 3:11	These were only shadows that ended when Christ came. He is all you need to be saved.
One must deny the body and live in strict asceticism.	2:18–23	Asceticism is no help in conquering evil thoughts and desires; instead, it leads to pride.
Angels must be worshiped.	2:18	Angels are not to be worshiped; Christ alone is worthy of worship.
Christ could not be both human and divine.	1:15–20; 2:2, 3	Christ is God in the flesh; he is the eternal One, head of the body, first in everything, supreme.
One must obtain "secret knowledge" in order to be saved or perfected—and this was not available to everyone.	2:2, 18	God's secret is Christ himself, and he has been revealed to all.
One must adhere to human wisdom, tradition, and philosophies.	2:4, 8–10; 3:15–17	By themselves, these can be misleading and shallow because they have human origin; instead, we should remember what Christ taught and follow his words as our ultimate authority.
It is even better to combine aspects of several religions.	2:10	You have everything when you have Christ; he is all-sufficient.
There is nothing wrong with immorality.	3:1–11	Get rid of sin and evil because you have been chosen by God to live a new life as a representative of the Lord Jesus.

Romans 5:5; 1 Corinthians 13). Christians have no excuse for not loving, because Christian love is a decision to *act* in the best interests of others.

1:9-14 Paul was exposing a heresy in the Colossian church that was similar to *Gnosticism* (see the note on 2:4ff for more information). Gnostics valued the accumulation of knowledge, but Paul pointed out that knowledge in itself is empty. To be worth anything, it must lead to a changed life and right living. His prayer for the Colossians has two dimensions: (1) that they might be filled with the knowledge of God's will through all spiritual wisdom and understanding, and (2) that they would bear fruit in every good work, growing in the knowledge of God. Knowledge is not merely to be accumulated; it should give us direction for living. Paul wanted the Colossians to be wise, but he also wanted them to *use* their knowledge. Knowledge of God is not a secret that only a few can discover; it is open to everyone. God wants us to learn more about him, and also to put belief into practice by helping others.

1:9-14 Sometimes we wonder how to pray for missionaries and other leaders we have never met. Paul had never met the Colossians, but he faithfully prayed for them. His prayers teach us how to pray for others, whether we know them or not. We can request that they (1) understand God's will, (2) gain spiritual

wisdom, (3) please and honor God, (4) bear good fruit, (5) grow in the knowledge of God, (6) be filled with God's strength, (7) have great endurance and patience, (8) stay full of Christ's joy, and (9) give thanks always. All believers have these same basic needs. When you don't know how to pray for someone, use Paul's prayer pattern for the Colossians.

1:12-14 Paul lists five benefits God gives all believers through Christ: (1) he made us qualified to share in our inheritance (see also 2 Corinthians 5:21); (2) he rescued us from Satan's dominion of darkness and made us his children (see also 2:15); (3) he brought us into his eternal kingdom (see also Ephesians 1:5, 6); (4) he redeemed us—bought our freedom from sin and judgment (see also Hebrews 9:12); and (5) he forgave all our sins (see also Ephesians 1:7). Thank God for what you have received in Christ.

1:13 The Colossians feared the unseen forces of darkness, but Paul says that true believers have been transferred from darkness to light, from slavery to freedom, from guilt to forgiveness, and from the power of Satan to the power of God. We have been rescued from a rebel kingdom to serve the rightful King. Our conduct should reflect our new allegiance.

The Supremacy of Christ

[15]He is the image [n] of the invisible God, the firstborn over all creation. [16]For by him all things were created: things in heaven and on earth, visible and invisible, whether thrones or powers or rulers or authorities;[o] all things were created by him and for him. [17]He is before all things, and in him all things hold together. [18]And he is the head of the body, the church; he is the beginning and the firstborn from among the dead,[p] so that in everything he might have the supremacy. [19]For God was pleased to have all his fullness [q] dwell in him, [20]and through him to reconcile[r] to himself all things, whether things on earth or things in heaven, by making peace through his blood,[s] shed on the cross.

[21]Once you were alienated from God and were enemies in your minds because of[a] your evil behavior. [22]But now he has reconciled you by Christ's physical body through death to present you holy in his sight, without blemish and free from accusation[t]— [23]if you continue in your faith, established[u] and firm, not moved from the hope held out in the gospel. This is the gospel that you heard and that has been proclaimed to every creature under heaven, [v] and of which I, Paul, have become a servant.

a21 Or minds, as shown by

1:15
n 2Co 4:4

1:16
o Eph 1:20, 21

1:18
p Rev 1:5

1:19
q Jn 1:16

1:20
r 2Co 5:18
s Eph 2:13

1:22
t Eph 5:27

1:23
u Eph 3:17
v Ro 10:18

1:15, 16 This is one of the strongest statements about the divine nature of Christ found anywhere in the Bible. Jesus is not only equal to God (Philippians 2:6), he *is* God (John 10:30, 38; 12:45; 14:1–11); as the image of the invisible God, he is the exact representation of God. He not only reflects God, but he reveals God to us (John 1:18; 14:9); as the firstborn over all creation, he has all the priority and authority of the firstborn prince in a king's household. He came from heaven, not from the dust of the earth (1 Corinthians 15:47), and he is Lord of all (Romans 9:5; 10:11–13; Revelation 1:5; 17:14). He is completely holy (Hebrews 7:26–28; 1 Peter 1:19; 2:22; 1 John 3:5), and he has authority to judge the world (Romans 2:16; 2 Corinthians 5:10; 2 Timothy 4:1). Therefore, Christ is supreme over all creation, including the spirit world. We, like the Colossian believers, must believe in the deity of Jesus Christ (that Jesus is God) or our Christian faith is hollow, misdirected, and meaningless. This is a central truth of Christianity. We must oppose those who say that Jesus was merely a prophet or a good teacher.

1:15–23 In the Colossian church there were several misconceptions about Christ that Paul directly refuted: (1) Believing that matter is evil, false teachers argued that God would not have come to earth as a true human being in bodily form. Paul stated that Christ is the image—the exact likeness—of God, and is himself God, and yet he died on the cross as a human being. (2) They believed that God did not create the world, because he would not have created evil. Paul proclaimed that Jesus Christ, who was also God in the flesh, is the Creator of both heaven and earth. (3) They said that Christ was not the unique Son of God, but rather one of many intermediaries between God and people. Paul explained that Christ existed before anything else and is the firstborn of those resurrected. (4) They refused to see Christ as the source of salvation, insisting that people could find God only through special and secret knowledge. In contrast Paul openly proclaimed the way of salvation to be through Christ alone. Paul continued to bring the argument back to Christ. When we share the gospel, we too must keep the focus on Christ.

1:16 Because the false teachers believed that the physical world was evil, they thought that God himself could not have created it. If Christ were God, they reasoned, he would be in charge only of the spiritual world. But Paul explained that all the rulers, powers, thrones, and authorities of both the spiritual and physical worlds were created by and are under the authority of Christ himself. This includes not only the government but also the spiritual world that the heretics were so concerned about. Christ has no equal and no rival. He is the Lord of all.

1:17 God is not only the Creator of the world, but he is also its Sustainer. In him, everything is held together, protected, and prevented from disintegrating into chaos. Because Christ is the Sustainer of all life, none of us is independent from him. We are

all his servants who must daily trust him for protecting us, caring for us, and sustaining us.

1:18 Christ is the "firstborn from among the dead." Jesus was raised from death, and his resurrection proves his lordship over the material world. All who trust in Christ will also defeat death and rise again to live eternally with him (1 Corinthians 15:20; 1 Thessalonians 4:14). Because of Christ's death on the cross, he has been exalted and elevated to the status that was rightfully his (see Philippians 2:5–11). Because Christ is spiritually supreme in the universe, surely we should give him first place in all our thoughts and activities. See the second note on Luke 24:6, 7 for more about the significance of Christ's resurrection.

1:19 By this statement, Paul was refuting the Greek idea that Jesus could not be human and divine at the same time. Christ is fully human; he is also fully divine. Christ has always been God and always will be God. When we have Christ we have all of God in human form. Don't diminish any aspect of Christ—either his humanity or his divinity.

1:20 Christ's death provided a way for all people to come to God. It cleared away the sin that keeps us from having a right relationship with our Creator. This does not mean that everyone has been saved, but that the way has been cleared for anyone who will trust Christ to be saved. We can have peace with God and be reconciled to him by accepting Christ, who died in our place. Is there a distance between you and the Creator? Be reconciled to God. Come to him through Christ.

1:21 Because we were alienated from God, we were strangers to his way of thinking and were "enemies in our minds." Sin corrupted our way of thinking about God. Wrong thinking leads to sin, which further perverts and destroys our thoughts about him. When we were out of harmony with God, our natural condition was to be totally hostile to his standards. See Romans 1:21–32 for more on the perverted thinking of unbelievers.

1:21, 22 *No one* is good enough to save himself or herself. If we want to live eternally with Christ, we must depend totally on God's grace. This is true whether we have been murderers or honest, hardworking citizens. We have all sinned repeatedly, and *any* sin is enough to cause us to come to Jesus Christ for salvation and eternal life. Apart from Christ, there is no way for our sin to be forgiven and removed.

1:22 In order to answer the accusation that Jesus was only a spirit and not a true human being, Paul explained that Jesus' physical body actually died. Jesus suffered death fully as a human so that we could be assured that he died in our place. Jesus faced death as God so we can be assured that his sacrifice was complete and that he truly removed our sin.

1:22, 23 The way to be free from sin is to trust Jesus Christ to take it away. We must remain "established and firm" in the truth

Paul's Labor for the Church

1:24
w 2Co 1:5
1:25
x Eph 3:2

1:28
y Col 3:16
1:29
z 1Co 15:10
a Col 2:1
b Eph 1:19
2:1
c Col 1:29

24 Now I rejoice in what was suffered for you, and I fill up in my flesh what is still lacking in regard to Christ's afflictions, w for the sake of his body, which is the church. 25 I have become its servant by the commission God gave me x to present to you the word of God in its fullness— 26 the mystery that has been kept hidden for ages and generations, but is now disclosed to the saints. 27 To them God has chosen to make known among the Gentiles the glorious riches of this mystery, which is Christ in you, the hope of glory.

28 We proclaim him, admonishing y and teaching everyone with all wisdom, so that we may present everyone perfect in Christ. 29 To this end I labor, z struggling a with all his energy, which so powerfully works in me. b

2 I want you to know how much I am struggling c for you and for those at Laodicea, and for all who have not met me personally. 2 My purpose is that they may be encouraged in heart and united in love, so that they may have the full riches of complete understanding, in order that they may know the mystery of God, namely, Christ, 3 in whom are hidden all the

---

HOW TO PRAY FOR OTHER CHRISTIANS

1. Be thankful for their faith and changed lives (1:3).
2. Ask God to help them know what he wants them to do (1:9).
3. Ask God to give them deep spiritual understanding (1:9).
4. Ask God to help them live for him (1:10).
5. Ask God to give them more knowledge of himself (1:10).
6. Ask God to give them strength for endurance (1:11).
7. Ask God to fill them with joy, strength, and thankfulness (1:11, 12).

How many people in your life could be touched if you prayed in this way?

---

of the gospel, putting our confidence in Jesus alone to forgive our sins, to make us right with God, and to empower us to live the way he desires. When a judge in a court of law declares the defendant not guilty, the person has been acquitted of all the accusations or charges. Legally, it is as if he or she had never been accused. When God forgives our sins, our record is wiped clean. From his perspective, it is as though we had never sinned. God's solution is available to you. No matter what you have done or what you have been like, God's forgiveness is for you.

1:24 Paul's statement, "I fill up in my flesh what is still lacking in regard to Christ's afflictions," may mean that suffering is unavoidable in bringing the Good News of Christ to the world. When we suffer, Christ feels it with us. But this suffering can be endured joyfully because it changes lives and brings people into God's kingdom (see 1 Peter 4:1, 2, 12–19). For more about how Paul could rejoice despite his suffering, see the note on Philippians 1:29.

1:26, 27 The false teachers in the Colossian church believed that spiritual perfection was a secret and hidden plan that only a few privileged people could discover. Their secret plan was meant to be exclusive. Paul said that he was proclaiming the entire message of God, not just a part of the plan. He also called God's plan a "mystery that has been kept hidden for ages and generations," not in the sense that only a few would understand, but because it was hidden until Christ came. Through Christ it was made open to all. God's secret plan is "Christ in you, the hope of glory"—God planned to have his Son, Jesus Christ, live in the hearts of all who believe in him—even Gentiles like the Colossians. Do you know Christ? He is not hidden if you will come to him.

1:28, 29 The word *perfect* means mature or complete, not flawless. Paul wanted to see each believer mature spiritually. Like Paul, we must work wholeheartedly like an athlete, but we should not strive in our own strength alone. We have the power of God's Spirit working in us. We can learn and grow daily, motivated by love, and not by fear or pride, knowing that God gives the energy to become mature.

1:28, 29 Christ's message is for everyone; so everywhere Paul and Timothy went they brought the Good News to all who would listen. An effective presentation of the gospel includes *admonishing* (warning) and teaching. The warning is that without Christ, people are doomed to eternal separation from God. The teaching is that salvation is available through faith in Christ. As Christ works in you, tell others about him, warning and teaching them in love. Who do you know that needs to hear this message?

2:1 Laodicea was located a few miles northwest of Colosse. Like the church at Colosse, the Laodicean church was probably founded by one of Paul's converts while Paul was staying in Ephesus (Acts 19:10). The city was a wealthy center of trade and commerce, but later Christ would criticize the believers at Laodicea for their lukewarm commitment (Revelation 3:14–22). The fact that Paul wanted this letter to be passed on to the Laodicean church (4:16) indicates that false teaching may have spread there as well. Paul was counting on ties of love to bring the churches together to stand against this heresy and to encourage each other to remain true to God's plan of salvation in Christ. Our churches should be encouraging, unified communities committed to carrying out Christ's work.

treasures of wisdom and knowledge.[d] [4]I tell you this so that no one may deceive you by fine-sounding arguments. [5]For though I am absent from you in body, I am present with you in spirit[e] and delight to see how orderly[f] you are and how firm[g] your faith in Christ is.

Freedom From Human Regulations Through Life With Christ

[6]So then, just as you received Christ Jesus as Lord, continue to live in him, [7]rooted and built up in him, strengthened in the faith as you were taught, and overflowing with thankfulness.

[8]See to it that no one takes you captive through hollow and deceptive philosophy, which depends on human tradition and the basic principles of this world[h] rather than on Christ. [9]For in Christ all the fullness of the Deity lives in bodily form, [10]and you have been given fullness in Christ, who is the head over every power and authority. [11]In him you were also circumcised,[i] in the putting off of the sinful nature,[a] not with a circumcision done by the hands of men but with the circumcision done by Christ, [12]having been buried with him in baptism and raised with him through your faith in the power of God, who raised him from the dead.[j]

[a] 11 Or *the flesh*

2:3
[d] Ro 11:33

2:5
[e] 1Th 2:17
[f] 1Co 14:40
[g] 1Pe 5:9

2:8
[h] Gal 4:3

2:11
[i] Ro 2:29

2:12
[j] Ac 2:24

2:4ff The problem that Paul was combating in the Colossian church was similar to *Gnosticism* (from the Greek word for *knowledge*). This *heresy* (a teaching contrary to Biblical doctrine) undermined Christianity in several basic ways: (1) It insisted that important secret knowledge was hidden from most believers; Paul, however, said that Christ provides all the knowledge we need. (2) It taught that the body was evil; Paul countered that God himself lived in a body—that is, he was embodied in Jesus Christ. (3) It contended that Christ only seemed to be human, but was not; Paul insisted that Jesus is fully human and fully God.

Gnosticism became fashionable in the second century. Even in Paul's day, these ideas sounded attractive to many, and exposure to such teachings could easily seduce a church that didn't know Christian doctrine well. Similar teachings still pose significant problems for many in the church today. We combat heresy by becoming thoroughly acquainted with God's Word through personal study and sound Bible teaching.

2:4 Christian faith provides a growth track into knowledge of the truth, but along the way, how do we guard against being deceived by lies that are masquerading as "fine-sounding arguments"?

If your growth track is too narrow, you become thickheaded and insular—no one can teach you a thing. Before long, you can't teach anyone around you, for no one is listening. You are isolated. Love disappears from your life.

If your track is too wide and every idea is an exciting new possibility, you'll waste a lot of time just keeping on track and risk some dangerous detours.

The key is centering on Christ and grounding yourself in his Word. Learn daily about the Savior. Study the Bible. Develop your theological knowledge. Stay humble and curious about the amazing complexity of the world God has made. Ask lots of questions about the assumptions behind ideas new to you. Press toward wisdom. Pray for understanding. God has given us minds for learning—never quit using yours.

2:6, 7 Receiving Christ as Lord of your life is the beginning of life with Christ. But you must continue to follow his leadership by being rooted, built up, and strengthened in the faith. Christ wants to guide you and help you with your daily problems. You can live for Christ by (1) committing your life and submitting your will to him (Romans 12:1, 2); (2) seeking to learn from him, his life, and his teachings (3:16); and (3) recognizing the Holy Spirit's power in you (Acts 1:8; Galatians 5:22).

2:7 Paul uses the illustration of our being rooted in Christ. Just as plants draw nourishment from the soil through their roots, so we draw our life-giving strength from Christ. The more we draw our strength from him, the less we will be fooled by those who falsely claim to have life's answers. If Christ is our strength, we will be free from human regulations.

2:8 Paul writes against any philosophy of life based only on human ideas and experiences. Paul himself was a gifted philosopher, so he is not condemning philosophy. He is condemning teaching that credits humanity, not Christ, with being the answer to life's problems. That approach becomes a false religion. There are many man-made approaches to life's problems that totally disregard God. To resist heresy you must use your mind, keep your eyes on Christ, and study God's Word.

2:9 Again Paul asserts Christ's deity. "In Christ all the fullness of the Deity lives in bodily form" means that all of God was in Christ's human body. When we have Christ we have everything we need for salvation and right living. See the note on 1:15, 16 for more on the divine nature of Christ.

2:10 Look around you. People are searching for something to give their lives a boost. Few people seem content within themselves. A strange and often hard-to-identify inner vacuum gives most people an uneasy sense of incompleteness. Christ fills that vacuum! As Jesus' person is fully divine, so we, united by faith to Jesus, find personal fulfillment in him: "You have been given fullness in Christ."

When you know Jesus Christ, you don't need to seek God by means of other religions, cults, or unbiblical philosophies as the Colossians were doing. Christ alone holds the answers to the true meaning of life, because he *is* life. Christ is the unique source of knowledge and power for the Christian life. No Christian needs anything in addition to what Christ has provided to be saved. Some days may not feel like it, but in Jesus, the vacuum is gone; the full power and presence of God have taken up residence in your mind and heart. You are a new person, equipped for life and satisfied in God. Take some risks—God will guide you. Give more generously—God will supply. Love more freely—God will energize you. Say "can do" more often—God will amaze you.

2:11 Jewish males were circumcised as a sign of the Jews' covenant with God (Genesis 17:9–14). With the death of Christ, circumcision was no longer necessary. So now our commitment to God is written on our hearts, not our bodies. Christ sets us free from our evil desires by a spiritual operation, not a bodily one. God removes the old nature and gives us a new nature.

2:11, 12 In this passage, circumcision is related to baptism; therefore, some see baptism as the New Testament sign of the covenant, identifying the person with the covenant community. Baptism parallels the death, burial, and resurrection of Christ, and it also portrays the death and burial of our sinful old way of life followed by resurrection to new life in Christ. Remembering that our old sinful life is dead and buried with Christ gives us a powerful motive to resist sin. Not wanting the desires of our past to come back to power again, we can consciously choose to treat our desires as if they were dead. Then we can continue to enjoy our wonderful new life with Christ (see Galatians 3:27 and Colossians 3:1–4).

2:14
k Eph 2:15

2:15
l Eph 6:12

2:16
m Ro 14:3, 4
n Ro 14:5

2:17
o Heb 8:5

¹³When you were dead in your sins and in the uncircumcision of your sinful nature,ᵃ God made youᵇ alive with Christ. He forgave us all our sins, ¹⁴having canceled the written code, with its regulations,ᵏ that was against us and that stood opposed to us; he took it away, nailing it to the cross. ¹⁵And having disarmed the powers and authorities,ˡ he made a public spectacle of them, triumphing over them by the cross.ᶜ

¹⁶Therefore do not let anyone judge youᵐ by what you eat or drink, or with regard to a religious festival,ⁿ a New Moon celebration or a Sabbath day. ¹⁷These are a shadow of the things that were to come;ᵒ the reality, however, is found in Christ. ¹⁸Do not let anyone who delights in false humility and the worship of angels disqualify you for the prize. Such a person goes

ᵃ 13 Or *your flesh*   ᵇ 13 Some manuscripts *us*   ᶜ 15 Or *them in him*

SALVATION THROUGH FAITH

		Religion by Self-Effort	Salvation by Faith
	Goal	Please God by our own good deeds	Trust in Christ and then live to please God
	Means	Practice, diligent service, discipline, and obedience, in hope of reward	Confess, submit, and commit ourselves to Christ's control
	Power	Good, honest effort through self-determination	The Holy Spirit in us helps us do good work for Christ's kingdom
	Control	Self-motivation; self-control	Christ is in us; we are in Christ
	Results	Chronic guilt, apathy, depression, failure, constant desire for approval	Joy, thankfulness, love, guidance, service, forgiveness

Salvation by faith in Christ sounds too easy for many people. They would rather think that they have done something to save themselves. Their religion becomes one of self-effort that leads either to disappointment or pride, but finally to eternal death. Christ's simple way is the only way, and it alone leads to eternal life.

2:13–15 Before we believed in Christ, our nature was evil. We disobeyed, rebelled, and ignored God (even at our best, we did not love him with all our heart, soul, and mind). The Christian, however, has a new nature. God has crucified the old rebellious nature (Romans 6:6) and replaced it with a new loving nature (3:9, 10). The penalty of sin died with Christ on the cross. God has declared us not guilty, and we need no longer live under sin's power. God does not take us out of the world or make us robots—we will still feel like sinning, and sometimes we will sin. The difference is that before we were saved, we were slaves to our sinful nature; but now we are free to live for Christ (see Galatians 2:20).

2:14 The written code that was canceled was the legal demands of the Old Testament law. The law opposed us by its demands for payment for our sin. Though no one can be saved by merely keeping that code, the moral truths and principles in the Old Testament still teach and guide today.

2:14 We can enjoy our new life in Christ because we have joined him in his death and resurrection. Our evil desires, our bondage to sin, and our love of sin died with him. Now, joining him in his resurrection life, we may have unbroken fellowship with God and freedom from sin. Our debt for sin has been paid in full; our sins are swept away and forgotten by God; and we can be clean and new. For more on the difference between our new life in Christ and our old sinful nature, read Ephesians 4:23, 24 and Colossians 3:3–15.

2:15 Who are these spiritual powers and authorities? Several suggestions have been made, including (1) demonic powers, (2) the gods of the powerful nations, (3) angels (highly regarded by the heretical teachers), or (4) the government of Rome. Since Paul did not identify who these rulers and authorities were, it could be any one of them, or all four. What Christ "disarmed" on the cross was any embodiment of rebellion in the world—whether that be Satan and his demons, false idols of pagan religious, evil world governments, or even God's good angels when they become objects of worship (as in the Colossian heresy). This "disarming" occurred when Jesus died on the cross, like stripping a defeated enemy of armor on the battlefield. Evil no longer has any power

over believers because Christ has disarmed it. Paul already had told the Colossians, "He has rescued us from the dominion of darkness and brought us into the kingdom of the Son" (1:13).

2:16 "What you eat or drink" probably refers to the Jewish dietary laws. The festivals mentioned are Jewish holy days celebrated annually, monthly (New Moon), and weekly (the Sabbath). These rituals distinguished the Jews from their pagan neighbors. Failure to observe them could be easily noticed by those who were keeping track of what others did. But we should not let ourselves be judged by the opinions of others, because Christ has set us free.

2:16, 17 Paul told the Colossian Christians not to let others criticize their diet or their religious ceremonies. Instead of outward observance, believers should focus on faith in Christ alone. Our worship, traditions, and ceremonies can help bring us close to God, but we should never criticize fellow Christians whose traditions and ceremonies differ from ours. More important than how we worship is that we worship Christ. Don't let anyone judge you. You are responsible to Christ.

2:17 Old Testament laws, holidays, and feasts pointed toward Christ. Paul calls them a "shadow" of the reality that was to come—Christ himself. When Christ came, he dispelled the shadow. If we have Christ, we have what we need to know and please God.

2:18 The false teachers were claiming that God was far away and could be approached only through various levels of angels. They taught that people had to worship angels in order, eventually, to reach God. This is unscriptural; the Bible teaches that angels are God's servants, and it forbids worshiping them (Exodus 20:3, 4; Revelation 22:8, 9). As you grow in your Christian faith, let God's Word be your guide, not the opinions of other people.

2:18 The expression "unspiritual mind" means that these people had a self-made religion. The false teachers were trying to deny the significance of the body by saying that it was evil, but their desire for attention from others showed that, in reality, they were obsessed with the physical realm.

into great detail about what he has seen, and his unspiritual mind puffs him up with idle notions. ¹⁹He has lost connection with the Head, from whom the whole body, supported and held together by its ligaments and sinews, grows as God causes it to grow. ᵖ

²⁰Since you died with Christ to the basic principles of this world, �q why, as though you still belonged to it, do you submit to its rules: ²¹"Do not handle! Do not taste! Do not touch!"? ²²These are all destined to perish ʳ with use, because they are based on human commands and teachings. ˢ ²³Such regulations indeed have an appearance of wisdom, with their self-imposed worship, their false humility and their harsh treatment of the body, but they lack any value in restraining sensual indulgence.

2. What Christians should do

Rules for Holy Living

3 Since, then, you have been raised with Christ, set your hearts on things above, where Christ is seated at the right hand of God. ²Set your minds on things above, not on earthly things. ³For you died, ᵗ and your life is now hidden with Christ in God. ⁴When Christ, who is your ᵃ life, appears, then you also will appear with him in glory. ᵘ

⁵Put to death, therefore, whatever belongs to your earthly nature: sexual immorality,

ᵃ4 Some manuscripts *our*

2:19
ᵖEph 4:16
2:20
qGal 4:3, 9
2:22
ʳ1Co 6:13
ˢMt 15:9; Tit 1:14

3:3
ʳRo 6:2
3:4
ᵘ1Jn 3:2
3:5
ᵛEph 5:3
ʷEph 5:5

2:19 The fundamental problem with the false teachers was that they were not connected to Christ, the Head of the body of believers. If they had been joined to him, they could not have taught false doctrine or lived immorally. Anyone who teaches about God without being connected to him by faith should not be trusted.

2:20 The "basic principles" are the beliefs of pagans. See 2:8 for more on Paul's view of non-Christian philosophy.

2:20; 3:1 How do we die with Christ, and how are we raised with him? When a person becomes a Christian, he or she is given new life through the power of the Holy Spirit. See the notes on 2:11, 12 and 2:13–15 for further information.

2:20–23 People should be able to see a difference between the way Christians and non-Christians live. Still, we should not expect instant maturity in new Christians. Christian growth is a lifelong process. Although we have a new nature, we don't automatically think all good thoughts and have all pure attitudes when we become new people in Christ. But if we keep listening to God, we will be changing all the time. As you look over the last year, what changes for the better have you seen in your thoughts and attitudes? Change may be slow, but your life will change significantly if you trust God to change you.

2:20–23 We cannot reach up to God by following rules of pious self-denial, by observing rituals, or by practicing religion. Paul isn't saying all rules are bad (see the note on Galatians 2:15, 16). But no keeping of laws or rules will earn salvation. The Good News is that God reaches down to human beings, and he asks for our response. Man-made religions focus on human effort; Christianity focuses on Christ's work. Believers must put aside sinful desires, but doing so is the by-product of our new life in Christ, not the reason for our new life. Our salvation does not depend on our own discipline and rule keeping, but on the power of Christ's death and resurrection.

2:22, 23 We can guard against man-made religions by asking these questions about any religious group: (1) Does it stress man-made rules and taboos rather than God's grace? (2) Does it foster a critical spirit toward others, or does it exercise discipline discreetly and lovingly? (3) Does it stress formulas, secret knowledge, or special visions more than the Word of God? (4) Does it elevate self-righteousness, honoring those who keep the rules, rather than elevating Christ? (5) Does it neglect Christ's universal church, claiming to be an elite group? (6) Does it teach humiliation of the body as a means to spiritual growth rather than focusing on the growth of the whole person? (7) Does it disregard the family rather than holding it in high regard as the Bible does?

2:23 To the Colossians, the discipline demanded by the false teachers seemed good, and legalism still attracts many people today. Following a long list of religious rules requires strong self-discipline and can make a person appear moral, but religious rules cannot change a person's heart. Only the Holy Spirit can do that.

3:1ff In chapter 2, Paul exposed the wrong reasons for self-denial. In chapter 3, he explains true Christian behavior—putting on the new self by accepting Christ and regarding the earthly nature as dead. We change our moral and ethical behavior by letting Christ live within us, so that he can shape us into what we *should* be.

3:1, 2 Setting our hearts on things above means striving to put heaven's priorities into daily practice. Setting our minds on things above means concentrating on the eternal rather than the temporal. See Philippians 4:9 and Colossians 3:15 for more on Christ's rule in our hearts and minds.

3:2, 3 "For you died" means that we should have as little desire for improper worldly desires as a dead person would have. The Christian's real home is where Christ lives (John 14:2, 3). This truth provides a different perspective on our lives here on earth. To "set your minds on things above" means to look at life from God's perspective and to seek what he desires. This provides the antidote to materialism; we gain the proper perspective on material goods when we take God's view of them. It also provides the antidote to sensuality. By seeking what Christ desires, we have the power to break our obsession with pleasure and leisure activities. But it also provides the antidote to empty religiosity because following Christ means loving and serving in this world. Regard the world around you as God does; then you will live in harmony with him.

3:3 What does it mean that a believer's life is "hidden with Christ"? *Hidden* means concealed and safe. This is not only a future hope, but an accomplished fact right now. Our service and conduct do not earn our salvation, but they are results of our salvation. Take heart that your salvation is sure, and live each day for Christ.

3:4 Christ gives us power to live for him now, and he gives us hope for the future—he will return. In the rest of this chapter Paul explains how Christians should act *now* in order to be prepared for Christ's return.

3:5 We should consider ourselves dead and unresponsive to sexual immorality, impurity, lust, evil desires, and greed. The warning in this verse is not against sex, but against sexual perversion. Where is the line between the two?

The Bible everywhere celebrates heterosexual, monogamous marriage as the proper situation for sexual fulfillment. Christian men and women should be open to true love—and to sexual intimacy—within the commitment to lifelong fidelity. That is God's way. The rest is dangerous and futile. Stay away. Sexual sin and perversion will drain your energies and turn your heart away from God.

3:8
x Eph 4:22
y Eph 4:29

3:9
z Eph 4:22, 25

3:10
a Ro 12:2; Eph 4:23

3:11
b Gal 3:28
c Eph 1:23

3:12
d Php 2:3
e Gal 5:22, 23

3:13
f Eph 4:32

3:14
g Eph 4:3

impurity, lust, evil desires and greed, *v* which is idolatry. *w* 6 Because of these, the wrath of God is coming. *a* 7 You used to walk in these ways, in the life you once lived. 8 But now you must rid yourselves *x* of all such things as these: anger, rage, malice, slander, and filthy language from your lips. *y* 9 Do not lie to each other, *z* since you have taken off your old self with its practices 10 and have put on the new self, which is being renewed *a* in knowledge in the image of its Creator. 11 Here there is no Greek or Jew, circumcised or uncircumcised, barbarian, Scythian, slave or free, *b* but Christ is all, *c* and is in all.

12 Therefore, as God's chosen people, holy and dearly loved, clothe yourselves with compassion, kindness, humility, *d* gentleness and patience. *e* 13 Bear with each other and forgive whatever grievances you may have against one another. Forgive as the Lord forgave you. *f* 14 And over all these virtues put on love, which binds them all together in perfect unity. *g*

a 6 Some early manuscripts *coming on those who are disobedient*

FROM DEATH TO LIFE
What happens when we accept Christ

The Bible uses many illustrations to teach what happens when we choose to let Jesus be Lord of our lives. Following are some of the most vivid pictures:

1. Because Christ died for us, we have been crucified with him.

Romans 6:2–13; 7:4–6
2 Corinthians 5:14
Galatians 2:20; 5:24; 6:14
Colossians 2:20; 3:3–5
1 Peter 2:24

2. Our old, rebellious nature died with Christ.

Romans 6:6; 7:4–6
Colossians 3:9, 10

3. Christ's resurrection guarantees our new life now and eternal life with him later.

Romans 6:4, 11
Colossians 2:12, 13; 3:1, 3

This process is acted out in baptism (Colossians 2:12), based on our faith in Christ: (1) The old sinful nature dies (crucified). (2) We are ready to receive a new life (buried). (3) Christ gives us new life (resurrected).

3:6 The "wrath of God" refers to God's judgment on these kinds of behavior, culminating with future and final punishment of evil. When tempted to sin, remember that you must one day stand before God.

3:8–10 We must rid ourselves of all evil practices and immorality. Then we can commit ourselves to what Christ teaches. Paul was appealing to the commitment the believers had made and urging them to remain true to their confession of faith. They were to rid themselves of the old life and "put on" the new way of living given by Christ and guided by the Holy Spirit. If you have made such a commitment to Christ, are you remaining true to it?

3:9 Lying to one another disrupts unity by destroying trust. It tears down relationships and may lead to serious conflict in a church. So don't exaggerate statistics, pass on rumors or gossip, or say things to build up your own image. Be committed to telling the truth.

Jesus wants to clean your life and your church of sexual sin and verbal sin. There is no place in the kingdom of God for hedonistic sexual experimentation or for gossip, rage, and backbiting. In their place, witness to the world like a lighthouse on a stormy night by displaying love, faith, and hope.

3:10 What does it mean to "put on the new self"? It means that your conduct should match your faith. If you are a Christian, you should act like it. To be a Christian means more than just making good resolutions and having good intentions; it means taking the right actions. This is a straightforward step that is as simple as putting on your clothes. You must rid yourself of all evil practices and immorality. Then you can commit yourself to what Christ teaches. If you have made such a commitment to Christ, are you remaining true to it? What old clothes do you need to strip off?

3:10 Every Christian is in a continuing education program. The more we know of Christ and his work, the more we are being changed to be like him. Because this process is lifelong, we must never stop learning and obeying. There is no justification for drifting along, but there is an incentive to find the rich treasures of growing in him. It takes practice, ongoing review, patience, and concentration to keep in line with his will.

3:11 The Christian church should have no barriers of nationality, race, education level, social standing, wealth, gender, religion, or power. Christ breaks down all barriers and accepts all people who come to him. Nothing should keep us from telling others about Christ or accepting into our fellowship any and all believers (Ephesians 2:14, 15). Christians should be building bridges, not walls.

3:12–17 Paul offers a strategy to help us live for God day by day: (1) imitate Christ's compassionate, forgiving attitude (3:12, 13); (2) let love guide your life (3:14); (3) let the peace of Christ rule in your heart (3:15); (4) always be thankful (3:15); (5) keep God's Word in you at all times (3:16); (6) live as Jesus Christ's representative (3:17).

3:13 The key to forgiving others is remembering how much God has forgiven you. Is it difficult for you to forgive someone who has wronged you a little when God has forgiven you so much? Realizing God's infinite love and forgiveness can help you love and forgive others. Let God worry about the wrongs you've suffered. Don't quench your life in bitter feuding; live renewed in love and joy.

3:14 All the virtues that Paul encourages us to develop are perfectly bound together by love. As we clothe ourselves with these virtues, the last garment we are to put on is love, which holds all of the others in place. To practice any list of virtues without practicing love will lead to distortion, fragmentation, and stagnation (1 Corinthians 13:3).

3:14, 15 Christians should live in peace. To live in peace does not mean that suddenly all differences in opinion are eliminated, but it does require that loving Christians work together despite their differences. Such love is not a feeling, but a decision to meet others' needs (see 1 Corinthians 13). To live in love leads to peace between individuals and among the members of the body of believers. Do problems in your relationships with other Christians cause open conflicts or mutual silence? Consider what you can do to heal those relationships with love.

¹⁵Let the peace of Christ rule in your hearts, since as members of one body you were called to peace. And be thankful. ¹⁶Let the word of Christ dwell in you richly as you teach and admonish one another with all wisdom, and as you sing psalms, hymns and spiritual songs with gratitude in your hearts to God. *h* ¹⁷And whatever you do, *i* whether in word or deed, do it all in the name of the Lord Jesus, giving thanks to God the Father through him.

3:16
h Eph 5:19

3:17
i 1Co 10:31

Rules for Christian Households

¹⁸Wives, submit to your husbands, as is fitting in the Lord.

¹⁹Husbands, love your wives and do not be harsh with them.

²⁰Children, obey your parents in everything, for this pleases the Lord.

²¹Fathers, do not embitter your children, or they will become discouraged.

²²Slaves, obey your earthly masters in everything; and do it, not only when their eye is on you and to win their favor, but with sincerity of heart and reverence for the Lord. ²³Whatever you do, work at it with all your heart, as working for the Lord, not for men, ²⁴since you know that you will receive an inheritance from the Lord as a reward. It is the Lord Christ you are serving. ²⁵Anyone who does wrong will be repaid for his wrong, and there is no favoritism. *j*

4 Masters, provide your slaves with what is right and fair, because you know that you also have a Master in heaven.

3:25
j Ac 10:34

3:15 The word *rule* comes from the language of athletics: Paul tells us to let Christ's peace be umpire or referee in our hearts. Our hearts are the center of conflict because there our feelings and desires clash—our fears and hopes, distrust and trust, jealousy and love. How can we deal with these constant conflicts and live as God wants? Paul explains that we must decide between conflicting elements by using the rule of peace—which choice will promote peace in our souls and in our churches? For more on the peace of Christ, see Philippians 4:9.

3:16 Although the early Christians had access to the Old Testament and freely used it, they did not yet have the New Testament or any other Christian books to study. Their stories and teachings about Christ were memorized and passed on from person to person. Sometimes the teachings were set to music, and so music became an important part of Christian worship and education.

3:16 Thankful people can worship wholeheartedly. Gratitude opens our hearts to God's peace and enables us to put on love. Discontented people constantly calculate what's wrong with their lot in life.

To increase your thankfulness, take an inventory of all you have (including your relationships, memories, abilities, and family, as well as material possessions). Use the inventory for prayers of gratitude. On Sunday, before worship, quit rushing around; instead, take time to reflect on reasons for thanks. Declare Sunday as your "thanks, faith, and hope" day. Celebrate God's goodness to you, and ask in prayer for all your needs for the week ahead.

3:17 Doing "all in the name of the Lord Jesus" means bringing honor to Christ in every aspect and activity of daily living. As a Christian, you represent Christ at all times—wherever you go and whatever you say. What impression do people have of Christ when they see or talk with you? What changes would you make in your life in order to honor Christ?

3:18—4:1 Paul gives rules for three sets of household relationships: (1) husbands and wives, (2) parents and children, and (3) masters and slaves. In each case there is mutual responsibility to submit and love, to obey and encourage, to work hard and be fair. Examine your family and work relationships. Do you relate to others as God intended? See Ephesians 5:21—6:9 for similar instructions.

3:18, 19 Why is submission of wives to husbands "fitting in the Lord"? This may have been good advice for Christian women, newly freed in Christ, who found submission difficult. Paul told them that they should willingly follow their husbands' leadership in Christ. But Paul had words for husbands as well: "Husbands, love your wives and do not be harsh with them." It may also have been true that Christian men, used to the Roman custom of giving

unlimited power to the head of the family, were not used to treating their wives with respect and love. Real spiritual leadership involves service. Just as Christ served the disciples, even to the point of washing their feet, so the husband is to serve his wife. This means putting aside his own interests in order to care for his wife. A wise and Christ-honoring husband will not abuse his leadership role. At the same time, a wise and Christ-honoring wife will not try to undermine her husband's leadership. Either approach causes disunity and friction in marriage. For more on submission, see the notes on Ephesians 5:21–33.

3:20, 21 Children must be handled with care. They need firm discipline administered in love. Parents should not alienate them by nagging, deriding, or destroying their self-respect so that they lose heart.

However, the opposite problem occurs when parents are afraid to correct a child for fear of stifling some aspect of his or her personality or losing his or her love. Single parents or parents who cannot spend much time with a child may be prone to indulgence. But such children, especially, need the security of guidance and structure. Boundaries and guidelines will not embitter a child. Instead, they will set the child free to live securely within the boundaries.

3:22—4:1 Paul does not condemn or condone slavery, but explains that Christ transcends all divisions between people. Slaves are told to work hard as though their master were Christ himself (3:22–25); but masters should be just and fair (4:1). Perhaps Paul was thinking specifically of Onesimus and Philemon—the slave and master whose conflict lay behind the letter to Philemon (see the book of Philemon). Philemon was a slave owner in the Colossian church, and Onesimus had been his slave (4:9).

3:23 Since the creation, God has given us work to do. If we could regard our work as an act of worship or service to God, such an attitude would take some of the drudgery and boredom out of it. We could work without complaining or resentment if we would treat our job problems as the cost of discipleship.

4:1 Masters were to provide what was right and fair. Similarly today, employers should pay fair wages and treat their employees justly. Paul's instructions encourage responsibility and integrity on the job. Christian employees should do their jobs as if Jesus Christ were their supervisor. And Christian employers should treat their employees fairly and with respect. Can you be trusted to do your best, even when the boss is not around? Do you work hard and with enthusiasm? Do you treat your employees as people, not machines? Employers should pay fair wages and treat their employees justly. Leaders should take care of their volunteers and not abuse them. If you have responsibility over others, make sure you do what is just and fair. Remember that no matter

Further Instructions

4:3
k Eph 6:19, 20

4:5
l Eph 5:15
m Eph 5:16

4:6
n Mk 9:50
o 1Pe 3:15

4:9
p Phm 10

4:10
q Ac 4:36

2 Devote yourselves to prayer, being watchful and thankful. 3 And pray for us, too, that God may open a door for our message, so that we may proclaim the mystery of Christ, for which I am in chains. k 4 Pray that I may proclaim it clearly, as I should. 5 Be wise l in the way you act toward outsiders; make the most of every opportunity. m 6 Let your conversation be always full of grace, seasoned with salt, n so that you may know how to answer everyone. o

Final Greetings

7 Tychicus will tell you all the news about me. He is a dear brother, a faithful minister and fellow servant in the Lord. 8 I am sending him to you for the express purpose that you may know about our a circumstances and that he may encourage your hearts. 9 He is coming with Onesimus, p our faithful and dear brother, who is one of you. They will tell you everything that is happening here.

10 My fellow prisoner Aristarchus sends you his greetings, as does Mark, the cousin of Barnabas. q (You have received instructions about him; if he comes to you, welcome him.) 11 Jesus, who is called Justus, also sends greetings. These are the only Jews among my fellow workers for the kingdom of God, and they have proved a comfort to me. 12 Epaphras, who is

a 8 Some manuscripts that he may know about your

SINS VS. SIGNS OF LOVE	Sins of Sexual Attitude and Behavior	Sins of Speech	Signs of Love
	Sexual immorality	Anger/Rage	Compassion
	Impurity	Malice	Kindness
	Lust	Slander	Humility
	Evil desires	Filthy language	Gentleness
	Greed	Lying	Patience
			Forgiveness

In Colossians 3:5 Paul tells us to put to death the things found in list 1. In 3:8, 9 he tells us to rid ourselves of the things found in list 2. In 3:12, 13 we're told to clothe ourselves with the things found in list 3. List 1 deals with sins of sexual attitudes and behavior—they are particularly destructive because of what they do to destroy any group or church. List 2 deals with sins of speech—these are the relationship breakers. List 3 contains the relationship builders, which we are to express as members of Christ's body.

---

whom you work for, and no matter who works for you, the One you ultimately should want to please is your Father in heaven. You are accountable to him.

4:2 Have you ever grown tired of praying for something or someone? Paul says we should "devote" ourselves to prayer and be "watchful" in prayer. Our persistence is an expression of our faith that God answers our prayers. Faith shouldn't die if the answers come slowly, for the delay may be God's way of working his will in our lives. When you feel tired of praying, know that God is present, always listening, always answering—maybe not in ways you had hoped, but in ways that he knows are best.

4:3 The "mystery of Christ" is Christ's Good News of salvation, the gospel. The whole focus of Paul's life was to tell others about Christ, explaining and preaching this wonderful mystery.

4:4 Paul asked for prayer that he could proclaim the Good News about Christ clearly, and we can request prayer to do the same. No matter what approach to evangelism we use, whether emphasizing lifestyle and example or whether building relationships, we should never obscure the message of the gospel.

4:5 We should be wise in our contacts with nonbelievers ("outsiders"), making the most of our opportunities to tell them the Good News of salvation. What opportunities do you have?

4:6 When we tell others about Christ, it is important always to be gracious in what we say. No matter how much sense the message makes, we lose our effectiveness if we are not courteous. Just as we like to be respected, we must respect others if we want them to listen to what we have to say. "Seasoned with salt"

means that what we say should be "tasty" and should encourage further dialogue.

4:7 Tychicus was one of Paul's personal representatives and probably the bearer of the letters to the Colossians and Ephesians (see also Ephesians 6:21, 22). He accompanied Paul to Jerusalem with the collection for the church (Acts 20:4).

4:10 Aristarchus was a Thessalonian who accompanied Paul on his third missionary journey. He was with Paul in the riot at Ephesus (Acts 19:29). He and Tychicus were with Paul in Greece (Acts 20:4). Aristarchus went to Rome with Paul (Acts 27:2). Mark started out with Paul and Barnabas on their first missionary journey (Acts 12:25), but he left in the middle of the trip for unknown reasons (Acts 13:13). Barnabas and Mark were relatives, and when Paul refused to take Mark on another journey, Barnabas and Mark journeyed together to preach the Good News (Acts 15:37–41). Mark also worked with Peter (Acts 12:12, 13; 1 Peter 5:13). Later, Mark and Paul were reconciled (Philemon 24). Mark wrote the Gospel of Mark. His Profile is in Acts 12, p. 1835.

4:12 Epaphras founded the Colossian church (see the note on 1:7), and his report to Paul in Rome caused Paul to write this letter. Epaphras was a hero of the Colossian church, one of the believers who helped keep the church together despite growing troubles. His earnest prayers for the believers show his deep love and concern for them.

one of you and a servant of Christ Jesus, sends greetings. He is always wrestling in prayer for you,ʳ that you may stand firm in all the will of God, mature and fully assured. ¹³I vouch for him that he is working hard for you and for those at Laodicea and Hierapolis. ¹⁴Our dear friend Luke,ˢ the doctor, and Demasᵗ send greetings. ¹⁵Give my greetings to the brothers at Laodicea, and to Nympha and the church in her house. ᵘ

¹⁶After this letter has been read to you, see that it is also read in the church of the Laodiceans and that you in turn read the letter from Laodicea.

¹⁷Tell Archippus: ᵛ "See to it that you complete the work you have received in the Lord."

¹⁸I, Paul, write this greeting in my own hand. ʷ Remember ˣ my chains. Grace be with you.ʸ

4:12
ʳRo 15:30

4:14
ˢ2Ti 4:11
ᵗ2Ti 4:10

4:15
ᵘRo 16:5

4:17
ᵛPhm 2

4:18
ʷ1Co 16:21
ˣHeb 13:3
ʸHeb 13:25

		RULES OF SUBMISSION
Wives, submit to your husbands (3:18).	*Husbands*, love your wives and don't be harsh with them (3:19).	
Children, always obey your parents (3:20).	*Fathers*, do not embitter your children, or they will become discouraged (3:21).	
Slaves, obey your earthly masters (3:22).	*Masters*, be just and fair to your slaves (4:1).	
(*Employees*, work hard for your employers.)	(*Employers*, be just and fair with your employees.)	

The New Testament includes many instructions concerning relationships. Most people read these instructions for the other person and ignore the ones that apply to themselves. But you can't control another person's behavior, only your own. Start by following your own instructions and not insisting on the obedience of others first.

4:13 Laodicea was located a few miles northwest of Colosse; Hierapolis was about five miles north of Laodicea. See the note on 2:1 for more about Laodicea.

4:14 Luke spent much time with Paul, not only accompanying him on most of his third missionary journey, but sitting with him in the prison at Rome. Luke wrote the Gospel of Luke and the book of Acts. His Profile is in Acts 17, p. 1853. Demas was faithful for a while, but then he deserted Paul, having "loved this world" (2 Timothy 4:10).

4:15 The early Christians often met in homes. Church buildings were not common until the third century.

4:16 Some suggest that the letter from Laodicea may be the book of Ephesians, because the letter to the Ephesians was circulated to all the churches in Asia Minor. It is also possible that there was a special letter to the Laodiceans, of which we have no record today. Paul wrote several letters that have been lost (see, for example, 2 Corinthians 2:3 and note).

4:17 Paul's letter to Philemon is also addressed to Archippus (Philemon 2). Paul called him a "fellow soldier." He may have been a Roman soldier who had become a member of the Colossian church, or he may have been Philemon's son.

4:17 Paul encouraged Archippus to make sure that he completed the work he had received in the Lord. There are many ways for

us to leave our work unfinished. We can easily get sidetracked morally, we can become exhausted and stop, we can get mad and quit, or we can let it slide and leave it up to others. We should see to it that we finish God's assignments, completing the work we have received.

4:18 Paul usually dictated his letters to a scribe, and then often ended with a short note in his own handwriting (see also 1 Corinthians 16:21; Galatians 6:11). This assured the recipients that false teachers were not writing letters in Paul's name. It also gave the letters a personal touch.

4:18 To understand the letter to the Colossians, we need to know that the church was facing pressure from a heresy that promised deeper spiritual life through secret knowledge (an early form of Gnosticism). The false teachers were destroying faith in Christ by undermining Christ's humanity and divinity.

Paul makes it clear in Colossians that Christ alone is the source of our spiritual life, the Head of the body of believers. Christ is Lord of both the physical and spiritual worlds. The path to deeper spiritual life is not through religious duties, special knowledge, or secrets; it is only through a clear connection with the Lord Jesus Christ. We must never let anything come between us and our Savior.

SLOWLY they walk, one by one, scattering the leaves and trampling the grass under measured and heavy steps. The minister's words still echoing in their minds, they hear workmen moving toward the terrible place, preparing to cover the casket of their loved one. Death, the enemy, has torn the bonded relationships of family and friends, leaving only memories . . . and tears . . . and loneliness.

But like a golden shaft of sun piercing the winter sky, a singular truth shatters the oppressive gloom: Death is not the end! Christ is the victor over death, and there is the hope of resurrection through him.

As with every member of the human family, first-century Christians came face to face with their mortality. Many of them met early deaths at the hands of those who hated Christ and all allied with him. Whether at the hands of zealous Jews (like Paul before his conversion), angry Greeks, or ruthless Roman authorities, persecution included stonings, beatings, crucifixions, torture, and death. To be a follower of Christ meant to give up everything.

Paul established the church in Thessalonica during his second missionary journey (about A.D. 51). He wrote this letter a short time later to encourage the young believers there. He wanted to assure them of his love, to praise them for their faithfulness during persecution, and to remind them of their hope—the sure return of their Lord and Savior.

Paul begins this letter with a note of affirmation, thanking God for the strong faith and good reputation of the Thessalonians (1:1–10). Then Paul reviews their relationship—how he and his companions brought the gospel to them (2:1–12), how they accepted the message (2:13–16), and how he longed to be with them again (2:17–20). Because of his concern, he had sent Timothy to encourage them in their faith (3:1–13).

Paul then presents the core of his message—exhortation and comfort. He challenges them to please God in their daily living by avoiding sexual immorality (4:1–8), loving each other (4:9, 10), and living as good citizens in a sinful world (4:11, 12).

Paul comforts the Thessalonians by reminding them of the hope of resurrection (4:13–18). Then he warns them to be prepared at all times, for Jesus Christ could return at any moment. When Christ returns, those Christians who are alive and those who have died will be raised to new life (5:1–11).

Paul then gives the Thessalonians a handful of reminders on how to prepare themselves for the second coming: Warn the idle (5:14), encourage the timid (5:14), help the weak (5:14), be patient with everyone (5:14), be kind to everyone (5:15), be joyful always (5:16), pray continually (5:17), give thanks (5:18), test everything that is taught (5:20, 21), and avoid evil (5:22). Paul concludes his letter with two benedictions and a request for prayer.

As you read this letter, listen carefully to Paul's practical advice for Christian living. And when burdened by grief and overwhelmed by sorrow, take hope in the reality of Christ's return, resurrection, and eternal life!

VITAL STATISTICS

PURPOSE:
To strengthen the Thessalonian Christians in their faith and give them the assurance of Christ's return

AUTHOR:
Paul

ORIGINAL AUDIENCE:
The church at Thessalonica

DATE WRITTEN:
Approximately A.D. 51 from Corinth; one of Paul's earliest letters

SETTING:
The church at Thessalonica was very young, having been established only two or three years before this letter was written. The Thessalonian Christians needed to mature in their faith. In addition, there was a misunderstanding concerning Christ's second coming—some thought Christ would return immediately; thus, they were confused when their loved ones died because they expected Christ to return beforehand. Also, believers were being persecuted.

KEY VERSE:
"We believe that Jesus died and rose again and so we believe that God will bring with Jesus those who have fallen asleep in him" (4:14).

KEY PEOPLE:
Paul, Timothy, Silas

KEY PLACE:
Thessalonica

SPECIAL FEATURES:
Paul received from Timothy a favorable report about the Thessalonians. However, Paul wrote this letter to correct their misconceptions about the resurrection and the second coming of Christ.

THE BLUEPRINT

1. Faithfulness to the Lord
   (1:1—3:13)
2. Watchfulness for the Lord
   (4:1—5:28)

Paul and his companions were faithful to bring the gospel to the Thessalonians in the midst of persecution. The Thessalonians had only recently become Christians, and yet they had remained faithful to the Lord, despite the fact that the apostles were not with them. Others have been faithful in bringing God's Word to us. We must remain faithful and live in the expectation that Christ will return at any time.

MEGATHEMES

THEME	EXPLANATION	IMPORTANCE
Persecution	Paul and the new Christians at Thessalonica experienced persecution because of their faith in Christ. We can expect trials and troubles as well. We need to stand firm in our faith in the midst of trials, being strengthened by the Holy Spirit.	The Holy Spirit helps us to remain strong in faith, able to show genuine love to others and maintain our moral character even when we are being persecuted, slandered, or oppressed.
Paul's Ministry	Paul expressed his concern for this church even while he was being slandered. Paul's commitment to share the gospel in spite of difficult circumstances is a model we should follow.	Paul not only delivered his message, but gave of himself. In our ministries, we must become like Paul—faithful and bold, yet sensitive and self-sacrificing.
Hope	One day all believers, both those who are alive and those who have died, will be united with Christ. To those Christians who die before Christ's return, there is hope—the hope of the resurrection of the body.	If we believe in Christ, we will live with him forever. All those who belong to Jesus Christ—from throughout history—will be present with him at his second coming. We can be confident that we will be with loved ones who have trusted in Christ.
Being Prepared	No one knows the time of Christ's return. We are to live moral and holy lives, ever watchful for his coming. Believers must not neglect daily responsibilities, but always work and live to please the Lord.	The gospel is not only what we believe but also what we must live. The Holy Spirit leads us in faithfulness, so we can avoid lust and fraud. Live as though you expect Christ's return at any time. Don't be caught unprepared.

LOCATION OF THESSALONICA

Paul visited Thessalonica on his second and third missionary journeys. It was a seaport and trade center located on the Egnatian Way, a busy international highway. Paul probably wrote his two letters to the Thessalonians from Corinth.

1. Faithfulness to the Lord

1 Paul, Silas[a] and Timothy,

To the church of the Thessalonians in God the Father and the Lord Jesus Christ:

Grace and peace to you. [b]

Thanksgiving for the Thessalonians' Faith

1:2
[a] Ro 1:8

2 We always thank God for all of you,[a] mentioning you in our prayers. 3 We continually remember before our God and Father your work produced by faith, your labor prompted by love, and your endurance inspired by hope in our Lord Jesus Christ.

4 For we know, brothers loved by God, that he has chosen you, 5 because our gospel came to you not simply with words, but also with power, with the Holy Spirit and with deep conviction. You know how we lived among you for your sake. 6 You became imitators of us[b] and

1:6
[b] 1Co 4:16

of the Lord; in spite of severe suffering, you welcomed the message with the joy given by the Holy Spirit. 7 And so you became a model to all the believers in Macedonia and Achaia. 8 The

1:8
[c] Ro 1:8; 10:18

Lord's message rang out from you not only in Macedonia and Achaia—your faith in God has become known everywhere. [c] Therefore we do not need to say anything about it, 9 for they

---

[a] 1 Greek *Silvanus*, a variant of *Silas*   [b] 1 Some early manuscripts *you from God our Father and the Lord Jesus Christ*

1:1 Paul and his companions probably arrived in Thessalonica in the early summer of A.D. 50. They planted the first Christian church in that city, but had to leave in a hurry because their lives were threatened (Acts 17:1–10). At the first opportunity, probably when he stopped at Corinth, Paul sent Timothy back to Thessalonica to see how the new believers were doing. Timothy returned to Paul with good news: the Christians in Thessalonica were remaining firm in the faith and were unified. But the Thessalonians did have some questions about their new faith. Paul had not had time to answer all their questions during his brief visit, and in the meantime, other questions had arisen. So Paul wrote this letter to answer their questions and to commend them on their faithfulness to Christ.

1:1 For more information on Paul, see his Profile in Acts 9, p. 1825. Timothy's Profile is in 1 Timothy, p. 2037. Silas accompanied Paul on his second missionary journey (Acts 15:36—17:15). He helped Paul establish the church in Thessalonica (Acts 17:1–9). He is also mentioned in 2 Corinthians 1:19, 2 Thessalonians 1:1, and in 1 Peter 5:12. Silas's Profile is found in Acts 16, p. 1847.

1:1 Thessalonica was the capital and largest city (about 200,000 population) of the Roman province of Macedonia. The most important Roman highway (the Egnatian Way)—extending from Rome all the way to the Orient—went through Thessalonica. This highway, along with the city's thriving seaport, made Thessalonica one of the wealthiest and most flourishing trade centers in the Roman empire. Recognized as a free city, Thessalonica was allowed self-rule and was exempted from most of the restrictions placed by Rome on other cities in the empire. With its international flavor, however, came many pagan religions and cultural influences that challenged the faith of the young Christians there.

1:3 The Thessalonians had stood firm when they were persecuted (1:6; 3:1–4, 7, 8). Paul commended these young Christians for their work produced by faith, labor prompted by love, and endurance inspired by hope. These characteristics are the marks of effective Christians in any age.

1:4 Paul reminded the Thessalonians of their status as God's "chosen" ones. Very few issues cause more confusion and even arguments among Christians than the issue of election (being chosen by God). It is difficult to simultaneously embrace God's sovereignty in choosing us and our human responsibility in choosing to follow him. Even though we may not be able to completely comprehend how these two truths can coexist, we can say the following: *Being chosen* comes from the heart of God (not our minds), should be an incentive to please God (not ignore him), and should give birth to gratitude (not complacency). *Human responsibility* requires that we actively confess Christ as Lord, focus on living to please him, and share the gospel with others.

God's choice of us energizes us to obey and to serve. Our choice of God challenges us to build lives worthy of him. As you consider God's divine selection of you, how do you respond?

1:5 The gospel came "with power;" it had a powerful effect on the Thessalonians. Whenever the Bible is heard and obeyed, lives are changed! Christianity is more than a collection of interesting facts; it is the power of God to every one who believes. What has God's power done in your life since you first believed?

1:5 The Holy Spirit changes people when they believe the gospel. When we tell others about Christ, we must depend on the Holy Spirit to open their eyes and convince them that they need salvation. God's power changes people—not our cleverness or persuasion. Without the work of the Holy Spirit, our words are meaningless. The Holy Spirit not only convicts people of sin but also assures them of the truth of the gospel. (For more information on the Holy Spirit, see John 14:23–26; 15:26, 27; and the notes on John 3:6 and Acts 1:5.)

1:5 Paul wrote, "You know how we lived among you for your sake." The Thessalonians had seen that what Paul, Silas, and Timothy were preaching was true because these men had lived it. Does your life confirm or contradict what you say you believe?

1:6 The message of salvation, though welcomed with great joy, brought the Thessalonians severe suffering because it led to persecution from both Jews and Gentiles (3:2–4; Acts 17:5). Many believers today think that pain is the exception in the Christian life. When suffering occurs, they say, "Why me?" They feel as though God deserted them, or perhaps they accuse him of not being as dependable as they thought he should be. In reality, the world is sinful, so even believers suffer. God allows some Christians to become martyrs for the faith, and he allows others to survive persecution. Rather than asking, "Why me?" we should ask, "Why not me?" Our faith and the values of this world are on a collision course. If we expect pain and suffering to come, we will not be shocked when they occur. We can take comfort in knowing that Jesus also suffered. He understands our fears, our weaknesses, and our disappointments (Hebrews 2:16–18; 4:14–16). He promised never to leave us (Matthew 28:18–20), and he intercedes on our behalf (Hebrews 7:24, 25). In times of pain, persecution, or suffering, trust confidently in Christ.

1:9, 10 All of us should respond to the Good News as the Thessalonians did: *turn* to God, *serve* God, and *wait* for his Son, Christ, to return from heaven. We should turn from sin to God because Christ is coming to judge the earth. We should be fervent in our service because we have little time before Christ returns. We should be prepared for Christ to return because we don't know when he will come.

themselves report what kind of reception you gave us. They tell how you turned to God from idols *d* to serve the living and true God, ¹⁰ and to wait for his Son from heaven, whom he raised from the dead *e*—Jesus, who rescues us from the coming wrath. *f*

Paul's Ministry in Thessalonica

2 You know, brothers, that our visit to you *g* was not a failure. ² We had previously suffered *h* and been insulted in Philippi, as you know, but with the help of our God we dared to tell you his gospel in spite of strong opposition. ³ For the appeal we make does not spring from error or impure motives, nor are we trying to trick you. ⁴ On the contrary, we speak as men approved by God to be entrusted with the gospel. We are not trying to please men *i* but God, who tests our hearts. ⁵ You know we never used flattery, nor did we put on a mask to cover up greed—God is our witness. *j* ⁶ We were not looking for praise from men, not from you or anyone else.

As apostles *k* of Christ we could have been a burden to you, ⁷ but we were gentle among you, like a mother caring for her little children. ⁸ We loved you so much that we were delighted to share with you not only the gospel of God but our lives as well, *l* because you had become so dear to us. ⁹ Surely you remember, brothers, our toil and hardship; we worked night and day in order not to be a burden to anyone *m* while we preached the gospel of God to you.

¹⁰ You are witnesses, *n* and so is God, of how holy, righteous and blameless we were among you who believed. ¹¹ For you know that we dealt with each of you as a father deals with his own children, ¹² encouraging, comforting and urging you to live lives worthy of God, who calls you into his kingdom and glory.

¹³ And we also thank God continually *o* because, when you received the word of God,

1:9
d 1Co 12:2
1:10
e Ac 2:24
f Ro 5:9

2:1
g 1Th 1:5, 9
2:2
h Ac 16:22; Php 1:30
2:4
i Gal 1:10
2:5
j Ro 1:9
2:6
k 1Co 9:1, 2
2:8
l 2Co 12:15
2:9
m 2Th 3:8
2:10
n 1Th 1:5
2:13
o 1Th 1:2

1:10 Paul emphasized Christ's second coming throughout this book. Because the Thessalonian church was being persecuted, Paul encouraged them to look forward to the deliverance that Christ would bring. A believer's hope is in the return of Jesus, our great God and Savior (Titus 2:13). Our perspective on life remains incomplete without this hope. Just as surely as Christ was raised from the dead and ascended into heaven, he will return (Acts 1:11).

2:1, 2 "Our visit to you" refers to Paul's first visit to Thessalonica recorded in Acts 17:1–9. The Thessalonians knew that Paul had been imprisoned in Philippi just prior to coming to Thessalonica (see Acts 16:11—17:1). Fear of imprisonment did not keep Paul from preaching the gospel. If God wants us to do something, he will give us the strength and courage to boldly speak out for him despite any obstacles that may come our way. Boldness is not reckless impulsiveness. Boldness requires courage to press through fears and do what is right. How can we be more bold? Like the apostles, we need to pray for that kind of courage. To gain boldness, you can pray for the Holy Spirit's power, look for opportunities to talk about Christ, and start right where you are being bolder in even small ways.

2:3 This pointed statement may be a response to accusations from the Jewish leaders who had stirred up the crowds (Acts 17:5). Paul did not seek money, fame, or popularity by sharing the gospel. He demonstrated the sincerity of his motives by showing that he and Silas had suffered for sharing the gospel in Philippi. People become involved in ministry for a variety of reasons, not all of them good or pure. When their bad motives are exposed, all of Christ's work suffers. When you get involved in ministry, do so out of love for Christ and others.

2:4–8 In trying to persuade people, we may be tempted to alter our position just enough to make our message more palatable or to use flattery or praise. Paul never changed his *message* to make it more acceptable, but he did tailor his *methods* to each audience. Although our presentation must be altered to be appropriate to the situation, the truth of the gospel must never be compromised.

2:5 It's disgusting to hear a person butter up someone. Flattery is phony, and it is a false cover-up for a person's real intentions. Christians should not be flatterers. Those who proclaim God's truth have a special responsibility to be honest. Are you honest and straightforward in your words and actions? Or do you tell people what they want to hear in order to get what you want or to get ahead?

2:6–8 When Paul was with the Thessalonians, he didn't flatter them, didn't seek their praise, and didn't become a burden to them. He and Silas completely focused their efforts on presenting God's message of salvation to the Thessalonians. This was important! The Thessalonian believers had their lives changed by God, not Paul; it was Christ's message they believed, not Paul's. When we witness for Christ, our focus should not be on the impressions we make. As true ministers of Christ, we should point to him, not to ourselves.

2:7 Gentleness is often overlooked as a personal trait in our society. Power and assertiveness gain more respect, even though no one likes to be bullied. Gentleness is love in action—being considerate, meeting the needs of others, allowing time for the other person to talk, and being willing to learn. It is an essential trait for both men and women. Maintain a gentle attitude in your relationships with others.

2:9 Although Paul had the right to receive financial support from the people he taught, he supported himself as a tentmaker (Acts 18:3) so that he wouldn't be a burden to the new Thessalonian believers.

2:11 No loving father would neglect the safety of his children, allowing them to walk into circumstances that might be harmful or fatal. In the same way, we must take new believers under our wing until they are mature enough to stand firm in their faith. We must help new Christians become strong enough to influence others for the sake of the gospel.

2:12 By his words and example, Paul encouraged the Thessalonians to live in such a way that would be worthy of God. Is there anything about your daily life that would embarrass God? What do people think of God from watching you?

2:13 Paul said that the word of God continued to work in the believers' lives. Paul knew that God's words are not mere sermons or documents but a real source of transforming power. This Bible you hold in your hands is full of real and living power. Its words are transforming lives all over the world every day. Read it. Encourage fellow believers to read it. Encourage non-Christian friends to read it. All who do so, truly seeking to learn, will be touched by its power. They will never be the same.

2:14
p Ac 17:5

2:15
q Ac 2:23

2:16
r Ac 13:45, 50
s Mt 23:32

which you heard from us, you accepted it not as the word of men, but as it actually is, the word of God, which is at work in you who believe. ¹⁴For you, brothers, became imitators of God's churches in Judea, which are in Christ Jesus: You suffered from your own countrymen *p* the same things those churches suffered from the Jews, ¹⁵who killed the Lord Jesus *q* and the prophets and also drove us out. They displease God and are hostile to all men ¹⁶in their effort to keep us from speaking to the Gentiles *r* so that they may be saved. In this way they always heap up their sins to the limit. *s* The wrath of God has come upon them at last. *a*

Paul's Longing to See the Thessalonians

2:17
t 1Co 5:3
u 1Th 3:10

2:18
v Ro 1:13

2:19
w 2Co 1:14

3:1
x ver 5
y Ac 17:15

3:3
z Ac 9:16

¹⁷But, brothers, when we were torn away from you for a short time (in person, not in thought), *t* out of our intense longing we made every effort to see you. *u* ¹⁸For we wanted to come to you—certainly I, Paul, did, again and again—but Satan stopped us. *v* ¹⁹For what is our hope, our joy, or the crown in which we will glory *w* in the presence of our Lord Jesus when he comes? Is it not you? ²⁰Indeed, you are our glory and joy.

3 So when we could stand it no longer, *x* we thought it best to be left by ourselves in Athens. *y* ²We sent Timothy, who is our brother and God's fellow worker *b* in spreading the gospel of Christ, to strengthen and encourage you in your faith, ³so that no one would be unsettled by these trials. You know quite well that we were destined for them. *z* ⁴In fact, when we were with you, we kept telling you that we would be persecuted. And it turned out that

a 16 Or *them fully*   *b 2* Some manuscripts *brother and fellow worker*; other manuscripts *brother and God's servant*

THE EVENTS OF CHRIST'S RETURN

1. Christ will return visibly, with a loud command.
2. There will be an unmistakable cry from an angel.
3. There will be a trumpet fanfare such as has never been heard.
4. Believers in Christ who are dead will rise from their graves.
5. Believers who are alive will be caught up in the clouds to meet Christ.

While Christians have often disagreed about what events will lead up to the return of Christ, there has been less disagreement about what will happen once Christ does return.

2:14 Just as the Jewish Christians in Jerusalem were persecuted by other Jews, so the Gentile Christians in Thessalonica were persecuted by their fellow Gentiles. Persecution is discouraging, especially when it comes from your own people. When you take a stand for Christ, you may face opposition, disapproval, and ridicule from your neighbors, friends, and even family members.

2:14 When Paul refers to the Jews, he is talking about certain Jews who opposed his preaching of the gospel. He does not mean all Jews. Many of Paul's converts were Jewish. Paul himself was a Jew (2 Corinthians 11:22).

2:15 Having believed the Good News and accepted new life in Christ, apparently many Thessalonians thought that they would be protected from death until Christ returned. Then, when believers began to die under persecution, some Thessalonian Christians started to question their faith. Many of Paul's comments throughout this letter were addressed to these people, as he explained what happens when believers die (see 4:13ff).

2:15, 16 Why were so many Jews opposed to Christianity? (1) Although the Jewish religion had been declared legal by the Roman government, it still had a tenuous relationship with the government. At this time, Christianity was viewed as a sect of Judaism. The Jews were afraid that reprisals leveled against the Christians might be expanded to include them. (2) The Jewish leaders thought Jesus was a false prophet, and they didn't want his teachings to spread. (3) The leaders feared that if many Jews were drawn away, their own political position might be weakened. (4) Jews were proud of their special status as God's chosen people and resented the fact that Gentiles could be full members within the Christian church.

2:18 Satan is real. He is called "the god of this age" (2 Corinthians 4:4) and "the ruler of the kingdom of the air" (Ephesians 2:2). We don't know exactly what hindered Paul from returning to

Thessalonica—opposition, illness, travel complications, or a direct attack by Satan—but Satan worked in some way to keep him away. Many of the difficulties that prevent us from accomplishing God's work can be attributed to Satan (see Ephesians 6:12).

2:20 The ultimate reward for Paul's ministry was not money, prestige, or fame, but new believers whose lives had been changed by God through the preaching of the gospel. This was why he longed to see them. No matter what ministry God has given to you, your highest reward and greatest joy should be those who come to believe in Christ and are growing in him.

3:1-3 Some think that troubles are always caused by sin or a lack of faith. Trials may be a part of God's plan for believers. Experiencing problems and persecutions can build character (James 1:2-4), perseverance (Romans 5:3-5), and sensitivity toward others who also face trouble (2 Corinthians 1:3-7). Problems are unavoidable for God's people. Your troubles may be a sign of effective Christian living.

3:2-5 Because Paul could not return to Thessalonica (2:18), he sent Timothy as his representative. According to Acts 17:10, Paul left Thessalonica and went to Berea. When trouble broke out in Berea, some Christians took Paul to Athens, while Silas and Timothy stayed behind (Acts 17:13-15). Then Paul directed Silas and Timothy to join him in Athens. Later Paul sent Timothy to encourage the Thessalonian Christians to be strong in their faith in the face of persecution and other troubles.

3:4 Some people turn to God with the hope of escaping suffering on earth. But God doesn't promise that. Instead he gives us power to grow through our sufferings. The Christian life involves obedience to Christ despite temptations and hardships.

way, as you well know. ⁵For this reason, when I could stand it no longer, I sent to find out about your faith. I was afraid that in some way the tempter might have tempted you and our efforts might have been useless. *a*

Timothy's Encouraging Report

⁶But Timothy has just now come to us from you and has brought good news about your faith and love. He has told us that you always have pleasant memories of us and that you long to see us, just as we also long to see you. ⁷Therefore, brothers, in all our distress and persecution we were encouraged about you because of your faith. ⁸For now we really live, since you are standing firm in the Lord. ⁹How can we thank God enough for you *b* in return for all the joy we have in the presence of our God because of you? ¹⁰Night and day we pray *c* most earnestly that we may see you again and supply what is lacking in your faith.

¹¹Now may our God and Father himself and our Lord Jesus clear the way for us to come to you. ¹²May the Lord make your love increase and overflow for each other *d* and for everyone else, just as ours does for you. ¹³May he strengthen your hearts so that you will be blameless *e* and holy in the presence of our God and Father when our Lord Jesus comes with all his holy ones.

2. Watchfulness for the Lord
Living to Please God

4 Finally, brothers, we instructed you how to live in order to please God, as in fact you are living. Now we ask you and urge you in the Lord Jesus to do this more and more. ²For you know what instructions we gave you by the authority of the Lord Jesus.

³It is God's will that you should be sanctified: that you should avoid sexual immorality; *f* ⁴that each of you should learn to control his own body *a* in a way that is holy and honorable, ⁵not in passionate lust *g* like the heathen, *h* who do not know God; ⁶and that in this matter no one should wrong his brother or take advantage of him. The Lord will punish men for all

a4 Or *learn to live with his own wife*; or *learn to acquire a wife*

3:5
a Gal 2:2

3:9
b 1Th 1:2

3:10
c 2Ti 1:3

3:12
d 1Th 4:9, 10

3:13
e 1Co 1:8

4:3
f 1Co 6:18

4:5
g Ro 1:26
h Eph 4:17

3:5 Satan ("the tempter") is the most powerful of the evil spirits. His power can affect both the spiritual world (Ephesians 2:1–3; 6:10–12) and the physical world (2 Corinthians 12:7–10). Satan even tempted Jesus (Matthew 4:1–11). But Jesus defeated Satan when he died on the cross for our sins and rose again to bring us new life. At the proper time God will overthrow Satan forever (Revelation 20:7–10).

3:7, 8 During persecution or pressure, believers should encourage one another. Christians who stand firm in the Lord are an encouragement to ministers and teachers (who can see the benefit of their work in those who remain faithful), and also an encouragement to those who are new in their faith (who can learn from the steadfastness of the mature).

3:9, 10 It brings great joy to a Christian to see another person come to faith in Christ and mature in that faith. Paul experienced this joy countless times. He thanked God for those who had come to know Christ and for their strong faith. He also prayed for their continued growth. If new Christians have brought you joy, thank God for them and support them as they continue to grow in the faith. Likewise, have you benefited from the ministry of others? Has someone's guidance and faithfulness stimulated you to grow in Christ? Consider how you may bring some word of encouragement or some thoughtful gift. Let that important person know that you have followed his or her example by being faithful to Christ.

3:11 Paul wanted to return to Thessalonica. We have no record that he was able to do so; but when he was traveling through Asia on his third journey, he was joined by Aristarchus and Secundus, who were from Thessalonica (Acts 20:4, 5).

3:12 If we are full of God's love, it will overflow to others. It's not enough merely to be courteous to others; we must actively and persistently show love to them. Our love should be growing continually. If your capacity to love has remained unchanged for some time, ask God to fill you again with his never-ending supply. Then look for opportunities to express his love.

3:13 "When our Lord Jesus comes with all his holy ones" refers to the second coming of Christ when he will establish his eternal kingdom. At that time, Christ will gather all believers, those who have died and those who are alive, into one united family under his rule. All believers of all times, including these Thessalonian believers, will be with Christ in his kingdom.

4:1–8 Sexual standards were very low in the Roman empire, and in many societies today they are not any higher. The temptation to engage in sexual intercourse outside the marriage relationship has always been powerful. Giving in to that temptation can have disastrous results. Sexual sins always hurt someone: individuals, families, businesses, churches. Besides the physical consequences, there are also spiritual consequences. For more on why sexual sin is so harmful, see the note on 1 Corinthians 6:18.

4:1–8 Sexual desires and activities must be placed under Christ's control. God created sex for procreation and pleasure, and as an expression of love between a husband and wife. Sexual experience must be limited to the marriage relationship to avoid hurting ourselves, our relationship to God, and our relationships with others.

4:3 Being *sanctified* or made holy is the process of living the Christian life. The Holy Spirit works in us, conforming us into the image of Christ (Romans 8:29).

4:4, 5 Paul said that lustful passions should not control God's people. Some argue that if they've already sinned by having lustful thoughts, they might as well go ahead with lustful actions too. Acting out sinful desires is harmful in several ways: (1) It causes people to excuse sin rather than to stop sinning; (2) it destroys marriages; (3) it is deliberate rebellion against God's Word; and (4) it always hurts someone else in addition to the sinner. Sinful action is more dangerous than sinful desire, so desires should not be acted out. Nevertheless, sinful desire is just as damaging to righteousness. Left unchecked, wrong desires will result in wrong actions and will turn people away from God.

4:6
i Heb 13:4

4:7
j Lev 11:44

4:8
k Ro 5:5

4:9
l 1Th 5:1

4:10
m 1Th 1:7
n 1Th 3:12

4:11
o Eph 4:28;
2Th 3:10-12

4:13
p Eph 2:12

such sins, *i* as we have already told you and warned you. 7For God did not call us to be impure, but to live a holy life. *j* 8Therefore, he who rejects this instruction does not reject man but God, who gives you his Holy Spirit. *k*

9Now about brotherly love we do not need to write to you, *l* for you yourselves have been taught by God to love each other. 10And in fact, you do love all the brothers throughout Macedonia. *m* Yet we urge you, brothers, to do so more and more. *n*

11Make it your ambition to lead a quiet life, to mind your own business and to work with your hands, *o* just as we told you, 12so that your daily life may win the respect of outsiders and so that you will not be dependent on anybody.

The Coming of the Lord

13Brothers, we do not want you to be ignorant about those who fall asleep, or to grieve like the rest of men, who have no hope. *p* 14We believe that Jesus died and rose again and so we believe that God will bring with Jesus those who have fallen asleep in him. 15According

CHECKLIST FOR ENCOURAGERS	Reference	Example	Suggested Application
The command to "encourage" others is found throughout the Bible. In 5:11–23, Paul gives many specific examples of how we can encourage others.	5:11	Build each other up.	Point out to someone a quality you appreciate in him or her.
	5:12	Respect leaders.	Look for ways to cooperate.
	5:13	Hold leaders in highest regard.	Hold back your next critical comments about those in positions of responsibility. Say "thank you" to your leaders for their efforts.
	5:13	Live in peace.	Search for ways to get along with others.
	5:14	Warn the idle.	Challenge someone to join you in a project.
	5:14	Encourage the timid.	Encourage those who are timid by reminding them of God's promises.
	5:14	Help the weak.	Support those who are weak by loving them and praying for them.
	5:14	Be patient.	Think of a situation that tries your patience, and plan ahead of time how you can stay calm.
	5:15	Resist revenge.	Instead of planning to get even with those who mistreat you, do good to them.
	5:16	Be joyful.	Remember that even in the midst of turmoil, God is in control.
	5:17	Pray continually.	God is always with you—talk to him.
	5:18	Give thanks.	Make a list of all the gifts God has given you, giving thanks to God for each one.
	5:19	Do not put out the Spirit's fire.	Cooperate with the Spirit the next time he prompts you to participate in a Christian meeting.
	5:20	Do not treat prophecies with contempt.	Receive God's word from those who speak for him.
	5:22	Avoid every kind of evil.	Avoid situations where you will be drawn into temptation.
	5:23	Count on God's constant help.	Realize that the Christian life is to be lived not in our own strength but through God's power.

4:11, 12 Christian living is more than simply loving other Christians. We must be responsible in all areas of life. Some of the Thessalonian Christians had adopted a life of idleness, depending on others for handouts. Some Greeks looked down on manual labor. So Paul told the Thessalonians to work hard and live a quiet life. You can't be effective in sharing your faith with others if they don't respect you. Whatever you do, do it faithfully and be a positive force in society.

4:13ff The Thessalonians were wondering why many of their fellow believers had fallen asleep (died) and what would happen to them when Christ returned. Paul wanted the Thessalonians to understand that death is not the end of the story. When Christ returns, all believers—dead and alive—will be reunited, never to suffer or die again.

4:15 What did Paul mean when he wrote, "according to the Lord's own word"? Either this was something that the Lord had revealed directly to Paul, or it was a teaching of Jesus that had been passed along orally by the apostles and other Christians.

4:15–18 Knowing exactly *when* the dead will be raised, in relation to the other events at the second coming, is not as important as knowing why Paul wrote these words—to challenge believers to comfort and encourage one another when loved ones die. This passage can be a great comfort when any believer dies. The same love that should unite believers in this life (4:9) will unite believers when Christ returns and reigns for eternity.

4:15–18 Because Jesus Christ came back to life, so will all believers. All Christians, including those living when Christ returns, will live with Christ forever. Therefore, we need not to the Lord's own word, we tell you that we who are still alive, who are left till the coming of the Lord, will certainly not precede those who have fallen asleep. 16For the Lord himself will come down from heaven, with a loud command, with the voice of the archangel and with the trumpet call of God,*q* and the dead in Christ will rise first.*r* 17After that, we who are still alive and are left*s* will be caught up together with them in the clouds*t* to meet the Lord in the air. And so we will be with the Lord forever. 18Therefore encourage each other with these words.

5 Now, brothers, about times and dates we do not need to write to you,*u* 2for you know very well that the day of the Lord will come like a thief in the night.*v* 3While people are saying, "Peace and safety," destruction will come on them suddenly, as labor pains on a pregnant woman, and they will not escape.

4But you, brothers, are not in darkness so that this day should surprise you like a thief. 5You are all sons of the light and sons of the day. We do not belong to the night or to the darkness. 6So then, let us not be like others, who are asleep, but let us be alert and self-controlled. 7For those who sleep, sleep at night, and those who get drunk, get drunk at night. 8But since we belong to the day, let us be self-controlled, putting on faith and love as a breastplate,*w* and the hope of salvation as a helmet. 9For God did not appoint us to suffer wrath but to receive salvation through our Lord Jesus Christ.*x* 10He died for us so that, whether we are awake or asleep, we may live together with him. 11Therefore encourage one another and build each other up, just as in fact you are doing.

Final Instructions

12Now we ask you, brothers, to respect those who work hard among you, who are over you in the Lord and who admonish you. 13Hold them in the highest regard in love because of their work. Live in peace with each other. 14And we urge you, brothers, warn those who are idle,*y* encourage the timid, help the weak, be patient with everyone. 15Make sure that nobody pays back wrong for wrong, but always try to be kind to each other*z* and to everyone else.

16Be joyful always; 17pray continually; 18give thanks in all circumstances, for this is God's will for you in Christ Jesus.

4:16
q Mt 24:31
r 1Co 15:23

4:17
s 1Co 15:52
t Ac 1:9

5:1
u 1Th 4:9

5:2
v 2Pe 3:10

5:8
w Eph 6:14

5:9
x 2Th 2:13, 14

5:14
y 2Th 3:6, 7, 11

5:15
z Gal 6:10; Eph 4:32

---

despair when loved ones die or world events take a tragic turn. God will turn our tragedies to triumphs, our poverty to riches, our pain to glory, and our defeat to victory. All believers throughout history will stand reunited in God's very presence, safe and secure. As Paul comforted the Thessalonians with the promise of the resurrection, so we should comfort and reassure each other with this great hope.

4:16 An *archangel* is a high or holy angel appointed to a special task. Michael is the only archangel mentioned in the New Testament (see Jude 9).

5:1 "Times and dates" refers to the knowledge of what will happen in the future, specifically to the return of Christ.

5:1–3 Efforts to determine the date of Christ's return are foolish. Don't be misled by anyone who claims to know. We are told here that no one knows and that even believers will be surprised. The Lord will return suddenly and unexpectedly, warns Paul, so be ready! Because no one knows when Jesus will come back to earth, we should be prepared at all times. Suppose he were to return today. How would he find you living? Are you ready to meet him? Live each day prepared to welcome Christ.

5:2 The "day of the Lord" is a future time when God will intervene directly and dramatically in world affairs. Predicted and discussed often in the Old Testament (Isaiah 13:6–12; Joel 2:28–32; Zephaniah 1:14–18), the day of the Lord will include both punishment and blessing. Christ will judge sin and set up his eternal kingdom.

5:4, 5 It is good that we don't know exactly when Christ will return. If we knew the precise date, we might be tempted to be lazy in our work for Christ. Worse yet, we might plan to keep sinning and then turn to God right at the end. Heaven is not our only goal; we have work to do here. Christians must keep on doing God's work until death or until we see the unmistakable return of our Savior.

5:8 For more about the Christian's armor, see Ephesians 6:13–17.

5:9–11 As you near the end of a long race, your legs ache, your throat burns, and your whole body cries out for you to stop. This is when friends and fans are most valuable. Their encouragement helps you push through the pain to the finish line. In the same way, Christians are to encourage one another. A word of encouragement offered at the right moment can be the difference between finishing well and collapsing along the way. Look around you. Be sensitive to others' need for encouragement, and offer supportive words or actions.

5:12 "Those who work hard among you, who are over you in the Lord" probably refers to elders and deacons in the church.

5:12, 13 How can you show respect to and hold in the "highest regard" your pastor and other church leaders? Express your appreciation, tell them how you have been helped by their leadership and teaching, and thank them for their ministry in your life. If you say nothing, how will they know where you stand? Remember, they need and deserve your support and love.

5:14 Don't loaf around with the idle; warn them. Don't yell at the timid and weak; encourage and help them. At times it can be difficult to distinguish between idleness and timidity. Two people may be doing nothing—one out of laziness and the other out of shyness or fear of doing something wrong. The key to ministry is sensitivity: sensing the condition of each person and offering the appropriate remedy for each situation. You can't effectively help until you know the problem. You can't apply the medicine until you know where the wound is.

5:16–18 Our joy, prayers, and thankfulness should not fluctuate with our circumstances or feelings. Obeying these three commands—be joyful, pray continually, and give thanks—often goes against our natural inclinations. When we make a conscious decision to do what God says, however, we will begin to see people in a new perspective. When we do God's will, we will find it easier to be joyful and thankful.

5:19
a Eph 4:30

19Do not put out the Spirit's fire;*a* 20do not treat prophecies with contempt. 21Test everything. Hold on to the good. 22Avoid every kind of evil.

5:24
b 1Co 1:9

23May God himself, the God of peace, sanctify you through and through. May your whole spirit, soul and body be kept blameless at the coming of our Lord Jesus Christ. 24The one who calls you is faithful*b* and he will do it.

5:27
c Col 4:16

25Brothers, pray for us. 26Greet all the brothers with a holy kiss. 27I charge you before the Lord to have this letter read to all the brothers. *c*
28The grace of our Lord Jesus Christ be with you.

5:17 We cannot spend all our time on our knees, but it is possible to have a prayerful attitude at all times. This attitude is built upon acknowledging our dependence on God, realizing his presence within us, and determining to obey him fully. Then we will find it natural to pray frequent, spontaneous, short prayers. A prayerful attitude is not a substitute for regular times of prayer but should be an outgrowth of those times.

5:18 Paul was not teaching that we should thank God *for* everything that happens to us, but *in* everything. Evil does not come from God, so we should not thank him for it. But when evil strikes, we can still be thankful for God's presence and for the good that he will accomplish through the distress.

5:19 By warning us not to "put out the Spirit's fire," Paul means that we should not ignore or toss aside the gifts the Holy Spirit gives. Here, he mentions prophecy (5:20); in 1 Corinthians 14:39, he mentions tongues. Sometimes spiritual gifts are controversial, and they may cause division in a church. Rather than trying to solve the problems, some Christians prefer to smother the gifts. This impoverishes the church. We should not stifle the Holy Spirit's work in anyone's life but encourage the full expression of these gifts to benefit the whole body of Christ.

5:20, 21 We shouldn't make fun of those who don't agree with what we believe ("treat prophecies with contempt"), but we should always "test everything," checking their words against the Bible. We are on dangerous ground if we laugh at a person who speaks the truth. Instead we should carefully check out what people say, accepting what is true and rejecting what is false.

5:22–24 Christians cannot avoid every kind of evil because we live in a sinful world. We can, however, make sure that we don't give evil a foothold by avoiding tempting situations and concentrating on obeying God.

5:23 The spirit, soul, and body refer not so much to the distinct parts of a person as to the entire being of a person. This expression is Paul's way of saying that God must be involved in *every* aspect of life. It is wrong to think that we can separate the spiritual life from everything else, obeying God only in some ethereal sense or living for him only one day each week. Christ must control *all* of us, not just a "religious" part.

5:27 For every Christian to hear this letter, it had to be read in a public meeting—there were not enough copies to circulate. Paul wanted to make sure that everyone had the opportunity to hear his message because he was answering important questions and offering needed encouragement.

5:28 The Thessalonian church was young, and they needed help and encouragement. Both the persecution they faced and the temptations of their pagan culture were potential problems for these new Christians. Paul wrote, therefore, to strengthen their faith and bolster their resistance to persecution and temptation. We too have a responsibility to help new believers, and to make sure that they continue in their faith and don't become sidetracked by wrong beliefs or practices. First Thessalonians can better equip us to help our brothers and sisters in Christ.

2 THESSALONIANS

thing. Hold on to the good. ... Avoid every kind of evil.
... May God himself, the God of peace, sanctify you through and through. May your whole
spirit, soul, and body be kept blameless at the coming of our Lord Jesus Christ. ... The one
who calls you is faithful ... and he will do it.

VITAL STATISTICS

PURPOSE:
To clear up the confusion about the second coming of Christ

AUTHOR:
Paul

ORIGINAL AUDIENCE:
The church at Thessalonica

DATE WRITTEN:
Approximately A.D. 51 or 52, a few months after 1 Thessalonians, from Corinth

SETTING:
Many in the church were confused about the timing of Christ's return. Because of mounting persecution, they thought the day of the Lord must be imminent, and they interpreted Paul's first letter to say that the second coming would be at any moment. In light of this misunderstanding, many persisted in being idle and disorderly, with the excuse of waiting for Christ's return.

KEY VERSE:
"May the Lord direct your hearts into God's love and Christ's perseverance" (3:5).

KEY PEOPLE:
Paul, Silas, Timothy

KEY PLACE:
Thessalonica

SPECIAL FEATURES:
This is a follow-up letter to 1 Thessalonians. In this letter, Paul indicates various events that must precede the second coming of Christ.

"BUT I thought he said . . . ," "I'm sure he meant . . . ," "It is clear to me that we should . . . ," "I disagree. I think we must . . ."

Effective communication is difficult; often the message sent is *not* the message received in the home, marketplace, neighborhood, or church. Even when clearly stated or written, words can be misinterpreted and misunderstood, especially when filtered through the sieve of prejudices and preconceptions.

Paul faced this problem with the Thessalonians. He had written them earlier to help them grow in the faith, comforting and encouraging them by affirming the reality of Christ's return. Just a few months later, however, word came from Thessalonica that some had misunderstood Paul's teaching about the second coming. His announcement that Christ could come at any moment had caused some to stop working and just wait, rationalizing their idleness by pointing to Paul's teaching. Adding fuel to this fire was the continued persecution of the church. Many felt that indeed this must be the "day of the Lord."

Responding quickly, Paul sent a second letter to this young church. In it he gave further instruction concerning the second coming and the day of the Lord (2:1, 2). Second Thessalonians, therefore, continues the subject of 1 Thessalonians and is a call to continued courage and consistent conduct.

The letter begins with Paul's trademark—a personal greeting and a statement of thanksgiving for their faith (1:1–3). He mentions their perseverance in spite of their persecution and trials (1:4) and uses this situation to broach the subject of Christ's return. At that time, Christ will vindicate the righteous who endure and will punish the wicked (1:5–12).

Paul then directly answers the misunderstanding concerning the timing of the events of the end times. He tells them not to listen to rumors and reports that the day of the Lord has already begun (2:1, 2) because a number of events must occur before Christ returns (2:3–12). Meanwhile, they should stand firm for Christ's truth (2:13–15), receive God's encouragement and hope (2:16, 17), pray for strength and for the spread of the Lord's message (3:1–5), and warn those who are idle (3:6–15). Paul ends with personal greetings and a benediction (3:16–18).

Almost 2,000 years later, we stand much closer to the time of Christ's return; but we also would be wrong to see his imminent appearance as an excuse for idle waiting and heavenward gazing. Being prepared for his coming means spreading the gospel, reaching out to those in need, and building the church, his body. As you read 2 Thessalonians, then, see clearly the reality of his return and your responsibility to live for him until that day.

THE BLUEPRINT

1. The bright hope of Christ's return (1:1—2:17)
2. Living in the light of Christ's return (3:1–18)

Paul wrote to encourage those who were facing persecution and to correct a misunderstanding about the timing of Christ's return. The teaching about the Lord's return promoted idleness in this young church. The imminent coming of Christ should never make us idle; we should be even more busy—living purely, using our time well, and working for his kingdom. We must work not only during easy times when it is convenient but also during difficult times. Christians must patiently watch for Christ's return and work for him while they wait.

MEGATHEMES

THEME	EXPLANATION	IMPORTANCE
Persecution	Paul encouraged the church to persevere in spite of troubles and trials. God will bring victory to his faithful followers and judge those who persecute them.	God promises to reward our faith by giving us his power and helping us bear persecution. Suffering for our faith will strengthen us to serve Christ. We must be faithful to him.
Christ's Return	Since Paul had said that the Lord could come at any moment, some of the Thessalonian believers had stopped working in order to wait for Christ.	Christ will return and bring total victory to all who trust in him. If we are ready, we need not be concerned about *when* he will return. We should stand firm, keep working, and wait for Christ.
Great Rebellion	Before Christ's return, there will be a great rebellion against God led by the man of lawlessness (the antichrist). God will remove all the restraints on evil before he brings judgment on the rebels. The antichrist will attempt to deceive many.	We should not be afraid when we see evil increase. God is in control, no matter how evil the world becomes. God guards us during Satan's attacks. We can have victory over evil by remaining faithful to God.
Persistence	Because church members had quit working and become disorderly and disobedient, Paul chastised them for their idleness. He called on them to show courage and true Christian conduct.	We must never get so tired of doing right that we quit. We can be persistent by making the most of our time and talents. Our endurance will be rewarded.

1. The bright hope of Christ's return

1 Paul, Silas[a] and Timothy,[a]

1:1
a 1 Th 1:1

To the church of the Thessalonians in God our Father and the Lord Jesus Christ:

2 Grace and peace to you from God the Father and the Lord Jesus Christ.

a 1 Greek *Silvanus*, a variant of *Silas*

1:1 Paul wrote this letter from Corinth less than a year after he had written 1 Thessalonians. He and his companions, Timothy and Silas, had visited Thessalonica on Paul's second missionary journey (Acts 17:1–10). They established the church there, but Paul had to leave suddenly because of persecution. This prompted him to write his first letter (1 Thessalonians), which contains words of comfort and encouragement. Paul then heard how the Thessalonians had responded to this letter. The good news was that they were continuing to grow in their faith. But the bad news was that false teachings about Christ's return were spreading, leading many to quit their jobs and wait for the end of the world. So Paul wrote to them again. While the purpose of Paul's first letter was to comfort the Thessalonians with the assurance of Christ's second coming, the purpose of his second letter is to correct false teaching about the second coming.

1:1 Paul, Silas, and Timothy were together in Corinth (Acts

18:5). Paul wrote this letter on behalf of all three of them. Paul often included Timothy as a cosender of his letters (see Philippians 1:1; Colossians 1:1; 1 Thessalonians 1:1). For more information about Paul, see his Profile in Acts 9, p. 1825. Silas's Profile is in Acts 15, p. 1847, and Timothy's Profile is found in 1 Timothy, p. 2037.

1:1 Thessalonica was the capital and largest city of the Roman province of Macedonia. The most important Roman highway—extending from Rome to the Orient—went through Thessalonica. This highway, along with the city's thriving seaport, made Thessalonica one of the wealthiest and most flourishing trade centers in the Roman empire. Recognized as a free city, Thessalonica was allowed self-rule and was exempted from most of the restrictions placed by Rome on other cities. Because of this open climate, however, the city had many pagan religions and cultural influences that challenged the Christians' faith.

Thanksgiving and Prayer

³We ought always to thank God for you, brothers, and rightly so, because your faith is growing more and more, and the love every one of you has for each other is increasing. ^b ⁴Therefore, among God's churches we boast about your perseverance and faith in all the persecutions and trials you are enduring. ^c

⁵All this is evidence^d that God's judgment is right, and as a result you will be counted worthy of the kingdom of God, for which you are suffering. ⁶God is just: He will pay back trouble to those who trouble you ⁷and give relief to you who are troubled, and to us as well. This will happen when the Lord Jesus is revealed from heaven in blazing fire with his powerful angels.^e ⁸He will punish those who do not know God and do not obey the gospel of our Lord Jesus.^f ⁹They will be punished with everlasting destruction^g and shut out from the presence of the Lord and from the majesty of his power ¹⁰on the day he comes to be glorified in his holy people and to be marveled at among all those who have believed. This includes you, because you believed our testimony to you.

¹¹With this in mind, we constantly pray for you, that our God may count you worthy^h of his calling, and that by his power he may fulfill every good purpose of yours and every act prompted by your faith. ⁱ ¹²We pray this so that the name of our Lord Jesus may be glorified in you, and you in him, according to the grace of our God and the Lord Jesus Christ.^a

The Man of Lawlessness

2 Concerning the coming of our Lord Jesus Christ and our being gathered to him,^j we ask you, brothers, ²not to become easily unsettled or alarmed by some prophecy, report or letter supposed to have come from us, saying that the day of the Lord has already come.

^a *12* Or *God and Lord, Jesus Christ*

1:3 ^b1Th 3:12
1:4 ^c1Th 2:14
1:5 ^dPhp 1:28
1:7 ^e1Th 4:16; Jude 14
1:8 ^fRo 2:8
1:9 ^gPhp 3:19
1:11 ^hver 5 ⁱ1Th 1:3
2:1 ^jMk 13:27; 1Th 4:15-17

1:3ff Regardless of the contents of Paul's letters, his style was affirming. Paul began most of his letters by stating what he most appreciated about his readers and the joy he felt because of their faith in God. We also should look for ways to encourage and build up other believers. For more on encouragement, see the note in 1 Timothy 4:12–16.

1:4 The keys to surviving persecution and trials are perseverance and faith. When faced with crushing troubles, we can have faith that God is using our trials for our good and for his glory. Knowing that God is fair and just will give us patience in our suffering because we know that he has not forgotten us. In God's perfect timing, he will relieve our suffering and punish those who persecute us. Do you trust God's timing? That is the first step toward growing in endurance and faithfulness.

1:4–6 Paul had been persecuted during his first visit to Thessalonica (Acts 17:5–9). No doubt those who had responded to his message and had become Christians were continuing to be persecuted by both Jews and Gentiles. In Paul's first letter to the Thessalonians, he had said that Christ's return would bring deliverance from persecution for the believers and judgment on the persecutors. But this caused the people to expect Christ's return right away to rescue and vindicate them. So Paul had to point out that while waiting for God's kingdom, believers could and should grow in their endurance and faithfulness through the hardships they were suffering.

1:5 As we live for Christ, we will experience troubles because we are trying to be God's people in a perverse world. Some people say that troubles are the result of sin or lack of faith, but Paul teaches that they may be a part of God's plan for believers. Our problems can help us look upward and forward, instead of inward (Mark 13:35, 36; Philippians 3:13, 14), they can build strong character (Romans 5:3, 4), and they can provide us with opportunities to comfort others who also are struggling (2 Corinthians 1:3–5). Your troubles may be an indication that you are taking a stand for Christ. When you do so, you are experiencing the privilege of showing that you are worthy of God's kingdom (see also 1:11).

1:5–7 The relief mentioned by Paul has two dimensions. We can gain relief in knowing that our sufferings are strengthening us, making us ready for Christ's kingdom. We can also gain relief in the fact that one day everyone will stand before God. At that time, wrongs will be righted, judgment will be pronounced, and evil will be terminated.

1:9 The "everlasting destruction" that Paul describes is the lake of fire (see Revelation 20:14)—the place of eternal separation from God. Those people who will be separated from God in eternity will no longer have any hope for salvation.

1:11, 12 Our "calling" from God, as Christians, is to become like Christ (Romans 8:29). This is a gradual, lifelong process that will be completed when we see Christ face-to-face (1 John 3:2). To be "worthy" of this calling means to *want* to do what is right and good (as Christ would). We aren't perfect yet, but we're moving in that direction as God works in us.

2:1ff Paul describes the end of the world and Christ's second coming. He says that great suffering and trouble lie ahead, but evil will not prevail because Christ will return to judge all people. Although Paul presents a few signs of the end times, his emphasis, like Jesus' (Mark 13), is the need for each person to prepare for Christ's return by living rightly day-by-day. If we are ready, we won't have to be concerned about the preceding events or the timing of Christ's return. God controls all events. (See 1 Thessalonians 4 and 5 for Paul's earlier teaching on this subject.)

2:1, 2 In the Bible, the *day of the Lord* is used in two ways: it can mean the end times (beginning with Christ's birth and continuing until today), and it can mean the final judgment day (in the future). Because some false teachers were saying that judgment day had come, many believers were waiting expectantly for their vindication and for relief from suffering. But judgment day had not yet come; other events would have to happen first.

2:2 "Prophecy, report or letter" could refer to the fact that false teaching had come from: (1) someone claiming to have had a divine revelation; (2) someone passing on a teaching as though it were from Paul; or (3) someone distributing a letter supposedly written by Paul.

2:3
k Eph 5:6-8
l Da 7:25

2:4
m 1Co 8:5
n Isa 14:13, 14

³Don't let anyone deceive you ᵏ in any way, for ⌐that day will not come⌐ until the rebellion occurs and the man of lawlessnessᵃ is revealed, ˡ the man doomed to destruction. ⁴He will oppose and will exalt himself over everything that is called God ᵐ or is worshiped, so that he sets himself up in God's temple, proclaiming himself to be God. ⁿ

⁵Don't you remember that when I was with you I used to tell you these things? ⁶And now you know what is holding him back, so that he may be revealed at the proper time. ⁷For the secret power of lawlessness is already at work; but the one who now holds it back will continue to do so till he is taken out of the way. ⁸And then the lawless one will be revealed, whom the Lord Jesus will overthrow with the breath of his mouth and destroy by the splendor of his

ᵃ3 Some manuscripts *sin*

LOCATION OF THESSALONICA
After Paul visited Thessalonica on his second missionary journey, he went on to Berea, Athens, and Corinth (Acts 17—18). From Corinth, Paul wrote his two letters to the Thessalonian church.

2:3 Throughout history there have been individuals who epitomized evil and who were hostile to everything Christ stands for (see 1 John 2:18; 4:3; 2 John 7). These antichrists have lived in every generation and will continue to work their evil. Then just before Christ's second coming, "the man of lawlessness . . . the man doomed to destruction," a completely evil man, will arise. He will be Satan's tool, equipped with Satan's power (2:9). This lawless man will be *the* antichrist.

It is dangerous, however, to label any person as the antichrist and to try to predict Christ's coming based on that assumption. Paul mentions the antichrist, not so we might attempt to identify him, but so we might be ready for anything that threatens our faith. If our faith is strong, we don't need to be afraid of what lies ahead, because we know that this lawless man has already been defeated by God, no matter how powerful he becomes or how terrible our situation seems. God is in control, and he will be victorious. Our task is to be prepared for Christ's return and to spread the gospel so that even more people will also be prepared.

2:3ff When Paul first wrote to the Thessalonians, they were in danger of losing hope in the second coming. Then they shifted to the opposite extreme—some of them thought that Jesus would be coming at any minute and so they stopped being productive for God. Paul tried to restore the balance by describing certain events that would happen before Christ's return.

2:6, 7 Who holds back the lawless one? We do not know for certain. Three possibilities have been suggested: (1) government and law, which help to curb evil; (2) the ministry and activity of the church and the effects of the gospel; or (3) the Holy Spirit. The Bible is not clear on who this restrainer is, only that he will not restrain forever. But we should not fear this time when the restraint is removed—God is far stronger than the man of lawlessness, and God will save his people.

2:7 "The secret power of lawlessness is already at work" means that the work that this antichrist will do is already going on. *Secret* means something no one can discover, but something God will reveal. *Lawlessness* is the hidden, subtle, underlying force from which all sin springs. Civilization still has a veneer of decency through law enforcement, education, science, and reason. Although we are horrified by criminal acts, we have yet to see the real horror of complete lawlessness. This will happen when "the one who now holds it back . . . is taken out of the way." Why will God allow this to happen? To show people and nations their own sinfulness, and to show them by bitter experience the true alternative to the lordship of Christ. People totally without God can act no better than vicious animals. Lawlessness, to a certain extent, is already going on, but the man of lawlessness has not yet been revealed.

coming. ⁹The coming of the lawless one will be in accordance with the work of Satan displayed in all kinds of counterfeit miracles, signs and wonders,° ¹⁰and in every sort of evil that deceives those who are perishing. They perish because they refused to love the truth and so be saved. ¹¹For this reason God sends them a powerful delusion so that they will believe the lie ¹²and so that all will be condemned who have not believed the truth but have delighted in wickedness.ᵖ

2:9
°Jn 4:48

2:12
ᵖRo 1:32

Stand Firm

¹³But we ought always to thank God for you, brothers loved by the Lord, because from the beginning God chose youᵃ �q to be saved through the sanctifying work of the Spiritʳ and through belief in the truth. ¹⁴He called you to this through our gospel, that you might share in the glory of our Lord Jesus Christ. ¹⁵So then, brothers, stand firmˢ and hold to the teachingsᵇ we passed on to you,ᵗ whether by word of mouth or by letter.

¹⁶May our Lord Jesus Christ himself and God our Father, who loved us and by his grace gave us eternal encouragement and good hope, ¹⁷encourage your hearts and strengthen you in every good deed and word.

2:13
qEph 1:4
ʳ1Pe 1:2

2:15
ˢ1Co 16:13
ᵗ1Co 11:2

2. Living in the light of Christ's return
Request for Prayer

3 Finally, brothers, pray for us that the message of the Lord may spread rapidly and be honored, just as it was with you. ²And pray that we may be delivered from wicked and evil men,ᵘ for not everyone has faith. ³But the Lord is faithful,ᵛ and he will strengthen and protect you from the evil one. ⁴We have confidence in the Lord that you are doing and will continue to do the things we command. ⁵May the Lord direct your heartsʷ into God's love and Christ's perseverance.

3:2
ᵘRo 15:31

3:3
ᵛ1Co 1:9

3:5
ʷ1Ch 29:18

ᵃ13 Some manuscripts *because God chose you as his firstfruits*   ᵇ15 Or *traditions*

2:9 This lawless one will use "counterfeit miracles, signs and wonders" to deceive and draw a following. Miracles from God can help strengthen our faith and lead people to Christ, but all miracles are not necessarily from God. Christ's miracles were significant, not just because of their power, but because of their purpose—to help, to heal, and to point us to God. The man of lawlessness will have power to do amazing things, but his power will be from Satan. He will use this power to destroy and to lead people away from God and toward himself. If any so-called religious personality draws attention only to himself or herself, his or her work is not from God.

2:10–12 Does God cause people to be deceived? To understand God's allowing such deception, we must first understand God's nature. (1) God himself is good (Psalm 11:7). (2) God created a good world that fell because of humanity's sin (Romans 5:12). (3) Someday God will recreate the world and it will be good again (Revelation 21:1). (4) God is stronger than evil (Matthew 13:41–43; Revelation 19:11–21). (5) God allows evil and thus has control over it. God did not create evil, and he offers help to those who wish to overcome it (Matthew 11:28–30). (6) God uses everything—both good and evil—for his good purposes (Genesis 50:20; Romans 8:28).

The Bible reveals a God who hates all evil and will one day do away with it completely and forever (Revelation 20:10–15). God does not entice anyone to become evil. Those committed to evil, however, may be used by God to sin even more in order to hasten their deserved judgment (see Exodus 11:10). We don't need to understand every detail of how God works in order to

have perfect confidence in his absolute power over evil and his total goodness toward us.

2:13 Paul consistently taught that salvation begins and ends with God. We can do nothing to be saved on our own merit—we must accept God's gift of salvation (see the note on Ephesians 1:4). There is no other way to receive forgiveness from sin. Paul is encouraging the Thessalonian believers by reminding them that they were chosen by God from the beginning. *Sanctification* is the process of Christian growth through which the Holy Spirit makes us like Christ (Romans 8:29). See the note on 1:11, 12.

2:14 God worked through Paul and his companions to tell the Good News so that people could share in Christ's glory. It may seem strange that God works through us—fallible, unfaithful, untrustworthy human creatures. But he has given us the fantastic privilege of accomplishing his great mission—telling the world how to find salvation.

2:15 Paul knew that the Thessalonians would face pressure from persecutions, false teachers, worldliness, and apathy to waver from the truth and to leave the faith. So he urged them to "stand firm" and hold on to the truth they had been taught both through his letters and in person. We also may face persecution, false teachings, worldliness, and apathy. We should hold on to the truth of Christ's teachings because our lives depend on it. Never forget the reality of Christ's life and love!

3:1–3 Beneath the surface of the routine of daily life, a fierce struggle among invisible spiritual powers is being waged. Our main defense is prayer that God will protect us from the evil one and that he will strengthen us. (See also comments on Ephesians 6:10–19 concerning our armor for spiritual warfare.) The following guidelines can help you prepare for and survive satanic attacks: (1) take the threat of spiritual attack seriously; (2) pray for strength and help from God; (3) study the Bible to recognize Satan's style and tactics; (4) memorize Scripture so it will be a source of help no matter where you are; (5) associate with those who speak the truth; and (6) practice what you are taught by sound spiritual leaders.

Warning Against Idleness

6 In the name of the Lord Jesus Christ, we command you, brothers, to keep away from every brother who is idle and does not live according to the teaching[a] you received from us. 7 For you yourselves know how you ought to follow our example. We were not idle when we were with you, 8 nor did we eat anyone's food without paying for it. On the contrary, we worked[x] night and day, laboring and toiling so that we would not be a burden to any of you. 9 We did this, not because we do not have the right to such help,[y] but in order to make ourselves a model for you to follow. 10 For even when we were with you, we gave you this rule: "If a man will not work,[z] he shall not eat."

11 We hear that some among you are idle. They are not busy; they are busybodies.[a] 12 Such people we command and urge in the Lord Jesus Christ to settle down and earn the bread they eat.[b] 13 And as for you, brothers, never tire of doing what is right.[c]

14 If anyone does not obey our instruction in this letter, take special note of him. Do not associate with him, in order that he may feel ashamed. 15 Yet do not regard him as an enemy, but warn him as a brother.

Final Greetings

16 Now may the Lord of peace[d] himself give you peace at all times and in every way. The Lord be with all of you.

17 I, Paul, write this greeting in my own hand,[e] which is the distinguishing mark in all my letters. This is how I write.

18 The grace of our Lord Jesus Christ be with you all.[f]

a 6 Or tradition

3:8
x Ac 18:3
3:9
y 1Co 9:4-14
3:10
z 1Th 4:11
3:11
a 1Ti 5:13
3:12
b 1Th 4:11
3:13
c Gal 6:9
3:16
d Ro 15:33
3:17
e 1Co 16:21
3:18
f Ro 16:20

3:6–10 Paul was writing here about the person who is lazy. Paul explained that when he and his companions were in Thessalonica, they worked hard, buying what they needed rather than becoming a burden to any of the believers. The rule they followed was, "If a man will not work, he shall not eat." There's a difference between leisure and laziness. Relaxation and recreation provide a necessary and much needed balance to our lives; when it is time to work, however, Christians should jump right in. We should make the most of our talent and time, doing all we can to provide for ourselves and our dependents. Rest when you should be resting, and work when you should be working.

3:6–15 Some people in the Thessalonian church were falsely teaching that because Christ would return any day, people should set aside their responsibilities, quit work, do no future planning, and just wait for the Lord. But their lack of activity only led them into sin. They became a burden to the church which was supporting them, they wasted time that could have been used for helping others, and they became "busybodies" (3:11). These church members may have thought that they were being more spiritual by not working, but Paul tells them to be responsible and get back to work. Being ready for Christ means obeying him in every area of life. Because we know that Christ is coming, we must live in such a way that our faith and our daily practice will please him when he arrives.

3:11, 12 A "busybody" is a gossip. An idle person who doesn't work ends up filling his or her time with less than helpful activities, like gossip. Rumors and hearsay are tantalizing, exciting to hear, and make us feel like insiders. But they tear people down. If you often find your nose in other people's business, you may be underemployed. Look for a task to do for Christ or for your family, and get to work.

3:14, 15 Paul counseled the church to stop supporting financially and associating with those who persisted in idleness. Hunger and loneliness can be very effective ways to make the idle person become productive. Paul was not advising coldness or cruelty, but tough love to help a person become responsible.

3:18 The book of 2 Thessalonians is especially meaningful for those who are being persecuted or are under pressure because of their faith. In chapter 1 we are told what suffering can do for us. In chapter 2 we are assured of final victory. In chapter 3 we are encouraged to continue living responsibly in spite of difficult circumstances. Christ's return is more than a doctrine; it is a promise. It is not just for the future; it has a vital impact on how we live now.

1 TIMOTHY

VITAL STATISTICS

PURPOSE:
To give encouragement and instruction to Timothy, a young leader

AUTHOR:
Paul

ORIGINAL AUDIENCE:
Timothy, Paul's son in the faith

DATE WRITTEN:
Approximately A.D. 64, from Rome or Macedonia (possibly Philippi), probably just prior to Paul's final imprisonment in Rome

SETTING:
Timothy was one of Paul's closest companions. Paul had sent Timothy to the church at Ephesus to counter the false teaching that had arisen there (1:3, 4). Timothy probably served for a time as a leader in the church at Ephesus. Paul hoped to visit Timothy (3:14, 15; 4:13), but in the meantime, he wrote this letter to give Timothy practical advice about the ministry.

KEY VERSE:
"Don't let anyone look down on you because you are young, but set an example for the believers in speech, in life, in love, in faith and in purity" (4:12).

KEY PEOPLE:
Paul, Timothy

KEY PLACE:
Ephesus

SPECIAL FEATURES:
First Timothy is a personal letter and a handbook of church administration and discipline.

WITHOUT trying, we model our values. Parents in particular demonstrate to their children what they consider important and valuable. "Like father, like son" is not just a well-worn cliché; it is a truth repeated in our homes. And experience proves that children often follow the life-styles of their parents, repeating their successes and mistakes.

Timothy is a prime example of one who was influenced by godly relatives. His mother, Eunice, and grandmother, Lois, were Jewish believers who helped shape his life and promote his spiritual growth (2 Timothy 1:5; 3:15). The first "second generation" Christian mentioned in the New Testament, Timothy became Paul's protégé and pastor of the church at Ephesus. As a young minister, Timothy faced all sorts of pressures, conflicts, and challenges from the church and his surrounding culture. To counsel and encourage Timothy, Paul sent this very personal letter.

Paul wrote 1 Timothy in about A.D. 64, probably just prior to his final Roman imprisonment. Because he had appealed to Caesar, Paul had been sent as a prisoner to Rome (see Acts 25—28). Most scholars believe that Paul was released about A.D. 62 (possibly because the "statute of limitations" had expired), and that during the next few years he was able to travel. During this time, he wrote 1 Timothy and Titus. Soon, however, Emperor Nero began his campaign to eliminate Christianity. It is believed that during this time Paul was imprisoned again and eventually executed. During this second Roman imprisonment, Paul wrote 2 Timothy. Titus and the two letters to Timothy comprise what are called the "Pastoral Letters."

Paul's first letter to Timothy affirms their relationship (1:2). Paul begins his fatherly advice, warning Timothy about false teachers (1:3—11) and urging him to hold on to his faith in Christ (1:12—20). Next, Paul considers public worship, emphasizing the importance of prayer (2:1—7) and order in church meetings (2:8—15). This leads to a discussion of the qualifications of church leaders—overseers and deacons. Here Paul lists specific criteria for each office (3:1—16).

Paul speaks again about false teachers, telling Timothy how to recognize them and respond to them (4:1—16). Next, he gives practical advice on pastoral care to the young and old (5:1, 2), widows (5:3—16), elders (5:17—25), and slaves (6:1, 2). Paul concludes by exhorting Timothy to guard his motives (6:3—10), to stand firm in his faith (6:11, 12), to live above reproach (6:13—16), and to minister faithfully (6:17—21).

First Timothy holds many lessons. If you are a church leader, take note of Paul's relationship with this young disciple—his careful counsel and guidance. Measure yourself against the qualifications that Paul gives for overseers and deacons. If you are young in the faith, follow the example of godly Christian leaders like Timothy, who imitated Paul's life. If you are a parent, remind yourself of the profound effect a Christian home can have on family members. A faithful mother and grandmother led Timothy to Christ, and Timothy's ministry helped change the world.

THE BLUEPRINT

1. Instructions on right belief (1:1—20)
2. Instructions for the church (2:1—3:16)
3. Instructions for elders (4:1—6:21)

Paul advised Timothy on such practical topics as qualifications for church leaders, public worship, confronting false teaching, and how to treat various groups of people within the church. Right belief and right behavior are critical for anyone who desires to lead or serve effectively in the church. We should all believe rightly, participate in church actively, and minister to one another lovingly.

MEGATHEMES

THEME	EXPLANATION	IMPORTANCE
Sound Doctrine	Paul instructed Timothy to preserve the Christian faith by teaching sound doctrine and modeling right living. Timothy had to oppose false teachers, who were leading church members away from belief in salvation by faith in Jesus Christ alone.	We must know the truth in order to defend it. We must cling to the belief that Christ came to save us. We should stay away from those who twist the words of the Bible for their own purposes.
Public Worship	Prayer in public worship must be done with a proper attitude toward God and fellow believers.	Christian character must be evident in every aspect of worship. We must rid ourselves of any anger, resentment, or offensive behavior that might disrupt worship or damage church unity.
Church Leadership	Paul gives specific instructions concerning the qualifications for church leaders so that the church might honor God and operate smoothly.	Church leaders must be wholly committed to Christ. If you are a new or young Christian, don't be anxious to become a leader in the church. Seek to develop your Christian character first. Be sure to seek God, not your own ambition.
Personal Discipline	It takes discipline to be a leader in the church. Timothy, like all pastors, had to guard his motives, minister faithfully, and live above reproach. Any pastor must keep morally and spiritually fit.	To stay in good spiritual shape, you must discipline yourself to study God's Word and to obey it. Put your spiritual abilities to work!
Caring Church	The church has a responsibility to care for the needs of all its members, especially the sick, the poor, and the widowed. Caring must go beyond good intentions.	Caring for the family of believers demonstrates our Christlike attitude and exhibits genuine love to nonbelievers.

1. Instructions on right belief

1:1
a Col 1:27

1 Paul, an apostle of Christ Jesus by the command of God our Savior and of Christ Jesus our hope,a

1:2
b Ac 16:1

2 To Timothy b my true son in the faith:

Grace, mercy and peace from God the Father and Christ Jesus our Lord.

1:1 This letter was written to Timothy in A.D. 64 or 65, after Paul's first imprisonment in Rome (Acts 28:16–31). Apparently Paul had been out of prison for several years, and during that time he had revisited many churches in Asia and Macedonia. When he and Timothy returned to Ephesus, they found widespread false teaching in the church. Paul had warned the Ephesian elders to be on guard against the false teachers who inevitably would come after he had left (Acts 20:17–31). Paul sent Timothy to lead the Ephesian church while he moved on to Macedonia. From there Paul wrote this letter of encouragement and instruction to help Timothy deal with the difficult situation in the Ephesian church. Later, Paul was arrested again and brought back to a Roman prison.

1:1 Paul calls himself an *apostle*, meaning *one who is sent*. Paul was sent by Jesus Christ to bring the message of salvation to the Gentiles (Acts 9:1–20). He was an apostle "by the command of God" because in Acts 13:2, the Holy Spirit, through the prophets, said, "Set apart for me Barnabas and Saul [Paul] for the work to which I have called them." From Romans 16:25, 26 and Titus 1:3, it is obvious that Paul regarded his commission as direct from God. For more information on Paul, see his Profile in Acts 9, p. 1825.

Warning Against False Teachers of the Law

3As I urged you when I went into Macedonia, stay there in Ephesus so that you may command certain men not to teach false doctrines *c* any longer 4nor to devote themselves to myths *d* and endless genealogies. These promote controversies rather than God's work—which is by faith. 5The goal of this command is love, which comes from a pure heart*e* and a good conscience and a sincere faith. 6Some have wandered away from these and turned to meaningless talk. 7They want to be teachers of the law, but they do not know what they are talking about or what they so confidently affirm.

8We know that the law is good*f* if one uses it properly. 9We also know that law*a* is made not for the righteous but for lawbreakers and rebels, the ungodly and sinful, the unholy and irreligious; for those who kill their fathers or mothers, for murderers, 10for adulterers and perverts, for slave traders and liars and perjurers—and for whatever else is contrary to the sound doctrine *g* 11that conforms to the glorious gospel of the blessed God, which he entrusted to me. *h*

The Lord's Grace to Paul

12I thank Christ Jesus our Lord, who has given me strength, that he considered me faithful, appointing me to his service. 13Even though I was once a blasphemer and a persecutor*i* and a violent man, I was shown mercy because I acted in ignorance and unbelief. 14The grace of our Lord was poured out on me abundantly, along with the faith and love that are in Christ Jesus.

15Here is a trustworthy saying*j* that deserves full acceptance: Christ Jesus came into the

a9 Or that the law

1:3
*c*Gal 1:6, 7
1:4
*d*Tit 1:14
1:5
*e*2Ti 2:22

1:8
*f*Ro 7:12
1:10
*g*2Ti 4:3; Tit 1:9
1:11
*h*Gal 2:7

1:13
*i*Ac 8:3

1:15
*j*2Ti 2:11

1:3, 4 Paul first visited Ephesus on his second missionary journey (Acts 18:19–21). Later, on his third missionary journey, he stayed there for almost three years (Acts 19; 20). Ephesus, along with Rome, Corinth, Antioch, and Alexandria, was one of the major cities in the Roman empire. It was a center for the commerce, politics, and religions of Asia Minor, and the location of the temple dedicated to the goddess Artemis (Diana).

1:3, 4 The church at Ephesus may have been plagued by the same heresy that was threatening the church at Colosse—the teaching that to be acceptable to God, a person had to discover certain hidden knowledge and had to worship angels (Colossians 2:8, 18). The false teachers were motivated by their own interests rather than Christ's. They embroiled the church in endless and irrelevant questions and controversies, taking precious time away from the study of the truth. Stay away from religious speculation and pointless theological arguments. Such exercises may seem harmless at first, but they have a way of sidetracking us from the central message of the gospel—the person and work of Jesus Christ. They expend time we should use to share the gospel with others, and they don't help people grow in the faith. Avoid anything that keeps you from doing God's work.

1:3–7 Many leaders and authorities today demand allegiance, some of whom would even have us turn from Christ to follow them. When they seem to know the Bible, their influence can be dangerously subtle. They are modern-day false teachers. How can you recognize false teachers? (1) They teach what is contrary to the truth found in Scripture (1:3; 1:6, 7; 4:1–3). (2) They promote trivial and divisive controversies instead of helping people come to Jesus (1:4). (3) They aren't concerned about personal evidence of God's presence in their lives, spending their time on "meaningless talk" instead (1:6). (4) Their motivation is to make a name for themselves (1:7). To protect yourself from the deception of false teachers, learn what the Bible teaches and remain steadfast in your faith in Christ alone.

1:6 Arguing about details of the Bible can send us off on interesting but irrelevant tangents and cause us to miss the intent of God's message. The false teachers at Ephesus constructed vast speculative systems and then argued about the minor details of their wholly imaginary ideas. We should allow nothing to distract

us from the Good News of salvation in Jesus Christ, the main point of Scripture. We should know what the Bible says, apply it to our lives daily, and teach it to others. When we do this, we will be able to evaluate all teachings in light of the central truth about Jesus.

1:7–11 The false teachers wanted to become famous as teachers of God's law, but they didn't even understand the law's purpose. The law was not meant to give believers a list of commands for every occasion, but to show unbelievers their sin and bring them to God. For more of what Paul taught about our relationship to law, see Romans 5:20, 21; 13:9, 10; Galatians 3:24–29.

1:10 "Perverts" may refer to homosexuals. Some people attempt to legitimize homosexuality as an acceptable alternative lifestyle. Even some Christians say people have a right to choose their sexual preference. But the entire Bible (both in the Old and New Testaments) calls homosexual behavior sin (see Leviticus 18:22; Romans 1:18–32; 1 Corinthians 6:9–11). We must be careful, however, to condemn only the practice, and not the people. People who live this lifestyle can be forgiven and their lives can be transformed. The church should be a haven of forgiveness and healing for repentant homosexuals without compromising its stance against homosexual behavior. For more on this subject see the notes on Romans 1:26, 27.

1:12–17 People can feel so guilt-ridden by their past that they think God could never forgive and accept them. But consider Paul's past. He had scoffed at the teachings of Jesus ("a blasphemer") and had hunted down and murdered God's people ("a persecutor and a violent man") before coming to faith in Christ (Acts 9:1–9). God forgave Paul and used Paul mightily for his kingdom. No matter how shameful your past, God also can forgive and use you.

1:14 Paul's boldness in Christ can be intimidating. We may feel that our faith in God and our love for Christ and for others will always be inadequate. We will experience times of failure. But we can remain confident that Christ will help our faith and love grow as our relationship with him deepens. Paul's prayer for the Philippians applies to us also: "He who began a good work in you will carry it on to completion until the day of Christ Jesus" (Philippians 1:6).

1:15 Here Paul summarizes the Good News: Jesus came into the world to save sinners, and no sinner is beyond his saving power.

world to save sinners—of whom I am the worst. [16]But for that very reason I was shown mercy so that in me, the worst of sinners, Christ Jesus might display his unlimited patience as an example for those who would believe on him and receive eternal life. [17]Now to the King eternal, immortal, invisible, the only God, be honor and glory for ever and ever. Amen.

1:18
k 1Ti 4:14
l 2Ti 2:3

[18]Timothy, my son, I give you this instruction in keeping with the prophecies once made about you,*k* so that by following them you may fight the good fight,*l* [19]holding on to faith and a good conscience. Some have rejected these and so have shipwrecked their faith. [20]Among them are Hymenaeus*m* and Alexander,*n* whom I have handed over to Satan to be taught not to blaspheme.

1:20
m 2Ti 2:17
n 2Ti 4:14

2. Instructions for the church
Instructions on Worship

2:2
o Ezr 6:10; Ro 13:1

2 I urge, then, first of all, that requests, prayers, intercession and thanksgiving be made for everyone— [2]for kings and all those in authority,*o* that we may live peaceful and quiet lives in all godliness and holiness. [3]This is good, and pleases God our Savior, [4]who wants all

---

(See Luke 5:32 for Jesus' purpose for being on earth.) Jesus didn't come merely to show us how to live better lives or challenge us to be better people. He came to offer us salvation that leads to eternal life. Have you accepted his offer?

1:15 Paul was not nearly as interested in creating an image as he was in being an example. He did not hesitate to share his past, because he knew his failures would allow others to have hope. At times we hesitate to share our past struggles with others because we are afraid it will tarnish our image. Paul demonstrated that lowering our guard can be an important step in communicating the gospel. People will not believe the gospel is important if they can't see that it is crucial in your life. How has Christ shown patience with you? Did he stay with you when you doubted and rebelled? Did he remain faithful when you ignored his prior claim on your life? Did he love you when you disregarded his Word and his church? Remember that his patience is unlimited for those who love him. Don't be afraid to let others know what Christ has done for you.

1:18 Paul highly valued the gift of prophecy (1 Corinthians 14:1). Through prophecy important messages of warning and encouragement came to the church. Just as pastors are ordained and set apart for ministry in church today, Timothy had been set apart for ministry when elders laid their hands on him (see 4:14). Apparently at this ceremony, several believers had prophesied about Timothy's gifts and strengths. These words from the Lord must have encouraged Timothy throughout his ministry.

1:19 How can you hold on to a good conscience? Treasure your faith in Christ more than anything else and do what you know is right. Each time you deliberately ignore your conscience, you are hardening your heart. Over a period of time your capacity to tell right from wrong will diminish. As you walk with God, he will speak to you through your conscience, letting you know the difference between right and wrong. Be sure to act on those inner tugs so that you do what is right—then your conscience will remain clear.

1:20 We don't know who Alexander was—he may have been an associate of Hymenaeus. Hymenaeus's error is explained in 2 Timothy 2:17, 18. He weakened people's faith by teaching that the resurrection had already occurred. Paul says that he handed both of these men over to Satan, meaning that Paul had removed them from the fellowship of the church. Paul did this so that they would see their error and repent. The ultimate purpose of this punishment was correction. The church today is too often lax in disciplining Christians who deliberately sin. Deliberate disobedience should be responded to quickly and sternly to prevent the entire congregation from being affected. But discipline must be done in a way that tries to bring the offender back to Christ and into the loving embrace of the church. The

definition of discipline includes these words: strengthening, purifying, training, correcting, perfecting. Condemnation, suspicion, withholding of forgiveness, or permanent exile should not be a part of church discipline.

2:1-4 Although God is all-powerful and all-knowing, he has chosen to let us help him change the world through our prayers. How this works is a mystery to us because of our limited understanding, but it is a reality. Paul based his instruction about prayer for *everyone* on his conviction that God's invitation for salvation extends equally to all people. The word *everyone* captures the nature of the gospel. The world that God loves includes every person (John 3:16). He loves us as individuals whom he knows intimately (Psalm 139:13–18). Paul urges us to pray for everyone. Our earnest prayers will have powerful results (James 5:16).

2:2 We should pray for those in authority around the world so that their societies will be conducive to the spread of the gospel. Paul's command to pray for kings is remarkable considering that Nero, a notoriously cruel ruler, was emperor at this time (A.D. 54–68). When Paul wrote this letter, persecution was a growing threat to believers. Later, when Nero needed a scapegoat for the great fire that destroyed much of Rome in A.D. 64, he blamed the Roman Christians so as to take the focus off himself. Then persecution erupted throughout the Roman empire. Not only were Christians denied certain privileges in society, some were even publicly butchered, burned, or fed to animals.

2:4 Both Peter and Paul said that God wants all to be saved (see 2 Peter 3:9). This does not mean that all *will* be saved, because the Bible makes it clear that many reject Christ (Matthew 25:31–46; John 12:44–50; Hebrews 10:26–29). The gospel message has a universal scope; it is not directed only to people of one race, one sex, or one national background. God loves the whole world and sent his Son to save sinners. No one is outside God's mercy or beyond the reach of his offer of salvation.

men to be saved and to come to a knowledge of the truth. *p* 5 For there is one God and one mediator *q* between God and men, the man Christ Jesus, 6 who gave himself as a ransom for all men—the testimony *r* given in its proper time. 7 And for this purpose I was appointed a herald and an apostle—I am telling the truth, I am not lying—and a teacher of the true faith to the Gentiles.

8 I want men everywhere to lift up holy hands *s* in prayer, without anger or disputing.

9 I also want women to dress modestly, with decency and propriety, not with braided hair or gold or pearls or expensive clothes, *t* 10 but with good deeds, appropriate for women who profess to worship God.

11 A woman should learn in quietness and full submission. 12 I do not permit a woman to teach or to have authority over a man; she must be silent. 13 For Adam was formed first, then Eve. *u* 14 And Adam was not the one deceived; it was the woman who was deceived and became a sinner. *v* 15 But women *a* will be saved *b* through childbearing—if they continue in faith, love and holiness with propriety.

a 15 Greek *she*   *b 15* Or *restored*

2:4
p 2Ti 2:25

2:5
q Gal 3:20

2:6
r 1Co 1:6

2:8
s Ps 134:2

2:9
t 1Pe 3:3

2:13
u 1Co 11:8

2:14
v Ge 3:1-6, 13;
2Co 11:3

2:5, 6 Though some people think there are many ways to God, in practice, each person must choose a single way. We can stand on one side of a gorge and discuss the possibility of many bridges across the abyss, but if we are determined to cross, we will have to commit to one bridge. Those who insist that there are many bridges to God usually fit one of the following categories: (1) They have not personally committed to any "bridge." They are surprised that their belief in multiple ways does not exempt them from having to choose one. (2) Their belief in "many ways to God" hides their true belief that finding God doesn't really matter at all. (3) They are convinced that arguing for "many ways to God" will insure that they won't be wrong. If there is only one way, their generalized belief will presumably have included it. (4) They have decided that believing in "many ways to God" requires less work than going to the trouble of actually considering the claims of various religious systems.

The facts remain: We human beings are separated from God by sin and we need a Savior—a way across the abyss of sin and back to God. Only one person in the universe is our Mediator and can stand between us and God and bring us together again—Jesus, who is both God and man. Jesus' sacrifice brought new life to all people. Have you let him bridge the gap between you and God?

2:7 Paul describes himself as a herald or preacher. He was given the special privilege of announcing the gospel to the Gentiles. He gives his credentials as an apostle in 1 Corinthians 15:7–11.

2:8 Besides displeasing God, anger and strife make prayer difficult. That is why Jesus said that we should interrupt our prayers, if necessary, to make peace with others (Matthew 5:23, 24). God wants us to obey him immediately and thoroughly. Our goal should be to have a right relationship with God and also with others.

2:9, 10 It is not unscriptural for a woman to want to be attractive. Today, however, to what degree should women take this advice about fixing their hair or wearing gold, pearls, or expensive clothes? Paul was not prohibiting these things; he was simply saying that women should not be drawing attention to themselves through these things. Modesty and decency are the key words. All women would do well to remember that beauty begins on the inside. A gentle, modest, loving character gives a light to the face that cannot be duplicated by even the best cosmetics. A carefully groomed and well-decorated exterior is artificial and cold unless inner beauty is present. The general rule for both women and men emphasizes that both behavior and dress must express submission to and respect for Jesus Christ.

2:9–15 To understand these verses, we must understand the situation in which Paul and Timothy worked. In first-century Jewish culture, women were not allowed to study. When Paul said that women should *learn* in quietness and full submission, he was offering them an amazing new opportunity to learn God's

Word. That they were to listen and learn quietly and submissively referred to an attitude of quietness and composure (not total silence). In addition, Paul himself acknowledges that women publicly prayed and prophesied (1 Corinthians 11:5). Apparently, however, the women in the Ephesian church were abusing their newly acquired Christian freedom. Because these women were new converts, they did not yet have the necessary experience, knowledge, or Christian maturity to teach those who already had extensive scriptural education.

2:12 Some interpret this passage to mean that women should never teach in the assembled church; however, commentators point out that Paul did not forbid women from ever teaching. Paul's commended coworker, Priscilla, taught Apollos, the great preacher (Acts 18:24–26). Paul frequently mentioned other women who held positions of responsibility in the church. Phoebe worked in the church (Romans 16:1). Mary, Tryphena, and Tryphosa were the Lord's workers (Romans 16:6, 12), as were Euodia and Syntyche (Philippians 4:2). Paul was very likely prohibiting the Ephesian women, not all women, from teaching (see the note on 2:9–15).

Paul did not want the Ephesian women to teach because they didn't yet have enough knowledge or experience. The Ephesian church had a particular problem with false teachers. Evidently the women were especially susceptible to the false teachings (2 Timothy 3:1–9) because they did not yet have enough biblical knowledge to discern the truth. In addition, some of the women were apparently flaunting their newfound Christian freedom by wearing inappropriate clothing (2:9). Paul was telling Timothy not to put anyone (in this case, women) into a position of leadership who was not yet mature in the faith (see 3:6; 5:22). The same principle applies to churches today (see the note on 3:6).

2:13, 14 In previous letters Paul had discussed male/female roles in marriage (Ephesians 5:21–33; Colossians 3:18, 19). Here he talks about male/female roles within the church. Some scholars see these verses about Adam and Eve as an illustration of what was happening in the Ephesian church. Just as Eve had been deceived in the Garden of Eden, so the women in the church were being deceived by false teachers. And just as Adam was the first human created by God, so the men in the church in Ephesus should be the first to speak and teach, because they had more training. This view, then, stresses that Paul's teaching here is not universal, but applies to churches with similar problems. Other scholars, however, contend that the roles Paul points out are God's design for his created order—God established these roles to maintain harmony in both the family and the church.

2:14 Paul is not excusing Adam for his part in the fall (Genesis 3:6, 7, 17–19). On the contrary, in his letter to the Romans Paul places the primary blame for humanity's sinful nature on Adam (Romans 5:12–21).

2:15 There are several ways to understand the phrase, being "saved through childbearing": (1) Man sinned, so men were

TIMOTHY

Painful lessons are usually doorways to new opportunities. Even the apostle Paul had much to learn. Shortly after his disappointing experience with John Mark, Paul recruited another eager young man, Timothy, to be his assistant. Paul's intense personality may have been too much for John Mark to handle. It could easily have created the same problem for Timothy. But Paul seems to have learned a lesson in patience from his old friend Barnabas. As a result, Timothy became a "son" to Paul.

Timothy probably became a Christian after Paul's first missionary visit to Lystra (Acts 16:1–5). Timothy already had solid Jewish training in the Scriptures from his mother and grandmother. By Paul's second visit, Timothy had grown into a respected disciple of Jesus. He did not hesitate to join Paul and Silas on their journey. His willingness to be circumcised as an adult is clearly a mark of his commitment. (Timothy's mixed Greek/Jewish background could have created problems on their missionary journeys, because many of their audiences would be made up of Jews who were concerned about the strict keeping of this tradition. Timothy's submission to the rite of circumcision helped to avoid that potential problem.)

Beyond the tensions created by his mixed racial background, Timothy seemed to struggle with a naturally timid character and a sensitivity to his youthfulness. Unfortunately, many who share Timothy's character traits are quickly written off as too great a risk to deserve much responsibility. By God's grace, Paul saw great potential in Timothy. Paul demonstrated his confidence in Timothy by entrusting him with important responsibilities. Paul sent Timothy as his personal representative to Corinth during a particularly tense time (1 Corinthians 4:14–17). Although Timothy was apparently ineffective in that difficult mission, Paul did not give up on him. Timothy continued to travel with Paul.

Our last pictures of Timothy come from the most personal letters in the New Testament: 1 and 2 Timothy. The aging apostle Paul was near the end of his life, but his burning desire to continue his mission had not dimmed. Paul was writing to one of his closest friends—they had traveled, suffered, cried, and laughed together. They shared the intense joy of seeing people respond to the Good News and the agonies of seeing the gospel rejected and distorted. Paul left Timothy in Ephesus to oversee the young church there (1 Timothy 1:3, 4). He wrote to encourage Timothy and give him needed direction. These letters have provided comfort and help to countless other "Timothys" through the years. When you face a challenge that seems beyond your abilities, read 1 and 2 Timothy, and remember that others have shared your experience.

Strengths and accomplishments:	• Became a believer after Paul's first missionary journey and joined him for his other two journeys • Was a respected Christian in his hometown • Was Paul's special representative on several occasions • Received two personal letters from Paul • Probably knew Paul better than any other person, becoming like a son to Paul
Weaknesses and mistakes:	• Struggled with a timid and reserved nature • Allowed others to look down on his youthfulness • Was apparently unable to correct some of the problems in the church at Corinth when Paul sent him there
Lessons from his life:	• Youthfulness should not be an excuse for ineffectiveness • Our inadequacies and inabilities should not keep us from being available to God
Vital statistics:	• Where: Lystra • Occupations: Missionary, pastor • Relatives: Mother: Eunice. Grandmother: Lois. Greek father. • Contemporaries: Paul, Silas, Luke, Mark, Peter, Barnabas
Key verses:	"I have no one else like him [Timothy], who takes a genuine interest in your welfare. For everyone looks out for his own interests, not those of Jesus Christ. But you know that Timothy has proved himself, because as a son with his father he has served with me in the work of the gospel" (Philippians 2:20–22).

Timothy's story is told in Acts, starting in chapter 16. He is also mentioned in Romans 16:21; 1 Corinthians 4:17; 16:10, 11; 2 Corinthians 1:1, 19; Philippians 1:1; 2:19–23; Colossians 1:1; 1 Thessalonians 1:1–10; 2:3, 4; 3:2–6; 1 and 2 Timothy; Philemon 1; Hebrews 13:23.

---

condemned to painful labor. Woman sinned, so women were condemned to pain in childbearing. Both men and women, however, can be saved through trusting Christ and obeying him. (2) Women who fulfill their God-given roles are demonstrating true commitment and obedience to Christ. One of the most important roles for a wife and mother is to care for her family. (3) The

childbearing mentioned here refers to the birth of Jesus Christ. Women (and men) are saved spiritually because of the most important birth, that of Christ himself. (4) From the lessons learned through the trials of childbearing, women can develop qualities that teach them about love, trust, submission, and service.

Overseers and Deacons

3 Here is a trustworthy saying: If anyone sets his heart on being an overseer,[a] he desires a noble task. [2] Now the overseer must be above reproach,[w] the husband of but one wife, temperate, self-controlled, respectable, hospitable, able to teach,[x] [3] not given to drunkenness, not violent but gentle, not quarrelsome, not a lover of money. [4] He must manage his own family well and see that his children obey him with proper respect.[y] [5] (If anyone does not know how to manage his own family, how can he take care of God's church?) [6] He must not be a recent convert, or he may become conceited[z] and fall under the same judgment as the devil. [7] He must also have a good reputation with outsiders, so that he will not fall into disgrace and into the devil's trap.[a]

[8] Deacons, likewise, are to be men worthy of respect, sincere, not indulging in much wine, and not pursuing dishonest gain. [9] They must keep hold of the deep truths of the faith with a clear conscience.[b] [10] They must first be tested; and then if there is nothing against them, let them serve as deacons.

[11] In the same way, their wives[b] are to be women worthy of respect, not malicious talkers[c] but temperate and trustworthy in everything.

[12] A deacon must be the husband of but one wife and must manage his children and his household well. [13] Those who have served well gain an excellent standing and great assurance in their faith in Christ Jesus.

[14] Although I hope to come to you soon, I am writing you these instructions so that, [15] if I

a *1* Traditionally *bishop*; also in verse 2   **b** *11* Or *way, deaconesses*

3:2
w Tit 1:6-8
x 2Ti 2:24

3:4
y Tit 1:6

3:6
z 1Ti 6:4

3:7
a 2Ti 2:26

3:9
b 1Ti 1:19

3:11
c Tit 2:3

3:1 To be a church leader ("overseer") is a heavy responsibility because the church belongs to the living God. The word *overseer* can refer to a pastor, church leader, or presiding elder. It is good to want to be a spiritual leader, but the standards are high. Paul enumerates some of the qualifications here. Church leaders should not be elected because they are popular, nor should they be allowed to push their way to the top. Instead they should be chosen by the church because of their respect for the truth, both in what they believe and in how they live. Do you hold a position of spiritual leadership, or would you like to be a leader some day? Check yourself against Paul's standard of excellence. Those with great responsibility must meet high expectations.

3:1–13 All believers, even if they never plan to be church leaders, should strive to follow these guidelines because they are consistent with what God says is true and right. For example, some people are effectively "able to teach" who never teach or lead formally at church. Their lessons are passed on to one or two others. They become mentors of spiritual truth. Paul described this intimate kind of teaching in 2 Timothy 2:2, "The things you have heard me say in the presence of many witnesses entrust to reliable men who will also be qualified to teach others." More is learned through living than through lectures. If you have been able to communicate your faith clearly to another person, you have demonstrated teaching at its best. In measuring your ability to teach, don't consider how many students you have had; instead, ask how much truth you have passed on to even one student whom God has brought your way.

3:2 Paul's statement that each overseer should have only one wife prohibits both polygamy and promiscuity. This does not prohibit an unmarried person from becoming an elder or a widowed elder from remarrying.

3:4, 5 Christian workers and volunteers sometimes make the mistake of being so involved in their work that they neglect their families, and especially the firm discipline of their children. Spiritual leadership, however, must begin at home. If a man is not willing to care for, discipline, and teach his children, he is not qualified to lead the church. Don't allow your volunteer activities to detract from your family responsibilities.

3:6 New believers should become secure and strong in the faith before taking leadership roles in the church. Too often, in a church desperate for workers, new believers are placed in positions of responsibility prematurely. New faith needs time to mature. New believers should have a place of service, but they

should not be put into leadership positions until they are firmly grounded in their faith, with a solid Christian lifestyle and a knowledge of the Word of God.

3:6 Younger believers who are selected for office need to beware of the damaging effects of pride. Pride can seduce emotions and cloud reason. It can make those who are immature susceptible to the influence of unscrupulous people. Pride and conceit were the devil's downfall, and he uses pride to trap others.

3:7 People outside the church should speak well of those who would lead in the church. The good reputation with outsiders that Paul required is realized when Christians act as dependable friends and good neighbors. How we carry out our duties as citizens, neighbors, and friends facilitates or frustrates our ability to communicate the gospel. Do you have friends who are not believers? Does your conduct help or hinder the cause of Christ? As the church carries out its mission in an increasingly secular world, the church needs those who build bridges with unbelievers in order to bring them the gospel.

3:8–13 *Deacon* means "one who serves." This position was possibly begun by the apostles in the Jerusalem church (Acts 6:1–6) to care for the physical needs of the congregation— at that time it was the needs of the Greek-speaking widows. Deacons were leaders in the church, and their qualifications resemble those of the overseers. In some churches today, the office of deacon has lost its importance. New Christians are often asked to serve in this position, but that is not the New Testament pattern. Paul says that potential deacons should have high qualifications and should be very carefully chosen.

3:11 *Wives* can refer to women helpers or deaconesses. It could also mean wives of deacons, or female leaders of the church (such as Phoebe, the deaconess mentioned in Romans 16:1). In either case, Paul expected the behavior of prominent women in the church to be just as responsible and blameless as that of prominent men.

3:14, 15 The Bible is the written form of what God expects us to know and do. God chose Paul to carry out one phase of the plan. Through Paul, the inspired teaching was written down. As such, it was passed on to Timothy. Then, it was passed on to others. Later, it was passed on to us. Times have changed, but the original authority remains. Because the Bible is from God, it must be studied seriously, understood thoroughly, and applied faithfully. Paul intended this letter to teach believers how to conduct themselves. We would do well to read carefully.

3:15
d ver 5

3:16
e Jn 1:14

am delayed, you will know how people ought to conduct themselves in God's household, which is the church *d* of the living God, the pillar and foundation of the truth. ¹⁶Beyond all question, the mystery of godliness is great:

> He*a* appeared in a body,*b* *e*
> was vindicated by the Spirit,
> was seen by angels,
> was preached among the nations,
> was believed on in the world,
> was taken up in glory.

3. Instructions for elders
Instructions to Timothy

4:1
f Jn 16:13

4:2
g Eph 4:19

4:3
h Ge 1:29
i Ro 14:6

4:6
j 1Ti 1:10

4:8
k 1Ti 6:6

4 The Spirit *f* clearly says that in later times some will abandon the faith and follow deceiving spirits and things taught by demons. ²Such teachings come through hypocritical liars, whose consciences have been seared as with a hot iron. *g* ³They forbid people to marry and order them to abstain from certain foods, which God created *h* to be received with thanksgiving *i* by those who believe and who know the truth. ⁴For everything God created is good, and nothing is to be rejected if it is received with thanksgiving, ⁵because it is consecrated by the word of God and prayer.

⁶If you point these things out to the brothers, you will be a good minister of Christ Jesus, brought up in the truths of the faith *j* and of the good teaching that you have followed. ⁷Have nothing to do with godless myths and old wives' tales; rather, train yourself to be godly. ⁸For physical training is of some value, but godliness has value for all things, *k* holding promise for both the present life and the life to come.

⁹This is a trustworthy saying that deserves full acceptance ¹⁰(and for this we labor and strive), that we have put our hope in the living God, who is the Savior of all men, and especially of those who believe.

a 16 Some manuscripts *God*   *b 16* Or *in the flesh*

3:16 In this short hymn, Paul affirms the humanity and divinity of Christ. By so doing he reveals the heart of the gospel, "the mystery of godliness" (the secret of how we become godly). "Appeared in a body"—Jesus was a man; Jesus' incarnation is the basis of our being right with God. "Was vindicated by the Spirit"—Jesus' resurrection showed that the Holy Spirit's power was in him (Romans 8:11). "Was seen by angels" and "was taken up in glory"—Jesus is divine. We can't please God on our own; we must depend on Christ. As a man, Jesus lived a perfect life, and so he is a perfect example of how to live. As God, Jesus gives us the power to do what is right. It is possible to live a godly life—through following Christ.

4:1 The "later times" began with Christ's resurrection and will continue until his return when he will set up his kingdom and judge all humanity.

4:1, 2 False teachers were and still are a threat to the church. Jesus and the apostles repeatedly warned against them (see, for example, Mark 13:21–23; Acts 20:28–31; 2 Thessalonians 2:1–12; 2 Peter 3:3–7). It is not enough that a teacher appears to know what he is talking about, is disciplined and moral, or says that he is speaking for God. If his words contradict the Bible, his teaching is false. Like Timothy, we must guard against any teaching that causes believers to dilute or reject any aspect of their faith. Such false teaching can be very direct or extremely subtle. Believers ought to respond quickly when they sense false teaching being promoted. The truth does not mind honest questions. Sometimes the source may prove to be ignorant of the error and appreciate the correction. But a firm warning may at least keep potential victims from the disastrous results of apostasy that Paul described. For how to spot false teaching, see the note on 1:3–7.

4:1–5 Paul said the false teachers were hypocritical liars who encouraged people to follow "deceiving spirits and things taught by demons." The danger that Timothy faced in Ephesus seems to have come from certain people in the church who were following some Greek philosophers who taught that the body was evil and

that only the soul mattered. The false teachers refused to believe that the God of creation was good, because his very contact with the physical world would have soiled him. Though these Greek-influenced church members honored Jesus, they could not believe he was truly human. Paul knew that their teachings, if left unchecked, would greatly distort Christian truth.

Satan deceives people by offering a clever imitation of the real thing. The false teachers gave stringent rules (such as forbidding people to marry or to eat certain foods). This made them appear self-disciplined and righteous. Their strict disciplines for the body, however, could not remove sin (see Colossians 2:20–23). We must not be unduly impressed by a teacher's style or credentials; we must look to his teaching about Jesus Christ. His conclusions about Christ show the source of his message.

4:4, 5 In opposition to the false teachers, Paul affirmed that everything God created is good (see Genesis 1). We should ask for God's blessing on his created gifts that give us pleasure and thank him for them. This doesn't mean that we should abuse what God has made (for example, gluttony abuses God's gift of good food, lust abuses God's gift of love, and murder abuses God's gift of life). Instead of abusing, we should enjoy these gifts by using them to serve and honor God. Have you thanked God for the good gifts he has given? Are you using the gifts in ways pleasing to you *and* to God?

4:7–10 Are you in shape both physically and spiritually? In our society, much emphasis is placed on physical fitness, but spiritual health (godliness) is even more important. Our physical health is susceptible to disease and injury, but faith can sustain us through any tragedy. To train ourselves to be godly, we must develop our faith by using our God-given abilities in the service of the church (see 4:14–16). Are you developing your spiritual muscles?

4:10 Christ is the Savior for all, but his salvation becomes effective only for those who trust him.

11Command and teach these things. 12Don't let anyone look down on you because you are young, but set an example[l] for the believers in speech, in life, in love, in faith[m] and in purity. 13Until I come, devote yourself to the public reading of Scripture, to preaching and to teaching. 14Do not neglect your gift, which was given you through a prophetic message[n] when the body of elders laid their hands on you.

15Be diligent in these matters; give yourself wholly to them, so that everyone may see your progress. 16Watch your life and doctrine closely. Persevere in them, because if you do, you will save both yourself and your hearers.

Advice About Widows, Elders and Slaves

5 Do not rebuke an older man harshly,[o] but exhort him as if he were your father. Treat younger men as brothers, 2older women as mothers, and younger women as sisters, with absolute purity.

3Give proper recognition to those widows who are really in need. 4But if a widow has children or grandchildren, these should learn first of all to put their religion into practice by caring for their own family and so repaying their parents and grandparents,[p] for this is pleasing to God. 5The widow who is really in need and left all alone puts her hope in God and continues night and day to pray[q] and to ask God for help. 6But the widow who lives for pleasure is dead even while she lives. 7Give the people these instructions,[r] too, so that no one may be open to blame. 8If anyone does not provide for his relatives, and especially for his immediate family, he has denied[s] the faith and is worse than an unbeliever.

4:12
*Tit 2:7
*m*1Ti 1:14

4:14
*n*1Ti 1:18

5:1
*o*Lev 19:32

5:4
*p*Eph 6:1, 2

5:5
*q*Lk 2:37
5:7
*r*1Ti 4:11
5:8
*s*Tit 1:16

4:12 Timothy was a young pastor. It would have been easy for older Christians to look down on him because of his youth. He had to earn the respect of his elders by setting an example in his speech, life, love, faith, and purity. Regardless of your age, God can use you. Whether you are young or old, don't think of your age as a handicap. Live so others can see Christ in you.

4:12–16 Apparently Timothy needed some encouragement. Most likely, so do many people around us. Each day we have many opportunities to support and inspire family members, fellow workers, and even total strangers. People need help and affirmation all along the way. Paul modeled six important principles to help us encourage others: (1) Begin with encouragement. People who know we will encourage them will be happy to work with us. (2) Expect of others only what you expect of yourself. People will resist being held to unfair standards. (3) Develop expectations of others with consideration for their skills, maturity, and experience. People will reject or fail to meet expectations that do not fit them. Be patient with distracted or slow learners. (4) Monitor your expectations of others. Changing circumstances sometimes require revised or reduced expectations. (5) Clarify your expectations with others. People are not likely to hit a target that no one has identified. (6) End with encouragement. People love to be thanked for a job well done.

4:13 The "Scripture" referred to here is, in fact, the Old Testament. We must make sure to emphasize the entire Bible, both the Old and the New Testaments. There are rich rewards in studying the people, events, prophecies, and principles of the Old Testament.

4:14 Highly skilled and talented athletes lose their abilities if their muscles aren't toned by constant use. Likewise, we will lose our spiritual gifts if we don't put them to work. Our talents are improved by exercise, but failing to use them causes them to waste away from lack of practice and nourishment. What gifts and abilities has God given you? Use them regularly in serving God and others. (See Romans 12:1–8; 2 Timothy 1:6–8 for more on using well the abilities God has given us.)

4:16 We must be on constant guard against falling into sin that can so easily destroy us. Yet we must watch what we believe ("doctrine") just as closely. Wrong beliefs can quickly lead us into sin and heresy. We should be on guard against those who would persuade us that how we live is more important than what we believe. We should keep a close watch on both, staying true to the faith.

5:2 Men in the ministry can avoid improper attitudes toward women by treating them as family members. If men see women as fellow members in God's family, they will protect them and help them grow spiritually.

5:3ff Paul wanted Christian families to be as self-supporting as possible. He insisted that children and grandchildren take care of the widows in their families (5:4); he suggested that younger widows remarry and start new families (5:14); he ordered the church not to support lazy members who refused to work (2 Thessalonians 3:10). Nevertheless, when necessary, the believers pooled their resources (Acts 2:44–47); they gave generously to help disaster-ridden churches (1 Corinthians 16:1–4); they took care of a large number of widows (Acts 6:1–6). The church has always had limited resources and has always had to balance financial responsibility with generosity. It only makes sense for members to work as hard as they can and to be as independent as possible, so they can adequately care for themselves and for less fortunate members. When church members are both responsible and generous, everyone's needs will be met.

5:3–5 Because there were no pensions, no social security, no life insurance, and few honorable jobs for women, widows were usually unable to support themselves. The responsibility for caring for the helpless naturally falls first on their families—the people whose lives are most closely linked with theirs. Paul stresses the importance of families caring for the needs of widows, and not leaving it for the church—so the church can care for those widows who have no families. A widow who had no children or other family members to support her was doomed to poverty. From the beginning, the church took care of its widows, who in turn gave valuable service to the church.

The church should support those who have no families and should also help the elderly, young, disabled, ill, or poverty-stricken with their emotional and spiritual needs. Often families who are caring for their own helpless members have heavy burdens. They may need extra money, a listening ear, a helping hand, or a word of encouragement. Interestingly, those who are helped often turn around and help others, turning the church into more of a caring community. Don't wait for people to ask. Take the initiative and look for ways to serve them.

5:8 Healthy homes remain the best possible training environment for children. When it comes to caring for relatives and honoring parents, children take most of their cues by watching how Mom and Dad honor the grandparents. If our children see the way we, as parents, care for our parents, they will understand

5:10
r Lk 7:44

⁹No widow may be put on the list of widows unless she is over sixty, has been faithful to her husband,ᵃ ¹⁰and is well known for her good deeds, such as bringing up children, showing hospitality, washing the feetʳ of the saints, helping those in trouble and devoting herself to all kinds of good deeds.

¹¹As for younger widows, do not put them on such a list. For when their sensual desires overcome their dedication to Christ, they want to marry. ¹²Thus they bring judgment on

5:13
u 2Th 3:11

themselves, because they have broken their first pledge. ¹³Besides, they get into the habit of being idle and going about from house to house. And not only do they become idlers, but

5:14
v 1Co 7:9

also gossips and busybodies,ᵘ saying things they ought not to. ¹⁴So I counsel younger widows to marry,ᵛ to have children, to manage their homes and to give the enemy no opportunity for slander. ¹⁵Some have in fact already turned away to follow Satan.

5:16
w ver 3-5

¹⁶If any woman who is a believer has widows in her family, she should help them and not let the church be burdened with them, so that the church can help those widows who are really in need. ʷ

5:18
x 1Co 9:7-9
y Lev 19:13;
Dt 24:14, 15;
Mt 10:10

¹⁷The elders who direct the affairs of the church well are worthy of double honor, especially those whose work is preaching and teaching. ¹⁸For the Scripture says, "Do not muzzle the ox while it is treading out the grain,"ᵇ ˣ and "The worker deserves his wages."ᶜ ʸ ¹⁹Do not entertain an accusation against an elder unless it is brought by two or three witnesses.

5:20
z Tit 1:13

²⁰Those who sin are to be rebukedᶻ publicly, so that the others may take warning.

5:21
a 1Ti 6:13

²¹I charge you, in the sight of God and Christ Jesusᵃ and the elect angels, to keep these instructions without partiality, and to do nothing out of favoritism.

²²Do not be hasty in the laying on of hands, and do not share in the sins of others. Keep yourself pure.

ᵃ 9 Or *has had but one husband*   ᵇ 18 Deut. 25:4   ᶜ 18 Luke 10:7

---

the importance of such honor for us in the future. Healthy, practical honor becomes a priceless gift that one generation gives to another. Disrespect and lack of care provide harmful examples that will eventually turn on us. The warning in the verse is ominous indeed.

5:9–16 Apparently some older widows had been "put on the list of widows," meaning that they had taken a vow committing themselves to work for the church in exchange for financial support. Paul lists a few qualifications for these church workers—these widows should be at least 60 years old, should have been faithful to their husbands, and should be well known for their kind deeds. Younger widows should not be included in this group because they might desire to marry again and thus have to break their pledge (5:11, 12).

Three out of four wives today eventually are widowed, and many of the older women in our churches have lost their husbands. Does your church provide an avenue of service for these women? Could you help match their gifts and abilities with your church's needs? Often their maturity and wisdom can be of great service in the church.

5:10 "Washing the feet of the saints" means to help and serve other believers with humility, following the example of Jesus, who washed the feet of his disciples at the Last Supper (John 13:1–17).

5:15 "Turned away to follow Satan" refers to the immoral conduct that identified these women with their pagan neighbors.

5:17 Preaching and teaching are closely related. Preaching is proclaiming the Word of God and confronting listeners with the truth of Scripture. Teaching is explaining the truth in Scripture, helping learners understand difficult passages, and helping them apply God's Word to daily life. Paul says that these elders are worthy of double honor. Unfortunately, however, we often take them for granted by not providing adequately for their needs or by subjecting them to heavy criticism. Think of how you can honor your leaders who work hard at preaching and teaching.

5:17, 18 Faithful church leaders should be supported and appreciated. Too often they are targets for criticism because the congregation has unrealistic expectations. How do you treat your church leaders? Do you enjoy finding fault, or do

you show your appreciation? Do they receive enough financial support to allow them to live without worry and to provide for the needs of their families? Jesus and Paul emphasized the importance of supporting those who lead and teach us (see Galatians 6:6 and the notes on Luke 10:7 and 1 Corinthians 9:4–10). Our ministers deserve to know that we are giving to them cheerfully, gratefully, and generously.

5:19–21 Church leaders are not exempt from sin, faults, and mistakes. But they are often criticized for the wrong reasons—minor imperfections, failure to meet someone's expectations, personality clashes. Thus Paul said that accusations should not even be heard unless two or three witnesses confirm them. Sometimes church leaders should be confronted about their behavior, and sometimes they should be rebuked. But all rebuking must be done fairly and lovingly, and for the purpose of restoration.

5:21 Church leadership is a heavy responsibility. As difficult as it might be, Timothy was not to waver on any of Paul's instructions (and particularly the instructions about rebuking elders). Any needed discipline or rebuke must be administered without regard to Timothy's personal inclinations or favoritism. Likewise, leadership in the church today must be handled with maturity, faithfulness, godliness, and lack of favoritism. The health of a body of believers is far more important than playing favorites with someone who is not meeting the standards set forth here.

5:22, 24, 25 Paul says that a church should never be in a hurry about choosing its leaders, especially the pastor, because major problems or sins might be overlooked. It is a serious responsibility to choose church leaders. They must have strong faith and be morally upright, having the qualities described in 3:1–13 and Titus 1:5–9. Not everyone who wants to be a church leader is eligible. Be certain of an applicant's qualifications before asking him or her to take a leadership position.

23 Stop drinking only water, and use a little wine because of your stomach and your frequent illnesses.

24 The sins of some men are obvious, reaching the place of judgment ahead of them; the sins of others trail behind them. 25 In the same way, good deeds are obvious, and even those that are not cannot be hidden.

6 All who are under the yoke of slavery should consider their masters worthy of full respect,*b* so that God's name and our teaching may not be slandered.*c* 2 Those who have believing masters are not to show less respect for them because they are brothers. Instead, they are to serve them even better, because those who benefit from their service are believers, and dear to them. These are the things you are to teach and urge on them.*d*

6:1
b Tit 2:9; 1Pe 2:18
c Tit 2:5, 8

6:2
d 1Ti 4:11

Love of Money

3 If anyone teaches false doctrines and does not agree to the sound instruction of our Lord Jesus Christ and to godly teaching, 4 he is conceited and understands nothing. He has an unhealthy interest in controversies and quarrels about words that result in envy, strife, malicious talk, evil suspicions 5 and constant friction between men of corrupt mind, who have been robbed of the truth and who think that godliness is a means to financial gain.

6 But godliness with contentment*e* is great gain. 7 For we brought nothing into the world, and we can take nothing out of it.*f* 8 But if we have food and clothing, we will be content with that. 9 People who want to get rich fall into temptation and a trap and into many foolish and harmful desires that plunge men into ruin and destruction. 10 For the love of money is a root of all kinds of evil. Some people, eager for money, have wandered from the faith and pierced themselves with many griefs.

6:6
e Heb 13:5

6:7
f Job 1:21

Paul's Charge to Timothy

11 But you, man of God, flee from all this, and pursue righteousness, godliness, faith, love, endurance and gentleness. 12 Fight the good fight*g* of the faith. Take hold of the eternal life to which you were called when you made your good confession in the presence of many witnesses. 13 In the sight of God, who gives life to everything, and of Christ Jesus, who while testifying before Pontius Pilate*h* made the good confession, I charge you*i* 14 to keep this command without spot or blame until the appearing of our Lord Jesus Christ, 15 which God will bring about in his own time—God, the blessed and only Ruler,*j* the King of kings and Lord of lords, 16 who alone is immortal and who lives in unapproachable light, whom no one has seen or can see. To him be honor and might forever. Amen.

6:12
g 1Ti 1:18

6:13
h Jn 18:33-37
i 1Ti 5:21

6:15
j 1Ti 1:17

5:23 It is unclear why Paul gave this advice to Timothy. Perhaps contaminated water had led to Timothy's indigestion and so he should stop drinking only water. Whatever the reason, this statement is not an invitation to overindulgence or alcoholism.

6:1, 2 In Paul's culture there was a great social and legal gulf separating masters and slaves. But as Christians, masters and slaves became spiritual equals, brothers and sisters in Christ Jesus (Galatians 3:28). Paul did not speak against the institution of slavery, but he gave guidelines for Christian slaves and Christian masters. His counsel for the master/slave relationship can be applied to the employer/employee relationship today. Employees should work hard, showing respect for their employers. In turn, employers should be fair (Ephesians 6:5–9; Colossians 3:22–25). Our work should reflect our faithfulness to and love for Christ.

6:3–5 Paul told Timothy to stay away from those who just wanted to make money from preaching, and from those who strayed from the sound teachings of the gospel into quarrels that caused strife in the church. A person's understanding of the finer points of theology should not become the basis for lording it over others or for making money. Stay away from people who just want to argue.

6:6 This statement is the key to spiritual growth and personal fulfillment. We should honor God and center our desires on him ("godliness," see Matthew 6:33), and we should be content with what God is doing in our lives (see Philippians 4:11–13).

6:6–10 Despite overwhelming evidence to the contrary, most people still believe that money brings happiness. Rich people craving greater riches can be caught in an endless cycle that only ends in ruin and destruction. How can you keep away from the love of money? Paul gives us some guidelines: (1) realize that one day riches will all be gone (6:7, 17); (2) be content with what you have (6:8); (3) monitor what you are willing to do to get more money (6:9, 10); (4) love people more than money (6:11); (5) love God's work more than money (6:11); (6) freely share what you have with others (6:18). (See Proverbs 30:7–9 for more on avoiding the love of money.)

6:8, 9 It is often helpful to distinguish between *needs* and *wants*. We may have all we need to live but let ourselves become anxious and discontented over what we merely want. Like Paul, we can choose to be content without having all that we want. The only alternative is to be a slave to our desires.

6:11, 12 Paul uses active and forceful verbs to describe the Christian life: flee, pursue, fight, take hold. Some think Christianity is a passive religion that advocates waiting for God to act. But we must have an *active* faith, training, working hard, sacrificing, and doing what we know is right. Is it time for action on your part? Christian service, like athletics, requires training and sacrifice. Our discipline and obedience largely define whether or not we will be contributors or merely spectators. How would other believers rank your contributing role on Christ's team?

6:13 Jesus' trial before Pilate is recorded in the Gospels: Matthew 27:11–26; Mark 15:1–15; Luke 23:1–25; John 18:28—19:16.

6:17
k Lk 12:20, 21
l Ac 14:17

¹⁷Command those who are rich in this present world not to be arrogant nor to put their hope in wealth,*ᵏ* which is so uncertain, but to put their hope in God, who richly provides us with everything for our enjoyment.*ˡ* ¹⁸Command them to do good, to be rich in good deeds, and to be generous and willing to share. ¹⁹In this way they will lay up treasure for themselves as a firm foundation for the coming age, so that they may take hold of the life that is truly life.

6:20
m 2Ti 1:12, 14

²⁰Timothy, guard what has been entrusted*ᵐ* to your care. Turn away from godless chatter and the opposing ideas of what is falsely called knowledge, ²¹which some have professed and in so doing have wandered from the faith.*ⁿ*

6:21
n 2Ti 2:18

Grace be with you.

6:17–19 Ephesus was a wealthy city, and the Ephesian church probably had many wealthy members. Paul advised Timothy to deal with any potential problems by teaching that having riches carries great responsibility. If you have been blessed with wealth, then thank the Lord. Don't be proud and don't trust in your money. Use your money to do good. Be rich in good works, generous, and ready to share. No matter how much money you have, your life should demonstrate that God controls the wealth that he has placed under your care.

6:21 The book of 1 Timothy provides guiding principles for local churches, including rules for public worship and qualifica-

tions for overseers (elders, pastors), deacons, and special church workers (widows). Paul tells the church leaders to correct incorrect doctrine and to deal lovingly and fairly with all people in the church. The church is not organized simply for the sake of organization, but so that Christ can be honored and glorified. While studying these guidelines, don't lose sight of what is most important in the life of the church—knowing God, working together in loving harmony, and taking God's Good News to the world.

VITAL STATISTICS

PURPOSE:
To give final instructions and encouragement to Timothy, pastor of the church at Ephesus

AUTHOR:
Paul

ORIGINAL AUDIENCE:
Timothy

DATE WRITTEN:
Approximately A.D. 66 or 67, from prison in Rome. After a year or two of freedom, Paul was arrested again and executed under Emperor Nero.

SETTING:
Paul was virtually alone in prison; only Luke was with him. Paul wrote this letter to pass the torch to the new generation of church leaders. He also asked for visits from his friends and for his books, especially the parchments—possibly parts of the Old Testament, the Gospels, and other biblical manuscripts.

KEY VERSE:
"Do your best to present yourself to God as one approved, a workman who does not need to be ashamed and who correctly handles the word of truth" (2:15).

KEY PEOPLE:
Paul, Timothy, Luke, Mark, and others

KEY PLACES:
Rome, Ephesus

SPECIAL FEATURES:
Because this is Paul's last letter, it reveals his heart and his priorities—sound doctrine, steadfast faith, confident endurance, and lasting love.

"FAMOUS last words" is more than a cliché. When notable men and women of influence are about to die, the world waits to hear their final words of insight and wisdom. Then those quotes are repeated worldwide. This is also true with a dying loved one. Gathered at his or her side, the family strains to hear every whispered syllable of blessing, encouragement, and advice, knowing that this will be the final message.

One of the most knowledgeable, influential, and beloved men of history is the apostle Paul. And we have his famous last words.

Paul was facing death. He was not dying of a disease in a sterile hospital with loved ones gathered nearby. He was very much alive, but his condition was terminal. Convicted as a follower of Jesus of Nazareth, Paul sat in a cold Roman prison, cut off from the world, with just a visitor or two and his writing materials. Paul knew that soon he would be executed (4:6), so he wrote his final thoughts to his "son" Timothy, passing to him the torch of leadership, reminding him of what was truly important, and encouraging him in the faith. Imagine how Timothy must have read and reread every word; this was the last message from his beloved mentor, Paul. Because of the situation and the recipient, this is the most intimate and moving of all Paul's letters and his last.

Paul's introduction is tender, and every phrase exudes the love he has for Timothy (1:1–5). He then reminds Timothy of the qualities necessary for a faithful minister of Jesus Christ (1:6—2:13). Timothy should remember his call and use his gifts with boldness (1:6–12), keep to the truth (1:13–18), prepare others to follow him in the ministry (2:1, 2), be disciplined and ready to endure suffering (2:3–7), and keep his eyes and mind focused on Christ (2:8–13). Paul challenges Timothy to hold to sound doctrine, reject error and avoid godless chatter, correctly handle the word of truth (2:14–19), and keep his life pure (2:20–26).

Next, Paul warns Timothy of the opposition that he and other believers would face in the last days from self-centered people who use the church for their own gain and teach false doctrines (3:1–9). Paul tells Timothy to be prepared for these unfaithful people by remembering his example (3:10, 11), understanding the real source of the opposition (3:12, 13), and finding strength and power in the Word of God (3:14–17). Then Paul gives Timothy a stirring charge: to preach the Word (4:1–4) and to fulfill his ministry until the end (4:5–8).

Paul concludes with personal requests and items of information. In these final words, he reveals his loneliness and his strong love for his brothers and sisters in Christ (4:9–22).

There has never been another person like Paul, the missionary apostle. He was a man of deep faith, undying love, constant hope, tenacious conviction, and profound insight. And he was inspired by the Holy Spirit to give us God's message. As you read 2 Timothy, know that you are reading the last words of this great man of God—his last words to Timothy and to all who would claim to follow Christ. Recommit yourself to stand courageously for the truth, knowing the Word and being empowered by the Holy Spirit.

THE BLUEPRINT

1. Foundations of Christian service
   (1:1—2:26)
2. Difficult times for Christian service
   (3:1—4:22)

Paul gives helpful advice to Timothy to remain solidly grounded in Christian service and to endure suffering during the difficult days to come. It is easy for us to serve Christ for the wrong reasons: because it is exciting, rewarding, or personally enriching. Without a proper foundation, however, we will find it easy to quit during difficult times. All believers need a strong foundation for their service, because Christian service does not get easier as we grow older, and it will become no easier as the time of Christ's return grows closer.

MEGATHEMES

THEME	EXPLANATION	IMPORTANCE
Boldness	In the face of opposition and persecution, Timothy was to carry out his ministry without fear or shame. Paul urged him to utilize boldly the gifts of preaching and teaching that the Holy Spirit had given him.	The Holy Spirit helps us to be wise and strong. God honors our confident testimony even when we suffer. To get over our fear of what people might say or do, we must take our eyes off of people and look only to God.
Faithfulness	Christ was faithful to all of us in dying for our sin. Paul was a faithful minister even when he was in prison. Paul urged Timothy to maintain not only sound doctrine but also loyalty, diligence, and endurance.	We can count on opposition, suffering, and hardship as we serve Christ. But this shows that our faithfulness is having an effect on others. As we trust Christ, he counts us worthy to suffer, and he will give us the strength we need to be steadfast.
Preaching and Teaching	Paul and Timothy were active in preaching and teaching the Good News about Jesus Christ. Paul encouraged Timothy not only to carry the torch of truth but also to train others, passing on to them sound doctrine and enthusiasm for Christ's mission.	We must prepare people to transmit God's Word to others so that they in turn might pass it on. Does your church carefully train others to teach?
Error	In the final days before Christ returns, there will be false teachers, spiritual dropouts, and heretics. The remedy for error is to have a solid program for teaching Christians.	Because of deception and false teaching, we must be disciplined and ready to reject error. Know the Word of God as your sure defense against error and confusion.

1. Foundations of Christian service

1

1:1
a 2Co 1:1

Paul, an apostle of Christ Jesus by the will of God, a according to the promise of life that is in Christ Jesus,

1:2
b 1Ti 1:2

2 To Timothy, my dear son: b

Grace, mercy and peace from God the Father and Christ Jesus our Lord.

1:1 This letter has a somber tone. Paul had been imprisoned for the last time, and he knew he would soon die. Unlike Paul's first imprisonment in Rome, when he was in a house (Acts 28:16, 23, 30) where he continued to teach, this time he was probably confined to a cold dungeon, awaiting his death (4:6–8). Emperor Nero had begun a major persecution in A.D. 64 as part of his plan to pass the blame for the great fire of Rome from himself to the Christians. This persecution spread across the empire and included social ostracism, public torture, and murder. As Paul was waiting to die, he wrote a letter to his dear friend Timothy, a younger man who was like a son to him (1:2). Written in approximately A.D. 66/67, these are the last words we have from Paul.

1:1 When we are united with Christ, life takes on both immediate and eternal dimensions. Paul's use of the phrase, "the promise of life that is in Christ Jesus," can apply to the life that Jesus gives

immediately to those who trust him, as well as to the life fully realized in eternity. On one hand, Paul said, "If anyone is in Christ, he is a new creation" (2 Corinthians 5:17). So new life begins at conversion. Yet on the other hand, we "wait eagerly for our adoption as sons, the redemption of our bodies" (Romans 8:23). The present experience we enjoy provides a foretaste of our complete redemption at Christ's return. When we struggle with difficulties in this life, remember that the best is yet to come.

1:2 Paul's second letter to Timothy was written about two to four years after his first letter. Timothy had been Paul's traveling companion on the second and third missionary journeys, and Paul had left him in Ephesus to help the church there (1 Timothy 1:3, 4). For more information on Timothy, see his Profile in 1 Timothy, p. 2037. For more information on the great missionary, Paul, see his Profile in Acts 9, p. 1825.

Encouragement to Be Faithful

³ I thank God,*c* whom I serve, as my forefathers did, with a clear conscience, as night and day I constantly remember you in my prayers. ⁴ Recalling your tears, I long to see you,*d* so that I may be filled with joy. ⁵ I have been reminded of your sincere faith,*e* which first lived in your grandmother Lois and in your mother Eunice*f* and, I am persuaded, now lives in you also. ⁶ For this reason I remind you to fan into flame the gift of God, which is in you through the laying on of my hands.*g* ⁷ For God did not give us a spirit of timidity,*h* but a spirit of power, of love and of self-discipline.

⁸ So do not be ashamed to testify about our Lord, or ashamed of me his prisoner.*i* But join with me in suffering for the gospel, by the power of God, ⁹ who has saved us and called us to a holy life—not because of anything we have done but because of his own purpose and grace. This grace was given us in Christ Jesus before the beginning of time, ¹⁰ but it has now been revealed through the appearing of our Savior, Christ Jesus, who has destroyed death and has brought life and immortality to light through the gospel. ¹¹ And of this gospel I was appointed a herald and an apostle and a teacher.*j* ¹² That is why I am suffering as I am. Yet I am not ashamed, because I know whom I have believed, and am convinced that he is able to guard*k* what I have entrusted to him for that day.

1:3 *c* Ro 1:8
1:4 *d* 2Ti 4:9
1:5 *e* 1Ti 1:5 *f* Ac 16:1
1:6 *g* 1Ti 4:14
1:7 *h* Ro 8:15
1:8 *i* Eph 3:1
1:11 *j* 1Ti 2:7
1:12 *k* 1Ti 6:20

1:3 Paul consistently prayed for Timothy, his friend, his fellow traveler, his son in the faith, and a strong leader in the Christian church. Although the two men were separated from each other, their prayers provided a source of mutual encouragement. We too should pray consistently for others, especially for those who do God's work. On your prayer list, include your pastor, other church leaders, and missionaries around the world. They need your prayers.

1:4 We don't know when Paul and Timothy last parted, but it was probably when Paul was arrested and taken to Rome for his second imprisonment. The tears they shed at parting revealed the depth of their relationship.

1:5 Timothy's mother and grandmother, Eunice and Lois, were early Christian converts, possibly through Paul's ministry in their home city, Lystra (Acts 16:1). They had communicated their strong Christian faith to Timothy, even though his father was probably not a believer. Don't hide your light at home; our families are fertile fields for planting gospel seeds. Let your parents, children, spouse, brothers, and sisters know of your faith in Jesus, and be sure they see Christ's love, helpfulness, and joy in you.

1:6 At the time of his ordination, Timothy had received special gifts of the Spirit to enable him to serve the church (see 1 Timothy 4:14). In telling Timothy to "fan into flame the gift of God," Paul was encouraging him to persevere. Timothy did not need new revelations or new gifts; he needed the courage and self-discipline to hang on to the truth and to use the gifts he had already received (see 1:13, 14). If Timothy would step out boldly in faith and proclaim the gospel once again, the Holy Spirit would go with him and give him power. When you use the gifts God has given you, you will find that God will give you the power you need to accomplish whatever task he gives you.

1:6 Clearly Timothy's spiritual gift had been given to him when Paul and the elders had laid their hands on him and set him apart for ministry (see 1 Timothy 4:14). God gives all Christians gifts to use to build up the body of Christ (see 1 Corinthians 12:4–31), and he gives special gifts to some through church leaders, who serve as God's instruments.

1:6, 7 Timothy was experiencing great opposition to his message and to himself as a leader. His youth, his association with Paul, and his leadership had come under fire from believers and nonbelievers alike. Paul urged him to be bold. When we allow people to intimidate us, we neutralize our effectiveness for God. The power of the Holy Spirit can help us overcome our fear

of what some might say or do to us, so that we can continue to do God's work.

1:7 Paul mentions three characteristics of the effective Christian leader: power, love, and self-discipline. These are available to us because the Holy Spirit lives in us. Follow his leading each day so that your life will more fully exhibit these characteristics. See Galatians 5:22, 23 for a list of the by-products of the Holy Spirit living in us.

1:8 In this time of mounting persecution, Timothy may have been afraid to continue preaching the gospel. His fears were based on fact, because believers were being arrested and executed. Paul told Timothy to expect suffering—Timothy, like Paul, would be jailed for preaching the gospel (Hebrews 13:23). But Paul promised Timothy that God would give him strength and that he would be ready when it was his turn to suffer. Even when there is no persecution, sharing our faith in Christ can be difficult. Fortunately we, like Paul and Timothy, can rely on the Holy Spirit to give us courage. Don't be ashamed to testify of your personal faith in Jesus Christ.

1:9, 10 In these verses Paul gives a brief summary of the gospel. God loves us, called us, and sent Christ to die for us. We can have eternal life through faith in him, because he broke the power of death with his resurrection. We do not deserve to be saved, but God offers us salvation anyway. What we must do is believe in him and accept his offer.

1:12 In spite of the suffering that might have caused Paul to despair, he affirmed his confidence in God's protection. This was not a claim to strong faith; rather, it was a trust in one so powerful that even a weak faith was sufficient. Paul based his confidence in Christ on his intimate relationship with him. Paul knew the one in whom he trusted with personal knowledge; he knew Christ so well that no earthly experience could break the bond of love by which Christ held him. If your situation looks bleak, give your concerns to Christ because you know him and love him. Realize that he will guard all you have entrusted to him until the day of his return. For more on our security in Christ, see Romans 8:38, 39.

1:12 The phrase "guard what I have entrusted to him" could mean: (1) Paul knew that God would protect the souls of those converted through his preaching; (2) Paul trusted God to guard his own soul until Christ's second coming; or (3) Paul was confident that, though he was in prison and facing death, God would carry out the gospel ministry through others such as Timothy. Paul may have expressed his confidence to encourage Timothy, who was undoubtedly discouraged by the problems in Ephesus and fearful of persecution. Even in prison, Paul knew that God was still in control. No matter what setbacks or problems we face, we can trust fully in God.

1:13
l Tit 1:9
m 1Ti 1:14

¹³What you heard from me, keep *l* as the pattern of sound teaching, with faith and love in Christ Jesus. *m* ¹⁴Guard the good deposit that was entrusted to you—guard it with the help of the Holy Spirit who lives in us.

¹⁵You know that everyone in the province of Asia has deserted me, including Phygelus and Hermogenes.

¹⁶May the Lord show mercy to the household of Onesiphorus, because he often refreshed me and was not ashamed of my chains. ¹⁷On the contrary, when he was in Rome, he searched hard for me until he found me. ¹⁸May the Lord grant that he will find mercy from the Lord on that day! You know very well in how many ways he helped me in Ephesus.

2:1
n Eph 6:10
2:3
o 1Ti 1:18

2:5
p 1Co 9:25

2 You then, my son, be strong *n* in the grace that is in Christ Jesus. ²And the things you have heard me say in the presence of many witnesses entrust to reliable men who will also be qualified to teach others. ³Endure hardship with us like a good soldier *o* of Christ Jesus. ⁴No one serving as a soldier gets involved in civilian affairs—he wants to please his commanding officer. ⁵Similarly, if anyone competes as an athlete, he does not receive the victor's crown *p* unless he competes according to the rules. ⁶The hardworking farmer should be the first to receive a share of the crops. ⁷Reflect on what I am saying, for the Lord will give you insight into all this.

2:8
q Ro 2:16

⁸Remember Jesus Christ, raised from the dead, descended from David. This is my gospel, *q* ⁹for which I am suffering even to the point of being chained like a criminal. But God's word is not chained. ¹⁰Therefore I endure everything for the sake of the elect, that they too may obtain the salvation that is in Christ Jesus, with eternal glory.

1:13, 14 Timothy was in a time of transition. He had been Paul's bright young helper; soon he would be on his own as leader of a church in a difficult environment. Although his responsibilities were changing, Timothy was not without help. He had everything he needed to face the future, if he would hold on tightly to the Lord's resources. When you are facing difficult transitions, follow Paul's advice to Timothy and look back at your experience. Who is the foundation of your faith? How can you build on that foundation? What gifts has the Holy Spirit given you? Use the gifts you have been given.

1:15, 16 Nothing more is known about Phygelus and Hermogenes, who evidently opposed Paul's ministry. These men serve as a warning that even leaders can fall. Onesiphorus was mentioned as a positive example in contrast to these men.

2:1 How can someone be strong in grace? Grace means undeserved favor. Just as we are saved by grace (Ephesians 2:8, 9), we should live by grace (Colossians 2:6). This means trusting completely in Christ and *his* grace, and not trying to live for Christ in our strength alone. Receive and utilize Christ's power. He will give you the strength to do his work.

2:2 If the church were to consistently follow this advice, it would expand geometrically as well-taught believers would teach others and commission them, in turn, to teach still others. Disciples need to be equipped to pass on their faith; our work is not done until new believers are able to make disciples of others (see Ephesians 4:12, 13).

2:3 The body of Christ contains all believers who have ever lived, not just those who are alive now. When we suffer, we share in a common experience, not just with those alive today, but with all those who have ever suffered for the sake of the gospel. All the martyrs, missionaries, and pioneers of the faith had to face what we face. Let us have the same courage, commitment, and willingness to renounce worldly pleasure in order to serve God. Can you face the challenge? "Therefore, since we are surrounded by such a great cloud of witnesses, let us throw off everything that hinders and the sin that so easily entangles, and let us run with perseverance the race marked out for us" (Hebrews 12:1).

2:3–7 As Timothy preached and taught, he would face suffering, but he should be able to endure. Paul used a comparison with soldiers, athletes, and farmers who must discipline themselves and be willing to sacrifice to achieve the results they want. Like soldiers, we have to give up worldly security and endure rigorous discipline. Like athletes, we must train hard and follow the rules.

Like farmers, we must work extremely hard and be patient. But we keep going despite suffering because of the thought of victory, the vision of winning, and the hope of harvest. We will see that our suffering is worthwhile when we achieve our goal of glorifying God, winning people to Christ, and one day living eternally with him.

2:7 Paul told Timothy to reflect on his words, and God would give him insight. God speaks through the Bible, his Word, but we need to be open and receptive to him. As you read the Bible, ask God to show you his timeless truths and the application to your life. Then consider what you have read by thinking it through and meditating on it. God will give you understanding.

2:8 False teachers were a problem in Ephesus (see Acts 20:29, 30; 1 Timothy 1:3–11). At the heart of false teaching is an incorrect view of Christ. In Timothy's day many asserted that Christ was divine but not human—God but not man. These days we often hear that Jesus was human but not divine—man but not God. Either view destroys the good news that Jesus Christ has taken our sins on himself and has reconciled us to God. In this verse, Paul firmly states that Jesus is fully man ("descended from David") and fully God ("raised from the dead"). This is an important doctrine for all Christians. For more on this key concept see the note on Philippians 2:5–7.

2:9 Paul was in chains in prison because of the gospel he preached. The truth about Jesus is no more popular in our day than in Paul's, but it still reaches receptive hearts. When Paul said that Jesus was God, he angered the Jews who had condemned Jesus for blasphemy; many Jews, however, became followers of Christ (1 Corinthians 1:24). He angered the Romans who worshiped the emperor as god; but even some in Caesar's household turned to Jesus (Philippians 4:22). When Paul said Jesus was human, he angered the Greeks who thought divinity was soiled if it had any contact with humanity; still many Greeks accepted the faith (Acts 11:20, 21). The truth that Jesus is one person with two united natures has never been easy to understand, but that doesn't make it untrue. The truth of God's Word is being believed by people every day and changing their lives for eternity. Despite the opposition, continue to proclaim Christ. Some will listen and believe.

2:10 When Paul says "obtain the salvation," is he contradicting grace? Salvation is not something that can be earned, as Paul taught in Ephesians 2:8, 9. Paul is referring to being faithful to the end, not to a way to earn salvation.

[11]Here is a trustworthy saying:

> If we died with him,
>   we will also live with him;
> [12] if we endure,
>   we will also reign with him.
> If we disown him,
>   he will also disown us;[r]
> [13] if we are faithless,
>   he will remain faithful,[s]
>   for he cannot disown himself.

2:12
[r]Mt 10:33

2:13
[s]Nu 23:19; Ro 3:3

A Workman Approved by God

[14]Keep reminding them of these things. Warn them before God against quarreling about words; it is of no value, and only ruins those who listen. [15]Do your best to present yourself to God as one approved, a workman who does not need to be ashamed and who correctly handles the word of truth. [16]Avoid godless chatter, because those who indulge in it will become more and more ungodly. [17]Their teaching will spread like gangrene. Among them are Hymenaeus [t] and Philetus, [18]who have wandered away from the truth. They say that the resurrection has already taken place, and they destroy the faith of some. [19]Nevertheless, God's solid foundation stands firm, sealed with this inscription: "The Lord knows those who are his,"[a][u] and, "Everyone who confesses the name of the Lord must turn away from wickedness."

2:17
[t]1Ti 1:20

2:19
[u]Jn 10:14

[20]In a large house there are articles not only of gold and silver, but also of wood and clay; some are for noble purposes and some for ignoble. [v] [21]If a man cleanses himself from the latter, he will be an instrument for noble purposes, made holy, useful to the Master and prepared to do any good work. [w]

2:20
[v]Ro 9:21

2:21
[w]2Ti 3:17

[a] 19 Num. 16:5 (see Septuagint)

2:11–13 This is probably an early Christian hymn. God is faithful to his children. Although we may suffer great hardships here, God promises that someday we will live eternally with him. What will this involve? It means believers will live in Christ's kingdom, and that we will share in the administration of that kingdom. This truth comforted Paul as he went through suffering and death. Are you facing hardships? Don't turn away from God—he promises you a wonderful future with him. For more information about living eternally with God, see Matthew 16:24–27; 19:28–30; Luke 22:28–30; Romans 5:17; 6:8; 8:10, 11, 17; 1 Corinthians 15:42–58; Colossians 3:3, 4; 1 Thessalonians 4:13–18; Revelation 3:21; 21:1—22:21.

2:13 Jesus is faithful. He will stay by our side even when we have endured so much that we seem to have no faith left. We may be faithless at times, but Jesus is faithful to his promise to be with us "to the very end of the age" (Matthew 28:20). Refusing Christ's help will break our communication with God, but he will never turn his back on us even though we may turn our backs on him.

2:14–16 Paul urged Timothy to remind the believers not to argue over unimportant details ("quarreling about words") or have foolish discussions ("godless chatter") because such arguments are confusing, useless, and even harmful. False teachers loved to cause strife and divisions by their meaningless quibbling over unimportant details (see 1 Timothy 6:3–5). To handle the word of truth correctly, we must study what the Word of God says so we can understand what it means.

2:15 Because God will examine what kind of workers we have been for him, we should build our lives on his Word and build his Word into our lives—it alone tells us how to live for him and serve him. Believers who ignore the Bible will certainly be ashamed at the judgment. Consistent and diligent study of God's Word is vital; otherwise we will be lulled into neglecting God and our true purpose for living.

2:16 In important areas of Christian teaching, we must carefully work through our disagreements. But when we bicker long hours over words and theories that are not central to the Christian faith and life, we only provoke anger and hurt feelings. Even if "godless chatter" reaches a resolution, it gains little ground for the kingdom. Learning and discussing are not bad unless they keep believers constantly focusing on false doctrine or unhelpful trivialities. Don't let anything keep you from your work for and service to God.

2:17, 18 Hymenaeus was also mentioned in 1 Timothy 1:20. Paul had handed Hymenaeus over to Satan because his false teaching concerning the resurrection was destroying some people's faith.

2:18 The false teachers were denying the resurrection of the body. They believed that when a person became a Christian, he or she was spiritually reborn, and that was the only resurrection there would ever be. To them, resurrection was symbolic and spiritual, not physical. Paul clearly taught, however, that believers will be resurrected after they die, and that their bodies as well as their souls will live eternally with Christ (1 Corinthians 15:35ff; 2 Corinthians 5:1–10; 1 Thessalonians 4:15–18). We should not try to shape the doctrines of Scripture to match our opinions. If we do, we are putting ourselves above God. Instead, our beliefs should be consistent with God's Word.

2:19 False teachers still spout lies. Some distort the truth, some dilute it, and some simply delete it by saying that God's truth no longer applies. But no matter how many people follow the liars, the solid foundation of God's truth never changes, is never shaken, and will never fade. When we follow God's truth, we will live God's way.

2:20, 21 Here Paul urged Timothy to be the kind of person Christ could use for his noblest purposes. Don't settle for less than God's highest and best. Allow him to use you as an instrument of his will. You do this by staying close to him and keeping yourself pure so that sin and its consequences do not get in the way of what God could do in your life. While God can redeem any situation, how much better it is to stay close to Christ and ready to be used by him at a moment's notice.

2:22
x 1Ti 1:5

22 Flee the evil desires of youth, and pursue righteousness, faith, love and peace, along with those who call on the Lord out of a pure heart. x 23 Don't have anything to do with foolish and stupid arguments, because you know they produce quarrels. 24 And the Lord's servant must not quarrel; instead, he must be kind to everyone, able to teach, not resentful.

2:26
y 1Ti 3:7

25 Those who oppose him he must gently instruct, in the hope that God will grant them repentance leading them to a knowledge of the truth, 26 and that they will come to their senses and escape from the trap of the devil, y who has taken them captive to do his will.

2. Difficult times for Christian service
Godlessness in the Last Days

3:1
z 1Ti 4:1

3:2
a Ro 1:30

3 But mark this: There will be terrible times in the last days. z 2 People will be lovers of themselves, lovers of money, boastful, proud, abusive, disobedient to their parents, a ungrateful, unholy, 3 without love, unforgiving, slanderous, without self-control, brutal, not lovers of the good, 4 treacherous, rash, conceited, lovers of pleasure rather than lovers of God— 5 having a form of godliness but denying its power. Have nothing to do with them.

3:8
b Ex 7:11
c 1Ti 6:5

3:9
d Ex 7:12

6 They are the kind who worm their way into homes and gain control over weak-willed women, who are loaded down with sins and are swayed by all kinds of evil desires, 7 always learning but never able to acknowledge the truth. 8 Just as Jannes and Jambres opposed Moses, b so also these men oppose the truth—men of depraved minds, c who, as far as the faith is concerned, are rejected. 9 But they will not get very far because, as in the case of those men, d their folly will be clear to everyone.

2:22 Running away is sometimes considered cowardly. But wise people realize that removing themselves physically from temptation often can be the most courageous action to take. Timothy, a young man, was warned to flee anything that produced evil thoughts. Do you have a recurring temptation that you find difficult to resist? Remove yourself physically from any situation that stimulates your desire to sin. Knowing when to run is as important in spiritual battle as knowing when and how to fight. (See also 1 Timothy 6:11.)

2:23–26 As a teacher, Timothy helped those who were confused about the truth. Paul's advice to Timothy, and to all who teach God's truth, is to be kind and gentle, patiently and courteously explaining the truth. Good teaching never promotes quarrels or foolish arguments. Whether you are teaching Sunday school, leading a Bible study, or preaching in church, remember to listen to people's questions and treat them respectfully, while avoiding foolish debates. If you do this, those who oppose you will be more willing to hear what you have to say and perhaps turn from their error.

3:1 Paul's reference to the "last days" reveals his sense of urgency. The last days began after Jesus' resurrection when the Holy Spirit came upon the believers at Pentecost. The "last days" will continue until Christ's second coming. This means that *we* are living in the last days. So we should make the most of the time that God has given us (Ephesians 5:16; Colossians 4:5).

3:1ff In many parts of the world today, being a Christian is not especially difficult—people aren't jailed for reading the Bible or executed for preaching Christ. (However, this kind of persecution is very real for many believers.) Paul's descriptive list of behavior in the last days describes our society—even, unfortunately, the behavior of many Christians. Check your life against Paul's list. Don't give in to society's pressures. Don't settle for comfort without commitment. Stand up against evil by living as God would have his people live.

3:4 Why is it so tempting to love pleasure rather than God? Pleasure is something we can control; God cannot be controlled. Most pleasures can be obtained easily; love for God requires effort and sometimes sacrifice. Pleasure benefits us now; the benefits of loving God are often in the future. Pleasure has a narcotic effect; it takes our minds off ourselves and our problems. Love for God reminds us of our needs and our responsibilities. Pleasure cooperates with pride. It makes us feel good when we look good in the eyes of others. To love God we must lay aside

our pride and our accomplishments. Have you chosen to love pleasure, or to love God? How do you know?

3:5 The "form" or appearance of godliness includes going to church, knowing Christian doctrine, using Christian clichés, and following a community's Christian traditions. Such practices can make a person look good, but if the inner attitudes of belief, love, and worship are lacking, the outer appearance is meaningless. Paul warns us not to be deceived by people who only appear to be Christians. It may be difficult to distinguish them from true Christians at first, but their daily behavior will give them away. The characteristics described in 3:2–4 are unmistakable.

3:6, 7 Because of their cultural background, women in the Ephesian church had received no formal religious training. They enjoyed their new freedom to study Christian truths, but their eagerness to learn made them a target for false teachers. Paul warned Timothy to watch out for men who would take advantage of these women. New believers need to grow in their knowledge of the Word, because ignorance can make them vulnerable to deception.

3:7 This verse is not opposing study and learning; it is warning about ineffective learning. It is possible to be a perpetual student and never graduate to putting theory into practice. But honest seekers and true students look for answers. Remember this as you study God's Word. Seek to find God's truth and will for your life. Then do as he says.

3:8, 9 According to tradition, Jannes and Jambres were two of the magicians who had counterfeited Moses' miracles before Pharaoh (Exodus 7:11, 12). Paul explained that just as Moses had exposed and defeated them (Exodus 8:18, 19), God would overthrow the false teachers who were plaguing the Ephesian church.

3:9 We can hide our sin for a while, but eventually the truth will be revealed. Sooner or later, distraction, opposition, anger, or fatigue will wear us down, and our true hearts will be exposed. The trials of life will conspire against our efforts to maintain a religious front. We can't pick when and where we will be tested by adversity. Build your character carefully because it will come out under stress. Live each day as if your actions will one day be known to everyone. It is useless, in the middle of a test, to acknowledge that you should have prepared. Now is the time to change anything you wouldn't want revealed later.

Paul's Charge to Timothy

¹⁰ You, however, know all about my teaching,ᵉ my way of life, my purpose, faith, patience, love, endurance, ¹¹persecutions, sufferings—what kinds of things happened to me in Antioch, Iconium and Lystra, the persecutions I endured. Yet the Lord rescued me from all of them. ¹²In fact, everyone who wants to live a godly life in Christ Jesus will be persecuted, ¹³while evil men and impostors will go from bad to worse,ᶠ deceiving and being deceived. ¹⁴But as for you, continue in what you have learned and have become convinced of, because you know those from whom you learned it,ᵍ ¹⁵and how from infancy you have known the holy Scriptures,ʰ which are able to make you wise for salvation through faith in Christ Jesus. ¹⁶All Scripture is God-breathed ⁱ and is useful for teaching, rebuking, correcting and training in righteousness, ¹⁷so that the man of Godʲ may be thoroughly equipped for every good work.ᵏ

4 In the presence of God and of Christ Jesus, who will judge the living and the dead,ˡ and in view of his appearing and his kingdom, I give you this charge:ᵐ ²Preachⁿ the Word; be prepared in season and out of season; correct, rebuke ᵒ and encourage—with great patience and careful instruction. ³For the time will come when men will not put up with sound doctrine.ᵖ Instead, to suit their own desires, they will gather around them a great number of teachers to say what their itching ears want to hear. ⁴They will turn their ears away from the truth and turn aside to myths. ⁵But you, keep your head in all situations, endure hardship, do the work of an evangelist,�q discharge all the duties of your ministry.

3:10
ᵉ 1Ti 4:6

3:13
ᶠ 2Ti 2:16

3:14
ᵍ 2Ti 1:13

3:15
ʰ Jn 5:39

3:16
ⁱ 2Pe 1:20, 21

3:17
ʲ 1Ti 6:11
ᵏ 2Ti 2:21

4:1
ˡ Ac 10:42
ᵐ 1Ti 5:21

4:2
ⁿ 1Ti 4:13
ᵒ 1Ti 5:20; Tit 1:13

4:3
ᵖ 1Ti 1:10

4:5
q Ac 21:8

3:11 In Lystra, Timothy's hometown, Paul had been stoned and left for dead (Acts 14:19); and this was only one incident among many. In 2 Corinthians 11:23–33 Paul summarized his lifetime of suffering for the sake of the gospel. Paul mentioned his suffering here to contrast his experience with that of the pleasure-seeking false teachers.

3:12 In this charge, Paul told Timothy that people who obey God and live for Christ will be persecuted. Don't be surprised when people misunderstand, criticize, and even try to hurt you because of what you believe and how you live. Don't give up. Continue to live as you know you should. God is the only one you need to please.

3:13 Don't expect false teachers and evil people to reform and change on their own. Left alone, they will go from bad to worse. If you have the opportunity, correct them so as to bring them back to faith in Christ. Fight for the truth, especially to protect younger Christians.

3:14 Besieged by false teachers and the inevitable pressures of a growing ministry, Timothy could easily have abandoned his faith or modified his doctrine. Once again Paul counseled Timothy to look to his past, and to hold to the basic teachings about Jesus that are eternally true. Like Timothy, we are surrounded by false teachings. But we must not allow our society to distort or crowd out God's eternal truth. Spend time every day reflecting on the foundation of your Christian faith found in God's Word, the great truths that build up your life.

3:15 Timothy was one of the first second-generation Christians: He became a Christian not because an evangelist preached a powerful sermon, but because his mother and grandmother had taught him the holy Scriptures when he was a small child (1:5). A parent's work is vitally important. At home and in church, we should realize that teaching small children is both an opportunity and a responsibility. Jesus wanted little children to come to him (Matthew 19:13–15). Like Timothy's mother and grandmother, Eunice and Lois, do your part in leading children to Christ.

3:15 For Timothy, the "holy Scriptures" was the Old Testament. The Old Testament is important because it points to Jesus Christ. At the same time, faith in Christ makes the whole Bible intelligible.

3:16 The Bible is not a collection of stories, fables, myths, or merely human ideas about God. It is not a human book. Through the Holy Spirit, God revealed his person and plan to certain believers, who wrote down his message for his people (2 Peter 1:20, 21). This process is known as *inspiration*. The writers wrote from their own personal, historical, and cultural contexts. Although they used

their own minds, talents, language, and style, they wrote what God wanted them to write. Scripture is completely trustworthy because God was in control of its writing. Its words are entirely authoritative for our faith and lives. The Bible is "God-breathed." Read it, and use its teachings to guide your conduct.

3:16, 17 The whole Bible is God's inspired Word. Because it is inspired and trustworthy, we should *read* it and *apply* it to our lives. The Bible is our standard for testing everything else that claims to be true. It is our safeguard against false teaching and our source of guidance for how we should live. It is our only source of knowledge about how we can be saved. God wants to show you what is true and equip you to live for him. How much time do you spend in God's Word? Read it regularly to discover God's truth and to become confident in your life and faith. Develop a plan for reading the whole Bible, not just the familiar passages.

3:17 In our zeal for the *truth* of Scripture, we must never forget its *purpose*—to equip us to do good. We should not study God's Word simply to increase our knowledge or to prepare us to win arguments. We should study the Bible so that we will know how to do Christ's work in the world. Our knowledge of God's Word is not useful unless it strengthens our faith and leads us to do good.

4:1, 2 It was important for Timothy to preach the gospel so that the Christian faith could spread throughout the world. We believe in Christ today because people like Timothy were faithful to their mission. It is still vitally important for believers to spread the gospel. Half of the total number of people who have ever lived are alive today, and most of them do not know Christ. He is coming soon, and he wants to find his faithful believers ready for him. It may be inconvenient to take a stand for Christ or to tell others about his love, but preaching the Word of God is the most important responsibility the church and its members have been given. Be prepared for, courageous in, and sensitive to God-given opportunities to tell the Good News.

4:2 "Be prepared in season and out of season" means to always be ready to serve God in any situation, whether or not it is convenient. Be sensitive to the opportunities God gives you.

4:2 Paul told Timothy to "correct, rebuke, and encourage." It is difficult to accept correction, to be told we have to change. But no matter how much the truth hurts, we must be willing to listen to it so we can more fully obey God.

4:3–5 Many speakers, teachers, and writers talk about the pursuit of knowledge. But often they don't want knowledge; they want power. Such people won't listen to "sound doctrine." Instead, they "turn their ears away from the truth and turn aside

4:6
r Php 2:17
s Php 1:23

4:8
t 2Ti 1:12

⁶ For I am already being poured out like a drink offering,ʳ and the time has come for my departure. ˢ ⁷ I have fought the good fight, I have finished the race, I have kept the faith. ⁸ Now there is in store for me the crown of righteousness, which the Lord, the righteous Judge, will award to me on that dayᵗ—and not only to me, but also to all who have longed for his appearing.

Personal Remarks

4:10
u Col 4:14

4:11
v Col 4:14
w 2Ti 1:15

⁹ Do your best to come to me quickly, ¹⁰ for Demas,ᵘ because he loved this world, has deserted me and has gone to Thessalonica. Crescens has gone to Galatia, and Titus to Dalmatia. ¹¹ Only Lukeᵛ is with me. ʷ Get Mark and bring him with you, because he is helpful to me in my ministry. ¹² I sent Tychicus to Ephesus. ¹³ When you come, bring the cloak that I left with Carpus at Troas, and my scrolls, especially the parchments.

4:14
x Ac 19:33

¹⁴ Alexander ˣ the metalworker did me a great deal of harm. The Lord will repay him for what he has done. ¹⁵ You too should be on your guard against him, because he strongly opposed our message.

to myths." You can see this everywhere—from liberal churches to university campuses. People claiming to have a bit more enlightenment than what the dusty Bible has to say; people claiming to improve on God's words. Such people have several things in common: (1) *They do not tolerate the truth.* They have no interest or respect for absolute truth or any standard for judgment. (2) *They reject truth for sensationalism.* They want truth that fits their situation and makes sense for them. What they feel, what works for them, what seems compelling—that is their truth and they claim an absolute right to it. No one should even attempt to tell them differently. (3) *They gather viewpoints to suit their selfish desires.* Although they profess objectivity, their only defense for their viewpoints is that those viewpoints suit their desires.

Such teachers have a following because they are telling people "what their itching ears want to hear." These people are following myths. Be careful. False teaching can be found in many places—even inside the doors of some churches. Like Timothy, you must "keep your head in all situations" and seek God's Word for the truth.

4:5 To keep cool when you are jarred and jolted by people or circumstances, don't react quickly. In any work of ministry that you undertake, keeping a clear mind in every situation makes you morally alert to temptation, resistant to pressure, and vigilant when facing heavy responsibility.

4:6–8 As he neared the end of his life, Paul could confidently say that he had been faithful to his call. Thus he faced death calmly, knowing that he would be rewarded by Christ. Is your life preparing you for death? Do you share Paul's confident expectation of meeting Christ? The good news is that the heavenly reward is not just for giants of the faith, like Paul, but for all who are eagerly looking forward to Jesus' second coming. Paul gave these words to encourage Timothy, and us, that no matter how difficult the fight seems—keep fighting. When we are with Jesus Christ, we will discover that it was all worth it.

4:8 In Roman athletic games, a laurel wreath would be given to each winner. A symbol of triumph and honor, it was the most coveted prize in ancient Rome. This is probably what Paul was referring to when he spoke of a "crown." But his would be a crown of righteousness. See 2 Corinthians 5:10 and the note on Matthew 19:27 for more on the rewards awaiting us for our faith and deeds. Although Paul would not receive an earthly reward, he would be rewarded in heaven. Whatever we may face—discouragement, persecution, or death—we know we will receive rewards with Christ in heaven.

4:9, 10 Paul was virtually alone and probably lonely. No one had come to his trial to speak in his defense (4:16), and Demas had left the faith (4:10). Crescens and Titus had left, but not for the same reasons as Demas. Paul did not criticize or condemn them. Demas had been one of Paul's coworkers (Colossians 4:14; Philemon 24), but he had deserted Paul because he "loved this world." In other words, Demas loved worldly values and

worldly pleasures. There are two ways to love the world. God loves the world as he created it and as it could be if it were rescued from evil. Others, like Demas, love the world as it is, sin and all. Do you love the world as it could be if justice were done, the hungry were fed, and people loved one another? Or do you love what the world has to offer—wealth, power, pleasure—even if gaining it means hurting people and neglecting the work God has given you to do?

4:11, 12 Mentioning Demas reminded Paul of more faithful coworkers. Luke had traveled much with Paul, writing both the Gospel of Luke and the book of Acts (much of which is a first-hand account). Tychicus, one of his most trusted companions (Acts 20:4; Ephesians 6:21; Colossians 4:7; Titus 3:12), had already left for Ephesus.

That Paul requested for Timothy to bring Mark might give us pause. Mark had left Paul and Barnabas on the first missionary journey, and this had greatly upset Paul (Acts 13:13; 15:36–41), causing a rift between Paul and Barnabas that was so severe that they parted company. Somewhere along the line, Paul had given Mark a second chance and Mark had proven to be a worthy helper. We don't have all the details in Mark's changed life or Paul's change of heart, but Paul realized that people can change.

There's a lesson in these few words. We should allow people to grow up and not hold them back from ministry or leadership for faults in the past that have now been corrected. When we encourage someone and open our minds to the possibility that he or she has changed and matured, we may be salvaging a significant ministry. Mark went on not only to be Paul's good friend and a trusted Christian leader (Colossians 4:10; Philemon 24), but he also wrote the Gospel of Mark.

4:13 Paul's arrest probably had occurred so suddenly that he had not been allowed to return home to gather his personal belongings. Because he was a prisoner in a damp and chilly dungeon, Paul asked Timothy to bring him his cloak. Even more than the cloak, Paul wanted his parchments. These may have included parts of the Old Testament, the Gospels, copies of his own letters, or other important documents.

4:14, 15 Alexander may have been a witness against Paul at his trial. He may have been the Alexander mentioned in 1 Timothy 1:20.

16At my first defense, no one came to my support, but everyone deserted me. May it not be held against them. y 17But the Lord stood at my side and gave me strength, so that through me the message might be fully proclaimed and all the Gentiles might hear it. And I was delivered from the lion's mouth. 18The Lord will rescue me from every evil attack z and will bring me safely to his heavenly kingdom. To him be glory for ever and ever. Amen. a

4:16
y Ac 7:60

4:18
z Ps 121:7
a Ro 11:36

Final Greetings

19Greet Priscilla a and Aquila and the household of Onesiphorus. 20Erastus b stayed in Corinth, and I left Trophimus sick in Miletus. 21Do your best to get here before winter. Eubulus greets you, and so do Pudens, Linus, Claudia and all the brothers.

22The Lord be with your spirit. c Grace be with you.

4:20
b Ac 19:22

4:22
c Gal 6:18

a 19 Greek Prisca, a variant of Priscilla

4:17 With his mentor in prison and his church in turmoil, Timothy was probably not feeling very brave. Paul may have been subtly telling Timothy that the Lord had called Timothy to preach, and would give him the courage to continue to do so. God always gives us the strength to do what he has commanded. This strength may not be evident, however, until we step out in faith and actually begin doing the task.

4:18 Here Paul was affirming his belief in eternal life after death. Paul knew the end was near, and he was ready for it. Paul was confident in God's power even as he faced death. Anyone facing a life and death struggle can be comforted knowing that God will bring each believer safely through death to his heavenly kingdom.

4:19, 20 Priscilla and Aquila were fellow Christian leaders with whom Paul had lived and worked (Acts 18:2, 3). Onesiphorus visited and encouraged Paul in jail. Erastus was one of Paul's trusted companions (Acts 19:22), as was Trophimus (Acts 20:4; 21:29).

4:19–22 Paul ended the final chapter in his book and in his life by greeting those who were closest to him. Although Paul had spent most of his life traveling, he had developed close and last-

ing friendships. Too often, we rush through our days, barely touching anyone's life. Do you have a Paul—a mentor or teacher who provides leadership, accountability, and encouragement? Do you have a Priscilla or Aquila—a coworker or peer who prays with you in times of stress, loves you, and supports you? Do you have a Timothy—a younger leader whom you are helping, encouraging, and discipling? Like Paul, we should take time to weave our lives into others' through close personal relationships.

4:22 As Paul reached the end of his life, he could look back and know he had been faithful to God's call. Now it was time to pass the torch to the next generation, preparing leaders to take his place so that the world would continue to hear the life-changing message of Jesus Christ. Timothy was Paul's living legacy, a product of Paul's faithful teaching, discipleship, and example. Because of Paul's work with many believers, including Timothy, the world is filled with believers today who are also carrying on the work. What legacy will you leave behind? Whom are you training to carry on your work? It is our responsibility to do all we can do to keep the gospel message alive for the next generation.

TITUS

THE VACUUM produced when a strong leader departs can devastate a movement, organization, or institution. Having been dependent on his or her skill, style, and personality, associates and subordinates flounder or vie for control. Soon efficiency and vitality are lost, and decline and demise follow. Often this pattern is repeated in churches. A great speaker or teacher gathers a following, and soon a church is flourishing. It is alive, vital, and effective. Lives are being changed and people led into the kingdom. But when this person leaves or dies, with him or her goes the drive and the heart of the organization.

People flocked to hear Paul's teaching. Educated, articulate, motivated, and filled with the Holy Spirit, this man of God faithfully proclaimed the Good News throughout the Roman empire; lives were changed and churches begun. But Paul knew that the church must be built on Christ, not on a person. And he knew that eventually he would not be there to build, encourage, discipline, and teach. So he trained young pastors to assume leadership in the churches after he was gone. Paul urged them to center their lives and preaching on the Word of God (2 Timothy 3:16, 17) and to train others to carry on the ministry (2 Timothy 2:2).

Titus was a Greek believer. Taught and nurtured by Paul, he stood before the leaders of the church in Jerusalem as a living example of what Christ was doing among the Gentiles (Galatians 2:1–3). Like Timothy, he was one of Paul's trusted traveling companions and closest friends. Later he became Paul's special ambassador (2 Corinthians 7:5–16) and eventually the overseer of the churches on Crete (Titus 1:5). Slowly and carefully, Paul developed Titus into a mature Christian and a responsible leader. The letter to Titus was a step in this discipleship process. As with Timothy, Paul told Titus how to organize and lead the churches.

Paul begins his letter with a longer than usual greeting and introduction, outlining the leadership progression: Paul's ministry (1:1–3), Titus's responsibilities (1:4, 5), and those leaders whom Titus would appoint and train (1:5). Paul then lists pastoral qualifications (1:6–9) and contrasts faithful elders with the false leaders and teachers (1:10–16).

Next, Paul emphasizes the importance of good deeds in the life of the Christian, telling Titus how to relate to the various age groups in the church (2:2–6). He urges Titus to be a good example of a mature believer (2:7, 8) and to teach with courage and conviction (2:9–15). He then discusses the general responsibilities of Christians in society: Titus should remind the people of these (3:1–8), and he should avoid divisive arguments (3:9–11). Paul concludes with a few matters of itinerary and personal greetings (3:12–15).

Paul's letter to Titus is brief, but it is an important link in the discipleship process, helping a young man grow into leadership in the church. As you read this pastoral letter, you will gain insight into the organization and life of the early church, and you will find principles for structuring contemporary churches. But you should also see how to be a responsible Christian leader. Read the letter to Titus and determine, like Paul, to train men and women to lead and teach others.

VITAL STATISTICS

PURPOSE:
To advise Titus in his responsibility of supervising the churches on the island of Crete

AUTHOR:
Paul

ORIGINAL AUDIENCE:
Titus, a Greek, probably converted to Christ through Paul's ministry (he had become Paul's special representative to the island of Crete)

DATE WRITTEN:
Approximately A.D. 64, around the same time 1 Timothy was written; probably from Macedonia when Paul traveled between his Roman imprisonments

SETTING:
Paul sent Titus to organize and oversee the churches on Crete. This letter tells Titus how to do this job.

KEY VERSE:
"The reason I left you in Crete was that you might straighten out what was left unfinished and appoint elders in every town, as I directed you" (1:5).

KEY PEOPLE:
Paul, Titus

KEY PLACES:
Crete, Nicopolis

SPECIAL FEATURES:
Titus is very similar to 1 Timothy with its instructions to church leaders.

THE BLUEPRINT

1. Leadership in the church (1:1–16)
2. Right living in the church (2:1–15)
3. Right living in society (3:1–15)

Paul calls for church order and right living on an island known for laziness, gluttony, lying, and evil. The Christians are to be self-disciplined as individuals, and they must be orderly as people who form one body, the church. We need to obey this message in our day when discipline is not respected or rewarded by our society. Although others may not appreciate our efforts, we must live upright lives, obey the government, and control our speech. We should live together peacefully in the church and be living examples of our faith to contemporary society.

MEGATHEMES

THEME	EXPLANATION	IMPORTANCE
A Good Life	The Good News of salvation is that we can't be saved by living a good life; we are saved only by faith in Jesus Christ. But the gospel transforms people's lives, so that they eventually perform good deeds. Our service won't save us, but we are saved to serve.	A good life is a witness to the gospel's power. As Christians, we must have commitment and discipline to serve. Are you putting your faith into action by serving others?
Character	Titus's responsibility in Crete was to appoint elders to maintain proper organization and discipline, so Paul listed the qualities needed for the eldership. Their conduct in their homes revealed their fitness for service in the church.	It's not enough to be educated or to have a loyal following to be Christ's kind of leader. You must have self-control, spiritual and moral fitness, and Christian character. Who you are is just as important as what you can do.
Church Relationships	Church teaching must relate to various groups. Older Christians were to teach and to be examples to younger men and women. People of every age and group have a lesson to learn and a role to play.	Right living and right relationships go along with right doctrine. Treat relationships with other believers as an outgrowth of your faith.
Citizenship	Christians must be good citizens in society, not just in church. Believers must obey the government and work honestly.	How you fulfill your civic duties is a witness to the watching world. Your community life should reflect Christ's love as much as your church life does.

1. Leadership in the church

1 Paul, a servant of God and an apostle of Jesus Christ for the faith of God's elect and the knowledge of the truth that leads to godliness— ²a faith and knowledge resting on the hope of eternal life,ᵃ which God, who does not lie, promised before the beginning of time, ³and at his appointed season he brought his word to lightᵇ through the preaching entrusted to me by the command of God our Savior,

⁴To Titus,ᶜ my true son in our common faith:

Grace and peace from God the Father and Christ Jesus our Savior.

1:2
ᵃ2Ti 1:1

1:3
ᵇ2Ti 1:10

1:4
ᶜ2Co 2:13

1:1 Paul wrote this letter between his first and second imprisonments in Rome (before he wrote 2 Timothy) to guide Titus in working with the churches on the island of Crete. Paul had visited Crete with Titus and had left him there to minister (1:5). Crete had a strong pagan influence because this small island may have been a training center for Roman soldiers. Therefore, the church in Crete needed strong Christian leadership.

1:1 Paul called himself "an apostle." Even though Paul was not one of the original 12, he was specially called by God to bring the Good News to the Gentiles (see Acts 9:1–16 for an account of his call). The word *apostle* means messenger or missionary. "God's elect" refers to God's choice of his people, the church. For more information on Paul, see his Profile in Acts 9, p. 1825.

1:1 In one short phrase, Paul gives insight into his reason for living. The process begins with the proclamation of *faith*, continues with *knowledge* of the truth, which is then shown by people living in *godliness*. Paul wanted men and women to be mature in Jesus Christ. This was his ultimate objective by which he evaluated all he did.

How would your church evaluate its ultimate objectives? What specific goals, ministries, and service opportunities bring believers

to faith, spiritual maturity, and godliness? Do established members reflect good Christian conduct and desire for Christian service?

How would you describe your purpose in life? To what are you devoted? Are you willing to share your faith, teach the truth, and live a godly life for all to see?

1:2 Apparently lying was commonplace in Crete (1:12). Paul made it clear at the start that God does not lie. The foundation of our faith is trust in God's character. Because God *is* truth, he is the *source* of all truth, and he cannot lie. Believing in him leads to *godliness*, living a God-honoring lifestyle (1:1). The eternal life that God has promised will be ours, because he keeps his promises. Build your faith on the foundation of a trustworthy God who never lies.

1:3 God is called "our Savior," as is Jesus Christ (1:4). "God" here refers to the Father. Jesus did the work of salvation by dying for our sins and, therefore, he is our Savior. God planned the work of salvation, and he forgives us our sins. Both the Father and the Son acted to save us from our sins.

1:4 Titus, a Greek, was one of Paul's most trusted and dependable coworkers. Paul had sent Titus to Corinth on several special missions to help the church in its troubles (2 Corinthians 7; 8). Paul and Titus also had traveled together to Jerusalem

Titus's Task on Crete

1:6
*d*1Ti 3:2
1:7
*e*1Co 4:1

1:8
*f*1Ti 3:2
1:9
*g*1Ti 1:10

⁵ The reason I left you in Crete was that you might straighten out what was left unfinished and appoint*a* elders in every town, as I directed you. ⁶An elder must be blameless,*d* the husband of but one wife, a man whose children believe and are not open to the charge of being wild and disobedient. ⁷Since an overseer*b* is entrusted with God's work,*e* he must be blameless—not overbearing, not quick-tempered, not given to drunkenness, not violent, not pursuing dishonest gain. ⁸Rather he must be hospitable,*f* one who loves what is good, who is self-controlled, upright, holy and disciplined. ⁹He must hold firmly to the trustworthy message as it has been taught, so that he can encourage others by sound doctrine*g* and refute those who oppose it.

*a*5 Or *ordain*   *b*7 Traditionally *bishop*

TITUS GOES TO CRETE
Tradition says that after Paul was released from prison in Rome (before his second and final Roman imprisonment), he and Titus traveled together for a while. They stopped in Crete, and when it was time for Paul to go, he left Titus behind to help the churches there.

(Galatians 2:3) and Crete (1:5). Paul left Titus in Crete to lead the new churches that were springing up on the island. Titus is last mentioned by Paul in 2 Timothy 4:10, Paul's final recorded letter. Titus had leadership ability, so Paul gave him leadership responsibility, urging him to use his abilities well.

1:5 Crete, a small island in the Mediterranean Sea, had a large population of Jews. The churches there were probably founded by Cretan Jews who had been in Jerusalem at Pentecost (Acts 2:11), more than 30 years before Paul wrote this letter. The unfinished work refers to establishing correct teaching and appointing elders in every town. Paul had appointed elders in various churches during his journeys (Acts 14:23). He could not stay in each church, but he knew that these new churches needed strong spiritual leadership. The men chosen were to lead the churches by teaching sound doctrine, helping believers mature spiritually, and equipping them to live for Jesus Christ despite opposition.

1:5–9 Paul briefly describes some qualifications that the elders or overseers should have. Paul had given Timothy a similar set of instructions for the church in Ephesus (see 1 Timothy 3:1–7; 5:22). Notice that most of the qualifications involve character, not knowledge or skill. A person's lifestyle and relationships provide a window into his or her character. Consider these qual-

ifications as you evaluate a person for a position of leadership in your church. It is important to have leaders who can effectively preach God's Word; it is even more important to have those who can live out God's Word and be examples for others to follow.

1:8 One qualification for an elder was that he must "be hospitable." Christian leaders must be known for their hospitality. In the early days of Christianity, traveling evangelists and teachers were helped by Christians who housed and fed them. We would benefit from inviting people to eat with us—visitors, fellow church members, young people, those in need. Giving hospitality is very important today because so many people struggle with loneliness. In our self-centered society, we can show that we care by being hospitable. Christians were not to entertain false teachers (2 John 1:10), but this prohibition did not apply to non-Christians in general. God wants us to be generous, courteous, and hospitable with non-Christians; through our friendship, some may be won to Christ.

¹⁰For there are many rebellious people, mere talkers ʰ and deceivers, especially those of the circumcision group. ¹¹They must be silenced, because they are ruining whole households by teaching things they ought not to teach—and that for the sake of dishonest gain. ¹²Even one of their own prophets ⁱ has said, "Cretans are always liars, evil brutes, lazy gluttons." ¹³This testimony is true. Therefore, rebuke them sharply, so that they will be sound in the faithʲ ¹⁴and will pay no attention to Jewish myths ᵏ or to the commands of those who reject the truth. ¹⁵To the pure, all things are pure, but to those who are corrupted and do not believe, nothing is pure. In fact, both their minds and consciences are corrupted. ¹⁶They claim to know God, but by their actions they deny him. ˡ They are detestable, disobedient and unfit for doing anything good.

1:10
ʰ1Ti 1:6

1:12
ⁱAc 17:28

1:13
ʲTit 2:2

1:14
ᵏ1Ti 1:4

1:16
ˡ1Jn 2:4

2. Right living in the church
What Must Be Taught to Various Groups

2 You must teach what is in accord with sound doctrine. ²Teach the older men to be temperate, worthy of respect, self-controlled, and sound in faith,ᵐ in love and in endurance.
³Likewise, teach the older women to be reverent in the way they live, not to be slanderers or addicted to much wine, but to teach what is good. ⁴Then they can train the younger women to love their husbands and children, ⁵to be self-controlled and pure, to be busy at home, to be kind, and to be subject to their husbands,ⁿ so that no one will malign the word of God.

2:2
ᵐTit 1:13

2:5
ⁿEph 5:22

1:10 "The circumcision group" were the *Judaizers*, Jews who taught that the Gentiles had to obey all the Jewish laws before they could become Christians. This regulation confused new Christians and caused problems in many churches where Paul had preached the Good News. Paul wrote letters to several churches to help them understand that Gentile believers did not have to become Jews first in order to be Christians—God accepts anyone who comes to him in faith (see Romans 1:17; Galatians 3:2–7). Although the Jerusalem council had dealt with this issue (see Acts 15), devout Jews who refused to believe in Jesus still tried to cause problems in the Christian churches. Church leaders must be alert and take action on anything that divides Christians.

1:10–14 Paul warned Titus to be on the lookout for people who teach wrong doctrines and lead others into error. Some false teachers are simply confused—they speak their misguided opinions without checking them against the Bible. Others have evil motives—they pretend to be Christians only because they can get more money ("dishonest gain"), additional business, or a feeling of power from being a leader in the church. Jesus and the apostles repeatedly warned against false teachers (see Mark 13:22; Acts 20:29; 2 Thessalonians 2:3–12; 2 Peter 3:3–7) because their teachings attack the foundations of truth and integrity upon which the Christian faith is built. You can recognize false teachers because they will (1) focus more attention on themselves than on Christ; (2) ask you to do something that will compromise or dilute your faith; (3) de-emphasize the divine nature of Christ or the inspiration of the Bible; or (4) urge believers to make decisions based more on human judgment than on prayer and Biblical guidelines.

1:12 Paul was quoting a line from a poem by Epimenides, a poet and philosopher who had lived in Crete 600 years earlier. Some Cretans had a bad reputation and were known for lying. Paul used this familiar phrase to make the point that Titus's ministry and leadership were very much needed.

1:15 Some people see good all around them, while others see nothing but evil. What is the difference? Our souls become filters through which we perceive goodness or evil. The pure (those who have Christ in control of their lives) learn to see goodness and purity even in this evil world. But corrupt and unbelieving people find evil in everything because their evil minds and hearts color even the good they see and hear. Whatever you choose to fill your mind with will affect the way you think and act. Turn your thoughts to God and his Word, and you will discover more

and more goodness, even in this evil world. A mind filled with good has little room for what is evil (see Philippians 4:8).

1:16 Many people claim to know God. How can we know if they really do? We will not know for certain in this life, but a glance at their lifestyles will quickly tell us what they value and whether they have ordered their lives around kingdom priorities. Our conduct speaks volumes about what we believe (see 1 John 2:4–6). What do people know about God and about your faith by watching your life?

2:1 Notice the emphasis on "sound doctrine" in Paul's instructions to Titus. This is the *content* of our faith. But how can you recognize wholesome teaching? When a teaching is sound, it combines correct knowledge and understanding with consistent practice. It must be found in the Bible, keep Jesus Christ central, result in consistently good behavior and actions, and promote spiritual health in ourselves and others.

Believers must be grounded in the truths of the Bible—then they won't be swayed by the powerful oratory of false teachers, the possible devastation of tragic circumstances, or the pull of emotions. Those responsible for preaching and teaching must challenge people to understand sound doctrine. Learn the Bible, study theology, apply Biblical principles, and *live* what you learn.

2:2–8 Having people of all ages in the church makes it strong, but it also brings potential for problems. Paul gave Titus counsel on how to help various groups of people. The older people should teach the younger by words *and* by example. This is how values are passed on from generation to generation. Does your church carry out this basic function?

2:2, 5 Self-control is an important aspect of living the Christian life. The Christian community, then and now, is made up of people from differing backgrounds and viewpoints, making conflict inevitable. We live in a pagan and often hostile world. To stay above reproach, believers need wisdom and discernment to be discreet, and to master their wills, tongues, and passions so that Christ would not be dishonored. How's your self-control?

2:3–5 Women who were new Christians were to learn how to have harmony in their homes by watching older women who had been Christians for some time. We have the same need today. Younger wives and mothers should learn to live in a Christian manner—loving their husbands and caring for their children—through observing exemplary women of God. If you are of an age or position where people look up to you, make sure that your example is motivating younger believers to live in a way that honors God.

⁶Similarly, encourage the young men to be self-controlled. ⁷In everything set them an example *o* by doing what is good. In your teaching show integrity, seriousness ⁸and soundness of speech that cannot be condemned, so that those who oppose you may be ashamed because they have nothing bad to say about us.

2:9
p Eph 6:5
2:10
q Mt 5:16
2:12
r 2Ti 3:12

⁹Teach slaves to be subject to their masters in everything, *p* to try to please them, not to talk back to them, ¹⁰and not to steal from them, but to show that they can be fully trusted, so that in every way they will make the teaching about God our Savior attractive. *q*

¹¹For the grace of God that brings salvation has appeared to all men. ¹²It teaches us to say "No" to ungodliness and worldly passions, and to live self-controlled, upright and godly lives *r* in this present age, ¹³while we wait for the blessed hope—the glorious appearing of our great God and Savior, Jesus Christ, ¹⁴who gave himself for us to redeem us from all wickedness and to purify for himself a people that are his very own, eager to do what is good.

¹⁵These, then, are the things you should teach. Encourage and rebuke with all authority. Do not let anyone despise you.

3. Right living in society
Doing What Is Good

3 Remind the people to be subject to rulers and authorities, to be obedient, to be ready to do whatever is good, ²to slander no one, *s* to be peaceable and considerate, and to show true humility toward all men.

³At one time we too were foolish, disobedient, deceived and enslaved by all kinds of passions and pleasures. We lived in malice and envy, being hated and hating one another.

2:6 This advice given to young men was very important. In ancient Greek society, the role of the husband/father was not viewed as a nurturing role, but merely as a functional one. Many young men today have been raised in families where fathers have neglected their responsibilities to their wives and children. Husbands and fathers who are good examples of Christian living are important role models for young men who need to *see* how it is done.

2:7, 8 Paul urged Titus to be a good example to those around him so that others might see Titus's good deeds and imitate him. Paul's life would give his words greater impact. If you want someone to act a certain way, be sure that you live that way yourself. Then you will earn the right to be heard, and your life will reinforce what you teach.

2:8 Paul counseled Titus to be above criticism in how he taught. This quality of integrity comes from careful Bible study and listening before speaking. This is especially important when teaching or confronting others about spiritual or moral issues. If we are impulsive, unreasonable, and confusing, we are likely to start arguments rather than to convince people of the truth.

2:9, 10 Slavery was common in Paul's day. Paul did not condemn slavery in any of his letters, but he advised slaves and masters to be loving and responsible in their conduct (see also Ephesians 6:5–9). The standards set by Paul can help any employee/employer relationship. Employees should always do their best work and be trustworthy, not just when the employer is watching. Businesses lose millions of dollars a year to employee theft and time-wasting. If all Christian employees would follow Paul's advice at work, what a transformation it would make!

2:12, 13 Paul brings out two aspects of Christian living that must be stressed today. "Live . . . while we wait for the blessed hope." Both aspects of *living* and *waiting* are essential to our Christian sanity in this present evil age. The living is made bearable because we live for God—seeking to build his kingdom with whatever gifts he has given us. And it is that very kingdom to which we are looking forward. As we live and look forward, we anticipate three great benefits of Christ's return: (1) Christ's personal presence—we look forward to being with him. (2) Redemption from our sinful nature—we long for the end of the battle with sin and our perfection in Christ. (3) Restoration of creation—we anticipate the complete rule of grace when the image of God will

be fully realized in people and when the created order will be restored.

2:14 Christ's redeeming us opens the way for him to purify us. *Redeem* means to purchase our release from the captivity of sin with a ransom (see Mark 10:45 for more on Christ as our ransom). We are not only free from the sentence of death for our sin, but we are also purified from sin's influence as we grow in Christ.

2:15 Paul told Titus to teach the Scriptures as well as to live them. We must also teach, encourage, and correct others when necessary. We can easily feel afraid when others are older, more influential in the community, or wealthier. Like Titus, we should not let ourselves be threatened when we are trying to minister to others or provide leadership in the church.

3:1 As Christians, our first allegiance is to Jesus as Lord, but we must obey our government and its leaders as well. Christians are not above the law. Obeying the civil law is only the beginning of our Christian responsibility; we must do what we can to be good citizens. (See Acts 5:29 and Romans 13:1ff for more on the Christian's attitude toward government.)

3:2 How does one "show true humility"? Humility is a very elusive character trait, yet the Bible regards it as a highly important quality. Jesus referred to himself as "gentle and humble in heart" (Matthew 11:29). In Romans 12:3, Paul wrote the clearest definition of humility apart from Jesus' own example: "Do not think of yourself more highly than you ought, but rather think of yourself with sober judgment, in accordance with the measure of faith God has given you."

Humility, then, boils down to having an honest estimate of ourselves before God. We show false humility when we project negative worth on our abilities and efforts. We show pride when we inflate the value of our efforts or look down on others. True humility seeks to view our character and accomplishments honestly. Recognizing that we have succeeded in an effort need not be pride.

3:3 Following a life of pleasure and giving in to every sensual desire leads to slavery. Many think freedom consists in doing anything they want. But this path leads to a slavish addiction to sensual gratification. A person is no longer free, but is a slave to what his or her body dictates (2 Peter 2:19). Christ frees us from the desires and control of sin. Have you been released?

⁴But when the kindness and love of God our Savior appeared,ᵗ ⁵he saved us, not because of righteous things we had done, but because of his mercy. He saved us through the washing of rebirth and renewal by the Holy Spirit, ⁶whom he poured out on us generously through Jesus Christ our Savior, ⁷so that, having been justified by his grace, we might become heirs having the hopeᵘ of eternal life. ⁸This is a trustworthy saying.ᵛ And I want you to stress these things, so that those who have trusted in God may be careful to devote themselves to doing what is good. ʷ These things are excellent and profitable for everyone.

⁹But avoid foolish controversies and genealogies and arguments and quarrelsˣ about the law, because these are unprofitable and useless. ¹⁰Warn a divisive person once, and then warn him a second time. After that, have nothing to do with him. ¹¹You may be sure that such a man is warped and sinful; he is self-condemned.

Final Remarks

¹²As soon as I send Artemas or Tychicusʸ to you, do your best to come to me at Nicopolis, because I have decided to winter there. ¹³Do everything you can to help Zenas the lawyer and Apollosᶻ on their way and see that they have everything they need. ¹⁴Our people must learn to devote themselves to doing what is good,ᵃ in order that they may provide for daily necessities and not live unproductive lives.

¹⁵Everyone with me sends you greetings. Greet those who love us in the faith. Grace be with you all.ᵇ

3:4	ᵗTit 2:11
3:7	ᵘRo 8:24
3:8	ᵛ1Ti 1:15 ʷTit 2:14
3:9	ˣ1Ti 1:4
3:12	ʸAc 20:4
3:13	ᶻAc 18:24
3:14	ᵃver 8
3:15	ᵇCol 4:18

3:4–8 Paul summarized what Christ does for us when he saves us. We move from a life full of sin to one where we are led by God's Holy Spirit. *All* our sins, not merely some, are washed away. Washing refers to the water of baptism, which is a sign of salvation. In becoming a Christian, the believer acknowledges Christ as Lord and recognizes Christ's saving work. We gain eternal life with all its treasures. We have *renewal* by the Holy Spirit, and he continually renews our hearts. None of this occurs because we earned or deserved it; it is all God's gift.

3:4–6 All three persons of the Trinity are mentioned in these verses because all three participate in the work of salvation. Based upon the redemptive work of his Son, the Father forgives and sends the Holy Spirit to wash away our sins and continually renew us.

3:8 In this chapter, Paul stressed that believers must devote themselves to doing good. Paul understood good works as faithful service, acts of charity, and involvement in civil affairs. While good works can't save us or even increase God's love for us, they are true indications of our faith and love for Christ. Paul did not make this aspect of discipleship optional. Service to others is a requirement. Everyone who is a Christian should be involved. Does your church encourage everyone's involvement and service? What can your church do to help every member identify the good works he or she should be doing?

3:9 Paul warned Titus, as he warned Timothy, not to get involved in foolish and unprofitable arguments (2 Timothy 2:14). This does not mean we should refuse to study, discuss, and examine different interpretations of difficult Bible passages. Paul is warning against petty quarrels, not honest discussion that leads to wisdom. If foolish arguments develop, it is best to turn the discussion back to a helpful direction or politely excuse yourself.

3:9 The false teachers were basing their heresies on spiritual pedigrees and speculations about the Jewish laws (see 1 Timothy 1:3, 4). Similar to the methods used by false teachers in Ephesus

and Colosse, they were building their case on genealogies of angels. We should avoid false teachers, not even bothering to react to their pretentious positions. Overreaction sometimes gives more attention to their points of view.

3:10, 11 A person must be warned when he or she is causing division that threatens the unity of the church. This warning should not be a heavy-handed action, but it is intended to correct the individual's divisive nature and restore him or her to fellowship. A person who refuses to be corrected should be put outside the fellowship. As Paul said, that person is "self-condemned"— he or she is sinning and knows it. (See also Matthew 18:15–18 and 2 Thessalonians 3:14, 15 for help in handling such problems in the church.)

3:12 The city of Nicopolis was on the western coast of Greece. Artemas or Tychicus would take over Titus's work on the island of Crete so Titus could meet Paul in Nicopolis. Tychicus was another of Paul's trusted companions (Acts 20:4; Ephesians 6:21; Colossians 4:7). Titus would have to leave soon because sea travel was dangerous in the winter months.

3:13 Apollos was a famous Christian preacher. A native of Alexandria in North Africa, he became a Christian in Ephesus and was trained by Aquila and Priscilla (Acts 18:24–28; 1 Corinthians 1:12).

3:15 The letters of Paul to Titus and Timothy are his last writings and mark the end of his life and ministry. These letters are rich treasures for us today because they give vital information for church leadership. They provide a strong model for elders, pastors, and other Christian leaders as they develop younger leaders to carry on the work, following Paul's example of preparing Timothy and Titus to carry on his ministry. For practical guidelines on church leadership and problem solving, carefully study the principles found in these letters.

PHILEMON

AT THE foreman's signal, the giant ball is released, and with dynamite force and a reverberating crash, it meets the wall, snapping bricks like twigs and scattering pieces of mortar. Repeatedly, the powerful pendulum works, and soon the barrier has been reduced to rubble. Then it is carted away so that construction can begin.

Life has many walls and fences that divide, separate, and compartmentalize. Not made of wood or stone, they are personal obstructions, blocking people from each other and from God. But Christ came as the great wall remover, tearing down the sin partition that separates us from God and blasting the barriers that keep us from each other. His death and resurrection opened the way to eternal life to bring all who believe into the family of God (see Ephesians 2:14–18).

Roman, Greek, and Jewish cultures were littered with barriers, as society assigned people to classes and expected them to stay in their place—men and women, slave and free, rich and poor, Jews and Gentiles, Greeks and barbarians, pious and pagan. But with the message of Christ, the walls came down, and Paul could declare, "Here there is no Greek or Jew, circumcised or uncircumcised, barbarian, Scythian, slave or free, but Christ is all, and is in all" (Colossians 3:11).

This life-changing truth forms the backdrop for the letter to Philemon. One of three personal letters in the Bible, the letter to Philemon is Paul's personal plea for a slave. Onesimus "belonged" to Philemon, a member of the Colossian church and Paul's friend. But Onesimus, the slave, had stolen from his master and had run away. He had run to Rome, where he had met Paul, and there he had responded to the Good News and had come to faith in Christ (verse 10). So Paul wrote to Philemon and reintroduced Onesimus to him, explaining that he was sending him back, not just as a slave but as a brother (verses 11, 12, 16). Tactfully he asked Philemon to accept and forgive his brother (verses 10, 14, 15, 20). The barriers of the past and the new ones erected by Onesimus's desertion and theft should divide them no longer—they are one in Christ.

This small book is a masterpiece of grace and tact and a profound demonstration of the power of Christ and of true Christian fellowship in action. What barriers stand in your home, neighborhood, and church? What separates you from fellow believers? Race? Status? Wealth? Education? Personality? As with Philemon, God calls you to seek unity, breaking down those walls and embracing your brothers and sisters in Christ.

VITAL STATISTICS

PURPOSE:
To convince Philemon to forgive his runaway slave, Onesimus, and to accept him as a brother in the faith

AUTHOR:
Paul

ORIGINAL AUDIENCE:
Philemon, who was probably a wealthy member of the Colossian church

DATE WRITTEN:
Approximately A.D. 60, during Paul's first imprisonment in Rome, at about the same time Ephesians and Colossians were written

SETTING:
Slavery was very common in the Roman empire, and evidently some Christians had slaves. Paul does not condemn the institution of slavery in his writings, but he makes a radical statement by calling this slave Philemon's brother in Christ.

KEY VERSES:
"Perhaps the reason he was separated from you for a little while was that you might have him back for good—no longer as a slave, but better than a slave, as a dear brother. He is very dear to me but even dearer to you, both as a man and as a brother in the Lord" (verses 15, 16).

KEY PEOPLE:
Paul, Philemon, Onesimus

KEY PLACES:
Colosse, Rome

SPECIAL FEATURES:
This is a private, personal letter to a friend.

THE BLUEPRINT

1. Paul's appreciation of Philemon (verses 1–7)
2. Paul's appeal for Onesimus (verses 8–25)

Paul pleads on behalf of Onesimus, a runaway slave. Paul's intercession for him illustrates what Christ has done for us. As Paul interceded for a slave, so Christ intercedes for us, slaves to sin. As Onesimus was reconciled to Philemon, so we are reconciled to God through Christ. As Paul offered to pay the debts of a slave, so Christ paid our debt of sin. Like Onesimus, we must return to God our Master and serve him.

MEGATHEMES

THEME	EXPLANATION	IMPORTANCE
Forgiveness	Philemon was Paul's friend and the legal owner of the slave Onesimus. Paul asked Philemon not to punish Onesimus but to forgive and restore him as a new Christian brother.	Christian relationships must be full of forgiveness and acceptance. Can you forgive those who have wronged you?
Barriers	Slavery was widespread in the Roman empire, but no one is lost to God or beyond his love. Slavery was a barrier between people, but Christian love and fellowship are to overcome such barriers.	In Christ we are one family. No walls of racial, economic, or political differences should separate us. Let Christ work through you to remove barriers between Christian brothers and sisters.
Respect	Paul was a friend of both Philemon and Onesimus. He had the authority as an apostle to tell Philemon what to do. Yet Paul chose to appeal to his friend in Christian love rather than to order him what to do.	Tactful persuasion accomplishes a great deal more than commands when dealing with people. Remember to exhibit courtesy and respect in your relationships.

1. Paul's appreciation of Philemon

[1] Paul, a prisoner *a* of Christ Jesus, and Timothy our brother,

To Philemon our dear friend and fellow worker, *b* [2] to Apphia our sister, to Archippus *c* our fellow soldier *d* and to the church that meets in your home: *e*

[3] Grace to you and peace from God our Father and the Lord Jesus Christ.

Thanksgiving and Prayer

[4] I always thank my God as I remember you in my prayers, [5] because I hear about your faith in the Lord Jesus and your love for all the saints. *f* [6] I pray that you may be active in sharing your faith, so that you will have a full understanding of every good thing we have in Christ. [7] Your love has given me great joy and encouragement, because you, brother, have refreshed the hearts of the saints.

1:1
a Eph 3:1
b Php 2:25
1:2
c Col 4:17
d Php 2:25
e Ro 16:5
1:5
f Col 1:4

---

1 Paul wrote this letter from Rome in about A.D. 60, when he was under house arrest (see Acts 28:30, 31). Onesimus was a domestic slave who belonged to Philemon, a wealthy man and a member of the church in Colosse. Onesimus had run away from Philemon and had made his way to Rome where he met Paul, who apparently led him to Christ (verse 10). Paul convinced Onesimus that running from his problems wouldn't solve them, and he persuaded Onesimus to return to his master. Paul wrote this letter to Philemon to ask him to be reconciled to his runaway slave.

1 For more information on Paul's life, see his Profile in Acts 9, p. 1825. Timothy's name is included with Paul's in 2 Corinthians, 1 Thessalonians, 2 Thessalonians, Philippians, Colossians, and Philemon—the last three of these letters are from a group known as the "Prison Letters." Timothy was one of Paul's trusted companions; Paul wrote two letters to him—1 and 2 Timothy. See Timothy's Profile in 1 Timothy, p. 2037.

1 Philemon was a Greek landowner living in Colosse. He had been converted under Paul's ministry, and the Colossian church met in his home. Onesimus was one of Philemon's slaves.

2 Apphia may have been Philemon's wife. Archippus may have been Philemon's son, or perhaps an elder in the Colossian

church. In either case, Paul included him as a recipient of the letter, possibly so Archippus could read the letter with Philemon and encourage him to take Paul's advice.

2 The early churches often would meet in people's homes. Because of sporadic persecutions and the great expense involved, church buildings were typically not constructed at this time.

4–7 Like cold water on a long hike, this Christian brother, Philemon, knew how to be refreshing. He was able to revive and restore his brothers and sisters in the faith. His love and generosity had replenished and stimulated them. Philemon also encouraged Paul by his love and loyalty. Are you a refreshing influence on others, or do your attitude and temperament add to the burden they carry? Instead of draining others' energy and motivation with complaints and problems, replenish their spirits by encouragement, love, and a helpful attitude.

6 Paul's prayer for Philemon was setting the stage for the request Paul would make in this letter. Philemon was active in his faith and generous in sharing its blessings. As he gained fuller understanding of all that Christ had done on his behalf, this knowledge should cause him to respond appropriately to Paul's request regarding Onesimus. Are you active and effective in sharing with others your faith, your resources, and your love?

2. Paul's appeal for Onesimus

⁸Therefore, although in Christ I could be bold and order you to do what you ought to do, ⁹yet I appeal to you on the basis of love. I then, as Paul—an old man and now also a prisoner of Christ Jesus— ¹⁰I appeal to you for my son Onesimus, ᵃ who became my son while I was in chains. ¹¹Formerly he was useless to you, but now he has become useful both to you and to me.

ᵃ 10 Onesimus means useful.

ONESIMUS

God must have a special love for runaways. The pages of Scripture record dozens of people who were prone to flight. From Adam and Eve's attempt to elude God, through Jacob's escape from his brother, past generations of God's people on the run, to that inner circle of disciples who fled from the garden when Jesus was captured, the Bible is a collection of runaway lives. God's special love for runaways is beautifully illustrated in the life of a slave named Onesimus.

We are not told why Onesimus ran away from Philemon's house in Colosse. Eventually, he and Paul were united in Rome. Though we might crave details, Paul simply wrote that Onesimus became a follower of Jesus. Later, his spiritual growth caused Paul to call him a "faithful and dear brother" (Colossians 4:9).

Eventually, Paul and Onesimus decided it was time for the runaway slave to return home. Paul wrote a letter of explanation to his friend Philemon, assuring him that Onesimus would now serve him wholeheartedly. Although the culture of the day gave masters complete control over their slaves and although severe punishment usually faced a runaway, Paul challenged Philemon to think of Onesimus more as a brother than as a slave. Paul took responsibility for any restitution Philemon might require of Onesimus. As difficult as it might be for him, Onesimus, the runaway slave turned believer, had to return and face his old life as a new person.

When God finds runaways, he often sends them back to the very places and people from which they ran in the first place. As God has become real in your life, how has your past come into new perspective? Are there still situations from your past that need to be resolved? In what ways has your relationship with Christ given you new opportunities and resources to face what you used to run away from?

Strengths and accomplishments:	• Tracked down and listened to the apostle Paul's message • Grew into an able believer and assistant to Paul while in Rome • Returned to his previous master as a willing slave
Weakness and mistake:	• Ran away from his master, Philemon
Lessons from his life:	• God is in the radical forgiveness business • We cannot run from God and hope to escape
Vital statistics:	• Where: Colosse • Occupation: Slave
Key verses:	"Perhaps the reason he was separated from you for a little while was that you might have him back for good—no longer as a slave, but better than a slave, as a dear brother. He is very dear to me but even dearer to you, both as a man and as a brother in the Lord" (Philemon 15, 16).

Onesimus is mentioned in Colossians 4:9 and is the subject of Paul's letter to Philemon.

8, 9 Because Paul was an elder and an apostle, he could have used his authority with Philemon, commanding him to deal kindly with his runaway slave. But Paul based his request not on his own authority, but on Philemon's Christian commitment. Paul wanted Philemon's heartfelt, not grudging, obedience. When you know something is right and you have the power to demand it, do you appeal to your authority or to the other person's commitment?

Paul provides a good example of how to deal with conflict between Christians. When reconciling a separation or mediating a dispute, trust must be rebuilt between the conflicting parties. Notice the steps that Paul used to help rebuild the trust: (1) He identified with those involved, calling Philemon "brother" and Onesimus "my son." (2) He requested, not ordered, Philemon to do the right thing. (3) He sought Philemon's voluntary consent, not his submission to rules or authority. (4) He appealed to Christian love, not to power or authority. (5) He agreed to absorb the loss and pay any cost for restoration. Instead of overusing power or position, use Paul's approach to rebuild a trusting relationship.

10 A master had the legal right to kill a runaway slave, so Onesimus feared for his life. Paul wrote this letter to Philemon to help him understand his new relationship with Onesimus, who was now a Christian brother, not a mere possession. "Who became my son" means that Onesimus had become a Christian.

10ff From his prison cell, Paul had led Onesimus to the Lord. Paul asked Philemon to forgive his runaway slave who had become a Christian, and even going beyond forgiveness, to accept Onesimus as a brother. As Christians, we should forgive as we have been forgiven (Matthew 6:12; Ephesians 4:31, 32). True forgiveness means that we treat the one we've forgiven as we would want to be treated. Is there someone you say you have forgiven, but who still needs your kindness?

¹²I am sending him—who is my very heart—back to you. ¹³I would have liked to keep him with me so that he could take your place in helping me while I am in chains for the gospel. ¹⁴But I did not want to do anything without your consent, so that any favor you do will be spontaneous and not forced. *g* ¹⁵Perhaps the reason he was separated from you for a little while was that you might have him back for good— ¹⁶no longer as a slave, but better than a slave, as a dear brother. *h* He is very dear to me but even dearer to you, both as a man and as a brother in the Lord.

¹⁷So if you consider me a partner, *i* welcome him as you would welcome me. ¹⁸If he has done you any wrong or owes you anything, charge it to me. ¹⁹I, Paul, am writing this with my own hand. I will pay it back—not to mention that you owe me your very self. ²⁰I do wish, brother, that I may have some benefit from you in the Lord; refresh my heart in Christ. ²¹Confident of your obedience, I write to you, knowing that you will do even more than I ask.

²²And one thing more: Prepare a guest room for me, because I hope to be *j* restored to you in answer to your prayers. *k*

²³Epaphras, *l* my fellow prisoner in Christ Jesus, sends you greetings. ²⁴And so do Mark, *m* Aristarchus, Demas and Luke, my fellow workers.

²⁵The grace of the Lord Jesus Christ be with your spirit.

1:14 *g* 2Co 9:7

1:16 *h* 1Ti 6:2

1:17 *i* 2Co 8:23

1:22 *j* Php 1:25
k 2Co 1:11

1:23 *l* Col 1:7

1:24 *m* Ac 12:12

11–15 *Onesimus* means "useful." Paul used a play on words, saying that Onesimus had not been much use to Philemon in the past, but had become very useful to both Philemon and Paul. Although Paul wanted to keep Onesimus with him, he was sending Onesimus back, requesting that Philemon accept him not only as a forgiven runaway servant, but also as a brother in Christ.

15, 16 Slavery was widespread throughout the Roman empire. In these early days, Christians did not have the political power to change the slavery system. Paul didn't condemn or condone slavery, but he worked to transform relationships. The gospel begins to change social structures by changing the *people* within those structures. (See also 1 Corinthians 7:20–24; Ephesians 6:5–9; Colossians 3:22—4:1 for more on master/slave relationships.)

16 What a difference Onesimus's status as a Christian made in his relationship to Philemon. He was no longer merely a slave, but he was also a brother. That meant that both Onesimus and Philemon were members of God's family—equals in Christ. A Christian's status as a member of God's family transcends all other distinctions among believers. Do you look down on any fellow Christians? Remember, they are your equals before Christ (Galatians 3:28). How you treat your brothers and sisters in Christ's family reflects your true Christian commitment.

17 Paul called Philemon his "partner," but he did not mean a partner in the business sense of the word. Philemon was a partner in grace. Paul and Philemon shared the same experience in Jesus Christ of being saved; in that sense, they were equals. Too often our relationships in the church don't possess true partnership but reflect merely tolerance of one another. Do you have room in your heart to welcome other believers warmly? Treat them as partners in God's grace and love, not just fellow workers. Let your common interests in Christ and your common feeling of gratitude for Christ's love knit you together with others.

17–19 Paul genuinely loved Onesimus. Paul showed his love by personally guaranteeing payment for any stolen goods or wrongs for which Onesimus might be responsible. Paul's investment in the life of this new believer certainly encouraged and strengthened Onesimus's faith. Are there young believers who need you to demonstrate such self-sacrifice toward them? Be grateful when you can invest in the lives of others, helping them with Bible study, prayer, encouragement, support, and friendship.

19 Philemon owed himself to Paul, meaning that Paul had led Philemon to Christ. Because Paul was Philemon's spiritual father, he was hoping that Philemon would feel a debt of gratitude that he would repay by accepting Onesimus with a spirit of forgiveness.

22 Paul was released from prison soon after writing this letter, but the Bible doesn't say whether or not he returned to Colosse.

23 Epaphras was well known to the Colossians because he had founded the church there (Colossians 1:7). He was a hero to this church, helping to hold it together in spite of growing persecution and struggles with false doctrine. His report to Paul about the problems in Colosse had prompted Paul to write his letter to the Colossians. Epaphras's greetings to and prayers for the Colossian Christians reveal his deep love for them (Colossians 4:12, 13). He may have been in prison with Paul for preaching the gospel.

24 Mark, Aristarchus, Demas, and Luke are also mentioned in Colossians 4:10, 14. Mark had accompanied Paul and Barnabas on their first missionary journey (Acts 12:25ff). Mark also wrote the Gospel of Mark. Luke had accompanied Paul on his third missionary journey and was the writer of the Gospel of Luke and the book of Acts. Demas had been faithful to Paul for a while but later deserted him (see 2 Timothy 4:10).

25 Paul urged Philemon to be reconciled to his slave, receiving him as a brother and fellow member of God's family. *Reconciliation* means reestablishing relationship. Christ has reconciled us to God and to others. Many barriers come between people—race, social status, sex, personality differences—but Christ can break down these barriers. Jesus Christ changed Onesimus's relationship to Philemon from slave to brother. Christ can transform our most hopeless relationships into deep and loving friendships.

HEBREWS

CONSCIENTIOUS consumers shop for value, the best products for the money. Wise parents desire only the best for their children, nourishing their growing bodies, minds, and spirits. Individuals with integrity seek the best investment of time, talents, and treasures. In every area, to settle for less would be wasteful, foolish, and irresponsible. Yet it is a natural pull to move toward what is convenient and comfortable.

Judaism was not second-rate or easy. Divinely designed, it was the best religion, expressing true worship and devotion to God. The commandments, the rituals, and the prophets described God's promises and revealed the way to forgiveness and salvation. But Christ came, fulfilling the Law and the Prophets, conquering sin, shattering all barriers to God, freely providing eternal life.

This message was difficult for Jews to accept. Although they had sought the Messiah for centuries, they were entrenched in thinking and worshiping in traditional forms. Following Jesus seemed to repudiate their marvelous heritage and Scriptures. With caution and questions they listened to the gospel, but many rejected it and sought to eliminate this "heresy." Those who did accept Jesus as the Messiah often found themselves slipping back into familiar routines, trying to live a hybrid faith.

Hebrews is a masterful document written to Jews who were evaluating Jesus or struggling with this new faith. The message of Hebrews is that Jesus is better, Christianity is superior, Christ is supreme and completely sufficient for salvation.

Hebrews begins by emphasizing that the old (Judaism) and the new (Christianity) are both religions revealed by God (1:1–3). In the doctrinal section that follows (1:4—10:18), the writer shows how Jesus is superior to angels (1:4—2:18), superior to their leaders (3:1—4:13), and superior to their priests (4:14—7:28). Christianity surpasses Judaism because it has a better covenant (8:1–13), a better sanctuary (9:1–10), and a more sufficient sacrifice for sins (9:11—10:18).

Having established the superiority of Christianity, the writer moves on to the practical implications of following Christ. The readers are exhorted to hold on to their new faith, encourage each other, and look forward to Christ's return (10:19–25). They are warned about the consequences of rejecting Christ's sacrifice (10:26–31) and reminded of the rewards for faithfulness (10:32–39). Then the author explains how to live by faith, giving illustrations of the faithful men and women in Israel's history (11:1–40) and giving encouragement and exhortation for daily living (12:1–17). This section ends by comparing the old covenant with the new (12:18–29). The writer concludes with moral exhortations (13:1–17), a request for prayer (13:18, 19), and a benediction and greetings (13:20–25).

Whatever you are considering as the focus of life, Christ is better. He is the perfect revelation of God, the final and complete sacrifice for sin, the compassionate and understanding mediator, and the *only* way to eternal life. Read Hebrews and begin to see history and life from God's perspective. Then give yourself unreservedly and completely to Christ.

VITAL STATISTICS

PURPOSE:
To present the sufficiency and superiority of Christ

AUTHOR:
Paul, Luke, Barnabas, Apollos, Silas, Philip, Priscilla, and others have been suggested because the name of the author is not given in the Biblical text itself. Whoever it was speaks of Timothy as "brother" (13:23).

ORIGINAL AUDIENCE:
Hebrew Christians (perhaps second-generation Christians, see 2:3) who may have been considering a return to Judaism, perhaps because of immaturity, stemming from a lack of understanding of Biblical truths

DATE WRITTEN:
Probably before the destruction of the temple in Jerusalem in A.D. 70 because the religious sacrifices and ceremonies are referred to in the book, but no mention is made of the temple's destruction

SETTING:
These Jewish Christians were probably undergoing fierce persecution, socially and physically, both from Jews and from Romans. Christ had not returned to establish his kingdom, and the people needed to be reassured that Christianity was true and that Jesus was indeed the Messiah.

KEY VERSE:
"The Son is the radiance of God's glory and the exact representation of his being, sustaining all things by his powerful word. After he had provided purification for sins, he sat down at the right hand of the Majesty in heaven" (1:3).

KEY PEOPLE:
Old Testament men and women of faith (chapter 11)

THE BLUEPRINT

A. THE SUPERIORITY OF CHRIST
(1:1—10:18)
1. Christ is greater than the angels
2. Christ is greater than Moses
3. Christ is greater than the Old Testament priesthood
4. The new covenant is greater than the old

The superiority of Christ over everyone and everything is clearly demonstrated by the author. Christianity supersedes all other religions and can never be surpassed. Where can one find anything better than Christ? Living in Christ is having the best there is in life. All competing religions are deceptions or cheap imitations.

B. THE SUPERIORITY OF FAITH
(10:19—13:25)

Jews who had become Christians in the first century were tempted to fall back into Judaism because of uncertainty, the security of custom, and persecution. Today believers are also tempted to fall back into legalism, fulfilling minimum religious requirements rather than pressing on in genuine faith. We must strive to live by faith each day.

MEGATHEMES

THEME	EXPLANATION	IMPORTANCE
Christ Is Superior	Hebrews reveals Jesus' true identity as God. Jesus is the ultimate authority. He is greater than any religion or any angel. He is superior to any Jewish leader (such as Abraham, Moses, or Joshua) and superior to any priest. He is the complete revelation of God.	Jesus alone can forgive our sin. He has secured our forgiveness and salvation by his death on the cross. We can find peace with God and real meaning for life by believing in Christ. We should not accept any alternative to or substitute for him.
High Priest	In the Old Testament, the high priest represented the Jews before God. Jesus Christ links us with God. There is no other way to reach God. Because Jesus Christ lived a sinless life, he is the perfect substitute to die for our sin. He is our perfect representative with God.	Jesus guarantees our access to God the Father. He intercedes for us so we can boldly come to the Father with our needs. When we are weak, we can come confidently to God for forgiveness and ask for his help.
Sacrifice	Christ's sacrifice was the ultimate fulfillment of all that the Old Testament sacrifices represented—God's forgiveness for sin. Because Christ is the perfect sacrifice for our sin, our sins are completely forgiven—past, present, and future.	Christ removed sin, which barred us from God's presence and fellowship. But we must accept his sacrifice for us. By believing in him, we are no longer guilty but cleansed and made whole. His sacrifice clears the way for us to have eternal life.
Maturity	Though we are saved from sin when we believe in Christ, we are given the task of going on and growing in our faith. Through our relationship with Christ, we can live blameless lives, be set aside for his special use, and develop maturity.	The process of maturing in our faith takes time. Daily commitment and service produce maturity. When we are mature in our faith, we are not easily swayed or shaken by temptations or worldly concerns.
Faith	Faith is confident trust in God's promises. God's greatest promise is that we can be saved through Jesus.	If we trust in Jesus Christ for our complete salvation, he will transform us completely. A life of obedience and complete trust is pleasing to God.
Endurance	Faith enables Christians to face trials. Genuine faith includes the commitment to stay true to God when we are under fire. Endurance builds character and leads to victory.	We can have victory in our trials if we don't give up or turn our back on Christ. Stay true to Christ and pray for endurance.

A. THE SUPERIORITY OF CHRIST (1:1—10:18)

The relationship of Christianity to Judaism was a critical issue in the early church. The author clears up confusion by carefully explaining how Christ is superior to angels, Moses, and high priests. The new covenant is shown to be far superior to the old. This can be a great encouragement to us and help us avoid drifting away from our faith in Christ.

1. Christ is greater than the angels

1:1
a Nu 12:6, 8

1:3
b Jn 1:14

1:4
c Php 2:9, 10

1 In the past God spoke to our forefathers through the prophets at many times and in various ways,*a* 2 but in these last days he has spoken to us by his Son, whom he appointed heir of all things, and through whom he made the universe. 3 The Son is the radiance of God's glory*b* and the exact representation of his being, sustaining all things by his powerful word. After he had provided purification for sins, he sat down at the right hand of the Majesty in heaven. 4 So he became as much superior to the angels as the name he has inherited is superior to theirs. *c*

5 For to which of the angels did God ever say,

CHRIST AND THE ANGELS	Hebrews passage	Old Testament passage	How Christ is superior to angels
	1:5, 6	Psalm 2:7	Christ is called "Son" of God, a title never given to an angel.
	1:7, 14	Psalm 104:4	Angels are important but are still only servants under God.
	1:8, 9	Psalm 45:6	Christ's kingdom is forever.
	1:10	Psalm 102:25	Christ is the Creator of the world.
	1:13	Psalm 110:1	Christ is given unique honor by God.

The writer of Hebrews quotes from the Old Testament repeatedly in demonstrating Christ's greatness in comparison to the angels. This audience of first-century Jewish Christians had developed an imbalanced belief in angels and their role. Christ's lordship is affirmed without disrespect to God's valued angelic messengers.

1:1 The book of Hebrews describes in detail how Jesus Christ not only fulfills the promises and prophecies of the Old Testament, but how Jesus Christ is better than everything in the Jewish system of thought. The Jews accepted the Old Testament, but most of them rejected Jesus as the long-awaited Messiah. The recipients of this letter seem to have been Jewish Christians. They were well versed in Scripture, and they had professed faith in Christ. Whether through doubt, persecution, or false teaching, however, they may have been in danger of giving up their Christian faith and returning to Judaism.

The authorship of this book is uncertain. Several names have been suggested, including Luke, Barnabas, Apollos, Priscilla, and Paul. Most scholars do not believe that Paul was the author, because the writing style of Hebrews is quite different from that of his letters. In addition, Paul identified himself in his other letters and appealed to his authority as an apostle, whereas this writer of Hebrews, who never gives his or her name, appeals to eyewitnesses of Jesus' ministry for authority. Nevertheless, the author of Hebrews evidently knew Paul well. Hebrews was probably written by one of Paul's close associates who often heard him preach.

1:1, 2 God used many approaches to send his messages to people in Old Testament times. He spoke to Isaiah in visions (Isaiah 6), to Jacob in a dream (Genesis 28:10–22), and to Abraham and Moses personally (Genesis 18; Exodus 31:18). Jewish people familiar with these stories would not have found it hard to believe that God was still revealing his will, but it was astonishing for them to think that God had revealed *himself* by speaking through his Son, Jesus Christ. Jesus is the fulfillment and culmination of God's revelation through the centuries. When we know him, we have all we need to be saved from our sin and to have a perfect relationship with God.

1:2 Jesus was God's agent in creating the world: "By him all things were created" (Colossians 1:16). As followers of Christ, we may give easy assent to this truth but deny it in practice. We may believe that Christ knows and controls the laws of heaven (pertaining to salvation and spiritual growth), but we may act each day as though our financial, family, or medical problems are beyond his

reach. If Jesus could create the universe, then no part of life is out of his control. Do not exclude Jesus' wisdom and the Bible's guidance in your complex problems of life. No expert, professor, doctor, lawyer, or financial advisor knows more about your ultimate security and well-being than Jesus does. Go first to God for advice. Talk to him in prayer and listen to him in his Word. He can sustain you in times of stress. From that perspective you can evaluate all the other wisdom and help made available to you.

1:3 Not only is Jesus the exact representation of God, but he is God himself—the very God who spoke in Old Testament times. He is eternal; he worked with the Father in creating the world (John 1:3; Colossians 1:16). He is the full revelation of God. You can have no clearer view of God than by looking at Christ. Jesus Christ is the complete expression of God in a human body.

1:3 The book of Hebrews links God's saving power with his creative power. In other words, the power that brought the universe into being and that keeps it operating (provides purification for) our sins. How mistaken we would be to ever think that God couldn't forgive us. No sin is too big for the Ruler of the universe to handle. He can and will forgive us when we come to him through his Son. That Jesus *sat down* means that the work was complete. Christ's sacrifice was final.

1:4 The name Jesus inherited that is superior to others is "Son of God." This name given to him by his Father is greater than the names and titles of the angels.

1:4ff False teachers in many of the early churches taught that God could be approached only through angels. Instead of worshiping God directly, followers of these heretics revered angels. Hebrews clearly denounces such teaching as false. Some thought of Jesus as the highest angel of God. But Jesus is not a superior angel; and, in any case, angels are not to be worshiped (see Colossians 2:18; Revelation 19:1–10). We should not regard any intermediaries or authorities as greater than Christ. Jesus is God. He alone deserves our worship.

"You are my Son;
today I have become your Father^a"^{b}?^{d}

Or again,

"I will be his Father,
and he will be my Son"^{c}?

^{6}And again, when God brings his firstborn into the world, he says,

"Let all God's angels worship him."$^{d\ e}$

^{7}In speaking of the angels he says,

"He makes his angels winds,
his servants flames of fire."$^{e\ f}$

^{8}But about the Son he says,

"Your throne, O God, will last for ever and ever,
and righteousness will be the scepter of your kingdom.
^{9}You have loved righteousness and hated wickedness;
therefore God, your God, has set you above your companions
by anointing you with the oil^g of joy."^{f}

^{10}He also says,

"In the beginning, O Lord, you laid the foundations of the earth,
and the heavens are the work of your hands.
^{11}They will perish, but you remain;
they will all wear out like a garment.^{h}
^{12}You will roll them up like a robe;
like a garment they will be changed.
But you remain the same,
and your years will never end."^{g}

^{13}To which of the angels did God ever say,

"Sit at my right hand
until I make your enemies
a footstool for your feet"^{h}?^{i}

^{14}Are not all angels ministering spirits^j sent to serve those who will inherit salvation?

1:5
^{d}Ps 2:7

1:6
^{e}Dt 32:43 (LXX and DSS); Ps 97:7

1:7
^{f}Ps 104:4

1:9
^{g}Isa 61:1, 3

1:11
^{h}Isa 34:4

1:13
^{i}Ps 110:1

1:14
^{j}Ps 103:20

^{a}5 Or *have begotten you* ^{b}5 Psalm 2:7 ^{c}5 2 Samuel 7:14; 1 Chron. 17:13 ^{d}6 Deut. 32:43 (see Dead Sea Scrolls and Septuagint) ^{e}7 Psalm 104:4 ^{f}9 Psalm 45:6,7 ^{g}12 Psalm 102:25-27 ^{h}13 Psalm 110:1

1:5, 6 Jesus is God's firstborn Son. In Jewish families the first-born son held the place of highest privilege and responsibility. The Jewish Christians reading this message would understand that as God's firstborn, Jesus was superior to any created being.

1:10–12 The author of Hebrews quotes Psalm 102:25–27. In the quotation, he regards God as the speaker and applies the words to the Son Jesus. The earth and heavens rolled up like a robe reveals that the earth is not permanent or indestructible (a position held by many Greek and Roman philosophies). Jesus' authority is established over all of creation, so we dare not treat any created object or earthly resource as more important than he is. When we spend more time on ourselves than on serving Christ, we treat ourselves (his creation) as being more important than our Creator. When we regard our finances, rather than our faith in Christ, as the basis for security, we give higher status to an earthly resource than we do to God. Rather than trusting in changeable and temporary resources, trust in God, who is eternal.

1:11, 12 Because the readers of Hebrews (Jewish Christians) had experienced the rejection of their fellow Jews, they often felt isolated. Many were tempted to exchange the changeless Christ for their familiar old faith. The writer of Hebrews warned them not to do this: Christ is our *only* security in a changing world. Whatever may happen in this world, Christ remains forever changeless. If we trust him, we are absolutely secure, because we stand on the firmest foundation in the universe—Jesus Christ. A famous hymn captures this truth: "On Christ the solid rock I stand, all other ground is sinking sand."

1:12 What does it mean that Christ is changeless ("you remain the same")? It means that Christ's character will never change. He persistently shows his love to us. He is always fair, just, and merciful to us who are so undeserving. Be thankful that Christ is changeless—he will always help you when you need it and offer forgiveness when you fall.

1:14 Angels are God's messengers, spiritual beings created by God and under his authority (Colossians 1:16). They have several functions: serving believers (1:14), protecting the helpless (Matthew 18:10), proclaiming God's messages (Revelation 14:6–12), and executing God's judgment (Acts 12:1–23; Revelation 20:1–3).

Warning to Pay Attention

2:2
k Ac 7:53
2:3
l Heb 10:29
m Lk 1:2
2:4
n 1Co 12:4
o Eph 1:5

2 We must pay more careful attention, therefore, to what we have heard, so that we do not drift away. 2For if the message spoken by angels k was binding, and every violation and disobedience received its just punishment, 3how shall we escape if we ignore such a great salvation? l This salvation, which was first announced by the Lord, was confirmed to us by those who heard him. m 4God also testified to it by signs, wonders and various miracles, and gifts of the Holy Spirit n distributed according to his will. o

Jesus Made Like His Brothers

5It is not to angels that he has subjected the world to come, about which we are speaking. 6But there is a place where someone has testified:

> "What is man that you are mindful of him,
> the son of man that you care for him?
> 7 You made him a littlea lower than the angels;
> you crowned him with glory and honor
> 8 and put everything under his feet."b p

2:8
p Ps 8:4-6;
1Co 15:25
2:9
q Ac 2:33
r Php 2:7-9
s Jn 3:16

In putting everything under him, God left nothing that is not subject to him. Yet at present we do not see everything subject to him. 9But we see Jesus, who was made a little lower than the angels, now crowned with glory and honor q because he suffered death, r so that by the grace of God he might taste death for everyone. s

a 7 Or him for a little while; also in verse 9   b 8 Psalm 8:4-6

LESSONS FROM CHRIST'S HUMANITY

Christ is the perfect human leader . . . . and he wants to lead you
model . . . . and he is worth imitating
sacrifice. . . . . . . and he died for you
conqueror . . . . . and he conquered death to give you eternal life
High Priest . . . . and he is merciful, loving, and understanding

God, in Christ, became a living, breathing human being. Hebrews points out many reasons why this is so important.

2:1–3 The author called his readers to pay attention to the truth they had heard so that they wouldn't drift away into false teachings. Paying careful attention is hard work. It involves focusing our minds, bodies, and senses. Listening to Christ means not merely hearing, but also obeying (see James 1:22–25). We must listen carefully and be ready to carry out his instructions.

2:1 These early believers were in danger of falling away from following Jesus. They had heard the words of the gospel, but those words had not sunk in. People raised in believing families and churches risk the same danger today. They hear the words and more or less agree, but mental assent to Christ's leadership is insufficient to be Christ's disciple. Are you a Sunday school teacher, a small group leader, or a club leader? Don't assume that people who comply and conform are truly committed to Christ. Get to know each person who attends your group and challenge each with the truth and implications of commitment to Christ. Don't surrender anyone to casual belief.

2:2, 3 "The message spoken by angels" refers to the teaching that angels, as messengers for God, had brought the law to Moses (see Galatians 3:19). A central theme of Hebrews is that Christ is infinitely greater than all other proposed ways to God. The author was saying that the faith of his Jewish readers was good, but faith must point to Christ. Just as Christ is greater than angels, so Christ's message is more important than theirs. No one will escape God's punishment if he or she is indifferent to the salvation offered by Christ.

2:3 Eyewitnesses to Jesus' ministry had handed down his teachings to the readers of this book. These readers were second-generation believers who had not seen Christ in the flesh. They are like us; we have not seen Jesus personally. We base our belief

in Jesus on the eyewitness accounts recorded in the Bible. See John 20:29 for Jesus' encouragement to those who believe without ever having seen him.

2:4 "God also testified to it" continues the thought from 2:3. Those who had heard Jesus speak and then had passed on his words also had the truth of their words confirmed by "signs, wonders and various miracles, and gifts of the Holy Spirit." In the book of Acts, miracles and gifts of the Spirit authenticated the gospel wherever it was preached (see Acts 9:31–42; 14:1–20). Paul, who discussed spiritual gifts in Romans 12, 1 Corinthians 12—14, and Ephesians 4, taught that their purpose is to build up the church, making it strong and mature. When we see the gifts of the Spirit in an individual or congregation, we know that God is truly present. As we receive God's gifts, we should thank him for them and put them to use in the church.

2:8, 9 God put Jesus in charge of everything, and Jesus revealed himself to us. We do not yet see Jesus reigning on earth, but we can picture him in his heavenly glory. When you are confused by present events and anxious about the future, remember Jesus' true position and authority. He is Lord of all, and one day he will rule on earth as he does now in heaven. This truth can give stability to your decisions day by day.

2:9, 10 God's grace to us led Christ to his death. Jesus did not come into the world to gain status or political power, but to suffer and die so that we could have eternal life ("bringing many sons to glory"). If it is difficult for us to identify with Christ's servant attitude, perhaps we need to evaluate our own motives. Are we more interested in power or participation, domination or service, getting or giving?

¹⁰In bringing many sons to glory, it was fitting that God, for whom and through whom everything exists,ᵗ should make the author of their salvation perfect through suffering. ¹¹Both the one who makes men holy and those who are made holy are of the same family. So Jesus is not ashamed to call them brothers. ᵘ ¹²He says,

> "I will declare your name to my brothers;
>   in the presence of the congregation I will sing your praises."ᵃ ᵛ

¹³And again,

> "I will put my trust in him."ᵇ

And again he says,

> "Here am I, and the children God has given me."ᶜ ʷ

¹⁴Since the children have flesh and blood, he too shared in their humanityˣ so that by his death he might destroyʸ him who holds the power of death—that is, the devilᶻ— ¹⁵and free those who all their lives were held in slavery by their fear of death. ¹⁶For surely it is not angels he helps, but Abraham's descendants. ¹⁷For this reason he had to be made like his brothersᵃ in every way, in order that he might become a merciful and faithful high priestᵇ in service to God, and that he might make atonement forᵈ the sins of the people. ¹⁸Because he himself suffered when he was tempted, he is able to help those who are being tempted.ᶜ

2. Christ is greater than Moses

3 Therefore, holy brothers,ᵈ who share in the heavenly calling, fix your thoughts on Jesus, the apostle and high priest whom we confess. ²He was faithful to the one who appointed him, just as Moses was faithful in all God's house. ³Jesus has been found worthy of greater honor than Moses, just as the builder of a house has greater honor than the house

ᵃ*12* Psalm 22:22   ᵇ*13* Isaiah 8:17   ᶜ*13* Isaiah 8:18   ᵈ*17* Or *and that he might turn aside God's wrath, taking away*

2:10 ᵗRo 11:36

2:11 ᵘJn 20:17

2:12 ᵛPs 22:22

2:13 ʷIsa 8:18

2:14 ˣJn 1:14
ʸ1Co 15:54-57
ᶻ1Jn 3:8

2:17 ᵃPhp 2:7
ᵇHeb 4:14, 15

2:18 ᶜHeb 4:15

3:1 ᵈHeb 2:11

2:10 How was Jesus made perfect through suffering? Jesus' suffering made him a perfect leader, or pioneer, of our salvation (see the notes on 5:8 and 5:9). Jesus did not need to suffer for his own salvation, because he was God in human form. His perfect obedience (which led him down the road of suffering) demonstrates that he was the complete sacrifice for us. Through suffering, Jesus completed the work necessary for our own salvation. Our suffering can make us more sensitive servants of God. People who have known pain are able to reach out with compassion to others who hurt. If you have suffered, ask God how your experience can be used to help others.

2:11–13 We who have been set apart for God's service, cleansed, and made holy (sanctified) by Jesus now have the same Father he has, so he has made us his brothers and sisters. Various psalms look forward to Christ and his work in the world. Here the writer quotes a portion of Psalm 22, a Messianic psalm. Because God has adopted all believers as his children, Jesus calls them his brothers and sisters.

2:14, 15 Jesus had to become human ("flesh and blood") so that he could die and rise again, in order to destroy the devil's power over death (Romans 6:5–11). Only then could Christ deliver those who had lived in constant fear of death, and free them to live for him. When we belong to God, we need not fear death, because we know that death is only the doorway into eternal life (1 Corinthians 15).

2:14, 15 Christ's death and resurrection set us free from the fear of death because death has been defeated. Every person must die, but death is not the end; instead, it is the doorway to a new life. All who dread death should have the opportunity to know the hope that Christ's victory brings. How can you share this truth with those close to you?

2:16, 17 In the Old Testament, the high priest was the mediator between God and his people. His job was to regularly offer animal sacrifices according to the law and to intercede with God for forgiveness for the people's sins. Jesus Christ is now our high priest. He came to earth as a human being; therefore, he under-

stands our weaknesses and shows mercy to us. He has *once and for all* paid the penalty for our sins by his own sacrificial death (atonement), and he can be depended on to restore our broken relationship with God. We are released from sin's domination over us when we commit ourselves fully to Christ, trusting completely in what he has done for us (see the note on 4:14 for more about Jesus as the great high priest).

2:18 Knowing that Christ suffered pain and faced temptation helps us face our trials. Jesus understands our struggles because he faced them as a human being. We can trust Christ to help us survive suffering and overcome temptation. When you face trials, go to Jesus for strength and patience. He understands your needs and is able to help (see 4:14–16).

3:1 This verse would have been especially meaningful to Jewish Christians. For Jews, the highest human authority was the high priest. For Christians, the highest human authorities were God's apostles. Jesus, God's apostle (meaning "one who is sent") and high priest, is the ultimate authority in the church.

3:1 The writer says to "fix your thoughts on Jesus," to ponder carefully and focus on the true significance of Jesus. How much do we do that? In our age of sound bites, fast food, and quick-fix solutions, very few people take time to think about anything or anyone. In Jesus we have one to whom we should listen (God's messenger), through whom we come to the Father (high priest), and to whom we give obedience (he is entrusted with God's entire house). When you think about the significance and superiority of Jesus, how does it affect your life today? your decisions? your actions?

3:2, 3 To the Jewish people, Moses was a great hero; he had led their ancestors, the Israelites, from Egyptian bondage to the border of the promised land. He also had written the first five books of the Old Testament, and he was the prophet through whom God had given the law; therefore, Moses was the greatest prophet in the Scriptures. But Jesus is worthy of greater honor as the central figure of faith than Moses, who was merely a human servant. Jesus is more than human; he is God himself (1:3). As Moses led

3:5
e Ex 14:31
f Nu 12:7

3:6
g Heb 1:2
h 1Co 3:16
i Ro 5:2

itself. [4] For every house is built by someone, but God is the builder of everything. [5] Moses was faithful as a servant *e* in all God's house, *f* testifying to what would be said in the future. [6] But Christ is faithful as a son *g* over God's house. And we are his house, *h* if we hold on to our courage and the hope *i* of which we boast.

Warning Against Unbelief

[7] So, as the Holy Spirit says:

> "Today, if you hear his voice,
> [8] do not harden your hearts
> as you did in the rebellion,
>   during the time of testing in the desert,
> [9] where your fathers tested and tried me
>   and for forty years saw what I did.
> [10] That is why I was angry with that generation,
>   and I said, 'Their hearts are always going astray,
>   and they have not known my ways.'

3:11
j Heb 4:3, 5

> [11] So I declared on oath in my anger,
>   'They shall never enter my rest.' *j* "a

[12] See to it, brothers, that none of you has a sinful, unbelieving heart that turns away from the living God. [13] But encourage one another daily, as long as it is called Today, so that none

3:14
k ver 6

3:15
l ver 7, 8

of you may be hardened by sin's deceitfulness. [14] We have come to share in Christ if we hold firmly *k* till the end the confidence we had at first. [15] As has just been said:

> "Today, if you hear his voice,
>   do not harden your hearts
>   as you did in the rebellion." b *l*

3:16
m Nu 14:2

3:17
n Ps 106:26

3:18
o Nu 14:20-23

[16] Who were they who heard and rebelled? Were they not all those Moses led out of Egypt? *m* [17] And with whom was he angry for forty years? Was it not with those who sinned, whose bodies fell in the desert? *n* [18] And to whom did God swear that they would never enter his rest *o* if not to those who disobeyed c ? [19] So we see that they were not able to enter, because of their unbelief.

a 11 Psalm 95:7-11   b 15 Psalm 95:7,8   c 18 Or *disbelieved*

---

the people of Israel out of Egyptian bondage, so Christ leads us out of sin's slavery. Why settle for Moses, the author of Hebrews asks, when you can have Jesus Christ, who appointed Moses?

3:5 Moses was faithful to God's calling not only to deliver Israel but also to prepare the way for the Messiah ("testifying to what would be said in the future"). All the Old Testament believers also served to prepare the way. Thus, knowing the Old Testament is the best foundation for understanding the New Testament. In reading the Old Testament, we see (1) how God used people to accomplish his purposes, (2) how God used events and personalities to illustrate important truths, (3) how, through prophets, God announced the Messiah, and (4) how, through the system of sacrifices, God prepared people to understand the Messiah's work. If you include the Old Testament in your regular Bible reading, the New Testament will grow clearer and more meaningful to you.

3:6 Because Christ lives in us as believers, we can remain courageous and hopeful to the end. We are not saved by being steadfast and firm in our faith, but our courage and hope do reveal that our faith is real. Without this enduring faithfulness, we could easily be blown away by the winds of temptation, false teaching, or persecution. (See also 3:14.)

3:7–15 This passage refers to the Israelites who had hardened their hearts in the desert. A hardened heart is as useless as a hardened lump of clay or a hardened loaf of bread. Nothing can restore it and make it useful. The writer of Psalm 95 warns against hardening our hearts as Israel did in the desert by continuing to resist God's will (Exodus 17:7; Numbers 13; 14; 20). The people were so convinced that God couldn't deliver them that they simply lost their faith in him. People with hardened hearts are so stubbornly set in their ways that they cannot turn to God. This does not happen suddenly

or all at once; it is the result of a series of choices to disregard God's will. Let people know that those who resist God long enough, God will toss aside like hardened bread, useless and worthless.

3:11 God's *rest* has several meanings in Scripture: (1) the seventh day of creation and the weekly Sabbath commemorating it (Genesis 2:2; Hebrews 4:4–9); (2) the promised land of Canaan (Deuteronomy 12:8–12; Psalm 95); (3) peace with God now because of our relationship with Christ through faith (Matthew 12:28; Hebrews 4:1, 3, 8–11); and (4) our future eternal life with Christ (Hebrews 4:8–11). All of these meanings were probably familiar to the Jewish Christian readers of Hebrews. We can apply the verses as a warning about God's anger in the face of human rebellion against his kingdom. By rejecting God's provision (Christ) and not enduring in our faith, we miss the opportunity for spiritual rest.

3:12–14 Our hearts turn away from the living God when we stubbornly refuse to believe him. If we persist in our unbelief, God will eventually leave us alone in our sin. But God can give us new hearts, new desires, and new spirits (Ezekiel 36:22–27). To prevent having an unbelieving heart, stay in fellowship with other believers, talk daily about your mutual faith, be aware of the deceitfulness of sin (it attracts but also destroys), and encourage each other with love and concern.

3:15–19 The Israelites failed to enter the promised land because they did not believe in God's protection, and they did not believe that God would help them conquer the giants in the land (see Numbers 14; 15). So God sent them into the desert to wander for 40 years. This was an unhappy alternative to the wonderful gift he had planned for them. Lack of trust in God always prevents us from receiving his best.

A Sabbath-Rest for the People of God

4 Therefore, since the promise of entering his rest still stands, let us be careful that none of you be found to have fallen short of it. *p* 2 For we also have had the gospel preached to us, just as they did; but the message they heard was of no value to them, because those who heard did not combine it with faith. **a** 3 Now we who have believed enter that rest, just as God has said,

> "So I declared on oath in my anger,
> 'They shall never enter my rest.'" **b** *q*

And yet his work has been finished since the creation of the world. 4 For somewhere he has spoken about the seventh day in these words: "And on the seventh day God rested from all his work." **c** *r* 5 And again in the passage above he says, "They shall never enter my rest."

6 It still remains that some will enter that rest, and those who formerly had the gospel preached to them did not go in, because of their disobedience. *s* 7 Therefore God again set a certain day, calling it Today, when a long time later he spoke through David, as was said before:

> "Today, if you hear his voice,
> do not harden your hearts." **d** *t*

8 For if Joshua had given them rest, God would not have spoken later about another day. 9 There remains, then, a Sabbath-rest for the people of God; 10 for anyone who enters God's rest also rests from his own work, just as God did from his. *u* 11 Let us, therefore, make every effort to enter that rest, so that no one will fall by following their example of disobedience. *v*

12 For the word of God is living and active. *w* Sharper than any double-edged sword, *x* it penetrates even to dividing soul and spirit, joints and marrow; it judges the thoughts and attitudes of the heart. *y* 13 Nothing in all creation is hidden from God's sight. *z* Everything is uncovered and laid bare before the eyes of him to whom we must give account.

a 2 Many manuscripts *because they did not share in the faith of those who obeyed* **b** 3 Psalm 95:11; also in verse 5
c 4 Gen. 2:2 **d** 7 Psalm 95:7,8

### Cross references (margin)

4:1 *p* Heb 12:15
4:3 *q* Ps 95:11
4:4 *r* Ex 20:11
4:6 *s* Heb 3:18
4:7 *t* Ps 95:7, 8
4:10 *u* ver 4
4:11 *v* Heb 3:18
4:12 *w* Jer 23:29 *x* Eph 6:17 *y* 1Co 14:24, 25
4:13 *z* Ps 33:13-15

4:1–3 Some of the Jewish Christians who received this letter may have been on the verge of turning back from their promised rest in Christ, just as the people in Moses' day had turned back from the promised land. In both cases, the difficulties of the present moment overshadowed the reality of God's promise, and the people doubted that God would fulfill his promises. When we trust our own efforts instead of Christ's power, we too are in danger of turning back. Our own efforts are never adequate; only Christ can see us through.

4:2 The Israelites of Moses' day illustrate a problem facing many who fill our churches today. They know a great deal about Christ, but they do not know him personally—they don't combine their knowledge with faith. Let the Good News about Christ benefit your life. Believe in him and then act on what you know. Trust in Christ and do what he says.

4:4 God rested on the seventh day, not because he was tired, but to indicate the completion of creation. The world was perfect, and God was well satisfied with it. This rest is a foretaste of our eternal joy when creation will be renewed and restored, every mark of sin will be removed, and the world will be made perfect again. Our Sabbath-rest in Christ begins when we trust him to complete his good and perfect work in us (see the note on 3:11).

4:6, 7 God had given the Israelites the opportunity to enter Canaan, but they disobeyed and failed to enter (Numbers 13; 14). Now God offers us the opportunity to enter his ultimate place of rest—he invites us to come to Christ. To enter his rest, you must believe that God has this relationship in mind for you; you must stop trying to create it; you must trust in Christ for it; and you must determine to obey him. *Today* is the best time to find peace with God. Tomorrow may be too late.

4:8–11 God wants us to enter his rest. For the Israelites of Moses' time, this rest was the earthly rest to be found in the promised land. For Christians, it is peace with God now and eternal life on a new earth later. We do not need to wait for the next life to enjoy God's rest and peace; we may have it daily now! Our daily rest in the Lord will not end with death, but will become an eternal rest in the place that Christ is preparing for us (John 14:1–4).

4:10 Busy people often work especially hard the week before vacation, tying up loose ends so they can relax. Students usually have their final exams right before semester breaks. When we know a rest is coming, we put extra effort into finishing our work.

Healthy Christians love the work God has given them, doing it with passion and gusto, putting all their strength and care into it. But Christians love God's promise of heaven's rest even more and look forward to God's rest with great joy. Today, renew your effort to work hard for God. Rest is coming. Relish the thought.

4:11 If Jesus has provided for our rest through faith, why must we "make every effort to enter that rest"? This is not the struggle of doing good in order to appreciate and benefit from salvation, nor is it a mystical struggle to overcome selfishness. It refers to making every effort to obtain what God has already provided. Salvation is not to be taken for granted; to appropriate the gift God offers requires decision and commitment.

4:12 The Word of God is not simply a collection of words from God, a vehicle for communicating ideas; it is living, life-changing, and dynamic as it works in us. With the incisiveness of a surgeon's knife, God's Word reveals who we are and what we are not. It penetrates the core of our moral and spiritual life. It discerns what is within us, both good and evil. The demands of God's Word require decisions. We must not only listen to the Word; we must also let it shape our lives.

4:13 Nothing can be hidden from God. He knows about everyone everywhere, and everything about us is wide open to his all-seeing eyes. God sees all we do and knows all we think. Even when we are unaware of his presence, he is there. When we try to hide from him, he sees us. We can have no secrets from God. It is comforting to realize that although God knows us intimately, he still loves us.

3. Christ is greater than the Old Testament priesthood
Jesus the Great High Priest

4:14
a Heb 3:1

4:15
b 2Co 5:21

[14]Therefore, since we have a great high priest who has gone through the heavens,*a* Jesus the Son of God, let us hold firmly to the faith we profess. *a* [15]For we do not have a high priest who is unable to sympathize with our weaknesses, but we have one who has been tempted in every way, just as we are—yet was without sin.*b* [16]Let us then approach the throne of grace with confidence, so that we may receive mercy and find grace to help us in our time of need.

5:1
c Heb 8:3

5:2
d Heb 7:28

5 Every high priest is selected from among men and is appointed to represent them in matters related to God, to offer gifts and sacrifices*c* for sins. [2]He is able to deal gently with those who are ignorant and are going astray, since he himself is subject to weakness. *d* [3]This is why he has to offer sacrifices for his own sins, as well as for the sins of the people.

5:4
e Ex 28:1

5:5
f Jn 8:54
g Ps 2:7

[4]No one takes this honor upon himself; he must be called by God, just as Aaron was. *e* [5]So Christ also did not take upon himself the glory*f* of becoming a high priest. But God said to him,

> "You are my Son;
>   today I have become your Father.*b"c g*

5:6
h Ps 110:4

[6]And he says in another place,

> "You are a priest forever,
>   in the order of Melchizedek."*d h*

a 14 Or *gone into heaven*   *b* 5 Or *have begotten you*   *c* 5 Psalm 2:7   *d* 6 Psalm 110:4

THE CHOICES OF MATURITY

Mature Choices	Versus	Immature Choices
Teaching others	rather than	just being taught
Developing depth of understanding	rather than	struggling with the basics
Self-evaluation	rather than	self-criticism
Seeking unity	rather than	promoting disunity
Desiring spiritual challenges	rather than	desiring entertainment
Careful study and observation	rather than	opinions and halfhearted efforts
Active faith	rather than	cautious apathy and doubt
Confidence	rather than	fear
Feelings and experiences evaluated in the light of God's Word	rather than	experiences evaluated according to feelings

One way to evaluate spiritual maturity is by looking at the choices we make. The writer of Hebrews notes many of the ways these choices change with personal growth.

4:14 Christ is superior to the priests, and his priesthood is superior to their priesthood. To the Jews, the high priest was the highest religious authority in the land. He alone entered the Holy of Holies in the temple once a year to make atonement for the sins of the whole nation (Leviticus 16). Like the high priest, Jesus mediates between God and us. As humanity's representative, he intercedes for us before God. As God's representative, he assures us of God's forgiveness. Jesus has more authority than the Jewish high priests because he is truly God and truly man. Unlike the high priest who could go before God only once a year, Christ is always at God's right hand, interceding for us. He is always available to hear us when we pray.

4:15 Jesus is like us because he experienced a full range of temptations throughout his life as a human being. We can be comforted knowing that Jesus faced temptation—he can sympathize with us. We can be encouraged knowing that Jesus faced temptation without giving in to sin. He shows us that we do not have to sin when facing the seductive lure of temptation. Jesus is the only perfect human being who has ever lived.

4:16 Prayer is our approach to God, and we are to come "with confidence." Some Christians approach God meekly with heads hung low, afraid to ask him to meet their needs. Others pray flippantly, giving little thought to what they say. Come with reverence because he is your King. But also come with bold assurance because he is your Friend and Counselor.

5:4-6 This chapter stresses both Christ's divine appointment and his humanity. The writer uses two Old Testament verses to show Christ's divine appointment—Psalms 2:7 and 110:4. At the time this book was written, the Romans selected the high priest in Jerusalem. In the Old Testament, however, God chose Aaron, and only Aaron's descendants could be high priests. Christ, like Aaron, was chosen and called by God.

5:6 Melchizedek was a priest of Salem (now called Jerusalem). His Profile is found in Genesis 16, p. 29. Melchizedek's position is explained in Hebrews 7.

7 During the days of Jesus' life on earth, he offered up prayers and petitions with loud cries and tears *i* to the one who could save him from death, and he was heard because of his reverent submission.*j* 8 Although he was a son, he learned obedience from what he suffered *k* 9 and, once made perfect, he became the source of eternal salvation for all who obey him 10 and was designated by God to be high priest *l* in the order of Melchizedek.

Warning Against Falling Away

11 We have much to say about this, but it is hard to explain because you are slow to learn. 12 In fact, though by this time you ought to be teachers, you need someone to teach you the elementary truths of God's word all over again. You need milk, not solid food! *m* 13 Anyone who lives on milk, being still an infant, is not acquainted with the teaching about righteousness. 14 But solid food is for the mature, *n* who by constant use have trained themselves to distinguish good from evil.

6 Therefore let us leave *o* the elementary teachings *p* about Christ and go on to maturity, not laying again the foundation of repentance from acts that lead to death, *a* *q* and of faith in God, 2 instruction about baptisms, the laying on of hands, the resurrection of the dead, and eternal judgment. 3 And God permitting, *r* we will do so.

4 It is impossible for those who have once been enlightened, *s* who have tasted the heavenly gift, *t* who have shared in the Holy Spirit, *u* 5 who have tasted the goodness of the word of God and the powers of the coming age, 6 if they fall away, to be brought back to repentance, because *b* to their loss they are crucifying the Son of God all over again and subjecting him to public disgrace.

a 1 Or *from useless rituals*   *b* 6 Or *repentance while*

5:7 /Mt 27:46, 50 /Mk 14:36
5:8 *k* Php 2:8
5:10 *l* ver 5
5:12 *m* 1Co 3:2
5:14 *n* 1Co 2:6
6:1 *o* Php 3:12-14 *p* Heb 5:12 *q* Heb 9:14
6:3 *r* Ac 18:21
6:4 *s* Heb 10:32 *t* Eph 2:8 *u* Gal 3:2

5:7 Jesus was in great agony as he prepared to face death (Luke 22:41–44). Although Jesus cried out to God, asking to be delivered, he was prepared to suffer humiliation, separation from his Father, and death in order to do God's will. At times we will undergo trials, not because we want to suffer, but because we want to obey God. Let Jesus' obedience sustain and encourage you in times of trial. You will be able to face anything if you know that Jesus Christ is with you.

5:7 Have you ever felt that God didn't hear your prayers? Be sure you are praying with reverent submission, willing to do what God wants. God responds to his obedient children.

5:8 Jesus' human life was not a script that he passively followed. It was a life that he chose freely (John 10:17, 18). It was a continuous process of making the will of God the Father his own. Jesus chose to obey, even though obedience led to suffering and death. Because Jesus obeyed perfectly, even under great trial, he can help us obey, no matter how difficult obedience seems to be.

5:9 Christ was always morally perfect. By obeying, he demonstrated his perfection to us, not to God or to himself. In the Bible, *perfection* usually means completeness or maturity. By sharing our experience of suffering, Christ shared our human experience completely. He is now able to offer eternal salvation to those who obey him. See Philippians 2:5–11 for Christ's attitude as he took on human form.

5:9 The "eternal salvation" we have been offered means the elimination of a verdict on our sin, the setting aside of judgment, and the award of undeserved membership in God's family. It is a change in destiny, an awakening of hope, an overcoming of death. Salvation turns a person toward heaven and inaugurates a life of discipleship with the living Christ. It is God's vote for you, God's invitation to you, God's energy invested in you. Salvation is the reason you can smile in the morning and rest in the evening. God loves you, and you belong to him.

5:12, 13 These Jewish Christians were immature. Some of them should have been teaching others, but they had not even applied the basics to their own lives. They were reluctant to move beyond age-old traditions, established doctrines, and discussion of the basics. They wouldn't be able to understand the high-priestly role of Christ unless they moved out of their comfortable position, cut some of their Jewish ties, and stopped trying to blend in with their culture. Commitment to Christ moves people out of their comfort zones.

5:12–14 In order to grow from infant Christians to mature Christians, we must learn discernment. We must train our consciences, our senses, our minds, and our bodies to distinguish good from evil. Can you recognize temptation before it traps you? Can you tell the difference between a correct use of Scripture and a mistaken one?

5:14 Our capacity to feast on deeper knowledge of God ("solid food") is determined by our spiritual growth. Too often we want God's banquet before we are spiritually capable of digesting it. As you grow in the Lord and put into practice what you have learned, your capacity to understand will also grow.

6:1, 2 Certain elementary teachings are essential for all believers to understand. Those basics include the importance of faith, the foolishness of trying to be saved by good deeds, the meaning of baptism and spiritual gifts, and the facts of resurrection and eternal life. To go on to maturity in our understanding, we need to move beyond (but not away from) the basic teachings to a more complete understanding of the faith. And this is what the author intends for his readers to do (6:3). Mature Christians should be teaching new Christians the basics. Then, acting on what they know, the mature will learn even more from God's Word.

6:3 These Christians needed to move beyond the basics of their faith to an understanding of Christ as the perfect high priest and the fulfillment of all the Old Testament prophecies. Rather than arguing about the respective merits of Judaism and Christianity, they needed to depend on Christ and live effectively for him.

6:4–6 In the first century, a pagan who investigated Christianity and then went back to paganism made a clean break with the church. But for Jewish Christians who decided to return to Judaism, the break was less obvious. Their lifestyle remained relatively unchanged. But by deliberately turning away from Christ, they were cutting themselves off from God's forgiveness. Those who persevere in believing are true saints; those who continue to reject Christ are unbelievers, no matter how well they behave.

6:6 This verse points to the danger of the Hebrew Christians returning to Judaism and thus committing apostasy. Some apply this verse today to superficial believers who renounce their Christianity, or to unbelievers who come close to salvation and then turn away. Either way, those who reject Christ will not be saved. Christ died once for all. He will not be crucified again. Apart from his cross, there is no other possible way of salvation. However, the author does not indicate that his readers were in danger of

7 Land that drinks in the rain often falling on it and that produces a crop useful to those for whom it is farmed receives the blessing of God. 8 But land that produces thorns and thistles is worthless and is in danger of being cursed. In the end it will be burned.

9 Even though we speak like this, dear friends, we are confident of better things in your case—things that accompany salvation. 10 God is not unjust; he will not forget your work and the love you have shown him as you have helped his people and continue to help them. v 11 We want each of you to show this same diligence to the very end, in order to make your hope w sure. 12 We do not want you to become lazy, but to imitate those who through faith and patience inherit what has been promised.

6:10
v Mt 10:40, 42;
1Th 1:3

6:11
w Heb 3:6

ABRAHAM IN THE NEW TESTAMENT			
Abraham was an ancestor of Jesus Christ.	Matthew 1:1, 2, 17; Luke 3:23, 34	Jesus Christ was human; he was born into the line of Abraham, whom God had chosen to be the father of a great nation through which the whole world would be blessed. We are blessed because of what Jesus Christ, Abraham's descendant, did for us.
Abraham was the father of the Jewish nation.	Matthew 3:9; Luke 3:8; Acts 13:26; Romans 4:1; 11:1; 2 Corinthians 11:22; Hebrews 6:13, 14	God wanted to set apart a nation for himself, a nation that would tell the world about him. He began with a man of faith who, though old and childless, believed God's promise of innumerable descendants. We can trust God to do the impossible when we have faith.
Abraham, because of his faith, now sits in the kingdom with Christ.	Matthew 8:11; Luke 13:28; 16:23–31	Abraham followed God, and now he is enjoying his reward—eternity with God. We will one day meet Abraham because we have been promised eternity as well.
God is Abraham's God; thus, Abraham is alive with God.	Matthew 22:32; Mark 12:26; Luke 20:37; Acts 7:32	As Abraham lives forever, we will live forever, because we, like Abraham, have chosen the life of faith.
Abraham received great promises from God.	Luke 1:55, 72, 73; Acts 3:25; 7:17, 18; Galatians 3:6, 14–16; Hebrews 6:13–15	Many of the promises God made to Abraham seemed impossible to be realized, but Abraham trusted God. The promises to believers in God's Word also seem too incredible to believe, but we can trust God to keep all his promises.
Abraham followed God.	Acts 7:2–8; Hebrews 11:8, 17–19	Abraham followed God's leading from his homeland to an unknown territory, which became the Jews' promised land. When we follow God, even before he makes all his plans clear to us, we will never be disappointed.
God blessed Abraham because of his faith.	Romans 4; Galatians 3:6–9, 14–19; Hebrews 11:8, 17–19; James 2:21–24	Abraham showed faith in times of disappointment, trial, and testing. Because of Abraham's faith, God counted him righteous and called him his "friend." God accepts us because of our faith.
Abraham is the father of all those who come to God by faith.	Romans 9:6–8; Galatians 3:6–9, 14–29	The Jews are Abraham's children, and Christ was his descendant. We are Christ's brothers and sisters; thus, all believers are Abraham's children and God's children. Abraham was righteous because of his faith; we are made righteous through faith in Christ. The promises made to Abraham apply to us because of Christ.

renouncing Christ (see 6:9). He is warning against hardness of heart that would make repentance inconceivable for the sinner.

6:7, 8 The writer uses an analogy from agriculture to make a simple point. Real seeds (the gospel) given genuine care by the farmer (God) and planted in a fertile field (your heart and life) will produce a bountiful crop (spiritual maturity). Weeds (temptations) threaten to overwhelm the crop. If the field produces only weeds, then the seeds are lost and the field ruined.

An unproductive Christian life falls under God's condemnation. You have been watered by God's grace with clear and abundant teaching and preaching. What excuse do you have for a useless or unproductive life? Don't be a Christian in name only. Make sure your life bears fruit.

6:10 It's easy to get discouraged, thinking that God has forgotten us. But God is never unjust. He never forgets or overlooks our hard work for him. Presently you may not be receiving rewards and acclaim, but God knows your efforts of love and ministry. Let God's love for you and his intimate knowledge of your service for him bolster you as you face disappointment and rejection here on earth.

6:11, 12 Hope keeps the Christian from becoming lazy or feeling bored. Like an athlete, train hard and run well, remembering the reward that lies ahead (Philippians 3:14).

The Certainty of God's Promise

13When God made his promise to Abraham, since there was no one greater for him to swear by, he swore by himself,ˣ 14saying, "I will surely bless you and give you many descendants."ᵃ 15And so after waiting patiently, Abraham received what was promised.

16Men swear by someone greater than themselves, and the oath confirms what is said and puts an end to all argument.ʸ 17Because God wanted to make the unchanging nature of his purpose very clear to the heirs of what was promised,ᶻ he confirmed it with an oath. 18God did this so that, by two unchangeable things in which it is impossible for God to lie, we who have fled to take hold of the hope offered to us may be greatly encouraged. 19We have this hope as an anchor for the soul, firm and secure. It enters the inner sanctuary behind the curtain, 20where Jesus, who went before us, has entered on our behalf. ᵃ He has become a high priest forever, in the order of Melchizedek.ᵇ

6:13
ˣGe 22:16; Lk 1:73

6:16
ʸEx 22:11
6:17
ᶻHeb 11:9

6:20
ᵃHeb 4:14
ᵇHeb 5:6

Melchizedek the Priest

7 This Melchizedek was king of Salem and priest of God Most High. He met Abraham returning from the defeat of the kings and blessed him,ᶜ 2and Abraham gave him a tenth of everything. First, his name means "king of righteousness"; then also, "king of Salem" means "king of peace." 3Without father or mother, without genealogy, without beginning of days or end of life, like the Son of God he remains a priest forever.

4Just think how great he was: Even the patriarch Abraham gave him a tenth of the plunder!ᵈ 5Now the law requires the descendants of Levi who become priests to collect a tenth from the people ᵉ—that is, their brothers—even though their brothers are descended from Abraham. 6This man, however, did not trace his descent from Levi, yet he collected a tenth from Abraham and blessed him who had the promises.ᶠ 7And without doubt the lesser person is blessed by the greater. 8In the one case, the tenth is collected by men who die; but in the other case, by him who is declared to be living.ᵍ 9One might even say that Levi, who collects the tenth, paid the tenth through Abraham, 10because when Melchizedek met Abraham, Levi was still in the body of his ancestor.

7:1
ᶜGe 14:18-20

7:4
ᵈGe 14:20
7:5
ᵉNu 18:21, 26
7:6
ᶠRo 4:13
7:8
ᵍHeb 5:6; 6:20

Jesus Like Melchizedek

11If perfection could have been attained through the Levitical priesthood (for on the basis of it the law was given to the people),ʰ why was there still need for another priest to come—one in the order of Melchizedek, not in the order of Aaron? 12For when there is a

7:11
ʰver 18, 19;
Heb 8:7

ᵃ14 Gen. 22:17

6:15 Abraham waited patiently—it was 25 years from the time God had promised him a son (Genesis 17:16) to Isaac's birth (Genesis 21:1–3). Because our trials and temptations are often so intense, they seem to last for an eternity. Both the Bible and the testimony of mature Christians encourage us to wait for God to act in his timing, even when our needs seem too great to wait any longer.

6:17 God's promises are unchanging and trustworthy because God is unchanging and trustworthy. When promising Abraham a son, God took an oath in his own name. The oath was as good as God's name, and God's name was as good as his divine nature.

6:18, 19 These two unchangeable things are God's nature and his promise. God embodies all truth; therefore, he cannot lie. Because God is truth, you can be secure in his promises; you don't need to wonder if he will change his plans. Our hope is secure and immovable, anchored in God, just as a ship anchor holds firmly to the seabed. To the true seeker who comes to God in belief, God gives an unconditional promise of acceptance. When you ask God with openness, honesty, and sincerity to save you from your sins, he will do it. This truth should give you encouragement, assurance, and confidence.

6:19, 20 This curtain hung between the Holy Place and the Most Holy Place, the two innermost rooms of the temple. This curtain prevented anyone from entering, gazing into, or even getting a fleeting glimpse of the interior of the Most Holy Place (see also 9:1–8). The high priest could enter there only once a year to stand before God's presence and atone for the sins of the entire nation.

But Christ is in God's presence at all times, not just once a year, as the high priest who can continually intercede for us.

7:2ff The writer uses this story from Genesis 14:18–20 to show that Christ is even greater than Abraham, father of the Jewish nation, and Levi (Abraham's descendant). Therefore, the Jewish priesthood (made up of Levi's descendants) was inferior to Melchizedek's priesthood (a type of Christ's priesthood).

7:3–10 Melchizedek was a priest of God Most High (see the note on Genesis 14:18 and his Profile in Genesis 16, p. 29). He is said to remain a priest forever (see also Psalm 110:4), because his priesthood has no record of beginning or ending—he was a priest of God in Salem (Jerusalem) long before the nation of Israel and the regular priesthood began.

7:7 The "lesser person is blessed by the greater" means a person who has the power to bless is always greater than the person that he or she blesses.

7:11–17 Jesus' high-priestly role was superior to that of any priest of Levi, because the Messiah was a priest of a higher order (Psalm 110:4). If the Jewish priests and their laws had been able to save people, why would God need to send Christ as a priest, who came not from the tribe of Levi (the priestly tribe), but from the tribe of Judah? The animal sacrifices had to be repeated, and they offered only temporary forgiveness; but Christ's sacrifice was offered once, and it offers total and permanent forgiveness. Under the new covenant, the Levitical priesthood was canceled in favor of Christ's role as high priest. Because Christ is our high priest, we need to pay attention to him. No minister, leader, or Christian friend can substitute for Christ's work and for his role in our salvation.

7:13
/ver 11

7:14
/Isa 11:1

7:17
kPs 110:4

change of the priesthood, there must also be a change of the law. [13]He of whom these things are said belonged to a different tribe,[i] and no one from that tribe has ever served at the altar. [14]For it is clear that our Lord descended from Judah,[j] and in regard to that tribe Moses said nothing about priests. [15]And what we have said is even more clear if another priest like Melchizedek appears, [16]one who has become a priest not on the basis of a regulation as to his ancestry but on the basis of the power of an indestructible life. [17]For it is declared:

> "You are a priest forever,
>   in the order of Melchizedek."[a][k]

7:18
/Ro 8:3
7:19
mRo 3:20
nHeb 4:16
7:21
oPs 110:4

[18]The former regulation is set aside because it was weak and useless[l] [19](for the law made nothing perfect),[m] and a better hope is introduced, by which we draw near to God.[n]

[20]And it was not without an oath! Others became priests without any oath, [21]but he became a priest with an oath when God said to him:

> "The Lord has sworn
>   and will not change his mind:
>   'You are a priest forever.'"[a][o]

[22]Because of this oath, Jesus has become the guarantee of a better covenant.

7:25
pRo 8:34

[23]Now there have been many of those priests, since death prevented them from continuing in office; [24]but because Jesus lives forever, he has a permanent priesthood. [25]Therefore he is able to save completely[b] those who come to God through him, because he always lives to intercede for them.[p]

7:26
qHeb 4:14
7:27
rHeb 5:1
7:28
sHeb 5:2
tHeb 2:10

[26]Such a high priest meets our need—one who is holy, blameless, pure, set apart from sinners, exalted above the heavens. [q][27]Unlike the other high priests, he does not need to offer sacrifices[r] day after day, first for his own sins, and then for the sins of the people. He sacrificed for their sins once for all when he offered himself. [28]For the law appoints as high priests men who are weak;[s] but the oath, which came after the law, appointed the Son, who has been made perfect[t] forever.

[a]17,21 Psalm 110:4   [b]25 Or forever

7:18, 19 The law was not intended to save people or to make them perfect, but to point out sin (see Romans 3:20; 5:20) and to point toward Christ (see Galatians 3:24, 25). Salvation comes through Christ, whose sacrifice brings forgiveness for our sins. Being ethical, working diligently to help others, and giving to charitable causes are all commendable, but all of our good deeds cannot save us or make us right with God.

7:19 How can you draw near to God? The Bible makes it clear that your own body is God's temple. Your spirit needs and wants closeness with God. You want to know the living God personally, not as an idea or concept, not as a distant monarch. You can draw near to God through prayer, worship, and Bible meditation. You need not live like a monk, but you probably need more prayer in your life. The habit of worship has become a convenience to be wedged between sports and other recreations. Instead, make worship your top priority. Bible meditation may include verse memory, songs, and quiet personal reading. The Bible is the word of God for you. Use it every day and you will draw nearer and nearer to God.

7:22–24 Jesus has a permanent priesthood. He should be everyone's ultimate authority for spiritual life. In our culture today, however, many people have advisors and counselors whom they elevate almost to the role of priest. People look to political leaders, lawyers, physicians, insurance agents, and financial advisors to provide hope, long life, and security against all disasters. Many Christians regard the advice of priests and ministers, Christian friends, and even pop musicians before they consider the words of Jesus written in the Bible. Make sure your first allegiance and priority is to know and follow the advice given by Jesus.

7:25 No one can add to what Jesus did to save us; our past, present, and future sins are all forgiven, and Jesus is with the Father as a sign that our sins are forgiven. As our high priest, Christ is our advocate, the mediator between us and God. He looks after our interests and intercedes for us with God. The Old Testament high priest went before God once a year to plead for

the forgiveness of the nation's sins; Christ makes perpetual intercession before God for us. Christ's continuous presence in heaven with the Father assures us that our sins have been paid for and forgiven (see Romans 8:33, 34; Hebrews 2:17, 18; 4:15, 16; 9:24). This wonderful assurance frees us from guilt and from fear of failure. If you are a Christian, remember that Christ has paid the price for your sins once and for all (see also 9:24–28).

7:27 In Old Testament times when animals were sacrificed, they were cut into pieces, the parts were washed, the fat was burned, the blood was sprinkled, and the meat was boiled. Blood was demanded as atonement for sins, and God accepted animal blood to cover the people's sins (Leviticus 17:11). Because of the sacrificial system, the Israelites were generally aware that sin costs someone something and that they themselves were sinful. Many people take Christ's work on the cross for granted. They don't realize how costly it was for Jesus to secure our forgiveness—it cost him his life and painful, temporary separation from his Father (Matthew 27:46; 1 Peter 1:18, 19).

Because Jesus died *once for all,* he brought the sacrificial system to an end. He forgave sins—past, present, and future. The Jews did not need to go back to the old system because Christ, the perfect sacrifice, completed the work of redemption. You don't have to look for another way to have your sins forgiven—Christ was the final sacrifice for you.

7:28 So much is attributed to Jesus in this chapter that it might appear that there is nothing you need to do, or can do, to make salvation a reality for you. And that is true. Jesus has done it all. Nothing you do can improve his work. Nothing you do adds to God's acceptance of Jesus' sacrifice.

So how do the benefits of Jesus' sacrifice become yours? You accept the gift of salvation by faith, trusting entirely in Jesus for salvation. You can do that now through a simple prayer: "Dear God, I trust in Jesus alone. Please forgive my sins through him, and give me the eternal life secured by him. Amen."

4. The new covenant is greater than the old
The High Priest of a New Covenant

8 The point of what we are saying is this: We do have such a high priest, who sat down at the right hand of the throne of the Majesty in heaven, 2 and who serves in the sanctuary, the true tabernacle u set up by the Lord, not by man.

3 Every high priest is appointed to offer both gifts and sacrifices, v and so it was necessary for this one also to have something to offer. 4 If he were on earth, he would not be a priest, for there are already men who offer the gifts prescribed by the law. 5 They serve at a sanctuary that is a copy w and shadow x of what is in heaven. This is why Moses was warned when he was about to build the tabernacle: "See to it that you make everything according to the pattern shown you on the mountain." a y 6 But the ministry Jesus has received is as superior to theirs as the covenant of which he is mediator is superior to the old one, and it is founded on better promises.

7 For if there had been nothing wrong with that first covenant, no place would have been sought for another. z 8 But God found fault with the people and said b:

> "The time is coming, declares the Lord,
>   when I will make a new covenant
> with the house of Israel
>   and with the house of Judah.
> 9 It will not be like the covenant
>   I made with their forefathers
> when I took them by the hand
>   to lead them out of Egypt,

a5 Exodus 25:40   b8 Some manuscripts may be translated *fault and said to the people.*

8:2
u Heb 9:11, 24

8:3
v Heb 5:1

8:5
w Heb 9:23
x Col 2:17
y Ex 25:40

8:7
z Heb 7:11, 18

8:4 Under the old Jewish system, priests were chosen only from the tribe of Levi, and sacrifices were offered daily on the altar for forgiveness of sins (see 7:12–14). This system would not have allowed Jesus to be a priest, because he was from the tribe of Judah. But his perfect sacrifice ended all need for further priests and sacrifices.

The use of the present tense, "there are already men who offer the gifts" indicates that this book was written before A.D. 70 when the temple in Jerusalem was destroyed, ending the sacrifices.

8:5 The pattern for the tabernacle built by Moses was given by God. It was a pattern of the spiritual reality of Christ's sacrifice, and thus it looked forward to the future reality. There is no tabernacle in heaven of which the earthly one is a copy, but rather the earthly tabernacle was an expression of eternal, theological principles. Because the temple at Jerusalem had not yet been destroyed, using the worship system there as an example would have had a great impact on this original audience.

8:8–12 This passage is a quotation of Jeremiah 31:31–34, which compares the new covenant with the old. The old covenant was the covenant of law between God and Israel. The new and better way is the covenant of grace—Christ's offer to forgive our sins and bring us to God through his sacrificial death. This covenant is new in extent—it goes beyond Israel and Judah to include all the Gentile nations. It is new in application because it is written on our hearts and in our minds. It offers a new way to forgiveness, not through animal sacrifice but through faith. Have you entered into this new covenant and begun walking in the better way?

8:10 If our hearts are not changed, following God's rules will be unpleasant and difficult. We will rebel against being told how to live. The Holy Spirit, however, gives us new desires, helping us *want* to obey God (see Philippians 2:12, 13). With new hearts, we find that serving God is our greatest joy.

8:10, 11 Under God's new covenant, God's law is inside us. It is no longer an external set of rules and principles. The Holy Spirit reminds us of Christ's words, activates our consciences, influences our motives and desires, and makes us want to obey. Now doing God's will is something we desire with all our heart and mind.

8:13 Some of the Jewish believers were clinging to the obsolete old ways instead of embracing Christ's new covenant. All the joy of newfound faith and all the relief of fresh forgiveness had given way to a kind of boredom that was never supposed to be. Growth had stopped. What should be done if this happens to you?

Realize that life in Christ is never complete. Heaven promises completeness; until then, growth is the normal pattern. Growth often endures seasons of drought and drabness. That's also normal. Think about what you are doing that might be spiritually ineffective or obsolete. The key to growth includes daily devotion to Christ through Bible study and prayer. Perhaps you need to intensify your study and find helps that provide more substance. Perhaps you need to grow by engaging in new areas of service that express your faith. Seek God for how he would have you keep growing in your faith.

9:5 *Cherubim* are mighty angels. One of the functions of the cherubim was to serve as guardians. These angels guarded the entrances to both the tree of life (Genesis 3:24) and the Most Holy Place (Exodus 26:31–33). With their wings "overshadowing the atonement cover," these two gold statues were believed to support God's invisible presence (Ezekiel 9:3; 10:4, 18). Here they are called "the cherubim of the Glory," referring to God's glory which hovered over the ark of the covenant (Exodus 40:34–36; Leviticus 16:2).

9:6–8 The high priest could enter the Most Holy Place (9:3; or the "inner room," 9:7), the innermost room of the tabernacle, one day each year to atone for the nation's sins. The Most Holy Place was a small room that contained the ark of the covenant (a gold-covered chest containing the original stone tablets on which the Ten Commandments were written, a jar of manna, and Aaron's staff). The top of the chest served as the "atonement cover" (the altar) on which the blood would be sprinkled by the high priest on the Day of Atonement. The Most Holy Place was the most sacred spot on earth for the Jews. Only the high priest could enter—the other priests and the common people were forbidden to come into the room. Their only access to God was through the high priest, who would offer a sacrifice and use the animal's blood to atone first for his own sins and then for the people's sins (see also 10:19).

because they did not remain faithful to my covenant,
and I turned away from them,

declares the Lord.

8:10
a Heb 10:16

¹⁰ This is the covenant I will make with the house of Israel
after that time, declares the Lord.
I will put my laws in their minds
and write them on their hearts. *a*
I will be their God,
and they will be my people.

8:11
b Isa 54:13; Jn 6:45

¹¹ No longer will a man teach his neighbor,
or a man his brother, saying, 'Know the Lord,'
because they will all know me,*b*
from the least of them to the greatest.

8:12
c Heb 10:17

¹² For I will forgive their wickedness
and will remember their sins no more.*c*"*a*

8:13
d 2Co 5:17

¹³By calling this covenant "new," he has made the first one obsolete;*d* and what is obsolete and aging will soon disappear.

a 12 Jer. 31:31-34

THE OLD AND NEW COVENANTS	Reference	The Old Covenant under Moses	The New Covenant in Christ	Application
Like pointing out the similarities and differences between the photograph of a person and the actual person, the writer of Hebrews shows the connection between the old Mosaic covenant and the new Messianic covenant. He proves that the old covenant was a shadow of the real Christ.	8:3, 4	Gifts and sacrifices by those guilty of sin	Self-sacrifice by the guiltless Christ	Christ died for you
	8:5, 6, 10–12	Focused on a physical building where one goes to worship	Focuses on the reign of Christ in believers' hearts	God is directly involved in your life
	8:5, 6, 10–12	A shadow	A reality	Not temporal, but eternal
	8:6	Limited promises	Limitless promises	We can trust God's promises to us
	8:8, 9	Failed agreement by people	Faithful agreement by Christ	Christ has kept the agreement where people couldn't
	9:1	External standards and rules	Internal standards—a new heart	God sees both actions and motives—we are accountable to God, not rules
	9:7	Limited access to God	Unlimited access to God	God is personally available
	9:9, 10	Legal cleansing	Personal cleansing	God's cleansing is complete
	9:11–14; 24–28	Continual sacrifice	Conclusive sacrifice	Christ's sacrifice was perfect and final
	9:22	Forgiveness earned	Forgiveness freely given	We have true and complete forgiveness
	9:24–28	Repeated yearly	Completed by Christ's death	Christ's death can be applied to our sin
	9:26	Available to some	Available to all	Available to you

9:10 The people had to keep the Old Testament dietary laws and ceremonial cleansing laws until Christ came with God's new and better way.

9:12 This imagery comes from the Day of Atonement rituals described in Leviticus 16. *Redemption* refers to the process of paying the price (ransom) to free a slave. Through his own death, Christ freed us from the slavery of sin forever.

9:12–14 Though you know Christ, you may believe that you have to work hard to make yourself good enough for God. But rules and rituals have never cleansed people's hearts. By Jesus' blood alone (1) we have our consciences cleansed, (2) we are freed from death's sting and can live to serve God, and (3) we are freed from sin's power. If you are carrying a load of guilt because you are finding that you can't be good enough for God, take another look at Jesus'

death and what it means for you. Christ can heal your conscience and deliver you from the frustration of trying to earn God's favor. Bring your guilt-ridden life to Christ, confess your inability to clean up your own conscience, ask him to forgive you. Thank him for his deliverance. God can forgive you and clear your record.

9:13, 14 When the people sacrificed animals, God considered the people's faith and obedience, cleansed them from sin, and made them *ceremonially* acceptable according to Old Testament law. But Christ's sacrifice transforms our lives and hearts and makes us clean on the inside. His sacrifice is infinitely more effective than animal sacrifices. No barrier of sin or weakness on our part can stifle his forgiveness.

Worship in the Earthly Tabernacle

9 Now the first covenant had regulations for worship and also an earthly sanctuary. [e] [2] A tabernacle was set up. In its first room were the lampstand, the table [f] and the consecrated bread; this was called the Holy Place. [3] Behind the second curtain was a room called the Most Holy Place, [g] [4] which had the golden altar of incense [h] and the gold-covered ark of the covenant. [i] This ark contained the gold jar of manna, [j] Aaron's staff that had budded, and the stone tablets of the covenant. [5] Above the ark were the cherubim of the Glory, overshadowing the atonement cover. [a] But we cannot discuss these things in detail now.

[6] When everything had been arranged like this, the priests entered regularly [k] into the outer room to carry on their ministry. [7] But only the high priest entered the inner room, and that only once a year, and never without blood, which he offered for himself [l] and for the sins the people had committed in ignorance. [8] The Holy Spirit was showing by this that the way [m] into the Most Holy Place had not yet been disclosed as long as the first tabernacle was still standing. [9] This is an illustration for the present time, indicating that the gifts and sacrifices being offered were not able to clear the conscience of the worshiper. [10] They are only a matter of food and drink [n] and various ceremonial washings—external regulations applying until the time of the new order.

The Blood of Christ

[11] When Christ came as high priest of the good things that are already here, [b] [o] he went through the greater and more perfect tabernacle [p] that is not man-made, that is to say, not a part of this creation. [12] He did not enter by means of the blood of goats and calves; but he entered the Most Holy Place once for all by his own blood, having obtained eternal redemption. [13] The blood of goats and bulls and the ashes of a heifer sprinkled on those who are ceremonially unclean sanctify them so that they are outwardly clean. [14] How much more, then, will the blood of Christ, who through the eternal Spirit offered himself unblemished to God, cleanse our consciences from acts that lead to death, [c] so that we may serve the living God!

[15] For this reason Christ is the mediator of a new covenant, that those who are called may receive the promised eternal inheritance—now that he has died as a ransom to set them free from the sins committed under the first covenant.

[16] In the case of a will, [d] it is necessary to prove the death of the one who made it, [17] because a will is in force only when somebody has died; it never takes effect while the one who made it is living. [18] This is why even the first covenant was not put into effect without blood. [q] [19] When Moses had proclaimed every commandment of the law to all the people, he took the blood of calves, together with water, scarlet wool and branches of hyssop, and sprinkled the scroll and all the people. [20] He said, "This is the blood of the covenant, which God has commanded you to keep." [e] [r] [21] In the same way, he sprinkled with the blood both the tabernacle and everything used in its ceremonies. [22] In fact, the law requires that nearly everything be cleansed with blood, [s] and without the shedding of blood there is no forgiveness. [t]

[23] It was necessary, then, for the copies [u] of the heavenly things to be purified with these sacrifices, but the heavenly things themselves with better sacrifices than these. [24] For Christ

Cross references

9:1 [e] Ex 25:8
9:2 [f] Ex 25:23-29
9:3 [g] Ex 26:31-33
9:4 [h] Ex 30:1-5; [i] Ex 25:10-22; [j] Ex 16:32, 33
9:6 [k] Nu 28:3
9:7 [l] Heb 5:2, 3
9:8 [m] Jn 14:6; Heb 10:19, 20
9:10 [n] Col 2:16
9:11 [o] Heb 10:1; [p] Heb 8:2
9:18 [q] Ex 24:6-8
9:20 [r] Ex 24:8; Mt 26:28
9:22 [s] Lev 8:15; [t] Lev 17:11
9:23 [u] Heb 8:5

a5 Traditionally *the mercy seat*   b11 Some early manuscripts *are to come*   c14 Or *from useless rituals*   d16 Same Greek word as *covenant* ; also in verse 17   e20 Exodus 24:8

9:14 Sinful deeds are more than just wrong actions; ironically, these also include our attempts to reach God by being good enough! Our culture glorifies self-effort and personal achievement. It defines a successful person as one who obtains certain goals: financial security, health and fitness, and the respect of others. But here the Bible gives us a different picture of successful living: accept Jesus' sacrifice for your sin, abandon the futility of sinful deeds, and let the blood of Christ purify your conscience (see 10:19–22).

9:15 People in Old Testament times were saved through Christ's sacrifice, although that sacrifice had not yet happened. In offering unblemished animal sacrifices, they were anticipating Christ's coming and his death for sin. There was no point in returning to the sacrificial system now that Christ had come and had become the final, perfect sacrifice.

9:22 Why does forgiveness require the shedding of blood? This is no arbitrary decree on the part of a bloodthirsty God, as some have suggested. There is no greater symbol of life than blood;

blood keeps us alive. Jesus shed his blood—gave his life—for our sins so that we wouldn't have to experience spiritual death, eternal separation from God. Jesus is the source of life, not death. He gave his own life to pay our penalty for us so that we might live. After shedding his blood for us, Christ rose from the grave and proclaimed victory over sin and death.

9:23 In a way that we don't fully understand, the earthly tabernacle was a copy and symbol of heavenly realities. This purification of the heavenly things can best be understood as referring to Christ's spiritual work for us in heaven (see the note on 8:5).

9:24 Among references to priests, tabernacles, sacrifices, and other ideas unfamiliar to us, we come to this description of Christ as our mediator, appearing in God's presence on our behalf. We can relate to this role and be encouraged by it. Christ is on our side at God's side. He is our Lord and Savior. He is not there to convince or remind God that our sins are forgiven, but to present both our needs and our service for him as an offering (see 7:25).

9:24–28 All people die physically, but Christ died so that we

9:24
v Heb 8:2

9:25
w ver 7, 8

9:26
x Heb 7:27

9:27
y Ge 3:19
z 2Co 5:10

9:28
a 1Pe 2:24

did not enter a man-made sanctuary that was only a copy of the true one; v he entered heaven itself, now to appear for us in God's presence. 25 Nor did he enter heaven to offer himself again and again, the way the high priest enters the Most Holy Place every year with blood that is not his own. w 26 Then Christ would have had to suffer many times since the creation of the world. But now he has appeared once for all x at the end of the ages to do away with sin by the sacrifice of himself. 27 Just as man is destined to die once, y and after that to face judgment, z 28 so Christ was sacrificed once to take away the sins of many people; and he will appear a second time, not to bear sin, a but to bring salvation to those who are waiting for him.

Christ's Sacrifice Once for All

10:1
b Heb 9:11

10:3
c Heb 9:7

10:5
d 1Pe 2:24

10 The law is only a shadow of the good things b that are coming—not the realities themselves. For this reason it can never, by the same sacrifices repeated endlessly year after year, make perfect those who draw near to worship. 2 If it could, would they not have stopped being offered? For the worshipers would have been cleansed once for all, and would no longer have felt guilty for their sins. 3 But those sacrifices are an annual reminder of sins, c 4 because it is impossible for the blood of bulls and goats to take away sins.

5 Therefore, when Christ came into the world, he said:

> "Sacrifice and offering you did not desire,
>   but a body you prepared for me; d
> 6 with burnt offerings and sin offerings
>   you were not pleased.

10:7
e Jer 36:2
f Ps 40:6-8

> 7 Then I said, 'Here I am—it is written about me in the scroll e—
>   I have come to do your will, O God.'" a f

8 First he said, "Sacrifices and offerings, burnt offerings and sin offerings you did not desire, nor were you pleased with them" (although the law required them to be made). 9 Then he said, "Here I am, I have come to do your will." He sets aside the first to establish the second. 10 And by that will, we have been made holy through the sacrifice of the body g of Jesus Christ once for all.

10:10
g 1Pe 2:24

a 7 Psalm 40:6-8 (see Septuagint)

---

would not have to die spiritually. We can have wonderful confidence in his saving work for us, doing away with sin—past, present, and future. He has forgiven our past sin—when he died on the cross, he sacrificed himself once for all (9:26); he has given us the Holy Spirit to help us deal with present sin—he appears for us now in heaven as our high priest (9:24); and he promises to return (9:28) and raise us to eternal life in a world where sin will be banished.

9:26 The "end of the ages" refers to the time of Christ's coming to earth in fulfillment of the Old Testament prophecies. Christ ushered in the new era of grace and forgiveness. We are still living in the "end of the ages." The day of the Lord has begun and will be completed at Christ's return.

9:27 Judgment is not a popular theme today, but the Bible teaches that judgment is coming. Do you look forward to Christ's return, or do you see it as a threat? As sure as death itself, judgment awaits. At God's judgment there will be no higher court of appeal should the verdict not be to your liking. If you hope for a favorable verdict in this court, put your hope entirely on Jesus. Pray today—now if you haven't before—for the freedom and pardon Jesus has won for you. Then rejoice that God's judgment of you will be based on the perfect life of his Son, Jesus. After that, tell others, for many will face an unfavorable judgment without Jesus.

10:3 When people gathered for the offering of sacrifices on the Day of Atonement, they were reminded of their sins, and they undoubtedly felt guilty all over again. What they needed most was forgiveness—the permanent, powerful, sin-destroying forgiveness we have from Christ. When we confess a sin to him, we need never think of it again. Christ has forgiven us, and the sin no longer exists. See 1 John 1:9.

10:4 Animal sacrifices could not take away sins; they provided only a temporary way to deal with sin until Jesus came to deal

with sin permanently. How, then, were people forgiven in Old Testament times? Because Old Testament believers were following God's command to offer sacrifices, he graciously forgave them when, by faith, they made their sacrifices. But that practice looked forward to Christ's perfect sacrifice. Christ's way was superior to the Old Testament way because the old way only pointed to what Christ would do to take away sins.

10:5-10 This quotation is not cited in any other New Testament book. However, it is a central teaching of the Old Testament that God desires obedience and a right heart, not empty compliance to the sacrifice system (see the chart in Hosea 7, p. 1403). The writer of Hebrews applies to Christ the words of the psalmist in Psalm 40:6-8. Christ came to offer his body on the cross for us as a sacrifice that is completely acceptable to God. God's new and living way for us to please him is not by keeping laws or even by abstaining from sin. It is by coming to him in faith to be forgiven, and then following him in loving obedience.

10:5-10 The costly sacrifice of an animal's life impressed upon the sinner the seriousness of his or her own sin before God. Because Jesus shed his own blood for us, his sacrifice is infinitely greater than any Old Testament offering. Considering the immeasurable gift he gave us, we should respond by giving him our devotion and service.

10:9 Setting aside the first system in order to establish a far better one meant doing away with the system of sacrifices contained in the ceremonial law. It didn't mean eliminating God's *moral* law (the Ten Commandments). The ceremonial law prepared people for Christ's coming. With Christ's death and resurrection, that system was no longer needed. And through Christ we can fulfill the moral law as we let him live in us.

¹¹Day after day every priest stands and performs his religious duties; again and again he offers the same sacrifices, which can never take away sins. ʰ ¹²But when this priest had offered for all time one sacrifice for sins, he sat down at the right hand of God. ¹³Since that time he waits for his enemies to be made his footstool, ¹⁴because by one sacrifice he has made perfect ⁱ forever those who are being made holy.

¹⁵The Holy Spirit also testifies to us about this. First he says:

¹⁶ "This is the covenant I will make with them
        after that time, says the Lord.
    I will put my laws in their hearts,
        and I will write them on their minds."ᵃʲ

¹⁷Then he adds:

    "Their sins and lawless acts
        I will remember no more."ᵇ ᵏ

¹⁸And where these have been forgiven, there is no longer any sacrifice for sin.

10:11
ʰver 1, 4

10:14
ⁱver 1

10:16
ʲJer 31:33

10:17
ᵏHeb 8:12

B. THE SUPERIORITY OF FAITH (10:19—13:25)

Moving from argument to instruction, the author cites many examples of those who have demonstrated faith throughout history. Living by faith is far better than merely fulfilling rituals and rules. This can challenge us to grow in faith and to live in obedience to God each day.

A Call to Persevere

¹⁹Therefore, brothers, since we have confidence to enter the Most Holy Place ˡ by the blood of Jesus, ²⁰by a new and living way opened for us through the curtain, ᵐ that is, his body, ²¹and since we have a great priest over the house of God, ²²let us draw near to God with a sincere heart in full assurance of faith, having our hearts sprinkled to cleanse us from a guilty conscienceⁿ and having our bodies washed with pure water. ²³Let us hold unswervingly to the hope we profess, for he who promised is faithful. ᵒ ²⁴And let us consider how we may spur one another on toward love and good deeds. ²⁵Let us not give up meeting

10:19
ˡEph 2:18
10:20
ᵐHeb 9:3
10:22
ⁿEze 36:25
10:23
ᵒ1Co 1:9

ᵃ16 Jer. 31:33   ᵇ17 Jer. 31:34

10:11, 12 Christ's work is contrasted with the work of the Jewish priests. The priests' work was never finished, so they always had to stand and offer sacrifices; Christ's sacrifice (dying in our place) is finished, so he is seated. The priests repeated the sacrifices often; Christ sacrificed once for all. The sacrifice system couldn't completely remove sin; Christ's sacrifice effectively cleansed us.

10:12 If the Jewish readers of this book were to return to the old Jewish system, they would be implying that Christ's sacrifice wasn't enough to forgive their sins. Adding anything to his sacrifice or taking anything from it denies its validity. Any system to gain salvation through good deeds is essentially rejecting the significance of Christ's death and spurning the Holy Spirit's work. Beware of anyone who tells you that Christ's sacrifice still leaves you incomplete or that something else is needed to make you acceptable to God. When we believe in Christ, he makes us completely right with God. Our loving relationship leads us to follow him in willing obedience and service. He is pleased with our service, but we cannot be saved by our good deeds.

10:14 We have been made perfect, yet we are "being made holy." Through his death and resurrection, Christ, once for all, made us believers perfect in God's sight. At the same time, he is making them holy (progressively cleansed and set apart for his special use) in their daily pilgrimage here. We should not be surprised, ashamed, or shocked that we still need to grow. God is not finished with us. We can encourage this growth process by deliberately applying Scripture to all areas of our lives, by accepting the discipline and guidance Christ provides, and by giving him control of our desires and goals.

10:17 The writer concludes his argument with this powerful statement that God will never again remember our sins. Christ

forgives completely, so there is no need to confess our past sins repeatedly. As believers, we can be confident that the sins we confess and renounce are forgiven and forgotten.

10:19 The Most Holy Place in the temple was sealed from view by a curtain (10:20). Only the high priest could enter this holy room, and he did so only once a year on the Day of Atonement when he offered the sacrifice for the nation's sins. But Jesus' death removed the curtain, and all believers may walk into God's presence at any time (see also 6:19, 20).

10:21, 22 How is it possible for us to go right into the presence of God? We come not halfheartedly or with improper motives or pretense, but with pure, individual, and sincere worship. We can know that we have sincere hearts if we evaluate our thoughts and motives according to his Word (see 4:12). Christians can approach God boldly, free from our guilty consciences and in full assurance because of the work of Jesus Christ. We can go to God without doubting, knowing that he will hear and answer us. Under the new covenant, our hearts and consciences are cleansed completely, not partially or temporarily (see 9:14). Our clean consciences allow us to enter God's presence with boldness. Finally, the imagery of our bodies having been "washed with pure water" actually pictures an inward cleansing. Just as baptism is an outward sign that represents the purification that Christ does inside us, so this washing speaks of an internal cleansing from sin. Once cleansed, we can approach God.

10:22–25 We have significant privileges associated with our new life in Christ: (1) We have personal access to God through Christ and can draw near to him without an elaborate system (10:22); (2) we may grow in faith, overcome doubts and questions, and deepen our relationship with God (10:23); (3) we may enjoy motivation from one another (10:24); (4) we may worship together (10:25).

10:25
p Ac 2:42

10:26
q Nu 15:30;
2Pe 2:20

10:27
r Isa 26:11

10:28
s Heb 2:2

10:29
t Heb 6:6
u Eph 4:30

10:30
v Dt 32:35
w Dt 32:36

10:32
x Heb 6:4
y Php 1:29, 30

10:33
z 1Co 4:9
a Php 4:14

10:38
b Ro 1:17; Gal 3:11

together,*p* as some are in the habit of doing, but let us encourage one another—and all the more as you see the Day approaching.

26 If we deliberately keep on sinning*q* after we have received the knowledge of the truth, no sacrifice for sins is left, 27 but only a fearful expectation of judgment and of raging fire*r* that will consume the enemies of God. 28 Anyone who rejected the law of Moses died without mercy on the testimony of two or three witnesses.*s* 29 How much more severely do you think a man deserves to be punished who has trampled the Son of God under foot,*t* who has treated as an unholy thing the blood of the covenant that sanctified him, and who has insulted the Spirit*u* of grace? 30 For we know him who said, "It is mine to avenge; I will repay,"*a v* and again, "The Lord will judge his people."*b w* 31 It is a dreadful thing to fall into the hands of the living God.

32 Remember those earlier days after you had received the light,*x* when you stood your ground in a great contest in the face of suffering.*y* 33 Sometimes you were publicly exposed to insult and persecution;*z* at other times you stood side by side with those who were so treated.*a* 34 You sympathized with those in prison and joyfully accepted the confiscation of your property, because you knew that you yourselves had better and lasting possessions.

35 So do not throw away your confidence; it will be richly rewarded. 36 You need to persevere so that when you have done the will of God, you will receive what he has promised. 37 For in just a very little while,

"He who is coming will come and will not delay.
38   But my righteous one*c* will live by faith.*b*
And if he shrinks back,
      I will not be pleased with him."*d*

39 But we are not of those who shrink back and are destroyed, but of those who believe and are saved.

a 30 Deut. 32:35   *b 30* Deut. 32:36; Psalm 135:14   *c 38* One early manuscript *But the righteous*   *d 38* Hab. 2:3,4

10:25 To neglect Christian meetings is to give up the encouragement and help of other Christians. We gather together to share our faith and to strengthen one another in the Lord. As we get closer to the "Day" when Christ will return, we will face many spiritual struggles, and even times of persecution. Anti-Christian forces will grow in strength. Difficulties should never be excuses for missing church services. Rather, as difficulties arise, we should make an even greater effort to be faithful in attendance.

10:26 When people deliberately reject Christ's offer of salvation, they reject God's most precious gift. They ignore the leading of the Holy Spirit, the one who communicates to us God's saving love. This warning was given to Jewish Christians who were tempted to reject Christ for Judaism, but it applies to anyone who rejects Christ for another religion or, having understood Christ's atoning work, deliberately turns away from it (see also Numbers 15:30, 31 and Mark 3:28–30). The point is that there is no other acceptable sacrifice for sin than the death of Christ on the cross. If someone deliberately rejects the sacrifice of Christ after clearly understanding the gospel teaching about it, then there is no way for that person to be saved, because God has not provided any other name under heaven by which we can be saved (see Acts 4:12).

10:29 How have people insulted the Holy Spirit? The sacrifice of Christ is tied with the Holy Spirit; therefore, to scorn Christ's sacrifice is to insult the Holy Spirit by arrogantly rejecting him. The Holy Spirit is a person, not just a force or influence. To reject him is to cut off the means of God's acceptance. This is equivalent to blasphemy against the Holy Spirit (see Matthew 12:31, 32). Deserving of great punishment are those who insult the Holy Spirit who brings God's mercy.

10:31 God's power is awesome, and his punishment terrible. These words give us a glimpse into the holiness of God. He is sovereign; his power is unlimited; he will do as he promises. This judgment is for those who have rejected God's mercy. For them, falling into God's hands will be a dreadful experience. They will have no more excuses. They will discover that they were wrong, but it will be too late. For those who accept Christ's love and accept his salvation, however, the coming judgment is no cause for worry. Being saved through his grace, they have nothing to fear (see 1 John 4:18).

10:32–36 Hebrews encourages believers to persevere in their Christian faith and conduct when facing persecution and pressure. We don't usually think of suffering as good for us, but it can build our character and our patience. During times of great stress, we may feel God's presence more clearly and find help from Christians we never thought would care. Knowing that Jesus is with us in our suffering and that he will return one day to put an end to all pain helps us grow in our faith and our relationship with him (see Romans 5:3–5).

10:35–38 The Bible gives us a clear choice between two life directions. Because life often forks off in two directions, you must take the higher road, even though it looks more difficult and treacherous. That road gets steep in places. The climb takes a toll on your energy. It gets lonely. Not many on it, but more than you imagined, and some because of your example. It gets slippery; Satan blows ice on the narrow passages. Despite its dangers, the higher road is bound for the peak, and you'll make it—God has a lifeline around you. When you are tempted to falter in your faith or to turn back from following Christ, keep focused on what he has done for you and what he offers in the future (see Romans 8:12–25; Galatians 3:10–13). Then keep climbing.

10:36 For the time being, these believers needed patient endurance, that is, to persevere, to hold firm. Because Christ lives in us, we can have that kind of perseverance. Jesus predicted that his followers would be severely persecuted by those who hated him (Matthew 10:22). In the midst of terrible persecution, they could have hope, however, knowing that salvation was theirs. Times of trial serve to sift true Christians from false or fair-weather Christians. When you are pressured to give up and turn your back on Christ, remember the benefits of standing firm and continue to live for Christ. Perseverance is not a way to be saved but the evidence that you are really committed to Jesus.

By Faith

11 Now faith is being sure of what we hope for and certain of what we do not see.[c] 2 This is what the ancients were commended for.[d]

3 By faith we understand that the universe was formed at God's command,[e] so that what is seen was not made out of what was visible.

4 By faith Abel offered God a better sacrifice than Cain did. By faith he was commended as a righteous man, when God spoke well of his offerings.[f] And by faith he still speaks, even though he is dead.

5 By faith Enoch was taken from this life, so that he did not experience death; he could not be found, because God had taken him away.[g] For before he was taken, he was commended as one who pleased God. 6 And without faith it is impossible to please God, because anyone who comes to him must believe that he exists and that he rewards those who earnestly seek him.

7 By faith Noah, when warned about things not yet seen, in holy fear built an ark[h] to save his family. By his faith he condemned the world and became heir of the righteousness that comes by faith.

8 By faith Abraham, when called to go to a place he would later receive as his inheritance, obeyed and went,[i] even though he did not know where he was going. 9 By faith he made his home in the promised land like a stranger in a foreign country; he lived in tents,[j] as did Isaac and Jacob, who were heirs with him of the same promise.[k] 10 For he was looking forward to the city[l] with foundations, whose architect and builder is God.

11 By faith Abraham, even though he was past age—and Sarah herself was barren[m]—was enabled to become a father because he[a] considered him faithful who had made the promise. 12 And so from this one man, and he as good as dead,[n] came descendants as numerous as the stars in the sky and as countless as the sand on the seashore.

[a] 11 Or *By faith even Sarah, who was past age, was enabled to bear children because she*

11:1 [c] 2Co 4:18
11:2 [d] ver 4, 39
11:3 [e] Ge 1
11:4 [f] Ge 4:4; 1Jn 3:12
11:5 [g] Ge 5:21-24
11:7 [h] Ge 6:13-22
11:8 [i] Ge 12:1-4; Ac 7:2-4
11:9 [j] Ge 12:8 [k] Heb 6:17
11:10 [l] Heb 12:22
11:11 [m] Ge 17:17-19; 18:11-14
11:12 [n] Ro 4:19

11:1 Do you remember how you felt when you were very young and your birthday approached? You were excited and anxious. You knew you would certainly receive gifts and other special treats. But some things would be a surprise. Birthdays combine assurance and anticipation, and so does faith! Faith is the confidence based on past experience that God's new and fresh surprises will surely be ours.

11:1 Two words describe faith: *sure* and *certain*. These two qualities need a secure beginning and ending point. The beginning point of faith is believing in God's character—he *is* who he says. The end point is believing in God's promises—he will *do* what he says. When we believe that God will fulfill his promises even though we don't see those promises materializing yet, we demonstrate true faith (see John 20:24–31).

11:3 God called the universe into existence out of nothing; he declared that it was to be, and it was. Our faith is in the God who created the entire universe by his word. God's word has awesome power. When he speaks, do you listen and respond? How can you better prepare yourself to respond to God's word?

11:4 Cain and Abel were Adam and Eve's first two sons. Abel offered a sacrifice that pleased God, while Cain's sacrifice was unacceptable. Abel's Profile is found in Genesis 6, p. 15. Cain's Profile is in Genesis 7, p. 17. Abel's sacrifice (an animal substitute) was more acceptable to God, both because it was a blood sacrifice and, most important, because of Abel's attitude when he offered it.

11:6 Believing that God exists is only the beginning; even the demons believe that much (James 2:19, 20). God will not settle for mere acknowledgment of his existence. He wants your faith to lead to a personal, dynamic relationship.

But does faith make sense, really? Do you believe because faith makes sense, or because faith doesn't need to make sense? Some Christians think people cannot understand God and should not try. Others believe that nothing true is irrational, including true faith. The truth is, God gave us minds that should be developed and used. To ignore intellectual growth is to live a stunted and naive life. God wants our trust and faith, even while we

ponder and wonder about so many matters mysterious to us. Even so, we do not believe in a void nor leap into the dark. Faith is reasonable, though reason alone cannot explain the whole of it. So use your mind to think things through. But leave room for the unexplainable works of God.

11:6 Sometimes we wonder about the fate of those who haven't heard of Christ and have not even had a Bible to read. God assures us that all who honestly seek him—who act in faith on the knowledge of God that they possess—will be rewarded. When you tell others the gospel, encourage them to be honest and diligent in their search for truth. Those who hear the gospel are responsible for what they have heard (see 2 Corinthians 6:1, 2).

11:7 Noah experienced rejection because he was different from his neighbors. God commanded him to build a huge boat in the middle of dry land, and although God's command seemed foolish, Noah obeyed. Noah's obedience made him appear strange to his neighbors, just as the new beliefs of Jewish Christians undoubtedly made them stand out. As you obey God, don't be surprised if others regard you as "different." Your obedience makes their disobedience stand out. Remember, if God asks you to do something, he will give you the necessary strength to carry out that task. For more information on Noah, see his Profile in Genesis 8, p. 19.

11:8–10 Abraham's life was filled with faith. At God's command, he left home and went to another land—obeying without question (Genesis 12:1ff). He believed the covenant that God made with him (Genesis 12:2, 3; 13:14–16; 15:1–6). In obedience to God, Abraham was even willing to sacrifice his son Isaac (Genesis 22:1–19). Do not be surprised if God asks you to give up secure, familiar surroundings in order to carry out his will. For further information on Abraham, see his Profile in Genesis 18, p. 33.

11:11, 12 Sarah was Abraham's wife. They were unable to have children through many years of their marriage. God promised Abraham a son, but Sarah doubted that she could become pregnant in her old age. At first she laughed, but afterwards, she believed (Genesis 18). For more information on Sarah, see her Profile in Genesis 19, p. 35.

11:13
o Ge 23:4

¹³All these people were still living by faith when they died. They did not receive the things promised; they only saw them and welcomed them from a distance. And they admitted that they were aliens and strangers on earth. *o* ¹⁴People who say such things show that they are looking for a country of their own. ¹⁵If they had been thinking of the country they had left, they would have had opportunity to return. ¹⁶Instead, they were longing for a better country—a heavenly one. Therefore God is not ashamed to be called their God,*p* for he has prepared a city for them.

11:16
p Ex 3:6, 15

11:17
q Ge 22:1-10

¹⁷By faith Abraham, when God tested him, offered Isaac as a sacrifice. *q* He who had received the promises was about to sacrifice his one and only son, ¹⁸even though God had said to him, "It is through Isaac that your offspring*a* will be reckoned."*b* *r* ¹⁹Abraham reasoned that God could raise the dead, and figuratively speaking, he did receive Isaac back from death.

11:18
r Ge 21:12

²⁰By faith Isaac blessed Jacob and Esau in regard to their future.

²¹By faith Jacob, when he was dying, blessed each of Joseph's sons, and worshiped as he leaned on the top of his staff.

11:22
s Ge 50:24, 25

²²By faith Joseph, when his end was near, spoke about the exodus of the Israelites from Egypt and gave instructions about his bones. *s*

11:23
t Ex 2:2
u Ex 1:16, 22

²³By faith Moses' parents hid him for three months after he was born,*t* because they saw he was no ordinary child, and they were not afraid of the king's edict. *u*

11:24
v Ex 2:10, 11

²⁴By faith Moses, when he had grown up, refused to be known as the son of Pharaoh's daughter. *v* ²⁵He chose to be mistreated along with the people of God rather than to enjoy the pleasures of sin for a short time. ²⁶He regarded disgrace *w* for the sake of Christ as of

11:26
w Heb 13:13

a 18 Greek *seed*   *b 18* Gen. 21:12

11:13 That we are "aliens and strangers" on earth may be an awareness forced on us by circumstances. It may come late in life or as the result of difficult times. But this world is not our home. We cannot live here forever (see also 1 Peter 1:1). It is best for us not to be so attached to this world's desires and possessions that we can't move out at God's command.

11:13–16 These people of faith died without receiving all that God had promised, but they never lost their vision of heaven ("a better country—a heavenly one"). Many Christians become frustrated and defeated because their needs, wants, expectations, and demands are not immediately met when they believe in Christ. They become impatient and want to quit. Are you discouraged because the achievement of your goal seems far away? Take courage from these heroes of faith who lived and died without seeing the fruit of their faith on earth and yet continued to believe (see 11:36–39).

11:17–19 Abraham was willing to give up his son when God commanded him to do so (Genesis 22:1–19). God did not let Abraham take Isaac's life, because God had given the command in order to test Abraham's faith. Instead of taking Abraham's son, God gave Abraham a whole nation of descendants through Isaac. If you are afraid to trust God with your most prized possession, dream, or person, pay attention to Abraham's example. Because Abraham was willing to give up everything for God, he received back more than he could have imagined. What we receive, however, is not always immediate, or in the form of material possessions. Material things should be among the least satisfying of rewards. Our best and greatest rewards await us in eternity.

11:20 Isaac was the son who had been promised to Abraham and Sarah in their old age. It was through Isaac that God fulfilled his promise to eventually give Abraham countless descendants. Isaac had twin sons, Jacob and Esau. God chose the younger son, Jacob, through whom to continue the fulfillment of his promise to Abraham. For more information on Isaac, see his Profile in Genesis 22, p. 39.

11:21 Jacob was Isaac's son and Abraham's grandson. Jacob's sons became the fathers of Israel's 12 tribes. Even when Jacob (also called "Israel") was dying in a strange land, he believed the promise that Abraham's descendants would be like the sand on the seashore and that Israel would become a great nation (Genesis 48:1–22). True faith helps us see beyond the grave. For more information on Jacob and Esau, see their Profiles in Genesis 26, p. 49 and 27, p. 51.

11:22 Joseph, one of Jacob's sons, was sold into slavery by his jealous brothers (Genesis 37). Eventually, Joseph was sold again, this time to an official of the Pharaoh of Egypt. Because of Joseph's faithfulness to God, however, he was given a top-ranking position in Egypt. Although Joseph could have used that position to build a personal empire, he remembered God's promise to Abraham. After he had been reconciled to his brothers, Joseph brought his family to be near him and requested that his bones be taken to the promised land when the Jews eventually left Egypt (Genesis 50:24, 25). Faith means trusting in God and doing what he wants, regardless of the circumstances or consequences. For more information on Joseph, see his Profile in Genesis 37, p. 71.

11:23 Moses' parents trusted God to protect their son's life. They were not merely proud parents; they were believers who had faith that God would care for him. As a parent, have you trusted God enough to take care of your children? God has a plan for every person, and your important task is to pray for your children and prepare them to do the work God has planned for them to do. Faith allows us to entrust even our children to God.

11:24–28 Moses became one of Israel's greatest leaders, a prophet, and a lawgiver. But when he was born, his people were slaves in Egypt, and the Egyptian officials had ordered that all Hebrew baby boys were to be killed. Moses was spared, however, and Pharaoh's daughter raised Moses in Pharaoh's own household (Exodus 1; 2)! It took faith for Moses to give up his place in the palace, but he could do it because he saw the fleeting nature of great wealth and prestige. It is easy to be deceived by the temporary benefits of wealth, popularity, status, and achievement, and to be blind to the long-range benefits of God's kingdom. Faith helps us look beyond the world's value system to see the eternal values of God's kingdom. For more information on Moses, see his Profile in Exodus 14, p. 117.

11:26 True wealth is eternal. Consider the most powerful or well-known people in our world—how many got where they are by being humble, self-effacing, and gentle? Not many! But in the life to come, the last will be first—if they got in last place by choosing to follow Jesus. Hebrews has a critical message for earth-loving Christians. Don't forfeit eternal rewards for temporary benefits. Like Moses, be willing to make sacrifices now for greater rewards later (Matthew 6:19–21).

greater value than the treasures of Egypt, because he was looking ahead to his reward. 27 By faith he left Egypt,ˣ not fearing the king's anger; he persevered because he saw him who is invisible. 28 By faith he kept the Passover and the sprinkling of blood, so that the destroyer of the firstborn would not touch the firstborn of Israel.ʸ

29 By faith the people passed through the Red Seaᵃ as on dry land; but when the Egyptians tried to do so, they were drowned. ᶻ

30 By faith the walls of Jericho fell, after the people had marched around them for seven days.

31 By faith the prostitute Rahab, because she welcomed the spies, was not killed with those who were disobedient.ᵇ ᵃ

32 And what more shall I say? I do not have time to tell about Gideon, Barak, Samson, Jephthah, David, Samuel and the prophets, 33 who through faith conquered kingdoms,ᵇ administered justice, and gained what was promised; who shut the mouths of lions,ᶜ 34 quenched the fury of the flames, and escaped the edge of the sword; whose weakness was turned to strength; and who became powerful in battle and routed foreign armies. ᵈ 35 Women received back their dead, raised to life again.ᵉ Others were tortured and refused to be released, so that they might gain a better resurrection. 36 Some faced jeers and flogging, ᶠ while still others were chained and put in prison. 37 They were stonedᶜ; they were sawed in two; they were put to death by the sword. They went about in sheepskins and goatskins, ᵍ destitute, persecuted and mistreated— 38 the world was not worthy of them. They wandered in deserts and mountains, and in cavesʰ and holes in the ground.

39 These were all commended for their faith, yet none of them received what had been promised. 40 God had planned something better for us so that only together with us would they be made perfect.

God Disciplines His Sons

12 Therefore, since we are surrounded by such a great cloud of witnesses, let us throw off everything that hinders and the sin that so easily entangles, and let us runⁱ with

ᵃ29 That is, Sea of Reeds   ᵇ31 Or *unbelieving*   ᶜ37 Some early manuscripts *stoned; they were put to the test;*

11:27 ˣEx 12:50, 51

11:28 ʸEx 12:21-23

11:29 ᶻEx 14:21-31

11:31 ᵃJos 6:22-25

11:33 ᵇ2Sa 7:11 ᶜDa 6:22

11:34 ᵈJdg 15:8

11:35 ᵉ1Ki 17:22, 23

11:36 ᶠJer 20:2

11:37 ᵍ2Ki 1:8

11:38 ʰ1Ki 18:4

12:1 ⁱ1Co 9:24

11:31 When Joshua planned the conquest of Jericho, he sent spies to investigate the fortifications of the city. The spies met Rahab, who had two strikes against her—she was a Gentile and a prostitute. But she showed that she had faith in God by welcoming the spies and by trusting God to spare her and her family when the city was destroyed. Faith helps us turn around and do what is right regardless of our past or the disapproval of others. For more information on Rahab, see her Profile in Joshua 3, p. 309.

11:32-35 The Old Testament records the lives of the various people who experienced these great victories. Joshua and Deborah conquered kingdoms (the book of Joshua; Judges 4; 5). Nehemiah administered justice (the book of Nehemiah). Daniel was saved from the mouths of lions (Daniel 6). Shadrach, Meshach, and Abednego were kept from harm in the furious flames of a fiery furnace (Daniel 3). Elijah escaped the edge of the swords of evil Queen Jezebel's henchmen (1 Kings 19:2ff). Hezekiah regained strength after sickness (2 Kings 20). Gideon was powerful in battle (Judges 7). A widow's son was brought back to life by the prophet Elisha (2 Kings 4:8–37).

We, too, can experience victory through faith in Christ. Our victories over oppressors may be like those of the Old Testament saints, but more likely, our victories will be directly related to the role God wants us to play. Even though our bodies deteriorate and die, we will live forever because of Christ. In the promised resurrection, even death will be defeated and Christ's victory will be made complete.

11:32-40 These verses summarize the lives of other great men and women of faith. Some experienced outstanding victories, even over the threat of death. But others were severely mistreated, tortured, and even killed. Having a steadfast faith in God does not guarantee a happy, carefree life. On the contrary, our faith almost guarantees us some form of abuse from the world. While we are on earth, we may never see the purpose of our suffering. But we know

that God will keep his promises to us. Do you believe that God will keep his promises to you?

11:35–39 Many think that pain is the exception in the Christian life. When suffering occurs, they say, "Why me?" They feel as though God deserted them, or perhaps they accuse him of not being as dependable as they thought. In reality, however, we live in an evil world filled with suffering, even for believers. But God is still in control. He allows some Christians to become martyrs for the faith, and he allows others to survive persecution. Rather than asking, "Why me?" it is much more helpful to ask, "Why not me?" Our faith and the values of this world are on a collision course. If we expect pain and suffering to come, we will not be shocked when it hits. But we can also take comfort in knowing that Jesus also suffered. He understands our fears, our weaknesses, and our disappointments (see 2:16–18; 4:14–16). He promised never to leave us (Matthew 28:18–20), and he intercedes on our behalf (7:24, 25). In times of pain, persecution, or suffering we should trust confidently in Christ.

11:39, 40 Hebrews 11 has been called faith's hall of fame. No doubt the author surprised his readers by this conclusion: these mighty Jewish heroes did not receive all that God had promised because they died before Christ came. In God's plan, they and the Christian believers (who were also enduring much testing) would be rewarded together. Once again Hebrews shows that Christianity offers a better way than Judaism.

11:40 There is a solidarity among believers (see 12:23). Old and New Testament believers will be glorified together. Not only are we one in the body of Christ with all those alive, but we are also one with all those who ever lived. It takes all of us to be perfect in him.

12:1 This "great cloud of witnesses" is composed of the people described in chapter 11. Their faithfulness is a constant encouragement to us. We do not struggle alone, and we are not the first to struggle with the problems we face. Others have run the race

12:2
j Php 2:8, 9

12:3
k Gal 6:9

perseverance the race marked out for us. ²Let us fix our eyes on Jesus, the author and perfecter of our faith, who for the joy set before him endured the cross,*j* scorning its shame, and sat down at the right hand of the throne of God. ³Consider him who endured such opposition from sinful men, so that you will not grow weary *k* and lose heart.

⁴In your struggle against sin, you have not yet resisted to the point of shedding your blood. ⁵And you have forgotten that word of encouragement that addresses you as sons:

> "My son, do not make light of the Lord's discipline,
>   and do not lose heart when he rebukes you,

12:6
l Ps 94:12

> ⁶ because the Lord disciplines those he loves,*l*
>   and he punishes everyone he accepts as a son."*a*

12:7
m Dt 8:5

12:8
n 1Pe 5:9

12:9
o Nu 16:22
p Isa 38:16

12:11
q Jas 3:17, 18

12:13
r Pr 4:26
s Gal 6:1

⁷Endure hardship as discipline; God is treating you as sons. *m* For what son is not disciplined by his father? ⁸If you are not disciplined (and everyone undergoes discipline),*n* then you are illegitimate children and not true sons. ⁹Moreover, we have all had human fathers who disciplined us and we respected them for it. How much more should we submit to the Father of our spirits*o* and live!*p* ¹⁰Our fathers disciplined us for a little while as they thought best; but God disciplines us for our good, that we may share in his holiness. ¹¹No discipline seems pleasant at the time, but painful. Later on, however, it produces a harvest of righteousness and peace *q* for those who have been trained by it.

¹²Therefore, strengthen your feeble arms and weak knees. ¹³"Make level paths for your feet,"*b r* so that the lame may not be disabled, but rather healed. *s*

Warning Against Refusing God

12:14
t Mt 5:8

12:15
u Gal 5:4

¹⁴Make every effort to live in peace with all men and to be holy; without holiness no one will see the Lord. *t* ¹⁵See to it that no one misses the grace of God *u* and that no bitter root

a6 Prov. 3:11,12   *b13* Prov. 4:26

---

and won, and their witness stirs us to run and win also. What an inspiring heritage we have!

12:1 Long-distance runners work hard to build endurance and strength. On race day, their clothes are lightweight and their bodies lean. To run the race that God has set before us, we must also strip off the excess weight that slows us down. How can we do that? (1) Choose friends who are also committed to the race. Wrong friends will have values and activities that may deter you from the course. Much of your own weight may result from the crowd you run with. Make wise choices. (2) Drop certain activities. That is, for you at this time these may be weight. Try dropping them for a while; then check the results in your life. (3) Get help for addictions that disable you. If you have a secret "weight" such as pornography, gambling, or alcohol, admit your need and get help today.

12:1–4 The Christian life involves hard work. It requires us to give up whatever endangers our relationship with God, to run with endurance, and to struggle against sin with the power of the Holy Spirit. To live effectively, we must keep our eyes on Jesus. We will stumble if we look away from him to stare at ourselves or at the circumstances surrounding us. We should be running for Christ, not ourselves, and we must always keep him in sight.

12:3 When we face hardship and discouragement, it is easy to lose sight of the big picture. But we're not alone; there is help. Many have already made it through life, enduring far more difficult circumstances than we have experienced. Suffering is the training ground for Christian maturity. It develops our patience and makes our final victory sweet.

12:4 These readers were facing difficult times of persecution, but none of them had yet died for their faith. Because they were still alive, the writer urged them to continue to run their race. Just as Christ did not give up, neither should they.

12:5–11 Who loves his child more—the father who allows the child to do what will harm him, or the one who corrects, trains, and even punishes the child to help him learn what is right? It's never pleasant to be corrected and disciplined by God, but his discipline is a sign of his deep love for us. When God corrects

you, see it as proof of his love and ask him what he is trying to teach you.

12:11 We may respond to discipline in several ways: (1) We can accept it with resignation; (2) we can accept it with self-pity, thinking we really don't deserve it; (3) we can be angry and resentful toward God; or (4) we can accept it gratefully, as the appropriate response we owe a loving Father.

12:12, 13 God is not only a disciplining parent but also a demanding coach who pushes us to our limits and requires our lives to be disciplined. Although we may not feel strong enough to push on to victory, we will be able to accomplish it as we follow Christ and draw on his strength. Then we can use our growing strength to help those around us who are weak and struggling.

12:12, 13 The word *therefore* is a clue that what follows is important! We must not live with only our own survival in mind. Others will follow our example, and we have a responsibility to them if we are living for Christ, as we claim to be. Does your example make it easier for others to believe in and follow Christ, and to mature in him? Or would those who follow you end up confused and misled?

12:14 The readers were familiar with the ceremonial cleansing ritual that prepared them for worship, and they knew that they had to be holy or clean in order to enter the temple. Sin always blocks our vision of God; so if we want to see God, we must renounce sin and obey him (see Psalm 24:3, 4). Holiness is coupled with living in peace. A right relationship with God leads to right relationships with fellow believers. Although we will not always feel loving toward all other believers, we must pursue peace as we become more Christlike.

12:15 Like a small root that grows into a great tree, bitterness springs up in our hearts and overshadows even our deepest Christian relationships. A "bitter root" comes when we allow disappointment to grow into resentment, or when we nurse grudges over past hurts. Bitterness brings with it jealousy, dissension, and immorality. When the Holy Spirit fills us, however, he can heal the hurt that causes bitterness.

grows up to cause trouble and defile many. [16]See that no one is sexually immoral, or is godless like Esau, who for a single meal sold his inheritance rights as the oldest son. [v] [17]Afterward, as you know, when he wanted to inherit this blessing, he was rejected. He could bring about no change of mind, though he sought the blessing with tears. [w]

[18]You have not come to a mountain that can be touched and that is burning with fire; to darkness, gloom and storm; [x] [19]to a trumpet blast or to such a voice speaking words that those who heard it begged that no further word be spoken to them, [y] [20]because they could not bear what was commanded: "If even an animal touches the mountain, it must be stoned." [a z] [21]The sight was so terrifying that Moses said, "I am trembling with fear." [b]

[22]But you have come to Mount Zion, to the heavenly Jerusalem, [a] the city of the living God. You have come to thousands upon thousands of angels in joyful assembly, [23]to the church of the firstborn, whose names are written in heaven. You have come to God, the judge of all men, to the spirits of righteous men made perfect, [b] [24]to Jesus the mediator of a new covenant, and to the sprinkled blood that speaks a better word than the blood of Abel.

[25]See to it that you do not refuse him who speaks. If they did not escape when they refused him who warned them on earth, how much less will we, if we turn away from him who warns us from heaven? [c] [26]At that time his voice shook the earth, [d] but now he has promised, "Once more I will shake not only the earth but also the heavens." [c e] [27]The words "once more" indicate the removing of what can be shaken—that is, created things—so that what cannot be shaken may remain.

[28]Therefore, since we are receiving a kingdom that cannot be shaken, let us be thankful, and so worship God acceptably with reverence and awe, [29]for our "God is a consuming fire." [d f]

Concluding Exhortations

13 Keep on loving each other as brothers. [g] [2]Do not forget to entertain strangers, for by so doing some people have entertained angels without knowing it. [h] [3]Remember those in prison [i] as if you were their fellow prisoners, and those who are mistreated as if you yourselves were suffering.

[a]20 Exodus 19:12,13   [b]21 Deut. 9:19   [c]26 Haggai 2:6   [d]29 Deut. 4:24

### Cross references (margin)

12:16
[v]Ge 25:29-34

12:17
[w]Ge 27:30-40

12:18
[x]Dt 4:11

12:19
[y]Ex 20:19

12:20
[z]Ex 19:12, 13

12:22
[a]Gal 4:26

12:23
[b]Php 3:12

12:25
[c]Heb 2:2, 3

12:26
[d]Ex 19:18
[e]Hag 2:6

12:29
[f]Dt 4:24

13:1
[g]Ro 12:10

13:2
[h]Ge 18:1-33

13:3
[i]Col 4:18

12:16, 17 Esau's story shows us that mistakes and sins sometimes have lasting consequences (Genesis 25:29–34; 27:36). Even repentance and forgiveness do not always eliminate sins consequences. How often do you make decisions based on what you want now, rather than on what you need in the long run? Evaluate the long-range effects of your decisions and actions.

12:18–24 What a contrast between the people's terrified approach to God at Mount Sinai and their joyful approach at Mount Zion! What a difference Jesus has made! Before Jesus came, God seemed distant and threatening. After Jesus came, God welcomes us through Christ into his presence. Accept God's invitation!

12:22 As Christians, we are citizens of the heavenly Jerusalem right now, because Christ rules our lives, the Holy Spirit is always with us, and we experience close fellowship with other believers. The full and ultimate rewards and reality of the heavenly Jerusalem are depicted in Revelation 21.

12:27–29 Eventually the world will crumble, and only God's kingdom will last. Those who follow Christ are part of this unshakable kingdom, and they will withstand the shaking, sifting, and burning. When we feel unsure about the future, we can take confidence from these verses. No matter what happens here, our future is built on a solid foundation that cannot be destroyed. Don't put your confidence in what will be destroyed; instead, build your life on Christ and his unshakable kingdom. (See Matthew 7:24–29 for the importance of building on a solid foundation.)

12:28 Here are five ways we can be thankful: (1) We can be thankful that God answers our prayers (Isaiah 65:24; John 11:41). (2) We can be thankful for God's provision for our needs (1 Thessalonians 5:17, 18; 1 Timothy 4:4, 5). (3) We can be thankful for God's blessings (1 Chronicles 16:34; Philippians 4:6). (4) We can be thankful for God's character and wondrous works (Psalm 7:17; 2 Corinthians 9:15; Revelation 11:17). (5) We can be

thankful for our brothers and sisters in Christ (1 Corinthians 1:4; Ephesians 1:16; Philippians 1:3–5).

12:29 There is a big difference between the flame of a candle and the roaring blast of a forest fire. We cannot even stand near a raging fire. Even with sophisticated fire-fighting equipment, a consuming fire is often beyond human control. God is not within our control either. We cannot force him to do anything for us through our prayers. He cannot be contained. Yet, he is a God of compassion. He has saved us from sin, and he will save us from death. But everything that is worthless and sinful will be consumed by the fire of his wrath. Only what is good, dedicated to God, and righteous will remain.

13:1–5 Real love for others produces tangible actions: (1) kindness to strangers (13:2); (2) empathy for those who are in prison and those who have been mistreated (13:3); (3) respect for your marriage vows (13:4); and (4) contentment with what you have (13:5). Make sure that your love runs deep enough to affect your hospitality, empathy, fidelity, and contentment.

13:2 Three Old Testament people "entertained angels without knowing it": (1) Abraham (Genesis 18:1ff), (2) Gideon (Judges 6:11ff), and (3) Manoah (Judges 13:2ff). Some people say they cannot be hospitable because their homes are not large enough or nice enough. But even if you have no more than a table and two chairs in a rented room, there are people who would be grateful to spend time in your home. Are there visitors to your church with whom you could share a meal? Do you know single people who would enjoy an evening of conversation? Is there any way your home could meet the needs of traveling missionaries? Hospitality simply means making other people feel comfortable and at home.

13:3 We are to have empathy for those in prison, especially for (but not limited to) Christians imprisoned for their faith. Jesus said that his true followers would represent him as they visit

13:4
/ 1Co 6:9

13:5
k Php 4:11

4 Marriage should be honored by all, and the marriage bed kept pure, for God will judge the adulterer and all the sexually immoral. / 5 Keep your lives free from the love of money and be content with what you have, k because God has said,

"Never will I leave you;
     never will I forsake you." a

6 So we say with confidence,

"The Lord is my helper; I will not be afraid.
     What can man do to me?" b

13:7
/ ver 17, 24
m Heb 6:12

7 Remember your leaders, / who spoke the word of God to you. Consider the outcome of their way of life and imitate m their faith. 8 Jesus Christ is the same yesterday and today and forever.

13:9
n Eph 4:14

9 Do not be carried away by all kinds of strange teachings. n It is good for our hearts to be strengthened by grace, not by ceremonial foods, which are of no value to those who eat them. o 10 We have an altar from which those who minister at the tabernacle have no right to eat. o

13:10
o 1Co 9:13

13:11
p Ex 29:14

11 The high priest carries the blood of animals into the Most Holy Place as a sin offering, but the bodies are burned outside the camp. p 12 And so Jesus also suffered outside the city gate to make the people holy through his own blood. 13 Let us, then, go to him outside the camp, bearing the disgrace he bore. 14 For here we do not have an enduring city, but we are looking for the city that is to come. q

13:14
q Php 3:20

a 5 Deut. 31:6   b 6 Psalm 118:6,7

---

those in prison (Matthew 25:36). Prisons are a mission field— believers can send in evangelists and Bible teachers. Prison systems are political projects—Christian voices are needed regarding justice and mercy in funding, staff training, and rehabilitative programs. Prisons are an international problem— through multinational Christian agencies, believers can help victims in other countries. Compassion for suffering people demands no less. There is a wide open field of ways to obey this command to "remember those in prison."

13:4 Giving honor to marriage will require the utmost in Christian conviction and sensitivity. Modern social theory may redefine the family, and the new definitions may be far from its biblical foundation. What can you do? Witness to the depth of God's love for you by keeping your marriage happy and strong. Remain faithful—in body and in mind. Pray for your spouse. Honor biblical marriage (consenting man-woman unions) by resisting political pressure to recognize and legalize other sexual preferences. Teach children the biblical meaning of marriage. Pray early for their own eventual spouses and families. Make marriage enrichment the goal of your small group discussions and study. Encourage the marriages around you to stay strong as well.

13:5, 6 How can we learn to be content? Strive to live with less rather than desiring more; give away out of your abundance rather than accumulating more; relish what you have rather than resent what you're missing. We become content when we realize God's sufficiency for our needs. Christians who become materialistic are saying by their actions that God can't take care of them— or at least that he won't take care of them the way they want. Insecurity can lead to the love of money, whether we are rich or poor. The only antidote is to trust God to meet all our needs. See God's love expressed in what he has provided, and remember that money and possessions will all pass away. (See Philippians 4:11 for more on contentment, and 1 John 2:17 for the futility of earthly desires.)

13:7 If you are a Christian, you owe much to others who have taught you and modeled for you what you needed to know about the gospel and Christian living. Continue following the good examples of those who have invested themselves in you by investing your life through evangelism, service, and Christian education.

13:8 Though human leaders have much to offer, we must keep our eyes on Christ, our ultimate leader. Unlike any human leaders, he will never change. Christ has been and will be the same forever. In a changing world we can trust our unchanging Lord.

13:9 Apparently some were teaching that keeping the Old Testament ceremonial laws and rituals (such as not eating certain foods) was important to salvation. But these laws were useless for conquering a person's evil thoughts and desires (Colossians 2:23). The laws could influence conduct, but they could not change the heart. Lasting changes in conduct begin when the Holy Spirit lives in each person.

13:13 The Jewish Christians were being ridiculed and persecuted by Jews who didn't believe in Jesus the Messiah. Most of the book of Hebrews tells them how Christ is greater than the sacrificial system. Here the writer drives home the point of his lengthy argument: It may be necessary to leave the "camp" and suffer with Christ. To be outside the camp meant to be unclean— in the days of the exodus, those who were ceremonially unclean had to stay outside the camp. But Jesus suffered humiliation and uncleanness outside the Jerusalem gates on their behalf. The time had come for Jewish Christians to declare their loyalty to Christ above any other loyalty, to choose to follow the Messiah whatever suffering that might entail. They needed to move outside the safe confinement of their past, their traditions, and their ceremonies to live for Christ. What holds you back from complete loyalty to Jesus Christ?

13:14 Christians love their families, spouses, jobs, and churches—but their sights should be set ahead beyond the horizon. Christians are activists, invested in witnessing to a needy world—but they take frequent glances toward a promised community still to come. Christians are gardeners and builders, shaping environments, turning weed pits into floral splendor, painting and patching and clearing—but they know God is building something far more beautiful and breathtaking just for them. Christians should be characterized by looking forward to the future. We should not be attached to this world, because all that we are and have here is temporary. We should not love our present home so much that we lose sight of God's future blessing. Don't store up your treasures here; store them in heaven (Matthew 6:19–21).

¹⁵Through Jesus, therefore, let us continually offer to God a sacrifice of praise—the fruit of lips ʳ that confess his name. ¹⁶And do not forget to do good and to share with others, for with such sacrifices God is pleased.

¹⁷Obey your leaders and submit to their authority. They keep watch over you as men who must give an account. Obey them so that their work will be a joy, not a burden, for that would be of no advantage to you.

¹⁸Pray for us. ˢ We are sure that we have a clear conscience and desire to live honorably in every way. ¹⁹I particularly urge you to pray so that I may be restored to you soon. ᵗ

²⁰May the God of peace, ᵘ who through the blood of the eternal covenant ᵛ brought back from the dead our Lord Jesus, that great Shepherd of the sheep, ²¹equip you with everything good for doing his will, and may he work in us ʷ what is pleasing to him, through Jesus Christ, to whom be glory for ever and ever. Amen.

²²Brothers, I urge you to bear with my word of exhortation, for I have written you only a short letter. ˣ

²³I want you to know that our brother Timothy has been released. If he arrives soon, I will come with him to see you.

²⁴Greet all your leadersʸ and all God's people. Those from Italy send you their greetings.
²⁵Grace be with you all.

13:15 ʳHos 14:2

13:18 ˢ1Th 5:25
13:19 ᵗPhm 22
13:20 ᵘRo 15:33
ᵛZec 9:11
13:21 ʷPhp 2:13

13:22 ˣ1Pe 5:12

13:24 ʸver 7, 17

13:15 Our lips should confess God's name in praise. Yet, in your typical day, how many times do you hear God's name used profanely? Christians should turn their frequency toward praise! Praise God early in the day before the rush, then again in the hurried middle, and at the end as business winds down. Offer Jesus a continual sacrifice of praise.

13:15, 16 Since these Jewish Christians, because of their witness to the Messiah, no longer worshiped with other Jews, they should consider praise and acts of service their sacrifices— ones they could offer anywhere, anytime. This must have reminded them of the prophet Hosea's words, "Forgive all our sins and receive us graciously, that we may offer the fruit of our lips" (Hosea 14:2). A "sacrifice of praise" today would include thanking Christ for his sacrifice on the cross and telling others about it. Acts of kindness and sharing are particularly pleasing to God, even when they go unnoticed by others.

13:17 The task of church leaders is to help people mature in Christ. Cooperative followers greatly ease the burden of leadership. Does your conduct give your leaders reason to report joyfully about you?

13:18, 19 The writer recognizes the need for prayer. Christian leaders are especially vulnerable to criticism from others, pride (if they succeed), depression (if they fail), and Satan's constant

efforts to destroy their work for God. The leaders in your church have been placed in that position by a loving God who has entrusted them with the responsibility of caring for you. Your leaders need your prayers! For whom should you regularly pray?

13:21 This verse includes two significant results of Christ's death and resurrection. God works in us to make us the kind of people that would please him, and he equips us to do the kind of *work* that would please him. Let God change you from within and then use you to help others.

13:23 We have no record of Timothy's imprisonment, but we know that he had been in prison because it states here that he had been released. For more about Timothy, see his Profile in 1 Timothy 2, p. 2037.

13:24, 25 Hebrews is a call to Christian maturity. It was addressed to first-century Jewish Christians, but it applies to Christians of any age or background. Christian maturity means making Christ the beginning and end of our faith. To grow in maturity, we must center our lives on him, not depending on religious ritual, not falling back into sin, not trusting in ourselves, and not letting anything come between us and Christ. Christ is sufficient and superior.

"MIRACULOUS!" . . . "Revolutionary!" . . . "Greatest ever!" We are inundated by a flood of extravagant claims as we channel surf the television or flip magazine pages. The messages leap out at us. The products assure that they are new, improved, fantastic, and capable of changing our lives. For only a few dollars, we can have "cleaner clothes," "whiter teeth," "glamorous hair," and "tastier food." Automobiles, perfume, diet drinks, and mouthwash are guaranteed to bring happiness, friends, and the good life. And just before an election, no one can match the politicians' promises. But talk is cheap, and too often we soon realize that the boasts were hollow, quite far from the truth.

"Jesus is the answer!" . . . "Believe in God!" . . . "Follow me to church!" Christians also make great claims but are often guilty of belying them with their actions. Professing to trust God and to be his people, they cling tightly to the world and its values. Possessing all the right answers, they contradict the gospel with their lives.

With energetic style and crisp, well-chosen words, James confronts this conflict head-on. It is not enough to talk the Christian faith, he says; we must live it. "What good is it, my brothers, if a man claims to have faith but has no deeds? Can such faith save him?" (2:14). The proof of the reality of our faith is a changed life.

Genuine faith will inevitably produce good deeds. This is the central theme of James' letter, around which he supplies practical advice on living the Christian life.

James begins his letter by outlining some general characteristics of the Christian life (1:1–27). Next, he exhorts Christians to act justly in society (2:1–13). He follows this practical advice with a theological discourse on the relationship between faith and action (2:14–26). Then James shows the importance of controlling one's speech (3:1–12). In 3:13–18, James distinguishes two kinds of wisdom—earthly and heavenly. Then he encourages his readers to turn from evil desires and obey God (4:1–12). James reproves those who trust in their own plans and possessions (4:13—5:6). Finally, he exhorts his readers to be patient with each other (5:7–11), to be straightforward in their promises (5:12), to pray for each other (5:13–18), and to help each other remain faithful to God (5:19, 20).

This letter could be considered a how-to book on Christian living. Confrontation, challenges, and a call to commitment await you in its pages. Read James and become a *doer* of the Word (1:22–25).

VITAL STATISTICS

PURPOSE:
To expose hypocritical practices and to teach right Christian behavior

AUTHOR:
James, Jesus' brother, a leader in the Jerusalem church

ORIGINAL AUDIENCE:
First-century Jewish Christians residing in Gentile communities outside Palestine

DATE WRITTEN:
Probably A.D. 49, prior to the Jerusalem council held in A.D. 50

SETTING:
This letter expresses James' concern for persecuted Christians who were once part of the Jerusalem church.

KEY VERSE:
"But someone will say, 'You have faith; I have deeds.' Show me your faith without deeds, and I will show you my faith by what I do" (2:18).

THE BLUEPRINT

1. Genuine religion (1:1–27)
2. Genuine faith (2:1—3:12)
3. Genuine wisdom (3:13—5:20)

James wrote to Jewish Christians who had been scattered throughout the Mediterranean world because of persecution. In their hostile surroundings they were tempted to let intellectual agreement pass for true faith. This letter can have rich meaning for us as we are reminded that genuine faith transforms lives. We are encouraged to put our faith into action. It is easy to say we have faith, but true faith will produce loving actions toward others.

MEGATHEMES

THEME	EXPLANATION	IMPORTANCE
Living Faith	James wants believers not only to hear the truth but also to put it into action. He contrasts empty faith (claims without conduct) with faith that works. Commitment to love and to serve others is evidence of true faith.	Living faith makes a difference. Make sure your faith is more than just a statement; it should also result in action. Seek ways of putting your faith to work.
Trials	In the Christian life there are trials and temptations. Successfully overcoming these adversities produces maturity and strong character.	Don't resent troubles when they come. Pray for wisdom; God will supply all you need to face persecution or adversity. He will give you patience and keep you strong in times of trial.
Law of Love	We are saved by God's gracious mercy, not by keeping the law. But Christ gave us a special command: "You shall love your neighbor as yourself" (Matthew 19:19). We are to love and serve those around us.	Keeping the law of love shows that our faith is vital and real. When we show love to others, we are overcoming our own selfishness.
Wise Speech	Wisdom shows itself in wise speech. God holds us responsible for the results of our destructive words. The wisdom of God that helps control the tongue can help control all our actions.	Accepting God's wisdom will affect your speech. Your words will convey true humility and lead to peace. Think before you speak and allow God to give you self-control.
Wealth	James taught Christians not to compromise with worldly attitudes about wealth. Because the glory of wealth fades, Christians should store up God's treasures through sincere service. Christians must not show partiality to the wealthy or be prejudiced against the poor.	All of us are accountable for how we use what we have. We should not hoard wealth but be generous toward others. In addition, we should not be impressed by the wealthy nor look down on those who are poor.

1. Genuine religion

1 James,[a] a servant of God[b] and of the Lord Jesus Christ,

To the twelve tribes scattered[c] among the nations:

Greetings.

Trials and Temptations

[2] Consider it pure joy, my brothers, whenever you face trials of many kinds, [3] because you know that the testing of your faith develops perseverance. [4] Perseverance must finish its work so that you may be mature and complete, not lacking anything. [5] If any of you lacks wisdom, he should ask God,[d] who gives generously to all without finding fault, and it will be

1:1
[a] Ac 15:13
[b] Tit 1:1
[c] Jn 7:35

1:5
[d] 1Ki 3:9, 10;
Pr 2:3-6

1:1 The writer of this letter, a leader of the church in Jerusalem (see Acts 12:17; 15:13), was James, Jesus' brother, not James the apostle. The book of James was one of the earliest letters, probably written before A.D. 50. After Stephen was martyred (Acts 7:55—8:3), persecution increased, and Christians in Jerusalem were scattered throughout the Roman world. There were thriving Jewish-Christian communities in Rome, Alexandria, Cyprus, and cities in Greece and Asia Minor. Because these early believers did not have the support of established Christian churches, James wrote to them as a concerned leader, to encourage them in their faith during those difficult times.

1:2, 3 James doesn't say *if* you face trials, but *whenever* you face them. He assumes that we will have trials and that it is possible to profit from them. The point is not to pretend to be happy when we face pain, but to have a positive outlook ("consider it pure joy") because of what trials can produce in our lives. James tells us to turn our hardships into times of learning. Tough times can teach us perseverance. For other passages dealing with perseverance (also called patience and steadfastness), see Romans 2:7; 5:3–5; 8:24, 25; 2 Corinthians 6:3–7; 2 Peter 1:2–9.

1:2–4 We can't really know the depth of our character until we see how we react under pressure. It is easy to be kind to others when everything is going well, but can we still be kind when others

are treating us unfairly? God wants to make us mature and complete, not to keep us from all pain. Instead of complaining about our struggles, we should see them as opportunities for growth. Thank God for promising to be with you in rough times. Ask him to help you solve your problems or to give you the strength to endure them. Then be patient. God will not leave you alone with your problems; he will stay close and help you grow.

1:5 By *wisdom*, James is talking not only about knowledge, but about the ability to make wise decisions in difficult circumstances. Whenever we need wisdom, we can pray to God, and he will generously supply what we need. Christians don't have to grope around in the dark, hoping to stumble upon answers. We can ask for God's wisdom to guide our choices.

1:5 The wisdom that we need has three distinct characteristics:

(1) *It is practical.* The wisdom from God relates to life even during the most trying times. It is not a wisdom isolated from suffering and trials. This wisdom is the tool by which trials are overcome. An intelligent person may have profound ideas, but a wise person puts profound ideas into action. Intelligence will allow someone to describe several reasons why the car broke down. The wise person chooses the most likely reason and proceeds to take action.

(2) *It is divine.* God's wisdom goes beyond common sense.

1:6
e Mk 11:24

given to him. 6 But when he asks, he must believe and not doubt, *e* because he who doubts is like a wave of the sea, blown and tossed by the wind. 7 That man should not think he will receive anything from the Lord; 8 he is a double-minded man, unstable in all he does.

1:10
f 1Co 7:31

9 The brother in humble circumstances ought to take pride in his high position. 10 But the one who is rich should take pride in his low position, because he will pass away like a wild flower. *f* 11 For the sun rises with scorching heat and withers the plant; its blossom falls and its beauty is destroyed. In the same way, the rich man will fade away even while he goes about his business.

12 Blessed is the man who perseveres under trial, because when he has stood the test, he will receive the crown of life that God has promised to those who love him.

13 When tempted, no one should say, "God is tempting me." For God cannot be tempted by evil, nor does he tempt anyone; 14 but each one is tempted when, by his own evil desire, he

---

Common sense does not lead us to choose joy in the middle of trials. This wisdom begins with respect for God, leads to living by God's direction, and results in the ability to tell right from wrong. It is a wisdom that James will describe at length in chapter 3.

(3) *It is Christlike.* Asking for wisdom is ultimately asking to be like Christ. The Bible identifies Christ as the "wisdom of God" (1 Corinthians 1:24; 2:1–7).

1:6 To "believe and not doubt" means not only believing in the existence of God, but also believing in his loving care. It includes relying on God and expecting that he will hear and answer when we pray. We must put away our critical attitude when we come to him. God does not grant every thoughtless or selfish request. We must have confidence that God will align our desires with his purposes. For more on this concept, read the note on Matthew 21:22.

1:6 A mind that wavers is not completely convinced that God's way is best. It treats God's Word like any human advice, and it retains the option to disobey. It vacillates between allegiance to subjective feelings, the world's ideas, and God's commands. If your faith is new, weak, or struggling, remember that you can trust God. Then be loyal to him. To stabilize your wavering or doubtful mind, commit yourself wholeheartedly to God.

1:6–8 If you have ever seen the constant rolling of huge waves at sea, you know how restless they are—subject to the forces of wind, gravity, and tide. Doubt leaves a person as unsettled as the restless waves. If you want to stop being tossed about, rely on God to show you what is best for you. Ask him for wisdom, and trust that he will give it to you. Then your decisions will be sure and solid.

1:9 Christianity brings a new dignity to the poor and not-so-influential people of this world. That dignity is most apparent in the church, where there are not (or should not be) any class distinctions. All believers share the distinction and dignity of being changed by the gospel and being charged with the mission of taking that same Good News to the rest of the world. Believers know they have dignity before God because Christ died for them. Mary, the mother of Jesus, is a great example of this truth. The dignity that she displayed when she realized what God had done for her is seen in her prayer of praise, called the *Magnificat* (Luke 1:46–55). Whatever our social or economic situation, James challenges us to see beyond it to our eternal advantages. What we can have in Jesus Christ outweighs anything in this life. Knowing him gives us our high position, where we find our true dignity.

1:9–11 The poor should be glad that riches mean nothing to God; otherwise these people would be considered unworthy. The rich should be glad that money means nothing to God, because money is easily lost. We find true wealth by developing our spiritual life, not by developing our financial assets. God is interested in what is lasting (our souls), not in what is temporary (our money and possessions). See Mark 4:18, 19 for Jesus' words on this subject. Strive to treat each person as Christ would treat him or her.

1:10, 11 If wealth, power, and status mean nothing to God, why do we attribute so much importance to them and so much honor to those who possess them? Do your material possessions give you goals and your only reason for living? If they were gone, what would be left? What you have in your heart, not your bank account, matters to God and endures for eternity.

1:12 The crown of life is like the victory wreath given to winning athletes (see 1 Corinthians 9:25). God's crown of life is not glory and honor here on earth, but the reward of eternal life—living with God forever. The way to be in God's winners' circle is by loving him and staying faithful even under pressure.

1:12–15 Temptation comes from evil desires inside us, not from God. It begins with an evil thought and becomes sin when we dwell on the thought and allow it to become an action. Like a snowball rolling downhill, sin grows more destructive the more we let it have its way. The best time to stop a temptation is before it is too strong or moving too fast to control. See Matthew 4:1–11; 1 Corinthians 10:13; and 2 Timothy 2:22 for more about escaping temptation.

1:13, 14 People who live for God often wonder why they still have temptations. Does God tempt them? God *tests* people, but he does not *tempt* them by trying to seduce them into sin. God allows Satan to tempt people, however, in order to refine their faith and to help them grow in their dependence on Christ. We can resist the temptation to sin by turning to God for strength and choosing to obey his Word.

1:13–15 It is easy to blame others and make excuses for evil thoughts and wrong actions. Excuses include (1) it's the other person's fault; (2) I couldn't help it; (3) everybody's doing it; (4) it was just a mistake; (5) nobody's perfect; (6) the devil made me do it; (7) I was pressured into it; (8) I didn't know it was wrong; (9) God is tempting me. A person who makes excuses is trying to shift the blame from himself or herself to something or someone else. A Christian, on the other hand, accepts responsibility for his or her wrongs, confesses them, and asks God for forgiveness.

is dragged away and enticed. [15]Then, after desire has conceived, it gives birth to sin;[g] and sin, when it is full-grown, gives birth to death.

[16]Don't be deceived, my dear brothers. [17]Every good and perfect gift is from above, coming down from the Father of the heavenly lights, who does not change like shifting shadows. [18]He chose to give us birth[h] through the word of truth, that we might be a kind of firstfruits[i] of all he created.

Listening and Doing

[19]My dear brothers, take note of this: Everyone should be quick to listen, slow to speak[j] and slow to become angry, [20]for man's anger does not bring about the righteous life that God desires. [21]Therefore, get rid of all moral filth and the evil that is so prevalent and humbly accept the word planted in you, which can save you.

[22]Do not merely listen to the word, and so deceive yourselves. Do what it says. [23]Anyone who listens to the word but does not do what it says is like a man who looks at his face in a mirror [24]and, after looking at himself, goes away and immediately forgets what he looks like. [25]But the man who looks intently into the perfect law that gives freedom,[k] and continues to do this, not forgetting what he has heard, but doing it—he will be blessed in what he does.[l]

[26]If anyone considers himself religious and yet does not keep a tight rein on his tongue, he deceives himself and his religion is worthless. [27]Religion that God our Father accepts as pure and faultless is this: to look after[m] orphans and widows in their distress and to keep oneself from being polluted by the world.

2. Genuine faith
Favoritism Forbidden

2 My brothers, as believers in our glorious[n] Lord Jesus Christ, don't show favoritism. [2]Suppose a man comes into your meeting wearing a gold ring and fine clothes, and a poor man in shabby clothes also comes in. [3]If you show special attention to the man wearing fine clothes and say, "Here's a good seat for you," but say to the poor man, "You stand

1:15 [g]Job 15:35; Ps 7:14

1:18 [h]Jn 1:13 [i]Rev 14:4

1:19 [j]Pr 10:19

1:25 [k]Jas 2:12 [l]Jn 13:17

1:27 [m]Mt 25:36

2:1 [n]1Co 2:8

1:17 The Bible often compares goodness with light and evil with darkness. For other passages where God is pictured as light, see Psalm 27:1, Isaiah 60:19–22, John 1:1–14.

1:18 First-century Christians were the first generation to believe in Jesus Christ as Messiah. James called them "a kind of firstfruits of all he created." The Jewish leaders would be well aware of the practice of offering the first crops to ripen just prior to harvest as an act of worship, and also as a blessing on the rest of the harvest (see Deuteronomy 26:9–11). In 1 Corinthians 15:20, Paul refers to Christ as the firstfruits of those who have died.

1:19 When we talk too much and listen too little, we communicate to others that we think our ideas are much more important than theirs. James wisely advises us to reverse this process. Put a mental stopwatch on your conversations and keep track of how much you talk and how much you listen. When people talk with you, do they feel that their viewpoints and ideas have value?

1:19, 20 These verses speak of anger that erupts when our egos are bruised—"*I* am hurt"; "*My* opinions are not being heard." When injustice and sin occur, we *should* become angry because others are being hurt. But we should not become angry when we fail to win an argument or when we feel offended or neglected. Selfish anger never helps anybody.

1:21 James advises us to get rid of all that is wrong in our lives and "humbly accept" the salvation message we have received ("the word planted in you"), because it alone can save us.

1:22–25 It is important to listen to what God's Word says, but it is much more important to obey it, to *do* what it says. We can measure the effectiveness of our Bible study time by the effect it has on our behavior and attitudes. Do you put into action what you have studied?

1:25 It seems paradoxical that a law could give us freedom, but God's law offers us a true reflection of our sinful condition and gives us the opportunity to ask for God's forgiveness (see Romans 7:7, 8). As Christians, we are saved by God's grace, and salvation frees us from sin's control. As believers, we are free to live as God created

us to live. Of course, this does not mean that we are free to do as we please (see 1 Peter 2:16). We are now free to obey God.

1:26 See the notes in chapter 3 for more on taming the tongue. No matter how spiritual we may think we are, we all could control our speech more effectively.

1:27 In the first century, orphans and widows had very little means of economic support. Unless a family member was willing to care for them, they were reduced to begging, selling themselves as slaves, or starving. By caring for these powerless people, the church put God's Word into practice. When we give with no hope of receiving in return, we show what it means to serve others.

1:27 To keep ourselves from being polluted by the world, we need to commit ourselves to Christ's ethical and moral system, not the world's. We are not to adapt to the world's value system, which is based on money, power, and pleasure. True faith means nothing if we are contaminated with such values.

2:1ff In this chapter James argues against favoritism and for the necessity of good deeds. He presents three principles of faith: (1) Commitment is an essential part of faith. You cannot be a Christian simply by affirming the right doctrines or agreeing with Biblical facts (2:19). You must commit your mind and heart to Christ. (2) Right actions are the natural by-products of true faith. A genuine Christian will have a changed life (2:18). (3) Faith without good deeds doesn't do anybody any good—it is useless (2:14–17). James's teachings are consistent with Paul's teaching that we receive salvation by faith alone. Paul emphasizes the purpose of faith—to bring salvation. James emphasizes the results of faith—a changed life.

2:1–7 James condemns acts of favoritism. Often we treat a well-dressed, impressive-looking person better than someone who looks shabby. We do this because we would rather identify with successful people than with apparent failures. The irony, as James reminds us, is that the supposed winners may have gained their impressive lifestyle at our expense. In addition, the rich find it difficult to identify with the Lord Jesus, who came as a humble servant. Are you easily impressed by status, wealth, or fame? Are you partial to the "haves" there" or "Sit on the floor by my feet," [4] have you not discriminated among yourselves and become judges with evil thoughts?

[5] Listen, my dear brothers: Has not God chosen those who are poor in the eyes of the world to be rich in faith [o] and to inherit the kingdom he promised those who love him? [6] But you have insulted the poor. [p] Is it not the rich who are exploiting you? Are they not the ones who are dragging you into court? [7] Are they not the ones who are slandering the noble name of him to whom you belong?

[8] If you really keep the royal law found in Scripture, "Love your neighbor as yourself," [a] [q] you are doing right. [9] But if you show favoritism, you sin and are convicted by the law as lawbreakers. [10] For whoever keeps the whole law and yet stumbles at just one point is guilty of breaking all of it. [r] [11] For he who said, "Do not commit adultery," [b] also said, "Do not murder." [c] [s] If you do not commit adultery but do commit murder, you have become a lawbreaker.

[12] Speak and act as those who are going to be judged by the law that gives freedom, [t] [13] because judgment without mercy will be shown to anyone who has not been merciful. Mercy triumphs over judgment!

[a] 8 Lev. 19:18   [b] 11 Exodus 20:14; Deut. 5:18   [c] 11 Exodus 20:13; Deut. 5:17

2:5
[o] Lk 12:21
2:6
[p] 1Co 11:22

2:8
[q] Lev 19:18
2:10
[r] Mt 5:19
2:11
[s] Ex 20:13
2:12
[t] Jas 1:25

SHOWING FAVORITISM
Why it is wrong to show favoritism to the wealthy:

1. It is inconsistent with Christ's teachings.
2. It results from evil thoughts.
3. It insults people made in God's image.
4. It is a by-product of selfish motives.
5. It goes against the Biblical definition of love.
6. It shows a lack of mercy to those less fortunate.
7. It is hypocritical.
8. It is sin.

---

while ignoring the "have nots"? This attitude is sinful. God views all people as equals, and if he favors anyone, it is the poor and the powerless. We should follow his example.

2:2–4 Why is it wrong to judge a person by his or her economic status? Wealth may indicate intelligence, wise decisions, and hard work. On the other hand, it may mean only that a person had the good fortune of being born into a wealthy family. Or it can even be the sign of greed, dishonesty, and selfishness. By honoring someone just because he or she dresses well, we are making appearance more important than character. Sometimes we do this because (1) poverty makes us uncomfortable; we don't want to face our responsibilities to those who have less than we do; (2) we want to be wealthy too, and we hope to use the rich person as a means to that end; (3) we want the rich person to join our church and help support it financially. All these motives are selfish; they view neither the rich nor the poor person as a human being in need of fellowship. If we say that Christ is our Lord, then we must live as he requires, showing no favoritism and loving all people regardless of whether they are rich or poor.

2:2–4 We are often partial to the rich because we mistakenly assume that riches are a sign of God's blessing and approval. But God does not promise us earthly rewards or riches; in fact, Christ calls us to be ready to suffer for him and give up everything in order to hold on to eternal life (Matthew 6:19–21; 19:28–30; Luke 12:14–34; Romans 8:15–21; 1 Timothy 6:17–19). We will have untold riches in eternity if we are faithful in our present life (Luke 6:35; John 12:23–25; Galatians 6:7–10; Titus 3:4–8).

2:5 When James speaks about the poor, he is talking about those who have no money and also about those whose simple values are despised by much of our affluent society. Perhaps the "poor" people prefer serving to managing, human relationships to financial security, peace to power. This does not mean that the poor will automatically go to heaven and the rich to hell. Poor people, however, are usually more aware of their powerlessness. Thus it is often easier for them to acknowledge their need for salvation. One of the greatest barriers to salvation for the rich is pride.

For the poor, bitterness can often bar the way to acceptance of salvation.

2:8 The *royal law* is the law of our great King Jesus Christ, who said, "Love each other as I have loved you" (John 15:12). This law, originally summarized in Leviticus 19:18, is the basis for all the laws of how people should relate to one another. Christ reinforced this truth in Matthew 22:37–40, and Paul taught it in Romans 13:8 and Galatians 5:14.

2:8, 9 We must treat all people as we would want to be treated. We should not ignore the rich, because then we would be withholding our love. But we must not favor them for what they can do for us, while ignoring the poor who can offer us seemingly so little in return.

2:10 Christians must not use this verse to justify sinning. We dare not say: "Because I can't keep every demand of God, why even try?" James reminds us that if we've broken just one law, we are sinners. We can't decide to keep part of God's law and ignore the rest. You can't break the law a little bit; if you have broken it at all, you need Christ to pay for your sin. Measure yourself, not someone else, against God's standards. Ask for forgiveness where you need it, and then renew your effort to put your faith into practice.

2:12 As Christians we are saved by God's free gift (grace) through faith, not by keeping the law. But as Christians, we are also required to obey Christ. The apostle Paul taught "for we must all appear before the judgment seat of Christ" (2 Corinthians 5:10) to be judged for our conduct. God's grace does not cancel our duty to obey him; it gives our obedience a new basis. The law is no longer an external set of rules, but it is a "law that gives freedom"—one we joyfully and willingly carry out, because we love God and because we have the power of his Holy Spirit to carry it out (see 1:25).

2:13 Only God in his mercy can forgive our sins. We can't earn forgiveness by forgiving others. But when we withhold forgiveness from others after having received it ourselves, we show that we don't understand or appreciate God's mercy toward us (see Matthew 6:14, 15; 18:21ff; Ephesians 4:31, 32).

Faith and Deeds

¹⁴What good is it, my brothers, if a man claims to have faith but has no deeds?ᵘ Can such faith save him? ¹⁵Suppose a brother or sister is without clothes and daily food. ¹⁶If one of you says to him, "Go, I wish you well; keep warm and well fed," but does nothing about his physical needs, what good is it?ᵛ ¹⁷In the same way, faith by itself, if it is not accompanied by action, is dead.

¹⁸But someone will say, "You have faith; I have deeds."

Show me your faith without deeds, and I will show you my faith by what I do. ʷ ¹⁹You believe that there is one God.ˣ Good! Even the demons believe that—and shudder.

²⁰You foolish man, do you want evidence that faith without deeds is uselessᵃ? ²¹Was not our ancestor Abraham considered righteous for what he did when he offered his son Isaac on the altar?ʸ ²²You see that his faith and his actions were working together,ᶻ and his faith was made complete by what he did. ²³And the scripture was fulfilled that says, "Abraham believed God, and it was credited to him as righteousness,"ᵇ ᵃ and he was called God's friend. ᵇ ²⁴You see that a person is justified by what he does and not by faith alone.

²⁵In the same way, was not even Rahab the prostitute considered righteous for what she did when she gave lodging to the spies and sent them off in a different direction?ᶜ ²⁶As the body without the spirit is dead, so faith without deeds is dead.

Taming the Tongue

3 Not many of you should presume to be teachers, my brothers, because you know that we who teach will be judged more strictly. ²We all stumble ᵈ in many ways. If anyone is never at fault in what he says, he is a perfect man,ᵉ able to keep his whole body in check.

³When we put bits into the mouths of horses to make them obey us, we can turn the whole animal. ᶠ ⁴Or take ships as an example. Although they are so large and are driven by strong winds, they are steered by a very small rudder wherever the pilot wants to go. ⁵Likewise the tongue is a small part of the body, but it makes great boasts.ᵍ Consider what a great forest is set on fire by a small spark. ⁶The tongue also is a fire,ʰ a world of evil among the parts of the body. It corrupts the whole person,ⁱ sets the whole course of his life on fire, and is itself set on fire by hell.

⁷All kinds of animals, birds, reptiles and creatures of the sea are being tamed and have been tamed by man, ⁸but no man can tame the tongue. It is a restless evil, full of deadly poison.ʲ

ᵃ20 Some early manuscripts *dead*   ᵇ23 Gen. 15:6

2:14 ᵘMt 7:26
2:16 ᵛ1Jn 3:17, 18
2:18 ʷJas 3:13
2:19 ˣDt 6:4
2:21 ʸGe 22:9, 12
2:22 ᶻHeb 11:17
2:23 ᵃGe 15:6; Ro 4:3
ᵇ2Ch 20:7; Isa 41:8
2:25 ᶜHeb 11:31
3:2 ᵈ1Ki 8:46
ᵉMt 12:37
3:3 ᶠPs 32:9
3:5 ᵍPs 12:3, 4
3:6 ʰPr 16:27
ⁱMt 15:11, 18, 19
3:8 ʲPs 140:3

2:14 When someone claims to have faith, what he or she may have is intellectual assent—agreement with a set of Christian teachings—and as such it would be incomplete faith. True faith transforms our conduct as well as our thoughts. If our lives remain unchanged, we don't truly believe the truths we claim to believe.

2:17 We cannot earn our salvation by serving and obeying God. But such actions show that our commitment to God is real. Deeds of loving service are not a substitute for, but rather a verification of, our faith in Christ.

2:18 At first glance, this verse seems to contradict Romans 3:28, "man is justified by faith apart from observing the law." Deeper investigation, however, shows that the teachings of James and Paul are not at odds. While it is true that our good deeds can never earn salvation, true faith always results in a changed life and good deeds. Paul speaks against those who try to be saved by deeds instead of true faith; James speaks against those who confuse mere intellectual assent with true faith. After all, even demons know who Jesus is, but they don't obey him (2:19). True faith involves a commitment of your whole self to God.

2:21–24 James says that Abraham was "considered righteous" for what he *did*. Paul says he was justified because he *believed* God (Romans 4:1–5). James and Paul are not contradicting but complementing each other. Let's not conclude that the truth is a blending of these two statements. We are not justified by what we do in any way. True faith always results in deeds, but the deeds do not justify us. Faith brings us salvation; active obedience demonstrates that our faith is genuine.

2:25 Rahab lived in Jericho, a city the Israelites conquered as they entered the promised land (Joshua 2). When Israel's spies came to the city, she hid them and helped them escape. In this way she demonstrated faith in God's purpose for Israel. As a result, she and her family were saved when the city was destroyed. Hebrews 11:31 lists Rahab among the heroes of faith.

3:1 Teaching was a highly valued and respected profession in Jewish culture, and many Jews who embraced Christianity wanted to become teachers. James warned that although it is good to aspire to teach, the teachers' responsibility is great because their words and example affect others' spiritual lives. If you are in a teaching or leadership role, how are you affecting those you lead?

3:2, 3 What you say and what you *don't* say are both important. Proper speech is not only saying the right words at the right time, but it is also controlling your desire to say what you shouldn't. Examples of an untamed tongue include gossiping, putting others down, bragging, manipulating, false teaching, exaggerating, complaining, flattering, and lying. Before you speak, ask, "Is what I want to say true? Is it necessary? Is it kind?"

3:6 James compares the damage the tongue can do to a raging fire—the tongue's wickedness has its source in hell itself. The uncontrolled tongue can do terrible damage. Satan uses the tongue to divide people and pit them against one another. Idle and hateful words are damaging because they spread destruction quickly, and no one can stop the results once they are spoken. We dare not be careless with what we say, thinking we can apologize later, because even if we do, the scars remain. A few words spoken in anger can destroy a relationship that took years to build. Before you speak, remember that words are like fire—you can neither control nor reverse the damage they can do.

3:8 If no human being can control the tongue, why bother trying?

3:9
k Ge 1:26, 27

9 With the tongue we praise our Lord and Father, and with it we curse men, who have been made in God's likeness. k 10 Out of the same mouth come praise and cursing. My brothers, this should not be. 11 Can both fresh water and salt a water flow from the same spring? 12 My brothers, can a fig tree bear olives, or a grapevine bear figs? Neither can a salt spring produce fresh water.

3. Genuine wisdom
Two Kinds of Wisdom

3:13
l Jas 2:18

13 Who is wise and understanding among you? Let him show it l by his good life, by deeds done in the humility that comes from wisdom. 14 But if you harbor bitter envy and selfish ambition in your hearts, do not boast about it or deny the truth. 15 Such "wisdom" does not come down from heaven but is earthly, unspiritual, of the devil. 16 For where you have envy and selfish ambition, there you find disorder and every evil practice.

3:17
m Ro 12:9

3:18
n Pr 11:18

17 But the wisdom that comes from heaven is first of all pure; then peace-loving, considerate, submissive, full of mercy and good fruit, impartial and sincere. m 18 Peacemakers who sow in peace raise a harvest of righteousness. n

Submit Yourselves to God

4:1
o Ro 7:23

4 What causes fights and quarrels among you? Don't they come from your desires that battle o within you? 2 You want something but don't get it. You kill and covet, but you cannot have what you want. You quarrel and fight. You do not have, because you do not ask

a 11 Greek *bitter* (see also verse 14)

SPEECH

When our speech is motivated by	It is full of
Satan	Bitter envy
	Selfish ambition
	Earthly concerns and desires
	Unspiritual thoughts and ideas
	Disorder
	Evil
God and his wisdom.	Mercy
	Love for others
	Peace
	Consideration for others
	Submission
	Sincerity, impartiality
	Righteousness

Even if we may not achieve perfect control of our tongues, we can still learn enough control to reduce the damage our words can do. It is better to fight a fire than to go around setting new ones! Remember that we are not fighting the tongue's fire in our own strength. The Holy Spirit will give us increasing power to monitor and control what we say, so that when we are offended, the Spirit will remind us of God's love, and we won't react in a hateful manner. When we are criticized, the Spirit will heal the hurt, and we won't lash out.

3:9–12 Our contradictory speech often puzzles us. At times our words are right and pleasing to God, but at other times they are violent and destructive. Which of these speech patterns reflects our true identity? The tongue gives us a picture of our basic human nature. We were made in God's image, but we have also fallen into sin. God works to change us from the inside out. When the Holy Spirit purifies a heart, he gives self-control so that the person will speak words that please God.

3:13–18 Have you ever known anyone who claimed to be wise but who acted foolishly? True wisdom can be measured by the depth of a person's character. Just as you can identify a tree by the type of fruit it produces, you can evaluate your wisdom by the way you act. Foolishness leads to disorder, but wisdom leads to peace and goodness. Are you tempted to escalate the conflict, pass on the gossip, or fan the fire of discord? Careful, winsome speech and wise, loving words are the seeds of peace. God loves peacemakers (Matthew 5:9).

3:14, 15 "Bitter envy and selfish ambition" are inspired by the devil. It is easy for us to be drawn into wrong desires by the pressures of society and sometimes even by well-meaning Christians. By listening to the advice: "Assert yourself," "Go for it," "Set high goals," we can be drawn into greed and destructive competitiveness. Seeking God's wisdom delivers us from the need to compare ourselves to others and to want what they have.

4:1–3 Conflicts and disputes among believers are always harmful. James explains that these quarrels result from evil desires battling within us—we want more possessions, more money, higher status, more recognition. When we want badly enough to fulfill these desires, we fight in order to do so. Instead of aggressively grabbing what we want, we should submit ourselves to God, ask God to help us get rid of our selfish desires, and trust him to give us what we really need.

4:2, 3 James mentions the most common problems in prayer: not asking, asking for the wrong things, asking for the wrong reasons. Do you talk to God at all? When you do, what do you talk about? Do you ask only to satisfy your desires? Do you seek God's approval for what you already plan to do? Your prayers will become powerful when you allow God to change your desires so that they perfectly correspond to his will for you (1 John 3:21, 22).

God. [3] When you ask, you do not receive, because you ask with wrong motives, that you may spend what you get on your pleasures.

[4] You adulterous people, don't you know that friendship with the world is hatred toward God? [p] Anyone who chooses to be a friend of the world becomes an enemy of God. [q] [5] Or do you think Scripture says without reason that the spirit he caused to live in us envies intensely? [a] [6] But he gives us more grace. That is why Scripture says:

> "God opposes the proud
> but gives grace to the humble." [b] [r]

[7] Submit yourselves, then, to God. Resist the devil, [s] and he will flee from you. [8] Come near to God and he will come near to you. Wash your hands, [t] you sinners, and purify your hearts, you double-minded. [u] [9] Grieve, mourn and wail. Change your laughter to mourning and your joy to gloom. [10] Humble yourselves before the Lord, and he will lift you up.

[11] Brothers, do not slander one another. [v] Anyone who speaks against his brother or judges him speaks against the law and judges it. When you judge the law, you are not keeping it, but sitting in judgment on it. [12] There is only one Lawgiver and Judge, the one who is able to save and destroy. [w] But you—who are you to judge your neighbor? [x]

Boasting About Tomorrow

[13] Now listen, you who say, "Today or tomorrow we will go to this or that city, spend a year there, carry on business and make money." [y] [14] Why, you do not even know what will happen tomorrow. What is your life? You are a mist that appears for a little while and then vanishes. [z] [15] Instead, you ought to say, "If it is the Lord's will, [a] we will live and do this or that." [16] As it is, you boast and brag. All such boasting is evil. [b] [17] Anyone, then, who knows the good he ought to do and doesn't do it, sins. [c]

a [5] Or that God jealously longs for the spirit that he made to live in us; or that the Spirit he caused to live in us longs jealously   b [6] Prov. 3:34

4:4 p 1 Jn 2:15   q Jn 15:19

4:6 r Pr 3:34

4:7 s 1 Pe 5:6-9

4:8 t Isa 1:16   u Jas 1:8

4:11 v 1 Pe 2:1

4:12 w Mt 10:28   x Ro 14:4

4:13 y Pr 27:1

4:14 z Job 7:7

4:15 a Ac 18:21

4:16 b 1 Co 5:6

4:17 c Lk 12:47; Jn 9:41

4:3, 4 There is nothing wrong with wanting a pleasurable life. God gives us good gifts that he wants us to enjoy (1:17; Ephesians 4:7; 1 Timothy 4:4, 5). But having friendship with the world involves seeking pleasure at others' expense or at the expense of obeying God. Pleasure that keeps us from pleasing God is sinful; pleasure from God's rich bounty is good.

4:4-6 The cure for evil desires is humility (see Proverbs 16:18, 19; 1 Peter 5:5, 6). Pride makes us self-centered and leads us to conclude that we deserve all we can see, touch, or imagine. It creates greedy appetites for far more than we need. We can be released from our self-centered desires by humbling ourselves before God, realizing that all we really need is his approval. When the Holy Spirit fills us, we see that this world's seductive attractions are only cheap substitutes for what God has to offer.

4:5 This verse may mean that because of our fallen nature, we have a tendency toward envy. James is not quoting a specific verse or passage—he is summing up a teaching of Scripture. See Romans 6:6-8 and Galatians 5:17-21 for more on the human tendency toward envy and discontent.

4:7 Although God and the devil are at war, we don't have to wait until the end to see who will win. God has *already* defeated Satan (Revelation 12:10-12), and when Christ returns, the devil and all he stands for will be eliminated forever (Revelation 20:10-15). Satan is here now, however, and he is trying to win us over to his evil cause. With the Holy Spirit's power, we can resist the devil, and he will flee from us.

4:7-10 How can you come near to God? James gives five ways: (1) *Submit to God* (4:7). Yield to his authority and will, commit your life to him and his control, and be willing to follow him. (2) *Resist the devil* (4:7). Don't allow Satan to entice and tempt you. (3) *Wash your hands . . . and purify your hearts* (that is, lead a pure life) (4:8). Be cleansed from sin, replacing your desire to sin with your desire to experience God's purity. (4) *Grieve and mourn and wail* in sincere sorrow for your sins (4:9). Don't be afraid to express deep heartfelt sorrow for what you have done. (5) *Humble yourself before the Lord*, and he will lift you up (4:10; 1 Peter 5:6).

4:10 Humbling ourselves means recognizing that our worth comes from God alone. To be humble involves working with his power according to his guidance, not with our own independent effort. Although we do not deserve God's favor, he reaches out to us in love and gives us worth and dignity, despite our human shortcomings.

4:11, 12 Jesus summarized the law as love for God and neighbor (Matthew 22:37-40), and Paul said that love demonstrated toward a neighbor would fully satisfy the law (Romans 13:6-10). When we fail to love, we are actually breaking God's law. Examine your attitude and actions toward others. Do you build people up or tear them down? When you're ready to criticize someone, remember God's law of love and say something good instead. Saying something beneficial to others will cure you of finding fault and increase your ability to obey God's law of love.

4:13-16 It is good to have goals, but goals can disappoint us if we leave God out of them. There is no point in making plans as though God does not exist because the future is in his hands. The beginning of good planning is to ask: "What would I like to be doing ten years from now? One year from now? Tomorrow? How will I react if God steps in and rearranges my plans?" We can plan ahead, but we must hold on to our plans loosely. If we put God's desires at the center of our planning, he will never disappoint us.

4:14 Life is short no matter how many years we live. Don't be deceived into thinking that you have lots of remaining time to live for Christ, to enjoy your loved ones, or to do what you know you should. Live for God today! Then, no matter when your life ends, you will have fulfilled God's plan for you.

4:17 We tend to think that *doing* wrong is sin. But James tells us that sin is also *not* doing right. (These two kinds of sin are sometimes called sins of commission and sins of omission.) It is a sin to lie; it can also be a sin to know the truth and not tell it. It is a sin to speak evil of someone; it is also a sin to avoid him or her when you know he or she needs your friendship. We should be willing to help as the Holy Spirit guides us. If God has directed you to do a kind act, to render a service, or to restore a relationship, do it. You will experience a renewed and refreshed vitality to your Christian faith.

Warning to Rich Oppressors

5:1
d Lk 6:24

5:2
e Job 13:28;
Mt 6:19, 20

5:4
f Lev 19:13
g Dt 24:15

5 Now listen, you rich people, *d* weep and wail because of the misery that is coming upon you. ² Your wealth has rotted, and moths have eaten your clothes. *e* ³ Your gold and silver are corroded. Their corrosion will testify against you and eat your flesh like fire. You have hoarded wealth in the last days. ⁴ Look! The wages you failed to pay the workmen *f* who mowed your fields are crying out against you. The cries *g* of the harvesters have reached the ears of the Lord Almighty. ⁵ You have lived on earth in luxury and self-indulgence. You have fattened yourselves in the day of slaughter. *a* ⁶ You have condemned and murdered innocent men, who were not opposing you.

Patience in Suffering

5:7
h Dt 11:14

⁷ Be patient, then, brothers, until the Lord's coming. See how the farmer waits for the land to yield its valuable crop and how patient he is for the autumn and spring rains. *h* ⁸ You too,

a 5 Or yourselves as in a day of feasting

FAITH THAT WORKS

James offers a larger number of similarities to the Sermon on the Mount than any other book in the New Testament. James relied heavily on Jesus' teachings.

Lesson	Reference
When your life is full of difficulties and persecutions, be glad. A reward awaits you.	James 1:2 Matthew 5:10–12
When your endurance is fully developed, you will be perfect, mature, and complete, lacking.	James 1:4 Matthew 5:48
Ask God, and he will answer.	James 1:5; 5:15 Matthew 7:7–12
Those who are humble (who don't amount to much by the world's standards) should rejoice in their position as those whom God loves.	James 1:9 Matthew 5:3
Watch out for your anger. . . . It can be dangerous.	James 1:19, 20 Matthew 5:22
Be merciful to others, as God is merciful to you.	James 2:13 Matthew 5:7; 6:14
Your faith must express itself in helping others.	James 2:14–16 Matthew 7:21–23
Blessed are the peacemakers; they sow in peace and reap a harvest of righteousness.	James 3:17, 18 Matthew 5:9
You cannot serve God *and* money, pleasures, or evil. Friendship with the world is hatred toward God.	James 4:4 Matthew 6:24
When you humble yourself and realize your dependence on God, he will lift you up.	James 4:10 Matthew 5:3, 4
Don't slander or speak evil against others; these go against God's command to love one another.	James 4:11 Matthew 7:1, 2
Treasures on earth will only rot and fade away—store up eternal treasures in heaven.	James 5:2, 3 Matthew 6:19
Be patient in suffering, as God's prophets were patient.	James 5:10 Matthew 5:12
Be honest in your speech; just say a simple yes or no so that you can always be trusted.	James 5:12 Matthew 5:33–37

5:1–6 James proclaims the worthlessness of riches, not the worthlessness of the rich. Today's money will be worthless when Christ returns, so we should spend our time accumulating the kind of treasures that will be worthwhile in God's eternal kingdom. Money is not the problem; Christian leaders need money to live and to support their families; missionaries need money to help them spread the gospel; churches need money to do their work effectively. It is the *love* of money that leads to evil (1 Timothy 6:10) and causes some people to oppress others in order to get more. This is a warning to all Christians who are tempted to adopt worldly standards rather than God's standards (Romans 12:1, 2) as well as an encouragement to all those who are oppressed by the rich. Also read Matthew 6:19–21 to see what Jesus says about riches.

5:6 *Innocent men* were defenseless persons, probably poor laborers. Poor people who could not pay their debts were thrown in

prison or forced to sell all their possessions. At times, they were even forced to sell their family members into slavery. With no opportunity to work off their debts, poor people often died of starvation. God called this murder. Hoarding money, exploiting employees, and living self-indulgently will not escape God's notice.

5:7, 8 The farmer must wait patiently for his crops to grow; he cannot hurry the process. But he does not take the summer off and hope that all goes well in the fields. There is much work to do to ensure a good harvest. In the same way, we must wait patiently for Christ's return. We cannot make him come back any sooner. But while we wait, there is much work that we can do to advance God's kingdom. Both the farmer and the Christian must live by faith, looking toward the future reward for their labors. Don't live as if Christ will never come. Work faithfully to build his kingdom—the King *will* come when the time is right.

be patient and stand firm, because the Lord's coming is near. [9]Don't grumble against each other, brothers,[i] or you will be judged. The Judge is standing at the door![j]

[10]Brothers, as an example of patience in the face of suffering, take the prophets[k] who spoke in the name of the Lord. [11]As you know, we consider blessed those who have persevered. You have heard of Job's perseverance and have seen what the Lord finally brought about.[l] The Lord is full of compassion and mercy.

[12]Above all, my brothers, do not swear—not by heaven or by earth or by anything else. Let your "Yes" be yes, and your "No," no, or you will be condemned.[m]

The Prayer of Faith

[13]Is any one of you in trouble? He should pray. Is anyone happy? Let him sing songs of praise. [14]Is any one of you sick? He should call the elders of the church to pray over him and anoint him with oil[n] in the name of the Lord. [15]And the prayer offered in faith will make the sick person well; the Lord will raise him up. If he has sinned, he will be forgiven. [16]Therefore confess your sins to each other and pray for each other so that you may be healed. The prayer of a righteous man is powerful and effective.

[17]Elijah was a man just like us.[o] He prayed earnestly that it would not rain, and it did not rain on the land for three and a half years.[p] [18]Again he prayed, and the heavens gave rain, and the earth produced its crops.[q]

[19]My brothers, if one of you should wander from the truth and someone should bring him back,[r] [20]remember this: Whoever turns a sinner from the error of his way will save[s] him from death and cover over a multitude of sins.[t]

5:9 [i]Jas 4:11 [j]Mt 24:33
5:10 [k]Mt 5:12
5:11 [l]Job 42:10, 12-17
5:12 [m]Mt 5:34-37
5:14 [n]Mk 6:13
5:17 [o]Ac 14:15 [p]1Ki 17:1; Lk 4:25
5:18 [q]1Ki 18:41-45
5:19 [r]Mt 18:15
5:20 [s]Ro 11:14 [t]1Pe 4:8

5:9 When things go wrong, we tend to grumble against and blame others for our miseries (see the second note on Genesis 3:11–13). Blaming others is easier than owning our share of the responsibility, but it can be both destructive and sinful. Before you judge others for their shortcomings, remember that Christ the Judge will come to evaluate each of us (Matthew 7:1–5; 25:31–46). He will not let us get away with shifting the blame to others.

5:10, 11 Many prophets suffered and were persecuted, such as Moses, Elijah, and Jeremiah. For a complete list of those persecuted, see the chart in 2 Chronicles 19, p. 672. For more on the topic of suffering, see the notes on Job 1:1ff; 2:10; 3:23–26; 4:7, 8; 42:17; and Job's Profile in Job 2, p. 771.

5:12 A person with a reputation for exaggeration or lying often can't get anyone to believe him on his word alone. Christians should never become like that. Always be honest so that others will believe your simple yes or no. By avoiding lies, half-truths, and omissions of the truth, you will become known as a trustworthy person.

5:14, 15 James is referring to someone who is incapacitated physically. In Scripture, oil was both a medicine (see the parable of the Good Samaritan in Luke 10:30–37) and a symbol of the Spirit of God (as used in anointing kings, see 1 Samuel 16:1–13). Thus oil can represent both the medical and the spiritual spheres of life. Christians should not separate the physical and the spiritual—Jesus Christ is Lord over both the body and the spirit.

5:14, 15 People in the church are not alone. Members of Christ's body should be able to count on others for support and prayer, especially when they are sick or suffering. The elders should be on call to respond to the illness of any member, and the church should stay alert to pray for the needs of all its members.

5:15 "The prayer offered in faith" does not refer to the faith of the sick person, but to the faith of the people praying. God heals, faith doesn't, and all prayers are subject to God's will. But our prayers are part of God's healing process. That is why God often waits for our prayers of faith before intervening to heal a person.

5:16 Christ has made it possible for us to go directly to God for forgiveness. But confessing our sins to each other still has an important place in the life of the church. (1) If we have sinned against an individual, we must ask him or her to forgive us. (2) If our sin has affected the church, we must confess it publicly. (3) If we need loving support as we struggle with a sin, we should confess that sin to those who are able to provide that support. (4) If, after confessing a private sin to God, we still don't feel his forgiveness, we may wish to confess that sin to a fellow believer and hear him or her assure us of God's pardon. In Christ's kingdom, every believer is a priest to other believers (1 Peter 2:9).

5:16–18 The Christian's most powerful resource is communion with God through prayer. The results are often greater than we thought were possible. Some people see prayer as a last resort to be tried when all else fails. This approach is backward. Prayer should come first. Because God's power is infinitely greater than ours, it only makes sense to rely on it—especially because God encourages us to do so.

5:17 For more about the great prophet Elijah, read his Profile in 1 Kings 18, p. 527.

5:19, 20 Clearly this person who has wandered from the truth is a believer who has fallen into sin—one who is no longer living a life consistent with his or her beliefs. Christians disagree over whether or not it is possible for people to lose their salvation, but all agree that those who move away from their faith are in serious trouble and need to repent. James urges Christians to help backsliders return to God. By taking the initiative, praying for the person, and acting in love, we can meet the person where he or she is and bring him or her back to God and his forgiveness.

5:20 The book of James emphasizes faith in action. Right living is the evidence and result of faith. The church must serve with compassion, speak lovingly and truthfully, live in obedience to God's commands, and love one another. The body of believers ought to be an example of heaven on earth, drawing people to Christ through love for God and each other. If we truly believe God's Word, we will *live* it day by day. God's Word is not merely something we read or think about, but something we do. Belief, faith, and trust must have hands and feet—ours!

1 PETER

CRUSHED, overwhelmed, devastated, torn—these waves of feelings wash over those who suffer, obliterating hope and threatening to destroy them. Suffering has many forms—physical abuse, debilitating disease, social ostracism, persecution. The pain and anguish tempt a person to turn back, to surrender, to give in.

Many first-century followers of Christ were suffering and being abused and persecuted for believing in and obeying Jesus. Beginning in Jerusalem at the hands of their Jewish brothers, the persecution spread to the rest of the world— wherever Christians gathered. It climaxed when Rome determined to rid the empire of the "Christ-ones"—those who would not bow to Caesar.

Peter knew persecution firsthand. Beaten and jailed, he had been threatened often. He had seen fellow Christians die and the church scattered. But he knew Christ, and nothing could shake his confidence in his risen Lord. So Peter wrote to the church scattered and suffering for the faith, giving comfort and hope, and urging continued loyalty to Christ.

Peter begins by thanking God for salvation (1:2–6). He explains to his readers that trials will refine their faith (1:7–9). They should believe in spite of their circumstances; for many in past ages believed in God's plan of salvation, even the prophets of old who wrote about it but didn't understand it. But now salvation has been revealed in Christ (1:10–13).

In response to such a great salvation, Peter commands them to live holy lives (1:14–16), to reverently fear and trust God (1:17–21), to be honest and loving (1:22—2:1), and to become like Christ (2:1–3).

Jesus Christ, as "a chosen and precious cornerstone" upon whom the church is to be built (2:4, 6), is also the stone that was rejected, causing those who are disobedient to stumble and fall (2:7, 8). But the church, built upon this Stone, is to be God's holy priesthood (2:9, 10).

Next, Peter explains how believers should live during difficult times (2:11— 4:11). Christians should be above reproach (2:12–17), imitating Christ in all their social roles—masters and servants, husbands and wives, church members and neighbors (2:18—3:17). Christ should be our model for obedience to God in the midst of great suffering (3:18—4:11).

Peter then outlines the right attitude to have about persecution: Expect it (4:12), be thankful for the privilege of suffering for Christ (4:13–18), and trust God for deliverance (4:19).

Next, Peter gives some special instructions: Elders should care for God's flock (5:1–4), younger men should be submissive to those who are older (5:5, 6), and everyone should trust God and resist Satan (5:7–11).

Peter concludes by introducing Silas and by sending personal greetings, possibly from the church in Rome, and from Mark (5:12–14).

When you suffer for doing what is right, remember that following Christ is a costly commitment. When persecuted for your faith, rejoice that you have been counted worthy to suffer for your Lord. He suffered for us; as his followers, we should expect nothing less. As you read 1 Peter, remember that trials will come to refine your faith. When they come, remain faithful to God.

VITAL STATISTICS

PURPOSE:
To offer encouragement to suffering Christians

AUTHOR:
Peter

ORIGINAL AUDIENCE:
Jewish Christians driven out of Jerusalem and scattered throughout Asia Minor

DATE WRITTEN:
Approximately A.D. 62–64, possibly from Rome

SETTING:
Peter was probably in Rome when the great persecution under Emperor Nero began. (Eventually Peter was executed during this persecution.) Throughout the Roman empire, Christians were being tortured and killed for their faith, and the church in Jerusalem was being scattered.

KEY VERSE:
"These have come so that your faith . . . may be proved genuine and may result in praise, glory and honor when Jesus Christ is revealed" (1:7).

KEY PEOPLE:
Peter, Silas, Mark

KEY PLACES:
Jerusalem, Rome, and the regions of Pontus, Galatia, Cappadocia, Asia Minor, and Bithynia

SPECIAL FEATURES:
Peter used several images that were very special to him because Jesus had used them when he had revealed certain truths to Peter. Peter's name (which means "rock") had been given to him by Jesus. Peter's conception of the church— a spiritual house composed of living stones built upon Christ as the foundation—had come from Christ. Jesus had encouraged Peter to care for the church as a shepherd tending the flock. Thus, it is not surprising to see Peter using living stones (2:5–9) and shepherds and sheep (2:25; 5:2, 4) to describe the church.

THE BLUEPRINT

1. God's great blessings to his people (1:1—2:10)
2. The conduct of God's people in the midst of suffering (2:11—4:19)
3. The shepherding of God's people in the midst of suffering (5:1–14)

Peter wrote to Jewish Christians who were experiencing persecution for their faith. He wrote to comfort them with the hope of eternal life and to challenge them to continue living holy lives. Those who suffer for being Christians become partners with Christ in his suffering. As we suffer, we must remember that Christ is both our hope in the midst of suffering and our example of how to endure suffering faithfully.

MEGATHEMES

THEME	EXPLANATION	IMPORTANCE
Salvation	Our salvation is a gracious gift from God. God chose us out of his love for us, Jesus died to pay the penalty for our sin, and the Holy Spirit cleansed us from sin when we believed. Eternal life is a wonderful gift for those who trust in Christ.	Our safety and security are in God. If we experience joy in relationship with Christ now, how much greater will our joy be when he returns and we see him face to face. Such a hope shuld motivate us to serve Christ with greater commitment.
Persecution	Peter offers faithful believers comfort and hope. We should expect ridicule, rejection, and suffering because we are Christians. Persecution makes us stronger because it refines our faith. We can face persecution victoriously, as Christ did, if we rely on him.	Christians still suffer for what they believe. We should expect persecution, but we don't have to be terrified by it. The fact that we will live eternally with Christ should give us the confidence, patience, and hope to stand firm even when we are persecuted.
God's Family	We are privileged to belong to God's family, a community with Christ as the founder and foundation. Everyone in this community is related—we are all brothers and sisters, loved equally by God.	Because Christ is the foundation of our family, we must be devoted, loyal, and faithful to him. By obeying him, we show that we are his children. We must accept the challenge to live differently from the society around us.
Family Life	Peter encouraged the wives of unbelievers to submit to their husbands' authority as a means of winning them to Christ. He urged all family members to treat others with sympathy, love, compassion, and humility.	We must treat our families lovingly. Though it's never easy, willing service is the best way to influence loved ones. To gain the strength we need for self-discipline and submission, we need to pray for God's help.
Judgment	God will judge everyone with perfect justice. We all will face God. He will punish evildoers and those who persecute God's people. Those who love him will be rewarded with life forever in his presence.	Because all are accountable to God, we can leave judgment of others to him. We must not hate or resent those who persecute us. We should realize that we will be held responsible for how we live each day.

1. God's great blessings to his people

1 Peter, an apostle of Jesus Christ,

To God's elect, strangers in the world, scattered throughout Pontus, Galatia, Cappadocia, Asia and Bithynia, ²who have been chosen according to the foreknowledge of God the Father, through the sanctifying work of the Spirit,ᵃ for obedience to Jesus Christ and sprinkling by his blood:

Grace and peace be yours in abundance.

1:2
ᵃ 2Th 2:13

1:1 The apostle Peter wrote this letter to encourage believers who would likely face trials and persecution under Emperor Nero. During most of the first century, Christians were not hunted down and killed throughout the Roman empire. They could, however, expect social and economic persecution from three main sources: the Romans, the Jews, and their own families. All would very likely be misunderstood; some would be harassed; a few would be tortured and even put to death.

The legal status of Christians in the Roman empire was unclear. Many Romans still thought of Christians as members of a Jewish sect, and because the Jewish religion was legal, they considered Christianity legal also—as long as Christians complied with the empire's laws. However, they became the target of persecution when they refused to worship the emperor as a god, refused to worship at pagan temples (so business for these moneymaking enterprises dropped wherever Christianity took hold), or exposed and rejected the horrible immorality of pagan culture.

Many Jews did not appreciate being legally associated with Christians. As the book of Acts frequently records, Jews occasionally harmed Christians physically, drove them out of town, or attempted to turn Roman officials against them. Saul, later the great apostle Paul, was an early Jewish persecutor of Christians.

THE CHURCHES OF PETER'S LETTER

Peter addressed his letter to the churches located throughout Bithynia, Pontus, Asia, Galatia, and Cappadocia. Paul had evangelized many of these areas; other areas had churches that were begun by the Jews who were in Jerusalem on the day of Pentecost and heard Peter's powerful sermon (see Acts 2:9–11).

Another source of persecution was the Christian's own family. Under Roman law, the head of the household had absolute authority over all its members. Unless the ruling male became a Christian, the wife, children, and servants who were believers might well face extreme hardship. If they were sent away, they would have no place to turn but the church; if they were beaten, no court of law would uphold their interests.

Peter may have been writing especially for new Christians and those planning to be baptized. Peter wanted to warn them about what lay ahead, and they needed his encouraging words to help them face opposition. This letter is still helpful for any Christians facing trials. Many Christians around the world are living under governments more repressive than the Roman empire of the first century. Christians everywhere are subject to misunderstanding, ridicule, and even harassment by unbelieving friends, employers, and family members. None of us is exempt from catastrophe, pain, illness, and death—trials that, like persecution, make us lean heavily on God's grace. For today's readers, as well as for Peter's original audience, the theme of this letter is *hope*.

1:1 Peter (also called Simon and Cephas) was one of the 12 disciples chosen by Jesus (Mark 1:16–18; John 1:42) and, with James and John, was part of the inner group that Jesus singled out for special training and fellowship. Peter was one of the first to recognize Jesus as the Messiah, God's Son, and Jesus gave him a special leadership role in the church (Matthew 16:16–19; Luke 22:31, 32; John 21:15–19). Although during Jesus' trial Peter denied knowing Jesus, Peter repented and became a great apostle. For more information on Peter, see his Profile in Matthew 27, p. 1595.

1:1 This letter is addressed to "God's elect, strangers in the world," or to the Jewish Christians scattered throughout the world as a result of persecution against believers in and around Jerusalem. The first believers and leaders of the early church were Jews. When they became Christians, they didn't give up their Jewish heritage, just as you didn't give up your nationality when you became a follower of Christ. Because of persecution, these believers had been scattered throughout the Roman world (this scattering is described in Acts 8:1–4). Persecution didn't

stop the spread of the gospel; instead, persecution served as a way to introduce the Good News to the whole empire. Thus the churches to whom Peter wrote also included Gentile Christians.

1:2 Peter encouraged his readers by this strong declaration that they were *chosen* by God the Father. At one time, only the nation of Israel could claim to be God's chosen people; but through Christ, all believers—Jews and Gentiles—belong to God. Our salvation and security rest in God's merciful choice; no trials or persecutions can take away the eternal life he gives to those who believe in him.

1:2 This verse mentions all three members of the Trinity—God the Father, God the Son (Jesus Christ), and God the Holy Spirit. All members of the Trinity work to bring about our salvation. The Father chose us before we chose him (Ephesians 1:4). Jesus Christ the Son died for us while we were still sinners (Romans 5:6–10). The Holy Spirit brings us the benefits of salvation and sets us apart (sanctifies us) for God's service (2 Thessalonians 2:13).

1:2 How did God "choose" us? Don't we make our own choices? God alone originates and accomplishes our salvation because of his grace; we do nothing to earn it. Being "chosen" in no way removes the necessity for people to choose to follow. The fact that God knows all events and decisions beforehand, even ordains them beforehand, does not mean that he forces the actions of his creatures or leaves them with no choice. Instead, God's foreknowledge means that he took the initiative and chose people before they had done anything to deserve it. God had intimate knowledge of these future believers; he knew who would believe, and he knew them personally. Those chosen ones were known by God the Father as a father knows his children, except that God knew about them from eternity past. God is not trapped in time—what he knows is from eternity past into eternity future. Believers are chosen, but not against their will. When the time comes, they accept the gospel message.

Praise to God for a Living Hope

³Praise be to the God and Father of our Lord Jesus Christ! In his great mercy^b he has given us new birth into a living hope through the resurrection of Jesus Christ from the dead,^c ⁴and into an inheritance that can never perish, spoil or fade—kept in heaven for you, ⁵who through faith are shielded by God's power^d until the coming of the salvation that is ready to be revealed in the last time. ⁶In this you greatly rejoice, though now for a little while you may have had to suffer grief in all kinds of trials.^e ⁷These have come so that your faith—of greater worth than gold, which perishes even though refined by fire—may be proved genuine^f and may result in praise, glory and honor when Jesus Christ is revealed. ⁸Though you have not seen him, you love him; and even though you do not see him now, you believe in him^g and are filled with an inexpressible and glorious joy, ⁹for you are receiving the goal of your faith, the salvation of your souls.^h

¹⁰Concerning this salvation, the prophets, who spoke of the grace that was to come to you, searched intently and with the greatest care, ¹¹trying to find out the time and circumstances to which the Spirit of Christⁱ in them was pointing when he predicted the sufferings of Christ and the glories that would follow. ¹²It was revealed to them that they were not serving themselves but you, when they spoke of the things that have now been told you by those who have preached the gospel to you by the Holy Spirit sent from heaven. Even angels long to look into these things.

Be Holy

¹³Therefore, prepare your minds for action; be self-controlled; set your hope fully on the grace to be given you when Jesus Christ is revealed. ¹⁴As obedient children, do not conform^j

1:3
^bJas 1:18
^c1Co 15:20

1:5
^dJn 10:28

1:6
^eJas 1:2

1:7
^fJas 1:3

1:8
^gJn 20:29

1:9
^hRo 6:22

1:11
ⁱ2Pe 1:21

1:14
^jRo 12:2

1:3 The term *new birth* refers to spiritual birth (regeneration)—the Holy Spirit's act of bringing believers into God's family. Jesus used this concept of new birth when he explained salvation to Nicodemus (see John 3). This term is a wonderful metaphor of new life from God. You cannot be a Christian without a fresh beginning based on the salvation Christ brings. To be born again is a magnificent gift from God.

1:3–5 Do you need encouragement? Peter's words offer joy and hope in times of trouble, and he bases his confidence on what God has done for us in Christ Jesus. We're called into a *living* hope of eternal life (1:3). Our hope is not only for the future; eternal life begins when we trust Christ and join God's family. God will help us remain true to our faith through whatever difficult times we must face. The "last time" is the judgment day of Christ described in Romans 14:10 and Revelation 20:11–15. No matter what trials or persecution you may face, your soul cannot be harmed if you have accepted Christ's gift of salvation. You will receive the promised rewards.

1:4 The Jews had looked forward to an inheritance in the promised land of Canaan (Numbers 32:19; Deuteronomy 2:12; 19:9). Although the nation had received that right of inheritance, eventually they defiled their faith through the influence of foreign nations. The people's sins had caused the promise to become only a fading memory. Christians now look forward to another inheritance—eternal life in the eternal city of God. God has reserved the inheritance; it will never fade or decay; it will be unstained by sin. The best part is that *you* have an inheritance if you have trusted Christ as your Savior.

1:6 Why were Christians the target of persecution? (1) They refused to worship the emperor as a god and thus were viewed as atheists and traitors. (2) They refused to worship at pagan temples, so business for these moneymaking enterprises dropped wherever Christianity took hold. (3) They didn't support the Roman ideals of self, power, and conquest; and the Romans scorned the Christian ideal of self-sacrificing service. (4) They exposed and rejected the horrible immorality of pagan culture.

1:6, 7 Peter mentions trials and suffering several times in this letter: 1:6, 7; 3:13–17; 4:12–19; 5:9. All believers face such trials when they let their light shine into the darkness. We must accept trials as part of the refining process that burns away impurities and prepares us to meet Christ. As gold is heated, impurities float to the

top and can be skimmed off. Likewise, our trials, struggles, and persecutions refine and strengthen our faith, making us useful to God. Instead of asking, "Why me?" we should respond to suffering with a new set of responses: (1) *Confidence* that God knows, plans, and directs our lives for the good. It's hard to calculate sometimes, but God always provides his love and strength for us. God leads us toward a better future. (2) *Perseverance* when facing grief, anger, sorrow, and pain. We express our grief, but we don't give in to bitterness and despair. (3) *Courage* because with Jesus as Brother and Savior, we need not be afraid. He who suffered for us will not abandon us. Jesus carries us through everything.

1:8, 9 Jesus had said to his disciple Thomas, who came to believe after touching the resurrected Christ: "Because you have seen me, you have believed; blessed are those who have not seen and yet have believed" (John 20:29). Peter, having heard those words, repeats them here: "Though you have not seen him, you love him." That faith brings both salvation and the promise of a day when pain will end and perfect justice begin. Faith will be rewarded and evil will be punished. But what should we do until then? The Bible's answer is simple but not easy: Because we know the future, we must faithfully serve God here and now. If today that means resolving a conflict, mending a hurt, working a dull job, confronting a belligerent child, rebuilding a marriage, or just waiting for guidance—do it all with the joy of God, who will return with his reward!

1:11 The Spirit of Christ is another name for the Holy Spirit. Before Jesus left his ministry on earth to return to heaven, he promised to send the Holy Spirit, the Counselor, to teach, help, and guide his followers (John 14:15–17, 26; 16:7). The Holy Spirit would tell them all about Jesus and would reveal his glory (John 15:26; 16:14). The Old Testament prophets, writing under the Holy Spirit's inspiration (2 Peter 1:20, 21), described the coming of the Messiah. The New Testament apostles, through the inspiration of the same Spirit, preached the crucified and risen Lord.

1:13, 14 The imminent return of Christ should motivate us to live for him. This means being mentally alert ("prepare your minds for action"), disciplined ("self-controlled"), and focused ("set your hope fully"). Are you ready to meet Christ, living as God's obedient child?

1:14–16 The God of Israel and of the Christian church is holy—he sets the standard for morality. Unlike the Roman gods, he is

1:15
k 2Co 7:1

1:16
l Lev 11:44, 45

1:17
m Heb 12:28

1:18
n 1Co 6:20

1:22
o Heb 13:1

1:23
p Jn 1:13

1:25
q Isa 40:6-8

2:2
r 1Co 3:2

2:3
s Heb 6:5

to the evil desires you had when you lived in ignorance. 15But just as he who called you is holy, so be holy in all you do; k 16for it is written: "Be holy, because I am holy."a l

17Since you call on a Father who judges each man's work impartially, live your lives as strangers here in reverent fear. m 18For you know that it was not with perishable things such as silver or gold that you were redeemed n from the empty way of life handed down to you from your forefathers, 19but with the precious blood of Christ, a lamb without blemish or defect. 20He was chosen before the creation of the world, but was revealed in these last times for your sake. 21Through him you believe in God, who raised him from the dead and glorified him, and so your faith and hope are in God.

22Now that you have purified yourselves by obeying the truth so that you have sincere love for your brothers, love one another deeply, o from the heart. b 23For you have been born again, p not of perishable seed, but of imperishable, through the living and enduring word of God. 24For,

> "All men are like grass,
>   and all their glory is like the flowers of the field;
>   the grass withers and the flowers fall,
> 25   but the word of the Lord stands forever."c q

And this is the word that was preached to you.

2 Therefore, rid yourselves of all malice and all deceit, hypocrisy, envy, and slander of every kind. 2Like newborn babies, crave pure spiritual milk, r so that by it you may grow up in your salvation, 3now that you have tasted that the Lord is good. s

a 16 Lev. 11:44,45; 19:2   b 22 Some early manuscripts from a pure heart   c 25 Isaiah 40:6-8

---

not warlike, adulterous, or spiteful. Unlike the gods of the pagan cults popular in the first century, he is not bloodthirsty or promiscuous. He is a God of mercy and justice who cares personally for each of his followers. Our holy God expects us to imitate him by following his high moral standards. Like him, we should be both merciful and just; like him, we should sacrifice ourselves for others.

1:15, 16 After people commit their lives to Christ, they usually still feel a pull back to their old ways. Peter tells us to be like our heavenly Father—holy in everything we do. Holiness means being totally devoted or dedicated to God, set aside for his special use and set apart from sin and its influence. We're to be set apart and different, not blending in with the crowd, yet not being different just for the sake of being different. What makes us different are God's qualities in our lives. Our focus and priorities must be his. All this is in direct contrast to our old ways (1:14). We cannot become holy on our own, but God gives us his Holy Spirit to help us obey and to give us power to overcome sin. Don't use the excuse that you can't help slipping into sin. Call on God's power to free you from sin's grip.

1:17 "Reverent fear" is the healthy respect of a believer for the all-powerful God. Because God is the Judge of all the earth, we dare not ignore him or treat him casually. We should not assume that our privileged status as God's children gives us freedom to do whatever we want. We should not be spoiled children, but grateful children who love to show respect for our heavenly Father.

1:18, 19 A slave was "redeemed" when someone paid money to buy his or her freedom. God redeemed us from the tyranny of sin, not with money, but with the precious blood of his own Son (Romans 6:6, 7; 1 Corinthians 6:20; Colossians 2:13, 14; Hebrews 9:12). We cannot escape from sin on our own; only the life of God's Son can free us.

1:20 Christ's sacrifice for our sins was not an afterthought, not something God decided to do when the world spun out of control. This plan was set in motion by the all-knowing, eternal God long before the world was created. What a comfort it must have been to Jewish believers to know that Christ's coming and his work of salvation were planned by God long before the world

began. This assured them that the law was not being scrapped because it didn't work, but that both the law and the coming of Christ were part of God's eternal plan.

1:22 "Sincere love" involves selfless giving; a self-centered person can't truly love. God's love and forgiveness free you to take your eyes off yourselves and to meet others' needs. By sacrificing his life, Christ showed that he truly loves you. Now you can love others by following his example and giving of yourself sacrificially.

1:24, 25 Quoting Isaiah 40:6–8, Peter reminds believers that everything in this life—possessions, accomplishments, people—will eventually fade away and disappear. Only God's will, word, and work are permanent. We must stop grasping the temporary, and begin focusing our time, money, and energy on the permanent—the word of God and our eternal life in Christ.

2:2, 3 One characteristic all children share is that they want to grow up—to be like big brother or sister or like their parents. When we are born again, we become spiritual newborn babies. If we are healthy, we will yearn to grow. How sad it is that some people never grow up. The need for milk is a natural instinct for a baby, and it signals the desire for nourishment that will lead to growth. Once we see our need for God's Word and begin to find nourishment in Christ, our spiritual appetite will increase, and we will start to mature. How strong is your desire for God's Word?

The Living Stone and a Chosen People

4 As you come to him, the living Stone—rejected by men but chosen by God and precious to him— 5 you also, like living stones, are being built into a spiritual house to be a holy priesthood, offering spiritual sacrifices acceptable to God through Jesus Christ.ᵗ 6 For in Scripture it says:

> "See, I lay a stone in Zion,
> a chosen and precious cornerstone,
> and the one who trusts in him
> will never be put to shame."ᵃ ᵘ

2:5
ᵗ Php 4:18

2:6
ᵘ Isa 28:16

7 Now to you who believe, this stone is precious. But to those who do not believe,

> "The stone the builders rejected
> has become the capstone,ᵇ "ᶜ ᵛ

8 and,

> "A stone that causes men to stumble
> and a rock that makes them fall."ᵈ ᵂ

2:7
ᵛ Ps 118:22

2:8
ᵂ Isa 8:14
ˣ Ro 9:22

They stumble because they disobey the message—which is also what they were destined for.ˣ

9 But you are a chosen people,ʸ a royal priesthood, a holy nation, a people belonging to God, that you may declare the praises of him who called you out of darkness into his wonderful light.ᶻ 10 Once you were not a people, but now you are the people of God;ᵃ once you had not received mercy, but now you have received mercy.

2:9
ʸ Dt 10:15
ᶻ Ac 26:18

2:10
ᵃ Hos 1:9, 10

2. The conduct of God's people in the midst of suffering

11 Dear friends, I urge you, as aliens and strangers in the world, to abstain from sinful desires, which war against your soul.ᵇ 12 Live such good lives among the pagans that, though they accuse you of doing wrong, they may see your good deedsᶜ and glorify Godᵈ on the day he visits us.

2:11
ᵇ Jas 4:1

2:12
ᶜ Php 2:15
ᵈ Mt 5:16

a6 Isaiah 28:16   *b7* Or *cornerstone*   *c7* Psalm 118:22   *d8* Isaiah 8:14

2:4–8 In describing the church as God's spiritual house, Peter drew on several Old Testament texts familiar to his Jewish Christian readers: Psalm 118:22; Isaiah 8:14; 28:16. Peter's readers would have understood the living stones to be Israel; then Peter applied the image of "stone" to Christ. Once again Peter showed that the church does not cancel the Jewish heritage, but fulfills it.

2:4–8 Peter portrays the church as a living, spiritual house, with Christ as the foundation and cornerstone and each believer as a stone. Paul portrays the church as a body, with Christ as the head and each believer as a member (see, for example, Ephesians 4:15, 16). Both pictures emphasize *community*. One stone is not a temple or even a wall; one body part is useless without the others. In our individualistic society, it is easy to forget our interdependence with other Christians. When God calls you to a task, remember that he is also calling others to work with you. Together your individual efforts will be multiplied. Look for those people and join with them to build a beautiful house for God.

2:5 What are the "spiritual sacrifices" that we offer to God? When sacrificing an animal according to God's law, a priest would kill the animal, cut it in pieces, and place it on the altar. Sacrifice was important, but even in the Old Testament God made it clear that obedience from the heart was much more important (see 1 Samuel 15:22; Psalm 40:6; Amos 5:21–24). God wants us, his "holy priesthood," to offer ourselves as living and spiritual sacrifices—daily laying aside our own desires and following him, putting all our energy and resources at his disposal, and trusting him to guide us.

2:6–8 No doubt Peter often thought of Jesus' words to him right after he confessed that Jesus was "the Christ, the Son of the living God": "You are Peter, and on this rock I will build my church, and the gates of Hades will not overcome it" (Matthew 16:16–18). What is the stone that really counts in the building of the church? Peter answers: Christ himself. Jesus Christ is called "the stone that causes men to stumble and a rock that makes them fall."

Some will stumble over Christ because they reject him or refuse to believe that he is who he says he is. But Psalm 118:22 says that "the stone the builders rejected has become the capstone," the most important part of God's building, the church. What are the characteristics of Christ, the cornerstone? (1) He is completely trustworthy; (2) he is precious to believers; (3) and, though rejected by some, he is the most important part of the church. People who refuse to believe in Christ have made the greatest mistake of their lives. They have stumbled over the one person who could save them and give meaning to their lives, and they have fallen into God's hands for judgment.

2:9 Christians sometimes speak of "the priesthood of all believers." In Old Testament times, people did not approach God directly. A priest acted as intermediary between God and sinful human beings. With Christ's victory on the cross, that pattern changed. Now we can come directly into God's presence without fear (Hebrews 4:16), and we are given the responsibility of bringing others to him also (2 Corinthians 5:18–21). When we are united with Christ as members of his body, we join in his priestly work of reconciling God and man.

2:9, 10 People often base their self-concept on their accomplishments. But our relationship with Christ is far more important than our jobs, successes, wealth, or knowledge. We have been chosen by God as his very own, and we have been called to represent him to others. Remember that your value comes from being one of God's children, not from what you can achieve. We have worth because of what *God does*, not because of what you do.

2:11 As believers, we are "aliens and strangers" in this world, because our real home is with God. Heaven is not the pink-cloud-and-harp existence popular in cartoons. Heaven is where God lives. Life in heaven operates according to God's principles and values, and it is eternal and unshakable. Heaven came to earth in the symbolism of the Jewish sanctuary (the tabernacle and

must keep his tongue from evil
and his lips from deceitful speech.
¹¹ He must turn from evil and do good;
he must seek peace and pursue it.
¹² For the eyes of the Lord are on the righteous
and his ears are attentive to their prayer,
but the face of the Lord is against those who do evil."ᵃ ᵘ

¹³Who is going to harm you if you are eager to do good?ᵛ ¹⁴But even if you should suffer for what is right, you are blessed. ʷ "Do not fear what they fearᵇ; do not be frightened."ᶜ ¹⁵But in your hearts set apart Christ as Lord. Always be prepared to give an answerˣ to everyone who asks you to give the reason for the hope that you have. But do this with gentleness and respect, ¹⁶keeping a clear conscience,ʸ so that those who speak maliciously against your good behavior in Christ may be ashamed of their slander.ᶻ ¹⁷It is better, if it is God's will, to suffer for doing good than for doing evil. ¹⁸For Christ died for sinsᵃ once for all, the righteous for the unrighteous, to bring you to God. He was put to death in the bodyᵇ but made alive by the Spirit, ¹⁹through whomᵈ also he went and preached to the spirits in prison ²⁰who disobeyed long ago when God waited patiently in the days of Noah while the ark was being built.ᶜ In it only a few people, eight in all, were savedᵈ through water, ²¹and this water symbolizes baptism that now saves youᵉ also—not the removal of dirt from the body but the pledgeᵉ of a good conscience toward God. It saves you by the resurrection of Jesus Christ,ᶠ ²²who has gone into heaven and is at God's right hand—with angels, authorities and powers in submission to him. ᵍ

3:12
ᵘ Ps 34:12-16

3:13
ᵛ Pr 16:7

3:14
ʷ 1Pe 2:19, 20

3:15
ˣ Col 4:6

3:16
ʸ Heb 13:18
ᶻ 1Pe 2:12, 15

3:18
ᵃ 1Pe 2:21
ᵇ Col 1:22

3:20
ᶜ Ge 6:3, 5, 13, 14
ᵈ Heb 11:7

3:21
ᵉ Tit 3:5
ᶠ 1Pe 1:3

3:22
ᵍ Ro 8:38

ᵃ12 Psalm 34:12-16   ᵇ14 Or *not fear their threats*   ᶜ14 Isaiah 8:12   ᵈ18,19 Or *alive in the spirit,* ¹⁹*through which*   ᵉ21 Or *response*

SUBMISSION
Submission is:

Functional	a distinguishing of our roles and the work we are called to do
Relational	a loving acknowledgement of another's value as a person
Reciprocal	a mutual, humble cooperation with one another
Universal	an acknowledgment by the church of the all-encompassing lordship of Jesus Christ

Submission is voluntarily cooperating with someone, first out of love and respect for God and then out of love and respect for that person. Submitting to unbelievers is difficult, but it is a vital part of leading them to Jesus Christ. We are not called to submit to nonbelievers to the point that we compromise our relationship with God, but we must look for every opportunity to humbly serve in the power of God's Spirit.

3:11 Too often we see peace as merely the absence of conflict, and we think of peacemaking as a passive role. But an effective peacemaker actively pursues peace. He or she builds good relationships, knowing that peace is a by-product of commitment. The peacemaker anticipates problems and deals with them before they occur. When conflicts arise, he or she brings them into the open and deals with them before they grow unmanageable. Making peace is hard work, but it results in God's blessing.

3:15 Some Christians believe that faith is a personal matter that should be kept to oneself. It is true that we shouldn't be boisterous or obnoxious in sharing our faith, but we should always be ready to give an answer, gently and respectfully, when asked about our faith, our lifestyle, or our Christian perspective. Can others see your hope in Christ? Are you prepared to tell them what Christ has done in your life?

3:16 You may not be able to keep people from slandering you, but you can at least stop supplying them with ammunition. As long as you do what is right, their accusations will be empty and will only embarrass them. Keep your conduct above criticism!

3:18–20 The meaning of preaching "to the spirits in prison" is not completely clear, and commentators have explained it in different ways. The traditional interpretation is that between his death and resurrection, Christ announced salvation to God's faithful followers who had been waiting for their salvation during the whole Old Testament era. Some think that this passage says that Christ's Spirit was in Noah as Noah preached to those imprisoned

by sin (but now in hell). Still others say that Christ went to Hades to proclaim his victory and final condemnation to the fallen angels imprisoned there since Noah's day (see 2 Peter 2:4).

In any case, the passage shows that Christ's Good News of salvation and victory is not limited. While some Bible passages, such as this one, may remain unclear, we can discover certain truths from them along with the context of the rest of Scripture. In this passage, we discover that: (1) God speaks. While we puzzle over what, where, and how, we can see that God is communicating to the world. (2) God triumphs. Christ victoriously preached, indicating his power, control, and transcendence over all creation. (3) God saves. God exerts himself to rescue those who desire him. This mysterious passage tells us at least this much—and that is indeed.

3:21 Peter says that Noah's salvation *through water* symbolized baptism, a ceremony involving water. In baptism we identify with Jesus Christ, who separates us from the lost and gives us new life. It is not the ceremony that saves us; instead, the ceremony is evidence of our faith in Christ's death and resurrection. Baptism is the symbol of the cleansing that happens in the hearts of those who believe (Romans 6:3–5; Galatians 3:27; Colossians 2:12). By identifying themselves with Christ through baptism, Peter's readers could resist turning back, even under the pressure of persecution. Public baptism would keep them from the temptation to renounce their faith.

Living for God

4 Therefore, since Christ suffered in his body, arm yourselves also with the same attitude, because he who has suffered in his body is done with sin. ²As a result, he does not live the rest of his earthly life for evil human desires, but rather for the will of God. ³For you have spent enough time in the past *h* doing what pagans choose to do—living in debauchery, lust, drunkenness, orgies, carousing and detestable idolatry. ⁴They think it strange that you do not plunge with them into the same flood of dissipation, and they heap abuse on you. ⁵But they will have to give account to him who is ready to judge the living and the dead.*i* ⁶For this is the reason the gospel was preached even to those who are now dead,*j* so that they might be judged according to men in regard to the body, but live according to God in regard to the spirit.

⁷The end of all things is near.*k* Therefore be clear minded and self-controlled so that you can pray. ⁸Above all, love each other deeply, because love covers over a multitude of sins.*l* ⁹Offer hospitality to one another without grumbling. ¹⁰Each one should use whatever gift he has received to serve others,*m* faithfully administering God's grace in its various forms. ¹¹If anyone speaks, he should do it as one speaking the very words of God. If anyone serves, he should do it with the strength God provides, so that in all things God may be praised through Jesus Christ. To him be the glory and the power for ever and ever. Amen.

Suffering for Being a Christian

¹²Dear friends, do not be surprised at the painful trial you are suffering, as though something strange were happening to you. ¹³But rejoice that you participate in the sufferings of Christ, so that you may be overjoyed when his glory is revealed.*n* ¹⁴If you are insulted because of the name of Christ, you are blessed, for the Spirit of glory and of God rests on you. ¹⁵If you suffer, it should not be as a murderer or thief or any other kind of criminal, or even

4:3
h Eph 2:2

4:5
i Ac 10:42; 2Ti 4:1

4:6
j 1Pe 3:19

4:7
k Ro 13:11

4:8
l Pr 10:12

4:10
m Ro 12:6, 7

4:13
n Ro 8:17

4:1, 2 Suffering helps us be like Christ, yet people will do anything to avoid pain. Followers of Christ, however, should be willing and prepared to do God's will and to suffer for it if necessary. We can overcome sin when we focus on Christ and what he wants us to do. Pain and danger reveal our true values. Anyone who suffers for doing good and still faithfully obeys in spite of suffering has made a clean break with sin.

4:3, 4 People whose lives change radically at conversion may experience contempt from his or her old friends. They may be scorned not only because they refuse to participate in certain activities, but also because their priorities have changed and they are now heading in the opposite direction. Their lives incriminate their friends' sinful activities. Mature Christians should help new believers resist such pressures of opposition by helping them to be faithful to Christ, surrounding them as new friends, and encouraging them to develop new habits and activities that are not only enjoyable but positive for their spiritual growth.

4:5 The basis of salvation is our belief in Jesus (Acts 16:31), but the basis for judgment is how we have lived. All people will be judged: believers for the rewards they will receive; unbelievers for punishment. Those who inflict persecution are marked for punishment when they stand before God. All will give an account to God, so we must be ready. This may give you a new perspective on your activities and actions today. Are you prepared to explain them to God?

4:5, 6 Many people in the early church had concerns about life after death. In Thessalonica, Christians worried that loved ones who died before Christ's return might never see Christ (1 Thessalonians 4:13–18). Peter's readers needed to be reminded that the dead (both the faithful and their oppressors) would be judged. The judgment will be perfectly fair, he pointed out, because even the dead have heard the gospel (see also 3:18, 19). The Good News was first announced when Jesus Christ preached on the earth, but it has been operating since before the creation of the world (Ephesians 1:4), and it affects all people, the dead as well as the living.

4:7–9 We should live expectantly because Christ is coming. Getting ready to meet Christ involves continually growing in love for

God and for others (see Jesus' summary of the law in Matthew 22:37–40). It is important to pray regularly, and it is also important to reach out to needy people. Your possessions, status, and power will mean nothing in God's kingdom, but you will spend eternity with other people. Invest your time and talents where they will make an eternal difference.

4:9 For more about hospitality, see the note on Romans 12:13.

4:10, 11 Our abilities should be faithfully used in serving others; none are for our own exclusive enjoyment. Some people, well aware of their abilities, believe that they have the right to use their abilities as they please. Others feel that they have no special talents at all. Peter addresses both groups in these verses. Everyone has some gifts; find yours and use them. Peter mentions speaking and serving. Paul lists these and other abilities in Romans 12:6–8; 1 Corinthians 12:8–11; Ephesians 4:11. Even as you seek to discover your gifts, if you see a need in the church, seek to meet it. You may find gifts in areas you might not have guessed!

4:11 How is God praised when we use our abilities? When we use them as he directs, to help others, they will see Jesus in us and praise him for the help they have received. Peter may have been thinking of Jesus' words, "Let your light shine before men, that they may see your good deeds and praise your Father in heaven" (Matthew 5:16).

4:14–16 Again Peter brings to mind Jesus' words: "Blessed are you when people insult you, persecute you and falsely say all kinds of evil against you because of me" (Matthew 5:11). Christ will send his Spirit to strengthen those who are persecuted for their faith. Peter creates no illusions; God's plan for your life may include pain and hardship. When trouble comes, don't be surprised.

This does not mean that all suffering is the result of good Christian conduct. Peter says to distinguish between suffering for being a believer and suffering for doing wrong things. For example, a Christian may think he is being picked on for his faith when it is obvious to everyone else that his own unpleasant behavior is the cause of his problems. It may take careful thought or wise counsel to determine the real cause of our suffering. We can be assured, however, that whenever we suffer because of our loyalty to Christ, he will be with us all the way.

4:16
o Ac 5:41

4:18
p Lk 23:31

as a meddler. [16]However, if you suffer as a Christian, do not be ashamed, but praise God that you bear that name. *o* [17]For it is time for judgment to begin with the family of God; and if it begins with us, what will the outcome be for those who do not obey the gospel of God? [18]And,

> "If it is hard for the righteous to be saved,
>   what will become of the ungodly and the sinner?"*a p*

[19]So then, those who suffer according to God's will should commit themselves to their faithful Creator and continue to do good.

3. The shepherding of God's people in the midst of suffering
To Elders and Young Men

5:1
q Lk 24:48
r Rev 1:9

5:2
s 1Ti 3:3

5:3
t Eze 34:4

5:5
u Jas 4:6

5 To the elders among you, I appeal as a fellow elder, a witness*q* of Christ's sufferings and one who also will share in the glory to be revealed:*r* [2]Be shepherds of God's flock that is under your care, serving as overseers—not because you must, but because you are willing, as God wants you to be; not greedy for money,*s* but eager to serve; [3]not lording it over*t* those entrusted to you, but being examples to the flock. [4]And when the Chief Shepherd appears, you will receive the crown of glory that will never fade away.

[5]Young men, in the same way be submissive to those who are older. All of you, clothe yourselves with humility toward one another, because,

> "God opposes the proud
>   but gives grace to the humble."*b u*

a 18 Prov. 11:31   *b 5* Prov. 3:34

4:16 It is not shameful to suffer for being a Christian. When Peter and John were persecuted for preaching the Good News, they rejoiced because such persecution was a mark of God's approval of their work (Acts 5:41). Don't seek out suffering, and don't try to avoid it. Instead, keep on doing what is right regardless of the suffering it might bring.

4:17, 18 This refers not to final judgment but to God's refining discipline (Hebrews 12:7). God often allows believers to sin and then experience the consequences. He does this for several reasons: (1) to show us our potential for sinning, (2) to encourage us to turn from sin and more constantly depend on him, (3) to prepare us to face other, even stronger temptations in the future, and (4) to help us stay faithful and keep on trusting him. If believers need earthly discipline (judgment) from God, how much more will unbelievers receive it? If it is hard for the righteous to be saved (only because of God's mercy), what chance have those who reject Christ?

4:19 Everywhere the Bible counsels that we trust God—in good times and bad, during sunny skies and thunderclouds, when we have a pocket full of change and a pocket full of sawdust. How does trust work? (1) *Trust overcomes fear.* Genuine trust in God says, "Whatever mess I'm in, my heavenly Father will lead me.". (2) *Trust overcomes depression.* No matter how overwhelming the situation or how low it makes you feel, God can draw you back to the light. (3) *Trust overcomes hate.* When careless or cruel people hurt you, sometimes irreparably, you can hate forever or you can trust God, but you can't do both. God is there to steady even the worst situation—always with a promise, always with hope. Commit your life to him for safekeeping. Rely on him when you face your worst circumstances.

5:1 Elders were church officers providing supervision, protection, discipline, instruction, and direction for the other believers. *Elder* simply means "older." Both Greeks and Jews gave positions of great honor to wise older men, and the Christian church continued this pattern of leadership. Elders carried great responsibility, and they were expected to be good examples.

5:1, 2 Peter, one of Jesus' 12 disciples, was one of the three who saw Christ's glory at the transfiguration (Mark 9:1–13; 2 Peter 1:16–18). Often the spokesman for the apostles, Peter witnessed Jesus' death and resurrection, preached at Pentecost,

and became a pillar of the Jerusalem church. But writing to the elders, he identified himself as a fellow elder, not a superior. He asked them to "be shepherds of God's flock," exactly what Jesus had told him to do (John 21:15–17). Peter was taking his own advice as he worked along with the other elders in caring for God's faithful people. His identification with the elders is a powerful example of Christian leadership, where authority is based on service, not power (Mark 10:42–45).

5:2–5 Peter describes several characteristics of good leaders in the church: (1) They realize they are caring for God's flock, not their own; (2) they lead out of eagerness to serve, not out of obligation; (3) they are concerned for what they can give, not for what they can get; (4) they lead by example, not force. All of us lead others in some way. Whatever our role, our leadership should be in line with these characteristics.

5:4 The Chief Shepherd is Jesus Christ. This refers to his second coming, when he will judge all people and give rewards to his faithful followers. The "crown," while metaphorical, pictures the glory believers will receive that is eternal and unchanging. What better motivation for selfless service! What better motivation for keeping the faith in the face of suffering and temptation!

5:5 Both young and old can benefit from Peter's instructions. Pride often keeps older people from trying to understand young people and keeps young people from listening to those who are older. Peter told both young and old to be humble and to serve each other. Young men should follow the leadership of older men, who should lead by example. Respect those who are older than you, listen to those younger than you, and be humble enough to admit that you can learn from each other.

6 Humble yourselves, therefore, under God's mighty hand, that he may lift you up in due time. *v* 7 Cast all your anxiety on him because he cares for you.

8 Be self-controlled and alert. Your enemy the devil prowls around like a roaring lion looking for someone to devour. 9 Resist him, standing firm in the faith, because you know that your brothers throughout the world are undergoing the same kind of sufferings. *w*

10 And the God of all grace, who called you to his eternal glory in Christ, after you have suffered a little while, will himself restore you and make you strong, *x* firm and steadfast. 11 To him be the power for ever and ever. Amen.

Final Greetings

12 With the help of Silas, *a* whom I regard as a faithful brother, I have written to you briefly, *y* encouraging you and testifying that this is the true grace of God. Stand fast in it.

13 She who is in Babylon, chosen together with you, sends you her greetings, and so does my son Mark. *z* 14 Greet one another with a kiss of love. *a*

Peace *b* to all of you who are in Christ.

a 12 Greek *Silvanus*, a variant of *Silas*

5:6
v Jas 4:10

5:9
w Ac 14:22

5:10
x 2Th 2:17

5:12
y Heb 13:22

5:13
z Ac 12:12

5:14
a Ro 16:16
b Eph 6:23

5:6 We often worry about our position and status, hoping to get proper recognition for what we do. But Peter advises us to remember that God's recognition counts more than human praise. God is able and willing to bless us according to his timing. Humbly obey God regardless of present circumstances, and in his good time—either in this life or in the next—he will lift you up.

5:7 Carrying your worries, stresses, and daily struggles by yourself shows that you have not trusted God fully with your life. It takes humility, however, to recognize that God cares, to admit your need, and to let others in God's family help you. Sometimes we think that struggles caused by our own sin and foolishness are not God's concern. But when we turn to God in repentance, he will bear the weight even of those struggles. Letting God have your anxieties calls for action, not passivity. Don't submit to circumstances, but to the Lord who controls circumstances.

5:8, 9 Lions attack sick, young, or straggling animals; they choose victims who are alone or not alert. Peter warns us to watch out for Satan when we are suffering or being persecuted. If you are feeling alone, weak, helpless, and cut off from other believers, or if you are so focused on your troubles that you forget to watch for danger, those are the times when you are especially vulnerable to Satan's attacks. During times of suffering, seek other Christians for support. Keep your eyes on Christ, and resist the devil. Then, says James, "he will flee from you" (James 4:7).

5:10 When we are suffering, we often feel as though our pain will never end. Peter gave these faithful Christians the wider perspective. In comparison with eternity, their suffering would last only "a little while." Some of Peter's readers would be strengthened and delivered in their own lifetimes. Others would be released from their suffering through death. All of God's faithful followers are assured of an eternal life with Christ where there will be no suffering (Revelation 21:4).

5:12 Silas was one of the men chosen to deliver the letter from the Jerusalem council to the church in Antioch (Acts 15:22). He accompanied Paul on his second missionary journey (Acts 15:40—18:11), is mentioned by Paul in the salutation of Paul's letters to the Thessalonians (1 Thessalonians 1:1; 2 Thessalonians 1:1), and ministered with Timothy in Corinth (2 Corinthians 1:19).

5:13 *Babylon* has been broadly understood by believers to be a reference to Rome. Just as the nation of Israel had been under captivity to Babylon, so the Christians as the new Israel were exiles in a foreign land.

5:13 Mark, also called John Mark, was known to many of this letter's readers because he had traveled widely (Acts 12:25—13:13; 15:36–41) and was recognized as a leader in the church (Colossians 4:10; Philemon 24). Mark was probably with the disciples at the time of Jesus' arrest (Mark 14:51, 52). Tradition says that Peter was Mark's main source of information when Mark wrote his Gospel.

5:14 Peter wrote this letter just before the cruel Emperor Nero began persecuting Christians in Rome and throughout the empire. Afraid for his life, Peter had three times denied even knowing Jesus (John 18:15–27). But here, having learned how to stand firm in an evil world, he encouraged other Christians who were facing persecution for their faith. Peter himself lived by the words he wrote because he was martyred for his faith. Those who stand for Christ will be persecuted because the world is ruled by Christ's greatest enemy. But just as the small group of early believers stood against persecution, so we must be willing to stand for our faith with the patience, endurance, and courage that Peter exhibited.

2 PETER

WARNINGS have many forms: lights, signs, sights, sounds, smells, feelings, and written words. With varied focus, their purpose is the same—to advise alertness and give notice of imminent danger. Responses to these warnings will also vary—from disregard and neglect to evasive or corrective action. How a person reacts to a warning is usually determined by the situation and the source. One reacts differently to an impending storm than to an onrushing automobile, and the counsel of a trusted friend is heeded more than advice from a stranger or the fearful imaginings of a child.

Second Peter is a letter of warning—from an authority none other than the courageous, experienced, and faithful apostle. And it is the last communication from this great warrior of Christ. Soon thereafter he would die, martyred for his faith.

Previously Peter had written to comfort and encourage believers in the midst of suffering and persecution—an external onslaught. But three years later, in this letter containing his last words, he wrote to warn them of an internal attack—complacency and heresy. He spoke of holding fast to the nonnegotiable facts of the faith, of growing and maturing in the faith, and of rejecting all who would distort the truth. To follow this advice would ensure Christ-honoring individuals and Christ-centered churches.

After a brief greeting (1:1), Peter gives the antidote for stagnancy and short-sightedness in the Christian life (1:2–11). Then he explains that his days are numbered (1:12–15) and that the believers should listen to his messages and the words of Scripture (1:16–21).

Next, Peter gives a blunt warning about false teachers (2:1–22). They will become prevalent in the last days (2:1, 2); they will do or say anything for money (2:3); they will spurn the things of God (2:2, 10, 11); they will do whatever they feel like doing (2:12–17); they will be proud and boastful (2:18, 19); they will be judged and punished by God (2:3–10, 20–22).

Peter concludes his brief letter by explaining why he has written it (3:1–18): to remind them of the words of the prophets and apostles that predicted the coming of false teachers, to give the reasons for the delay in Christ's return (3:1–13), and to encourage them to beware of heresies and to grow in their faith (3:14–18).

Addressed to those who "have received a faith as precious as ours," 2 Peter could have been written to us. Our world is filled with false prophets and teachers, who claim to have the truth and who clamor for attention and allegiance. Listen carefully to Peter's message and heed his warning. Determine to grow in your knowledge of Christ and to reject all those who preach anything inconsistent with God's Word.

VITAL STATISTICS

PURPOSE:
To warn Christians about false teachers and to exhort them to grow in their faith in and knowledge of Christ

AUTHOR:
Peter

ORIGINAL AUDIENCE:
The church at large

DATE WRITTEN:
Approximately A.D. 67, three years after 1 Peter was written, possibly from Rome

SETTING:
Peter knew that his time on earth was limited (1:13, 14), so he wrote about what was on his heart, warning believers of what would happen when he was gone—especially about the presence of false teachers. He reminded his readers of the unchanging truth of the gospel.

KEY VERSE:
"His divine power has given us everything we need for life and godliness through our knowledge of him who called us by his own glory and goodness" (1:3).

KEY PEOPLE:
Peter, Paul

SPECIAL FEATURES:
The date and destination are uncertain, and the authorship has been disputed. Because of this, 2 Peter was the last book admitted to the canon of the New Testament Scripture. Also, there are similarities between 2 Peter and Jude.

THE BLUEPRINT

1. Guidance for growing Christians (1:1–21)
2. Danger to growing Christians (2:1–22)
3. Hope for growing Christians (3:1–18)

While Peter wrote his first letter to teach about handling persecution (trials from without), he wrote this letter to teach about handling heresy (trials from within). False teachers are often subtly deceitful. Believers today must still be vigilant against falling into false doctrine, heresy, and cult activity. This letter gives us clues to help detect false teaching.

MEGATHEMES

THEME	EXPLANATION	IMPORTANCE
Diligence	If our faith is real, it will be evident in our godly behavior. If people are diligent in Christian growth, they won't backslide or be deceived by false teachers.	Growth is essential. It begins with faith and culminates in love for others. To keep growing we need to know God, keep on following him, and remember what he taught us. We must remain diligent in faithful obedience and Christian growth.
False Teachers	Peter warns the church to beware of false teachers. These teachers were proud of their position, promoted sexual sin, and advised against keeping the Ten Commandments. Peter countered them by pointing to the Spirit-inspired Scriptures as our authority.	Christians need discernment to be able to resist false teachers. God can rescue us from their lies if we stay true to his Word, the Bible, and reject those who distort the truth.
Christ's Return	One day Christ will create a new heaven and earth, where we will live forever. As Christians, our hope is in this promise. But with Christ's return comes his judgment on all who refuse to believe.	The cure for complacency, lawlessness, and heresy is found in the confident assurance that Christ will return. God is still giving unbelievers time to repent. To be ready, Christians must keep on trusting and resist the pressure to give up waiting for Christ's return.

1. Guidance for growing Christians

1 Simon Peter, a servant *a* and apostle of Jesus Christ,

To those who through the righteousness of our God and Savior Jesus Christ *b* have received a faith as precious as ours:

2 Grace and peace be yours in abundance through the knowledge of God and of Jesus our Lord.

Making One's Calling and Election Sure

3 His divine power *c* has given us everything we need for life and godliness through our knowledge of him who called us *d* by his own glory and goodness. 4 Through these he has given us his very great and precious promises, *e* so that through them you may participate in the divine nature and escape the corruption in the world caused by evil desires.

5 For this very reason, make every effort to add to your faith goodness; and to goodness, knowledge; 6 and to knowledge, self-control; and to self-control, perseverance; and to perseverance, godliness; 7 and to godliness, brotherly kindness; and to brotherly kindness, love. 8 For if you possess these qualities in increasing measure, they will keep you from being

1:1
a Ro 1:1
b Tit 2:13

1:3
c 1Pe 1:5
d 1Th 2:12

1:4
e 2Co 7:1

1:1 First Peter was written just before the time that the Roman Emperor Nero began his persecution of Christians. Second Peter was written two or three years later (between A.D. 66-68), after persecution had intensified. First Peter was a letter of encouragement to the Christians who suffered, but 2 Peter focuses on the church's internal problems, especially on the false teachers who were causing people to doubt their faith and turn away from Christianity. Second Peter combats their heresies by denouncing the evil motives of the false teachers and reaffirming Christianity's truths—the authority of Scripture, the primacy of faith, and the certainty of Christ's return.

1:2 Many believers want an abundance of God's grace and peace, but they are unwilling to put forth the effort to get to know him better through Bible study and prayer. To enjoy the privileges God offers us freely, we have "the knowledge of God and of Jesus our Lord."

1:3, 4 The power to grow doesn't come from within us, but from God. Because we don't have the resources to be truly

godly, God allows us to "participate in the divine nature" in order to keep us from sin and help us live for him. When we are born again, God by his Spirit empowers us with his own moral goodness. See John 3:6; 14:17–23; 2 Corinthians 5:21; and 1 Peter 1:22, 23.

1:5–9 Faith must be more than belief in certain facts; it must result in action, growth in Christian character, and the practice of moral discipline, or it will die away (James 2:14–17). Peter lists several of faith's actions: learning to know God better, developing perseverance, doing God's will, loving others. These actions do not come automatically; they require hard work. They are not optional; all of them must be a continual part of the Christian life. We don't finish one and start on the next, but we work on them all together. God empowers and enables us, but he also gives us the responsibility to learn and to grow.

1:6 False teachers were saying that self-control was not needed because deeds do not help the believer anyway (2:19). It is true that deeds cannot save us, but it is absolutely false to think they are unimportant. We are saved so that we can grow to resemble Christ and so that we can serve others. God wants to produce his character in us. But to do this, he demands our discipline and effort. As we obey Christ who guides us by his Spirit, we will develop self-control, not only with respect to food and drink, but also with respect to our emotions.

1:8
f Jn 15:2

1:9
g Eph 5:26

ineffective and unproductive *f* in your knowledge of our Lord Jesus Christ. 9But if anyone does not have them, he is nearsighted and blind, and has forgotten that he has been cleansed from his past sins. *g*

10Therefore, my brothers, be all the more eager to make your calling and election sure. For if you do these things, you will never fall, 11and you will receive a rich welcome into the eternal kingdom of our Lord and Savior Jesus Christ.

Prophecy of Scripture

1:12
h 1Jn 2:21

1:13
i 2Co 5:1, 4

1:14
j 2Ti 4:6
k Jn 21:18, 19

1:16
l Mt 17:1-8

1:17
m Mt 3:17

12So I will always remind you of these things, *h* even though you know them and are firmly established in the truth you now have. 13I think it is right to refresh your memory as long as I live in the tent of this body, *i* 14because I know that I will soon put it aside, *j* as our Lord Jesus Christ has made clear to me. *k* 15And I will make every effort to see that after my departure you will always be able to remember these things.

16We did not follow cleverly invented stories when we told you about the power and coming of our Lord Jesus Christ, but we were eyewitnesses of his majesty. *l* 17For he received honor and glory from God the Father when the voice came to him from the Majestic Glory, saying, "This is my Son, whom I love; with him I am well pleased." *a m* 18We ourselves heard this voice that came from heaven when we were with him on the sacred mountain.

1:19
n Ps 119:105
o Rev 22:16

1:21
p 2Ti 3:16
q Ac 1:16

19And we have the word of the prophets made more certain, and you will do well to pay attention to it, as to a light *n* shining in a dark place, until the day dawns and the morning star *o* rises in your hearts. 20Above all, you must understand that no prophecy of Scripture came about by the prophet's own interpretation. 21For prophecy never had its origin in the will of man, but men spoke from God *p* as they were carried along by the Holy Spirit. *q*

a 17 Matt. 17:5; Mark 9:7; Luke 9:35

1:9 Our faith must go beyond what we believe; it must become a dynamic part of all we do, resulting in good fruit and spiritual maturity. Salvation does not depend on good deeds, but it results in good deeds. A person who claims to be saved while remaining unchanged does not understand faith or what God has done for him or her.

1:10 Peter wanted to rouse the complacent believers who had listened to the false teachers and believed that because salvation is not based on good deeds they could live any way they wanted. If you truly belong to the Lord, Peter wrote, your hard work will prove it. If you're not working to develop the qualities listed in 1:5–7, you may not belong to him. If you are the Lord's—and your hard work backs up your claim to be chosen by God ("calling and election")—you will be able to resist the lure of false teaching or glamorous sin. What does your life say about your faith?

1:12–15 Outstanding coaches constantly review the basics of the sport with their teams, and good athletes can execute the fundamentals consistently well. Believers must not neglect the basics of their faith, even as they go on to study deeper truths. Just as an athlete needs constant practice, Christians need constant reminders of the fundamentals of our faith and of how we came to believe in the first place. Don't allow yourself to be bored or impatient with messages on the basics of the Christian life. Instead, take the attitude of an athlete who continues to practice and refine the basics.

1:13, 14 Peter knew that he would die soon. Many years before, Christ had prepared Peter for the kind of death Peter would face (see John 21:18, 19). At this time, Peter knew that his death was at hand. Peter was martyred for the faith in about A.D. 68. According to one tradition, he was crucified upside down, at his own request, because he did not feel worthy to die in the same manner as his Master.

1:16–18 Peter is referring to the transfiguration where Jesus' divine identity was revealed to him and two other disciples, James and John (see Matthew 17:1–8; Mark 9:2–8; Luke 9:28–36).

1:16–21 This section is a strong statement on the inspiration of Scripture. Peter affirms that the Old Testament prophets wrote God's messages. He puts himself and the other apostles in the same category, because they also proclaim God's truth. The Bible is not a collection of fables or human ideas about God. It is God's very words given *through* people *to* people. Peter emphasized his authority as an eyewitness as well as the God-inspired authority of Scripture to prepare the way for his harsh words against the false teachers. If these wicked men were contradicting the apostles and the Bible, their message could not be from God.

1:19 Christ is the "morning star," and when he returns, he will shine in his full glory. Until that day we have Scripture as a light and the Holy Spirit to illuminate Scripture for us and guide us as we seek the truth. For more on Christ as the morning star, see Luke 1:78; Ephesians 5:14; Revelation 2:28; 22:16.

1:20, 21 "Men spoke from God as they were carried along by the Holy Spirit" means that Scripture did not come from the creative work of the prophets' own invention or interpretation. God inspired the writers, so their message is authentic and reliable. God used the talents, education, and cultural background of each writer (they were not mindless robots); and God cooperated with the writers in such a way to ensure that the message he intended was faithfully communicated in the very words they wrote.

2. Danger to growing Christians
False Teachers and Their Destruction

2 But there were also false prophets among the people, just as there will be false teachers among you. They will secretly introduce destructive heresies, even denying the sovereign Lord *r* who bought them—bringing swift destruction on themselves. [2] Many will follow their shameful ways and will bring the way of truth into disrepute. [3] In their greed these teachers will exploit you *s* with stories they have made up. Their condemnation has long been hanging over them, and their destruction has not been sleeping.

[4] For if God did not spare angels when they sinned, but sent them to hell,*a* putting them into gloomy dungeons *b* to be held for judgment; *t* [5] if he did not spare the ancient world when he brought the flood on its ungodly people, but protected Noah, a preacher of righteousness, and seven others; *u* [6] if he condemned the cities of Sodom and Gomorrah by burning them to ashes, *v* and made them an example of what is going to happen to the ungodly; [7] and if he rescued Lot, *w* a righteous man, who was distressed by the filthy lives of lawless men [8] (for that righteous man, living among them day after day, was tormented in his righteous soul by the lawless deeds he saw and heard)— [9] if this is so, then the Lord knows how to rescue godly men from trials and to hold the unrighteous for the day of judgment, while continuing their punishment. *c* [10] This is especially true of those who follow the corrupt desire of the sinful nature *d* and despise authority.

Bold and arrogant, these men are not afraid to slander celestial beings;*x* [11] yet even angels, although they are stronger and more powerful, do not bring slanderous accusations against such beings in the presence of the Lord. *y* [12] But these men blaspheme in matters they do not understand. They are like brute beasts, creatures of instinct, born only to be caught and destroyed, and like beasts they too will perish. *z*

[13] They will be paid back with harm for the harm they have done. Their idea of pleasure is

a4 Greek *Tartarus*   *b4* Some manuscripts *into chains of darkness*   *c9* Or *unrighteous for punishment until the day of judgment*   *d10* Or *the flesh*

**Cross-references (right margin):**
- 2:1 *r* Jude 4
- 2:3 *s* 2Co 2:17
- 2:4 *t* Jude 6; Rev 20:1, 2
- 2:5 *u* 1Pe 3:20
- 2:6 *v* Ge 19:24, 25
- 2:7 *w* Ge 19:16
- 2:10 *x* Jude 8
- 2:11 *y* Jude 9
- 2:12 *z* Jude 10

2:1 Jesus had told the disciples that false teachers would come (Matthew 24:11; Mark 13:22, 23). Peter had heard these words, and at this time he was seeing them come true. Just as false prophets had contradicted the true prophets in Old Testament times (see, for example, Jeremiah 23:16–40; 28:1–17), telling people only what they wanted to hear, so false teachers were twisting Christ's teachings and the words of his apostles. These teachers were belittling the significance of Jesus' life, death, and resurrection. Some claimed that Jesus couldn't be God; others claimed that he couldn't have been a real man. These teachers allowed and even encouraged all kinds of wrong and immoral acts, especially sexual sin. We must be careful to avoid false teachers today. Any book, tape series, or TV message must be evaluated according to God's Word. Beware of special meanings or interpretations that belittle Christ or his work.

2:1-3 Peter gives three warning signs for identifying false teachers:

(1) *Shameful ways*. Do their lives contain or condone immoral practices? Does the group listening to the false teachers have a lot of immoral sexual relationships?

(2) *Greed*. Teachers have a right to financial support (1 Corinthians 9:1–14; Galatians 6:6; 1 Timothy 5:17, 18), but is money the teacher's or group's prime motivation? Before you send money to any cause, evaluate it carefully. Is the teacher or preacher clearly serving God or merely promoting his/her own interests? Will the person or organization use the money to promote valid ministry, or will it merely finance further promotions or extravagant lifestyles?

(3) *Lying*. Is the leader offended when you ask for the scriptural backing behind his/her statements? Does he/she fudge on the facts when asked for evidence?

Believers today would do well to heed Peter's warnings against false teachers; the danger is great.

2:4-6 If God did not spare angels, or people who lived before the flood, or the citizens of Sodom and Gomorrah, he would not spare these false teachers. These words that promised justice were a great comfort to those who were oppressed. God will

punish all evildoers. These words also served as a warning to wanderers to not stray away from the truth. Some people would have us believe that God will save all people because he is so loving. But it is foolish to think that God will cancel the last judgment. Don't ever minimize the certainty of God's judgment on those who rebel against him.

2:7-9 Just as God rescued Lot from Sodom, so he is able to rescue us from the temptations and trials we face in a wicked world. Lot was not sinless, but he put his trust in God and was spared when Sodom was destroyed. For more information on Lot, see his Profile in Genesis 14, p. 27. God also will judge those who cause the temptations and trials, so we need never worry about justice being done.

2:10-12 The *celestial beings* may be angels, all the glories of the unseen world, or more probably, fallen angels. A similar passage is found in Jude 8–10. Whoever they are, the false teachers slandered the spiritual realities they did not understand, taking Satan's power lightly and claiming to have the ability to judge evil. Many in our world today mock the supernatural. They deny the reality of the spiritual world and claim that only what can be seen and felt is real. Like the false teachers of Peter's day, they are fools who will be proven wrong in the end. Don't take Satan and his supernatural powers of evil lightly, and don't become arrogant about how defeated he will be. Although Satan will be destroyed completely, he is at work now trying to render Christians complacent and ineffective.

2:13, 14 The feast may have been part of the celebration of the Lord's Supper—a full meal that ended with Communion. The false teachers, although they were sinning openly, took part in these meals with everyone else in the church. In one of the greatest of hypocritical acts, they attended a sacred feast designed to promote love and unity among believers, while at the same time they gossiped and slandered those who disagreed with their opinions. As Paul told the Corinthians, "Therefore, whoever eats the bread or drinks the cup of the Lord in an unworthy manner will be guilty of sinning against the body and blood of the Lord" (1 Corinthians 11:27). These men were guilty of more than false teaching

2:13
a Ro 13:13
b 1Co 11:20, 21
2:15
c Nu 22:4-20

to carouse in broad daylight. *a* They are blots and blemishes, reveling in their pleasures while they feast with you. *a b* 14With eyes full of adultery, they never stop sinning; they seduce the unstable; they are experts in greed—an accursed brood! 15They have left the straight way and wandered off to follow the way of Balaam *c* son of Beor, who loved the wages of wickedness. 16But he was rebuked for his wrongdoing by a donkey—a beast without speech—who spoke with a man's voice and restrained the prophet's madness.

2:17
d Jude 12
2:18
e Jude 16
2:19
f Ro 6:16
2:20
g 2Pe 1:2
h Mt 12:45

2:22
i Pr 26:11

17These men are springs without water *d* and mists driven by a storm. Blackest darkness is reserved for them. 18For they mouth empty, boastful words *e* and, by appealing to the lustful desires of sinful human nature, they entice people who are just escaping from those who live in error. 19They promise them freedom, while they themselves are slaves of depravity— for a man is a slave to whatever has mastered him. *f* 20If they have escaped the corruption of the world by knowing *g* our Lord and Savior Jesus Christ and are again entangled in it and overcome, they are worse off at the end than they were at the beginning. *h* 21It would have been better for them not to have known the way of righteousness, than to have known it and then to turn their backs on the sacred command that was passed on to them. 22Of them the proverbs are true: "A dog returns to its vomit,"*b i* and, "A sow that is washed goes back to her wallowing in the mud."

3. Hope for growing Christians
The Day of the Lord

3:1
j 2Pe 1:13

3 Dear friends, this is now my second letter to you. I have written both of them as reminders *j* to stimulate you to wholesome thinking. 2I want you to recall the words spoken in the past by the holy prophets and the command given by our Lord and Savior through your apostles.

3:3
k 2Pe 2:10
3:4
l Eze 12:22
3:5
m Ge 1:6, 9
n Ps 24:2
3:7
o ver 10, 12
3:8
p Ps 90:4
3:9
q Heb 10:37

3First of all, you must understand that in the last days scoffers will come, scoffing and following their own evil desires. *k* 4They will say, "Where is this 'coming' he promised? *l* Ever since our fathers died, everything goes on as it has since the beginning of creation." 5But they deliberately forget that long ago by God's word *m* the heavens existed and the earth was formed out of water and by water. *n* 6By these waters also the world of that time was deluged and destroyed. 7By the same word the present heavens and earth are reserved for fire, *o* being kept for the day of judgment and destruction of ungodly men.

8But do not forget this one thing, dear friends: With the Lord a day is like a thousand years, and a thousand years are like a day. *p* 9The Lord is not slow in keeping his promise, *q* as some understand slowness. He is patient with you, not wanting anyone to perish, but everyone to come to repentance.

a 13 Some manuscripts *in their love feasts*   *b* 22 Prov. 26:11

---

and promoting evil pleasures; they were guilty of leading others away from God's Son, Jesus.

2:15 Balaam was hired by a pagan king to curse Israel. He did what God told him to do for a time (Numbers 22—24), but eventually his evil motives and desire for money won out (Numbers 25:1–3; 31:16). Like the false teachers of Peter's day, Balaam used religion for personal advancement, a sin that God does not take lightly.

2:19 A person is a slave to whatever controls him or her. Many believe that freedom means doing anything we want. But no one is ever completely free in that sense. If we refuse to follow God, we will follow our own sinful desires and become enslaved to what our bodies want. If we submit our lives to Christ, he will free us from slavery to sin. Christ frees us to serve him, a freedom that results in our ultimate good.

2:20–22 Peter is speaking of a person who has learned about Christ and how to be saved, and has even been positively influenced by Christians, but then rejects the truth and returns to his or her sin. This person is worse off than before, because he or she has rejected the only way out of sin, the only way of salvation. Like a person sinking in quicksand who refuses to grab the rope thrown to him or her, the one who turns away from Christ casts aside his or her only means of escape (see the note on Luke 11:24–26).

3:3, 4 "In the last days" scoffers will say that Jesus is never coming back, but Peter refutes their argument by explaining

God's mastery over time. The "last days" is the time between Christ's first and second comings; thus we, like Peter, live in the last days. We must do the work to which God has called us and believe that he will return as he promised.

3:7 In Noah's day the earth was judged by water; at the second coming it will be judged by fire. This fire is described in Revelation 19:20; 20:10–15.

3:8, 9 God may have seemed slow to these believers as they faced persecution every day and longed to be delivered. But God is not slow; he just is not on *our* timetable (Psalm 90:4). Jesus is waiting so that more sinners will repent and turn to him. We must not sit and wait for Christ to return, but we should live with the realization that time is short and that we have important work to do. Be ready to meet Christ any time, even today; yet plan your course of service as though he may not return for many years.

10 But the day of the Lord will come like a thief. The heavens will disappear with a roar; the elements will be destroyed by fire, and the earth and everything in it will be laid bare.[a] [r]

11 Since everything will be destroyed in this way, what kind of people ought you to be? You ought to live holy and godly lives 12 as you look forward[s] to the day of God and speed its coming.[b] That day will bring about the destruction of the heavens by fire, and the elements will melt in the heat. 13 But in keeping with his promise we are looking forward to a new heaven and a new earth,[t] the home of righteousness.

14 So then, dear friends, since you are looking forward to this, make every effort to be found spotless, blameless and at peace with him. 15 Bear in mind that our Lord's patience means salvation, just as our dear brother Paul also wrote you with the wisdom that God gave him. [u] 16 He writes the same way in all his letters, speaking in them of these matters. His letters contain some things that are hard to understand, which ignorant and unstable[v] people distort, as they do the other Scriptures, to their own destruction.

17 Therefore, dear friends, since you already know this, be on your guard so that you may not be carried away by the error of lawless men and fall from your secure position. [w] 18 But grow in the grace and knowledge of our Lord and Savior Jesus Christ. To him be glory both now and forever! Amen.

a 10 Some manuscripts be burned up   b 12 Or as you wait eagerly for the day of God to come

3:10 [r] Mt 24:35

3:12 [s] 1Co 1:7

3:13 [t] Isa 65:17; 66:22; Rev 21:1

3:15 [u] Eph 3:3

3:16 [v] 2Pe 2:14

3:17 [w] Rev 2:5

3:10, 11 The day of the Lord is the day of God's judgment on the earth. Here it is used in reference to Christ's return. Christ's second coming will be sudden and terrible for those who do not believe in him. But if we are morally clean and spiritually alert, it won't come as a surprise. For other prophetic pictures of the day of the Lord, see Isaiah 34:4; Joel 3:15, 16; Matthew 24; Mark 13; Luke 21; Revelation 6:12–17. Realizing that the earth is going to be burned up, we should put our confidence in what is lasting and eternal and not be bound to earth and its treasures or pursuits. Do you spend more of your time piling up possessions, or striving to develop Christlike character?

3:13 God's purpose for people is not destruction but re-creation (see Isaiah 66:22; Revelation 21; 22). God will purify the heavens and earth with fire; then he will create them anew. We can joyously look forward to the restoration of God's good world.

3:14 We should not become lazy and complacent because Christ has not yet returned. Instead, we should live in eager expectation of his coming. What would you like to be doing when Christ returns? That is how you should be living each day.

3:15, 16 By the time of Peter's writing, Paul's letters already had a widespread reputation. Notice that Peter spoke of Paul's letters as if they were on a level with "the other Scriptures." Already the early church was thinking of Paul's letters as inspired by God.

3:15–18 Peter and Paul had very different backgrounds and personalities, and they preached from different viewpoints. Paul emphasized salvation by grace, not law, while Peter preferred to talk about Christian life and service. The two men did not contradict each other, however, and they always held each other in high esteem. The false teachers intentionally misused Paul's writings by distorting them to condone lawlessness. No doubt this made the teachers popular, because people always like to have their favorite sins justified, but the net effect was to totally destroy Paul's message. Paul may have been thinking of teachers like these when he wrote in Romans 6:15: "What then? Shall we sin because we are not under law but under grace? By no means!" Peter warned his readers to avoid the mistakes of those wicked teachers by growing in the grace and knowledge of Jesus. The better we know Jesus, the less attractive false teaching will be.

3:18 Peter concludes this brief letter as he began, by urging his readers to grow in the grace and knowledge of the Lord and Savior Jesus Christ—to get to know him better and better. This is the most important step in refuting false teachers. No matter where we are in our spiritual journey, no matter how mature we are in our faith, the sinful world always will challenge our faith. We still have much room for growth. If every day we find some way to draw closer to Christ, we will be prepared to stand for truth in any and all circumstances.

"A GOOD man . . . yes . . . perhaps one of the best who ever lived . . . but just a man," say many. Others disagree, claiming that he suffered from delusions of grandeur—a "messiah complex." And the argument rages over the true identity of this man called Jesus. Suggestions have ranged from "simple teacher" to "egomaniac" and "misguided fool." Whoever he was, all would agree that Jesus left his mark on history.

Hearing these discussions, even Christians can begin to wonder and doubt. Is Jesus really God? Did he come to save sinners like us? Does God care about me?

First John was written to dispel doubts and to build assurance by presenting a clear picture of Christ. Entering history, Jesus was and is God in the flesh and God in focus—seen, heard, and touched by the author of this letter, John the apostle. John walked and talked with Jesus, saw him heal, heard him teach, watched him die, met him arisen, and saw him ascend. John knew God—he had lived with him and had seen him work. And John enjoyed fellowship with the Father and the Son all the days of his life.

The elder statesman in the church, John wrote this letter to his "dear children." In it he presented God as light, as love, and as life. He explained in simple and practical terms what it means to have fellowship with God.

At the same time, false teachers had entered the church, denying the incarnation of Christ. John wrote to correct their serious errors. So John's letter is a model for us to follow as we combat modern heresies.

John opens this letter by presenting his credentials as an eyewitness of the Incarnation and by stating his reason for writing (1:1–4). He then presents God as "light," symbolizing absolute purity and holiness (1:5–7), and he explains how believers can walk in the light and have fellowship with God (1:8–10). If they do sin, Christ is their defender (2:1, 2). John urges them to obey Christ fully and to love all the members of God's family (2:3–17). He warns his readers of "antichrists" and the antichrist who will try to lead them away from the truth (2:18–29).

In the next section, John presents God as "love"—giving, dying, forgiving, and blessing (3:1—4:21). God *is* love, and because God loves us, he calls us his children and makes us like Christ (3:1, 2). This truth should motivate us to live close to him (3:3–6). We can be sure of our family relationship with God when our lives are filled with good deeds and love for others (3:7–24). Again, John warns of false teachers who twist the truth. We should reject these false teachers (4:1–6) as we continue to live in God's love (4:7–21).

In the last section, John presents God as "life" (5:1–21). God's life is in his Son. To have his Son is to have eternal life.

Do you know God? Do you know Christ? Do you know that you have eternal life? First John was written to help you know the reality of God in your life through faith in Christ, to assure you that you have eternal life, and to encourage you to remain in fellowship with the God who is light and love. Read this letter written by one overwhelmed by God's love, and with renewed confidence, pass on his love to others.

VITAL STATISTICS

PURPOSE:
To reassure Christians in their faith and to counter false teachings

AUTHOR:
The apostle John

ORIGINAL AUDIENCE:
The letter is untitled and was written to no particular church. It was sent as a pastoral letter to several Gentile congregations.

DATE WRITTEN:
Probably between A.D. 85 and 90 from Ephesus

SETTING:
John was an older man and perhaps the only surviving apostle at this time. He had not yet been banished to the island of Patmos, where he would live in exile. As an eyewitness of Christ, he wrote authoritatively to give this new generation of believers assurance and confidence in God and in their faith.

KEY VERSE:
"I write these things to you who believe in the name of the Son of God so that you may know that you have eternal life" (5:13).

KEY PEOPLE:
John, Jesus

SPECIAL FEATURES:
John is the apostle of love, and love is mentioned throughout this letter. There are a number of similarities between this letter and John's Gospel—in vocabulary, style, and main ideas. John uses brief statements and simple words, and he features sharp contrasts—light and darkness, truth and error, God and Satan, life and death, and love and hate.

THE BLUEPRINT

1. God is light
   (1:1—2:27)
2. God is love
   (2:28—4:21)
3. God is life
   (5:1–21)

John wrote about the most vital aspects of faith so that his readers would know Christian truth from error. He emphasizes the basics of faith so that we can be confident in our faith. In our dark world, God is light. In our cold world, God brings the warmth of love. In our dying world, God brings life. When we lack confidence, these truths bring us certainty.

MEGATHEMES

THEME	EXPLANATION	IMPORTANCE
Sin	Even Christians sin. Sin requires God's forgiveness, and Christ's death provides it for us. Determining to live according to God's standards in the Bible shows that our life is being transformed.	We cannot deny our sin nature, maintain that we are "above" sinning, or minimize the consequences of sin in our relationship with God. We must resist the attraction of sin, yet we must confess when we do sin.
Love	Christ commands us to love others as he loved us. This love is evidence that we are truly saved. God is the Creator of love; he cares that his children love each other.	Love means putting others first and being unselfish. Love is action—showing others we care—not just saying it. To show love we must give sacrificially of our time and money to meet the needs of others.
Family of God	We become God's children by believing in Christ. God's life in us enables us to love our fellow family members.	How we treat others shows who our Father is. Live as a faithful, loving family member.
Truth and Error	Teaching that the physical body does not matter, false teachers encouraged believers to throw off moral restraints. They also taught that Christ wasn't really a man and that we must be saved by having some special mystical knowledge. The result was that people became indifferent to sin.	God is truth and light, so the more we get to know him, the better we can keep focused on the truth. Don't be led astray by any teaching that denies Christ's deity or humanity. Check the message; test the claims.
Assurance	God is in control of heaven and earth. Because his word is true, we can have assurance of eternal life and victory over sin. By faith we can be certain of our eternal destiny with him.	Assurance of our relationship with God is a promise, but it is also a way of life. We build our confidence by trusting in God's Word and in Christ's provision for our sin.

1. God is light
The Word of Life

1 That which was from the beginning, which we have heard, which we have seen with our eyes, [a] which we have looked at and our hands have touched [b]—this we proclaim concerning the Word of life. [2] The life appeared; [c] we have seen it and testify to it, and we proclaim to you the eternal life, which was with the Father and has appeared to us. [3] We proclaim to you what we have seen and heard, so that you also may have fellowship with us.

1:1
[a] Jn 1:14
[b] Jn 20:27

1:2
[c] Jn 1:1-4

1:1 First John was written by John, one of Jesus' original 12 disciples. He was probably "the disciple whom Jesus loved" (John 21:20) and, along with Peter and James, he had a special relationship with Jesus. This letter was written between A.D. 85-90 from Ephesus, before John's exile to the island of Patmos (see Revelation 1:9). Jerusalem had been destroyed in A.D. 70, and Christians were scattered throughout the empire. By the time John wrote this letter, Christianity had been around for more than a generation. It had faced and survived severe persecution. The main problem confronting the church at this time was declining commitment: many believers were conforming to the world's standards, failing to stand up for Christ, and compromising their faith. False teachers were plentiful, and they were accelerating the church's downward slide away from the Christian faith.

John wrote this letter to put believers back on track, to show the difference between light and darkness (truth and error), and to encourage the church to grow in genuine love for God and for one another. He also wrote to assure true believers that they possessed eternal life and to help them know that their faith was

genuine—so they could enjoy all the benefits of being God's children. For more about John, see his Profile in John 13, p. XXX.

1:1–5 John opens his first letter to the churches similar to the way he began his Gospel, emphasizing that Christ ("the Word of life") is eternal, that God came into the world as a human, that he, John, was an eyewitness to Jesus' life. John had lived with Jesus, having personal, physical contact with Jesus. He knew beyond any doubt that Jesus brings light and life.

1:3 As an eyewitness to Jesus' ministry, John was qualified to teach the truth about him. The readers of this letter had not seen and heard Jesus themselves, but they could trust that what John wrote was accurate. We are like those second- and third-generation Christians. Though we have not personally seen, heard, or touched Jesus, we have the New Testament record of his eyewitnesses, and we can trust that they spoke the truth about him. See John 20:29.

1:3, 4 John writes about having fellowship with other believers. There are three principles behind true Christian fellowship. First, our fellowship is grounded in the testimony of God's Word. Without this underlying strength, togetherness is impossible.

And our fellowship is with the Father and with his Son, Jesus Christ. ⁴We write this to make our ⁴ joy complete.

Walking in the Light

1:5
ᵈ1Jn 3:11
1:6
ᵉ2Co 6:14
1:7
ᶠHeb 9:14

⁵This is the message we have heard ᵈ from him and declare to you: God is light; in him there is no darkness at all. ⁶If we claim to have fellowship with him yet walk in the darkness, ᵉ we lie and do not live by the truth. ⁷But if we walk in the light, as he is in the light, we have fellowship with one another, and the blood of Jesus, his Son, purifies us from all ᵇ sin. ᶠ

ᵃ4 Some manuscripts *your*   ᵇ7 Or *every*

JOHN COUNTERS FALSE TEACHINGS	John counters two major threads in the false teachings of the heretics in this letter:
	1:6, 8, 10 . . . . They denied the reality of sin. John said that if we continue in sin, we can't claim to belong to God. If we say we have no sin, we are only fooling ourselves and refusing to live according to the truth.
	2:22; 4:1–3 . . . . They denied that Jesus was the Messiah—God in the flesh. John said that if we believe that Jesus was God incarnate and trust him for our salvation, we are children of God.

Second, it is mutual, depending on the unity of believers. Third, it is renewed daily through the Holy Spirit. True fellowship combines social and spiritual interaction, and it is made possible only through a living relationship with Christ.

1:5, 6 Light represents what is good, pure, true, holy, and reliable. Darkness represents what is sinful and evil. The statement "God is light" means that God is perfectly holy and true and that he alone can guide us out of the darkness of sin. Light is also related to truth in that light exposes whatever exists, whether it is good or bad. In the dark, good and evil look alike; in the light, they can be clearly distinguished. Just as darkness cannot exist in the presence of light, sin cannot exist in the presence of a holy God. If we want to have a relationship with God, we must put aside our sinful ways of living. To claim that we belong to him but then to go out and live for ourselves is hypocrisy. Christ will expose and judge such deceit.

1:6 Here John was confronting the first of three claims of the false teachers: that we can have fellowship with God and go on living in spiritual darkness. False teachers who thought that the physical body was evil or worthless taught one of two approaches to behavior: either they insisted on denying bodily desires through rigid discipline, or they approved of gratifying every physical lust because the body was going to be destroyed anyway. Obviously the second approach was more popular! Here John is saying that no one can claim to be a Christian and still live in evil and immorality. We can't love God and court sin at the same time.

1:7 How does Jesus' blood purify us from every sin? In Old Testament times, believers symbolically transferred their sins to an animal, which they then sacrificed (see a description of this ceremony in Leviticus 4). The animal died in their place to pay for their sin and to allow them to continue living in God's favor. God graciously forgave them because of their faith in him, and because they obeyed his commandments concerning the sacrifice. Those sacrifices anticipated the day when Christ would completely remove sin. Real cleansing from sin came with Jesus, the "Lamb of God, who takes away the sin of the world" (John 1:29). Sin, by its very nature, brings death—that is a fact as certain as the law of gravity. Jesus did not die for his own sins; he had none. Instead, by a transaction that we may never fully understand, he died for the sins of the world. When we commit our lives to Christ and thus identify ourselves with him, his death becomes ours. He has paid the penalty for our sins, and his blood has purified us. Just as Christ rose from the grave, we rise to a new life of fellowship with him (Romans 6:4).

1:8 Here John was attacking the second claim of the false teachers: that people had no natural tendency toward sin, that they were "without sin," and that they were then incapable of sinning. This is a lie. The false teachers refused to take sin seriously. They wanted to be considered Christians, but they saw no need to confess and repent. The death of Christ did not mean much to them because they didn't think they needed it. Instead of repenting and being purified by Christ's blood, they were encouraging sin among believers. In this life we are always capable of sinning, so we should never let down our guard.

1:8–10 The false teachers not only denied that sin breaks fellowship with God (1:6) and that they had a sinful nature (1:8), but they also denied that their conduct involved any sin at all (1:10). That was a lie that ignored one basic truth: All people are sinners by nature and by practice. At conversion all our sins are forgiven—past, present, and future. Yet even after we become Christians, we still sin and still need to confess. This kind of confession is not offered to gain God's acceptance, but to remove the barrier to fellowship that our sin has put between us and him. It is difficult, however, for many people to admit their faults and shortcomings, even to God. It takes humility and honesty to recognize our weaknesses, and most of us would rather pretend that we are strong. But we need not fear revealing our sins to God—he knows them already. He will not push us away, no matter what we've done. Instead he will draw us to himself.

⁸If we claim to be without sin, *g* we deceive ourselves and the truth is not in us. *h* ⁹If we confess our sins, he is faithful and just and will forgive us our sins and purify us from all unrighteousness. ¹⁰If we claim we have not sinned, we make him out to be a liar *i* and his word has no place in our lives.

2 My dear children, I write this to you so that you will not sin. But if anybody does sin, we have one who speaks to the Father in our defense *j*—Jesus Christ, the Righteous One. ²He is the atoning sacrifice for our sins, *k* and not only for ours but also for *a* the sins of the whole world.

³We know that we have come to know him if we obey his commands. ⁴The man who says, "I know him," but does not do what he commands is a liar, and the truth is not in him. *l* ⁵But if anyone obeys his word, *m* God's love *b* is truly made complete in him. *n* This is how we know we are in him: ⁶Whoever claims to live in him must walk as Jesus did. *o*

⁷Dear friends, I am not writing you a new command but an old one, which you have had since the beginning. *p* This old command is the message you have heard. ⁸Yet I am writing you a new command; its truth is seen in him and you, because the darkness is passing and the true light *q* is already shining.

⁹Anyone who claims to be in the light but hates his brother is still in the darkness. ¹⁰Whoever loves his brother lives in the light, *r* and there is nothing in him *c* to make him stumble. ¹¹But whoever hates his brother is in the darkness and walks around in the darkness; he does not know where he is going, because the darkness has blinded him.

a2 Or He is the one who turns aside God's wrath, taking away our sins, and not only ours but also   *b5 Or word, love for God*   *c10 Or it*

**Cross references (right margin):**

1:8
g Jas 3:2
h 1Jn 2:4

1:10
i 1Jn 5:10

2:1
j Ro 8:34; Heb 7:25

2:2
k Ro 3:25

2:4
l 1Jn 1:6, 8

2:5
m Jn 14:21, 23
n 1Jn 4:12

2:6
o 1Pe 2:21

2:7
p 2Jn 5, 6

2:8
q Jn 1:9

2:10
r 1Jn 3:14

1:9 Confession is supposed to free us to enjoy fellowship with Christ. It should ease our consciences and lighten our cares. But some Christians do not understand how it works. They feel so guilty that they confess the same sins over and over; then they wonder if they might have forgotten something. Other Christians believe that God forgives them when they confess, but if they died with unconfessed sins, they would be forever lost. These Christians do not understand that God *wants* to forgive us. He allowed his beloved Son to die just so he could offer us pardon. When we come to Christ, he forgives all the sins we have committed or will ever commit. We don't need to confess the sins of the past all over again, and we don't need to fear that God will reject us if we don't keep our slate perfectly clean. Of course we should continue to confess our sins, but not because failure to do so will make us lose our salvation. Our relationship with Christ is secure. Instead, we should confess so that we can enjoy maximum fellowship and joy with him.

True confession also involves a commitment not to continue in sin. We wouldn't be genuinely confessing our sins to God if we planned to commit them again and just wanted temporary forgiveness. We should also pray for strength to defeat temptation the next time we face it.

1:9 If God has forgiven us for our sins because of Christ's death, why must we confess our sins? In admitting our sins and receiving Christ's cleansing, we are: (1) agreeing with God that our sin truly is sin and that we are willing to turn from it, (2) ensuring that we don't conceal our sins from him and consequently from ourselves, and (3) recognizing our tendency to sin and relying on his power to overcome it.

2:1 John uses the address "dear children" in a warm, fatherly way. He is not talking down to his readers but is showing affection for them. At this writing, John was a very old man. He had spent almost all his life in ministry, and many of his readers were indeed his spiritual children.

2:1, 2 To people who are feeling guilty and condemned, John offers reassurance. They know they have sinned, and Satan (called "the accuser" in Revelation 12:10) is demanding the death penalty. When you feel this way, don't give up hope—the best defense attorney in the universe is pleading your case. Jesus Christ, your advocate, your defender, is the Judge's Son. He has already suffered your penalty in your place. You can't be tried for a case that is no longer on the docket. United with Christ, you are as safe as he is. Don't be afraid to ask Christ to plead your case—he has already won it (see Romans 8:33, 34; Hebrews 7:24, 25).

2:2 Jesus Christ is the atoning sacrifice for our sins (see also 4:10). He is our defense attorney. He can stand before God as our mediator because his death satisfied the wrath of God against sin and paid the death penalty for our sin. Thus Christ both satisfies God's requirement and removes our sin. In him we are forgiven and purified.

2:2 Sometimes it is difficult to forgive those who wrong us. Imagine how hard it would be to forgive all people, no matter what they had done! This is what God has done in Jesus. No one, no matter what sin has been committed, is beyond forgiveness. All a person has to do is turn from sin, receive Christ's forgiveness, and commit his or her life to him.

2:3–6 How can you be sure that you belong to Christ? This passage gives two ways to know: if you do what Christ says and live as Christ wants. What does Christ tell us to do? John answers in 3:23: "to believe in the name of his Son, Jesus Christ, and to love one another." True Christian faith results in loving behavior; that is why John says that the way we act can give us assurance that we belong to Christ.

2:6 To "walk as Jesus did" or living as Christ did doesn't mean choosing 12 disciples, performing great miracles, and being crucified. We cannot merely copy Christ's life—much of what Jesus did had to do with his identity as God's Son, the fulfillment of his special role in dying for sin, and the cultural context of the first-century Roman world. To walk today as Christ did we must obey his teachings and follow his example of complete obedience to God and loving service to people.

2:7, 8 The commandment to love others is both old and new. It is old because it comes from the Old Testament (Leviticus 19:18). It is new because Jesus interpreted it in a radically new way (John 13:34, 35). In the Christian church, love is not only expressed by showing respect; it is also expressed through self-sacrifice and servanthood (John 15:13). In fact, it can be defined as "selfless giving," reaching beyond friends to enemies and persecutors (Matthew 5:43–48). Love should be the unifying force and the identifying mark of the Christian community. Love is the key to walking in the light, because we cannot grow spiritually while we hate others. Our growing relationship with God will result in growing relationships with others.

2:9–11 Does this mean that if you dislike someone you aren't a Christian? These verses are not talking about disliking a disagreeable Christian brother or sister. There will always be people we will

¹² I write to you, dear children,
  because your sins have been forgiven on account of his name.
¹³ I write to you, fathers,
  because you have known him who is from the beginning.
I write to you, young men,
  because you have overcome the evil one.
I write to you, dear children,
  because you have known the Father.
¹⁴ I write to you, fathers,
  because you have known him who is from the beginning.
I write to you, young men,
  because you are strong,ˢ
  and the word of God lives in you,ᵗ
  and you have overcome the evil one.

2:14
ˢEph 6:10
ᵗJn 5:38

Do Not Love the World

2:15
ᵘRo 12:2
2:16
ᵛPr 27:20
2:17
ʷ1Co 7:31

¹⁵Do not love the world or anything in the world.ᵘ If anyone loves the world, the love of the Father is not in him. ¹⁶For everything in the world—the cravings of sinful man, the lust of his eyesᵛ and the boasting of what he has and does—comes not from the Father but from the world. ¹⁷The world and its desires pass away,ʷ but the man who does the will of God lives forever.

A BOOK OF CONTRASTS

One of the distinct features of John's writing style was his habit of noting both sides of a conflict. He wrote to show the difference between real Christianity and anything else. Here are some of his favorite contrasts.

Contrast between	Passage
Light and darkness	1:5
The new command and the old command	2:7, 8
Loving the Father and loving the world	2:15, 16
Christ and antichrist	2:18, 22
Truth and lies	2:20, 21
Children of God and children of the devil	3:1–10
Eternal life and eternal death	3:14
Love and hatred	3:15, 16
True teaching and false teaching	4:1–3
Love and fear	4:18, 19
Having life and not having life	5:11, 12

---

not like as well as others. John's words focus on the attitude that causes us to ignore or despise others, to treat them as irritants, competitors, or enemies. Christian love is not a feeling but a choice. We can choose to be concerned with people's well-being and treat them with respect, whether or not we feel affection toward them. If we choose to love others, God will help us express our love.

2:12–14 John was writing to believers of all ages. The "dear children" had experienced forgiveness through Jesus. The older men ("fathers") were mature in the faith and had a long-standing relationship with Christ. The young men had battled with Satan's temptations and had won. Each stage of life in the Christian pilgrimage builds upon the other. As children learn about Christ, they grow in their ability to win battles with temptation. As young adults move from victory to victory, they grow in their relationship with Christ. Older adults, having known Christ for years, have developed the wisdom needed to teach young people and start the cycle all over again. Has your Christian growth reached the maturity level appropriate for your stage in life?

2:15, 16 Some people think that worldliness is limited to external behavior—the people we associate with, the places we go, the activities we enjoy. Worldliness is also internal because it begins in the heart and is characterized by three attitudes: (1) *the cravings of sinful man*—preoccupation with gratifying physical desires; (2) *the lust of his eyes*—craving and accumulating things, bowing to the god of materialism; and (3) *boasting of what he has and does*—obsession with one's status or importance. When the serpent tempted Eve (Genesis 3:6), he tempted her in these areas. Also, when the devil tempted Jesus in the desert, these were his three areas of attack (see Matthew 4:1–11).

By contrast, God values self-control, a spirit of generosity, and a commitment to humble service. It is possible to give the impression of avoiding worldly pleasures while still harboring worldly attitudes in one's heart. It is also possible, like Jesus, to love sinners and spend time with them while maintaining a commitment to the values of God's kingdom. What values are most important to you? Do your actions reflect the world's values or God's values?

2:17 When the desire for possessions and sinful pleasures feels so intense, we probably doubt that these objects of desire will all one day pass away. It may be even more difficult to believe that the person who does the will of God will live forever. But this was John's conviction based on the facts of Jesus' life, death, resurrection, and promises. Knowing that this evil world will end can give you the courage to deny yourself temporary pleasures in this world in order to enjoy what God has promised for eternity.

Warning Against Antichrists

18Dear children, this is the last hour; and as you have heard that the antichrist is coming,ˣ even now many antichrists have come. This is how we know it is the last hour. 19They went out from us, but they did not really belong to us. For if they had belonged to us, they would have remained with us; but their going showed that none of them belonged to us.ʸ

20But you have an anointingᶻ from the Holy One, and all of you know the truth.ᵃ 21I do not write to you because you do not know the truth, but because you do know itᵃ and because no lie comes from the truth. 22Who is the liar? It is the man who denies that Jesus is the Christ. Such a man is the antichrist—he denies the Father and the Son. 23No one who denies the Son has the Father; whoever acknowledges the Son has the Father also.

24See that what you have heard from the beginning remains in you. If it does, you also will remain in the Son and in the Father.ᵇ 25And this is what he promised us—even eternal life.

26I am writing these things to you about those who are trying to lead you astray. 27As for you, the anointing you received from him remains in you, and you do not need anyone to teach you. But as his anointing teaches you about all things and as that anointing is real, not counterfeit—just as it has taught you, remain in him.

2. God is love
Children of God

28And now, dear children, continue in him, so that when he appearsᶜ we may be confidentᵈ and unashamed before him at his coming.

29If you know that he is righteous,ᵉ you know that everyone who does what is right has been born of him.

2:18 ˣ1Jn 4:3
2:19 ʸ1Co 11:19
2:20 ᶻ2Co 1:21
2:21 ᵃ2Pe 1:12
2:24 ᵇJn 14:23
2:28 ᶜ1Jn 3:2 ᵈ1Jn 4:17
2:29 ᵉ1Jn 3:7

ᵃ**20** Some manuscripts *and you know all things*

2:18–23 John is talking about the last days, the time between Christ's first and second comings. The first-century readers of 1 John lived in the last days, and so do we. During this time, antichrists (false teachers who pretend to be Christians and who lure weak members away from Christ) will appear. Finally, just before the world ends, one great antichrist will arise (Revelation 13; 19:20; 20:10). We do not need to fear these evil people, however. The Holy Spirit shows us their errors, so we will not be deceived. However, we must teach God's Word clearly and carefully to the peripheral, weak members among us so that they won't fall prey to these teachers who "come to you in sheep's clothing, but inwardly they are ferocious wolves" (Matthew 7:15).

2:19 The antichrists were not total strangers to the church; they once had been in the church, but they did not really belong to it. John does not say why they left; it is clear that their reasons for joining in the first place were wrong. Some people may call themselves Christians for less than the best reasons. Perhaps going to church is a family tradition. Maybe they like the social and business contacts they make there. Or possibly going to church is a long-standing habit, and they have never stopped to ask themselves why they do it. What is your main reason for being a Christian? Unless it is a Christ-centered reason, you may not really belong. You don't have to settle for less than the best. You can become personally acquainted with Jesus Christ and become a loyal, trustworthy follower.

2:20 *Anointing* usually refers to the pouring out of special olive oil. Oil was used to consecrate kings and special servants for service (1 Samuel 16:1, 13), and also was used by the church when someone was sick (James 5:14). "You have an anointing from the Holy One" could read, "The Holy Spirit has been given to you by the Father and the Son." When a person becomes a Christian, he or she receives the Holy Spirit. One way the Holy Spirit helps the believer and the church is by communicating truth. Jesus is the truth (John 14:6), and the Holy Spirit guides believers to him (John 16:13). People who are opposed to Christ are also opposed to his truth, and the Holy Spirit is not working in their lives. When we are led by the Spirit, we can stand against false teachers and the antichrist. Ask the Spirit to guide you each day (see 2:27).

2:22, 23 Apparently the antichrists in John's day were claiming faith in God while denying and opposing Christ. To do so, John

firmly states, is impossible. Because Jesus is God's Son and the Messiah, to deny Christ is to reject God's way of revealing himself to the world. A person who accepts Christ as God's Son, however, accepts God the Father at the same time. The two are one and cannot be separated. Many cultists today call themselves Christians, but they deny that Jesus is divine. We must expose these heresies and oppose such teachings so that the weak believers among us do not succumb to their teachings.

2:24 These Christians had heard the gospel, very likely from John himself. They knew that Christ was God's Son, that he died for their sins and was raised to give them new life, and that he would return and establish his kingdom in its fullness. But their fellowship was being infiltrated by teachers who denied these basic doctrines of the Christian faith, and some of the believers were in danger of succumbing to false arguments. John encouraged them to hold on to the Christian truth they heard at the beginning of their walk with Christ. It is important to grow in our knowledge of the Lord, to deepen our understanding through careful study, and to teach these truths to others. But no matter how much we learn, we must never abandon the basic truths about Christ. Jesus will always be God's Son, and his sacrifice for our sins is permanent. No truth will ever contradict these teachings in the Bible.

2:26, 27 Christ had promised to send the Holy Spirit to teach his followers and to remind them of all that Christ had taught (John 14:26). As a result, Christians have the Holy Spirit within them ("the anointing") to keep them from going astray. In addition, they have the God-inspired Scriptures, against which they can test questionable teachings. To stay true to Christ, we must follow his Word and his Spirit. Let the Holy Spirit help you discern truth from error. For more about who the Holy Spirit is and what he does, see the notes on John 3:6; Acts 1:5; and Ephesians 1:13, 14.

2:27 Christ lives (remains) in us through the Holy Spirit, and we also live in Christ. This means that we place our total trust in him, rely on him for guidance and strength, and live as he wants us to live. It implies a personal, life-giving relationship. John uses the same idea in John 15:5, where he speaks of Christ as the vine and his followers as the branches (see also 3:24; 4:15).

2:28, 29 The visible proof of being a Christian is right behavior. Many people do good deeds but don't have faith in Jesus Christ. Others claim to have faith but rarely produce good deeds. A defi-

3:1
f Jn 1:12
g Jn 16:3

3:2
h Ro 8:29; 2Pe 1:4

3 How great is the love the Father has lavished on us, that we should be called children of God! *f* And that is what we are! The reason the world does not know us is that it did not know him. *g* 2 Dear friends, now we are children of God, and what we will be has not yet been made known. But we know that when he appears, *a* we shall be like him, *h* for we shall see him as he is. 3 Everyone who has this hope in him purifies himself, just as he is pure.

3:4
i 1Jn 5:17

3:5
j 2Co 5:21

3:7
k 1Jn 2:26

3:8
l Jn 8:44

3:9
m 1Jn 5:18

4 Everyone who sins breaks the law; in fact, sin is lawlessness. *i* 5 But you know that he appeared so that he might take away our sins. And in him is no sin. *j* 6 No one who lives in him keeps on sinning. No one who continues to sin has either seen him or known him.

7 Dear children, do not let anyone lead you astray. *k* He who does what is right is righteous, just as he is righteous. 8 He who does what is sinful is of the devil, *l* because the devil has been sinning from the beginning. The reason the Son of God appeared was to destroy the devil's work. 9 No one who is born of God will continue to sin, *m* because God's seed remains in him; he cannot go on sinning, because he has been born of God. 10 This is how we know who the children of God are and who the children of the devil are: Anyone who does not do what is right is not a child of God; nor is anyone who does not love his brother.

Love One Another

3:11
n 1Jn 1:5
o Jn 13:34, 35

11 This is the message you heard *n* from the beginning: We should love one another. *o* 12 Do not be like Cain, who belonged to the evil one and murdered his brother. And why did he murder him? Because his own actions were evil and his brother's were righteous. 13 Do not be surprised, my brothers, if the world hates you. 14 We know that we have passed from death to life, because we love our brothers. Anyone who does not love remains in death.

a 2 Or *when it is made known*

---

cit in either faith or right behavior will be a cause for shame when Christ returns. Because true faith always results in good deeds, those who claim to have faith *and* who consistently do what is right are true believers. Good deeds cannot produce salvation (see Ephesians 2:8, 9), but they are necessary proof that true faith is actually present (James 2:14–17).

3:1 As believers, our self-worth is based on the fact that God loves us and calls us his children. We are his children *now*, not just sometime in the distant future. Knowing that we are his children should encourage us to live as Jesus did. For other references about being part of God's family, see Romans 8:14–17; Galatians 3:26, 27; 4:6, 7.

3:1ff Verse 1 tells us who we are—members of God's family ("children of God"). Verse 2 tells us who we are becoming—reflections of God. The rest of the chapter tells us what we have as we grow to resemble God: (1) victory over sin (3:4–9); (2) love for others (3:10–18); and (3) confidence before God (3:19–24).

3:2, 3 The Christian life is a process of becoming more and more like Christ (see Romans 8:29). This process will not be complete until we see Christ face-to-face (1 Corinthians 13:12; Philippians 3:21), but knowing that it is our ultimate destiny should motivate us to purify ourselves. To purify means to keep morally straight, free from the corruption of sin. God also purifies us, but there is action we must take to remain morally fit (see 1 Timothy 5:22; James 4:8; 1 Peter 1:22).

3:4ff There is a difference between committing a sin and continuing to sin. Even the most faithful believers sometimes commit sins, but they do not cherish a particular sin or continually choose to commit it. A believer who commits a sin can repent, confess it, and find forgiveness. A person who continues to sin, by contrast, is not sorry for what he or she is doing. Thus this person never confesses and never receives forgiveness. Such a person is in opposition to God, no matter what religious claims he or she makes.

3:5 Under the Old Testament sacrifice system, a lamb without blemish was offered as a sacrifice for sin. Jesus is "the Lamb of God, who takes away the sin of the world" (John 1:29). Because Jesus lived a perfect life and sacrificed himself for our sins, we can be completely forgiven (2:2). We can look back to his death for us and know that we need never suffer eternal death (1 Peter 1:18–20).

3:8, 9 We all have areas where temptation is strong and habits are hard to conquer. These weaknesses give the devil a foothold, so we must deal with our areas of vulnerability. If we are struggling with a particular sin, however, these verses are not directed at us, even if for the time we seem to keep on sinning. John is not talking about people whose victories are still incomplete; he is talking about people who make a practice of sinning and look for ways to justify it.

Three steps are necessary to find victory over prevailing sin: (1) seek the power of the Holy Spirit and God's Word; (2) stay away from tempting situations; and (3) seek the help of the body of Christ—be open to their willingness to hold you accountable and to pray for you.

3:9 "No one who is born of God will continue to sin" means that true believers do not make a practice of sinning, nor do they become indifferent to God's moral law. All believers still sin, but they are working to gain victory over sin. "God's seed remains in him" means that true believers do not make a practice of sinning because God's new life has been born into them.

3:9 We are "born of God" when the Holy Spirit lives in us and gives us Jesus' new life. Being born again is more than a fresh start; it is a rebirth, receiving a new family name based on Christ's death for us. When this happens, God forgives us and totally accepts us; the Holy Spirit gives us new minds and hearts, lives in us, and begins helping us to become like Christ. Our perspective changes too because we have a mind that is renewed day by day by the Holy Spirit (see Romans 12:2; Ephesians 4:22–24). So we must begin to think and act differently. See John 3:1–21 for more on being born again.

3:12, 13 Cain killed his brother, Abel, when God accepted Abel's offering and not his (Genesis 4:1–16). Abel's offering showed that Cain was not giving his best to God, and Cain's jealous anger drove him to murder. People who are morally upright expose and shame those who aren't. If we live for God, the world will often hate us, because we make them painfully aware of their immoral way of living.

15Anyone who hates his brother is a murderer,ᵖ and you know that no murderer has eternal life in him. �q

16This is how we know what love is: Jesus Christ laid down his life for us. And we ought to lay down our lives for our brothers. 17If anyone has material possessions and sees his brother in need but has no pity on him,ʳ how can the love of God be in him?ˢ 18Dear children, let us not love with words or tongue but with actions and in truth.ᵗ 19This then is how we know that we belong to the truth, and how we set our hearts at rest in his presence 20whenever our hearts condemn us. For God is greater than our hearts, and he knows everything.

21Dear friends, if our hearts do not condemn us, we have confidence before God 22and receive from him anything we ask, ᵘ because we obey his commands and do what pleases him. 23And this is his command: to believe in the name of his Son, Jesus Christ, and to love one another as he commanded us.ᵛ 24Those who obey his commands live in him, and he in them. And this is how we know that he lives in us: We know it by the Spirit he gave us.

Test the Spirits

4 Dear friends, do not believe every spirit, but test the spirits to see whether they are from God, because many false prophets have gone out into the world. ʷ 2This is how you can recognize the Spirit of God: Every spirit that acknowledges that Jesus Christ has come in the flesh is from God,ˣ 3but every spirit that does not acknowledge Jesus is not from God. This is the spirit of the antichrist,ʸ which you have heard is coming and even now is already in the world.

4You, dear children, are from God and have overcome them, because the one who is in you is greater than the one who is in the world. 5They are from the world ᶻ and therefore speak from the viewpoint of the world, and the world listens to them. 6We are from God,

3:15
ᵖMt 5:21, 22
qGal 5:20, 21

3:17
ʳDt 15:7, 8
ˢ1Jn 4:20

3:18
ᵗRo 12:9

3:22
ᵘMt 7:7

3:23
ᵛJn 13:34

4:1
ʷ2Pe 2:1

4:2
ˣ1Co 12:3

4:3
ʸ2Jn 7

4:5
ᶻJn 15:19

3:15 John echoes Jesus' teaching that whoever hates another person is a murderer at heart (Matthew 5:21, 22). Christianity is a religion of the heart; outward compliance alone is not enough. Bitterness against someone who has wronged you is an evil cancer within you and will eventually destroy you. Don't let a "bitter root" (Hebrews 12:15) grow in you or your church.

3:16 Real love is an action, not a feeling. It produces selfless, sacrificial giving. The greatest act of love is giving oneself for others. How can we lay down our lives? By serving others with no thought of receiving anything in return. Sometimes it is easier to say we'll die for others than to truly live for them—this involves putting others' desires first. Jesus taught this same principle of love in John 15:13.

3:17, 18 These verses give an example of how to lay down our lives for others—to help those in need. This is strikingly similar to James's teaching (James 2:14–17). How clearly do your actions say you really love others? Are you as generous as you should be with your money, possessions, and time?

3:19, 20 Many are afraid that they don't love others as they should. They feel guilty because they think they are not doing enough to show proper love to Christ. Their consciences bother them. John has these people in mind in this letter. How do we escape the gnawing accusations of our consciences? Not by ignoring them or rationalizing our behavior, but by setting our hearts on God's love. When we feel guilty, we should remind ourselves that God knows our motives as well as our actions. His voice of assurance is stronger than the accusing voice of our conscience. If we are in Christ, he will not condemn us (Romans 8:1; Hebrews 9:14, 15). So if you are living for the Lord but feeling that you are not good enough, remind yourself that God is greater than your conscience.

3:21, 22 If your conscience is clear, you can come to God without fear, confident that your requests will be heard. John reaffirms Jesus' promise that whatever we ask for will be given to us (Matthew 7:7; see also Matthew 21:22; John 9:31; 15:7). You

will receive if you obey and do what pleases him because you will then be asking in line with God's will. Of course this does not mean that you can have anything you want, like instant riches. If you are truly seeking God's will, there are some requests you will not make.

3:23 In the Bible, a person's name stands for his or her character. It represents who he or she really is. We are to believe not only in Jesus' words, but also in his very person as the Son of God. Moreover, to believe "in the name" means to pattern your life after Christ's, to become more like him by uniting yourself with him. And if we are living like Christ, we will "love one another."

3:24 The mutual relationship, living in Christ as he lives in us, shows itself in Christians who keep these three essential commands: (1) believe in Christ, (2) love the brothers and sisters, and (3) live morally upright lives. The Spirit's presence is not only spiritual and mystical, but it is also practical. Our conduct verifies his presence.

4:1, 2 "Do not believe every spirit, but test the spirits" means that we shouldn't believe everything we hear just because someone says it is a message inspired by God. There are many ways to test teachers to see if their message is truly from the Lord. One is to check to see if their words match what God says in the Bible. Other tests include their commitment to the body of believers (2:19), their lifestyles (3:23, 24), and the fruit of their ministries (4:6). But the most important test of all, says John, is what they believe about Christ. Do they teach that Jesus is fully God and fully man? Our world is filled with voices claiming to speak for God. Give them these tests to see if they are indeed speaking God's truth.

4:3 The antichrist will be a person who epitomizes all that is evil, and he will be readily received by an evil world. He is more fully described in 2 Thessalonians 2:3–12 and Revelation 13. The "spirit of the antichrist" is already here (see the note on 2:18–23). Those who reject Christ are unknowingly or consciously siding with the spirit of the antichrist.

4:4 It is easy to be frightened by the wickedness we see all around us and overwhelmed by the problems we face. Evil is obviously much stronger than we are. John assures us, however, that God is even stronger. He will conquer all evil—and his Spirit and his Word live in our hearts!

4:6
a Jn 8:47

and whoever knows God listens to us; but whoever is not from God does not listen to us. *a* This is how we recognize the Spirit *a* of truth and the spirit of falsehood.

God's Love and Ours

4:7
b 1Jn 3:11

4:9
c Jn 3:16, 17;
1Jn 5:11

4:10
d Ro 5:8, 10
e 1Jn 2:2

4:12
f Jn 1:18
g 1Jn 2:5

7 Dear friends, let us love one another, *b* for love comes from God. Everyone who loves has been born of God and knows God. 8 Whoever does not love does not know God, because God is love. 9 This is how God showed his love among us: He sent his one and only Son *b* into the world that we might live through him. *c* 10 This is love: not that we loved God, but that he loved us *d* and sent his Son as an atoning sacrifice for *c* our sins. *e* 11 Dear friends, since God so loved us, we also ought to love one another. 12 No one has ever seen God; *f* but if we love one another, God lives in us and his love is made complete in us. *g*

a 6 Or spirit   *b* 9 Or his only begotten Son   *c* 10 Or as the one who would turn aside his wrath, taking away

---

HERESIES

Most of the eyewitnesses to Jesus' ministry had died by the time John composed this letter. Some of the second- or third-generation Christians began to have doubts about what they had been taught about Jesus. Some Christians with a Greek background had a hard time believing that Jesus was human as well as divine, because in Platonic thought the spirit was all-important. The body was only a prison from which one desired to escape. Heresies developed from a uniting of this kind of Platonic thought and Christianity.

A particularly widespread false teaching, later called *Docetism* (from a Greek word meaning "to seem"), held that Jesus was actually a spirit who only appeared to have a body. In reality he cast no shadow and left no footprints; he was God but not man. Another heretical teaching, related to *Gnosticism* (from a Greek word meaning "knowledge", held that all physical matter was evil, the spirit was good, and only the intellectually enlightened could enjoy the benefits of religion. Both groups found it hard to believe in a Savior who was fully human.

John answers these false teachers as an eyewitness to Jesus' life on earth. He saw Jesus, talked with him, touched him—he knew that Jesus was more than a mere spirit. In the very first sentence of his letter, John establishes that Jesus had been alive before the world began and also that he lived as a man among men and women. In other words, he was both divine and human.

Through the centuries, many heretics have denied that Jesus was both God and man. In John's day people had trouble believing he was human; today more people have problems seeing him as God. But Jesus' divine-human nature is the pivotal issue of Christianity. Before you accept what religious teachers say about any topic, listen carefully to what they believe about Jesus. To deny either his divinity or his humanity is to consider him less than Christ, the Savior.

4:6 False teachers are popular with the world because, like the false prophets of the Old Testament, they tell people what they want to hear. John warns that Christians who faithfully teach God's Word will not win any popularity contests in the world. People don't want to hear their sins denounced; they don't want to listen to demands that they change their behavior. A false teacher will be well received by non-Christians.

4:7ff Everyone believes that love is important, but love is usually thought of as a feeling. In reality, love is a choice and an action, as 1 Corinthians 13:4–7 shows. God is the source of our love: He loved us enough to sacrifice his Son for us. Jesus is our example of what it means to love; everything he did in life and death was supremely loving. The Holy Spirit gives us the power to love; he lives in our hearts and makes us more and more like Christ. God's love always involves a choice and an action, and our love should be like his. How well do you display your love for God in the choices you make and the actions you take?

4:8 John says, "God is love," not "Love is God." Our world, with its shallow and selfish view of love, has turned these words around and contaminated our understanding of love. The world thinks that love is what makes a person feel good and that it is all right to sacrifice moral principles and others' rights in order to obtain such "love." But that isn't real love; it is the exact opposite—selfishness. And God is not that kind of "love." Real love is like God, who is holy, just, and perfect. If we truly know God, we will love as he does.

4:9 Jesus is God's *only* Son. While all believers are sons and daughters of God, only Jesus lives in this special unique relationship (see John 1:18; 3:16).

4:9, 10 Love explains (1) why God creates—because he loves, he creates people to love; (2) why God cares—because he loves them, he cares for sinful people; (3) why we are free to choose—God wants a loving response from us; (4) why Christ died—his love for us caused him to seek a solution to the problem of sin; and (5) why we receive eternal life—God's love expresses itself to us forever.

4:10 Nothing sinful or evil can exist in God's presence. He is absolute goodness. He cannot overlook, condone, or excuse sin as though it never happened. He loves us, but his love does not make him morally lax. If we trust in Christ, however, we will not have to bear the penalty for our sins (1 Peter 2:24). We will be acquitted (Romans 5:18) by his atoning sacrifice.

4:12 If no one has ever seen God, how can we ever know him? John in his Gospel said, "God the One and Only, who is at the Father's side, has made him known" (John 1:18). Jesus is the complete expression of God in human form and he has revealed God to us. When we love one another, the invisible God reveals himself to others through us, and his love is made complete.

4:12 Some people simply enjoy being with others. They make friends with strangers easily and are always surrounded by friends. Other people are shy or reserved. They have a few friends, but are frequently uncomfortable talking with people they don't know or mingling in crowds. Shy people don't need to become extroverts in order to love others. John isn't telling us *how many* people to love, but *how much* to love the people we already know. Our job is to love faithfully the people God has given us to love, whether there are two or two hundred of them. If God sees that we are ready to love others, he will bring them to us. No matter how shy we are, we don't need to be afraid of the love commandment. God provides us the strength to do what he asks.

¹³We know that we live in him and he in us, because he has given us of his Spirit. ¹⁴And we have seen and testify that the Father has sent his Son to be the Savior of the world. ¹⁵If anyone acknowledges that Jesus is the Son of God,ʰ God lives in him and he in God. ¹⁶And so we know and rely on the love God has for us.

God is love.ⁱ Whoever lives in love lives in God, and God in him. ¹⁷In this way, love is made complete among us so that we will have confidence on the day of judgment, because in this world we are like him. ¹⁸There is no fear in love. But perfect love drives out fear,ʲ because fear has to do with punishment. The one who fears is not made perfect in love.

¹⁹We love because he first loved us. ²⁰If anyone says, "I love God," yet hates his brother, he is a liar.ᵏ For anyone who does not love his brother, whom he has seen, cannot love God, whom he has not seen. ²¹And he has given us this command: Whoever loves God must also love his brother.

3. God is life
Faith in the Son of God

5 Everyone who believes that Jesus is the Christˡ is born of God,ᵐ and everyone who loves the father loves his child as well.ⁿ ²This is how we know that we love the children of God: by loving God and carrying out his commands. ³This is love for God: to obey his commands.ᵒ And his commands are not burdensome, ⁴for everyone born of God overcomes the world. This is the victory that has overcome the world, even our faith. ⁵Who is it that overcomes the world? Only he who believes that Jesus is the Son of God.

⁶This is the one who came by water and bloodᵖ—Jesus Christ. He did not come by water only, but by water and blood. And it is the Spirit who testifies, because the Spirit is the truth. ⁷For there are three that testify: ⁸theª Spirit, the water and the blood; and the three are in agreement. ⁹We accept man's testimony, but God's testimony is greater because it is the testimony of God,�q which he has given about his Son. ¹⁰Anyone who believes in the Son of God has this testimony in his heart.ʳ Anyone who does not believe God has made him out to be a liar,ˢ because he has not believed the testimony God has given about his Son. ¹¹And this is the testimony: God has given us eternal life, and this life is in his Son. ¹²He who has the Son has life; he who does not have the Son of God does not have life.ᵗ

4:15	ʰRo 10:9
4:16	ⁱver 8
4:18	ʲRo 8:15
4:20	ᵏ1Jn 2:4
5:1	ˡ1Jn 2:22
	ᵐ1Jn 2:23
	ⁿJn 8:42
5:3	ᵒJn 14:15
5:6	ᵖJn 19:34
5:9	qMt 3:16, 17;
	Jn 8:17, 18
5:10	ʳRo 8:16
	ˢJn 3:33
5:12	ᵗJn 3:15, 16, 36

ª*7,8* Late manuscripts of the Vulgate *testify in heaven: the Father, the Word and the Holy Spirit, and these three are one. ⁸And there are three that testify on earth: the* (not found in any Greek manuscript before the fourteenth century)

4:13 When we become Christians, we receive the Holy Spirit. God's presence in our lives is proof that we really belong to him. He also gives us the power to love (Romans 5:5; 8:9; 2 Corinthians 1:22). Rely on that power as you reach out to others. As you do so, you will gain confidence. See also Romans 8:16.

4:17 The day of judgment is that time when all people will appear before Christ and be held accountable for their actions. With God living in us through Christ, we have no reason to fear this day, because we have been saved from punishment. Instead, we can look forward to the day of judgment, because it will mean the end of sin and the beginning of a face-to-face relationship with Jesus Christ.

4:18 If we ever are afraid of the future, eternity, or God's judgment, we can remind ourselves of God's love. We know that he loves us perfectly (Romans 8:38, 39). We can resolve our fears first by focusing on his immeasurable love for us, and then by allowing him to love others through us. His love will quiet your fears and give you confidence.

4:19 God's love is the source of all human love, and it spreads like fire. In loving his children, God kindles a flame in their hearts. In turn, they love others, who are warmed by God's love through them.

4:20, 21 It is easy to say we love God when that love doesn't cost us anything more than weekly attendance at religious services. But the real test of our love for God is how we treat the people right in front of us—our family members and fellow

believers. We cannot truly love God while neglecting to love those who are created in his image.

5:1, 2 When we become Christians, we become part of God's family, with fellow believers as our brothers and sisters. It is God who determines who the other family members are, not us. We are simply called to accept and love them. How well do you treat your fellow family members?

5:3, 4 Jesus never promised that obeying him would be easy. But the hard work and self-discipline of serving Christ is no burden to those who love him. At this time, there was a false teaching in circulation that said Jesus was "the Christ" only between his baptism and his death—that is, he was merely human until he was baptized, at which time "the Christ" then descended upon him but then later left him before his death on the cross. But if Jesus died only as a man, he could not have taken upon himself the sins of the world, and Christianity would be an empty religion. Only an act of God could take away the punishment that we deserve for our sin.

5:6–8 The phrase "came by water and blood" may refer to Jesus' baptism and his crucifixion. At this time, there was a false teaching in circulation that said Jesus was "the Christ" only between his baptism and his death—that is, he was merely human until he was baptized, at which time "the Christ" then descended upon him but then later left him before his death on the cross. But if Jesus died only as a man, he could not have taken upon himself the sins of the world, and Christianity would be an empty religion. Only an act of God could take away the punishment that we deserve for our sin.

5:7–9 The Gospels twice record God's clear declaration that Jesus was his Son—at Jesus' baptism (Matthew 3:16, 17), and at his transfiguration (Matthew 17:5).

5:12 Whoever believes in God's Son has eternal life. He is all you need. You don't need to *wait* for eternal life, because it begins the moment you believe. You don't need to *work* for it, because it is already yours. You don't need to *worry* about it, because you have been given eternal life by God himself—and it is guaranteed.

Concluding Remarks

¹³I write these things to you who believe in the name of the Son of God so that you may know that you have eternal life. ¹⁴This is the confidence ^u we have in approaching God: that if we ask anything according to his will, he hears us. ¹⁵And if we know that he hears us—whatever we ask—we know that we have what we asked of him.

¹⁶If anyone sees his brother commit a sin that does not lead to death, he should pray and God will give him life. ^v I refer to those whose sin does not lead to death. There is a sin that leads to death. ^w I am not saying that he should pray about that. ¹⁷All wrongdoing is sin, ^x and there is sin that does not lead to death.

¹⁸We know that anyone born of God does not continue to sin; the one who was born of God keeps him safe, and the evil one cannot harm him. ¹⁹We know that we are children of God, and that the whole world is under the control of the evil one. ²⁰We know also that the Son of God has come and has given us understanding, ^y so that we may know him who is true. ^z And we are in him who is true—even in his Son Jesus Christ. He is the true God and eternal life.

²¹Dear children, keep yourselves from idols. ^a

5:14
^u1Jn 3:21

5:16
^vJas 5:15
^wHeb 6:4-6

5:17
^x1Jn 3:4

5:20
^yLk 24:45
^zJn 17:3

5:21
^a1Co 10:14

5:13 Some people *hope* that they will receive eternal life. John says we can *know* we have it. Our certainty is based on God's promise that he has given us eternal life through his Son. This is true whether you feel close to God or far away from him. Eternal life is not based on feelings, but on facts. You can know that you have eternal life if you believe God's truth. If you aren't sure that you are a Christian, ask yourself: "Have I honestly committed my life to him as my Savior and Lord?" If so, you know by faith that you are indeed a child of God.

5:14, 15 The emphasis here is on God's will, not our will. When we communicate with God, we don't demand what we want; rather we discuss with him what *he* wants for us. If we align our prayers to his will, he will listen; and we can be certain that if he listens, he will give us a definite answer. Start praying with confidence!

5:16, 17 Commentators differ widely in their thoughts about what this sin that leads to death is, and whether the death it causes is physical or spiritual. Paul wrote that some Christians had died because they took Communion "in an unworthy manner" (1 Corinthians 11:27–30), and Ananias and Sapphira were struck dead when they lied to God (Acts 5:1–11). Blasphemy against the Holy Spirit results in spiritual death (Mark 3:29), and the book of Hebrews describes the spiritual death of the person who turns against Christ (Hebrews 6:4–6). John was probably referring to the people who had left the Christian fellowship and joined the antichrists. By rejecting the only way of salvation, these people were putting themselves out of reach of prayer. In most cases, however, even if we knew what the terrible sin is, we would have no sure way of knowing whether a certain person had committed it. Therefore we should continue praying for our loved ones and for our Christian brothers and sisters, leaving the judgment up to God. Note that John says, "I am not saying that he should pray about that," rather than "You cannot pray about that." He recognized the lack of certainty.

5:18, 19 Christians commit sins, of course, but they ask God to forgive them, and then they continue serving him. God has freed believers from their slavery to Satan, and he keeps them safe from Satan's continued attacks. The rest of the world does not have the Christian's freedom to obey God. Unless they come to Christ in faith, they have no choice but to obey Satan. There is no middle ground; people either belong to God and obey him, or they live under Satan's control.

5:21 An idol is anything that substitutes for the true faith, anything that robs Christ of his full deity and humanity, any human idea that claims to be more authoritative than the Bible, any loyalty that replaces God at the center of our lives.

5:21 John presents a clear picture of Christ. What we think about Jesus Christ is central to our teaching, preaching, and living. Jesus is the God-man, fully God and fully human at the same time. He came to earth to die in our place for our sins. Through faith in him, we are given eternal life and the power to do his will. What is your answer to the most important question you could ever ask—Who is Jesus Christ?

2 JOHN

VITAL STATISTICS

PURPOSE:
To emphasize the basics of following Christ—truth and love—and to warn against false teachers

AUTHOR:
The apostle John

ORIGINAL AUDIENCE:
To "the chosen lady" and her children—or possibly to a local church

DATE WRITTEN:
About the same time as 1 John, approximately A.D. 90 from Ephesus

SETTING:
Evidently this woman and her family were involved in one of the churches that John was overseeing—they had developed a strong friendship with John. John was warning her of the false teachers who were becoming prevalent in some of the churches.

KEY VERSE:
"And this is love: that we walk in obedience to his commands. As you have heard from the beginning, his command is that you walk in love" (verse 6).

KEY PEOPLE:
John, the chosen lady, and her children

TRUTH and love are frequently discussed in our world but seldom practiced.

From politicians to marketers, people conveniently ignore or conceal facts and use words to enhance positions or sell products. Perjury is common, and integrity and credibility are endangered species. Words, twisted in meaning and torn from context, have become mere tools for ego building. It is not surprising that we have to "swear" to tell the truth.

And what about love? Our world is filled with its words: Popular songs, greeting cards, media counselors, and romantic novels shower us with notions and dreams of ethereal, idyllic relationships and feelings. Real love, however, is scarce—selfless giving, caring, sharing, and even dying. We yearn to love and be loved, but we see few living examples of real love. Plentiful are those who grasp, hoard, and watch out for "number one."

Christ is the antithesis of society's prevailing values, that is, falsehood and self-centeredness—for *he is truth and love* in person. Therefore, all who claim loyalty to him must be committed to these ideals—following the truth and living the truth, reflecting love and acting with love toward one another.

The apostle John had seen Truth and Love firsthand—he had been with Jesus. So affected was this disciple that all of his writings, from the Gospel to the book of Revelation, are filled with this theme: Truth and love are vital to the Christian and are inseparable in the Christian life. Second John, his brief letter to a dear friend, is no different. John says to live in the truth and obey God (verse 4), watch out for deceivers (verse 7), and love God and each other (verse 6).

Second John will take just a few minutes to read, but its message should last a lifetime. As you reflect on these few paragraphs penned by the wise and aged follower of Christ, recommit yourself to being a person of truth, of love, and of obedience.

THE BLUEPRINT

1. Watch out for false teachers (verses 1–11)
2. John's final words (verses 12, 13)

False teachers were a dangerous problem for the church to which John was writing. His warning against showing hospitality to false teachers may sound harsh and unloving to many today. Yet these men were teaching heresy that could seriously harm many believers—for eternity.

MEGATHEMES

THEME	EXPLANATION	IMPORTANCE
Truth	Following God's Word, the Bible, is essential to Christian living because God is truth. Christ's true followers consistently obey his truth.	To be loyal to Christ's teaching, we must seek to know the Bible, but we may never twist its message to our own needs or purposes or encourage others who misuse it.
Love	Christ's command is for Christians to love one another. This is the basic ingredient of true Christianity.	To obey Christ fully, we must believe his command to love others. Helping, giving, and meeting needs put love into practice.
False Leaders	We must be wary of religious leaders who are not true to Christ's teaching. We should not give them a platform to spread false teaching.	Don't encourage those who are opposed to Christ. Politely remove yourself from association with false leaders. Be aware of what is being taught in your church.

1. Watch out for false teachers

1:1
a 3Jn 1
b Jn 8:32

¹ The elder,ᵃ

To the chosen lady and her children, whom I love in the truth—and not I only, but also all who know the truth ᵇ— ² because of the truth, which lives in us and will be with us forever:

³ Grace, mercy and peace from God the Father and from Jesus Christ, the Father's Son, will be with us in truth and love.

1:4
c 3Jn 3, 4
1:5
d 1Jn 3:11
1:6
e 1Jn 2:5

⁴ It has given me great joy to find some of your children walking in the truth,ᶜ just as the Father commanded us. ⁵ And now, dear lady, I am not writing you a new command but one we have had from the beginning. ᵈ I ask that we love one another. ⁶ And this is love:ᵉ that we walk in obedience to his commands. As you have heard from the beginning, his command is that you walk in love.

⁷ Many deceivers, who do not acknowledge Jesus Christ as coming in the flesh, have gone

1 The "elder" is John, one of Jesus' 12 disciples and the writer of the Gospel of John, three letters, and the book of Revelation. For more information about John, see his Profile in John 13, p. 1771. This letter was written shortly after 1 John to warn about false teachers. The salutation, "to the chosen lady and her children," could refer to a specific woman, or to a church whose identity is no longer known. John may have written this from Ephesus.

1, 2 John wrote this second letter (which probably fit on one sheet of papyrus) to warn believers against inadvertently supporting false teachers. The number of itinerant evangelists and teachers had grown by the end of the first century; mixed in with the legitimate missionaries were others who were promoting heretical ideas about Christ and the gospel. Little has changed in two thousand years. Advocates of unorthodox beliefs still exist and still attempt to confuse and deceive the people of God. This letter, 2 John, should serve as a wake-up call to believers to be alert, to be careful, and to be solidly grounded in the faith. Are you prepared to recognize false doctrine?

3, 4 The "truth" is the truth about Jesus Christ, as opposed to the lies of the false teachers (see 1 John 2:21–23). John refers to truth five times in the first four verses of this brief letter. In contrast to so many in our culture who dogmatically deny truth ("There are no ultimate realities") or absurdly define it according to personal preference ("Your truth is your truth and my truth is my truth"), John declared the existence of an Absolute. God is

that ultimate standard by which all else can be judged. God is true, his words and ways are true, and whatever or whoever contradicts or opposes him is false, deceptive, and dangerous. Christian leaders, teachers, and parents must engage now in the difficult but critical battle for truth. To paraphrase a familiar saying: "All that is required for Deception to triumph is for the people of the Truth to do nothing." Begin an intentional campaign to teach those under your care how to distinguish between truth and error.

5, 6 The statement that Christians should love one another is a recurrent New Testament theme. Yet love for one's neighbor is an old command, first appearing in the third book of Moses (Leviticus 19:18). We can show love in many ways: by avoiding prejudice and discrimination; by accepting people; by listening, helping, giving, serving, and refusing to judge. Knowing God's command is not enough. We must put it into practice, walking "in obedience to his commands." (See also Matthew 22:37–39 and 1 John 2:7, 8.)

7 In John's day, many false teachers taught that spirit was good and matter was evil; therefore, they reasoned that Jesus could not have been both God and man. In strong terms, John warns against this kind of teaching. Many false teachers still promote an understanding of Jesus that is not Biblical. These teachers are dangerous because they distort the truth and undermine the foundations of Christian faith. They may use the right words but change the meanings.

out into the world. ᶠ Any such person is the deceiver and the antichrist. ⁸Watch out that you do not lose what you have worked for, but that you may be rewarded fully. ⁹Anyone who runs ahead and does not continue in the teaching of Christ does not have God; whoever continues in the teaching has both the Father and the Son.ᵍ ¹⁰If anyone comes to you and does not bring this teaching, do not take him into your house or welcome him. ʰ ¹¹Anyone who welcomes him shares in his wicked work.

1:7
ᶠ1Jn 4:1
1:9
ᵍ1Jn 2:23
1:10
ʰRo 16:17

2. John's final words

¹²I have much to write to you, but I do not want to use paper and ink. Instead, I hope to visit you and talk with you face to face,ⁱ so that our joy may be complete.

1:12
ⁱ3Jn 13, 14

¹³The children of your chosen sister send their greetings.

---

7 The term translated "deceivers" can also be translated "impostors"; it carries the idea of leading another astray. Notice that the verse refers to "many" such charlatans and pretenders. The great danger of deceitful leaders is that they seem so sincere and believable. They are not easy to spot in a crowd. Usually they are winsome and attractive; otherwise, how would they gather people to themselves? We do not want to become paranoid and suspicious about everyone we meet, but we do need to be wise in evaluating the character and conduct of those who would seek to influence people. The way your teachers live shows a lot about what they believe about Christ. For more on testing teachers, see 1 John 4:1.

8 To "be rewarded fully" refers not to salvation but to the rewards of loyal service. All who value the truth and persistently hold to it will win their full reward. Those who live for themselves and justify their self-centeredness by teaching false doctrines will lose that reward (see Matthew 7:21–23).

10 John instructed the believers not to show hospitality to false teachers. They were to do nothing that would encourage the heretics in their propagation of falsehoods. In addition, if believers were to invite them in, such action would show that they were approving of what the false teachers said and did. John is condemning the support of those who are dedicated to opposing the true teachings of God, not condemning hospitality to unbelievers. John adds that a person who supports a false teacher in any way shares in the teacher's evil work.

13 False teaching is serious business, and we dare not overlook it. It is so serious that John wrote this letter to warn against it. Because our world has so many false teachings, we might be tempted to take many of them lightly. Instead, we should realize the dangers they pose and actively refuse to give heresies any foothold.

3 JOHN

BY SPECIAL invitation or with a surprise knock, company arrives and with them comes the promise of soiled floors, extra laundry, dirty dishes, altered schedules, personal expense, and inconvenience. From sharing a meal to providing a bed, *hospitality* costs . . . in time, energy, and money. But how we treat others reflects our true values—what is really important to us. Do we see people as objects or inconveniences, or as unique creations of a loving God? And which is more important to God, a person or a carpet? Perhaps the most effective way to demonstrate God's values and Christ's love to others is to invite and welcome guests into our homes.

For Gaius, hospitality was a habit, and his reputation for friendship and generosity, especially to traveling teachers and missionaries (verse 5), had spread. To affirm and thank Gaius for his Christian life-style, and to encourage him in his faith, John wrote this personal note.

John's format for this letter centers around three men: Gaius, the example of one who follows Christ and loves others (verses 1–8); Diotrephes, the self-proclaimed church leader who does not reflect God's values (verses 9–11); and Demetrius, who also follows the truth (verse 12). John encourages Gaius to practice hospitality, continue to walk in the truth, and do what is right.

Although this is a personal letter, we can look over the shoulder of Gaius and apply its lessons to our life. As you read 3 John, with which man do you identify? Are you a Gaius, generously giving to others? a Demetrius, loving the truth? or a Diotrephes, looking out for yourself and your things? Determine to reflect Christ's values in your relationships, opening your home and touching others with his love.

VITAL STATISTICS

PURPOSE:
To commend Gaius for his hospitality and to encourage him in his Christian life

AUTHOR:
The apostle John

ORIGINAL AUDIENCE:
Gaius, a prominent Christian in one of the churches known to John

DATE WRITTEN:
Approximately A.D. 90 from Ephesus

SETTING:
Church leaders traveled from town to town helping to establish new congregations. They depended on the hospitality of fellow believers. Gaius was one who welcomed these leaders into his home.

KEY VERSE:
"Dear friend, you are faithful in what you are doing for the brothers, even though they are strangers to you" (verse 5).

KEY PEOPLE:
John, Gaius, Diotrephes, Demetrius

THE BLUEPRINT

1. God's children live by the standards of the gospel (verses 1–12)
2. John's final words (verses 13–15)

John wrote to commend Gaius, who was taking care of traveling teachers and missionaries, and to warn against people like Diotrephes, who was proud and refused to listen to spiritual leaders in authority. If we are to live in the truth of the gospel, we must look for ways to support pastors, Christian workers, and missionaries today. All Christians should work together to support God's work both at home and around the world.

MEGATHEMES

THEME	EXPLANATION	IMPORTANCE
Hospitality	John wrote to encourage those who were kind to others. Genuine hospitality for traveling Christian workers was needed then and is still important today.	Faithful Christian teachers and missionaries need our support. Whenever you can extend hospitality to others, it will make you a partner in their ministry.
Pride	Diotrephes not only refused to offer hospitality but also set himself up as a church boss. Pride disqualified him from being a real leader.	Christian leaders must shun pride and its effects on them. Be careful not to misuse your position of leadership.
Faithfulness	Gaius and Demetrius were commended for their faithful work in the church. They were held up as examples of faithful, selfless servants.	Don't take for granted Christian workers who serve faithfully. Be sure to encourage them so they won't grow weary of serving.

1. God's children live by the standards of the gospel

¹The elder,ᵃ

To my dear friend Gaius, whom I love in the truth.

²Dear friend, I pray that you may enjoy good health and that all may go well with you, even as your soul is getting along well. ³It gave me great joy to have some brothers come and tell about your faithfulness to the truth and how you continue to walk in the truth. ᵇ ⁴I have no greater joy than to hear that my childrenᶜ are walking in the truth.

⁵Dear friend, you are faithful in what you are doing for the brothers, even though they are strangers to you.ᵈ ⁶They have told the church about your love. You will do well to send them on their way in a manner worthy of God. ⁷It was for the sake of the Name that they went out, receiving no help from the pagans. ᵉ ⁸We ought therefore to show hospitality to such men so that we may work together for the truth.

⁹I wrote to the church, but Diotrephes, who loves to be first, will have nothing to do with us. ¹⁰So if I come, I will call attention to what he is doing, gossiping maliciously about us. Not satisfied with that, he refuses to welcome the brothers. He also stops those who want to do so and puts them out of the church.

¹¹Dear friend, do not imitate what is evil but what is good.ᶠ Anyone who does what is good is from God. Anyone who does what is evil has not seen God. ¹²Demetrius is well spoken of by everyoneᵍ—and even by the truth itself. We also speak well of him, and you know that our testimony is true. ʰ

1:1
ᵃ2Jn 1

1:3
ᵇ2Jn 4
1:4
ᶜ1Co 4:15

1:5
ᵈRo 12:13

1:7
ᵉAc 20:33, 35

1:11
ᶠPs 37:27
1:12
ᵍ1Ti 3:7
ʰJn 21:24

---

1 This letter provides us an important glimpse into the life of the early church. Third John, addressed to Gaius, highlights the need for showing hospitality to traveling preachers and other believers. It also warns against a would-be church dictator.

1 The "elder," John, was one of Jesus' 12 disciples and the writer of the Gospel of John, three letters, and the book of Revelation. For more information about John, see his Profile in John 13, p. 1771. We have no further information about Gaius, but he is someone whom John loved dearly. Perhaps Gaius had shared his home and hospitality with John at some time during John's travels. If so, John would have appreciated his actions, because traveling preachers depended on expressions of hospitality to survive (see Matthew 10:11–16).

2 John was concerned for Gaius's physical *and* spiritual well-being. This was the opposite of the popular heresy that taught the separation of spirit and matter and despised the physical side of life. Today, many people still fall into this way of thinking. This non-Christian attitude logically leads to one of two responses: neglect of the body and physical health, or indulgence of the body's sinful desires. God is concerned for both your body and your soul. As a responsible Christian, you should neither neglect nor indulge yourself, but care for your physical needs and discipline your body so that you are at your best for God's service.

4 John wrote about "my children" because, as a result of his preaching, he was the spiritual father of many, including Gaius.

5, 6 In the church's early days, traveling prophets, evangelists, and teachers ("the brothers") were helped on their way by people like Gaius who housed and fed them. Hospitality is a lost art in many churches today. We would do well to invite more people for meals—fellow church members, young people, traveling missionaries, those in need, visitors. This is an active and much-appreciated way to show your love. In fact it is probably more important today. Because of our individualistic, self-centered society, many lonely people wonder if anyone cares whether they live or die. If you find such a lonely person, show him or her that *you* care!

7 The traveling missionaries neither asked for nor accepted anything from nonbelievers. This was not intended to be a criticism of unbelievers, but a statement of how things ought to be.

Imagine the awkwardness of a Christian worker's requesting funds or lodging from the very people he or she was trying to reach! Instead, it is the responsibility of churches and Christian individuals to support those who are called by God to full-time vocational ministry. In that way, unbelievers will not be questioning the missionaries' motives for preaching. God's true preachers do not preach to make money but to fulfill their calling and express their love for God. It is the church's responsibility to care for Christian workers; this should never be left to nonbelievers. Don't just discard the next missionary fund-raising letter you receive. That appeal may be God's invitation for you to become a partner in a new gospel venture.

8 When you help someone who is spreading the gospel, you are in a very real way a partner in the ministry. This is the other side of the principle in 2 John 10 (see the note there). Not everyone should go to the mission field; those who work for Christ at home are vital to the ministry of those who go and who need support. We can support missionaries by praying for them and by giving our money, hospitality, and time.

9 This letter to which John refers was neither 1 or 2 John, but another letter that no longer exists.

9, 10 All we know about Diotrephes is that he wanted to control the church. John denounced (1) his refusal to have anything to do with other spiritual leaders, (2) his slander of the leaders, (3) his bad example in refusing to welcome any gospel teachers, and (4) his attempt to excommunicate those who opposed his leadership. Sins such as pride, jealousy, and slander are still present in the church, and when a leader makes a habit of encouraging sin and discouraging right actions, he or she must be stopped. If no one speaks up, great harm can come to the church. We must confront sin in the church; if we ignore it, it will continue to grow. A true Christian leader is a servant, not an autocrat!

12 We know nothing about Demetrius except that he may have carried this letter from John to Gaius. The book of Acts mentions an Ephesian silversmith named Demetrius who opposed Paul (Acts 19:24ff), but this is probably another man. In contrast to the corrupt Diotrephes, Demetrius had a high regard for truth. John personified truth as a witness to Demetrius's character and teaching. In other words, if truth could speak, it would speak on Demetrius's behalf. When Demetrius arrived, Gaius certainly opened his home to him.

2. John's final words

[13]I have much to write you, but I do not want to do so with pen and ink. [14]I hope to see you soon, and we will talk face to face.

Peace to you. The friends here send their greetings. Greet the friends there by name.

---

14 Whereas 2 John emphasizes the need to refuse hospitality to false teachers, 3 John urges continued hospitality to those who teach the truth. Hospitality is a strong sign of support for people and their work. It means giving them of your resources so their stay will be comfortable and their work and travel easier. Actively look for creative ways to show hospitality to God's workers. It may be in the form of a letter of encouragement, a gift, financial support, an open home, or prayer.

JUDE

TO PROTECT from harm, to guard from attack, to repulse enemies—for centuries rugged defenders have built walls, launched missiles, and waged wars, expending material and human resources in the battle to save nations and cities. And with total commitment and courageous abandon, individuals have fought for their families. It is a rule of life that we fight for survival, defending with all our strength what is most precious to us, from every real or imagined attack.

God's Word and the gift of eternal life have infinite value and have been entrusted to Christ's faithful followers. Many people live in opposition to God and his followers. They twist God's words, seeking to deceive and destroy the unwary. But God's truth must go forth, carried and defended by those who have committed their lives to his Son. It is an important task, an awesome responsibility, and a profound privilege to have this commission.

This was Jude's message to Christians everywhere. Opposition would come and godless teachers would arise, but Christians should "contend for the faith" (verse 3) by rejecting all falsehood and immorality (verses 4–19), remembering God's mighty acts of rescue and punishment (verses 5–11, 14–16) and the warnings of the apostles (verses 17–19). His readers are to build up their own faith through prayer (verse 20), keeping close to Christ (verse 21), helping others (verses 22, 23), and hating sin (verse 23). Then Jude concludes with a glorious benediction of praise to God (verses 24, 25).

How much do you value God's Word, the fellowship of the church, and obedience to Jesus Christ? Many false teachers are waiting to destroy your Christ-centered life, the credibility of God's Word, and the unity of the body of Christ. Read Jude and determine to stand firm in your faith and defend God's truth at all costs. *Nothing* is more valuable.

THE BLUEPRINT

1. The danger of false teachers (verses 1–16)
2. The duty to fight for God's truth (verses 17–25)

Jude wrote to motivate Christians everywhere to action. He wanted them to recognize the dangers of false teaching, to protect themselves and other believers, and to win back those who had already been deceived. Jude was writing against godless teachers who were saying that Christians could do as they pleased without fear of God's punishment. While few teach this heresy openly in the church today, many in the church act as though this were true. This letter contains a warning against living a nominal Christian life.

MEGATHEMES

THEME	EXPLANATION	IMPORTANCE
False Teachers	Jude warns against false teachers and leaders who reject the lordship of Christ, undermine the faith of others, and lead them astray. These leaders and any who follow them will be punished.	We must staunchly defend Christian truth. Make sure that you avoid leaders and teachers who distort the Bible to suit their own purposes. Genuine servants of God will faithfully portray Christ in their words and conduct.
Apostasy	Jude also warns against apostasy—turning away from Christ. We are to remember that God punishes rebellion against him. We must be careful not to drift away from a faithful commitment to Christ.	Those who do not seek to know the truth in God's Word are susceptible to apostasy. Christians must guard against any false teachings that would distract them from the truth preached by the apostles and written in God's Word.

1. The danger of false teachers

1:1
a Ac 1:13

¹Jude, *a* a servant of Jesus Christ and a brother of James,

To those who have been called, who are loved by God the Father and kept by*a* Jesus Christ:

²Mercy, peace and love be yours in abundance.

The Sin and Doom of Godless Men

1:3
b Tit 1:4

³Dear friends, although I was very eager to write to you about the salvation we share,*b* I felt I had to write and urge you to contend for the faith that was once for all entrusted to the saints. ⁴For certain men whose condemnation was written about *b* long ago have secretly

a 1 Or for; or in   b 4 Or men who were marked out for condemnation

---

1 Jude's letter focuses on *apostasy*—when people turn away from God's truth and embrace false teachings. Jude reminded his readers of God's judgment on those who had left the faith. This letter warns against false teachers—in this case, probably Gnostic teachers (see the note on Colossians 2:4ff for a description of the Gnostic heresy). Gnostics opposed two of the basic tenets of Christianity—the incarnation of Christ and the call to Christian ethics. Jude wrote to combat these false teachings and to encourage true doctrine and right conduct.

1 Jude was a brother of James, who was one of the leaders in the early church. Both of these men were Jesus' half brothers. Mary was their mother, and Joseph was their father. Although Mary was Jesus' true mother, God was Jesus' true Father.

3 Jude emphasizes the important relationship between correct doctrine and true faith. The truth of the Bible must not be compromised, because it gives us the real facts about Jesus and salvation. The Bible is inspired by God and should never be twisted or manipulated; when it is, we can become confused over right and wrong and lose sight of the only path that leads to eternal life. Before writing about salvation, then, Jude felt he had to set his readers back on the right track, calling them back to the basics of their faith. Then the way to salvation would be clearer. *Saints* refers to all believers.

3 How do ordinary Christians "contend for the faith" today? Think about these ideas:

(1) We can contend for the faith by knowing the truth. We do that by studying the Bible. Don't ever imagine that pastors and seminary professors hold a monopoly on this task. Without study, you cannot know what to defend. You must understand the basic doctrines of the faith so that you can recognize false

doctrines and prevent wrong teaching from undermining your faith and hurting others.

(2) We can contend for the faith as we grow personally with Christ. While knowledge is important, your personal relationship with Christ is essential. Through that relationship, God has given you the Holy Spirit as a teacher. Unattached to God, you may know everything, but understand nothing. Attached to Christ, you are given spiritual understanding as well as experiences with Christ that underscore your faith.

(3) We can contend for the faith by remaining unified on the essentials. While Christians can certainly disagree on many non-essentials (music in worship, methods of worship, methods of outreach), we must always defend the truth of the basics of our faith as found in God's Word.

4 Even some of our churches today have false ("godless") teachers who "have secretly slipped in" and are twisting the Bible's teachings to justify their own opinions, lifestyle, or wrong behavior. In doing this, they may gain temporary freedom to do as they wish, but they will discover that in distorting Scripture they are playing with fire. God will judge them for excusing, tolerating, and promoting sin.

4 Many first-century false teachers were teaching that Christians could do whatever they liked without fear of God's punishment. They had a light view of God's holiness and his justice. Paul refuted this same kind of false teaching in Romans 6:1–23. Even today, some Christians minimize the sinfulness of sin, believing that how they live has little to do with their faith. But what a person truly believes will show up in how he or she acts. Those who truly have faith will show it by their deep respect for God and their sincere desire to live according to the principles in his Word.

slipped in among you. *c* They are godless men, who change the grace of our God into a license for immorality and deny Jesus Christ our only Sovereign and Lord. *d*

5 Though you already know all this, I want to remind you that the Lord *a* delivered his people out of Egypt, but later destroyed those who did not believe. 6 And the angels who did not keep their positions of authority but abandoned their own home—these he has kept in darkness, bound with everlasting chains for judgment on the great Day. *e* 7 In a similar way, Sodom and Gomorrah and the surrounding towns gave themselves up to sexual immorality and perversion. They serve as an example of those who suffer the punishment of eternal fire.

8 In the very same way, these dreamers pollute their own bodies, reject authority and slander celestial beings. *f* 9 But even the archangel Michael, *g* when he was disputing with the devil about the body of Moses, did not dare to bring a slanderous accusation against him, but said, "The Lord rebuke you!" 10 Yet these men speak abusively against whatever they do not understand; and what things they do understand by instinct, like unreasoning animals—these are the very things that destroy them. *h*

11 Woe to them! They have taken the way of Cain; they have rushed for profit into Balaam's error; they have been destroyed in Korah's rebellion. *i*

12 These men are blemishes at your love feasts, eating with you without the slightest qualm—shepherds who feed only themselves. They are clouds without rain, blown along by the wind;*j* autumn trees, without fruit and uprooted *k*—twice dead. 13 They are wild waves of the sea,*l* foaming up their shame; *m* wandering stars, for whom blackest darkness has been reserved forever.

14 Enoch,*n* the seventh from Adam, prophesied about these men: "See, the Lord is coming with thousands upon thousands of his holy ones*o* 15 to judge everyone, and to convict all the ungodly of all the ungodly acts they have done in the ungodly way, and of all the harsh words ungodly sinners have spoken against him." 16 These men are grumblers and faultfinders; they follow their own evil desires; they boast*p* about themselves and flatter others for their own advantage.

a 5 Some early manuscripts *Jesus*

1:4
*c*Gal 2:4
*d*2Pe 2:1

1:6
*e*2Pe 2:4, 9

1:8
*f*2Pe 2:10
1:9
*g*Da 10:13, 21
1:10
*h*2Pe 2:12

1:11
*i*Nu 16:1-3, 31-35

1:12
*j*Eph 4:14
*k*Mt 15:13
1:13
*l*Isa 57:20
*m*Php 3:19

1:14
*n*Ge 5:18, 21-24
*o*Dt 33:2

1:16
*p*2Pe 2:18

5–7 Jude gave three examples of rebellion: (1) the children of Israel—who, although they were delivered from Egypt, refused to trust God and enter the promised land (Numbers 14:26–39); (2) the angels—although they were once pure, holy, and living in God's presence, some gave in to pride and joined Satan to rebel against God (2 Peter 2:4); (3) the cities of Sodom and Gomorrah—the inhabitants were so full of sin that God wiped them off the face of the earth (Genesis 19:1–29). If the chosen people, angels, and sinful cities were punished, how much more would these false teachers be severely judged?

7 Many people don't want to believe that God sentences people to "eternal fire" for rejecting him. But this is clearly taught in Scripture. Sinners who don't seek forgiveness from God will face eternal separation from him. Jude warns all who rebel against, ignore, or reject God.

8 The "celestial beings" here are probably angels. Just as the men of Sodom insulted angels (Genesis 19), these false teachers scoffed at any authority. For information on the danger of insulting even the fallen angels, see the note on 2 Peter 2:10–12.

9 This incident is not recorded in any other place in Scripture. Moses' death is recorded in Deuteronomy 34. Here Jude may have been making use of an ancient book called *The Assumption of Moses*.

10 False teachers claimed to possess secret knowledge that gave them authority. Their "knowledge" of God was esoteric—mystical and beyond human understanding. The nature of God *is* beyond our understanding, but God, in his grace, has chosen to reveal himself to us—in his Word, and supremely in Jesus Christ.

Therefore, we must seek to know all we can about what he has revealed, even though we cannot fully comprehend God with our finite human minds. Beware of those who claim to have all the answers and who belittle what they do not understand.

11 Jude gives three examples of men who did whatever they wanted (verse 10)—Cain, who murdered his brother out of vengeful jealousy (Genesis 4:1–16); Balaam, who prophesied out of greed, not out of obedience to God's command (Numbers 22—24); Korah, who rebelled against God's divinely appointed leaders, wanting the power for himself (Numbers 16:1–35). These stories illustrate attitudes that are typical of false teachers—pride, selfishness, jealousy, greed, lust for power, and disregard of God's will.

12 When the Lord's Supper was celebrated in the early church, believers would eat a full meal before taking part in Communion with the sharing of the bread and wine. The meal was called a "love feast," and it was designed to be a sacred time of fellowship to prepare one's heart for Communion. In several of the churches, however, this meal had turned into a time of gluttony and drunken revelry. In Corinth, for example, some people hastily gobbled food while others went hungry (1 Corinthians 11:20–22). No church function should be an occasion for selfishness, gluttony, greed, disorder, or other sins that destroy unity or take one's mind away from the real purpose for gathering together.

12 The false teachers were "twice dead." They were useless "trees" because they weren't producing fruit. They weren't even believers, so they would be rooted up and burned.

14 Enoch is mentioned briefly in Genesis 5:21–24. This quotation is from an apocryphal book called the book of Enoch.

14 Jesus is also mentioned as coming with angels ("holy ones") in Matthew 16:27 and 24:31. Daniel 7:10 speaks of God judging humanity in the presence of ten thousand times ten thousand angels.

2. The duty to fight for God's truth
A Call to Persevere

1:17
q 2Pe 3:2

1:18
r 1Ti 4:1

1:20
s Col 2:7

1:21
t Tit 2:13; 2Pe 3:12

1:23
u Am 4:11;
Zec 3:2-5

1:24
v Col 1:22

1:25
w Ro 11:36

¹⁷But, dear friends, remember what the apostles of our Lord Jesus Christ foretold. *q* ¹⁸They said to you, "In the last times *r* there will be scoffers who will follow their own ungodly desires." ¹⁹These are the men who divide you, who follow mere natural instincts and do not have the Spirit.

²⁰But you, dear friends, build yourselves up *s* in your most holy faith and pray in the Holy Spirit. ²¹Keep yourselves in God's love as you wait *t* for the mercy of our Lord Jesus Christ to bring you to eternal life.

²²Be merciful to those who doubt; ²³snatch others from the fire and save them; *u* to others show mercy, mixed with fear—hating even the clothing stained by corrupted flesh.

Doxology

²⁴To him who is able to keep you from falling and to present you before his glorious presence without fault *v* and with great joy— ²⁵to the only God our Savior be glory, majesty, power and authority, through Jesus Christ our Lord, before all ages, now and forevermore! Amen. *w*

---

17 Other apostles also warned about false teachers—see Acts 20:29; 1 Timothy 4:1; 2 Timothy 3:1–5; 2 Peter 2:1–3; 2 John 7.

18 The *last times* is a common phrase referring to the time between Jesus' first and second comings. We live in the last times.

21 To "keep yourselves in God's love" means to live close to God and his people, not listening to false teachers who would try to pull you away from him (John 15:9, 10).

22, 23 Bringing people to Jesus saves them from God's judgment. We can do this through compassion and kindness. To hate "even the clothing stained by corrupted flesh" means that we are to hate the sin, but we must witness to and love the sinner. Unbelievers, no matter how successful they seem by worldly standards, are lost and in need of salvation. We should not take witnessing lightly—it is a matter of life and death.

23 In trying to find common ground with those to whom we witness, we must be careful not to fall into the quicksand of compromise. When reaching out to others, we must be sure that our own footing is safe and secure. Be careful not to become so much like non-Christians that no one can tell who you are or what you believe. Influence them for Christ—don't allow them to influence you to sin!

24, 25 As the letter begins, so it ends—with assurance. God keeps believers from falling prey to false teachers. Although false teachers are widespread and dangerous, we don't have to be afraid if we trust God and are rooted and grounded in him.

24, 25 To be sinless and perfect ("without fault") will be the ultimate condition of the believer when he or she finally sees Christ face-to-face. When Christ appears, and we are given our new bodies, we will be like Christ (1 John 3:2). Coming into Christ's presence will be more wonderful than we could ever imagine!

24, 25 The audience to whom Jude wrote was vulnerable to heresies and to temptations toward immoral living. Jude encouraged the believers to remain firm in their faith and trust in God's promises for their future. This was all the more important because they were living in a time of increased apostasy. We too are living in the last days, much closer to the end than were the original readers of this letter. We too are vulnerable to doctrinal error. We too are tempted to give in to sin. Although much false teaching is around us, we need not be afraid or give up in despair—God can keep us from falling, and he guarantees that if we remain faithful, he will bring us into his presence and give us everlasting joy.

REVELATION

VITAL STATISTICS

PURPOSE:
To reveal the full identity of Christ and to give warning and hope to believers

AUTHOR:
The apostle John

ORIGINAL AUDIENCE:
The seven churches in Asia and all believers everywhere

DATE WRITTEN:
Approximately A.D. 95 from Patmos

SETTING:
Most scholars believe that the seven churches of Asia to whom John writes were experiencing the persecution that took place under Emperor Domitian (A.D. 90–95). It seems that the Roman authorities had exiled John to the island of Patmos (off the coast of Asia). John, who had been an eyewitness of the incarnate Christ, had a vision of the glorified Christ. God also revealed to John what would take place in the future—judgment and the ultimate triumph of God over evil.

KEY VERSE:
"Blessed is the one who reads the words of this prophecy, and blessed are those who hear it and take to heart what is written in it, because the time is near" (1:3).

KEY PEOPLE:
John, Jesus

KEY PLACES:
Patmos, the seven churches, the new Jerusalem

SPECIAL FEATURES:
Revelation is written in "apocalyptic" form—a type of Jewish literature that uses symbolic imagery to communicate hope (in the ultimate triumph of God) to those in the midst of persecution. The events are ordered according to literary, rather than strictly chronological, patterns.

WITH tiny wrinkles and cries, he entered the world and, wrapped in strips of cloth, took his first nap on a bed of straw. Subject to time and to parents, he grew to manhood in Roman-occupied Palestine, his gentle hands becoming strong and calloused in Joseph's woodworking shop. As a man, he walked through the countryside and city, touching individuals, preaching to crowds, and training 12 men to carry on his work. At every step he was hounded by those seeking to rid the world of his influence. Finally, falsely accused and tried, he was condemned to a disgraceful execution by foreign hands. And he died—spat upon, cursed, pierced by nails, and hung heavenward for all to deride. Jesus, the God-man, gave his life completely so that all might live.

At God's appointed time, the risen and ascended Lord Jesus will burst onto the world scene. Then everyone will know that Jesus is Lord of the universe! Those who love him will rejoice, greeting their Savior with hearts overflowing into songs of praise. But his enemies will be filled with fear. Allied with Satan, the enemies of Christ will marshal their legions against Christ and his armies. But who can withstand God's wrath? Christ will win the battle and reign victorious forever! Jesus, the humble suffering servant, is also the powerful, conquering King and Judge.

Revelation is a book of hope. John, the beloved apostle and eyewitness of Jesus, proclaimed that the victorious Lord would surely return to vindicate the righteous and judge the wicked. But Revelation is also a book of warning. Things were not as they should have been in the churches, so Christ called the members to commit themselves to live in righteousness.

Although Jesus gave this revelation of himself to John nearly 2,000 years ago, it still stands as a comfort and challenge to God's people today. We can take heart as we understand John's vision of hope: Christ will return to rescue his people and settle accounts with all who defy him.

John begins this book by explaining how he received this revelation from God (1:1–20). He then records specific messages from Jesus to the seven churches in Asia (2:1—3:22). Suddenly, the scene shifts as a mosaic of dramatic and majestic images bursts into view before John's eyes. This series of visions portrays the future rise of evil, culminating in the antichrist (4:1—18:24). Then follows John's recounting of the triumph of the King over all kings, the wedding of the Lamb, the final judgment, and the coming of the new Jerusalem (19:1—22:5). Revelation concludes with the promise of Christ's soon return (22:6–21), and John breathes a prayer that has been echoed by Christians through the centuries: "Amen. Come, Lord Jesus" (22:20).

As you read the book of Revelation, marvel with John at the wondrous panorama of God's revealed plan. Listen as Christ warns the churches, and root out any sin that blocks your relationship with him. Be full of hope, knowing that God is in control, Christ's victory is assured, and all who trust him will be saved.

THE BLUEPRINT

A. LETTERS TO THE CHURCHES
   (1:1—3:22)

The vision John received opens with instructions for him to write to seven churches. He both commends them for their strengths and warns them about their flaws. Each letter was directed to a church then in existence but also speaks to conditions in the church throughout history. Both in the church and in our individual lives, we must constantly fight against the temptation to become loveless, immoral, lenient, compromising, lifeless, or casual about our faith. The letters make it clear how our Lord feels about these qualities.

B. MESSAGE FOR THE CHURCH
   (4:1—22:21)
   1. Worshiping God in heaven
   2. Opening the seven seals
   3. Sounding the seven trumpets
   4. Observing the great conflict
   5. Pouring out the seven plagues
   6. Seizing the final victory
   7. Making all things new

This revelation is both a warning to Christians who have grown apathetic and an encouragement to those who are faithfully enduring the struggles in this world. It reassures us that good will triumph over evil, gives us hope as we face difficult times, and gives guidance when we are wavering in our faith. Christ's message to the church is a message of hope for all believers in every generation.

MEGATHEMES

THEME	EXPLANATION	IMPORTANCE
God's Sovereignty	God is sovereign. He is greater than any power in the universe. God is not to be compared with any leader, government, or religion. He controls history for the purpose of uniting true believers in loving fellowship with him.	Though Satan's power may temporarily increase, we are not to be led astray. God is all-powerful. He is in control. He will bring his true family safely into eternal life. Because he cares for us, we can trust him with our very life.
Christ's Return	Christ came to earth as a "Lamb," the symbol of his perfect sacrifice for our sin. He will return as the triumphant "Lion," the rightful ruler and conqueror. He will defeat Satan, settle accounts with all those who reject him, and bring his faithful people into eternity.	Assurance of Christ's return gives suffering Christians the strength to endure. We can look forward to his return as king and judge. Since no one knows the time when he will appear, we must be ready at all times by keeping our faith strong.
God's Faithful People	John wrote to encourage the church to resist the demands to worship the Roman emperor. He warns all God's faithful people to be devoted only to Christ. Revelation identifies who the faithful people are and what they should be doing until Christ returns.	You can take your place in the ranks of God's faithful people by believing in Christ. Victory is sure for those who resist temptation and make loyalty to Christ their top priority.
Judgment	One day God's anger toward sin will be fully and completely unleashed. Satan will be defeated with all of his agents. False religion will be destroyed. God will reward the faithful with eternal life, but all who refuse to believe in him will face eternal punishment.	Evil and injustice will not prevail forever. God's final judgment will put an end to these. We need to be certain of our commitment to Jesus if we want to escape this great final judgment. No one who rejects Christ will escape God's punishment.
Hope	One day God will create a new heaven and a new earth. All believers will live with him forever in perfect peace and security. Those who have already died will be raised to life. These promises for the future bring us hope.	Our great hope is that what Christ promises will come true. When we have confidence in our final destination, we can follow Christ with unwavering dedication no matter what we must face. We can be encouraged by hoping in Christ's return.

A. LETTERS TO THE CHURCHES (1:1—3:22)

Near the end of his life, John received a vision from Christ, which he recorded for the benefit of the seven churches in Asia and for Christians throughout history. This is the only book in the Bible that promises a blessing to those who listen to its words and do what it says.

Prologue

1 The revelation of Jesus Christ, which God gave him to show his servants what must soon take place. He made it known by sending his angel *a* to his servant John, [2] who testifies to everything he saw—that is, the word of God and the testimony of Jesus Christ. *b* [3] Blessed is the one who reads the words of this prophecy, and blessed are those who hear it and take to heart what is written in it, *c* because the time is near.

1:1
a Rev 22:16

1:2
b 1Co 1:6

1:3
c Lk 11:28

Greetings and Doxology

[4] John,

To the seven churches in the province of Asia:

Grace and peace to you from him who is, and who was, and who is to come, and from the seven spirits *a* before his throne, [5] and from Jesus Christ, who is the faithful witness, the firstborn from the dead, *d* and the ruler of the kings of the earth.

1:5
d Col 1:18

a 4 Or *the sevenfold Spirit*

1:1 Revelation is a book about the future *and* about the present. It offers future hope to all believers, especially those who have suffered for their faith, by proclaiming Christ's final victory over evil and the reality of eternal life with him. It also gives present guidance as it teaches us about Jesus Christ and how we should live for him now. Through graphic pictures we learn that (1) Jesus Christ is coming again, (2) evil will be judged, and (3) the dead will be raised to judgment, resulting in eternal life or eternal destruction.

1:1 According to tradition, John, the author, was the only one of Jesus' original twelve disciples who was not killed for the faith. He also wrote the Gospel of John and the letters of 1, 2, and 3 John. When he wrote Revelation, John was in exile on the island of Patmos in the Aegean Sea, sent there by the Romans for his witness about Jesus Christ. For more information on John, see his Profile in John 13, p. 1771.

1:1 This book is the revelation *of, concerning,* and *from* Jesus Christ. God gave the revelation of his plan to Jesus Christ, who, in turn, revealed it to John. The book of Revelation unveils Christ's full identity and God's plan for the end of the world, and it focuses on Jesus Christ, his second coming, his victory over evil, and the establishment of his kingdom. As you read and study Revelation, don't focus so much on the timetable of the events or the details of John's imagery that you miss the main message—the infinite love, power, and justice of the Lord Jesus Christ.

1:1 The book of Revelation is *apocalyptic* (meaning uncovered, unveiled, or revealed) in style. This style of ancient literature usually featured spectacular and mysterious imagery, and such literature was written under the name of an ancient hero. John was acquainted with Jewish apocalyptic works, but his book is different in several ways: (1) He uses his own name rather than the name of an ancient hero; (2) he denounces evil and exhorts people to high Christian standards; (3) he offers hope rather than gloom. John was not a psychic attempting to predict the future; he was a prophet of God describing what God had shown him.

1:1 For more about angels, see the note on 5:11.

1:1 Jesus gave his message to John in a vision, allowing John to see and record certain future events so they could be an encouragement to all believers. The vision includes many signs and symbols that convey the essence of what is to happen. What John saw, in most cases, was indescribable, so he used illustrations to show what it was *like*. When reading this symbolic language, we don't have to understand every detail—John himself didn't. Instead, realize that John's imagery shows us that Christ is indeed the glorious and victorious Lord of all.

1:1–3 The book of Revelation reveals future events, but there is not the gloomy pessimism we might expect. The drama of these

unfolding events is spectacular, but there is nothing to fear if you are on the winning side. When you think about the future, walk with confidence because Christ, the victor, walks with you.

1:3 Revelation is a book of prophecy that is both *prediction* (foretelling future events) and *proclamation* (preaching about who God is and what he will do). Prophecy is more than telling the future. Behind the predictions are important principles about God's character and promises. As we read, we will get to know God better so that we can trust him completely.

1:3 The typical news reports—filled with violence, scandal, and political haggling—are depressing, and we may wonder where the world is heading. God's plan for the future, however, provides inspiration and encouragement because we know he will intervene in history to conquer evil. John encourages churches to read this book aloud so everyone can hear it, apply it ("take to heart what is written in it"), and be assured of the fact that God will triumph.

1:3 When John says, "the time is near," he is urging his readers to be ready at all times for the Last Judgment and the establishment of God's kingdom. We do not know when these events will occur, but we must always be prepared. They will happen quickly, and there will be no second chance to change sides.

1:4 Jesus told John to write to seven churches that knew and trusted him and had read his earlier letters (see 1:11). The letters were addressed so that they could be read and passed on in a systematic fashion, following the main Roman road clockwise around the province of Asia (now called Turkey).

1:4 The "seven spirits" is another name for the Holy Spirit. The number seven is used throughout Revelation to symbolize completeness and perfection. For more about the Holy Spirit, see the notes on John 3:6 and Acts 1:5.

1:4–6 The Trinity—the Father ("him who is, and who was, and who is to come"), the Holy Spirit ("the seven spirits"), and the Son (Jesus Christ)—is the source of all truth (John 14:6, 17; 1 John 2:27; Revelation 19:11). Thus we can be assured that John's message is reliable and is God's word to us.

1:5 Others had risen from the dead—people whom the prophets, Jesus, and the apostles brought back to life during their ministries—but later those people died again. Jesus was the first who rose from the dead in an imperishable body (1 Corinthians 15:20), never to die again. He is the firstborn from the dead.

1:5, 6 Many hesitate to witness about their faith in Christ because they don't feel the change in their lives has been spectacular enough. But you qualify as a witness for Jesus because of what he has done for you, not because of what you have done for him. Christ demonstrated his great love by setting us free from our sins

To him who loves us and has freed us from our sins by his blood, 6 and has made us to be a kingdom and priests to serve his God and Father—to him be glory and power for ever and ever! Amen.

1:7
e Zec 12:10

7 Look, he is coming with the clouds,
    and every eye will see him,
        even those who pierced him;
    and all the peoples of the earth will mourn*e* because of him.

So shall it be! Amen.

1:8
f Rev 4:8

8 "I am the Alpha and the Omega," says the Lord God, "who is, and who was, and who is to come, the Almighty."*f*

INTERPRETING THE BOOK OF REVELATION	Approach	Description	Challenge	Caution
	Preterist View	John is writing to encourage Christians in his own day who are experiencing persecution from the Roman empire.	To gain the same kind of encouragement John's first readers gained from the vivid images of God's sovereignty	Do not forget that most biblical prophecy has both an immediate and a future application.
	Futurist View	Except for the first three chapters, John is describing events that will occur at the end of history.	To see in contemporary events many of the characteristics John describes and realize that the end could come at any time	Do not assume that we have "figured out" the future, since Jesus said that no one will know the day of his return before it happens.
	Historicist View	The book of Revelation is a presentation of history from John's day until the second coming of Christ and beyond.	To note the consistency of human evil throughout history and recognize that names may change but the rebellion against God has not	Be careful before identifying current events or leaders as fulfilling aspects of the book of Revelation.
	Idealist View	The book of Revelation is a symbolic representation of the continual struggle of good and evil. It does not refer to any particular historical events. It is applicable at any point in history.	To gain insight into the past, to prepare for the future, and to live obediently and confidently in the present	Do not avoid the book because it is difficult. Try to understand Revelation within its broader literary context.

Over the centuries, four main approaches to interpreting the book of Revelation have developed. Each approach has had capable supporters, but none has proved itself the only way to read this book. However, the most basic application question for each approach can be summarized by asking yourself, Will this help me become a better follower of Jesus Christ today?

through his death on the cross ("freed us from our sins by his blood"), guaranteeing us a place in his kingdom, and making us priests to administer God's love to others. The fact that the all-powerful God has offered eternal life to you is nothing short of spectacular.

1:5–7 Jesus is portrayed as an all-powerful King, victorious in battle, glorious in peace. He is not just a humble earthly teacher, he is the glorious God. When you read John's description of the vision, keep in mind that his words are not just good advice; they are truth from the King of kings. Don't just read his words for their interesting and amazing portrayal of the future. Let the truth about Christ penetrate your life, deepen your faith in him, and strengthen your commitment to follow him no matter what the cost.

1:7 John is announcing the return of Jesus to earth (see also Matthew 24; Mark 13; 1 Thessalonians 4:15–18). Jesus' second coming will be *visible* and *victorious*. All people will see him arrive (Mark 13:26), and they will *know* it is Jesus. When he

comes, he will conquer evil and judge all people according to their deeds (20:11–15).

1:7 "Those who pierced him" could refer to the Roman soldiers who pierced Jesus' side as he hung on the cross or to the Jews who were responsible for his death. John saw Jesus' death with his own eyes, and he never forgot the horror of it (see John 19:34, 35; see also Zechariah 12:10).

1:8 *Alpha* and *Omega* are the first and last letters of the Greek alphabet. The Lord God is the beginning and the end. God the Father is the eternal Lord and Ruler of the past, present, and future (see also 4:8; Isaiah 44:6; 48:12–15). Without him you have nothing that is eternal, nothing that can change your life, nothing that can save you from sin. Is the Lord your reason for living, "the Alpha and the Omega" of your life? Honor the One who is the beginning and the end of all existence, wisdom, and power.

One Like a Son of Man

⁹I, John, your brother and companion in the suffering and kingdom and patient enduranceg that are ours in Jesus, was on the island of Patmos because of the word of God and the testimony of Jesus. ¹⁰On the Lord's Day I was in the Spirit, and I heard behind me a loud voice like a trumpet,ʰ ¹¹which said: "Write on a scroll what you see and send it to the seven churches: to Ephesus, Smyrna, Pergamum, Thyatira, Sardis, Philadelphia and Laodicea."

¹²I turned around to see the voice that was speaking to me. And when I turned I saw seven golden lampstands, ⁱ ¹³and among the lampstands was someone "like a son of man,"ᵃ ʲ dressed in a robe reaching down to his feet and with a golden sash around his chest. ᵏ ¹⁴His head and hair were white like wool, as white as snow, and his eyes were like blazing fire.ˡ ¹⁵His feet were like bronze glowing in a furnace,ᵐ and his voice was like the sound of rushing waters.ⁿ ¹⁶In his right hand he held seven stars,ᵒ and out of his mouth came a sharp double-edged sword.ᵖ His face was like the sun shining in all its brilliance.

ᵃ13 Daniel 7:13

1:9 g 2Ti 2:12
1:10 h Rev 4:1
1:12 i Ex 25:31-40
1:13 j Eze 1:26; Da 7:13 k Da 10:5
1:14 l Da 7:9; 10:6
1:15 m Da 10:6 n Eze 43:2
1:16 o Rev 2:1 p Heb 4:12

THE SEVEN CHURCHES
The seven churches were located on a major Roman road. A letter carrier would leave the island of Patmos (where John was exiled), arriving first at Ephesus. He would travel north to Smyrna and Pergamum, turn southeast to Thyatira, and continue on to Sardis, Philadelphia, and Laodicea—in the exact order in which the letters were dictated.

1:9 Patmos was a small rocky island in the Aegean Sea, about 50 miles offshore from the city of Ephesus on the Asia Minor seacoast (see map).

1:9 The Christian church was facing severe persecution. Almost all believers were socially, politically, or economically suffering because of this empire-wide persecution, and some were even being killed for their faith. John was exiled to Patmos because he refused to stop preaching the gospel. We may not face persecution for our faith as the early Christians did, but even with our freedom few of us have the courage to share God's Word with others. If we hesitate to share our faith during easy times, how will we do during times of persecution?

1:12, 13 The seven golden lampstands are the seven churches in Asia (1:11, 20), and Jesus stands among them. No matter what the churches face, Jesus protects them with his all-encompassing love and reassuring power. Through his Spirit, Jesus Christ is still among the churches today. When a church faces persecution, it should remember Christ's deep love and compassion. When a church is wracked by internal strife and conflict, it should remember Christ's concern for purity and his intolerance of sin.

1:13, 14 This man "like a son of man" is Jesus himself. The title *Son of Man* occurs many times in the New Testament in reference to Jesus as the Messiah. John recognized Jesus because he lived with him for three years and had seen him both as the Galilean preacher and as the glorified Son of God at the transfiguration (Matthew 17:1–8). Here Jesus appears as the mighty Son of Man. His white hair indicates his wisdom and divine nature (see also Daniel 7:9); his blazing eyes symbolize judgment of all evil; the golden sash around his chest reveals him as the high priest who goes into God's presence to obtain forgiveness of sin for those who have believed in him.

Revelation will challenge your mental picture of Jesus Christ. What forms your impression of him right now—famous paintings, movies, Sunday school art? Do you ever picture Jesus with a gold sash and snow white, woolly hair? Do his eyes flash fire and his feet glow like bronze? When you imagine Jesus speaking to you, does his voice thunder like mighty ocean waves? Reevaluate the way you think of Jesus as you read and study Revelation. Allow his powerful presence to transform your life.

1:16 The sword in Jesus' mouth symbolizes the power and force

1:17
qDa 8:17, 18
rIsa 41:4

1:18
sRo 6:9
tRev 20:1

¹⁷When I saw him, I fell at his feetq as though dead. Then he placed his right hand on me and said: "Do not be afraid. I am the First and the Last.r ¹⁸I am the Living One; I was dead,s and behold I am alive for ever and ever! And I hold the keys of death and Hades.t

¹⁹"Write, therefore, what you have seen, what is now and what will take place later. ²⁰The mystery of the seven stars that you saw in my right hand and of the seven golden lampstands is this: The seven stars are the angelsa of the seven churches, and the seven lampstands are the seven churches.

a20 Or messengers

A JOURNEY THROUGH THE BOOK OF REVELATION
Revelation is a complex book, and it has baffled interpreters for centuries. We can avoid a great deal of confusion by understanding the literary structure of this book. This approach will allow us to understand the individual scenes within the overall structure of Revelation and keep us from getting unnecessarily bogged down in the details of each vision. John gives hints throughout the book to indicate a change of subject, or a flashback to an earlier scene.

In chapter 1, John relates the circumstances that led to the writing of this book (1:1–20). In chapters 2 and 3, Jesus gives special messages to the seven churches of Asia Minor (2:1–3:22).

Suddenly, John is caught up into heaven, where he sees a vision of God Almighty on his throne. All of Christ's followers and the heavenly angels are worshiping God (4:1–11). John watches as God gives a scroll with seven seals to the worthy Lamb, Jesus Christ (5:1–14). The Lamb begins to open the seals one by one. As each seal is opened, a new vision appears.

As the first four seals are opened, riders appear on horses of different colors: war, famine, disease, and death are in their path (6:1–8). As the fifth seal is opened, John sees those in heaven who have been martyred for their faith in Christ (6:9–11).

A set of contrasting images appears at the opening of the sixth seal. On one side, there is a great earthquake, stars fall from the sky, and the sky rolls up like a scroll (6:12–17). On the other side, multitudes are before the throne, worshiping and praising God and the Lamb (7:1–17).

Finally, the seventh seal is opened (8:1–5), unveiling a series of God's judgments announced by seven angels with seven trumpets. The first four angels bring hail, fire, a burning mountain, and a falling star—the sun and moon are darkened (8:6–13). The fifth trumpet announces the coming of locusts with the power to sting (9:1–12). The sixth trumpet heralds the coming of an army of warriors on horses (9:13–21). In 10:1–11, John is given a little scroll to eat. Following this, John is commanded to measure the temple of God (11:1, 2). He sees two witnesses, who proclaim God's judgment on the earth for three and a half years (11:3–14).

Finally, the seventh trumpet sounds, calling the rival forces of good and evil to the final battle. On one side is Satan and his forces; on the other side stands Jesus Christ with his forces (11:15—13:18). In the midst of this call to battle, John sees three angels announcing the final judgment (14:6–13). Two angels begin to reap this harvest of judgment on the earth (14:14–20). Following on the heels of these two angels are seven more angels, who pour out God's judgment on the earth from seven bowls (15:1—16:21). One of these angels from the group of seven reveals to John a vision of a "great prostitute" called Babylon (symbolizing the Roman Empire), riding a scarlet beast (17:1–18). After the defeat of Babylon (18:1–24), a great multitude in heaven shouts praise to God for his mighty victory (19:1–10).

The final three chapters of the book of Revelation catalog the events that finalize Christ's victory over the enemy: Satan's 1,000-year imprisonment (20:1–10), the final judgment (20:11–15), and the creation of a new earth and a new Jerusalem (21:1—22:6). An angel then gives John final instructions concerning the visions John has seen and what to do once he has written them all down (22:7–11).

Revelation concludes with the promise of Christ's soon return, an offer to drink of the water of life that flows through the great street of the new Jerusalem, and a warning to those who read the book (22:12–21). May we pray with John, "Amen. Come, Lord Jesus" (22:20).

The Bible ends with a message of warning and hope for men and women of every generation. Christ is victorious, and all evil has been done away with. As you read the book of Revelation, marvel at God's grace in the salvation of the saints and his power over the evil forces of Satan, and remember the hope of this victory to come.

---

of his message. His words of judgment are as sharp as swords (Isaiah 49:2; Hebrews 4:12).

1:17, 18 As the Roman government stepped up its persecution of Christians, John must have wondered if the church could survive and stand against the opposition. But Jesus appeared in glory and splendor, reassuring John that he and his fellow believers had access to God's strength to face these trials. If you are facing difficult problems, remember that the power available to John and the early church is also available to you (see 1 John 4:4).

1:17, 18 Our sins have convicted and sentenced us, but Jesus holds the keys of death and Hades. He alone can free us from eternal bondage to Satan. He alone has the power and authority to set us free from sin's control. Believers don't have to fear Hades or death, because Christ holds the keys to both. All we must do is turn from sin and turn to him in faith. When we attempt to control

our lives and disregard God, we set a course that leads directly to hell. But when we place our lives in Christ's hands, he restores us now and resurrects us later to an eternal, peaceful relationship with him.

1:20 Who are the "angels of the seven churches"? Some say that they are angels designated to guard the churches; others say that they are elders or pastors of the local churches. Because the seven letters in chapters 2 and 3 contain reprimands, it is doubtful that these angels are heavenly messengers. If these are earthly leaders or messengers, they are accountable to God for the churches they represent.

To the Church in Ephesus

2 "To the angel[a] of the church in Ephesus write:

These are the words of him who holds the seven stars in his right hand[u] and walks among the seven golden lampstands:[v] [2]I know your deeds,[w] your hard work and your perseverance. I know that you cannot tolerate wicked men, that you have tested[x] those who claim to be apostles but are not, and have found them false.[y] [3]You have persevered and have endured hardships for my name, and have not grown weary.

[4]Yet I hold this against you: You have forsaken your first love. [5]Remember the height from which you have fallen! Repent and do the things you did at first. If you do not repent, I will come to you and remove your lampstand from its place. [6]But you have this in your favor: You hate the practices of the Nicolaitans, which I also hate.

[7]He who has an ear, let him hear[z] what the Spirit says to the churches. To him who overcomes, I will give the right to eat from the tree of life,[a] which is in the paradise of God.

a 1 Or *messenger*; also in verses 8, 12 and 18

2:1
u Rev 1:16
v Rev 1:12, 13

2:2
w Rev 3:1, 8, 15
x 1Jn 4:1
y 2Co 11:13

2:7
z Mt 11:15; Rev 3:6, 13, 22
a Ge 2:9; Rev 22:2, 14, 19

2:1 Ephesus was the capital of Asia Minor, a center of land and sea trade, and, along with Alexandria and Antioch in Syria, one of the three most influential cities in the eastern part of the Roman empire. The temple to Artemis, one of the ancient wonders of the world, was located in this city, and a major industry was the manufacture of images of this goddess (see Acts 19:21–41). Paul ministered in Ephesus for three years and warned the Ephesians that false teachers would come and try to draw people away from the faith (see Acts 20:29–31). False teachers did indeed cause problems in the Ephesian church, but the church resisted them, as we can see from Paul's letter to them (see the book of Ephesians). John spent much of his ministry in this city and knew that they had resisted false teaching (2:2).

2:1 The one who "walks among the seven golden lampstands" (the seven churches) is Jesus (1:11–13). He holds the "seven stars in his right hand" (messengers of the churches), indicating his power and authority over the churches and their leaders. Ephesus had become a large, proud church, and Jesus' message would remind them that he alone is the head of the body of believers.

2:1ff Does God care about your church? If you are tempted to doubt it, look more closely at these seven letters. The Lord of the universe knew each of these churches and its precise situation. In each letter, Jesus told John to write about specific people, places, and events. He praised believers for their successes and told them how to correct their failures. Just as Jesus cared for each of these churches, he cares for yours. He wants it to reach its greatest potential. The group of believers with whom you worship and serve is God's vehicle for changing the world. Take it seriously—God does.

2:2 Over a long period of time, the church in Ephesus had steadfastly refused to tolerate sin among its members. This was not easy in a city noted for immoral sexual practices associated with the worship of the goddess Artemis. We also are living in times of widespread sin and sexual immorality. It is popular to be open-minded toward many types of sin, calling them personal choices or alternative lifestyles. But when the body of believers begins to tolerate sin in the church, it is lowering the standards and compromising the church's witness. Remember that God's approval is infinitely more important than the world's. Use God's Word, not what people around you are willing to accept, to set the standards for what is right or wrong.

2:2, 3 Christ commended the church at Ephesus for (1) working hard, (2) persevering, (3) resisting sin, (4) critically examining the claims of false apostles, and (5) enduring hardships without becoming weary. Every church should have these characteristics. But these good efforts should spring from our love for Jesus Christ. Both Jesus and John stressed love for one another as an authentic proof of the gospel (John 13:34; 1 John 3:18, 19). In the battle to maintain sound teaching and moral and doctrinal purity, it is possible to lose a charitable spirit. Prolonged conflict can weaken or destroy our patience and affection. In defending our faith, guard against any structure or rigidity that weakens love.

2:4 Paul had once commended the church at Ephesus for its love for God and others (Ephesians 1:15), but many of the church founders had died, and many of the second-generation believers had lost their zeal for God. They were a busy church—the members did much to benefit themselves and the community—but they were acting out of the wrong motives. Work for God must be motivated by love for God or it will not last.

2:4, 5 Just as when a man and woman fall in love, so also new believers rejoice at their newfound forgiveness. But when we lose sight of the seriousness of sin, we begin to lose the thrill of our forgiveness (see 2 Peter 1:9). In the first steps of your Christian life, you may have had enthusiasm without knowledge. Do you now have knowledge without enthusiasm? Both are necessary if we are to keep love for God intense and untarnished (see Hebrews 10:32, 35). Do you love God with the same fervor as when you were a new Christian?

2:5 For Jesus to "remove your lampstand from its place" would mean the church would cease to be an effective church. Just as the seven-branched candlestick in the temple gave light for the priests to see, the churches were to give light to their surrounding communities. But Jesus warned them that their lights could go out. In fact, Jesus himself would extinguish any light that did not fulfill its purpose. The church had to repent of its sins.

2:6 The Nicolaitans were believers who compromised their faith in order to enjoy some of the sinful practices of Ephesian society. The name *Nicolaitans* is held by some to be roughly the Greek equivalent of the Hebrew word for "Balaamites." Balaam was a prophet who had induced the Israelites to carry out their lustful desires (see 2:14 and Numbers 31:16). When we want to take part in an activity that we know is wrong, we may make excuses to justify our behavior, saying that it isn't as bad as it seems or that it won't hurt our faith. Christ has strong words for those who look for excuses to sin.

2:6 Through John, Jesus commended the church at Ephesus for hating the wicked practices of the Nicolaitans. Note that they didn't hate the people, just their sinful actions. We should accept and love all people but refuse to tolerate all evil. God cannot tolerate sin, and he expects us to stand against it. The world needs Christians who will stand for God's truth and point people toward right living.

2:7 Two trees had been in the Garden of Eden—the tree of life and the tree of the knowledge of good and evil (see Genesis 2:9). Eating from the tree of life brought eternal life with God; eating from the tree of knowledge brought realization of good and evil. When Adam and Eve ate from the tree of knowledge, they disobeyed God's command. So they were excluded from Eden and barred from eating from the tree of life. Eventually, evil will be destroyed and believers will be brought into a restored paradise. In the new earth, everyone will eat from the tree of life and will live forever.

To the Church in Smyrna

2:8
b Rev 1:17

8 "To the angel of the church in Smyrna write:

These are the words of him who is the First and the Last,[b] who died and came to life

2:9
c Jas 2:5
d Rev 3:9

2:10
e Da 1:12, 14

again. 9 I know your afflictions and your poverty—yet you are rich![c] I know the slander of those who say they are Jews and are not,[d] but are a synagogue of Satan. 10 Do not be afraid of what you are about to suffer. I tell you, the devil will put some of you in prison to test you, and you will suffer persecution for ten days.[e] Be faithful, even to the point of death, and I will give you the crown of life.

2:11
f Rev 21:8

11 He who has an ear, let him hear what the Spirit says to the churches. He who overcomes will not be hurt at all by the second death.[f]

To the Church in Pergamum

2:12
g Rev 1:16

12 "To the angel of the church in Pergamum write:

These are the words of him who has the sharp, double-edged sword.[g] 13 I know where you live—where Satan has his throne. Yet you remain true to my name. You did

---

THE NAMES OF JESUS IN REVELATION

Reference	Jesus' Name	Reference	Jesus' Name
1:8	The Alpha and the Omega	5:5	The Root of David
1:8	Lord God	5:6	Lamb
1:8	The Almighty	7:17	Shepherd
1:13	The Son of Man	12:10	Christ
1:17	The First and the Last	19:11	Faithful and True
1:18	The Living One	19:13	The Word of God
2:18	The Son of God	19:16	King of kings
3:14	The faithful and true witness	19:16	Lord of lords
5:5	The Lion of the tribe of Judah	22:16	The Morning Star

Scattered among the vivid images of the book of Revelation is a large collection of names for Jesus. Each one tells something of his character and highlights a particular aspect of his role within God's plan of redemption.

2:8 The city of Smyrna was about 25 miles north of Ephesus. It was nicknamed "Port of Asia" because it had an excellent harbor on the Aegean Sea. The church in this city struggled against two hostile forces: a Jewish population strongly opposed to Christianity, and a non-Jewish population that was loyal to Rome and supported emperor worship. Persecution and suffering were inevitable in an environment like this.

2:9, 10 Persecution comes from Satan, not from God. Satan, the devil, will cause believers to be thrown into prison and even killed. But believers need not fear death, because it will only result in their receiving the crown of life. Satan may harm their earthly bodies, but he can do them no spiritual harm. The "synagogue of Satan" means that these Jews were serving Satan's purposes, not God's, when they gathered to worship. "Ten days" means that although persecution would be intense, it would be relatively short. It would have a definite beginning and end, and God would remain in complete control.

2:9–11 Pain is part of life, but it is never easy to suffer, no matter what the cause. Jesus commended the church at Smyrna for its faith in suffering. He then encouraged the believers that they need not fear the future if they remained faithful. If you are experiencing difficult times, don't let them turn you away from God. Instead let them draw you toward greater faithfulness. Trust God and remember your heavenly reward (see also 22:12–14).

2:10 Smyrna was famous for its athletic games. A crown was the victory wreath, the trophy for the champion at the games. If we have been faithful, we will receive the prize of victory—eternal life (James 1:12). The message to the Smyrna church was to remain faithful during their suffering because God is in control and his promises are reliable. Jesus never says that by being faithful to him we will avoid troubles, suffering, and persecution.

Rather, we must be faithful to him *in* our sufferings. Only then will our faith prove to be genuine. We remain faithful by keeping our eyes on Christ and on what he promises us now and in the future (see Philippians 3:13, 14; 2 Timothy 4:8).

2:11 Believers and unbelievers alike experience physical death. All people will be resurrected, but believers will be resurrected to eternal life with God while unbelievers will be resurrected to be punished with a second death, eternal separation from God (see also 20:14; 21:8, 27; 22:15).

2:12 The city of Pergamum was built on a hill 1,000 feet above the surrounding countryside, creating a natural fortress. It was a sophisticated city, a center of Greek culture and education, with a 200,000-volume library. But it was also the center of four cults, and it rivaled Ephesus in its worship of idols. The city's chief god was Asclepius, whose symbol was a serpent, and who was considered the god of healing. People came to Pergamum from all over the world to seek healing from this god.

2:12 Just as the Romans used their swords for authority and judgment, Jesus' sharp, double-edged sword represents God's ultimate authority and judgment. It may also represent God's future separation of believers from unbelievers. Unbelievers cannot experience the eternal rewards of living in God's kingdom.

2:13 As the center for four idolatrous cults (Zeus, Dionysius, Asclepius, and Athene), Pergamum was called the city "where Satan has his throne." Surrounded by worship of Satan and the Roman emperor as god, the church at Pergamum refused to renounce their faith, even when Satan's worshipers martyred one of their members. Standing firm against the strong pressures and temptations of society is never easy, but the alternative is deadly (2:11).

2:13–15 It was not easy to be a Christian in Pergamum. Believers experienced great pressure to compromise or leave the faith. (For not renounce your faith in me,[h] even in the days of Antipas, my faithful witness, who was put to death in your city—where Satan lives.

[14] Nevertheless, I have a few things against you: You have people there who hold to the teaching of Balaam,[i] who taught Balak to entice the Israelites to sin by eating food sacrificed to idols and by committing sexual immorality. [15] Likewise you also have those who hold to the teaching of the Nicolaitans. [16] Repent therefore! Otherwise, I will soon come to you and will fight against them with the sword of my mouth.[j]

[17] He who has an ear, let him hear what the Spirit says to the churches. To him who overcomes, I will give some of the hidden manna. I will also give him a white stone with a new name written on it, known only to him who receives it.[k]

To the Church in Thyatira

[18] "To the angel of the church in Thyatira write:

These are the words of the Son of God, whose eyes are like blazing fire and whose feet are like burnished bronze.[l] [19] I know your deeds, your love and faith, your service and perseverance, and that you are now doing more than you did at first.

[20] Nevertheless, I have this against you: You tolerate that woman Jezebel,[m] who calls herself a prophetess. By her teaching she misleads my servants into sexual immorality and the eating of food sacrificed to idols. [21] I have given her time to repent of her immorality, but she is unwilling.[n] [22] So I will cast her on a bed of suffering, and I will make those who commit adultery with her suffer intensely, unless they repent of her ways. [23] I will strike her children dead. Then all the churches will know that I am he who

2:13
[h] Rev 14:12

2:14
[i] 2Pe 2:15

2:16
[j] 2Th 2:8; Rev 1:16

2:17
[k] Rev 19:12

2:18
[l] Rev 1:14, 15

2:20
[m] 1Ki 16:31; 21:25; 2Ki 9:7

2:21
[n] Rev 9:20

---

information on the Nicolaitans, see the first note on 2:6.) Nothing is known about Antipas except that he did *not* compromise. He was faithful, and he died for his faith. Apparently, however, some in the church were tolerating those who taught or practiced what Christ opposed. Compromise can be defined as a blending of the qualities of two different things or a concession of principles. Cooperate with people as much as you can, but avoid any alliance, partnership, or participation that could lead to immoral practices.

2:14 There is room for differences of opinion among Christians in some areas, but there is no room for heresy and moral impurity. Your town might not participate in idol feasts, but it probably has pornography, sexual sin, cheating, gossiping, and lying. Don't tolerate sin by bowing to the pressure to be open-minded.

2:14–16 Balak was a king who feared the large number of Israelites traveling through his country, so he hired Balaam to pronounce a curse on them. Balaam refused at first, but an offer of money changed his mind (Numbers 22—24). Later Balaam influenced the Israelites to turn to idol worship (Numbers 31:16; also see 2 Peter 2:15; Jude 11). Here Christ rebuked the church for tolerating those who, like Balaam, lead people away from God.

2:16 This sword is God's judgment against rebellious nations (19:15, 21) and all forms of sin. See also the note on 1:16 and the second note on 2:12.

2:17 "Hidden manna" suggests the spiritual nourishment that the faithful believers will receive. As the Israelites traveled toward the promised land, God provided manna from heaven for their physical nourishment (Exodus 16:13–18). Jesus, as the bread of life (John 6:51), provides spiritual nourishment that satisfies our deepest hunger.

2:17 It is unclear what the white stones are or exactly what the names on each will be. Because they relate to the hidden manna, they may be symbols of the believer's eternal nourishment, or eternal life. The stones are significant because each will bear the new name of every person who truly believes in Christ. They are the evidence that a person has been accepted by God and declared worthy to receive eternal life. A person's name represented his or her character. God will give us new names and new hearts.

2:18 Thyatira was a working man's town, with many trade guilds for cloth making, dyeing, and pottery. Lydia, Paul's first convert in Philippi, was a merchant from Thyatira (Acts 16:14). The city was basically secular, with no focus on any particular religion.

2:19 The believers in Thyatira were commended for growing in good deeds. We should not feel satisfied when our church only rejoices in the salvation of its members or in the comfort of gathering for worship. We should grow in love, faith, and acts of service. Because the times are critical, we must spend our days wisely and faithfully.

2:20 A woman in the church in Thyatira was teaching that immorality was not a serious matter for believers. Her name may have been Jezebel, or John may have used the name Jezebel to symbolize the kind of evil she was promoting. Jezebel, a pagan queen of Israel, was considered the most evil woman who ever lived (see 1 Kings 19:1, 2; 21:1–15; 2 Kings 9:7–10, 30–37; and her Profile in 1 Kings 21, p. 537).

2:20 Why is sexual immorality serious? Sex outside marriage always hurts someone. It hurts God because it shows that we prefer to satisfy our desires our own way instead of according to God's Word, or to satisfy them now instead of waiting for his timing. It hurts others because it violates the commitment so necessary to a relationship. It hurts us because it often brings disease to our bodies and adversely affects our personalities. Sexual immorality has tremendous power to destroy families, churches, and communities because it destroys the integrity on which these relationships are built. God wants to protect us from hurting ourselves and others; thus we are to have no part in sexual immorality, even if our culture accepts it.

2:20 In pagan temples, meat was often offered to idols. Then the meat that wasn't burned was sold to shoppers in the temple marketplace. Eating food offered to idols wasn't wrong in itself, but it could violate the principle of sensitivity toward weaker Christian brothers and sisters who would be bothered by it (see 1 Corinthians 8 and the note on Romans 14:2). Jezebel was obviously more concerned about her own selfish pleasure and freedom than about the needs and concerns of fellow believers.

2:21 Jezebel was unwilling to repent. "Repent" means to change our mind and direction from following our way to following God's way, from sin and its disastrous consequences to God and eternal life. In his mercy, God has given us time to decide to follow him. Only our stubborn willfulness stands in the way.

2:23 We cannot hide from Christ; he knows what is in our hearts and minds, and still he loves us. The sins we try to hide from God need to be confessed to him.

2:23
o Jer 11:20;
Ac 1:24; Ro 8:27
2:24
p Ac 15:28

searches hearts and minds, *o* and I will repay each of you according to your deeds. ²⁴Now I say to the rest of you in Thyatira, to you who do not hold to her teaching and have not learned Satan's so-called deep secrets (I will not impose any other burden on you): *p* ²⁵Only hold on to what you have until I come.

²⁶To him who overcomes and does my will to the end, I will give authority over the nations—

2:27
q Isa 30:14

> ²⁷ 'He will rule them with an iron scepter;
>   he will dash them to pieces like pottery'ᵃ *q* —

just as I have received authority from my Father. ²⁸I will also give him the morning star. ²⁹He who has an ear, let him hear what the Spirit says to the churches.

To the Church in Sardis

3:1
r Rev 1:4
s Rev 1:16
t Rev 2:2

3 "To the angel *b* of the church in Sardis write:

These are the words of him who holds the seven spirits *c r* of God and the seven stars. *s* I know your deeds; *t* you have a reputation of being alive, but you are dead. ²Wake up! Strengthen what remains and is about to die, for I have not found your

a 27 Psalm 2:9   *b* 1 Or *messenger*; also in verses 7 and 14   *c* 1 Or *the sevenfold Spirit*

THE LETTERS TO THE SEVEN CHURCHES

Church	Reference	Commendation	Rebuke	Action
Ephesus	2:1–7	Hard work, perserverance	Forsaken first love	Remember and repent
Smyrna	2:8–11	Suffered persecution, poverty	None	Don't fear; be faithful
Pergamum	2:12–17	True to the faith	Tolerate compromise	Repent
Thyatira	2:18–29	Love, faith, service	Tolerate immorality	Repent
Sardis	3:1–6	Effective	Superficial	Wake up; repent
Philadelphia	3:7–13	Faithful	None	Hold on
Laodicea	3:14–22	None	Lukewarm	Be earnest and repent

This summary of the letters to the seven churches shows us the qualities our churches should seek and those we should avoid.

2:24, 25 The "deep secrets" of Satan were either false teaching advocated by heretics, or secret insights by so-called believers "guaranteed" to promote deeper spiritual life. What was the appeal of such teaching? It may have been appealing to hear that what happens in the body is inconsequential; therefore, it is not sinful to fulfill sexual desires outside of marriage. Another appeal to the "deep secrets" may have been the sense of pride that such knowledge stimulated in those seeking it. We should hold tightly to the basics of our Christian faith and view with extreme caution any new teaching that turns us away from the Bible, the fellowship of our church, or our basic confession of faith.

2:26, 27 Christ says that those who overcome (those who remain faithful until the end and continue to please God) will rule over Christ's enemies and reign with him as he judges evil (see also Psalm 2:8, 9; Isaiah 30:14; Jeremiah 19:11; 1 Corinthians 6:2, 3; Revelation 12:5; 19:15; 20:3, 4 for more about God's judgment).

2:28 Christ is called the morning star in 2:28, 22:16, and 2 Peter 1:19. A morning star appears just before dawn, when the night is coldest and darkest. When the world is at its bleakest point, Christ will burst onto the scene, exposing evil with his light of truth and bringing his promised reward.

3:1 The wealthy city of Sardis was actually in two locations. The older section of the city was on a mountain, and, when its population outgrew the spot, a newer section was built in the valley below.

3:1 The "seven spirits of God" is another name for the Holy Spirit. The seven stars are the messengers, or leaders, of the churches (see 2:1).

3:1 The problem in the Sardis church was not heresy, but spiritual death. In spite of its reputation for being active, Sardis was infested with sin. Its deeds were evil and its clothes soiled. The Spirit has no words of commendation for this church that looked so good on the outside but was so corrupt on the inside.

Even though Christ called Sardis a dead church, he also affirmed the handful of people who were faithful believers. Christ loves to defeat death. If you find yourself in a dead church, make sure you preserve your own faithfulness. Ask God to intervene. Ask God to help you find other believers, and pray together for an awakening of your church.

deeds complete in the sight of my God. [3] Remember, therefore, what you have received and heard; obey it, and repent. But if you do not wake up, I will come like a thief, [u] and you will not know at what time I will come to you.

[4] Yet you have a few people in Sardis who have not soiled their clothes. [v] They will walk with me, dressed in white, [w] for they are worthy. [5] He who overcomes will, like them, be dressed in white. I will never blot out his name from the book of life, but will acknowledge his name before my Father and his angels. [6] He who has an ear, let him hear [x] what the Spirit says to the churches.

To the Church in Philadelphia

[7] "To the angel of the church in Philadelphia write:

These are the words of him who is holy and true, [y] who holds the key of David. [z] What he opens no one can shut, and what he shuts no one can open. [8] I know your deeds. See, I have placed before you an open door that no one can shut. I know that you have little strength, yet you have kept my word and have not denied my name. [9] I will make those who are of the synagogue of Satan, [a] who claim to be Jews though they are not, but are liars—I will make them come and fall down at your feet [b] and acknowledge that I have loved you. [10] Since you have kept my command to endure patiently, I will also keep you [c] from the hour of trial that is going to come upon the whole world to test those who live on the earth. [d]

[11] I am coming soon. Hold on to what you have, [e] so that no one will take your crown. [f] [12] Him who overcomes I will make a pillar [g] in the temple of my God. Never again will he leave it. I will write on him the name of my God [h] and the name of the city of my God, the new Jerusalem, which is coming down out of heaven from my God; and I will also write on him my new name. [13] He who has an ear, let him hear what the Spirit says to the churches.

To the Church in Laodicea

[14] "To the angel of the church in Laodicea write:

These are the words of the Amen, the faithful and true witness, the ruler of God's creation. [i] [15] I know your deeds, that you are neither cold nor hot. I wish you were either

3:3
[u] 2Pe 3:10

3:4
[v] Jude 23
[w] Rev 6:11

3:6
[x] Rev 2:7

3:7
[y] 1Jn 5:20
[z] Isa 22:22

3:9
[a] Rev 2:9
[b] Isa 49:23

3:10
[c] 2Pe 2:9
[d] Rev 6:10

3:11
[e] Rev 2:25
[f] Rev 2:10

3:12
[g] Gal 2:9
[h] Rev 22:4

3:14
[i] Col 1:16, 18

3:3 The church at Sardis was urged to go back to what they first heard and believed, to get back to the basics of the faith. It is important to grow in our knowledge of the Lord, to deepen our understanding through careful study. But no matter how much we learn, we must never abandon the basic truths. No new truth from God will ever contradict these Biblical teachings.

The church was also told to wake up. Their wealth and comfort had lulled them to sleep. Their self-satisfaction caused them to die spiritually. Not only had they wandered from the apostles' teaching, but they were no longer growing in faith or evangelism. They lacked compassionate service to others and had no unity or love. Are you watchful and alert? If God has given you a place of responsibility to teach, lead, or serve, use that position to encourage those around you to be spiritually awake and morally prepared.

3:5 To be "dressed in white" means to be set apart for God and made pure. Christ promises future honor and eternal life to those who stand firm in their faith. The names of all believers are registered in the book of life. This book symbolizes God's knowledge of who belongs to him. All such people are guaranteed a listing in the book of life and are introduced to the hosts of heaven as belonging to Christ (see Luke 12:8, 9).

3:7 Philadelphia was founded by the citizens of Pergamum. The community was built in a frontier area as a gateway to the central plateau of Asia Minor. Philadelphia's residents kept barbarians out of the region and brought in Greek culture and language. The city was destroyed by an earthquake in A.D. 17, and aftershocks kept the people so worried that most of them lived outside the city limits.

3:7 The key of David represents Christ's authority to open the door of invitation into his future kingdom. After the door is opened, no one can close it—salvation is assured. Once it is closed, no one can open it—judgment is certain.

3:10 Some believe that "I will also keep you from the hour of trial" means there will be a future time of great tribulation from which true believers will be spared. Others interpret this to mean that the church will go through the time of tribulation and that God will keep them strong in the midst of it. Still others believe this refers to times of great distress in general, the church's suffering through the ages. We cannot interpret from this verse when or for how long Christians will experience "the hour of trial." Today, millions of Christians are suffering and dying at the hands of godless tyrants throughout the world. To them, the time of testing has already begun. Whenever Christians suffer, Christ promises protection of their eternal souls (see Luke 21:17–19).

3:11 Christians have differing gifts, abilities, experience, and maturity. God doesn't expect us all to be and act the same, but he does expect us to "hold on" to what we have, to persevere in using our resources for him. The Philadelphians are commended for their effort to obey (3:8) and encouraged to hold tightly to whatever strength they have. You may be a new believer and feel that your faith and spiritual strength are little. Use what you have to live for Christ, and God will commend you.

3:12 The new Jerusalem is the future dwelling of the people of God (21:2). We will have a new citizenship in God's future kingdom. Everything will be new, pure, and secure.

3:14 Laodicea was the wealthiest of the seven cities, known for its banking industry, manufacture of wool, and a medical school that produced eye salve. But the city had always had a problem with its water supply. At one time an aqueduct was built to bring water to the city from hot springs. But by the time the water reached the city, it was neither hot nor refreshingly cool—only lukewarm. The church had become as bland as the tepid water that came into the city.

3:15 Lukewarm water makes a disgusting drink. The church in

3:17
j Hos 12:8; 1Co 4:8

3:19
k Heb 12:5, 6

3:20
l Lk 12:36

3:21
m Mt 19:28

3:22
n Rev 2:7

4:1
o Rev 1:10
p Rev 11:12
q Rev 1:19

4:2
r Rev 1:10

one or the other! [16]So, because you are lukewarm—neither hot nor cold—I am about to spit you out of my mouth. [17]You say, 'I am rich; I have acquired wealth and do not need a thing.'*j* But you do not realize that you are wretched, pitiful, poor, blind and naked. [18]I counsel you to buy from me gold refined in the fire, so you can become rich; and white clothes to wear, so you can cover your shameful nakedness; and salve to put on your eyes, so you can see.

[19]Those whom I love I rebuke and discipline.*k* So be earnest, and repent. [20]Here I am! I stand at the door and knock. If anyone hears my voice and opens the door,*l* I will come in and eat with him, and he with me.

[21]To him who overcomes, I will give the right to sit with me on my throne,*m* just as I overcame and sat down with my Father on his throne. [22]He who has an ear, let him hear*n* what the Spirit says to the churches."

B. MESSAGE FOR THE CHURCH (4:1—22:21)

Moving from the conditions within the churches in Asia to the future of the universal church, John sees the course of coming events in a way similar to Daniel and Ezekiel. Many of these passages contain clear spiritual teachings, but others seem beyond our ability to understand. The clear teaching of this book is that God will defeat all evil in the end. We must live in obedience to Jesus Christ, the coming Conqueror and Judge.

1. Worshiping God in heaven

The Throne in Heaven

4 After this I looked, and there before me was a door standing open in heaven. And the voice I had first heard speaking to me like a trumpet*o* said, "Come up here,*p* and I will show you what must take place after this."*q* [2]At once I was in the Spirit,*r* and there before

---

Laodicea had become lukewarm and thus distasteful and repugnant. The believers didn't take a stand for anything; indifference had led to idleness. By neglecting to do anything for Christ, the church had become hardened and self-satisfied, and it was destroying itself. There is nothing more disgusting than a half-hearted, in-name-only Christian who is self-sufficient. Don't settle for following God halfway. Let Christ fire up your faith and get you into the action.

3:17 Some believers falsely assume that numerous material possessions are a sign of God's spiritual blessing. Laodicea was a wealthy city, and the church was also wealthy. But what the Laodiceans could see and buy had become more valuable to them than what is unseen and eternal. Wealth, luxury, and ease can make people feel confident, satisfied, and complacent. But no matter how much you possess or how much money you make, you have nothing if you don't have a vital relationship with Christ. How does your current level of wealth affect your spiritual desire? Instead of centering your life primarily on comfort and luxury, find your true riches in Christ.

3:18 Laodicea was known for its great wealth—but Christ told the Laodiceans to buy their gold from him (real spiritual treasures). The city was proud of its cloth and dyeing industries—but Christ told them to purchase white clothes from him (his righteousness). Laodicea prided itself on its precious eye salve that healed many eye problems—but Christ told them to get medicine from him to heal their eyes so they could see the truth (John 9:39). Christ was showing the Laodiceans that true value was not in material possessions, but in a right relationship with God. Their possessions and achievements were valueless compared with the everlasting future of Christ's kingdom.

3:19 God would discipline this lukewarm church unless it turned from its indifference toward him. God's purpose in discipline is not to punish, but to bring people back to him. Are you lukewarm in your devotion to God? God may discipline you to help you out of your uncaring attitude, but he uses only loving discipline. You can avoid God's discipline by drawing near to him again through confession, service, worship, and studying his Word. Just as the spark of love can be rekindled in marriage, so the Holy Spirit can reignite our zeal for God when we allow him to work in our hearts.

3:20 The Laodicean church was complacent and rich. They felt self-satisfied, but they didn't have Christ's presence among them.

Christ knocked at the door of their hearts, but they were so busy enjoying worldly pleasures that they didn't notice that he was trying to enter. The pleasures of this world—money, security, material possessions—can be dangerous, because their temporary satisfaction makes us indifferent to God's offer of lasting satisfaction. If you find yourself feeling indifferent to church, to God, or to the Bible, you have begun to shut God out of your life. Leave the door of your heart constantly open to God, and you won't need to worry about hearing his knock. Letting him in is your only hope for lasting fulfillment.

3:20 Jesus is knocking on the door of our hearts every time we sense we should turn to him. Jesus wants to have fellowship with us, and he wants us to open up to him. He is patient and persistent in trying to get through to us—not breaking and entering, but knocking. He allows us to decide whether or not to open our lives to him. Do you intentionally keep his life-changing presence and power on the other side of the door?

3:22 At the end of each letter to these churches, the believers were urged to listen and take to heart what was written to them. Although a different message was addressed to each church, all the messages contain warnings and principles for everyone. Which letter speaks most directly to your church? Which has the greatest bearing on your own spiritual condition at this time? How will you respond?

4:1 Chapters 4 and 5 record glimpses into Christ's glory. Here we see into the throne room of heaven. God is on the throne and orchestrating all the events that John will record. The world is not spinning out of control; the God of creation will carry out his plans as Christ initiates the final battle with the forces of evil. John shows us heaven before showing us earth so that we will not be frightened by future events.

4:1 The voice John had first heard that sounded like a trumpet blast was the voice of Christ (see 1:10, 11).

4:2 Four times in the book of Revelation John says he was "in the Spirit" (1:10; 4:2; 17:3; 21:10). This expression means that the Holy Spirit was giving him a vision—showing him situations and events he could not have seen with mere human eyesight. All true prophecy comes from God through the Holy Spirit (2 Peter 1:20, 21).

me was a throne in heaven[s] with someone sitting on it. [3]And the one who sat there had the appearance of jasper and carnelian. A rainbow, resembling an emerald, encircled the throne. [4]Surrounding the throne were twenty-four other thrones, and seated on them were twenty-four elders.[t] They were dressed in white and had crowns of gold on their heads. [5]From the throne came flashes of lightning, rumblings and peals of thunder.[u] Before the throne, seven lamps[v] were blazing. These are the seven spirits[a][w] of God. [6]Also before the throne there was what looked like a sea of glass,[x] clear as crystal.

In the center, around the throne, were four living creatures, and they were covered with eyes, in front and in back. [7]The first living creature was like a lion, the second was like an ox, the third had a face like a man, the fourth was like a flying eagle.[y] [8]Each of the four living creatures had six wings[z] and was covered with eyes all around, even under his wings. Day and night they never stop saying:

> "Holy, holy, holy
> is the Lord God Almighty,[a]
> who was, and is, and is to come."[b]

[9]Whenever the living creatures give glory, honor and thanks to him who sits on the throne and who lives for ever and ever, [10]the twenty-four elders fall down before him[c] who sits on the throne, and worship him who lives for ever and ever. They lay their crowns before the throne and say:

> [11] "You are worthy, our Lord and God,
> to receive glory and honor and power,[d]
> for you created all things,
> and by your will they were created
> and have their being."

The Scroll and the Lamb

5 Then I saw in the right hand of him who sat on the throne a scroll with writing on both sides[e] and sealed with seven seals. [2]And I saw a mighty angel proclaiming in a loud voice, "Who is worthy to break the seals and open the scroll?" [3]But no one in heaven or on earth or under the earth could open the scroll or even look inside it. [4]I wept and wept

[a]5 Or *the sevenfold Spirit*

4:2
[s] Isa 6:1

4:4
[t] Rev 11:16

4:5
[u] Rev 8:5
[v] Zec 4:2
[w] Rev 1:4

4:6
[x] Rev 15:2

4:7
[y] Eze 1:10

4:8
[z] Isa 6:2
[a] Rev 1:8
[b] Rev 1:4

4:10
[c] Rev 5:8, 14

4:11
[d] Rev 5:12

5:1
[e] Eze 2:9, 10

4:4 Who are these 24 elders? Because there were 12 tribes of Israel in the Old Testament and 12 apostles in the New Testament, the 24 elders in this vision probably represent all the redeemed of God for all time (both before and after Christ's death and resurrection). They symbolize all those—both Jews and Gentiles—who are now part of God's family. The 24 elders show us that *all* the redeemed of the Lord are worshiping him.

4:5 In Revelation, lightning and thunder are connected with significant events in heaven. They remind us of the lightning and thunder at Mount Sinai when God gave the people his laws (Exodus 19:16). The Old Testament often uses such imagery to reflect God's power and majesty (Psalm 77:18).

4:5 The "seven spirits of God" is another name for the Holy Spirit. See also Zechariah 4:2–6, where the seven lamps are equated with the one Spirit.

4:6 Glass was very rare in New Testament times, and crystal-clear glass was virtually impossible to find (see 1 Corinthians 13:12). The "sea of glass" highlights both the magnificence and holiness of God.

4:6, 7 Just as the Holy Spirit is seen symbolically in the seven lighted lamps, so the "four living creatures" represent the attributes (the qualities and character) of God. These creatures were not real animals. Like the cherubim (the highest order of the angels), they guard God's throne, lead others in worship, and proclaim God's holiness. God's attributes symbolized in the

animal-like appearance of these four creatures are majesty and power (the lion), faithfulness (the ox), intelligence (the man), and sovereignty (the eagle). The Old Testament prophet Ezekiel saw four similar creatures in one of his visions (Ezekiel 1:5–10).

4:9 John describes these scenes in such detail because Christians in the first century came from many backgrounds. Not all of them understood Jewish history or knew the glory of the temple. Revelation instructs us in worship. It shows us where, why, and how to praise God. Worship takes our minds off our problems and focuses them on God. Worship leads us from individual meditation to corporate worship. Worship causes us to consider and appreciate God's character. Worship lifts our perspective from the earthly to the heavenly.

4:11 The point of this chapter is summed up in this verse: All creatures in heaven and earth will praise and honor God because he is the Creator and Sustainer of everything.

5:1ff Chapter 5 continues the glimpse into heaven begun in chapter 4.

5:1 In John's day, books were written on scrolls—pieces of papyrus or vellum up to 30 feet long, rolled up and sealed with clay or wax. The scroll that John sees contains the full account of what God has in store for the world. The seven seals indicate the importance of its contents. The seals are located throughout the scroll so that as each one is broken, more of the scroll can be read to reveal another phase of God's plan for the end of the world. Only Christ is worthy to break the seals and open the scroll (5:3–5).

5:5
f Ge 49:9

because no one was found who was worthy to open the scroll or look inside. ⁵Then one of the elders said to me, "Do not weep! See, the Lion *f* of the tribe of Judah, the Root of David, has triumphed. He is able to open the scroll and its seven seals."

⁶Then I saw a Lamb, looking as if it had been slain, standing in the center of the throne, encircled by the four living creatures and the elders. He had seven horns and seven eyes, which are the seven spirits *a* of God sent out into all the earth. ⁷He came and took the scroll

5:8
g Rev 14:2

from the right hand of him who sat on the throne. ⁸And when he had taken it, the four living creatures and the twenty-four elders fell down before the Lamb. Each one had a harp *g* and they were holding golden bowls full of incense, which are the prayers of the saints. ⁹And

5:9
h Ps 40:3
i 1Co 6:20

they sang a new song: *h*

> "You are worthy to take the scroll
>   and to open its seals,
> because you were slain,
>   and with your blood you purchased *i* men for God
>   from every tribe and language and people and nation.
> ¹⁰ You have made them to be a kingdom and priests to serve our God,
>   and they will reign on the earth."

5:11
j Da 7:10

¹¹Then I looked and heard the voice of many angels, numbering thousands upon thousands, and ten thousand times ten thousand. *j* They encircled the throne and the living creatures and the elders. ¹²In a loud voice they sang:

> "Worthy is the Lamb, who was slain,
> to receive power and wealth and wisdom and strength
> and honor and glory and praise!"

5:13
k Php 2:10

¹³Then I heard every creature in heaven and on earth and under the earth *k* and on the sea, and all that is in them, singing:

a 6 Or *the sevenfold Spirit*

5:5 The Lion, Jesus, proved himself worthy to break the seals and open the scroll by living a perfect life of obedience to God, dying on the cross for the sins of the world, and rising from the dead to show his power and authority over evil and death. Only Christ conquered sin, death, hell, and Satan himself; so only he can be trusted with the world's future. The Root of David refers to Jesus being from David's family line, thus fulfilling the promise of the Messiah in the Old Testament.

5:5, 6 Jesus Christ is pictured as both a Lion (symbolizing his authority and power) and a Lamb (symbolizing his submission to God's will). One of the elders calls John to look at the Lion, but when John looks he sees a Lamb. Christ the Lamb was the perfect sacrifice for the sins of all mankind; therefore, only he can save us from the terrible events revealed by the scroll. Christ the Lamb won the greatest battle of all. He defeated all the forces of evil by dying on the cross. The role of Christ the Lion will be to lead the battle where Satan is finally defeated (19:19–21). Christ the Lion is victorious because of what Christ the Lamb has already done. We will participate in his victory not because of our effort or goodness, but because he has promised eternal life to all who believe in him.

5:6 John sees the Lamb "looking as if it had been slain;" the wounds inflicted on Jesus' body during his trial and crucifixion could still be seen (see John 20:24–31). Jesus was called the Lamb of God by John the Baptist (John 1:29). In the Old Testament, lambs were sacrificed to atone for sins: the Lamb of God died as the final sacrifice for all sins (see Isaiah 53:7; Hebrews 10:1–12, 18).

5:6 The horns symbolize strength and power (see 1 Kings 22:11; Zechariah 1:18). Although Christ is a sacrificial lamb, he is in no way weak. He was killed, but now he lives in God's strength and power. In Zechariah 4:2–10, the eyes are equated with the seven lamps and the one Spirit.

5:9, 10 People from every nation are praising God before his throne. God's message of salvation and eternal life is not limited

to a specific culture, race, or country. Anyone who comes to God in repentance and faith is accepted by him and will be part of his kingdom. Don't allow prejudice or bias to keep you from sharing Christ with others. Christ welcomes all people into his kingdom.

5:9, 10 The song of God's people praises Christ's work. He (1) was slain, (2) purchased them with his blood, (3) gathered them into a kingdom, (4) made them priests, and (5) appointed them to reign on the earth. Jesus has already died and paid the penalty for sin. He is now gathering us into his kingdom and making us priests. In the future we will reign with him. Worship God and praise him for what he has done, what he is doing, and what he will do for all who trust in him. When we realize the glorious future that awaits us, we will find the strength to face our present difficulties.

5:10 The believers' song praises Christ for bringing them into the kingdom and making them kings and priests. While now we are sometimes despised and mocked for our faith (John 15:17–27), in the future we will reign over all the earth (Luke 22:29, 30). Christ's death made all believers priests of God—the channels of blessing between God and mankind (1 Peter 2:5–9).

5:11 Angels are spiritual beings created by God who help carry out his work on earth. They bring messages (Luke 1:26–28), protect God's people (Daniel 6:22), offer encouragement (Genesis 16:7ff), give guidance (Exodus 14:19), bring punishment (2 Samuel 24:16), patrol the earth (Ezekiel 1:9–14), and fight the forces of evil (2 Kings 6:16–18; Revelation 20:1). There are both good and evil angels (12:7), but because evil angels are allied with Satan, they have considerably less power and authority than good angels. Eventually, the main role of the good angels will be to offer continuous praise to God (see also 19:1–3).

"To him who sits on the throne and to the Lamb
be praise and honor and glory and power,
for ever and ever!"

14 The four living creatures said, "Amen," and the elders fell down and worshiped. *l*

5:14
l Rev 4:10

2. Opening the seven seals
The Seals

6 I watched as the Lamb opened the first of the seven seals. Then I heard one of the four living creatures say in a voice like thunder, "Come!" **2** I looked, and there before me was a white horse! *m* Its rider held a bow, and he was given a crown, *n* and he rode out as a conqueror bent on conquest.

6:2
m Rev 19:11
n Zec 6:11

3 When the Lamb opened the second seal, I heard the second living creature *o* say, "Come!" **4** Then another horse came out, a fiery red one. Its rider was given power to take peace from the earth and to make men slay each other. To him was given a large sword.

6:3
o Rev 4:7

5 When the Lamb opened the third seal, I heard the third living creature *p* say, "Come!" I looked, and there before me was a black horse! Its rider was holding a pair of scales in his hand. **6** Then I heard what sounded like a voice among the four living creatures, saying, "A quart *a* of wheat for a day's wages, *b* and three quarts of barley for a day's wages, *b* and do not damage *q* the oil and the wine!"

6:5
p Rev 4:7
6:6
q Rev 9:4

7 When the Lamb opened the fourth seal, I heard the voice of the fourth living creature *r* say, "Come!" **8** I looked, and there before me was a pale horse! *s* Its rider was named Death, and Hades was following close behind him. They were given power over a fourth of the earth to kill by sword, famine and plague, and by the wild beasts of the earth.

6:7
r Rev 4:7
6:8
s Zec 6:3

9 When he opened the fifth seal, I saw under the altar the souls of those who had been slain *t* because of the word of God and the testimony they had maintained. **10** They called out in a loud voice, "How long, *u* Sovereign Lord, holy and true, *v* until you judge the inhabitants of the earth and avenge our blood?" **11** Then each of them was given a white robe, and they were told to wait a little longer, until the number of their fellow servants and brothers who were to be killed as they had been was completed. *w*

6:9
t Rev 20:4
6:10
u Zec 1:12
v Rev 3:7
6:11
w Heb 11:40

a 6 Greek *a choinix* (probably about a liter)   *b 6* Greek *a denarius*

5:14 The scene in chapter 5 shows us that only the Lamb, Jesus Christ, is worthy to open the scroll (the events of history). Jesus, not Satan, holds the future. Jesus Christ is in control, and he alone is worthy to set into motion the events of the last days of history.

6:1ff This is the first of three seven-part judgments. The trumpets (chapters 8; 9) and the bowls (chapter 16) are the other two. As each seal is opened, Christ the Lamb sets in motion events that will bring about the end of human history. This scroll is not completely opened until the seventh seal is broken (8:1). The contents of the scroll reveal mankind's depravity and portray God's authority over the events of human history.

6:2ff Four horses appear as the first four seals are opened. The horses represent God's judgment of people's sin and rebellion. God is directing human history—even using his enemies to accomplish his purposes. The four horses are a foretaste of the final judgments yet to come. Some view this chapter as a parallel to the Olivet Discourse (see Matthew 24). The imagery of four horses is also found in Zechariah 6:1–8.

6:2–8 Each of the four horses is a different color. Some assume that the white horse represents victory and that its rider must be Christ (because Christ later rides to victory on a white horse—19:11). But because the other three horses relate to judgment and destruction, this rider on a white horse would most likely not be Christ. The four are part of the unfolding judgment of God, and it would be premature for Christ to ride forth as conqueror. The other horses represent different kinds of judgment: red for warfare and bloodshed; black for famine; pale for death. The high prices of wheat and barley illustrate famine conditions. But the worst is yet to come.

6:4 Complete peace will only come when Christ returns. The picture in Revelation of the coming persecutions and natural disasters is gloomy, but ultimately it is cause for great joy. When

believers see these events happening, they will know that their Messiah's return is coming soon, and they can look forward to his reign of justice and peace. Rather than being terrified by what is happening in our world, we should confidently await Christ's return to bring justice and restoration to his people.

6:8 It is not clear whether Hades was on a separate horse than Death or merely rode along with Death, but the riders described in verses 2–8 are commonly referred to as the four horsemen of the Apocalypse. The four riders are given power over one-fourth of the earth, indicating that God is still limiting his judgment—it is not yet complete. With these judgments there is still time for unbelievers to turn to Christ and away from their sin. In this case, the limited punishment not only demonstrates God's wrath on sin, but also his merciful love in giving people yet another opportunity to turn to him before he brings final judgment. We must not presume upon God's patience. Our repentance must be visible and authentic. In what ways does your life reflect new and different behavior?

6:9 The altar represents the altar of sacrifice in the temple, where animals were sacrificed to atone for sins. Instead of the animals' blood at the base of the altar, John saw the souls of martyrs who had died for preaching the gospel. These martyrs were told that still more would lose their lives for their belief in Christ (6:11). In the face of warfare, famine, persecution, and death, Christians will be called on to stand firmly for what they believe. Only those who endure to the end will be rewarded by God (Mark 13:13).

6:9–11 The martyrs are eager for God to bring justice to the earth, but they are told to wait. God is not waiting until a certain number is reached, but he is promising that those who suffer and die for their faith will not be forgotten. Rather, they will be singled out by God for special honor. We may wish for justice immediately, as these martyrs did, but we must be patient. God

6:12
x Rev 16:18
y Mt 24:29

6:13
z Rev 8:10

6:14
a Jer 4:24

6:17
b Zep 1:14, 15;
Rev 16:14
c Ps 76:7

¹²I watched as he opened the sixth seal. There was a great earthquake. ˣ The sun turned black ʸ like sackcloth made of goat hair, the whole moon turned blood red, ¹³and the stars in the sky fell to earth, ᶻ as late figs drop from a fig tree when shaken by a strong wind. ¹⁴The sky receded like a scroll, rolling up, and every mountain and island was removed from its place. ᵃ

¹⁵Then the kings of the earth, the princes, the generals, the rich, the mighty, and every slave and every free man hid in caves and among the rocks of the mountains. ¹⁶They called to the mountains and the rocks, "Fall on us and hide us from the face of him who sits on the throne and from the wrath of the Lamb! ¹⁷For the great day ᵇ of their wrath has come, and who can stand?" ᶜ

144,000 Sealed

7 After this I saw four angels standing at the four corners of the earth, holding back the four winds of the earth to prevent any wind from blowing on the land or on the sea or on

EVENTS IN REVELATION DESCRIBED ELSEWHERE IN THE BIBLE	Other Reference	Revelation Reference	Event
	Ezekiel 1:22–28	4:2, 3; 10:1–3	Glowing rainbow around God's throne
	Isaiah 53:7	5:6–8	Christ is pictured as a Lamb
	Psalm 96	5:9–14	New song
	Zechariah 1:7–11; 6:1–8	6:1–8	Horses and riders
	Isaiah 2:19–22	6:12; 8:5; 11:13	Earthquake
	Joel 2:28–32; Acts 2:14–21	6:12	Moon turns blood red
	Mark 13:21–25	6:13	Stars falling from the sky
	Isaiah 34:1–4	6:14	Sky rolled up like a scroll
	Zephaniah 1:14–18; 1 Thessalonians 5:1–3	6:15–17	God's inescapable wrath
	Jeremiah 49:35–39	7:1	Four winds of judgment
	Luke 8:26–34	9:1, 2; 17:3–8	Abyss (bottomless pit)
	Joel 1:2—2:11	9:3–11	Plague of locusts
	Luke 21:20–24	11:1, 2	Trampling of the holy city of Jerusalem
	Zechariah 4	11:3–6	Two olive trees as witnesses
	Daniel 7	13:1–10	A beast coming out of the sea
	2 Thessalonians 2:7–14	13:11–15	Astounding signs and miracles done by the evil beast
	Jeremiah 25:15–29	14:9–12	Drinking the cup of God's wrath
	Isaiah 21:1–10	18:2, 3	"Babylon" falls
	Matthew 22:1–14	19:5–8	Wedding supper of the Lamb
	Ezekiel 38; 39	20:7–10	Conflict with Gog and Magog
	John 5:19–30	20:11–15	Judging of all people
	Ezekiel 37:21–28	21:3	God lives among his people
	Isaiah 25:1–8	21:4	Our tears will be wiped away forever
	Genesis 2:8–14	22:1, 2	Tree of life
	1 Corinthians 13:11, 12	22:3–5	We will see God face to face
	Daniel 7:18–28	22:5	Believers will reign with God forever

works according to his own timetable, and he promises justice. No suffering for the sake of God's kingdom, however, is wasted.

6:12 The sixth seal changes the scene back to the physical world. The first five judgments were directed toward specific areas, but this judgment is universal. Everyone will be afraid when the earth itself trembles.

6:15–17 At the sight of God sitting on the throne, all human beings, great and small, will be terrified, calling for the mountains to fall on them so that they will not have to face the judgment of the Lamb. This vivid picture was not intended to frighten believers. For them, the Lamb is a gentle Savior. But those generals,

emperors, or kings who previously showed no fear of God and arrogantly flaunted their unbelief will find that they were wrong, and in that day they will have to face God's wrath. No one who has rejected God can survive the day of his wrath, but those who belong to Christ can receive a reward rather than punishment. Do you belong to Christ? If so, you need not fear these final days.

7:1ff The sixth seal has been opened, and the people of the earth have tried to hide from God, saying, "Who can stand?" (6:12–17). Just when all hope seems lost, four angels hold back the four winds of judgment until God's people are sealed as his own. Only then will God open the seventh seal (8:1).

any tree. ²Then I saw another angel coming up from the east, having the seal of the living God. He called out in a loud voice to the four angels who had been given power to harm the land and the sea: ³"Do not harm *d* the land or the sea or the trees until we put a seal on the foreheads *e* of the servants of our God." ⁴Then I heard the number *f* of those who were sealed: 144,000 *g* from all the tribes of Israel.

7:3
d Rev 6:6
e Rev 22:4

7:4
f Rev 9:16
g Rev 14:1, 3

> ⁵ From the tribe of Judah 12,000 were sealed,
>   from the tribe of Reuben 12,000,
>   from the tribe of Gad 12,000,
> ⁶ from the tribe of Asher 12,000,
>   from the tribe of Naphtali 12,000,
>   from the tribe of Manasseh 12,000,
> ⁷ from the tribe of Simeon 12,000,
>   from the tribe of Levi 12,000,
>   from the tribe of Issachar 12,000,
> ⁸ from the tribe of Zebulun 12,000,
>   from the tribe of Joseph 12,000,
>   from the tribe of Benjamin 12,000.

The Great Multitude in White Robes

⁹After this I looked and there before me was a great multitude that no one could count, from every nation, tribe, people and language, *h* standing before the throne and in front of the Lamb. They were wearing white robes and were holding palm branches in their hands. ¹⁰And they cried out in a loud voice:

> "Salvation belongs to our God, *i*
> who sits on the throne,
> and to the Lamb."

¹¹All the angels were standing around the throne and around the elders and the four living creatures. *j* They fell down on their faces before the throne and worshiped God, ¹²saying:

> "Amen!
> Praise and glory

7:2 A seal on a scroll or document identified and protected its contents. God places his own seal on his followers, identifying them as his own and guaranteeing his protection over their souls. This shows how valuable we are to him. Our physical bodies may be beaten, maimed, or even destroyed, but *nothing* can harm our souls when we have been sealed by God. See Ephesians 1:13 for the seal of the Holy Spirit.

7:3 God's seal is placed on the foreheads of his servants. This seal is the exact opposite of the mark of the beast explained in 13:16. These two marks place the people in two distinct categories—those owned by God and those owned by Satan.

7:4–8 The number 144,000 is 12 x 12 x 1,000, symbolizing completeness—*all* God's followers will be brought safely to him; not one will be overlooked or forgotten. God seals these believers either by withdrawing them from the earth (this is called the Rapture) or by giving them special strength and courage to make it through this time of great persecution. Even though many believers have to undergo persecution, the seal does not necessarily guarantee protection from physical harm—many will die (see 6:11)—but God will protect them from spiritual harm. No matter what happens, they will be brought to their reward of eternal life. Their destiny is secure. These believers will not fall away from God even though they may undergo intense persecution.

    This is not saying that 144,000 individuals must be sealed before the persecution comes, but that when persecution begins, the faithful will have already been sealed (marked by God) and they will remain true to him until the end.

7:4–8 This is a different list from the usual listing of the 12 tribes in the Old Testament, because it is a symbolic list of God's true

followers. (1) Judah is mentioned first because Judah is both the tribe of David and of Jesus the Messiah (Genesis 49:8–12; Matthew 1:1). (2) Levi had no tribal allotment because of the Levites' work for God in the temple (Deuteronomy 18:1), but here the tribe is given a place as a reward for faithfulness. (3) Dan is not mentioned because it was known for rebellion and idolatry, traits unacceptable for God's followers (Genesis 49:17). (4) The two tribes representing Joseph (usually called Ephraim and Manasseh, after Joseph's sons) are here called Joseph and Manasseh because of Ephraim's rebellion. See Genesis 49 for the story of the beginning of these 12 tribes.

7:9 Who is this great multitude? While some interpreters identify it as the martyrs described in 6:9, it may also be the same group as the 144,000 just mentioned (7:4–8). The 144,000 were sealed by God before the great time of persecution; the great multitude was brought to eternal life, as God had promised. Before, they were being prepared; now, they are victorious. This multitude in heaven is composed of all those who remained faithful to God throughout the generations. No true believer ever need worry about which group he or she will be in. God includes and protects each of us, and we are guaranteed a place in his presence.

7:10 People try many methods to remove the guilt of sin—good deeds, intellectual pursuits, and even casting blame on others. The multitude in heaven, however, praises God, saying that salvation comes from him and from the Lamb. Salvation from sin's penalty can come only through Jesus Christ. Have you had the guilt of sin removed in the only way possible?

7:11 More information about the elders is found in the note on 4:4. The four living creatures are explained further in the note on 4:6, 7.

and wisdom and thanks and honor
and power and strength
be to our God for ever and ever.
Amen!"*k*

7:12
k Rev 5:12-14

13Then one of the elders asked me, "These in white robes—who are they, and where did they come from?"

14I answered, "Sir, you know."

And he said, "These are they who have come out of the great tribulation; they have washed their robes and made them white in the blood of the Lamb.*l* 15Therefore,

7:14
l Heb 9:14; 1Jn 1:7

7:15
m Rev 21:3

"they are before the throne of God
and serve him day and night in his temple;
and he who sits on the throne will spread his tent over them.*m*

7:16
n Isa 49:10

16 Never again will they hunger;
never again will they thirst.
The sun will not beat upon them,
nor any scorching heat.*n*

7:17
o Ps 23:1; Jn 10:11
p Isa 25:8; Rev 21:4

17 For the Lamb at the center of the throne will be their shepherd;*o*
he will lead them to springs of living water.
And God will wipe away every tear from their eyes."*p*

The Seventh Seal and the Golden Censer

8:1
q Rev 6:1

8 When he opened the seventh seal,*q* there was silence in heaven for about half an hour. 2And I saw the seven angels who stand before God, and to them were given seven trumpets.

8:3
r Rev 5:8
s Ex 30:1-6

8:4
t Ps 141:2

3Another angel, who had a golden censer, came and stood at the altar. He was given much incense to offer, with the prayers of all the saints,*r* on the golden altar*s* before the throne. 4The smoke of the incense, together with the prayers of the saints, went up before God*t* from the angel's hand. 5Then the angel took the censer, filled it with fire from the altar, and hurled it on the earth; and there came peals of thunder, rumblings, flashes of lightning and an earthquake.

7:14 "The great tribulation" has been explained in several ways. Some believe it refers to the suffering of believers through the ages; others believe that there is a specific time of intense tribulation yet to come. In either case, these believers come through their times of suffering by remaining loyal to God. Because they remain faithful, God will give them eternal life with him (7:17).

7:14 It is difficult to imagine how blood could make any cloth white, but the blood of Jesus Christ is the world's greatest purifier because it removes the stain of sin. White symbolizes sinless perfection or holiness, which can be given to people only by the death of the sinless Lamb of God on our behalf. This is a picture of how we are saved through faith (see Isaiah 1:18; Romans 3:21–26).

7:16, 17 God will provide for his children's needs in their eternal home where there will be no hunger, thirst, or pain, and he will wipe away all tears. When you are suffering or torn apart by sorrow, take comfort in this promise of complete protection and relief.

7:17 In verses 1–8 we see the believers receiving a seal to protect them through a time of great tribulation and suffering; in verses 9–17 we see the believers finally with God in heaven. All who have been faithful through the ages are singing before God's throne. Their tribulations and sorrows are over: no more tears for sin, for all sins are forgiven; no more tears for suffering, for all suffering is over; no more tears for death, for all believers have been resurrected to die no more.

8:1 There was silence in heaven for about half an hour. With all the activity, this dramatic pause must have seemed to last for an eternity. During this time, the only activity was the prayers of the saints (8:3, 4). We must seek God in times of silence. How proper for us to be quiet and honor God for his power and might. Take time each day to be silent and exalt God. Silence also conveys trust and confidence in God (see Isaiah 30:15). We can trust God that he will give us strength and provide the justice against oppressors that we seek.

8:1, 2 When the seventh seal is opened, the seven trumpet judgments are revealed. In the same way, the seventh trumpet will announce the seven bowl judgments in 11:15 and 16:1–21. The trumpet judgments, like the seal judgments, are only partial. God's final and complete judgment has not yet come.

8:3–5 A censer filled with live coals was used in temple worship. Incense was poured on the coals, and the sweet-smelling smoke drifted upwards, symbolizing believers' prayers ascending to God (see Exodus 30:7–9).

The angel then threw the censer down upon the earth. This symbolizes the judgment of God released on earth in answer to the prayers of the saints for justice for those who had oppressed and killed them. This shows that judgment, vindication, and revenge are in God's hands, not ours (see Matthew 5:38; Romans 12:9; 1 Peter 3:9). No matter how strong the desire to exact revenge and retaliate at our enemies, our work is to pray to God for his justice.

3. Sounding the seven trumpets

The Trumpets

6 Then the seven angels who had the seven trumpets prepared to sound them.

7 The first angel sounded his trumpet, and there came hail and fire *u* mixed with blood, and it was hurled down upon the earth. A third of the earth was burned up, a third of the trees were burned up, and all the green grass was burned up. *v*

8 The second angel sounded his trumpet, and something like a huge mountain, *w* all ablaze, was thrown into the sea. A third of the sea turned into blood, *x* 9 a third of the living creatures in the sea died, and a third of the ships were destroyed.

10 The third angel sounded his trumpet, and a great star, blazing like a torch, fell from the sky *y* on a third of the rivers and on the springs of water *z* — 11 the name of the star is Wormwood. *a* A third of the waters turned bitter, and many people died from the waters that had become bitter. *a*

12 The fourth angel sounded his trumpet, and a third of the sun was struck, a third of the moon, and a third of the stars, so that a third of them turned dark. A third of the day was without light, and also a third of the night.

13 As I watched, I heard an eagle that was flying in midair *b* call out in a loud voice: "Woe! Woe! Woe *c* to the inhabitants of the earth, because of the trumpet blasts about to be sounded by the other three angels!"

9 The fifth angel sounded his trumpet, and I saw a star that had fallen from the sky to the earth. *d* The star was given the key to the shaft of the Abyss. *e* 2 When he opened the Abyss, smoke rose from it like the smoke from a gigantic furnace. The sun and sky were darkened by the smoke from the Abyss. 3 And out of the smoke locusts came down upon the earth and were given power like that of scorpions *f* of the earth. 4 They were told not to harm *g* the grass of the earth or any plant or tree, *h* but only those people who did not have the seal of God on their foreheads. 5 They were not given power to kill them, but only to torture them for five months. *i* And the agony they suffered was like that of the sting of a scorpion when it strikes a man. 6 During those days men will seek death, but will not find it; they will long to die, but death will elude them. *j*

7 The locusts looked like horses prepared for battle. On their heads they wore something like crowns of gold, and their faces resembled human faces. 8 Their hair was like women's hair, and their teeth were like lions' teeth. *k* 9 They had breastplates like breastplates of iron, and the sound of their wings was like the thundering of many horses and chariots rushing

a 11 That is, Bitterness

8:7 *u* Eze 38:22 *v* Rev 9:4

8:8 *w* Jer 51:25 *x* Rev 16:3

8:10 *y* Isa 14:12; Rev 9:1 *z* Rev 16:4

8:11 *a* Jer 9:15; 23:15

8:13 *b* Rev 14:6; 19:17 *c* Rev 9:12; 11:14

9:1 *d* Rev 8:10 *e* Lk 8:31

9:3 *f* ver 5, 10

9:4 *g* Rev 6:6 *h* Rev 8:7

9:5 *i* ver 10

9:6 *j* Jer 8:3

9:8 *k* Joel 1:6

8:6 The trumpet blasts have three purposes: (1) to warn that judgment is certain, (2) to call the forces of good and evil to battle, and (3) to announce the return of the King, the Messiah. These warnings urge us to make sure our faith is firmly fixed on Christ.

8:7–12 Since only one-third of the earth is destroyed by these trumpet judgments, this is only a partial judgment from God. His full wrath is yet to be unleashed.

8:11 Wormwood is a plant with a very bitter taste, and it stands for the bitterness of God's judgment.

8:13 Habakkuk used the image of a vulture to symbolize swiftness and destruction (see Habakkuk 1:8). The picture here is of a strong, powerful bird flying over all the earth, warning of the terrors yet to come. While both believers and unbelievers experience the terrors described in verses 7–12, the "inhabitants of the earth" are the unbelievers who will meet spiritual harm through the next three trumpet judgments. God has guaranteed believers protection from spiritual harm (7:2, 3).

8:13 In 6:10, the martyrs call out to God, "How long . . . until you judge the inhabitants of the earth and avenge our blood?" As we see the world's wickedness, we too may cry out to God, "How long?" In the following chapters, the judgment comes at last. We may be distressed and impatient, but God has his plan and his timing, and we must learn to trust him to know what is best. Judgment is coming—be sure of that. Thank God for the time he has given you to turn from sin. Use the available time to work to help others turn to him.

9:1 It is not known whether this "star" that fell from heaven is Satan, a fallen angel, Christ, or a good angel. Most likely it is a good angel, because the key to the shaft of the Abyss (bottomless pit) is normally held by Christ (1:17, 18), and it was temporarily given to this other being from heaven (see also 20:1). This being, whoever he may be, is still under God's control and authority. The Abyss represents the place of the demons and of Satan, the king of demons (9:11). See also Luke 8:31 for another reference to the Abyss.

9:3 The prophet Joel described a locust plague as a foreshadowing of the "day of the LORD," meaning God's coming judgment (Joel 2:1–10). In the Old Testament, locusts were symbols of destruction because they destroyed vegetation. Here, however, they symbolize an invasion of demons called to torture people who do not believe in God. The limitations placed on the demons (they could only torment people for five months) show that they are under God's authority.

9:3ff Most likely these locusts are demons—evil spirits ruled by Satan who tempt people to sin. They were not created by Satan, because God is the Creator of all; rather, they are fallen angels who joined Satan in his rebellion. God limits what they can do; they can do nothing without his permission. Their main purpose on earth is to prevent, distort, or destroy people's relationship with God. Because they are corrupt and degenerate, their appearance reflects the distortion of their spirits. While it is important to recognize their evil activity so we can stay away from them, we must avoid any curiosity about or involvement with demonic forces or with the occult.

9:9
l Joel 2:5

9:11
m ver 1, 2

9:12
n Rev 8:13

9:14
o Rev 16:12

9:16
p Rev 7:4

9:20
q 1Co 10:20
r Ps 115:4-7

10:1
s Mt 17:2

10:4
t Da 8:26

into battle. *l* 10They had tails and stings like scorpions, and in their tails they had power to torment people for five months. 11They had as king over them the angel of the Abyss, *m* whose name in Hebrew is Abaddon, and in Greek, Apollyon. *a*

12The first woe is past; two other woes are yet to come. *n*

13The sixth angel sounded his trumpet, and I heard a voice coming from the horns *b* of the golden altar that is before God. 14It said to the sixth angel who had the trumpet, "Release the four angels who are bound at the great river Euphrates." *o* 15And the four angels who had been kept ready for this very hour and day and month and year were released to kill a third of mankind. 16The number of the mounted troops was two hundred million. I heard their number. *p*

17The horses and riders I saw in my vision looked like this: Their breastplates were fiery red, dark blue, and yellow as sulfur. The heads of the horses resembled the heads of lions, and out of their mouths came fire, smoke and sulfur. 18A third of mankind was killed by the three plagues of fire, smoke and sulfur that came out of their mouths. 19The power of the horses was in their mouths and in their tails; for their tails were like snakes, having heads with which they inflict injury.

20The rest of mankind that were not killed by these plagues still did not repent of the work of their hands; they did not stop worshiping demons, *q* and idols of gold, silver, bronze, stone and wood—idols that cannot see or hear or walk. *r* 21Nor did they repent of their murders, their magic arts, their sexual immorality or their thefts.

The Angel and the Little Scroll

10 Then I saw another mighty angel coming down from heaven. He was robed in a cloud, with a rainbow above his head; his face was like the sun, *s* and his legs were like fiery pillars. 2He was holding a little scroll, which lay open in his hand. He planted his right foot on the sea and his left foot on the land, 3and he gave a loud shout like the roar of a lion. When he shouted, the voices of the seven thunders spoke. 4And when the seven thunders spoke, I was about to write; but I heard a voice from heaven say, "Seal up what the seven thunders have said and do not write it down." *t*

a 11 *Abaddon* and *Apollyon* mean *Destroyer.* *b* 13 That is, projections

---

9:11 The locust-demons have a leader whose name in Hebrew and in Greek means *destroyer.* It may be a play on words by John to show that those who worshiped the great god Apollo worshiped only a demon.

9:13 The altar in the temple had four projections, one at each corner, and these were called the horns of the altar (see Exodus 27:2).

9:14 The word "angels" here means fallen angels or demons. These four unidentified demons will be exceedingly evil and destructive. But note that they do not have the power to release themselves and do their evil work on earth. Instead, they are held back by God and will be released at a specific time, doing only what he allows them to do.

9:15 Here one-third of all people are killed. In 6:7, 8, one-fourth of mankind was killed. Thus, over one-half of the people in the world will have been killed by God's great judgments. Even more would have been killed if God had not set limits on the destruction.

9:16 In John's day, this number of mounted troops in an army was inconceivable, but today there are countries and alliances that could easily amass this many soldiers. This huge army, led by the four demons, will be sent out to destroy one-third of the earth's population. But the judgment is still not complete.

9:20, 21 These people were so hardhearted that even plagues did not drive them to God. People don't usually fall into immorality and evil suddenly—they slip into it a little bit at a time until, hardly realizing what has happened, they are irrevocably mired in their wicked ways. Any person who allows sin to take root in his or her life can find himself or herself in this predicament. Temptation entertained today becomes sin tomorrow, then a habit the next day, then death and separation from God forever (see James 1:15). To think you could never become this evil is the first step

toward a hard heart. Acknowledge your need to confess your sin before God.

10:1–6 The purpose of this mighty angel is clear—to announce the final judgments on the earth. His right foot on the sea and left foot on the land (10:2) indicate that his words deal with all creation, not just a limited part as did the seal and trumpet judgments. The seventh trumpet (11:15) will usher in the seven bowl judgments, which will bring an end to the present world. When this universal judgment comes, God's truth will prevail.

10:2 We see two scrolls in Revelation. The first contains a revelation of judgments against evil (5:1ff). The contents of the second little scroll are not indicated, but it also may contain a revelation of judgment.

10:2 This powerful angel conveyed his high rank and his authority from God by straddling the land and the sea. His huge size contrasts with the smallness of God's enemies. When things are going bad in your life, remember that this angel represents the kind of power that is on your side. God's angelic forces are with you (Matthew 18:10; Hebrews 1:14). Keep your problems in their proper perspective by remembering that God's power is available to you to deal with your problems.

10:4 Throughout history people have wanted to know what would happen in the future, and God reveals some of it in this book. But John was stopped from revealing certain parts of his vision. An angel also told the prophet Daniel that some visions he saw were not to be revealed yet to everyone (Daniel 12:9), and Jesus told his disciples that the time of the end is known by no one but God (Mark 13:32, 33). God has revealed all we need to know to live for him now. In our desire to be ready for the end, we must not place more emphasis on speculation about the last days than on living for God while we wait.

5 Then the angel I had seen standing on the sea and on the land raised his right hand to heaven. u 6 And he swore by him who lives for ever and ever, who created the heavens and all that is in them, the earth and all that is in it, and the sea and all that is in it, v and said, "There will be no more delay! w 7 But in the days when the seventh angel is about to sound his trumpet, the mystery of God will be accomplished, just as he announced to his servants the prophets."

8 Then the voice that I had heard from heaven x spoke to me once more: "Go, take the scroll that lies open in the hand of the angel who is standing on the sea and on the land."

9 So I went to the angel and asked him to give me the little scroll. He said to me, "Take it and eat it. It will turn your stomach sour, but in your mouth it will be as sweet as honey." y 10 I took the little scroll from the angel's hand and ate it. It tasted as sweet as honey in my mouth, but when I had eaten it, my stomach turned sour. 11 Then I was told, "You must prophesy again about many peoples, nations, languages and kings."

The Two Witnesses

11 I was given a reed like a measuring rod z and was told, "Go and measure the temple of God and the altar, and count the worshipers there. 2 But exclude the outer court; a do not measure it, because it has been given to the Gentiles. b They will trample on the holy city for 42 months. c 3 And I will give power to my two witnesses, and they will prophesy for 1,260 days, clothed in sackcloth." 4 These are the two olive trees d and the two lampstands that stand before the Lord of the earth. 5 If anyone tries to harm them, fire comes from their mouths and devours their enemies. e This is how anyone who wants to harm them must die. f 6 These men have power to shut up the sky so that it will not rain during the time they are prophesying; and they have power to turn the waters into blood and to strike the earth with every kind of plague as often as they want.

7 Now when they have finished their testimony, the beast that comes up from the Abyss will attack them, g and overpower and kill them. 8 Their bodies will lie in the street of the great city, which is figuratively called Sodom and Egypt, where also their Lord was crucified. 9 For three and a half days men from every people, tribe, language and nation will gaze on their bodies and refuse them burial. 10 The inhabitants of the earth will gloat over them and will celebrate by sending each other gifts, h because these two prophets had tormented those who live on the earth.

10:5
u Da 12:7

10:6
v Rev 4:11
w Rev 16:17

10:8
x ver 4

10:9
y Jer 15:16;
Eze 2:8-3:3

11:1
z Eze 40:3;
Rev 21:15

11:2
a Eze 40:17, 20
b Lk 21:24
c Rev 13:5

11:4
d Ps 52:8;
Jer 11:16;
Zec 4:3, 11

11:5
e 2Ki 1:10
f Nu 16:29, 35

11:7
g Da 7:21

11:10
h Est 9:19, 22

10:7 By saying that "the mystery of God will be accomplished," John was pointing to God's removal of all evil and the final exaltation of Christ as Lord. This pronouncement would bring fear to God's enemies. For God's chosen ones, however, it would bring hope and peace. Do you really long for Christ's return? Do you long for God and his people to be vindicated? Believers ought to pray for God's justice to be carried out and his plan fulfilled. We should want Christ to come because of the triumph of his kingdom—not because things are bad or because we want out of our struggles. Pray expectantly for the fulfillment of God's plan.

10:9, 10 The prophet Ezekiel also had a vision in which he was told to eat a scroll filled with judgments against the nation of Israel (Ezekiel 3:1ff). The taste was sweet in his mouth, but the scroll's contents brought destruction—just like the scroll John was told to eat. God's Word is sweet to us as believers because it brings encouragement, but it sours our stomach because of the coming judgment we must pronounce on unbelievers.

11:1ff This temple is most likely a symbol of the church (all true believers), because there will be no temple in the new Jerusalem (21:22). John measured the temple to show that God is building walls of protection around his people to spare them from spiritual harm, and that there is a place reserved for all believers who remain faithful to God.

11:1, 2 Those worshiping inside the temple will be protected spiritually, but those outside will face great suffering. This is a way of saying that true believers will be protected through persecution, but those who refuse to believe will be destroyed.

11:3 These two witnesses bear strong resemblance to Moses and Elijah, two of God's mighty prophets. With God's power, Moses

called plagues down upon the nation of Egypt (see Exodus 8—11). Elijah defeated the prophets of Baal (1 Kings 18). Both of these men appeared with Christ at his transfiguration (see Matthew 17:1–7).

11:3 In the book of Revelation, numbers are likely to have symbolic rather than literal meanings. The 42 months or 1,260 days equal 3 1/2 years. As half of the perfect number 7, 3 1/2 can indicate incompletion, imperfection, or even evil. Notice the events predicted for this time period: there is trouble (Daniel 12:7), the holy city is trampled (11:2), the woman takes refuge in the desert (12:6), and the devil-inspired beast exercises his authority (13:5). Some commentators link the 3 1/2 years with the period of famine in the days of Elijah (Luke 4:25; James 5:17). Since Malachi predicted the return of Elijah before the Last Judgment (Malachi 4:5), and since the events in Daniel and Revelation pave the way for the second coming, perhaps John was making this connection. It is possible, of course, that the 3 1/2 years are literal. If so, we will clearly recognize when the 3 1/2 years are over! Whether symbolic or literal, however, they indicate that evil's reign will have a definite end.

11:7 This beast could be Satan or an agent of Satan.

11:8, 9 Jerusalem, once the great city and the capital of Israel, is now enemy territory. It is compared with Sodom and with Egypt, both well known for their evil. At the time of John's writing, Jerusalem had been destroyed by the Romans in A.D. 70, nearly a million Jews had been slaughtered, and the temple treasures had been carried off to Rome.

11:10 As representatives of every believer who has witnessed for Jesus Christ, the two final, faithful witnesses are a picture of both invincibility and vulnerability. They win, they lose, they win again. Truth remains victorious, even though human channels

11:11
i Eze 37:5, 9, 10, 14

11:12
j Ac 1:9

11:13
k Rev 6:12

11:15
l Rev 12:10
m Da 2:44

11:16
n Rev 4:4

11:17
o Rev 19:6

11:18
p Rev 19:5

11:19
q Rev 15:5, 8
r Rev 16:21

¹¹But after the three and a half days a breath of life from God entered them, *i* and they stood on their feet, and terror struck those who saw them. ¹²Then they heard a loud voice from heaven saying to them, "Come up here." And they went up to heaven in a cloud, *j* while their enemies looked on.

¹³At that very hour there was a severe earthquake *k* and a tenth of the city collapsed. Seven thousand people were killed in the earthquake, and the survivors were terrified and gave glory to the God of heaven.

¹⁴The second woe has passed; the third woe is coming soon.

The Seventh Trumpet

¹⁵The seventh angel sounded his trumpet, and there were loud voices in heaven, which said:

> "The kingdom of the world has become the kingdom of our Lord and of his
>   Christ, *l*
> and he will reign for ever and ever." *m*

¹⁶And the twenty-four elders, *n* who were seated on their thrones before God, fell on their faces and worshiped God, ¹⁷saying:

> "We give thanks to you, Lord God Almighty,
>   the One who is and who was,
> because you have taken your great power
>   and have begun to reign. *o*
> ¹⁸ The nations were angry;
>   and your wrath has come.
> The time has come for judging the dead,
>   and for rewarding your servants the prophets
> and your saints and those who reverence your name,
>   both small and great *p*—
> and for destroying those who destroy the earth."

¹⁹Then God's temple *q* in heaven was opened, and within his temple was seen the ark of his covenant. And there came flashes of lightning, rumblings, peals of thunder, an earthquake and a great hailstorm. *r*

---

fall. Their message—and God's plan—march on in spite of death, for even death proves to be a defeated foe.

Seldom do we face the possibility of death when we share our faith. Why should Satan threaten our lives when fear of embarrassment or rejection is enough to keep us silent? But if Jesus has truly changed our lives, we will find a way to let others know. Not to witness represents more than just fear; it also reveals selfishness. Have those near you heard what Jesus has done for you?

11:13 The ultimate goal of God's saving plan is that everything in creation will glorify him. "Glory" refers to the splendor, radiance, and magnificence of God. It refers not only to God in his essential nature but to the praiseworthy effects of what God has accomplished. We glorify God because his glory is true and real, and we acknowledge his greatness. In so doing, we see our rightful position as his servants. When we glorify him in our singing, our speaking, and our living, we experience some of his transcendence and thus edify and uplift our own spirits. Glorifying God prompts us to moral action and loving service.

11:15 The seventh trumpet is sounded, announcing the arrival of the King. There is now no turning back. The coming judgments are no longer partial, but complete in their destruction. God is in control, and he unleashes his full wrath on the evil world that refuses to turn to him (9:20, 21). When his wrath begins, there will be no escape.

11:16 For more on the 24 elders, see the note on 4:4.

11:18 In the Bible, God gives rewards to his people accord-

ing to what they deserve. Throughout the Old Testament, obedience often brought reward in this life (Deuteronomy 28), but obedience and immediate reward are not always linked. If they were, good people would always be rich, and suffering would always be a sign of sin. If we were quickly rewarded for every faithful deed, we would soon think we were pretty good. Before long, we would be doing many good deeds for purely selfish reasons. While it is true that God will reward us for our earthly deeds (see 20:12), our greatest reward will be eternal life in his presence.

11:19 In Old Testament days, the ark of the covenant was the most sacred treasure of the Israelite nation. For more information about the ark, see the note on Exodus 37:1.

4. Observing the great conflict
The Woman and the Dragon

12 A great and wondrous sign appeared in heaven: a woman clothed with the sun, with the moon under her feet and a crown of twelve stars on her head. ²She was pregnant and cried out in pain as she was about to give birth. ³Then another sign appeared in heaven: an enormous red dragon with seven heads and ten horns ˢ and seven crowns on his heads. ⁴His tail swept a third of the stars out of the sky and flung them to the earth. ᵗ The dragon stood in front of the woman who was about to give birth, so that he might devour her child the moment it was born. ⁵She gave birth to a son, a male child, who will rule all the nations with an iron scepter. And her child was snatched up to God and to his throne. ⁶The woman fled into the desert to a place prepared for her by God, where she might be taken care of for 1,260 days.

⁷And there was war in heaven. Michael and his angels fought against the dragon, and the dragon and his angels fought back. ⁸But he was not strong enough, and they lost their place in heaven. ⁹The great dragon was hurled down—that ancient serpentᵘ called the devil, or Satan, who leads the whole world astray.ᵛ He was hurled to the earth,ʷ and his angels with him. ¹⁰Then I heard a loud voice in heavenˣ say:

"Now have come the salvation and the power and the kingdom of our God,
and the authority of his Christ.
For the accuser of our brothers,ʸ
who accuses them before our God day and night,
has been hurled down.
¹¹ They overcame him
by the blood of the Lamb
and by the word of their testimony;

12:3
ˢ Rev 13:1

12:4
ᵗ Da 8:10

12:9
ᵘ Ge 3:1-7
ᵛ Rev 20:3, 8, 10
ʷ Jn 12:31

12:10
ˣ Rev 11:15
ʸ Job 1:9-11;
Zec 3:1

12:1—14:20 The seventh trumpet (11:15) ushers in the bowl judgments (15:1—16:21), but in the intervening chapters (12—14), John sees the conflict between God and Satan. He sees the source of all sin, evil, persecution, and suffering on the earth, and he understands why the great battle between the forces of God and Satan must soon take place. In these chapters the nature of evil is exposed, and Satan is seen in all his wickedness.

12:1–6 The woman represents God's faithful people who have been waiting for the Messiah; the crown of 12 stars represents the 12 tribes of Israel. God set apart the Jews for himself (Romans 9:4, 5), and that nation gave birth to the Messiah. The male child (12:5) is Jesus, born to a devout Jew named Mary (Luke 1:26–33). Evil King Herod immediately tried to destroy the infant Jesus (Matthew 2:13–20). Herod's desire to kill this newborn king, whom he saw as a threat to his throne, was motivated by Satan (the red dragon), who wanted to kill the world's Savior. The heavenly pageant of Revelation 12 shows that Christ's quiet birth in the town of Bethlehem had cosmic significance.

12:3, 4 The enormous red dragon, Satan, has seven heads, ten horns, and seven crowns, representing his power and the kingdoms of the world over which he rules. The stars that plunged to earth with him are usually considered to be the angels who fell with Satan and became his demons. According to Hebrew tradition, one-third of all the angels in heaven fell with Satan. For more on demons, see the notes on 9:3ff and Mark 5:1–20.

12:6 The desert represents a place of spiritual refuge and protection from Satan. Because God aided the woman's escape into the desert, we can be sure that he offers security to all true believers. Satan always attacks God's people, but God keeps them spiritually secure. Some will experience physical harm, but all will be protected from spiritual harm. God will not let Satan take the souls of God's true followers. When Satan's attacks seem overpowering, remember that God is ruler over all. Trust him.

12:6 The 1,260 days (3 1/2 years) is the same length of time that the dragon is allowed to exercise his authority (13:5) and that the holy city is trampled (see the second note on 11:3).

12:7 This event fulfills Daniel 12:1ff. Michael is a high-ranking angel. One of his responsibilities is to guard God's community of believers.

12:7ff Much more happened at Christ's birth, death, and resurrection than most people realize. A war between the forces of good and evil was under way. With Christ's resurrection, Satan's ultimate defeat was assured. Some believe that Satan's fall to earth took place at Jesus' resurrection or ascension and that the 1,260 days (3 1/2 years) is a symbolic way of referring to the time between Christ's first and second comings. Others say that Satan's defeat will occur in the middle of a literal seven-year tribulation period, following the rapture of the church and preceding the second coming of Christ and the beginning of Christ's 1,000-year reign. Whatever the case, we must remember that Christ is victorious—Satan has already been defeated because of Christ's death on the cross (12:10–12).

12:9 The devil is not a symbol or legend; he is very real. Originally Satan was an angel of God, but through his own pride, he became corrupt. The devil is God's enemy, and he constantly tries to hinder God's work, but he is limited by God's power and can do only what he is permitted to do (Job 1:6—2:8). The name *Satan* means "accuser" (12:10). He actively looks for people to attack (1 Peter 5:8, 9). Satan likes to pursue believers who are vulnerable in their faith, who are spiritually weak, or who are isolated from other believers.

Even though God permits the devil to do his work in this world, God is still in control. And Jesus has complete power over Satan—he defeated Satan when he died and rose again for the sins of mankind. One day Satan will be bound forever, never again to do his evil work (see 20:10).

12:10 Many believe that until this time, Satan still had access to God (see the note on Job 1:7ff). But here his access is forever barred (see also 9:1). He can no longer accuse people before God (see how Satan made accusations about Job before God in Job 1:6ff).

12:11 The critical blow to Satan came when the Lamb, Jesus Christ, shed his blood for our sins. The victory is won by sacri-

12:11
z Lk 14:26

they did not love their lives so much
as to shrink from death.z

12:12
a Ps 96:11;
Rev 18:20
b Rev 10:6

12 Therefore rejoice, you heavensa
and you who dwell in them!
But woe to the earth and the sea,b
because the devil has gone down to you!
He is filled with fury,
because he knows that his time is short."

12:13
c ver 5

12:14
d Ex 19:4
e Da 7:25

13When the dragon saw that he had been hurled to the earth, he pursued the woman who had given birth to the male child.c 14The woman was given the two wings of a great eagle,d so that she might fly to the place prepared for her in the desert, where she would be taken care of for a time, times and half a time,e out of the serpent's reach. 15Then from his mouth the serpent spewed water like a river, to overtake the woman and sweep her away with the torrent. 16But the earth helped the woman by opening its mouth and swallowing the river that the dragon had spewed out of his mouth. 17Then the dragon was enraged at the woman and went off to make warf against the rest of her offspringg—those who obey God's commandmentsh and hold to the testimony of Jesus. 1And the dragona stood on the shore of the sea.

12:17
f Rev 11:7
g Ge 3:15
h Rev 14:12

13:1
i Da 7:1-6

The Beast out of the Sea

13:2
j Rev 2:13

And I saw a beast coming out of the sea.i He had ten horns and seven heads, with ten crowns on his horns, and on each head a blasphemous name. 2The beast I saw resembled a leopard, but had feet like those of a bear and a mouth like that of a lion. The dragon gave the beast his power and his throne and great authority.j 3One of the heads of the beast seemed

a 1 Some late manuscripts And I

---

fice—Christ's death in our place to pay the penalty for our sin, and the sacrifices we make because of our faith in him. As we face the battle with Satan, we should not fear it or try to escape from it, but we should loyally serve Christ, who alone brings victory (see Romans 8:34–39).

12:12 The devil begins to step up his persecution because he knows that "his time is short." We are living in the last days, and Satan's work has become more intense. Even though the devil is very powerful, as we can see by the condition of our world, he is always under God's control. One of the reasons God allows Satan to work evil and bring temptation is so that those who pretend to be Christ's followers will be weeded out from Christ's true believers. Knowing that the last great confrontation with Jesus is near, Satan is desperately trying to recruit as great an enemy force as possible for this final battle.

12:17 While the woman (12:1) represents faithful Jews and the child (12:5) represents Christ, the rest of her offspring could be either Jewish believers or, most likely, all believers.

12:17 The apostle Paul tells us that we are in a spiritual battle (Ephesians 6:10–12). John says that the war is still being waged, but the outcome has already been determined. Satan and his followers have been defeated and will be destroyed. Nevertheless, Satan is battling daily to bring more into his ranks and to keep his own from defecting to God's side. Those who belong to Christ have gone into battle on God's side, and he has guaranteed them victory. God will not lose the war, but we must make certain not to lose the battle for our own souls. Don't waver in your commitment to Christ. A great spiritual battle is being fought, and there is no time for indecision.

13:1 This beast was initially identified with Rome, because the Roman empire, in its early days, encouraged an evil lifestyle, persecuted believers, and opposed God and his followers. But the beast also symbolizes the antichrist—not Satan, but someone under Satan's power and control. This antichrist looks like a combination of the four beasts that Daniel saw centuries earlier in a vision (Daniel 7). As the dragon (12:17) is in opposition to God, so the beast from the sea is against Christ and may be seen as Satan's false messiah. The early Roman empire was strong and

also anti-Christ (or against Christ's standards); many other individual powers throughout history have been anti-Christ. Many Christians believe that Satan's evil will culminate in a final antichrist who will focus all the powers of evil against Jesus Christ and his followers.

13:1ff Chapter 13 introduces Satan's (the dragon's) two evil accomplices: (1) the beast out of the sea (13:1ff) and (2) the beast out of the earth (13:11ff). Together, the three evil beings form an unholy trinity in direct opposition to the holy Trinity of God the Father, God the Son, and God the Holy Spirit.

When Satan tempted Jesus in the desert, he wanted Jesus to show his power by turning stones into bread, to do miracles by jumping from a high place, and to gain political power by worshiping him (see Matthew 4:1–11). Satan's plan was to rule the world through Jesus, but Jesus refused to do Satan's bidding. Thus Satan turns to the fearsome beasts described in Revelation. To the beast out of the sea he gives political power. To the beast out of the earth he gives power to do miracles. Both beasts work together to capture the control of the whole world. This unholy trinity—the dragon, the beast out of the sea, and the false prophet (see 16:13)—unite in a desperate attempt to overthrow God, but their efforts are doomed to failure. See what becomes of them in 19:19–21 and 20:10.

13:3ff Because the beast, the antichrist, is a false messiah, he will be a counterfeit of Christ and will even stage a false resurrection (13:14). People will follow and worship him because they will be awed by his power and miracles (13:3, 4). He will unite the world under his leadership (13:7, 8), and he will control the world economy (13:16, 17). People are impressed by power and will follow those who display it forcefully or offer it to their followers. But those who follow the beast will only be fooling themselves: He will use his power to manipulate others, to point to himself, and to promote evil plans. God, by contrast, uses his infinitely greater power to love and to build up. Don't be misled by claims of great miracles or reports about a resurrection or reincarnation of someone claiming to be Christ. When Jesus returns, he will reveal himself to everyone (Matthew 24:23–28).

to have had a fatal wound, but the fatal wound had been healed. The whole world was astonished[k] and followed the beast. [4] Men worshiped the dragon because he had given authority to the beast, and they also worshiped the beast and asked, "Who is like the beast? Who can make war against him?"

[5] The beast was given a mouth to utter proud words and blasphemies[l] and to exercise his authority for forty-two months.[m] [6] He opened his mouth to blaspheme God, and to slander his name and his dwelling place and those who live in heaven. [7] He was given power to make war[n] against the saints and to conquer them. And he was given authority over every tribe, people, language and nation. [8] All inhabitants of the earth will worship the beast—all whose names have not been written in the book of life[o] belonging to the Lamb that was slain from the creation of the world.[a]

[9] He who has an ear, let him hear.[p]

[10] If anyone is to go into captivity,
    into captivity he will go.
If anyone is to be killed[b] with the sword,
    with the sword he will be killed.

This calls for patient endurance and faithfulness on the part of the saints.[q]

The Beast out of the Earth

[11] Then I saw another beast, coming out of the earth. He had two horns like a lamb, but he spoke like a dragon. [12] He exercised all the authority of the first beast on his behalf, and made the earth and its inhabitants worship the first beast, whose fatal wound had been healed. [13] And he performed great and miraculous signs,[r] even causing fire to come down from heaven to earth in full view of men. [14] Because of the signs[s] he was given power to do on behalf of the first beast, he deceived[t] the inhabitants of the earth. He ordered them to set up an image in honor of the beast who was wounded by the sword and yet lived. [15] He was given power to give breath to the image of the first beast, so that it could speak and cause all who refused to worship the image to be killed. [16] He also forced everyone, small and great, rich and poor, free and slave, to receive a mark on his right hand or on his forehead, [17] so that no one could buy or sell unless he had the mark, which is the name of the beast or the number of his name.[u]

[a] 8 Or written from the creation of the world in the book of life belonging to the Lamb that was slain   [b] 10 Some manuscripts anyone kills

13:3
[k] Rev 17:8

13:5
[l] Da 7:8, 11, 20, 25
[m] Rev 11:2

13:7
[n] Rev 11:7

13:8
[o] Rev 3:5

13:9
[p] Rev 2:7

13:10
[q] Rev 14:12

13:13
[r] Mt 24:24

13:14
[s] 2Th 2:9, 10
[t] Rev 12:9

13:17
[u] Rev 14:11

13:5 The power given to the beast will be limited by God. He will allow the beast to exercise authority only for a short time. Even while the beast is in power, God will still be in control (11:15; 12:10–12).

13:7 The beast will conquer God's people and rule over them, but he will not be able to harm them spiritually. He will establish worldwide dominance and demand that everyone worship him. And many *will* worship him—everyone except true believers. Refusal to worship the beast will result in temporary suffering for God's people, but they will be rewarded with eternal life in the end.

13:8 See the note on 3:5 for more information on the book of life.

13:10 In this time of persecution, being faithful to Christ could bring imprisonment and even execution. Some believers will be hurt or killed. But all that the beast and his followers will be able to do to believers is harm them physically; no spiritual harm will come to those whose faith in God is sincere. All believers will enter God's presence perfected and purified by the blood of the Lamb (7:9–17).

13:10 The times of great persecution that John saw will provide an opportunity for believers to exercise patient endurance and faithfulness. The tough times we face right now are also opportunities for spiritual growth. Don't fall into Satan's trap and turn away from God when hard times come. Instead, use those tough times as opportunities for testifying for God (see Philippians 1:28, 29).

13:11ff The first beast came out of the sea (13:1), but this second beast comes out of the earth. Later identified as the false prophet (16:13; 19:20), he is a counterfeit of the Holy Spirit. He seems to do good, but the purpose of his miracles is to deceive.

13:14 Throughout the Bible we see miracles performed as proofs of God's power, love, and authority. But here we see counterfeit miracles performed to deceive. This is a reminder of Pharaoh's magicians, who duplicated Moses' signs in Egypt. True signs and miracles point us to Jesus Christ, but miracles alone can be deceptive. That is why we must ask with respect to each miracle we see: Is this consistent with what God says in the Bible? The second beast here gains influence through the signs and wonders that he can perform on behalf of the first beast. The second beast orders the people to worship an image in honor of the first beast—a direct flouting of the second commandment (Exodus 20:4–6). Allowing the Bible to guide our faith and practice will keep us from being deceived by false signs, however convincing they appear to be. Any teaching that contradicts God's Word is false.

13:16–18 This mark of the beast is designed to mock the seal that God places on his followers (7:2, 3). Just as God marks his people to save them, so Satan's beast marks his people to save them from the persecution that Satan will inflict upon God's followers. Identifying this particular mark is not as important as identifying the purpose of the mark. Those who accept it show their allegiance to Satan, their willingness to operate within the economic system he promotes, and their rebellion against God. To refuse the mark means to commit oneself entirely to God, preferring death to compromising one's faith in Christ.

13:16, 17 In every generation, Christians need to maintain a healthy skepticism about society's pleasures and rewards. In our educational, economic, and civic structures, there are incentives and rewards. Cooperating Christians must always support what is good and healthy about our society, but we must stand against

13:18
v Rev 17:9

[18]This calls for wisdom. v If anyone has insight, let him calculate the number of the beast, for it is man's number. His number is 666.

The Lamb and the 144,000

14:1
w Rev 5:6

14:2
x Rev 1:15
y Rev 5:8

14:3
z Rev 5:9

14:4
a Rev 3:4
b Rev 5:9

14:5
c Ps 32:2; Zep 3:13

14 Then I looked, and there before me was the Lamb, w standing on Mount Zion, and with him 144,000 who had his name and his Father's name written on their foreheads. [2]And I heard a sound from heaven like the roar of rushing waters x and like a loud peal of thunder. The sound I heard was like that of harpists playing their harps. y [3]And they sang a new song z before the throne and before the four living creatures and the elders. No one could learn the song except the 144,000 who had been redeemed from the earth. [4]These are those who did not defile themselves with women, for they kept themselves pure. a They follow the Lamb wherever he goes. They were purchased from among men b and offered as firstfruits to God and the Lamb. [5]No lie was found in their mouths; c they are blameless.

The Three Angels

[6]Then I saw another angel flying in midair, and he had the eternal gospel to proclaim to those who live on the earth—to every nation, tribe, language and people. [7]He said in a loud voice, "Fear God and give him glory, because the hour of his judgment has come. Worship him who made the heavens, the earth, the sea and the springs of water."

sin. In some cases, such as Satan's system described here, the system or structure becomes so evil that there is no way to cooperate with it.

13:18 The meaning of this number has been discussed more than that of any other part of the book of Revelation. The three sixes have been said to represent many things, including the number of man or the unholy trinity of Satan, the first beast, and the false prophet (16:13). If the number seven is considered to be the perfect number in the Bible, and if three sevens represent complete perfection, then the number 666 falls completely short of perfection. The first readers of this book probably applied the number to the Emperor Nero, who symbolized all the evils of the Roman empire. (The Greek letters of Nero's name represent numbers that total 666.) Whatever specific application the number is given, the number symbolizes the worldwide dominion and complete evil of this unholy trinity designed to undo Christ's work and overthrow him.

14:1ff Chapter 13 described the onslaught of evil that will occur when Satan and his helpers control the world. Chapter 14 gives a glimpse into eternity to show believers what awaits them if they endure. The Lamb is the Messiah. Mount Zion, often another name for Jerusalem, the capital of Israel, is contrasted with the worldly empire. The 144,000 represent believers who have endured persecutions on earth and now are ready to enjoy the eternal benefits and blessings of life with God forever. The three angels contrast the destiny of believers with that of unbelievers.

14:4 These people are true believers whose robes have been washed and made white in Christ's blood (7:14) through his death ("purchased from among men"). In the Old Testament, idolatry was often portrayed as spiritual adultery (see the book of Hosea). Their purity is best understood symbolically, mean-

ing that they are free from involvement with the pagan world system. To remain spiritually pure means resisting the seductions and idolatries of the present world—power, wealth, and sexual immorality. To do so requires daily application of God's Word, for it has a purifying effect on the mind and heart. It requires great resolution not to give in to these temptations.

Following Christ, the Lamb, "wherever he goes" requires heroic effort to carry out Christ's commission to face oppression and even death if required. Too many shrink back when the work is difficult or the future looks bleak. Join those who take their stand with Christ and against sin.

"Firstfruits" refers to the act of dedicating the first part of the harvest as holy to God (Exodus 23:19; see also James 1:18).

14:6, 7 Some believe that this is a final, worldwide appeal to all people to recognize the one true God. No one will have the excuse of never hearing God's truth. Others, however, see this as an announcement of judgment rather than as an appeal. The people of the world have had their chance to proclaim their allegiance to God, and now God's great judgment is about to begin. If you are reading this, you have already heard God's truth. You know that God's final judgment will not be put off forever. Have you joyfully received the everlasting Good News? Have you confessed your sins and trusted in Christ to save you? If so, you have nothing to fear from God's judgment. The Judge of all the earth is your Savior!

8A second angel followed and said, "Fallen! Fallen is Babylon the Great,*d* which made all the nations drink the maddening wine of her adulteries."

9A third angel followed them and said in a loud voice: "If anyone worships the beast and his image*e* and receives his mark on the forehead or on the hand, 10he, too, will drink of the wine of God's fury,*f* which has been poured full strength into the cup of his wrath. *g* He will be tormented with burning sulfur in the presence of the holy angels and of the Lamb. 11And the smoke of their torment rises for ever and ever. *h* There is no rest day or night for those who worship the beast and his image, or for anyone who receives the mark of his name." 12This calls for patient endurance on the part of the saints*i* who obey God's commandments and remain faithful to Jesus.

13Then I heard a voice from heaven say, "Write: Blessed are the dead who die in the Lord*j* from now on."

"Yes," says the Spirit, "they will rest from their labor, for their deeds will follow them."

The Harvest of the Earth

14I looked, and there before me was a white cloud, and seated on the cloud was one "like a son of man"*a* with a crown*k* of gold on his head and a sharp sickle in his hand. 15Then another angel came out of the temple and called in a loud voice to him who was sitting on the cloud, "Take your sickle*l* and reap, because the time to reap has come, for the harvest *m* of the earth is ripe." 16So he who was seated on the cloud swung his sickle over the earth, and the earth was harvested.

17Another angel came out of the temple in heaven, and he too had a sharp sickle. 18Still another angel, who had charge of the fire, came from the altar and called in a loud voice to him who had the sharp sickle, "Take your sharp sickle and gather the clusters of grapes from the earth's vine, because its grapes are ripe." 19The angel swung his sickle on the earth, gathered its grapes and threw them into the great winepress of God's wrath. *n* 20They were trampled in the winepress outside the city,*o* and blood flowed out of the press, rising as high as the horses' bridles for a distance of 1,600 stadia. *b*

a 14 Daniel 7:13   *b 20* That is, about 180 miles (about 300 kilometers)

14:8 *d* Isa 21:9; Jer 51:8

14:9 *e* Rev 13:14

14:10 *f* Isa 51:17 *g* Rev 18:6

14:11 *h* Isa 34:10

14:12 *i* Rev 13:10

14:13 *j* 1Co 15:18; 1Th 4:16

14:14 *k* Rev 6:2

14:15 *l* Joel 3:13 *m* Jer 51:33

14:19 *n* Rev 19:15

14:20 *o* Heb 13:12

14:8 Babylon was the name of both an evil city and an immoral empire, a world center for idol worship. Babylon ransacked Jerusalem and carried the people of Judah into captivity (see 2 Kings 24 and 2 Chronicles 36). Just as Babylon was the Jews' worst enemy, the Roman empire was the worst enemy of the early Christians. John, who probably did not dare speak against Rome openly, applied the name *Babylon* to this enemy of God's people (Rome)—and, by extension, to all God's enemies of all times.

14:9–11 Those who worship the beast, accept his mark and operate according to his world economic system will ultimately face God's judgment. Our world values money, power, and pleasure over God's leadership. To get what the world values, many people disown God and violate Christian principles. Thus they must drink of the wine of God's wrath (see Psalm 75; Isaiah 51:17).

14:11 The ultimate result of sin is unending separation from God. Because human beings are created in God's image with an inborn thirst for fellowship with him, separation from God will be the ultimate torment and misery. Sin always brings misery, but in this life we can choose to repent and restore our relationship with God. In eternity there will no longer be opportunity for repentance. If in this life we choose to be independent of God, in the next life we will be separated from him forever. Nobody is forced to choose eternal separation from God, and nobody suffers this fate by accident. Jesus invites all of us to open the door of our hearts to him (3:20). If we do this, we will enjoy everlasting fellowship with him.

14:12 This news about God's ultimate triumph should encourage God's people to remain faithful through every trial and persecution. They can do this, God promises, by trusting in Jesus and obeying the commands found in his Word. The secret to enduring, therefore, is trust and obedience. Trust God to give you patience to endure even the small trials you face daily; obey him even when obedience is unattractive or dangerous.

14:13 While it is true that money, fame, and belongings can't be taken with us from this life, God's people *can* produce fruit that survives even death. God will remember our love, kindness, and faithfulness, and those who accept Christ through our witness will join us in the new earth. Be sure that your values are in line with God's values, and decide today to produce fruit that lasts forever.

14:14–16 This is an image of judgment: Christ is separating the faithful from the unfaithful like a farmer harvesting his crops. This is a time of joy for the Christians who have been persecuted and martyred—they will receive their long-awaited reward. Christians should not fear the Last Judgment. Jesus said, "I tell you the truth, whoever hears my word and believes him who sent me has eternal life and will not be condemned; he has crossed over from death to life" (John 5:24).

14:19 A winepress was a large vat or trough where grapes were collected and then smashed. The juice flowed out of a duct that led into a large holding vat. The winepress is often used in the Bible as a symbol of God's wrath and judgment against sin (Isaiah 63:3–6; Lamentations 1:15; Joel 3:12, 13). The distance of 1,600 stadia equals about 180 miles, approximately the north-south length of Palestine.

To those unaccustomed to vivid descriptions of God's anger in judgment, these are disturbing images. People dislike the idea of other people, even evil ones, being trampled like grapes. The depth and length of the blood flow provides a sickening scene of the immensity of God's judgment. But unless we face the necessity of God's judgment, we will never see our desperate need for his mercy. A God with only a grandfatherly kindness would not inspire our repentance, obedience, or worship. God has promised a harsh harvest for those who reject him. Those who know God well enough to fear his wrath know God well enough to desire his grace. The crushing wrath of God is coming. Blessed are those who have had their sins forgiven, and blessed are those who lead others to God's mercy.

5. Pouring out the seven plagues
Seven Angels With Seven Plagues

15 I saw in heaven another great and marvelous sign: *p* seven angels with the seven last plagues—last, because with them God's wrath is completed. ²And I saw what looked like a sea of glass *q* mixed with fire and, standing beside the sea, those who had been victorious over the beast and his image *r* and over the number of his name. They held harps given them by God ³and sang the song of Moses the servant of God and the song of the Lamb:

> "Great and marvelous are your deeds, *s*
>   Lord God Almighty.
> Just and true are your ways,
>   King of the ages.
> ⁴ Who will not fear you, O Lord, *t*
>   and bring glory to your name?
> For you alone are holy.
> All nations will come
>   and worship before you,
> for your righteous acts have been revealed."

⁵After this I looked and in heaven the temple, that is, the tabernacle of the Testimony, *u* was opened. ⁶Out of the temple came the seven angels with the seven plagues. *v* They were dressed in clean, shining linen and wore golden sashes around their chests. ⁷Then one of the four living creatures *w* gave to the seven angels seven golden bowls filled with the wrath of God, who lives for ever and ever. ⁸And the temple was filled with smoke from the glory of God and from his power, and no one could enter the temple *x* until the seven plagues of the seven angels were completed.

The Seven Bowls of God's Wrath

16 Then I heard a loud voice from the temple saying to the seven angels, *y* "Go, pour out the seven bowls of God's wrath on the earth."

²The first angel went and poured out his bowl on the land, *z* and ugly and painful sores broke out on the people who had the mark of the beast and worshiped his image.

³The second angel poured out his bowl on the sea, and it turned into blood like that of a dead man, and every living thing in the sea died. *a*

⁴The third angel poured out his bowl on the rivers and springs of water, and they became blood. *b* ⁵Then I heard the angel in charge of the waters say:

> "You are just in these judgments,
>   you who are and who were, the Holy One,
> because you have so judged;

Margin references

15:1
p Rev 12:1, 3

15:2
q Rev 4:6
r Rev 13:14

15:3
s Ps 111:2

15:4
t Jer 10:7

15:5
u Nu 1:50

15:6
v ver 1

15:7
w Rev 4:6

15:8
x Ex 40:34, 35

16:1
y Rev 15:1

16:2
z Rev 8:7

16:3
a Ex 7:17-21

16:4
b Ex 7:17-21

15:1 The seven last plagues are also called the seven bowl judgments. They actually begin in chapter 16. Unlike the previous plagues, these are universal, and they will culminate in the abolition of all evil ("with them God's wrath is completed") and the end of the world.

15:3, 4 The song of Moses celebrated Israel's deliverance from Egypt (Exodus 15). The song of the Lamb celebrates the ultimate deliverance of God's people from the power of Satan.

15:5–8 The *tabernacle of Testimony* is a Greek translation for the Hebrew "Tent of Meeting" (see Exodus 40:34, 35). The imagery brings us back to the time of the exodus in the desert when the ark of the covenant (the symbol of God's presence among his people) resided in the tabernacle. The angels' garments are reminiscent of the high priest's clothing, showing that they are free from corruption, immorality, and injustice. The smoke that fills the temple is the manifestation of God's glory and power. There is no escape from this judgment.

15:8 John saw the temple filled with the glory and power of God. The key to God's eternal glory and power is his holiness (4:8). God's glory is not only his strength but also his perfect moral character. God will never do anything that is not morally perfect. This reassures us that we can trust him, yet it places a demand on us. Our desire to be holy (dedicated to God and morally pure) is our only suitable response. Our eternal reign with Christ won't begin until all evil is destroyed by his judgment. We must wait for his timetable to be revealed.

16:1ff The bowl judgments are God's final and complete judgments on the earth. The end has come. There are many similarities between the bowl judgments and the trumpet judgments (8:6—11:19), but there are three main differences: (1) These judgments are complete whereas the trumpet judgments are partial; (2) the trumpet judgments still give unbelievers the opportunity to repent, but the bowl judgments do not; and (3) mankind is indirectly affected by several of the trumpet judgments but directly attacked by all the bowl judgments.

6 for they have shed the blood of your saints and prophets,
and you have given them blood to drink[c] as they deserve."

7And I heard the altar respond:

"Yes, Lord God Almighty,
true and just are your judgments."[d]

8The fourth angel poured out his bowl on the sun, and the sun was given power to scorch people with fire. 9They were seared by the intense heat and they cursed the name of God, who had control over these plagues, but they refused to repent and glorify him.[e]

10The fifth angel poured out his bowl on the throne of the beast,[f] and his kingdom was plunged into darkness. Men gnawed their tongues in agony 11and cursed[g] the God of heaven because of their pains and their sores, but they refused to repent of what they had done.

12The sixth angel poured out his bowl on the great river Euphrates,[h] and its water was dried up to prepare the way for the kings from the East.[i] 13Then I saw three evil[a] spirits that looked like frogs; they came out of the mouth of the dragon,[j] out of the mouth of the beast and out of the mouth of the false prophet. 14They are spirits of demons[k] performing miraculous signs, and they go out to the kings of the whole world, to gather them for the battle[l] on the great day of God Almighty.

15"Behold, I come like a thief! Blessed is he who stays awake and keeps his clothes with him, so that he may not go naked and be shamefully exposed."

16Then they gathered the kings together to the place that in Hebrew is called Armageddon.

17The seventh angel poured out his bowl into the air, and out of the temple came a loud voice from the throne, saying, "It is done!"[m] 18Then there came flashes of lightning, rumblings, peals of thunder and a severe earthquake. No earthquake like it has ever occurred since man has been on earth,[n] so tremendous was the quake. 19The great city split into three parts, and the cities of the nations collapsed. God remembered[o] Babylon the Great and gave her the cup filled with the wine of the fury of his wrath.[p] 20Every island fled away and the mountains could not be found.[q] 21From the sky huge hailstones of about a hundred pounds each fell upon men. And they cursed God on account of the plague of hail,[r] because the plague was so terrible.

a 13 Greek *unclean*

16:6 [c]Isa 49:26
16:7 [d]Rev 15:3
16:9 [e]Rev 11:13
16:10 [f]Rev 13:2
16:11 [g]ver 9, 21
16:12 [h]Rev 9:14 [i]Isa 41:2
16:13 [j]Rev 12:3
16:14 [k]1 Ti 4:1 [l]Rev 17:14
16:17 [m]Rev 21:6
16:18 [n]Da 12:1
16:19 [o]Rev 18:5 [p]Rev 14:10
16:20 [q]Rev 6:14
16:21 [r]Ex 9:23-25

16:6 The angel acclaimed God for his justice in dealing with those who had killed the martyrs. God's wrath may be hard for us to accept. In a moral universe, however, God must ultimately oppose and destroy evil. Those who join the revolt against God suffer with their leaders.

We must avoid the misconception that God must be fair and kind in his dealings with humanity. This view of justice is merely a projection of a human idea. People who believe this notion appeal to tolerance and forgiveness and assume that God must play by our rules. In reality, God sets his own standard of justice. He uses his power according to his own moral perfection. Thus, whatever he chooses or decrees is fair, even if we don't understand it or like it. Those who rebel and reject God are not rejecting a "lifestyle option"; they are rejecting truth and justice itself.

16:7 The significance of the altar itself responding is that *everyone and everything* will be praising God, acknowledging his righteousness and perfect justice.

16:9-21 We know that the people realize that these judgments come from God because they curse him for sending them. But they still refuse to recognize God's authority and repent of their sins. Christians should not be surprised at the hostility and hardness of heart of unbelievers. Even when the power of God is fully and completely revealed, many will still refuse to repent. Don't wait until "just the right time" before turning to God. Do it now while you still have the chance. If you continually ignore God's warnings, you will eventually be unable to hear him at all.

16:12 The Euphrates River was a natural protective boundary against the empires to the east (Babylon, Assyria, Persia). If it dried up, nothing could hold back invading armies. The armies from the east symbolize unhindered judgment.

16:13, 14 These spirits of demons performing miraculous signs who come out of the mouths of the unholy trinity unite the rulers of the world for battle against God. The imagery of the demons coming out of the mouths of the three evil rulers signifies the verbal enticements and propaganda that will draw many people to their evil cause. For more about demons, see the note on 9:3ff.

16:15 Christ will return unexpectedly (1 Thessalonians 5:1–6), so we must be ready when he returns. We can prepare ourselves by standing firm in temptation and by being committed to God's moral standards. In what ways does your life show either your readiness or your lack of preparation for Christ's return?

16:16 This battlefield called Armageddon is near the city of Megiddo (southeast of the modern port of Haifa), which guarded a large plain in northern Israel. It is a strategic location near a prominent international highway leading north from Egypt through Israel, along the coast, and on to Babylon. Megiddo overlooked the entire plain southward toward Galilee and westward toward the mountains of Gilboa.

16:16 Sinful people will unite to fight against God in a final display of rebellion. Many are already united against Christ and his people—those who stand for truth, peace, justice, and morality. Your personal battle with evil foreshadows the great battle pictured here, where God will meet evil and destroy it once and for all. Be strong and courageous as you battle against sin and evil: You are fighting on the winning side.

16:17-21 For more information on Babylon and what it represents in Revelation, see the note on 14:8. The city's division into three sections is a symbol of its complete destruction.

6. Seizing the final victory
The Woman on the Beast

17:1
s Rev 16:19
t Rev 19:2
u Jer 51:13

17:3
v Rev 12:6, 14

17:4
w Jer 51:7

17 One of the seven angels who had the seven bowls came and said to me, "Come, I will show you the punishment s of the great prostitute,t who sits on many waters. u 2 With her the kings of the earth committed adultery and the inhabitants of the earth were intoxicated with the wine of her adulteries."

3 Then the angel carried me away in the Spirit into a desert. v There I saw a woman sitting on a scarlet beast that was covered with blasphemous names and had seven heads and ten horns. 4 The woman was dressed in purple and scarlet, and was glittering with gold, precious stones and pearls. She held a golden cup w in her hand, filled with abominable things and the filth of her adulteries. 5 This title was written on her forehead:

MYSTERY

BABYLON THE GREAT

THE MOTHER OF PROSTITUTES

AND OF THE ABOMINATIONS OF THE EARTH.

6 I saw that the woman was drunk with the blood of the saints, the blood of those who bore testimony to Jesus.

When I saw her, I was greatly astonished. 7 Then the angel said to me: "Why are you astonished? I will explain to you the mystery of the woman and of the beast she rides, which has the seven heads and ten horns. 8 The beast, which you saw, once was, now is not, and will

---

BLESSINGS IN REVELATION
Seven times in Revelation, God promises blessings upon the believers.

Reference	Verse
1:3	"Blessed is the one who reads the words of this prophecy, and blessed are those who hear it and take to heart what is written in it, because the time is near."
14:13	"Blessed are the dead in the Lord from now on. . . . They will rest from their labor, for their deeds will follow them."
16:15	"Behold, I come like a thief! Blessed is he who stays awake and keeps his clothes with him, so that he may not go naked and and be shamefully exposed."
19:9	"Blessed are those who are invited to the wedding supper of the Lamb!"
20:6	"Blessed and holy are those who have part in the first resurrection. The second death has no power over them, but they will be priests of God and of Christ and will reign with him for a thousand years."
22:7	"Behold, I am coming soon! Blessed is he who keeps the words of the prophecy written in this book."
22:14	"Blessed are those who wash their robes, that they may have the right to the tree of life and may go through the gates into the city."

17:1ff The destruction of Babylon mentioned in 16:17–21 is now described in greater detail. The "great prostitute," called Babylon, represents the early Roman empire with its many gods and the blood of Christian martyrs on its hands. The water stands for either sea commerce or a well-watered (well-provisioned) city. The great prostitute represents the seductiveness of the governmental system that uses immoral means to gain its own pleasure, prosperity, and advantage. In contrast to the prostitute, Christ's bride, the church, is pure and obedient (19:6—9). The wicked city of Babylon contrasts with the heavenly city of Jerusalem (21:10—22:5). The original readers probably rather quickly identified Babylon with Rome, but Babylon also symbolizes any system that is hostile to God (see 17:5).

17:3 The angel took John into the desert to see the prostitute in her reality. (The scarlet beast is either the dragon of 12:3, or the beast from the sea described in 13:1.) Sometimes we can only get a clear view of reality when we step back from our daily lives and see the patterns of evil and sin around us. Retreats, conferences, and days of prayer and fasting can help us extricate ourselves from jobs, newspapers, and television and bring us to new spiritual heights. Take time to view the reality of your life and evaluate its direction and activities. Do these glorify God and renew you to serve others?

17:6 Throughout history, people have been killed for their faith. Over the last century, millions have been killed by oppressive governments, and many of those victims were believers. The woman's drunkenness shows her pleasure in her evil accomplishments and her false feeling of triumph over the church. But every martyr who has fallen before her sword has only served to strengthen the faith of the church. Persecution is by no means a thing of the past. Christians in many parts of the world know that faith in Christ amounts to a death sentence. Believers who live in places free of such persecution must not forget to pray for their brothers and sisters in Christ in those difficult parts of the world.

17:8 In chapter 12 we met the dragon (Satan). In chapter 13 we saw the beast from the sea and the power he received from Satan. In chapters 14—16 we see God's great judgments. In this chapter, a scarlet beast similar to the beast and the dragon appears as an ally of the great prostitute. The phrase, "was, now is not, and will come" means that the beast was alive, died, and then came back to life. The beast's resurrection symbolizes the persistence of evil. This resurgence of evil power will convince many to join forces with the beast, but those who choose the side of evil condemn themselves to the devil's fate—eternal torment.

17:8 For more information on the book of life, see the note on 3:5.

come up out of the Abyss and go to his destruction.[x] The inhabitants of the earth whose names have not been written in the book of life from the creation of the world will be astonished[y] when they see the beast, because he once was, now is not, and yet will come.

9"This calls for a mind with wisdom.[z] The seven heads are seven hills on which the woman sits. 10 They are also seven kings. Five have fallen, one is, the other has not yet come; but when he does come, he must remain for a little while. 11 The beast who once was, and now is not,[a] is an eighth king. He belongs to the seven and is going to his destruction.

12"The ten horns you saw are ten kings who have not yet received a kingdom, but who for one hour will receive authority as kings along with the beast. 13 They have one purpose and will give their power and authority to the beast. 14 They will make war[b] against the Lamb, but the Lamb will overcome them because he is Lord of lords and King of kings[c]—and with him will be his called, chosen and faithful followers."

15 Then the angel said to me, "The waters you saw, where the prostitute sits, are peoples, multitudes, nations and languages. 16 The beast and the ten horns you saw will hate the prostitute. They will bring her to ruin and leave her naked;[d] they will eat her flesh and burn her with fire.[e] 17 For God has put it into their hearts to accomplish his purpose by agreeing to give the beast their power to rule, until God's words are fulfilled.[f] 18 The woman you saw is the great city[g] that rules over the kings of the earth."

The Fall of Babylon

18 After this I saw another angel[h] coming down from heaven. He had great authority, and the earth was illuminated by his splendor.[i] 2 With a mighty voice he shouted:

> "Fallen! Fallen is Babylon the Great!
> She has become a home for demons
> and a haunt for every evil[a] spirit,
> a haunt for every unclean and detestable bird.[j]
> 3 For all the nations have drunk
> the maddening wine of her adulteries.[k]
> The kings of the earth committed adultery with her,
> and the merchants of the earth grew rich from her excessive luxuries."

4 Then I heard another voice from heaven say:

> "Come out of her, my people,[l]
> so that you will not share in her sins,
> so that you will not receive any of her plagues;

[a]2 Greek *unclean*

Cross references (right margin):
17:8
[x] Rev 13:10
[y] Rev 13:3
17:9
[z] Rev 13:18
17:11
[a] ver 8
17:14
[b] Rev 16:14
[c] 1Ti 6:15
17:16
[d] Eze 16:37, 39
[e] Rev 18:8
17:17
[f] Rev 10:7
17:18
[g] Rev 16:19
18:1
[h] Rev 17:1
[i] Eze 43:2
18:2
[j] Isa 13:21, 22; Jer 50:39
18:3
[k] Rev 14:8
18:4
[l] Jer 50:8; 2Co 6:17

17:9-11 Here John is referring to Rome, the city famous for its seven hills. Many say that this city also symbolized all evil in the world—any person, religion, group, government, or structure that opposed Christ. Whatever view is taken of the seven hills and seven kings, this section indicates the climax of Satan's struggle against God. Evil's power is limited, and its destruction is on the horizon.

17:12 As we ponder the identity of the seven kings and the emergence of the ten kings, we must see John's theme of worldly power and its ultimate ineffectiveness against God and his people. Their authority only lasts "for one hour," meaning a brief moment, symbolizing its brevity and ultimate destruction. As Christians, have we become infatuated with the worldly power of movie stars, sports celebrities, political coalitions, and world economic forces? Are you craving the power and prestige that position, wealth, and connections offer? If so, you are an easy target for Satan's great deception. Worldly power is Satan's trap; the desire for it can turn us away from God. Worship only God and make it your strongest desire to serve him.

17:16 In a dramatic turn of events, the prostitute's allies turn on her and destroy her. This is how evil operates. Destructive by its very nature, it discards its own adherents when they cease to serve its purposes. An unholy alliance is an uneasy alliance because each partner puts its own interests first.

17:17 No matter what happens, we must trust that God is still in charge, that God overrules all the plans and intrigues of the evil one, and that God's plans will happen just as he says. God even uses people opposed to him as tools to execute his will. Although he allows evil to permeate this present world, the new earth will never know sin.

18:1ff This chapter shows the complete destruction of Babylon, John's metaphorical name for the evil world power and all it represents. Everything that tries to block God's purposes will come to a violent end. For more information on how the book of Revelation uses the name *Babylon*, see the note on 14:8.

18:2, 3 Merchants in the Roman empire grew rich by exploiting the sinful pleasures of their society. Many business people today do the same thing. Businesses and governments are often based on greed, money, and power. Many bright individuals are tempted to take advantage of an evil system to enrich themselves. Christians are warned to stay free from the lure of money, status, and the good life. We are to live according to the values Christ exemplified: service, giving, self-sacrifice, obedience, and truth.

18:4-8 The people of Babylon had lived in luxury and pleasure. The city boasted, "I sit as queen . . . and I will never mourn." The powerful, wealthy people of this world are susceptible to this same attitude. A person who is financially comfortable often feels invulnerable, secure, and in control, feeling no need for God or anyone else. This kind of attitude defies God, and his judgment

18:5
m Jer 51:9

18:6
n Ps 137:8;
Jer 50:15, 29

18:7
o Eze 28:2-8
p Zep 2:15

18:8
q Rev 17:16

18:9
r Rev 19:3

18:11
s Eze 27:27

18:12
t Rev 17:4

18:13
u Eze 27:13

5 for her sins are piled up to heaven,*m*
and God has remembered her crimes.
6 Give back to her as she has given;
pay her back*n* double for what she has done.
Mix her a double portion from her own cup.
7 Give her as much torture and grief
as the glory and luxury she gave herself.*o*
In her heart she boasts,
'I sit as queen; I am not a widow,
and I will never mourn.'*p*
8 Therefore in one day her plagues will overtake her:
death, mourning and famine.
She will be consumed by fire,*q*
for mighty is the Lord God who judges her.

9 "When the kings of the earth who committed adultery with her and shared her luxury see the smoke of her burning,*r* they will weep and mourn over her. 10 Terrified at her torment, they will stand far off and cry:

"'Woe! Woe, O great city,
O Babylon, city of power!
In one hour your doom has come!'

11 "The merchants*s* of the earth will weep and mourn over her because no one buys their cargoes any more— 12 cargoes of gold, silver, precious stones and pearls; fine linen, purple, silk and scarlet cloth; every sort of citron wood, and articles of every kind made of ivory, costly wood, bronze, iron and marble;*t* 13 cargoes of cinnamon and spice, of incense, myrrh and frankincense, of wine and olive oil, of fine flour and wheat; cattle and sheep; horses and carriages; and bodies and souls of men. *u*

HOW CAN A PERSON KEEP AWAY FROM THE EVIL SYSTEM?
Here are some suggestions:

1. People must always be more important than products.
2. Keep away from pride in your own programs, plans, and successes.
3. Remember that God's will and Word must never be compromised.
4. People must always be considered above the making of money.
5. Do what is right, no matter what the cost.
6. Be involved in businesses that provide worthwhile products or services—not just things that feed the world's desires.

---

against it is harsh. We are told to avoid Babylon's sins. If you are financially secure, don't become complacent and deluded by the myth of self-sufficiency. Use your resources to help others and advance God's kingdom.

18:9, 10 Those who are tied to the world's system will lose everything when it collapses. What they have worked for a lifetime to build up will be destroyed in one hour. Those who work only for material rewards will have nothing when they die or when their possessions are destroyed. What can we take with us to the new earth? Our faith, our Christian character, and our relationships with other believers. These are more important than any amount of money, power, or pleasure.

18:9–19 Those who are in control of various parts of the economic system will mourn at Babylon's fall. The political leaders will mourn because they were the overseers of Babylon's wealth and were in a position to enrich themselves greatly. The merchants will mourn because Babylon, the greatest customer for their goods, will be gone. The sea captains will no longer have anywhere to bring their goods because the merchants will have nowhere to sell them. The fall of the evil world system affects all who enjoyed and depended on it. No one will remain unaffected by Babylon's fall.

18:11–14 The voice from heaven (18:4) continued to prophesy against the greedy merchants. This list of various merchandise

illustrates the extreme materialism of this society. Few of these goods were necessities—most are luxuries. Even people had become commodities—the "bodies and souls of men" were sold as slaves to Babylon. The desire for nonessential luxuries had driven these merchants. Yet, how many of these luxuries listed are in *your* home? Most people will find that they own almost everything on this list. We are people who truly live in great luxury. We, too, are in danger of being absorbed in possessions and pleasure. Make sure that your desires lead you in the right direction. Put boundaries on them. Don't go after everything you see. Keep your desires on serving God and building his kingdom by helping others.

18:11–19 God's people should not live for money, because money will be worthless in eternity. And they should keep on guard constantly against greed, a sin that is always ready to take over their lives. God wants us to work and to provide for our families, and he commands the proper use of money. But when the desire for money fills our lives, it becomes a false god. Don't be enslaved by the desire for wealth.

14"They will say, 'The fruit you longed for is gone from you. All your riches and splendor have vanished, never to be recovered.' 15The merchants who sold these things and gained their wealth from her will stand far off, terrified at her torment. They will weep and mourn 16and cry out:

> "'Woe! Woe, O great city,
>> dressed in fine linen, purple and scarlet,
>> and glittering with gold, precious stones and pearls!v
> 17 In one hour such great wealth has been brought to ruin!'

"Every sea captain, and all who travel by ship, the sailors, and all who earn their living from the sea,w will stand far off. 18When they see the smoke of her burning, they will exclaim, 'Was there ever a city like this great city?'x 19They will throw dust on their heads,y and with weeping and mourning cry out:

> "'Woe! Woe, O great city,
>> where all who had ships on the sea
>> became rich through her wealth!
>> In one hour she has been brought to ruin!
> 20 Rejoice over her, O heaven!z
>> Rejoice, saints and apostles and prophets!
>> God has judged her for the way she treated you.'"

21Then a mighty angel picked up a boulder the size of a large millstone and threw it into the sea,a and said:

> "With such violence
>> the great city of Babylon will be thrown down,
>> never to be found again.
> 22 The music of harpists and musicians, flute players and trumpeters,
>> will never be heard in you again.b
> No workman of any trade
>> will ever be found in you again.
> The sound of a millstone
>> will never be heard in you again.c
> 23 The light of a lamp
>> will never shine in you again.
> The voice of bridegroom and bride
>> will never be heard in you again.d
> Your merchants were the world's great men.e
>> By your magic spell all the nations were led astray.
> 24 In her was found the blood of prophets and of the saints,f
>> and of all who have been killed on the earth."

Hallelujah!

19 After this I heard what sounded like the roar of a great multitudeg in heaven shouting:

> "Hallelujah!
> Salvationh and glory and poweri belong to our God,
> 2   for true and just are his judgments.
> He has condemned the great prostitute
>> who corrupted the earth by her adulteries.
> He has avenged on her the blood of his servants."

18:16 vRev 17:4
18:17 wEze 27:28-30
18:18 xRev 13:4
18:19 yJos 7:6
18:20 zJer 51:48
18:21 aJer 51:63
18:22 bEze 26:13 cJer 25:10
18:23 dJer 7:34; 16:9 eIsa 23:8
18:24 fRev 17:6
19:1 gRev 11:15 hRev 7:10 iRev 4:11

19:1ff Praise is the heartfelt response to God by those who love him. The more you get to know God and realize what he has done, the more you will respond with praise. Praise is at the heart of true worship. Let your praise of God flow out of your realization of who he is and how much he loves you.

19:1, 2 The identity of this great prostitute is explained in the note on 17:1ff.

19:1–8 A great multitude in heaven initiates the chorus of praise to God for his victory (19:1–3). Then the 24 elders (identified in the note on 4:4) join the chorus (19:4). Finally, the great choir of heaven once again praises God—the wedding of the Lamb has come (19:6–8). See Matthew 25:1–13 where Christ compares the coming of his kingdom to a wedding for which we must be prepared.

19:3
i Isa 34:10;
Rev 14:11

³And again they shouted:

"Hallelujah!
The smoke from her goes up for ever and ever."*i*

19:4
k Rev 4:4
l Rev 4:6

⁴The twenty-four elders *k* and the four living creatures *l* fell down and worshiped God, who was seated on the throne. And they cried:

"Amen, Hallelujah!"

19:5
m Ps 134:1

⁵Then a voice came from the throne, saying:

"Praise our God,
    all you his servants,*m*
you who fear him,
    both small and great!"

19:6
n Rev 11:15

⁶Then I heard what sounded like a great multitude,*n* like the roar of rushing waters and like loud peals of thunder, shouting:

"Hallelujah!
    For our Lord God Almighty reigns.

19:7
o Mt 22:2; Eph 5:32
p Rev 21:2, 9

⁷ Let us rejoice and be glad
    and give him glory!
For the wedding of the Lamb*o* has come,
    and his bride*p* has made herself ready.
⁸ Fine linen, bright and clean,
    was given her to wear."

(Fine linen stands for the righteous acts of the saints.)

19:9
q Lk 14:15

⁹Then the angel said to me, "Write: 'Blessed are those who are invited to the wedding supper of the Lamb!'"*q* And he added, "These are the true words of God."

19:10
r Rev 22:9

¹⁰At this I fell at his feet to worship him. But he said to me, "Do not do it! I am a fellow servant with you and with your brothers who hold to the testimony of Jesus. Worship God!*r* For the testimony of Jesus is the spirit of prophecy."

The Rider on the White Horse

19:11
s Rev 6:2
t Rev 3:14

¹¹I saw heaven standing open and there before me was a white horse, whose rider *s* is called Faithful and True.*t* With justice he judges and makes war. ¹²His eyes are like blazing

19:12
u Rev 1:14
v Rev 6:2

fire,*u* and on his head are many crowns. *v* He has a name written on him that no one knows but himself. ¹³He is dressed in a robe dipped in blood,*w* and his name is the Word of God.

19:13
w Isa 63:2, 3

¹⁴The armies of heaven were following him, riding on white horses and dressed in fine

---

19:7, 8 This is the culmination of human history—the judgment of the wicked and the wedding of the Lamb and his bride, the church. The church consists of all faithful believers from all time. The bride's clothing stands in sharp contrast to the gaudy clothing of the great prostitute of 17:4 and 18:16. The bride's clothing is the righteousness of the saints. These righteous acts are not religious deeds done by believers to their merit, but they reflect the work of Christ to save us (7:9, 14).

19:10 The angel did not accept John's homage and worship because only God is worthy of worship. Like John, it would be easy for us to become overwhelmed by this prophetic pageant. But Jesus is the central focus of God's revelation and his redemptive plan (as announced by the prophets). As you read the book of Revelation, don't get bogged down in all the details of the awesome visions; remember that the overarching theme in all the visions is the ultimate victory of Jesus Christ over evil.

19:11 The name "Faithful and True" contrasts with the faithless and deceitful Babylon described in chapter 18.

19:11–21 John's vision shifts again. Heaven opens and Jesus appears, this time not as a Lamb, but as a warrior on a white horse (symbolizing victory). Jesus came first as a Lamb to be a

sacrifice for sin, but he will return as a Conqueror and King to execute judgment (2 Thessalonians 1:7–10). Jesus' first coming brought forgiveness; his second will bring judgment. The battle lines have been drawn between God and evil, and the world is waiting for the King to ride onto the field.

19:12 Although Jesus is called "Faithful and True" (19:11), "Word of God" (19:13), and "KING OF KINGS AND LORD OF LORDS" (19:16), this verse implies that no name can do him justice. He is greater than any description or expression the human mind can devise.

19:13 For more about the symbolism of Jesus' clothes being dipped in blood, see the second note on 7:14.

linen, white and clean. ¹⁵Out of his mouth comes a sharp sword with which to strike down˟ the nations. "He will rule them with an iron scepter."ᵃ He treads the winepress of the fury of the wrath of God Almighty. ¹⁶On his robe and on his thigh he has this name written:

KING OF KINGS AND LORD OF LORDS.

¹⁷And I saw an angel standing in the sun, who cried in a loud voice to all the birds flying in midair, "Come,ʸ gather together for the great supper of God, ¹⁸so that you may eat the flesh of kings, generals, and mighty men, of horses and their riders, and the flesh of all people,ᶻ free and slave, small and great."

¹⁹Then I saw the beast and the kings of the earthᵃ and their armies gathered together to make war against the rider on the horse and his army. ²⁰But the beast was captured, and with him the false prophet who had performed the miraculous signs on his behalf.ᵇ With these signs he had deluded those who had received the mark of the beast and worshiped his image. The two of them were thrown alive into the fiery lakeᶜ of burning sulfur. ²¹The rest of them were killed with the sword that came out of the mouth of the rider on the horse, and all the birds gorged themselves on their flesh.

The Thousand Years

20 And I saw an angel coming down out of heaven, having the keyᵈ to the Abyss and holding in his hand a great chain. ²He seized the dragon, that ancient serpent, who is the devil, or Satan, and bound him for a thousand years.ᵉ ³He threw him into the Abyss, and locked and sealedᶠ it over him, to keep him from deceiving the nationsᵍ anymore until the thousand years were ended. After that, he must be set free for a short time.

⁴I saw thronesʰ on which were seated those who had been given authority to judge. And I

ᵃ15 Psalm 2:9

19:15 ˟Isa 11:4

19:17 ʸEze 39:17
19:18 ᶻEze 39:18-20

19:19 ᵃRev 16:14, 16
19:20 ᵇRev 13:12
ᶜDa 7:11

20:1 ᵈRev 1:18
20:2 ᵉ2Pe 2:4
20:3 ᶠDa 6:17
ᵍRev 12:9
20:4 ʰDa 7:9

19:15 This scene provides a graphic display of the wrath of God. It shows God's anger and judgment against sin and against those who have constantly rejected Christ as the means of forgiveness and reconciliation. God's wrath exists alongside his mercy. In each generation, there must be balanced preaching and teaching about God's grace and his anger against sin.

In our day, however, teaching about God's love and tolerance have become so predominant that God's anger seems to be mythical. Such a portrayal of God hardly warns people away from sin. Teaching about God's wrath may be watered down by some, but it is nevertheless real and will be terrible for those who have steadfastly refused him (1 Thessalonians 1:10). In your study and teaching, do not emphasize God's mercy to the exclusion of his wrath.

19:16 This title indicates our God's sovereignty. Most of the world is worshiping the beast, the antichrist, whom they believe has all power and authority. Then suddenly out of heaven rides Christ and his army of angels—the "KING OF KINGS AND LORD OF LORDS." His entrance signals the end of the false powers.

19:17 This "great supper of God" is a grim contrast to the wedding supper of the Lamb (19:9). One is a celebration; the other is devastation.

19:19 The beast is identified in the note on 13:1.

19:19–21 The battle lines have been drawn, and the greatest confrontation in the history of the world is about to begin. The beast (the antichrist) and the false prophet have gathered the governments and armies of the earth under the antichrist's rule. The enemy armies believe they have come of their own volition; in reality, God has summoned them to battle in order to defeat them. That they would even presume to fight against God shows how their pride and rebellion have perverted their thinking. There really is no fight, however, because the victory was won when Jesus died on the cross for sin and rose from the dead. Thus the evil leaders are immediately captured and sent to their punishment, and the forces of evil are annihilated.

19:20 The fiery lake of burning sulfur is the final destination of the wicked. This lake is different from the Abyss (bottomless pit) referred to in 9:1. The antichrist and the false prophet are thrown into the fiery lake. Then their leader, Satan himself, will be thrown into that lake (20:10), and finally death and Hades (20:14). After-

ward, everyone whose name is not recorded in the book of life will be thrown into the lake of fire (20:15).

20:1 The angel and the Abyss (bottomless pit) are explained in the notes on 9:1 and 19:20.

20:2 The dragon, Satan, is discussed in more detail in the notes on 12:3, 4 and 12:9. The dragon is not bound as punishment—that occurs in 20:10—but so that he cannot deceive the nations.

20:2–4 The 1,000 years are often referred to as the *Millennium* (Latin for *1,000*). Just how and when this 1,000 years takes place is understood differently among Christian scholars. The three major positions on this issue are called postmillennialism, premillennialism, and amillennialism.

(1) *Postmillennialism* looks for a literal 1,000-year period of peace on earth ushered in by the church. At the end of the 1,000 years, Satan will be unleashed once more, but then Christ will return to defeat him and reign forever. Christ's second coming will not occur until after the 1,000-year period.

(2) *Premillennialism* also views the 1,000 years as a literal time period, but holds that Christ's second coming initiates his 1,000-year reign and that this reign occurs before the final removal of Satan.

(3) *Amillennialism* understands the 1,000-year period to be symbolic of the time between Christ's ascension and his return. This Millennium is the reign of Christ in the hearts of believers and in his church; thus it is another way of referring to the church age. This period will end with the second coming of Christ.

These different views about the Millennium need not cause division and controversy in the church, because each view acknowledges what is most crucial to Christianity—Christ will return, defeat Satan, and reign forever! Whatever and whenever the Millennium is, Jesus Christ will unite all believers; therefore, we should not let this issue divide us.

20:3 John doesn't say why God releases Satan for a little while, but it is part of God's plan for judging the world. Perhaps it is to expose those who rebel against God in their hearts and confirm those who are truly faithful to God. Whatever the reason, Satan's release results in the final destruction of all evil (20:12–15).

20:4 The beast's mark is explained in the note on 13:16–18.

20:4
i Rev 6:9
j Rev 13:16

saw the souls of those who had been beheaded *i* because of their testimony for Jesus and because of the word of God. They had not worshiped the beast or his image and had not received his mark on their foreheads or their hands. *j* They came to life and reigned with Christ a thousand years. 5 (The rest of the dead did not come to life until the thousand years were ended.) This is the first resurrection. 6 Blessed and holy are those who have part in the first resurrection. The second death *k* has no power over them, but they will be priests of God and of Christ and will reign with him for a thousand years.

20:6
k Rev 2:11

Satan's Doom

20:8
l Eze 38:2

20:9
m Eze 38:9, 16

7 When the thousand years are over, Satan will be released from his prison 8 and will go out to deceive the nations in the four corners of the earth—Gog and Magog *l*—to gather them for battle. In number they are like the sand on the seashore. 9 They marched across the breadth of the earth and surrounded *m* the camp of God's people, the city he loves. But fire came down from heaven and devoured them. 10 And the devil, who deceived them, was thrown into the lake of burning sulfur, where the beast and the false prophet had been thrown. They will be tormented day and night for ever and ever.

The Dead Are Judged

11 Then I saw a great white throne and him who was seated on it. Earth and sky fled from his presence, and there was no place for them. 12 And I saw the dead, great and small, standing before the throne, and books were opened. Another book was opened, which is the

---

THE BEGINNING AND THE END

Genesis	Revelation
The sun is created....................	The sun is not needed.
Satan is victorious...................	Satan is defeated.
Sin enters the human race.	Sin is banished.
People run and hide from God.	People are invited to live with God forever.
People are cursed...................	The curse is removed.
Tears are shed, with sorrow for sin......	No more sin, no more tears or sorrow.
The garden and earth are cursed.	God's city is glorified; the earth is made new.
Paradise is lost.	Paradise is regained.
People are doomed to death...........	Death is defeated; believers live forever with God.

The Bible records for us the beginning of the world and the end of the world. The story of mankind, from beginning to end—from the fall into sin to redemption and God's ultimate victory over evil—is found in the pages of the Bible.

20:5, 6 Christians hold two basic views concerning this first resurrection. (1) Some believe that the first resurrection is spiritual (in our hearts at salvation), and that the Millennium is our spiritual reign with Christ between his first and second comings. During this time, we are priests of God because Christ reigns in our hearts. In this view, the second resurrection is the bodily resurrection of all people for judgment. (2) Others believe that the first resurrection occurs after Satan has been set aside. It is a physical resurrection of believers who then reign with Christ on the earth for a literal 1,000 years. The second resurrection occurs at the end of this Millennium in order to judge unbelievers who have died.

20:6 The second death is spiritual death—everlasting separation from God (see 21:8).

20:7–9 Gog and Magog symbolize all the forces of evil that band together to battle God. Noah's son, Japheth, had a son named Magog (Genesis 10:2). Ezekiel presents Gog as a leader of forces against Israel (Ezekiel 38; 39).

20:9 This is not a typical battle where the outcome is in doubt during the heat of the conflict. Here there is no contest. Two mighty forces of evil—those of the beast (19:19) and of Satan (20:8)—unite to do battle against God. The Bible uses just two verses to describe each battle—the evil beast and his forces are captured and thrown into the fiery lake (19:20, 21), and fire from

heaven devours Satan and his attacking armies (20:9, 10). For God, it is as easy as that. There will be no doubt, no worry, no second thoughts for believers about whether they have chosen the right side. If you are with God, you will experience this tremendous victory with Christ.

20:10 Satan's power is not eternal—he will meet his doom. He began his evil work in mankind at the beginning (Genesis 3:1–6) and continues it today, but he will be destroyed when he is thrown into the lake of burning sulfur. The devil will be released from the Abyss ("his prison," 20:7), but he will never be released from the fiery lake. He will never be a threat to anyone again.

20:12–15 At the judgment, the books will be opened. The book of life contains the names of those who have put their trust in Christ to save them. These books also contain the recorded deeds of everyone, good or evil. Everyone's life will be reviewed and evaluated. No one is saved by deeds, but deeds are seen as clear evidence of a person's actual relationship with God. Jesus will look at how we have handled gifts, opportunities, and responsibilities. God's gracious gift of salvation does not free us from the requirement of faithful obedience and service. Each of us must serve Christ in the best way we know and live each day knowing the books will one day be opened.

book of life. The dead were judged according to what they had done[n] as recorded in the books. [13]The sea gave up the dead that were in it, and death and Hades gave up the dead that were in them, and each person was judged according to what he had done. [14]Then death[o] and Hades were thrown into the lake of fire. The lake of fire is the second death. [15]If anyone's name was not found written in the book of life, he was thrown into the lake of fire.

7. Making all things new
The New Jerusalem

21 Then I saw a new heaven and a new earth,[p] for the first heaven and the first earth had passed away, and there was no longer any sea. [2]I saw the Holy City, the new Jerusalem, coming down out of heaven from God,[q] prepared as a bride beautifully dressed for her husband. [3]And I heard a loud voice from the throne saying, "Now the dwelling of God is with men, and he will live with them. They will be his people, and God himself will be with them and be their God. [4]He will wipe every tear from their eyes. There will be no more death[r] or mourning or crying or pain,[s] for the old order of things has passed away."

[5]He who was seated on the throne[t] said, "I am making everything new!" Then he said, "Write this down, for these words are trustworthy and true."[u]

[6]He said to me: "It is done.[v] I am the Alpha and the Omega,[w] the Beginning and the End. To him who is thirsty I will give to drink without cost from the spring of the water of life.[x] [7]He who overcomes will inherit all this, and I will be his God and he will be my son. [8]But the cowardly, the unbelieving, the vile, the murderers, the sexually immoral, those who practice magic arts, the idolaters and all liars—their place will be in the fiery lake of burning sulfur. This is the second death."

[9]One of the seven angels who had the seven bowls full of the seven last plagues[y] came and said to me, "Come, I will show you the bride, the wife of the Lamb." [10]And he carried me away in the Spirit[z] to a mountain great and high, and showed me the Holy City, Jerusalem, coming down out of heaven from God. [11]It shone with the glory of God,[a] and its brilliance

20:12
[n]Mt 16:27

20:14
[o]1Co 15:26

21:1
[p]2Pe 3:13

21:2
[q]Heb 11:10;
Rev 3:12

21:4
[r]1Co 15:26
[s]Isa 35:10

21:5
[t]Rev 4:9; 20:11
[u]Rev 19:9

21:6
[v]Rev 16:17
[w]Rev 1:8
[x]Jn 4:10

21:9
[y]Rev 15:1, 6, 7

21:10
[z]Rev 1:10

21:11
[a]Rev 22:5

20:14 Death and Hades are thrown into the lake of fire. God's judgment is finished. The lake of fire is the ultimate destination of everything wicked—Satan, the beast, the false prophet, the demons, death, Hades, and all those whose names are not recorded in the book of life because they did not place their faith in Jesus Christ. John's vision does not permit any gray areas in God's judgment. If by faith we have not identified with Christ, confessing him as Lord, there will be no hope, no second chance, no other appeal.

21:1 The earth as we know it will not last forever, but after God's great judgment, he will create a new earth (see Romans 8:18–21; 2 Peter 3:7–13). God had also promised Isaiah that he would create a new and eternal earth (Isaiah 65:17; 66:22). The sea is gone as well; in John's time, the sea was viewed as dangerous and changeable. It was also the source of the beast (13:1). We don't know how the new earth will look or where it will be, but God and his followers—those whose names are written in the book of life—will be united to live there forever. Will you be there?

21:2, 3 The new Jerusalem is where God lives among his people. Instead of our going up to meet him, he comes down to be with us, just as God became man in Jesus Christ and lived among us (John 1:14). Wherever God reigns, there is peace, security, and love.

21:3, 4 Have you ever wondered what eternity will be like? The "Holy City, the new Jerusalem" is described as the place where God will "wipe every tear from their eyes." Forevermore, there will be no death, pain, sorrow, or crying. What a wonderful truth! No matter what you are going through, it's not the last word—God has written the final chapter, and it is about true fulfillment and eternal joy for those who love him. We do not know as much as we would like, but it is enough to know that eternity with God will be more wonderful than we could ever imagine.

21:5 God is the Creator. The Bible begins with the majestic story of his creation of the universe, and it concludes with his creation of a new heaven and a new earth. This is a tremendous hope and

encouragement for the believer. When we are with God, with our sins forgiven and our future secure, we will be like Christ. We will be made perfect like him.

21:6 Just as God finished the work of creation (Genesis 2:1–3) and Jesus finished the work of redemption (John 19:30), so the Trinity will finish the entire plan of salvation by inviting the redeemed into a new creation.

21:6 For more about the water of life, see the note on 22:1.

21:7, 8 The "cowardly" are the fearful ones who abandon Christ at the threats of the beast. They fear persecution so badly that they choose temporary personal safety over eternal life with God. They are put in the same list as the unbelieving, the vile, the murderers, the liars, the idolaters, the sexually immoral, and those practicing magic arts.

By contrast, people who overcome "stand firm to the end" (Mark 13:13). They will receive the blessings that God promised: (1) eating from the tree of life (2:7), (2) escaping from the lake of fire (the "second death," 2:11), (3) receiving a special name (2:17), (4) having authority over the nations (2:26), (5) being included in the book of life (3:5), (6) being a pillar in God's spiritual temple (3:12), and (7) sitting with Christ on his throne (3:21). To follow Christ requires boldness and bravery to stand for him when oppression occurs. Pray for courage to do what is right no matter what pressure you face. Keep clearly in mind the heavenly reward of Christ so that you won't be tempted to turn away. Those who can endure the testing of evil and remain faithful will be rewarded by God.

21:8 The lake is explained in the notes on 19:20 and 20:14. The second death is spiritual death, meaning either eternal torment or destruction. In either case, it is permanent separation from God.

21:10ff The rest of the chapter is a stunning description of the new city of God. The vision is symbolic and shows us that our new home with God will defy description. We will not be disappointed by it in any way.

21:12
b Eze 48:30-34

was like that of a very precious jewel, like a jasper, clear as crystal. [12]It had a great, high wall with twelve gates, and with twelve angels at the gates. On the gates were written the names of the twelve tribes of Israel. *b* [13]There were three gates on the east, three on the north, three on the south and three on the west. [14]The wall of the city had twelve foundations, and on them were the names of the twelve apostles of the Lamb.

[15]The angel who talked with me had a measuring rod of gold to measure the city, its gates and its walls. [16]The city was laid out like a square, as long as it was wide. He measured the city with the rod and found it to be 12,000 stadia *a* in length, and as wide and high as it is long.

21:19
c Isa 54:11, 12

[17]He measured its wall and it was 144 cubits *b* thick, *c* by man's measurement, which the angel was using. [18]The wall was made of jasper, and the city of pure gold, as pure as glass. [19]The foundations of the city walls were decorated with every kind of precious stone. *c* The first foundation was jasper, the second sapphire, the third chalcedony, the fourth emerald, [20]the fifth sardonyx, the sixth carnelian, the seventh chrysolite, the eighth beryl, the ninth topaz, the tenth chrysoprase, the eleventh jacinth, and the twelfth amethyst. *d* [21]The twelve gates were twelve pearls, each gate made of a single pearl. The great street of the city was of pure gold, like transparent glass.

21:22
d Jn 4:21, 23

21:23
e Isa 24:23;
60:19, 20

21:24
f Isa 60:3, 5

21:25
g Isa 60:11
h Zec 14:7;
Rev 22:5

21:27
i Isa 52:1;
Rev 22:14, 15

[22]I did not see a temple *d* in the city, because the Lord God Almighty and the Lamb are its temple. [23]The city does not need the sun or the moon to shine on it, for the glory of God gives it light, *e* and the Lamb is its lamp. [24]The nations will walk by its light, and the kings of the earth will bring their splendor into it. *f* [25]On no day will its gates ever be shut, *g* for there will be no night there. *h* [26]The glory and honor of the nations will be brought into it. [27]Nothing impure will ever enter it, nor will anyone who does what is shameful or deceitful, *i* but only those whose names are written in the Lamb's book of life.

a 16 That is, about 1,400 miles (about 2,200 kilometers)   *b 17* That is, about 200 feet (about 65 meters)   *c 17* Or *high*
d 20 The precise identification of some of these precious stones is uncertain.

WHAT WE KNOW ABOUT ETERNITY

Description	Reference
A place prepared for us	John 14:2, 3
Unlimited by physical properties (1 Corinthians 15:35–49)	John 20:19, 26
We will be like Jesus.	1 John 3:2
We will have new bodies	1 Corinthians 15
A wonderful experience	1 Corinthians 2:9
A new environment	Revelation 21:1
A new experience of God's presence (1 Corinthians 13:12)	Revelation 21:3
New emotions	Revelation 21:4
No more death	Revelation 21:4

The Bible devotes much less space to describing eternity than it does to convincing people that eternal life is available as a free gift from God. Most of the brief descriptions of eternity would be more accurately called hints, since they use terms and ideas from present experience to describe what we cannot fully grasp until we are there ourselves. These references hint at aspects of what our future will be like if we have accepted Christ's gift of eternal life.

21:12–14 The new Jerusalem is a picture of God's future home for his people. The 12 tribes of Israel (21:12) probably represent all the faithful in the Old Testament; the twelve apostles (21:14) represent the church. Thus, both believing Gentiles and Jews who have been faithful to God will live together in the new earth.

21:15–17 The city's measurements are symbolic of a place that will hold all God's people. These measurements are all multiples of 12, the number for God's people: There were 12 tribes in Israel, and 12 apostles who started the church. The walls are 144 (12 x 12) cubits (216 feet) thick; there are 12 layers in the walls, and 12 gates in the city; and the length, width, and height are all the same, 12,000 stadia (1,400 miles). The new Jerusalem is a perfect cube, the same shape as the Most Holy Place in the temple (1 Kings 6:20). These measurements illustrate that this new home will be perfect for us.

21:18–21 The picture of walls made of jewels reveals that the new Jerusalem will be a place of purity and durability—it will last forever.

21:22–24 The temple, the center of God's presence among his

people, was the primary place of worship. No temple is needed in the new city, however, because God's presence will be everywhere. God will be the light in the new Jerusalem. Light represents what is good, pure, true, holy, and reliable. Darkness represents what is sinful and evil. That God's glory illuminates the city means that the city will be enveloped by him, who is perfectly holy and true. Light is also related to truth in that it exposes whatever exists. Just as darkness cannot exist in the presence of light, so sin cannot exist in the presence of a holy God. The city will be completely without sin and evil. We will be able to worship God throughout the city; nothing will hinder us from being with him.

21:25–27 Not everyone will be allowed into the new Jerusalem, but "only those whose names are written in the Lamb's book of life." (The book of life is explained in the notes on 3:5 and 20:12–15.) Don't think that you will get in because of your background, personality, or good behavior. Eternal life is available to you only because of what Jesus, the Lamb, has done. Trust him today to secure your citizenship in his new creation.

The River of Life

22 Then the angel showed me the river of the water of life, as clear as crystal, flowing[j] from the throne of God and of the Lamb 2 down the middle of the great street of the city. On each side of the river stood the tree of life,[k] bearing twelve crops of fruit, yielding its fruit every month. And the leaves of the tree are for the healing of the nations.[l] 3 No longer will there be any curse.[m] The throne of God and of the Lamb will be in the city, and his servants will serve him. 4 They will see his face,[n] and his name will be on their foreheads. 5 There will be no more night. They will not need the light of a lamp or the light of the sun, for the Lord God will give them light.[o] And they will reign for ever and ever.

6 The angel said to me,[p] "These words are trustworthy and true. The Lord, the God of the spirits of the prophets, sent his angel to show his servants the things that must soon take place."

Jesus Is Coming

7 "Behold, I am coming soon! Blessed[q] is he who keeps the words of the prophecy in this book."

8 I, John, am the one who heard and saw these things. And when I had heard and seen them, I fell down to worship at the feet[r] of the angel who had been showing them to me. 9 But he said to me, "Do not do it! I am a fellow servant with you and with your brothers the prophets and of all who keep the words of this book. Worship God!"[s]

10 Then he told me, "Do not seal up[t] the words of the prophecy of this book, because the time is near. 11 Let him who does wrong continue to do wrong; let him who is vile continue to be vile; let him who does right continue to do right; and let him who is holy continue to be holy."[u]

12 "Behold, I am coming soon! My reward is with me,[v] and I will give to everyone according to what he has done. 13 I am the Alpha and the Omega, the First and the Last, the Beginning and the End.

14 "Blessed are those who wash their robes, that they may have the right to the tree of life and may go through the gates into the city. 15 Outside[w] are the dogs,[x] those who practice

22:1	[j] Eze 47:1
22:2	[k] Rev 2:7
	[l] Eze 47:12
22:3	[m] Zec 14:11
22:4	[n] Mt 5:8
22:5	[o] Rev 21:23
22:6	[p] Rev 1:1
22:7	[q] Rev 1:3
22:8	[r] Rev 19:10
22:9	[s] Rev 19:10
22:10	[t] Da 8:26
22:11	[u] Eze 3:27
22:12	[v] Isa 40:10
22:15	[w] Gal 5:19-21
	[x] Php 3:2

22:1 The water of life is a symbol of eternal life. Jesus used this same image with the Samaritan woman (John 4:7–14). It pictures the fullness of life with God and the eternal blessings that come when we believe in him and allow him to satisfy our spiritual thirst (see 22:17).

22:2 This tree of life is like the tree of life in the Garden of Eden (Genesis 2:9). After Adam and Eve sinned, they were forbidden to eat from the tree of life because they could not have eternal life as long as they were under sin's control. But because of the forgiveness of sin through the blood of Jesus, there will be no evil or sin in this city. We will be able to eat freely from the tree of life when sin's control over us is destroyed and our eternity with God is secure.

22:2 Why would the nations need to be healed if all evil is gone? John is quoting from Ezekiel 47:12, where water flowing from the temple produces trees with healing leaves. He is not implying that there will be illness in the new earth; he is emphasizing that the water of life produces health and strength wherever it goes.

22:3 "No longer will there be any curse" means that nothing accursed will be in God's presence. This fulfills Zechariah's prophecy (see Zechariah 14:11).

22:8, 9 Hearing or reading an eyewitness account is the next best thing to seeing the event yourself. John witnessed the events reported in Revelation and wrote them down so we could see and believe as he did. If you have read this far, you have seen. Have you also believed?

22:8, 9 The first of the Ten Commandments is "You shall have no other gods before me" (Exodus 20:3). Jesus said that the greatest command of Moses' laws was "Love the Lord your God with all your heart and with all your soul and with all your mind" (Matthew 22:37). Here, at the end of the Bible, this truth is reiterated. The angel instructs John to worship God, and worship is a major emphasis in Revelation. The first step toward meaningful worship is a desire to know God. If we thirst for him, the Bible

promises that he will provide for us and satisfy our needs. Would you like your worship to be completely transformed? Confess any sins that might be hindering your fellowship with God. Then ask God to stir your heart, to instill within you an unquenchable thirst to know him. Meditate upon how God has revealed himself in the Bible, and ask him to reveal himself to you again. When you see God in a new way, worship will be your only fitting response.

22:10, 11 The angel tells John what to do after his vision is over. Instead of sealing up what he has written, as Daniel was commanded to do (Daniel 12:4–12), the book is to be left open so that all can read and understand. Daniel's message was sealed because it was not a message for Daniel's time. But the book of Revelation was a message for John's time, and it is relevant today. As Christ's return gets closer, there is a greater polarization between God's followers and Satan's followers. We must read the book of Revelation, hear its message, and be prepared for Christ's imminent return.

22:12–14 Those who wash their robes are those who seek to purify themselves from a sinful way of life. They strive daily to remain faithful and ready for Christ's return. This concept is also explained in the second note on 7:14.

22:14 In Eden, Adam and Eve were barred from any access to the tree of life because of their sin (Genesis 3:22–24). In the new earth, God's people will eat from the tree of life because their sins have been removed by Christ's death and resurrection. Those who eat the fruit of this tree will live forever. If Jesus has forgiven your sins, you will have the right to eat from this tree. For more on this concept, see the first note on 22:2.

22:15 Jesus will exclude from the holy city "everyone who loves and practices falsehood." These are people whose lives have gone so wrong that they resemble Satan, who deceived the whole world (12:9; 13:13–15; 16:14). They are hypocrites, trying to live one way while pretending to believe another. They are like the Nicolaitans, mentioned in 2:15, who were among the believers but magic arts, the sexually immoral, the murderers, the idolaters and everyone who loves and practices falsehood.

22:16
y Rev 1:1
z Rev 5:5

16"I, Jesus, *y* have sent my angel to give you *a* this testimony for the churches. I am the Root *z* and the Offspring of David, and the bright Morning Star."

17The Spirit and the bride say, "Come!" And let him who hears say, "Come!" Whoever is thirsty, let him come; and whoever wishes, let him take the free gift of the water of life.

22:18
a Dt 4:2; Pr 30:6

18I warn everyone who hears the words of the prophecy of this book: If anyone adds anything to them, *a* God will add to him the plagues described in this book. 19And if anyone takes words away from this book of prophecy, God will take away from him his share in the tree of life and in the holy city, which are described in this book.
20He who testifies to these things says, "Yes, I am coming soon."
Amen. Come, Lord Jesus.

22:21
b Ro 16:20

21The grace of the Lord Jesus be with God's people. *b* Amen.
a 16 The Greek is plural.

---

compromised their faith in order to also include worship of the Roman emperor. John records Jesus' statement that Satan is the father of lies (John 8:44).

Today we see leaders who twist the truth to serve their purposes. Many people have lost the ability to distinguish what's true from what they wish was true. Dishonest people soon begin to believe the lies they construct around themselves. Then they lose the ability to tell the difference between truth and lies. By believing your own lies, you deceive yourself, you alienate yourself from God, and you lose credibility in all your relationships. In the long run, honesty wins out.

22:16 Jesus is both David's "Root" and "Offspring." As the Creator of all, Jesus existed long before David. As a human, however, he was one of David's direct descendants (see Isaiah 11:1–5; Matthew 1:1–17). As the Messiah, he is the "bright Morning Star," the light of salvation to all.

22:17 Both the Holy Spirit and the bride, the church, extend the invitation to all the world to come to Jesus and experience the joys of salvation in Christ.

22:17 When Jesus met the Samaritan woman at the well, he told her of the living water that he could supply (John 4:10–15). This image is used again as Christ invites anyone to come and drink of the water of life. The gospel is unlimited in scope—all people everywhere may come. Salvation cannot be earned, but God gives it freely. We live in a world desperately thirsty for living water, and many are dying of thirst. But it's still not too late. Let us invite everyone to come and drink.

22:18, 19 This warning is given to those who might purposefully distort the message in this book. Moses gave a similar warning in Deuteronomy 4:1–4. We too must handle the Bible with care and great respect so that we do not distort its

message, even unintentionally. We should be quick to put its principles into practice in our lives. No human explanation or interpretation of God's Word should be elevated to the same authority as the text itself.

22:20 We don't know the day or the hour, but Jesus is coming soon and unexpectedly. This is good news to those who trust him, but a terrible message for those who have rejected him and stand under judgment. *Soon* means at any moment, and we must be ready for him, always prepared for his return. Would Jesus' sudden appearance catch you off guard?

22:21 Revelation closes human history as Genesis opened it—in paradise. But there is one distinct difference in Revelation—evil is gone forever. Genesis describes Adam and Eve walking and talking with God; Revelation describes people worshiping God face to face. Genesis describes a garden with an evil serpent; Revelation describes a perfect city with no evil. The Garden of Eden was destroyed by sin; but paradise is recreated in the new Jerusalem.

The book of Revelation ends with an urgent request: "Come, Lord Jesus." In a world of problems, persecution, evil, and immorality, Christ calls us to endure in our faith. Our efforts to better our world are important, but their results cannot compare with the transformation that Jesus will bring about when he returns. He alone controls human history, forgives sin, and will recreate the earth and bring lasting peace.

Revelation is, above all, a book of hope. It shows that no matter what happens on earth, God is in control. It promises that evil will not last forever. And it depicts the wonderful reward that is waiting for all those who believe in Jesus Christ as Savior and Lord.

This section includes:
How to Become a Christian
How to Follow Up with a New Believer
Mining the Treasures of the *Life Application Study Bible*
So You've Been Asked to Speak . . .
Taking the Step to Application

How to Become a Christian

As a believer, you will have the opportunity to talk to others about your faith. At times you will find a person who wants to know how he or she can become a Christian. Following is a guide you can use to help a person understand what it means to begin a relationship with Christ.

FACT: You were created by a loving God. You have great value. God loves you and wants to have a personal relationship with you.

SET-UP: Explain to the person that the world tells us that we are accidents of nature. We began as ooze in a pond, evolved into apes, and finally into humans. We live, we die, so we should grab for all we can get in this life—after all, that's the only way to fulfillment. In contrast, the Bible tells us that we are *not* accidents. We were created by a loving God who knew about us before we were born. We are here for a purpose, and we can find ultimate fulfillment by finding a relationship with him.

Read the following verses and make the following points:

God created you.

Psalm 139:13–16. *For you created my inmost being; you knit me together in my mother's womb. I praise you because I am fearfully and wonderfully made; your works are wonderful, I know that full well. My frame was not hidden from you when I was made in the secret place. When I was woven together in the depths of the earth, your eyes saw my unformed body. All the days ordained for me were written in your book before one of them came to be.*

God knew you before you were born—even while you were in your mother's womb. He knew all about your family and your life until now. [Be sensitive that some people have had difficult circumstances in their lives. Explain that God has not been absent, but has been drawing this person to himself.] He wants to give you a brand new start and a new way of living. He can do that when you give him your life. Why would you do that? Because . . .

God wants to have a personal relationship with you.

John 17:3. *Now this is eternal life: that they may know you, the only true God, and Jesus Christ, whom you have sent.*

God is not some "force," an unspeaking or unseeing idol, or merely another name for your own self-esteem. Instead, God is a person, your Creator, who created you to be in relationship with him. Why? Because . . .

God loves you.

John 3:16. *For God so loved the world that he gave his one and only Son, that whoever believes in him shall not perish but have eternal life.*

You can turn your life over to God's control because he loves you and wants the very best for you. In fact, he loves you so much that he gave his Son, Jesus, to die on the cross for you. I'll explain more about that in a minute. I just want you to realize that when you trust God, you are actually trusting the One who created you. When you turn your life over to him, you are giving your life to the One who knows you inside out. Don't you think that's a good place to put your trust?

FACT: Your sin keeps you from having a personal relationship with God.

SET-UP: Most people don't understand the concept of sin. We live in a fairly amoral world that believes each person can decide what is right, what is true, and what is "moral"—whatever that might mean. Television and movies don't help with their portrayals of happy people blatantly living sinful lives. You will probably need to explain that God has set some standards about right and wrong, and that there is such a thing as "sin."

What is sin?

James 4:17. *Anyone, then, who knows the good he ought to do and doesn't do it, sins.*

1 John 3:4. *Everyone who sins breaks the law; in fact, sin is lawlessness.*

God is holy and perfect; people are sinful. You probably know that for yourself—if you tried to be perfect for a day, you'd quickly discover that you couldn't do it. [Here you can draw a picture of a chasm, with a stick figure on one side and the word "God" on the other. Put the word "sin" in the chasm and explain further.] Sin means not understanding or even caring about what is "right." You defy God when you know what is right and then refuse to do it.

Who has sinned?

Romans 3:23. *For all have sinned and fall short of the glory of God.*

Romans 5:17. *By the trespass of the one man, death reigned through that one man.*

The Bible says "all have sinned." We simply cannot help it—we're human. When Adam sinned (way back in the Garden of Eden in the book of Genesis), sin entered the human race and sinfulness is part of our nature. You might be asking, "So what?"

What's so bad about sin?

Romans 6:23. *The wages of sin is death.*

Isaiah 59:2. *Your iniquities have separated you from your God.*

Sin leads to death. That's a big problem! Because God is perfect, he cannot have anything to do with us because we are sinners. He wants to have a personal relationship with us but he can't because of sin! So what did God do?

FACT: Only through Jesus Christ can you have a personal relationship with God.

SET-UP: Sometimes people don't understand the concept of having a "relationship" with a being they cannot see or touch. Yet it is a reality. That's why Jesus Christ came. He was a human being who lived on this earth so that we could understand what God is like. At this point you may discover that the person has lots of questions (for example, "How can God be God and also Jesus?"), the details of which can send you off the point. If that happens, explain that you don't have all of the answers to some of those kinds of questions—in fact, some questions are simply unanswerable because we humans cannot completely understand God and how he works. Explain that having a relationship with Christ is a spiritual reality that must be experienced, and that doing so will answer a lot of questions. The key questions to deal with at this point in the discussion include:

Why Jesus Christ?

John 14:6. *Jesus answered, "I am the way and the truth and the life. No one comes to the Father except through me."*

Remember how God can't have anything to do with us because of sin? Well, he decided to deal with our sin. Problem was, he had made it clear throughout the Old Testament that sin leads to death. In the Old Testament, people sacrificed animals as a way to show how sorry they were for their sins. And that was only temporary. God's plan all along was to send his Son, Jesus—a perfect human being—to be the final and ultimate sacrifice.

Why did Jesus have to die?

1 Peter 3:18. *For Christ died for sins once for all, the righteous for the unrighteous, to bring you to God. He was put to death in the body but made alive by the Spirit.*

Jesus died to take the penalty our sins deserved. In essence, he took our punishment so that we wouldn't have to! Now, because of Jesus, the way is prepared for us to be able to have a personal relationship with a holy God. [At this point, you can draw a cross in the chasm, connecting the two sides. On the cross, write the word "Jesus." This visually shows that Jesus is the only way to God. Also add that Jesus did not stay dead. He rose from the dead, which is a promise to us that we will also rise from the dead and go to heaven to be with him.] So what do you need to do next?

FACT: You must personally respond by trusting Jesus Christ as Savior and Lord.

SET-UP: The fact of salvation means nothing unless a person accepts it for himself or herself. Emphasize that even if the person grew up in church, he or she still needs to accept Jesus personally. Also emphasize that even if the person has led a terrible life, no one is too bad for God—a person does not have to "clean up his act" before coming to Christ. In fact, Jesus died to take away all that sin and to help the person start anew. So emphasize that being good is not good enough, yet no one is too bad to be able to be forgiven—God wants all people to come to him. All people need to trust in Jesus in order to be saved. So what kind of response should a person have? Talk about the following:

You respond with belief in Christ.

Romans 10:9, 10. *That if you confess with your mouth, "Jesus is Lord," and believe in your heart that God raised him from the dead, you will be saved. For it is with your heart that you believe and are justified, and it is with your mouth that you confess and are saved.*

You simply need to believe. That doesn't mean that you don't have any questions or that you understand everything. It simply means recognizing that you are indeed a sinner in need of a Savior. You recognize that you cannot be good enough for a perfect God on your own. And you understand that God loved you so much that he sent Jesus to save you. If you believe that, say so.

You respond by receiving Christ.

John 1:12. *Yet to all who received him, to those who believed in his name, he gave the right to become children of God.*

"Receiving Christ" means acknowledging your belief in Christ, inviting him to come into your life, turning to God from your present way of living (repentance), and then beginning the adventure of letting God direct your life! And the moment you ask, it's done. Jesus has come in!

QUESTION: Would you like to accept Jesus as your Savior?

SET-UP: If the person is ready, explain that he or she can express belief and trust in Christ through prayer. Prayer is simply talking to God. He knows what a person means even when it is difficult to express. Tell the person that he or she may use their own words, or they can repeat the following prayer after you:

> *Dear God, I know that my sin has separated me from you. Thank you that Jesus Christ died in my place. I ask Jesus to forgive my sin and to come into my life. Please begin to direct my life. Thank you for giving me eternal life. In Jesus' name, Amen.*

That's it! You can officially welcome this person into God's family—your new brother or sister in Christ!

Just as a baby is not born and then left to fend for himself, so a newborn believer in God's family needs some guidance. As the one who introduced him or her to Christ, you should attempt to help this new believer grow. The following pages will show you how.

How to Follow Up with a New Believer

Helping a New Believer Take the Next Steps in the Christian Life

If you have had the privilege of helping someone make the step of faith and accept Jesus as Savior, you want to continue that relationship if possible by offering some help to that new believer about the basics of the Christian faith. Your friend may wonder: "What does 'being a Christian' mean? How does it make a difference in my life? What should I be doing differently from now on?" This section gives you fourteen discussion points to use with a new believer. You don't need to (and shouldn't) cover all of these points in one sitting. These are designed to be discussion points that you can use over the course of several weeks as part of discipling someone in understanding the basic tenets of the Christian faith and ways they can keep growing.

Tell your friend that you would like to get together regularly (in person, by phone, by e-mail, by instant messaging, whatever works) over the next few weeks to talk about the next steps in his or her walk with God. After you've worked out a schedule, give the person a first assignment—to get a Bible (if he or she doesn't already have one—or doesn't have one in an easy-to-read translation). You might offer to go with the person, as the first trip to a Christian bookstore and its wide array of Bibles can be a bit daunting. Or even better—purchase a Bible yourself and give it as a gift. Also ask the person to get a journal in which to record some of the material you will be sharing as well as some of his or her own thoughts.

You can use each numbered point below as a basis for each meeting, or divide up the material as you wish. Read the Bible verses. As you meet together, help your friend find the verses in the Bible and underline them. Encourage him or her to ask whatever questions come to mind. You may not know all the answers. If you don't, be honest and say, "I don't know the answer to that question, but I'll do some research and see what I can find out." Then do what you can to try to answer that question to the best of your ability.

Also realize that God will do his work in his timing. Don't expect a new believer to suddenly get rid of all vices (not swear anymore, quit smoking, and change his or her wardrobe the very next day after accepting Christ). Part of your discipleship process will be to help him or her learn how to be sensitive to God's leading. You will need to be sensitive as well—to know what to say and when to say it, and what not to say until the time is right. Commit yourself to praying daily for this new believer!

Here are the points to discuss:

1. You can be assured of your salvation.
You recently became a Christian, but you may have experienced doubts about what really happened to you. So I want to share with you some assurances that God gives in the Bible.

> **God assures you that Jesus Christ has come into your life.**
>
> John 14:20. *On that day you will realize that I am in my Father, and you are in me, and I am in you.*

> **God assures you that your sins have been forgiven.**
>
> Colossians 2:13, 14. *God made you alive with Christ. He forgave us all our sins, having canceled the written code, with its regulations, that was against us and that stood opposed to us; he took it away, nailing it to the cross.*

> **God assures you that you have eternal life.**
>
> 1 John 5:13. *I write these things to you who believe in the name of the Son of God so that you may know that you have eternal life.*

ASSIGNMENT: In your journal, write a description of when, where, and how you became a Christian. Make a note of the assurances that God has given you today.

2. You can know that you are loved unconditionally.
No matter what else may be going on in your life, no matter what acceptance or rejection you may be facing from others, you can know that God has completely accepted you and loves you unconditionally.

> **God loves you, chose you, and adopts you into his own family.**
>
> Ephesians 1:4, 5. *For he chose us in him before the creation of the world to be holy and blameless in his sight. In love he predestined us to be adopted as his sons through Jesus Christ, in accordance with his pleasure and will.*

ASSIGNMENT: Write about what it means to you to be a part of God's family and to be loved unconditionally.

3. You have a new life in Christ.
What's next? God has given you a new life, but don't expect to be different all at once. Just as a new baby has to grow and learn, so God is going to work in you and help you to grow.

You have begun a relationship that will continue the rest of your life.

Colossians 2:6, 7. *So then, just as you received Christ Jesus as Lord, continue to live in him, rooted and built up in him, strengthened in the faith as you were taught, and overflowing with thankfulness.*

ASSIGNMENT: Write how it feels to know that God has given you a new life. What does that mean to you personally?

4. You have the privilege of prayer.

Just as good friends can talk to each other, so God, your heavenly Father, wants you to talk to him. And, while you may not understand it right now, you'll find that he "talks" to you as well.

You can pray to God about anything and everything. He wants to hear from you.

Philippians 4:6. *Do not be anxious about anything, but in everything, by prayer and petition, with thanksgiving, present your requests to God.*

ASSIGNMENT: Commit yourself to getting used to talking to God. Start out with about three minutes a day of focused time talking to God. Talk to him as you would to a friend. In your journal, begin a list of the things you're talking to God about and the concerns that you're bringing to him.

5. You have the treasure of God's Word.

When you buy a new gadget, you usually get an instruction manual. With your new life in Christ, you need God's instruction manual, the Bible. In fact, the communication you "hear" from God will often come as you read his Word.

You can trust God's Word.

2 Timothy 3:16. *All Scripture is God-breathed and is useful for teaching, rebuking, correcting and training in righteousness.*

ASSIGNMENT: Commit yourself to spending five minutes a day reading the Bible. Begin in the book of Mark (in the New Testament) and read about Jesus. As a result of something you read, write in your journal something you learned or something you need to do.

6. You have a great friend in Jesus, so get to know him!

As you're reading in the book of Mark, you've been learning more about Jesus. In essence, Jesus is God put into focus for human eyes. Jesus came in order to show us God and then to take the punishment for our sins.

Only because of Jesus do you have a personal relationship with God.

Colossians 1:19, 20. *For God was pleased to have all his fullness dwell in him, and through him to reconcile to himself all things, whether things on earth or things in heaven, by making peace through his blood, shed on the cross.*

ASSIGNMENT: Write a prayer to Jesus, thanking him for all he did for you.

7. You have a new lifestyle.

A good foundation is essential for a house to stand strong. Jesus wants you to know that obeying God will give your life a solid foundation.

You show your love for Jesus by doing as he says.

John 14:15. *If you love me, you will obey what I command.*

Philippians 2:13. *For it is God who works in you to will and to act according to his good purpose.*

ASSIGNMENT: In your journal, write one area of your life where you are obeying God and one where you think you are not. Ask God to show you what he wants you to do, and then to give you the strength to do it.

8. God will help you to follow and obey him.

As a Christian, you have been given the Holy Spirit. He will give you insight into what God is like and what he wants you to do.

God gives you his Holy Spirit to enable you to live the Christian life.

John 14:26. *But the Counselor, the Holy Spirit, whom the Father will send in my name, will teach you all things and will remind you of everything I have said to you.*

ASSIGNMENT: Write down one question that you'd like the Holy Spirit to help you with. Now take a couple of minutes and just talk to God about it.

9. You can resist temptation.
Becoming a Christian is like switching sides in a battle. You used to be on Satan's side and now you're on God's side—and Satan isn't happy about it! He wants to try to trip you up and tempt you to disobey God.

You're not alone in temptation. God promises to show the way out.

1 Corinthians 10:13. *No temptation has seized you except what is common to man. And God is faithful; he will not let you be tempted beyond what you can bear. But when you are tempted, he will also provide a way out so that you can stand up under it.*

ASSIGNMENT: List three temptations that Satan often uses on you. Now thank God ahead of time that he will show you how not to give in next time.

10. You can continue to receive forgiveness.
As a child in God's family, you'll still mess up. But God's love for you is so great that he will continue to forgive you.

When you mess up, go to God and ask him to forgive you.

1 John 1:9. *If we confess our sins, he is faithful and just and will forgive us our sins and purify us from all unrighteousness.*

ASSIGNMENT: Write down ways that you have disobeyed God recently. Look at each one and confess it through prayer. Then cross out each sin. Let this remind you of God's loving forgiveness. Commit to obey him in the future.

11. You have the privilege of worship.
When you became a Christian, you joined a family—sometimes called "the body of Christ," which means you're now "related" to Christians all over the world! You need to join a portion of that family by beginning to attend a local church.

You need the church to help you continue to grow.

Hebrews 10:25. *Let us not give up meeting together, as some are in the habit of doing, but let us encourage one another—and all the more as you see the Day approaching.*

ASSIGNMENT: Go with some friends or family to church this week. List two ways you worshiped God.

12. You can let others know about what Christ has done for you.
If you found a really great doctor, or a helpful mechanic, or even a terrific diet, you probably would tell your closest friend about it. Since you've found the One who forgives sin and gives you a new life, don't you think that's something you ought to share?

The news you have to share is the best news anyone could hear!

Romans 1:16. *I am not ashamed of the gospel, because it is the power of God for the salvation of everyone who believes: first for the Jew, then for the Gentile.*

ASSIGNMENT: Write down the name of one person who needs to know Jesus Christ. Start praying for that person to become a Christian. Ask a Christian friend to pray with you for the person and to help you learn how to share your faith with him or her.

13. Take time to memorize Scripture.
To fight a battle you need powerful equipment. The Holy Spirit will use the power of God's Word like a sword to defeat Satan. A great strategy is to memorize Scripture so you always have it with you.

Memorized verses will give you comfort and help you in temptation.

Ephesians 6:17. *Take the . . . sword of the Spirit, which is the word of God.*

ASSIGNMENT: Review the verses you've underlined in your Bible. Choose one or two favorites and begin to memorize them.

14. Realize your long-term goal—to be like Christ.
You've been a Christian for a short time now, and you're learning that you have a lifelong relationship with Christ. So what's your long-range goal? Becoming like Christ!

Fortunately, you don't do this alone. God works in you to help you become more like his Son.

Philippians 1:6. *He who began a good work in you will carry it on to completion until the day of Christ Jesus.*

Psalm 119:105. *Your word is a lamp to my feet and a light for my path.*

ASSIGNMENT: Make a list of at least five ways you want to become more like Jesus. Spend time asking God to help you. Remind yourself to read this part of your journal in one month to check on your spiritual growth.

Mining the Treasures of the *Life Application Study Bible*

As a believer in Christ, you will often be asked questions about your faith—sometimes these are honest seekers with tough questions that have bothered them; sometimes they're questions used by the questioners in hopes of tripping you up. In either case, it helps to be prepared with answers, or at least to know where to find the answers. *The Life Application Study Bible* notes were written not only to help explain the contents of the Bible and to get people started in thinking about application, but also to answer some of these key questions.

The treasures are here, and so we have mined them for you by guiding you to the notes that best answer questions in the following twenty-five categories. The references noted after each question are for the note(s) that will best help you to answer that question. (A number in parentheses indicates that there is more than one note on that particular Scripture.)

BELIEF
Why should I believe? *See notes on Genesis 15:6; Exodus 9:12.*
What does it mean to "believe" in Jesus? *See note on John 3:16(3).*

BIBLE
Why should I read the Bible? *See notes on 2 Chronicles 17:7–9; 34:31; Psalm 119:19.*
Why should I trust the Bible? *See notes on Psalm 33:4; Proverbs 16:22; 2 Peter 1:16–21.*
Why do you call the Bible God's Word? *See note on 2 Timothy 3:16, 17.*
How is the Bible different from other religious literature? *See note on 2 Timothy 3:16.*

CHURCH
How should I choose a church? *See notes on 1 Corinthians 3:10, 11; 1 Peter 5:8, 9.*
If eternal life is free, what's this 10 percent I keep hearing about? *See notes on Deuteronomy 14:22, 23; 2 Corinthians 8:10–15; 8:12(1 and 2).*
Isn't participation in church an option? *See note on Luke 4:16.*

DEATH
What happens when people die? *See notes on Hebrews 2:14, 15 (1 and 2); 1 Thessalonians 4:15–18.*
How can I be ready to die? *See notes on Genesis 50:24; Psalm 23:4.*

DEVIL
Is the devil real? *See notes on Job 1:6–12; Matthew 4:1(2).*
What does the devil do? *See notes on Genesis 3:5; 3:6.*
How powerful is the devil? *See note on Joshua 6:2–5.*

FAITH
How strong does my faith have to be? *See notes on Matthew 17:17–20; Luke 17:6; Romans 14:1ff.*
Is faith enough? That seems too easy. *See notes on 2 Kings 5:12; Matthew 3:9, 10; Philippians 3:2, 3(2); James 2:1ff.*
How can I tell others about my faith? *See notes on Exodus 3:16, 17; Revelation 1:5, 6.*

FORGIVENESS
How can I know that God forgives me? *See notes on Psalm 32:1, 2; Isaiah 1:18; Hebrews 10:17; 1 John 1:9(1).*

FUTURE

What can God tell me about the future? *See notes on Job 19:25–27; Matthew 24:3ff; John 14:19–21; Revelation 21:7, 8; 22:20.*
How is the world going to end? *See notes on Mark 13:5–7; Luke 12:40; 1 John 2:18–23.*

GOD

What is God really like? *See notes on Genesis 1:1; 18:14; Numbers 14:17–20; Deuteronomy 27:15–26; Psalm 34:9, 10; 36:5–8; 99:5; John 14:5, 6; 2 Thessalonians 2:10–12.*
What are idols and what's wrong with them? *See notes on Exodus 20:1–6; 32:4, 5; 1 Kings 18:29.*
Isn't God only all about rules? *See note on Isaiah 5:11–13.*

GOSPEL

What is the gospel? *See notes on Matthew 4:23, 24; John 3:16(1); Romans 1:3–5; 1 Corinthians 15:3, 4.*

GRACE

What is grace? *See note on Ephesians 1:7, 8.*
How important it is to have God's grace? *See note on Nehemiah 9:28–31.*

HEAVEN/HELL

What does the Bible really say about heaven? *See notes on Mark 12:24; 1 Corinthians 2:9; 1 Peter 2:11.*
What does the Bible really say about hell? *See notes on Matthew 25:46; 2 Thessalonians 1:9; Jude 1:7; Revelation 20:14.*

HOLY SPIRIT

Who is the Holy Spirit? *See notes on Psalm 48:14; John 14:15, 16; 14:17ff; Acts 1:5.*

JESUS

How do we know Jesus wasn't just a really great teacher? *See notes on Matthew 17:5; Luke 24:6, 7(2); John 5:31ff; Philippians 2:5–11(1).*
What do you mean when you say Jesus is God? *See notes on Hebrews 1:1, 2; 1:3(1).*
What did Jesus do for me? *See notes on Mark 15:31; 2 Corinthians 5:21; Colossians 1:12–14; Hebrews 9:22.*

LIFE

What does God really want from me? *See notes on Numbers 9:23; Judges 21:25; Proverbs 13:6; Ecclesiastes 1:8–11; 1 John 4:20, 21.*
Doesn't God want me to be perfect? How can I do that? *See notes on Matthew 5:48; Romans 5:20; Hebrews 10:14.*
How can I "commit" my life to God? *See notes on Proverbs 16:3; 1 Peter 1:14–16(2).*
If I am a Christian, how am I supposed to live? *See notes on Exodus 23:24, 25; Joshua 1:5; John 17:18; Romans 13:1ff; 1 Peter 1:8, 9.*

OLD TESTAMENT

The Old Testament seems so—*old*. How much of it really applies to me today? *See notes on Deuteronomy 4:8; Matthew 5:17–20; Acts 21:23, 24(2).*
How do the Old and New Testaments relate? *See notes on Leviticus 1:2(2); Matthew 13:52; Hebrews 3:5.*

ONLY ONE WAY

How can Christians insist that Jesus is the only way to God? *See notes on John 6:67, 68; Acts 4:12; 1 Timothy 2:5, 6; 2 Timothy 4:3–5; Hebrews 10:26.*
Why isn't just being "good" good enough? *See note on Colossians 1:21, 22; Hebrews 7:28; 9:14.*

OTHER RELIGIONS

How can you say that devout people who follow other religions are wrong? *See notes on Colossians 2:20–23(2); 2:22, 23; 2 John 1:1, 2; 1:3, 4.*
What makes Christianity any different from the rest of religions? *See notes on Hebrews 7:25; 1 John 5:12; 5:13.*

PRAYER

What good does prayer do? *See notes on 2 Chronicles 6:19–42; Psalm 4:3; Mark 9:29.*

If God knows everything, why pray? *See notes on Isaiah 38:1–5; Acts 1:12, 13.*

How should I pray? *See notes on Jonah 2:1ff; Mark 11:22, 23; Hebrews 4:16; 1 John 5:14, 15.*

REPENTANCE/CONFESSION

Why are confession and repentance necessary? *See notes on Leviticus 5:5; 2 Samuel 12:14(1); Matthew 3:1, 2(1); 1 John 1:9(1 and 2).*

SIN

What is sin? *See note on James 4:17.*

Why is sin dangerous? What's the big deal? *See notes on 2 Samuel 11:1ff; 1 Kings 11:9, 10; 1 Chronicles 21:13, 14; 21:14; 12 6:12, 13(1); 1 Thessalonians 4:4, 5; Revelation 9:20, 21.*

Why should I call myself a sinner when I can think of a lot of people who are *really* bad? *See note on Romans 3:23.*

How could a loving God send sincere people to hell? *See notes on Deuteronomy 7:2; Romans 1:18–20(1 and 2).*

Can someone be too sinful to be saved? *See notes on 2 Chronicles 33:12, 13; Psalm 51:1ff; 51:1–7.*

SPIRITUAL GIFTS

What are spiritual gifts? Does everyone have one? *See notes on Romans 12:6(1); 12:6–8; Ephesians 4:11, 12.*

SUFFERING

Why do bad things happen to good people? *See notes on Job 1:1ff; 2:10; Acts 12:2–11; Romans 8:28.*

How does God help me deal with the problems in my life? *See notes on Exodus 5:22, 23; Job 5:17–26; Psalm 106:40–42; Philippians 1:29; 1 Thessalonians 3:1–3; Hebrews 11:35–39.*

TEMPTATION

How does the devil tempt me? *See notes on Luke 4:3(1 and 2).*

Why does the devil tempt me? *See note on Genesis 3:1–6.*

At what point does temptation become sin? *See note on Matthew 4:1ff(1).*

How do I handle temptation? *See notes on Matthew 26:40, 41; Luke 4:1–13; 1 Corinthians 10:13.*

TRINITY

Why isn't the Trinity like believing in three gods? *See notes on Matthew 3:16, 17; Mark 1:10, 11; Acts 1:4, 5.*

So You've Been Asked to Speak . . .

Chances are you're going to find yourself faced with the task of leading a Bible study, giving a devotional, offering a short talk, or teaching a Sunday school class. Or perhaps you will be given the responsibility for leading a small group study and you won't know where to begin.

The *Life Application Study Bible* is an inexhaustible resource of information. If you follow some of the steps and hints below, you'll be able to put together a talk that is both informative and challenging—to any audience, at any time.

Ways to Use the Life Application Study Bible as a Research Tool
Using the Master Index

If you need to cover a topic, take a quick trip to the Master Index and look up the topic. There you will find notes on that topic (with a phrase that gives you an idea of the content of the note) as well as any charts or personality profiles on that topic. (See the Sample Lesson below to get an idea how this would work.)

Focusing on a Book of the Bible

For studying a Bible book, the *Life Application Study Bible* has plenty of overview material to help. Simply start at the beginning of the book you're studying. For example, if you're working through Jonah with your Bible study group or preparing to speak about that book, use the introductory material to get a sense of the time frame, the author and reason for writing, and an introduction that places the book into a contemporary setting. Study the Blueprint to understand how the book is laid out. Read the Megathemes and discover the main themes of that book and their importance. Many books also include overview maps with key events noted to give you the geographical context and flow.

Focusing on a Particular Passage

If you have been assigned a verse or passage of Scripture to discuss, use the life application notes, cross-references, and section headings to help you put the passage into context. If you don't find a note on that particular verse, consider the topic that you want to discuss and go to the index to look up the topic and other notes that will give further insight.

Using the Cross-References

The cross-references are an often-missed resource. For example, if you're studying the life of David or of Solomon, you can use the cross-references in the inside column beside the text to send you to the same account recorded in 2 Samuel or in 1 Chronicles.

Studying the Personality Profiles

The Personality Profiles are a nearly inexhaustible resource of study ideas. In a women's Bible study, you could work your way through the profiles of women. Or you could study the profiles ahead of time and do a topical study based on the life lessons for various women (using them like case studies). You can study all the people in a particular book, compare various kings or apostles, or even study the Bible characters by age (for example, choosing some of the more elderly faithful followers, such as Simeon and Anna, for an older group).

Employing the Charts as Visual Aids

The charts are designed to be simple and to summarize Bible data and teachings. They will give you an overview of a topic either from a specific book or the Bible as a whole. You could do an entire study from one chart or series of charts. For example, the charts in Proverbs pull together scattered verses on similar topics. These would be helpful in discussing key topics covered in Proverbs. In addition, the Bible includes several large charts that give sweeping overviews on various topics.

Seeing the Big Picture of Jesus by Using the Harmony of the Gospels

In studying a Gospel or the life of Christ, the Harmony of the Gospels presents his story in chronological order (the events are numbered, and the numbers also appear in the text) and will show you where the same stories appear in other Gospels. (The Harmony of the Gospels is located after the Gospel of John.) In addition, none of the footnotes have been repeated—so the notes you read in Matthew on the feeding of the five thousand will be different from the notes you read about that same story elsewhere. Use the Harmony to help you get a full picture of an event by seeing it from the different perspectives of all who wrote about the same event. Read the same accounts in different Gospels. Notice the differing details. Consider the point of view of the authors.

Getting a Wider Perspective by Using the Harmony of Kings and Chronicles

In a study of the books of Kings or Chronicles, the Harmony of the Kings and Chronicles (located between the books of 1 and 2 Kings) will give you a visual timeline for when the various kings ruled, tell whether accounts of their reigns are recorded in other books, and show the prophet who was preaching at the time. Similarly, if you're studying any of the prophetic books, you can use the Harmony to learn about what was going on in the kingdom to which the prophet had been called to speak. This will give you great insight into why the prophet spoke as he did.

Sampling the Maps

If your group is interested in maps, use the maps in the Gospels (in conjunction with the Harmony) to trace Jesus' steps throughout his ministry. Use the maps of Paul's journeys and follow his footsteps across Asia Minor and on to Rome. Use the maps in Genesis to help your readers visualize the whereabouts of the people they are studying.

Those are just a few suggestions for using the resources in the Life Application Study Bible. The following section takes you through steps for planning a topical talk using the Master Index.

A Sample Lesson in Six Easy Steps

You've been given the assignment to give a talk to a group about the importance of prayer in a Christian's life.

STEP ONE: Pray.
Begin by asking God to guide you as you put together your talk. Ask him to give you insight and wisdom. Ask him to guide the process and give you the right words to say.

STEP TWO: Anticipate questions.
List questions your group might have about this topic, focusing on particular issues that may be important to them at this time. (For example, if a family is facing a difficult illness and God doesn't seem to be answering their request, you will need to be prepared to discuss the issue of unanswered prayer.)

STEP THREE: Prepare an outline.
Keeping in mind the questions from step two, begin an outline. Three points are usually good. Give an introduction (an anecdote, a question, an example). List the three points you want to make about prayer. Give an application-oriented conclusion (see the article, "Taking the Step to Application" on the following pages).

STEP FOUR: Go to the Master Index.
Look up "Prayer" in the Master Index. You'll find a long list of notes on various verses. Whittle it down by looking at the topic sentence for each note; then jot down the locations of notes you think might fit into your outline. Also notice that the Master Index lists three charts that focus on prayer and three Personality Profiles that include life lessons on the topic of prayer. Make a note of the page numbers for these.

STEP FIVE: Read the passages, notes, and other helpful materials.
Now refer to your jotted list and read the notes, charts, and profiles. When you find Bible verses and significant points in the notes that you want to use, write them on your three-point outline.

STEP SIX: Put it all together.
Now make your points flow together. Write transition sentences between points. Finally, add a conclusion that challenges your listeners to take the message to heart and let it make a difference in their lives.

Taking the Step to Application

Whether you are studying the Bible for yourself or teaching it to others, moving toward application is the most important part of the studying and teaching process. You see, just having information about what is in the Bible is not enough (even Satan knew enough of the Bible to be able to quote it—Matthew 4:1–11). Understanding the context or the concepts is not enough. Even being able to see that it is relevant to today's world is not enough. For the Bible to really make a difference in our lives, we need to (1) receive the message personally, (2) reflect on our lives and identify what needs to change as a result of God's Word, and (3) lay out a plan to make that change. Taking the step to application means that we finish our Bible study or go away from a lesson asking:

Now that I know what God wants me to do, how am I going to start doing it?

Application is the step between *knowing* what the Bible says and *doing* what it says. While the truths of the Bible never change, people's life situations are different and are constantly changing. You must continue to study the Bible and learn the new things God wants you to learn. And when you teach, you may be able to tell your listeners how *you* are applying certain principles from God's Word, but at the same time you need to give them the tools and the opportunity to apply the Bible to *their own* life situations. So how do you do that? We have developed a Bible study system called the Pyramid. Using the nine sets of questions in the Pyramid, you will be able to study the Bible and then apply its principles more practically and thoroughly to your personal life situations.

LIFE APPLICATION PYRAMID

Each step is described in detail below, followed by the questions you should ask yourself as you work your way over the Pyramid toward application. After point 5, at the top of the Pyramid, we offer an example of how your study might look. Then follow points 6 to 9 down the other side of the Pyramid. We have provided an example here as well, although these points will vary greatly for each individual.

1. People
Begin by identifying the people in the passage, the characters who are actively involved. Sometimes no specific individuals or groups will be named (such as when you're reading Proverbs or Romans). But don't forget the author and the original audience. Note the people and learn something about them. (For example, if you're reading Isaiah's message to Moab, look up the "Moabites" in the Master Index and read the notes to better understand the people in this passage.) So you should ask,

  • Who are all the people in this passage?
  • How are these people like people in my world?
  • What characteristics of these people do I see in myself?

2. Place
Next, consider Place. This step puts the passage in its original setting, the historical and cultural context. You can learn about Place by again using the Master Index and looking up the notes (and often the maps). The more you know about the culture, history, and problems of the people in the passage, the more you will be able to find parallels to your life today. Ask,

  • What is the setting of this passage?
  • What are the significant details in the history, culture, and geography?
  • What are the similarities to my world?

3. Plot
This step answers the question "What's happening?" Usually you can discover this by the context of the passage and book. The notes in the section you're reading will also help you to unravel the plot of a particular passage. Ask,

  • What is happening in this passage?
  • What is the conflict or tension?
  • What would I have done in this situation?
  • How is this similar to what is happening in my life or in the world today?

4. Point
Before you can determine what something in the Bible means for you today, you must first ascertain the meaning for the original audience. The events recorded in the Bible happened to real people at specific times in history. Real audiences heard the parables, and real churches received the epistles. Therefore, carefully consider the cultural context (what you learned in the first three steps) to find the particular lessons that God wanted to teach these people. A clear understanding of the Point can prevent damaging misapplication and is invaluable for determining the timeless truths in the passage. To determine the Point, ask,

- What was the intended message for the original audience?
- What did the people in the passage learn?
- What did God want them to do?
- What was God's solution to the problem?

5. Principles

The next step is to determine what transferable principles are embedded in the passage. The Point and Principles may be exactly the same—or may be indirectly related. The Principles are the distilled essence of a passage. You should ask,

- What is the message for all of humankind?
- What are the timeless truths?
- What is the moral of the story?

Here are possible answers for Acts 27:27–44 for the first five steps up the Bible study Pyramid.

> PEOPLE: Luke (the author, included in the "we" passage), Paul, the sailors, other prisoners, soldiers guarding the other prisoners, the army officer guarding Paul (Julius, see 27:1), God.
>
> PLACE: on ship, sailing across the Adriatic Sea (27:27), near the island of Malta (28:1), during a terrible storm, as Paul and other Roman prisoners were being taken to Rome for trial; the journey was undertaken "after the Fast" (27:9), so it may have been October, a time when dangerous storms could arise suddenly.
>
> PLOT: Paul had warned that the trip would be disastrous (27:9, 10), but the pilot and centurion didn't listen and determined to sail anyway. When the terrible storm arose, Paul encouraged everyone (27:22) and told them what to do; this time the Roman crew listened (27:31–38). Paul also thanked God in front of everyone (27:35). When the ship began to break up, the soldiers were about to kill their prisoners (so they wouldn't escape), but the centurion guarding Paul stopped them (27:43).
>
> POINT: Paul was confident of God's protection and care, even during a life-threatening storm. This confidence freed Paul to encourage others, even his captors, and to give a clear testimony of his faith in Christ.
>
> PRINCIPLES: God is present and in control of all our "storms"; we can take courage and have hope because we know that God is with us and he cares for us. Even when we are going through difficult times, we should encourage and help others and give clear evidence of our faith.

Now you've made it up one side of the Pyramid. The path to the top of the Pyramid narrows to a single point and a few principles, but the paths going down the other side are diverse and varied for each person and for each situation. Points 6 to 9 are as follows:

6. Present

This step expands the areas of application for the Point and Principles that you have extracted so far. A different kind of thinking is required because you are expanding possibilities and adding your life to the principles. Here you describe the significant implications of these timeless truths for life at home, school, job, and in your neighborhood. This step brings the truth into your context, into today's world, here and now. The meaning for the original audience may be clear, but the implications for the present may be rich and varied. Ask,

- What do these principles mean for my society and culture?
- How is this relevant?
- What back then is similar to today?
- How can I make the timeless truth timely?

7. Parallels

This step is similar to Present, except that it is very personal, addressing specific life situations, fears, hopes, and relationships. This is the time to explore all the areas of life where the truth might apply. Thus, you should ask,

- What does this truth mean for me?
- Where are my areas of need, conviction, and opportunity?
- Where in my life might this truth possibly apply?

8. Priorities

After surfacing application areas, select one that you consider to be most important—one that God is nudging you about. This is one of the more difficult steps—it can be easy to start rationalizing or to make excuses. But to truly get God's Word into your life and grow as a believer, you need to listen when God speaks. In taking this step, you are answering the question, "So what?"; that is, what does this passage say about how I should change? This involves asking these tough questions:

- How should I adjust my priorities?
- What should I change about my values, beliefs, attitudes, or character?
- What about my thoughts and motives should change?
- What kind of person does God want me to become?

9. Plan

After pinpointing what needs to change, you need to take action. You need to answer the question, "Now what?" and put truth into practice by determining to change and then making plans to live differently. Planning involves selecting a goal, breaking it down into bite-size pieces, and getting moving! These questions will help:

- What does God want me to do about what I have learned?
- What steps will get me to that goal?
- What should be my first step? How should I get started?

Here are possible answers for Acts 27:27–44 for the last four steps, down the Bible study Pyramid. While the answers in Steps 1 through 5 are pretty straightforward, the answers in Steps 6 through 9 will vary greatly from person to person, so these are merely suggestions:

PRESENT: I'm not a prisoner of a foreign government being taken to trial by ship in a terrible storm, but I do have rough seas in my life. I have a conflict with my daughter's teacher, a problem with one of my company's clients, and other difficult situations.

PARALLELS: The main parallel to my life is Paul's attitude in the middle of the crisis—he remained calm, gave instructions, encouraged everyone, and was a positive example of a follower of Christ. In both the problem at school and the one at work, I need to explain my case calmly and confidently. But in doing this, I should be positive and helpful, not negative, hateful, or divisive.

PRIORITIES: My natural tendency is to get angry and tell someone off when I think he or she is wrong, or to shout orders without being sensitive to the feelings of others. I think that God wants me to be more patient and understanding. Perhaps through the *way* I communicate, I can be a positive witness for Christ.

PLAN: With the conflict at school, I need to speak directly to the teacher (not write a letter) and explain my position carefully, calmly, and with concern for the feelings of the teacher. I will make an appointment, write out my points beforehand so I won't get off on tangents and get upset, and carefully explain my position while letting the teacher know that I respect him.

Remember, a big difference stands between *knowing* and *doing*, and another big difference between *teaching* and *doing*. So as you begin taking the steps to application in both your personal study and in your teaching, ask yourself:

Am I doing what God wants me to do?
Am I obeying him?

Be honest in your self-evaluation. Applying the Bible begins *now*, with *you*. James wrote:

Do not merely listen to the word, and so deceive yourselves. Do what it says. Anyone who listens to the word but does not do what it says is like a man who looks at his face in a mirror and, after looking at himself, goes away and immediately forgets what he looks like. But the man who looks intently into the perfect law that gives freedom, and continues to do this, not forgetting what he has heard, but doing it—he will be blessed in what he does (James 1:22–25).

This article is adapted from Dave Veerman, *How to Apply the Bible* (Wheaton, IL: Tyndale House Publishers, 1993). Books are available at www.lifeapplicationbible.com.

JAN 1	Day 1	Genesis 1:1—2:3	**20**	Day 51	Numbers 14:5–45
2	Day 2	Genesis 2:15—3:24	**21**	Day 52	Numbers 21:4–9
3	Day 3	Genesis 4:1–16	**22**	Day 53	Numbers 22:5–38
4	Day 4	Genesis 6:9–22	**23**	Day 54	Deuteronomy 29:1–29
5	Day 5	Genesis 7:1–24	**24**	Day 55	Deuteronomy 30:1–20
6	Day 6	Genesis 8:1–22	**25**	Day 56	Deuteronomy 31:1–8
7	Day 7	Genesis 9:1–17	**26**	Day 57	Deuteronomy 34:1–12
8	Day 8	Genesis 11:1–9	**27**	Day 58	Joshua 1:1–18
9	Day 9	Genesis 12:1–9; 17:1–8	**28**	Day 59	Joshua 2:1–24
10	Day 10	Genesis 18:1–15	**MAR 1**	Day 60	Joshua 3:1–17
11	Day 11	Genesis 19:15–29	**2**	Day 61	Joshua 5:13—6:27
12	Day 12	Genesis 21:8–21	**3**	Day 62	Joshua 7:1–26
13	Day 13	Genesis 22:1–19	**4**	Day 63	Joshua 10:1–15
14	Day 14	Genesis 24:1–27	**5**	Day 64	Joshua 23:1–16
15	Day 15	Genesis 24:28–67	**6**	Day 65	Joshua 24:1–31
16	Day 16	Genesis 25:19–34	**7**	Day 66	Judges 4:4–24
17	Day 17	Genesis 27:1–40	**8**	Day 67	Judges 6:1–40
18	Day 18	Genesis 28:10–22	**9**	Day 68	Judges 7:1–25
19	Day 19	Genesis 29:14–30	**10**	Day 69	Judges 13:1–25
20	Day 20	Genesis 32:1—33:16	**11**	Day 70	Judges 14:1–20
21	Day 21	Genesis 37:1–36	**12**	Day 71	Judges 15:1–20
22	Day 22	Genesis 39:1–23	**13**	Day 72	Judges 16:1–21
23	Day 23	Genesis 40:1–23	**14**	Day 73	Judges 16:22–31
24	Day 24	Genesis 41:1–36	**15**	Day 74	Ruth 1:1–22
25	Day 25	Genesis 41:37–57	**16**	Day 75	Ruth 2:1–23
26	Day 26	Genesis 42:1–38	**17**	Day 76	Ruth 3:1–18
27	Day 27	Genesis 43:1–34	**18**	Day 77	Ruth 4:1–22
28	Day 28	Genesis 44:1–34	**19**	Day 78	1 Samuel 1:1–28
29	Day 29	Genesis 45:1–28	**20**	Day 79	1 Samuel 3:1–21
30	Day 30	Genesis 49:1–33	**21**	Day 80	1 Samuel 8:1–5
31	Day 31	Exodus 1:8—2:10	**22**	Day 81	1 Samuel 8:6–22
FEB 1	Day 32	Exodus 2:11–25	**23**	Day 82	1 Samuel 9:1–21
2	Day 33	Exodus 3:1–22	**24**	Day 83	1 Samuel 10:1–27
3	Day 34	Exodus 4:1–17	**25**	Day 84	1 Samuel 14:1–23
4	Day 35	Exodus 5:1–23	**26**	Day 85	1 Samuel 16:1–13
5	Day 36	Exodus 6:1–13	**27**	Day 86	1 Samuel 17:1–31
6	Day 37	Exodus 7:1–14	**28**	Day 87	1 Samuel 17:32–58
7	Day 38	Exodus 7:15—9:7	**29**	Day 88	1 Samuel 18:1–30
8	Day 39	Exodus 9:8—10:29	**30**	Day 89	1 Samuel 20:1–42
9	Day 40	Exodus 11:1–10; 12:29–36	**31**	Day 90	1 Samuel 24:1–22
10	Day 41	Exodus 13:17—14:31	**APR 1**	Day 91	1 Samuel 25:1–42
11	Day 42	Exodus 15:22–27; 17:1–7	**2**	Day 92	1 Samuel 28:1–25
12	Day 43	Exodus 16:1–36	**3**	Day 93	2 Samuel 5:1–12
13	Day 44	Exodus 18:1–27	**4**	Day 94	2 Samuel 9:1–13
14	Day 45	Exodus 19:1–25	**5**	Day 95	2 Samuel 11:1–27
15	Day 46	Exodus 20:1–22	**6**	Day 96	2 Samuel 12:1–25
16	Day 47	Exodus 32:1–29	**7**	Day 97	2 Samuel 13:1–19
17	Day 48	Exodus 40:1–38	**8**	Day 98	2 Samuel 13:20–39
18	Day 49	Numbers 12:1–16	**9**	Day 99	2 Samuel 15:1–37
19	Day 50	Numbers 13:1—14:4	**10**	Day 100	2 Samuel 18:1–18

TABLE OF WEIGHTS AND MEASURES

BIBLICAL UNIT		APPROXIMATE AMERICAN EQUIVALENT	APPROXIMATE METRIC EQUIVALENT
WEIGHTS			
talent	(60 minas)	75 pounds	34 kilograms
mina	(50 shekels)	1 1/4 pounds	0.6 kilogram
shekel	(2 bekas)	2/5 ounce	11.5 grams
pim	(2/3 shekel)	1/3 ounce	7.6 grams
beka	(10 gerahs)	1/5 ounce	5.5 grams
gerah		1/50 ounce	0.6 gram
LENGTH			
cubit		18 inches	0.5 meter
span		9 inches	23 centimeters
handbreadth		3 inches	8 centimeters
CAPACITY **Dry Measure**			
cor [homer]	(10 ephahs)	6 bushels	220 liters
lethek	(5 ephahs)	3 bushels	110 liters
ephah	(10 omers)	3/5 bushel	22 liters
seah	(1/3 ephah)	7 quarts	7.3 liters
omer	(1/10 ephah)	2 quarts	2 liters
cab	(1/18 ephah)	1 quart	1 liter
Liquid Measure			
bath	(1 ephah)	6 gallons	22 liters
hin	(1/6 bath)	4 quarts	4 liters
log	(1/72 bath)	1/3 quart	0.3 liter

The figures of the table are calculated on the basis of a shekel equaling 11.5 grams, a cubit equaling 18 inches and an ephah equaling 22 liters. The quart referred to is either a dry quart (slightly larger than a liter) or a liquid quart (slightly smaller than a liter)., whichever is applicable. The ton referred to in the footnotes is the American ton of 2,000 pounds.

This table is based upon the best available information, but it is not intended to be mathematically precise; like the measurement equivalents in the footnotes, it merely gives approximate amounts and distances. Weight and measures differed somewhat at various times and places in the ancient world. There is uncertainty particularly about the ephah and the bath; further discoveries may give more light on these units of capacity.

ABBREVIATIONS IN THE MASTER INDEX

Following is a list of abbreviations in the Master Index:

BOOKS OF THE BIBLE

Genesis . . . . Gn	Isaiah . . . . Is	Romans . . . . Rom
Exodus . . . . Ex	Jeremiah . . . . Jer	1 Corinthians . . . . 1 Cor
Leviticus Lv	Lamentations . . . . Lam	2 Corinthians . . . . 2 Cor
Numbers . . . . Nm	Ezekiel . . . . Ez	Galatians . . . . Gal
Deuteronomy . . . . Dt	Daniel . . . . Dn	Ephesians . . . . Eph
Joshua . . . . Jos	Hosea . . . . Hos	Philippians . . . . Phil
Judges . . . . Jgs	Joel . . . . Jl	Colossians . . . . Col
Ruth . . . . Ru	Amos . . . . Am	1 Thessalonians . . . . 1 Thes
1 Samuel . . . . 1 Sm	Obadiah . . . . Ob	2 Thessalonians . . . . 2 Thes
2 Samuel . . . . 2 Sm	Jonah . . . . Jon	1 Timothy . . . . 1 Tm
1 Kings . . . . 1 Kgs	Micah . . . . Mi	2 Timothy . . . . 2 Tm
2 Kings . . . . 2 Kgs	Nahum . . . . Na	Titus . . . . Ti
1 Chronicles . . . . 1 Chr	Habakkuk . . . . Hb	Philemon . . . . Phlm
2 Chronicles . . . . 2 Chr	Zephaniah . . . . Zep	Hebrews . . . . Heb
Ezra . . . . Ezr	Haggai . . . . Hg	James . . . . Jas
Nehemiah . . . . Neh	Zechariah . . . . Zec	1 Peter . . . . 1 Pt
Esther . . . . Est	Malachi . . . . Mal	2 Peter . . . . 2 Pt
Job . . . . Jb	Matthew . . . . Mt	1 John . . . . 1 Jn
Psalms . . . . Ps	Mark . . . . Mk	2 John . . . . 2 Jn
Proverbs . . . . Prv	Luke . . . . Lk	3 John . . . . 3 Jn
Ecclesiastes . . . . Eccl	John . . . . Jn	Jude . . . . Jude
Song of Songs . . . . Song	Acts . . . . Acts	Revelation . . . . Rv

This is an index to the notes, charts, maps, and personality profiles in the *Life Application Study Bible*. Every entry concerning a note has a Bible reference and a page number; every entry concerning a chart, map, or personality profile has a page number. In some instances, a Bible reference is followed by a number in parentheses to indicate that there is more than one note on that particular Scripture. For example, Rv 1:1(2) means that the reader should look up the second note with the heading of 1:1 in Revelation. In most cases, the entries follow in biblical/canonical order (i.e., from Genesis to Revelation). In some cases, however, the entries follow a chronological order—this is especially true with important people in the Bible. Following the general index are special indexes: Index to Charts, Index to Maps and Index to Personality Profiles. Because of the emphasis on application in the *Life Application Study Bible,* these indexes are helpful guides for personal and group Bible study, sermon preparation, or teaching.

CHAOS

CHARACTER

CHARACTER PROFILES

CHARACTERISTICS

CHARIOTS

CHEEK

CHEMOSH (Moabite god)

CHERISH

CHERUBIM

CHESTPIECE

CHIEF PRIESTS

CHILDBIRTH

CHILDLESSNESS

CHILDREN

FAITHFULNESS

FALSE PROPHET, THE

FALSE TEACHERS, TEACHINGS & PROPHETS

FAME
     see POPULARITY

FAMILY, FAMILIES

FAMILY REDEEMER

FAMILY TREE
     see GENEALOGIES

FAMINE

FANTASIES

FARM, FARMERS, FARMING

FASTING

RELUCTANCE

REMEMBER, REMEMBERING

REMINDERS

REMNANT

RENEWAL

REPENTANCE

REPETITION

REPLACEMENT

REPRESENTATIVES

REPULSIVE

REPUTATION

REQUESTS

RESCUE

RESENTMENT

SIN DESERT

SINAI, MOUNT

SINCERITY

SINGING, SONGS

SINGLE-MINDEDNESS

SINGLENESS

INDEX TO CHARTS

Maps in the Gospels concerning Jesus' ministry are given in chronological order—see Harmony of the Gospels.

INDEX TO PERSONALITY PROFILES

The personality profiles are listed in alphabetical order. The name of the book where the profile appears is also noted.

ABANDON(ED) *to withdraw one's protection, support, or help; to forsake*
he will not *a* or destroy you . . . Dt 4:31
and will not *a* my people Israel. . . . 1 Kgs 6:13
compassion you did not *a* them . . . Neh 9:19
you will not *a* me to the grave, . . . Ps 16:10
you will not *a* me to the grave, . . . Acts 2:27
persecuted, but not *a;* struck down, . . . 2 Cor 4:9
in later times some will *a* the faith . . . 1 Tm 4:1

ABBA *Aramaic for "daddy"; see FATHER*
"*A,* Father," he said, "everything is . . . Mk 14:36
And by him we cry, "*A,* Father." . . . Rom 8:15
the Spirit who calls out, "*A,* Father . . . Gal 4:6

ABHOR(S) *to detest or loathe; see HATE*
of your idols, and I will *a* you. . . . Lv 26:30
Utterly *a* and detest it, . . . Dt 7:26
I *a* the assembly of evildoers . . . Ps 26:5
I hate and *a* falsehood . . . Ps 119:163
and *a* those who rise up against you . . . Ps 139:21
The LORD *a* dishonest scales, . . . Prv 11:1
I *a* the pride of Jacob . . . Am 6:8
You who *a* idols, do you rob . . . Rom 2:22

ABILITY, ABLE *marked by power, intelligence, competence, skill, giftedness*
The LORD was not *a* . . . Nm 14:16
for it is he who gives you the *a* . . . Dt 8:18
that we should be *a* to give . . . 1 Chr 29:14
who is *a* to build a temple for him, . . . 2 Chr 2:6
According to their *a* they gave . . . Ezr 2:69
and gold will not be *a* to save them . . . Ez 7:19
the God we serve is *a* to save us . . . Dn 3:17
walk in pride he is *a* to humble. . . . Dn 4:37
Do you believe that I am *a* . . . Mt 9:28
one talent, each according to his *a* . . . Mt 25:15
will try to enter and will not be *a* to . . . Lk 13:24
to build and was not *a* to finish. . . . Lk 14:30
none of your adversaries will be *a* . . . Lk 21:15
disciples, each according to his *a,* . . . Acts 11:29
will be *a* to separate us . . . Rom 8:39
for the Lord is *a* to make him stand . . . Rom 14:4
to him who is *a* to establish you . . . Rom 16:25
far beyond our *a* to endure, . . . 2 Cor 1:8
were able, and even beyond their *a.* . . . 2 Cor 8:3
God is *a* to make all grace abound . . . 2 Cor 9:8
him who is *a* to do immeasurably . . . Eph 3:20
you may be *a* to stand your ground, . . . Eph 6:13
respectable, hospitable, *a* to teach, . . . 1 Tm 3:2
and am convinced that he is *a* . . . 2 Tm 1:12
he is *a* to help those who are being . . . Heb 2:18
he is *a* to save completely . . . Heb 7:25
To him who is *a* to keep you . . . Jude 1:24
He is *a* to open the scroll . . . Rv 5:5

ABOLISH(ED)(ING) *to do away with; to destroy completely*
I will *a* from the land, . . . Hos 2:18
that I have come to *a* the Law . . . Mt 5:17
the offense of the cross has been *a.* . . . Gal 5:11
by *a* in his flesh the law . . . Eph 2:15

ABOMINATION *anything extremely repulsive to God*
set up the *a* that causes desolation. . . .

Dn 11:31
a that causes desolation is set up, . . . Dn 12:11
the holy place 'the *a* that causes . . . Mt 24:15
you see 'the *a* that causes . . . Mk 13:14

ABOUND(ING) *to have more than enough*
slow to anger, *a* in love . . . Ex 34:6
a in love and forgiving sin . . . Nm 14:18
slow to anger and *a* in love. . . . Neh 9:17
a in love to all who call to you. . . . Ps 86:5
slow to anger, *a* in love . . . Ps 86:15
slow to anger and *a* in love, . . . Jl 2:13
slow to anger and *a* in love, . . . Jon 4:2
able to make all grace *a* to you, . . . 2 Cor 9:8
that your love may *a* more . . . Phil 1:9

ABSTAIN(S) *to refrain from something by one's own choice*
he must *a* from wine and other . . . Nm 6:3
them to *a* from food polluted . . . Acts 15:20
thanks to God; and he who *a,* . . . Rom 14:6
to *a* from sinful desires, . . . 1 Pt 2:11

ABUNDANCE, ABUNDANT *great or plentiful amount*
Seven years of great *a* are coming . . . Gn 41:29
will grant you *a* prosperity . . . Dt 28:11
and *a* showers fall on mankind. . . . Jb 36:28
but you brought us to a place of *a* . . . Ps 66:12
You gave *a* showers, O God; . . . Ps 68:9
gave them water as *a* as the seas; . . . Ps 78:15
I will bless her with *a* provisions; . . . Ps 132:15
will celebrate your *a* goodness . . . Ps 145:7
works his land will have *a* food, . . . Prv 12:11
but the *a* of a rich man . . . Eccl 5:12
and delight in her overflowing *a* . . . Is 66:11
given more, and he will have an *a.* . . . Mt 13:12
consist in the *a* of his possessions. . . . Lk 12:15
who receive God's *a* provision . . . Rom 5:17
Grace and peace be yours in *a.* . . . 1 Pt 1:2
yours in *a* through the knowledge . . . 2 Pt 1:2
peace and love be yours in *a.* . . . Jude 1:2

ACCEPT(ABLE)(ANCE)(ED)(S) *to receive or approve with favor*
will you not be *a?* But if you do not . . . Gn 4:7
Do not *a* a bribe, . . . Ex 23:8
and I will *a* his prayer and not deal . . . Jb 42:8
the LORD *a* my prayer. . . . Ps 6:9
The wise in heart *a* commands, . . . Prv 10:8
Listen to advice and *a* instruction, . . . Prv 19:20
is more *a* to the LORD . . . Prv 21:3
no prophet is *a* in his hometown. . . . Lk 4:24
whoever *a* anyone I send *a* me; . . . Jn 13:20
what will their *a* be but life . . . Rom 11:15
A one another, then, just . . . Rom 15:7
you a gospel other than what you *a,* . . . Gal 1:9
humbly *a* the word planted in you, . . . Jas 1:21

ACCESS *the right to enter or approach*
through whom we have gained *a* . . . Rom 5:2
For through him we both have *a* . . . Eph 2:18

ACCOUNT *description of facts or events; a report*
to give *a* on the day of judgment . . . Mt 12:36
each of us will give an *a* of himself . . . Rom 14:12
of him to whom we must give *a.* . . . Heb 4:13

ACCOUNTABLE *to be held responsible*
and I will hold you *a* for his blood. . . . Ez 3:18
but I will hold the watchman *a* . . . Ez 33:6

and will hold them *a* for my flock. . . . Ez 34:10
Do not hold us *a* for killing . . . Jon 1:14
and the whole world held *a* to God. . . . Rom 3:19

ACCUSATION(S) *a charge of wrongdoing*
Do not entertain an *a* . . . 1 Tm 5:19
do not bring slanderous *a* . . . 2 Pt 2:11

ACCUSE(S), ACCUSING *to charge with wrongdoing*
Let him who *a* God answer him! . . . Jb 40:2
Do not *a* a man for no reason . . . Prv 3:30
and don't *a* people falsely . . . Lk 3:14
and their thoughts now *a,* . . . Rom 2:15
who *a* them before our God day . . . Rv 12:10

ACCUSER *one who makes a charge of wrongdoing*
Your *a* is Moses, on whom your . . . Jn 5:45
For the *a* of our brothers, . . . Rv 12:10

ACKNOWLEDGE(D)(S) *to express gratitude for; to recognize as being valid or having power; to confess*
for he *a* my name. . . . Ps 91:14
in all your ways *a* him, . . . Prv 3:6
Only *a* your guilt . . . Jer 3:13
let us press on to *a* him. . . . Hos 6:3
Whoever *a* me before men, . . . Mt 10:32
a him before my Father in heaven. . . . Mt 10:32
a that God's way was right, . . . Lk 7:29
whoever *a* me before men, . . . Lk 12:8
whoever *a* the Son has the Father . . . 1 Jn 2:23
Every spirit that *a* that Jesus Christ . . . 1 Jn 4:2
If anyone *a* that Jesus is the Son . . . 1 Jn 4:15

ACT(S), ACTION(S) *deed; the process of doing*
tell of all his wonderful *a* . . . 1 Chr 16:9
proclaim your mighty *a,* . . . Ps 71:16
tell of all his wonderful *a.* . . . Ps 105:2
Who can proclaim the mighty *a* . . . Ps 106:2
It is time for you to *a,* O LORD; . . . Ps 119:126
they will tell of your mighty *a.* . . . Ps 145:4
Praise him for his *a* of power; . . . Ps 150:2
all our righteous *a* are like filthy . . . Is 64:6
not to do your '*a* of righteousness' . . . Mt 6:1
wisdom is proved right by her *a.* . . . Mt 11:19
has stirred most of them to *a.* . . . 2 Cor 9:2
Each one should test his own *a.* . . . Gal 6:4
but by their *a* they deny him. . . . Ti 1:16
if it is not accompanied by *a,* . . . Jas 2:17
minds for *a;* be self-controlled; . . . 1 Pt 1:13

ADMONISH(ING) *to warn or give advice*
a and teaching everyone . . . Col 1:28
and *a* one another with all wisdom, . . . Col 3:16
you in the Lord and who *a* you. . . . 1 Thes 5:12

ADOPTED, ADOPTION *to take another's child into one's own family*
as we wait eagerly for our *a* as sons, . . . Rom 8:23
Theirs is the *a* as sons; theirs . . . Rom 9:4
In love he predestined us to be *a* . . . Eph 1:5

ADULTERER(S), ADULTERESS *one who commits adultery*
both the *a* and the adulteress must . . . Lv 20:10
she is loved by another and is an *a.* . . . Hos 3:1
idolaters nor *a* nor male prostitutes . . . 1 Cor 6:9
for murderers, for *a* and perverts, . . . 1 Tm 1:10
God will judge the *a* . . . Heb 13:4

ADULTEROUS *given to physical or spiritual adultery*
in this *a* and sinful generation, . . . Mk 8:38
You *a* people, don't you know that . . . Jas 4:4

ADULTERY *voluntary sexual intercourse between a married person and someone other than the lawful spouse; symbolic of idolatry*
You shall not commit *a* . . . Ex 20:14
that it was said, 'Do not commit *a*.' . . . Mt 5:27
lustfully has already committed *a* . . . Mt 5:28
the divorced woman commits *a* . . . Mt 5:32
murder, *a*, sexual immorality, theft . . . Mt 15:19
marries another woman commits *a* . . . Mt 19:9
do not commit *a*, do not steal, . . . Mt 19:18
theft, murder, *a*, greed, malice, . . . Mk 7:21
woman was caught in the act of *a*. . . . Jn 8:4
of the earth committed *a* with her, . . . Rv 18:3

AFFLICT(ED) *to oppress, trouble, mistreat; to bring low*
and *a* Job with painful sores . . . Jb 2:7
but gives the *a* their rights. . . . Jb 36:6
he does not ignore the cry of the *a*. . . . Ps 9:12
Before I was *a* I went astray, . . . Ps 119:67
and in faithfulness you have *a* me. . . . Ps 119:75
will have compassion on his *a* ones. . . . Is 49:13
smitten by him, and. . . . Is 53:4

AFFLICTION(S) *great suffering that produces sorrow*
bread of *a*, because you left Egypt . . . Dt 16:3
he lifted the needy out of their *a* . . . Ps 107:41
of adversity and the water of *a*, . . . Is 30:20
in the furnace of *a*. . . . Is 48:10
For he does not willingly bring *a* . . . Lam 3:33
patient in *a*, faithful in prayer. . . . Rom 12:12
lacking in regard to Christ's *a*, . . . Col 1:24

AFRAID *to be fearful or apprehensive about an unwanted or uncertain situation; see FEAR*
and I was *a* because I was naked; . . . Gn 3:10
Do not be *a*, for I am with you; . . . Gn 26:24
Then Moses was *a* and thought, . . . Ex 2:14
because he was *a* to look at God. . . . Ex 3:6
Do not be *a*; do not be discouraged . . . Dt 1:21
Do not be fainthearted or *a*; . . . Dt 20:3
of whom shall I be *a*? . . . Ps 27:1
When I am *a*, I will trust in you. . . . Ps 56:3
in God I trust; I will not be *a*. . . . Ps 56:4
lie down, you will not be *a*; . . . Prv 3:24
I will trust and not be *a*. . . . Is 12:2
Do not tremble, do not be *a*. . . . Is 44:8
Do not be *a* of them, for I am . . . Jer 1:8
You of little faith, why are you so *a*. . . Mt 8:26
be *a* of the One who can destroy . . . Mt 10:28
So don't be *a*; you are worth more . . . Mt 10:31
Don't be *a*; just believe. . . . Mk 5:36
they were *a* as they entered . . . Lk 9:34
hearts be troubled and do not be *a*. . . . Jn 14:27
beside me and said, 'Do not be *a*, . . . Acts 27:24
Do not be arrogant, but be *a*. . . . Rom 11:20
Lord is my helper; I will not be *a*. . . . Heb 13:6

AGE(S) *long period of time; a measure of history or culture*
the mystery hidden for long *a* past, . . . Rom 16:25
that in the coming *a* he might show . . . Eph 2:7
which for *a* past was kept hidden . . . Col 1:26
that has been kept hidden for *a* . . . Col 1:26
King of the *a*. . . . Rv 15:3

AGED *having lived a long time; old*
Is not wisdom found among the *a*? . . . Jb 12:12
children are a crown to the *a*, . . . Prv 17:6

ALIEN(S) *strangers, sojourners, foreigners; see STRANGE*
Do not mistreat an *a* . . . Ex 22:21
know how it feels to be *a*, . . . Ex 23:9
are to have the same law for the *a* . . . Lv 24:22

The LORD watches over the *a*. . . Ps 146:9
as *a* and strangers in the world, . . . 1 Pt 2:11

ALIENATED *made enemies of; caused to turn away; estranged*
by law have been *a* from Christ; . . . Gal 5:4
Once you were *a* from God . . . Col 1:21

ALIVE *having life; active; aware*
LORD brings death and makes *a*; . . . 1 Sm 2:6
vision of angels, who said he was *a*. . . . Lk 24:23
convincing proofs that he was *a*. . . . Acts 1:3
but *a* to God in Christ Jesus. . . . Rom 6:11
so in Christ all will be made *a*. . . . 1 Cor 15:22
made us *a* with Christ . . . Eph 2:5

ALPHA *first letter of Greek alphabet; figurative of beginning or first one*
I am the *A* and the Omega, . . . Rv 1:8
I am the *A* and the Omega, . . . Rv 21:6
I am the *A* and the Omega, . . . Rv 22:13

ALTAR *place of worship where sacrifices are offered or incense burned*
Then Noah built an *a* to the LORD . . . Gn 8:20
So he built an *a* there to the LORD . . . Gn 12:7
where he built an *a* to the LORD . . . Gn 13:18
Abraham built an *a* there . . . Gn 22:9
Isaac built an *a* there and called . . . Gn 26:25
and build an *a* there to God, . . . Gn 35:1
Moses built an *a* and called it . . . Ex 17:15
Build an *a* of acacia wood, . . . Ex 27:1
Make an *a* of acacia wood . . . Ex 30:1
They made the *a* of incense out . . . Ex 37:25
an *a* to the LORD your God, an *a* . . . Dt 27:5
on Mount Ebal an *a* to the LORD, . . . Jos 8:30
built an imposing *a* there . . . Jos 22:10
So Gideon built an *a* to the LORD . . . Jgs 6:24
the next day the people built an *a* . . . Jgs 21:4
he built an *a* there to the LORD. . . . 1 Sm 7:17
Then Saul built an *a* to the LORD; . . . 1 Sm 14:35
David built an *a* to the LORD . . . 2 Sm 24:25
sacrifices on the *a* he had built . . . 1 Kgs 12:33
O *a*, *a*! This is what the LORD . . . 1 Kgs 13:2
He set up an *a* for Baal . . . 1 Kgs 16:32
he repaired the *a* of the LORD . . . 1 Kgs 18:30
So Uriah the priest built an *a* . . . 2 Kgs 16:11
David built an *a* to the LORD . . . 1 Chr 21:26
made a bronze *a* twenty cubits . . . 2 Chr 4:1
the golden *a*; the tables . . . 2 Chr 4:19
He repaired the *a* of the LORD . . . 2 Chr 15:8
You must worship before one *a* . . . 2 Chr 32:12
he restored the *a* of the LORD . . . 2 Chr 33:16
to build the *a* of the God of Israel . . . Ezr 3:2
taken with tongs from the *a*. . . . Is 6:6
the *a* was in front of the temple. . . . Ez 40:47
if you are offering your gift at the *a* . . . Mt 5:23
found an *a* with this inscription: . . . Acts 17:23
We have an *a* from which those . . . Heb 13:10
I saw under the *a* the souls . . . Rv 6:9

AMBASSADOR(S) *representative; spokesperson*
We are therefore Christ's *a*, . . . 2 Cor 5:20
for which I am an *a* in chains. . . . Eph 6:20

AMBITION *aspiration to achieve a particular goal, good or bad*
It has always been my *a* . . . Rom 15:20
fits of rage, selfish *a*, dissensions, . . . Gal 5:20
preach Christ out of selfish *a*, . . . Phil 1:17
Do nothing out of selfish *a* . . . Phil 2:3
Make it your *a* to lead a quiet life, . . . 1 Thes 4:11
and selfish *a* in your hearts, . . . Jas 3:14
where you have envy and selfish *a*, . . . Jas 3:16

ANGEL(S) *spiritual being; messenger of God*
The *a* of the LORD found Hagar . . . Gn 16:7
But the *a* of the LORD called out . . . Gn 22:11
I am sending an *a* ahead of you . . . Ex 23:20
When the donkey saw the *a* . . . Nm 22:23
The *a* of the LORD went up . . . Jgs 2:1

Gideon realized that it was the *a* . . . Jgs 6:22
Manoah said to the *a* of the LORD . . . Jgs 13:15
The *a* of the LORD was then . . . 2 Sm 24:16
The *a* of the LORD came back . . . 1 Kgs 19:7
That night the *a* of the LORD went . . . 2 Kgs 19:35
The *a* of the LORD encamps . . . Ps 34:7
command his *a* concerning you . . . Ps 91:11
He struggled with the *a* . . . Hos 12:4
an *a* of the Lord appeared . . . Mt 2:13
command his *a* concerning you, . . . Mt 4:6
of the age, and the harvesters are *a*. . . . Mt 13:39
The *a* will come and separate . . . Mt 13:49
For I tell you that their *a* . . . Mt 18:10
prepared for the devil and his *a* . . . Mt 25:41
for an *a* of the Lord came . . . Mt 28:2
God sent the *a* Gabriel . . . Lk 1:26
An *a* of the Lord appeared to them, . . . Lk 2:9
command his *a* concerning you . . . Lk 4:10
for they are like the *a*. . . . Lk 20:36
An *a* from heaven appeared to him . . . Lk 22:43
his face was like the face of an *a*. . . . Acts 6:15
Suddenly an *a* of the Lord . . . Acts 12:7
you not know that we will judge *a*? . . . 1 Cor 6:3
in the tongues of men and of *a*, . . . 1 Cor 13:1
Satan himself masquerades as an *a* . . . 2 Cor 11:14
or an *a* from heaven should preach . . . Gal 1:8
and the worship of *a* disqualify you . . . Col 2:18
as much superior to the *a* . . . Heb 1:4
Let all God's *a* worship him. . . . Heb 1:6
Are not all *a* ministering spirits . . . Heb 1:14
made him a little lower than the *a*; . . . Heb 2:7
some people have entertained *a* . . . Heb 13:2
Even *a* long to look . . . 1 Pt 1:12
For if God did not spare *a* . . . 2 Pt 2:4
a who did not keep their positions . . . Jude 1:6

ANGER, ANGRY *strong feeling of displeasure or hostility*
You unleashed your burning *a*; . . . Ex 15:7
My *a* will be aroused, and I will kill . . . Ex 22:24
alone so that my *a* may burn . . . Ex 32:10
Turn from your fierce *a*; relent . . . Ex 32:12
his *a* burned and he threw . . . Ex 32:19
slow to *a*, abounding in love . . . Ex 34:6
then in my *a* I will be hostile . . . Lv 26:28
slow to *a*, abounding in love . . . Nm 14:18
has turned my *a* away . . . Nm 25:11
LORD's *a* was aroused that day . . . Nm 32:10
feared the *a* and wrath . . . Dt 9:19
In furious *a* and in great wrath . . . Dt 29:28
Burning with *a*, he went up . . . Jgs 14:19
David burned with *a* . . . 2 Sm 12:5
Great is the LORD's *a* that burns . . . 2 Kgs 22:13
slow to *a* and abounding in love. . . . Neh 9:17
Kiss the Son, lest he be *a* . . . Ps 2:12
For his *a* lasts only a moment, . . . Ps 30:5
Time after time he restrained his *a* . . . Ps 78:38
slow to *a*, abounding in love . . . Ps 86:15
We are consumed by your *a* . . . Ps 90:7
For forty years I was *a* . . . Ps 95:10
slow to *a*, abounding in love. . . . Ps 103:8
a harsh word stirs up *a*. . . . Prv 15:1
A fool gives full vent to his *a*, . . . Prv 29:11
An *a* man stirs up dissension, . . . Prv 29:22
so stirring up *a* produces strife. . . . Prv 30:33
slow to *a* and abounding in love, . . . Jon 4:2
But I tell you that anyone who is *a* . . . Mt 5:22
"In your *a* do not sin": Do not let . . . Eph 4:26
slow to speak and slow to become *a* . . . Jas 1:19
man's *a* does not bring about . . . Jas 1:20

ANGUISH *great pain or suffering*
In my *a* I cried to the LORD, . . . Ps 118:5
Oh, my *a*, my *a*! . . . Jer 4:19
a day of distress and *a*, . . . Zep 1:15
nations will be in *a* and perplexity . . . Lk 21:25
in *a*, he prayed more earnestly, . . . Lk 22:44
and unceasing *a* in my heart. . . . Rom 9:2

ANOINT(ED)(ING) *to pour oil upon; used for healing or consecration to sacred duty; used for burial; figurative for divine appointment; see OIL*
use it to a the Tent of Meeting, . . . Ex 30:26
A Aaron and his sons . . . Ex 30:30
some of the a oil on Aaron's head . . . Lv 8:12
A him leader over my people Israel . . . 1 Sm 9:16
to a you king over his people Israel; . . . 1 Sm 15:1
what the LORD says: I a you king . . . 2 Kgs 9:3
Do not touch my a ones; . . . 1 Chr 16:22
a him before the LORD to be ruler . . . 1 Chr 29:22
You a my head with oil; . . . Ps 23:5
by a you with the oil of joy. . . . Ps 45:7
Do not touch my a ones; . . . Ps 105:15
because the LORD has a me . . . Is 61:1
prophecy and to a the most holy. . . . Dn 9:24
the A One will be cut off . . . Dn 9:26
because he has a me . . . Lk 4:18
how God a Jesus of Nazareth . . . Acts 10:38
by a you with the oil of joy. . . . Heb 1:9
and a him with oil in the name . . . Jas 5:14
you have an a from the Holy One, . . . 1 Jn 2:20

ANTICHRIST *opponent of Christ; the personification of evil*
have heard that the a is coming, . . . 1 Jn 2:18
a man is the a he denies . . . 1 Jn 2:22
of the a, which you have heard is . . . 1 Jn 4:3
person is the deceiver and the a. . . . 2 Jn 1:7

ANXIETY, ANXIOUS *uneasiness; fearful or worried*
An a heart weighs a man down, . . . Prv 12:25
drunkenness and the a of life, . . . Lk 21:34
Do not be a about anything, . . . Phil 4:6
Cast all your a on him . . . 1 Pt 5:7

APOSTLE(S) *messenger or "sent one"; generally but not exclusively applied to the original 12 disciples of Christ and to Paul*
twelve designating them a . . . Mk 3:14
I will send them prophets and a, . . . Lk 11:49
so he was added to the eleven a. . . . Acts 1:26
signs were done by the a. . . . Acts 2:43
as I am the a to the Gentiles, . . . Rom 11:13
Am I not an a? Have I not seen . . . 1 Cor 9:1
God has appointed first of all a, . . . 1 Cor 12:28
For I am the least of the a . . . 1 Cor 15:9
masquerading as a of Christ. . . . 2 Cor 11:13
The things that mark an a signs, . . . 2 Cor 12:12
of Peter as an a to the Jews, . . . Gal 2:8
built on the foundation of the a . . . Eph 2:20
It was he who gave some to be a, . . . Eph 4:11
was appointed a herald and an a . . . 1 Tm 2:7
I was appointed a herald and an a . . . 2 Tm 1:11
a and high priest whom we confess. . . . Heb 3:1
names of the twelve a of the Lamb. . . . Rv 21:14

APPEAR(ED)(ING)(S) *to come into sight or public view*
to one place, and let dry ground a. . . . Gn 1:9
I a in the cloud over the atonement . . . Lv 16:2
glory of the LORD a at the Tent . . . Nm 14:10
Who can stand when he a? . . . Mal 3:2
an angel of the Lord a to him . . . Mt 1:20
of the Son of Man will a in the sky, . . . Mt 24:30
false prophets will a and perform . . . Mk 13:22
An angel of the Lord a to them, . . . Lk 2:9
of God was going to a at once. . . . Lk 19:11
and that he a to Peter, . . . 1 Cor 15:5
we must all a before the judgment . . . 2 Cor 5:10
When Christ, who is your life, a, . . . Col 3:4
until the a of our Lord Jesus Christ, . . . 1 Tm 6:14
through the a of our Savior, . . . 2 Tm 1:10
to all who have longed for his a. . . . 2 Tm 4:8
the glorious a of our great God . . . Ti 2:13
now to a for us in God's presence. . . . Heb 9:24
And when the Chief Shepherd a, . . . 1 Pt 5:4

But we know that when he a, . . . 1 Jn 3:2

APPEARANCE(S) *outward or visible aspect of someone or something*
Man looks at the outward a, . . . 1 Sm 16:7
his a was so disfigured beyond that . . . Is 52:14
in his a that we should desire him. . . . Is 53:2
Stop judging by mere a, . . . Jn 7:24
God does not judge by external a . . . Gal 2:6

APPOINT(ED) *to ordain or designate*
a them to have authority over you . . . Dt 1:15
a your love and faithfulness . . . Ps 61:7
I was a from eternity, . . . Prv 8:23
an end will still come at the a time. . . . Dn 11:27
For the revelation awaits an a time; . . . Hb 2:3
Chose you and a you to go . . . Jn 15:16
At the a time I will return, . . . Rom 9:9
For God did not a us . . . 1 Thes 5:9
and a elders in every town, . . . Ti 1:5

APPROVAL, APPROVE(D)(S) *to have or express a favorable opinion of*
Your journey has the LORD's a. . . . Jgs 18:6
the Father has placed his seal of a. . . . Jn 6:27
if you know his will and a . . . Rom 2:18
and a what God's will is . . . Rom 12:2
pleasing to God and a by men. . . . Rom 14:18
Greet Apelles, tested and a . . . Rom 16:10
to show which of you have God's a . . . 1 Cor 11:19
who commends himself who is a, . . . 2 Cor 10:18
trying to win the a of men, . . . Gal 1:10
as men a by God to be entrusted . . . 1 Thes 2:4
to present yourself to God as one a, . . . 2 Tm 2:15

ARK *commonly, a portable wooden chest or box; of Noah, a large boat; of the covenant, a sacred housing for the law of Moses*
So make yourself an a . . . Gn 6:14
and put in the a the Testimony, . . . Ex 25:21
put the tablets in the a I had made, . . . Dt 10:5
The a of God was captured, . . . 1 Sm 4:11
that the a remained at Kiriath . . . 1 Sm 7:2
They brought the a of the LORD . . . 2 Sm 6:17
There was nothing in the a . . . 1 Kgs 8:9
out his hand to steady the a, . . . 1 Chr 13:9
Put the sacred a in the temple that . . . 2 Chr 35:3
This a contained the gold jar . . . Heb 9:4
in holy fear built an a . . . Heb 11:7
within his temple was seen the a . . . Rv 11:19

ARM(S) *upper limb of the body; figurative of power or might*
Is the LORD's a too short? . . . Nm 11:23
hand and an outstretched a, . . . Dt 4:34
mighty hand and outstretched a, . . . Dt 7:19
underneath are the everlasting a. . . . Dt 33:27
it was your right hand, your a, . . . Ps 44:3
his right hand and his holy a . . . Ps 98:1
her a are strong for her tasks. . . . Prv 31:17
He gathers the lambs in his a . . . Is 40:11
outstretched a I made the earth . . . Jer 27:5
And he took the children in his a, . . . Mk 10:16
strengthen your feeble a . . . Heb 12:12
a yourselves also with the same . . . 1 Pt 4:1

ARMIES, ARMY *large band of men organized and armed for war; any large multitude devoted to a cause*
Philistine that he should defy the a . . . 1 Sm 17:26
No king is saved by the size of his a . . . Ps 33:16
a large and mighty a comes, . . . Jl 2:2
a of heaven were following him, . . . Rv 19:14

ARMOR *weapons of war or self-defense; figurative of spiritual resources*
deeds of darkness and put on the a . . . Rom 13:12
Put on the full a of God . . . Eph 6:11

Therefore put on the full a of God, . . . Eph 6:13

ARROGANCE, ARROGANT *feeling or attitude of superiority shown by presumptuous manners or claims; see PRIDE*
or let your mouth speak such a, . . . 1 Sm 2:3
The a cannot stand . . . Ps 5:5
May the a be put to shame . . . Ps 119:78
I hate pride and a, . . . Prv 8:13
A lips are unsuited to a fool . . . Prv 17:7
a man—"Mocker" is his name; . . . Prv 21:24
lewdness, envy, slander, a and folly . . . Mk 7:22
God-haters, insolent, a . . . Rom 1:30
Do not be a, but be afraid. . . . Rom 11:20
slander, gossip, a and disorder. . . . 2 Cor 12:20
in this present world not to be a . . . 1 Tm 6:17

ASCEND(ED)(ING) *to go or move upward*
and the angels of God were a . . . Gn 28:12
Who will a into heaven to get it . . . Dt 30:12
Who may a the hill of the LORD? . . . Ps 24:3
When you a on high, . . . Ps 68:18
I will a to heaven; . . . Is 14:13
I will a above the tops of the clouds . . . Is 14:14
and the angels of God a . . . Jn 1:51
of Man a to where he was before! . . . Jn 6:62
For David did not a to heaven, . . . Acts 2:34
'Who will a into heaven?' " . . . Rom 10:6
When he a on high, . . . Eph 4:8

ASHAMED *feeling of shame, guilt, or disgrace; see SHAME*
If anyone is a of me and my words . . . Mk 8:38
I am not a of the gospel, . . . Rom 1:16
So do not be a to testify about our . . . 2 Tm 1:8
who does not need to be a . . . 2 Tm 2:15

ASHES *burnt residue; denotes grief, repentance, or humiliation*
and repent in dust and a. . . . Jb 42:6
ago in sackcloth and a. . . . Mt 11:21

ASLEEP *state of body rest; figurative for dull to spiritual things; see SLEEP*
who have fallen a in Christ are lost. . . . 1 Cor 15:18
be ignorant about those who fall a, . . . 1 Thes 4:13

ASSURANCE, ASSURED *characterized by full conviction or confidence; made certain*
the will of God, mature and fully a. . . . Col 4:12
with a sincere heart in full a of faith . . . Heb 10:22

ASTRAY *wandering; lost; on the wrong path; see STRAYED*
Before I was afflicted I went a, . . . Ps 119:67
ignores correction leads others a. . . . Prv 10:17
whoever is led a by them is not . . . Prv 20:1
We all, like sheep, have gone a, . . . Is 53:6
their shepherds have led them a . . . Jer 50:6
you so that you will not go a. . . . Jn 16:1
For you were like sheep going a, . . . 1 Pt 2:25
do not let anyone lead you a. . . . 1 Jn 3:7

ATONE(D) *to reconcile; to make amends for an offense*
to the LORD to a for your lives. . . . Ex 30:15
And the bloodshed will be a for. . . . Dt 21:8
guilt of Eli's house will never be a . . . 1 Sm 3:14
for a sin offering to a for all Israel, . . . 2 Chr 29:24
faithfulness sin is a for; . . . Prv 16:6
guilt is taken away and your sin a . . . Is 6:7
your dying day this sin will not be a . . . Is 22:14
then, will Jacob's guilt be a for, . . . Is 27:9
an end to sin, to a for wickedness, . . . Dn 9:24

ATONEMENT *the reconciliation of God and mankind; making amends for an offense; cleansing*
Make an a cover of pure gold . . . Ex 25:17
Once a year Aaron shall make a . . . Ex 30:10
it is the blood that makes a . . . Lv 17:11
this seventh month is the Day of A. . . . Lv 23:27

and made *a* for the Israelites. . . . Nm 25:13
presented him as a sacrifice of *a*, . . . Rom 3:25
that he might make *a* for the sins . . . Heb 2:17

ATTITUDE(S) *state of mind or feeling with regard to some matter*
new in the *a* of your minds; . . . Eph 4:23
Your *a* should be the same . . . Phil 2:5
it judges the thoughts and *a* . . . Heb 4:12
yourselves also with the same *a*, . . . 1 Pt 4:1

AUTHORITIES, AUTHORITY *persons having rightful power; the right to govern; the freedom or ability to act*
because he taught as one who had *a* . . .
    Mt 7:29
the Son of Man has *a* on earth . . . Mt 9:6
All in heaven and on earth has . . . Mt 28:18
a to lay it down and *a* . . . Jn 10:18
the Father has set by his own *a*. . . . Acts 1:7
that the law has *a* over a man only . . . Rom 7:1
a that exist have been established . . . Rom 13:1
for the *a* are God's servants, . . . Rom 13:6
to have a sign of *a* on her head. . . . 1 Cor 11:10
he has destroyed all dominion, *a* . . . 1 Cor
    15:24
and *a* in the heavenly realms, . . . Eph 3:10
but against the rulers, against the *a*, . . . Eph
    6:12
thrones or powers or rulers or *a*; . . . Col 1:16
having disarmed the powers and *a*, . . . Col 2:15
for kings and all those in *a*, . . . 1 Tm 2:2
to teach or to have *a* over a man; . . . 1 Tm 2:12
Encourage and rebuke with all *a*. . . . Ti 2:15
people to be subject to rulers and *a*, . . . Ti 3:1
your leaders and submit to their *a*. . . . Heb
    13:17
a and powers in submission to him. . . . 1 Pt
    3:22

AVENGE(S), AVENGING *to take revenge or punish an evildoer; see VENGEANCE*
sword upon you to *a* the breaking . . . Lv 26:25
It is mine to *a*; I will repay. . . . Dt 32:35
and from *a* yourself with your own . . . 1 Sm
    25:26
O LORD, the God who *a*, . . . Ps 94:1
The LORD is a jealous and *a* God; . . . Na 1:2
It is mine to *a*; I will repay, . . . Rom 12:19
It is mine to *a*; I will repay, . . . Heb 10:30
of the earth and *a* our blood? . . . Rv 6:10

AVENGER *someone who takes revenge or punishes an evildoer*
the *a* of blood may kill the accused . . .
    Nm 35:27
find protection from the *a* of blood. . . . Jos 20:3
to silence the foe and the *a*. . . . Ps 8:2

AVOID(S) *to depart from or stay away from*
A it, do not travel on it; . . . Prv 4:15
of the LORD a man *a* evil. . . . Prv 16:6
The highway of the upright *a* evil; . . . Prv 16:17
It is to a man's honor to *a* strife, . . . Prv 20:3
so *a* a man who talks too much. . . . Prv 20:19
who fears God will *a* all extremes. . . . Eccl 7:18
you should *a* sexual immorality; . . . 1 Thes 4:3
A every kind of evil. . . . 1 Thes 5:22
A godless chatter, because those . . . 2 Tm 2:16
But *a* foolish controversies . . . Ti 3:9

AWE *amazement; reverential fear*
So all the people stood in *a* . . . 1 Sm 12:18
they held the king in *a*, . . . 1 Kgs 3:28
Dominion and *a* belong to God; . . . Jb 25:2
I stand in *a* of your laws. . . . Ps 119:120
Therefore stand in *a* of God. . . . Eccl 5:7
will stand in *a* of the God of Israel. . . . Is 29:23
and have no *a* of me, . . . Jer 2:19
they will be in *a* and will tremble . . . Jer 33:9
I stand in *a* of your deeds, . . . Hb 3:2
and stood in *a* of my name. . . . Mal 2:5
they were filled with *a*; . . . Mt 9:8
The neighbors were all filled with *a* . . . Lk 1:65

They were filled with *a* and said, . . . Lk 5:26
They were all filled with *a* . . . Lk 7:16
Everyone was filled with *a*, . . . Acts 2:43
acceptably with reverence and *a*, . . . Heb 12:28

AWESOME *amazing; characterized by reverential fear*
and said, "How *a* is this place! . . . Gn 28:17
a in glory, . . . Ex 15:11
among will see how *a* is the work . . . Ex 34:10
or by great and *a* deeds, . . . Dt 4:34
is among you, is a great and *a* God. . . . Dt 7:21
the great God, mighty and *a*, . . . Dt 10:17
revere this glorious and *a* name . . . Dt 28:58
performed the *a* deeds that Moses . . . Dt 34:12
like an angel of God, very *a*. . . . Jgs 13:6
a wonders by driving out nations . . . 2 Sm 7:23
a wonders by driving out nations . . . 1 Chr
    17:21
of heaven, the great and *a* God, . . . Neh 1:5
and *a*, and fight for your brothers, . . . Neh 4:14
the great, mighty and *a* God, . . . Neh 9:32
again display your *a* power . . . Jb 10:16
God comes in *a* majesty. . . . Jb 37:22
let your right hand display *a* deeds. . . . Ps 45:4
How *a* is the LORD Most High, . . . Ps 47:2
us with *a* deeds of righteousness, . . . Ps 65:5
to God, "How *a* are your deeds! . . . Ps 66:3
You are *a*, O God, . . . Ps 68:35
he is more *a* than all who surround . . . Ps 89:7
praise your great and *a* name . . . Ps 99:3
and *a* deeds by the Red Sea. . . . Ps 106:22
holy and *a* is his name. . . . Ps 111:9
of the power of your *a* works, . . . Ps 145:6
when you did *a* things that we did . . . Is 64:3
Their rims were high and *a*, . . . Ez 1:18
dazzling statue, *a* in appearance. . . . Dn 2:31
O Lord, the great and *a* God, . . . Dn 9:4
The LORD will be *a* to them . . . Zep 2:11

BABIES, BABY *infant child; youngest of a group; figurative of immature Christians; see INFANTS*
The *b* jostled each other within her . . . Gn 25:22
She opened it and saw the *b*. . . . Ex 2:6
So the woman took the *b* . . . Ex 2:9
I had a *b* while she was there . . . 1 Kgs 3:17
Can a mother forget the *b* . . . Is 49:15
the *b* leaped in her womb, . . . Lk 1:41
the time came for the *b* to be born, . . . Lk 2:6
You will find a *b* wrapped in strips . . . Lk 2:12
the *b*, who was lying in the manger. . . . Lk 2:16
also bringing *b* to Jesus . . . Lk 18:15
when her *b* is born she forgets . . . Jn 16:21
them to throw out their newborn *b* . . . Acts
    7:19
Like newborn *b*, crave pure . . . 1 Pt 2:2

BACKSLIDING(S) *moral lapse; see UNFAITHFUL*
your *b* will rebuke you. . . . Jer 2:19
I will cure you of *b*. . . . Jer 3:22
and their *b* many. . . . Jer 5:6
For our *b* is great; . . . Jer 14:7
You keep on *b*. . . . Jer 15:6
them from all their sinful *b*, . . . Ez 37:23

BAPTISM(S), BAPTIZE(D), BAPTIZING *Christian sacrament; a ritual washing with water, symbolizing a cleansing from sin, linked with repentance and admission into the community of faith; symbolic for being filled with the Holy Spirit; see WASH*
He will *b* you with the Holy Spirit . . . Mt 3:11
b them in the name of the Father . . . Mt 28:19
and preaching a *b* of repentance . . . Mk 1:4
believes and is *b* will be saved, . . . Mk 16:16
because they had been *b* by John. . . . Lk 7:29
But I have a *b* to undergo, . . . Lk 12:50
John's *b* was it from heaven, . . . Lk 20:4
spent some time with them, and *b*. . . . Jn 3:22
to the place where John had been *b* . . .

Jn 10:40
For John *b* with water, . . . Acts 1:5
beginning from John's *b* . . . Acts 1:22
Repent and be *b*, every one of you, . . . Acts 2:38
Why shouldn't I be *b*? . . . Acts 8:36
after the *b* that John preached . . . Acts 10:37
you will be *b* with the Holy Spirit. . . . Acts 11:16
and *b* to all the people of Israel. . . . Acts 13:24
members of her household were *b*, . . . Acts
    16:15
he and all his family were *b*. . . . Acts 16:33
though he knew only the *b* of John. . . . Acts
    18:25
did you receive?" "John's *b*," . . . Acts 19:3
Were you *b* into the name of Paul? . . . 1 Cor
    1:13
They were all *b* into Moses . . . 1 Cor 10:2
For we were all *b* by one Spirit . . . 1 Cor 12:13
what will those do who are *b* . . . 1 Cor 15:29
with him through *b* into death . . . Rom 6:4
one Lord, one faith, one *b*; . . . Eph 4:5
having been buried with him in *b* . . . Col 2:12
instruction about *b*, the laying . . . Heb 6:2

BARREN *unproductive, unfruitful, especially in childbearing*
Sarai was *b*; she had no children. . . . Gn 11:30
her womb, but Rachel was *b*. . . . Gn 29:31
He settles the *b* woman . . . Ps 113:9
Sing, O *b* woman . . . Is 54:1
children, because Elizabeth was *b*; . . . Lk 1:7
Be glad, O *b* woman, . . . Gal 4:27
and Sarah herself was *b* . . . Heb 11:11

BEAR(ING)(S) *to carry or support; to suffer under the weight of; to give as testimony*
punishment is more than I can *b*. . . . Gn 4:13
house I have built *b* your Name. . . . 1 Kgs 8:43
like a burden too heavy to *b*. . . . Ps 38:4
who daily *b* our burdens. . . . Ps 68:19
and he will *b* their iniquities. . . . Is 53:11
A good tree cannot *b* bad fruit, . . . Mt 7:18
branch that does *b* fruit he prunes . . . Jn 15:2
glory, that you *b* much fruit, . . . Jn 15:8
in order that we might *b* fruit . . . Rom 7:4
ought to *b* with the failings . . . Rom 15:1
tempted beyond what you can *b*. . . . 1 Cor
    10:13
b with one another in love. . . . Eph 4:2
b fruit in every good work, . . . Col 1:10
B with each other and forgive . . . Col 3:13
outside the camp, *b* the disgrace he . . . Heb
    13:13

BEAST(S) *evil creature that ravishes the earth in the end times*
Four great *b*, each different . . . Dn 7:3
him calculate the number of the *b*, . . . Rv 13:18
people who had the mark of the *b* . . . Rv 16:2
who had received the mark of the *b* . . .
    Rv 19:20

BEAUTIFUL, BEAUTY *lovely, handsome, or pleasing to the eye; excellence*
that the daughters of men were *b*, . . . Gn 6:2
I know what a *b* woman you are. . . . Gn 12:11
The girl was very *b*, a virgin; . . . Gn 24:16
of Rebekah, because she is *b*. . . . Gn 26:7
Rachel was lovely in form, and *b*. . . . Gn 29:17
that bears *b* fawns. . . . Gn 49:21
How *b* are your tents, O Jacob, . . . Nm 24:5
among the captives a *b* woman . . . Dt 21:11
saw in the plunder a *b* robe . . . Jos 7:21
was an intelligent and *b* woman, . . . 1 Sm 25:3
The woman was very *b*, . . . 2 Sm 11:2
the *b* sister of Absalom son . . . 2 Sm 13:1
and she became a *b* woman. . . . 2 Sm 14:27
throughout Israel for a *b* girl . . . 1 Kgs 1:3
The girl was very *b*; she took care . . . 1 Kgs 1:4
order to display her *b* to the people . . . Est 1:11
for *b* young virgins for the king. . . . Est 2:2
her with her *b* treatments . . . Est 2:9
Can you bind the *b* Pleiades? . . . Jb 38:31

land were there found women as *b* . . . Jb 42:15
to gaze upon the *b* of the LORD . . . Ps 27:4
LORD's enemies will be like the *b* . . . Ps 37:20
The king is enthralled by your *b*; . . . Ps 45:11
It is *b* in its loftiness, . . . Ps 48:2
From Zion, perfect in *b*, . . . Ps 50:2
lust in your heart after her *b* . . . Prv 6:25
is a *b* woman who shows no . . . Prv 11:22
filled with rare and *b* treasures. . . . Prv 24:4
is deceptive, and *b* is fleeting; . . . Prv 31:30
He has made everything *b* . . . Eccl 3:11
If you do not know, most *b* . . . Song 1:8
my *b* one, and come with me. . . . Song 2:10
How *b* you are, my darling! . . . Song 4:1
most *b* of women? . . . Song 5:9
most *b* of women? . . . Song 6:1
How *b* you are and how pleasing, . . . Song 7:6
instead of *b*, branding. . . . Is 3:24
of the LORD will be *b* . . . Is 4:2
to the fading flower, his glorious *b*, . . . Is 28:1
Your eyes will see the king in his *b* . . . Is 33:17
How *b* on the mountains . . . Is 52:7
He had no *b* or majesty . . . Is 53:2
to bestow on them a crown of *b* . . . Is 61:3
the most *b* inheritance . . . Jer 3:19
so *b* and delicate. . . . Jer 6:2
with fruit *b* in form. . . . Jer 11:16
Egypt is a *b* heifer, . . . Jer 46:20
the perfection of *b*, . . . Lam 2:15
They were proud of their *b* jewelry . . . Ez 7:20
and became the most *b* of jewels. . . . Ez 16:7
and a *b* crown on your head. . . . Ez 16:12
But you trusted in your *b* . . . Ez 16:15
lofty shrines and degraded your *b*, . . . Ez 16:25
and honey, the most *b* of all lands. . . . Ez 20:6
and honey, most *b* of all lands . . . Ez 20:15
and *b* crowns on their heads. . . . Ez 23:42
I am perfect in *b*. . . . Ez 27:3
they brought your *b* to perfection. . . . Ez 27:11
draw their swords against your *b* . . . Ez 28:7
with *b* branches overshadowing . . . Ez 31:3
It was majestic in *b*, . . . Ez 31:7
who sings love songs with a *b* voice . . .
   Ez 33:32
Its leaves were *b*, its fruit abundant . . . Dn 4:12
with *b* leaves and abundant fruit, . . . Dn 4:21
to the east and toward the *B* Land. . . . Dn 8:9
will establish himself in the *B* Land . . . Dn 11:16
He will also invade the *B* Land. . . . Dn 11:41
How attractive and *b* they will be! . . . Zec 9:17
which look *b* on the outside . . . Mt 23:27
She has done a *b* thing to me. . . . Mt 26:10
temple was adorned with *b* stones . . . Lk 21:5
carried to the temple gate called *B*, . . . Acts 3:2
at the temple gate called *B*, . . . Acts 3:10
How *b* are the feet . . . Rom 10:15
blossom falls and its *b* is destroyed. . . . Jas
   1:11
Your *b* should not come . . . 1 Pt 3:3

BEGINNING *a point of coming into existence; a
starting point*
In the *b* God created the heavens . . . Gn 1:1
In the *b* you laid the foundations . . . Ps 102:25
of the LORD is the *b* of wisdom; . . . Ps 111:10
of the LORD is the *b* of knowledge . . . Prv 1:7
of the LORD is the *b* of wisdom, . . . Prv 9:10
fathom what God has done from *b* . . . Eccl 3:11
Has it not been told you from the *b* . . . Is 40:21
I make known the end from the *b*, . . . Is 46:10
All these are the *b* of birth pains. . . . Mt 24:8
investigated everything from the *b*, . . . Lk 1:3
In the *b* was the Word, . . . Jn 1:1
That which was from the *b*, . . . 1 Jn 1:1
and the Omega, the *B* and the End. . . . Rv 21:6
and the Last, the *B* and the End. . . . Rv 22:13

BELIEVE(D)(S), BELIEVING *to trust in; to hold
a firm conviction about*
Abram *b* the LORD, and he . . . Gn 15:6
What if they do not *b* me . . . Ex 4:1
signs before the people, and they *b*. . . . Ex 4:31

I did not *b* these things until I came . . . 1 Kgs
   10:7
But I did not *b* what they said . . . 2 Chr 9:6
of his wonders, they did not *b*. . . . Ps 78:32
A simple man *b* anything, . . . Prv 14:15
Who has *b* our message . . . Is 53:1
The Ninevites *b* God. . . . Jon 3:5
that you would not *b*, . . . Hb 1:5
one of these little ones who *b* in me . . . Mt 18:6
If you *b*, you will receive whatever . . . Mt 21:22
from the cross, and we will *b* in him . . .
   Mt 27:42
Repent and *b* the good news! . . . Mk 1:15
ruler, "Don't be afraid; just *b*." . . . Mk 5:36
is possible for him who *b*. . . . Mk 9:23
one of these little ones who *b* in me . . . Mk 9:42
b that what he says will happen, . . . Mk 11:23
the cross, that we may see and *b*. . . . Mk 15:32
Whoever *b* and is baptized will be . . . Mk 16:16
is she who has *b* that what the Lord . . . Lk 1:45
so that they may not *b* and be saved. . . .
   Lk 8:12
just *b*, and she will be healed. . . . Lk 8:50
to *b* all that the prophets have . . . Lk 24:25
that through him all men might *b*. . . . Jn 1:7
to those who *b* in his name, . . . Jn 1:12
that whoever *b* in him shall not . . . Jn 3:16
b him who sent me has eternal life . . . Jn 5:24
for you do not *b* the one he sent. . . . Jn 5:38
If you *b* Moses, you would believe . . . Jn 5:46
to *b* in the one he has sent. . . . Jn 6:29
he who *b* in me will never be . . . Jn 6:35
and *b* in him shall have eternal life, . . . Jn 6:40
he who *b* has everlasting life. . . . Jn 6:47
his own brothers did not *b* in him. . . . Jn 7:5
Whoever *b* in me, as the Scripture . . . Jn 7:38
if you do not *b* that I am the one I . . . Jn 8:24
Do you *b* in the Son of Man? . . . Jn 9:35
you do not *b* because you are not . . . Jn 10:26
He who *b* in me will live, even . . . Jn 11:25
I *b* that you are the Christ, . . . Jn 11:27
Did I not tell you that if you *b*, . . . Jn 11:40
they still would not *b* in him. . . . Jn 12:37
Jesus cried out, "When a man *b* . . . Jn 12:44
does happen you will *b* that I am . . . Jn 13:19
Don't you *b* that I am in the Father . . . Jn 14:10
This makes us *b* that you came . . . Jn 16:30
that the world may *b* that you have . . . Jn 17:21
he testifies so that you also may *b*. . . . Jn 19:35
He saw and *b*. . . . Jn 20:8
Stop doubting and *b*. . . . Jn 20:27
not *b* that he really was a disciple. . . . Acts 9:26
about him that everyone who *b* . . . Acts 10:43
him everyone who *b* is justified . . . Acts 13:39
were appointed for eternal life *b*. . . . Acts 13:48
They replied, "*B* in the Lord Jesus, . . . Acts
   16:31
the Holy Spirit when you *b*? . . . Acts 19:2
I *b* everything that agrees . . . Acts 24:14
Agrippa, do you *b* the prophets? . . . Acts 26:27
for the salvation of everyone who *b* . . . Rom
   1:16
faith in Jesus Christ to all who *b*. . . . Rom 3:22
Scripture say? "Abraham *b* God, . . . Rom 4:3
he is the father of all who *b* . . . Rom 4:11
righteousness for everyone who *b*. . . . Rom
   10:4
Lord, who has *b* our message? . . . Rom 10:16
so that all nations might *b* . . . Rom 16:26
preached to save those who *b*. . . . 1 Cor 1:21
sanctified through her *b* husband. . . . 1 Cor 7:14
right to take a *b* wife along with us, . . . 1 Cor
   9:5
Otherwise, you have *b* in vain. . . . 1 Cor 15:2
or by *b* what you heard? Are you . . . Gal 3:2
might be given to those who *b*. . . . Gal 3:22
of Christ not only to *b* on him, . . . Phil 1:29
We *b* that Jesus died and rose again . . . 1 Thes
   4:14
delusion so that they will *b* the lie . . . 2 Thes
   2:11

was *b* on in the world, . . . 1 Tm 3:16
and especially of those who *b*. . . . 1 Tm 4:10
Those who have *b* masters are not . . . 1 Tm 6:2
because I know whom I have *b*, . . . 2 Tm 1:12
a man whose children *b* . . . Ti 1:6
comes to him must *b* that he exists . . . Heb
   11:6
But when he asks, he must *b* . . . Jas 1:6
Even the demons *b* that . . . Jas 2:19
You *b* that there is one God. . . . Jas 2:19
that says, "Abraham *b* God, . . . Jas 2:23
to you who *b*, this stone is precious . . . 1 Pt 2:7
to *b* in the name of his Son, . . . 1 Jn 3:23
Dear friends, do not *b* every spirit, . . . 1 Jn 4:1
Everyone who *b* that Jesus is . . . 1 Jn 5:1
Only he who *b* that Jesus is the Son . . .
   1 Jn 5:5
Anyone who *b* in the Son . . . 1 Jn 5:10
things to you who *b* in the name . . . 1 Jn 5:13

BELIEVER(S) *someone who trusts, has faith in,
or holds firm convictions about someone or
something*
Obadiah was a devout *b* . . . 1 Kgs 18:3
of his words many more became *b*. . . . Jn 4:41
among the *b* (a group numbering . . . Acts 1:15
All the *b* were together . . . Acts 2:44
All the *b* were one in heart . . . Acts 4:32
And all the *b* used to meet together . . . Acts
   5:12
he called the *b* and the widows . . . Acts 9:41
The circumcised *b* who had come . . . Acts
   10:45
the circumcised *b* criticized him . . . Acts 11:2
along with some other *b*, . . . Acts 15:2
Then some of the *b* who belonged . . . Acts 15:5
To the Gentile *b* in Antioch, . . . Acts 15:23
whose mother was a Jewess and a *b* . . . Acts
   16:1
If you consider me a *b* in the Lord . . . Acts
   16:15
for the Gentile *b*, we have written . . . Acts 21:25
to judge a dispute between *b*? . . . 1 Cor 6:5
brother has a wife who is not a *b* . . . 1 Cor 7:12
is for *b*, not for unbelievers. . . . 1 Cor 14:22
What does a *b* have in common . . . 2 Cor 6:15
who belong to the family of *b*. . . . Gal 6:10
a model to all the *b* in Macedonia . . . 1 Thes 1:7
set an example for the *b* in speech, . . . 1 Tm
   4:12
any woman who is a *b* has widows . . . 1 Tm
   5:16
benefit from their service are *b*, . . . 1 Tm 6:2
b in our glorious Lord Jesus Christ, . . . Jas 2:1
Love the brotherhood of *b*, . . . 1 Pt 2:17

BELONG(ING)(S) *to be the property of a
person or thing*
Do not interpretations *b* to God? . . . Gn 40:8
for the Israelites *b* to me . . . Lv 25:55
b to the LORD; it is holy . . . Lv 27:30
of any man, for judgment *b* to God. . . . Dt 1:17
LORD your God *b* the heavens, . . . Dt 10:14
The secret things *b* . . . Dt 29:29
To God *b* wisdom and power; . . . Jb 12:13
Dominion and awe *b* to God; . . . Jb 25:2
Everything under heaven *b* to me. . . . Jb 41:11
for dominion *b* to the LORD . . . Ps 22:28
for the kings of the earth *b* to God; . . . Ps 47:9
Indeed, our shield *b* to the LORD, . . . Ps 89:18
and the mountain peaks *b* to him. . . . Ps 95:4
To him *b* eternal praise. . . . Ps 111:10
The highest heavens *b* . . . Ps 115:16
for these people do not *b* . . . Jer 5:10
For every living soul *b* to me, . . . Ez 18:4
You *b* to your father, the devil, . . . Jn 8:44
As it is, you do not *b* to the world, . . . Jn 15:19
called to *b* to Jesus Christ. . . . Rom 1:6
that you might *b* to another, . . . Rom 7:4
of Christ, he does not *b* to Christ. . . . Rom 8:9
each member *b* to all the others. . . . Rom 12:5
we live or die, we *b* to the Lord. . . . Rom 14:8

but he must *b* to the Lord. . . . 1 Cor 7:39
when he comes, those who *b* . . 1 Cor 15:23
If you *b* to Christ, then you are . . . Gal 3:29
Those who *b* to Christ Jesus have . . . Gal 5:24
We do not *b* to the night . . . 1 Thes 5:5
But since we *b* to the day, let us be . . . 1 Thes 5:8
a holy nation, a people *b* to God, . . . 1 Pt 2:9
then is how we know that we *b* . . . 1 Jn 3:19
Salvation *b* to our God, . . . Rv 7:10

BENEFIT(S) *advantages or blessings*
Can a man be of *b* to God? . . . Jb 22:2
and forget not all his *b*. . . . Ps 103:2
Surely it was for my *b* . . . Is 38:17
you have reaped the *b* of their labor . . . Jn 4:38
the *b* you reap leads to holiness, . . . Rom 6:22
All this is for your *b*, . . . 2 Cor 4:15

BETRAY(ED)(S) *to turn away from a friend; deliver to the enemy*
nor will I ever *b* my faithfulness. . . . Ps 89:33
A gossip *b* a confidence, . . . Prv 11:13
do not *b* another man's confidence, . . . Prv 25:9
Brother will *b* brother to death, . . . Mt 10:21
the truth, one of you will *b* me. . . . Mt 26:21
for I have *b* innocent blood. . . . Mt 27:4

BIND(S) *to fasten or tie together; see BOUND*
and *b* them on your foreheads. . . . Dt 6:8
and *b* up their wounds. . . . Ps 147:3
b them around your neck, . . . Prv 3:3
B them upon your heart forever; . . . Prv 6:21
B them on your fingers; . . . Prv 7:3
when the LORD *b* up the bruises . . . Is 30:26
me to *b* up the brokenhearted, . . . Is 61:1
whatever you *b* on earth will be . . . Mt 16:19

BITTER(NESS) *having a taste that is sharp and unpleasant; expression of severe pain, grief, or regret*
along with *b* herbs, and bread made . . . Ex 12:8
Each heart knows its own *b*, . . . Prv 14:10
and *b* to the one who bore him. . . . Prv 17:25
what is *b* tastes sweet. . . . Prv 27:7
full of cursing and *b*. . . . Rom 3:14
Get rid of all *b*, rage and anger, . . . Eph 4:31

BLAMELESS(LY) *innocent; without guilt*
b among the people of his time, . . . Gn 6:9
walk before me and be *b*. . . . Gn 17:1
You must be *b* before the LORD . . . Dt 18:13
I have been *b* before him . . . 2 Sm 22:24
to the *b* you show yourself *b*, . . . 2 Sm 22:26
This man was *b* and upright; . . . Jb 1:1
one on earth like him; he is *b* . . . Jb 1:8
and your *b* ways your hope? . . . Jb 4:6
God does not reject a *b* man . . . Jb 8:20
if I were *b*, it would pronounce me . . . Jb 9:20
Although I am *b*, . . . Jb 9:21
He destroys both the *b* . . . Jb 9:22
though righteous and *b!* . . . Jb 12:4
gain if your ways were *b?*. . . Jb 22:3
he will know that I am *b* . . . Jb 31:6
He whose walk is *b* . . . Ps 15:2
I have been *b* before him . . . Ps 18:23
to the *b* you show yourself *b*, . . . Ps 18:25
Then will I be *b*, . . . Ps 19:13
for I have led a *b* life; . . . Ps 26:1
But I lead a *b* life; . . . Ps 26:11
The days of the *b* are known . . . Ps 37:18
Consider the *b*, observe the upright . . . Ps 37:37
from those whose walk is *b*. . . . Ps 84:11
I will be careful to lead a *b* life . . . Ps 101:2
house with *b* heart. . . . Ps 101:2
he whose walk is *b* . . . Ps 101:6
Blessed are they whose ways are *b*, . . . Ps 119:1
May my heart be *b* . . . Ps 119:80
a shield to those whose walk is *b*, . . . Prv 2:7
and the *b* will remain in it; . . . Prv 2:21
of the *b* makes a straight way . . . Prv 11:5

in those whose ways are *b*. . . . Prv 11:20
Better a poor man whose walk is *b* . . . Prv 19:1
The righteous man leads a *b* life; . . . Prv 20:7
Better a poor man whose walk is *b* . . . Prv 28:6
b will receive a good inheritance. . . . Prv 28:10
He whose walk is *b* is kept safe, . . . Prv 28:18
You were *b* in your ways . . . Ez 28:15
commandments and regulations *b*. . . . Lk 1:6
so that you will be *b* on the day . . . 1 Cor 1:8
world to be holy and *b* in his sight. . . . Eph 1:4
any other blemish, but holy and *b*. . . . Eph 5:27
and *b* until the day of Christ, . . . Phil 1:10
so that you may become *b* and pure . . . Phil 2:15
and *b* we were among you who . . . 1 Thes 2:10
hearts so that you will be *b*. . . . 1 Thes 3:13
and body be kept *b* at the coming . . . 1 Thes 5:23
An elder must be *b*, the husband of . . . Ti 1:6
he must be *b* not overbearing, . . . Ti 1:7
b, pure, set apart from sinners, . . . Heb 7:26
effort to be found spotless, *b* . . . 2 Pt 3:14
found in their mouths; they are *b*. . . . Rv 14:5

BLASPHEME(D)(S), BLASPHEMING *to dishonor or address God with irreverence*
Do not *b* God or curse the ruler . . . Ex 22:28
of the Israelite woman *b* the Name . . . Lv 24:11
anyone who *b* the name . . . Lv 24:16
native-born or alien, *b* the LORD, . . . Nm 15:30
of the king of Assyria have *b* me. . . . 2 Kgs 19:6
Who is it you have insulted and *b?* . . . 2 Kgs 19:22
of the king of Assyria have *b* me. . . . Is 37:6
Who is it you have insulted and *b?* . . . Is 37:23
my name is constantly *b*. . . . Is 52:5
your fathers *b* me by forsaking me: . . . Ez 20:27
"This fellow is *b!*" . . . Mt 9:3
He's *b!* Who can forgive sins . . . Mk 2:7
whoever *b* against the Holy Spirit . . . Mk 3:29
but anyone who *b* against the Holy . . . Lk 12:10
robbed temples nor *b* our goddess. . . . Acts 19:37
I tried to force them to *b*. . . . Acts 26:11
name is *b* among the Gentiles . . . Rom 2:24
over to Satan to be taught not to *b*. . . . 1 Tm 1:20
these men *b* in matters they do not . . . 2 Pt 2:12
He opened his mouth to *b* God, . . . Rv 13:6

BLASPHEMER, BLASPHEMIES, BLASPHEMY *one who dishonors God; words or actions that dishonor God*
Take the *b* outside the camp. . . . Lv 24:14
they took the *b* outside the camp . . . Lv 24:23
or when they committed awful *b*. . . . Neh 9:18
and *b* will be forgiven men, . . . Mt 12:31
Look, now you have heard the *b*. . . . Mt 26:65
and *b* of men will be forgiven them. . . . Mk 3:28
You have heard the *b*. . . . Mk 14:64
Who is this fellow who speaks *b?* . . . Lk 5:21
replied the Jews, "but for *b*, . . . Jn 10:33
words of *b* against Moses . . . Acts 6:11
I was once a *b* and a persecutor . . . 1 Tm 1:13
and *b* and to exercise his authority . . . Rv 13:5

BLEMISH(ES) *defect or flaw*
be without defect or *b* . . . Lv 22:21
or wrinkle or any other *b*, . . . Eph 5:27
without *b* and free from accusation . . . Col 1:22
a lamb without *b* or defect. . . . 1 Pt 1:19
and *b*, reveling in their pleasures . . . 2 Pt 2:13
These men are *b* at your love feasts . . . Jude 1:12

BLESS(ES) *to honor in worship; to offer approval or encouragement*
I will *b* those who *b* you, . . . Gn 12:3
not let you go unless you *b* me. . . . Gn 32:26
He will love you and *b* you . . . Dt 7:13
B all his skills, O LORD, . . . Dt 33:11
the LORD *b* his people with peace. . . . Ps 29:11

and *b* him all day long. . . . Ps 72:15
and richly *b* all who call on him, . . . Rom 10:12
B those who persecute you; *b* . . . Rom 12:14

BLESSED *happy or wonderful; praiseworthy; bringing pleasure or divine favor*
May those who bless you be *b* . . . Nm 24:9
B is the man . . . Ps 1:1
B are all who take refuge in him. . . . Ps 2:12
B is the man . . . Ps 32:2
B is the nation whose God is . . . Ps 33:12
B is the man . . . Ps 40:4
B is he who has regard for the weak . . . Ps 41:1
B are those whose strength is . . . Ps 84:5
B are those who have learned . . . Ps 89:15
B is the man you discipline, . . . Ps 94:12
B are they who maintain justice, . . . Ps 106:3
B is the man who fears the LORD, . . . Ps 112:1
B is he who comes in the name . . . Ps 118:26
B are they whose ways are . . . Ps 119:1
B is the man . . . Ps 127:5
B is the man who finds wisdom, . . . Prv 3:13
B is the man who listens to me, . . . Prv 8:34
A faithful man will be richly *b*, . . . Prv 28:20
but *b* is he who keeps the law. . . . Prv 29:18
Her children arise and call her *b*; . . . Prv 31:28
B are all who wait for him! . . . Is 30:18
Then all the nations will call you *b*, . . . Mal 3:12
But now we call the arrogant *b*. . . . Mal 3:15
saying: "*B* are the poor in spirit, . . . Mt 5:3
B are those who mourn, . . . Mt 5:4
B are the meek, . . . Mt 5:5
B are those who hunger . . . Mt 5:6
B are the merciful, . . . Mt 5:7
B are the pure in heart, . . . Mt 5:8
B are the peacemakers, . . . Mt 5:9
B are those who are persecuted . . . Mt 5:10
B are you when people insult you, . . . Mt 5:11
on all generations will call me *b*, . . . Lk 1:48
B is he who comes in the name . . . Jn 12:13
It is more *b* to give than to receive . . . Acts 20:35
while we wait for the *b* hope . . . Ti 2:13
B is the man who perseveres . . . Jas 1:12
B is the one who reads the words . . . Rv 1:3
B is he who keeps the words . . . Rv 22:7
B are those who wash their robes, . . . Rv 22:14

BLESSING(S) *happiness; praise; divine favor or heavenly reward*
so that I may give you my *b* . . . Gn 27:4
proclaim on Mount Gerizim the *b*, . . . Dt 11:29
turned the curse into a *b* for you, . . . Dt 23:5
This is the *b* that Moses the man . . . Dt 33:1
all the words of the law—the *b* . . . Jos 8:34
B crown the head of the righteous, . . . Prv 10:6
The *b* of the LORD brings wealth, . . . Prv 10:22
there will be showers of *b*. . . . Ez 34:26
shared in the Jews' spiritual *b*, . . . Rom 15:27

BLIND(ED) *to be without sight; to lack spiritual discernment*
a *b* man leads a *b* man, both will fall . . . Mt 15:14
Woe to you, *b* guides! You say, . . . Mt 23:16
a *b* man, Bartimaeus (that is, . . . Mk 10:46
Can a *b* man lead a *b* man? . . . Lk 6:39
I was *b* but now I see! . . . Jn 9:25
"He has *b* their eyes . . . Jn 12:40
The god of this age has *b* the minds . . . 2 Cor 4:4

BLOOD(SHED)(THIRSTY) *fluid in the circulatory system; signifies human life; of animals, used in priestly sacrifices; of Christ, effective for the forgiveness of sins; on hands or head, symbolic of guilt*
Your brother's *b* cries out to me . . . Gn 4:10
Whoever sheds the *b* of man, . . . Gn 9:6
and when I see the *b*, I will pass . . . Ex 12:13
This is the *b* of the covenant that . . . Ex 24:8
take its *b* behind the curtain . . . Lv 16:15
For the life of a creature is in the *b*, . . . Lv 17:11

eat the *b*, because the *b* is the life, . . . Dt 12:23
b and deceitful men . . . Ps 5:6
my life with *b* men, . . . Ps 26:9
b and deceitful men . . . Ps 55:23
save me from *b* men. . . . Ps 59:2
for precious is their *b* in his sight. . . . Ps 72:14
Away from me, you *b* men! . . . Ps 139:19
hands that shed innocent *b*, . . . Prv 6:17
B men hate a man of integrity . . . Prv 29:10
pleasure in the *b* of bulls and lambs . . . Is 1:11
on him who keeps his sword from *b* . . . Jer 48:10
did not hate *b*, *b* will pursue you. . . . Ez 35:6
to him who builds a city with *b* . . . Hb 2:12
This is my *b* of the covenant, . . . Mt 26:28
I am innocent of this man's *b*, . . . Mt 27:24
This is my *b* of the covenant, . . . Mk 14:24
drops of *b* falling to the ground. . . . Lk 22:44
of the Son of Man and drink his *b*, . . . Jn 6:53
of strangled animals and from *b*. . . . Acts 15:20
innocent of the *b* of all men. . . . Acts 20:26
of atonement, through faith in his *b* . . . Rom 3:25
have now been justified by his *b*, . . . Rom 5:9
cup is the new covenant in my *b*; . . . 1 Cor 11:25
we have redemption through his *b*, . . . Eph 1:7
near through the *b* of Christ. . . . Eph 2:13
by making peace through his *b*, . . . Col 1:20
once a year, and never without *b*, . . . Heb 9:7
once for all by his own *b*, . . . Heb 9:12
This is the *b* of the covenant, . . . Heb 9:20
of *b* there is no forgiveness. . . . Heb 9:22
word than the *b* of Abel. . . . Heb 12:24
but with the precious *b* of Christ, . . . 1 Pt 1:19
and the *b* of Jesus, his Son, . . . 1 Jn 1:7
has freed us from our sins by his *b*, . . . Rv 1:5
with your *b* you purchased men . . . Rv 5:9
white in the *b* of the Lamb. . . . Rv 7:14
him by the *b* of the Lamb . . . Rv 12:11
He is dressed in a robe dipped in *b*, . . . Rv 19:13

BLOT(S) *to erase or cover up*
then *b* me out of the book you have . . . Ex 32:32
I, even I, am he who *b* out . . . Is 43:25
b out my transgressions. . . . Ps 51:1
I will never *b* out his name . . . Rv 3:5

BOAST(S) *to brag; a prideful statement; see BRAG*
armor should not *b* like one who . . . 1 Kgs 20:11
My soul will *b* in the LORD; . . . Ps 34:2
In God we make our *b* all day long, . . . Ps 44:8
Do not *b* about tomorrow, . . . Prv 27:1
or the rich man *b* of his riches, . . . Jer 9:23
let him who *b* boast about this: . . . Jer 9:24
Let him who boasts *b* in the Lord. . . . 1 Cor 1:31
I do not inwardly burn? If I must *b*, . . . 2 Cor 11:30
May I never *b* except in the cross . . . Gal 6:14
not by works, so that no one can *b*. . . . Eph 2:9

BODIES, BODY *a person's physical being; a corpse; a group of people*
their *b* will rise. . . . Is 26:19
What are these wounds on your *b*? . . . Zec 13:6
afraid of those who kill the *b* . . . Mt 10:28
"Take and eat; this is my *b* . . . Mt 26:26
spirit is willing, but the *b* is weak. . . . Mt 26:41
"Take it; this is my *b*." . . . Mk 14:22
"This is my *b* given for you; . . . Lk 22:19
wash his feet; his whole *b* is clean. . . . Jn 13:10
to offer your *b* as living sacrifices, . . . Rom 12:1
Do not offer the parts of your *b* . . . Rom 6:13
us has one *b* with many members, . . . Rom 12:4
not know that your *b* are members . . . 1 Cor 6:15
not know that your *b* is a temple . . . 1 Cor 6:19

Therefore honor God with your *b*. . . . 1 Cor 6:20
This is my *b*, which is for you; . . . 1 Cor 11:24
The *b* is a unit, though it is made up . . . 1 Cor 12:12
a natural *b*, it is raised a spiritual *b*. . . . 1 Cor 15:44
which is his *b*, the fullness . . . Eph 1:23
we are all members of one *b*. . . . Eph 4:25
to love their wives as their own *b*. . . . Eph 5:28
we are members of his *b*. . . . Eph 5:30
Christ will be exalted in my *b*, . . . Phil 1:20
sake of his *b*, which is the church. . . . Col 1:24

BOLD(NESS) *fearless before danger; self-assured*
you made me *b* and stouthearted. . . . Ps 138:3
A wicked man puts up a *b* front, . . . Prv 21:29
the righteous are as *b* as a lion. . . . Prv 28:1
of the man's *b* he will get up . . . Lk 11:8
to speak your word with great *b*. . . . Acts 4:29

BOOK(S) *literary work; written record or account*
against me I will blot out of my *b*. . . . Ex 32:33
Do not let this *B* of the Law depart . . . Jos 1:8
I have found the *B* of the Law . . . 2 Kgs 22:8
They read from the *B* of the Law . . . Neh 8:8
May they be blotted out of the *b*. . . . Ps 69:28
Of making many *b* there is no end, . . . Eccl 12:12
and the *b* were opened. . . . Dn 7:10
name is found written in the *b*. . . . Dn 12:1
which are not recorded in this *b*. . . . Jn 20:30
for the *b* that would be written. . . . Jn 21:25
whose names are in the *b* of life. . . . Phil 4:3
never blot out his name from the *b* . . . Rv 3:5
b was opened, which is the *b* . . . Rv 20:12
was not found written in the *b*. . . . Rv 20:15
written in the Lamb's *b* of life. . . . Rv 21:27
him the plagues described in this *b*. . . . Rv 22:18

BORN AGAIN *given new life by the Holy Spirit, analogous to birth*
kingdom of God unless he is *b* a. . . . Jn 3:3
my saying, 'You must be *b* a . . . Jn 3:7
For you have been *b* a, . . . 1 Pt 1:23

BOUGHT *purchased or redeemed*
which he *b* with his own blood. . . . Acts 20:28
You are not your own; you were *b* . . . 1 Cor 6:20
You were *b* at a price; do not . . . 1 Cor 7:23
the sovereign Lord who *b* them . . . 2 Pt 2:1

BOUND *held fast; under physical restraint or moral obligation; see BIND*
Let no foreigner who has *b* himself . . . Is 56:3
bind on earth will be *b* in heaven, . . . Mt 16:19
bind on earth will be *b* in heaven, . . . Mt 18:18
by law a married woman is *b* . . . Rom 7:2
A woman is *b* to her husband . . . 1 Cor 7:39
b with everlasting chains . . . Jude 1:6
and *b* him for a thousand years. . . . Rv 20:2

BOUNDARY, BOUNDS *border; limit; dividing line*
your southern *b* will start . . . Nm 34:3
Do not move an ancient *b* stone . . . Prv 23:10
who move *b* stones. . . . Hos 5:10
all our troubles my joy knows no *b*. . . . 2 Cor 7:4

BOUNTY *free and abundant giving; generous yield*
than the *b* of the age-old hills. . . . Gn 49:26
heavens, the storehouse of his *b*, . . . Dt 28:12
he had given her out of his royal *b*. . . . 1 Kgs 10:13
You crown the year with your *b*, . . . Ps 65:11
from your *b*, O God, you provided . . . Ps 68:10
rejoice in the *b* of the LORD . . . Jer 31:12

BRAG *to boast; a prideful statement; see BOAST*
and *b* about your freewill offerings . . . Am 4:5
b about your relationship to God; . . . Rom 2:17
You who *b* about the law, . . . Rom 2:23
As it is, you boast and *b*. . . . Jas 4:16

BRANCH(ES) *limb of a (family) tree; figurative of offspring or of disciples*
In that day the *B* of the LORD will . . . Is 4:2
up to David a righteous *B*, . . . Jer 23:5
I will make a righteous *B* sprout . . . Jer 33:15
going to bring my servant, the *B*. . . . Zec 3:8
is the man whose name is the *B*, . . . Zec 6:12
while every *b* that does bear fruit . . . Jn 15:2
No *b* can bear fruit by itself; . . . Jn 15:4
I am the vine; you are the *b*. . . . Jn 15:5
if God did not spare the natural *b*, . . . Rom 11:21

BREAD *basic staple in diet of ancient Israel; signifies livelihood*
and *b* made without yeast. . . . Ex 12:8
the Feast of Unleavened *B*; . . . Ex 23:15
Put the *b* of the Presence . . . Ex 25:30
that man does not live on *b* alone . . . Dt 8:3
Men ate the *b* of angels; . . . Ps 78:25
but give me only my daily *b*. . . . Prv 30:8
Cast your *b* upon the waters, . . . Eccl 11:1
Why spend money on what is not *b* . . . Is 55:2
tell these stones to become *b*. . . . Mt 4:3
Man does not live on *b* alone, . . . Mt 4:4
Give us today our daily *b*. . . . Mt 6:11
Jesus took *b*, gave thanks . . . Mt 26:26
tell this stone to become *b*. . . . Lk 4:3
We have only five loaves of *b* . . . Lk 9:13
For the *b* of God is he who comes . . . Jn 6:33
Jesus declared, "I am the *b* of life. . . . Jn 6:35
I am the *b* that came . . . Jn 6:41
I am the *b* of life. . . . Jn 6:48
I am the living *b* that came . . . Jn 6:51
This *b* is my flesh, which I will give . . . Jn 6:51
took the *b* and gave it to them, . . . Jn 21:13
And is not the *b* that we break . . . 1 Cor 10:16
took *b*, and when he had given . . . 1 Cor 11:23

BREAK(ING)(S), BROKE *to fracture; to shatter; to violate or transgress; to force a way through*
he must not *b* his word . . . Nm 30:2
fall on us for *b* the oath we swore . . . Jos 9:20
I will never *b* my covenant . . . Jgs 2:1
and a gentle tongue can *b* a bone. . . . Prv 25:15
A bruised reed he will not *b*, . . . Is 42:3
and like a hammer that *b* a rock . . . Jer 23:29
oath by *b* the covenant. . . . Ez 16:59
the oath by *b* the covenant. . . . Ez 17:18
do not *b* faith with the wife . . . Mal 2:15
A bruised reed he will not *b*, . . . Mt 12:20
took bread, gave thanks and *b* it, . . . Mt 26:26
to the *b* of bread and to prayer. . . . Acts 2:42
They *b* bread in their homes . . . Acts 2:46
week we came together to *b* bread. . . . Acts 20:7
the bread that we *b* a participation . . . 1 Cor 10:16
when he had given thanks, he *b* it . . . 1 Cor 11:24
at just one point is guilty of *b* all . . . Jas 2:10
Everyone who sins *b* the law; . . . 1 Jn 3:4
Who is worthy to *b* the seals . . . Rv 5:2

BROKEN(NESS) *fractured or shattered; violated or transgressed against*
not one of them will be *b*. . . . Ps 34:20
The sacrifices of God are a *b* spirit; . . . Ps 51:17
of three strands is not quickly *b*. . . . Eccl 4:12
and wail in *b* of spirit. . . . Is 65:14
on that stone will be *b* to pieces, . . . Lk 20:18
the law of Moses may not be *b*, . . . Jn 7:23
the Scripture cannot be *b* . . . Jn 10:35
Not one of his bones will be *b*, . . . Jn 19:36
they were *b* off because of unbelief, . . . Rom 11:20

BROTHER(HOOD)(LY)(S) *male sibling; fellow believer*

"Am I my *b*'s keeper?" . . . Gn 4:9
and a *b* is born for adversity. . . . Prv 17:17
a friend who sticks closer than a *b*. . . . Prv 18:24
neighbor nearby than a *b* far away. . . . Prv 27:10
and be reconciled to your *b*; . . . Mt 5:24
remove the speck from your *b*'s eye. . . . Mt 7:5
If your *b* sins against you, . . . Mt 18:15
Whoever does God's will is my *b* . . . Mk 3:35
If your *b* sins, rebuke him, . . . Lk 17:3
devoted to one another in *b* love. . . . Rom 12:10
or obstacle in your *b*'s way. . . . Rom 14:13
not by your eating destroy your *b* . . . Rom 14:15
anything else that will cause your *b* . . . Rom 14:21
if what I eat causes my *b* to fall . . . 1 Cor 8:13
Now about *b* love we do not need . . . 1 Thes 4:9
away from every *b* who is idle . . . 2 Thes 3:6
as an enemy, but warn him as a *b*. . . . 2 Thes 3:15
but better than a slave, as a dear *b*. . . . Phlm 1:16
Suppose a *b* or sister is . . . Jas 2:15
Anyone who speaks against his *b* . . . Jas 4:11
Love the *b* of believers, fear God, . . . 1 Pt 2:17
and to godliness, *b* kindness; . . . 2 Pt 1:7
hates his *b* is still in the darkness. . . . 1 Jn 2:9
is anyone who does not love his *b*. . . . 1 Jn 3:10
who hates his *b* is a murderer, . . . 1 Jn 3:15
For anyone who does not love his *b* . . . 1 Jn 4:20
If anyone sees his *b* commit a sin . . . 1 Jn 5:16

BUILD(S), BUILT *to erect, construct*

Are you the one to *b* me a house . . . 2 Sm 7:5
he began to *b* the temple . . . 1 Kgs 6:1
So Solomon *b* the temple . . . 1 Kgs 6:14
unless the LORD *b* the house, . . . Ps 127:1
The wise woman *b* her house, . . . Prv 14:1
a time to tear down and a time to *b*, . . . Eccl 3:3
is like a wise man who *b* his house . . . Mt 7:24
and on this rock I will *b* my church, . . . Mt 16:18
is like a man who *b* a house . . . Lk 6:49
does not live in temples *b* by hands. . . . Acts 17:24
which can *b* you up and give you . . . Acts 20:32
neighbor for his good, to *b* him up. . . . Rom 15:2
If what he has *b* survives, he will . . . 1 Cor 3:14
one should be careful how he *b*. . . . 1 Cor 3:10
Knowledge puffs up, but love *b* up. . . . 1 Cor 8:1
excel in gifts that *b* up the church. . . . 1 Cor 14:12
in heaven, not *b* by human hands. . . . 2 Cor 5:1
b on the foundation of the apostles . . . Eph 2:20
the body of Christ may be *b* up . . . Eph 4:12
grows and *b* itself up in love, . . . Eph 4:16
live in him, rooted and *b* up in him, . . . Col 2:7
one another and *b* each other up, . . . 1 Thes 5:11
are being *b* into a spiritual house . . . 1 Pt 2:5
b yourselves up in your most holy . . . Jude 1:20

BUILDER(S) *a person who erects or constructs*

The stone the *b* rejected . . . Ps 118:22
The stone the *b* rejected . . . Mt 21:42
The stone the *b* rejected . . . Mk 12:10
The stone the *b* rejected . . . Lk 20:17
the stone you *b* rejected, . . . Acts 4:11
I laid a foundation as an expert *b*, . . . 1 Cor 3:10
the *b* of a house has greater honor . . . Heb 3:3
God is the *b* of everything. . . . Heb 3:4

whose architect and *b* is God. . . . Heb 11:10
The stone the *b* rejected . . . 1 Pt 2:7

BUILDING *walled structure built for permanent use; figurative, of the church*

you are God's field, God's *b*. . . . 1 Cor 3:9
we have a *b* from God, an eternal . . . 2 Cor 5:1
him the whole *b* is joined together . . . Eph 2:21

BURDEN(S) *that which is borne, physically or spiritually*

like a *b* too heavy to bear. . . . Ps 38:4
who daily bears our *b*. . . . Ps 68:19
What a heavy *b* God has laid . . . Eccl 1:13
my yoke is easy and my *b* is light. . . . Mt 11:30
down with *b* they can hardly carry, . . . Lk 11:46
to us not to *b* you with anything . . . Acts 15:28
from being a *b* to you in any way, . . . 2 Cor 11:9
and I will not be a *b* to you, . . . 2 Cor 12:14
Carry each other's *b*, . . . Gal 6:2
day in order not to be a *b* to anyone . . . 1 Thes 2:9
so that we would not be a *b* to any . . . 2 Thes 3:8
not a *b*, for that would be . . . Heb 13:17

BURDENED *bearing a heavy load, physically or spiritually*

have not *b* you with grain offerings . . . Is 43:23
But you have *b* me with your sins . . . Is 43:24
How have I *b* you? Answer me. . . . Mi 6:3
all you who are weary and *b*, . . . Mt 11:28
are in this tent, we groan and are *b*, . . . 2 Cor 5:4
do not let yourselves be *b* again . . . Gal 5:1
not let the church be *b* with them, . . . 1 Tm 5:16

BURIED, BURY *interred with funeral ceremonies; figurative, of self-denial and submission to Christ*

I will die, and there I will be *b*. . . . Ru 1:17
and let the dead *b* their own dead. . . . Mt 8:22
Let the dead *b* their own dead, . . . Lk 9:60
b with him through baptism . . . Rom 6:4
that he was *b*, that he was raised . . . 1 Cor 15:4
having been *b* with him in baptism . . . Col 2:12

BURN(ED)(ING), BURNT *consume by fire; as sacrifices (burnt offerings); with destructiveness; for purification; in hell; as a martyr; with passion*

he sacrificed *b* offerings on it. . . . Gn 8:20
as a *b* offering on one . . . Gn 22:2
and *b* offerings to present . . . Ex 10:25
brought a *b* offering and other . . . Ex 18:12
so that the lamps may be kept *b*. . . . Ex 27:20
Place the altar of *b* offering in front . . . Ex 40:6
If the offering is a *b* offering . . . Lv 1:3
the fire must be kept *b* on the altar. . . . Lv 6:9
and *b* their idols in the fire. . . . Dt 7:5
offered to the LORD *b* offerings . . . Jos 8:31
offer the second bull as a *b* offering . . . Jgs 6:26
But if you prepare a *b* offering, . . . Jgs 13:16
offered a thousand *b* offerings . . . 1 Kgs 3:4
year Solomon sacrificed *b* offerings . . . 1 Kgs 9:25
and the *b* offerings he made . . . 1 Kgs 10:5
Israel to sacrifice *b* offerings on it, . . . Ezr 3:2
You, O LORD, keep my lamp *b*; . . . Ps 18:28
long will your jealousy *b* like fire? . . . Ps 79:5
you will heap *b* coals on his head, . . . Prv 25:22
for sacrificing *b* offerings . . . Ez 43:18
you will heap *b* coals on his head. . . . Rom 12:20
to marry than to *b* with passion. . . . 1 Cor 7:9
alive into the fiery lake of *b* sulfur. . . . Rv 19:20

CALL(ED)(ING)(S) *to make a request or demand; to designate or name; a divine summons; an occupation of vocation*

she shall be *c* 'woman,' . . . Gn 2:23

he blessed them and *c* them "man" . . . Gn 5:2
c on the name of the LORD. . . . Gn 12:8
there he *c* upon the name . . . Gn 21:33
c on the name of the LORD. . . . Gn 26:25
"Here I am; you *c* me." . . . 1 Sm 3:5
I will *c* on the name of the LORD. . . . 1 Kgs 18:24
c on the name of the LORD his . . . 2 Kgs 5:11
to the LORD, *c* on his name; . . . 1 Chr 16:8
if my people, who are *c* . . . 2 Chr 7:14
This poor man *c*, and the LORD . . . Ps 34:6
to the LORD, *c* on his name; . . . Ps 105:1
Then I *c* on the name of the LORD . . . Ps 116:4
c on the name of the LORD. . . . Ps 116:13
near to all who *c* on him, . . . Ps 145:18
and *c* them each by name. . . . Ps 147:4
children arise and *c* her blessed; . . . Prv 31:28
Woe to those who *c* evil good . . . Is 5:20
to the LORD, *c* on his name; . . . Is 12:4
A voice of one *c*: . . . Is 40:3
c on him while he is near. . . . Is 55:6
for my house will be *c* . . . Is 56:7
Before they *c* I will answer; . . . Is 65:24
C to me and I will answer you . . . Jer 33:3
that all of them may *c* on the name . . . Zep 3:9
They will *c* on my name . . . Zec 13:9
come to *c* the righteous, . . . Mt 9:13
I have not come to *c* the righteous, . . . Mk 2:17
Cheer up! On your feet! He's *c* you . . . Mk 10:49
I have not come to *c* the righteous, . . . Lk 5:32
He *c* his own sheep by name . . . Jn 10:3
all whom the Lord our God will *c*. . . . Acts 2:39
to arrest all who *c* on your name. . . . Acts 9:14
among those who *c* on this name? . . . Acts 9:21
c to be an apostle and set apart . . . Rom 1:1
among those who are *c* to belong . . . Rom 1:6
loved by God and *c* to be saints: . . . Rom 1:7
who have been *c* according . . . Rom 8:28
And those he predestined, he also *c* . . . Rom 8:30
and richly blesses all who *c* on him, . . . Rom 10:12
gifts and his *c* are irrevocable. . . . Rom 11:29
c to be an apostle of Christ Jesus . . . 1 Cor 1:1
in Christ Jesus and *c* to be holy, . . . 1 Cor 1:2
but to those whom God has *c*, . . . 1 Cor 1:24
of what you were when you were *c*. . . . 1 Cor 1:26
God has *c* us to live in peace. . . . 1 Cor 7:15
and to which God has *c* him. . . . 1 Cor 7:17
deserting the one who *c* you . . . Gal 1:6
from birth and *c* me by his grace, . . . Gal 1:15
You, my brothers, were *c* to be free . . . Gal 5:13
the hope to which he has *c* you, . . . Eph 1:18
worthy of the *c* you have received. . . . Eph 4:1
as you were *c* to one hope . . . Eph 4:4
of one body you were *c* to peace. . . . Col 3:15
For God did not *c* us to be impure, . . . 1 Thes 4:7
The one who *c* you is faithful . . . 1 Thes 5:24
may count you worthy of his *c*, . . . 2 Thes 1:11
He *c* you to this through our gospel . . . 2 Thes 2:14
life to which you were *c* . . . 1 Tm 6:12
who has saved us and *c* us . . . 2 Tm 1:9
along with those who *c* . . . 2 Tm 2:22
that those who are *c* may receive . . . Heb 9:15
But just as he who *c* you is holy, . . . 1 Pt 1:15
of him who *c* you out of darkness . . . 1 Pt 2:9
to this you were *c* so that you may . . . 1 Pt 3:9
who *c* you to his eternal glory . . . 1 Pt 5:10
of him who *c* us by his own glory . . . 2 Pt 1:3
all the more eager to make your *c* . . . 2 Pt 1:10
To those who have been *c*, . . . Jude 1:1

CAPTIVE(S) *prisoner; someone held against their will*

you led *c* in your train; . . . Ps 68:18
to proclaim freedom for the *c* . . . Is 61:1
full of bitterness and *c* to sin. . . . Acts 8:23
we take *c* every thought . . . 2 Cor 10:5

he led *c* in his train . . . Eph 4:8
See to it that no one takes you *c* . . . Col 2:8
who has taken them *c* to do his will. . . . 2 Tm
2:26

CAPTIVITY *imprisonment, exile; subjection or subservience*
because they will go into *c* . . . . Dt 28:41
So Judah went into *c*, away . . . 2 Kgs 25:21
Israel and Judah back from *c* . . . Jer 30:3
So Judah went into *c*, away . . . Jer 52:27
I will bring them back from *c* . . . Ez 29:14

CARE(S), CARING *to show due concern, regard, or oversight; also its opposite—undue anxiety or worry*
It is a land the LORD your God *c* . . . Dt 11:12
she *c* not that her labor was in vain, . . .
Jb 39:16
the son of man that you *c* for him? . . . Ps 8:4
Cast your *c* on the LORD . . . Ps 55:22
You *c* for the land and water it; . . . Ps 65:9
no one *c* for my life. . . . Ps 142:4
what is man that you *c* for him, . . . Ps 144:3
A righteous man *c* for the needs . . . Prv 12:10
The righteous *c* about justice . . . Prv 29:7
when there are many *c*, . . . Eccl 5:3
because there is no one who *c* . . . Jer 12:11
Zion for whom no one *c* . . . Jer 30:17
He *c* for those who trust in him, . . . Na 1:7
deal under the *c* of many doctors . . . Mk 5:26
him to an inn and took *c* of him. . . Lk 10:34
I don't fear God or *c* about men, . . . Lk 18:4
and *c* nothing for the sheep. . . . Jn 10:13
Jesus said, "Take *c* of my sheep." . . . Jn 21:16
but he feeds and *c* for it, just . . . Eph 5:29
like a mother *c* for her little . . . 1 Thes 2:7
how can he take *c* of God's church . . . 1 Tm 3:5
practice by *c* for their own family . . . 1 Tm 5:4
what has been entrusted to your *c*. . . . 1 Tm
6:20
the son of man that you *c* for him? . . . Heb 2:6
of God's flock that is under your *c*, . . . 1 Pt 5:2
on him because he *c* for you. . . . 1 Pt 5:7

CAREFUL *meticulous; scrupulously attentive*
Be *c* not to say anything to Jacob, . . . Gn 31:24
Be *c* to do everything I have said . . . Ex 23:13
be *c* to follow my decrees. . . . Lv 18:4
Be *c* not to forget the covenant . . . Dt 4:23
be *c* to obey so that it may go well . . . Dt 6:3
Be *c* to obey all the law my servant . . . Jos 1:7
if only your sons are *c* in all they do . . . 1 Kgs
8:25
I will be *c* to lead a blameless life . . . Ps 101:2
But if you are *c* to obey me, . . . Jer 17:24
will follow my decrees and be *c* . . . Ez 11:20
Give *c* thought to your ways. . . . Hg 1:5
Be *c* not to do your 'acts . . . Mt 6:1
each one should be *c* how he builds . . . 1 Cor
3:10
Be very *c*, then, how you live . . . Eph 5:15

CARRIED, CARRY(ING) *to lift and move a burden; to transport*
and how I *c* you on eagles' wings . . . Ex 19:4
goat will *c* on itself all their sins . . . Lv 16:22
and fail to *c* out all my commands . . . Lv 26:15
how the LORD your God *c* you, . . . Dt 1:31
I have made you and I will *c* you; . . . Is 46:4
and *c* our sorrows, . . . Is 53:4
he lifted them up and *c* them . . . Is 63:9
and *c* our diseases. . . . Mt 8:17
anyone who does not *c* his cross . . . Lk 14:27
c his own cross, he went out . . . Jn 19:17
c each other's burdens, . . . Gal 6:2
for each one should *c* his own load. . . . Gal 6:5
Do not be *c* away by all kinds . . . Heb 13:9
as they were *c* along by the Holy . . . 2 Pt 1:21
so that you may not be *c* away . . . 2 Pt 3:17
loving God and *c* out his . . . 1 Jn 5:2

CAST(ING) *to direct (a glance); to throw off (a restraint); to shape molten metal*

Do not make *c* idols. . . . Ex 34:17
He is to *c* lots for the two goats . . . Lv 16:8
and *c* lots for my clothing. . . . Ps 22:18
C your cares on the LORD . . . Ps 55:22
The lot is *c* into the lap, . . . Prv 16:33
C the lot settles disputes . . . Prv 18:18
C your bread upon the waters, . . . Eccl 11:1
divided up his clothes by *c* lots. . . . Mt 27:35
and *c* lots for my clothing. . . . Jn 19:24
C all your anxiety on him . . . 1 Pt 5:7

CATCH(ES), CAUGHT *to get entangled; to seize and hold firmly*
there in a thicket he saw a ram *c* . . . Gn 22:13
He *c* the wise in their craftiness, . . . Jb 5:13
let down the nets for a *c*. . . . Lk 5:4
from now on you will *c* men. . . . Lk 5:10
He *c* the wise in their craftiness . . . 1 Cor 3:19
who fourteen years ago was *c* up . . . 2 Cor 12:2
and are left will be *c* up together . . . 1 Thes 4:17

CERTAIN(TY) *sure; freedom from any doubt*
so that you may know the *c* . . . Lk 1:4
They knew with *c* that I came . . . Jn 17:8
word of the prophets made more *c*, . . . 2 Pt
1:19

CHAFF *the husk on a seed of grain*
They are like *c* . . . Ps 1:4
May they be like *c* before the wind, . . . Ps 35:5
became like *c* on a threshing floor . . . Dn 2:35
up the *c* with unquenchable fire. . . . Mt 3:12

CHAIN(ED)(S) *to confine or secure; to obstruct; metal links*
for which I am an ambassador in *c*. . . . Eph
6:20
Remember my *c*. . . . Col 4:18
and was not ashamed of my *c* . . . 2 Tm 1:16
But God's word is not *c*. . . . 2 Tm 2:9
with everlasting *c* for judgment . . . Jude 1:6

CHANGE(D) *to transform; to shift, exchange or transfer*
you will be *c* into a different person . . . 1 Sm
10:6
of Israel does not lie or *c* his mind; . . . 1 Sm
15:29
and will not *c* his mind: . . . Ps 110:4
If you really *c* your ways . . . Jer 7:5
My heart is *c* within me; . . . Hos 11:8
I the LORD do not *c*. . . . Mal 3:6
unless you *c* and become like little . . . Mt 18:3
we will all be *c* in a flash, . . . 1 Cor 15:51
and will not *c* his mind: . . . Heb 7:21
who does not *c* like shifting . . . Jas 1:17

CHEER(FUL)(S) *to instill with hope, joy, hilarity, or comfort*
but a kind word *c* him up. . . . Prv 12:25
A happy heart makes the face *c*, . . . Prv 15:13
the *c* heart has a continual feast . . . Prv 15:15
A *c* look brings joy to the heart, . . . Prv 15:30
A *c* heart is good medicine, . . . Prv 17:22
for God loves a *c* giver. . . . 2 Cor 9:7

CHILD(REN) *young person between infancy and youth; offspring or descendants*
punishing the *c* for the sin . . . Ex 20:5
Teach them to your *c* . . . Dt 4:9
Impress them on your *c*. . . . Dt 6:7
them to your *c*, talking about them . . . Dt 11:19
nor *c* put to death for their fathers; . . . Dt 24:16
so that you and your *c* may live . . . Dt 30:19
Perhaps my *c* have sinned . . . Jb 1:5
From the lips of *c* and infants . . . Ps 8:2
forefathers to teach their *c*, . . . Ps 78:5
Children's *c* are a crown . . . Prv 17:6
blessed are his *c* after him. . . . Prv 20:7
Even a *c* is known by his actions, . . . Prv 20:11
Train a *c* in the way he should go, . . . Prv 22:6
Folly is bound up in the heart of a *c* . . . Prv 22:15
not withhold discipline from a *c*; . . . Prv 23:13
c left to himself disgraces his mother. . . . Prv
29:15

Her *c* arise and call her blessed; . . . Prv 31:28
The virgin will be with *c* . . . Is 7:14
For to us a *c* is born, . . . Is 9:6
and a little *c* will lead them. . . . Is 11:6
As a mother comforts her *c*, . . . Is 66:13
Tell it to your *c*, . . . Jl 1:3
the hearts of the fathers to their *c*, . . . Mal 4:6
The virgin will be with *c* . . . Mt 1:23
how to give good gifts to your *c*, . . . Mt 7:11
and revealed them to little *c*. . . . Mt 11:25
He called a little *c* and had him . . . Mt 18:2
Let the little *c* come to me, . . . Mt 19:14
From the lips of *c* and infants . . . Mt 21:16
one of these little *c* in my name . . . Mk 9:37
And he took the *c* in his arms, . . . Mk 10:16
C will rebel against their parents . . . Mk 13:12
and blessed is the *c* you will bear! . . . Lk 1:42
And the *c* grew and became strong . . . Lk 1:80
and revealed them to little *c*. . . . Lk 10:21
the right to become *c* of God . . . Jn 1:12
The promise is for you and your *c* . . . . Acts 2:39
with our spirit that we are God's *c*. . . . Rom
8:16
When I was a *c*, I talked like a *c*, . . . 1 Cor 13:11
Brothers, stop thinking like *c*. . . . 1 Cor 14:20
parents, but parents for their *c*. . . . 2 Cor 12:14
C, obey your parents in the Lord, . . . Eph 6:1
do not exasperate your *c*; instead, . . . Eph 6:4
C, obey your parents in everything, . . . Col 3:20
Fathers, do not embitter your *c*, . . . Col 3:21
and see that his *c* obey him . . . 1 Tm 3:4
and must manage his *c* and his . . . 1 Tm 3:12
bringing up *c*, showing hospitality, . . . 1 Tm
5:10
and the *c* God has given me. . . . Heb 2:13
that we should be called *c* of God! . . . 1 Jn 3:1
who loves the father loves his *c* . . . 1 Jn 5:1

CHOOSE(S), CHOSE(N) *to decide or select; to be selected for a sovereign purpose*
So Lot *c* for himself the whole plain . . . Gn 13:11
Now *c* life, so that you . . . Dt 30:19
then *c* for yourselves this day . . . Jos 24:15
the people he *c* for his inheritance. . . . Ps 33:12
C my instruction instead of silver, . . . Prv 8:10
to *c* understanding rather . . . Prv 16:16
to whom the Son *c* to reveal him. . . . Mt 11:27
for many are invited, but few are *c* . . . Mt 22:14
to whom the Son *c* to reveal him. . . . Lk 10:22
Mary has *c* what is better, . . . Lk 10:42
the Christ of God, the *C* One. . . . Lk 23:35
If anyone *c* to do God's will, . . . Jn 7:17
You did not *c* me, but I *c* you . . . Jn 15:16
But God *c* the foolish things . . . 1 Cor 1:27
he *c* us in him before the creation . . . Eph 1:4
from the beginning God *c* you . . . 2 Thes 2:13
He was *c* before the creation . . . 1 Pt 1:20
But you are a *c* people, a royal . . . 1 Pt 2:9

CHRIST *the Messiah; the Son of God*
was born Jesus, who is called *C*. . . . Mt 1:16
Peter answered, "You are the *C*, . . . Mt 16:16
Who is he that condemns? *C* Jesus, . . . Rom
8:34
C died for nothing!" You foolish . . . Gal 2:21
as *C* is the head of the church, . . . Eph 5:23
to live is *C* and to die is gain. . . . Phil 1:21
which is *C* in you, the hope of glory . . . Col 1:27
and your life is now hidden with *C* . . . Col 3:3
Jesus *C* is the same yesterday . . . Heb 13:8
believes that Jesus is the *C* is born . . . 1 Jn 5:1

CHRISTIAN(S) *follower of Jesus the Messiah (Christ)*
The disciples were called *C* first . . . Acts 11:26
you can persuade me to be a *C*? . . . Acts 26:28
as a *C*, do not be ashamed, . . . 1 Pt 4:16

CHURCH *"assembly" or "called out ones"; the body of believers gathered to worship Jesus*
and on this rock I will build my *c*, . . . Mt 16:18
if he refuses to listen even to the *c*, . . .
Mt 18:17

Be shepherds of the *c* of God, . . . Acts 20:28
of mine to judge those outside the *c*. . . 1 Cor 5:12
but he who prophesies edifies the *c*. . . . 1 Cor 14:4
to excel in gifts that build up the *c*. . . . 1 Cor 14:12
done for the strengthening of the *c*. . . . 1 Cor 14:26
because I persecuted the *c* of God. . . . 1 Cor 15:9
how intensely I persecuted the *c* . . . Gal 1:13
as Christ is the head of the *c*, . . . Eph 5:23
he is the head of the body, the *c*; . . . Col 1:18
the sake of his body, which is the *c*. . . . Col 1:24

CIRCUMCISE(D), CIRCUMCISION *to remove the foreskin of male children, signifying Israel's covenant relationship with God*
Every male among you shall be *c*. . . . Gn 17:10
C your hearts, therefore, . . . Dt 10:16
and *c* the Israelites at Gibeath . . . Jos 5:3
C has value if you observe the law, . . . Rom 2:25
and *c* is *c* of the heart, by the Spirit, . . . Rom 2:29
C is nothing and uncircumcision is . . . 1 Cor 7:19
that if you let yourselves be *c*, . . . Gal 5:2

CITIZEN(S)(SHIP) *person owing allegiance to and deriving protection from a sovereign state*
I had to pay a big price for my *c*. . . . Acts 22:28
excluded from *c* in Israel . . . Eph 2:12
but fellow *c* with God's people . . . Eph 2:19
But our *c* is in heaven. . . . Phil 3:20

CLEAN *pure; without guilt or moral corruption; without ceremonial defilement; see UNCLEAN*
seven of every kind of *c* animal, . . . Gn 7:2
the camp to a place ceremonially *c*, . . . Lv 4:12
you will be *c* from all your sins. . . . Lv 16:30
He who has *c* hands and a pure . . . Ps 24:4
with hyssop, and I will be *c*; . . . Ps 51:7
I am *c* and without sin"? . . . Prv 20:9
I will sprinkle *c* water on you, . . . Ez 36:25
are willing, you can make me *c*. . . . Mt 8:2
the house unoccupied, swept *c*. . . . Mt 12:44
You *c* the outside of the cup . . . Mt 23:25
Jesus declared all foods *"c."*) . . . Mk 7:19
to wash his feet; his whole body is *c* . . . Jn 13:10
are already *c* because of the word . . . Jn 15:3
impure that God has made *c*. . . . Acts 10:15
All food is *c*, but it is wrong . . . Rom 14:20

CLEANSE(D)(S), CLEANSING *to make clean or pure*
and *c* me from my sin. . . . Ps 51:2
C me with hyssop, and I will be . . . Ps 51:7
Blows and wounds *c* away evil, . . . Prv 20:30
c her by the washing with water . . . Eph 5:26
If a man *c* himself from the latter, . . . 2 Tm 2:21
c our consciences from acts that . . . Heb 9:14
requires that nearly everything be *c* . . . Heb 9:22
having our hearts sprinkled to *c* us . . . Heb 10:22
has forgotten that he has been *c* . . . 2 Pt 1:9

COLD *seasonal (like winter); lacking warmth; indifferent*
Like *c* water to a weary soul . . . Prv 25:25
anyone gives even a cup of *c* water . . . Mt 10:42
the love of most will grow *c*, . . . Mt 24:12

COMFORT(ED)(S) *to encourage, help, and strengthen*
He will *c* us in the labor . . . Gn 5:29
You have given me *c* . . . Ru 2:13
sympathize with him and *c* him. . . . Jb 2:11

rod and your staff, they *c* me. . . . Ps 23:4
and *c* me once again. . . . Ps 71:21
My *c* in my suffering is this: . . . Ps 119:50
May your unfailing love be my *c*, . . . Ps 119:76
C, *c* my people, . . . Is 40:1
For the LORD *c* his people . . . Is 49:13
I, even I, am he who *c* you. . . . Is 51:12
to *c* all who mourn, . . . Is 61:2
As a mother *c* her child, . . . Is 66:13
there is none to *c* her. . . . Lam 1:2
you have already received your *c*. . . . Lk 6:24
of compassion and the God of all *c*, . . . 2 Cor 1:3
so that we can *c* those . . . 2 Cor 1:4
through Christ our *c* overflows. . . . 2 Cor 1:5
But God, who *c* the downcast, . . . 2 Cor 7:6
if any *c* from his love, . . . Phil 2:1

COMFORTER(S) *a person who encourages, helps, and strengthens*
miserable *c* are you all! . . . Jb 16:2
for *c*, but I found none. . . . Ps 69:20
and they have no *c*; . . . Eccl 4:1
O my *C* in sorrow, . . . Jer 8:18

COMMAND(ED) *to issue a charge or directive*
Noah did all that the LORD *c* him. . . . Gn 7:5
Do not add to what I *c* you . . . Dt 4:2
The LORD *c* us to obey all these . . . Dt 6:24
Have I not *c* you? Be strong . . . Jos 1:9
Obey me and do everything I *c* you . . . Jer 11:4
mighty are those who obey his *c*. . . . Jl 2:11
love me, you will obey what I *c*. . . . Jn 14:15
My *c* is this: Love each other . . . Jn 15:12
Lord has *c* that those who preach . . . 1 Cor 9:14
law is summed up in a single *c*: . . . Gal 5:14
goal of this *c* is love, which comes . . . 1 Tm 1:5
universe was formed at God's *c*, . . . Heb 11:3
I am not writing you a new *c* . . . 1 Jn 2:7
this is his *c*: to believe in the name . . . 1 Jn 3:23

COMMANDMENT(S), COMMANDS *a charge or directive; a gracious provision of God's law or religious instruction*
who love me and keep my *c*. . . . Ex 20:6
Keep my *c* and follow them. . . . Lv 22:31
to you his covenant, the Ten *C*, . . . Dt 4:13
who love me and keep my *c*. . . . Dt 5:10
These *c* that I give you today are . . . Dt 6:6
those who love him and keep his *c*, . . . Dt 7:9
But be very careful to keep the *c* . . . Jos 22:5
those who love him and obey his *c*, . . . Neh 1:5
for I delight in your *c* . . . Ps 119:47
All your *c* are trustworthy; . . . Ps 119:86
Your *c* make me wiser . . . Ps 119:98
and all your *c* are true. . . . Ps 119:151
for all your *c* are righteous. . . . Ps 119:172
but keep my *c* in your heart, . . . Prv 3:1
For these *c* are a lamp, . . . Prv 6:23
Fear God and keep his *c*, . . . Eccl 12:13
all who love him and obey his *c*, . . . Dn 9:4
This is the first and greatest *c*. . . . Mt 22:38
There is no *c* greater than these. . . . Mk 12:31
A new *c* I give you: Love one . . . Jn 13:34
which is the first *c* with a promise . . . Eph 6:2
This is love for God: to obey his *c*. . . . 1 Jn 5:3

COMMEND(ABLE)(ED)(S) *to entrust for care or preservation; to praise; praiseworthy*
The people *c* all the men who . . . Neh 11:2
and those who saw me *c* me, . . . Jb 29:11
One generation will *c* your works . . . Ps 145:4
of the wise *c* knowledge, . . . Prv 15:2
So I *c* the enjoyment of life, . . . Eccl 8:15
master *c* the dishonest manager . . . Lk 16:8
c by the brothers to the grace . . . Acts 15:40
do what is right and he will *c* you. . . . Rom 13:3
I *c* to you our sister Phoebe, . . . Rom 16:1
beginning to *c* ourselves again? . . . 2 Cor 3:1
the truth plainly we *c* ourselves . . . 2 Cor 4:2
trying to *c* ourselves to you again, . . . 2 Cor 5:12

as servants of God we *c* ourselves . . . 2 Cor 6:4
with some who *c* themselves. . . . 2 Cor 10:12
I ought to have been *c* by you, . . . 2 Cor 12:11
This is what the ancients were *c* for . . . Heb 11:2
By faith he was *c* as a righteous . . . Heb 11:4
he was *c* as one who pleased God. . . . Heb 11:5
These were all *c* for their faith, . . . Heb 11:39
and to *c* those who do right. . . . 1 Pt 2:14
For it is *c* if a man bears up . . . 1 Pt 2:19
you endure it, this is *c* before God. . . . 1 Pt 2:20

COMMIT(S), COMMITTED *to perpetrate; to obligate or pledge oneself to something*
You shall not *c* adultery. . . . Ex 20:14
and *c* yourselves to the LORD . . . 1 Sm 7:3
Into your hands I *c* my spirit; . . . Ps 31:5
C your way to the LORD; . . . Ps 37:5
C to the LORD whatever you do, . . . Prv 16:3
a wicked man *c* a hundred crimes . . . Eccl 8:12
that it was said, 'Do not *c* adultery.' . . . Mt 5:27
All things have been *c* to me . . . Mt 11:27
into your hands I *c* my spirit. . . . Lk 23:46
c them to the Lord, . . . Acts 14:23
where they had been *c* to the grace . . . Acts 14:26
I *c* you to God and to the word . . . Acts 20:32
I am simply discharging the trust *c* . . . 1 Cor 9:17
And he has *c* to us the message . . . 2 Cor 5:19
to God's will should *c* themselves . . . 1 Pt 4:19

COMPANION(S) *friend or fellow participant*
your God, has set you above your *c* . . . Ps 45:7
my *c*, my close friend, . . . Ps 55:13
My *c* attacks his friends; . . . Ps 55:20
but a *c* of fools suffers harm. . . . Prv 13:20
A man of many *c* may come to ruin . . . Prv 18:24
a *c* of gluttons disgraces his father. . . . Prv 28:7
c of prostitutes squanders his . . . Prv 29:3
your God, has set you above your *c* . . . Heb 1:9
your brother and *c* in the suffering . . . Rv 1:9

COMPASSION(ATE) *loving sympathy; empathy*
the LORD, the *c* and gracious God . . . Ex 34:6
he will show you mercy, have *c* . . . Dt 13:17
gracious and *c*, slow to anger . . . Neh 9:17
O Lord, are a *c* and gracious God, . . . Ps 86:15
and crowns you with love and *c*. . . . Ps 103:4
Your *c* is great, O LORD; . . . Ps 119:156
LORD is gracious and *c*, . . . Ps 145:8
says the LORD, who has *c* on you. . . . Is 54:10
that you are a gracious and *c* God, . . . Jon 4:2
show mercy and *c* to one another. . . . Zec 7:9
When he saw the crowds, he had *c* . . . Mt 9:36
he had *c* on them and healed their . . . Mt 14:14
I have *c* for these people; . . . Mt 15:32
Jesus had *c* on them and touched . . . Mt 20:34
I will have *c* on whom I have *c* . . . Rom 9:15
the Father of *c* and the God . . . 2 Cor 1:3
Be kind and *c* to one another, . . . Eph 4:32
and *c*, then make my joy complete . . . Phil 2:1
clothe yourselves with *c*, kindness, . . . Col 3:12
The Lord is full of *c* and mercy. . . . Jas 5:11
love as brothers, be *c* and humble. . . . 1 Pt 3:8

COMPEL(S), COMPELLED *to force; to urge*
and the spirit within me *c* me; . . . Jb 32:18
And now, *c* by the Spirit, . . . Acts 20:22
I cannot boast, for I am *c* to preach. . . . 1 Cor 9:16
For Christ's love *c* us, because we . . . 2 Cor 5:14

COMPLAINING *protesting; making a formal allegation against a party*
Do everything without *c* or arguing . . . Phil 2:14

COMPLETE *having all necessary parts; finished; thorough*
your hands, and your joy will be *c*. . . . Dt 16:15
That joy is mine, and it is now *c*. . . . Jn 3:29
and that your joy may be *c*. . . . Jn 15:11

will receive, and your joy will be c. . . . Jn 16:24
May they be brought to c unity . . . Jn 17:23
c the task the Lord Jesus has given . . . Acts 20:24
then make my joy c . . . Phil 2:2
to it that you c the work you have . . . Col 4:17
so that you may be mature and c, . . . Jas 1:4
his faith was made c by what he did . . . Jas 2:22
We write this to make our joy c. . . . 1 Jn 1:4
God's love is truly made c in him. . . . 1 Jn 2:5
his love is made c in us. . . . 1 Jn 4:12
love is made c among us . . . 1 Jn 4:17
to face, so that our joy may be c. . . . 2 Jn 1:12

CONCEIVE(D)(S) *to become pregnant; to devise or imagine*
c trouble gives birth . . . Ps 7:14
from the time my mother c me. . . . Ps 51:5
what is c in her is from the Holy . . . Mt 1:20
no mind has c . . . 1 Cor 2:9
after desire has c, it gives birth . . . Jas 1:15

CONDEMN(ATION)(ED)(ING)(S) *to declare guilty; conviction of guilt; censure*
the innocent and c the guilty. . . . Dt 25:1
c the guilty and bringing . . . 1 Kgs 8:32
the foes of the righteous will be c. . . . Ps 34:21
and c the innocent to death. . . . Ps 94:21
the guilty and c the innocent . . . Prv 17:15
Who is he that will c me? . . . Is 50:9
of c and reproach; you will never . . . Jer 42:18
and horror, of c and reproach. . . . Jer 44:12
you would not have c the innocent. . . . Mt 12:7
and by your words you will be c. . . . Mt 12:37
whoever does not believe will be c . . . Mk 16:16
Do not c, and you will not be . . . Lk 6:37
Son into the world to c the world, . . . Jn 3:17
yet in c him they fulfilled the words . . . Acts 13:27
judge the other, you are c yourself, . . . Rom 2:1
why am I still c as a sinner? . . . Rom 3:7
followed one sin and brought c, . . . Rom 5:16
there is now no c for those who are . . . Rom 8:1
Who is he that c? Christ Jesus, . . . Rom 8:34
disciplined so that we will not be c . . . 1 Cor 11:32
Their c has long been hanging . . . 2 Pt 2:3
presence whenever our hearts c us. . . . 1 Jn 3:20
certain men whose c was written . . . Jude 1:4

CONFESS(ED)(ES)(ING)(ION) *to admit or acknowledge (sin or faith); creedal statement*
But if they will c their sins . . . Lv 26:40
they turn back and c your name, . . . 2 Chr 6:24
I c the sins we Israelites, including . . . Neh 1:6
I c my iniquity; . . . Ps 38:18
whoever c and renounces them . . . Prv 28:13
C their sins, they were baptized . . . Mt 3:6
fail to c, but confessed freely, . . . Jn 1:20
they would not c their faith . . . Jn 12:42
and openly c their evil deeds. . . . Acts 19:18
That if you c with your mouth, . . . Rom 10:9
obedience that accompanies your c . . . 2 Cor 9:13
every tongue c that Jesus Christ is . . . Phil 2:11
called when you made your good c . . . 1 Tm 6:12
and, "Everyone who c the name . . . 2 Tm 2:19
Therefore c your sins to each other . . . Jas 5:16
If we c our sins, he is faithful . . . 1 Jn 1:9

CONFIDENCE, CONFIDENT *being sure of something; without doubt*
And the people gained c . . . 2 Chr 32:8
Should not your piety be your c . . . Jb 4:6
even then will I be c. . . . Ps 27:3
I am still c of this: . . . Ps 27:13
my c since my youth. . . . Ps 71:5
for the LORD will be your c . . . Prv 3:26
A gossip betrays a c, . . . Prv 11:13
do not betray another man's c, . . . Prv 25:9
Her husband has full c in her . . . Prv 31:11

a source of c for the people of Israel . . . Ez 29:16
put no c in a friend. . . . Mi 7:5
I had c in all of you, that you would . . . 2 Cor 2:3
Such c as this is ours . . . 2 Cor 3:4
Therefore we are always c . . . 2 Cor 5:6
We are c, I say, and would prefer . . . 2 Cor 5:8
If anyone is c that he belongs . . . 2 Cor 10:7
God with freedom and c. . . . Eph 3:12
day until now, being c of this, . . . Phil 1:6
and who put no c in the flesh . . . Phil 3:3
We have c in the Lord that you are . . . 2 Thes 3:4
till the end the c we had at first. . . . Heb 3:14
the throne of grace with c, . . . Heb 4:16
we are c of better things . . . Heb 6:9
since we have c to enter the Most . . . Heb 10:19
So do not throw away your c; . . . Heb 10:35
that when he appears we may be c . . . 1 Jn 2:28
we have c before God and receive . . . 1 Jn 3:21
us so that we will have c on the day . . . 1 Jn 4:17

CONFORM(ED)(ITY)(S) *to make similar or the same; to give one thing the characteristics of something else*
c to the standards of the nations . . . Ez 5:7
but have c to the standards . . . Ez 11:12
predestined to be c to the likeness . . . Rom 8:29
Do not c any longer to the pattern . . . Rom 12:2
in c with the purpose of his will, . . . Eph 1:11
to the sound doctrine that c . . . 1 Tm 1:11
do not c to the evil desires you had . . . 1 Pt 1:14

CONSCIENCE(S) *one's moral sensitivity or scruples*
I have done this with a clear c . . . Gn 20:5
have on his c the staggering burden . . . 1 Sm 25:31
my c will not reproach me as long . . . Jb 27:6
to keep my c clear before God . . . Acts 24:16
their c also bearing witness, . . . Rom 2:15
my c confirms it in the Holy Spirit . . . Rom 9:1
punishment but also because of c. . . . Rom 13:5
My c is clear, but that does not . . . 1 Cor 4:4
since their c is weak, it is defiled. . . . 1 Cor 8:7
without raising questions of c, . . . 1 Cor 10:25
Our c testifies that we have . . . 2 Cor 1:12
to every man's c in the sight of God . . . 2 Cor 4:2
and I hope it is also plain to your c. . . . 2 Cor 5:11
and a good c and a sincere faith. . . . 1 Tm 1:5
holding on to faith and a good c. . . . 1 Tm 1:19
truths of the faith with a clear c . . . 1 Tm 3:9
whose c have been seared . . . 1 Tm 4:2
as my forefathers did, with a clear c . . . 2 Tm 1:3
their minds and c are corrupted. . . . Ti 1:15
able to clear the c of the worshiper. . . . Heb 9:9
to cleanse us from a guilty c . . . Heb 10:22
We are sure that we have a clear c . . . Heb 13:18
and respect, keeping a clear c, . . . 1 Pt 3:16
the pledge of a good c toward God. . . . 1 Pt 3:21

CONSECRATE(D) *to set apart or devote to God*
C to me every firstborn male. . . . Ex 13:2
the place will be c by my glory. . . . Ex 29:43
c it and all its furnishings, . . . Ex 40:9
So he c Aaron and his garments . . . Lv 8:30
C yourselves and be holy, . . . Lv 20:7
C the fiftieth year and proclaim . . . Lv 25:10
fellow Levites are to c yourselves . . . 1 Chr 15:12
c this temple so that my Name may . . . 2 Chr 7:16

is to be c to the Lord"), . . . Lk 2:23
because it is c by the word of God . . . 1 Tm 4:5

CONSUME(S), CONSUMING *to destroy (as by fire); to waste or burn away*
For the LORD your God is a c fire, . . . Dt 4:24
for zeal for your house c me, . . . Ps 69:9
Zeal for your house will c me. . . . Jn 2:17
and awe, for our "God is a c fire." . . . Heb 12:29

CONTEMPT *to arouse disgust, scorn, disdain*
He who oppresses the poor shows c . . . Prv 14:31
He who mocks the poor shows c . . . Prv 17:5
When wickedness comes, so does c . . . Prv 18:3
O priests, who show c for my name. . . . Mal 1:6
Or do you show c for the riches . . . Rom 2:4
do not treat prophecies with c. . . . 1 Thes 5:20

CONTENT(MENT) *to be pleased, satisfied, willing; satisfaction*
If only we had been c to stay . . . Jos 7:7
and their years in c. . . . Jb 36:11
The righteous eat to their hearts' c, . . . Prv 13:25
one rests c, untouched by trouble. . . . Prv 19:23
yet his eyes were not c . . . Eccl 4:8
like one bringing c. . . . Song 8:10
to be c whatever the circumstances . . . Phil 4:11
I have learned the secret of being c . . . Phil 4:12
and clothing, we will be c with that. . . . 1 Tm 6:8
But godliness with c is great gain. . . . 1 Tm 6:6
and be c with what you have, . . . Heb 13:5

CONTRITE *grieving and penitent for sin*
a broken and c heart, . . . Ps 51:17
also with him who is c and lowly . . . Is 57:15
he who is humble and c in spirit, . . . Is 66:2

CONVICT(ION) *to find or prove guilty of an offense; feelings of guilt*
with those who c the guilty, . . . Prv 24:25
he will c the world of guilt in regard . . . Jn 16:8
the Holy Spirit and with deep c. . . . 1 Thes 1:5
and to c all the ungodly . . . Jude 1:15

CORNERSTONE *essential part of a building's foundation; metaphor for Christ*
or who laid its c . . . Jb 38:6
a precious c for a sure foundation; . . . Is 28:16
rock will be taken from you for a c, . . . Jer 51:26
From Judah will come the c, . . . Zec 10:4
Christ Jesus himself as the chief c. . . . Eph 2:20
a chosen and precious c, . . . 1 Pt 2:6

CORRECT(ED)(ING)(ION)(S) *to set right with remedies, revisions, or reforms*
things you do not accept my c . . . Lv 26:23
Blessed is the man whom God c; . . . Jb 5:17
Do you mean to c what I say, . . . Jb 6:26
He makes them listen to c . . . Jb 36:10
contends with the Almighty c him? . . . Jb 40:2
How my heart spurned c! . . . Prv 5:12
Whoever c a mocker invites insult; . . . Prv 9:7
whoever ignores c leads others . . . Prv 10:17
he who hates c is stupid. . . . Prv 12:1
whoever heeds c is honored. . . . Prv 13:18
whoever heeds c shows prudence. . . . Prv 15:5
he who hates c will die. . . . Prv 15:10
A mocker resents c; . . . Prv 15:12
whoever heeds c gains . . . Prv 15:32
The rod of c imparts wisdom, . . . Prv 29:15
A servant cannot be c . . . Prv 29:19
they did not respond to c. . . . Jer 2:30
crushed them, but they refused c. . . . Jer 5:3
LORD its God or responded to c. . . . Jer 7:28
C me, LORD, but only with justice . . . Jer 10:24
she accepts no c. . . . Zep 3:2
you will fear me and accept c! . . . Zep 3:7

c, rebuke and encourage . . . 2 Tm 4:2
c and training in righteousness, . . . 2 Tm 3:16

CORRUPT(ED)(ION)(S) *to go from good to bad, physically or morally*
Now the earth was *c* in God's sight . . . Gn 6:11
They are *c*, their deeds are vile; . . . Ps 14:1
they have together become *c*; . . . Ps 14:3
keep *c* talk far from your lips. . . . Prv 4:24
who goes about with a *c* mouth, . . . Prv 6:12
A *c* witness mocks at justice, . . . Prv 19:28
and a bribe *c* the heart. . . . Eccl 7:7
Bad company *c* good character. . . . 1 Cor 15:33
wronged no one, we have *c* no one, . . . 2 Cor 7:2
but to those who are *c* and do not . . . Ti 1:15
It *c* the whole person, . . . Jas 3:6
escape the *c* in the world caused . . . 2 Pt 1:4
If they have escaped the *c* . . . 2 Pt 2:20

COUNSEL *advice; policy, plan, or action; to advise*
First seek the *c* of the LORD. . . . 1 Kgs 22:5
walk in the *c* of the wicked . . . Ps 1:1
You guide me with your *c*, . . . Ps 73:24
despised the *c* of the Most High. . . . Ps 107:11
C and sound judgment are mine; . . . Prv 8:14
Plans fail for lack of *c*, . . . Prv 15:22
wonderful in *c* and magnificent . . . Is 28:29
So I *c* younger widows to marry, . . . 1 Tm 5:14
I *c* you to buy from me gold refined . . . Rv 3:18

COURAGE(OUS) *mental or moral strength; see* DISCOURAGE
Be strong and *c*. . . . Dt 31:6
and *c*, because you will lead these . . . Jos 1:6
commanded you? Be strong and *c*. . . . Jos 1:9
Be strong and *c*. . . . Jos 10:25
Act with *c*, and may the LORD be . . . 2 Chr 19:11
with these words: "Be strong and *c*. . . . 2 Chr 32:7
said to them: "Take *c*! . . . Mt 14:27
When they saw the *c* of Peter . . . Acts 4:13
Take *c*! As you have testified . . . Acts 23:11
now I urge you to keep up your *c*, . . . Acts 27:22
stand firm in the faith; be men of *c*; . . . 1 Cor 16:13
will have sufficient *c* so that now . . . Phil 1:20
if we hold on to our *c* and the hope . . . Heb 3:6

COVENANT(S) *agreement or promise between two or more parties; see* PROMISE
I now establish my *c* with you . . . Gn 9:9
I will confirm my *c* between me . . . Gn 17:2
if you obey me fully and keep my *c*, . . . Ex 19:5
declared to you his *c*, the Ten . . . Dt 4:13
you who keep your *c* of love . . . 1 Kgs 8:23
He remembers his *c* forever, . . . 1 Chr 16:15
who keeps his *c* of love . . . Neh 1:5
He remembers his *c* forever, . . . Ps 105:8
when I will make a new *c* . . . Jer 31:31
I will make a *c* of peace with them; . . . Ez 37:26
the wife of your marriage *c*. . . . Mal 2:14
blood of the *c*, which is poured out . . . Mt 26:28
This is my blood of the *c*, . . . Mk 14:24
This cup is the new *c* in my blood, . . . Lk 22:20
theirs the divine glory, the *c*, . . . Rom 9:4
for the women represent two *c*. . . . Gal 4:24
as the *c* of which he is mediator . . . Heb 8:6
Christ is the mediator of a new *c*, . . . Heb 9:15

COVER(ED)(S) *to hide from sight or knowledge; to be of sufficient scope so as to include or top something else*
Make an atonement *c* of pure gold . . . Ex 25:17
and *c* you with my hand . . . Ex 33:22
in the cloud over the atonement *c*. . . . Lv 16:2
and did not *c* up my iniquity. . . . Ps 32:5
He will *c* you with his feathers, . . . Ps 91:4
but love *c* over all wrongs. . . . Prv 10:12
He who *c* over an offense promotes . . . Prv 17:9

c you with the shadow of my hand . . . Is 51:16
whose sins are *c*. . . . Rom 4:7
and *c* over a multitude of sins. . . . Jas 5:20
love *c* over a multitude of sins. . . . 1 Pt 4:8

COVET(ED)(ING) *to wrongfully desire what belongs to another*
You shall not *c* your neighbor's . . . Ex 20:17
and no one will *c* your land . . . Ex 34:24
You shall not *c* your neighbor's . . . Dt 5:21
Do not *c* the silver and gold . . . Dt 7:25
weighing fifty shekels, I *c* them . . . Jos 7:21
They *c* fields and seize them, . . . Mi 2:2
I have not *c* anyone's silver or gold . . . Acts 20:33
"Do not steal," "Do not *c*," . . . Rom 13:9

CREATE(D) *to bring into being; to form, make, produce; see* CREATION, MAKE
In the beginning God *c* the heavens . . . Gn 1:1
So God *c* man in his own image, . . . Gn 1:27
and the earth when they were *c*. . . . Gn 2:4
C in me a pure heart, O God, . . . Ps 51:10
For you *c* my inmost being; . . . Ps 139:13
for he commanded and they were *c* . . . Ps 148:5
Behold, I will *c* new heavens . . . Is 65:17
for I will *c* Jerusalem to be a delight . . . Is 65:18
The LORD will *c* a new thing . . . Jer 31:22
one Father? Did not one God *c* us? . . . Mal 2:10
His purpose was to *c* . . . Eph 2:15
c to be like God in true . . . Eph 4:24
For by him all things were *c*: . . . Col 1:16
for everything God *c* is good, . . . 1 Tm 4:4
a kind of firstfruits of all he *c*. . . . Jas 1:18
and by your will they were *c*. . . . Rv 4:11

CREATION *something that is created; the world and universe; the act of bringing something into existence; see* CREATE
hidden since the *c* of the world. . . . Mt 13:35
of *c* God 'made them male . . . Mk 10:6
and preach the good news to all *c*. . . . Mk 16:15
me before the *c* of the world. . . . Jn 17:24
The *c* waits in eager expectation . . . Rom 8:19
he is a new *c*; the old has gone, . . . 2 Cor 5:17
what counts is a new *c*. . . . Gal 6:15
God, the firstborn over all *c*. . . . Col 1:15
that is to say, not a part of this *c*. . . . Heb 9:11
chosen before the *c* of the world, . . . 1 Pt 1:20

CREATOR *Maker; see* CREATE; *see* MAKER
C of heaven and earth. . . . Gn 14:19
Remember your *C* . . . Eccl 12:1
the *C* of the ends of the earth. . . . Is 40:28
in knowledge in the image of its *C*. . . . Col 3:10

CREATURE(S) *created being or animal*
bring into the ark two of all living *c*, . . . Gn 6:19
again will I destroy all living *c*, . . . Gn 8:21
For the life of a *c* is in the blood, . . . Lv 17:11
the life of every *c* is its blood, . . . Lv 17:14
the earth is full of your *c*. . . . Ps 104:24
and who gives food to every *c*. . . . Ps 136:25
was what looked like four living *c*. . . . Ez 1:5
beside each *c* with its four faces. . . . Ez 1:15
The first living *c* was like a lion, . . . Rv 4:7

CROSS *a structure consisting of an upright post with a cross beam, used as an instrument of death; the means by which atonement was made between God and humanity*
anyone who does not take his *c* . . . Mt 10:38
take up his *c* and follow me. . . . Mt 16:24
take up his *c* daily and follow me. . . . Lk 9:23
anyone who does not carry his *c* . . . Lk 14:27
Carrying his own *c*, he went out . . . Jn 19:17
to death by nailing him to the *c*. . . . Acts 2:23
lest the *c* of Christ be emptied . . . 1 Cor 1:17
offense of the *c* has been abolished. . . . Gal 5:11
persecuted for the *c* of Christ. . . . Gal 6:12
both of them to God through the *c*, . . . Eph 2:16
he took it away, nailing it to the *c*. . . . Col 2:14

triumphing over them by the *c*. . . . Col 2:15
set before him endured the *c*, . . . Heb 12:2

CROWN(ED)(S) *the top of the head; emblem encircling the head worn by victors, priests, or royalty*
and *c* him with glory and honor. . . . Ps 8:5
and *c* me with love and compassion . . . Ps 103:4
he *c* the humble with salvation. . . . Ps 149:4
present you with a *c* of splendor. . . . Prv 4:9
blessing *c* him who is willing to sell. . . . Prv 11:26
noble character is her husband's *c*, . . . Prv 12:4
the prudent are *c* with knowledge. . . . Prv 14:18
Gray hair is a *c* of splendor; . . . Prv 16:31
Children's children are a *c* . . . Prv 17:6
everlasting joy will *c* their heads. . . . Is 35:10
to bestow on them a *c* of beauty . . . Is 61:3
and a beautiful *c* on your head. . . . Ez 16:12
then twisted together a *c* of thorns . . . Mt 27:29
The soldiers twisted together a *c* . . . Jn 19:2
it to get a *c* that will last forever. . . . 1 Cor 9:25
and long for, my joy and *c*, . . . Phil 4:1
or the *c* in which we will glory . . . 1 Thes 2:19
he does not receive the victor's *c* . . . 2 Tm 2:5
you *c* him with glory and honor . . . Heb 2:7
you will receive the *c* . . . 1 Pt 5:4
I will give you the *c* of life. . . . Rv 2:10
had *c* of gold on their heads. . . . Rv 4:4
They lay their *c* before the throne . . . Rv 4:10
ten horns and seven *c* on his heads. . . . Rv 12:3
and on his head are many *c*. . . . Rv 19:12

CRUCIFIED, CRUCIFY *to execute or nail to the cross; to put to death*
to be mocked and flogged and *c*. . . . Mt 20:19
of Man will be handed over to be *c*. . . . Mt 26:2
They all answered, "*C* him!" . . . Mt 27:22
and handed him over to be *c*. . . . Mt 27:26
Then they led him away to *c* him. . . . Mt 27:31
whom you *c*, both Lord and Christ . . . Acts 2:36
For we know that our old self was *c* . . . Rom 6:6
we preach Christ *c*: a stumbling . . . 1 Cor 1:23
I have been *c* with Christ . . . Gal 2:20

CUP *drinking vessel; figurative for tangible consolation, salvation of Christ, the wrath of God, or drunkenness*
my *c* overflows. . . . Ps 23:5
from that *c*, the goblet of my wrath, . . . Is 51:22
the *c* that made you stagger; . . . Is 51:22
anyone gives even a *c* of cold water . . . Mt 10:42
Can you drink the *c* I am going . . . Mt 20:22
You clean the outside of the *c* . . . Mt 23:25
Then he took the *c*, gave thanks . . . Mt 26:27
may this *c* be taken from me. . . . Mt 26:39
Is not the *c* of thanksgiving . . . 1 Cor 10:16

CURSE(D)(S), CURSING *to pronounce a sentence; a condemnation or judgment*
C is the ground because of you; . . . Gn 3:17
Now you are under a *c* . . . Gn 4:11
Never again will the ground . . . Gn 8:21
and whoever curses you I will *c*; . . . Gn 12:3
Anyone who *c* his father . . . Ex 21:17
before you today a blessing and a *c* . . . Dt 11:26
hung on a tree is under God's *c*. . . . Dt 21:23
C God and die!" . . . Jb 2:9
They may *c*, but you will bless; . . . Ps 109:28
The LORD's *c* is on the house . . . Prv 3:33
bless those who *c* you, pray . . . Lk 6:28
Their mouths are full of *c* . . . Rom 3:14
persecute you; bless and do not *c* . . . Rom 12:14
When we are *c*, we bless; . . . 1 Cor 4:12
on observing the law are under a *c*, . . . Gal 3:10
the same mouth come praise and *c*. . . . Jas 3:10
No longer will there be any *c*. . . . Rv 22:3

DARK(NESS) *devoid of light; nightfall; blackened; in spiritual terms, secret, closed, or blinded*

d was over the surface of the deep, . . . Gn 1:2
he separated the light from the *d*. . . . Gn 1:4
and total *d* covered all Egypt . . . Ex 10:22
approached the thick *d* where God . . . Ex 20:21
the LORD turns my *d* into light. . . . 2 Sm 22:29
There is no *d* place, no deep . . . Jb 34:22
d clouds were under his feet. . . . Ps 18:9
my God turns my *d* into light. . . . Ps 18:28
the pestilence that stalks in the *d*, . . . Ps 91:6
Even in *d* light dawns . . . Ps 112:4
even the *d* will not be dark to you; . . . Ps 139:12
the way of the wicked is like deep *d* . . . Prv 4:19
She gets up while it is still *d*; . . . Prv 31:15
Do not stare at me because I am *d*, . . . Song 1:6
and light for *d*, . . . Is 5:20
I will turn the *d* into light . . . Is 42:16
I form the light and create *d*, . . . Is 45:7
then your light will rise in the *d*, . . . Is 58:10
and release from *d*, . . . Is 61:1
The sun will be turned to *d* . . . Jl 2:31
the people living in *d* . . . Mt 4:16
how great is that *d!* "No one can . . . Mt 6:23
are bad, your body also is full of *d*. . . . Lk 11:34
and *d* came over the whole land . . . Lk 23:44
The light shines in the *d*, . . . Jn 1:5
but men loved *d* instead of light . . . Jn 3:19
in the *d* does not know where he is . . . Jn 12:35
The sun will be turned to *d* . . . Acts 2:20
a light for those who are in the *d*, . . . Rom 2:19
who said, "Let light shine out of *d*, . . . 2 Cor 4:6
fellowship can light have with *d*? . . . 2 Cor 6:14
For you were once *d*, but now you . . . Eph 5:8
out of *d* into his wonderful light. . . . 1 Pt 2:9
as to a light shining in a *d* place, . . . 2 Pt 1:19
Blackest *d* is reserved for them. . . . 2 Pt 2:17
in him there is no *d* at all. . . . 1 Jn 1:5
in *d*, bound with everlasting chains . . . Jude 1:6
for whom blackest *d* has been . . . Jude 1:13

DAY(S) *daylight; a 24-hour period; a specified time or period in the distance*

God called the light "*d*," . . . Gn 1:5
so on the seventh *d* he rested . . . Gn 2:2
the people rested on the seventh *d*. . . . Ex 16:30
Remember the Sabbath *d* . . . Ex 20:8
meditate on it *d* and night, . . . Jos 1:8
all the *d* of my life, . . . Ps 23:6
have made my *d* a mere . . . Ps 39:5
Better is one *d* in your courts . . . Ps 84:10
The length of our *d* is seventy years . . .
　Ps 90:10
Teach us to number our *d* aright, . . . Ps 90:12
proclaim his salvation *d* after *d* . . . Ps 96:2
As for man, his *d* are like grass, . . . Ps 103:15
This is the *d* the LORD has made; . . . Ps 118:24
Creator in the *d* of your youth, . . . Eccl 12:1
and to his blessings in the last *d* . . . Hos 3:5
I will pour out my Spirit in those *d*. . . . Jl 2:29
Will not the *d* of the LORD be . . . Am 5:20
The *d* of the LORD is near . . . Ob 1:15
The great *d* of the LORD is near . . . Zep 1:14
joined with the LORD in that *d* . . . Zec 2:11
A *d* of the LORD is coming . . . Zec 14:1
dreadful *d* of the LORD comes. . . . Mal 4:5
up to the *d* of Noah entered the ark; . . . Mt 24:38
Give us each *d* our daily bread. . . . Lk 11:3
in his *d* will be like the lightning, . . . Lk 17:24
The *d* will come upon you . . . Lk 19:43
by the prophet Joel: " 'In the last *d*, . . . Acts
　2:17
D after *d*, in the temple courts . . . Acts 5:42
examined the Scriptures every *d* . . . Acts 17:11
man considers every *d* alike. . . . Rom 14:5
his spirit saved on the *d* of the Lord . . . 1 Cor
　5:5
we are being renewed *d* by *d*. . . . 2 Cor 4:16
I spent a night and a *d* . . . 2 Cor 11:25
for you know very well that the *d* . . . 1 Thes 5:2

so that this *d* should surprise you . . . 1 Thes
　5:4
saying that the *d* of the Lord has . . . 2 Thes 2:2
will be terrible times in the last *d*. . . . 2 Tm 3:1
in these last *d* he has spoken to us . . . Heb 1:2
that in the last *d* scoffers will come, . . . 2 Pt 3:3
With the Lord a *d* is like . . . 2 Pt 3:8
d of the Lord will come like a thief. . . . 2 Pt 3:10
For the great *d* of their wrath has . . . Rv 6:17
on the great *d* of God Almighty. . . . Rv 16:14

DEACON(S) *person called to serve others in need; leader in the church*

together with the overseers and *d*: . . . Phil 1:1
D, likewise, are to be men worthy . . . 1 Tm 3:8
against them, let them serve as *d* . . . 1 Tm
　3:10
A *d* must be the husband of . . . 1 Tm 3:12

DEAD *without (physical or spiritual) life; see DEATH, DIE*

who eats anything found *d* . . . Lv 17:15
or spiritist or who consults the *d*. . . . Dt 18:11
Why consult the *d* on behalf . . . Is 8:19
and let the *d* bury their own *d*. . . . Mt 8:22
He has risen from the *d* . . . Mt 28:7
For this son of mine was *d* . . . Lk 15:24
rise from the *d* on the third day, . . . Lk 24:46
count yourselves *d* to sin . . . Rom 6:11
do who are baptized for the *d*? . . . 1 Cor 15:29
you were *d* in your transgressions . . . Eph 2:1
and the *d* in Christ will rise first. . . . 1 Thes 4:16
is not accompanied by action, is *d*. . . . Jas 2:17
so faith without deeds is *d*. . . . Jas 2:26
Blessed are the *d* who die . . . Rv 14:13
And I saw the *d*, great and small, . . . Rv 20:12

DEATH *cessation of (physical or spiritual) life; see DEAD, DIE*

kills him shall surely be put to *d*. . . . Ex 21:12
the murderer shall be put to *d*. . . . Nm 35:16
set before you life and *d*, . . . Dt 30:19
if anything but *d* separates you . . . Ru 1:17
D is naked before God; . . . Jb 26:6
the valley of the shadow of *d*, . . . Ps 23:4
for your sake we face *d* all day long . . .
　Ps 44:22
What man can live and not see *d*, . . . Ps 89:48
is the *d* of his saints. . . . Ps 116:15
all who hate me love *d*. . . . Prv 8:36
he who pursues evil goes to his *d*. . . . Prv
　11:19
but in the end it leads to *d*. . . . Prv 14:12
D and Destruction lie open . . . Prv 15:11
but in the end it leads to *d*. . . . Prv 16:25
tongue has the power of life and *d*, . . . Prv
　18:21
do not be a willing party to his *d*. . . . Prv 19:18
and save his soul from *d*. . . . Prv 23:14
for *d* is the destiny of every man; . . . Eccl 7:2
he will swallow up *d* forever. . . . Is 25:8
he poured out his life unto *d*, . . . Is 53:12
pleasure in the *d* of the wicked? . . . Ez 18:23
Where, O *d*, are your plagues? . . . Hos 13:14
he has crossed over from *d* to life. . . . Jn 5:24
delivered over to *d* for our sins . . . Rom 4:25
and in this way *d* came to all men, . . . Rom
　5:12
d reigned from the time of Adam . . . Rom 5:14
Jesus were baptized into his *d*? . . . Rom 6:3
For the wages of sin is *d*, . . . Rom 6:23
me from this body of *d*? . . . Rom 7:24
put to *d* the misdeeds of the body, . . . Rom
　8:13
your sake we face *d* all day long; . . . Rom 8:36
For since *d* came through a man, . . . 1 Cor
　15:21
The last enemy to be destroyed is *d* . . . 1 Cor
　15:26
Where, O *d*, is your sting? . . . 1 Cor 15:55
who has destroyed *d* and has . . . 2 Tm 1:10
him who holds the power of *d* . . . Heb 2:14

There is a sin that leads to *d*. . . . 1 Jn 5:16
And I hold the keys of *d* and Hades . . . Rv 1:18
The second *d* has no power . . . Rv 20:6
The lake of fire is the second *d*. . . . Rv 20:14
Then *d* and Hades were thrown . . . Rv 20:14
There will be no more *d* . . . Rv 21:4
This is the second *d*. . . . Rv 21:8

DEBT(S) *that which is owed to someone; see DEBTOR*

seven years you must cancel *d*. . . . Dt 15:1
the year for canceling *d*, is near, . . . Dt 15:9
the upper one as security for a *d*, . . . Dt 24:6
or in *d* or discontented gathered . . . 1 Sm 22:2
of the poor is seized for a *d*. . . . Jb 24:9
or puts up security for *d*; . . . Prv 22:26
Forgive us our *d*, . . . Mt 6:12
that he had be sold to repay the *d*. . . . Mt 18:25
canceled the *d* and let him go. . . . Mt 18:27
into prison until he could pay the *d* . . .
　Mt 18:30
I canceled all that *d* of yours . . . Mt 18:32
so he canceled the *d* of both. . . . Lk 7:42
Let no *d* remain outstanding, . . . Rom 13:8
continuing *d* to love one another, . . . Rom 13:8

DEBTOR(S) *one in debt or under obligation; see DEBT*

for *d* as for creditor. . . . Is 24:2
Will not your *d* suddenly arise? . . . Hb 2:7
as we also have forgiven our *d*. . . . Mt 6:12
called in each one of his master's *d*. . . . Lk 16:5

DECEIT *deliberate concealment of the truth; dishonesty; trickery*

with their tongue they speak *d*. . . . Ps 5:9
nor was any *d* in his mouth. . . . Is 53:9
He will cause *d* to prosper, . . . Dn 8:25
nor will *d* be found in their mouths. . . . Zep
　3:13
greed, malice, *d*, lewdness, envy, . . . Mk 7:22
You are full of all kinds of *d* . . . Acts 13:10
murder, strife, *d* and malice. . . . Rom 1:29
their tongues practice *d*. . . . Rom 3:13
yourselves of all malice and all *d*, . . . 1 Pt 2:1
and no *d* was found in his mouth. . . . 1 Pt 2:22

DECEITFUL(NESS) *dishonest; misrepresenting the truth*

for their *d* is in vain. . . . Ps 119:118
The heart is *d* above all things . . . Jer 17:9
Their heart is *d*, . . . Hos 10:2
and the *d* of wealth choke it, . . . Mt 13:22
the *d* of wealth and the desires . . . Mk 4:19
men are false apostles, *d* workmen, . . . 2 Cor
　11:13
of men in their *d* scheming. . . . Eph 4:14
is being corrupted by its *d* desires; . . . Eph 4:22
of you may be hardened by sin's *d*. . . . Heb
　3:13
and his lips from *d* speech. . . . 1 Pt 3:10
who does what is shameful or *d*, . . . Rv 21:27

DECEIVE(D)(S), DECEIVING *to mislead; to misrepresent the truth*

The serpent *d* me, and I ate. . . . Gn 3:13
d his neighbor about something . . . Lv 6:2
Do not *d* one another. . . . Lv 19:11
A truthful witness does not *d*, . . . Prv 14:5
or use your lips to *d*. . . . Prv 24:28
is a man who *d* his neighbor . . . Prv 26:19
Do not *d* yourselves, thinking, . . . Jer 37:9
garment of hair in order to *d*. . . . Zec 13:4
Watch out that no one *d* you. . . . Mt 24:4
'I am he,' and will *d* many. . . . Mk 13:6
Watch out that you are not *d*, . . . Lk 21:8
and flattery they *d* the minds . . . Rom 16:18
Do not *d* yourselves. . . . 1 Cor 3:18
the kingdom of God? Do not be *d*: . . . 1 Cor 6:9
Eve was *d* by the serpent's cunning . . . 2 Cor
　11:3
when he is nothing, he *d* himself. . . . Gal 6:3
Do not be *d*: God cannot be . . . Gal 6:7
Let no one *d* you with empty words . . . Eph 5:6

this so that no one may *d* you . . . Col 2:4
Don't let anyone *d* you in any way, . . . 2 Thes 2:3
And Adam was not the one *d*; . . . 1 Tm 2:14
follow *d* spirits and things taught . . . 1 Tm 4:1
to worse, deceiving and being *d*. . . . 2 Tm 3:13
d and enslaved by all kinds . . . Ti 3:3
Don't be *d*, my dear brothers. . . . Jas 1:16
we *d* ourselves and the truth is not . . . 1 Jn 1:8
he *d* the inhabitants of the earth. . . . Rv 13:14
him from the nations anymore . . . Rv 20:3

DECEIVER(S) *one who leads others astray*
when wicked *d* surround me . . . Ps 49:5
while he was still alive that *d* said, . . . Mt 27:63
and *d*, especially those . . . Ti 1:10
Any such person is the *d* . . . 2 Jn 1:7

DECREE(D)(S) *to decide and declare; a thing decided and declared*
my commands, my *d* and my laws . . . Gn 26:5
There the LORD made a *d* . . . Ex 15:25
inform them of God's *d* and laws. . . . Ex 18:16
Israelites all the *d* the LORD has . . . Lv 10:11
and be careful to follow my *d*. . . . Lv 18:4
confirmed it to Jacob as a *d*, . . . 1 Chr 16:17
I will proclaim the *d* of the LORD: . . . Ps 2:7
Awake, my God; *d* justice. . . . Ps 7:6
He *d* statutes for Jacob . . . Ps 78:5
this is a *d* for Israel, . . . Ps 81:4
teach me your *d*. . . . Ps 119:12
I delight in your *d*; . . . Ps 119:16
and I meditate on your *d*. . . . Ps 119:48
My heart is set on keeping your *d* . . . Ps 119:112
he gave a *d* that will never pass . . . Ps 148:6
LORD your God *d* this disaster . . . Jer 40:2
happen if the Lord has not *d* it? . . . Lam 3:37
and this is the *d* the Most High has . . . Dn 4:24
Augustus issued a *d* that a census . . . Lk 2:1
Son of Man will go as it has been *d*, . . . Lk 22:22
know God's righteous *d* that those . . . Rom 1:32

DEDICATE(D), DEDICATION *to set apart for a purpose, often spiritual; the act of setting apart*
he has been *d* by the anointing oil . . . Lv 21:12
thus defiling the hair he has *d*, . . . Nm 6:9
He must *d* himself to the LORD . . . Nm 6:12
shave off the hair that he *d*. . . . Nm 6:18
d to the LORD to do the work . . . Nm 18:6
and all the Israelites dedicate the temple . . . 1 Kgs 8:63
You have now *d* yourselves . . . 2 Chr 29:31
They *d* it and set its doors in place, . . . Neh 3:1
for a man to *d* something rashly . . . Prv 20:25
came the Feast of *D* at Jerusalem. . . . Jn 10:22
sensual desires overcome their *d* . . . 1 Tm 5:11

DEED(S) *a feat or exploit; legal document defining ownership*
or on earth who can do the *d* . . . Dt 3:24
or by great and awesome *d*, . . . Dt 4:34
and by him *d* are weighed. . . . 1 Sm 2:3
his marvelous *d* among all peoples. . . . 1 Chr 16:24
Because he takes note of their *d*, . . . Jb 34:25
and telling of all your wonderful *d*. . . . Ps 26:7
right hand display awesome *d*. . . . Ps 45:4
with awesome *d* of righteousness, . . . Ps 65:5
How awesome are your *d*! . . . Ps 66:3
day I declare your marvelous *d*. . . . Ps 71:17
who alone does marvelous *d*. . . . Ps 72:18
I will tell of all your *d*. . . . Ps 73:28
men tell of your wonderful *d*. . . . Ps 75:1
I will remember the *d* of the LORD . . . Ps 77:11
the praiseworthy *d* of the LORD, . . . Ps 78:4
no *d* can compare with yours. . . . Ps 86:8
or your righteous *d* in the land . . . Ps 88:12
May your *d* be shown . . . Ps 90:16
For you make me glad by your *d*, . . . Ps 92:4
his marvelous *d* among all peoples. . . . Ps 96:3
and his wonderful *d* for men, . . . Ps 107:8

Glorious and majestic are his *d*, . . . Ps 111:3
and I will proclaim your great *d*. . . . Ps 145:6
and sealed the *d*, had it witnessed, . . . Jer 32:10
that they may see your good *d* . . . Mt 5:16
He has performed mighty *d* . . . Lk 1:51
we are getting what our *d* deserve. . . . Lk 23:41
prove their repentance by their *d*. . . . Acts 26:20
you do, whether in word or *d*, . . . Col 3:17
and strengthen you in every good *d* . . . 2 Thes 2:17
rich in good *d*, and to be generous . . . 1 Tm 6:18
on toward love and good *d*. . . . Heb 10:24
claims to have faith but has no *d*? . . . Jas 2:14
they may see your good *d* . . . 1 Pt 2:12
I know your *d*, your love and faith, . . . Rv 2:19
I know your *d*; you have . . . Rv 3:1
for their *d* will follow them. . . . Rv 14:13
Great and marvelous are your *d*, . . . Rv 15:3

DEEP *primeval chaos; sea; ocean; great depth; see DEPTH*
was over the surface of the *d*, . . . Gn 1:2
Now the springs of the *d* . . . Gn 8:2
D calls to *d* . . . Ps 42:7
to Simon, "Put out into *d* water, . . . Lk 5:4
all things, even the *d* things . . . 1 Cor 2:10
hold of the *d* truths of the faith . . . 1 Tm 3:9

DEFEND(ED)(ING)(S) *to protect; to thwart an attack*
He *d* the cause of the fatherless . . . Dt 10:18
With his own hands he *d* his cause. . . . Dt 33:7
d the fatherless and the oppressed, . . . Ps 10:18
He will *d* the afflicted . . . Ps 72:4
Rise up, O God, and *d* your cause; . . . Ps 74:22
How long will you *d* the unjust . . . Ps 82:2
D the cause of the weak . . . Ps 82:3
D my cause and redeem me; . . . Ps 119:154
d the rights of the poor and needy . . . Prv 31:9
D the cause of the fatherless, . . . Is 1:17
They do not *d* the cause . . . Is 1:23
your God, who *d* his people: . . . Is 51:22
they do not *d* the rights of the poor. . . . Jer 5:28
He *d* the cause of the poor . . . Jer 22:16
He will vigorously *d* their cause . . . Jer 50:34
now accusing, now even *d* them.) . . . Rom 2:15
or *d* and confirming the gospel, . . . Phil 1:7

DEFENDER, DEFENSE *one who thwarts an attack; protection*
the *d* is not guilty of bloodshed; . . . Ex 22:2
Awake, and rise to my *d*! . . . Ps 35:23
to the fatherless, a *d* of widows, . . . Ps 68:5
for their *D* is strong; . . . Prv 23:11
here for the *d* of the gospel. . . . Phil 1:16
speaks to the Father in our *d* . . . 1 Jn 2:1

DELIGHT(ED)(FUL)(ING)(S) *something that gives great pleasure; to enjoy*
and I will take no *d* in the pleasing . . . Lv 26:31
The LORD will again *d* in you . . . Dt 30:9
Does the LORD *d* . . . 1 Sm 15:22
But his *d* is in the law of the LORD . . . Ps 1:2
and *d* in his salvation. . . . Ps 35:9
D yourself in the LORD . . . Ps 37:4
You do not *d* in sacrifice, . . . Ps 51:16
I *d* in your decrees; . . . Ps 119:16
and *d* in mankind. . . . Prv 8:31
but accurate weights are his *d*. . . . Prv 11:1
he *d* in men who are truthful. . . . Prv 12:22
A king *d* in a wise servant, . . . Prv 14:35
for your love is more *d* than wine. . . . Song 1:2
We rejoice and *d* in you; . . . Song 1:4
How *d* is your love, my sister, . . . Song 4:10
the one I love, in whom I *d*; . . . Mt 12:18
in my inner being I *d* in God's law; . . . Rom 7:22
Love does not *d* in evil . . . 1 Cor 13:6

DELIVER(ANCE)(ED)(ER)(S) *to rescue, liberate, or redeem; to turn over or give up to*
and no one can *d* out of my hand. . . . Dt 32:39
From the LORD comes *d*. . . . Ps 3:8
is my rock, my fortress and my *d*; . . . Ps 18:2
A horse is a vain hope for *d*; . . . Ps 33:17
he *d* me from all my fears. . . . Ps 34:4
he *d* them from the wicked . . . Ps 37:40
You are my help and my *d*; . . . Ps 40:17
For he will *d* the needy who cry out . . . Ps 72:12
of the goodness of your love, *d* me. . . . Ps 109:21
have *d* my soul from death, . . . Ps 116:8
d me according to your promise. . . . Ps 119:170
but *d* us from the evil one. . . . Mt 6:13
He was *d* over to death for our sins . . . Rom 4:25
The *d* will come from Zion; . . . Rom 11:26

DEMON(S) *an evil spirit*
to *d*, which are not God . . . Dt 32:17
and in your name drive out *d* . . . Mt 7:22
d begged Jesus, "If you drive us . . . Mt 8:31
And when the *d* was driven out, . . . Mt 9:33
and they say, 'He has a *d*.' . . . Mt 11:18
Jesus rebuked the *d*, and it came . . . Mt 17:18
but he would not let the *d* speak . . . Mk 1:34
The *d* begged Jesus, "Send us . . . Mk 5:12
to drive the *d* out of her daughter. . . . Mk 7:26
In my name they will drive out *d*; . . . Mk 16:17
there was a man possessed by a *d*, . . . Lk 4:33
wine, and you say, 'He has a *d*.' . . . Lk 7:33
driven by the *d* into solitary places. . . . Lk 8:29
the *d* threw him to the ground . . . Lk 9:42
When the *d* left, the man who had . . . Lk 11:14
I am not possessed by a *d*, . . . Jn 8:49
Can a *d* open the eyes of the blind . . . Jn 10:21
neither angels nor *d*, neither . . . Rom 8:38
of pagans are offered to *d*, . . . 1 Cor 10:20
spirits and things taught by *d*. . . . 1 Tm 4:1
Good! Even the *d* believe that . . . Jas 2:19
they did not stop worshiping *d*, . . . Rv 9:20
of *d* performing miraculous signs, . . . Rv 16:14
She has become a home for *d* . . . Rv 18:2

DEMON-POSSESSED *controlled or indwelt by an evil spirit*
those suffering severe pain, the *d*, . . . Mt 4:24
many who were *d* were brought . . . Mt 8:16
two *d* men coming . . . Mt 8:28
man who was *d* and could not talk . . . Mt 9:32
they brought him a *d* man who was . . . Mt 12:22
brought to Jesus all the sick and *d*. . . . Mk 1:32
what had happened to the *d* man . . . Mk 5:16
met by a *d* man from the town. . . . Lk 8:27
the people how the *d* man had been . . . Lk 8:36
"You are *d*," the crowd answered. . . . Jn 7:20
that you are a Samaritan and *d*? . . . Jn 8:48
Many of them said, "He is *d* . . . Jn 10:20
Jesus over those who were *d*. . . . Acts 19:13

DENIED, DENIES, DENY(ING) *to reject, disavow, or refuse to accept as true*
Do not *d* justice to your poor . . . Ex 23:6
till I die, I will not *d* my integrity. . . . Jb 27:5
but *d* justice to the innocent. . . . Is 5:23
to *d* a man his rights . . . Lam 3:35
and *d* justice to the oppressed. . . . Am 2:7
he must *d* himself and take up his . . . Mt 16:24
But he *d* it before them all. . . . Mt 26:70
you will *d* three times that you . . . Lk 22:34
he has *d* the faith and is worse . . . 1 Tm 5:8
a form of godliness but *d* its power. . . . 2 Tm 3:5
by their actions they *d* him. . . . Ti 1:16
It is the man who *d* that Jesus is . . . 1 Jn 2:22
No one who *d* the Son has . . . 1 Jn 2:23
my word and have not *d* my name. . . . Rv 3:8

DEPART(ED)(S)(URE) *to leave or go away; to deviate from; to separate from*
The scepter will not *d* from Judah, . . . Gn 49:10

The glory has *d* from Israel . . . 1 Sm 4:21
and naked I will *d*. . . . Jb 1:21
I have not *d* from your laws, . . . Ps 119:102
and as he comes, so he *d* . . . Eccl 5:15
D from me, you who are cursed, . . . Mt 25:41
I desire to *d* and be with Christ, . . . Phil 1:23
the time has come for my *d* . . . 2 Tm 4:6
after my *d* you will always be able . . . 2 Pt 1:15

DEPRAVED *marked by corruption or evil*
ways you soon became more *d* . . . Ez 16:47
and prostitution she was more *d* . . . Ez 23:11
he gave them over to a *d* mind, . . . Rom 1:28
in a crooked and *d* generation, . . . Phil 2:15
oppose the truth—men of *d* minds, . . . 2 Tm 3:8

DEPTH(S) *bottomless pit; vastness; deep waters; see DEEP*
Out of the *d* I cry to you, O LORD; . . . Ps 130:1
any powers, neither height nor *d*, . . . Rom 8:39
the *d* of the riches of the wisdom . . . Rom 11:33

DESCEND(ED)(ING) *to go or come down*
of God were ascending and *d* on it. . . . Gn 28:12
the Spirit of God *d* like a dove . . . Mt 3:16
the Spirit *d* on him like a dove. . . . Mk 1:10
and *d* on the Son of Man. . . . Jn 1:51
or 'Who will *d* into the deep?' . . . Rom 10:7
except that he also *d* to the lower, . . . Eph 4:9
For it is clear that our Lord *d* . . . Heb 7:14

DESIRE(S) *to have a longing for; to wish or request*
and also *d* for gaining wisdom, . . . Gn 3:6
Your *d* will be for your husband, . . . Gn 3:16
at your door; it *d* to have you, . . . Gn 4:7
anything you *d* from me I will do . . . 2 Sm 19:38
give you the *d* of your heart. . . . Ps 37:4
Sacrifice and offering you did not *d* . . . Ps 40:6
earth has nothing I *d* besides you . . . Ps 73:25
who satisfies your *d* with good things, . . . Ps 103:5
satisfy the *d* of every living thing. . . . Ps 145:16
What a man *d* is unfailing love; . . . Prv 19:22
do not *d* their company; . . . Prv 24:1
appearance that we should *d* him. . . . Is 53:2
For I *d* mercy, not sacrifice, . . . Hos 6:6
learn what this means: 'I *d* mercy, . . . Mt 9:13
set on what that nature *d*; . . . Rom 8:5
to gratify the *d* of the sinful nature. . . . Rom 13:14
But eagerly *d* the greater gifts. . . . 1 Cor 12:31
and you will not gratify the *d* . . . Gal 5:16
being corrupted by its deceitful *d*; . . . Eph 4:22
impurity, lust, evil *d* and greed, . . . Col 3:5
their sensual *d* overcome their . . . 1 Tm 5:11
and harmful *d* that plunge men . . . 1 Tm 6:9
Flee the evil *d* of youth, . . . 2 Tm 2:22
are swayed by all kinds of evil *d*, . . . 2 Tm 3:6
Sacrifice and offering you did not *d* . . . Heb 10:5
and sin offerings you did not *d*, . . . Heb 10:8
to abstain from sinful *d*, which war . . . 1 Pt 2:11
in the world caused by evil *d*. . . . 2 Pt 1:4
to the lustful *d* of sinful human . . . 2 Pt 2:18
The world and its *d* pass away, . . . 1 Jn 2:17
they follow their own evil *d*; . . . Jude 1:16
will follow their own ungodly *d*. . . . Jude 1:18

DESPISE(D)(S) *to scorn or regard as unworthy, sometimes with malice*
So Esau *d* his birthright. . . . Gn 25:34
Why did you *d* the word . . . 2 Sm 12:9
God is mighty, but does not *d* men; . . . Jb 36:5
by men and *d* by the people. . . . Ps 22:6
O God, you will not *d* . . . Ps 51:17
but fools *d* wisdom and discipline. . . . Prv 1:7
do not *d* the LORD's discipline . . . Prv 3:11
He who *d* his neighbor sins, . . . Prv 14:21
who ignores discipline *d* himself, . . . Prv 15:32
do not *d* your mother . . . Prv 23:22
He was *d* and rejected by men, . . . Is 53:3
devoted to the one and *d* the other. . . . Mt 6:24
of this world and the *d* things . . . 1 Cor 1:28

Or do you *d* the church of God . . . 1 Cor 11:22
Do not let anyone *d* you. . . . Ti 2:15

DESTROY(ED)(S) *to kill, annihilate; to cause devastation or ruin*
floodwaters on the earth to *d* all life . . . Gn 6:17
will there be a flood to *d* the earth. . . . Gn 9:11
you today that you will surely be *d*. . . . Dt 8:19
complacency of fools will *d* them; . . . Prv 1:32
the unfaithful are *d* . . . Prv 11:3
mouth the godless *d* his neighbor, . . . Prv 11:9
listens to him will be *d* forever. . . . Prv 21:28
but one sinner *d* much good. . . . Eccl 9:18
his kingdom will not be *d*, . . . Dn 6:26
of the One who can *d* both soul . . . Mt 10:28
I will *d* this man-made temple . . . Mk 14:58
to *d* us? I know who you are . . . Lk 4:34
only to steal and kill and *d*; . . . Jn 10:10
But Saul began to *d* the church. . . . Acts 8:3
so that the sinful nature may be *d* . . . 1 Cor 5:5
for whom Christ died, is *d* . . . 1 Cor 8:11
The last enemy to be *d* is death. . . . 1 Cor 15:26
abandoned; struck down, but not *d*. . . . 2 Cor 4:9
who has *d* death and has brought . . . 2 Tm 1:10
the elements will be *d* by fire, . . . 2 Pt 3:10
Since everything will be *d* . . . 2 Pt 3:11
later *d* those who did not believe. . . . Jude 1:5
destroying those who *d* the earth. . . . Rv 11:18

DESTRUCTION *ruin, failure*
and you will be the cause of their *d* . . . Nm 32:15
Pride goes before *d*, . . . Prv 16:18
he who builds a high gate invites *d*. . . . Prv 17:19
Where, O grave, is your *d*? . . . Hos 13:14
broad is the road that leads to *d*, . . . Mt 7:13
it collapsed and its *d* was complete . . . Lk 6:49
except the one doomed to *d* . . . Jn 17:12
from that nature will reap *d*; . . . Gal 6:8
Their destiny is *d*, their god is their . . . Phil 3:19
d will come on them suddenly, . . . 1 Thes 5:3
punished with everlasting *d* . . . 2 Thes 1:9
is revealed, the man doomed to *d*. . . . 2 Thes 2:3
that plunge men into ruin and *d*. . . . 1 Tm 6:9
bringing swift *d* on themselves. . . . 2 Pt 2:1
of judgment and *d* of ungodly men. . . . 2 Pt 3:7
out of the Abyss and go to his *d*. . . . Rv 17:8

DEVIL *Satan; the personification of evil*
the desert to be tempted by the *d*. . . . Mt 4:1
the enemy who sows them is the *d*. . . . Mt 13:39
the eternal fire prepared for the *d* . . . Mt 25:41
then the *d* comes and takes away . . . Lk 8:12
of you is a *d*!" (He meant Judas, . . . Jn 6:70
You belong to your father, the *d*, . . . Jn 8:44
the *d* had already prompted Judas . . . Jn 13:2
You are a child of the *d* . . . Acts 13:10
and do not give the *d* a foothold. . . . Eph 4:27
stand against the *d*'s schemes. . . . Eph 6:11
under the same judgment as the *d*. . . . 1 Tm 3:6
and escape from the trap of the *d*, . . . 2 Tm 2:26
the *d* and free those who all their . . . Heb 2:14
but is earthly, unspiritual, of the *d*. . . . Jas 3:15
Resist the *d*, and he will flee . . . Jas 4:7
Your enemy the *d* prowls . . . 1 Pt 5:8
because the *d* has been sinning . . . 1 Jn 3:8
who does what is sinful is of the *d*, . . . 1 Jn 3:8
and who the children of the *d* are: . . . 1 Jn 3:10
with the *d* about the body of Moses . . . Jude 1:9
the *d* will put some of you in prison . . . Rv 2:10
that ancient serpent called the *d* . . . Rv 12:9
the *d* has gone down to you! . . . Rv 12:12
that ancient serpent, who is the *d*, . . . Rv 20:2
And the *d*, who deceived them, . . . Rv 20:10

DEVOTE(D) *to consecrate or set apart*
Now *d* your heart and soul . . . 1 Chr 22:19

Levites so they could *d* themselves . . . 2 Chr 31:4
For Ezra had *d* himself to the study . . . Ezr 7:10
Yet if you *d* your heart to him . . . Jb 11:13
Guard my life, for I am *d* to you. . . . Ps 86:2
for who is he who will *d* himself . . . Jer 30:21
You will *d* their ill-gotten gains . . . Mi 4:13
or he will be *d* to the one . . . Mt 6:24
from me is Corban' (that is, a gift *d* . . . Mk 7:11
They *d* themselves . . . Acts 2:42
Paul *d* himself exclusively . . . Acts 18:5
Be *d* to one another . . . Rom 12:10
so that you may *d* yourselves . . . 1 Cor 7:5
Her aim is to be *d* to the Lord . . . 1 Cor 7:34
and they have *d* themselves . . . 1 Cor 16:15
for yourselves how *d* to us you are. . . . 2 Cor 7:12
D yourselves to prayer, being . . . Col 4:2
nor to *d* themselves to myths . . . 1 Tm 1:4
d yourself to the public reading . . . 1 Tm 4:13
may be careful to *d* themselves . . . Ti 3:8

DEVOUR(ED)(ING)(S) *to consume or destroy*
Must the sword *d* forever? . . . 2 Sm 2:26
the sword *d* one as well as another. . . . 2 Sm 11:25
but a foolish man *d* all he has. . . . Prv 21:20
But all who devour you will be *d*; . . . Jer 30:16
They *d* widows' houses . . . Mk 12:40
keep on biting and *d* each other, . . . Gal 5:15
lion looking for someone to *d* . . . 1 Pt 5:8

DEVOUT *deeply sincere in religious faith*
Obadiah was a *d* believer . . . 1 Kgs 18:3
d men are taken away, . . . Is 57:1
Simeon, who was righteous and *d*. . . . Lk 2:25
his family were *d* and God-fearing; . . . Acts 10:2
a *d* soldier who was one of his attendants . . . Acts 10:7
and *d* converts to Judaism followed . . . Acts 13:43
He was a *d* observer of the law . . . Acts 22:12

DIE(D)(S) *to cease living; see DEAD, DEATH*
when you eat of it you will surely *d* . . . Gn 2:17
you must not touch it, or you will *d*. . . . Gn 3:3
Every firstborn son in Egypt will *d*, . . . Ex 11:5
Where you *d* I will *d*, and there I . . . Ru 1:17
each is to *d* for his own sins. . . . 2 Kgs 14:6
Saul *d* because he was unfaithful . . . 1 Chr 10:13
If a man *d*, will he live again? . . . Jb 14:14
He will *d* for lack of discipline, . . . Prv 5:23
fools *d* for lack of judgment. . . . Prv 10:21
he who hates correction will *d*. . . . Prv 15:10
with the rod, he will not *d*. . . . Prv 23:13
a time to be born and a time to *d*, . . . Eccl 3:2
everyone will *d* for his own sin; . . . Jer 31:30
that wicked man will *d* for his sin, . . . Ez 3:18
soul who sins is the one who will *d*. . . . Ez 18:4
Why will you *d*, O house of Israel? . . . Ez 18:31
O wicked man, you will surely *d*, . . . Ez 33:8
for all who draw the sword will *d* . . . Mt 26:52
The time came when the beggar *d* . . . Lk 16:22
you will *d* in your sin. . . . Jn 8:21
in me will live, even though he *d*; . . . Jn 11:25
But if it *d*, it produces many seeds. . . . Jn 12:24
we were still powerless, Christ *d* . . . Rom 5:6
by no means! We *d* to sin; . . . Rom 6:2
if we *d*, we *d* to the Lord. . . . Rom 14:8
that Christ *d* for our sins according . . . 1 Cor 15:3
in Adam all *d*, so in Christ all will . . . 1 Cor 15:22
d for all, and therefore all *d*. . . . 2 Cor 5:14
to live is Christ and to *d* is gain. . . . Phil 1:21
Since you *d* with Christ . . . Col 2:20
We believe that Jesus *d* . . . 1 Thes 4:14
He *d* for us so that, whether we are . . . 1 Thes 5:10
now that he has *d* as a ransom . . . Heb 9:15

Just as man is destined to *d* once, . . . Heb 9:27
so that we might *d* to sins . . . 1 Pt 2:24
For Christ *d* for sins once for all, . . . 1 Pt 3:18

DIFFER(ING)(S) *to be unlike or distinct in nature; different*
Do not have two *d* weights . . . Dt 25:13
Do not have two *d* measures . . . Dt 25:14
D weights and *d* measures . . . Prv 20:10
The LORD detests *d* weights, . . . Prv 20:23
and star *d* from star in splendor. . . . 1 Cor 15:41

DIFFERENCE(S), DIFFERENT *distinguishing characteristic; dissimilar, not alike*
my servant Caleb has a *d* spirit . . . Nm 14:24
you will be changed into a *d* person . . . 1 Sm 10:6
Can I tell the *d* between what is . . . 2 Sm 19:35
so that they may learn the *d* . . . 2 Chr 12:8
each one *d* from the other, . . . Est 1:7
whose customs are *d* from those . . . Est 3:8
they teach that there is no *d* . . . Ez 22:26
are to teach my people the *d* . . . Ez 44:23
Jesus appeared in a *d* form . . . Mk 16:12
There is no *d*, for all have sinned . . . Rom 3:22
For there is no *d* between Jew . . . Rom 10:12
We have *d* gifts, according . . . Rom 12:6
For who makes you *d* . . . 1 Cor 4:7
to be *d* among you to show which . . . 1 Cor 11:19
There are *d* kinds of gifts, . . . 1 Cor 12:4
or a *d* gospel from the one you . . . 2 Cor 11:4
and are turning to a *d* gospel . . . Gal 1:6
whatever they were makes no *d* . . . Gal 2:6
he is no *d* from a slave, . . . Gal 4:1
are said belonged to a *d* tribe, . . . Heb 7:13
and sent them off in a *d* direction? . . . Jas 2:25

DILIGENCE, DILIGENT *earnest; hardworking; dutiful; careful; persevering in doing good*
The work is being carried on with *d* . . . Ezr 5:8
but *d* hands bring wealth. . . . Prv 10:4
D hands will rule, . . . Prv 12:24
the *d* man prizes his possessions. . . . Prv 12:27
of the *d* are fully satisfied. . . . Prv 13:4
The plans of the *d* lead to profit . . . Prv 21:5
Be *d* in these matters; give yourself . . . 1 Tm 4:15
to show this same *d* to the very end . . . Heb 6:11

DISCERN(ED)(ING)(MENT) *to discover; to recognize; the ability to discover or recognize*
So give your servant a *d* heart . . . 1 Kgs 3:9
I will give you a wise and *d* heart, . . . 1 Kgs 3:12
Who can *d* his errors? . . . Ps 19:12
I am your servant; give me *d* . . . Ps 119:125
You *d* my going out and my lying . . . Ps 139:3
let the *d* get guidance . . . Prv 1:5
preserve sound judgment and *d*, . . . Prv 3:21
To the *d* all of them are right; . . . Prv 8:9
on the lips of the *d*, . . . Prv 10:13
knowledge comes easily to the *d*. . . . Prv 14:6
in the heart of the *d* . . . Prv 14:33
The *d* heart seeks knowledge, . . . Prv 15:14
The wise in heart are called *d*, . . . Prv 16:21
A rebuke impresses a man of *d* . . . Prv 17:10
A *d* man keeps wisdom in view, . . . Prv 17:24
and *d* if he holds his tongue. . . . Prv 17:28
heart of the *d* acquires knowledge; . . . Prv 18:15
rebuke a *d* man, and he will gain . . . Prv 19:25
He who keeps the law is a *d* son, . . . Prv 28:7
a poor man who has *d* sees . . . Prv 28:11
because they are spiritually *d*. . . . 1 Cor 2:14
you may be able to *d* what is best . . . Phil 1:10

DISCIPLE(S) *follower of some doctrine or teacher*
He called his twelve *d* to him . . . Mt 10:1
these little ones because he is my *d*, . . . Mt 10:42

Therefore go and make *d* . . . Mt 28:19
withdrew with his *d* to the lake, . . . Mk 3:7
Then the *d* went out and preached . . . Mk 16:20
he called his *d* to him and chose . . . Lk 6:13
his own life he cannot be my *d*. . . . Lk 14:26
everything he has cannot be my *d*. . . . Lk 14:33
and his *d* put their faith in him. . . . Jn 2:11
many of his *d* turned back . . . Jn 6:66
to my teaching, you are really my *d* . . . Jn 8:31
men will know that you are my *d* . . . Jn 13:35
The *d* were called Christians first . . . Acts 11:26

DISCIPLINE(D)(S) *to punish, guide, instruct; punishment, guidance, instruction*
made you hear his voice to *d* you. . . . Dt 4:36
listen to them when they *d* him, . . . Dt 21:18
so do not despise the *d* . . . Jb 5:17
You rebuke and *d* men for their sin; . . . Ps 39:11
Does he who *d* nations not punish? . . . Ps 94:10
but fools despise wisdom and *d*. . . . Prv 1:7
do not despise the LORD's *d* . . . Prv 3:11
You will say, "How I hated *d*! . . . Prv 5:12
He will die for lack of *d*, . . . Prv 5:23
and the corrections of *d* . . . Prv 6:23
He who heeds *d* shows the way . . . Prv 10:17
Whoever loves *d* loves knowledge, . . . Prv 12:1
He who ignores *d* comes to poverty . . . Prv 13:18
who loves him is careful to *d* him. . . . Prv 13:24
A fool spurns his father's *d*, . . . Prv 15:5
Stern *d* awaits him who leaves . . . Prv 15:10
He who ignores *d* despises himself, . . . Prv 15:32
D your son, for in that there is hope . . . Prv 19:18
the rod of *d* will drive it far . . . Prv 22:15
Do not withhold *d* from a child; . . . Prv 23:13
get wisdom, *d* and understanding. . . . Prv 23:23
D your son, and he will give you . . . Prv 29:17
would not listen or respond to *d*. . . . Jer 17:23
I will *d* you but only with justice; . . . Jer 30:11
would not listen or respond to *d*. . . . Jer 32:33
I will *d* you but only with justice; . . . Jer 46:28
we are being *d* so that we will not . . . 1 Cor 11:32
do not make light of the Lord's *d*, . . . Heb 12:5
Those whom I love I rebuke and *d*. . . . Rv 3:19

DISCOURAGE(D) *to hinder; to deprive of courage or hope; see COURAGE*
they *d* the Israelites . . . Nm 32:9
Do not be afraid; do not be *d*. . . . Dt 1:21
Do not be afraid; do not be *d*. . . . Dt 31:8
Do not be terrified; do not be *d*, . . . Jos 1:9
Do not be afraid or *d*. . . . Jos 8:1
Do not be afraid or *d*. . . . 1 Chr 22:13
or *d*, for the LORD God, . . . 1 Chr 28:20
or *d* because of this vast army. . . . 2 Chr 20:15
Do not be afraid; do not be *d*. . . . 2 Chr 20:17
or *d* because of the king of Assyria . . . 2 Chr 32:7
to you, and you are *d*; . . . Jb 4:5
he will not falter or be *d* . . . Is 42:4
to be *d* because of my sufferings . . . Eph 3:13
children, or they will become *d*. . . . Col 3:21

DISCRETION *good judgment; prudence in behavior, speech, and dress*
May the LORD give you *d* . . . 1 Chr 22:12
knowledge and *d* to the young . . . Prv 1:4
D will protect you, . . . Prv 2:11
that you may maintain *d* . . . Prv 5:2
I possess knowledge and *d*. . . . Prv 8:12
a beautiful woman who shows no *d*. . . . Prv 11:22

DISGRACE(FUL)(S) *to be a source of shame; to cause to lose favor or standing; the condition of one fallen from grace or honor*
during harvest is a *d* son. . . . Prv 10:5
When pride comes, then comes *d*, . . . Prv 11:2

a *d* wife is like decay in his bones. . . . Prv 12:4
but sin is a *d* to any people. . . . Prv 14:34
wise servant will rule over a *d* son, . . . Prv 17:2
is a son who brings shame and *d* . . . Prv 19:26
of gluttons *d* his father. . . . Prv 28:7
but a child left to himself *d* his mother . . . Prv 29:15
want to expose her to public *d*, . . . Mt 1:19
of suffering *d* for the Name. . . . Acts 5:41
and if it is a *d* for a woman . . . 1 Cor 11:6
it is a *d* to him, but that . . . 1 Cor 11:14
for it is *d* for a woman to speak . . . 1 Cor 14:35
so that he will not fall into *d* . . . 1 Tm 3:7
and subjecting him to public *d*. . . . Heb 6:6
He regarded *d* for the sake . . . Heb 11:26

DISHONEST *unfair, deceptive; characterized by lack of truth*
trustworthy men who hate *d* gain . . . Ex 18:21
Do not use *d* standards . . . Lv 19:35
They turned aside after *d* gain . . . 1 Sm 8:3
The LORD abhors *d* scales, . . . Prv 11:1
D money dwindles away, . . . Prv 13:11
and *d* scales do not please him. . . . Prv 20:23
The righteous detest the *d*; . . . Prv 29:27
are set only on *d* gain, . . . Jer 22:17
By your many sins and *d* trade . . . Ez 28:18
The merchant uses *d* scales; . . . Hos 12:7
and cheating with *d* scales, . . . Am 8:5
Shall I acquit a man with *d* scales, . . . Mi 6:11
master commended the *d* manager . . . Lk 16:8
whoever is *d* with very little will . . . Lk 16:10
wine, and not pursuing *d* gain . . . 1 Tm 3:8
not violent, not pursuing *d* gain. . . . Ti 1:7

DISHONOR(ED)(S) *to degrade or bring shame upon*
Do not *d* your father . . . Lv 18:7
for that would *d* a close relative; . . . Lv 20:19
he must not *d* his father's bed. . . . Dt 22:30
Cursed is the man who *d* his father . . . Dt 27:16
and so the name of my God. . . . Prv 30:9
do not *d* your glorious throne. . . . Jer 14:21
their *d* will never be forgotten. . . . Jer 20:11
are those who *d* their fathers' bed; . . . Ez 22:10
For a son *d* his father, . . . Mi 7:6
I honor my Father and you *d* me. . . . Jn 8:49
do you *d* God by breaking the law? . . . Rom 2:23
You are honored, we are *d*! . . . 1 Cor 4:10
with his head covered *d* his head. . . . 1 Cor 11:4
her head uncovered *d* her head . . . 1 Cor 11:5
it is sown in *d*, it is raised in glory; . . . 1 Cor 15:43
through glory and *d*, bad report . . . 2 Cor 6:8

DISSENSION(S) *disagreement; contentious arguing*
he always stirs up *d*. . . . Prv 6:14
and a man who stirs up *d* . . . Prv 6:19
Hatred stirs up *d*, . . . Prv 10:12
A hot-tempered man stirs up *d*, . . . Prv 15:18
A perverse man stirs up *d*, . . . Prv 16:28
A greedy man stirs up *d*, . . . Prv 28:25
An angry man stirs up *d*, . . . Prv 29:22
debauchery, not in *d* and jealousy. . . . Rom 13:13
selfish ambition, *d*, factions . . . Gal 5:20

DISTRESS(ED) *suffering grief or misery; a troubling or painful situation*
in their *d* they turned to the LORD . . . 2 Chr 15:4
In my *d* I called to the LORD; . . . Ps 18:6
In your *d* you called and I rescued . . . Ps 81:7
I call on the LORD in my *d*, . . . Ps 120:1
"In my *d* I called to the LORD, . . . Jon 2:2
For then there will be great *d*, . . . Mt 24:21
how *d* I am until it is completed! . . . Lk 12:50
If your brother is *d* . . . Rom 14:15
after orphans and widows in their *d* . . . Jas 1:27

DIVIDE(D), DIVIDING *to separate into parts; to partition*
They *d* my garments among them . . . Ps 22:18

household *d* against itself will not . . . Mt 12:25
they *d* up his clothes by casting lots . . .
　Lk 23:34
Is Christ *d?* Was Paul crucified . . . 1 Cor 1:13
destroyed the barrier, the *d* wall . . . Eph 2:14
it penetrates even to *d* soul . . . Heb 4:12

DIVINE *holy; eternal*
his eternal power and *d* nature . . . Rom 1:20
they have *d* power . . . 2 Cor 10:4
you may participate in the *d* nature . . . 2 Pt 1:4

DIVISION(S) *separation into parts; partitioning*
on earth? No, I tell you, but *d*. . . . Lk 12:51
to watch out for those who cause *d* . . . Rom
　16:17
another so that there may be no *d* . . . 1 Cor
　1:10
there are *d* among you, . . . 1 Cor 11:18
so that there should be no *d* . . . 1 Cor 12:25

DIVORCE(D)(S) *to dissolve a marriage; to end
a relationship*
or *d* from their husbands, . . . Lv 21:7
not marry a widow, a *d* woman, . . . Lv 21:14
daughter becomes a widow or is *d*, . . . Lv 22:13
or *d* woman will be binding on her. . . . Nm 30:9
he must not *d* her as long as he lives . . .
　Dt 22:19
He can never *d* her as long . . . Dt 22:29
and he writes her a certificate of *d*, . . . Dt 24:1
after he had *d* his wives Hushim . . . 1 Chr 8:8
is your mother's certificate of *d* . . . Is 50:1
If a man *d* his wife . . . Jer 3:1
faithless Israel her certificate of *d* . . . Jer 3:8
not marry widows or *d* women; . . . Ez 44:22
"I hate *d*," says the LORD God . . . Mal 2:16
he had in mind to *d* her quietly. . . . Mt 1:19
Anyone who *d* his wife must give . . . Mt 5:31
for a man to *d* his wife for any . . . Mt 19:3
man give his wife a certificate of *d* . . . Mt 19:7
permitted you to *d* your wives . . . Mt 19:8
Is it lawful for a man to *d* his wife? . . . Mk 10:2
a man to write a certificate of *d* . . . Mk 10:4
Anyone who *d* his wife . . . Mk 10:11
Anyone who *d* his wife . . . Lk 16:18
And a husband must not *d* his wife. . . . 1 Cor
　7:11
Are you married? Do not seek a *d*. . . . 1 Cor
　7:27

DOCTRINE(S) *teaching, instruction*
not to teach false *d* any longer . . . 1 Tm 1:3
to the sound *d* that conforms . . . 1 Tm 1:10
Watch your life and *d* closely. . . . 1 Tm 4:16
If anyone teaches false *d* . . . 1 Tm 6:3
men will not put up with sound *d*. . . . 2 Tm 4:3
can encourage others by sound *d* . . . Ti 1:9
is in accord with sound *d*. . . . Ti 2:1

DOUBT(ING)(S) *to lack confidence in; uncertainty*
he said, "why did you *d?*" . . . Mt 14:31
if you have faith and do not *d*, . . . Mt 21:21
and does not *d* in his heart . . . Mk 11:23
why do *d* rise in your minds? . . . Lk 24:38
Stop *d* and believe. . . . Jn 20:27
the man who has *d* is condemned . . . Rom
　14:23
he who *d* is like a wave of the sea, . . . Jas 1:6
Be merciful to those who *d*; . . . Jude 1:22

DRINK(ING)(S) *to take in liquids; something to
be imbibed; see DRUNK*
of a hin of wine as a *d* offering. . . . Ex 29:40
He must not *d* grape juice . . . Nm 6:3
from those who kneel down to *d*. . . . Jgs 7:5
that someone would get me a *d* . . . 2 Sm 23:15
D water from your own cistern, . . . Prv 5:15
and champions at mixing *d*, . . . Is 5:22
Can you *d* the cup I am going to *d* . . . Mt 20:22
saying, "*D* from it, all of you. . . . Mt 26:27
when they *d* deadly poison, . . . Mk 16:18
Take life easy; eat, *d* and be merry . . . Lk 12:19

Everyone who *d* this water will be . . . Jn 4:13
and *d* my blood has eternal life, . . . Jn 6:54
let him come to me and *d*. . . . Jn 7:37
Shall I not *d* the cup the Father has . . . Jn 18:11
God is not a matter of eating and *d*, . . . Rom
　14:17
and drank the same spiritual *d*; . . . 1 Cor 10:4
or *d* the cup of the Lord . . . 1 Cor 11:27
were all given the one Spirit to *d*. . . . 1 Cor
　12:13
being poured out like a *d* offering . . . Phil 2:17
being poured out like a *d* offering, . . . 2 Tm 4:6
too, will *d* of the wine of God's fury . . .
　Rv 14:10
to *d* without cost from the spring . . . Rv 21:6

DRUNK(ENNESS), DRUNKARD(S) *intoxicated;
one who drinks to excess; see DRINK*
Eli thought she was *d* and said . . . 1 Sm 1:13
for *d* and gluttons become poor, . . . Prv 23:21
Like a thornbush in a *d*'s hand . . . Prv 26:9
and a *d*, a friend of tax collectors . . . Mt 11:19
weighed down with dissipation, *d* . . . Lk 21:34
men are not *d*, as you suppose. . . . Acts 2:15
and *d*, not in sexual immorality . . . Rom 13:13
or a slanderer, a *d* or a swindler. . . . 1 Cor 5:11
nor the greedy nor *d* nor slanderers . . . 1 Cor
　6:10
factions and envy; *d*, orgies, . . . Gal 5:21
Do not get *d* on wine, which leads . . . Eph 5:18
not given to *d*, not violent . . . 1 Tm 3:3
living in debauchery, lust, *d*, orgies, . . . 1 Pt 4:3

DUST *specks or clumps of earthy matter; earth*
man from the *d* of the ground . . . Gn 2:7
for *d* you are . . . Gn 3:19
and repent in *d* and ashes. . . . Jb 42:6
you lay me in the *d* of death. . . . Ps 22:15
he remembers that we are *d*. . . . Ps 103:14
all come from *d*, and to *d* all return. . . . Eccl
　3:20
shake the *d* off your feet . . . Mt 10:14
was of the *d* of the earth, . . . 1 Cor 15:47

DUTIES, DUTY *rightful obligations*
for this is the whole *d* of man. . . . Eccl 12:13
I have fulfilled my *d* to God . . . Acts 23:1
husband should fulfill his marital *d* . . . 1 Cor 7:3
discharge all the *d* of your ministry . . . 2 Tm 4:5

DWELL(S) *to reside*
for me, and I will *d* among them. . . . Ex 25:8
the one to build me a house to *d* in? . . . 2 Sm
　7:5
But will God really *d* on earth? . . . 1 Kgs 8:27
I will *d* in the house of the LORD . . . Ps 23:6
d in the land and enjoy safe pasture . . . Ps 37:3
holy place where the Most High *d*. . . . Ps 46:4
I long to *d* in your tent forever . . . Ps 61:4
He who *d* in the shelter . . . Ps 91:1
wisdom, *d* together with prudence; . . . Prv 8:12
of us can *d* with the consuming fire . . . Is 33:14
do not *d* on the past. . . . Is 43:18
nor does his word *d* in you, . . . Jn 5:38
so that Christ may *d* in your hearts . . . Eph 3:17
to have all his fullness *d* in him, . . . Col 1:19
the word of Christ *d* in you richly . . . Col 3:16

DWELLING(S) *a place to live in*
I will put my *d* place among you, . . . Lv 26:11
from heaven, your holy *d* place, . . . Dt 26:15
Lord, you have been our *d* place . . . Ps 90:1
will be welcomed into eternal *d*. . . . Lk 16:9
to be clothed with our heavenly *d*, . . . 2 Cor 5:2
to become a *d* in which God lives . . . Eph 2:22

EAGER *enthusiastic or impatient desire or
interest*
and works with *e* hands. . . . Prv 31:13
The creation waits in *e* expectation . . . Rom
　8:19
Since you are *e* to have spiritual . . . 1 Cor 14:12
my brothers, be *e* to prophesy, . . . 1 Cor 14:39

a people that are his very own, *e* . . . Ti 2:14
greedy for money, but *e* to serve; . . . 1 Pt 5:2

EAR(S) *organ of hearing, also representing a
person's understanding*
Give *e* to my words, O LORD, . . . Ps 5:1
and his *e* are attentive to their cry; . . . Ps 34:15
turning your *e* to wisdom . . . Prv 2:2
If a man shuts his *e* to the cry . . . Prv 21:13
Like one who seizes a dog by the *e* . . . Prv
　26:17
He who has *e*, let him hear. . . . Mt 11:15
no *e* has heard, . . . 1 Cor 2:9
if the *e* should say, "Because I am . . . 1 Cor
　12:16
to say what their itching *e* want . . . 2 Tm 4:3
his *e* are attentive to their prayer, . . . 1 Pt 3:12
He who has an *e*, let him hear what . . . Rv 2:7

EASIER, EASY *involving little difficultly or
discomfort*
For my yoke is *e* and my burden is . . . Mt 11:30
It is *e* for heaven and earth . . . Lk 16:17
it is *e* for a camel to go . . . Lk 18:25

EAT(ING)(S) *to take in through the mouth as
food; to ingest*
You are free to *e* from any tree . . . Gn 2:16
E it in haste; it is the LORD's . . . Ex 12:11
these are the ones you may *e*: . . . Lv 11:2
None of you may *e* blood, . . . Lv 17:12
He gave you manna to *e* . . . Dt 8:16
Out of the eater, something to *e*; . . . Jgs 14:14
and does not *e* the bread of idleness . . . Prv
　31:27
and the lion will *e* straw like the ox, . . . Is 65:25
e what is before you, *e* this scroll; . . . Ez 3:1
You give them something to *e*. . . . Mt 14:16
Take and *e*; this is my body. . . . Mt 26:26
where I may *e* the Passover . . . Mk 14:14
what you will *e*; or about your body . . . Lk 12:22
bread from heaven to *e*. . . . Jn 6:31
If anyone *e* of this bread, he will live . . . Jn 6:51
faith allows him to *e* everything, . . . Rom 14:2
not by your *e* destroy your brother . . . Rom
　14:15
about *e* food sacrificed to idols: . . . 1 Cor 8:4
if what I *e* causes my brother to fall . . . 1 Cor
　8:13
E anything sold in the meat market . . . 1 Cor
　10:25
For whenever you *e* this bread . . . 1 Cor 11:26
man will not work, he shall not *e*. . . . 2 Thes
　3:10

EDIFICATION, EDIFIED, EDIFIES *the building
up and encouraging of, morally or spiritually*
leads to peace and to mutual *e*. . . . Rom 14:19
but he who prophesies *e* the church . . . 1 Cor
　14:4
but the other man is not *e*. . . . 1 Cor 14:17

ELDER(S) *an older, wise person; leaders given
governing authority because of age, character,
or experience; see OVERSEER, SHEPHERD*
rejected the advice the *e* gave him . . . 1 Kgs
　12:8
holding to the tradition of the *e*. . . . Mk 7:3
gift to the *e* by Barnabas . . . Acts 11:30
and Barnabas appointed *e* for them . . . Acts
　14:23
the apostles and *e* about this . . . Acts 15:2
and *e* in Jerusalem for the people . . . Acts 16:4
They went to the chief priests and *e* . . . Acts
　23:14
to Caesarea with some of the *e* . . . Acts 24:1
when the body of *e* laid their hands . . . 1 Tm
　4:14
The *e* who direct the affairs . . . 1 Tm 5:17
an accusation against an *e* . . . 1 Tm 5:19
and appoint *e* in every town, . . . Ti 1:5
He should call the *e* of the church . . . Jas 5:14
among you, I appeal as a fellow *e*, . . . 1 Pt 5:1
seated on them were twenty-four *e*. . . . Rv 4:4

ELECT(ION) *chosen by God for his purpose*
the sake of the *e* those days will be . . . Mt 24:22
miracles to deceive even the *e* . . . Mt 24:24
and they will gather his *e* . . . Mt 24:31
sake of the *e*, whom he has chosen, . . . Mk 13:20
and miracles to deceive the *e* . . . Mk 13:22
gather his *e* from the four winds, . . . Mk 13:27
God's purpose in *e* might stand: . . . Rom 9:11
it did not obtain, but the *e* did. . . . Rom 11:7
but as far as *e* is concerned, . . . Rom 11:28
and Christ Jesus and the *e* angels, . . . 1 Tm 5:21
everything for the sake of the *e*, . . . 2 Tm 2:10
Christ for the faith of God's *e* . . . Ti 1:1
To God's *e*, strangers in the world, . . . 1 Pt 1:1
to make your calling and *e* sure. . . . 2 Pt 1:10

ENABLE(D)(S) *to teach the skill or provide the power or means to succeed*
e you to walk with heads held high. . . . Lv 26:13
And the LORD *e* her to conceive, . . . Ru 4:13
to *e* us to serve him without fear . . . Lk 1:74
unless the Father has *e* him. . . . Jn 6:65
other tongues as the Spirit *e* them. . . . Acts 2:4
e your servants to speak your word . . . Acts 4:29
and *e* him to gain the goodwill . . . Acts 7:10
by the power that *e* him . . . Phil 3:21
was *e* to become a father . . . Heb 11:11

ENCOURAGE(D)(MENT), ENCOURAGING *to strengthen or stimulate*
E him, because he will lead Israel . . . Dt 1:38
and *e* and strengthen him, . . . Dt 3:28
But the men of Israel *e* one another . . . Jgs 20:22
Say this to *e* Joab. . . . 2 Sm 11:25
Now go out and *e* your men. . . . 2 Sm 19:7
But my mouth would *e* you; . . . Jb 16:5
you *e* them, and you listen . . . Ps 10:17
They *e* each other in evil plans, . . . Ps 64:5
e the oppressed. . . . Is 1:17
to the dreams you *e* them to have. . . . Jer 29:8
Barnabas (which means Son of *E*), . . . Acts 4:36
e them to remain true to the faith. . . . Acts 14:22
to *e* and strengthen the brothers. . . . Acts 15:32
for the disciples and, after *e* them, . . . Acts 20:1
men Paul thanked God and was *e*. . . . Acts 28:15
if it is *e*, let him *e*; . . . Rom 12:8
e of the Scriptures we might have . . . Rom 15:4
I am greatly *e*; in all our troubles . . . 2 Cor 7:4
how we are, and that he may *e* you. . . . Eph 6:22
If you have any *e* from being united . . . Phil 2:1
My purpose is that they may be *e* . . . Col 2:2
and that he may *e* your hearts. . . . Col 4:8
e, comforting and urging you . . . 1 Thes 2:12
to strengthen and *e* you . . . 1 Thes 3:2
persecution we were *e* about you . . . 1 Thes 3:7
Therefore *e* each other . . . 1 Thes 4:18
those who are idle, *e* the timid, . . . 1 Thes 5:14
and by his grace gave us eternal *e* . . . 2 Thes 2:16
rebuke and *e* with great patience . . . 2 Tm 4:2
so that he can *e* others . . . Ti 1:9
e the young men to be . . . Ti 2:6
E and rebuke with all authority. . . . Ti 2:15
But *e* one another daily, as long . . . Heb 3:13
but let us *e* one another . . . Heb 10:25

END *cessation, death, or destruction; goal toward which something is heading*
then I will keep them to the *e*. . . . Ps 119:33
Such is the *e* of all who go . . . Prv 1:19
but in the *e* she is bitter as gall, . . . Prv 5:4

At the *e* of your life you will groan, . . . Prv 5:11
but in the *e* it leads to death. . . . Prv 14:12
and joy may *e* in grief. . . . Prv 14:13
but in the *e* it leads to death. . . . Prv 16:25
and in the *e* you will be wise. . . . Prv 19:20
will not be blessed at the *e*. . . . Prv 20:21
In the *e* it bites like a snake . . . Prv 23:32
for what will you do in the *e* . . . Prv 25:8
in the *e* gain more favor . . . Prv 28:23
he will bring grief in the *e*. . . . Prv 29:21
done from beginning to *e*. . . . Eccl 3:11
making many books there is no *e*, . . . Eccl 12:12
The *e!* The *e* has come . . . Ez 7:2
firm to the *e* will be saved. . . . Mt 10:22
nations, and then the *e* will come. . . . Mt 24:14
but the *e* will not come right away . . . Lk 21:9
Christ is the *e* of the law . . . Rom 10:4
the *e* will come, when he hands . . . 1 Cor 15:24
Omega, the Beginning and the *E*. . . . Rv 21:6
the Last, the Beginning and the *E*. . . . Rv 22:13

ENDURANCE, ENDURE(D)(S) *the ability to withstand hardship or adversity; to carry on despite suffering*
May his name *e* forever; . . . Ps 72:17
his righteousness *e* forever; . . . Ps 112:9
for we have *e* much contempt. . . . Ps 123:3
and all the hardships he *e*. . . . Ps 132:1
His love *e* forever. . . . Ps 136:1
Truthful lips *e* forever, . . . Prv 12:19
for riches do not *e* forever, . . . Prv 27:24
everything God does will *e* forever; . . . Eccl 3:14
to an end, but it will itself *e* forever. . . . Dn 2:44
made for yourself a name that *e* . . . Dn 9:15
who can *e* the day of his coming? . . . Mal 3:2
through *e* and the encouragement . . . Rom 15:4
when we are persecuted, we *e* it; . . . 1 Cor 4:12
which produces in you patient *e* . . . 2 Cor 1:6
in great *e*; in troubles, hardships . . . 2 Cor 6:4
his righteousness *e* forever. . . . 2 Cor 9:9
might so that you may have great *e* . . . Col 1:11
and your *e* inspired by hope . . . 1 Thes 1:3
faith, love, *e* and gentleness. . . . 1 Tm 6:11
E hardship with us like a good . . . 2 Tm 2:3
Therefore I *e* everything . . . 2 Tm 2:10
patience, love, *e*, persecutions, . . . 2 Tm 3:10
head in all situations, *e* hardship, . . . 2 Tm 4:5
and sound in faith, in love and in *e*. . . . Ti 2:2
E hardship as discipline; God is . . . Heb 12:7
set before him *e* the cross, . . . Heb 12:2
a beating for doing wrong and *e* it? . . . 1 Pt 2:20
and patient *e* that are ours in Jesus, . . . Rv 1:9
and have *e* hardships for my name, . . . Rv 2:3
kept my command to *e* patiently, . . . Rv 3:10

ENEMIES, ENEMY *foe—personal, national, or spiritual*
in the presence of my *e*. . . . Ps 23:5
hand until I make your *e* . . . Ps 110:1
his *e* live at peace with him. . . . Prv 16:7
Do not gloat when your *e* falls; . . . Prv 24:17
If your *e* is hungry, give him food . . . Prv 25:21
but an *e* multiplies kisses. . . . Prv 27:6
of a thief is his own *e*; . . . Prv 29:24
a man's *e* are the members . . . Mi 7:6
Love your *e* and pray . . . Mt 5:44
a man's *e* will be the members . . . Mt 10:36
Love your *e*, do good . . . Lk 6:27
But love your *e*, do good to them, . . . Lk 6:35
to overcome all the power of the *e*; . . . Lk 10:19
hand until I make your *e* . . . Lk 20:43
For if, when we were God's *e*, . . . Rom 5:10
If your *e* is hungry, feed him; . . . Rom 12:20
reign until he has put all his *e* . . . 1 Cor 15:25
The last *e* to be destroyed is death. . . . 1 Cor 15:26
many live as *e* of the cross of Christ . . . Phil 3:18
and to give the *e* no opportunity . . . 1 Tm 5:14

hand until I make your *e* . . . Heb 1:13
for his *e* to be made his footstool, . . . Heb 10:13
Your *e* the devil prowls . . . 1 Pt 5:8

ENJOY(MENT) *to delight in; the experience of delight*
and so that you may *e* long life. . . . Dt 6:2
dwell in the land and *e* safe pasture. . . . Ps 37:3
ill-gotten gain will *e* a long life. . . . Prv 28:16
better for a man than to *e* his work, . . . Eccl 3:22
and why am I depriving myself of *e* . . . Eccl 4:8
and that you may *e* long life . . . Eph 6:3
us with everything for our *e* . . . 1 Tm 6:17
rather than to *e* the pleasures of sin . . . Heb 11:25
I pray that you may *e* good health . . . 3 Jn 1:2

ENLIGHTENED *free from ignorance and misinformation, especially regarding spiritual understanding*
that the eyes of your heart may be *e* . . . Eph 1:18
for those who have once been *e*, . . . Heb 6:4

ENTICE(D)(S) *to tempt artfully by arousing hope or desire*
do not be *e* into bowing . . . Dt 4:19
or you will be *e* to turn away . . . Dt 11:16
your closest friend secretly *e* you, . . . Dt 13:6
Jeroboam *e* Israel away . . . 2 Kgs 17:21
If my heart has been *e* by a woman, . . . Jb 31:9
so that my heart was secretly *e* . . . Jb 31:27
Be careful that no one *e* you . . . Jb 36:18
My son, if sinners *e* you, . . . Prv 1:10
A violent man *e* his neighbor . . . Prv 16:29
desire, he is dragged away and *e*. . . . Jas 1:14
they *e* people who are just escaping . . . 2 Pt 2:18
who taught Balak to *e* the Israelites . . . Rv 2:14

ENTRUST(ED) *to commit to another with confidence*
Where is the flock that was *e* to you . . . Jer 13:20
Jesus would not *e* himself to them, . . . Jn 2:24
but has *e* all judgment to the Son, . . . Jn 5:22
they have been *e* with the very . . . Rom 3:2
of teaching to which you were *e*. . . . Rom 6:17
as those *e* with the secret things . . . 1 Cor 4:1
by God to be *e* with the gospel. . . . 1 Thes 2:4
of the blessed God, which he *e* . . . 1 Tm 1:11
guard what has been *e* to your care. . . . 1 Tm 6:20
able to guard what I have *e* to him . . . 2 Tm 1:12
the presence of many witnesses *e* . . . 2 Tm 2:2
light through the preaching *e* to me . . . Ti 1:3
Since an overseer is *e* . . . Ti 1:7
he *e* himself to him who judges . . . 1 Pt 2:23
not lording it over those *e* to you, . . . 1 Pt 5:3
once for all *e* to the saints. . . . Jude 1:3

ENVIOUS, ENVY *jealous; resentment aroused by another's advantage or possessions*
I will make them *e* . . . Dt 32:21
Do not *e* a violent man . . . Prv 3:31
but *e* rots the bones. . . . Prv 14:30
Do not let your heart *e* sinners, . . . Prv 23:17
Do not *e* wicked men, . . . Prv 24:1
or be *e* of the wicked, . . . Prv 24:19
malice, deceit, lewdness, *e*, slander . . . Mk 7:22
They are full of *e*, murder, strife, . . . Rom 1:29
I will make you *e* . . . Rom 10:19
arouse my own people to *e* . . . Rom 11:14
It does not *e*, it does not boast, . . . 1 Cor 13:4
factions and *e*; drunkenness, orgies . . . Gal 5:21
that some preach Christ out of *e* . . . Phil 1:15
quarrels about words that result in *e*, . . . 1 Tm 6:4
lived in malice and *e*, being hated . . . Ti 3:3
But if you harbor bitter *e* . . . Jas 3:14
where you have *e* and selfish . . . Jas 3:16
e, and slander of every kind. . . . 1 Pt 2:1

ESCAPE(D)(S), ESCAPING *to get away from; avoid, evade*
from the Sovereign LORD comes *e* . . . Ps 68:20
through knowledge the righteous *e* . . . Prv 11:9
but a righteous man *e* trouble. . . . Prv 12:13
think you will *e* God's judgment? . . . Rom 2:3
only as one *e* through the flames. . . . 1 Cor 3:15
woman, and they will not *e*. . . . 1 Thes 5:3
and *e* from the trap of the devil, . . . 2 Tm 2:26
how shall we *e* if we ignore such . . . Heb 2:3
If they did not *e* when they refused . . . Heb 12:25
and *e* the corruption in the world . . . 2 Pt 1:4
they entice people who are just *e* . . . 2 Pt 2:18

ESTABLISH(ED)(ES) *to make firm or stable; to prove*
But I will *e* my covenant with you, . . . Gn 6:18
the sign of the covenant I have *e* . . . Gn 9:17
But my covenant I will *e* with Isaac . . . Gn 17:21
also *e* my covenant with them . . . Ex 6:4
the LORD himself will *e* a house . . . 2 Sm 7:11
I will *e* your royal throne . . . 1 Kgs 9:5
I will *e* his kingdom forever . . . 1 Chr 28:7
he *e* order in the heights of heaven. . . . Jb 25:2
e the work of our hands for us . . . Ps 90:17
a throne is *e* through righteousness. . . . Prv 16:12
LORD, you *e* peace for us; . . . Is 26:12
till he *e* justice on earth. . . . Is 42:4
God and sought to *e* their own, . . . Rom 10:3
able to *e* you by my gospel . . . Rom 16:25
sets aside the first to *e* the second. . . . Heb 10:9

ESTEEMED *to value or appreciate*
to be *e* is better than silver or gold. . . . Prv 22:1
he was despised, and we *e* him not. . . . Is 53:3

ETERNAL(LY), ETERNITY *perpetual; forever; characterized by abiding fellowship with God; see EVERLASTING*
the name of the LORD, the *E* God. . . . Gn 21:33
The *e* God is your refuge, . . . Dt 33:27
of the LORD's *e* love for Israel, . . . 1 Kgs 10:9
with *e* pleasures at your right hand. . . . Ps 16:11
you have granted him *e* blessings . . . Ps 21:6
you are from all *e*. . . . Ps 93:2
To him belongs *e* praise. . . . Ps 111:10
Your word, O LORD, is *e*; . . . Ps 119:89
all your righteous laws are *e*. . . . Ps 119:160
I was appointed from *e*, . . . Prv 8:23
also set *e* in the hearts of men; . . . Eccl 3:11
Then man goes to his *e* home . . . Eccl 12:5
LORD, the LORD, is the Rock *e*. . . . Is 26:4
he is the living God, the *e* King. . . . Jer 10:10
His kingdom is an *e* kingdom; . . . Dn 4:3
two feet and be thrown into *e* fire. . . . Mt 18:8
good thing must I do to get *e* life? . . . 9:16
into the *e* fire prepared for the devil . . . Mt 25:41
be forgiven; he is guilty of an *e* sin. . . . Mk 3:29
what must I do to inherit *e* life? . . . Mk 10:17
him shall not perish but have *e* life. . . . Jn 3:16
spring of water welling up to *e* life. . . . Jn 4:14
believes him who sent me has *e* life . . . Jn 5:24
that by them you possess *e* life. . . . Jn 5:39
but for food that endures to *e* life, . . . Jn 6:27
believes in him shall have *e* life, . . . Jn 6:40
and drinks my blood has *e* life, . . . Jn 6:54
You have the words of *e* life. . . . Jn 6:68
I give them *e* life, and they shall . . . Jn 10:28
in this world will keep it for *e* life. . . . Jn 12:25
that his command leads to *e* life. . . . Jn 12:50
his *e* power and divine nature . . . Rom 1:20
and immortality, he will give *e* life. . . . Rom 2:7
righteousness to bring *e* life . . . Rom 5:21
but the gift of God is *e* life . . . Rom 6:23
from the Spirit will reap *e* life. . . . Gal 6:8
believe on him and receive *e* life. . . . 1 Tm 1:16
Take hold of the *e* life . . . 1 Tm 6:12
resting on the hope of *e* life, . . . Ti 1:2
heirs having the hope of *e* life. . . . Ti 3:7
he became the source of *e* salvation . . . Heb 5:9

of the dead, and *e* judgment. . . . Heb 6:2
having obtained *e* redemption. . . . Heb 9:12
the promised *e* inheritance . . . Heb 9:15
of the *e* covenant brought back . . . Heb 13:20
and we proclaim to you the *e* life, . . . 1 Jn 1:2
what he promised us—even *e* life. . . . 1 Jn 2:25
God has given us *e* life, . . . 1 Jn 5:11
you may know that you have *e* life. . . . 1 Jn 5:13
Christ to bring you to *e* life. . . . Jude 1:21

EVERLASTING *perpetual or enduring through all time; see ETERNAL*
and remember the *e* covenant . . . Gn 9:16
an *e* covenant between me and you . . . Gn 17:7
e possession to your descendants . . . Gn 48:4
and the fruitfulness of the *e* hills; . . . Dt 33:15
from *e* to *e* you are God. . . . Ps 90:2
to Israel as an *e* covenant: . . . Ps 105:10
Your righteousness is *e* . . . Ps 119:142
and lead me in the way *e*. . . . Ps 139:24
Your kingdom is an *e* kingdom, . . . Ps 145:13
E Father, Prince of Peace. . . . Is 9:6
e joy will crown their heads. . . . Is 35:10
The LORD is the *e* God, . . . Is 40:28
e joy will crown their heads. . . . Is 51:11
I have loved you with an *e* love; . . . Jer 31:3
His kingdom will be an *e* kingdom, . . . Dn 7:27
O LORD, are you not from *e*? . . . Hb 1:12
the truth, he who believes has *e* life. . . . Jn 6:47
punished with *e* destruction . . . 2 Thes 1:9
bound with *e* chains for judgment . . . Jude 1:6

EVIL *morally bad or wrong; something that causes harm or distress; see EVILDOER*
of the knowledge of good and *e*. . . . Gn 2:9
how prone these people are to *e*. . . . Ex 32:22
Then the Israelites did *e* in the eyes . . . Jgs 2:11
he feared God and shunned *e*. . . . Jb 1:1
not a God who takes pleasure in *e*; . . . Ps 5:4
I will fear no *e*, . . . Ps 23:4
keep your tongue from *e*, . . . Ps 34:13
Turn from *e* and do good; . . . Ps 34:14
those who love the LORD hate *e*, . . . Ps 97:10
To fear the LORD is to hate *e*; . . . Prv 8:13
A fool finds pleasure in *e* conduct, . . . Prv 10:23
he who pursues *e* goes to his death. . . . Prv 11:19
If a man pays back *e* for good, . . . Prv 17:13
for the man has no future hope, . . . Prv 24:20
Woe to those who call *e* good . . . Is 5:20
but deliver us from the *e* one. . . . Mt 6:13
When an *e* spirit comes out . . . Mt 12:43
out of the heart come *e* thoughts, . . . Mt 15:19
Everyone who does *e* hates . . . Jn 3:20
"Let us do *e* that good may result"? . . . Rom 3:8
Hate what is *e*; cling . . . Rom 12:9
Do not repay anyone *e* for *e*. . . . Rom 12:17
Love does not delight in *e* . . . 1 Cor 13:6
of money is a root of all kinds of *e*. . . . 1 Tm 6:10
Flee the *e* desires of youth, . . . 2 Tm 2:22
you have overcome the *e* one. . . . 1 Jn 2:13

EVILDOER(S) *one who does evil; see EVIL*
saying goes, 'From *e* come evil . . . 1 Sm 24:13
Deliver me from *e*, . . . Ps 59:2
the LORD will banish with the *e*. . . . Ps 125:5
but terror to *e*. . . . Prv 21:15
you *e!* 'Therefore everyone who . . . Mt 7:23
Away from me, all you *e!* . . . Lk 13:27

EXALT(ED)(S) *to elevate; to glorify; to raise in rank or power*
my father's God, and I will *e* him. . . . Ex 15:2
he humbles and he *e*. . . . 1 Sm 2:7
E be God, the Rock, my Savior! . . . 2 Sm 22:47
God is *e* in his power. . . . Jb 36:22
Be *e*, O LORD, in your strength; . . . Ps 21:13
I will *e* you, O LORD, . . . Ps 30:1
let us *e* his name together. . . . Ps 34:3
I will be *e* among the nations, . . . Ps 46:10

I will be *e* in the earth. . . . Ps 46:10
he brings one down, he *e* another. . . . Ps 75:7
you are *e* far above all gods. . . . Ps 97:9
you are my God, and I will *e* you. . . . Ps 118:28
Esteem her, and she will *e* you; . . . Prv 4:8
Righteousness *e* a nation, . . . Prv 14:34
Do not *e* yourself in the king's . . . Prv 25:6
have played the fool and *e* yourself, . . . Prv 30:32
e, and the train of his robe filled . . . Is 6:1
The lowly will be *e* and the *e* will be . . . Ez 21:26
For whoever *e* himself will be . . . Mt 23:12
For everyone who *e* himself will be . . . Lk 14:11
E to the right hand of God, . . . Acts 2:33
God *e* him to his own right hand . . . Acts 5:31
always Christ will be *e* in my body, . . . Phil 1:20
Therefore God *e* him . . . Phil 2:9

EXAMPLE(S) *object lesson or warning; copy or type*
In everything he followed the *e*. . . 2 Kgs 14:3
and make him an *e* and a byword. . . . Ez 14:8
have set you an *e* that you should . . . Jn 13:15
Follow my *e*, as I follow the *e* . . . 1 Cor 11:1
Join with others in following my *e*, . . . Phil 3:17
how you ought to follow our *e*. . . . 2 Thes 3:7
as an *e* for those who would believe . . . 1 Tm 1:16
set an *e* for the believers in speech, . . . 1 Tm 4:12
In everything set them an *e* . . . Ti 2:7
as an *e* of patience in the face . . . Jas 5:10
leaving you an *e*, that you should . . . 1 Pt 2:21
to you, but being *e* to the flock. . . . 1 Pt 5:3
as an *e* of those who suffer . . . Jude 1:7

EXCUSE *to justify or make an apology for; the justification offered*
who are treacherous without *e*. . . . Ps 25:3
they have no *e* for their sin. . . . Jn 15:22
so that men are without *e*. . . . Rom 1:20
You, therefore, have no *e*, . . . Rom 2:1

EXHORT *to incite by argument or advice; urge strongly*
but *e* him as if he were your father. . . . 1 Tm 5:1

EXPECT(ED)(ING), EXPECTATION *to consider probable or certain; hope; assurance*
all he *e* from his power comes . . . Prv 11:7
You *e* much, but see, it turned out . . . Hg 1:9
at an hour when you do not *e* him. . . . Mt 24:44
and lend to them without *e* . . . Lk 6:35
waits in eager *e* for the sons . . . Rom 8:19
I eagerly *e* and hope that I will . . . Phil 1:20
but only a fearful *e* of judgment . . . Heb 10:27

EYE(S) *organ of sight; also represents one's understanding*
good for food and pleasing to the *e*, . . . Gn 3:6
you are to take life for life, *e* for *e*, . . . Ex 21:24
the *e* of the LORD your God are . . . Dt 11:12
right in the *e* of the LORD. . . . Dt 12:25
for a bribe blinds the *e* of the wise . . . Dt 16:19
life for life, *e* for *e*, tooth for tooth, . . . Dt 19:21
you were once small in your own *e*, . . . 1 Sm 15:17
For the *e* of the LORD range . . . 2 Chr 16:9
My *e* are ever on the LORD, . . . Ps 25:15
Does he who formed the *e* not see? . . . Ps 94:9
My *e* will be on the faithful . . . Ps 101:6
Open my *e* that I may see . . . Ps 119:18
my *e* away from worthless things; . . . Ps 119:37
I lift up my *e* to the hills . . . Ps 121:1
your *e* saw my unformed body, . . . Ps 139:16
Do not be wise in your own *e*; . . . Prv 3:7
The *e* of the LORD are everywhere . . . Prv 15:3
to open *e* that are blind, . . . Is 42:7
Your *e* are too pure to look on evil; . . . Hb 1:13
If your right *e* causes you to sin, . . . Mt 5:29
E for *e*, and tooth for tooth. . . . Mt 5:38
The *e* is the lamp of the body. . . . Mt 6:22

of sawdust in your brother's *e* . . . Mt 7:3
He was taken up before their very *e*, . . . Acts 1:9
No *e* has seen, . . . 1 Cor 2:9
I am not an *e*, I do not belong . . . 1 Cor 12:16
of an *e*, at the last trumpet. . . . 1 Cor 15:52
So we fix our *e* not on what is seen, . . . 2 Cor 4:18
favor when their *e* is on you, . . . Eph 6:6
not only when their *e* is on you . . . Col 3:22
Let us fix our *e* on Jesus, the author . . . Heb 12:2
poor in the *e* of the world to be rich . . . Jas 2:5
For the *e* of the Lord are . . . 1 Pt 3:12
and every *e* will see him, . . . Rv 1:7
wipe away every tear from their *e*. . . . Rv 7:17

FACE(S) *countenance; also represents one's presence*
It is because I saw God *f* to *f*, . . . Gn 32:30
Moses hid his *f*, because he was . . . Ex 3:6
would speak to Moses *f* to *f*, . . . Ex 33:11
was not aware that his *f* was radiant . . . Ex 34:29
The LORD spoke to you *f* to *f* out . . . Dt 5:4
Israel: "Come, meet me *f* to *f*." . . . 2 Chr 25:17
Let the light of your *f* shine upon us . . . Ps 4:6
Your *f*, LORD, I will seek. . . . Ps 27:8
Let your *f* shine on your servant; . . . Ps 31:16
and the light of your *f*, . . . Ps 44:3
Hide your *f* from my sins . . . Ps 51:9
make your *f* shine upon us, . . . Ps 80:3
I hid my *f* from you for a moment, . . . Is 54:8
and he will speak with you *f* to *f*. . . . Jer 34:3
Each of the four had the *f* of a man, . . . Ez 1:10
His *f* shone like the sun, . . . Mt 17:2
the appearance of his *f* changed, . . . Lk 9:29
then we shall see *f* to *f*. . . . 1 Cor 13:12
could not look steadily at the *f* . . . 2 Cor 3:7
the glory of God in the *f* of Christ. . . . 2 Cor 4:6
His *f* was like the sun shining . . . Rv 1:16

FAIL(ED)(S) *to fall short; fade away; disappear; disappoint*
and *f* to carry out all my commands . . . Lv 26:15
has been fulfilled; not one has *f*. . . . Jos 23:14
you will never *f* to have a man . . . 1 Kgs 2:4
Not one word has *f*. . . . 1 Kgs 8:56
He will not *f* you or forsake you . . . 1 Chr 28:20
my covenant with him will never *f* . . . Ps 89:28
Plans *f* for lack of counsel, . . . Prv 15:22
my righteousness will never *f*. . . . Is 51:6
for his compassions never *f*. . . . Lam 3:22
Simon, that your faith may not *f* . . . Lk 22:32
Love never *f*. . . . 1 Cor 13:8
unless, of course, you *f* the test? . . . 2 Cor 13:5

FAINT(HEARTED) *weak in body and spirit; to lose strength or courage*
Do not be *f* or afraid; do not be . . . Dt 20:3
shall add, "Is any man afraid or *f*? . . . Dt 20:8
they will walk and not be *f*. . . . Is 40:31

FAITH *reliance, loyalty, or complete trust in God or someone else*
Have *f* in the LORD your God . . . 2 Chr 20:20
If you do not stand firm in your *f*, . . . Is 7:9
but the righteous will live by his *f* . . . Hb 2:4
by breaking *f* with one another? . . . Mal 2:10
and do not break *f* with the wife . . . Mal 2:15
in your spirit, and do not break *f*. . . . Mal 2:16
O you of little *f*? So do not worry, . . . Mt 6:30
anyone in Israel with such great *f*. . . . Mt 8:10
He replied, "You of little *f*, . . . Mt 8:26
When Jesus saw their *f*, he said . . . Mt 9:2
he said, "your *f* has healed you." . . . Mt 9:22
According to your *f* will it be done . . . Mt 9:29
there because of their lack of *f*. . . . Mt 13:58
Woman, you have great *f*! . . . Mt 15:28
if you have *f* as small as a mustard . . . Mt 17:20
if you have *f* and do not doubt, . . . Mt 21:21
Daughter, your *f* has healed you. . . . Mk 5:34

he was amazed at their lack of *f*. . . . Mk 6:6
"Have *f* in God," Jesus answered. . . . Mk 11:22
he rebuked them for their lack of *f* . . . Mk 16:14
what Jesus did, put their *f* . . . Jn 11:45
anyone who has *f* in me will do . . . Jn 14:12
By *f* in the name of Jesus, this man . . . Acts 3:16
full of *f* and of the Holy Spirit; . . . Acts 6:5
of priests became obedient to the *f*. . . . Acts 6:7
saw that he had *f* to be healed . . . Acts 14:9
the door of *f* to the Gentiles. . . . Acts 14:27
for he purified their hearts by *f*. . . . Acts 15:9
and have *f* in our Lord Jesus. . . . Acts 20:21
to the obedience that comes from *f*. . . . Rom 1:5
The righteous will live by *f*. . . . Rom 1:17
comes through *f* in Jesus Christ . . . Rom 3:22
his *f* is credited as righteousness. . . . Rom 4:5
the righteousness that comes by *f*. . . . Rom 4:13
Therefore, the promise comes by *f*, . . . Rom 4:16
we have been justified through *f*, . . . Rom 5:1
a righteousness that is by *f*; . . . Rom 9:30
f comes from hearing the message, . . . Rom 10:17
let him use it in proportion to his *f*. . . . Rom 12:6
but another man, whose *f* is weak, . . . Rom 14:2
and if I have a *f* that can move . . . 1 Cor 13:2
And now these three remain: *f*, . . . 1 Cor 13:13
because it is by *f* you stand firm. . . . 2 Cor 1:24
We live by *f*, not by sight. . . . 2 Cor 5:7
Jesus that we may be justified by *f* . . . Gal 2:16
would justify the Gentiles by *f*, . . . Gal 3:8
The righteous will live by *f*. . . . Gal 3:11
that we might be justified by *f*, . . . Gal 3:24
that counts is *f* expressing itself . . . Gal 5:6
through *f* in him we may approach . . . Eph 3:12
one Lord, one *f*, one baptism; . . . Eph 4:5
to all this, take up the shield of *f*, . . . Eph 6:16
continue in your *f*, established . . . Col 1:23
Father your work produced by *f*, . . . 1 Thes 1:3
evil men, for not everyone has *f*. . . . 2 Thes 3:2
and so have shipwrecked their *f*. . . . 1 Tm 1:19
he has denied the *f* and is worse . . . 1 Tm 5:8
pursue righteousness, godliness, *f*, . . . 1 Tm 6:11
Fight the good fight of the *f*. . . . 1 Tm 6:12
finished the race, I have kept the *f*. . . . 2 Tm 4:7
may be active in sharing your *f*, . . . Phlm 1:6
But my righteous one will live by *f*. . . . Heb 10:38
f is being sure of what we hope for . . . Heb 11:1
And without *f* it is impossible . . . Heb 11:6
the author and perfecter of our *f*, . . . Heb 12:2
so *f* without deeds is dead. . . . Jas 2:26

FAITHFUL(NESS) *firm in adherence; loyal; worthy of trust; devotion*
f, maintaining love to thousands, . . . Ex 34:6
your God is God; he is the *f* God, . . . Dt 7:9
To the *f* you show yourself *f*, . . . 2 Sm 22:26
The LORD preserves the *f*, . . . Ps 31:23
he is *f* in all he does. . . . Ps 33:4
your *f* to the skies. . . . Ps 36:5
and will not forsake his *f* ones. . . . Ps 37:28
I speak of your *f* and salvation. . . . Ps 40:10
God sends his love and his *f* . . . Ps 57:3
your *f* reaches to the skies. . . . Ps 57:10
Love and *f* meet together; . . . Ps 85:10
to anger, abounding in love and *f*. . . . Ps 86:15
mouth I will make your *f* known . . . Ps 89:1
My *f* love will be with him, . . . Ps 89:24
f continues through all . . . Ps 100:5
will be on the *f* in the land, . . . Ps 101:6
the *f* of the LORD endures forever. . . . Ps 117:2
The LORD is *f* to all his promises . . . Ps 145:13
the LORD, who remains *f* forever. . . . Ps 146:6
Let love and *f* never leave you; . . . Prv 3:3

Through love and *f* sin is atoned for . . . Prv 16:6
but a *f* man who can find? . . . Prv 20:6
Love and *f* keep a king safe; . . . Prv 20:28
A *f* man will be richly blessed, . . . Prv 28:20
and *f* instruction is on her tongue. . . . Prv 31:26
great is your *f*. . . . Lam 3:23
Who then is the *f* and wise servant, . . . Mt 24:45
You have been *f* with a few things; . . . Mt 25:21
then is the *f* and wise manager, . . . Lk 12:42
lack of faith nullify God's *f*? . . . Rom 3:3
patient in affliction, *f* in prayer. . . . Rom 12:12
his Son Jesus Christ our Lord, is *f*. . . . 1 Cor 1:9
my son whom I love, who is *f* . . . 1 Cor 4:17
And God is *f*; he will not let you be . . . 1 Cor 10:13
But as surely as God is *f*, . . . 2 Cor 1:18
patience, kindness, goodness, *f*, . . . Gal 5:22
the Lord is *f*, and he will strengthen . . . 2 Thes 3:3
themselves to their *f* Creator . . . 1 Pt 4:19
he is *f* and just and will forgive us . . . 1 Jn 1:9
his called, chosen and *f* followers. . . . Rv 17:14
whose rider is called *F* and True. . . . Rv 19:11

FALL(EN)(ING)(S) *to drop down; to drop wounded or dead; to descend as from the sky; to experience defeat or ruin: collapse; to stumble or stray (morally)*
How the mighty have *f*! . . . 2 Sm 1:19
though he stumble, he will not *f*, . . . Ps 37:24
he will never let the righteous *f*. . . . Ps 55:22
of those who insult you *f* on me. . . . Ps 69:9
The LORD upholds all those who *f*. . . . Ps 145:14
For lack of guidance a nation *f*, . . . Prv 11:14
Whoever trusts in his riches will *f*, . . . Prv 11:28
Do not gloat when your enemy *f*; . . . Prv 24:17
he who hardens his heart *f*. . . . Prv 28:14
How you have *f* from heaven, . . . Is 14:12
The grass withers and the flowers *f*, . . . Is 40:7
yet it did not *f*, because it had its . . . Mt 7:25
of the word, he quickly *f* away. . . . Mt 13:21
He who *f* on this stone will be . . . Mt 21:44
I saw Satan *f* like lightning . . . Lk 10:18
a house divided against itself will *f*. . . . Lk 11:17
say to the mountains, "*F* on us!" . . . Lk 23:30
a kernel of wheat *f* to the ground . . . Jn 12:24
To his own master he stands or *f*. . . . Rom 14:4
and a number of you have *f* asleep. . . . 1 Cor 11:30
though some have *f* asleep. . . . 1 Cor 15:6
who have *f* asleep in Christ are lost. . . . 1 Cor 15:18
of those who have *f* asleep. . . . 1 Cor 15:20
and *f* short of the glory of God, . . . Rom 3:23
you have *f* away from grace. . . . Gal 5:4
precede those who have *f* asleep. . . . 1 Thes 4:15
if they *f* away, to be brought back . . . Heb 6:6
able to keep you from *f*. . . . Jude 1:24

FALSE(HOOD)(LY) *dishonest; intentionally untrue; misleading; faithless*
You shall not give *f* testimony . . . Ex 20:16
Do not spread *f* reports. . . . Ex 23:1
Have nothing to do with a *f* charge . . . Ex 23:7
Do not swear *f* by my name . . . Lv 19:12
You shall not give *f* testimony . . . Dt 5:20
left of your answers but *f*! . . . Jb 21:34
If I have walked in *f* . . . Jb 31:5
f rather than speaking the truth. . . . Ps 52:3
I hate and abhor *f*, . . . Ps 119:163
but a *f* witness tells lies. . . . Prv 12:17
The righteous hate what is *f*, . . . Prv 13:5
but a *f* witness pours out lies. . . . Prv 14:5
but a *f* witness is deceitful. . . . Prv 14:25
A *f* witness will not go unpunished, . . . Prv 19:5
A *f* witness will perish, . . . Prv 21:28
is the man who gives *f* testimony . . . Prv 25:18
Keep *f* and lies far from me; . . . Prv 30:8
who foils the signs of *f* prophets . . . Is 44:25
they fill you with *f* hopes. . . . Jer 23:16
f say all kinds of evil against you . . . Mt 5:11

Watch out for *f* prophets. . . . Mt 7:15
theft, *f* testimony, slander. . . . . Mt 15:19
not steal, do not give *f* testimony, . . . Mt 19:18
and many *f* prophets will appear . . . Mt 24:11
do not give *f* testimony, do not . . . Mk 10:19
For *f* Christs and *f* prophets will . . . Mk 13:22
and don't accuse people *f* . . . Lk 3:14
their fathers treated the *f* prophets. . . . Lk 6:26
not steal, do not give *f* testimony, . . . Lk 18:20
in whom there is nothing *f*. . . . Jn 1:47
found to be *f* witnesses about God, . . . 1 Cor 15:15
For such men are *f* apostles, . . . 2 Cor 11:13
some *f* brothers had infiltrated our . . . Gal 2:4
each of you must put off *f* . . . Eph 4:25
whether from *f* motives or true, . . . Phil 1:18
anyone who delights in *f* humility . . . Col 2:18
not to teach *f* doctrines any longer . . . 1 Tm 1:3
If anyone teaches *f* doctrines . . . 1 Tm 6:3
ideas of what is *f* called knowledge, . . . 1 Tm 6:20
also *f* prophets among the people, . . . 2 Pt 2:1
many *f* prophets have gone out . . . 1 Jn 4:1
Spirit of truth and the spirit of *f*. . . . 1 Jn 4:6
out of the mouth of the *f* prophet. . . . Rv 16:13
with him the *f* prophet who had . . . Rv 19:20
and the *f* prophet had been thrown. . . . Rv 20:10
everyone who loves and practices *f* . . . Rv 22:15

FAMILIES, FAMILY *a household unit of related people, possibly extending to an entire clan or tribe*
God sets the lonely in *f*, . . . Ps 68:6
greedy man brings trouble to his *f*, . . . Prv 15:27
she provides food for her *f*, . . . Prv 31:15
to your *f* and tell them how much . . . Mk 5:19
go back and say good-by to my *f*. . . . Lk 9:61
in one *f* divided against each other, . . . Lk 12:52
He and all his *f* were devout . . . Acts 10:2
and all his *f* were baptized. . . . Acts 16:33
he and his whole *f*. . . . Acts 16:34
He must manage his own *f* well . . . 1 Tm 3:4
how to manage his own *f*, . . . 1 Tm 3:5
practice by caring for their own *f* . . . 1 Tm 5:4
and especially for his immediate *f*, . . . 1 Tm 5:8

FAMINE *scarcity of food*
Now there was a *f* in the land, . . . Gn 12:10
Now there was a *f* in the land . . . Gn 26:1
seven years of *f* will follow them. . . . Gn 41:30
the judges ruled, there was a *f* . . . Ru 1:1
Now the *f* was severe in Samaria, . . . 1 Kgs 18:2
but a *f* of hearing the words . . . Am 8:11
or persecution or *f* or nakedness . . . Rom 8:35

FAST(ING) *to abstain from food, especially as a religious discipline*
and humbled myself with *f*. . . . Ps 35:13
When you *f*, do not look somber . . . Mt 6:16
were worshiping the Lord and *f*, . . . Acts 13:2
and *f*, committed them to the Lord . . . Acts 14:23

FATHER(S) *male parent or male ancestor; a mentor or provider; God's role in relation to his children; see ABBA*
this reason a man will leave his *f* . . . Gn 2:24
You will be the *f* of many nations. . . . Gn 17:4
for the sin of the *f* to the third . . . Ex 20:5
Honor your *f* and your mother, . . . Ex 20:12
Anyone who attacks his *f* . . . Ex 21:15
Do not dishonor your *f* . . . Lv 18:7
you must respect his mother and *f*, . . . Lv 19:3
If anyone curses his *f* or mother, . . . Lv 20:9
carried you, as a *f* carries his son, . . . Dt 1:31
Honor your *f* and your mother, . . . Dt 5:16
son who does not obey his *f* . . . Dt 21:18
Is he not your *F*, your Creator, . . . Dt 32:6
I will be his *f*, and he will be my son . . . 2 Sm 7:14
today I have become your *F*. . . . Ps 2:7

A *f* to the fatherless, a defender . . . Ps 68:5
A wise son brings joy to his *f*, . . . Prv 10:1
A wise son heeds his *f*'s instruction, . . . Prv 13:1
A fool spurns his *f*'s discipline, . . . Prv 15:5
A foolish son brings grief to his *f* . . . Prv 17:25
A foolish son is his *f*'s ruin, . . . Prv 19:13
Listen to your *f*, who gave you life, . . . Prv 23:22
f of a righteous man has great joy; . . . Prv 23:24
He who robs his *f* or mother . . . Prv 28:24
Everlasting, *F*, Prince of Peace. . . . Is 9:6
the son not share the guilt of his *f*? . . . Ez 18:19
hearts of the children to their *f*; . . . Mal 4:6
and praise your *F* in heaven. . . . Mt 5:16
Our *F* in heaven, . . . Mt 6:9
yet your heavenly *F* feeds them. . . . Mt 6:26
Anyone who loves his *f* . . . Mt 10:37
no one knows the *F* except the Son . . . Mt 11:27
Honor your *f* and mother . . . Mt 15:4
this reason a man will leave his *f* . . . Mt 19:5
the hearts of the *f* to their children . . . Lk 1:17
had to be in my *F*'s house? . . . Lk 2:49
Which of you *f*, if your son asks . . . Lk 11:11
f against son and son against *f*, . . . Lk 12:53
and does not hate his *f* and mother, . . . Lk 14:26
How dare you turn my *F*'s house . . . Jn 2:16
The *F* loves the Son and has placed . . . Jn 3:35
My *F* is always at his work . . . Jn 5:17
No one has seen the *F*. . . . Jn 6:46
You do not know me or my *F*, . . . Jn 8:19
speak just what the *F* has taught me . . . Jn 8:28
The only *F* we have is God himself . . . Jn 8:41
can snatch them out of my *F*'s hand. . . . Jn 10:29
In my *F*'s house are many rooms; . . . Jn 14:2
No one comes to the *F*. . . Jn 14:6
As the *F* has loved me, . . . Jn 15:9
he is the *f* of all who believe . . . Rom 4:11
And by him we cry, *"Abba, F."* . . . Rom 8:15
I will be a *F* to you, . . . 2 Cor 6:18
this reason a man will leave his *f* . . . Eph 5:31
Honor your *f* and mother . . . Eph 6:2
F, do not exasperate your children; . . . Eph 6:4
to the glory of God the *F*. . . . Phil 2:11
F, do not embitter your children, . . . Col 3:21
what son is not disciplined by his *f*? . . . Heb 12:7

FATHERLESS *without a father; orphaned*
He defends the cause of the *f* . . . Dt 10:18
the *f* and the widows who live . . . Dt 14:29
Do not deprive the alien or the *f* . . . Dt 24:17
Leave it for the alien, the *f* . . . Dt 24:19
the alien, the *f* and the widow, . . . Dt 26:12
A father to the *f*, a defender . . . Ps 68:5
Defend the cause of the weak and *f* . . . Ps 82:3
or encroach on the fields of the *f*, . . . Prv 23:10

FAULT(S) *moral weakness less serious than a vice; responsibility for wrongdoing*
I have found no *f* in him. . . . 1 Sm 29:3
Forgive my hidden *f* . . . Ps 19:12
and show him his *f*, just . . . Mt 18:15
of God without *f* in a crooked . . . Phil 2:15
generously to all without finding *f*, . . . Jas 1:5
his glorious presence without *f* . . . Jude 1:24

FAVOR *kindness; approval; friendly regard from a superior*
The LORD looked with *f* on Abel . . . Gn 4:4
But Noah found *f* in the eyes . . . Gn 6:8
and you have found *f* with me. . . . Ex 33:12
if I have found *f* in your eyes, . . . Ex 34:9
I will look on you with *f* . . . Lv 26:9
if I have found *f* in your eyes . . . Nm 11:15
If now I have found *f* in your eyes, . . . Jgs 6:17
in *f* with the LORD and with men. . . . 1 Sm 2:26
and I too will show you the same *f* . . . 2 Sm 2:6

If I have found *f* with you, O king, . . . Est 7:3
May the *f* of the Lord our God rest . . . Ps 90:17
and receives *f* from the LORD. . . . Prv 8:35
Many curry *f* with a ruler, . . . Prv 19:6
proclaim the year of the LORD's *f* . . . Is 61:2
called one *F* and the other Union, . . . Zec 11:7
Mary, you have found *f* with God. . . . Lk 1:30
to men on whom his *f* rests. . . . Lk 2:14
and in *f* with God and men. . . . Lk 2:52
to proclaim the year of the Lord's *f* . . . Lk 4:19
now is the time of God's *f*, . . . 2 Cor 6:2

FAVORITISM *showing special favor; partiality*
and do not show *f* to a poor man . . . Ex 23:3
to the poor or *f* to the great, . . . Lv 19:15
true it is that God does not show *f* . . . Acts 10:34
For God does not show *f*. . . . Rom 2:11
and there is no *f* with him. . . . Eph 6:9
for his wrong, and there is no *f*. . . . Col 3:25
and to do nothing out of *f*. . . . 1 Tm 5:21
Lord Jesus Christ, don't show *f*. . . . Jas 2:1
But if you show *f*, you sin . . . Jas 2:9

FEAR(ED)(S) *profound reverence and awe toward God; an emotion of dread or alarm caused by danger; timidity; see AFRAID*
F the LORD your God, serve him . . . Dt 6:13
but to *f* the LORD your God, . . . Dt 10:12
learn to *f* the LORD your God . . . Dt 31:12
you might always *f* the LORD . . . Jos 4:24
Now *f* the LORD and serve him . . . Jos 24:14
If you *f* the LORD and serve . . . 1 Sm 12:24
when he rules in the *f* of God, . . . 2 Sm 23:3
let the *f* of the LORD be upon you. . . . 2 Chr 19:7
who instructed him in the *f* of God. . . . 2 Chr 26:5
he *f* God and shunned evil. . . . Jb 1:1
a man who *f* God and shuns evil. . . . Jb 1:8
Serve the LORD with *f* . . . Ps 19:9
The *f* of the LORD is pure, . . . Ps 2:11
I will *f* no evil, . . . Ps 23:4
whom shall I *f*? . . . Ps 27:1
Let all the earth *f* the LORD; . . . Ps 33:8
he delivered me from all my *f*. . . . Ps 34:4
F the LORD, you his saints, . . . Ps 34:9
Therefore we will not *f*, . . . Ps 46:2
You alone are to be *f*. . . . Ps 76:7
that I may *f* your name. . . . Ps 86:11
great as the *f* that is due you. . . . Ps 90:11
You will not *f* the terror of night, . . . Ps 91:5
f of the LORD is the beginning . . . Ps 111:10
is the man who *f* the LORD, . . . Ps 112:1
Let those who *f* the LORD say: . . . Ps 118:4
Blessed are all who *f* the LORD, . . . Ps 128:1
of those who *f* him; . . . Ps 145:19
delights in those who *f* him, . . . Ps 147:11
f of the LORD is the beginning . . . Prv 1:33
and be at ease, without *f* of harm. . . . Prv 1:7
To *f* the LORD is to hate evil; . . . Prv 8:13
f of the LORD is the beginning . . . Prv 9:10
The *f* of the LORD adds length . . . Prv 10:27
A wise man *f* the LORD . . . Prv 14:16
He who *f* the LORD has a secure . . . Prv 14:26
f of the LORD teaches a man . . . Prv 15:33
through the *f* of the LORD a man . . . Prv 16:6
The *f* of the LORD leads to life: . . . Prv 19:23
Humility and the *f* of the LORD . . . Prv 22:4
F of man will prove to be a snare, . . . Prv 29:25
she has no *f* for her household; . . . Prv 31:21
a woman who *f* the LORD is . . . Prv 31:30
F God and keep his . . . Eccl 12:13
delight in the *f* of the LORD. . . . Is 11:3
the *f* of the LORD is the key . . . Is 33:6
Be strong, do not *f*; . . . Is 35:4
So do not *f*, for I am with you; . . . Is 41:10
and says to you, Do not *f*; . . . Is 41:13
F not, for I have redeemed you; . . . Is 43:1
Do not *f* the reproach of men . . . Is 51:7
you will have nothing to *f*. . . . Is 54:14
those who *f* the LORD talked . . . Mal 3:16

I will show you whom you should f: . . . Lk 12:5
we know what it is to f the Lord, . . . 2 Cor 5:11
conflicts on the outside, f within. . . . 2 Cor 7:5
to work out your salvation with f . . . Phil 2:12
But perfect love drives out f, . . . 1 Jn 4:18
to others show mercy, mixed with f . . . Jude
1:23
F God and give him glory, . . . Rv 14:7

FEAST(ING)(S) *a large, elaborate meal;*
banquet
the cheerful heart has a continual f. . . Prv
15:15
than a house full of f, with strife. . . . Prv 17:1
I hate, I despise your religious f; . . . Am 5:21
pleasures while they f with you. . . . 2 Pt 2:13
men are blemishes at your love f, . . . Jude 1:12

FEEBLE *weak*
you have strengthened f hands. . . . Jb 4:3
Strengthen the f hands, . . . Is 35:3
strengthen your f arms . . . Heb 12:12

FELLOWSHIP *friendship; association; compan-*
ionship
burnt offerings and f offerings, . . . Ex 20:24
If someone's offering is a f offering, . . . Lv 3:1
who has called you into f . . . 1 Cor 1:9
out of your f the man who did this? . . . 1 Cor
5:2
what f can light have with darkness . . . 2 Cor
6:14
and the f of the Holy Spirit be . . . 2 Cor 13:14
and Barnabas the right hand of f . . . Gal 2:9
if any f with the Spirit, . . . Phil 2:1
the f of sharing in his sufferings, . . . Phil 3:10
And our f is with the Father . . . 1 Jn 1:3
so that you also may have f with us. . . .
1 Jn 1:3
claim to have f with him yet walk . . . 1 Jn 1:6
we have f with one another, . . . 1 Jn 1:7

FERVOR *intensity of feeling or expression*
and he spoke with great f . . . Acts 18:25
but keep your spiritual f, serving . . . Rom 12:11

FIGHT(ING)(S), FOUGHT *to actively oppose or*
combat, as with weapons; to gain by struggle
The LORD will f for you; you need . . . Ex 14:14
going before you, will f for you, . . . Dt 1:30
the LORD your God himself will f . . . Dt 3:22
Surely the LORD was f for Israel! . . . Jos 10:14
the LORD your God f for you, . . . Jos 23:10
because he f the LORD's battles. . . . 1 Sm 25:28
Our God will f for us! . . . Neh 4:20
f against those who f against me. . . . Ps 35:1
my servants would f . . . Jn 18:36
I do not f like a man beating the air. . . . 1 Cor
9:26
The weapons we f . . . 2 Cor 10:4
them you may f the good f, . . . 1 Tm 1:18
Fight the good f of the faith. . . . 1 Tm 6:12
fought the good f, I have finished . . . 2 Tm 4:7
What causes f and quarrels . . . Jas 4:1

FIND(S), FOUND *to come upon after a search;*
to attain or reach (a goal or conclusion); to
discover by study or experiment; to experience
be sure that your sin will f you out. . . .
Nm 32:23
you will f him if you look for him . . . Dt 4:29
If you seek him, he will be f by you; . . . 1 Chr
28:9
sought God eagerly, and he was f . . . 2 Chr
15:15
f refuge in the shadow . . . Ps 36:7
My soul f rest in God alone; . . . Ps 62:1
under his wings you will f refuge; . . . Ps 91:4
who f great delight . . . Ps 112:1
like one who f great spoil. . . . Ps 119:162
Blessed is the man who f wisdom, . . . Prv 3:13
and those who seek me f me. . . . Prv 8:17
those who plan what is good f love . . . Prv
14:22

He who f a wife f what is good . . . Prv 18:22
if you f it, there is a future hope . . . Prv 24:14
A wife of noble character who can f . . . Prv
31:10
Seek the LORD while he may be f; . . . Is 55:6
and you will f rest for your souls. . . . Jer 6:16
and f me when you seek me . . . Jer 29:13
seek and you will f; knock . . . Mt 7:7
Whoever f his life will lose it, . . . Mt 10:39
and you will f rest for your souls. . . . Mt 11:29
loses his life for me will f it. . . . Mt 16:25
seek and you will f; knock . . . Lk 11:9
he who seeks f; and to him who . . . Lk 11:10
go after the lost sheep until he f it? . . . Lk 15:4
and search carefully until she f it? . . . Lk 15:8
is alive again; he was lost and is f. . . . Lk 15:24
come in and go out, and f pasture. . . . Jn 10:9
Salvation is f in no one else, . . . Acts 4:12

FINISH(ED) *bring to completion; completed or*
perfected
seventh day God had f the work he . . . Gn 2:2
him who sent me and to f his work. . . . Jn 4:34
that the Father has given me to f, . . . Jn 5:36
the drink, Jesus said, "It is f." . . . Jn 19:30
if only I may f the race . . . Acts 20:24
Now f the work, so that your eager . . . 2 Cor
8:11
I have f the race, I have kept . . . 2 Tm 4:7
Perseverance must f its work . . . Jas 1:4

FIRE *chemical reaction that releases heat and*
light; intensity of feeling: enthusiasm; severe
trial or ordeal; symbolic of hell
in flames of f from within a bush. . . . Ex 3:2
in a pillar of f to give them light, . . . Ex 13:21
f on the altar must be kept burning; . . . Lv 6:12
F came out from the presence . . . Lv 9:24
suddenly a chariot of f . . . 2 Kgs 2:11
and his tongue is a consuming f. . . . Is 30:27
my word like f," declares . . . Jer 23:29
four men walking around in the f, . . . Dn 3:25
stick snatched from the f? . . . Zec 3:2
For he will be like a refiner's f . . . Mal 3:2
you with the Holy Spirit and with f . . . Mt 3:11
will be in danger of the f of hell. . . . Mt 5:22
and be thrown into eternal f. . . . Mt 18:8
into the eternal f prepared . . . Mt 25:41
where the f never goes out. . . . Mk 9:43
you with the Holy Spirit and with f. . . . Lk 3:16
I have come to bring f on the earth, . . .
Lk 12:49
to be tongues of f that separated . . . Acts 2:3
Do not put out the Spirit's f; . . . 1 Thes 5:19
for our "God is a consuming f." . . . Heb 12:29
set on f by a small spark. . . . Jas 3:5
the elements will be destroyed by f, . . . 2 Pt
3:10
suffer the punishment of eternal f. . . . Jude 1:7
snatch others from the f . . . Jude 1:23
and his eyes were like blazing f. . . . Rv 1:14
The lake of f is the second death. . . . Rv 20:14

FIRST *highest; earliest; most prominent;*
preferred to something else
and there was morning—the f day. . . . Gn 1:5
and where he had f built an altar. . . . Gn 13:4
f offspring of every womb belongs . . . Ex 34:19
F seek the counsel of the LORD . . . 1 Kgs 22:5
f to present his case seems right, . . . Prv 18:17
I am the f and I am the last; . . . Is 44:6
F go and be reconciled . . . Mt 5:24
But seek f his kingdom . . . Mt 6:33
f take the plank out . . . Mt 7:5
But many who are f will be last, . . . Mt 19:30
last will be f, and the f will be last. . . . Mt 20:16
wants to be f must be your slave . . . Mt 20:27
This is the f and greatest . . . Mt 22:38
F clean the inside of the cup . . . Mt 23:26
And the gospel must f be preached . . .
Mk 13:10
him be the f to throw a stone . . . Jn 8:7

disciples were called Christians f . . . Acts 11:26
f for the Jew, then for the Gentile. . . . Rom 1:16
is by faith from f to last, . . . Rom 1:17
which is the f commandment . . . Eph 6:2
and the dead in Christ will rise f. . . . 1 Thes 4:16
We love because he f loved us. . . . 1 Jn 4:19
I am the F and the Last. . . . Rv 1:17

FIRSTBORN *eldest*
Every f son in Egypt will die, . . . Ex 11:5
Redeem all your f sons. . . . Ex 34:20
I will also appoint him my f, . . . Ps 89:27
and she gave birth to her f, a son. . . . Lk 2:7
that he might be the f . . . Rom 8:29
image of the invisible God, the f . . . Col 1:15
and the f from among the dead, . . . Col 1:18
when God brings his f . . . Heb 1:6
of the f, whose names are written . . . Heb 12:23
who is the faithful witness, the f . . . Rv 1:5

FIRSTFRUITS *first brought forth; first of the*
harvest
the Feast of Harvest with the f . . . Ex 23:16
Bring the best of the f of your soil . . . Ex 23:19
who have the f of the Spirit, . . . Rom 8:23
Christ, the f; then, when he comes, . . . 1 Cor
15:23
offered as f to God and the Lamb. . . . Rv 14:4

FLATTER(ING)(S)(Y) *to praise excessively out*
of self-interest
nor will I f any man; . . . Jb 32:21
their f lips speak with deception. . . . Ps 12:2
For in his own eyes he f himself . . . Ps 36:2
But then they would f him . . . Ps 78:36
and a f mouth works ruin. . . . Prv 26:28
than he who has a f tongue. . . . Prv 28:23
Whoever f his neighbor . . . Prv 29:5
or f divinations among the people . . . Ez 12:24
With f he will corrupt those who . . . Dn 11:32
and f they deceive the minds . . . Rom 16:18
You know we never used f, . . . 1 Thes 2:5
f others for their own advantage. . . . Jude 1:16

FLESH *the soft tissue of the body; the carnal*
aspect of human nature; humanity, in general
and f of my f; . . . Gn 2:23
With him is only the arm of f, . . . 2 Chr 32:8
yet in my f I will see God; . . . Jb 19:26
of stone and give them a heart of f . . . Ez 11:19
of stone and give you a heart of f . . . Ez 36:26
and the two will become one f? . . . Mt 19:5
The Word became f and made his . . . Jn 1:14
This bread is my f, which I will give . . . Jn 6:51
All f is not the same: Men have one . . . 1 Cor
15:39
For our struggle is not against f . . . Eph 6:12
do evil, those mutilators of the f. . . . Phil 3:2
come in the f is from God, . . . 1 Jn 4:2
the clothing stained by corrupted f. . . . Jude
1:23

FLOURISH(ES)(ING) *to grow luxuriantly, pros-*
per, thrive
f in the house of God; . . . Ps 52:8
In his days the righteous will f; . . . Ps 72:7
and all evildoers f, . . . Ps 92:7
The righteous will f like a palm tree . . . Ps 92:12
but the root of the righteous f. . . . Prv 12:12
but the tent of the upright will f. . . . Prv 14:11

FOLLOW(ED)(ING)(S) *to pursue or go after; to*
imitate or strive for
Do not f the crowd in doing wrong. . . . Ex 23:2
and be careful to f my decrees. . . . Lv 18:4
they have not f me wholeheartedly, . . .
Nm 32:11
he f the LORD wholeheartedly. . . . Dt 1:36
Learn them and be sure to f them. . . . Dt 5:1
f carefully all the words of this law . . . Dt 17:19
he f the LORD, the God of Israel, . . . Jos 14:14
he did not f the LORD completely, . . . 1 Kgs 11:6
he f the advice of the young men . . . 2 Chr
10:14

Surely goodness and love will f me . . . Ps 23:6
I rejoice in f your statutes . . . Ps 119:14
and I f your commands. . . . Ps 119:166
f me," Jesus said, "and I will make . . . Mt 4:19
I will f you wherever you go. . . . Mt 8:19
and Matthew got up and f him. . . . Mt 9:9
and take up his cross and f me. . . . Mt 16:24
We have left everything to f you! . . . Mt 19:27
But Peter f him at a distance, . . . Mt 26:58
take up his cross daily and f me. . . . Lk 9:23
Whoever f me will never walk . . . Jn 8:12
his sheep f him because they know . . . Jn 10:4
I know them, and they f me. . . . Jn 10:27
Whoever serves me must f me; . . . Jn 12:26
Then he said to him, "F me!" . . . Jn 21:19
F my example, as I f . . . 1 Cor 11:1
F the way of love and eagerly . . . 1 Cor 14:1
Join with others in f my example, . . . Phil 3:17
ourselves a model for you to f . . . 2 Thes 3:9
by f them you may fight the good . . . 1 Tm 1:18
that you should f in his steps. . . . 1 Pt 2:21
They f the Lamb wherever he goes. . . . Rv 14:4

FOLLY *lack of good sense; foolishness; wicked or lewd behavior; see FOOL*
a quick-tempered man displays f. . . . Prv 14:29
A man's own f ruins his life, . . . Prv 19:3
so a little f outweighs wisdom . . . Eccl 10:1
envy, slander, arrogance and f. . . . Mk 7:22
their f will be clear to everyone. . . . 2 Tm 3:9

FOOL(S) *one who is lacking judgment, sense, or understanding; see FOLLY*
his name is F, and folly goes . . . 1 Sm 25:25
The f says in his heart, . . . Ps 14:1
but f despise wisdom and discipline . . . Prv 1:7
but f he holds up to shame. . . . Prv 3:35
and a chattering f comes to ruin. . . . Prv 10:10
and whoever spreads slander is a f. . . . Prv 10:18
The way of a f seems right to him, . . . Prv 12:15
A f shows his annoyance at once, . . . Prv 12:16
but the heart of f blurts out folly. . . . Prv 12:23
but f detest turning from evil. . . . Prv 13:19
but a companion of f suffers harm. . . . Prv 13:20
A f's talk brings a rod to his back, . . . Prv 14:3
F mock at making amends for sin, . . . Prv 14:9
but a f is hotheaded and reckless. . . . Prv 14:16
but the folly of f yields folly. . . . Prv 14:24
A f spurns his father's discipline, . . . Prv 15:5
than a f in his folly. . . . Prv 17:12
use is money in the hand of a f, . . . Prv 17:16
To have a f for a son brings grief; . . . Prv 17:21
Even a f is thought wise . . . Prv 17:28
A f finds no pleasure . . . Prv 18:2
A f's mouth is his undoing, . . . Prv 18:7
but every f is quick to quarrel. . . . Prv 20:3
Do not speak to a f; . . . Prv 23:9
Wisdom is too high for a f; . . . Prv 24:7
Do not answer a f according . . . Prv 26:4
Answer a f according to his folly, . . . Prv 26:5
is a proverb in the mouth of a f. . . . Prv 26:7
so a f repeats his folly. . . . Prv 26:11
for a f than for him. . . . Prv 26:12
Though you grind a f in a mortar, . . . Prv 27:22
He who trusts in himself is a f, . . . Prv 28:26
A f gives full vent to his anger, . . . Prv 29:11
for a f than for him. . . . Prv 29:20
than to listen to the song of f. . . . Eccl 7:5
so is the laughter of f. . . . Eccl 7:6
F are put in many high positions, . . . Eccl 10:6
But anyone who says, 'You f!' . . . Mt 5:22
You blind f! Which is greater: . . . Mt 23:17
they became f and exchanged . . . Rom 1:22
he should become a "f" . . . 1 Cor 3:18
We are f for Christ, but you are . . . 1 Cor 4:10

FOOLISH(NESS) *lacking good sense; behavior befitting a fool*
but a f son grief to his mother. . . . Prv 10:1
her own hands the f one tears hers . . . Prv 14:1

but a f man despises his mother. . . . Prv 15:20
A f son brings grief to his father . . . Prv 17:25
A f son is his father's ruin, . . . Prv 19:13
practice is like a f man who built . . . Mt 7:26
of them were f and five were wise. . . . Mt 25:2
You f people! Did not the one who . . . Lk 11:40
He said to them, "How f you are, . . . Lk 24:25
Has not God made f the wisdom . . . 1 Cor 1:20
of the cross is f to those who are . . . 1 Cor 1:18
God chose the f things of the world . . . 1 Cor 1:27
for they are f to him, and he cannot . . . 1 Cor 2:14
of this world is f in God's sight. . . . 1 Cor 3:19
died for nothing!" You f Galatians! . . . Gal 3:1
should there be obscenity, f talk . . . Eph 5:4
Therefore do not be f, . . . Eph 5:17
But avoid f controversies . . . Ti 3:9

FOREIGNER(S) *a person belonging to a foreign country*
give praise to God except this f? . . . Lk 17:18
I am a f to the speaker, . . . 1 Cor 14:11
f to the covenants of the promise, . . . Eph 2:12
you are no longer f and aliens, . . . Eph 2:19

FOREKNEW, FOREKNOWLEDGE *to know beforehand; to predetermine*
to you by God's set purpose and f; . . . Acts 2:23
For those God f he . . . Rom 8:29
not reject his people, whom he f. . . . Rom 11:2
to the f of God the Father, . . . 1 Pt 1:2

FORESAW *saw in advance*
Scripture f that God would justify . . . Gal 3:8

FORGAVE, FORGIVE(NESS)(S), FORGIVING *to pardon or acquit of sins; acquittal*
I ask you to f your brothers the sins . . . Gn 50:17
Now f my sin once more . . . Ex 10:17
But now, please f their sin . . . Ex 32:32
and f wickedness, rebellion and sin. . . . Ex 34:7
abounding in love and f sin . . . Nm 14:18
But you are a f God, gracious . . . Neh 9:17
F my hidden faults. . . . Ps 19:12
f my iniquity, though it is great. . . . Ps 25:11
you f our transgressions . . . Ps 65:3
you f their iniquities . . . Ps 78:38
deliver us and f our sins . . . Ps 79:9
You are f and good, O Lord, . . . Ps 86:5
you were to f our sins . . . Ps 99:8
He f all my sins . . . Ps 103:3
But with you there is f; . . . Ps 130:4
The Lord our God is merciful and f . . . Dn 9:9
pardons sin and f the transgression . . . Mi 7:18
F us our debts, . . . Mt 6:12
For if you f men when they sin . . . Mt 6:14
authority on earth to f sins. . . . Mt 9:6
many times shall I f my brother . . . Mt 18:21
out for many for the f of sins. . . . Mt 26:28
of repentance for the f of sins. . . . Mk 1:4
Who can f sins but God alone? . . . Mk 2:7
anything against anyone, f him, . . . Mk 11:25
salvation through the f of their sins, . . . Lk 1:77
of repentance for the f of sins. . . . Lk 3:3
F, and you will be forgiven. . . . Lk 6:37
Who is this who even f sins? . . . Lk 7:49
f everyone who sins against us. . . . Lk 11:4
rebuke him, and if he repents, f him . . . Lk 17:3
Jesus said, "Father, f them, . . . Lk 23:34
and f of sins will be preached . . . Lk 24:47
that he might give repentance and f . . . Acts 5:31
believes in him receives f of sins . . . Acts 10:43
that through Jesus the f . . . Acts 13:38
so that they may receive f of sins . . . Acts 26:18
you ought to f and comfort him, . . . 2 Cor 2:7
through his blood, the f of sins, . . . Eph 1:7
to one another, f each other, . . . Eph 4:32
in whom we have redemption, the f . . . Col 1:14
F as the Lord f you. . . . Col 3:13

the shedding of blood there is no f. . . . Heb 9:22
and just and will f us our sins . . . 1 Jn 1:9

FORGET(S)(TING), FORGOT(TEN) *to be unable to remember; to disregard intentionally*
Be careful not to f the covenant . . . Dt 4:23
you f the God who gave you birth. . . . Dt 32:18
God has even f some of your sin. . . . Jb 11:6
all the nations that f God. . . . Ps 9:17
Do not f the helpless. . . . Ps 10:12
If we had f the name of our God . . . Ps 44:20
Consider this, you who f God, . . . Ps 50:22
and f not all his benefits. . . . Ps 103:2
I will never f your precepts, . . . Ps 119:93
My son, do not f my teaching, . . . Prv 3:1
do not f my words or swerve . . . Prv 4:5
that you the LORD your Maker, . . . Is 51:13
Yet not one of them is f by God. . . . Lk 12:6
F what is behind and straining . . . Phil 3:13
he will not f your work . . . Heb 6:10
Do not f to entertain strangers, . . . Heb 13:2
And do not f to do good . . . Heb 13:16
immediately f what he looks like. . . . Jas 1:24
and has f that he has been cleansed . . . 2 Pt 1:9
But do not f this one thing, . . . 2 Pt 3:8

FORM(ED) *a shape; to create or fashion*
the LORD God f the man . . . Gn 2:7
Now the LORD God had f out . . . Gn 2:19
for he knows how we are f, . . . Ps 103:14
or how the body is f in a mother's . . . Eccl 11:5
Shall what is f say to him who f it, . . . Is 29:16
but f it to be inhabited . . . Is 45:18
he who f me in the womb . . . Is 49:5
f marred beyond human likeness . . . Is 52:14
Before I f you in the womb I knew . . . Jer 1:5
Shall what is f say to him who f it, . . . Rom 9:20
of childbirth until Christ is f in you, . . . Gal 4:19
For Adam was f first, then Eve. . . . 1 Tm 2:13
having a f of godliness . . . 2 Tm 3:5
understand that the universe was f. . . . Heb 11:3
and the earth was f out of water . . . 2 Pt 3:5

FORSAKE(N) *to quit, abandon, leave behind, cease from*
he will never leave you nor f you. . . . Dt 31:6
I will never leave you nor f you. . . . Jos 1:5
Far be it from us to f the LORD . . . Jos 24:16
but if you f him, he will f you. . . . 2 Chr 15:2
my God, why have you f me? . . . Ps 22:1
Though my father and mother f me . . . Ps 27:10
I have never seen the righteous f. . . . Ps 37:25
he will never f his inheritance. . . . Ps 94:14
Let the wicked f his way . . . Is 55:7
my God, why have you f me? . . . Mt 27:46
never will I f you. . . . Heb 13:5
You have f your first love. . . . Rv 2:4

FOUNDATION(S), FOUNDED *base on which something is built; to build on a solid base*
In the beginning you laid the f . . . Ps 102:25
a precious cornerstone for a sure f; . . . Is 28:16
he f the world by his wisdom . . . Jer 10:12
because it had its f on the rock. . . . Mt 7:25
For if he lays the f and is not able . . . Lk 14:29
building on someone else's f . . . Rom 15:20
I laid a f as an expert builder, . . . 1 Cor 3:10
For no one can lay any f other . . . 1 Cor 3:11
built on the f of the apostles . . . Eph 2:20
the pillar and f of the truth. . . . 1 Tm 3:15
God's solid f stands firm, . . . 2 Tm 2:19
O Lord, you laid the f of the earth, . . . Heb 1:10
not laying again the f of repentance . . . Heb 6:1
and it is f on better promises. . . . Heb 8:6

FOUNTAIN *source; spring of water*
For with you is the f of life; . . . Ps 36:9
The fear of the LORD is a f of life, . . . Prv 14:27
the f of wisdom is a bubbling brook. . . . Prv 18:4
On that day a f will be opened . . . Zec 13:1

FREE(D)(DOM)(LY) *voluntary; without restraint; without cost; to set at liberty*
You are *f* to eat from any tree . . . Gn 2:16
you have *f* me from my chains. . . . Ps 116:16
and he answered by setting me *f*. . . . Ps 118:5
for you have set my heart *f*. . . . Ps 119:32
The LORD sets prisoners *f*, . . . Ps 146:7
then do this, my son, to *f* yourself, . . . Prv 6:3
and to our God, for he will *f* pardon . . . Is 55:7
to proclaim *f* for the captives . . . Is 61:1
Freely you have received, *f* give. . . . Mt 10:8
me to proclaim *f* for the prisoners . . . Lk 4:18
and the truth will set you *f*. . . . Jn 8:32
and are justified *f* by his grace . . . Rom 3:24
anyone who has died has been *f*. . . Rom 6:7
You have been set *f* from sin . . . Rom 6:18
of life set me *f* from the law of sin . . . Rom 8:2
into the glorious *f* of the children . . . Rom 8:21
although if you can gain your *f*, . . . 1 Cor 7:21
whether Jews or Greeks, slave or *f* . . . 1 Cor 12:13
the Spirit of the Lord is, there is *f*. . . . 2 Cor 3:17
slave nor *f*, male nor female, . . . Gal 3:28
for freedom that Christ has set us *f*. . . . Gal 5:1
But do not use your *f* to indulge . . . Gal 5:13
which he has *f* given us . . . Eph 1:6
into the perfect law that gives *f*, . . . Jas 1:25
but do not use your *f* as a cover-up . . . 1 Pt 2:16
has *f* us from our sins by his blood, . . . Rv 1:5

FRIEND(S) *intimate companion or associate; one attached to another by affection or esteem*
as a man speaks with his *f*. . . . Ex 33:11
descendants of Abraham your *f*? . . . 2 Chr 20:7
and a gossip separates close *f*. . . . Prv 16:28
the matter separates close *f*. . . . Prv 17:9
A *f* loves at all times, . . . Prv 17:17
there is a *f* who sticks closer . . . Prv 18:24
Wounds from a *f* can be trusted . . . Prv 27:6
Do not forsake your *f* and the *f* . . . Prv 27:10
you descendants of Abraham my *f*, . . . Is 41:8
a *f* of tax collectors and "sinners." . . . Mt 11:19
him the bread because he is his *f*, . . . Lk 11:8
that he lay down his life for his *f*. . . . Jn 15:13
If you let this man go, you are no *f* . . . Jn 19:12
and he was called God's *f*. . . . Jas 2:23
Anyone who chooses to be a *f* . . . Jas 4:4

FRUIT *product of a plant; the effect or consequence of one's work; product; result; offspring*
Should I give up my *f*, so good . . . Jgs 9:11
which yields its *f* in season . . . Ps 1:3
The *f* of the righteous is a tree . . . Prv 11:30
From the *f* of his lips a man is filled . . . Prv 12:14
He who tends a fig tree will eat its *f* . . . Prv 27:18
from his roots a Branch will bear *f*. . . . Is 11:1
and fill all the world with *f*. . . . Is 27:6
The *f* of righteousness will be peace . . . Is 32:17
and never fails to bear *f*. . . . Jer 17:8
reap the *f* of unfailing love, . . . Hos 10:12
that we may offer the *f* of our lips. . . . Hos 14:2
showed me: a basket of ripe *f* . . . Am 8:1
Produce *f* in keeping . . . Mt 3:8
By their *f* you will recognize them. . . . Mt 7:16
a tree good and its *f* will be good, . . . Mt 12:33
does not produce good *f* will be cut . . . Lk 3:9
nor does a bad tree bear good *f*. . . . Lk 6:43
and he went to look for *f* on it, . . . Lk 13:6
branch in me that bears no *f*, . . . Jn 15:2
and bear *f*—*f* that will last. . . . Jn 15:16
in order that we might bear *f* . . . Rom 7:4
But the *f* of the Spirit is love, joy, . . . Gal 5:22
with the *f* of righteousness that . . . Phil 1:11
bearing *f* in every good work, . . . Col 1:10
the *f* of lips that confess his name. . . . Heb 13:15

and good *f*, impartial and sincere. . . . Jas 3:17
of *f*, yielding its *f* every month. . . . Rv 22:2

FRUITFUL *bearing fruit; abundantly productive*
Be *f* and increase in number . . . Gn 1:22
Be *f* and increase in number . . . Gn 9:1
be *f* and increase in number. . . . Gn 35:11
the Israelites were *f* and multiplied . . . Ex 1:7
Your wife will be like a *f* vine . . . Ps 128:3
prunes so that it will be even more *f*. . . . Jn 15:2
this will mean *f* labor for me. . . . Phil 1:22

FULFILL(ED)(MENT)(S) *to complete or perform as promised; to measure up or satisfy*
Does he promise and not *f*? . . . Nm 23:19
Every promise has been *f*; . . . Jos 23:14
to God, who *f* his purpose for me. . . . Ps 57:2
and *f* my vows day after day. . . . Ps 61:8
I will *f* my vows to the LORD . . . Ps 116:14
The LORD will *f* his purpose . . . Ps 138:8
He *f* the desires of those who fear . . . Ps 145:19
but a longing *f* is a tree of life. . . . Prv 13:12
A longing *f* is sweet to the soul, . . . Prv 13:19
than to make a vow and not *f* it. . . . Eccl 5:5
far-off land, a man to *f* my purpose. . . . Is 46:11
when I will *f* the gracious promise . . . Jer 33:14
place to *f* what the Lord had said . . . Mt 1:22
so was *f* what the Lord had said . . . Mt 2:15
us to do this to *f* all righteousness. . . . Mt 3:15
f what was said . . . Mt 4:14
come to abolish them but to *f* them. . . . Mt 5:17
This was to *f* what was spoken . . . Mt 8:17
This was to *f* what was spoken . . . Mt 12:17
In them is *f* the prophecy of Isaiah: . . . Mt 13:14
place to *f* what was spoken . . . Mt 21:4
the Scriptures be *f* that say it . . . Mt 26:54
by Jeremiah the prophet was *f*: . . . Mt 27:9
Today this scripture is *f* . . . Lk 4:21
This was to *f* the word . . . Jn 12:38
But this is to *f* the scripture: . . . Jn 13:18
But this is to *f* what is written . . . Jn 15:25
words he had spoken would be *f*: . . . Jn 18:9
the Scripture might be *f* which said, . . . Jn 19:24
to be *f* which the Holy Spirit spoke . . . Acts 1:16
loves his fellowman has *f* the law. . . . Rom 13:8
Therefore love is the *f* of the law. . . . Rom 13:10
husband should *f* his marital duty . . . 1 Cor 7:3
And the scripture was *f* that says, . . . Jas 2:23

FULL(NESS) *containing all that is wanted, needed, or possible*
gifts of the earth and its *f*. . . . Dt 33:16
them into the chest until it was *f*. . . . 2 Chr 24:10
whose quiver is *f* of them. . . . Ps 127:5
He who is *f* loathes honey, . . . Prv 27:7
Her husband has *f* confidence . . . Prv 31:11
the whole earth is *f* of his glory. . . . Is 6:3
for the earth will be *f* . . . Is 11:9
Jesus, *f* of the Holy Spirit, . . . Lk 4:1
From the *f* of his grace we have all . . . Jn 1:16
may have life, and have it to the *f*. . . . Jn 10:10
known to be *f* of the Spirit . . . Acts 6:3
a man *f* of faith and of the Holy . . . Acts 6:5
But Stephen, *f* of the Holy Spirit, . . . Acts 7:55
f of the Holy Spirit and faith, . . . Acts 11:24
greater riches will their *f* bring! . . . Rom 11:12
the *f* of him who fills everything . . . Eph 1:23
to the measure of all the *f* of God. . . . Eph 3:19
to the whole measure of the *f*. . . . Eph 4:13
to have all his *f* dwell in him, . . . Col 1:19
to you the word of God in its *f*. . . . Col 1:25
in Christ all the *f* of the Deity lives . . . Col 2:9

FURIOUS, FURY *wrath; fierceness*
In *f* anger and in great wrath . . . Dt 29:28
and in *f* subdued nations . . . Is 14:6
and a mighty arm in anger and *f*. . . Jer 21:5
where I banish them in my *f* anger . . . Jer 32:37

will drink of the wine of God's *f*, . . . Rv 14:10
with the wine of the *f* of his wrath. . . . Rv 16:19
the winepress of the *f* of the wrath . . . Rv 19:15

GAIN(ED)(S) *to win; to derive advantage from; winnings or profits*
And I will *g* glory through Pharaoh . . . Ex 14:17
With God we will *g* the victory, . . . Ps 60:12
the man who *g* understanding, . . . Prv 3:13
pay attention and *g* understanding. . . . Prv 4:1
You who are simple, *g* prudence; . . . Prv 8:5
A kindhearted woman *g* respect, . . . Prv 11:16
heeds correction *g* understanding. . . . Prv 15:32
he who hates ill-gotten *g* will enjoy . . . Prv 28:16
in the end *g* more favor . . . Prv 28:23
but a man of lowly spirit *g* honor. . . . Prv 29:23
to *g* for himself everlasting renown . . . Is 63:12
have *g* the renown that is still yours . . . Jer 32:20
that you are trying to *g* time, . . . Dn 2:8
for a man if he *g* the whole world, . . . Mt 16:26
standing firm you will *g* life. . . . Lk 21:19
through whom we have *g* access . . . Rom 5:2
but have not love, I *g* nothing. . . . 1 Cor 13:3
to live is Christ and to die is *g*. . . . Phil 1:21
that I may *g* Christ and be found . . . Phil 3:8
have served well *g* an excellent . . . 1 Tm 3:13
godliness is a means to financial *g*. . . . 1 Tm 6:5
with contentment is great *g*. . . . 1 Tm 6:6

GARDEN(ER) *plot of ground where plants are cultivated; one who cultivates plants*
the LORD God planted a *g* . . . Gn 2:8
put him in the *G* of Eden to work it . . . Gn 2:15
You are a *g* locked up, my sister, . . . Song 4:12
You will be like a well-watered *g*, . . . Is 58:11
They will be like a well-watered *g*, . . . Jer 31:12
in Eden, the *g* of God; . . . Ez 28:13
of Eden in the *g* of God. . . . Ez 31:9
true vine, and my Father is the *g*. . . . Jn 15:1

GATE(S) *opening in a city wall, often protected by barriers and towers; place of judicial decisions, announcements, and trade*
Lift up your heads, O you *g*; . . . Ps 24:7
Enter his *g* with thanksgiving . . . Ps 100:4
Open for me the *g* of righteousness . . . Ps 118:19
husband is respected at the city *g*, . . . Prv 31:23
works bring her praise at the city *g*. . . . Prv 31:31
Your *g* will always stand open, . . . Is 60:11
Pass through, pass through the *g*! . . . Is 62:10
For wide is the *g* and broad is . . . Mt 7:13
the *g* of Hades will not overcome it . . . Mt 16:18
not enter the sheep pen by the *g*, . . . Jn 10:1
also suffered outside the city *g* . . . Heb 13:12
On the *g* were written the names . . . Rv 21:12
The twelve *g* were twelve pearls, . . . Rv 21:21
On no day will its *g* ever be shut, . . . Rv 21:25
may go through the *g* into the city. . . . Rv 22:14

GATHER(ED)(S) *to bring together; to harvest; to assemble*
and he who *g* little did not have too . . . Ex 16:18
and *g* us from the nations, . . . Ps 106:47
he *g* the exiles of Israel. . . . Ps 147:2
He who *g* crops in summer is a wise . . . Prv 10:5
Who has *g* up the wind . . . Prv 30:4
and *g* the exiles of Israel; . . . Is 11:12
He *g* the lambs in his arms . . . Is 40:11
and all nations will *g* in Jerusalem . . . Jer 3:17
I myself will *g* the remnant . . . Jer 23:3
who scattered Israel will *g* them . . . Jer 31:10
G together, *g* together, . . . Zep 2:1
At that time I will *g* you; . . . Zep 3:20
I will *g* all the nations to Jerusalem . . . Zec 14:2
he who does not *g* with me scatters . . . Mt 12:30
then *g* the wheat and bring it . . . Mt 13:30

longed to *g* your children together, . . . Mt 23:37
and they will *g* his elect . . . Mt 24:31
g where I have not scattered seed? . . . Mt 25:26
All the nations will be *g* before him . . . Mt 25:32
and *g* his elect from the four winds, . . .
   Mk 13:27
and to *g* the wheat into his barn, . . . Lk 3:17
and he who does not *g* with me, . . . Lk 11:23
longed to *g* your children together, . . . Lk 13:34
and he who *g* little did not have too . . . 2 Cor
   8:15
Lord Jesus Christ and our being *g* . . . 2 Thes
   2:1
Then they *g* the kings together . . . Rv 16:16

GAVE, GIVE(N)(S), GIVING *to grant, bestow, or
provide; to yield or produce*
She also *g* some to her husband, . . . Gn 3:6
Abram *g* him a tenth of everything. . . . Gn 14:20
g him success in whatever he did. . . . Gn 39:23
You shall not *g* false testimony . . . Ex 20:16
The rich are not to *g* more . . . Ex 30:15
he *g* him the two tablets . . . Ex 31:18
and *g* you peace. . . . Nm 6:26
The LORD our God *g* us all . . . Dt 2:36
He *g* you manna to eat in the desert . . . Dt 8:16
G generously to him and do . . . Dt 15:10
The LORD *g* them rest . . . Jos 21:44
then I will *g* him to the LORD . . . 1 Sm 1:28
The LORD *g* Solomon wisdom, . . . 1 Kgs 4:29
According to their ability they *g* . . . Ezr 2:69
LORD *g* and the LORD has taken . . . Jb 1:21
g joy to the heart. . . . Ps 19:8
The unfolding of your words *g* light; . . .
   Ps 119:130
but *g* grace to the humble. . . . Prv 3:34
One man *g* freely, yet gains . . . Prv 11:24
good news *g* health to the bones. . . . Prv 15:30
of a man who *g* gifts. . . . Prv 19:6
but the righteous *g* without sparing . . . Prv
   21:26
My son, *g* me your heart . . . Prv 23:26
if he is thirsty, *g* him water to drink . . . Prv
   25:21
is a righteous man who *g* way . . . Prv 25:26
He who *g* to the poor will lack . . . Prv 28:27
but *g* me only my daily bread. . . . Prv 30:8
G her the reward she has earned, . . . Prv 31:31
He *g* strength to the weary . . . Is 40:29
I will *g* you a new heart . . . Ez 36:26
so that your *g* may be in secret. . . . Mt 6:4
G us today our daily bread. . . . Mt 6:11
and all these things will be *g* to you . . . Mt 6:33
Ask and it will be *g* to you; . . . Mt 7:7
Freely you have received, freely *g*. . . . Mt 10:8
if anyone *g* even a cup of cold water . . .
   Mt 10:42
Whoever has will be *g* more, . . . Mt 13:12
I will *g* you the keys . . . Mt 16:19
G to Caesar what is Caesar's, . . . Mt 22:21
Jesus took bread, *g* thanks . . . Mt 26:26
in a loud voice, he *g* up his spirit. . . . Mt 27:50
g them authority over evil spirits. . . . Mk 6:7
G, and it will be given to you. . . . Lk 6:38
kingdom of God has been *g* to you, . . . Lk 8:10
Father in heaven *g* the Holy Spirit . . . Lk 11:13
saying, "This is my body *g* for you; . . . Lk 22:19
he *g* the right to become children . . . Jn 1:12
so loved the world that he *g* his one . . . Jn 3:16
even so the Son *g* life to whom he is . . . Jn 5:21
The Spirit *g* life; the flesh counts . . . Jn 6:63
I *g* them eternal life, and they shall . . . Jn 10:28
A new commandment I *g* you: . . . Jn 13:34
he will *g* you another Counselor . . . Jn 14:16
leave with you; my peace I *g* you. . . . Jn 14:27
the cup the Father has *g* me? . . . Jn 18:11
g many convincing proofs that he . . . Acts 1:3
they *g* to anyone as he had need. . . . Acts 2:45
them by *g* the Holy Spirit to them, . . . Acts 15:8
blessed to *g* than to receive. . . . Acts 20:35
Therefore God *g* them . . . Rom 1:24

the Holy Spirit, whom he has *g* us. . . . Rom 5:5
not spare his own Son, but *g* him up . . . Rom
   8:32
the letter kills, but the Spirit *g* life. . . . 2 Cor 3:6
and has *g* us the Spirit as a deposit, . . . 2 Cor
   5:5
g us the ministry of reconciliation: . . . 2 Cor
   5:18
also excel in this grace of *g*. . . . 2 Cor 8:7
Each man should *g* what he has . . . 2 Cor 9:7
to each one of us grace has been *g* . . . Eph 4:7
shared with me in the matter of *g* . . . Phil 4:15
who *g* himself as a ransom . . . 1 Tm 2:6
who *g* himself for us to redeem us . . . Ti 2:14
Let us not *g* up meeting together, . . . Heb 10:25
into the perfect law that *g* freedom, . . . Jas 1:25
but *g* grace to the humble. . . . Jas 4:6
We know it by the Spirit he *g* us. . . . 1 Jn 3:24

GENERATION(S) *group of people born and
living about the same time; offspring having a
common parent or parents and constituting a
single step in the line of descent*
a covenant for all *g* to come: . . . Gn 9:12
after you for the *g* to come, . . . Gn 17:7
a thousand *g* of those . . . Ex 20:6
until the whole *g* of those who had . . .
   Nm 32:13
covenant of love to a thousand *g* . . . Dt 7:9
such is the *g* of those who seek him . . . Ps 24:6
tell of them to the next *g*. . . . Ps 48:13
faithfulness known through all *g*. . . . Ps 89:1
your renown endures through all *g*. . . .
   Ps 102:12
Let this be written for a future *g*, . . . Ps 102:18
he commanded, for a thousand *g*, . . . Ps 105:8
the *g* of the upright will be blessed . . . Ps 112:2
dominion endures through all *g*. . . . Ps 145:13
my salvation through all *g* . . . Is 51:8
his dominion endures from *g* to *g*. . . . Dn 4:3
O unbelieving and perverse *g*, . . . Mt 17:17
this *g* will certainly not pass away . . . Mt 24:34
now on all *g* will call me blessed, . . . Lk 1:48
Jesus said, "This is a wicked *g*. . . . Lk 11:29
Save yourselves from this corrupt *g* . . . Acts
   2:40
not made known to men in other *g* . . . Eph 3:5
fault in a crooked and depraved *g*, . . . Phil 2:15
been kept hidden for ages and *g*, . . . Col 1:26

GENTILE(S) *person of a non-Jewish nation or
non-Jewish faith; pagan or heathen*
and a light for the *G*, . . . Is 42:6
See, I will beckon to the *G*, . . . Is 49:22
a light for revelation to the *G* . . . Lk 2:32
on by the *G* until the times . . . Lk 21:24
to carry my name before the *G* . . . Acts 9:15
been poured out even on the *G*. . . . Acts 10:45
of eternal life, we now turn to the *G* . . . Acts
   13:46
I have made you a light for the *G*, . . . Acts
   13:47
From now on I will go to the *G*. . . . Acts 18:6
As for the *G* believers, we have . . . Acts 21:25
and in all Judea, and to the *G* also, . . . Acts
   26:20
first for the Jew, then for the *G*. . . . Rom 1:16
when *G*, who do not have the law, . . . Rom 2:14
and *G* alike are all under sin. . . . Rom 3:9
Is he not the God of *G* too? Yes, . . . Rom 3:29
to the *G* to make Israel envious. . . . Rom 11:11
block to Jews and foolishness to *G*, . . . 1 Cor
   1:23
the gospel the *G* are heirs together . . . Eph 3:6
to the *G* the unsearchable riches . . . Eph 3:8

GENTLE(NESS) *kind, mild-mannered*
Even the most *g* and sensitive man . . . Dt 28:54
And after the fire came a *g* whisper . . . 1 Kgs
   19:12
Will he speak to you with *g* words? . . . Jb 41:3
A *g* answer turns away wrath, . . . Prv 15:1

and a *g* tongue can break a bone. . . . Prv 25:15
g and riding on a donkey, . . . Zec 9:9
for I am *g* and humble in heart, . . . Mt 11:29
g and riding on a donkey, . . . Mt 21:5
or in love and with a *g* spirit? . . . 1 Cor 4:21
By the meekness and *g* of Christ, . . . 2 Cor 10:1
faithfulness, *g* and self-control. . . . Gal 5:23
Be completely humble and *g*; . . . Eph 4:2
Let your *g* be evident to all. . . . Phil 4:5
kindness, humility, *g* and patience. . . . Col 3:12
but we were *g* among you, . . . 1 Thes 2:7
not violent but *g*, not quarrelsome, . . . 1 Tm 3:3
faith, love, endurance and *g*. . . . 1 Tm 6:11
the unfading beauty of a *g* . . . 1 Pt 3:4
But do this with *g* and respect, . . . 1 Pt 3:15

GIFT(ED)(S) *a present; a sacrifice; anything
given voluntarily, at no cost*
bring *g* to the One to be feared. . . . Ps 76:11
He has scattered abroad his *g* . . . Ps 112:9
A *g* opens the way for the giver . . . Prv 18:16
A *g* given in secret soothes anger, . . . Prv 21:14
of *g* he does not give. . . . Prv 25:14
in all his toil—this is the *g* of God. . . . Eccl 3:13
and presented him with *g* of gold . . . Mt 2:11
if you are offering your *g* . . . Mt 5:23
Father in heaven give good *g* . . . Mt 7:11
to give good *g* to your children, . . . Lk 11:13
If you knew the *g* of God . . . Jn 4:10
wait for the *g* my Father promised, . . . Acts 1:4
And you will receive the *g* . . . Acts 2:38
and *g* to the poor have come up . . . Acts 10:4
So if God gave them the same *g* . . . Acts 11:17
for God's *g* and his call are . . . Rom 11:29
We have different *g*, according . . . Rom 12:6
but the *g* of God is eternal life . . . Rom 6:23
If a man's *g* is prophesying, . . . Rom 12:6
each man has his own *g* from God; . . . 1 Cor
   7:7
Now about spiritual *g*, brothers, . . . 1 Cor 12:1
and eagerly desire spiritual *g*, . . . 1 Cor 14:1
excel in *g* that build up the church. . . . 1 Cor
   14:12
he is a prophet or spiritually *g*, . . . 1 Cor 14:37
the *g* is acceptable according . . . 2 Cor 8:12
He has scattered abroad his *g* . . . 2 Cor 9:9
be to God for his indescribable *g*! . . . 2 Cor
   9:15
it is the *g* of God—not by works, . . . Eph 2:8
and gave *g* to men. . . . Eph 4:8
not neglect your *g*, . . . 1 Tm 4:14
you to fan into flame the *g* of God, . . . 2 Tm 1:6
and *g* of the Holy Spirit distributed . . . Heb 2:4
who have tasted the heavenly *g*, . . . Heb 6:4
indicating that the *g* and sacrifices . . . Heb 9:9
and perfect *g* is from above, . . . Jas 1:17
with you of the gracious *g* of life, . . . 1 Pt 3:7
should use whatever *g* he has . . . 1 Pt 4:10
let him take the free *g* of the water . . . Rv 22:17

GLAD(NESS) *experiencing or exhibiting joy
and pleasure; providing joy and pleasure*
his heart will be *g* when he sees you . . . Ex 4:14
and you saw it and were *g*. . . . 1 Sm 19:5
g in heart for all the good things . . . 1 Kgs 8:66
heavens rejoice, let the earth be *g*; . . . 1 Chr
   16:31
So they sang praises with *g* . . . 2 Chr 29:30
let all who take refuge in you be *g*; . . . Ps 5:11
I will be *g* and rejoice in you; . . . Ps 9:2
Let Jacob rejoice and Israel be *g*! . . . Ps 14:7
Therefore my heart is *g* . . . Ps 16:9
made him *g* with the joy . . . Ps 21:6
I will be *g* and rejoice in your love, . . . Ps 31:7
Rejoice in the LORD and be *g*, . . . Ps 32:11
shout for joy and *g*; . . . Ps 35:27
rejoice and be *g* in you; . . . Ps 40:16
music of the strings makes you *g*. . . . Ps 45:8
They are led in with joy and *g*; . . . Ps 45:15
Let me hear joy and *g*; . . . Ps 51:8
let Jacob rejoice and Israel be *g*! . . . Ps 53:6
The righteous will be *g* . . . Ps 58:10

the hills are clothed with *g*. . . . Ps 65:12
May the nations be *g* and sing . . . . Ps 67:4
But may the righteous be *g* . . . Ps 68:3
The poor will see and be *g* . . . Ps 69:32
rejoice and be *g* in you; . . . Ps 70:4
for joy and be *g* all our days. . . . Ps 90:14
Make us *g* for as many days . . . Ps 90:15
For you make me *g* by your deeds, . . . Ps 92:4
heavens rejoice, let the earth be *g*; . . . Ps 96:11
LORD reigns, let the earth be *g*; . . . Ps 97:1
Worship the LORD with *g*; . . . Ps 100:2
let us rejoice and be *g* in it. . . . Ps 118:24
then my heart will be *g*; . . . Prv 23:15
May your father and mother be *g*; . . . Prv 23:25
a righteous one can sing and be *g*. . . . Prv 29:6
sun than to eat and drink and be *g*. . . . Eccl 8:15
Go, eat your food with *g*, . . . Eccl 9:7
let us rejoice and be *g* . . . Is 25:9
and the parched land will be *g*; . . . Is 35:1
G and joy will overtake them, . . . Is 35:10
But be *g* and rejoice forever . . . Is 65:18
be *g*, because great is your reward . . . Mt 5:12
But we had to celebrate and be *g*, . . . Lk 15:32
and the reaper may be *g* together. . . . Jn 4:36
my day; he saw it and was *g*. . . . Jn 8:56
for your sake I am *g* I was not there . . . Jn 11:15
you would be *g* that I am going . . . Jn 14:28
Therefore my heart is *g* . . . Acts 2:26
he was *g* and encouraged them all . . . Acts 11:23
they were *g* and honored the word . . . Acts 13:48
news made all the brothers very *g*. . . . Acts 15:3
were *g* for its encouraging message. . . . Acts 15:31
We are *g* whenever we are weak . . . 2 Cor 13:9
Let us rejoice and be *g* . . . Rv 19:7

GLORIFIED, GLORIFY *to give honor or praise (as in worship); to exalt*
G the LORD with me; . . . Ps 34:3
my lips will *g* you. . . . Ps 63:3
and *g* him with thanksgiving. . . . Ps 69:30
I will *g* your name forever. . . . Ps 86:12
I will *g* the place of my feet. . . . Is 60:13
Let the LORD be *g*, . . . Is 66:5
day I am *g* will be a memorable day . . . Ez 39:13
and *g* him who lives forever. . . . Dn 4:34
and exalt and *g* the King of heaven, . . . Dn 4:37
since Jesus had not yet been *g*. . . . Jn 7:39
Jesus replied, "If I *g* myself, . . . Jn 8:54
glory so that God's Son may be *g* . . . Jn 11:4
after Jesus was *g* did they realize . . . Jn 12:16
come for the Son of Man to be *g*. . . . Jn 12:23
I have *g* it, and will *g* it again . . . Jn 12:28
Son of Man *g* and God is *g* in him. . . . Jn 13:31
G your Son, that your Son may . . . Jn 17:1
death by which Peter would *g* God. . . . Jn 21:19
our fathers, has *g* his servant Jesus. . . . Acts 3:13
they neither *g* him as God . . . Rom 1:21
those he justified, he also *g* . . . Rom 8:30
and mouth you may *g* the God . . . Rom 15:6
comes to be *g* in his holy people . . . 2 Thes 1:10
of our Lord Jesus may be *g* in you, . . . 2 Thes 1:12
him from the dead and *g* him, . . . 1 Pt 1:21
and *g* God on the day he visits us. . . . 1 Pt 2:12
they refused to repent and *g* him. . . . Rv 16:9

GLORIOUS *possessing or deserving glory; splendid*
not revere this *g* and awesome . . . Dt 28:58
and praise your *g* name. . . . 1 Chr 29:13
and his place of rest will be *g*. . . . Ps 11:10
for he has done *g* things; . . . Ps 12:5
they are the *g* ones . . . Ps 16:3

to the fading flower, his *g* beauty, . . . Ps 28:1
to make his law great and *g*. . . . Ps 42:21
All *g* is the princess . . . Ps 45:13
and I will adorn my *g* temple. . . . Ps 60:7
who sent his *g* arm of power . . . Ps 63:12
from your lofty throne, holy and *g*. . . . Ps 63:15
g temple, where our fathers praised . . . Ps 64:11
Praise be to his *g* name forever; . . . Ps 72:19
G things are said of you, . . . Ps 87:3
G and majestic are his deeds, . . . Ps 111:3
of the *g* splendor of your majesty, . . . Ps 145:5
the *g* splendor of your kingdom. . . . Ps 145:12
the LORD will be beautiful and *g*, . . . Is 4:2
do not dishonor your *g* throne. . . . Jer 14:21
A *g* throne, exalted . . . Jer 17:12
how broken the *g* staff! . . . Jer 48:17
the Son of Man sits on his *g* throne, . . . Mt 19:28
appeared in *g* splendor, talking . . . Lk 9:31
of the great and *g* day of the Lord. . . . Acts 2:20
and brought into the *g* freedom . . . Rom 8:21
of the Spirit be even more *g*? . . . 2 Cor 3:8
to the praise of his *g* grace, . . . Eph 1:6
g Father, may give you the Spirit . . . Eph 1:17
of his *g* riches he may strengthen . . . Eph 3:16
so that they will be like his *g* body. . . . Phil 3:21
to his *g* riches in Christ Jesus. . . . Phil 4:19
all power according to his *g* might . . . Col 1:11
among the Gentiles the *g* riches . . . Col 1:27
to the *g* gospel of the blessed God, . . . 1 Tm 1:11
the *g* appearing of our great God . . . Ti 2:13
believers in our *g* Lord Jesus Christ . . . Jas 2:1
with an inexpressible and *g* joy, . . . 1 Pt 1:8
before his *g* presence without fault . . . Jude 1:24

GLORY *great honor, praise, and thanksgiving offered in worship; splendor and majestic beauty*
And I will gain *g* through Pharaoh . . . Ex 14:17
there was the *g* of the LORD . . . Ex 16:10
the *g* of the LORD settled . . . Ex 24:16
Moses said, "Now show me your *g* . . . Ex 33:18
the *g* of the LORD filled . . . Ex 40:34
LORD our God has shown us his *g* . . . Dt 5:24
My son, give *g* to the LORD, . . . Jos 7:19
The *g* has departed from Israel . . . 1 Sm 4:21
and crowned him with *g* and honor . . . Ps 8:5
The heavens declare the *g* of God; . . . Ps 19:1
that the King of *g* may come in. . . . Ps 24:7
the place where your *g* dwells. . . . Ps 26:8
ascribe to the LORD *g* . . . Ps 29:1
Sing the *g* of his name; . . . Ps 66:2
the whole earth be filled with his *g*. . . . Ps 72:19
This is the *g* of all his saints. . . . Ps 149:9
it is to his *g* to overlook an offense. . . . Prv 19:11
It is the *g* of God to conceal . . . Prv 25:2
over all the *g* will be a canopy. . . . Is 4:5
the whole earth is full of his *g*. . . . Is 6:3
they will see the *g* of the LORD, . . . Is 35:2
the *g* of the LORD will be revealed . . . Is 40:5
I will not give my *g* to another . . . Is 42:8
Let them give *g* to the LORD . . . Is 42:12
They will proclaim my *g* . . . Is 66:19
and saw the *g* of the LORD filling . . . Ez 44:4
knowledge of the *g* of the LORD, . . . Hb 2:14
in his Father's *g* with his angels, . . . Mt 16:27
of the sky, with power and great *g*. . . . Mt 24:30
sit on his throne in heavenly *g*. . . . Mt 25:31
and the *g* of the Lord shone . . . Lk 2:9
saying, "*G* to God in the highest, . . . Lk 2:14
of him when he comes in his *g* . . . Lk 9:26
they saw his *g* and the two men . . . Lk 9:32
these things and then enter his *g*? . . . Lk 24:26
We have seen his *g*, the *g* of the One . . . Jn 1:14
I am not seeking *g* for myself; . . . Jn 8:50
for God's *g* so that God's Son may . . . Jn 11:4

so that the Son may bring *g* . . . Jn 14:13
The God of *g* appeared . . . Acts 7:2
exchanged the *g* of the immortal . . . Rom 1:23
and fall short of the *g* of God, . . . Rom 3:23
in his faith and gave *g* to God, . . . Rom 4:20
that we may also share in his *g*. . . . Rom 8:17
theirs the divine *g*, the covenants, . . . Rom 9:4
riches of his *g* known to the objects . . . Rom 9:23
To him be the *g* forever! Amen. . . . Rom 11:36
Therefore I *g* in Christ Jesus . . . Rom 15:17
to the only wise God be *g* forever . . . Rom 16:27
whatever you do, do it all for the *g* . . . 1 Cor 10:31
in letters on stone, came with *g*, . . . 2 Cor 3:7
comparison with the surpassing *g*. . . . 2 Cor 3:10
to overflow to the *g* of God. . . . 2 Cor 4:15
us an eternal *g* that far outweighs . . . 2 Cor 4:17
Christ in you, the hope of *g*. . . . Col 1:27
also will appear with him in *g*. . . . Col 3:4
be honor and *g* for ever and ever. . . . 1 Tm 1:17
To him be *g* for ever and ever. . . . 2 Tm 4:18
The Son is the radiance of God's *g* . . . Heb 1:3
you crowned him with *g* and honor . . . Heb 2:7
to whom be *g* for ever and ever. . . . Heb 13:21
g and honor when Jesus Christ is . . . 1 Pt 1:7
To him be the *g* and the power . . . 1 Pt 4:11
overjoyed when his *g* is revealed. . . . 1 Pt 4:13
for the Spirit of *g* and of God rests . . . 1 Pt 4:14
will share in the *g* to be revealed: . . . 1 Pt 5:1
of *g* that will never fade away. . . . 1 Pt 5:4
you to his eternal *g* in Christ, . . . 1 Pt 5:10
of him who called us by his own *g* . . . 2 Pt 1:3
came to him from the Majestic *G*, . . . 2 Pt 1:17
To him be *g* both now and forever! . . . 2 Pt 3:18
to the only God our Savior be *g*, . . . Jude 1:25
to him be *g* and power for ever . . . Rv 1:6
the living creatures give *g*, . . . Rv 4:9
to receive *g* and honor and power, . . . Rv 4:11
Fear God and give him *g*, . . . Rv 14:7
g and power belong to our God, . . . Rv 19:1
It shone with the *g* of God, . . . Rv 21:11
for the *g* of God gives it light, . . . Rv 21:23

GODLINESS, GODLY *devotion to God; piety*
that the LORD has set apart the *g* . . . Ps 4:3
G sorrow brings repentance that . . . 2 Cor 7:10
jealous for you with a *g* jealousy. . . . 2 Cor 11:2
and quiet lives in all *g* and holiness. . . . 1 Tm 2:2
but *g* has value for all things, . . . 1 Tm 4:8
and who think that *g* is a means . . . 1 Tm 6:5
and pursue righteousness, *g*, faith, . . . 1 Tm 6:11
everyone who wants to live a *g* life . . . 2 Tm 3:12
and to perseverance, *g*; . . . 2 Pt 1:6
You ought to live holy and *g* lives . . . 2 Pt 3:11

GODS *powerless pagan deity; image or idol*
You shall have no other *g* . . . Ex 20:3
You shall have no other *g* . . . Dt 5:7
For all the *g* of the nations are idols . . . 1 Chr 16:26
"I said, 'You are "*g*"; . . . Ps 82:6
have said you are *g*'? If he called . . . Jn 10:34
He says that man-made *g* are no *g* . . . Acts 19:26

GOOD *kind; profitable; excellent; fitting or appropriate; morally right*
God saw that the light was *g*, . . . Gn 1:4
And God saw that it was *g*. . . . Gn 1:10
And God saw that it was *g*. . . . Gn 1:12
And God saw that it was *g*. . . . Gn 1:18
And God saw that it was *g*. . . . Gn 1:21
And God saw that it was *g*. . . . Gn 1:25
he had made, and it was very *g*. . . . Gn 1:31
and the tree of the knowledge of *g* . . . Gn 2:9
pleasing to the eye and *g* for food. . . . Gn 2:9

It is not *g* for the man to be alone. . . . Gn 2:18
become like one of us, knowing *g* . . . Gn 3:22
but God intended it for *g* . . . Gn 50:20
He is *g;* his love endures . . . 2 Chr 7:3
doing what was *g* and right . . . 2 Chr 31:20
there is no one who does *g* . . . Ps 14:1
Taste and see that the LORD is *g;* . . . Ps 34:8
Turn from evil and do *g;* . . . Ps 34:14
Trust in the LORD and do *g;* . . . Ps 37:3
for your name is *g.* . . . Ps 52:9
there is no one who does *g,* . . . Ps 53:3
no *g* thing does he withhold . . . Ps 84:11
You are forgiving, O Lord . . . Ps 86:5
For the LORD is *g* and his love . . . Ps 100:5
satisfies your desires with *g* things, . . .
   Ps 103:5
G will come to him who is . . . Ps 112:5
You are *g,* and what you do is *g;* . . . Ps 119:68
How *g* and pleasant it is . . . Ps 133:1
The LORD is *g* to all; . . . Ps 145:9
How *g* it is to sing praises . . . Ps 147:1
you will win favor and a *g* name . . . Prv 3:4
Do not withhold *g* . . . Prv 3:27
He who seeks *g* finds *g* will, . . . Prv 11:27
A *g* man leaves an inheritance . . . Prv 13:22
those who plan what is *g* find love . . . Prv 14:22
on the wicked and the *g.* . . . Prv 15:3
and how *g* is a timely word! . . . Prv 15:23
g news gives health to the bones. . . . Prv 15:30
A cheerful heart is *g* medicine, . . . Prv 17:22
He who finds a wife finds what is *g* . . . Prv
   18:22
It is not *g* to have zeal . . . Prv 19:2
A *g* name is more desirable . . . Prv 22:1
She brings him *g,* not harm, . . . Prv 31:12
whether it is *g* or evil. . . . Eccl 12:14
Woe to those who call evil *g* . . . Is 5:20
You who bring *g* tidings . . . Is 40:9
the feet of those who bring *g* news, . . . Is 52:7
Neither can you do *g* . . . Jer 13:23
has showed you, O man, what is *g.* . . . Mi 6:8
sun to rise on the evil and the *g,* . . . Mt 5:45
Father in heaven give *g* gifts . . . Mt 7:11
Likewise every *g* tree bears *g* fruit, . . . Mt 7:17
A *g* tree cannot bear bad fruit, . . . Mt 7:18
The *g* man brings *g* things out . . . Mt 12:35
Still other seed fell on *g* soil, . . . Mt 13:8
and collected the *g* fish in baskets, . . . Mt 13:48
There is only One who is *g.* . . . Mt 19:17
both *g* and bad, and the wedding . . . Mt 22:10
Well done, *g* and faithful servant! . . . Mt 25:21
Repent and believe the *g* news! . . . Mk 1:15
No one is *g* except God alone. . . . Mk 10:18
I bring you *g* news . . . Lk 2:10
does not produce *g* fruit will be . . . Lk 3:9
The *g* man brings *g* things out . . . Lk 6:45
Salt is *g,* but if it loses its saltiness, . . . Lk 14:34
Well done, my *g* servant! . . . Lk 19:17
I am the *g* shepherd. . . . Jn 10:11
there is no one who does *g,* . . . Rom 3:12
want to do, I agree that the law is *g.* . . . Rom
   7:16
for the *g* of those who love him, . . . Rom 8:28
his *g,* pleasing and perfect will. . . . Rom 12:2
Hate what is evil; cling to what is *g.* . . . Rom
   12:9
It is *g* for a man not to marry. . . . 1 Cor 7:1
Bad company corrupts *g* character . . . 1 Cor
   15:33
you will abound in every *g* work. . . . 2 Cor 9:8
us not become weary in doing *g,* . . . Gal 6:9
in Christ Jesus to do *g* works, . . . Eph 2:10
that he who began a *g* work . . . Phil 1:6
bearing fruit in every *g* work, . . . Col 1:10
have a *g* reputation with outsiders, . . . 1 Tm 3:7
For everything God created is *g,* . . . 1 Tm 4:4
Fight the *g* fight of the faith. . . . 1 Tm 6:12
equipped for every *g* work. . . . 2 Tm 3:17
I have fought the *g* fight, I have . . . 2 Tm 4:7
loves what is *g,* who is . . . Ti 1:8
God disciplines us for our *g,* . . . Heb 12:10

you have tasted that the Lord is *g.* . . . 1 Pt 2:3
Live such *g* lives among the pagans . . . 1 Pt
   2:12

GOSPEL *good news*
I am not ashamed of the *g,* . . . Rom 1:16
duty of proclaiming the *g* of God, . . . Rom
   15:16
to preach the *g* not with words . . . 1 Cor 1:17
rather than hinder the *g* of Christ. . . . 1 Cor
   9:12
you of the *g* I preached to you, . . . 1 Cor 15:1
light of the *g* of the glory of Christ, . . . 2 Cor 4:4
your confession of the *g* . . . 2 Cor 9:13
a different *g* which is really no *g* . . . Gal 1:7
comes from the *g* of peace. . . . Eph 6:15
in a manner worthy of the *g* . . . Phil 1:27
by God to be entrusted with the *g.* . . . 1 Thes
   2:4
do not obey the *g* of our Lord Jesus . . . 2 Thes
   1:8
immortality to light through the *g.* . . . 2 Tm
   1:10
he had the eternal *g* to proclaim . . . Rv 14:6

GRACE *God's free and unmerited favor for
sinful humanity*
lips have been anointed with *g,* . . . Ps 45:2
will be a garland to *g* your head . . . Prv 1:9
an ornament to *g* your neck. . . . Prv 3:22
but gives *g* to the humble. . . . Prv 3:34
She will set a garland of *g* . . . Prv 4:9
Though *g* is shown to the wicked, . . . Is 26:10
forfeit the *g* that could be theirs. . . . Jon 2:8
of Jerusalem a spirit of *g* . . . Zec 12:10
the *g* of God was upon him. . . . Lk 2:40
who came from the Father, full of *g* . . . Jn 1:14
and much *g* was upon them all. . . . Acts 4:33
a man full of God's *g* and power, . . . Acts 6:8
saw the evidence of the *g* of God, . . . Acts
   11:23
them to continue in the *g* of God. . . . Acts 13:43
message of his *g* by enabling them . . . Acts
   14:3
they had been committed to the *g* . . . Acts
   14:26
We believe it is through the *g* . . . Acts 15:11
by the brothers to the *g* of the Lord . . . Acts
   15:40
to those who by *g* had believed. . . . Acts 18:27
testifying to the gospel of God's *g.* . . . Acts
   20:24
to God and to the word of his *g,* . . . Acts 20:32
and are justified freely by his *g* . . . Rom 3:24
be by *g* and may be guaranteed . . . Rom 4:16
access by faith into this *g* . . . Rom 5:2
came by the *g* of the one man, . . . Rom 5:15
where sin increased, *g* increased . . . Rom 5:20
on sinning so that *g* may increase? . . . Rom 6:1
you are not under law, but under *g.* . . . Rom
   6:14
there is a remnant chosen by *g.* . . . Rom 11:5
But by the *g* of God I am what I am . . . 1 Cor
   15:10
his *g* to me was not without effect. . . . 1 Cor
   15:10
wisdom but according to God's *g.* . . . 2 Cor
   1:12
so that the *g* that is reaching more . . . 2 Cor
   4:15
not to receive God's *g* in vain. . . . 2 Cor 6:1
also to completion this act of *g* . . . 2 Cor 8:6
able to make all *g* abound to you, . . . 2 Cor 9:8
of the surpassing *g* God has given . . . 2 Cor
   9:14
My *g* is sufficient for you, . . . 2 Cor 12:9
from birth and called me by his *g,* . . . Gal 1:15
when they recognized the *g* given . . . Gal 2:9
you have fallen away from *g.* . . . Gal 5:4
to the praise of his glorious *g,* . . . Eph 1:6
it is by *g* you have been saved. . . . Eph 2:5
by the gift of God's *g* given me . . . Eph 3:7

all of you share in God's *g* with me. . . . Phil 1:7
conversation be always full of *g,* . . . Col 4:6
be strong in the *g* that is . . . 2 Tm 2:1
having been justified by his *g,* . . . Ti 3:7
G to you and peace . . . Phlm 1:3
find *g* to help us in our time of need . . . Heb
   4:16
the throne of *g* with confidence, . . . Heb 4:16
who has insulted the Spirit of *g.* . . . Heb 10:29
but gives *g* to the humble. . . . Jas 4:6
But he gives us more *g.* . . . Jas 4:6
gives *g* to the humble. . . . 1 Pt 5:5
But grow in the *g* and knowledge . . . 2 Pt 3:18

GRACIOUS *of a merciful or compassionate
nature; kind*
the compassionate and *g* God, . . . Ex 34:6
and be *g* to you; . . . Nm 6:25
But you are a forgiving God, *g* . . . Neh 9:17
May God be *g* to us and bless us . . . Ps 67:1
a pure heart and whose speech is *g* . . . Prv
   22:11
Yet the LORD longs to be *g* to you . . . Is 30:18

GRASS *plant of the field; symbolic of the
shortness of life*
As for man, his days are like *g,* . . . Ps 103:15
All men are like *g,* . . . Is 40:6
If that is how God clothes the *g* . . . Mt 6:30
All men are like *g,* . . . 1 Pt 1:24

GRAVE(S) *burial place*
who touches a human bone or a *g,* . . .
   Nm 19:16
day no one knows where his *g* is. . . . Dt 34:6
Their throat is an open *g;* . . . Ps 5:9
will redeem my life from the *g;* . . . Ps 49:15
Her house is a highway to the *g,* . . . Prv 7:27
I am going to open your *g* . . . Ez 37:12
Where, O *g,* is your destruction? . . . Hos 13:14
are in their *g* will hear his voice . . . Jn 5:28
Take off the *g* clothes . . . Jn 11:44
you will not abandon me to the *g,* . . . Acts 2:27
Their throats are open *g;* . . . Rom 3:13

GRIEF(S), GRIEVE(D) *deep mental anguish; to
be sorrowful*
O God, do see trouble and *g;* . . . Ps 10:14
but a foolish son *g* to his mother. . . . Prv 10:1
and joy may end in *g.* . . . Prv 14:13
To have a fool for a son brings *g;* . . . Prv 17:21
the more knowledge, the more *g.* . . . Eccl 1:18
and *g* his Holy Spirit. . . . Is 63:10
Though he brings *g,* he will show . . . Lam 3:32
but your *g* will turn to joy. . . . Jn 16:20
do not *g* the Holy Spirit of God, . . . Eph 4:30
or to *g* like the rest of men, . . . 1 Thes 4:13
pierced themselves with many *g.* . . . 1 Tm 6:10
had to suffer *g* in all kinds of trials. . . . 1 Pt 1:6

GROAN(S), GROANING *to make a deep moan;
expression of pain or grief*
God heard their *g* and he . . . Ex 2:24
'Why are you *g?'* you shall say, . . . Ez 21:7
that the whole creation has been *g* . . . Rom
   8:22
g inwardly as we wait eagerly . . . Rom 8:23
with *g* that words cannot express. . . . Rom 8:26
For while we are in this tent, we *g* . . . 2 Cor 5:4

GROUND *soil, earth, or territory*
God called the dry *g* "land," . . . Gn 1:10
Cursed is the *g* because of you; . . . Gn 3:17
blood cries out to me from the *g.* . . . Gn 4:10
where you are standing is holy *g.* . . . Ex 3:5
walked through the sea on dry *g.* . . . Ex 15:19
and like a root out of dry *g.* . . . Is 53:2
fall to the *g* apart from the will . . . Mt 10:29
and hid your talent in the *g.* . . . Mt 25:25
to write on the *g* with his finger. . . . Jn 8:6
you may be able to stand your *g,* . . . Eph 6:13

GUARANTEE(ING) *assurance for the fulfillment
of a promise*
as a deposit, *g* what is to come. . . . 2 Cor 1:22

who is a deposit *g* our inheritance . . . Eph 1:14
Jesus has become the *g* . . . Heb 7:22

GUIDANCE, GUIDE(S) *the act or process of giving direction; one who gives direction*
of cloud to *g* them on their way . . . Ex 13:21
In your strength you will *g* them . . . Ex 15:13
cease to *g* them on their path, . . . Neh 9:19
He *g* me in paths of righteousness . . . Ps 23:3
g me in your truth and teach me, . . . Ps 25:5
He *g* the humble in what is right . . . Ps 25:9
he will be our *g* even to the end. . . . Ps 48:14
and *g* the nations of the earth. . . . Ps 67:4
You *g* me with your counsel, . . . Ps 73:24
even there your hand will *g* me, . . . Ps 139:10
and let the discerning get *g* . . . Prv 1:5
I *g* you in the way of wisdom . . . Prv 4:11
When you walk, they will *g* you; . . . Prv 6:22
The integrity of the upright *g* them, . . . Prv 11:3
For lack of *g* a nation falls, . . . Prv 11:14
A wise man's heart *g* his mouth, . . . Prv 16:23
for waging war you need *g*, . . . Prv 24:6
The LORD will *g* you always; . . . Is 58:11
Woe to you, blind *g*! You say, . . . Mt 23:16
You blind *g*! You strain out a gnat . . . Mt 23:24
he will *g* you into all truth. . . . Jn 16:13

GUILT(Y) *being responsible for an offense or wrongdoing*
does not leave the *g* unpunished; . . . Ex 34:7
It is a *g* offering. . . . Lv 5:15
your *g* is taken away and your sin . . . Is 6:7
the stain of your *g* is still before me . . . Jer 2:22
Why does the son not share the *g* . . . Ez 18:19
Spirit will never be forgiven; he is *g* . . . Mk 3:29
Can any of you prove me *g* of sin? . . . Jn 8:46
in an unworthy manner will be *g* . . . 1 Cor 11:27
and would no longer have felt *g* . . . Heb 10:2
to cleanse us from a *g* conscience . . . Heb 10:22
at just one point is *g* of breaking all . . . Jas 2:10

HADES *place of the dead; see HELL*
the gates of *H* will not overcome it. . . . Mt 16:18
And I hold the keys of death and *H* . . . Rv 1:18
H was following close behind him. . . . Rv 6:8
and *H* gave up the dead that were . . . Rv 20:13
H were thrown into the lake of fire. . . . Rv 20:14

HALLOWED *consecrated; holy or set apart for sacred use; see HOLINESS*
h be your name, . . . Mt 6:9
h be your name, . . . Lk 11:2

HAPPIER, HAPPY *enjoying well-being and contentment*
The women will call me *h*. . . . Gn 30:13
Then Leah said, "How *h* I am! . . . Gn 30:13
they drank and they were *h*. . . . 1 Kgs 4:20
How *h* your men must be! . . . 1 Kgs 10:8
Haman went out that day *h* . . . Est 5:9
the king to the dinner and be *h* . . . Est 5:14
I'll always be *h* and never have . . . Ps 10:6
may they be *h* and joyful. . . . Ps 68:3
as a *h* mother of children. . . . Ps 113:9
h is he who repays you . . . Ps 137:8
A *h* heart makes the face cheerful, . . . Prv 15:13
better for men than to be *h* . . . Eccl 3:12
to accept his lot and be *h* . . . Eccl 5:19
When times are good, be *h*; . . . Eccl 7:14
Be *h*, young man, while you are . . . Eccl 11:9
Jonah was very *h* about the vine. . . . Jon 4:6
and glad occasions and *h* festivals . . . Zec 8:19
he is *h* about that one sheep . . . Mt 18:13
those who are *h*, as if they were not . . . 1 Cor 7:30
she is *h* if she stays as she is . . . 1 Cor 7:40
yet now I am *h*, not because you . . . 2 Cor 7:9
delighted to see how *h* Ti was, . . . 2 Cor 7:13
Is anyone *h*? Let him sing songs . . . Jas 5:13

HAPPINESS *a state of well-being and contentment*
bring *h* to the wife he has married. . . . Dt 24:5
For the Jews it was a time of *h* . . . Est 8:16
my eyes will never see *h* again. . . . Jb 7:7
gives wisdom, knowledge and *h*, . . . Eccl 2:26
Come and share your master's *h*! . . . Mt 25:21
Come and share your master's *h*! . . . Mt 25:23

HARD, HARDEN(ED)(ING)(S) *cruel or harsh; difficult or tough; (to make) permanent or firm*
Is anything too *h* for the LORD? . . . Gn 18:14
I will *h* his heart so that he will not . . . Ex 4:21
But the LORD *h* Pharaoh's heart, . . . Ex 10:20
came to test him with *h* questions. . . . 1 Kgs 10:1
do not *h* your hearts as you did . . . Ps 95:8
All *h* work brings a profit, . . . Prv 14:23
he who *h* his heart falls into trouble . . . Prv 28:14
Nothing is too *h* for you. . . . Jer 32:17
They made their hearts as *h* as flint . . . Zec 7:12
it is *h* for a rich man . . . Mt 19:23
your hearts were *h* that Moses . . . Mk 10:5
disciples said, "This is a *h* teaching. . . . Jn 6:60
of *h* work we must help the weak, . . . Acts 20:35
It is *h* for you to kick . . . Acts 26:14
he hardens whom he wants to . . . Rom 9:18
Israel has experienced a *h* in part . . . Rom 11:25
woman who has worked very *h* . . . Rom 16:12
We work *h* with our own hands. . . . 1 Cor 4:12
imprisonments and riots; in *h* work . . . 2 Cor 6:5
in them due to the *h* of their hearts. . . . Eph 4:18
to respect those who work *h* . . . 1 Thes 5:12
do not *h* your hearts . . . Heb 3:8
your *h* work and your . . . Rv 2:2

HARDSHIP(S) *difficult or tough experiences and situations*
go through many *h* to enter . . . Acts 14:22
Shall trouble or *h* or persecution . . . Rom 8:35
in troubles, in *h* and distresses; . . . 2 Cor 6:4
in insults, in *h*, in persecutions, . . . 2 Cor 12:10
Endure *h* with us like a good . . . 2 Tm 2:3
endure *h*, do the work . . . 2 Tm 4:5
Endure *h* as discipline; . . . Heb 12:7
and have endured *h* for my name, . . . Rv 2:3

HARVEST *the activity of gathering a crop, or the crop itself; often used as spiritual image*
the Feast of *H* with the firstfruits . . . Ex 23:16
God will bless you in all your *h* . . . Dt 16:15
during *h* is a disgraceful son. . . . Prv 10:5
The *h* is past, . . . Jer 8:20
for the *h* is ripe. . . . Jl 3:13
h is plentiful but the workers are . . . Mt 9:37
He told them, "The *h* is plentiful, . . . Lk 10:2
at the fields! They are ripe for *h*. . . . Jn 4:35
if we reap a material *h* from you? . . . 1 Cor 9:11
the *h* of your righteousness. . . . 2 Cor 9:10
at the proper time we will reap a *h* . . . Gal 6:9
it produces a *h* of righteousness . . . Heb 12:11
in peace raise a *h* of righteousness. . . . Jas 3:18
for the *h* of the earth is ripe. . . . Rv 14:15

HATE(D)(S), HATRED *to dislike or detest, often with enmity or malice; strong emotional aversion; detestable; see ABHOR*
Do not *h* your brother . . . Lv 19:17
you *h* all who do wrong. . . . Ps 5:5
too much to detect or *h* his sin. . . . Ps 36:2
righteousness and *h* wickedness; . . . Ps 45:7
those who love the LORD *h* evil, . . . Ps 97:10
therefore I *h* every wrong path. . . . Ps 119:104
I *h* and abhor falsehood . . . Ps 119:163
Do I not *h* those who *h* you, . . . Ps 139:21
There are six things the LORD *h*, . . . Prv 6:16
To fear the LORD is to *h* evil; . . . Prv 8:13
rebuke a mocker or he will *h* you; . . . Prv 9:8

H stirs up dissension, . . . Prv 10:12
The righteous *h* what is false, . . . Prv 13:5
He who spares the rod *h* his son, . . . Prv 13:24
than a fattened calf with *h*. . . . Prv 15:17
but he who *h* bribes will live. . . . Prv 15:27
too much of you, and he will *h* you. . . . Prv 25:17
A lying tongue *h* those it hurts, . . . Prv 26:28
Bloodthirsty men *h* a man . . . Prv 29:10
a time to love and a time to *h*, . . . Eccl 3:8
I *h* robbery and iniquity. . . . Is 61:8
Since you did not *h* bloodshed, . . . Ez 35:6
H evil, love good; . . . Am 5:15
loved Jacob, but Esau I have *h*, . . . Mal 1:3
"I *h* divorce," says the LORD God . . . Mal 2:16
your neighbor and *h* your enemy. . . . Mt 5:43
All men will *h* you because of me, . . . Mt 10:22
Blessed are you when men *h* you, . . . Lk 6:22
do good to those who *h* you, . . . Lk 6:27
does not *h* his father and mother, . . . Lk 14:26
Everyone who does evil *h* the light, . . . Jn 3:20
while the man who *h* his life . . . Jn 12:25
keep in mind that it *h* me first. . . . Jn 15:18
Jacob I loved, but Esau I *h*. . . . Rom 9:13
H what is evil; cling to what is good . . . Rom 12:9
no one ever *h* his own body, . . . Eph 5:29
righteousness and *h* wickedness; . . . Heb 1:9
with the world is *h* toward God? . . . Jas 4:4
h his brother is still in the darkness. . . . 1 Jn 2:9
"I love God," yet *h* his brother, . . . 1 Jn 4:20

HEAD(S) *top part of the body; seat of the intellect; place of honor; the ranking member; seat of authority*
he will crush your *h*, . . . Gn 3:15
my *h* were shaved, my strength . . . Jgs 16:17
a *h* taller than any of the others. . . . 1 Sm 9:2
Absalom's *h* got caught in the tree. . . . 2 Sm 18:9
You anoint my *h* with oil; . . . Ps 23:5
Lift up your *h*, O you gates; . . . Ps 24:7
is like precious oil poured on the *h*, . . . Ps 133:2
Blessings crown the *h* . . . Prv 10:6
will heap burning coals on his *h*, . . . Prv 25:22
everlasting joy will crown their *h*. . . . Is 35:10
and the helmet of salvation on his *h* . . . Is 59:17
his blood will be on his own *h*. . . . Ez 33:4
of Man has no place to lay his *h*. . . . Mt 8:20
stand up and lift up your *h*, . . . Lk 21:28
crown of thorns and put it on his *h*. . . . Jn 19:2
Your blood be on your own *h*! . . . Acts 18:6
will heap burning coals on his *h*. . . . Rom 12:20
and the *h* of Christ is God. . . . 1 Cor 11:3
her *h* uncovered dishonors her *h* . . . 1 Cor 11:5
And the *h* cannot say to the feet, . . . 1 Cor 12:21
him to be *h* over everything . . . Eph 1:22
For the husband is the *h* of the wife . . . Eph 5:23
And he is the *h* of the body, . . . Col 1:18
keep your *h* in all situations, . . . 2 Tm 4:5
and had crowns of gold on their *h*. . . . Rv 4:4
with a crown of gold on his *h* . . . Rv 14:14
and on his *h* are many crowns. . . . Rv 19:12

HEAL(ED)(ING)(S) *to mend, cure, make whole; return to original state of health*
for I am the LORD, who *h* you. . . . Ex 15:26
and see that he is completely *h*. . . . Ex 21:19
please *h* her!" The LORD replied . . . Nm 12:13
I have wounded and I will *h*, . . . Dt 32:39
you will be *h*, and you will know . . . 1 Sm 6:3
and seen your tears; I will *h* you. . . . 2 Kgs 20:5
their sin and will *h* their land. . . . 2 Chr 7:14
heard Hezekiah and *h* the people. . . . 2 Chr 30:20
he injures, but his hands also *h*. . . . Jb 5:18
h me, for my bones are in agony. . . . Ps 6:2
h me, for I have sinned against you . . . Ps 41:4
and *h* all your diseases; . . . Ps 103:3
He sent forth his word and *h* them; . . . Ps 107:20
He *h* the brokenhearted . . . Ps 147:3

the tongue of the wise brings *h*. . . . Prv 12:18
a trustworthy envoy brings *h*. . . . Prv 13:17
The tongue that brings *h* is a tree . . . Prv 15:4
sweet to the soul and *h* to the bones . . . Prv 16:24
a time to kill and a time to *h*, . . . Eccl 3:3
he will strike them and *h* them. . . . Is 19:22
respond to their pleas and *h* them. . . . Is 19:22
and *h* the wounds he inflicted. . . . Is 30:26
and by his wounds we are *h*. . . . Is 53:5
seen his ways, but I will *h* him; . . . Is 57:18
H me, O LORD, and I will be *h*; . . . Jer 17:14
We would have *h* Babylon, . . . Jer 51:9
or seek the young, or *h* the injured, . . . Zec 11:16
rise with *h* in its wings. . . . Mal 4:2
and *h* every disease and sickness . . . Mt 4:23
said to him, "I will go and *h* him." . . . Mt 8:7
If I only touch his cloak, I will be *h*. . . Mt 9:21
to *h* every disease and sickness. . . . Mt 10:1
H the sick, raise the dead, . . . Mt 10:8
Is it lawful to *h* on the Sabbath? . . . Mt 12:10
and turn, and I would *h* them. . . . Mt 13:15
on them and *h* their sick. . . . Mt 14:14
And her daughter was *h* . . . Mt 15:28
but they could not *h* him. . . . Mt 17:16
followed him, and he *h* them there. . . . Mt 19:2
to him at the temple, and he *h* them . . . Mt 21:14
and Jesus *h* many who had various . . . Mk 1:34
if he would *h* him on the Sabbath. . . . Mk 3:2
hands on her so that she will be *h* . . . Mk 5:23
on a few sick people and *h* them. . . . Mk 6:5
said Jesus, "your faith has *h* you." . . . Mk 10:52
to me: 'Physician, *h* yourself!' . . . Lk 4:23
hands on each one, he *h* them. . . . Lk 4:40
and to be *h* of their sicknesses. . . . Lk 5:15
to see if he would *h* on the Sabbath. . . . Lk 6:7
him to come and *h* his servant. . . . Lk 7:3
years, but no one could *h* her. . . . Lk 8:43
kingdom of God and to *h* the sick. . . . Lk 9:2
h the boy and gave him back . . . Lk 9:42
H the sick who are there . . . Lk 10:9
Jesus had *h* on the Sabbath. . . . Lk 13:14
Is it lawful to *h* on the Sabbath . . . Lk 14:3
when he saw he was *h*, came back, . . . Lk 17:15
your sight; your faith has *h* you. . . . Lk 18:42
touched the man's ear and *h* him. . . . Lk 22:51
begged him to come and *h* his son, . . . Jn 4:47
angry with me for *h* the whole man . . . Jn 7:23
nor turn and I would *h* them. . . . Jn 12:40
him that has given this complete *h* . . . Acts 3:16
and are asked how he was *h*, . . . Acts 4:9
Stretch out your hand to *h* . . . Acts 4:30
evil spirits, and all of them were *h*. . . . Acts 5:16
paralytics and cripples were *h* . . . Acts 8:7
said to him, "Jesus Christ *h* you. . . . Acts 9:34
h all who were under the power . . . Acts 10:38
saw that he had faith to be *h* . . . Acts 14:9
placed his hands on him and *h* him. . . . Acts 28:8
to another gifts of *h* . . . 1 Cor 12:9
also those having gifts of *h*, . . . 1 Cor 12:28
may not be disabled, but rather *h*. . . . Heb 12:13
for each other so that you may be *h*. . . . Jas 5:16
by his wounds you have been *h*. . . . 1 Pt 2:24
but the fatal wound had been *h*. . . . Rv 13:3

HEAR(D)(ING)(S) *to perceive sound; to be informed of; obedient to*
God *h* their groaning and he . . . Ex 2:24
The nations will *h* and tremble; . . . Ex 15:14
I will *h*, for I am compassionate. . . . Ex 22:27
Then the Egyptians will *h* about it! . . . Nm 14:13
H the disputes between your . . . Dt 1:16
has anything like it ever been *h* of? . . . Dt 4:32
H, O Israel: The LORD our God, . . . Dt 6:4
The rest of the people will *h* of this . . . Dt 19:20
must *h* it and learn . . . Dt 31:13
of the country will *h* about this . . . Jos 7:9
as we have *h* with our own ears. . . . 2 Sm 7:22

H the supplication of your servant . . . 1 Kgs 8:30
O LORD, and *h*; open your eyes, . . . 2 Kgs 19:16
then will I *h* from heaven . . . 2 Chr 7:14
Oh, that I had someone to *h* me! . . . Jb 31:35
My ears had *h* of you . . . Jb 42:5
he who implanted the ear not *h*? . . . Ps 94:9
Today, if you *h* his voice, . . . Ps 95:7
or you may *h* your servant cursing . . . Eccl 7:21
Be ever *h*, but never understanding . . . Is 6:9
I am staggered by what I *h*, . . . Is 21:3
that day the deaf will *h* the words . . . Is 29:18
your ears will *h* a voice behind you, . . . Is 30:21
Have you not *h*? . . . Is 40:21
H me, you who know what is right, . . . Is 51:7
nor his ear too dull to *h*. . . . Is 59:1
while they are still speaking I will *h* . . . Is 65:24
Who has ever *h* of such a thing? . . . Is 66:8
who have ears but do not *h*; . . . Jer 5:21
Who has ever *h* anything like this? . . . Jer 18:13
so the word I speak and give . . . Ez 33:7
Dry bones, *h* the word . . . Ez 37:4
the deaf *h*, the dead are raised, . . . Mt 11:5
will be ever *h* but never . . . Mt 13:14
h what you *h* but did not *h* it . . . Mt 13:17
answered Jesus, "is this: '*H*, . . . Mk 12:29
the deaf *h*, the dead are raised, . . . Lk 7:22
in the dark will be *h* in the daylight, . . . Lk 12:3
whoever *h* my word and believes . . . Jn 5:24
and what I have *h* from him I tell . . . Jn 8:26
reason you do not *h* is that you do . . . Jn 8:47
he wanted to *h* the word of God. . . . Acts 13:7
gathered to *h* the word of the Lord. . . . Acts 13:44
We want to *h* you again . . . Acts 17:32
is not those who *h* the law who are . . . Rom 2:13
they *h* without someone preaching . . . Rom 10:14
no ear has *h*, . . . 1 Cor 2:9
where would the sense of *h* be? . . . 1 Cor 12:17
He *h* inexpressible things, . . . 2 Cor 12:4
What you *h* from me, keep . . . 2 Tm 1:13
what their itching ears want to *h*. . . . 2 Tm 4:3
Today, if you *h* his voice, . . . Heb 3:7
not forgetting what he has *h*, . . . Jas 1:25
according to his will, he *h* us. . . . 1 Jn 5:14
If anyone *h* my voice and opens . . . Rv 3:20
am the one who *h* and saw these . . . Rv 22:8

HEART(S) *organ that circulates the blood; the vital center of one's being, emotions, and sensibilities*
But I will harden his *h* . . . Ex 4:21
Do not hate your brother in your *h*. . . . Lv 19:17
or let them slip from your *h* as long . . . Dt 4:9
LORD your God with all your *h* . . . Dt 6:5
Circumcise your *h*, therefore, . . . Dt 10:16
Fix these words of mine in your *h* . . . Dt 11:18
observe them with all your *h* . . . Dt 26:16
to the LORD with all your *h*, . . . 1 Sm 7:3
God changed Saul's *h*, . . . 1 Sm 10:9
sought out a man after his own *h* . . . 1 Sm 13:14
but the LORD looks at the *h*. . . . 1 Sm 16:7
for the LORD searches every *h* . . . 1 Chr 28:9
all whose *h* were willing brought . . . 2 Chr 29:31
you, O LORD, with all my *h*; . . . Ps 9:1
The fool says in his *h*, . . . Ps 14:1
Therefore my *h* is glad . . . Ps 16:9
and the meditation of my *h* . . . Ps 19:14
he give you the desire of your *h* . . . Ps 20:4
who has clean hands and a pure *h*, . . . Ps 24:4
examine my *h* and my mind; . . . Ps 26:2
will give you the desires of your *h*. . . . Ps 37:4
Create in me a pure *h*, O God, . . . Ps 51:10
The fool says in his *h*, . . . Ps 53:1
to those who are pure in *h*. . . . Ps 73:1
give me an undivided *h*, . . . Ps 86:11

that we may gain a *h* of wisdom. . . . Ps 90:12
do not harden your *h* as you did . . . Ps 95:8
and seek him with all their *h*. . . . Ps 119:2
I have hidden your word in my *h* . . . Ps 119:11
Search me, O God, and know my *h* . . . Ps 139:23
write them on the tablet of your *h*. . . . Prv 3:3
Trust in the LORD with all your *h* . . . Prv 3:5
hold of my words with all your *h*; . . . Prv 4:4
Above all else, guard your *h*, . . . Prv 4:23
Hope deferred makes the *h* sick, . . . Prv 13:12
Even in laughter the *h* may ache, . . . Prv 14:13
A happy *h* makes the face cheerful, . . . Prv 15:13
h of the righteous weighs its . . . Prv 15:28
My son, if your *h* is wise, . . . Prv 23:15
and keep your *h* on the right path. . . . Prv 23:19
so a man's *h* reflects the man. . . . Prv 27:19
also set eternity in the *h* of men; . . . Eccl 3:11
wise *h* will know the proper time . . . Eccl 8:5
banish anxiety from your *h* . . . Eccl 11:10
I looked for the one my *h* loves; . . . Song 3:1
Place me like a seal over your *h*, . . . Song 8:6
and carries them close to his *h*; . . . Is 40:11
wash the evil from your *h* . . . Jer 4:14
of Israel is uncircumcised in *h*. . . . Jer 9:26
The *h* is deceitful above all things . . . Jer 17:9
I will give them a *h* to know me, . . . Jer 24:7
when you seek me with all your *h*. . . . Jer 29:13
I will give them singleness of *h* . . . Jer 32:39
and get a new *h* and a new spirit. . . . Ez 18:31
I will give you a new *h* . . . Ez 36:26
He will turn the *h* of the fathers . . . Mal 4:6
Blessed are the pure in *h*, . . . Mt 5:8
adultery with her in his *h*. . . . Mt 5:28
treasure is, there your *h* will be . . . Mt 6:21
for I am gentle and humble in *h*, . . . Mt 11:29
of the *h* the mouth speaks. . . . Mt 12:34
out of the mouth come from the *h*, . . . Mt 15:18
the Lord your God with all your *h* . . . Mt 22:37
but God knows your *h*. . . . Lk 16:15
Were not our *h* burning within us . . . Lk 24:32
not have the love of God in your *h*. . . . Jn 5:42
Do not let your *h* be troubled. . . . Jn 14:1
All the believers were one in *h* . . . Acts 4:32
true to the Lord with all their *h*. . . . Acts 11:23
for he purified their *h* by faith. . . . Acts 15:9
The Lord opened her *h* to respond . . . Acts 16:14
their foolish *h* were darkened. . . . Rom 1:21
of the law are written on their *h*, . . . Rom 2:15
is circumcision of the *h*, . . . Rom 2:29
will expose the motives of men's *h*. . . . 1 Cor 4:5
put his Spirit in our *h* as a deposit, . . . 2 Cor 1:22
we do not lose *h*. . . . 2 Cor 4:1
shine in our *h* to give us the light . . . 2 Cor 4:6
eyes of your *h* may be enlightened . . . Eph 1:18
dwell in your *h* through faith. . . . Eph 3:17
make music in your *h* to the Lord, . . . Eph 5:19
set your *h* on things above, . . . Col 3:1
the peace of Christ rule in your *h*, . . . Col 3:15
work at it with all your *h*, . . . Col 3:23
which comes from a pure *h*. . . . 1 Tm 1:5
call on the Lord out of a pure *h*. . . . 2 Tm 2:22
do not harden your *h* . . . Heb 3:8
and write them on their *h*. . . . Heb 8:10
I will put my laws in their *h*, . . . Heb 10:16
For God is greater than our *h*, . . . 1 Jn 3:20

HEAVEN(LY)(S) *sky and stars above; place of eternal bliss; pertaining to God in the highest*
In the beginning God created the *h* . . . Gn 1:1
with a tower that reaches to the *h*, . . . Gn 11:4
Creator of *h* and earth. . . . Gn 14:19
with its top reaching to *h*, . . . Gn 28:12
that I have spoken to you from *h*; . . . Ex 20:22
from *h*, your holy dwelling place, . . . Dt 26:15
Who will ascend into *h* to get it . . . Dt 30:12
the highest *h*, cannot contain you. . . . 1 Kgs 8:27

Hear from *h*, your dwelling place, . . . 1 Kgs 8:30

up to *h* in a whirlwind, . . . 2 Kgs 2:1

then will I hear from *h* . . . 2 Chr 7:14

him a little lower than the *h* beings . . . Ps 8:5

The *h* declare the glory of God; . . . Ps 19:1

Be exalted, O God, above the *h*; . . . Ps 57:5

the *h* are the work of your hands. . . . Ps 102:25

as high as the *h* are above the earth, . . . Ps 103:11

is your love, higher than the *h*; . . . Ps 108:4

If I go up to the *h*, you are there; . . . Ps 139:8

As the *h* are higher than the earth, . . . Is 55:9

H is my throne, . . . Is 66:1

coming with the clouds of *h*. . . . Dn 7:13

for the kingdom of *h* is near. . . . Mt 3:2

At that moment *h* was opened, . . . Mt 3:16

because great is your reward in *h*, . . . Mt 5:12

Father in *h*, hallowed be your name . . . Mt 6:9

up for yourselves treasures in *h*, . . . Mt 6:20

Lord,' will enter the kingdom of *h*, . . . Mt 7:21

bind on earth will be bound in *h*, . . . Mt 16:19

and you will have treasure in *h*. . . . Mt 19:21

H and earth will pass away, . . . Mt 24:35

and coming on the clouds of *h* . . . Mt 26:64

he was taken up into *h* . . . Mk 16:19

saw Satan fall like lightning from *h*. . . . Lk 10:18

that your names are written in *h*. . . . Lk 10:20

in *h* over one sinner who repents . . . Lk 15:7

and you will have treasure in *h*, . . . Lk 18:22

left them and was taken up into *h*. . . . Lk 24:51

No one has ever gone into *h* . . . Jn 3:13

down from *h* not to do my will . . . Jn 6:38

Then a voice came from *h*, . . . Jn 12:28

has been taken from you into *h*, . . . Acts 1:11

the prophet says: " '*H* is my throne . . . Acts 7:49

looked up to *h* and saw the glory . . . Acts 7:55

a light from *h* flashed around him. . . . Acts 9:3

disobedient to the vision from *h*. . . . Acts 26:19

to be clothed with our *h* dwelling, . . . 2 Cor 5:2

ago was caught up to the third *h* . . . 2 Cor 12:2

in the *h* realms with every spiritual . . . Eph 1:3

at his right hand in the *h* realms, . . . Eph 1:20

who ascended higher than all the *h*, . . . Eph 4:10

But our citizenship is in *h*. . . . Phil 3:20

bring me safely to his *h* kingdom. . . . 2 Tm 4:18

priest who has gone through the *h*, . . . Heb 4:14

from sinners, exalted above the *h*. . . . Heb 7:26

and shadow of what is in *h*. . . . Heb 8:5

to the *h* Jerusalem, the city . . . Heb 12:22

who has gone into *h* . . . 1 Pt 3:22

ago by God's word the *h* existed . . . 2 Pt 3:5

The *h* will disappear with a roar; . . . 2 Pt 3:10

we are looking forward to a new *h* . . . 2 Pt 3:13

Then I heard every creature in *h* . . . Rv 5:13

God's temple in *h* was opened, . . . Rv 11:19

And there was war in *h*. . . . Rv 12:7

this I looked and in *h* the temple, . . . Rv 15:5

of a great multitude in *h* shouting: . . . Rv 19:1

I saw *h* standing open . . . Rv 19:11

Then I saw a new *h* and a new earth . . . Rv 21:1

coming down out of *h* from God. . . . Rv 21:10

HEIR(S) *one who inherits or is entitled to inherit property; see INHERITANCE, HERITAGE*

then we are *h*—*h* of God . . . Rom 8:17

and *h* according to the promise. . . . Gal 3:29

God has made you also an *h*. . . . Gal 4:7

gospel the Gentiles are *h* together . . . Eph 3:6

whom he appointed *h* of all things, . . . Heb 1:2

as *h* with you of the gracious gift . . . 1 Pt 3:7

HELL *place of the dead; place of eternal punishment; see HADES*

will be in danger of the fire of *h*. . . . Mt 5:22

body to be thrown into *h*. . . . Mt 5:29

for your whole body to go into *h*. . . . Mt 5:30

destroy both soul and body in *h*. . . . Mt 10:28

and be thrown into the fire of *h*. . . . Mt 18:9

as much a son of *h* as you are. . . . Mt 23:15

you escape being condemned to *h*? . . . Mt 23:33

than with two hands to go into *h*, . . . Mk 9:43

have two feet and be thrown into *h*. . . . Mk 9:45

two eyes and be thrown into *h*, . . . Mk 9:47

has power to throw you into *h*. . . . Lk 12:5

In *h*, where he was in torment, . . . Lk 16:23

and is itself set on fire by *h*. . . . Jas 3:6

when they sinned, but sent them to *h*, . . . 2 Pt 2:4

HELP(ED)(ER)(FUL)(ING)(S) *to give assistance or support; to give relief to; one who gives aid (coworker); assistance*

I will make a *h* suitable for him. . . . Gn 2:18

leave it there; be sure you *h* him . . . Ex 23:5

h him as you would an alien . . . Lv 25:35

who rides on the heavens to *h* you . . . Dt 33:26

you are the *h* of the fatherless. . . . Ps 10:14

I cried to my God for *h*. . . . Ps 18:6

my God, I called to you for *h* . . . Ps 30:2

he is our *h* and our shield. . . . Ps 33:20

an ever-present *h* in trouble. . . . Ps 46:1

the afflicted who have no one to *h*. . . . Ps 72:12

H us, O God our Savior, . . . Ps 79:9

for the *h* of man is worthless. . . . Ps 108:12

he is their *h* and shield. . . . Ps 115:9

where does my *h* come from? . . . Ps 121:1

his friend can *h* him up. . . . Eccl 4:10

I will strengthen you and *h* you; . . . Is 41:10

depths of the grave I called for *h*, . . . Jon 2:2

h me overcome my unbelief! . . . Mk 9:24

will not lift one finger to *h* them. . . . Lk 11:46

always doing good and *h* the poor. . . . Acts 9:36

Come over to Macedonia and *h* us . . . Acts 16:9

he was a great *h* to those who . . . Acts 18:27

of hard work we must *h* the weak, . . . Acts 20:35

I have had God's *h* to this very day, . . . Acts 26:22

the Spirit *h* us in our weakness. . . . Rom 8:26

those able to *h* others, those . . . 1 Cor 12:28

For I know your eagerness to *h*, . . . 2 Cor 9:2

only what is *h* for building others . . . Eph 4:29

h those in trouble and devoting . . . 1 Tm 5:10

she should *h* them and not let . . . 1 Tm 5:16

Lord is my *h*; I will not be afraid. . . . Heb 13:6

HERITAGE *inheritance or legacy; birthright; see HEIR, INHERITANCE*

you have given me the *h* . . . Ps 61:5

Your statutes are my *h* forever; . . . Ps 119:111

Sons are a *h* from the LORD, . . . Ps 127:3

HID(DEN)(ING), HIDE(S) *to put out of sight; to conceal for shelter or protection; to keep secret*

and they *h* from the LORD God . . . Gn 3:8

she *h* him for three months. . . . Ex 2:2

I will *h* my face from them, . . . Dt 31:17

because she *h* the spies we sent. . . . Jos 6:17

has *h* himself among the baggage. . . . 1 Sm 10:22

I *h* a hundred of the LORD's . . . 1 Kgs 18:13

she *h* the child from Athaliah . . . 2 Chr 22:11

and brings *h* things to light. . . . Jb 28:11

h me in the shadow of your wings . . . Ps 17:8

Forgive my *h* faults. . . . Ps 19:12

he will *h* me in the shelter . . . Ps 27:5

You are my *h* place; . . . Ps 32:7

I will utter *h* things, things from of old . . . Ps 78:2

I have *h* your word in my heart . . . Ps 119:11

for I *h* myself in you. . . . Ps 143:9

and search for it as for *h* treasure, . . . Prv 2:4

rebuke than *h* love. . . . Prv 27:5

to power, men go into *h*. . . . Prv 28:12

one from whom men *h* their faces . . . Is 53:3

I *h* my face from you for a moment, . . . Is 54:8

your sins have *h* his face from you, . . . Is 59:2

He reveals deep and *h* things; . . . Dn 2:22

A city on a hill cannot be *h*. . . . Mt 5:14

or *h* that will not be made known. . . . Mt 10:26

because you have *h* these things . . . Mt 11:25

I will utter things *h* . . . Mt 13:35

of heaven is like treasure *h* . . . Mt 13:44

and *h* your talent in the ground. . . . Mt 25:25

For whatever is *h* is meant . . . Mk 4:22

of the mystery *h* for long ages past, . . . Rom 16:25

a wisdom that has been *h* . . . 1 Cor 2:7

for ages past was kept *h* in God, . . . Eph 3:9

the mystery that has been kept *h* . . . Col 1:26

in whom are *h* all the treasures . . . Col 2:3

and your life is now *h* with Christ . . . Col 3:3

By faith Moses' parents *h* him . . . Heb 11:23

HIGH *elevated; lofty or noble; foremost in rank*

He was priest of God Most *H*, . . . Gn 14:18

God Most *H*, Creator of heaven . . . Gn 14:22

the unfailing love of the Most *H* . . . Ps 21:7

you are all sons of the Most *H*. . . . Ps 82:6

I will make myself like the Most *H*. . . . Is 14:14

know that the Most *H* is sovereign . . . Dn 4:17

Jesus, Son of the Most *H* God? . . . Mk 5:7

and priest of God Most *H*. . . . Heb 7:1

HOLINESS, HOLY *worthy of worship or veneration; sacred; divine; consecrated or set apart for sacred use; living according to a highly moral spiritual system; see HALLOWED*

the seventh day and made it *h*. . . . Gn 2:3

you are standing is *h* ground. . . . Ex 3:5

kingdom of priests and a *h* nation. . . . Ex 19:6

the Sabbath day by keeping it *h*. . . . Ex 20:8

Place from the Most *H* Place. . . . Ex 26:33

I am the LORD, who makes you *h*. . . . Ex 31:13

and be *h*, because I am *h*. . . . Lv 11:44

Given to the LORD becomes *h*. . . . Lv 27:9

they must not touch the *h* things . . . Nm 4:15

Your camp must be *h*, . . . Dt 23:14

from heaven, your *h* dwelling place . . . Dt 26:15

because you did not uphold my *h* . . . Dt 32:51

He is a *h* God; he is a jealous God. . . . Jos 24:19

not denied the words of the *H* One. . . . Jb 6:10

Who may stand in his *h* place? . . . Ps 24:3

in the splendor of his *h*. . . . Ps 96:9

H, *h*, *h* is the LORD Almighty; . . . Is 6:3

it will be called the Way of *H*. . . . Is 35:8

I will show my greatness and my *h*, . . . Ez 38:23

the *H* One of God!" "Be quiet!" . . . Mk 1:24

and know that you are the *H* One . . . Jn 6:69

prophets in the *H* Scriptures . . . Rom 1:2

to righteousness leading to *h*. . . . Rom 6:19

as living sacrifices, *h* and pleasing . . . Rom 12:1

in Christ Jesus and called to be *h*, . . . 1 Cor 1:2

perfecting *h* out of reverence . . . 2 Cor 7:1

by the Spirit to God's *h* apostles . . . Eph 3:5

death to present you *h* in his sight, . . . Col 1:22

us to be impure, but to live a *h* life. . . . 1 Thes 4:7

quiet lives in all godliness and *h*. . . . 1 Tm 2:2

to lift up *h* hands in prayer, . . . 1 Tm 2:8

saved us and called us to a *h* life . . . 2 Tm 1:9

you have known the *h* Scriptures, . . . 2 Tm 3:15

upright, *h* and disciplined. . . . Ti 1:8

that we may share in his *h*. . . . Heb 12:10

is written: "Be *h*, because I am *h*." . . . 1 Pt 1:16

a spiritual house to be a *h* priesthood, . . . 1 Pt 2:5

You ought to live *h* and godly lives . . . 2 Pt 3:11

H, *h*, is the Lord God . . . Rv 4:8

HONEST(Y) *displaying truthfulness and integrity; upright; not deceptive or fraudulent; sincerity*

Use *h* scales and *h* weights, . . . Lv 19:36

and *h* weights and measures, . . . Dt 25:15

they acted with complete *h*. . . . 2 Kgs 12:15

let God weigh me in *h* scales . . . Jb 31:6

truthful witness gives *h* testimony, . . . Prv 12:17

HONOR(ED)(S), HONORABLE, HONORABLY *to treat with respect or reverence; having a good reputation; characterized by integrity*
H your father and your mother, . . . Ex 20:12
trust in me enough to *h* me . . . Nm 20:12
Those who *h* me I will *h*, . . . 1 Sm 2:30
Wealth and *h* come from you; . . . 1 Chr 29:12
and crowned him with glory and *h*. . . . Ps 8:5
when what is vile is *h* among men. . . . Ps 12:8
but *h* those who fear the LORD, . . . Ps 15:4
the LORD bestows favor and *h*; . . . Ps 84:11
H the LORD with your wealth, . . . Prv 3:9
whoever heeds correction is *h*. . . . Prv 13:18
to the needy *h* God. . . . Prv 14:31
and humility comes before *h*. . . . Prv 15:33
is to a man's *h* to avoid strife, . . . Prv 20:3
is it honorable to seek one's own *h*. . . . Prv 25:27
and *h* me with their lips, . . . Is 29:13
own house is a prophet without *h*. . . . Mt 13:57
H your father and mother . . . Mt 15:4
These people *h* me with their lips, . . . Mt 15:8
h your father and mother, . . . Mt 19:19
they love the place of *h* at banquets . . . Mt 23:6
own house is a prophet without *h*. . . . Mk 6:4
do not take the place of *h*, . . . Lk 14:8
that all may *h* the Son just . . . Jn 5:23
does so to gain *h* for himself, . . . Jn 7:18
My Father will *h* the one who . . . Jn 12:26
H one another above yourselves. . . . Rom 12:10
Therefore *h* God with your body. . . . 1 Cor 6:20
if one part is *h*, every part rejoices . . . 1 Cor 12:26
H your father and mother . . . Eph 6:2
body in a way that is holy and *h*, . . . 1 Thes 4:4
well are worthy of double *h*, . . . 1 Tm 5:17
you crowned him with glory and *h* . . . Heb 2:7
Marriage should be *h* by all, . . . Heb 13:4
and desire to live *h* in every way. . . . Heb 13:18
h and thanks to him who sits . . . Rv 4:9

HOPE(S) *to desire something with confident expectation of its fulfillment*
Though he slay me, yet will I *h* . . . Jb 13:15
No one whose *h* is in you . . . Ps 25:3
A horse is a vain *h* for deliverance; . . . Ps 33:17
Put your *h* in God, . . . Ps 42:5
my *h* comes from him. . . . Ps 62:5
for I have put my *h* in your word. . . . Ps 119:74
and in his word I put my *h*. . . . Ps 130:5
O Israel, put your *h* in the LORD, . . . Ps 130:7
whose *h* is in the LORD his God, . . . Ps 146:5
who put their *h* in his unfailing love . . . Ps 147:11
H deferred makes the heart sick, . . . Prv 13:12
There is surely a future *h* for you, . . . Prv 23:18
but those who *h* in the LORD . . . Is 40:31
plans to give you *h* and a future. . . . Jer 29:11
and therefore I have *h*: . . . Lam 3:21
to your fortress, O prisoners of *h*; . . . Zec 9:12
character; and character, *h*. . . . Rom 5:4
in *h* that the creation itself will be . . . Rom 8:20
if we *h* for what we do not yet have, . . . Rom 8:25
Be joyful in *h*, patient in affliction, . . . Rom 12:12
of the Scriptures we might have *h*. . . . Rom 15:4
May the God of *h* fill you . . . Rom 15:13
always *h*, always perseveres. . . . 1 Cor 13:7
now these three remain: faith, *h* . . . 1 Cor 13:13
Christ in you, the *h* of glory. . . . Col 1:27
and your endurance inspired by *h* . . . 1 Thes 1:3
and the *h* of salvation as a helmet. . . . 1 Thes 5:8
resting on the *h* of eternal life, . . . Ti 1:2
while we wait for the blessed *h* . . . Ti 2:13
We have this *h* as an anchor . . . Heb 6:19
unswervingly to the *h* we profess, . . . Heb 10:23
faith is being sure of what we *h* for . . . Heb 11:1

HOUR *time of day; a particular time*
knows when his *h* will come: . . . Eccl 9:12

you by worrying can add a single *h* . . . Mt 6:27
the Son of Man will come at an *h* . . . Lk 12:40
The *h* has come for the Son of Man . . . Jn 12:23
for this very reason I came to this *h* . . . Jn 12:27

HOUSE(HOLD) *a building that serves as living quarters; a family line, including ancestors and descendants*
lamb for his family, one for each *h*. . . . Ex 12:3
the door of his *h* until morning. . . . Ex 12:22
shall not covet your neighbor's *h*. . . . Ex 20:17
he is faithful in all my *h*. . . . Nm 12:7
desire on your neighbor's *h* . . . Dt 5:21
my *h*, we will serve the LORD. . . . Jos 24:15
LORD himself will establish a *h* . . . 2 Sm 7:11
and his *h* be established forever. . . . 1 Chr 17:23
We will not neglect the *h* . . . Neh 10:39
I will dwell in the *h* of the LORD . . . Ps 23:6
dwell in the *h* of the LORD . . . Ps 27:4
for zeal for your *h* consumes me, . . . Ps 69:9
a doorkeeper in the *h* of my God . . . Ps 84:10
Let us go to the *h* of the LORD. . . . Ps 122:1
Unless the LORD builds the *h*, . . . Ps 127:1
Her *h* is a highway to the grave, . . . Prv 7:27
than share a *h* with a quarrelsome . . . Prv 21:9
a *h* of prayer for all nations. . . . Is 56:7
will flow out of the LORD's *h* . . . Jl 3:18
is like a wise man who built his *h* . . . Mt 7:24
My *h* will be called a *h* of prayer, . . . Mt 21:13
If a *h* is divided against itself, . . . Mk 3:25
My *h* will be called . . . Mk 11:17
sweep the *h* and search carefully . . . Lk 15:8
Today salvation has come to this *h*, . . . Lk 19:9
How dare you turn my Father's *h* . . . Jn 2:16
In my Father's *h* are many rooms; . . . Jn 14:2
you will be saved—you and your *h* . . . Acts 16:31
the church that meets at their *h*. . . . Rom 16:5
people and members of God's *h*, . . . Eph 2:19
manage his children and his *h* well. . . . 1 Tm 3:12
the builder of a *h* has greater honor . . . Heb 3:3
built into a spiritual *h* to be a holy . . . 1 Pt 2:5

HUMBLE(D)(S) *not proud or arrogant; having a spirit of submission or deference; to bring into submission*
Now Moses was a very *h* man, . . . Nm 12:3
he *h* and he exalts. . . . 1 Sm 2:7
will *h* themselves and pray . . . 2 Chr 7:14
You save the *h* . . . Ps 18:27
He guides the *h* in what is right . . . Ps 25:9
he crowns the *h* with salvation. . . . Ps 149:4
but gives grace to the *h*. . . . Prv 3:34
He *h* those who dwell on high, . . . Is 26:5
he who is *h* and contrite in spirit, . . . Is 66:2
for I am gentle and *h* in heart, . . . Mt 11:29
whoever *h* himself like this child is . . . Mt 18:4
whoever exalts himself will be *h*, . . . Mt 23:12
Be completely *h* and gentle; . . . Eph 4:2
he *h* himself . . . Phil 2:8
but gives grace to the *h*. . . . Jas 4:6
H yourselves before the Lord, . . . Jas 4:10
but gives grace to the *h*. . . . 1 Pt 5:5
H yourselves, . . . 1 Pt 5:6

HUMILITY *the state of being humble; lack of pride*
of truth, *h* and righteousness; . . . Ps 45:4
but with *h* comes wisdom. . . . Prv 11:2
and *h* comes before honor. . . . Prv 15:33
but *h* comes before honor. . . . Prv 18:12
H and the fear of the LORD . . . Prv 22:4
Seek righteousness, seek *h*; . . . Zep 2:3
I served the Lord with great *h* . . . Acts 20:19
but in *h* consider others better . . . Phil 2:3
let anyone who delights in false *h* . . . Col 2:18
their false *h* and their harsh . . . Col 2:23
h, gentleness and patience. . . . Col 3:12
and to show true *h* toward all men. . . . Ti 3:2

in the *h* that comes from wisdom. . . . Jas 3:13
clothe yourselves with *h* . . . 1 Pt 5:5

HUNGER, HUNGRY *to crave food; any craving or strong desire*
In their *h* you gave them bread . . . Neh 9:15
carry the sheaves, but still go *h*. . . . Jb 24:10
and fills the *h* with good things. . . . Ps 107:9
and gives food to the *h*. . . . Ps 146:7
to satisfy his *h* when he is starving. . . . Prv 6:30
and the shiftless man goes *h*. . . . Prv 19:15
If your enemy is *h*, give him food . . . Prv 25:21
to the *h* even what is bitter tastes . . . Prv 27:7
not to share your food with the *h* . . . Is 58:7
but gives his food to the *h*, . . . Ez 18:7
Blessed are those who *h* . . . Mt 5:6
I do not want to send them away *h*, . . . Mt 15:32
For I was *h* and you gave me . . . Mt 25:35
He has filled the *h* with good things . . . Lk 1:53
Blessed are you who *h* now, . . . Lk 6:21
comes to me will never go *h*, . . . Jn 6:35
If your enemy is *h*, feed him; . . . Rom 12:20
To this very hour we go *h* . . . 1 Cor 4:11
sleepless nights and *h*; in purity, . . . 2 Cor 6:5
I have known *h* and thirst . . . 2 Cor 11:27
whether well fed or *h*, . . . Phil 4:12
Never again will they *h*; . . . Rv 7:16

HUSBAND(S) *married man; protector and provider; figurative of Christ*
Her *h*'s brother shall take her . . . Dt 25:5
of noble character is her *h*'s crown, . . . Prv 12:4
Her *h* has full confidence in her . . . Prv 31:11
Her *h* is respected at the city gate, . . . Prv 31:23
Her *h* also, and he praises her: . . . Prv 31:28
For your Maker is your *h* . . . Is 54:5
the LORD, "for I am your *h*. . . . Jer 3:14
"I have no *h*," she replied. . . . Jn 4:17
a married woman is bound to her *h* . . . Rom 7:2
and each woman her own *h*. . . . 1 Cor 7:2
wife must not separate from her *h*. . . . 1 Cor 7:10
A woman is bound to her *h* as long . . . 1 Cor 7:39
promised you to one *h*, to Christ, . . . 2 Cor 11:2
woman than of her who has a *h*. . . . Gal 4:27
submit to your *h* as to the Lord. . . . Eph 5:22
For the *h* is the head of the wife . . . Eph 5:23
and the wife must respect her *h*. . . . Eph 5:33
h ought to love their wives . . . Eph 5:28
submit to your *h*, as is fitting . . . Col 3:18
the *h* of but one wife, temperate, . . . 1 Tm 3:2
A deacon must be the *h* of . . . 1 Tm 3:12
has been faithful to her *h*, . . . 1 Tm 5:9
An elder must be blameless, the *h* . . . Ti 1:6
the younger women to love their *h* . . . Ti 2:4
same way be submissive to your *h* . . . 1 Pt 3:1
H, in the same way be considerate . . . 1 Pt 3:7

HYPOCRISY, HYPOCRITE(S) *pretense of piety; insincerity; a person who puts on a false appearance of virtue; a pretender*
nor do I consort with *h*; . . . Ps 26:4
as the *h* do in the synagogues . . . Mt 6:2
when you pray, do not be like the *h* . . . Mt 6:5
do not look somber as the *h* do, . . . Mt 6:16
You *h*, first take the plank out . . . Mt 7:5
You *h*! Isaiah was right . . . Mt 15:7
their evil intent, said, "You *h*, . . . Mt 22:18
of the law and Pharisees, you *h*! . . . Mt 23:13
you *h*! You are like whitewashed . . . Mt 23:27
assign him a place with the *h*, . . . Mt 24:51
when he prophesied about you *h*, . . . Mk 7:6
But Jesus knew their *h*. . . . Mk 12:15
yeast of the Pharisees, which is *h*. . . . Lk 12:1
The Lord answered them, "You *h*! . . . Lk 13:15
The other Jews joined him in his *h*, . . . Gal 2:13
by their *h* even Barnabas was led . . . Gal 2:13
h, envy, and slander of every kind. . . . 1 Pt 2:1

IDLE(NESS) *unemployed; lacking worth; vain; inactivity; laziness*
They are not just *i* words for you . . . Dt 32:47

Will your *i* talk reduce men . . . Jb 11:3
and does not eat the bread of *i*. . . . Prv 31:27
if his hands are *i*, the house leaks. . . . Eccl 10:18
at evening let not your hands be *i*, . . . Eccl 11:6
as you please or speaking *i* words, . . . Is 58:13
mind puffs him up with *i* notions. . . . Col 2:18
those who are *i*, encourage . . . 1 Thes 5:14
away from every brother who is *i* . . . 2 Thes 3:6
We were not *i* when we were . . . 2 Thes 3:7
We hear that some among you are *i* . . . 2 Thes 3:11
they get into the habit of being *i* . . . 1 Tm 5:13

IDOL(S) *image used as an object of worship; false god*
make for yourself an *i* in the form . . . Ex 20:4
made it into an *i* cast in the shape . . . Ex 32:4
angered him with their detestable *i*. . . . Dt 32:16
aroused his jealousy with their *i*. . . . Ps 78:58
As for an *i*, a craftsman casts it, . . . Is 40:19
He nails down the *i*. . . . Is 41:7
All who make *i* are nothing, . . . Is 44:9
he makes an *i* and bows down to it. . . . Is 44:15
sacrificed their children to their *i*, . . . Ez 23:39
Of what value is an *i*, . . . Hb 2:18
to abstain from food polluted by *i*, . . . Acts 15:20
abstain from food sacrificed to *i*, . . . Acts 21:25
Now about food sacrificed to *i*: . . . 1 Cor 8:1
We know that an *i* is nothing at all . . . 1 Cor 8:4
children, keep yourselves from *i*. . . . 1 Jn 5:21
to sin by eating food sacrificed to *i*. . . . Rv 2:14

IDOLATER(S), IDOLATRY *those who worship idols; blind worship or admiration of an undeserving object*
and arrogance like the evil of *i*. . . . 1 Sm 15:23
or the greedy and swindlers, or *i*. . . . 1 Cor 5:10
Neither the sexually immoral nor *i* . . . 1 Cor 6:9
my dear friends, flee from *i* . . . 1 Cor 10:14
and debauchery; . . . witchcraft; . . . Gal 5:20
greedy person such a man is an *i* . . . Eph 5:5
evil desires and greed, which is *i*. . . . Col 3:5
orgies, carousing and detestable *i*. . . . 1 Pt 4:3

IGNORANT *without education or knowledge; unaware*
for there are some who are *i* of God . . . 1 Cor 15:34
to deal gently with those who are *i* . . . Heb 5:2
good you should silence the *i* talk . . . 1 Pt 2:15
which *i* and unstable people distort . . . 2 Pt 3:16

IMAGE(S) *man-made figure or idol; a likeness or reflection*
Let us make man in our *i*, . . . Gn 1:26
So God created man in his own *i*, . . . Gn 1:27
for in the *i* of God . . . Gn 9:6
Cursed is the man who carves an *i* . . . Dt 27:15
All who worship *i* are put to shame, . . . Ps 97:7
What *i* will you compare him to? . . . Is 40:18
His *i* are a fraud; . . . Jer 10:14
King Nebuchadnezzar made an *i* . . . Dn 3:1
of the immortal God for *i* made . . . Rom 1:23
since he is the *i* and glory of God; . . . 1 Cor 11:7
glory of Christ, who is the *i* of God. . . . 2 Cor 4:4
He is the *i* of the invisible God, . . . Col 1:15
in knowledge in the *i* of its Creator. . . . Col 3:10
them to set up an *i* in honor . . . Rv 13:14

IMITATE, IMITATORS *to follow as a pattern, model, or example; to copy; those who follow another's example*
Therefore I urge you to *i* me. . . . 1 Cor 4:16
Be *i* of God, therefore, . . . Eph 5:1
You became *i* of us and of the Lord . . . 1 Thes 1:6
became *i* of God's churches . . . 1 Thes 2:14
but to *i* those who through faith . . . Heb 6:12
of their way of life and *i* their faith. . . . Heb 13:7
do not *i* what is evil but what is . . . 3 Jn 1:11

IMMORAL(ITY) *behavior contrary to Biblical moral principles*
in sexual *i* with Moabite women, . . . Nm 25:1
keeping you from the *i* woman, . . . Prv 6:24
Because Israel's *i* mattered so little . . . Jer 3:9
murder, adultery, sexual *i*, theft, . . . Mt 15:19
sexual *i*, theft, murder, adultery, . . . Mk 7:21
from sexual *i*, from the meat . . . Acts 15:20
animals and from sexual *i*. . . . Acts 15:29
animals and from sexual *i*. . . . Acts 21:25
not in sexual *i* and debauchery, . . . Rom 13:13
reported that there is sexual *i* . . . 1 Cor 5:1
to associate with sexually *i* people . . . 1 Cor 5:9
Neither the sexually *i* nor idolaters . . . 1 Cor 6:9
The body is not meant for sexual *i*, . . . 1 Cor 6:13
We should not commit sexual *i*, . . . 1 Cor 10:8
sexual *i*, impurity and debauchery; . . . Gal 5:19
must not be even a hint of sexual *i*, . . . Eph 5:3
No *i*, impure or greedy person . . . Eph 5:5
sexual *i*, impurity, lust, evil desires . . . Col 3:5
that you should avoid sexual *i*; . . . 1 Thes 4:3
See that no one is sexually *i*, . . . Heb 12:16
the adulterer and all the sexually *i*. . . . Heb 13:4
grace of our God into a license for *i* . . . Jude 1:4
gave themselves up to sexual *i* . . . Jude 1:7
and by committing sexual *i*. . . . Rv 2:14
misleads my servants into sexual *i* . . . Rv 2:20
their sexual *i* or their thefts. . . . Rv 9:21
the murderers, the sexually *i*, . . . Rv 21:8
the sexually *i*, the murderers, . . . Rv 22:15

IMMORTAL(ITY) *imperishable; exempt from death*
along that path is *i*. . . . Prv 12:28
glory of the *i* God for images made . . . Rom 1:23
honor and *i*, he will give eternal life . . . Rom 2:7
and the mortal with *i*, . . . 1 Cor 15:53
and the mortal with *i*, . . . 1 Cor 15:54
Now to the King eternal, *i*, . . . 1 Tm 1:17
Lord of lords, who alone is *i* . . . 1 Tm 6:16
and *i* to light through the gospel. . . . 2 Tm 1:10

IMPERISHABLE *not subject to physical decay or dissolution*
it is raised *i*; it is sown in dishonor, . . . 1 Cor 15:42
nor does the perishable inherit the *i* . . . 1 Cor 15:50
not of perishable seed, but of *i*, . . . 1 Pt 1:23

IMPOSSIBLE *incapable of occurring; having little likelihood of happening*
Nothing will be *i* for you. . . . Mt 17:20
With man this is *i*, . . . Mt 19:26
For nothing is *i* with God. . . . Lk 1:37
What is *i* with men is possible . . . Lk 18:27
it was *i* for death to keep its hold . . . Acts 2:24
It is *i* for those who have once been . . . Heb 6:4
things in which it is *i* for God to lie, . . . Heb 6:18
because it is *i* for the blood of bulls . . . Heb 10:4
without faith it is *i* to please God, . . . Heb 11:6

INCREASE(D)(S), INCREASING *to multiply, augment, enrich; enlargement in size, extent*
Be fruitful and *i* in number . . . Gn 1:22
I will greatly *i* your pains . . . Gn 3:16
be fruitful and *i* in number upon it . . . Gn 8:17
though your riches *i*, . . . Ps 62:10
oppresses the poor to *i* his wealth . . . Prv 22:16
and a man of knowledge *i* strength; . . . Prv 24:5
Of the *i* of his government . . . Is 9:7
Because of the *i* of wickedness, . . . Mt 24:12
said to the Lord, "*I* our faith!" . . . Lk 17:5
when the number of disciples was *i*, . . . Acts 6:1
of disciples in Jerusalem *i* rapidly, . . . Acts 6:7
But the word of God continued to *i* . . . Acts 12:24
But where sin *i*, grace *i* all the more . . . Rom 5:20

the Lord make your love *i*. . . . 1 Thes 3:12
one of you has for each other is *i*. . . . 2 Thes 1:3
these qualities in *i* measure, . . . 2 Pt 1:8

INFANTS *children in the earliest period of life; see BABIES*
From the lips of children and *i*. . . . Ps 8:2
From the lips of children and *i*. . . . Mt 21:16
but as worldly—mere *i* in Christ. . . . 1 Cor 3:1
In regard to evil be *i*, . . . 1 Cor 14:20
Then we will no longer be *i*, . . . Eph 4:14

INFIRMITIES *frailties; diseases; personal failings*
Surely he took up our *i*. . . . Is 53:4
He took up our *i* . . . Mt 8:17

INHERIT(ANCE) *to receive as a legacy or promise; to come into possession of or receive as a rightful heir; the acquisition of a possession from past generations; see HEIR, HERITAGE*
I will give it to you as an *i*, . . . Lv 20:24
because he will lead Israel to *i* it. . . . Dt 1:38
the LORD is their *i*, as the LORD . . . Dt 4:20
to be the people of his *i*, . . . Dt 10:9
people to *i* the land I swore . . . Jos 1:6
two-and-a-half tribes their *i* east . . . Jos 14:3
surely I have a delightful *i*. . . . Ps 16:6
the people he chose for his *i*. . . . Ps 33:12
But the meek will *i* the land . . . Ps 37:11
the righteous will *i* the land . . . Ps 37:29
and gave their land as an *i*, . . . Ps 136:21
A good man leaves an *i* . . . Prv 13:22
The LORD will *i* Judah . . . Zec 2:12
for they will *i* the earth. . . . Mt 5:5
as much and will *i* eternal life. . . . Mt 19:29
blessed by my Father; take your *i*, . . . Mt 25:34
what must I do to *i* eternal life? . . . Mk 10:17
what must I do to *i* eternal life? . . . Lk 18:18
the wicked will not *i* the kingdom . . . 1 Cor 6:9
blood cannot *i* the kingdom of God . . . 1 Cor 15:50
who is a deposit guaranteeing our *i* . . . Eph 1:14
has any *i* in the kingdom of Christ . . . Eph 5:5
you to share in the *i* of the saints . . . Col 1:12
you know that you will receive an *i* . . . Col 3:24
receive the promised eternal *i*. . . . Heb 9:15
and into an *i* that can never perish, . . . 1 Pt 1:4
He who overcomes will *i* all this, . . . Rv 21:7

INIQUITIES, INIQUITY *sin, implying perversion of heart and wickedness of purpose*
forgive my *i*, though it is great. . . . Ps 25:11
and did not cover up my *i*, . . . Ps 32:5
Wash away all my *i*. . . . Ps 51:2
and blot out all my *i*. . . . Ps 51:9
he forgave their *i*. . . . Ps 78:38
or repay us according to our *i*. . . . Ps 103:10
he was crushed for our *i*; . . . Is 53:5
and he will bear their *i*. . . . Is 53:11
But your *i* have separated . . . Is 59:2
and hurl all our *i* into the depths . . . Mi 7:19

INNOCENT *free from guilt or sin*
do not put an *i* or honest person . . . Ex 23:7
acquitting the *i* and condemning . . . Dt 25:1
hands that shed *i* blood, . . . Prv 6:17
It is not good to punish an *i* man, . . . Prv 17:26
shrewd as snakes and as *i* as doves. . . . Mt 10:16
for I have betrayed *i* blood. . . . Mt 27:4
I am *i* of this man's blood," he said. . . . Mt 27:24
declare to you today that I am *i* . . . Acts 20:26
what is good, and *i* about what is . . . Rom 16:19
but that does not make me *i*. . . . 1 Cor 4:4

INSIGHT *discernment of the true nature of a situation; seeing intuitively*
Solomon wisdom and very great *i*, . . . 1 Kgs 4:29
I have more *i* than all my teachers, . . . Ps 119:99
listen well to my words of *i*, . . . Prv 5:1

There is no wisdom, no *i*, no plan . . . Prv 21:30
more in knowledge and depth of *i*, . . . Phil 1:9
for the Lord will give you *i* . . . 2 Tm 2:7

INSTRUCTION(S) *teaching that calls for obedience*
Listen, my son, to your father's *i* . . . Prv 1:8
Listen, my sons, to a father's *i*; . . . Prv 4:1
Hold on to *i*, do not let it go; . . . Prv 4:13
Choose my *i* instead of silver, . . . Prv 8:10
Listen to my *i* and be wise; . . . Prv 8:33
A wise son heeds his father's *i*, . . . Prv 13:1
He who scorns *i* will pay for it, . . . Prv 13:13
Whoever gives heed to *i* prospers, . . . Prv 16:20
and pleasant words promote *i*. . . . Prv 16:21
Listen to advice and accept *i*, . . . Prv 19:20
Apply your heart to *i* . . . Prv 23:12
or prophecy or word of *i*? . . . 1 Cor 14:6
or a word of *i*, a revelation, . . . 1 Cor 14:26
up in the training and *i* of the Lord. . . . Eph 6:4
he who rejects this *i* does not reject . . . 1 Thes 4:8
If anyone does not obey our *i* . . . 2 Thes 3:14
I give you this *i* in keeping . . . 1 Tm 1:18
I am writing you these *i* so that, . . . 1 Tm 3:14
to the sound of *i* of our Lord Jesus . . . 1 Tm 6:3
with great patience and careful *i*. . . . 2 Tm 4:2

INTEGRITY *honesty; without compromise or corruption*
or your *i* that you are going . . . Dt 9:5
if you walk before me in *i* of heart . . . 1 Kgs 9:4
the heart and are pleased with *i*. . . . 1 Chr 29:17
because he was a man of *i*. . . . Neh 7:2
And he still maintains his *i*, . . . Jb 2:3
Are you still holding on to your *i*? . . . Jb 2:9
reconsider, for my *i* is at stake. . . . Jb 6:29
till I die, I will not deny my *i*. . . . Jb 27:5
according to my *i*, O Most High. . . . Ps 7:8
May *i* and uprightness protect me, . . . Ps 25:21
In my *i* you uphold me . . . Ps 41:12
David shepherded them with *i* . . . Ps 78:72
The man of *i* walks securely, . . . Prv 10:9
The *i* of the upright guides them, . . . Prv 11:3
Righteousness guards the man of *i*, . . . Prv 13:6
or to flog officials for their *i*. . . . Prv 17:26
Bloodthirsty men hate a man of *i* . . . Prv 29:10
my mouth has uttered in all *i* . . . Is 45:23
no one pleads his case with *i*. . . . Is 59:4
we know you are a man of *i* . . . Mt 22:16
we know you are a man of *i* . . . Mk 12:14
your teaching show *i*, seriousness . . . Ti 2:7

INTERCEDE(S), INTERCEDING *to plead someone's case*
but the Spirit himself *i* for us . . . Rom 8:26
because the Spirit *i* for the saints . . . Rom 8:27
hand of God and is also *i* for us. . . . Rom 8:34
he always lives to *i* for them. . . . Heb 7:25

INTERCESSION *the act of pleading someone's case*
and made *i* for the transgressors, . . . Is 53:12
i and thanksgiving be made . . . 1 Tm 2:1

INTERPRET(S), INTERPRETATION *to explain the meaning of something; to translate; explanation*
I had a dream, and no one can *i* it. . . . Gn 41:15
you cannot *i* the signs of the times. . . . Mt 16:3
and to still another the *i* of tongues. . . . 1 Cor 12:10
Do all *i*? But eagerly desire . . . 1 Cor 12:30
he *i*, so that the church may be . . . 1 Cor 14:5
pray that he may *i* what he says. . . . 1 Cor 14:13
a revelation, a tongue or an *i*. . . . 1 Cor 14:26
about by the prophet's own *i*. . . . 2 Pt 1:20

INVISIBLE *hidden; imperceptible*
of the world God's *i* qualities . . . Rom 1:20
He is the image of the *i* God, . . . Col 1:15
and on earth, visible and *i*, . . . Col 1:16
immortal, *i*, the only God, . . . 1 Tm 1:17
because he saw him who is *i* . . . Heb 11:27

JEALOUS(Y) *apprehensive of the loss of another's affection; vigilant in guarding something; feelings of envy or bitterness*
the LORD your God, am a *j* God, . . . Ex 20:5
God is a consuming fire, a *j* God. . . . Dt 4:24
He is a holy God; he is a *j* God. . . . Jos 24:19
How long will your *j* burn like fire? . . . Ps 79:5
for *j* arouses a husband's fury, . . . Prv 6:34
its *j* unyielding as the grave. . . . Song 8:6
I will direct my *j* anger against you, . . . Ez 23:25
the LORD will be *j* for his land . . . Jl 2:18
LORD is a *j* and avenging God; . . . Na 1:2
In the fire of his *j* . . . Zep 1:18
consumed by the fire of my *j* anger. . . . Zep 3:8
I am very *j* for Jerusalem and Zion, . . . Zec 1:14
debauchery, not in dissension and *j* . . . Rom 13:13
For since there is *j* and quarreling . . . 1 Cor 3:3
trying to arouse the Lord's *j*? . . . 1 Cor 10:22
j, outbursts of anger, factions, . . . 2 Cor 12:20
hatred, discord, *j*, fits of rage, . . . Gal 5:20

JOIN(ED) *to bring together; unite*
and do not *j* with the rebellious, . . . Prv 24:21
J them together into one stick . . . Ez 37:17
Many nations will be *j* . . . Zec 2:11
Therefore what God has *j* together, . . . Mt 19:6
They all *j* together constantly . . . Acts 1:14
to *j* me in my struggle by praying . . . Rom 15:30
him the whole building is *j* together . . . Eph 2:21
and held together . . . Eph 4:16
j with me in suffering for the gospel . . . 2 Tm 1:8

JOY(FUL)(OUS) *emotion evoked by well-being, success or good fortune: gladness or delight; see OVERJOYED*
shouted for *j* and fell facedown. . . . Lv 9:24
with *j* songs and with tambourines . . . 1 Sm 18:6
j and glad in heart . . . 1 Kgs 8:66
and sheep, for there was *j* in Israel. . . . 1 Chr 12:40
with *j* how willingly your people . . . 1 Chr 29:17
while many others shouted for *j*. . . . Ezr 3:12
for the *j* of the LORD is your . . . Neh 8:10
the city of Susa held a *j* celebration. . . . Est 8:15
may no shout of *j* be heard in it. . . . Jb 3:7
he sees God's face and shouts for *j*; . . . Jb 33:26
and all the angels shouted for *j*? . . . Jb 38:7
me with *j* in your presence, . . . Ps 16:11
sackcloth and clothed me with *j*, . . . Ps 30:11
shout for *j* and gladness; . . . Ps 35:27
They are led in with *j* and gladness; . . . Ps 45:15
to me the *j* of your salvation . . . Ps 51:12
the nations be glad and sing for *j*, . . . Ps 67:4
the trees of the forest will sing for *j*; . . . Ps 96:12
and *j* on the upright in heart. . . . Ps 97:11
they are the *j* of my heart. . . . Ps 119:111
tormentors demanded songs of *j*; . . . Ps 137:3
and sing for *j* on their beds. . . . Ps 149:5
A wise son brings *j* to his father, . . . Prv 10:1
A cheerful look brings *j* . . . Prv 15:30
and drink your wine with a *j* heart, . . . Eccl 9:7
let your heart give you *j* in the days . . . Eccl 11:9
With *j* you will draw water . . . Is 12:3
the *j* harp is silent. . . . Is 24:8
Gladness and *j* will overtake them, . . . Is 35:10
Sing for *j*, O heavens, . . . Is 44:23
everlasting *j* will crown their heads . . . Is 51:11
You will go out in *j* . . . Is 55:12
then you will find your *j* . . . Is 58:14
out of the *j* of their hearts, . . . Is 65:14
will bring an end to the sounds of *j* . . . Jer 7:34
Sing with *j* for Jacob; . . . Jer 31:7
J and gladness are gone . . . Jer 48:33

the *j* of the whole earth? . . . Lam 2:15
not *j*, upon the mountains. . . . Ez 7:7
j of mankind is withered away . . . Jl 1:12
I will be *j* in God my Savior. . . . Hb 3:18
and at once receives it with *j*. . . . Mt 13:20
in his *j* went and sold all he had . . . Mt 13:44
the baby in my womb leaped for *j*. . . . Lk 1:44
news of great *j* that will be . . . Lk 2:10
The seventy-two returned with *j* . . . Lk 10:17
still did not believe it because of *j* . . . Lk 24:41
returned to Jerusalem with great *j*. . . . Lk 24:52
and that your *j* may be complete. . . . Jn 15:11
but your grief will turn to *j*. . . . Jn 16:20
So there was great *j* in that city. . . . Acts 8:8
And the disciples were filled with *j* . . . Acts 13:52
What has happened to all your *j*? . . . Gal 4:15
j, peace, patience, kindness, . . . Gal 5:22
I always pray with *j* . . . Phil 1:4
then make my *j* complete . . . Phil 2:2
For what is our hope, our *j*, . . . 1 Thes 2:19
Be *j* always; pray continually; . . . 1 Thes 5:16
by anointing you with the oil of *j*. . . . Heb 1:9
for the *j* set before him endured . . . Heb 12:2
thousands of angels in *j* assembly, . . . Heb 12:22
Consider it pure *j*, my brothers, . . . Jas 1:2
to mourning and your *j* to gloom. . . . Jas 4:9
without fault and with great *j* . . . Jude 1:24

JUDGE(D)(S), JUDGING *to pass sentence, punish or condemn; one appointed to do this; see JUDGMENT*
May the LORD *j* between you . . . Gn 16:5
Will not the *J* of all the earth do . . . Gn 18:25
The LORD will *j* his people . . . Dt 32:36
Then the LORD raised up *j*, . . . Jgs 2:16
May the LORD *j* between you . . . 1 Sm 24:12
for he comes to *j* the earth. . . . 1 Chr 16:33
plead with my *J* for mercy. . . . Jb 9:15
J me, O LORD, according . . . Ps 7:8
and justified when you *j*. . . . Ps 51:4
it is I who *j* uprightly. . . . Ps 75:2
Rise up, O God, *j* the earth, . . . Ps 82:8
He will *j* the world in righteousness . . . Ps 96:13
To show partiality in *j* is not good: . . . Prv 24:23
If a king *j* the poor with fairness, . . . Prv 29:14
He will *j* between the nations . . . Is 2:4
For the LORD is our *j*, . . . Is 33:22
Almighty, you who *j* righteously . . . Jer 11:20
by their own standards I will *j* them . . . Ez 7:27
I will *j* between one sheep . . . Ez 34:17
sit to *j* all the nations on every side. . . . Jl 3:12
Her leaders *j* for a bribe, . . . Mi 3:11
Do not *j*, or you too will be judged. . . . Mt 7:1
And he has given him authority to *j* . . . Jn 5:27
Stop *j* by mere appearances, . . . Jn 7:24
For I did not come to *j* the world, . . . Jn 12:47
a day when he will *j* the world . . . Acts 17:31
day when God will *j* men's secrets . . . Rom 2:16
then, why do you *j* your brother? . . . Rom 14:10
not *j* by external appearance . . . Gal 2:6
who will *j* the living and the dead, . . . 2 Tm 4:1
come to God, the *j* of all men, . . . Heb 12:23
who teach will be *j* more strictly. . . . Jas 3:1
who are you to *j* your neighbor? . . . Jas 4:12
on a Father who *j* each man's work . . . 1 Pt 1:17
to him who is ready to *j* the living . . . 1 Pt 4:5
The dead were *j* according . . . Rv 20:12

JUDGMENT(S) *to pass sentence upon; condemn; to act or decide as a judge; to form a negative opinion about; good sense; the final judgment by God; see JUDGE*
of any man, for *j* belongs to God. . . . Dt 1:17
May you be blessed for your good *j*. . . . 1 Sm 25:33
the wicked will not stand in the *j*, . . . Ps 1:5

Teach me knowledge and good *j*, . . . Ps 119:66
preserve sound *j* and discernment, . . . Prv 3:21
man who commits adultery lacks *j*; . . . Prv 6:32
but fools die for lack of *j*. . . . Prv 10:21
he defies all sound *j*. . . . Prv 18:1
God will bring every deed into *j*, . . . Eccl 12:14
By oppression and *j* he was taken . . . Is 53:8
he will bring *j* on all mankind . . . Jer 25:31
pronounced *j* in favor of the saints . . . Dn 7:22
my *j* flashed like lightning . . . Hos 6:5
So I will come near to you for *j*. . . . Mal 3:5
on the day of *j* than for that town. . . . Mt 10:15
have to give account on the day of *j* . . .
    Mt 12:36
but has entrusted all *j* to the Son, . . . Jn 5:22
For *j* I have come into this world, . . . Jn 9:39
Now is the time for *j* on this world; . . . Jn 12:31
to sin and righteousness and *j*: . . . Jn 16:8
self-control and the *j* to come, . . . Acts 24:25
you who pass *j* on someone else, . . . Rom 2:1
How unsearchable his *j*, . . . Rom 11:33
rather think of yourself with sober *j* . . . Rom
    12:3
stand before God's *j* seat. . . . Rom 14:10
appear before the *j* seat of Christ, . . . 2 Cor 5:10
fall under the same *j* as the devil. . . . 1 Tm 3:6
to die once, and after that to face *j*, . . . Heb 9:27
but only a fearful expectation of *j* . . . Heb 10:27
For it is time for *j* to begin . . . 1 Pt 4:17
being kept for the day of *j* . . . 2 Pt 3:7
have confidence on the day of *j*, . . . 1 Jn 4:17
bound with everlasting chains for *j*. . . . Jude 1:6
because the hour of his *j* has come. . . . Rv 14:7

JUST(LY); JUST(LY) *conforming to a standard of correctness; righteous; see JUSTICE, UNJUST*
j as the LORD, the God . . . Dt 6:3
and honey, *j* as the LORD, . . . Dt 27:3
j as he delighted in your fathers, . . . Dt 30:9
and all his ways are *j*. . . . Dt 32:4
They are not *j* idle words for you . . . Dt 32:47
doing what was *j* and right . . . 2 Sm 8:15
doing what was *j* and right . . . 1 Chr 18:14
and said, "The LORD is *j*." . . . 2 Chr 12:6
and laws that are *j* and right, . . . Neh 9:13
Will you condemn the *j*? . . . Jb 34:17
Elihu said: "Do you think this is *j*? . . . Jb 35:2
For the LORD loves the *j* . . . Ps 37:28
Do you rulers indeed speak *j*? . . . Ps 58:1
for you rule the peoples *j* . . . Ps 67:4
what is *j* and right. . . . Ps 99:4
of his hands are faithful and *j*; . . . Ps 111:7
I have done what is righteous and *j*; . . .
    Ps 119:121
doing what is right and *j* and fair; . . . Prv 1:3
for he guards the course of the *j* . . . Prv 2:8
will understand what is right and *j* . . . Prv 2:9
All the words of my mouth are *j*; . . . Prv 8:8
and rulers make laws that are *j*; . . . Prv 8:15
The plans of the righteous are *j*, . . . Prv 12:5
To do what is right and *j* . . . Prv 21:3
even when the plea of the needy is *j* . . . Is 32:7
They ask me for *j* decisions . . . Is 58:2
if in a truthful, *j* and righteous way . . . Jer 4:2
and deal with each other *j*, . . . Jer 7:5
what the LORD says: Do what is *j* . . . Jer 22:3
He did what was right and *j*, . . . r 22:15
do what is *j* and right in the land. . . . Jer 23:5
he will do what is *j* and right . . . Jer 33:15
who does what is *j* and right. . . . Ez 18:5
Since the son has done what is *j* . . . Ez 18:19
and does what is *j* and right, . . . Ez 18:21
The way of the Lord is not *j*. . . . Ez 18:25
and does what is *j* and right, . . . Ez 18:27
and does what is *j* and right . . . Ez 33:14
But it is their way that is not *j*. . . . Ez 33:17
and does what is *j* and right, . . . Ez 33:19
and oppression and do what is *j* . . . Ez 45:9
does is right and all his ways are *j* . . . Dn 4:37
To act *j* and to love mercy . . . Mi 6:8
We are punished *j*, . . . Lk 23:41

as to be *j* and the one who justifies . . . Rom
    3:26
God is *j*: He will pay back trouble . . . 2 Thes 1:6
received its *j* punishment, . . . Heb 2:2
himself to him who judges *j*. . . . 1 Pt 2:23
and *j* and will forgive us our sins . . . 1 Jn 1:9
J and true are your ways, . . . Rv 15:3
You are *j* in these judgments, . . . Rv 16:5
for true and *j* are his judgments. . . . Rv 19:2

JUSTICE *fairness, correctness; equity; see
JUST*
Dan will provide *j* for his people . . . Gn 49:16
do not pervert *j* by siding . . . Ex 23:2
Do not deny *j* to your poor people . . . Ex 23:6
Do not pervert *j* or show partiality. . . . Dt 16:19
the alien or the fatherless of *j*, . . . Dt 24:17
and I would see that he gets *j*, . . . 2 Sm 15:4
came to the king asking for *j*, . . . 2 Sm 15:6
for discernment in administering *j*, . . . 1 Kgs
    3:11
the Hall of *J*, where he was to judge . . . 1 Kgs
    7:7
to maintain *j* and righteousness. . . . 1 Kgs 10:9
experts in matters of law and *j*, . . . Est 1:13
Does God pervert *j*? . . . Jb 8:3
though I call for help, there is no *j*. . . . Jb 19:7
I will ascribe *j* to my Maker. . . . Jb 36:3
Awake, my God; decree *j*. . . . Ps 7:6
he will govern the peoples with *j*. . . . Ps 9:8
j of your cause like the noonday . . . Ps 37:6
j are the foundation of your throne; . . . Ps 89:14
I will sing of your love and *j*; . . . Ps 101:1
Blessed are they who maintain *j*, . . . Ps 106:3
I know that the LORD secures *j* . . . Ps 140:12
and his mouth should not betray *j*. . . . Prv
    16:10
or to deprive the innocent of *j*. . . . Prv 18:5
When *j* is done, it brings joy . . . Prv 21:15
poor oppressed in a district, and *j* . . . Eccl 5:8
he looked for *j*, but saw bloodshed; . . . Is 5:7
and withhold *j* from the oppressed of . . .
    Is 10:2
I will make *j* the measuring line . . . Is 28:17
For the LORD is a God of *j*. . . . Is 30:18
and he will bring *j* to the nations. . . . Is 42:1
there is no *j* in their paths. . . . Is 59:8
We look for *j*, but find none; . . . Is 59:11
For I, the LORD, love *j*; . . . Is 61:8
I will discipline you but only with *j*; . . . Jer
    30:11
mistreat the alien, denying them *j*. . . . Ez 22:29
I will shepherd the flock with *j*. . . . Ez 34:16
But let *j* roll on like a river, . . . Am 5:24
or "Where is the God of *j*?" . . . Mal 2:17
important matters of the law—*j*, . . . Mt 23:23
And will not God bring about *j*. . . . Lk 18:7
humiliation he was deprived of *j*. . . . Acts 8:33
He did this to demonstrate his *j*, . . . Rom 3:25

**JUSTIFICATION, JUSTIFIED, JUSTIFIES,
JUSTIFY(ING)** *the act, process, or state of
being declared right with God*
you condemn me to *j* yourself? . . . Jb 40:8
and *j* when you judge. . . . Ps 51:4
my righteous servant will *j* many, . . . Is 53:11
But he wanted to *j* himself, . . . Lk 10:29
rather than the other, went home *j*. . . . Lk 18:14
and are *j* freely by his grace . . . Rom 3:24
For we maintain that a man is *j*. . . . Rom 3:28
If, in fact, Abraham was *j* by works, . . . Rom
    4:2
and was raised to life for our *j*. . . . Rom 4:25
since we have been *j* through faith, . . . Rom 5:1
those he called, he also *j*; those he *j*, . . . Rom
    8:30
heart that you believe and are *j*, . . . Rom 10:10
in Christ Jesus that we may be *j* . . . Gal 2:16
Clearly no one is *j* before God . . . Gal 3:11
to Christ that we might be *j* by faith . . . Gal 3:24
so that, having been *j* by his grace, . . . Ti 3:7
You see that a person is *j* . . . Jas 2:24

KEEP(ING)(S), KEPT *to guard or protect*
May the LORD *k* watch . . . Gn 31:49
the Sabbath day by *k* it holy, . . . Dt 5:12
your God will *k* his covenant . . . Dt 7:12
K his commands and obey him; . . . Dt 13:4
your God and *k* his commands . . . Dt 30:10
and to *k* his commands, decrees . . . Dt 30:16
and to *k* the commands, . . . 1 Kgs 8:58
you who *k* your covenant of love . . . 2 Chr 6:14
the LORD and *k* his commands, . . . 2 Chr 34:31
You have *k* your promise . . . Neh 9:8
who *k* his oath . . . Ps 15:4
You, O LORD, *k* my lamp burning . . . Ps 18:28
in *k* them there is great reward. . . . Ps 19:11
Blessed are they who *k* his statutes . . . Ps 119:2
can a young man *k* his way pure? . . . Ps 119:9
My heart is set on *k* your decrees . . .
    Ps 119:112
k them within your heart; . . . Prv 4:21
a fool is thought wise if he *k* silent, . . . Prv
    17:28
a time to *k* and a time . . . Eccl 3:6
and *k* his commandments, . . . Eccl 12:13
You will *k* in perfect peace . . . Is 26:3
In your love you *k* me . . . Is 38:17
and be careful to *k* my laws. . . . Ez 20:19
who *k* his covenant of love . . . Dn 9:4
Therefore the prudent man *k* quiet . . . Am 5:13
Produce fruit in *k* with repentance. . . . Mt 3:8
these I have *k*," the young man . . . Mt 19:20
k watch over their flocks at night. . . . Lk 2:8
and *k* your lamps burning, . . . Lk 12:35
tries to *k* his life will lose it, . . . Lk 17:33
Yet not one of you *k* the law. . . . Jn 7:19
if anyone *k* my word, he will never . . . Jn 8:51
He will *k* you strong to the end, . . . 1 Cor 1:8
K God's commands is what counts. . . . 1 Cor
    7:19
is not easily angered, it *k* no record . . . 1 Cor
    13:5
let us *k* in step with the Spirit. . . . Gal 5:25
Make every effort to *k* the unity . . . Eph 4:3
to *k* away from every brother who . . . 2 Thes
    3:6
K yourself pure. . . . 1 Tm 5:22
k your head in all situations, . . . 2 Tm 4:5
K your lives free from the love . . . Heb 13:5
If you really *k* the royal law found . . . Jas 2:8
able to *k* his whole body in check. . . . Jas 3:2
spoil or fade *k* in heaven for you, . . . 1 Pt 1:4
Lord is not slow in *k* his promise, . . . 2 Pt 3:9
K yourselves in God's love . . . Jude 1:21
able to *k* you from falling . . . Jude 1:24
Blessed is he who *k* the words . . . Rv 22:7

KEYS *instruments that are turned to open or
close locks; symbolic of authority, power, and
control*
I will give you the *k* of the kingdom . . . Mt 16:19
And I hold the *k* of death . . . Rv 1:18

KILL(ED)(S) *to take life (manslaughter if accidental, murder if deliberate)*
his brother Abel and *k* him. . . . Gn 4:8
the LORD *k* every firstborn . . . Ex 13:15
but whoever *k* a man must be put . . . Lv 24:21
who has *k* someone accidentally . . . Nm 35:11
They *k* your prophets, who had . . . Neh 9:26
a time to *k* and a time to heal, . . . Eccl 3:3
I *k* you with the words . . . Hos 6:5
k the body but cannot *k* the soul. . . . Mt 10:28
They will *k* him, and on the third . . . Mt 17:23
You *k* the author of life, . . . Acts 3:15
for the letter *k*, but the Spirit gives . . . 2 Cor 3:6

KIND(S) *showing sympathy and understanding; benevolent; gentle; classification or division; see KINDNESS*
animals, each according to its *k*. . . . Gn 1:24
but a *k* word cheers him up. . . . Prv 12:25
blessed is he who is *k* to the needy. . . . Prv
    14:21

whoever is *k* to the needy honors . . . Prv 14:31
by being *k* to the oppressed. . . . Dn 4:27
because he is *k* to the ungrateful . . . Lk 6:35
There are different *k* of gifts, . . . 1 Cor 12:4
Love is patient, love is *k*. . . . 1 Cor 13:4
Be *k* and compassionate . . . Eph 4:32

KINDNESS(ES) *benevolence, favorable disposition; see KIND*
and show *k* to my master Abraham . . . Gn 24:12
has not stopped showing his *k* . . . Ru 2:20
to whom I can show God's *k*? . . . 2 Sm 9:3
he shows unfailing *k* . . . 2 Sm 22:51
did not remember your many *k*, . . . Ps 106:7
but with everlasting *k* . . . Is 54:8
I will tell of the *k* of the LORD . . . Is 63:7
I led them with cords of human *k*, . . . Hos 11:4
Consider therefore the *k* . . . Rom 11:22
understanding, patience and *k*; . . . 2 Cor 6:6
peace, patience, *k*, goodness, . . . Gal 5:22
yourselves with compassion, *k*, . . . Col 3:12
brotherly *k*; and to brotherly *k*, . . . 2 Pt 1:7

KINGDOM(S) *rule or realm; dominion of a king*
you will be for me a *k* of priests . . . Ex 19:6
to tear the *k* out of Solomon's hand . . . 1 Kgs 11:31
God over all the *k* of the earth. . . . 2 Kgs 19:15
so that all *k* on earth may know . . . 2 Kgs 19:19
and his *k* rules over all. . . . Ps 103:19
God over all the *k* of the earth. . . . Is 37:16
After you, another *k* will rise, . . . Dn 2:39
His *k* is an eternal *k*; . . . Dn 4:3
Most High is sovereign over the *k* . . . Dn 4:17
great beasts are four *k* that will rise . . . Dn 7:17
Repent, for the *k* of heaven is near . . . Mt 3:2
preaching the good news of the *k*, . . . Mt 4:23
for theirs is the *k* of heaven. . . . Mt 5:3
great in the *k* of heaven. . . . Mt 5:19
your *k* come, . . . Mt 6:10
But seek first his *k* . . . Mt 6:33
least in the *k* of heaven is greater . . . Mt 11:11
Every *k* divided against itself will . . . Mt 12:25
knowledge of the secrets of the *k* . . . Mt 13:11
The *k* of heaven is like a man who . . . Mt 13:24
the keys of the *k* of heaven; . . . Mt 16:19
the *k* of heaven is like a king who . . . Mt 18:23
because of the *k* of heaven. . . . Mt 19:12
for the *k* of heaven belongs to such . . . Mt 19:14
for a rich man to enter the *k* of God . . . Mt 19:24
the other at your left in your *k*. . . . Mt 20:21
the prostitutes are entering the *k* . . . Mt 21:31
rise against nation, and *k* against *k* . . . Mt 24:7
gospel of the *k* will be preached . . . Mt 24:14
the *k* prepared for you . . . Mt 25:34
The *k* of God is near. . . . Mk 1:15
The secret of the *k* . . . Mk 4:11
I will give you, up to half my *k*. . . . Mk 6:23
You are not far from the *k* of God . . . Mk 12:34
who was himself waiting for the *k* . . . Mk 15:43
The *k* of God is near you. . . . Lk 10:9
the good news of the *k* . . . Lk 16:16
he was waiting for the *k* of God. . . . Lk 23:51
My *k* is not of this world. . . . Jn 18:36
going to restore the *k* to Israel? . . . Acts 1:6
For the *k* of God is not a matter . . . Rom 14:17
the wicked will not inherit the *k* . . . 1 Cor 6:9
hands over the *k* to God the Father . . . 1 Cor 15:24
live like this will not inherit the *k* . . . Gal 5:21
bring me safely to his heavenly *k* . . . 2 Tm 4:18
we are receiving a *k* that cannot be . . . Heb 12:28
to inherit the *k* he promised those . . . Jas 2:5
has made us to be a *k* and priests . . . Rv 1:6
the *k* of the world has become the *k* . . . Rv 11:15

KINGS *sovereign rulers (often God)*
The *k* of the earth take their stand . . . Ps 2:2
k will bring you gifts. . . . Ps 68:29

and *k* will shut their mouths . . . Is 52:15
he sets up *k* and deposes them. . . . Dn 2:21
ten horns are ten *k* who will come . . . Dn 7:24
and you will be brought before *k* . . . Lk 21:12
for *k* and all those in authority, . . . 1 Tm 2:2
the King of *k* and Lord of lords, . . . 1 Tm 6:15
and the ruler of the *k* of the earth. . . . Rv 1:5
he is Lord of lords and King of *k* . . . Rv 17:14

KISS(ED)(ES) *to touch or caress with the lips as a sign of affection, greeting, or respect*
K the Son, lest he be angry . . . Ps 2:12
is like a *k* on the lips. . . . Prv 24:26
but an enemy multiplies *k*. . . . Prv 27:6
with the *k* of his mouth . . . Song 1:2
Judas said, "Rabbi!" and *k* him. . . . Mk 14:45
k them and poured perfume . . . Lk 7:38
Greet one another with a holy *k*. . . . Rom 16:16

KNEE(S) *joint in the middle part of the human leg*
all whose *k* have not bowed . . . 1 Kgs 19:18
steady the *k* that give way; . . . Is 35:3
Before me every *k* will bow; . . . Is 45:23
times a day he got down on his *k* . . . Dn 6:10
he fell at Jesus' *k* and said, . . . Lk 5:8
every *k* will bow before me; . . . Rom 14:11
name of Jesus every *k* should bow, . . . Phil 2:10
your feeble arms and weak *k*. . . . Heb 12:12

KNEEL, KNELT *to bend or rest upon one or both knees, demonstrating deference, respect, or supplication*
But Mordecai would not *k* down . . . Est 3:2
let us *k* before the LORD our . . . Ps 95:6
a ruler came and *k* before him . . . Mt 9:18
The woman came and *k* before him . . . Mt 15:25
a man approached Jesus and *k* . . . Mt 17:14
k down and prayed, "Father, . . . Lk 22:41
he *k* down with all of them . . . Acts 20:36
there on the beach we *k* to pray. . . . Acts 21:5
For this reason I *k* . . . Eph 3:14

KNEW, KNOW(ING)(N)(S) *to discern, recognize, acknowledge, learn; to be intimately familiar with; to have sexual intercourse with; see KNOWLEDGE*
and you will be like God, *k* good . . . Gn 3:5
you will *k* that I am the LORD . . . Ex 6:7
and the Egyptians will *k* that I am . . . Ex 14:4
teach me your ways so I may *k* you . . . Ex 33:13
the whole world will *k* that there is . . . 1 Sm 17:46
heart (for you alone *k* the hearts . . . 1 Kgs 8:39
I *k* that my Redeemer lives, . . . Jb 19:25
If only I *k* where to find him; . . . Jb 23:3
But he *k* the way that I take; . . . Jb 23:10
Those who *k* your name will trust . . . Ps 9:10
Be still, and *k* that I am God; . . . Ps 46:10
LORD has made his salvation *k* . . . Ps 98:2
for he *k* how we are formed, . . . Ps 103:14
Search me, O God, and *k* my heart; . . . Ps 139:23
no man *k* when his hour will come: . . . Eccl 9:12
k the end from the beginning, . . . Is 46:10
you in the womb I *k* you, . . . Jer 1:5
his brother, saying, 'K the LORD,' . . . Jer 31:34
they will *k* that I am the LORD; . . . Ez 6:10
let your left hand *k* what your right . . . Mt 6:3
for your Father *k* what you need . . . Mt 6:8
tell them plainly, 'I never *k* you. . . . Mt 7:23
or hidden that will not be made *k*. . . . Mt 10:26
Jesus *k* their thoughts . . . Mt 12:25
No one *k* about that day or hour, . . . Mt 24:36
himself to them, for he *k* all men. . . . Jn 2:24
we speak of what we *k*, . . . Jn 3:11
Then you will *k* the truth, . . . Jn 8:32
I *k* my sheep and my sheep *k* me . . . Jn 10:14
Now that you *k* these things, . . . Jn 13:17

all men will *k* that you are my . . . Jn 13:35
I have made you *k* to them, . . . Jn 17:26
It is not for you to *k* the times . . . Acts 1:7
since what may be *k* about God is . . . Rom 1:19
Lord, you *k* everyone's heart. . . . Acts 1:24
You have made *k* to me the paths . . . Acts 2:28
apart from law, has been made *k*, . . . Rom 3:21
We do not *k* what we ought to pray . . . Rom 8:26
Who has *k* the mind of the Lord? . . . Rom 11:34
the gospel where Christ was not *k*, . . . Rom 15:20
through its wisdom did not *k* him, . . . 1 Cor 1:21
For I resolved to *k* nothing . . . 1 Cor 2:2
For we *k* in part and we prophesy . . . 1 Cor 13:9
or rather are *k* by God . . . Gal 4:9
I want to *k* Christ and the power . . . Phil 3:10
order that they may *k* the mystery . . . Col 2:2
punish those who do not *k* God . . . 2 Thes 1:8
because I *k* whom I have believed, . . . 2 Tm 1:12
The Lord *k* those who are his," and . . . 2 Tm 2:19
because they will all *k* me, . . . Heb 8:11
k what will happen tomorrow. . . . Jas 4:14
than to have *k* it and then . . . 2 Pt 2:21
This is how we *k* we are in him: . . . 1 Jn 2:5
not *k* us is that it did not *k* him. . . . 1 Jn 3:1
This is how we *k* who the children . . . 1 Jn 3:10
This is how we *k* what love is: . . . 1 Jn 3:16
We *k* it by the Spirit he gave us. . . . 1 Jn 3:24
does not love does not *k* God, . . . 1 Jn 4:8
so that you may *k* that you have . . . 1 Jn 5:13
We *k* that anyone born . . . 1 Jn 5:18
I *k* your deeds, your hard work . . . Rv 2:2

KNOCK *to strike a hard object with the knuckles in order to get attention*
k and the door will be opened . . . Mt 7:7
I stand at the door and *k*. . . . Rv 3:20

KNOWLEDGE *the state or fact of knowing; learning; awareness; sum of what has been learned or discovered; see KNEW*
the tree of the *k* of good and evil. . . . Gn 2:9
and *k*, that I may lead this people, . . . 2 Chr 1:10
counsel with words without *k*? . . . Jb 38:2
night after night they display *k*. . . . Ps 19:2
Does he who teaches man lack *k*? . . . Ps 94:10
Such *k* is too wonderful for me, . . . Ps 139:6
k and discretion to the young . . . Prv 1:4
of the LORD is the beginning of *k*, . . . Prv 1:7
and *k* will be pleasant to your soul. . . . Prv 2:10
k rather than choice gold, . . . Prv 8:10
k of the Holy One is understanding . . . Prv 9:10
Wise men store up *k*, . . . Prv 10:14
Whoever loves discipline loves *k*, . . . Prv 12:1
The discerning heart seeks *k*, . . . Prv 15:14
heart of the discerning acquires *k*; . . . Prv 18:15
to have zeal without *k*, . . . Prv 19:2
through *k* its rooms are filled . . . Prv 24:4
but the advantage of *k* is this: . . . Eccl 7:12
full of the *k* of the LORD . . . Is 11:9
are destroyed from lack of *k*. . . . Hos 4:6
filled with the *k* of the glory . . . Hb 2:14
The *k* of the secrets of the kingdom . . . Mt 13:11
with a thorough *k* of the Scriptures . . . Acts 18:24
worthwhile to retain the *k* of God, . . . Rom 1:28
but their zeal is not based on *k*. . . . Rom 10:2
riches of the wisdom and *k* of God! . . . Rom 11:33
k puffs up, but love builds up. . . . 1 Cor 8:1
can fathom all mysteries and all *k*, . . . 1 Cor 13:2
where there is *k*, it will pass away. . . . 1 Cor 13:8
light of the *k* of the glory of God . . . 2 Cor 4:6

to know this love that surpasses *k* . . . Eph 3:19
and more in *k* and depth of insight, . . . Phil 1:9
all the treasures of wisdom and *k.* . . . Col 2:3
and to come to a *k* of the truth. . . . 1 Tm 2:4
ideas of what is falsely called *k,* . . . 1 Tm 6:20
and to goodness, *k;* and to *k,* . . . 2 Pt 1:5
grow in the grace and *k* of our Lord . . . 2 Pt 3:18

LABOR(ING) *to work to produce goods and services; the process of such work; strenuous effort*
to oppress them with forced *l,* . . . Ex 1:11
Six days you shall *l* and do all your . . . Ex 20:9
its builders *l* in vain. . . . Ps 127:1
You will eat the fruit of your *l;* . . . Ps 128:2
but laziness ends in slave *l.* . . . Prv 12:24
and your *l* on what does not satisfy . . . Is 55:2
They do not *l* or spin. . . . Mt 6:28
have reaped the benefits of their *l.* . . . Jn 4:38
rewarded according to his own *l.* . . . 1 Cor 3:8
because you know that your *l* . . . 1 Cor 15:58
you who have no *l* pains; . . . Gal 4:27
day of Christ that I did not run or *l* . . . Phil 2:16
they will rest from their *l,* . . . Rv 14:13

LACK(ED)(ING)(S) *to be in need of*
and you have not *l* anything. . . . Dt 2:7
them in the desert; they *l* nothing, . . . Neh 9:21
who commits adultery *l* judgment; . . . Prv 6:32
he who chases fantasies *l* judgment . . . Prv 12:11
is a man who *l* self-control. . . . Prv 25:28
Never be *l* in zeal, but keep your . . . Rom 12:11
any of you *l* wisdom, he should ask . . . Jas 1:5

LAID, LAY(ING)(S) *to place in a resting position*
and his sons shall *l* their hands . . . Ex 29:10
He is to *l* his hand on the head . . . Lv 1:4
whom is the spirit, and *l* your hand . . . Nm 27:18
Who can *l* a hand on the LORD's . . . 1 Sm 26:9
on the man himself do not *l* a finger . . . Jb 1:12
and *l* up his words in your heart. . . . Jb 22:22
See, I *l* a stone in Zion, . . . Is 28:16
and the LORD has *l* on him . . . Is 53:6
of Man has no place to *l* his head. . . . Mt 8:20
Come and see the place where he *l.* . . . Mt 28:6
took his body and *l* it in a tomb. . . . Mk 6:29
and *l* his hands on each one, . . . Lk 4:40
and *l* the foundation on rock. . . . Lk 6:48
The good shepherd *l* down his life . . . Jn 10:11
that he *l* down his life . . . Jn 15:13
at the *l* on of the apostles' hands, . . . Acts 8:18
I *l* in Zion a stone that causes men . . . Rom 9:33
no one can *l* any foundation other . . . 1 Cor 3:11
Do not be hasty in the *l* on of hands . . . 1 Tm 5:22
through the *l* on of my hands . . . 2 Tm 1:6
not *l* again the foundation . . . Heb 6:1
And we ought to *l* down our lives . . . 1 Jn 3:16
They *l* their crowns . . . Rv 4:10

LAMB(S)('S) *young sheep*
God himself will provide the *l* . . . Gn 22:8
and slaughter the Passover *l.* . . . Ex 12:21
are to eat the *l,* together . . . Nm 9:11
he took the ewe *l* that belonged . . . 2 Sm 12:4
The wolf will live with the *l,* . . . Is 11:6
he was led like a *l* to the slaughter, . . . Is 53:7
I am sending you out like *l* . . . Lk 10:3
L of God, who takes away the sin . . . Jn 1:29
Jesus said, "Feed my *l.*" . . . Jn 21:15
as a *l* before the shearer is silent, . . . Acts 8:32
our Passover *l,* has been sacrificed. . . . 1 Cor 5:7
Then I saw a *L,* looking . . . Rv 5:6
Worthy is the *L,* who was slain, . . . Rv 5:12
white in the blood of the *L.* . . . Rv 7:14

to the wedding supper of the *L!* . . . Rv 19:9
written in the *L* book of life. . . . Rv 21:27

LAMENT *loud mourning or wailing*
took up this *l* concerning Saul . . . 2 Sm 1:17
Take up a *l* concerning the princes . . . Ez 19:1

LAMP(S) *container for burning oil to produce light*
You, O LORD, keep my *l* burning; . . . Ps 18:28
Your word is a *l* to my feet . . . Ps 119:105
For these commands are a *l,* . . . Prv 6:23
and her *l* does not go out at night. . . . Prv 31:18
The eye is the *l* of the body. . . . Mt 6:22
be like ten virgins who took their *l* . . . Mt 25:1
No one lights a *l* and hides it . . . Lk 8:16
the throne, seven *l* were blazing. . . . Rv 4:5
They will not need the light of a *l* . . . Rv 22:5

LAMPSTAND(S) *pedestal supporting a lamp*
Make a *l* of pure gold . . . Ex 25:31
He made ten gold *l* . . . 2 Chr 4:7
I see a solid gold *l* with a bowl . . . Zec 4:2
In its first room were the *l,* . . . Heb 9:2
when I turned I saw seven golden *l,* . . . Rv 1:12
and remove your *l* from its place. . . . Rv 2:5

LAND *dry earth; real estate; nation; Canaan, the Promised Land*
God called the dry ground *"l,"* . . . Gn 1:10
and go to the *l* I will show you, . . . Gn 12:1
a *l* flowing with milk and honey . . . Ex 3:8
l on which your feet have walked . . . Jos 14:9
their sin and will heal their *l* . . . 2 Chr 7:14
But the meek will inherit the *l* . . . Ps 37:11
my portion in the *l* of the living. . . . Ps 142:5
cut off from the *l* of the living; . . . Is 53:8
and bring you back into your own *l.* . . . Ez 36:24

LANGUAGE(S) *the expression of ideas with words; the particular set of such expressions characteristic of an ethnic group*
Now the whole world had one *l* . . . Gn 11:1
there the LORD confused the *l* . . . Gn 11:9
There is no speech or *l* . . . Ps 19:3
When he lies, he speaks his native *l* . . . Jn 8:44
heard them speaking in his own *l,* . . . Acts 2:6
slander, and filthy *l* from your lips. . . . Col 3:8
from every tribe and *l* and people . . . Rv 5:9

LAST(ING)(S) *to endure; final*
During the *l* watch of the night . . . Ex 14:24
of the Israelites, as a *l* covenant. . . . Lv 24:8
For his anger *l* only a moment, . . . Ps 30:5
and Jerusalem: In the *l* days . . . Is 2:2
and with the *l* I am he. . . . Is 41:4
I am the first and I am the *l;* . . . Is 44:6
In the *l* days . . . Mi 4:1
But many who are first will be *l,* . . . Mt 19:30
beginning with the *l* ones hired . . . Mt 20:8
must be the very *l,* and the servant . . . Mk 9:35
a loud cry, Jesus breathed his *l.* . . . Mk 15:37
and I will raise him up at the *l* day. . . . Jn 6:40
and bear fruit—fruit that will *l.* . . . Jn 15:16
In the *l* days, God says, . . . Acts 2:17
is by faith from first to *l,* . . . Rom 1:17
l enemy to be destroyed is death. . . . 1 Cor 15:26
of an eye, at the *l* trumpet. . . . 1 Cor 15:52
had better and *l* possessions. . . . Heb 10:34
In the *l* times there will be . . . Jude 1:18
I am the First and the *L.* . . . Rv 1:17

LAUGH(ED)(S)(TER) *to show joy or scorn at something amusing; the expression of such joy*
Abraham fell facedown; he *l* . . . Gn 17:17
So Sarah *l* to herself as she thought, . . . Gn 18:12
The One enthroned in heaven *l;* . . . Ps 2:4
But you, O LORD, *l* at them; . . . Ps 59:8
Our mouths were filled with *l,* . . . Ps 126:2
Even in *l* the heart may ache, . . . Prv 14:13
a time to weep and a time to *l,* . . . Eccl 3:4

Change your *l* to mourning . . . Jas 4:9
Woe to you who *l* now, . . . Lk 6:25

LAVISHED *gave generously*
of God's grace that he *l* on us . . . Eph 1:8
great is the love the Father has *l* . . . 1 Jn 3:1

LAW(S) *universal principle; governing authority; binding decree; the body of God-given decrees imparted by Moses*
and be careful to obey my *l,* . . . Lv 25:18
to obey all this *l* before the LORD . . . Dt 6:25
Take this Book of the *L* . . . Dt 31:26
of the *L* depart from your mouth; . . . Jos 1:8
walk before me according to my *l,* . . . 2 Chr 6:16
Ezra the priest brought the *L.* . . . Neh 8:2
and on his *l* he meditates day . . . Ps 1:2
The *l* of the LORD is perfect, . . . Ps 19:7
your *l* is within my heart. . . . Ps 40:8
wonderful things in your *l.* . . . Ps 119:18
for your *l* is my delight. . . . Ps 119:77
but blessed is he who keeps the *l.* . . . Prv 29:18
The *l* will go out from Zion, . . . Is 2:3
To the *l* and to the testimony! . . . Is 8:20
I will put my *l* in their minds . . . Jer 31:33
they are a *l* to themselves . . . Hb 1:7
as flint and would not listen to the *l* . . . Zec 7:12
that I have come to abolish the *L* . . . Mt 5:17
sums up the *L* and the Prophets. . . . Mt 7:12
stroke of a pen to drop out of the *L.* . . . Lk 16:17
All who sin apart from the *l* will . . . Rom 2:12
apart from *l,* has been made known . . . Rom 3:21
because you are not under *l,* . . . Rom 6:14
released from the *l* so that we serve . . . Rom 7:6
For what the *l* was powerless to do . . . Rom 8:3
Christ is the end of the *l* . . . Rom 10:4
love is the fulfillment of the *l.* . . . Rom 13:10
and the power of sin is the *l.* . . . 1 Cor 15:56
The *l,* introduced 430 years later, . . . Gal 3:17
then, was the purpose of the *l?* . . . Gal 3:19
obligated to obey the whole *l.* . . . Gal 5:3
The entire *l* is summed up . . . Gal 5:14
by the Spirit, you are not under *l.* . . . Gal 5:18
We know that the *l* is good . . . 1 Tm 1:8
I will put my *l* in their minds . . . Heb 8:10
The *l* is only a shadow . . . Heb 10:1
intently into the perfect *l* that gives . . . Jas 1:25

LAWGIVER *human or divine author or dispenser of law*
the LORD is our *l,* . . . Is 33:22
There is only one *L* and Judge, . . . Jas 4:12

LAWLESS(NESS) *without regard for law*
and the man of *l* is revealed, . . . 2 Thes 2:3
And then the *l* one will be revealed . . . 2 Thes 2:8
Their sins and *l* acts . . . Heb 10:17
sins breaks the law; in fact, sin is *l.* . . . 1 Jn 3:4

LAZINESS, LAZY *unwillingness or lack of desire to work; idle*
They are *l;* that is why they are . . . Ex 5:8
L hands make a man poor, . . . Prv 10:4
l ends in slave labor. . . . Prv 12:24
L brings on deep sleep, . . . Prv 19:15
he is too *l* to bring it back . . . Prv 26:15
If a man is *l,* the rafters sag; . . . Eccl 10:18
replied, 'You wicked, *l* servant!' . . . Mt 25:26
liars, evil brutes, *l* gluttons. . . . Ti 1:12
We do not want you to become *l,* . . . Heb 6:12

LEAD(S), LED *to guide by direction or example; to go first*
In your unfailing love you will *l.* . . . Ex 15:13
the LORD your God *l* you all . . . Dt 8:2
now appoint a king to *l* us, . . . 1 Sm 8:5
his wives *l* him astray. . . . 1 Kgs 11:3
he *l* me beside quiet waters, . . . Ps 23:2
l me in a straight path . . . Ps 27:11
and *l* me in the way everlasting. . . . Ps 139:24

ignores correction / others astray. . . . Prv 10:17
and a little child will / them. . . . Is 11:6
he gently / those that have young. . . . Is 40:11
those who / many to righteousness, . . . Dn 12:3
I / you forty years in the desert . . . Am 2:10
Then Jesus was / by the Spirit . . . Mt 4:1
And / us not into temptation, . . . Mt 6:13
and broad is the road that / . . . Mt 7:13
till he / justice to victory. . . . Mt 12:20
If a blind man / a blind man, . . . Mt 15:14
they / him away to crucify him. . . . Mt 27:31
sheep by name and / them out. . . . Jn 10:3
which / to death, or to obedience, . . . Rom 6:16
those who are / by the Spirit . . . Rom 8:14
always / us in triumphal procession . . . 2 Cor
   2:14
So the law was put in charge to / us . . . Gal
   3:24
But if you are / by the Spirit, . . . Gal 5:18
do not let anyone / you astray. . . . 1 Jn 3:7

LEADER(S)(SHIP) *guidance by direction or example*
by divisions under the / of Moses . . . Nm 33:1
Samuel was / of Israel at Mizpah. . . . 1 Sm 7:6
I have been your / from my youth . . . 1 Sm 12:2
may another take his place of / . . . . Ps 109:8
if it is /, let him govern diligently; . . . Rom 12:8
Remember your /, who spoke . . . Heb 13:7

LEAP(ED)(S) *jump*
My heart / for joy . . . Ps 28:7
Then will the lame / like a deer, . . . Is 35:6
/ like calves released from the stall. . . . Mal 4:2
heard Mary's greeting, the baby / . . . Lk 1:41
Rejoice in that day and / for joy, . . . Lk 6:23

LEARN(ED)(ING)(S) *to discover or come to know; to develop the habit of; instruction or education*
L them and be sure to follow them. . . . Dt 5:1
/ to fear the LORD your God . . . Dt 31:12
as I / your righteous laws. . . . Ps 119:7
Long ago I / from your statutes . . . Ps 119:152
let the wise listen and add to their /, . . . Prv 1:5
/ to do right! . . . Is 1:17
of the world / righteousness. . . . Is 26:9
who overthrows the / of the wise . . . Is 44:25
yoke upon you and / from me, . . . Mt 11:29
How did this man get such / . . . Jn 7:15
Whatever you have / or received . . . Phil 4:9
for I have / to be content whatever . . . Phil 4:11
that each of you should / . . . 1 Thes 4:4
A woman should / in quietness . . . 1 Tm 2:11
always / but never able . . . 2 Tm 3:7
continue in what you have / . . . 2 Tm 3:14
he / obedience from what he suffered . . . Heb
   5:8

LEFT *side toward west when facing north (opposite of right)*
turn from it to the right or to the /, . . . Jos 1:7
Do not swerve to the right or the /; . . . Prv 4:27
do not let your / hand know what . . . Mt 6:3
on his right and the goats on his /. . . . Mt 25:33

LEND(ER)(S) *to allow another to use temporarily; to loan; one who loans*
freely / him whatever he needs. . . . Dt 15:8
who / his money without usury . . . Ps 15:5
are always generous and / freely; . . . Ps 37:26
to the poor / to the LORD, . . . Prv 19:17
the borrower is servant to the /. . . . Prv 22:7
He does not / at usury . . . Ez 18:8
if you / to those from whom you . . . Lk 6:34

LEPROSY, LEPROUS *severe skin disease; f igurative of moral or spiritual disease*
and when he took it out, it was /, . . . Ex 4:6
and saw that she had /; . . . Nm 12:10
was a valiant soldier, but he had /. . . . 2 Kgs 5:1
men with / at the entrance . . . 2 Kgs 7:3
those who have / are cured, . . . Mt 11:5
ten men who had / met him. . . . Lk 17:12

LIAR(S) *one who lies*
and if the witness proves to be a /, . . . Dt 19:18
I am considered a /; . . . Jb 34:6
the mouths of / will be silenced. . . . Ps 63:11
All men are /. . . . Ps 116:11
better to be poor than a / . . . Prv 19:22
will rebuke you and prove you a / . . . Prv 30:6
the offspring of /? . . . Is 57:4
If a / and deceiver comes and says, . . . Mi 2:11
for he is a / and the father of lies. . . . Jn 8:44
Let God be true, and every man a /. . . . Rom 3:4
Cretans are always /, evil brutes, . . . Ti 1:12
we make him out to be a / . . . 1 Jn 1:10
not do what he commands is a /, . . . 1 Jn 2:4
Who is the /? It is the man who . . . 1 Jn 2:22
yet hates his brother, he is a /. . . . 1 Jn 4:20
God has made him out to be a /, . . . 1 Jn 5:10
magic arts, the idolaters and all / . . . Rv 21:8

LIE(D)(S), LYING *to deliberately tell an untruth; to recline; to have sexual intercourse with*
Do not / with a man . . . Lv 18:22
God is not a man, that he should /, . . .
   Nm 23:19
when you / down and when you get . . . Dt 6:7
the Glory of Israel does not / . . . 1 Sm 15:29
I will / down and sleep in peace, . . . Ps 4:8
You destroy those who tell /; . . . Ps 5:6
His mouth is full of curses and / . . . Ps 10:7
Everyone / to his neighbor; . . . Ps 12:2
me / down in green pastures, . . . Ps 23:2
and your lips from speaking /. . . . Ps 34:13
I will not / to David . . . Ps 89:35
whose mouths are full of /, . . . Ps 144:8
when you / down, you will not be . . . Prv 3:24
a false witness who pours out / . . . Prv 6:19
he who pours out / will not go free. . . . Prv 19:5
A fortune made by a / tongue . . . Prv 21:6
A / tongue hates those it hurts, . . . Prv 26:28
leopard will / down with the goat, . . . Is 11:6
for we have made a / our refuge . . . Is 28:15
Your lips have spoken /, . . . Is 59:3
like a bow, to shoot /; . . . Jer 9:3
They have taught their tongues to / . . . Jer 9:5
The prophets are prophesying / . . . Jer 14:14
They commit adultery and live a / . . . Jer 23:14
they will / down in good grazing . . . Ez 34:14
for he is a liar and the father of /. . . . Jn 8:44
You have not / to men but to God. . . . Acts 5:4
exchanged the truth of God for a /, . . . Rom
   1:25
Do not / to each other, . . . Col 3:9
which God, who does not /, . . . Ti 1:2
because no / comes from the truth. . . .
   1 Jn 2:21
No / was found in their mouths; . . . Rv 14:5

LIFE, LIVES *period from birth to death; vitality; spiritual existence transcending death; salvation; see LIVE*
into his nostrils the breath of /, . . . Gn 2:7
of the garden were the tree of / . . . Gn 2:9
to destroy all / under the heavens, . . . Gn 6:17
Never again will all / be cut . . . Gn 9:11
you are to take / for /, eye for eye, . . . Ex 21:23
the / of every creature is its blood. . . . Lv 17:14
because the blood is the /, . . . Dt 12:23
I set before you today / . . . Dt 30:15
that the light of / may shine on him. . . .
   Jb 33:30
known to me the path of /; . . . Ps 16:11
LORD is the stronghold of my / . . . Ps 27:1
Whoever of you loves / . . . Ps 34:12
For with you is the fountain of /; . . . Ps 36:9
let me know how fleeting is my /. . . . Ps 39:4
Because your love is better than /, . . . Ps 63:3
they be blotted out of the book of / . . . Ps 69:28
With long / will I satisfy him . . . Ps 91:16
preserve my / according to your word . . .
   Ps 119:25
will prolong your / many years . . . Prv 3:2

for it is the wellspring of /. . . . Prv 4:23
adulteress preys upon your very /. . . . Prv 6:26
of the righteous is a fountain of /, . . . Prv 10:11
He who guards his lips guards his /, . . . Prv
   13:3
The fear of the LORD leads to /: . . . Prv 19:23
LORD makes his / a guilt offering, . . . Is 53:10
he will see the light of / . . . Is 53:11
that a man's / is not his own; . . . Jer 10:23
you redeemed my /. . . . Lam 3:58
some to everlasting /, others . . . Dn 12:2
you brought my / up from the pit, . . . Jon 2:6
Is not / more important than food, . . . Mt 6:25
and narrow the road that leads to /, . . . Mt 7:14
Whoever finds his / will lose it, . . . Mt 10:39
and on the third day be raised to /. . . . Mt 16:21
better for you to enter / maimed . . . Mt 18:8
thing must I do to get eternal /? . . . Mt 19:16
to give his / as a ransom for many. . . . Mt 20:28
a man's / does not consist . . . Lk 12:15
In him was /, and that / was . . . Jn 1:4
believes in him may have eternal /. . . . Jn 3:15
of water welling up to eternal /. . . . Jn 4:14
raises the dead and gives them /, . . . Jn 5:21
For as the Father has / in himself, . . . Jn 5:26
Jesus declared, "I am the bread of / . . . Jn 6:35
he who believes has everlasting /. . . . Jn 6:47
You have the words of eternal /. . . . Jn 6:68
but will have the light of /. . . . Jn 8:12
and I lay down my / for the sheep. . . . Jn 10:15
I give them eternal /, and they shall . . . Jn 10:28
I am the resurrection and the /. . . . Jn 11:25
The man who loves his / will lose it, . . .
   Jn 12:25
am the way and the truth and the /. . . . Jn 14:6
God has raised this Jesus to /, . . . Acts 2:32
was raised to / for our justification. . . . Rom
   4:25
shall we be saved through his /! . . . Rom 5:10
but the gift of God is eternal / . . . Rom 6:23
also give / to your mortal bodies . . . Rom 8:11
convinced that neither death nor /, . . . Rom
   8:38
If only for this / we have hope . . . 1 Cor 15:19
I urge you to live a / worthy . . . Eph 4:1
as you hold out the word of / . . . Phil 2:16
whose names are in the book of /. . . . Phil 4:3
order that you may live a / worthy . . . Col 1:10
your / is now hidden with Christ . . . Col 3:3
quiet / in all godliness and holiness. . . . 1 Tm
   2:2
for both the present / and the /. . . . 1 Tm 4:8
Take hold of the eternal / . . . 1 Tm 6:12
hold of the / that is truly /. . . . 1 Tm 6:19
destroyed death and has brought / . . . 2 Tm
   1:10
to live a godly / in Christ Jesus will . . . 2 Tm
   3:12
crown of / that God has promised . . . Jas 1:12
Let him show it by his good /, . . . Jas 3:13
the purity and reverence of your /. . . . 1 Pt 3:2
Whoever would love / . . . 1 Pt 3:10
given us everything we need for / . . . 2 Pt 1:3
we have passed from death to /, . . . 1 Jn 3:14
Jesus Christ laid down his / for us. . . .
   1 Jn 3:16
has given us eternal /, and this / is . . . 1 Jn 5:11
the right to eat from the tree of /, . . . Rv 2:7
and I will give you the crown of /. . . . Rv 2:10
name from the book of /, . . . Rv 3:5
was opened, which is the book of /. . . .
   Rv 20:12
from the spring of the water of /. . . . Rv 21:6
me the river of the water of /, . . . Rv 22:1
may have the right to the tree of / . . . Rv 22:14

LIFT(ED)(ING)(S) *to raise to a higher position*
and all the people / their hands . . . Neh 8:6
be / up, you ancient doors, . . . Ps 24:7
as I / up my hands . . . Ps 28:2
He / me out of the slimy pit, . . . Ps 40:2

has / up his heel against me.... Ps 41:9
in your name I will / up my hands.... Ps 63:4
and / the needy from the ash heap; ... Ps 113:7
I / up my eyes to the hills ... Ps 121:1
L up your hands in the sanctuary ... Ps 134:2
may the / up of my hands be like ... Ps 141:2
for to you I / up my soul.... Ps 143:8
/ up your voice with a shout, ... Is 40:9
he / them up and carried them ... Is 63:9
Let us / up our hearts and our ... Lam 3:41
they will / you up in their hands, ... Mt 4:6
stand up and / up your heads, ... Lk 21:28
Moses / up the snake in the desert, ... Jn 3:14
When you have / up the Son ... Jn 8:28
when I am / up from the earth, ... Jn 12:32
everywhere to / up holy hands ... 1 Tm 2:8
the Lord, and he will / you up.... Jas 4:10
that he may / you up in due time.... 1 Pt 5:6

LIGHT(S) *daytime, brightness, illumination;
exposure to truth*
"Let there be /," and there was /.... Gn 1:3
in a pillar of fire to give them /, ... Ex 13:21
it so that they / the space in front ... Ex 25:37
What is the way to the abode of /? ... Jb 38:19
Let the / of your face shine upon us ... Ps 4:6
my God turns my darkness into /.... Ps 18:28
giving / to the eyes.... Ps 19:8
LORD is my / and my salvation ... Ps 27:1
in your / we see /.... Ps 36:9
who walk in the / of your presence, ... Ps 89:15
He wraps himself in / ... Ps 104:2
and a / for my path.... Ps 119:105
The unfolding of your words gives /; ...
Ps 119:130
for darkness is as / to you.... Ps 139:12
till the full / of day.... Prv 4:18
let us walk in the / of the LORD.... Is 2:5
have seen a great /; ... Is 9:2
and a / for the Gentiles, ... Is 42:6
I form the / and create darkness, ... Is 45:7
Arise, shine, for your / has come, ... Is 60:1
LORD will be your everlasting /, ... Is 60:19
and brilliant / surrounded him. ... Ez 1:27
the LORD will be my /.... Mi 7:8
You are the / of the world.... Mt 5:14
your whole body will be full of /... Mt 6:22
yoke is easy and my burden is /.... Mt 11:30
his clothes became as white as the /... Mt
17:2
and the moon will not give its /; ... Mt 24:29
those who come in can see the /.... Lk 8:16
and that life was the / of men.... Jn 1:4
The true / that gives / ... Jn 1:9
but men loved darkness instead of /... Jn 3:19
he said, "I am the / of the world.... Jn 8:12
Walk while you have the /, ... Jn 12:35
I have come into the world as a /, ... Jn 12:46
I have made you a / ... Acts 13:47
darkness and put on the armor of /.... Rom
13:12
made his / shine in our hearts ... 2 Cor 4:6
Or what fellowship can / have ... 2 Cor 6:14
masquerades as an angel of /.... 2 Cor 11:14
You are all sons of the / ... 1 Thes 5:5
and who lives in unapproachable /... 1 Tm
6:16
of darkness into his wonderful /.... 1 Pt 2:9
as to a / shining in a dark place, ... 2 Pt 1:19
God is /; in him there is no ... 1 Jn 1:5
But if we walk in the /, ... 1 Jn 1:7
Anyone who claims to be in the /... 1 Jn 2:9
for the glory of God gives it /, ... Rv 21:23

LIGHTNING *the flash of light produced by a
discharge of atmospheric electricity*
and / flashed down to the ground.... Ex 9:23
with hailstones and bolts of /.... Ps 18:12
it was bright, and / flashed out of it. ... Ez 1:13
his face like /, his eyes like flaming ... Dn 10:6
For as the / that comes from the east ...
Mt 24:27

I saw Satan fall like / from heaven.... Lk 10:18
From the throne came flashes of /, ... Rv 4:5

LIKENESS *similarity, resemblance*
man in our image, in our /, ... Gn 1:26
I will be satisfied with seeing your / ...
Ps 17:15
his form marred beyond human /... Is 52:14
Son in the / of sinful man ... Rom 8:3
to be conformed to the / of his Son, ... Rom
8:29
his / with ever-increasing glory, ... 2 Cor 3:18
being made in human /.... Phil 2:7
who have been made in God's /.... Jas 3:9

LIMIT *boundary; end*
his understanding has no /.... Ps 147:5
for God gives the Spirit without /.... Jn 3:34

LIPS *folds of flesh surrounding the mouth*
From the / of children and infants ... Ps 8:2
his praise will always be on my /.... Ps 34:1
May my / overflow with praise, ... Ps 119:171
the poison of vipers is on their /.... Ps 140:3
keep watch over the door of my /.... Ps 141:3
on the / of the discerning, ... Prv 10:13
who conceals his hatred has lying /, ... Prv
10:18
/ of the righteous know what is ... Prv 10:32
He who guards his / guards his life, ... Prv 13:3
honest answer is like a kiss on the /.... Prv
24:26
are fervent / with an evil heart.... Prv 26:23
For I am a man of unclean /, ... Is 6:5
with foreign / and strange tongues ... Is 28:11
and honor me with their /, ... Is 29:13
From the / of children ... Mt 21:16
The poison of vipers is on their /.... Rom 3:13
and filthy language from your /.... Col 3:8
the fruit of / that confess his name.... Heb
13:15
and his / from deceitful speech.... 1 Pt 3:10

LISTEN(ED)(ING)(S) *to hear; to pay attention*
/ to his voice, and hold fast to him.... Dt 30:20
Speak, LORD, for your servant is / ... 1 Sm 3:9
came to / to Solomon's wisdom, ... 1 Kgs 4:34
And all the people / attentively ... Neh 8:3
but a wise man / to advice.... Prv 12:15
He who answers before / ... Prv 18:13
when I spoke, no one /.... Is 66:4
And whether they / or fail to / ... Ez 2:5
We have not / to your servants ... Dn 9:6
earth to / to Solomon's wisdom, ... Mt 12:42
Son, whom I love. L to him!" ... Mk 9:7
at the Lord's feet / to what he said. ... Lk
10:39
My sheep / to my voice; ... Jn 10:27
you must / to everything he tells ... Acts 3:22
Everyone should be quick to /, ... Jas 1:19
Do not merely / to the word, ... Jas 1:22
whoever knows God / to us; ... 1 Jn 4:6
not from God does not / to us.... 1 Jn 4:6

LIVE(S), LIVING *to be alive or come to life; to
endure a period of time; to gain eternal life; see
LIFE*
and the man became a / being.... Gn 2:7
tree of life and eat, and / forever.... Gn 3:22
so that you may / long ... Ex 20:12
for no one may see me and /.... Ex 33:20
who is bitten can look at it and /.... Nm 21:8
as you / by keeping all his decrees ... Dt 6:2
to teach you that man does not / ... Dt 8:3
If a man dies, will he / again? ... Jb 14:14
I know that my Redeemer /, ... Jb 19:25
Who may / on your holy hill? ... Ps 15:1
the world, and all who / in it; ... Ps 24:1
Let me / that I may praise you, ... Ps 119:175
Better to / on a corner of the roof ... Prv 21:9
a / dog is better off than a dead lion ... Eccl 9:4
But your dead will /; ... Is 26:19
cut off from the land of the /; ... Is 53:8
hear me, that your soul may /.... Is 55:3

he who / forever, whose name is holy ...
Is 57:15
the spring of / water, ... Jer 2:13
what looked like four / creatures.... Ez 1:5
LORD says: As surely as I /, ... Ez 17:19
can these bones /?" I said, ... Ez 37:3
Seek the LORD and /, ... Am 5:6
but the righteous will / by his faith ... Hb 2:4
I will / among you and you will... Zec 2:11
On that day / water will flow out ... Zec 14:8
Man does not / on bread alone, ... Mt 4:4
the God of the dead but of the /.... Mt 22:32
I am the / bread that came ... Jn 6:51
streams of / water will flow ... Jn 7:38
for he / with you and will be in you. ... Jn 14:17
Because I /, you also will /.... Jn 14:19
does not / in temples built by hands ... Acts
17:24
For in him we / and move ... Acts 17:28
The righteous will / by faith.... Rom 1:17
but the life he /, he / to God.... Rom 6:10
I know that nothing good / in me, ... Rom 7:18
if the Spirit of God / in you.... Rom 8:9
to offer your bodies as / sacrifices, ... Rom
12:1
For none of us / to himself alone ... Rom 14:7
We / by faith, not by sight. ... 2 Cor 5:7
I will / with them and walk ... 2 Cor 6:16
The life I / in the body, I / by faith ... Gal 2:20
Since we / by the Spirit, let us keep ... Gal 5:25
to / is Christ and to die is gain.... Phil 1:21
order that you may / a life worthy ... Col 1:10
we instructed you how to / in order ... 1 Thes
4:1
L in peace with each other.... 1 Thes 5:13
who wants to / a godly life ... 2 Tm 3:12
and to / self-controlled, upright ... Ti 2:12
For the word of God is / and active.... Heb 4:12
but because Jesus / forever, ... Heb 7:24
to fall into the hands of the / God.... Heb 10:31
But my righteous one will / by faith ... Heb
10:38
Make every effort to / in peace ... Heb 12:14
/ your lives as strangers here ... 1 Pt 1:17
through the / and enduring word ... 1 Pt 1:23
/ in harmony with one another; ... 1 Pt 3:8
Whoever / in love / in God, ... 1 Jn 4:16
I am the L One; I was dead, ... Rv 1:18
the throne, were four / creatures, ... Rv 4:6
to springs of / water.... Rv 7:17

LONELY *unhappy from being alone*
God sets the / in families, ... Ps 68:6
Jesus often withdrew to / places ... Lk 5:16

LONG(ED)(ING)(INGS)(S) *to earnestly desire;
the content of such desire; extending a considerable distance*
with /, and a despairing heart.... Dt 28:65
How / will you waver ... 1 Kgs 18:21
my body / for you, ... Ps 63:1
the / of the wicked will come ... Ps 112:10
My soul is consumed with /... Ps 119:20
I meditate on it all day /... Ps 119:97
/ for your commands.... Ps 119:131
I / for your salvation, O LORD, ... Ps 119:174
my spirit faints with /... Ps 143:7
but a / fulfilled is a tree of life. ... Prv 13:12
in the morning my spirit / for you.... Is 26:9
Yet the LORD / to be gracious ... Is 30:18
look on these things with /... Ez 23:27
I / to redeem them ... Hos 7:13
righteous men / to see what you see ...
Mt 13:17
how often I have /... Mt 23:37
The bridegroom was a / time ... Mt 25:5
and / to eat what fell from the rich ... Lk 16:21
As / as it is day, we must do ... Jn 9:4
since I have been / for many years ... Rom
15:23
that if a man has / hair, ... 1 Cor 11:14
/ to be clothed with our heavenly ... 2 Cor 5:2

to grasp how wide and / and high . . . Eph 3:18
God can testify how I / for all . . . Phil 1:8
to all who have / for his appearing. . . . 2 Tm 4:8
they were / for a better country . . . Heb 11:16
Even angels / to look . . . 1 Pt 1:12

LOOK(ED)(ING)(S) *to use the sense of sight; to
expect; to anticipate with pleasure; to explore*
Lot's wife / back, and she became . . . Gn 19:26
anyone who is bitten can / at it . . . Nm 21:8
Kadesh Barnea to / over the land. . . . Nm 32:8
you will find him if you / for him . . . Dt 4:29
because they had / into the ark . . . 1 Sm 6:19
is on everyone who / to him, . . . Ezr 8:22
not to / lustfully at a girl. . . . Jb 31:1
Those who / to him are radiant; . . . Ps 34:5
who / at the earth, and it trembles; . . .
    Ps 104:32
who stoops down to / . . . Ps 113:6
My eyes fail, I / for your promise; . . . Ps 119:82
As the eyes of slaves / to the hand . . . Ps 123:2
on high, he / upon the lowly, . . . Ps 138:6
they will / for me but will not find . . . Prv 1:28
Let your eyes / straight ahead, . . . Prv 4:25
A cheerful / brings joy to the heart, . . . Prv
    15:30
I / for the one my heart loves; . . . Song 3:1
do not / to the Holy One of Israel, . . . Is 31:1
Lift your eyes and / to the heavens: . . . Is 40:26
Then you will / and be radiant, . . . Is 60:5
Yet you have the brazen / . . . Jer 3:3
I / for a man among them who . . . Ez 22:30
for my sheep and / after them. . . . Ez 34:11
I / and saw the glory . . . Ez 44:4
I / up and there before me was . . . Dn 10:5
Your eyes are too pure to / on evil; . . . Hb 1:13
he I, and made the nations tremble. . . . Hb 3:6
They will / on me, the one they . . . Zec 12:10
See that you do not / down on one . . . Mt 18:10
which / beautiful on the outside . . . Mt 23:27
'L, here is the Christ!' or, 'L, . . . Mk 13:21
You are / for Jesus the Nazarene. . . . Mk 16:6
Why do you / at the speck . . . Lk 6:41
and / back is fit for service . . . Lk 9:62
L at my hands and my feet. . . . Lk 24:39
he said, "L, the Lamb of God!" . . . Jn 1:36
open your eyes and / at the fields! . . . Jn 4:35
why do you / down on your brother . . . Rom
    14:10
You are / only on the surface . . . 2 Cor 10:7
Each of you should / not only . . . Phil 2:4
For everyone / out . . . Phil 2:21
Not that I am / for a gift, . . . Phil 4:17
We were not / for praise from men, . . . 1 Thes
    2:6
Don't let anyone / down on you . . . 1 Tm 4:12
But the man who / intently . . . Jas 1:25
long to / into these things. . . . 1 Pt 1:12
as you / forward to the day of God . . . 2 Pt 3:12
I saw a Lamb, / as if it had been . . . Rv 5:6

LOOSE *to set free; to forgive*
Your rigging hangs l: . . . Is 33:23
and whatever you / on earth will be . . . Mt 16:19
and whatever you / on earth will be . . . Mt 18:18

LOSE(S), LOSS, LOST *to no longer possess;
beyond reach; ruined physically or morally; lacking eternal salvation*
Our brothers have made us / heart. . . . Dt 1:28
I had nearly / my foothold. . . . Ps 73:2
Do not / heart because of these two . . . Is 7:4
My people have been / sheep; . . . Jer 50:6
for the / and bring back the strays. . . . Ez 34:16
But if the salt / its saltiness, . . . Mt 5:13
Whoever finds his life will / it, . . . Mt 10:39
and yet / or forfeit his very self? . . . Lk 9:25
you has a hundred sheep and / one . . . Lk 15:4
has ten silver coins and / one. . . . Lk 15:8
is alive again; he was / and is found . . . Lk 15:24
to seek and to save what was l. . . . Lk 19:10
he will suffer l; he himself will be . . . 1 Cor 3:15

Therefore we do not / heart. . . . 2 Cor 4:16
I consider everything a / compared . . . Phil 3:8
will not grow weary and / heart. . . . Heb 12:3
that you do not / what you have . . . 2 Jn 1:8

LOTS *small stones or other devices used for
making choices, in process similar to throwing
dice or drawing straws*
Joshua then cast / for them . . . Jos 18:10
and cast / for my clothing. . . . Ps 22:18
They cast / for my people . . . Jl 3:3
divided up his clothes by casting l. . . . Mt 27:35
Then they cast l, and the lot fell . . . Acts 1:26

LOVE(D)(S), LOVING *strong affection, desire,
or devotion*
This is how you can show your / . . . Gn 20:13
showing / to a thousand generations . . . Ex 20:6
but / your neighbor as yourself. . . . Lv 19:18
Because he / your forefathers . . . Dt 4:37
generations of those who / him . . . Dt 7:9
and / the alien, giving him food . . . Dt 10:18
L the LORD your God . . . Dt 11:1
because the LORD your God / you . . . Dt 23:5
to / the LORD your God, to walk . . . Jos 22:5
You hate me! You don't really / me . . . Jgs
    14:16
he fell in / with a woman . . . Jgs 16:4
"How can you say, 'I / you,' . . . Jgs 16:15
who / you and who is better to you . . . Ru 4:15
Your / for me was wonderful, . . . 2 Sm 1:26
You / those who hate you . . . 2 Sm 19:6
of the LORD's eternal / for Israel, . . . 1 Kgs 10:9
/ many foreign women . . . 1 Kgs 11:1
his / endures forever. . . . 1 Chr 16:34
I will never take my / away . . . 1 Chr 17:13
Remember the great / promised . . . 2 Chr 6:42
Because of the / of your God . . . 2 Chr 9:8
for his / endures forever. . . . 2 Chr 20:21
slow to anger and abounding in l. . . . Neh 9:17
or to water his earth and show his l. . . .
    Jb 37:13
save me because of your unfailing l. . . . Ps 6:4
Surely goodness and / will follow . . . Ps 23:6
I / the house where you live, . . . Ps 26:8
I will be glad and rejoice in your l, . . . Ps 31:7
Whoever of you / life . . . Ps 34:12
Your l, O LORD, reaches . . . Ps 36:5
may those who / your salvation . . . Ps 40:16
You / righteousness and hate . . . Ps 45:7
You / evil rather than good, . . . Ps 52:3
God sends his / and his faithfulness . . . Ps 57:3
in the morning I will sing of your l; . . . Ps 59:16
Because your / is better than life, . . . Ps 63:3
or withheld his / from me! . . . Ps 66:20
Mount Zion, which he l. . . . Ps 78:68
L and faithfulness meet together; . . . Ps 85:10
the LORD / the gates of Zion . . . Ps 87:2
Is your / declared in the grave, . . . Ps 88:11
declare that your / stands firm . . . Ps 89:2
I will maintain my / to him forever, . . . Ps 89:28
slow to anger, abounding in l. . . . Ps 103:8
and out of his great / he relented. . . . Ps 106:45
to the LORD for his unfailing / . . . Ps 107:8
I / the LORD, for he heard my voice . . . Ps 116:1
The earth is filled with your l, . . . Ps 119:64
Oh, how I / your law! . . . Ps 119:97
to those who / your name. . . . Ps 119:132
for he grants sleep to those he l. . . . Ps 127:2
for with the LORD is unfailing / . . . Ps 130:7
He is my / God and my fortress, . . . Ps 144:2
and / toward all he has made. . . . Ps 145:13
the LORD disciplines those he l, . . . Prv 3:12
you ever be captivated by her l. . . . Prv 5:19
let's drink deep of / till morning; . . . Prv 7:18
rebuke a wise man and he will / you . . . Prv 9:8
/ covers over all wrongs. . . . Prv 10:12
Whoever / discipline / knowledge, . . . Prv 12:1
of vegetables where there is / Prv 15:17
A friend / at all times, . . . Prv 17:17
Do not / sleep or you will grow poor . . . Prv
    20:13

He who / pleasure will become poor . . . Prv
    21:17
A man who / wisdom brings joy . . . Prv 29:3
a time to / and a time to hate, . . . Eccl 3:8
Whoever / money never has money . . . Eccl
    5:10
his banner over me is l. . . . Song 2:4
Tell him I am faint with l. . . . Song 5:8
Many waters cannot quench l; . . . Song 8:7
In your / you kept me from the pit . . . Is 38:17
to / the name of the LORD, . . . Is 56:6
For I, the LORD, / justice; . . . Is 61:8
how as a bride you / me . . . Jer 2:2
I / foreign gods, . . . Jer 2:25
They greatly / to wander; . . . Jer 14:10
so great is his unfailing l. . . . Lam 3:32
saw that you were old enough for l, . . . Ez 16:8
more than one who sings / songs . . . Ez 33:32
Go, show your / to your wife again, . . . Hos 3:1
Your / is like the morning mist, . . . Hos 6:4
you / the wages of a prostitute . . . Hos 9:1
When Israel was a child, I / him, . . . Hos 11:1
you who hate good and / evil; . . . Mi 3:2
he will quiet you with his l, . . . Zep 3:17
This is my Son, whom I l; . . . Mt 3:17
L your neighbor and hate your . . . Mt 5:43
L the Lord your God . . . Mt 22:37
L your neighbor as yourself. . . . Mt 22:39
the / of most will grow cold, . . . Mt 24:12
so / the world that he gave his one . . . Jn 3:16
reason my Father / me is that I lay . . . Jn 10:17
Lord, the one you / is sick. . . . Jn 11:3
The man who / his life will lose it, . . . Jn 12:25
disciples, if you / one another. . . . Jn 13:35
If you / me, you will obey what I . . . Jn 14:15
This is my command: L each other. . . .
    Jn 15:17
have / them even as you have / me. . . . Jn 17:23
because God has poured out his / . . . Rom 5:5
for the good of those who / him, . . . Rom 8:28
L must be sincere. . . . Rom 12:9
L your neighbor as yourself. . . . Rom 13:9
prepared for those who / him . . . 1 Cor 2:9
Knowledge puffs up, but / builds up . . . 1 Cor
    8:1
L is patient, / is kind. . . . 1 Cor 13:4
But the greatest of these is / . . . 1 Cor 13:13
Do everything in l. . . . 1 Cor 16:14
to let you know the depth of my / . . . 2 Cor 2:4
For Christ's / compels us, . . . 2 Cor 5:14
who / me and gave himself for me. . . . Gal 2:20
is faith expressing itself through l. . . . Gal 5:6
rather, serve one another in l. . . . Gal 5:13
But the fruit of the Spirit is l, joy, . . . Gal 5:22
being rooted and established in l, . . . Eph 3:17
and to know this / that surpasses . . . Eph 3:19
bearing with one another in l. . . . Eph 4:2
/ your wives, just as Christ loved . . . Eph 5:25
who / us and by his grace gave us . . . 2 Thes
    2:16
in life, in l, in faith and in purity. . . . 1 Tm 4:12
For the / of money is a root . . . 1 Tm 6:10
unholy, without l, unforgiving, . . . 2 Tm 3:3
faith, patience, l, endurance, . . . 2 Tm 3:10
women to / their husbands . . . Ti 2:4
may spur one another on toward / . . . Heb
    10:24
the Lord disciplines those he l, . . . Heb 12:6
you have not seen him, you / him; . . . 1 Pt 1:8
/ one another deeply, . . . 1 Pt 1:22
L the brotherhood of believers, . . . 1 Pt 2:17
Whoever would / life . . . 1 Pt 3:10
/ covers over a multitude of sins. . . . 1 Pt 4:8
and to brotherly kindness, l. . . . 2 Pt 1:7
God's / is truly made complete . . . 1 Jn 2:5
Do not / the world or anything . . . 1 Jn 2:15
How great is the / the Father has . . . 1 Jn 3:1
God is l. . . . 1 Jn 4:16
There is no fear in l. . . . 1 Jn 4:18
We / because he first loved us. . . . 1 Jn 4:19
You have forsaken your first l. . . . Rv 2:4

LOVELY *having pleasing or attractive qualities; beautiful; inspiring love*
but Rachel was *l* in form, . . . Gn 29:17
and nobles, for she was *l* to look at. . . . Est 1:11
How *l* is your dwelling place, . . . Ps 84:1
Dark am I, yet *l*, . . . Song 1:5
he is altogether *l*. . . . Song 5:16
l as Jerusalem, . . . Song 6:4
l young women and strong young . . . Am 8:13
whatever is *l*, whatever is . . . Phil 4:8

LOVER(S) *one who loves, especially in a one-to-one relationship*
My *l* is to me a sachet of myrrh . . . Song 1:13
is my *l* among the young men. . . . Song 2:3
My *l* is mine and I am his; . . . Song 2:16
Let my *l* come into his garden . . . Song 4:16
drink your fill, O *l*. . . . Song 5:1
if you find my *l*, . . . Song 5:8
Where has your *l* gone, . . . Song 6:1
that I have stored up for you, my *l*. . . . Song 7:13
leaning on her *l?* . . . Song 8:5
Come away, my *l*, . . . Song 8:14
as a prostitute with many *l* . . . Jer 3:1
Your *l* despise you; . . . Jer 4:30
Among all her *l* . . . Lam 1:2
but you give gifts to all your *l*, . . . Ez 16:33
she lusted after her *l*, the Assyrians . . . Ez 23:5
I handed her over to her *l*, . . . Ez 23:9
I will stir up your *l* against you, . . . Ez 23:22
She said, 'I will go after my *l*, . . . Hos 2:5
lewdness before the eyes of her *l*; . . . Hos 2:10
Ephraim has sold herself to *l*. . . . Hos 8:9
not quarrelsome, not a *l* of money. . . . 1 Tm 3:3
People will be *l* of themselves, . . . 2 Tm 3:2

LOWLY *humble, meek, of low social status*
The *l* he sets on high, . . . Jb 5:11
on high, he looks upon the *l*, . . . Ps 138:6
but a man of *l* spirit gains honor. . . . Prv 29:23
also with him who is contrite and *l*. . . Is 57:15
He chose the *l* things of this world . . . 1 Cor 1:28

LUST(S) *inappropriate and excessive desire or craving*
Do not *l* in your heart . . . Prv 6:25
God gave them over to shameful *l*. . . . Rom 1:26
not in passionate *l* like the heathen, . . . 1 Thes 4:5
in debauchery, *l*, drunkenness, . . . 1 Pt 4:3
the *l* of his eyes and the boasting . . . 1 Jn 2:16

MADE, MAKE(S), MAKING *to create, prepare, or fashion; to bring about; see CREATE*
So God *m* the expanse . . . Gn 1:7
God saw all that he had *m*, . . . Gn 1:31
I will *m* a helper suitable for him. . . . Gn 2:18
was grieved that he had *m* man . . . Gn 6:6
m yourself an ark of cypress wood; . . . Gn 6:14
that day the LORD *m* a covenant . . . Gn 15:18
six days the LORD *m* the heavens . . . Ex 20:11
who *m* you and formed you? . . . Dt 32:6
You have *m* heaven and earth. . . . 2 Kgs 19:15
the God of Israel, who *m* heaven . . . 2 Chr 2:12
You *m* the heavens, . . . Neh 9:6
of the LORD were the heavens *m*, . . . Ps 33:6
The sea is his, for he *m* it, . . . Ps 95:5
but the LORD *m* the heavens. . . . Ps 96:5
It is he who *m* us, and we are his; . . . Ps 100:3
This is the day the LORD has *m*; . . . Ps 118:24
who *m* the great lights . . . Ps 136:7
I am fearfully and wonderfully *m*; . . . Ps 139:14
He has *m* everything beautiful . . . Eccl 3:11
It is I who *m* the earth . . . Is 45:12
he who fashioned and *m* the earth, . . . Is 45:18
Has not my hand *m* all these things . . . Is 66:2
But God *m* the earth by his power; . . . Jer 10:12
and outstretched arm I *m* the earth . . . Jer 27:5
you have *m* the heavens . . . Jer 32:17

LORD says, he who *m* the earth, . . . Jer 33:2
He *m* the earth by his power; . . . Jer 51:15
(he who *m* the Pleiades and Orion, . . . Am 5:8
who *m* the sea and the land. . . . Jon 1:9
Through him all things were *m*; . . . Jn 1:3
The God who *m* the world . . . Acts 17:24
through whom he *m* the universe. . . . Heb 1:2
it that you *m* everything according . . . Heb 8:5
Worship him who *m* the heavens, . . . Rv 14:7

MAJESTIC, MAJESTY *grand; greatness or splendor of character; the sovereignty and power of God; a title used in speaking of or to a sovereign monarch*
In the greatness of your *m* . . . Ex 15:7
has shown us his glory and his *m*, . . . Dt 5:24
In *m* he is like a firstborn bull; . . . Dt 33:17
and on the clouds in his *m*. . . . Dt 33:26
Splendor and *m* are before him; . . . 1 Chr 16:27
if it pleases your *m*, grant me my . . . Est 7:3
he thunders with his *m* voice. . . . Jb 37:4
and clothe yourself in honor and *m* . . . Jb 40:10
how *m* is your name in all the earth . . . Ps 8:1
the voice of the LORD is *m*. . . . Ps 29:4
In your *m* ride forth victoriously . . . Ps 45:4
whose *m* is over Israel, . . . Ps 68:34
more *m* than mountains rich . . . Ps 76:4
The LORD reigns, he is robed in *m* . . . Ps 93:1
clothed with splendor and *m*. . . . Ps 104:1
Arrayed in holy *m*, . . . Ps 110:3
of the glorious splendor of your *m*, . . . Ps 145:5
m as troops with banners. . . . Song 6:4
m as the stars in procession? . . . Song 6:10
and the splendor of his *m!* . . . Is 2:10
west they acclaim the LORD's *m*. . . . Is 24:14
and regard not the *m* of the LORD. . . . Is 26:10
men to hear his *m* voice . . . Is 30:30
or *m* to attract us to him, . . . Is 53:2
can be compared with you in *m?* . . . Ez 31:2
and for the glory of my *m?* . . . Dn 4:30
and he will be clothed with *m* . . . Zec 6:13
will be robbed of her divine . . . Acts 19:27
to write to His *M* about him. . . . Acts 25:26
and from the *m* of his power . . . 2 Thes 1:9
hand of the *M* in heaven. . . . Heb 1:3
of the throne of the *M* in heaven, . . . Heb 8:1
but we were eyewitnesses of his *m*. . . . 2 Pt 1:16
only God our Savior be glory, *m*, . . . Jude 1:25

MAKER *God; see CREATOR*
Can a man be more pure than his *M* . . . Jb 4:17
He is the *M* of the Bear and Orion, . . . Jb 9:9
my *M* would soon take me away. . . . Jb 32:22
no one says, 'Where is God my *M*, . . . Jb 35:10
kneel before the LORD our *M*; . . . Ps 95:6
the *M* of heaven and earth. . . . Ps 115:15
Let Israel rejoice in their *M*; . . . Ps 149:2
poor shows contempt for their *M*, . . . Prv 14:31
The LORD is the *M* of them all. . . . Prv 22:2
the *M* of all things. . . . Eccl 11:5
so their *M* has no compassion . . . Is 27:11
to him who quarrels with his *M*, . . . Is 45:9
the Holy One of Israel, and its *M*: . . . Is 45:11
For your *M* is your husband . . . Is 54:5
for he is the *M* of all things, . . . Jer 10:16
Israel has forgotten his *M*. . . . Hos 8:14

MALICE *hatred; ill will; malevolence*
adultery, greed, *m*, deceit, . . . Mk 7:22
murder, strife, deceit and *m*. . . . Rom 1:29
the yeast of *m* and wickedness, . . . 1 Cor 5:8
along with every form of *m*. . . . Eph 4:31
m, slander, and filthy language . . . Col 3:8
rid yourselves of all *m* . . . 1 Pt 2:1

MAN(KIND)('S), MEN('S) *the entire human race; also can refer to an adult human male*
Let us make *m* in our image, . . . Gn 1:26
God formed the *m* from the dust . . . Gn 2:7
God took the *m* and put . . . Gn 2:15
for the *m* to be alone . . . Gn 2:18
she was taken out of *m*. . . . Gn 2:23

daughter of *m* were beautiful, . . . Gn 6:2
grieved that he had made *m* . . . Gn 6:6
Whoever sheds the blood of *m*, . . . Gn 9:6
m does not live on bread . . . Dt 8:3
a *m* after his own heart . . . 1 Sm 13:14
he is not a *m* that he . . . 1 Sm 15:29
at the things *m* looks at. . . . 1 Sm 16:7
M born of woman is of few . . . Jb 14:1
If a *m* dies, will he live . . . Jb 14:14
Blessed is the *m* who does . . . Ps 1:1
nations know they are but *m*. . . . Ps 9:20
Blessed is the *m* whose sin . . . Ps 32:2
and sees all *m*; . . . Ps 33:13
Blessed is the *m* who makes . . . Ps 40:4
As for *m*, his days are like grass . . . Ps 103:15
Blessed is the *m* who fears . . . Ps 112:1
can a young *m* keep his . . . Ps 119:9
Blessed is the *m* whose quiver . . . Ps 127:5
Blessed is the *m* who finds . . . Prv 3:13
that seems right to a *m*, . . . Prv 14:12
A *m* steps are directed by . . . Prv 20:24
way of a *m* with a maiden. . . . Prv 30:19
and all *m* together will see it. . . . Is 40:5
a *m* of sorrows, . . . Is 53:3
I looked for a *m* . . . Ez 22:30
M does not live on bread . . . Mt 4:4
will make you fishers of *m* . . . Mt 4:19
your light shine before *m* . . . Mt 5:16
if you forgive *m* when . . . Mt 6:14
acknowledges me before *m* . . . Mt 10:32
a *m* will leave his father . . . Mt 19:5
are but rules taught by *m*. . . . Mk 7:7
And all *m* will see God's salvation . . . Lk 3:6
Blessed are you when *m* . . . Lk 6:22
life was the light of *m*. . . . Jn 1:4
m loved darkness instead . . . Jn 3:19
will draw all *m* to myself . . . Jn 12:32
all *m* will know that you . . . Jn 13:35
obey God rather than *m!* . . . Acts 5:29
entered the world through one *m* . . . Rom 5:12
is wiser than *m* wisdom, . . . 1 Cor 1:25
not rest on *m* wisdom, . . . 1 Cor 2:5
spiritual *m* makes judgments . . . 1 Cor 2:15
all things to all *m* . . . 1 Cor 9:22
head of every *m* is Christ, . . . 1 Cor 11:3
tongues of *m* and of angels . . . 1 Cor 13:1
When I became a *m*, . . . 1 Cor 13:11
death came through a *m*, . . . 1 Cor 15:21
first *m* Adam became a . . . 1 Cor 15:45
we try to persuade *m*. . . . 2 Cor 5:11
sent not from *m* nor by *m* . . . Gal 1:1
create in himself one new *m* . . . Eph 2:15
and gave gifts to *m*. . . . Eph 4:8
a *m* will leave his father . . . Eph 5:31
found in appearance as a *m*, . . . Phil 2:8
wants all *m* to be saved . . . 1 Tm 2:4
younger *m* as brothers . . . 1 Tm 5:2
entrust to reliable *m* . . . 2 Tm 2:2
has appeared to all *m* . . . Ti 2:11
that the *m* of God may be . . . 2 Tm 3:17
what is *m* that you are . . . Heb 2:6
is selected from among *m* . . . Heb 5:1
as *m* is destined to die . . . Heb 9:27
but *m* spoke from God . . . 2 Pt 1:21
dwelling of God is with *m*, . . . Rv 21:3

MANNA *miraculous food supply given to Israel in the wilderness, symbolic of spiritual nourishment*
people of Israel called the bread *m*. . . . Ex 16:31
He gave you *m* to eat in the desert, . . . Dt 8:16
Your forefathers ate the *m* . . . Jn 6:49
I will give some of the hidden *m* . . . Rv 2:17

MARKETPLACE(S) *central area in ancient cities where business was transacted*
they love to be greeted in the *m* . . . Mt 23:7
are like children sitting in the *m* . . . Lk 7:32

MARRIAGE *the state of being married; see MARRIED*
neither marry nor be given in *m*; . . . Mt 22:30

marrying and giving in *m*, . . . Mt 24:38
she is released from the law of *m*. . . . Rom 7:2
by all, and the *m* bed kept pure, . . . Heb 13:4

MARRIED, MARRIES, MARRY *united in wedlock; figurative of any close union (often with God); see MARRIAGE*
happiness to the wife he has *m*. . . . Dt 24:5
brother shall take her and *m* her . . . Dt 25:5
you have *m* foreign women, . . . Ezr 10:10
an unloved woman who is *m*, . . . Prv 30:23
anyone who *m* the divorced woman . . . Mt 5:32
and *m* another woman commits . . . Mt 19:9
resurrection people will neither *m* . . . Mt 22:30
It is good for a man not to *m*. . . . 1 Cor 7:1
control themselves, they should *m*, . . . 1 Cor 7:9
Are you *m*? Do not seek a divorce. . . . 1 Cor 7:27
But a *m* man is concerned about . . . 1 Cor 7:33
They forbid people to *m* . . . 1 Tm 4:3

MARVEL(ED)(ING), MARVELOUS *to express wonder or amazement*
his *m* deeds among all peoples. . . . 1 Chr 16:24
God's voice thunders in *m* ways; . . . Jb 37:5
who alone does *m* deeds. . . . Ps 72:18
and it is *m* in our eyes. . . . Ps 118:23
but will it seem *m* to me? . . . Zec 8:6
and it is *m* in our eyes'? . . . Mt 21:42
mother *m* at what was said about . . . Lk 2:33
While everyone was *m* . . . Lk 9:43
and to be *m* at among all those who . . . 2 Thes 1:10
in heaven another great and *m* sign . . . Rv 15:1
Great and *m* are your deeds, . . . Rv 15:3

MASTER(ED)(S) *one in authority or leadership; employer; teacher; lord or Lord; to exercise control over*
to have you, but you must *m* it. . . . Gn 4:7
he refreshes the spirit of his *m*. . . . Prv 25:13
you will no longer call me 'my *m*.' . . . Hos 2:16
No one can serve two *m*. . . . Mt 6:24
nor a servant above his *m*. . . . Mt 10:24
that servant whose *m* finds him . . . Mt 24:46
"His *m* replied, 'Well done, . . . Mt 25:21
For sin shall not be your *m*, . . . Rom 6:14
To his own *m* he stands or falls. . . . Rom 14:4
but I will not be *m* by anything. . . . 1 Cor 6:12
obey your earthly *m* with respect . . . Eph 6:5
you know that you also have a *M* . . . Col 4:1
useful to the *M* and prepared . . . 2 Tm 2:21
subject to their *m* in everything, . . . Ti 2:9
a slave to whatever has *m* him. . . . 2 Pt 2:19

MATURE, MATURITY *fully developed, physically, mentally, emotionally, or spiritually*
and pleasures, and they do not *m*. . . . Lk 8:14
a message of wisdom among the *m*, . . . 1 Cor 2:6
of us who are *m* should take such . . . Phil 3:15
firm in all the will of God, *m* . . . Col 4:12
But solid food is for the *m*, . . . Heb 5:14
about Christ and go on to *m*, . . . Heb 6:1
work so that you may be *m* . . . Jas 1:4

MEANINGLESS *lacking any apparent purpose; see VAIN*
"*M! M!*" says the Teacher. . . . Eccl 1:2
from these and turned to *m* talk. . . . 1 Tm 1:6

MEASURE(D)(S) *a basis or standard for comparison; to gauge or regulate the specific dimensions of; due portion*
Do not have two differing *m* . . . Dt 25:14
though I know not its *m*. . . . Ps 71:15
Who has *m* the waters . . . Is 40:12
if the heavens above can be *m* . . . Jer 31:37
A good *m*, pressed down . . . Lk 6:38
to the *m* of all the fullness of God. . . . Eph 3:19
to the whole *m* of the fullness . . . Eph 4:13
Go and *m* the temple of God . . . Rv 11:1

MEDIATOR *one who intercedes between opposing parties*
and one *m* between God and men, . . . 1 Tm 2:5
of which he is *m* is superior . . . Heb 8:6
For this reason Christ is the *m* . . . Heb 9:15
to Jesus the *m* of a new covenant, . . . Heb 12:24

MEDITATE(S), MEDITATION *to contemplate; to think deeply about*
and on his law he *m* day and night. . . . Ps 1:2
of my mouth and the *m* of my heart . . . Ps 19:14
we *m* on your unfailing love. . . . Ps 48:9
I will *m* on all your works . . . Ps 77:12
May my *m* be pleasing to him, . . . Ps 104:34
I *m* on your precepts . . . Ps 119:15
then I will *m* on your wonders. . . . Ps 119:27
I *m* on it all day long. . . . Ps 119:97
that I may *m* on your promises. . . . Ps 119:148
I will *m* on your wonderful works. . . . Ps 145:5

MEDIUM *one through whom it is thought the dead communicate with the living*
A man or woman who is a *m* . . . Lv 20:27
"Find me a woman who is a *m*," . . . 1 Sm 28:7

MEET(ING)(S) *come together; encounter; satisfy; fulfill*
When can I go and *m* with God? . . . Ps 42:2
Love and faithfulness *m* together; . . . Ps 85:10
prepare to *m* your God, O Israel. . . . Am 4:12
them in the clouds to *m* the Lord . . . 1 Thes 4:17
Such a high priest *m* our need . . . Heb 7:26
Let us not give up *m* together, . . . Heb 10:25

MEEK(NESS) *gentle, humble*
But the *m* will inherit the land . . . Ps 37:11
the *m* and humble, . . . Zep 3:12
Blessed are the *m*, . . . Mt 5:5
By the *m* and gentleness of Christ, . . . 2 Cor 10:1

MEMBERS *parts of a larger whole such as a body or social group (often of the church)*
a man's enemies are the *m* . . . Mi 7:6
law at work in the *m* of my body, . . . Rom 7:23
of us has one body with many *m*, . . . Rom 12:4
not know that your bodies are *m* . . . 1 Cor 6:15
But God has combined the *m* . . . 1 Cor 12:24
m together of one body, . . . Eph 3:6
as *m* of one body you were called . . . Col 3:15

MERCIFUL, MERCY *forgiving; compassionate*
m on whom I will have *m*, . . . Ex 33:19
the LORD your God is a *m* God; . . . Dt 4:31
of the LORD, for his *m* is great; . . . 2 Sm 24:14
But in your great *m* you did not put . . . Neh 9:31
for he has heard my cry for *m*. . . . Ps 28:6
Have *m* on me, O God, have *m* . . . Ps 57:1
Has God forgotten to be *m*? . . . Ps 77:9
renounces them finds *m*. . . . Prv 28:13
and *m* he redeemed them; . . . Is 63:9
for I am *m*,' declares the LORD, . . . Jer 3:12
For I desire *m*, not sacrifice, . . . Hos 6:6
LORD God Almighty will have *m* . . . Am 5:15
To act justly and to love *m* . . . Mi 6:8
but delight to show *m*. . . . Mi 7:18
in wrath remember *m*. . . . Hb 3:2
show *m* and compassion . . . Zec 7:9
for they will be shown *m*. . . . Mt 5:7
'I desire *m*, not sacrifice,' you . . . Mt 12:7
Shouldn't you have had *m* . . . Mt 18:33
justice, *m* and faithfulness. . . . Mt 23:23
His *m* extends to those who fear . . . Lk 1:50
Be *m*, just as your Father is *m*. . . . Lk 6:36
I will have *m* on whom I have *m*, . . . Rom 9:15
so that he may have *m* on them all. . . . Rom 11:32
brothers, in view of God's *m*, . . . Rom 12:1
if it is showing *m*, let him do it . . . Rom 12:8
who is rich in *m*, made us alive . . . Eph 2:4

I was shown *m* because I acted . . . 1 Tm 1:13
we had done, but because of his *m*. . . . Ti 3:5
so that we may receive *m* . . . Heb 4:16
judgment without *m* will be shown . . . Jas 2:13
M triumphs over judgment! . . . Jas 2:13
full of compassion and *m*. . . . Jas 5:11
In his great *m* he has given us new . . . 1 Pt 1:3
once you had not received *m*, . . . 1 Pt 2:10
Be *m* to those who doubt; snatch . . . Jude 1:22

MESSAGE, MESSENGER *communication between two people or between God and humanity; one who brings a message*
Who has believed our *m* . . . Is 53:1
I will send my *m*, who will prepare . . . Mal 3:1
Lord, who has believed our *m*. . . . Jn 12:38
You know the *m* God sent . . . Acts 10:36
for they received the *m* . . . Acts 17:11
faith comes from hearing the *m*, . . . Rom 10:17
For the *m* of the cross is . . . 1 Cor 1:18
My *m* and my preaching were not . . . 1 Cor 2:4
to us the *m* of reconciliation. . . . 2 Cor 5:19
a *m* of Satan, to torment me. . . . 2 Cor 12:7
firmly to the trustworthy *m* . . . Ti 1:9
the *m* they heard was of no value . . . Heb 4:2
because they disobey the *m* . . . 1 Pt 2:8

MIGHT(Y) *strength, power, authority; very great, extraordinary; see POWER*
of the hand of the *M* One of Jacob, . . . Gn 49:24
of my *m* hand he will drive them . . . Ex 6:1
he brought you out with a *m* hand . . . Dt 7:8
the great God, *m* and awesome, . . . Dt 10:17
one has ever shown the *m* power . . . Dt 34:12
Then he pushed with all his *m*, . . . Jgs 16:30
How the *m* have fallen! . . . 2 Sm 1:19
with all their *m* before the LORD, . . . 2 Sm 6:5
the names of David's *m* men: . . . 2 Sm 23:8
Power and *m* are in your hand, . . . 2 Chr 20:6
the great, *m* and awesome God, . . . Neh 9:32
God is *m*, but does not despise men . . . Jb 36:5
we will sing and praise your *m*. . . . Ps 21:13
upon your side, O *m* one; . . . Ps 45:3
vindicate me by your *m*. . . . Ps 54:1
he is my *m* rock, my refuge. . . . Ps 62:7
who thunders with *m* voice. . . . Ps 68:33
proclaim your *m* acts, . . . Ps 71:16
The King is *m*, he loves justice . . . Ps 99:4
LORD will extend your *m* scepter . . . Ps 110:2
with a *m* hand and outstretched . . . Ps 136:12
they will tell of your *m* acts. . . . Ps 145:4
all men may know of your *m* acts . . . Ps 145:12
like a *m* flame. . . . Song 8:6
Wonderful Counselor, *M* God, . . . Is 9:6
your Redeemer, the *M* One . . . Is 60:16
m to save. . . . Is 63:1
Where are your zeal and your *m*? . . . Is 63:15
with me like a *m* warrior; . . . Jer 20:11
your purposes and *m* are your . . . Jer 32:19
I will rule over you with a *m* hand . . . Ez 20:33
he is *m* to save. . . . Zep 3:17
Not by *m* nor by power, . . . Zec 4:6
like the working of his *m* strength, . . . Eph 1:19
in the Lord and in his *m* power. . . . Eph 6:10
power according to his glorious *m* . . . Col 1:11
To him be honor and *m* forever. . . . 1 Tm 6:16
therefore, under God's *m* hand, . . . 1 Pt 5:6

MILK *liquid that female mammals feed their young; figurative of spiritual food, abundance, and salvation*
a land flowing with *m* and honey . . . Ex 3:8
a young goat in its mother's *m*. . . . Ex 23:19
as churning the *m* produces butter, . . . Prv 30:33
Come, buy wine and *m* . . . Is 55:1
I gave you *m*, not solid food, . . . 1 Cor 3:2
babies, crave pure spiritual *m*, . . . 1 Pt 2:2

MIND(ED)(FUL)(S) *human faculty of reflective thinking (often used of emotions as well)*
that he should change his *m*. . . . Nm 23:19
of mine in your hearts and *m*; . . . Dt 11:18

devotion and with a willing *m*, . . . 1 Chr 28:9
who searches *m* and hearts, . . . Ps 7:9
what is man that you are *m* of him, . . . Ps 8:4
examine my heart and my *m;* . . . Ps 26:2
and will not change his *m:* . . . Ps 110:4
him whose *m* is steadfast, . . . Is 26:3
I will put my law in their *m* . . . Jer 31:33
all your soul and with all your *m.* . . . Mt 22:37
God my Savior, for he has been *m* . . . Lk 1:48
Then he opened their *m* . . . Lk 24:45
believers were one in heart and *m.* . . . Acts 4:32
he gave them over to a depraved *m* . . . Rom 1:28
I myself in my *m* am a slave . . . Rom 7:25
to the sinful nature have their *m* set . . . Rom 8:5
by the renewing of your *m.* . . . Rom 12:2
you may be perfectly united in *m* . . . 1 Cor 1:10
no *m* has conceived . . . 1 Cor 2:9
spirit prays, but my *m* is unfruitful. . . . 1 Cor 14:14
god of this age has blinded the *m* . . . 2 Cor 4:4
be of one *m*, live in peace. . . . 2 Cor 13:11
new in the attitude of your *m;* . . . Eph 4:23
Their *m* is on earthly things. . . . Phil 3:19
Set your *m* on things above, . . . Col 3:2
to *m* your own business . . . 1 Thes 4:11
What is man that you are *m* of him, . . . Heb 2:6
and will not change his *m:* . . . Heb 7:21
I will put my laws in their *m* . . . Heb 8:10
prepare your *m* for action; . . . 1 Pt 1:13
be clear *m* and self-controlled . . . 1 Pt 4:7
I am he who searches hearts and *m*, . . .
   Rv 2:23

MINISTER(ING)(S), MINISTRY *one who
serves or assists someone else; exercise of
one's gifts and resources*
will *m* to me. . . . Ps 101:6
to prayer and the *m* of the word. . . . Acts 6:4
as *m* of a new covenant . . . 2 Cor 3:6
God's mercy we have this *m*, . . . 2 Cor 4:1
gave us the *m* of reconciliation: . . . 2 Cor 5:18
who was at work in the *m* of Peter . . . Gal 2:8
discharge all the duties of your *m* . . . 2 Tm 4:5
Are not all angels *m* spirits sent . . . Heb 1:14
But the *m* Jesus has received is . . . Heb 8:6

MIRACLE(S), MIRACULOUS *divine act unexplainable by the laws of nature; see SIGN,
WONDERS*
'Perform a *m*,' then say to Aaron, . . . Ex 7:9
his *m*, and the judgments he . . . 1 Chr 16:12
to remember the *m* you performed . . . Neh 9:17
m that cannot be counted. . . . Jb 5:9
I will remember your *m* of long ago . . .
   Ps 77:11
He did *m* in the sight . . . Ps 78:12
they gave no thought to your *m;* . . . Ps 106:7
out demons and perform many *m?* . . . Mt 7:22
most of his *m* had been performed, . . .
   Mt 11:20
generation asks for a *m* sign! . . . Mt 12:39
And he did not do many *m* there . . . Mt 13:58
does *m!* Isn't this the carpenter? . . . Mk 6:2
and *m* to deceive the elect . . . Mk 13:22
For if the *m* that were performed . . . Lk 10:13
for all the *m* they had seen: . . . Lk 19:37
hoped to see him perform some *m*. . . . Lk 23:8
Unless you people see *m* signs . . . Jn 4:48
disciples may see the *m* you do. . . . Jn 7:3
m I do in my Father's name speak . . . Jn 10:25
the evidence of the *m* themselves. . . . Jn 14:11
Jesus did many other *m* signs . . . Jn 20:30
accredited by God to you by *m*, . . . Acts 2:22
m signs were done by the apostles. . . . Acts 2:43
God did extraordinary *m* . . . Acts 19:11
by the power of signs and *m*, . . . Rom 15:19
Jews demand *m* signs and Greeks . . . 1 Cor 1:22
to another *m* powers, . . . 1 Cor 12:10

and *m* were done among you . . . 2 Cor 12:12
work *m* among you because you . . . Gal 3:5
in all kinds of counterfeit *m*, . . . 2 Thes 2:9
it by signs, wonders and various *m*, . . . Heb 2:4

MIRROR *surface capable of reflecting light*
but a poor reflection as in a *m;* . . . 1 Cor 13:12
a man who looks at his face in a *m* . . . Jas 1:23

MISERY *a condition of mental or emotional
unhappiness or distress*
I have indeed seen the *m* . . . Ex 3:7
he could bear Israel's *m* no longer. . . . Jgs 10:16
in their *m* they will earnestly seek . . . Hos 5:15
ruin and *m* mark their ways, . . . Rom 3:16
of the *m* that is coming upon you. . . . Jas 5:1

MISTREAT(ED) *to treat in a harmful or disre-
spectful manner*
Do not *m* an alien or oppress him, . . . Ex 22:21
m the fatherless and the widow. . . . Ez 22:7
pray for those who *m* you. . . . Lk 6:28
to be *m* along with the people . . . Heb 11:25
destitute, persecuted and *m* . . . Heb 11:37
who are *m* as if you yourselves . . . Heb 13:3

MOCK(ED)(ER)(ERS)(ING)(S) *to ridicule; to
make fun of*
or sit in the seat of *m*. . . . Ps 1:1
All who see me *m* me; . . . Ps 22:7
The arrogant *m* me . . . Ps 119:51
corrects a *m* invites insult; . . . Prv 9:7
if you are a *m*, you alone will suffer . . . Prv 9:12
He who *m* the poor shows . . . Prv 17:5
Wine is a *m* and beer a brawler; . . . Prv 20:1
M stir up a city, . . . Prv 29:8
The eye that *m* a father, . . . Prv 30:17
face from *m* and spitting. . . . Is 50:6
knelt in front of him and *m* him. . . . Mt 27:29
who will *m* him and spit on him, . . . Mk 10:34
not be deceived: God cannot be *m*. . . . Gal 6:7

MOMENT *brief period of time; an instant*
the joy of the godless lasts but a *m*. . . . Jb 20:5
for his wrath can flare up in a *m*. . . . Ps 2:12
For his anger lasts only a *m*, . . . Ps 30:5
but a lying tongue lasts only a *m*. . . . Prv 12:19
For a brief *m* I abandoned you, . . . Is 54:7
or a nation be brought forth in a *m?* . . . Is 66:8
and *m* troubles are achieving . . . 2 Cor 4:17
We did not give in to them for a *m*, . . . Gal 2:5

MONEY *standardized medium for the exchange
of goods and services; coins*
Dishonest *m* dwindles away, . . . Prv 13:11
Whoever loves *m* never has *m* . . . Eccl 5:10
and you who have no *m*, . . . Is 55:1
You cannot serve both God and *M*. . . . Mt 6:24
Judas threw the *m* into the temple . . . Mt 27:5
no bread, no *m*, no extra tunic. . . . Lk 9:3
part of the *m* for himself, . . . Acts 5:2
set aside a sum of *m* in keeping . . . 1 Cor 16:2
not quarrelsome, not a lover of *m*. . . . 1 Tm 3:3
For the love of *m* is a root . . . 1 Tm 6:10
lovers of *m*, boastful, proud, . . . 2 Tm 3:2
free from the love of *m* . . . Heb 13:5

MOON *heavenly body revolving around the
earth*
you established the sun and *m*. . . . Ps 74:16
be established forever like the *m*, . . . Ps 89:37
The *m* marks off the seasons, . . . Ps 104:19
nor the *m* by night. . . . Ps 121:6
the *m* and stars to govern the night; . . .
   Ps 136:9
Praise him, sun and *m*, . . . Ps 148:3
fair as the *m*, bright as the sun, . . . Song 6:10
and the *m* to blood . . . Jl 2:31
and the *m* will not give its light; . . . Mt 24:29
and the *m* to blood . . . Acts 2:20
m another and the stars another; . . . 1 Cor 15:41
a New *M* celebration or a Sabbath . . . Col 2:16
the whole *m* turned blood red, . . . Rv 6:12

city does not need the sun or the *m* . . .
   Rv 21:23

MORNING *beginning of a day; dawn*
and there was *m* the first day. . . . Gn 1:5
In the *m* you will say, "If only it . . . Dt 28:67
he is like the light of *m* at sunrise . . . 2 Sm 23:4
In the *m*, O LORD, . . . Ps 5:3
blesses his neighbor early in the *m*, . . . Prv 27:14
O *m* star, son of the dawn! . . . Is 14:12
They are new every *m;* . . . Lam 3:23
and the *m* star rises in your hearts. . . . 2 Pt 1:19
I will also give him the *m* star. . . . Rv 2:28

MORTAL *human; subject to death*
for he is *m;* his days will be . . . Gn 6:3
Do you see as a *m* sees? . . . Jb 10:4
also give life to your *m* bodies . . . Rom 8:11
and the *m* with immortality. . . . 1 Cor 15:53
that what is *m* may be swallowed . . . 2 Cor 5:4

MOTHER('S) *female parent*
and *m* and be united to his wife, . . . Gn 2:24
because she would become the *m* . . . Gn 3:20
Honor your father and your *m*, . . . Ex 20:12
If anyone curses his father or *m*, . . . Lv 20:9
who does not obey his father and *m* . . .
   Dt 21:18
arose a *m* in Israel. . . . Jgs 5:7
Each year his *m* made him a little . . . 1 Sm 2:19
Naked I came from my *m* womb, . . . Jb 1:21
as a happy *m* of children. . . . Ps 113:9
and do not forsake your *m* teaching . . . Prv 1:8
do not despise your *m* . . . Prv 23:22
a child left to himself disgraces his *m*. . . . Prv 29:15
that scorns obedience to a *m*, . . . Prv 30:17
from his *m* womb, . . . Eccl 5:15
the body is formed in a *m* womb, . . . Eccl 11:5
Can a *m* forget the baby . . . Is 49:15
As a *m* comforts her child, . . . Is 66:13
a daughter rises up against her *m*, . . . Mi 7:6
or *m* more than me is not worthy . . . Mt 10:37
He replied to him, "Who is my *m*, . . . Mt 12:48
Honor your father and *m* . . . Mt 15:4
and *m* and be united to his wife, . . . Mt 19:5
Blessed is the *m* who gave you . . . Lk 11:27
time into his *m* womb to be born! . . . Jn 3:4
to the disciple, "Here is your *m*." . . . Jn 19:27
is above is free, and she is our *m*. . . . Gal 4:26
and *m* and be united to his wife, . . . Eph 5:31
Honor your father and *m* . . . Eph 6:2
like a *m* caring for her little . . . 1 Thes 2:7

MOTHER-IN-LAW *female parent of spouse*
Ruth told her *m* about the one . . . Ru 2:19
a daughter-in-law against her *m* . . . Mt 10:35

MOTIVE(S) *an emotion or desire that urges a
person to act in a certain way*
and understands every *m* . . . 1 Chr 28:9
but *m* are weighed by the LORD. . . . Prv 16:2
will expose the *m* of men's hearts. . . . 1 Cor 4:5
whether from false *m* or true, . . . Phil 1:18
spring from error or impure *m*, . . . 1 Thes 2:3
because you ask with wrong *m*, . . . Jas 4:3

MOUNT(AIN)(AINS) *large mass of earth rising
above the surrounding terrain*
And he stayed on the *m* forty days . . . Ex 24:18
face to face out of the fire on the *m*. . . . Dt 5:4
But as a *m* erodes and crumbles . . . Jb 14:18
righteousness is like the mighty *m*, . . . Ps 36:6
the *m* fall into the heart of the sea, . . . Ps 46:2
in the city of our God, his holy *m*. . . . Ps 48:1
Before the *m* were born . . . Ps 90:2
enthroned on the *m* of assembly, . . . Is 14:13
every *m* and hill made low; . . . Is 40:4
How beautiful on the *m* . . . Is 52:7
Though the *m* be shaken . . . Is 54:10
the *m* and hills . . . Is 55:12
You were on the holy *m* of God; . . . Ez 28:14
let us go up to the *m* of the LORD, . . . Mi 4:2

stand on the *M* of Olives, . . . Zec 14:4
the devil took him to a very high *m* . . . Mt 4:8
say to this *m*, 'Move from here . . . Mt 17:20
are in Judea flee to the *m*. . . . Mt 24:16
with him and led them up a high *m*, . . . Mk 9:2
every *m* and hill made low. . . . Lk 3:5
they will say to the *m*, "Fall on us!" . . . Lk 23:30
the Father neither on this *m* . . . Jn 4:21
were with him on the sacred *m*. . . . 2 Pt 1:18
They called to the *m* and the rocks, . . . Rv 6:16

MOURN(ING)(S) *to grieve; sorrow*
a time to *m* and a time to dance, . . . Eccl 3:4
to comfort all who *m*, . . . Is 61:2
I will turn their *m* into gladness; . . . Jer 31:13
as one *m* for an only child, . . . Zec 12:10
Blessed are those who *m*, . . . Mt 5:4
m with those who . . . om 12:15
There will be no more death or *m* . . . Rv 21:4

MOUTH(S) *the natural opening through which one speaks and food is taken into the body; sometimes figurative of God's communication and word to humanity*
comes from the *m* of the LORD. . . . Dt 8:3
I will put my words in his *m*, . . . Dt 18:18
it is in your *m* and in your heart . . . Dt 30:14
of the Law depart from your *m*; . . . Jos 1:8
m to *m*, eyes to eyes, hands . . . 2 Kgs 4:34
resolved that my *m* will not sin. . . . Ps 17:3
May the words of my *m* . . . Ps 19:14
He put a new song in my *m*, . . . Ps 40:3
would flatter him with their *m*, . . . Ps 78:36
sweeter than honey to my *m!* . . . Ps 119:103
The *m* of the righteous is a fountain . . . Prv 10:11
A wise man's heart guides his *m*, . . . Prv 16:23
praise you, and not your own *m*; . . . Prv 27:2
Do not be quick with your *m*, . . . Eccl 5:2
with the kisses of his *m* . . . Song 1:2
come near to me with their *m* . . . Is 29:13
For the *m* of the LORD has spoken . . . Is 40:5
I have put my words in your *m* . . . Is 51:16
so he did not open his *m*. . . . Is 53:7
my word that goes out from my *m*: . . . Is 55:11
With their *m* they express devotion . . . Ez 33:31
and from his *m* men should seek . . . Mal 2:7
comes from the *m* of God. . . . Mt 4:4
overflow of the heart the *m* speaks. . . . Mt 12:34
into a man's *m* does not make him . . . Mt 15:11
That if you confess with your *m*, . . . Rom 10:9
and *m* you may glorify the God . . . Rom 15:6
talk come out of your *m*, . . . Eph 4:29
bits into the *m* of horses . . . Jas 3:3
and no deceit was found in his *m*. . . . 1 Pt 2:22
and out of his *m* came a sharp . . . Rv 1:16
I am about to spit you out of my *m*. . . . Rv 3:16
Out of his *m* comes a sharp sword . . . Rv 19:15

MOVE(D) *to change position physically, mentally, or spiritually*
everyone whose heart God had *m* . . . Ezr 1:5
it cannot be *m*. . . . Ps 93:1
Do not *m* an ancient boundary . . . Prv 23:10
he was deeply *m* in spirit . . . Jn 11:33
and *m* and have our being. . . . Acts 17:28
have a faith that can *m* mountains, . . . 1 Cor 13:2
Let nothing *m* you. . . . 1 Cor 15:58

MULTITUDE(S) *large crowd*
and the *m* of heaven worship you. . . . Neh 9:6
who trust in the *m* of their chariots . . . Is 31:1
M who sleep in the dust . . . Dn 12:2
M, *m* in the valley of decision! . . . Jl 3:14
and cover over a *m* of sins. . . . Jas 5:20
me was a great *m* that no one could . . . Rv 7:9

MURDER(ED)(ER)(ERS) *the unlawful killing of one human being by another, especially with premeditated malice; killer*
You shall not *m*. . . . Ex 20:13
A man tormented by the guilt of *m* . . . Prv 28:17
Do not *m*, and anyone who . . . Mt 5:21

m, adultery, sexual immorality, . . . Mt 15:19
of those who *m* the prophets. . . . Mt 23:31
He was a *m* from the beginning, . . . Jn 8:44
now you have betrayed and *m* him . . . Acts 7:52
"Do not *m*," "Do not steal," . . . Rom 13:9
for *m*, for adulterers and perverts, . . . 1 Tm 1:9
adultery," also said, "Do not *m*." . . . Jas 2:11
to the evil one and *m* his brother. . . . 1 Jn 3:12
the *m*, the sexually immoral, . . . Rv 21:8

MYSTERIES, MYSTERY *secret; riddle; something hidden by God for a set time*
Can you fathom the *m* of God? . . . Jb 11:7
to the king the *m* he has asked . . . Dn 2:27
you to be ignorant of this *m*, . . . Rom 11:25
to the revelation of the *m* hidden . . . Rom 16:25
can fathom all *m* and all knowledge . . . 1 Cor 13:2
he utters *m* with his spirit. . . . 1 Cor 14:2
I tell you a *m*: We will not all sleep, . . . 1 Cor 15:51
to us the *m* of his will according . . . Eph 1:9
the *m* made known to me . . . Eph 3:3
This *m* is that through the gospel . . . Eph 3:6
the administration of this *m*, . . . Eph 3:9
This is a profound *m* . . . Eph 5:32
I will fearlessly make known the *m* . . . Eph 6:19
the *m* that has been kept hidden . . . Col 1:26
in order that they may know the *m* . . . Col 2:2
so that we may proclaim the *m* . . . Col 4:3
the *m* of godliness is great: . . . 1 Tm 3:16
m of the seven stars that you saw . . . Rv 1:20
the *m* of God will be accomplished, . . . Rv 10:7
explain to you the *m* of the woman . . . Rv 17:7

NAKED *nude, without clothes; exposed*
The man and his wife were both *n*, . . . Gn 2:25
N I came from my mother's womb, . . . Jb 1:21
when you see the *n*, to clothe him, . . . Is 58:7
are clothed, we will not be found *n*. . . . 2 Cor 5:3

NAME(S) *word by which a person or thing is known; one's reputation or essential nature (often of God)*
man to see what he would *n* them; . . . Gn 2:19
to call on the *n* of the LORD . . . Gn 4:26
so that we may make a *n* . . . Gn 11:4
I will make your *n* great, . . . Gn 12:2
Jacob said, "Please tell me your *n*." . . . Gn 32:29
You shall not misuse the *n* . . . Ex 20:7
for the LORD, whose *n* is Jealous, . . . Ex 34:14
choose as a dwelling for his *N* . . . Dt 12:11
of his great *n* the LORD will not . . . 1 Sm 12:22
which is called by the *N*, the name . . . 2 Sm 6:2
will build the temple for my *N*. . . . 1 Kgs 5:5
you said, 'My *N* shall be there,' . . . 1 Kgs 8:29
my people, who are called by my *n*, . . . 2 Chr 7:14
how majestic is your *n* . . . Ps 8:1
Those who know your *n* will trust . . . Ps 9:10
to the LORD the glory due his *n*; . . . Ps 29:2
let us exalt his *n* together. . . . Ps 34:3
Sing the glory of his *n*; . . . Ps 66:2
my inmost being, praise his holy *n*. . . . Ps 103:1
but to your *n* be the glory, . . . Ps 115:1
I will praise your *n* for ever . . . Ps 145:1
and calls them each by *n*. . . . Ps 147:4
you will win favor and a good *n* . . . Prv 3:4
n of the LORD is a strong tower; . . . Prv 18:10
A good *n* is more desirable . . . Prv 22:1
A good *n* is better . . . Eccl 7:1
your *n* is like perfume poured out. . . . Song 1:3
and calls them each by *n*. . . . Is 40:26
I am the LORD; that is my *n!* . . . Is 42:8
I will give them an everlasting . . . Is 56:5
do something for the sake of your *n* . . . Jer 14:7

of my *n* I did what would keep it . . . Ez 20:9
everyone whose *n* is found written . . . Dn 12:1
the LORD is his *n* of renown! . . . Hos 12:5
on the *n* of the LORD will be saved . . . Jl 2:32
call on the *n* of the LORD . . . Zep 3:9
O priests, who show contempt for my *n*. . . . Mal 1:6
and you are to give him the *n* Jesus, . . . Mt 1:21
hallowed be your *n*, . . . Mt 6:9
or three come together in my *n*, . . . Mt 18:20
For many will come in my *n*, . . . Mt 24:5
them in the *n* of the Father . . . Mt 28:19
gives you a cup of water in my *n* . . . Mk 9:41
but rejoice that your *n* are written . . . Lk 10:20
He calls his own sheep by *n* . . . Jn 10:3
I will do whatever you ask in my *n*, . . . Jn 14:13
for there is no other *n* . . . Acts 4:12
Everyone who calls on the *n* . . . Rom 10:13
him the *n* that is above every *n*, . . . Phil 2:9
whose *n* are in the book of life. . . . Phil 4:3
do it all in the *n* of the Lord Jesus, . . . Col 3:17
as the *n* he has inherited is superior . . . Heb 1:4
him with oil in the *n* of the Lord. . . . Jas 5:14
believe in the *n* of the Son of God . . . 1 Jn 5:13
stone with a new *n* written on it, . . . Rv 2:17
I will never blot out his *n* . . . Rv 3:5
I will also write on him my new *n*. . . . Rv 3:12
and his *n* is the Word of God. . . . Rv 19:13
but only those whose *n* are written . . . Rv 21:27

NATION(S) *group of people defined by geography or ethnic origin*
I will make you into a great *n* . . . Gn 12:2
You will be the father of many *n*. . . . Gn 17:4
and all *n* on earth will be blessed . . . Gn 18:18
of all *n* you will be my treasured . . . Ex 19:5
What other *n* is so great . . . Dt 4:7
drives out before you many *n* . . . Dt 7:1
You will rule over many *n* . . . Dt 15:6
I will scatter you among the *n*, . . . Neh 1:8
Why do the *n* conspire . . . Ps 2:1
Blessed is the *n* whose God is . . . Ps 33:12
I will be exalted among the *n*, . . . Ps 46:10
your salvation among all *n*. . . . Ps 67:2
Scatter the *n* who delight in war. . . . Ps 68:30
Declare his glory among the *n*, . . . Ps 96:3
but they mingled with the *n* . . . Ps 106:35
He will judge the *n*, heaping up . . . Ps 110:6
The LORD is exalted over all the *n* . . . Ps 113:4
Righteousness exalts a *n*, . . . Prv 14:34
and all *n* will stream to it. . . . Is 2:2
among the *n* what he has done, . . . Is 12:4
Surely the *n* are like a drop . . . Is 40:15
and he will bring justice to the *n*. . . . Is 42:1
a house of prayer for all *n*. . . . Is 56:7
N will come to your light, . . . Is 60:3
To a *n* that did not call on my name . . . Is 65:1
a *n* be brought forth in a moment? . . . Is 66:8
you as a prophet to the *n*. . . . Jer 1:5
and all *n* will gather in Jerusalem . . . Jer 3:17
I will bring them out from the *n* . . . Ez 34:13
n will know that I am the LORD, . . . Ez 36:23
and they will never again be two *n* . . . Ez 37:22
Ephraim mixes with the *n*; . . . Hos 7:8
a byword among the *n*. . . . Jl 2:17
N will not take up sword . . . Mi 4:3
I have decided to assemble the *n*, . . . Zep 3:8
and the desired of all *n* will come, . . . Hg 2:7
n will take firm hold of one Jew . . . Zec 8:23
He will proclaim peace to the *n*. . . . Zec 9:10
he will proclaim justice to the *n*. . . . Mt 12:18
N will rise against *n*, . . . Mt 24:7
whole world as a testimony to all *n*, . . . Mt 24:14
All the *n* will be gathered . . . Mt 25:32
and make disciples of all *n*, . . . Mt 28:19
a house of prayer for all *n*'? . . . Mk 11:17
Why do the *n* rage . . . Acts 4:25
who will arise to rule over the *n*; . . . Rom 15:12
All *n* will be blessed through you. . . . Gal 3:8

a royal priesthood, a holy n, . . . 1 Pt 2:9
from every n, tribe, people . . . Rv 7:9
All n will come . . . Rv 15:4
The n will walk by its light, . . . Rv 21:24
are for the healing of the n. . . . Rv 22:2

NATURAL *conforming to a usual or ordinary course of nature; operating in the physical rather than the supernatural realm*
you are weak in your n selves. . . . Rom 6:19
If there is a n body, there is . . . 1 Cor 15:44

NATURE *inherent character or essence*
his eternal power and divine n . . . Rom 1:20
lives in me, that is, in my sinful n. . . . Rom 7:18
do not live according to the sinful n . . . Rom 8:4
freedom to indulge the sinful n; . . . Gal 5:13
The acts of the sinful n are obvious: . . . Gal 5:19
Jesus have crucified the sinful n . . . Gal 5:24
Who, being in very n God, . . . Phil 2:6
whatever belongs to your earthly n . . . Col 3:5
you may participate in the divine n . . . 2 Pt 1:4

NEED(S)(Y) *requirement, especially for physical survival*
toward the poor and n in your land. . . . Dt 15:11
and lifts the n from the ash heap; . . . 1 Sm 2:8
Israel according to each day's n, . . . 1 Kgs 8:59
and n from those who rob them. . . . Ps 35:10
The LORD hears the n . . . Ps 69:33
he will deliver the n who cry out, . . . Ps 72:12
when I was in great n, he saved me. . . . Ps 116:6
and upholds the cause of the n. . . . Ps 140:12
for I am in desperate n; . . . Ps 142:6
to the n honors God. . . . Prv 14:31
and do not crush the n in court, . . . Prv 22:22
and extends her hands to the n. . . . Prv 31:20
he will satisfy your n . . . Is 58:11
So when you give to the n, . . . Mt 6:2
for your Father knows what you n . . . Mt 6:8
they gave to anyone as he had n. . . . Acts 2:45
with God's people who are in n. . . . Rom 12:13
say to the hand, "I don't n you!" . . . 1 Cor 12:21
something to share with those in n. . . . Eph 4:28
God will meet all your n according . . . Phil 4:19
to those widows who are really in n . . . 1 Tm 5:3
grace to help us in our time of n. . . . Heb 4:16
does nothing about his physical n, . . . Jas 2:16
sees his brother in n but has no pity . . . 1 Jn 3:17

NEGLECT(ED) *to disregard, overlook, or ignore*
Be careful not to n the Levites . . . Dt 12:19
Be careful not to n this matter. . . . Ezr 4:22
We will not n the house of our God . . . Neh 10:39
Do not n anything you have . . . Est 6:10
But you have n the more important . . . Mt 23:23
you n justice and the love of God. . . . Lk 11:42
for us to n the ministry of the word . . . Acts 6:2
Do not n your gift, which was . . . 1 Tm 4:14

NEIGHBOR('S) *member of one's community*
give false testimony against your n. . . . Ex 20:16
You shall not covet your n wife, . . . Ex 20:17
Do not defraud your n or rob him. . . . Lv 19:13
but love your n as yourself. . . . Lv 19:18
not move your n boundary stone . . . Dt 19:14
who does his n no wrong . . . Ps 15:3
Do not plot harm against your n, . . . Prv 3:29
who lacks judgment derides his n, . . . Prv 11:12
against your n without cause, . . . Prv 24:28
Seldom set foot in your n house . . . Prv 25:17
gives false testimony against his n. . . . Prv 25:18

better a n nearby than a brother far . . . Prv 27:10
If a man loudly blesses his n . . . Prv 27:14
Whoever flatters his n . . . Prv 29:5
No longer will a man teach his n, . . . Jer 31:34
Love your n and hate your enemy. . . . Mt 5:43
and 'love your n as yourself.' . . . Mt 19:19
Each of us should please his n . . . Rom 15:2
and speak truthfully to his n, . . . Eph 4:25
No longer will a man teach his n, . . . Heb 8:11
Love your n as yourself, . . . Jas 2:8

NEW *fresh; original; different than before; unfamiliar; successor*
He put a n song in my mouth, . . . Ps 40:3
Sing to the LORD a n song, . . . Ps 98:1
there is nothing n under the sun. . . . Eccl 1:9
and n things I declare; . . . Is 42:9
you will be called by a n name . . . Is 62:2
n heavens and a n earth. . . . Is 65:17
when I will make a n covenant . . . Jer 31:31
They are n every morning; . . . Lam 3:23
and get a n heart and a n spirit. . . . Ez 18:31
and every n day he does not fail, . . . Zep 3:5
Neither do men pour n wine . . . Mt 9:17
they will speak in n tongues; . . . Mk 16:17
after drinking old wine wants the n . . . Lk 5:39
This cup is the n covenant . . . Lk 22:20
A n commandment I give you: . . . Jn 13:34
the full message of this n life. . . . Acts 5:20
the Father, we too may live a n life. . . . Rom 6:4
old yeast that you may be a n batch . . . 1 Cor 5:7
This cup is the n covenant . . . 1 Cor 11:25
as ministers of a n covenant . . . 2 Cor 3:6
he is a n creation; the old has gone, . . . 2 Cor 5:17
and have put on the n self, . . . Col 3:10
when I will make a n covenant . . . Heb 8:8
by a n and living way opened for us . . . Heb 10:20
Jesus the mediator of a n covenant, . . . Heb 12:24
great mercy he has given us n birth . . . 1 Pt 1:3
to a n heaven and a n earth, . . . 2 Pt 3:13
stone with a n name written on it, . . . Rv 2:17
the n Jerusalem, which is coming . . . Rv 3:12
I saw a n heaven and a n earth, . . . Rv 21:1

NEWS *information, often concerning recent events (often of the Good News or gospel)*
He will have no fear of bad n; . . . Ps 112:7
is good n from a distant land. . . . Prv 25:25
the feet of those who bring good n, . . . Is 52:7
me to preach good n to the poor. . . . Is 61:1
Repent and believe the good n! . . . Mk 1:15
preach the good n to all creation. . . . Mk 16:15
proclaiming the good n that Jesus . . . Acts 5:42
feet of those who bring good n! . . . Rom 10:15

NIGHT(S) *period of darkness between sunset and sunrise; figurative of suffering, sorrow, or sin*
and the darkness he called "n." . . . Gn 1:5
and by n in a pillar of fire . . . Ex 13:21
filled with dread both n and day, . . . Dt 28:66
who gives songs in the n, . . . Jb 35:10
on his law he meditates day and n. . . . Ps 1:2
n after n they display knowledge. . . . Ps 19:2
at n his song is with me . . . Ps 42:8
of you through the watches of the n . . . Ps 63:6
I remembered my songs in the n. . . . Ps 77:6
You will not fear the terror of n, . . . Ps 91:5
through the watches of the n, . . . Ps 119:148
the moon and stars to govern the n; . . . Ps 136:9
and her lamp does not go out at n. . . . Prv 31:18
Watchman, what is left of the n? . . . Is 21:11
and your n will become like . . . Is 58:10
After fasting forty days and forty n . . . Mt 4:2
three n in the belly of a huge fish, . . . Mt 12:40

watch over their flocks at n. . . . Lk 2:8
and spent the n praying to God. . . . Lk 6:12
He came to Jesus at n and said, . . . Jn 3:2
N is coming, when no one can work . . . Jn 9:4
Lord will come like a thief in the n. . . . 1 Thes 5:2
We do not belong to the n . . . 1 Thes 5:5
for there will be no n there. . . . Rv 21:25

NOBLE *possessing high moral qualities*
you are a woman of n character. . . . Ru 3:11
My heart is stirred by a n theme . . . Ps 45:1
of n character is her husband's . . . Prv 12:4
good soil stands for those with a n . . . Lk 8:15
of clay some pottery for n purposes . . . Rom 9:21
whatever is n, whatever is right, . . . Phil 4:8
some are for n purposes . . . 2 Tm 2:20

NOTHING *not anything; lack of existence*
offerings that cost me n. . . . 2 Sm 24:24
in the desert; they lacked n, . . . Neh 9:21
earth has n I desire besides you . . . Ps 73:25
N is too hard for you . . . Jer 32:17
apart from me you can do n. . . . Jn 15:5

OATH *an appeal to God to witness the truth of a statement*
up to the land I promised on o . . . Ex 33:1
or takes an o to obligate himself . . . Nm 30:2
promised on o to your forefathers, . . . Dt 6:18
and kept the o he swore . . . Dt 7:8
you this day and sealing with an o, . . . Dt 29:12
So I declared on o in my anger, . . . Ps 95:11
The LORD swore an o to David, . . . Ps 132:11
because you took an o before God. . . . Eccl 8:2
Do not break your o, but keep . . . Mt 5:33

OBEDIENCE, OBEDIENT *submissiveness to authority; following orders; see OBEY*
and the o of the nations is his. . . . Gn 49:10
of o to the LORD's commands. . . . Jgs 2:17
in o to the law and the commands, . . . 2 Chr 31:21
If you are willing and o, . . . Is 1:19
with them and was o to them. . . . Lk 2:51
Sabbath in o to the commandment. . . . Lk 23:56
of priests became o to the faith. . . . Acts 6:7
but that you yourself are living in o . . . Acts 21:24
to the o that comes from faith. . . . Rom 1:5
also through the o of the one man . . . Rom 5:19
if you would stand the test and be o . . . 2 Cor 2:9
once your o is complete. . . . 2 Cor 10:6
thought to make it o to Christ. . . . 2 Cor 10:5
and became o to death . . . Phil 2:8
to be o, to be ready . . . Ti 3:1
Confident of your o, I write to you, . . . Phlm 1:21
he learned o from what he suffered . . . Heb 5:8
for o to Jesus Christ and sprinkling . . . 1 Pt 1:2
As o children, do not conform . . . 1 Pt 1:14
that we walk in o to his commands. . . . 2 Jn 1:6

OBEY(ED)(ING)(S) *to submit to authority; to follow orders; see OBEDIENCE*
blessed, because you have o me. . . . Gn 22:18
Now if you o me fully and keep my . . . Ex 19:5
the LORD has said; we will o. . . . Ex 24:7
You must o my laws and be careful . . . Lv 18:4
and be careful to o my laws, . . . Lv 25:18
We will listen and o . . . Dt 5:27
careful to o so that it may go well . . . Dt 6:3
us to o all these decrees . . . Dt 6:24
if you faithfully o the commands I . . . Dt 11:13
Keep his commands and o him; . . . Dt 13:4
son who does not o his father . . . Dt 21:18
If you fully o the LORD your God . . . Dt 28:1
and o him with all your heart . . . Dt 30:2
if you o the LORD your God . . . Dt 30:10
children to o carefully all the words . . . Dt 32:46
to o all the law my servant Moses . . . Jos 1:7
we fully o Moses, so we will o . . . Jos 1:17

in all his ways, to *o* his commands, . . . Jos 22:5
the LORD our God and *o* him. . . . Jos 24:24
To *o* is better than sacrifice, . . . 1 Sm 15:22
and to *o* the words of the covenant . . . 2 Chr 34:31
and remember to *o* his precepts, . . . Ps 103:18
I will *o* your word. . . . Ps 119:17
I have promised to *o* your words. . . . Ps 119:57
therefore I *o* them. . . . Ps 119:129
I would not *o* my teachers . . . Prv 5:13
He who *o* instructions guards his . . . Prv 19:16
I gave them this command: *O* me, . . . Jer 7:23
we will *o* the LORD our God, . . . Jer 42:6
for the man who *o* them will live . . . Ez 20:11
who love him and *o* his commands, . . . Dn 9:4
Jonah *o* the word of the LORD . . . Jon 3:3
the nations that have not *o* me. . . . Mi 5:15
the winds and the waves *o* him! . . . Mt 8:27
to enter life, *o* the commandments . . . Mt 19:17
to *o* everything I have commanded . . . Mt 28:20
hear the word of God and *o* it. . . . Lk 11:28
you will *o* what I command. . . . Jn 14:15
If you *o* my commands, you will . . . Jn 15:10
and they have *o* your word. . . . Jn 17:6
We must *o* God rather than men! . . . Acts 5:29
through angels but have not *o* it. . . . Acts 7:53
it is those who *o* the law who will . . . Rom 2:13
and yet *o* the law will condemn you . . . Rom 2:27
body so that you *o* its evil desires. . . . Rom 6:12
slaves to the one whom you *o* . . . Rom 6:16
in leading the Gentiles to *o* God . . . Rom 15:18
obligated to *o* the whole law. . . . Gal 5:3
o your parents in the Lord, . . . Eph 6:1
o your earthly masters with respect . . . Eph 6:5
as you have always *o* not only . . . Phil 2:12
and see that his children *o* him . . . 1 Tm 3:4
eternal salvation for all who *o* him . . . Heb 5:9
o and went, even though he did not . . . Heb 11:8
O your leaders and submit . . . Heb 13:17
purified yourselves by *o* the truth . . . 1 Pt 1:22
for those who do not *o* the gospel . . . 1 Pt 4:17
if anyone *o* his word, God's love is . . . 1 Jn 2:5
Those who *o* his commands live . . . 1 Jn 3:24
love for God: to *o* his commands. . . . 1 Jn 5:3
those who *o* God's commandments . . . Rv 12:17
the saints who *o* God's . . . Rv 14:12

OBSERVE, OBSERVING *to notice; to follow or obey; to watch over or protect*
You must *o* my Sabbaths. . . . Ex 31:13
the land itself must *o* a sabbath . . . Lv 25:2
O them carefully, for this will show . . . Dt 4:6
O the commands of the LORD . . . Dt 8:6
If you carefully *o* all these . . . Dt 11:22
principle? On that of *o* the law? . . . Rom 3:27
a man is not justified by *o* the law, . . . Gal 2:16
you receive the Spirit by *o* the law, . . . Gal 3:2
All who rely on *o* the law are . . . Gal 3:10

OFFENSE(S), OFFENSIVE *violation of a moral code; something that outrages moral sensibilities*
it is to his glory to overlook an *o*. . . . Prv 19:11
swept away your *o* like a cloud, . . . Is 44:22
For our *o* are many in your sight, . . . Is 59:12
Repent! Turn away from all your *o*; . . . Ez 18:30
Our *o* and sins weigh us down, . . . Ez 33:10
In that case the *o* of the cross has . . . Gal 5:11
See if there is any *o* way in me, . . . Ps 139:24

OFFER(ED)(ING)(INGS) *to present for acceptance; a gift or sacrifice*
of the soil as an *o* to the LORD. . . . Gn 4:3
a burnt *o* on one of the mountains I . . . Gn 22:2
provide the lamb for the burnt *o*, . . . Gn 22:8
If you bring a grain *o* baked . . . Lv 2:4
a sin *o* for the sin he has committed . . . Lv 4:3
It is a guilt *o*. . . . Lv 5:15
and consumed the burnt *o* . . . Lv 9:24

to fulfill a vow or as a freewill *o*, . . . Lv 22:18
And Saul offered up the burnt *o*. . . . 1 Sm 13:9
Does the LORD delight in burnt *o* . . . 1 Sm 15:22
and goats for the Passover *o*, . . . 2 Chr 35:7
O right sacrifices . . . Ps 4:5
Sacrifice and *o* you did not desire, . . . Ps 40:6
I will sacrifice a thank *o* to you . . . Ps 116:17
Stop bringing meaningless *o*! . . . Is 1:13
I *o* my back to those who beat me, . . . Is 50:6
the LORD makes his life a guilt *o*, . . . Is 53:10
of God rather than burnt *o*. . . . Hos 6:6
do we rob you?' "In tithes and *o*. . . . Mal 3:8
if you are *o* your gift at the altar . . . Mt 5:23
is more important than all burnt *o* . . . Mk 12:33
Do not *o* the parts of your body . . . Rom 6:13
likeness of sinful man to be a sin *o*. . . . Rom 8:3
to *o* your bodies as living sacrifices, . . . Rom 12:1
as a fragrant *o* and sacrifice to God. . . . Eph 5:2
I am being poured out like a drink *o* . . . Phil 2:17
are a fragrant *o*, an acceptable . . . Phil 4:18
once for all when he *o* himself. . . . Heb 7:27
he enter heaven to *o* himself again . . . Heb 9:25
Sacrifice and *o* you did not desire, . . . Heb 10:5
By faith Abel *o* God a better . . . Heb 11:4
when God tested him, *o* Isaac . . . Heb 11:17
o spiritual sacrifices acceptable . . . 1 Pt 2:5

OFFSPRING *descendants; children*
and between your *o* and hers; . . . Gn 3:15
To your *o* I will give this land. . . . Gn 12:7
I will make your *o* like the dust . . . Gn 13:16
and through your *o* all nations . . . Gn 26:4
The first *o* of every womb . . . Ex 13:2
Through the *o* the LORD gives . . . Ru 4:12
I will pour out my Spirit on your *o*, . . . Is 44:3
he will see his *o* and prolong his . . . Is 53:10
own poets have said, 'We are his *o*.' . . . Acts 17:28
said to him, "So shall your *o* be." . . . Rom 4:18
who are regarded as Abraham's *o*. . . . Rom 9:8

OIL *a greasy vegetable or mineral liquid substance with various uses; often used for anointing; symbolic of divine blessing; see ANOINT*
and the jug of *o* did not run dry, . . . 1 Kgs 17:16
Then the *o* stopped flowing. . . . 2 Kgs 4:6
You anoint my head with *o*; . . . Ps 23:5
by anointing you with the *o* of joy, . . . Ps 45:7
o to make his face shine, . . . Ps 104:15
It is like precious *o* poured . . . Ps 133:2
loves wine and *o* will never be . . . Prv 21:17
soothed with *o* . . . Is 1:6
the *o* of gladness . . . Is 61:3
but did not take any *o* with them. . . . Mt 25:3
pouring on *o* and wine . . . Lk 10:34
by anointing you with the *o* of joy. . . . Heb 1:9

OLD(ER) *aged; former (associated with the past); worn out; obsolete; invalid*
the *o* will serve the younger. . . . Gn 25:23
gray hair the splendor of the *o*. . . . Prv 20:29
pour new wine into *o* wineskins. . . . Mt 9:17
your *o* men will dream dreams. . . . Acts 2:17
that our *o* self was crucified with . . . Rom 6:6
the *o* has gone, the new has come! . . . 2 Cor 5:17

OLIVE(S) *mideastern fruit used mainly for oil; often symbolic of Israel*
beak was a freshly plucked *o* leaf! . . . Gn 8:11
stand on the Mount of *O*, . . . Zec 14:4
sitting on the Mount of *O*, . . . Mt 24:3
and you, though a wild *o* shoot, . . . Rom 11:17
a fig tree bear *o*, or a grapevine bear . . . Jas 3:12
These are the two *o* trees . . . Rv 11:4

OMEGA *last letter of Greek alphabet; figurative of end*
I am the Alpha and the *O*, . . . Rv 1:8
I am the Alpha and the *O*, . . . Rv 21:6
I am the Alpha and the *O*, . . . Rv 22:13

ONE *of the same substance; singular; first in a series; unique*
and they will become *o* flesh . . . Gn 2:24
shall be *o* flock and *o* shepherd . . . Jn 10:16
I and the Father are *o*. . . . Jn 10:30
that all of them may be *o*, . . . Jn 17:21
for you are all *o* in Christ Jesus. . . . Gal 3:28
o new man out of the two, . . . Eph 2:15
o Lord, *o* faith, *o* baptism; . . . Eph 4:5
o mediator between God and men, . . . 1 Tm 2:5

OPEN(ED)(S) *to move from a closed position; to make accessible; to make more discerning*
when you eat of it your eyes will be *o*. . . . Gn 3:5
yet he did not *o* his mouth; . . . Is 53:7
knock and the door will be *o* to you. . . . Mt 7:7
What he *o* no one can shut, . . . Rv 3:7
I saw heaven standing *o* . . . Rv 19:11

OPPORTUNITY *favorable circumstance or advantage*
Now you have a second *o* . . . 1 Sm 18:21
watched for an *o* to hand him over. . . . Mt 26:16
and has had an *o* to defend himself . . . Acts 25:16
seizing the *o* afforded . . . Rom 7:8
as we have *o*, let us do good . . . Gal 6:10
making the most of every *o*, . . . Eph 5:16
make the most of every *o*. . . . Col 4:5
to give the enemy no *o* for slander. . . . 1 Tm 5:14

OPPOSE(D)(S), OPPOSING, OPPOSITION *to be actively against*
I to think that I could *o* God? . . . Acts 11:17
to Antioch, I *o* him to his face, . . . Gal 2:11
the *o* ideas of what is falsely called . . . 1 Tm 6:20
doctrine and refute those who *o* it. . . . Ti 1:9
so that those who *o* you may be . . . Ti 2:8
Consider him who endured such *o* . . . Heb 12:3
God *o* the proud . . . Jas 4:6

OPPRESS(ED)(ES)(ION)(OR) *to treat cruelly or unjustly*
Do not mistreat an alien or *o* him, . . . Ex 22:21
as they groaned under those who *o* . . . Jgs 2:18
The LORD is a refuge for the *o*, . . . Ps 9:9
he will crush the *o* . . . Ps 72:4
He will rescue them from *o* . . . Ps 72:14
the rights of the poor and *o*. . . . Ps 82:3
Redeem me from the *o* of men, . . . Ps 119:134
He upholds the cause of the *o* . . . Ps 146:7
He who *o* the poor shows contempt . . . Prv 14:31
He who *o* the poor . . . Prv 22:16
and deprive all the *o* of their rights. . . . Prv 31:5
encourage the *o*. . . . Is 1:17
He was *o* and afflicted, . . . Is 53:7
If you do away with the yoke of *o*, . . . Is 58:9
hand of his *o* the one who has been . . . Jer 22:3
they *o* the poor and needy . . . Ez 22:29
the Most High and *o* his saints . . . Dn 7:25
You *o* the righteous and take bribes . . . Am 5:12
Do not *o* the widow . . . Zec 7:10
o for lack of a shepherd. . . . Zec 10:2
who *o* the widows . . . Mal 3:5
to release the *o*, . . . Lk 4:18

ORPHAN(S) *child whose parents have died*
advantage of a widow or an *o*. . . . Ex 22:22
will not leave you as *o*; I will come . . . Jn 14:18
to look after *o* and widows . . . Jas 1:27

OUTSIDERS *unbelievers; non-Christians*
wise in the way you act toward *o*; . . . Col 4:5
daily life may win the respect of *o* . . . 1 Thes 4:12
also have a good reputation with *o*, . . . 1 Tm 3:7

OVERCAME, OVERCOME(S) *to gain a superior position over; to conquer*
and the gates of Hades will not *o* it. . . . Mt 16:18
to *o* all the power of the enemy; . . . Lk 10:19
But take heart! I have *o* the world. . . . Jn 16:33
Do not be *o* by evil, but *o* evil . . . Rom 12:21
because you have *o* the evil one. . . . 1 Jn 2:13
are from God and have *o* them, . . . 1 Jn 4:4
everyone born of God *o* the world. . . . 1 Jn 5:4
is the victory that has *o* the world, . . . 1 Jn 5:4
To him who *o*, I will give the right . . . Rv 2:7
Him who *o* I will make a pillar . . . Rv 3:12
as I *o* and sat down with my Father . . . Rv 3:21
They *o* him by the blood of the Lamb . . . Rv 12:11
but the Lamb will *o* them . . . Rv 17:14
He who *o* will inherit all this, . . . Rv 21:7

OVERFLOW(ING)(S) *to spread or flow beyond certain limits; abundant*
my cup *o*. . . . Ps 23:5
and your carts *o* with abundance. . . . Ps 65:11
May my lips *o* with praise, . . . Ps 119:171
then your barns will be filled to *o*, . . . Prv 3:10
and my eyes *o* with tears. . . . Lam 1:16
out of the *o* of the heart the mouth . . . Mt 12:34
Jesus Christ, *o* to the many! Again, . . . Rom 5:15
also through Christ our comfort *o*. . . . 2 Cor 1:5
to *o* to the glory of God. . . . 2 Cor 4:15
their *o* joy and their extreme . . . 2 Cor 8:2
o in many expressions of thanks . . . 2 Cor 9:12

OVERJOYED *filled with joy; see JOY*
they saw the star, they were *o*. . . . Mt 2:10
The disciples were *o* . . . Jn 20:20
she was so *o* she ran back . . . Acts 12:14
so that you may be *o* . . . 1 Pt 4:13

OVERSEER(S) *supervisor; church leader; see ELDER, SHEPHERD*
the Holy Spirit has made you *o*. . . . Acts 20:28
together with the *o* and deacons: . . . Phil 1:1
Now the *o* must be above reproach, . . . 1 Tm 3:2
Since an *o* is entrusted . . . Ti 1:7
returned to the Shepherd and *O*. . . . 1 Pt 2:25

OVERWHELMED, OVERWHELMING *to render helpless, overcome, overpower*
the torrents of destruction *o* me. . . . 2 Sm 22:5
My guilt has *o* me . . . Ps 38:4
When we were *o* by sins, . . . Ps 65:3
When an *o* scourge sweeps by, . . . Is 28:15
My soul is *o* with sorrow . . . Mt 26:38
People were *o* with amazement. . . . Mk 7:37
they were *o* with wonder . . . Mk 9:15
so that he will not be *o* . . . 2 Cor 2:7

PAGANS *person claiming no belief in Judaism or Christianity*
Do not even *p* do that? Be perfect, . . . Mt 5:47
do not keep on babbling like *p*, . . . Mt 6:7
For the *p* run after all these things, . . . Mt 6:32
that does not occur even among *p*: . . . 1 Cor 5:1
You know that when you were *p*, . . . 1 Cor 12:2
such good lives among the *p* that, . . . 1 Pt 2:12
in the past doing what *p* choose . . . 1 Pt 4:3

PAID, PAY(MENT)(S) *to compensate for goods received or services rendered*
They will *p* for their sins . . . Lv 26:43
no *p* is ever enough . . . Ps 49:8
If a man *p* back evil for good, . . . Prv 17:13
man must *p* the penalty; . . . Prv 19:19

I'll *p* that man back for what he did . . . Prv 24:29
that her sin has been *p* for, . . . Is 40:2
give me my *p*; but if not, keep it. . . . Zec 11:12
He agreed to *p* them a denarius . . . Mt 20:2
Is it right to *p* taxes to Caesar . . . Mt 22:17
be content with your *p*. . . . Lk 3:14
I will *p* back four times the amount . . . Lk 19:8
This is also why you *p* taxes, . . . Rom 13:6
sure that nobody *p* back wrong . . . 1 Thes 5:15

PAIN(FUL)(S) *physical, mental, or emotional suffering*
with *p* you will give birth . . . Gn 3:16
and *p* toil of our hands caused . . . Gn 5:29
and his heart was filled with *p*. . . . Gn 6:6
How *p* are honest words! . . . Jb 6:25
my joy in unrelenting *p* . . . Jb 6:10
may be chastened on a bed of *p* . . . Jb 15:18
Why is my *p* unending, . . . Jer 4:19
neighbors who are *p* briers . . . Ez 28:24
these are the beginning of birth *p*. . . . Mt 24:8
woman giving birth to a child has *p* . . . Jn 16:21
as in the *p* of childbirth right up . . . Rom 8:22
I would not make another *p* visit . . . 2 Cor 2:1
again in the *p* of childbirth . . . Gal 4:19
as labor *p* on a pregnant woman, . . . 1 Thes 5:3
seems pleasant at the time, but *p*. . . . Heb 12:11
up under the *p* of unjust suffering . . . 1 Pt 2:19
at the *p* trial you are suffering, . . . 1 Pt 4:12
or mourning or crying or *p*, . . . Rv 21:4

PARABLES *a brief story using physical symbols to illustrate a spiritual truth*
I will open my mouth in *p*, . . . Ps 78:2
I will open my mouth in *p*, . . . Mt 13:35
but to others I speak in *p*, . . . Lk 8:10

PARDON(ED)(S) *to spare a guilty person the punishment deserved; to forgive*
as you have *p* them from the time . . . Nm 14:19
p everyone who sets his heart . . . 2 Chr 30:18
Why do you not *p* my offenses . . . Jb 7:21
and to our God, for he will freely *p*. . . . Is 55:7
I will *p*. . . . Jl 3:21
who *p* sin and forgives . . . Mi 7:18

PARENTS *a person's mother and father*
wealth are inherited from *p*, . . . Prv 19:14
children will rebel against their *p* . . . Mt 10:21
left home or wife or brothers or *p* . . . Lk 18:29
You will be betrayed even by *p*, . . . Lk 21:16
Neither this man nor his *p* sinned, . . . Jn 9:3
they disobey their *p*; they are . . . Rom 1:30
Children, obey your *p* in the Lord, . . . Eph 6:1
disobedient to their *p*, ungrateful, . . . 2 Tm 3:2

PARTIAL(ITY) *inclined to favor one person more than another; biased*
do not show *p* to the poor . . . Lv 19:15
Do not show *p* in judging; . . . Dt 1:17
our God there is no injustice or *p* . . . 2 Chr 19:7
who shows no *p* to princes . . . Jb 34:19
It is not good to be *p* to the wicked . . . Prv 18:5
have shown *p* in matters of the law . . . Mal 2:9
and that you do not show *p* . . . Lk 20:21

PASS(ED)(ING), PAST *to proceed from one place or time to another*
and when I see the blood, I will *p* . . . Ex 12:13
you with my hand until I have *p* by. . . . Ex 33:22
all who *p* by will be appalled . . . 1 Kgs 9:8
for they quickly *p*, and we fly away. . . . Ps 90:10
When you *p* through the waters, . . . Is 43:2
dominion that will not *p* away, . . . Dn 7:14
will certainly not *p* away . . . Mt 24:34
Heaven and earth will *p* away, . . . Mt 24:35
saw him, *p* by on the other side. . . . Lk 10:32
in the *p* was written to teach us, . . . Rom 15:4
world in its present form is *p* away. . . . 1 Cor 7:31

there is knowledge, it will *p* away. . . . 1 Cor 13:8
For what I received I *p* on to you . . . 1 Cor 15:3
which for ages *p* was kept hidden . . . Eph 3:9
In the *p* God spoke . . . Heb 1:1
he will *p* away like a wild flower. . . . Jas 1:10
The world and its desires *p* away, . . . 1 Jn 2:17

PASSION(ATE)(S) *intense emotion*
Their *p* smolders all night; . . . Hos 7:6
the sinful *p* aroused . . . Rom 7:5
better to marry than to burn with *p*. . . . 1 Cor 7:9
crucified the sinful nature with its *p* . . . Gal 5:24
not in *p* lust like the heathen, . . . 1 Thes 4:5
and enslaved by all kinds of *p* . . . Ti 3:3

PASSOVER *historic event (when God's judgment passed over the Hebrews); meal commemorating the Hebrews' liberation from slavery in Egypt*
Eat it in haste; it is the LORD's *P*. . . . Ex 12:11
Have the Israelites celebrate the *P*. . . Nm 9:2
celebrate the *P* of the LORD your . . . Dt 16:1
Celebrate the *P* to the LORD . . . 2 Kgs 23:21
the exiles celebrated the *P*. . . . Ezr 6:19
our *P* lamb, has been sacrificed. . . . 1 Cor 5:7
he kept the *P* and the sprinkling . . . Heb 11:28

PASTURE(S) *plot of land suitable for grazing cattle*
He makes me lie down in green *p*, . . . Ps 23:2
dwell in the land and enjoy safe *p*. . . . Ps 37:3
and we are the people of his *p*, . . . Ps 95:7
I will *p* them on the mountains . . . Ez 34:13
P the flock marked for slaughter. . . . Zec 11:4
come in and go out, and find *p*. . . . Jn 10:9

PATH(S) *trail, often worn by footsteps*
known to me the *p* of life; . . . Ps 16:11
He guides me in *p* of righteousness . . . Ps 23:3
teach me your *p*; . . . Ps 25:4
lead me in a straight *p* . . . Ps 27:11
and a light for my *p*. . . . Ps 119:105
and he will make your *p* straight. . . . Prv 3:6
Make level *p* for your feet . . . Prv 4:26
and he examines all his *p*, . . . Prv 5:21
along the *p* of justice, . . . Prv 8:20
along that *p* is immortality. . . . Prv 12:28
the *p* of the upright is a highway. . . . Prv 15:19
from the *p* of understanding . . . Prv 21:16
In the *p* of the wicked lie thorns . . . Prv 22:5
The *p* of the righteous is level; . . . Is 26:7
ask for the ancient *p*, . . . Jer 6:16
so that we may walk in his *p*. . . . Mi 4:2
make straight *p* for him. . . . Mt 3:3
fell along the *p*, and the birds came . . . Mt 13:4
to guide our feet into the *p* of peace . . . Lk 1:79
to me the *p* of life; . . . Acts 2:28
no stumbling block in anyone's *p*, . . . 2 Cor 6:3

PATIENCE, PATIENT(LY) *endurance; hopeful forbearance*
What prospects, that I should be *p*? . . . Jb 6:11
I waited *p* for the LORD; . . . Ps 40:1
A *p* man has great understanding, . . . Prv 14:29
Better a *p* man than a warrior, . . . Prv 16:32
A man's wisdom gives him *p*; . . . Prv 19:11
Through a *p* ruler can be persuaded . . . Prv 25:15
Is it not enough to try the *p* of men? . . . Is 7:13
I waited *p* till dawn, . . . Is 38:13
Yet I will wait *p* for the day . . . Hb 3:16
and *p*, not realizing that God's . . . Rom 2:4
we do not yet have, we wait for it *p*. . . . Rom 8:25
bore with great *p* the objects . . . Rom 9:22
Be joyful in hope, *p* in affliction, . . . Rom 12:12
Love is *p*, love is kind. . . . 1 Cor 13:4
produces in you endurance . . . 2 Cor 1:6
understanding, *p* and kindness; . . . 2 Cor 6:6
joy, peace, *p*, kindness, goodness, . . . Gal 5:22
humble and gentle; be *p*, . . . Eph 4:2
humility, gentleness and *p*. . . . Col 3:12
with great *p* and careful instruction . . . 2 Tm 4:2

Be *p*, then, brothers, . . . Jas 5:7
He is *p* with you, not wanting . . . 2 Pt 3:9
p endurance that are ours in Jesus, . . . Rv 1:9
kept my command to endure *p*, . . . Rv 3:10
This calls for *p* endurance . . . Rv 13:10

PATTERN *design; plan; customary mode of behavior*
according to the *p* shown you . . . Ex 25:40
who was a *p* of the one to come. . . . Rom 5:14
longer to the *p* of this world, . . . Rom 12:2
keep as the *p* of sound teaching, . . . 2 Tm 1:13
according to the *p* shown you . . . Heb 8:5

PEACE(FUL) *state of calm; freedom from strife or discord; harmony in personal relationship*
I will grant *p* in the land, . . . Lv 26:6
him I am making my covenant of *p* . . . Nm 25:12
So the land had *p* for forty years, . . . Jgs 3:11
and the land had *p* for eighty years. . . . Jgs 3:30
And there was *p* between Israel . . . 1 Sm 7:14
may there be the LORD's *p* forever . . . 1 Kgs 2:33
and I will grant Israel *p* . . . 1 Chr 22:9
I have no *p*, no quietness; . . . Jb 3:26
LORD blesses his people with *p*. . . . Ps 29:11
seek *p* and pursue it. . . . Ps 34:14
there is a future for the man of *p*. . . . Ps 37:37
righteousness and *p* kiss each other . . . Ps 85:10
I am a man of *p*; . . . Ps 120:7
Pray for the *p* of Jerusalem: . . . Ps 122:6
A heart at *p* gives life to the body, . . . Prv 14:30
his enemies live at *p* with him. . . . Prv 16:7
Better a dry crust with *p* and quiet . . . Prv 17:1
a time for war and a time for *p*. . . . Eccl 3:8
Everlasting Father, Prince of *P*. . . . Is 9:6
You will keep in perfect *p* . . . Is 26:3
The fruit of righteousness will be *p*; . . . Is 32:17
your *p* would have been like a river, . . . Is 48:18
punishment that brought us *p* was . . . Is 53:5
nor my covenant of *p* be removed, . . . Is 54:10
and be led forth in *p*; . . . Is 55:12
P, p, to those far and near, . . . Is 57:19
The way of *p* they do not know; . . . Is 59:8
'*P, p*,' they say, . . . Jer 6:14
"*P*," when there is no *p*, . . . Ez 13:10
I will make a covenant of *p* . . . Ez 34:25
And he will be their *p*. . . . Mi 5:5
He walked with me in *p* . . . Mal 2:6
I did not come to bring *p*, . . . Mt 10:34
to guide our feet into the path of *p* . . . Lk 1:79
on earth *p* to men on whom his . . . Lk 2:14
P I leave with you; my *p* . . . Jn 14:27
so that in me you may have *p*. . . . Jn 16:33
we have *p* with God . . . Rom 5:1
by the Spirit is life and *p*; . . . Rom 8:6
God has called us to live in *p*. . . . 1 Cor 7:15
a God of disorder but of *p*. . . . 1 Cor 14:33
joy, *p*, patience, kindness, . . . Gal 5:22
he himself is our *p*, who has made . . . Eph 2:14
comes from the gospel of *p*. . . . Eph 6:15
the *p* of God, which transcends all . . . Phil 4:7
by making *p* through his blood, . . . Col 1:20
Let the *p* of Christ rule . . . Col 3:15
While people are saying, "*P*. . . 1 Thes 5:3
the God of *p*, sanctify you through . . . 1 Thes 5:23
that we may live *p* and quiet lives . . . 1 Tm 2:2
righteousness, faith, love and *p*, . . . 2 Tm 2:22
"king of Salem" means "king of *p*." . . . Heb 7:2
effort to live in *p* with all men . . . Heb 12:14
May the God of *p*, who . . . Heb 13:20
he must seek *p* and pursue it. . . . 1 Pt 3:11
blameless and at *p* with him. . . . 2 Pt 3:14
power to take *p* from the earth . . . Rv 6:4

PERCEIVE, PERCEIVING *to understand*
you *p* my thoughts from afar. . . . Ps 139:2
not he who weighs the heart *p* it? . . . Prv 24:12

you will be ever seeing but never *p*. . . . Mt 13:14

PERFECT(ER)(ING)(ION) *whole, complete*
As for God, his way is *p*; . . . 2 Sm 22:31
one *p* in knowledge is with you. . . . Jb 36:4
The law of the LORD is *p*, . . . Ps 19:7
From Zion, *p* in beauty, . . . Ps 50:2
To all *p* I see a limit; . . . Ps 119:96
but my dove, my *p* one, is unique, . . . Song 6:9
for in *p* faithfulness . . . Is 25:1
You will keep in *p* peace . . . Is 26:3
the *p* of beauty, . . . Lam 2:15
had given you made your beauty *p*, . . . Ez 16:14
full of wisdom and *p* in beauty. . . . Ez 28:12
answered, "If you want to be *p*, . . . Mt 19:21
his good, pleasing and *p* will. . . . Rom 12:2
but when *p* comes, the imperfect . . . 1 Cor 13:10
p holiness out of reverence for God . . . 2 Cor 7:1
for my power is made *p* . . . 2 Cor 12:9
and our prayer is for your *p*. . . . 2 Cor 13:9
or have already been made *p*, . . . Phil 3:12
binds them all together in *p* unity. . . . Col 3:14
the author of their salvation *p* . . . Heb 2:10
what he suffered and, once made *p*, . . . Heb 5:9
If *p* could have been attained . . . Heb 7:11
useless (for the law made nothing *p* . . . Heb 7:19
and more *p* tabernacle that is not . . . Heb 9:11
make *p* those who draw . . . Heb 10:1
he has made *p* forever those who . . . Heb 10:14
the author and *p* of our faith, . . . Heb 12:2
spirits of righteous men made *p*, . . . Heb 12:23
Every good and *p* gift is from above . . . Jas 1:17
into the *p* law that gives freedom, . . . Jas 1:25
But *p* love drives out fear, . . . 1 Jn 4:18

PERISH(ABLE)(ED)(ES)(ING) *to be lost or destroyed, either physically or spiritually; to pass away*
And if I *p*, I *p*. . . . Est 4:16
but the way of the wicked will *p*. . . . Ps 1:6
Those who are far from you will *p*; . . . Ps 73:27
They will *p*, but you remain; . . . Ps 102:26
and he who pours out lies will *p*. . . . Prv 19:9
A false witness will *p*, . . . Prv 21:28
when the wicked *p*, the righteous . . . Prv 28:28
the wisdom of the wise will *p*, . . . Is 29:14
that will not serve you will *p*; . . . Is 60:12
unless you repent, you too will all *p* . . . Lk 13:3
But not a hair of your head will *p*. . . . Lk 21:18
whoever believes in him shall not *p* . . . Jn 3:16
eternal life, and they shall never *p*; . . . Jn 10:28
foolishness to those who are *p*, . . . 1 Cor 1:18
The body that is sown is *p*, . . . 1 Cor 15:42
it is veiled to those who are *p*. . . . 2 Cor 4:3
They will *p*, but you remain; . . . Heb 1:11
into an inheritance that can never *p* . . . 1 Pt 1:4
which *p* even though refined by fire . . . 1 Pt 1:7
not wanting anyone to *p*, . . . 2 Pt 3:9

PERSECUTE(D), PERSECUTION(S) *to harass constantly; oppress*
for men *p* me without cause. . . . Ps 119:86
Blessed are those who are *p* . . . Mt 5:10
and pray for those who *p* you, . . . Mt 5:44
or hardship or *p* or famine . . . Rom 8:35
Bless those who *p* you; bless . . . Rom 12:14
when we are *p*, we endure it; . . . 1 Cor 4:12
in hardships, in *p*, in difficulties. . . . 2 Cor 12:10
faith in all the *p* and trials you are . . . 2 Thes 1:4
life in Christ Jesus will be *p*, . . . 2 Tm 3:12
destitute, *p* and mistreated . . . Heb 11:37

PERSEVERANCE, PERSEVERE(D)(S), PERSEVERING *patient endurance of hardship; persisting in a state or enterprise in spite of difficulties and discouragement*
we know that suffering produces *p*; . . . Rom 5:3

trusts, always hopes, always *p*. . . . 1 Cor 13:7
into God's love and Christ's *p*. . . . 2 Thes 3:5
You need to *p* so that . . . Heb 10:36
he *p* because he saw him who is . . . Heb 11:27
run with *p* the race marked out . . . Heb 12:1
the testing of your faith develops *p*. . . . Jas 1:3
P must finish its work . . . Jas 1:4
Blessed is the man who *p* . . . Jas 1:12
p; and to *p*, godliness; . . . 2 Pt 1:6

PERSUADE(D), PERSUASIVE *to convince*
trying to *p* Jews and Greeks. . . . Acts 18:4
being fully *p* that God had power . . . Rom 4:21
not with wise and *p* words, . . . 1 Cor 2:4
is to fear the Lord, we try to *p* men. . . . 2 Cor 5:11

PERVERSION, PERVERT(ED)(S) *departure from what is natural, reasonable, or morally right*
sexual relations with it; that is a *p*. . . . Lv 18:23
What they have done is a *p*; . . . Lv 20:12
Do not *p* justice or show partiality. . . . Dt 16:19
and accepted bribes and *p* justice. . . . 1 Sm 8:3
to *p* the course of justice. . . . Prv 17:23
the due penalty for their *p*. . . . Rom 1:27
are trying to *p* the gospel of Christ. . . . Gal 1:7
for murderers, for adulterers and *p*, . . . 1 Tm 1:10
up to sexual immorality and *p*. . . . Jude 1:7

PIERCE(D) *to penetrate with a sharp instrument*
and *p* his ear with an awl. . . . Ex 21:6
they have *p* my hands and my feet. . . . Ps 22:16
but my ears you have *p*; . . . Ps 40:6
Reckless words *p* like a sword, . . . Prv 12:18
But he was *p* for our transgressions, . . . Is 53:5
look on me, the one they have *p*, . . . Zec 12:10
a sword will *p* your own soul too. . . . Lk 2:35
even those who *p* him; . . . Rv 1:7

PILLAR(S) *structural support; stone slabs built to pagan deities; strong leader*
and she became a *p* of salt. . . . Gn 19:26
ahead of them in a *p* of cloud . . . Ex 13:21
and John, those reputed to be *p*, . . . Gal 2:9
the *p* and foundation of the truth. . . . 1 Tm 3:15
who overcomes I will make a *p* . . . Rv 3:12

PIT *natural or dug-out hole in the earth; grave*
falls into the *p* he has made. . . . Ps 7:15
He lifted me out of the slimy *p*, . . . Ps 40:2
for a prostitute is a deep *p* . . . Prv 23:27
If a man digs a *p*, he will fall into it; . . . Prv 26:27
me from the *p* of destruction; . . . Is 38:17
a blind man, both will fall into a *p*. . . . Mt 15:14

PITIED, PITY *to sympathize; to feel compassion*
He will take *p* on the weak . . . Ps 72:13
But *p* the man who falls . . . Eccl 4:10
when he saw him, he took *p* on him . . . Lk 10:33
we are to be *p* more than all men. . . . 1 Cor 15:19

PLAGUE(D)(S) *widespread calamity or epidemic; sometimes a divine judgment; figurative of great suffering*
When famine or *p* comes . . . 2 Chr 6:28
they are not *p* by human ills. . . . Ps 73:5
All day long I have been *p*; . . . Ps 73:14
nor the *p* that destroys at midday. . . . Ps 91:6
Where, O death, are your *p*? . . . Hos 13:14
full of the seven last *p* came . . . Rv 21:9
to him the *p* described in this book. . . . Rv 22:18

PLAN(NED)(S) *a scheme for making or doing something*
no *p* of yours can be thwarted. . . . Jb 42:2
and make all your *p* succeed. . . . Ps 20:4
p of the LORD stand firm forever, . . . Ps 33:11

The things you *p* for us . . . Ps 40:5
those who *p* what is good find love . . . Prv 14:22
Many are the *p* in a man's heart, . . . Prv 19:21
Make *p* by seeking advice; . . . Prv 20:18
Surely, as I have *p*, so it will be, . . . Is 14:24
to hide their *p* from the LORD, . . . Is 29:15
those who carry out *p* that are not . . . Is 30:1
But the noble man makes noble *p*, . . . Is 32:8
what I have *p*, that will I do. . . . Is 46:11
Or do I make my *p* in a worldly . . . 2 Cor 1:17
predestined according to the *p* . . . Eph 1:11
God had *p* something better for us . . . Heb 11:40

PLANTED *sown with seeds; established*
the LORD God had *p* a garden . . . Gn 2:8
He is like a tree *p* by streams . . . Ps 1:3
out of her earnings she *p* a vineyard . . . Prv 31:16
He will be like a tree *p* by the water . . . Jer 17:8
I will *p* Israel in their own land, . . . Am 9:15
Father has not *p* will be pulled . . . Mt 15:13
was a landowner who *p* a vineyard. . . . Mt 21:33
I *p* the seed, Apollos watered it, . . . 1 Cor 3:6
Who *p* a vineyard and does not eat . . . 1 Cor 9:7
humbly accept the word *p* in you, . . . Jas 1:21

PLEASANT *satisfying to the senses*
and how *p* is his land, . . . Gn 49:15
for me in *p* places; . . . Ps 16:6
how *p* and fitting to praise him! . . . Ps 147:1
knowledge will be *p* to your soul. . . . Prv 2:10
and *p* words promote instruction. . . . Prv 16:21
Tell us *p* things, . . . Is 30:10
that you always have *p* memories . . . 1 Thes 3:6
No discipline seems *p* at the time, . . . Heb 12:11

PLEASE(D)(S), PLEASING *to make glad; to satisfy*
trees that were *p* to the eye . . . Gn 2:9
LORD was *p* to make you his own. . . . 1 Sm 12:22
He does whatever he *p*. . . . Jb 23:13
This will *p* the LORD more . . . Ps 69:31
May my meditation be *p* to him, . . . Ps 104:34
he does whatever *p* him. . . . Ps 115:3
but the prayer of the upright *p* him. . . . Prv 15:8
but those of the pure are *p* to him. . . . Prv 15:26
and dishonest scales do not *p* him. . . . Prv 20:23
man who *p* God will escape her, . . . Eccl 7:26
How much more *p* is your love . . . Song 4:10
and I will do all that I *p*. . . . Is 46:10
your sacrifices do not *p* me. . . . Jer 6:20
and I give it to anyone I *p* . . . Jer 27:5
whom I love; with him I am well *p* . . . Mt 3:17
The wind blows wherever it *p*. . . . Jn 3:8
for I seek not to *p* myself . . . Jn 5:30
by the sinful nature cannot *p* God. . . . Rom 8:8
p to God this is your spiritual . . . Rom 12:1
of the weak and not to *p* ourselves. . . . Rom 15:1
So we make it our goal to *p* him, . . . 2 Cor 5:9
or of God? Or am I trying to *p* men . . . Gal 1:10
find out what *p* the Lord . . . Eph 5:10
an acceptable sacrifice, *p* to God. . . . Phil 4:18
and may *p* him in every way: . . . Col 1:10
how to live in order to *p* God, . . . 1 Thes 4:1
This is good, and *p* God our Savior, . . . 1 Tm 2:3
wants to *p* his commanding officer. . . . 2 Tm 2:4
to try to *p* them, not to talk back . . . Ti 2:9
I will not be *p* with him. . . . Heb 10:38
faith it is impossible to *p* God, . . . Heb 11:6
for with such sacrifices God is *p*. . . . Heb 13:16

may he work in us what is *p* to him, . . . Heb 13:21
whom I love; with him I am well *p* . . . 2 Pt 1:17

PLEASURE(S) *enjoyable sensation or emotion; a source of delight or joy*
you do not take *p* in burnt offerings . . . Ps 51:16
His *p* is not in the strength . . . Ps 147:10
A fool finds *p* in evil conduct, . . . Prv 10:23
A fool finds no *p* in understanding . . . Prv 18:2
He who loves *p* will become poor; . . . Prv 21:17
I take no *p* in the death . . . Ez 33:11
Father, for this was your good *p*. . . . Lk 10:21
in accordance with his *p* and will . . . Eph 1:5
the widow who lives for *p* is dead . . . 1 Tm 5:6
lovers of *p* rather than lovers . . . 2 Tm 3:4
by all kinds of passions and *p*. . . . Ti 3:3
rather than to enjoy the *p* of sin . . . Heb 11:25
may spend what you get on your *p*. . . . Jas 4:3
reveling in their *p* while they feast . . . 2 Pt 2:13

PONDER(ED) *to think deeply; to meditate*
and *p* what he has done. . . . Ps 64:9
they are *p* by all who delight . . . Ps 111:2
but I will *p* your statutes. . . . Ps 119:95
up all these things and *p* them . . . Lk 2:19

POOR *having little or no wealth and few possessions; humble; see POVERTY*
Leave them for the *p* and the alien. . . . Lv 19:10
there should be no *p* among you, . . . Dt 15:4
There will always be *p* people . . . Dt 15:11
So the *p* have hope, . . . Jb 5:16
frustrate the plans of the *p*, . . . Ps 14:6
This *p* man called, and the LORD . . . Ps 34:6
You rescue the *p* from those too . . . Ps 35:10
Yet I am *p* and needy; . . . Ps 40:17
O God, you provided for the *p*. . . . Ps 68:10
maintain the rights of the *p* . . . Ps 82:3
scattered abroad his gifts to the *p*, . . . Ps 112:9
He raises the *p* from the dust . . . Ps 113:7
the LORD secures justice for the *p* . . . Ps 140:12
Lazy hands make a man *p*, . . . Prv 10:4
to be *p*, yet has great wealth. . . . Prv 13:7
The *p* are shunned . . . Prv 14:20
oppresses the *p* shows contempt . . . Prv 14:31
who mocks the *p* shows contempt . . . Prv 17:5
better to be *p* than a liar. . . . Prv 19:22
not love sleep or you will grow *p*; . . . Prv 20:13
Rich and *p* have this in common: . . . Prv 22:2
for he shares his food with the *p*. . . . Prv 22:9
Better a *p* man whose walk is . . . Prv 28:6
to the *p* will lack nothing, . . . Prv 28:27
defend the rights of the *p*, . . . Prv 31:9
Better a *p* but wise youth . . . Eccl 4:13
to deprive the *p* of their rights . . . Is 10:2
You have been a refuge for the *p*, . . . Is 25:4
me to preach good news to the *p*. . . . Is 61:1
He defended the cause of the *p* . . . Jer 22:16
They trample on the heads of the *p* . . . Am 2:7
you women who oppress the *p* . . . Am 4:1
saying: "Blessed are the *p* in spirit, . . . Mt 5:3
the good news is preached to the *p*. . . . Mt 11:5
your possessions and give to the *p*, . . . Mt 19:21
The *p* you will always have . . . Mt 26:11
me to preach good news to the *p*. . . . Lk 4:18
invite the *p*, the crippled, the lame, . . . Lk 14:13
also saw a *p* widow put . . . Lk 21:2
You will always have the *p* . . . Jn 12:8
doing good and helping the *p* . . . Acts 9:36
If I give all I possess to the *p* . . . 1 Cor 13:3
yet for your sakes he became *p*, . . . 2 Cor 8:9
continue to remember the *p*, . . . Gal 2:10
and a *p* man in shabby clothes . . . Jas 2:2
not God chosen those who are *p* . . . Jas 2:5

POSSESSION(S) *property; something owned*
to give you this land to take *p* of it . . . Gn 15:7
I will give it to you as a *p* . . . Ex 6:8
nations you will be my treasured *p*. . . . Ex 19:5
to be his people, his treasured *p*. . . . Dt 7:6

take *p* of the land the LORD your . . . Jos 1:11
the ends of the earth your *p*. . . . Ps 2:8
go, sell your *p* and give to the poor, . . . Mt 19:21
consist in the abundance of his *p*. . . . Lk 12:15
now I give half of my *p* to the poor, . . . Lk 19:8
any of his *p* was his own, . . . Acts 4:32
what I want is not your *p* but you. . . . 2 Cor 12:14
of those who are God's *p* . . . Eph 1:14
yourselves had better and lasting *p*. . . . Heb 10:34
If anyone has material *p* . . . 1 Jn 3:17

POSSIBLE *capable of existing or of being done*
but with God all things are *p*. . . . Mt 19:26
if it is *p*, may this cup be taken . . . Mt 26:39
Everything is *p* for him who . . . Mk 9:23
If it is *p*, as far as it depends on you, . . . Rom 12:18
to everyone, to win as many as *p* . . . 1 Cor 9:19
by all *p* means I might save some. . . . 1 Cor 9:22

POUR(ED)(S) *to send forth; to flow freely*
I am *p* out like water, . . . Ps 22:14
till the Spirit is *p* upon us . . . Is 32:15
I will *p* out my Spirit . . . Is 44:3
So I said I would *p* out my wrath . . . Ez 20:8
I will *p* out my Spirit on all people. . . . Jl 2:28
I will *p* out on the house of David . . . Zec 12:10
p out so much blessing that you . . . Mal 3:10
which is *p* out for many . . . Mt 26:28
And no one *p* new wine . . . Lk 5:37
I will *p* out my Spirit on all people. . . . Acts 2:17
of the Holy Spirit had been *p* out . . . Acts 10:45
because God has *p* out his love . . . Rom 5:5
even if I am being *p* out like a drink . . . Phil 2:17
whom he *p* out on us generously . . . Ti 3:6
and *p* out his bowl on the land, . . . Rv 16:2

POTTER *one who makes earthenware pots, dishes, or other vessels from clay*
Can the pot say of the *p*, . . . Is 29:16
Does the clay say to the *p*, . . . Is 45:9
We are the clay, you are the *p*; . . . Is 64:8
Like clay in the hand of the *p*, . . . Jer 18:6
Does not the *p* have the right . . . Rom 9:21

POVERTY *the state of being poor; lack or the means of providing material needs; see POOR*
The LORD sends *p* and wealth; . . . 1 Sm 2:7
p will come on you like a bandit . . . Prv 6:11
who ignores discipline comes to *p* . . . Prv 13:18
but mere talk leads only to *p*. . . . Prv 14:23
as surely as haste leads to *p*, . . . Prv 21:5
fantasies will have his fill of *p*. . . . Prv 28:19
give me neither *p* nor riches, . . . Prv 30:8
let them drink and forget their *p* . . . Prv 31:7
she out of her *p* put in all she had . . . Lk 21:4
and their extreme *p* welled up . . . 2 Cor 8:2
through his *p* might become rich. . . . 2 Cor 8:9
I know your afflictions and your *p* . . . Rv 2:9

POWER(FUL)(LESS)(S) *the strength or authority to act or to accomplish something; see MIGHT*
was majestic in *p*. . . . Ex 15:6
out of Egypt with great *p* . . . Ex 32:11
Spirit of God came upon him in *p*, . . . 1 Sm 10:10
the LORD came upon David in *p* . . . 1 Sm 16:13
P and might are in your hand, . . . 2 Chr 20:6
God is exalted in his *p*. . . . Jb 36:22
with the saving of his right hand. . . . Ps 20:6
and beheld your *p* and your glory. . . . Ps 63:2
Your arm is endued with *p*; . . . Ps 89:13
of the *p* of your awesome works, . . . Ps 145:6
Great is our Lord and mighty in *p*; . . . Ps 147:5
Praise him for his acts of *p*; . . . Ps 150:2
The tongue has the *p* of life . . . Prv 18:21
A wise man has great *p*, . . . Prv 24:5
the Sovereign LORD comes with *p* . . . Is 40:10
But God made the earth by his *p*; . . . Jer 10:12

With my great *p* and outstretched . . . Jer 27:5
and the earth by your great *p* . . . Jer 32:17
nor by *p*, but by my Spirit, . . . Zec 4:6
do not know the Scriptures or the *p* . . .
  Mt 22:29
on the clouds of the sky, with *p* . . . Mt 24:30
After me will come one more *p* . . . Mk 1:7
and the *p* of the Most High will . . . Lk 1:35
to Galilee in the *p* of the Spirit, . . . Lk 4:14
he gave them *p* and authority . . . Lk 9:1
clothed with *p* from on high. . . . Lk 24:49
you will receive *p* when the Holy . . . Acts 1:8
With great *p* the apostles . . . Acts 4:33
with the Holy Spirit and *p*, . . . Acts 10:38
it is the *p* of God for the salvation . . . Rom 1:16
his eternal *p* and divine nature . . . Rom 1:20
when we were still *p*, Christ died . . . Rom 5:6
For what the law was *p* to do . . . Rom 8:3
nor any *p*, neither height nor depth . . . Rom
  8:38
that I might display my *p* in you . . . Rom 9:17
cross of Christ be emptied of its *p*. . . . 1 Cor
  1:17
a demonstration of the Spirit's *p*, . . . 1 Cor 2:4
all dominion, authority and *p*. . . . 1 Cor 15:24
to show that this all-surpassing *p* is . . . 2 Cor
  4:7
for my *p* is made perfect . . . 2 Cor 12:9
weakness, yet he lives by God's *p*. . . . 2 Cor
  13:4
according to his *p* that is at work . . . Eph 3:20
and the *p* of his resurrection . . . Phil 3:10
strengthened with all *p* according . . . Col 1:11
whether thrones or *p* or rulers . . . Col 1:16
in blazing fire with his *p* angels. . . . 2 Thes 1:7
form of godliness but denying its *p*. . . . 2 Tm
  3:5
sustaining all things by his *p* word. . . . Heb 1:3
might destroy him who holds the *p* . . . Heb 2:14
The prayer of a righteous man is *p* . . . Jas 5:16
His divine *p* has given us . . . 2 Pt 1:3
p and authority, through Jesus . . . Jude 1:25
to receive glory and honor and *p*, . . . Rv 4:11
and glory and *p* belong to our God, . . . Rv 19:1
The second death has no *p* . . . Rv 20:6

PRACTICE *to do or perform frequently; to apply*
but they do not put them into *p*. . . . Ez 33:31
into *p* is like a wise man who built . . . Mt 7:24
for they do not *p* what they preach. . . . Mt 23:3
or seen in me—put it into *p*. . . . Phil 4:9
to put their religion into *p* by caring . . . 1 Tm
  5:4

PRAISE(D)(S), PRAISING *to worship,*
commend, or give honor to
He is my God, and I will *p* him, . . . Ex 15:2
Oh, *p* the greatness of our God! . . . Dt 32:3
The LORD lives! *P* be to my Rock . . . 2 Sm
  22:47
is the LORD and most worthy of *p*; . . . 1 Chr
  16:25
that we may glory in your *p*. . . . 1 Chr 16:35
four thousand are to *p* the LORD . . . 1 Chr 23:5
P be to you, O LORD, . . . 1 Chr 29:10
they raised their voices in *p* . . . 2 Chr 5:13
took their places to *p* the LORD, . . . Ezr 3:10
Ezra *p* the LORD, the great God; . . . Neh 8:6
may the name of the LORD be *p*. . . . Jb 1:21
I will *p* you, O LORD, . . . Ps 9:1
I will sing *p* to your name. . . . Ps 18:49
it is fitting for the upright to *p* him. . . . Ps 33:1
his *p* will always be on my lips. . . . Ps 34:1
a hymn of *p* to our God. . . . Ps 40:3
for I will yet *p* him, . . . Ps 42:5
the nations will *p* you for ever . . . Ps 45:17
sing to him a psalm of *p*. . . . Ps 47:7
I will *p* you as long as I live, . . . Ps 63:4
P awaits you, O God, in Zion; . . . Ps 65:1
make his *p* glorious. . . . Ps 66:2
I will *p* God's name in song . . . Ps 69:30
My mouth is filled with your *p*, . . . Ps 71:8

the poor and needy *p* your name. . . . Ps 74:21
I will *p* you, O Lord my God, . . . Ps 86:12
The heavens *p* your wonders, . . . Ps 89:5
Sing to the LORD, *p* his name; . . . Ps 96:2
to you, O LORD, I will sing *p*. . . . Ps 101:1
not yet created may *p* the LORD: . . . Ps 102:18
P the LORD, O my soul; . . . Ps 103:1
Sing to him, sing *p* to him; . . . Ps 105:2
P the LORD, all you nations; . . . Ps 117:1
Let me live that I may *p* you, . . . Ps 119:175
I *p* you because I am fearfully . . . Ps 139:14
P be to the LORD my Rock, . . . Ps 144:1
is the LORD and most worthy of *p*; . . . Ps 145:3
Let every creature *p* his holy name . . .
  Ps 145:21
how pleasant and fitting to *p* him! . . . Ps 147:1
Let them *p* the name of the LORD, . . . Ps 148:13
his *p* in the assembly of the saints. . . . Ps 149:1
Let another *p* you, and not your . . . Prv 27:2
man is tested by the *p* he receives. . . . Prv
  27:21
let her works bring her *p* . . . Prv 31:31
we will *p* your love more than wine . . . Song 1:4
his *p* from the ends of the earth, . . . Is 42:10
and a garment of *p* . . . Is 61:3
Then Daniel *p* the God of heaven . . . Dn 2:19
and *p* your Father in heaven. . . . Mt 5:16
you have ordained *p*'? . . . Mt 21:16
the people saw it, they also *p* God. . . . Lk 18:43
seeing what had happened, *p* God . . . Lk 23:47
for they loved *p* from men more . . . Jn 12:43
p God and enjoying the favor . . . Acts 2:47
speaking in tongues and *p* God. . . . Acts 10:46
If you are *p* God with your spirit, . . . 1 Cor
  14:16
might be for the *p* of his glory. . . . Eph 1:12
offer to God a sacrifice of *p* . . . Heb 13:15
With the tongue we *p* our Lord . . . Jas 3:9
happy? Let him sing songs of *p*. . . . Jas 5:13
that in all things God may be *p* . . . 1 Pt 4:11

PRAY(ED)(ING) *to communicate with God; see*
PRAYER
is near us whenever we *p* to him? . . . Dt 4:7
the LORD by failing to *p* for you. . . . 1 Sm 12:23
when they *p* toward this place. . . . 1 Kgs 8:30
And Elisha *p*, "O LORD, . . . 2 Kgs 6:17
will humble themselves and *p* . . . 2 Chr 7:14
and *p* for the well-being of the king . . . Ezr 6:10
we *p* to our God and posted a guard . . . Neh 4:9
My servant Jb will *p* for you, . . . Jb 42:8
let everyone who is godly *p* . . . Ps 32:6
P for the peace of Jerusalem: . . . Ps 122:6
got down on his knees and *p*, . . . Dn 6:10
I *p* to the LORD my God . . . Dn 9:4
From inside the fish Jonah *p* . . . Jon 2:1
and *p* for those who persecute you, . . . Mt 5:44
And when you *p*, do not be like . . . Mt 6:5
up on a mountainside by himself to *p*. . . .
  Mt 14:23
hands on them and *p* for them. . . . Mt 19:13
Sit here while I go over there and *p* . . .
  Mt 26:36
with his face to the ground and *p*, . . . Mt 26:39
off to a solitary place, where he *p*. . . . Mk 1:35
p that if possible the hour might . . . Mk 14:35
them that they should always *p* . . . Lk 18:1
P that you will not fall . . . Lk 22:40
he looked toward heaven and *p*: . . . Jn 17:1
After they *p*, the place where they . . . Acts 4:31
who *p* and laid their hands on them . . . Acts 6:6
they *p* for them that they might . . . Acts 8:15
do not know what we ought to *p* for, . . . Rom
  8:26
in my struggle by *p* to God for me. . . . Rom
  15:30
in a tongue should *p* that he may . . . 1 Cor
  14:13
I *p* also that the eyes . . . Eph 1:18
I *p* that out of his glorious riches he . . . Eph
  3:16

And *p* in the Spirit on all occasions . . . Eph 6:18
p for us, too, that God may open . . . Col 4:3
Be joyful always; *p* continually; . . . 1 Thes 5:17
in mind, we constantly *p* for you, . . . 2 Thes
  1:11
one of you in trouble? He should *p*. . . . Jas 5:13
p for each other so that you may be . . . Jas
  5:16
self-controlled so that you can *p*. . . . 1 Pt 4:7
up in your most holy faith and *p* . . . Jude 1:20

PRAYER(S) *communication with God; see*
PRAY
for their *p* reached heaven, . . . 2 Chr 30:27
be merciful to me and hear my *p*. . . . Ps 4:1
the LORD accepts my *p*. . . . Ps 6:9
Give ear to my *p* . . . Ps 17:1
O you who hear *p*, . . . Ps 65:2
but the *p* of the upright pleases him . . . Prv
  15:8
but he hears the *p* of the righteous. . . . Prv
  15:29
a house of *p* for all nations. . . . Is 56:7
receive whatever you ask for in *p*. . . . Mt 21:22
This kind can come out only by *p*. . . . Mk 9:29
and for a show make lengthy *p*. . . . Mk 12:40
to the breaking of bread and to *p*. . . . Acts 2:42
patient in affliction, faithful in *p*. . . . Rom 12:12
you may devote yourselves to *p*. . . . 1 Cor 7:5
as you help us by your *p*. . . . 2 Cor 1:11
and our *p* is for your perfection. . . . 2 Cor 13:9
but in everything, by *p* and petition . . . Phil 4:6
yourselves to *p*, being watchful . . . Col 4:2
to lift up holy hands in *p*, . . . 1 Tm 2:8
by the word of God and *p*. . . . 1 Tm 4:5
p offered in faith will make the sick . . . Jas 5:15
so that nothing will hinder your *p*. . . . 1 Pt 3:7
and his ears are attentive to their *p*, . . . 1 Pt
  3:12
which are the *p* of the saints. . . . Rv 5:8

PREACH(ED)(ING) *to speak publicly on a reli-*
gious theme; see PROCLAIM
me to *p* good news to the poor. . . . Is 61:1
As you go, *p* this message: . . . Mt 10:7
they do not practice what they *p*. . . . Mt 23:3
wherever the gospel is *p* . . . Mk 14:9
and *p* the good news to all creation. . . .
  Mk 16:15
p the gospel and healing people . . . Lk 9:6
had been scattered *p* the word . . . Acts 8:4
devoted himself exclusively to *p*, . . . Acts 18:5
hindrance he *p* the kingdom . . . Acts 28:31
am so eager to *p* the gospel . . . Rom 1:15
hear without someone *p* to them? . . . Rom
  10:14
to *p* the gospel where Christ was . . . Rom
  15:20
wisdom, but we *p* Christ crucified: . . . 1 Cor
  1:23
and my *p* were not with wise . . . 1 Cor 2:4
Woe to me if I do not *p* the gospel! . . . 1 Cor
  9:16
so that after I have *p* to others, . . . 1 Cor 9:27
For we do not *p* ourselves, . . . 2 Cor 4:5
p peace to you who were far away . . . Eph 2:17
I give you this charge: *P* the Word; . . . 2 Tm 4:2
the public reading of Scripture, to *p* . . . 1 Tm
  4:13
this is the word that was *p* to you. . . . 1 Pt 1:25
and *p* to the spirits in prison who . . . 1 Pt 3:19

PRECEPTS *rules of conduct; moral instruc-*
tions
The *p* of the LORD are right, . . . Ps 19:8
and remember to obey his *p*. . . . Ps 103:18
that they might keep his *p* . . . Ps 105:45
all his *p* are trustworthy. . . . Ps 111:7
I meditate on your *p* . . . Ps 119:15
for I have sought out your *p*. . . . Ps 119:45
I will never forget your *p*, . . . Ps 119:93
See how I love your *p*; . . . Ps 119:159

for I have chosen your *p*. . . . Ps 119:173

PRECIOUS *of great worth*
They are more *p* than gold, . . . Ps 19:10
P in the sight of the LORD . . . Ps 116:15
How *p* to me are your thoughts, . . . Ps 139:17
for wisdom is more *p* than rubies, . . . Prv 8:11
but with the *p* blood of Christ, . . . 1 Pt 1:19
but chosen by God and *p* to him . . . 1 Pt 2:4
a chosen and *p* cornerstone, . . . 1 Pt 2:6
Christ have received a faith as *p* . . . 2 Pt 1:1
us his very great and *p* promises, . . . 2 Pt 1:4

PREDESTINED *predetermined by God*
And those he *p*, he also called; . . . Rom 8:30
In love he *p* us to be adopted . . . Eph 1:5
having been *p* according . . . Eph 1:11

PREPARE(D) *to make ready or suitable for a specific purpose*
to bring you to the place I have *p*. . . . Ex 23:20
You *p* a table before me . . . Ps 23:5
p to meet your God, O Israel. . . . Am 4:12
who will *p* the way before me. . . . Mal 3:1
P the way for the Lord, . . . Mt 3:3
the kingdom *p* for you . . . Mt 25:34
there to *p* a place for you. . . . Jn 14:2
of his wrath *p* for destruction? . . . Rom 9:22
what God has *p* for those who love . . . 1 Cor 2:9
and *p* to do any good work. . . . 2 Tm 2:21
be *p* in season and out of season; . . . 2 Tm 4:2
Therefore, *p* your minds for action; . . . 1 Pt 1:13
Always be *p* to give an answer . . . 1 Pt 3:15

PRESENCE *the state of being near; often expressing nearness to God*
The LORD replied, "My *P* will go . . . Ex 33:14
Out of the brightness of his *p* . . . 2 Sm 22:13
LORD removed them from his *p*, . . . 2 Kgs 17:23
one of us can stand in your *p*. . . . Ezr 9:15
with the joy of your *p*. . . . Ps 21:6
in the *p* of my enemies. . . . Ps 23:5
the shelter of your *p* you hide them . . . Ps 31:20
Do not cast me from your *p* . . . Ps 51:11
who walk in the light of your *p*, . . . Ps 89:15
our secret sins in the light of your *p* . . . Ps 90:8
Where can I flee from your *p*? . . . Ps 139:7
so were we in your *p*, O LORD. . . . Is 26:17
Should you not tremble in my *p*? . . . Jer 5:22
that we may live in his *p*. . . . Hos 6:2
The earth trembles at his *p*, . . . Na 1:5
you will fill me with joy in your *p*. . . . Acts 2:28
have in the *p* of our God . . . 1 Thes 3:9
and shut out from the *p* of the Lord . . . 2 Thes 1:9
rest in his *p* whenever our hearts . . . 1 Jn 3:19
before his glorious *p* without fault . . . Jude 1:24

PRESENT *the here and now; to introduce or display; to offer or make a gift of; near at hand*
life or death or the *p* or the future . . . 1 Cor 3:22
of the *p* crisis, I think that it is good . . . 1 Cor 7:26
so that I might *p* you as a pure . . . 2 Cor 11:2
and to *p* her to himself . . . Eph 5:27
holding promise for both the *p* life . . . 1 Tm 4:8
Do your best to *p* yourself to God . . . 2 Tm 2:15
and to *p* you before his glorious . . . Jude 1:24

PRIDE *an excessively high opinion of oneself; conceit; see PROUD, ARROGANCE*
I hate *p* and arrogance, . . . Prv 8:13
P goes before destruction, . . . Prv 16:18
A man's *p* brings him low, . . . Prv 29:23
God will bring down their *p* . . . Is 25:11
The LORD has sworn by the *P* . . . Am 8:7
in you; I take great *p* in you. . . . 2 Cor 7:4
Then he can take *p* in himself, . . . Gal 6:4
ought to take *p* in his high position. . . . Jas 1:9

PRIEST(HOOD)(S) *religious official; descendant of Levi in charge of Israel's sacrificial system*
He was *p* of God Most High, . . . Gn 14:18
you will be for me a kingdom of *p* . . . Ex 19:6
You are a *p* forever, . . . Ps 110:4
p are to sacrifice his burnt offering . . . Ez 46:2
faithful high *p* in service to God, . . . Heb 2:17
and high *p* whom we confess. . . . Heb 3:1
have a great high *p* who has gone . . . Heb 4:14
You are a *p* forever, . . . Heb 5:6
Son of God he remains a *p* forever. . . . Heb 7:3
lives forever, he has a permanent *p*. . . . Heb 7:24
We do have such a high *p*, . . . Heb 8:1
Day after day every *p* stands . . . Heb 10:11
you are a chosen people, a royal *p*, . . . 1 Pt 2:9
to be a kingdom and *p* . . . Rv 5:10
but they will be *p* of God . . . Rv 20:6

PRISON(ER)(ERS) *state or place of confinement or captivity (physical or spiritual)*
he leads forth the *p* with singing; . . . Ps 68:6
groans of the *p* come before you; . . . Ps 79:11
p suffering in iron chains, . . . Ps 107:10
Set me free from my *p*, . . . Ps 142:7
The LORD sets *p* free, . . . Ps 146:7
to free captives from *p* . . . Is 42:7
I was in *p* and you came to visit me . . . Mt 25:36
me to proclaim freedom for the *p* . . . Lk 4:18
and making me a *p* of the law of sin . . . Rom 7:23
declares that the whole world is a *p* . . . Gal 3:22
the *p* of Christ Jesus for the sake . . . Eph 3:1
others were chained and put in *p*, . . . Heb 11:36
spirits in *p* who disobeyed long ago . . . 1 Pt 3:19
Satan will be released from his *p* . . . Rv 20:7

PROCLAIM(ED)(ING) *to announce officially; see PREACH*
and I will *p* my name, the LORD, . . . Ex 33:19
and *p* liberty throughout the land . . . Lv 25:10
and *p* it to us so we may obey it? . . . Dt 30:12
p his salvation day after day. . . . 1 Chr 16:23
p among the nations what he has . . . Ps 9:11
the skies *p* the work of his hands. . . . Ps 19:1
They will *p* his righteousness . . . Ps 22:31
p aloud your praise . . . Ps 26:7
I *p* righteousness in the great . . . Ps 40:9
the heavens *p* his righteousness, . . . Ps 50:6
was the company of those who *p* it: . . . Ps 68:11
P the power of God, . . . Ps 68:34
to *p* your love in the morning . . . Ps 92:2
p his salvation day after day. . . . Ps 96:2
The heavens *p* his righteousness, . . . Ps 97:6
and I will *p* your great deeds. . . . Ps 145:6
and *p* his praise in the islands. . . . Is 42:12
to *p* freedom for the captives . . . Is 61:1
lift up a banner and *p* it; . . . Jer 50:2
He will *p* peace to the nations. . . . Zec 9:10
in your ear, *p* from the roofs. . . . Mt 10:27
and he will *p* justice to the nations. . . . Mt 12:18
me to *p* freedom for the prisoners . . . Lk 4:18
and *p* the good news that Jesus is . . . Acts 5:42
unknown I am going to *p* . . . Acts 17:23
the word of faith we are *p*: . . . Rom 10:8
I have fully *p* the gospel of Christ. . . . Rom 15:19
you *p* the Lord's death . . . 1 Cor 11:26
that has been *p* to every creature . . . Col 1:23
Pray that I may *p* it clearly, . . . Col 4:4
me the message might be fully *p* . . . 2 Tm 4:17

PROFANE(D) *to speak irreverently; to desecrate or treat with contempt*
and so *p* the name of your God. . . . Lv 19:12
Do not *p* my holy name. . . . Lv 22:32
the nations they *p* my holy name, . . . Ez 36:20
Why do we *p* the covenant . . . Mal 2:10

PROFIT(ABLE) *gain; benefit; usefulness*
for she is more *p* than silver . . . Prv 3:14
All hard work brings a *p*, . . . Prv 14:23
The plans of the diligent lead to *p* . . . Prv 21:5
She sees that her trading is *p*, . . . Prv 31:18
which can *p* him nothing? . . . Is 44:10
not peddle the word of God for *p*. . . . 2 Cor 2:17
was to my *p* I now consider loss . . . Phil 3:7
These things are excellent and *p* . . . Ti 3:8

PROGRESS *improvement; movement toward completion*
continue with all of you for your *p* . . . Phil 1:25
so that everyone may see your *p*. . . . 1 Tm 4:15

PROMISE(D)(S) *to pledge or give assurance; see COVENANT*
did for Sarah what he had *p*. . . . Gn 21:1
And I have *p* to bring you up out . . . Ex 3:17
for the LORD has *p* good things . . . Nm 10:29
Does he *p* and not fulfill? . . . Nm 23:19
your God will bless you as he has *p* . . . Dt 15:6
one of all the LORD's good *p* . . . Jos 21:45
The LORD has kept the *p* he made . . . 1 Kgs 8:20
failed of all the good *p* he gave . . . 1 Kgs 8:56
man who does not keep his *p* . . . Neh 5:13
have kept your *p* because you are . . . Neh 9:8
Has his *p* failed for all time? . . . Ps 77:8
he *p* peace to his people, his saints . . . Ps 85:8
I have *p* to obey your words. . . . Ps 119:57
Your *p* preserves my life. . . . Ps 119:50
The LORD is faithful to all his *p* . . . Ps 145:13
to send you what my Father has *p*; . . . Lk 24:49
The *p* is for you and your children . . . Acts 2:39
What God our fathers he has . . . Acts 13:32
Since we have these *p*, dear friends, . . . 2 Cor 7:1
holding *p* for both the present life . . . 1 Tm 4:8
p before the beginning of time, . . . Ti 1:2
When God made his *p* to Abraham . . . Heb 6:13
and it is founded on better *p*. . . . Heb 8:6
for he who *p* is faithful. . . . Heb 10:23
you will receive what he has *p*. . . . Heb 10:36
him faithful who had made the *p*. . . . Heb 11:11
the crown of life that God has *p* . . . Jas 1:12
the kingdom he *p* those who love . . . Jas 2:5
us his very great and precious *p*, . . . 2 Pt 1:4
"Where is this 'coming' he *p*? . . . 2 Pt 3:4
Lord is not slow in keeping his *p*, . . . 2 Pt 3:9

PROPHECIES, PROPHECY *spoken or written communication from God, often but not always of a predictive nature*
to seal up vision and *p* . . . Dn 9:24
where there are *p*, they will cease; . . . 1 Cor 13:8
gifts, especially the gift of *p*. . . . 1 Cor 14:1
do not treat *p* with contempt. . . . 1 Thes 5:20
you must understand that no *p* . . . 2 Pt 1:20
the words of the *p* of this book: . . . Rv 22:18

PROPHESIED, PROPHESIES, PROPHESY *to give a prophecy; see PROPHECIES*
the Spirit rested on them, they *p*, . . . Nm 11:25
the prophet who *p* peace will be . . . Jer 28:9
daughters of your people who *p* out . . . Ez 13:17
P to these bones and say to them, . . . Ez 37:4
Your sons and daughters will *p*, . . . Jl 2:28
Lord, did we not *p* in your name, . . . Mt 7:22
and they spoke in tongues and *p*. . . . Acts 19:6
know in part and we *p* in part, . . . 1 Cor 13:9
my brothers, be eager to *p*, . . . 1 Cor 14:39

PROPHET(S) *one who gives a prophecy; see PROPHECIES*
that all the LORD's people were *p* . . . Nm 11:29
If a *p*, or one who foretells . . . Dt 13:1
up for them a *p* like you . . . Dt 18:18
and he will know that there is a *p* . . . 2 Kgs 5:8
but Elisha, the *p* who is in Israel, . . . 2 Kgs 6:12
do my *p* no harm. . . . 1 Chr 16:22
I am against the *p* who steal . . . Jer 23:30
they will know that a *p* has been . . . Ez 2:5

I was neither a *p* nor a prophet's . . . Am 7:14
that day every *p* will be ashamed . . . Zec 13:4
I will send you the *p* Elijah . . . Mal 4:5
come to abolish the Law or the *P*; . . . Mt 5:17
Anyone who receives a *p* . . . Mt 10:41
except the sign of the *p* Jonah. . . . Mt 12:39
you who kill the *p* and stone those . . . Mt 23:37
false Christs and false *p* will appear . . .
    Mt 24:24
of the *p* might be fulfilled. . . . Mt 26:56
will be called a *p* of the Most High; . . . Lk 1:76
a *p*, Anna, the daughter of Phanuel, . . . Lk 2:36
no *p* is accepted in his hometown. . . . Lk 4:24
A great *p* has appeared among us, . . . Lk 7:16
Indeed, all the *p* from Samuel on, . . . Acts 3:24
God will send you a *p* like me . . . Acts 7:37
All the *p* testify about him that . . . Acts 10:43
the Law of Moses and from the *P*. . . . Acts
    28:23
to which the Law and the *P* testify. . . . Rom
    3:21
they have killed your *p* . . . Rom 11:3
second *p*, third teachers, then . . . 1 Cor 12:28
The spirits of *p* are subject . . . 1 Cor 14:32
foundation of the apostles and *p*, . . . Eph 2:20
some to be *p*, some . . . Eph 4:11
through the *p* at many times . . . Heb 1:1
Concerning this salvation, the *p*, . . . 1 Pt 1:10
word of the *p* made more certain, . . . 2 Pt 1:19
spoken in the past by the holy *p* . . . 2 Pt 3:2
because many false *p* have gone out . . .
    1 Jn 4:1
Rejoice, saints and apostles and *p*! . . . Rv 18:20

PROSPER(ED)(ITY)(OUS)(S)   *to succeed or
thrive; to flourish; to cause others to succeed;
economic well-being*
so that you may live and *p* . . . Dt 5:33
will grant you abundant *p* . . . Dt 28:11
pleased the LORD to make you *p* . . . Dt 28:63
that you may *p* in everything you . . . Dt 29:9
I set before you today life and *p*, . . . Dt 30:15
Then you will be *p* and successful. . . . Jos 1:8
the LORD made him *p* again . . . Jb 42:10
Whatever he does *p*. . . . Ps 1:3
when I saw the *p* of the wicked. . . . Ps 73:3
blessings and *p* will be yours. . . . Ps 128:2
and bring you *p*. . . . Prv 3:2
A generous man will *p*; . . . Prv 11:25
but *p* is the reward of the righteous. . . . Prv
    13:21
he who cherishes understanding *p*. . . . Prv 19:8
finds life, *p* and honor. . . . Prv 21:21
who conceals his sins does not *p*, . . . Prv 28:13
he who trusts in the LORD will *p*. . . . Prv 28:25
I bring *p* and create disaster; . . . Is 45:7
of the LORD will *p* in his hand. . . . Is 53:10
Why does the way of the wicked *p*? . . . Jer 12:1

PROSTITUTE(S), PROSTITUTION   *one who
solicits and accepts payment for sexual intercourse*
and not *p* yourselves by going . . . Nm 15:39
for the *p* reduces you to a loaf . . . Prv 6:26
like a *p* and with crafty intent. . . . Prv 7:10
of *p* squanders his wealth. . . . Prv 29:3
engaging in *p* from their youth. . . . Ez 23:3
you must not be a *p* or be intimate . . . Hos 3:3
engage in *p* but not increase, . . . Hos 4:10
and the *p* are entering the kingdom . . . Mt 21:31
male *p* nor homosexual offenders . . . 1 Cor 6:9
of Christ and unite them with a *p*? . . . 1 Cor
    6:15
you the punishment of the great *p*, . . . Rv 17:1

PROTECT(ED)(ION)(S)   *to shield from danger*
about in your camp to *p* you . . . Dt 23:14
He *p* us on our entire journey . . . Jos 24:17
he has given us a wall of *p* in Judah . . . Ezr 9:9
Spread your *p* over them, . . . Ps 5:11
you will *p* me from trouble . . . Ps 32:7
your truth always *p* me. . . . Ps 40:11

The LORD will *p* him . . . Ps 41:2
I will *p* him, for he acknowledges . . . Ps 91:14
The LORD *p* the simplehearted; . . . Ps 116:6
p me from men of violence, . . . Ps 140:1
Discretion will *p* you, . . . Prv 2:11
forsake wisdom, and she will *p* you; . . . Prv 4:6
p them by the power of your name . . . Jn 17:11
It always *p*, always trusts, . . . 1 Cor 13:7
and *p* you from the evil one. . . . 2 Thes 3:3

PROUD   *arrogant or haughty; having excessive
self-esteem; see PRIDE*
has haughty eyes and a *p* heart, . . . Ps 101:5
but the *p* he knows from afar. . . . Ps 138:6
The LORD detests all the *p* . . . Prv 16:5
than to share plunder with the *p*. . . . Prv 16:19
Do not be *p*, but be willing . . . Rom 12:16
it does not boast, it is not *p*. . . . 1 Cor 13:4
lovers of money, boastful, *p*, . . . 2 Tm 3:2
God opposes the *p* . . . Jas 4:6

PROVIDE(D)(S), PROVISION   *to supply*
God himself will *p* the lamb . . . Gn 22:8
O God, you *p* for the poor. . . . Ps 68:10
He *p* food for those who fear him; . . . Ps 111:5
He *p* redemption for his people; . . . Ps 111:9
she *p* food for her family . . . Prv 31:15
because I *p* water in the desert . . . Is 43:20
and *p* clothing for the naked. . . . Ez 18:7
who receive God's abundant *p* . . . Rom 5:17
p a way out so that you can stand . . . 1 Cor
    10:13
If anyone must *p* . . . 1 Tm 5:8
who richly *p* us with everything . . . 1 Tm 6:17
in order that they may *p* . . . Ti 3:14

PRUDENCE, PRUDENT   *sound judgment;
discretion*
You who are simple, gain *p*; . . . Prv 8:5
but a *p* man overlooks an insult. . . . Prv 12:16
Every *p* man acts out of knowledge . . . Prv
    13:16
a *p* man gives thought to his steps. . . . Prv
    14:15
whoever heeds correction shows *p*. . . . Prv
    15:5
but a *p* wife is from the LORD. . . . Prv 19:14
The *p* see danger and take refuge, . . . Prv 27:12
Therefore the *p* man keeps quiet . . . Am 5:13

PUNISH(ED)(ES)(MENT)   *to impose a penalty*
you have *p* us less than our sins . . . Ezr 9:13
It is not good to *p* an innocent man, . . . Prv
    17:26
if you *p* him with the rod, he will . . . Prv 23:13
I will *p* the world for its evil, . . . Is 13:11
the *p* that brought us peace was . . . Is 53:5
Your wickedness will *p* you; . . . Jer 2:19
I will *p* you as your deeds deserve, . . . Jer
    21:14
and *p* those who are complacent, . . . Zep 1:12
Then they will go away to eternal *p* . . . Mt 25:46
Such men will be *p* most severely. . . . Mk 12:40
and does things deserving *p* will be . . .
    Lk 12:48
wrath to bring *p* on the wrongdoer. . . . Rom
    13:4
disobedience received its just *p*, . . . Heb 2:2
to be *p* who has trampled the Son . . . Heb
    10:29
and he *p* everyone he accepts . . . Heb 12:6
by him to *p* those who do wrong . . . 1 Pt 2:14

PURE, PURIFIED, PURIFIES, PURIFY, PURITY
*free from contamination; ritually clean; guiltless;
chaste*
to the *p* you show yourself *p*, . . . 2 Sm 22:27
The fear of the LORD is *p*, . . . Ps 19:9
who has clean hands and a *p* heart, . . . Ps 24:4
Create in me a *p* heart, O God, . . . Ps 51:10
can a young man keep his way *p*? . . . Ps 119:9
can say, "I have kept my heart *p*; . . . Prv 20:9
Come out from it and be *p*, . . . Is 52:11
long will they be incapable of *p*? . . . Hos 8:5

Your eyes are too *p* to look on evil; . . . Hb 1:13
Blessed are the *p* in heart, . . . Mt 5:8
for he *p* their hearts by faith. . . . Acts 15:9
in *p*, understanding, patience . . . 2 Cor 6:6
us *p* ourselves from everything that . . . 2 Cor
    7:1
I might present you as a *p* virgin . . . 2 Cor 11:2
whatever is *p*, whatever is lovely, . . . Phil 4:8
which comes from a *p* heart . . . 1 Tm 1:5
in life, in love, in faith and in *p*. . . . 1 Tm 4:12
as sisters, with absolute *p*. . . . 1 Tm 5:2
Keep yourself *p*. . . . 1 Tm 5:22
To the *p*, all things are *p*, . . . Ti 1:15
to *p* for himself a people that are . . . Ti 2:14
and the marriage bed kept *p*, . . . Heb 13:4
comes from heaven is first of all *p*; . . . Jas 3:17
you sinners, and *p* your hearts, . . . Jas 4:8
Now that you have *p* yourselves . . . 1 Pt 1:22
when they see the *p* and reverence . . . 1 Pt 3:2
of Jesus, his Son, *p* us from all sin. . . . 1 Jn 1:7
and *p* us from all unrighteousness. . . . 1 Jn 1:9
who has this hope in him *p* himself, . . . 1 Jn 3:3

PURPOSE(D)(S)   *intention; objective; God's
predetermined will*
I have raised you up for this very *p*, . . . Ex 9:16
he is mighty, and firm in his *p*. . . . Jb 36:5
he thwarts the *p* of the peoples. . . . Ps 33:10
but it is the LORD's *p* that prevails . . . Prv 19:21
and achieve the *p* for which I sent it . . . Is 55:11
great are your *p* and mighty are . . . Jer 32:19
handed over to you by God's set *p*. . . . Acts 2:23
have been called according to his *p*. . . . Rom
    8:28
I raised you up for this very *p*, . . . Rom 9:17
who has made us for this very *p* . . . 2 Cor 5:5
be zealous, provided the *p* is good, . . . Gal 4:18
which he *p* in Christ, to be put . . . Eph 1:9
according to his eternal *p* which he . . . Eph
    3:11
and to act according to his good *p*. . . . Phil 2:13
but because of his own *p* and grace. . . . 2 Tm
    1:9

PURSUE(S)   *to follow in order to seize, overtake or kill; to seek*
seek peace and *p* it. . . . Ps 34:14
he loves those who *p* righteousness . . . Prv
    15:9
wicked man flees though no one *p*, . . . Prv 28:1
who did not *p* righteousness, . . . Rom 9:30
and *p* righteousness, godliness, . . . 1 Tm 6:11
he must seek peace and *p* it. . . . 1 Pt 3:11

QUARREL(ING)(S)(SOME)   *angry argument;
complaint*
but a patient man calms a *q*. . . . Prv 15:18
Starting a *q* is like breaching a dam; . . . Prv
    17:14
a *q* wife is like a constant dripping. . . . Prv
    19:13
in a *q* not his own. . . . Prv 26:17
so is a *q* man for kindling strife. . . . Prv 26:21
without gossip a *q* dies down. . . . Prv 26:20
Woe to him who *q* with his Maker, . . . Is 45:9
For since there is jealousy and *q* . . . 1 Cor 3:3
What causes fights and *q* . . . Jas 4:1

QUENCH(ED)   *to extinguish (as with water)*
Many waters cannot *q* love; . . . Song 8:7
nor will their fire be *q*, . . . Is 66:24
and the fire is not *q*. . . . Mk 9:48

QUIET(NESS)   *peaceful; calm or still*
he leads me beside *q* waters, . . . Ps 23:2
Better a dry crust with peace and *q* . . . Prv 17:1
The *q* words of the wise are more . . . Eccl 9:17
in *q* and trust is your strength, . . . Is 30:15
Therefore the prudent man keeps *q* . . . Am 5:13
he will *q* you with his love, . . . Zep 3:17
it your ambition to lead a *q* life, . . . 1 Thes 4:11
beauty of a gentle and *q* spirit, . . . 1 Pt 3:4

RACE *competition of speed or endurance*
The *r* is not to the swift . . . Eccl 9:11
if only I may finish the *r* . . . Acts 20:24
that in a *r* all the runners run, . . . 1 Cor 9:24
I have finished the *r,* I have kept . . . 2 Tm 4:7
perseverance the *r* marked out . . . Heb 12:1

RADIANCE, RADIANT *brightness (especially of God's glory)*
he was not aware that his face was *r* . . . Ex 34:29
Those who look to him are *r;* . . . Ps 34:5
her to himself as a *r* church, . . . Eph 5:27
The Son is the *r* of God's glory . . . Heb 1:3

RAIN(BOW) *precipitation; colors formed by the refraction and reflection of the sun's rays in raindrops or water vapor*
from now I will send *r* on the earth . . . Gn 7:4
I have set my *r* in the clouds, . . . Gn 9:13
and I will send *r* on the land. . . . 1 Kgs 18:1
and sends *r* on the righteous . . . Mt 5:45
They are clouds without *r,* . . . Jude 1:12

RAISED, RISE(N) *to move or cause to move upward or to a higher position; to resurrect; see RESURRECTION*
R in the presence of the aged, . . . Lv 19:32
a scepter will *r* out of Israel. . . . Nm 24:17
their bodies will *r* . . . . Is 26:19
he will be *r* and lifted up . . . Is 52:13
of righteousness will *r* with healing . . . Mal 4:2
on the third day he will be *r* to life . . . Mt 17:23
After three days I will *r* again. . . . Mt 27:63
He is not here; he has *r,* just . . . Mt 28:6
the deaf hear, the dead are *r,* . . . Lk 7:22
those who have done good will *r* . . . Jn 5:29
But God *r* him from the dead, . . . Acts 2:24
was *r* to life for our justification. . . . Rom 4:25
in your heart that God *r* him . . . Rom 10:9
that he was *r* on the third day . . . 1 Cor 15:4
the dead in Christ will *r* first. . . . 1 Thes 4:16

RANSOM(ED) *price paid for release from captivity*
and the *r* of the LORD will return. . . . Is 35:10
Was my arm too short to *r* you? . . . Is 50:2
and to give his life as a *r* for many. . . . Mt 20:28
as a *r* to set them free . . . Heb 9:15

READ(ING)(S) *to examine and grasp the meaning of written characters, words, or sentences*
He *r* in their hearing all the words . . . 2 Kgs 23:2
They *r* from the Book of the Law . . . Neh 8:8
and *r* to the people from the scroll . . . Jer 36:6
known and *r* by everybody. . . . 2 Cor 3:2
to the public *r* of Scripture, . . . 1 Tm 4:13
Blessed is the one who *r* the words . . . Rv 1:3

REAP(ER)(S) *to harvest; to obtain as the result of effort*
will *r* with songs of joy. . . . Ps 126:5
who sows righteousness *r* a sure . . . Prv 11:18
and *r* the whirlwind. . . . Hos 8:7
r the fruit of unfailing love, . . . Hos 10:12
and the *r* may be glad together. . . . Jn 4:36
generously will also *r* generously. . . . 2 Cor 9:6
A man *r* what he sows. . . . Gal 6:7

REASON(ED) *to discuss; to think; the cause of an event; the basis or motive for an action*
Come now, let us *r* together, . . . Is 1:18
For this *r* a man will leave his . . . Mt 19:5
it was for this very *r* I came . . . Jn 12:27
They hated me without *r.* . . . Jn 15:25
to give the *r* for the hope that you . . . 1 Pt 3:15
thought like a child, I *r* like a child. . . . 1 Cor 13:11

REBEL(LED)(LING)(LION)(S) *to take up arms against; to oppose, disobey*
Only do not *r* against the LORD. . . . Nm 14:9
and do not *r* against his commands, . . . 1 Sm 12:14

For *r* is like the sin of divination, . . . 1 Sm 15:23
and *r* against the Most High; . . . Ps 78:56
children will *r* against their parents . . . Mt 10:21
will not come until the *r* occurs . . . 2 Thes 2:3
but for lawbreakers and *r,* . . . 1 Tm 1:9

REBUKE(D)(ING)(S) *to criticize or reprove sharply*
r a wise man and he will love you. . . . Prv 9:8
r a discerning man, and he will gain . . . Prv 19:25
It is better to heed a wise man's *r* . . . Eccl 7:5
never to *r* you again. . . . Is 54:9
he *r* them for their lack of faith . . . Mk 16:14
If your brother sins, *r* him, . . . Lk 17:3
Do not *r* an older man harshly, . . . 1 Tm 5:1
Those who sin are to be *r* publicly, . . . 1 Tm 5:20
r, correcting and training . . . 2 Tm 3:16
correct, *r* and encourage . . . 2 Tm 4:2
Encourage and *r* with all authority. . . . Ti 2:15
do not lose heart when he *r* you, . . . Heb 12:5
Those whom I love I *r* . . . Rv 3:19

RECEIVE(D)(S) *to gain or take possession of; to believe or accept as true; to welcome*
they have *r* their reward in full. . . . Mt 6:2
everyone who asks *r;* he who seeks . . . Mt 7:8
Freely you have *r,* freely give. . . . Mt 10:8
anyone who will not *r* the kingdom . . . Mk 10:15
Yet to all who *r* him, . . . Jn 1:12
and said, "*R* the Holy Spirit. . . . Jn 20:22
you will *r* power when the Holy . . . Acts 1:8
you will *r* the gift of the Holy Spirit . . . Acts 2:38
believes in him *r* forgiveness of sins . . . Acts 10:43
It is more blessed to give than to *r* . . . Acts 20:35
but you *r* the Spirit of sonship. . . . Rom 8:15
For I *r* from the Lord what I . . . 1 Cor 11:23
just as you *r* Christ Jesus as Lord, . . . Col 2:6
believe on him and *r* eternal life. . . . 1 Tm 1:16
should not think he will *r* anything . . . Jas 1:7
and *r* from him anything we ask, . . . 1 Jn 3:22
to *r* glory and honor and power, . . . Rv 4:11
to *r* power and wealth and wisdom . . . Rv 5:12

RECONCILE(D), RECONCILIATION *to restore harmony between persons*
First go and be *r* to your brother; . . . Mt 5:24
how much more, having been *r,* . . . Rom 5:10
and gave us the ministry of *r:* . . . 2 Cor 5:18
in this one body to *r* both of them . . . Eph 2:16
him to *r* to himself all things, . . . Col 1:20

RECORD(ED) *to set down in writing; something that relates past events*
Oh, that my words were *r,* . . . Jb 19:23
If you, O LORD, kept a *r* of sins, . . . Ps 130:3
which are not *r* in this book. . . . Jn 20:30
is not easily angered, it keeps no *r* . . . 1 Cor 13:5

REDEEM(ED)(ER), REDEMPTION *to buy back, repurchase; to rescue (often from sin) with a ransom*
will *r* you with an outstretched arm . . . Ex 6:6
I know that my *R* lives, . . . Jb 19:25
O LORD, my Rock and my *R.* . . . Ps 19:14
r us because of your unfailing love. . . . Ps 44:26
No man can *r* the life of another . . . Ps 49:7
Let the *r* of the LORD say this . . . Ps 107:2
He himself will *r* Israel . . . Ps 130:8
But only the *r* will walk there, . . . Is 35:9
your *R,* the Holy One of Israel: . . . Is 48:17
I will *r* them from death. . . . Hos 13:14
because your *r* is drawing near. . . . Lk 21:28
as sons, the *r* of our bodies. . . . Rom 8:23
under law, to *r* those under law, . . . Gal 4:5
In him we have *r* through his blood . . . Eph 1:7
you were sealed for the day of *r.* . . . Eph 4:30

for us to *r* us from all wickedness . . . Ti 2:14
or gold that you were *r* . . . 1 Pt 1:18

REFINE *to remove impurities*
See, I will *r* and test them, . . . Jer 9:7
I will *r* them like silver . . . Zec 13:9
and *r* them like gold and silver. . . . Mal 3:3

REFRESHED, REFRESHES, REFRESHING *restored, revived, renewed*
r others will himself be *r.* . . . Prv 11:25
that times of *r* may come . . . Acts 3:19

REFUGE *shelter; safety; sanctuary*
towns to be your cities of *r,* . . . Nm 35:11
The eternal God is your *r,* . . . Dt 33:27
wings you have come to take *r.* . . . Ru 2:12
Blessed are all who take *r* in him. . . . Ps 2:12
The LORD is a *r* for the oppressed, . . . Ps 9:9
God is my rock, in whom I take *r.* . . . Ps 18:2
find *r* in the shadow of your wings. . . . Ps 36:7
God is our *r* and strength, . . . Ps 46:1
He is my *r* and my fortress, . . . Ps 91:2
and for his children it will be a *r.* . . . Prv 14:26
a *r* in times of trouble. . . . Na 1:7

REIGN(S) *to rule with supreme authority; see RULE*
God *r* over the nations; . . . Ps 47:8
mountain where God chooses to *r,* . . . Ps 68:16
The LORD *r,* let the earth be glad; . . . Ps 97:1
The LORD *r,* / let the nations tremble; . . . Ps 99:1
He will *r* on David's throne . . . Is 9:7
See, a king will *r* in righteousness . . . Is 32:1
Your God *r!* . . . Is 52:7
and he will *r* over the house . . . Lk 1:33
Therefore do not let sin *r* . . . Rom 6:12
For he must *r* until he has put all . . . 1 Cor 15:25
we will also *r* with him. . . . 2 Tm 2:12
and he will *r* for ever and ever. . . . Rv 11:15
will *r* with him for a thousand years . . . Rv 20:6

REJECT(ED)(S) *to refuse to accept*
it is not you they have *r,* . . . 1 Sm 8:7
For the LORD will not *r* his people . . . Ps 94:14
The stone the builders *r* . . . Ps 118:22
He was despised and *r* by men, . . . Is 53:3
The stone the builders *r* . . . Mt 21:42
but he who *r* me *r* him who sent me . . . Lk 10:16
whoever *r* the Son will not see life, . . . Jn 3:36
I ask then: Did God *r* his people? . . . Rom 11:1
nothing is to be *r* if it is received . . . 1 Tm 4:4
r by men but chosen by God . . . 1 Pt 2:4
The stone the builders *r* . . . 1 Pt 2:7

REJOICE(S), REJOICING *to take joy in or give joy to*
shall *r* in everything you have put . . . Dt 12:7
Let the heavens *r,* let the earth be . . . 1 Chr 16:31
and there *r* in your salvation. . . . Ps 9:14
but *r* comes in the morning. . . . Ps 30:5
let the afflicted hear and *r.* . . . Ps 34:2
come, let us *r* in him. . . . Ps 66:6
let us *r* and be glad in it. . . . Ps 118:24
I *r* in following your statutes . . . Ps 119:14
Let Israel *r* in their Maker; . . . Ps 149:2
may you *r* in the wife of your youth . . . Prv 5:18
stumbles, do not let your heart *r,* . . . Prv 24:17
the wilderness will *r* and blossom. . . . Is 35:1
so will your God *r* over you. . . . Is 62:5
he will *r* over you with singing. . . . Zep 3:17
R greatly, O Daughter of Zion! . . . Zec 9:9
and my spirit *r* in God my Savior, . . . Lk 1:47
R in that day and leap for joy, . . . Lk 6:23
but *r* that your names are written . . . Lk 10:20
And we *r* in the hope of the glory . . . Rom 5:2
Rejoice with those who *r;* mourn . . . Rom 12:15
delight in evil but *r* with the truth. . . . 1 Cor 13:6
sorrowful, yet always *r;* poor, . . . 2 Cor 6:10
Finally, my brothers, *r* in the Lord! . . . Phil 3:1
Let us *r* and be glad . . . Rv 19:7

RELENTED, RELENTS *to let up*
the LORD *r* and did not bring . . . Ex 32:14
and out of his great love he *r*. . . . Ps 106:45
and he *r* from sending calamity. . . . Jl 2:13
a God who *r* from sending calamity . . . Jon 4:2

REMAIN *to continue unchanged*
But you *r* the same, . . . Ps 102:27
R in me, and I will *r* in you. . . . Jn 15:4
And now these three *r*: faith, . . . 1 Cor 13:13
he will *r* faithful, . . . 2 Tm 2:13
They will perish, but you *r*; . . . Heb 1:11
just as it has taught you, *r* in him. . . . 1 Jn 2:27

REMEMBER(ED)(S), REMEMBRANCE *to have a person or event come to mind; to keep in mind*
I will *r* my covenant between me . . . Gn 9:15
he *r* his covenant with Abraham, . . . Ex 2:24
R the Sabbath day . . . Ex 20:8
R that you were slaves in Egypt . . . Dt 5:15
R, O LORD, your great mercy . . . Ps 25:6
On my bed I *r* you; . . . Ps 63:6
R the people you purchased of old, . . . Ps 74:2
I will *r* the deeds of the LORD; . . . Ps 77:11
he *r* that we are dust. . . . Ps 103:14
for their sake he *r* his covenant . . . Ps 106:45
he *r* his covenant forever. . . . Ps 111:5
R your Creator . . . Eccl 12:1
and *r* your sins no more. . . . Is 43:25
The former things will not be *r*, . . . Is 65:17
and will *r* their sins no more. . . . Jer 31:34
given for you; do this in *r* of me. . . . Lk 22:19
which is for you; do this in *r* of me . . . 1 Cor 11:24
we should continue to *r* the poor, . . . Gal 2:10
I thank my God every time I *r* you. . . . Phil 1:3
R Jesus Christ, raised . . . 2 Tm 2:8
and will *r* their sins no more. . . . Heb 8:12

REMNANT *something left over (often with regards to Israel's regathering from exile)*
has been gracious in leaving us a *r* . . . Ezr 9:8
time to reclaim the *r* that is left . . . Is 11:11
I myself will gather the *r* . . . Jer 23:3
inheritance to the *r* of this people. . . . Zec 8:12
the present time there is a *r* chosen . . . Rom 11:5

RENEW(AL)(ED)(ING) *to restore; to make new spiritually*
and *r* a steadfast spirit within me. . . . Ps 51:10
that your youth is *r* like the eagle's. . . . Ps 103:5
will *r* their strength. . . . Is 40:31
You found *r* of your strength, . . . Is 57:10
transformed by the *r* of your mind. . . . Rom 12:2
yet inwardly we are being *r* day . . . 2 Cor 4:16
of rebirth and *r* by the Holy Spirit, . . . Ti 3:5

REPAID, REPAY *to settle a debt; to reward a favor or punish a wrong*
It is mine to avenge; I will *r*. . . . Dt 32:35
or *r* us according to our iniquities. . . . Ps 103:10
How can I *r* the LORD . . . Ps 116:12
to 'sinners,' expecting to be *r* in full . . . Lk 6:34
you will be *r* at the resurrection . . . Lk 14:14
Do not *r* anyone evil for evil. . . . Rom 12:17
Anyone who does wrong will be *r*. . . . Col 3:25
Do not *r* evil with evil. . . . 1 Pt 3:9

REPENT(ANCE)(S) *to experience sorrow for and seek to change wrong behavior*
and *r* in dust and ashes. . . . Jb 42:6
In *r* and rest is your salvation, . . . Is 30:15
If you *r*, I will restore you . . . Jer 15:19
R! Turn away from all your . . . Ez 18:30
R, for the kingdom of heaven is . . . Mt 3:2
a baptism of *r* for the forgiveness . . . Mk 1:4
call the righteous, but sinners to *r*. . . . Lk 5:32
unless you *r*, you too will all perish. . . . Lk 13:3
in heaven over one sinner who *r* . . . Lk 15:7
rebuke him, and if he *r*, forgive him . . . Lk 17:3
Peter replied, "*R* and be baptized, . . . Acts 2:38
all people everywhere to *r*. . . . Acts 17:30

and prove their *r* by their deeds. . . . Acts 26:20
kindness leads you toward *r*? . . . Rom 2:4
Godly sorrow brings *r* that leads . . . 2 Cor 7:10
but everyone to come to *r*. . . . 2 Pt 3:9
R and do the things you did at first. . . . Rv 2:5

RESCUE(D)(S) *to save from danger or harm*
come quickly to my *r*; . . . Ps 31:2
R me from the mire, . . . Ps 69:14
R me from my enemies, O LORD, . . . Ps 143:9
The righteous man is *r*. . . . Prv 11:8
been able to *r* you from the lions? . . . Dn 6:20
Who will *r* me from this body . . . Rom 7:24
himself for our sins to *r* us . . . Gal 1:4
For he has *r* us from the dominion . . . Col 1:13
who *r* us from the coming wrath. . . . 1 Thes 1:10
how to *r* godly men from trials . . . 2 Pt 2:9

RESIST *to actively oppose*
I tell you, Do not *r* an evil person. . . . Mt 5:39
R the devil, and he will flee . . . Jas 4:7
R him, standing firm in the faith, . . . 1 Pt 5:9

RESPECT *to give honor to; to show high regard for*
Each of you must *r* his mother . . . Lv 19:3
show *r* for the elderly and revere . . . Lv 19:32
and the wife must *r* her husband. . . . Eph 5:33
obey your earthly masters with *r*. . . . Eph 6:5
so that your daily life may win the *r* . . . 1 Thes 4:12
to *r* those who work hard . . . 1 Thes 5:12
are to be men worthy of *r*, sincere, . . . 1 Tm 3:8
are to be women worthy of *r*, . . . 1 Tm 3:11
Show proper *r* to everyone: . . . 1 Pt 2:17
But do this with gentleness and *r*, . . . 1 Pt 3:16

REST(ED) *freedom from activity or labor; peace of mind or spirit; to take relief or respite; see SABBATH*
so on the seventh day he *r*. . . . Gn 2:2
the seventh day is a Sabbath of *r*, . . . Ex 31:15
The land is to have a year of *r*. . . . Lv 25:5
who will be a man of peace and *r*, . . . 1 Chr 22:9
and there the weary are at *r*. . . . Jb 3:17
my body also will *r* secure, . . . Ps 16:9
My soul finds *r* in God alone; . . . Ps 62:1
will *r* in the shadow . . . Ps 91:1
They shall never enter my *r*. . . . Ps 95:11
a little folding of the hands to *r*. . . . Prv 6:10
and his place of *r* will be glorious. . . . Is 11:10
and you will find *r* for your souls. . . . Jer 6:16
and burdened, and I will give you *r*. . . . Mt 11:28
They shall never enter my *r*. . . . Heb 3:11
for anyone who enters God's *r*. . . . Heb 4:10
they will *r* from their labor, . . . Rv 14:13

RESTORE(S) *to replace; to renew or revive; to return*
he *r* my soul. . . . Ps 23:3
R to me the joy of your salvation . . . Ps 51:12
R me, and I will return, . . . Jer 31:18
R us to yourself, O LORD, . . . Lam 5:21
The LORD will *r* the splendor . . . Na 2:2
are spiritual should *r* him gently. . . . Gal 6:1
will himself *r* you and make you . . . 1 Pt 5:10

RESTRAINT *control of impulses and desires*
of knowledge uses words with *r*, . . . Prv 17:27
have the wisdom to show *r*. . . . Prv 23:4
no revelation, the people cast off *r*; . . . Prv 29:18

RESURRECTION *rising from the dead; see RAISED*
who say there is no *r*, came to him . . . Mt 22:23
at the *r*, whose wife will she be . . . Mt 22:28
and after Jesus' *r* they went . . . Mt 27:53
Jesus said to her, "I am the *r*. . . . Jn 11:25
he spoke of the *r* of the Christ, . . . Acts 2:31
to testify to the *r* of the Lord Jesus, . . . Acts 4:33

good news about Jesus and the *r*. . . . Acts 17:18
also be united with him in his *r*. . . . Rom 6:5
some of you say that there is no *r* . . . 1 Cor 15:12
power of his *r* and the fellowship . . . Phil 3:10
say that the *r* has already taken . . . 2 Tm 2:18
so that they might gain a better *r*. . . . Heb 11:35
It saves you by the *r* of Jesus Christ . . . 1 Pt 3:21
This is the first *r*. . . . Rv 20:5
those who have part in the first *r*. . . . Rv 20:6

RETURN(ED)(S) *to go back, physically, mentally, or spiritually (involving repentance)*
and to dust you will *r*. . . . Gn 3:19
If you *r* to the LORD, then your . . . 2 Chr 30:9
joy before I go to the place of no *r*, . . . Jb 10:21
R to us, O God Almighty! . . . Ps 80:14
will *r* with songs of joy, . . . Ps 126:6
A remnant will *r*, a remnant . . . Is 10:21
the ransomed of the LORD will *r*. . . . Is 35:10
When the LORD *r* to Zion, . . . Is 52:8
It will not *r* to me empty, . . . Is 55:11
But you must *r* to your God; . . . Hos 12:6
R, O Israel, to the LORD your . . . Hos 14:1
r to me with all your heart, . . . Jl 2:12
yet you have not *r* to me, . . . Am 4:6
finds him doing so when he *r*. . . . Mt 24:46
now you have *r* to the Shepherd . . . 1 Pt 2:25

REVEAL(ED)(S) *to make known; see REVELATION*
but the things *r* belong to us . . . Dt 29:29
He *r* the deep things of darkness . . . Jb 12:22
the glory of the LORD will be *r*, . . . Is 40:5
the arm of the LORD been *r*? . . . Is 53:1
I *r* myself to those who did not ask . . . Is 65:1
He *r* deep and hidden things; . . . Dn 2:22
and *r* his thoughts to man, . . . Am 4:13
and *r* them to little children. . . . Mt 11:25
with the glory that will be *r* in us. . . . Rom 8:18
but now *r* and made known . . . Rom 16:26
but God has *r* it to us by his Spirit. . . . 1 Cor 2:10
was pleased to *r* his Son in me . . . Gal 1:16
happen when the Lord Jesus is *r*. . . . 2 Thes 1:7
and the man of lawlessness is *r*, . . . 2 Thes 2:3
but was *r* in these last times . . . 1 Pt 1:20
overjoyed when his glory is *r*. . . . 1 Pt 4:13

REVELATION(S) *something revealed by God; see REVEAL*
Where there is no *r*, the people cast . . . Prv 29:18
For the *r* awaits an appointed time; . . . Hb 2:3
a light for *r* to the Gentiles . . . Lk 2:32
according to the *r*, . . . Rom 16:25
I bring you some *r* or knowledge . . . 1 Cor 14:6
a *r*, a tongue or an interpretation. . . . 1 Cor 14:26
on to visions and *r* from the Lord. . . . 2 Cor 12:1
of these surpassingly great *r*, . . . 2 Cor 12:7
I received it by *r* from Jesus Christ. . . . Gal 1:12
I went in response to a *r*. . . . Gal 2:2
you the Spirit of wisdom and *r*, . . . Eph 1:17
mystery made known to me by *r*, . . . Eph 3:3
r of Jesus Christ, which God gave . . . Rv 1:1

REVERE(NCE)(NT) *to adore, highly respect; to worship*
and have *r* for my sanctuary. . . . Lv 19:30
so that they may learn to *r* me . . . Dt 4:10
to *r* the LORD your God always. . . . Dt 14:23
in *r* will I bow down . . . Ps 5:7
let all the people of the world *r* him . . . Ps 33:8
of the earth will *r* your glory. . . . Ps 102:15
God does it so that men will *r* him. . . . Eccl 3:14
with God-fearing men, who are *r*. . . . Eccl 8:12
cities of ruthless nations will *r* you. . . . Is 25:3
Who should not *r* you, . . . Jer 10:7
because we did not *r* the LORD. . . . Hos 10:3

But for you who *r* my name, . . . Mal 4:2
perfecting holiness out of *r* for God . . . 2 Cor 7:1
to one another out of *r* for Christ. . . . Eph 5:21
women to be *r* in the way they live, . . . Ti 2:3
as strangers here in *r* fear. . . . 1 Pt 1:17
and those who *r* your name, . . . Rv 11:18

REVIVE *to bring or come back to life (often of spiritual life)*
r us, and we will call on your name. . . . Ps 80:18
Will you not *r* us again, . . . Ps 85:6
and to *r* the heart of the contrite. . . . Is 57:15
After two days he will *r* us; . . . Hos 6:2

REWARD(ED)(S) *to compensate for good or evil*
your very great *r*. . . . Gn 15:1
May the LORD *r* you well . . . 1 Sm 24:19
in keeping them there is great *r*. . . . Ps 19:11
children a *r* from him. . . . Ps 127:3
are wise, your wisdom will *r* you; . . . Prv 9:12
he who respects a command is *r*. . . . Prv 13:13
prosperity is the *r* of the righteous. . . . Prv 13:21
Give her the *r* she has earned, . . . Prv 31:31
See, his *r* is with him, . . . Is 40:10
to *r* a man according to his conduct . . . Jer 17:10
because great is your *r* in heaven, . . . Mt 5:12
they have received their *r* in full. . . . Mt 6:5
and each will be *r* according . . . 1 Cor 3:8
know that the Lord will *r* everyone . . . Eph 6:8
an inheritance from the Lord as a *r*. . . . Col 3:24
your confidence; it will be richly *r*. . . . Heb 10:35
that he *r* those who earnestly seek . . . Heb 11:6
he was looking ahead to his *r*. . . . Heb 11:26
I am coming soon! My *r* is with me . . . Rv 22:12

RICH *wealthy; abundant; see RICHES, WEALTH*
does not favor the *r* over the poor, . . . Jb 34:19
overawed when a man grows *r*, . . . Ps 49:16
loves wine and oil will never be *r*. . . . Prv 21:17
R and poor have this in common: . . . Prv 22:2
Do not wear yourself out to get *r*; . . . Prv 23:4
A stingy man is eager to get *r* . . . Prv 28:22
a *r* store of salvation and wisdom . . . Is 33:6
it is hard for a *r* man . . . Mt 19:23
but has sent the *r* away empty. . . . Lk 1:53
But woe to you who are *r*, . . . Lk 6:24
for himself but is not *r* toward God . . . Lk 12:21
Jesus saw the *r* putting their gifts . . . Lk 21:1
poverty welled up in *r* generosity. . . . 2 Cor 8:2
he was *r*, yet for your sakes he . . . 2 Cor 8:9
love for us, God, who is *r* in mercy, . . . Eph 2:4
want to get *r* fall into temptation . . . 1 Tm 6:9
to do good, to be *r* in good deeds, . . . 1 Tm 6:18
you *r* people, weep and wail . . . Jas 5:1

RICHES *wealth; abundant resources; see RICH, WEALTH*
despite his *r*, does not endure; . . . Ps 49:12
though your *r* increase, . . . Ps 62:10
as one rejoices in great *r*. . . . Ps 119:14
Whoever trusts in his *r* will fall, . . . Prv 11:28
is more desirable than great *r*; . . . Prv 22:1
give me neither poverty nor *r*, . . . Prv 30:8
Where will you leave your *r*? . . . Is 10:3
to you the *r* of the nations will . . . Is 60:5
the depth of the *r* of the wisdom . . . Rom 11:33
to the Gentiles the unsearchable *r* . . . Eph 3:8

RIGHT(S) *correct; that to which one has a just claim; correct by divine declaration; opposite of left; see RIGHTEOUS*
But if you do not do what is *r*, . . . Gn 4:7
the Judge of all the earth do *r*? . . . Gn 18:25
Your *r* hand, O LORD, . . . Ex 15:6
do not turn aside to the *r* . . . Dt 5:32

and doing what is *r* in his eyes. . . . Dt 13:18
to distinguish between *r* and wrong . . . 1 Kgs 3:9
For David had done what was *r* . . . 1 Kgs 15:5
and laws that are just and *r*, . . . Neh 9:13
eternal pleasures at your *r* hand. . . . Ps 16:11
and your *r* hand sustains me; . . . Ps 18:35
The precepts of the LORD are *r*, . . . Ps 19:8
For the word of the LORD is *r* . . . Ps 33:4
so that you are proved *r* . . . Ps 51:4
your *r* hand upholds me. . . . Ps 63:8
maintain the *r* of the poor . . . Ps 82:3
ten thousand at your *r* hand, . . . Ps 91:7
his *r* hand and his holy arm . . . Ps 98:1
Sit at my *r* hand . . . Ps 110:1
Your statutes are forever *r*; . . . Ps 119:144
may my *r* hand forget its skill. . . . Ps 137:5
Do not swerve to the *r* or the left; . . . Prv 4:27
There is a way that seems *r* . . . Prv 14:12
The first to present his case seems *r* . . . Prv 18:17
for the *r* of all who are destitute. . . . Prv 31:8
How *r* they are to adore you! . . . Song 1:4
reject the wrong and choose the *r*. . . . Is 7:15
to deprive the poor of their *r* . . . Is 10:2
Whether you turn to the *r* . . . Is 30:21
who takes hold of your *r* hand . . . Is 41:13
my *r* hand spread out the heavens; . . . Is 48:13
to the help of those who gladly do *r* . . . Is 64:5
and do what is just and *r* in the land . . . Jer 23:5
The ways of the LORD are *r*; . . . Hos 14:9
If your *r* eye causes you to sin, . . . Mt 5:29
know what your *r* hand is doing, . . . Mt 6:3
Sit at my *r* hand . . . Mt 22:44
He will put the sheep on his *r*. . . . Mt 25:33
he gave the *r* to become children . . . Jn 1:12
So that you may be proved *r* . . . Rom 3:4
Does not the potter have the *r*. . . . Rom 9:21
Don't we have the *r* to food . . . 1 Cor 9:4
parents in the Lord, for this is *r*. . . . Eph 6:1
whatever is *r*, whatever is pure, . . . Phil 4:8
never tire of doing what is *r*. . . . 2 Thes 3:13
down at the *r* hand of the Majesty . . . Heb 1:3
if you should suffer for what is *r*, . . . 1 Pt 3:14
I will give the *r* to eat from the tree . . . Rv 2:7
let him who does *r* continue to do *r* . . . Rv 22:11

RIGHTEOUS(NESS) *acting in a morally correct manner; correct by divine declaration; see RIGHT, UNRIGHTEOUS, UPRIGHT*
and he credited it to him as *r*. . . . Gn 15:6
Will you sweep away the *r* . . . Gn 18:23
He does not take his eyes off the *r*; . . . Jb 36:7
nor sinners in the assembly of the *r*. . . . Ps 1:5
He will judge the world in *r*; . . . Ps 9:8
He guides me in paths of *r*. . . . Ps 23:3
The LORD loves *r* and justice; . . . Ps 33:5
My tongue will speak of your *r*. . . . Ps 35:28
Better the little that the *r* have . . . Ps 37:16
but the *r* give generously; . . . Ps 37:21
yet I have never seen the *r* forsaken . . . Ps 37:25
I proclaim *r* in the great assembly; . . . Ps 40:9
your right hand is filled with *r*. . . . Ps 48:10
he will never let the *r* fall. . . . Ps 55:22
us with awesome deeds of *r*, . . . Ps 65:5
Your *r* reaches to the skies, O God, . . . Ps 71:19
r and peace kiss each other. . . . Ps 85:10
R and justice are the foundation . . . Ps 89:14
He will judge the world in *r*. . . . Ps 96:13
This was credited to him as *r*. . . . Ps 106:31
and his *r* endures forever. . . . Ps 111:3
Open for me the gates of *r*; . . . Ps 118:19
as I learn your *r* laws. . . . Ps 119:7
Surely the *r* will praise your name . . . Ps 140:13
for no one living is *r* before you. . . . Ps 143:2
The LORD is *r* in all his ways . . . Ps 145:17
but he blesses the home of the *r*. . . . Prv 3:33
of the *r* is like the first gleam . . . Prv 4:18

The mouth of the *r* is a fountain . . . Prv 10:11
The tongue of the *r* is choice silver, . . . Prv 10:20
what the *r* desire will be granted. . . . Prv 10:24
The prospect of the *r* is joy, . . . Prv 10:28
The fruit of the *r* is a tree of life, . . . Prv 11:30
A *r* man cares for the needs . . . Prv 12:10
R exalts a nation, . . . Prv 14:34
but he hears the prayer of the *r*. . . . Prv 15:29
Better a little with *r* . . . Prv 16:8
the *r* run to it and are safe. . . . Prv 18:10
The father of a *r* man has great joy; . . . Prv 23:24
but the *r* are as bold as a lion. . . . Prv 28:1
The *r* care about justice . . . Prv 29:7
There is not a *r* man on earth . . . Eccl 7:20
but with *r* he will judge the needy, . . . Is 11:4
the people of the world learn *r*. . . . Is 26:9
The fruit of *r* will be peace; . . . Is 32:17
you with my *r* right hand. . . . Is 41:10
You heavens above, rain down *r*; . . . Is 45:8
Listen to me, you who pursue *r*, . . . Is 51:1
He put on *r* as his breastplate, . . . Is 59:17
and arrayed me in a robe of *r*, . . . Is 61:10
and all our *r* acts are like filthy rags . . . Is 64:6
up to David a *r* Branch, . . . Jer 23:5
The *r* man, if he sins, will not be . . . Ez 33:12
and those who lead many to *r*, . . . Dn 12:3
but the *r* will live by his faith . . . Hb 2:4
r like a never-failing stream! . . . Am 5:24
I will see his *r*. . . . Mi 7:9
Seek *r*, seek humility; . . . Zep 2:3
the sun of *r* will rise with healing . . . Mal 4:2
those who hunger and thirst for *r*, . . . Mt 5:6
rain on the *r* and the unrighteous. . . . Mt 5:45
But seek first his kingdom and his *r*. . . . Mt 6:33
For I have not come to call the *r*, . . . Mt 9:13
Then the *r* will shine like the sun . . . Mt 13:43
to eternal punishment, but the *r*. . . . Mt 25:46
will be a resurrection of both the *r* . . . Acts 24:15
Paul discoursed on *r*, self-control . . . Acts 24:25
For in the gospel a *r* from God is . . . Rom 1:17
There is no one *r*, not even one; . . . Rom 3:10
This *r* from God comes . . . Rom 3:22
faith was credited to him as *r*. . . . Rom 4:9
body to him as instruments of *r*. . . . Rom 6:13
and have become slaves to *r*. . . . Rom 6:18
did not pursue *r*, have obtained it, . . . Rom 9:30
is the ministry that brings *r*! . . . 2 Cor 3:9
that in him we might become the *r* . . . 2 Cor 5:21
his *r* endures forever. . . . 2 Cor 9:9
for if *r* could be gained . . . Gal 2:21
and it was credited to him as *r*. . . . Gal 3:6
created to be like God in true *r*. . . . Eph 4:24
with the breastplate of *r* in place, . . . Eph 6:14
not having a *r* of my own that . . . Phil 3:9
and pursue *r*, faith, love and peace, . . . 2 Tm 2:22
correcting and training in *r*, . . . 2 Tm 3:16
is in store for me the crown of *r*, . . . 2 Tm 4:8
became heir of the *r* that comes . . . Heb 11:7
sow in peace raise a harvest of *r*. . . . Jas 3:18
The prayer of a *r* man is powerful . . . Jas 5:16
die to sins and live for *r*; . . . 1 Pt 2:24
the eyes of the Lord are on the *r*, . . . 1 Pt 3:12
and a new earth, the home of *r*. . . . 2 Pt 3:13
it is hard for the *r* to be saved, . . . 1 Pt 4:18

RIVER(S) *natural stream of water emptying into another body of water; symbolic of blessing*
There is a *r* whose streams make . . . Ps 46:4
By the *r* of Babylon we sat . . . Ps 137:1
I will extend peace to her like a *r*, . . . Is 66:12
grow on both banks of the *r*. . . . Ez 47:12
Then the angel showed me the *r*. . . . Rv 22:1

ROCK *large stone or cliff; symbolic of shelter or safety*
of the Shepherd, the *R* of Israel, . . . Gn 49:24
Strike the *r*, and water will come . . . Ex 17:6

O LORD, my *R* and my Redeemer . . . Ps 19:14
he set my feet on a *r* . . . Ps 40:2
lead me to the *r* that is higher . . . Ps 61:2
the LORD, is the *R* eternal. . . . Is 26:4
to the *r* from which you were cut . . . Is 51:1
you were watching, a *r* was cut out, . . . Dn 2:34
man who built his house on the *r*. . . . Mt 7:24
and on this *r* I will build my church . . . Mt 16:18
and a *r* that makes them fall, . . . Rom 9:33

ROD(S) *straight wooden stick, used as walking stick, weapon, royal scepter, or measuring device; figurative of divine authority*
your *r* and your staff, . . . Ps 23:4
He who spares the *r* hates his son, . . . Prv 13:24
r of correction imparts wisdom, . . . Prv 29:15
the earth with the *r* of his mouth; . . . Is 11:4
Three times I was beaten with *r*, . . . 2 Cor 11:25

ROOM(S) *area enclosed by walls, floor, and ceiling*
But when you pray, go into your *r*, . . . Mt 6:6
there was no *r* for them in the inn. . . . Lk 2:7
because you have no *r* for my word . . . Jn 8:37
In my Father's house are many *r*; . . . Jn 14:2
Make *r* for us in your hearts. . . . 2 Cor 7:2

ROOT(ED) *part of plant extending downward from seed into ground, providing stability and nourishment; to be firmly established; to pull up and destroy*
and like a *r* out of dry ground. . . . Is 53:2
already at the *r* of the trees, . . . Mt 3:10
But since he has no *r*, he lasts only . . . Mt 13:21
if the *r* is holy, so are the branches. . . . Rom 11:16
The *R* of Jesse will spring up, . . . Rom 15:12
being *r* and established in love, . . . Eph 3:17
of money is a *r* of all kinds of evil. . . . 1 Tm 6:10
I am the *R* and the Offspring . . . Rv 22:16

RULE(S) *law; standard of conduct; to enforce such laws; to exercise leadership over; see REIGN*
let them *r* over the fish of the sea . . . Gn 1:26
and he will *r* over you. . . . Gn 3:16
No, we want a king to *r* over us . . . 1 Sm 12:12
You will *r* them with an iron . . . Ps 2:9
and he *r* over the nations. . . . Ps 22:28
He *r* forever by his power, . . . Ps 66:7
for you *r* the peoples justly . . . Ps 67:4
A wise servant will *r* . . . Prv 17:2
r on *r*, *r* on *r*; . . . Is 28:10
is made up only of *r* taught by men. . . . Is 29:13
and will sit and *r* on his throne. . . . Zec 6:13
their teachings are but *r* taught . . . Mt 15:9
one who *r* like the one who serves. . . . Lk 22:26
are summed up in this one *r*: . . . Rom 13:9
arise to *r* over the nations; . . . Rom 15:12
and mercy to all who follow this *r*, . . . Gal 6:16
far above all *r* and authority, . . . Eph 1:21
the peace of Christ *r* in your hearts, . . . Col 3:15
he competes according to the *r*. . . . 2 Tm 2:5
He will *r* them with an iron scepter; . . . Rv 2:27
who will *r* all the nations . . . Rv 12:5

RULER(S) *person with authority to lead or enforce laws; powerful spiritual being*
and the *r* gather together . . . Ps 2:2
You made him *r* over the works . . . Ps 8:6
When you sit to dine with a *r*, . . . Prv 23:1
reduces the *r* of this world . . . Is 40:23
and righteousness your *r*, . . . Is 60:17
one who will be *r* over Israel, . . . Mi 5:2
for out of you will come a *r*. . . . Mt 2:6
and their *r* did not recognize Jesus, . . . Acts 13:27
of this age or of the *r* of this age, . . . 1 Cor 2:6
of the *r* of the kingdom of the air, . . . Eph 2:2
should be made known to the *r*. . . . Eph 3:10
or powers or *r* or authorities; . . . Col 1:16
God, the blessed and only *R*, . . . 1 Tm 6:15

RUN(NERS)(NING) *to move forward rapidly; to flow*
champion rejoicing to *r* his course. . . . Ps 19:5
r down on Aaron's beard, . . . Ps 133:2
the righteous *r* to it and are safe. . . . Prv 18:10
they will *r* and not grow weary, . . . Is 40:31
Do not go *r* off after them. . . . Lk 17:23
that in a race all the *r* run, . . . 1 Cor 9:24
that I was *r* or had *r* my race . . . Gal 2:2
You were *r* a good race. . . . Gal 5:7
let us *r* with perseverance the race . . . Heb 12:1

SABBATH(-REST)(S) *seventh day of week, divinely set apart for rest and worship; see REST*
"Remember the *S* day" . . . Ex 20:8
the land itself must observe a *s* . . . Lv 25:2
if you call the *S* a delight . . . Is 58:13
through the grainfields on the *S* . . . Mt 12:1
then, a *S* for the people of God. . . . Heb 4:9

SACKCLOTH *coarse cloth worn as symbol of repentance or sorrow*
you removed my *s* and clothed me . . . Ps 30:11
in fasting, and in *s* and ashes. . . . Dn 9:3
would have repented long ago in *s* . . . Mt 11:21

SACRIFICE(D)(S) *to offer something to God for worship or payment for sin*
S him there as a burnt offering . . . Gn 22:2
To obey is better than *s*, . . . 1 Sm 15:22
S and offering you did not desire, . . . Ps 40:6
You do not delight in *s*, . . . Ps 51:16
Let them *s* thank offerings . . . Ps 107:22
The LORD detests the *s* . . . Prv 15:8
time that the daily *s* is abolished . . . Dn 12:11
For I desire mercy, not *s*, . . . Hos 6:6
are to abstain from food *s* to idols, . . . Acts 15:29
to offer your bodies as living *s*, . . . Rom 12:1
our Passover lamb, has been *s* . . . 1 Cor 5:7
as a fragrant offering and *s* to God. . . . Eph 5:2
an acceptable *s*, pleasing to God. . . . Phil 4:18
away with sin by the *s* of himself. . . . Heb 9:26
S and offering you did not desire, . . . Heb 10:5
there is no longer any *s* for sin. . . . Heb 10:18
offer to God a *s* of praise . . . Heb 13:15
offering spiritual *s* acceptable . . . 1 Pt 2:5
He is the atoning *s* for our sins, . . . 1 Jn 2:2
as an atoning *s* for our sins. . . . 1 Jn 4:10

SAFE(TY) *free from danger; see SECURE*
make me dwell in *s*. . . . Ps 4:8
he will keep me *s* in his dwelling; . . . Ps 27:5
the righteous run to it and are *s*. . . . Prv 18:10
in the LORD is kept *s*. . . . Prv 29:25
so that all may lie down in *s*. . . . Hos 2:18
kept them *s* by that name you gave . . . Jn 17:12
people are saying, "Peace and *s*, . . . 1 Thes 5:3
born of God keeps him *s*, . . . 1 Jn 5:18

SAINTS *those declared righteous by God*
He will guard the feet of his *s*, . . . 1 Sm 2:9
Sing to the LORD, you *s* of his; . . . Ps 30:4
is the death of his *s*. . . . Ps 116:15
his praise in the assembly of the *s*. . . . Ps 149:1
the *s* of the Most High will receive . . . Dn 7:18
intercedes for the *s* in accordance . . . Rom 8:27
not know that the *s* will judge . . . 1 Cor 6:2
of his glorious inheritance in the *s*, . . . Eph 1:18
which are the prayers of the *s*. . . . Rv 5:8

SALVATION *deliverance from danger or difficulty; deliverance from the power or penalty of sin; see SAVE*
he has become my *s*. . . . Ex 15:2
my shield and the horn of my *s*, . . . 2 Sm 22:3
my heart rejoices in your *s*. . . . Ps 13:5
The LORD is my light and my *s* . . . Ps 27:1
and delight in his *s*. . . . Ps 35:9
I speak of your faithfulness and *s*. . . . Ps 40:10
Restore to me the joy of your *s* . . . Ps 51:12
He alone is my rock and my *s*; . . . Ps 62:2

your *s* among all nations. . . . Ps 67:2
may your *s*, O God, protect me. . . . Ps 69:29
of your *s* all day long, . . . Ps 71:15
and grant us your *s*. . . . Ps 85:7
Surely his *s* is near those who fear . . . Ps 85:9
to the Rock of our *s*. . . . Ps 95:1
proclaim his *s* day after day. . . . Ps 96:2
I will lift up the cup of *s* . . . Ps 116:13
he has become my *s*. . . . Ps 118:14
My eyes fail, looking for your *s*, . . . Ps 119:123
S is far from the wicked, . . . Ps 119:155
I wait for your *s*, O LORD, . . . Ps 119:166
I will clothe her priests with *s*, . . . Ps 132:16
he crowns the humble with *s*. . . . Ps 149:4
from the wells of *s*. . . . Is 12:3
In repentance and rest is your *s*, . . . Is 30:15
I will grant *s* to Zion, . . . Is 46:13
and my *s* will not be delayed. . . . Is 46:13
and in the day of *s* I will help you; . . . Is 49:8
But my *s* will last forever, . . . Is 51:6
my *s* through all generations. . . . Is 51:8
for my *s* is close at hand . . . Is 56:1
so his own arm worked *s* for him, . . . Is 59:16
and the helmet of *s* on his head; . . . Is 59:17
but you will call your walls *S* . . . Is 60:18
me with garments of *s* . . . Is 61:10
S comes from the LORD . . . Jon 2:9
He has raised up a horn of *s* for us . . . Lk 1:69
give his people the knowledge of *s* . . . Lk 1:77
For my eyes have seen your *s*, . . . Lk 2:30
Today *s* has come to this house, . . . Lk 19:9
for *s* is from the Jews. . . . Jn 4:22
S is found in no one else, . . . Acts 4:12
to know that God's *s* has been sent . . . Acts 28:28
for the *s* of everyone who believes: . . . Rom 1:16
s has come to the Gentiles . . . Rom 11:11
because our *s* is nearer now . . . Rom 13:11
and in the day of *s* I helped you. . . . 2 Cor 6:2
brings repentance that leads to *s* . . . 2 Cor 7:10
word of truth, the gospel of your *s*. . . . Eph 1:13
Take the helmet of *s* and the sword . . . Eph 6:17
to work out your *s* with fear . . . Phil 2:12
wise for *s* through faith . . . 2 Tm 3:15
of God that brings *s* has appeared . . . Ti 2:11
to serve those who will inherit *s*? . . . Heb 1:14
escape if we ignore such a great *s*? . . . Heb 2:3
of their *s* perfect through suffering. . . . Heb 2:10
case—things that accompany *s*. . . . Heb 6:9
of your faith, the *s* of your souls. . . . 1 Pt 1:9
Concerning this *s*, the prophets, . . . 1 Pt 1:10
by it you may grow up in your *s*, . . . 1 Pt 2:2
S belongs to our God, . . . Rv 7:10
have come the *s* and the power . . . Rv 12:10

SANCTIFIED, SANCTIFY(ING) *to cleanse or set apart for sacred use; to declare or make holy*
S them by the truth; your word is . . . Jn 17:17
among all those who are *s*. . . . Acts 20:32
to God, *s* by the Holy Spirit. . . . Rom 15:16
But you were washed, you were *s*, . . . 1 Cor 6:11
and the unbelieving wife has been *s* . . . 1 Cor 7:14
s you through and through. . . . 1 Thes 5:23
blood of the covenant that *s* him, . . . Heb 10:29
through the *s* work of the Spirit, . . . 1 Pt 1:2

SANCTUARY *area or structure declared holy by God and set apart for sacred use*
and have reverence for my *s*, . . . Lv 19:30
LORD, who may dwell in your *s*? . . . Ps 15:1
I have seen you in the *s* . . . Ps 63:2
me till I entered the *s* of God; . . . Ps 73:17
looked down from his *s* on high, . . . Ps 102:19
Lift up your hands in the *s* . . . Ps 134:2
Praise God in his *s*; . . . Ps 150:1
I will put my *s* among them forever . . . Ez 37:26

It enters the inner s . . . Heb 6:19
enter a man-made s that was only . . . Heb 9:24

SANG, SING(ING), SUNG *to produce words along with musical sounds; see SONG*
and the Israelites s this song . . . Ex 15:1
Then Israel s this song: . . . Nm 21:17
David s to the LORD the words . . . 2 Sm 22:1
So they s praises with gladness . . . 2 Chr 29:30
thanksgiving they s to the LORD: . . . Ezr 3:11
while the morning stars s together . . . Jb 38:7
let them ever s for joy. . . . Ps 5:11
S joyfully to the LORD, you . . . Ps 33:1
I will s and make music. . . . Ps 57:7
I s in the shadow of your wings. . . . Ps 63:7
S to the glory of his name; . . . Ps 66:2
he leads forth the prisoners with s; . . . Ps 68:6
Come, let us s for joy to the LORD . . . Ps 95:1
S to the LORD a new song, . . . Ps 98:1
I will s of your love and justice; . . . Ps 101:1
S us one of the songs of Zion! . . . Ps 137:3
They will enter Zion with s; . . . Is 35:10
S, O barren woman, . . . Is 54:1
he will rejoice over you with s. . . . Zep 3:17
When they had s a hymn, they . . . Mt 26:30
Silas were praying and s hymns . . . Acts 16:25
S and make music in your heart . . . Eph 5:19
and as you s psalms, hymns . . . Col 3:16
Is anyone happy? Let him s songs . . . Jas 5:13
And they s a new song: . . . Rv 5:9
and s the song of Moses the servant . . . Rv 15:3

SAT, SIT(S)(TING) *to be seated; to take a position of authority; see SEAT*
when you s at home . . . Dt 6:7
or s in the seat of mockers. . . . Ps 1:1
s enthroned between the cherubim, . . . Ps 99:1
By the rivers of Babylon we s . . . Ps 137:1
You know when I s and when I rise . . .
   Ps 139:2
I delight to s in his shade, . . . Song 2:3
He s enthroned above the circle . . . Is 40:22
Every man will s under his own . . . Mi 4:4
to s at my right or left is not for me . . .
   Mt 20:23
the Son of Man s at the right hand . . . Mt 26:64
who s at the Lord's feet listening . . . Lk 10:39
in my kingdom and s on thrones, . . . Lk 22:30
S at my right hand . . . Heb 1:13
who s down at the right hand . . . Heb 8:1
right to s with me on my throne, . . . Rv 3:21
thanks to him who s on the throne . . . Rv 4:9

SATISFIED, SATISFIES, SATISFY *to please or appease; to fulfill an obligation*
The poor will eat and be s; . . . Ps 22:26
My soul will be s as with the richest . . . Ps 63:5
who s your desires with good things, . . .
   Ps 103:5
for he s the thirsty . . . Ps 107:9
may her breasts s you always, . . . Prv 5:19
the desires of the diligent are fully s . . . Prv
   13:4
are three things that are never s, . . . Prv 30:15
whoever loves wealth is never s . . . Eccl 5:10
he will see the light of life and be s . . . Is 53:11
and your labor on what does not s? . . . Is 55:2
They all ate and were s, . . . Mt 14:20
for you will be s. . . . Lk 6:21

SAVE(D)(S) *to rescue or preserve from danger; to deliver from sin; see SALVATION*
that your own right hand can s you. . . .
   Jb 40:14
who s the upright in heart. . . . Ps 7:10
You s the humble . . . Ps 18:27
They cried to you and were s; . . . Ps 22:5
s me in your unfailing love. . . . Ps 31:16
for God will s Zion . . . Ps 69:35
and s the needy from death. . . . Ps 72:13
Surely he will s you . . . Ps 91:3
They forgot the God who s them, . . . Ps 106:21
in mortal men, who cannot s. . . . Ps 146:3

will s you also from the adulteress, . . . Prv 2:16
Turn to me and be s, . . . Is 45:22
it cannot s him from his troubles. . . . Is 46:7
of the LORD is not too short to s, . . . Is 59:1
How then can we be s? . . . Is 64:5
and we are not s . . . Jer 8:20
but you will have s yourself. . . . Ez 3:19
of the righteous man will not s him . . . Ez 33:12
on the name of the LORD will be s; . . . Jl 2:32
the God we serve is able to s us . . . Dn 3:17
he is mighty to s. . . . Zep 3:17
I will s my people . . . Zec 8:7
he will s his people from their sins . . . Mt 1:21
firm to the end will be s . . . Mt 10:22
wants to s his life will lose it, . . . Mt 16:25
believes and is baptized will be s, . . . Mk 16:16
to seek and to s what was lost. . . . Lk 19:10
but to s the world through him. . . . Jn 3:17
come to judge the world, but to s it. . . .
   Jn 12:47
on the name of the Lord will be s. . . . Acts 2:21
how much more shall we be s . . . Rom 5:9
only the remnant will be s. . . . Rom 9:27
the Israelites is that they may be s. . . . Rom
   10:1
on the name of the Lord will be s. . . . Rom
   10:13
so all Israel will be s, as it is written: . . . Rom
   11:26
will suffer loss; he himself will be s, . . . 1 Cor
   3:15
whether you will s your husband? . . . 1 Cor
   7:16
For it is by grace you have been s, . . . Eph 2:8
came into the world to s sinners . . . 1 Tm 1:15
He s us through the washing . . . Ti 3:5
but of those who believe and are s. . . . Heb
   10:39
of his way will s him from death . . . Jas 5:20
It s you by the resurrection . . . 1 Pt 3:21
others from the fire and s them; . . . Jude 1:23

SAVIOR *one who delivers from trouble, sin, or judgment (usually refers to Jesus Christ)*
stronghold, my refuge and my s . . . 2 Sm 22:3
Exalted be God, the Rock, my S! . . . 2 Sm
   22:47
Exalted be God my S! . . . Ps 18:46
for you are God my S, . . . Ps 25:5
my S and my God. . . . Ps 42:11
Praise be to the Lord, to God our S, . . .
   Ps 68:19
Restore us again, O God our S, . . . Ps 85:4
You have forgotten God your S; . . . Is 17:10
he will send them a s and defender, . . . Is 19:20
and apart from me there is no s . . . Is 43:11
know that I, the LORD, am your S, . . . Is 60:16
See, your S comes! . . . Is 62:11
and so he became their S. . . . Is 63:8
its S in times of distress, . . . Jer 14:8
I wait for God my S; . . . Mi 7:7
and my spirit rejoices in God my S, . . . Lk 1:47
know that this man really is the S . . . Jn 4:42
his body, of which he is the S. . . . Eph 5:23
we eagerly await a S from there, . . . Phil 3:20
who is the S of all men, . . . 1 Tm 4:10
through the appearing of our S, . . . 2 Tm 1:10
appearing of our great God and S, . . . Ti 2:13
and love of God our S appeared, . . . Ti 3:4
through Jesus Christ our S, . . . Ti 3:6
eternal kingdom of our Lord and S . . . 2 Pt 1:11
and knowledge of our Lord and S . . . 2 Pt 3:18
Son to be the S of the world. . . . 1 Jn 4:14
to the only God our S be glory, . . . Jude 1:25

SCATTER(ED)(S) *to disperse in many directions*
The LORD will s you . . . Dt 4:27
I will s you among the nations, . . . Neh 1:8
he will assemble the s people . . . Is 11:12
for I have s you to the four winds . . . Zec 2:6
I s them among the peoples, . . . Zec 10:9

he who does not gather with me s. . . . Mt 12:30
and the sheep of the flock will be s. . . . Mt 26:31
who had been s preached the word . . . Acts 8:4
To the twelve tribes s . . . Jas 1:1

SCHEMES *plans (always with a negative connotation)*
a heart that devises wicked s, . . . Prv 6:18
For we are not unaware of his s. . . . 2 Cor 2:11
stand against the devil's s. . . . Eph 6:11

SCORN(ED)(ING)(S) *to ridicule, make light of*
s by men and despised . . . Ps 22:6
an object of s to my accusers; . . . Ps 109:25
He who s instruction will pay for it, . . . Prv
   13:13
you will bear the s of the nations. . . . Mi 6:16
him endured the cross, s its shame, . . . Heb
   12:2

SCRIPTURE(S) *the Law; the writings of Moses; the entire collection of the books of the Bible*
said in all the S concerning himself. . . .
   Lk 24:27
These are the S that testify about . . . Jn 5:39
Does not the S say that the Christ . . . Jn 7:42
and the S cannot be broken . . . Jn 10:35
examined the S every day to see . . . Acts 17:11
yourself to the public reading of S, . . . 1 Tm
   4:13
All S is God-breathed . . . 2 Tm 3:16
that no prophecy of S came about . . . 2 Pt 1:20

SEA *the body of salt water covering most of the earth, or any large body of salt water*
Who will cross the s to get it . . . Dt 30:13
and wider than the s. . . . Jb 11:9
The s is his, for he made it, . . . Ps 95:5
the wicked are like the tossing s, . . . Is 57:20
iniquities into the depths of the s. . . . Mi 7:19
as the waters cover the s. . . . Hb 2:14
His rule will extend from s to s . . . Zec 9:10
who doubts is like a wave of the s, . . . Jas 1:6
The s gave up the dead that were . . . Rv 20:13
and there was no longer any s. . . . Rv 21:1

SEAL(ED) *to confirm, certify, or make secure; a device that prevents entry; symbol or mark of office*
Place me like a s over your heart, . . . Song 8:6
and s the words of the scroll . . . Dn 12:4
God the Father has placed his s . . . Jn 6:27
set his s of ownership on us, . . . 2 Cor 1:22
you were marked in him with a s, . . . Eph 1:13
with whom you were s for the day . . . Eph 4:30
When he opened the seventh s, . . . Rv 8:1
Do not s up the words . . . Rv 22:10

SEARCH(ES) *to investigate or examine thoroughly*
for the LORD s every heart . . . 1 Chr 28:9
s your hearts and be silent. . . . Ps 4:4
who s minds and hearts, . . . Ps 7:9
S me, O God, and know my heart; . . . Ps 139:23
I will s for the one my heart loves. . . . Song 3:2
I myself will s for my sheep . . . Ez 34:11
I will s for the lost and bring back . . . Ez 34:16
and s carefully until she finds it? . . . Lk 15:8
And he who s our hearts knows . . . Rom 8:27
The Spirit s all things, . . . 1 Cor 2:10

SEASON(ED) *one of four divisions of the year; a period of time; to enhance flavor or add zest*
which yields its fruit in s . . . Ps 1:3
full of grace, s with salt, . . . Col 4:6
be prepared in s and out of s; . . . 2 Tm 4:2

SEAT(ED) *place where one sits; position of authority; see SAT*
or sit in the s of mockers. . . . Ps 1:1
I saw the Lord s on a throne, . . . Is 6:1
and the Ancient of Days took his s . . . Dn 7:9
say to you, 'Give this man your s.' . . . Lk 14:9
before the judgment s of Christ, . . . 2 Cor 5:10

and *s* him at his right hand . . . Eph 1:20
and *s* us with him in the heavenly . . . Eph 2:6
s on the cloud was one "like a son . . . Rv 14:14

SECRET(S) *hidden or unexplained; kept from the knowledge of others*
The *s* things belong . . . Dt 29:29
since he knows the *s* of the heart? . . . Ps 44:21
when I was made in the *s* place. . . . Ps 139:15
but a trustworthy man keeps a *s*. . . . Prv 11:13
so that your giving may be in *s*. . . . Mt 6:4
The *s* of the kingdom . . . Mk 4:11
No, we speak of God's *s* wisdom, . . . 1 Cor 2:7
we have renounced *s* and shameful . . . 2 Cor 4:2
what the disobedient do in *s*. . . . Eph 5:12
I have learned the *s* . . . Phil 4:12
Satan's so-called deep *s* (I will not . . . Rv 2:24

SECURE *free from danger or fear; see SAFE*
beloved of the LORD rest *s* in him, . . . Dt 33:12
my body also will rest *s*, . . . Ps 16:9
His heart is *s*, he will have no fear; . . . Ps 112:8
an anchor for the soul, firm and *s*. . . . Heb 6:19
and fall from your *s* position. . . . 2 Pt 3:17

SEED(S) *part of plant that produces new plant; embryo; symbolic of descendants or hope of future growth*
so that it yields *s* for the sower . . . Is 55:10
A farmer went out to sow his *s*. . . . Mt 13:3
of heaven is like a mustard *s*, . . . Mt 13:31
But if it dies, it produces many *s*. . . . Jn 12:24
I planted the *s*, Apollos watered it, . . . 1 Cor 3:6
he who supplies *s* to the sower . . . 2 Cor 9:10
then you are Abraham's *s*, . . . Gal 3:29
not of perishable *s*, . . . 1 Pt 1:23

SEEK(ING), SOUGHT *to search for; to request; to aim or try*
if from there you *s* the LORD your . . . Dt 4:29
If you *s* him, he will be found . . . 1 Chr 28:9
themselves and pray and *s* my face . . . 2 Chr 7:14
I *s* the LORD, and he answered me . . . Ps 34:4
s his face always. . . . Ps 105:4
and *s* him with all their heart. . . . Ps 119:2
I have *s* your face with all my heart; . . . Ps 119:58
and those who *s* me find me. . . . Prv 8:17
those who *s* the LORD understand . . . Prv 28:5
S the LORD while he may be . . . Is 55:6
found by those who did not *s* me. . . . Is 65:1
You will *s* me and find me . . . Jer 29:13
the Lord you are *s* will come . . . Mal 3:1
But *s* first his kingdom . . . Mt 6:33
s and you will find . . . Mt 7:7
For the Son of Man came to *s*. . . . Lk 19:10
Nobody should *s* his own good, . . . 1 Cor 10:24
rewards those who earnestly *s* him. . . . Heb 11:6
he must *s* peace and pursue it. . . . 1 Pt 3:11

SELF-CONTROL(LED) *restraint exercised over one's own impulses, desires, or emotions; temperance*
is a man who lacks *s*. . . . Prv 25:28
you because of your lack of *s*. . . . 1 Cor 7:5
faithfulness, gentleness and *s*. . . . Gal 5:23
let us be *s*, putting on faith and love . . . 1 Thes 5:8
s, respectable, hospitable, . . . 1 Tm 3:2
to live *s*, upright and godly lives . . . Ti 2:12
prepare your minds for action; be *s*; . . . 1 Pt 1:13
and *s* so that you can pray. . . . 1 Pt 4:7
and to knowledge, *s*; and to *s*, . . . 2 Pt 1:6

SELFISH *concerned for self at expense of others*
An unfriendly man pursues *s* ends; . . . Prv 18:1
fits of rage, *s* ambition, dissensions, . . . Gal 5:20
Do nothing out of *s* ambition . . . Phil 2:3

you have envy and *s* ambition, . . . Jas 3:16

SELL(ING), SOLD *to exchange for something of value, usually money*
First *s* me your birthright. . . . Gn 25:31
Are not two sparrows *s* for a penny . . . Mt 10:29
then in his joy went and *s* all he had . . . Mt 13:44
s everything you have . . . Mk 10:21
buying and *s*, planting and building . . . Lk 17:28
I am unspiritual, *s* as a slave to sin. . . . Rom 7:14
or *s* unless he had the mark, . . . Rv 13:17

SEND(ING), SENT *to cause to go; to commission*
S forth your light and your truth, . . . Ps 43:3
"Here am I. *S* me!" . . . Is 6:8
achieve the purpose for which I *s* it. . . . Is 55:11
See, I will *s* my messenger, . . . Mal 3:1
to *s* out workers into his harvest . . . Mt 9:38
he *s* them out two by two . . . Mk 6:7
I am *s* you out like sheep . . . Mt 10:16
He has *s* me to proclaim freedom . . . Lk 4:18
and he *s* them out to preach . . . Lk 9:2
There came a man who was *s* . . . Jn 1:6
is to do the will of him who *s* me . . . Jn 4:34
but if I go, I will *s* him to you. . . . Jn 16:7
must do the work of him who *s* me. . . . Jn 9:4
As you *s* me into the world, . . . Jn 17:18
Father has *s* me, I am *s* you. . . . Jn 20:21
can they preach unless they are *s*? . . . Rom 10:15
For Christ did not *s* me to baptize, . . . 1 Cor 1:17

SEPARATE(D)(S) *to divide; to end an association; to go in different directions; to set apart for a special purpose*
and a gossip *s* close friends. . . . Prv 16:28
But your iniquities have *s* . . . Is 59:2
has joined together, let man not *s*. . . . Mt 19:6
as a shepherd *s* the sheep . . . Mt 25:32
Who shall *s* us from the love . . . Rom 8:35
and be *s*, says the Lord. . . . 2 Cor 6:17
at that time you were *s* from Christ, . . . Eph 2:12

SERVANT(S) *one who works for or is in subjection to another; see SERVE*
Speak, for your *s* is listening. . . . 1 Sm 3:10
Have you considered my *s* Job? . . . Jb 1:8
By them is your *s* warned; . . . Ps 19:11
Keep your *s* also from willful sins; . . . Ps 19:13
The LORD redeems his *s*; . . . Ps 34:22
you his *s* who do his will. . . . Ps 103:21
wise *s* will rule over a disgraceful . . . Prv 17:2
and the borrower is a *s* to the lender. . . . Prv 22:7
But you, O Israel, my *s*, . . . Is 41:8
my righteous *s* will justify . . . Is 53:11
so will I do in behalf of my *s*; . . . Is 65:8
Who then is the faithful and wise *s*, . . . Mt 24:45
'Well done, good and faithful *s*! . . . Mt 25:21
I am the Lord's *s*," Mary answered. . . . Lk 1:38
No *s* can serve two masters. . . . Lk 16:13
should say, 'We are unworthy *s*; . . . Lk 17:10
and where I am, my *s* also will be. . . . Jn 12:26
longer call you *s*, because a servant . . . Jn 15:15
taking the very nature of a *s*, . . . Phil 2:7
of which I, Paul, have become a *s*. . . . Col 1:23
his *s* flames of fire. . . . Heb 1:7

SERVE(D)(S), SERVING *to work for or be in subjection to another; see SERVANT*
to *s* the LORD your God . . . Dt 10:12
this day whom you will *s*, . . . Jos 24:15
to the LORD and *s* him only, . . . 1 Sm 7:3
the God we *s* is able to save us . . . Dn 3:17
No one can *s* two masters. . . . Mt 6:24
but to *s*, and to give his life . . . Mt 20:28
But I am among you as one who *s*. . . . Lk 22:27
And he is not *s* by human hands, . . . Acts 17:25

your spiritual fervor, *s* the Lord. . . . Rom 12:11
rather, *s* one another in love. . . . Gal 5:13
as if you were *s* the Lord, not men, . . . Eph 6:7
It is the Lord Christ you are *s*. . . . Col 3:24
Those who have *s* well gain . . . 1 Tm 3:13
so that we may *s* the living God! . . . Heb 9:14
If anyone *s*, he should do it . . . 1 Pt 4:11
greedy for money, but eager to *s*; . . . 1 Pt 5:2

SERVICE *see SERVE, SERVANT*
fit for *s* in the kingdom . . . Lk 9:62
Be dressed ready for *s* . . . Lk 12:35
There are different kinds of *s*, . . . 1 Cor 12:5
God's people for works of *s*, . . . Eph 4:12
and faith, your *s* and perseverance, . . . Rv 2:19

SEVEN *number between six and eight; symbolic of perfection*
Take with you *s* of every kind . . . Gn 7:2
march around the city *s* times, . . . Jos 6:4
s that are detestable to him: . . . Prv 6:16
comes, there will be *s* sevens . . . Dn 9:25
not *s* times, but seventy-seven times. . . . Mt 18:22
To the *s* churches in the province of Asia: . . . Rv 1:4
opened the first of the *s* seals . . . Rv 6:1

SEXUAL(LY) *related to human reproduction and physical attraction*
Anyone who has *s* relations . . . Ex 22:19
Do not have *s* relations with . . . Lv 18:20
murder, adultery, *s* immorality, . . . Mt 15:19
to associate with *s* immoral people . . . 1 Cor 5:9
he who sins *s* sins against his own . . . 1 Cor 6:18
Flee from *s* immorality. . . . 1 Cor 6:18
should not commit *s* immorality, . . . 1 Cor 10:8
even a hint of *s* immorality, . . . Eph 5:3
s immorality, impurity, lust, . . . Col 3:5
that you should avoid *s* immorality . . . 1 Thes 4:3
the adulterer and all the *s* immoral. . . . Heb 13:4
the murderers, the *s* immoral, . . . Rv 21:8

SHADOW *shade cast by object blocking light; hint; an omen*
hide me in the *s* of your wings . . . Ps 17:8
through the valley of the *s* of death, . . . Ps 23:4
will rest in the *s* of the Almighty. . . . Ps 91:1
covered you with the *s* of my hand . . . Is 51:16
These are a *s* of the things that . . . Col 2:17
and *s* of what is in heaven. . . . Heb 8:5
The law is only a *s* . . . Heb 10:1

SHAKE(N) *to cause to move in short, quick motions; to cause distress*
I will not be *s*. . . . Ps 16:8
he is my fortress, I will never be *s*. . . . Ps 62:2
all who see them will *s* their heads . . . Ps 64:8
let the earth *s*. . . . Ps 99:1
Though the mountains be *s* . . . Is 54:10
I will once more *s* the heavens . . . Hg 2:6
and the heavenly bodies will be *s*. . . . Mt 24:29
s together and running over, . . . Lk 6:38
that what cannot be *s* may remain. . . . Heb 12:27

SHAME(D)(FUL) *disgrace, humiliation, often at hands of an enemy; see ASHAMED*
their faces are never covered with *s* . . . Ps 34:5
not be put to *s* because of me, . . . Ps 69:6
that is his folly and his *s*. . . . Prv 18:13
every goldsmith is *s* by his idols. . . . Jer 10:14
never again will my people be *s*. . . . Jl 2:26
trusts in him will never be put to *s*. . . . Rom 9:33
things of the world to *s* the wise; . . . 1 Cor 1:27
have renounced secret and *s* ways; . . . 2 Cor 4:2
endured the cross, scorning its *s*, . . . Heb 12:2

SHARE(D)(S), SHARING *to participate in; to give a part to; a portion*
All will *s* alike. . . . 1 Sm 30:24
for he *s* his food with the poor. . . . Prv 22:9
The son will not *s* the guilt . . . Ez 18:20
and *s* your master's happiness! . . . Mt 25:21
The man with two tunics should *s* . . . Lk 3:11
but they *s* everything they had. . . . Acts 4:32
as you *s* in our sufferings, . . . 2 Cor 1:7
for your generosity in *s* with them . . . 2 Cor 9:13
something to *s* with those in need. . . . Eph 4:28
the fellowship of *s* in his sufferings, . . . Phil 3:10
you to *s* in the inheritance . . . Col 1:12
that you might *s* in the glory . . . 2 Thes 2:14
and to be generous and willing to *s*. . . . 1 Tm 6:18
you may be active in *s* your faith, . . . Phlm 1:6
that we may *s* in his holiness. . . . Heb 12:10
to do good and to *s* with others, . . . Heb 13:16
from him his *s* in the tree of life . . . Rv 22:19

SHEEP('S) *animal similar to goat, producing wool; figurative of God's people*
What then is this bleating of *s* . . . 1 Sm 15:14
we are considered as *s* . . . Ps 44:22
we are his people, the *s* . . . Ps 100:3
I have strayed like a lost *s*. . . . Ps 119:176
We all, like *s*, have gone astray, . . . Is 53:6
as a *s* before her shearers is silent, . . . Is 53:7
I myself will search for my *s* . . . Ez 34:11
and the *s* will be scattered, . . . Zec 13:7
They come to you in *s* clothing, . . . Mt 7:15
helpless, like *s* without a shepherd. . . . Mt 9:36
I am sending you out like *s* . . . Mt 10:16
If any of you has a *s* and it falls . . . Mt 12:11
he is happier about that one *s* . . . Mt 18:13
as a shepherd separates the *s* . . . Mt 25:32
He calls his own *s* by name . . . Jn 10:3
and I lay down my life for the *s*. . . . Jn 10:15
My *s* listen to my voice; I know . . . Jn 10:27

SHELTER *place of protection*
In the *s* of your presence you hide . . . Ps 31:20
take refuge in the *s* of your wings. . . . Ps 61:4
in the *s* of the Most High . . . Ps 91:1
Wisdom is a *s* . . . Eccl 7:12
a *s* from the storm . . . Is 25:4

SHEPHERD(S) *caretaker of sheep; figurative of religious leaders; see ELDER, OVERSEER*
the God who has been my *s* . . . Gn 48:15
will not be like sheep without a *s*. . . . Nm 27:17
commanded to *s* my people Israel, . . . 2 Sm 7:7
LORD is my *s*, I shall not be in want. . . . Ps 23:1
be their *s* and carry them forever. . . . Ps 28:9
He tends his flock like a *s*; . . . Is 40:11
Woe to the *s* who are destroying . . . Jer 23:1
will watch over his flock like a *s*. . . . Jer 31:10
scattered because there was no *s*, . . . Ez 34:5
Woe to the worthless *s*, . . . Zec 11:17
Strike the *s*, . . . Zec 13:7
who will be the *s* of my people . . . Mt 2:6
there were *s* living out in the fields . . . Lk 2:8
The good *s* lays down his life . . . Jn 10:11
there shall be one flock and one *s*. . . . Jn 10:16
that great *S* of the sheep, equip you . . . Heb 13:20
And when the Chief *S* appears, . . . 1 Pt 5:4

SHIELD *defensive armor*
I am your *s*, . . . Gn 15:1
my *s* and the horn of my salvation. . . . 2 Sm 22:3
But you are a *s* around me, . . . Ps 3:3
with your favor as with a *s*. . . . Ps 5:12
LORD is my strength and my *s*; . . . Ps 28:7
For the LORD God is a sun and *s*; . . . Ps 84:11
his faithfulness will be your *s* . . . Ps 91:4
You are my refuge and my *s*; . . . Ps 119:114
my *s*, in whom I take refuge, . . . Ps 144:2

he is a *s* to those who take refuge . . . Prv 30:5
to all this, take up the *s* of faith, . . . Eph 6:16

SHINE(S), SHINING, SHONE *to give off light*
the LORD make his face *s* . . . Nm 6:25
that the light of life may *s* on him. . . . Jb 33:30
Let the light of your face *s* upon us, . . . Ps 4:6
s ever brighter till the full light . . . Prv 4:18
Arise, *s*, for your light has come, . . . Is 60:1
let your light *s* before men, . . . Mt 5:16
the righteous will *s* like the sun . . . Mt 13:43
glory of the Lord *s* around them, . . . Lk 2:9
The light *s* in the darkness, . . . Jn 1:5
made his light *s* in our hearts . . . 2 Cor 4:6
and Christ will *s* on you. . . . Eph 5:14
in which you *s* like stars . . . Phil 2:15
as to a light *s* in a dark place, . . . 2 Pt 1:19
His face was like the sun *s* . . . Rv 1:16
It *s* with the glory of God, . . . Rv 21:11

SHORT *lacking height, time, or other qualities or substances*
Is the LORD's arm too *s*? . . . Nm 11:23
Was my arm too *s* to ransom you? . . . Is 50:2
If those days had not been cut *s*, . . . Mt 24:22
and fall *s* of the glory of God, . . . Rom 3:23
brothers, is that the time is *s*. . . . 1 Cor 7:29
of you be found to have fallen *s* of it . . . Heb 4:1

SHOUT *to speak loudly and forcefully*
s to God with cries of joy. . . . Ps 47:1
let us *s* aloud to the Rock . . . Ps 95:1
S for joy to the LORD, all the earth . . . Ps 98:4
wake up and *s* for joy. . . . Is 26:19
the mute tongue *s* for joy. . . . Is 35:6
He will not *s* or cry out, . . . Is 42:2
s aloud, O earth beneath. . . . Is 44:23
S, Daughter of Jerusalem! . . . Zec 9:9

SHOW(ED) *to display or demonstrate*
Moses said, "Now *s* me your glory . . . Ex 33:18
the faithful you *s* yourself faithful, . . . 2 Sm 22:26
S the wonder of your great love, . . . Ps 17:7
S me the way I should go, . . . Ps 143:8
s me your face, . . . Song 2:14
the holy God will *s* himself holy . . . Is 5:16
I will *s* myself holy among them . . . Ez 28:25
I will *s* wonders in the heavens . . . Jl 2:30
s mercy and compassion . . . Zec 7:9
he *s* them his hands and feet. . . . Lk 24:40
ages he might *s* the incomparable . . . Eph 2:7
I will *s* you my faith by what I do. . . . Jas 2:18
This is how God *s* his love . . . 1 Jn 4:9
to others *s* mercy, mixed with fear . . . Jude 1:23

SHUT *to close*
what he opens no one can *s*, . . . Is 22:22
they will never be *s*, day or night, . . . Is 60:11
and he *s* the mouths of the lions. . . . Dn 6:22
On no day will its gates ever be *s*, . . . Rv 21:25

SICK(NESS) *ill; in bad health*
Hope deferred makes the heart *s*, . . . Prv 13:12
and healing every disease and *s* . . . Mt 4:23
who need a doctor, but the *s*. . . . Mt 9:12
Heal the *s*, raise the dead, cleanse . . . Mt 10:8
I was *s* and you looked after me, . . . Mt 25:36
of you *s*? He should call the elders . . . Jas 5:14

SIGHT *the ability to see; something seen; range of vision; judgment, evaluation*
For a thousand years in your *s* . . . Ps 90:4
Precious in the *s* of the LORD . . . Ps 116:15
The blind receive *s*, the lame walk, . . . Mt 11:5
this world is foolishness in God's *s*. . . . 1 Cor 3:19
We live by faith, not by *s*. . . . 2 Cor 5:7
which is of great worth in God's *s*. . . . 1 Pt 3:4

SIGN(S) *divinely ordained event pointing to something larger or more important; miracle; see MIRACLE, WONDERS*

let them serve as *s* to mark seasons . . . Gn 1:14
This is the *s* of the covenant I am . . . Gn 9:12
and it will be the *s* of the covenant . . . Gn 17:11
the Lord himself will give you a *s*: . . . Is 7:14
I gave them my Sabbaths as a *s* . . . Ez 20:12
he performs *s* and wonders . . . Dn 6:27
At that time the *s* of the Son . . . Mt 24:30
these *s* will accompany those who . . . Mk 16:17
This will be a *s* to you: You will . . . Lk 2:12
Jesus did many other miraculous *s* . . . Jn 20:30
and *s* on the earth below, . . . Acts 2:19
are a *s*, not for believers . . . 1 Cor 14:22
s, wonders and miracles . . . 2 Cor 12:12

SILENCE(D), SILENT *absence of sound*
For if you remain *s* at this time, . . . Est 4:14
When I kept *s*, . . . Ps 32:3
a fool is thought wise if he keeps *s*, . . . Prv 17:28
a time to be *s* and a time to speak, . . . Eccl 3:7
as a sheep before her shearers is *s*, . . . Is 53:7
For Zion's sake I will not keep *s*, . . . Is 62:1
let all the earth be *s* before him. . . . Hb 2:20
so that every mouth may be *s* . . . Rom 3:19
good you should *s* the ignorant talk . . . 1 Pt 2:15
there was *s* in heaven . . . Rv 8:1

SIMPLE(HEARTED) *foolish, lacking good sense; absence of hypocrisy*
making wise the *s*. . . . Ps 19:7
The LORD protects the *s*; . . . Ps 116:6
it gives understanding to the *s*. . . . Ps 119:130
A *s* man believes anything, . . . Prv 14:15

SIN(NED)(NING)(S) *violation of conscience or of divine law; missing the mark; falling short of God's perfect standard; see SINFUL*
s is crouching at your door; . . . Gn 4:7
But if they will confess their *s* . . . Lv 26:40
But anyone who *s* defiantly, . . . Nm 15:30
be sure that your *s* will find you . . . Nm 32:23
each is to die for his own *s*. . . . Dt 24:16
I have *s* greatly in what I have done . . . 2 Sm 24:10
for there is no one who does not *s* . . . 1 Kgs 8:46
and will forgive their *s* and will heal . . . 2 Chr 7:14
our *s* are higher than our heads . . . Ezr 9:6
In your anger do not *s*; . . . Ps 4:4
your servant also from willful *s*; . . . Ps 19:13
whose *s* are covered. . . . Ps 32:1
Then I acknowledged my *s* to you . . . Ps 32:5
and cleanse me from my *s* . . . Ps 51:2
If I had cherished *s* in my heart, . . . Ps 66:18
does not treat us as our *s* deserve . . . Ps 103:10
that I might not *s* against you. . . . Ps 119:11
let no *s* rule over me. . . . Ps 119:133
the cords of his *s* hold him fast. . . . Prv 5:22
Though your *s* are like scarlet, . . . Is 1:18
they parade their *s* like Sodom; . . . Is 3:9
is taken away and your *s* atoned . . . Is 6:7
we have indeed *s* against you. . . . Jer 14:20
and remembers your *s* no more. . . . Is 43:25
your *s* have hidden his face . . . Is 59:2
like the wind our *s* sweep us away. . . . Is 64:6
and will remember their *s* no more . . . Jer 31:34
soul who *s* is the one who will die. . . . Ez 18:4
who pardons *s* and forgives . . . Mi 7:18
See, I have taken away your *s*, . . . Zec 3:4
if you do not forgive men their *s*, . . . Mt 6:15
If your brother *s* against you, . . . Mt 18:15
If your hand causes you to *s*, . . . Mk 9:43
who takes away the *s* of the world! . . . Jn 1:29
If any one of you is without *s*, . . . Jn 8:7
everyone who sins is a slave to *s*. . . . Jn 8:34
so that your *s* may be wiped out, . . . Acts 3:19
be baptized and wash your *s* away, . . . Acts 22:16
for all have *s* and fall short . . . Rom 3:23

whose *s* are covered. . . . Rom 4:7
as *s* entered the world . . . Rom 5:12
where *s* increased, grace increased . . . Rom 5:20
By no means! We died to *s; . . .* Rom 6:2
For the wages of *s* is death, . . . Rom 6:23
that does not come from faith is *s. . . .* Rom 14:23
died for our *s* according . . . 1 Cor 15:3
The sting of death is *s, . . .* 1 Cor 15:56
God made him who had no *s* to be *s . . .* 2 Cor 5:21
if someone is caught in a *s, . . .* Gal 6:1
dead in your transgressions and *s, . . .* Eph 2:1
us all our *s,* having canceled . . . Col 2:13
just as we are—yet was without *s. . . .* Heb 4:15
If we deliberately keep on *s . . .* Heb 10:26
the pleasures of *s* for a short time. . . . Heb 11:25
and will remember their *s* no more . . . Heb 8:12
of bulls and goats to take away *s. . . .* Heb 10:4
of the truth, no sacrifice for *s* is left, . . . Heb 10:26
and the *s* that so easily entangles, . . . Heb 12:1
it gives birth to *s; and s, . . .* Jas 1:15
ought to do and doesn't do it, *s. . . .* Jas 4:17
Therefore confess your *s . . .* Jas 5:16
and cover over a multitude of *s. . . .* Jas 5:20
He himself bore our *s* in his body . . . 1 Pt 2:24
If we claim to be without *s, . . .* 1 Jn 1:8
But if anybody does *s,* we have one . . . 1 Jn 2:1
No one who lives in him keeps on *s . . .* 1 Jn 3:6
There is a *s* that leads to death. . . . 1 Jn 5:16

SINCERE, SINCERITY *truthful; without deceit or hypocrisy*
ate together with glad and *s* hearts, . . . Acts 2:46
Love must be *s. . . .* Rom 12:9
speak before God with *s, . . .* 2 Cor 2:17
and with *s* of heart, just . . . Eph 6:5
but with *s* of heart and reverence . . . Col 3:22
a good conscience and a *s* faith. . . . 1 Tm 1:5
near to God with a *s* heart . . . Heb 10:22
the truth so that you have *s* love . . . 1 Pt 1:22

SINFUL *transgression of God's laws; see SIN*
Surely I was *s* at birth, . . . Ps 51:5
s from the time my mother . . . Ps 51:5
from me, Lord; I am a *s* man! . . . Lk 5:8
we were controlled by the *s* nature, . . . Rom 7:5
Son in the likeness of *s* man . . . Rom 8:3
if you live according to the *s* nature . . . Rom 8:13
to gratify the desires of the *s* nature . . . Rom 13:14
The acts of the *s* nature are obvious . . . Gal 5:19
Jesus have crucified the *s* nature . . . Gal 5:24
in the putting off of the *s* nature, . . . Col 2:11
abstain from *s* desires, which war . . . 1 Pt 2:11
He who does what is *s* is . . . 1 Jn 3:8

SINNER(S) *one who transgresses; see SIN*
or stand in the way of *s . . .* Ps 1:1
My son, if *s* entice you, . . . Prv 1:10
Do not let your heart envy *s . . .* Prv 23:17
come to call the righteous, but *s. . . .* Mt 9:13
in heaven over one *s* who repents . . . Lk 15:7
God, have mercy on me, a *s. . . .* Lk 18:13
While we were still *s,* Christ died . . . Rom 5:8
convinced by all that he is a *s . . .* 1 Cor 14:24
came into the world to save *s . . .* 1 Tm 1:15
Whoever turns a *s* from the error . . . Jas 5:20

SLANDER(ED)(ERS) *to deliberately lie in order to cause harm*
Do not go about spreading *s . . .* Lv 19:16
and has no *s* on his tongue, . . . Ps 15:3
and whoever spreads *s* is a fool. . . . Prv 10:18
They are gossips, *s,* God-haters, . . . Rom 1:30
when we are *s,* we answer kindly. . . . 1 Cor 4:13
nor the greedy nor drunkards nor *s . . .* 1 Cor 6:10

outbursts of anger, factions, *s, . . .* 2 Cor 12:20
rage and anger, brawling and *s, . . .* Eph 4:31
the enemy no opportunity for *s. . . .* 1 Tm 5:14
to *s* no one, to be peaceable . . . Ti 3:2
in Christ may be ashamed of their *s . . .* 1 Pt 3:16
afraid to *s* celestial beings; . . . 2 Pt 2:10

SLAVE(RY)(S) *one held in servitude to another*
The Israelites groaned in their *s . . .* Ex 2:23
As the eyes of *s* look to the hand . . . Ps 123:2
wants to be first must be your *s . . .* Mt 20:27
everyone who sins is a *s* to sin. . . . Jn 8:34
that we should no longer be *s* to sin . . . Rom 6:6
I am unspiritual, sold as a *s* to sin. . . . Rom 7:14
s nor free, male nor female, . . . Gal 3:28
were in *s* under the basic principles . . . Gal 4:3
S, obey your earthly masters . . . Eph 6:5
a man is a *s* to whatever has . . . 2 Pt 2:19

SLEEP(ER)(ING)(S) *rest; mental dullness; laziness; figurative for death; see ASLEEP*
the man to fall into a deep *s; . . .* Gn 2:21
Abram fell into a deep *s, . . .* Gn 15:12
it under his head and lay down to *s. . . .* Gn 28:11
I will lie down and *s* in peace, . . . Ps 4:8
will neither slumber nor *s. . . .* Ps 121:4
for he grants *s* to those he loves. . . . Ps 127:2
he who *s* during harvest is . . . Prv 10:5
The *s* of a laborer is sweet, . . . Eccl 5:12
suddenly, do not let him find you *s. . . .* Mk 13:36
We will not all *s,* but we will all be . . . 1 Cor 15:51
Wake up, O *s, . . .* Eph 5:14
For those who *s,* *s* at night, . . . 1 Thes 5:7

SLOW *not fast or hasty*
and gracious God, *s* to anger, . . . Ex 34:6
s to speak and *s* to become angry, . . . Jas 1:19
The Lord is not *s* in keeping his . . . 2 Pt 3:9

SOLDIER *person associated with active military duty*
as a *s* at his own expense? . . . 1 Cor 9:7
with us like a good *s* of Christ Jesus . . . 2 Tm 2:3

SON(S) *male child or descendant; spiritual heir; relationship of Jesus to God the Father*
"You are my *S;* today I have . . . Ps 2:7
to us a *s* is given, . . . Is 9:6
"This is my *S,* whom I love; . . . Mt 3:17
"You are the Christ, the *S* of the" . . . Mt 16:16
he was a *s,* he learned obedience . . . Heb 5:8
No one who denies *S* has the Father; . . . 1 Jn 2:23

SONG(S) *musical composition; see SANG*
LORD is my strength and my *s; . . .* Ex 15:2
who gives *s* in the night, . . . Jb 35:10
He put a new *s* in my mouth, . . . Ps 40:3
Sing to the LORD a new *s; . . .* Ps 96:1
come before him with joyful *s. . . .* Ps 100:2
Sing us one of the *s* of Zion! . . . Ps 137:3
burst into *s,* O mountains! . . . Is 49:13
with psalms, hymns and spiritual *s. . . .* Eph 5:19
Is anyone happy? Let him sing *s . . .* Jas 5:13
And they sang a new *s: . . .* Rv 5:9

SORROW(S) *mental, physical, or emotional anguish*
My eyes grow weak with *s; . . .* Ps 6:7
a man of *s,* and familiar . . . Is 53:3
I have great *s* and unceasing . . . Rom 9:2
Godly *s* brings repentance that . . . 2 Cor 7:10

SOUL(S) *person's essential self; that part of a person that is eternal*
with all your *s* and with all your . . . Dt 6:5
he restores my *s. . . .* Ps 23:3

so my *s* pants for you, O God. . . . Ps 42:1
Why are you downcast, O my *s? . . .* Ps 42:11
Find rest, O my *s,* in God alone; . . . Ps 62:5
Praise the LORD, O my *s; . . .* Ps 103:1
and he who wins *s* is wise. . . . Prv 11:30
A longing fulfilled is sweet to the *s, . . .* Prv 13:19
he who guards his *s* stays far . . . Prv 22:5
your *s* will delight in the richest . . . Is 55:2
and my *s* is downcast within me. . . . Lam 3:20
kill the body but cannot kill the *s. . . .* Mt 10:28
and you will find rest for your *s. . . .* Mt 11:29
yet forfeits his *s?* Or what can . . . Mt 16:26
even to dividing *s* and spirit, . . . Heb 4:12
even as your *s* is getting along well. . . . 3 Jn 1:2

SOUND *sensation perceived by the sense of hearing; healthy or whole; logically valid*
and his wife heard the *s . . .* Gn 3:8
preserve *s* judgment . . . Prv 3:21
Suddenly a *s* like the blowing . . . Acts 2:2
if the trumpet does not *s* a clear call . . . 1 Cor 14:8
the trumpet will *s,* the dead will . . . 1 Cor 15:52
to the *s* doctrine that conforms . . . 1 Tm 1:10
is in accord with *s* doctrine. . . . Ti 2:1

SOVEREIGN *supreme in power or authority (usually of God)*
your mighty acts, O *S* LORD; . . . Ps 71:16
S LORD will wipe away the tears . . . Is 25:8
The Spirit of the *S* LORD is on me, . . . Is 61:1
to the LORD: "Ah, *S* LORD, . . . Jer 32:17
that the Most High is . . . Dn 4:25
denying the *s* Lord who bought . . . 2 Pt 2:1
and deny Jesus Christ our only *S . . .* Jude 1:4

SOW(ER)(N)(S) *to scatter seeds in planting a crop; to cause a given effect*
Those who *s* in tears . . . Ps 126:5
he who *s* righteousness reaps a sure . . . Prv 11:18
They *s* the wind . . . Hos 8:7
they do not *s* or reap or store away . . . Mt 6:26
A farmer went out to *s* his seed. . . . Mt 13:3
along the path, where the word is *s. . . .* Mk 4:15
so that the *s* and the reaper may be . . . Jn 4:36
The body that is *s* is perishable, . . . 1 Cor 15:42
Whoever *s* sparingly will . . . 2 Cor 9:6
A man reaps what he *s. . . .* Gal 6:7

SPARE(S) *to refrain from destroying or punishing; more than what is needed*
s my people—this is my request. . . . Est 7:3
He who *s* the rod hates his son, . . . Prv 13:24
He who did not *s* his own Son, . . . Rom 8:32
For if God did not *s* angels . . . 2 Pt 2:4

SPEND, SPENT *to use up or pay out; to exhaust or consume*
do not *s* your strength on women, . . . Prv 31:3
Why *s* money on what is not bread, . . . Is 55:2
After he had *s* everything, . . . Lk 15:14
So I will very gladly *s . . .* 2 Cor 12:15

SPIRIT(S) *invisible, nonmaterial part of humans; supernatural being (third person of Trinity); other lesser supernatural beings; see SPIRITUAL*
and the *S* of God was hovering . . . Gn 1:2
My *S* will not contend . . . Gn 6:3
and put the *S* on the seventy elders. . . . Nm 11:25
filled with the *s* of wisdom . . . Dt 34:9
the *S* of God came upon him . . . 1 Sm 10:10
inherit a double portion of your *s, . . .* 2 Kgs 2:9
By your *S* you admonished them . . . Neh 9:30
Into your hands I commit my *s; . . .* Ps 31:5
saves those who are crushed in *s. . . .* Ps 34:18
and renew a steadfast *s* within me. . . . Ps 51:10
or take your Holy *S* from me. . . . Ps 51:11
Where can I go from your *S? . . .* Ps 139:7
till the *S* is poured upon us . . . Is 32:15
him who is contrite and lowly in *s, . . .* Is 57:15

and grieved his Holy S. . . . Is 63:10
you a new heart and put a new s . . . Ez 36:26
I will pour out my S on all people. . . . Jl 2:28
but by my S, says the LORD . . . Zec 4:6
to be with child through the Holy S. . . Mt 1:18
will baptize you with the Holy S . . . Mt 3:11
he saw the S of God descending . . . Mt 3:16
led by the S into the desert . . . Mt 4:1
saying: "Blessed are the poor in s, . . . Mt 5:3
against the S will not be forgiven. . . . Mt 12:31
s is willing, but the body is weak. . . . Mt 26:41
The Holy S will come upon you, . . . Lk 1:35
into your hands I commit my s. . . . Lk 23:46
a man is born of water and the S, . . . Jn 3:5
God is s, and his worshipers must . . . Jn 4:24
The S gives life; the flesh counts . . . Jn 6:63
Up to that time the S had not been . . . Jn 7:39
But the Counselor, the Holy S, . . . Jn 14:26
But when he, the S of truth, comes, . . .
    Jn 16:13
and said, "Receive the Holy S . . . Jn 20:22
of them were filled with the Holy S . . . Acts 2:4
that you have lied to the Holy S . . . Acts 5:3
will be baptized with the Holy S. . . . Acts 11:16
And if anyone does not have the S . . . Rom 8:9
the S helps us in our weakness. . . . Rom 8:26
present, I am with you in s. . . . 1 Cor 5:3
body is a temple of the Holy S, . . . 1 Cor 6:19
to another distinguishing between s, . . . 1 Cor
    12:10
The s of prophets are subject . . . 1 Cor 14:32
but with the S of the living God, . . . 2 Cor 3:3
the letter kills, but the S gives life. . . . 2 Cor 3:6
and has given us the S as a deposit, . . . 2 Cor
    5:5
But the fruit of the S is love, joy, . . . Gal 5:22
let us keep in step with the S. . . . Gal 5:25
from the S will reap eternal life. . . . Gal 6:8
with a seal, the promised Holy S, . . . Eph 1:13
There is one body and one S . . . Eph 4:4
do not grieve the Holy S of God, . . . Eph 4:30
Instead, be filled with the S. . . . Eph 5:18
the sanctifying work of the S . . . 2 Thes 2:13
beauty of a gentle and quiet s, . . . 1 Pt 3:4
carried along by the Holy S. . . . 2 Pt 1:21
test the s to see whether they are . . . 1 Jn 4:1
holy faith and pray in the Holy S. . . . Jude 1:20

SPIRITUAL *having to do with God, the human
spirit, or other supernatural spirits; see SPIRIT*
to God—this is your s act of worship. . . . Rom
    12:1
expressing s truths in s words. . . . 1 Cor 2:13
Now about s gifts, brothers, . . . 1 Cor 12:1
of love and eagerly desire s gifts, . . . 1 Cor 14:1
a natural body, it is raised a s body. . . . 1 Cor
    15:44
with every s blessing in Christ. . . . Eph 1:3
with psalms, hymns and s songs. . . . Eph 5:19
and against the s forces of evil . . . Eph 6:12
are being built into a s house . . . 1 Pt 2:5

SPLENDOR *majesty; glory*
the glory and the majesty and the s, . . . 1 Chr
    29:11
of the north he comes in golden s; . . . Jb 37:22
clothe yourself with s and majesty. . . . Ps 45:3
S and majesty are before him; . . . Ps 96:6
of the glorious s of your majesty, . . . Ps 145:5
Gray hair is a crown of s; . . . Prv 16:31
for he has endowed you with s. . . . Is 55:5
Who is this, robed in s, . . . Is 63:1
His s was like the sunrise; . . . Hb 3:4
appeared in glorious s, talking . . . Lk 9:31
and destroy by the s of his coming. . . . 2 Thes
    2:8

STAND(ING)(S), STOOD *to take an upright
position; to maintain a specified position or
posture; to endure*
where you are s is holy ground. . . . Ex 3:5
S firm and you will see . . . Ex 14:13

So the sun s still, . . . Jos 10:13
s firm and see the deliverance . . . 2 Chr 20:17
in the end he will s upon the earth. . . . Jb 19:25
or s in the way of sinners . . . Ps 1:1
Therefore the wicked will not s . . . Ps 1:5
Who may s in his holy place? . . . Ps 24:3
and gave me a firm place to s. . . . Ps 40:2
that your love s firm forever, . . . Ps 89:2
Therefore s in awe of God. . . . Eccl 5:7
If you do not s firm in your faith, . . . Is 7:9
but the word of our God s forever. . . . Is 40:8
s before me in the gap on behalf . . . Ez 22:30
Who can s when he appears? . . . Mal 3:2
divided against itself will not s. . . . Mt 12:25
By s firm you will gain life. . . . Lk 21:19
for the Lord is able to make him s. . . . Rom
    14:4
out so that you can s up under it. . . . 1 Cor
    10:13
Therefore, my dear brothers, s firm . . . 1 Cor
    15:58
Be on your guard; s firm in the faith . . . 1 Cor
    16:13
S firm then, with the belt . . . Eph 6:14
But the Lord s at my side . . . 2 Tm 4:17
because when he has s the test, . . . Jas 1:12
but the word of the Lord s forever . . . 1 Pt 1:25
Resist him, s firm in the faith, . . . 1 Pt 5:9
Here I am! I s at the door . . . Rv 3:20

STAR(S) *heavenly body*
A s will come out of Jacob; . . . Nm 24:17
while the morning s sang together . . . Jb 38:7
We saw his s in the east . . . Mt 2:2
in which you shine like s . . . Phil 2:15
the morning s rises in your hearts. . . . 2 Pt 1:19
I will also give him the morning s. . . . Rv 2:28
and the bright Morning S. . . . Rv 22:16

STEADFAST *unchanging; dependable*
and renew a s spirit within me. . . . Ps 51:10
My heart is s, O God, . . . Ps 57:7
They are s for ever and ever, . . . Ps 111:8
him whose mind is s, . . . Is 26:3
and make you strong, firm and s. . . . 1 Pt 5:10

STEAL, STOLEN *to take another's property
without permission; see THIEF*
You shall not s. . . . Ex 20:15
he must return what he has s . . . Lv 6:4
You have s my heart, my sister, . . . Song 4:9
do not s, do not give false . . . Mt 19:18
has been stealing must s no longer, . . . Eph
    4:28

STEP(S) *the action of moving the foot when
walking; a person's customary mode of behavior; see WALK, WAY*
prudent man gives thought to his s. . . . Prv
    14:15
but the LORD determines his s. . . . Prv 16:9
it is not for man to direct his s. . . . Jer 10:23
let us keep in s with the Spirit. . . . Gal 5:25
that you should follow in his s. . . . 1 Pt 2:21

STILL *without sound; without motion*
So the sun stood s, . . . Jos 10:13
Be s, and know that I am God; . . . Ps 46:10
its waves mount up, you s them. . . . Ps 89:9
said to the waves, "Quiet! Be s!" . . . Mk 4:39

STONE(D)(S) *hardened mineral or rock; figurative of Christ or of hardened hearts*
Chisel out two s tablets like . . . Ex 34:1
your neighbor's boundary s set up . . . Dt 19:14
will not strike your foot against a s. . . .
    Ps 91:12
The s the builders rejected . . . Ps 118:22
not move an ancient boundary s . . . Prv 22:28
a s that causes men to stumble . . . Is 8:14
See, I lay a s in Zion, . . . Is 28:16
remove from them their heart of s . . . Ez 11:19
out of these s God can raise up . . . Mt 3:9
will give him a s? Or if he asks . . .

not one s here will be left . . . Mt 24:2
tell this s to become bread. . . . Lk 4:3
the first to throw a s at her. . . . Jn 8:7
stumbled over the "stumbling s." . . . Rom 9:32
silver, costly s, wood, hay or straw, . . . 1 Cor
    3:12
not on tablets of s but on tablets . . . 2 Cor 3:3
once I was s, three times I was . . . 2 Cor 11:25
They were s; they were sawed . . . Heb 11:37
also, like living s, are being built . . . 1 Pt 2:5
also give him a white s . . . Rv 2:17

STOP *to cease from thought or action*
s and consider God's wonders. . . . Jb 37:14
S doing wrong, . . . Is 1:16
S grumbling among yourselves, . . . Jn 6:43
S judging by mere appearances, . . . Jn 7:24
S doubting and believe. . . . Jn 20:27
Therefore let us s passing judgment . . . Rom
    14:13
Brothers, s thinking like children. . . . 1 Cor
    14:20

STORE(D) *to gather a supply of*
and s up my commands within you, . . . Prv 2:1
Wise men s up knowledge, . . . Prv 10:14
a rich s of salvation and wisdom . . . Is 33:6
not s up for yourselves treasures . . . Mt 6:19
or reap or s away in barns, . . . Mt 6:26
out of the good s up in his heart, . . . Lk 6:45
from the hope that is s up for you . . . Col 1:5
Now there is in s for me the crown . . . 2 Tm 4:8

STRAIGHT *free of curves; free of obstacles; in
keeping with divine law*
and he will make your paths s. . . . Prv 3:6
and lead you along s paths. . . . Prv 4:11
Let your eyes look s ahead, . . . Prv 4:25
make s in the wilderness . . . Is 40:3
Make s the way for the Lord. . . . Jn 1:23
They have left the s way . . . 2 Pt 2:15

STRANGE(R)(RS) *unusual; foreigner; see
ALIEN*
I am a s on earth; . . . Ps 119:19
with foreign lips and s tongues . . . Is 28:11
I was a s and you invited me in, . . . Mt 25:35
But they will never follow a s; . . . Jn 10:5
Do not forget to entertain s, . . . Heb 13:2
as aliens and s in the world, . . . 1 Pt 2:11
They think it s that you do not . . . 1 Pt 4:4

STRAYED, STRAYS *to wander from a given
area or group or beyond established limits; to
deviate from what is right; see ASTRAY,
WANDER*
I have s like a lost sheep. . . . Ps 119:176
A man who s from the path . . . Prv 21:16
for the lost and bring back the s. . . . Ez 34:16

STREAM(S) *flow of water, smaller than a river*
He is like a tree planted by s . . . Ps 1:3
is a river whose s make glad . . . Ps 46:4
righteousness like a never-failing s! . . . Am 5:24
s of living water will flow . . . Jn 7:38

STRENGTH(EN)(ENED)(ENING) *capacity for
endurance; see STRONG*
The LORD is my s and my song; . . . Ex 15:2
all your soul and with all your s . . . Dt 6:5
In your hands are s and power . . . 1 Chr 29:12
for the joy of the LORD is your s. . . . Neh 8:10
I love you, O LORD, my s. . . . Ps 18:1
The LORD is my s and my shield; . . . Ps 28:7
God is our refuge and s, . . . Ps 46:1
O my S, I sing praise to you; . . . Ps 59:17
but God is the s of my heart . . . Ps 73:26
Blessed are those whose s is in you, . . . Ps 84:5
The LORD is my s and my song; . . . Ps 118:14
not in the s of the horse, . . . Ps 147:10
a man of knowledge increases s; . . . Prv 24:5
Ants are creatures of little s, . . . Prv 30:25
and in the great s of their horsemen . . . Is 31:1
S the feeble hands, . . . Is 35:3
will renew their s. . . . Is 40:31

I will *s* you and help you; . . . Is 41:10
or the strong man boast of his *s* . . . Jer 9:23
The Sovereign LORD is my *s*; . . . Hb 3:19
all your mind and with all your *s*. . . . Mk 12:30
have turned back, *s* your brothers. . . . Lk 22:32
of God is stronger than man's *s*. . . 1 Cor 1:25
done for the *s* of the church. . . . 1 Cor 14:26
is like the working of his mighty *s*, . . . Eph 1:19
of his glorious riches he may *s* you . . . Eph 3:16
through him who gives me *s*. . . . Phil 4:13
being *s* with all power according . . . Col 1:11
and *s* you in every good deed . . . 2 Thes 2:17
whose weakness was turned to *s*; . . . Heb 11:34
s your feeble arms and weak knees. . . . Heb 12:12

STRIFE, STRIVE *conflict between persons; to exert much effort*
than a house full of feasting, with *s*. . . Prv 17:1
It is to a man's honor to avoid *s*, . . . Prv 20:3
(and for this we labor and *s*), . . . 1 Tm 4:10
s, malicious talk, evil suspicions . . . 1 Tm 6:4

STRONG(ER) *having the capacity for endurance or exertion; see STRENGTH*
before you nations greater and *s* . . . Dt 4:38
Be *s* and courageous. . . . Dt 31:6
March on, my soul; be *s*! . . . Jgs 5:21
So be *s*, show yourself a man, . . . 1 Kgs 2:2
The LORD *s* and mighty, . . . Ps 24:8
a *s* fortress to save me. . . . Ps 31:2
The name of the LORD is a *s* tower . . . Prv 18:10
her arms are *s* for her tasks. . . . Prv 31:17
or the battle to the *s*, . . . Eccl 9:11
for love is as *s* as death, . . . Song 8:6
he will divide the spoils with the *s*, . . . Is 53:12
or the *s* man boast of his strength . . . Jer 9:23
can anyone enter a *s* man's house . . . Mt 12:29
And the child grew and became *s*; . . . Lk 2:40
We who are *s* ought to bear . . . Rom 15:1
of God is *s* than man's strength. . . . 1 Cor 1:25
be *s* in the Lord and in his mighty . . . Eph 6:10
be *s* in the grace that is . . . 2 Tm 2:1
restore you and make you *s*, . . . 1 Pt 5:10

STRONGHOLD(S) *place or means of protection or refuge; Satan's power*
He is my *s*, my refuge and my . . . 2 Sm 22:3
the horn of my salvation, my *s*. . . . Ps 18:2
my *s* and my deliverer, . . . Ps 144:2
have divine power to demolish *s*. . . . 2 Cor 10:4

STUMBLE(S), STUMBLING *to lose one's footing; to fall*
put a *s* block in front of the blind, . . . Lv 19:14
though he *s*, he will not fall, . . . Ps 37:24
and my feet from *s*, . . . Ps 56:13
and nothing can make them *s*. . . . Ps 119:165
and your foot will not *s*; . . . Prv 3:23
when he *s*, do not let your heart . . . Prv 24:17
a stone that causes men to *s* . . . Is 8:14
but the rebellious *s* in them. . . . Hos 14:9
teaching have caused many to *s*; . . . Mal 2:8
in Zion a stone that causes men to *s* . . . Rom 9:33
a *s* block to Jews and foolishness . . . 1 Cor 1:23
freedom does not become a *s* block . . . 1 Cor 8:9
Do not cause anyone to *s*, . . . 1 Cor 10:32
and yet *s* at just one point is guilty . . . Jas 2:10
We all *s* in many ways. . . . Jas 3:2
nothing in him to make him *s*. . . . 1 Jn 2:10

SUBJECT(ED) *to bring under control or dominion*
For the creation was *s* . . . Rom 8:20
of prophets are *s* to the control . . . 1 Cor 14:32
then the Son himself will be made *s*. . . 1 Cor 15:28
and to be *s* to their husbands, . . . Ti 2:5

SUBMISSION, SUBMISSIVE, SUBMIT *voluntary yielding to another; accountability*
Everyone must *s* himself . . . Rom 13:1

necessary to *s* to the authorities, . . . Rom 13:5
to *s* to such as these . . . 1 Cor 16:16
S to one another out of reverence . . . Eph 5:21
Wives, *s* to your husbands, . . . Col 3:18
learn in quietness and full *s*. . . . 1 Tm 2:11
How much more should we *s* . . . Heb 12:9
Obey your leaders and *s* . . . Heb 13:17
then peace-loving, considerate, *s*, . . . Jas 3:17
S yourselves, then, to God. . . . Jas 4:7
s yourselves to your masters . . . 1 Pt 2:18
in the same way be *s* . . . 1 Pt 3:1

SUCCEED, SUCCESS(FUL) *to achieve a favorable outcome*
and gave him *s* in whatever he did. . . . Gn 39:23
that you may be *s* wherever you go. . . . Jos 1:7
In everything he did he had great *s*, . . . 1 Sm 18:14
you will have *s* if you are careful . . . 1 Chr 22:13
but skill will bring *s*. . . . Eccl 10:10
and make all your plans *s*. . . . Ps 20:4
but with many advisers they *s*. . . . Prv 15:22
and your plans will *s*. . . . Prv 16:3

SUFFER(ING)(INGS)(S) *to endure hardship or experience loss*
those who *s* he delivers . . . Jb 36:15
of sorrows, and familiar with *s*. . . . Is 53:3
Is any *s* like my *s* . . . Lam 1:12
the Son of Man must *s* many things . . . Mk 8:31
but we also rejoice in our *s*, . . . Rom 5:3
share in his *s* in order that we may . . . Rom 8:17
If one part *s*, every part *s* with it; . . . 1 Cor 12:26
to *s* for him, since you are going . . . Phil 1:29
the fellowship of sharing in his *s*, . . . Phil 3:10
of their salvation perfect through *s*. . . . Heb 2:10
to *s* for doing good . . . 1 Pt 3:17
at the painful trial you are *s*, . . . 1 Pt 4:12

SUN *star around which the earth revolves*
So the *s* stood still, . . . Jos 10:13
For the LORD God is a *s* . . . Ps 84:11
the *s* will not harm you by day, . . . Ps 121:6
the *s* to govern the day, . . . Ps 136:8
there is nothing new under the *s*. . . . Eccl 1:9
the *s* of righteousness will rise . . . Mal 4:2
He causes his *s* to rise on the evil . . . Mt 5:45
the righteous will shine like the *s* . . . Mt 13:43
His face shone like the *s*, . . . Mt 17:2
Do not let the *s* go . . . Eph 4:26
The city does not need the *s* . . . Rv 21:23

SURE *certain; inevitable*
you may be *s* that your sin will find . . . Nm 32:23
Be *s* to keep the commands . . . Dt 6:17
But be *s* to fear the LORD . . . 1 Sm 12:24
The ordinances of the LORD are *s* . . . Ps 19:9
cornerstone for a *s* foundation; . . . Is 28:16
of this you can be *s*: No immoral, . . . Eph 5:5
faith is being *s* of what we hope for . . . Heb 11:1
to make your calling and election *s*. . . . 2 Pt 1:10

SURPASS(ED)(ES)(ING) *to become superior to*
praise him for his *s* greatness. . . . Ps 150:2
but you *s* them all. . . . Prv 31:29
unless your righteousness *s* that . . . Mt 5:20
He who comes after me has *s* me . . . Jn 1:15
to know this love that *s* knowledge . . . Eph 3:19
the *s* greatness of knowing Christ . . . Phil 3:8

SUSTAIN(ING)(S) *to support or maintain; to keep in existence*
and your right hand *s* me; . . . Ps 18:35
and he will *s* you; . . . Ps 55:22
and *s* the fatherless and the widow, . . . Ps 146:9

I am he, I am he who will *s* you. . . . Is 46:4
s all things by his powerful word. . . . Heb 1:3

SWEAR, SWORE, SWORN *to affirm by solemn oath or binding commitment*
Do not *s* falsely by my name . . . Lv 19:12
or *s* by what is false. . . . Ps 24:4
by me every tongue will *s*. . . . Is 45:23
Do not *s* at all: either by heaven, . . . Mt 5:34
for him to *s* by, he *s* by himself . . . Heb 6:13
The Lord has *s* . . . Heb 7:21
Above all, my brothers, do not *s* . . . Jas 5:12

SWEET(ER)(NESS) *pleasing to the taste*
they are *s* than honey, . . . Ps 19:10
How *s* are your words . . . Ps 119:103
Stolen water is *s*; . . . Prv 9:17
A longing fulfilled is *s* to the soul, . . . Prv 13:19
also that wisdom is *s* to your soul; . . . Prv 24:14
Your lips drop *s* as the honeycomb, . . . Song 4:11
The sleep of a laborer is *s*, . . . Eccl 5:12
It tasted as *s* as honey in my mouth . . . Rv 10:10

SWIFT *fast; occurring suddenly*
they are *s* to shed blood. . . . Prv 1:16
The race is not to the *s* . . . Eccl 9:11
Their feet are *s* to shed blood; . . . Rom 3:15
bringing *s* destruction . . . 2 Pt 2:1

SWORD(S) *handheld weapon with long blade; symbolic of war or persecution*
s which turned every . . . Gn 3:24
You come against me with *s* . . . 1 Sm 17:45
therefore, the *s* will never depart . . . 2 Sm 12:10
Reckless words pierce like a *s*, . . . Prv 12:18
Nation will not take up *s* . . . Is 2:4
Beat your plowshares into *s* . . . Jl 3:10
come to bring peace, but a *s*. . . . Mt 10:34
all who draw the *s* will die by the *s*. . . . Mt 26:52
a *s* will pierce your own soul too. . . . Lk 2:35
for he does not bear the *s* . . . Rom 13:4
of salvation and the *s* of the Spirit, . . . Eph 6:17
Sharper than any double-edged *s*, . . . Heb 4:12

TABERNACLE(S) *tent designated for worship in Moses' time, later replaced by temple; sometimes used of God's dwelling among his people; see TENT*
the glory of the LORD filled the *t*. . . . Ex 40:34
the LORD's Feast of *T* begins, . . . Lv 23:34
the true *t* set up by the Lord, . . . Heb 8:2
and more perfect *t* that is not . . . Heb 9:11
that is, the *t* of the Testimony, . . . Rv 15:5

TABLE(S) *flat-topped furniture item with numerous uses*
You prepare a *t* before me . . . Ps 23:5
changers and overturned their *t*. . . . Jn 2:15
word of God in order to wait on *t*. . . . Acts 6:2

TABLET(S) *writing surface*
he gave him the two *t*. . . . Ex 31:18
and put the *t* in the ark I had made, . . . Dt 10:5
write them on the *t* of your heart. . . . Prv 3:3
not on *t* of stone but on *t* . . . 2 Cor 3:3

TAKE(N)(S), TAKING, TOOK *to get possession of; to seize or capture*
land to *t* possession of it. . . . Gn 15:7
T off your sandals, . . . Ex 3:5
you are to *t* life for life, eye for eye, . . . Ex 21:23
Do not *t* advantage of a widow . . . Ex 22:22
do not add to it or *t* away from it. . . . Dt 12:32
I will never *t* my love away . . . 1 Chr 17:13
Blessed are all who *t* refuge in him. . . . Ps 2:12
You are not a God who *t* pleasure . . . Ps 5:4
and *t* away all my sins. . . . Ps 25:18
be strong and *t* heart . . . Ps 27:14
for he will *t* nothing with him . . . Ps 49:17
or *t* your Holy Spirit from me. . . . Ps 51:11

afterward you will *t* me into glory. . . . Ps 73:24
added to it and nothing *t* from it. . . . Eccl 3:14
your guilt is *t* away and your sin . . . Is 6:7
Surely he *t* up our infirmities . . . Is 53:4
and *t* to heart all the words I speak . . . Ez 3:10
I *t* no pleasure in the death . . . Ez 33:11
anyone who does not *t* his cross . . . Mt 10:38
T my yoke upon you and learn . . . Mt 11:29
even what he has will be *t* from him . . .
　　Mt 13:12
one will be *t* and the other left. . . . Mt 24:40
saying, "*T* and eat; this is my body . . . Mt 26:26
T this cup from me. . . . Mk 14:36
he was *t* up into heaven . . . Mk 16:19
　　　　　　　　　　　　　　who *t*
away the sin of the world! . . . Jn 1:29
No one *t* it from me, but I lay it . . . Jn 10:18
I *t* the very nature of a servant, . . . Phil 2:7
for which Christ Jesus *t* hold of me. . . . Phil
　　3:12
T hold of the eternal life . . . 1 Tm 6:12
And if anyone *t* words away . . . Rv 22:19

TASTE(D) *to detect flavor; to experience*
T and see that the LORD is good; . . . Ps 34:8
sweet are your words to my *t,* . . . Ps 119:103
it *t* as sweet as honey in my mouth. . . . Ez 3:3
Do not *t!* Do not touch!"? . . . Col 2:21
the grace of God he might *t* death . . . Heb 2:9
now that you have *t* that the Lord . . . 1 Pt 2:3

TAUGHT, TEACH(ER)(ERS)(ES)(ING)(INGS) *to*
impart knowledge or skill
and will *t* you what to say. . . . Ex 4:12
t me your ways so I may know you . . . Ex 33:13
T them to your children . . . Dt 4:9
T them the right way to live, . . . 1 Kgs 8:36
t them how to worship the LORD. . . . 2 Kgs
　　17:28
and *t* them his way. . . . Ps 25:9
I will *t* transgressors your ways, . . . Ps 51:13
T us to number our days aright, . . . Ps 90:12
Does he who *t* man lack . . . Ps 94:10
I have more insight than all my *t,* . . . Ps 119:99
for you yourself have *t* me. . . . Ps 119:102
T me to do your will, . . . Ps 143:10
My son, do not forget my *t,* . . . Prv 3:1
guard my *t* as the apple of your eye. . . . Prv 7:2
No longer will a man *t* his neighbor . . . Jer
　　31:34
t these commands will be called . . . Mt 5:19
he *t* as one who had authority, . . . Mt 7:29
A student is not above his *t,* . . . Mt 10:24
t them to obey everything I have . . . Mt 28:20
said to him, "Lord, *t* us to pray, . . . Lk 11:1
for the Holy Spirit will *t* you . . . Lk 12:12
loves me, he will obey my *t.* . . . Jn 14:23
have *t* you publicly and from house . . . Acts
　　20:20
who *t* others, do you not *t* yourself? . . . Rom
　　2:21
in the past was written to *t* us, . . . Rom 15:4
and there by every wind of *t* . . . Eph 4:14
but in words *t* by the Spirit, . . . 1 Cor 2:13
respectable, hospitable, able to *t,* . . . 1 Tm 3:2
also be qualified to *t* others. . . . 2 Tm 2:2
is God-breathed and is useful for *t,* . . . 2 Tm
　　3:16
around them a great number of *t* . . . 2 Tm 4:3
It *t* us to say "No" to ungodliness . . . Ti 2:12
by this time you ought to be *t,* . . . Heb 5:12
leave the elementary *t* about Christ . . . Heb 6:1
No longer will a man *t* his neighbor . . . Heb
　　8:11
know that we who *t* will be judged . . . Jas 3:1
you do not need anyone to *t* you. . . . 1 Jn 2:27

TEAR(S) *secretion from tear duct, usually*
caused by sorrow ; see WEEP
Those who sow in *t* . . . Ps 126:5
and your eyes from *t,* . . . Jer 31:16
she began to wet his feet with her *t.* . . . Lk 7:38

and now say again even with *t,* . . . Phil 3:18
He will wipe every *t* . . . Rv 21:4

TEMPERATE *self-controlled, moderate*
t, self-controlled, respectable, . . . 1 Tm 3:2
Teach the older men to be *t,* . . . Ti 2:2

TEMPLE(S) *structure that replaced tabernacle*
as place of worship; figurative of human body
and of Christ
began to build the *t* of the LORD. . . . 1 Kgs 6:1
the cloud filled the *t* of the LORD. . . . 1 Kgs 8:10
and to seek him in his *t.* . . . Ps 27:4
and the train of his robe filled the *t.* . . . Is 6:1
cloud filled the *t,* and the court was . . . Ez 10:4
glory of the LORD entered the *t* . . . Ez 43:4
But the LORD is in his holy *t;* . . . Hb 2:20
that one greater than the *t* is here. . . . Mt 12:6
of the *t* was torn in two from top . . . Mt 27:51
In the *t* courts he found men selling . . . Jn 2:14
does not live in *t* built by hands. . . . Acts 17:24
that you yourselves are God's *t* . . . 1 Cor 3:16
you not know that your body is a *t* . . . 1 Cor 6:19
I did not see a *t* in the city, . . . Rv 21:22

TEMPT(ATION)(ED) *to entice someone to sin;*
cause of enticement
into the desert to be *t* by the devil. . . . Mt 4:1
And lead us not into *t,* . . . Mt 6:13
pray so that you will not fall into *t.* . . . Mt 26:41
again so that Satan will not *t* you . . . 1 Cor 7:5
No *t* has seized you except what is . . . 1 Cor
　　10:13
yourself, or you also may be *t.* . . . Gal 6:1
want to get rich fall into *t* . . . 1 Tm 6:9
able to help those who are being *t.* . . . Heb 2:18
but we have one who has been *t* . . . Heb 4:15
For God cannot be *t* by evil, . . . Jas 1:13

TEN(TH) *number between nine and eleven,*
basis of decimal system; often figurative;
percentage designated as tithe; see TITHE
Abram gave him a *t* of everything. . . . Gn 14:20
covenant, the *T* Commandments, . . . Dt 4:13
Be sure to set aside a *t* . . . Dt 14:22
t thousand at your right hand, . . . Ps 91:7
t horns are *t* kings who will come . . . Dn 7:24
will be like *t* virgins who took . . . Mt 25:1
suppose a woman has *t* silver coins . . . Lk 15:8
I fast twice a week and give a *t* . . . Lk 18:12
patriarch Abraham gave him a *t* . . . Heb 7:4

TENT(S) *portable housing made of cloth or*
skins; figurative of mortal body; see TABERNA-
CLE
and pitched his *t* near Sodom. . . . Gn 13:12
Set up the tabernacle, the *T* . . . Ex 40:2
than dwell in the *t* of the wicked. . . . Ps 84:10
Enlarge the place of your *t,* . . . Is 54:2
that if the earthly *t* we live . . . 2 Cor 5:1
as long as I live in the *t* of this body, . . . 2 Pt
　　1:13

TERRIFIED, TERRIFY, TERRIFYING *very fear-*
ful; to cause fear or dread;horrific
Do not be *t* by them, . . . Dt 7:21
walking on the lake, they were *t.* . . . Mt 14:26
they fell facedown to the ground, *t.* . . . Mt 17:6
they were *t,* and exclaimed, . . . Mt 27:54
They were *t* and asked each other, . . . Mk 4:41

TERROR *fear or dread*
very day I will begin to put the *t* . . . Dt 2:25
You will not fear the *t* of night, . . . Ps 91:5
live in constant *t* every day . . . Is 51:13
T will be far removed; . . . Is 54:14
Men will faint from *t,* apprehensive . . . Lk 21:26
For rulers hold no *t* . . . Rom 13:3

TEST(ED)(ING)(S) *to examine in order to*
determine quality, value, or character
Some time later God *t* Abraham. . . . Gn 22:1
Do not *t* the LORD your God . . . Dt 6:16
when he has *t* me, I will come forth . . .
　　Jb 23:10

T me, O LORD, and try me, . . . Ps 26:2
They willfully put God to the *t* . . . Ps 78:18
t me and know my anxious . . . Ps 139:23
but the LORD *t* the heart. . . . Prv 17:3
man is *t* by the praise he receives. . . . Prv 27:21
a *t* stone, . . . Is 28:16
I have *t* you in the furnace . . . Is 48:10
but in the time of *t* they fall away. . . . Lk 8:13
and the fire will *t* the quality . . . 1 Cor 3:13
We should not *t* the Lord, . . . 1 Cor 10:9
unless, of course, you fail the *t?* . . . 2 Cor 13:5
but God, who *t* our hearts. . . . 1 Thes 2:4
during the time of *t* in the desert, . . . Heb 3:8
By faith Abraham, when God *t* him . . . Heb
　　11:17
because when he has stood the *t,* . . . Jas 1:12
t the spirits to see whether they are . . . 1 Jn 4:1

TESTIFIES, TESTIFY *to bear witness; to*
present evidence for or against a person or
thing; see TESTIMONY, WITNESS
Do not *t* against your neighbor . . . Prv 24:28
a witness to *t* concerning that light, . . . Jn 1:7
There is another who *t* in my favor, . . . Jn 5:32
he will *t* about me. And you . . . Jn 15:26
All the prophets *t* about him that . . . Acts 10:43
The Spirit himself *t* . . . Rom 8:16
ashamed to *t* about our Lord, . . . 2 Tm 1:8
t that the Father has sent his Son . . . 1 Jn 4:14

TESTIMONY *evidence given by a witness; see*
TESTIFIES
You shall not give false *t* . . . Ex 20:16
only on the *t* of witnesses. . . . Nm 35:30
and to the *t!* If they do not speak . . . Is 8:20
preached in the whole world as a *t* . . . Mt 24:14
not give false *t,* honor your father . . . Lk 18:20
We know that his *t* is true. . . . Jn 21:24
and by the word of their *t;* . . . Rv 12:11

THANK(FUL)(FULNESS)(S)(SGIVING) *to*
express gratitude or appreciation
Give *t* to the LORD, call . . . 1 Chr 16:8
assigned two large choirs to give *t.* . . . Neh
　　12:31
I will give you *t* in the great . . . Ps 35:18
we give *t,* for your Name is near; . . . Ps 75:1
Let us come before him with *t* . . . Ps 95:2
give *t* to him and praise his name. . . . Ps 100:4
are my God, and I will give you *t;* . . . Ps 118:28
Give *t* to the LORD, for he is good. . . . Ps 136:1
as God nor gave *t* to him, . . . Rom 1:21
when he had given *t,* he broke it . . . 1 Cor
　　11:24
t be to God! He gives us the victory . . . 1 Cor
　　15:57
T be to God for his indescribable . . . 2 Cor 9:15
I *t* my God every time I remember . . . Phil 1:3
by prayer and petition, with *t,* . . . Phil 4:6
taught, and overflowing with *t.* . . . Col 2:7
And be *t.* . . . Col 3:15
give *t* in all circumstances, . . . 1 Thes 5:18
let us be *t,* and so worship God . . . Heb 12:28

THIEF, THIEVES *one who steals; see STEAL*
A *t* must certainly make restitution . . . Ex 22:3
and where *t* break in and steal. . . . Mt 6:19
at what hour the *t* was coming, . . . Lk 12:39
day of the Lord will come like a *t* . . . 1 Thes 5:2
or *t* or any other kind of criminal, . . . 1 Pt 4:15

THINK(ING) *to use one's mind; see THOUGHT*
I *t* of you through the watches . . . Ps 63:6
What do you *t* about the Christ? . . . Mt 22:42
Do not *t* of yourself more highly . . . Rom 12:3
Brothers, stop *t* like children. . . . 1 Cor 14:20
praiseworthy—*t* about such things . . . Phil 4:8
to stimulate you to wholesome *t.* . . . 2 Pt 3:1

THIRST(S)(Y) *desire or need to drink; any*
strong desire or craving
My soul *t* for God, . . . Ps 42:2
for he satisfies the *t.* . . . Ps 107:9
Come, all you who are *t,* . . . Is 55:1

Blessed are those who hunger and *t* . . . Mt 5:6
I was *t* and you gave me something . . .
   Mt 25:35
the water I give him will never *t*. . . . Jn 4:14
If anyone is *t*, let him come to me . . . Jn 7:37
never again will they *t*. . . . Rv 7:16
To him who is *t* I will give to drink . . . Rv 21:6

THORN(S) *spiny plant; a source of irritation or suffering*
It will produce *t* and thistles . . . Gn 3:18
fell among *t*, which grew up . . . Mt 13:7
then twisted together a crown of *t* . . . Mt 27:29
there was given me a *t* in my flesh, . . . 2 Cor 12:7

THOUGHT(S) *product of thinking; see THINK*
The LORD knows the *t* of man; . . . Ps 94:11
test me and know my anxious *t* . . . Ps 139:23
a prudent man gives *t* to his steps. . . . Prv 14:15
For my *t* are not your *t*, . . . Is 55:8
I talked like a child, I *t* like a child, . . . 1 Cor 13:11
it judges the *t* and attitudes . . . Heb 4:12

THREE *number between two and four, often figurative*
the testimony of two or *t* witnesses. . . .
   Dt 19:15
There are *t* things that are never . . . Prv 30:15
of *t* strands is not quickly broken. . . . Eccl 4:12
Weren't there *t* men that we tied up . . . Dn 3:24
so the Son of Man will be *t* days . . . Mt 12:40
I will put up *t* shelters—one . . . Mt 17:4
or *t* come together in my name, . . . Mt 18:20
you will disown me *t* times. . . . Mt 26:34
After *t* days I will rise again. . . . Mt 27:63
And now these *t* remain: faith, . . . 1 Cor 13:13
For there are *t* that testify: . . . 1 Jn 5:7

THRONE *seat of power for king or deity*
your *t* will be established forever . . . 2 Sm 7:16
God is seated on his holy *t*. . . . Ps 47:8
justice are the foundation of your *t*; . . . Ps 89:14
Heaven is my *t*, . . . Is 66:1
His *t* was flaming with fire, . . . Dn 7:9
Son of Man sits on his glorious *t*, . . . Mt 19:28
prophet says: " 'Heaven is my *t*, . . . Acts 7:49
Let us then approach the *t* of grace . . . Heb 4:16
at the right hand of the *t* of God. . . . Heb 12:2
the right to sit with me on my *t*, . . . Rv 3:21
They lay their crowns before the *t*. . . . Rv 4:10
Then I saw a great white *t* . . . Rv 20:11

TIME(S) *occasion or duration of an event*
come to royal position for such a *t* . . . Est 4:14
a stronghold in *t* of trouble. . . . Ps 9:9
My *t* are in your hands; . . . Ps 31:15
A friend loves at all *t*, . . . Prv 17:17
There is a *t* for everything, . . . Eccl 3:1
to him for a *t*, times and half a *t*. . . . Dn 7:25
cannot interpret the signs of the *t*. . . . Mt 16:3
how many *t* shall I forgive my . . . Mt 18:21
Jesus replied, "My *t* has not yet . . . Jn 2:4
It is not for you to know the *t* . . . Acts 1:7
understanding the present *t*. . . . Rom 13:11
brothers, is that the *t* is short. . . . 1 Cor 7:29
now is the *t* of God's favor, . . . 2 Cor 6:2
Jesus before the beginning of *t*, . . . 2 Tm 1:9
and he will appear a second *t*, . . . Heb 9:28
for all *t* one sacrifice for sins, . . . Heb 10:12
For it is *t* for judgment to begin . . . 1 Pt 4:17

TITHE(S), TITHING *one-tenth of any property or produce; see TEN*
A *t* of everything from the land, . . . Lv 27:30
give to the Levites all the *t* in Israel . . .
   Nm 18:21
'How do we rob you?' In *t* . . . Mal 3:8

TODAY *present day or age*
T, if you hear his voice, . . . Ps 95:7
Give us *t* our daily bread. . . . Mt 6:11
T in the town of David a Savior has . . . Lk 2:11

t you will be with me in paradise. . . . Lk 23:43
t I have become your Father. . . . Acts 13:33
daily, as long as it is called *T*, . . . Heb 3:13
Christ is the same yesterday and *t* . . . Heb 13:8

TOMORROW *day following today*
Do not boast about *t*, . . . Prv 27:1
for *t* we die! . . . Is 22:13
Therefore do not worry about *t*, . . . Mt 6:34
Today or *t* we will go to this . . . Jas 4:13

TONGUE(S) *part of mouth enabling speech; language; special language given to Christians by the Holy Spirit*
I am slow of speech and *t*. . . . Ex 4:10
our *t* with songs of joy. . . . Ps 126:4
keep your *t* from evil . . . Ps 34:13
my *t* will sing of your righteousness . . .
   Ps 51:14
My *t* will tell of your righteous acts . . . Ps 71:24
May my *t* cling to the roof . . . Ps 137:6
Before a word is on my *t* . . . Ps 139:4
but he who holds his *t* is wise. . . . Prv 10:19
he whose *t* is deceitful falls . . . Prv 17:20
He who guards his mouth and his *t* . . . Prv 21:23
A lying *t* hates those it hurts, . . . Prv 26:28
with foreign lips and strange *t* . . . Is 28:11
than he who has a flattering *t*. . . . Prv 28:23
and the stammering *t* will be fluent . . . Is 32:4
by me every *t* will swear. . . . Is 45:23
the prophets who wag their own *t* . . . Jer 23:31
and began to speak in other *t* . . . Acts 2:4
their *t* practice deceit. . . . Rom 3:13
every *t* will confess to God. . . . Rom 14:11
If I speak in the *t* of men . . . 1 Cor 13:1
speaks in a *t* does not speak to men . . . 1 Cor 14:2
than ten thousand words in a *t*. . . . 1 Cor 14:19
and do not forbid speaking in *t*. . . . 1 Cor 14:39
every *t* confess that Jesus Christ is . . . Phil 2:11
does not keep a tight rein on his *t*, . . . Jas 1:26
Likewise the *t* is a small part . . . Jas 3:5
or *t* but with actions and in truth. . . . 1 Jn 3:18

TORMENT(ED)(ORS) *intense suffering or pain, often linked with divine judgment*
our *t* demanded songs of joy; . . . Ps 137:3
also come to this place of *t*. . . . Lk 16:28
a messenger of Satan, to *t* me. . . . 2 Cor 12:7
They will be *t* day and night . . . Rv 20:10

TOUCH(ED)(ES) *to perceive by feeling; to come into contact with; to influence*
you must not *t* it, or you will die. . . . Gn 3:3
Whoever *t* the mountain shall . . . Ex 19:12
Do not *t* my anointed ones; . . . Ps 105:15
With it he *t* my mouth and said, . . . Is 6:7
for whoever *t* you the apple . . . Zec 2:8
If I only *t* his cloak, I will be healed . . . Mt 9:21
"Who *t* me?" Jesus asked. . . . Lk 8:45
T no unclean thing, . . . 2 Cor 6:17
Do not taste! Do not *t*!"? . . . Col 2:21
looked at and our hands have *t* . . . 1 Jn 1:1

TRADITION(S) *the handing down of stories, customs, or values by oral or written means or by example*
Why do your disciples break the *t* . . . Mt 15:2
are holding on to the *t* of men. . . . Mk 7:8
zealous for the *t* of my fathers. . . . Gal 1:14
which depends on human *t* . . . Col 2:8

TRAIN(ED)(ING) *to teach so as to make fit or qualified*
T a child in the way he should go, . . . Prv 22:6
nor will they *t* for war anymore. . . . Is 2:4
in the games goes into strict *t*. . . . 1 Cor 9:25
up in the *t* and instruction . . . Eph 6:4
rather, *t* yourself to be godly. . . . 1 Tm 4:7
correcting and *t* in righteousness, . . . 2 Tm 3:16
they can *t* the younger women . . . Ti 2:4
by constant use have *t* themselves . . . Heb 5:14

TRANSFORM(ED) *to change in appearance or character*
be *t* by the renewing of your mind. . . . Rom 12:2
are being *t* into his likeness . . . 2 Cor 3:18
will *t* our lowly bodies . . . Phil 3:21

TRANSGRESSED, TRANSGRESSION(S) *to go beyond a boundary; to violate one's conscience or God's law*
innocent of great *t*. . . . Ps 19:13
whose *t* are forgiven, . . . Ps 32:1
blot out my *t*. . . . Ps 51:1
so far has he removed our *t* from us . . .
   Ps 103:12
But he was pierced for our *t*, . . . Is 53:5
All Israel has *t* your law . . . Dn 9:11
who pardons sin and forgives the *t* . . . Mi 7:18
whose *t* are forgiven, . . . Rom 4:7
Rather, because of their *t*, . . . Rom 11:11
you were dead in your *t* and sins, . . . Eph 2:1

TREASURE(D)(S) *valuable object (physical or spiritual)*
you will be my *t* possession. . . . Ex 19:5
I have *t* the words . . . Jb 23:12
Ill-gotten *t* are of no value, . . . Prv 10:2
up for yourselves *t* on earth, . . . Mt 6:19
of heaven is like *t* hidden in a field. . . . Mt 13:44
But Mary *t* up all these things . . . Lk 2:19
But we have this *t* in jars of clay . . . 2 Cor 4:7
in whom are hidden all the *t* . . . Col 2:3
In this way they will lay up *t* . . . 1 Tm 6:19

TREAT(ED)(ING) *to behave in a particular way toward a person or thing*
The alien living with you must be *t* . . . Lv 19:34
he does not *t* us as our sins deserve . . .
   Ps 103:10
t your slaves in the same way. . . . Eph 6:9
do not *t* prophecies with contempt. . . . 1 Thes 5:20
T younger men as brothers, . . . 1 Tm 5:1
who has *t* as an unholy thing . . . Heb 10:29
as discipline; God is *t* you as sons. . . . Heb 12:7
and *t* them with respect . . . 1 Pt 3:7

TREE(S) *large, woody plant; often figurative*
and the *t* of the knowledge of good . . . Gn 2:9
of the garden were the *t* of life . . . Gn 2:9
hung on a *t* is under God's curse. . . . Dt 21:23
One day the *t* went out . . . Jgs 9:8
He is like a *t* planted by streams . . . Ps 1:3
righteous will flourish like a palm *t*, . . .
   Ps 92:12
Then all the *t* of the forest will sing . . . Ps 96:12
She is a *t* of life to those who . . . Prv 3:18
For as the days of a *t*, . . . Is 65:22
I the LORD bring down the tall *t* . . . Ez 17:24
to sit under his vine and fig *t*, . . . Zec 3:10
every *t* that does not produce good . . . Mt 3:10
they look like *t* walking around. . . . Mk 8:24
killed by hanging him on a *t*. . . . Acts 5:30
be grafted into their own olive *t*! . . . Rom 11:24
My brothers, can a fig *t* bear olives, . . . Jas 3:12
side of the river stood the *t* of life, . . . Rv 22:2

TREMBLE(D)(S), TREMBLING *to shake uncontrollably, usually from fear*
The nations will hear and *t*; . . . Ex 15:14
in smoke, they *t* with fear. . . . Ex 20:18
The earth *t* and quaked, . . . 2 Sm 22:8
T before him, all the earth! . . . 1 Chr 16:30
he who looks at the earth, and it *t*, . . .
   Ps 104:32
and *t* at my word. . . . Is 66:2
Should you not *t* in my presence? . . . Jer 5:22
set me *t* on my hands and knees. . . . Dn 10:10
he looked, and made the nations *t*. . . . Hb 3:6
out your salvation with fear and *t*, . . . Phil 2:12

TRIAL(S) *spiritual test*
saw with your own eyes the great *t*, . . . Dt 7:19
who have stood by me in my *t*. . . . Lk 22:28

most severe *t*, their overflowing . . . 2 Cor 8:2
is the man who perseveres under *t*, . . . Jas 1:12
at the painful *t* you are suffering, . . . 1 Pt 4:12
whenever you face *t* of many kinds, . . . Jas 1:2
how to rescue godly men from *t* . . . 2 Pt 2:9
you from the hour of *t* that is going . . . Rv 3:10

TRIBE(S) *family divisions of Israel or other
people groups*
All these are the twelve *t* of Israel, . . . Gn 49:28
See, the Lion of the *t* of Judah, . . . Rv 5:5
to every nation, *t*, language . . . Rv 14:6

TRIBULATION(S) *trouble (often punishment
from God); period of great suffering in last days*
who have come out of the great *t*; . . . Rv 7:14

TRIUMPH(AL)(ED)(ING)(S) *to win; to defeat*
nor let my enemies *t* over me. . . . Ps 25:2
in the end he will look in *t* . . . Ps 112:8
When the righteous *t*, there is great . . . Prv
    28:12
their kings led in *t* procession. . . . Is 60:11
us in *t* procession in Christ . . . 2 Cor 2:14
of them, *t* over them by the cross. . . . Col 2:15
Mercy *t* over judgment! What . . . Jas 2:13
of Judah, the Root of David, has *t* . . . Rv 5:5

TROUBLE(D)(S) *to disturb mentally or physically; affliction, distress*
God has made me forget all my *t* . . . Gn 41:51
Yet man is born to *t* . . . Jb 5:7
a stronghold in times of *t*. . . . Ps 9:9
you will protect me from *t* . . . Ps 32:7
A righteous man may have many *t*, . . . Ps 34:19
he is their stronghold in time of *t*. . . . Ps 37:39
I am *t* by my sin. . . . Ps 38:18
an ever-present help in *t*. . . . Ps 46:1
and call upon me in the day of *t*; . . . Ps 50:15
spoke when I was in *t*. . . . Ps 66:14
I will be with him in *t*, . . . Ps 91:15
I was overcome by *t* and sorrow. . . . Ps 116:3
Though I walk in the midst of *t*, . . . Ps 138:7
righteous man is rescued from *t*, . . . Prv 11:8
He who brings *t* on his family will . . . Prv 11:29
but the wicked have their fill of *t*. . . . Prv 12:21
one rests content, untouched by *t*. . . . Prv
    19:23
If you falter in times of *t*, . . . Prv 24:10
It will be a time of *t* for Jacob, . . . Jer 30:7
a refuge in times of *t*. . . . Na 1:7
Each day has enough *t* of its own. . . . Mt 6:34
began to be deeply distressed and *t*. . . .
    Mk 14:33
Do not let your hearts be *t*. . . . Jn 14:1
In this world you will have *t*. . . . Jn 16:33
Shall *t* or hardship or persecution . . . Rom 8:35
those who marry will face many *t* . . . 1 Cor 7:28
who comforts us in all our *t*, . . . 2 Cor 1:4
and momentary *t* are achieving . . . 2 Cor 4:17
one of you in *t*? He should pray. . . . Jas 5:13

TRUE *consistent with fact or reality; consistent
with God's special revelation; faithful, loyal; see
TRUTH*
and everything he says comes *t*. . . . 1 Sm 9:6
of the LORD is right and *t*; . . . Ps 33:4
and your law is *t*. . . . Ps 119:142
All your words are *t*; . . . Ps 119:160
teaching you *t* and reliable words, . . . Prv 22:21
But the LORD is the *t* God; . . . Jer 10:10
only if his prediction comes *t*. . . . Jer 28:9
who will trust you with *t* riches? . . . Lk 16:11
The *t* light that gives light . . . Jn 1:9
when the *t* worshipers will worship . . . Jn 4:23
on my own, but he who sent me is *t*. . . . Jn 7:28
I am the *t* vine, and my Father is . . . Jn 15:1
testimony, and his testimony is *t*. . . . Jn 19:35
all to remain *t* to the Lord . . . Acts 11:23
Let God be *t*, and every man a liar. . . . Rom 3:4
whatever is *t*, whatever is noble, . . . Phil 4:8
and the *t* light is already shining. . . . 1 Jn 2:8
He is the *t* God and eternal life. . . . 1 Jn 5:20
These words are trustworthy and *t*. . . . Rv 22:6

TRUST(ED)(S) *to place one's confidence in; to
hope; that which has been entrusted*
and will always put their *t* in you. . . . Ex 19:9
you did not *t* in the LORD your . . . Dt 1:32
to *t* in the LORD when he says, . . . 2 Kgs 18:30
What he *t* in is fragile; . . . Jb 8:14
If I have put my *t* in gold . . . Jb 31:24
Those who know your name will *t* . . . Ps 9:10
Some *t* in chariots and some . . . Ps 20:7
In you our fathers put their *t*; . . . Ps 22:4
my heart *t* in him, and I am helped. . . . Ps 28:7
surrounds the man who *t* in him. . . . Ps 32:10
for we *t* in his holy name. . . . Ps 33:21
T in the LORD and do good; . . . Ps 37:3
who makes the LORD his *t*, . . . Ps 40:4
Even my close friend, whom I *t*, . . . Ps 41:9
I do not *t* in my bow, . . . Ps 44:6
those who *t* in their wealth . . . Ps 49:6
of those who *t* in themselves, . . . Ps 49:13
but *t* in his great wealth . . . Ps 52:7
in God I *t*; I will not be afraid. . . . Ps 56:4
T in him at all times, O people; . . . Ps 62:8
or *t* in his deliverance. . . . Ps 78:22
blessed is the man who *t* in you. . . . Ps 84:12
my God, in whom I *t*. . . . Ps 91:2
and so will all who *t* in them. . . . Ps 115:8
O house of Israel, *t* in the LORD . . . Ps 115:9
than to *t* in man. . . . Ps 118:8
and so will all who *t* in them. . . . Ps 135:18
T in the LORD with all your heart . . . Prv 3:5
Whoever *t* in his riches will fall, . . . Prv 11:28
the stronghold in which they *t*. . . . Prv 21:22
He who *t* in himself is a fool, . . . Prv 28:26
whoever *t* in the LORD is kept safe . . . Prv 29:25
I will *t* and not be afraid. . . . Is 12:2
we *t* in him, and he saved us. . . . Is 25:9
in quietness and *t* is your strength, . . . Is 30:15
But those who *t* in idols, . . . Is 42:17
the fortified cities in which you *t*. . . . Jer 5:17
do not *t* your brothers. . . . Jer 9:4
and *t* in false gods. . . . Jer 13:25
Since you *t* in your deeds . . . Jer 48:7
you *t* in your riches and say, . . . Jer 49:4
But you *t* in your beauty . . . Ez 16:15
but then he *t* in his righteousness . . . Ez 33:13
because he had *t* in his God. . . . Dn 6:23
Do not *t* a neighbor; . . . Mi 7:5
who *t* in the name of the LORD. . . . Zep 3:12
t with very little can also be *t*. . . . Lk 16:10
Put your *t* in the light . . . Jn 12:36
T in God; *t* also in me. . . . Jn 14:1
but *t* God who justifies the wicked, . . . Rom 4:5
one who *t* in him will never be put . . . Rom 9:33
discharging the *t* committed . . . 1 Cor 9:17
always protects, always *t*, . . . 1 Cor 13:7
but to show that they can be fully *t*, . . . Ti 2:10
I will put my *t* in him. . . . Heb 2:13

TRUSTWORTHY *dependable; worthy of being
trusted*
you are God! Your words are *t*, . . . 2 Sm 7:28
these men were considered *t*. . . . Neh 13:13
All your commands are *t*; . . . Ps 119:86
but a *t* man keeps a secret. . . . Prv 11:13
So if you have not been *t*. . . . Lk 16:11
one who by the Lord's mercy is *t*. . . . 1 Cor
    7:25
but temperate and *t* in everything. . . . 1 Tm
    3:11
must hold firmly to the *t* message . . . Ti 1:9
This is a *t* saying. . . . Ti 3:8
These words are *t* and true. . . . Rv 22:6

TRUTH *reality; actuality; see TRUE*
tested to see if you are telling the *t*. . . .
    Gn 42:16
guide me in your *t* and teach me, . . . Ps 25:5
and I walk continually in your *t* . . . Ps 26:3
your *t* always protect me. . . . Ps 40:11
Send forth your light and your *t*, . . . Ps 43:3
Surely you desire *t* . . . Ps 51:6
and I will walk in your *t*; . . . Ps 86:11

and the peoples in his *t*. . . . Ps 96:13
to all who call on him in *t*. . . . Ps 145:18
Buy the *t* and do not sell it; . . . Prv 23:23
I, the LORD, speak the *t*; . . . Is 45:19
t has stumbled in the streets, . . . Is 59:14
do not your eyes look for *t*? . . . Jer 5:3
T has perished; it has vanished . . . Jer 7:28
what is written in the Book of *T*. . . . Dn 10:21
will be called the City of *T*, . . . Zec 8:3
I tell you the *t*, until heaven . . . Mt 5:18
I tell you the *t*, whatever you bind . . . Mt 18:18
Jesus said to them, "I tell you the *t*, . . .
    Mt 21:31
of God in accordance with the *t*. . . . Mt 22:16
from the Father, full of grace and *t*. . . . Jn 1:14
and *t* came through Jesus Christ. . . . Jn 1:17
But whoever lives by the *t* comes . . . Jn 3:21
worship the Father in spirit and *t*, . . . Jn 4:23
and he has testified to the *t*. . . . Jn 5:33
Then you will know the *t*, . . . Jn 8:32
I am the way and the *t* and the life. . . . Jn 14:6
with you forever—the Spirit of *t*. . . . Jn 14:17
But when he, the Spirit of *t*, comes, . . . Jn 16:13
them by the *t*; your word is . . . Jn 17:17
"What is *t*?" Pilate asked. . . . Jn 18:38
of men who suppress the *t*. . . . Rom 1:18
who reject the *t* and follow evil, . . . Rom 2:8
in evil but rejoices with the *t*. . . . 1 Cor 13:6
setting forth the *t* plainly we . . . 2 Cor 4:2
so that the *t* of the gospel might . . . Gal 2:5
Instead, speaking the *t* in love, . . . Eph 4:15
with the belt of *t* buckled . . . Eph 6:14
understood God's grace in all its *t*. . . . Col 1:6
because they refused to love the *t*. . . . 2 Thes
    2:10
to come to a knowledge of the *t*. . . . 1 Tm 2:4
the pillar and foundation of the *t*. . . . 1 Tm 3:15
correctly handles the word of *t*. . . . 2 Tm 2:15
never able to acknowledge the *t*. . . . 2 Tm 3:7
will turn their ears away from the *t*. . . . 2 Tm 4:4
received the knowledge of the *t*, . . . Heb 10:26
birth through the word of *t*, . . . Jas 1:18
of you should wander from the *t*. . . . Jas 5:19
by obeying the *t* so that you have . . . 1 Pt 1:22
established in the *t* you now have. . . . 2 Pt 1:12
we lie and do not live by the *t*. . . . 1 Jn 1:6
and all of you know the *t*. . . . 1 Jn 2:20
or tongue but with actions and in *t*. . . .
    1 Jn 3:18
we know that we belong to the *t*, . . . 1 Jn 3:19
is how we recognize the Spirit of *t* . . . 1 Jn 4:6
of your children walking in the *t*, . . . 2 Jn 1:4
my children are walking in the *t*. . . . 3 Jn 1:4

TRY(ING) *to attempt; to test*
Test me, O LORD, and *t* me, . . . Ps 26:2
t hard to be reconciled to him . . . Lk 12:58
will *t* to enter and will not be able . . . Lk 13:24
t to excel in gifts that build up . . . 1 Cor 14:12
We are not *t* to commend ourselves . . . 2 Cor
    5:12
We are not *t* to please men but God . . . 1 Thes
    2:4
always *t* to be kind to each other . . . 1 Thes 5:15
to *t* to please them, not to talk back . . . Ti 2:9
t to find out the time . . . 1 Pt 1:11

TURN(ED)(S) *to change direction or state; to
change allegiance*
If you *t* away from following him, . . . Nm 32:15
do not *t* aside to the right . . . Dt 5:32
and *t* to the LORD your God . . . Dt 30:10
the LORD *t* my darkness into light . . . 2 Sm
    22:29
May he *t* our hearts to him, . . . 1 Kgs 8:58
his wives *t* his heart . . . 1 Kgs 11:4
but now the tables were *t*. . . . Est 9:1
All have *t* aside, . . . Is 14:3
You *t* my wailing into dancing; . . . Ps 30:11
T from evil and do good; . . . Ps 34:14
and sinners will *t* back to you. . . . Ps 51:13
A gentle answer *t* away wrath, . . . Prv 15:1

when he is old he will not *t* from it. . . . Prv 22:6
You *t* things upside down, . . . Is 29:16
Whether you *t* to the right . . . Is 30:21
T to me and be saved, . . . Is 45:22
each of us has *t* to his own way; . . . Is 53:6
I will *t* their mourning . . . Jer 31:13
The sun will be *t* to darkness . . . Jl 2:31
He will *t* the hearts of the fathers . . . Mal 4:6
you on the right cheek, *t* . . . Mt 5:39
And when you have *t* back, . . . Lk 22:32
nor *t* and I would heal them. . . . Jn 12:40
but your grief will *t* to joy. . . . Jn 16:20
Repent, then, and *t* to God, . . . Acts 3:19
Whoever *t* a sinner from the error . . . Jas 5:20
He must *t* from evil and do good; . . . 1 Pt 3:11

UNBELIEF, UNBELIEVER(S), UNBELIEVING *lack of faith (usually due to rebellion against God); see UNFAITHFUL*
O *u* and perverse generation, . . . Mt 17:17
help me overcome my *u!* . . . Mk 9:24
they were broken off because of *u*, . . . Rom 11:20
But if the *u* leaves, let him do so. . . . 1 Cor 7:15
however, is for believers, not for *u*. . . . 1 Cor 14:22
this age has blinded the minds of *u*, . . . 2 Cor 4:4
Do not be yoked together with *u*. . . . 2 Cor 6:14
the faith and is worse than an *u*. . . . 1 Tm 5:8
able to enter, because of their *u*. . . . Heb 3:19
But the cowardly, the *u*, the vile, . . . Rv 21:8

UNCLEAN *according to the law of Moses, unfit for human consumption, use in worship, or social contact; see CLEAN*
and two of every kind of *u* animal, . . . Gn 7:2
ruined! For I am a man of *u* lips, . . . Is 6:5
Touch no *u* thing! . . . Is 52:11
never eaten anything impure or *u*. . . . Acts 10:14
fully convinced that no food is *u* . . . Rom 14:14

UNDERSTAND(ING)(S), UNDERSTOOD *to comprehend, realize, discernment*
and *u* every motive . . . 1 Chr 28:9
Does not long life bring *u?* . . . Jb 12:12
How great is God—beyond our *u!* . . . Jb 36:26
Surely I spoke of things I did not *u*, . . . Jb 42:3
When I tried to *u* all this, . . . Ps 73:16
it gives *u* to the simple. . . . Ps 119:130
who by his *u* made the heavens, . . . Ps 136:5
his *u* has no limit. . . . Ps 147:5
Then you will *u* what is right . . . Prv 2:9
lean not on your own *u*; . . . Prv 3:5
a man of *u* holds his tongue. . . . Prv 11:12
A patient man has great *u*, . . . Prv 14:29
whoever heeds correction gains *u*. . . . Prv 15:32
to choose *u* rather than silver! . . . Prv 16:16
U is a fountain of life . . . Prv 16:22
a man of *u* is even-tempered. . . . Prv 17:27
four that I do not *u*: . . . Prv 30:18
so you cannot *u* the work of God, . . . Eccl 11:5
u with their hearts, . . . Is 6:10
the Spirit of wisdom and of *u*, . . . Is 11:2
Who has *u* the mind of the LORD, . . . Is 40:13
that he *u* and knows me, . . . Jer 9:24
stretched out the heavens by his *u*. . . . Jer 10:12
u with their hearts . . . Mt 13:15
and ever hearing but never *u*; . . . Mk 4:12
with all your *u* and with all your . . . Mk 12:33
who heard him was amazed at his *u* . . . Lk 2:47
so they could *u* the Scriptures. . . . Lk 24:45
the darkness has not *u* it. . . . Jn 1:5
Do you *u* what you are reading? . . . Acts 8:30
being *u* from what has been made, . . . Rom 1:20
there is no one who *u*, . . . Rom 3:11
I do not *u* what I do. . . . Rom 7:15
those who have not heard will *u*. . . . Rom 15:21

and he cannot *u* them, . . . 1 Cor 2:14
on us with all wisdom and *u*. . . . Eph 1:8
but *u* what the Lord's will is. . . . Eph 5:17
By faith we *u* that the universe was . . . Heb 11:3
of God, which transcends all *u*, . . . Phil 4:7
through all spiritual wisdom and *u*. . . . Col 1:9
some things that are hard to *u*, . . . 2 Pt 3:16

UNFAILING *never ceasing; unending; dependable*
he shows *u* kindness . . . 2 Sm 22:51
But I trust in your *u* love; . . . Ps 13:5
he shows *u* kindness . . . Ps 18:50
May your *u* love rest upon us, . . . Ps 33:22
according to your *u* love; . . . Ps 51:1
Has his *u* love vanished forever? . . . Ps 77:8
May your *u* love come to me, . . . Ps 119:41
What a man desires is *u* love; . . . Prv 19:22
yet my *u* love for you will not be . . . Is 54:10
so great is his *u* love. . . . Lam 3:32

UNFAITHFUL(NESS) *lacking faith; guilty of adultery; see BACKSLIDING, UNBELIEF*
the *u* are trapped by evil desires. . . . Prv 11:6
the way of the *u* is hard. . . . Prv 13:15
and multiplies the *u* among men. . . . Prv 23:28
except for marital *u*, causes her . . . Mt 5:32

UNGODLINESS, UNGODLY *moral corruption; impiety; see WICKED*
powerless, Christ died for the *u*. . . . Rom 5:6
It teaches us to say "No" to *u* . . . Ti 2:12
of what is going to happen to the *u*; . . . 2 Pt 2:6

UNITED, UNITY *to bring together, forming one body; agreement, harmony*
and mother and be *u* to his wife, . . . Gn 2:24
is when brothers live together in *u!* . . . Ps 133:1
May they be brought to complete *u* . . . Jn 17:23
If we have been *u* with him like this . . . Rom 6:5
effort to keep the *u* of the Spirit . . . Eph 4:3
from being *u* with Christ, . . . Phil 2:1
encouraged in heart and in *u* in love, . . . Col 2:2
them all together in perfect *u*. . . . Col 3:14

UNIVERSE *all of created matter*
in order to fill the whole *u*.) . . . Eph 4:10
which you shine like stars in the *u* . . . Phil 2:15
and through whom he made the *u*. . . . Heb 1:2
understand that the *u* was formed . . . Heb 11:3

UNJUST *unfair; not conforming to any standard of correctness; see JUST*
That God is *u* in bringing his wrath . . . Rom 3:5
What then shall we say? Is God *u?* . . . Rom 9:14
up under the pain of *u* suffering . . . 1 Pt 2:19

UNRIGHTEOUS *wicked; see RIGHTEOUS*
rain on the righteous and the *u*. . . . Mt 5:45
and to hold the *u* for the day . . . 2 Pt 2:9

UNSEARCHABLE *beyond our comprehension*
How *u* his judgments, . . . Rom 11:33
preach to the Gentiles the *u* riches . . . Eph 3:8

UNSTABLE *wavering in purpose or intent*
he is a double-minded man, *u* . . . Jas 1:8
they seduce the *u*; they are experts . . . 2 Pt 2:14
ignorant and *u* people distort, . . . 2 Pt 3:16

UNWORTHY *without merit, undeserving*
I am *u* of all the kindness . . . Gn 32:10
should say, 'We are *u* servants,' . . . Lk 17:10
Lord in an *u* manner will be guilty . . . 1 Cor 11:27

UPHOLD(ING)(S) *to support*
but the LORD *u* the righteous. . . . Ps 37:17
and *u* the cause of the needy. . . . Ps 140:12
The LORD *u* all those who fall . . . Ps 145:14
I will *u* you with my righteous right . . . Is 41:10
Not at all! Rather, we *u* the law. . . . Rom 3:31

UPRIGHT *moral, honorable; see RIGHTEOUS*
This man was blameless and *u*; . . . Jb 1:1

who saves the *u* in heart. . . . Ps 7:10
Good and *u* is the LORD; . . . Ps 25:8
it is fitting for the *u* to praise him. . . . Ps 33:1
and joy on the *u* in heart. . . . Ps 97:11
He holds victory in store for the *u*, . . . Prv 2:7
but takes the *u* into his confidence. . . . Prv 3:32
an *u* man gives thought to his ways. . . . Prv 21:29
who is self-controlled, *u*, holy . . . Ti 1:8

USEFUL *helpful; beneficial*
doing something *u* . . . Eph 4:28
u to the Master and prepared . . . 2 Tm 2:21
Scripture is God-breathed and is *u* . . . 2 Tm 3:16
now he has become *u* both to you . . . Phlm :11

USELESS *not helpful or beneficial*
our preaching is *u* . . . 1 Cor 15:14
Formerly he was *u* to you, . . . Phlm :11
faith without deeds is *u?* . . . Jas 2:20

VAIN *empty, worthless, futile; see MEANINGLESS*
A horse is a *v* hope for deliverance; . . . Ps 33:17
its builders labor in *v*. . . . Ps 127:1
Otherwise, you have believed in *v*. . . . 1 Cor 15:2
labor in the Lord is not in *v*. . . . 1 Cor 15:58
not to receive God's grace in *v*. . . . 2 Cor 6:1

VALUABLE, VALUE(D) *possessing worth*
and lacks nothing of *v*. . . . Prv 31:11
When he found one of great *v*, . . . Mt 13:46
And how much more *v* you are . . . Lk 12:24
What is highly *v* among men is . . . Lk 16:15
For physical training is of some *v*, . . . 1 Tm 4:8
as of greater *v* than the treasures . . . Heb 11:26
appears for a little while and then *v*. . . . Jas 4:14

VENGEANCE *punishment for wrongdoing; see AVENGE*
to carry out the LORD's *v* on them . . . Nm 31:3
For the LORD has a day of *v*, . . . Is 34:8
The LORD takes *v* on his foes . . . Na 1:2

VICTORIES, VICTORY *overcoming of an enemy; the state of having triumphed*
He gives his king great *v*; . . . 2 Sm 22:51
great is his joy in the *v* you give! . . . Ps 21:1
With God we will gain the *v*, . . . Ps 60:12
but many advisers make *v* sure. . . . Prv 11:14
Death has been swallowed up in *v* . . . 1 Cor 15:54
He gives us the *v* through our Lord . . . 1 Cor 15:57
This is the *v* that has overcome . . . 1 Jn 5:4

VINDICATED *to prove right or innocent; to avenge*
I know I will be *v*. . . . Jb 13:18
was *v* by the Spirit, . . . 1 Tm 3:16

VINE *woody trailing plant (usually grape vine); often figurative*
Your wife will be like a fruitful *v* . . . Ps 128:3
one of you will eat from his own *v* . . . Is 36:16
I am the true *v*, and my Father is . . . Jn 15:1

VIOLENCE, VIOLENT *physical force with intent to cause injury*
though he had done no *v*, . . . Is 53:9
not *v* but gentle, not quarrelsome, . . . 1 Tm 3:3

VISION(S) *supernatural revelation, including a dream or trance, consisting of symbolic images, often accompanied by interpretation*
I reveal myself to him in *v*, . . . Nm 12:6
to seal up *v* and prophecy . . . Dn 9:24
your young men will see *v*. . . . Jl 2:28
disobedient to the *v* from heaven. . . . Acts 26:19

VOICE *communication that comes through the mouth; figurative of God speaking to his people*
listen to his *v*, and hold fast to him. . . . Dt 30:20
and can your *v* thunder like his? . . . Jb 40:9
Their *v* goes out into all the earth, . . . Ps 19:4
Today, if you hear his *v*, . . . Ps 95:7
your ears will hear a *v* behind you, . . . Is 30:21
a *v* of one calling in the desert, . . . Mk 1:3
are in their graves will hear his *v* . . . Jn 5:28
and the sheep listen to his *v*. . . . Jn 10:3
Their *v* has gone out . . . Rom 10:18
Today, if you hear his *v*, . . . Heb 3:7
If anyone hears my *v* and opens . . . Rv 3:20

WAGE(S) *payment for work; recompense for actions*
who defraud laborers of their *w*, . . . Mal 3:5
for the worker deserves his *w*. . . . Lk 10:7
For the *w* of sin is death, . . . Rom 6:23
and "The worker deserves his *w*." . . . 1 Tm 5:18

WAIT(ED)(ING) *to stay, serve, or attend to; to patiently anticipate*
I *w* patiently for the LORD; . . . Ps 40:1
I *w* for the LORD, my soul waits, . . . Ps 130:5
Blessed are all who *w* for him! . . . Is 30:18
w for the gift my Father promised, . . . Acts 1:4
as we *w* eagerly for our adoption . . . Rom 8:23
and to *w* for his Son from heaven, . . . 1 Thes 1:10
while we *w* for the blessed hope . . . Ti 2:13
to those who are *w* for him. . . . Heb 9:28

WALK(ED)(ING)(S) *to advance by moving the feet; a person's usual mode of behavior; see STEP, WAY*
Enoch *w* with God; then he was no . . . Gn 5:24
I will *w* among you and be your . . . Lv 26:12
and when you *w* along the road, . . . Dt 6:7
to *w* in all his ways, to love him, . . . Dt 10:12
which your feet have *w* will be your . . . Jos 14:9
to *w* in all his ways, . . . Jos 22:5
who does not *w* in the counsel . . . Ps 1:1
He whose *w* is blameless . . . Ps 15:2
Even though I *w* . . . Ps 23:4
I will *w* about in freedom, . . . Ps 119:45
When you *w*, they will guide you; . . . Prv 6:22
He who *w* with the wise grows wise . . . Prv 13:20
so that we may *w* in his paths. . . . Is 2:3
let us *w* in the light of the LORD. . . . Is 2:5
saying, "This is the way; *w* in it." . . . Is 30:21
they will *w* and not be faint. . . . Is 40:31
I see four men *w* around in the fire, . . . Dn 3:25
Do two *w* together . . . Am 3:3
w on the water and came toward Jesus. . . . Mt 14:29
'Get up, take your mat and *w*'? . . . Mk 2:9
A man who *w* by day will not . . . Jn 11:9
with him yet *w* in the darkness, . . . 1 Jn 1:6
But if we *w* in the light, . . . 1 Jn 1:7
of your children *w* in the truth, . . . 2 Jn :4

WALL(S) *partition enclosing a building or dividing rooms; something causing separation*
let us rebuild the *w* of Jerusalem, . . . Neh 2:17
but you will call your *w* Salvation . . . Is 60:18
the dividing *w* of hostility, . . . Eph 2:14
By faith the *w* of Jericho fell, . . . Heb 11:30

WANDER(ED) *to stray; to move about without direction; to stray from accepted standards; see ASTRAY*
he made them *w* in the desert forty . . . Nm 32:13
go to look for the one that *w* off? . . . Mt 18:12
have *w* from the faith and pierced . . . 1 Tm 6:10
one of you should *w* from the truth . . . Jas 5:19

WANT(ING)(S) *to desire or wish; to lack or do without*
We *w* a king over us. . . . 1 Sm 8:19
weighed on the scales and found *w*. . . . Dn 5:27

whoever *w* to become great . . . Mt 20:26
For whoever *w* to save his life will . . . Mk 8:35
whoever *w* to become great . . . Mk 10:43
For what I *w* to do I do not do, . . . Rom 7:15
Do you *w* to be free from fear . . . Rom 13:3
who *w* to know Christ and the power . . . Phil 3:10
who *w* all men to be saved . . . 1 Tm 2:4
with you, not *w* anyone to perish, . . . 2 Pt 3:9

WAR(S) *armed conflict; symbolic of spiritual conflict*
Then the land had rest from *w*. . . . Jos 11:23
He makes *w* cease to the ends . . . Ps 46:9
the nations who delight in *w*. . . . Ps 68:30
nor will they train for *w* anymore. . . . Is 2:4
W will continue until the end, . . . Dn 9:26
You will hear of *w* and rumors of *w*, . . . Mt 24:6
which *w* against your soul. . . . 1 Pt 2:11
And there was *w* in heaven. . . . Rv 12:7

WARN(ED)(INGS) *to inform of coming danger*
but *w* them solemnly and let them . . . 1 Sm 8:9
By them is your servant *w*; . . . Ps 19:11
O my people, and I will *w* you . . . Ps 81:8
I *w* you today that you made a fatal . . . Jer 42:19
and you do not *w* him or speak out . . . Ez 3:18
Who *w* you to flee . . . Mt 3:7
but to *w* you, as my dear children. . . . 1 Cor 4:14
and were written down as *w* for us, . . . 1 Cor 10:11
brothers, *w* those who are idle, . . . 1 Thes 5:14
an enemy, but *w* him as a brother. . . . 2 Thes 3:15
W them before God . . . 2 Tm 2:14
and then *w* him a second time. . . . Ti 3:10
when *w* about things not yet seen, . . . Heb 11:7
I *w* everyone who hears the words . . . Rv 22:18

WASH(ED)(ING) *to cleanse with water; to be cleansed spiritually; see BAPTISM*
w me, and I will be whiter . . . Ps 51:7
in vain have I *w* my hands . . . Ps 73:13
and began to *w* his disciples' feet, . . . Jn 13:5
be baptized and *w* your sins away, . . . Acts 22:16
you were *w*, you were sanctified, . . . 1 Cor 6:11
cleansing her by the *w* with water . . . Eph 5:26
us through the *w* of rebirth . . . Ti 3:5
and having our bodies *w* . . . Heb 10:22
W your hands, you sinners, . . . Jas 4:8
and, "A sow that is *w* goes back . . . 2 Pt 2:22
Blessed are those who *w* their robes . . . Rv 22:14

WATCH(ER)(ES)(ING) *to observe; to be alert to physical or spiritual danger*
O *w* of men? . . . Jb 7:20
The eye of the adulterer *w* for dusk; . . . Jb 24:15
of you through the *w* of the night. . . . Ps 63:6
or like a *w* in the night. . . . Ps 90:4
he who *w* over you will not slumber . . . Ps 121:3
Unless the LORD *w* over the city, . . . Ps 127:1
keep *w* over the door of my lips. . . . Ps 141:3
The LORD *w* over the alien . . . Ps 146:9
when you sleep, they will *w* . . . Prv 6:22
Whoever *w* the wind will not plant; . . . Eccl 11:4
will *w* over his flock like a shepherd . . . Jer 31:10
Therefore keep *w*, because you do . . . Mt 24:42
W and pray so that you will not fall . . . Mt 26:41
keeping *w* over their flocks at night . . . Lk 2:8
whose master finds them *w* . . . Lk 12:37
W your life and doctrine closely. . . . 1 Tm 4:16
They keep *w* over you . . . Heb 13:17

WATER(S) *colorless liquid sustaining plant and animal life; symbolic of blessing*
all the *w* was changed into blood. . . . Ex 7:20
there was no *w* for the community, . . . Nm 20:2
like a tree planted by streams of *w*, . . . Ps 1:3

I am poured out like *w*, . . . Ps 22:14
he leads me beside quiet *w*, . . . Ps 23:2
As the deer pants for streams of *w*, . . . Ps 42:1
if he is thirsty, give him *w* to drink. . . . Prv 25:21
Cast your bread upon the *w*, . . . Eccl 11:1
Many *w* cannot quench love; . . . Song 8:7
as the *w* cover the sea. . . . Is 11:9
With joy you will draw *w* . . . Is 12:3
like streams of *w* in the desert . . . Is 32:2
When you pass through the *w*, . . . Is 43:2
come to the *w*; . . . Is 55:1
and lead them beside springs of *w*. . . . Is 49:10
I will sprinkle clean *w* on you, . . . Ez 36:25
On that day living *w* will flow out . . . Zec 14:8
walked on the *w* and came toward Jesus. . . . Mt 14:29
anyone who gives you a cup of *w* . . . Mk 9:41
unless he is born of *w* and the Spirit. . . . Jn 3:5
he would have given you living *w*. . . . Jn 4:10
washing with *w* through the word, . . . Eph 5:26
our bodies washed with pure *w*. . . . Heb 10:22
this *w* symbolizes baptism that now . . . 1 Pt 3:21
These men are springs without *w* . . . 2 Pt 2:17
come by *w* only, but by *w* . . . 1 Jn 5:6
to springs of living *w*. . . . Rv 7:17
cost from the spring of the *w* of life. . . . Rv 21:6

WAY(S) *path; method of moving from place to place; manner; condition; a person's usual mode of behavior; see STEP, WALK*
and show them the *w* to live . . . Ex 18:20
teach me your *w* so I may know . . . Ex 33:13
and all his *w* are just. . . . Dt 32:4
in all his *w*, to obey his commands, . . . Jos 22:5
I will teach you the *w* that is good . . . 1 Sm 12:23
But he knows the *w* that I take; . . . Jb 23:10
or stand in the *w* of sinners . . . Ps 1:1
All the *w* of the LORD are loving . . . Ps 25:10
Commit your *w* to the LORD; . . . Ps 37:5
I will teach transgressors your *w*, . . . Ps 51:13
Teach me your *w*, O LORD, . . . Ps 86:11
can a young man keep his *w* pure? . . . Ps 119:9
See if there is any offensive *w* in me . . . Ps 139:24
The LORD is righteous in all his *w*. . . . Ps 145:17
in all your *w* acknowledge him, . . . Prv 3:6
There is a *w* that seems right . . . Prv 14:12
All a man's *w* seem innocent . . . Prv 16:2
Train a child in the *w* he should go, . . . Prv 22:6
and the *w* of a man with a maiden. . . . Prv 30:19
He will teach us his *w*, . . . Is 2:3
saying, "This is the *w*; walk in it." . . . Is 30:21
you in the *w* you should go. . . . Is 48:17
each of us has turned to his own *w*; . . . Is 53:6
Let the wicked forsake his *w* . . . Is 55:7
The *w* of the LORD are right; . . . Hos 14:9
Prepare the *w* for the Lord, . . . Mt 3:3
I am the *w* and the truth . . . Jn 14:6
any there who belonged to the *W*, . . . Acts 9:2
they invent *w* of doing evil; . . . Rom 1:30
also provide a *w* out so that you can . . . 1 Cor 10:13
Follow the *w* of love and eagerly . . . 1 Cor 14:1
and may please him in every *w*; . . . Col 1:10
who has been tempted in every *w*, . . . Heb 4:15
We all stumble in many *w*. . . . Jas 3:2

WEAK(ER) *frail; feeble; unable to withstand persuasion or temptation; see WEAKNESS*
is he who has regard for the *w*; . . . Ps 41:1
Defend the cause of the *w* . . . Ps 82:3
spirit is willing, but the body is *w*. . . . Mt 26:41
Accept him whose faith is *w*, . . . Rom 14:1
to bear with the failings of the *w* . . . Rom 15:1
God chose the *w* things . . . 1 Cor 1:27
become a stumbling block to the *w*. . . . 1 Cor 8:9
That is why many among you are *w*. . . . 1 Cor 11:30

seem to be *w* are indispensable, . . . 1 Cor 12:22
For when I am *w*, then I am strong. . . . 2 Cor 12:10
them with respect as the *w* partner . . . 1 Pt 3:7
your feeble arms and *w* knees. . . . Heb 12:12

WEAKNESS(ES) *shortcoming; see WEAK*
the Spirit helps us in our *w*. . . . Rom 8:26
and the *w* of God is stronger . . . 1 Cor 1:25
it is sown in *w*, it is raised in power; . . . 1 Cor 15:43
for my power is made perfect in *w* . . . 2 Cor 12:9
he was crucified in *w*, yet he lives . . . 2 Cor 13:4
unable to sympathize with our *w*, . . . Heb 4:15

WEALTH *a great supply of resources or valuable material possessions; see RICH, RICHES*
gives you the ability to produce *w*, . . . Dt 8:18
he heaps up *w*, not knowing who . . . Ps 39:6
Honor the LORD with your *w*, . . . Prv 3:9
but diligent hands bring *w*. . . . Prv 10:4
W is worthless in the day of wrath, . . . Prv 11:4
to be poor, yet has great *w*. . . . Prv 13:7
whoever loves *w* is never satisfied . . . Eccl 5:10
all the *w* of his house for love, . . . Song 8:7
and the deceitfulness of *w* choke it, . . . Mt 13:22
away sad, because he had great *w*. . . . Mk 10:22
nor to put their hope in *w*, . . . 1 Tm 6:17
Your *w* has rotted, and moths have . . . Jas 5:2

WEARY *without strength, endurance, or spiritual resources*
they will run and not grow *w*, . . . Is 40:31
all you who are *w* and burdened, . . . Mt 11:28
Let us not become *w* in doing good, . . . Gal 6:9

WEEP(ING), WEPT *to cry; to express deep sorrow; see TEAR*
w may remain for a night, . . . Ps 30:5
He who goes out *w*, . . . Ps 126:6
of Babylon we sat and *w* . . . Ps 137:1
a time to *w* and a time to laugh, . . . Eccl 3:4
Rachel *w* for her children . . . Jer 31:15
where there will be *w* and gnashing . . . Mt 8:12
Blessed are you who *w* now, . . . Lk 6:21
And he went outside and *w* bitterly . . . Lk 22:62
Jesus *w*. . . . Jn 11:35

WEIGH(ED)(S) *to determine the weight of; to evaluate or consider; to be burdensome*
An anxious heart *w* a man down, . . . Prv 12:25
but the LORD *w* the heart. . . . Prv 21:2
You have been *w* on the scales . . . Dn 5:27
others should *w* carefully what is . . . 1 Cor 14:29

WHIRLWIND *a small rotating windstorm of limited extent; a violent destructive force*
to take Elijah up to heaven in a *w*, . . . 2 Kgs 2:1
and reap the *w*. . . . Hos 8:7

WHISPER(ED) *to speak softly in order to hide information or maintain privacy*
And after the fire came a gentle *w*. . . . 1 Kgs 19:12
He stilled the storm to a *w*; . . . Ps 107:29
speak in the daylight; what is *w*. . . Mt 10:27

WHOLE *complete, entire*
Now the *w* world had one language . . . Gn 11:1
Although the *w* earth is mine, . . . Ex 19:5
of the LORD fills the *w* earth, . . . Num 14:21
gives you the *w* land he promised . . . Dt 19:8
the *w* world will know that there is . . . 1 Sm 17:46
and will keep the *w* Law that my . . . 2 Kgs 21:8
may the *w* earth be filled . . . Ps 72:19
for this is the *w* duty of man. . . . Eccl 12:13
the *w* earth is full of his glory. . . . Is 6:3
the *w* world will be consumed, . . . Zep 1:18
will be king over the *w* earth. . . . Zec 14:9
the *w* tithe into the storehouse, . . . Mal 3:10
for a man if he gains the *w* world, . . . Mt 16:26
will be preached in the *w* world . . . Mt 24:14

to wash his feet; his *w* body is clean . . . Jn 13:10
the *w* world would not have room . . . Jn 21:25
proclaim to you the *w* will of God. . . . Acts 20:27
whom I serve with my *w* heart . . . Rom 1:9
and the *w* world held accountable . . . Rom 3:19
know that the *w* creation has been . . . Rom 8:22
If the *w* body were an ear, . . . 1 Cor 12:17
For whoever keeps the *w* law . . . Jas 2:10
but also for the sins of the *w* world. . . . 1 Jn 2:2

WHOLEHEARTEDLY *enthusiastically, without reservation*
for they followed the LORD *w*. . . . Nm 32:12
with your servants who continue *w* . . . 1 Kgs 8:23
for they had given freely and *w* . . . 1 Chr 29:9
and *w* in the fear of the LORD. . . . 2 Chr 19:9
he sought his God and worked *w*. . . . 2 Chr 31:21
you *w* obeyed the form of teaching . . . Rom 6:17
Serve *w*, as if you were serving . . . Eph 6:7

WICKED(NESS) *evil; morally corrupt; ungodly; see UNGODLINESS*
The LORD saw how great man's *w* . . . Gn 6:5
Now the men of Sodom were *w* . . . Gn 13:13
not to harbor this *w* thought: . . . Dt 15:9
Eli's sons were *w* men; they had no . . . 1 Sm 2:12
in Israel! Don't do this *w* thing. . . . 2 Sm 13:12
and turn from their *w* ways, . . . 2 Chr 7:14
walk in the counsel of the *w* . . . Ps 1:1
Why does the *w* man revile God? . . . Ps 10:13
The *w* freely strut about . . . Ps 12:8
Many are the woes of the *w*, . . . Ps 32:10
but the Lord laughs at the *w*, . . . Ps 37:13
You love righteousness and hate *w*; . . . Ps 45:7
Even from birth the *w* go astray; . . . Ps 58:3
when I saw the prosperity of the *w*, . . . Ps 73:3
the longings of the *w* will come . . . Ps 112:10
Salvation is far from the *w*, . . . Ps 119:155
Let the *w* fall into their own nets, . . . Ps 141:10
but he frustrates the ways of the *w*. . . . Ps 146:9
Do not set foot on the path of the *w* . . . Prv 4:14
a heart that devises *w* schemes, . . . Prv 6:18
w are brought down by their own . . . Prv 11:5
The *w* will not go unpunished, . . . Prv 11:21
the kindest acts of the *w* are cruel. . . . Prv 12:10
keeping watch on the *w* . . . Prv 15:3
A *w* man puts up a bold front, . . . Prv 21:29
w man flees though no one pursues, . . . Prv 28:1
the *w* detest the upright. . . . Prv 29:27
breath of his lips he will slay the *w*. . . . Is 11:4
He was assigned a grave with the *w* . . . Is 53:9
Let the *w* forsake his way . . . Is 55:7
But the *w* are like the tossing sea, . . . Is 57:20
O LORD, we acknowledge our *w* . . . Jer 14:20
to the *w* man, 'You will surely die,' . . . Ez 33:14
to atone for *w*, to bring . . . Dn 9:24
but the *w* will continue to be *w*. . . . Dn 12:10
w and adulterous generation asks . . . Mt 12:39
Because of the increase of *w*, . . . Mt 24:12
and you, with the help of *w* men, . . . Acts 2:23
who suppress the truth by their *w*, . . . Rom 1:18
but trusts God who justifies the *w*, . . . Rom 4:5
not know that the *w* will not inherit . . . 1 Cor 6:9
what do righteousness and *w* have . . . 2 Cor 6:14
of the Lord must turn away from *w* . . . 2 Tm 2:19
loved righteousness and hated *w*; . . . Heb 1:9
For I will forgive their *w* . . . Heb 8:12
who loved the wages of *w*. . . . 2 Pt 2:15

WIDE *covering a large area*
Open *w* your mouth and I will fill it . . . Ps 81:10
For *w* is the gate and broad is . . . Mt 7:13
my children—open *w* your hearts . . . 2 Cor 6:13
to grasp how *w* and long and high . . . Eph 3:18

WIDOW(S) *woman whose husband has died*
Do not take advantage of a *w* . . . Ex 22:22
cause of the fatherless and the *w*, . . . Dt 10:18
to the fatherless, a defender of *w*, . . . Ps 68:5
plead the case of the *w*. . . . Is 1:17
their *w* were being overlooked . . . Acts 6:1
to the unmarried and the *w* I say: . . . 1 Cor 7:8
to those *w* who are really . . . 1 Tm 5:3
look after orphans and *w* . . . Jas 1:27

WIFE, WIVES, WIVES' *married woman*
and be united to his *w*, . . . Gn 2:24
But Lot's *w* looked back, . . . Gn 19:26
shall not covet your neighbor's *w*, . . . Ex 20:17
happiness to the *w* he has married. . . . Dt 24:5
in the *w* of your youth. . . . Prv 5:18
He who finds a *w* finds what is . . . Prv 18:22
quarrelsome *w* is like a constant . . . Prv 19:13
w of noble character who can find? . . . Prv 31:10
take to yourself an adulterous *w* . . . Hos 1:2
for a man to divorce his *w* for any . . . Mt 19:3
Remember Lot's *w!* Whoever tries . . . Lk 17:32
how he can please his *w* . . . 1 Cor 7:33
W, submit to your husbands . . . Eph 5:22
must love his *w* as he loves himself, . . . Eph 5:33
with godless myths and old *w* tales . . . 1 Tm 4:7
words by the behavior of their *w*, . . . 1 Pt 3:1
I will show you the bride, the *w* . . . Rv 21:9

WILL(ING) *desire; decision-making capacity; by choice, without reluctance*
grant me a *w* spirit, to sustain me. . . . Ps 51:12
Teach me to do your *w*, . . . Ps 143:10
Yet it was the LORD's *w* . . . Is 53:10
your *w* be done . . . Mt 6:10
does the *w* of my Father . . . Mt 12:50
her wings, but you were not *w*. . . . Mt 23:37
The spirit is *w*, but the body . . . Mt 26:41
If anyone chooses to do God's *w*, . . . Jn 7:17
to you the whole *w* of God. . . . Acts 20:27
understand what the Lord's *w* is. . . . Eph 5:17
for it is God who works in you to *w* . . . Phil 2:13
God's *w* that you should be sanctified: . . . 1 Thes 4:3
for this is God's *w* for you . . . 1 Thes 5:18
and to be generous and *w* to share. . . . 1 Tm 6:18
has taken them captive to do his *w*. . . . 2 Tm 2:26
I have come to do your *w*, O God . . . Heb 10:7
everything good for doing his *w*, . . . Heb 13:21
If it is the Lord's *w*, . . . Jas 4:15
anything according to his *w*, . . . 1 Jn 5:14

WIND(S) *forceful movement of air*
that the *w* blows away. . . . Ps 1:4
He makes *w* his messengers, . . . Ps 104:4
meaningless, a chasing after the *w*; . . . Eccl 2:11
gather his elect from the four *w*, . . . Mt 24:31
Even the *w* and the waves obey . . . Mk 4:41
The *w* blows wherever it pleases. . . . Jn 3:8
and there by every *w* of teaching . . . Eph 4:14

WINE *fermented grape juice*
w that gladdens the heart of man, . . . Ps 104:15
W is a mocker and beer a brawler; . . . Prv 20:1
Do not gaze at *w* when it is red, . . . Prv 23:31
your love is more delightful than *w*. . . . Song 1:2
Come, buy *w* and milk . . . Is 55:1
Neither do men pour new *w* . . . Mt 9:17
When the *w* was gone, Jesus . . . Jn 2:3

not to eat meat or drink w . . . Rom 14:21
on w, which leads to debauchery. . . . Eph 5:18
a little w because of your stomach . . . 1 Tm
  5:23

WING(S) *feathered appendage of a bird that
enables flight; under one's protection*
and how I carried you on eagles' w . . . Ex 19:4
hide me in the shadow of your w . . . Ps 17:8
They will soar on w like eagles; . . . Is 40:31
of them had four faces and four w . . . Ez 1:6
rise with healing in its w. . . . Mal 4:2
hen gathers her chicks under her w, . . .
  Lk 13:34
the four living creatures had six w . . . Rv 4:8

WISDOM *ability to make good use of knowledge; ability to recognize right from wrong;
good judgment; see WISE*
God gave Solomon w and very . . . 1 Kgs 4:29
of the LORD is the beginning of w; . . .
  Ps 111:10
but with humility comes w. . . . Prv 11:2
w is found in those who take advice . . . Prv
  13:10
get w, discipline and understanding . . . Prv
  23:23
A man who loves w brings joy . . . Prv 29:3
The rod of correction imparts w, . . . Prv 29:15
Spirit of w and of understanding, . . . Is 11:2
he founded the world by his w . . . Jer 10:12
and to fear your name is w . . . Mi 6:9
And Jesus grew in w and stature, . . . Lk 2:52
the depth of the riches of the w . . . Rom 11:33
not with words of human w, . . . 1 Cor 1:17
who has become for us w from God . . . 1 Cor
  1:30
are hidden all the treasures of w . . . Col 2:3
indeed have an appearance of w, . . . Col 2:23
of you lacks w, he should ask God, . . . Jas 1:5
in the humility that comes from w . . . Jas 3:13

WISE(R) *shrewd; see WISDOM*
He catches the w in their craftiness . . . Jb 5:13
making w the simple. . . . Ps 19:7
Do not be w in your own eyes; . . . Prv 3:7
rebuke a w man and he will love . . . Prv 9:8
he who wins souls is w. . . . Prv 11:30
A w son heeds his father's . . . Prv 13:1
A w man's heart guides his mouth, . . . Prv
  16:23
Even a fool is thought w . . . Prv 17:28
Those who are w will shine like . . . Dn 12:3
hidden these things from the w . . . Mt 11:25
I will destroy the wisdom of the w; . . . 1 Cor
  1:19
of God is w than man's wisdom, . . . 1 Cor 1:25
able to make you w for salvation . . . 2 Tm 3:15
Who is w and understanding . . . Jas 3:13

WITHER(S) *to dry or shrivel up*
whose leaf does not w. . . . Ps 1:3
In times of disaster they will not w; . . .
  Ps 37:19
The grass w and the flowers fall, . . . Is 40:7

WITNESS(ES) *person who gives testimony;
see TESTIFIES*
by the testimony of two or three w. . . . Dt 19:15
truthful w gives honest testimony, . . . Prv 12:17
he came only as a w to the light. . . . Jn 1:8
and you will be my w in Jerusalem, . . . Acts 1:8

WOMAN, WOMEN *female human being*
God made a w from . . . Gn 2:22
between you and the w, . . . Gn 3:15
sexual relations with both a w . . . Lv 18:17
as one lies with a w, . . . Lv 20:13
the captives a beautiful w . . . Dt 21:11
w must not wear men's . . . Dt 22:5
a w of noble character . . . Ru 3:11
Man born of w is of few . . . Jb 14:1
A kindhearted w gains respect, . . . Prv 11:16
a wise w builds her house, . . . Prv 14:1

O barren w, you who never . . . Is 54:1
looks at a w lustfully . . . Mt 5:28
among those born of w, . . . Mt 11:11
a w whose little daughter . . . Mk 7:25
Blessed are you among w, . . . Lk 1:42
what kind of a w is this . . . Lk 7:39
a Samaritan w came . . . Jn 4:7
a w caught in adultery. . . . Jn 8:3
not a few prominent w. . . . Acts 17:4
w exchanged natural relations . . . Rom 1:26
a married w is bound to . . . Rom 7:2
each w her own husband . . . 1 Cor 7:2
an unmarried w or virgin . . . 1 Cor 7:34
the head of the w is man, . . . 1 Cor 11:3
his Son, born of a w, . . . Gal 4:4
older w as mothers, . . . 1 Tm 5:2
any w who is a believer . . . 1 Tm 5:16
teach the older w to be . . . Ti 2:3
the holy w of the past . . . 1 Pt 3:5
he pursued the w who had . . . Rv 12:13

WOMB *uterus*
Naked I came from my mother's w, . . . Jb 1:21
in my mother's w. . . . Ps 139:13
the baby in my w leaped for joy. . . . Lk 1:44
into his mother's w to be born! . . . Jn 3:4

WONDERFUL *marvelous, amazing, extraordinary*
tell of all his w acts. . . . 1 Chr 16:9
things too w for me to know. . . . Jb 42:3
for he showed his w love to me . . . Ps 31:21
tell of all his w acts. . . . Ps 105:2
w things in your law. . . . Ps 119:18
Such knowledge is too w for me, . . . Ps 139:6
your works are w, . . . Ps 139:14
W Counselor, Mighty God, . . . Is 9:6
with all the w things he was doing. . . . Lk 13:17
out of darkness into his w light. . . . 1 Pt 2:9

WONDERS *divine act that transcends the
known laws of nature; see MIRACLE, SIGN*
with all the w that I will perform . . . Ex 3:20
awesome w by driving out nations . . . 2 Sm
  7:23
I will tell of all your w. . . . Ps 9:1
I will show w in the heavens . . . Jl 2:30
many miraculous signs and w . . . Acts 5:12
also testified to it by signs, . . . Heb 2:4

WORD(S) *combination of letters communicat-
ing an understood meaning; special revelation
from God*
but on every w that comes . . . Dt 8:3
Fix these w of mine in your hearts . . . Dt 11:18
I have hidden your w in my heart . . . Ps 119:11
Your w is a lamp to my feet . . . Ps 119:105
but a kind w cheers him up. . . . Prv 12:25
Pleasant w are a honeycomb, . . . Prv 16:24
A w aptly spoken . . . Prv 25:11
The w of the wise are like goads, . . . Eccl 12:11
so is my w that goes out . . . Is 55:11
"Is not my w like fire," declares . . . Jer 23:29
but on every w that comes . . . Mt 4:4
for every careless w they have . . . Mt 12:36
but my w will never pass away. . . . Mt 24:35
was the W, and the W was . . . Jn 1:1
You have the w of eternal life. . . . Jn 6:68
them by the truth; your w is truth. . . . Jn 17:17
and the ministry of the w. . . . Acts 6:4
of the Spirit, which is the w of God. . . . Eph
  6:17
as you hold out the w of life . . . Phil 2:16
Let the w of Christ dwell . . . Col 3:16
and who correctly handles the w . . . 2 Tm 2:15
For the w of God is living . . . Heb 4:12
Do not merely listen to the w, . . . Jas 1:22
And we have the w of the prophets . . . 2 Pt 1:19
And if anyone takes w away . . . Rv 22:19

WORK(S) *to exert effort for any given purpose;
useless human efforts to gain acceptance from
God*
day he rested from all his w. . . . Gn 2:2

Six days do your w, . . . Ex 23:12
the skies proclaim the w . . . Ps 19:1
how awesome his w in man's behalf . . . Ps 66:5
Do not w for food that spoils, . . . Jn 6:27
we must do the w of him who sent . . . Jn 9:4
in fact, Abraham was justified by w . . . Rom 4:2
in all things God w for the good . . . Rom 8:28
test the quality of each man's w. . . . 1 Cor 3:13
not by w, so that no one can boast. . . . Eph 2:9
to prepare God's people for w . . . Eph 4:12
that he who began a good w . . . Phil 1:6
continue to w out your salvation . . . Phil 2:12
and to w with your hands, . . . 1 Thes 4:11
If a man will not w, he shall not eat . . . 2 Thes
  3:10
equipped for every good w. . . . 2 Tm 3:17
he will not forget your w . . . Heb 6:10

WORLD *the earth and its inhabitants; unbelievers and their value systems*
for the w is mine, and all that is in it . . .
  Ps 50:12
the whole w will be consumed, . . . Zep 1:18
You are the light of the w. . . . Mt 5:14
for a man if he gains the whole w . . . Mt
  16:26
into all the w and preach the good . . . Mk 16:15
who takes away the sin of the w! . . . Jn 1:29
so loved the w that he gave his one . . . Jn 3:16
he said, "I am the light of the w. . . . Jn 8:12
In this w you will have trouble. . . . Jn 16:33
not of the w any more than I am . . . Jn 17:14
My kingdom is not of this w. . . . Jn 18:36
the whole w held accountable . . . their words to
  the ends of the w. . . . Rom 10:18
the wisdom of this w is foolishness . . . 1 Cor
  3:19
that the saints will judge the w? . . . 1 Cor 6:2
that God was reconciling the w . . . 2 Cor 5:19
For we brought nothing into the w, . . . 1 Tm 6:7
the w was not worthy of them. . . . Heb 11:38
but also for the sins of the whole w. . . . 1 Jn 2:2
born of God overcomes the w. . . . 1 Jn 5:4

WORSHIP *to express praise and devotion*
w the LORD in the splendor . . . 1 Chr 16:29
Come, let us bow down in w, . . . Ps 95:6
w the LORD with gladness; . . . Ps 100:2
and have come to w him. . . . Mt 2:2
and his worshipers must w in spirit . . . Jn 4:24
perfect those who draw near to w. . . . Heb 10:1

WORTH(LESS)(Y) *value*
For great is the LORD and most w . . . 1 Chr
  16:25
Wealth is w in the day of wrath, . . . Prv 11:4
She is w far more than rubies. . . . Prv 31:10
are w more than many sparrows. . . . Mt 10:31
I am no longer w to be called your . . . Lk 15:19
sufferings are not w comparing . . . Rom 8:18
to live a life w of the calling you . . . Eph 4:1
Jesus has been found w . . . Heb 3:3
himself and his religion is w. . . . Jas 1:26
of greater w than gold, . . . 1 Pt 1:7
Who is w to break the seals . . . Rv 5:2

WOUNDS *physical, mental, or emotional injury*
w from a friend can be trusted . . . Prv 27:6
and by his w we are healed. . . . Is 53:5

WRATH *extreme displeasure, anger*
Surely your w against men brings . . . Ps 76:10
A gentle answer turns away w, . . . Prv 15:1
at the w of the LORD Almighty, . . . Is 13:13
the cup of his w, . . . Is 51:17
filled with the wine of my w. . . . Jer 25:15
maintains his w against his enemies . . . Na 1:2
The w of God is being revealed . . . Rom 1:18
you are storing up w . . . Rom 2:5
saved from God's w through him! . . . Rom 5:9
God did not appoint us to suffer w . . . 1 Thes
  5:9
the fury of the w of God Almighty. . . . Rv 19:15

WRITE, WRITTEN, WROTE *to form characters or symbols (such as words) on a surface with an instrument (as a pen)*
And he *w* on the tablets the words . . . Ex 34:28
W them on the doorframes . . . Dt 6:9
careful to do everything *w* in it. . . . Jos 1:8
it is *w* about me in the scroll. . . . Ps 40:7
w them on the tablet of your heart. . . . Prv 7:3
everyone whose name is found *w* . . . Dn 12:1
but rejoice that your names are *w* . . . Lk 10:20
must be fulfilled that is *w* about me . . . Lk 24:44
these are *w* that you may believe . . . Jn 20:31
Do not go beyond what is *w*. . . . 1 Cor 4:6
w not with ink but with the Spirit . . . 2 Cor 3:3
and *w* them on their hearts. . . . Heb 8:10
whose names are *w* in heaven. . . . Heb 12:23
I will also *w* on him my new name. . . . Rv 3:12
but only those whose names are *w* . . . Rv 21:27

WRONG(ED)(S) *immoral; unjust; unfair*
Do not follow the crowd in doing *w* . . . Ex 23:2
unthinkable that God would do *w*, . . . Jb 34:12

but love covers over all *w*. . . . Prv 10:12
not rather be *w?* Why not rather . . . 1 Cor 6:7
angered, it keeps no record of *w*. . . .
  1 Cor 13:5
to his face, because he was clearly in the *w*. . . .
  Gal 2:11
that nobody pays back *w* for *w*, . . . 1 Thes
  5:15

YOKE(D) *wooden crossbar linking two load-pulling animals*
and the heavy *y* he put on us, . . . 1 Kgs 12:4
Take my *y* upon you and learn . . . Mt 11:29
Do not be *y* together . . . 2 Cor 6:14
be burdened again by a *y* . . . Gal 5:1

YOUNG(ER) *being in the early part of life or growth*
I was *y* and now I am old, . . . Ps 37:25
How can a *y* man keep his way . . . Ps 119:9
The glory of *y* men is their strength . . . Prv
  20:29

he gently leads those that have *y*. . . . Is 40:11
your *y* men will see visions. . . . Jl 2:28
down on you because you are *y*, . . . 1 Tm 4:12
Treat *y* men as brothers, older . . . 1 Tm 5:1
Then they can train the *y* women . . . Ti 2:4
I write to you, *y* men, . . . 1 Jn 2:13

YOUTH *young person*
so that your *y* is renewed like . . . Ps 103:5
Creator in the days of your *y*, . . . Eccl 12:1
Flee the evil desires of *y*, . . . 2 Tm 2:22

ZEAL(OUS) *enthusiastic and diligent devotion: fervor*
for *z* for your house consumes me, . . . Ps 69:9
to have *z* without knowledge, . . . Prv 19:2
I will be *z* for my holy name. . . . Ez 39:25
their *z* is not based on knowledge. . . . Rom 10:2
Never be lacking in *z*, . . . Rom 12:11
fine to be *z*, provided the purpose is . . . Gal
  4:18

Map 1: WORLD OF THE PATRIARCHS

Caspian Sea

Mt Ararat
Araxes R.
Lake Urmia

BABYLONIANS

Nippur
Erech (Uruk)
Ur

Possible location of Biblical "Ur of the Chaldeans," where Abraham's migration began

Nineveh
Nuzi
Asshur
Tigris R.
Babylon
Euphrates
Mari
Tadmor
Haran
PADDAN ARAM

ARABIA

Persian Gulf

Abraham's journeys

HITTITES

Hattusha

TAURUS MTS
Carchemish
Aleppo
Ebla
Ugarit
Byblos

Damascus
Hazor
Shechem
Ai
Hebron
Zoar?
Kadesh Barnea

Possible location of Sodom and Gomorrah

Megiddo
Dothan
Bethel
Beersheba
Gerar
Succoth
On (Heliopolis)

Red Sea

SINAI

EGYPTIANS

Nile R.

Zoan (Tanis)
Noph (Memphis)

Kittim (Cyprus)

The Great Sea

Black Sea

Troy

Aegean Sea

Knossus
Caphtor (Crete)

Mycenae

0   100   200   300 mi.
0   100 200 300 400 km

© 2000 Zondervan

© 2000 Zondervan

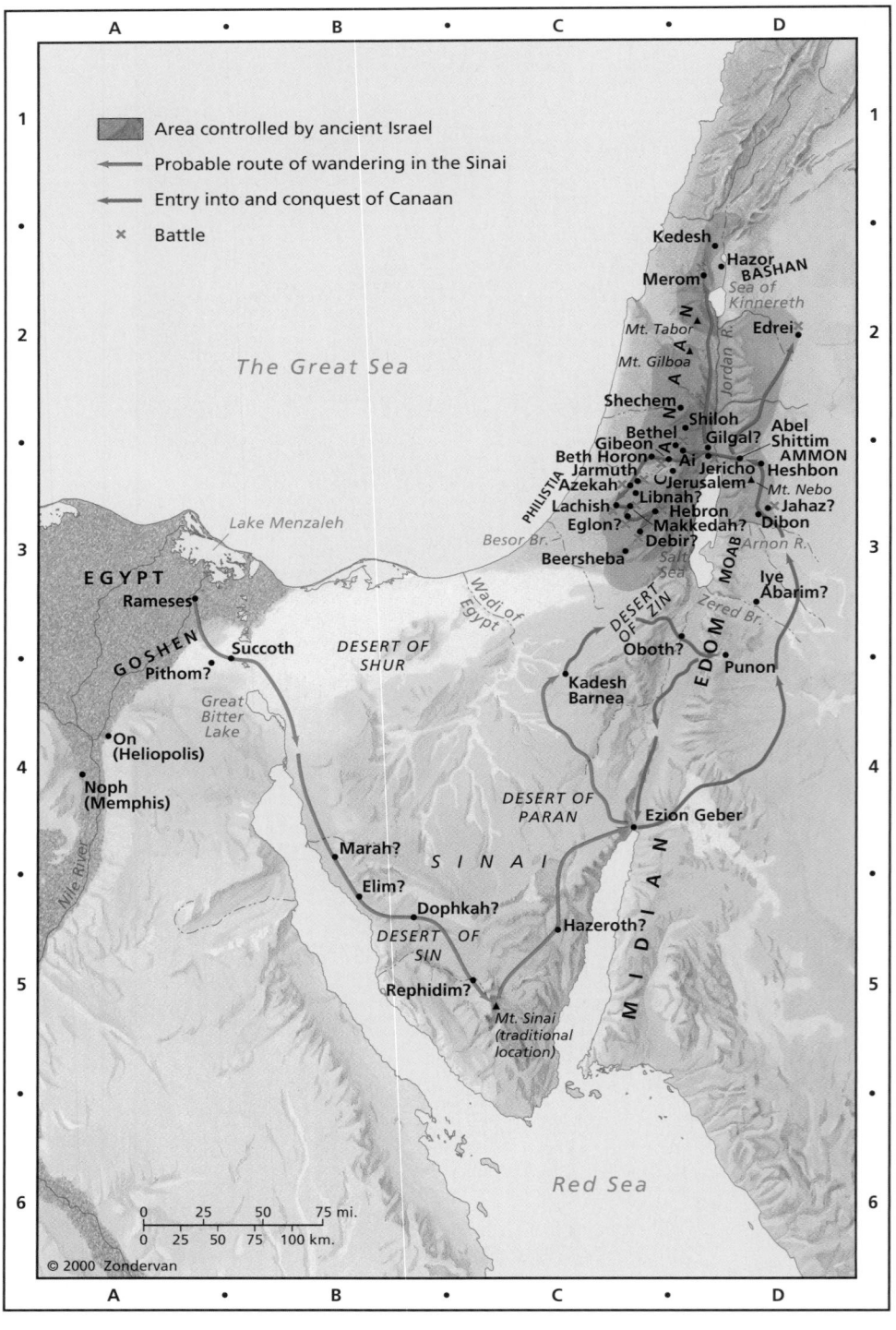

Map 3: EXODUS AND CONQUEST OF CANAAN

Area controlled by ancient Israel
Probable route of wandering in the Sinai
Entry into and conquest of Canaan
× Battle

A • **B** • **C** • **D**

The Great Sea

Kedesh
Hazor BASHAN
Merom
Sea of Kinnereth
Mt. Tabor
Edrei
Mt. Gilboa
Jordan R.
Shechem
CANAAN
Shiloh
Bethel
Gilgal?
Abel Shittim
Gibeon
AMMON
Beth Horon
Ai
Jericho
Heshbon
Jarmuth
Jerusalem
Mt. Nebo
Azekah
Libnah?
Jahaz?
Lachish
Hebron
Dibon
Eglon?
Makkedah?
Debir?
Arnon R.
Beersheba
Salt Sea
MOAB
Iye Abarim?
Besor Br.
Zered Br.
DESERT OF ZIN
Lake Menzaleh
Wadi of Egypt
Oboth?
Punon
EGYPT
EDOM
Rameses
Succoth
DESERT OF SHUR
Kadesh Barnea
GOSHEN
Pithom?
Great Bitter Lake
On (Heliopolis)
Noph (Memphis)
DESERT OF PARAN
Ezion Geber
Nile River
Marah?
SINAI
Elim?
MIDIAN
Dophkah?
Hazeroth?
DESERT OF SIN
Rephidim?
Mt. Sinai (traditional location)
PHILISTIA

Red Sea

0   25   50   75 mi.
0 25 50 75 100 km.

© 2000 Zondervan

A • **B** • **C** • **D**

⊙ Cities of refuge
• Other cities

Damascus

ARAM

Mt. Hermon

Litani R.

Pharpar R.

Ijon

Tyre

Dan

ASHER

NAPHTALI

Kedesh

Hazor

Acco

Cabul

Merom

EAST

Rimmon

Sea of Kinnereth

Golan

Ashtaroth

The Great Sea

ZEBULUN

Mt. Tabor

Yarmuk R.

Dor

Mt. Moreh

MANASSEH

Edrei

Megiddo

ISSACHAR

Kishon R.

Jezreel

Taanach

Beth Shan

Ramoth Gilead

MANASSEH

Jabesh Gilead

Tirzah

Jordan R.

Samaria

Mt. Ebal

Jabbok R.

Mahanaim?

Mt. Gerizim

Shechem

Succoth

Joppa

Aphek

Shiloh

DAN

EPHRAIM

Jazer?

GAD

Mizpah

Bethel

Rabbah

Gezer

Gibeon

BENJAMIN

Gilgal

AMMON

Ashdod

Kiriath Jearim

Jericho

Heshbon

Bezer

Ekron

Jerusalem

Mt. Nebo

Gath

Beth Shemesh

Bethlehem

Ashkelon

REUBEN

Hebron

Gaza

Lachish

En Gedi

Dibon

Eglon?

JUDAH

Salt Sea

Arnon R.

Aroer

Gerar

Ziklag

Beersheba

MOAB

Hormah

SIMEON

Zered Br.

EDOM

0	10	20	30 mi.
0	10	20	30 40 km.

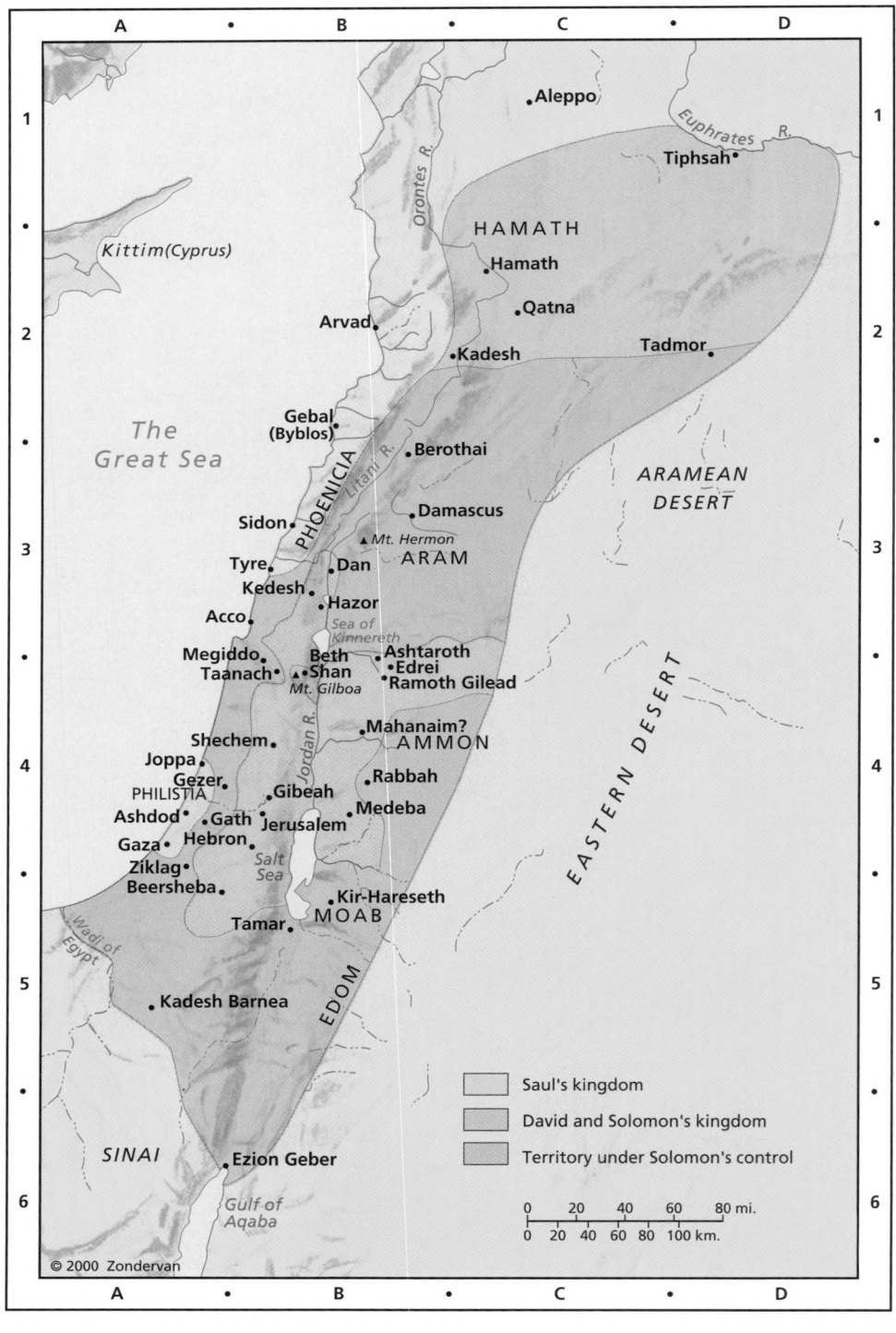

Map 5: KINGDOM OF DAVID AND SOLOMON

Aleppo
Euphrates R.
Tiphsah

Orontes R.

HAMATH
Hamath

Kittim (Cyprus)

Qatna

Arvad

Kadesh
Tadmor

The
Great Sea

Gebal
(Byblos)

Litani R.
Berothai

ARAMEAN
DESERT

PHOENICIA
Damascus

Sidon

▲ Mt. Hermon

Tyre
Dan
ARAM

Kedesh

Acco
Hazor

Sea of
Kinnereth

Megiddo
Beth
Ashtaroth
Taanach
▲ Shan
Edrei
Mt. Gilboa
Ramoth Gilead

Mahanaim?
Shechem
AMMON

Joppa
Jordan R.
Gezer
Rabbah
PHILISTIA
Gibeah
Ashdod
Gath
Medeba
Jerusalem
Gaza
Hebron
Ziklag
Salt
Sea
Beersheba
Kir-Hareseth
Tamar
MOAB

EASTERN DESERT

Wadi of Egypt

EDOM

Kadesh Barnea

SINAI

Ezion Geber

Gulf of
Aqaba

Saul's kingdom

David and Solomon's kingdom

Territory under Solomon's control

0   20   40   60   80 mi.
0 20 40 60 80 100 km.

© 2000 Zondervan

Map 6: KINGDOMS OF ISRAEL AND JUDAH

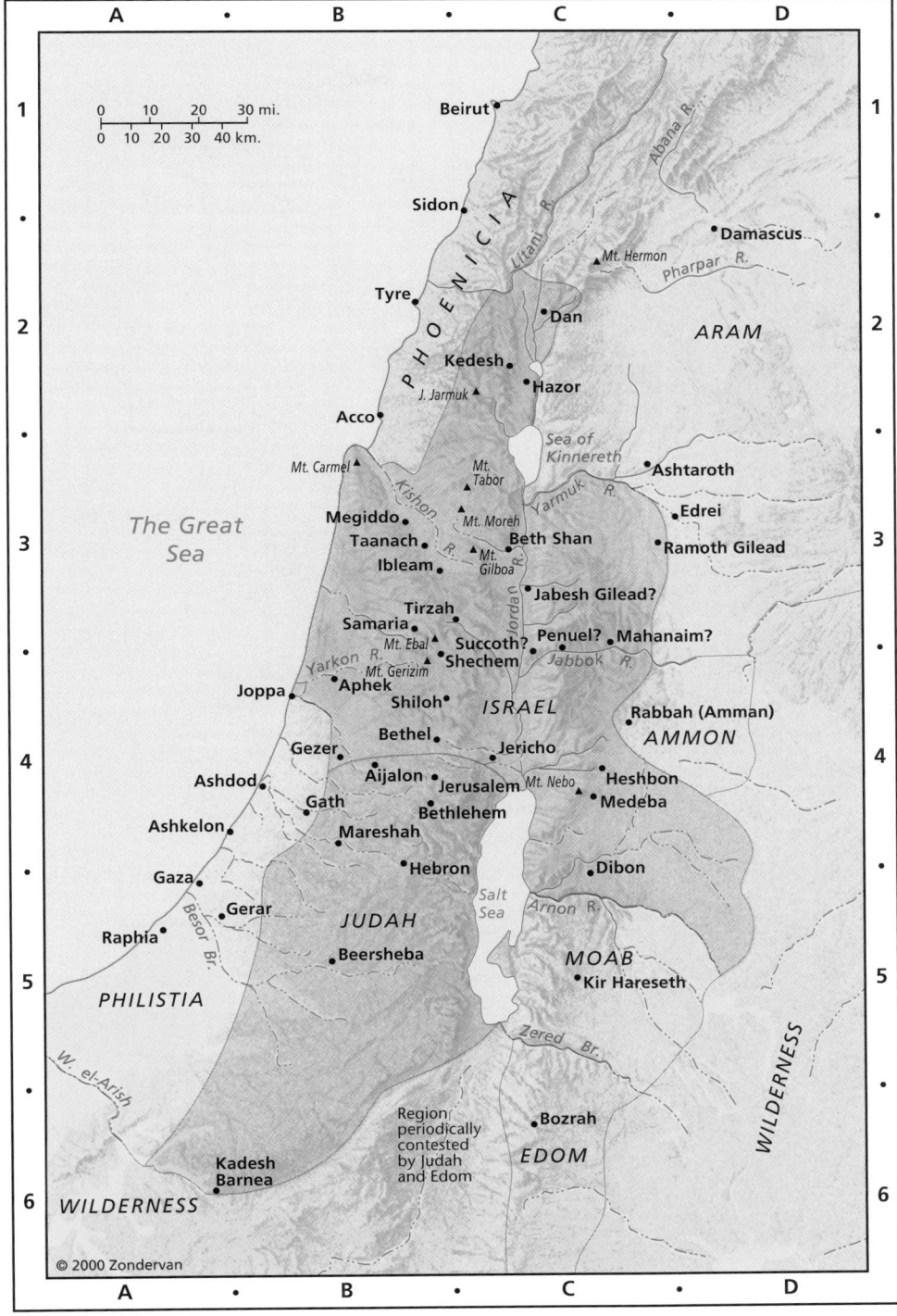

0 10 20 30 mi.
0 10 20 30 40 km.

Beirut

Sidon

Damascus

Mt. Hermon

Tyre

Dan

ARAM

Kedesh

Hazor

J. Jarmuk

Acco

Sea of
Kinnereth

Ashtaroth

Mt. Carmel

Mt.
Tabor

Edrei

Kishon

Mt. Moreh

Megiddo

Ramoth Gilead

Taanach

Beth Shan

Ibleam

Mt.
Gilboa

Jabesh Gilead?

Tirzah

Samaria

Penuel?

Mahanaim?

Mt. Ebal

Succoth?

Shechem

Mt. Gerizim

Jabbok R.

Yarkon R.

Joppa

Aphek

Shiloh

ISRAEL

Rabbah (Amman)

Bethel

AMMON

Gezer

Jericho

Ashdod

Aijalon

Jerusalem

Mt. Nebo

Heshbon

Gath

Medeba

Bethlehem

Ashkelon

Mareshah

Gaza

Hebron

Dibon

Gerar

JUDAH

Salt
Sea

Arnon R.

Raphia

Beersheba

MOAB

Kir Hareseth

PHILISTIA

Zered Br.

W. el-Arish

Region
periodically
contested
by Judah
and Edom

Bozrah

EDOM

WILDERNESS

Kadesh
Barnea

WILDERNESS

The Great
Sea

PHOENICIA

Abana R.

Pharpar R.

Litani R.

Yarmuk R.

Jordan R.

Besor Br.

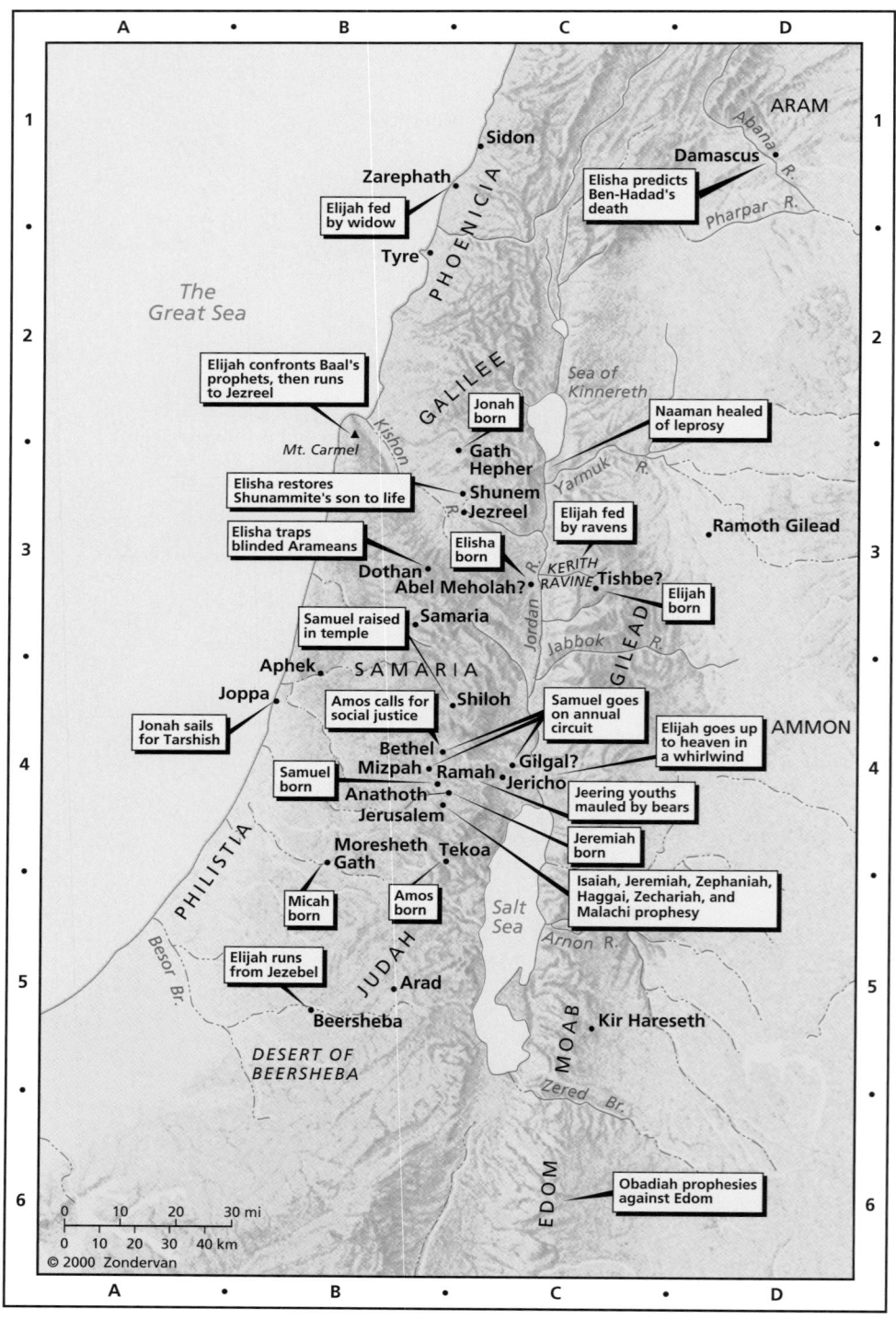

ARAM

Sidon

Zarephath

Elijah fed by widow

Damascus

Elisha predicts Ben-Hadad's death

Pharpar R.

Tyre

PHOENICIA

The Great Sea

GALILEE

Sea of Kinnereth

Elijah confronts Baal's prophets, then runs to Jezreel

Mt. Carmel

Kishon

Jonah born

Gath Hepher

Naaman healed of leprosy

Yarmuk R.

Elisha restores Shunammite's son to life

Shunem

Jezreel

Elijah fed by ravens

Ramoth Gilead

Elisha traps blinded Arameans

Dothan

Elisha born

KERITH RAVINE

Tishbe?

Elijah born

Abel Meholah?

Jordan R.

Jabbok R.

GILEAD

Samuel raised in temple

Samaria

SAMARIA

Aphek

Amos calls for social justice

Shiloh

Samuel goes on annual circuit

AMMON

Joppa

Jonah sails for Tarshish

Bethel

Mizpah

Ramah

Gilgal?

Jericho

Elijah goes up to heaven in a whirlwind

Samuel born

Anathoth

Jerusalem

Jeering youths mauled by bears

Jeremiah born

Moresheth Gath

Tekoa

Isaiah, Jeremiah, Zephaniah, Haggai, Zechariah, and Malachi prophesy

Micah born

Amos born

Salt Sea

PHILISTIA

Besor Br.

Elijah runs from Jezebel

JUDAH

Arad

MOAB

Kir Hareseth

Arnon R.

Beersheba

DESERT OF BEERSHEBA

Zered Br.

EDOM

Obadiah prophesies against Edom

0   10   20   30 mi
0   10   20   30   40 km
© 2000 Zondervan

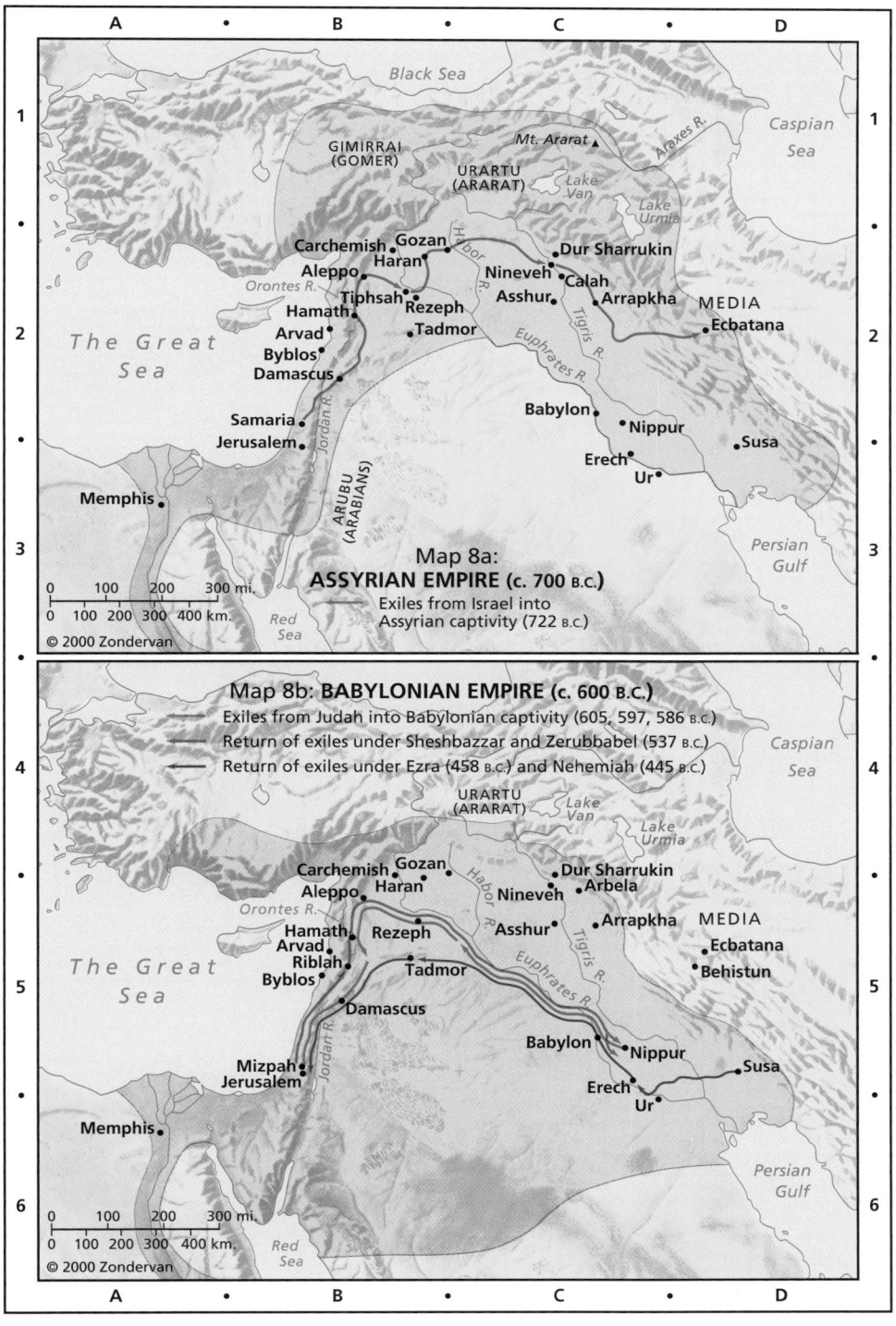

Map 8: ASSYRIAN AND BABYLONIAN EMPIRES

Map 8a: ASSYRIAN EMPIRE (c. 700 B.C.)

Black Sea

GIMIRRAI (GOMER)

Mt. Ararat

URARTU (ARARAT)

Araxes R.

Caspian Sea

Lake Van

Lake Urmia

Carchemish
Gozan
Haran
Aleppo
Dur Sharrukin
Nineveh
Calah
Asshur
Arrapkha
Tiphsah
Rezeph
Hamath
Tadmor
Arvad
Byblos
Damascus

MEDIA
Ecbatana

Orontes R.
Hbor
Tigris R.
Euphrates R.

The Great Sea

Samaria
Jerusalem

Jordan R.

ARUBU (ARABIANS)

Babylon
Nippur
Erech
Ur
Susa

Memphis

Persian Gulf

0   100   200   300 mi.
0 100 200 300 400 km.

Exiles from Israel into
Assyrian captivity (722 B.C.)

© 2000 Zondervan

Red Sea

Map 8b: BABYLONIAN EMPIRE (c. 600 B.C.)

— Exiles from Judah into Babylonian captivity (605, 597, 586 B.C.)
— Return of exiles under Sheshbazzar and Zerubbabel (537 B.C.)
— Return of exiles under Ezra (458 B.C.) and Nehemiah (445 B.C.)

Caspian Sea

URARTU (ARARAT)

Lake Van

Lake Urmia

Carchemish
Gozan
Aleppo
Haran
Dur Sharrukin
Nineveh
Arbela
Asshur
Arrapkha
Hamath
Rezeph
Arvad
Riblah
Tadmor
Byblos
Damascus

MEDIA
Ecbatana
Behistun

Orontes R.
Habor R.
Tigris R.
Euphrates R.

The Great Sea

Mizpah
Jerusalem

Jordan R.

Babylon
Nippur
Erech
Ur
Susa

Memphis

Persian Gulf

0   100   200   300 mi.
0 100 200 300 400 km.

© 2000 Zondervan

Red Sea

Map 9: HOLY LAND IN THE TIME OF JESUS

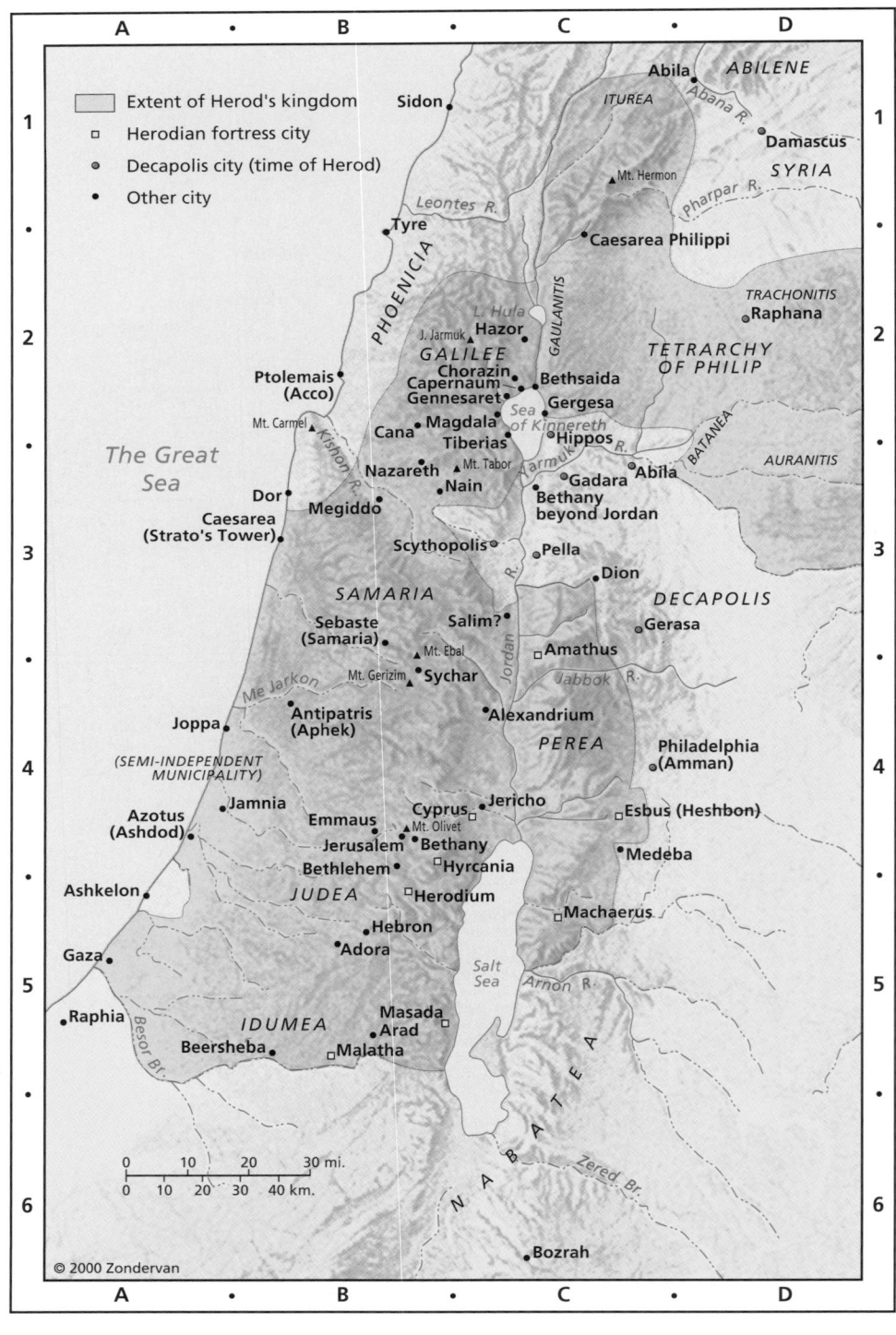

Extent of Herod's kingdom
□ Herodian fortress city
● Decapolis city (time of Herod)
● Other city

Abila
ABILENE
Sidon
ITUREA
Abana R.
Damascus
Mt. Hermon
SYRIA
Leontes R.
Pharpar R.
Tyre
Caesarea Philippi
PHOENICIA
TRACHONITIS
Raphana
L. Hula
Hazor
J. Jarmuk
GALILEE
GAULANITIS
TETRARCHY
OF PHILIP
Ptolemais
(Acco)
Chorazin
Capernaum
Bethsaida
Gennesaret
Gergesa
Mt. Carmel
Sea
of
Kinnereth
Cana
Magdala
Hippos
BATANEA
Tiberias
AURANITIS
Kishon R.
The Great
Sea
Nazareth
Mt. Tabor
Nain
Jarmuk R.
Gadara
Abila
Dor
Bethany
beyond Jordan
Caesarea
(Strato's Tower)
Megiddo
Scythopolis
Pella
Dion
SAMARIA
DECAPOLIS
Sebaste
(Samaria)
Salim?
Gerasa
Mt. Ebal
Amathus
Me Jarkon
Mt. Gerizim
Sychar
Jabbok R.
Joppa
Antipatris
(Aphek)
Alexandrium
PEREA
Philadelphia
(Amman)
(SEMI-INDEPENDENT
MUNICIPALITY)
Jamnia
Cyprus
Jericho
Esbus (Heshbon)
Azotus
(Ashdod)
Emmaus
Mt. Olivet
Jerusalem
Bethany
Medeba
Bethlehem
Hyrcania
Ashkelon
JUDEA
Herodium
Machaerus
Hebron
Adora
Gaza
Salt
Sea
Arnon R.
Raphia
IDUMEA
Masada
Arad
Besor Br.
Beersheba
Malatha
N
A
B
A
T
E
A
Zered Br.
0   10   20   30 mi.
0 10 20 30 40 km.

© 2000 Zondervan

Bozrah

Map 10: JERUSALEM IN THE TIME OF JESUS

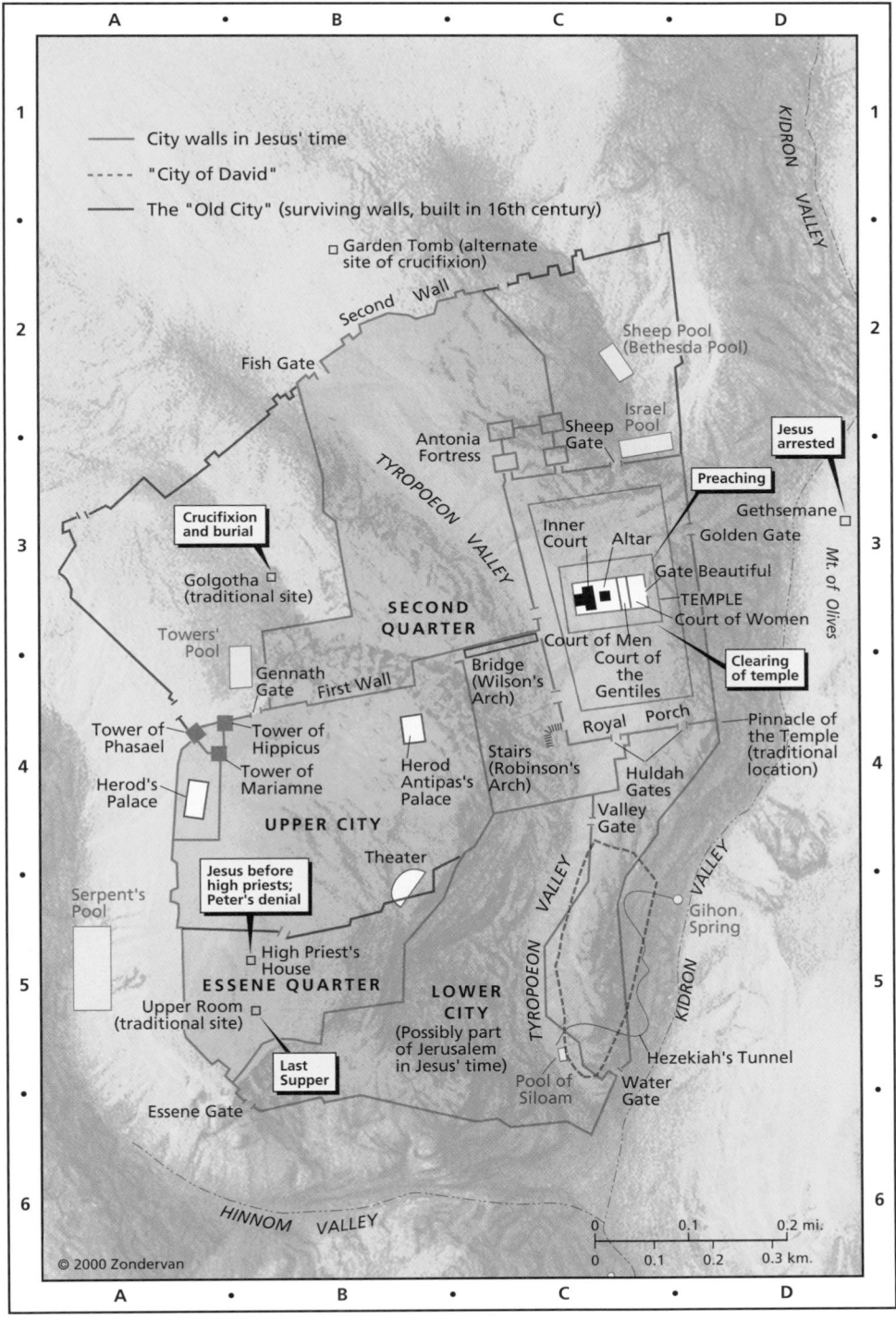

A • **B** • **C** • **D**

—— City walls in Jesus' time

----- "City of David"

—— The "Old City" (surviving walls, built in 16th century)

KIDRON VALLEY

□ Garden Tomb (alternate site of crucifixion)

Second Wall

Sheep Pool (Bethesda Pool)

Fish Gate

Israel Pool

Antonia Fortress

Sheep Gate

Jesus arrested

Preaching

TYROPOEON VALLEY

Gethsemane □

Crucifixion and burial

Inner Court

Altar

Golden Gate

Gate Beautiful

Golgotha (traditional site) □

SECOND QUARTER

TEMPLE
Court of Women

Mt. of Olives

Towers' Pool

Gennath Gate

First Wall

Bridge (Wilson's Arch)

Court of Men
Court of the Gentiles

Clearing of temple

Royal Porch

Pinnacle of the Temple (traditional location)

Tower of Phasael

Tower of Hippicus

Tower of Mariamne

Herod Antipas's Palace

Stairs (Robinson's Arch)

Huldah Gates

Herod's Palace

UPPER CITY

Valley Gate

Theater

Jesus before high priests; Peter's denial

Serpent's Pool

TYROPOEON VALLEY

KIDRON VALLEY

Gihon Spring

High Priest's House □

ESSENE QUARTER

LOWER CITY (Possibly part of Jerusalem in Jesus' time)

Upper Room (traditional site) □

Hezekiah's Tunnel

Last Supper

Pool of Siloam

Water Gate

Essene Gate

HINNOM VALLEY

© 2000 Zondervan

| 0 | | 0.1 | | 0.2 mi. |
| 0 | 0.1 | 0.2 | | 0.3 km. |

A • **B** • **C** • **D**

A · B · C · D

— International transportation artery
— Regional roadway

0   10   20   30 mi.
0   10   20 30 40 km.

PHOENICIA

▲ Mt. Hermon

Transfiguration?
(possible site)

Tyre •
Heals Canaanite
woman's daughter

• Caesarea Philippi

Predicts his
death

Sermon on
the Mount?

The
Great Sea

Heals the centurion's servant,
a paralytic, and Peter's
mother-in-law; restores
Jairus's daughter to life

Heals blind Man;
feeds 5,000?

Korazin •

Ptolemais •
(Acco)

Turns water
into wine

GALILEE

• Bethsaida
Capernaum

Heals man
with demons
(Mk 5:1; Lk 8:26)

Cana •

Magdala •

Sea
of
Galilee

• Khersa
(Gergesa?)

Transfiguration?
(traditional site)

Tiberias •

Walks on water;
quiets storm

Nazareth •

Mt.
▲ Tabor

Yarmuk

Gadara •

Heals men
with demons
(Mt 8:28)

Spends boyhood

• Nain

Restores widow's
son to life

Bethany beyond
Jordan?

DECAPOLIS

Caesarea •
(Strato's Tower)

Baptism
(possible site)

Salim? •

• Gerasa

SAMARIA

Jordan R.

Jabbok R.

Talks with
woman
at well

• Sychar
▲ Mt. Gerizim

PEREA

Raises Lazarus from dead;
anointed in Simon the
Leper's house

Tempted?

Ascends
into heaven

Baptism
(traditional site)

Clears
temple

Jericho •

• Bethany beyond Jordan?

Emmaus? •

▲ Mt. of Olives

• Bethany
Jerusalem

Heals blind Bartimaeus;
calls Zacchaeus down
from tree

Appears to two
after resurrection

• Bethlehem

JUDEA

Birth

Salt
Sea

• Machaerus

Crucifixion and
resurrection

© 2000 Zondervan

A · B · C · D

Map 12: APOSTLES' EARLY TRAVELS

CILICIA
•Tarsus

0   20   40   60 mi.
0   20   40   60   80 km.

Disciples first
called Christians

•Antioch
Seleucia•   Aleppo •

SYRIA

•Hamath

*The
Great Sea*

•Byblos

Cyprus

Orontes R.

Litani R.

Sidon•   •Damascus

•Tyre   •Caesarea Philippi

Ptolemais•   Capernaum
GALILEE   •
        Sea of Galilee

Cornelius
baptized

Caesarea •   Samaria
        (Sebaste)   Simon the
Peter sees vision;   •Sychar   sorcerer
restores Tabitha   Mt. Gerizim•   baptized
to life   SAMARIA   *Jabbok R.*

Peter   Joppa •   •Lydda
heals   Emmaus•
Aeneas   Stephen
    martyred
Azotus•   •Jerusalem
Betogabris•
Gaza • Bethsura•
        JUDEA   Salt
        Sea

Philip meets eunuch
(traditional location)

Euphrates R.

- - - - - Paul's trip to Damascus and
return to Jerusalem

– – – – Philip's first journey

――――― Philip's second journey

――――― Paul's flight from Grecian Jews

――――→ Peter's journey

――――― Paul and Barnabas's trip to
Jerusalem and return to Antioch

――――― Mark and Barnabas's trip to Cyprus

© 2000 Zondervan

GERMANIA

GALLIA

DALMATIA

A · B · C · D

1

ITALY

Adriatic Sea

Corsica

Rome
Forum of Appius
Three Taverns
Puteoli

2

MACE

Ber

Sardinia

EPIRUS

Tyrrhenian Sea

Rhegium

3

Ionian Sea

A

Sicily

Syracuse

NUMIDIA

Malta

AFRICA

4

T h e

TRIPOLITANIA

5

First Missionary Journey (A.D. 46–48)

Second Missionary Journey (A.D. 49–52)

Third Missionary Journey (A.D. 53–57)

Trip to Rome (A.D. 59–60)

© 2000 Zondervan

6

A · B · C · D

E · F · G · H

1

DACIA

MOESIA

Black Sea

THRACE

Philippi
hipolis Neapolis

Apollonia
Samothrace
Thessalonica
Olympus
Aegean
Sea
Troas **MYSIA**
Assos
Mitylene **Pergamum**
Kios Thyatira **ASIA**
Sardis Philadelphia
elphi Smyrna **LYDIA** **PHRYGIA**
nth Ephesus
Athens *Samos*
Laodicea **Colosse**
nchrea Miletus
arta
Patmos
Cos Cnidus
Attalia
LYCIA
Patara
Rhodes Myra

Pisidian
Antioch **LYCAONIA**
Iconium
Lystra Derbe
PISIDIA
Tarsus
PAMPHYLIA
Perga

GALATIA

CAPPADOCIA

COMMAGENE

CILICIA Issus
Antioch Aleppo
Seleucia

Euphrates R.

SYRIA

Cyprus Salamis
Paphos

hoenix *Crete*
Lasea Salmone
Fair Havens

Great   Sea

YRENAICA

EGYPT

Sidon
PHOENICIA Damascus
Tyre **ABILENE**
Ptolemais
Caesarea
JUDEA Jerusalem
Jordan R.

Salt Sea

ARABIA

Nile R.

0   100   200 mi.
0 100 200 300 km.

Red Sea

E · F · G · H

2

3

4

5

6

Roman Empire by the time of Julius Caesar (44 B.C.)

Territory added by Augustus Caesar (A.D. 14)

Territory added by Trajan (A.D. 117)

Territory temporarily annexed by Rome

© 2000 Zondervan